ARCHBOLD

CRIMINAL PLEADING, EVIDENCE AND PRACTICE

2009

SWEET & MAXWELL

THOMSON REUTERS

1st	Edition	..	1822	..	By	J. F. Archbold		
2nd	,,	..	1825	..	,,	,,		
3rd	,,	..	1829	..	,,	,,		
4th	,,	..	1831	..	,,	John Jervis		
5th	,,	..	1834	..	,,	,,		
6th	,,	..	1835	..	,,	,,		
7th	,,	..	1838	..	,,	,,		
8th	,,	..	1841	..	,,	,,		
9th	,,	..	1843	..	,,	,,		
10th	,,	..	1846	..	,,	W. N. Welsby		
11th	,,	..	1849	..	,,	,,		
12th	,,	..	1853	..	,,	,,		
13th	,,	..	?	..	,,	,,		
14th	,,	..	1859	..	,,	,,		
15th	,,	..	1862	..	,,	,,		
16th	,,	..	1867	..	,,	W. Bruce		
17th	,,	..	1871	..	,,	,,		
18th	,,	..	1875	..	,,	,,		
19th	,,	..	1878	..	,,	,,		
20th	,,	..	1886	..	,,	,,		
21st	,,	..	1893	..	,,	,,		
22nd	,,	..	1900	..	,,	W. F. Craies	and G. Stephenson	
23rd	,,	..	1905	..	,,	,,		
24th	,,	..	1910	..	,,	,,	and H. D. Roome	
25th	,,	..	1918	..	,,	H. D. Roome	and R. E. Ross	
26th	,,	..	1922	..	,,	,,	,,	
27th	,,	..	1927	..	,,	,,	,,	
28th	,,	..	1931	..	,,	R. E. Ross	and T. R. F. Butler	
29th	,,	..	1934	..	,,	,,	,,	
30th	,,	..	1938	..	,,	,,	and M. Turner	
31st	,,	..	1943	..	,,	T. R. F. Butler	and M. Garsia	
32nd	,,	..	1949	..	,,	,,	,,	
33rd	,,	..	1954	..	,,	,,	,,	
34th	,,	..	1959	..	,,	,,	,,	
35th	,,	..	1962	..	,,	,,	,,	
36th	,,	..	1966	..	,,	,,	,,	
37th	,,	..	1969	..	,,	,,	,,	
38th	,,	..	1973	..	,,	,,	and S. G. Mitchell	
39th	,,	..	1976	..	,,	S. G. Mitchell		
40th	,,	..	1979	..	,,	,,		
41st	,,	..	1982	..	,,	,,	and P. J. Richardson	
42nd	,,	..	1985	..	,,	,,	,,	
43rd	,,	..	1988	..	,,	,,	,,	and D. A. Thomas
1992	Edition				Editor:	P. J. Richardson		
1993	Edition				,,	,,		
1994	Edition				,,	,,		
1995	Edition				,,	,,		
1996	Edition				,,	,,		
1997	Edition				,,	,,		
1998	Edition				,,	,,		
1999	Edition				,,	,,		
2000	Edition				,,	,,		
2001	Edition				,,	,,		
2002	Edition				,,	,,		
2003	Edition				,,	,,		
2004	Edition				,,	,,		
2005	Edition				,,	,,		
2006	Edition				,,	,,		
2007	Edition				,,	,,		
2008	Edition				,,	,,		
2009	Edition				,,	,,		

EDITOR

P.J. RICHARDSON, LL.M. (LOND.), Dip. Crim. (CANTAB.)
of Gray's Inn and the Inner Temple, Barrister

CONTRIBUTING EDITORS

WILLIAM CARTER, B.A. (OXON.)
of Gray's Inn, Barrister

JULIAN CHRISTOPHER, B.A. Hons (CANTAB.)
of Gray's Inn, Barrister

MRS JUSTICE DOBBS, B.Sc., LL.M., Ph.D. (LOND.)

BEN EMMERSON, Q.C., LL.B. (BRISTOL)
of the Middle Temple, Barrister

MARTIN EVANS, B.A. (SUSSEX), Dip. Law (CITY)
of the Middle Temple, Barrister

DANNY FRIEDMAN, LL.M. (LOND.)
of the Middle Temple and the Inn of Court of Northern Ireland, Barrister

NICHOLAS HILLIARD, Q.C., M.A. (OXON.)
of the Middle Temple, Barrister

MARK LUCRAFT, Q.C., B.A. (KENT)
of the Inner Temple, Barrister

HELEN MALCOLM, Q.C., M.A. (OXON.)
of Gray's Inn and the Inner Temple, Barrister

CLARE MONTGOMERY, Q.C., LL.B. (LOND.)
of Gray's Inn, Barrister

ANTONY SHAW, Q.C., B.A. (OXON.)
of the Middle Temple, Barrister

STEPHEN SHAY, B.A. (OXON.)
of the Middle Temple, Barrister

HIS HONOUR JUDGE PETER THORNTON, Q.C., B.A. (CANTAB.)
Senior Circuit Judge, Central Criminal Court

JAMES TURNER, Q.C., LL.B. Hons (HULL)
of the Inner Temple, Barrister

PREFACE TO THE 2009 EDITION

It has been a recurring theme of the preface to this work that there is far too much criminal legislation. The willingness of the Labour government to continue its practice of legislating by trial-and-error has shown no sign of abating even in its eleventh year in office. The *Serious Crime Act* 2007 rounded off 2007, only to be followed onto the statute book within a matter of months by the *Criminal Justice and Immigration Act* 2008. But for the *Criminal Justice Act* 2003, the 2008 Act would have been, by some way, the most substantial piece of criminal legislation ever enacted. The two statutes combined comprise 493 sections and 66 schedules. The explosion in legislative activity is evidenced by the fact that until 2005 the criminal law section of the fourth edition *Halsbury's Statutes* was accommodated in a single volume (volume 12). In that year, volume 12 was reissued in two parts, and, just three years on, it has become necessary to reissue it in four parts. It is not just quantity, but quality. The state of the criminal statute book is a disgrace. The 2008 Act is the usual hotchpotch of measures, with no theme, with much of the detail tucked away from close scrutiny in the schedules, and consisting in large part of textual amendment of earlier legislation. Much of the amendment is by way of undoing this government's earlier legislation—youth penalties, bail, committal for sentence (a series of amendments of amendments in the 2003 Act that are not yet in force), dangerous offenders and release from prison. On top of all this, there are great tracts of legislation that have either not been brought into force or have been abandoned: see, for example, the *Sexual Offences (Protected Material) Act* 1997, the extension of imprisonment to 18-year-olds (*Criminal Justice and Court Services Act* 2000), the sending for trial provisions in the 2003 Act, the increase in magistrates' courts' sentencing powers in the same Act, intermittent custody (introduced, then abandoned) and custody plus (also in the 2003 Act) and drinking banning orders in the *Violent Crime Reduction Act* 2006. The difficulties that face judges and practitioners are further compounded by the fact that each batch of amendments is accompanied by a raft of transitional, transitory and saving provisions, the effect of which is that in various areas (community sentences, custodial sentences, release from custody, confiscation, sexual offences, incitement), there are two or more versions of the law which will apply according to the date of the conduct in question.

As ever, the higher courts have been busy over the last year. Notable decisions of the House of Lords include *R. v. Kennedy* (manslaughter), *R. v. Abdroikov*; *R. v. Green*; *R. v. Williamson* (persons working within criminal justice system serving on juries), *R. v. Clarke and McDaid* (trial on indictment a nullity without an indictment, which includes a signature), *R. v. Davis* (common law embargo on anonymous witnesses), *R. v. Rahman* (joint enterprise in murder (again)), and the trio of confiscation cases (*R. v. May*, *Jennings v. CPS* and *R. v. Green*). The knee-jerk reaction of the government to *Davis* was to legislate (*Criminal Evidence (Witness Anonymity) Act* 2008), so as to reverse the effect of the decision. As to the confiscation cases, they provided some cause for optimism that a measure of proportionality would be introduced to the operation of the legislation at the level of the Court of Appeal. Decisions such as those in *R. v. Shabir*, *R. v. Morgan*; *R. v. Bygrave* and *R. v. Sivaraman* provided some basis for supposing that such optimism was well founded. On the other hand, in *R. v. Waller*, the Court of Appeal upheld what must rank as one of the most extravagant prosecution applications to date. The impression that is given is that certain prosecuting authorities see the confiscation legislation as a means of generating revenue. There is an urgent need for the courts to curb such excessive claims as the legislation, properly interpreted, undoubtedly permits them to do. The alternative is the embarrassment of having the corrective applied by the European Court of Human Rights.

All of these changes, together with a host of others, have been incorporated into this edition. In consequence of Parliament's abolition of the offence of blasphemy (formerly chapter 27), there have been some relatively minor changes to the ordering of the material. What was chapter 33 (money laundering) has become chapter 26, what was chapter 26 (drugs) has become chapter 27 and what was chapter 34 (conspiracy, encouragement and attempt) has become chapter 33.

I would like to express my thanks to the team of authors for all their hard work in assisting in preparing this edition. Their many years of experience as practitioners at the very forefront of the profession are reflected throughout the pages of this work.

As with every edition, it is a pleasure to place on record how deeply indebted I am to the in-house editors at the publishers without whom none of this would have been possible. Hannah George has gone from strength to strength in supervising the production of the main work, whilst Kacey Mann has continued as the supplement editor (a task that included production of two of the largest supplements ever produced for this work). They make for a truly remarkable team—hugely efficient and skilful, tireless and hard-working (through a night or weekend when necessary), endlessly loyal, patient and charming throughout. It goes without saying that they have made my task immensely more straightforward. It has been the greatest of pleasures to have worked with them. I readily acknowledge, however, that there are many others who are involved in the process of producing a work of this scale. I would like to express my appreciation of the contribution made by each one of them.

In addition, I would like to thank Sean Redmond, who has indexed this edition, and Fiona Mullen for updating the tables.

23 Essex Street — P.J.R.
London WC2 — 16.10.2008

CONTENTS

ABBREVIATIONS OF LAW REPORTS

The dates denote the period covered by the reports or the latest editions of textbooks. Current series are marked with an asterisk (*).

A.C.	Law Reports, Appeal Cases, 1875–90
[1891] A.C.	Law Reports, Appeal Cases (1891 onwards).*
A. & E.	Adolphus and Ellis's Reports, Q.B. 1834–40.
A.L.R.	Australian Law Reports 1834–40.
All E.R.	All England Reports.*
Andr.	Andrews' Reports, K.B. 1737–38.
App.Cas.	Law Reports, Appeal Cases (1891 onwards).*
Ass.	Assisarum Liber. 1–50 Edward 3, 1327–77.
Atk.	Atkyns' Reports, Chancery. 1736–54.
Austr.Com.L.R.	Commonwealth Law Reports (Australia).
B.C.C.	British Company Cases.
B.C.L.C.	Butterworths Company Law Cases.
B.T.C.	British Tax Cases.
B. & Ad.	Barnewall and Adolphus's Reports, K.B. 1830–34.
B. & Ald.	Barnewall and Alderson's Reports, K.B. 1817–22.
B. & B.	Broderip and Bingham's Reports, C.P. 1819–22.
B. & C.	Barnewall and Cresswell's Report, K.B. 1822–30.
B. & P.	Bosanquet and Puller's Reports, C.P. 1796–1804.
B. & P.N.R.	Bosanquet and Puller's New Reports, C.P. 1804–7.
B. & S.	Best and Smith's Reports, Q.B. 1861–70.
Bac.Abr.	Bacon's Abridgement. (1832).
Bac.Elem.	Bacon's Elements of the Common Law. (1639.)
Barnard. K.B.	Barnardiston's Reports, K.B. 1926–34.
Beav.	Beavan's Reports, Rolls Court. 1838–66.
Bell	Bell's Crown Cases 1858–60.
Bing	Bingham's Reports, C.P. 1822–34.
Bing. N.C.	Bingham's New Cases, C.P. 1834–40.
Bl.Com.	Blackstone's Commentaries.
Bli. (N.S.)	Bligh's Reports, New Series. 1827–37.
Br.Abr.	Brooke's Abridgment. (1586.)
Bracton	Bracton de Legibus Angliæ. (1640.)
Bro.Ent.	Brown's Book of Entries. (1675–74.)
Bro.P.C.	Brown's Parliament Cases. 1702–1800.
Bull.N.P.	Buller's Nisi Prius. (1817.)
Bulst.	Bulstrode's Reports, K.B. 1610–25.
Burn	Burn's Justice of the Peace. (1869.)
Burr	Burrow's Reports, K.B. 1757–71.
C.B.	Common Bench Reports. 1840–56.
C.B. (N.S.)	Common Bench Reports, N.S. 1856–65.
C.C.C.Sess.Pap.	Central Criminal Court Cases. 1834–1913.
C.C.R.	Crown Cases Reserved.
C.D.	Collection of decisions of the European Commission of Human Rights.
C. & K.	Carrington and Kirwan's Reports, N.P. 1843–50.
C.L.C.	Current Law Consolidation.
C.L.R.	Irish Common Law Reports. 1850–66; Commonwealth Law Reports (Australia). 1903.*
C.L.Y.	Current Law Year Book.
C. & Mar.	Carrington and Marshman's Reports, N.P. 1840–42.
C.M. & R.	Crompton, Meeson and Roscoe's Reports, Ex. 1834–36.
C. & P.	Carrington and Payne's Reports, N.P. 1828–41.

C.O.D.	Crown Office Digest.*
C.P.D.	Law Reports, Common Pleas Division. 1875–80.
Cab. & Ell.	Cababé and Ellis Q.B. Reports. 1882–85.
Cald.	Caldecott's Magistrates' Cases, K.B. 1776–85.
Camp.	Campbell's Reports, Nisi Prius. 1808–16.
Can.Cr.Cas.	Canadian Criminal Cases. 1898.*
Cape S.C.	Supreme Court Reports, Cape Colony. 1880–1910.
Carr.C.L. (*or* Supp.)	Carrington's Criminal Law Supplement. 1828.
Carth.	Carthew's Reports, K.B. 1686–1701.
Cas.t.H.	Cases temp. Hardwicke, K.B. 1733–38.
Cas.temp.Holt	Modern Reports, Vol. 11. 1702–10.
[1891] Ch.	Law Reports, Chancery (1891 onwards).*
Ch.D.	Law Reports, Chancery Division. 1876–90.
Chit.Cr.L.	Chitty's Criminal Law. (1826).
Chit.Rep. (*or* K.B.)	Chitty's Reports, Bail Court. 1770–1822.
Cl. & F.	Clark and Finelly's Reports, H.L. 1831–46.
Co.Ent.	Coke's Entries. (1671.)
Co.Inst.	Coke's Institutes.
Co.Lit.	Coke on Littleton (1 Inst.)
Co.Rep.	Coke's Reports. 1572–1616.
Com.	Comyns. 1695–1741.
Comb.	Comberbach's Reports, K.B. 1685–99.
Com.Dig.	Comyn's Digest. (1822.)
Costs L.R.	Costs Law Reports. (1997.)*
Cowp.	Cowper's Reports, K.B. 1774–78.
Cox	Cox's Criminal Cases. 1843–1945.
Cr.App.R.	Criminal Appeal Reports. (1908.)*
Cr.App.R.(S.)	Criminal Appeal Reports (Sentencing). (1979.)
Cr.M. & R.	Crompton, Meeson and Roscoe's Exch. Reports. 1834–36.
Cr. & D.	Crawford and Dix's Irish Circuit Court Cases. 1839–49.
Cr. & J.	Crompton and Jervis's Exch. Reports. 1830–32.
Cr. & M.	Crompton and Meeson's Exch. Reports. 1832–34.
Crim.L.R.	Criminal Law Review.*
Cro.Car.	Croke's K.B. Reports temp. Charles I (3 Cro.).
Cro.Eliz.	Croke's K.B. Reports temp. Elizabeth I (1 Cro.).
Cro.Jac.	Croke's K.B. Reports temp. James I (2 Cro.).
Crom.	Crompton's Authorite et Jurisdiction des Courts. (1637.)
CSP	Current Sentencing Practice. (1982.)*
D. & B.	Dearsley and Bell's Crown Cases. 1856–58.
D. & R.	Dowling and Ryland's K.B. Reports. 1821–27.
D. & R.N.P.	Dowling and Ryland's N.P. Cases. 1822–23.
D.R.	Decisions and Reports of the European Commission of Human Rights.
Dalt.	Dalton's Sheriffs (1700) *or* Countrey Justice. (1746.)
Dav. & M.	Davison and Merivale's Reports, Q.B. 1843–44.
Deacon Cr.L.	Deacon's Criminal Law. (1831.)
Dears.	Dearsly's Crown Cases. 1852–56.
Dears. & B.	Dearsly and Bell's Crown Cases. 1856–58.
Den.	Denison's Crown Cases. 1844–52.
Den. & P.	Denison and Pearce's Crown Cases. 1844–52.
Dick. Q.S.	Dickinson Quarter Sessions Guide. (1845.)
Doct. & Stu.	St. German's Doctor and Student.
Doug.	Douglas' King Bench Reports. 1778–85.
Dow. P.C.	Dowling's Practice Cases. 1830–41.
Dow. & Ry.	Dowling and Ryland's K.B. Reports. 1821–27.
Dow. & Ry.N.P.	Dowling and Ryland's N.P. Cases. 1822–23.
Dowl.	Dowling's Bail Court Cases. 1830–42.
Dy.	Dyer's King's Bench Reports. 1513–82.

E. & B.	Ellis and Blackburn's Q.B. Reports. 1852–58.
E.B. & E.	Ellis, Blackburn and Ellis' Q.B. Reports. 1858.
E. & E.	Ellis and Ellis, Q.B. Reports. 1858–61.
E.H.R.L.R.	European Human Rights Law Review. (1996).
E.H.R.R.	European Human Rights Reports.
E.M.L.R.	Entertainment and Media Law Reports. (1993.)*
E.R.	English Reports Reprint.
East	East's King's Bench Reports. 1801–12.
East P.C.	East's Pleas of the Crown. 1803.
Eng.Rep.	English Reports Reprint. 1378–1865.
Esp.	Espinasse's Nisi Prius Reports. 1793–1807.
Ex.	Exchequer Reports. 1848–56.
Ex.D.	Law Reports, Exchequer Division. 1875–80.
F. & F.	Foster and Finlason's Nisi Prius Reports. 1856–67.
Fitzh.Abr.	Fitzherbert's Abirdgment. (1577.)
Fitzh.N.B.	Fitzherbert's New Natura Brevium.
Fort.K.B.	Fortescue's King's Bench Reports. 1695–1738.
Fost.	Foster's Crown Cases. 1743–61.
Fox & Sm.	Fox and Smith's Irish King's Bench Reports. 1822–24.
Fraser	Session Cases, 5th Series. 1898–1906.
G. & D.	Gale and Davison's Q.B. Reports. 1841–43.
Gibson	Gibson's Codex Juris Ecclesiastici. (1761.)
Gilb.Ev.	Gilbert's Law of Evidence. (1777.)
H.Bl.	H. Blackstone's Common Pleas Reports. 1788–96.
H.L.C.	House of Lords' Cases (Clark). 1847–66.
H. & C.	Hurlstone and Coltman's Exch. Reports. 1862–66.
H. & N.	Hurlstone and Norman's Exch. Reports. 1856–62.
Hag.Adm.	Haggard's Admiralty Reports. 1822–28.
Hag.Con.	Haggard's Consistory Reports. 1789–1821.
Hale	Hale's History of Pleas of the Crown. (1800.)
Hale's Summary	Hale's Pleas of the Crown. (1773.)
Har. & Woll.	Harrison and Wollaston's K.B. Reports. 1835–36.
Hare.	Hare's Vice-Chancellor's Reports. 1841–53.
Harg.St.Tr.	Hargrave's State Trials. (1776.)
Hawk.	Hawkin's Pleas of the Crown. (1824.)
Het.	Hetley's Common Pleas Reports. 1627–32.
Hob.	Hobart's King's Bench Reports. 1603–25.
Holborne's Reading	Holborne's Reading on the Statute of Treasons. (1681, printed with Bacon's Cases of Treason.)
Holt	Holt's King's Bench Reports. 1688–1710.
Holt N.P.	Holt's Nisi Prius Reports. 1815–17.
H.R.L.J.	Human Rights Law Journal
Imm.A.R.	Immigration Appeal Reports.
Inst.	Coke's Institutes.
Ir.C.L.	Irish Common Law Reports. 1850–66.
Ir.Circ.R.	Cases on the Six Circuits. 1841–43.
Ir.L.R.	Irish Law Reports. 1838–50. The Law Reports, Ireland. 1878.*
Ir.L.T.	Irish Law Times. 1867.*
Ir.Law Rep.	Irish Law Reports. 1838–50.
Ir.Law Rec.	Irish Law Recorder. 1827–38.
[1894] Ir.R.	Irish Law Reports (1893 onwards).*
Ir.R.Ch.	Irish Reports, Chancery. 1866–78.
Ir.Rep.C.L.	Irish Reports, Common Law. 1866–78.
Irvine	Irvine's Justiciary Cases, Scotland. 1852–67.
J.C.	Justiciary Cases, Scotland. 1916.*

J.P. .... Justice of the Peace. 1837.*
J. & H. .... Johnson and Hemming's Vice-Ch. Reports. 1859–62.
Jac. .... Jacob's Chancery Reports. 1821–22.
Jebb .... Jebb's Irish Crown Cases. 1822–40.
Jur. .... The Jurist. 1837–54.

[1901] K.B. .... Law Reports, King's Bench (1901 onwards).
Keb. .... Keble's King's Bench Reports. 1661–79.
Kel.J. .... Sir John Kelyng's Crown Cases. 1662–69.
Kel.W. .... Wm. Kelynge's Chancery Reports. 1730–36.

L.J.Newsp. .... Law Journal Newspaper. 1866.
L.J.Bk. .... Law Journal Bankruptcy. 1832–80.
L.J.Ch. .... Law Journal Chancery. 1831–1946.
L.J.C.P. .... Law Journal Common Pleas. 1831–75.
L.J.Exch. .... Law Journal Exchequer. 1831–75.
L.J.M.C. .... Law Journal Magistrates' Cases. 1831–96.
L.J.(o.s.) .... The Law Journal, Old Series. 1822–31.
L.J.P. .... Law Journal, Probate, Divorce and Admiralty. 1875–1946.
L.J.P.C. .... Law Journal, Privy Council. 1865–1946.
L.J.P.D. & A. .... Law Journal, Probate, Divorce and Admiralty. 1866–75.
L.J.P. & M. .... Law Journal, Probate and Matrimonial. 1860–65.
L.J.Q.B. (*or* K.B.) .... Law Journal, Queen's Bench *or* King's Bench. 1831–1946.
[1947] L.J.R. .... Law Journal Reports. 1947–49.
L.R.A. & E. .... Law Reports, Admiralty and Ecclesiastical. 1865–75.
L.R.C.C.R. .... Law Reports, Crown Cases Reserved. 1865–75.
L.R.C.P. .... Law Reports, Common Pleas. 1865–75.
L.R.Ex. .... Law Reports, Exchequer. 1865–75.
L.R.H.L. .... Law Report, English and Irish Appeal Cases. 1865–75.
L.R.Ir. .... Law Reports, Ireland. 1876–93.
L.R.P.C. .... Law Reports, Privy Council Appeal Cases. 1865–75.
L.R.P. & D. (*or* M.) .... Law Reports, Probate and Divorce. 1865–75.
L.R.Q.B. .... Law Reports, Queen's Bench. 1865–75.
L.T. .... Law Times Reports. 1859–1947.
L.T.J. .... Law Times Journal. 1845–1965.
L.T. (o.s.) .... Law Times, Old Series. 1843–59.
L. & C. .... Leigh and Cave's Crown Cases. 1861–65.
Ld.Ken. .... Kenyon's King Bench Reports. 1753–59.
Ld.Raym. .... Lord Raymond's Reports. 1694–1732.
Leach .... Leach's Crown Cases. 1730–1815.
Leon .... Leonard's King's Bench Reports. 1540–1615.
Lev. .... Levinz's King's Bench Reports. 1660–97.
Lew. .... Lewin's Court Cases. 1822–38.
Lofft .... Lofft's King's Bench Reports. 1772–74.

M. & M. .... Moody and Malkin's Nisi Prius Reports. 1826–30.
M. & Rob. .... Moody and Robinson's N.P. Reports. 1830–44.
M. & S. .... Maule and Selwyn's King's Bench Reports. 1813–17.
M. & W. .... Meeson and Welsby's Exchequer Reports. 1836–47.
Man. & G. .... Manning and Granger's C.P. Reports. 1840–44.
Man. & Ry. .... Manning and Ryland's K.B. Reports. 1827–30.
Man. L.R. .... Manitoba Law Reports. 1883.*
Marsh .... Marshall's Common Pleas Reports. 1814–16.
Mass. .... Massachusetts Reports.
McCl. & Y. .... McClelland and Younge's Exchequer Reports. 1824–25.

Wolf. & B. .... Wolferstan and Bristow's Election Cases. 1859–65.
Wood's Inst. .... Wood's Institutes of the Laws of England. (1772.)

Y.B. .... Year Books. The Year Books are usually referred to by the year of each King's reign, the initial letter of his name, and the folio and number of the *placita, e.g.,* 34 H. VI, 25, 3. The initial letter of the name of the term in which the case was decided is sometimes prefixed, *e.g.*, H. 34 H. VI, 25, 3. This abbreviation is also used for the Yearbook of the European Convention on Human Rights.

This abbreviation is also used for the Yearbook of the European Convention on Human Rights.

SERVICE INFORMATION

Archbold: Criminal Pleading, Evidence and Practice consists of one main text volume (including the tables and index). This volume is re-issued annually, and is updated by cumulative supplements and *Archbold News*.

Quoted matter and commentary

Material set out in smaller type is quoted from legislation or other sources, and is printed as amended. Details of amendments are set out immediately after each section or group of sections printed. Where relevant, details of commencement and transitional provisions are included.

Material set out in larger type is commentary.

Cumulative supplements

Three cumulative supplements, containing updating material for the main volume, are published in each year as part of the service.

The back cover of each supplement highlights important developments that have been included for the first time in that supplement. Such material is marked in the text of the supplement by a **bold** star in the margin. ★

Paragraph numbering

Paragraphs are numbered throughout the text of *Archbold*. Where reference is made to a particular paragraph, please check the corresponding paragraph in the current cumulative supplement for updating on any recent developments on this point.

Archbold News

Published 10 times each year, *Archbold News* contains:

Cases in Brief—short notes of recent cases
Cases in Detail—longer discussions of the more important decisions
Legislation—early warning of the effect of new statutes
Feature—a short article covering a topic of practical interest to *Archbold* subscribers
In Practice/News—coverage of statutory instruments, commencement orders and other relevant practice news.

From time to time other features are included.

Publisher's Note

All suggestions, comments and notices of error should be addressed to the House Editor, Archbold, Sweet & Maxwell Ltd, 100 Avenue Rd, London NW3 3PF.

Law Reports

From the first issue of 2001, all cases included in Sweet & Maxwell law reports have been given a unique citation. This takes the form of, *e.g.*, [2001] 1 Cr.App.R.(S.) 1 for the first case reported in [2001] 1 Cr.App.R.(S.), [2001] 1 Cr.App.R.(S.) 2 for the second case reported in [2001] 1 Cr.App.R.(S.), and so on. References in this work to cases reported in any series of law reports published by Sweet & Maxwell from the beginning of 2001 are to the case number, **not** to the page number. The particular series of law reports cited in this work and which are affected by this change are the Criminal Appeal Reports (Cr.App.R.), the Criminal Appeal (Sentencing) Reports (Cr.App.R.(S.)), the Road Traffic Reports (R.T.R.), the Administrative Court Digest and the European Human Rights Reports (E.H.R.R.).

The case number assigned by Sweet & Maxwell is distinct from, and bears no relation to, the neutral citation number: see Practice Direction (Judgments: Form and citation) [2001] 1 W.L.R. 194.

TABLE OF STATUTES

Northern Ireland

TABLE OF NON-UK STATUTORY MATERIAL

TABLE OF EUROPEAN AND INTERNATIONAL TREATIES AND CONVENTIONS

TABLE OF EUROPEAN DIRECTIVES AND REGULATIONS

Regulations

Directives

TABLE OF STATUTORY INSTRUMENTS

Great Britain

Northern Ireland

TABLE OF CASES

[1992] 3 All E.R. 897; [1994] E.C.C. 362; (1992) 156 J.P.N. 746; (1992) 136 S.J.L.B. 197 23–87

Att.-Gen.'s Reference (No.1 of 1992), Re [1993] 1 W.L.R. 274; [1993] 2 All E.R. 190; (1993) 96 Cr. App. R. 298; [1993] Crim. L.R. 274; (1992) 136 S.J.L.B. 304 20–27

Att.-Gen.'s Reference (No.2 of 1992), Re [1994] Q.B. 91; [1993] 3 W.L.R. 982; [1993] 4 All E.R. 683; (1993) 97 Cr. App. R. 429; (1994) 158 J.P. 741; [1993] R.T.R. 337; (1994) 158 J.P.N. 552; (1993) 90(27) L.S.G. 36; (1993) 143 N.L.J. 919; (1993) 137 S.J.L.B. 152 . . . . 17–84, 17–95, 32–22

Att.-Gen.'s Reference (No.3 of 1992), Re [1994] 1 W.L.R. 409; (1994) 98 Cr. App. R. 383; [1994] R.T.R. 122; [1994] Crim. L.R. 348; (1993) 143 N.L.J. 1675; (1993) 137 S.J.L.B. 278 . . . . 23–23, 28–74, 33–128

Att.-Gen.'s Reference (No.22 of 1992), Re, *sub nom.* R. *v.* Thomas (Steven Mark) [1994] 1 All E.R. 105; (1993) 97 Cr. App. R. 275; (1993) 14 Cr. App. R. (S.) 435; [1993] Crim. L.R. 227 . . . . 7–122, 7–369c

Att.-Gen.'s Reference (No.3 of 1993), Re, *sub nom.* R. *v.* W (Richard Kenneth) (1994) 98 Cr. App. R. 84; (1993) 14 Cr. App. R. (S.) 739; [1993] Crim. L.R. 472 7–367

Att.-Gen.'s Reference (No.19 of 1993), Re, *sub nom.* R. *v.* Downey (Conor Edward) (1994) 15 Cr. App. R. (S.) 760; [1994] Crim. L.R. 535 28–28

Att.-Gen.'s Reference (No.1 of 1994), Re [1995] 1 W.L.R. 599; [1995] 2 All E.R. 1007; (1995) 159 J.P. 584; [1995] Env. L.R. 356; 93 L.G.R. 349; (1995) 159 J.P.N. 387; (1995) 92(10) L.S.G. 37; (1995) 139 S.J.L.B. 56 . 17–66

Att.-Gen.'s Reference (No.3 of 1994), Re [1998] A.C. 245; [1997] 3 W.L.R. 421; [1997] 3 All E.R. 936; [1998] 1 Cr. App. R. 91; [1997] Crim. L.R. 829; (1997) 94(36) L.S.G. 44; (1997) 147 N.L.J. 1185; (1997) 141 S.J.L.B. 189, HL; affirming in part [1996] Q.B. 581; [1996] 2 W.L.R. 412; [1996] 2 All E.R. 10; [1996] 1 Cr. App. R. 351; [1996] 2 F.L.R. 1; (1996) 29 B.M.L.R. 99; [1996] Crim. L.R. 268; (1995) 145 N.L.J. 1777; (1996) 140 S.J.L.B 17–24, 19–16

Att.-Gen.'s Reference (No.48 of 1994), Re, *sub nom.* R. *v.* Jeffrey (Robert Allan) (1995) 16 Cr. App. R. (S.) 980; [1995] Crim. L.R. 515 5–286

Att.-Gen.'s Reference (No.2 of 1995) (Unduly Lenient Sentence), Re, *sub nom.* R. *v.* S (David William) [1996] 1 Cr. App. R. (S.) 274; [1995] Crim. L.R. 835 . . . . 5–77b

Att.-Gen.'s Reference (Nos.14, 15 and 16 of 1995), Re, *sub nom.* R. *v.* Ward (Michael Grainger); R. *v.* Howarth (Jeremy John); R. *v.* Hendry (George), *The Times*, April 10 1997 . . . . 30–215c

Att.-Gen.'s Reference (Nos.32 and 33 of 1995), Re, *sub nom.* R. *v.* Pegg (Shane Robin); R. *v.* Martin (Mark Anthony) [1996] 2 Cr. App. R. (S.) 346 . . . 21–92

Att.-Gen.'s Reference (Nos.62, 63 and 64 of 1995), Re, *sub nom.* R. *v.* O'Halloran (Paul Gerrard); R. *v.* Cameron (Clarence Raymond); R. *v.* Wood (Jane Leslie) [1996] 2 Cr. App. R. (S.) 223 5–103

Att.-Gen.'s Reference (No.7 of 1996), Re, *sub nom.* R. *v.* Hodgeon (Robert Christopher) [1997] 1 Cr. App. R. (S.) 399; [1997] Crim. L.R. 64 5–291

Att.-Gen.'s Reference (No.32 of 1996), Re, *sub nom.* R. *v.* Whittaker (Steven Alan) [1997] 1 Cr. App. R. (S.) 261; [1996] Crim. L.R. 917; (1996) 93(38) L.S.G. 42 5–288

Att.-Gen.'s Reference (No.33 of 1996), Re, *sub nom.* R. *v.* Latham (Daniel George) [1997] 2 Cr. App. R. (S.) 10; [1997] Crim. L.R. 140 . . . . 7–369e

Att.-Gen.'s Reference (No.40 of 1996), Re, *sub nom.* R. *v.* Robinson (Mark Leslie) [1997] 1 Cr. App. R. (S.) 357; [1997] Crim. L.R. 69 . . . . 7–369d

Att.-Gen.'s Reference (No.60 of 1996), Re, *sub nom.* R. *v.* Hartnett (Michael Christopher) [1997] 2 Cr. App. R. (S.) 198 19–194

Att.-Gen.'s Reference (No.7 of 1997), Re, *sub nom.* R. *v.* Fearon (Robert) [1998] 1 Cr. App. R. (S.) 268; [1997] Crim. L.R. 908 . . . . 5–46, 7–136

Att.-Gen.'s Reference (Nos.48 and 49 of 1997), Re, *sub nom.* R. *v.* Day (Mark Allen); R. *v.* Drady (Elliott John) [1998] 2 Cr. App. R. (S.) 392 5–63

Att.-Gen.'s Reference (No.1 of 1998), Re (1999) 163 J.P. 390; (1999) 163 J.P.N. 473; (1998) 95(37) L.S.G. 36; (1998) 142 S.J.L.B. 250 . . . . 25–469a

Att.-Gen.'s Reference (No.3 of 1998), Re [2000] Q.B. 401; [1999] 3 W.L.R. 1194; [1999] 3 All E.R. 40; [1999] 2 Cr. App. R. 214; (1999) 49 B.M.L.R. 124; [1999] Crim. L.R. 986; (1999) 96(19) L.S.G. 27; (1999) 149 N.L.J. 522; (1999) 143 S.J.L.B. 130 . . . . 4–174a, 4–468, 17–77

Att.-Gen.'s Reference (No.17 of 1998), Re, *sub nom.* R. *v.* Stokes (Ellen Marie) [1999] 1 Cr. App. R. (S.) 407; (1999) 163 J.P. 279; [1999] Crim. L.R. 92; (1999) 163 J.P.N. 234 . . . . 7–369d

Hall (Andrew Mark) [2007] EWCA Crim 195; [2007] 2 Cr. App. R. (S.) 42 . 5–81a, 28–28

Hall (Billy Paul) [2004] EWCA Crim 2671; [2005] 1 Cr. App. R. (S.) 118; [2005] Crim. L.R. 152 ... 5–884a

Hall (Edward Leonard) (1985) 81 Cr. App. R. 260; [1985] Crim. L.R. 377; (1985) 82 L.S.G. 1485; (1985) 136 N.L.J. 604; (1985) 128 S.J. 283 ... 21–311

Hall (Geoffrey) [1973] Q.B. 126; [1972] 3 W.L.R. 381; [1972] 2 All E.R. 1009; (1972) 56 Cr. App. R. 547; [1972] Crim. L.R. 453; (1972) 116 S.J. 598 ... 21–71, 21–72, 21–74

Hall (Michael) [1968] 2 Q.B. 788; [1968] 3 W.L.R. 359; [1968] 2 All E.R. 1009; (1968) 52 Cr. App. R. 528; (1968) 132 J.P. 417; [1968] Crim. L.R. 403; (1968) 112 S.J. 621 ... 1–150, 4–104

Hall (Michael Daniel) (1986) 8 Cr. App. R. (S.) 458 ... 5–363

Hall (Terence) (1984) 6 Cr. App. R. (S.) 321; [1985] Crim. L.R. 54 ... 5–75

Hall (Terry) [2002] EWCA Crim 1881 ... 7–82

Hall *v.* Cotton [1987] Q.B. 504; [1986] 3 W.L.R. 681; [1986] 3 All E.R. 332; (1986) 83 Cr. App. R. 257; (1986) 83 L.S.G. 3340; (1986) 130 S.J. 785 ... 24–6, 24–13, 24–50, 24–88

Hall-Chung (Teon) (2007) 151 S.J.L.B. 1020 ... 12–17, 12–18, , 13–9, 15–424

Hall's Estate, Re (1852) 22 L.J. Ch. 177 ... 9–24

Hallam (James Edward) [1957] 1 Q.B. 569; [1957] 2 W.L.R. 521; [1957] 1 All E.R. 665; (1957) 41 Cr. App. R. 111; (1957) 121 J.P. 254; (1957) 101 S.J. 268 ... 17–49, 23–76

Halliday (1889) 61 L.T. 701 ... 19–11

Halliwell (Peter Ian) (1990–91) 12 Cr. App. R. (S.) 692; [1991] Crim. L.R. 723 5–415

Halliwell *v.* Counsell (1878) 38 L.T. 176 ... 19–48

Halloren (Barry Philip) [2004] EWCA Crim 233; [2004] 2 Cr. App. R. (S.) 57; [2004] Crim. L.R. 392 ... 31–113

Halpin [1996] Crim. L.R. 112 ... 27–74

Halpin (John Francis) [1975] Q.B. 907; [1975] 3 W.L.R. 260; [1975] 2 All E.R. 1124; (1975) 61 Cr. App. R. 97; [1975] Crim. L.R. 453; (1975) 119 S.J. 541 9–70

Halton (1824) Ry. & M. 78 ... 4–166

Ham (1995) 36 B.M.L.R. 169 ... 15–490

Ham (Benjamin Albert) (1997) 36 B.M.L.R. 169 ... 15–371

Hamadi [2008] Crim. L.R. 635 ... 8–123p

Hamand (Graham Alan) (1986) 82 Cr. App. R. 65; [1985] Crim. L.R. 375; (1985) 82 L.S.G. 156 ... 1 7–87, 15–408, 15–505

Hambery (Cyril) [1977] Q.B. 924; [1977] 2 W.L.R. 999; [1977] 3 All E.R. 561; (1977) 65 Cr. App. R. 233; (1977) 121 S.J. 270 ... 4–253, 4–263, 7–100

Hambleton *v.* Callinan [1968] 2 Q.B. 427; [1968] 3 W.L.R. 235; [1968] 2 All E.R. 943; (1968) 132 J.P. 461; (1968) 112 S.J. 503 ... 27–68

Hamilton, 26 Cox 157; 13 Cr.App.R. 32; 118 L.T. 180 ... 8–147

Hamilton (1849) 7 St. Tr. (n.s.) 1130 ... 25–36

Hamilton [1972] Crim. L.R. 266 ... 4–376

Hamilton (Erroll) (1998) 95(30) L.S.G. 25; (1998) 142 S.J.L.B. 214 ... 8–138

Hamilton (Simon Austin) [2007] EWCA Crim 2062; [2008] Q.B. 224; [2008] 2 W.L.R. 107; [2008] 1 All E.R. 1103; [2008] 1 Cr. App. R. 13; [2008] Crim. L.R. 225; (2007) 104(34) L.S.G. 28; (2007) 157 N.L.J. 1234 ... 20–243

Hamilton (Winston) (1991) 92 Cr. App. R. 54; (1991) 155 J.P. 264; [1990] Crim. L.R. 806; (1990) 154 J.P.N. 692 ... 21–379

Hamilton-Johnson *v.* RSPCA, *sub nom.* Hamilton-Johnson *v.* Royal Society for the Prevention of Cruelty to Animals [2000] 2 Cr. App. R. (S.) 390; (2000) 164 J.P. 345; (2000) 164 J.P.N. 484; (2000) 97(20) L.S.G. 42 ... 2–179, 6–34

Hammersley (John Richard); R. *v.* Bellson (Samuel); R. *v.* Heath (Trevor Ernest) (1958) 42 Cr. App. R. 207 ... 28–8, 33–21, 33–25, 33–61

Hammersmith & City Railway Co *v.* Brand, *sub nom.* Brand and Wife *v.* Hammersmith & City Railway Co; Brand *v.* Hammersmith & City Railway Co (1869–70) L.R. 4 H.L. 171, HL; reversing (1866–67) L.R. 2 Q.B. 223, Ex Chamber; reversing (1865–66) L.R. 1 Q.B. 130 ... 31–46

Hammersmith Juvenile Court Ex p. O (A Minor) (1988) 86 Cr. App. R. 343; (1987) 151 J.P. 639; [1987] Crim. L.R. 343 ... 1–75r, 1–75w, 4–93

Hammond (Leslie Walter) [1941] 3 All E.R. 318; (1943) 28 Cr. App. R. 84 . 4–270, 15–378

Hammond *v.* DPP, *sub nom.* DPP *v.* Hammond [2004] EWHC 69 (Admin); (2004) 168 J.P. 601; (2004) 168 J.P.N. 877 ... 16–125, 29–34a

Wilkes v. Hungerford Market Co. (1835) 2 Bing.(n.c.) 281; 1 Hodg. 281; 5 L.J. C.P. 23; 2 Scott 446 31–40
Wilkins (Betty Margaret) [1975] 2 All E.R. 734; (1974) 60 Cr. App. R. 300; [1975] Crim. L.R. 343 .... 7–63, 21–313
Wilkins (Paul Edward) (1995) 16 Cr. App. R. (S.) 49 5–48
Wilkinson (William) [1996] 1 Cr. App. R. 81 .... 4–67a
Wilkinson *v.* CPS, *sub nom.* Wilkinson *v.* DPP (1998) 162 J.P. 591; [1998] Crim. L.R. 743; [1998] C.O.D. 367; (1998) 162 J.P.N. 625 10–11
Wilkinson *v.* Lord Chancellor's Department, *sub nom.* Wilkinson *v.* Official Solicitor; Wilkinson *v.* S [2003] EWCA Civ 95; [2003] 1 W.L.R. 1254; [2003] 2 All E.R. 184; [2003] C.P. Rep. 37; [2003] 1 F.C.R. 741; (2003) 100(12) L.S.G. 29; (2003) 147 S.J.L.B. 178 .... 12–158, 16–60, 16–74, 28–115, 28–125
Wilkinson *v.* S. *See* Wilkinson *v.* Lord Chancellor's Department
Willcock, *The Times*, March 31, 1982 7–355
Wille (Bryan James) (1988) 86 Cr. App. R. 296 21–45
Willer (Mark Edward) (1986) 83 Cr. App. R. 225; [1987] R.T.R. 22 17–128
Willesden Justices Ex p. Clemmings (1988) 87 Cr. App. R. 280; (1988) 152 J.P.N. 46 .... 4–67a
Willesden Juvenile Court Ex p. Brent LBC [1988] 2 F.L.R. 95; 86 L.G.R. 197; [1988] Fam. Law 341; (1988) 152 J.P.N. 686 4–13
William *v.* Worall (1838) 8 C. & P. 380 14–60
William C Leitch Bros Ltd, Re (No.1) [1932] 2 Ch. 71 30–120
Williams (1871) Cox 684 19–147
Williams (Alan Davis) *v.* DPP [1991] 1 W.L.R. 1160; [1991] 3 All E.R. 651; (1991) 93 Cr. App. R. 319; (1992) 156 J.P. 804; [1991] R.T.R. 214; [1991] C.O.D. 500; (1991) 141 N.L.J. 564; (1991) 135 S.J. 508 .... 4–118, 4–143, 4–146
Williams (Alan Geoffrey) (1987) 84 Cr. App. R. 274 4–447
Williams (Barry Anthony); R. *v.* Davis (Frank O'Neill) [1992] 1 W.L.R. 380; [1992] 2 All E.R. 183; (1992) 95 Cr. App. R. 1; [1992] Crim. L.R. 198 18–7, 19–10
Williams (Carl) [1982] 1 W.L.R. 1398; [1982] 3 All E.R. 1092; (1982) 75 Cr. App. R. 378; (1982) 4 Cr. App. R. (S.) 239; [1982] Crim. L.R. 762; (1982) 126 S.J. 690 .... 5–118, 7–122, 7–132
Williams (Clarence Ivor) (1987) 84 Cr. App. R. 299; [1987] Crim. L.R. 198 .... 13–32, 19–129
Williams (David) [1998] Crim. L.R. 495 8–102
Williams (Gary Ian) [2001] EWCA Crim 932; (2001) 98(19) L.S.G. 36; (2001) 145 S.J.L.B. 86 7–52
Williams (Gary John) *v.* DPP; O'Hare (Edward Martin) *v.* DPP [1993] 3 All E.R. 365; (1994) 98 Cr. App. R. 209; [1994] R.T.R. 61; [1993] Crim. L.R. 775 .... 15–519, 15–524, 15–527
Williams (Gladstone) [1987] 3 All E.R. 411; (1984) 78 Cr. App. R. 276; [1984] Crim. L.R. 163; (1984) 81 L.S.G. 278 .... 7–54, 17–11, 17–12, 17–16, 17–44, 19–49, 19–166a, 19–169, 19–260, 19–275
Williams (Harold Leon) [1971] 1 W.L.R. 1029; [1971] 2 All E.R. 444; (1971) 55 Cr. App. R. 275; (1971) 115 S.J. 484 .... 25–461, 25–468
Williams (Henry) (1927) 19 Cr. App. R. 67 7–357
Williams (Hugh) [2003] EWCA Crim 3200; (2003) 147 S.J.L.B. 1305 14–31
Williams (John) (1913) 8 Cr. App. R. 133 8–96
Williams (John Owen) (1910) 4 Cr. App. R. 89 19–304
Williams (Kevin John) (1991) 92 Cr. App. R. 158; (1991) 155 J.P. 365; [1991] Crim. L.R. 205; (1990) 154 J.P.N. 836 .... 28–19, 28–27
Williams (M.), (92/6329/W5), unreported, April 15, 1994 4–320
Williams (Mark Alexander) (1992) 156 J.P. 776; (1992) 156 J.P.N. 330 15–488
Williams (Melanie Jane) [2001] EWCA Crim 2362; [2002] 1 Cr. App. R. (S.) 125 27–85
Williams (Noel) *v.* Queen, The [1997] 1 W.L.R. 548; (1997) 141 S.J.L.B. 84 14–42
Williams (Owen Richard) [1923] 1 K.B. 340; (1924) 17 Cr. App. R. 56 20–15
Williams (Paul David) (1992) 156 J.P. 325 7–129
Williams (Richard) *v.* DPP (1992) 95 Cr. App. R. 415; (1992) 156 J.P. 804; [1992] Crim. L.R. 503; (1992) 156 J.P.N. 427 .... 24–113, 24–114
Williams (Robert Charles) [2006] EWCA Crim 2530; [2007] 1 Cr. App. R. (S.) 107 24–127
Williams (Roy Brian) [1978] Q.B. 373; [1977] 2 W.L.R. 400; [1977] 1 All E.R. 874; (1977) 64 Cr. App. R. 106; [1977] Crim. L.R. 305; (1977) 121 S.J. 135 .... 4–98, 7–355

TABLE OF EUROPEAN HUMAN RIGHTS CASES

TABLE OF PRACTICE DIRECTIONS

Practice Directions relating to Civil Procedure Rules (SI 1998/3132)

ABBREVIATIONS OF LEGISLATION

The following abbreviations have been adopted throughout.

AFA	Armed Forces Act
CAA	Criminal Appeal Act
CDA	Crime and Disorder Act
CDDA	Company Directors Disqualification Act
CEMA	Customs and Excise Management Act
CJA	Criminal Justice Act
CJCSA	Criminal Justice and Court Services Act
CJIA	Criminal Justice and Immigration Act
CJPA	Criminal Justice and Police Act
CJPOA	Criminal Justice and Public Order Act
CLA	Criminal Law Act
CPIA	Criminal Procedure and Investigations Act
C(S)A	Crime (Sentences) Act
CYPA	Children and Young Persons Act
DTA	Drug Trafficking Act
DTOA	Drug Trafficking Offences Act
ECHR	European Convention on Human Rights
FSMA	Financial Services and Markets Act
MCA	Magistrates' Courts Act
MHA	Mental Health Act
PACE	Police and Criminal Evidence
PCA	Proceeds of Crime Act
PCCA	Powers of Criminal Courts Act
PCC(S)A	Powers of Criminal Courts (Sentencing) Act
PJA	Police and Justice Act
RIPA	Regulation of Investigatory Powers Act
RSA	Road Safety Act
RSC	Rules of the Supreme Court (Revision)
RTA	Road Traffic Act
RTOA	Road Traffic Offenders Act
SCA	Serious Crime Act
SOA	Sexual Offences Act
SOCPA	Serious Organised Crime and Police Act
VCRA	Violent Crime Reduction Act
YJCEA	Youth Justice and Criminal Evidence Act

Chapter 1

THE INDICTMENT

I. DEFINITION

A bill of indictment is a written or printed accusation of crime made at the suit of the Crown against one or more persons. The circumstances in which a bill of indictment may be preferred are specified in section 2(2) of the *Administration of Justice* **1–1**

(Miscellaneous Provisions) Act 1933, which identifies the foundation procedures to be followed in that regard (see *post*, § 1-204). The bill of indictment becomes an actual indictment when it is signed in accordance with section 2(1) of that Act (*post*, § 1-231). As to the proper form of an indictment, see *post*, §§ 1-108 *et seq.*, and see *post*, §§ 1-190 *et seq.* as to certain objections that may be taken to an indictment and the means by which certain defects in connection with indictments may be cured. As to the extent to which defects in the relevant procedures and requirements may affect the validity of an indictment or of a conviction, and as to whether a valid conviction of an indictable offence can take place in the Crown Court in the absence of an indictment, see generally *post*, §§ 1-35, 1-195 *et seq.*, and 7-97a.

II. NATURE OF INDICTABLE OFFENCES

A. WHEN AN INDICTMENT LIES

(1) General

1-2 An indictment is the ordinary common law remedy for all treasons, misprisions of treasons and offences of a public nature: 2 Hawk. c. 25, ss.1, 4. It is also the means by which certain offences created by or under statute are brought before the Crown Court for trial.

(2) Breach of common law duty

1-3 An indictment lies at common law for a breach of duty which is not a mere private injury but an outrage on the moral duties of society, *e.g.* neglect to provide sufficient food, medical aid or other necessaries, for a person unable to provide for himself, and for whom the defendant is obliged by duty or contract to provide, where such neglect injures the health of that person, whether the person injured is of extreme age (*R. v. Instan* [1893] 1 Q.B. 450), or of tender years (*R. v. Senior* [1899] 1 Q.B. 283 at 289), or is the defendant's servant (*R. v. Smith* (1865) L. & C. 607), or apprentice (*R. v. Smith* (1837) 8 C. & P. 153), or is a person of unsound mind (*R. v. Pelham* [1846] 8 Q.B. 959). The common law is strengthened by statutory provisions, *e.g. Offences against the Person Act* 1861, s.26 (servants and apprentices); *CYPA* 1933, s.1 (persons under 16); *MHA* 1983, s.127 (persons of unsound mind). It being a democratic principle, however, that it is for Parliament and not the executive or judges to determine whether conduct not previously regarded as criminal should be treated as such, statute is now to be regarded as the sole source of new offences: *R. v. Jones*; *Ayliffe v. DPP*; *Swain v. Same* [2007] 1 A.C. 136, HL; and *R. (Gentle) v. Prime Minister* [2008] 2 W.L.R. 879, HL (at [40]) (and see *post*, § 1-4a).

Unless a statute specifically so provides, or the case is one in which the common law, in the criminal context, imposes a duty or responsibility on one person to act in a particular way towards another, then a mere omission to act cannot make the person, who so fails to do something, guilty of a criminal offence: see *R. v. Miller* [1983] 2 A.C. 161, HL, where the appellant was held liable for his reckless omission to take steps to nullify a risk of damage to property which had been created by his own earlier inadvertent act (see further *post*, §§ 23-10, 23-31). The House of Lords approached the facts on the basis that—unlike the case of the mere bystander—the appellant had a duty to act.

(3) Acts prejudicing the public

1-4 An indictment lies at common law for any act of wilful negligence which endangers human life or health: *Williams v. East India Co.* (1802) 3 East 192; *Shillito v. Thompson* (1875) 1 Q.B.D. 12; or against an innkeeper for failing to provide a traveller with food and lodging without reasonable excuse, on being tendered a reasonable price; the question of what amounts to a reasonable excuse being a question of fact for the jury: *R. v. Higgins* [1948] 1 K.B. 165, 32 Cr.App.R. 113, CCA.

An indictment also lies for all nuisances of a public nature, though occasioned by an act in itself innocent, if the creation of the nuisance is the probable consequence of the act: *R. v. Moore* (1832) 3 B. & Ad. 184; and see 1 Hawk. c. 75, ss.6, 7. As to the offence of public nuisance generally, see *post*, §§ 31-40 *et seq.*

(4) Customary international law

Although crimes recognised under customary international law have been assimilated into domestic criminal law, assimilation is not automatic and must be provided for by domestic statute: *R. v. Jones*; *Ayliffe v. DPP*; *Swain v. Same* [2007] 1 A.C. 136, HL; and *R. (Gentle) v. Prime Minister* [2008] 2 W.L.R. 879, HL (at [40]) (and see *ante*, § 1–3). **1–4a**

(5) Intention to commit offences

Mere intention to commit an offence is not indictable (see *Hope v. Brown* [1954] 1 W.L.R. 250), except in the case of high treason: 25 Edw. 3, st. 5, c. 2 (see *post*, § 25–1), but see *post*, §§ 33–1 *et seq.* as to conspiracy. **1–5**

(6) Attempts to commit offences

See *post*, §§ 33–119 *et seq.* **1–5a**

(7) Incitement and secondary participation

See *post*, §§ 33–78 *et seq.* as to incitement; and see *post*, §§ 18–1 *et seq.* as to aiding, abetting, counselling and procuring. **1–5b**

(8) Disobedience to statutes

Where a statute has declared any act or omission to be treason, felony, misprision of treason or misdemeanour, an indictment lies in respect of such act or omission. Even though a statute does not use express terms describing the nature of the offence, if it prohibits a matter of public grievance to the liberties and securities of the subject, or commands a matter of public convenience (such as the repairing of highways or the like), all acts or omissions contrary to the prohibition or command of the statute are misdemeanours at common law, punishable on indictment by unlimited fine, unless such method of procedure manifestly appears to be excluded by the statute: 2 Hawk. c. 25, s.4; *R. v. Wright* (1758) 1 Burr. 543; *R. v. Hall* [1891] 1 Q.B. 747; *R. v. Lennox-Wright* [1973] Crim.L.R. 529, CCC (H.H. Judge Lawson Q.C.). In *R. v. Horseferry Road JJ., ex p. Independent Broadcasting Authority* [1987] Q.B. 54, DC, it was held that the "doctrine of contempt of statute" was no more than a rule of construction. **1–6**

> "Among the factors which will have to be considered are (i) whether the duty is mandatory or prohibitory; (ii) whether the statute is ancient or modern; for in ancient statutes it was far more common than it is today for offences not to be defined, but to leave enforcement, for example, to a common informer; and (iii) whether there are any other means of enforcing the duty. In the case of a mandatory duty imposed by a modern statute, enforceable by way of judicial review, the inference that Parliament did not intend to create an offence in the absence of an express provision to that effect is, nowadays, almost irresistible. [Counsel for the IBA] ... argued that the rule as stated in *Hawkins' Pleas of the Crown* has ceased to exist: *cessante ratione legis cessat lex ipsa*. I do not find it necessary to go that far; for, as I have said, the 'rule' or 'doctrine' never was more than a rule of construction. It is not a substantive rule of law. The only difference between today and 1716 ... is that it is easier to infer in the case of a modern statute that Parliament does not intend to create an offence unless it says so. There is no longer any presumption, if indeed, there ever were, that a breach of duty imposed by statute is indictable. Nowadays the presumption, if any, is the other way: although I would prefer to say that it requires clear language, or a very clear inference, to create a crime" (*per* Lloyd J. at p. 72).

Effect of repeal on subsequent proceedings

See the *Interpretation Act* 1978, ss.15– 17 (Appendix B–15 *et seq.*). **1–6a**

Effect of expiry on subsequent proceedings

The provisions of the *Interpretation Act* 1978 do not apply to the case of a statute which has expired by effluxion of time. In the case of expiry, the particular statute must be considered to see whether it is intended that it should be in force for any—and if so for what—purposes after expiry. See, for example, *Wicks v. DPP* [1947] A.C. 362, HL. **1–6b**

(9) Creation of new offences

Where a statute makes a new offence of conduct which was in no way prohibited by **1–7** the common law, and appoints a particular manner of proceeding against the offender, as by commitment, or action of debt, or information, etc., without mentioning an indictment, it seems to be settled that the statute will not maintain an indictment, because the mentioning only of the other methods of proceeding impliedly excludes that of indictment: 2 Hawk. c. 25, s.4; *R. v. Kakelo* [1923] 2 K.B. 793, 17 Cr.App.R. 150, CCA.

(10) Where a statute provides a special remedy

1–8 Where a statute prescribes a new penalty or remedy for an offence which is already an offence at common law, the remedy at common law is not taken away except by express negative words (*e.g.* "and not otherwise": *Crofton's Case* (1670) 1 Mod.Rep. 34) and the prosecutor has the option of proceeding either by indictment at common law or by the mode specified by the statute: *R. v. Richard Carlile* (1819) 3 B. & Ald. 161; and see *Maxwell on The Interpretation of Statutes*, 12th ed., p. 195. If the prohibition and the penalty are all in one and the same clause, no indictment will lie unless it be one of the remedies named in the statute; but if they are in separate and distinct clauses an indictment will lie on the prohibitory clause: *R. v. Hall* [1891] 1 Q.B. 747; *Saunders v. Holborn District Board of Works* [1895] 1 Q.B. 64. Where a new offence is created by a statute and a penalty is annexed to it by a separate and substantive clause, it is not necessary for the prosecutor to sue for the penalty but he may proceed on the prior clause on the ground of its being a misdemeanour: *R. v. Buchanan* [1846] 8 Q.B. 883. Where a statute, in one clause, declares an act to be a *public nuisance*, it is indictable, though a subsequent clause subjects it to a pecuniary penalty recoverable by "information, bill, plaint, or action at law", or makes it abatable: *R. v. Crawshaw* (1860) 8 Cox 375.

Provision against more than one punishment

1–8a The *Interpretation Act* 1978, s.18 (Appendix B–18) provides for the situation where an act or omission constitutes an offence under two or more Acts of Parliament, or both under an Act and at common law. If a statute describes an offence created by an earlier statute, and affixes to it a different punishment, varying the procedure, and giving an appeal where there was no appeal before, the prosecutor must proceed for the offence under the later statute: *Michell v. Brown* (1858) 1 E. & E. 267.

(11) Disobedience to subordinate legislation

1–9 Disobedience to an order relating to quarantine, made under statutory authority, has been held to be an indictable misdemeanour at common law: *R. v. Harris* (1791) 4 T.R. 202, explained in *R. v. Hall* [1891] 1 Q.B. 747 at 765. Where a statute, the matter of which concerns the public in general, delegates power to make orders under it, disobedience to an order made in pursuance of such power is an indictable misdemeanour at common law: *R. v. Walker* (1875) L.R. 10 Q.B. 355. Where a statute gives power to make regulations, a regulation made under the power becomes, for the purposes of obedience or disobedience, a provision of the statute: *Willingale v. Norris* [1909] 1 K.B. 57 at 64, DC.

Modern drafting practice is to spell out in the enabling legislation the extent to which offences may be created by the subordinate legislation and to specify whether such offences may be made triable on indictment: see, for example, the *Civil Aviation Act* 1982, s.61(1), (2). An alternative is for the enabling statute to provide that non-compliance with the subordinate legislation is an offence: see, for example, the *Criminal Justice (International Co-operation) Act* 1990, s.13(5), *post*, § 25–490. It is unlikely that a court would hold, where some such drafting technique has not been used, that non-compliance with modern subordinate legislation is a criminal offence: see *R. v. Horseferry Road JJ., ex. p. Independent Broadcasting Authority*, *ante*, § 1–6.

See *post*, §§ 4–350 and 9–27 *et seq.* as to the need to prove the making and publication of a statutory instrument.

Challenging the validity of subordinate legislation

1–9a The defendant to a criminal charge may raise as a defence thereto the contention that subordinate legislation under which he is being prosecuted, or an administrative decision made thereunder, is *ultra vires* and unlawful; and no distinction is to be drawn between legislation or a decision that is bad on its face (substantive invalidity) and that which is bad for procedural irregularity; the burden is on the defendant to establish on a balance of probabilities that the legislation or decision was invalid; but, in every case, it is necessary to examine the particular statutory context to determine whether a court has jurisdiction to rule on a defence based on such alleged invalidity; the statutory context might preclude such challenges in certain situations (as to which, see *R. v. Wicks* [1998] A.C. 92, HL, and *Quietlynn Ltd v. Plymouth City Council* [1988] Q.B. 114, DC): *Boddington v. British Transport Police* [1999] 2 A.C. 143, HL.

In the absence of express provision, the courts presume that even the most general statutory words are intended to be subject to the basic rights of the individual; *a fortiori* where the words merely delegate a power to legislate: *General Mediterranean Holdings S.A. v. Patel* [2000] 1 W.L.R. 272, QBD (Toulson J.). To similar effect, see *R. v. Secretary of State for the Home Department, ex p. Leech (No. 2)* [1994] Q.B. 198, CA (Civ. Div.), *R. v. Lord Chancellor, ex p. Witham* [1998] Q.B. 575, DC, and *R. v. Secretary of State for the Home Department, ex p. Simms* [2000] 2 A.C. 115, HL.

(12) Private injuries

An indictment will not lie at common law for a mere private injury against an individual: *R. v. Atkins* (1765) 3 Burr. 1706. The remedy for such injuries is by action only, unless they in some measure concern the Crown, or are accompanied by circumstances which amount to a breach of the peace. Nor will an indictment lie for the infringement of a right common only to the inhabitants of a particular district: 1 Hawk. c. 76, s.1; *Austin's case* (1672) 1 Vent. 189; *R. v. Thrower* (1672) 1 Vent. 208. Further, an indictment will not lie for the infringement of rights which are merely private, though regulated by a public statute: *R. v. Richards* (1800) 8 T.R. 634; nor for an act prohibited by a private statute, which tends merely to the damage of a particular individual: *R. v. Pawlyn* (1664) 1 Sid. 208; nor will it lie for a mere breach of the byelaws or customs of a corporation: *R. v. Sharples* (1792) 4 T.R. 777. **1–10**

B. CLASSIFICATION OF OFFENCES

(1) By mode of trial

The *CLA* 1977 (ss.14– 26 and Scheds 1– 4) introduced a straightforward classification of all offences, namely, those triable: (a) only on indictment; (b) only summarily; and (c) either way. The 1977 provisions were repealed (except for s.15 and Sched. 1, both now repealed in part, and s.17, now repealed) by the *MCA* 1980. The 1980 Act is essentially consolidating and it preserves the classification established by the 1977 Act. **1–11**

For definitions of the terms "indictable offence", "summary offence", and "offence triable either way", see the *Interpretation Act* 1978, Sched. 1 (Appendix B–28).

Notwithstanding the apparently straightforward division of offences into three categories, section 22 of the *MCA* 1980 makes provision for certain offences triable either way to be tried only summarily if the value involved is small (*post*, §§ 1–75i *et seq.*), section 40 of the *CJA* 1988 (*post*, § 1–75ai) makes provision for certain summary offences to be included in an indictment in the circumstances there specified, section 41 of that Act (*post*, § 1–75am), pending its prospective repeal, makes provision for certain summary offences to be "committed" for trial and to be dealt with by the Crown Court otherwise than on indictment, sections 51 and 51A of the *CDA* 1998 (*post*, §§ 1–17 *et seq.*) make provision for certain summary offences to be "sent" for trial, and paragraph 6 of Schedule 3 to that Act (*post*, §§ 1–17 *et seq.*) makes provision for the Crown Court to deal, otherwise than on indictment, with summary offences that have been "sent" for trial.

As to the mode of trial for offences of aiding, abetting, counselling or procuring, see *post*, § 18–4.

(2) Felony and misdemeanor

Criminal Law Act 1967, ss.1, 12(5), (6)

1–12 **1.**—(1) All distinctions between felony and misdemeanour are hereby abolished.

(2) Subject to the provisions of this Act, on all matters on which a distinction has previously been made between felony and misdemeanour, including mode of trial, the law and practice in relation to all offences cognisable under the law of England and Wales (including piracy) shall be the law and practice applicable at the commencement of this Act in relation to misdemeanour.

12.—(5) Subject to any express amendment or repeal made by this Act, the following provisions shall have effect in relation to any Act passed before this Act:—

(a) any enactment creating an offence by directing it to be felony shall be read as directing it to be an offence … ; [*remainder of paragraph not printed*]

(b) any enactment relating to felonious stealing shall be read as referring merely to stealing;

(c) nothing in this Part of this Act shall affect the punishment provided for an offence by the enactments specially relating to that offence.

(6) In this Part of this Act references to felony shall not be taken as including treason; but the procedure on trials for treason or misprision of treason shall be the same as the procedure as altered by this Act on trials for murder.

(3) Arrestable offence

1–13 The classification of offences as "non-arrestable", "arrestable" and "serious arrestable" has, with effect from January 1, 2006, been removed by amendments to the *PACE Act* 1984 effected by the *SOCPA* 2005. In consequence, all offences are now arrestable, but the exercise of the power of arrest is subject to the conditions set out in the amended provisions of the 1984 Act, and subject to the Code of Practice for the Statutory Power of Arrest by Police Officers (Code G (Appendix A–204 *et seq.*)), promulgated pursuant to that Act. Specific distinctions are drawn between the power of a constable to arrest without a warrant and the power of other persons to arrest without a warrant. See generally, *post*, §§ 15–152 *et seq.*

III. SENDINGS, TRANSFERS AND COMMITTALS FOR TRIAL OF INDICTABLE OFFENCES

A. BACKGROUND

1–14 Originally, all cases tried on indictment before the Crown Court had either been the subject of committal proceedings, or resulted from the grant of leave to prefer a voluntary bill of indictment. However, the *CJA* 1987 introduced a transfer procedure in place of committal proceedings for cases of serious or complex fraud (see *post*, § 1–41). This formed part of a legislative scheme inspired by the *Fraud Trials Committee Report* (HMSO 1986), chaired by Lord Roskill. The transfer procedure was extended, by the *CJA* 1991, to cover certain cases involving children as victims or witnesses of certain sex offences or offences of violence (see *post*, § 1–53).

The *CDA* 1998 then abolished committal proceedings for offences triable only on indictment and created instead a procedure for those who are charged with such offences (together with related either way and summary offences) to be "sent" to the Crown Court for trial. This developed and implemented recommendations of the Royal Commission on Criminal Procedure 1981 (Cmnd. 8092), the Royal Commission on Criminal Justice 1993 (Cm. 2263), and the Narey Report, *Review of Delay in the Criminal Justice System* (1997).

If and when the provisions of Schedule 3 to the *CJA* 2003 are fully in force, all cases of the types that would previously have been subject to either the transfer or sending procedures will be sent to the Crown Court for trial, pursuant to provisions of the *CDA* 1998, as amended by the 2003 Act, as will all charges of offences in respect of which it is determined under the new allocation procedures in a magistrates' court that any trial should take place in the Crown Court. Committal proceedings will, thus, be completely abolished. This is part of the package of measures intended to bring about the "closer alignment" between the magistrates' courts and the Crown Court proposed in the Government Paper, *Justice for All* (2002).

The purpose of the transfer and sending provisions is to speed the progress of serious cases, with the effect of transferring the jurisdiction for management of the same from magistrates' courts to the Crown Court, so that the plea and directions hearing should take place much earlier in the life of the case, with Crown Court judges responsible for the review and management of the progress and readiness of the case for trial: *R. (Snelgrove) v. Woolwich Crown Court* [2005] 1 Cr.App.R. 18, DC.

B. SENDINGS FOR TRIAL

(1) Introduction

Pending the commencement of the substitution by the *CJA* 2003 of new sections 51 to 51E of the *CDA* 1998 for the original section 51, that section provides for offenders charged with offences triable only on indictment (and related either way and summary offences) to be "sent" to the Crown Court for trial: see *post*, § 1–17. The substituted sections (*post*, §§ 1–18 *et seq.*), when they come into force, will amend that procedure and will extend its ambit, as explained *ante*, § 1–14. **1–15**

Section 52 (*post*, § 1–24) supplements the primary provisions, and gives effect to Schedule 3 (*post*, § 1–27), which contains the detailed procedural provisions, including provision for the taking of depositions from reluctant witnesses, the use of such depositions, the procedure where no offence forming the basis for a sending remains and the power of the Crown Court to deal with summary offences. Sections 52A and 52B of the 1998 Act, when they are in force, will impose reporting restrictions in respect of allocation and sending proceedings and create offences in respect of the breach of those restrictions (*post*, § 1–25).

As to the first appearance in the Crown Court following a sending, see *post*, § 1–36, and as to the service of the prosecution evidence following a sending, see *post*, § 1–37.

Once the case is at the Crown Court, the defendant may apply for the dismissal of any charge on which he has been sent for trial, as to which see paragraph 2 of Schedule 3 to the 1998 Act (*post*, § 1–28), and see further *post*, §§ 1–38 *et seq*. Paragraph 3 of Schedule 3 imposes reporting restrictions in respect of dismissal applications and creates offences in respect of the breach of those restrictions.

(2) Sending of cases to the Crown Court

Crime and Disorder Act 1998, ss.50A, 51–51E

[Order of consideration for either-way offences

50A.—(1) Where an adult appears or is brought before a magistrates' court charged with an either-way offence (the "relevant offence"), the court shall proceed in the manner described in this section. **1–16**

(2) If notice is given in respect of the relevant offence under section 51B or 51C below, the court shall deal with the offence as provided in section 51 below.

(3) Otherwise—

(a) if the adult (or another adult with whom the adult is charged jointly with the relevant offence) is or has been sent to the Crown Court for trial for an offence under section 51(2)(a) or 51(2)(c) below—

(i) the court shall first consider the relevant offence under subsection (3), (4), (5) or, as the case may be, (6) of section 51 below and, where applicable, deal with it under that subsection;

(ii) if the adult is not sent to the Crown Court for trial for the relevant offence by virtue of sub-paragraph (i) above, the court shall then proceed to deal with the relevant offence in accordance with sections 17A to 23 of the 1980 Act;

(b) in all other cases—

(i) the court shall first consider the relevant offence under sections 17A to 20 (excluding subsections (8) and (9) of section 20) of the 1980 Act;

(ii) if, by virtue of sub-paragraph (i) above, the court would be required to proceed in relation to the offence as mentioned in section 17A(6), 17B(2)(c) or 20(7) of that Act (indication of guilty plea), it shall proceed as so required (and, accordingly, shall not consider the offence under section 51 or 51A below);

(iii) if sub-paragraph (ii) above does not apply—

(a) the court shall consider the relevant offence under sections 51 and 51A below and, where applicable, deal with it under the relevant section;

(b) if the adult is not sent to the Crown Court for trial for the relevant offence by virtue of paragraph (a) of this sub-paragraph, the court shall then proceed to deal with the relevant offence as contemplated by section 20(9) or, as the case may be, section 21 of the 1980 Act.

(4) Subsection (3) above is subject to any requirement to proceed as mentioned in subsections (2) or (6)(a) of section 22 of the 1980 Act (certain offences where value involved is small).

(5) Nothing in this section shall prevent the court from committing the adult to the Crown Court for sentence pursuant to any enactment, if he is convicted of the relevant offence.]

[This section is inserted by the *CJA* 2003, s.41, and Sched. 3, paras 15 and 17, which come into force on a day or days to be appointed: *ibid*., s.336(3) and (4).]

No committal proceedings for indictable-only offences

1–17 **51.**—(1) *Where an adult appears or is brought before a magistrates' court ("the court") charged with an offence triable only on indictment ("the indictable-only offence"), the court shall send him forthwith to the Crown Court for trial—*

(a) *for that offence, and*

(b) *for any either-way or summary offence with which he is charged which fulfils the requisite conditions (as set out in subsection (11) below).*

(2) *Where an adult who has been sent for trial under subsection (1) above subsequently appears or is brought before a magistrates' court charged with an either-way or summary offence which fulfils the requisite conditions, the court may send him forthwith to the Crown Court for trial for the either-way or summary offence.*

(3) *Where—*

(a) *the court sends an adult for trial under subsection (1) above;*

(b) *another adult appears or is brought before the court on the same or a subsequent occasion charged jointly with him with an either-way offence; and*

(c) *that offence appears to the court to be related to the indictable-only offence,*

the court shall where it is the same occasion, and may where it is a subsequent occasion, send the other adult forthwith to the Crown Court for trial for the either-way offence.

(4) *Where a court sends an adult for trial under subsection (3) above, it shall at the same time send him to the Crown Court for trial for any either-way or summary offence with which he is charged which fulfils the requisite conditions.*

(5) *Where—*

(a) *the court sends an adult for trial under subsection (1) or (3) above; and*

(b) *a child or young person appears or is brought before the court on the same or a subsequent occasion charged jointly with the adult with an indictable offence for which the adult is sent for trial,*

the court shall, if it considers it necessary in the interests of justice to do so, send the child or young person forthwith to the Crown Court for trial for the indictable offence.

(6) *Where a court sends a child or young person for trial under subsection (5) above, it may at the same time send him to the Crown Court for trial for any either-way or summary offence with which he is charged which fulfils the requisite conditions.*

(7) *The court shall specify in a notice the offence or offences for which a person is sent for trial under this section and the place at which he is to be tried; and a copy of the notice shall be served on the accused and given to the Crown Court sitting at that place.*

(8) *In a case where there is more than one indictable-only offence and the court includes an either-way or a summary offence in the notice under subsection (7) above, the court shall specify in that notice the indictable-only offence to which the either-way offence or, as the case may be, the summary offence appears to the court to be related.*

(9) *The trial of the information charging any summary offence for which a person is sent for trial under this section shall be treated as if the court had adjourned it under section 10 of the 1980 Act and had not fixed the time and place for its resumption.*

(10) *In selecting the place of trial for the purpose of subsection (7) above, the court shall have regard to—*

(a) *the convenience of the defence, the prosecution and the witnesses;*

(b) *the desirability of expediting the trial; and*

(c) *any direction given by or on behalf of the Lord Chief Justice with the concurrence of the Lord Chancellor under section 75(1) of the* Supreme Court Act *1981.*

(11) *An offence fulfils the requisite conditions if—*

(a) *it appears to the court to be related to the indictable-only offence; and*

(b) *in the case of a summary offence, it is punishable with imprisonment or involves obligatory or discretionary disqualification from driving.*

(12) *For the purposes of this section—*

(a) *"adult" means a person aged 18 or over, and references to an adult include references to a corporation;*

(b) *"either-way offence" means an offence which, if committed by an adult, is triable either on indictment or summarily;*

(c) *an either-way offence is related to an indictable-only offence if the charge for the either-way offence could be joined in the same indictment as the charge for the indictable-only offence;*

(d) *a summary offence is related to an indictable-only offence if it arises out of circumstances which are the same as or connected with those giving rise to the indictable-only offence.*

[New ss.51 to 51E (*post*) are substituted for this section by the *CJA* 2003, s.41, and Sched. 3, paras 15 and 18. The insertion of the new s.51A, except subs. (3)(a) to (c), came into force on April 4, 2005, as did the insertion of the new sections 51D and 51E, but only in relation to cases sent under section 51A(3)(d): *Criminal Justice Act 2003 (Commencement No. 8 and Transitional and Saving Provisions) Order* 2005 (S.I. 2005 No. 950). The new provisions otherwise come into force on a day or days to be appointed, any further information as to which will be noted in the supplement to this work.]

[Sending cases to the Crown Court: adults

51.—(1) Where an adult appears or is brought before a magistrates' court ("the court") charged with an offence and any of the conditions mentioned in subsection (2) below is satisfied, the court shall send him forthwith to the Crown Court for trial for the offence. **1–18**

(2) Those conditions are—

(a) that the offence is an offence triable only on indictment other than one in respect of which notice has been given under section 51B or 51C below;

(b) that the offence is an either-way offence and the court is required under section 20(9)(b), 21, 23(4)(b) or (5) or 25(2D) of the *Magistrates' Courts Act* 1980 to proceed in relation to the offence in accordance with subsection (1) above;

(c) that notice is given to the court under section 51B or 51C below in respect of the offence.

(3) Where the court sends an adult for trial under subsection (1) above, it shall at the same time send him to the Crown Court for trial for any either-way or summary offence with which he is charged and which—

(a) (if it is an either-way offence) appears to the court to be related to the offence mentioned in subsection (1) above; or

(b) (if it is a summary offence) appears to the court to be related to the offence mentioned in subsection (1) above or to the either-way offence, and which fulfils the requisite condition (as defined in subsection (11) below).

(4) Where an adult who has been sent for trial under subsection (1) above subsequently appears or is brought before a magistrates' court charged with an either-way or summary offence which—

(a) appears to the court to be related to the offence mentioned in subsection (1) above; and

(b) (in the case of a summary offence) fulfils the requisite condition,

the court may send him forthwith to the Crown Court for trial for the either-way or summary offence.

(5) Where—

(a) the court sends an adult ("A") for trial under subsection (1) or (3) above;

(b) another adult appears or is brought before the court on the same or a subsequent occasion charged jointly with A with an either-way offence; and

(c) that offence appears to the court to be related to an offence for which A was sent for trial under subsection (1) or (3) above,

the court shall where it is the same occasion, and may where it is a subsequent occasion, send the other adult forthwith to the Crown Court for trial for the either-way offence.

(6) Where the court sends an adult for trial under subsection (5) above, it shall at the same time send him to the Crown Court for trial for any either-way or summary offence with which he is charged and which—

(a) (if it is an either-way offence) appears to the court to be related to the offence for which he is sent for trial; and

(b) (if it is a summary offence) appears to the court to be related to the offence for which he is sent for trial or to the either-way offence, and which fulfils the requisite condition.

(7) Where—

(a) the court sends an adult ('A') for trial under subsection (1), (3) or (5) above; and

(b) a child or young person appears or is brought before the court on the same or a subsequent occasion charged jointly with A with an indictable offence for which A is sent for trial under subsection (1), (3) or (5) above, or an indictable offence which appears to the court to be related to that offence,

the court shall, if it considers it necessary in the interests of justice to do so, send the child or young person forthwith to the Crown Court for trial for the indictable offence.

(8) Where the court sends a child or young person for trial under subsection (7) above, it may at the same time send him to the Crown Court for trial for any indictable or summary offence with which he is charged and which—

(a) (if it is an indictable offence) appears to the court to be related to the offence for which he is sent for trial; and

(b) (if it is a summary offence) appears to the court to be related to the offence for which he is sent for trial or to the indictable offence, and which fulfils the requisite condition.

(9) Subsections (7) and (8) above are subject to sections 24A and 24B of the *Magistrates' Courts Act* 1980 (which provide for certain cases involving children and young persons to be tried summarily).

(10) The trial of the information charging any summary offence for which a person is sent for trial under this section shall be treated as if the court had adjourned it under section 10 of the 1980 Act and had not fixed the time and place for its resumption.

(11) A summary offence fulfils the requisite condition if it is punishable with imprisonment or involves obligatory or discretionary disqualification from driving.

(12) In the case of an adult charged with an offence—

(a) if the offence satisfies paragraph (c) of subsection (2) above, the offence shall be dealt with under subsection (1) above and not under any other provision of this section or section 51A below;

(b) subject to paragraph (a) above, if the offence is one in respect of which the court is required to, or would decide to, send the adult to the Crown Court under—

(i) subsection (5) above; or

(ii) subsection (6) of section 51A below,

the offence shall be dealt with under that subsection and not under any other provision of this section or section 51A below.

(13) The functions of a magistrates' court under this section, and its related functions under section 51D below, may be discharged by a single justice.]

[As to the insertion of this section, see the note to the original s.51, *ante*, § 1–17.]

[Sending cases to the Crown Court: children and young persons

1–19 **51A.**—(1) This section is subject to sections 24A and 24B of the *Magistrates' Courts Act* 1980 (which provide for certain offences involving children or young persons to be tried summarily).

(2) Where a child or young person appears or is brought before a magistrates' court ("the court") charged with an offence and any of the conditions mentioned in subsection (3) below is satisfied, the court shall send him forthwith to the Crown Court for trial for the offence.

(3) Those conditions are—

(a) that the offence falls within subsection (12) below;

(b) that the offence is such as is mentioned in subsection (1) of section 91 of the

Powers of Criminal Courts (Sentencing) Act 2000 (other than one mentioned in paragraph (d) below in relation to which it appears to the court as mentioned there) and the court considers that if he is found guilty of the offence it ought to be possible to sentence him in pursuance of subsection (3) of that section;

(c) that notice is given to the court under section 51B or 51C below in respect of the offence;

(d) that the offence is a specified offence (within the meaning of section 224 of the *Criminal Justice Act* 2003) and it appears to the court that if he is found guilty of the offence the criteria for the imposition of a sentence under section 226(3) or 228(2) of that Act would be met.

(4) Where the court sends a child or young person for trial under subsection (2) above, it may at the same time send him to the Crown Court for trial for any indictable or summary offence with which he is charged and which—

(a) (if it is an indictable offence) appears to the court to be related to the offence mentioned in subsection (2) above; or

(b) (if it is a summary offence) appears to the court to be related to the offence mentioned in subsection (2) above or to the indictable offence, and which fulfils the requisite condition (as defined in subsection (9) below).

(5) Where a child or young person who has been sent for trial under subsection (2) above subsequently appears or is brought before a magistrates' court charged with an indictable or summary offence which—

(a) appears to the court to be related to the offence mentioned in subsection (2) above; and

(b) (in the case of a summary offence) fulfils the requisite condition,

the court may send him forthwith to the Crown Court for trial for the indictable or summary offence.

(6) Where—

(a) the court sends a child or young person ("C") for trial under subsection (2) or (4) above; and

(b) an adult appears or is brought before the court on the same or a subsequent occasion charged jointly with C with an either-way offence for which C is sent for trial under subsection (2) or (4) above, or an either-way offence which appears to the court to be related to that offence,

the court shall where it is the same occasion, and may where it is a subsequent occasion, send the adult forthwith to the Crown Court for trial for the either-way offence.

(7) Where the court sends an adult for trial under subsection (6) above, it shall at the same time send him to the Crown Court for trial for any either-way or summary offence with which he is charged and which—

(a) (if it is an either-way offence) appears to the court to be related to the offence for which he was sent for trial; and

(b) (if it is a summary offence) appears to the court to be related to the offence for which he was sent for trial or to the eitherway offence, and which fulfils the requisite condition.

(8) The trial of the information charging any summary offence for which a person is sent for trial under this section shall be treated as if the court had adjourned it under section 10 of the 1980 Act and had not fixed the time and place for its resumption.

(9) A summary offence fulfils the requisite condition if it is punishable with imprisonment or involves obligatory or discretionary disqualification from driving.

(10) In the case of a child or young person charged with an offence—

(a) if the offence satisfies any of the conditions in subsection (3) above, the offence shall be dealt with under subsection (2) above and not under any other provision of this section or section 51 above;

(b) subject to paragraph (a) above, if the offence is one in respect of which the requirements of subsection (7) of section 51 above for sending the child or young person to the Crown Court are satisfied, the offence shall be dealt with under that subsection and not under any other provision of this section or section 51 above.

(11) The functions of a magistrates' court under this section, and its related functions under section 51D below, may be discharged by a single justice.

(12) An offence falls within this subsection if—

(a) it is an offence of homicide;

(b) each of the requirements of section 51A(1) of the *Firearms Act* 1968 would be satisfied with respect to—
   (i) the offence; and
   (ii) the person charged with it,

if he were convicted of the offence; or

(c) section 29(3) of the *Violent Crime Reduction Act* 2006 (minimum sentences in certain cases of using someone to mind a weapon) would apply if he were convicted of the offence.]

[As to the insertion of this section, which as at September 20, 2008, was in force to a limited extent only, see the details in the note to the original s.51, *ante*, § 1-17. Subs. (12) is printed as amended and repealed in part by the *VCRA* 2006, ss.49 and 65, and Scheds 1, para. 5, and 5.]

[Notices in serious or complex fraud cases

1-20 **51B.**—(1) A notice may be given by a designated authority under this section in respect of an indictable offence if the authority is of the opinion that the evidence of the offence charged—

(a) is sufficient for the person charged to be put on trial for the offence; and
(b) reveals a case of fraud of such seriousness or complexity that it is appropriate that the management of the case should without delay be taken over by the Crown Court.

(2) That opinion must be certified by the designated authority in the notice.

(3) The notice must also specify the proposed place of trial, and in selecting that place the designated authority must have regard to the same matters as are specified in paragraphs (a) to (c) of section 51D(4) below.

(4) A notice under this section must be given to the magistrates' court at which the person charged appears or before which he is brought.

(5) Such a notice must be given to the magistrates' court before any summary trial begins.

(6) The effect of such a notice is that the functions of the magistrates' court cease in relation to the case, except—

(a) for the purposes of section 51D below;
(b) as provided by paragraph 2 of Schedule 3 to the *Access to Justice Act* 1999; and
(c) as provided by section 52 below.

(7) The functions of a designated authority under this section may be exercised by an officer of the authority acting on behalf of the authority.

(8) A decision to give a notice under this section shall not be subject to appeal or liable to be questioned in any court (whether a magistrates' court or not).

(9) In this section "designated authority" means

(a) the Director of Public Prosecutions;
(b) the Director of the Serious Fraud Office;
(c) the Director of Revenue and Customs Prosecutions;
(d) ...; or
(e) the Secretary of State.]

[Subs. (9) is printed as amended by the *Commissioners for Revenue and Customs Act* 2005, s.50(6), and Sched. 4, para. 69. As to the insertion of this section, see the note to the original s.51, *ante*, § 1-17.]

[Notices in certain cases involving children

1-21 **51C.**—(1) A notice may be given by the Director of Public Prosecutions under this section in respect of an offence falling within subsection (3) below if he is of the opinion—

(a) that the evidence of the offence would be sufficient for the person charged to be put on trial for the offence;
(b) that a child would be called as a witness at the trial; and
(c) that, for the purpose of avoiding any prejudice to the welfare of the child, the case should be taken over and proceeded with without delay by the Crown Court.

(2) That opinion must be certified by the Director of Public Prosecutions in the notice.

(3) This subsection applies to an offence—

(a) which involves an assault on, or injury or a threat of injury to, a person;
(b) under section 1 of the *Children and Young Persons Act* 1933 (cruelty to persons under 16);

(c) under the *Sexual Offences Act* 1956, the *Protection of Children Act* 1978 or the *Sexual Offences Act* 2003;

(d) of kidnapping or false imprisonment, or an offence under section 1 or 2 of the *Child Abduction Act* 1984;

(e) which consists of attempting or conspiring to commit, or of aiding, abetting, counselling, procuring or inciting the commission of, an offence falling within paragraph (a), (b), (c) or (d) above.

(4) Subsections (4), (5) and (6) of section 51B above apply for the purposes of this section as they apply for the purposes of that.

(5) The functions of the Director of Public Prosecutions under this section may be exercised by an officer acting on behalf of the Director.

(6) A decision to give a notice under this section shall not be subject to appeal or liable to be questioned in any court (whether a magistrates' court or not).

(7) In this section "child" means—

(a) a person who is under the age of 17; or

(b) any person of whom a video recording (as defined in section 63(1) of the *Youth Justice and Criminal Evidence Act* 1999) was made when he was under the age of 17 with a view to its admission as his evidence in chief in the trial referred to in subsection (1) above.]

[As to the insertion of this section, see the note to the original s.51, *ante*, § 1–17. The reference in subs. (3)(e) to the common law offence of incitement has effect as a reference to the offences under the *SCA* 2007, Pt 2: 2007 Act, s.63(1), and Sched. 6, para. 36.]

[Notice of offence and place of trial

51D.—(1) The court shall specify in a notice— **1–22**

(a) the offence or offences for which a person is sent for trial under section 51 or 51A above; and

(b) the place at which he is to be tried (which, if a notice has been given under section 51B above, must be the place specified in that notice).

(2) A copy of the notice shall be served on the accused and given to the Crown Court sitting at that place.

(3) In a case where a person is sent for trial under section 51 or 51A above for more than one offence, the court shall specify in that notice, for each offence—

(a) the subsection under which the person is so sent; and

(b) if applicable, the offence to which that offence appears to the court to be related.

(4) Where the court selects the place of trial for the purposes of subsection (1) above, it shall have regard to—

(a) the convenience of the defence, the prosecution and the witnesses;

(b) the desirability of expediting the trial; and

(c) any direction given by or on behalf of the Lord Chief Justice with the concurrence of the Lord Chancellor under section 75(1) of the *Supreme Court [Senior Courts] Act* 1981].

[As to the insertion of this section, which as at September 20, 2008, was in force to a limited extent only, see the note to the original s.51, *ante*, § 1–17. The *Supreme Court Act* 1981 is renamed the *Senior Courts Act* 1981 as from a day to be appointed: *Constitutional Reform Act* 2005, s.59(5), and Sched. 11, para. 1(2).]

[Interpretation of sections 50A to 51D

51E. For the purposes of sections 50A to 51D above— **1–23**

(a) "adult" means a person aged 18 or over, and references to an adult include a corporation;

(b) "either-way offence" means an offence triable either way;

(c) an either-way offence is related to an indictable offence if the charge for the either-way offence could be joined in the same indictment as the charge for the indictable offence;

(d) a summary offence is related to an indictable offence if it arises out of circumstances which are the same as or connected with those giving rise to the indictable offence.]

[As to the insertion of this section, which as at September 20, 2008, was in force to a limited extent only, see the note to the original s.51, *ante*, § 1–17.]

The procedure for sending cases for trial under section 51 of the 1998 Act applies as much to a situation where a defendant is charged with an offence within that section on a second or subsequent appearance before a magistrates' court as where he faces such a charge on his first appearance; the relevant wording is general in this respect: *R. (Salubi) v. Bow Street Magistrates' Court*; *R. (Harmer) v. Commrs for Customs and Excise*; *R. (Ojutaleyo) v. Bournmouth Crown Court*; *R. (Boucher) v. Luton Crown Court* [2002] 2 Cr.App.R. 40, DC.

The duty of the court under section 51 to send cases to the Crown Court does not preclude it from staying the proceedings as an abuse of process, although this will only rarely be appropriate (instances of which may include the addition of an unmeritorious indictable only charge for an improper tactical purpose); novel or complex points should normally be left for resolution in the Crown Court or High Court: *ibid*.

Rule 12.1 of the *Criminal Procedure Rules* 2005 (S.I 2005 No. 384) (not printed in this work) lists the documents that must be sent to the Crown Court by a magistrates' court when there is a sending under section 51 and specifies the time within which those documents must be sent.

In *R. v. McGrath* [2004] 1 Cr.App.R. 15, CA, it was said, *obiter*, that given the plain unqualified obligation on magistrates' courts, imposed by section 51, to send relevant cases for trial, and the fact that the requirements as to the contents of notices of such sending is adjectival to that section, it might be difficult to argue that the existence of the substantive duty in any case depends on proper compliance with the duties as to the giving of notice. However, that was not to say that a failure to fulfil the notice requirements might not give rise to due process arguments if prejudice or unfairness were occasioned.

Section 51(7) (and, prospectively, section 51D) requires the offences for which a person is sent for trial to be specified in a notice that is to be served on the accused and given to the Crown Court; such a notice should, at least as a matter of good practice, either summarise the offences so as to particularise them adequately, or cross-refer to documents which are to be sent to the Crown Court and which do set out adequate particulars of the charges sent, such as a memorandum of the relevant entry in the register of the magistrates' court, or (if the charge has not been amended) the charge sheet, but inadequacy in this regard will not invalidate the sending for trial: *Bentham v. Governor of H.M. Prison Wandsworth* [2006] Crim.L.R. 855, DC. See *post*, § 1–40 as to the potential significance of any such inadequacy in relation to an application for dismissal pursuant to Schedule 3 to the 1998 Act, and see generally *post*, §§ 1–35, 1–195 *et seq.* and 2–8, as to the potential consequences of non-compliance with procedural requirements.

As to the choice of location of the Crown Court to be specified in a notice given under section 51 of the 1998 Act, see *post*, § 2–18. As to the power of the Crown Court to alter the place for trial that has been specified in a notice given under section 51 or section 51D of the 1998 Act, see section 76 of the *Supreme Court [Senior Courts] Act* 1981 (renamed, as from a day to be appointed, by the *Constitutional Reform Act* 2005, s.59, and Sched. 11, para. 1) and *R. v. Croydon Crown Court, ex p. Britton*, *post*, § 2–13.

As to the conflict between section 51A of the 1998 Act and section 24 of the *MCA* 1980, and as to the approach to be followed in applying those provisions, see *post*, § 1–75m.

(3) Supplementary provision

Crime and Disorder Act 1998, s.52

Provisions supplementing section 51 [and 51A]

1–24 **52.**—(1) Subject to section 4 of the *Bail Act* 1976, section 41 of the 1980 Act, regulations under section 22 of the 1985 Act and section 25 of the 1994 Act, the court may send a person for trial under section 51 [or 51A] above—

(a) in custody, that is to say, by committing him to custody there to be safely kept until delivered in due course of law; or

(b) on bail in accordance with the *Bail Act* 1976, that is to say, by directing him to appear before the Crown Court for trial.

(2) Where—

(a) the person's release on bail under subsection (1)(b) above is conditional on his providing one or more sureties; and

(b) in accordance with subsection (3) of section 8 of the *Bail Act* 1976, the court fixes the amount in which a surety is to be bound with a view to his entering into his recognisance subsequently in accordance with subsections (4) and (5) or (6) of that section,

the court shall in the meantime make an order such as is mentioned in subsection (1)(a) above.

(3) The court shall treat as an indictable offence for the purposes of section 51 [or 51A] above an offence which is mentioned in the first column of Schedule 2 to the 1980 Act (offences for which the value involved is relevant to the mode of trial) unless it is clear to the court, having regard to any representations made by the prosecutor or the accused, that the value involved does not exceed the relevant sum.

(4) In subsection (3) above "the value involved" and "the relevant sum" have the same meanings as in section 22 of the 1980 Act (certain offences triable either way to be tried summarily if value involved is small).

(5) A magistrates' court may adjourn any proceedings under section 51 [or 51A] above, and if it does so shall remand the accused.

(6) Schedule 3 to this Act (which makes further provision in relation to persons sent to the Crown Court for trial under section 51 [or 51A] above) shall have effect.

[The references in square brackets to section 51A are inserted by the *CJA* 2003, s.41, and Sched. 3, paras 68 and 69. Those insertions took effect from May 9, 2005, in relation to cases sent for trial under section 51A(3)(d) of the 1998 Act (*ante*, § 1–19): *Criminal Justice Act 2003 (Commencement No. 9) Order* 2005 (S.I. 2005 No. 1267). For all other purposes they will take effect on a day or days to be appointed.]

(4) Reporting restrictions

Crime and Disorder Act 1998, ss.52A, 52B

[Restrictions on reporting

52A.—(1) Except as provided by this section, it shall not be lawful— **1–25**

(a) to publish in the United Kingdom a written report of any allocation or sending proceedings in England and Wales; or

(b) to include in a relevant programme for reception in the United Kingdom a report of any such proceedings,

if (in either case) the report contains any matter other than that permitted by this section.

(2) Subject to subsections (3) and (4) below, a magistrates' court may, with reference to any allocation or sending proceedings, order that subsection (1) above shall not apply to reports of those proceedings.

(3) Where there is only one accused and he objects to the making of an order under subsection (2) above, the court shall make the order if, and only if, it is satisfied, after hearing the representations of the accused, that it is in the interests of justice to do so.

(4) Where in the case of two or more accused one of them objects to the making of an order under subsection (2) above, the court shall make the order if, and only if, it is satisfied, after hearing the representations of the accused, that it is in the interests of justice to do so.

(5) An order under subsection (2) above shall not apply to reports of proceedings under subsection (3) or (4) above, but any decision of the court to make or not to make such an order may be contained in reports published or included in a relevant programme before the time authorised by subsection (6) below.

(6) It shall not be unlawful under this section to publish or include in a relevant programme a report of allocation or sending proceedings containing any matter other than that permitted by subsection (7) below—

(a) where, in relation to the accused (or all of them, if there are more than one), the magistrates' court is required to proceed as mentioned in section 20(7) of the 1980 Act, after the court is so required;

(b) where, in relation to the accused (or any of them, if there are more than one), the court proceeds other than as mentioned there, after conclusion of his trial or, as the case may be, the trial of the last to be tried.

(7) The following matters may be contained in a report of allocation or sending proceedings published or included in a relevant programme without an order under subsection (2) above before the time authorised by subsection (6) above—

(a) the identity of the court and the name of the justice or justices;
(b) the name, age, home address and occupation of the accused;
(c) in the case of an accused charged with an offence in respect of which notice has been given to the court under section 51B above, any relevant business information;
(d) the offence or offences, or a summary of them, with which the accused is or are charged;
(e) the names of counsel and solicitors engaged in the proceedings;
(f) where the proceedings are adjourned, the date and place to which they are adjourned;
(g) the arrangements as to bail;
(h) whether a right to representation funded by the Legal Services Commission as part of the Criminal Defence Service was granted to the accused or any of the accused.

(8) The addresses that may be published or included in a relevant programme under subsection (7) above are addresses—
(a) at any relevant time; and
(b) at the time of their publication or inclusion in a relevant programme.

(9) The following is relevant business information for the purposes of subsection (7) above—
(a) any address used by the accused for carrying on a business on his own account;
(b) the name of any business which he was carrying on on his own account at any relevant time;
(c) the name of any firm in which he was a partner at any relevant time or by which he was engaged at any such time;
(d) the address of any such firm;
(e) the name of any company of which he was a director at any relevant time or by which he was otherwise engaged at any such time;
(f) the address of the registered or principal office of any such company;
(g) any working address of the accused in his capacity as a person engaged by any such company;

and here "engaged" means engaged under a contract of service or a contract for services.

(10) Subsection (1) above shall be in addition to, and not in derogation from, the provisions of any other enactment with respect to the publication of reports of court proceedings.

(11) In this section—

"allocation or sending proceedings" means, in relation to an information charging an indictable offence—
(a) any proceedings in the magistrates' court at which matters are considered under any of the following provisions—
(i) sections 19 to 23 of the 1980 Act;
(ii) section 51, 51A or 52 above;
(b) any proceedings in the magistrates' court before the court proceeds to consider any matter mentioned in paragraph (a) above; and
(c) any proceedings in the magistrates' court at which an application under section 25(2) of the 1980 Act is considered;

"publish", in relation to a report, means publish the report, either by itself or as part of a newspaper or periodical, for distribution to the public;

"relevant programme" means a programme included in a programme service (within the meaning of the *Broadcasting Act* 1990);

"relevant time" means a time when events giving rise to the charges to which the proceedings relate occurred.]

[Offences in connection with reporting

1–26 **52B.**—(1) If a report is published or included in a relevant programme in contravention of section 52A above, each of the following persons is guilty of an offence—
(a) in the case of a publication of a written report as part of a newspaper or periodical, any proprietor, editor or publisher of the newspaper or periodical;
(b) in the case of a publication of a written report otherwise than as part of a newspaper or periodical, the person who publishes it;
(c) in the case of the inclusion of a report in a relevant programme, any body corporate which is engaged in providing the service in which the programme is

included and any person having functions in relation to the programme corresponding to those of the editor of a newspaper.

(2) A person guilty of an offence under this section is liable on summary conviction to a fine not exceeding level 5 on the standard scale.

(3) Proceedings for an offence under this section shall not, in England and Wales, be instituted otherwise than by or with the consent of the Attorney General.

(4) Proceedings for an offence under this section shall not, in Northern Ireland, be instituted otherwise than by or with the consent of the Attorney General for Northern Ireland.

(5) Subsection (11) of section 52A above applies for the purposes of this section as it applies for the purposes of that section.]

[Sections 52A and 52B are inserted by the *CJA* 2003, s.41, and Sched. 3, para. 19(1), which come into force on a day or days to be appointed: *ibid.*, s.336(3) and (4).]

(5) Procedure

Crime and Disorder Act 1998, Sched. 3

Section 52(6) SCHEDULE 3

PROCEDURE WHERE PERSONS ARE SENT FOR TRIAL UNDER SECTION 51

Regulations

1. The Attorney General shall by regulations [*see* post, *§ 1–37 as to the relevant regulations*] provide that, where a person is sent for trial under section 51 [or 51A] of this Act on any charge or charges, copies of the documents containing the evidence on which the charge or charges are based shall, ... **1–27**

(a) be served on that person; and

(b) be given to the Crown Court sitting at the place specified in the notice under *subsection (7) of that section* [section 51D of this Act],

before the expiry of the period prescribed by the regulations; but the judge may at his discretion extend or further extend that period.

(2) The regulations may make provision as to the procedure to be followed on an application for the extension or further extension of a period under sub-paragraph (1) above [*sic*].

Applications for dismissal

2.—(1) A person who is sent for trial under section 51 [or 51A] of this Act on any charge or charges may, at any time— **1–28**

(a) after he is served with copies of the documents containing the evidence on which the charge or charges are based; and

(b) before he is arraigned (and whether or not an indictment has been preferred against him),

apply orally or in writing to the Crown Court sitting at the place specified in the notice under *subsection (7) of that section* [section 51D of this Act] for the charge, or any of the charges, in the case to be dismissed.

(2) The judge shall dismiss a charge (and accordingly quash any count relating to it in any indictment preferred against the applicant) which is the subject of any such application if it appears to him that the evidence against the applicant would not be sufficient for him to be properly convicted.

(3) No oral application may be made under sub-paragraph (1) above unless the applicant has given to the Crown Court sitting at the place in question written notice of his intention to make the application.

(4) *Oral evidence may be given on such an application only with the leave of the judge or by his order; and the judge shall give leave or make an order only if it appears to him, having regard to any matters stated in the application for leave, that the interests of justice require him to do so.*

(5) *If the judge gives leave permitting, or makes an order requiring, a person to give oral evidence, but that person does not do so, the judge may disregard any document indicating the evidence that he might have given.*

(6) If the charge, or any of the charges, against the applicant is dismissed—

(a) no further proceedings may be brought on the dismissed charge or charges except by means of the preferment of a voluntary bill of indictment; and

(b) unless the applicant is in custody otherwise than on the dismissed charge or charges, he shall be discharged.

(7) Criminal Procedure Rules may make provision for the purposes of this paragraph [*see* post, *§ 1–39 for the relevant rules*] and, without prejudice to the generality of this sub-paragraph, may make provision—

(a) as to the time or stage in the proceedings at which anything required to be done is to be done (unless the court grants leave to do it at some other time or stage);

(b) as to the contents and form of notices or other documents;

(c) as to the manner in which evidence is to be submitted; and

(d) as to persons to be served with notices or other material.

Reporting restrictions

1–29 3.—(1) Except as provided by this paragraph, it shall not be lawful—

(a) to publish in *Great Britain* [the United Kingdom] a written report of an application under paragraph 2(1) above; or

(b) to include in a relevant programme for reception in *Great Britain* [the United Kingdom] a report of such an application,

if (in either case) the report contains any matter other than that permitted by this paragraph.

(2) An order that sub-paragraph (1) above shall not apply to reports of an application under paragraph 2(1) above may be made by the judge dealing with the application.

(3) Where in the case of two or more accused one of them objects to the making of an order under sub-paragraph (2) above, the judge shall make the order if, and only if, he is satisfied, after hearing the representations of the accused, that it is in the interests of justice to do so.

(4) An order under sub-paragraph (2) above shall not apply to reports of proceedings under sub-paragraph (3) above, but any decision of the court to make or not to make such an order may be contained in reports published or included in a relevant programme before the time authorised by sub-paragraph (5) below.

(5) It shall not be unlawful under this paragraph to publish or include in a relevant programme a report of an application under paragraph 2(1) above containing any matter other than that permitted by sub-paragraph (8) below where the application is successful.

(6) Where—

(a) two or more persons were jointly charged; and

(b) applications under paragraph 2(1) above are made by more than one of them,

sub-paragraph (5) above shall have effect as if for the words "the application is" there were substituted the words "all the applications are".

(7) It shall not be unlawful under this paragraph to publish or include in a relevant programme a report of an unsuccessful application at the conclusion of the trial of the person charged, or of the last of the persons charged to be tried.

(8) The following matters may be contained in a report published or included in a relevant programme without an order under sub-paragraph (2) above before the time authorised by sub-paragraphs (5) and (6) above, that is to say—

(a) the identity of the court and the name of the judge;

(b) the names, ages, home addresses and occupations of the accused and witnesses;

[(bb) where the application made by the accused under paragraph 2(1) above relates to a charge for an offence in respect of which notice has been given to the court under section 51B of this Act, any relevant business information;]

(c) the offence or offences, or a summary of them, with which the accused is or are charged;

(d) the names of counsel and solicitors engaged in the proceedings;

(e) where the proceedings are adjourned, the date and place to which they are adjourned;

(f) the arrangements as to bail;

(g) whether a right to representation funded by the Legal Services Commission as part of the Criminal Defence Service was granted to the accused or any of the accused.

(9) The addresses that may be published or included in a relevant programme under sub-paragraph (8) above are addresses—

(a) at any relevant time; and
(b) at the time of their publication or inclusion in a relevant programme.

[(9A) The following is relevant business information for the purposes of sub-paragraph (8) above—

(a) any address used by the accused for carrying on a business for his own account;
(b) the name of any business which he was carrying on on his own account at any relevant time;
(c) the name of any firm in which he was a partner at any relevant time or by which he was engaged at any such time;
(d) the address of any such firm;
(e) the name of any company of which he was a director at any relevant time or by which he was otherwise engaged at any such time;
(f) the address of the registered or principal office of any such company;
(g) any working address of the accused in his capacity as a person engaged by any such company;

and here "engaged" means engaged under a contract of service or a contract for services.]

(10) [*Summary offence of publication of report or inclusion thereof in relevant programme in breach of para. 6.*]

(11) Proceedings for an offence under this paragraph shall not, in England and Wales, be instituted otherwise than by or with the consent of the Attorney General.

[(11A) [*Northern Ireland.*]]

(12) Sub-paragraph (1) above shall be in addition to, and not in derogation from, the provisions of any other enactment with respect to the publication of reports of court proceedings.

(13) In this paragraph—

"publish", in relation to a report, means publish the report, either by itself or as part of a newspaper or periodical, for distribution to the public;

"relevant programme" means a programme included in a programme service (within the meaning of the *Broadcasting Act* 1990);

"relevant time" means a time when events giving rise to the charges to which the proceedings relate occurred.

Power of justice to take depositions etc.

4.—(1) Sub-paragraph (2) below applies where a justice of the peace for any commission area is satisfied that— **1–30**

(a) any person in England and Wales ("the witness") is likely to be able to make on behalf of the prosecutor a written statement containing material evidence, or produce on behalf of the prosecutor a document or other exhibit likely to be material evidence, for the purposes of proceedings for an offence for which a person has been sent for trial under section 51 [or 51A] of this Act by a magistrates' court for that area; and
(b) it is in the interests of justice to issue a summons under this paragraph to secure the attendance of the witness to have his evidence taken as a deposition or to produce the document or other exhibit.

(2) In such a case the justice shall issue a summons directed to the witness requiring him to attend before a justice at the time and place appointed in the summons, and to have his evidence taken as a deposition or to produce the document or other exhibit.

(3)–(5) [*Further process to secure attendance (arrest warrant, etc.).*]

(6) Where—

(a) a summons is issued under sub-paragraph (2) above or a warrant is issued under sub-paragraph (3) or (5) above; and
(b) the summons or warrant is issued with a view to securing that the witness has his evidence taken as a deposition,

the time appointed in the summons or specified in the warrant shall be such as to enable the evidence to be taken as a deposition before the relevant date.

(7), (8) [*Punishment for refusal to give evidence.*]

(9) If in pursuance of this paragraph a person has his evidence taken as a deposition, the chief executive to the justice concerned shall as soon as is reasonably practicable send a copy of the deposition to the prosecutor and the Crown Court.

(10) If in pursuance of this paragraph a person produces an exhibit which is a

document, the chief executive to the justice concerned shall as soon as is reasonably practicable send a copy of the document to the prosecutor and the Crown Court.

(11) If in pursuance of this paragraph a person produces an exhibit which is not a document, the chief executive to the justice concerned shall as soon as is reasonably practicable inform the prosecutor and the Crown Court of that fact and of the nature of the exhibit.

(12) In this paragraph—

"prescribed" means prescribed by Criminal Procedure Rules;

"the relevant date" *has the meaning given by paragraph 1(2) above* [means the expiry of the period referred to in paragraph 1(1) above].

Use of depositions as evidence

1–31 5.—(1) Subject to sub-paragraph (3) below, sub-paragraph (2) below applies where in pursuance of paragraph 4 above a person has his evidence taken as a deposition.

(2) Where this sub-paragraph applies the deposition may without further proof be read as evidence on the trial of the accused, whether for an offence for which he was sent for trial under section 51 [or 51A] of this Act or for any other offence arising out of the same transaction or set of circumstances.

(3) Sub-paragraph (2) above does not apply if—

(a) it is proved that the deposition was not signed by the justice by whom it purports to have been signed;

(b) the court of trial at its discretion orders that sub-paragraph (2) above shall not apply; or

(c) a party to the proceedings objects to sub-paragraph (2) above applying.

Power of Crown Court to deal with summary offence

1–32 6.—(1) This paragraph applies where a magistrates' court has sent a person for trial under section 51 [or 51A] of this Act for offences which include a summary offence.

(2) If the person is convicted on the indictment, the Crown Court shall consider whether the summary offence is related to the *offence that is triable only on indictment or, as the case may be, any of the offences that are so triable* [indictable offence for which he was sent for trial or, as the case may be, any of the indictable offences for which he was so sent].

(3) If it considers that the summary offence is so related, the court shall state to the person the substance of the offence and ask him whether he pleads guilty or not guilty.

(4) If the person pleads guilty, the Crown Court shall convict him, but may deal with him in respect of the summary offence only in a manner in which a magistrates' court could have dealt with him.

(5) If he does not plead guilty, the powers of the Crown Court shall cease in respect of the summary offence except as provided by sub-paragraph (6) below.

(6) If the prosecution inform the court that they would not desire to submit evidence on the charge relating to the summary offence, the court shall dismiss it.

(7) The Crown Court shall inform the chief executive to the magistrates' court of the outcome of any proceedings under this paragraph.

(8) If the summary offence is one to which section 40 of the *Criminal Justice Act* 1988 applies, the Crown Court may exercise in relation to the offence the power conferred by that section; but where the person is tried on indictment for such an offence, the functions of the Crown Court under this paragraph in relation to the offence shall cease.

(9) Where the Court of Appeal allows an appeal against conviction of an *indictable-only* [indictable] offence which is related to a summary offence of which the appellant was convicted under this paragraph—

(a) it shall set aside his conviction of the summary offence and give the clerk of the magistrates' court notice that it has done so; and

(b) it may direct that no further proceedings in relation to the offence are to be undertaken;

and the proceedings before the Crown Court in relation to the offence shall thereafter be disregarded for all purposes.

(10) A notice under sub-paragraph (9) above shall include particulars of any direction given under paragraph (b) of that sub-paragraph in relation to the offence.

(11) [*Repealed.*]

(12) An offence is related to another offence for the purposes of this paragraph if it arises out of circumstances which are the same as or connected with those giving rise to the other offence.

Procedure where no indictable-only offence remains

7.—(1) Subject to paragraph 13 below, this paragraph applies where— **1–33**

(a) a person has been sent for trial under section 51 [or 51A] of this Act but has not been arraigned; and

(b) the person is charged on an indictment which (following amendment of the indictment, or as a result of an application under paragraph 2 above, or for any other reason) includes no *offence that is triable only on indictment* [main offence].

(2) Everything that the Crown Court is required to do under the following provisions of this paragraph must be done with the accused present in court.

(3) The court shall cause to be read to the accused each [remaining] count of the indictment that charges an offence triable either way.

(4) The court shall then explain to the accused in ordinary language that, in relation to each of those offences, he may indicate whether (if it were to proceed to trial) he would plead guilty or not guilty, and that if he indicates that he would plead guilty the court must proceed as mentioned in sub-paragraph (6) below.

(5) The court shall then ask the accused whether (if the offence in question were to proceed to trial) he would plead guilty or not guilty.

(6) If the accused indicates that he would plead guilty the court shall proceed as if he had been arraigned on the count in question and had pleaded guilty.

(7) If the accused indicates that he would plead not guilty, or fails to indicate how he would plead, the court shall *consider* [decide] whether the offence is more suitable for summary trial or for trial on indictment.

(8) Subject to sub-paragraph (6) above, the following shall not for any purpose be taken to constitute the taking of a plea—

(a) asking the accused under this paragraph whether (if the offence were to proceed to trial) he would plead guilty or not guilty;

(b) an indication by the accused under this paragraph of how he would plead.

[(9) In this paragraph, a "main offence" is—

(a) an offence for which the person has been sent to the Crown Court for trial under section 51(1) of this Act; or

(b) an offence—

(i) for which the person has been sent to the Crown Court for trial under subsection (5) of section 51 or subsection (6) of section 51A of this Act ("the applicable subsection"); and

(ii) in respect of which the conditions for sending him to the Crown Court for trial under the applicable subsection (as set out in paragraphs (a) to (c) of section 51(5) or paragraphs (a) and (b) of section 51A(6)) continue to be satisfied.]

8.—(1) Subject to paragraph 13 below, this paragraph applies in a case where—

(a) a person has been sent for trial under section 51 [or 51A] of this Act but has not been arraigned;

(b) he is charged on an indictment which (following amendment of the indictment, or as a result of an application under paragraph 2 above, or for any other reason) includes *no offence that is triable only on indictment* [main offence (within the meaning of paragraph 7 above)];

(c) he is represented by a legal representative;

(d) the Crown Court considers that by reason of his disorderly conduct before the court it is not practicable for proceedings under paragraph 7 above to be conducted in his presence; and

(e) the court considers that it should proceed in his absence.

(2) In such a case—

(a) the court shall cause to be read to the representative each [remaining] count of the indictment that charges an offence triable either way;

(b) the court shall ask the representative whether (if the offence in question were to proceed to trial) the accused would plead guilty or not guilty;

(c) if the representative indicates that the accused would plead guilty the court shall proceed as if the accused had been arraigned on the count in question and had pleaded guilty;

(d) if the representative indicates that the accused would plead not guilty, or fails to indicate how the accused would plead, the court shall *consider* [decide] whether the offence is more suitable for summary trial or for trial on indictment.

(3) Subject to sub-paragraph (2)(c) above, the following shall not for any purpose be taken to constitute the taking of a plea—

(a) asking the representative under this section whether (if the offence were to proceed to trial) the accused would plead guilty or not guilty;

(b) an indication by the representative under this paragraph of how the accused would plead.

9.—(1) This paragraph applies where the Crown Court is required by paragraph 7(7) or 8(2)(d) above to *consider* [decide] the question whether an offence is more suitable for summary trial or for trial on indictment.

(2) *Before considering the question, the court shall afford first the prosecutor and then the accused an opportunity to make representations as to which mode of trial would be more suitable.*

(3) *In considering the question, the court shall have regard to—*

(a) *any representations made by the prosecutor or the accused;*

(b) *the nature of the case;*

(c) *whether the circumstances make the offence one of a serious character;*

(d) *whether the punishment which a magistrates' court would have power to impose for it would be adequate; and*

(e) *any other circumstances which appear to the court to make it more suitable for the offence to be dealt tried in one way rather than the other.*

[(2) Before deciding the question, the court—

(a) shall give the prosecution an opportunity to inform the court of the accused's previous convictions (if any); and

(b) shall give the prosecution and the accused an opportunity to make representations as to whether summary trial or trial on indictment would be more suitable.

(3) In deciding the question, the court shall consider—

(a) whether the sentence which a magistrates' court would have power to impose for the offence would be adequate; and

(b) any representations made by the prosecution or the accused under sub-paragraph (2)(b) above,

and shall have regard to any allocation guidelines (or revised allocation guidelines) issued as definitive guidelines under section 170 of the *Criminal Justice Act* 2003.

(4) Where—

(a) the accused is charged on the same occasion with two or more offences; and

(b) it appears to the court that they constitute or form part of a series of two or more offences of the same or a similar character;

sub-paragraph (3)(a) above shall have effect as if references to the sentence which a magistrates' court would have power to impose for the offence were a reference to the maximum aggregate sentence which a magistrates' court would have power to impose for all of the offences taken together.

(5) In this paragraph any reference to a previous conviction is a reference to—

(a) a previous conviction by a court in the United Kingdom, or

(b) *a previous finding of guilt in—*

(i) *any proceedings under the* Army Act *1955, the* Air Force Act *1955 or the* Naval Discipline Act *1957 (whether before a court-martial or any other court or person authorised under any of those Acts to award a punishment in respect of any offence), or*

(ii) *any proceedings before a Standing Civilian Court.*

[(b) a previous conviction of a service offence within the meaning of the *Armed Forces Act* 2006 ("conviction" here including anything that under section 376(1) and (2) of that Act is to be treated as a conviction)].]

10.—(1) This paragraph applies (unless excluded by paragraph 15 below) where the Crown Court considers that an offence is more suitable for summary trial.

(2) *The court shall explain to the accused in ordinary language—*

(a) *that it appears to the court more suitable for him to be tried summarily for the offence, and that he can either consent to be so tried or, of he wishes, be tried by a jury; and*

(b) *that if he is tried summarily and is convicted by the magistrates' court, he may be committed for sentence to the Crown Court under section 3 of the* Powers of Criminal Courts (Sentencing) Act *2000 if the convicting court is of such opinion as is mentioned in subsection (2) of that section.*

[(2) The court shall explain to the accused in ordinary language—

(a) that it appears to the court more suitable for him to be tried summarily for the offence;

(b) that he can either consent to be so tried or, if he wishes, be tried on indictment; and

(c) in the case of a specified offence (within the meaning of section 224 of the *Criminal Justice Act* 2003), that if he is tried summarily and is convicted by the court, he may be committed for sentence to the Crown Court under section 3A of the *Powers of Criminal Courts (Sentencing) Act* 2000 if the committing court is of such opinion as is mentioned in subsection (2) of that section.]

(3) After explaining to the accused as provided by sub-paragraph (2) above the court shall ask him whether he wishes to be tried summarily or *by a jury* [on indictment], and—

(a) if he indicates that he wishes to be tried summarily, shall remit him for trial to a magistrates' court acting for the place where he was sent to the Crown Court for trial;

(b) if he does not give such an indication, shall retain its functions in relation to the offence and proceed accordingly.

11. If the Crown Court considers that an offence is more suitable for trial on indictment, the court—

(a) shall tell the accused that it has decided that it is more suitable for him to be tried for the offence *by a jury* [on indictment]; and

(b) shall retain its functions in relation to the offence and proceed accordingly.

12.—(1) *Where the prosecution is being carried on by the Attorney General, the Solicitor General or the Director of Public Prosecutions and he applies for an offence which may be tried on indictment to be so tried—*

(a) *sub-paragraphs (4) to (8) of paragraph 7, sub-paragraphs (2)(b) to (d) and (3) of paragraph 8 and paragraphs 9 to 11 above shall not apply; and*

(b) *the Crown Court shall retain its functions in relation to the offence and proceed accordingly.*

(2) *The power of the Director of Public Prosecutions under this paragraph to apply for an offence to be tried on indictment shall not be exercised except with the consent of the Attorney General.*

13.—(1) This paragraph applies, in place of paragraphs 7 to 12 above, in the case of a child or young person who—

(a) has been sent for trial under section 51 [or 51A] of this Act but has not been arraigned; and

(b) is charged on an indictment which (following amendment of the indictment, or as a result of an application under paragraph 2 above, or for any other reason) includes no *offence that is triable only on indictment* [main offence].

(2) The Crown Court shall remit the child or young person for trial to a magistrates' court acting for the place where he was sent to the Crown Court for trial *unless—*

(a) *he is charged with such an offence as is mentioned in subsection (1) or (2) of section 91 of the* Powers of Criminal Courts (Sentencing) Act *2000 (punishment of certain grave crimes) and the Crown Court considers that if he is found guilty of the offence it ought to be possible to sentence him in pursuance of subsection (3) of that section; or*

(b) *he is charged jointly with an adult with an offence triable either way and the Crown Court considers it necessary in the interests of justice that they both be tried for the offence in the Crown Court.*

(3) *In sub-paragraph (2) above "adult" has the same meaning as in section 51 of this Act.*

[(3) In this paragraph, a "main offence" is—

(a) an offence for which the child or young person has been sent to the Crown Court for trial under section 51A(2) of this Act; or

(b) an offence—

(i) for which the child or young person has been sent to the Crown Court for trial under subsection (7) of section 51 of this Act; and

(ii) in respect of which the conditions for sending him to the Crown Court for trial under that subsection (as set out in paragraphs (a) and (b) of that subsection) continue to be satisfied.]

Procedure for determining whether offences of criminal damage etc. are summary offences

14.—(1) This paragraph applies where the Crown Court has to determine, for the **1–34** purposes of this Schedule, whether an offence which is listed in the first column of Schedule 2 to the 1980 Act (offences for which the value involved is relevant to the mode of trial) is a summary offence.

(2) The court shall have regard to any representations made by the prosecutor or the accused.

(3) If it appears clear to the court that the value involved does not exceed the relevant sum, it shall treat the offence as a summary offence.

(4) If it appears clear to the court that the value involved exceeds the relevant sum, it shall treat the offence as an indictable offence.

(5) If it appears to the court for any reason not clear whether the value involved does or does not exceed the relevant sum, the court shall ask the accused whether he wishes the offence to be treated as a summary offence.

(6) Where sub-paragraph (5) above applies—

(a) if the accused indicates that he wishes the offence to be treated as a summary offence, the court shall so treat it;

(b) if the accused does not give such an indication, the court shall treat the offence as an indictable offence.

(7) In this paragraph "the value involved" and "the relevant sum" have the same meanings as in section 22 of the 1980 Act (certain offences triable either way to be tried summarily if value involved is small).

Power of Crown Court, with consent of legally-represented accused, to proceed in his absence

1–35 15.—(1) The Crown Court may proceed in the absence of the accused in accordance with such of the provisions of paragraphs 9 to 14 above as are applicable in the circumstances if—

(a) the accused is represented by a legal representative who signifies to the court the accused's consent to the proceedings in question being conducted in his absence; and

(b) the court is satisfied that there is good reason for proceeding in the absence of the accused.

(2) Sub-paragraph (1) above is subject to the following provisions of this paragraph which apply where the court exercises the power conferred by that sub-paragraph.

(3) If, where the court has *considered* [decided] as required by paragraph 7(7) or 8(2)(d) above, it appears to the court that an offence is more suitable for summary trial, paragraph 10 above shall not apply and—

(a) if the legal representative indicates that the accused wishes to be tried summarily, the court shall remit the accused for trial to a magistrates' court acting for the place where he was sent to the Crown Court for trial;

(b) if the legal representative does not give such an indication, the court shall retain its functions and proceed accordingly.

(4) If, where the court has *considered* [decided] as required by paragraph 7(7) or 8(2)(d) above, it appears to the court that an offence is more suitable for trial on indictment, paragraph 11 above shall apply with the omission of paragraph (a).

(5) Where paragraph 14 above applies and it appears to the court for any reason not clear whether the value involved does or does not exceed the relevant sum, sub-paragraphs (5) and (6) of that paragraph shall not apply and—

(a) the court shall ask the legal representative whether the accused wishes the offence to be treated as a summary offence;

(b) if the legal representative indicates that the accused wishes the offence to be treated as a summary offence, the court shall so treat it;

(c) if the legal representative does not give such an indication, the court shall treat the offence as an indictable offence.

[This Schedule is printed as amended and repealed in part by the *Access to Justice Act* 1999, ss.67(1), 90(1) and 106, Sched. 13, para. 179, and Sched. 15, Pt V(7); the *PCC(S)A* 2000, s.165(1), and Sched. 9, para. 201; the *CJA* 2003, ss.130 and 331, and Sched. 36, para. 73; the *Courts Act (Consequential Amendments) Order* 2004 (S.I. 2004 No. 2035); and the *SOCPA* 2005, s.169(4). As from a day or days to be appointed, the italicised words in paras 1 to 11, 13 and 15, and the whole of para. 12, are repealed, and the words in square brackets inserted or substituted, by the *CJA* 2003, ss.41 and 332, Sched. 3, paras 20, 68, 71 and 72, and Sched. 37, Pt 4; save that the *AFA* 2006, s.378(1), and Sched. 16, para. 155, replace, as from a day to be appointed, the prospectively inserted para. 9(5)(b) (in italics) with a new para. 9(5)(b) (in square brackets).]

In paragraph 6(2) of Schedule 3 (*ante*, § 1–32), the words "so triable" are to be taken to mean "triable on indictment" and not "triable only on indictment". Thus, where charges for a summary offence and an either-way offence are sent for trial with a charge for an indictable-only offence, pursuant to section 51 of the 1998 Act, but, in the event, the indictment contains no count charging an indictable-only offence and the defendant indicates, pursuant to paragraph 7(6) of Schedule 3 (*ante*, § 1–33), that he would plead guilty to the either-way offence charged on the indictment, the Crown Court has power under paragraph 6 to deal with the summary offence, provided that the court considers it to be "related to" the either-way offence: *R. v. Nembhard*, 166 J.P. 363, CA. For a criticism of this decision see *Criminal Law Week* at 2002/08/26. The prospective amendment removes the issue.

As to whether section 66 of the *Courts Act* 2003 confers power on a judge of the Crown Court to deal with a summary offence that comes within paragraph 6(5) of Schedule 3 (*ante*, § 1–32), see *post*, § 2–8.

In *R. v. Haye* [2003] Crim.L.R. 287, CA, it was held that where a person who has been sent for trial under section 51 has not been arraigned and is charged on an indictment that includes no offence that is triable only on indictment, a complete failure to carry out the mode of trial procedure required in such circumstances by paragraphs 7 to 11 of Schedule 3 (*ante*, § 1–33) will render any subsequent proceedings in the Crown Court (including a plea of guilty) a nullity. In *R. v. Ashton*; *R. v. Draz*; *R. v. O'Reilly* [2006] 2 Cr.App.R. 15, CA, the court declined to follow this approach, refusing to grant leave to appeal against a conviction resulting from a purported application of the procedure under paragraph 7 in relation to an offence triable either way in circumstances where no offence triable only on indictment had been sent for trial and where no indictment was in existence, and holding that there had been a mere procedural defect which had not resulted in a lack of jurisdiction or substantive invalidity. That decision was treated in *R. v. Thwaites* (2006) 150 S.J. 1568, CA, as having superseded the approach in *R. v. Haye* (even though it had not been made on a substantive appeal), resulting in the upholding of a conviction where there had been a failure to follow the procedure prescribed by paragraph 7 of Schedule 3, in a case which came within sub-paragraph (1) of that paragraph. However, the approach in *R. v. Ashton*; *R. v. Draz*; *R. v. O'Reilly* has now been overruled by the House of Lords in *R. v. Clarke and McDaid* [2008] 2 Cr.App.R. 2, as to which see *post*, §§ 1–161 *et seq.*, 1–195 *et seq.*, and 1–232. In that regard, the words of paragraph 7(1)(b) of Schedule 3 predicate the procedure under paragraph 7 on the existence of an indictment. The validity of what is done depends, therefore, on the existence of a valid indictment.

For the rules setting out the procedure relating to dismissal applications, see further *post*, §§ 1–38 *et seq.*, and see *post*, § 1–40 as to the proper approach in deciding such an application, and as to the possibility of challenges to any such decision.

(6) First appearance in Crown Court

Criminal Procedure Rules 2005 (S.I. 2005 No. 384), r.12.2

Time for first appearance of accused sent for trial

12.2. A Crown Court officer to whom notice has been given under section 51(7) of the *Crime and Disorder Act* 1998, shall list the first Crown Court appearance of the person to whom the notice relates in accordance with any directions given by the magistrates' court. **1–36**

(7) Service of prosecution evidence

The *Crime and Disorder Act 1998 (Service of Prosecution Evidence) Regulations* 2005 (S.I. 2005 No. 902), *post*, were made under paragraph 1 of Schedule 3 to the 1998 Act (*ante*, § 1–27). They came into force on April 4, 2005 (reg. 1). Previous regulations as to the time for service of prosecution evidence were revoked (reg. 7). **1–37**

Paragraph 1 of Schedule 3 to the 1998 Act also provides that the judge may extend or further extend the period provided for service under the regulations, and, pursuant to paragraph 2 of that schedule, regulation 3 of the regulations (*post*) sets out the procedure in this regard. These provisions, unlike certain other provisions which deal with extensions of time, do not specifically state whether or not there is power to extend the relevant time if the application for an extension is made after the expiry of the relevant period. After conflicting first instance decisions on the point, it was held in *Fehily v. Governor of Wandsworth Prison* [2003] 1 Cr.App.R. 10, DC, in respect of the identically worded previous regulations, that there is power to extend retrospectively the time limited for service of the prosecution evidence in a section 51 case.

S.I. 2005 No. 902, regs 2–6

2. Where a person is sent for trial under section 51 of the1998 Act on any charge or charges, copies of the documents containing the evidence on which the charge or charges are based, shall, no later than 70 days after the date on which the person was sent for trial or, in the case of a person committed to custody under section 52(1)(a) of the Act, no later than 50 days after that date, be:

(a) served on that person; and

(b) given to the Crown Court sitting at the place specified in the notice under subsection (7) of that section.

3. The prosecutor may apply orally or in writing to the Crown Court sitting at the place specified in the notice under section 51(7) of the 1998 Act for the period prescribed by regulation 2 to be extended or, where that period has already been extended, for it to be further extended.

4. Where the prosecutor proposes to make an oral application under regulation 3 above, he shall give notice in writing of his intention to the appropriate officer of the Crown Court; and a copy thereof shall be given at the same time to the person sent for trial.

5. Any written application made under regulation 3 above shall be sent by the prosecutor to the appropriate officer of the Crown Court specifying the grounds for the application; and a copy thereof shall be given at the same time to the person sent for trial who may make written representations in response within 3 days of service of the application on him.

6. Where an application under regulation 3 is determined otherwise than at an oral hearing, the appropriate officer of the Crown Court shall, as soon as reasonably practicable, send to all the parties to the case a notice of the outcome of the application.

(8) Dismissal applications

Procedure and evidence

1–38 The procedural rules relating to dismissal applications made pursuant to paragraph 2 of Schedule 3 to the *CDA* 1998 are now found in Part 13 of the *Criminal Procedure Rules* 2005 (S.I. 2005 No. 384), which came into effect on April 4, 2005.

Rule 13.2(6) of the 2005 rules requires that a notice of intention to make a dismissal application shall be accompanied by "a copy of any material upon which the applicant relies". The use which may properly be made of "material" that is not in the form of admissible evidence was considered in *R. (Snelgrove) v. Woolwich Crown Court* [2005] 1 Cr.App.R. 18, DC.

The dismissal application may be made orally if appropriate notice is given in accordance with paragraph 2(3) of Schedule 3 (*ante*, § 1–28) and Part 13 of the 2005 rules (*post*), but oral evidence may only be given with the leave of the judge, in the circumstances described in paragraph 2(4) of Schedule 3, and after appropriate notice has been given in accordance with Part 13 of the 2005 rules.

Criminal Procedure Rules 2005 (S.I. 2005 No. 384), Pt 13

Interpretation of this Part

1–39 **13.1.** In this Part:

"notice of transfer" means a notice referred to in section 4(1) of the *Criminal Justice Act* 1987 or section 53(1) of the *Criminal Justice Act* 1991; and

"the prosecution" means the authority by or on behalf of whom notice of transfer was given under the 1987 or 1991 Acts, or the authority by or on behalf of whom documents were served under paragraph 1 of Schedule 3 to the *Crime and Disorder Act* 1998.

Written notice of oral application for dismissal

13.2.—(1) Where notice of transfer has been given under the *Criminal Justice Act* 1987 or the *Criminal Justice Act* 1991, or a person has been sent for trial under the *Crime and Disorder Act* 1998, and the person concerned proposes to apply orally— **1–39a**

(a) under section 6(1) of the 1987 Act;

(b) under paragraph 5(1) of Schedule 6 to the 1991 Act; or

(c) under paragraph 2(1) of Schedule 3 to the 1998 Act

for any charge in the case to be dismissed, he shall give notice of his intention in writing to the Crown Court officer at the place specified by the notice of transfer under the 1987 or 1991 Acts or the notice given under section 51(7) of the 1998 Act as the proposed place of trial. Notice of intention to make an application under the 1987 or 1991 Acts shall be in the form set out in the Practice Direction.

(2) Notice of intention to make an application shall be given—

(a) in the case of an application to dismiss charges transferred under the 1987 Act, not later than 28 days after the day on which notice of transfer was given;

(b) in the case of an application to dismiss charges transferred under the 1991 Act, not later than 14 days after the day on which notice of transfer was given; and

(c) in the case of an application to dismiss charges sent under the 1998 Act, not later than 14 days after the day on which the documents were served under paragraph 1 of Schedule 3 to that Act,

and a copy of the notice shall be given at the same time to the prosecution and to any person to whom the notice of transfer relates or with whom the applicant for dismissal is jointly charged.

(3) The time for giving notice may be extended, either before or after it expires, by the Crown Court, on an application made in accordance with paragraph (4).

(4) An application for an extension of time for giving notice shall be made in writing to the Crown Court officer, and a copy thereof shall be given at the same time to the prosecution and to any other person to whom the notice of transfer relates or with whom the applicant for dismissal is jointly charged. Such an application made in proceedings under the 1987 or 1991 Acts shall be in the form set out in the Practice Direction.

(5) The Crown Court officer shall give notice in the form set out in the Practice Direction of the judge's decision on an application under paragraph (3)—

(a) to the applicant for dismissal;

(b) to the prosecution; and

(c) to any other person to whom the notice of transfer relates or with whom the applicant for dismissal is jointly charged.

(6) A notice of intention to make an application under section 6(1) of the 1987 Act, paragraph 5(1) of Schedule 6 to the 1991 Act or paragraph 2(1) of Schedule 3 to the 1998 Act shall be accompanied by a copy of any material on which the applicant relies and shall—

(a) specify the charge or charges to which it relates;

(b) state whether the leave of the judge is sought under section 6(3) of the 1987 Act, paragraph 5(4) of Schedule 6 to the 1991 Act or paragraph 2(4) of Schedule 3 to the 1998 Act to adduce oral evidence on the application, indicating what witnesses it is proposed to call at the hearing; and

(c) in the case of a transfer under the 1991 Act, confirm in relation to each such witness that he is not a child to whom paragraph 5(5) of Schedule 6 to that Act applies.

(7) Where leave is sought from the judge for oral evidence to be given on an application, notice of his decision, indicating what witnesses are to be called if leave is granted, shall be given in writing by the Crown Court officer to the applicant for dismissal, the prosecution and to any other person to whom the notice of transfer relates or with whom the applicant for dismissal is jointly charged. Notice of a decision in proceedings under the 1987 or 1991 Acts shall be in the form set out in the Practice Direction.

(8) Where an application for dismissal under section 6(1) of the 1987 Act, paragraph 5(1) of Schedule 6 to the 1991 Act or paragraph 2(1) of Schedule 3 to the 1998 Act is to be made orally, the Crown Court officer shall list the application for hearing before a judge of the Crown Court and the prosecution shall be given the opportunity to be represented at the hearing.

Written application for dismissal

13.3.—(1) Application may be made for dismissal under section 6(1) of the *Criminal Justice Act* 1987, paragraph 5(1) of Schedule 6 to the *Criminal Justice Act* 1991 or paragraph 2(1) of **1–39b**

Schedule 3 to the *Crime and Disorder Act* 1998 without an oral hearing. Such an application shall be in writing, and in proceedings under the 1987 or 1991 Acts shall be in the form set out in the Practice Direction.

(2) The application shall be sent to the Crown Court officer and shall be accompanied by a copy of any statement or other document, and identify any article, on which the applicant for dismissal relies.

(3) A copy of the application and of any accompanying documents shall be given at the same time to the prosecution and to any other person to whom the notice of transfer relates or with whom the applicant for dismissal is jointly charged.

(4) A written application for dismissal shall be made—

(a) not later than 28 days after the day on which notice of transfer was given under the 1987 Act;

(b) not later than 14 days after the day on which notice of transfer was given under the 1991 Act; or

(c) not later than 14 days after the day on which documents required by paragraph 1 of Schedule 3 to the 1998 Act were served

unless the time for making the application is extended, either before or after it expires, by the Crown Court; and rule 13.2(4) and (5) shall apply for the purposes of this paragraph as if references therein to giving notice of intention to make an oral application were references to making a written application under this rule.

Prosecution reply

1–39c **13.4.**—(1) Not later than seven days from the date of service of notice of intention to apply orally for the dismissal of any charge contained in a notice of transfer or based on documents served under paragraph 1 of Schedule 3 to the *Crime and Disorder Act* 1998, the prosecution may apply to the Crown Court under section 6(3) of the *Criminal Justice Act* 1987, paragraph 5(4) of Schedule 6 to the *Criminal Justice Act* 1991 or paragraph 2(4) of Schedule 3 to the 1998 Act for leave to adduce oral evidence at the hearing of the application, indicating what witnesses it is proposed to call.

(2) Not later than seven days from the date of receiving a copy of an application for dismissal under rule 13.3, the prosecution may apply to the Crown Court for an oral hearing of the application.

(3) An application under paragraph (1) or (2) shall be served on the Crown Court officer in writing and, in the case of an application under paragraph (2), shall state whether the leave of the judge is sought to adduce oral evidence and, if so, shall indicate what witnesses it is proposed to call. Where leave is sought to adduce oral evidence under paragraph 5(4) of Schedule 6 to the 1991 Act, the application should confirm in relation to each such witness that he is not a child to whom paragraph 5(5) of that Schedule applies. Such an application in proceedings under the 1987 or 1991 Acts shall be in the form set out in the Practice Direction.

(4) Notice of the judge's determination upon an application under paragraph (1) or (2), indicating what witnesses (if any) are to be called shall be served in writing by the Crown Court officer on the prosecution, on the applicant for dismissal and on any other party to whom the notice of transfer relates or with whom the applicant for dismissal is jointly charged. Such a notice in proceedings under the 1987 or 1991 Acts shall be in the form set out in the Practice Direction.

(5) Where, having received the material specified in rule 13.2 or, as the case may be, rule 13.3, the prosecution proposes to adduce in reply thereto any written comments or any further evidence, the prosecution shall serve any such comments, copies of the statements or other documents outlining the evidence of any proposed witnesses, copies of any further documents and, in the case of an application to dismiss charges transferred under the 1991 Act, copies of any video recordings which it is proposed to tender in evidence, on the Crown Court officer not later than 14 days from the date of receiving the said material, and shall at the same time serve copies thereof on the applicant for dismissal and any other person to whom the notice of transfer relates or with whom the applicant is jointly charged. In the case of a defendant acting in person, copies of video recordings need not be served but shall be made available for viewing by him.

(6) The time for—

(a) making an application under paragraph (1) or (2) above; or

(b) serving any material on the Crown Court officer under paragraph (5) above

may be extended, either before or after it expires, by the Crown Court, on an application made in accordance with paragraph (7) below.

(7) An application for an extension of time under paragraph (6) above shall be made in writing and shall be served on the Crown Court officer, and a copy thereof shall be served at the same time on to the applicant for dismissal and on any other person to whom the notice of transfer relates or with whom the applicant for dismissal is jointly charged. Such an application in proceedings under the 1987 or 1991 Acts shall be in the form set out in the Practice Direction.

Determination of applications for dismissal—procedural matters

13.5.—(1) A judge may grant leave for a witness to give oral evidence on an application for dismissal notwithstanding that notice of intention to call the witness has not been given in accordance with the foregoing provisions of this Part. **1–39d**

(2) Where an application for dismissal is determined otherwise than at an oral hearing, the Crown Court officer shall as soon as practicable, send to all the parties to the case written notice of the outcome of the application. Such a notice in proceedings under the 1987 and 1991 Acts shall be in the form set out in the Practice Direction.

Service of documents

13.6. [*Revoked by* Criminal Procedure (Amendment) Rules *2007 (S.I. 2007 No. 699).*] **1–39e**

As to the service of documents, see now Part 4 of the 2005 rules, *post*, §§ 2–207 *et seq.*

Proper approach on dismissal application, and challenges to decisions

The test to be applied on a dismissal application is that which is set out in paragraph 2(2) of Schedule 3 to the *CDA* 1998, *ante*, § 1–28. It has been said that this test, as originally set out in section 6(1) of the *CJA* 1987 (*post*, § 1–50), requires application of the criteria commonly applied on a submission of "no case to answer" (as to which see *post*, §§ 4–293 *et seq.*): *R. v. X.* [1989] Crim.L.R. 726, Crown Court (Henry J.); and *R. v. Thompson and Hanson*, *post*. **1–40**

The relevant words also require the judge to take into account the whole of the evidence against a defendant. It is not appropriate for the judge to view any evidence in isolation from its context and other evidence, any more than it is appropriate to derive a meaning from a single document or from a number of documents without regard to the remainder of the document or the other connected documents before the court. Nor is the judge bound to assume that a jury might make every possible inference capable of being drawn from a document against the defendant. The judge must decide not only whether there is any evidence to go to a jury, but whether that evidence is sufficient for a jury properly to convict. That exercise requires him to assess the weight of the evidence. This is not to say that the judge is entitled to substitute himself for the jury. The question for him is not whether the defendant should be convicted on the evidence put forward by the prosecution, but the sufficiency of that evidence. Where the evidence is largely documentary, and the case depends on the inferences or conclusions to be drawn from it, the judge must assess the inferences or conclusions that the prosecution propose to ask the jury to draw from the documents, and decide whether it appears to him that the jury could properly draw those inferences and come to those conclusions: *R. (Inland Revenue Commrs) v. Crown Court at Kingston* [2001] 4 All E.R. 721, DC.

It was said (*ibid.*) that the words of the legislation demonstrate that Parliament intended judges to have a wide margin of appreciation in dealing with dismissal applications and that a challenge to decisions in that regard will only succeed if the decision is perverse and one that no reasonable judge could have reached. It was also said that when giving reasons for his decision a judge is not obliged to consider every document referred to and to summarise his conclusions on it. Those remarks were made in the context of an application for judicial review of a decision to dismiss transferred charges, in which no issue was raised as to the existence of the judicial review jurisdiction in such cases. Similarly, in *R. v. Snaresbrook Crown Court, ex p. Director of Serious Fraud Office*, *The Times*, October 26, 1998, DC, where it was said that a challenge to a decision to dismiss a transferred charge should be made by way of judicial review, rather than by way of the voluntary bill of indictment procedure, the availability of the jurisdiction was not in issue. However, in *R. (Snelgrove) v. Woolwich Crown Court*

[2005] 1 Cr.App.R. 18, DC, it was held that judicial review does not lie in respect of a decision of the Crown Court on a dismissal application pursuant to the 1998 Act, as to which see further *post*, § 7–12. That decision was followed in *R. (O.) v. Central Criminal Court*, unreported, January 27, 2006, DC ([2006] EWHC 256 (Admin.)), rejecting an additional argument based on Article 5(4) of the ECHR. Further, the prosecution's right of appeal against a ruling "in relation to a trial on indictment" under section 58 of the *CJA* 2003 does not extend to a ruling dismissing charges sent for trial under section 51 of the 1998 Act: *R. v. Thompson and Hanson* [2007] 1 Cr.App.R. 15, and *post*, § 7–244. These decisions would appear to have equal applicability in respect of dismissal applications in cases that are before the Crown Court as a result of the notice of transfer procedures.

In *Bentham v. Governor of H.M. Prison Wandsworth* (as to which see *ante*, § 1–23), it was said (*obiter*) that, in the absence of improper prejudice to the accused person, a failure to identify offences adequately in the notice required by section 51(7) of the *CDA* 1998 (*ante*, § 1–17) would not justify dismissal of those charges if the relevant particulars could be ascertained from the other documentation provided to the accused person and the Crown Court. As to the potential consequences generally of non-compliance with procedural requirements, see *ante*, § 1–35, and *post*, §§ 1–161 *et seq.*, 1–195 *et seq.* and 2–8.

C. TRANSFERS FOR TRIAL

(1) Serious fraud cases

(a) *Notices of transfer*

Criminal Justice Act 1987, ss.4, 5

Notices of transfer and designated authorities

1–41 **4.**—(1) *If—*

(a) *a person has been charged with an indictable offence; and*

(b) *in the opinion of an authority designated by subsection (2) below or of one of such an authority's officers acting on the authority's behalf the evidence of the offence charged—*

(i) *would be sufficient for the person charged to be committed for trial; and*

(ii) *reveals a case of fraud of such seriousness or complexity that it is appropriate that the management of the case should without delay be taken over by the Crown Court; and*

(c) *before the magistrates' court in whose jurisdiction the offence has been charged begins to inquire into the case as examining justices the authority or one of the authority's officers acting on the authority's behalf gives the court a notice (in this Act referred to as a "notice of transfer") certifying that opinion,*

the functions of the magistrates' court shall cease in relation to the case, except as provided by section 5(3), (7A) and (8) below and by paragraph 2 of Schedule 3 to the Access to Justice Act *1999.*

(2) *The authorities mentioned in subsection (1) above (in this Act referred to as "designated authorities") are—*

(a) *the Director of Public Prosecutions;*

(b) *the Director of the Serious Fraud Office;*

(c) *the Commissioners of Revenue and Customs;*

(d) *…; and*

(e) *the Secretary of State.*

(3) *A designated authority's decision to give notice of transfer shall not be subject to appeal or liable to be questioned in any court.*

(4) *This section and sections 5 and 6 below shall not apply in any case in which section 51 of the* Crime and Disorder Act *1998 (no committal proceedings for indictable-only offences) applies.*

[This section is printed as amended by the *CJA* 1988, s.144(1), (2); the *Legal Aid Act* 1988, s.45(1), (3), and Sched. 5, para. 22; the *CJPOA* 1994, Sched. 9, para. 29; the *CDA* 1998, s.119, and Sched. 8, para. 65; the *Access to Justice Act* 1999, s.24, and Sched. 4, para. 39; and the *Commissioners for Revenue and Customs Act* 2005, s.50(1).

With effect from a day to be appointed it is repealed by the *CJA* 2003, s.41, and Sched. 3, para. 58(1) and (2), and s.332, and Sched. 37, Pt 4. It will, in effect, be replaced by the new scheme of sending for trial, *ante*, § 1–14.]

The decision to transfer a case to the Crown Court under section 4 is, notwithstanding section 4(3), susceptible to judicial review if one of the pre-conditions in section 4(1) has not been satisfied: *R. v. Salford Magistrates' Court, ex p. Gallagher* [1994] Crim.L.R. 374, DC (relief refused in the exercise of the court's discretion).

A notice of transfer can precede determination of mode of trial, but cannot reverse it: see *R. v. Fareham Youth Court and Morey, ex p. CPS*, 163 J.P. 812, DC, *post*, § 1–73.

Where justices were assured by the prosecution in open court on the day when mode of trial proceedings were due to take place that the prosecution intended to issue a notice of transfer under section 4 of the Act, they could lawfully adjourn the mode of trial proceedings although all parties were ready to proceed: *R. v. Stevenage JJ., ex p. Johl, The Times*, December 1, 1989, DC.

Notices of transfer—procedure

5.—(1) *A notice of transfer shall specify the proposed place of trial and in selecting that place the designated authority shall have regard to the considerations to which section 7 of the* Magistrates' Courts Act *1980 requires a magistrates' court committing a person for trial to have regard when selecting the place at which he is to be tried.* **1–42**

(2) *A notice of transfer shall specify the charge or charges to which it relates and include or be accompanied by such additional matter as regulations under subsection (9) below may require.*

(3) *If a magistrates' court has remanded a person to whom a notice of transfer relates in custody, it shall have power, subject to section 4 of the* Bail Act *1976 and regulations under section 22 of the* Prosecution of Offences Act *1985—*

(a) *to order that he shall be safely kept in custody until delivered in due course of law; or*

(b) *to release him on bail in accordance with the* Bail Act *1976, that is to say, by directing him to appear before the Crown Court for trial;*

and where his release on bail is conditional on his providing one or more surety or sureties and, in accordance with section 8(3) of the Bail Act *1976 the court fixes the amount in which the surety is to be bound with a view to his entering into his recognizance subsequently in accordance with subsections (4) and (5) or (6) of that section, the court shall in the meantime make an order such as is mentioned in paragraph (a) of this subsection.*

(4) *If the conditions specified in subsection (5) below are satisfied, a court may exercise the powers conferred by subsection (3) above in relation to a person charged without his being brought before it in any case in which by virtue of section 128(3A) of the* Magistrates' Courts Act *1980 it would have power further to remand him on an adjournment such as is mentioned in that subsection.*

(5) *The conditions mentioned in subsection (4) above are—*

(a) *that the person charged has given his written consent to the powers conferred by subsection (3) above being exercised without his being brought before the court; and*

(b) *that the court is satisfied that, when he gave his consent, he knew that the notice of transfer had been issued.*

(6) *Where notice of transfer is given after a person to whom it relates has been remanded on bail to appear before a magistrates' court on an appointed day, the requirement that he shall so appear shall cease on the giving of the notice, unless the notice states that it is to continue.*

(7) *Where the requirement that a person to whom the notice of transfer relates shall appear before a magistrates' court ceases by virtue of subsection (6) above, it shall be his duty to appear before the Crown Court at the place specified by the notice of transfer as the proposed place of trial or at any place substituted for it by a direction under section 76 of the* Supreme Court [Senior Courts] Act *1981.*

(7A) *If the notice states that the requirement is to continue, when a person to whom the notice relates appears before the magistrates' court, the court shall have—*

(a) *the powers and duty conferred on a magistrates' court by subsection (3) above, but subject as there provided; and*

(b) *power to enlarge, in the surety's absence, a recognizance conditioned in accordance with section 128(4)(a) of the* Magistrates' Courts Act *1980 so that the surety is bound to secure that the person charged appears also before the Crown Court.*

(8) *For the purposes of the* Criminal Procedure (Attendance of Witnesses) Act *1965—*

(a) *any magistrates' court for the petty sessions area for which the court from which a case was transferred sits shall be treated as examining magistrates; and*

(b) *a person indicated in the notice of transfer as a proposed witness shall be treated as a person who has been examined by the court.*

(9)–(11) [Provision for regulations as to notices of transfer.]

[Subss. (1)–(8) are printed as amended by the *CJA* 1988, s.144(1), (3), (4). Subs. (9) is amended by, and subs. (9A) is inserted by, the *CPIA* 1996, s.45(1)–(3). With effect from days to be appointed, (i) the name of the 1981 Act in subs. (7) is amended by substitution of the words in the square brackets: *Constitutional Reform Act* 2005, s.59, and Sched. 11, para. 1(2); and (ii) the whole section is repealed by the *CJA* 2003, ss.41 and 332, Sched. 3, para. 58(1) and (2), and Sched. 37, Pt 4.]

Transfer to specified Crown Court centres

1–43 The proposed place of trial specified in the transfer notice, pursuant to section 5(1) of the 1987 Act, must be identified in accordance with paragraph III.21.10 of the consolidated criminal practice direction (*post,* § 2–18).

Notice of transfer regulations

1–44 The *Criminal Justice Act 1987 (Notice of Transfer) Regulations* 1988 (S.I. 1988 No. 1691) were made by the Attorney-General under section 5(9) of the 1987 Act. The relevant provisions are set out below.

S.I. 1988 No. 1691, regs 2–6

Interpretation

1–45 **2.** In these Regulations—

"designated authority" means an authority designated by section 4(2) of the *Criminal Justice Act* 1987; and

"notice of transfer" means a notice given under section 4(1) of that Act.

Notice of transfer

3. A notice of transfer given by or on behalf of a designated authority shall be in Form 1 in the Schedule to these Regulations, or in a form to the like effect.

Notice to defendant

4. Where a notice of transfer is given by or on behalf of a designated authority, a copy of the notice shall be given by or on behalf of the authority to any person to whom the notice of transfer relates (or, if he is acting by a solicitor, to his solicitor) together with—

(a) a notice in Form 2 in the Schedule to these Regulations, or in a form to the like effect; and

(b) a statement of the evidence on which any charge to which the notice of transfer relates is based.

Notice to Crown Court

5. Where a notice of transfer is given by or on behalf of a designated authority, a copy of the notice shall be given by or on behalf of the authority to the appropriate officer of the Crown Court sitting at the place specified by the notice of transfer as the proposed place of trial together with—

(a) a copy of the notice referred to in paragraph (a) of regulation 4 above and copies of the material enclosed with that notice; and

(b) the statement referred to in paragraph (b) of that regulation.

Notice to prison governor etc.

6. Where a notice of transfer is given by or on behalf of a designated authority, a copy of the notice shall be given by or on behalf of the authority to any person who has custody of any person to whom the notice of transfer relates together with a copy of the notice referred to in paragraph (a) of regulation 4 above.

The Schedule to the regulations (amended by the *Criminal Justice Act 1987 (Notice of Transfer) (Amendment) Regulations* 1997 (S.I. 1997 No. 737), and the *Criminal Justice Acts 1987 and 1991 (Notice of Transfer) (Amendment) Regulations* 2001 (S.I. 2001 No. 444)) contains the following specimen forms: **1–46**

- Notice of transfer of case to the Crown Court (Form 1);
- Notice to person to whom a notice of transfer relates (Form 2);
- Consent form for persons remanded in custody (Form 3).

Whereas regulation 4 requires a notice of transfer to be accompanied by a notice in Form 2, and paragraph 5 of that form refers to the enclosure of "a list of witnesses ... together with in each case copies of the statements or other documents outlining the evidence of those witnesses", the requirement for an outline of the evidence of a witness could be satisfied by an outline provided by a person other than the witness; but prosecutors in serious fraud cases should not regard themselves as free from a duty to provide full details of the evidence to be called; a bare outline would not suffice: *R. v. Cheung* [1999] 8 *Archbold News* 3, CA.

The statement of evidence

In *R. v. X* [1989] Crim.L.R. 726, Crown Court, Henry J. expressed the following view as to the content of a statement of evidence given pursuant to regulation 4(b), *ante*, § 1–45. **1–47**

> "In serious fraud cases the case is always likely to depend to a greater or lesser extent on inference, and it seems to me to be ... positively desirable that the inferences which the prosecution say should be drawn from the direct evidence should be included in their statement of evidence so that, first, the defendant may make a fully-informed decision whether to apply to dismiss and, second, that in his written submissions or material he originally files in support of an oral application he may deal with the whole of the case against him at that stage and not have to foresee the inferences that will be sought to be drawn."

(The above passage is taken from the transcript of the judgment and does not appear in the *Criminal Law Review* report.)

It is desirable that the statement of evidence should be as close to the final case statement as can be achieved at the time it is drafted: *R. v. Saunders*, CCC, unreported, November 6, 1989, (Henry J.).

Notice of transfer rules

Procedural rules relating to proceedings where a notice of transfer is given are now found in Part 11 of the *Criminal Procedure Rules* 2005 (S.I. 2005 No. 384), which came into effect on April 4, 2005. **1–48**

Criminal Procedure Rules 2005 (S.I. 2005 No. 384), Pt 11

TRANSFER FOR TRIAL OF SERIOUS FRAUD CASES OR CASES INVOLVING CHILDREN

Interpretation of this Part

11.1.—(1) In this part: **1–49**

"notice of transfer" means a notice referred to in section 4(1) of the *Criminal Justice Act* 1987 or section 53(1) of the *Criminal Justice Act* 1991.

(2) Where this Part requires a document to be given or sent, or a notice to be communicated in writing, it may, with the consent of the addressee, be sent by electronic communication.

(3) Electronic communication means a communication transmitted (whether from one person to another, from one device to another or from a person to a device or vice versa)—

(a) by means of an electronic communications network (within the meaning of the *Communications Act* 2003); or

(b) by other means but while in an electronic form.

Transfer on bail

11.2.—(1) Where a person in respect of whom notice of transfer has been given— **1–49a**

(a) is granted bail under section 5(3) or (7A) of the *Criminal Justice Act* 1987 by the magistrates' court to which notice of transfer was given; or

(b) is granted bail under paragraph 2(1) or (7) of Schedule 6 to the *Criminal Justice Act* 1991 by the magistrates' court to which notice of transfer was given,

the magistrates' court officer shall give notice thereof in writing to the governor of the prison or remand centre to which the said person would have been committed by that court if he had been committed in custody for trial.

(2) Where notice of transfer is given under section 4(1) of the 1987 Act in respect of a corporation the magistrates' court officer shall give notice thereof to the governor of the prison to which would be committed a male over 21 committed by that court in custody for trial.

Notice where person removed to hospital

1–49b **11.3.** Where a transfer direction has been given by the Secretary of State under section 47 or 48 of the *Mental Health Act* 1983 in respect of a person remanded in custody by a magistrates' court and, before the direction ceases to have effect, notice of transfer is given in respect of that person, the magistrates' court officer shall give notice thereof in writing—

(a) to the governor of the prison to which that person would have been committed by that court if he had been committed in custody for trial; and

(b) to the managers of the hospital where he is detained.

Variation of arrangements for bail

1–49c **11.4.**—(1) A person who intends to make an application to a magistrates' court under section 3(8) of the *Bail Act* 1976 as that subsection has effect under section 3(8A) of that Act shall give notice thereof in writing to the magistrates' court officer, and to the designated authority or the defendant, as the case may be, and to any sureties concerned.

(2) Where, on an application referred to in paragraph (1), a magistrates' court varies or imposes any conditions of bail, the magistrates' court officer shall send to the Crown Court officer a copy of the record made in pursuance of section 5 of the 1976 Act relating to such variation or imposition of conditions.

Documents etc. to be sent to Crown Court

1–49d **11.5.** As soon as practicable after a magistrates' court to which notice of transfer has been given has discharged the functions reserved to it under section 4(1) of the *Criminal Justice Act* 1987 or section 53(3) of the *Criminal Justice Act* 1991, the magistrates' court officer shall send to the Crown Court officer—

(a) a list of the names, addresses and occupations of the witnesses;

(b) a copy of the record made in pursuance of section 5 of the *Bail Act* 1976 relating to the grant of [*sic*] withholding of bail in respect of the accused;

(c) any recognizance entered into by any person as surety for the accused together with a statement of any enlargement thereof;

(d) a copy of any representation order previously made in the case; and

(e) a copy of any application for a representation order previously made in the case which has been refused.

(b) *Dismissal applications*

Criminal Justice Act 1987, s.6

Applications for dismissal

1–50 **6.**—(1) *Where notice of transfer has been given, any person to whom the notice relates, at any time before he is arraigned (and whether or not an indictment has been preferred against him), may apply orally or in writing to the Crown Court sitting at the place specified by the notice of transfer as the proposed place of trial for the charge, or any of the charges, in the case to be dismissed; and the judge shall dismiss a charge (and accordingly quash a count relating to it in any indictment preferred against the applicant) if it appears to him that the evidence against the applicant would not be sufficient for a jury properly to convict him.*

(2) *No oral application may be made under subsection (1) above unless the applicant has given the Crown Court sitting at the place specified by the notice of transfer as the proposed place of trial written notice of his intention to make the application.*

(3) *Oral evidence may be given on such an application only with the leave of the judge or by his order, and the judge shall give leave or make an order only if it appears to him, having regard to any matters stated in the application for leave, that the interests of justice require him to do so.*

(4) *If the judge gives leave permitting, or makes an order requiring, a person to give oral evidence, but he does not do so, the judge may disregard any document indicating the evidence that he might have given.*

(5) *Dismissal of the charge, or all the charges, against the applicant shall have the same effect as a refusal by examining magistrates to commit for trial, except that no further proceedings may be brought on a dismissed charge except by means of the preferment of a voluntary bill of indictment.*

(6) [Provision for Criminal Procedure Rules.]

[This section is printed as substituted by the *CJA* 1988, s.144(1), (5). The reference in subs. (6) to the *Criminal Procedure Rules* was substituted by the *Courts Act 2003 (Consequential Amendments) Order* 2004 (S.I. 2004 No. 2035). With effect from a day to be appointed, the whole section is repealed by the *CJA* 2003, ss.41 and 332, Sched. 3, para. 58(1) and (2), and Sched. 37, Pt 4.]

Procedure and evidence

The procedural rules and evidential principles relating to dismissal applications that are made under section 6 of the *CJA* 1987 are now the same as in respect of dismissal applications made under paragraph 2 of Schedule 3 to the *CDA* 1998, as to which see *ante*, §§ 1–38 *et seq.* **1–51**

Criteria to be applied on application, and challenges to decisions

The relevant principles are the same as those which apply in respect of dismissal applications made under paragraph 2 of Schedule 3 to the *CDA* 1998, as to which see *ante*, § 1–40. **1–52**

(2) Cases involving children

(a) *Notices of transfer*

Criminal Justice Act 1991, s.53 and Sched. 6

Notices of transfer in certain cases involving children

53.—(1) *If a person has been charged with an offence to which section 32(2) of the 1988 Act applies (sexual offences and offences involving violence or cruelty) and the Director of Public Prosecutions is of the opinion—* **1–53**

(a) *that the evidence of the offence would be sufficient for the person charged to be committed for trial;*

(b) *that a child who is alleged—*

(i) *to be a person against whom the offence was committed; or*

(ii) *to have witnessed the commission of the offence,*

will be called as a witness at the trial; and

(c) *that, for the purpose of avoiding any prejudice to the welfare of the child, the case should be taken over and proceeded with without delay by the Crown Court,*

a notice ("notice of transfer") certifying that opinion may be given by or on behalf of the Director to the magistrates' court in whose jurisdiction the offence has been charged.

(2) *A notice of transfer shall be given before the magistrates' court begins to inquire into the case as examining justices.*

(3) *On the giving of a notice of transfer the functions of the magistrates' court shall cease in relation to the case except as provided by paragraphs 2 and 3 of Schedule 6 to this Act or by paragraph 2 of Schedule 3 to the* Access to Justice Act *1999.*

(4) *The decision to give a notice of transfer shall not be subject to appeal or liable to be questioned in any court.*

(5) *Schedule 6 to this Act (which makes further provision in relation to notices of transfer) shall have effect.*

(6) *In this section "child" means a person who—*

(a) *in the case of an offence falling within section 32(2)(a) or (b) of the 1988 Act, is under fourteen years of age or, if he was under that age when any such video recording as is mentioned in section 32A(2) of that Act was made in respect of him, is under fifteen years of age; or*

(b) *in the case of an offence falling within section 32(2)(c) of that Act, is under seventeen years of age or, if he was under that age when any such video recording was made in respect of him, is under eighteen years of age.*

(7) *Any reference in* subsection (6) *above to an offence falling within paragraph (a), (b) or (c) of section 32(2) of that Act includes a reference to an offence which consists of attempting or conspiring to commit, or of aiding, abetting, counselling, procuring or inciting the commission of, an offence falling within that paragraph.*

(8) *This section shall not apply in any case in which section 51 of the* Crime and Disorder Act *1998 (no committal proceedings for indictable-only offences) applies.*

[This section is printed as amended by the *CJPOA* 1994, Sched. 9, para. 49; the *CDA* 1998, s.119, and Sched. 8, para. 93; and the *Access to Justice Act* 1999, s.24, and Sched. 4, para. 47. The reference in subs. (7) to the common law offence of incitement has effect as a reference to the offences under the *SCA* 2007, Pt 2: 2007 Act, s.63(1), and Sched. 6, para. 36. With effect from a further day to be appointed, the whole section is repealed by the *CJA* 2003, ss.41 and 332, Sched. 3, para. 62(1) and (2), and Sched. 37, Pt 4. It will, in effect, be replaced by the new scheme of sending for trial, *ante*, §§ 1–14 *et seq.*]

By analogy with the reasoning in *R. v. Salford Magistrates' Court, ex p. Gallagher* [1994] Crim.L.R. 374, DC, *ante*, § 1–41, it seems likely that a decision to transfer a case to the Crown Court under section 53 is, notwithstanding section 53(4), susceptible to judicial review if one of the pre-conditions in section 53(1) has not been satisfied.

The reference in subsection (1) to "the 1988 Act" is to the *CJA* 1988. Sections 32(2) and 32A of that Act were repealed by the *YJCEA* 1999. No consequential amendment was made to this section, but it is submitted that, in order that this section should retain any meaning, it is possible, by reference to the *Interpretation Act* 1978, s.17(2) (Appendix B–17), to construe the reference to section 32(2) as a reference to section 35(3) of the 1999 Act (*post*, § 8–123c) (see also s.21 of the 1999 Act, *post*, § 8–55c), with section 35(3)(a) coinciding with section 32(2)(c), and section 35(c) and (d) coinciding with section 32(2)(a) and (b). Section 32(2) did not apply to offences of kidnapping, false imprisonment or child abduction under the *Child Abduction Act* 1984. It is submitted, however, that the terms of section 17(2) of the 1978 Act ("with or without modification") are broad enough to cover this, but that, for the purposes of subsection (6), such offences should be bracketed with paragraphs (a) and (b) of section 32(2), rather than with paragraph (c). As to section 32A, the corresponding provision under the 1999 Act for the video-recording of evidence is section 27 (*post*, § 8–55k).

A notice of transfer can precede determination of mode of trial, but cannot reverse it: see *R. v. Fareham Youth Court and Morey, ex p. CPS*, 163 J.P. 812, DC, *post*, § 1–73. As to adjournment of mode of trial proceedings to enable service of a notice of transfer, see *ante*, § 1–41.

There should be no transfer to the Crown Court for trial of a defendant aged under 18 unless the prosecution could conclude that a magistrates' court would be likely to find that the case fell within the requirements of seriousness set out in section 24 of the *MCA* 1980 (*post*, § 1–75m), and thereby commit the matter for trial in the Crown Court (but now see also section 51A of the *CDA* 1998, *ante*, § 1–19); a decision to transfer a case involving children should only be taken for grave offences: *R. v. T. and K.* [2001] 1 Cr.App.R. 32, CA.

SCHEDULE 6

NOTICES OF TRANSFER: PROCEDURE IN LIEU OF COMMITTAL

Contents of notice of transfer

1–54 1.—(1) *A notice of transfer shall specify the proposed place of trial; and in selecting that place the Director of Public Prosecutions shall have regard to the considerations to which a magistrates' court committing a person for trial is required by section 7 of the 1980 Act to have regard when selecting the place at which he is to be tried.*

(2) *A notice of transfer shall specify the charge or charges to which it relates and include or be accompanied by such additional material as regulations under paragraph 4 below may require.*

Remand

2.—(1) *If a magistrates' court has remanded in custody a person to whom a notice of transfer relates, it shall have power, subject to section 4 of the* Bail Act *1976, section 25 of the* Criminal Justice and Public Order Act *1994 and regulations under section 22 of the* Prosecution of Offences Act *1985*— **1–55**

(a) *to order that he shall be safely kept in custody until delivered in due course of law; or*

(b) *to release him on bail in accordance with the* Bail Act *1976, that is to say, by directing him to appear before the Crown Court for trial.*

(2) *Where*—

(a) *a person's release on bail under paragraph (b) of sub-paragraph (1) above is conditional on his providing one or more sureties; and*

(b) *in accordance with subsection (3) of section 8 of the* Bail Act *1976, the court fixes the amount in which a surety is to be bound with a view to his entering into his recognisance subsequently in accordance with subsections (4) and (5) or (6) of that section,*

the court shall in the meantime make an order such as is mentioned in paragraph (a) of that sub-paragraph.

(3) *If the conditions specified in sub-paragraph (4) below are satisfied, a court may exercise the powers conferred by sub-paragraph (1) above in relation to a person charged without his being brought before it in any case in which by virtue of subsection (3A) of section 128 of the 1980 Act it would have the power further to remand him on an adjournment such as is mentioned in that subsection.*

(4) *The conditions referred to in sub-paragraph (3) above are*—

(a) *that the person in question has given his consent to the powers conferred by sub-paragraph (1) above being exercised without his being brought before the court; and*

(b) *that the court is satisfied that, when he gave his consent, he knew that the notice of transfer had been issued.*

(5) *Where a notice of transfer is given after a person to whom it relates has been remanded on bail to appear before a magistrates' court on an appointed day, the requirement that he shall so appear shall cease on the giving of the notice unless the notice states that it is to continue.*

(6) *Where that requirement ceases by virtue of sub-paragraph (5) above, it shall be the duty of the person in question to appear before the Crown Court at the place specified by the notice of transfer as the proposed place of trial or at any place substituted for it by a direction under section 76 of the* Supreme Court [Senior Courts] Act *1981.*

(7) *If, in a case where the notice states that the requirement mentioned in sub-paragraph (5) above is to continue, a person to whom the notice relates appears before the magistrates' court, the court shall have*—

(a) *the powers and duties conferred on a magistrates' court by sub-paragraph (1) above but subject as there provided; and*

(b) *power to enlarge, in the surety's absence, a recognisance conditioned in accordance with section 128(4)(a) of the 1980 Act so that the surety is bound to secure that the person charged appears also before the Crown Court.*

Witnesses

3. [Identical to *Criminal Justice Act* 1987, s.5(8), *ante*, § 1–42.]

Regulations

4. [Provision for regulations as to notices of transfer.]

Applications for dismissal

5.—(1) *Where a notice of transfer has been given, any person to whom the notice relates may, at any time before he is arraigned (and whether or not an indictment has been preferred against him), apply orally or in writing to the Crown Court sitting at the place specified by the notice of transfer as the proposed place of trial for the charge, or any of the charges, in the case to be dismissed.* **1–56**

(2) *The judge shall dismiss a charge (and accordingly quash a count relating to it in any indictment preferred against the applicant) which is the subject of any such application if it*

appears to him that the evidence against the applicant would not be sufficient for a jury properly to convict him.

(3) *No oral application may be made under sub-paragraph (1) above unless the applicant has given the Crown Court mentioned in that sub-paragraph written notice of his intention to make the application.*

(4) [Identical to *Criminal Justice Act* 1987, s.6(3), *ante*, § 1–50.]

(5) *No leave or order under sub-paragraph (4) above shall be given or made in relation to oral evidence from a child (within the meaning of section 53 of this Act) who is alleged—*

(a) *to be a person against whom an offence to which the notice of transfer relates was committed; or*

(b) *to have witnessed the commission of such an offence.*

(6) *If the judge gives leave permitting, or makes an order requiring, a person to give oral evidence, but that person does not do so, the judge may disregard any document indicating the evidence that he might have given.*

(7) [Identical to *Criminal Justice Act* 1987, s.6(5), *ante*, § 1–50.]

(8) [Provision for rules of court.]

Reporting restrictions

1–57 6. [Identical to *CDA* 1998, Sched. 3, para. 3, *ante*, § 1–29, save: (i) for the prospective amendments to para. 3, made by the *CJA* 2003 and shown in square brackets; (ii) for references to "paragraph 5" in lieu of references to "paragraph 2" throughout; (iii) for references to "sub-paragraphs (5) and (7)" in lieu of references to "sub-paragraphs (5) and (6)" in sub-paragraph (8); and (iv) the wording of sub-paragraph (8)(g) is "whether legal aid was granted to the accused or any of the accused".]

Avoidance of delay

1–58 7.—(1) *Where a notice of transfer has been given in relation to any case—*

(a) *the Crown Court before which the case is to be tried; and*

(b) *any magistrates' court which exercises any functions under paragraph 2 or 3 above or section 20(4) of the* Legal Aid Act *1988 in relation to the case,*

shall, in exercising any of its powers in relation to the case, have regard to the desirability of avoiding prejudice to the welfare of any relevant child witness that may be occasioned by unnecessary delay in bringing the case to trial.

(2) *In this paragraph "child" has the same meaning as in section 53 of this Act and "relevant child witness" means a child who will be called as a witness at the trial and who is alleged—*

(a) *to be a person against whom an offence to which the notice of transfer relates was committed; or*

(b) *to have witnessed the commission of such an offence.*

8. [Amends *Administration of Justice (Miscellaneous Provisions) Act* 1933, s.2(2), *ante*, § 1–204.]

9. [Repealed by *Access to Justice Act* 1999, s.106 and Sched. 15, Pt I.]

[Paras 4 and 6(8) (substitution of "(7)" for "(6)") were amended by the *CPIA* 1996, s.45(4)–(9). The reference to "Rules of court" in para. 5(8) was substituted by the *Courts Act 2003 (Consequential Amendments) Order* 2004 (S.I. 2004 No. 2035). As from a day to be appointed, the whole schedule is repealed by the *CJA* 2003, ss.41 and 332, Sched. 3, para. 62(1) and (2), and Sched. 37, Pt 4.]

Transfer to specified Crown Court centres

1–59 The proposed place of trial specified in the transfer notice, pursuant to paragraph 1(1) of Schedule 6 to the 1991 Act, must be identified in accordance with the requirements of paragraph III.21.11 of the consolidated criminal practice direction, *post*, § 2–18.

Notice of transfer regulations

1–60 The *Criminal Justice Act 1991 (Notice of Transfer) Regulations* 1992 (S.I. 1992 No. 1670) were made by the Attorney-General in exercise of the powers conferred on him by section 53(5) of, and paragraph 4 of Schedule 6 to, the 1991 Act.

Regulation 1(1) provides for the commencement of the regulations on October 1, 1992. Regulation 1(2) provides that "the Director" means the Director of Public Prosecutions and that "notice of transfer" means a notice served under section 53(1).

S.I. 1992 No. 1670, regs 2–5

Notice of transfer

2. A notice of transfer served by or on behalf of the Director shall be in Form 1 in the Schedule to these Regulations, or in a form to the like effect. **1–61**

Notice to defendant

3. Where a notice of transfer is served by or on behalf of the Director, a copy of the notice shall be given by or on behalf of the Director to any person to whom the notice of transfer relates (or, if he is acting by a solicitor, to his solicitor) together with—

(a) a notice in Form 2 in the Schedule to these Regulations, or in a form to the like effect; and

(b) subject to regulation 3A below, copies of the documents containing the evidence (including oral evidence) on which any charge to which the notice of transfer relates is based.

3A. There shall be no requirement for copies of any documents referred to in the documents sent with the notice of transfer as having already been supplied to accompany the copy of the notice of transfer given in accordance with regulation 3 above.

Notice to Crown Court

4. Where a notice of transfer is served by or on behalf of the Director, a copy of the notice shall be given by or on behalf of the Director to the appropriate officer of the Crown Court sitting at the place specified by the notice of transfer as the proposed place of trial together with—

(a) a copy of the notice referred to in paragraph (a) of regulation 3 above and copies of the material enclosed with that notice; and

(b) copies of the documents referred to in paragraph (b) of that regulation, including both those which accompanied the copy of the notice of transfer given to the person to whom the notice relates and those which had already been supplied.

Notice to prison governor etc.

5. Where a notice of transfer is served by or on behalf of the Director, a copy of the notice shall be given by or on behalf of the Director to any person who has custody of any person to whom the notice of transfer relates together with a copy of the notice referred to in paragraph (a) of regulation 3 above.

[Regs 3 and 4 are printed as amended by the *Criminal Justice Act 1991 (Notice of Transfer) (Amendment) Regulations* 1998 (S.I. 1998 No. 461), which also inserted reg. 3A.]

The Schedule contains forms corresponding to the forms in the Schedule to S.I. 1988 No. 1691 (*ante*, § 1–46); form 2 was amended by S.I. 1998 No. 461, *ante*.

Notice of transfer rules

See *ante*, §§ 1–48 *et seq.*, for details of the rules which now apply to all proceedings where a notice of transfer is given. **1–62**

(b) *Dismissal applications*

Procedure and evidence

The procedural rules and evidential principles relating to dismissal applications that are made under paragraph 5 of Schedule 6 to the *CJA* 1991 (*ante*, § 1–56) are now the same as in respect of dismissal applications made under paragraph 2 of Schedule 3 to the *CDA* 1998, as to which see *ante*, §§ 1–38 *et seq.* **1–63**

Criteria to be applied on application, and challenges to decisions

The relevant principles are the same as those which apply in respect of dismissal applications made under paragraph 2 of Schedule 3 to the *CDA* 1998, as to which see *ante*, § 1–40. **1–64**

D. COMMITTALS FOR TRIAL

(1) Introduction

1-65 The conventional process through which a case passes before any charge comes before the Crown Court on indictment is: determination of mode of trial, followed by committal proceedings to determine whether there is a case to answer, and, if there is, committal of the case to the Crown Court. These procedures take place in the magistrates' courts, pursuant to the provisions of the *MCA* 1980, with the voluntary bill of indictment procedure being available as an alternative in exceptional cases instead of proceedings before the magistrates, or where the magistrates have determined that there is no case to answer (*post*, §§ 1–226 *et seq.*). As to committal proceedings generally, see *post*, §§ 2–11, 4–20 and 10–9 to 10–40. See also *post*, §§ 1–73 *et seq.*

The scope of the investigation in committal proceedings has been limited by amendments to the 1980 Act over the years, and in certain classes of case the committal process has been replaced by the summary "transfer for trial" and "sending for trial" procedures, as to which see *ante*, §§ 1–14 *et seq.*, in which any preliminary issue as to whether there is a case to answer is dealt with in the Crown Court by way of a "dismissal" application. When the provisions of Schedule 3 to the *CJA* 2003 are fully in force, the committal process will be abolished completely and replaced by the substituted "sending for trial" provisions of sections 51 to 51E of the *CDA* 1998. However, mode of trial procedures in the magistrates' courts will continue to exist, albeit in an amended form.

(2) Determination of mode of trial

1-66 Adults who appear or are brought before a magistrates' court charged with an offence triable only on indictment must always be sent forthwith to the Crown Court for trial in accordance with section 51 of the *CDA* 1998, as to which see *ante*, §§ 1–17 *et seq*. The position of a child or young person who is jointly tried with such an adult must also be considered in accordance with the provisions of section 51. As to the transfer of cases in which notices of transfer have been served pursuant to section 4 of the *CJA* 1987 (serious fraud), or section 53 of the *CJA* 1991 (certain cases involving children as a victim or witness), pending the prospective repeal of those provisions, see *ante*, §§ 1–41 *et seq*.

Once section 50A of the *CDA* 1998 is in force, a magistrates' court before whom an adult charged with an either-way offence appears or is brought must proceed in accordance with that section, as to which see *ante*, § 1–16. See *post*, § 1–75ad as to what is an either-way offence.

If, in the case of an adult who appears or is brought before a magistrates' court charged with an either-way offence, the matter has not been dealt with by a transfer or sending for trial in accordance with the above mentioned provisions, the court is required to proceed as follows.

(a) *Statutory provisions*

Procedure for indication of intention as to plea

Magistrates' Courts Act 1980, ss.17A–17E

Initial procedure: accused to indicate intention as to plea

1-67 **17A.**—(1) This section shall have effect where a person who has attained the age of 18 years appears or is brought before a magistrates' court on an information charging him with an offence triable either way.

(2) Everything that the court is required to do under the following provisions of this section must be done with the accused present in court.

(3) The court shall cause the charge to be written down, if this has not already been done, and to be read to the accused.

(4) The court shall then explain to the accused in ordinary language that he may indicate whether (if the offence were to proceed to trial) he would plead guilty or not guilty, and that if he indicates that he would plead guilty—

(a) the court must proceed as mentioned in subsection (6) below; and

(b) *he may be committed for sentence to the Crown Court under section 3 of the* Powers of Criminal Courts (Sentencing) Act *2000 if the court is of such opinion as is mentioned in subsection (2) of that section* [he may (unless section 17D(2) below were to apply) be committed for sentence to the Crown Court under section 3 or (if applicable) 3A of the *Powers of Criminal Courts (Sentencing) Act* 2000 if the court is of such opinion as is mentioned in subsection (2) of the applicable section].

(5) The court shall then ask the accused whether (if the offence were to proceed to trial) he would plead guilty or not guilty.

(6) If the accused indicates that he would plead guilty the court shall proceed as if—

(a) the proceedings constituted from the beginning the summary trial of the information; and

(b) section 9(1) above was complied with and he pleaded guilty under it.

(7) If the accused indicates that he would plead not guilty section 18(1) below shall apply.

(8) If the accused in fact fails to indicate how he would plead, for the purposes of this section and section 18(1) below he shall be taken to indicate that he would plead not guilty.

(9) Subject to subsection (6) above, the following shall not for any purpose be taken to constitute the taking of a plea—

(a) asking the accused under this section whether (if the offence were to proceed to trial) he would plead guilty or not guilty;

(b) an indication by the accused under this section of how he would plead.

[(10) If in respect of the offence the court receives a notice under section 51B or 51C of the *Crime and Disorder Act* 1998 (which relate to serious or complex fraud cases and to certain cases involving children respectively), the preceding provisions of this section and the provisions of section 17B below shall not apply, and the court shall proceed in relation to the offence in accordance with section 51 or, as the case may be, section 51A of that Act.]

[This section was inserted by the *CPIA* 1996, s.49(1) and (2). It is printed as amended by the *PCC(S)A* 2000, s.165(1), and Sched. 9, para. 62. As from a day or days to be appointed, the *CJA* 2003, s.41, and Sched. 3, paras 1 and 2 (as itself amended by the *CJIA* 2008, s.53, and Sched. 13, paras 1 and 2), amend subs. (4)(b), by substituting the words in square brackets, and insert subs. (10).]

Intention as to plea: absence of accused

17B.—(1) This section shall have effect where— **1–68**

(a) a person who has attained the age of 18 years appears or is brought before a magistrates' court on an information charging him with an offence triable either way,

(b) the accused is represented by a legal representative,

(c) the court considers that by reason of the accused's disorderly conduct before the court it is not practicable for proceedings under section 17A above to be conducted in his presence, and

(d) the court considers that it should proceed in the absence of the accused.

(2) In such a case—

(a) the court shall cause the charge to be written down, if this has not already been done, and to be read to the representative;

(b) the court shall ask the representative whether (if the offence were to proceed to trial) the accused would plead guilty or not guilty;

(c) if the representative indicates that the accused would plead guilty the court shall proceed as if the proceedings constituted from the beginning the summary trial of the information, and as if section 9(1) above was complied with and the accused pleaded guilty under it;

(d) if the representative indicates that the accused would plead not guilty section 18(1) below shall apply.

(3) If the representative in fact fails to indicate how the accused would plead, for the purposes of this section and section 18(1) below he shall be taken to indicate that the accused would plead not guilty.

(4) Subject to subsection (2)(c) above, the following shall not for any purpose be taken to constitute the taking of a plea—

(a) asking the representative under this section whether (if the offence were to proceed to trial) the accused would plead guilty or not guilty;

(b) an indication by the representative under this section of how the accused would plead.

Intention as to plea: adjournment

1–69 **17C.** A magistrates' court proceeding under section 17A or 17B above may adjourn the proceedings at any time, and on doing so on any occasion when the accused is present may remand the accused, and shall remand him if—

(a) on the occasion on which he first appeared, or was brought, before the court to answer to the information he was in custody or, having been released on bail, surrendered to the custody of the court; or

(b) he has been remanded at any time in the course of proceedings on the information;

and where the court remands the accused, the time fixed for the resumption of proceedings shall be that at which he is required to appear or be brought before the court in pursuance of the remand or would be required to be brought before the court but for section 128(3A) below.

[Sections 17B and 17C were inserted by the *CPIA* 1996, s.49(1) and (2).]

[Maximum penalty under section 17A(6) or 17B(2)(c) for certain offences

1–70 **17D.**—(1) If—

(a) the offence is a scheduled offence (as defined in section 22(1) below);

(b) the court proceeds in relation to the offence in accordance with section 17A(6) or 17B(2)(c) above; and

(c) the court convicts the accused of the offence,

the court shall consider whether, having regard to any representations made by him or by the prosecutor, the value involved (as defined in section 22(10) below) appears to the court to exceed the relevant sum (as specified for the purposes of section 22 below).

(2) If it appears to the court clear that the value involved does not exceed the relevant sum, or it appears to the court for any reason not clear whether the value involved does or does not exceed the relevant sum—

(a) subject to subsection (4) below, the court shall not have power to impose on the accused in respect of the offence a sentence in excess of the limits mentioned in section 33(1)(a) below; and

(b) sections 3 and 4 of the *Powers of Criminal Courts (Sentencing) Act* 2000 shall not apply as regards that offence.

(3) Subsections (9) to (12) of section 22 below shall apply for the purposes of this section as they apply for the purposes of that section (reading the reference to subsection (1) in section 22(9) as a reference to subsection (1) of this section).

(4) Subsection (2)(a) above does not apply to an offence under section 12A of the *Theft Act* 1968 (aggravated vehicle-taking).]

[Functions under sections 17A to 17D capable of exercise by single justice

1–71 **17E.**—(1) The functions of a magistrates' court under sections 17A to 17D above may be discharged by a single justice.

(2) Subsection (1) above shall not be taken as authorising—

(a) the summary trial of an information (otherwise than in accordance with section 17A(6) or 17B(2)(c) above); or

(b) the imposition of a sentence,

by a magistrates' court composed of fewer than two justices.]

[Sections 17D and 17E are inserted, as from a day to be appointed, by the *CJA* 2003, s.41, and Sched. 3, paras 1 and 3.]

1–72 As to the proper application of section 3 of the *PCC(S)A* 2000 (committal for sentence) where an intention to plead guilty is indicated by or on behalf of the accused during the "plea before venue" procedure, see *post*, § 5–29. See also, *post*, § 5–30, as to the need for magistrates to make clear whether the option of committal for sentence is being left open when adjourning for reports after a guilty plea has been indicated.

The procedure provided for by section 22(1) and (2) of the *MCA* 1980 (*post*, § 1–75i), as to mode of trial for certain offences where the value involved is small, is to be taken to prevail over the procedure provided for by section 17A of the same Act in such cases: *R. v. Kelly* [2001] R.T.R. 5, CA. This decision provides a pragmatic solution in respect of a problem that arises from what appears to be an oversight in the drafting of section 17A, and the consequential amendment of section 18(1) of the 1980 Act (*post*, § 1–73). Section 18(1) provides that section 22 has effect once a not guilty plea has been indicated under section 17A. The question arises as to whether section 22 can have effect in any other situation. Section 17A(6) makes provision as to the situation where a guilty plea is indicated, but this provision makes no reference to section 22. In the case under consideration by the court this had led to a defendant who had indicated a guilty plea in a small value case being committed to the Crown Court for sentence, section 22 never having been engaged and the offence charged thus having been treated as an either way offence.

As to the provisions for advance disclosure in a magistrates' court also taking precedence over the plea before venue provisions, see *R. v. Calderdale Magistrates' Court, ex p. Donahue and Cutler* [2001] Crim.L.R. 141, DC (*post*, § 12–118).

Procedure for determining mode of trial of offences triable either way

Magistrates' Courts Act 1980, s.18

Initial procedure on information for offence triable either way

18.—(1) Sections 19 to 23 below shall have effect where a person who has attained the age of 18 years appears or is brought before a magistrates' court on an information charging him with an offence triable either way and— **1–73**

(a) he indicates under section 17A above that (if the offence were to proceed to trial) he would plead not guilty, or

(b) his representative indicates under section 17B above that (if the offence were to proceed to trial) he would plead not guilty.

(2) Without prejudice to section 11(1) above everything that the court is required to do under sections 19 to 22 below must be done before any evidence is called and, subject to subsection (3) below and section 23 below, with the accused present in court.

(3) The court may proceed in the absence of the accused in accordance with such of the provisions of sections 19 to 22 below as are applicable in the circumstances if they consider that by reason of his disorderly conduct before them it is not practicable for the proceedings to be conducted in his presence; and subsections (3) to (5) of section 23 below, so far as applicable, shall have effect in relation to proceedings conducted in the absence of the accused by virtue of this subsection (references in those subsections to the person representing the accused being for this purpose read as references to the person, if any, representing him).

(4) A magistrates' court proceeding under sections 19 to 23 below may adjourn the proceedings at any time, and on doing so on any occasion when the accused is present may remand the accused, and shall remand him if—

(a) on the occasion on which he first appeared, or was brought, before the court to answer to the information he was in custody or, having been released on bail surrendered to the custody of the court; or

(b) if he has been remanded at any time in the course of proceedings on the information;

and where the court remands the accused, the time fixed for the resumption of the proceedings shall be that at which he is required to appear or be brought before the court in pursuance of the remand or would be required to be brought before the court but for section 128(3A) below.

(5) The functions of a magistrates' court under sections 19 to 23 below may be discharged by a single justice, but *the foregoing provision shall not be taken to authorise the summary trial of an information by a magistrates' court composed of less than two justices* [this subsection shall not be taken as authorizing—

(a) the summary trial of an information (otherwise than in accordance with section 20(7) below); or

(b) the imposition of a sentence,

by a magistrates' court composed of fewer than two justices].

[This section is printed as amended by the *CJA* 1982, Sched. 9; the *CJA* 1991, s.68, and Sched. 8, para. 6(1)(a); and the *CPIA* 1996, s.49(3). As from a day to be appointed, the *CJA* 2003, s.41, and Sched. 3, paras 1 and 4, amend subs. (5) by substituting the words in square brackets for the italicised words.]

Section 11(1) of the 1980 Act contains general provisions as to the non-appearance of the accused.

For section 128(3A), see *post*, § 3–148.

The stage of the proceedings at which a defendant charged with an offence triable either way must have attained the age provided for in section 18(1) of the 1980 Act, so as to enable him to elect trial by jury, is the occasion when the court makes its decision as to which mode of trial should be adopted. It is not the occasion when the defendant first appears before the youth court to answer the information: *R. v. Islington North Juvenile Court, ex p. Daley* [1983] 1 A.C. 347, HL. If mode of trial has been decided upon, the fact that the defendant reaches the relevant age before any trial actually takes place does not enable a committal for trial then to take place: *R. v. Nottingham JJ., ex p. Taylor* [1992] 1 Q.B. 557, 93 Cr.App.R. 365, DC. The taking of a plea from a defendant who is under the age of 18 amounts to a decision as to mode of trial: *R. v. West London JJ., ex p. Siley-Winditt* [2000] Crim.L.R. 926, DC. See section 25(5) to (7) of the 1980 Act (*post*, §§ 1–75v *et seq.*) for the limited statutory power to redetermine the mode of trial of a defendant who was under the relevant age at the time of the original determination of mode of trial.

As to the circumstances in which a person under the age of 18 is to be committed for trial, see *post*, §§ 1–75m *et seq.*

As to the ascertainment of age, see *post*, § 19–326.

As to the adjournment of mode of trial proceedings where the prosecution give an assurance that they intend to issue a notice of transfer, see *ante*, § 1–41. Once the decision has been made to try a case summarily and, in the case of an adult, there is consent to being so tried, it is too late to serve a notice of transfer: *R. v. Fareham Youth Court and Morey, ex p. CPS*, 163 J.P. 812, DC.

Magistrates' Courts Act 1980, s.19

Court to begin by considering which mode of trial appears more suitable

1–74 **19.**—(1) *The court shall consider whether, having regard to the matters mentioned in subsection (3) below and any representations made by the prosecutor or the accused, the offence appears to the court more suitable for summary trial or for trial on indictment.*

(2) *Before so considering, the court—*

(a) [repealed by *CPIA* 1996, s.49(4)];

(b) *shall afford first the prosecutor and then the accused an opportunity to make representations as to which mode of trial would be more suitable.*

(3) *The matters to which the court is to have regard under subsection (1) above are the nature of the case; whether the circumstances make the offence one of serious character; whether the punishment which a magistrates' court would have power to inflict for it would be adequate; and any other circumstances which appear to the court to make it more suitable for the offence to be tried in one way rather than the other.*

(4) *If the prosecution is being carried on by the Attorney General, the Solicitor General or the Director of Public Prosecutions and he applies for the offence to be tried on indictment, the preceding provisions of this section and sections 20 and 21 below shall not apply, and the court shall proceed to inquire into the information as examining justices.*

(5) *The power of the Director of Public Prosecutions under subsection (4) above to apply for an offence to be tried on indictment shall not be exercised except with the consent of the Attorney General.*

[Decision as to allocation

19.—(1) The court shall decide whether the offence appears to it more suitable for summary trial or for trial on indictment.

(2) Before making a decision under this section, the court—

(a) shall give the prosecution an opportunity to inform the court of the accused's previous convictions (if any); and

(b) shall give the prosecution and the accused an opportunity to make representations as to whether summary trial or trial on indictment would be more suitable.

(3) In making a decision under this section, the court shall consider—

(a) whether the sentence which a magistrates' court would have power to impose for the offence would be adequate; and

(b) any representations made by the prosecution or the accused under subsection (2)(b) above, and shall have regard to any allocation guidelines (or revised allocation guidelines) issued as definitive guidelines under section 170 of the *Criminal Justice Act* 2003.

(4) Where—

(a) the accused is charged with two or more offences; and

(b) it appears to the court that the charges for the offences could be joined in the same indictment or that the offences arise out of the same or connected circumstances,

subsection (3)(a) above shall have effect as if references to the sentence which a magistrates' court would have power to impose for the offence were a reference to the maximum aggregate sentence which a magistrates' court would have power to impose for all of the offences taken together.

(5) In this section any reference to a previous conviction is a reference to—

(a) a previous conviction by a court in the United Kingdom; or

(b) a previous [conviction of a service offence within the meaning of the *Armed Forces Act* 2006 ("conviction" here including anything that under section 376(1) and (2) of that Act is to be treated as a conviction)] *finding of guilt in—*

(i) *any proceedings under the* Army Act *1955, the* Air Force Act *1955* or the Naval Discipline Act *1957 (whether before a court-martial or any other court or person authorised under any of those Acts to award a punishment in respect of any offence); or*

(ii) *any proceedings before a Standing Civilian Court.*

(6) If, in respect of the offence, the court receives a notice under section 51B or 51C of the *Crime and Disorder Act* 1998 (which relate to serious or complex fraud cases and to certain cases involving children respectively), the preceding provisions of this section and sections 20, 20A and 21 below shall not apply, and the court shall proceed in relation to the offence in accordance with section 51(1) of that Act.]

[Subs. (5) of the original section was added by the *Prosecution of Offences Act* 1985, Sched. 1, para. 2. As from a day to be appointed, a new section 19 (in square brackets) is substituted for the original section (italicised) by the *CJA* 2003, s.41, and Sched. 3, paras 1 and 5. In subs. (5) of the new section, the words in square brackets are inserted, and the italicised words are omitted, as from a day to be appointed: *AFA* 2006, s.378(1), and Sched. 16, para. 88.]

The court should not be given, and should not take into account, any information as **1–75** to the defendant's previous convictions (*R. v. Colchester JJ., ex p. North East Essex Building Co. Ltd* [1977] 1 W.L.R. 1109, DC), but the position in this regard will be different when the substituted section comes into force.

Trial on indictment is not more suitable than summary trial merely because one of jointly charged defendants indicates that he will elect trial on indictment in any event: *R. v. Brentwood JJ., ex p. Nicholls* [1992] 1 A.C. 1, HL.

There are situations when it is foreseen that contested issues as to the disclosure of sensitive material will arise, such as to make it desirable for the matter to be dealt with on indictment: *R. v. Bromley JJ., ex p. Smith and Wilkins*; *R. v. Wells Street Stipendiary Magistrate, ex p. King* [1995] 2 Cr.App.R. 285, DC. However, magistrates' courts can properly decide issues as to non-disclosure of material on the grounds of public interest immunity and should not, as a matter of invariable practice, decline jurisdiction in such cases because of the existence of such an issue; no distinction is to be drawn in this regard as between lay justices and a professional magistrate; the normal practice should be for the trial to be conducted before the same bench as has conducted any application for non-disclosure; only in the case of highly prejudicial material having been disclosed to the bench during such an application should the bench disqualify itself; this would be exceptional, especially because any successor bench would need to be apprised of the same material: *R. v. Stipendiary Magistrate for Norfolk, ex p. Taylor*, 161 J.P. 773, DC. It is submitted that the need, in a magistrates' court, for the ultimate fact-finding body to be apprised of prejudicial material may in itself provide a justification for the matter to go to the Crown Court in such a case.

The prosecution should not invite justices to deal with serious offences summarily, even though such a course may be convenient and expeditious: *R. v. Coe*, 53 Cr.App.R. 66, CA; *R. v. Norfolk JJ., ex p. DPP* [1950] 2 K.B. 558 at 567, 34 Cr.App.R. 120 at

126, DC. *Cf. R. v. McLean, ex p. Metropolitan Police Commr* [1975] Crim.L.R. 289, DC (magistrate's acceptance of jurisdiction not unreasonable, appropriate penalties had been imposed).

When deciding whether to accept jurisdiction, the circumstances of the case as alleged by the prosecution should be considered in the light of: (i) the limited sentencing powers of magistrates' courts; and (ii) the consolidated criminal practice direction (*post*, § 1–75u). Thus, it was held to be inappropriate for the magistrates to have accepted jurisdiction in *R. v. Northamptonshire Magistrates' Court, ex p. Commrs of Customs and Excise* [1994] Crim.L.R. 598, DC (fraudulent evasion of nearly £200,000 of VAT, with unrecovered property of high value); *R. v. Horseferry Road Magistrates' Court, ex p. DPP* [1997] C.O.D. 89, DC (possession of 114 Ecstasy tablets with intent to supply); and *R. v. Stamford Magistrates' Court, ex p. DPP* [1998] C.O.D. 10, DC (burglary by breaking into dormitory of school at night). But, an assault committed by banging the victim's head against part of a building cannot be said to involve "the use of a weapon", within the meaning of the practice direction: *R. v. Derby JJ., ex p. DPP*, *The Times*, August 17, 1999, DC.

As to the power of magistrates to commit for sentence in a case in which no new information has emerged after they have accepted jurisdiction, and as to the exercise of that power, see *post*, §§ 5–24, 5–29.

Magistrates' Courts Act 1980, ss.20, 20A

Procedure where summary trial appears more suitable

1–75a **20.**—(1) *If, where the court has considered as required by section 19(1) above, it appears to the court that the offence is more suitable for summary trial, the following provisions of this section shall apply (unless excluded by section 23 below).*

(2) *The court shall explain to the accused in ordinary language—*

(a) *that it appears to the court more suitable for him to be tried summarily for the offence, and that he can either consent to be so tried or, if he wishes, be tried by a jury; and*

(b) *that if he is tried summarily and is convicted by the court, he may be committed for sentence to the Crown Court under section 3 of the* Powers of Criminal Courts (Sentencing) Act *2000 if the convicting court is of such opinion as mentioned in subsection (2) of that section.*

(3) *After explaining to the accused as provided by subsection (2) above the court shall ask him whether he consents to be tried summarily or wishes to be tried by a jury, and—*

(a) *if he consents to be tried summarily, shall proceed to the summary trial of the information;*

(b) *if he does not consent, shall proceed to inquire into the information as examining justices.*

[20.—(1) If the court decides under section 19 above that the offence appears to it more suitable for summary trial, the following provisions of this section shall apply (unless they are excluded by section 23 below).

(2) The court shall explain to the accused in ordinary language—

(a) that it appears to the court more suitable for him to be tried summarily for the offence;

(b) that he can either consent to be so tried or, if he wishes, be tried on indictment; and

(c) that if he is tried summarily and is convicted by the court, he may be committed for sentence to the Crown Court under section 3 or (if applicable) section 3A of the *Powers of Criminal Courts (Sentencing) Act* 2000 if the court is of such opinion as is mentioned in subsection (2) of the applicable section.

(3) The accused may then request an indication ("an indication of sentence") of whether a custodial sentence or non-custodial sentence would be more likely to be imposed if he were to be tried summarily for the offence and to plead guilty.

(4) If the accused requests an indication of sentence, the court may, but need not, give such an indication.

(5) If the accused requests and the court gives an indication of sentence, the court shall ask the accused whether he wishes, on the basis of the indication, to reconsider the indication of plea which was given, or is taken to have been given, under section 17A or 17B above.

(6) If the accused indicates that he wishes to reconsider the indication under section 17A or 17B above, the court shall ask the accused whether (if the offence were to proceed to trial) he would plead guilty or not guilty.

(7) If the accused indicates that he would plead guilty the court shall proceed as if—

(a) the proceedings constituted from that time the summary trial of the information; and

(b) section 9(1) above were complied with and he pleaded guilty under it.

(8) Subsection (9) below applies where—

(a) the court does not give an indication of sentence (whether because the accused does not request one or because the court does not agree to give one);

(b) the accused either—

(i) does not indicate, in accordance with subsection (5) above, that he wishes; or

(ii) indicates, in accordance with subsection (5) above, that he does not wish, to reconsider the indication of plea under section 17A or 17B above; or

(c) the accused does not indicate, in accordance with subsection (6) above, that he would plead guilty.

(9) The court shall ask the accused whether he consents to be tried summarily or wishes to be tried on indictment and—

(a) if he consents to be tried summarily, shall proceed to the summary trial of the information; and

(b) if he does not so consent, shall proceed in relation to the offence in accordance with section 51(1) of the *Crime and Disorder Act* 1998.]

[Procedure where summary trial appears more suitable: supplementary

20A.—(1) Where the case is dealt with in accordance with section 20(7) above, no court (whether a magistrates' court or not) may impose a custodial sentence for the offence unless such a sentence was indicated in the indication of sentence referred to in section 20 above. **1–75b**

(2) Subsection (1) above is subject to sections 3A(4), 4(8) and 5(3) of the *Powers of Criminal Courts (Sentencing) Act* 2000.

(3) Except as provided in subsection (1) above—

(a) an indication of sentence shall not be binding on any court (whether a magistrates' court or not); and

(b) no sentence may be challenged or be the subject of appeal in any court on the ground that it is not consistent with an indication of sentence.

(4) Subject to section 20(7) above, the following shall not for any purpose be taken to constitute the taking of a plea—

(a) asking the accused under section 20 above whether (if the offence were to proceed to trial) he would plead guilty or not guilty; or

(b) an indication by the accused under that section of how he would plead.

(5) Where the court gives an indication of sentence under section 20 above, it shall cause each such indication to be entered in the register.

(6) In this section and in section 20 above, references to a custodial sentence are to a custodial sentence within the meaning of section 76 of the *Powers of Criminal Courts (Sentencing) Act* 2000, and references to a non-custodial sentence shall be construed accordingly.]

[The original section 20 (italicised) is printed as amended by the *CJA* 1991, s.100, and Sched. 11, para. 25; and the *PCC(S)A* 2000, s.165(1), and Sched. 9, para. 63. As from a day to be appointed, new sections 20 and 20A (both in square brackets) are substituted for that section by the *CJA* 2003, s.41, and Sched. 3, paras 1 and 6 (as itself amended by the *CJIA* 2008, s.53, and Sched. 13, paras 1 and 3).]

As to section 3 of the 2000 Act (see the original s.20(2)(b)) and as to the need for an accurate explanation of its effect to be given before an election for summary trial is made, see *post*, §§ 5–24, 5–29.

Consequences of failure to follow prescribed procedure

Failure to comply with the procedure stipulated by sections 18 to 21 of the 1980 Act may result in any ensuing proceedings being held to be a nullity: see *R. v. Simons*, 37 Cr.App.R. 120, CCA, and *R. v. Cardiff Magistrates' Court, ex p. Cardiff* **1–75c**

City Council, *The Times*, February 24, 1987, DC (*certiorari* granted to quash acquittal where defendant had not been put to his election, so that summons could be reheard after defendant had been put to his election). See also *post*, §§ 1–209 *et seq.* as to the consequences of an invalid committal, and, as to validity generally, see *ante*, § 1–35, and *post*, §§ 1–161 *et seq.* and 1–195 *et seq.*

Application to change election

1–75d Magistrates have a discretion to permit a change of election as to mode of trial. When considering how to exercise that discretion a fundamental question is whether the defendant properly understood the nature and significance of the choice which he had made at his initial election. Unless he had such an understanding, he should be permitted to re-elect. On an application to change an election for summary trial, where a not guilty plea has been entered, the facts that prosecution witnesses are ready to give evidence and that it is undesirable to delay the trial further are not relevant to the understanding of the applicant, but once it is established that he understood the nature and significance of his original choice these are matters that can properly be taken into account in the exercise of the justices' discretion: *R. v. Bourne JJ., ex p. Cope* [1989] C.O.D. 304, DC. An accused person is not lightly to be deprived of a right to trial by jury: *R. v. Craske, ex p. Metropolitan Police Commr* [1957] 2 Q.B. 591, DC. Where an accused has been permitted to withdraw a guilty plea (at to which, see *post*, §§ 2–200, 4–186 and 4–187), or where an equivocal plea of guilty has not been accepted, it is inescapable that the accused should be given the right to choose whether or not to consent to summary trial afresh. The fact that the magistrates consider the case more suitable for summary trial is irrelevant in such circumstances: *R. v. Birmingham JJ., ex p. Hodgson* [1985] Q.B. 1131, 81 Cr.App.R. 231, DC; *R. v. Bow Street Magistrate, ex p. Welcombe*, *The Times*, May 7, 1992, DC.

Election as to mode of trial where defendants jointly charged

1–75e The right of election in section 20(3) is given to each accused individually and is not intended to be affected by the nature of any different election made by his co-accused. It is not the case that if one of a number of jointly charged defendants elects trial on indictment, all must be treated as if bound by that election: *R. v. Brentwood JJ., ex p. Nicholls* [1992] 1 A.C. 1, HL. See also *ante*, § 1–75.

Substitution of summary only charge

1–75f The prosecution do not need leave to offer no evidence on an either way charge in respect of which the defendant has elected for trial on indictment and the Divisional Court will not grant judicial review of a summary only charge arising out of the same facts in such circumstances, provided that the offences are not grave ones and that the powers of the justices *vis-à-vis* sentence are appropriate: *R. v. Canterbury and St Augustine JJ., ex p. Klisiak* [1982] Q.B. 398, 72 Cr.App.R. 250, DC. This will be the position even where the sole purpose of the substitution is to deprive the defendant of a jury trial. In the absence of bad faith, the only basis for judicial review can be on the question of appropriateness of the particular charge for summary trial: *R. v. Liverpool Stipendiary Magistrate, ex p. Ellison* [1990] R.T.R. 220, DC. See also *R. v. Barking Magistrates, ex p. DPP* [1993] C.O.D. 108, DC.

Addition or substitution of charge triable only on indictment

1–75g Where a defendant is charged with an "either way" offence, justices cannot refuse to issue an additional summons alleging an offence triable only on indictment merely because the prosecutor's reason for adding the new charge is to ensure that the case is heard in the Crown Court, provided that the justices are satisfied that the course proposed by the prosecutor is proper and appropriate in the light of the facts put before them. However, once the justices have decided to try the original charge summarily, any later application to add a charge triable only on indictment should be scrutinised with particular care so that the earlier decision to deal with the matter summarily is not improperly frustrated. It is only in an exceptional case that the Divisional Court will interfere with a bona fide exercise by the justices of their discretion in such a matter: *R. v. Redbridge JJ., ex p. Whitehouse*, 94 Cr.App.R. 332, DC. See also *post*, § 4–60.

Magistrates' Courts Act 1980, s.21

Procedure where trial on indictment appears more suitable

21. *If, where the court has considered as required by section 19(1) above, it appears to the court that the offence is more suitable for trial on indictment, the court shall tell the accused that the court has decided that it is more suitable for him to be tried for the offence by a jury, and shall proceed to inquire into the information as examining justices.* **1–75h**

[**21.** If the court decides under section 19 above that the offence appears to it more suitable for trial on indictment, the court shall tell the accused that the court has decided that it is more suitable for him to be tried on indictment, and shall proceed in relation to the offence in accordance with section 51(1) of the *Crime and Disorder Act* 1998.]

[As from a day to be appointed, a new section 21 (in square brackets) is substituted for the original section (italicised) by the *CJA* 2003, s.41, and Sched. 3, paras 1 and 7.]

Magistrates who have decided that trial on indictment is appropriate do not thereafter begin the committal procedure of inquiring into the case by simply hearing an application to stay the proceedings for abuse of process. The application for the stay and the committal inquiry are separate matters. It is desirable that the same magistrates should adjudicate on both matters, where both arise, but this is not essential unless the application for a stay is made after the magistrates begin to inquire into the case as examining justices: *R. v. Worcester Magistrates' Court, ex p. Bell*, 157 J.P. 921, DC.

Magistrates' Courts Act 1980, s.22

Certain offences triable either way to be tried summarily if value involved is small

22.—(1) If the offence charged by the information is one of those mentioned in the first column of Schedule 2 to this Act (in this section referred to as "scheduled offences") then, ... the court shall, before proceeding in accordance with section 19 above, consider whether, having regard to any representations made by the prosecutor or the accused, the value involved (as defined in subsection (10) below) appears to the court to exceed the relevant sum. **1–75i**

For the purposes of this section the relevant sum is £5,000.

(2) If, where subsection (1) above applies, it appears to the court clear that, for the offence charged, the value involved does not exceed the relevant sum, the court shall proceed as if the offence were triable only summarily, and sections 19 to 21 above shall not apply.

(3) If, where subsection (1) above applies, it appears to the court clear that, for the offence charged, the value involved exceeds the relevant sum, the court shall thereupon proceed in accordance with section 19 above in the ordinary way without further regard to the provisions of this section.

(4) If, where subsection (1) above applies, it appears to the court for any reason not clear whether, for the offence charged, the value involved does or does not exceed the relevant sum, the provisions of subsections (5) and (6) below shall apply.

(5) The court shall cause the charge to be written down, if this has not already been done, and read to the accused, and shall explain to him in ordinary language—

- (a) that he can, if he wishes, consent to be tried summarily for the offence and that if he consents to be so tried, he will definitely be tried in that way; and
- (b) that if he is tried summarily and is convicted by the court, his liability to imprisonment or a fine will be limited as provided in section 33 below.

(6) After explaining to the accused as provided by subsection (5) above the court shall ask him whether he consents to be tried summarily and—

- (a) if he so consents, shall proceed in accordance with subsection (2) above as if that subsection applied;
- (b) if he does not so consent, shall proceed in accordance with subsection (3) above as if that subsection applied.

(7) [*Repealed by* Criminal Justice Act *1988, s.170(2) and Sched. 16.*]

(8) Where a person is convicted by a magistrates' court of a scheduled offence, it shall not be open to him to appeal to the Crown Court against the conviction on the ground that the convicting court's decision as to the value involved was mistaken.

(9) If, where subsection (1) above applies, the offence charged is one with which the accused is charged jointly with a person who has not attained the age of 18 years, the reference

in that subsection to any representations made by the accused shall be read as including any representations made by the person under 18.

(10) In this section "the value involved," in relation to any scheduled offence, means the value indicated in the second column of Schedule 2 to this Act, measured as indicated in the third column of that Schedule; and in that Schedule "the material time" means the time of the alleged offence.

(11) Where—

(a) the accused is charged on the same occasion with two or more scheduled offences and it appears to the court that they constitute or form part of a series of two or more offences of the same or a similar character; or

(b) the offence charged consists in incitement to commit two or more scheduled offences,

this section shall have effect as if any reference in it to the value involved were a reference to the aggregate of the values involved.

(12) Subsection (8) of section 12A of the *Theft Act* 1968 (which determines when a vehicle is recovered) shall apply for the purposes of paragraph 3 of Schedule 2 to this Act as it applies for the purposes of that section.

[This section is printed as amended by the *CJA* 1988, s.38(3); the *CJA* 1991, s.68, and Sched. 8, para. 6(1)(a) and (b); the *Aggravated Vehicle-Taking Act* 1992, s.2(2); and the *CJPOA* 1994, ss.46(1) and 168(3), and Sched. 11. The reference in subs. (11) to the common law offence of incitement has effect as a reference to the offences under the *SCA* 2007, Pt 2: 2007 Act, s.63(1), and Sched. 6, para. 5(a).]

1–75j For sentencing powers on summary conviction in pursuance of section 22(2), see section 33, *post*, § 1–75ab. For Schedule 2 to the 1980 Act, see *post*, § 1–75k. Section 22 is mandatory: see *R. v. Braden*, 87 Cr.App.R. 289, CA.

The procedure provided for by section 22 is to be taken to prevail over the "plea before venue" procedure: see *ante*, § 1–72.

Section 22(10) defines "the value involved" by reference to Schedule 2 to the 1980 Act, which makes express provision as to the value of damage being measured by the open market replacement cost where the property has been damaged beyond repair (*post*, § 1–75k); consequential loss is therefore irrelevant to the assessment of the value of damage for the purposes of section 22: *R. v. Colchester Magistrates' Court, ex p. Abbott*, 165 J.P. 386, DC. Where a charge alleged destruction of an experimental maize crop, the district judge had been entitled to conclude that by reason of the investment that had gone into its production the value of the crop had been greater than that of a like crop of ordinary maize, and that, because there was no open market in the property in question, it was not clear whether the value exceeded the relevant sum; thus the case came within section 22(4): *R. (DPP) v. Prestatyn Magistrates' Court* [2002] Crim.L.R. 924, DC.

It is not necessary for justices to hear evidence as to value; whether they should or not is a matter for their discretion: *R. v. Canterbury and St Augustine JJ., ex p. Klisiak* [1982] Q.B. 398, 72 Cr.App.R. 250, DC. In *R. v. Brentwood JJ., ex p. Nicholls* (*ante*, § 1–75e), the House of Lords said, *obiter*, that it was quite apparent that the procedure set out in subsections (4) to (6) (value not clear) refers to accused persons individually and not to accused persons collectively.

As to the situation where several accused have between them caused damage well in excess of the relevant sum, but the prosecution assert that each accused has individually caused damage of a value well under the relevant sum, see *R. v. Salisbury Magistrates' Court, ex p. Martin*, 84 Cr.App.R. 248, DC, where the prosecution's formula for arriving at an upper limit of the damage caused by each individual was approved.

The words "constitute or form part of a series of offences of the same or a similar character" in subsection (11)(a) also appeared in the now repealed subsection (7), and the cases decided in the context of subsection (7) may provide some guidance as to how the courts will interpret subsection (11)(a): see the commentary on section 40 of the *CJA* 1988, *post*, §§ 1–75aj *et seq.*, where those cases are considered.

Magistrates' Courts Act 1980, Sched. 2

Section 22

SCHEDULE 2

OFFENCES FOR WHICH THE VALUE INVOLVED IS RELEVANT TO THE MODE OF TRIAL

1–75k

Offence	*Value involved*	*How measured*
1. Offences under section 1 of the *Criminal Damage Act* 1971 (destroying or damaging property), excluding any offence committed by destroying or damaging property by fire.	As regards property alleged to have been destroyed, its value.	What the property would probably have cost to buy in the open market at the material time.
	As regards property alleged to have been damaged, the value of the alleged damage.	(a) If immediately after the material time the damage was capable of repair— (i) what would probably then have been the market price for the repair of the damage, or (ii) what the property alleged to have been damaged would probably have cost to buy in the open market at the material time, whichever is the less; or (b) if immediately after the material time the damage was beyond repair, what the said property would probably have cost to buy in the open market at the material time.
2. The following offences, namely— (a) aiding, abetting, counselling or procuring the commission of any offence mentioned in paragraph 1 above; (b) attempting to commit any offence so mentioned; and (c) inciting another to commit any offence so mentioned.	The value indicated in paragraph 1 above for the offence alleged to have been aided, abetted, counselled or procured, or attempted or incited.	As for the corresponding entry in paragraph 1 above.

3. Offences under section 12A of the *Theft Act* 1968 (aggravated vehicle-taking) where no allegation is made under subsection (1)(b) other than of damage, whether to the vehicle or other property or both.	The total value of the damage alleged to have been caused.	(1) In the case of damage to any property other than the vehicle involved in the offence, as for the corresponding entry in paragraph 1 above, substituting a reference to the time of the accident concerned for any reference to the material time. (2) In the case of damage to the vehicle involved in the offence— (a) if immediately after the vehicle was recovered the damage was capable of repair— (i) what would probably then have been the market price for the repair of the damage, or (ii) what the vehicle would probably have cost to buy in the open market immediately before it was unlawfully taken, whichever is the less; or (b) if immediately after the vehicle was recovered the damage was beyond repair, what the vehicle would probably have cost to buy in the open market immediately before it was unlawfully taken.

[Paragraph 3 of this Schedule was inserted by the *Aggravated Vehicle-Taking Act* 1992, s.2(1), with effect from April 1, 1992 (S.I. 1992 No. 764). The reference in para. 2 to the common law offence of incitement has effect as a reference to the offences under the *SCA* 2007, Pt 2: 2007 Act, s.63(1), and Sched. 6, para. 5(b).]

Proceedings in absence of accused

1–75l Section 23 of the *MCA* 1980 (as amended, and as further amended prospectively, by the *CJA* 2003) makes provision for the conduct of proceedings for determining mode of trial in the absence of the accused where he is legally represented and his legal representative indicates his consent to such course. See also *post*, § 1–75x.

Magistrates' Courts Act 1980, ss.24–24D

Summary trial of information against child or young person for indictable offence

1–75m **24.**—(1) *Where a person under the age of 18 years appears or is brought before a magistrates' court on an information charging him with an indictable offence other than one falling within subsection (1B) below, he shall be tried summarily unless—*

(a) … *the offence is such as is mentioned in subsection (1) or (2) of section 91 of the* Powers of Criminal Courts (Sentencing) Act *2000 (under which young persons convicted on indictment of certain grave crimes may be sentenced to be detained for long periods) and the court considers that if he is found guilty of the offence it ought to be possible to sentence him in pursuance of subsection (3) of that section; or*

(b) *he is charged jointly with a person who has attained the age of 18 years and the court considers it necessary in the interests of justice to commit them both for trial;*

and accordingly in a case falling within paragraph (a) or (b) of this subsection the court shall commit the accused for trial if either it is of opinion that there is sufficient evidence to put him on trial or it has power under section 6(2) above so to commit him without consideration of the evidence.

[(1) Where a person under the age of 18 years appears or is brought before a magistrates' court on an information charging him with an indictable offence he shall, subject to sections 51 and 51A of the *Crime and Disorder Act* 1998 and to sections 24A and 24B below, be tried summarily.]

(1A) *Where a magistrates' court—*

(a) *commits a person under the age of 18 for trial for an offence falling within subsection (1B) below; or*

(b) *in a case falling within subsection (1)(a) above, commits such a person for trial for an offence, the court may also commit him for trial for any other indictable offence with which he is charged at the same time if the charges for both offences could be joined in the same indictment.*

(1B) *An offence falls within this subsection if—*

(a) *it is an offence of homicide;*

(b) *each of the requirements of section 51A(1) of the* Firearms Act *1968 would be satisfied with respect to—*

(i) *the offence; and*

(ii) *the person charged with it,*

if he were convicted of the offence; or

(c) *section 29(3) of the* Violent Crime Reduction Act *2006 (minimum sentences in certain cases of using someone to mind a weapon) would apply if he were convicted of the offence.*

(2) *Where, in a case falling within subsection (1)(b) above, a magistrates' court commits a person under the age of 18 years for trial for an offence with which he is charged jointly with a person who has attained that age, the court may also commit him for trial for any other indictable offence with which he is charged at the same time (whether jointly with the person who has attained that age or not) if the charges for both offences could be joined in the same indictment.*

(3) If ontrying a person summarily in pursuance of subsection (1) above the court finds him guilty, it may impose a fine of an amount not exceeding £1,000 or may exercise the same powers as it could have exercised if he had been found guilty of an offence for which, but for section 89(1) of *the said Act of 2000* [the *Powers of Criminal Courts (Sentencing) Act* 2000], it could have sentenced him to imprisonment for a term not exceeding—

(a) the maximum term of imprisonment for the offence on conviction on indictment; or

(b) six months,

whichever is the less.

(4) In relation to a person under the age of 14 subsection (3) above shall have effect as if for the words "£1,000" there were substituted the words "£250" …

[This section is printed as amended, and repealed in part, by the *CJA* 1982, Sched. 14, para. 47; the *CJA* 1991, s.101(2), and Sched. 13; the *CJPOA* 1994, s.168(2), (3), and Scheds 10, para. 40, and 11; the *CDA* 1998, ss.47(6) and 119, and Sched. 8, para. 40; the *PCC(S)A* 2000, s.165(1), and Sched. 9, para. 64; the *CJA* 2003, s.42(1) and (2); and the *VCRA* 2006, ss.49 and 65, and Scheds 1, para. 1, and 5. The references to the age of 18 years were substituted by the *CJA* 1991, s.68, and Sched. 8, para. 6(1)(a). As from a day to be appointed, subs. (1) (printed in italics) is replaced by subs. (1) (printed in square brackets), subss. (1A), (1B) and (2) are repealed and the italicised words in subs. (3) are replaced by the words in square brackets, by the *CJA* 2003, ss.41 and 332, Sched. 3, paras 1 and 9 (as itself amended by the *CJIA* 2008, s.53, and Sched. 13, para. 5), and Sched. 37, Pt 4.]

[Child or young person to indicate intention as to plea in certain cases

24A.—(1) This section applies where— **1–75n**

(a) a person under the age of 18 years appears or is brought before a magistrates' court on an information charging him with an offence other than one falling within section 51A(12) of the *Crime and Disorder Act* 1998 ('the 1998 Act'); and

(b) but for the application of the following provisions of this section, the court would be required at that stage, by virtue of section 51(7) or (8) or 51A(3)(b), (4) or (5) of the 1998 Act to determine, in relation to the offence, whether to send the person to the Crown Court for trial (or to determine any matter, the effect of which would be to determine whether he is sent to the Crown Court for trial).

(2) Where this section applies, the court shall, before proceeding to make any such determination as is referred to in subsection (1)(b) above (the "relevant determination"), follow the procedure set out in this section.

(3) Everything that the court is required to do under the following provisions of this section must be done with the accused person in court.

(4) The court shall cause the charge to be written down, if this has not already been done, and to be read to the accused.

(5) The court shall then explain to the accused in ordinary language that he may

indicate whether (if the offence were to proceed to trial) he would plead guilty or not guilty, and that if he indicates that he would plead guilty—

(a) the court must proceed as mentioned in subsection (7) below; and

(b) (in cases where the offence is one mentioned in section 91(1) of the *Powers of Criminal Courts (Sentencing) Act* 2000) he may be sent to the Crown Court for sentencing under section 3B or (if applicable) 3C of that Act if the court is of such opinion as is mentioned in subsection (2) of the applicable section.

(6) The court shall then ask the accused whether (if the offence were to proceed to trial) he would plead guilty or not guilty.

(7) If the accused indicates that he would plead guilty, the court shall proceed as if—

(a) the proceedings constituted from the beginning the summary trial of the information; and

(b) section 9(1) above was complied with and he pleaded guilty under it,

and, accordingly, the court shall not (and shall not be required to) proceed to make the relevant determination or to proceed further under section 51 or (as the case may be) section 51A of the 1998 Act in relation to the offence.

(8) If the accused indicates that he would plead not guilty, the court shall proceed to make the relevant determination and this section shall cease to apply.

(9) If the accused in fact fails to indicate how he would plead, for the purposes of this section he shall be taken to indicate that he would plead not guilty.

(10) Subject to subsection (7) above, the following shall not for any purpose be taken to constitute the taking of a plea—

(a) asking the accused under this section whether (if the offence were to proceed to trial) he would plead guilty or not guilty;

(b) an indication by the accused under this section of how he would plead.]

[Intention as to plea by child or young person: absence of accused

1–75o **24B.**—(1) This section shall have effect where—

(a) a person under the age of 18 years appears or is brought before a magistrates' court on an information charging him with an offence other than one falling within section 51A(12) of the *Crime and Disorder Act* 1998;

(b) but for the application of the following provisions of this section, the court would be required at that stage to make one of the determinations referred to in paragraph (b) of section 24A(1) above ("the relevant determination");

(c) the accused is represented by a legal representative;

(d) the court considers that by reason of the accused's disorderly conduct before the court it is not practicable for proceedings under section 24A above to be conducted in his presence; and

(e) the court considers that it should proceed in the absence of the accused.

(2) In such a case—

(a) the court shall cause the charge to be written down, if this has not already been done, and to be read to the representative;

(b) the court shall ask the representative whether (if the offence were to proceed to trial) the accused would plead guilty or not guilty;

(c) if the representative indicates that the accused would plead guilty the court shall proceed as if the proceedings constituted from the beginning the summary trial of the information, and as if section 9(1) above was complied with and the accused pleaded guilty under it;

(d) if the representative indicates that the accused would plead not guilty the court shall proceed to make the relevant determination and this section shall cease to apply.

(3) If the representative in fact fails to indicate how the accused would plead, for the purposes of this section he shall be taken to indicate that the accused would plead not guilty.

(4) Subject to subsection (2)(c) above, the following shall not for any purpose be taken to constitute the taking of a plea—

(a) asking the representative under this section whether (if the offence were to proceed to trial) the accused would plead guilty or not guilty;

(b) an indication by the representative under this section of how the accused would plead.]

[Intention as to plea by child or young person: adjournment

1–75p **24C.**—(1) A magistrates' court proceeding under section 24A or 24B above may adjourn the proceedings at any time, and on doing so on any occasion when the accused is present may remand the accused.

(2) Where the court remands the accused, the time fixed for the resumption of proceedings shall be that at which he is required to appear or be brought before the court in pursuance of the remand or would be required to be brought before the court but for section 128(3A) below.]

[Functions under sections 24A to 24C capable of exercise by single justice

24D.—(1) The functions of a magistrates' court under sections 24A to 24C above may be discharged by a single justice. **1–75q**

(2) Subsection (1) above shall not be taken as authorising—

(a) the summary trial of an information (other than a summary trial by virtue of section 24A(7) or 24B(2)(c) above); or

(b) the imposition of a sentence,

by a magistrates' court composed of fewer than two justices.]

[Sections 24A to 24D are inserted, as from a day to be appointed, by the *CJA* 2003, s.41, and Sched. 3, paras 1 and 10.]

Section 89(1) of the *PCC(S)A* 2000 (see s.24(3)) contains a general prohibition on sentencing persons under 21 years of age to imprisonment. **1–75r**

In *CPS v. South East Surrey Youth Court* [2006] 2 Cr.App.R.(S.) 26, DC, the court highlighted the existence of an apparent conflict between the requirements of section 24 of the 1980 Act in its present form (*ante*, § 1–75m) and those of section 51A of the *CDA* 1998 (*ante*, § 1–19), in so far as that section is now in force. It was held that neither provision can be ignored, but, pending the coming into force of the new section 24(1), justices should bear in mind, (i) that the policy of the legislature is that those who are under 18 should, wherever possible, be tried in a youth court, which is best designed for their needs, (ii) the guidance in *R. v. Lang*, *post*, §§ 5–302 *et seq.*, particularly in relation to non-serious specified offences, (iii) the need, in relation to those under 18, to be particularly rigorous before concluding that there is a significant risk of serious harm by the commission of further offences, such a conclusion being unlikely to be appropriate in the absence of a pre-sentence report from a young offender team, (iv) that in most cases where a non-serious specified offence is charged, an assessment of dangerousness will not be appropriate until after conviction, when, if the dangerousness criteria are met, the defendant may be committed for sentence, and (v) that when a youth is charged jointly with an adult, a judgment will be called for as between the desirability of those jointly accused being tried together and of young offenders being tried in the youth court; considerations relevant to this judgment will be the age and maturity of the youth, comparative culpability, their previous convictions and whether separate trials would be feasible without injustice or undue inconvenience to witnesses.

Under (the original) section 24(1) the court is not obliged to consider the evidence but merely to decide on the basis of representations from both sides whether the gravity of the charges requires the additional sentencing powers of the Crown Court. Good character can weigh with the justices when deciding on the adequacy of their powers: *R. v. South Hackney Juvenile Court, ex p. R.B. and C.B.*, 77 Cr.App.R. 294, DC; but previous convictions are also relevant, as they would affect a judge's decision whether, and for how long, to impose a sentence under section 91 of the Act of 2000, in the event of a conviction: *R. (Tullet) v. Medway Magistrates' Court*, 167 J.P. 541, DC (not following *R. v. Hammersmith Juvenile Court, ex p. O.*, 86 Cr.App.R. 343, DC).

Where a person under the age of 18 years is committed for trial for one offence pursuant to section 24(1)(a), a count alleging another indictable matter that does not satisfy the test for committal for trial pursuant to that section may be included in the indictment, provided that the rules are satisfied as to addition of charges in respect of which there has been no committal and in respect of joinder, and provided that any charge in the magistrates' court in respect of the offence that has not been committed for trial has been withdrawn, so as to disapply section 24(1) in relation to that charge: *R. v. S. (Paul John)* [1999] 1 Cr.App.R. 1, CA.

Where the Crown Court has remitted the case of a child or young person found guilty before it to the youth court for sentence, pursuant to section 8(2) of the *PCC(S)A*

2000 (*post*, § 5–35), the youth court has no power to commit the case back to the Crown Court pursuant to sections 6 and 24 of the 1980 Act, although the power did exist in such a case to commit back for sentence under (the now repealed) section 37 of the 1980 Act: *R. v. Allen and Lambert*, 163 J.P. 841, DC and CA.

In *R. (D.) v. Sheffield Youth Court*, unreported, March 6, 2008, DC ([2008] EWHC 601 (Admin.)), where a defendant under the age of 18 had been jointly charged with an adult with a "grave" crime for the purposes of the *PCC(S)A* 2000, s.91, it was held that the justices should have considered whether to commit for trial pursuant to section 24(1), and should have done so before allowing the defendant to enter a plea of guilty (which amounted to an acceptance of summary jurisdiction by the court), but that failures in these respects should not render subsequent steps invalid. In reaching this decision, the court adopted the approach in *R. v. Herefordshire JJ., ex p. J., post*, § 1–75w, and the general principles identified in the authorities cited at §§ 1–195 *et seq.*, *post*, as to the consequences of defects remaining uncorrected.

As to re-determination of mode of trial after a decision has been made under section 24, see *post*, §§ 1–75v *et seq.*

The appropriate method of challenging a decision to commit a defendant aged under 18 for trial in the Crown Court under section 24 is by way of application for judicial review, rather than by way of an application to the Crown Court for a stay on the basis of abuse of process; the Crown Court is not equipped to investigate such issues as whether the lower court misdirected itself as to the principles to be applied; but the position might be different where there was a patent lack of jurisdiction to commit: *R. v. A.H.*, 167 J.P. 30, CA. It is submitted that where there was a patent lack of jurisdiction, the application to the Crown Court should be by way of a motion to quash the indictment (*post*, §§ 1–209 *et seq.*), rather than by way of an application for a stay on the basis of abuse of process. Thus, the distinction can be seen to be between a committal which is valid, albeit liable to be quashed on judicial review, and one that is so defective as to be a nullity.

On an application for judicial review of a decision to commit under section 24(1)(a) it is not sufficient for the High Court to conclude that it would have made a different decision if exercising the power in accordance with the appropriate priciples (as to which see *post*, § 1–75s); it can only interfere if one of the conventional grounds for judicial review exists: *R. (D.) v. Sheffield Youth Court*; *R. (N.) v. Sheffield Youth Court*, 167 J.P. 159, QBD (Stanley Burnton J.).

As to the question of age and the precise time at which it becomes relevant, see *ante*, § 1–73.

Jurisdiction to be declined where detention a possibility

1–75s In *R. v. Corcoran*, 8 Cr.App.R.(S.) 118, CA, it was stressed that justices should give effect to section 24(1)(a): jurisdiction should be declined where a person is charged with such a serious offence that long term detention under the *PCC(S)A* 2000, s.91 (*post*, § 5–358) is a possibility. In considering whether such a disposal is a possibility, magistrates are entitled to proceed on a "worst case scenario" basis, even if such a disposal is unlikely: *R. v. Sheffield Youth JJ., ex p. M.* [1998] 1 F.L.R. 929, DC. See also *R. v. Billam*, 82 Cr.App.R. 347 at 351, CA, and *R. v. Learmonth*, 10 Cr.App.R.(S.) 229, CA. In such a case the court has no alternative to committing the defendant for trial, and there is no substance in any argument that the Crown Court is not a suitable place to deal with a child, relevant provisions of international conventions affecting the manner in which the trial should be conducted but not the decision as to whether it should be in the youth court or the Crown Court: *R. v. Devizes Youth Court, ex p. A.*, 164 J.P. 330, DC. To a similar effect, see *R. v. C. (a Minor), The Times*, July 5, 2000, CA, and see also *R. v. North Hampshire Youth Court, ex p. DPP*, 164 J.P. 377, DC. For a criticism of these decisions, see the commentary at *Criminal Law Week* 2000/27/2, and see the concerns expressed in *R. v. B. (Child: Mode of trial for indecency), The Times*, February 27, 2001, CA.

A difference in approach then emerged in cases such as *R. (D.) v. Manchester City*

Youth Court [2002] 1 Cr.App.R.(S.) 135, QBD (Gage J.), and *R. (M.) v. Waltham Forest Youth Court*; *R. (W.) v. Thetford Youth Court* [2003] 1 Cr.App.R.(S.) 67, DC, where it was held that the words "ought to be possible" in section 24(1)(a) of the 1980 Act are to be taken to mean "a real possibility", rather than "a vague or theoretical possibility", and that whether, in a given case, detention for a long period pursuant to section 91 of the 2000 Act is a "real possibility" must be decided in the context of a proper appreciation of the legislative framework relating to the sentencing of offenders under 18, which includes sections 100 to 107 of the 2000 Act (*post*, §§ 5–348 *et seq.*), making a section 91 disposal "very much a long-stop reserved for very serious offences". That approach was also followed and developed in cases such as *R. (W.) v. Southampton Youth Court*; *R. (K.) v. Wirral Borough Magistrates Court* [2003] 1 Cr.App.R.(S.) 87, DC (where it was also pointed out that the Crown Court, in deciding what sentence is appropriate, is not bound by the fact that the justices have declined jurisdiction), *R. (D.) v Sheffield Youth Court*; *R. (N.) v. Sheffield Youth Court*, *ante* § 1–75r, and *CPS v. Redbridge Youth Court*, 169 J.P. 393, DC.

In *R. (H., A. and O.) v. Southampton Youth Court* [2005] 2 Cr.App.R.(S.) 30, DC, the principles that had emerged were summarised and applied. It was said that the general policy of the legislature is that those who are under 18 years of age, and in particular children under 15 years of age, should, whenever possible, be tried in a youth court; it is further the policy that, generally speaking, first-time offenders aged 12 to 14, and all offenders under 12, should not be detained in custody, and decisions as to jurisdiction should have regard to the fact that the exceptional power to detain for grave offences under section 91 of the 2000 Act should not be used to water down the general principle. The court also said that those under 15 will rarely attract a period of detention, and, even more rarely those under 12; in every case where it has to apply section 24, the court should ask itself whether there is a real prospect, having regard to his or her age, that the defendant whose case it is considering might require a sentence of, or in excess of, two years, or, alternatively, whether, although the sentence might be less than two years, there is some unusual feature of the case which justifies declining jurisdiction, bearing in mind that the absence of a power to impose a detention and training order because the defendant is under 15 is not such an unusual feature (as to which, see also *R. v. A.H.*, 167 J.P. 30, CA).

In *R. (W.) v. Brent Youth Court CPS (interested party)*, 170 J.P. 198, DC, it was said that when applying these principles the youth court should be assisted by the advocates or the court's legal adviser, that where several defendants are charged together the position of each of them is to be considered separately, and that to make a satisfactory decision the court must have all the necessary information before it, *viz.* (i) the factual allegation (which must be assumed to be true, unless manifestly not), it being the duty of the advocates to ensure that the summary is scrupulously fair and balanced, (ii) any undisputed mitigation that will be available to the defendant, including any indication of an intention to plead guilty, (iii) the defendant's previous record, accurately described, (iv) the correct approach, as set out in the authorities, and (v) any relevant sentencing guidelines (and, where there are no guidelines from the Sentencing Guidelines Council, any relevant published advice of the Sentencing Advisory Panel, provided that the court recognises that such advice does not carry legal force).

In applying section 24 of the 1980 Act, pending the coming into force of the new subsection (1), the court must also apply section 51A of the *CDA* 1998, as to which see *CPS v. South East Surrey Youth Court*, *ante*, § 1–75r.

See further *post*, § 5–359, as to the type of case that will now come within section 91.

Juvenile charged jointly with adult

See, generally, the principles explained at § 1–75r, *ante*. In order to satisfy section 24(1)(b) of the Act it is not necessary for an adult and a juvenile, who are jointly charged, to appear together before the court at any time: *R. v. Coventry City JJ., ex p. M.* [1992] Crim.L.R. 810, DC. The decision in respect of the juvenile may be made in the absence of the older defendant once a valid decision has been made, by a court with jurisdiction, to commit the older defendant for trial. In so construing the section, the court concluded that a dictum to a different effect in *R. v. Doncaster Crown Court, ex p. CPS*, 85 Cr.App.R. 1, DC, was too wide. **1–75t**

If two people are charged in separate informations with an offence of aggravated vehicle-taking, one being charged with driving the vehicle and the other charged with allowing himself to be carried in that vehicle, they are properly to be regarded as being jointly charged for the purposes of section 24: *ex p. Allgood*, *The Times*, November 25, 1994, DC.

Once a juvenile has been validly committed for trial with an adult, he must be tried in the Crown Court even if the adult pleads guilty (*cf.* section 29 of the 1980 Act, *post*, § 1–75y).

As to the sending to the Crown Court for trial, without committal proceedings, of a child or young person who is charged jointly with an adult with an indictable offence for which the adult is sent for trial without committal proceedings, see section 51(5) of the *CDA* 1998 (*ante*, § 1–17).

(b) *Practice direction*

Introduction

1–75u The mode of trial provisions of the practice direction (*post*) have been superseded by parts of the Sentencing Guidelines Council's guideline on sentencing in magistrates' courts (Appendix K–147 *et seq.*), but only in relation to the specific offences dealt with in that guideline. The substance of the provisions of the practice direction which are superseded is not, therefore, printed in this work. The guideline also contains guidance relevant to mode of trial in respect of a range of offences that were not mentioned in the practice direction.

Practice Direction (Criminal Procedings: Consolidation), para. V.51
[2002] 1 W.L.R. 2870

Mode of trial

V.51.1 The purpose of these guidelines is to help magistrates decide whether or not to commit defendants charged with "either way" offences for trial in the Crown Court. Their object is to provide guidance not direction. They are not intended to impinge on a magistrate's duty to consider each case individually and on its own particular facts. These guidelines apply to all defendants aged 18 and above.

General mode of trial considerations

V.51.2 Section 19 of the *Magistrates' Courts Act* 1980 requires magistrates to have regard to the following matters in deciding whether an offence is more suitable for summary trial or trial on indictment: (a) the nature of the case; (b) whether the circumstances make the offence one of a serious character; (c) whether the punishment which a magistrates' court would have power to inflict for it would be adequate; (d) any other circumstances which appear to the court to make it more suitable for the offence to be tried in one way rather than the other; (e) any representations made by the prosecution or the defence.

V.51.3 Certain general observations can be made: (a) the court should never make its decision on the grounds of convenience or expedition; (b) the court should assume for the purpose of deciding mode of trial that the prosecution version of the facts is correct; (c) the fact that the offences are alleged to be specimens is a relevant consideration (although, it has to be borne in mind that difficulties can arise in sentencing in relation to specimen counts (see *R. v. Clark* [1996] 2 Cr.App.R. 282 and *R. v. Kidd* [1998] 1 W.L.R. 604)); the fact that the defendant will be asking for other offences to be taken into consideration, if convicted, is not; (d) where cases involve complex questions of fact or difficult questions of law, including difficult issues of disclosure of sensitive material, the court should consider committal for trial; (e) where two or more defendants are jointly charged with an offence each has an individual right to elect his mode of trial; (f) in general, except where otherwise stated, either way offences should be tried summarily unless the court considers that the particular case has one or more of the features set out in paragraphs 51.4 to 51.18 and that its sentencing powers are insufficient; (g) the court should also consider its power to commit an offender for sentence under sections 3 and 4 of the *Powers of Criminal Courts (Sentencing) Act* 2000, if information emerges during the course of the hearing which leads it to conclude that the offence is so serious, or the offender such a risk to the public, that its powers to sentence him are inadequate. This means that committal for sentence is no longer determined by reference to the character and antecedents of the offender.

Features relevant to individual offences

V.51.4 Where reference is made in these guidelines to property or damage of "high value" it means a figure equal to at least twice the amount of the limit (currently £5,000) imposed by statute on a magistrates' court when making a compensation order.

Burglary: dwelling-house

V.51.5 [*See now the "Introduction"*, ante, *and the Sentencing Guidelines Council's guideline on sentencing in magistrates' courts (Appendix K–149 and K–150).*] NOTE: Attention is drawn to paragraph 28(c) of Schedule 1 to the *Magistrates' Courts Act* 1980 by which offences of burglary in a dwelling cannot be tried summarily if any person in the dwelling was subjected to violence or the threat of violence.

Burglary: non-dwelling

V.51.6 Cases should be tried summarily unless the court considers that one or more of the following features is present in the case *and* that its sentencing powers are insufficient. Magistrates should take account of their powers under sections 3 and 4 of the *Powers of Criminal Courts (Sentencing) Act* 2000 to commit for sentence: see paragraph 51.3(g). (a) Entry of a pharmacy or doctor's surgery. (b) Fear is caused or violence is done to anyone lawfully on the premises (*e.g.* night-watchman, security guard). (c) The offence has professional hallmarks. (d) Vandalism on a substantial scale. (e) The unrecovered property is of high value: see paragraph 51.4 for definition of "high value". (f) The offence is racially motivated.

Theft and fraud

V.51.7 [*Identical to first two sentences of para. 51.6*, ante.] (a) Breach of trust by a person in a position of substantial authority, or in whom a high degree of trust is placed. (b) Theft or fraud which has been committed or disguised in a sophisticated manner. (c) Theft or fraud committed by an organised gang. (d) The victim is particularly vulnerable to theft or fraud, *e.g.* the elderly or infirm. (e) [*As para. 51.6 (e)*, ante.]

Handling

V.51.8 [*See now the "Introduction"*, ante, *and the Sentencing Guidelines Council's guideline on sentencing in magistrates' courts (Appendix K–151 and K–152).*]

Social security frauds

V.51.9 [*See now the "Introduction"*, ante, *and the Sentencing Guidelines Council's guideline on sentencing in magistrates' courts (Appendix K–154).*]

Violence (sections 20 and 47 of the Offences against the Person Act 1861)

V.51.10 [*See now the "Introduction"*, ante, *and the Sentencing Guidelines Council's guideline on sentencing in magistrates' courts (Appendix K–156 and K–157).*] NOTE: The same considerations apply to cases of domestic violence.

Public Order Act offences

V.51.11 [*Identical to first two sentences of para. 51.6,* ante.] (a) Cases of *violent disorder* should generally be committed for trial. (b) [*As to affray, see now the "Introduction"*, ante, *and the Sentencing Guidelines Council's guideline on sentencing in magistrates' courts (Appendix K–163).*]

Violence to and neglect of children

V.51.12 [*See now the "Introduction"*, ante, *and the Sentencing Guidelines Council's guideline on sentencing in magistrates' courts (Appendix K–162).*]

Indecent assault

V.51.13 [*See now the "Introduction"*, ante, *and the Sentencing Guidelines Council's guideline on sentencing in magistrates' courts (Appendix K–167).*]

Unlawful sexual intercourse

V.51.14 [*Identical to first two sentences of para. 51.6,* ante.] (a) Wide disparity of age. (b) Breach of position of trust. (c) The victim is particularly vulnerable. NOTE: Unlawful sexual intercourse with a girl *under* 13 is triable only on indictment.

Drugs

V.51.15 Class A. [*See now the "Introduction"*, ante, *and the Sentencing Guidelines Council's guideline on sentencing in magistrates' courts (Appendix K–175 and K–176).*]

V.51.16 Class B. [*See now the "Introduction",* ante, *and the Sentencing Guidelines Council's guideline on sentencing in magistrates' courts (Appendix K–177).*]

Dangerous driving and aggravated vehicle taking

V.51.17 [*See now the "Introduction",* ante, *and the Sentencing Guidelines Council's guideline on sentencing in magistrates' courts (Appendix K–179 to K–181).*]

Criminal damage

V.51.18 [*See now the "Introduction",* ante, *and the Sentencing Guidelines Council's guideline on sentencing in magistrates' courts (Appendix K–182 and K–183).*] NOTE: offences set out in Schedule 2 to the *Magistrates' Courts Act* 1980 (which includes offences of criminal damage which do not amount to arson) *must* be tried summarily if the value of the property damaged or destroyed is £5,000 or less.

(3) Changing from summary trial to committal proceedings, and vice versa

Magistrates' Courts Act 1980, s.25

Power to change from summary trial to committal proceedings, and vice versa

1–75v **25.**—(1) Subsections (2) to *(4)* [2D] below shall have effect where a person who has attained the age of 18 years appears or is brought before a magistrates' court on an information charging him with an offence triable either way.

(2) *Where the court has (otherwise than in pursuance of section 22(2) above) begun to try the information summarily, the court may, at any time before the conclusion of the evidence for the prosecution, discontinue the summary trial and proceed to inquire into the information as examining justices and, on doing so, shall adjourn the hearing.*

[(2) Where the court is required under section 20(9) above to proceed to the summary trial of the information, the prosecution may apply to the court for the offence to be tried on indictment instead.

(2A) An application under subsection (2) above—

(a) must be made before the summary trial begins; and

(b) must be dealt with by the court before any other application or issue in relation to the summary trial is dealt with.

(2B) The court may grant an application under subsection (2) above but only if it is satisfied that the sentence which a magistrates' court would have power to impose for the offence would be inadequate.

(2C) Where—

(a) the accused is charged on the same occasion with two or more offences; and

(b) it appears to the court that they constitute or form part of a series of two or more offences of the same or a similar character,

subsection (2B) above shall have effect as if references to the sentence which a magistrates' court would have power to impose for the offence were a reference to the maximum aggregate sentence which a magistrates' court would have power to impose for all of the offences taken together.

(2D) Where the court grants an application under subsection (2) above, it shall proceed in relation to the offence in accordance with section 51(1) of the *Crime and Disorder Act* 1998.]

(3) *Where the court has begun to inquire into the information as examining justices, then, if at any time during the inquiry it appears to the court, having regard to any representations made in the presence of the accused by the prosecutor, or made by the accused, and to the nature of the case, that the offence is after all more suitable for summary trial, the court may, after doing as provided in subsection (4) below, ask the accused whether he consents to be tried summarily and, if he so consents, may subject to subsection (3A) below proceed to try the information summarily.*

(3A) *Where the prosecution is being carried on by the Attorney-General or the Solicitor General, the court shall not exercise the power conferred by subsection (3) above without his consent and, where the prosecution is being carried on by the Director of Public Prosecutions, shall not exercise that power if the Attorney-General directs that it should not be exercised.*

(4) *Before asking the accused under subsection (3) above whether he consents to be tried summarily, the court shall in ordinary language—*

(a) *explain to him that it appears to the court more suitable for him to be tried summarily for the offence, but that this can only be done if he consents to be so tried; and*

(b) *unless it has already done so, explain to him, as provided in section 20(2)(b) above, about the court's power to commit to the Crown Court for sentence.*

(5) *Where a person under the age of 18 years appears or is brought before a magistrates' court on an information charging him with an indictable offence other than one falling within section 24(1B) above, and the court—*

(a) *has begun to try the information summarily on the footing that the case does not fall within paragraph (a) or (b) of section 24 above and must therefore be tried summarily, as required by the said section 24(1); or*

(b) *has begun to inquire into the case as examining justices on the footing that the case does so fall,*

subsection (6) or (7) below, as the case may be, shall have effect.

(6) *If, in a case falling within subsection (5)(a) above, it appears to the court at any time before the conclusion of the evidence for the prosecution that the case is after all one which under the said section 24(1) ought not to be tried summarily, the court may discontinue the summary trial and proceed to inquire into the information as examining justices and, on doing so, shall adjourn the hearing.*

(7) *If, in a case falling within subsection (5)(b) above, it appears to the court at any time during the inquiry that the case is after all one which under the said section 24(1) ought to be tried summarily, the court may proceed to try the information summarily.*

(8) *If the court adjourns the hearing under subsection (2) or (6) above it may (if it thinks fit) do so without remanding the accused.*

[This section is printed as amended by the *Prosecution of Offences Act* 1985, Scheds 1 and 2; the *CJA* 1991, s.68, and Sched. 8, para. 6(1)(a); the *CPIA* 1996, s.47, and Sched. 1, para. 5; and the *CJA* 2003, s.42(1) and (3). The amendments of subss. (2) and (6) and the insertion of subs. (8), effected by the 1996 Act, apply only in relation to alleged offences into which no criminal investigation had begun before April 1, 1997: S.I. 1997 Nos 682 and 683 (*post*, § 10–9). As from a day or days to be appointed, the *CJA* 2003, s.41, and Sched. 3, paras 1 and 11, (i) substitute for the reference to subs. (4) in subs. (1) the reference in square brackets; (ii) substitute new subss. (2) to (2D), printed in square brackets, for the original subs. (2); and (iii), together with *ibid.*, s.332 and Sched. 37, Pt 4, repeal subss. (3) to (8).]

See *ante*, § 1–73 as to the stage of the proceedings at which the defendant must have attained the age of 18. **1–75w**

Save where a change of election by the defendant is permitted (*ante*, § 1–75d), once mode of trial has been decided pursuant to the provisions of sections 18 to 24 of the 1980 Act, any decision as to change of mode of trial is governed by section 25; justices have no inherent jurisdiction to revisit the issue: *R. (DPP) v. Camberwell Green Youth Court*, 168 J.P. 157, DC (disapproving dicta to the contrary in *R. v. Newham Juvenile Court, ex p. F (a Minor)*, 84 Cr.App.R. 81, DC); even if further charges arising out of the same incident have been laid and are to be committed to the Crown Court: *R. v. St Helens Magistrates' Court, ex p. Critchley* [1988] Crim.L.R. 311, DC.

It has been held that justices have not "begun to try the information summarily" (within subsection (2)), merely because the defendant has consented to a summary trial (*R. v. Southend JJ., ex p. Wood, The Times*, March 8, 1986, DC), and pleaded "not guilty" (*R. v. St Helens Magistrates' Court, ex p. Critchley, ante*). However, in *R. v. Hammersmith Juvenile Court, ex p. O.*, 86 Cr.App.R. 343, DC, it was said that a defendant's trial had begun by reason of his "not guilty" pleas, but this dictum would appear to be *obiter* in the light of the further conclusion of the court that, in any event, the material relied upon to justify a re-determination of the mode of trial (as to which, see *post*) had not been such as to justify that course. As to when a trial begins, see also *post*, § 4–93.

When justices disagree and the case is put back for re-hearing it cannot be said that the evidence for the prosecution has been concluded, so as to exclude the power under subsection (2) of section 25: *R. v. Coventry City JJ., ex p. Wilson* [1981] Crim.L.R. 787, DC.

There is no power to act under subsection (2) once a plea of guilty has been accepted: *R. v. Dudley JJ., ex p. Gillard* [1986] A.C. 442, HL, and *R. v. Telford JJ., ex p. Darlington* 87 Cr.App.R. 194, DC. Similarly, the court may not act pursuant to subsection (6) after a valid plea of guilty has been accepted, and an unequivocal plea of guilty in a youth court by a properly identified defendant is valid, even if no proper consideration has been given under section 24(1)(a) of the *MCA* 1980 to the question of whether the charge falls within section 91 of the *PCC(S)A* 2000 (*post*, § 5–358): *R. v. Herefordshire JJ., ex p. J., The Times*, May 4, 1998, DC (an approach to validity that was followed in *R. (D.) v. Sheffield Youth Court, ante*, § 1–75r).

A court is not entitled to use its powers under section 25 merely because it disagrees with an earlier decision by a differently constituted bench to accept summary jurisdiction (*R. v. Birmingham Stipendiary Magistrate, ex p. Webb*, 95 Cr.App.R. 75, DC), or for the purpose of enabling the joint trial of the accused with co-defendants who have elected trial (*R. v. West Norfolk JJ., ex p. McMullen* [1993] C.O.D. 25, DC, and *R. v. Bradford Magistrates' Court, ex p. Grant*, 163 J.P. 717, DC); to exercise the power for the latter purpose would be a device to avoid the effect of *R. v. Brentwood JJ., ex p. Nicholls* [1992] 1 A.C. 1, HL (*ante*, § 1–75).

In *R. (K.) v. Leeds Youth Court*, 165 J.P. 694, DC, it was held that "a change of circumstances", such as to justify the exercise of the power in subsection (6), will include not only the emergence of new material in the course of the evidence, but also situations where, as the evidence unfolds, the manner in which it is presented by the witness or witnesses is, of itself, of a nature which justifies the conclusion that the original decision as to mode of trial is no longer appropriate. Similarly, the jurisdiction conferred by subsections (5) and (7) to reconsider whether the case ought to be tried summarily may be exercised at any time after the enquiry by the magistrates' court has begun, and is not fettered by a previous decision which the examination by the court shows to be wrong; any concern that the exercise of that power would be, in effect, to act as an appellate court in respect of the initial decision as to mode of trial would be too limited an approach: *R. (R.) v. Manchester City Youth Court*, 170 J.P. 217, QBD (Ouseley J.). For a criticism of the first of these decisions, see *Criminal Law Week* 2001/38/5.

(4) Power to issue summons to accused

Magistrates' Courts Act 1980, s.26

Power to issue summons to accused in certain circumstances

1–75x **26.**—(1) *Where—*

(a) *in the circumstances mentioned in section 23(1)(a) above the court is not satisfied that there is good reason for proceeding in the absence of the accused; or*

(b) *subsection (4)(b) or (5) of section 23 or subsection (2) or (6) of section 25 above applies, and the court adjourns the hearing in pursuance of that subsection without remanding the accused,*

the justice or any of the justices of which the court is composed may issue a summons directed to the accused requiring his presence before the court.

(2) *If the accused is not present at the time and place appointed—*

(a) *in a case within subsection (1)(a) above, for the proceedings under section 19(1) or 22(1) above, as the case may be; or*

(b) *in a case within subsection (1)(b) above, for the resumption of the hearing,*

the court may issue a warrant for his arrest.

[(1) Where, in the circumstances mentioned in section 23(1)(a) above, the court is not satisfied that there is good reason for proceeding in the absence of the accused, the justice or any of the justices of which the court is composed may issue a summons directed to the accused requiring his presence before the court.

(2) In a case within subsection (1) above, if the accused is not present at the time and place appointed for the proceedings under section 19 or section 22(1) above, the court may issue a warrant for his arrest.]

[As from a day to be appointed, new subss. (1) and (2) (printed in square brackets) are substituted for the original section (italicised) by the *CJA* 2003, s.41, and Sched 3, paras 1 and 12.]

(5) Remittal to youth court

Magistrates' Courts Act 1980, s.29

Power to remit person under 18 for trial to youth court

29.—(1) Where— **1–75y**

(a) a person under the age of 18 years ("the juvenile") appears or is brought before a magistrates' court other than a youth court on an information jointly charging him and one or more other persons with an offence; and

(b) that other person, or any of those other persons, has attained that age,

subsection (2) below shall have effect notwithstanding proviso (a) in section 46(1) of the *Children and Young Persons Act* 1933 (which would otherwise require the charge against the juvenile to be heard by a magistrates' court other than a youth court).

In the following provisions of this section "the older accused" means such one or more of the accused as have attained the age of 18 years.

(2) If—

(a) the court proceeds to the summary trial of the information in the case of both or all of the accused, and the older accused or each of the older accused pleads guilty; or

(b) the court—

(i) in the case of the older accused or each of the older accused, *proceeds to inquire into the information as examining justices and either commits him for trial or discharges him* [sends him to the Crown Court for trial under section 51 or 51A of the *Crime and Disorder Act* 1998]; and

(ii) in the case of the juvenile, proceeds to the summary trial of the information,

then, if in either situation the juvenile pleads not guilty, the court may before any evidence is called in his case remit him for trial to a youth court acting for the same place as the remitting court or for the place where he habitually resides.

(3) A person remitted to a youth court under subsection (2) above shall be brought before and tried by a youth court accordingly.

(4) Where a person is so remitted to a youth court—

(a) he shall have no right of appeal against the order of remission; and

(b) the remitting court may, subject to section 25 of the *Criminal Justice and Public Order Act* 1994, give such directions as appear to be necessary with respect to his custody or for his release on bail until he can be brought before the youth court.

(5) The preceding provisions of this section shall apply in relation to a corporation as if it were an individual who has attained the age of 18 years.

[The references in this section to the age of 18 years were substituted for references to the age of 17 by the *CJA* 1991, s.68 and Sched. 8, para. 6(1)(a). The references to a youth court were substituted for references to a juvenile court by *ibid.*, s.100 and Sched. 11, para. 40. Subs. (4)(b) is printed as amended by the *CJPOA* 1994, s.168(2), and Sched. 10, para. 41. The words in square brackets in subs. (2)(b)(i) are substituted for the words in italics by the *CJA* 2003, s.41, and Sched. 3, para. 51(1) and (5). That substitution came into force on May 9, 2005, but only in relation to cases sent for trial under s.51 or 51A(3)(d) of the *CDA* 1998 (as to which see *ante*, §§ 1–17, 1–18): *Criminal Justice Act 2003 (Commencement No. 9) Order* 2005 (S.I. 2005 No. 1267). The substitution otherwise comes into effect on a day or days to be appointed.]

Where the decision is taken not to commit for trial any jointly charged adult, it is the duty of the magistrates to decide whether the case against the juvenile comes within section 24(1)(a) of the 1980 Act (*ante*, § 1–75m) and, if it does, to proceed against him as examining justices; otherwise it should proceed to summary trial; in the event of a plea of not guilty it may remit the matter to a youth court for trial, pursuant to section 29(2), but the powers under section 25(5) to (7) of the 1980 Act (*ante*, §§ 1–75v *et seq.*) should also be borne in mind; in the event of a plea of guilty or a conviction after a plea of not guilty, the court should normally remit the question of sentence to a youth court, pursuant to section 8(2) of the *PCC(S)A* 2000 (*post*, § 5–35); but there is no jurisdiction to remit the juvenile to a youth court for that court to decide the issue under section 24(1)(a): *R. v. Haringey JJ., ex p. Fawzy* [1998] 1 Cr.App.R. 411, DC. **1–75z**

(6) Penalties on summary conviction

Magistrates' Courts Act 1980, s.32

Penalties on summary conviction for offences triable either way

1–75aa **32.**—(1) On summary conviction of any of the offences triable either way listed in Schedule 1 to this Act a person shall be liable to imprisonment for a term not exceeding *6 months* [12 months] or to a fine not exceeding the prescribed sum or both, except that—

(a) a magistrates' court shall not have power to impose imprisonment for an offence so listed if the Crown Court would not have that power in the case of an adult convicted of it on indictment; ...

(c) [*repealed by* Criminal Attempts Act *1981, Sched.*].

(2) For any offence triable either way which is not listed in Schedule 1 to this Act, being an offence under a relevant enactment, the maximum fine which may be imposed on summary conviction shall by virtue of this subsection be the prescribed sum unless the offence is one for which by virtue of an enactment other than this subsection a larger fine may be imposed on summary conviction.

(3) Where, by virtue of any relevant enactment, a person summarily convicted of an offence triable either way would, apart from this section, be liable to a maximum fine of one amount in the case of a first conviction and of a different amount in the case of a second or subsequent conviction, subsection (2) above shall apply irrespective of whether the conviction is a first, second or subsequent one.

(4) Subsection (2) above shall not affect so much of any enactment as (in whatever words) makes a person liable on summary conviction to a fine not exceeding a specified amount for each day on which a continuing offence is continued after conviction or the occurrence of any other specified event.

(5) Subsection (2) above shall not apply on summary conviction of any of the following offences:—

(a) offences under section 5(2) of the *Misuse of Drugs Act* 1971 (having possession of a controlled drug) where the controlled drug in relation to which the offence was committed was a Class B or Class C drug;

(b) offences under the following provisions of that Act, where the controlled drug in relation to which the offence was committed was a Class C drug, namely—

(i) section 4(2) (production, or being concerned in the production, of a controlled drug);

(ii) section 4(3) (supplying or offering a controlled drug or being concerned in the doing of either activity by another);

(iii) section 5(3) (having possession of a controlled drug with intent to supply it to another);

(iv) section 8 (being the occupier, or concerned in the management, of premises and permitting or suffering certain activities to take place there);

(v) section 12(6) (contravention of direction prohibiting practitioner etc. from possessing, supplying etc. controlled drugs); or

(vi) section 13(3) (contravention of direction prohibiting practitioner etc. from prescribing, supplying etc. controlled drugs).

(6) Where, as regards any offence triable either way, there is under any enactment (however framed or worded) a power by subordinate instrument to restrict the amount of the fine which on summary conviction can be imposed in respect of that offence—

(a) subsection (2) above shall not affect that power or override any restriction imposed in the exercise of that power; and

(b) the amount to which that fine may be restricted in the exercise of that power shall be any amount less than the maximum fine which could be imposed on summary conviction in respect of the offence apart from any restriction so imposed.

(7) [*Repealed by* Criminal Justice Act *1988, s.170(2) and Sched. 16.*]

(8) In subsection (5) above "controlled drug", "Class B drug" and "Class C drug" have the same meaning as in the *Misuse of Drugs Act* 1971.

(9) In this section—

"fine" includes a pecuniary penalty but does not include a pecuniary forfeiture or pecuniary compensation;

"the prescribed sum" means £5000 or such sum as is for the time being substituted in this definition by an order in force under section 143(1) below;

"relevant enactment" means an enactment contained in the *Criminal Law Act* 1977 or in any Act passed before, or in the same session as, that Act.

[This section is printed as amended by the *SCA* 2007, ss.63(2) and 92, Sched. 6, para. 55(1) and (2), and Sched. 14; and as amended, as from a day to be appointed, by the *CJA* 2003, s.282(1) (substitution of "12 months" for "6 months" in subs. (1); but not in relation to any offence committed before date of commencement: s.282(4)).]

On October 1, 1992, the "prescribed sum" was increased from £2,000 to £5,000, but only in relation to offences committed on or after that date: *CJA* 1991, s.17(2)(c), Sched. 12, para. 6, and *Criminal Justice Act 1991 (Commencement No. 3) Order* 1992 (S.I. 1992 No. 333).

Magistrates' Courts Act 1980, s.33

Maximum penalties on summary conviction in pursuance of section 22

33.—(1) Where in pursuance of subsection (2) of section 22 above a magistrates' court proceeds to the summary trial of an information, then, if the accused is summarily convicted of the offence— **1–75ab**

(a) subject to subsection (3) below the court shall not have power to impose on him in respect of that offence imprisonment for more than *3 months* [51 weeks] or a fine greater than level 4 on the standard scale; and

(b) section 3 of the *Powers of Criminal Courts (Sentencing) Act* 2000 shall not apply as regards that offence.

(2) In subsection (1) above "fine" includes a pecuniary penalty but does not include a pecuniary forfeiture or pecuniary compensation.

(3) Paragraph (a) of subsection (1) above does not apply to an offence under section 12A of the *Theft Act* 1968 (aggravated vehicle-taking).

[Subs. (3) and the introductory words in para. (a) of subs. (1) were inserted by the *Aggravated Vehicle-Taking Act* 1992, s.2(3). The reference to "level 4 on the standard scale" was substituted for "£1,000" by the *CJA* 1991, s.17(3), and Sched. 4, Pt II. Subs. (1)(b) is printed as amended by the *PCC(S)A* 2000, s.165(1), and Sched. 9, para. 65. As from a day to be appointed, the words in square brackets are substituted for the words in italics by the *CJA* 2003, s.304, and Sched. 32, paras 25 and 27. The prospective repeal of subs. (1)(b) by *ibid*., ss.41 and 332, Sched. 3, paras 1 and 13, and Sched. 37, Pt 4, has itself been repealed by the *CJIA* 2008, ss.53, 148(1) and 149, Sched. 13, paras 1 and 6, Sched. 26, paras 59 and 77, and Sched. 28, Pt 4.]

For section 3 of the 2003 Act, see *post*, § 5–24.

Penalty on summary conviction for offences triable either way under subordinate legislation

Section 51 of the *CJA* 1988, which is not set out in this work, makes provision as to maximum penalties in respect of offences triable either way under subordinate legislation. **1–75ac**

(7) Offences triable either way

Introduction

The definition of the expression "offence triable either way" is provided by the *Interpretation Act* 1978, Sched. 1 (Appendix B–28). Most such offences are identifiable by virtue of the fact that the statute creating the offence specifically provides for punishment on summary conviction and for punishment on conviction on indictment. Apart from such express provision, section 17 of the *MCA* 1980 provides that certain offences (listed in Schedule 1) which appear from the offence-creating provision to be indictable only (*e.g*. s.15 of the *Theft Act* 1968) can in fact be tried either way. **1–75ad**

Specific offences

Magistrates' Courts Act 1980, s.17 and Sched. 1

Certain offences triable either way

17.—(1) The offences listed in Schedule 1 to this Act shall be triable either way. **1–75ae**

(2) Subsection (1) above is without prejudice to any other enactment by virtue of which any offence is triable either way.

SCHEDULE 1

OFFENCES TRIABLE EITHER WAY BY VIRTUE OF SECTION 17

1–75af 1. Offences at common law of public nuisance.

1A. An offence at common law of outraging public decency. [*Inserted by* CJA *2003, s.320.*]

2. [*Repealed by* Statute Law (Repeals) Act *2008, s.1(1), and Sched. 1, Pt 3.*]

3. Offences consisting in contravention of section 13 of the *Statutory Declaration Act* 1835 (administration by a person of an oath etc. touching matters in which he has no jurisdiction).

4. Offences under section 36 of the *Malicious Damage Act* 1861 (obstructing engines or carriages on railways).

5. Offences under the following provisions of the *Offences against the Person Act* 1861—

(a)–(j) [*sections 16 (threats to kill), 20 (inflicting bodily injury, with or without a weapon), 26 (not providing apprentices or servants with food, etc.), 27 (abandoning or exposing child), 34 (doing or omitting to do anything so as to endanger railway passengers), 36 (assaulting a clergyman at a place of worship, etc.), 38 (assault with intent to resist apprehension), 47 (assault occasioning actual bodily harm), 57 (bigamy) and 60 (concealing the birth of a child) (paras (a) to (j) respectively)*].

6. Offences under section 20 of the *Telegraph Act* 1868 (disclosing or intercepting messages).

7. Offences under section 13 of the *Debtors Act* 1869 (transactions intended to defraud creditors).

8. Offences under section 5 of the *Public Stores Act* 1875 (obliteration of marks with intent to conceal).

9. Offences under section 12 of the *Corn Returns Act* 1882 (false returns).

10. [*Repealed by* Electricity Act *1989, s.112(4) and Sched. 18.*]

11. Offences under section 3 of the *Submarine Telegraph Act* 1885 (damaging submarine cables).

12. Offences under section 13 of the *Stamp Duties Management Act* 1891 (offences in relation to dies and stamps).

13. Offences under section 8(2) of the *Cremation Act* 1902 (making false representations etc. with a view to procuring the burning of any human remains).

14. All offences under the *Perjury Act* 1911 except offences under—

(a) section 1 (perjury in judicial proceedings);

(b) section 3 (false statements etc. with reference to marriage);

(c) section 4 (false statements etc. as to births or deaths).

15. [*Repealed by* Statute Law (Repeals) Act *1989, s.1(1) and Sched. 1, Pt I.*]

16. Offences under section 17 of the *Deeds of Arrangement Act* 1914 (trustee making preferential payments).

17. Offences under section 3(4) of the *Checkweighing in Various Industries Act* 1919 (false statements). [*1919 Act repealed by* Wages Act *1986.*]

18. Offences under section 8(2) of the *Census Act* 1920 (disclosing census information).

19. Offences under section 36 of the *Criminal Justice Act* 1925 (forgery of passports etc.).

20. Offences under section 11 of the *Agricultural Credits Acts* 1928 (frauds by farmers).

21. [*Repealed by* Statute Law (Repeals) Act *1989, s.1(1) and Sched. 1, Pt I.*]

22. [*Repealed by* Postal Services Act 2000 (Consequential Modifications No. 1) Order *2001 (S.I. 2001 No. 1149), Art. 3(2) and Sched. 2.*]

23. Offences under the following provisions of the *Sexual Offences Act* 1956—

(a) section 6 (unlawful sexual intercourse with a girl under 16);

(b) section 13 (indecency between men);

(c) section 26 (permitting a girl under 16 to use premises for sexual intercourse).

24. [*Repealed by* Statute Law (Repeals) Act *1989, s.1(1) and Sched. 1, Pt I.*]

25. [*Repealed by* Housing (Consequential Provisions) Act *1985, s.3(1) and Sched. 1.*]

26. The following offences under the *Criminal Law Act* 1967—

(a) offences under section 4 (1) (assisting offenders); and

(b) offences under section 5(1) (concealing arrestable offences and giving false information),

where the offence to which they relate is triable either way.

27. Offences under section 4(1) of the *Sexual Offences Act* 1967 (procuring others to commit homosexual acts).

28. All indictable offences under the *Theft Act* 1968 except—

(a) robbery, aggravated burglary, blackmail and assault with intent to rob;

(b) burglary comprising the commission of, or an intention to commit, an offence which is triable only on indictment;

(c) burglary in a dwelling if any person in the dwelling was subjected to violence or the threat of violence.

29. Offences under the following provisions of the *Criminal Damage Act* 1971—

section 1(1) (destroying or damaging property);
section 1(1) and (3) (arson);
section 2 (threats to destroy or damage property);
section 3 (possessing anything with intent to destroy or damage property).

30. Offences in relation to stamps issued for the purpose of national insurance under the provisions of any enactments as applied to those stamps.

31. Uttering any forged document the forgery of which is an offence listed in this Schedule. [*The offences to which this paragraph relates were those referred to in paragraph 15, now repealed.*]

32. Committing an indecent assault upon a person whether male or female.

33. Aiding, abetting, counselling or procuring the commission of any offence listed in the preceding paragraphs of this Schedule except paragraph 26.

34. [*Repealed by* Criminal Attempts Act *1981, Sched.*]

35. [*Repealed by* SCA *2007, ss.63(2) and 92, Sched. 6, para. 55(1) and (4), and Sched. 14.*]

Paragraph 28(c) is is not limited to situations where violence is used to effect the burglary; it is wide enough to embrace cases where violence is used towards the occupant of premises who tries to restrain the offender, and matters of scale or degree play no part in the operation of the provision: *R. v. McGrath* [2004] 1 Cr.App.R. 15, CA.

Aiding and abetting

See section 44(2) of the *MCA* 1980, *post*, § 18–4. **1–75ag**

(8) Joinder of certain summary offences in an indictment

The effect of the *CJA* 1988, ss.37 and 39, was to convert the offences of taking a conveyance without authority, common assault and battery into summary offences. In limited circumstances, however, section 40 of the 1988 Act permits the joinder of such offences and certain other summary offences in an indictment. **1–75ah**

Criminal Justice Act 1988, s.40

Power to join in indictment count for common assault etc.

40.—(1) A count charging a person with a summary offence to which this section applies may be included in an indictment if the charge— **1–75ai**

(a) is founded on the same facts or evidence as a count charging an indictable offence; or

(b) is part of a series of offences of the same or similar character as an indictable offence which is also charged,

but only if (in either case) the facts or evidence relating to the offence *were disclosed to a magistrates' court inquiring into the offence as examining justices or* are disclosed by material which, in pursuance of regulations made under paragraph 1 of Schedule 3 to the *Crime and Disorder Act* 1998 (procedure where person sent for trial under section 51 [or 51A]), has been served on the person charged.

(2) Where a count charging an offence to which this section applies is included in an indictment, the offence shall be tried in the same manner as if it were an indictable offence; but the Crown Court may only deal with the offender in respect of it in a manner in which a magistrates' court could have dealt with him.

(3) The offences to which this section applies are—

(a) common assault;

(aa) an offence under section 90(1) of the *Criminal Justice Act* 1991 (assaulting a prisoner custody officer);

(ab) an offence under section 13(1) of the *Criminal Justice and Public Order Act* 1994 (assaulting a secure training centre custody officer);

(b) an offence under section 12(1) of the *Theft Act* 1968 (taking motor vehicle or other conveyance without authority etc.);

(c) an offence under section 103(1)(b) of the *Road Traffic Act* 1988 (driving a motor vehicle while disqualified);

(d) an offence mentioned in the first column of Schedule 2 to the *Magistrates' Courts Act* 1980 (criminal damage etc.) which would otherwise be triable only summarily by virtue of section 22(2) of that Act; and

(e) any summary offence specified under subsection (4) below.

(4) The Secretary of State may by order made by statutory instrument specify for the purposes of this section any summary offence which is punishable with imprisonment or involves obligatory or discretionary disqualification from driving.

(5) [*Statutory instrument procedure.*]

[This section is printed as amended by the *Road Traffic (Consequential Provisions) Act* 1988, s.4, and Sched. 3, para. 39; the *CJPOA* 1994, s.168(2), and Sched. 9, para. 35; the *CPIA* 1996, s.47, and Sched. 1, para. 34; and the *CDA* 1998, s.119, and Sched. 8, para. 66. The amendment of subs. (1) by the 1996 Act applies only in relation to alleged offences into which no criminal investigation had begun before April 1, 1997: S.I. 1997 Nos 682 & 683 (*post*, § 10–9). As from a day or days to be appointed, the words in italics in subs. (1) are repealed and the words in square brackets in that subsection are inserted: *CJA* 2003, ss.41 and 332, Sched. 3, para. 60(1) and (7), and Sched. 37, Pt 4. The insertion came into force on May 9, 2005, but only in relation to cases sent for trial under s.51(A)(3)(d) of the *CDA* 1998 (as to which see *ante*, § 1–17): *Criminal Justice Act 2003 (Commencement No. 9) Order* 2005 (S.I. 2005 No. 1267).]

1–75aj For Schedule 2 to the 1980 Act, see *ante*, § 1–75k.

A count charging a summary offence listed in section 40(3) of the *CJA* 1988 may only be included in an indictment in the circumstances permitted by section 40(1) and (2) of that Act, namely, where there has been a committal for trial by examining justices, or a sending for trial pursuant to section 51 of the *CDA* 1998; section 40 does not permit the inclusion of a count charging such an offence in an indictment where there has been a transfer for trial; proviso (iA) to section 2(2) of the *Administration of Justice (Miscellaneous Provisions) Act* 1933 (*post*, § 1–204), which allows the inclusion in an indictment of counts founded on material that accompanies a notice of transfer "being counts which may lawfully be joined in the same indictment", does not therefore justify the inclusion of a count charging a summary offence of the type listed in section 40(3) of the 1988 Act, albeit founded on material accompanying the relevant notice of transfer, because such a count may not "lawfully be joined" where the circumstances do not bring the case within section 40(1) and (2) of the 1988 Act: *R. v. T. and K.* [2001] 1 Cr.App.R. 32, CA (confirming the correctness of views expressed in *R. v. Wrench* [1996] 1 Cr.App.R. 340, CA).

It is not permissible to include in an indictment a count charging a summary offence that is not listed in section 40(3): *R. v. Ashton*; *R. v. Draz*; *R. v. O'Reilly* [2006] 2 Cr.App.R. 15, CA. See further *post*, § 2–8.

Section 40 is a procedural provision enabling the inclusion in an indictment in certain circumstances of a count charging a summary offence together with a count validly charging an indictable offence; if the conditions for inclusion are met, the Crown Court can proceed to try the summary offence, notwithstanding an acquittal at some point during the trial in respect of the indictable offence, because an acquittal does not have the effect of amending the indictment or retrospectively invalidating the satisfaction of the conditions for the inclusion of the summary matter: *R. v. Plant* [2008] 2 Cr.App.R. 27, CA.

The reference to "common assault" in section 40(3) should be construed to include an offence of battery: *R. v. Lynsey* [1995] 2 Cr.App.R. 667, CA.

In *R. v. Alden* [2002] 2 Cr.App.R.(S.) 74, CA, it was held that where, following committal for trial, a count of simple criminal damage on which the defendant has not been committed for trial is included in an indictment, section 40 of the 1988 Act will have no relevance where the committing magistrates have not gone through the procedure prescribed by section 22 of the *MCA* 1980 (*ante*, § 1–75i) and, thus, have not concluded that the value involved is below the relevant sum to enable them to commit for trial, with the result that the Crown Court will not be restricted to the maximum sentence that could have been imposed by the magistrates for that offence. In reaching this decision the court appears to have (i) been influenced by the decision in *R. v. Fennell* (*post*, § 23–14) to the effect that criminal damage offences below the relevant value remain offences that are triable either way, although justices are obliged to treat them, in certain circumstances, "as if" they are summary only offences, and (ii) not followed the unreasoned earlier decision in *R. v. McKechnie, Gibbons and Dixon*, 94 Cr.App.R. 51, CA, which had treated a criminal damage charge as if it had been included in the indictment pursuant to section 40 of the 1988 Act in the sort of circumstances under consideration. However, in *R. v. Gwynn* [2003] 2 Cr.App.R.(S.) 41, CA, it was held that where, following a sending for trial under section 51 of the *CDA* 1998 (*ante*, § 1–17), the indictment includes a count of criminal damage in respect of which there is no dispute that the value is below the amount specified in section 22 of the 1980 Act, section 40 of the 1988 Act operates to limit the sentencing powers of the Crown Court. In reaching that decision the court purported to distinguish the decision in *R. v. Alden*, by reference to Schedule 3 to the 1998 Act. The validity of this purported distinction is challenged in the commentary at *Criminal Law Week* 2003/06/4, where it is argued that the court in *R. v. Gwynn* reached the right result, but for the wrong reasons. It is also argued there, and in a commentary at *Criminal Law Week* 2002/15/6, that *R. v. Alden* was itself wrongly decided.

The fact that a charge which is only triable summarily has been adjourned *sine die* in the magistrates' court does not prevent the addition to an indictment, pursuant to section 40, of a count charging the same offence: *R. v. King* [1992] Crim.L.R. 47, CA. See further *post*, § 4–144.

A summary offence cannot be included in an indictment pursuant to section 40 if its only connection with the other offences charged in that indictment is with another summary offence that is itself validly joined. There must be an appropriate nexus with an indictable offence in the indictment to satisfy the section: *R. v. Callaghan*, 94 Cr.App.R. 226, CA. Where a count has been misjoined in breach of section 40, any conviction thereon will be quashed, but convictions on other counts in the indictment will not be affected: *ibid.*; and *R. v. Smith (B.P.)* [1997] 1 Cr.App.R. 390, CA (*cf.* the effect of a breach of the rules as to joinder, *post*, §§ 1–161 *et seq.*). The wording of section 40(1) bears a close resemblance to the wording of the rules as to joinder (see *post*, §§ 1–154 *et seq.* for the rules and the cases decided thereon.)

In *R. v. Simon* [1992] Crim.L.R. 444, CA (the summary report is not completely accurate), it was held that for the purposes of section 40(1) an offence of taking a convey- **1–75ak**
ance without authority was "founded on the same facts" as an offence of robbery where those offences formed part of a continuous series of events during an evening of criminality. In *R. v. Bird* [1995] Crim.L.R. 745, CA, it was held that a summary charge of driving whilst disqualified was "founded on the same facts or evidence" as a charge of possession of an offensive weapon, where a wooden pole had been found in a motor car that was being driven by a disqualified driver. This decision is criticised in the *Criminal Law Review* commentary, where the wording of section 40(1)(a) of the 1988 Act is contrasted with the wider wording of section 41(1)(b) of the same Act (*post*, § 1–75am). In *R. v. Cox* [2001] 5 *Archbold News* 2, the Court of Appeal (on a leave application) considered these criticisms, but held that the questioned phrase refers to a situation where there is a sufficient factual or evidential overlap to make it both just and convenient for the relevant offences to be tried together, and would certainly apply where the evidence of facts going to establish the summary offence would be admissible as part of the narrative leading up to the commission of the indictable offence (driving whilst disqualified properly joined to charge of witness intimidation where latter offence arose from threats made to arresting officer).

In *R. v. Smith (B.P.)*, *ante*, it was held that an offence of driving a conveyance taken without authority on January 14, 1996 and an offence of driving whilst disqualified on the same date were not part of a series of offences of the same or a similar character as an offence of dangerous driving on February 26, 1996. The court concluded that it was always the intention of Parliament that summary offences should be tried by magistrates and that the language of section 40 ought not to be strained to defeat that intention. See also, *R. v. Lewis*, 95 Cr.App.R. 131, CA (common assault on police officer at police station not properly joined with earlier threats to kill former girlfriend and her cohabitee).

The phrase "is one of two or more offences with which the accused is charged on the same occasion and which appear to the court to constitute or form part of a series of two or more offences of the same or a similar character" formed part of the repealed section 22(7) of the *MCA* 1980 (now s.22(11), *ante*, § 1–75i) and, in that context, was interpreted in a rather more restrictive way than the rules as to joinder. See *Re Prescott*, 70 Cr.App.R. 244, CA (Civ. Div.) (charges of assault on a police officer and criminal damage to his uniform were not offences of a similar character and did not form part of a series); *R. v. Hatfield JJ., ex p. Castle*, 71 Cr.App.R. 287, DC (assault on a police officer, obstruction of a police officer, using threatening words and behaviour held to have nothing in common with allegation of criminal damage to the officer's uniform); and *R. v. Tottenham JJ., ex p. Tibble*, 73 Cr.App.R. 55, DC (common assault and criminal damage not of similar character).

1–75al In *ex p. Tibble*, the court considered the relevance of *Ludlow v. Metropolitan Police Commr* [1971] A.C. 29, HL (the leading authority on the rules as to joinder, *post*, § 1–158), when construing section 22(7) and concluded that certain of the principles there enunciated in the context of the *Indictment Rules* were of no assistance. The word "similar" in section 22(7) was held to mean literally similar types of offence involving damage to property. It was stated that *R. v. Leicester JJ., ex p. Lord* [1980] Crim.L.R. 581, DC (the high-water mark of the "*Ludlow*" approach to s.22(7)), was decided *per incuriam* (*Prescott* and *ex p. Castle*, *ante*, having been decided but not cited) and should not be followed. In *R. v. St Helens Magistrates' Court, ex p. McClorie*, 78 Cr.App.R. 1, DC, it was held that where a defendant had broken into an enclosed yard, damaging a padlock worth £5, and on being apprehended in the yard within minutes by a police officer had caused damage to the extent of £15 to the officer's watch, a series of offences had been committed within the meaning of section 22(7). This decision was distinguished on its facts in *R. v. Braden*, 87 Cr.App.R. 289, CA, where it was held that an offence of criminal damage to a cell door was not part of a series of offences, within section 22(7), when the other offences relied upon were criminal damage to cars on the highway, caused in the course of parking an hour previously. The court emphasised the lapse in time and the difference in location.

Section 40(2) does not preclude the making of an order under section 5 of the *Criminal Procedure (Insanity) Act* 1964 where the defendant is found unfit to plead, but is found to have done the act constituting the summary offence: see *R. v. Southwark Crown Court, ex p. Koncar* [1998] 1 Cr.App.R. 321, CA, *post*, § 4–175b.

As to the effect of section 40(2) where the defendant falls to be sentenced for two or more summary offences, see *R. v. James* [2008] 1 Cr.App.R.(S.) 44, CA (*post*, § 4–456).

(9) Committal for trial of summary offence connected with either way offence

Criminal Justice Act 1988, s.41

Power of Crown Court to deal with summary offence where person committed for either way offence

1–75am **41.**—(1) *Where a magistrates' court commits a person to the Crown Court for trial on indictment for an offence triable either way or a number of such offences, it may also commit him for trial for any summary offence with which he is charged and which—*

(a) *is punishable with imprisonment or involves obligatory or discretionary disqualification from driving; and*

(b) *arises out of circumstances which appear to the court to be the same as or connected with those giving rise to the offence, or one of the offences, triable either way,*

whether or not evidence relating to that summary offence appears on the depositions or written statements in the case; and the trial of the information charging the summary offence shall then be treated as if the magistrates' court had adjourned it under section 10 of the Magistrates' Courts Act *1980 and had not fixed the time and place for its resumption.*

(2) *Where a magistrates' court commits a person to the Crown Court for trial on indictment for a number of offences triable either way and exercises the power conferred by subsection (1) above in respect of a summary offence, the magistrates' court shall give the Crown Court and the person who is committed for trial a notice stating which of the offences triable either way appears to the court to arise out of circumstances which are the same as or connected with those giving rise to the summary offence.*

(3) *A magistrates' court's decision to exercise the power conferred by subsection (1) above shall not be subject to appeal or liable to be questioned in any court.*

(4) *The committal of a person under this section in respect of an offence to which section 40 above applies shall not preclude the exercise in relation to the offence of the power conferred by that section; but where he is tried on indictment for such an offence, the functions of the Crown Court under this section in relation to the offence shall cease.*

[(4A) *The committal of a person under this section in respect of an offence to which section 40 above applies shall not prevent him being found guilty of that offence under section 6(3) of the* Criminal Law Act *1967 (alternative verdicts on trial on indictment); but where he is convicted under that provision of such an offence, the functions of the Crown Court under this section in relation to the offence shall cease.*]

(5) *If he is convicted on the indictment, the Crown Court shall consider whether the conditions specified in subsection (1) above were satisfied.*

(6) *If it considers that they were satisfied, it shall state to him the substance of the summary offence and ask him whether he pleads guilty or not guilty.*

(7) *If he pleads guilty, the Crown Court shall convict him, but may deal with him in respect of that offence only in a manner in which a magistrates' court could have dealt with him.*

(8) *If he does not plead guilty, the Crown Court may try him for the offence, but may deal with him only in a manner in which a magistrates' court could have dealt with him.*

(10) *The Crown Court shall inform the designated officer for the magistrates' court of the outcome of any proceedings under this section.*

(11) *Where the Court of Appeal allows an appeal against conviction of an offence triable either way which arose out of circumstances which were the same as or connected with those giving rise to a summary offence of which the appellant was convicted under this section—*

(a) *it shall set aside his conviction of the summary offence and give the designated officer for the magistrates' court notice that it has done so; and*

(b) *it may direct that no further proceedings in relation to the offence are to be undertaken;*

and the proceedings before the Crown Court in relation to the offence shall thereafter be disregarded for all purposes.

(12) *A notice under subsection (11) above shall include particulars of any direction given under paragraph (b) of that subsection in relation to the offence.*

(13) [*Repealed.*]

[This section is printed as amended and repealed in part by the *Access to Justice Act* 1999, ss.90(1) and 106, and Scheds 13, para. 137, and 15, Pt V(7); and the *Courts Act* 2003, s.109(1) and (3), Sched. 8, para. 303, and Sched. 10. As from days to be appointed: (i) subs. (4A) is inserted: *Domestic Violence, Crime and Victims Act* 2004, s.58(1), and Sched. 10, para. 28; and (ii) the whole section is repealed: *CJA* 2003, ss.41 and 332, Sched. 3, para. 60(1) and (8), and Sched. 37, Pt 4.]

The section has no application in respect of an offence triable only on indictment: *R. v. Miall* [1992] 1 Q.B. 836, 94 Cr.App.R. 258, DC and CA (but see s.51(1)(b) of the *CDA* 1998 in respect of matters sent for trial under that section). In *R. v. Foote*, 94 Cr.App.R. 82, CA, it was held that there was no power under this section to include any summary only charge in the indictment, or to deal with any such charge in the Crown Court on a contested basis, or to deal with it if the defendant is not convicted of a charge on the indictment. However, the substitution of a new subsection (8), and the repeal of subsection (9), by the *Courts Act* 2003, now enables the Crown Court to try a summary charge on a contested basis under section 41. In so trying a contested summary charge the judge of the Crown Court will exercise the powers conferred by section 66 of the 2003 Act (*post*, § 2–8). By reason of subsection (5), prior conviction of a charge on the indictment would still appear to be a condition precedent for the exercise of the power under subsection (8). In this regard, see *ante*, § 1–35, and *post*, §§ 1–195 *et seq.*, **1–75an** as to the consequences of a defect being left uncorrected. A conviction "on the indictment", for the purposes of subsection (5), includes a conviction of a summary offence that has been added to the indictment pursuant to section 40, even if there has been no conviction of any offence triable either way: *R. v. Bird* [1995] Crim.L.R. 745, CA.

As to subsections (3) and (5), see also *R. v. Miall, ante*. It was held that the Crown Court's function under subsection (5) is confined to considering whether paragraphs (a) and (b) of subsection (1) have been complied with. It is not its function to consider whether there has been a committal for trial of an either way offence within the opening words of the subsection. If there has not been, then any purported committal for trial of a summary offence pursuant to the subsection will be a nullity, but the remedy is not an "appeal against conviction" to the Court of Appeal (the Crown Court not having erred), but an application for judicial review. This leaves open the question of what the Crown Court is to do if it appears that the committal is invalid because the sole offence committed for trial is triable only on indictment. It is submitted that the answer may lie in the concluding words of paragraph (b) which refers to "the offence ... triable either way": can the Crown Court be satisfied that this condition is met if the offence in question is not so triable? To this extent, it is submitted the decision in *Miall* may be wrong; that there is no appeal against conviction to the Court of Appeal is clearly right, but the reason is that the *CAA* 1968 confers a right of appeal against conviction on indictment only (see s.1(1) thereof, *post*, § 7–36).

As to the power to commit for sentence on summary matters when committing for sentence on other matters, see *post*, § 5–25.

IV. AGAINST WHOM AN INDICTMENT LIES

A. GENERAL

Natural persons

1–76 An indictment lies against all persons who actually commit, or who procure, or assist in, the commission of an indictable offence, or who knowingly harbour a traitor or assist persons who have committed an offence. All persons who aid, abet, counsel or procure the offence are treated as principal offenders: see *post*, §§ 18–2 *et seq*.

1–77 As to gender and number in an Act of Parliament, see the *Interpretation Act* 1978, s.6 (Appendix B–6).

Corporations

1–78 No difficulty arises where the legislation creating an offence makes express provision for criminal liability on the part of corporations, since a corporation has a legal personality that is separate from its members. However, problems can arise as to the liability of corporations in respect of offences where no express provision is made for such liability. See also *post*, § 1–81b, in respect of partnerships and other bodies, and as to the possibility of transfer of criminal liability between entities that are not individuals.

General provision is made by the *Interpretation Act* 1978. Subject to the appearance of a contrary intention, the word "person" in a statute or subordinate legislation is to be construed as including "a body of persons corporate or unincorporate": see ss.5 and 11, and Scheds 1 and 2, Pt I, para. 4(5) (Appendix B–5).

In determining when a contrary intent is to be inferred, regard needs to be had to the common law development of the principles governing corporate liability for crimes. It is important also to distinguish between the law which determines the offences of which a corporation may be convicted (*e.g.* conspiracy to defraud but not murder, *post*) and the principles which govern the liability of a corporation for an offence of which it can be convicted. As to the latter, see *post*, §§ 17–30 *et seq*. In summary, liability will depend on whether the offence is one for which there is vicarious liability (see *post*, § 17–25), or, if there is not, whether the prohibited act by the natural person can be attributed to the company.

As to the former, this is a branch of the law to which the attitude of the courts has in the passage of time undergone a process of development: see *per* Hallett J. in *DPP v.*

Kent and Sussex Contractors Ltd [1944] 1 K.B. 146 at 157, DC. The general principles and problems were referred to in *Meridian Global Funds Management Asia Ltd v. Securities Commission* [1995] 2 A.C. 500, PC, *post*, § 17–31.

In *R. v. ICR Haulage Co. Ltd* [1944] K.B. 551, 30 Cr.App.R. 31, CCA, a limited company had been convicted of a common law conspiracy to defraud. On appeal it was contended that a company could not be guilty of an offence involving as an essential ingredient *mens rea* in the restricted sense of a dishonest or criminal mind. *Held*, that a limited company can as a general rule be indicted for its criminal acts which from the very necessity of the case must be performed by human agency and which in given circumstances become the acts of the company, and that for this purpose there was no distinction between an intention or other function of the mind and any other form of activity. Exceptions to this general rule exist: such exceptions include "cases in which, from its very nature, the offence cannot be committed by a corporation, as, for example, perjury, an offence which cannot be vicariously committed [but see *Odyssey Re (London) Ltd (formerly Sphere Drake Insurance plc) v. OIC Run-Off Ltd (formerly Orion Insurance Co. plc)*, *The Times*, March 17, 2000, CA (Civ. Div.), where it was said, in the context of civil proceedings, that the evidence of an individual given on behalf of a company is capable, as a matter of law, of being treated as the evidence of the company and that the company, as well as the individual, may be guilty of perjury if he gives false evidence], or bigamy, an offence which a limited company, not being a natural person, cannot commit vicariously or otherwise" (at pp. 554, 34). A further exception to the general rule "comprises offences of which murder is an example, where the only punishment the court can impose is corporal, the basis on which this exception rests being that the court will not stultify itself by embarking on a trial in which, if a verdict of guilty is returned, no effective order by way of sentence can be made" (*ibid.*). See also *Hawke v. Hulton* [1909] 2 K.B. 93, DC. **1–79**

Persuasive authority that a corporation may be convicted of manslaughter at common law is to be found in *R. v. P&O European Ferries (Dover) Ltd*, 93 Cr.App.R. 72, CCC (Turner J.). This was also assumed to be the law in *R. v. H.M. Coroner for East Kent, ex p. Spooner*, 88 Cr.App.R. 10, DC; and it is implicit in the decision in *Att.-Gen.'s Reference (No. 2 of 1999)* [2000] 2 Cr.App.R. 207, CA (*post*, § 19–109), that a corporation can indeed be convicted of manslaughter. However, the common law offence of manslaughter by gross negligence has now been abolished in respect of corporations and other specified entities (save in respect of deaths in custody, and subject to transitional and saving provisions) by the *Corporate Manslaughter and Corporate Homicide Act* 2007, s.20, and replaced, by section 1 of that Act, with a statutory offence. The relevant provisions are set out at §§ 19–117 *et seq.*, *post*. **1–80**

In *Richmond LBC v. Pinn and Wheeler Ltd* [1989] R.T.R. 354, DC, the court was concerned with an offence contrary to subordinate legislation made under the *Road Traffic Regulation Act* 1984, an ingredient of which was "driving". The court considered the *Interpretation Act* 1978 but held that "a contrary intention" appeared as the act of driving a motor vehicle is a physical act which can be performed only by natural persons. It is submitted that this overlooks the fact that all corporate activity is performed through human agency. The test, it is submitted, is not whether the prohibited act can only be performed by a natural person, but whether it is one which it is possible for the agent to commit while acting as such. If it is clear that the prohibited act is one which could only be done by the actor acting in his personal capacity, then corporate liability will be excluded. Bigamy and rape would seem to be the clearest examples. If a corporation can commit manslaughter (which may be committed by an act of driving), it seems illogical that it cannot commit a regulatory offence, an ingredient of which is driving.

On the question of whose acts, intention, knowledge, etc. a corporation can be held liable for, if at all, see *post*, §§ 17–30 *et seq*. **1–81**

As to the general procedure to be followed when a corporation is charged with an indictable offence, see *post*, § 1–242 and §§ 4–101, 4–102. See also rule 2.5(1) of the *Criminal Procedure Rules* 2005 (S.I. 2005 No. 384), *post*, § 2–206.

Consequences of winding-up or administration petition or order

The *Insolvency Act* 1986 contains prohibitions on the commencement or pursuit of **1–81a** proceedings against a company in respect of which a petition for an administration order has been presented (s.10), or an administration order has been made (s.11), or a winding-up order has been made (s.130), save with the leave of the court that is dealing with the insolvency proceedings. Section 126 of the 1986 Act makes provision for the making of applications to stay other proceedings against a company in respect of which a winding-up petition has been presented. In *R. v. Dickson and Wright*, 94 Cr.App.R. 7, the Court of Appeal assumed (without deciding the point) that by reason of section 130 the prosecution of a company in liquidation was improperly brought where leave of the court that had made the winding-up order had not been sought before the prosecution was commenced. In *Re Rhondda Waste Disposal Ltd* [2001] Ch. 57, CA (Civ. Div.), it was held that the prohibitions in sections 10 and 11 of the 1986 Act include prohibition on the commencement or pursuit, without leave, of criminal proceedings, but that when the public interest so dictates such leave ought readily to be given; the interests of the creditors of the company should not be treated as effectively trumping all other considerations.

Partnerships and other bodies

1–81b Many of the considerations and procedures in relation to the liability to prosecution of corporations (as to which, see *ante*, §§ 1–78 *et seq.*) apply also in respect of partnerships and other bodies. In *R. v. W. Stevenson & Sons (a Partnership)*; *R. v. Bick* [2008] 2 Cr.App.R. 14, CA, various complexities relating specifically to partnerships were considered and it was held that: (i) certain statutes expressly and validly impose criminal liability on a partnership separately from any liability imposed on individual partners; (ii) where there is no express provision for separate partnership liability, difficult questions may arise as to whether a partnership can have separate liability, and the inclusion of "a body of persons corporate or unincorporated" in the definition of "person" in the *Interpretation Act* 1978 (as to which, see *ante*, § 1–78) is subject to the qualification of "the appearance of a contrary intention", so as to make the particular context of crucial importance; and (iii) for individual partners or their assets to be at risk, in the absence of specific statutory provision, they must be prosecuted in their own names.

In *R. v. R.L. and J.F.*, unreported, August 28, 2008, CA ([2008] EWCA Crim 1970), the same approach was held to be applicable to the ascertainment of the liability of unincorporated associations generally, partnerships being a particular type of unincorporated association. As was acknowledged (at [11]), there are probably almost as many different types of unincorporated association as there are forms of human activity. It was held that although specific legislative provision for criminal liability on the part of such associations is made in some statutes, the absence of such specific provision, whether in respect of liability or procedure, is not necessarily determinative. Accordingly, it was held that a members' golf club could be prosecuted for the either-way offence, contrary to the *Water Resources Act* 1991, s.85, of causing polluting matter to enter controlled waters. Whilst the court made clear that a contrary intent, within the 1978 Act, might well be inferred in the case of an offence involving *mens rea*, it further decided that in the case of offences of strict liability such as that under consideration, any or all of the individual members could be prosecuted in their own names as principal offenders, and this was so notwithstanding an absence of personal culpability. This was subject only to the possibility of such a prosecution being stayed in the case of oppression as an abuse of process. It is submitted that this may go too far. Officers' liability provisions, such as that in the *Health Act* 2006, s.76(6) (to which the court referred, and which makes an officer or member of an unincorporated association that is guilty of an offence under the Act equally guilty where the offence is proved to have been attributable to "any neglect" on his part), are premised on a parliamentary view that the officer or member would not, as such, be guilty of the offence in the absence of such provision. There is no such specific provision in the 1991 Act, but section 217(3) was a more general provision (commonly found in regulatory legislation) to the effect that where the commission by any person of an offence is due to the act or default of some other person, that other person may also be charged and convicted of the offence. Here, as the court said (at [29]), the natural defendant was the landowner, *i.e.* the club. Individual members should have been liable to prosecution only where it could be shown that the club's lapse was due to their act or default.

An order made by the Secretary of State, pursuant to paragraph 30 of Schedule 2 to the *National Health Service and Community Care Act* 1990, transferring all "property, rights and liabilities" of a dissolved N.H.S. trust to another trust did not have the effect of transferring potential criminal liabilities: *R. v. Pennine Acute Hospitals N.H.S. Trust* [2004] 1 All E.R. 1324, CA.

B. EXEMPTIONS

(1) Aliens

British law is not generally construed as applying to the acts of aliens on land outside **1-82**
the dominions of the Crown or at sea, except within British territorial waters, or on British ships, or in cases of piracy *jure gentium* (*post*, §§ 25–38 *et seq.*). This rule does not apply to treason if the alien has resided in the dominions of the Crown and still remains under a duty of allegiance to the sovereign: *Joyce v. DPP* [1946] A.C. 347, *post*, § 2–36 and §§ 25–10 *et seq.*

A British subject cannot naturalise himself as a subject of a foreign state at war with this country so as to exempt himself from criminal liability for treason: *R. v. Lynch* [1903] 1 K.B. 444.

An alien resident within the dominions of the Crown is guilty of treason if he joins an invading force of his countrymen, when the royal forces have temporarily retired, for strategical or other reasons: *De Jager v. Att.-Gen. of Natal* [1907] A.C. 326. An alien friend is subject to indictment for offences committed in England (*R. v. Barronet and Allain* (1852) 1 E. & B. 1), or upon British ships within the Admiralty jurisdiction (see *post*, §§ 2–69 *et seq.*), and for piracy *jure gentium* (see *post*, §§ 25–38 *et seq.*; 1 Hawk. c. 17, s.5; *Att.-Gen. of Hong Kong v. Kwok a Sing* (1873) L.R. 5 C.P. 179, 199). The burden of proof that the accused person is an alien appears to lie upon him (see *R. v. Macdonald* (1747) 18 St.Tr. 857), except perhaps where the offence is committed outside the realm, but see *R. v. Jameson* [1896] 2 Q.B. 425. The liability of an alien enemy is not clearly ascertained: see *R. v. Johnson* (1805) 6 East 583 at 593; 1 Hawk. c. 17, s.6.

Various statutes make specific provision as to jurisdiction over aliens in respect of offences committed abroad, such as offences under the *War Crimes Act* 1991 (not printed in this work), breaches of certain Geneva Conventions (*post*, § 19–367), certain terrorist offences (*post*, § 25–149), hostage-taking (*post*, § 25–159) and torture (*post*, § 19–349) (considered in the context of extradition proceedings against a former head of state of a foreign power in *R. v. Bow Street Metropolitan Stipendiary Magistrate, ex p. Pinochet Ugarte (No. 3)* [2000] 1 A.C. 147, HL).

See also, generally, *post*, §§ 2–33 *et seq.*

(2) Diplomatic and international immunities

Diplomatic missions

Certain articles of the Vienna Convention on Diplomatic Relations 1961 have the **1-83**
force of law in the United Kingdom by virtue of section 2(1) of the *Diplomatic Privileges Act* 1964. Those articles (set out in Schedule 1) apply only to permanent missions and not to ad hoc missions: *R. v. Governor of Pentonville Prison, ex p. Teja* [1971] 2 Q.B. 274, DC. Under Article 31, a "diplomatic agent" (defined in Article 1) enjoys immunity from criminal jurisdiction and he is not obliged to give evidence as a witness. Under Article 38(1), read in conjunction with section 2(2) of the Act, a diplomatic agent who is a citizen of the United Kingdom and Colonies, or permanently resident in the United Kingdom, enjoys immunity only in respect of "official acts performed in the exercise of his functions", the meaning of which phrase was considered in *R. v. Bow Street Stipendiary Magistrate, ex p. Pinochet Ugarte (No. 3)* [2000] 1 A.C. 147, HL, *post*, § 1–88. As to the immunity of members of the family of a diplomatic agent who form part of his household, members of staff of a diplomatic mission and members of

the family of such staff, and private servants of members of the mission, see Articles 1, 37 and 38. See also section 2(6) of the 1964 Act and the *Diplomatic Privileges (British Nationals) Order* 1999 (S.I. 1999 No. 670).

Although Article 39 provides that a person entitled to diplomatic immunity should enjoy that immunity from the moment that he enters the receiving state, no such immunity can arise unless (a) the Foreign and Commonwealth Office has been notified by the sending state of the appointment as a member of its diplomatic mission of the person claiming immunity, and (b) that appointment has been accepted in the United Kingdom; diplomatic immunity cannot be conferred by the unilateral action of the sending state; this is the position even though Articles 2, 4 and 10 of the Vienna Convention, which deal with such matters, are not set out in Schedule 1 to the 1964 Act: *R. v. Governor of Pentonville Prison, ex p. Teja, ante*; *R. v. Lambeth JJ., ex p. Yusufu* [1985] Crim.L.R. 510, DC; and *R. v. Governor of Pentonville Prison, ex p. Osman (No. 2)* [1989] C.O.D. 446.

When the functions of a person enjoying privileges and immunities have come to an end, such privileges and immunities shall normally cease at the moment when he leaves the country, or on the expiry of a reasonable period in which to do so, but shall subsist until that time, even in the case of armed conflict. However, with respect to acts performed by such a person in the exercise of his functions as a member of a mission, immunity shall continue to subsist: Article 39(2).

1–84 Article 40 gives immunity to a diplomatic agent who is not accredited to the Court of St James but who is passing through, or is in, the United Kingdom while he is proceeding to take up or to return to his post in some other state, or is returning to his own country. This immunity extends to members of the diplomat's family who are accompanying him, or travelling separately to join him or return to their own country. It is not limited to the situation where the diplomatic agent is in transit between his home state and the state where he is posted, and the purpose for which the diplomat is in the United Kingdom is irrelevant: *R. v. Guildhall Magistrates' Court, ex p. Jarrett-Thorpe*, *The Times*, October 6, 1977, DC. A contrary view of the proper construction of Article 40 seems to have been taken in *ex p. Yusufu, ante*, although it may be that the two cases are not irreconcilable on their facts. Whether or not a diplomatic agent is proceeding to take up or return to his post is a question of fact: *ex p. Teja, ante*.

European Court of Human Rights

1–84a The *European Court of Human Rights (Immunities and Privileges) Order* 2000 (S.I. 2000 No. 1817) confers various privileges and immunities on certain judges and officials of the European Court of Human Rights, and on persons participating in proceedings before that court or the Committee of Ministers of the Council of Europe.

Commonwealth Secretariat

1–85 See the *Commonwealth Secretariat Act* 1966, s.1 and Sched., Pt I.

Consular and commonwealth quasi-consular posts

1–85a See the *Consular Relations Act* 1968, ss.2, 3 and 12.

Conference attendance

1–85b See the *International Organisations Act* 1968, s.6 (foreign government representatives attending United Kingdom conferences).

Waiver of immunity

1–86 Under Article 32 of the Vienna Convention, immunity may be expressly waived by the sending state. Waiver by a head of mission, or by any person for the time being performing his functions, is deemed to be a waiver by the sending state: *Diplomatic Privileges Act* 1964, s.2(3). A conviction obtained against a person entitled to immunity will be quashed where there has been no waiver: *R. v. Madan* [1961] 2 Q.B. 1, 45 Cr.App.R. 80, CCA.

Certificates as evidence

Under section 4 of the *Diplomatic Privileges Act* 1964, paragraph 9 of the Schedule to the *Commonwealth Secretariat Act* 1966, section 11 of the *Consular Relations Act* 1968 and section 8 of the *International Organisations Act* 1968, if in any proceedings a question arises whether or not a person is entitled to immunity by virtue of the legislation concerned, a certificate issued by or under the authority of the Secretary of State stating any fact relating to that question shall be conclusive evidence of that fact. Certificates relate only to questions of fact, and all questions of law are for the court. The effect of such certificates was considered in detail in *R. v. Governor of Pentonville Prison, ex p. Osman (No. 2), ante*, § 1–83. As to the court applying to a minister of the Crown for information as to recognition of diplomatic status, see *Engelke v. Musmann* [1928] A.C. 433, HL. **1–86a**

(3) Sovereign and state immunity

The Sovereign is immune from criminal jurisdiction. Such immunity does not extend to deposed or exiled sovereigns who happen to be within the jurisdiction: *R. v. Mary, Queen of Scots* (1586) 1 St.Tr. 1161. **1–87**

State Immunity Act 1978, s.20(1), (2)

20.—(1) Subject to the provisions of this section and to any necessary modifications, the *Diplomatic Privileges Act* 1964 shall apply to— **1–88**

(a) a sovereign or other head of State;

(b) members of his family forming part of his household; and

(c) his private servants,

as it applies to the head of a diplomatic mission, to members of his family forming part of his household and to his private servants.

(2) The immunities and privileges conferred by virtue of subsection (1)(a) and (b) above shall not be subject to the restrictions by reference to nationality or residence mentioned in Article 37(1) or 38 in Schedule 1 to the said Act of 1964.

As to the 1964 Act, see *ante*, §§ 1–83 *et seq.*

The concepts of sovereign immunity and immunity in respect of acts of state were considered in *R. v. Bow Street Metropolitan Stipendiary Magistrate, ex p. Pinochet Ugarte (No. 3)* [2000] 1 A.C. 147, HL, where it was held that whilst a former head of state enjoys continuing immunity in respect of acts done as part of his official function as head of state, those functions could not include the commission or authorisation of torture, which since the International Convention against Torture and other Cruel, Inhuman or Degrading Treatment or Punishment 1984 has been established as an international crime and one of the features of which is that it can only be committed by a person acting in an official capacity. It is impossible that international law could accept as "official", conduct which it has itself prohibited and criminalised.

In *R. (Alamieyeseigha) v. CPS* [2006] Crim.L.R. 669, DC, it was held that whether a head of a member state of a federal state is entitled to immunity under section 20 will depend on whether the state itself is entitled to state immunity, which is a case sensitive issue, and in respect of which certain relevant factors are identified in the judgment.

(4) Visiting forces

By the *Visiting Forces Act* 1952, s.3 (as amended), a member of a visiting force or of a civilian component of such force is not, in certain situations, liable to be tried by a United Kingdom court for certain offences. **1–89**

(5) Children under 10

Children and Young Persons Act 1933, s.50

Age of criminal responsibility

50. It shall be conclusively presumed that no child under the age of ten years can be guilty of any offence. **1–90**

[This section is printed as amended by the *CYPA 1963*, s.16(1).]

As to the ascertainment of age, see *post*, § 19–326.

(6) Children between 10 and 14

1–91 Section 34 of the *CDA* 1998 abolished the "rebuttable presumption of criminal law that a child aged 10 or over is incapable of committing an offence". This had the effect of abolishing both the presumption of *doli incapax* and the availability of that doctrine as a common law defence: *R. v. T.* [2008] 2 Cr.App.R. 17, CA (rejecting a tentative suggestion in *DPP v. P.* [2008] 1 W.L.R. 1005, DC, that only the presumption had been abolished). However, *DPP v. P.* remains an important authority as to the process which a judge should adopt before deciding whether to continue with a trial against a child in respect of whose capacity to understand the nature of the alleged wrongdoing there are doubts (as to which, see *post*, § 4–73).

See *post*, § 1–92, as to certain notification obligations in respect of the institution of criminal proceedings against children who have attained the age of 10.

As to the ascertainment of age, see *post*, § 19–326.

(7) Children aged 14 or over

1–92 A person who decides to lay an information against a person whom he has reason to believe has attained the age of 14 and is under the age of 18, is under a duty to give notice of the decision to the appropriate local authority: *CYPA* 1969, ss.5(8) and 70(1). Section 34(2) of the 1969 Act (as amended by the *CJCSA* 2000, s.74, and Sched. 7, para. 4(1)(a) and (2), and the *Offender Management Act 2007 (Consequential Amendments) Order* 2008 (S.I. 2008 No. 912), art. 3, and Sched. 1, para. 3(1) and (2)(a), and as read together with S.I. 1970 No. 1882) provides that, in relation to a person who has attained the age of 10 and is under the age of 17, no proceedings for an offence shall be begun in any court unless the person proposing to begin the proceedings has given notice of the proceedings to an officer of a local probation board, or an officer of a provider of probation services, acting in the area for which the court acts, in addition to giving any notice required by section 5(8). In *DPP v. Cottier* [1996] 2 Cr.App.R. 410, DC, it was held that these requirements had both been satisfied by the giving of oral notice as soon as reasonably practicable after the decision to institute the proceedings had been made (in respect of section 5(8)) and before the first court appearance (in respect of section 34(2)), albeit after the date of charge, and that, in any event, failure to comply with the notice provisions of either section would not invalidate the proceedings, since the requirements are directory and not mandatory (followed in *R. v. Marsh* [1997] 1 W.L.R. 649, CA). (As to the principles to be applied to the ascertainment of the consequences of non-compliance with procedural requirements, see now *post*, §§ 1–195 *et seq*.)

(8) Persons of unsound mind

1–93 Every person of the age of discretion is, unless the contrary is proved, presumed by law to be sane, and to be accountable for his actions: *R. v. Layton* (1849) 4 Cox 149. See, generally, Chapter 17, *post*.

(9) Offenders assisting investigations and prosecutions

Serious Organised Crime and Police Act 2005, s.71

Assistance by offender: immunity from prosecution

1–94 **71.**—(1) If a specified prosecutor thinks that for the purposes of the investigation or prosecution of any offence it is appropriate to offer any person immunity from prosecution he may give the person a written notice under this subsection (an "immunity notice").

(2) If a person is given an immunity notice, no proceedings for an offence of a description specified in the notice may be brought against that person in England and Wales or Northern Ireland except in circumstances specified in the notice.

(3) An immunity notice ceases to have effect in relation to the person to whom it is given if the person fails to comply with any conditions specified in the notice.

(4) Each of the following is a specified prosecutor—

(a) the Director of Public Prosecutions;

(b) the Director of Revenue and Customs Prosecutions;

(c) the Director of the Serious Fraud Office;

(d) the Director of Public Prosecutions for Northern Ireland;

(e) a prosecutor designated for the purposes of this section by a prosecutor mentioned in paragraphs (a) to (d).

(5) The Director of Public Prosecutions or a person designated by him under subsection (4)(e) may not give an immunity notice in relation to proceedings in Northern Ireland.

(6) The Director of Public Prosecutions for Northern Ireland or a person designated by him under subsection (4)(e) may not give an immunity notice in relation to proceedings in England and Wales.

(7) An immunity notice must not be given in relation to an offence under section 188 of the *Enterprise Act* 2002 (cartel offences).

See section 72 of the same Act (*post*, § 15–344) as to the power to give an undertaking to any person that information of a specified description will not be used against him in any proceedings. **1–95**

C. Indicting Extradited Persons

(1) Introduction

The *Extradition Act* 1989 was repealed as from January 1, 2004 (*Extradition Act 2003 (Commencement and Savings) Order* 2003 (S.I. 2003 No. 3103), *Extradition Act 2003 (Commencement and Savings) (Amendment) Order* 2003 (S.I. 2003 No. 3258), and *Extradition Act 2003 (Commencement and Savings) (Amendment No. 2) Order* 2003 (S.I. 2003 No. 3312)) by the *Extradition Act* 2003, ss.218 and 220, and Sched. 4. The provisions of the 2003 Act that govern the prosecution of persons extradited to the United Kingdom are set out in the following paragraphs. **1–96**

Extradition Act 2003, ss.146–151

Dealing with person for other offences

146.—(1) This section applies if a person is extradited to the United Kingdom from a category 1 territory in pursuance of a Part 3 warrant. **1–97**

(2) The person may be dealt with in the United Kingdom for an offence committed before his extradition only if—

(a) the offence is one falling within subsection (3), or

(b) the condition in subsection (4) is satisfied.

(3) The offences are—

(a) the offence in respect of which the person is extradited;

(b) an offence disclosed by the information provided to the category 1 territory in respect of that offence;

(c) an extradition offence in respect of which consent to the person being dealt with is given on behalf of the territory in response to a request made by the appropriate judge;

(d) an offence which is not punishable with imprisonment or another form of detention;

(e) an offence in respect of which the person will not be detained in connection with his trial, sentence or appeal;

(f) an offence in respect of which the person waives the right that he would have (but for this paragraph) not to be dealt with for the offence.

(4) The condition is that the person has been given an opportunity to leave the United Kingdom and—

(a) he has not done so before the end of the permitted period, or

(b) he has done so before the end of the permitted period and has returned to the United Kingdom.

(5) The permitted period is 45 days starting with the day on which the person arrives in the United Kingdom.

[This section is printed as amended by the *PJA* 2006, s.42, and Sched. 13, para. 23.]

Effect of consent to extradition to the United Kingdom

147.—(1) This section applies if— **1–98**

(a) a person is extradited to the United Kingdom from a category 1 territory in pursuance of a Part 3 warrant;

(b) the person consented to his extradition to the United Kingdom in accordance with the law of the category 1 territory.

(2) Section 146(2) does not apply if the conditions in subsection (3) or the conditions in subsection (4) are satisfied.

(3) The conditions are that—

(a) under the law of the category 1 territory, the effect of the person's consent is to waive his right under section 146(2);

(b) the person has not revoked his consent in accordance with that law, if he is permitted to do so under that law.

(4) The conditions are that—

(a) under the law of the category 1 territory, the effect of the person's consent is not to waive his right under section 146(2);

(b) the person has expressly waived his right under section 146(2) in accordance with that law;

(c) the person has not revoked his consent in accordance with that law, if he is permitted to do so under that law;

(d) the person has not revoked the waiver of his right under section 146(2) in accordance with that law, if he is permitted to do so under that law.

Extradition offences

1–99 **148.**—(1) Conduct constitutes an extradition offence in relation to the United Kingdom if these conditions are satisfied—

(a) the conduct occurs in the United Kingdom;

(b) the conduct is punishable under the law of the relevant part of the United Kingdom with imprisonment or another form of detention for a term of 12 months or a greater punishment.

(2) Conduct also constitutes an extradition offence in relation to the United Kingdom if these conditions are satisfied—

(a) the conduct occurs outside the United Kingdom;

(b) the conduct constitutes an extra-territorial offence punishable under the law of the relevant part of the United Kingdom with imprisonment or another form of detention for a term of 12 months or a greater punishment.

(3) But subsections (1) and (2) do not apply in relation to conduct of a person if—

(a) he has been convicted by a court in the United Kingdom of the offence constituted by the conduct, and

(b) he has been sentenced for the offence.

(4) Conduct also constitutes an extradition offence in relation to the United Kingdom if these conditions are satisfied—

(a) the conduct occurs in the United Kingdom;

(b) a sentence of imprisonment or another form of detention for a term of 4 months or a greater punishment has been imposed in the United Kingdom in respect of the conduct.

(5) Conduct also constitutes an extradition offence in relation to the United Kingdom if these conditions are satisfied—

(a) the conduct occurs outside the United Kingdom;

(b) the conduct constitutes an extra-territorial offence;

(c) a sentence of imprisonment or another form of detention for a term of 4 months or a greater punishment has been imposed in the United Kingdom in respect of the conduct.

(6) The relevant part of the United Kingdom is the part of the United Kingdom in which the relevant proceedings are taking place.

(7) The relevant proceedings are the proceedings in which it is necessary to decide whether conduct constitutes an extradition offence.

(8) Subsections (1) to (5) apply for the purposes of sections 142 to 147.

[This section is printed as amended by the *PJA* 2006, s.42, and Sched. 13, para. 2(6).]

The appropriate judge

1–100 **149.**—(1) The appropriate judge is—

(a) in England and Wales, a District Judge (Magistrates' Courts), a justice of the peace or a judge entitled to exercise the jurisdiction of the Crown Court;

(b), (c) [*Scotland*; *Northern Ireland*].

(2) This section applies for the purposes of sections 142 to 147.

Dealing with person for other offences: Commonwealth countries etc.

150.—(1) This section applies if— **1–101**

(a) a person is extradited to the United Kingdom from a category 2 territory under law of the territory corresponding to Part 2 of this Act, and

(b) the territory is a Commonwealth country, a British overseas territory or the Hong Kong Special Administrative Region of the People's Republic of China.

(2) The person may be dealt with in the United Kingdom for an offence committed before his extradition only if—

(a) the offence is one falling within subsection (3), or

(b) the condition in subsection (6) is satisfied.

(3) The offences are—

(a) the offence in respect of which the person is extradited;

(b) a lesser offence disclosed by the information provided to the category 2 territory in respect of that offence;

(c) an offence in respect of which consent to the person being dealt with is given by or on behalf of the relevant authority.

(4) An offence is a lesser offence in relation to another offence if the maximum punishment for it is less severe than the maximum punishment for the other offence.

(5) The relevant authority is—

(a) if the person has been extradited from a Commonwealth country, the government of the country;

(b) if the person has been extradited from a British overseas territory, the person administering the territory;

(c) if the person has been extradited from the Hong Kong Special Administrative Region of the People's Republic of China, the government of the Region.

(6) The condition is that the protected period has ended.

(7) The protected period is 45 days starting with the first day after his extradition to the United Kingdom on which the person is given an opportunity to leave the United Kingdom.

(8) A person is dealt with in the United Kingdom for an offence if—

(a) he is tried there for it;

(b) he is detained with a view to trial there for it.

Dealing with person for other offences: other category 2 territories

151.—(1) This section applies if— **1–102**

(a) a person is extradited to the United Kingdom from a category 2 territory under law of the territory corresponding to Part 2 of this Act, and

(b) the territory is not one falling within section 150(1)(b).

(2) The person may be dealt with in the United Kingdom for an offence committed before his extradition only if—

(a) the offence is one falling within subsection (3), or

(b) the condition in subsection (4) is satisfied.

(3) The offences are—

(a) the offence in respect of which the person is extradited;

(b) an offence disclosed by the information provided to the category 2 territory in respect of that offence;

(c) an offence in respect of which consent to the person being dealt with is given on behalf of the territory.

(4) The condition is that—

(a) the person has returned to the territory from which he was extradited, or

(b) the person has been given an opportunity to leave the United Kingdom.

(5) A person is dealt with in the United Kingdom for an offence if—

(a) he is tried there for it;

(b) he is detained with a view to trial there for it.

Extradition Act 2003, ss.153, 154

Return of person acquitted or not tried

1-103 **153.**—(1) This section applies if—

(a) a person is accused in the United Kingdom of the commission of an offence;

(b) the person is extradited to the United Kingdom in respect of the offence from—

(i) a category 1 territory under law of the territory corresponding to Part 1 of this Act, or

(ii) a category 2 territory under law of the territory corresponding to Part 2 of this Act;

(c) the condition in subsection (2) or the condition in subsection (3) is satisfied.

(2) The condition is that—

(a) proceedings against the person for the offence are not begun before the end of the required period, which is 6 months starting with the day on which the person arrives in the United Kingdom on his extradition, and

(b) before the end of the period of 3 months starting immediately after the end of the required period the person asks the Secretary of State to return him to the territory from which he was extradited.

(3) The condition is that—

(a) at his trial for the offence the person is acquitted or is discharged under any of the provisions specified in subsection (4), and

(b) before the end of the period of 3 months starting immediately after the date of his acquittal or discharge the person asks the Secretary of State to return him to the territory from which he was extradited.

(4) The provisions are—

(a) section 12(1) of the *Powers of Criminal Courts (Sentencing) Act* 2000;

(b), (c) [*Scotland*; *Northern Ireland*].

(5) The Secretary of State must arrange for him to be sent back, free of charge and with as little delay as possible, to the territory from which he was extradited to the United Kingdom in respect of the offence.

(6) [*Scotland*.]

Restriction on bail where undertaking given by Secretary of State

1-104 **154.**—(1) This section applies in relation to a person if—

(a) the Secretary of State has given an undertaking in connection with the person's extradition to the United Kingdom, and

(b) the undertaking includes terms that the person be kept in custody until the conclusion of any proceedings against him in the United Kingdom for an offence.

(2) A court, judge or justice of the peace may grant bail to the person in the proceedings only if the court, judge or justice of the peace considers that there are exceptional circumstances which justify it.

Category 1 territories and category 2 territories are those which are designated as such by order made by the Secretary of State: ss.1 and 69. A Part 3 warrant is a warrant issued pursuant to section 142.

(2) General

1-104a In *R. v. Horseferry Road Magistrates' Court, ex p. Bennett* [1994] 1 A.C. 42, the House of Lords held that the High Court, in the exercise of its supervisory jurisdiction, has the power to inquire into the circumstances by which a person has been brought within the jurisdiction; and that where extradition procedures are available to bring an accused to the United Kingdom, but he has been forcibly brought within the jurisdiction in disregard of those procedures by a process to which the police of this country, or the prosecuting or other executive authorities, had been a knowing party, the courts would stay the prosecution on the basis that to proceed in such circumstances would be an abuse of process. (As to the reasoning behind this decision, see further *post*, § 4–55.) The responsibility of exercising this power in such circumstances should be that of the High Court, and if a serious question arises before magistrates as to the deliberate abuse of extradition procedures, an adjournment should be allowed so that an appropriate application can be made to the Divisional Court. Different considerations would arise in a case where no lawful extradition procedures were available (such as *R. v. Plymouth*

Magistrates' Court, ex p. Driver, 82 Cr.App.R. 85, DC), but their Lordships made it clear that they were expressing no opinion in relation to such a situation. For the application of this guidance, see *R. v. Horseferry Road Magistrates' Court, ex p. Bennett (No. 2)* [1995] 1 Cr.App.R. 147, DC (committal for trial quashed), *R. v. Staines Magistrates' Court, ex p. Westfallen; R. v. Same, ex p. Soper; R. v. Swindon Magistrates' Court, ex p. Nangle* [1998] 1 W.L.R. 652, DC (no abuse of process; see *post*, § 4–64), and *R. v. Mullen* [1999] 2 Cr.App.R. 143, CA (conviction quashed as trial an abuse of process; see *post*, § 4–64).

See *Pooley v. Whetham* (1880) 15 Ch.D. 435, as to the possibility of an improper motive for bringing extradition proceedings amounting to an abuse of the process of the court. **1–105**

The restrictions on the offences for which an extradited person may be tried do not justify any other departure from the normal rules of procedure: *R. v. Aubrey Fletcher, ex p. Ross-Munro* [1968] 1 Q.B. 620, DC. Accordingly, where such a person is properly being tried, there is no reason why further evidence which had not been used in the extradition proceedings could not be used at trial to support the charge.

In *R. v. Davidson*, 64 Cr.App.R. 209, CA, an appeal was brought on the basis that the trial judge had wrongly refused an application to quash an indictment; the basis of the application, apparently, being a contention that the defendant had been extradited from West Germany contrary to the laws of that country and that the charges which he faced were not within a restriction that the extraditing court had purported to impose. The Court of Appeal held that the only legitimate concern of the English court in a case where the defendant has been extradited to England is to ensure that the offences for which he is to be tried are such as are permitted under English extradition legislation. As the facts on which the extradition had been grounded disclosed the offences for which the defendant was tried, the charges on which he was tried had not fallen foul of the restrictions imposed under English extradition law and the English court was not concerned with any decision of the foreign court which had ordered the extradition or with the contents of any treaty between the two countries. This case was decided before the 1989 Act came into force and before the decision in *ex p. Bennett, ante*, § 1–104a. In any event, the courts must, it is submitted, at the very least be entitled to investigate the circumstances in which a fugitive is returned to the United Kingdom to the extent that such an inquiry may be necessary to determine whether the relevant statutory provisions, now found in the 2003 Act, apply and have been complied with. **1–106**

In *R. v. Corrigan* [1931] 1 K.B. 527, CCA, it was held that the burden is on the accused to establish that the extradition laws operate to bar a prosecution for a particular offence in a particular case. However, the contrary viewpoint does not appear to have been argued in the case. **1–107**

V. THE FORM OF AN INDICTMENT

A. Rules as to Indictments

The statutory provisions as to indictments are to be found in the *Indictments Act* 1915, and in section 2 of the *Administration of Justice Act* 1933. Those provisions are supplemented by rules 6 to 10 of the *Indictments (Procedure) Rules* 1971 (S.I. 1971 No. 2084), and by the *Criminal Procedure Rules* 2005 (S.I. 2005 No. 384), as amended (as to which rules, see generally, *post*, §§ 2–204 *et seq.*). The *Indictment Rules* 1971 have been revoked by the *Criminal Procedure (Amendment) Rules* 2007 (S.I. 2007 No. 699), which (by rule 9) inserted a new Part 14 in the 2005 rules to make fresh provision as to the form, content, signature and service of indictments. Rule 2.1(5) of the 2005 rules (inserted by rule 4 of the 2007 rules) provides that the rules in the new Part 14 apply in cases in which one of the events listed in sub-paragraphs (a) to (d) of rule 14.1(1) (*post*, § 1–224) takes place on or after April 2, 2007, and that in other cases the rules replaced by those rules apply. As to the previous rules, see the 2007 edition of this work. **1–108**

The legislative provisions as to indictments are supplemented by parts of the Lord Chief Justice's consolidated criminal practice direction, as amended, which is referred to **1–109** as the "Practice Direction" in the 2005 rules: see the definition in rule 2.2, *post*, § 2–206. The jurisdictional basis for that practice direction is explained at § 2–1, *post*.

As to the prescribed forms of indictment, see *post*, §§ 1–115, 1–119 and 1–120.

As to the consequences of a breach of the various rules as to indictments, see *post*, §§ 1–195 *et seq.*

B. DRAWING THE INDICTMENT

(1) General

1–110 The drafting of an indictment always requires care and attention and often requires the exercise of considerable thought and skill. "Simple" cases can give rise to difficult drafting problems. The fact that the original charge is straightforward does not mean either that it is the appropriate charge or that it should be the only charge in the indictment. The Court of Appeal has expressed concern about the number of cases involving defective indictments—see *R. v. Newland* [1988] Q.B. 402, 87 Cr.App.R. 118, CA, and *R. v. Hodgson and Pollin* (*post*, § 1–117), in both of which cases the court made it clear that the indictment is no mere formality and emphasised that it is the responsibility of counsel to ensure that the indictment is in proper form before arraignment. As to the importance of the existence of a valid indictment, see also *R. v. Clarke and McDaid*, *post*, § 1–196.

1–111 Paragraph IV.34.1 of the *Practice Direction (Criminal Proceedings: Consolidation)* [2002] 1 W.L.R. 2870, as substituted by *Practice Direction (Criminal Proceedings: Arraignment)* [2008] 1 W.L.R. 154, apart from summarising the effect of rules 14.1 and 14.2(5) of the *Criminal Procedure Rules* 2005 (S.I. 2005 No. 384), as amended (*post*, §§ 1–223 and 1–115 respectively), states that where the prosecutor intends to include in the draft indictment counts which differ materially from, or are additional to, those on which the defendant was sent or committed for trial then the defendant should be given as much notice as possible, usually by service of a draft indictment, or a provisional draft indictment, at the earliest opportunity.

As to the responsibility and discretion that the Crown has in respect of the determination of the order in which defendants are named in an indictment, see *R. v. Cairns, Zaidi and Chaudhary* [2003] 1 Cr.App.R. 38, CA, *post*, § 1–176.

See further, *post*, §§ 1–204 *et seq.* as to the preferment and signing of indictments.

If counsel for the prosecution considers that the indictment requires amendment, he should apply to the court for the necessary order before arraignment, having given as much notice as possible to the defence. As to amendment of the indictment, see *post*, §§ 1–147 *et seq.*

(2) Number of counts

1–112 As to the power to include more than one count in an indictment, and as to the criteria to be satisfied in that regard, see *post*, §§ 1–115, 1–154 *et seq.*, 1–204 *et seq.*

In complicated cases, where the indictment contains a large number of counts involving a number of defendants, the prosecution should seriously consider dividing the trial into such parts as will enable the jury to grasp and retain the evidence properly: *R. v. Shaw and Agard*, 28 Cr.App.R. 138, CCA. The following guidance is given in *Practice Direction (Criminal Proceedings: Consolidation)* [2002] 1 W.L.R. 2870, as substituted by *Practice Direction (Criminal Proceedings: Arraignment)* [2008] 1 W.L.R. 154:

> **IV.34.3** Save in the special circumstances described in the following paragraphs of this practice direction, it is undesirable that a large number of counts should be contained in one indictment. Where defendants on trial have a variety of offences alleged against them then in the interests of effective case management it is the court's responsibility to exercise its powers in accordance with the overriding objective set out in Part 1 of the *Criminal Procedure Rules* 2005. The prosecution may be required to identify a selection of counts on which the trial should proceed, leaving a decision to be taken later whether to try any of the remainder. Where an indictment contains substantive counts and one or more related conspiracy counts the court will expect the prosecution to justify the joinder. Failing justification the prosecution should be required to choose whether to proceed on the substantive counts or on the conspiracy counts. In any event, if there is a conviction on any counts that are tried then those that have been

postponed can remain on the file marked "not to be proceeded with without the leave of the court". In the event that a conviction is later quashed on appeal, the remaining counts can be tried. Where necessary the court has power to order that an indictment be divided and some counts removed to a separate indictment.

For the relevant following paragraphs of the practice direction, see *post*, §§ 1–120a, 1–140. As to Part 1 of the 2005 rules and the overriding objective, see *post*, §§ 4–84a *et seq*. See *post*, §§ 1–147, 1–166 *et seq*. as to severance.

As to the principles identified in paragraph IV.34.3, see *R. v. Hudson*, 36 Cr.App.R. 94, CCA; *R. v. Novac*, 65 Cr.App.R. 107 at 118, CA; *R. v. Thorne*, 66 Cr.App.R. 6, CA; *R. v. Cohen, The Independent*, July 29, 1992, CA, and *R. v. Kellard* [1995] 2 Cr.App.R. 134, CA. See also *post*, §§ 1–180, 33–63 and Appendix N–2, N–15.

Common sense should be used in deciding what charges should be included; trivial offences should not be included: *R. v. Ambrose*, 57 Cr.App.R. 538 at 540, CA.

Where a prolonged course of offending is alleged, a lengthy indictment may be necessary in order that the judge should be able to pass a sentence (in the event of conviction) which adequately reflects the offender's criminality: *R. v. Canavan*; *R. v. Kidd*; *R. v. Shaw* [1998] 1 Cr.App.R. 79, CA. See also *R. v. Evans (Cheryl)* [2000] 1 Cr.App.R.(S.) 144, CA, and *R. v. B.T.* [2002] 2 Cr.App.R.(S.) 2, CA. However, see the power that now exists under rule 14.2(2) of the *Criminal Procedure Rules* 2005 (S.I. 2005 No. 384) to charge more than one incident in a single count in certain circumstances (*post*, § 1–115), and see *post*, §§ 1–139 *et seq.*, as to the application of that rule. See also the power under section 17 of the *Domestic Violence, Crime and Victims Act* 2004 to direct the trial of certain counts by a judge alone in specified circumstances (*post*, § 4–267h), and see *post*, §§ 1–120 *et seq.*, as to the application of that rule. As to the sentencing problems that may arise if the number of offences charged is insufficient to reflect the alleged criminality, see *post*, § 5–68. As to the related problem of identifying the relevant incident when specimen charges are laid, see *post*, §§ 1–131 *et seq.*

(3) No count necessary for attempt

Where a defendant is indicted for an offence, it is not necessary to add another count for an attempt to commit it; the jury may acquit him of the offence charged and find him guilty of the attempt: *CLA* 1967, s.6(3), (4), *post*, § 4–455. **1–113**

(4) Inconsistent counts

An indictment may contain counts in which the allegations made in one count are inconsistent with the allegations made in another count. In such a case, both counts may properly be pursued and left to the jury as alternatives if there is a case to answer made out on each. It is then for the jury to decide which, if either, of the counts is made out: *R. v. Bellman* [1989] A.C. 836, HL. **1–113a**

(5) Single count appropriate to cover alternative modes of participation

See *R. v. Gaughan*, 155 J.P. 235, CA, *post*, § 18–32, and *R. v. Tirnaveanu* [2007] 2 Cr.App.R. 23, CA, but see also *post*, §§ 4–391 *et seq*. **1–113b**

C. CONTENTS

An indictment consists of the commencement, the statement of offence, the particulars of an offence and a signature. It should also be dated. **1–114**

(1) Commencement

See *post*, §§ 1–115, 1–119 *et seq.*, as to the prescribed forms for an indictment, and as to the words by which an indictment is commenced. No problem arises as to venue, since in England and Wales there is a single Crown Court (which is a superior court of record: *Supreme Court [Senior Courts] Act* 1981 (renamed as from a day to be appointed by the *Constitutional Reform Act* 2005, s.59(5), and Sched. 11, para. 1(2)), ss.1(1) and 45(1), *post*, § 2–29), but see *post*, § 2–11 as to allocation of business. This court has exclusive jurisdiction in trials on indictment: *ibid.*, s.46. **1–114a**

(2) Statement and particulars of offence(s) and signature

Indictments Act 1915, s.3

1–114b **3.**—(1) Every indictment shall contain, and shall be sufficient if it contains, a statement of the specific offence or offences with which the accused person is charged, together with such particulars as may be necessary for giving reasonable information as to the nature of the charge.

(2) Notwithstanding any rule of law or practice, an indictment shall, subject to the provisions of this Act, not be open to objection in respect of its form or contents if it is framed in accordance with the rules under this Act.

As to the revocation of the *Indictment Rules* 1971 and the replacement of those rules, in respect of the form and content of an indictment, by the new Part 14 of the *Criminal Procedure Rules* 2005 (S.I. 2005 No. 384), see *ante*, § 1–108.

Criminal Procedure Rules 2005 (S.I. 2005 No. 384), r.14.2

Form and content of indictment

1–115 **14.2.**—(1) An indictment must be in one of the forms set out in the Practice Direction and must contain, in a paragraph called a "count"—

(a) a statement of the offence charged that—
  (i) describes the offence in ordinary language, and
  (ii) identifies any legislation that creates it; and
(b) such particulars of the conduct constituting the commission of the offence as to make clear what the prosecutor alleges against the defendant.

(2) More than one incident of the commission of the offence may be included in a count if those incidents taken together amount to a course of conduct having regard to the time, place or purpose of commission.

(3) An indictment may contain more than one count if all the offences charged—
(a) are founded on the same facts; or
(b) form or are a part of a series of offences of the same or a similar character.

(4) The counts must be numbered consecutively.

(5) An indictment may contain—
(a) any count charging substantially the same offence as one—
  (i) specified in the notice of the offence or offences for which the defendant was sent for trial,
  (ii) on which the defendant was committed for trial, or
  (iii) specified in the notice of transfer given by the prosecutor; and
(b) any other count based on the prosecution evidence already served which the Crown Court may try.

[This rule is printed as substituted by the *Criminal Procedure (Amendment) Rules* 2007 (S.I. 2007 No. 699), r.9.]

See *ante*, § 1–108, as to the relevant commencement and transitional provisions.

For the forms of indictment that have been prescribed by the practice direction, pursuant to rule 14.2(1), see *post*, §§ 1–119, 1–120, and see further *post*, §§ 1–120a, 1–120b, as to the situation where it is sought to have certain counts tried by a judge alone. As to the charges that an indictment may contain, see (in addition to rule 14.2(5)), section 2(2) of the *Administration of Justice (Miscellaneous Provisions) Act* 1933, *post*, §§ 1–204 *et seq.*, and section 40 of the *CJA* 1988, *ante*, § 1–75ai. As to the charging of more than one incident in a single count, pursuant to rule 14.2(2), see *post*, §§ 1–139 *et seq.* As to the joinder of counts, pursuant to rule 14.2(3), see further *post*, §§ 1–154 *et seq.*

As to the potential consequences of defects in indictments, see *post*, §§ 1–195 *et seq.*

Statement of offence

1–116 As to the need to describe the offence in ordinary language and to identify any legislation that creates the offence, see rule 14.2(1)(a) of the 2005 rules, *ante*, § 1–115. See *R. v. Mandair* [1995] 1 A.C. 208, HL, as to the importance of the identification of any legislation that creates the offence (and see *R. v. Hodgson and Pollin*, *ante*, § 1–110, and *post*, § 1–117).

Particulars of offence

1–117 As to the need to provide particulars which make clear the conduct which is alleged to constitute the commission of the offence charged, see section 3(1) of the 1915 Act (*ante*, § 1–114b) and rule 14.2(1)(b) of the 2005 rules (*ante*, § 1–115). As to the purpose of the provision of particulars, see *post*, § 33–47. See *post*, §§ 1–121 *et seq.*, as to certain specific averments.

If the particulars in an indictment are thought to be inadequate, and if the prosecution do not voluntarily give further particulars, an application should be made to the court for an order requiring the prosecution to give such further particulars as may be necessary to enable the defence to know the case that it has to meet: *R. v. Savage*; *DPP v. Parmenter* [1992] 1 A.C. 699 at 737, HL. In some cases, it may be appropriate for the judge to direct the giving of such further particulars even though no application is made: *R. v. Warburton-Pitt*, 92 Cr.App.R. 136, CA. Further particulars should be reduced to writing: *ibid.* (where an offence charged depends on allegations which could be put on several different footings it is incumbent on the prosecution to particularise the facts on which it relies in support of their allegations).

In *R. v. Litanzios* [1999] Crim.L.R. 667, CA, it was said that a count for cheating the public revenue should be drafted with sufficient detail to inform the court and the defence as to the exact nature of the factual allegation, and so as to eliminate the possibility of a conviction on either of two alternative bases, but see *post*, §§ 1–139 *et seq.* In this regard, see also *R. v. Carr* [2000] 2 Cr.App.R. 149, CA (unfortunate that judge had not ordered particulars to be given in such a situation when pre-trial request for same had not been met); and *post*, §§ 4–391 *et seq.* See also *post*, §§ 1–131 *et seq.*, as to the need for particularity where specimen charges are laid, and as to the importance of the provision of particulars in the context of the right to a fair trial under Article 6 of the ECHR.

In *R. v. Hodgson and Pollin* [2008] 2 Cr.App.R. 35, CA, the relevant statement of offence had read "Inflicting grievous bodily harm, contrary to section 18 of the *Offences against the Person Act* 1861", and the particulars alleged that the appellants had "unlawfully inflicted grievous bodily harm" on the victim. The count was sloppily drawn in that it did not identify in either the statement of offence, or the particulars of offence, the intent that was alleged (*cf.* the specimen at § 19–201, *post*, and see *ante*, § 1–110 as to the responsibility of prosecuting counsel in this regard). However, it was held that the requirement to provide a "statement of the specific offence" had been satisfied by the express reference to section 18, and the requirements as to particulars had been satisfied because it is implicit, where section 18 is charged with no specific reference to intent, that what is alleged is an intent to cause grievous bodily harm, rather than the less common intent to resist or prevent lawful apprehension or detainer (see *post*, § 19–199). Although the count was defective, it was not a nullity, and the appellants, who had pleaded guilty, had not been the subject of an unsafe conviction, because all concerned had known and intended that the pleas would be an admission of an intent to cause grievous bodily harm. See further *post*, §§ 1–195 *et seq.*, as to the potential consequences of defects being left uncorrected.

The particularity required of a count alleging conspiracy has frequently given rise to difficulty: see generally, *post*, §§ 33–45 *et seq.*, but see also *R. v. Bolton*, 94 Cr.App.R. 74, CA (need to allege course of conduct agreed upon) (*post*, § 33–5), and *R. v. Patel*, *The Independent*, September 2, 1991, CA (89 04351 S1) (conspiracy relating to controlled drugs) (*post*, §§ 33–19, 33–20).

Where the prosecution case is that the defendant committed an offence either as a principal or as a secondary party, but cannot say which, one count may be laid to cover the alternative modes of participation, and if particulars are sought the prosecution are entitled to allege the two modes of participation in the alternative. See further *ante*, § 1–113b and *post*, § 18–32.

For examples of the application of the general principles in relation to other specific averments and situations, see *post*, §§ 1–121 *et seq.*

Signature and date

Although section 3(1) of the *Indictments Act* 1915 (*ante*, § 1–114b) provides that an indictment shall be sufficient if it contains an appropriate statement of offence and **1–118** particulars of offence, section 2(1) of the *Administration of Justice (Miscellaneous Provisions) Act* 1933 (*post*, § 1–231) requires that a bill of indictment *shall* be signed by a proper officer of the court, whereupon it becomes an indictment. Rule 14.1(3)(a) of the *Criminal Procedure Rules* 2005 (S.I. 2005 No. 384) (*post*, § 1–224) also now requires that the draft indictment *must* be signed and dated before it becomes an indictment. Rule 4(1) of the now repealed *Indictment Rules* 1971 required that: "An indictment shall be in the form in Schedule 1 to these rules or in a form substantially to the like effect." Rule 14.2 of the 2005 rules requires that: "An indictment must be in one of the forms set out in the Practice Direction", but contains no saving in respect of a form substantially to the like effect. The forms of indictment prescribed by both the 1971 and 2005 rules all conclude with the signature of a Crown Court officer. In *R. v. Laming*, 90 Cr.App.R. 450, CA, an indictment that was subject to the 1971 rules had been signed on its front page, rather than at its conclusion. It was held that the rules were "directory rather than mandatory", that the bill of indictment had been signed with the intention of validating it and that it was therefore valid, although the practice of signing the document otherwise than where indicated on the prescribed forms was strongly discouraged. As to the general approach now in respect of the consequences of defects in indictments, see *post*, §§ 1–195 *et seq.*, and as to the application of that approach where the bill of indictment has not been signed at all, see *post*, §§ 1–231 *et seq.*

Prescribed forms of indictment and their use

1–119 Two specimen forms of indictment have now been inserted in Annex D to the practice direction and, pursuant to rule 14.2(1), *ante*, § 1–115, the indictment in every case must now be in one of those forms. The first, which is printed below, is the form for a standard indictment.

Practice Direction (Criminal Proceedings: Consolidation), Annex D
(as inserted by Practice Direction (Criminal Proceedings: Further Directions [2007] 1 W.L.R. 1790)
Form of indictment
(Criminal Procedure Rules, Part 14)

INDICTMENT

IN THE CROWN COURT AT ....
THE QUEEN v. ....
charged as follows:—

STATEMENT OF OFFENCE

[*e.g. Theft, contrary to section 1(1) of the* Theft Act *1968*.]

PARTICULARS

[*e.g. A.B. on the 1st day of January, 2007, stole a bag belonging to S.M.*]

Date ....
Crown Court officer

NOTE: The specimen wording given in the square brackets is not included in the practice direction. If there is more than one count the counts must be numbered consecutively (rule 14.2(4) of the 2005 rules, *ante*, § 1–115).

1–120 The second prescribed form of indictment that has been inserted in Annex D to the practice direction, but which is not printed here, is for use where an order is made under section 17(2) of the *Domestic Violence, Crime and Victims Act* 2004 (order for trial of some counts to be conducted without a jury), *post*, § 4–267h. It divides the indictment into two parts after the standard words of commencement, the first being headed "PART 1" and containing counts numbered in the standard way. This is followed by a part headed "PART 2", which is divided into sections, the first of which is headed "Section 1: counts associated with Count 1 in Part 1 of this indictment". That heading is followed by counts numbered 1.1, 1.2, 1.3 etc. Counts associated with other counts in Part 1 of the indictment are then set out with the same style of section heading and count numbering. The form concludes with a date and signature, in the same manner as in the standard form. Guidance is also given in the practice direction (*post*) as to the use of the special form of indictment.

Practice Direction (Criminal Proceedings: Consolidation), paras IV.34.4–IV.34.9 (as inserted by Practice Direction (Criminal Proceedings: Arraignment) [2008] 1 W.L.R. 154)

Multiple offending: trial by jury and then by judge alone

IV.34.4 Under sections 17 to 21 of the *Domestic Violence, Crime and Victims Act* 2004 the court may order that the trial of certain counts will be by jury in the usual way and, if the jury convicts, that other associated counts will be tried by judge alone. The use of this power is likely to be appropriate where justice cannot be done without charging a large number of separate offences and the allegations against the defendant appear to fall into distinct groups by reference to the identity of the victim, by reference to the dates of the offences, or by some other distinction in the nature of the offending conduct alleged. **1–120a**

IV.34.5 In such a case it is essential to make clear from the outset the association asserted by the prosecutor between those counts to be tried by a jury and those counts which it is proposed should be tried by judge alone, if the jury convict on the former. A special form of indictment is prescribed for this purpose.

IV.34.6 An order for such a trial may be made only at a preparatory hearing. It follows that where the prosecutor intends to invite the court to order such a trial it will normally be appropriate to proceed as follows. The draft indictment served under *Criminal Procedure Rule* 14.1(1) should be in the form appropriate to such a trial. It should be accompanied by an application under *Criminal Procedure Rule* 15.1 for a preparatory hearing. This will ensure that the defendant is aware at the earliest possible opportunity of what the prosecution propose and of the proposed association of counts in the indictment. It is undesirable for a draft indictment in the usual form to be served where the prosecutor expects to apply for a two stage trial and hence, of necessity, for permission to amend the indictment at a later stage in order that it may be in the special form.

IV.34.7 On receipt of a draft two part indictment a Crown Court officer should sign it at the end of Part Two. At the start of the preparatory hearing the defendant should be arraigned on all counts in Part One of the indictment. Arraignment on Part Two need not take place until after there has been either a guilty plea to, or finding of guilt on, an associated count in Part One of the indictment.

IV.34.8 If the prosecution application is successful, the prosecutor should prepare an abstract of the indictment, containing the counts from Part One only, for use in the jury trial. Preparation of such an abstract does not involve "amendment" of the indictment. It is akin to where a defendant pleads guilty to certain counts in an indictment and is put in the charge of the jury on the remaining counts only.

IV.34.9 If the prosecution application for a two stage trial is unsuccessful, the prosecutor may apply to amend the indictment to remove from it any counts in Part Two which would make jury trial on the whole indictment impracticable and to revert to a standard form of indictment. It will be a matter for the court whether arraignment on outstanding counts takes place at the preparatory hearing, or at a future date.

Paragraphs IV.34.6 to IV.34.9 of the consolidated criminal practice direction were substituted for paragraphs IV.34.6 and IV.34.7 of the previous version, with effect from December 3, 2007. The revision corrects the mistake in the previous version that was highlighted in the 2008 edition of this work, but in its stead it introduces the notion of arraignment in stages (see paragraph IV.34.7). As to the drawbacks and questionable legality of such a practice, see the commentary in *Criminal Law Week* 2007/45/3. **1–120b**

In many cases which would come within section 17 of the 2004 Act the prosecution may wish, and be entitled, to adduce before the jury the evidence relating to the counts that could be tried by a judge alone, in order to strengthen the case on the counts that are before the jury. In such a case it might be thought that there would be little if any benefit in obtaining an order under section 17. The power under rule 14.2(2) of the *Criminal Procedure Rules* 2005 (S.I. 2005 No. 384) to include more than one incident of the commission of an offence in a single count (*ante*, § 1–115) may also serve to limit the cases in which section 17 of the 2004 Act will be of utility, although the use of section 17 in preference to that power would take account of some of the issues highlighted at §§ 1–139 *et seq., post*.

D. SPECIFIC AVERMENTS

1–121 The following paragraphs refer to certain authorities in which the courts have considered particular averments. Some of these authorities are of considerable antiquity and, when drafting an indictment, it should be borne in mind that the extent to which the dicta in any of the authorities referred to is relevant may well depend upon the particular facts of the case under consideration. Above all else, the requirements of section 3(1) of the *Indictments Act* 1915 (*ante*, § 1–114) and rule 14.2(1) of the *Criminal Procedure Rules* 2005 (*ante*, § 1–115) should be complied with. See also *ante*, § 1–117.

(1) Property

Ownership or occupation of property

1–122 Where it is common knowledge that the property named in an indictment belongs to some person or institution (*e.g.* in the case of an outstanding work of art), it may be unnecessary to particularise the ownership of the property; but where the property is of a common or undistinctive type, for the sake of clarity, and in order that the defendant may know exactly with what he is charged, the name of the owner should be stated in the particulars of offence: *R. v. Gregory*, 56 Cr.App.R. 441, CA. Where, however, the ownership of property is unknown, it is common practice and unobjectionable to aver the theft of property "belonging to a person unknown".

Description of property

1–122a As to the degree of particularity required in a count of theft when describing the property alleged to have been stolen, see *post*, §§ 21–7, 21–56.

(2) Trading companies

1–123 Trading companies may be described by their corporate name, whether incorporated under company law legislation or not. The existence of a company under its corporate name is sufficiently proved by parol evidence that it has carried on business under that name: *R. v. Langton* (1876) 2 Q.B.D. 296. But it is preferable to prove the existence and name of an incorporated company by the certificate of incorporation given where the correctness of such matters is relevant: *R. v. May*, 64 J.P. 570.

(3) Description of persons

1–124 The accused should be described in the indictment by his forename and surname: see 2 Hale 175. But these need not necessarily be stated correctly, provided that he is described in a manner which is reasonably sufficient to identify him.

The surname may be such as the accused has usually been known by or acknowledged; and if there be a doubt as to which one of two names is his real surname, the second may be added in the indictment, thus: "Richard Wilson, otherwise called Richard Layer".

In indictments for offences against the person or property of individuals, the forename and surname of the person injured should be stated, if known: 2 Hawk. c. 25, ss.71, 72. A new-born child may be sufficiently described as "... a child then recently born to A.B. and not named".

Where the person injured has a name of dignity as a peer, baronet, or knight, he should be described by it. "His Royal Highness the Duke of Cambridge" has been considered sufficient without setting forth any of his forenames: *R. v. Frost* (1855) Dears. 474.

Rule 8 of the *Indictment Rules* 1971 (now repealed, as to which see *ante*, § 1–108) provided that it shall be sufficient to describe a person whose name is not known as a person unknown. Although no rule in these terms appears in the *Criminal Procedure Rules* 2005 (S.I. 2005 No. 384), the effect thereof would appear to be encompassed by section 3 of the *Indictments Act* 1915 (*ante*, § 1–114b), and by rule 14.2(1) of the 2005 rules (*ante*, § 1–115).

(4) Certainty as to age of person injured

Where it is essential to constitute the offence that the person injured should have been under a certain age, the person should be stated in *every* relevant count of the indictment to be under that age: *R. v. Martin* (1843) 9 C. & P. 213, and *R. v. Sarah Waters* (1848) 1 Den. 356. **1–124a**

(5) Date and place

In *R. v. Wallwork*, 42 Cr.App.R. 153, CCA, it was held that there is no necessity to identify in the indictment the place where an offence is alleged to have taken place unless it is material to the charge. As to date, there is old authority for the proposition that the proper practice is to state in the indictment the date on which the offence is alleged to have been committed: *R. v. Hollond* (1841) 5 T.R. 607; *R. v. Aylett* (1785) 1 T.R. 63 at 69; *R. v. Haynes* (1815) 4 M. & Sel. 214. Quite apart from these authorities, however, it will usually be necessary to identify in the indictment the date when the offence charged is said to have occurred in order to satisfy section 3 of the *Indictments Act* 1915 (*ante*, § 1–114b), and rule 14.2(1) of the *Criminal Procedure Rules* 2005 (S.I. 2005 No. 384) (*ante*, § 1–115). For the same reason, it will sometimes be necessary to particularise the place where the offence is alleged to have taken place. It is in fact the invariable practice to have some reference to the date in an indictment. **1–125**

The date specified should be the day of the month, the month and year when the offence is alleged to have been committed. **1–126**

When an offence of unlawful killing is charged in a case where the fatal injury was caused on a date earlier than the death, it is the date of the death that should be shown on the indictment because the offence is not complete until the death occurs.

Where a time is limited for preferring an indictment, the time laid should appear to be within the time so limited (see *R. v. Brown* (1828) M. & M. 163) and in such a case, despite the general rule in *R. v. Dossi*, 13 Cr.App.R. 158, CCA (*post*, § 1–127), the prosecution should not be entitled to rely on any earlier date that may appear from the evidence if that date is not within the relevant time limit. See also *R. v. Pritchett* and *R. v. Tirnaveanu*, *post*, § 1–130.

Where the exact date of the offence is not known the date should be stated as being on or about a particular date, or on a day unknown between two stated dates, so as to isolate the date of the offence alleged as accurately as possible. Unless the offence is a "continuous" one (*post*, § 1–133), the date of the offence should not be given merely as between two stated dates because this may give rise to problems of duplicity, *post*, §§ 1–135 *et seq*.

See also the *CYPA* 1933, s.14(4), *post*, § 19–323 (continuous offences against children), and *post*, § 1–133.

Materiality of averment as to date and place

In *R. v. Wallwork*, *ante*, § 1–125, it was held that the lack of precision as to place in the particulars did not invalidate the indictment because the place of commission of the offence was not material to the charge. **1–127**

Despite the old authorities to the effect that the date of the offence must be shown in the indictment it never seems to have been necessary for the date shown to be proved by the evidence unless time is of the essence of the offence.

In other cases, if the time stated were prior to the finding of the indictment, a variance between the indictment and evidence of the time when the offence was committed was not material: 2 Co. Inst. 318; 3 Co. Inst. 230; *Sir H. Vane's Case* (1662) Kel.(J.) 16; *R. v. Aylett*, *ante*; *R. v. Dossi*, *ante*. In *Dossi* it was held that a date specified in an indictment is not a material matter unless it is an essential part of the alleged offence; the defendant may be convicted although the jury finds that the offence was committed on a date other than that specified in the indictment. Amendment of the indictment is unnecessary, although it will be good practice to do so (provided there is no prejudice, *post*) where it is clear on the evidence that if the offence was committed at all it was committed on a day other than that specified.

1–128 The prosecution should not be allowed to depart from an allegation that an offence was committed on a particular day in reliance on the principle in *Dossi* if there is a risk that the defendant has been misled as to the allegation he has to answer or that he would be prejudiced in having to answer a less specific allegation: see *Wright v. Nicholson*, 54 Cr.App.R. 38, DC; *R. v. Robson* [1992] Crim.L.R. 655, CA. See *post*, § 1–132d, as to the importance of the provision of such particulars in the context of the right to a fair trial under Article 6 of the ECHR.

1–129 In *R. v. Hartley* [1972] 2 Q.B. 1, 56 Cr.App.R. 189, CA, the court observed that where the words "on or about [the date]" are used, the offence must be shown to have been committed "within some period which has reasonable approximation to the date mentioned in the indictment". However this dictum was *obiter* and should not be taken as more than an indication of the desirability of identifying the relevant date as accurately as possible so that the defendant is not misled as to the case which he has to meet.

1–130 For further examples of circumstances in which it has been held that a variance between the evidence and the particulars was immaterial, see *R. v. Bonner* [1974] Crim.L.R. 479, CA; *R. v. Browning* [1974] Crim.L.R. 714, CA; *R. v. Fernandes* [1996] 1 Cr.App.R. 175, CA; and *Kay v. Biggs*, *The Independent (C.S.)*, November 23, 1998, DC. For examples of allegations as to time, or time and place, being held to be material, see *R. v. Radcliffe* [1990] Crim.L.R. 524, CA (an essential ingredient of the offence charged related to the age of victim); *R. v. Allamby and Medford*, 59 Cr.App.R. 189, CA (having an offensive weapon in a public place, *post*, § 24–107); and *R. v. Maher*, *The Times*, February 17, 1995, CA (convictions quashed where based on general allegations rather than on specific evidence relating to the particular occasions charged).

In *R. v. Pritchett* [2008] Crim.L.R. 214, CA, the dates pleaded in the indictment in respect of a continuous offence (as to which see *post*, § 1–133) included a period before the statutory provision creating the offence had come into force. On appeal it was held that, because the prosecution could have proved the charge if they were able to prove that the offence was committed during that part of the indictment period when the relevant statutory provision was in force, the indictment did not fall within the category identified in *R. v. Ayres* [1984] A.C. 447, HL (*post*, § 7–46), where the particulars "disclose no criminal offence whatsoever or charge some offence which has been abolished, in which case the indictment could fairly be described as a nullity". In that sense, the pleading of the dates had not been a material averment (as to which, see *Dossi*, *ante*, § 1–127), but it was held that the indictment was nevertheless irregular and, in order to decide whether the conviction was safe, it was necessary to consider, for example, the possibility that the jury had convicted only by reference to conduct occurring before the date when the relevant statutory provision came into force. However, the position was held to be different in *R. v. Tirnaveanu* [2007] 2 Cr.App.R. 23, CA, where during the time span covered by the relevant count the nature of the relevant offence had been changed by a substitution of the statutory wording which created the offence. The conviction was quashed on the basis that the one charge had improperly alleged two quite different offences (as to which, see *post*, § 1–136) and, in any event, the prosecution did not suggest that they could prove the commission of an offence on the basis explained in *Pritchett*.

Specimen charges; identifying the incident charged

1–131 A further problem can arise if evidence is put before the jury of a number of incidents occurring within the date span specified in a particular count (or relied upon by the prosecution) where any one of those incidents, if proved, could amount to the offence charged. Quite apart from the difficulties that a defendant may have in such a case in knowing precisely which incident to concentrate his defence upon, there is the risk that some members of the jury will found a conviction on one incident while other members of the jury will found a conviction on a different incident. (See *post*, §§ 4–391 *et seq.* for a discussion of a similar problem in other contexts, and see *ante*, §§ 1–116, 1–117 generally, and as to the practice of seeking further particulars.) Furthermore, the judge who passes sentence will not know which incident the jury have found proved. This problem can arise where specimen charges only are laid. The facts of *R. v. Shore*, 89 Cr.App.R. 32, CA, illustrate these difficulties. The defendant was charged with four counts of indecent assault against four different girls, the date span in each count being one of several years. The defendant was a school teacher and evidence was adduced of indecent acts by him against the four girls in three particular situations, namely during P.E. lessons, on a bus during school trips and at swimming lessons. No attempt was made to tie any count to any particular allegation. The Court of Appeal appears to have regarded this as unobjectionable, but it is submitted that such an approach is objectionable in that the allegations and the resulting convictions were too vague. The judge could not have known whether the jury were satisfied about one particular incident or about a course of conduct, or, indeed, about which type of incident.

In such circumstances, there is no reason why there should not be one count for each situation in which any particular child was alleged to have been assaulted. Where a child's statement refers not to situations but to particular occasions (a birthday, a holiday, a time when his or her mother was in hospital), the counts can be drafted to make clear what offences are being alleged. Where the prosecution does relate particular counts to particular incidents, it is incumbent on the judge in summing up to relate the evidence to the particular counts: see *R. v. Farrugia*, *The Times*, January 18, 1988, CA. This approach was followed by the Court of Appeal in *R. v. Rackham* [1997] 2 Cr.App.R. 222, where convictions in respect of alleged sexual assaults on children over a lengthy period of time were quashed on the ground that the trial judge should have acceded to a request for better identification of the specific incidents to which the various counts related. The court concluded that in such a case the indictment should be drawn or exemplified with as much particularity as the circumstances of the case will admit and that a difficulty in being precise in every respect is not a reason for not being precise when it is possible to be so. The decision in *R. v. Shore*, *ante*, it was said, reflected no more than that if a defendant chooses to meet general charges without objection he cannot easily raise lack of particularity in the Court of Appeal. Similarly, in *R. v. Donnelly* [1998] Crim.L.R. 131, CA, it was suggested that the Court of Appeal will not countenance an appeal on the basis that the evidence (as opposed to the charge itself) disclosed more than one offence, unless either an application in that regard was made to the trial judge, or defence counsel was flagrantly incompetent, but see *Criminal Law Week* 1998/05/4 for a criticism of that approach. **1–132**

Where a child speaks of a number of incidents with no distinguishing features, a convenient course, in order to establish the systematic conduct of the accused, is to have a number of counts, each, apart from the first, alleging "on an occasion other than that alleged in [the previous counts]". The overriding principle is that the number of counts in the indictment should fairly reflect the alleged criminality (*R. v. Canavan*; *R. v. Kidd*; *R. v. Shaw* [1998] 1 Cr.App.R. 79, CA), otherwise sentencing problems may arise: *post*, § 5–68. It should not be too difficult in most cases to settle an indictment which steers a safe course between prejudicial uncertainty and overloading: *R. v. Rackham*, *ante*.

Further examples of the problems that can arise are to be found in *R. v. Evans* [1995] Crim.L.R. 245, CA, and *R. v. Maher*, *ante*, § 1–130. See also *R. v. Litanzios*, *ante*, § 1–117.

Where the evidence does reveal the commission of more than one offence, then, subject to the rule 14.2(2) of the *Criminal Procedure Rules* 2005 (S.I. 2005 No. 384) (as to which, see *post*, §§ 1–139 *et seq.*), it may be necessary for the prosecution to apply for the count to be amended, *e.g.* in a case of theft by striking out all but one article from the particulars, or by splitting the count into separate counts, as in *R. v. Radley*, 58 Cr.App.R. 394, CA (*post*, § 1–152). If this is not done, the count may be susceptible to an application that it be stayed as an abuse of process, because it would be unfair to try the defendant upon it, and any conviction may be susceptible to appeal on that basis, and/or on the basis that the defendant was convicted of an offence that was not disclosed by the evidence (*e.g.* one theft of £10,000 rather than 10 offences of theft of £1,000), and/or on the basis that the count was bad for uncertainty. **1–132a**

The dangers addressed above appear to be the sort of problems that the general rule **1–132b** against duplicity was designed to address, in situations where the count itself was construed as alleging more than one offence: see *post*, § 1–136. In *R. v. Jones (J.)*, 59 Cr.App.R. 120, CA, it was held that a count charging affray in different streets and at different times was in breach of the then rule against duplicity, but said that even if the count had not itself been defective in this way the evidence, when led by the Crown, disclosed separate offences of affray and should then either have been split by amendment, or the Crown should have been required to elect upon which offence the trial should proceed. In *R. v. Greenfield*, 57 Cr.App.R. 849, CA, it was said that where more than one offence is disclosed by the evidence the additional evidence is, *prima facie*, irrelevant and should be excluded unless its admission can be justified by reference to some established principle. In *R. v. Mintern* (2004) 148 S.J. 146, CA, it was said that if a count is not bad for duplicity, but the evidence reveals the existence of two or more offences, then special precautions may need to be taken to ensure that "the difficulties of duplicity" are avoided.

1–132c The rule against duplicity has now been "recast" by rule 14.2(2) of the 2005 rules (*ante*, § 1–115), so as to widen the categories in which more than one incident of the commission of an offence may be included in a single count, with the consequence that evidence of more than one offence will be admitted in circumstances where the prosecution are permitted to proceed in accordance with that rule. However, certain of the issues highlighted above may need to be considered when deciding whether to seek to utilise the rule and/or when objection is taken to its use. In this regard, see generally *post*, §§ 1–139 *et seq*.

1–132d Article 6(3)(a) of the ECHR (*post*, § 16–57) requires special attention to be paid to the notification of the accusation to the defendant; particulars of the offence play a crucial role in the criminal process, in that it is from the moment of their service that the suspect is formally put on notice of the factual and legal basis of the charges against him; the right to be informed "in detail" of the cause of the accusation refers to the material facts which found the accusation, and the legal qualification of those facts; the provision of detailed information is an essential prerequisite of fair proceedings; the amount of detail will depend on the particular circumstances, but it must be sufficient for the accused to understand fully the extent of the charges against him so as to enable him to prepare a proper defence; where there is a change in the nature of the accusation, the accused must be duly and fully informed thereof and must be provided with adequate time and facilities to react to the change and to organise his defence on the basis of the revised allegation; the duty to inform the accused of the nature of the accusation rests on the prosecution and cannot be complied with passively by making information available without bringing this to the attention of the defence: *Mattocia v. Italy* (2003) 36 E.H.R.R. 47, ECtHR (on the particular facts, it was found that the applicant had been denied his rights under Article 6(3)(a) on a charge of rape of a mentally handicapped child where the information in the accusation was characterised by vagueness as to essential details concerning time and place, was repeatedly contradicted and amended during the course of the trial, and where no allowance had been made to the applicant when confronted with "yet another new version of events" late in the trial). To a similar effect, see *Pélissier and Sassi v. France* 30 E.H.R.R. 715, ECtHR, and *Sadak v. Turkey* (2003) 36 E.H.R.R. 26, ECtHR.

Continuous offence

1–133 It is not an essential characteristic of a single criminal offence that the prohibited act or omission took place once and for all on a single day, since it can take place continuously or intermittently over a period of time and still remain a single offence: *Chiltern D.C. v. Hodgetts* [1983] A.C. 120, HL. Upholding a conviction for failure to comply with an enforcement notice, the House said that the offence should be alleged to have been committed between the date when compliance with the notice was first required and the date when the information was laid or the notice complied with, whichever was the earlier. See also *post*, §§ 1–137, 19–323.

(6) Value

1–134 It is unnecessary to state value, except where it is of the essence of the offence such as an offence against the *Insolvency Act* 1986, s.360(1)(a) (*post*, § 30–185).

(7) Immaterial averments—surplusage

Allegations which are not essential to constitute the offence and which may be omitted without affecting the charge, or vitiating the indictment, do not require proof and may be rejected as surplusage: *R. v. Barraclough* [1906] 1 K.B. 201 at 210. Similarly, the Crown need only prove sufficient of the particulars to constitute the offence charged, *e.g.* the theft of one of the several articles charged in the count or the theft of part of a sum of money (see also *R. v. Hancock* [1996] 2 Cr.App.R. 554, CA, *post*, § 33–47), but the problem identified at §§ 4–391 *et seq.*, *post*, should be borne in mind. **1–134a**

E. DUPLICITY

(1) Introduction

The general principle in respect of what has come to be known as the rule against duplicity is that the indictment must not be double; that is to say, no one count of the indictment should charge the defendant with having committed two or more separate offences. That principle was set out explicitly in rule 4(2) of the *Indictment Rules* 1971 (now repealed, as to which, see *ante*, § 1–108), and is implicit in rule 14.2(1) of the *Criminal Procedure Rules* 2005 (S.I. 2005 No. 384) (*ante*, § 1–115), in that the rule requires a count to contain a statement and particulars of the offence (in the singular). **1–135**

Although the general rule is easy to state, its application has not always been easy and has resulted, historically, in the drawing of some fine distinctions and in decisions that are difficult to reconcile with each other, as to which, see the 2007 edition of this work at §§ 1–135 *et seq.* Certain common law "exceptions" to the general rule also emerged (seemingly for pragmatic reasons) in respect of situations concerning "continuous taking", or "general deficiency", as to which, see the 2007 edition of this work at §§ 1–143 *et seq.* Those common law "exceptions" have now, in effect, been subsumed within rule 14.2(2) of the 2005 rules (*ante*, § 1–115), as have many of the situations in which the courts have previously held that there has not been a breach of the general rule against duplicity, but rule 14.2(2) goes still further in making inroads on the general rule. For discussion thereof, see *post*, §§ 1–139 *et seq.*

(2) Analysis of the general rule and its purpose

The question of whether a count breaches the general rule against duplicity is a question relating to the form of the count, not to the underlying evidence: *R. v. Greenfield*, 57 Cr.App.R. 849, CA; *R. v. West* [1948] 1 K.B. 709, 32 Cr.App.R. 152, CCA; *R. v. Davey and Davey*, 45 Cr.App.R. 11, CCA; and *cf. R. v. Griffiths* [1966] 1 Q.B. 589, 49 Cr.App.R. 279, CCA. Thus, if the particulars set out in the count allege only one offence, the fact that the evidence at trial may reveal more than one offence does not make the count bad for duplicity. In *R. v. Browning* [1974] Crim.L.R. 714, CA, it was said that "the question which arises when an issue of duplicity is raised is one of substance and not of form", but that comment appears to be inconsistent with what is said in the earlier cases and seems to have been *obiter*, as well as *per incuriam*. **1–136**

It was held in *Greenfield*, *ante*, that in order to determine an issue as to whether a count is bad for duplicity it will usually be unnecessary to look further than the count itself, but if particulars have been requested and given (as to which, see *ante*, § 1–117) they too should be considered. Further, if particulars have been requested and refused, the judge may look at the evidence upon which the indictment is said to be founded, *semble* because a refusal to provide particulars is usually justified by an assertion that the particulars will be apparent from that evidence. It might be thought that these latter points do not sit entirely comfortably with the assertion that duplicity depends on the form of the count, not on the underlying evidence.

In any event, even though a count may not be bad for duplicity merely because the underlying evidence in respect of a count discloses more than one offence, valid grounds for objection may nevertheless exist in some such situations on different grounds, as to which see *ante*, §§ 1–131 *et seq.* Such an objection will, in reality, be based on the same principles as those which have been said to found the rule against duplicity (*post*).

In *R. v. Wilmot*, 24 Cr.App.R. 63, CCA, it was held that an information must not charge offences in the alternative, since the defendant cannot then know with precision with what he is charged and of what he is convicted and may on a future occasion be prevented from pleading *autrefois convict*. In *Ministry of Agriculture, Fisheries & Food v. Nunn Corn (1987) Ltd* [1990] Crim.L.R. 268, DC, the court said that the question of duplicity is one of fact and degree and stated that the purpose of the rule against duplicity is to enable a defendant to know the case he has to meet in relation to matters such as submissions of no case to answer or pleas in mitigation and is a rule of elementary fairness. In *Amos v. DPP* [1988] R.T.R. 198, DC, it was said (at p. 203) that uncertainty in the mind of the defendant is the vice against which the rule against duplicity is aimed and that the rule is a salutary one, designed to counter a true risk that there may be confusion in the presenting and the meeting of charges which are mixed up and uncertain. Indeed, reasonable information and clarity in respect of a charge are required by section 3(1) of the *Indictments Act* 1915 (*ante*, § 1–114) and rule 4.2(1) of the *Criminal Procedure Rules* 2005 (S.I. 2005 No. 384) (*ante*, § 1–115). Furthermore, see *Mattioca v. Italy* (2003) 36 E.H.R.R. 47, ECtHR (*ante*, § 1–132d), as to the requirements of Article 6(3)(a) of the ECHR in this regard.

(3) Application of the general rule

1–137 A given count on an indictment cannot be bad for duplicity if the details set out in that count allege only a single offence. In this regard, an important point to bear in mind is that it is not necessarily an essential ingredient of a single criminal offence that the prohibited act or omission took place once and for all on one occasion: see, for example, *Chiltern D.C. v. Hodgetts* [1983] A.C. 120, HL, *ante*, § 1–133 (failure to comply with planning enforcement notice is a continuing offence). However, where a count charges an offence other than a continuing offence as having been committed "on divers days" it will usually be construed as alleging more than one offence: see *R. v. Thompson*, 9 Cr.App.R. 252, CCA; *R. v. Robertson*, 25 Cr.App.R. 208, CCA.

Issues of construction will often arise as to whether a particular offence-creating provision creates one offence, or more than one offence. For example, it has been held that section 22(1) of the *Theft Act* 1968 creates only one offence, although that offence can be committed by doing one of a number of acts, and with one of two alternative mental states: see *post*, §§ 21–272 *et seq*. Similarly, an Act may create a single offence of failing to discharge a duty, which duty can be breached by a number of different failures: *Health and Safety Executive v. Spindle Select Ltd.*, *The Times*, December 9, 1996, DC (s.33(1)(a) of the *Health and Safety at Work etc. Act* 1974 creates a single offence of failure to comply with a duty to which the accused is subject by virtue of ss.2 to 7 of that Act). Likewise, the *CJPOA* 1994, s.68(1), creates one offence (aggravated trespass) that may be committed with various different intents: *Nelder v. DPP*, *The Times*, June 11, 1998, DC. As to alternative modes of participation being alleged within a single count, see *R. v. Gaughan*, 155 J.P. 235, CA, *ante*, § 1–113b, and *post*, § 18–32. Rule 7 of the *Indictment Rules* 1971 (printed at § 1–120 in the 2007 edition of this work) provided specific authority to set out such alternatives in an indictment charging the relevant offence, but the revocation of that rule (as to which, see *ante*, § 1–108) seems unlikely to have affected the legitimacy of charging such alternatives in a single count, provided that it alleges only one offence. However, the various reported authorities indicate that even where the pleading of alternatives in one count would not breach the rule against duplicity it will be necessary to consider whether the general principles upon which that rule is founded nevertheless require separate counts. See further *ante*, § 1–136, and *post*, §§ 1–140 *et seq.*, in this regard.

See also *R. v. Asif*, 82 Cr.App.R. 123, CA (*post*, § 25–517), for another type of situation in which only one offence was held to have been charged (under s.72(8) of the *Value Added Tax Act* 1994), even though the relevant count set out allegations that could have founded charges for more than one offence of a type other than the offence actually charged, but see *R. v. Choudhury* [1996] 2 Cr.App.R. 484, CA (*post*, § 25–517), as to the need to consider separate counts in such a situation.

Laying several overt acts in a count for high treason is not duplicitous (Kel.(J.) 8), because the offence consists of the compassing, etc., of the death of the sovereign, and the overt acts are merely evidence (see *post*, § 25–7).

Many examples can be found in the reported authorities where it has been held that an allegation involving more than one event amounts to an allegation of only one offence, on the basis that the relevant events are incidents of a single activity, or single transaction (see the 2007 edition of this work at §§ 1–136a *et seq.*). However, assault and battery are separate and distinct offences and a charge alleging that the defendant did "unlawfully assault and batter" the victim is, therefore, bad for duplicity, even though only one activity is alleged: *DPP v. Taylor*; *DPP v. Little* [1992] 1 Q.B. 645, 95 Cr.App.R. 28, DC. But if the relevant assault is alleged to have involved the use of physical force on the victim a charge alleging "assault by beating" would not fall foul of the rule against duplicity: *ibid.* **1–138**

The reported decisions in relation to single activity, or single transaction, cases are in certain respects difficult to reconcile with the general principles and with each other. It was of little help to the draftsman of an indictment that, in this regard, the question of whether more than one offence is disclosed has been said to be "a matter of fact and degree", as to which see *R. v. Jones (J.)*, 59 Cr.App.R. 120, CA, and *Ministry of Agriculture, Fisheries & Food v. Nunn Corn (1987) Ltd.*, *ante*, § 1–136. Again, irrespective of the strict position in respect of duplicity it has always been necessary to consider the general underlying principles of fairness and clarity when deciding whether to use more than one count, as to which see *ante*, §§ 1–131 *et seq.*, and 1–136, and *post*, §§ 1–140 *et seq.*

Many of the problems and anomalies in relation to the situations addressed in the reported decisions have now been overcome by the creation of rule 14.2(2) of the *Criminal Procedure Rules* 2005 (S.I. 2005 No. 384) (*ante*, § 1–115), but that rule itself creates certain problems, as to which see *post*, §§ 1–140 *et seq.*

(4) Rule 14.2(2) of the Criminal Procedure Rules 2005 (S.I. 2005 No. 384)

Rule 14.2(2) of the 2005 rules (*ante*, § 1–115) provides that "more than one incident of the commission of the offence may be included in a count if those incidents taken together amount to a course of conduct having regard to the time, place or purpose of commission." As to the commencement of that rule, see *ante*, § 1–108. The rule is supplemented by new paragraphs IV.34.10 to IV.34.14 of the consolidated criminal practice direction. **1–139**

Practice Direction (Criminal Proceedings: Consolidation), paras IV.34.10–IV.34.14 (as inserted by Practice Direction (Criminal Proceedings: Arraignment) [2008] 1 W.L.R. 154)

Multiple offending: count charging more than one incident

IV.34.10 Rule 14.2(2) of the *Criminal Procedure Rules* 2005 allows a single count to allege more than one incident of the commission of an offence in certain circumstances. Each incident must be of the same offence. The circumstances in which such a count may be appropriate include, but are not limited to, the following: (a) the victim on each occasion was the same, or there was no identifiable individual victim as, for example, in a case of the unlawful importation of controlled drugs or of money laundering; (b) the alleged incidents involved a marked degree of repetition in the method employed or in their location, or both; (c) the alleged incidents took place over a clearly defined period, typically (but not necessarily) no more than about a year; (d) in any event, the defence is such as to apply to every alleged incident without differentiation. Where what is in issue differs between different incidents, a single "multiple incidents" count will not be appropriate, though it may be appropriate to use two or more such counts according to the circumstances and to the issues raised by the defence. **1–140**

IV.34.11 Even in circumstances such as those set out in paragraph IV.34.8, there may be occasions on which a prosecutor chooses not to use such a count, in order to bring the case within section 75(3)(a) of the *Proceeds of Crime Act* 2002 (criminal lifestyle established by conviction of three or more offences in the same proceedings): for example, because section 75(2)(c) of that Act does not apply (criminal lifestyle established by an offence committed over a period of at least six months). Where the prosecutor proposes such a course it is unlikely that Part 1 of the *Criminal Procedure Rules* 2005 (the overriding objective) will require an indictment to contain a single "multiple incidents" count in place of a larger number of counts, subject to the general principles set out in paragraph IV.34.3.

IV.34.12 For some offences, particularly sexual offences, the penalty for the offence may have changed during the period over which the alleged incidents took place. In such a case, additional "multiple incidents" counts should be used so that each count only alleges incidents to which the same maximum penalty applies.

IV.34.13 In some cases, such as money laundering or theft, there will be documented evidence of individual incidents but the sheer number of these will make it desirable to cover them in a single count. Where the indictment contains a count alleging multiple incidents of the commission of such offences, and during the course of the trial it becomes clear that the jury may bring in a verdict in relation to a lesser amount than that alleged by the prosecution, it will normally be desirable to direct the jury that they should return a partial verdict with reference to that lesser amount.

IV.34.14 In other cases, such as sexual or physical abuse, a complainant may be in a position only to give evidence of a series of similar incidents without being able to specify when or the precise circumstances in which they occurred. In these cases, a "multiple incidents" count may be desirable. If on the other hand, the complainant is able to identify particular incidents of the offence by reference to a date or other specific event, but alleges that in addition there were other incidents which the complainant is unable to specify, then it may be desirable to include separate counts for the identified incidents and a "multiple incidents" count or counts alleging that incidents of the same offence occurred "many" times. Using a "multiple incidents" count may be an appropriate alternative to using "specimen" counts in some cases where repeated sexual or physical abuse is alleged. The choice of count will depend on the particular circumstances of the case and should be determined bearing in mind the implications for sentencing set out in [*R. v. Canavan*; *R. v. Kidd*; *R. v. Shaw* [1998] 1 Cr.App.R. 79, CA].

Application of the rule and potential problems arising from it

1–141 The new rule 14 was inserted in the 2005 rules by the *Criminal Procedure (Amendment) Rules* 2007 (S.I. 2007 No. 699), as to which see *ante*, § 1–108. The explanatory note to the 2007 rules states that in "some circumstances the new rules allow more than one incident of the same offence to be charged in a single paragraph of an indictment, which was not explicitly permitted" by the former rules. An explanatory memorandum published with the 2007 rules says that the new rule 14.2(2) "recasts" the rule against duplicity. The new rule clearly encompasses the "exceptions" that had developed under the common law and encompasses the forms of count previously held to be permissible under the single activity or single transaction principles, but the use of the expression "course of conduct" is likely to open the door far wider (*cf*. the approach of the courts to the expression "course of conduct" in the *Protection from Harassment Act* 1997 (*post*, §§ 19–277a *et seq*.)).

The explanatory memorandum also states that the Criminal Procedure Rule Committee was "satisfied that the new rule reflects what judgments of the House of Lords in the past have found consistent with fundamental principles of fairness." It does not identify which judgments the committee had in mind in that regard and the only obvious candidate is *DPP v. Merriman* [1973] A.C. 584, HL. Indeed, the use of the formula "time, place or purpose" in rule 14.2(2) is clearly derived from the speech of Lord Diplock in *Merriman* (at p. 607). However, in *Merriman* their Lordships were not concerned with the bundling together in a single count of a number of separate offences committed by one person, but were concerned with the propriety of joinder in a single count (charging wounding with intent) of two defendants, even if they had been acting independently of each other. Further, no reference was made by their Lordships to "a course of conduct".

1–142 Examples of the potential use of the new rule given in the explanatory memorandum are the person who launders the proceeds of drug trafficking in comparatively small weekly sums, week after week (as to which, see *R. v. Middleton and Rourke*, unreported, January 31, 2008, CA ([2008] EWCA Crim. 233) (*post*, § 26–11)), or the person who has assaulted the same victim in the same way repeatedly over a period of time. The second example is probably inspired by the decision in *R. v. Cox* [1998] Crim.L.R. 810, CA (*post*, § 4–393), where a whole range of different types of behaviour was lumped together in a single count of assault. Further examples are given in the practice direction. The explanatory memorandum states that the committee took account among other things of the potential under the old rules for a perceived unfairness to a victim of multiple offending where out of many alleged offences only a few are prosecuted as examples, giving the impression that the victim's distress has been underestimated or that he or she has not been believed. However, no reference is made to the well known problems which can arise where more than one offence is disclosed by the evidence called in respect of a single count (as to which see *ante*, §§ 1–131 *et seq.*), or to the purpose that the rule against duplicity was designed to meet (*ante*, § 1–136). No explanation is given as to why any perceived unfairness to victims cannot be dealt with by the use of more counts, which would also avoid the limitations on sentencing in respect of a single count. The more similar the different offences (and hence the greater the supposed justification for putting them in a single count), the easier it would be to prepare a multi-count indictment, particularly in the age of the word processor. Further, whilst it remains to be seen how, if at all, section 17 of the *Domestic Violence, Crime and Victims Act* 2004 (*post*, § 4–267h) is operated in practice (jury to try sample counts, with judge to try remainder, as to which, see *ante*, §§ 1–120 *et seq.*), it is plain that if a prosecutor seeks to take advantage of rule 14.2(2) of the 2005 rules there will be no scope for the operation of section 17 of the 2004 Act.

The various practical difficulties involved in charging several incidents of the commission of an offence in a single count need to be addressed. How is the count to be worded? How is the defendant to plead if he admits certain allegations, but not others? How are the jury to be directed? Is it enough that they are sure of any one incident and, if so, must they be agreed as to one and the same incident (as to which, see *post*, §§ 4–391 *et seq.*)? How is it to be known on what basis the jury have convicted? How is it to be known whether the defendant can plead *autrefois acquit* or *convict* in respect of any relevant allegation in the future? What if there are different defences to the different allegations, and what if the evidence differs? Some of these potential problems (and others) are addressed in the practice direction, but not all are answered. **1–143**

The power to include more than one incident of the commission of an offence in a single count does not mean that it is appropriate for this to be done in every case where the criteria set out in rule 14.2(2) are satisfied. Indeed, even under the old regime prosecutors were urged to consider carefully in every case whether it was proper to take advantage of any "exception" that might be available to the rule against duplicity. In this regard, see *ante*, § 1–137, and, for example, *R. v. Nicklin*, 64 Cr.App.R. 205, CA, *post*, § 21–273. See also *R. v. Bristol Crown Court, ex p. Willets* [1985] Crim.L.R. 219, DC, and the commentary thereon, the commentary on *R. v. Ward* [1988] Crim.L.R. 57, CA, and *R. v. Jackson, The Guardian*, November 20, 1991, CA (91 05435 X3), *post*, § 21–8. In *R. v. Lawson*, 36 Cr.App.R. 30, Assizes, one of the leading cases on "general deficiency", Lynskey J. said:

> "I agree that in the ordinary case, where it is possible to trace the individual items and to prove a conversion of individual property and money, it is undesirable that one should include them all in a count alleging a general deficiency. Such a count may be bad for uncertainty, but in a case like this, where individual items cannot be traced in detail, but where the evidence makes it clear that there has been a fraudulent conversion, the prosecution are entitled to frame their counts in the way in which they have been framed here."

Those comments were approved and adopted in *R. v. Tomlin* [1954] 2 Q.B. 274, 38 Cr.App.R. 82, CCA (at pp. 282, 89–90).

Examples are given in the practice direction of situations in which the use of rule 14.2(2) may not be appropriate, even though the criteria set out in that rule may be satisfied. However, its use may be objectionable in other situations. Common sense, fairness and good practice will frequently dictate that separate instances of the same offence should be charged separately. It is submitted that the sort of issues highlighted at §§ 1–131 *et seq.*, *ante*, and the requirements of Article 6(3) of the ECHR (*ante*, § 1–132d), should be borne in mind in this regard. Distinct allegations for what are in fact distinct transactions have the advantage that the defendant will know exactly what is alleged against him, the jury will be clear as to their task, the risks arising from different defences or the evidence varying in relation to different allegations or the jurors taking a different view of the evidence or the witnesses will be eliminated, and, in the event of convictions the court will know exactly what level of offending the defendant has been found guilty of. **1–144**

(5) Taking the objection

1–145 See generally *post*, §§ 1–190 *et seq.* In a given case there may be an application to quash the indictment, or a count in the indictment, on the basis that it is bad for duplicity.

If the relevant count satisfies the criteria set out in rule 14.2(2) of the 2005 rules it does not follow that it will necessarily be fair to proceed to trial on that basis, as to which, see *ante*, §§ 1–139 *et seq.* In such a situation it may be possible, by way of an application for a stay on the basis of abuse of process (*post*, §§ 4–48 *et seq.*), to challenge the fairness of the prosecution proceeding in that way, but section 3(2) of the *Indictments Act* 1915 (*ante*, § 1–114b) should be borne in mind. However, that section must, it is submitted, be construed in accordance with section 3(1) of the *Human Rights Act* 1998 (*post*, § 16–15) if to do otherwise would result in a breach of Article 6 of the ECHR (*post*, § 16–57). In that event, see also section 7 of the 1915 Act (*post*, § 1–190).

As to the potential consequences of leaving a defect uncorrected, see *post*, §§ 1–195 *et seq.*, and, in particular, the reference to *R. v. Marchese*, at § 1–196. As to appeals to the Court of Appeal, see *post*, § 7–78.

(6) Can amendment provide a remedy?

1–146 In view of the clear provisions of section 5 of the *Indictments Act* 1915 (*post*, § 1–147), where at any stage of the trial an application is made to quash a count on the ground of duplicity the court has the power to cure the defect (if it can be done fairly at that stage) by permitting the necessary amendment, which may involve splitting the count, or removing words from it: see *R. v. Jones (J.)*, 59 Cr.App.R. 120, CA, and *R. v. Mintern* (2004) 148 S.J. 146, CA. Similarly, amendment may be used to remedy any unfairness that might otherwise be created in a particular case by the framing of a charge in accordance with rule 14.2(2) of the 2005 rules.

F. AMENDMENT

Indictments Act 1915, s.5

1–147 **5.**—(1) Where, before trial, or at any stage of a trial, it appears to the court that the indictment is defective, the court shall make such order for the amendment of the indictment as the court thinks necessary to meet the circumstances of the case, unless, having regard to the merits of the case, the required amendments cannot be made without injustice …

(2) Where an indictment is so amended, a note of the order for amendment shall be endorsed on the indictment, and the indictment shall be treated for the purposes of the trial and for the purposes of all proceedings in connection therewith as having been signed by the proper officer in the amended form.

(3) Where, before trial, or at any stage of a trial, the court is of opinion that a person accused may be prejudiced or embarrassed in his defence by reason of being charged with more than one offence in the same indictment, or that for any other reason it is desirable to direct that the person should be tried separately for any one or more offences charged in an indictment, the court may order a separate trial of any count or counts of such indictment.

(4) Where, before trial, or at any stage of a trial, the court is of opinion that the postponement of the trial of a person accused is expedient as a consequence of the exercise of any power of the court under this Act to amend an indictment or to order a separate trial of a count, the court shall make such order as to the postponement of the trial as appears necessary.

(5) Where an order of the court is made under this section for a separate trial or for the postponement of a trial—

(a) if such an order is made during a trial the court may order that the jury (if there is one) be discharged from giving a verdict on the count or counts the trial of which is postponed or on the indictment, as the case may be; and

(b) the procedure on the separate trial of a count shall be the same in all respects as if the count had been found in a separate indictment, and the procedure on the postponed trial shall be the same in all respects (if the jury has been discharged under paragraph (a)) as if the trial had not commenced; and

(c) the court may make such order … as to granting the accused person bail, and as to the enlargement of recognizances and otherwise as the court thinks fit.

(6) Any power of the court under this section shall be in addition to and not in derogation of any other power of the court for the same or similar purposes.

[This section is printed as amended, and repealed in part, by the *Administration of Justice (Miscellaneous Provisions) Act* 1933, ss.1 and 2, and Sched. 2; the *Bail Act* 1976, s.12(1), and Sched. 2; the *Prosecution of Offences Act* 1985, s.31(6), and Sched. 2; and the *CJA* 2003, s.331, and Sched. 36, para. 40.]

As to the application of section 5(3), see *post*, §§ 1–166 *et seq.*

Incidental points

Where no application to amend the indictment has been made by either side, the judge, in exercising his discretion whether to direct an amendment or not, should invite the parties, and in particular the defence, to express their views on the matter before deciding to do so: *R. v. West* [1948] 1 K.B. 709, 32 Cr.App.R. 152, CCA, and see also *R. v. Gregory*, 56 Cr.App.R. 441, CA. **1–148**

Where an amendment of a substantial nature is made after arraignment, it is desirable that the arraignment should be repeated on the indictment as amended. No harm can be done if a judge unnecessarily directs a second arraignment: *R. v. Radley*, 58 Cr.App.R. 394, CA. Re-arraignment is unnecessary where the amended indictment merely reproduces the original allegations in a different form, albeit including a number of new counts: *R. v. Fyffe* [1992] Crim.L.R. 442, CA.

For the purpose of exercising the powers of amendment in section 5 of the 1915 Act there is no distinction to be drawn between an indictment preferred as a result of a committal for trial and an indictment preferred as a result of leave being given by a High Court judge under the provisions of the *Administration of Justice (Miscellaneous Provisions) Act* 1933: *R. v. Walters*, 69 Cr.App.R. 115, CA; *R. v. Ismail*, 92 Cr.App.R. 92, CA (as to which see further, *post*, § 1–215); *R. v. Wells* [1995] 2 Cr.App.R. 417, CA; and *R. v. Allcock* [1999] 1 Cr.App.R. 227, CA.

The failure to endorse a note of an amendment on the indictment, as required by section 5(2), is not something which, in itself, invalidates the amendment: *R. v. Ismail*, *ante*, but see generally *post*, §§ 1–195 *et seq.*, as to the consequences of a defect being left uncorrected.

When an amendment may be made

The appellate courts have shown an increasing willingness to allow amendments of substance to be made, and the more recent decisions cannot be reconciled with certain of the earlier ones. In *R. v. Radley*, *ante*, the court observed that, as no amendment should be made if it could not be made without injustice, the trial court ought to give a fairly liberal meaning to the language of section 5(1) of the 1915 Act. **1–149**

As to the significance of Article 6(3) of the ECHR in relation to the change of an accusation against a defendant, see *Mattocia v. Italy* (2003) 36 E.H.R.R. 47, ECtHR, *ante*, § 1–132d.

In *R. v. Osieh* [1996] 2 Cr.App.R. 145, CA, it was said, *obiter*, that, notwithstanding the restrictions imposed by section 2(2) of the *Administration of Justice (Miscellaneous Provisions) Act* 1933 (*post*, § 1–204), the power to amend an indictment, once it has been preferred, extends to the addition of a count or counts charging offences that are not disclosed in the committal evidence but which are disclosed by evidence subsequently served. In *R. v. Swaine* [2001] Crim.L.R. 166, CA, it was held that an indictment may be amended after a jury have disagreed and before retrial so as to add a count based on a committal for trial which occurred after the first trial. It is submitted that a more principled approach would have been to prefer a fresh indictment to combine the charges from the two committals, or to obtain a voluntary bill.

In *R. v. Hemmings* [2000] 1 Cr.App.R. 360, CA, it was held that where an appeal is allowed by the Court of Appeal and a retrial ordered by that court, pursuant to section 7 of the *CAA* 1968 (*post*, § 7–112), the indictment upon which the retrial takes place pursuant to that order, and which is preferred pursuant to section 8 of the 1968 Act (*post*, § 7–113), may be amended to include counts charging offences in respect of which the retrial could not, by reason of the prohibition in section 7(2) of the 1968 Act, have been ordered by the Court of Appeal and which could not have been included on the indictment when it was preferred. In reaching its conclusion, the court sought to draw a distinction between the power to prefer, or direct the preferment of, an indictment, and the power to amend the indictment after it has been preferred. It held that section 7(2) of the 1968 Act neither explicitly, nor implicitly, proscribes the making of such an amendment. That left the question of whether the indictment could be said to be "defective", within the meaning of section 5 of the *Indictments Act* 1915, so as to provide the jurisdictional basis for amendment. The court took the view that if an indictment preferred pursuant to the direction of a High Court judge under the "voluntary bill" procedure could be defective (as to which, see *R. v. Wells*, *post*, § 1–150), there was no reason why the position should be different in the situation under consideration, although it also accepted that a distinction exists in respect of the voluntary bill procedure in that there is no statutory limitation on the offences that may be included in the original bill of indictment that is preferred pursuant to the leave given by the High Court judge.

In the 2000 edition of this work the correctness of the above-mentioned dictum in *R. v. Osieh* was doubted and it was submitted that it was inconsistent with decisions in certain other authorities that were there identified. The question was posed as to how an indictment can be properly described as "defective", so as to give jurisdiction for the court to allow an amendment, where the alleged defect is that the indictment does not include certain charges that could not lawfully have been included in it at the time when it was originally preferred. In *Hemmings* the court rejected this criticism, saying of the question posed in that criticism (which also arose on the facts under consideration in *Hemmings* itself) simply that "the interests of justice and fairness (and in particular the interests of the defendants) required that [the indictment] should be amended".

In *R. v. Adams and Davy* [2001] 7 *Archbold News* 2, CA, it was said that it may be questioned how real the difference really is in practice between the two positions discussed above; if the evidence relied on to support the charge is new, quite separate and different from the material before the magistrates' court, then as likely as not that could only give rise to a new case altogether and, whether by application of the principle asserted in the 2000 edition of this work or as a matter of general fairness, the court may be likely to rule against amendment, leaving the Crown to institute separate proceedings if desired; if, however, the application to amend does no more than take forward a case already laid on the evidence, reformulating it, possibly with the assistance of some additional evidence, it is doubtful whether it would be improper to amend the indictment. Indeed, as was acknowledged in *Osieh*, an amendment will only be permitted if it can be made without injustice and the fact that a proposed amendment raises, for the first time, a charge not foreshadowed in the committal evidence may provide a basis for refusing to permit it, or for permitting it only subject to the grant of an adjournment. Likewise, it was emphasised in *Hemmings* that the power to permit an amendment in the situation there under consideration must be exercised in accordance with the underlying purpose of section 7 of the 1968 Act, namely to permit the court to order a retrial to ensure that justice is done, while at the same time protecting the defendant by ensuring that he is not put in a worse position than at the original trial (thus, indictment lawfully amended where original conspiracy charge replaced, at the suggestion of defence counsel, by charges of substantive offences founded on the conduct on which the original conspiracy charge had been based).

There is no power to amend an indictment to add a count charging a summary offence that is not listed in section 40(3) of the *CJA* 1988 (*ante*, § 1–75ai): *R. v. Ashton*; *R. v. Draz*; *R. v. O'Reilly* [2006] 2 Cr.App.R. 15, CA. See further *post*, § 2–8.

1–150 The present position as to the exercise of the power to permit amendments is largely set out in the judgment of the Court of Appeal in *R. v. Johal and Ram*, 56 Cr.App.R. 348, where reference is made to several of the earlier authorities. The effect of section 5(1) is, therefore, as follows (the word "indictment" including "count" where there is more than one count).

(1) An indictment may be defective ("defect" in this context connoting "lack of" or "want": *R. v. Palmer* [2002] Crim.L.R. 973, CA) not only when it is bad on its

face (*e.g.* because of duplicity, *ante*, §§ 1–135 *et seq.*, or because of misjoinder, *post*, §§ 1–154 *et seq.*), but also, for example:

(a) when it does not accord with the evidence before the magistrates either because of inaccuracies or deficiencies in the indictment or because the indictment charges offences not disclosed in that evidence or fails to charge an offence which is disclosed therein: *R. v. Martin* [1962] 1 Q.B. 221, 45 Cr.App.R. 199, CCA;

(b) when for such reasons it does not accord with the evidence given at the trial: *R. v. Hall* [1968] 2 Q.B. 787, 52 Cr.App.R. 528, CA; *R. v. Johal and Ram*, *ante*;

(c) when the evidence led in support of the indictment discloses more than one offence: *R. v. Jones (J.)* (see *ante*, § 1–132b); and *R. v. Stanley*, *The Independent*, November 27, 1998, CA (allegation of fraudulent evasion of VAT based on allegations of provision of two distinct and separate pieces of false information; desirable that issue of whether defendant guilty, if at all, of one or both of distinct allegations should be resolved by a jury rather than judge—*cf.* the situation discussed *post*, § 21–11);

(d) when it has been preferred under the voluntary bill procedure and does not include a charge in respect of an offence disclosed on the material before the judge who granted leave to prefer the voluntary bill: *R. v. Wells*, *ante*, and *R. v. Allcock*, *ante*;

(e) when it does not include as a defendant a person who might properly be joined in the indictment: *R. v. Ismail*, 92 Cr.App.R. 92, CA (amendment of indictment preferred under the voluntary bill procedure to add a defendant who had been committed for trial on the same charge—see further, *post*, § 1–215), and *R. v. Palmer*, *ante* (indictment amended to add a defendant who was committed for trial on the same charge after that indictment had been signed – it was not necessary to prefer a further compendious indictment in accordance with the practice described at § 1–218, *post*).

(2) The court has power to order an amendment which involves the substitution of a different offence for that originally charged in the indictment, or even the inclusion of an additional count for an offence not previously charged: *R. v. Johal and Ram*, *ante*.

(3) An amendment of any kind, including the addition or substitution of a count, may be made at any stage of the trial *provided* that, having regard to the circumstances of the case and the power of the court to direct a separate trial of any accused or to postpone the trial, the amendment can be made without injustice: *R. v. Smith*, 34 Cr.App.R. 168, CCA; *R. v. Johal and Ram*, *ante*; *R. v. Harris*, 62 Cr.App.R. 28, CA. In *R. v. Sheffield Stipendiary Magistrate, ex p. DPP*, *The Independent (C.S.)*, November 27, 2000, DC, it was held that in adjudicating on an application to amend an information which, if granted, may necessitate an adjournment, it is appropriate for a magistrates' court to have regard to the spirit of the new civil procedure rules, and, in particular, to the consideration that inefficiency in the conduct of litigation may prejudice litigants in other cases by leading to a risk that their cases will be delayed (*cf.* now the *Criminal Procedure Rules* 2005 (S.I. 2005 No. 384), Pt 1, *post*, §§ 4–84a *et seq.*). The facts of the case were fairly extreme and it remains to be seen what, if any, impact the case has in respect of applications to amend indictments. **1–151**

(4) An application for an amendment to meet the evidence before the magistrates should be made before arraignment, after notice given to the defence, but can be made later: *R. v. Johal and Ram*, *ante*, and cases cited therein.

(5) The longer the interval between arraignment and amendment, the less likely it is that the amendment can be made without injustice: *R. v. Johal and Ram*, *ante*.

(6) In the case of an immaterial averment an amendment can be made after verdict, though this is not necessary: see *R. v. Dossi*, 13 Cr.App.R. 158, CCA, *ante*, § 1–127).

(7) The power of amendment may be used to cure misjoinder, but any proceedings on the indictment prior to such an amendment *may* be a nullity—see further *post*, §§ 1–161 *et seq.* and 1–195 *et seq.*

1–152 Although each case will depend very much on its own facts, the following summary of certain cases where the appellate court has considered the propriety of an amendment may assist on the question of whether an amendment can be made without injustice.

(1) *R. v. Teong Sun Chuah and Teong Tatt Chuah* [1991] Crim.L.R. 463, CA (appropriate charges substituted for inappropriate charges at the end of prosecution case; no injustice as substance of allegation unchanged; defence merely deprived of technical acquittal). See also *R. v. Tirado*, 59 Cr.App.R. 80, CA.

(2) *R. v. Radley*, 58 Cr.App.R. 394, CA (single count indictment alleging conspiracy to defraud amended after prosecution opening by addition of counts to cater for the possibility that more than one conspiracy had existed; the case was made easier for the jury and no injustice resulted from the amendment at the stage at which it occurred).

(3) *R. v. Bonner* [1974] Crim.L.R. 479, CA (amendment to date after start of summing up; such late amendments should be made only after particular care has been taken to ensure that defence has had ample opportunity to consider whether witnesses should be recalled or further evidence called).

(4) *R. v. Nelson*, 65 Cr.App.R. 119, CA (statement of offence defective in that it omitted to refer to statute alleged to have been contravened, as to which, see *ante*, § 1–116; amendment even after verdict would have been permissible).

1–153 (5) *R. v. Collison*, 71 Cr.App.R. 249, CA (amendment by adding a count after the jury's initial retirement upheld; for the circumstances, see *post*, § 4–455).

(6) *R. v. O'Connor* [1997] Crim.L.R. 516, CA (wrong to permit addition of further count in order to put prosecution case on different basis, after submission of no case; defendant deprived of putting his case in way that he would have done if prosecution put in that way from outset).

(7) *R. v. Newington*, 91 Cr.App.R. 247, CA (the court questioned whether it is ever wise to exercise the power to amend during a summing up, especially in a long and complex case; when such a course is pursued it must inevitably deprive defence counsel of the opportunity to address the jury on the implications of the amendment; furthermore, there is a risk of the judge being unequal to the task of properly adjusting his summing up to accommodate the change brought about by amendment).

(8) *R. v. Piggott and Litwin* [1999] 2 Cr.App.R. 320, CA (where successful submission of no case made at close of prosecution evidence, wrong to permit amendment of indictment to allege different offence in respect of which prima facie case did exist but which necessitated discharge of jury and new trial because some evidence on original charge inadmissible on new charge; prosecution of second trial an abuse of process).

G. JOINDER

(1) Joinder of counts in one indictment

Indictments Act 1915, s.4

1–154 **4.** Subject to the provisions of the rules under this Act charges ... for more than one misdemeanour ... may be joined in the same indictment.

[This section is printed as repealed in part by the *CJA* 1948, s.83(3), Sched. 10, Pt I; and the *CLA* 1967, s.10(2), Sched. 3, Pt III.]

By virtue of the *CLA* 1967, s.1(2) (*ante*, § 1–12), this applies to all offences triable on indictment.

Rule 14.2(3) of the *Criminal Procedure Rules* 2005 (S.I. 2005 No. 384) (*ante*, § 1–115), which repeats in substance the now repealed rule 9 of the *Indictment Rules* 1971 (S.I. 1971 No. 1253) (and the predecessor to that rule), provides that an indictment may contain more than one count if all the offences charged (a) are founded on the same facts, or (b) form or are part of a series of offences of the same or a similar character. As to the commencement of rule 14.2(3) and transitional provisions, see *ante*, § 1–108.

In many of the authorities no clear distinction is drawn between the topics of joinder and severance, but in view of the decision in *R. v. Newland* [1988] Q.B. 402, 87 Cr.App.R. 118, CA (*post*, § 1–161) as to the effect of misjoinder, it is important to consider these two matters in separate stages, but see also *post*, §§ 1–195 *et seq*. See *post*, §§ 1–166 *et seq*., as to the severance of properly joined counts.

The appellate courts have repeatedly drawn attention to the rules as to joinder and to the necessity of observing them. See, *e.g.*, *R. v. Taylor*, 18 Cr.App.R. 25, CCA; *R. v. Clarke*, *ibid.*, 166, CCA; *R. v. Tyreman*, 19 Cr.App.R. 4, CCA; *R. v. Newland*, *ante*.

Different defendants in separate counts

It has been said, *obiter*, in respect of one of the predecessors to the present rule **1–155**
14.2(3), that it was concerned with the joinder of charges against one accused and not with the joinder of counts against two or more accused charged with separate offences: see *R. v. Tizzard and Ruxton* [1962] 2 Q.B. 608, 46 Cr.App.R. 82, CCA, and *R. v. Assim* [1966] 2 Q.B. 249, 50 Cr.App.R. 224, CCA. However, no reasoned explanation was given in this regard. Even if the rule has no direct application, there would appear to be no reason why the principles set out therein should not be applied when deciding whether counts against different accused may be properly joined in one indictment. Indeed, the guidance given in *R. v. Assim*, *ante*, amounts to much the same as rule 14.2(3).

As to the joinder of two or more defendants in one count, see *post*, § 1–164.

See *post*, § 1–165 as to specific considerations relating to the joinder of persons who have been separately committed for trial.

Handling stolen goods

For specific statutory provision relating to the joinder of charges and persons in re- **1–156**
spect of handling items that have been stolen in one theft, see section 27(1) of the *Theft Act* 1968, *post*, § 21–277.

"founded on the same facts"

The question whether the charges are "founded on the same facts", such as to justify **1–157**
joinder pursuant to rule 14.2(3) of the 2005 rules, should be tested by asking whether the charges have a common factual origin; if the "subsidiary" charge could not be alleged but for the facts which give rise to the "primary" charge, the charges are founded on the same facts for the purpose of the rule and may legitimately be joined in the same indictment: *R. v. Barrell and Wilson*, 69 Cr.App.R. 250, CA (count charging attempt to pervert the course of justice held to be properly joined with counts of affray and assault occasioning actual bodily harm where first of those charges based on allegation of trying to bribe witness for the prosecution in respect of other two charges). In one sense, it is perhaps difficult to see how the offences in *R. v. Barrell and Wilson* can truly be said to have had a common factual origin, and in *R. v. Barnes*, 83 Cr.App.R. 38, CA, the court, having considered that decision, seems to have doubted the propriety of joinder of counts of wounding and perjury where the allegation of wounding was based on the confession of the appellant to that offence when giving evidence on behalf of his brother, who had originally been charged with it, and where the allegation of perjury was based on an alternative allegation that the confession was untrue.

Other examples of the application of the principles relating to joinder of offences founded on the same facts are:

(1) *R. v. Conti*, 58 Cr.App.R. 387, CA (charges of assault occasioning actual bodily harm, possessing offensive weapon and possessing a prohibited drug properly joined where allegation was that C had taken the drug for the purpose of getting himself into suitable frame of mind to commit the assault);

(2) *R. v. Williams* [1993] Crim.L.R. 533, CA (charge of indecent assault on a girl

improperly joined with charge of false imprisonment of same girl on a later date; although indecent assault committed on same occasion as false imprisonment might be said to be founded on the same facts, different where the charges arise out of separate incidents and are not of similar character, despite an evidential nexus); and

(3) *R. v. Lockley and Sainsbury* [1997] Crim.L.R. 455, CA (charge of dangerous driving not properly joined with charge of conspiracy to commit burglary, where driving charge arose out of the dangerous condition of the car allegedly used in the course of the burglary; the defective nature of the vehicle could have been alleged without any reference to the facts giving rise to the charge of conspiracy to burgle and the charge of dangerous driving did not arise out of the facts which established the conspiracy to burgle).

The requirements of section 40(1)(a) of the *CJA* 1988, *ante*, § 1–75ai (joinder of certain summary offences), are similar to the requirements of rule 14.2(3) in respect of joinder of offences founded on the same facts. Authorities dealing with this aspect of section 40 are cited at § 1–75ak, *ante*.

"series of offences of the same or a similar character"

1–158 The question whether particular charges "form or are part of a series of offences of the same or a similar character", such as to justify joinder pursuant to rule 14.2(3) of the 2005 rules, has also been considered in a number of authorities. The fact that evidence in relation to one count was not admissible in relation to another count under the old "similar fact" principle did not necessarily mean that those counts could not properly be joined pursuant to this limb of the rule: see *R. v. Kray*, 53 Cr.App.R. 569, CA, and *Ludlow v. Metropolitan Police Commr* [1971] A.C. 29, HL.

In *Kray* it was held: (a) that two offences may constitute a "series" within the meaning of the rule, and (b) that although the relevant part of the rule does not require the offences to arise out of the same facts or be part of a system of conduct before joinder can be sanctioned, a sufficient nexus must nevertheless exist between the relevant offences; such a nexus is clearly established if evidence of one offence would be admissible on the trial of the other, but the rule is not confined to such cases; all that is necessary to satisfy the rule is that the offences should exhibit such similar features as to establish a prima facie case that they can properly and conveniently be tried together in the interests of justice, which include, in addition to the interests of the defendants, those of the Crown, witnesses and the public; a further relevant factor is the prejudice likely to arise in the second trial from extensive press reports of the first trial if the offences are tried separately. It was further held (at p. 575) that it is not desirable that the rule should be given an unduly restricted meaning, since any risk of injustice can be avoided by the exercise of the judge's discretion to sever the indictment (as to which, see *post*, §§ 1–166 *et seq.*). (For a rather more restrictive approach to a similarly phrased provision in section 22 of the *MCA* 1980, see *ante*, §§ 1–75ak *et seq.*)

In *Ludlow v. Metropolitan Police Commr*, *ante*, the House of Lords, having considered the previous law and practice, held, in respect of rule 3 of the *Indictment Rules* 1915 (now rule 14.2(3) of the 2005 rules), that (a) two offences can constitute a series, and (b) both the law and the facts should be taken into account when deciding whether offences are similar or dissimilar in character. They concluded that, in respect of the limb of the rule then under consideration, there must be a *series* of offences of a similar character; for this purpose there must be some nexus between the offences; nexus is a feature of similarity which in all the circumstances of the case enables the offences to be described as a series. Applying these principles to the facts of the case before them (charge of attempted larceny from a public house in Acton and a charge of robbery at a different public house in Acton 16 days later), it was held that the joinder had been proper; the offences charged were similar in both law and fact; they had the same essential ingredient of actual or attempted theft; they involved neighbouring public houses, and the time interval was only 16 days. Their Lordships also cited, with implicit approval, the dictum in *Kray*, *ante*, that the operation of the relevant part of the rule is not restricted to cases where the evidence on one charge is admissible on the other(s) and expressly approved the dictum that the rule should not be given an unduly restricted meaning.

Examples of the application of the principles expounded in *Kray* and *Ludlow* are: **1–159**

(1) *R. v. Clayton-Wright*, 33 Cr.App.R. 22, CCA (albeit decided before *Kray* and *Ludlow*) (counts charging arson of a vessel, arson of the vessel with intent to prejudice its insurers, attempting to obtain money from the insurers by false pretences in respect of the insurance on the vessel, and obtaining money by false pretences from other insurers by pretending that a mink coat had been stolen from appellant's car, had been properly joined; the nexus of fraudulent acts to the prejudice of insurers was sufficient);

(2) *R. v. Harward*, 73 Cr.App.R. 168, CA (count charging conspiracy to defraud banks by unlawful use of cheque cards improperly joined with count of dishonest handling relating to recording equipment; the common element of "dishonesty" was not a sufficient nexus); and

(3) *R. v. Marsh*, 83 Cr.App.R. 165, CA (not necessary to establish both legal and factual similarity in order to justify joinder, but in respect of, on the one hand, charges of reckless driving and causing criminal damage thereby, and, on the other, a charge of assault arising out of a separate incident, common element of violence not a legal similarity and of insufficient factual similarity to establish appropriate nexus; violence to property distinguished from violence to the person in this regard).

The relevant principles were also reviewed in *R. v. McGlinchey*, 78 Cr.App.R. 282, CA, and in *R. v. Mariou* [1992] Crim.L.R. 511, CA, but in both cases there appears to be a failure to distinguish between the topics of joinder and severance.

The question whether two sets of alleged offences can be described as a "series", for the purposes of the rule, should not be approached by reference to the dictionary definition of that word; if an appropriate nexus exists to bring the charges within the rules even offences separated by a period of nine years could be said to form a series; a coincidence in point of time, like a coincidence in point of location, may be an important factor in determining whether or not particular offences can be regarded as being or forming part of a series, but every case must depend on its own facts; where the evidence on one such group of charges is properly admissible on the trial of others, a sufficient nexus exists despite any lapse of time between the relevant incidents: *R. v. Baird*, 97 Cr.App.R. 308, CA. **1–160**

In *R. v. C.*, *The Times*, February 4, 1993, CA, the appellant had been convicted of offences of rape and attempted rape of his daughter. It was held that where two or more counts alleged against a defendant were of a broadly similar character and there was but one single victim, generally it would not merely be permissible for the counts to be joined pursuant to the rule, but, additionally, it would seldom be appropriate for the trial judge to exercise his discretion to order severance. Their Lordships expressed no final view, but said, however, it might be that the rule had been stretched towards, or even to, its limits to accommodate counts that were separated in time by 11 years.

Where no nexus based on mutual admissibility of evidence exists, time is a relevant factor for consideration but is not determinative; thus a sufficient nexus may exist between offences alleged to have taken place many years apart, but the greater the interval, the clearer must be the nexus: *R. v. O'Brien*, *The Times*, March 23, 2000 CA (where alleged offences separated by 19 years, and evidence not mutually admissible, no sufficient nexus arose from fact that all matters related to allegations made by pupils at school where defendant was the headmaster).

The requirements of section 40(1)(b) of the *CJA* 1988, *ante*, § 1–75ai (joinder of certain summary offences), are similar to the requirements of rule 14.2(3) in respect of joinder of offences that form or are part of a series of offences of the same or a similar character. Authorities dealing with this aspect of section 40 are cited at §§ 1–75aj, 1–75ak, *ante*.

(2) The effect of misjoinder in contravention of rule 14.2(3)

In *R. v. Newland* [1988] Q.B. 402, 87 Cr.App.R. 118, CA, it was held that misjoinder **1–161** of offences in contravention of rule 9 of the *Indictment Rules* 1971 (S.I. 1971 No. 1253) (now r.14.2(3) of the 2005 rules) cannot be cured by a direction for separate trials of the misjoined counts; the power to give such a direction, pursuant to section 5(3) of the *Indictments Act* 1915 (*ante*, § 1–147), applies only to a valid indictment and an indictment containing misjoined charges is not a valid indictment because section 4 of the 1915 Act (*ante*, § 1–154) provides, in effect, that an indictment may only contain more than one count if the joinder complies with rules made under the Act. It had also been argued that, in any event, a direction for separate trials pursuant to section 5(3) of the 1915 Act would not cure the invalidity because, on a proper construction of that section and section 5(5), there would still be only one (misjoined) indictment, albeit there would be separate trials. However, a misjoined indictment, although invalid, is not a nullity because it can be cured by amendment, pursuant to section 5(1) of the 1915 Act (*ante*, § 1–147), so as to remove one or more of the counts. In order to proceed on the counts so removed it would be necessary for the prosecution either to obtain leave to prefer a voluntary bill or, alternatively, to commence fresh proceedings in respect of the offences charged in any such count. It was, accordingly, further held in *Newland* that if a court proceeds to try a misjoined indictment, or purports to cure the misjoinder by directing separate trials, the proceedings will be a nullity and any resulting convictions, including those resulting from guilty pleas will be quashed. *Newland* was followed in *R. v. O'Reilly*, 90 Cr.App.R. 40, CA, where the defect in the indictment was cured after guilty pleas had been entered, but the defendant had not been rearraigned; his pleas had been entered to an invalid indictment and the convictions were all quashed, although a *venire de novo* was ordered, but see now *post*, § 1–163.

1–162 *Newland* was also referred to in *R. v. Lombardi*, 88 Cr.App.R. 179, CA, where it was held that counts based on evidence which was before the committing justices, but in respect of which there was no committal, could be the proper subject of an indictment, pursuant to the proviso to section 2(2) of the *Administration of Justice (Miscellaneous Provisions) Act* 1933 (*post*, § 1–204) only if they were in substitution for, or in addition to, counts in respect of which there had been a committal and only if they could lawfully be joined, pursuant to what is now rule 14.2(3) of the 2005 rules, in the indictment which was the subject of that committal. In *Lombardi*, one indictment had been preferred to cover the charges upon which the appellant had been committed and a second indictment had been preferred containing charges based on evidence that had been before the justices but upon which the appellant had not been committed and which could not be joined with the counts in the first indictment without breaching the rule. This second indictment was held to be invalid. As to section 2(2) of the 1933 Act, see further *post*, §§ 1–216 *et seq*.

In *R. v. Follett* [1989] Q.B. 338, 88 Cr.App.R. 310, CA, a court consisting of the same members as that which had decided *Lombardi*, embarked upon an extensive review of the authorities relating to misjoinder. As to their alternative solution where an indictment has misjoined counts, see *post*, § 1–207.

The consequences of proceeding on a misjoined indictment have also been considered in the context of section 40 of the *CJA* 1988, where it has been held in a number of authorities that the wrongful addition of a "summary only" charge to an indictment does not invalidate the whole indictment. In *R. v. Callaghan*, 94 Cr.App.R. 226, CA, *ante*, § 1–75aj, the wrongful addition of a "summary only" charge led to the quashing of the conviction on that charge, but the convictions in respect of the other counts in the indictment were upheld, a distinction being drawn between the effect of misjoinder in breach of section 40 and the effect of a misjoinder in breach of the predecessor to rule 14.2(3). On the facts, the Court of Appeal held that there had been no breach of the rule. In *R. v. Lewis*, 95 Cr.App.R. 131, CA, *ante*, § 1–75ak, all of the convictions were quashed, but the position seems to have been different because, on the facts, there was a misjoinder that appears to have amounted to a breach of both section 40 and of the predecessor to rule 14.2(3). However, in *R. v. Simon* [1992] Crim.L.R. 444, CA, *ante*, § 1–75ak, the court appears to have regarded *Callaghan* and *Lewis* as conflicting decisions.

1–163 In *R. v. Smith (B.P.)* [1997] 1 Cr.App.R. 390, CA, the court followed *Callaghan* to the extent of holding that the validity of the conviction for an indictable offence was not affected by the quashing of a conviction for a summary offence that had not been joined in accordance with section 40 of the 1988 Act. However, the court went on to express the view that no proper distinction can be drawn between the effect of misjoinder under section 40 and misjoinder under the predecessor to rule 14.2(3) and that *Newland*, *ante*, was wrongly decided in so far as it held that misjoinder in breach of that rule would invalidate all convictions on the indictment. In reaching this conclusion, the court reviewed the decision in *Lewis*, *ante*, but did not consider the distinction, referred to above, that may be drawn between the situation in that case and the situation in *Callaghan*. Furthermore, the court did not explain how it is to be decided which of two charges that are joined in breach of the rule is to be regarded as the misjoined charge; this difficulty does not arise in respect of misjoinder under section 40 of a summary charge and, it is submitted, provides a valid distinction between the effect of breach of the two provisions. Although *obiter* in respect of what is now rule 14.2(3), the decision in *Smith* was applied in *R. v. Lockley and Sainsbury* [1997] Crim.L.R. 455, CA, where charges had been misjoined in breach of that rule. The report does not indicate that any consideration was given to the difficulty highlighted above or to any question of the application of the doctrine of *stare decisis*.

The question of the present status of the decision in *Newland* was also canvassed in *R. v. S. (Paul John)* [1999] 1 Cr.App.R. 1, CA, but the court did not find it necessary to resolve the issue.

The matter was then considered (*obiter*) in *R. v. Ashton*; *R. v. Draz*; *R. v. O'Reilly* [2006] 2 Cr.App.R. 15, CA, where the court was of the view that *Newland* would now be decided differently in so far as it suggests that misjoinder renders any subsequent trial a nullity. However, the correctness of that view must be open to serious doubt in the light of the fact that certain aspects of the approach to validity propounded therein have now been overruled by the House of Lords in *R. v. Clarke and McDaid* [2008] 2 Cr.App.R. 2. As to the correct approach, see now *post*, §§ 1–195 *et seq.* On the basis of that approach, it can be argued that: (i) just as a signature on the bill of indictment (*post*, § 1–196), or a consent to prosecution in certain cases (*post*, § 2–244), is a condition precedent to the existence of a valid indictment, and there cannot be a valid trial without a valid indictment (*R. v. Clarke and McDaid*), so also, on a proper construction of section 4 of the *Indictments Act* 1915 (*ante*, § 1–154) and rule 14.2(3) of the *Criminal Procedure Rules* 2005 (S.I. 2005 No. 384) (*ante*, § 1–154), compliance with the requirements as to the inclusion of a number of counts in one indictment is a condition precedent to the validity of the indictment; (ii) compliance with the rules as to joinder permits that which would otherwise be impermissible; it is thus a matter that goes to substantive validity and is not to be equated to a mere procedural defect, the consequence of which is to be judged simply by reference to considerations such as prejudice or substantive merit; and (iii) since there can be no valid indictment containing more than one count in the absence of compliance with the said statutory provisions, Parliament must be taken to have intended that there can be no valid trial in the absence of compliance with the statutory condition precedent. The importance of ensuring proper joinder was mentioned in *R. v. Clarke and McDaid* (at [7]) and the decision in *Newland* was mentioned in passing (at [8]).

(3) Joinder of two or more defendants in one count

All persons concerned in committing an offence, whether as principals or by assistance or encouragement (see *post*, Chap. 18), can be charged together in one count with that offence, although they may each be charged in separate counts or indictments: 2 Hale 173; *R. v. Atkinson* (1706) 1 Salk. 382; *Young v. R.* (1798) 3 Term Rep. 98; and see the speech of Lord Diplock in *DPP v. Merriman* [1973] A.C. 584 at 606, HL. **1–164**

A charge against two or more defendants in a single count is joint and several. If, therefore, in the case of any particular defendant the evidence at the trial proves that he was guilty of the offence but was acting on his own, and not in concert with any other, he can nevertheless be convicted on the count as laid: *DPP v. Merriman*, *ante*.

As to the joinder of persons separately committed, transferred or sent for trial, see *post*, § 1–165, and as to separate trials for persons who have been jointly charged, or charged with different offences in the same indictment, see *post*, § 1–166.

(4) Joinder of persons separately committed for trial

1–165 See *R. v. Groom* [1977] Q.B. 6, 62 Cr.App.R. 242, CA, and *R. v. Townsend* [1997] 2 Cr.App.R. 540, CA, *post*, §§ 1–218 *et seq.*

As to the power to amend a charge contained in an indictment preferred in accordance with the voluntary bill procedure so as to add the name of a defendant who has been separately committed for trial on the same charge, see *R. v. Ismail*, 92 Cr.App.R. 92, CA, and *post*, § 1–215.

(5) Separate trials of counts lawfully joined and of defendants jointly charged

The power to order severance

1–166 The fact that charges are lawfully joined in one indictment, or that defendants are jointly charged, does not necessarily mean that it will be proper to try those charges or defendants together. Section 5(3) of the *Indictments Act* 1915 (*ante*, § 1–147) gives the power to order a separate trial of any count or counts in an indictment where, before trial or at any stage of a trial, the court is of the opinion that a person accused may be prejudiced or embarrassed in his defence by reason of being charged with more than one offence in the same indictment, or where for any other reason it is desirable to direct that the person should be tried separately for any one or more offences charged in an indictment.

It is submitted that section 5(3) includes the power to order separate trials of defendants who are jointly charged in one count because such a charge is joint and several and therefore alleges separate offences against the defendants: see *DPP v. Merriman* [1973] A.C. 584, HL. In any event, the authorities show that the courts have a power to order separate trials against defendants who are jointly charged in one count and that the principles upon which the court acts in such cases are the same as those upon which it acts in respect of separate trials of separate counts: see, for example, *R. v. Gibbins and Proctor*, 13 Cr.App.R. 134, CCA, *R. v. Bywaters*, 17 Cr.App.R. 66, CCA, *R. v. Grondkowski and Malinowski* [1946] K.B. 369, 31 Cr.App.R. 116, CCA, and *R. v. Wilson* [1958] Crim.L.R. 475, CCA. For particular considerations in respect of separate trials as between defendants, see *post*, §§ 1–176 *et seq.*

Section 5(5) of the *Indictments Act* 1915 (*ante*, § 1–147) gives the court a specific power to discharge the jury if an order for separate trials is made pursuant to section 5 during the course of a trial. It also provides, *inter alia*, that the procedure on the separate trial of a severed count shall be the same in all respects as if the count had been found in a separate indictment.

1–167 It is to be noted that an order for separate trials may be made "before trial, or at any stage of a trial". This provision would appear to permit a judge to postpone a decision on severance if necessary, or to change his original ruling if the course which the trial takes justifies such a change (see the authorities cited, *post*, §§ 1–173 *et seq.*). It will also sometimes happen that the necessity to make an application for separate trials will not arise until part way through a trial. In some cases it will be of assistance to have a ruling on questions of severance in advance of the trial date. See *post*, §§ 4–84a *et seq.* as to pre-trial reviews generally, and see *post*, §§ 4–84m, 4–84t, as to the consideration of questions as to severance or joinder at a preparatory hearing. In *R. v. Wright*, 90 Cr.App.R. 325, CA, an application for severance had been refused by one judge at a pre-trial review. The different trial judge refused to reconsider the question, regarding the matter as concluded by the decision of the first judge. The Court of Appeal held that the decision of the first judge did not bind the second, although the latter was not obliged to hear the same point argued again if nothing material had changed. It is submitted that a judge should also entertain a fresh application for severance if some matter which is clearly material to the issue was not put before the first judge, even though there has been no actual change of circumstances.

The general approach to severance

1–168 The discretion given to a trial judge to order separate trials is a wide one, but like all discretions it must be exercised judicially: *R. v. Gibbins and Proctor*, *ante*. The Court of Appeal will not readily interfere with the exercise of that discretion unless it can be shown to have been exercised other than on the basis of the usual and proper principles: *R. v. Blackstock*, 70 Cr.App.R. 34, CA; *R. v. Wells*, 92 Cr.App.R. 24, CA; *R. v. Dixon*, 92 Cr.App.R. 43, CA; *R. v. Cannan*, 92 Cr.App.R. 16, CA. The application of the general principles will depend to a great extent on the individual facts of particular cases.

In *Ludlow v. Metropolitan Police Commr* [1971] A.C. 29, HL (*ante*, § 1–158), the "discretion aspect" of the problem was considered by Lord Pearson.

> "The judge has no duty to direct separate trials under section 5(3) unless in his opinion there is some special feature of the case which would make a joint trial of the several counts prejudicial or embarrassing to the accused and separate trials are required in the interests of justice. In some cases the offences charged may be too numerous and complicated (*R. v. King* [1897] 1 Q.B. 214; *R. v. Bailey* (1924) 18 Cr.App.R. 42) or too difficult to disentangle (*R. v. Norman* [1915] 1 K.B. 341) so that a joint trial of all the counts is likely to cause confusion and the defence may be embarrassed or prejudiced. In other cases objection may be taken to the inclusion of a count on the ground that it is of a scandalous nature and likely to arouse in the minds of the jury hostile feelings against the accused: see *R. v. Southern* (1930) 22 Cr.App.R. 6, at 9; *R. v. Muir* (1938) 26 Cr.App.R. 164" (at p. 41).

(See *post*, § 1–180, as to severance of long and unduly complicated cases, and see *post*, §§ 1–170 *et seq.*, in relation to severance of charges alleging sexual misconduct.)

The mere fact that evidence is admissible on one count and inadmissible on another is not in itself a ground for ordering the counts to be tried separately; but where it would be difficult in the course of a summing up to distinguish the evidence relating to the respective counts, and there is, therefore, a risk that the jury when considering one count may be unable to disregard the evidence relating to another count, there is a ground for ordering separate trials: *R. v. Sims* [1946] K.B. 531, 31 Cr.App.R. 158, CCA. It could also be argued that the considerations outlined by Lord Cross in *DPP v. Boardman* [1975] A.C. 421, HL, *post*, § 1–170, would have equal validity in certain cases that are not of a sexual, or particularly scandalous, nature.

In *R. v. Blackstock*, *ante*, when dismissing an appeal against the refusal of the trial judge to order separate trials of pairs of robbery and firearm charges, where the evidence on one pair of charges was not admissible on the other, the Court of Appeal said:

> "Every trial judge is familiar with the requirement, where more counts than one of a similar kind are joined in an indictment, of adding a warning to the jury that they must not add all the counts together and convict because there is more than one count in the indictment, or use the evidence on one count as evidence on the other. They should consider each count separately in the light of the evidence upon that particular count against the accused person, but no other. Juries have shown themselves well able over the years to follow such a direction and apply it" (at p. 37).

This decision was followed in *R. v. McGlinchey*, 78 Cr.App.R. 282, CA (refusal of **1–169**
trial judge to sever count of dishonest handling of photographic equipment from counts of burglary and handling of credit card stolen in the burglary, upheld), where an argument based on dicta in *Boardman*, to the effect that the judge should have exercised his discretion in favour of severance in respect of the evidentially unrelated counts, was held to be ill-founded. It was said that the dicta in *Boardman*, a case concerning allegations of sexual misconduct, cannot be taken as casting doubt on the principles expressed in *Ludlow* (*ante*, § 1–168) and should not be regarded as being intended to apply beyond circumstances such as those then before the House of Lords. See also *R. v. Mariou* [1992] Crim.L.R. 511, CA, *R. v. Dixon*, 92 Cr.App.R. 43, CA, and *R. v. Cannan*, 92 Cr.App.R. 16, CA (*post*, §§ 1–171 *et seq.*) in this regard. Sexual misconduct cases may, therefore, merit separate consideration: see *post*, §§ 1–170 *et seq*.

In *R. v. Wells*, *ante*, the Court of Appeal found no reason to interfere with the exercise by the trial judge of his discretion (refusal to sever two groups of charges arising from two separate drugs raids at appellant's premises) on the particular facts of the case (prejudice and complexity had been relied upon), but indicated that each case depends on its own facts and that other considerations might have applied if the charges had amounted to an allegation that the appellant was a "drugs baron".

Ordinarily, if offences are properly joined, a defendant does not have the right to have the indictment severed merely because he might wish to give evidence in respect of one count and not another; while the right of a defendant not to give evidence must be recognised, and weight may be given to his desires, it should be borne in mind that he could change his mind about giving evidence and applications to sever might be made for tactical reasons; it is a matter for the discretion of the trial judge: *R. v. Phillips (D.M.)*, 86 Cr.App.R. 18, CA. In this regard, see now also the right discussed at §§ 16–69 *et seq., post.*

For guidance on the practice to be followed in a case where the question of the admissibility of "bad character" evidence may affect the decision as to severance, see *post*, §§ 1–173 *et seq.*

As to the practice of severing a count of conspiracy from related substantive counts, see *post*, §§ 33–58 *et seq.*

The approach to severance in cases alleging scandalous conduct

1–170 The scandalous nature of one or more of the offences alleged was mentioned by Lord Pearson in *Ludlow* (*ante*, § 1–168) as a factor that might justify the ordering of separate trials for counts that are properly joined, but in respect of which the evidence on one is not admissible on the other. In *R. v. Sims* [1946] K.B. 531, 31 Cr.App.R. 158, CCA, Lord Goddard C.J. said, "... in such a case as the present [allegations of homosexual misconduct], however, it is asking too much to expect any jury when considering one charge to disregard the evidence on the others, and if such evidence is inadmissible, the prejudice created by it would be too great for any direction to overcome" (at pp. 536, 164). Dicta to similar effect are to be found in the speeches in *DPP v. Boardman* [1975] A.C. 421, HL:

> "When in a case of this sort, the prosecution wishes to adduce 'similar facts' evidence which the defence says is inadmissible, the question ... ought, if possible, to be decided in the absence of the jury at the outset of the trial and if ... the evidence is inadmissible and the accused is being charged in the same indictment with offences against other men the charges relating to the different persons ought to be tried separately. If they are tried together the judge will, of course, have to tell the jury that in considering whether the accused is guilty of the offence alleged against him by A, they must put out of mind the fact—which they know—that B and C are making similar allegations against him. But, as the Court of Criminal Appeal said in *Sims*, it is asking too much of any jury to tell them to perform mental gymnastics of that sort. If the charges are tried together it is inevitable that the jurors will be influenced, consciously or unconsciously, by the fact that the accused is being charged not with a single offence against one person but with three separate offences against three persons. It is said ... that to order separate trials in all these cases would be highly inconvenient. If and so far as this is true it is a reason for doubting the wisdom of the general rule [of exclusion]. But so long as there is that general rule, the courts ought to strive to give effect to it loyally and not, while paying lip service to it, in effect let in the inadmissible evidence by trying all the charges together" (*per* Lord Cross at p. 459).

1–171 In many cases the considerations mentioned by Lord Cross in *Boardman* proved to be determinative in the exercise of the discretion as to whether separate trials should be ordered in cases of allegations concerning sexual misconduct. In this regard, see also *R. v. Novac*, 65 Cr.App.R. 107, CA, *R. v. Wilmot*, 89 Cr.App.R. 341, CA, and *R. v. Brooks*, 92 Cr.App.R. 36, CA.

However, in a number of subsequent cases, the Court of Appeal upheld the refusal of trial judges to order separate trials of charges of sexual offences, purporting to apply to the individual facts of each case the general principles stated in such decisions as *Ludlow*, *Blackstock*, and *McGlinchey* (cited *ante*, § 1–168), although those decisions themselves suggest that particular considerations may apply in cases of a scandalous or sexual nature: see *R. v. Dixon*, 92 Cr.App.R. 43, and *R. v. Cannan*, 92 Cr.App.R. 16, CA. In *Cannan*, the court did acknowledge that in sexual cases trial judges may well often order separate trials in the exercise of their discretion, but said that decisions based on individual facts should not be erected into binding authorities. Trenchant academic criticism of the way in which the discretion as to the ordering of separate trials was exercised on the facts of *Dixon* and *Cannan* is to be found in the commentaries at [1990] Crim.L.R. 335 and 869.

What was, nevertheless, clear was that no problem as to the exercise of the discretion as to severance would arise in a case where the evidence on each count would be admissible on the other; in such a case there would be no point in ordering separate trials. It is therefore important when dealing with an application to order separate trials of two charges to ascertain whether the evidence on each charge is admissible on the other. (For practical guidance as to the procedure that should be followed in this regard, see *post*, §§ 1–173 *et seq.*) In *DPP v. P.* [1991] 2 A.C. 447, HL, the two certified questions were:

> "(1) where a father or step-father is charged with sexually abusing a young daughter of the family, is evidence that he has also similarly abused other young children of the family admissible (assuming there to be no collusion) in support of such charge in the absence of any other 'striking similarities'; and (2) where a defendant is charged with sexual offences against more than one child or young person, is it necessary in the absence of 'striking similarities' for the charges to be tried separately?"

In the course of a speech with which the rest of their Lordships agreed, Lord Mackay L.C. set out the test to be applied in answering the first certified question (now superseded by the "bad character" provisions of the *CJA* 2003, *post*, Chapter 13). His Lordship went on to say that the answer to the second certified question is "no", provided that there is a relationship between the offences of the kind described in his answer to the first certified question. Unfortunately, his Lordship did not say in terms whether or not charges of the type under consideration may properly be tried together in the absence of a relationship of this kind.

In the subsequent decisions of *R. v. Tickner* [1992] Crim.L.R. 44, and *R. v. Smith* **1–172** [1992] Crim.L.R. 445, the Court of Appeal again rejected, on the basis of the individual facts, appeals based on the refusal of trial judges to order separate trials of sexual charges in which the evidence on the various charges had not been mutually admissible, but in neither case does the court appear to have addressed the implications of the answer to the second certified question in *DPP v. P.*, *ante*. However, in *R. v. Christou (G.)* [1997] A.C. 117, HL, the answer to the second certified question was prayed in aid in support of a contention that in cases of sexual abuse of children where the evidence of one child is not admissible in support of allegations by another child, the judge's discretion should always be exercised in favour of severance. In a speech with which the rest of their Lordships agreed, Lord Taylor C.J., having reviewed the authorities, concluded that the relevant principles had been correctly explained in *R. v. Cannan*, *ante*. The appropriateness of separate trials will depend on the particular facts of each case. Judges will often consider it right to order separate trials but to hold that either generally or in respect of any particular class of case the judge must so order would be to fetter the discretion given by statute. The relevant factors will vary from case to case, but the essential criterion is the achievement of a fair resolution of the issues. That requires fairness to the accused but also to the prosecution and those involved in it. Some, but by no means an exhaustive list, of the factors which may need to be considered are: how discrete or inter-related are the factors giving rise to the counts; the impact of ordering two or more trials on the defendant and his family, on the victims and their families and on press publicity; and importantly, whether directions the judge can give to the jury will suffice to secure a fair trial if the counts are tried together. In relation to that last factor, his Lordship stated that jury trials are conducted on the basis that the judge's directions of law are to be applied faithfully and experience shows that juries, where counts are jointly tried, do follow the judge's directions and consider the counts separately.

For further examples of the application of the principles by the courts, see *R. v. Musquera* [1999] Crim.L.R. 857, CA, and *R. v. Thomas (Paul Karl)* (2006) 150 S.J. 1251, CA, and see the commentaries on those decisions at *Criminal Law Week* 2000/08/1 and 2006/35/3, respectively.

As to the importance, where there are two or more complainants and no question of cross-admissibility, of a specific direction to the jury as to the need to give separate consideration not only to each count but also to each complainant, see *R. v. D.* [2004] 1 Cr.App.R. 19, CA.

See also *R. v. C.*, *The Times*, February 4, 1993, CA, *ante*, § 1–160.

Procedural guidance where evidence on joined charge may be admissible under "bad character" rules

In *Boardman* (*ante*, § 1–170), Lord Cross said that issues as to severance and similar **1–173** fact evidence (now bad character evidence) ought, if possible, to be decided at the outset of the trial. The resolution of these issues may well affect the approach adopted by counsel on both sides to various matters during the course of the trial. However, in *R. v. Scarrott* [1978] Q.B. 1016, 65 Cr.App.R. 125, CA, Scarman L.J. offered guidance to trial judges as to how to approach the issues of severance and admissibility in two stages. "The first phase is before arraignment when a defendant submits that the indictment should be severed ... the next phase is when the judge's ruling is sought as to the admissibility of the similar fact evidence." At the time the judge rules upon the question of severance "he is taking no final decision as to the admissibility of evidence." Scarman L.J. thereafter explains that if the application for severance is rejected and a multi-count indictment has to be tried, it does not follow that the evidence given will be admissible on all counts contained in the indictment. Similarly, if an application for severance is upheld, it is still open to the Crown, at the appropriate moment, to adduce evidence relating to the other (and now put aside) counts as admissible evidence on the count(s) being tried; it will then be for the judge to rule, in accordance with the laws of evidence whether the evidence is admissible or not.

1–174 Where a judge has ruled at the outset of a trial that evidence of a previous offence is admissible on a "similar fact" (now "bad character") basis, but the evidence given during the trial destroys the basis for that ruling, the correct course (assuming that the jury have been made aware of the previous offence) is to discharge the jury: *R. v. Naylor* [1998] Crim.L.R. 662, CA. A similar course should be considered where an application for separate trials has been refused on a "bad character" basis, which is subsequently undermined. In *R. v. Wells*, 92 Cr.App.R. 24, CA, which was not a case of sexual misconduct, the trial judge had deferred a ruling on the "similar fact" point until the end of all the evidence. The Court of Appeal said that the trial judge then had three choices:

> "first, at that stage, to discharge the jury, if he decided that the evidence on the first batch [of counts] was not admissible on the second batch and that a firm direction could not remove the prejudice; second, to allow the trial to proceed, but give the usual direction on separate consideration; or, third, to direct the jury that the evidence on the first batch of counts was admissible as probative of the second batch and, logically, vice versa" (at p. 29).

See also *R. v. Dixon*, 92 Cr.App.R. 43, CA, for a further example of a trial judge declining to give a definitive ruling on a "similar fact" issue when ruling on an application for separate trials.

1–175 The procedural guidance given in *Boardman* and *Scarrott* was considered in *R. v. Wilmot*, 89 Cr.App.R. 341, CA, where the defendant was charged with a series of rapes. At the outset of the trial, the judge ruled in favour of severance and against the suggested admissibility of evidence in relation to one offence in proof of another. After the complainant in the first trial had been cross-examined and the issue in the case had become apparent, counsel for the prosecution invited the judge to reconsider his ruling. This the judge did. In the light of what the issue now appeared to be (and having regard also to the fact that in the intervening two days, two of the total of five alleged victims had been traced by the police and were then, therefore, available to give evidence) the judge revised his earlier ruling. The solution adopted was not simply to admit the evidence of the other offences on the first trial but to discharge the jury on the first trial and order a new trial with the counts being tried together. This, in effect, achieved the best of both worlds at a small price, namely two or three wasted court days: this was inevitable on the basis of the material put before the trial judge on the original application. The Court of Appeal entirely approved of the course taken.

As to the test for the admission of bad character evidence, see Chapter 13, *post*.

See also *post*, §§ 13–105 *et seq.* as to contamination of, or collusion between, complainants.

Severance as between defendants

1–176 The general principles (*ante*, § 1–166) apply when questions arise as to separate trials as between different defendants, whether jointly charged or charged with different offences in the same indictment. However, certain issues commonly arise in such cases.

In *R. v. Moghal*, 65 Cr.App.R. 56, CA (an appeal based on the fact that separate trials *had* taken place), it was said that it is only in exceptional cases that separate trials should be ordered for two or more defendants who are jointly charged with participation in one offence. Similarly, it was said in *R. v. Lake*, 64 Cr.App.R. 172 at 175, CA, that it has been accepted for a long time in English practice that there are powerful public reasons why joint offences should be tried jointly; the importance is not merely the saving of time and money; it also affects the desirability that the same verdict and the same treatment shall be returned against all those concerned in the same offence; if joint offences were widely to be tried as separate offences, all sorts of inconsistencies might arise; accordingly, it is accepted practice that a joint offence can properly be tried jointly, even though this will involve inadmissible evidence being given before the jury and the possible prejudice which may result from that; the practice requires that the trial judge should warn the jury that such evidence is not admissible as against a particular defendant or defendants. The court recognised that there could be exceptions to the general practice and that the application of general principles will be affected by the facts of individual cases. Observations to similar effect were made in *R. v. Josephs and Christie*, 65 Cr.App.R. 253 at 255, CA.

In the majority of cases it is in the public interest that defendants who are jointly indicted should be tried together: *R. v. Hoggins*, 51 Cr.App.R. 444, CA. However, in long or complicated cases it may be desirable to order separate trials: see *post*, § 1–180.

In *R. v. Pieterson and Holloway* [1995] 2 Cr.App.R. 11, CA, the trial judge had refused to abort the trial part way through and order separate trials where one of two defendants claimed to be prejudiced by the fact that the joint trial prevented him from calling as a witness his co-defendant, who had not given evidence in his own defence—appeal dismissed. In *R. v. Eriemo* [1995] 2 Cr.App.R. 206, CA, it was said, *obiter*, that a defence of duress by a co-accused would not in itself be a sufficient justification for separate trials and that the interests of justice in such cases may well dictate that defendants be tried together so that the whole truth may be put before the jury.

There is no rule of law that separate trials should be ordered where an essential part **1–177**
of one defendant's defence amounts to an attack on a co-defendant, but the matter is one which the judge should take into account in deciding whether to order separate trials or not: *R. v. Grondkowski and Malinowski* [1946] K.B. 369, 13 Cr.App.R. 164, CCA. See also *R. v. Miller*, 36 Cr.App.R. 169, Assizes (Devlin J.) (observations on desirability of trying co-conspirators together).

It will be a rare case in which those charged with a conspiracy can properly, in the interests of justice, be granted a separate trial; there is a considerable risk with separate trials in such circumstances and on such a charge that the respective juries would hear a different account of events from the defendants they are trying, with a distinct possibility of a miscarriage of justice; the trial court has a discretion, to be exercised in the interests of justice, to order separate trials, but the fact that one defendant is likely to give evidence adverse to a co-defendant, after that co-defendant, will not of itself normally require separate trials, that being a common feature of trials where "cut-throat" defences are being run: *R. v. Cairns, Zaidi and Chaudhary* [2003] 1 Cr.App.R. 38, CA. See also *post*, § 4–315.

In *R. v. Sullivan*, *The Times*, March 18, 2003, CA, where the appellant had been charged with murder and false imprisonment, and his two co-accused had been charged with manslaughter, false imprisonment and obstructing a coroner, all arising out of the same sequence of events, it was held that the refusal of the appellant's various applications for separate trials had been correct and that the case was "crying out" for all three defendants to be tried together, notwithstanding that (i) the defence of the co-defendants was that the appellant was solely responsible for the victim's death and that any relevant actions on their parts had been the result of duress by the appellant, (ii) the co-defendants were permitted to adduce evidence that was prejudicial to the appellant to support their defences, and (iii) the co-defendants were given a more general licence to adduce evidence of the appellant's bad character once he had put his character in issue by attacking the character of one of them.

However, the fact that certain evidence which would not be admissible in the case of one defendant tried alone will be admissible in a joint trial (for reasons such as those explained in the authorities summarised *post*, § 13–72), albeit subject to a direction that it is not admissible evidence as against one of the defendants, requires careful consideration on an application for separate trials.

In *R. v. Hoggins*, *ante*, two defendants who were charged with murder sought to blame each other. They were convicted and appealed on the ground that the trial judge should have ordered separate trials in view of the consideration introduced by *Murdoch v. Taylor* [1965] A.C. 574, HL, that the court had no discretion to limit the cross-examination of a defendant who had given evidence against a co-defendant. *Held*, dismissing the appeal, this was only one factor to be taken into consideration, and that it must be weighed against the interests of the defendant seeking to cross-examine and of the public in the proper administration of justice. Likewise, the likelihood of one defendant being exposed to cross-examination as to his criminal record on behalf of another defendant is just one matter to be considered; the interests of witnesses who would have to give evidence about, for example, sexual matters, should also be taken into account in an assessment of the requirements of the interests of justice when separate trials are sought: *R. v. Edwards and Lake (deceased)* [1998] Crim.L.R. 756, CA. However, where a co-defendant was entitled to cross-examine the appellant on the contents of an interview which had been ruled inadmissible for prosecution purposes, and where counsel for the co-defendant made it clear that she intended so to cross-examine, the prejudice was such as to justify a departure from the general practice of trying co-conspirators together and, in those circumstances, the judge should have granted separate trials: *R. v. O'Boyle*, 92 Cr.App.R. 202, CA. See also *post*, § 15–387.

1–178 Although there is no firm rule, it will often be appropriate to order separate trials where an indictment contains a count that A assaulted B, together with a count that C assaulted A. If a joint trial were to take place in such a case and either defendant gave evidence in his own defence, counsel for the Crown could cross-examine him to bring out evidence against the other defendant, rather than adduce such evidence by examination-in-chief. This situation would be prejudicial to a defendant against whom such evidence was adduced and is to be distinguished from the situation that arises where defendants are jointly charged with the same offence and run cut-throat defences, which enables counsel for the Crown to cross-examine each about the other. In the latter situation, the prejudice would arise from the nature of the respective defences. In the first situation, the avoidance of unusual prejudice will normally outweigh the convenience of not having to call the same witnesses at two separate trials: *R. v. Johnson (A.)* [1995] 2 Cr.App.R. 1, CA.

The prejudice to co-defendants from incriminating remarks made in interview can sometimes be mitigated by suitable editing, as to which, see *post*, §§ 4–282 and 15–390.

1–179 In *R. v. Pervez and Khan* [1983] Crim.L.R. 108, CA, the court said that the question of severance should be raised and determined before consideration of questions of admissibility of alleged confession statements made by defendants. It is submitted that the court must have overlooked the fact that whether the trial of defendants should be severed may well depend upon the admissibility of one or more confession statements. Indeed, the fact that an alleged confession by A was highly prejudicial to B might be B's only ground for asking for a separate trial. If A's statement was held inadmissible, the ground for B's application would disappear.

As to the question whether separate trials are appropriate in a case where not all of the defendants are of good character, but those who are of good character are entitled to a full direction in that regard, see *R. v. Vye*; *R. v. Wise*; *R. v. Stephenson*, 97 Cr.App.R. 134, CA, *post*, §§ 4–406 *et seq.*

As to the question whether a child or young person who is indicted with an adult should be tried alone, and as to the stage at which that should be considered, see *post*, § 4–96a.

See *post*, § 9–92, as to the effect of a change of plea by a co-defendant in certain circumstances.

Unduly long and complicated cases

1–180 The desirability of trying joint offenders together, or of trying counts together which are properly joined in one indictment according to the rules, may often be outweighed by the difficulties which could arise from the jury having to deal with a number of issues or a great volume of evidence or both. In *R. v. Novac*, 65 Cr.App.R. 107 at 118, the Court of Appeal said that nothing short of absolute necessity could justify the imposition of the burdens of a very long trial. The court added that, in a jury trial, brevity and simplicity are the hand-maidens of justice; length and complexity its enemies. See also *ante*, § 1–112, and *post*, § 33–63, and see the overriding objective set out in the *Criminal Procedure Rules* 2005 (S.I. 2005 No. 384), rule 1.1(2)(e), *post*, § 4–84b, and the protocol for the control and management of heavy fraud and other complex cases (Appendix N–1).

On some occasions, little if any extra court time is likely to be taken up by separate trials, even of defendants charged with the same offence. The evidence common to all defendants, which alone has to be repeated, may not be disputed and may often be admitted. Moreover, an acquittal on the first trial may lead to the Crown offering no evidence on a subsequent trial. A conviction may lead to a plea of guilty in a subsequent trial. Considerable public expense is saved by reducing the number of solicitors and counsel attending each day.

[The next paragraph is § 1–190.]

H. Objections to Indictment

(1) General

Indictments Act 1915, s.7

7. Nothing in this Act shall prevent an indictment being open to objection if it contravenes or fails to comply with … any other enactment: …. **1–190**

[This section is printed as repealed in part by the *Administration of Justice (Miscellaneous Provisions) Act* 1933, s.2.]

There are many matters which may result in objection being taken to an indictment. Such objection may be taken because of some defect in the indictment itself, or because of some defect in the procedure followed in the preferment of that indictment or the pursuit of it. For example, an indictment will be open to objection in the following situations:

(a) if it has been preferred otherwise than in accordance with the provisions of section 2(2) of the *Administration of Justice (Miscellaneous Provisions) Act* 1933 (see *post*, §§ 1–204 *et seq.*);

(b) if it is drafted otherwise than in accordance with the *Criminal Procedure Rules* 2005 (see *ante*, §§ 1–114 *et seq.*), *e.g.* if it is insufficiently, or incorrectly, particularised (see *ante*, §§ 1–114 *et seq.*), if it breaches the rule against duplicity, or is otherwise unfair (see *ante*, §§ 1–135 *et seq.*), or if it contains counts that cannot properly be joined in the same indictment (see *ante*, §§ 1–154 *et seq.*);

(c) if a draft indictment has not been served on the Crown Court officer within the time permitted by rule 14.1 of the 2005 rules (see *post*, §§ 1–224, 1–225);

(d) if it has not been signed, as required by section 2(1) of the *Administration of Justice (Miscellaneous Provisions) Act* 1933 (see *post*, §§ 1–231 *et seq.*);

(e) if the time limits for the beginning of trials have not been complied with (see *post*, § 4–1);

(f) if it charges an offence that is not known to law (see *post* §§ 1–236 and 7–75); **1–191**

(g) if it charges an offence that is not triable on indictment and which does not satisfy the requirements of section 40 of the *CJA* 1988 (see *ante*, §§ 1–75ai *et seq.*);

(h) if it charges an offence in respect of which any necessary consents to the institution or continuation of the prosecution have not been obtained (see *post*, §§ 1–212 and 1–244 *et seq.*, and, in respect of companies in liquidation, see *ante*, § 1–81a) or in respect of which any necessary notification of a decision to bring proceedings has not been given (see *ante*, § 1–94);

(i) if it charges an offence in respect of which any relevant limitation period had expired before the commencement of the prosecution (see *post*, §§ 1–199 *et seq.*);
(j) if it would amount to an abuse of process to permit the prosecution to pursue it (see *post*, §§ 4–47 *et seq.*);
(k) if it charges the defendant with an offence for which he has already been convicted or acquitted or pardoned (see *post*, §§ 4–114 *et seq.*);
(l) if it charges a person who is immune from prosecution or whose acts at the relevant time are not susceptible to the jurisdiction of the Crown or who, by reason of age, was incapable in law of committing an offence at the relevant time (see *ante*, §§ 1–82 *et seq.*, and *post*, § 4–111);
(m) if it charges a person, who has been extradited from abroad, with an offence that was not covered by the extradition proceedings (see *ante*, §§ 1–96 *et seq.*).

The original version of the above list was referred to, with apparent approval, in *R. v. Central Criminal Court and Nadir, ex p. Director of Serious Fraud Office*, 96 Cr.App.R. 248 at 252, DC.

(2) Means by which objection may be taken

1–192 The most usual means of taking objection to an indictment, or any count in an indictment, is by way of a motion to quash; as to which, see *post*, §§ 1–236 *et seq.* Section 2(3) of the *Administration of Justice (Miscellaneous Provisions) Act* 1933 (*post*, § 1–221) specifically provides that an indictment preferred otherwise than in accordance with the provisions of section 2(2) of that Act shall be liable to be quashed. However, in some circumstances judicial review of an underlying committal, transfer or sending for trial may be appropriate. See further *post*, §§ 1–209 *et seq.*

The proper way to challenge an indictment on the basis of abuse of process is to seek a stay of that indictment or of the relevant counts: *R. v. Central Criminal Court, ex p. Randle and Pottle*, 92 Cr.App.R. 323, DC.

The usual time to move to quash an indictment is before the defendant has pleaded to it, but see the authorities cited *post*, § 1–240. Section 2(3)(b) of the 1933 Act (*post*, § 1–221) sets out certain limitations on the quashing of counts pursuant to section 2(3) if no application to quash was made at the trial. In certain cases it may be cost effective, and assist in the efficient administration of the courts, if applications to quash the indictment are dealt with at a preliminary hearing by the trial judge; the substantive trial being adjourned to a later date if the application to quash is refused. See *post*, §§ 4–84m, 4–84t as to the consideration of questions of joinder or severance at preparatory hearings.

See *post*, §§ 4–111, 4–112 as to the ways in which objection may be taken on a point of jurisdiction; and see *post*, §§ 4–153 *et seq.* as to the method of entering a plea in bar.

(3) Dealing with the objection

1–193 If an application to quash, made either before or during trial, is well founded, the judge should quash the indictment (or, in an appropriate case, the relevant part thereof) unless the defect complained of does not go to jurisdiction and can be cured without any undue prejudice to the defendant. As to the curing of defects, see *post*, § 1–194. See also *post*, §§ 1–238 *et seq.*

As to whether a particular defect is such as to render an application to quash well founded, see generally *ante*, §§ 1–35, 1–161 *et seq.*, and *post*, §§ 1–195 *et seq.*

If an objection based on abuse of process is well founded, the indictment, or relevant part thereof, should be stayed: *R. v. Central Criminal Court, ex p. Randle and Pottle*, *ante*. In *ex p. Randle and Pottle* mention is made of the possibility of the existence of a power to remove the stay if, for example, the court had been misled when granting it.

An indictment is not an indivisible entity and a court has an inherent jurisdiction to stay an indictment in part, in an appropriate case, where there are a number of counts or a number of defendants: *R. v. Munro*, 97 Cr.App.R. 183, CA. See further *post*, § 1–220.

(4) Curing the defect

Certain defects cannot be cured, *e.g.* if the indictment has been preferred otherwise than in accordance with section 2(2) of the *Administration of Justice (Miscellaneous Provisions) Act* 1933 (*post*, §§ 1–204 *et seq.*), or if any relevant limitation period has expired before the commencement of the prosecution. **1–194**

If the indictment is defective because it has not been served in draft on the Crown Court officer (preferred) within the permitted time, the judge may, in a proper case, give leave to prefer it out of time, *post*, §§ 1–224, 1–225. If it is defective because it has not been signed, the proper officer of the court may sign it to cure the defect, but as to the validity of any proceedings that take place on the indictment before it is signed, see *post*, § 1–232. An adjournment will solve any problem created by a case being listed for trial before the expiration of the period set out in rule 39.1 of the *Criminal Procedure Rules* 2005 (S.I. 2005 No. 384) (*post*, § 4–1). Defects resulting from breaches of Part 14 of the 2005 rules can be dealt with by the giving of any necessary further particulars or by the giving of leave to make suitable amendments, pursuant to section 5 of the *Indictments Act* 1915, provided that no improper prejudice would be caused to the defendant by taking such a course. Further ways in which a defect caused by misjoinder can be dealt with and the effect of such a defect are explained in the authorities referred to *ante*, §§ 1–161 *et seq.*, and *post*, § 1–207.

(5) Consequences of a defect being left uncorrected

A defect in an indictment (*e.g.* in relation to form, jurisdiction, time for preferring) may provide a foundation for an appeal to the Court of Appeal, either under section 1 of the *CAA* 1968 (*post*, §§ 7–36 *et seq.*) or, if the indictment is invalid, pursuant to the inherent discretion which that court has to quash any conviction resulting from an invalid indictment: *Crane v. DPP* [1921] 2 A.C. 299, HL; *R. v. Newland* [1988] Q.B. 402, 87 Cr.App.R. 118, CA. However, the provisions of section 2(3)(b) of the *Administration of Justice (Miscellaneous Provisions) Act* 1933 (*post*, § 1–221) and the authorities which criticise the practice of taking an objection to the form of an indictment for the first time in the Court of Appeal (*post*, § 1–240) should be kept in mind. See the checklist of possible objections, *ante*, § 1–190. **1–195**

The Court of Appeal has no jurisdiction on appeal to amend a defective indictment, but it is not every defect in an indictment or in procedure that will result in the quashing of a conviction. No conviction can stand if the underlying proceedings were a nullity, but it is not every uncorrected defect that will have such a consequence. If the particular defect does not render the proceedings a nullity, the existence of the defect will not necessarily result in the quashing of a conviction. In many of the older cases, the outcome depended upon whether the provision creating the relevant procedure was construed as being mandatory, or merely directory; see, for example, the authorities referred to *post*, §§ 1–225 (time within which indictment to be preferred) and 4–2 (maximum and minimum periods between committal and trial). However, in *R. v. Immigration Appeal Tribunal, ex p. Jeyeanthan*; *Ravichandran v. Secretary of State for the Home Department* [2000] 1 W.L.R. 354, CA (Civ. Div.), it was held that, as a matter of general principle, in determining the effect of non-compliance with a procedural requirement laid down by statute or regulation, the court should consider what the legislator had intended to be the consequence of non-compliance, in the context of the circumstances of the particular case, rather than merely considering whether the requirement is to be categorised as directory or mandatory. Lord Woolf M.R., in his judgment in that case, also made the point that procedural requirements exist for good reason, saying:

> "It must be remembered that procedural requirements are designed to further the interests of justice and any consequence which would achieve a result contrary to those interests should be treated with considerable reservation" (at p. 359H).

This approach was also adopted in *Att.-Gen.'s Reference (No. 3 of 1999)* [2001] 2 A.C. 91, HL, *R. v. Sekhon* [2003] 1 Cr.App.R. 34, CA, and *R. v. Soneji* [2006] 1 A.C. 340, HL. In *Seal v. Chief Constable of South Wales Police* [2005] 1 W.L.R. 3183, CA (Civ. Div.), it was said, referring to those decisions, that there is no doubt that in the present day the courts will strive anxiously to interpret procedural provisions flexibly where that furthers the interests of justice, but that where Parliament has made it absolutely clear what the consequences are of a failure to take a particular step, it is not for the courts to import a discretion or flexibility that is not there. That approach was upheld by the House of Lords on appeal; although Parliament had not expressly indicated that the effect of the relevant procedural irregularity was to invalidate the proceedings in question, it was plain, as a matter of construction, that compliance with the specified procedure was a precondition of any effective proceedings and did not admit of any flexibility; it was not the task of the court to decide whether the existence of the protection which that provided for the defendant was necessary or desirable: *Seal v. Chief Constable of South Wales Police* [2007] 1 W.L.R. 1910, HL.

1–196 In *R. v. Ashton*; *R. v. Draz*; *R. v. O'Reilly* [2006] 2 Cr.App.R. 15 (decided prior to the decision of the House of Lords in *Seal*), the Court of Appeal drew a distinction between the situation where a court acts without jurisdiction (in which case the proceedings will "usually" be invalid) and the situation where there has been a breakdown in the procedures whereby a case progresses through the courts. It held that in the case of a procedural failure the court should first ask itself whether the intention of the legislature was that any act done following that procedural failure should be invalid and if the answer to that question is in the negative, then the court should go on to consider the interests of justice generally, and most particularly whether there is a real possibility that either the prosecution or the defence may suffer prejudice on account of the procedural failure; if there is such a risk, the court must decide whether it is just to allow the proceedings to continue. One problem that arises from this approach is in determining whether the particular defect has been such as to go to the jurisdiction of the court, or whether it is merely procedural. In this regard, it was said in *Sekhon*, *ante*, that:

> "The purpose of rules of procedure is not usually to give or take away a court's jurisdiction. It is the substantive provisions of the legislation creating the power or duty of the court which have given the jurisdiction .... What the procedural provisions are doing is to provide a convenient and just machinery enabling the court to exercise its jurisdiction.
>
> The procedural provisions can be, but usually are not, conditions that have to be fulfilled to give the court jurisdiction. More usually procedural provisions do no more than: (a) enable the court if they are complied with to make orders to require something to be done if it has not been done in accordance with the statutory provisions; or, (b) in the same circumstances to dismiss the proceedings" (at [21]).

Another problem is in determining what the intention of the legislature is to be taken to be in respect of a merely procedural failure in the particular circumstances of a given case. In *R. v. Ashton*; *R. v. Draz*; *R. v. O'Reilly*, the Court of Appeal, when applying to the factual situation before it the test that it had stated, did not seem to consider that an apparent statutory requirement for the existence of an indictment went either to the jurisdiction of the court to deal with a case in the absence of an indictment, or indicated an intention on the part of the legislature that proceedings without an indictment should be invalid: see further *ante*, § 1–35. In reaching its decision, the court departed from a long line of previous authority to the effect that proceedings will be a nullity in the absence of a valid indictment, concluding that the outcome of those previous cases would have been different if they had been decided by reference to the principles in *Soneji* and *Sekhon*. Those previous authorities included *R. v. Thomson and Clein*, 61 Cr.App.R. 108, CA (*post*, §§ 1–206 *et seq.*, and 1–214), *R. v. Cairns*, 87 Cr.App.R. 287, CA (*post*, § 1–214), *R. v. Morais*, 87 Cr.App.R. 9, CA (*post*, § 1–232), and *R. v. Newland* [1988] Q.B. 402, 87 Cr.App.R. 118, CA (*ante*, §§ 1–161 *et seq.*).

However, in *R. v. Clarke and McDaid* [2008] 2 Cr.App.R. 2, the House of Lords overturned the decision of the court below, which had regarded itself as bound by *R. v. Ashton*; *R. v. Draz*; *R. v. O'Reilly*, to dismiss an appeal against conviction in a case where there had been no signed indictment, but otherwise no improper prejudice to the appellant. This was the same situation as that which had resulted in the quashing of the conviction in *Morais* (*ante*, and *post*, § 1–232). The House of Lords held that on a proper construction of the relevant legislation (*post*, § 1–231) in the context of the situation under consideration, it was an inescapable conclusion that Parliament intended that a bill of indictment should not become an indictment until it had been duly signed and that there could be no valid trial on indictment in the absence of an indictment. Their Lordships approved of the approach that had been adopted by the Court of Appeal in *Morais* (at [9], [20] and [42]), in effect concluding that, as a matter of statutory construction, the requirement as to the signing of the bill of indictment was a condition precedent to the existence of a valid indictment and that the existence of a valid indictment is itself a condition precedent to a valid trial on indictment. The matter is one of substantive validity and jurisdiction, in respect of which considerations of prejudice and substantive merits are irrelevant. Lord Bingham commented that "if the state exercises its coercive power to put a citizen on trial for serious crime a degree of formality is not out of place" (at [17]). As Lord Brown observed, "the problem is easily enough avoided and will only occur if the Crown is at fault" (at [40]). Lord Bingham also said that "the decisions in *R. v. Sekhon* and *R. v. Soneji* are valuable and salutary, but the effect of the sea-change that they wrought has been exaggerated and they do not warrant a wholesale jettisoning of all rules affecting procedure irrespective of their legal effect" (at [20]). Lord Rodger said that "the true significance of the decision in *Soneji* lies ... in the approval of the view that any classification into mandatory or directory is the end of the relevant inquiry, not the beginning, and that the better test is to ask 'whether it was a purpose of the legislation that an act done in breach of the provision should be invalid'" (at [28]). See also *ante*, §§ 1–190 *et seq.*, and the individual topics to which cross-references are there given.

In *R. v. Marchese* [2008] 2 Cr.App.R. 12, CA, it was held, having considered the principles in *R. v. Clarke and McDaid*, that if a count is bad for duplicity (*ante*, §§ 1–135 *et seq.*), it does not automatically follow that a conviction on that count will be quashed; the relevant question remains whether the duplicity resulted in a risk of injustice to the defendant (in respect of which, see the principles at § 1–136).

For detailed consideration of the approach of the Court of Appeal to appeals against conviction based on allegations that the indictment was defective, see *post*, §§ 7–75 *et seq.* (appeals under the *CAA* 1968, s.2), and § 7–103 and §§ 7–289 *et seq.* (appeals involving the residual jurisdiction of the Court of Appeal to quash a conviction where the proceedings were a nullity). **1–197**

As to the possibility of issuing a writ of *venire de novo* where there has been an invalid trial, see *post*, §§ 7–352 *et seq.*, but this will not usually be done where, for example, a significant part of a sentence has already been served as a result of the invalid trial (as in *R. v. Newland* and *R. v. Clarke and McDaid*).

I. JURISDICTION UNAFFECTED

Indictments Act 1915, s.8

8.—(1) Nothing in this Act or the rules thereunder shall affect the law or practice relating to the jurisdiction of a court or the place where an accused person can be tried, nor prejudice or diminish in any respect the obligation to establish by evidence according to law any acts, omissions, or intentions which are legally necessary to constitute the offence with which the person accused is charged, nor otherwise affect the laws of evidence in criminal cases. **1–198**

(2) In this Act, unless the context otherwise requires, the expression "the court" means the court before which any indictable offence is tried or prosecuted.

(3) The provisions of this Act relating to indictments shall apply to ... any pleas, replication, or other criminal pleading, with such modifications as may be made by rules under this Act.

[This section is printed as repealed in part by the *CLA* 1967, s.10(2), Sched. 3, Pt III; and the *CLA* 1977, s.65(5), Sched. 13.]

VI. TIME FOR COMMENCEMENT OF PROSECUTION

A. AT COMMON LAW

At common law, there is no time limit for commencing a suit by the Crown; and therefore, in all cases where a time is not limited by statute, a prosecution may be commenced at any length of time after the offence. However, delay in commencing or **1–199** pursuing a prosecution may amount to an abuse of the process of the court: see *post*, §§ 4–47 *et seq*.

B. STATUTORY LIMITATIONS ON THE PROSECUTION OF OFFENCES

(1) General time limits

Magistrates' Courts Act 1980, s.127

Limitation of time

1–200 **127.**—(1) Except as otherwise expressly provided by any enactment and subject to subsection (2) below, a magistrates' court shall not try an information or hear a complaint unless the information was laid, or the complaint made, within 6 months from the time when the offence was committed, or the matter of complaint arose.

(2) Nothing in—

(a) subsection (1) above; or

(b) subject to subsection (4) below, any other enactment (however framed or worded) which, as regards any offence to which it applies, would but for this section impose a time-limit on the power of a magistrates' court to try an information summarily or impose a limitation on the time for taking summary proceedings,

shall apply in relation to any indictable offence.

(3) Without prejudice to the generality of paragraph (b) of subsection (2) above, that paragraph includes enactments which impose a time-limit that applies only in certain circumstances (for example, where the proceedings are not instituted by or with the consent of the Director of Public Prosecutions or some other specified authority).

(4) Where, as regards any indictable offence, there is imposed by any enactment (however framed or worded, and whether falling within subsection (2)(b) above or not) a limitation on the time for taking proceedings on indictment for that offence no summary proceedings for that offence shall be taken after the latest time for taking proceedings on indictment.

1–200a As to the new method by which a "public prosecutor" may, by virtue of section 29 of the *CJA* 2003, institute criminal proceedings (issue and service of documents called a "written charge" and a "requisition"), see *post*, § 1–203. Sections 30 and 31 of the 2003 Act make further provision as to the procedure to be followed in that regard and in respect of the procedure for the laying of an information, as does Part 7 of the *Criminal Procedure Rules* 2005 (S.I. 2005 No. 384), as substituted by the *Criminal Procedure (Amendment) Rules* 2008 (S.I. 2008 No. 2076), para. 8, and Sched. 1. Section 30(5) of the 2003 Act makes provision to the effect that, except where the context otherwise requires, any reference in any prior enactment (i) which is or includes a reference to an information within the meaning of section 1 of the *MCA* 1980, or to the laying of such an information, is to be read as including a reference to a written charge or to the issue of a written charge, and (ii) which is or includes a reference to a summons under section 1 of that Act or to a justice of the peace issuing such a summons is to be read as including a reference to a requisition or to a public prosecutor issuing a requisition. As to the extent to which these provisions of the 2003 Act are in force, see *post*, § 1–203.

1–201 As to the procedure to be followed for the laying of a valid written information or complaint, see *R. v. Manchester Stipendiary Magistrate, ex p. Hill* [1983] A.C. 328, HL. It was said, *per curiam*, in *Schiavo v. Anderton* [1987] Q.B. 20, 83 Cr.App.R. 228, DC, that although an information may be laid either orally or in writing it must be an information designed for the purpose of initiating criminal proceedings; a deliberate act which commences in the conventional sense a prosecution which ultimately will have the effect of bringing an offence and an offender before the court. In *R. v. Enfield Magistrates' Court, ex p. Caldwell*, 161 J.P. 336, DC, it was held that where an arrest warrant was issued upon an information laid within the time limit prescribed by section 127 of the 1980 Act, and the accused was thereafter arrested and charged after the expiration of that period, the proceedings against him were commenced by the laying of the information and were not out of time; the later charging may have been otiose (the defendant had argued that the information had been laid for the purpose only of effecting his arrest, as demonstrated by the fact that he was subsequently charged with the same matter, and did not manifest an intention to begin proceedings). See *Criminal Law Week* 1997/14/17 for a critical analysis of this decision. See also *R. v. Hull*, *post*, § 1–203.

If, on evidence of whatever nature before the court, justices doubt the date of the information, such that it could have been laid outside the time limit, they should decline jurisdiction; it is a matter for their determination in accordance with the ordinary criminal standard of proof: *Atkinson v. DPP*, 168 J.P. 472, DC (considering the system in use for the laying of informations by the police and the issue of summonses by magistrates' courts, *viz.* that the information date would be dictated by the date when the police first make an entry of an alleged offence on the computer system to which both they and the courts have access, but that entry can be added to, or corrected, and it is only when the police consider that all the necessary details to constitute an information are included that they "validate" the entry, at which point someone in the magistrates' court may issue a summons).

An information had been laid by fax within the relevant time when it could be properly inferred that it had been retrievable within that time, whether or not it had in fact been retrieved; whether it had been so retrievable was a matter to be established by inference or otherwise; in the absence of contrary evidence, fax headers and transmission sheets are capable of establishing the necessary facts: *Department for Environment, Food and Rural Affairs v. Rockall* [2007] 3 All E.R. 258, DC.

Where an information for a summary offence is laid within the statutory time limit, but, as a result of a failure to serve the summons, a fresh information is laid outside the time limit, there is no jurisdiction to try a summons resulting from the fresh information: *R. v. Network Sites Ltd, ex p. London Borough of Havering* [1997] Crim.L.R. 595, DC. However, more than one summons may be issued on the basis of an information laid within the time limit (*ex p. Fielding*, 25 J.P. 759, DC), and a second summons issued after the expiration of the time limit will be valid if the information upon which it was based was laid within the time limit: *R. v. Clerkenwell Magistrates' Court, ex p. Ewing*, *The Times*, June 3, 1987, DC.

As to steps that have been held sufficient to satisfy the requirement that an information be laid within six months of the commission of an offence, see also *R. v. Pontypridd Juvenile Magistrates' Court, ex p. B.* [1988] Crim.L.R. 842, DC; and *R. v. Kennett JJ., ex p. Humphrey and Wyatt* [1993] Crim.L.R. 787, DC.

By reason of the definition of "indictable offence" in Schedule 1 to the *Interpretation Act* 1978 (Appendix B–28), "indictable offence" in section 127(2) includes an offence triable either way: *Kemp v. Liebherr-GB Ltd* [1987] 1 All E.R. 885, DC.

A judge of the Crown Court exercising the powers of a district judge (magistrates' courts), pursuant to section 66 of the *Courts Act* 2003, is bound by the time limit in section 127: see *R. v. Ashton*; *R. v. Draz*; *R. v. O'Reilly* [2006] 2 Cr.App.R. 15, CA, and *post*, § 2–8.

As to the power to amend an information that has been laid within the general six month time limit, so as to allege outside that time limit a different summary offence, and as to the exercise of that power, see *R. v. Newcastle upon Tyne JJ., ex p. John Bryce (Contractors) Ltd* [1976] 1 W.L.R. 517, DC, *Simpson v. Roberts*, *The Times*, December 21, 1984, DC, *R. v. Scunthorpe JJ., ex p. McPhee and Gallagher*, 162 J.P. 635, DC (and the commentary thereon at *Criminal Law Week* 1998/10/02), *Ward v. London Borough of Barking and Dagenham* [1999] Crim.L.R. 920, DC (unfair to permit amendment outside the six-month period where information drafted in such a way that impossible to understand from it precisely what offence alleged), *R. v. Thames Magistrates' Court, ex p. Stevens*, 164 J.P. 233, DC, *Shaw v. DPP*, 171 J.P. 254, DC (permissible where substituted charge alleged the "same misdoing", but should not be permitted where unrepresented and absent defendant not given advance notice, and substituted charge carried possibility of prison sentence), *R. v. Ashton*; *R. v. Draz*; *R. v. O'Reilly* (*ante*), and *R. (Thornhill) v. Uxbridge Magistrates' Court and CPS*, 172 J.P. 297, QBD (Silber J.) (distinct difference found to exist between the original charge of failing to provide a specimen of urine and the improperly amended charge of failing to provide a specimen of breath). See also *post*, § 1–202.

It is not permissible to amend an information after the expiration of the time limit so as to substitute a subsidiary company for its parent company, a separate legal entity (as opposed to correcting a misdescription of the company originally charged); to permit such a course would amount to the preferment of a charge against a new defendant outside the time limit: *Sainsbury's Supermarkets Ltd and J. Sainsbury plc v. H.M. Courts Service (South West Region, Devon and Cornwall area), Plymouth City Council (interested party)*, 170 J.P. 690, DC.

Section 127 of the 1980 Act provides a bar on the *trial* of an information that has not been laid within six months from the time when the offence was committed, not a bar on the *laying* of an information in such circumstances; where, therefore, an information alleges that a summary offence has been committed on a date more than six months prior to the date on which the information was laid, but could have alleged its commission on a date within the six-month period (because particular offence is a continuing one), amendment of the information is permissible, after the expiry of the time limit, so as to allege a date within the time limit, if that can be done without unfairness: *R. v. Blackburn JJ., ex p. Holmes* [2000] Crim.L.R. 300, DC (not unfair to allow amendment when accused had been under no misapprehension as to what he was alleged to have done).

In so far as the effect of section 731(2) of the *Companies Act* 1985 (section 1128 of *Companies Act* 2006) might otherwise be to impose a time limit on the summary prosecution of offences triable either way under that Act, such effect is nullified by section 127(2) of the 1980 Act: *R. v. Thames Magistrates' Court, ex p. Horgan* [1998] 2 Cr.App.R. 47, DC.

See *post*, § 1–203, as to the calculation of time.

(2) Particular provisions as to time

1–202 Details of time limits imposed by particular statutes in relation to the commencement of prosecutions are dealt with together with the offences to which they relate.

The principles applicable in respect of an application to amend an information so as to allege a different offence outside the general time limit provided by section 127(1) of the *MCA* 1980 (*ante*, § 1–201) apply equally when it is sought to amend a charge in circumstances where the institution of new proceedings would be barred by a specific provision as to time; so long as the new allegation arises out of the same, or substantially the same, facts and there is no possible prejudice to the conduct of the defence as a result of the delay, and provided it is in the interests of justice, the court has a discretion to permit an amendment; it is for the justices to balance the important public interest of ensuring that prosecuting authorities commence proceedings within prescribed time limits and of seeing that those alleged to have contravened important statutory provisions are prosecuted: *R. v. Newcastle upon Tyne Magistrates' Court, ex p. Poundstretchers Ltd* [1998] C.O.D. 256, DC.

Where a statute prohibits the institution of a prosecution for an offence after the expiry of a specified period "from its discovery by the prosecutor", discovery does not import any investigation or confirmation of the facts, and so discovering the offence should be taken to mean discovering grounds sufficient to found a reasonable belief that an offence has been committed: *Tesco Stores Ltd v. London Borough of Harrow*, 167 J.P. 657, DC.

As to the time within which a bill of indictment must be preferred, see *post*, §§ 1–224 *et seq*.

As to the time limits for beginning trials on indictment, see *post*, § 4–1.

As to custody time limits, see *post*, §§ 1–266 *et seq*., and §§ 3–56 *et seq*.

See also the right to trial within a reasonable time, guaranteed by Articles 5(3) and 6(1) of the ECHR, as implemented by the *Human Rights Act* 1998, *post*, §§ 16–43, 16–54, 16–57 and 16–73.

C. COMMENCEMENT OF PROSECUTION

1–203 The commencement of the prosecution is the laying of the information or complaint, or the preferring of the indictment when there are no proceedings in the magistrates' court; or, it would seem, the arrest of the accused person or the application for a summons or warrant in respect of the offence: see 2 Hale 72; *R. v. West* [1898] 1 Q.B. 174 at 177. See also *Thorpe v. Priestnall* [1897] 1 Q.B. 159 at 162; *Robertson v. Page* [1943] S.C. (5) 32; *R. v. Hughes*, 43 J.P. 556; and *R. v. O'Connor* [1913] 1 K.B. 557. However, the mere issuing of a warrant to apprehend the accused has been held not to be a commencement of the prosecution, unless it is shown to have been executed within the time limited for the commencement of the prosecution: *R. v. Hull* (1860) 2 F. & F. 16. Proof of the existence of a warrant to apprehend the accused is not evidence of the commencement of such a prosecution, although the warrant was issued within the period limited for the commencement of a prosecution and although it recites the laying of the information. The information itself must be given in evidence: *R. v. Parker* (1864) L. & C. 459. See also *R. v. Casbolt* (1869) 11 Cox 385. *Cf.* the *Prosecution of Offences Act* 1985, s.15(2) (*post*, § 1–265), and the *PCA* 2002, s.85, *post*, § 5–646. The process referred to in section 2 of the *Administration of Justice (Miscellaneous Provisions) Act* 1933 (*post*, §§ 1–204; 1–221) as preferring a bill of indictment is now described in rule 14.1(1) of the *Criminal Procedure Rules* 2005 (S.I. 2005 No. 384) (*post*, § 1–224) as service of a draft indictment on the Crown Court officer.

Section 29 of the *CJA* 2003 creates a new method by which a "public prosecutor" may institute criminal proceedings (issue and service of documents called a "written charge" and a "requisition"). The definition of "public prosecutor" is set out in subsections (5) (as amended by the *SOCPA* 2005, s.59, and Sched. 4, para. 196, and the *Commissioners for Revenue and Customs Act* 2005, s.50(1) and (6), and Sched. 4, para. 130) and (6). Subsection (4) provides that, in consequence of the new procedure, a public prosecutor is not to have the power to lay an information for the purpose of obtaining the issue of a summons under section 1 of the *MCA* 1980. See *ante*, § 1–200a, as to further provisions in respect of this new method of instituting criminal proceedings. The relevant provisions of the 2003 Act are in force to a specified and limited extent, in respect of certain prosecutors, offences and locations: see the *Criminal Justice Act 2003 (Commencement No. 16) Order* 2007 (S.I. 2007 No. 1999) and the *Criminal Justice Act 2003 (Commencement No. 21) Order* 2008 (S.I. 2008 No. 1424).

The answer to the question of when proceedings are instituted or begun may vary according to the context of the particular statutory provision and its purpose: *DPP v. Cottier* [1996] 2 Cr.App.R. 410, DC (as to which, see *ante*, § 1–94).

As to when "proceedings" can be said to have been "instituted" in relation to the obtaining of any necessary consents from the Attorney-General, see *post*, § 1–248.

Section 15(2) of the *Prosecution of Offences Act* 1985 (*post*, § 1–265) identifies the various events that amount to the institution of proceedings for the purposes of Part 1 of that Act.

As to when an information is laid for the purpose of section 127 of the *MCA* 1980 (*ante*, § 1–200), see *ante*, § 1–201.

The time is calculated by excluding the day on which the offence is said to have been committed, and including the day on which the prosecution begins: *Radcliffe v. Bartholomew* [1892] 1 Q.B. 161. Sundays are included in computing the time unless expressly excluded: *R. v. Middlesex JJ.* (1843) 2 Dowl. (n.s.) 719 at 724. An amendment of an information does not necessarily prevent the information as originally laid from being the commencement of the prosecution unless a different offence is charged: *R. v. Wakeley*, 14 Cr.App.R. 121, CCA. In Acts passed since 1850, "month" means calendar month: *Interpretation Act* 1978, Sched. 1 (Appendix B–28).

As to when time begins to run for the purposes of the requirement in Article 6 of the ECHR for trial within a reasonable time, see the authorities cited at § 16–73, *post*.

VII. PREFERRING THE BILL OF INDICTMENT

A. When a Bill of Indictment may be Preferred

Administration of Justice (Miscellaneous Provisions) Act 1933, s.2(2)

2.—(2) Subject as hereinafter provided no bill of indictment charging any person with an indictable offence shall be preferred unless either— **1–204**

(a) the person charged has been *committed* [sent] for trial for the offence; or (aa) *the offence is specified in a notice of transfer under section 4 of the* Criminal Justice Act *1987 (serious and complex fraud); or*

(ab) *the offence is specified in a notice of transfer under* section 53 *of the* Criminal Justice Act *1991 (violent or sexual offences against children); or*

(ac) *the person charged has been sent for trial for the offence under section 51 (no committal proceedings for indictable-only offences) of the* Crime and Disorder Act *1998 ("the 1998 Act"); or*

(b) the bill is preferred by the direction of the Court of Criminal Appeal or by the direction or with the consent of a judge of the High Court ... ; or

(c) the bill is preferred under section 22B(3)(a) of the *Prosecution of Offences Act* 1985.

Provided that—

(i) *where the person charged has been committed for trial, the bill of indictment against him may include, either in substitution for or in addition to counts charging the offence for which he was committed, any counts founded on facts or evidence disclosed to the magistrates' court inquiring into that offence as examining justices, being counts which may lawfully be joined in the same indictment;*

[(i) where the person charged has been sent for trial, the bill of indictment against him may include, either in substitution for or in addition to any count charging an offence specified in the notice under section 57D(1) [*sic*] of the *Crime and Disorder Act* 1998, any counts founded on material which, in pursuance of regulations made under paragraph 1 of Schedule 3 to that Act, was served on the person charged, being counts which may lawfully be joined in the same indictment;]

(iA) *in a case to which paragraph (aa) or (ab) above applies, the bill of indictment may include, either in substitution for or in addition to any count charging an offence specified in the notice of transfer, any counts founded on material that accompanied the copy of that notice which, in pursuance of regulations under the relevant provision, was given to the person charged, being counts which may lawfully be joined in the same indictment;*

(iB) *in a case to which paragraph (ac) above applies, the bill of indictment may include, either in substitution for or in addition to any count charging an offence specified in the notice under section 51(7) of the 1998 Act, any counts founded on material which, in pursuance of regulations made under paragraph 1 of Schedule 3 to that Act, was served on the person charged, being counts which may be lawfully joined in the same indictment;*

(ii) a charge of a previous conviction of an offence ... may, notwithstanding that it was not included in *the committal* [such notice] or in any such direction or consent as aforesaid, be included in any bill of indictment;

and in paragraph (iA) above "the relevant provision" means section 5(9) of the Criminal Justice Act *1987 in a case to which paragraph (aa) above applies, and paragraph 4 of Schedule 6 to the* Criminal Justice Act *1991 in a case to which paragraph (ab) above applies.*

[This subsection is printed as amended and repealed in part by the *CAA* 1964, s.5, Sched. 2; the *CAA* 1966; the *Supreme Court Act* 1981, s.152(1), Sched. 5; the *Prosecution of Offences Act* 1985, s.31(6), Sched. 2; the *CJA* 1987, s.15, Sched. 2, para.1(1) and (2); the *CJA* 1988, s.170(1), Sched. 15, para. 10; the *CJA* 1991, s.53, Sched. 6, para. 8; the *Statute Law (Repeals) Act* 1993, s.1 and Sched. 1; the *CPIA* 1996, s.47, and Sched. 1, para. 17; and the *CDA* 1998, s.119 and Sched. 8, para. 5. The amendment of proviso (i) effected by the 1996 Act applies only in relation to alleged offences into which no criminal investigation had begun before April 1, 1997: S.I. 1997 Nos 682 & 683 (*post*, § 10–9). The words in italics are repealed and the words in square brackets are substituted or inserted by the *CJA* 2003, ss.41 and 332, Sched. 3, para. 34(1) and (2), and Sched. 37, Pt 4. Of those changes, the substitution of the word "sent" in para. (a) and the substitution of proviso (i) came into force on May 9, 2005, but only in relation to cases sent for trial under s.51A(3)(d) of the *CDA* 1998, and the substitution of the words "such notice" in proviso (ii) came into force on the same date, but only in relation to cases sent for trial under s.51 or s.51A(3)(d) of the *CDA* 1998: *Criminal Justice Act 2003 (Commencement No. 9) Order* 2005 (S.I. 2005 No. 1267). For all other purposes the amendments effected by the 2003 Act come into force on a day or days to be appointed.]

For section 2(1) of the 1933 Act, which makes provision as to the preferment and signing of indictments, see *post*, § 1–231. See also rule 14.1 of the *Criminal Procedure Rules* 2005 (S.I. 2005 No. 384), *post*, § 1–223, which, unlike the 1933 Act, refers to service of a draft indictment on the Crown Court officer, rather than to a bill of indictment being preferred. For section 2(3) of the 1933 Act, which makes provision for the quashing of indictments preferred otherwise than in accordance with section 2(2), see *post*, § 1–221, and see the general principles at §§ 1–195 *et seq.*, *ante*. The opening words of section 2(3) might be thought to provide some indication of the consequence intended by Parliament in respect of a failure to satisfy the criteria and requirements of section 2(2), although the words "be liable" arguably qualify the imperative effect of the word "shall". As to the foundation requirements for the counts which appear on the substantive indictment, see also rule 14.1(5) of the 2005 rules (*ante*, § 1–115). 1–205

The words "the offence", in section 2(2) of the 1933 Act, do not require that the count in the indictment shall be framed exactly as the committal (or transfer, or sent) charge, but only that there is no *substantial* departure from the original charge. The dropping of the words "and with others unknown" on a conspiracy charge is not a substantial departure: *R. v. McDonnell* [1966] 1 Q.B. 233, 50 Cr.App.R. 5, Assizes (Nield J.).

As to the requirement for notice to be given to the defendant as soon as possible of any intention by the prosecutor to include in the draft indictment counts which differ materially from, or are additional to, those on which the defendant was committed for trial, see paragraph IV.34.1 of the consolidated criminal practice direction, *ante*, § 1–111.

Power to join certain summary offences in an indictment

See section 40 of the *CJA* 1988, *ante*, § 1–75ai. 1–205a

Indictment based on committal

If an indictment, or any count on an indictment, is quashed, no further indictment containing the charges that have been quashed may be preferred on the strength of an original committal, the force of that committal having been spent. Accordingly, a judge who is not a High Court judge will have no power to grant leave to prefer a further indictment in such circumstances. This was one of the reasons given by the Court of Appeal in *R. v. Thompson and Clein*, 61 Cr.App.R. 108, CA, for holding that proceedings on such a further indictment had been a nullity (but see now *ante*, §§ 1–195 *et seq.*). However, the court preferred to found its decision on the ground that an indictment can be preferred only once on the basis of one committal. *Thompson and Clein* was referred to in the judgment of the court in *R. v. Newland* [1988] Q.B. 402, 87 Cr.App.R. 118, CA, where it was said that a judge who is not a High Court judge has no power to grant leave to prefer a fresh indictment containing counts which have been deleted from a misjoined indictment (*ante*, §§ 1–161 *et seq.*). 1–206

The remedy for the Crown in such a situation was said to be to obtain leave to prefer a "voluntary bill" of indictment in accordance with the provisions of section 2(2)(b) of the 1933 Act (as to which, see *ante*, § 1–162, and *post*, §§ 1–213 *et seq.*). However, in *R. v. Follett* [1989] Q.B. 338, 88 Cr.App.R. 310, CA, the authorities were extensively reviewed and it was held that where an indictment is invalid, because it transgresses rule 9 of the *Indictment Rules* 1971, a judge of any status, sitting in the Crown Court, may give leave to the Crown to prefer two or more fresh indictments out of time, each of which complies with rule 9 and with section 2(2) of the 1933 Act; the original defective indictment being stayed rather than being quashed or amended by deletion of counts. *Newland* and *Thompson and Clein* were distinguished and explained on the basis that where the first indictment has been quashed (*Thompson and Clein*) or amended by the deletion of one or more counts (*Newland*) the prosecution cannot then produce, or pursue, a second indictment based on the same committal containing the same matters as those which were covered by the quashed indictment, or the deleted counts, because the committal will have been, so to speak, spent. 1–207

1–208 In reaching this decision, the court adopted the narrower, rather than the wider, reason given for the decision in *Thompson and Clein* and referred to *Poole v. R.* [1961] A.C. 223, PC, as authority for the proposition that there can be in existence at the same time two indictments against the same person for the same offence or for offences based on the same facts. *R. v. Groom* [1977] Q.B. 6, 62 Cr.App.R. 242, CA, and the *Practice Direction (Indictment—Joinder of Counts)*, 62 Cr.App.R. 251, CA (now replaced by paragraph IV.34.2 of the consolidated criminal practice direction, *post*, §§ 1–218, 1–219), were cited as authority for the proposition that there can be more than one indictment based on a single committal for any given charge, although it seems to have been appreciated that the practice direction was wider than the decision in *Groom*, on which it was based. Lord Lane C.J. went on in *Follett* to say:

> "The only limitations on indictments based on a single committal are these. First, the indictment or indictments should be preferred in the time laid down by the rules, or such further time in respect of which the trial judge gives leave. Secondly, the offences in the indictment must be offences in respect of which the accused has been committed for trial or are offences in respect of which he may be charged in addition to or substitution for those offences for which he has been committed for trial—the proviso to section 2(2) of the Act of 1933. Thirdly the offences charged in a single indictment must be properly joined in that single indictment" (at pp. 345, 316).

As to misjoinder and its effects, see further *ante*, §§ 1–161 *et seq.* and 1–195 *et seq.* As to the proviso to section 2(2) of the Act of 1933, see *post*, §§ 1–216 *et seq.*, and as to the time for preferring a bill of indictment, see *post*, §§ 1–224 *et seq.*

Nothing in section 2(2) of the 1933 Act can be said to prohibit the joinder in one indictment of charges which have been the subjects of separate committal proceedings: *R. v. Wilson (S. C.)*, 58 Cr.App.R. 169, CA. *See post*, §§ 1–218 *et seq.* as to the joinder of persons or charges separately committed (or transferred) for trial.

Committal defective

1–209 It has been held that it is only on a valid committal that an indictment can be properly founded. If an indictment is founded on an invalid committal it will be liable to be quashed and any proceedings upon that indictment will be a nullity: *R. v. Gee* [1936] 2 K.B. 442, 25 Cr.App.R. 198, CCA. See further the 1997 edition of this work, at §§ 10–19, 10–20, as to the application of this principle, and see *R. v. Coleshill JJ., ex p. Davies* [1971] 1 W.L.R. 1684, DC, *R. v. L. and W.* [1971] Crim.L.R. 481, Assizes (Thomson J.) (defect in procedures then required for committal of person under age of 17 who was jointly charged with a person over that age), and *R. v. A.H.*, 167 J.P. 30, CA, *ante*, § 1–75r. However, these and the following authorities must now be considered in the light of the principles explained *ante*, §§ 1–195 *et seq.*, and see *ante*, § 1–205.

1–210 In *R. v. Lamb* [1968] 1 W.L.R. 1946, CA, it was held that there had been no valid committal where the justices had purported to commit the defendant on a charge alleging an offence not known to law at the relevant time. Similarly, where justices committed for trial on a charge in respect of which there was no jurisdiction to commit: *R. v. Braden*, 87 Cr.App.R. 289, CA (*ante*, § 1–75j).

The fact that the magistrates' court's certificate, following a committal for trial to the Crown Court, stated that the committal had been under legislation not then in force (*viz.* the *MCA* 1980) so far as those proceedings were concerned, did not invalidate the committal: *R. v. Hall*, 74 Cr.App.R. 67, CA. *Hall* was applied in *R. v. Carey*, 76 Cr.App.R. 152, CA, where it was held that the fact that the certificate of committal for trial was not signed by one of the examining justices as required by rule 58(8) of the *Magistrates' Courts Rules* 1968, did not invalidate the committal. It is the validity of the committal itself, rather than the accuracy of the certificate, that is important. See also *R. v. Nelson Group Services (Maintenance) Ltd* [1999] 1 W.L.R. 1526, CA, *post*, § 1–242.

1–211 A failure to follow the prescribed procedure may render a committal invalid, especially if the failure relates directly to the rights of the accused: see *R. v. Barnet Magistrates' Court, ex p. Wood* [1993] Crim.L.R. 78, DC. See also *R. v. Simons*, 37 Cr.App.R. 120, CCA (defendant not put to his election as to mode of trial), and *ante*, § 1–75c.

It has been held that a court is not entitled to quash an indictment because an examination of the evidence leads to the conclusion that the prosecution would fail. Also, that where a count follows a committal charge the court is not entitled to look at the evidence to see whether or not there was evidence to justify the committal: *R. v. Chairman of London County Sessions, ex p. Downes* [1954] 1 Q.B. 1, 37 Cr.App.R. 148, *post* § 4–47 (as endorsed by the Court of Appeal in *R. v. Plant* [2008] 2 Cr.App.R. 27 (at [20]); *R. v. Brooker* [1976] Crim.L.R. 573, CA; *R. v. Jones (J.)*, 59 Cr.App.R. 120, CA; and *R. v. Central Criminal Court and Nadir, ex p. Director of Serious Fraud Office*, 96 Cr.App.R. 248 at 252. See also *R. v. McDonnell* [1966] 1 Q.B. 233, 50 Cr.App.R. 5 (Nield J.).

However, in *R. v. Bedwellty JJ., ex p. Williams* [1997] A.C. 225, HL, it was held (following the decision in the Northern Irish case of *Neill v. North Antrim Magistrates' Court*, 97 Cr.App.R. 121, HL) that, despite dicta to the contrary in various previous English cases, the Divisional Court should exercise its power to quash a committal for trial where the committal has been much influenced by inadmissible evidence, even though some admissible evidence was before the justices. Their Lordships also resolved an issue left open in *Neill* by holding that, in a clear case, a committal for trial should also be quashed on the basis of insufficiency of evidence, even where further evidence to establish a prima facie case could be put before the Crown Court. Their Lordships emphasised that in both situations the discretion to grant *certiorari* should only be exercised on solid grounds (emphasised in the subsequent case of *R. v. Whitehaven JJ., ex p. Thompson* [1999] C.O.D. 15, DC) and that the question of whether justices were correct in finding, on admissible evidence, a case to justify committal, will often be more appropriately dealt with on a submission of no case at the close of the prosecution evidence in the Crown Court, or even on a pre-trial application grounded on abuse of process. The possibility of the Crown Court quashing the indictment on the basis of invalidity of the committal does not appear to have been canvassed. In *R. v. Dorset Magistrates' Court, ex p. Cox* [1997] C.O.D. 86, QBD (apparently decided without reference to the *Bedwellty* case), one of the reasons given for the refusal to grant judicial review of a committal for trial was that the applicant had not exhausted all his avenues of challenge in that his application to the Crown Court to quash the indictment had yet to be heard. 1–212

The *Bedwellty JJ.* decision was applied in *R. v. Belmarsh Magistrates' Court, ex p. Gilligan* [1998] 1 Cr.App.R. 14, DC, where certain material was held to have been inadmissible in evidence and, accordingly, the committal on certain charges was quashed.

It should be noted that the court has a discretion whether to grant a remedy in judicial review proceedings, whereas, it is submitted, the absence of prejudice to the defendant is irrelevant on a motion to quash the indictment if any irregularity in the committal proceedings that is relied upon is sufficient to render those proceedings a nullity (*cf. R. v. Clarke and McDaid, ante*, § 1–196).

For a committal for trial under section 6(2) of the *MCA* 1980 (*post*, § 10–9) to be valid, all that is necessary is that the magistrates' court is satisfied that all the evidence tendered by the prosecution falls within section 5A(3) of that Act (*post*, § 10–15) and that no submission of no case is made; the fact that a statement essential to support the charge is omitted from the papers is irrelevant: *R. v. Harding (deceased)* [1998] Crim.L.R. 877, CA.

In the event of a failure by the prosecution to comply with its pre-committal disclosure obligations (*post*, §§ 12–47 *et seq.*), the remedy is not to quash the committal proceedings; it lies in the hands of the trial judge who is best placed to assess the effect of the non-disclosure; the right to a fair trial, guaranteed by Article 6 of the ECHR (*post*, § 16–57) relates to the proceedings taken as a whole; a flaw at one stage of the proceedings may be rectified at the next: *R. v. Bow Street Magistrates' Court, ex p. Finch and Bossino* [1999] 10 *Archbold News* 1, DC.

Where some consent that is required to the institution of proceedings is not obtained, the whole of any trial that takes place, including the committal proceedings, is a nullity and a conviction which occurs in such circumstances will be quashed: *R. v. Angel*, 52 Cr.App.R. 280, CA; *R. v. Pearce*, 72 Cr.App.R. 295, CA (*post*, § 1–244).

Indictment based on transfer or sending

1–212a There would seem to be no reason why, as in the case of committal proceedings (*ante*, §§ 1–209 *et seq.*), section 2(2) of the 1933 Act should not be interpreted so as enable an indictment to be founded only on valid transfer or sending procedures, thus enabling an application to be made to quash an indictment founded on a purported transfer or sending procedure which was in fact so defective as to be a nullity, but see *ante*, §§ 1–195 *et seq.*, 1–205. Again, as in respect of a defective committal, any such application would be in addition to any right to apply to quash the transfer or sending by way of judicial review, as to which see *R. v. Salford Magistrates' Court, ex p. Gallagher* [1994] Crim.L.R. 374, DC, *ante*, § 1–41. However, once there has been a transfer or sending to the Crown Court the only way to challenge the sufficiency of the evidence, in advance of the substantive trial, is by way of a dismissal application in that court and a decision made in respect of such an application is not susceptible of judicial review, as to which see *ante*, § 1–40, and *post*, § 7–10. Defects in the notice required by the sending procedure will not invalidate the sending: see *Bentham v. Governor of H.M. Prison Wandsworth* [2006] Crim.L.R. 855, DC, *ante*, § 1–23.

Indictment based on voluntary bill

1–213 As to the procedure for the preferment of a bill of indictment with the consent of a judge of the High Court, see the *Indictments (Procedure) Rules* 1971, *post*, §§ 1–226 *et seq.* A bill preferred in this way is commonly referred to as a "voluntary bill".

In *Brooks v. DPP* [1994] 1 A.C. 568, the Privy Council was concerned with the preferment of a voluntary bill where the charge had been dismissed in committal proceedings. A balanced approach was called for; the decision of the magistrates should be treated with the greatest respect; there must be exceptional circumstances to warrant a prosecution. Where an application was made for a voluntary bill when there had been no committal proceedings it should be borne in mind that such proceedings are an important element for the protection of the accused, while regard must also be had to the interests of the Crown acting on behalf of the community. In *R. v. DPP, ex p. Moran* [1999] 3 *Archbold News* 3, DC, it was held that the prosecution had been justified in seeking a voluntary bill where there had been persistent, deliberate and orchestrated attempts to frustrate and delay, if not to sabotage altogether, old-style committal proceedings by means of late, unannounced and technical objections. See also *post*, § 1–227.

A defendant should not be deprived of the opportunity of making an application for the dismissal of a charge sent for trial under section 51 of the *CDA* 1998 (*ante*, §§ 1–17 *et seq.*) by the device of obtaining the consent of a judge of the High Court for the preferment of a voluntary bill of indictment: *R. v. X. and Y.* [1999] 5 *Archbold News* 4, CCC (The Recorder of London).

1–214 Where a bill has been preferred with the consent of a judge of the High Court, the Court of Appeal will not inquire into the exercise of the judge's discretion, so long as it is clear that he had jurisdiction to deal with the application for leave to prefer the bill: *R. v. Rothfield*, 26 Cr.App.R. 103, CCA. See also *R. v. Raymond* [1981] Q.B. 910, 72 Cr.App.R. 151, CA. The Divisional Court has no jurisdiction to review the decision of a High Court judge to give leave to prefer a voluntary bill: *R. v. Manchester Crown Court, ex p. Williams and Simpson* [1990] Crim.L.R. 654, DC (*ex p. Moran*, *ante*, was an attempt to review a prosecutor's decision to seek leave).

A judge who is not a judge of the High Court has no jurisdiction to direct or consent to the preferment of a voluntary bill and, if he purports to do so, any proceedings on the indictment that results will be a nullity: *R. v. Thompson and Clein*, 61 Cr.App.R. 108, CA. *Thompson and Clein* was applied in *R. v. Cairns*, 87 Cr.App.R. 287, CA, where the defendant having been committed for trial on seven charges, a voluntary bill was subsequently preferred by leave of a High Court judge in respect of a further charge. The circuit judge at trial authorised the preferment of a new indictment containing all eight charges. It was held that this indictment was a nullity and that only a judge of the High Court or the Court of Appeal had jurisdiction to authorise such a course. *Cf.* the practice approved in *R. v. Follett* [1989] Q.B. 338, 88 Cr.App.R. 310, CA, *ante*,

§ 1–207, and see *R. v. Wells* and *R. v. Allcock*, *ante*, § 1–150, as to the power to amend an indictment preferred under the voluntary bill procedure so as to add a count charging an offence disclosed on the material that had been before the High Court judge who granted leave to prefer the bill. As to questions of validity, see now also *ante*, §§ 1–195 *et seq.*, 1–205.

A judge who is not a judge of the High Court does have power to amend an indictment preferred under the voluntary bill procedure so as to add a defendant who has been separately committed for trial on the same charge: *R. v. Ismail*, 92 Cr.App.R. 92, CA. See also *post*, §§ 1–218 *et seq.* **1–215**

As to the preferment of a voluntary bill in respect of a charge which a defendant already faces on another indictment, see *post*, §§ 1–218 *et seq.*

Counts included pursuant to the proviso to section 2(2) of the 1933 Act

A charge upon which a defendant has not been committed (transferred or sent) for trial cannot properly be included in the indictment, pursuant to the proviso, unless he has been validly committed (transferred or sent) for trial on some charge: *R. v. Lamb* [1968] 1 W.L.R. 1946, CA. **1–216**

As to the inclusion of other counts, pursuant to the proviso, where the defendant is under the age of 18 and has been committed for trial only in respect of a matter coming within section 91 of the *PCC(S)A* 2000, see *R. v. S. (Paul John)* [1999] 1 Cr.App.R. 1, CA, *ante*, § 1–75r.

The charges that may be lawfully added are not confined to charges similar to the committal charge: *R. v. Roe*, 51 Cr.App.R. 10, CA. However, a charge based on evidence or material within the scope of the proviso can, if there was no committal (or sending, or transfer) for trial on that charge, only be the proper subject of an indictment if it is in substitution for or in addition to counts in respect of which there was a committal *and* if it can be lawfully joined in the indictment which was the subject of the committal: *R. v. Lombardi*, 88 Cr.App.R. 179, CA, *ante*, § 1–162. The only circumstances in which a judge is entitled to look at the committal evidence to see whether that material supports a count is where a new charge has been added under the proviso: *R. v. McDonnell* [1966] 1 Q.B. 233, 50 Cr.App.R. 5, Assizes (Nield J.), and *R. v. Jones (J.)*, 59 Cr.App.R. 120 at 126, CA (but see the authorities cited at §§ 1–211, 1–212, *ante*, and see *R. v. Greenfield*, 57 Cr.App.R. 849, CA, *ante*, § 1–136).

The proviso to section 2(2) is not complied with if there is no prima facie case on the evidence or material within the scope of the proviso that it was *the defendant* who committed the offence that is included in the indictment in purported reliance on that proviso. A prima facie case that *someone* committed that offence is not sufficient: *R. v. Dixon*, 92 Cr.App.R. 43, CA.

Where justices have refused to commit on a particular charge, it is open to the prosecution to include in the indictment a count based on that charge without the leave of a judge, but, if the defence object, it is for the judge at trial to rule whether the count comes within proviso (i) to section 2(2) of the 1933 Act, and to disallow it if it does not: *R. v. Morry* [1946] K.B. 153, 31 Cr.App.R. 19, CCA. As to the respect that should be accorded to the decisions of magistrates, see *R. v. Dawson and Wenlock*, 44 Cr.App.R. 87 at 91, CCA. See also *Brooks v. DPP* [1994] 1 A.C. 568, PC, *ante*, § 1–213.

Proviso (iA) does not justify the inclusion in an indictment of a count charging a summary offence founded upon material accompanying a notice of transfer: see *R. v. T. and K.* [2001] 1 Cr.App.R. 32, CA, *ante*, § 1–75aj.

The court has inherent jurisdiction to ensure that the alteration of the original charge when it becomes a count in the indictment, or the addition of further counts, even though they are founded on evidence or material within the scope of the proviso, is not unfair to the defendant: see *R. v. Nisbet* [1972] 1 Q.B. 36, 55 Cr.App.R. 490, CA. See, however, the observations of Lord Dilhorne in *DPP v. Humphrys* [1977] A.C. 1, HL, as to the undesirability of judges refusing to try indictments preferred according to law; and the observations of Lords Diplock and Scarman in *R. v. Sang* [1980] A.C. 402 at 436, 452, 455, HL. These observations must apply equally to individual counts in an **1–217** indictment. See *post*, §§ 4–47 *et seq.*, as to the power of the court to prevent a prosecution from proceeding.

As to whether there is power to add by amendment a count charging an offence that is only disclosed by material served after committal, see *ante*, § 1–149.

As to the power to add counts to an indictment that has been preferred pursuant to the voluntary bill procedure (which practice is not encompassed by the proviso to section 2(2) of the 1933 Act), see *ante*, § 1–150.

Joinder of persons or charges separately committed or transferred for trial

1–218 The practice of joining in the same indictment persons who had been separately committed for trial for offences which can lawfully be charged in counts in the same indictment was approved by the Court of Appeal in *R. v. Groom* [1977] Q.B. 6, 62 Cr.App.R. 242 (and see *R. v. Bell*, 78 Cr.App.R. 305, CA). Prior to *Groom*, the practice had been confined to cases in which the committals had taken place before the indictment in respect of any one committal had been signed. In a subsequent practice direction an extension of the circumstances in which the practice could be applied was approved. That practice direction has now been incorporated in the consolidated criminal practice direction.

Practice Direction (Criminal Proceedings: Consolidation), para. IV.34.2 (as substituted by Practice Direction (Criminal Proceedings: Arraignment) [2008] 1 W.L.R. 154)

IV.34.2 There is no rule of law or practice which prohibits two indictments being in existence at the same time for the same offence against the same person and on the same facts. But the court will not allow the prosecution to proceed on both indictments. They cannot be tried together and the court will require the prosecution to elect the one on which the trial will proceed. Where different defendants have been separately sent or committed for trial for offences which can lawfully be charged in the same indictment then it is permissible to join in one indictment counts based on the separate sendings or committals for trial even if an indictment based on one of them already has been signed. Where necessary the court should be invited to exercise its powers of amendment under section 5 of the *Indictments Act* 1915.

1–219 In holding that the practice (in either form) does not constitute a contravention of section 2(2) of the *Administration of Justice (Miscellaneous Provisions) Act* 1933, the court explained in *Groom* that the purpose of section 2(2) is to prescribe the two circumstances in which an indictment may be preferred and to enable counts to be added to or substituted for a charge or charges on which the defendant named on the indictment had been committed for trial but, in respect of any such additional or substituted count, to ensure that the defendant will not have to answer to a count charging an offence which is not disclosed by the facts or evidence made known to him by the documents founding his committal. The subsection has no relevance to counts charging defendants separately committed and joined in the same indictment unless the indictment includes a count against a defendant charging him with an offence for which he was not committed and which is not disclosed in the documents founding his committal. The addition of a count in which a defendant is *not* charged cannot in relation to *that* defendant infringe section 2(2) because in relation to *that* count the indictment is not against him.

1–220 Section 2(2) of the 1933 Act imposes no prohibition on the joinder of counts based on a committal for trial with counts based on a transfer for trial. That provision identifies the circumstances in which a bill of indictment may be preferred, and limits the counts to those disclosed in the documents founding committal or transfer, but it does not deal with joinder: *R. v. Townsend* [1997] 2 Cr.App.R. 540, CA. See also *ante*, § 1–208.

In *R. v. Munro*, 97 Cr.App.R. 183, CA, the appellant had pleaded guilty to the counts on an indictment, but his co-defendants had pleaded not guilty. A further defendant had then been apprehended and a second indictment preferred against all defendants under the voluntary bill procedure. The first indictment had been stayed save insofar as it charged the appellant and he was sentenced on the guilty pleas that he had entered to it. The other defendants were dealt with on the second indictment. It was held that the partial stay of the first indictment had been within the power of the trial judge and had been a proper exercise of that power. It was further held that there had not been a breach of the requirement, set out in the practice direction, *ante*, § 1–218, that where there are two indictments against a defendant charging the same matter the prosecution must elect as to which is to be proceeded upon; there had been no second indictment in existence against the appellant at the time when he had entered his pleas and those pleas, which had not been withdrawn, remained effective. In the event of any attempt to try the appellant on the duplicate charges that had been included against him on the second indictment a plea of *autrefois convict* would be available to him.

For the power to amend an existing indictment so as to join a defendant who has been separately committed for trial on the same charge, see *R. v. Ismail*, 92 Cr.App.R. 92, CA, and *R. v. Palmer* [2002] Crim.L.R. 973, CA, *ante*, § 1–150.

Administration of Justice (Miscellaneous Provisions) Act 1933, s.2(3)–(8) and Sched. 2

2.—(3) If a bill of indictment preferred otherwise than in accordance with the provisions of the last foregoing subsection has been signed by the proper officer of the court, the indictment shall be liable to be quashed: **1–221**

Provided that—

(a) if the bill contains several counts, and the said provisions have been complied with as respects one or more of them, those counts only that were wrongly included shall be quashed under this subsection; and

(b) where a person who has been *committed* [sent] for trial is convicted on any indictment or any count of an indictment, that indictment or count shall not be quashed under this subsection in any proceedings on appeal, unless application was made at the trial that it should be so quashed.

(4), (5) [*Repealed by* Courts Act *1971, Sched. 11.*]

(6) [*Power to make rules. See* post, *§ 1–223 for such rules.*]

(7) … nothing in this section shall affect any enactment restricting the right to prosecute in particular classes of case.

(8) [*Gives effect to schedule of amendments and repeals.*]

[The opening words of subs. (7) were repealed by the *Statute Law (Repeals) Act* 1993, s.1, and Sched. 1. In subs. (3)(b) the word in square brackets is substituted for the word in italics by the *CJA* 2003, s.41, and Sched. 3, para. 34(1)and (3). That substitution came into effect on May 9, 2005, but only in relation to cases sent for trial under s.51 or 51A(3)(d) of the *CDA* 1998: *Criminal Justice Act 2003 (Commencement No. 9) Order* 2005 (S.I. 2005 No. 1267). For all other purposes the substitution will come into force on a day to be appointed.]

SCHEDULE 2

Consequential adaptations of enactments

1. References in any enactment to the preferment of a bill of indictment before or the finding of an indictment by a grand jury shall (whatever words are used) include respectively references to the preferment and signing of a bill of indictment under this Act.

2.–4. [*Repealed.*]

For section 2(2) of the 1933 Act and the authorities thereon, see *ante*, §§ 1–204 *et seq.* **1–222**
As to the foundation requirements for the counts which appear on the substantive indictment, see also rule 14.1(5) of the *Criminal Procedure Rules* 2005 (S.I. 2005 No. 384) (*ante*, § 1–115). As to the general principles relating to the consequences of uncorrected defects, see *ante*, §§ 1–195 *et seq.*

Proviso (b) to section 2(3) has no application where an indictment is defective for some reason other than contravention of subsection (2): see, for example, *R. v. Wilmot*, 24 Cr.App.R. 63, CCA (duplicity). In *R. v. Nisbet*, 55 Cr.App.R. 490, CA, *ante*, § 1–217, the court expressed the view, *obiter*, that it had an inherent jurisdiction to prevent injustice by quashing convictions in respect of counts added to or substituted for the committal charge, even though they were founded on the evidence contained in the depositions, and despite the fact that no application to quash was made at trial.

B. RULES AS TO PROCEDURE

1–223 The procedure as to the preferment of bills of indictment is regulated by the *Indictments (Procedure) Rules* 1971 (S.I. 1971 No. 2084), made pursuant to section 2(6) of the *Administration of Justice (Miscellaneous Provisions) Act* 1933 (*ante*, § 1–221), and by Part 14 of the *Criminal Procedure Rules* 2005 (*post*), which replaces certain of the 1971 rules.

Criminal Procedure Rules 2005 (S.I. 2005 No. 384), r.14.1

Signature and service of indictment

1–224 **14.1.**—(1) The prosecutor must serve a draft indictment on the Crown Court officer not more than 28 days after—

(a) service on the defendant and on the Crown Court officer of copies of the documents containing the evidence on which the charge or charges are based, in a case where the defendant is sent for trial;

(b) a High Court judge gives permission to serve a draft indictment;

(c) the Court of Appeal orders a retrial; or

(d) the committal or transfer of the defendant for trial.

(2) The Crown Court may extend the time limit, even after it has expired.

(3) Unless the Crown Court otherwise directs, the court officer must—

(a) sign and date the draft, which then becomes an indictment; and

(b) serve a copy of the indictment on all parties.

[This rule is printed as substituted by the *Criminal Procedure (Amendment) Rules* 2007 (S.I. 2007 No. 699), r.9, and Sched. 2.]

1–225 As to the signing of an indictment, see further *post*, §§ 1–231 *et seq*.

As to the requirement for notice to be given to the defendant as soon as possible of any intention by the prosecutor to include in the draft indictment counts which differ materially from, or are additional to, those on which the defendant was committed for trial, see paragraph IV.34.1 of the consolidated criminal practice direction, *ante*, § 1–111.

The procedural rules as to the method of, and time for, preferring a bill of indictment were previously set out in rules 14.1 and 14.2 of the original version of the 2005 rules; they simply repeated provisions to the same effect in the *Indictments (Procedure) Rules* 1971 (*ante*) (as amended). As to the substitution of the present revised Part 14, and as to its commencement and transitional provisions, see *ante*, § 1–108. The process referred to in the previous rules, and still referred to in section 2 of the *Administration of Justice (Miscellaneous Provisions) Act* 1933 (*ante*, §§ 1–204; 1–221), as preferring a bill of indictment is now described in rule 14.1(1) of the 2005 rules as service of a draft indictment on the Crown Court officer.

The power to extend time in the original version of the 1971 rules made no express reference to that power being available once the initial time limit had expired. In *R. v. Sheerin*, 64 Cr.App.R. 68, CA, however, the rule in that original form was held to confer power to extend time even after it had expired (a matter put beyond dispute by subsequent amendment), and that power was held to have been lawfully exercised where the size of the case and the need to involve counsel made the delay understandable and where the delay had caused no prejudice to the defence. The court encouraged the making of applications for an extension within the initial 28 day period where the size of the case makes the need for further time virtually inevitable, but made it clear that prosecuting authorities should not think that they have a licence to delay or that leave to prefer the indictment out of time, or to prefer a voluntary bill of indictment, will always be granted.

As with the previous version of the rules, the present rules would appear to permit the court to grant an extension of time of its own volition, without any application being made by the prosecutor. The previous version of the rules required an application for an extension of time for preferring a bill of indictment to be made in writing, unless a judge of the Crown Court otherwise directed, and further required such an application to include (i) a statement of the reasons why an extension was necessary and (ii) if made after the expiry of the primary period, a statement of the reasons why the application was not made within that period. The new rules are silent as to the procedure to be adopted in respect of the making of an application for an extension of time. In any event, the granting an extension is, it is submitted, the exercise of a judicial power and, as such, it must be founded on good reasons. Under the previous version of the rules, the Crown Court officer could grant a first extension of up to 28 days, but no such power is expressed in the new rule 14.1 and that rule appears to draw a distinction between the "Crown Court officer" and the "Crown Court". As to the meaning of "court" and "court officer", see rule 2.2(1) of the 2005 rules, *post*, § 2–206.

In *R. v. Soffe*, 75 Cr.App.R. 133, CA, it was said in relation to rule 5 (in its original form) that the accused has no right to make representations in respect of any application for an extension of time, but that decision was reached by analogy with the practice that then existed in respect of the procedure for obtaining leave to prefer a voluntary bill of indictment, which has itself now changed (see *post*, § 1–227). It was also said that a breach of those rules does not constitute a material irregularity in the course of a trial or in any way invalidate the proceedings. This view was relied upon by the Court of Appeal in *R. v. Farooki*, 77 Cr.App.R. 257, when dismissing an appeal based on the fact that an indictment had been signed out of time without leave having been obtained from a judge. In *R. v. Clarke and McDaid* [2008] 2 Cr.App.R. 2, HL, it was said (at [14]) that the cases of *Sheerin*, *Soffe* and *Farooki*, exemplify situations where errors relating to indictments fall squarely into the procedural category, as to which see *ante*, §§ 1–195 *et seq*. See also the overriding objective in Part 1 of the 2005 rules, *post*, § 4–84a.

A bill of indictment must be preferred before it can be signed: section 2(1) of the *Administration of Justice (Miscellaneous Provisions) Act* 1933 (*post*, § 1–231). The fundamental distinction between the preferment of a bill and the signing of that bill was explained in *R. v. Stewart*, 91 Cr.App.R. 301, CA, and confirmed in *R. v. Clarke and McDaid*, *ante*. See further *post*, § 1–232. It was also said in *Stewart* that it would be of assistance in preventing applications being made on an erroneous basis if those responsible for indictments, in particular the appropriate officers of the court, were to record on the bill the date of preferment, and of any extension.

The High Court has no jurisdiction to entertain an application for judicial review of a refusal to extend the time for preferring a bill of indictment: *R. v. Isleworth Crown Court, ex p. King* [1992] C.O.D. 298, DC.

Voluntary bill procedure

Indictments (Procedure) Rules 1971, r.2

2. In these Rules— **1–226**

"the appropriate officer" means such officer as may be designated for the purpose in question by arrangements made by or on behalf of the Lord Chancellor;

"the Act" means the *Administration of Justice (Miscellaneous Provisions) Act* 1933;

"committal proceedings" means proceedings before a magistrates' court acting as examining justices;

"sending for trial" means the sending of a person by a magistrates' court to the Crown Court for trial under section 51 of the *Crime and Disorder Act* 1998;

"committal documents" means evidence falling within section 5A(3) of the *Magistrates' Courts Act* 1980 and tendered at any committal proceedings:

"given documents" means documents given to the Crown Court under paragraph 1 of Schedule 3 to the *Crime and Disorder Act* 1998 where a person is sent for trial under section 51 of that Act;

Provided that any requirement of these Rules that an application should be accompanied by a copy of any committal documents or given documents shall, as respects documents mentioned in paragraphs (b) and (d) of section 5A(3) of the *Magistrates' Courts Act* 1980 or paragraph 1 of Schedule 3 to the *Crime and Disorder Act* 1998, be satisfied if a copy of such parts only of those documents as are, in the opinion of the applicant, material, accompanies the application, and the application contains an express statement to that effect.

By virtue of rule 3 of the *Indictments (Procedure) (Amendment) Rules* 1997 (S.I. 1997 No. 711), in any case where committal proceedings have taken place before April 1, 1997, or where the committal proceedings are not ones to which Schedules 1 and 2 to the *CPIA* 1996 apply (*i.e.* those in respect of which no criminal investigation had begun before April 1, 1997), the expression "committal documents" in the rules shall mean the depositions made and other evidence tendered at those proceedings, whether or not they would have fallen within section 5A(3) of the *MCA* 1980 (*post*, § 10–15).

Indictments (Procedure) Rules 1971, r.6

1–226a **6.** An application under section 2(2)(b) of the Act for consent to the preferment of a bill of indictment may be made to a judge of the High Court.

Rules 6 to 10 of the 1971 rules and rule 14.3 of the 2005 rules are concerned with what are commonly referred to as applications for voluntary bills. The history of the procedure provided for in the 1971 rules is detailed in *R. v. Raymond* [1981] Q.B. 910, 72 Cr.App.R. 151, CA. See also *ante*, §§ 1–213 *et seq.* as to the exercise of the power, and generally.

Practice Direction (Criminal Proceedings: Consolidation), para. IV.35
[2002] 1 W.L.R. 2870

Voluntary bills of indictment

1–227 **IV.35.1** Section 2(2)(b) of the *Administration of Justice (Miscellaneous Provisions) Act* 1933 allows the preferment of a bill of indictment by the direction or with the consent of a judge of the High Court. Bills so preferred are known as voluntary bills.

IV.35.2 Applications for such consent must not only comply with each paragraph of the *Indictments (Procedure) Rules* 1971 (S.I. 1971 No. 2084), but must also be accompanied by (a) a copy of any charges on which the defendant has been committed for trial; (b) a copy of any charges on which his committal for trial was refused by the magistrates' court; (c) a copy of any existing indictment which has been preferred in consequence of his committal; (d) a summary of the evidence or other document which (i) identifies the counts in the proposed indictment on which he has been committed for trial (or which are substantially the same as charges on which he has been so committed), and (ii) in relation to each other count in the proposed indictment, identifies the pages in the accompanying statements and exhibits where the essential evidence said to support that count is to be found; (e) marginal markings of the relevant passages on the pages of the statement and exhibits identified under (d)(ii). These requirements should be complied with in relation to each defendant named in the indictment for which consent is sought, whether or not it is proposed to prefer any new count against him.

IV.35.3 The preferment of a voluntary bill is an exceptional procedure. Consent should only be granted where good reason to depart from the normal procedure is clearly shown and only where the interests of justice, rather than considerations of administrative convenience, require it.

IV.35.4 Neither the 1933 Act nor the 1971 Rules expressly require a prosecuting authority applying for consent to the preferment of a voluntary bill to give notice of the application to the prospective defendant or to serve on him a copy of documents delivered to the judge; nor is it expressly required that the prospective defendant have any opportunity to make any submissions to the judge, whether in writing or orally.

IV.35.5 The prosecuting authorities for England and Wales have issued revised guidance to prosecutors on the procedures to be adopted in seeking judicial consent to the preferment of voluntary bills. These procedures direct prosecutors (a) on the making of application for consent to preferment of a voluntary bill, forthwith to give notice to the prospective defendant that such application has been made; (b) at about the same time, to serve on the prospective defendant a copy of all the documents delivered to the judge (save to the extent that they have already been served on him); (c) to inform the prospective defendant that he may make submissions in writing to the judge, provided that he does so within nine working days of the giving of notice under (a) above. Prosecutors will be directed that those procedures should be followed unless there are good grounds for not doing so, in which case prosecutors will inform the judge that the procedures have not been followed and seek his leave to dispense with all or any of them. Judges should not give leave to dispense unless good grounds are shown.

IV.35.6 A judge to whom application for consent to the preferment of a voluntary bill is made will, of course, wish to consider carefully the documents submitted by the prosecutor and any written submissions timeously made by the prospective defendant, and may properly seek any necessary amplification. The judge may invite oral submissions from either party, or accede to a request for an opportunity to make such oral submissions, if the judge considers it necessary or desirable to receive such oral submissions in order to make a sound and fair decision on the application. Any such oral submissions should be made on notice to the other party, who should be allowed to attend.

Indictments (Procedure) Rules 1971, rr.7, 8

7. Every such application shall be in writing, and shall be signed by the applicant or his solicitor. **1–228**

8. Every such application—

(a) shall be accompanied by the bill of indictment which it is proposed to prefer and, unless the application is made by or on behalf of the Director of Public Prosecutions, shall also be accompanied by an affidavit by the applicant, or, if the applicant is a corporation, by an affidavit by some director or officer of the corporation, that the statements contained in the application are, to the best of the deponent's knowledge, information and belief, true;

(b) shall state whether or not any application has previously been made under these Rules or any Rules revoked by these Rules and whether there have been any committal proceedings, and the result of any such application or proceedings; and

(c) shall state whether there has been any sending for trial and any application for dismissal under paragraph 2 of Schedule 3 to the *Crime and Disorder Act* 1998, and the result of any such application.

[Rule 8 is printed as amended by the *Indictments (Procedure) (Amendment) Rules* 2000 (S.I. 2000 No. 3360).]

Rule 8 does not require a Crown Prosecutor to support an application to a High Court judge for a voluntary bill of indictment with an affidavit deposing to the truth of the statements in the application, since section 1(6) of the *Prosecution of Offences Act* 1985 (*post*, § 1–252) confers on Crown Prosecutors "all the powers of the Director (of Public Prosecutions) as to the institution and conduct of proceedings": *ex p. Bray, The Times*, October 7, 1986, DC.

In *R. v. Coleville-Scott* [1990] Crim.L.R. 871, CA, it was held to be proper to combine an application and the affidavit in support thereof in one document. Further, there could be no objection to the judge indicating his assent to the application by signing the draft bill, rather than the application.

On an application for leave, disclosure should be made of, *inter alia*, any previous grant of bail resulting from a refusal to extend a custody time limit: *R. v. Birmingham Crown Court, ex p. Bell*; *R. v. Same, ex p. Brown and Francis* [1997] 2 Cr.App.R. 363, DC.

Indictments (Procedure) Rules 1971, rr.9, 10

9.—(1) Where there have been no committal proceedings and no sending for trial, the application shall state the reason why it is desired to prefer a bill without such proceedings and— **1–229**

(a) there shall accompany the application proofs of the evidence of the witnesses whom it is proposed to call in support of the charges; and

(b) the application shall embody a statement that the evidence shown by the proofs will be available at the trial and that the case disclosed by the proofs is, to the best of the knowledge, information and belief of the applicant, substantially a true case.

(2) Where there have been committal proceedings, and the justice or justices have refused to commit the accused for trial, or there has been a sending for trial, and the charge or charges have been withdrawn or dismissed, the application shall be accompanied by—

(a) a copy of the committal documents or given documents; and

(b) proofs of any evidence which it is proposed to call in support of the charges so far as that evidence is not contained in the committal documents or given documents;

and the application shall embody a statement that the evidence shown by the proofs and (except so far as may be expressly stated to the contrary in the application) the evidence shown by the committal documents or given documents, will be available at the trial and that the case disclosed by the committal documents or given documents and proofs is, to the best of the knowledge, information and belief of the applicant, substantially a true case.

(3) Where the accused has been committed or sent for trial the application shall state why the application is made and shall be accompanied by proofs of any evidence which it is proposed to call in support of the charges, so far as that evidence is not contained in the committal documents or given documents, and, unless the committal documents or given documents have already been transmitted to the judge to whom the application is made, shall also be accompanied by a copy of the committal documents or given documents; and the application shall embody a statement that the evidence shown by the proofs will be available at the trial, and that the case disclosed by the committal documents or given documents and proofs is, to the best of the knowledge, information and belief of the applicant, substantially a true case.

1–230 **10.** Unless the judge otherwise directs in any particular case, his decision on the application shall be signified in writing on the application without requiring the attendance before him of the applicant or of any of the witnesses, and if the judge thinks fit to require the attendance of the applicant or of any of the witnesses, their attendance shall not be in open court.

Unless the judge gives a direction to the contrary, where an applicant is required to attend as aforesaid, he may attend by a solicitor or by counsel.

[Rule 9 is printed as amended by S.I. 1997 No. 711 (*ante*, § 1–226).]

See *R. v. Coleville-Scott*, *ante*, § 1–228.

C. SIGNING OF INDICTMENT

Administration of Justice (Miscellaneous Provisions) Act 1933, s.2(1)

1–231 **2.**—(1) Subject to the provisions of this section, a bill of indictment charging any person with an indictable offence may be preferred by any person before a court in which the person charged may lawfully be indicted for that offence, and where a bill of indictment has been so preferred the proper officer of the court shall, if he is satisfied that the requirements of the next following subsection have been complied with, sign the bill, and it shall thereupon become an indictment and be proceeded with accordingly:

Provided that if the judge ... of the court is satisfied that the said requirements have been complied with, he may, on the application of the prosecutor or of his own motion, direct the proper officer to sign the bill and the bill shall be signed accordingly.

[Printed as repealed in part by the *Courts Act* 1971, s.56, and Sched. 11.]

1–232 For section 2(2), see *ante*, §§ 1–204 *et seq.*

The bill of indictment does not become an indictment until it is signed in accordance with the provisions of section 2(1): see *post*. See also rule 14.1(3)(a) of the *Criminal Procedure Rules* 2005 (S.I. 2005 No. 384) (*ante*, § 1–224), which now provides that the document referred to in rule 14.1 as a draft indictment becomes an indictment once it has been signed and dated by the court officer. In *R. v. Morais*, 87 Cr.App.R. 9, CA, where the indictment had not been signed, the proceedings that had taken place were held to be a nullity, even though a judge of the High Court had given leave to prefer the indictment in accordance with the provisions of section 2(2)(b) of that Act (*ante*, §§ 1–204, 1–213 *et seq.*).

In *R. v. Jackson* [1997] 2 Cr.App.R. 497, CA, the original indictment contained misjoined counts so the judge had directed that new separate bills of indictment be preferred and that, pursuant to section 2(1) of the 1993 Act, such new bills be signed. The proper officer of the court, however, omitted to sign the new bills. The Court of Appeal, distinguishing *Morais*, held that the unsigned indictments, and the proceedings upon them, were not nullities. Where the judge had satisfied himself that the requirements of section 2(2) of the 1933 Act had been satisfied in respect of the bills of indictment that he had directed to be signed, the signature of the proper officer of the court was no more than a meaningless formality and should be deemed to exist. Some support for this approach may be found in *R. v. Sidoli* (1824) 1 Lew. 55.

In *R. v. Clarke and McDaid* [2008] 2 Cr.App.R. 2, the House of Lords upheld the correctness of the decision in *R. v. Morais*. As a matter of statutory construction, the relevant legislation (*ante*, § 1–231) requires a bill of indictment to be signed before it becomes an indictment, so without satisfaction of that condition precedent there can be no valid indictment, and without a valid indictment there can be no valid trial on indictment. The late signing of the indictment during the course of the trial in the case under consideration was held to have made no difference to the invalidity of the proceedings. For further details of that decision, and generally as to the consequences of defects being left uncorrected, see *ante*, §§ 1–195 *et seq.* The decision in *R. v. Jackson* was also endorsed in *R. v. Clarke and McDaid*, as turning on the special facts of the case (at [10]). Further, the decision in *R. v. Laming*, *ante*, § 1–118 (conviction upheld although indictment signed in wrong place) was approved, and the error in that case was said to exemplify the type of errors which fall into the procedural category (at [14]). Such errors will, it seems, have no adverse consequences in the absence of prejudice being demonstrated on the facts of the individual case.

The fundamental distinction between the preferment of a bill of [service of a draft] indictment and the signing of the bill, which converts it into an indictment, was explained in *R. v. Stewart*, 91 Cr.App.R. 301, CA (and confirmed in *R. v. Clarke and McDaid*, *ante*), and it was pointed out that the time limits set out in the relevant rules (*ante*, § 1–224) relate to the preferment, not the signing, of a bill. It was also said that the situation which had resulted in the appeal might not have arisen if, when the bill was signed, the date had been added. That would have removed any uncertainty as to when it was signed. It would also have been of assistance, the court said, if the date of preferment and of the extension of time that had been granted had been recorded on the bill. Those responsible for indictments, in particular the appropriate officers of the court, should consider such steps in the future so as to prevent application being made on an erroneous basis.

Where the appropriate officer of the Crown Court is in doubt whether or not to sign **1–233**
an indictment he should refer the matter to a judge for his decision. If the judge directs the officer not to sign the indictment the position will be the same as if there had been no committal for trial: *R. v. Chairman of London County Sessions, ex p. Downes* [1954] 1 Q.B. 1, 37 Cr.App.R. 148, DC, and see *post*, § 1–241. In *R. v. Abdul Karim*, unreported, June 23, 1975, CCC, the appropriate officer referred to Judge Hines the question whether he should sign a bill of indictment which followed the committal charge but where the only deposition was to the effect that the deponent had read and verified the truth of a statement, which was not attached to the committal documents. There was, therefore, no evidence of the commission of the offence disclosed. Judge Hines, applying *ex p. Downes* (*ante*), decided that the principles relating to the refusal to sign a bill of indictment must be the same as those relating to the quashing of an indictment. He had, therefore, no power to go behind the committal charge and must direct that the indictment should be signed. The judge observed that to rule otherwise would give the officer a discretion not possessed by the court, and would involve requiring him in every case where a count followed a committal charge to determine whether the evidence justified the committal. As to the power of the court, see, however, *ante*, §§ 1–211, 1–212.

D. Copy of Indictment for Parties and Judge

As to the requirement for the court officer to serve a copy of the indictment upon all **1–234**
parties, see rule 14.1(3) of the *Criminal Procedure Rules* 2005 (S.I. 2005 No. 384), *ante*, § 1–224. As to the requirement for notice to be given to the defendant as soon as possible of any intention by the prosecutor to include in the draft indictment counts which differ materially from, or are additional to, those on which the defendant was committed for trial, see paragraph IV.34.1 of the consolidated criminal practice direction, *ante*, § 1–111.

Those engaged in the defence should obtain a copy of the indictment at the earliest **1–235**
possible moment: *R. v. Dickson*, 53 Cr.App.R. 263, CA.

The officer of the court should see that the judge has the actual indictment or an accurate abstract thereof before him: *R. v. Olivo*, 28 Cr.App.R. 173, CCA.

VIII. QUASHING AN INDICTMENT

A. Common Law

Indictments have been quashed because the facts stated in them did not amount to **1–236** an offence punishable by law: see *R. v. Burkett* (1738) Andr. 230; *R. v. Sarmon* (1758) 1 Burr. 516; *R. v. Wright* (1758) 1 Burr. 543; and *R. v. Philpotts* (1843) 1 C. & K. 112. In *R. v. Yates* (1872) 12 Cox 233, an indictment for libel was quashed, the expressions used in the alleged libel not being prima facie libellous, and the indictment containing no averments or innuendoes showing that those expressions were intended to impute improper conduct to the prosecutor.

An indictment is also liable to be quashed if it is defective in form and for a variety of other reasons, see generally *ante*, §§ 1–190, § 1–191. However, it is often possible for defects in the indictment to be cured. As to how particular defects may be cured, and as to the consequences of failure to cure particular defects, see generally, *ante*, §§ 1–192 *et seq.*

B. STATUTE

1–237 As to quashing an indictment which has been preferred otherwise than in accordance with section 2(2) of the *Administration of Justice (Miscellaneous Provisions) Act* 1933, see subsection (3) thereof, *ante*, § 1–221.

C. APPLICATION MADE BY PROSECUTION

1–238 If the application is made by the prosecution, the court will quash the indictment in all cases where it appears to be so defective that the defendant cannot be convicted on it, and where the prosecution appears to be bona fide, and not instituted from malicious motives, or for the purposes of oppression.

An application to quash may, it would seem, be made by the prosecution at any time before the defendant has been actually tried upon the indictment: see *R. v. Webb* (1764) 3 Burr. 1468. But if judgment has been given for the defendant on demurrer (see *post*, § 4–113), the indictment cannot afterwards be quashed at the instance of the prosecutor: *R. v. W. Smith*, 2 M. & Rob. 109.

1–239 Before an application to quash is made by the prosecution a new bill for the same offence must have been preferred against the defendant and signed: *R. v. Wynn* (1802) 2 East 226. See now *R. v. Thompson and Clein*, 61 Cr.App.R. 108, CA; *R. v. Follett* [1989] Q.B. 338, 88 Cr.App.R. 310, CA (*ante*, §§ 1–206 *et seq.*).

D. METHOD OF QUASHING

1–240 The proper time for making an application to quash is before plea pleaded (Fost. 231; *R. v. Chapple and Bolingbroke* (1892) 17 Cox 455; *R. v. Maywhort*, 39 Cr.App.R. 107, Assizes (Sellers J.)), but this, while just and convenient, is not essential (*R. v. Thompson*, 9 Cr.App.R. 252, CCA). Where it is clear that an indictment has been preferred and signed without jurisdiction, or has a substantial and apparent defect, the court will quash it on motion by the defendant *after* plea pleaded (*R. v. Heane* (1864) 4 B. & S. 947), even after the case for the prosecution has closed (*R. v. James* (1871) 12 Cox 127), although in a doubtful case it may leave him to test its validity by motion in arrest of judgment (*R. v. Sheares* (1798) 27 St.Tr. 255 at 266; *R. v. Lynch* [1903] 1 K.B. 444), or on appeal. Even if an objection that a count is bad for duplicity (*ante*, §§ 1–135 *et seq.*) is not taken until after the verdict, it may be taken in the Court of Appeal and may be a good ground of appeal: see *post*, § 7–78. As to the situation where the indictment is regular in form, but the evidence in support thereof discloses two or more offences, see *R. v. Donnelly*, *ante*, § 1–132, and see *ante* § 1–136.

In *R. v. Asif*, 82 Cr.App.R. 123, CA, the court disapproved of the practice of tactical postponement of a motion to quash on the ground of duplicity and said that the proper time for such an application is before the plea is taken, save in exceptional circumstances. See further, *ante*, § 1–192.

Section 2(3) of the *Administration of Justice (Miscellaneous Provisions) Act* 1933 (*ante*, § 1–221) contains a limited restriction on the quashing of indictments on appeal where no application to quash was made at trial.

1–241 The material that will be considered by the judge when dealing with an application to quash a count will depend upon the particular defect that is alleged to exist. For example, if it is asserted that the count is bad for duplicity (which is a matter of form) it will seldom be necessary or appropriate for the judge to look beyond the count itself; see further *ante*, § 1–136. However, other grounds for an application to quash may in some cases require consideration of the committal or transfer evidence (*e.g.* applications based on misjoinder, or on the addition of counts alleging matters upon which there has been no committal or transfer and which are not disclosed by the committal or transfer evidence). See generally *ante*, §§ 1–190 *et seq.* and the other paragraphs to which reference is there made.

IX. PROCEEDINGS AGAINST CORPORATIONS

Procedure on charge of offence against corporation

Magistrates' Courts Act 1980, s.46 and Sched. 3

46. The provisions of Schedule 3 to this Act shall have effect where a corporation is charged with an offence before a magistrates' court. **1–242**

SCHEDULE 3

Corporations

1.—(1) A magistrates' court may commit a corporation for trial by an order in writing empowering the prosecutor to prefer a bill of indictment in respect of the offence named in the order.

(2) An order under this paragraph shall not prohibit the inclusion in the bill of indictment of counts that under section 2 of the *Administration of Justice (Miscellaneous Provisions) Act* 1933 may be included in the bill in substitution for, or in addition to, counts charging the offence named in the order.

2. A representative may on behalf of a corporation—

(a) *make before examining justices such representations as could be made by an accused who is not a corporation;*

(b) consent to the corporation being tried summarily;

(c) enter a plea of guilty or not guilty on the trial by a magistrates' court of an information.

3.—(1) Where a representative appears, any requirement of this Act that anything shall be done in the presence of the accused, or shall be read or said to the accused, shall be construed as a requirement that that thing shall be done in the presence of the representative or read or said to the representative.

(2) Where a representative does not appear, any such requirement, and any requirement that the consent of the accused shall be obtained for summary trial, shall not apply.

4. [*Relates to pleas of guilty by post.*]

5. [*Repealed by* Criminal Justice Act *1991, s.101(2) and Sched. 13.*]

6. Subject to the preceding provisions of this Schedule, the provisions of this Act relating to the *inquiry into, and trial of,* [trial of] indictable offences shall apply to a corporation as they apply to an adult.

7. Where a corporation and an individual who has attained the age of 18 years are jointly charged before a magistrates' court with an offence triable either way, the court shall not try either of the accused summarily unless each of them consents to be so tried.

8. Subsection (6) of section 33 of the *Criminal Justice Act* 1925 shall apply to a representative for the purposes of this Schedule as it applies to a representative for the purposes of that section.

[This Schedule is printed as amended by the *CPIA* 1996, s.47, and Sched. 1, para. 13; and as prospectively amended, and repealed in part, from a day or days to be appointed, by the *CJA* 2003, ss.41 and 332, Sched. 3, para. 51(1) and (13), and Sched. 37, Pt 4 (repeal of para. 2(a), substitution in para. 6 of words in square brackets for the italicised words). The amendment of para. 2(a) that was effected by the 1996 Act applies only in relation to alleged offences into which no criminal investigation had begun before April 1, 1997: S.I. 1997 Nos 682 & 683 (*post*, § 10–9). The *CJA* 1991, s.68, and Sched. 8, para. 6(1)(a), substitutes "the age of 18 years" for the words "the age of 17" in each place where they occur in Part I of the 1980 Act. Although no specific provision is made in relation to such words in Schedule 3 to that Act, it is printed here with the substituted words in paragraph 7 because section 46, which gives effect to the Schedule, is within Part I.]

As to the application of Schedule 3 to proceedings against a partnership or an unincorporated association in respect of an offence under section 25 of the *SCA* 2007, see sections 31(6) and 32(5) of that Act respectively (*post*, §§ 5–876d, 5–886e).

The signature by committing magistrates of a certificate in the form appropriate for the committal for trial of an individual is sufficient compliance with paragraph 1(1); the act of committal is the oral determination in court and if that act is valid it cannot subsequently be invalidated by the use of an inappropriate form: *R. v. Nelson Group Services (Maintenance) Ltd* [1999] 1 W.L.R. 1526, CA (not following *R. v. H. Sherman Ltd* [1949] 2 K.B. 674, CCA). For a detailed criticism of this decision, see *Criminal Law Week* 1998/33/1. See also *ante*, § 1–210.

As to the susceptibility of corporations to prosecution, see *ante*, §§ 1–78 *et seq.*

For the service of summonses on corporations, see the *Criminal Procedure Rules* 2005 (S.I. 2005 No. 384), r.4.1 (*post*, § 2–207); and, as to representation, see *ibid.*, r.2.5(1) (*post*, § 2–206).

For the arraignment of a corporation at trial, see *post*, § 4–101.

For restrictions on the prosecution of insolvent corporations, see *ante*, § 1–81a.

No alteration of substantive law

1–243 Section 33 of the *CJA* 1925 (*post*, § 4–101) does not alter the substantive law so as to render a corporation liable to be indicted where previously it had not been so liable, but merely provides machinery to avoid the inconvenience arising from the fact that before 1925 a corporation could not be indicted at assizes: *R. v. Cory Bros. & Co. Ltd* [1927] 1 K.B. 810, Assize (Finlay J.). It is submitted that the same applies to the provisions of Schedule 3 to the 1980 Act (*ante*), which is in line of succession to the repealed subsections of section 33 of the Act of 1925.

X. POWERS OF THE ATTORNEY-GENERAL OVER PROSECUTIONS

A. WHEN SANCTION OF ATTORNEY-GENERAL NECESSARY

1–244 Certain prosecutions may not be instituted or pursued without the sanction of the Attorney-General.

Proceedings instituted without any necessary consent will be a nullity: *R. v. Pearce*, 72 Cr.App.R. 295, CA. See also *R. v. Angel*, *ante*, § 1–212, and see *post*, § 33–33. The decision in *R. v. Angel* was mentioned with apparent approval in *R. v. Clarke and McDaid* [2008] 2 Cr.App.R. 2, HL (at [42]), as to which, see further, *ante*, §§ 1–195 *et seq*.

Form of, and time for, consent to institution or continuation of proceedings

1–245 In *R. v. Cain and Schollick* [1976] Q.B. 496, 61 Cr.App.R. 186, CA, the Attorney-General's consent to a prosecution under the *Explosive Substances Act* 1883 was in the following terms: "In pursuance of my powers under the above-named Act I hereby consent to the prosecution of [the accused] of [address] for an offence or offences contrary to the provisions of the said Act." It was contended on appeal, *inter alia*, that the consent was not sufficiently detailed and in particular did not identify the consent with the charge before the magistrate. Further, it was said that a consent in such wide and general terms meant in effect that the Attorney-General, contrary to the requirements of the Act, was delegating his duty to another. This approach was rejected by the Court of Appeal:

> "… it is not necessary that the Attorney-General should have considered and approved every detail of the charge as it ultimately appears in the indictment. His duty is to consider the general circumstances of the case, and to decide whether any, and if he thinks fit, which, of the provisions of the Act can properly be pursued against the defendant … If he considers that the prosecutor should be at liberty to pursue any charge under the Act which is justified by the evidence, there is no constitutional objection to his giving consent in the wide terms adopted here. When consent is given in any terms it should be presumed that the Attorney-General has made the necessary and proper inquiries before giving that consent" (at pp. 502–503, 190, *per* Lord Widgery C.J.).

Consent to the prosecution of a person for an offence or offences contrary to identified provisions does not extend to the prosecution of that person for conspiring, contrary to section 1(1) of the *CLA* 1977, to contravene those provisions; see section 4(3) of that Act and *R. v. Pearce*, 72 Cr.App.R. 295, CA, *post*, § 33–33. **1–246**

Where a prosecution is instituted on the *fiat* of the Attorney-General it is sufficient to lodge the *fiat* with the clerk of the court of trial, and it need not be proved at the trial: *R. v. Dexter, Laidler and Coates* (1899) 19 Cox 360. See also *R. v. Metz*, 11 Cr.App.R. 164, CCA. **1–247**

See section 26 of the *Prosecution of Offences Act* 1985, *post*, § 1–279, as to the evidential status of a document purporting to be the consent of a Law Officer, the DPP or a Crown Prosecutor.

In *R. v. Whale and Lockton* [1991] Crim.L.R. 692, CA, it was held, following *R. v. Elliott*, 81 Cr.App.R. 115, CA, that for the purpose of obtaining the Attorney-General's consent to the institution of proceedings, such proceedings were instituted when the defendant "came to court to answer the charge" and that meant that proceedings were not instituted against the defendants until, following a number of occasions when the case was remanded, they were arraigned for the purpose of committal proceedings. The apparent inconsistency between these decisions and the decision in *Price v. Humphries* [1958] 2 Q.B. 353, DC (where it was held that proceedings were instituted when a summons was issued, following the laying of an information), was explained in *R. v. Bull*, 99 Cr.App.R. 193, CA, on the basis that section 25(2) of the *Prosecution of Offences Act* 1985 (*post*, § 1–278a) may be prayed in aid where the procedure adopted has been arrest, charge and production to court, rather than the procedure of laying an information and obtaining a summons. It would, therefore, appear that proceedings are indeed "instituted" when charges are laid, although the lack of any necessary consent to the institution of such charges at that time will only invalidate the charges in situations where section 25(2) of the 1985 Act has no application (*i.e.* where the information and summons procedure has been used). **1–248**

See also *ante*, § 1–203.

Solicitor-General

Any function of the Attorney-General, whether arising under an enactment or otherwise, may be exercised by the Solicitor-General: *Law Officers Act* 1997, s.1. Nothing in that section requires anything done by the Solicitor-General to be done in the name of the Solicitor-General instead of the name of the Attorney-General: *ibid.*, s.1(4)(b). **1–249**

B. INTERVENTION OF ATTORNEY-GENERAL

The Attorney-General, or the DPP under the special or general directions of the Attorney-General, was always entitled to take over and continue a private prosecution. See now section 6(2) of the *Prosecution of Offences Act* 1985, *post*, § 1–258. **1–250**

C. NOLLE PROSEQUI

Proceedings upon an indictment pending in any court may be stayed by the entry of a *nolle prosequi* at any time after the bill of indictment is signed and before judgment: *R. v. Dunn* (1843) 1 C. & K. 730; *R. v. Colling* (1847) 2 Cox 184; but not before the indictment has been preferred: *R. v. Wylie, Howe & McGuire*, 83 J.P. 295. A *nolle prosequi* can be entered only on the direction of the Attorney-General: *R. v. Rowlands* [1851] 17 Q.B. 671, but see *ante*, § 1–249. It has been said that this power of the Attorney-General is not subject to any control by the courts: *R. v. Comptroller of Patents* [1899] 1 Q.B. 909 at 914. However, that was before the development of judicial review in respect of decisions as to whether or not to prosecute, as to which see *post*, § 1–263. **1–251**

Either the prosecution or the accused person can apply to the Attorney-General for his direction that a *nolle prosequi* should be entered. Such application is made quite informally, *e.g.* by letter.

A *nolle prosequi* is now usually directed to be entered in cases where the accused person cannot be produced in court to plead or stand his trial owing to physical or mental incapacity which is expected to be permanent. A *nolle prosequi* may be entered as to one of several defendants: *R. v. Teal* (1809) 11 East 307.

A *nolle prosequi* puts an end to the prosecution (see *Gilchrist v. Gardener* (1891) 12 N.S.W.Rep.(Law) 184, and English authorities there cited), but does not operate as a bar or discharge or an acquittal on the merits: *Goddard v. Smith* (1704) 3 Salk. 245; *R. v. Ridpath* (1713) 10 Mod. 152, and the party remains liable to be re-indicted. It has been said that fresh process may be awarded on the same indictment (*Goddard v. Smith, ante*), but this dictum appears not to be law: see *R. v. Allen* (1862) 1 B. & S. 850; *R. v. Mitchel* (1848) 3 Cox 93.

XI. POWERS AND DUTIES OF PARTICULAR PROSECUTION AGENCIES

A. CROWN PROSECUTION SERVICE

(1) Establishment

Prosecution of Offences Act 1985, s.1

1–252 **1.**—(1) There shall be a prosecuting service for England and Wales (to be known as the "Crown Prosecution Service") consisting of—

(a) the Director of Public Prosecutions, who shall be head of the Service;

(b) the Chief Crown Prosecutors, designated under subsection (4) below, each of whom shall be the member of the Service responsible to the Director for supervising the operation of the Service in his area; and

(c) the other staff appointed by the Director under this section.

(2) [*Appointment of staff.*]

(3) The Director may designate any member of the Service who has a general qualification (within the meaning of section 71 of the *Courts and Legal Services Act* 1990) for the purposes of this subsection, and any person so designated shall be known as a Crown Prosecutor.

(4) [*Division of England and Wales into areas.*]

(5) [*Variation of division.*]

(6) Without prejudice to any functions which may have been assigned to him in his capacity as a member of the Service, every Crown Prosecutor shall have all the powers of the Director as to the institution and conduct of proceedings but shall exercise those powers under the direction of the Director.

(7) Where any enactment (whenever passed)—

(a) prevents any step from being taken without the consent of the Director or without his consent or the consent of another; or

(b) requires any step to be taken by or in relation to the Director;

any consent given by or, as the case may be, step taken by or in relation to, a Crown Prosecutor shall be treated, for the purposes of that enactment, as given by or, as the case may be, taken by or in relation to the Director.

[Subs. (3) is printed as amended by the *Courts and Legal Services Act* 1990, s.71, Sched. 10, para. 61(1).]

As to the effect of section 1(6), see *Ex p. Bray, The Times*, October 7, 1986, DC, *ante*, § 1–228.

Section 1(7) does not apply to the provisions of Part 10 of the *CJA* 2003 (retrial for serious offences), other than section 85(2)(a): s.92(1) of the 2003 Act (*post*, § 7–278).

Where the consent of the DPP is required as to the institution of proceedings there need not be an express written consent (although written consent is desirable) where the proceedings are instituted by a crown prosecutor, pursuant to section 1(6), if he has the consent requirement present to his mind when he decides that the prosecution is in the public interest and prepares the draft indictment for typing: *R. v. Jackson* [1997] Crim.L.R. 293, CA. As to when proceedings are "instituted", see *ante*, §§ 1–203, 1–248.

(2) Functions of Director of Public Prosecutions

Prosecution of Offences Act 1985, s.3

3.—(1) The Director shall discharge his functions under this or any other enactment under the superintendence of the Attorney-General. **1–253**

(2) It shall be the duty of the Director, subject to any provisions contained in the *Criminal Justice Act* 1987—

(a) to take over the conduct of all criminal proceedings, other than specified proceedings, instituted on behalf of a police force (whether by a member of that force or by any other person);

(aa) to take over the conduct of any criminal proceedings instituted by an immigration officer (as defined for the purposes of the *Immigration Act* 1971) acting in his capacity as such an officer;

(b) to institute and have the conduct of criminal proceedings in any case where it appears to him that—

(i) the importance or difficulty of the case makes it appropriate that proceedings should be instituted by him; or

(ii) it is otherwise appropriate for proceedings to be instituted by him;

(ba) to institute and have the conduct of any criminal proceedings in any case where the proceedings relate to the subject-matter of a report a copy of which has been sent to him under paragraph 23 or 24 of Schedule 3 to the *Police Reform Act* 2002 (reports on investigations into conduct of persons serving with the police);

(c) to take over the conduct of all binding over proceedings instituted on behalf of a police force (whether by a member of that force or by any other person);

(d) to take over the conduct of all proceedings begun by summons issued under section 3 of the *Obscene Publications Act* 1959 (forfeiture of obscene articles);

(e) to give, to such extent as he considers appropriate, advice to police forces on all matters relating to criminal offences;

(ea) to have the conduct of any extradition proceedings;

(eb) to give, to such extent as he considers appropriate, and to such persons as he considers appropriate, advice on any matters relating to extradition proceedings or proposed extradition proceedings;

(ec) to give, to such extent as he considers appropriate, advice to immigration officers on matters relating to criminal offences;

(f) to appear for the prosecution, when directed by the court to do so, on any appeal under—

(i) section 1 of the *Administration of Justice Act* 1960 (appeal from the High Court in criminal cases);

(ii) Part I or Part II of the *Criminal Appeal Act* 1968 (appeals from the Crown Court to the criminal division of the Court of Appeal and thence to the *House of Lords* [Supreme Court]); or

(iii) section 108 of the *Magistrates' Courts Act* 1980 (right of appeal to Crown Court) as it applies, by virtue of subsection (5) of section 12 of the *Contempt of Court Act* 1981, to orders made under section 12 (contempt of magistrates' courts);

(fa) to have the conduct of applications for orders under section 1C of the *Crime and Disorder Act* 1998 (orders made on conviction of certain offences)[, section 6 of the *Violent Crime Reduction Act* 2006 (orders on conviction in criminal proceedings)] and section 14A of the *Football Spectators Act* 1989 (banning orders made on conviction of certain offences);

(faa) where it appears to him appropriate to do so, to have the conduct of applications made by him for orders under section 14B of the *Football Spectators Act* 1989 (banning orders made on complaint);

(fb) where it appears to him appropriate to do so, to have the conduct of applications under section 1CA(3) of the *Crime and Disorder Act* 1998 for the variation or discharge of orders made under section 1C of that Act;

(fc) where it appears to him appropriate to do so, to appear on any application under section 1CA of that Act made by a person subject to an order under section 1C of that Act for the variation or discharge of the order;

[(fd) where it appears to him appropriate to do so, to have the conduct of applications under section 8(1)(b) of the *Violent Crime Reduction Act* 2006 for the variation or discharge of orders made under section 6 of that Act;

(fe) where it appears to him appropriate to do so, to appear on any application under section 8(1)(a) of that Act by a person subject to an order under section 6 of that Act for the variation or discharge of the order;]

(ff) to discharge such duties as are conferred on him by, or in relation to, Part 5 or Part 8 of the *Proceeds of Crime Act* 2002 (civil recovery of the proceeds etc., of unlawful conduct, civil recovery investigations and disclosure orders in relation to confiscation investigations);

(g) to discharge such other functions as may from time to time be assigned to him by the Attorney-General in pursuance of this paragraph.

(2A) Subsection 2(ea) above does not require the Director to have the conduct of any extradition proceedings in respect of a person if he has received a request not to do so and—

(a) in a case where the proceedings are under Part 1 of the *Extradition Act* 2003, the request is made by the authority which issued the Part 1 warrant in respect of the person;

(b) in a case where the proceedings are under Part 2 of that Act, the request is made on behalf of the territory to which the person's extradition has been requested.

(3) In this section—

"the court" means—

(a) in the case of an appeal to or from the criminal division of the Court of Appeal, that division;

(b) in the case of an appeal from a Divisional Court of the Queen's Bench Division, the Divisional Court; and

(c) in the case of an appeal against an order of a magistrates' court, the Crown Court;

"police force" means any police force maintained by a police authority under the *Police Act* 1996 and any other body of constables for the time being specified by order made by the Secretary of State for the purposes of this section; and

"specified proceedings" means proceedings which fall within any category for the time being specified by order made by the Attorney General for the purposes of this section.

(4) [*Procedure for making orders under subs. (3).*]

[This section is printed as amended, and repealed in part, by the *CJA* 1987, s.15, Sched. 2, para. 13; the *Police Act* 1996, s.103, and Sched. 7, para. 39; the *Police Act* 1997, s.134, and Sched. 9, para. 48; the *Immigration and Asylum Act* 1999, s.164; the *Police Reform Act* 2002, s.107(1), and Sched. 7, para. 10; the *Extradition Act* 2003, s.190(1) to (3); the *Anti-social Behaviour Act* 2003, ss.86(6) and 92, and Sched. 3; the *Asylum and Immigration (Treatment of Claimants, etc.) Act* 2004, s.7; the *SOCPA* 2005, ss.59, 140(5) and 174, and Scheds. 4, para. 47, and 17, Pt 2; the *VCRA* 2006, s.52(2), and Sched. 3, para. 15; and the *SCA* 2007, s.74(2), and Sched. 8, para. 149; and as amended, as from days to be appointed, by the *Constitutional Reform Act* 2005, s.40(4), and Sched. 9, para. 41(1) and (2) (substitution in subs. (2)(f) of words in square brackets for italicised words); and the *VCRA* 2006, ss.7(10) (insertion of words in square brackets in subs. (2)(fa)), and 8(7) (insertion of subs. (2)(fd) and (fe)).]

See section 38(3) and (4) of the *SOCPA* 2005, *post*, § 1–303, as to certain further functions of the Director in relation to advice, and the institution and conduct of criminal proceedings, in respect of matters within the scope of that section, and see the summary of section 39 of that Act, *post*, § 1–300.

1–254 As to the question of whether proceedings that result from the investigations of some individual or of some body, such as the Revenue and Customs or trading standards authorities, can be said to have been "instituted on behalf of a police force" so as to require the DPP to take over the conduct of those proceedings, pursuant to section 3(2), and so as to invalidate any proceedings not taken over, see *R. v. Ealing JJ., ex p. Dixon* [1990] 2 Q.B. 91, DC; *R. v. Stafford JJ., ex p. Customs and Excise Commrs* [1991] 2 Q.B. 339, DC; *R. v. Jackson* [1990] Crim.L.R. 55, Crown Court (H.H. Judge Laurie); *R. v. Croydon JJ., ex p. Holmberg* [1992] Crim.L.R. 892, DC; and *R. (Hunt) v. Criminal Cases Review Commission* [2001] 2 Cr.App.R. 6, DC.

See also the commentary *post*, §§ 3–100, 3–101, and the definition set out in section 15(2) of the 1985 Act, *post*, § 1–265.

The effect of section 6(1) of the 1985 Act, *post*, § 1–258, is to preclude a person from bringing a private prosecution in the cases covered by paragraphs (a), (c) and (d) in section 3(2), but not in the residuary category of cases covered by section 3(2)(b): *R. v.*

Bow Street Stipendiary Magistrate, ex p. South Coast Shipping Company Ltd, 96 Cr.App.R. 405, DC.

The DPP has no power to give an undertaking that he will not consent to the prosecution of a crime yet to be committed: *R. (Pretty) v. DPP* [2002] 1 A.C. 800, HL.

Specified police forces

See the *Prosecution of Offences Act 1985 (Specified Police Forces) Order* 1985 (S.I. 1985 No. 1956) which specifies various bodies of constables for the purposes of section 3 of the 1985 Act. **1–255**

Specified proceedings

See the *Prosecution of Offences Act 1985 (Specified Proceedings) Order* 1999 (S.I. 1999 No. 904). **1–255a**

(3) Rights of audience of Crown Prosecutors

Subsections (1) to (3E) of section 4 of the *Prosecution of Offences Act* 1985, which made provision as to the rights of audience of crown prosecutors, were repealed by the *Access to Justice Act* 1999, s.106, and Sched. 15, Pt II, with effect from July 31, 2000: *Access to Justice Act 1999 (Commencement No. 4 and Transitional Provisions) Order* 2000 (S.I. 2000 No. 1920). The present position as to the rights of audience of crown prosecutors is summarised at § 2–22, *post*. **1–256**

(4) Conduct of prosecutions on behalf of the service

Prosecution of Offences Act, 1985, s.5

5.—(1) The Director may at any time appoint a person who is not a Crown Prosecutor but who has a general qualification (within the meaning of section 71 of the *Courts and Legal Services Act* 1990) to institute or take over the conduct of such criminal proceedings or extradition proceedings as the Director may assign to him. **1–257**

(2) Any person conducting proceedings assigned to him under this section shall have all the powers of a Crown Prosecutor but shall exercise those powers subject to any instructions given to him by a Crown Prosecutor.

[This section is printed as amended by the *Courts and Legal Services Act* 1990, s.71, Sched. 10, para. 61(2); and the *Extradition Act* 2003, s.190(1) and (4).]

(5) Private prosecutions

Prosecution of Offences Act, 1985, s.6

6.—(1) Subject to subsection (2) below, nothing in this Part shall preclude any person from instituting any criminal proceedings or conducting any criminal proceedings to which the Director's duty to take over the conduct of proceedings does not apply. **1–258**

(2) Where criminal proceedings are instituted in circumstances in which the Director is not under a duty to take over their conduct, he may nevertheless do so at any stage.

The DPP does not have a duty, within the meaning of section 6(1), to take over the conduct of proceedings merely because he could have instituted those proceedings by reason of section 3(2)(b) (*ante*, § 1–253). Furthermore, section 6(1) is not subject to any implied limitation precluding a private prosecution on a serious charge in circumstances where the public prosecuting authorities have already instituted proceedings for a minor offence arising out of the same incident. Section 6(2) contemplates that the DPP may take over the conduct of proceedings instituted by a private prosecutor which he might otherwise have instituted himself and having taken over such proceedings he may discontinue them under section 23 (*post*, § 1–276) if the evidence is insufficient, or if the proceedings would be contrary to the public interest, or to avoid duplication, or for any other good reason. If it is too late to discontinue, he may offer no evidence or the Attorney-General may enter a *nolle prosequi*: *R. v. Bow Street Stipendiary Magistrate, ex p. South Coast Shipping Company Ltd*, 96 Cr.App.R. 405, DC.

Section 3(2)(b) has nothing to do with the discretion to take over a private prosecution and, further, it could not be right for the DPP to apply the same test when deciding whether to take over proceedings for the purpose of discontinuing them as that which he applies when deciding whether to institute or continue a prosecution (as to which, see *post*, § 1–262 and Appendix E–1 *et seq.*); the result of applying the same test would be to undermine the right of private prosecution, because it would result in the DPP stopping a private prosecution merely because it was not one that he would have initiated or continued; a policy of intervening only if there is clearly no case to answer, or if the public interest factors against a private prosecution outweigh those in favour, is not unlawful; but where there is more than one charge, the policy should be applied to each charge individually: *R. v. DPP, ex p. Duckenfield*; *R. v. Same, ex p. Murray*; *R. v. South Yorkshire Police Authority, ex p. Chief Constable of the South Yorkshire Police*; *R. v. Same, ex p. Duckenfield*; *R. v. Same, ex p. Murray* [2000] 1 W.L.R. 55, DC. See also *Raymond v. Att.-Gen.* [1982] Q.B. 839, 75 Cr.App.R. 34, CA (Civ. Div.); *Turner v. DPP*, 68 Cr.App.R. 70, QBD (Mars-Jones J.); and *R. v. DPP, ex p. Raymond*, 70 Cr.App.R. 233, CA (Civ. Div.), as to the similarly worded provision that was replaced by section 6(2).

1–259 In exercising the judicial discretion as to whether to issue a summons, a magistrate should at the very least ascertain: (i) whether the allegation is of an offence known to the law and, if so, whether the essential ingredients of the offence are prima facie present; (ii) that the offence alleged is not "out of time"; (iii) that the court has jurisdiction; and (iv) whether the informant has the necessary authority to prosecute; and it may also be necessary to consider whether the allegation is vexatious: *R. v. West London Metropolitan Stipendiary Magistrate, ex p. Klahn* [1979] 1 W.L.R. 933, DC. If the incident which gives rise to the prosecution has been investigated by a responsible prosecuting authority which is pursuing what it considers to be the appropriate charges, a magistrate should be slow (in the absence of special circumstances) to issue a summons for a more serious charge on the application of a private prosecutor, because such a course may be oppressive, and the possibility of the DPP taking over the private prosecution is a relevant factor: *R. v. Tower Bridge Metropolitan Stipendiary Magistrate, ex p. Chaudhry* [1994] Q.B. 340, 99 Cr.App.R. 170, DC. However, the fact that the DPP has discontinued or declined to bring charges in respect of a particular incident does not justify a requirement that special circumstances be shown before a summons is issued at the behest of a private prosecutor in respect of that incident; to conclude otherwise would result in a private prosecutor being wrongly constrained by the test applied by the CPS (as to which, see *ante*) and would emasculate the right to initiate a private prosecution: *R. (Charlson) v. Guildford Magistrates' Court* [2006] 1 W.L.R. 3494, QBD (Silber J.).

As to the propriety of bringing a private prosecution in a situation where there has already been a conviction for a lesser offence arising out of the same incident, see *R. v. Moxon-Tritsch*, *post*, § 4–59 (and see the principle explained in *R. v. Beedie*, *post*, § 4–58). As to the situation where an earlier summons has been withdrawn by the CPS after the defendant has agreed to be bound over or cautioned, see *R. v. Grays JJ., ex p. Low*, *Hayter v. L.*, and *Jones v. Whalley*, *post*, § 4–59.

The right to institute a private prosecution does not confer a right of access to police statements, reports and photographs held by the CPS: *R. v. DPP, ex p. Hallas*, 87 Cr.App.R. 340, DC. Further, those who provide material for the CPS are entitled to confidentiality in respect of such of that material as is not in the public domain: *Taylor v. Director of the Serious Fraud Office* [1999] 2 A.C. 177, HL. As to rights of audience, see *R. v. Southwark Crown Court, ex p. Tawfick, CPS intervening*, *post*, § 2–22.

In *R. v. Belmarsh Magistrates' Court, ex p. Watts* [1999] 2 Cr.App.R. 188, DC, *obiter* remarks were made as to a private prosecutor having the same "minister of justice" obligations as the public prosecuting authorities; but this applies only in relation to the actual conduct of the proceedings (duty of disclosure etc.), not to the motive for bringing them, as to which see also *post*, § 4–63a: *R. (Dacre and Associated Newspapers) v. City of Westminster Magistrates' Court* [2008] 8 *Archbold News* 2, DC ([2008] EWHC 1667 (Admin.)).

See also *ante*, § 1–254, and *post*, § 1–263.

(6) Delivery of recognizances, etc., to Director

Prosecution of Offences Act 1985, s.7

7.—(1) Where the Director or any Crown Prosecutor gives notice to any justice of the peace that he has instituted, or is conducting, any criminal proceedings, the justice shall— **1–260**

(a) at the prescribed time and in the prescribed manner; or

(b) in a particular case, at the time and in the manner directed by the Attorney General;

send him every recognizance, information, certificate, deposition, document and thing connected with those proceedings which the justice is required by law to deliver to the appropriate officer of the Crown Court.

(2) The Attorney General may make regulations for the purpose of supplementing this section; and in subsection (1) above "prescribed" means prescribed by the regulations.

(3) The Director or, as the case may be, Crown Prosecutor shall—

(a) subject to the regulations, cause anything which is sent to him under subsection (1) above to be delivered to the appropriate officer of the Crown Court; and

(b) be under the same obligation (on the same payment) to deliver to an applicant copies of anything so sent as that officer.

(4) It shall be the duty of the designated officer for every magistrates' court to send to the Director, in accordance with the regulations, a copy of the information and of any depositions and other documents relating to any case in which—

(a) a prosecution for an offence before the magistrates' court is withdrawn or is not proceeded with within a reasonable time;

(b) the Director does not have the conduct of the proceedings; and

(c) there is some ground for suspecting that there is no satisfactory reason for the withdrawal or failure to proceed.

[This section is printed as amended by the *Access to Justice Act* 1999, s.90(1), and Sched. 13, para. 130; and the *Courts Act* 2003, s.109(1), and Sched. 8, para. 287.]

(7) Bail applications

Prosecution of Offences Act 1985, s.7A

7A.—(1) The Director may designate, for the purposes of this section, members of the staff of the Crown Prosecution Service who are not Crown Prosecutors. **1–261**

(2) Subject to such exceptions (if any) as may be specified in the designation, a person so designated shall have such of the following as may be so specified, namely—

(a) the powers and rights of audience of a Crown Prosecutor in relation to—

(i) applications for, or relating to, bail in criminal proceedings;

(ii) the conduct of criminal proceedings in magistrates' courts other than trials of offences triable either way or offences which are punishable with imprisonment in the case of persons aged 21 or over;

(iii) the conduct of applications or other proceedings relating to preventative civil orders;

(iv) the conduct of proceedings (other than criminal proceedings) in, or in connection with, the discharge of functions assigned to the Director under section 3(2)(g) above;

(b) any powers of a Crown Prosecutor that do not involve the exercise of such rights of audience as are mentioned in paragraph (a) above but are exercisable in relation to the conduct of—

(i) criminal proceedings in magistrates' courts, or

(ii) applications or proceedings falling within paragraph (a)(iii) or (iv).

(3) A person so designated shall exercise any such powers subject to instructions given to him by the Director.

(4) Any such instructions may be given so as to apply generally.

(5) In this section—

"bail in criminal proceedings" has the same meaning as in the *Bail Act* 1976 (see section 1 of that Act);

"preventative civil orders" means—

(a) orders within section 3(2)(fa) to (fe) above;

(b) orders under section 5 or 5A of the *Protection from Harassment Act* 1997 (restraining orders); or

(c) orders under section 8 of the *Crime and Disorder Act* 1998 (parenting orders).

(5A) For the purposes of this section a trial begins with the opening of the prosecution case after the entry of a plea of not guilty and ends with the conviction or acquittal of the accused.

(7) [*Details to be included in Director's annual report under s.9.*]

(8) As from 1 May 2011 nothing in this section confers on persons designated under this section—

(a) any rights of audience, or

(b) any right to conduct litigation,

for the purposes of Part 3 of the *Legal Services Act* 2007 (reserved legal activities).

(9) As from that date the following provisions of that Act accordingly do not apply to persons designated under this section—

(a) paragraph 1(3) of Schedule 3 (exemption for persons with statutory rights of audience), and

(b) paragraph 2(3) of that Schedule (exemption for persons with statutory right to conduct litigation).

(10) The Attorney General may by order make such modifications in the application of any enactment (including this section) in relation to persons designated under this section as the Attorney General considers appropriate in consequence of, or in connection with, the matters provided for by subsections (8) and (9).

(11) The Attorney General may also by order amend subsection (2)(a)(ii) so as to omit the words "or offences which are punishable with imprisonment in the case of persons aged 21 or over".

(12) The power to make an order under subsection (10) or (11) is exercisable by statutory instrument, but a statutory instrument containing such an order may not be made unless a draft of the instrument has been laid before, and approved by a resolution of, each House of Parliament.

[This section is printed as substituted by the *CDA* 1998, s.53, for the original section, which was inserted by the *Courts and Legal Services Act* 1990, s.114. It is printed as amended, and repealed in part, by the *CJA* 2003, s.331, and Sched. 36, paras 49 and 50; and the *CJIA* 2008, ss.55(1)-(5) and 149, and Sched. 28, Pt 4.]

(8) Guidelines for Crown Prosecutors

Prosecution of Offences Act 1985, s.10

1–262 **10.**—(1) The Director shall issue a Code for Crown Prosecutors giving guidance on general principles to be applied by them—

(a) in determining, in any case—

(i) whether proceedings for an offence should be instituted or, where proceedings have been instituted, whether they should be discontinued; or

(ii) what charges should be preferred; and

(b) in considering, in any case, representations to be made by them to any magistrates' court about the mode of trial suitable for that case.

(2) The Director may from time to time make alterations in the Code.

(3) The provisions of the Code shall be set out in the Director's report under section 9 of this Act for the year in which the Code is issued; and any alteration in the Code shall be set out in his report under that section for the year in which the alteration is made.

1–263 Section 9 provides for an annual report to the Attorney-General which is to be laid before Parliament and published. For the current code, see Appendix E.

The creation of a policy not to institute prosecutions in certain situations is susceptible to judicial review and will be judged on the conventional bases for relief in such proceedings: see *R. v. Commr of the Police for the Metropolis, ex p. Blackburn* [1968] 2 Q.B. 118, CA (Civ. Div.). See also *R. (Pretty) v. DPP, ante*, § 1–254. A decision by the public prosecuting authorities not to institute a prosecution, or to discontinue a prosecution that they have instituted, is also susceptible to judicial review. Applications for such review have been successful in a number of reported cases (*R. v. DPP, ex p. C.* [1995] 1 Cr.App.R. 136, DC; *R. v. DPP, ex p. Jones* [2000] Crim.L.R. 858, DC; *R. v. DPP, ex p. Treadaway, The Times*, October 31, 1997, DC; *R. v. DPP, ex p. Manning* [2001] Q.B. 330, DC; and *R. (Joseph) v. DPP* [2001] Crim.L.R. 489, DC). There are two reported cases (*R. v. DPP, ex p. Panayiotu* [1997] C.O.D. 83, DC, and *R. v.*

DPP, ex p. Camelot Group Ltd [1998] C.O.D. 54, DC), and many other unreported cases, in which such applications have failed. What is clear from all of the cases is that the power to review a decision not to prosecute is one that is to be sparingly exercised. However, it has also been said (in *ex p. Manning*) that the standard of review should, nevertheless, not be set too high, since judicial review is the only means by which the citizen can seek redress against a decision not to prosecute. In *ex p. Camelot Group Ltd* (*ante*) it was said that the availability of the alternative remedy of the right to bring a private prosecution (*ante*, §§ 1–258 *et seq.*) may, where it is a realistic option, be a powerful factor, albeit not decisive, when judicial review is sought of a decision not to prosecute. Further general guidance as to the sort of factors to be taken into account was given in *R. (Dennis) v. DPP* [2007] 2 *Archbold News* 3, DC. In *R. (Da Silva) v. DPP*, 157 N.L.J. 31, DC, it was held that the approach laid down in *ex p. Manning* is compatible with the "careful scrutiny" approach required by Article 2 of the ECHR (*post*, § 16–36), as is the evidential test set out in the Code for Crown Prosecutors (Appendix E–6).

In a number of reported cases (identified at § 1–263 in the 2000 edition of this work) it has been said that a decision to institute a prosecution is also amenable to judicial review, but only in rare and exceptional situations (such as demonstrable fraud, corruption, *mala fides*, or failure to follow settled policy on the part of the decision-maker), and that judicial review may be particularly inappropriate where an alternative remedy exists in that the matters complained of could be considered by the criminal court on an application to stay the prosecution as an abuse of process. These *dicta* have been given added force by the decision of the House of Lords in *R. v. DPP, ex p. Kebilene* [2000] 2 A.C. 326. Their Lordships held (in respect of the specific basis of challenge in that case) that the *Human Rights Act* 1998 did not give rise to any legitimate expectation that, prior to that Act taking full effect, the DPP would exercise his discretion to consent to a prosecution in accordance with Article 6(2) of the ECHR (*post*, § 16–57); and (generally) that although section 29(3) of the *Supreme Court [Senior Courts] Act* 1981 (*post*, § 7–4, and renamed as from a day to be appointed by the *Constitutional Reform Act* 2005, s.59(5), and Sched. 11, para. 1(2)) is not intended to curtail the High Court's power to make orders against parties other than the Crown Court in respect of matters relating to trial on indictment, the policy underlying that Act is that criminal proceedings should not be subjected to delay by collateral challenges, and as a general rule the courts will, in accordance with that policy, refuse to entertain a judicial review application where the complaint could be raised within the criminal trial and appeal process. Their Lordships made it clear that judicial review is, however, available in an appropriate case in respect of a decision *not* to prosecute, because in such a situation there is no other remedy, and their Lordships distinguished the situation where judicial review of a decision to commit for trial is available in accordance with the principles explained in *R. v. Bedwellty JJ., ex p. Williams* [1997] A.C. 225, HL (*ante*, § 1–212).

As to the desirability of resolving through the criminal trial process, rather than by way of judicial review, a decision to prosecute that is alleged to have resulted from improper political pressure rather than from proper prosecutorial considerations, see *Sharma v. Brown-Antoine* [2007] 1 W.L.R. 780, PC.

There is no public law basis by which a prosecutorial decision to bring a charge of acquiring, etc., criminal property, contrary to section 329 of the *PCA* 2002 (*post*, § 26–13), rather than a charge of handling stolen goods, contrary to section 22 of the *Theft Act* 1968 (*post*, § 21–270), can be challenged in a case where the alleged facts fall within either offence; this is so even if the decision is outwith guidance issued by the prosecution authority to the effect that a charge under the 2002 Act should only be brought in a serious case: *R. (Wilkinson) v. DPP* [2007] 1 *Archbold News* 5, DC.

As to the appropriate test to be applied by the DPP when deciding whether to take over a private prosecution for the purpose of discontinuing the proceedings, see *ante*, § 1–258.

Charging standards for criminal offences

Apart from the guidelines, the CPS and the police have agreed to work together to **1–263a** produce charging standards for various types of criminal offences. They are intended: (a) to ensure greater fairness to individual defendants; and (b) to lessen the administrative burdens on the police, the CPS, the courts and the defence, by reducing the need to amend or substitute charges during the course of the proceedings. As to these, see also Appendix E–13 *et seq.*.

(9) Control of certain fees and expenses, etc., paid by the service

1–264 The *Prosecution of Offences Act* 1985, s.14 (as amended) confers power on the Attorney-General to make regulations in relation to the fees of any legal representative briefed to appear on behalf of the CPS in any criminal proceedings or extradition proceedings, and in relation to the costs and expenses of witnesses attending to give evidence at the instance of the service. The only regulations made under this section are the *Crown Prosecution Service (Witnesses', etc. Allowances) Regulations* 1988 (S.I. 1988 No. 1862).

(10) Interpretation of Part I

Prosecution of Offences Act 1985, s.15

1–265 **15.**—(1) In this Part—

"binding over proceedings" means any proceedings instituted (whether by way of complaint under section 115 of the *Magistrates' Courts Act* 1980 or otherwise) with a view to obtaining from a magistrates' court an order requiring a person to enter into a recognisance to keep the peace or to be of good behaviour;

"Director" means the Director of Public Prosecutions;

"extradition proceedings" means proceedings under the *Extradition Act* 2003;

"legal representative" means *an authorised advocate or authorised litigator, as defined by section 119(1) of the* Courts and Legal Services Act *1990* [a person who, for the purposes of the *Legal Services Act* 2007, is an authorised person in relation to an activity which constitutes the exercise of a right of audience or the conduct of litigation (within the meaning of that Act)];

"police force" has the same meaning as in section 3 of this Act;

"prosecution functions" means functions which by virtue of this Part become functions of the Director;

"public authority" has the same meaning as in section 17 of this Act;

"public prosecutor", "requisition" and "written charge" have the same meaning as in section 29 of the *Criminal Justice Act* 2003;

"Service" means the Crown Prosecution Service.

(2) For the purposes of this Part, proceedings in relation to an offence are instituted—

(a) where a justice of the peace issues a summons under section 1 of the *Magistrates' Courts Act* 1980, when the information for the offence is laid before him;

(b) where a justice of the peace issues a warrant for the arrest of any person under that section, when the information for the offence is laid before him;

(ba) where a public prosecutor issues a written charge and requisition for the offence, when the written charge and requisition are issued;

(c) where a person is charged with the offence after being taken into custody without a warrant, when he is informed of the particulars of the charge;

(d) where a bill of indictment is preferred under section 2 of the *Administration of Justice (Miscellaneous Provisions) Act* 1933 in a case falling within paragraph (b) of subsection (2) of that section, when the bill of indictment is preferred before the court;

and where the application of this subsection would result in there being more than one time for the institution of the proceedings, they shall be taken to have been instituted at the earliest of those times.

(3) For the purposes of this Part, references to the conduct of any proceedings include references to the proceedings being discontinued and to the taking of any steps (including the bringing of appeals and making of representations in respect of applications for bail) which may be taken in relation to them.

(4) For the purposes of sections 3(2)(b), 5, 6, 7(1) and 7A of this Act, binding over proceedings shall be taken to be criminal proceedings.

(5) For the purposes of section 5 of this Act, proceedings begun by summons issued

under section 3 of the *Obscene Publications Act* 1959 (forfeiture of obscene articles) shall be taken to be criminal proceedings.

(6) [*Not printed.*]

[This section is printed as amended, and repealed in part, by the *Courts and Legal Services Act* 1990, s.125(3), Sched. 18, para. 52(2) and s.125(7), Sched. 20; the *Extradition Act* 2003, s.190(1) and (6); the *CJA* 2003, s.331, and Sched. 36, para. 10; the *CJIA* 2008, s.55(6); and the *Statute Law (Repeals) Act* 2008, s.1(1), and Sched. 1, Pt 3; and as amended, as from a day to be appointed, by the *Legal Services Act* 2007, s.208(1), and Sched. 21, para. 64 (substitution in subs. (1) of words in square brackets for italicised words).]

In relation to subsection (2), see *ante*, § 1–254.

(11) Power of Secretary of State to set time limits in relation to preliminary stages of criminal proceedings

Prosecution of Offences Act 1985, s.22

22.—(1) The Secretary of State may by regulations make provision, with respect to any specified preliminary stage of proceedings for an offence, as to the maximum period— **1–266**

(a) to be allowed to the prosecution to complete that stage;

(b) during which the accused may, while awaiting completion of that stage, be—

(i) in the custody of a magistrates' court; or

(ii) in the custody of the Crown Court;

in relation to that offence.

(2) The regulations may, in particular—

(a) be made so as to apply only in relation to proceedings instituted in specified areas, or proceedings of, or against persons of, specified classes or descriptions;

(b) make different provision with respect to proceedings instituted in different areas, or different provision with respect to proceedings of, or against persons of, different classes or descriptions;

(c) make such provision with respect to the procedure to be followed in criminal proceedings as the Secretary of State considers appropriate in consequence of any other provision of the regulations;

(d) provide for the *Magistrates' Courts Act* 1980 and the *Bail Act* 1976 to apply in relation to cases to which custody or overall time limits apply subject to such modifications as may be specified (being modifications which the Secretary of State considers necessary in consequence of any provision made by the regulations); and

(e) make such transitional provision in relation to proceedings instituted before the commencement of any provision of the regulations as the Secretary of State considers appropriate.

(3) The appropriate court may, at any time before the expiry of a time limit imposed by the regulations, extend, or further extend, that limit; but the court shall not do so unless it is satisfied— **1–267**

(a) that the need for the extension is due to—

(i) the illness or absence of the accused, a necessary witness, a judge or a magistrate;

(ii) a postponement which is occasioned by the ordering by the court of separate trials in the case of two or more accused or two or more offences; or

(iii) some other good and sufficient cause; and

(b) that the prosecution has acted with all due diligence and expedition.

(4) Where, in relation to any proceedings for an offence, an overall time limit has expired before the completion of the stage of the proceedings to which the limit applies, the appropriate court shall stay the proceedings.

(5) Where—

(a) a person escapes from the custody of a magistrates' court or the Crown Court before the expiry of a custody time limit which applies in his case; or

(b) a person who has been released on bail in consequence of the expiry of a custody time limit—

(i) fails to surrender himself into the custody of the court at the appointed time; or

(ii) is arrested by a constable on a ground mentioned in section 7(3)(b) of the *Bail Act* 1976 (breach, or likely breach, of conditions of bail);

the regulations shall, so far as they provide for any custody time limit in relation to the preliminary stage in question, be disregarded.

(6) Subsection (6A) below applies where—

(a) a person escapes from the custody of a magistrates' court or the Crown Court; or

(b) a person who has been released on bail fails to surrender himself into the custody of the court at the appointed time;

and is accordingly at large for any period.

(6A) The following, namely—

(a) the period for which the person is unlawfully at large; and

(b) such additional period (if any) as the appropriate court may direct, having regard to the disruption of the prosecution occasioned by—

(i) the person's escape or failure to surrender; and

(ii) the length of the period mentioned in paragraph (a) above,

shall be disregarded, so far as the offence in question is concerned, for the purposes of the overall time limit which applies in his case in relation to the stage which the proceedings have reached at the time of the escape or, as the case may be, at the appointed time.

(6B) Any period during which proceedings for an offence are adjourned pending the determination of an appeal under Part 9 of the *Criminal Justice Act* 2003 shall be disregarded, so far as the offence is concerned, for the purposes of the overall time limit and the custody time limit which applies to the stage which the proceedings have reached when they are adjourned.

(7) Where a magistrates' court decides to extend, or further extend, a custody or overall time limit, or to give a direction under subsection (6A) above, the accused may appeal against the decision to the Crown Court.

(8) Where a magistrates' court refuses to extend, a custody or overall time limit, or to give a direction under subsection (6A) above, the prosecution may appeal against the refusal to the Crown Court.

(9) An appeal under subsection (8) above may not be commenced after the expiry of the limit in question; but where such an appeal is commenced before the expiry of the limit the limit shall be deemed not to have expired before the determination or abandonment of the appeal.

(10) Where a person is convicted of an offence in any proceedings, the exercise, in relation to any preliminary stage of those proceedings, of the power conferred by subsection (3) above shall not be called into question in any appeal against that conviction.

1–268 (11) In this section—

"appropriate court" means—

(a) where the accused has been committed for trial, *sent for trial under section 51 of the* Crime and Disorder Act *1998* [sent for trial] or indicted for the offence, the Crown Court; and

(b) in any other case, the magistrates' court specified in the summons or warrant in question or, where the accused has already appeared or been brought before a magistrates' court, a magistrates' court for the same area;

"custody" includes local authority accommodation to which a person is remanded or committed by virtue of section 23 of the *Children and Young Persons Act* 1969, and references to a person being committed to custody shall be construed accordingly;

"custody of the Crown Court" includes custody to which a person is committed in pursuance of—

(a) *section 6 of the* Magistrates' Courts Act *1980 (magistrates' court committing accused for trial); or*

(b) *section 43A of that Act (magistrates' court dealing with a person brought before it following his arrest in pursuance of a warrant issued by the Crown Court); or*

(c) *section 5(3)(a) of the* Criminal Justice Act *1987 (custody after transfer order in fraud case); or*

(d) *paragraph 2(1)(a) of Schedule 6 to the* Criminal Justice Act *1991 (custody after transfer order in certain cases involving children);*

["custody of the Crown Court" includes custody to which a person is committed in pursuance of—

(a) section 43A of the *Magistrates' Courts Act* 1980 (magistrates' court dealing with a person brought before it following his arrest in pursuance of a warrant issued by the Crown Court); or

(b) section 52 of the *Crime and Disorder Act* 1998 (provisions supplementing section 51);]

"custody of a magistrates' court" means custody to which a person is committed in pursuance of section 128 of the *Magistrates' Courts Act* 1980 (remand);

"custody time limit" means a time limit imposed by regulations made under subsection (1)(b) above or, where any such limit has been extended by a court under subsection (3) above, the limit as so extended;

"preliminary stage", in relation to any proceedings does not include any stage after the start of the trial (within the meaning given by subsections (11A) and (11B) below;

"overall time limit" means a time limit imposed by regulations made under subsection (1)(a) above or, where any such limit has been extended by a court under subsection (3) above, the limit as so extended; and

"specified" means specified in the regulations.

(11ZA) For the purposes of this section, proceedings for an offence shall be taken to begin when the accused is charged with the offence or, as the case may be, an information is laid charging him with the offence.

(11A) For the purposes of this section, the start of a trial on indictment shall be taken to occur at the time when a jury is sworn to consider the issue of guilt or fitness to plead or, if the court accepts a plea of guilty before the time when a jury is sworn, when that plea is accepted; but this is subject to section 8 of the *Criminal Justice Act* 1987 and section 30 of the *Criminal Procedure and Investigations Act* 1996 (preparatory hearings).

(11AA) The references in subsection (11A) above to the time when a jury is sworn include the time when that jury would be sworn but for the making of an order under Part 7 of the *Criminal Justice Act* 2003.

(11B) For the purposes of this section, the start of a summary trial shall be taken to occur—

(a) when the court begins to hear evidence for the prosecution at the trial or to consider whether to exercise its power under section 37(3) of the *Mental Health Act* 1983 (power to make hospital order without convicting the accused), or

(b) if the court accepts a plea of guilty without proceeding as mentioned above, when that plea is accepted.

(12) For the purposes of the application of any custody time limit in relation to a person who is in the custody of a magistrates' court or the Crown Court— **1–269**

(a) all periods during which he is in the custody of a magistrates' court in respect of the same offence shall be aggregated and treated as a single continuous period; and

(b) all periods during which he is in the custody of the Crown Court in respect of the same offence shall be aggregated and treated similarly.

(13) For the purposes of section 29(3) of the *Supreme Court Act* 1981 (High Court to have power to make prerogative orders in relation to jurisdiction of Crown Court in matters which do not relate to trial on indictment) the jurisdiction conferred on the Crown Court by this section shall be taken to be part of its jurisdiction in matters other than those relating to trial on indictment.

[This section is printed as amended by the *CJA* 1988, s.170, and Sched. 15, para. 104; the *CJA* 1991, s.100, and Sched. 11, para. 36; the *CJPOA* 1994, s.168(1), and Sched. 9, para. 27; the *CPIA* 1996, s.71(1)–(3); the *CDA* 1998, s.43; the *Access to Justice Act* 1999, s.67(3); and the *CJA* 2003, ss.70 and 331, and Sched. 36, paras 49 and 51. The words in square brackets in the definition of "appropriate court" and the definition in square brackets of "custody of the Crown Court" in subs. (11) are substituted for the italicised words by the *CJA* 2003, s.41, and Sched. 3, para. 57(1) and (5). The substitution of the definition of "custody of the Crown Court" came into force on May 9, 2005, but only in relation to cases sent for trial under s.51 or 51A(3)(d) of the *CDA* 1998, and the substitution of words in the definition of "appropriate Crown Court" came into force on the same date, but only in relation to cases sent for trial under s.51A(3)(d): *Criminal Justice Act 2003 (Commencement No. 9) Order* 2005 (S.I. 2005 No. 1267). For all other purposes, they come into force on a day or days to be appointed.]

Prosecution of Offences Act 1985, ss.22A, 22B

Additional time limits for persons under 18

1–269a **22A.**—(1) The Secretary of State may by regulations make provision—

(a) with respect to a person under the age of 18 at the time of his arrest in connection with an offence, as to the maximum period to be allowed for the completion of the stage beginning with his arrest and ending with the date fixed for his first appearance in court in connection with the offence ("the initial stage");

(b) with respect to a person convicted of an offence who was under that age at the time of his arrest for the offence or (where he was not arrested for it) the laying of the information charging him with it, as to the period within which the stage between his conviction and his being sentenced for the offence should be completed.

(2) Subsection (2) of section 22 above applies for the purposes of regulations under subsection (1) above as if—

(a) the reference in paragraph (d) to custody or overall time limits were a reference to time limits imposed by the regulations; and

(b) the reference in paragraph (e) to proceedings instituted before the commencement of any provisions of the regulations were a reference to a stage begun before that commencement.

(3) A magistrates' court may, at any time before the expiry of the time limit imposed by the regulations under subsection (1)(a) above ("the initial stage time limit"), extend, or further extend, that limit; but the court shall not do so unless it is satisfied—

(a) that the need for the extension is due to some good and sufficient cause; and

(b) that the investigation has been conducted, and (where applicable) the prosecution has acted, with all due diligence and expedition.

(4) Where the initial stage time limit (whether as originally imposed or as extended or further extended under subsection (3) above) expires before the person arrested is charged with the offence, he shall not be charged with it unless further evidence relating to it is obtained, and—

(a) if he is then under arrest, he shall be released;

(b) if he is then on bail under Part IV of the *Police and Criminal Evidence Act* 1984, his bail (and any duty or conditions to which it is subject) shall be discharged.

(5) Where the initial stage time limit (whether as originally imposed or as extended or further extended under subsection (3) above) expires after the person arrested is charged with the offence but before the date fixed for his first appearance in court in connection with it, the court shall stay the proceedings.

(6) Where—

(a) a person escapes from arrest; or

(b) a person who has been released on bail under Part IV of the *Police and Criminal Evidence Act* 1984 fails to surrender himself at the appointed time,

and is accordingly unlawfully at large for any period, that period shall be disregarded, so far as the offence in question is concerned, for the purposes of the initial stage time limit.

(7) Subsections (7) to (9) of section 22 above apply for the purposes of this section, at any time after the person arrested has been charged with the offence in question, as if any reference (however expressed) to a custody or overall time limit were a reference to the initial stage time limit.

(8) Where a person is convicted of an offence in any proceedings, the exercise of the power conferred by subsection (3) above shall not be called into question in any appeal against that conviction.

(9) Any reference in this section (however expressed) to a person being charged with an offence includes a reference to the laying of an information charging him with it.

Re-institution of proceedings stayed under section 22(4) or 22A(5)

1–269b **22B.**—(1) This section applies where proceedings for an offence ("the original proceedings") are stayed by a court under section 22(4) or 22A(5) of this Act.

(2) If—

(a) in the case of proceedings conducted by the Director, the Director or a Chief Crown Prosecutor so directs;

(b) in the case of proceedings conducted by the Director of the Serious Fraud Office, the Commissioners of Inland Revenue or the Commissioners of Customs and Excise, that Director or those Commissioners so direct; or

(c) in the case of proceedings not conducted as mentioned in paragraph (a) or (b) above, a person designated for the purpose by the Secretary of State so directs, fresh proceedings for the offence may be instituted within a period of three months (or such longer period as the court may allow) after the date on which the original proceedings were stayed by the court.

(3) Fresh proceedings shall be instituted as follows—

(a) where the original proceedings were stayed by the Crown Court, by preferring a bill of indictment;

(b) where the original proceedings were stayed by a magistrates' court, by laying an information.

(4) Fresh proceedings may be instituted in accordance with subsections (2) and (3)(b) above notwithstanding anything in section 127(1) of the *Magistrates' Courts Act* 1980 (limitation of time).

(5) Where fresh proceedings are instituted, anything done in relation to the original proceedings shall be treated as done in relation to the fresh proceedings if the court so directs or it was done—

(a) by the prosecutor in compliance or purported compliance with section 3, 4 or 7A of the *Criminal Procedure and Investigations Act* 1996; or

(b) by the accused in compliance or purported compliance with section 5 or 6 of that Act.

(6) Where a person is convicted of an offence in fresh proceedings under this section, the institution of those proceedings shall not be called into question in any appeal against that conviction.

[Ss.22A and 22B were inserted by the *CDA* 1998, ss.44 and 45 respectively. S.22B(5) is printed as amended by the *CJA* 2003, s.331, and Sched. 36, para. 17, in respect of which see the saving provision in the commencement details at § 12–54, *post*.]

Appeals

In connection with section 22(7) and (8) (appeals), see the *Criminal Procedure Rules* **1–269c**
2005 (S.I. 2005 No. 384), Pt 20 (*post*, § 2–169).

Requirements of the European Convention on Human Rights

The requirements of Articles 5(3) and 6(1) of the ECHR (*post*, §§ 16–43 *et seq.*, 16–57 **1–269ca**
and 16–73) have significance when considering the 1985 legislation in respect of time limits, as may be seen from *R. v. Manchester Crown Court, ex p. McDonald* [1999] 1 Cr.App.R. 409, DC, *post*, § 1–273.

In *Punzelt v. Czech Republic* (2001) 33 E.H.R.R. 49, ECtHR, the entitlement under Article 5(3) to trial within a reasonable time or release pending trial was considered. Following a general discussion as to situations where pre-trial detention may be justified despite the presumption of innocence, it was held that the persistence of a reasonable suspicion is the *sine qua non* of the lawfulness of pre-trial detention, but after a certain lapse of time it no longer suffices; it must then be established whether any other grounds continue to justify the deprivation of liberty; even where such other grounds are "relevant" and "sufficient" the European Court will seek to ascertain whether the national authorities have displayed "special diligence" in the conduct of the proceedings. Further, the "reasonable time" requirement in Article 5(3) is to be distinguished from that contained in Article 6(1); where, therefore, there has been a violation of Article 5(3) on account of lack of "special diligence" on the part of the authorities, it will not necessarily follow that there has been a violation of the reasonable time requirement in Article 6. To a similar effect, see *Ceský v. Czech Republic* (2001) 33 E.H.R.R. 8, ECtHR. As to the general principles, see also *Barfuss v. Czech Republic* (2002) 34 E.H.R.R. 37, ECtHR, *Kudla v. Poland* (2002) 35 E.H.R.R. 11, ECtHR, *Erdem v. Germany* (2002) 35 E.H.R.R. 15, ECtHR, *Jecius v. Lithuania* (2002) 35 E.H.R.R. 16, ECtHR, *Grisez v. Belgium* (2003) 36 E.H.R.R. 48, ECtHR, and *Kalashnikov v. Russia* (2003) 36 E.H.R.R. 34, ECtHR. See also *post*, §§ 4–66 *et seq*.

Notwithstanding the marked similarity between the language of section 22(3)(b) and that of the Strasbourg jurisprudence, the expiration of a custody time limit will not necessarily mean that the "reasonable time" has elapsed within which, for the purposes of Article 5(3), an accused must be tried or released pending trial: *R. (O.) v. Crown Court at Harrow* [2007] 1 A.C. 249, HL (continuation of detention of accused to whom section 25 of the *CJPOA* 1994 applies may be lawful despite expiration of custody time limit; however, their Lordships did not expect there would be many cases where bail is refused notwithstanding a refusal to extend a custody time limit, but did not give guidance as to the sort of situation in which an absence of "due diligence" within the meaning of section 22(3)(b) will, or will not, also amount to an absence of "special diligence" within the meaning of the Strasbourg jurisprudence – it is submitted that section 25 must not be construed in a manner that will prevent release on bail in circumstances where there has been a lack of special diligence; certainly, it must be read down so as not to impose a burden of proof on an accused person and so as not to inhibit judicial assessment and balancing of all the relevant circumstances, the words "exceptional circumstances" merely serving to remind the court of the risks normally posed by defendants to whom the section applies, as to which see *post*, § 3–55). See also *post*, § 1–270.

As to the impact of the Convention on the relevant procedures, see *Wildman v. DPP*, 165 J.P. 453, DC, *post*, § 1–272.

Overall time limits

1–269d The only regulations made pursuant to sections 22(1)(a) and 22A(1) were in respect of youth court time limits. However, those regulations have now been revoked, so that, as from April 22, 2003, there have been no overall time limits: *Prosecution of Offences (Youth Courts Time Limits) (Revocation and Transitional Provisions) Regulations* 2003 (S.I. 2003 No. 917).

Custody time limits: general and procedure

1–270 The regulations concerning custody time limits, made under section 22(1)(b) and (2), are set out *post*, §§ 3–56 *et seq.*

Generally, a defendant is entitled to be released on bail once a custody time limit, and any extension thereto, has expired, but an order of the court is necessary to secure such release; in the Crown Court such an order will be the result of the compliance by the prosecution with regulation 6 of the *Prosecution of Offences (Custody Time Limits) Regulations* 1987 (*post*, §§ 3–61 *et seq.*), but in default of such compliance it will be for the defendant to make a bail application or seek relief from the Divisional Court: *Olotu v. Home Office* [1997] 1 W.L.R. 328, CA (Civ. Div.).

By reason of regulation 6(6), the general right to release on bail once a custody time limit has expired is subject to the limitation on the right to bail imposed by section 25 of the *CJPOA* 1994 (*post*, § 3–55) in respect of the situations specified in that section, as to which see *R. (O.) v. Crown Court at Harrow*, *ante*. See also *post*, § 1–271.

Each charge attracts its own custody time limit: *R. v. Wirral District Magistrates' Court, ex p. Meikle* [1991] C.O.D. 2, DC. This principle is subject to two qualifications; first, the bringing of a new charge will not result in the commencement of a new custody time limit if the offence in the new charge is simply a restatement of the old offence with different particulars; the new offence must be a different offence in law if it is to attract a fresh time limit; secondly, the bringing of a new charge will be an abuse of process if the court is satisfied that (*per* Lord Hope) it has been brought solely for the purpose of substituting a new custody time limit, which issue can best be tested by requiring the prosecutor to demonstrate why, on the facts of the case, the bringing of the new charge is necessary, or that (*per* Lord Slynn) the way in which and the time at which the new charge is added or substituted, indicates that it is not done for the genuine purpose of introducing a new charge on a revised assessment of the case, but is done primarily to keep the accused in custody: *R. (Wardle) v. Crown Court at Leeds* [2002] 1 A.C. 754, HL (manslaughter is a different offence from murder; therefore, the substitution of a charge of manslaughter for murder attracted a new custody time limit, notwithstanding the circumstances were such that no extension of the custody time limits would have been granted). For a reasoned criticism of this decision, see *Criminal Law Week* 2001/11/2.

Once committal proceedings have started, magistrates' court custody time limits cease to have effect (see *post*, § 3–58). If such a time limit expires during an adjourned or an aborted committal hearing the prosecution do not need an extension of the time limit to keep the accused in custody: *R. v. Governor of Winson Green Prison, ex p. Trotter*, 94 Cr.App.R. 29, DC. The position is the same where a trial on indictment has commenced within the relevant custody time limit, but the jury have then been discharged and a retrial ordered; however, in such a situation the judge should be vigilant to protect the interests of the accused by fixing a speedy retrial, or considering the grant of bail or, even, a stay of the proceedings as an abuse: *R. v. Leeds Crown Court, ex p. Whitehead*, 164 J.P. 102, DC.

As to when magistrates can be said to have started enquiring into a case as examining magistrates, see *R. v. Worcester Magistrates, ex p. Bell* [1994] Crim.L.R. 133, DC. Where committal proceedings had been commenced regularly on the day before the expiry of the relevant custody time limit, an order quashing the committal and requiring the magistrates' court to consider the matter *de novo*, as the result of an irregularity during the proceedings, did not render the entire proceedings a nullity; accordingly the relevant custody time limit had not expired before the magistrates' court had begun to inquire into the information, within the meaning of regulation 4(5)(a) of the regulations (*post*, § 3–58): *Re Najam, The Independent (C.S.)*, October 19, 1998, DC (clarified by the commentary in *Criminal Law Week* 1998/37/3).

The commencement of a preparatory hearing, pursuant to various statutory provisions, has the effect of bringing to an end the operation of a custody time limit; it is therefore important to bear in mind the purpose of custody time limits in deciding when to commence such a hearing: *Re Kanaris* [2003] 2 Cr.App.R. 1, HL, *post*, § 4–85d.

Where a defendant is remanded in custody, time continues to run for the purposes of the custody time limit regime during any period when he is serving a custodial sentence in respect of another matter: *R. v. Peterborough Crown Court, ex p. L.* [2000] Crim.L.R. 470, DC.

Many difficulties in connection with custody time limits in the Crown Court can be avoided by holding an early plea and directions hearing at which a date is set for trial within the relevant time limit, with other directions tailored to fit that date; if it is impossible to fix a trial date at such hearing, the judge should direct that the trial be fixed for a date before the expiration of the time limit and that the matter be re-listed in the event of any problem in this regard; any potential time limit problem will then become apparent, and any necessary application for an extension made, sooner rather than later; there is a joint duty on the Crown Court and the prosecution to make such arrangements, the duty of the defence being to indicate which prosecution witnesses are required, so that their availability may be ascertained: see *R. v. Worcester Crown Court, ex p. Norman* [2000] 2 Cr.App.R. 33, DC, and *R. v. Sheffield Crown Court, ex p. Headley* [2000] 2 Cr.App.R. 1, DC. As to the fixing of trial dates, see further *post*, §§ 1–274 *et seq.* **1–270a**

The requirements of regulation 7 (*post*, § 3–64), as to the giving of notice of an application to extend a time limit, are directory, not mandatory; failure to comply therewith does not therefore preclude the exercise of the general discretion conferred by section 22(3) to extend a time limit "at any time ... before expiry": *R. v. Governor of Canterbury Prison, ex p. Craig* [1991] 2 Q.B. 195, 91 Cr.App.R. 7, DC (but see now *ante*, §§ 1–195 *et seq.*). In the course of his judgment in *ex p. Craig*, Watkins L.J. expressed the following views: **1–271**

(a) all custody periods begin at the close of the day during which a defendant is first remanded and expire at the relevant midnight thereafter;

(b) the standard of proof embodied in the requirements that the court be satisfied of various matters as a precondition of the exercise of its discretions respectively under section 22(3) and regulation 7(4) is the civil standard (agreed in *R. v. Manchester Crown Court, ex p. McDonald (and consolidated applications)* [1999] 1 Cr.App.R. 409, DC);

(c) where the prosecution is uncertain whether or not it will need to apply for an extension, it is strictly unnecessary to give a contingent notice of an intention to apply unless there is at least a high likelihood of an application becoming necessary;

(d) an application for habeas corpus is an inappropriate means of challenging a decision of justices to extend a custody time limit, when a specific right of appeal to the Crown Court is given by section 22(7) (see also *R. v. Folkestone Magistrates' Court, ex p. Bradley* [1994] C.O.D. 138, DC).

1–272 The requirement in section 22(3) that the court must be "satisfied" means that the court can never abdicate its responsibility by granting an extension on the nod, or simply because the parties agree or no objection is raised; the court must address its mind to the requirements of section 22(3), for which purpose it must be adequately and fully informed of the matters which may affect the decision; whether evidence will be necessary, or whether the court can rely on information supplied by the advocates, will depend on the nature and extent of any controversy; if, for example, the prosecutor outlines the history of the proceedings and suggests, without contradiction by the defence, that the prosecution has acted with all due diligence and expedition, the court will be more readily satisfied on that score than if that condition is the subject of a substantial contest; any application for the extension of custody time limits will call for careful consideration, and many will call for rigorous scrutiny; when ruling on such an application the court should not only state its decision, but also its reasons for reaching that decision (whichever way) and, if an extension is granted, for holding the conditions in section 22(3) to be fulfilled; where full argument has been heard and the court has given its decision, with reasons, the Divisional Court will be most reluctant to interfere, its role being confined to review, with relief being granted only on one of the familiar grounds for founding a successful application for judicial review: *ex p. McDonald* (*ante*) (summarising and explaining previous decisions). As to the need for evidence and reasoned decisions, and as to judicial review, see further *post*, § 1–272c.

Where there is an issue as to whether the prosecution have "acted with all due diligence" the court should be provided with a chronology, preferably agreed, showing the dates of all material events and orders: *R. v. Chelmsford Crown Court, ex p. Mills*, 164 J.P. 1, DC. Where an application is based on the size and complexity of the case, it is incumbent on the prosecution to give a detailed explanation as to what has been done and what is delaying preparation; further, it is good practice to give the grounds for the application in the notice of intention to make the application, although this is not required by rule 7: *R. v. Central Criminal Court, ex p. Marotta* [1999] C.O.D. 13, DC.

1–272a All applications for an extension should be listed in open court, with advocates (where possible, those instructed in the trial) attending; they should be fully instructed on all aspects of the case relating to the timetable, the nature of the case and any other matter relevant to the decision that has to be made; all advocates will be expected to be fully conversant with the judgment in *ex p. McDonald* (*ante*); however short the extension sought, each application must be fully considered; advocates should inform the court at least 24 hours before the hearing of the anticipated length thereof: *Practice Direction (Application to extend custody time limits)*, unreported, December 18, 1998, Western Circuit (Butterfield J.)—subsequently adopted also on the other circuits (see *Criminal Law Week* 1999/29/13).

As to the extent to which the coming into force of the *Human Rights Act* 1998 has affected the procedure previously adopted for dealing with extensions of custody time limits, see *ex p. McDonald*, *ante*, § 1–269c. It is not helpful to set out precisely what the approach should be as it will differ from case to case; the important point is that the procedure can be more informal than a normal trial process, which means that it is unnecessary to comply with the formal rules of evidence; the burden is on the Crown to obtain an extension and it must satisfy the court that the application is a proper one; the procedure must also enable the defendant to test the appropriateness of the application, bearing in mind the matters that are relied upon by the Crown; it is to be hoped that in the majority of cases it will be possible for the prosecution to make information available to the defence in advance of the application, which will allow them to be satisfied as to the propriety of the application; in so far as it is necessary for a defendant to test any aspect of the application, then the means must be provided to enable him to do that, but formal disclosure of the sort which is appropriate prior to trial will not normally be necessary: *Wildman v. DPP*, 165 J.P. 453, DC. This does not mean that the defence can require the prosecution to call witnesses in respect of any particular matter that the defence wish to criticise; it is for the prosecution to decide what evidence to call in support of their application and if they fail to call appropriate evidence their application will fail: *R. (Rippe) v. Chelmsford Crown Court* [2002] Crim.L.R. 485, DC. Further, it is open to a judge hearing an application for an extension to rely on transcripts of what has been said at earlier hearings, and on evidence given at such hearings, where there has been an opportunity at the earlier hearing for cross-examination and where it must have been apparent to the defence representatives that the issues then being discussed would in due course lead to an application for an extension of the custody time limit: *ibid*.

The opening words of section 22(3) allow of the making of an application for an extension of a time limit before the expiry of a period that has been extended by the court, as well as before the expiry of the original time limit: *R. (Haque) v. Central Criminal Court* [2003] 10 *Archbold News* 1, QBD (Mitting J.). There is no power, however, to grant an extension of a custody time limit after it has expired, but the expiry of one custody time limit is not a bar to detention under a different custody time limit at a later stage of the proceedings: *R. v. Sheffield JJ., ex p. Turner* [1991] 2 Q.B. 472, 93 Cr.App.R. 180, DC. Thus, where the Crown Court has refused to extend a custody time limit, the Divisional Court can provide no useful relief once the relevant time limit has expired, even if there would otherwise be grounds for granting relief to the prosecutor: *R. v. Croydon Crown Court, ex p. Commrs of Customs and Excise* [1997] 8 *Archbold News* 1, DC. Likewise, where an extension of a custody time limit is quashed, there is no power to reconsider the matter in accordance with the correct principles if the time limit has by then expired. However, the High Court, in exercise of its discretion as to whether to grant relief in respect of judicial review proceedings that have not been instituted promptly, will take account of any failure on the part of those acting for an applicant to bring such proceedings within a period that would enable the court below to reconsider an application for an extension: *R. (Siraju and Kabeya) v. Snaresbrook Crown Court*, unreported, August 14, 2001, QBD (Stanley Burnton J.). **1–272b**

It is on the occasion of an application for an extension of a custody time limit that the court must be satisfied as to the conditions for an extension being met; the court cannot abdicate its responsibility by assuming that the relevant matters have been considered on a previous occasion by another judge, or that the matter had been properly dealt with by counsel and that therefore the conditions must have been met; thus, where a date for trial beyond the relevant custody time limit has previously been fixed, it is not open to the judge who hears the application for an extension to assume that the judge who fixed the trial date would not have fixed that date unless he had been satisfied that the conditions for extending the time limit were satisfied: *ibid*. See also *post*, § 1–274a.

An application for an extension of a custody time limit must be made clearly and unmistakably so that the defence have the opportunity to raise any objections to the application; further, an order extending a time limit must be made clearly and unambiguously and cannot simply be inferred from other orders; all relevant dates and details must be clearly announced when such an order is made and the clerk of the court must ensure that a proper and permanent record is made: *R. v. Governor of Armley Prison, ex p. Ward*, *The Times*, November 23, 1990, DC.

If a judge in the Crown Court, in refusing to extend a custody time limit, acts on the basis of a fundamental error of fact, the appropriate procedure is to re-apply under section 22(3) of the 1985 Act to that judge or, if he is unavailable, to the senior judge at the relevant court centre; this should not be taken as a charter for inadequate preparation by the prosecution or for having a second bite at the cherry in other situations, and in the ordinary way a re-application would constitute an abuse: *R. v. Bradford Crown Court, ex p. Crossling* [2000] 1 Cr.App.R. 463, DC. **1–272c**

As to the need, indicated in *ex p. McDonald*, *ante*, for reasons to be given in respect of a decision as to whether or not to extend a custody time limit, elaborate or detailed reasons studded with authority are not necessary; what is called for is a succinct, summary and brief account by the judge of the crux of the decision and of why he has taken the view that he has on the submissions made to him: *R. v. Leeds Crown Court, ex p. Bagoutie*; *R. v. Same, ex p. Callaghan*, *The Times*, May 31, 1999, DC (CO/1211/99).

It will sometimes suffice, in giving reasons, for the judge to summarise the submissions made on one side or the other and to indicate that he accepts them: *R. v. Chelmsford Crown Court, ex p. Mills, ante*. In *R. v. Leeds Crown Court, ex p. Wilson* [1999] Crim.L.R. 738, DC, it was said that a failure by the judge at first instance to give reasons will not be fatal if the decision is otherwise reasonable. Principles expounded in other areas of the law as to the necessity for reasoned decisions, and the general requirement for reasoned decisions to be given in the Crown Court on appeals from decisions of magistrates, were considered in *R. v. Kingston Crown Court, ex p. Bell*, 164 J.P. 633, QBD (Jackson J.), in the context of appeals to the Crown Court from decisions of magistrates as to custody time limits: see further *post*, § 2–202. There is a particular need for a reasoned judgment where any "good and sufficient cause" identified is not one for which there is any authoritative precedent: *R. (Lake and Bennett) v. Northampton Crown Court* [2001] 3 *Archbold News* 2, DC. See also *Becciev v. Moldova* (2007) 45 E.H.R.R. 11, ECtHR, as to the need for, and purpose of, the giving of focused and acceptable reasons, so as to satisfy the requirements of Article 5(3) of the ECHR (*post*, § 16–43).

Although it might be desirable in principle for the case stated procedure to be used to challenge a decision of a judge to extend a custody time limit (as to which see *R. v. Central Criminal Court, ex p. Behbehani* [1994] Crim.L.R. 352, DC), the time scale of that procedure is such that its use might deprive an applicant of effective relief; the giving of a reasoned decision will facilitate the use of judicial review: *R. v. Leeds Crown Court, ex p. Briggs (No. 1)* [1998] 2 Cr.App.R. 413, DC. Section 22(13) enables the making of such a challenge by judicial review, albeit in respect of a decision of the Crown Court. To succeed on such a challenge it will be necessary to establish the existence of one of the conventional bases for judicial review; the mere fact that the judges hearing the challenge might have reached a different decision at first instance will not suffice: *R. v. Preston Crown Court, ex p. Campbell* [1999] C.O.D. 407, DC, and *Rippe*, *ante*, following *ex p. McDonald*, *ante*. It will rarely be appropriate to grant permission to apply for judicial review when the outcome has become academic because the proceedings have moved on, or would have moved on, to the next stage: *R. v. Leeds Crown Court, ex p. Whitehead*, *The Times*, September 16, 1998, DC. A stay of the underlying proceedings should not be granted pending a challenge in the High Court: *R. v. Merthyr Tydfil Crown Court, ex p. West and David*; *R. v. Same, ex p. Evans*; *R. v. Same, ex p. Allan and Allan* [1997] 5 *Archbold News* 2, DC (CO4481/96).

In *R. v. Bristol Crown Court, ex p. Commrs of Customs and Excise* [1990] C.O.D. 11, DC, it was held that section 22(13) permits the review of a decision made by the Crown Court, pursuant to S.I. 1987 No. 299, to admit a defendant to bail. As to judicial review of Crown Court proceedings generally, see *post*, §§ 2–159, 2–160, 7–4 *et seq*.

Criteria to be satisfied before extension granted

1–273 The criteria to be satisfied before an extension of a custody time limit may be granted are set out in section 22(3) of the 1985 Act (*ante*, § 1–267). See *R. v. Manchester Crown Court, ex p. McDonald* [1999] 1 Cr.App.R. 409, DC, *ante*, §§ 1–271, 1–272, as to the burden and standard of proof in this regard and as to the rigour with which each application should be scrutinised. The purpose of the relevant legislation was also analysed in both its domestic context and in the context of the requirements of the ECHR in *ex p. McDonald*. It was said that the overriding purposes of the legislation are (i) to ensure that periods for which unconvicted defendants are held in custody awaiting trial are as short as reasonably and practically possible; (ii) to oblige the prosecution to prepare cases for trial with all due diligence and expedition; and (iii) to invest the court with a power and duty to control any extension, and that any court making a decision on an application for an extension must be careful to give full weight to all of these important objectives.

Prior to its amendment by the *CDA* 1998, section 22(3) gave the court power to grant an extension if satisfied "(a) that there is good and sufficient cause for doing so, and (b) that the prosecution has acted with all due expedition". In *ex p. McDonald*, *ante* (as in *R. v. Luton Crown Court, ex p. Neaves* [1992] Crim.L.R. 721, DC), it was held that if, but only if, *both* these statutory criteria were satisfied the court could, in the exercise of its discretion (but need not) grant an extension. In *R. v. Central Criminal Court, ex p. Bennett, The Times*, January 25, 1999, DC (transcript CO/4518/98), it was held that although the illness of a prosecution witness provided good and sufficient cause for an extension of the custody time limit, that was irrelevant to what should have been the separate question of whether the prosecution had acted with all due expedition, and that the judge below had erred by considering the question of due expedition in the light of the existence of the good and sufficient cause, rather than separately. In reaching this decision, reference was made to observations of Lord Bingham C.J. in *ex p. McDonald*, as summarised, *ante*, as to the overriding objectives of the relevant legislation.

However, in *R. v. Leeds Crown Court, ex p. Bagoutie*; *R. v. Same, ex p. Callaghan, ante*, § 1-272, Lord Bingham C.J., with whom Ognall J. agreed, held that, on a proper construction, the statutory provision as to "due expedition" is linked to the provision as to "good and sufficient reason", in that, when seeking an extension, the Crown "must show that the need for the extension does not arise from lack of due expedition or diligence on its part". His Lordship said that this had not been made plain in *ex p. McDonald* because the issue had not arisen there, and went on to say that the court is not obliged "to refuse the extension ... because the prosecution is shown to have been guilty of avoidable delay where that delay has had no effect whatever on the ability of the prosecution and the defence to be ready for trial on a pre-determined trial date". The *ex p. Bagoutie* approach was followed in a number of subsequent authorities: see, in particular, *R. v. Kingston Crown Court, ex p. Bell*, 164 J.P. 633, QBD (Jackson J.), and *R. (Rippe) v. Chelmsford Crown Court, ante*, § 1-272.

The conflict of authority was considered in *R. (Gibson) v. Winchester Crown Court* [2004] 2 Cr.App.R. 14, DC, where the court came down in favour of *ex p. Bagoutie*. It came to this conclusion by reference to the allegedly absurd results that would follow from the opposite conclusion. Whilst the court conceded that the language of the subsection suggested the conclusion in *ex p. Bennett*, it declined to consult *Hansard* in accordance with *Pepper v. Hart* [1993] A.C. 593. Had it done so, it would have found that what was intended by Parliament was what is suggested by the language of the legislation (see H.C., vol. 77, cols 155–156; and H.L., vol. 459, col. 421). However, short of consideration of the issue by the House of Lords, the point must now be taken to be settled.

In *R. (Thomas) v. Central Criminal Court*; *R. (Stubbs) v. Same* [2007] 1 Cr.App.R. 7, DC, it was held that, notwithstanding the absence from section 22(3)(b) of the words "that the need for the extension is due to", which appear in respect of the criteria set out in paragraph (a), where an application for a further extension is made, paragraphs (a) and (b) work in tandem and are both focussed on the need for a further extension; thus, the defendant may only rely upon delay prior to the original extension if such delay is the root cause of the need to seek the further extension. In the course of the judgments, reference was made to earlier dicta in which attention was drawn to the intensity of the scrutiny required, both at first instance and upon review, in relation to matters concerning the liberty of the individual, but also to the dangers of satellite litigation and of disruption of the trial process where there is a failure to appreciate the primacy of the role of the judge at first instance in assessing the individual situation.

See also *Re Gilligan*; *R. v. Crown Court at Woolwich, ex p. Gilligan* [1998] 2 All E.R. 1, DC, where it was said that the requirement for the prosecution to have "acted with all due expedition" relates to the period up to the making of the application to extend the custody time limit, not to any delay that may result from granting the application, and that the requirement for "good and sufficient cause" relates to the period after any extension.

Many of the previous authorities in respect of the section 22(3) criteria were reviewed **1-274**
in *ex p. McDonald, ante*, where Lord Bingham C.J., giving the judgment of the court, said, in respect of the section in its original form, that:

> "The condition in section 22(3)(b) that the prosecution should have acted with all due expedition poses little difficulty of interpretation. The condition looks to the conduct of the

prosecuting authority (police, solicitors, counsel). To satisfy the court that this condition is met the prosecution need not show that every stage of preparation of the case has been accomplished as quickly and efficiently as humanly possible. That would be an impossible standard to meet, particularly when the court which reviews the history of the case enjoys the immeasurable benefit of hindsight. Nor should the history be approached on the unreal assumption that all involved on the prosecution side have been able to give the case in question their undivided attention. What the court must require is such diligence and expedition as would be shown by a competent prosecutor conscious of his duty to bring the case to trial as quickly as reasonably and fairly possible. In considering, whether that standard is met, the court will of course have regard to the nature and complexity of the case, the extent of preparation necessary, the conduct (whether co-operative or obstructive) of the defence, the extent to which the prosecutor is dependent on the co-operation of others outside his control and other matters directly and genuinely bearing on the preparation of the case for trial. It would be undesirable and unhelpful to compile a list of matters which it may be relevant to consider in deciding whether this condition is met. In deciding whether the condition is met, however, the court must bear in mind that the period ... specified in the regulations is a maximum, not a target; and that it is a period applicable to all cases. ... the court will not, in considering whether this condition is satisfied, pay attention to pretexts such as chronic staff shortages or ... overwork, sickness, absenteeism or matters of that kind.

Under section 22(3)(a) the court must be satisfied that there is good and sufficient cause for extending or further extending the maximum period of custody specified in the regulations. The seriousness of the offence with which the defendant is charged cannot of itself be good and sufficient cause within the section; nor can the need to protect the public. ... Nor ... can it be a good cause that the extension is only for a short period [as to which, see also *R. v. Sheffield Crown Court, ex p. Headley* [2000] 2 Cr.App.R. 1, DC]. ...

While it is possible to rule that some matters, such as those we have just mentioned, are incapable of amounting in law to good and sufficient cause for granting an extension, there is an almost infinite variety of matters which may, depending on the facts of a particular case, be capable of amounting to a good and sufficient cause. ... it would be facile to propose any test which would be applicable in all cases" (at pp. 414C–415C).

His Lordship went on to adopt the proposition that even where a "good cause" for an extension exists, the circumstances must be examined rigorously to determine whether the cause is also "sufficient" for any extension, and cited with approval a number of previous authorities, and passages from judgments in such authorities, in support of the proposition that unavailability of a suitable judge or court-room might, in special cases and upon particular facts, amount to a good and sufficient cause for an extension of some period, but emphasised that an application based on such matters should be approached with great caution to avoid the danger that the statutory purpose would be undermined by the too ready grant of applications based on such grounds. In this regard, see also *R. v. Norwich Crown Court, ex p. Stiller* [1992] C.O.D. 310, DC (lack of court room and judge not good and sufficient cause for extension where no indication when such facilities would be available), *R. v. Maidstone Crown Court, ex p. Schulz and Steinkeller* [1993] C.O.D. 183, DC (unreasonable to grant 14 day extension when judge had been told that earliest possible date was 93 days away), and *R. v. Stoke-on-Trent Crown Court, ex p. Marsden* [1999] C.O.D. 114, DC (where reliance placed on lack of suitable judge or court-room it was not enough that there was a clash with another case; it was necessary to show why other case should have priority).

In respect of the right to trial within a reasonable time, pursuant to Articles 5(3) and 6(1) of the ECHR, one area for particular enquiry is the manner in which the case has been dealt with by the administrative and judicial authorities, and in that regard contracting states cannot blame unacceptable delays on a general want of prosecutors or judges or courthouses or on chronic underfunding of the legal system, for it is generally incumbent on contracting states so to organise their legal systems as to ensure that the reasonable time requirement is honoured; but the courts are not required to shut their eyes to the practical realities of litigious life even in a reasonably well-organised legal system; thus it is not objectionable for a prosecutor to deal with cases according to what he reasonably regards as their priority, so as to achieve an orderly dispatch of business, and it must be accepted that a prosecutor cannot ordinarily devote his whole time to a single case; and the courts are entitled to draw up their lists of cases some time in advance; it might be necessary to wait for the availability of a judge possessing a special expertise, or of a courthouse with special facilities or security; and plans might be disrupted by unexpected illness or the pressure on a court might be increased by a sudden and unforeseen surge in business: *Dyer v. Watson*; *K. v. H.M. Advocate* [2004] 1 A.C. 379, PC (further discussed at § 4–64, *post*). As to the general obligation on contracting states to organise and fund their legal systems so as to ensure that the reasonable time requirements are honoured, see also *Baggetta v. Italy*, 10 E.H.R.R. 325, ECtHR, *Garyfallou Aebe v. Greece*, 28 E.H.R.R. 344, ECtHR, and *Mattocia v. Italy* (2003) 36 E.H.R.R. 47, ECtHR.

A trial should not be fixed for hearing on a date after the expiry of the relevant custody time limit without full inquiry as to whether it is possible to try the case before that time; however, if this appears to be impossible and a later date is fixed, a judge hearing a subsequent application for an extension of the time limit should be fully informed as to what occurred when the date was fixed; it will still be incumbent on him to investigate the possibility of an earlier trial before making a finding of "good and sufficient cause" on the basis of unavailability of court or judge; it is for the prosecution to satisfy the judge of reasons why, in a sensible world, an earlier trial is not possible: *R. v. Preston Crown Court, ex p. Barraclough* [1999] Crim.L.R. 973, DC. See also *R. v. Leeds Crown Court, ex p. Wilson* [1999] Crim.L.R. 738, DC (when considering the possibility of moving a trial to another location or of accelerating a hearing date, judges should be vigilant to ensure that court staff responsible for making the necessary inquiries and arrangements are fulfilling their duties scrupulously and keeping the representatives of the parties informed); and *R. (Bannister) v. Crown Court at Guildford and CPS*, unreported, January 29, 2004, DC ([2004] EWHC 221 (Admin.)) ("positive judicial intervention" using "all judicial means available" may be required to assist a trial date being found within the custody time limit). See also *ante*, §§ 1–270a, 1–272b. **1–274a**

In *R. (Gibson) v. Winchester Crown Court*, *ante*, § 1–273, it was said that before a court grants an extension because of the lack of availability of a courtroom, or of a particular judge required to try a case, it should go to considerable lengths to avoid having to do so; but the availability of a particular category of judge can be important to achieve justice in certain cases. In routine cases, the court said that the approach suggested in *R. (Bannister) v. Crown Court at Guildford and CPS* (chronic lack of resources cannot amount to "good and sufficient cause") may generally be appropriate; but that approach should not be taken to indicate that the availability of resources is irrelevant; the fact that they are limited cannot be ignored, and occasions will occur when pressures on the court are more intense than usual, and it is the task of the judge to take account of all relevant circumstances.

Where it is said that there are real pressures on a court which have been created by exceptional circumstances, the court should examine carefully the reasons for that situation and the proposed solution to it; it should then make a judgment as to whether it can properly be said that (a) the reasons are exceptional, and (b) the proposed steps to alleviate the situation appear to have a prospect of success; if it can, then there may be a good and sufficient cause for an extension, but if the delays which are being experienced by the court are not being alleviated by any steps that are being taken, the judge may be forced to conclude that there is a systemic failure, in which event listing difficulties in a routine case will not be a good and sufficient cause for an extension: *Kalonji v. Wood Green Crown Court* [2008] A.C.D. 11, DC. Although listing difficulties may amount to "good and sufficient cause" for extending a custody time limit in exceptional cases, this does not encompass routine listing difficulties due to the normal pressure of work on the Crown Court in routine cases: *R. (Miah) v. Crown Court at Snaresbrook*, unreported, October 19, 2006, QBD (Sullivan J.) ([2006] EWHC 2873 (Admin.)).

The fact that witnesses are professional investigators does not make their convenience (particularly with regard to other duties) irrelevant: *R. v. Leeds Crown Court, ex p. Wilson*, *ante*.

Whilst it is sensible to list some cases as "floaters", it is necessary to consider at an early stage what will happen to a floater that is not reached; not being reached as a floater cannot provide a "good and sufficient" cause for an extension of a custody time limit where the consequence is that the case goes to the back of the queue: *R. v. Bradford Crown Court, ex p. Leadbetter* [2000] 4 *Archbold News* 1, DC. Although the wording of the substituted section 22(3) tightens the circumstances in which an extension may be granted and makes it plain that the scales are weighted against an extension, the amendment does not restrict what may amount to a "good and sufficient cause"; an administrative error in listing may be such a cause; however, a judge should be the less easily persuaded that there is cause for granting an extension when the error is administrative and should only do so if satisfied that the difficulties in the way of a trial within the time limit are insuperable: *R. v. Manchester Crown Court (Minshull Street), ex p. S.*, unreported, August 23, 1999, QBD (Collins J.) (CO/3313/99).

In *R. v. Sheffield Crown Court, ex p. Headley* [2000] 2 Cr.App.R. 1, DC, it was said that matters relevant to the grant or refusal of bail cannot of themselves provide a good and sufficient cause for extending a custody time limit, but in *R. (Eliot) v. Reading Crown Court* [2002] 1 Cr.App.R. 3, DC, it was held that such matters were wholly irrelevant to the issue of good and sufficient cause and that the bail and custody time limit regimes are separate and different. However, it is not absolutely clear from this decision whether factors relevant to the grant or refusal of bail can be taken into account when exercising the discretion that arises as to whether to grant an extension once it is established that the conditions precedent for the granting of an extension have been made out. In *R. v. Manchester Crown Court (Minshull Street), ex p. S., ante*, it had been held that bail considerations could be taken into account at the discretion stage, but in *R. v. Worcester Crown Court, ex p. Norman* [2000] 2 Cr.App.R. 33, DC, there is an apparently clear statement by Smith J. (at p. 39D) that this is not permissible. Rose L.J. had presided over the court in *ex p. Norman* and had agreed with the judgment given by Smith J., but in *Eliot* his Lordship conceded that the relevant passage in the judgment of Smith J. had been obiter and was not an entirely accurate representation of the decision in *ex p. Headley*, on which Smith J. had relied. The reality is that this issue was not separately considered in *ex p. Headley*.

In *Re Gilligan, ante*, § 1–273, postponement of English proceedings pending the outcome of extradition proceedings, where the English proceedings would only be pursued if the extradition application failed, was held to amount to a good and sufficient cause for the extension of a custody time limit. The unexpected absence of a prosecution witness may also suffice: *ex p. Redfearn, post*, § 1–275.

The granting of a defence application to postpone a trial may give rise to a good and sufficient cause to extend a custody time limit: *Re C.*, 164 J.P. 693, DC. In one of the substantive applications considered in *ex p. McDonald, ante*, § 1–273, the wish of a defendant to be represented by counsel of his choice was held to have satisfied the requirement for a "good and sufficient cause". However, the Crown will not have satisfied the relevant conditions if the defence application for an adjournment has been necessitated by a lack of due diligence and expedition on the part of the prosecution: *McKay White v. DPP* [1989] Crim.L.R. 375, DC, and *R. v. Kingston Crown Court, ex p. Bell, ante*, § 1–273. The fact that a case has been delayed by reason of it having been taken out of the warned list at the request of, and for the convenience of, counsel for a co-defendant on bail, is not capable of amounting to a "good and sufficient cause" for extending a custody time limit: *R. (Lake and Bennett) v. Northampton Crown Court* [2001] 3 *Archbold News* 2, DC.

1–275 As to the requirement that "the prosecution has acted with all due expedition", see also *R. v. Norwich Crown Court, ex p. Smith*, unreported, June 25, 1991, DC (CO/0986/91) (entitlement of prosecution to serve only enough evidence to establish prima facie case for committal does not in itself mean lack of due expedition where delay is caused by decision of prosecution, for good reason, to obtain and serve substantial further evidence for purpose of committal); *R. v. Birmingham Crown Court, ex p. Ricketts* [1991] R.T.R. 105, DC (since "prosecution" includes the police, it is not just the period during which CPS have been seised of a matter that is relevant when considering whether prosecution has acted with due expedition); *R. v. Governor of Winchester Prison, ex p. Roddie*, 93 Cr.App.R. 190, DC (history of particular case must be measured against objective yardstick; not sufficient that understaffed police were doing their best; the test of due expedition is not the same as due diligence); *R. v. Birmingham Crown Court, ex p. Bell*; *R. v. Same, ex p. Brown and Francis* [1997] 2 Cr.App.R. 363, DC (question must be decided by reference to the expedition used in the stage of proceedings to which the particular time limit in issue relates; lack of expedition at some earlier stage need not be taken into account, although there may be factual situations where it will be necessary to look at past history, including the preferment of a voluntary bill and what has gone before, to determine whether, on particular facts, good and sufficient cause for extension exists); *ex p. Behbehani, ante*, § 1–272 (prosecution had not acted with all due expedition where there had been unwarranted delay in serving important evidence upon the defence, which had consequence of delay in the proceedings to enable defence to consider same); *R. v. Southwark Crown Court, ex p. DPP* [1999] Crim.L.R. 394, DC (alleged delay by prosecution in doing something which they had no obligation to do is irrelevant); *R. v. Leeds Crown Court, ex p. Briggs (No. 2)* [1998] 2 Cr.App.R. 424, DC, and *R. v. Leeds Crown Court, ex p. Whitehead*, *The Times*, September 16, 1998, DC (in case to be tried on indictment, if at all, the question is whether the prosecution could have acted so as to achieve the relevant form of committal within the relevant period, not whether they have at some point within that period failed to act with all due expedition); *R. v. Central Criminal Court, ex p. Johnson* [1999] 2 Cr.App.R. 51, DC (delay by independent science service is not a failure by the prosecution to act with due expedition, but obligation exists for prosecution to do everything possible to ensure evidence available on time, including making laboratory aware of relevant dates and time limits); *R. (Holland) v. Leeds Crown Court* [2003] Crim.L.R. 272, DC (clear failure to act with all due diligence and expedition where scientific evidence served so late that long-standing fixture had to be broken to enable the defence to deal with it; although forensic science service had acted diligently, being unaware of the relevant dates, the prosecuting authority had failed to communicate effectively with that service, with the defence and with the court; had the problem been raised earlier it was likely that the trial could have been re-fixed for a date earlier than the earliest date that was available once the matter in fact came to the attention of the court); and *R. v. Leeds Crown Court, ex p. Redfearn* [1998] C.O.D. 437, DC (unexpected absence of crucial prosecution witness capable of amounting to good and sufficient cause and did not in itself show failure to act with due expedition; prosecution could not be expected to act as nursemaid to all its witnesses—however, it is submitted that the prosecution should demonstrate that it has taken such steps as are reasonable in the particular circumstances to ensure attendance by its witnesses and it is submitted that various further *dicta* in this case are inconsistent with subsequent authorities and with the duty of disclosure required by the *CPIA* 1996 and by the common law).

(12) Discontinuance of proceedings in magistrates' courts

Prosecution of Offences Act 1985, s.23

23.—(1) Where the Director of Public Prosecutions has the conduct of proceedings for an offence, this section applies in relation to the preliminary stages of those proceedings. **1–276**

(2) In this section, "preliminary stage" in relation to proceedings for an offence does not include—

(a) *in the case of a summary offence,* any stage of the proceedings after the court has begun to hear evidence for the prosecution at *the trial* [a summary trial of the offence]; [or]

(b) *in the case of an indictable offence, any stage of the proceedings after—*

(i) *the accused has been committed for trial; or*

(ii) *the court has begun to hear evidence for the prosecution at a summary trial of the offence;*

[(b) any stage of the proceedings after the accused has been sent for trial for the offence;]

(c) *in the case of any offence, any stage of the proceedings after the accused has been sent for trial under section 51 of the* Crime and Disorder Act *1998 (no committal proceedings for indictable-only and related offences).*

(3) Where, at any time during the preliminary stages of the proceedings, the Director gives notice under this section to the designated officer for the court that he does not want the proceedings to continue, they shall be discontinued with effect from the giving of that notice but may be revived by notice given by the accused under subsection (7) below.

(4) Where, in the case of a person charged with an offence after being taken into custody without a warrant, the Director gives him notice, at a time when no magistrates'

court has been informed of the charge, that the proceedings against him are discontinued, they shall be discontinued with effect from the giving of that notice.

(5) The Director shall, in any notice given under subsection (3) above, give reasons for not wanting the proceedings to continue.

(6) On giving any notice under subsection (3) above the Director shall inform the accused of the notice and of the accused's right to require the proceedings to be continued; but the Director shall not be obliged to give the accused any indication of his reasons for not wanting the proceedings to continue.

(7) Where the Director has given notice under subsection (3) above, the accused shall, if he wants the proceedings to continue, give notice to that effect to the designated officer for the court within the prescribed period; and where notice is so given the proceedings shall continue as if no notice had been given by the Director under subsection (3) above.

(8) Where the designated officer for the court has been so notified by the accused he shall inform the Director.

(9) The discontinuance of any proceedings by virtue of this section shall not prevent the institution of fresh proceedings in respect of the same offence.

(10) In this section "prescribed" means prescribed by Criminal Procedure Rules.

[This section is printed as amended by the *CDA* 1998, s.119, and Sched. 8, para. 63; the *Access to Justice Act* 1999, s.90(1), and Sched. 13, para. 131; and the *Courts Act* 2003, s.109(1), and Sched. 8, para. 290. The words in square brackets in subs. (2) are substituted for the italicised words by the *CJA* 2003, s.41, and Sched. 3, para. 57(1) and (6). This substitution came into force on May 9, 2005, but only in relation to cases sent for trial under s.51A(3)(d) of the *CDA* 1998: *Criminal Justice Act 2003 (Commencement No. 9) Order* 2005 (S.I. 2005 No. 1267). For all other purposes it comes into force on a day to be appointed.]

As to the application of section 23 of the 1985 Act to proceedings conducted by the Director of Revenue and Customs Prosecutions, see the *Commissioners for Revenue and Customs Act* 2005, s.36(3), *post*, § 1–294, and the *SOCPA* 2005, s.38(5), *post*, § 1–303.

Objecting to the discontinuance of proceedings in a magistrates' court

Criminal Procedure Rules 2005 (S.I. 2005 No. 384), Pt 8

Time for objecting

1–277 **8.1.** The period within which an accused person may give notice under section 23(7) of the *Prosecution of Offences Act* 1985 that he wants proceedings against him to continue is 35 days from the date when the proceedings were discontinued under that section.

Form of notice

8.2. Notice under section 23(3), (4) or (7) of the *Prosecution of Offences Act* 1985 shall be given in writing and shall contain sufficient particulars to identify the particular offence to which it relates.

Duty of Director of Public Prosecutions

8.3. On giving notice under section 23(3) or (4) of the *Prosecution of Offences Act* 1985 the Director of Public Prosecutions shall inform any person who is detaining the accused person for the offence in relation to which the notice is given that he has given such notice and of the effect of the notice.

Duty of magistrates' court

8.4. On being given notice under section 23(3) of the *Prosecution of Offences Act* 1985 in relation to an offence for which the accused person has been granted bail by a court, a magistrates' court officer shall inform—

(a) any sureties of the accused; and

(b) any persons responsible for securing the accused's compliance with any conditions of bail

that he has been given such notice and of the effect of the notice.

[This part is printed as revoked in part by the *Criminal Procedure (Amendment) Rules* 2007 (S.I. 2007 No. 699), r.7.]

As to the service of notices, see Part 4 of the *Criminal Procedure Rules* 2005 (S.I. 2005 No. 384), *post*, §§ 2–207 *et seq.*

In *R. v. DPP, ex p. Cooke*, 95 Cr.App.R. 233, the Divisional Court considered whether a notice of discontinuance served pursuant to section 23 is the only means by which charges may now be discontinued in a magistrates' court. The CPS had withdrawn two "either way" charges and replaced them with charges that were triable only summarily. It was argued on behalf of the defendant that the CPS was in breach of section 23 in so acting, as no notice of discontinuance had been served and he had thus been deprived of his right under section 23(7) to insist that the case continue and be tried in the Crown Court. *Held*, section 23 created a power to discontinue proceedings additional to that already possessed by a prosecutor and was simply intended to provide a useful and economical procedure for proceedings to be discontinued without the need for a court hearing.

As to the power to make an order for costs after the service of a notice of discontinuance, see *DPP v. Denning* [1991] 2 Q.B. 532, 94 Cr.App.R. 272, DC, and *post*, § 6–54. A refusal to award costs to a defendant against whom proceedings have been discontinued may raise an issue under Article 6(2) of the ECHR: see *Leutscher v. Netherlands*, 24 E.H.R.R. 181, ECtHR, *post*, § 16–77.

Discontinuance by a public prosecuting authority does not give rise to a need for special circumstances to be established by a private prosecutor who seeks a summons alleging an offence arising out of the incident that led to the discontinued charge: *R. (Charlson) v. Guildford Magistrates' Court, ante*, § 1–259.

As to the exercise of the power of the DPP to take over a private prosecution for the purpose of discontinuing the proceedings, see *ante*, § 1–258.

As to the susceptibility to judicial review of a decision to discontinue, see *ante*, § 1–263.

(13) Discontinuance of proceedings in Crown Court

Prosecution of Offences Act 1985, s.23A

Discontinuance of proceedings after accused has been sent for trial

23A.—(1) This section applies where— 1–277a

(a) the Director of Public Prosecutions, or a public authority (within the meaning of section 17 of this Act), has the conduct of proceedings for an offence; and

(b) the accused has been sent for trial under *section 51 of the* Crime and Disorder Act *1998* for the offence.

(2) Where, at any time before the indictment is preferred, the Director or authority gives notice under this section to the Crown Court sitting at the place specified in the notice under section *51(7)* [51D(1)] of the *Crime and Disorder Act* 1998 that he or it does not want the proceedings to continue, they shall be discontinued with effect from the giving of that notice.

(3) The Director or authority shall, in any notice given under subsection (2) above, give reasons for not wanting the proceedings to continue.

(4) On giving any notice under subsection (2) above the Director or authority shall inform the accused of the notice; but the Director or authority shall not be obliged to give the accused any indication of his reasons for not wanting the proceedings to continue.

(5) The discontinuance of any proceedings by virtue of this section shall not prevent the institution of fresh proceedings in respect of the same offence.

[This section was inserted by the *CDA* 1998, s.119 and Sched. 8, para. 64. The reference to section 51 of the 1998 Act in subs. (1)(b) is omitted, and the reference to s.51D(1) of that Act in subs. (2) is substituted for the reference to s.51(7), by the *CJA* 2003, ss.41 and 332, Sched. 3, para. 57(1) and (2), and Sched. 37, Pt 4. The first of these amendments came into force on May 9, 2005, but only in relation to cases sent for trial under s.51 or 51A(3)(d) of the 1998 Act, and the second amendment came into force on the same date, but only in relation to cases sent for trial under s.51A(3)(d): *Criminal Justice Act 2003 (Commencement No. 9) Order* 2005 (S.I. 2005 No. 1267). For all other purposes the amendments come into force on a day to be appointed.]

As to the application of section 23A of the 1985 Act to proceedings conducted by the

Director of Revenue and Customs Prosecutions, see the *Commissioners for Revenue and Customs Act* 2005, s.36(3), *post*, § 1–294, and the *SOCPA* 2005, s.38(5) *post*, § 1–303.

(14) Restriction of vexatious prosecutions

1–278 See section 42 of the *Supreme Court [Senior Courts] Act* 1981 (renamed as from a day to be appointed by the *Constitutional Reform Act* 2005, s.59(5), and Sched. 11, para. 1(2)), as amended by section 24 of the *Prosecution of Offences Act* 1985.

(15) Consents to prosecutions, etc.

Prosecution of Offences Act 1985, s.25

1–278a **25.**—(1) This section applies to any enactment which prohibits the institution or carrying on of proceedings for any offence except—

(a) with the consent (however expressed) of a Law Officer of the Crown or the Director; or

(b) where the proceedings are instituted or carried on by or on behalf of a Law Officer of the Crown or the Director;

and so applies whether or not there are other exceptions to the prohibition (and in particular whether or not the consent is an alternative to the consent of any other authority or person).

(2) An enactment to which this section applies—

(a) shall not prevent the arrest without warrant, or the issue or execution of a warrant for the arrest, of a person for any offence, or the remand in custody or on bail of a person charged with any offence; and

(b) shall be subject to any enactment concerning the apprehension or detention of children or young persons.

(3) In this section "enactment" includes any provision having effect under or by virtue of any Act; and this section applies to enactments whenever passed or made.

As to the effect of section 25, see *R. v. Bull*, 99 Cr.App.R. 193, CA, *ante*, § 1–248.

(16) Consents to be admissible in evidence

Prosecution of Offences Act 1985, s.26

1–279 **26.** Any document purporting to be the consent of a Law Officer of the Crown, the Director or a Crown Prosecutor for, or to—

(a) the institution of any criminal proceedings; or

(b) the institution of criminal proceedings in any particular form;

and to be signed by a Law Officer of the Crown, the Director or, as the case may be, a Crown Prosecutor shall be admissible as prima facie evidence without further proof.

See *ante*, §§ 1–244 *et seq.* as to the form of a consent to the institution of criminal proceedings, and see *post*, § 4–352 as to the presumption that any necessary consents have been given.

B. SERIOUS FRAUD OFFICE

(1) Establishment and functions

1–280 The Serious Fraud Office was established by the *CJA* 1987, s.1(1).

See *ante*, §§ 1–41 *et seq.* and *post*, §§ 4–84m *et seq.* as to the provisions of the 1987 Act relating to the special procedures available in serious fraud prosecutions.

Criminal Justice Act 1987, s.1

The Serious Fraud Office

1–280a **1.**—(1) A Serious Fraud Office shall be constituted for England and Wales and Northern Ireland.

(2) The Attorney General shall appoint a person to be the Director of the Serious Fraud Office (referred to in this Part of this Act as "the Director"), and he shall discharge his functions under the superintendence of the Attorney General.

(3) The Director may investigate any suspected offence which appears to him on reasonable grounds to involve serious or complex fraud.

(4) The Director may, if he thinks fit, conduct any such investigation in conjunction either with the police or with any other person who is, in the opinion of the Director, a proper person to be concerned in it.

(5) The Director may—

(a) institute and have the conduct of any criminal proceedings which appear to him to relate to such fraud; and

(b) take over the conduct of any such proceedings at any stage.

(6) The Director shall discharge such other functions in relation to fraud as may from time to time be assigned to him by the Attorney General.

(6A) The Director has the functions conferred on him by, or in relation to, Part 5 or Part 8 of the *Proceeds of Crime Act* 2002 (civil recovery of the proceeds, etc., of unlawful conduct, civil recovery investigations and disclosure orders in relation to confiscation investigations).

(7) The Director may designate for the purposes of subsection (5) above any member of the Serious Fraud Office who is—

(a) a barrister in England and Wales or Northern Ireland;

(b) a solicitor of the Supreme Court; or

(c) a solicitor of the Supreme Court of Judicature of Northern Ireland.

(8) Any member so designated shall, without prejudice to any functions which may have been assigned to him in his capacity as a member of that Office, have all the powers of the Director as to the institution and conduct of proceedings but shall exercise those powers under the direction of the Director.

(9)–(11) [*Repealed by* Access to Justice Act *1999, s.106 and Sched. 15, Pt II.*]

(12), (13), (14) [*Relate to Northern Ireland.*]

(15) Schedule 1 to this Act shall have effect.

(16) For the purposes of this section (including that Schedule) references to the conduct of any proceedings include references to the proceedings being discontinued and to the taking of any steps (including the bringing of appeals and making of representations in respect of applications for bail) which may be taken in relation to them.

(17) [*Relates to Northern Ireland.*]

[This section is printed as amended by the *SCA* 2007, s.74(2), and Sched. 8, para. 152.]

Where there is the possibility of a prosecution in either this jurisdiction or abroad in respect of a particular matter, section 1(3) is not to be construed so as to impose a positive obligation on the Director to launch an investigation into that matter with a view to pre-empting extradition and trial abroad in a situation where there is some question of the rights of the prospective defendant under the ECHR being violated if a trial were to take place in the foreign jurisdiction; that would be a fanciful construction and would usurp the statutory obligation of the courts to resolve any such question as part of the extradition process: *R. (Bermingham) v. Director of the Serious Fraud Office* [2006] 3 All E.R. 239, DC.

When exercising his discretion under section 1 as to whether to pursue an investigation, in circumstances where an official of a foreign state who was allegedly complicit in the matter under investigation had allegedly made threats that steps would be taken which would damage the national security of the U.K. if the investigation were not halted, and having consulted the most expert sources available to him in that regard, the Director had been lawfully entitled to discontinue the investigation on the basis of a risk to life and national security; he had not surrendered his discretionary power of decision making to any third party, there is no principle that submission by a decision-maker to a threat is lawful only when it is demonstrated that there is no alternative course open, and it is not for the court to purport to decide whether the particular decision is right or wrong; the role of the court hearing an application to review such a decision is simply to decide whether the decision maker made a decision outside the lawful bounds of the discretion entrusted to him; in the instant case, there had been no procedural failing or error of law, and there was no basis for a conclusion that no reasonable decision-maker could have reached the same decision: *R. (Corner House Research) v. Director of the Serious Fraud Office (JUSTICE intervening)* [2008] 3 W.L.R. 568, HL.

Criminal Justice Act 1987, Sched. 1

SCHEDULE 1

THE SERIOUS FRAUD OFFICE

General

1–280b 1.–3. [*Not printed.*]

Procedure

4.—(1) Where any enactment (whenever passed) prohibits the taking of any step—

(a) except by the Director of Public Prosecutions or except by him or another; or

(b) without the consent of the Director of Public Prosecutions or without his consent or the consent of another,

it shall not prohibit the taking of any such step by the Director of the Serious Fraud Office.

(2) [*References to the Director of Public Prosecutions for Northern Ireland.*]

5.—(1) Where the Director has the conduct of any criminal proceedings in England and Wales, the Director of Public Prosecutions shall not in relation to those proceedings be subject to any duty by virtue of section 3(2) of the *Prosecution of Offences Act* 1985.

(2) [*Proceedings in Northern Ireland.*]

6.—(1) [*Corresponds to* Prosecution of Offences Act *1985, s.7(1),* ante, *§ 1–260.*]

(2) [*Proceedings in Northern Ireland.*]

(3) [*Corresponds to* Prosecution of Offences Act *1985, s.7(2) ante, § 1–260.*]

(4) [*Corresponds to* ibid., *s.7(3).*]

7. [*Power to make regulations requiring chief officers of police to supply Director with information as to offences.*]

8. [*Power to make provision by regulation as to fees of counsel and costs and expenses of witnesses and interpreters.*]

9.—(1) [*Procedure for making regulations.*]

(2) Any such regulations may make different provision with respect to different cases or classes of case.

[The above Schedule is printed as amended by the *CJA* 1988, s.166, and Sched. 15, para. 116.]

1–280c For regulations made under paragraph 8, see the *Serious Fraud Office (Witnesses', etc. Allowances) Regulations* 1988 (S.I. 1988 No. 1863).

(2) Investigation powers

Criminal Justice Act 1987, s.2

Director's investigation powers

1–281 **2.**—(1) The powers of the Director under this section shall be exercisable, but only for the purposes of an investigation under section 1 above, or, on a request made by an authority entitled to make such a request, in any case in which it appears to him that there is good reason to do so for the purpose of investigating the affairs, or any aspect of the affairs, of any person.

(1A) The authorities entitled to request the Director to exercise his powers under this section are—

(a) the Attorney General of the Isle of Man, Jersey or Guernsey, acting under legislation corresponding to section 1 of this Act and having effect in the Island whose Attorney-General makes the request; and

(b) the Secretary of State acting under section 15(2) of the *Crime (International Co-operation) Act* 2003, in response to a request received by him from a person mentioned in section 13(2) of that Act (an "overseas authority").

(1B) The Director shall not exercise his powers on a request from the Secretary of State acting in response to a request received from an overseas authority within subsection (1A)(b) above unless it appears to the Director on reasonable grounds that the offence in respect of which he has been requested to obtain evidence involves serious or complex fraud.

(2) The Director may by notice in writing require the person whose affairs are to be investigated ("the person under investigation") or any other person whom he has reason to believe has relevant information to answer questions or otherwise furnish information with respect to any matter relevant to the investigation at a specified place and either at a specified time or forthwith.

(3) The Director may by notice in writing require the person under investigation or any other person to produce at such place as may be specified in the notice and either forthwith or at such time as may be so specified, any specified documents which appear to the Director to relate to any matter relevant to the investigation or any documents of a specified description which appear to him so to relate; and—

(a) if any such documents are produced, the Director may—
 (i) take copies or extracts from them;
 (ii) require the person producing them to provide an explanation of any of them;

(b) if any such documents are not produced, the Director may require the person who was required to produce them to state, to the best of his knowledge and belief, where they are.

(4) Where, on information on oath laid by a member of the Serious Fraud Office, a justice of the peace is satisfied, in relation to any documents, that there are reasonable grounds for believing—

(a) that—
 (i) a person has failed to comply with an obligation under this section to produce them;
 (ii) it is not practicable to serve a notice under subsection (3) above in relation to them; or
 (iii) the service of such a notice in relation to them might seriously prejudice the investigation; and

(b) that they are on premises specified in the information,

he may issue such a warrant as is mentioned in subsection (5) below.

(5) The warrant referred to above is a warrant authorising any constable— **1–282**

(a) to enter (using such force as is reasonably necessary for the purpose) and search the premises, and

(b) to take possession of any documents appearing to be documents of the description specified in the information or to take in relation to any documents so appearing any other steps which may appear to be necessary for preserving them and preventing interference with them.

(6) Unless it is not practicable in the circumstances, a constable executing a warrant issued under subsection (4) above shall be accompanied by an appropriate person.

(6A) Where an appropriate person accompanies a constable, he may exercise the powers conferred by subsection (5) but only in the company, and under the supervision, of the constable.

(7) In this section "appropriate person" means—

(a) a member of the Serious Fraud Office; or

(b) some person who is not a member of that Office but whom the Director has authorised to accompany the constable.

(8) A statement by a person in response to a requirement imposed by virtue of this section may only be used in evidence against him—

(a) on a prosecution for an offence under subsection (14) below; or

(b) on a prosecution for some other offence where in giving evidence he makes a statement inconsistent with it.

(8AA) However, the statement may not be used against that person by virtue of paragraph (b) of subsection (8) unless evidence relating to it is adduced, or a question relating to it is asked, by or on behalf of that person in the proceedings arising out of the prosecution.

(8A)–(8D) [*Evidence for use by overseas authority.*]

(9) A person shall not under this section be required to disclose any information or produce any document which he would be entitled to refuse to disclose or produce on grounds of legal professional privilege in proceedings in the High Court, except that a lawyer may be required to furnish the name and address of his client.

(10) A person shall not under this section be required to disclose information or produce a document in respect of which he owes an obligation of confidence by virtue of carrying on any banking business unless—

(a) the person to whom the obligation of confidence is owed consents to the disclosure or production; or

(b) the Director has authorised the making of the requirement or, if it is impracticable for him to act personally, a member of the Serious Fraud Office designated by him for the purposes of that subsection has done so.

1–283 (11) Without prejudice to the power of the Director to assign functions to members of the Serious Fraud Office, the Director may authorise any competent investigator (other than a constable) who is not a member of that Office to exercise on his behalf all or any of the powers conferred by this section, but no such authority shall be granted except for the purpose of investigating the affairs, or any aspect of the affairs, of a person specified in the authority.

(12) No person shall be bound to comply with any requirement imposed by a person exercising powers by virtue of any authority granted under subsection (11) above unless he has, if required to do so, produced evidence of his authority.

(13) Any person who without reasonable excuse fails to comply with a requirement imposed on him under this section shall be guilty of an offence and liable on summary conviction to imprisonment for a term not exceeding six months or to a fine not exceeding level 5 on the standard scale or to both.

(14) A person who, in purported compliance with a requirement under this section—

(a) makes a statement which he knows to be false or misleading in a material particular; or

(b) recklessly makes a statement which is false or misleading in a material particular,

shall be guilty of an offence.

(15) A person guilty of an offence under subsection (14) above shall—

(a) on conviction on indictment, be liable to imprisonment for a term not exceeding two years or to a fine or to both; and

(b) on summary conviction, be liable to imprisonment for a term not exceeding *six* [12] months or to a fine not exceeding the statutory maximum, or to both.

1–284 (16) Where any person—

(a) knows or suspects that an investigation by the police or the Serious Fraud Office into serious or complex fraud is being or is likely to be carried out; and

(b) falsifies, conceals, destroys or otherwise disposes of, or causes or permits the falsification, concealment, destruction or disposal of documents which he knows or suspects are or would be relevant to such an investigation,

he shall be guilty of an offence unless he proves that he had no intention of concealing the facts disclosed by the documents from persons carrying out such an investigation.

(17) A person guilty of an offence under subsection (16) above shall—

(a) on conviction on indictment, be liable to imprisonment for a term not exceeding 7 years or to a fine or to both; and

(b) on summary conviction, be liable to imprisonment for a term not exceeding *6* [12] months or to a fine not exceeding the statutory maximum or to both.

(18) In this section, "documents" includes information recorded in any form and, in relation to information recorded otherwise than in legible form, references to its production include references to producing a copy of the information in legible form; and "evidence" (in relation to subsections (1A)(b), (8A) and (8C) above) includes documents and other articles.

(19) [*Relates to proceedings in Scotland and Northern Ireland.*]

[This section is printed as amended by the *CJA* 1988, s.143, and Sched. 15, paras 112 and 113; the *CJPOA* 1994, s.164(2); the *YJCEA* 1999, s.59, and Sched. 3, para. 20; the *CJPA* 2001, s.70, and Sched. 2, Pt 2, para. 23; the *CJA* 2003, s.12, and Sched. 1, paras 11 to 13; and the *Crime (International Co-operation) Act* 2003, s.91(1), and Sched. 5, paras 11 and 12. In subss. (15)(b) and (17)(b), "12" is substituted for "six" and "6" respectively, as from a day to be appointed, by the *CJA* 2003, s.282(2) and (3). The increase has no application to offences committed before the substitutions take effect: s.282(4).]

As to the potential involvement of the Serious Fraud Office when the Serious Organised Crime Agency becomes aware of conduct appearing to it to involve serious or complex fraud, see the *SOCPA* 2005, ss.2(3) and 38(3) (*post*, §§ 1–302, 1–303).

Section 2 of the 1987 Act was considered in *R. v. Director of Serious Fraud Office, ex p. Smith* [1993] A.C. 1, HL *post*, § 1–286. That decision, like certain of the other decisions referred to in the following commentary on section 2, pre-dates the amendment to that section effected by, *inter alia*, the insertion of subsection (8AA).

1–285 In *R. v. Serious Fraud Office, ex p. Maxwell (Kevin)*, *The Times*, October 9, 1992, DC, the defendant sought an order of mandamus to compel the Serious Fraud Office to comply with the common law duty of disclosure prior to his interview under section 2. It was held that, in accordance with section 1 of the 1987 Act, two concurrent forms of process were instigated by the Director of the Serious Fraud Office, *viz.* an investigative process and a judicial process; the proposed interview with the defendant pursuant to section 2 was part of the investigative process and there is no obligation on the investigator to show to the person interviewed any information already available; in some cases an investigator might find it fruitful or helpful to disclose such information, but in other cases it might be damaging; if the statutory investigator abused his powers, that could be corrected by judicial review. See also *post*, § 12–118. For the current law as to disclosure in respect of the judicial process, see *post*, §§ 12–45 *et seq.*

A letter of request to the Secretary of State from an overseas authority is confidential and no part of it may be disclosed without the consent of the requesting authority; thus, where such a request is referred to the Director of the Serious Fraud Office, pursuant to section 4(2A) of the *Criminal Justice (International Co-operation) Act* 1990 (repealed and replaced by the *Crime (International Co-operation) Act* 2003, s.15 (*post*, § 2–154)), and the Director, acting pursuant to section 2(1A)(b) of the 1987 Act, exercises the power available under section 2 of that Act to issue a notice, the recipient of the notice is not entitled to disclosure of the request, but justice to that person can normally be met by disclosure of general information as to the nature of the investigation; further, when such an overseas request for assistance is referred to the Director, the full range of powers under section 2 of the 1987 Act is available, and the power to obtain "information" is not cut down by the use of the word "evidence" in the 1990 Act; there is flexibility in the concept of evidence, and in the context of a criminal investigation the permissible area of inquiry must inevitably be wider than when the investigation is complete and the concern of the prosecution has become that of proving an already investigated charge: *R. (Evans) v. Director of the Serious Fraud Office* [2003] 1 W.L.R. 299, DC.

As to the obtaining by the Serious Fraud Office of transcripts of interviews conducted under compulsory procedures provided by legislation such as the *Companies Act* 1985 and the *Insolvency Act* 1986, see *Re Arrows Ltd (No. 4)* [1995] 2 A.C. 75, HL. It should be noted that Lord Browne-Wilkinson expressed "considerable doubts" whether, in using the word "documents" in section 2(3), Parliament directed its mind to documents other than those which formed part of the transactions under investigation (at p. 108A). This point appears to remain open.

In *R. (Energy Financing Team Ltd) v. Bow Street Magistrates' Court* [2006] 1 W.L.R. 1316, DC, it was held that, (i) before a warrant to search for and seize documents was sought, or issued under section 2(4), consideration should be given to whether some lesser measure, such as giving notice to produce documents under section 2(3), would suffice; and where such a notice would not suffice (*e.g.*, the documents might be destroyed), then consideration should be given to the possibility of obtaining the documents from an untainted source, such as a bank (although that might be impracticable, having regard to the needs of the investigation, where many inquiries of many institutions which might or might not be able to produce the information required would be involved); (ii) where an application was made under section 2(4), it was the duty of the applicant to give full assistance to the court and that included drawing attention to anything that militated against the issue of a warrant; (iii) where the warrant was sought pursuant to a request for mutual assistance, it need not reflect the precise wording of the letter(s) of request, it being for the Director of the Serious Fraud Office (who was even entitled to go further than the letter(s) of request) to decide how best to give effect to the request in furtherance of the overall investigation; (iv) notwithstanding the difficulties in identifying what documentation of value might be recovered where there was a continuing investigation into a substantial fraud, the warrant should be drafted with sufficient precision to enable both those who executed it and those whose property was affected by it to know whether any document or class of document fell within it (the requisite specificity being no less than would be required for a notice under section 2(3)); and, provided it went to support an investigation which had apparent merit, the fact that the terms of the warrant were wide would not mean that it was simply "fishing"; (v) it was desirable to give the court from whom the warrant was sought time to pre-read the material relied upon (*viz.* the sworn information, usually supported by the letter(s) of request and the draft warrant), and it was important, for the purposes of any subsequent review, for the director or his representative to be able to say whether or not this had been done; and if, at the hearing itself, the applicant for the warrant had supplemented the material already provided, possibly in response to questions from the court, this should be noted; (vi) if practicable, tape recording the decision of the court, which should be briefly reasoned, was clearly the best method of recording the decision; but if this was not practicable, the applicant for the warrant should prepare a note, which should then be submitted to the court for approval; (vii) where a warrant was issued, there was no jurisdiction to permit the party affected by it to invite the court to reconsider its decision, the proper remedy being judicial review; (viii) in deciding whether to grant relief, the High Court would always bear in mind that the seizure of documents pursuant to a warrant was an investigative step, perhaps best reconsidered either at, or even after, the trial; (ix) although it might often not be appropriate, even after execution of the warrant, to disclose to the person affected by it or his legal representatives all of the material laid before the court, the person affected had a right to be satisfied as to the legality of the procedure which had led to the execution of the warrant; and there should be an accommodating response to a request by the affected person or his legal representatives to see what had been laid before the court; in order to respond to such a request, it might be that permission for disclosure from an investigating authority abroad had to be sought and/ or that what was produced or said to the court might only be disclosed in an edited form; however, judicial control by way of judicial review could not operate effectively unless the party affected was in a position to take meaningful advice, and, if so advised, to seek relief from the court; and it was no answer to say that there was no general duty of disclosure in proceedings for judicial review.

See also *Marlwood Commercial Inc. v. Kozeny*; *Omega Group Holdings Ltd v. Kozeny*, *post*, § 1–290.

1–286 In *R. v. Director of the Serious Fraud Office, ex p. Johnson* [1993] C.O.D. 58, QBD (Auld J.), the applicant, who faced criminal charges, sought leave to apply for judicial review of a notice that had been served on his wife under section 2(2) of the 1987 Act. He contended that, by virtue of their marital relationship, his wife had a reasonable excuse within the meaning of section2(13) of the Act for refusing to comply with the notice. It was held, *inter alia*, that although section 80 of the *PACE Act* 1984 prevents a person from being compelled to give evidence against his or her spouse there is no analogous provision in the 1987 Act, that Act being a designedly draconian statute concerned with the investigation of fraud rather than the admissibility of evidence. Further, it was held inappropriate to create by judicial review a class of persons who would always have a reasonable excuse within section 2(13); the question whether the applicant's wife could rely on the defence of reasonable excuse in the particular circumstances of the case if criminal proceedings should be taken against her under that section should be decided by the court seised of those proceedings.

It having been decided in *ex p. Smith*, *ante*, § 1–284, that the powers of the Serious Fraud Office to compel answers to questions on pain of punishment continue after the person under investigation has been charged, it was said in *R. v. Metropolitan Stipendiary Magistrate, ex p. Serious Fraud Office*, *The Independent*, June 24, 1994, DC, that the defence of reasonable excuse under section 2(13) of the 1987 Act does not apply by reason only of the fact that the defendant has been charged. However, the court did not have the benefit of full argument, and in *Shannon v. U.K.* (2006) 42 E.H.R.R. 31, ECtHR, it was held that a requirement to attend an interview with financial investigators, and to answer questions, in connection with events in respect of which the person so required had been charged, was not compatible with the right not to incriminate oneself under Article 6 of the ECHR (*post*, § 16–57). The applicant had been convicted in the domestic courts in Northern Ireland of failing, without reasonable excuse, to answer questions (a defence based on the argument that the right not to incriminate himself amounted to a reasonable excuse having been rejected). This decision should have the effect of depriving the existing English authorities on the point of any continuing force. In any event, the question of whether the privilege against self incrimination could amount to a reasonable excuse, within the meaning of section 2(13) of the 1987 Act, was not an issue that had been decided in *ex p. Smith*.

(3) Pre-investigation powers in relation to bribery and corruption: foreign officers etc.

Criminal Justice Act 1987, s.2A

Director's pre-investigation powers in relation to bribery and corruption: foreign officers etc

2A.—(1) The powers of the Director under section 2 are also exercisable for the purpose of enabling him to determine whether to start an investigation under section 1 in a case where it appears to him that conduct to which this section applies may have taken place. **1–286a**

(2) But—

(a) the power under subsection (2) of section 2 is so exercisable only if it appears to the Director that for the purpose of enabling him to make that determination it is expedient to require any person appearing to him to have relevant information to do as mentioned in that subsection, and

(b) the power under subsection (3) of that section is so exercisable only if it appears to the Director that for that purpose it is expedient to require any person to do as mentioned in that subsection.

(3) Accordingly, where the powers of the Director under section 2 are exercisable in accordance with subsections (1) and (2) above—

(a) the reference in subsection (2) of that section to the person under investigation or any other person whom the Director has reason to believe has relevant information is to be read as a reference to any such person as is mentioned in subsection (2)(a) above,

(b) the reference in subsection (3) of that section to the person under investigation or any other person is to be read as a reference to any such person as is mentioned in subsection (2)(b) above, and

(c) any reference in subsection (2), (3) or (4) of that section to the investigation is to be read as a reference to the making of any such determination as is mentioned in subsection (1) above.

(4) Any reference in section 2(16) to the carrying out of an investigation by the Serious Fraud Office into serious or complex fraud includes a reference to the making of any such determination as is mentioned in subsection (1) above.

(5) This section applies to any conduct which, as a result of section 108 of the *Anti-terrorism, Crime and Security Act* 2001 (bribery and corruption: foreign officers etc.), constitutes a corruption offence (wherever committed).

(6) The following are corruption offences for the purposes of this section—

(a) any common law offence of bribery;

(b) the offences under section 1 of the *Public Bodies Corrupt Practices Act* 1889 (corruption in office); and

(c) the offences under section 1 of the *Prevention of Corruption Act* 1906 (corrupt transactions with agents).

[This section was inserted by the *CJIA* 2008, s.59.]

(4) Disclosure of information

Criminal Justice Act 1987, s.3

Disclosure of information

3.—(1) Where any information to which section 18 of the *Commissioners for Revenue and Customs Act* 2005 would apply but for section 18(2) has been disclosed by Her Majesty's Revenue and Customs to any member of the Serious Fraud Office for the purposes of any prosecution of an offence relating to a former Inland Revenue matter, that information may be disclosed by any member of the Serious Fraud Office— **1–287**

(a) for the purposes of any prosecution of which that Office has the conduct;

(b) to the Revenue and Customs Prosecutions Office for the purposes of any prosecution of an offence relating to a former Inland Revenue matter; and

(c) to the Director of Public Prosecutions for Northern Ireland for the purposes of any prosecution of an offence relating to inland revenue,

but not otherwise.

(2) Where the Serious Fraud Office has the conduct of any prosecution of an offence which does not relate to inland revenue, the court may not prevent the prosecution from relying on any evidence under section 78 of the *Police and Criminal Evidence Act* 1984

(discretion to exclude unfair evidence) by reason only of the fact that the information concerned was disclosed by Her Majesty's Revenue and Customs for the purposes of any prosecution of an offence relating to a former Inland Revenue matter.

(3) Where any information is subject to an obligation of secrecy imposed by or under any enactment other than an enactment contained in the *Taxes Management Act* 1970, the obligation shall not have effect to prohibit the disclosure of that information to any person in his capacity as a member of the Serious Fraud Office but any information disclosed by virtue of this subsection may only be disclosed by a member of the Serious Fraud Office for the purposes of any prosecution in England and Wales, Northern Ireland or elsewhere and may only be disclosed by such a member if he is designated by the Director for the purposes of this subsection.

(4) Without prejudice to his power to enter into agreements apart from this subsection, the Director may enter into a written agreement for the supply of information to or by him subject, in either case, to an obligation not to disclose the information concerned otherwise than for a specified purpose.

1-288 (5) Subject to subsections (1) and (3) above and to any provision of an agreement for the supply of information which restricts the disclosure of the information supplied, information obtained by any person in his capacity as a member of the Serious Fraud Office may be disclosed by any member of that Office designated by the Director for the purposes of this subsection—

(a) to any government department or Northern Ireland department or other authority or body discharging its functions on behalf of the Crown (including the Crown in right of Her Majesty's Government in Northern Ireland);
(b) to any competent authority;
(c) for the purposes of any criminal investigation or criminal proceedings whether in the United Kingdom or elsewhere; and
(d) for the purposes of assisting any public or other authority for the time being designated for the purposes of this paragraph by an order made by the Secretary of State to discharge any functions which are specified in the order.

(6) [*List of "competent authorities".*]

(7) [*Supplements subsection (5)(d).*]

(8) In subsections (1) and (2) "former Inland Revenue matter" means a matter listed in Schedule 1 to the *Commissioners for Revenue and Customs Act* 2005 except for paragraphs 2, 10, 13, 14, 15, 17, 19, 28, 29 and 30.

[This section is printed as amended by the *Crime (International Co-operation) Act* 2003, s.80 (subss. (5) and (6)); and by the *Commissioners for Revenue and Customs Act* 2005, s.50(6), and Sched. 4, para. 35.]

1-289 The Serious Fraud Office has no general power to disclose to a company's liquidators information obtained, under statutory powers of search and seizure, when investigating a fraud involving that company: *Morris v. Director of the Serious Fraud Office* [1993] Ch. 372, Ch D.

Where a member of the Serious Fraud Office intends to disclose to another government department, pursuant to section 3(5), information obtained under a compulsory process, it is normally incumbent upon the Serious Fraud Office to give notice to the person from whom the information was obtained, with a reasonable time being allowed for him to make representations or (if so advised) to apply to the court. There will be cases where the desirability of such a course will be overridden by other factors. In the absence of advance notice, notice should be given as soon as possible after the disclosure for the same purposes. If the intended purpose of disclosure falls within the normal functions of the recipient authority, whether civil litigation or something else, the circumstances in which a potential claimant will have any legitimate cause for complaint will be minimal: *R. (Kent Pharmaceuticals Ltd) v. Director of the Serious Fraud Office* [2005] 1 W.L.R. 1302, CA (Civ Div.).

1-290 In *Marlwood Commercial Inc. v. Kozeny*; *Omega Group Holdings Ltd v. Kozeny* [2005] 1 W.L.R. 104, CA (Civ. Div.), the court considered an application by a party to civil proceedings for permission to provide to the Director of the Serious Fraud Office, in compliance with a request made under section 2 of the 1987 Act (which was itself made as a result of a request pursuant to the *Criminal Justice (International Co-operation) Act* 1990), documents disclosed by another party pursuant to its obligations in the civil proceedings and which had been brought to England for that purpose. It was held that section 3(3) of the 1987 Act does not override rule 31.22 of the *Civil Procedure Rules* 1998 (S.I. 1998 No. 3132), which restricts the use that may be made of documents disclosed in civil proceedings. The application was allowed in the particular circumstances, and general guidance was given.

C. REVENUE AND CUSTOMS PROSECUTIONS OFFICE

(1) Establishment

The Revenue and Customs Prosecutions Office was established by the *Commissioners for Revenue and Customs Act* 2005, the long title to which describes it as "an Act to make provision for the appointment of Commissioners to exercise functions presently vested in the Commissioners of Inland Revenue and the Commissioners of Customs and Excise; for the establishment of a Revenue and Customs Prosecutions Office; and for connected purposes". As to this Act, see also *post*, § 25–386. **1–291**

Commissioners for Revenue and Customs Act 2005, s.34

The Revenue and Customs Prosecutions Office

34.—(1) The Attorney General shall appoint an individual as Director of Revenue and Customs Prosecutions. **1–292**

(2) The Director may, with the approval of the Minister for the Civil Service as to terms and conditions of service, appoint staff.

(3) The Director and his staff may together be referred to as the Revenue and Customs Prosecutions Office.

(4) Schedule 3 (which makes provision about the Office) shall have effect.

(2) Functions

Commissioners for Revenue and Customs Act 2005, ss.35–39

Functions

35.—(1) The Director— **1–293**

(a) may institute and conduct criminal proceedings in England and Wales relating to a criminal investigation by the Revenue and Customs, and

(b) shall take over the conduct of criminal proceedings instituted in England and Wales by the Revenue and Customs.

(2) The Director shall provide such advice as he thinks appropriate, to such persons as he thinks appropriate, in relation to—

(a) a criminal investigation by the Revenue and Customs, or

(b) criminal proceedings instituted in England and Wales relating to a criminal investigation by the Revenue and Customs.

(3) In this section a reference to the Revenue and Customs is a reference to—

(a) the Commissioners,

(b) an officer of Revenue and Customs, and

(c) a person acting on behalf of the Commissioners or an officer of Revenue and Customs.

(4) The Attorney General may by order assign to the Director a function of—

(a) instituting criminal proceedings,

(b) assuming the conduct of criminal proceedings, or

(c) providing legal advice.

(4A) [*Identical to* CJA *1987, s.1(6A)*, ante, *§ 1–280a*.]

(5) In this section—

(a) a reference to the institution of criminal proceedings shall be construed in accordance with section 15(2) of the *Prosecution of Offences Act* 1985, and

(b) "criminal investigation" means any process—

(i) for considering whether an offence has been committed,

(ii) for discovering by whom an offence has been committed, or

(iii) as a result of which an offence is alleged to have been committed.

[This section is printed as amended by the *SCA* 2007, s.74(2), and Sched. 8, para. 165.]

See section 38 of the *SOCPA* 2005, *post*, § 1–303, as to certain further functions of the Director in relation to advice, and the institution and conduct of criminal proceedings, in respect of matters within the scope of that section. See also section 40 of that Act, *post*, § 3–99.

Functions: supplemental

1–294 **36.**—(1) The Director shall discharge his functions under the superintendence of the Attorney General.

(2) The Director or an individual designated under section 37 or 39 or appointed under section 38 must have regard to the Code for Crown Prosecutors issued by the Director of Public Prosecutions under section 10 of the *Prosecution of Offences Act* 1985—

(a) in determining whether proceedings for an offence should be instituted,

(b) in determining what charges should be preferred,

(c) in considering what representations to make to a magistrates' court about mode of trial, and

(d) in determining whether to discontinue proceedings.

(3) Sections 23 and 23A of the *Prosecution of Offences Act* 1985 (power to discontinue proceedings) shall apply (with any necessary modifications) to proceedings conducted by the Director under this Act as they apply to proceedings conducted by the Director of Public Prosecutions.

(4) A power of the Director under an enactment to institute proceedings may be exercised to institute proceedings in England and Wales only.

As to the power to discontinue proceedings, see also section 38(5) of the *SOCPA* 2005, *post*, § 1–303, in respect of proceedings conducted by the Director pursuant to that section.

Prosecutors

1–295 **37.**—(1) The Director may designate a member of the Office (to be known as a "Revenue and Customs Prosecutor") to exercise any function of the Director under or by virtue of section 35 (excluding any function mentioned in subsection (4A) of that section).

(2) An individual may be designated as a Prosecutor only if he has a general qualification within the meaning of section 71 of the *Courts and Legal Services Act* 1990 (qualification for judicial appointments).

(3) A Prosecutor shall act in accordance with any instructions of the Director.

[This section is printed as amended by the *SCA* 2007, s.74(2), and Sched. 8, para. 166.]

The reference in section 37(1) to section 35 has effect as if it included a reference to section 38 of the *SOCPA* 2005 (*post*, § 1–303): s.38(6) of that Act.

Conduct of prosecutions on behalf of the Office

1–296 **38.**—(1) An individual who is not a member of the Office may be appointed by the Director to exercise any function of the Director under or by virtue of section 35 in relation to—

(a) specified criminal proceedings, or

(b) a specified class or description of criminal proceedings.

(1A) An individual who is not a member of the Office may be appointed by the Director to appear in—

(a) specified proceedings, or

(b) a specified class or description of proceedings,

in which the Director or a prosecutor would otherwise appear by virtue of section 302A of the *Proceeds of Crime Act* 2002 (cash recovery proceedings).

(2) An individual may be appointed under this section only if he has a general qualification within the meaning of section 71 of the *Courts and Legal Services Act* 1990 (qualifications for judicial appointments).

(3) An individual appointed under this section shall act in accordance with any instructions of—

(a) the Director, or

(b) a Prosecutor.

[This section is printed as amended by the *SCA* 2007, s.84(3).]

The reference in section 38(1) to section 35 has effect as if it included a reference to section 38 of the *SOCPA* 2005 (*post*, § 1–303): s.38(6) of that Act.

Designation of non-legal staff

39.—(1) The Director may designate a member of the Office— **1–297**

(a) to conduct summary bail applications, and

(b) to conduct other ancillary magistrates' criminal proceedings.

(1A) The Director may designate a member of the Office to appear in—

(a) specified proceedings, or

(b) a specified class or description of proceedings,

in which the Director or a prosecutor would otherwise appear by virtue of section 302A of the *Proceeds of Crime Act* 2002 (cash recovery proceedings).

(2) In carrying out a function for which he is designated under this section an individual shall have the same powers and rights of audience as a Prosecutor.

(3) In subsection (1)—

(a) "summary bail application" means an application for bail made in connection with an offence—

(i) which is not triable only on indictment, and

(ii) in respect of which the accused has not been sent to the Crown Court for trial, and

(b) "ancillary magistrates' criminal proceedings" means criminal proceedings other than trials in a magistrates' court.

(4) An individual designated under this section shall act in accordance with any instructions of—

(a) the Director, or

(b) a Prosecutor.

[This section is printed as amended by the *SCA* 2007, s.84(4).]

(3) Confidentiality of information

Commissioners for Revenue and Customs Act 2005, ss.40, 41

Confidentiality

40.—(1) The Revenue and Customs Prosecutions Office may not disclose information which— **1–298**

(a) is held by the Prosecutions Office in connection with any of its functions, and

(b) relates to a person whose identity is specified in the disclosure or can be deduced from it.

(2) But subsection (1)—

(a) does not apply to a disclosure which—

(i) is made for the purposes of a function of the Prosecutions Office, and

(ii) does not contravene any restriction imposed by the Director,

(b) does not apply to a disclosure made to Her Majesty's Revenue and Customs in connection with a function of the Revenue and Customs (within the meaning of section 25),

(c) does not apply to a disclosure made for the purposes of a criminal investigation or criminal proceedings (whether or not within the United Kingdom),

(ca) does not apply to a disclosure made for the purposes of—

(i) the exercise of any functions of the prosecutor under Parts 2, 3 and 4 of the *Proceeds of Crime Act* 2002,

(ii) the exercise of any functions of the Serious Organised Crime Agency under that Act,

(iii) the exercise of any functions of the Director of Public Prosecutions, the Director of the Serious Fraud Office, the Director of Public Prosecutions for Northern Ireland or the Scottish Ministers under, or in relation to, Part 5 or 8 of that Act,

(iv) the exercise of any functions of an officer of Revenue and Customs, an accredited financial investigator or a constable under Chapter 3 of Part 5 of that Act, or

(v) investigations or proceedings outside the United Kingdom which have led or may lead to the making of an external order within the meaning of section 447 of that Act,

(cb) does not apply to a disclosure of information obtained in the exercise of functions under the *Proceeds of Crime Act* 2002 if the disclosure is made for the purposes of the exercise of a function which the Secretary of State thinks is a public function and which he designates by order,

(d) does not apply to a disclosure which in the opinion of the Director is desirable for the purpose of safeguarding national security,

(e) does not apply to a disclosure made in pursuance of an order of a court,

(f) does not apply to a disclosure made with the consent of each person to whom the information relates, and

(g) is subject to any other enactment.

(3) A person commits an offence if he contravenes subsection (1).

(4) Subsection (3) does not apply to the disclosure of information about internal administrative arrangements of the Revenue and Customs Prosecutions Office (whether relating to a member of the Office or to another person).

(5) It is a defence for a person charged with an offence under this section of disclosing information to prove that he reasonably believed—

(a) that the disclosure was lawful, or

(b) that the information had already and lawfully been made available to the public.

(6) In this section a reference to the Revenue and Customs Prosecutions Office includes a reference to—

(a) former members of the Office, and

(b) persons who hold or have held appointment under section 38.

(7) A person guilty of an offence under this section shall be liable—

(a) on conviction on indictment, to imprisonment for a term not exceeding two years, to a fine or to both, or

(b) on summary conviction, to imprisonment for a term not exceeding 12 months, to a fine not exceeding the statutory maximum or to both.

(8) A prosecution for an offence under this section may be instituted in England and Wales only—

(a) by the Director of Revenue and Customs Prosecutions, or

(b) with the consent of the Director of Public Prosecutions.

(9) A prosecution for an offence under this section may be instituted in Northern Ireland only—

(a) by the Commissioners, or

(b) with the consent of the Director of Public Prosecutions for Northern Ireland.

(10) In the application of this section to Scotland or Northern Ireland the reference in subsection (7)(b) to 12 months shall be taken as a reference to six months.

(10A) [*Procedure for making an order under subs. (2)(cb).*]

(11) In subsection (2) the reference to an enactment does not include—

(a) an Act of the Scottish Parliament or an instrument made under such an Act, or

(b) an Act of the Northern Ireland Assembly or an instrument made under such an Act.

[This section is printed as amended by the *SCA* 2007, ss.74(2) and 79, and Scheds 8, para. 167, and 11, para. 16.]

In relation to an offence under this section committed before the commencement of section 282 of the *CJA* 2003 (short sentences), the reference in subsection (7)(b) to "12 months" shall have effect as if it were a reference to "six months": *Commissioners for Revenue and Customs Act* 2005, s.55(7).

Disclosure of information to Director of Revenue and Customs Prosecutions

1–299 **41.**—(1) A person specified in subsection (2) may disclose information held by him to the Director for a purpose connected with a specified investigation or prosecution or for the purposes of the exercise by the Director of his functions under the *Proceeds of Crime Act* 2002.

(2) Those persons are—

(a) a constable,

(b) the Director General of the National Criminal Intelligence Service,

(c) the Director General of the National Crime Squad,

(d) the Director of the Serious Fraud Office,

(e) the Director General of the Serious Organised Crime Agency,

(f) the Director of Public Prosecutions,

(g) the Director of Public Prosecutions for Northern Ireland, and

(h) such other persons as the Attorney General may specify by order.

(3) An order under subsection (2)(h)—

(a) may specify a person only if, or in so far as, he appears to the Attorney General to be exercising public functions,

(b) may include transitional or incidental provision,

(c) shall be made by statutory instrument, and

(d) shall not be made unless a draft has been laid before, and approved by resolution of, each House of Parliament.

(4) [*Persons having functions in Northern Ireland.*]

(5) [*Application to Scotland.*]

(6) Nothing in this section authorises the making of a disclosure which—

(a) contravenes the *Data Protection Act* 1998, or

(b) is prohibited by Part 1 of the *Regulation of Investigatory Powers Act* 2000.

[This section is printed as amended by the *SCA* 2007, s.74(2), and Sched. 8, para. 168.]

D. SERIOUS ORGANISED CRIME AGENCY

(1) Establishment and functions

The *SOCPA* 2005 creates, by section 1, *post*, a body corporate to be known as the Serious Organised Crime Agency ("SOCA"). That body has functions as to, *inter alia*, the prevention, detection, reduction and mitigation of the consequences of serious organised crime, as provided for by section 2, *post*. If, in exercising its function of preventing and detecting serious organised crime, SOCA becomes aware of conduct appearing to it to involve serious or complex fraud, it may continue to exercise that function in relation to the fraud in question only with the agreement of the Director, or an authorised officer of, the SFO, or if the SFO declines to act in relation to it (s.2(3)). Certain other functions are specified in sections 3 and 5, and section 5 also confers the power on SOCA to institute criminal proceedings. **1–300**

Section 38, *post*, § 1–303, makes provision for the giving of advice by the Director of Revenue and Customs Prosecutions in relation to criminal investigations conducted by SOCA relating to "designated" offences, and in relation to criminal proceedings that arise out of any such investigation. That section also permits the Director of Revenue and Customs Prosecutions to institute and conduct any criminal proceedings in relation to a designated offence investigated by SOCA, and requires him to take over the conduct of any criminal proceedings that have been instituted by SOCA in respect of any such offence. Identical provision is made by the same section in respect of the rights and duties of the DPP as to advice and prosecution in relation to non-designated offences that have been investigated by SOCA, save that the obligation to take over criminal proceedings does not apply when the Director of the SFO has the conduct of the same. Section 39 makes provision for the ascertainment of whether an offence is "designated".

Section 10 confers power on the Secretary of State to issue codes of practice relating to the exercise by SOCA of any of its functions, and SOCA is required, by section 4(3), to have regard to any such code in exercising any function to which it relates. Sections 32 and 33 make provision regulating the disclosure by SOCA of information obtained by it in connection with the exercise of any of its functions, and section 35 imposes restrictions on further disclosure by those to whom disclosure is made pursuant to section 33. Section 34 makes provision relaxing certain inhibitions on the disclosure of information by others if that disclosure is made to SOCA for the purpose of the exercise by it of any of its functions. Section 36 imposes a duty on every chief officer of police to keep SOCA informed of any information relating to crime in his police area that appears to him to be relevant to the exercise by SOCA of any of its functions, and section 37 imposes a duty on any constable, officer of Revenue and Customs, and any coastguard or member of the armed forces to assist SOCA in the exercise of its functions in relation to serious organised crime.

Serious Organised Crime and Police Act 2005, ss.1, 2, 2A

Establishment of Serious Organised Crime Agency

1.—(1) There shall be a body corporate to be known as the Serious Organised Crime Agency ("SOCA"). **1–301**

(2) Schedule 1 makes provision about the constitution, members and staff of SOCA and other matters relating to it.

(3) [*Provision for abolition of NCIS, and its Service Authority, and National Crime Squad, and its Service Authority.*]

Functions of SOCA as to serious organised crime

1–302 **2.**—(1) SOCA has the functions of—

(a) preventing and detecting serious organised crime, and

(b) contributing to the reduction of such crime in other ways and to the mitigation of its consequences.

(2) SOCA's functions under subsection (1) are exercisable subject to subsections (3) to (5) (but subsection (3) does not apply to Scotland).

(3) If, in exercising its function under subsection (1)(a), SOCA becomes aware of conduct appearing to SOCA to involve serious or complex fraud, SOCA may thereafter exercise that function in relation to the fraud in question only—

(a) with the agreement of the Director, or an authorised officer, of the Serious Fraud Office, or

(b) if the Serious Fraud Office declines to act in relation to it.

(4) If, in exercising its function under subsection (1)(a), SOCA becomes aware of conduct appearing to SOCA to involve revenue fraud, SOCA may thereafter exercise that function in relation to the fraud in question only with the agreement of the Commissioners.

(5) Before exercising its function under subsection (1)(b) in any way in relation to revenue fraud, SOCA must consult the Commissioners.

(6) The issue of whether SOCA's function under subsection (1)(a) continued to be exercisable in any circumstances within subsection (3) or (4) may not be raised in any criminal proceedings.

(7) In this section "revenue fraud" includes fraud relating to taxes, duties and national insurance contributions.

(8) In this Chapter "the Commissioners" means the Commissioners for Her Majesty's Revenue and Customs.

Functions of SOCA as to the recovery of assets

1–302a **2A.** SOCA has the functions conferred on it (whether directly or through its staff) by the *Proceeds of Crime Act* 2002 (functions relating to the recovery of assets).

[This section was inserted by the *SCA* 2007, s.74(2), and Sched. 8, para. 169.]

(2) Prosecution of offences

Serious Organised Crime and Police Act 2005, s.38

Prosecution of offences investigated by SOCA

1–303 **38.**—(1) The Director of Revenue and Customs Prosecutions—

(a) may institute and conduct criminal proceedings in England and Wales that arise out of a criminal investigation by SOCA relating to a designated offence, and

(b) must take over the conduct of criminal proceedings instituted by SOCA in England and Wales in respect of a designated offence.

(2) The Director of Revenue and Customs Prosecutions must provide such advice as he thinks appropriate, to such persons as he thinks appropriate, in relation to—

(a) a criminal investigation by SOCA relating to a designated offence, or

(b) criminal proceedings instituted in England and Wales that arise out of such an investigation.

(3) The Director of Public Prosecutions—

(a) may institute and conduct criminal proceedings in England and Wales that arise out of a criminal investigation by SOCA relating to a non-designated offence, and

(b) must take over the conduct of criminal proceedings instituted by SOCA in England and Wales in respect of such an offence.

But paragraph (b) does not apply where the Director of the Serious Fraud Office has the conduct of the proceedings.

(4) The Director of Public Prosecutions must provide such advice as he thinks appropriate, to such persons as he thinks appropriate, in relation to—

(a) a criminal investigation by SOCA relating to a non-designated offence, or

(b) criminal proceedings instituted in England and Wales that arise out of such an investigation.

(5) Sections 23 and 23A of the *Prosecution of Offences Act* 1985 (power to discontinue proceedings) apply (with any necessary modifications) to proceedings conducted by the Director of Revenue and Customs Prosecutions in accordance with this section as they apply to proceedings conducted by the Director of Public Prosecutions.

(6) In the *Commissioners for Revenue and Customs Act* 2005—

(a) section 37(1) (prosecutors), and

(b) section 38(1) (conduct of prosecutions by appointed persons),

have effect as if the reference to section 35 of that Act included a reference to this section.

(7) For the purposes of this section and section 39—

(a) "criminal investigation" means any process—

(i) for considering whether an offence has been committed,

(ii) for discovering by whom an offence has been committed, or

(iii) as a result of which an offence is alleged to have been committed;

(b) an offence is a "designated offence" if criminal proceedings instituted by SOCA in respect of the offence fall (or, as the case may be, would fall) to be referred to the Director of Revenue and Customs Prosecutions by virtue of directions under section 39(1);

(c) "non-designated offence" means an offence which is not a designated offence;

(d) a reference to the institution of criminal proceedings is to be construed in accordance with section 15(2) of the *Prosecution of Offences Act* 1985; and

(e) a reference to the institution of proceedings by SOCA includes a reference to their institution by the Director General of SOCA or a person authorised by him.

Special powers of designated staff

Sections 43 to 49 of the 2005 Act confer power on the Director General of SOCA to designate members of the staff of SOCA as one or more of (i) a person having the powers of a constable, (ii) a person having the customs powers of an officer of Revenue and Customs, and (iii) a person having the powers of an immigration officer (which powers may be subject to limitations specified in the designation and which may have effect for a specified period or without limit of time), and make further provision as to those powers. Section 50 contains further supplementary provisions. **1–304**

Section 51 creates summary offences of assaulting, resisting, or wilfully obstructing a designated person acting in the exercise of a relevant power (or a person who is assisting a designated person in the exercise of such a power). A person will also be guilty of a summary offence under that section if, with intent to deceive, he impersonates a designated person, or makes a statement or does an act calculated falsely to suggest that he is a designated person, or that he has powers as a designated person that exceed the powers he actually has.

CHAPTER 2

THE CRIMINAL JURISDICTION OF THE CROWN COURT

I. THE CROWN COURT

A. INTRODUCTION

The Crown Court was created by the *Courts Act* 1971 to replace courts of Assize and Quarter Sessions. The status, jurisdiction and manning of the court is now governed by the *Supreme Court Act* 1981 and by certain of the *Criminal Procedure Rules* 2005 (S.I. 2005 No. 384), as amended, as to which see generally *post*, §§ 2–204 *et seq*. As from a day to be appointed, the 1981 Act is renamed the *Senior Courts Act* 1981: *Constitutional Reform Act* 2005, s.59(5), and Sched. 11, paras 1 and 26. Provision as to practice and procedure is also made by the consolidated criminal practice direction, as amended and supplemented from time to time. The power of the Lord Chief Justice to give such directions (with the concurrence of the Lord Chancellor) was originally provided by section 75 of the 1981 Act, but is now to be found in section 74 of the *Courts Act* 2003. **2–1**

B. STATUS

The Crown Court is part of the Supreme Court, having such jurisdiction as is conferred on it by the 1981 Act or any other Act: *Supreme Court Act* 1981, s.1(1). It is a superior court of record: *ibid*. s.45(1) (*post*, § 2–29). **2–2**

When the Crown Court sits in the City of London, it shall be known as the Central Criminal Court: *ibid*. s.8(3), *post*, § 2–3.

As from a day to be appointed, the Supreme Court of England and Wales is renamed the Senior Courts of England and Wales: *Constitutional Reform Act* 2005, s.59(1); and the 1981 Act is renamed the *Senior Courts Act* 1981 (*ante*, § 2–1).

C. CONSTITUTION

(1) Judges of the Crown Court

Supreme Court [Senior Courts] Act 1981, s.8

The Crown Court

2–3 **8.**—(1) The jurisdiction of the Crown Court shall be exercisable by—

(a) any judge of the High Court; or

(b) any Circuit judge, Recorder or District Judge (Magistrates' Courts); or

(c) subject to and in accordance with the provisions of sections 74 and 75(2), a judge of the High Court, Circuit judge or Recorder sitting with not more than four justices of the peace,

and any such persons when exercising the jurisdiction of the Crown Court shall be judges of the Crown Court.

(2) A justice of the peace is not disqualified from acting as a judge of the Crown Court merely because the proceedings are not at a place within the local justice area to which he is assigned, or because the proceedings are not related to that area in any other way.

(3) When the Crown Court sits in the City of London it shall be known as the Central Criminal Court; and the Lord Mayor of the City and any Alderman of the City shall be entitled to sit as judges of the Central Criminal Court with any judge of the High Court, Circuit judge, Recorder or District Judge (Magistrates' Courts).

[This section is printed as amended by the *Courts Act* 2003, ss.65(1) and 109(1), and Sched. 8, para. 259. As to the renaming of the 1981 Act, see *ante*, § 2–1.]

As to justices of the peace acting as judges of the Crown Court, see, *post* §§ 2–4 *et seq.*

Supreme Court [Senior Courts] Act 1981, ss.73, 74

General provisions

2–4 **73.**—(1) Subject to the provisions of section 8(1)(c), 74 and 75(2) as respects courts comprising justices of the peace, all proceedings in the Crown Court shall be heard and disposed of before a single judge of that court.

(2) Rules of court may authorise or require a judge of the High Court, Circuit judge or Recorder, in such circumstances as are specified by the rules, at any stage to continue with any proceedings with a court from which any one or more of the justices initially constituting the court has withdrawn, or is absent for any reason.

(3) Where a judge of the High Court, Circuit judge or Recorder sits with justices of the peace he shall preside, and—

(a) the decision of the Crown Court may be a majority decision; and

(b) if the members of the court are equally divided, the judge of the High Court, Circuit judge or Recorder shall have a second and casting vote.

[Subs. (2) is printed as amended by the *Courts Act 2003 (Consequential Amendments) Order* 2004 (S.I. 2004 No. 2035). As to the renaming of the 1981 Act, see *ante*, § 2–1.]

When the Crown Court includes justices, the judge in announcing a decision of the court, should make clear that the justices have been consulted: *R. v. Newby*, 6 Cr.App.R.(S.) 148, CA.

Appeals and committals for sentence

2–5 **74.**—(1) On any hearing by the Crown Court—

(a) of any appeal;

…

the Crown Court shall consist of a judge of the High Court or a Circuit judge or a Recorder who, subject to the following provisions of this section, shall sit with not less than two nor more than four justices of the peace.

(2) [*Rules of court may, with respect to hearings within subs. (1), provide for number (within limits in subs. (1)) and qualification of justices.*]

(3) [*Rules of court may authorise or require judge to start or continue hearing with a court not comprising requisite number of justices.*]

(4), (5) [*Lord Chancellor's power to direct that subss. (1) and (2) shall not apply.*]

(5A) Before exercising any functions under subsection (4), the Lord Chancellor must consult the Lord Chief Justice.

(6) No decision of the Crown Court shall be questioned on the ground that the court was not constituted as required by or under subsections (1) and (2) unless objection was taken by or on behalf of a party to the proceedings not later than the time when the proceedings were entered on, or when the alleged irregularity began.

(7) [*Rules of court may make provision for disqualification of justices concerned in proceedings in court below; and for validity of proceedings notwithstanding participation of disqualified person.*]

(8) The Lord Chief Justice may nominate a judicial office holder (as defined in section 109(4) of the *Constitutional Reform Act* 2005) to exercise his functions under this section.

[The words omitted from subs. (1) were repealed by the *Access to Justice Act* 1999, ss.79 and 106, and Sched. 15, Pt V(4). Subss. (5A) and (8) were inserted by the *Constitutional Reform Act* 2005, s.15(1), and Sched. 4, paras 114 and 133. As to the renaming of the 1981 Act, see *ante*, § 2–1.]

For the respective functions of judges and justices on appeal, see *post*, § 2–201.

Criminal Procedure Rules 2005 (S.I. 2005 No. 384), r.63.10 (as substituted by the Criminal Procedure (Amendment) Rules 2008 (S.I. 2008 No. 2076), r.14 and Sched. 2)

Constitution of the Crown Court

63.10. On the hearing of an appeal— **2–6**

(a) the general rule is that the Crown Court must comprise—

(i) a judge of the High Court, a circuit judge or a recorder, and

(ii) no less than two and no more than four justices of the peace, none of whom took part in the decision under appeal; and

(b) if the appeal is from a youth court—

(i) each justice of the peace must be qualified to sit as a member of a youth court, and

(ii) the Crown Court must include a man and a woman; but

(c) the Crown Court may include only one justice of the peace and need not include both a man and a woman if—

(i) the presiding judge decides that otherwise the start of the appeal hearing will be delayed unreasonably, or

(ii) one or more of the justices of the peace who started hearing the appeal is absent.

As to the commencement provisions for the substituted rule 63.10, see rule 2.1(12) of the 2005 Rules, *post*, § 2–206. **2–7**

Rule 63.10 is subject to any direction given pursuant to section 74(4) of the *Supreme Court [Senior Courts] Act* 1981, *ante*, § 2–5, as to the requisite number and qualifications of justices.

If there is any doubt whether it is appropriate for a particular justice to sit on an appeal when he has been involved in any way with the matter below, it should be mentioned at the outset that the justice had been so involved, so that the parties can make submissions: *R. v. Bristol Crown Court, ex p. Cooper* [1989] 1 W.L.R. 878, DC.

(2) Additional powers

Courts Act 2003, s.66

Judges having powers of District Judges (Magistrates' Courts)

66.—(1) Every holder of a judicial office specified in subsection (2) has the powers of a justice of the peace who is a District Judge (Magistrates' Courts) in relation to— **2–8**

(a) criminal causes and matters, and

(b) [*family proceedings*].

(2) The offices are—

(a) judge of the High Court;

(b) deputy judge of the High Court;

(c) Circuit judge;

(d) Deputy Circuit judge;
(e) recorder.

(3) For the purposes of section 45 of the 1933 Act, every holder of a judicial office specified in subsection (2) is qualified to sit as a member of a youth court.

(4) [*Family proceedings*.]

The "1933 Act" is the *CYPA* 1933: *Courts Act* 2003, s.107(1).

Section 66 enables judges of the Crown Court to deal with cases normally reserved to magistrates' courts when disposing of related cases in the Crown Court. In *R. v. Ashton*; *R. v. Draz*; *R. v. O'Reilly* [2006] 2 Cr.App.R. 15, CA, the section was held to permit a judge of the Crown Court, absent improper prejudice to the accused, to reconstitute himself as a district judge to determine mode of trial where there has been an irregularity in getting a defendant before the Crown Court, and then, if appropriate, to commit the offender for sentence to the Crown Court and, finally, to sit again as a judge of the Crown Court to deal with the committal for sentence. It was held that this procedure (unlike the procedure adopted in *R. v. Bullock* [1964] 1 Q.B. 481, 47 Cr.App.R. 288, CCA, *post*, § 5–34) did not amount to a court committing to itself for sentence, because, when acting under section 66, the judge of the Crown Court is acting as a judge of a magistrates' court. It remains to be seen whether this reasoning would also entitle a judge of the Crown Court to try a summary matter to which paragraph 6(5) of Schedule 3 to the *CDA* 1998 applies, notwithstanding that paragraph 6(5) provides that the powers of the Crown Court shall cease in such a case (*ante*, § 1–32). In this regard it should be borne in mind that the 2003 Act replaced section 41(8) of the *CJA* 1988 (which contained wording that was to the same effect as the wording in the 1998 Act) with a provision which now permits the "Crown Court" to try a summary offence in the circumstances in which that section is engaged, albeit it may only deal with the defendant in a manner in which a magistrates' court could have dealt with him (*ante*, § 1–75am). The explanatory notes to the 2003 Act strongly suggest that section 66 is intended to be used in the section 41(8) situation, although the wording of section 41(8) makes it clear that the judge who is exercising the powers of a district judge (magistrates' courts) will be acting as a judge of the Crown Court when exercising those powers; he does not act as a judge of a magistrates' court, but simply exercises the powers of such a judge in his capacity as a judge of the Crown Court. This analysis, it is submitted, throws doubt on the correctness of the decision in *R. v. Ashton*; *R. v. Draz*; *R. v. O'Reilly*. Although various aspects of that decision were considered by the House of Lords in *R. v. Clarke and McDaid* [2008] 2 Cr.App.R. 2, *ante*, § 1–196, this particular issue was not addressed.

A district judge (magistrates' court) does not have the power to try a summary charge brought outside a statutory time limit for such a charge, and section 66 of the 2003 Act does not, in itself, confer any wider powers in that regard on a judge of the Crown Court: *R. v. Ashton*; *R. v. Draz*; *R. v. O'Reilly, ante*.

(3) Mode of address

2–9 Apart from judges of the High Court, any judge sitting as a deputy High Court judge under the *Supreme Court Act* 1981 (prospectively renamed the *Senior Courts Act* 1981: see *ante*, § 2–2), s.9, any judge sitting at the Central Criminal Court and any senior circuit judge who is the honorary recorder of the city in which he sits shall be addressed as "My Lord" or "My Lady", as the case may be; otherwise, judges of the Crown Court should be addressed as "Your Honour" when sitting in open court: *Practice Direction (Criminal Proceedings: Consolidation)* [2002] 1 W.L.R. 2870 (para. IV.30).

(4) Duties of Crown Court officers

Supreme Court [Senior Courts] Act 1981, s.82

2–10 **82.**—(1) The officers of the Crown Court shall be responsible for the keeping of the records of the proceedings of the court, the signing of indictments, the notification to the parties or their legal advisers of the place and time appointed for any proceedings, and such other formal or administrative matters as may be specified by directions given by the Lord Chancellor after consulting the Lord Chief Justice.

(2) Officers of the Crown Court shall in particular give effect to any orders or directions of the court for taking into custody, and detaining, any person committing contempt of court, and shall execute any order or warrant duly issued by the court for the committal of any person to prison for contempt of court.

(3) The Lord Chief Justice may nominate a judicial office holder (as defined in section 109(4) of the *Constitutional Reform Act* 2005) to exercise his functions under this section.

[This section is printed as amended by the *Constitutional Reform Act* 2005, s.15(1), and Sched. 4, paras 114 and 135. As to the renaming of the 1981 Act, see *ante*, § 2–1.]

D. Allocation of Business and Location of Crown Court Sittings

(1) Statutory provisions

Magistrates' Courts Act 1980, s.7

Place of trial on indictment

7. *A magistrates' court committing a person for trial shall specify the place at which he is to be tried, and in selecting that place shall have regard to—* **2–11**

(a) *the convenience of the defence, the prosecution and the witnesses,*

(b) *the expediting of the trial, and*

(c) *any direction given by or on behalf of the Lord Chief Justice with the concurrence of the Lord Chancellor under section 4(5) of the* Courts Act *1971.*

[As from a day to be appointed, this section is repealed: *CJA* 2003, ss.41 and 332, Sched. 3, para. 51(1) and (3), and Sched. 37, Pt 4.]

The reference to section 4(5) of the 1971 Act should be construed as a reference to section 75(1) of the 1981 Act: *Interpretation Act* 1978, s.17(2)(a) (Appendix B–17).

As to the requirement to specify a place for trial in notices of transfer relating to (i) serious and complex fraud, and (ii) certain cases concerning children, see, respectively, the *CJA* 1987, s.5(1), *ante*, § 1–42, and the *CJA* 1991, Sched. 6, para. 1(1), *ante*, § 1–54. As to the requirement to specify a place for trial in a notice of sending for trial under the *CDA* 1998, prior to its prospective amendment by the *CJA* 2003, see section 51(7) and (10) of the 1998 Act, *ante*, § 1–17, and see section 51D of that Act, as prospectively inserted by the 2003 Act, *ante*, § 1–22.

Supreme Court [Senior Courts] Act 1981, ss.75, 76

Allocation of cases according to composition of court, etc.

75.—(1) The cases or classes of cases in the Crown Court suitable for allocation respectively to a judge of the High Court Circuit judge, Recorder or District Judge (Magistrates' Courts), and all other matters relating to the distribution of Crown Court business, shall be determined in accordance with directions given by or on behalf of the Lord Chief Justice with the concurrence of the Lord Chancellor. **2–12**

(2) Subject to section 74(1), the cases or classes of cases in the Crown Court suitable for allocation to a court comprising justices of the peace (including those by way of trial on indictment which are suitable for allocation to such a court) shall be determined in accordance with directions given by or on behalf of the Lord Chief Justice with the concurrence of the Lord Chancellor.

[This section is printed as amended by the *Courts Act* 2003, s.109(1), and Sched. 8, para. 261. As to the renaming of the 1981 Act, see *ante*, § 2–1.]

Committal [Sending] for trial: alteration of place of trial

76.—(1) Without prejudice to the provisions of this Act about the distribution of Crown Court business, the Crown Court may give directions, or further directions, altering the place of any trial on indictment, whether by *varying the decision of the magistrates' court under section 7 of the* Magistrates' Courts Act *1980 or by substituting some other place for the place specified in a notice under a relevant transfer provision (notices of transfer from magistrates' courts to Crown Court)* [substituting some other place for the place specified in a notice under section 51D(1) of the *Crime and Disorder Act* 1998 (a "section 51D notice")] or by varying a previous decision of the Crown Court. **2–13**

(2) Directions under subsection (1) may be given on behalf of the Crown Court by an officer of the court.

(2A) Where a preparatory hearing has been ordered under section 7 of the *Criminal Justice Act* 1987, directions altering the place of trial may be given under subsection (1) above at any time before the time when the jury are sworn.

(2B) The reference in subsection (2A) to the time when the jury are sworn includes the time when the jury would be sworn but for the making of an order under Part 7 of the *Criminal Justice Act* 2003.

(3) The defendant or the prosecutor, if dissatisfied with the place of trial as *fixed by the magistrates' court, as specified in a notice under a relevant transfer provision* [specified in a section 51D notice] or as fixed by the Crown Court, may apply to the Crown Court for a direction, or further direction, varying the place of trial; and the court shall take the matter into consideration and may comply with or refuse the application, or give a direction not in compliance with the application, as the court thinks fit.

(4) [*Repealed by* Courts Act *2003, s.86(3).*]

(5) *In this section "a relevant transfer provision" means—*

(a) *section 4 of the* Criminal Justice Act *1987, or*

(b) *section 53 of the* Criminal Justice Act *1991.*

[This section is printed as amended by the *CJA* 1987, s.15, and Sched. 2, para. 10; the *CJPOA* 1994, Sched. 9, para. 17; and the *CJA* 2003, s.331, and Sched. 36, para. 47; and as amended and repealed in part, as from a day to be appointed, by the *CJA* 2003, ss.41, and 332, Sched. 3, para. 54(1) and (2), and Sched. 37, Pt 4 (insertion of words in square brackets, omission of italicised words). As to the renaming of the 1981 Act, see *ante*, § 2–1.]

The Crown Court has power to give a direction under this section, altering the place of trial where a person has been sent for trial under section 51 of the *CDA* 1998 (*ante*, § 1–17), notwithstanding the absence of specific reference to that section, pending the coming into force of certain of the amendments made by the *CJA* 2003: *R. v. Croydon Crown Court, ex p. Britton*, 164 J.P. 729, QBD.

Supreme Court [Senior Courts] Act 1981, s.78

Sittings

2–14 **78.**—(1) Any Crown Court business may be conducted at any place in England or Wales and the sittings of the Crown Court at any place may be continuous or intermittent or occasional.

(2) Judges of the Crown Court may sit simultaneously to take any number of different cases in the same or different places, and may adjourn cases from place to place at any time.

(3) The places at which the Crown Court sits and the days and times at which the Crown Court sits at any place, shall be determined in accordance with directions given by the Lord Chancellor after consulting the Lord Chief Justice.

(4) The Lord Chief Justice may nominate a judicial office holder (as defined in section 109(4) of the *Constitutional Reform Act* 2005) to exercise his functions under this section.

[This section is printed as amended by the *Constitutional Reform Act* 2005, s.15(1), and Sched. 4, paras 114 and 134. As to the renaming of the 1981 Act, see *ante*, § 2–1.]

Sunday sittings

2–15 At common law, Sunday was a *dies non juridicus*: *Re N. (Infants)* [1967] Ch. 512, Ch D (Stamp J.); but there seems to be no reason why a direction under section 78(3) should not extend to a sitting on Sunday.

(2) Practice directions

2–16 With effect from June 6, 2005, the consolidated criminal practice direction (as to which see *ante*, § 2–1) was amended by the substitution of the following directions regarding the classification and allocation of business in the Crown Court.

Practice Direction (Criminal Proceedings: Consolidation), paras III.21, IV.31, IV.32 and IV.33 [2002] 1 W.L.R. 2870 (as substituted by Practice Direction (Crown Court: Classification and Allocation of Business) [2005] 1 W.L.R. 2215)

CLASSIFICATION OF CROWN COURT BUSINESS AND ALLOCATION TO CROWN COURT CENTRES

Classification

2–17 **III.21.1** For the purposes of trial in the Crown Court offences are classified as follows:

Class 1: (a) misprision of treason and treason felony; (b) murder; (c) genocide; (d) torture, hostage taking and offences under the *War Crimes Act* 1991; (e) an offence under the *Official Secrets Acts*; (f) manslaughter; (g) infanticide; (h) child destruction; (i) abortion (section 58 of the *Offences against the Person Act* 1861); (j) sedition; (k) an offence under section 1 of the *Geneva Conventions Act* 1957; (l) mutiny; (m) piracy; (n) soliciting, incitement, attempt or conspiracy to commit any of the above offences.

Class 2: (a) rape; (b) sexual intercourse with a girl under 13; (c) incest with girl under 13; (d) assault by penetration; (e) causing a person to engage in sexual activity, where penetration is involved; (f) rape of a child under 13; (g) assault of a child under 13 by penetration; (h) causing or inciting a child under 13 to engage in sexual activity, where penetration is involved; (i) sexual activity with a person with a mental disorder, where penetration is involved; (j) inducement to procure sexual activity with a mentally disordered person where penetration is involved; (k) paying for sexual services of a child where child is under 13 and penetration is involved; (l) committing an offence with intent to commit a sexual offence, where the offence is kidnapping or false imprisonment; (m) soliciting, incitement, attempt or conspiracy to commit any of the above offences.

Class 3: all other offences not listed in classes 1 or 2.

Cases committed, transferred or sent for trial

III.21.2 The magistrates' court, upon either committing a person for trial under section 6 of the *Magistrates' Courts Act* 1980, or sending a person under section 51 of the *Crime and Disorder Act* 1998, shall: (a) if the offence or any of the offences is included in Class 1, specify the most convenient location of the Crown Court where a High Court judge, or, where a circuit judge duly authorised by the Lord Chief Justice to try class 1 cases, regularly sits; (b) if the offence or any of the offences is included in class 2, specify the most convenient location of the Crown Court where a judge duly authorised to try class 2 cases regularly sits. These courts on each circuit will be identified by the presiding judges, with the concurrence of the Lord Chief Justice. (c) Where an offence is in class 3 the magistrates' court shall specify the most convenient location of the Crown Court. Where a case is transferred under section 4 of the *Criminal Justice Act* 1987 or section 53 of the *Criminal Justice Act* 1991, the authority shall, in specifying the proposed place of trial in the notice of transfer, comply with the provisions of this paragraph. **2–18**

III.21.3 In selecting the most convenient location of the Crown Court the justices shall have regard to the considerations referred to in section 7 of the *Magistrates' Courts Act* 1980 and section 51(10) of the *Crime and Disorder Act* 1998 and the location or locations of the Crown Court designated by a presiding judge as the location to which cases should normally be committed from their court.

III.21.4 Where on one occasion a person is committed in respect of a number of offences all the committals shall be to the same location of the Crown Court and that location shall be the one where a High Court judge regularly sits if such a location is appropriate for any of the offences.

Committals following breach

III.21.5 Where, in the Crown Court, a community order or an order for conditional discharge has been made, or a suspended sentence has been passed, and the offender is subsequently found or alleged to be in breach before a magistrates' court which decides to commit the offender to the Crown Court, he shall be committed in accordance with paragraphs III.21.6, III.21.7 or III.21.8

III.21.6 He shall be committed to the location of the Crown Court where the order was made or the suspended sentence was passed, unless it is inconvenient, impracticable or inappropriate to do so in all the circumstances.

III.21.7 If, for whatever reason, he is not so committed and the order was made or sentence passed by a High Court judge, he shall be committed to the most convenient location of the Crown Court where a High Court judge regularly sits.

III.21.8 In all other cases he shall be committed to the most convenient location of the Crown Court.

III.21.9 In selecting the most convenient location of the Crown Court, the justices shall have regard to the locations of the Crown Court designated by a presiding judge as the locations to which cases should normally be committed from their court.

Notice of transfer in cases of serious or complex fraud

III.21.10 Where a notice of transfer is served under section 4 of the *Criminal Justice Act* 1987 the proposed place of trial to be specified in the notice shall be one of the Crown Court centres designated by the senior presiding judge.

Notice of transfer in child witness cases

III.21.11 Where a notice of transfer is served under section 53 of the *Criminal Justice Act* 1991 (child witness cases) the proposed place of trial to be specified in accordance with paragraph 1(1) of Schedule 6 to the Act shall be a Crown Court centre which is equipped with live television link facilities.

Transfer of cases from one circuit to another

2–19 **IV.31.1** An application that a case be transferred from one circuit to another should not be granted unless the judge is satisfied that: (a) the approval of the presiding judges and regional director for each region/circuit has been obtained, or (b) the case may be transferred under general arrangements approved by the presiding judges and regional directors.

Transfer of proceedings between locations of the Crown Court

IV.32.1 Without prejudice to the provisions of section 76 of the *Supreme Court Act* 1981 (committal for trial: alteration of place of trial) directions may be given for the transfer from one location of the Crown Court to another of: (a) appeals; (b) proceedings on committal for sentence or to be dealt with.

IV.32.2 Such directions may be given in a particular case by an officer of the Crown Court, or generally, in relation to a class or classes of case, by the presiding judge or a judge acting on his behalf.

IV.32.3 If dissatisfied with such directions given by an officer of the Crown Court, any party to the proceedings may apply to a judge of the Crown Court who may hear the application in chambers.

ALLOCATION OF BUSINESS WITHIN THE CROWN COURT

General

2–20 **IV.33.1** Cases in class 1 may only be tried by: (1) a High Court judge, or (2) a circuit judge or deputy High Court judge or deputy circuit judge provided (a) that, in all cases save attempted murder, such judge is authorised by the Lord Chief Justice to try murder cases, or in the case of attempted murder, to try murder or attempted murder, and (b) the presiding judge has released the case for trial by such a judge.

IV.33.2 Cases in class 2 may be tried by: (1) a High Court judge; (2) a circuit judge or deputy High Court judge or deputy circuit judge or a recorder, provided that in all cases such judge is authorised to try class 2 cases by the Lord Chief Justice and the case has been assigned to the judge by or under the direction of either the presiding judge or resident judge in accordance with guidance given by the presiding judges.

IV.33.3 Cases in class 3 may be tried by a High Court Judge, or in accordance with guidance given by the presiding judges, a circuit judge, a deputy circuit judge or a recorder. A case in class 3 shall not be listed for trial by a High Court judge except with the consent of a presiding judge.

IV.33.4 Appeals from decisions of magistrates shall be heard by: (a) a resident judge, or (b) a circuit judge, nominated by the resident judge, who regularly sits at the Crown Court centre, or (c) an experienced recorder or deputy circuit judge specifically approved by or under the direction of the presiding judges for the purpose, or (d) where no circuit judge or recorder satisfying the requirements above is available and it is not practicable to obtain the approval of the presiding judges, by a circuit judge, recorder or deputy circuit judge selected by the resident judge to hear a specific case or cases listed on a specific day.

IV.33.5 Committals following breach (such as a matter in which a community order has been made, or a suspended sentence passed) should, where possible, be listed before the judge who originally dealt with the matter, or, if not, before a judge of the same or higher level.

Applications for removal of a driving disqualification

2–21 **IV.33.6** Application should be made to the location of the Crown Court where the order of disqualification was made.

Absence of resident judge

IV.33.7 A resident judge must appoint a deputy to exercise his functions when he is absent from his centre.

Guidance issued by the senior presiding judge and the presiding judges

IV.33.8 For the just, speedy and economical disposal of the business of the circuits or a circuit, the senior presiding judge or the presiding judges, with the approval of the senior presiding judge, may issue guidance to resident judges in relation to the allocation and management of the work at their court.

IV.33.9 With the approval of the senior presiding judge, general directions may be given by the presiding judges of the South Eastern Circuit concerning the distribution and allocation of business of all classes of case at the Central Criminal Court.

An allegation of arson being reckless as the endangerment of life should be listed in front of a full-time judge: *R. v. Jones (Stephen)*, *The Times*, May 20, 1999, CA.

E. RIGHTS OF AUDIENCE AND COURT DRESS

Rights of audience

Rights of audience before the Crown Court are governed by Part II of the *Courts and Legal Services Act* 1990: s.27(1). The Act does not affect the court's right to refuse to hear a person (for reasons which apply to him as an individual) who would otherwise have a right of audience before that court in those proceedings, although reasons for such refusal must be given: s.27(4),(5). The Act effectively limits rights of audience in the Crown Court for legal or other representatives to: (a) practising barristers; (b) solicitors approved by the Law Society to exercise rights of audience in criminal courts or all courts; and (c) persons granted similar rights by any body designated by Order in Council for that purpose: s.27(2), (9). **2–22**

Part II of the 1990 Act was substantially amended by the *Access to Justice Act* 1999. The qualification regulations and rules of conduct of the Bar Council and of the Law Society no longer govern the granting of rights of audience, as opposed to the exercise thereof. Instead, a new section 31 (substituted for the original sections 31 to 33 by section 36 of the 1999 Act) deems every barrister and every solicitor to have been granted by the Bar Council and the Law Society respectively a right of audience in every court in relation to all proceedings, such right to be exercisable in accordance with the qualification regulations and rules of conduct of those bodies approved under section 27.

Certificates of attainment for solicitor advocates (criminal courts, civil courts or all courts) are considered and issued by the Law Society approximately every two months. Lists of solicitor advocates are circulated to all locations of the Crown Court on a regular basis.

Section 37 of the 1999 Act inserts section 31A into the 1990 Act. This provides for the rights of audience of barristers and solicitors in employment, including in particular those employed in the Crown Prosecution Service. Any qualification regulation or rule of conduct which limits the courts before which or the proceedings in which they may exercise their rights, or limits the circumstances in which they may exercise their rights by requiring them to be accompanied by some other person when exercising them, is to have no effect if there is no corresponding limitation on those who are not employed. Section 38 of the 1999 Act inserts section 31B into the 1990 Act. This provides for the rights of audience of barristers and solicitors employed by or under the Legal Services Commission. Any rule of an authorised body which prohibits or limits the exercise of those rights by members of the body who are employees has no effect where the prohibition or limitation is on the exercise thereof otherwise than on the instructions of solicitors or other persons acting for members of the public, and the rules do not impose the same prohibition or limitation on members of the body who are not employees.

The Crown Court has a discretion to allow a private individual to conduct a private prosecution before it, but it is likely that such discretion will be exercised only rarely: *R. v. Southwark Crown Court, ex p. Tawfick, CPS intervening*, *The Times*, December 1, 1994, DC (considering s.27(2)(c)).

[The next paragraph is § 2–28.]

Court dress of advocates

Practice Direction (Criminal Proceedings: Consolidation), para. I.1.1 [2002] 1 W.L.R. 2870 (as amended by Practice Direction (Court Dress) (No. 4) [2008] 1 W.L.R. 357)

Court dress

2–28 **I.1.1** In magistrates' courts advocates appear without robes or wigs. In all other courts, Queen's Counsel wear a short wig and a silk (or stuff) gown over a court coat with bands, junior counsel wear a short wig and stuff gown with bands. Solicitors and other advocates authorised under the *Courts and Legal Services Act* 1990 wear a black solicitor's gown with bands; they may wear short wigs in circumstances where they would be worn by Queen's counsel or junior counsel.

The wearing of wigs and gowns may be dispensed with by way of a special measures direction pursuant to section 26 of the *YJCEA* 1999, *post*, § 8–55j, and the wearing of business suits is all that is required for matters that are dealt with in chambers, as to which, see *post*, § 2–153.

II. THE GENERAL JURISDICTION OF THE CROWN COURT

Supreme Court [Senior Courts] Act 1981, ss.45, 46, 46A

General jurisdiction of the Crown Court

2–29 **45.**—(1) The Crown Court shall be a superior court of record.

(2) Subject to the provisions of this Act, there shall be exercisable by the Crown Court—

(a) all such appellate and other jurisdiction as is conferred on it by or under this or any other Act; and

(b) all such other jurisdiction as was exercisable by it immediately before the commencement of this Act.

(3) Without prejudice to subsection (2), the jurisdiction of the Crown Court shall include all such powers and duties as were exercisable or fell to be performed by it immediately before the commencement of this Act.

(4) Subject to section 8 of the *Criminal Procedure (Attendance of Witnesses) Act* 1965 (substitution in criminal cases of procedure in that Act for procedure by way of *subpoena*) and to any provision contained in or having effect under this Act, the Crown Court shall, in relation to the attendance and examination of witnesses, any contempt of court, the enforcement of its orders and all other matters incidental to its jurisdiction, have the like powers, rights, privileges and authority as the High Court.

(5) The specific mention elsewhere in this Act of any jurisdiction covered by subsections (2) and (3) shall not derogate from the generality of those subsections.

For the purposes of section 45(4), matters are "incidental to" the jurisdiction of the Crown Court only when the powers to be exercised relate to the proper dispatch of the business before it and are directly linked to the exercise of its jurisdiction and statutory functions: *Re Trinity Mirror plc* [2008] 2 Cr.App.R. 1, CA (no general or inherent power to grant injunction to protect identity of defendant's children, who were not victims or witnesses, as to which, see also *post*, § 4–18).

Exclusive jurisdiction of Crown Court in trial on indictment

2–30 **46.**—(1) All proceedings on indictment shall be brought before the Crown Court.

(2) The jurisdiction of the Crown Court with respect to proceedings on indictment shall include jurisdiction in proceedings on indictment for offences wherever committed, and in particular proceedings on indictment for offences within the jurisdiction of the Admiralty of England.

Offences committed on ships and abroad

2–31 **46A.** Sections 280, 281, and 282 of the *Merchant Shipping Act* 1995 (offences on ships and abroad by British citizens and others) apply in relation to other offences under the law of England and Wales as they apply in relation to offences under that Act or instruments under that Act.

[S.46A was inserted by the *Merchant Shipping Act* 1995, s.314(2), and Sched. 13, para. 59(1). As to the renaming of the 1981 Act, see *ante*, § 2–1.]

For sections 280 to 282 of the 1995 Act, see *post*, §§ 2–64 *et seq.*

Supreme Court [Senior Courts] Act 1981, s.79

Practice and procedure in connection with indictable offences and appeals

79.—(1) All enactments and rules of law relating to procedure in connection with indictable offences shall continue to have effect in relation to proceedings in the Crown Court. **2–32**

(2) Without prejudice to the generality of subsection (1), that subsection applies in particular to—

(a) the practice by which, on any one indictment, the taking of pleas, the trial by jury and the pronouncement of judgment may respectively be by or before different judges;

(b) the release, after respite of judgment, of a convicted person on recognizance to come up for judgment if called on, but meanwhile to be of good behaviour;

(c) the manner of trying any question relating to the breach of a recognizance;

(d) the manner of execution of any sentence on conviction, or the manner in which any other judgment or order given in connection with trial on indictment may be enforced.

(3) [*Appeals: see* post, *§ 2–184.*]

[As to the renaming of the 1981 Act, see *ante*, § 2–1.]

III. JURISDICTION IN RESPECT OF ACTS PERFORMED ABROAD AND IN RESPECT OF FOREIGN NATIONALS

A. GENERAL PRINCIPLES

The primary basis of English criminal jurisdiction is territorial, it being the function of the English criminal courts to maintain the Queen's peace within her realm: see *Board of Trade v. Owen* [1957] A.C. 602, HL (*per* Lord Tucker at p. 625). It followed, therefore, that, statutory exceptions apart, the courts were not concerned with conduct abroad: see *Cox v. Army Council* [1963] A.C. 48, HL ("the whole body of the criminal law of England deals only with acts committed in England", *per* Viscount Simonds at p. 67). Accordingly, there is a well-established presumption in construing a statute creating an offence that, in the absence of clear words to the contrary, it is not intended to make conduct taking place outside the territorial jurisdiction of the Crown an offence triable in an English court: *Air India v. Wiggins*, 71 Cr.App.R. 213, HL (*per* Lord Diplock at p. 217). The presumption against a Parliamentary intention to make acts done by foreigners abroad offences triable by English courts is even stronger: *ibid.* and *R. v. Jameson* [1896] 2 Q.B. 425. **2–33**

Where the definition of an offence includes both certain conduct of the accused and certain consequences resulting therefrom, the traditional common law view as to whether the offence was committed within the jurisdiction was that it was to be so regarded if the essence or the gist of the offence occurred within the jurisdiction: see *R. v. Harden* [1963] 1 Q.B. 8, 46 Cr.App.R. 90, CCA. This rule of jurisdiction was sometimes known as the "last act" rule: see *R. v. Manning* [1998] 2 Cr.App.R. 461, CA.

The more modern view is epitomised by the *obiter* opinion of Lord Diplock in *Treacy v. DPP* [1971] A.C. 537, HL. His Lordship said that the absence of any geographical limitation in the definition of statutory offences means that the existence and extent of any such limitation is to be discovered by applying some presumption as to Parliament's intention extraneous to the definition. The source of such a presumption can only be the rules of international comity, which do not call for more than that each sovereign state should refrain from punishing persons for their conduct within the territory of another state where that conduct has had no harmful consequences within the territory of the state that imposes the punishment. Consequently, where the definition of an offence contains a requirement that the described conduct should be followed by described consequences, it is sufficient to constitute the offence if either the conduct of the accused, or its consequences, take place in England or Wales.

2–34 Lord Diplock's view was fully reflected in the decision of the Privy Council in *Somchai Liangsiriprasert v. Government of the United States of America* [1991] 1 A.C. 225, in which Lord Griffiths said (at p. 251) that crime having ceased to be largely local in origin and effect, the common law must now face this new reality. It was held that there was nothing in precedent, comity or good sense to inhibit the common law from regarding as justiciable in England inchoate crimes committed abroad which are intended to result in the commission of criminal offences in England. The Court of Appeal has subsequently accepted this to be the law of England and Wales: *R. v. Sansom* [1991] 2 Q.B. 130, 92 Cr.App.R. 115, CA. The court was concerned with the statutory offence of conspiracy contrary to the *CLA* 1977, holding that it could not have been the intention of Parliament to alter the common law rules without specific words. There is no reason to suppose that any different view would be applied to an attempt or incitement.

After some vacillation (see *Manning*, *ante*), the Court of Appeal has now adopted the more modern approach. In *R. v. Smith (Wallace Duncan) (No. 4)* [2004] 2 Cr.App.R. 17, CA, it was held that where a substantial measure of the activities constituting a crime takes place within the jurisdiction, then the courts of England and Wales have jurisdiction to try the crime, save only where it can seriously be argued on a reasonable view that these activities should, on the basis of international comity, be dealt with by another country; in particular, it was held that it is not necessary that the "final act" or the "gist" of the offence should occur within the jurisdiction.

Apart from the above, if a person abroad commits an offence in England through the agency of another, innocent or guilty, he is liable to be indicted in this country: see *R. v. Baxter* [1972] Q.B. 1, 55 Cr.App.R. 214, CA; *DPP v. Stonehouse* [1978] A.C. 55, HL. In *Liangsiriprasert*, *ante*, it was held to be immaterial that the agents who committed the acts relied on were law officers who intended to hand L. over to justice.

Where the *actus reus* of the crime is committed within the jurisdiction, it is immaterial that the intent that is an element of the offence is to do something outside the jurisdiction: *R. v. Hornett* [1975] R.T.R. 256, CA (uttering documents with intent to defraud); *R. v. El-Hakkaoui*, 60 Cr.App.R. 281, CA (possession of firearms with intent to endanger life).

B. ACTS COMMITTED WITHIN DIPLOMATIC AND CONSULAR PREMISES

2–35 The building occupied by a foreign embassy or consulate and the land upon which it stands are part of the territory of the receiving state. Notwithstanding this, diplomatic premises and consular premises are inviolable and the local authorities may enter them only with the consent of the head of the mission, see the *Diplomatic Privileges Act* 1964, Sched. 1, arts 1(i) and 22 and the *Consular Relations Act* 1968, Sched. 1, art. 1, para. 1(j).

In *R. v. Nejad*, unreported, January 1981, CCC, a group of foreign nationals had invaded the Iranian Embassy in London and held a number of persons hostage. It was common ground that no question of jurisdiction arose on the indictment, which included counts of murder, of unlawful imprisonment and of possessing firearms with intent to endanger life. See also *Kamara v. DPP* [1974] A.C. 104, HL; and *Radwan v. Radwan* [1973] Fam. 24, Fam D (Cumming-Bruce J.).

C. ACTS PERFORMED ABROAD BY FOREIGN NATIONALS

2–36 A foreigner is not liable under English law for an offence committed on land abroad except in the case of treason, where the foreigner has previously resided within the dominions of the Crown and at the time of the treasonable act still owes allegiance to the Crown, *e.g.* by being in possession of a British passport: *Joyce v. DPP* [1946] A.C. 347, HL. See also *ante*, § 1–82. There is also a possible exception in the case of a person who within the three months last past has belonged to the crew of a British merchant ship (see *Merchant Shipping Act* 1995, s.282, *post*, § 2–68, but see *R. v. Anderson*, L.R. 1 C.C.R. 161).

D. PARTICULAR OFFENCES

(1) Sexual offences

(a) *Sexual Offences (Conspiracy and Incitement) Act 1996*

The *Sexual Offences (Conspiracy and Incitement) Act* 1996 made it an offence to conspire to commit, or to incite the commission of, certain sexual acts abroad against children. The Act came into force on October 1, 1996: s.7(2) and the *Sexual Offences (Conspiracy and Incitement) Act 1996 (Commencement) Order* 1996 (S.I. 1996 No. 2262); but nothing in either section 1 (conspiracy) or section 2 (incitement) applied to any act or event occurring before that date. Section 1 was repealed by the *Criminal Justice (Terrorism and Conspiracy) Act* 1998, s.9(1), (2), and Sched. 1, Pt II, para. 9(1), and Sched. 2, Pt II. For conspiracies to commit offences outside the United Kingdom, see now the more general provision in section 1A of the *CLA* 1977 (*post*, § 33–22), which was inserted by section 5(1) of the 1998 Act. It has, however, no application to an agreement entered into before the day on which the 1998 Act received Royal Assent (September 4, 1998): s.1A(14). It follows, therefore, that section 1 of the 1996 Act continues to apply to acts and events occurring in the period from October 1, 1996, to September 3, 1998. For the text thereof, see § 34–22a in the 1998 edition of this work. **2–36a**

Sexual Offences (Conspiracy and Incitement) Act 1996, ss.2, 3

Incitement to commit certain sexual acts outside the United Kingdom

2.—(1) This section applies where— **2–36b**

(a) any act done by a person in England and Wales would amount to the offence of incitement to commit a listed sexual offence but for the fact that what he had in view would not be an offence triable in England and Wales,

(b) the whole or part of what he had in view was intended to take place in a country or territory outside the United Kingdom, and

(c) what he had in view would involve the commission of an offence under the law in force in that country or territory.

(2) Where this section applies—

(a) what he had in view is to be treated as that listed sexual offence for the purposes of any charge of incitement brought in respect of that act, and

(b) any such charge is accordingly triable in England and Wales.

(3) Any act *of incitement* [done] by means of a message (however communicated) is to be treated as done in England and Wales if the message is sent or received in England and Wales.

Sections 1 and 2: supplementary

3.—(1) Conduct punishable under the law in force in any country or territory is an offence under that law for the purposes of section 2, however it is described in that law. **2–36c**

(2) Subject to subsection (3), a condition in section … 2(1)(c) is to be taken to be satisfied unless, not later than rules of court may provide, the defence serve on the prosecution a notice—

(a) stating that, on the facts as alleged with respect to what the accused had in view, the condition is not in their opinion satisfied,

(b) showing their grounds for that opinion, and

(c) requiring the prosecution to show that it is satisfied.

(3) [*Repealed by* Criminal Justice (Terrorism and Conspiracy) Act *1998, s.9(1) and Sched. 1, para. 9.*]

(4) The court, if it thinks fit, may permit the defence to require the prosecution to show that the condition is satisfied without the prior service of a notice under subsection (2).

(5) In the Crown Court the question whether the condition is satisfied is to be decided by the judge alone.

(6) In any proceedings in respect of any offence triable by virtue of section … 2, it is immaterial to guilt whether or not the accused was a British citizen at the time of any act or other event proof of which is required for conviction of the offence.

(7) [*Repealed by* Criminal Justice (Terrorism and Conspiracy) Act *1998, s.9(1) and Sched. 1, para. 9.*]

(8) References to an offence of incitement to commit a listed sexual offence include an offence triable in England and Wales as such an incitement by virtue of section 2 (without prejudice to subsection (2) of that section).

(9) Subsection (8) applies to references in any enactment, instrument or document (except those in section 2 of this Act and in Part I of the *Criminal Law Act* 1977).

[Sections 2 and 3 are printed as amended and repealed in part by the *Criminal Justice (Terrorism and Conspiracy) Act* 1998, s.9(1), and Sched. 1, para. 9; and as amended, as from a day to be appointed, by the *SCA* 2007, s.63(2), and Sched. 6, para. 60 (substitution in s.2(3) of word in square brackets for words in italics). The references in ss.2(1) and (2), and 3(8) to the common law offence of incitement have effect as references to the offences under the 2007 Act, Pt 2: s.63(1), and Sched. 6, para. 30.]

Sexual Offences (Conspiracy and Incitement) Act 1996, Sched.

Section 5 SCHEDULE

LISTED SEXUAL OFFENCES

England and Wales

2–36d 1.—(1) In relation to England and Wales, the following are listed sexual offences:

(a) [*repealed by* Sexual Offences Act *2003, s.140 and Sched. 7*];

(b) an offence under any of sections 1 to 12, 14 and 15 to 26 of the *Sexual Offences Act* 2003.

(2) Sub-paragraph (1)(b) does not apply where the victim of the offence has attained the age of sixteen years.

2. [*Northern Ireland*.]

[This Schedule is printed as amended by the *SOA* 2003, s.139, and Sched. 6, para. 35.]

(b) *Sexual Offences Act 2003*

2–36e The jurisdiction of the courts in England and Wales and Northern Ireland was extended in respect of certain sexual offences by section 7 of the *Sex Offenders Act* 1997, which came into force on September 1, 1997. That section was repealed and replaced by the original version of section 72 of the *SOA* 2003, with effect from May 1, 2004 (*Sexual Offences Act 2003 (Commencement) Order* 2004 (S.I. 2004 No. 874)). A new section 72 (*post*) was then substituted by the *CJIA* 2008, s.72(1), with effect from July 14, 2008 (*Criminal Justice and Immigration Act 2008 (Commencement No. 2 and Transitional and Savings Provisions) Order* 2008 (S.I. 2008 No. 1586)). The terms of the various substantive provisions, and the details of the offences to which they relate, are not identical, so it is important to ensure that any prosecution is brought under the provision which was in force at the date of the alleged offending. There are no specific transitional provisions, but none of the provisions can have retrospective effect, and liability under a repealed provision in respect of the period when it was in force is preserved generally by section 16 of the *Interpretation Act* 1978 (Appendix B–16).

Sexual Offences Act 2003, s.72

Offences outside the United Kingdom

2–36f **72.**—(1) If—

(a) a United Kingdom national does an act in a country outside the United Kingdom, and

(b) the act, if done in England and Wales *or Northern Ireland*, would constitute a sexual offence to which this section applies,

the United Kingdom national is guilty in *that part of the United Kingdom* [England and Wales] of that sexual offence.

(2) If—

(a) a United Kingdom resident does an act in a country outside the United Kingdom,

(b) the act constitutes an offence under the law in force in that country, and

(c) the act, if done in England and Wales *or Northern Ireland*, would constitute a sexual offence to which this section applies,

the United Kingdom resident is guilty in *that part of the United Kingdom* [England and Wales] of that sexual offence.

(3) If—

(a) a person does an act in a country outside the United Kingdom at a time when the person was not a United Kingdom national or a United Kingdom resident,

(b) the act constituted an offence under the law in force in that country,

(c) the act, if done in England and Wales *or Northern Ireland*, would have constituted a sexual offence to which this section applies, and

(d) the person meets the residence or nationality condition at the relevant time,

proceedings may be brought against the person in *that part of the United Kingdom* [England and Wales] for that sexual offence as if the person had done the act there.

(4) The person meets the residence or nationality condition at the relevant time if the person is a United Kingdom national or a United Kingdom resident at the time when the proceedings are brought.

(5) An act punishable under the law in force in any country constitutes an offence under that law for the purposes of subsections (2) and (3) however it is described in that law.

(6) The condition in subsection (2)(b) or (3)(b) is to be taken to be met unless, not later than rules of court may provide, the defendant serves on the prosecution a notice—

(a) stating that, on the facts as alleged with respect to the act in question, the condition is not in the defendant's opinion met,

(b) showing the grounds for that opinion, and

(c) requiring the prosecution to prove that it is met.

(7) But the court, if it thinks fit, may permit the defendant to require the prosecution to prove that the condition is met without service of a notice under subsection (6).

(8) In the Crown Court the question whether the condition is met is to be decided by the judge alone.

(9) In this section—

"country" includes territory;

"United Kingdom national" means an individual who is—

(a) a British citizen, a British overseas territories citizen, a British National (Overseas) or a British Overseas citizen;

(b) a person who under the *British Nationality Act* 1981 is a British subject; or

(c) a British protected person within the meaning of that Act;

"United Kingdom resident" means an individual who is resident in the United Kingdom.

(10) Schedule 2 lists the sexual offences to which this section applies.

[This section is printed as substituted by the *CJIA* 2008, s.72(1) (*ante*, § 2–36e); and as amended, as from a day to be appointed, by the *Sexual Offences (Northern Ireland Consequential Amendments) Order* 2008 (S.I. 2008 No. 1779) (in subss. (1), (2) and (3), repeal of words in italics and insertion of words in square brackets).]

Sexual Offences Act 2003, Sched. 2

SCHEDULE 2

SEXUAL OFFENCES TO WHICH SECTION 72 APPLIES

England and Wales

1. In relation to England and Wales, the following are sexual offences to which section 72 applies— **2–36g**

(a) an offence under any of sections 5 to 19, 25 and 26 and 47 to 50;

(b) an offence under any of sections 1 to 4, 30 to 41 and 61 where the victim of the offence was under 18 at the time of the offence;

(c) an offence under section 62 or 63 where the intended offence was an offence against a person under 18;

(d) an offence under—

(i) section 1 of the *Protection of Children Act* 1978 (indecent photographs of children), or

(ii) section 160 of the *Criminal Justice Act* 1988 (possession of indecent photograph of child).

2. [*Northern Ireland.*]

General

3. A reference in paragraph 1 *or 2(1)* to an offence includes—

(a) a reference to an attempt, conspiracy or incitement to commit that offence; and

(b) a reference to aiding and abetting, counselling or procuring the commission of that offence.

[This Schedule is printed as amended (with effect from July 14, 2008 (*ante*, § 2–36e)) by the *CJIA* 2008, ss.72(2) and (3) and 149, and Sched. 28, Pt 5. As from a day to be appointed, para. 2 and the italicised words in para. 3 are repealed by S.I. 2008 No. 1779 (*ante*, § 2–36f). The reference in para. 3 to the common law offence of incitement has effect as a reference to the offences under the *SCA* 2007, Pt 2: 2007 Act, s.63(1), and Sched. 6, para. 47.]

For details of the offences under the *SOA* 2003, see Chapter 20, *post*.

(2) Offences of dishonesty and blackmail

Criminal Justice Act 1993, ss.1–6

PART I

JURISDICTION

Offences to which this Part applies

2–37 **1.**—(1) This Part applies to two groups of offences—

(a) any offence mentioned in subsection (2) (a "Group A offence"); and

(b) any offence mentioned in subsection (3) (a "Group B offence").

(2) The Group A offences are—

(a) an offence under any of the following provisions of the *Theft Act* 1968—

section 1 (theft);

section 17 (false accounting);

section 19 (false statements by company directors, etc.);

section 21 (blackmail);

section 22 (handling stolen goods);

section 24A (retaining credits from dishonest sources, etc.)

(bb) offence under any of the following provisions of the *Fraud Act* 2006—

(i) section 1 (fraud);

(ii) section 6 (possession etc. of articles for use in frauds);

(iii) section 7 (making or supplying articles for use in frauds);

(iv) section 9 (participating in fraudulent business carried on by sole trader etc.);

(v) section 11 (obtaining services dishonestly);

(c) an offence under any of the following provisions of the *Forgery and Counterfeiting Act* 1981—

section 1 (forgery);

section 2 (copying a false instrument);

section 3 (using a false instrument);

section 4 (using a copy of a false instrument);

section 5 (offences which relate to money orders, share certificates, passports, etc.);

section 14 (offences of counterfeiting notes and coins);

section 15 (offences of passing etc counterfeit notes and coins);

section 16 (offences involving the custody or control of counterfeit notes and coins);

section 17 (offences involving the making or custody or control of counterfeiting materials and implements);

section 20 (prohibition of importation of counterfeit notes and coins);

section 21 (prohibition of exportation of counterfeit notes and coins);

(ca) an offence under section 25 of the *Identity Cards Act* 2006;

(d) the common law offence of cheating in relation to the public revenue.

(3) The Group B offences are—

(a) conspiracy to commit a Group A offence;

(b) conspiracy to defraud;

(c) attempting to commit a Group A offence;

(d) incitement to commit a Group A offence.

(4)–(6) [*Power to amend subs. (2) or (3) by order.*]

[This section is printed as amended, and repealed in part, by the *Theft (Amendment) Act* 1996, s.3; the *Criminal Justice Act 1993 (Extension of Group A Offences) Order* 2000 (S.I. 2000 No. 1878); the *Identity Cards Act* 2006, s.30(1); and the *Fraud Act* 2006, s.14(1) and (3), Sched. 1, para. 24, and Sched. 3. The reference in subs. (3)(d) to the common law offence of incitement has effect as a reference to the offences under the *SCA* 2007, Pt 2: 2007 Act, s.63(1), and Sched. 6, para. 21(a).]

Jurisdiction in respect of Group A offences

2.—(1) For the purposes of this Part, "relevant event", in relation to any Group A offence, means (subject to subsection (1A)) any act or omission or other event (including any result of one or more acts or omissions) proof of which is required for conviction of the offence. **2–38**

(1A) In relation to an offence under section 1 of the *Fraud Act* 2006 (fraud), "relevant event" includes—

(a) if the fraud involved an intention to make a gain and the gain occurred, that occurrence;

(b) if the fraud involved an intention to cause a loss or to expose another to a risk of loss and the loss occurred, that occurrence.

(2) For the purpose of determining whether or not a particular event is a relevant event in relation to a Group A offence, any question as to where it occurred is to be disregarded.

(3) A person may be guilty of a Group A offence if any of the events which are relevant events in relation to the offence occurred in England and Wales.

[This section is printed as amended by the *Fraud Act* 2006, s.14(1), and Sched. 1, para. 25.]

Questions immaterial to jurisdiction in the case of certain offences

3.—(1) A person may be guilty of a Group A or Group B offence whether or not— **2–39**

(a) he was a British citizen at any material time;

(b) he was in England and Wales at any such time.

(2) On a charge of conspiracy to commit a Group A offence, or on a charge of conspiracy to defraud in England and Wales, the defendant may be guilty of the offence whether or not—

(a) he became a party to the conspiracy in England and Wales;

(b) any act or omission or other event in relation to the conspiracy occurred in England and Wales.

(3) On a charge of attempting to commit a Group A offence, the defendant may be guilty of the offence whether or not—

(a) the attempt was made in England and Wales;

(b) it had an effect in England and Wales.

(4) Subsection (1)(a) does not apply where jurisdiction is given to try the offence in question by an enactment which makes provision by reference to the nationality of the person charged.

(5) Subsection (2) does not apply in relation to any charge under the *Criminal Law Act* 1977 brought by virtue of section 1A of that Act.

(6) Subsection (3) does not apply in relation to any charge under the *Criminal Attempts Act* 1981 brought by virtue of section 1A of that Act.

Rules for determining certain jurisdictional questions relating to the location of events

4. In relation to a Group A or Group B offence— **2–40**

(a) there is an obtaining of property in England and Wales if the property is either despatched from or received at a place in England and Wales; and

(b) there is a communication in England and Wales of any information, instruction, request, demand or other matter if it is sent by any means—

(i) from a place in England and Wales to a place elsewhere; or

(ii) from a place elsewhere to a place in England and Wales.

Conspiracy, attempt and incitement

5.—(1) [*Repealed by* Criminal Justice (Terrorism and Conspiracy) Act *1998, s.9(2) and Sched. 2.*] **2–41**

(2) [*See § 33–121,* post.]

(3) A person may be guilty of conspiracy to defraud if—

(a) a party to the agreement constituting the conspiracy, or a party's agent, did anything in England and Wales in relation to the agreement before its formation, or

(b) a party to it became a party in England and Wales (by joining it either in person or through an agent), or

(c) a party to it, or a party's agent, did or omitted anything in England and Wales in pursuance of it,

and the conspiracy would be triable in England and Wales but for the fraud which the parties to it had in view not being intended to take place in England and Wales.

(4) A person may be guilty of incitement to commit a Group A offence if the incitement—

(a) takes place in England and Wales; and

(b) would be triable in England and Wales but for what the person charged had in view not being an offence triable in England and Wales.

(5) Subsections (3) and (4) are subject to section 6.

[The reference in subs. (3)(d) to the common law offence of incitement has effect as a reference to the offences under the *SCA* 2007, Pt 2: 2007 Act, s.63(1), and Sched. 6, para. 21(b).]

Relevance of external law

2–42 **6.**—(1) A person is guilty of an offence triable ... by virtue of section 5(3), only if the pursuit of the agreed course of conduct would at some stage involve—

(a) an act or omission by one or more of the parties, or

(b) the happening of some other event,

constituting an offence under the law in force where the act, omission or other event was intended to take place.

(2) A person is guilty of an offence triable by virtue of section 1A of the *Criminal Attempts Act* 1981, or by virtue of section 5(4), only if what he had in view would involve the commission of an offence under the law in force where the whole or any part of it was intended to take place.

(3) Conduct punishable under the law in force in any place is an offence under that law for the purpose of this section, however it is described in that law.

(4) Subject to subsection (6), a condition specified in subsection (1) or (2) shall be taken to be satisfied unless, not later than rules of court may provide, the defence serve on the prosecution a notice—

(a) stating that, on the facts as alleged with respect to the relevant conduct, the condition is not in their opinion satisfied;

(b) showing their grounds for that opinion; and

(c) requiring the prosecution to show that it is satisfied.

(5) In subsection (4) "the relevant conduct" means—

(a) where the condition in subsection (1) is in question, the agreed course of conduct; and

(b) where the condition in subsection (2) is in question, what the defendant had in view.

(6) The court, if it thinks fit, may permit the defence to require the prosecution to show that the condition is satisfied without the prior service of a notice under subsection (4).

(7) In the Crown Court, the question whether the condition is satisfied shall be decided by the judge alone.

(8) [*Amends* Criminal Justice Act *1987, s.9(3).*]

2–43 [The words omitted from subs. (1) were repealed by the *Criminal Justice (Terrorism and Conspiracy) Act* 1998, s.9(1) and Sched. 1, para. 7(2).]

Part I came into force on June 1, 1999: *Criminal Justice Act 1993 (Commencement No. 10) Order* 1999 (S.I. 1999 No. 1189), and *Criminal Justice 1993 (Commencement No. 11) Order* 1999 (S.I. 1999 No. 1499). It is not retrospective. Section 78(5) provides that nothing in any provision in Part I applies to any act, omission or other event occurring before the coming into force of that provision. The old jurisdictional limits governing the relevant offences will continue to apply to prosecutions begun after the commencement date, if they relate to conduct occurring before that date.

Since jurisdiction depends upon establishing where certain acts take place, section 4 lays down rules for determining where an obtaining of property or a communication takes place.

Jurisdiction over Group A offences. By virtue of section 2, the court has jurisdiction to try a Group A offence where any one of the constituent elements of the offence occurs in England and Wales. Section 3(1) emphasises that a person may be guilty of a Group A offence, whether or not he was in England and Wales at any material time, and whether or not he was a British citizen at any such time (subject only to the exception in s.3(4)). **2–44**

Jurisdiction over Group B offences—conspiracy. As a result of the extension of jurisdiction over Group A offences, the courts will also have extended jurisdiction over conspiracies to commit Group A offences. Thus a conspiracy to commit a Group A offence will be triable in England and Wales provided that the agreed course of conduct would, if carried out in accordance with the parties' intentions, result in one of the constituent elements of the Group A offence occurring in England and Wales. Section 3 provides that it is immaterial to the courts' jurisdiction over conspiracies to commit Group A offences and conspiracies to defraud in England and Wales that a defendant was not in England or Wales at the material time, or that he was not a British citizen at the material time (s.3(1)) (subject to the exception in s.3(4)), or that he did not join the conspiracy in England or Wales, or that no act or omission or other event in relation to the conspiracy took place in England or Wales (s.3(2)). Section 3(2) does not apply, however, where the charge is brought by virtue of section 1A of the *CLA* 1977. **2–45**

Section 5(3) extends the jurisdiction of the courts over offences of conspiracy to defraud where the fraud the parties had in view was not intended to take place in England or Wales. The jurisdiction depends on proof that pursuit of the agreed course of conduct would involve conduct punishable under the law in force in the place where the conduct was intended to take place. The relevant external law may be proved by the procedure described in section 6(4)–(7). The prosecution must also prove either that a conspirator or his agent joined the conspiracy in England or Wales, or that a conspirator or his agent did something in relation to the agreement before its formation, or did or omitted anything in pursuance of the agreement after its formation, in England and Wales.

Jurisdiction over Group B offences—offences under the *SCA* 2007, Pt 2. The extension of jurisdiction over Group A offences has also given the courts extended jurisdiction over an offence of encouraging or assisting Group A offences (*SCA* 2007, Pt 2). Encouraging or assisting a Group A offence will be triable in England and Wales provided that what the defendant had in view would involve one of the constituent elements of the Group A offence occurring in England and Wales. Section 3(1) of the 1993 Act provides that a defendant may be convicted of encouraging or assisting a Group A offence whether or not he was in England and Wales at any material time and whether or not he was a British citizen at any such time (subject to s.3(4)). **2–46**

Section 5(4) stipulates that a person may be guilty of encouraging or assisting a Group A offence if the encouragement or assistance took place in England and Wales, and would be triable in England and Wales but for the fact that what the person charged had in view was not an offence triable in England and Wales. This is subject to the requirement that the conduct he had in view would involve the commission of an offence under the law in force where the whole or any part of it was to take place: ss.5(5), 6.

Jurisdiction over Group B offences—attempts. An attempt to commit a Group A offence will be triable in England and Wales provided that the attempt, if completed, would involve one of the constituent elements of the Group A offence occurring in England and Wales. Section 3 provides that the defendant may be convicted of an attempt to commit a Group A offence whether or not he was in England and Wales and whether or not he was a British citizen at the material time (subject to s.3(4)) and whether or not the attempt was made in England and Wales or had an effect in England and Wales: s.3(3). **2–47**

In addition, section 5(2) inserts a new section 1A in the *Criminal Attempts Act* 1981 which gives the courts extended jurisdiction in relation to certain attempts: section 1A applies to any attempt where a person does an act in England and Wales that would be more than merely preparatory to the commission of a Group A offence but for the fact that that offence, if completed, would not be an offence triable in England and Wales. However, a person will only be guilty of an offence triable by virtue of section 1A of the *Criminal Attempts Act* 1981 if what he had in view would involve the commission of an offence under the law in force where the whole or any part of it was intended to take place: s.1A(4). As to proof of the relevant law, see section 6 of the 1993 Act.

(3) Conspiracy, incitement and attempt

2–48 As to conspiracy, see *post*, §§ 33–21 *et seq.*, 33–40. As to encouragement and assistance, see *post*, §§ 33–106 *et seq.* As to attempt, see *post*, § 33–133.

Conspiracy, incitement and attempt to commit a Group A offence within the *CJA* 1993, s.1, are Group B offences within that section; for the jurisdiction over Group B offences and for the extended jurisdiction over certain incitements and attempts, see *ante*, §§ 2–45 *et seq.*

In *R. v. Tompkins* [2007] Crim.L.R. 235, CA, it was held that the courts of England and Wales have jurisdiction to try a charge of incitement to distribute indecent photographs of children where the person doing the inciting is at all material times within the jurisdiction and the distribution was to occur, at least in part within the jurisdiction, notwithstanding that the person incited was outside the jurisdiction. See also *ante*, §§ 2–36a *et seq.*

(4) Offences connected with aircraft

Civil Aviation Act 1982, s.92

2–49 **92.**—(1) Any act or omission taking place on board a British-controlled aircraft or (subject to subsection (1A) below) a foreign aircraft while in flight elsewhere than in or over the United Kingdom which, if taking place in, or in a part of, the United Kingdom, would constitute an offence under the law in force in, or in that part of, the United Kingdom shall constitute that offence; but this subsection shall not apply to any act or omission which is expressly or impliedly authorised by or under that law when taking place outside the United Kingdom.

(1A) Subsection (1) above shall only apply to an act or omission which takes place on board a foreign aircraft where—

(a) the next landing of the aircraft is in the United Kingdom, and

(b) in the case of an aircraft registered in a country other than the United Kingdom, the act or omission would, if taking place there, also constitute an offence under the law in force in that country.

(2) Subject to any provision to the contrary in any Act passed after 14th July 1967, no proceedings for any offence under the law in force in, or in a part of, the United Kingdom committed on board an aircraft while in flight elsewhere than in or over the United Kingdom (other than an offence under, or under any instrument made under, any of the air navigation enactments) shall be instituted—

(a) in England and Wales, except by or with the consent of the Director of Public Prosecutions; or

(b) [*Northern Ireland*];

but, [*relates to Northern Ireland*].

(2A) The requirement in subsection (1A)(b) above shall be taken to be met unless, not later than the rules of court may provide, the defence serve on the prosecution a notice—

(a) stating that, on the facts as alleged with respect to the act or omission, the requirement is not in their opinion met;

(b) showing the grounds for their opinion; and

(c) requiring the prosecution to prove that it is met.

(2B) The court, if it thinks fit, may permit the defence to require the prosecution to prove that the requirement is met without the prior service of a notice under subsection (2A) above.

(2C) In the Crown Court the question whether the requirement is met is to be decided by the judge alone.

(3) For the purpose of conferring jurisdiction, any offence under the law in force in, or

in a part of, the United Kingdom committed on board an aircraft in flight shall be deemed to have been committed in any place in the United Kingdom (or, as the case may be, in that part thereof) where the offender may for the time being be.

(4) For the purposes of this section the period during which an aircraft is in flight shall be deemed to include any period from the moment when power is applied for the purpose of the aircraft taking off on a flight until the moment when the landing run (if any) at the termination of that flight ends; and any reference in this section to an aircraft in flight shall include a reference to an aircraft during any period when it is on the surface of the sea or land but not within the territorial limits of any country.

(5) In this section, except where the context otherwise requires— **2–50**

"aircraft" means any aircraft, whether or not a British-controlled aircraft, other than—

(a) a military aircraft; or

(b) subject to section 101(1)(b) below, an aircraft which, not being a military aircraft, belongs to or is exclusively employed in the service of Her Majesty in right of the United Kingdom;

"the air navigation enactments" mean the enactments contained in section 60 to 62, 72 to 77, 81 to 83, 87 and 97 of this Act;

"British-controlled aircraft" means an aircraft—

(a) which is for the time being registered in the United Kingdom; or

(b) which is not for the time being registered in any country but in the case of which either the operator of the aircraft or each person entitled as owner to any legal or beneficial interest in it satisfies the following requirements, namely—

(i) that he is a person qualified to be the owner of a legal or beneficial interest in an aircraft registered in the United Kingdom; and

(ii) that he resides or has his principal place of business in the United Kingdom; or

(c) which, being for the time being registered in some other country, is for the time being chartered by demise to a person who, or to persons each of whom, satisfies the requirements aforesaid;

"military aircraft" means—

(a) an aircraft of the naval, military or air forces of any country; or

(b) any other aircraft in respect of which there is in force a certificate issued in accordance with any Order in Council in force under section 60, 87, 89, 91, 101(1)(a) or 107(2) of this Act that the aircraft is to be treated for the purposes of that Order in Council as a military aircraft; and a certificate of the Secretary of State that any aircraft is or is not a military aircraft for the purposes of this section shall be conclusive evidence of the fact certified.

(6) [*Northern Ireland*.]

[This section is printed as amended by the *Civil Aviation (Amendment) Act* 1996, s.1.]

See also the *Aviation Security Act* 1982, Pt I (*post*, §§ 25–177 *et seq.*); and the *Aviation and Maritime Security Act* 1990, s.1 (*post*, § 25–198).

(5) Homicide

Offences against the Person Act 1861, s.9

9. Where any murder or manslaughter shall be committed on land out of the United Kingdom, whether within the Queen's dominions or without, and whether the person killed were a subject of Her Majesty or not, every offence committed by any subject of Her Majesty, in respect of any such case, whether the same shall amount to the offence of murder or of manslaughter ... may be dealt with, inquired of, tried, determined and punished ... in England or Ireland .... Provided, that nothing herein contained shall prevent any person from being tried in any place out of England or Ireland for any murder or manslaughter committed out of England or Ireland, in the same manner as such person might have been tried before the passing of this Act. **2–51**

[This section is printed as amended by the *CLA* 1967, s.10(2) and Sched. 3.]

A British subject, therefore, who, in a foreign country, within the dominion of a foreign power, murders either a British subject or a foreigner is triable in England under the express provisions of this section: see *R. v. Azzopardi* (1843) 6 St.Tr.(n.s.) 21, and *R. v. Page* [1954] 1 Q.B. 170, 37 Cr.App.R. 189, Ct-MAC.

Offences against the Person Act 1861, s.10

2–52 **10.** Where any person, being criminally stricken, poisoned, or otherwise hurt upon the sea, or at any place out of England or Ireland, shall die of such stroke, poisoning, or hurt in England or Ireland, or, being criminally stricken, poisoned, or otherwise hurt in any place in England or Ireland, shall die of such stroke, poisoning or hurt upon the sea, or at any place out of England or Ireland, every offence committed in respect of any such case, whether the same shall amount to the offence of murder or of manslaughter, ... may be dealt with, inquired of, tried, determined, and punished ... in England or Ireland.

[This section is printed as amended by the *CLA* 1967, s.10(1), Sched. 2, para. 6 and Sched. 3.]

"Ireland" means Northern Ireland: see the *Irish Free State (Consequential Adaptation of Enactments) Order* 1923 (S.R. & O. 1923 No. 405).

Section 10 apparently applies to British subjects only, not to foreigners: see *R. v. Lewis* (1857) Dears. & B. 82; *R. v. Jameson* [1896] 2 Q.B. 425, *per* Lord Russell C.J. at p. 430.

(6) Offences in connection with taxation etc. in the E.C.

Criminal Justice Act 1993, s.71

2–53 **71.**—(1) A person who, in the United Kingdom, assists or induces conduct outside the United Kingdom which involves the commission of a serious offence against the law of another member State is guilty of an offence under this section if—

(a) the offence involved is one consisting in or including the contravention of provisions of the law of that member State which relate to any of the matters specified in subsection (2);

(b) the offence involved is one consisting in or including the contravention of other provisions of that law so far as they have effect in relation to any of those matters; or

(c) the conduct is such as to be calculated to have an effect in that member State in relation to any of those matters.

(2) The matters mentioned in subsection (1) are—

(a) the determination, discharge or enforcement of any liability for a Community duty or tax;

(b) the operation of arrangements under which reliefs or exemptions from any such duty or tax are provided or sums in respect of any such duty or tax are repaid or refunded;

(c) the making of payments in pursuance of Community arrangements made in connection with the regulation of the market for agricultural products and the enforcement of the conditions of any such payments;

(d) the movement into or out of any member State of anything in relation to the movement of which any Community instrument imposes, or requires the imposition of, any prohibition or restriction; and

(e) such other matters in relation to which provision is made by any Community instrument as the Secretary of State may by order specify.

(3) For the purposes of this section—

(a) an offence against the law of a member State is a serious offence if provision is in force in that member State authorising the sentencing, in some or all cases, of a person convicted of that offence to imprisonment for a maximum term of 12 months or more; and

(b) the question whether any conduct involves the commisison of such an offence shall be determined according to the law in force in the member State in question at the time of the assistance or inducement.

(4) In any proceedings against any person for an offence under this section it shall be a defence for that person to show—

(a) that the conduct in question would not have involved the commission of an offence against the law of the member State in question but for circumstances of which he had no knowledge; and

(b) that he did not suspect or anticipate the existence of those circumstances and did not have reasonable grounds for doing so.

(5) For the purposes of any proceedings for an offence under this section, a certificate purporting to be issued by or on behalf of the government of another member State which contains a statement, in relation to such times as may be specified in the certificate—

(a) that a specified offence existed against the law of that member State;

(b) that an offence against the law of that member State was a serious offence within the meaning of this section;

(c) that such an offence consists in or includes the contravention of particular provisions of the law of that member State;

(d) that specified provisions of the law of that member State relate to, or are capable of having an effect in relation to, particular matters;

(e) that specified conduct involved the commission of a particular offence against the law of that member State, or

(f) that a particular effect in that member State in relation to any matter would result from specified conduct,

shall, in the case of a statement falling within paragraphs (a) to (d), be conclusive of the matters stated and, in the other cases, be evidence, and in Scotland sufficient evidence, of the matters stated.

(6) A person guilty of an offence under this section shall be liable—

(a) on summary conviction, to a penalty of the statutory maximum or to imprisonment for a term not exceeding *six* [12] months or to both; or

(b) on conviction on indictment, to a penalty of any amount or to imprisonment for a term not exceeding seven years or to both.

(7) Sections 145 to 152 and 154 of the *Customs and Excise Management Act* 1979 (general provisions as to legal proceedings) shall apply as if this section were contained in that Act; and that an offence under this section shall be treated for all purposes as an offence for which a person is liable to be arrested under the customs and excise Acts.

(8) [*Making of statutory instruments.*]

(9) In this section—

"another member State" means a member State other than the United Kingdom;

"Community duty or tax" means any of the following, that is to say—

(a) any Community customs duty;

(b) an agricultural levy of the Economic Community;

(c) value added tax under the law of another member State;

(d) any duty or tax on tobacco products, alcoholic liquors or hydrocarbon oils which, in another member State, corresponds to any excise duty;

(e) any duty, tax or other charge not falling within paragraphs (a) to (d) of this definition which is imposed by or in pursuance of any Community instrument on the movement of goods into or out of any member State;

"conduct" includes acts, omissions and statements;

"contravention" includes a failure to comply; and

"the customs and excise Acts" has the same meaning as in the *Customs and Excise Management Act* 1979.

(10) References in this section, in relation to a Community instrument, to the movement of anything into or out of a member State include references to the movement of anything between member States and to the doing of anything which falls to be treated for the purposes of that instrument as involving the entry into, or departure from, the territory of the Community of any goods (within the meaning of that Act of 1979).

[In subs. (6)(a), "12" is substituted for "six", as from a day to be appointed, by the *CJA* 2003, s.282(2) and (3). The increase has no application to offences committed before the substitution takes effect: s.282(4).]

This section enables the United Kingdom to take action against fraud perpetrated against the European Community. *Inter alia*, it has been used to deal with transit frauds involving continental lorry drivers and hauliers, which are increasingly common. See Don Mavin, "The European dimension for the Duty Men" (1998) 142 S.J. 344. **2–54**

For sections 145 to 152 and 154 of the 1979 Act, see *post*, §§ 25–427 *et seq*.

(7) Offences by servants of the Crown

Criminal Justice Act 1948, s.31(1)

31.—(1) Any British subject employed under Her Majesty's Government in the United **2–55**

Kingdom in the service of the Crown who commits, in a foreign country, when acting or purporting to act in the course of his employment, any offence which, if committed in England, would be punishable on indictment, shall be guilty of an offence ... and subject to the same punishment, as if the offence had been committed in England.

[The words omitted from subs. (1) and subss. (2) and (3) were repealed by the *CJA* 1948, Sched. 3, Pt III.]

See *Hastings and Folkestone Glassworks Ltd v. Kalson* [1949] 1 K.B. 214 at 221 and 222.

See also *post*, § 25–382.

(8) Slave trade

2–56 By section 26 of the *Slave Trade Act* 1873, offences in connection with the slave trade are deemed, for all purposes of and incidental to the jurisdiction of any court, to have been committed either in the place in which the offence was committed or in any place in which the person guilty of the offence may for the time being be.

[The next paragraph is § 2–63.]

(9) Offences under the Merchant Shipping Act 1995

Merchant Shipping Act 1995, ss.279–281

Jurisdiction in relation to offences

2–63 **279.**—(1) For the purpose of conferring jurisdiction, any offence under this Act shall be deemed to have been committed in any place in the United Kingdom where the offender may for the time being be.

(2) [*Irrelevant to criminal proceedings.*]

(3) The jurisdiction under subsections (1) and (2) above shall be in addition to and not in derogation of any jurisdiction or power of a court under any other enactment.

Jurisdiction over ships lying off coasts

2–64 **280.**—(1) Where the area within which a court in any part of the United Kingdom has jurisdiction is situated on the coast of any sea or abuts on or projects into any bay, channel, lake, river or other navigable water the court shall have jurisdiction as respects offences under this Act over any vessel being on, or lying or passing off, that coast or being in or near that bay, channel, lake, river or navigable water and over all persons on board that vessel or for the time being belonging to it.

(2) The jurisdiction under subsection (1) above shall be in addition to and not in derogation of any jurisdiction or power of a court under the *Magistrates' Courts Act* 1980 or the *Magistrates' Courts (Northern Ireland) Order* 1981.

Jurisdiction in case of offences on board ship

2–65 **281.** Where any person is charged with having committed any offence under this Act then—

(a) if he is a British citizen and is charged with having committed it—
   (i) on board any United Kingdom ship on the high seas,
   (ii) in any foreign port or harbour, or
   (iii) on board any foreign ship to which he does not belong; or

(b) if he is not a British citizen and is charged with having committed it on board any United Kingdom ship on the high seas;

and he is found within the jurisdiction of any court in any part of the United Kingdom which would have had jurisdiction in relation to the offence if it had been committed on board a United Kingdom ship within the limits of its ordinary jurisdiction to try the offence that court shall have jurisdiction to try the offence as if it had been so committed.

2–66 "British citizen" has the same meaning as in the *British Nationality Act* 1981: s.313(1).

For the extension of sections 280 and 281 to other offences, see the *Supreme Court [Senior Courts] Act* 1981 (renamed on the coming into force of the *Constitutional Reform Act* 2005, s.59(5), and Sched. 11, paras 1 and 26), s.46A, *ante*, § 2–31.

There appears to be a substantial drafting error in section 281; this section's predecessor (section 686 of the *Merchant Shipping Act* 1894, as amended) referred to a British citizen being charged with an offence committed "on board a British ship on the high seas or in any foreign port or harbour" (as to which, see *R. v. Cumberworth*, 89 Cr.App.R. 187, CA). Because of the drafting style adopted in the 1995 Act, there appears to be no requirement that the offence be on a British ship (or any ship) if it is committed in a foreign port or harbour. This was surely unintentional; for otherwise, it would purport to confer jurisdiction on the English courts over any conduct which would be an offence by English law committed within any "port or harbour" in the world, regardless of whether it was committed on board ship or not, and regardless of the nationality of the ship if it was committed on board ship.

The words "is found" refer to the time of trial: *R. v. Lopez*; *R. v. Sattler* (1858) Dears. & B. 525.

The words "on board any ship to which he does not belong" should be given their ordinary meaning in the context of the provision: *R. v. Kelly* [1982] A.C. 665, HL. Those persons "belong to" a vessel who have some reasonably permanent attachment to it. The phrase is wide enough to include not only the master and crew but also persons who are on the ship for a substantial time for some other purpose, *e.g.* scientists or engineers engaged in exploration or survey. The words do not include passengers on a passenger ferry who were only on the ship for a short voyage: *ibid.*

In *R. v. Liverpool JJ., ex p. Molyneux* [1972] 2 Q.B. 484, DC, it was said that a Commonwealth port could not be a "foreign" port; it seems unlikely that this could have been the legislative intention for the consequence would be that on the face of it, the jurisdiction of the English courts would be more extensive in relation to foreign ports and harbours than in relation to Commonwealth ports and harbours. The point may have little practical significance because it was held that "high seas" has the same meaning as when used with reference to the Admiralty jurisdiction, *i.e.* all oceans, seas, bays, channels, rivers, creeks and waters below low-water mark and "where great ships go", except such parts of such oceans, etc., as lie within the body of a county.

Particular offences

Apart from the general provisions set out above, some of the sections of the 1995 Act creating individual offences are specifically stated to apply to things done outside, as well as to things done within, the United Kingdom: see, for example, sections 14 and 15 (offences relating to a ship's British connection and offences relating to unregistered fishing vessels), and section 6 of the *Shipping and Trading Interests (Protection) Act* 1995 (provision of coastal shipping services in breach of prohibition). **2–67**

(10) Offences committed by British seamen

Merchant Shipping Act 1995, s.282

Offences committed by British seamen

282.—(1) Any act in relation to property or person done in or at any place (ashore or afloat) outside the United Kingdom by any master or seaman who at the time is employed in a United Kingdom ship, which, if done in any part of the United Kingdom, would be an offence under the law of any part of the United Kingdom, shall— **2–68**

(a) be an offence under that law, and

(b) be treated for the purposes of jurisdiction and trial as if it had been done within the jurisdiction of the Admiralty of England.

(2) Subsection (1) above also applies to a person who has been so employed within the period of three months expiring with the time when the act was done.

(3) Subsections (1) and (2) above apply to omissions as they apply to acts.

For the extension of section 282 to other offences, see section 46A of the *Supreme Court [Senior Courts] Act* 1981 (*ante*, § 2–31) (renamed as from a day to be appointed: *Constitutional Reform Act* 2005, s.59(5), and Sched. 11, para. 1).

(11) Offences in the Admiralty jurisdiction

General

The Crown Court has jurisdiction over offences committed within the jurisdiction of the Admiralty of England: see the 1981 Act, s.46(2) (*ante*, § 2–30). **2–69**

As to the geographical extent of the Admiralty jurisdiction, see *R. v. Liverpool JJ., ex p. Molyneux* (*ante*, § 2–66), and *post*, § 25–42. The jurisdiction covers offences committed within United Kingdom territorial waters, offences committed on British ships anywhere on the high seas (as defined in *R. v. Liverpool JJ., ex p. Molyneux*), and, by virtue of section 2 of the *Territorial Waters Jurisdiction Act* 1878, offences committed on foreign ships within the territorial waters of Her Majesty's dominions. For the meaning of "foreign ship", see section 7 of the 1878 Act. References in that Act in whatever terms to ships, vessels or boats or activities or places connected therewith are extended to include hovercraft or activities or places connected with hovercraft: *Hovercraft (Application of Enactments) Order* 1972 (S.I. 1972 No. 971).

Proceedings for an offence declared to be within the jurisdiction of the Admiralty by the 1878 Act are not to be instituted without the consent of one of Her Majesty's principal secretaries of state and his certificate that the institution of proceedings is in his opinion expedient: s.3. The giving of such consent and certificate are to be presumed unless disputed by the defendant; if disputed, the production of a document purporting to be signed by one of Her Majesty's principal secretaries of state, and containing such consent and certificate shall be sufficient evidence for all the purposes of the Act: s.4.

The fact that the municipal authorities of a foreign country may have concurrent jurisdiction does not oust the jurisdiction of the Admiralty: *R. v. Anderson* (1868) L.R. 1 C.C.R. 161. If great ships go to the place, proof that the tide ebbs and flows is unnecessary: *R. v. Allen* (1837) 1 Mood. 494. The jurisdiction extends to all persons on board the ship whether British subjects or foreigners: *R. v. Lopez*; *R. v. Sattler* (1858) Dears. & B. 525; *R. v. Lesley* (1860) Bell 220.

Artificial structures outside territorial waters, such as a disused anti-aircraft tower (*R. v. Bates*, unreported, October 21, 1968, Essex Assizes, Chapman J.), are not within the Admiralty jurisdiction and the position of light-houses outside territorial waters in relation to offences committed on them has not been clearly established: see Oppenheim's *International Law*, 9th ed., 1992, Vol. 1, para. 195.

Territorial sea

2–70 The area of territory can, for the purpose of jurisdiction over offences, be extended by exercise of the prerogative: *R. v. Kent JJ., ex p. Lye* [1967] 2 Q.B. 153, DC; *Post Office v. Estuary Radio* [1967] 1 W.L.R. 1396; or by Parliament. The *Territorial Sea Act* 1987, s.1(1) now provides that, subject to the provisions of the Act, the territorial sea adjacent to the United Kingdom shall for all purposes be 12 nautical miles and the baselines from which the breadth of the territorial sea is to be measured shall for all purposes be those established by Her Majesty by Order in Council. The Act is supplemented by the *Territorial Sea (Limits) Order* 1989 (S.I. 1989 No. 482) made under section 1(2) which establishes the seaward limits of the territorial sea adjacent to the United Kingdom in the narrow part of the Straits of Dover and in the vicinity of the Isle of Man.

Piracy

2–71 See *post*, §§ 25–42 *et seq.*

Offences against the safety of ships and fixed platforms

2–72 See the *Aviation and Maritime Security Act* 1990, Pt II, *post*, §§ 25–201 *et seq.*

Drug offences committed at sea

2–73 See sections 18 to 21 of the *Criminal Justice (International Co-operation) Act* 1990, *post*, §§ 25–497 *et seq.*

Proof of ship's nationality

2–74 The term "British ship" is defined in section 1(1) of the *Merchant Shipping Act* 1995. The definition includes a ship registered in the United Kingdom under Part II: as to the proof of information in the register of British ships established for all registrations of ships in the United Kingdom, see section 9(8) of the 1995 Act.

To prove that a ship is a British ship, it is not necessary to produce the register or a copy thereof; it is sufficient to show orally that she belongs to British owners and carries the British flag: *R. v. Allen* (1866) 10 Cox 406. Where it was stated by three witnesses that the vessel, on board of which an offence was alleged to have been committed, was a British ship of the port of Shields, and that she was sailing under the British flag, but no proof was given of the registration or ownership of that vessel, it was held that the court had jurisdiction, as the evidence was sufficient to prove that the vessel was British, and that being so, the court would have jurisdiction even if it had appeared that the vessel was not registered: *R. v. Seberg* (1870) L.R. 1 C.C.R. 264.

Offences by foreigners in foreign ships

As to offences committed within the territorial waters of Her Majesty's dominions, see the *Territorial Waters Jurisdiction Act* 1878 (*ante*, § 2–69). Apart from cases within this statute, piracy and any offences where the particular statute provides otherwise (*e.g.* the *Aviation and Maritime Security Act* 1990, s.9 (*post*, § 25–201)), the acts of a foreigner on board a foreign ship are not justiciable in this country. Thus a foreigner who kills an Englishman on board a foreign ship is not triable in England: *R. v. De Mattos* (1836) 7 C. & P. 458; *R. v. Lewis* (1857) Dears. & B. 182. This rule applies where the ship has been illegally seized as a slaver by a British vessel: *R. v. Serva* (1845) 1 Den. 104. **2–75**

The criminal law consolidation Acts of 1861

Each of these Acts contained a provision by which all indictable offences in those Acts committed within the jurisdiction of the Admiralty are to be subject to the same punishments as if they had been committed in England: *e.g.* the *Offences against the Person Act* 1861, s.68. These provisions, if they were not superfluous in 1861, are certainly redundant now. **2–76**

(12) Offshore activities

Petroleum Act 1998, s.10

Application of criminal law etc.

10.—(1) Her Majesty may by Order in Council provide that, in such cases and subject to such exceptions as may be prescribed by the Order, any act or omission which— **2–77**

(a) takes place on, under or above an installation in waters to which this section applies or any waters within 500 metres of any such installation; and

(b) would, if taking place in any part of the United Kingdom, constitute an offence under the law in force in that part,

shall be treated for the purposes of that law as taking place in that part.

(2) Her Majesty may by Order in Council provide that, in such cases and subject to such exceptions as may be prescribed by the Order, a constable shall on, under or above any installation in waters to which this section applies or any waters within 500 metres of such an installation have all the powers, protection and privileges which he has in the area for which he acts as constable.

(3) Subsection (2) is without prejudice to any other enactment or rule of law affording any power, protection or privilege to constables.

(4) Where a body corporate is guilty of an offence by virtue of an Order in Council under this section and that offence is proved to have been committed with the consent or connivance of, or to be attributable to any neglect on the part of, any director, manager, secretary or other similar officer of the body corporate or any person who was purporting to act in any such capacity, he as well as the body corporate shall be guilty of that offence and shall be liable to be proceeded against and punished accordingly.

(5) Where the affairs of a body corporate are managed by its members, subsection (4) shall apply in relation to acts and defaults of a member in connection with his functions of management as if he were a director of a body corporate.

(6) Proceedings for anything that is an offence by virtue of an Order in Council under this section may be taken, and the offence may for all incidental purposes be treated as having been committed, in any place in the United Kingdom.

(7) The waters to which this section applies are—

(a) the territorial sea adjacent to the United Kingdom;
(b) waters in any area designated under section 1(7) of the *Continental Shelf Act* 1964; and
(c) waters in any area specified under subsection (8).

(8) Her Majesty may from time to time by Order in Council specify any area which—
(a) is in a foreign sector of the continental shelf; and
(b) comprises any part of a cross-boundary field,

as an area as respects which the powers conferred by this section and section 11 are exercisable.

(9) In this section—

"cross-boundary field" means a field that extends across the boundary between waters falling within paragraph (a) or (b) of subsection (7) above and a foreign sector of the continental shelf;

"field" means a geological structure identified as such by Order in Council under subsection (8) above.

(10) This section applies to installations notwithstanding that they are for the time being in transit.

(11) [*Order in Council procedure.*]

2–78 The *Criminal Jurisdiction (Offshore Activities) Order* 1987 (S.I. 1987 No. 2198) was made under section 22 of the *Oil and Gas (Enterprise) Act* 1982, and, by virtue of the *Interpretation Act* 1978, s.17(2)(b) (Appendix B–17), has effect as if made under section 10. It applies to territorial waters of the United Kingdom and to waters in any area for the time being designated under section 1(7) of the *Continental Shelf Act* 1964: art. 2. Any act or omission which (a) takes place on, under or above an installation in waters to which the order applies or any waters within 500 metres of any such installation; and (b) would, if taking place in any part of the United Kingdom, constitute an offence under the law in force in that part, shall be treated for the purposes of that law as taking place in that part: art. 3. Article 4 provides that a constable shall on, under or above any installation in waters to which the order applies or any waters within 500 metres of such installation have all the powers, protection and privileges which he has in the area for which he acts as constable.

2–79 Section 12 contains restrictions on prosecutions for certain offences alleged to have been committed on, under or above an installation in waters to which section 10 applies, or any waters within 500 metres of such an installation, and for certain offences under the *Civil Aviation Act* 1982. Where the restriction applies, no proceedings are to be instituted without the consent of the DPP unless the offence is one which requires the consent of the Attorney-General.

Continental Shelf Act 1964, s.11(1)

2–80 **11.**—(1) Proceedings for any offence under another Act as applied by or under this Act may be taken, and the offence may for all incidental purposes be treated as having been committed in any place in the United Kingdom.

[Printed as amended by the *Oil and Gas (Enterprise) Act* 1982, Sched. 3.]

This provision covers offences under Part II of the *Coast Protection Act* 1949 and section 3 of the *Submarine Telegraph Act* 1885 (see sections 4 and 8 of the 1964 Act respectively).

Petroleum Act 1987

2–81 This Act made fresh provision for safety zones around offshore installations. Section 21 provides for the automatic establishment of safety zones and section 22 empowers the Secretary of State to establish a safety zone by order.

Section 23 places restrictions on vessels entering, or remaining in, a safety zone. Contravention of these restrictions is made an offence on the part of both the owner and master who are liable, on summary conviction, to a fine not exceeding the statutory maximum and, on conviction on indictment, to imprisonment not exceeding two years, or to a fine, or both. Proceedings may be taken, and the offence may for all incidental purposes be treated as having been committed, in any place in the United Kingdom (s.23(7)).

Section 24(3) provides that sections 21 to 23, so far as they apply to individuals, apply to them whether or not they are British citizens, and, so far as they apply to bodies corporate, apply to them whether or not they are incorporated in any part of the United Kingdom.

By virtue of the *Offshore Safety Act* 1992, s.1, sections 21 to 23 of the 1987 Act are "existing statutory provisions" within the meaning of Part I of the *Health and Safety at Work etc. Act* 1974.

Energy Act 2004

Section 84 of the 2004 Act makes provision for the designation of offshore areas as renewable energy zones, and sections 85 and 86 broadly correspond to sections 10 and 12 of the *Petroleum Act* 1998 (*ante*) in relation to renewable energy installations (as to which, see section 104(1) and (3) to (5)). Sections 95 to 98 of the 2004 Act correspond generally to sections 22 and 23 of the *Petroleum Act* 1987 (*ante*). **2–81a**

(13) Bribery and corruption

Anti-Terrorism, Crime and Security Act 2001, s.109

Bribery and corruption committed outside the U.K.

109.—(1) This section applies if— **2–82**

(a) a national of the United Kingdom or a body incorporated under the law of any part of the United Kingdom does anything in a country or territory outside the United Kingdom, and

(b) the act would, if done in the United Kingdom, constitute a corruption offence (as defined below).

(2) In such a case—

(a) the act constitutes the offence concerned, and

(b) proceedings for the offence may be taken in the United Kingdom.

(3) These are corruption offences—

(a) any common law offence of bribery;

(b) the offences under section 1 of the *Public Bodies Corrupt Practices Act* 1889 (corruption in office);

(c) the first two offences under section 1 of the *Prevention of Corruption Act* 1906 (bribes obtained by or given to agents).

(4) A national of the United Kingdom is an individual who is—

(a) a British citizen, a British overseas territories citizen, a British National (Overseas) or a British Overseas citizen,

(b) a person who under the *British Nationality Act* 1981 is a British subject, or

(c) a British protected person within the meaning of that Act.

[This section came into force on February 14, 2002: *Anti-Terrorism, Crime and Security Act 2001 (Commencement No. 3) Order* 2002 (S.I. 2002 No. 228). It is printed as amended by the *British Overseas Territories Act* 2002, s.2(3).]

(14) Miscellaneous

A range of other statutes make provision for the prosecution of conduct occurring abroad: see *post*, § 19–118 (corporate manslaughter), § 19–349 (torture), §§ 23–62 *et seq.* (explosives), §§ 25–1 *et seq.* (treason), §§ 25–55 *et seq.* (terrorism), §§ 25–155 *et seq.* (offences against United Nations personnel), §§ 25–216 *et seq.* and Appendix F (Channel tunnel), §§ 25–237 *et seq.* (foreign enlistment), §§ 25–310, 25–341 (official secrets), § 25–460 (customs and excise), and §§ 31–1, 31–7 (bigamy). **2–83**

[The next paragraph is § 2–153.]

IV. JURISDICTION IN CHAMBERS

Criminal Procedure Rules 2005 (S.I. 2005 No. 384), r.16.11

Crown Court hearings in chambers

2–153 **16.11.**—(1) The criminal jurisdiction of the Crown Court specified in the following paragraph may be exercised by a judge of the Crown Court sitting in chambers.

(2) The said jurisdiction is—

(a) hearing applications for bail;

(b) issuing a summons or warrant;

(c) hearing any application relating to procedural matters preliminary or incidental to criminal proceedings in the Crown Court, including applications relating to legal aid;

(d) jurisdiction under rules 12.2 (listing first appearance of accused sent for trial), 28.3 (application for witness summons), 63.2(5) (extending time for appeal against decision of magistrates' court), and 64.7 (application to state case for consideration of High Court);

(e) hearing an application under section 41(2) of the *Youth Justice and Criminal Evidence Act* 1999 (evidence of complainant's sexual history);

(f) hearing applications under section 22(3) of the *Prosecution of Offences Act* 1985 (extension or further extension of custody time limit imposed by regulations made under section 22(1) of that Act);

(g) hearing an appeal brought by an accused under section 22(7) of the 1985 Act against a decision of a magistrates' court to extend, or further extend, such a time limit, or brought by the prosecution under section 22(8) of the same Act against a decision of a magistrates' court to refuse to extend, or further extend, such a time limit;

(h) hearing appeals under section 1 of the *Bail (Amendment) Act* 1993 (against grant of bail by magistrates' court); and

(i) hearing appeals under section 16 of the *Criminal Justice Act* 2003 (against condition of bail imposed by magistrates' court).

As to the desirability, generally, of bail applications being heard in open court, and as to when such applications should be heard in chambers, see *R. (Malik) v. Central Criminal Court*, *post*, § 3–16.

For the general principle relating to the conduct of proceedings in open court and the limited justification for departing therefrom (other than in cases within rule 16.11), see *post*, §§ 4–3 *et seq.* For practical guidance as to when a judge may conduct proceedings in private, otherwise than pursuant to rule 16.11, see *Re Crook*, 93 Cr.App.R. 17, CA (*post*, § 4–6).

As to an application that all or part of a trial be conducted *in camera* for reasons of national security or for the protection of the identity of a witness or any other person, see rule 16.10 of the 2005 rules (*post*, § 4–7).

See also rule 32.4 of the 2005 rules (*post*, § 2–155) (exclusion of public in proceedings to obtain evidence for use overseas under the *Crime (International Co-operation) Act* 2003, s.15(1)).

V. JURISDICTION TO OBTAIN EVIDENCE FOR USE OVERSEAS

Crime (International Co-operation) Act 2003

2–154 Part 1 (ss.1– 51) of this Act (replacing provisions of the *Criminal Justice (International Co-operation) Act* 1990) is entitled "Mutual Assistance in Criminal Matters". Chapter 2 (ss.7– 28) is headed "Mutual Provision of Evidence", with sections 7 to 12 dealing with assistance in obtaining evidence from abroad, and sections 13 to 19 providing for the rendering of assistance to overseas authorities in the obtaining of evidence in the United Kingdom. Section 13 deals with the procedure for requests for assistance from overseas authorities. Section 14 sets out the powers of the Secretary of State to arrange for evidence to be obtained. Section 15(1) provides for the Secretary of State to nominate a court to receive any evidence to which the request relates, but the Secretary of State may refer a request to the Director of the Serious Fraud Office where it relates to an offence involving serious or complex fraud (s.15(2)), as to which see *ante*, § 1–281. Section 16 (as amended by the *SOCPA* 2005, s.111, and Sched. 7, para. 51) provides that Part 2 of the *PACE Act* 1984 (powers of entry, search and seizure) is to have effect as if references to indictable offences in section 8 of, and Schedule 1 to, that Act included any conduct which constitutes an offence under the law of a country outside the United Kingdom, and would, if it occurred in England and Wales, constitute an indictable offence. However, the section only has effect in limited circumstances (s.16(2)). Section 17 (as amended by the 2005 Act) makes provision for a justice of the peace to issue a warrant (to enter, search and seize) when certain conditions are fulfilled. Section 19 makes provision in relation to evidence seized pursuant to a warrant.

Schedule 1 (given effect by section 15) makes provision as to proceedings before a court nominated under section 15. It deals with the attendance of witnesses, the administration of oaths, persons entitled to appear, the exclusion of members of the public, privilege of witnesses, the forwarding of evidence obtained, the application of the *Bankers' Books Evidence Act* 1879, and costs.

In relation to the corresponding provisions of the 1990 Act, see *R. v. Secretary of State for the Home Department, ex p. Finivest SpA* [1997] 1 Cr.App.R. 257, DC ("evidence" is not to be confined to direct evidence for use at trial, as opposed to information which might lead to the discovery of evidence); and, in relation to references to the Director of the Serious Fraud Office, see *R. (Evans) v. Director of the Serious Fraud Office* [2003] 1 W.L.R. 299, DC (*ante*, § 1–285).

A court nominated to receive evidence pursuant to section 15 must be careful to ensure that legal professional privilege is not infringed, and must have regard to the rights conferred by Article 8(1) of the ECHR (*post*, § 16–101), although, as a general principle, privacy rights under that article are unlikely to prevail in the face of Article 8(2) where disclosure of documents or information is necessary for the prevention of crime; succinct reasons for decisions should also be given (as to which, see also *post*, § 2–202): *R. (Hafner) v. Westminster Magistrates' Court, The Times*, March 19, 2008, DC.

Rules of court

Where the court nominated under section 15 of the 2003 Act (*ante*) is the Crown Court, reference should be made to the *Criminal Procedure Rules* 2005 (S.I. 2005 No. 384), rules 32.4 (persons entitled to appear and take part in proceedings before a nominated court and exclusion of public) and 32.5 (record of proceedings to receive evidence before a nominated court). **2–155**

[The next paragraph is § 2–159.]

VI. APPELLATE JURISDICTION OF CROWN COURT IN CRIMINAL CASES

A. CONCURRENT JURISDICTION OF HIGH COURT

(1) Extent

Any party to a proceeding in a magistrates' court who is aggrieved by the conviction, order, or other determination may question the proceeding on the ground that it is wrong in law or is in excess of jurisdiction by applying to the justices to state a case for the opinion of the High Court on the question of law or jurisdiction involved: *Magistrates' Courts Act* 1980, s.111(1). On the making of such an application any right of the applicant to appeal against the decision to the Crown Court ceases: *ibid.* s.111(3) (*post*, § 2–174). For the powers of the High Court on an appeal by way of case stated, see the *Supreme Court [Senior Courts] Act* 1981 (as to the renaming of the 1981 Act, see *ante*, § 2–1), s.28A (as substituted by the *Access to Justice Act* 1999, s.61). **2–159**

A decision of a magistrates' court may also be challenged by way of an application for judicial review pursuant to section 31 of the 1981 Act (*post*, § 7–5). As to the principles on which relief will be granted on an application for judicial review, see *post*, § 7–13.

(2) Practice

The existence of a right of appeal to the Crown Court does not preclude a person **2–160** convicted of an offence by a magistrates' court from seeking relief by way of judicial review where the ground upon which relief is sought is procedural impropriety, unfairness or bias; *R. v. Peterborough JJ., ex p. Dowler* [1996] 2 Cr.App.R. 561, DC, should not be followed to the extent that it suggests that a party complaining of procedural unfairness should be denied permission to move for judicial review and left to whatever rights he might have in the Crown Court: *R. v. Hereford Magistrates' Court, ex p. Rowlands and Ingram*; *R. v. Harrow Youth Court, ex p. Prussia* [1997] 2 Cr.App.R. 340, DC. (The court added two notes of caution. First, permission should only be granted where the applicant advanced an apparently plausible case, which, if made good, might arguably be held to vitiate the proceedings in the lower court. Immaterial and minor deviations from best practice would not have that effect and the court should be respectful of discretionary decisions of magistrates' courts. Secondly, the granting of relief was discretionary; many factors would be relevant; the need of the applicant to make full disclosure of all matters relevant to the exercise of the discretion needed no emphasis, but the existence of a right of appeal to the Crown Court, particularly if unexercised, should not ordinarily count against either the giving of permission or the grant of relief.)

An applicant for judicial review must at the outset of any hearing before the High Court, inform the court if there is an appeal pending to the Crown Court: *R. v. Mid-Worcester JJ., ex p. Hart* [1989] C.O.D. 397, DC.

Where facts emerge after conviction, an appeal to the Crown Court is the correct procedure, because the Crown Court's power to investigate facts is not available to the High Court: *R. v. Huyton JJ., ex p. Roberts* [1988] C.O.D. 43.

In relation to sentence, a defendant may go to the High Court by either route: *R. v. Ealing JJ., ex p. Scrafield*, *The Times*, March 29, 1993, DC; but the High Court will grant relief in respect of a lawful sentence only in the most exceptional circumstances: see generally, *post*, § 7–16.

As to the choice between judicial review and case stated, if the decision has been made to seek relief in the High Court, see *R. v. Felixstowe JJ., ex p. Baldwin*, 72 Cr.App.R. 131, DC; *R. v. Morpeth Ward JJ., ex p. Ward*, 95 Cr.App.R. 215, DC ("judicial review ... should only be sought when the route prescribed by Parliament is for some reason inapposite or clearly inappropriate" *per* Brooke J. at p. 221; case stated "will be appropriate where identification of the facts as found is, or may be, critical to the resolution of the issue" *per* Mann L.J. at p.222); *DPP v. O'Connor*, 95 Cr.App.R. 135, DC (case stated appropriate where the issue arose from the exercise of the magistrates' discretion in drink-driving cases involving special reasons); *R. v. Derwentside JJ., ex p. Swift*; *R. v. Sunderland JJ., ex p. Bate* [1997] R.T.R. 89, DC (where challenge to conviction is based on insufficiency of evidence, better to proceed by case stated, particularly where a successful application can be made for a stay of sentence pending appeal); and *R. (P.) v. Liverpool City Magistrates*, 170 J.P. 453, QBD (Collins J.) (generally speaking, judicial review more appropriate where allegation of unfairness in the way justices conducted the case, whereas appeal by case stated more appropriate where allegation that justices misdirected themselves or otherwise erred in law; where case stated is the appropriate remedy it will generally be wrong to avoid the relevant time limit by seeking judicial review, as to which see also *R. (White) v. Crown Court at Blackfriars*, 172 J.P. 321, DC). It seems implicit in the decision in *Revitt v. DPP*, *post*, § 2–200, that an appeal against a refusal to permit the withdrawal of a guilty plea may be brought by way of judicial review or case stated. If the judicial review procedure is used in a situation where it is not clear which procedure is most appropriate, a safe course might be to initiate that procedure within the time limits for an appeal by case stated; in any event, rule 54.5 of the *Civil Procedure Rules* 1998 (S.I. 1998 No. 3132) requires that a claim for judicial review must be filed not simply within three months of the grounds arising, but "promptly" within that period.

B. RIGHTS OF APPEAL TO CROWN COURT

(1) General

Magistrates' Courts Act 1980, s.108

Right of appeal to the Crown Court

2–161 **108.**—(1) A person convicted by a magistrates' court may appeal to the Crown Court—

(a) if he pleaded guilty, against his sentence;

(b) if he did not, against the conviction or sentence.

(1A) Section 14 of the *Powers of Criminal Courts (Sentencing) Act* 2000 (under which a conviction of an offence for which an order for conditional or absolute discharge is made is deemed not to be a conviction except for certain purposes) shall not prevent an appeal under this section, whether against conviction or otherwise.

(2) A person sentenced by a magistrates' court for an offence in respect of which ... an order for conditional discharge has been previously made may appeal to the Crown Court against the sentence.

(3) In this section "sentence" includes any order made on conviction by a magistrates' court, not being—

(a) [*repealed by* Criminal Justice Act *1982, s.78 and Sched. 16*];

(b) an order for the payment of costs;

(c) an order under section 37(1) of the *Animal Welfare Act* 2006 (which enables a court to order the destruction of an animal); or

(d) an order made in pursuance of an enactment under which the court has no discretion as to the making of the order or its terms,

and also includes a declaration of relevance, within the meaning of section 23 of ... the *Football Spectators Act* 1989.

(4) Subsection 3(d) above does not prevent an appeal against a surcharge imposed under section 161A of the *Criminal Justice Act* 2003.

[This section is printed as amended, and repealed in part, by the *CJA* 1982, ss.66(2) and 78, and Sched. 16; the *Football Spectators Act* 1989, s.23(3)(c); the *CJA* 1991, s.101(2), and Sched. 13; the *CJPOA* 1994, Sched. 9, para. 16; the *CDA* 1998, s.119, and Sched. 8, para. 43; the *PCC(S)A* 2000, s.165, and Sched. 9, para. 71; the *Football (Disorder) Act* 2000, s.1(3), and Sched. 3; the *Domestic Violence, Crime and Victims Act* 2004, s.58(1), and Sched. 10, para. 10; the *VCRA* 2006, s.52(2), and Sched. 3, para. 14; and the *Animal Welfare Act* 2006, s.64, and Sched. 3, para. 10.]

As to procedure, see *post*, §§ 2–180 *et seq*.

A decision by the Crown Court determining sentence upon committal by the magistrates does not render the court *functus officio* if thereafter the offender appeals against his conviction: *R. v. Croydon Crown Court, ex p. Bernard*, 72 Cr.App.R. 29, DC. **2–162**

There is a right of appeal against a recommendation for deportation: *Immigration Act* 1971, s.6(5)(a); and against a driving disqualification, whether compulsory or discretionary, and whether for the offence itself or under the "totting up" provisions: *Road Traffic Offenders Act* 1988, s.38(1) (*post* § 32–200). A committal for sentence is not a "sentence": *R. v. London Sessions, ex p. Rogers* [1951] 2 K.B. 74, DC; nor is a refusal by a magistrates' court to vary or discharge a restraining order made under the *Protection from Harassment Act* 1997, s.5(4) (*post*, § 19–277f): *R. (Lee) v. Leeds Crown Court, The Independent (C.S.)*, October 30, 2006, DC ([2006] EWHC 2550 (Admin.)).

Schedules 3 (as originally enacted, and as substituted by the *CJA* 2003, s.304, and Sched. 32, para. 125), 5, 7 and 8 to the *PCC(S)A* 2000, and Schedule 8 to the 2003 Act all deal with breach, revocation and amendment of various forms of community sentence. All contain provisions for re-sentencing by a magistrates' court and all provide for a corresponding right of appeal to the Crown Court. For the details of these provisions, see *post*, Chapter 5.

(2) Appeal against binding over order

Magistrates' Courts (Appeals from Binding Over Orders) Act 1956, s.1(1)

1.—(1) Where under the *Justices of the Peace Act* 1361, or otherwise, a person is ordered by a magistrates' court (as defined in the *Magistrates' Courts Act* 1980) to enter into a recognisance with or without sureties to keep the peace or to be of good behaviour, he may appeal to the Crown Court. **2–163**

See *Hughes v. Holley*, *post*, § 2–179 (powers); and *Shaw v. Hamilton*, *post*, § 2–184 (procedure).

(3) Appeal against refusal to excuse from jury service

2–164 See *post*, § 4–230.

(4) Appeal under the Football Spectators Act 1989

Banning orders and declaration of relevance

Football Spectators Act 1989, s.22(7)

2–165 **22.**—(7) Any person aggrieved by the decision of a magistrates' court making a banning order under this section may appeal to the Crown Court against the decision.

[This subsection is printed as amended by the *Football (Disorder) Act* 2000, s.1(2) and Sched. 2, para. 10.]

2–166 A right of appeal lies in respect of a declaration of relevance made by a magistrates' court under the 1989 Act: *MCA* 1980, s.108(3), *ante*, § 2–161. A banning order made upon conviction of a relevant offence shall be quashed if the making of a declaration of relevance as respects that offence is reversed on appeal: *Football Spectators Act* 1989, s.23(4). See *post*, § 5–837.

(5) Appeal by parent or guardian

2–167 As to appeals by parents or guardians ordered to pay a fine, costs or compensation, see the *PCC(S)A* 2000, s.137(6), *post*, § 5–928. As to appeals by parents or guardians against orders binding them over, see *ibid.*, s.150(8), *post* § 5–932.

(6) Appeal in respect of custody time limits

2–168 For the right of appeal of the defendant and prosecution in respect of decisions to extend, or further extend, a custody time limit or overall time limit, or refusals to do so, see the *Prosecution of Offences Act* 1985, s.22(7), (8) (*ante*, § 1–267).

As to the custody time limit regulations, see *post*, §§ 3–56 *et seq.*

Criminal Procedure Rules 2005 (S.I. 2005 No. 384), Pt 20

Appeal to Crown Court against a decision of a magistrates' court in respect of a custody time limit

2–169 **20.1.**—(1) This rule applies—

(a) to any appeal brought by an accused, under section 22(7) of the *Prosecution of Offences Act* 1985, against a decision of a magistrates' court to extend, or further extend, a custody time limit imposed by regulations made under section 22(1) of the 1985 Act; and

(b) to any appeal brought by the prosecution, under section 22(8) of the 1985 Act, against a decision of a magistrates' court to refuse to extend, or further extend, such a time limit.

(2) An appeal to which this rule applies shall be commenced by the appellant's giving notice in writing of appeal—

(a) to the court officer for the magistrates' court which took the decision;

(b) if the appeal is brought by the accused, to the prosecutor and, if the prosecution is to be carried on by the Crown Prosecution Service, to the appropriate Crown Prosecutor;

(c) if the appeal is brought by the prosecution, to the accused; and

(d) to the Crown Court officer.

(3) The notice of an appeal to which this rule applies shall state the date on which the custody time limit applicable to the case is due to expire and, if the appeal is brought by the accused under section 22(7) of the 1985 Act, the date on which the custody time limit would have expired had the court decided not to extend or further extend that time limit.

(4) On receiving notice of an appeal to which this rule applies, the Crown Court officer shall enter the appeal and give notice of the time and place of the hearing to—

(a) the appellant;

(b) the other party to the appeal; and

(c) the court officer for the magistrates' court which took the decision.

(5) Without prejudice to the power of the Crown Court to give leave for an appeal to be

abandoned, an appellant may abandon an appeal to which this rule applies by giving notice in writing to any person to whom notice of the appeal was required to be given by paragraph (2) of this rule not later than the third day preceding the day fixed for the hearing of the appeal:

Provided that, for the purpose of determining whether notice was properly given in accordance with this paragraph, there shall be disregarded any Saturday and Sunday and any day which is specified to be a bank holiday in England and Wales under section 1(1) of the *Banking and Financial Dealings Act* 1971.

As to the procedure to be adopted on an appeal under section 22, see *R. v. Crown Court at Norwich, ex p. Parker and Ward*, 96 Cr.App.R. 68, DC; and see generally, *ante*, § 1–272. **2–170**

(7) Appeal under the Mental Health Act 1983

Where a magistrates' court makes a hospital or guardianship order against a defendant under the *MHA* 1983, s.37(3) (*post*, § 5–894) without convicting him, he has the same right of appeal as if it had been made on his conviction, and on any such appeal the Crown Court has the same powers as if the appeal had been against both conviction and sentence: *ibid.* s.45(1). Where such an order is made against a child or young person, an appeal may be brought by him or by his parent or guardian: *ibid.* s.45(2). **2–171**

(8) Appeal against grant of bail

See *post*, §§ 3–86 *et seq.* **2–172**

(9) Appeal against reporting restrictions

See section 44(11) of the *YJCEA* 1999 (*post*, § 4–29a) (appeal against order of magistrates' court dispensing with, or refusing to dispense with, restrictions on reporting of alleged offences involving persons under the age of 18 years). **2–172a**

(10) Appeal against drinking banning order

Violent Crime Reduction Act 2006, s.10

[Appeals

10.—(1) An appeal lies to the Crown Court against the making by a magistrates' court of a drinking banning order section 3 or 6. **2–172b**

(2) On such an appeal the Crown Court—

(a) may make such orders as may be necessary to give effect to its determination of the appeal;

(b) may also make such incidental or consequential orders as appear to it to be just.

(3) An order of the Crown Court made on an appeal under this section (other than one directing that an application be re-heard by a magistrates' court) shall be treated for the purposes of sections 5 and 8 as an order of the magistrates' court from which the appeal was brought.]

This section comes into force on a day to be appointed. As to drinking banning orders generally, see *post*, §§ 5–843a *et seq.*

C. REFERRING OF CASES BY CRIMINAL CASES REVIEW COMMISSION

Criminal Appeal Act 1995, s.11

Cases dealt with summarily in England and Wales

11.—(1) Where a person has been convicted of an offence by a magistrates' court in England and Wales, the Commission— **2–173**

(a) may at any time refer the conviction to the Crown Court, and

(b) (whether or not they refer the conviction) may at any time refer to the Crown Court any sentence imposed on, or in subsequent proceedings relating to, the conviction.

(2) A reference under subsection (1) of a person's conviction shall be treated for all purposes as an appeal by the person under section 108(1) of the *Magistrates' Courts Act* 1980 against the conviction (whether or not he pleaded guilty).

(3) A reference under subsection (1) of a sentence imposed on, or in subsequent

proceedings relating to, a person's conviction shall be treated for all purposes as an appeal by the person under section 108(1) of the *Magistrates' Courts Act* 1980 against—

(a) the sentence, and

(b) any other sentence imposed on, or in subsequent proceedings relating to, the conviction or any related conviction.

(4) On a reference under subsection (1) of a person's conviction the Commission may give notice to the Crown Court that any related conviction which is specified in the notice is to be treated as referred to the Crown Court under subsection (1).

(5) For the purposes of this section convictions are related if they are convictions of the same person by the same court on the same day.

(6) On a reference under this section the Crown Court may not award any punishment more severe than that awarded by the court whose decision is referred.

(7) The Crown Court may grant bail to a person whose conviction or sentence has been referred under this section; and any time during which he is released on bail shall not count as part of any term of imprisonment or detention under his sentence.

"The Commission" is the Criminal Cases Review Commission established under section 8 of the 1995 Act. For more detail in relation thereto, see *post*, §§ 7–154 *et seq.* As to the procedure on a reference, see *post*, § 2–180e.

For section 108 of the 1980 Act, see *ante*, § 2–161.

D. CESSATION AND ABANDONMENT OF RIGHT OF APPEAL

(1) Cessation of right of appeal

Magistrates' Courts Act 1980, s.111

Statement of case by magistrates' court

2–174 **111.**—(1) Any person who was a party to any proceeding before a magistrates' court or is aggrieved by the conviction, order, determination or other proceeding of the court may question the proceeding on the ground that it is wrong in law or is in excess of jurisdiction by applying to the justices composing the court to state a case for the opinion of the High Court on the question of law or jurisdiction involved; but a person shall not make an application under this section in respect of a decision against which he has a right of appeal to the High Court or which by virtue of any enactment passed after 31st December 1879 is final.

(2) An application under subsection (1) above shall be made within 21 days after the day on which the decision of the magistrates' court was given.

(3) For the purpose of subsection (2) above, the day on which the decision of the magistrates' court is given shall, where the court has adjourned the trial of an information after conviction, be the day on which the court sentences or otherwise deals with the offender.

(4) On the making of an application under this section in respect of a decision any rights of the applicant to appeal against the decision to the Crown Court shall cease.

(5), (6) [*Not printed.*]

As to appeal by way of case stated generally, see *ante*, §§ 2–159, 2–160.

The right to appeal to the Crown Court ceases only on the making of a valid application under section 111(1). An application is not valid unless it is made within the time limit in subsection (2); it can be regarded as having been made within the time limit if it is written and sent within the 21 days in such circumstances that in the normal course of events it would have arrived on time: *P. & M. Supplies (Essex) Ltd v. Hackney LBC* [1990] Crim.L.R. 569, DC.

Where proceedings in a magistrates' court are concluded with a decision as to costs, time runs from the date of that decision for the purposes of section 111(2) and (3): *Liverpool C.C. v. Worthington, The Times*, June 16, 1998, DC.

(2) Death of appellant pending appeal

2–175 See *Hawkins v. Bepey*, 70 Cr.App.R. 64, DC, and *R. v. Jefferies* [1969] 1 Q.B. 120, 52 Cr.App.R. 654, CA.

(3) Abandonment of appeal

Criminal Procedure Rules 2005 (S.I. 2005 No. 384), r.63.8

Abandoning an appeal

63.8.—(1) The appellant— **2–176**

(a) may abandon an appeal without the Crown Court's permission, by serving a notice of abandonment on—

(i) the magistrates' court officer,

(ii) the Crown Court officer, and

(iii) every other party before the hearing of the appeal begins; but

(b) after the hearing of the appeal begins, may only abandon the appeal with the Crown Court's permission.

(2) A notice of abandonment must be signed by or on behalf of the appellant.

(3) Where an appellant who is on bail pending appeal abandons an appeal—

(a) the appellant must surrender to custody as directed by the magistrates' court officer; and

(b) any conditions of bail apply until then.

[This rule is printed as substituted by the *Criminal Procedure (Amendment) Rules* 2008 (S.I. 2008 No. 2076), r.14, and Sched. 2.]

The form of notice of abandonment is provided by the consolidated criminal practice direction (see *post*, § 2–219); but, as to departure from the prescribed form and oral abandonment, see rule 63.9(d) (*post*, § 2–180h). As to the commencement provisions for the substituted rules, see rule 2.1(12), *post*, § 2–206.

The Crown Court cannot entertain an appeal once it has been validly abandoned, unless the abandonment is a nullity by reason of mistake or fraudulent inducement: *R. v. Essex Q.S. Appeals Committee, ex p. Larkin* [1962] 1 Q.B. 712, DC; and *R. v. Gloucester Crown Court, ex p. Betteridge*, 161 J.P. 721, DC (no jurisdiction to review sentence once leave given to abandon appeal). Nor can the Crown Court reinstate abandoned appeals, unless it is satisfied that the notice of abandonment was a nullity: *R. v. Knightsbridge Crown Court, ex p. Commrs of Customs and Excise* [1986] Crim.L.R. 324, DC.

Only in exceptional circumstances should a judge grant leave to abandon an appeal where the application is made after the hearing has commenced: *R. v. Manchester Crown Court, ex p. Welby*, 73 Cr.App.R. 248, DC.

As to whether abandonment may be implied from a failure by an appellant on bail to appear in accordance with the conditions of bail, see *R. (Hayes) v. Chelmsford Crown Court*, *post*, § 2–186.

Magistrates' Courts Act 1980, s.109

109.—(1) Where notice to abandon an appeal has been duly given by the appellant— **2–177**

(a) the court against whose decision the appeal was brought may issue process for enforcing that decision, subject to anything already suffered or done under it by the appellant; and

(b) the said court may, on the application of the other party to the appeal, order the appellant to pay to that party such costs as appear to the court to be just and reasonable in respect of expenses properly incurred by that party in connection with the appeal before notice of the abandonment was given to that party.

(2) In this section "appeal" means an appeal from a magistrates' court to the Crown Court, and the reference to a notice to abandon an appeal is a reference to a notice shown to the satisfaction of the magistrates' court to have been given in accordance with rules of court.

[This section is printed as amended by the *Courts Act* 2003, s.109(1), and Sched. 8, para. 234.]

As to the power of the Crown Court to make orders for costs on the abandonment of an appeal, see rule 78.1(4) of the *Criminal Procedure Rules* 2005 (S.I. 2005 No. 384), *post*, § 6–89.

E. POWERS OF THE CROWN COURT ON APPEAL

Supreme Court [Senior Courts] Act 1981, s.48

48.—(1) The Crown Court may, in the course of hearing any appeal, correct any error or mistake in the order or judgment incorporating the decision which is the subject of the appeal. **2–178**

(2) On the termination of the hearing of an appeal the Crown Court—

(a) may confirm, reverse or vary any part of the decision appealed against, including a determination not to impose a separate penalty in respect of an offence; or

(b) may remit the matter with its opinion thereon to the authority whose decision is appealed against; or

(c) may make such order in the matter as the court thinks just, and by such order exercise any power which the said authority might have exercised.

(3) Subsection (2) has effect subject to any enactment relating to any such appeal which expressly limits or restricts the powers of the court on the appeal.

(4) Subject to section 11(6) of the *Criminal Appeal Act* 1995, if the appeal is against a conviction or a sentence, the preceding provisions of this section shall be construed as including power to award any punishment, whether more or less severe than that awarded by the magistrates' court whose decision is appealed against, if that is a punishment which that magistrates' court might have awarded.

(5) This section applies whether or not the appeal is against the whole of the decision.

(6) In this section "sentence" includes any order made by a court when dealing with an offender, including—

(a) a hospital order under Part III of the *Mental Health Act* 1983, with or without a restriction order, and an interim hospital order under that Act; and

(b) a recommendation for deportation made when dealing with an offender.

(7) The fact that an appeal is pending against an interim hospital order under the said Act of 1983 shall not affect the power of the magistrates' court that made it to renew or terminate the order or to deal with the appellant on its termination; and where the Crown Court quashes such an order but does not pass any sentence or make any other order in its place the Court may direct the appellant to be kept in custody or released on bail pending his being dealt with by that magistrates' court.

(8) Where the Crown Court makes an interim hospital order by virtue of subsection (2)—

(a) the power of renewing or terminating the order and of dealing with the appellant on its termination shall be exercisable by the magistrates' court whose decision is appealed against and not by the Crown Court; and

(b) that magistrates' court shall be treated for the purposes of section 38(7) of the said Act of 1983 (absconding offenders) as the court that made the order.

[This section is printed as amended by the *Mental Health (Amendment) Act* 1982, Sched. 3; the *MHA* 1983, Sched. 4; the *CJA* 1988, s.156; and the *CAA* 1995, Sched. 2, para. 14. As to the renaming of the 1981 Act, see *ante*, § 2–1.]

2–179 Where there is an issue as to the precise nature of the charge of which the appellant was convicted, a document admissible under rule 6.4 of the *Criminal Procedure Rules* 2005 (S.I. 2005 No. 384) (*post*, § 9–75) is not to be treated as conclusive; the Crown Court is entitled also to look at other material bearing on the issue, including the original charge sheet, a letter asking for an extension of time in which to serve notice of appeal and the notice of appeal itself (signed by the appellant); it is also entitled to have regard to the way in which the records of magistrates' courts are made in practice: *Gill v. DPP (Note—1995)* [1998] R.T.R. 166, DC.

The substitution by the *CJA* 1988 of the words "any part of the decision appealed against, including a determination not to impose a separate penalty in respect of an offence" in subsection (2)(a) for the words "the decision appealed against" appears to put beyond doubt the decision in *Dutta v. Westcott* [1987] Q.B. 291, 84 Cr.App.R. 103, DC, *viz.*, on appeal against one of several convictions, the Crown Court has power to vary the sentences imposed by the justices for all the convictions. Subsection (2)(a) is wide enough to permit the Crown Court to make an award of costs against an unsuccessful appellant in respect of the proceedings in the magistrates' court: *Johnson v. RSPCA*, 164 J.P. 345, DC.

For section 11 of the *CAA* 1995, see *ante*, § 2–173.

If the Crown Court has acceded to an application for leave to abandon an appeal, there is no power to increase sentence: *R. v. Gloucester Crown Court, ex p. Betteridge*, 161 J.P. 721, DC.

In deciding what punishment the magistrates' court might have awarded under subsection (4) the material date is the date of sentencing by the magistrates and not the date of the disposal of the appeal. Thus the Crown Court has no power to make a sentence imposed by the magistrates consecutive to one imposed by another court after the sentence appealed against, but before the hearing of the appeal: *R. v. Portsmouth Crown Court, ex p. Ballard, The Times*, June 27, 1989, DC. As to the duty of the Crown Court when substituting on appeal a suspended sentence for a sentence of imprisonment, with regard to any period spent in custody pending appeal, see *Practice Direction (Criminal Proceedings: Consolidation)* [2002] 1 W.L.R. 2870, para. I.9. See also *R. v. Burn*, 63 Cr.App.R. 289, CA, and *R. v. Birmingham JJ., ex p. Wyatt*, 61 Cr.App.R. 306, DC.

As to the Crown Court dealing with a committal for sentence and an appeal against conviction in respect of the same matter, and as to the impropriety of the Crown Court committing to itself for sentence when dealing with an appeal, see *post*, § 5–34.

On an appeal against a binding over order under the 1956 Act (*ante*, § 2–163), the task of the Crown Court is to determine whether the magistrates were right to impose the order. Accordingly, it is not open to the Crown Court to allow the appeal on the ground that a pre-condition for making the order, namely a fear of repetition which had existed in the magistrates' court, had ceased to exist at the time of the appeal: *Hughes v. Holley*, 86 Cr.App.R. 130, DC.

F. PROCEDURE

(1) Rules of court

Criminal Procedure Rules 2005 (S.I. 2005 No. 384), Pt 63 (as substituted by the Criminal Procedure (Amendment) Rules 2008 (S.I. 2008 No. 2076), r.14, and Sched. 2)

When this Part applies

63.1.—(1) This Part applies where— **2–180**

(a) a defendant wants to appeal under—

(i) section 108 of the *Magistrates' Courts Act* 1980,

(ii) section 45 of the *Mental Health Act* 1983,

(iii) paragraph 10 of Schedule 3 to the *Powers of Criminal Courts (Sentencing) Act* 2000;

(b) the Criminal Cases Review Commission refers a defendant's case to the Crown Court under section 11 of the *Criminal Appeal Act* 1995;

(c) a prosecutor wants to appeal under—

(i) section 14A(5A) of the *Football Spectators Act* 1989, or

(ii) section 147(3) of the *Customs and Excise Management Act* 1979; or

(d) a person wants to appeal under—

(i) section 1 of the *Magistrates' Courts (Appeals from Binding Over Orders) Act* 1956,

(ii) section 12(5) of the *Contempt of Court Act* 1981,

(iii) regulation 3C or 3H of the *Costs in Criminal Cases (General) Regulations* 1986, or

(iv) section 22 of the *Football Spectators Act* 1989.

(2) A reference to an "appellant" in this Part is a reference to such a party or person.

Service of appeal notice

63.2.—(1) An appellant must serve an appeal notice on— **2–180a**

(a) the magistrates' court officer; and

(b) every other party.

(2) The appellant must serve the appeal notice—

(a) as soon after the decision appealed against as the appellant wants; but

(b) not more than 21 days after—

(i) sentence or the date sentence is deferred, whichever is earlier, if the appeal is against conviction or against a finding of guilt,

(ii) sentence, if the appeal is against sentence, or

(iii) the order or failure to make an order about which the appellant wants to appeal, in any other case.

(3) The appellant must—
(a) serve with the appeal notice any application for an extension of the time limit under this rule; and
(b) in that application, explain why the appeal notice is late.

Form of appeal notice

2–180b **63.3.** The appeal notice must be in writing and must—
(a) specify—
(i) the conviction or finding of guilt,
(ii) the sentence, or
(iii) the order, or the failure to make an order about which the appellant wants to appeal;
(b) summarise the issues;
(c) in an appeal against conviction—
(i) identify the prosecution witnesses whom the appellant will want to question if they are called to give oral evidence, and
(ii) say how long the trial lasted in the magistrates' court and how long the appeal is likely to last in the Crown Court;
(d) in an appeal against a finding that the appellant insulted someone or interrupted proceedings in the magistrates' court, attach—
(i) the magistrates' court's written findings of fact, and
(ii) the appellant's response to those findings;
(e) say whether the appellant has asked the magistrates' court to reconsider the case; and
(f) include a list of those on whom the appellant has served the appeal notice.

Duty of magistrates' court officer

2–180c **63.4.** The magistrates' court officer must—
(a) as soon as practicable serve on the Crown Court officer—
(i) the appeal notice and any accompanying application served by the appellant,
(ii) details of the parties including their addresses,
(iii) a copy of each magistrates' court register entry relating to the decision under appeal and to any application for bail pending appeal, and
(iv) any report received for the purposes of sentencing;
(b) keep any document or object exhibited in the proceedings in the magistrates' court, or arrange for it to be kept by some other appropriate person, until—
(i) 6 weeks after the conclusion of those proceedings, or
(ii) the conclusion of any proceedings in the Crown Court that begin within that 6 weeks; and
(c) provide the Crown Court with any document, object or information for which the Crown Court officer asks, within such period as the Crown Court officer may require.

Duty of person keeping exhibit

2–180d **63.5.** A person who, under arrangements made by the magistrates' court officer, keeps a document or object exhibited in the proceedings in the magistrates' court must—
(a) keep that exhibit until—
(i) 6 weeks after the conclusion of those proceedings, or
(ii) the conclusion of any proceedings in the Crown Court that begin within that 6 weeks,

unless the magistrates' court or the Crown Court otherwise directs; and
(b) provide the Crown Court with any such document or object for which the Crown Court officer asks, within such period as the Crown Court officer may require.

Reference by the Criminal Cases Review Commission

2–180e **63.6.**—(1) The Crown Court officer must, as soon as practicable, serve a reference by the Criminal Cases Review Commission on—
(a) the appellant;
(b) every other party; and

(c) the magistrates' court officer.

(2) The appellant may serve an appeal notice on—

(a) the Crown Court officer; and

(b) every other party,

not more than 21 days later.

(3) The Crown Court must treat the reference as the appeal notice if the appellant does not serve an appeal notice.

Hearings and decisions

63.7.—(1) The Crown Court as a general rule must hear in public an appeal or reference to which this Part applies, but— **2–180f**

(a) may order any hearing to be in private; and

(b) where a hearing is about a public interest ruling, must hold that hearing in private.

(2) The Crown Court officer must give as much notice as reasonably practicable of every hearing to—

(a) the parties;

(b) any party's custodian; and

(c) any other person whom the Crown Court requires to be notified.

(3) The Crown Court officer must serve every decision on—

(a) the parties;

(b) any other person whom the Crown Court requires to be served; and

(c) the magistrates' court officer and any party's custodian, where the decision determines an appeal.

(4) But where a hearing or decision is about a public interest ruling, the Crown Court officer must not—

(a) give notice of that hearing to; or

(b) serve that decision on,

anyone other than the prosecutor who applied for that ruling, unless the court otherwise directs.

Abandoning an appeal

63.8. [*See* ante, *§ 2–176*.] **2–180g**

Court's power to vary requirements under this Part

63.9. The Crown Court may— **2–180h**

(a) shorten or extend (even after it has expired) a time limit under this Part;

(b) allow an appellant to vary an appeal notice that that appellant has served;

(c) direct that an appeal notice be served on any person;

(d) allow an appeal notice or a notice of abandonment to be in a different form to one set out in the Practice Direction, or to be presented orally.

Constitution of the Crown Court

63.10. [*See* ante, *§ 2–6*.] **2–180i**

As to the commencement provisions for the substituted Part 63, see rule 2.1(12), *post*, § 2–206. **2–181**

The consolidated criminal practice direction sets out a form of notice of appeal (as to which, see also *post*, § 2–219), but rule 63.9 (*ante*) gives the Crown Court power to allow such notices to be in a different form, or to be presented orally.

(2) Practice direction

Practice Direction (Criminal Proceedings: Consolidation), para. V.52.2 [2002] 1 W.L.R. 2870

COMMITTAL FOR SENTENCE AND APPEALS TO CROWN COURT

V.52.2 Any case notes should be sent to the Crown Court when there is an appeal, thereby making them available to the judge if the judge requires them in order to decide before the hearing questions of listing or representation or the like. They will also be available to the court during the hearing if it becomes necessary or desirable for the court to see what happened in the lower court. On a committal for sentence or an appeal, any reasons given by the magistrates for their decision should be included with the notes. **2–182**

(3) Applications for leave to appeal against conviction out of time

2–183 In dealing with such applications: (a) the judge is entitled to take account of the apparent merits of the appeal; (b) the appellant has no right to an oral hearing; (c) no decision to list an application for oral hearing should be taken without prior consultation with the judge who has read the application and who decides whether oral representations should be made to him or to another judge in chambers; (d) the judge is under no general duty to give reasons for his decision to refuse leave: *R. v. Croydon Crown Court, ex p. Smith*, 77 Cr.App.R. 277, DC, decided under now repealed rules (but see the more modern tendency towards succinct reasons, exemplified by the authorities cited at § 1–272c, *ante*, and *post*, § 2–202).

(4) Appeal is by way of rehearing

Supreme Court [Senior Courts] Act 1981, s.79(3)

2–184 **79.**—(3) The customary practice and procedure with respect to appeals to the Crown Court and in particular any practice as to the extent to which an appeal is by way of rehearing of the case, shall continue to be observed.

[As to the renaming of the 1981 Act, see *ante*, § 2–1.]

An appeal to the Crown Court being by way of rehearing, there is no obligation on the prosecution to put their case in the same way as in the lower court and there is nothing objectionable about the Crown Court finding the case proved on a different basis to the finding in the lower court: *Hingley-Smith v. DPP* [1998] 1 *Archbold News* 2, DC; and, on an appeal against sentence it is open to the Crown Court to pass sentence on a different factual basis to that adopted in the magistrates' court; where, however, the court intends to depart from the magistrates' court's expressed view of the facts, this should be made plain to the appellant in order that he should have an opportunity to deal with the matter: *Bussey v. DPP* [1999] 1 Cr.App.R.(S.) 125, DC.

The rule that an appeal is by way of rehearing applies to appeals under the 1956 Act, *ante*, § 2–163. In order to make a binding over order in the first place the magistrates have to satisfy themselves on admissible material that unless steps are taken to prevent it there might be a breach of the peace. Accordingly, unless an appellant is prepared to admit the evidence which was before the magistrates, the facts which justified the making of the order must be strictly proved in the Crown Court by sworn evidence subject to cross-examination: *Shaw v. Hamilton*, 75 Cr.App.R. 288, DC. Similarly, if the justices have found special reasons to exist but have nevertheless imposed a period of disqualification, the Crown Court on an appeal by the defendant will have to re-hear the whole issue and consider afresh both the question of the existence of special reasons and, if they are found to exist, the question of whether to disqualify: *DPP v. O'Connor*, 95 Cr.App.R. 135 at 156–157, DC.

The fact that an appeal is by way of rehearing does not mean that the Crown Court must start with the information as originally laid in its unamended form (if it was amended). The rehearing is a rehearing of the evidence on the amended information. Further, the Crown Court has no jurisdiction to hear an appeal against the manner in which justices exercised their discretion to amend a charge in the course of proceedings before them. The question whether the amendment was properly made is a question which, if suitable for appeal at all, is eminently suitable for appeal to the High Court: *Fairgrieve v. Newman*, 82 Cr.App.R. 60, DC. The absence of jurisdiction in the Crown Court to amend an information on appeal is now regarded as well settled: *R. v. Swansea Crown Court, ex p. Stacey* [1990] R.T.R. 183, DC. Where, however, the defect is such that, if it had been noticed, the justices could have proceeded with the information as it stood under section 123 of the *MCA* 1980, because the defect was not material, nor capable of leading to injustice, the Crown Court may proceed likewise: *ibid.*

(5) Attendance and parties to the appeal

(a) *Appellant in person*

2–185 An appellant is entitled to appear in person and conduct his own appeal. A refusal to allow an appellant in person to make a speech after evidence in his own defence is a breach of natural justice: *R. v. Middlesex Crown Court, ex p. Riddle* [1975] Crim.L.R. 731, DC; *cf. R. v. Knightsbridge Crown Court, ex p. Martin* [1976] Crim.L.R. 463, DC.

(b) *Appellant who is represented need not attend*

An appellant represented by a legal representative on appeal against conviction is deemed to be present: *MCA* 1980, s.122. Accordingly, any appellant so represented is entitled to be absent and any application made to hear the appeal in his absence is unnecessary and merely a courtesy to the court: *R. v. Croydon Crown Court, ex p. Clair*, 83 Cr.App.R. 202, DC. **2–186**

Where the Crown Court concludes that a person who was convicted in the magistrates' court, who has given notice of appeal against conviction and who has been granted bail pending the appeal, but subject to a condition requiring him to surrender at the appeal hearing, is deliberately absenting himself from the appeal hearing, it is not open to the court to dismiss the appeal on the basis that it has been impliedly abandoned where counsel is present and ready to conduct the appeal; the remedy is to hear the appeal in the absence of the appellant: *R. (Hayes) v. Chelmsford Crown Court*, 167 J.P. 65, QBD (Henriques J.).

(c) *Appellant who fails to attend and give instructions*

Where an appellant fails to attend or to give instructions so that his legal representative cannot proceed, it is right for the Crown Court to proceed to hear the appeal in the absence of the appellant but in the presence of his counsel. Such failure to appear and instruct could not amount to notice to abandon the appeal: *R. v. Guildford Crown Court, ex p. Brewer*, 87 Cr.App.R. 265, DC. See also *Podmore v. DPP* [1997] C.O.D. 80, DC (where appellant is represented by counsel, Crown Court has no jurisdiction to dismiss appeal without hearing evidence and adjudicating upon it). As to abandonment, see *ante*, § 2–176. **2–187**

(d) *Re-opening appeal after appellant's failure to attend*

Judicial review does not lie to quash a decision of an inferior tribunal given without hearing the applicant where the tribunal had acted correctly but the applicant had been deprived of the opportunity to have his case heard solely through the fault of his own legal advisers: *R. v. Secretary of State for the Home Department, ex p. Al Mehdawi* [1990] 1 A.C. 876, HL, in effect overruling *R. v. Knightsbridge Crown Court, ex p. Johnson* [1986] Crim.L.R. 803, DC. In *ex p. Johnson, ante*, the Divisional Court said, *obiter*, that the Crown Court, in its jurisdiction inherited from Quarter Sessions, had a power to set aside its own order made in the absence of a party: see *R. v. County of London Q.S. Appeals Committee, ex p. Rossi* [1956] 1 Q.B. 683, CA (Civ. Div.), *per* Lord Denning at pp. 693–694. **2–188**

Where the appellant fails to attend because he has not been notified of the date of the hearing and the appeal is dismissed, it is doubtful that the judgment of the Crown Court would be regarded as regularly obtained: see *R. v. Liverpool Crown Court, ex p. Poole* [1997] C.O.D. 10, DC, where the court left the point open. To the extent that the court relied on *ex p. Johnson* for its conclusion that it was unnecessary to decide the point, it is to be regarded as of limited authority.

(e) *Non-attendance of prosecution advocate*

In *R. (CPS, Harrow) v. Portsmouth Crown Court* [2004] Crim.L.R. 224, DC, it was said that, where prosecution counsel had not been present when an appeal against conviction was called on, it had been unreasonable for the judge to have allowed the appeal without making enquiries as to where counsel was. There was a triangulation of interests to be served, those of the accused, the victim and the public. The prosecutor's non-appearance was just one factor to take into account: others were that there had been a previous adjournment at the instigation of the defence, the inconvenience that had been occasioned to the witnesses, who were the victims, the gravity of the offence, **2–189** and the fact that the appellant had already been convicted. More vigorous enquiries as to when counsel would be available would have resulted in only a short delay, and the judge could then have made his displeasure known to counsel (and, if necessary, counsel's head of chambers, the circuit leader or the Bar Council), rather than taking a step that was manifestly to the disadvantage of an innocent third party, namely the victims in the appeal.

(f) *Attendance of neither party to the appeal*

2–189a Where neither party attends by themselves or counsel, the proper course is to dismiss the appeal: *R. v. Guildford Crown Court, ex p. Brewer, ante.*

(6) Provision of notes of evidence

2–190 Under the *Legal Aid in Criminal and Care Proceedings (General) Regulations* 1989 (S.I. 1989 No. 344), there was an obligation on a justices' clerk to supply, on the application of the solicitor for a legally-aided appellant to the Crown Court, copies of any notes of evidence or depositions taken in the proceedings in the magistrates' court. In *R. v. Highbury Corner JJ., ex p. Hussein*, 84 Cr.App.R. 112, DC, it was held that in non-legal aid cases, there was no such obligation, but it was said to be desirable that there should be no difference in practice, and requests for notes by non-legally aided appellants should be viewed sympathetically where a proper reason was given.

The *Criminal Defence Service (General) (No. 2) Regulations* 2001 (S.I. 2001 No. 1437) (*post*, §§ 6–152 *et seq.*) contain no corresponding provision. The legal position would therefore seem to be that there is no obligation on a justices' clerk to supply notes of evidence in any case. See, however, *ante*, § 2–182.

(7) Adjournments

2–191 In *Arthur v. Stringer*, 84 Cr.App.R. 361, DC, it was held that since the power conferred on justices by section 10(3) of the *MCA* 1980 to adjourn after convicting a person and before sentencing him did not entitle them to adjourn for the sole purpose of allowing him to reach the age of 21 years so that they could pass a sentence which they could not pass when he was under 21, then equally the Crown Court upon an appeal from justices had no such power. Its powers were limited to those which the justices might have exercised when they passed sentence. It was implicit in section 10(3) of the 1980 Act that the power had to be exercised judicially. It was an abuse of the power to adjourn for no other purpose than to allow the defendant to become 21. It is a similar abuse to adjourn for no other purpose than to await a change in the substantive law, as it is a principle of the rule of law that the courts have to apply the law as it exists: *R. v. Walsall JJ., ex p. W.* [1990] 1 Q.B. 253, 90 Cr.App.R. 186, DC. It is submitted that different considerations may apply if an adjournment is sought pending an imminent clarification of the law in another case.

(8) Appeals against sentence

The proper approach

2–192 The function of the Crown Court is not to review the justices' decision and ask itself whether the sentence was within the ambit of their discretion; rather, it should ask itself what, on all the evidence, was the right sentence: *R. v. Swindon Crown Court, ex p. Murray*, 162 J.P. 36, DC. The court should go through the sentencing procedure without regard to the decision of the justices; having decided how the appellant ought to be sentenced, it should then see to what extent, if at all, this differs from the order made in the lower court. If the difference is trifling or insignificant, it should be ignored; if it is significant, the sentence should be varied to that extent: *R. v. Knutsford Crown Court, ex p. Jones*, 7 Cr.App.R.(S.) 448, DC. However, although the appeal is by way of rehearing, the court should take into account what has happened before the justices. A defendant's legitimate expectation that if reports were favourable to him he would not be sent to prison, cannot be subsequently ignored by the Crown Court on appeal: *R. v. Isleworth Crown Court, ex p. Irwin, The Times*, December 5, 1991, DC.

It is doubtful whether it would ever be appropriate for a sentence to be increased on appeal solely for the purpose of ensuring that the offender was on licence when released: *R. v. DPP, ex p. McGeary* [1999] 2 Cr.App.R.(S.) 263, DC.

Disputed issues of fact

If the proper factual basis for sentence is first raised in the magistrates' court and the magistrates hear evidence on the issue prior to committing for sentence, they should ensure that the Crown Court is informed of the facts and the Crown Court should sentence upon the basis of the facts as found by the justices: *Munroe v. DPP* [1988] Crim.L.R. 823, DC. See also *ante*, § 2–182. Where, however, the issue as to the proper basis of sentence is first raised in the Crown Court, the Crown Court has a discretion whether to remit the case to the magistrates' court or to determine the issue itself. In deciding which course to adopt, the Crown Court should have regard to the following matters: (a) the facts of the offence; (b) whether on a balance of probabilities, the defendant had raised the issue before the magistrates; (c) the fact, which was by no means conclusive, that the Crown Court would know that the magistrates had considered the defendant's record sufficiently serious to justify committing him for sentence; and (d) the delay which remitting the issue to the magistrates would inevitably cause with consequent detriment to the defendant and the administration of justice: *ibid.* **2–193**

If the Crown Court does decide to try the issue itself, the principles laid down in *Newton* (*post*, §§ 5–74 *et seq.*) as to the determination of such issues, apply to appeals: *Williams v. R.*, 77 Cr.App.R. 329, DC; as they do to committals for sentence: *Munroe v. DPP*, *ante*. Where necessary, the judge should remind the justices with whom he is sitting that they should put the appellant's record out of their minds when deciding the dispute as to facts: *ibid.*

(9) Change of plea—equivocal plea

Although the circumstances in which an appeal may properly lie to the Crown Court are defined in section 108 of the *MCA* 1980 (*ante*, § 2–161), not infrequently persons who have pleaded "guilty" before the magistrates "appeal" to the Crown Court in the hope of persuading the Crown Court that the plea of "guilty" was equivocal and that the proper course for the Crown Court is to remit the case to the magistrates with a direction that the "appellant" be allowed to change his plea to one of "not guilty". **2–194**

The situation usually arises in one or other of the following situations: either (a) the person has been convicted by the magistrates, *i.e.* the plea of guilty recorded and sentence passed, or (b) the person having pleaded "guilty" has been committed to the Crown Court for sentence.

(a) *Plea of guilty recorded and magistrates pass sentence*

General

If a plea of "guilty" tendered in a magistrates' court was an unequivocal plea (*i.e.* a plea which could not be described as a "guilty but ... " plea), then once sentence has been passed by the magistrates and the conviction is accordingly complete, it is too late for any court to entertain an application for a change of plea: *R. v. McNally*, 38 Cr.App.R. 90, CCA; *S. (an Infant) v. Manchester City Recorder* [1971] A.C. 481, HL. A plea is not equivocal because it is based upon incorrect or corrupted evidence: *R. v. Bolton JJ., ex p. Scally* [1991] 1 Q.B. 537, DC (relief was available on judicial review, *post*, § 7–14); *R. v. Burton upon Trent Magistrates' Court, ex p. Woolley*, *The Times*, November 17, 1994, DC. **2–195**

The Crown Court is entitled to inquire into the question of whether the plea entered before the magistrates was equivocal. But unless it is told something which prima facie raises the issue of an equivocal plea having been tendered before the magistrates, it ought not to set about making an inquiry: *R. v. Coventry Crown Court, ex p. Manson*, 67 Cr.App.R. 315, DC. The Crown Court must first hear evidence for, or on behalf of the appellant as to the basis on which the allegation of equivocality is founded: *R. v. Rochdale JJ., ex p. Allwork*, 73 Cr.App.R. 319, DC. The issue of equivocality is confined to what went on before the magistrates. If the evidence reveals that nothing occurred there to render the plea equivocal that is the end of the matter and the Crown Court will proceed to hear the appeal against sentence (if pursued). In the rare case of an appellant producing some prima facie and credible evidence tending to show that the plea before the magistrates was equivocal, the Crown Court should seek assistance from the magistrates' court. The chairman or the clerk (or both) should swear an affidavit as to what happened in the court and only after considering the affidavit(s) should the Crown Court decide the issue. Cases should not be remitted to the magistrates before their assistance has been sought.

2–196 *Ex p. Allwork* was approved and applied in *R. v. Plymouth JJ., ex p. Hart* [1986] Q.B. 950, 83 Cr.App.R. 81, DC. In *Hart*, the court reviewed all the authorities and concluded that where a defendant's case has been dealt with and disposed of in a magistrates' court on a guilty plea which he later asserts to have been equivocal, the Crown Court is, on appeal, entitled under the *Supreme Court [Senior Courts] Act* 1981 (as to the renaming of which, see *ante*, § 2–1), s.48(2) (*ante*, § 2–178) to order the magistrates' court to rehear the case provided that the Crown Court has conducted a proper inquiry into the circumstances of the acceptance of the plea by the justices. In order to decide safely whether a plea was equivocal the Crown Court must have sufficient evidence of what happened at the hearing in the magistrates' court when the defendant was convicted and sentenced:

> "Providing a proper inquiry into the issue of plea is made at the Crown Court the power to direct a rehearing arises and such an order must be obeyed. If dispute arises as to whether a proper inquiry was made at the Crown Court, that can only be resolved in this court. However, if everyone concerned in a matter of this kind acts responsibly and carefully that will not be necessary. I am not, of course, suggesting that a defendant may not come to this court to have the issue of plea decided rather than go to the Crown Court. ... But a defendant in the future may find it more expeditious and less costly to have the issue of plea effectively resolved in the Crown Court" (*per* Watkins L.J. at pp. 963–964, 93).

This question can be investigated and determined at any stage of the proceedings before an appeal has finally been disposed of: *R. v. Tottenham JJ., ex p. Rubens*, 54 Cr.App.R. 183, DC.

2–197 In *P. Foster (Haulage) Ltd v. Roberts*, 67 Cr.App.R. 305, DC, it was said that the Crown Court should ask itself three questions. (a) Was the plea itself equivocal? (b) If not, did anything occur during the proceedings which should have led the justices to consider whether they should exercise their discretion to invite or permit a change of plea? (c) If so, had it been shown that by not inviting a change of plea the justices had exercised their discretion wrongly? (Presumably, a failure to appreciate that there is a discretion to be exercised is equivalent to exercising it wrongly.) In relation to the second issue, the court said that if the defendant is legally represented, it will be rare that it can be said that it ought to have been apparent to justices that they should consider exercising their discretion to invite a change of plea. If, however, the mitigation is inconsistent with the legal ingredients of the offence, as here, or with the plea, as in *R. v. South Sefton JJ., ex p. Rabaca*, *The Times*, February 20, 1986, DC, they should do so. But a general assertion in mitigation that the defendant had behaved in such a way as would bring him within the benefit of a statutory defence (on a charge of failing to comply with an enforcement notice, contrary to the *Town and Country Planning Act* 1990, s.179(2), that the defendant had done "all he could"—see s.179(3)), without any express claim to entitlement to such defence, does not render a plea of guilty equivocal where the admitted facts are such as to make clear that the defence could not succeed (it being acknowledged that compliance did not depend on third parties, and was within the power of the defendant—difficulty in complying not being enough to raise the defence): *R. v. Warwick Crown Court, ex p. White* [1997] C.O.D. 418, DC.

A plea of guilty to an offence of failure to provide a specimen for analysis, contrary to section 7(6) of the *RTA* 1988 (*post*, § 32–93), is not rendered equivocal by the fact that the police failed to follow the procedure required by *DPP v. Warren* [1993] A.C. 319, HL, if the statement of facts read to the magistrates' court said nothing as to the detail of the procedure which was in fact followed, with the consequence that nothing was said to alert the justices to the fact that the procedure was in any way unlawful: *Ankrah v. DPP (Note—1996)* [1998] R.T.R. 169, DC.

Pleas of guilty were held to be equivocal in *R. v. Durham Q.S., ex p. Virgo* [1952] 2 Q.B. 1 (unrepresented defendant's statement to the court before sentence was inconsistent with plea); and *R. v. Blandford JJ., ex p. G (an infant)* [1967] 1 Q.B. 82, DC (statement of unrepresented defendant to police inconsistent with plea).

If the plea was not equivocal, the Crown Court has no jurisdiction to remit the matter even though it is satisfied, on making inquiry, that the defendant had not intended to plead guilty: *R. v. Marylebone JJ., ex p. Westminster City Council* [1971] 1 W.L.R. 567, DC.

Plea of guilty under duress

In *R. v. Huntingdon JJ., ex p. Jordan*, 73 Cr.App.R. 194, DC, a husband and wife appeared before a magistrates' court, pleaded guilty to theft and were sentenced. Thereafter, the wife appealed to the Crown Court against her conviction on the basis that her plea was procured by the duress of her husband, as indeed had been her conduct which resulted in the charge. It was held that the Crown Court had been wrong in holding that it had no jurisdiction to inquire into those alleged circumstances. **2–198**

Unequivocal pleas and pleas in bar

The Crown Court is entitled to consider an appeal or application to withdraw an unequivocal plea on the ground of a special plea in bar raised, such as *autrefois convict*. The rule that no person should be put in peril twice for the same offence is so fundamental that it is incumbent on the court to enquire into the circumstances to see whether the plea was justified: *Cooper v. New Forest District Council, The Times*, March 19, 1992, DC. **2–199**

Procedure

Rule 37.6 of the *Criminal Procedure Rules* 2005 (S.I. 2005 No. 384) (in identical terms to rule 39.3 (*post*, § 4–187a)) prescribes the procedure to be followed where a defendant seeks to vacate a plea of guilty entered in summary proceedings. Neither rule expressly applies to the situation in the Crown Court where a defendant seeks to change a plea of guilty entered in the magistrates' court on an appeal against sentence or a committal for sentence, but it is likely that the court would insist on a like procedure being adopted, and the defendant's legal representatives would be well advised to proceed as if the rule applied. It may be noted that the rules purport to restrict the circumstances in which an application to vacate a plea may be made to the time before "the final disposal of the case, whether by sentence or otherwise." It is submitted, however, that this cannot be taken to limit the jurisdiction of the Crown Court to inquire into a plea which is alleged to have been equivocal and in an appropriate case to remit the matter to the magistrates' court for a rehearing (*ante*, §§ 2–195, 2–196). **2–199a**

(b) *Plea of "guilty" followed by committal for sentence*

In summary proceedings, as in cases tried on indictment (see *post*, §§ 4–186, 4–187) the defendant may apply at any time before sentence to change his plea of guilty and it is for the court then to decide whether justice requires that that should be permitted: *S. (an Infant) v. Manchester City Recorder* [1971] A.C. 481, HL. As to the proper approach by magistrates to applications to change plea, or to change an election of summary trial, see *R. v. Craske, ex p. Commr of Police of the Metropolis* [1957] 2 Q.B. 591, DC; *R. v. Southampton JJ., ex p. Briggs* [1972] 1 W.L.R. 277, DC; *R. v. Birmingham JJ., ex p. Hodgson* [1985] Q.B. 1131, 81 Cr.App.R. 231, DC; *R. v. Bristol JJ., ex p. Sawyers* [1988] Crim.L.R. 754, DC; *R. v. Aldridge JJ., ex p. Till, The Times*, December 27, 1988, DC; *R. v. Eccles JJ., ex p. Fitzpatrick*, 89 Cr.App.R. 324, DC; *R. v. Bow Street Magistrate, ex p. Welcombe, The Times*, May 7, 1991, DC; and see *ante*, § 1–75d. **2–200**

The relevant principles were considered yet again in *Revitt v. DPP* [2007] 1 Cr.App.R. 19, DC, where it was held that a refusal to allow the withdrawal of an unequivocal plea of guilty, and to treat such plea as conclusive of guilt, does not breach the right of an accused person, under Article 6 of the ECHR, to be presumed innocent until proved guilty according to the law; however, a guilty plea can only bring an end to the presumption of innocence where it is unequivocal; and it is likely to be appropriate to permit the withdrawal of an unequivocal plea of guilty if it becomes apparent that the defendant did not appreciate the elements of the offence to which he was pleading, or if it becomes apparent that the facts relied upon by the prosecution do not add up to the offence charged, but such situations should be rare where a defendant is represented, and, where he is not represented, it is the duty of the court to make sure that the nature of the offence is made clear to him before a guilty plea is accepted; the onus is on a party seeking to vacate a guilty plea to demonstrate that justice requires such a course, and where an appeal is brought by the case stated procedure, rather than by way of judicial review, it is important to ensure that the case contains the facts needed to make good the grounds of appeal.

Where a defendant has unequivocally pleaded guilty at a magistrates' court and has been committed to the Crown Court for sentence, the Crown Court has power to entertain an application by the defendant to be allowed to change his plea. If the court after hearing the application refuses it, that is the end of the matter. If, however, it accedes to the application, the proper course is for the Crown Court to remit the case to the magistrates for trial on the basis of a "not guilty" plea: *R. v. Mutford and Lothingland JJ., ex p. Harber* [1971] 2 Q.B. 291, 55 Cr.App.R. 57, DC; and see *R. v. Isleworth Crown Court and Uxbridge Magistrates' Court, ex p. Buda* [2000] 1 Cr.App.R.(S.) 538, DC (discretion to permit change of plea of guilty entered under material mistake of fact). A consequence of this decision is the danger that defendants, content to plead guilty and be dealt with by justices, will endeavour to change their plea as soon as they realise that they are risking greater punishment on committal. That is a danger which should be borne in mind by the Crown Court when called upon to determine an application for a change of plea: "... the cases must be comparatively rare in which it would be proper at that stage to allow a change of plea": *ex p. Harber*, *ante*, at pp. 299, 64–65.

Justices are not entitled to reject a direction by the Crown Court that they enter a plea of not guilty where the defendant has been committed for sentence: *R. v. Camberwell Green JJ., ex p. Sloper*, 69 Cr.App.R. 1, DC, applying *R. v. Mutford and Lothingland JJ.*, *ante*.

(10) Function and duties of judges on appeals to the Crown Court

2–201 Where the Crown Court sits in its appellate capacity, the presiding judge shall be the judge of the High Court, Circuit judge or recorder, and shall have the casting vote: the *Supreme Court [Senior Courts] Act* 1981 (as to the renaming of which, see *ante*, § 2–1), s.73(3), *ante*, § 2–4. Justices of the peace sitting in the Crown Court are themselves judges of the Crown Court and must play a full part in all decisions, whether on interlocutory matters or sentence. However, in matters of law, lay justices must take a ruling from the presiding judge in precisely the same way as the jury is required to take his ruling when it retires to consider its verdict. Accordingly, where in the course of a trial the admissibility of a confession is challenged, it is proper for the presiding judge to retire with the justices and for them together to reach a decision on the facts within the framework of law explained by the judge: *R. v. Orpin* [1975] Q.B. 283, 59 Cr.App.R. 231, CA.

Where the court has a discretion as to the admissibility of evidence, it is for the justices to decide the issue as much as for the judge; where, however, the discretion could be exercised in only one lawful way, then it is for the judge so to decide and the justices are bound by such decision: *Cook v. DPP* [2001] Crim.L.R. 321, DC.

The judge in announcing a decision of the court, should make clear that the justices have been consulted: *R. v. Newby*, 6 Cr.App.R.(S.) 148, CA.

Where the respondent's counsel does not appear, it is inappropriate for the judge to conduct the respondent's case; for justice to be seen to be done, the judge must remain aloof from the proceedings: *R. v. Wood Green Crown Court, ex p. Taylor*, *The Times*, May 25, 1995, DC.

(11) Duty to give reasons

When the Crown Court is sitting in its appellate capacity, it is obliged to give reasons for its decisions. The court must say enough to demonstrate that it has identified the main contentious issues in the case and how it has resolved each of them. The reasoning required will depend upon the circumstances. In some cases a bald statement that the evidence of a particular witness is accepted will be sufficient. In others, reasons may have to be advanced to explain why apparently powerful points in favour of the unsuccessful party have been rejected. A failure to give reasons may amount to a denial of natural justice: *R. v. Harrow Crown Court, ex p. Dave*, 99 Cr.App.R. 114, DC; and *R. (Taylor) v. Maidstone Crown Court* [2004] A.C.D. 19, QBD (Silber J.). See also *R. v. Southwark Crown Court, ex p. Brooke* [1997] C.O.D. 81, DC (a sentence or two may suffice but some indication of the court's reasoning should be given); *Pullum v. CPS* [2000] C.O.D. 206, DC (on dismissal of an appeal against conviction, the minimum that the appellant is entitled to expect, even in a straightforward case, is a clear statement as to the issues which had to be resolved, and the basis upon which they had been resolved, identifying the evidence that had been accepted (applied in *Weightman v. DPP* [2007] R.T.R. 45, DC, where the Crown Court had failed to give a clear statement of the issues that it had to resolve, and the basis upon which it had resolved them, in respect of a defence under the *RTA* 1988, s.172(4), *post*, § 32–133)); *R. v. Inner London Crown Court, ex p. London Borough of Lambeth* [2000] Crim.L.R. 303, DC (duty applies equally where appeal allowed, but possible that the High Court will exercise its discretion differently according to who is seeking relief); and *Flannery v. Halifax Estate Agencies Ltd* [2000] 1 W.L.R. 377, CA (Civ. Div.) (failure to give reasons might be a good self-standing ground of appeal; the giving of reasons enabled the parties to know why they had won or lost, whether the court had properly directed itself and therefore whether there was any available appeal). 2–202

In *R. v. Kingston Crown Court, ex p. Bell*, 164 J.P. 633, QBD, Jackson J., having referred to *ex p. Dave* and other authorities not concerned with appeals to the Crown Court, concluded that a failure to give reasons will vitiate the Crown Court's decision unless the reasons are obvious, the case simple or the subject matter unimportant. It is submitted that a judge would be ill-advised to rely on this authority when dismissing an appeal to the Crown Court. It would only be in the most exceptional circumstances that a judge would be justified in describing an appeal as unimportant; and if the reasons are obvious or simple, they can be shortly stated. The giving of reasons also has the beneficial effect of concentrating the mind of the decision-maker on the relevant issues.

Where no reasons were given by a judge when dismissing an appeal, a note of the proceedings subsequently provided by him, which was unsupported by affidavit and not signed by the justices sitting on the appeal, was of no real weight. Reasons should be given contemporaneously with the decision so that the losing party could be sure that there was no *ex post facto* rationalisation: *R. v. Snaresbrook Crown Court, ex p. Input Management*, 163 J.P. 533, DC; and *R. (Taylor) v. Maidstone Crown Court, ante*.

As to the general desirability of giving reasons for decisions, see also *R. v. Southampton Crown Court, ex p. J. and P.* [1993] Crim.L.R. 962, DC (applied in *R. (Hafner) v. Westminster Magistrates' Court, ante*, § 2–154); and see *ante*, § 1–272c.

(12) Appellants liable to automatic deportation

As to the power of a court determining an appeal against conviction or sentence to direct the release of an appellant who is being detained as being liable to automatic deportation under section 32 of the *UK Borders Act* 2007, see *post*, § 7–242a. 2–202a

G. Enforcement of Decision of Crown Court

Magistrates' Courts Act 1980, s.110

110. After the determination by the Crown Court of an appeal from a magistrates' court the decision appealed against as confirmed or varied by the Crown Court, or any decision of the Crown Court substituted for the decision appealed against, may, without prejudice to the powers of the Crown Court to enforce the decision, be enforced— 2–203

(a) by the issue by the court by which the decision appealed against was given of any process that it could have issued if it had decided the case as the Crown Court decided it;

(b) so far as the nature of any process already issued to enforce the decision appealed against permits, by that process;

and the decision of the Crown Court shall have effect as if it had been made by the magistrates' court against whose decision the appeal is brought.

VII. CRIMINAL PROCEDURE RULES

Rule making power

2–204 The general power to make rules of court for the purpose of regulating and prescribing the practice and procedure to be followed in the criminal courts, which include the Crown Court, is now to be found in section 69 of the *Courts Act* 2003. Section 69 provides, *inter alia*, that such rules are to be called "Criminal Procedure Rules" and are to be made by a committee known as the Criminal Procedure Rule Committee. It also provides that the power to make or alter such rules is to be exercised with a view to securing that the criminal justice system is accessible, fair and efficient, and that the rules are both simple and simply expressed. The membership of the committee is provided for by sections 70 and 71 of the 2003 Act. Section 72 sets out the process to be followed in the making of Criminal Procedure Rules. An ancillary power to amend, repeal or revoke (by order) any enactment in order to facilitate the making of Criminal Procedure Rules, or in consequence of sections 69 to 72 of the 2003 Act, is conferred by section 73 of that Act.

Criminal Procedure Rules 2005 (S.I. 2005 No. 384)

2–205 The *Criminal Procedure Rules* 2005 (S.I. 2005 No. 384) were made pursuant to section 69 of the *Courts Act* 2003, and came into force on April 4, 2005. They are said, in the explanatory note published with them, to represent the first step in the creation of a new, consolidated criminal code. Part 1 (*post*, § 4–84b) contains the overriding objective of the rules. Part 2 (*post*, § 2–206) contains provisions for understanding and applying the rules (there is also a glossary at the end of the rules explaining some of the terms used in the rules). Part 3 (*post*, §§ 4–84c *et seq.*) contains new rules to facilitate the management of criminal cases by the court in accordance with the overriding objective. The main body of the rules (Parts 4– 78) (as originally made) was a consolidation of various previous rules of court. There have now been a number of sets of amending rules. Parts 2 (application of the rules), 4 (service), 5 (forms) and 75 (references to the European Court of Justice), which are of general application, are set out *post*. Where other of the rules are relevant, they are set out, or referred to (in their amended form), at the appropriate point in the text in this work.

Criminal Procedure Rules 2005 (S.I. 2005 No. 384), Pt 2

When the Rules apply

2–206 **2.1.**—(1) In general, the Criminal Procedure Rules apply—

(a) in all criminal cases in magistrates' courts and in the Crown Court; and

(b) in all cases in the criminal division of the Court of Appeal.

(2) If a rule applies only in one or two of those courts, the rule makes that clear.

(3) The Rules apply on and after 4th April, 2005, but do not affect any right or duty existing under the rules of court revoked by the coming into force of these Rules.

(4) The rules in Part 33 apply in all cases in which the defendant is charged on or after 6 November 2006 and in other cases if the court so orders.

(5) The rules in Part 14 apply in cases in which one of the events listed in subparagraphs (a) to (d) of rule 14.1(1) takes place on or after 2nd April 2007. In other cases the rules of court replaced by those rules apply.

(6) The rules in Part 28 apply in cases in which an application under rule 28.3 is made on or after 2nd April 2007. In other cases the rules replaced by those rules apply.

(7) The rules in Parts 65, 66, 67, 68, 69 and 70 apply where an appeal, application or reference, to which one of those Parts applies, is made on or after 1st October 2007. In other cases the rules replaced by those rules apply.

(8) The rules in Parts 57–62 apply in proceedings to which one of those Parts applies that begin on or after 1st April 2008. In such proceedings beginning before that date the rules in those Parts apply as if—

(a) the amendments made to them by the *Criminal Procedure (Amendment No. 3) Rules* 2007 had not been made; and

(b) references to the Director of the Assets Recovery Agency or to that Agency were references to the Serious Organised Crime Agency.

(9) The rules in Part 50 apply in cases in which the defendant is charged on or after 7th April 2008 and in other cases if the court so orders. Otherwise, the rules replaced by those rules apply.

(10) The rules in Part 74 apply where an appeal, application or reference, to which Part 74 applies, is made on or after 7th April 2008. In other cases the rules replaced by those rules apply.

(11) The rules in Part 7 apply in cases in which on or after 6th October 2008—

(a) a prosecutor serves an information on the court officer or presents it to a magistrates' court;

(b) a public prosecutor issues a written charge; or

(c) a person who is in custody is charged with an offence.

In other cases the rules replaced by those rules apply.

(12) The rules in Part 63 apply in cases in which the decision that is the subject of the appeal, or reference, to which that Part applies is made on or after 6th October 2008. In other cases the rules replaced by those rules apply.

[This rule is printed as amended by the *Criminal Procedure (Amendment No. 2) Rules* 2006 (S.I. 2006 No. 2636); the *Criminal Procedure (Amendment) Rules* 2007 (S.I. 2007 No. 699); the *Criminal Procedure (Amendment No. 2) Rules* 2007 (S.I. 2007 No. 2317); the *Criminal Procedure (Amendment No. 3) Rules* 2007 (S.I. 2007 No. 3662); and the *Criminal Procedure (Amendment) Rules* 2008 (S.I. 2008 No. 2076).]

Definitions

2.2.—(1) In these Rules, unless the context makes it clear that something different is meant:

"business day" means any day except Saturday, Sunday, Christmas Day, Boxing Day, Good Friday, Easter Monday or a bank holiday;

"court" means a tribunal with jurisdiction over criminal cases. It includes a judge, recorder, District Judge (Magistrates' Courts), lay justice and, when exercising their judicial powers, the Registrar of Criminal Appeals, a justices' clerk or assistant clerk;

"court officer" means the appropriate member of the staff of a court;

"live link" means an arrangement by which a person can see and hear, and be seen and heard by, the court when that person is not in court;

"Practice Direction" means the Lord Chief Justice's Consolidated Criminal Practice Direction, as amended; and

"public interest ruling" means a ruling about whether it is in the public interest to disclose prosecution material under sections 3(6), 7A(8) or 8(5) of the *Criminal Procedure and Investigations Act* 1996.

(2) Definitions of some other expressions are in the rules in which they apply.

[This rule is printed as amended by S.I. 2007 No. 2317 (*ante*).]

References to Acts of Parliament and to statutory instruments

2.3. In these Rules, where a rule refers to an Act of Parliament or to subordinate legislation by title and year, subsequent references to that Act or to that legislation in the rule are shortened: so, for example, after a reference to the *Criminal Procedure and Investigations Act* 1996 that Act is called "the 1996 Act"; and after a reference to the *Criminal Procedure and Investigations Act 1996 (Defence Disclosure Time Limits) Regulations* 1997 those Regulations are called "the 1997 Regulations".

The glossary

2.4. The glossary at the end of the Rules is a guide to the meaning of certain legal expressions used in them.

Representatives

2.5.—(1) Under these Rules, unless the context makes it clear that something different is meant, anything that a party may or must do may be done—

(a) by a legal representative on that party's behalf;
(b) by a person with the corporation's written authority, where that party is a corporation;
(c) with the help of a parent, guardian or other suitable supporting adult where that party is a defendant—
(i) who is under 18, or
(ii) whose understanding of what the case involves is limited.

(2) Anyone with a prosecutor's authority to do so may, on that prosecutor's behalf—
(a) serve on the magistrates' court officer, or present to a magistrates' court, an information under section 1 of the *Magistrates' Courts Act* 1980; or
(b) issue a written charge and requisition under section 29 of the *Criminal Justice Act* 2003.

[Rule 2.5 was inserted by S.I. 2008 No. 2076 (*ante*), r.5.]

Criminal Procedure Rules 2005 (S.I. 2005 No. 384), Pt 4 (as substituted by the Criminal Procedure (Amendment) Rules 2007 (S.I. 2007 No. 699), r.5 and Sched. 1)

When this Part applies

2–207 **4.1.** The rules in this Part apply to the service of every document in a case to which these Rules apply, subject to any special rules in other legislation (including other Parts of these Rules) or in the Practice Direction.

Methods of service

2–208 **4.2.** A document may be served by any of the methods described in rules 4.3 to 4.6 (subject to rule 4.7), or in rule 4.8.

Service by handing over a document

2–209 **4.3.**—(1) A document may be served on—
(a) an individual by handing it to him or her;
(b) a corporation by handing it to a person holding a senior position in that corporation;
(c) an individual or corporation who is legally represented in the case by handing it to that representative;
(d) the prosecution by handing it to the prosecutor or to the prosecution representative;
(e) the court officer by handing it to a court officer with authority to accept it at the relevant court office; and
(f) the Registrar of Criminal Appeals by handing it to a court officer with authority to accept it at the Criminal Appeal Office.

(2) If an individual is 17 or under, a copy of a document served under paragraph (1)(a) must be handed to his or her parent, or another appropriate adult, unless no such person is readily available.

Service by leaving or posting a document

2–210 **4.4.**—(1) A document may be served by leaving it at the appropriate address for service under this rule or by sending it to that address by first class post or by the equivalent of first class post.

(2) The address for service under this rule on—
(a) an individual is an address where it is reasonably believed that he or she will receive it;
(b) a corporation is its principal office, and if there is no readily identifiable principal office then any place where it carries on its activities or business;
(c) an individual or corporation who is legally represented in the case is that representative's office;
(d) the prosecution is the prosecutor's office;
(e) the court officer is the relevant court office; and
(f) the Registrar of Criminal Appeals is the Criminal Appeal Office, Royal Courts of Justice, Strand, London WC2A 2LL.

[Rule 4.4(2)(b) is printed as repealed in part by S.I. 2008 No. 2076 (*ante*, § 2–206), r.5.]

A note that follows rule 4.4 draws attention to the fact that in addition to service in England and Wales, for which these rules provide, service outside England and Wales may be allowed under other legislation, examples of which are there given.

Service through a document exchange

4.5. A document may be served by document exchange (DX) where— **2–211**

(a) the writing paper of the person to be served gives a DX box number; and

(b) that person has not refused to accept service by DX.

Service by fax, e-mail or other electronic means

4.6.—(1) A document may be served by fax, e-mail or other electronic means where— **2–212**

(a) the person to be served has given a fax, e-mail or other electronic address; and

(b) that person has not refused to accept service by that means.

(2) Where a document is served under this rule the person serving it need not provide a paper copy as well.

Documents that must be served only by handing them over, leaving or posting them

4.7.—(1) The documents listed in this rule may be served— **2–213**

(a) on an individual only under rule 4.3(1)(a) or rule 4.4(1) and (2)(a); and

(b) on a corporation only under rule 4.3(1)(b) or rule 4.4(1) and (2)(b).

(2) Those documents are—

(a) a summons, requisition or witness summons;

(b) notice of an order under section 25 of the *Road Traffic Offenders Act* 1988;

(c) a notice of registration under section 71(6) of that Act;

(d) a notice of discontinuance under section 23(4) of the *Prosecution of Offences Act* 1985;

(e) notice under rule 37.3(1) of the date, time and place to which the trial of an information has been adjourned, where it was adjourned in the defendant's absence;

(f) a notice of fine or forfeited recognizance required by rule 52.1(1);

(g) notice under section 86 of the *Magistrates' Courts Act* 1980 of a revised date to attend a means inquiry;

(h) notice of a hearing to review the postponement of the issue of a warrant of commitment under section 77(6) of the *Magistrates' Courts Act* 1980;

(i) a copy of the minute of a magistrates' court order required by rule 52.7(1);

(j) an invitation to make observations or attend a hearing under rule 53.1(2) on the review of a compensation order under section 133 of the *Powers of Criminal Courts (Sentencing) Act* 2000;

(k) any notice or document served under Part 19.

Service by person in custody

4.8.—(1) A person in custody may serve a document by handing it to the custodian addressed to the person to be served. **2–214**

(2) The custodian must—

(a) endorse it with the time and date of receipt;

(b) record its receipt; and

(c) forward it promptly to the addressee.

Service by another method

4.9.—(1) The court may allow service of a document by a method other than those described in rules 4.3 to 4.6 and in rule 4.8. **2–215**

(2) An order allowing service by another method must specify—

(a) the method to be used; and

(b) the date on which the document will be served.

Date of service

4.10.—(1) A document served under rule 4.3 or rule 4.8 is served on the day it is handed over. **2–216**

(2) Unless something different is shown, a document served on a person by any other method is served—

(a) in the case of a document left at an address, on the next business day after the day on which it was left;

(b) in the case of a document sent by first class post or by the equivalent of first class post, on the second business day after the day on which it was posted or despatched;

(c) in the case of a document served by document exchange, on the second business day after the day on which it was left at the addressee's DX or at a correspondent DX;

(d) in the case of a document transmitted by fax, e-mail or other electronic means, on the next business day after it was transmitted; and

(e) in any case, on the day on which the addressee responds to it if that is earlier.

(3) Unless something different is shown, a document produced by a court computer system is to be taken as having been sent by first class post or by the equivalent of first class post to the addressee on the business day after the day on which it was produced.

(4) In this Part "business day" means any day except Saturday, Sunday, Christmas Day, Boxing Day, Good Friday, Easter Monday or a bank holiday.

(5) Where a document is served on or by the court officer, "business day" does not include a day on which the court office is closed.

Proof of service

2–217 **4.11.** The person who serves a document may prove that by signing a certificate explaining how and when it was served.

Court's power to give directions about service

2–218 **4.12.**—(1) The court may specify the time as well as the date by which a document must be—

(a) served under rule 4.3 or rule 4.8; or

(b) transmitted by fax, e-mail or other electronic means if it is served under rule 4.6.

(2) The court may treat a document as served if the addressee responds to it even if it was not served in accordance with the rules in this Part.

Criminal Procedure Rules 2005 (S.I. 2005 No. 384), Pt 5

Forms

2–219 **5.1.** The forms set out in the Practice Direction shall be used as appropriate in connection with the rules to which they apply.

A table of relevant forms is set out at the beginning of Annex D to the *Practice Direction (Criminal Proceedings: Consolidation)* [2002] 1 W.L.R. 2870 (as inserted therein by *Practice Direction (Criminal Proceedings: Forms)* [2005] 1 W.L.R. 1479). Amendments to certain of the 2005 rules (*ante*, § 2–205) have necessitated corresponding amendments to the table of forms: *Practice Direction (Criminal Proceedings: Updated Forms)* [2006] 1 W.L.R. 1152; *Consolidated Criminal Practice Direction (Amendment No. 14) (Forms for use in Criminal Proceedings)* [2007] 1 Cr.App.R. 22; *Consolidated Criminal Practice Direction (Amendment No. 15)* [2007] 2 Cr.App.R. 20; *Practice Direction (Criminal Appeals: Forms)* [2007] 1 W.L.R. 2607; *Consolidated Practice Direction (Amendment) (No. 19)* [2008] 2 Cr.App.R. 16; and *Consolidated Criminal Practice Direction (Amendment No. 21) (Criminal Proceedings: Witness Anonymity Orders; Forms)*, unreported, August 29, 2008 (adding an appeal notice form and a notice of abandonment of appeal form for use in connection with Pt 63 of the 2005 rules (*ante*, §§ 2–180 *et seq.*)). The forms may be found at http://www.dca.gov.uk/criminal/procrules_fin/contents/formssection/formspage.htm.

Criminal Procedure Rules 2005 (S.I. 2005 No. 384), Pt 75

Reference to the European Court

2–220 **75.1.**—(1) In this rule "order" means an order referring a question to the European Court for a preliminary ruling under Article 234 of the Treaty establishing the European Community, Article 150 of the Treaty establishing Euratom or Article 41 of the Treaty establishing the Coal and Steel Community.

(2) An order may be made—

(a) by the Crown Court of its own motion or on application by a party to proceedings in the Crown Court; or

(b) by the Court of Appeal on application or otherwise, at any time before the determination of an appeal or application for leave to appeal under Part I of the Criminal Appeal Act 1968.

(3) An order shall set out in a schedule the request for the preliminary ruling of the European Court, and the court making the order may give directions as to the manner and form in which the schedule is to be prepared.

(4) When an order has been made, a copy shall be sent to the senior master of the Supreme Court (Queen's Bench Division) for transmission to the Registrar of the European Court.

(5) The Crown Court proceedings in which an order is made shall, unless the Crown Court otherwise determines, be adjourned until the European Court has given a preliminary ruling on the question referred to it.

(6) Nothing in paragraph (5) above shall be taken as preventing the Crown Court from deciding any preliminary or incidental question that may arise in the proceedings after an order is made and before a preliminary ruling is given by the European Court.

(7) No appeal or application for leave to appeal, in the course of which an order is made, shall, unless the Court of Appeal otherwise orders, be determined until the European Court has given a preliminary ruling on the question referred to it.

See also *Practice Direction (E.C. references: procedure)* [1997] 1 Cr. App. R. 452.

(b) by the Court of Appeal, on application or otherwise, at any time before the determination of an appeal or application for leave to appeal under Part I of the *Criminal Appeal Act* 1968.

(3) An order shall set out in a schedule the request for the preliminary ruling of the European Court, and the court making the order may give directions as to the manner and form in which the schedule is to be prepared.

(4) When an order has been made, a copy shall be sent to the senior master of the Supreme Court (Queen's Bench Division) for transmission to the Registrar of the European Court.

(5) The Crown Court proceedings in which an order is made shall, unless the Crown Court otherwise determines, be adjourned until the European Court has given a preliminary ruling on the question referred to it.

(6) Nothing in paragraph (5) above shall be taken as preventing the Crown Court from deciding any preliminary or incidental question that may arise in the proceedings after an order is made and before a preliminary ruling is given by the European Court.

(7) No appeal or application for leave to appeal, in the course of which an order is made, shall, unless the Court of Appeal otherwise orders, be determined until the European Court has given a preliminary ruling on the question referred to it.

See also *Practice Direction (E.C.J. references: procedure)* [1999] 1 Cr.App.R. 452.

Chapter 3

BAIL, APPEARANCE OF ACCUSED FOR TRIAL, PRESENCE DURING TRIAL

I. BAIL

A. General

(1) Introduction

Refusal or delay by any judge or magistrate to bail any person bailable is at common law an offence against the liberty of the subject: 4 Bl.Com. 297. It is also a violation of the *Habeas Corpus Act* 1679, and of the *Bill of Rights* 1688. But the duty of a magistrate as to admitting a defendant to bail is judicial, and not merely ministerial, and therefore an action will not lie against him without proof of malice for refusing to admit to bail a person charged with an offence, and entitled to be admitted to bail: *R. v. Badger* (1843) 4 Q.B. 468; *Linford v. Fitzroy* (1849) 13 Q.B. 240. **3–1**

(2) The Bail Act 1976

(a) *Introduction*

Bail in all criminal proceedings is to be granted in accordance with the Act: s.1(6). The Act does not affect bail granted in civil proceedings or recognizances to keep the peace or be of good behaviour. The Act has been extensively amended. **3–2**

(b) *Summary of the Act*

General right to bail (s.4 and Sched. 1)

Bail must be granted by a court to a person accused of an offence, or remanded after conviction for inquiries or a report, or brought before the court for breach of a requirement of a community order, if none of the exceptions specified in Schedule 1 applies. The court must consider whether bail should be granted on each occasion that the defendant is brought before it whether or not the defendant makes an application: see, in particular, Part IIA of Schedule 1. The general right to bail under section 4 does not apply to persons accused of homicide or rape in certain circumstances: see section 25 of the *CJPOA* 1994, *post*, § 3–55. **3–3**

Reasons for decision (s.5)

When a magistrates' court or the Crown Court refuses bail to a person to whom section 4 applies *or* imposes conditions on the grant of bail to such a person, the court is required (but see s.5(5) in relation to the Crown Court) to give reasons for its decision. **3–3a**

The conditions for which a reason must be given are any of those which may be imposed by virtue of section 3 of the Act.

When a court decides to grant bail to a person charged with certain serious offences it must, in certain circumstances, state the reasons for its decision: see Sched. 1, Pt I, para. 9A.

A custody officer who grants bail subject to conditions or varies the conditions of bail must give reasons, but there is no obligation on such an officer to give reasons for the withholding of bail: see ss.5 and 5A of the Act.

Abolition of personal recognizances (s.3)

3–3b The system of taking recognizances from persons granted bail in criminal proceedings is abolished.

Conditions of bail (s.3)

3–4 Section 3(4)–(7) sets out the types of condition which may be attached to the grant of bail in criminal proceedings.

When bail is granted to a person to whom section 4 applies, no condition may be attached unless it is considered necessary for the purpose of preventing absconding, the commission of an offence on bail or interference with witnesses, or for the purpose of obtaining medical or other reports. The conditions which may be imposed by a constable who grants bail are more limited: see s.3A(5).

(i) *Security (ss.3 and 5)*

A court or a police officer granting a person bail may require him to give security for his surrender to custody before release. Courts (or police) have an unfettered discretion as to the form of the security—the term is not defined in the Act.

(ii) *Other conditions (s.3)*

Courts (or police) should ensure that the defendant is able to comply with any condition(s) they intend to impose under section 3(6) and that such conditions are enforceable. A condition of bail sometimes imposed is that the defendant surrenders his passport. As this is a device to prevent the defendant from absconding abroad, it should be accompanied by a post-release condition stipulating that the defendant shall not leave Great Britain during the period of bail.

Remands for inquiries or medical reports

3–5 The general right to bail extends to persons remanded after conviction for inquiries or medical reports, but bail need not be granted if the court considers it impracticable for the inquiries or report to be made without keeping the defendant in custody.

(c) *Text of the Act*

Bail Act 1976, ss.1, 2

Meaning of "bail in criminal proceedings"

3–6 **1.**—(1) In this Act "bail in criminal proceedings" means—

(a) bail grantable in or in connection with proceedings for an offence to a person who is accused or convicted of the offence, or

(b) bail grantable in connection with an offence to a person who is under arrest for the offence or for whose arrest for the offence a warrant (endorsed for bail) is being issued, or

(c) bail grantable in connection with extradition proceedings in respect of an offence.

(2) In this Act "bail" means bail grantable under the law (including common law) for the time being in force.

(3) Except as provided by section 13 (3) of this Act, this section does not apply to bail in or in connection with proceedings outside England and Wales.

(4) [*Repealed by* CJPOA *1994, s.168(3) and Sched. 11.*]

(5) This section applies—

(a) whether the offence was committed in England or Wales or elsewhere, and

(b) whether it is an offence under the law of England and Wales, or of any other country or territory.

(6) Bail in criminal proceedings shall be granted (and in particular shall be granted unconditionally or conditionally) in accordance with this Act.

[This section is printed as amended by the *Extradition Act* 2003, s.198(1) and (2).]

Other definitions

2.—(1) In this Act, unless the context otherwise requires, "conviction" includes— **3–7**

(a) a finding of guilt,

(b) a finding that a person is not guilty by reason of insanity,

(c) a finding under section 11(1) of the *Powers of Criminal Courts (Sentencing) Act* 2000 (remand for medical examination) that the person in question did the act or made the omission charged, and

(d) a conviction of an offence for which an order is made discharging the offender absolutely or conditionally,

and "convicted" shall be construed accordingly.

(2) In this Act, unless the context otherwise requires—

"bail hostel" means premises for the accommodation of persons remanded on bail,

"child" means a person under the age of fourteen,

"court" includes a judge of a court, a justice of the peace ... and, in the case of a specified court, includes a judge or (as the case may be) justice having powers to act in connection with proceedings before that court,

"Courts-Martial Appeal rules" ["Court Martial Appeal rules"] means rules made under the *Courts-Martial (Appeals) Act* 1968,

"extradition proceedings" means proceedings under the *Extradition Act* 2003,

"offence" includes an alleged offence,

"probation hostel" means premises for the accommodation of persons who may be required to reside there by a community order under section 177 of the *Criminal Justice Act* 2003,

"prosecutor", in relation to extradition proceedings, means the person acting on behalf of the territory to which extradition is sought,

"surrender to custody" means, in relation to a person released on bail, surrendering himself into the custody of the court or of the constable (according to the requirements of the grant of bail) at the time and place for the time being appointed for him to do so,

"vary", in relation to bail, means imposing further conditions after bail is granted, or varying or rescinding conditions,

"young person" means a person who has attained the age of fourteen and is under the age of seventeen.

(3) Where an enactment (whenever passed) which relates to bail in criminal proceedings refers to the person bailed appearing before a court it is to be construed unless the context otherwise requires as referring to his surrendering himself into the custody of the court.

(4) Any reference in this Act to any other enactment is a reference thereto as amended, and includes a reference thereto as extended or applied, by or under any other enactment, including this Act.

[This section is printed as amended, and repealed in part, by the *CLA* 1977, Sched. 12; the *MCA* 1980, Sched. 7; the *CJA* 1988, Sched. 15; the *Extradition Act* 1989, s.36(3); the *PCC(S)A* 2000, s.165(1) and Sched. 9, para. 50; the *Extradition Act* 2003, s.198(1) and (3); the *Courts Act* 2003, s.109(3), and Sched. 10; and the *CJA* 2003, s.304, and Sched. 32, paras 20 and 21; and, as from a day to be appointed, by the *AFA* 2006, s.378(1), and Sched. 16, para. 73 (substitution of words in square brackets for italicised words).]

The *Courts Act* 1971, s.15, the *Justices of the Peace Act* 1949, s.15, and the *Supreme Court of Judicature (Consolidation) Act* 1925, s.99, have been repealed. The first and the third of these provisions have been replaced by section 84 of the *Supreme Court* **3–8**

[Senior Courts] Act 1981 (renamed as from a day to be appointed: *Constitutional Reform Act* 2005, s.59(5), and Sched. 11, para. 1): the second has been replaced by sections 144 and 145 of the *Magistrates' Courts Act* 1980.

As to "surrender to custody", see *post*, § 3–30.

Bail Act 1976, s.3

General provisions

3–9 **3.**—(1) A person granted bail in criminal proceedings shall be under a duty to surrender to custody, and that duty is enforceable in accordance with section 6 of this Act.

(2) No recognizance for his surrender to custody shall be taken from him.

(3) Except as provided by this section—

(a) no security for his surrender to custody shall be taken from him,

(b) he shall not be required to provide a surety or sureties for his surrender to custody, and

(c) no other requirement shall be imposed on him as a condition of bail.

(4) He may be required, before release on bail, to provide a surety or sureties to secure his surrender to custody.

(5) He may be required, before release on bail, to give security for his surrender to custody.

The security may be given by him or on his behalf.

(6) He may be required ... to comply, before release on bail or later, with such requirements as appear to the court to be necessary—

(a) to secure that he surrenders to custody,

(b) to secure that he does not commit an offence while on bail,

(c) to secure that he does not interfere with witnesses or otherwise obstruct the course of justice whether in relation to himself or any other person,

(ca) for his own protection or, if he is a child or young person, for his own welfare or in his own interests,

(d) to secure that he makes himself available for the purpose of enabling inquiries or a report to be made to assist the court in dealing with him for the offence,

(e) to secure that before the time appointed for him to surrender to custody, he attends an interview with *an authorised advocate or authorised litigator, as defined by section 119(1) of the* Courts and Legal Services Act *1990* [a person who, for the purposes of the *Legal Services Act* 2007, is an authorised person in relation to an activity which constitutes the exercise of a right of audience or the conduct of litigation (within the meaning of that Act)];

and, in any Act, "the normal powers to impose conditions of bail" means the powers to impose conditions under paragraph (a), (b), (c) or (ca) above.

(6ZAA) *Subject to section 3AA below, if he is a child or young person he may be required to comply with requirements imposed for the purpose of securing the electronic monitoring of his compliance with any other requirement imposed on him as a condition of bail.*

[(6ZAA) The requirements which may be imposed under subsection (6) include electronic monitoring requirements.

The imposition of electronic monitoring requirements is subject to section 3AA (in the case of a child or young person), section 3AB (in the case of other persons) and section 3AC (in all cases).

(6ZAB) In this section and sections 3AA to 3AC "electronic monitoring requirements" means requirements imposed for the purpose of securing the electronic monitoring of a person's compliance with any other requirement imposed on him as a condition of bail.]

(6ZA) Where he is required under subsection (6) above to reside in a bail hostel, he may also be required to comply with the rules of the hostel.

3–10 (6A) In the case of a person accused of murder the court granting bail shall, unless it considers that satisfactory reports on his mental condition have already been obtained, impose as conditions of bail—

(a) a requirement that the accused shall undergo examination by two medical practitioners for the purpose of enabling such reports to be prepared; and

(b) a requirement that he shall for that purpose attend such an institution or place as the court directs and comply with any other directions which may be given to him for that purpose by either of those practitioners.

(6B) Of the medical practitioners referred to in subsection (6A) above at least one shall be a practitioner approved for the purposes of section 12 of the *Mental Health Act* 1983.

(6C) Subsection (6D) below applies where—

(a) the court has been notified by the Secretary of State that arrangements for conducting a relevant assessment or, as the case may be, providing relevant follow-up have been made for the local justice area in which it appears to the court that the person referred to in subsection (6D) would reside if granted bail; and

(b) the notice has not been withdrawn.

(6D) In the case of a person ("P")—

(a) in relation to whom paragraphs (a) to (c) of paragraph 6B(1) of Part 1 of Schedule 1 to this Act apply (including where P is a person to whom the provisions of Part 1A of Schedule 1 apply);

(b) who, after analysis of the sample referred to in paragraph (b) of that paragraph, has been offered a relevant assessment or, if a relevant assessment has been carried out, has had relevant follow-up proposed to him; and

(c) who has agreed to undergo the relevant assessment or, as the case may be, to participate in the relevant follow-up,

the court, if it grants bail, shall impose as a condition of bail that P both undergo the relevant assessment and participate in any relevant follow-up proposed to him or, if a relevant assessment has been carried out, that P participate in the relevant follow-up.

(6E) In subsections (6C) and (6D) above—

(a) "relevant assessment" means an assessment conducted by a suitably qualified person of whether P is dependent upon or has a propensity to misuse any specified Class A drugs;

(b) "relevant follow-up" means, in a case where the person who conducted the relevant assessment believes P to have such a dependency or propensity, such further assessment, and such assistance or treatment (or both) in connection with the dependency or propensity, as the person who conducted the relevant assessment (or conducts any later assessment) considers to be suitable in P's case,

and in paragraph (a) above "Class A drug" and "misuse" have the same meaning as in the *Misuse of Drugs Act* 1971, and "specified" (in relation to a Class A drug) has the same meaning as in Part 3 of the *Criminal Justice and Court Services Act* 2000.

(6F) In subsection (6E)(a) above, "suitably qualified person" means a person who has such qualifications or experience as are from time to time specified by the Secretary of State for the purposes of this subsection.

(7) If a parent or guardian of a child or young person consents to be surety for the child or young person for the purposes of this subsection, the parent or guardian may be required to secure that the child or young person complies with any requirement imposed on him by virtue of subsection (6), (6ZAA) or (6A) above, but—

(a) no requirement shall be imposed on the parent or the guardian of a young person by virtue of this subsection where it appears that the young person will attain the age of seventeen before the time to be appointed for him to surrender to custody; and

(b) the parent or guardian shall not be required to secure compliance with any requirement to which his consent does not extend and shall not, in respect of those requirements to which his consent does extend, be bound in a sum greater than £50.

(8) Where a court has granted bail in criminal proceedings that court or, where the court has *committed* [sent] a person on bail to the Crown Court for trial or [committed him on bail to the Crown Court] to be sentenced or otherwise dealt with, that court or the Crown Court may on application— **3–11**

(a) by or on behalf of the person to whom bail was granted, or

(b) by the prosecutor or a constable,

vary the conditions of bail or impose conditions in respect of bail which has been granted unconditionally.

(8A) *Where a notice of transfer is given under a relevant transfer provision, subsection (8) above shall have effect in relation to a person in relation to whose case the notice is given as if he had been committed on bail to the Crown Court for trial.*

(8B) *Subsection (8) above applies where a court has sent a person on bail to the Crown Court for trial under section 51 of the* Crime and Disorder Act *1998 as it applies where a court has committed a person on bail to the Crown Court for trial.*

(9) This section is subject to subsection (3) of section 11 of the *Powers of Criminal Courts (Sentencing) Act* 2000 (conditions of bail on remand for medical examination).

(10) This section is subject, in its application to bail granted by a constable, to section 3A of this Act.

(10) *In subsection (8A) above "relevant transfer provision" means—*

(a) *section 4 of the* Criminal Justice Act *1987, or*

(b) *section 53 of the* Criminal Justice Act *1991.*

(10A) *Where a custody time limit has expired this section shall have effect as if—*

(a) *subsections (4) and (5) (sureties and security for his surrender to custody) were omitted;*

(b) *in subsection (6) (conditions of bail) for the words "before release on bail or later" there were substituted the words "after release on bail".*

[This section is printed as amended and repealed in part by the *CLA* 1977, Sched. 12; the *MCA* 1980, Sched. 7; the *Mental Health (Amendment) Act* 1982, s.34; the *MHA* 1983, Sched. 4; the *CJA* 1987, Sched. 2; the *CJA* 1988, s.131(1); the *CJPOA* 1994, ss.27(2) (insertion of first subs. (10)) and 168(1) and (3), and Sched. 9, para. 12 (insertion of second subs. (10)) and Sched. 11; the *CDA* 1998, ss.54(1) and 119, and Sched. 8, para. 37; the *PCC(S)A* 2000, s.165(1) and Sched. 9, para. 51; the *CJPA* 2001, s.131(1) and (3); the *CJA* 2003, ss.13(1), 19(1) and (2); the *Courts Act 2003 (Consequential Provisions) Order* 2005 (S.I. 2005 No. 886); and the *CJIA* 2008, s.52, and Sched. 12, paras 1 and 2. The *CJA* 2003, s.41, and Sched. 3, para. 48(1) and (2), substitute the word "sent" for "committed" in subs. (8); insert the further words in square brackets in the same subs.; and repeal subss. (8A), (8B) and the second subs. (10). The first of these amendments came into force on May 9, 2005, in relation to cases sent for trial under section 51A(3)(d) of the *CDA* 1998: *Criminal Justice Act 2003 (Commencement No. 9) Order* 2005 (S.I. 2005 No. 1267). Otherwise they come into force on a day to be appointed. The words in square brackets in subs. (6)(e) are substituted for the italicised words as from a day to be appointed: *Legal Services Act* 2007, s.208(1), and Sched. 21, paras 33 and 34. Subs. (6ZAA) (printed in italics) is substituted by subss. (6ZAA) and (6ZAB) (in square brackets) as from a further day to be appointed: *CJIA* 2008, s.51, and Sched. 11, paras 1 and 2.]

In a case to which a custody time limit applies, section 3 has effect as if subsection (10A) were inserted at the end thereof: *Prosecution of Offences (Custody Time Limits) Regulations* 1987 (S.I. 1987 No. 299), reg. 8 (as amended by S.I. 1995 No. 555), *post*, §§ 3–56, 3–65.

Section 17(2) of the *Drugs Act* 2005 provides that for the purposes of section 3(6D), a relevant assessment is to be treated as having been carried out if a person has attended an "initial assessment" and remained for its duration, and the initial assessor is satisfied that the initial assessment fulfilled the purposes of a relevant assessment. Subsection (4) provides that an initial assessor may disclose information relating to an initial assessment for the purpose of enabling a court considering an application for bail by the person concerned to determine whether subsection (2) applies. An "initial assessment" may be required under section 9 of the 2005 Act by a police officer where a sample is taken under section 63B of the *PACE Act* 1984 (*post*, § 15–243), analysis of the sample reveals the presence of a Class A drug, and certain other conditions are met. Before the person from whom the sample is taken is released from a police station, a police officer may require him to attend an initial assessment with a suitably qualified assessor for the purpose of (a) establishing whether he is dependent upon, or has a propensity to misuse, Class A drugs, (b) if the assessor thinks he has such dependency or propensity, establishing whether he might benefit from further assessment or from assistance or treatment, and (c) if the assessor thinks he might benefit from such assistance or treatment, providing advice, including as to the types of assistance or treatment available.

Conditions of bail

3–11a As to conditions of bail generally, see also Schedule 1, paragraph 8, *post*, § 3–49. As to the proper approach to objections to bail, see *post*, § 3–53. As to the grant of conditional bail on a charge of a non-imprisonable offence, see *R. v. Bournemouth Magistrates' Court, ex p. Cross*, 89 Cr.App.R. 90, DC.

Where a magistrates' court commits a person for trial on bail (*MCA* 1980, s.6(3)(b)) (*post*, § 3–133) the bail ceases (whatever form of words is used in the magistrates' order) when the defendant surrenders to the Crown Court, whether for the purposes of arraignment or otherwise; if the Crown Court releases him on bail thereafter, it is duty bound to consider the suitability of any conditions afresh, including the position of a surety; where, therefore, a judge granted bail "as heretofore" without considering the position of a surety required by the magistrates, this was ineffective for the purpose of renewing the suretyship as a condition of bail; but a judge who renewed a requirement for a security to be provided was not obliged to do more than consider the position of the defendant, to whom the obligation belonged; the fact that a third party had paid the security did not obligate the judge to inquire into the means of the third party: *R. v. Kent Crown Court, ex p. Jodka*, 161 J.P. 638, DC.

Ex p. Jodka was distinguished in *Choudhry v. Birmingham Crown Court and H.M. Revenue & Customs*; *Hanson v. Same*, 172 J.P. 33, DC. It was held that: (i) it is lawful for a recognizance in proceedings in the Crown Court to be expressed as being continuous until the conclusion of those proceedings; adjournments, orders for separate trials and other procedural events are not themselves capable of bringing the obligations of a surety to an end, nor do variations of bail give rise to the need for sureties to be taken afresh where they do not impact on the position of the surety; when a defendant previously on bail is allowed to remain on bail at the commencement of a trial, that is a fresh grant of bail rather than a continuance of previous bail, but at such a fresh grant there is no need to take sureties again if they have been taken on terms that made it clear they would continue until the conclusion of the proceedings; and (ii) it is perfectly valid and sensible for a judge, upon being informed that a surety wishes to withdraw and being asked to alter the conditions of bail so as to reduce the total amount of the required sureties, to refuse to do so unless a replacement can be found willing to stand as surety for the same amount; the situation might be different if the surety actually attended court and stated that he refused to be bound any longer, as in those circumstances it might come to the stage where the defendant would be remanded in custody until a substitute surety could be found. For criticism of the approach of the Crown Court and of the Divisional Court, see *Criminal Law Week* 2008/05/1. As to bail being made continuous where there is a surety, see also *R. v. Wells Street Magistrates' Court, ex p. Albanese*, 74 Cr.App.R. 180, DC (*post*, § 3–144).

In *R. (Stevens) v. Truro Magistrates' Court* [2002] 1 W.L.R. 144, DC, it was held that whereas Parliament had not limited the type of security that might be given under section 3(5) there was little doubt that what was envisaged was the lodging of some asset, whether in cash or kind, which could be readily forfeited on the defendant's non-appearance; but security could be given in less simple form if the justice of the case demanded it and it could be readily forfeited, in the event of non-appearance, without complicated disputes about third party rights; and whilst it was permissible for a third party to make available an asset to the defendant in order to enable him to give it as security, where a court failed to make clear the extent to which a third party's interest in registered land belonging to the defendant was the subject of the security, the security was to be interpreted as extending only to the defendant's beneficial interest; loose reference to "title deeds" in respect of registered land was likely to cause difficulty.

It is open to a court imposing a curfew condition also to impose a "doorstep condition" requiring the defendant during the hours of his curfew to present himself at the door of his premises if requested to do so by a police officer, provided only that this appeared necessary for securing any or all of the purposes listed in paragraphs (a) to (c) of subsection (6): *R. (CPS) v. Chorley JJ.*, 166 J.P. 764, DC.

In *McDonald v. Procurator Fiscal, Elgin, The Times*, April 17, 2003, the High Court of Justiciary held that whilst a bail condition requiring the defendant to remain in his dwelling at all times, save between 10 a.m. and midday, constituted a "restriction" on liberty, it did not amount to a "deprivation of liberty", so as to engage Article 5 of the ECHR (*post*, § 16–43).

Bail Act 1976, s.3AA

Electronic monitoring of compliance with bail conditions [Conditions for the imposition of electronic monitoring requirements: children and young persons]

3AA.—(1) A court *shall not impose on a child or young person a requirement under* **3–12**

section 3(6ZAA) above (an "electronic monitoring requirement") [may not impose electronic monitoring requirements on a child or young person] unless each of the following conditions is *satisfied* [met].

(2) The first condition is that the child or young person has attained the age of twelve years.

(3) The second condition is that—

(a) the child or young person is charged with or has been convicted of a violent or sexual offence, or an offence punishable in the case of an adult with imprisonment for a term of fourteen years or more; or

(b) he is charged with or has been convicted of one or more imprisonable offences which, together with any other imprisonable offences of which he has been convicted in any proceedings—

(i) amount, or

(ii) would, if he were convicted of the offences with which he is charged, amount,

to a recent history of repeatedly committing imprisonable offences while remanded on bail or to local authority accommodation.

(4) The third condition is that the court [is satisfied that the necessary provision for dealing with the person concerned can be made under arrangements for the electronic monitoring of persons released on bail that are currently available in each local justice area which is a relevant area]—

(a) *has been notified by the Secretary of State that electronic monitoring arrangements are available in each local justice area which is a relevant area; and*

(b) *is satisfied that the necessary provision can be made under those arrangements.*

(5) The fourth condition is that a youth offending team has informed the court that in its opinion the imposition of *such a requirement* [electronic monitoring requirements] will be suitable in the case of the child or young person.

(6) *Where a court imposes an electronic monitoring requirement, the requirement shall include provision for making a person responsible for the monitoring; and a person who is made so responsible shall be of a description specified in an order made by the Secretary of State.*

(7) *The Secretary of State may make rules for regulating—*

(a) *the electronic monitoring of compliance with requirements imposed on a child or young person as a condition of bail; and*

(b) *without prejudice to the generality of paragraph (a) above, the functions of persons made responsible for securing the electronic monitoring of compliance with such requirements.*

(8) *Rules under this section may make different provision for different cases.*

(9) *Any power of the Secretary of State to make an order or rules under this section shall be exercisable by statutory instrument.*

(10) *A statutory instrument containing rules made under this section shall be subject to annulment in pursuance of a resolution of either House of Parliament.*

(11) In this section "local authority accommodation" has the same meaning as in the *Children and Young Persons Act* 1969.

(12) *For the purposes of this section a local justice area is a relevant area in relation to a proposed electronic monitoring requirement if the court considers that it will not be practicable to secure the electronic monitoring in question unless electronic monitoring arrangements are available in that area.*

[This section is inserted by the *CJPA* 2001, s.131(2). It is printed as amended by the *Courts Act* 2003, s.109(1), and Sched. 8, para. 181. As from a day to be appointed, the words in square brackets are inserted, and the italicised words are omitted, by the *CJIA* 2008, s.51, and Sched. 11, paras 1 and 3.]

Bail Act 1976, ss.3AB, 3AC

[Conditions for the imposition of electronic monitoring requirements: other persons

3–12a **3AB.**—(1) A court may not impose electronic monitoring requirements on a person who has attained the age of seventeen unless each of the following conditions is met.

(2) The first condition is that the court is satisfied that without the electronic monitoring requirements the person would not be granted bail.

(3) The second condition is that the court is satisfied that the necessary provision for

dealing with the person concerned can be made under arrangements for the electronic monitoring of persons released on bail that are currently available in each local justice area which is a relevant area.

(4) If the person is aged seventeen, the third condition is that a youth offending team has informed the court that in its opinion the imposition of electronic monitoring requirements will be suitable in his case.]

[Electronic monitoring: general provisions

3AC.—(1) Where a court imposes electronic monitoring requirements as a condition of bail, the requirements must include provision for making a person responsible for the monitoring. **3–12b**

(2) A person may not be made responsible for the electronic monitoring of a person on bail unless he is of a description specified in an order made by the Secretary of State.

(3) The Secretary of State may make rules for regulating—

(a) the electronic monitoring of persons on bail;

(b) without prejudice to the generality of paragraph (a), the functions of persons made responsible for such monitoring.

(4) The rules may make different provision for different cases.

(5) Any power of the Secretary of State to make an order or rules under this section is exercisable by statutory instrument.

(6) A statutory instrument containing rules under this section shall be subject to annulment in pursuance of a resolution of either House of Parliament.

(7) For the purposes of section 3AA or 3AB a local justice area is a relevant area in relation to a proposed electronic monitoring requirement if the court considers that it will not be practicable to secure the electronic monitoring in question unless electronic monitoring arrangements are available in that area.

(8) Nothing in sections 3, 3AA or 3AB is to be taken to require the Secretary of State to ensure that arrangements are made for the electronic monitoring of persons released on bail.]

[Ss.3AB and 3AC are inserted, as from a day to be appointed, by the *CJIA* 2008, s.51, and Sched. 11, paras 1 and 4.]

Bail Act 1976, s.3A

General provisions

3A.—(1) Section 3 of this Act applies, in relation to bail granted by a custody officer under Part IV of the *Police and Criminal Evidence Act* 1984 or Part 3 of the *Criminal Justice Act* 2003 in cases where the normal powers to impose conditions of bail are available to him, subject to the following modifications. **3–13**

(2) Subsection (6) does not authorise the imposition of a requirement to reside in a bail hostel or any requirement under paragraph (d) or (e).

(3) Subsections (6ZAA), (6ZA) and (6A) to (6F) shall be omitted.

(4) For subsection (8), substitute the following—

"(8) Where a custody officer has granted bail in criminal proceedings he or another custody officer serving at the same police station may, at the request of the person to whom it was granted, vary the conditions of bail; and in doing so he may impose conditions or more onerous conditions.".

(5) Where a constable grants bail to a person no conditions shall be imposed under subsections (4), (5), (6) or (7) of section 3 of this Act unless it appears to the constable that it is necessary to do so … —

(a) for the purpose of preventing that person from failing to surrender to custody, or

(b) for the purpose of preventing that person from committing an offence while on bail, or

(c) for the purpose of preventing that person from interfering with witnesses or otherwise obstructing the course of justice, whether in relation to himself or any other person, or

(d) for that person's own protection or, if he is a child or young person, for his own welfare or in his own interests.

(6) Subsection (5) above also applies on any request to a custody officer under subsection (8) of section 3 of this Act to vary the conditions of bail.

[This section was inserted by the *CJPOA* 1994, s.27(3); and is printed as amended by the *CDA* 1998, s.54(3); the *CJPA* 2001, s.131(4); the *CJA* 2003, ss.13(2) and 19(1) and (3); and the *PJA* 2006, s.52, and Sched. 14, para. 5.]

Bail Act 1976, s.4

General right to bail of accused persons and others

3–14 **4.**—(1) A person to whom this section applies shall be granted bail except as provided in Schedule 1 to this Act.

(2) This section applies to a person who is accused of an offence when—

(a) he appears or is brought before a magistrates' court or the Crown Court in the course of or in connection with proceedings for the offence, or

(b) he applies to a court for bail or for a variation of the conditions of bail in connection with the proceedings.

This subsection does not apply as respects proceedings on or after a person's conviction of the offence … .

(2A) This section also applies to a person whose extradition is sought in respect of an offence, when—

(a) he appears or is brought before a court in the course of or in connection with extradition proceedings in respect of the offence, or

(b) he applies to a court for bail or for a variation of the conditions of bail in connection with the proceedings.

(2B) But subsection (2A) above does not apply if the person is alleged to have been convicted of the offence.

(3) This section also applies to a person who, having been convicted of an offence, appears or is brought before a magistrates' court or the Crown Court *to be dealt with* under—

[(za) Schedule 1 to the *Powers of Criminal Courts (Sentencing) Act* 2000 (referral orders: referral back to appropriate court),

(zb) Schedule 8 to that Act (breach of reparation order),]

(a) *Part 2 of Schedule 3 to the* Powers of Criminal Courts (Sentencing) Act *2000 (breach of certain youth community orders)* [Schedule 2 to the *Criminal Justice and Immigration Act* 2008 (breach, revocation or amendment of youth rehabilitation orders)], or

(b) Part 2 of Schedule 8 to the *Criminal Justice Act* 2003 (breach of requirements of community order).

(4) This section also applies to a person who has been convicted of an offence and whose case is adjourned by the court for the purpose of enabling inquiries or a report to be made to assist the court in dealing with him for the offence.

(5) Schedule 1 to this Act also has effect as respects conditions of bail for a person to whom this section applies.

(6) In Schedule 1 to this Act "the defendant" means a person to whom this section applies and any reference to a defendant whose case is adjourned for inquiries or a report is a reference to a person to whom this section applies by virtue of subsection (4) above.

(7) This section is subject to section 41 of the *Magistrates' Courts Act* 1980 (restriction of bail by magistrates' court in cases of treason).

(8) This section is subject to section 25 of the *Criminal Justice and Public Order Act* 1994 (exclusion of bail in cases of homicide and rape).

(8A) *Where a custody time limit has expired this section shall have effect as if, in subsection (1), the words "except as provided in Schedule 1 to this Act" were omitted.*

(9) In taking any decisions required by Part I or II of Schedule 1 to this Act, the considerations to which the court is to have regard include, so far as relevant, any misuse of controlled drugs by the defendant ("controlled drugs" and "misuse" having the same meanings as in the *Misuse of Drugs Act* 1971).

[This section is printed as amended, and repealed in part, by the *MCA* 1980, Sched. 7; the *CJA* 1991, s.100 and Sched. 11, para. 21; the *CJPOA* 1994, s.168(2) and Sched. 10, paras 32 and 33; the *PCC(S)A* 2000, s.165(1) and Sched. 9, para. 52; the *CJCSA* 2000, s.58; the *Extradition Act* 2003, s.198(1), (4) and (5); the *CJA* 2003, s.304, and Sched. 32, paras 20 and 22; and the *PJA* 2006, s.42, and Sched. 13, para. 34. It should be noted that the *YJCEA* 1999, s.67(3), and Sched. 6 provide for the repeal, as from a day to be appointed, of para. 32 of Sched. 10 to the 1994 Act (inserting subs. (8)). It is not clear whether this is an error, or, if not, what the intended effect is, for there is no corresponding repeal of subs. (8). It is submitted that the repeal of the amending provision alone would not have the effect of undoing the amendment itself. Once an amendment takes effect, the enactment amended is to be construed as if it had always been so enacted. Error is the most likely explanation, in that the reference should have been to para. 32 of Schedule 9 to the 1994 Act, which amended section 32A(3B) of the *CJA* 1988, that provision being itself repealed by Schedule 6 to the 1999 Act. The words in italics in subs. (3) are omitted, and the words in square brackets are inserted, as from a day to be appointed, by the *CJIA* 2008, ss.6(2) and (3) and 149, Sched. 4, paras 23 and 102, and Sched. 28, Pt 1. These amendments (other than the insertion of paras (za) and (zb)) are of no effect in relation to any offence committed before they come into force or any failure to comply with an order made in respect of an offence committed before they come into force: *ibid.*, s.148(2), and Sched. 27, para. 1(1). Paras (za) and (zb) apply to orders made before, as well as after, they come into force: *ibid.*, para. 1(2).]

In a case to which a custody time limit applies, section 4 has effect as if subsection (8A) were inserted at the end thereof: *Prosecution of Offences (Custody Time Limits) Regulations* 1987 (S.I. 1987 No. 299), reg. 8 (as amended by S.I. 1995 No. 555), *post*, §§ 3–56, 3–65. **3–15**

This section applies in relation to the grant of bail by the Court of Appeal under section 90 of the *CJA* 2003 (*post*, § 7–276) as if in subsection (2) the reference to the Crown Court included a reference to the Court of Appeal: s.90(4) of the 2003 Act.

No bail where sentence deferred

Where sentence is deferred under the *PCC(S)A* 2000, s.1, no question of bail arises: *R. v. Ross*, 86 Cr.App.R. 337, Crown Court (Judge Rubin). **3–15a**

Applications for bail

As to applications in the Crown Court for bail generally, see rules 19.18 and 19.22 of the *Criminal Procedure Rules* 2005 (S.I. 2005 No. 384), *post*, §§ 3–181 *et seq.* An applicant for bail is not entitled to be present on the hearing of his application unless the Crown Court gives him leave: *ibid.* r.19(5). See also *post*, § 3–53. **3–16**

As to the desirability of any evidence as to the defendant's previous convictions being submitted to the court in writing, rather than given *viva voce*, see *R. v. Dyson*, 29 Cr.App.R. 104, CCA; and of any newspaper reporting the case not including in the report any mention of the previous convictions, see *R. v. Fletcher*, 113 J.P. 365, CCA. Under the *Criminal Procedure Rules* 2005 (S.I. 2005 No. 384), r.16.11(1) and (2)(a) (*ante*, § 2–153), the Crown Court's jurisdiction in relation to the hearing of applications for bail may be exercised by a judge sitting in chambers. In *R. (Malik) v. Central Criminal Court* [2006] 4 All E.R. 1141, DC, it was held: (i) that this gave rise to a discretion, rather than create a presumption; (ii) that the presumption should be in favour of a hearing in open court, but that there would be cases where it would be necessary to depart from the principle of open justice in the interests of justice itself; whether it was necessary to do so was a question of judgment and not an exercise of discretion. The court distinguished between hearings "in chambers" and hearings "in private", although the Court of Appeal in *Clibbery v. Allan* [2002] Fam. 261, equated hearings in chambers with hearings in private, but distinguished them from secret hearings. A non-secret chambers hearing is one to which the public and press should be allowed access on request: see *per* Lord Woolf in *Hodgson v. Imperial Tobacco Ltd* [1998] 1 W.L.R. 1056 at 1071–1072, CA (Civ. Div.). In *Malik*, the court said there would be many cases where there are good reasons for the court to sit in chambers, and a few where it would need to sit in private (*i.e.* secret); among the former would be those where the delay involved in arranging a public hearing would defeat the purpose of the application; reasons for a private hearing may be that it would be necessary for the prosecution to rehearse a damaging case against the defendant or a co-defendant, that they may have to give detailed reasons for a fear that he would abscond, that they may have to detail his previous convictions, or they may have to reveal personal and confidential information about him or prosecution witnesses or others. The court added that whilst this might affect day-to-day practice in the Crown Court, it did not follow that bail hearings would have to be listed and called on in open court and then adjourned to chambers if, and only if, a case was made for doing so; applications could be listed on the provisional assumption that the interests of justice would call for a closed hearing, so long as there was the possibility of an application (normally by the parties, but also legitimately by the press or other third parties) being made to sit in public. As to there being no general requirement under Article 5 of the ECHR (right to liberty (*post*, § 16–43)) for a public hearing to determine the lawfulness of pre-trial detention, see *Reinprecht v. Austria* (2007) 44 E.H.R.R. 39, ECtHR.

A judge or magistrate who has considered an application for bail and made known his decision cannot be regarded as *functus officio* as soon as he has stopped speaking. Common sense should be applied in considering the question when in practical terms the occasion has come to an end. For example, if having just granted conditional bail, a magistrate recalled the defendant to the dock and imposed a further condition, no objection could properly be taken. Likewise, it was open to him to withdraw bail: *R. v. Governor of Ashford Remand Centre, ex p. Harris* [1984] Crim.L.R. 618, DC.

Renewed applications for bail

3–17 On making an application to the Crown Court relating to bail, the applicant shall inform the court of any earlier application to the High Court or the Crown Court relating to bail in the course of the same proceedings: *Criminal Procedure Rules* 2005 (S.I. 2005 No. 384), r.19.18, *post*, § 3–183.

The Divisional Court considered the question of the extent of the obligation of courts of first instance to entertain renewed applications for bail in a number of cases prior to the amendments to the 1976 Act effected by the *CJA* 1988. The general effect of the decisions was that a court was not bound to entertain an application for bail, after it had previously been refused, unless it was satisfied that there had been a material change of circumstances. A decision to refuse bail presupposed that the court had found as a fact that there were substantial grounds for believing that one of the events described in paragraph 2(a), (b) or (c) of Schedule 1 to the Act (*post*, § 3–48) would occur. A later court was bound to accept that finding of fact, otherwise it would be acting as an appellate court unless there was a material change of circumstances. Committal for trial *per se* did not constitute a material change of circumstances. See *R. v. Nottingham JJ., ex p. Davies* [1981] Q.B. 38, 71 Cr.App.R. 178, DC; *R. v. Reading Crown Court, ex p. Malik* [1981] Q.B. 451, 72 Cr.App.R. 146, DC; and *R. v. Slough JJ., ex p. Duncan*, 75 Cr.App.R. 384, DC.

3–18 The *CJA* 1988, s.154, inserted a new Part IIA into Schedule 1 to the 1976 Act: see *post*, § 3–51. It appears that the intention was to provide a statutory solution to the problem of renewed applications for bail. Clearly the statutory provisions have precedence over the previous case law where they apply.

The combined effect of section 4 and Part IIA of Schedule 1, it is submitted, is as follows. At the first hearing at which the defendant is a person to whom section 4 applies, the court shall grant him bail unless satisfied that one of the exceptions under Part I or II of Schedule 1 is established. At the first hearing, the defendant may support an application for bail with any relevant argument as to fact or law. The court must, however, consider the question of bail regardless of whether or not any application for bail is made.

If, at the first hearing, bail is refused, the defendant's case then falls within paragraph 1 of Part IIA and at each subsequent hearing while he is a person to whom section 4 applies, the court is bound to consider the question of bail. Applications for further remands in the absence of the defendant under section 128(3A) of the *MCA* 1980 (*post*, § 3–148) are not hearings within paragraph 1 of Part IIA of Schedule 1. At such a hearing, section 4 does not apply to him, for he neither appears, nor is brought, before the court and makes no application for bail: see *R. v. Dover and East Kent JJ., ex p. Dean* [1992] Crim.L.R. 33, DC.

Paragraph 2 of Part IIA provides that at the first hearing after that at which the court decided not to grant the defendant bail he may support an application for bail with any argument as to fact or law, whether or not he has advanced that argument previously.

Although the paragraph does not say so in terms, the "hearing" referred to is clearly referable to a hearing at which the defendant is a person to whom section 4 applies. It does not, therefore, include the hearing of an application for the remand of the defendant in his absence under section 128(3A) of the 1980 Act: see *ex p. Dean*, *ante*. This was not the actual point decided in *ex p. Dean*, although it seems plain that this was the Divisional Court's view. Any other construction would make complete nonsense of the legislation.

The apparent intention of the legislation was to provide for any argument being advanced on two occasions as of right; the second court being bound to consider the matter *de novo*. In practice, however, this will frequently not be the result of the legislation. Paragraph 2 applies to the first hearing after "that at which the court decided not to grant the defendant bail": it is not restricted to decisions made at a hearing where a bail application is made. A defendant who appears in court having been charged with armed robbery the previous day comes within section 4(1) of the Act: he should be granted bail unless the court decides otherwise. Almost invariably the court will decide otherwise and, often, without a bail application being made on his behalf. When he next appears before the court, an application for bail may be made and any argument in support thereof may be made as of right. If bail is refused, however, he has no *right* to advance the same arguments a second time: see *post*, § 3–19, as to whether he *may* do so. If no application for bail is made at the first hearing after that at which the court decided not to grant the defendant bail, paragraph 2 does not apply so as to confer a right to make an application at any subsequent hearing, whether or not an application was made when bail was originally refused. However he has such a right by common law: see *ex p. Dean*, *ante*. This was the actual point decided. The Divisional Court held that there was always a right to make an application for bail: whether the justices were obliged to entertain certain arguments was a separate issue. It is submitted that where no application has previously been made, any relevant argument may be placed before the court, and the provisions of Part IIA in no way derogate from this principle. **3–18a**

Where justices decided that a defendant need not be granted bail because it had not been practicable to obtain sufficient information to decide whether or not to grant it (see paragraph 5 of Part I of Schedule 1, *post*, § 3–48), that was not a decision not to grant it within paragraph 1 of Part IIA: *R. v. Calder JJ., ex p. Kennedy* [1992] Crim.L.R. 496, DC.

Paragraph 3 of Part IIA provides that at hearings subsequent to the first hearing after the hearing at which the court decided to refuse bail the court need not hear arguments as to fact or law which it has heard previously. This implies that it may do so. It is submitted, however, that here the former case law does have some application and that, on the basis of that case law, the court should not hear arguments as to fact or law which it has previously heard unless there has been such a change of circumstances as might have affected the earlier decision: to do otherwise would be to act in an appellate capacity, contrary to the decision in *R. v. Slough JJ., ex p. Duncan*, *ante*. **3–19**

Bail Act 1976, s.5

Supplementary provisions about decisions on bail

5.—(1) Subject to subsection (2) below, where— **3–20**

(a) a court or constable grants bail in criminal proceedings, or

(b) a court withholds bail in criminal proceedings from a person to whom section 4 of this Act applies, or

(c) a court, officer of a court or constable appoints a time or place or a different time or place for a person granted bail in criminal proceedings to surrender to custody, or

(d) a court or constable varies any conditions of bail or imposes conditions in respect of bail in criminal proceedings,

that court, officer or constable shall make a record of the decision in the prescribed manner and containing the prescribed particulars and, if requested to do so by the person in relation to whom the decision was taken, shall cause him to be given a copy of the record of the decision as soon as practicable after the record is made.

(2) Where bail in criminal proceedings is granted by endorsing a warrant of arrest for

bail the constable who releases on bail the person arrested shall make the record required by subsection (1) above instead of the judge or justice who issued the warrant.

(2A) Where a magistrates' court or the Crown Court grants bail in criminal proceedings to a person to whom section 4 of this Act applies after hearing representations from the prosecutor in favour of withholding bail, then the court shall give reasons for granting bail.

(2B) A court which is by virtue of subsection (2A) above required to give reasons for its decision shall include a note of those reasons in the record of its decision and, if requested to do so by the prosecutor, shall cause the prosecutor to be given a copy of the record of the decision as soon as practicable after the record if made.

(3) Where a magistrates' court or the Crown Court—

(a) withholds bail in criminal proceedings, or

(b) imposes conditions in granting bail in criminal proceedings, or

(c) varies any conditions of bail or imposes conditions in respect of bail in criminal proceedings,

and does so in relation to a person to whom section 4 of this Act applies, then the court shall ... give reasons for withholding bail or for imposing or varying the conditions.

3–21 (4) A court which is by virtue of subsection (3) above required to give reasons for its decision shall include a note of those reasons in the record of its decision and shall (except in a case where, by virtue of subsection (5) below, this need not be done) give a copy of that note to the person in relation to whom the decision was taken.

(5) The Crown Court need not give a copy of the note of the reasons for its decision to the person in relation to whom the decision was taken where that person *is represented by counsel or a solicitor* [has legal representation] unless his *counsel or solicitor* [legal representative] requests the court to do so.

(6) Where a magistrates' court withholds bail in criminal proceedings from a person who *is not represented by counsel or a solicitor* [does not have legal representation], the court shall—

(a) if it is *committing* [sending] him for trial to the Crown Court or if it issues a certificate under subsection (6A) below inform him that he may apply ... to the Crown Court to be granted bail; ...

3–22 (6A) Where in criminal proceedings—

(a) a magistrates' court remands a person in custody under [section 52(5) of the *Crime and Disorder Act* 1998,] section 11 of the *Powers of Criminal Courts (Sentencing) Act* 2000 (remand for medical examination) or any of the following provisions of the *Magistrates' Courts Act* 1980—

(i) *section 5 (adjournment of inquiry into offence);*

(ii) section 10 (adjournment of trial); or

[(iia) section 17C (intention as to plea: adjournment), or]

(iii) section 18 (initial procedure on information against adult for offence triable either way), [or

(iv) section 24C (intention as to plea by child or young person: adjournment)],

after hearing full argument on an application for bail from him; and

(b) either—

(i) it has not previously heard such argument on an application for bail from him in those proceedings; or

(ii) it has previously heard full argument from him on such an application but it is satisfied that there has been a change in his circumstances or that new considerations have been placed before it,

it shall be the duty of the court to issue a certificate in the prescribed form that they heard full argument on his application for bail before they refused the application.

(6B) Where the court issues a certificate under subsection (6A) above in a case to which paragraph (b)(ii) of that subsection applies, it shall state in the certificate the nature of the change of circumstances or the new considerations which caused it to hear a further fully argued bail application.

(6C) Where a court issues a certificate under subsection (6A) above it shall cause the person to whom it refuses bail to be given a copy of the certificate.

3–23 (7) Where a person has given security in pursuance of section 3(5) above and a court is satisfied that he failed to surrender to custody then, unless it appears that he had reasonable cause for his failure, the court may order the forfeiture of the security.

(8) If a court orders the forfeiture of a security under subsection (7) above, the court may declare that the forfeiture extends to such amount less than the full value of the security as it thinks fit to order.

(8A) An order under subsection (7) above shall, unless previously revoked, take effect at the end of twenty-one days beginning with the day on which it is made.

(8B) A court which has ordered the forfeiture of a security under subsection (7) above may, if satisfied on an application made by or on behalf of the person who gave it that he did after all have reasonable cause for his failure to surrender to custody, by order remit the forfeiture or declare that it extends to such amount less than the full value of the security as it thinks fit to order.

(8C) An application under subsection (8B) above may be made before or after the order for forfeiture has taken effect, but shall not be entertained unless the court is satisfied that the prosecution was given reasonable notice of the applicant's intention to make it.

(9) A security which has been ordered to be forfeited by a court under subsection (7) above shall, to the extent of the forfeiture— **3–24**

(a) if it consists of money, be accounted for and paid in the same manner as a fine imposed by that court would be;

(b) if it does not consist of money, be enforced by such magistrates' court as may be specified in the order.

(9A) Where an order is made under subsection (8B) above after the order for forfeiture of the security in question has taken effect, any money which would have fallen to be repaid or paid over to the person who gave the security if the order under subsection (8B) had been made before the order for forfeiture took effect shall be repaid or paid over to him.

(10) In this section "prescribed" means, in relation to the decision of a court or an officer of a court, prescribed by Civil Procedure Rules, *Courts-Martial* [Court Martial] appeal rules or Criminal Procedure Rules, as the case requires or, in relation to a decision of a constable, prescribed by direction of the Secretary of State.

(11) This section is subject, in its application to bail granted by a constable, to section 5A of this Act.

[This section is printed as amended, and repealed in part, by the *CLA* 1977, Sched. 12; the *CJA* 1982, s.60(3); the *CJPOA* 1994, s.27(4), and Sched. 3, para. 1; the *PCC(S)A* 2000, s.165(1), and Sched. 9, para. 53; the *CJPA* 2001, s.129(1); the *Courts Act* 2003, s.109(1), and Sched. 8, para. 182; and the *CJA* 2003, s.332, and Sched. 37, Pts 2 and 12. It is printed as further amended by *ibid.*, s.41, and Sched. 3, para. 48(1) and (3) (substitution of word in square brackets for italicised word in subs. (6)(a), insertion of words in square brackets in subs. (6A)(a), repeal of subs. (6A)(a)(i), insertion of sub-paras (iia) and (iv) in subs. (6A)(a)). Apart from the omission of subs. (6A)(a)(i) and the insertion of subs. (6A)(a)(iia) and (iv), the latter amendments came into force on May 9, 2005, in relation to cases sent for trial under section 51 or 51A(3)(d) of the *CDA* 1998: *Criminal Justice Act 2003 (Commencement No. 9) Order* 2005 (S.I. 2005 No. 1267). Otherwise these amendments come into force on a day to be appointed. It should be noted that some of these amendments are duplicated (more or less exactly) by paragraph 2 of Schedule 36 to the 2003 Act. The latter provisions have been ignored here on the ground that a court would be likely to construe the Act on the basis that the more specific provisions of Schedule 3 took precedence over the more general provisions of Schedule 36. As from a day to be appointed, the *AFA* 2006, s.378(1), and Sched. 16, para. 74, substitute the words in square brackets for the italicised words in subs. (10). As from a further day to be appointed, the *Legal Services Act* 2007, s.208(1), and Sched. 21, paras 33 and 35, substitute the words in square brackets for the italicised words in subs. (5).]

Section 5 should be read in conjunction with rule 19.18(8) of the *Criminal Procedure Rules* 2005 (S.I. 2005 No. 384), *post*, § 3–182.

Bail Act 1976, s.5A

Supplementary provisions in cases of police bail

5A.—(1) Section 5 of this Act applies, in relation to bail granted by a custody officer under Part IV of the *Police and Criminal Evidence Act* 1984 or Part 3 of the *Criminal Justice Act* 2003 in cases where the normal powers to impose conditions of bail are available to him, subject to the following modifications. **3–25**

(1A) Subsections (2A) and (2B) shall be omitted.

(2) For subsection (3) substitute the following—

"(3) Where a custody officer, in relation to any person,—

(a) imposes conditions in granting bail in criminal proceedings, or

(b) varies any conditions of bail or imposes conditions in respect of bail in criminal proceedings,

the custody officer shall … give reasons for imposing or varying the conditions.".

(3) For subsection (4) substitute the following—

"(4) A custody officer who is by virtue of subsection (3) above required to give reasons for his decision shall include a note of those reasons in the custody record and shall give a copy of that note to the person in relation to whom the decision was taken.".

(4) Subsections (5) and (6) shall be omitted.

[This section was inserted by the *CJPOA* 1994, s.27(4), and Sched. 3, para. 2; and is printed as amended, and repealed in part, by the *CJPA* 2001, s.129(2); the *CJA* 2003, s.332, and Sched. 37, Pt 2; and the *PJA* 2006, s.52, and Sched. 14, para. 5.]

Bail Act 1976, ss.5B, 6

Reconsideration of decisions granting bail

3–26 **5B.**—(A1) This section applies in any of these cases—

(a) a magistrates' court has granted bail in criminal proceedings in connection with an offence to which this section applies or proceedings for such an offence;

(b) a constable has granted bail in criminal proceedings in connection with proceedings for such an offence;

(c) a magistrates' court or a constable has granted bail in connection with extradition proceedings.

(1) The court or the appropriate court in relation to the constable may, on application by the prosecutor for the decision to be reconsidered—

(a) vary the conditions of bail,

(b) impose conditions in respect of bail which has been granted unconditionally, or

(c) withhold bail.

(2) The offences to which this section applies are offences triable on indictment and offences triable either way.

(3) No application for the reconsideration of a decision under this section shall be made unless it is based on information which was not available to the court or constable when the decision was taken.

(4) Whether or not the person to whom the application relates appears before it, the magistrates' court shall take the decision in accordance with section 4(1) (and Schedule 1) of this Act.

(5) Where the decision of the court on a reconsideration under this section is to withhold bail from the person to whom it was originally granted the court shall—

(a) if that person is before the court, remand him in custody, and

(b) if that person is not before the court, order him to surrender himself forthwith into the custody of the court.

(6) Where a person surrenders himself into the custody of the court in compliance with an order under subsection (5) above, the court shall remand him in custody.

(7) A person who has been ordered to surrender to custody under subsection (5) above may be arrested without warrant by a constable if he fails without reasonable cause to surrender to custody in accordance with the order.

(8) A person arrested in pursuance of subsection (7) above shall be brought as soon as practicable, and in any event within 24 hours after his arrest, before a justice of the peace … and the justice shall remand him in custody.

In reckoning for the purposes of this subsection any period of 24 hours, no account shall be taken of Christmas Day, Good Friday or any Sunday.

(8A) Where the court, on a reconsideration under this section, refuses to withhold bail from a relevant person after hearing representations from the prosecutor in favour of withholding bail, then the court shall give reasons for refusing to withhold bail.

(8B) In subsection (8A) above, "relevant person" means a person to whom section 4(1) (and Schedule 1) of this Act is applicable in accordance with subsection (4) above.

(8C) A court which is by virtue of subsection (8A) above required to give reasons for its decision shall include a note of those reasons in any record of its decision and, if requested to do so by the prosecutor, shall cause the prosecutor to be given a copy of any such record as soon as practicable after the record is made.

(9) Criminal Procedure rules shall include provision—

(a) requiring notice of an application under this section and of the grounds for it to be given to the person affected, including notice of the powers available to the court under it;

(b) for securing that any representations made by the person affected (whether in writing or orally) are considered by the court before making its decision; and

(c) designating the court which is the appropriate court in relation to the decision of any constable to grant bail.

[This section was inserted by the *CJPOA* 1994, s.30; and is printed as amended by the *CJPA* 2001, s.129(3); the *Extradition Act* 2003, s.198(1) and (6); and the *Courts Act* 2003, s.109(1), and Sched. 8, para. 183.]

As to the procedure on reconsideration, see *post*, § 3–166a.

Offence of absconding by person released on bail

6.—(1) If a person who has been released on bail in criminal proceedings fails without reasonable cause to surrender to custody he shall be guilty of an offence. **3–27**

(2) If a person who—

(a) has been released on bail in criminal proceedings, and

(b) having reasonable cause therefore, has failed to surrender to custody,

fails to surrender to custody at the appointed place as soon after the appointed time as is reasonably practicable he shall be guilty of an offence.

(3) It shall be for the accused to prove that he had reasonable cause for his failure to surrender to custody.

(4) A failure to give to a person granted bail in criminal proceedings a copy of the record of the decision shall not constitute a reasonable cause for that person's failure to surrender to custody.

(5) An offence under subsection (1) or (2) above shall be punishable either on summary conviction or as if it were a criminal contempt of court.

(6) Where a magistrates' court convicts a person of an offence under subsection (1) or (2) above the court may, if it thinks—

(a) that the circumstances of the offence are such that greater punishment should be inflicted for that offence than the court has power to inflict, or

(b) in a case where it *commits* [sends] that person for trial to the Crown Court for another offence that it would be appropriate for him to be dealt with for the offence under subsection (1) or (2) above by the court before which he is tried for the other offence,

commit him in custody or on bail to the Crown Court for sentence.

(7) A person who is convicted summarily of an offence under subsection (1) or (2) above and is not committed to the Crown Court for sentence shall be liable to imprisonment for a term not exceeding 3 months or to a fine not exceeding level 5 on the standard scale or to both and a person who is so committed for sentence or is dealt with as for such a contempt shall be liable to imprisonment for a term not exceeding 12 months or to a fine or to both. **3–28**

(8) In any proceedings for an offence under subsection (1) or (2) above a document purporting to be a copy of the part of the prescribed record which relates to the time and place appointed for the person specified in the record to surrender to custody and to be duly certified to be a true copy of that part of the record shall be evidence of the time and place appointed for that person to surrender to custody.

(9) For the purposes of subsection (8) above— **3–29**

(a) "the prescribed record" means the record of the decision of the court, officer or constable made in pursuance of section 5(1) of this Act;

(b) the copy of the prescribed record is duly certified if it is certified by the appropriate officer of the court or, as the case may be, by the constable who took the decision or a constable designated for the purpose by the officer in charge of the police station from which the person to whom the record relates was released;

(c) "the appropriate officer" of the court is—

(i) in the case of a magistrates' court, the *justices' chief executive* [designated officer of the court];

(ii) in the case of the Crown Court, such officer as may be designated for the purpose in accordance with arrangements made by the Lord Chancellor;

(iii) in the case of the High Court, such officer as may be designated for the purpose in accordance with arrangements made by the Lord Chancellor;
(iv) in the case of the Court of Appeal, the registrar of criminal appeals or such other officer as may be authorised by him to act for the purpose;
(v) in the case of the *Courts-Martial* [Court Martial] Appeal Court, the registrar or such other officer as may be authorised by him to act for the purpose.

(10) Section 127 of the *Magistrates' Courts Act* 1980 shall not apply in relation to an offence under subsection (1) or (2) above.

(11) Where a person has been released on bail in criminal proceedings and that bail was granted by a constable, a magistrates' court shall not try that person for an offence under subsection (1) or (2) above in relation to that bail (the "relevant offence") unless either or both of subsections (12) and (13) below applies.

(12) This subsection applies if an information is laid for the relevant offence within 6 months from the time of the commission of the relevant offence.

(13) This subsection applies if an information is laid for the relevant offence no later than 3 months from the time of the occurrence of the first of the events mentioned in subsection (14) below to occur after the commission of the relevant offence.

(14) Those events are—
(a) the person surrenders to custody at the appointed place;
(b) the person is arrested, or attends a police station, in connection with the relevant offence or the offence for which he was granted bail;
(c) the person appears or is brought before a court in connection with the relevant offence or the offence for which he was granted bail.

[This section is printed as amended by the *Access to Justice Act* 1999, s.90(1) and Sched. 13, para. 89; the *CJA* 2003, s.15(3); and the *Courts Act* 2003, s.109(1), and Sched. 8, para. 184. The italicised word in subs. (6)(b) is substituted by the word in square brackets by the *CJA* 2003, s.41, and Sched. 3, para. 48(1) and (4). This amendment came into force on May 9, 2005, in relation to cases sent for trial under section 51 or 51A(3)(d) of the *CDA* 1998: *Criminal Justice Act 2003 (Commencement No. 9) Order* 2005 (S.I. 2005 No. 1267). Otherwise it comes into force on a day to be appointed. The italicised words in subs. (9)(c)(v) are substituted by the words in square brackets as from a day to be appointed: *AFA* 2006, s.378(1), and Sched. 16, para. 75.]

As to "the standard scale", see *post*, § 5–403.

"Surrender to custody"

3–30 The offence of failing to surrender to custody is committed by a person who surrenders to custody late, even if only slightly (here, 30 minutes); the proper construction of the 1976 Act (considering, in particular, s.2(2) (*ante*, § 3–7)) is that surrendering to custody means surrendering at the appointed time and place; this cannot be glossed over so as to allow for some unidentified further margin by any permissible process of statutory interpretation: *R. v. Scott (Casim)*, 172 J.P. 149, CA (disapproving *R. v. Gateshead JJ., ex p. Usher* [1981] Crim.L.R. 491, DC (*de minimis* principle should be applied if defendant only marginally late)).

The obligation of a person on bail is to comply with the procedures of the court where he is due to appear and to report to the appropriate person. He is then in custody, being under an implied obligation not to leave without consent: if he does so, he is liable to be arrested under section 7(2): *DPP v. Richards* [1988] Q.B. 701, DC. It might be that courts would have to consider making it clear to persons who had reported to the appropriate officer that thereafter they were in custody and, even if they were allowed to sit in the concourse, they were not permitted to leave the building without consent. In *R. v. Central Criminal Court, ex p. Guney* [1996] A.C. 616, HL, it was held that when a defendant who has not previously surrendered to custody is arraigned, he thereby surrenders to the custody of the court.

The offence under section 6, consisting of a failure to answer bail, will not be committed by a person who fails to appear in answer to a summons: *R. v. Noble*, *The Times*, July 21, 2008, CA (see also *post*, § 28–58).

"Reasonable cause" for failure to answer bail

3–30a In *Laidlaw v. Atkinson*, *The Times*, August 2, 1986, DC, it was held that there was no reasonable cause for failure to surrender to custody where the defendant, because he handed his charge sheet to his solicitor without making any note of the date on which he was to surrender, mistakenly formed the opinion that he was to surrender on a later date. McCowan J. said that it was not suggested that the failure was deliberate. The reasons outlined played a part in the defendant's confusion and could be said to amount to mitigation, but there was no question of anything having arisen to prevent his attendance. The error was his responsibility. Whether a mistake by a solicitor (giving the defendant the wrong date) amounted to a reasonable excuse was a question of fact to be decided in all the circumstances of the particular case: *R. v. Liverpool City JJ., ex p. Santos*, *The Times*, January 23, 1997, DC.

Procedure

Where a defendant failed to appear at court one morning during the course of his trial (he had become very drunk the night before) the judge, at the conclusion of the trial dealt with the matter summarily as if it were contempt of court and sentenced him to three months' imprisonment. The Court of Appeal approved the course taken by the judge but reduced the sentence to one month: *R. v. Singh (Harbax)* [1979] Q.B. 319, 68 Cr.App.R. 108, CA. In dealing summarily with an offence under section 6 as if it were a criminal contempt, a judge is not precluded from activating a suspended sentence: *R. v. Tyson*, 68 Cr.App.R. 314, CA. **3–31**

In *Schiavo v. Anderton* [1987] Q.B. 20, 83 Cr.App.R. 228, DC, the court gave guidance as to the steps to be taken in the event of a failure by a defendant who had been granted bail to surrender to custody contrary to section 6. On a proper construction of section 6, Parliament intended the following effects:

(a) both the Crown Court and the magistrates' court each required, separately, a power to punish the offence of absconding;
(b) the offence is not subject to the general rule that trial was to be commenced by the laying of an information;
(c) the offence is not triable either way or on indictment;
(d) the offence is only triable by the court in respect of which a failure to surrender had occurred.

The offence is subject to the usual appellate procedures, and justices have power to commit to the Crown Court for sentence if satisfied that their own powers are insufficient: *ibid*. The court's guidance as to who should initiate proceedings, and as to the appropriate stage for dealing with a *Bail Act* offence has been overtaken by the consolidated criminal practice direction (*post*, §§ 3–32a *et seq*.). See, in particular, paragraphs I.13.5 to I.13.9.

The provision in section 6(5) for dealing with an offence contrary to section 6(1) "as if it were a criminal contempt of court" does not convert the offence into one of contempt; it merely provides an alternative procedure. The offence remains an offence contrary to section 6(1): *R. v. Lubega*, 163 J.P. 221, CA.

Practice direction

Paragraph 56 of the consolidated criminal practice direction has been replaced by a new paragraph 13, which was added at the end of Part I of the practice direction. The preamble declared it to have taken account of the decisions of the Court of Appeal in *R. v. McKinnon and White* [2003] 2 Cr.App.R.(S.) 29, CA (*post*, § 3–35), and of the House of Lords in *R. v. Jones (Anthony)* [2003] 1 A.C. 1 (*post*, § 3–197). Those parts of it which have been superseded by the Sentencing Guidelines Council's definitive guideline in relation to sentencing for offences under section 6 (Appendix K–107 *et seq*.) have been omitted. **3–32**

Practice Direction (Criminal Proceedings: Consolidation), para. I.13
[2004] 1 W.L.R. 589

Failure to surrender

I.13.1 The following directions take effect immediately. **3–32a**

I.13.2 The failure of the defendants [*sic*] to comply with the terms of their bail by not surrendering can undermine the administration of justice. It can disrupt proceedings. The resulting delays impact on victims, witnesses and other court users and also waste costs. A defendant's failure to surrender affects not only the case with which he is concerned, but also the courts' ability to administer justice more generally by damaging the confidence of victims, witnesses and the public in the effectiveness of the court system and the judiciary. It is, therefore most important that defendants who are granted bail appreciate the significance of the obligation to surrender to custody in accordance with the terms of their bail and that courts take appropriate action if they fail to do so.

I.13.3 There are at least three courses of action for the courts to consider taking:—

(a) imposing penalties for the failure to surrender;

(b) revoking bail or imposing more stringent bail conditions; and

(c) conducting trials in the absence of the defendant.

Penalties for failure to surrender

3–32b **I.13.4** …

I.13.5 … If there is no good reason for postponing dealing with the breach until after the trial, the breach should be dealt with as soon as practicable. If the disposal of the breach of bail is deferred, … bail should usually be revoked in the meantime (see I.13.14 to 16). In the case of offences which cannot, or are unlikely to, result in a custodial sentence, trial in the absence of the defendant may be a pragmatic sensible response to the situation (see I.13.17 to I.13.19). This is not a penalty for the *Bail Act* offence and a penalty may also be imposed for the *Bail Act* offence.

Initiating proceedings—bail granted by a police officer

I.13.6 When a person has been granted bail by a police officer to attend court and subsequently fails to surrender to custody, the decision whether to initiate proceedings for a section 6(1) or section 6(2) offence will be for the police/prosecutor.

I.13.7 The offence in this form is a summary offence and should be initiated as soon as practicable after the offence arises in view of the six month time limit running from the failure to surrender. It should be dealt with on the first appearance after arrest, unless an adjournment is necessary, as it will be relevant in considering whether to grant bail again.

Initiating proceedings—bail granted by a court

I.13.8 When a person has been granted bail by a court and subsequently fails to surrender to custody, on arrest that person should normally be brought as soon as appropriate before the court at which the proceedings in respect of which bail was granted are to be heard. (The six months time limit does not apply where bail was granted by the court.) Should the defendant commit another offence outside the jurisdiction of the bail court, the *Bail Act* offence should, where practicable, be dealt with by the new court at the same time as the new offence. If impracticable, the defendant may, if this is appropriate, be released formally on bail by the new court so that the warrant may be executed for his attendance before the first court in respect of the substantive and *Bail Act* offences.

I.13.9 Given that bail was granted by a court, it is more appropriate that the court itself should initiate the proceedings by its own motion. The court will be invited to take proceedings by the prosecutor, if the prosecutor considers proceedings are appropriate.

Conduct of proceedings

I.13.10 Proceedings under section 6 of the *Bail Act* 1976 may be conducted either as a summary offence or as a criminal contempt of court. Where the court is invited to take proceedings by the prosecutor, the prosecutor will conduct the proceedings and, if the matter is contested, call the evidence. Where the court initiates proceedings without such an invitation the same role can be played by the prosecutor at the request of the court, where this is practicable.

I.13.11 The burden of proof is on the defendant to prove that he had reasonable cause for his failure to surrender to custody (s.6(3) of the *Bail Act* 1976).

Proceedings to be progressed to disposal as soon as is practicable

I.13.12 If the court decides to proceed, the section 6 *Bail Act* 1976 offence should be concluded as soon as practicable.

I.13.13 [*Sentencing for a Bail Act offence*]

Relationship between the Bail Act offence and further remands on bail or in custody

I.13.14 When a defendant has been convicted of a *Bail Act* offence, the court should review the remand status of the defendant, including the conditions of that bail, in respect of the main proceedings for which bail had been granted. **3–32c**

I.13.15 Failure by the defendant to surrender or a conviction for failing to surrender to bail in connection with the main proceedings will be a significant factor weighing against the re-granting of bail or, in the case of offences which do not normally give rise to a custodial sentence, in favour of trial in the absence of the offender.

I.13.16 Whether or not an immediate custodial sentence has been imposed for the *Bail Act* offence, the court may, having reviewed the defendant's remand status, also remand the defendant in custody in the main proceedings.

Trials in absence

I.13.17 A defendant has a right, in general, to be present and to be represented at his trial. However, a defendant may choose not to exercise those rights by voluntarily absenting himself and failing to instruct his lawyers adequately so that they can represent him and, in the case of proceedings before the magistrates' court, there is an express statutory power to hear trials in the defendant's absence (s.11 of the *Magistrates' Courts Act* 1980). In such circumstances, the court has discretion whether the trial should take place in his/her absence. **3–32d**

I.13.18 The court must exercise its discretion to proceed in the absence of the defendant with the utmost care and caution. The overriding concern must be to ensure that such a trial is as fair as circumstances permit and leads to a just outcome.

I.13.19 Due regard should be had to the judgment of Lord Bingham in *R. v. Jones* [as to which, see *post*, § 3–198]. Other relevant considerations are the seriousness of the offence and likely outcome if the defendant is found guilty. If the defendant is only likely to be fined for a summary offence this can be relevant since the costs that a defendant might otherwise be ordered to pay as a result of an adjournment could be disproportionate. In the case of summary proceedings the fact that there can be an appeal that is a complete rehearing is also relevant, as is the power to re-open the case under section 142 of the *Magistrates' Courts Act* 1980.

As to the time limit on proceedings where bail was granted by the police, and the disapplication of the general time limit on proceedings for a summary offence, see subsections (10) to (14) of section 6 of the 1976 Act, *ante*. As to the position prior to the insertion of these provisions by the *CJA* 2003, see *Murphy v. DPP*, 91 Cr.App.R. 96, DC. **3–33**

In *France v. Dewsbury Magistrates' Court* [1988] Crim.L.R. 295, DC, it was held that it was not open to justices to proceed of their own motion to deal with a failure to answer to bail when at an earlier date a different court had agreed not to deal with the matter. On the earlier occasion, the justices, having heard the defendant's explanation, conferred and then told him that they accepted his explanation. His unconditional bail was renewed. The Divisional Court said that it was clear that the failure to answer to bail was being overlooked and would not be dealt with. It was then a case of *res judicata*. **3–34**

Affording an opportunity to be heard

As to the importance, where a court decides of its own motion to deal with a failure to answer bail as if it were a contempt of court, of affording the defendant an opportunity to give an explanation, and of inviting submissions from his counsel, see *R. v. Davis (Seaton Roy)*, 8 Cr.App.R.(S.) 64, CA. If the defendant is unrepresented the court should give him the chance of legal representation for the purposes of explaining why he absented himself, or at least the opportunity to explain himself: *ibid.* and *R. v. Woods*, 11 Cr.App.R.(S.) 551, CA. **3–34a**

Sentence

See now the Sentencing Guidelines Council's definitive guideline in relation to sentencing for offences under section 6 (Appendix K–107 *et seq.*). **3–35**

Appeal

An appeal lies as of right against any order or decision of the Crown Court in exercise of its power to deal with an offence under section 6(1) or (2) as a criminal contempt of court under section 6(5). This is the effect of the *Administration of Justice Act* 1960, s.13(1), (2)(bb) and (5)(a) (*post*, §§ 28–138 *et seq.*): *R. v. Maguire (Joseph)*, *The Times*, **3–36**

July 1, 1992, CA. In connection with such appeals, see RSC, Ord. 109 (as set out in Sched. 1 to the *Civil Procedure Rules* 1998 (S.I. 1998 No. 3132)), as amended by the *Civil Procedure (Amendment) Rules* 2000 (S.I. 2000 No. 221). This governs the giving of notice of appeal and the grant of bail pending appeal.

It was held in *R. v. Manchester Crown Court, ex p. Massey* [2000] 2 *Archbold News* 1, DC, that judicial review lies in respect of a decision of the Crown Court in relation to an offence under section 6(1). No counsel appeared in opposition to the application, and it is submitted that the decision is wrong as it overlooks the express provision made by section 13 of the 1960 Act, to which no reference was made.

Bail Act 1976, s.7

Liability to arrest for absconding or breaking conditions of bail

3–37 **7.**—(1) If a person who has been released on bail in criminal proceedings and is under a duty to surrender into the custody of a court fails to surrender at the time appointed for him to do so the court may issue a warrant for his arrest.

(1A) Subsection (1B) applies if—

(a) a person has been released on bail in connection with extradition proceedings,

(b) the person is under a duty to surrender into the custody of a constable, and

(c) the person fails to surrender to custody at the time apppointed for him to do so.

(1B) A magistrates' court may issue a warrant for the person's arrest.

(2) If a person who has been released on bail in criminal proceedings absents himself from the court at any time after he has surrendered into the custody of the court and before the court is ready to begin or to resume the hearing of the proceedings, the court may issue a warrant for his arrest; but no warrant shall be issued under this subsection where that person is absent in accordance with leave given to him by or on behalf of the court.

(3) A person who has been released on bail in criminal proceedings and is under a duty to surrender into the custody of a court may be arrested without warrant by a constable—

(a) if the constable has reasonable grounds for believing that that person is not likely to surrender to custody;

(b) if the constable has reasonable grounds for believing that that person is likely to break any of the conditions of his bail or has reasonable grounds for suspecting that that person has broken any of those conditions; or

(c) in a case where that person was released on bail with one or more surety or sureties, if a surety notifies a constable in writing that that person is unlikely to surrender to custody and that for that reason the surety wishes to be relieved of his obligations as a surety.

(4) A person arrested in pursuance of subsection (3) above—

(a) shall, except where he was arrested within 24 hours of the time appointed for him to surrender to custody, be brought as soon as practicable and in any event within 24 hours after his arrest before a justice of the peace ...; and

(b) in the said excepted case shall be brought before the court at which he was to have surrendered to custody.

(4A) A person who has been releaed on bail in connection with extradition proceedings and is under a duty to surender into the custody of a constable may be arrested without warrant by a constable on any of the grounds set out in paragraphs (a) to (c) of subsection (3).

(4B) A person arrested in pursuance of subsection (4A) above shall be brought as soon as practicable and in any event within 24 hours after his arrest before a justice of the peace for the petty sessions area in which he was arrested.

3–38 (5) A justice of the peace before whom a person is brought under subsection (4) or (4B) above may, subject to subsection (6) below, if of the opinion that that person—

(a) is not likely to surrender to custody, or

(b) has broken or is likely to break any condition of his bail,

remand him in custody or commit him to custody, as the case may require, or alternatively, grant him bail subject to the same or to different conditions, but if not of that opinion shall grant him bail subject to the same conditions (if any) as were originally imposed.

(6) Where the person so brought before the justice is a child or young person and the justice does not grant him bail, subsection (5) above shall have effect subject to the provisions of section 23 of the *Children and Young Persons Act* 1969 (remands to the care of local authorities).

(7) In reckoning for the purposes of this section any period of 24 hours, no account shall be taken of Christmas Day, Good Friday or any Sunday.

(7) *Where a custody time limit has expired this section shall have effect as if, in subsection (3), paragraphs (a) and (c) were omitted.*

[This section is printed as amended by the *CLA* 1977, Sched. 12; the *Extradition Act* 2003, s.198(1), and (7) to (11) (including by inserting the first of the subsections numbered (7)); and the *Courts Act* 2003, s.109(1), and Sched. 8, para. 185.]

In a case to which a custody time limit applies, section 7 has effect as if the second subsection (7) were inserted at the end thereof: *Prosecution of Offences (Custody Time Limits) Regulations* 1987 (S.I. 1987 No. 299), reg. 8, *post*, § 3–65.

For a corresponding provision conferring a power of arrest on officers of Revenue and Customs, see the *CJA* 1988, s.151, *post*, § 3–66a.

As to section 23 of the 1969 Act, see *post*, § 3–69.

In *R. v. Guildhall JJ., ex p. Prushinowski, The Times*, December 14, 1985, DC, it **3–39** was held that before a defendant who had been refused bail and who was the subject of a warrant of arrest applied to the Divisional Court for relief, he should first exhaust the remedy available to him in the Crown Court under the *Supreme Court [Senior Courts] Act* 1981, s.81 (*post*, § 3–175) (as to the renaming of this Act, see *ante*, § 3–8). The tentative view was expressed by Watkins L.J. that, in the absence of bias or ill-will, the court had no power to review the exercise of a justice's discretion under section 7(1).

Where a person arrested under this section is brought before a justice of the peace, pursuant to section 7(4)(a), the justice is bound to deal with the matter under subsection (5); he has no power to commit to the Crown Court in custody even in a case where bail was granted by the Crown Court: *R. v. Teesside Magistrates' Court, ex p. Ellison*, 165 J.P. 355, DC.

A justice of the peace, acting under section 7(5), had first to determine whether there had been a breach of any bail condition where that was alleged. No question of reasonable excuse arose at this stage. If there had been a breach, the next question was whether bail should be renewed, as to which any excuse for the breach would be relevant: *R. (Vickers) v. West London Magistrates' Court*, 167 J.P. 473, QBD (Gage J.).

Where a person arrested under section 7(3) is not brought before a justice within 24 hours, as required by section 7(4), he has an absolute right to be set free; bringing him within the precincts of a magistrates' court within 24 hours is not sufficient for this purpose: *R. v. Governor of Glen Parva Young Offender Institution, ex p. G. (a minor)* [1998] 2 Cr.App.R. 349, DC. Furthermore, the court must complete its investigation and decision-making under subsection (5) within the 24-hour period (from arrest) stipulated in subsection (4); there is no power to adjourn the proceedings and once that period has expired, everything done by the court thereafter is *ultra vires* and unlawful: *R. (Culley) v. Crown Court sitting at Dorchester*, 171 J.P. 373, QBD (Forbes J.) (in which the court observed, *obiter*, that a court would be entitled to conclude that there had been a breach of a curfew condition from the fact that the person concerned did not answer the door to his home when the police had knocked on it).

The procedure provided for by section 7(5) is not a trial or hearing governed by section 121 of the *MCA* 1980 requiring at least two justices: *R. v. Liverpool City JJ., ex p. DPP*, 95 Cr.App.R. 222, DC. A justice has no power to adjourn such a hearing: if he is not of the opinion that the case falls within either sub-paragraph (a) or (b) his duty is to release the arrested person on the same conditions as before: *ibid*. But neither section 7(5), nor section 121(6) of the *MCA* 1980 ("... the justices composing the court before which any proceedings take place shall be present during the whole of the proceedings ...") prevent a bench before whom the arrestee is originally brought from adjourning the matter for another bench to deal with later in the day where it is apparent that the first bench will not have time to deal with the matter: *R. (Hussain) v. Derby Magistrates' Court* [2001] 1 W.L.R. 2454, DC.

The procedure provided for by section 7(5) does not involve the determination of a criminal charge within Article 6(1) of the ECHR (*post*, § 16–57); and Article 5 (*post*, § 16–43) neither requires that the underlying facts relevant to the justice's decision need to be proved to the criminal standard, nor that the justice should be restricted to the consideration of admissible evidence. All that was necessary was that the justice, when forming his opinion, took proper account of the quality of the material upon which he was being asked to adjudicate, and afforded the defendant a proper opportunity to answer the material, by being allowed to cross-examine any witness who gave oral evidence and by being able to give evidence in person. As to the exception to the right to bail specified in paragraphs 6 and 5 of Parts I and II respectively of Schedule 1 to the 1976 Act (*viz.* that the defendant had been arrested under section 7(3)), this was not to be construed as meaning that the mere fact of an arrest under that subsection could justify a denial of bail; rather, it was to be construed as meaning that such an arrest could be taken into account in deciding whether any of the grounds for refusing bail set out in paragraph 2 of Part I or II had been made out: *R. (DPP) v. Havering Magistrates' Court*; *R. (McKeown) v. Wirral Borough Magistrates Court* [2001] 2 Cr.App.R. 2, DC.

Bail Act 1976, s.8

Bail with sureties

3–40 **8.**—(1) This section applies where a person is granted bail in criminal proceedings on condition that he provides one or more surety or sureties for the purpose of securing that he surrenders to custody.

(2) In considering the suitability for that purpose of a proposed surety, regard may be had (amongst other things) to—

(a) the surety's financial resources;

(b) his character and any previous convictions of his; and

(c) his proximity (whether in point of kinship, place of residence or otherwise) to the person for whom he is to be surety.

(3) Where a court grants a person bail in criminal proceedings on such a condition but is unable to release him because no surety or no suitable surety is available, the court shall fix the amount in which the surety is to be bound and subsections (4) and (5) below, or in a case where the proposed surety resides in Scotland subsection (6) below, shall apply for the purpose of enabling the recognizance of the surety to be entered into subsequently.

3–41 (4) Where this subsection applies the recognizance of the surety may be entered into before such of the following persons or descriptions of persons as the court may by order specify or, if it makes no such order, before any of the following persons, that is to say—

(a) where the decision is taken by magistrates' court, before a justice of the peace, a justices' clerk or a police officer who either is of the rank of inspector or above or is in charge of a police station or, if Criminal Procedure Rules so provide, by a person of such other description as is specified in the rules;

(b) where the decision is taken by the Crown Court, before any of the persons specified in paragraph (a) above or, if Criminal Procedure Rules so provide, by a person of such other description as is specified in the rules;

(c) where the decision is taken by the High Court or the Court of Appeal, before any of the persons specified in paragraph (a) above or, if Civil Procedure Rules or Criminal Procedure Rules so provide, by a person of such other description as is specified in the rules;

(d) where the decision is taken by the *Courts-Martial* [Court Martial] Appeal Court before any of the persons specified in paragraph (a) above or, if *Courts-Martial* [Court Martial] appeal rules so provide, by a person of such other description as is specified in the rules;

and Civil Procedure Rules, Criminal Procedure Rules or *Courts-Martial* [Court Martial] appeal rules may also prescribe the manner in which a recognizance which is to be entered into before such a person is to be entered into and the persons by whom and the manner in which the recognizance may be enforced.

3–42 (5) Where a surety seeks to enter into his recognizance before any person in accordance with subsection (4) above but that person declines to take his recognizance because he is not satisfied of the surety's suitability, the surety may apply to—

(a) the court which fixed the amount of the recognizance in which the surety was to be bound, or

(b) a magistrates' court,

for that court to take his recognizance and that court shall, if satisfied of his suitability, take his recognizance.

(6) Where this subsection applies, the court, if satisfied of the suitability of the proposed surety, may direct that arrangements be made for the recognizance of the surety to be entered into in Scotland before any constable, within the meaning of the *Police (Scotland) Act* 1967, having charge at any police office or station in like manner as the recognizance would be entered into in England or Wales.

(7) Where, in pursuance of subsection (4) or (6) above, a recognizance is entered into otherwise than before the court that fixed the amount of the recognizance, the same consequences shall follow as if it had been entered into before that court.

[This section is printed as amended by the *Courts Act* 2003, s.109(1), and Sched. 8, para. 186; and as amended, as from a day to be appointed, by the *AFA* 2006, s.378(1), and Sched. 16, para. 76 (substitution of words in square brackets for italicised words).]

Sureties

The bail must be of ability sufficient to answer for the sum in which they are bound: 2 Hawk. c. 15, s.4. It is for the magistrate or judge to act upon his discretion as to the sufficiency of the bail: *R. v. Saunders* (1849) 2 Cox 249; and the proposed bail may be examined upon oath as to his means. See *R. v. Hall* (1776) 2 W.Bl. 110. The court or magistrate may, at their discretion, order that reasonable notice shall be given to the prosecutor and the police, to enable him or them to inquire or object as to the sufficiency of the bail. It is not expedient to accept the solicitor of the accused as bail for his client: *R. v. Scott Jervis*, *The Times*, November 20, 1876, QBD. A person who has been indemnified by the accused person is not accepted as his bail. For the offence of agreeing to indemnify sureties in criminal proceedings, see the *Bail Act* 1976, s.9, *post*, § 3–46. Persons in custody cannot be bail. Infants cannot be bail. Personation of bail is an offence under the *Forgery Act* 1861, s.34 (*post*, § 22–63). **3–43**

Before a surety formally accepts the obligations imposed upon him it is the practice (a) to explain to him exactly what the obligations involve, (b) to ensure that he understands the obligations he is to undertake, (c) to ensure that he is still prepared to undertake the obligations and that he is worth the sum involved after all his debts are paid, and (d) to warn him of the consequences, which include possible imprisonment, if the defendant fails to appear when required to. **3–44**

As to when it may be necessary to review the position of a surety upon the defendant surrendering to the custody of the Crown Court, see *R. v. Kent Crown Court, ex p. Jodka*, and *Choudhry v. Birmingham Crown Court and H.M. Revenue & Customs*; *Hanson v. Same*, *ante*, § 3–11a.

If the condition of a recognizance entered into by a surety is broken, the recognizance may be forfeited, and on forfeiture the obligee becomes a debtor to the Crown for the sum in which he is bound: see *R. v. Southampton JJ., ex p. Green* [1976] Q.B. 11, CA, *per* Lord Denning M.R. at pp. 15, 19.

As to the considerations relevant to the exercise of the discretion, whether by a magistrates' court or by the Crown Court, see *post*, §§ 3–143 *et seq.*

As to notification of sureties of the date fixed for trial, or the likely date of trial, see *R. v. Reading Crown Court, ex p. Bello*, 92 Cr.App.R. 303, CA (Civ. Div.), *post*, § 3–144.

As to the procedure to be followed in the case of a surety who wishes to withdraw, see *Choudhry v. Birmingham Crown Court and H.M. Revenue & Customs*; *Hanson v. Same*, *ante*, § 3–11a.

Scottish sureties

Agreement has been reached on a procedure which it is suggested might be followed in cases where a court becomes aware, either from the defendant or from the police in Scotland, that a person in Scotland wishes to stand surety. This is as follows. The police in Scotland should be asked to make appropriate inquiries about the prospective surety to enable the court to decide on the person's suitability. It is for the English court alone to determine, from the information provided, whether the proposed surety is suitable and no discretion rests with the Scottish police officer concerned. If the court is satisfied of the surety's suitability, the clerk should write to the Scottish police officer explaining the procedure for taking the recognizance and enclosing the necessary forms. A specimen letter for the use of **3–45** courts has been agreed with the Scottish authorities. Three copies of the appropriate forms must accompany the letter, since stocks of these will not be held in Scotland. The court should complete each of the forms, leaving the Scottish police officer simply to obtain the surety's signature, to witness the signing, and to dispatch the appropriate documents in accordance with the instructions in the letter: see Home Office Circular No. 11/1978.

Bail Act 1976, s.9

Offence of agreeing to indemnify sureties in criminal proceedings

3–46 **9.**—(1) If a person agrees with another to indemnify that other against any liability which that other may incur as a surety to secure the surrender to custody of a person accused or convicted of or under arrest for an offence, he and that other person shall be guilty of an offence.

(2) An offence under subsection (1) above is committed whether the agreement is made before or after the person to be indemnified becomes a surety and whether or not he becomes a surety and whether the agreement contemplates compensation in money or in money's worth.

(3) Where a magistrates' court convicts a person of an offence under subsection (1) above the court may, if it thinks—

(a) that the circumstances of the offence are such that greater punishment should be inflicted for that offence than the court has power to inflict, or

(b) in a case where it *commits* [sends] that person for trial to the Crown Court for another offence, that it would be appropriate for him to be dealt with for the offence under subsection (1) above by the court before which he is tried for the other offence,

commit him in custody or on bail to the Crown Court for sentence.

(4) A person guilty of an offence under subsection (1) above shall be liable—

(a) on summary conviction, to imprisonment for a term not exceeding 3 months or to a fine not exceeding the prescribed sum or to both; or

(b) on conviction on indictment or if sentenced by the Crown Court on committal for sentence under subsection (3) above, to imprisonment for a term not exceeding 12 months or to a fine or to both.

(5) No proceedings for an offence under subsection (1) above shall be instituted except by or with the consent of the Director of Public Prosecutions.

[This section is printed as amended, as from a day to be appointed, by the *CJA* 2003, s.41, and Sched. 3, para. 48(1) and (5) (substitution of word in square brackets in subs. (3)(b) for italicised word). This amendment came into force on May 9, 2005, in relation to cases sent for trial under s.51 or 51A(3)(d) of the *CDA* 1998: *Criminal Justice Act 2003 (Commencement No. 9) Order* 2005 (S.I. 2005 No. 1267). Otherwise it comes into force on a day to be appointed.]

3–47 The reference to the "prescribed sum" was substituted by virtue of section 32(2) of the *MCA* 1980. The "prescribed sum" is currently £5,000: see s.32(9) of the 1980 Act, *ante*, § 1–75aa.

Bail Act 1976, s.9A

Bail decisions relating to persons aged under 18 who are accused of offences mentioned in Schedule 2 to the Magistrates' Courts Act 1980

3–47a **9A.**—(1) This section applies whenever—

(a) a magistrates' court is considering whether to withhold or grant bail in relation to a person aged under 18 who is accused of a scheduled offence; and

(b) the trial of that offence has not begun.

(2) The court shall, before deciding whether to withhold or grant bail, consider whether, having regard to any representations made by the prosecutor or the accused person, the value involved does not exceed the relevant sum for the purposes of section 22.

(3) The duty in subsection (2) does not apply in relation to an offence if—

(a) a determination under subsection (4) has already been made in relation to that offence; or

(b) the accused person is, in relation to any other offence of which he is accused which is not a scheduled offence, a person to whom Part 1 of Schedule 1 to this Act applies.

(4) If where the duty in subsection (2) applies it appears to the court clear that, for the

offence in question, the amount involved does not exceed the relevant sum, the court shall make a determination to that effect.

(5) In this section—

(a) "relevant sum" has the same meaning as in section 22(1) of the *Magistrates' Courts Act* 1980 (certain either way offences to be tried summarily if value involved is less than the relevant sum);

(b) "scheduled offence" means an offence mentioned in Schedule 2 to that Act (offences for which the value involved is relevant to the mode of trial); and

(c) "the value involved" is to be construed in accordance with section 22(10) to (12) of that Act.

[This section was inserted by the *CJIA* 2008, s.52, and Sched. 12, paras 1 and 3.]

Bail Act 1976, Sched. 1

SCHEDULE 1

PERSONS ENTITLED TO BAIL: SUPPLEMENTARY PROVISIONS

PART I

Defendants Accused or Convicted of Imprisonable Offences

Defendants to whom Part I applies

1.—(1) Subject to sub-paragraph (2), the following provisions of this Part of this Schedule apply to the defendant if— **3–48**

(a) the offence or one of the offences of which he is accused or convicted in the proceedings is punishable with imprisonment, or

(b) his extradition is sought in respect of an offence.

(2) But those provisions do not apply by virtue of sub-paragraph (1)(a) if the offence, or each of the offences punishable with imprisonment, is—

(a) a summary offence; or

(b) an offence mentioned in Schedule 2 to the *Magistrates' Courts Act* 1980 (offences for which the value involved is relevant to the mode of trial) in relation to which—

(i) a determination has been made under section 22(2) of that Act (certain either way offences to be tried summarily if value involved is less than the relevant sum) that it is clear that the value does not exceed the relevant sum for the purposes of that section; or

(ii) a determination has been made under section 9A(4) of this Act to the same effect.

Exceptions to right to bail

2.—(1) The defendant need not be granted bail if the court is satisfied that there are substantial grounds for believing that the defendant, if released on bail (whether subject to conditions or not) would—

(a) fail to surrender to custody, or

(b) commit an offence while on bail, or

(c) interfere with witnesses or otherwise obstruct the course of justice, whether in relation to himself or any other person.

(2) Where the defendant falls [within one or more of paragraphs 2A, 6 and] [[paragraph]] 6B of this Part of this Schedule, this paragraph shall not apply unless—

[(a) where the defendant falls within paragraph 2A, the court is satisfied as mentioned in sub-paragraph (1) of that paragraph;

(b) where the defendant falls within paragraph 6, the court is satisfied as mentioned in sub-paragraph (1) of that paragraph;]

(c) where the defendant falls within paragraph 6B, the court is satisfied as mentioned in paragraph 6A of this Part of this Schedule or paragraph 6A does not apply by virtue of paragraph 6C of this Part of this Schedule.

2A. *The defendant need not be granted bail if—*

(a) *the offence is an indictable offence or an offence triable either way; and*

(b) *it appears to the court that he was on bail in criminal proceedings on the date of the offence.*

[2A.—(1) If the defendant falls within this paragraph he may not be granted bail unless the court is satisfied that there is no significant risk of his committing an offence while on bail (whether subject to conditions or not).

(2) The defendant falls within this paragraph if—

(a) he is aged 18 or over, and

(b) it appears to the court that he was on bail in criminal proceedings on the date of the offence.]

2B. The defendant need not be granted bail in connection with extradition proceedings if—

(a) the conduct constituting the offence would, if carried out by the defendant in England and Wales, constitute an indictable offence or an offence triable either way; and

(b) it appears to the court that the defendant was on bail on the date of the offence.

3. The defendant need not be granted bail if the court is satisfied that the defendant should be kept in custody for his own protection or, if he is a child or young person, for his own welfare.

4. The defendant need not be granted bail if he is in custody in pursuance of *the* [a] sentence of a court or *of any authority acting under any of the Services Acts* [a sentence imposed by an officer under the *Armed Forces Act* 2006].

5. The defendant need not be granted bail where the court is satisfied that it has not been practicable to obtain sufficient information for the purpose of taking the decisions required by this Part of this Schedule for want of time since the institution of the proceedings against him.

6. *The defendant need not be granted bail if, having been released on bail in or in connection with the proceedings for the offence or the extradition proceedings, he has been arrested in pursuance of section 7 of this Act.*

[6.—(1) If the defendant falls within this paragraph, he may not be granted bail unless the court is satisfied that there is no significant risk that, if released on bail (whether subject to conditions or not), he would fail to surrender to custody.

(2) Subject to sub-paragraph (3) below, the defendant falls within this paragraph if—

(a) he is aged 18 or over, and

(b) it appears to the court that, having been released on bail in or in connection with the proceedings for the offence, he failed to surrender to custody.

(3) Where it appears to the court that the defendant had reasonable cause for his failure to surrender to custody, he does not fall within this paragraph unless it also appears to the court that he failed to surrender to custody at the appointed place as soon as reasonably practicable after the appointed time.

(4) For the purposes of sub-paragraph (3) above, a failure to give to the defendant a copy of the record of the decision to grant him bail shall not constitute a reasonable cause for his failure to surrender to custody.]

Exception applicable to drug users in certain areas

3–48a 6A. Subject to paragraph 6C below, a defendant who falls within paragraph 6B below may not be granted bail unless the court is satisfied that there is no significant risk of his committing an offence while on bail (whether subject to conditions or not).

6B.—(1) A defendant falls within this paragraph if—

(a) he is aged 18 or over;

(b) a sample taken—

(i) under section 63B of the *Police and Criminal Evidence Act* 1984 (testing for presence of Class A drugs) in connection with the offence; or

(ii) under section 161 of the *Criminal Justice Act* 2003 (drug testing after conviction of an offence but before sentence),

has revealed the presence in his body of a specified Class A drug;

(c) either the offence is one under section 5(2) or (3) of the *Misuse of Drugs Act* 1971 and relates to a specified Class A drug, or the court is satisfied that there are substantial grounds for believing—

(i) that misuse by him of any specified Class A drug caused or contributed to the offence; or

(ii) (even if it did not) that the offence was motivated wholly or partly by his intended misuse of such a drug; and

(d) the condition set out in sub-paragraph (2) below is satisfied or (if the court is considering on a second or subsequent occasion whether or not to grant bail) has been, and continues to be, satisfied.

(2) The condition referred to is that after the taking and analysis of the sample—

(a) a relevant assessment has been offered to the defendant but he does not agree to undergo it; or

(b) he has undergone a relevant assessment, and relevant follow-up has been proposed to him, but he does not agree to participate in it.

(3) In this paragraph and paragraph 6C below—

(a) "Class A drug" and "misuse" have the same meaning as in the *Misuse of Drugs Act* 1971;

(b) "relevant assessment" and "relevant follow-up" have the meaning given by section 3(6E) of this Act;

(c) "specified" (in relation to a Class A drug) has the same meaning as in Part 3 of the *Criminal Justice and Court Services Act* 2000.

6C. Paragraph 6A above does not apply unless—

(a) the court has been notified by the Secretary of State that arrangements for conducting a relevant assessment or, as the case may be, providing relevant follow-up have been made for the local justice area in which it appears to the court that the defendant would reside if granted bail; and

(b) the notice has not been withdrawn.

Exception applicable only to defendant whose case is adjourned for inquiries or a report

7. Where his case is adjourned for inquiries or a report, the defendant need not be granted bail if it appears to the court that it would be impracticable to complete the inquiries or make the report without keeping the defendant in custody. **3–49**

Restriction of conditions of bail

8.—(1) Subject to sub-paragraph (3) below, where the defendant is granted bail, no conditions shall be imposed under subsections (4) to (6B) or (7) (except subsection (6)(d) or (e)) of section 3 of this Act unless it appears to the court that it is necessary to do so—

(a) for the purpose of preventing the occurrence of any of the events mentioned in paragraph 2(1) of this Part of this Schedule, or

(b) for the defendant's own protection or, if he is a child or young person, for his own welfare or in his own interests.

(1A) No condition shall be imposed under section 3(6)(d) of this Act unless it appears to be necessary to do so for the purpose of enabling inquiries or a report to be made.

(2) Sub-paragraphs (1) and (1A) above also apply on any application to the court to vary the conditions of bail or to impose conditions in respect of bail which has been granted unconditionally.

(3) The restriction imposed by sub-paragraph (1A) above shall not apply to the conditions required to be imposed under section 3(6A) of this Act or operate to override the direction in section 11(3) of the *Powers of Criminal Courts (Sentencing) Act* 2000 to a magistrates' court to impose conditions of bail under section 3(6)(d) of this Act of the description specified in the said section 11(3) in the circumstances so specified.

Decisions under paragraph 2

9. In taking the decisions required by paragraph [2(1), or in deciding whether it is satisfied as mentioned in paragraph 2A(1), 6(1) or 6A] [[2(1) or 2A, or in deciding whether it is satisfied as mentioned in paragraph 6A]] of this Part of this Schedule, the court shall have regard to such of the following considerations as appear to it to be relevant, that is to say— **3–50**

(a) the nature and seriousness of the offence or default (and the probable method of dealing with the defendant for it),

(b) the character, antecedents, associations and community ties of the defendant,

(c) the defendant's record as respects the fulfilment of his obligations under previous grants of bail in criminal proceedings,

(d) except in the case of a defendant whose case is adjourned for inquiries or a report, the strength of the evidence of his having committed the offence or having defaulted,

as well as to any others which appear to be relevant.

9A. [*Repealed by* CJPA *2001, s.129(4)*.]

[9AA.—(1) This paragraph applies if—

(a) the defendant is under the age of 18, and

(b) it appears to the court that he was on bail in criminal proceedings on the date of the offence.

(2) In deciding for the purposes of paragraph 2(1) of this Part of this Schedule whether it is satisfied that there are substantial grounds for believing that the defendant, if released on bail (whether subject to conditions or not), would commit an offence while on bail, the court shall give particular weight to the fact that the defendant was on bail in criminal proceedings on the date of the offence.

9AB.—(1) Subject to sub-paragraph (2) below, this paragraph applies if—

(a) the defendant is under the age of 18, and

(b) it appears to the court that, having been released on bail in or in connection with the proceedings for the offence, he failed to surrender to custody.

(2) Where it appears to the court that the defendant had reasonable cause for his failure to surrender to custody, this paragraph does not apply unless it also appears to the court that he failed to surrender to custody at the appointed place as soon as reasonably practicable after the appointed time.

(3) In deciding for the purposes of paragraph 2(1) of this Part of this Schedule whether it is satisfied that there are substantial grounds for believing that the defendant, if released on bail (whether subject to conditions or not), would fail to surrender to custody, the court shall give particular weight to—

(a) where the defendant did not have reasonable cause for his failure to surrender to custody, the fact that he failed to surrender to custody, or

(b) where he did have reasonable cause for his failure to surrender to custody, the fact that he failed to surrender to custody at the appointed place as soon as reasonably practicable after the appointed time.

(4) For the purposes of this paragraph, a failure to give to the defendant a copy of the record of the decision to grant him bail shall not constitute a reasonable cause for his failure to surrender to custody.]

Cases under section 128A of Magistrates' Courts Act 1980

9B. Where the court is considering exercising the power conferred by section 128A of the *Magistrates' Courts Act* 1980 (power to remand in custody for more than eight clear days), it shall have regard to the total length of time which the accused would spend in custody if it were to exercise the power.

PART IA

Defendants Accused or Convicted of Imprisonable Offences to which Part 1 does not apply

Defendants to whom Part 1A applies

3–50a 1. The following provisions of this Part apply to the defendant if—

(a) the offence or one of the offences of which he is accused or convicted is punishable with imprisonment, but

(b) Part 1 does not apply to him by virtue of paragraph 1(2) of that Part.

Exceptions to right to bail

2. The defendant need not be granted bail if—

(a) it appears to the court that, having been previously granted bail in criminal proceedings, he has failed to surrender to custody in accordance with his obligations under the grant of bail; and

(b) the court believes, in view of that failure, that the defendant, if released on bail (whether subject to conditions or not) would fail to surrender to custody.

3. The defendant need not be granted bail if—

(a) it appears to the court that the defendant was on bail in criminal proceedings on the date of the offence; and

(b) the court is satisfied that there are substantial grounds for believing that the defendant, if released on bail (whether subject to conditions or not) would commit an offence while on bail.

4. The defendant need not be granted bail if the court is satisfied that there are substantial grounds for believing that the defendant, if released on bail (whether subject to conditions or not), would commit an offence while on bail by engaging in conduct that would, or would be likely to, cause—

(a) physical or mental injury to any person other than the defendant; or

(b) any person other than the defendant to fear physical or mental injury.

5. [*Identical to Pt I, para. 3.*]

6. The defendant need not be granted bail if he is in custody in pursuance of a sentence of a court or a sentence imposed by an officer under the *Armed Forces Act* 2006.

7. The defendant need not be granted bail if—

(a) having been released on bail in or in connection with the proceedings for the offence, he has been arrested in pursuance of section 7 of this Act; and

(b) the court is satisfied that there are substantial grounds for believing that the defendant, if released on bail (whether subject to conditions or not) would fail to surrender to custody, commit an offence while on bail or interfere with witnesses or otherwise obstruct the course of justice (whether in relation to himself or any other person).

8. The defendant need not be granted bail where the court is satisfied that it has not been practicable to obtain sufficient information for the purpose of taking the decisions required by this Part of this Schedule for want of time since the institution of the proceedings against him.

Application of paragraphs 6A to 6C of Part 1

9. Paragraphs 6A to 6C of Part 1 (exception applicable to drug users in certain areas and related provisions) apply to a defendant to whom this Part applies as they apply to a defendant to whom that Part applies.

PART II

Defendants Accused or Convicted of Non-Imprisonable Offences

Defendants to whom Part II applies

1. Where the offence or every offence of which the defendant is accused or convicted in the proceedings is one which is not punishable with imprisonment the following provisions of this Part of this Schedule apply. **3–51**

Exceptions to right to bail

2. The defendant need not be granted bail if—

(a) it appears to the court that, having been previously granted bail in criminal proceedings, he has failed to surrender to custody in accordance with his obligations under the grant of bail; and

(b) the court believes, in view of that failure, that the defendant, if released on bail (whether subject to conditions or not) would fail to surrender to custody.

3. The defendant need not be granted bail if the court is satisfied that the defendant should be kept in custody for his own protection or, if he is a child or young person, for his own welfare.

4. [*Identical to Pt I, para. 4 (including the prospective amendment)*, ante, *§ 3–48.*]

5. The defendant need not be granted bail if—

(a) having been released on bail in or in connection with the proceedings for the offence, he has been arrested in pursuance of section 7 of this Act; and

(b) the court is satisfied that there are substantial grounds for believing that the defendant, if released on bail (whether subject to conditions or not) would fail to surrender to custody, commit an offence on bail or interfere with witnesses or otherwise obstruct the course of justice (whether in relation to himself or any other person).

PART IIA

Decisions where Bail Refused on Previous Hearing

1. If the court decides not to grant the defendant bail, it is the court's duty to consider, at each subsequent hearing while the defendant is a person to whom section 4 above

applies and remains in custody, whether he ought to be granted bail.

2. At the first hearing after that at which the court decided not to grant the defendant bail he may support an application for bail with any argument as to fact or law that he desires (whether or not he has advanced that argument previously).

3. At subsequent hearings the court need not hear arguments as to fact or law which it has heard previously.

PART III

Interpretation

3–52 1. For the purposes of this Schedule the question whether an offence is one which is punishable with imprisonment shall be determined without regard to any enactment prohibiting or restricting the imprisonment of young offenders or first offenders.

2. References in this Schedule to previous grants of bail include—

(a) bail granted before the coming into force of this Act;

(b) as respects the reference in paragraph 2A of Part 1 of this Schedule (as substituted by section 14(1) of the *Criminal Justice Act* 2003), bail granted before the coming into force of that paragraph;

(c) as respects the references in paragraph 6 of Part 1 of this Schedule (as substituted by section 15(1) of the *Criminal Justice Act* 2003), bail granted before the coming into force of that paragraph;

(d) as respects the references in paragraph 9AA of Part 1 of this Schedule, bail granted before the coming into force of that paragraph;

(e) as respects the references in paragraph 9AB of Part 1 of this Schedule, bail granted before the coming into force of that paragraph;

(f) as respects the reference in paragraph 5 of Part 2 of this Schedule (as substituted by section 13(4) of the *Criminal Justice Act* 2003), bail granted before the coming into force of that paragraph.

3. References in this Schedule to a defendant's being kept in custody or being in custody include (where the defendant is a child or young person) references to his being kept or being in the care of a local authority in pursuance of a warrant of commitment under section 23 (1) of the *Children and Young Persons Act* 1969.

4. In this Schedule—

"court", in the expression "sentence of a court", includes a service court as defined in section 12(1) of the *Visiting Forces Act* 1952 and "sentence", in that expression, shall be construed in accordance with that definition;

"default", in relation to the defendant, means the default for which he is to be dealt with under Part 2 of Schedule 8 to the *Criminal Justice Act* 2003 (breach of requirement of order);

"the Services Acts" means the Army Act *1955, the* Air Force Act *1955 and the* Naval Discipline Act *1957*.

[This Schedule is printed as amended and repealed in part by the *MCA* 1980, Sched. 7; the *Mental Health (Amendment) Act* 1982, s.34; the *CJA* 1988, ss.153– 155; the *CJA* 1991, s.100 and Sched. 11, para. 22; the *CJPOA* 1994, ss.26, 168(2) and Sched. 10, para. 34; the *CDA* 1998, s.119 and Sched. 8, para. 38; the *PCC(S)A* 2000, s.165(1) and Sched. 9, para. 54; the *Extradition Act* 2003, s.198(1) and (12) to (14); the *CJA* 2003, ss.13(3) and (4), 19(1) and (4), 20, 304 and 331, Sched. 32, paras 20 and 23, and Sched. 36, paras 1 and 3; the *Courts Act 2003 (Consequential Provisions) Order* 2005 (S.I. 2005 No. 886); and the *CJIA* 2008, s.52, and Sched. 12, paras 1 and 4 to 6; and as amended, as from a day to be appointed (but see *post*), by the *CJA* 2003, ss.14(1) (substitution of para. 2A(1) and (2) in Pt I) and (2) (insertion of para. 9AA in Pt I) and 15(1) (substitution of para. 6 in Pt I) and (2) (insertion of para. 9AB in Pt I); and the *AFA* 2006, s.378(1) and (2), Sched. 16, para. 78, and Sched. 17 (substitution of words in square brackets in Pt 1, para. 4 (and like amendment in Pt II, para. 4) and omission of last definition in Pt III, para. 4). In relation to the amendments made by section 20 of the 2003 Act (insertion of para. 2(2) of Pt I and insertion of words in single square brackets in para. 9 of Pt I), in para. 2(2) the words in single square brackets do not have effect, and the word in double square brackets does have effect during any time prior to the commencement of sections 14 and 15(1) and (2), and in para. 9 the words in single square brackets do not have effect and the words in double square brackets do have effect at any such time: *Criminal Justice Act 2003 (Commencement No. 3 and Transitional Provisions) Order* 2004 (S.I. 2004 No. 829), art. 2(2). The *Criminal Justice Act 2003 (Commencement No. 14 and Transitional Provision) Order* 2006 (S.I. 2006 No. 3217) brought into force sections 14 and 15(1) and (2) on January 1, 2007, for the purposes only of any offence, (i) to which paragraph 2A(2)(b), 6(2)(b), 9AA(1)(b) or 9AB(1)(b) of Part 1 applies, and (ii) in relation to which the defendant is liable on conviction to a sentence of imprisonment for life, detention during Her Majesty's pleasure or custody for life; but the coming into force of section 14 has effect only where the offence to which paragraph 2A(2)(b) or 9AA(1)(b) applies was committed after December 31, 2006, and the coming into force of section 15(1) and (2) has effect only where the failure to surrender referred to in paragraph 6(2)(b) or 9AB(1)(b) occurred after that date: art. 3.]

Section 17(3) of the *Drugs Act* 2005 provides that for the purposes of paragraph 6B(2)(b) of Schedule 1 to the 1976 Act (*ante*, § 3–48), a relevant assessment is to be treated as having been carried out if a person has attended an initial assessment and remained for its duration, and the initial assessor is satisfied that the initial assessment fulfilled the purposes of a relevant assessment. Subsection (4) provides that an initial assessor may disclose information relating to an initial assessment for the purpose of enabling a court considering an application for bail by the person concerned to determine whether subsection (3) applies. As to "initial assessments", see *ante*, § 3–11, and for section 63B of the *PACE Act* 1984, see *post*, § 15–243.

Proper approach to objections to bail, imposition of conditions, etc.

The strict rules of evidence are inherently inappropriate in a court concerned to decide whether there are substantial grounds for believing something: *Re Moles* [1981] Crim.L.R. 170, DC. See also *R. v. Mansfield JJ., ex p. Sharkey* [1985] Q.B. 613, DC. **3–53**

In *ex p. Sharkey*, *ante*, it was held that the test for imposing a condition on the grant of bail under section 3(6) and paragraph 8 of Part I of Schedule 1 was whether the court perceived a real risk of one of the specified events occurring.

In *R. (Thompson) v. Central Criminal Court* [2006] A.C.D. 9, QBD (Collins J.), it was said that the issue under paragraph 2(1) of Part I of Schedule 1 was not as to whether bail should be granted, but was whether it was necessary for the defendant to be in custody (custody being necessary where the court decides that, whatever conditions can reasonably be imposed, there are nonetheless substantial grounds for believing that the defendant would fail to surrender, *etc.*); and for the purpose of deciding whether custody was necessary, the severity of the sentence risked was a matter to be taken into account, but the risk of absconding on account of the severity of the potential sentence had to be assessed in the light of other relevant factors. As to the imposition of conditions, his Lordship said that the question of bail must be determined in the round, involving consideration of the question whether suitable conditions would make it unnecessary to remand in custody.

A person charged with a serious offence, facing a severe penalty if convicted, may well have a powerful incentive to abscond or interfere with witnesses likely to give evidence against him; where there are reasonable grounds to infer that the grant of bail may lead to such a result, which cannot be effectively eliminated by the imposition of appropriate conditions, they will afford good grounds for refusing bail; but they do not do so of themselves, without more; they are factors relevant to the judgment whether, in all the circumstances, it is necessary to deprive the applicant of his liberty; whether or not that is the conclusion reached, clear and explicit reasons should be given: *Hurnam v. State of Mauritius* [2006] 1 W.L.R. 857, PC. In *Gault v. UK* (2008) 46 E.H.R.R. 48, ECtHR, the applicant had been denied bail pending her retrial for murder, following the quashing of her conviction, where she had been on bail prior to conviction. In all the circumstances, it was held that it was not possible to infer a greater risk of her absconding pending the retrial than there had been prior to the original trial from the mere fact that she had already been convicted once.

The fact that a trial will take place promptly is no reason for refusing bail: *Gault v. UK*, *ante*.

In *R. v. Kwame*, 60 Cr.App.R. 65, CA, a decision under the law prior to the 1976 Act, it was said that although granting bail on condition that the defendant does not drive was lawful, courts ought to consider whether it might have unexpected and possibly unjust results. Under the Act, the imposition of such a condition would have to be justified by reference to paragraphs 2 and 8 of Schedule 1. However, the note of caution sounded by the court would appear to be as relevant after the Act as before.

As to the grant of conditional bail on a charge of a non-imprisonable offence, see *R. v. Bournemouth Magistrates' Court, ex p. Cross*, 89 Cr.App.R. 90, DC.

Renewed applications for bail

3–54 Part IIA of Schedule 1 was added by the *CJA* 1988, s.154: see *ante*, § 3–18.

(3) Limitation on right to bail

Criminal Justice and Public Order Act 1994, s.25

No bail for defendants charged with or convicted of homicide or rape after previous conviction of such offences

3–55 **25.**—(1) A person who in any proceedings has been charged with or convicted of an offence to which this section applies in circumstances to which it applies shall be granted bail in those proceedings only if the court, or as the case may be, the constable considering the grant of bail is satisfied that there are exceptional circumstances which justify it.

(2) This section applies, subject to subsection (3) below, to the following offences, that is to say—

(a) murder;
(b) attempted murder;
(c) manslaughter;
(d) rape under the law of Scotland or Northern Ireland;
(e) an offence under section 1 of the *Sexual Offences Act* 1956 (rape);
(f) an offence under section 1 of the *Sexual Offences Act* 2003 (rape);
(g) an offence under section 2 of that Act (assault by penetration);
(h) an offence under section 4 of that Act (causing a person to engage in sexual activity without consent), where the activity caused involved penetration within subsection (4)(a) to (d) of that section;
(i) an offence under section 5 of that Act (rape of a child under 13);
(j) an offence under section 6 of that Act (assault of a child under 13 by penetration);
(k) an offence under section 8 of that Act (causing or inciting a child under 13 to engage in sexual activity), where an activity involving penetration within subsection (3)(a) to (d) of that section was caused;
(l) an offence under section 30 of that Act (sexual activity with a person with a mental disorder impeding choice), where the touching involved penetration within subsection (3)(a) to (d) of that section;
(m) an offence under section 31 of that Act (causing or inciting a person with a mental disorder impeding choice, to engage in sexual activity), where an activity involving penetration within subsection (3)(a) to (d) of that section was caused;
[(ma)–(mh) [*an offence under article 5 , 6 , 12 or 13 of the* Sexual Offences (Northern Ireland) Order *2008 (S.I. 2008 No. 1769), an offence under article 8 of that order where the activity caused involved penetration within paragraph (4)(a) to (d) of that article, an offence under article 15 of that order where an activity involving penetration within paragraph (2)(a) to (d) of that article was caused, an offence under article 43 of that order where the touching involved penetration within paragraph (3)(a) to (d) of that article or an offence under article 44 of that order where an activity involving penetration within paragraph (3)(a) to (d) of that article was caused*];]
(n) an attempt to commit an offence within any of paragraphs (d) to *(m)* [(mh)].

(3) This section applies to a person charged with or convicted of any such offence only if he has been previously convicted by or before a court in any part of the United Kingdom of any such offence or of culpable homicide and, in the case of a previous conviction of manslaughter or of culpable homicide, if he was then sentenced to imprisonment or, if he was then a child or young person, to long-term detention under any of the relevant enactments.

(4) This section applies whether or not an appeal is pending against conviction or sentence.

(5) In this section—

"conviction" includes—

(a) a finding that a person is not guilty by reason of insanity;

(b) a finding under section 4A(3) of the *Criminal Procedure (Insanity) Act* 1964 (cases of unfitness to plead) that a person did the act or made the omission charged against him; and

(c) a conviction of an offence for which an order is made discharging the offender absolutely or conditionally;

and "convicted" shall be construed accordingly; and

"the relevant enactments" means—

(a) as respects England and Wales, section 91 of the *Powers of Criminal Courts (Sentencing) Act* 2000;

(b), (c) [*Scotland and Northern Ireland*].

(6) This section does not apply in relation to proceedings instituted before its commencement.

[This section is printed as amended by the *CDA* 1998, s.56; the *PCC(S)A* 2000, s.165(1), and Sched. 9, para. 160; the *SOA* 2003, s.139, and Sched. 6, para. 32; and the *CJA* 2003, s.304, and Sched. 32, para. 67; and as amended, as from a day to be appointed, by the *Sexual Offences (Northern Ireland Consequential Amendments) Order* 2008 (S.I. 2008 No. 1779) (insertion of subs. (2)(ma)-(mh), substitution of "(mh)" for "(m)" in subs. (2)(n)).]

In *R. (O.) v. Crown Court at Harrow* [2007] 1 A.C. 249, HL, it was held that section 25(1) merely serves to remind the court of the risks normally posed by defendants to whom it applied, and it had no substantive effect upon the way in which bail applications (prior to the expiry of a custody time limit) would fall to be determined; to the extent that the provision appeared to impose a burden of proof on the defendant, this would only assume relevance where the court, having considered the matter under the 1976 Act, was left unsure as to bail; but such rare cases occupied the default position at which bail would have to be granted, from which it followed that section 25 should be read down under section 3 of the *Human Rights Act* 1998 (*post*, § 16–15) to that extent. Such reading down was necessary as it had been established that presumptions against bail were incompatible with Article 5(3) of the ECHR (*post*, § 16–43) (see *Ilijokov v. Bulgaria* [2001] 7 *Archbold News* 1, ECtHR). As to their Lordships' decision as to the application of section 25 where an application for an extension of a custody time limit has been refused, see *ante*, §§ 1–269ca, 1–270.

(4) Custody time limits

The *Prosecution of Offences (Custody Time Limits) Regulations* 1987 (S.I. 1987 No. 299) were made under sections 22(1) and (2) and 29(2) of the *Prosecution of Offences Act* 1985 (*ante*, §§ 1–266 *et seq.*) **3–56**

The regulations are printed as amended and revoked in part by S.I. 1988 No. 164; S.I. 1989 No. 767; S.I. 1989 No. 1107 (correcting an error in S.I. 1989 No. 767); S.I. 1991 No. 1515; S.I. 1995 No. 555; S.I. 1999 No. 2744; S.I. 2000 No. 3284 (all entitled *Prosecution of Offences (Custody Time Limits) (Amendment) Regulations*); the *Prosecution of Offences (Custody Time Limits) (Modification) Regulations* 1998 (S.I. 1998 No. 3037); and the *CPIA* 1996, s.71(4).

S.I. 1987 No. 299, regs 2, 4–8

Interpretation

2.—(1) In these Regulations— **3–57**

"the 1980 Act" means the *Magistrates' Courts Act* 1980;

"the 1985 Act" means the *Prosecution of Offences Act* 1985.

(2) In these Regulations, a reference to a person's first appearance in relation to proceedings in a magistrates' court for an offence is—

(a) in a case where that person has made an application under section 43B of the

1980 Act, a reference to the time when he appears before the court on the hearing of that application;

(b) in a case where that person appears or is brought before the court in pursuance of section 5B of the *Bail Act* 1976 and the decision which is to be, or has been, reconsidered under that section is the decision of a constable, a reference to the time when he so appears or is brought; and

(c) in any other case, a reference to the time when first he appears or is brought before the court on an information charging him with that offence.

(3) In these Regulations any reference to the start of the trial shall be construed in accordance with section 22(11A) and (11B) of the 1985 Act.

(4) Any maximum period set by these Regulations during which a person may be in the custody of a court does not include the day on which the custody commenced.

(5) A custody time limit which would, apart from this paragraph, expire on any of the days to which this paragraph applies shall be treated as expiring on the next preceding day which is not one of those days.

The days to which this paragraph applies are Saturday, Sunday, Christmas Day, Good Friday and any day which under the *Banking and Financial Dealings Act* 1971 is a bank holiday in England and Wales.

Where a defendant is remanded in custody, time continues to run for the purposes of the custody time limit regime during any period when he is serving a custodial sentence in respect of another matter: *R. v. Peterborough Crown Court, ex p. L.* [2000] Crim.L.R. 470, DC.

Custody time limits in magistrates' courts

3–58 **4.**—(1) … the maximum period during which a person accused of an indictable offence other than treason may be in the custody of a magistrates' court in relation to that offence while awaiting completion of any preliminary stage of the proceedings specified in the following provisions of this Regulation shall be as stated in those provisions.

(2) Except as provided in paragraph (3) below, in the case of an offence triable either way the maximum period of custody between the accused's first appearance and the start of summary trial or, as the case may be, the time when the court decides whether or not to commit the accused to the Crown Court for trial shall be 70 days ….

(3) In the case of an offence triable either way if, before the expiry of 56 days following the day of the accused's first appearance, the court decides to proceed to summary trial in pursuance of sections 19 to 24 of the 1980 Act the maximum period of custody between the accused's first appearance and the start of the summary trial shall be 56 days.

(4) In the case of an offence triable on indictment exclusively the maximum period of custody between the accused's first appearance and the time when the court decides whether or not to commit the accused to the Crown Court for trial, shall be 70 days … .

(4A) In the case of a summary offence, the maximum period of custody beginning with the date of the accused's first appearance and ending with the date of the start of the summary trial shall be 56 days.

(5) The foregoing provisions of this regulation shall have effect as if any reference therein to the time when the court decides whether or not to commit the accused to the Crown Court for trial were a reference—

(a) where a court proceeds to inquire into an information as examining justices in pursuance of section 6(1) of the 1980 Act, to the time when it begins to hear evidence for the prosecution at the inquiry;

(b) where a notice has been given under section 4(1)(c) of the *Criminal Justice Act* 1987 (in these Regulations referred to as a "notice of transfer"), to the date on which notice of transfer was given.

In regulation 4, the expression "offence triable either way" includes an offence which in the case of an adult would be triable only on indictment, but which, in the case of child or young offender, may be tried summarily: *R. v. Stratford Youth Court, ex p. S. (a Minor)* [1998] 1 W.L.R. 1758, DC.

Custody time limits in the Crown Court

3–59 **5.**—(1) [*Revoked by S.I. 1991 No. 1515.*]

(2) Where—

(a) a person accused of an indictable offence other than treason is committed to the Crown Court for trial; or

(b) a bill of indictment is preferred against a person under section 2(2)(b) of the *Administration of Justice (Miscellaneous Provisions) Act* 1933,

the maximum period during which he may be in the custody of the Crown Court in relation to that offence, or any other offence included in the indictment preferred against him, while awaiting the preliminary stage of the proceedings specified in the following provisions of this Regulation shall be as stated in those provisions.

(3) The maximum period of custody—

(a) between the time when the accused is committed for trial and the start of the trial; or

(b) where a bill of indictment is preferred against him under the said section 2(2)(b), between the preferment of the bill and the start of the trial,

shall, subject to the following provisions of this Regulation, be 112 days.

(4) Where, following a committal for trial, the bill of indictment preferred against the accused (not being a bill preferred under the said section 2(2)(b)) contains a count charging an offence for which he was committed for trial at that committal together with a count charging an offence for which he was committed for trial on a different occasion, paragraph (3) above applies in relation to each offence separately.

(5) Where, following a committal for trial, a bill of indictment is preferred under the said section 2(2)(b) and the bill does not contain a count charging an offence for which he was not committed for trial, the maximum period of custody between the preferment of the bill and the start of the trial shall be 112 days less any period, or the aggregate of any periods, during which the accused has, since the committal, been in the custody of the Crown Court in relation to an offence for which he was committed for trial.

(6) Where, following a committal for trial, the bill of indictment preferred against the accused (not being a bill preferred under the said section 2(2)(b)) contains a count charging an offence for which he was not committed for trial, the maximum period of custody— **3–60**

(a) between the preferment of the bill and the start of the trial, or

(b) if the count was added to the bill after its preferment, between that addition and the start of the trial,

shall be 112 days less any period, or the aggregate of any periods, during which he has, since the committal, been in the custody of the Crown Court in relation to an offence for which he was committed for trial.

(6A) The foregoing provisions of this regulation shall have effect, where notice of transfer is given in respect of a case, as if references to committal for trial and to offences for which a person was or was not committed for trial included references to the giving of notice of transfer and to charges contained or not contained in the notice of transfer.

(6B) Where an accused is sent for trial under section 51 of the *Crime and Disorder Act* 1998 ("the 1998 Act"), the maximum period of custody between the accused being sent to the Crown Court by a magistrates' court for an offence and the start of the trial in relation to it, shall be 182 days less any period, or the aggregate of any periods, during which the accused has, since that first appearance for the offence, been in the custody of the magistrates' court.

(6C) Where, following a sending for trial under section 51 of the 1998 Act, a bill of indictment is preferred under the said section 2(2)(b) and the bill does not contain a count charging an offence for which he was not sent for trial, the maximum period of custody between the preferment of the bill and the start of the trial shall be the maximum period of custody as provided for in paragraph (6B) above (after making any deductions required by that paragraph) less any period, or the aggregate of any periods, during which the accused has, since he was sent for trial, been in the custody of the Crown Court in relation to an offence for which he was sent for trial.

(6D) Where, following a sending for trial under section 51 of the 1998 Act, the bill of indictment preferred against the accused (not being a bill preferred under the said section 2(2)(b)) contains a count charging an offence for which he was not sent for trial, the maximum period of custody—

(a) between the preferment of the bill and the start of the trial, or

(b) if the count was added to the bill after its preferment, between that addition and the start of the trial,

shall be the maximum period of custody as provided for in paragraph (6B) above (after making any deductions required by that paragraph) less any period, or the aggregate of any periods, during which he has, since being sent for trial, been in the custody of the Crown Court in relation to the offence for which he was previously sent for trial.

Bail on expiry of Crown Court custody time limit

6.—(1) Subject to the following provisions of this Regulation where an accused who is in **3–61**

custody pending trial in the Crown Court has the benefit of a custody time limit under Regulation 5 above the prosecution shall—

(a) not less than 5 days before the expiry of the time limit give notice in writing to the appropriate officer of the Crown Court and to the accused or his representative stating whether or not it intends to ask the Crown Court to impose conditions on the grant of bail in respect of the accused and, if it intends to do so, the nature of the conditions to be sought; and

(b) make arrangements for the accused to be brought before the Crown Court within the period of 2 days preceding the expiry of the time limit.

3–62 (2) If the Crown Court is satisfied that it is not practicable in all the circumstances for the prosecution to comply with sub-paragraph (a) in paragraph (1) above, the Crown Court may direct that the prosecution need not comply with that sub-paragraph or that the minimum period of notice required by that sub-paragraph shall be such lesser minimum period as the Crown Court may specify.

(3) The prosecution need not comply with paragraph (1)(a) above if it has given notice under Regulation 7(2) below of its intention to make an application under section 22(3) of the 1985 Act.

(4) On receiving notice under paragraph (1)(a) above stating that the prosecution intends to ask the Crown Court to impose conditions on the grant of bail, the accused or his representative shall—

(a) give notice in writing to the appropriate officer of the Crown Court and to the prosecution that the accused wishes to be represented at the hearing of the application; or

(b) give notice in writing to the appropriate officer and to the prosecution stating that the accused does not oppose the application; or

(c) give to the appropriate officer, for the consideration of the Crown Court, a written statement of the accused's reasons for opposing the application, at the same time sending a copy of the statement to the prosecution.

3–63 (5) The Crown Court may direct that the prosecution need not comply with paragraph (1)(b) above.

(6) The Crown Court, on being notified that an accused who is in custody pending trial there has the benefit of a custody time limit under Regulation 5 above and that the time limit is about to expire, shall, subject to section 25 of the *Criminal Justice and Public Order Act* 1994 (exclusion of bail in cases of homicide and rape), grant him bail in accordance with the *Bail Act* 1976, as from the expiry of the time limit, subject to a duty to appear before the Crown Court for trial.

Once a custody time limit has expired without extension, the Crown Court is obliged to order the defendant's release on bail and may impose terms to be complied with after release: *Olotu v. Home Office* [1997] 1 W.L.R. 328, CA (Civ. Div.).

As to subjecting entitlement to bail on expiry of a custody time limit to section 25 of the *CJPOA* 1994 (*ante*, § 3–55), see *R. (O.) v. Crown Court at Harrow* [2007] 1 A.C. 249, HL (*ante*, §§ 1–269ca, 1–270).

Application for extension of custody time limit

3–64 **7.**—(1) An application to a court for the extension or further extension of a custody time limit under section 22(3) of the 1985 Act may be made orally or in writing.

(2) Subject to paragraphs (3) and (4) below the prosecution shall—

(a) not less than 5 days before making such an application in the Crown Court; and

(b) not less than 2 days before making such an application in a magistrates' court,

give notice in writing to the accused or his representative and to the proper officer of the court stating that it intends to make such an application.

(2A) In paragraph (2) above, "the proper officer of the court" means in relation to an application in the Crown Court the appropriate officer of the court and in relation to an application in a magistrates' court the clerk of the court.

(3) It shall not be necessary for the prosecution to comply with paragraph (2) above if the accused or his representative has informed the prosecution that he does not require such notice.

(4) If the court is satisfied that it is not practicable in all the circumstances for the prosecution to comply with paragraph (2) above, the court may direct that the prosecution need not comply with that paragraph or that the minimum period of notice required by that paragraph to be given shall be such lesser minimum period as the court may specify.

Application of Bail Act 1976

8.—(1) The *Bail Act* 1976 shall apply in relation to cases to which a custody time limit applies subject to the modifications specified in paragraph (2) below, being modifications necessary in consequence of the foregoing provisions of these Regulations. **3–65**

(2) [*See* ante, *§§ 3–11, 3–14, 3–38.*]

Each offence attracts its own time limit

See the cases cited *ante*, § 1–270. **3–65a**

Extension of time limits

See the cases cited *ante*, §§ 1–271 *et seq.* **3–65b**

Youth court time limits

The *Prosecution of Offences (Youth Courts Time Limits) Regulations* 1999 (S.I. 1999 No. 2743) were revoked by the *Prosecution of Offences (Youth Courts Time Limits) (Revocation and Transitional Provision) Regulations* 2003 (S.I. 2003 No. 917), as from April 22, 2003, so that there are no longer any maximum periods in relation to proceedings in youth courts. **3–65c**

(5) Provisions relating to Customs and Excise

Bail for persons in customs detention

See the amendment to section 114(2) of the *PACE Act* 1984 effected by section 150 of the *CJA* 1988: *post*, § 15–40. **3–66**

Criminal Justice Act 1988, s.151

Commissioners for Her Majesty's Revenue and Customs' power of arrest

151.—[(1) If— **3–66a**

(a) a person—

(i) has been released on bail in criminal proceedings for an offence falling within subsection (4) below; and

(ii) is under a duty to surrender into customs detention; and

(b) an officer of Revenue and Customs has reasonable grounds for believing that that person is not likely to surrender to custody,

he may be arrested without warrant by an officer of Revenue and Customs.

(2) A person arrested in pursuance of subsection (1) above shall be brought as soon as practicable and in any event within 24 hours after his arrest before a justice of the peace for the petty sessions area in which he was arrested.

(3) In reckoning for the purposes of subsection (2) above any period of 24 hours, no account shall be taken of Christmas Day, Good Friday or any Sunday.

(4) The offences that fall within this subsection are—

(a) an offence against section 5(2) of the *Misuse of Drugs Act* 1971 (possession of controlled drugs);

(b) a drug trafficking offence;

(c) a money laundering offence.]

(5) In this section and section 152 below "drug trafficking offence" means any offence which is specified in —

(a) paragraph 1 of Schedule 2 to the *Proceeds of Crime Act* 2002 (drug trafficking offences), or

(b) so far as it relates to that paragraph, paragraph 10 of that Schedule.

[(6) In this section "money laundering offence" means any offence which by virtue of section 415 of the *Proceeds of Crime Act* 2002 is a money laundering offence for the purposes of Part 8 of that Act.]

[This section is printed as amended by the *PCA* 2002, s.456, and Sched. 11, para. 17(1) and (3) to (6); and the *Commissioners for Revenue and Customs Act* 2005, s.50(1) and (2).]

Section 151(5) came into force on April 3, 1989: *Criminal Justice Act 1988 (Commencement No. 7) Order* 1989 (S.I. 1989 No. 264). The remainder of the section will come into force on a day to be appointed.

Subsections (1) to (3) correspond broadly to subsections (3) and (4) of section 7 of the *Bail Act* 1976, *ante*, § 3–37.

Criminal Justice Act 1988, s.152

Remands of suspected drug offenders to detention

3–67 **152.**—(1) Subject—

(a) to subsection (2) below; and

(b) to section 4 of the *Bail Act* 1976,

where—

(i) a person is brought before a magistrates' court on a charge of an offence against section 5(2) of the *Misuse of Drugs Act* 1971 or a drug trafficking offence; and

(ii) the court has power to remand him,

it shall have power, if it considers it appropriate to do so, to remand him to customs detention, that is to say, commit him to the custody of an officer of Revenue and Customs for a period not exceeding 192 hours.

(1A) In subsection (1) the power of a magistrates' court to remand a person to customs detention for a period not exceeding 192 hours includes power to commit the person to the custody of a constable to be detained for such a period.

(2) This section does not apply where a charge is brought against a person under the age of 17.

(3), (4) [*Northern Ireland.*]

[This section is printed as amended by the *Commissioners for Revenue and Customs Act* 2005, s.50(2); and the *Drugs Act* 2005, s.8.]

For the meaning of "drug trafficking offence", see section 151(5), *ante*, § 3–66a.

(6) Place of remand

(a) *Allocation of prisoners*

A decision of the Secretary of State as to the allocation of a particular prisoner which gave rise to a real danger that the prisoner might be denied a fair trial would be *ultra vires* section 12 of the *Prison Act* 1952 (prisoners to be committed to such prisons as the Secretary of State may from time to time direct); should his decision give rise to such a risk, relief should not be refused on the ground that an application to the trial judge to stay the proceedings on the ground of abuse of process was an adequate alternative remedy, as the relief sought (the quashing of the decision as to allocation) was different from the relief that would be sought from the trial judge, and it was only the High Court that could rule on the lawfulness of a decision of the Secretary of State: *R. v. Secretary of State for the Home Department, ex p. Quinn*, *The Times*, April 17, 1999, QBD (Richards J.).

(b) *Persons under 21 years*

Persons aged 17 to 20

Criminal Justice Act 1948, s.27

3–68 **27.**—(1) Where a court remands a person charged with or convicted of an offence or *commits him for trial or* [sends him to the Crown Court for trial or commits him there for] sentence and he is not less than seventeen but under twenty-one years old and is not released on bail, then, if the court has been notified by the Secretary of State that a remand centre is available for the reception from the court of persons of his class or description, it shall commit him to a remand centre and, if it has not been so notified, it shall commit him to a prison.

(2) Where a person is committed to a remand centre in pursuance of this section, the centre shall be specified in the warrant and he shall be detained there for the period for which he is remanded or until he is delivered thence in due course of law.

(3) In this section "court" includes a justice; and nothing in this section affects the provisions of section 128(7) of the *Magistrates' Courts Act* 1980 (which provides for remands to the custody of a constable).

[This section is printed as substituted by the *CYPA* 1969, Sched. 5; as subsequently amended by the *MCA* 1980, Sched. 7; and the *CJA* 2003, s.41, and Sched. 3, para. 35(1) and (2) (substitution of words in square brackets for italicised words in subs. (1)). The latter amendment came into force on May 9, 2005, in relation to cases sent for trial under section 51 or 51A(3)(d) of the *CDA* 1998: *Criminal Justice Act 2003 (Commencement No. 9) Order* 2005 (S.I. 2005 No. 1267). Otherwise it comes into force on a day to be appointed.]

For section 128(7) of the *MCA* 1980, see *post*, § 3–152.

Section 43 of the *Prison Act* 1952 makes provision for remand centres, being places for the detention of persons not less than 14 but under 21 years of age who are remanded or committed in custody for trial or sentence. Section 43(2) authorises the Secretary of State to direct the detention of a person under 21 but not less than 17 in a prison instead of a remand centre or vice versa and notwithstanding the provisions of section 27 of the 1948 Act. The *CJA* 2003, s.41, and Sched. 3, para. 36, amend section 43, so that pending their repeal by section 59 of, and paragraph 10(a)(ii) of Schedule 7 to, the *CJCSA* 2000, paragraph (c) of subsection (1), and paragraphs (b) and (c) of subsection (2), shall have effect as if references to being committed for trial were references to being sent for trial. This amendment came into force on May 9, 2005, in relation to cases sent for trial under section 51 or 51A(3)(d) of the *CDA* 1998: S.I. 2005 No. 1267 (*ante*). Otherwise it comes into force on a day to be appointed.

See also section 89 of the *PCC(S)A* 2000, *post*, § 5–278.

Persons under 17

Children and Young Persons Act 1969, s.23

Remands and committals to local authority accommodation

23.—(1) Where— **3–69**

(a) a court remands a child or young person charged with or convicted of one or more offences, or [[sends him for trial]] or commits him for trial or sentence; and

(b) he is not released on bail,

[*then, unless he is remanded to a remand centre or a prison in pursuance of subsection (4)(b) or (c) below*] the remand [[, sending]] or committal shall be to local authority accommodation; and in the following provisions of this section (except subsection (1A)), any reference (however expressed) to a remand shall be construed as including a reference to [[such]] a [[sending or]] committal.

(1A) Where a court remands a child or young person in connection with extradition proceedings and he is not released on bail the remand shall be to local authority accommodation.

(2) A court remanding a person to local authority accommodation shall designate the local authority who are to receive him; and that authority shall be—

(a) in the case of a person who is being looked after by a local authority, that authority; and

(b) in any other case, the local authority in whose area it appears to the court that he resides or the offence or one of the offences was committed.

(3) Where a person is remanded to local authority accommodation, it shall be lawful for any person acting on behalf of the designated authority to detain him. **3–70**

(4) Subject to subsections (5), (5ZA) and (5A) below, a court remanding a person to local authority accommodation may, after consultation with the designated authority, require that authority to comply with a security requirement, that is to say, a requirement that the person in question be placed and kept in secure accommodation.

(5) A court shall not impose a security requirement in relation to a person remanded in accordance with subsection (1) above except in respect of a child who has attained the age of twelve, or a young person, who (in either case) is of a prescribed description, and then only if—

(a) he is charged with or has been convicted of a violent or sexual offence, or an offence punishable in the case of an adult with imprisonment for a term of fourteen years or more; or

(b) he is charged with or has been convicted of one or more imprisonable offences which, together with any other imprisonable offences of which he has been convicted in any proceedings—

(i) amount, or

(ii) would, if he were convicted of the offences with which he is charged, amount,

to a recent history of repeatedly committing imprisonable offences while remanded on bail or to local authority accommodation,

and (in either case) the condition set out in subsection (5AA) below is satisfied.

(5ZA) A court shall not impose a security requirement in relation to a person remanded in accordance with subsection (1A) above unless—

(a) he has attained the age of twelve and is of a prescribed description;

(b) one or both of the conditions set out in subsection (5ZB) below is satisfied; and

(c) the condition set out in subsection (5AA) below is satisfied.

(5ZB) The conditions mentioned in subsection (5ZA)(b) above are—

(a) that the conduct constituting the offence to which the extradition proceedings relate would if committed in the United Kingdom constitute an offence punishable in the case of an adult with imprisonment for a term of fourteen years or more;

(b) that the person has previously absconded from the extradition proceedings or from proceedings in the United Kingdom or the requesting territory which relate to the conduct constituting the offence to which the extradition proceedings relate.

(5ZC) For the purposes of subsection (5ZB) above a person has absconded from proceedings if in relation to those proceedings—

(a) he has been released subject to a requirement to surrender to custody at a particular time and he has failed to surrender to custody at that time, or

(b) he has surrendered into the custody of a court and he has at any time absented himself from the court without its leave.

(5AA) The condition mentioned in subsections (5) and (5ZA) above is that the court is of the opinion, after considering all the options for the remand of the person, that only remanding him to local authority accommodation with a security requirement would be adequate—

(a) to protect the public from serious harm from him; or

(b) to prevent the commission by him of imprisonable offences.

(5A) A court shall not impose a security requirement in respect of a child or young person who is not legally represented in the court unless—

(a) he was granted a right to representation funded by the Legal Services Commission as part of the Criminal Defence Service but the right was withdrawn because of his conduct or because it appeared that his financial resources were such that he was not eligible to be granted such a right;

(aa) he applied for such representation and the application was refused because it appeared that his financial resources were such that he was not eligible to be granted a right to it; or

(b) having been informed of his right to apply for such representation and had the opportunity to do so, he refused or failed to apply.

3–71 [(4) *Where a court, after consultation with a probation officer, a social worker of a local authority social services department or a member of a youth offending team, declares a person to be one to whom subsection (5) below applies—*

(a) *it shall remand him to local authority accommodation and require him to be placed and kept in secure accommodation, if—*

(i) *it also, after such consultation, declares him to be a person to whom subsection (5A) below applies; and*

(ii) *it has been notified that secure accommodation is available for him;*

(b) *it shall remand him to a remand centre, if paragraph (a) above does not apply and it has been notified that such a centre is available for the reception from the court of persons to whom subsection (5) below applies; and*

(c) *it shall remand him to a prison, if neither paragraph (a) nor paragraph (b) above applies.*

(4A) *A court shall not declare a person who is not legally represented in the court to be a person to whom subsection (5) below applies unless*—[identical to subs. (5A)].

(5) *This subsection applies to a person who—*

(a) *is charged with or has been convicted of a violent or sexual offence, or an offence punishable in the case of an adult with imprisonment for a term of fourteen years or more; or*

(b) *has a recent history of absconding while remanded to local authority accommodation, and is charged with or has been convicted of an imprisonable offence alleged or found to have been committed while he was so remanded,*

if (in either case) the court is of opinion that only remanding him to a remand centre or prison, or to local authority accommodation with a requirement that he be placed and kept in secure accommodation, would be adequate to protect the public from serious harm from him.

(5AA) *The condition mentioned in subsection (5) above is that the court is of the opinion, after considering all the options for the remand of the person, that only remanding him to a remand centre or prison, or to local authority accommodation with a requirement that he be placed and kept in secure accommodation would be adequate—*

(a) *to protect the public from serious harm from him; or*

(b) *to prevent the commission by him of imprisonable offences.*

(5A) *This subsection applies to a person if the court is of opinion that, by reason of his physical or emotional immaturity or a propensity of his to harm himself, it would be undesirable for him to be remanded to a remand centre or a prison.*]

(6) Where a court [imposes a security requirement in respect of a person] *declares a person to be one to whom subsection (5) above applies*, it shall be its duty— **3–72**

(a) to state in open court that it is of such opinion as is mentioned in subsection (5AA) above; and

(b) to explain to him in open court and in ordinary language why it is of that opinion;

and a magistrates' court shall cause a reason stated by it under paragraph (b) above to be specified in the warrant of commitment and to be entered in the register.

(7) Subject to section 23AA below, a court remanding a person to local authority accommodation without imposing a security requirement *(that is to say, a requirement imposed under subsection (4)(a) above that the person be placed and kept in secure accommodation)* may, after consultation with the designated authority, require that person to comply with—

(a) any such conditions as could be imposed under section 3(6) of the *Bail Act* 1976 if he were then being granted bail; and

(b) any conditions imposed for the purpose of securing the electronic monitoring of his compliance with any other condition imposed under this subsection.

(7A) Where a person is remanded to local authority accommodation and a security requirement is imposed in respect of him—

(a) the designated local authority may, with the consent of the Secretary of State, arrange for the person to be detained, for the whole or any part of the period of the remand or committal, in a secure training centre; and

(b) his detention there pursuant to the arrangements shall be lawful.

(7B) Arrangements under subsection (7A) above may include provision for payments to be made by the authority to the Secretary of State.

(8) Where a court imposes on a person any such conditions as are mentioned in subsection (7) above, it shall be its duty to explain to him in open court and in ordinary language why it is imposing those conditions; and a magistrates' court shall cause a reason stated by it under this subsection to be specified in the warrant of commitment and to be entered in the register.

(9) A court remanding a person to local authority accommodation without imposing a security requirement may, after consultation with the designated authority, impose on that authority requirements—

(a) for securing compliance with any conditions imposed on that person under subsection (7) above; or

(b) stipulating that he shall not be placed with a named person.

(9A) *Where a person is remanded to local authority accommodation without the imposition of a security requirement, a relevant court may, on the application of the designated authority, declare him to be a person to whom subsection (5) above applies; and on its doing so, subsection (4) above shall apply.* **3–73**

(10) Where a person is remanded to local authority accommodation, a relevant court—

(a) may, on the application of the designated authority, impose on that person any such conditions as could be imposed under subsection (7) above if the court were then remanding him to such accommodation; and

(b) where it does so, may impose on that authority any requirements for securing compliance with the conditions so imposed.

(11) Where a person is remanded to local authority accommodation, a relevant court may, on the application of the designated authority or that person, vary or revoke any conditions or requirements imposed under subsection (7), (9) or (10) above.

(12) In this section—

"children's home" has the same meaning as in the *Care Standards Act* 2000;

"court" and "magistrates' court" include a justice;

"extradition proceedings" means proceedings under the *Extradition Act* 2003;

"imprisonable offence" means an offence punishable in the case of an adult with imprisonment;

"prescribed description" means a description prescribed by reference to age or sex or both by an order of the Secretary of State;

"relevant court" —

(a) in relation to a person remanded to local authority accommodation under subsection (1) above, means the court by which he was so remanded, or any magistrates' court having jurisdiction in the place where he is for the time being;

(b) in relation to a person remanded to local authority accommodation under subsection (1A) above, means the court by which he was so remanded;

"requesting territory" means the territory to which a person's extradition is sought in extradition proceedings;

"secure accommodation" means accommodation which is provided in a children's home in respect of which a person is registered under Part II of the *Care Standards Act* 2000 for the purpose of restricting liberty, and is approved for that purpose by the Secretary of State;

"sexual offence" means an offence specified in Part 2 of Schedule 15 to the *Criminal Justice Act* 2003;

"violent offence" means murder or an offence specified in Part 1 of Schedule 15 to the *Criminal Justice Act* 2003;

"young person" means a person who has attained the age of fourteen years and is under the age of seventeen years,

but, for the purposes of the definition of "secure accommodation", "local authority accommodation" includes any accommodation falling within section 61(2) of the *Criminal Justice Act* 1991.

3–74 (13) In this section—

(a) any reference to a person who is being looked after by a local authority shall be construed in accordance with section 22 of the *Children Act* 1989;

(b) any reference to consultation shall be construed as a reference to such consultation (if any) as is reasonably practicable in all the circumstances of the case; and

(c) any reference, in relation to a person charged with or convicted of a violent or sexual offence, to protecting the public from serious harm from him shall be construed as a reference to protecting members of the public from death or serious personal injury, whether physical or psychological, occasioned by further such offences committed by him.

(14) This section has effect subject to—

(a) [*repealed by* CDA *1998, s.120(2) and Sched. 10*];

(b) section 128(7) of that Act (remands to the custody of a constable for periods of not more than three days),

but section 128(7) shall have effect in relation to a child or young person as if for the reference to three clear days there were substituted a reference to 24 hours.

[This section is printed as substituted from October 1, 1992 by the *CJA* 1991, s.60(1); as subsequently amended by the *CJPOA* 1994, s.19(1); the *CDA* 1998, s.97; the *Access to Justice Act* 1999, s.24 and Sched. 4, paras 6 and 7; the *PCC(S)A* 2000, s.165(1) and Sched. 9, para. 38; the *Care Standards Act* 2000, s.116 and Sched. 4, para. 3; the *CJPA* 2001, ss.130(1)–(4), 132(1) and 133(1); the *Extradition Act* 2003, s.201(1) to (9); the *CJA* 2003, s.304, and Sched. 32, para. 15; and the *Criminal Defence Service Act* 2006, s.4(2) and (3); and as modified in relation to certain persons by the *CDA* 1998, s.98. As to the modifications, see *post*. It is further amended, as from a day to be appointed, by the *VCRA* 2006, s.61 (insertion of words in double square brackets in subs. (1)).]

Modifications

3–75 Section 98(7) of the *CDA* 1998 repealed section 62 of the *CJA* 1991, which effected temporary modifications to section 23 of the 1969 Act. Section 98(2) to (6) introduced new modifications, which "have effect ... in relation to any male person who (a) is of the age of 15 or 16; (b) is not of a description prescribed for the purposes of subsection (5) of" section 23; and (c) is not remanded in connection with proceedings under the *Extradition Act* 2003: s.98(1) (as amended by the *Extradition Act* 2003, s.201(1) and (10)). The *Secure Remands and Committals (Prescribed Description of Children and Young Persons) Order* 1999 (S.I. 1999 No. 1265) prescribes for the purposes of section 23(5), boys and girls aged 12, 13 or 14, and girls aged 15 or 16. The modifications (as further modified by the *CJPA* 2001, s.130(5)–(7)) are:

(a) the inclusion of the italicised words in square brackets in subsection (1);
(b) the substitution of subsections (4) to (5A) by the italicised subsections (4), (4A), (5), (5AA) and (5A) printed in square brackets;
(c) the substitution in subsection (6) of the words in square brackets by the italicised words;
(d) the insertion of the italicised words in subsection (7); and
(e) the inclusion of subsection (9A).

It was doubtful whether one of the modifications of the modifications introduced by the *CJPA* 2001 achieved its intended purpose. Section 130(6) provided for the substitution of subsection (5AA) (itself inserted by section 130(2)) by the italicised subsection (5AA). Since, however, there was no amendment to the substituted subsection (5) to correspond to the amendment to the original subsection (5) made by section 130(2) (substitution of new para. (b) to the end), it followed that the reference in the substituted subsection (5AA) to "The condition mentioned in subsection (5)" was meaningless. However, in *R. (M.) v. Inner London Crown Court* [2006] 1 W.L.R. 3406, DC, it was held that the substituted subsection (5) should be read as if it had been subject to an identical amendment as that made to the original subsection (5), such having been the obvious intent of the legislator.

Ancillary matters

As to section 128(7) of the *MCA* 1980, see *post*, § 3–152. As to section 61 of the *CJA* 1991, see *post*, § 3–78. **3–76**

For Schedule 15 to the 2003 Act, see *post*, § 5–299.

Section 22 of the *Children Act* 1989 (general duty of local authority in relation to children looked after by them) is not printed in this work.

Children and Young Persons Act 1969, s.23AA

Electronic monitoring of conditions of remand

23AA.—(1) A court shall not impose a condition on a person under section 23(7)(b) above (an "electronic monitoring condition") unless each of the following requirements is fulfilled. **3–76a**

(2) The first requirement is that the person has attained the age of twelve years.

(3) The second requirement is that—

(a) the person is charged with or has been convicted of a violent or sexual offence, or an offence punishable in the case of an adult with imprisonment for a term of fourteen years or more; or

(b) he is charged with or has been convicted of one or more imprisonable offences which, together with any other imprisonable offences of which he has been convicted in any proceedings—

(i) amount, or

(ii) would, if he were convicted of the offences with which he is charged, amount,

to a recent history of repeatedly committing imprisonable offences while remanded on bail or to local authority accommodation.

(4) The third requirement is that the court—

(a) *has been notified by the Secretary of State that electronic monitoring arrangements are available in each local justice area which is a relevant area; and*

(b) is satisfied that the necessary provision can be made under *those* arrangements [currently available in each local justice area which is a relevant area].

(5) The fourth requirement is that a youth offending team has informed the court that in its opinion the imposition of such a condition will be suitable in the person's case.

(6) Where a court imposes an electronic monitoring condition, the condition shall include provision for making a person responsible for the monitoring; and a person who is made so responsible shall be of a description specified in an order made by the Secretary of State.

(7) The Secretary of State may make rules for regulating—

(a) the electronic monitoring of compliance with conditions imposed under section 23(7)(a) above; and

(b) without prejudice to the generality of paragraph (a) above, the functions of persons made responsible for securing the electronic monitoring of compliance with such conditions.

(8) Subsections *(8) to (10)* [(4) to (7)] of section *3AA* [3AC] of the *Bail Act* 1976 (provision about rules and orders under that section) shall apply in relation to this section as they apply in relation to that section.

(9) For the purposes of this section a local justice area is a relevant area in relation to a proposed electronic monitoring condition if the court considers that it will not be practicable to secure the electronic monitoring in question unless electronic monitoring arrangements are available in that area.

[This section is inserted by the *CJPA* 2001, s.132(2). It is printed as amended by the *Courts Act* 2003, s.109(1), and Sched. 8, para. 135; and as amended, as from a day to be appointed, by the *CJIA* 2008, ss.148(1) and 149, Sched. 26, para. 5, and Sched. 29, Pt 4 (omission of italicised words, insertion of words in square brackets).]

Provision of accommodation for children in police protection or detention or on remand, etc.

3–77 Section 21(2) of the *Children Act* 1989 stipulates that every local authority shall receive, and provide accommodation for, children: (a) in police protection whom they are requested to receive under section 46(3)(f); (b) whom they are requested to receive under section 38(6) of the *PACE Act* 1984 (*post*, § 3–103); and (c) who are on remand under paragraph 7(5) of Schedule 7 to the *PCC(S)A* 2000 or section 23(1) (*ante*) of the 1969 Act or the subject of a supervision order imposing a local authority residence requirement under paragraph 5 of Schedule 6 to the Act of 2000. Note that in the *Children Act* 1989 "child" means a person under the age of 18: see section 105(1). Note also that section 21(2) of the 1989 Act is amended as from a day to be appointed by the *CJIA* 2008, s.6(1), and Sched. 4, paras 33 and 34, with the effect that (c), *ante*, will read: "(c) who are (i) on remand under section 23(1) (*ante*) of the 1969 Act, (ii) remanded to accommodation provided by or on behalf of a local authority by virtue of paragraph 21 of Schedule 2 to the *CJIA* 2008 (breach, etc., of youth rehabilitation orders), or (iii) the subject of a youth rehabilitation order imposing a local authority residence requirement or a youth rehabilitation order with fostering".

3–78 Section 61 of the 1991 Act imposes a duty on every local authority to secure that they are in a position to comply with any security requirement which may be imposed on them under section 23(4) (*ante*). A local authority may discharge this duty either by providing secure accommodation themselves or by making arrangements with other local authorities for the provision by them of such accommodation or by the making of arrangements with voluntary organisations or persons carrying on a registered children's home for the provision or use by them of such accommodation or by making arrangements with the Secretary of State for the use by them of a home provided by him under section 82(5) of the *Children Act* 1989.

3–79 Where a child or young person has been remanded or committed to local authority accommodation by a youth court or a magistrates' court other than a youth court, any application under section 25 of the *Children Act* 1989 that he be placed in secure accommodation shall be made to that court, notwithstanding anything in section 92(2) of that Act or section 65 of the *MCA* 1980: *CJA* 1991, s.60(3).

Applications under section 25 of the 1989 Act can be made only by the local authority looking after the child. They are applications for authorisation to keep a child the local authority is looking after in secure accommodation for a period greater than an aggregate of 72 hours in any 28-day period. Such applications may obviously relate to children who are already subjects of the criminal process, whether detained under section

38(6) of the *PACE Act* 1984 (*post*, § 3–103) or remanded to local authority accommodation under section 23 of the 1969 Act (*ante*). Such applications do not, however, themselves form part of the criminal process, although their outcome will have a direct bearing on what happens to the children concerned. Section 25 is not, therefore, printed in this work. Practitioners who are involved in applications under section 25, should make reference also to the *Children (Secure Accommodation) Regulations* 1991 (S.I. 1991 No. 1505) as amended by the *Children (Secure Accommodation) (Amendment) Regulations* 1992 (S.I. 1992 No. 2117), and the *Children Act (Miscellaneous Amendments) (England) Regulations* 2002 (S.I. 2002 No. 546). These, *inter alia*, regulate applications under section 25 and modify it in various ways according to which one of various categories a child belongs.

Procedural provision in relation to applications under section 25 of the *Children Act* 1989 is made by the *Magistrates' Courts (Children and Young Persons) Rules* 1992 (S.I. 1992 No. 2071), rr.13– 22.

Children and Young Persons Act 1969, ss.23A, 23B

Liability to arrest for breaking conditions of remand

23A.—(1) A person who has been remanded or committed to local authority accommodation and in respect of whom conditions under subsection (7) or (10) of section 23 of this Act have been imposed may be arrested without warrant by a constable if the constable has reasonable grounds for suspecting that that person has broken any of those conditions. **3–80**

(2) A person arrested under subsection (1) above—

(a) shall, except where he was arrested within 24 hours of the time appointed for him to appear before the court in pursuance of the remand or committal, be brought as soon as practicable and in any event within 24 hours after his arrest before a justice of the peace …; and

(b) in the said excepted case shall be brought before the court before which he was to have appeared.

In reckoning for the purposes of this subsection any period 24 hours, no account shall be taken of Christmas Day, Good Friday or any Sunday.

(3) A justice of the peace before whom a person is brought under subsection (2) above—

(a) if of the opinion that that person has broken any condition imposed on him under subsection (7) or (10) of section 23 of this Act shall remand him; and that section shall apply as if he was then charged with or convicted of the offence for which he had been remanded or committed;

(b) if not of that opinion shall remand him to the place to which he had been remanded or committed at the time of his arrest subject to the same conditions as those which had been imposed on him at that time.

[This section was inserted by the *CJPOA* 1994, s.23. It is printed as amended by the *Courts Act* 2003, s.109(1), and Sched. 8, para. 136.]

Report by local authority in certain cases where person remanded on bail

23B.—(1) Subsection (2) below applies where a court remands a person aged 10 or 11 on bail and either— **3–80a**

(a) the person is charged with or has been convicted of a serious offence, or

(b) in the opinion of the court the person is a persistent offender.

(2) The court may order a local authority to make an oral or written report specifying where the person is likely to be placed or maintained if he is further remanded to local authority accommodation.

(3) An order under subsection (2) above must designate the local authority which is to make the report; and that authority must be the local authority which the court would have designated under section 23(2) of this Act if the person had been remanded to local authority accommodation.

(4) An order under subsection (2) above must specify the period within which the local authority must comply with the order.

(5) The maximum period that may be so specified is seven working days.

(6) If the Secretary of State by order so provides, subsection (2) above also applies where—

(a) a court remands on bail any person who has attained the age of 12 and is under the age of 17,

(b) the requirement in section 23AA(3) of this Act is fulfilled, and
(c) in a case where he is remanded after conviction, the court is satisfied that the behaviour which constituted the offence was due, to a significant extent, to the circumstances in which the offender was living.

(7) In this section—

"serious offence" means an offence punishable in the case of an adult with imprisonment for a term of two years or more.

"working day" means any day other than—

(a) a Saturday or a Sunday,
(b) Christmas day or Good Friday, or
(c) a bank holiday in England and Wales under the *Banking and Financial Dealings Act* 1971.

[This section was inserted by the *Anti-social Behaviour Act* 2003, s.90.]

(7) Transfer to hospital of persons in custody otherwise than under sentence

Removal to hospital of certain prisoners

3–81 Section 47 of the *MHA* 1983 authorises the Secretary of State in certain circumstances to direct the transfer to hospital of prisoners under sentence. Section 48 (as amended by the *MHA* 2007, ss.1(4) and 5(1) and (3), and Sched. 1, paras 1 and 11) contains a similar power in the case of (a) persons detained in a prison or remand centre, not being persons serving a sentence of imprisonment or persons falling within paragraphs (b) to (d); (b) persons remanded in custody by a magistrates' court; (c) civil prisoners; and (d) persons detained under the *Immigration Act* 1971: see section 48(2). The power under section 48 may be exercised where (a) the Secretary of State is satisfied by reports from at least two registered medical practitioners that the person is suffering from mental disorder of a nature or degree that makes it appropriate for him to be detained in hospital for medical treatment and that he is in urgent need of such treatment and that appropriate medical treatment is available for him, and (b) he is of the opinion having regard to the public interest and all the circumstances that it is expedient to do so. A transfer direction ceases to have effect after 14 days unless it has been executed within that period: sections 47(2), 48(3). It has the same effect as a hospital order made in the case of the person in question: sections 47(3), 48(3).

When a transfer direction is given in respect of a person coming within section 48(2)(a) or (b) the Secretary of State must further direct that he shall be subject to the special restrictions in section 41 of the 1983 Act (*post*, § 5–898).

For the meaning of "mental disorder", see the *MHA* 1983, s.1(2) (*post*, § 5–887). Section 145 (as amended by the 2007 Act, s.7) defines "medical treatment" as including "nursing" and "psychological intervention and specialist mental health habilitation, rehabilitation and care" (subs. (1)), with subsection (4) providing that any reference to "medical treatment, in relation to mental disorder, shall be construed as a reference to medical treatment the purpose of which is to alleviate, or prevent a worsening of, the disorder or one of its symptoms or manifestations".

Powers of courts

3–82 Sections 51 and 52 of the *MHA* 1983 contain supplementary provisions in the case of persons subject to transfer directions who fall within paragraphs (a) and (b) respectively of section 48(2). *Inter alia*, they govern the powers of the court which is seised of the case of such a person. Section 51(3) governs the power of the Secretary of State to direct that a person coming within section 48(2)(a) be transferred back to a place where he might have been detained but for the transfer direction; as it has no relevance to the powers of the court, it is not printed here.

Mental Health Act 1983, s.51

Further provisions as to detained persons

3–83 **51.**—(1) This section has effect where a transfer direction has been given in respect of any such person as is described in paragraph (a) of section 48(2) above and that person is in this section referred to as "the detainee".

(2) The transfer direction shall cease to have effect when the detainee's case is disposed of by the court having jurisdiction to try or otherwise deal with him, but without prejudice to any power of that court to make a hospital order or other order under this Part of this Act in his case.

(3) [*Power of Secretary of State to direct patient's return to prison.*]

(4) If (no direction having been given under subsection (3) above) the court having jurisdiction to try or otherwise deal with the detainee is satisfied on the written or oral evidence of the responsible clinician—

(a) that the detainee no longer requires treatment in hospital for mental disorder; or

(b) that no effective treatment for his disorder can be given at the hospital to which he has been removed,

the court may order him to be remitted to any such place as is mentioned in subsection (3) above or, subject to section 25 of the *Criminal Justice and Public Order Act* 1994, released on bail and on his arrival at that place or, as the case may be, his release on bail the transfer direction shall cease to have effect.

(5) If (no direction or order having been given or made under subsection (3) or (4) above) it appears to the court having jurisdiction to try or otherwise deal with the detainee—

(a) that it is impracticable or inappropriate to bring the detainee before the court; and

(b) that the conditions set out in subsection (6) below are satisfied,

the court may make a hospital order (with or without a restriction order) in his case in his absence and, in the case of a person awaiting trial, without convicting him.

(6) A hospital order may be made in respect of a person under subsection (5) above if the court— **3–84**

(a) is satisfied, on the written or oral evidence of at least two registered medical practitioners, that—

(i) the detainee is suffering from mental disorder of a nature or degree which makes it appropriate for the patient to be detained in a hospital for medical treatment;

(ii) appropriate medical treatment is available for him; and

(b) is of the opinion, after considering any depositions or other documents required to be sent to the proper officer of the court, that it is proper to make such an order.

(7) Where a person committed to the Crown Court to be dealt with under section 43 above is admitted to a hospital in pursuance of an order under section 44 above, subsections (5) and (6) above shall apply as if he were a person subject to a transfer direction.

[This section is printed as amended by the *CJPOA* 1994, s.168(2), and Sched. 10, para. 51; and as amended by the *MHA* 2007, ss.1(4), 5(1) and (4) and 11(1) and (4), and Sched. 1, paras 1 and 12.]

As to hospital orders generally, see *post*, §§ 5–887 *et seq*. As to section 43 of the 1983 Act, see *post*, § 5–899; as to section 44 thereof, see *post*, § 5–900.

Mental Health Act 1983, s.52

Further provisions as to persons remanded by magistrates' courts

52.—(1) This section has effect where a transfer direction has been given in respect of any such person as is described in paragraph (b) of section 48(2) above; and that person is in this section referred to as "the accused". **3–85**

(2) Subject to subsection (5) below, the transfer direction shall cease to have effect on the expiration of the period of remand unless the accused is *committed* [sent] in custody to the Crown Court for trial or to be otherwise dealt with.

(3) Subject to subsection (4) below, the power of further remanding the accused under section 128 of the *Magistrates' Courts Act* 1980 may be exercised by the court without his being brought before the court; and if the court further remands the accused in custody (whether or not he is brought before the court) the period of remand shall, for the purposes of this section, be deemed not to have expired.

(4) The court shall not under subsection (3) above further remand the accused in his absence unless he has appeared before the court within the previous six months.

(5) If the magistrates' court is satisfied, on the written or oral evidence of the responsible clinician—

(a) that the accused no longer requires treatment in hospital for mental disorder; or

(b) that no effective treatment for his disorder can be given in the hospital to which he has been removed,

the court may direct that the transfer direction shall cease to have effect notwithstanding that the period of remand has not expired or that the accused is *committed* [sent] to the Crown Court as mentioned in subsection (2) above.

(6) If the accused is *committed* [sent] to the Crown Court as mentioned in subsection (2) above and the transfer direction has not ceased to have effect under subsection (5) above, section 51 above shall apply as if the transfer direction given in his case were a direction given in respect of a person falling within that section.

(7) [*See* post, *§ 10–13*.]

[This section is printed as amended by the *CJA* 2003, s.41, and Sched. 3, para. 55(1) and (3) (substitution of word in square brackets for italicised word in subss. (2), (5) and (6)). These amendments came into force on May 9, 2005, in relation to cases sent for trial under section 51 or 51A(3)(d) of the *CDA* 1998: *Criminal Justice Act 2003 (Commencement No. 9) Order* 2005 (S.I. 2005 No. 1267). Otherwise they come into force on a day to be appointed. Subs. (5) is printed as further amended by the *MHA* 2007, s.11(1) and (4).]

(8) Appeal against grant of bail

Bail (Amendment) Act 1993, s.1

Prosecution right of appeal

3–86 **1.**—(1) Where a magistrates' court grants bail to a person who is charged with, or convicted of, an offence punishable by imprisonment, the prosecution may appeal to a judge of the Crown Court against the granting of bail.

(1A) Where a magistrates' court grants bail to a person in connection with extradition proceedings, the prosecution may appeal to the High Court against the granting of bail.

(2) Subsection (1) above applies only where the prosecution is conducted—

(a) by or on behalf of the Director of Public Prosecutions; or

(b) by a person who falls within such class or description of person as may be prescribed for the purposes of this section by order made by the Secretary of State.

(3) An appeal under subsection (1) or (1A) may be made only if—

(a) the prosecution made representations that bail should not be granted; and

(b) the representations were made before it was granted.

(4) In the event of the prosecution wishing to exercise the right of appeal set out in subsection (1) or (1A) above, oral notice of appeal shall be given to the court which has granted bail at the conclusion of the proceedings in which bail has been granted and before the release from custody of the person concerned.

(5) Written notice of appeal shall thereafter be served on the court which has granted bail and the person concerned within two hours of the conclusion of such proceedings.

(6) Upon receipt from the prosecution of oral notice of appeal from its decision to grant bail the court which has granted bail shall remand in custody the person concerned, until the appeal is determined or otherwise disposed of.

3–87 (7) Where the prosecution fails, within the period of two hours mentioned in subsection (5) above, to serve one or both of the notices required by that subsection, the appeal shall be deemed to have been disposed of.

(8) The hearing of an appeal under subsection (1) or (1A) above against a decision of the court to grant bail shall be commenced within forty-eight hours, excluding weekends and any public holiday (that is to say, Christmas Day, Good Friday or a bank holiday), from the date on which oral notice of appeal is given.

(9) At the hearing of any appeal by the prosecution under this section, such appeal shall be by way of re-hearing, and the judge hearing any such appeal may remand the person concerned in custody or may grant bail subject to such conditions (if any) as he thinks fit.

(10) In relation to a child or young person (within the meaning of the *Children and Young Persons Act* 1969)—

(a) the reference in subsection (1) above to an offence punishable by imprisonment is to be read as a reference to an offence which would be so punishable in the case of an adult; and

(b) the references in subsections (6) and (9) above to remand in custody are to be read subject to the provisions of section 23 of the Act of 1969 (remands to local authority accommodation).

(11) [*Making of orders under subs. (2).*]

(12) In this section—

"extradition proceedings" means proceedings under the *Extradition Act* 2003;

"magistrates' court" and "court" in relation to extradition proceedings means a District Judge (Magistrates' Courts) designated in accordance with section 67 or section 139 of the *Extradition Act* 2003;

"prosecution" in relation to extradition proceedings means the person acting on behalf of the territory to which extradition is sought.

[This section is printed as amended by the *Extradition Act* 2003, s.200(1) to (9); the *CJA* 2003, s.18 (as to which, see *post*, § 3–87a); the *Constitutional Reform Act* 2005, s.15(1), and Sched. 4, para. 231; and the *PJA* 2006, s.42, and Sched. 13, para. 28.]

The *Bail (Amendment) Act 1993 (Prescription of Prosecuting Authorities) Order* 1994 (S.I. 1994 No. 1438); as amended by the *Postal Services Act 2000 (Consequential Modifications No. 1) Order* 2001 (S.I. 2001 No. 1149), Sched. 1, para. 102, the *Bail (Amendment) Act 1993 (Prescription of Prosecuting Authorities) (Amendment) Order* 2005 (S.I. 2005 No. 1129), and the *Secretaries of State for Children, Schools and Families, for Innovation, Universities and Skills and for Business, Enterprise and Regulatory Reform Order* 2007 (S.I. 2007 No. 3224), prescribes the following authorities for the purposes of section 1: the Director of the Serious Fraud Office and any person designated under section 1(7) of the *CJA* 1987; the Secretary of State for Business, Enterprise and Regulatory Reform; the Secretary of State for Social Security; a universal service provider (within the meaning of the *Postal Services Act* 2000) in connection with the provision of a universal postal service (within the meaning of that Act); and the Director of Revenue and Customs Prosecutions and any person designated under section 37(1) of the *Commissioners for Revenue and Customs Act* 2005.

For section 23 of the *CYPA* 1969, see *ante*, § 3–69.

The requirement that oral notice of appeal is given to the magistrates' court "at the conclusion of the proceedings" (s.1(4)), was satisfied where notice was given five minutes after the justices had withdrawn: *R. v. Isleworth Crown Court, ex p. Clarke* [1998] 1 Cr.App.R. 257, DC. Where the prosecution failed (by three minutes) to comply with subsection (5), subsection (7) did not operate to dispose of the appeal where they had used all due diligence and had allowed ample time to comply, but had been defeated by circumstances outside their control, and where there was no prejudice to the defendant (who was aware of their intention): *R. (Jeffrey) v. Warwick Crown Court* [2003] Crim.L.R. 190, QBD (Hooper J.). The hearing of the appeal must be commenced within 48 hours of the end of the day on which oral notice of appeal is given: *R. v. Middlesex Guildhall Crown Court, ex p. Okoli* [2000] 1 Cr.App.R. 1, DC (considering subs. (8)).

If the judge remands the defendant in custody, he should (unless the defendant was committed for trial at the same time as being granted bail) specify a date until which he is remanded in accordance with sections 128, 128A and 129 of the *MCA* 1980 (*post*, §§ 3–146 *et seq.*); failure to do so would result in the defendant being unlawfully detained once eight days had elapsed since the last appearance in front of the justices: *Re Bone*, 159 J.P. 111, DC; *Re Szakal* [2000] 1 Cr.App.R. 248, DC; and *Remice v. Governor of Belmarsh Prison* [2007] Crim.L.R. 796, DC (whilst ss.128 and 128A do not directly bind the Crown Court, that court should act consistently with them).

Transitional

In connection with the commencement of section 18 of the *CJA* 2003 (substituting subs. (1) and making a minor amendment to subs. (10)(a)), reference should be made to the saving provision in paragraph 3 of Schedule 2 to the *Criminal Justice Act 2003* **3–87a**

(Commencement No. 8 and Transitional and Saving Provisions) Order 2005 (S.I. 2005 No. 950).

S.I. 2005 No. 950, Sched. 2, para. 3

3–87b 3.—(1) In the case of any criminal proceedings falling under paragraph (2)—

(a) the coming into force of sections 18, 57 to 61, 67 to 72 and 74 of the 2003 Act confers no additional prosecution right of appeal;

(b) the coming into force of sections 309 and 310 of the 2003 Act confers no additional power to order a preparatory hearing on a judge of the Crown Court; and

(c) the coming into force of section 311 of the 2003 Act does not alter the jurisdiction in which reporting restrictions may apply in those proceedings.

(2) The criminal proceedings to which this paragraph applies are those in which one of the following occurred before 4th April 2005—

(a) the defendant was committed for trial;

(b) the proceedings were transferred to the Crown Court under section 53 of the *Criminal Justice Act* 1991 or section 4 of the *Criminal Justice Act* 1987;

(c) an order was made by a magistrates' court that the accused be sent for trial for an indictable only offence under section 51 of the *Crime and Disorder Act* 1998; or

(d) a bill of indictment was preferred by the direction or with the consent of a judge of the High Court.

Criminal Procedure Rules 2005 (S.I. 2005 No. 384), rr.19.16, 19.17

Lodging an appeal against a grant of bail by a magistrates' court

3–88 **19.16.**—(1) Where the prosecution wishes to exercise the right of appeal, under section 1 of the *Bail (Amendment) Act* 1993, to a judge of the Crown Court against a decision to grant bail, the oral notice of appeal must be given to the justices' clerk and to the person concerned, at the conclusion of the proceedings in which such bail was granted and before the release of the person concerned.

(2) When oral notice of appeal is given, the justices' clerk shall announce in open court the time at which such notice was given.

(3) A record of the prosecution's decision to appeal and the time the oral notice of appeal was given shall be made in the register and shall contain the particulars set out.

(4) Where an oral notice of appeal has been given the court shall remand the person concerned in custody by a warrant of commitment.

(5) On receipt of the written notice of appeal required by section 1(5) of the 1993 Act, the court shall remand the person concerned in custody by a warrant of commitment, until the appeal is determined or otherwise disposed of.

(6) A record of the receipt of the written notice of appeal shall be made in the same manner as that of the oral notice of appeal under paragraph (3).

3–89 (7) If, having given oral notice of appeal, the prosecution fails to serve a written notice of appeal within the two hour period referred to in section 1(5) of the 1993 Act the justices' clerk shall, as soon as practicable, by way of written notice (served by a court officer) to the persons in whose custody the person concerned is, direct the release of the person concerned on bail as granted by the magistrates' court and subject to any conditions which it imposed.

(8) If the prosecution serves notice of abandonment of appeal on a court officer, the justices' clerk shall, forthwith, by way of written notice (served by the court officer) to the governor of the prison where the person concerned is being held, or the person responsible for any other establishment where such a person is being held, direct his release on bail as granted by the magistrates' court and subject to any conditions which it imposed.

(9) A court officer shall record the prosecution's failure to serve a written notice of appeal, or its service of a notice of abandonments.

(10) Where a written notice of appeal has been served on a magistrates' court officer, he shall provide as soon as practicable to a Crown Court officer a copy of that written notice, together with—

(a) the notes of argument made by the court officer for the court under rule 19.10; and

(b) a note of the date, or dates, when the person concerned is next due to appear in the magistrates' court, whether he is released on bail or remanded in custody by the Crown Court.

(11) References in this rule to "the person concerned" are references to such a person within the meaning of section 1 of the 1993 Act.

Crown Court procedure on appeal against grant of bail by a magistrates' court

19.17.—(1) This rule shall apply where the prosecution appeals under section 1 of the *Bail (Amendment) Act* 1993 against a decision of a magistrates' court granting bail and in this rule "the person concerned" has the same meaning as in that Act. **3–90**

(2) The written notice of appeal required by section 1(5) of the 1993 Act shall be in the form set out in the Practice Direction and shall be served on—

(a) the magistrates' court officer; and

(b) the person concerned.

(3) The Crown Court officer shall enter the appeal and give notice of the time and place of the hearing to—

(a) the prosecution;

(b) the person concerned or his legal representative; and

(c) the magistrates' court officer.

(4) The person concerned shall not be entitled to be present at the hearing of the appeal unless he is acting in person or, in any other case of an exceptional nature, a judge of the Crown Court is of the opinion that the interests of justice require his [*sic*] to be present and gives him leave to be so.

(5) Where a person concerned has not been able to instruct a solicitor to represent him at the appeal, he may give notice to the Crown Court requesting that the Official Solicitor shall represent him at the appeal, and the court may, if it thinks fit, assign the Official Solicitor to act for the person concerned accordingly.

(6) At any time after the service of written notice of appeal under paragraph (2), the prosecution may abandon the appeal by giving notice in writing in the form set out in the Practice Direction.

(7) The notice of abandonment required by the preceding paragraph shall be served on— **3–91**

(a) the person concerned or his legal representative;

(b) the magistrates' court officer; and

(c) the Crown Court officer.

(8) Any record required by section 5 of the *Bail Act* 1976 (together with any note of reasons required by subsection (4) of that section to be included) shall be made by way of an entry in the file relating to the case in question and the record shall include the following particulars, namely—

(a) the effect of the decision;

(b) a statement of any condition imposed in respect of bail, indicating whether it is to be complied with before or after release on bail; and

(c) where bail is withheld, a statement of the relevant exception to the right to bail (as provided in Schedule 1 to the 1976 Act) on which the decision is based.

(9) The Crown Court officer shall, as soon as practicable after the hearing of the appeal, give notice of the decision and of the matters required by the preceding paragraph to be recorded to—

(a) the person concerned or his legal representative;

(b) the prosecution;

(c) the police;

(d) the magistrates' officer; and

(e) the governor of the prison or person responsible for the establishment where the person concerned is being held.

(10) Where the judge hearing the appeal grants bail to the person concerned, the provisions of rule 19.18(9) (informing the Court of any earlier application for bail) and rule 19.22 (conditions attached to bail granted by the Crown Court) shall apply as if that person had applied to the Crown Court for bail.

(11) The notices required by paragraphs (3), (5), (7) and (9) of this rule may be served under rule 4.6 (service by fax, e-mail or other electronic means) and the notice required by paragraph (3) may be given by telephone.

[This rule is printed as amended by the *Criminal Procedure (Amendment) Rules* 2007 (S.I. 2007 No. 699), r.14.]

(9) Appeal against condition of bail

Criminal Justice Act 2003, s.16

Appeal to Crown Court

3–91a **16.**—(1) This section applies where a magistrates' court grants bail to a person ("the person concerned") on adjourning a case under—

(a) section 10 of the *Magistrates' Courts Act* 1980 (adjournment of trial),

(b) section 17C of that Act (intention as to plea: adjournment),

(c) section 18 of that Act (initial procedure on information against adult for offence triable either way),

(d) section 24C of that Act (intention as to plea by child or young person: adjournment),

(e) section 52(5) of the *Crime and Disorder Act* 1998 (adjournment of proceedings under section 51 etc), or

(f) section 11 of the *Powers of Criminal Courts (Sentencing) Act* 2000 (remand for medical examination).

(2) Subject to the following provisions of this section, the person concerned may appeal to the Crown Court against any condition of bail falling within subsection (3).

(3) A condition of bail falls within this subsection if it is a requirement—

(a) that the person concerned resides away from a particular place or area,

(b) that the person concerned resides at a particular place other than a bail hostel,

(c) for the provision of a surety or sureties or the giving of a security,

(d) that the person concerned remains indoors between certain hours,

(e) imposed under section 3(6ZAA) of the 1976 Act (requirements with respect to electronic monitoring), or

(f) that the person concerned makes no contact with another person.

(4) An appeal under this section may not be brought unless subsection (5) or (6) applies.

(5) This subsection applies if an application to the magistrates' court under section 3(8)(a) of the 1976 Act (application by or on behalf of person granted bail) was made and determined before the appeal was brought.

(6) This subsection applies if an application to the magistrates' court—

(a) under section 3(8)(b) of the 1976 Act (application by constable or prosecutor), or

(b) under section 5B(1) of that Act (application by prosecutor),

was made and determined before the appeal was brought.

(7) On an appeal under this section the Crown Court may vary the conditions of bail.

(8) Where the Crown Court determines an appeal under this section, the person concerned may not bring any further appeal under this section in respect of the conditions of bail unless an application or a further application to the magistrates' court under section 3(8)(a) of the 1976 Act is made and determined after the appeal.

3–91b Section 21 of the 2003 Act provides that in Part 2 of that Act (ss.13– 21), "bail" means bail in criminal proceedings (within the meaning of the 1976 Act), "bail hostel" has the meaning given by section 2(2) of that Act (*ante*, § 3–7), "the 1976 Act" means the *Bail Act* 1976, and "vary" has the same meaning as in that Act (as to which see s.2(2)).

B. SPECIFIC PROVISIONS

(1) The police

(a) *The Police and Criminal Evidence Act 1984*

General

3–92 Part IV (ss.34– 52) of the *PACE Act* 1984 is entitled "Detention". It makes provision for the detention of persons after arrest: sections 34, 37, 38 and 41 to 44 impose an obligation to release a person on bail in certain circumstances. Section 47 is a general section relating to persons who are released on bail under Part IV.

As to the Code of Practice on the Detention, Treatment and Questioning of Persons by Police Officers, see Appendix A–38.

Police and Criminal Evidence Act 1984, s.34

Limitations on police detention

3–93 **34.**—(1) A person arrested for an offence shall not be kept in police detention except in accordance with the provisions of this Part of this Act.

(2) Subject to subsection (3) below, if at any time a custody officer—

(a) becomes aware, in relation to any person in police detention, that the grounds for the detention of that person have ceased to apply; and

(b) is not aware of any other grounds on which the continued detention of that person could be justified under the provisions of this Part of this Act,

it shall be the duty of the custody officer, subject to subsection (4) below, to order his immediate release from custody.

(3) No person in police detention shall be released except on the authority of a custody officer at the police station where his detention was authorised or, if it was authorised at more than one station, a custody officer at the station where it was last authorised.

(4) A person who appears to the custody officer to have been unlawfully at large when he was arrested is not to be released under subsection (2) above.

(5) A person whose release is ordered under subsection (2) above shall be released without bail unless it appears to the custody officer—

(a) that there is need for further investigation of any matter in connection with which he was detained at any time during the period of his detention; or

(b) that, in respect of any such matter, proceedings may be taken against him or he may be reprimanded or warned under section 65 of the *Crime and Disorder Act* 1998,

and, if it so appears, he shall be released on bail.

(6) For the purposes of this Part of this Act a person arrested under section 6D of the *Road Traffic Act* 1988 or section 30(2) of the *Transport and Works Act* 1992 is arrested for an offence.

(7) For the purposes of this Part a person who—

(a) attends a police station to answer to bail granted under section 30A,

(b) returns to a police station to answer to bail granted under this Part, or

(c) is arrested under section 30D or 46A,

is to be treated as arrested for an offence and that offence is the offence in connection with which he was granted bail.

[(8) Subsection (7) does not apply in relation to a person who is granted bail subject to the duty mentioned in section 47(3)(b) and who either—

(a) attends a police station to answer to such bail, or

(b) is arrested under section 46A for failing to do so,

(provision as to the treatment of such persons for the purposes of this Part being made by section 46ZA).]

[This section is printed as amended by the *Road Traffic (Consequential Provisions) Act* 1988, s.4 and Sched. 3, para. 27(2); the *CJPOA* 1994, s.29(3); the *CJCSA* 2000, s.56(2); the *Police Reform Act* 2002, s.53(1); the *Railways and Transport Safety Act* 2003, s.107, and Sched. 7, para. 12; and the *CJA* 2003, s.12, and Sched. 1, paras 1 and 5. Subs. (8) was inserted as from April 1, 2007 (but only in the local justice area of Lambeth and Southwark) (*Police and Justice Act 2006 (Commencement No. 2, Transitional and Saving Provisions) Order* 2007 (S.I. 2007 No. 709)) by the *PJA* 2006, s.46(1) and (2).]

Section 24B(1) and (2) of the *CJA* 2003 provide that in the case of a person arrested under section 24A for breach of a condition attached to a conditional caution, section 34(1) to (5) of the 1984 Act apply, "with such ... modifications as are necessary", as they apply in the case of a person arrested for an offence. As to when a person is in "police detention", see section 118(2) of the Act, *post*, § 15–27.

Police and Criminal Evidence Act 1984, s.35

Designated police stations

35.—(1) The chief officer of police for each police area shall designate the police stations in his area which, subject to sections 30(3) and (5), 30A(5) and 30D(2), are to be the stations in that area to be used for the purpose of detaining arrested persons. **3–94**

(2) A chief officer's duty under subsection (1) above is to designate police stations appearing to him to provide enough accommodation for that purpose.

(2A) The Chief Constable of the British Transport Police Force may designate police stations which (in addition to those designated under subsection (1) above) may be used for the purpose of detaining arrested persons.

(3) Without prejudice to section 12 of the *Interpretation Act* 1978 (continuity of duties) a chief officer—

(a) may designate a station which was not previously designated; and

(b) may direct that a designation of a station previously made shall cease to operate.

(4) In this Act "designated police station" means a police station for the time being designated under this section.

[This section is printed as amended by the *Anti-terrorism, Crime and Security Act* 2001, s.101, and Sched. 7, paras 11 and 12; and the *CJA* 2003, s.12, and Sched. 1, paras 1 and 6.]

For section 30 of the Act, see *post*, § 15–182. As to the modification of this section in its application to Revenue and Customs, see the *Police and Criminal Evidence Act 1984 (Application to Revenue and Customs) Order* 2007 (S.I. 2007 No. 3175), art. 9 (*post*, § 15–43).

Police and Criminal Evidence Act 1984, s.36

Custody officers at police station

3–95 **36.**—(1) One or more custody officers shall be appointed for each designated police station.

(2) [*Authority to appoint custody officers.*]

(3) *No officer may be appointed a custody officer unless he is of at least the rank of sergeant.*

[(3 No person may be appointed a custody officer unless—

(a) he is a police officer of at least the rank of sergeant; or

(b) he is a staff custody officer.]

(4) An officer of any rank may perform the functions of a custody officer at a designated police station if a custody officer is not readily available to perform them.

(5) Subject to the following provisions of this section and to section 39(2) below, none of the functions of a custody officer in relation to a person shall be performed by an *officer* [individual] who at the time when the function falls to be performed is involved in the investigation of an offence for which that person is in police detention at that time.

(6) Nothing in subsection (5) above is to be taken to prevent a custody officer—

(a) performing any function assigned to custody officers—

(i) by this Act; or

(ii) by a code of practice issued under this Act;

(b) carrying out the duty imposed on custody officers by section 39 below;

(c) doing anything in connection with the identification of a suspect; or

(d) doing anything under sections 7 and 8 of the *Road Traffic Act* 1988.

3–96 (7) Where an arrested person is taken to a police station which is not a designated police station, the functions in relation to him which at a designated police station would be the function of a custody officer shall be performed—

(a) by an officer [or a staff custody officer] who is not involved in the investigation of an offence for which he is in police detention, if *such an officer* [such a person] is readily available; and

(b) if no *such officer* [such person] is readily available, by the officer who took him to the station or any other officer.

(7A) Subject to subsection (7B), subsection (7) applies where a person attends a police station which is not a designated station to answer to bail granted under section 30A as it applies where a person is taken to such a station.

(7B) Where subsection (7) applies because of subsection (7A), the reference in subsection (7)(b) to the officer who took him to the station is to be read as a reference to the officer who granted him bail.

(8) References to a custody officer in [section 34 above or in] the following provisions of this Act include references to *an officer* [a person] other than a custody officer who is performing the functions of a custody officer by virtue of subsection (4) or (7) above.

(9) Where by virtue of subsection (7) above an officer of a force maintained by a police authority who took an arrested person to a police station is to perform the functions of a custody officer in relation to him, the officer shall inform an officer who—

(a) is attached to a designated police station; and

(b) is of at least the rank of inspector,

that he is to do so.

(10) The duty imposed by subsection (9) above shall be performed as soon as it is practicable to perform it.

[(11) In this section, "staff custody officer" means a person who has been designated as such under section 38 of the *Police Reform Act* 2002.]

[This section is printed as amended by the *Road Traffic (Consequential Provisions) Act* 1988, s.4 and Sched. 3, para. 27(3); and the *CJA* 2003, s.12, and Sched. 1, paras 1 and 7; and as amended, as from a day to be appointed, by the *SOCPA* 2005, s.121(1)–(6) (insertion of words in square brackets, omission of words in italics).]

As to the modification of this section in its application to Revenue and Customs, see S.I. 2007 No. 3175 (*ante*, § 3–94), art. 10 (*post*, § 15–43).

Section 24B(1) and (2) of the *CJA* 2003 provide that in the case of a person arrested under section 24A for breach of a condition attached to a conditional caution, section 36 applies, with the modifications to subsections (5) and (7) set out in subsection (3), and "with such further modifications as are necessary", as it applies in the case of a person arrested for an offence. The modifications specified in section 24B(3) are the substitution for the references to being involved in the investigation of an offence for which the person is in police detention, of references to being involved in the investigation of the offence in respect of which the person was given the conditional caution, or in investigating whether the person has failed, without reasonable excuse, to comply with any of the conditions attached to the conditional caution.

Section 36(1) means that the chief officer has a duty to appoint one custody officer for each designated police station. There is no duty to ensure that at each designated police station at least one custody officer is normally available to perform the functions of a custody officer: *Vince v. Chief Constable of Dorset Police* [1993] 1 W.L.R. 415, CA (Civ. Div.).

Police and Criminal Evidence Act 1984, s.37

Duties of custody officer before charge

37.—(1) Where— **3–97**

(a) a person is arrested for an offence—

(i) without a warrant; or

(ii) under a warrant not endorsed for bail ...

the custody officer at each police station where he is detained after his arrest shall determine whether he has before him sufficient evidence to charge that person with the offence for which he was arrested and may detain him at the police station for such period as is necessary to enable him to do so.

(2) If the custody officer determines that he does not have such evidence before him, the person arrested shall be released either on bail or without bail, unless the custody officer has reasonable grounds for believing that his detention without being charged is necessary to secure or preserve evidence relating to an offence for which he is under arrest or to obtain such evidence by questioning him.

(3) If the custody officer has reasonable grounds for so believing, he may authorise the person arrested to be kept in police detention.

(4) Where a custody officer authorises a person who has not been charged to be kept in police detention, he shall, as soon as is practicable, make a written record of the grounds for the detention.

(5) Subject to subsection (6) below, the written record shall be made in the presence of **3–98** the person arrested who shall at that time be informed by the custody officer of the grounds for his detention.

(6) Subsection (5) above shall not apply where the person arrested is, at the time when the written record is made—

(a) incapable of understanding what is said to him;

(b) violent or likely to become violent; or

(c) in urgent need of medical attention.

(7) Subject to section 41(7) below, if the custody officer determines that he has before him sufficient evidence to charge the person arrested with the offence for which he was arrested, the person arrested—

(a) shall be—

(i) released without charge and on bail, or

(ii) kept in police detention,

for the purpose of enabling the Director of Public Prosecutions to make a decision under section 37B below,

(b) shall be released without charge and on bail but not for that purpose,

(c) shall be released without charge and without bail, or

(d) shall be charged.

(7A) The decision as to how a person is to be dealt with under subsection (7) above shall be that of the custody officer.

(7B) Where a person is dealt with under subsection (7)(a) above, it shall be the duty of the custody officer to inform him that he is being released, or (as the case may be) detained to enable the Director of Public Prosecutions to make a decision under section 37B below.

(8) Where—

(a) a person is released under subsection (7)(b) or (c) above; and

(b) at the time of his release a decision whether he should be prosecuted for the offence for which he was arrested has not been taken,

it shall be the duty of the custody officer so to inform him.

(8A Subsection (8B) applies if the offence for which the person is arrested is one in relation to which a sample could be taken under section 63B below and the custody officer—

(a) is required in pursuance of subsection (2) above to release the person arrested and decides to release him on bail, or

(b) decides in pursuance of subsection (7)(a) or (b) above to release the person without charge and on bail.

(8B) The detention of the person may be continued to enable a sample to be taken under section 63B, but this subsection does not permit a person to be detained for a period of more than 24 hours after the relevant time.

(9) If the person arrested is not in a fit state to be dealt with under subsection (7) above, he may be kept in police detention until he is.

(10) The duty imposed on the custody officer under subsection (1) above shall be carried out by him as soon as practicable after the person arrested arrives at the police station or, in the case of a person arrested at the police station, as soon as practicable after the arrest.

3–99 (11)–(14) [*Repealed by* Criminal Justice Act *1991, s.101(2) , and Sched. 13.*]

(15) In this Part of this Act—

"arrested juvenile" means a person arrested with or without a warrant who appears to be under the age of 17.....

"endorsed for bail" means endorsed with a direction for bail in accordance with section 117(2) of the *Magistrates' Courts Act* 1980.

[This section is printed as amended, and repealed in part, by the *Children Act* 1989, s.108(7), and Sched. 15; the *CJPOA* 1994, ss.29(1) and (4)(a), and 168(3), and Sched. 11; the *CJA* 2003, s.28, and Sched. 2, paras 1 and 2; the *Drugs Act* 2005, s.23(1), and Sched. 1, paras 1 and 2; and the *PJA* 2006, ss.11 and 52, and Sched. 14, para. 9.]

Section 24B(1) and (2) of the *CJA* 2003 provide that in the case of a person arrested under section 24A for breach of a condition attached to a conditional caution, section 37(4) to (6) apply, "with such ... modifications as are necessary", as they apply in the case of a person arrested for an offence.

Sections 37 to 37B of the 1984 Act have effect, in relation to a person arrested following a criminal investigation by the Serious Organised Crime Agency relating to a designated offence, or by the Revenue and Customs, as if references to the Director of Public Prosecutions were references to the Director of Revenue and Customs Prosecutions: *SOCPA* 2005, s.40(1); and *Commissioners for Revenue and Customs Act* 2005, s.50(6), and Sched. 4, para. 30. As to "a designated offence", see s.38(7)(b) of the former Act: s.40(2).

As to the modified application of specified provisions of Part IV of the 1984 Act (including this section) where a person is arrested for an offence under a warrant issued in accordance with section 87(1)(a) of the *CJA* 2003 (arrest of a person acquitted of serious offence where fresh evidence available to support application for retrial) (*post*, § 7–273), or having been so arrested, is subsequently treated under section 34(7) (*ante*, § 3–93) as arrested for that offence, see section 87(4) to (8) of that Act, *post*, § 3–131c.

As to section 117 of the *MCA* 1980, see *post*, § 3–139.

In *Al Fayed v. Metropolitan Police Commr* [2005] 1 *Archbold News* 2, CA (Civ. Div.) ([2004] EWCA Civ. 1579) it was said that section 37(2) and (3) would be unworkable if, in a complicated investigation, a custody officer were required to ask for chapter and verse of the evidence and/or information that had prompted an officer to arrest a suspect before he, the custody officer, determined on detention without charge; whilst it is a custody officer's function to introduce an independent filter as to whether continued detention without charge is necessary, he is not required to inquire into the legality of an arrest and is entitled to assume that it was lawful (*DPP v. L.* [1999] Crim.L.R. 752, DC); he is entitled to have regard to the arresting officer's assessment of the need for arrest for the purpose of interview, and whilst he is not bound by that assessment, he is not required to test it forensically as if it were an adversarial process.

Power of police to charge on behalf of private individual

In *R. v. Ealing JJ., ex p. Dixon* [1990] 2 Q.B. 91, DC, it was held that a police officer, as custody officer acting under sections 37 and 38(1) had no power to charge a person or perform the other duties imposed by those sections on behalf of a private individual; and that, where a custody officer did charge someone, the Director of Public Prosecutions was bound to take over the conduct of the proceedings by virtue of section 3(2) of the *Prosecution of Offences Act* 1985 (*ante*, § 1–253) because they had been "instituted on behalf of a police force". **3–100**

The Divisional Court in *R. v. Stafford JJ., ex p. Customs and Excise Commrs* [1991] 2 Q.B. 339, declined to follow *ex p. Dixon*, concluding that it was wrongly decided. Watkins L.J., delivering a judgment with which Nolan J. agreed, said that the provisions of section 6 of the 1985 Act (*ante*, § 1–258) envisaged that persons other than the DPP might institute proceedings and prosecute. His Lordship said that the view of the legislation taken in *ex p. Dixon* was an incorrect one which would lead to the conclusion that a person such as a customs officer who investigated the commission of an offence, arrested a person and took him to a police station to be charged, thereby surrendered the prosecution of the proceedings to the DPP because the charging process, in stark opposition to the facts, deemed the proceedings to have been instituted on behalf of the police force. Proceedings could only be said to have been instituted on behalf of a police force when it was the police who had investigated, arrested and brought the arrested person to the custody officer. **3–101**

Police and Criminal Evidence Act 1984, ss.37A–37D

Guidance

37A.—(1) The Director of Public Prosecutions may issue guidance— **3–101a**

(a) for the purpose of enabling custody officers to decide how persons should be dealt with under section 37(7) above or 37C(2) or 37CA(2) below, and

(b) as to the information to be sent to the Director of Public Prosecutions under section 37B(1) below.

(2) The Director of Public Prosecutions may from time to time revise guidance issued under this section.

(3) Custody officers are to have regard to guidance under this section in deciding how persons should be dealt with under section 37(7) above or 37C(2) or 37CA(2) below.

(4) A report under section 9 of the *Prosecution of Offences Act* 1985 (report by DPP to Attorney General) must set out the provisions of any guidance issued, and any revisions to guidance made, in the year to which the report relates.

(5) The Director of Public Prosecutions must publish in such manner as he thinks fit—

(a) any guidance issued under this section, and

(b) any revisions made to such guidance.

(6) Guidance under this section may make different provision for different cases, circumstances or areas.

[This section was inserted by the *CJA* 2003, s.28, and Sched. 2, paras 1 and 3. It is printed as amended by the *PJA* 2006, s.10, and Sched. 6, paras 1 and 8(2).]

As to references to the "Director of Public Prosecutions" in this section and section 37B, *post*, see *ante*, § 3–99.

As to the unlawfulness of part of the guidance issued under this section, see *G. v. Chief Constable of West Yorkshire Police* (*ante*, § 3–99).

Consultation with the Director of Public Prosecutions

3–101b **37B.**—(1) Where a person is dealt with under section 37(7)(a) above, an officer involved in the investigation of the offence shall, as soon as is practicable, send to the Director of Public Prosecutions such information as may be specified in guidance under section 37A above.

(2) The Director of Public Prosecutions shall decide whether there is sufficient evidence to charge the person with an offence.

(3) If he decides that there is sufficient evidence to charge the person with an offence, he shall decide—

(a) whether or not the person should be charged and, if so, the offence with which he should be charged, and

(b) whether or not the person should be given a caution and, if so, the offence in respect of which he should be given a caution.

(4) The Director of Public Prosecutions shall give notice of his decision to an officer involved in the investigation of the offence.

(4A) Notice under subsection (4) above shall be in writing, but in the case of a person kept in police detention under section 37(7)(a) above it may be given orally in the first instance and confirmed in writing subsequently.

(5) If his decision is—

(a) that there is not sufficient evidence to charge the person with an offence, or

(b) that there is sufficient evidence to charge the person with an offence but that the person should not be charged with an offence or given a caution in respect of an offence,

a custody officer shall give the person notice in writing that he is not to be prosecuted.

(6) If the decision of the Director of Public Prosecutions is that the person should be charged with an offence, or given a caution in respect of an offence, the person shall be charged or cautioned accordingly.

(7) But if his decision is that the person should be given a caution in respect of the offence and it proves not to be possible to give the person such a caution, he shall instead be charged with the offence.

(8) For the purposes of this section, a person is to be charged with an offence either—

(a) when he is in police detention at a police station (whether because he has returned to answer bail, because he is detained under section 37(7)(a) above or for some other reason), or

(b) in accordance with section 29 of the *Criminal Justice Act* 2003.

(9) In this section "caution" includes—

(a) a conditional caution within the meaning of Part 3 of the *Criminal Justice Act* 2003, and

[(aa) a youth conditional caution within the meaning of Chapter 1 of Part 4 of the *Crime and Disorder Act* 1998;]

(b) a warning or reprimand under section 65 of *the* Crime and Disorder Act *1998* [that Act].

[This section was inserted by the *CJA* 2003, s.28, and Sched. 2, paras 1 and 3. It is printed as amended by the *PJA* 2006, s.52, and Sched. 10, para. 10; and as amended, as from a day to be appointed, by the *CJIA* 2008, s.148(1), and Sched. 26, para. 20(1) (insertion of subs. (9)(aa), substitution of words in square brackets in subs. (9)(b) for the words "*the* Crime and Disorder Act *1998*").]

Breach of bail following release under section 37(7)(a)

3–101c **37C.**—(1) This section applies where—

(a) a person released on bail under section 37(7)(a) above or subsection (2)(b) below is arrested under section 46A below in respect of that bail, and

(b) at the time of his detention following that arrest at the police station mentioned in section 46A(2) below, notice under section 37B(4) above has not been given.

(2) The person arrested—

(a) shall be charged, or

(b) shall be released without charge, either on bail or without bail.

(3) The decision as to how a person is to be dealt with under subsection (2) above shall be that of a custody officer.

(4) A person released on bail under subsection (2)(b) above shall be released on bail subject to the same conditions (if any) which applied immediately before his arrest.

[This section was inserted by the *CJA* 2003, s.28, and Sched. 2, paras 1 and 3.]

Breach of bail following release under section 37(7)(b)

37CA.—(1) This section applies where a person released on bail under section 37(7)(b) above or subsection (2)(b) below— **3–101ca**

(a) is arrested under section 46A below in respect of that bail, and

(b) is being detained following that arrest at the police station mentioned in section 46A(2) below.

(2) The person arrested—

(a) shall be charged, or

(b) shall be released without charge, either on bail or without bail.

(3) The decision as to how a person is to be dealt with under subsection (2) above shall be that of a custody officer.

(4) A person released on bail under subsection (2)(b) above shall be released on bail subject to the same conditions (if any) which applied immediately before his arrest.

[This section was inserted by the *PJA* 2006, s.10, and Sched. 6, paras 1 and 8(1).]

Release on bail under section 37: further provision

37D.—(1) Where a person is released on bail under section 37, 37C(2)(b) or 37CA(2)(b) above, a custody officer may subsequently appoint a different time, or an additional time, at which the person is to attend at the police station to answer bail. **3–101d**

(2) The custody officer shall give the person notice in writing of the exercise of the power under subsection (1).

(3) The exercise of the power under subsection (1) shall not affect the conditions (if any) to which bail is subject.

(4) Where a person released on bail under section 37(7)(a) or 37C(2)(b) above returns to a police station to answer bail or is otherwise in police detention at a police station, he may be kept in police detention to enable him to be dealt with in accordance with section 37B or 37C above or to enable the power under subsection (1) above to be exercised.

(4A) Where a person released on bail under section 37(7)(b) or 37CA(2)(b) above returns to a police station to answer bail or is otherwise in police detention at a police station, he may be kept in police detention to enable him to be dealt with in accordance with section 37CA above or to enable the power under subsection (1) above to be exercised.

(5) If the person mentioned in subsection (4) or (4A) above is not in a fit state to enable him to be dealt with as mentioned in that subsection or to enable the power under subsection (1) above to be exercised, he may be kept in police detention until he is.

(6) Where a person is kept in police detention by virtue of subsection (4), (4A), or (5) above, section 37(1) to (3) and (7) above (and section 40(8) below so far as it relates to section 37(1) to (3)) shall not apply to the offence in connection with which he was released on bail under section 37(7), 37C(2)(b) or 37CA(2)(b) above.

[This section was inserted by the *CJA* 2003, s.28, and Sched. 2, paras 1 and 3. It is printed as amended by the *PJA* 2006, s.10, and Sched. 6, paras 1, 9 and 10.]

Section 24B(5) of the *CJA* 2003 provides that section 37D(1) to (3) apply to a person released on bail under section 24A(2)(b) of the 2003 Act (following arrest for failure to comply with a conditional caution) as they apply to a person released on bail under section 37 of the 1984 Act.

Police and Criminal Evidence Act 1984, s.38

Duties of custody officer after charge

38.—(1) Where a person arrested for an offence otherwise than under a warrant endorsed for bail is charged with an offence, the custody officer shall, subject to section 25 of the *Criminal Justice and Public Order Act* 1994, order his release from police detention, either on bail or without bail, unless— **3–102**

(a) if the person arrested is not an arrested juvenile—

(i) his name or address cannot be ascertained or the custody officer has reasonable grounds for doubting whether a name or address furnished by him as his name or address is his real name or address;

(ii) the custody officer has reasonable grounds for believing that the person arrested will fail to appear in court to answer to bail;

(iii) in the case of a person arrested for an imprisonable offence, the custody officer has reasonable grounds for believing that the detention of the person arrested is necessary to prevent him from committing an offence;

(iiia) in a case where a sample may be taken from the person under section 63B below, the custody officer has reasonable grounds for believing that the detention of the person is necessary to enable the sample to be taken from him;

(iv) in the case of a person arrested for an offence which is not an imprisonable offence, the custody officer has reasonable grounds for believing that the detention of the person arrested is necessary to prevent him from causing physical injury to any other person or from causing loss of or damage to property;

(v) the custody officer has reasonable grounds for believing that the detention of the person arrested is necessary to prevent him from interfering with the administration of justice or with the investigation of offences or of a particular offence; or

(vi) the custody officer has reasonable grounds for believing that the detention of the person arrested is necessary for his own protection;

(b) if he is an arrested juvenile—

(i) any of the requirements of paragraph (a) above is satisfied (but, in the case of paragraph (a)(iiia) above, only if the arrested juvenile has attained the minimum age); or

(ii) the custody officer has reasonable grounds for believing that he ought to be detained in his own interests.

(2) If the release of a person arrested is not required by subsection (1) above, the custody officer may authorise him to be kept in police detention but may not authorise a person to be kept in police detention by virtue of subsection (1)(a)(iiia) after the end of the period of six hours beginning when he was charged with the offence.

(2A) The custody officer, in taking the decisions required by subsection (1)(a) and (b) above (except (a)(i) and (vi) and (b)(ii)), shall have regard to the same considerations as those which a court is required to have regard to in taking the corresponding decisions under paragraph 2(1) of Part I of Schedule 1 to the *Bail Act* 1976 (disregarding paragraph 2(2) of that Part).

(3) Where a custody officer authorises a person who has been charged to be kept in police detention, he shall, as soon as practicable, make a written record of the grounds for the detention.

3–103 (4), (5) [*Identical to s.37(5), (6),* ante, *§ 3–98, apart from references to subss. (5) and (4) in lieu of references to subss. (6) and (5) respectively*.]

(6) Where a custody officer authorises an arrested juvenile to be kept in police detention under subsection (1) above, the custody officer shall, unless he certifies—

(a) that, by reason of such circumstances as are specified in the certificate, it is impracticable for him to do so; or

(b) in the case of an arrested juvenile who has attained the age of 12 years, that no secure accommodation is available and that keeping him in other local authority accommodation would not be adequate to protect the public from serious harm from him,

secure that the arrested juvenile is moved to local authority accommodation.

(6A) In this section—

"local authority accommodation" means accommodation provided by or on behalf of a local authority (within the meaning of the *Children Act* 1989);

"minimum age" means the age specified in section 63B(3)(b) below;

"secure accommodation" means accommodation provided for the purpose of restricting liberty;

"sexual offence" means an offence specified in Part 2 of Schedule 15 to the *Criminal Justice Act* 2003;

"violent offence" means murder or an offence specified in Part 1 of that Schedule;

and any reference, in relation to an arrested juvenile charged with a violent or sexual offence, to protecting the public from serious harm from him shall be construed as a reference to protecting members of the public from death or serious personal injury, whether physical or psychological, occasioned by further such offences committed by him.

(6B) Where an arrested juvenile is moved to local authority accommodation under subsection (6) above, it shall be lawful for any person acting on behalf of the authority to detain him.

(7) A certificate made under subsection (6) above in respect of an arrested juvenile shall be produced to the court before which he is first brought thereafter.

(7A) In this section "imprisonable offence" has the same meaning as in Schedule 1 to the *Bail Act* 1976.

(8) In this Part of this Act "local authority" has the same meaning as in the *Children Act* 1989.

[This section is printed as amended by the *Children Act* 1989, s.108(5) and Sched. 13, para. 53(2), (3); the *CJA* 1991, s.59; the *CJPOA* 1994, ss.24, 28(1), (2), (3), (4) and 168(2), and Sched. 10, para. 54; the *PCC(S)A* 2000, s.165(1), and Sched. 9, para. 96; the *CJCSA* 2000, s.57(3); the *CJA* 2003, ss.5(1) and (2), 304 and 331, Sched. 32, para. 44, and Sched. 36, para. 5; and the *Drugs Act* 2005, s.23(1), and Sched. 1, paras 1 and 3.]

Section 24B(1) and (2) of the *CJA* 2003 provide that in the case of a person arrested under section 24A for breach of a condition attached to a conditional caution, section 38 applies, with the modification to subsection (1)(iii) and (iv) set out in subsection (3), and "with such further modifications as are necessary", as it applies in the case of a person arrested for an offence. The modification to subsection (1)(iii) and (iv) specified in section 24B(3) is the substitution of the words "charged with" for the words "arrested for".

As to the modification of this section in relation to a person charged with an offence in accordance with section 87(4) of the *CJA* 2003 (retrial for serious offences), see section 88 of that Act, *post*, § 3–131d.

Section 21(2) of the 1989 Act stipulates that every local authority shall receive, and provide accommodation for children whom they are requested to receive under section 38(6) of the 1984 Act. **3–104**

The reference to an "offence" in section 38(1) is to an arrestable offence: *Hutt v. Commr of Police of the Metropolis*, *The Times*, December 5, 2003, CA (Civ. Div.).

Where a local authority received a request from the police under section 38(6) to receive a juvenile, whom a custody officer had authorised under subsection (1) to be kept in police detention, the authority was under a duty, pursuant to section 21(2) of the *Children Act* 1989, to provide accommodation in response to such request, regardless of whether or not the juvenile was within its area at the time of the request, but there was no absolute duty to provide secure accommodation where such accommodation was requested, merely a duty to provide accommodation: *R. (M.) v. Gateshead M.B.C.* [2006] Q.B. 650, CA (Civ. Div.).

Where a custody officer was not satisfied with the proposed arrangements of the local authority for the secure detention of a juvenile, he was entitled in accordance with section 38(6) to refuse to transfer that juvenile into the care of the local authority. This is particularly so if the only accommodation available for the detention of the juvenile is insufficient to avoid the very consequences which led to the original decision to refuse bail. See *R. v. Chief Constable of Cambridgeshire, ex p. Michel*, 91 Cr.App.R. 325, DC.

In connection with section 38(6), see paragraph 16(7) of the Code of Practice for the Detention, Treatment and Questioning of Persons by Police Officers, see Appendix A–90.

Police and Criminal Evidence Act 1984, s.39

Responsibilities in relation to persons detained

39.—(1) Subject to subsections (2) and (4) below, it shall be the duty of the custody officer at a police station to ensure— **3–105**

(a) that all persons in police detention at that station are treated in accordance with this Act and any code of practice issued under it and relating to the treatment of persons in police detention; and

(b) that all matters relating to such persons which are required by this Act or by such codes of practice to be recorded are recorded in the custody records relating to such persons.

(2) If the custody officer, in accordance with any code of practice issued under this Act, transfers or permits the transfer of a person in police detention—

(a) to the custody of a police officer investigating an offence for which that person is in police detention; or

(b) to the custody of an officer who has charge of that person outside the police station,

the custody officer shall cease in relation to that person to be subject to the duty imposed on him by subsection (1)(a) above; and it shall be the duty of the officer to whom the transfer is made to ensure that he is treated in accordance with the provisions of this Act and of any such codes of practice as are mentioned in subsection (1) above.

3–106 (3) If the person detained is subsequently returned to the custody officer, it shall be the duty of the officer investigating the offence to report to the custody officer as to the manner in which this section and the codes of practice have been complied with while that person was in his custody.

(4) If an arrested juvenile is moved to local authority accommodation under section 38(6) above, the custody officer shall cease in relation to that person to be subject to the duty imposed on him by subsection (1) above.

(5) [*Repealed by* Children Act *1989, s.108(7) and Sched. 15.*]

(6) Where—

(a) an officer of higher rank than the custody officer [or, if the custody officer is a staff custody officer, any police officer or any police employee] gives directions relating to a person in police detention; and

(b) the directions are at variance—

(i) with any decision made or action taken by the custody officer in the performance of a duty imposed on him under this Part of this Act; or

(ii) with any decision or action which would but for the directions have been made or taken by him in the performance of such a duty,

the custody officer shall refer the matter at once to an officer of the rank of superintendent or above who is responsible for the police station for which the custody officer is acting as custody officer.

[(7) In subsection (6) above—

"police employee" means a person employed under section 15 of the *Police Act* 1996;

"staff custody officer" has the same meaning as in the *Police Reform Act* 2002.]

[This section is printed as amended by the *Children Act* 1989, s.108(5), and Sched. 13, para. 54; and, as from a day to be appointed, by the *SOCPA* 2005, s.121(1) and (7) (insertion of words in square brackets).]

Section 24B(1) and (2) of the *CJA* 2003 provide that in the case of a person arrested under section 24A for breach of a condition attached to a conditional caution, section 39 applies, with the modification to subsections (2) and (3) set out in subsection (3), and "with such further modifications as are necessary", as it applies in the case of a person arrested for an offence. The modification to subsections (2) and (3) specified in section 24B(3) is the substitution of references to a failure to comply with conditions attached to a conditional caution for the references to an offence.

Police and Criminal Evidence Act 1984, s.40

Review of police detention

3–107 **40.**—(1) Reviews of the detention of each person in police detention in connection with the investigation of an offence shall be carried out periodically in accordance with the following provisions of this section—

(a) in the case of a person who has been arrested and charged, by the custody officer; and

(b) in the case of a person who has been arrested but not charged, by an officer of at least the rank of inspector who has not been directly involved in the investigation.

(2) The officer to whom it falls to carry out a review is referred to in this section as a "review officer".

(3) Subject to subsection (4) below—

(a) the first review shall be not later than six hours after the detention was first authorised;

(b) the second review shall be not later than nine hours after the first;

(c) subsequent reviews shall be at intervals of not more than nine hours.

(4) A review may be postponed— 3–108

(a) if, having regard to all the circumstances prevailing at the latest time for it specified in subsection (3) above, it is not practicable to carry out the review at that time;

(b) without prejudice to the generality of paragraph (a) above—

(i) if at that time the person in detention is being questioned by a police officer and the review officer is satisfied that an interruption of the questioning for the purpose of carrying out the review would prejudice the investigation in connection with which he is being questioned; or

(ii) if at that time no review officer is readily available.

(5) If a review is postponed under subsection (4) above it shall be carried out as soon as practicable after the latest time specified for it in subsection (3) above.

(6) If a review is carried out after postponement under subsection (4) above, the fact that it was so carried out shall not affect any requirement of this section as to the time at which any subsequent review is to be carried out.

(7) The review officer shall record the reasons for any postponement of a review in the custody record.

(8) Subject to subsection (9) below, where the person whose detention is under review has not been charged before the time of the review, section 37(1) to (6) above shall have effect in relation to him, but with the modifications specified in subsection (8A).

(8A) The modifications are—

(a) the substitution of references to the person whose detention is under review for references to the person arrested;

(b) the substitution of references to the review officer for references to the custody officer; and

(c) in subsection (6), the insertion of the following paragraph after paragraph (a)—

"(aa) asleep;".

(9) Where a person has been kept in police detention by virtue of section 37(9) or 37D(5) above, section 37(1) to (6) shall not have effect in relation to him but it shall be the duty of the review officer to determine whether he is yet in a fit state. 3–109

(10) Where the person whose detention is under review has been charged before the time of the review, section 38(1) to (6B) above shall have effect in relation to him, but with the modifications specified in subsection (10A).

(10A) The modifications are—

(a) the substitution of a reference to the person whose detention is under review for any reference to the person arrested or to the person charged; and

(b) in subsection (5), the insertion of the following paragraph after paragraph (a)—

"(aa) asleep;".

(11) [*Identical to s.39(6),* ante, *§ 3–106, save that (1) references to* "review officer" *replace references to* "custody officer", *(2) the words* "in connection with the detention" *are added at the end of the subsection, and (3) there is no amendment corresponding to that made by the* Serious Organised Crime and Police Act *2005 to s.39(6)*.]

(12) Before determining whether to authorise a person's continued detention the review officer shall give— 3–110

(a) that person (unless he is asleep); or

(b) any solicitor representing him who is available at the time of the review,

an opportunity to make representations to him about the detention.

(13) Subject to subsection (14) below, the person whose detention is under review or his solicitor may make representations under subsection (12) above either orally or in writing.

(14) The review officer may refuse to hear oral representations from the person whose detention is under review if he considers that he is unfit to make such representations by reason of his condition or behaviour.

[This section is printed as amended by the *Police Reform Act* 2002, s.52; and the *CJA* 2003, s.28, and Sched. 2, para. 4.]

As to the modified application of specified provisions of Part IV of the 1984 Act (including this section) where a person is arrested for an offence under a warrant issued in accordance with section 87(1)(a) of the *CJA* 2003 (arrest of a person acquitted of serious offence where fresh evidence available to support application for retrial) (*post*, § 7–273), or having been so arrested, is subsequently treated under section 34(7) (*ante*, § 3–93) as arrested for that offence, see section 87(4) to (8) of that Act, *post*, § 3–131c.

Section 24B(4) of the *CJA* 2003 provides that section 40 applies to a person in police detention by virtue of section 24A of the 2003 Act (arrest for failure to comply with conditions of conditional caution) as it applies to a person in police detention in connection with the investigation of an offence, but modified so as (i) to omit subsections (8) and (8A), and (ii) to substitute, for the reference in subsection (9) to section 37(9) or 37D(5), of a reference to the second sentence of section 24A(5).

In connection with this section, see paragraph 15 of the Code of Practice for the Detention, Treatment and Questioning of Persons by Police Officers (Appendix A–85). A review under section 40 must be conducted in the physical presence of the detainee and may not be conducted by video link: *R. v. Chief Constable of Kent Constabulary, ex p. Kent Police Federation Joint Branch Board* [2000] 2 Cr.App.R. 196, DC. But see now, section 45A of the Act, *post*, § 3–124.

Police and Criminal Evidence Act 1984, s.40A

Use of telephone for review under s.40

3–110a **40A.**—(1) A review under section 40(1)(b) may be carried out by means of a discussion, conducted by telephone, with one or more persons at the police station where the arrested person is held.

(2) But subsection (1) does not apply if—

(a) the review is of a kind authorised by regulations under section 45A to be carried out using video-conferencing facilities; and

(b) it is reasonably practicable to carry it out in accordance with those regulations.

(3) Where any review is carried out under this section by an officer who is not present at the station where the arrested person is held—

(a) any obligation of that officer to make a record in connection with the carrying out of the review shall have effect as an obligation to cause another officer to make the record;

(b) any requirement for the record to be made in the presence of the arrested person shall apply to the making of that record by that other officer; and

(c) the requirements under section 40(12) and (13) above for—

(i) the arrested person, or

(ii) a solicitor representing him,

to be given any opportunity to make representations (whether in writing or orally) to that officer shall have effect as a requirement for that person, or such a solicitor, to be given an opportunity to make representations in a manner authorised by subsection (4) below.

(4) Representations are made in a manner authorised by this subsection—

(a) in a case where facilities exist for the immediate transmission of written representations to the officer carrying out the review, if they are made either—

(i) orally by telephone to that officer; or

(ii) in writing to that officer by means of those facilities; and

(b) in any other case, if they are made orally by telephone to that officer.

(5) In this section "video-conferencing facilities" has the same meaning as in section 45A below.

[This section was inserted by the *CJPA* 2001, s.73(1), (2). It is printed as amended by the *CJA* 2003, s.6.]

Police and Criminal Evidence Act 1984, s.41

Limits on period of detention without charge

3–111 **41.**—(1) Subject to the following provisions of this section and to sections 42 and 43 below, a person shall not be kept in police detention for more than 24 hours without being charged.

(2) The time from which the period of detention of a person is to be calculated (in this Act referred to as "the relevant time")—

(a) in the case of a person to whom this paragraph applies, shall be—

(i) the time at which that person arrives at the relevant police station; or

(ii) the time 24 hours after the time of that person's arrest,

whichever is the earlier;

(b) in the case of a person arrested outside England and Wales, shall be—

(i) the time at which that person arrives at the first police station to which he is taken in the police area in England or Wales in which the offence for which he was arrested is being investigated; or

(ii) the time 24 hours after the time of that person's entry into England and Wales,

whichever is the earlier;

(c) in the case of a person who—

(i) attends voluntarily at a police station; or

(ii) accompanies a constable to a police station without having been arrested,

and is arrested at the police station, the time of his arrest;

(ca) in the case of a person who attends a police station to answer to bail granted under section 30A, the time when he arrives at the police station;

(d) in any other case, except where subsection (5) below applies, shall be the time at which the person arrested arrives at the first police station to which he is taken after his arrest.

(3) Subsection (2)(a) above applies to a person if— **3–112**

(a) his arrest is sought in one police area in England and Wales;

(b) he is arrested in another police area; and

(c) he is not questioned in the area in which he is arrested in order to obtain evidence in relation to an offence for which he is arrested;

and in sub-paragraph (i) of that paragraph "the relevant police station" means the first police station to which he is taken in the police area in which his arrest was sought.

(4) Subsection (2) above shall have effect in relation to a person arrested under section 31 above as if every reference in it to his arrest or his being arrested were a reference to his arrest or his being arrested for the offence for which he was originally arrested.

(5) If—

(a) a person is in police detention in a police area in England and Wales ("the first area"); and

(b) his arrest for an offence is sought in some other police area in England and Wales ("the second area"); and

(c) he is taken to the second area for the purposes of investigating that offence, without being questioned in the first area in order to obtain evidence in relation to it,

the relevant time shall be—

(i) the time 24 hours after he leaves the place where he is detained in the first area; or

(ii) the time at which he arrives at the first police station to which he is taken in the second area,

whichever is the earlier.

(6) When a person who is in police detention is removed to hospital because he is in need of medical treatment, any time during which he is being questioned in hospital or on the way there or back by a police officer for the purpose of obtaining evidence relating to an offence shall be included in any period which falls to be calculated for the purposes of this Part of this Act, but any other time while he is in hospital or on his way there or back shall not be included. **3–113**

(7) Subject to subsection (8) below, a person who at the expiry of 24 hours after the relevant time is in police detention and has not been charged shall be released at that time either on bail or without bail.

(8) Subsection (7) above does not apply to a person whose detention for more than 24 hours after the relevant time has been authorised or is otherwise permitted in accordance with section 42 or 43 below.

(9) A person released under subsection (7) above shall not be re-arrested without a warrant for the offence for which he was previously arrested unless new evidence justifying a further arrest has come to light since his release, but this subsection does not prevent an arrest under section 46A below.

[This section is printed as amended by the *CJPOA* 1994, s.29(1), (4)(b); and the *CJA* 2003, s.12, and Sched. 1, paras 1 and 8.]

For section 31, see *post*, § 15–185. As to the modification of this section in its application to Revenue and Customs, see S.I. 2007 No. 3175 (*ante*, § 3–94), art. 11 (*post*, § 15–43).

Police and Criminal Evidence Act 1984, s.42

Authorisation of continued detention

3–114 **42.**—(1) Where a police officer of the rank of superintendent or above who is responsible for the police station at which a person is detained has reasonable grounds for believing that—

(a) the detention of that person without charge is necessary to secure or preserve evidence relating to an offence for which he is under arrest or to obtain such evidence by questioning him;

(b) an offence for which he is under arrest is an indictable offence; and

(c) the investigation is being conducted diligently and expeditiously,

he may authorise the keeping of that person in police detention for a period expiring at or before 36 hours after the relevant time.

(2) Where an officer such as is mentioned in subsection (1) above has authorised the keeping of a person in police detention for a period expiring less than 36 hours after the relevant time, such an officer may authorise the keeping of that person in police detention for a further period expiring not more than 36 hours after that time if the conditions specified in subsection (1) are still satisfied when he gives the authorisation.

(3) If it is proposed to transfer a person in police detention to another police area, the officer determining whether or not to authorise keeping him in detention under section (1) above shall have regard to the distance and the time the journey would take.

3–115 (4) No authorisation under subsection (1) above shall be given in respect of any person—

(a) more than 24 hours after the relevant time; or

(b) before the second review of his detention under section 40 above has been carried out.

(5) Where an officer authorises the keeping of a person in police detention under subsection (1) above, it shall be his duty—

(a) to inform that person of the grounds for his continued detention; and

(b) to record the grounds in that person's custody record.

(6) Before determining whether to authorise the keeping of a person in detention under subsection (1) or (2) above, an officer shall give—

(a) that person; or

(b) any solicitor representing him who is available at the time when it falls to the officer to determine whether to give the authorisation,

an opportunity to make representations to him about the detention.

(7) Subject to subsection (8) below, the person in detention or his solicitor may make representations under subsection (6) above either orally or in writing.

(8) The officer to whom it falls to determine whether to give the authorisation may refuse to hear oral representations from the person in detention if he considers that he is unfit to make such representations by reason of his condition or behaviour.

3–116 (9) Where—

(a) an officer authorises the keeping of a person in detention under subsection (1) above; and

(b) at the time of the authorisation he has not yet exercised a right conferred on him by section 56 or 58 below,

the officer—

(i) shall inform him of that right;

(ii) shall decide whether he should be permitted to exercise it;

(iii) shall record the decision in his custody record; and

(iv) if the decision is to refuse to permit the exercise of the right, shall also record the grounds for the decision in that record.

(10) Where an officer has authorised the keeping of a person who has not been charged in detention under subsection (1) or (2) above, he shall be released from detention, either on bail or without bail, not later than 36 hours after the relevant time, unless—

(a) he has been charged with an offence; or

(b) his continued detention is authorised or otherwise permitted in accordance with section 43 below.

(11) [*Identical to s.41(9),* ante, *§ 3–113, save that reference to* "subsection (10)" *replaces reference to* "subsection (7)".]

[Subs. (1) is printed as amended by the *CJA* 2003, s.7; and the *SOCPA* 2005, s.111, and Sched. 7, para. 43(1) and (7). Subs. (11) was subject to a like amendment as that made to section 41(9): *CJPOA* 1994, s.29(1), (4)(b).]

As to the modified application of specified provisions of Part IV of the 1984 Act (including this section) where a person is arrested for an offence under a warrant issued in accordance with section 87(1)(a) of the *CJA* 2003 (arrest of a person acquitted of serious offence where fresh evidence available to support application for retrial) (*post*, § 7–273), or having been so arrested, is subsequently treated under section 34(7) (*ante*, § 3–93) as arrested for that offence, see section 87(4) to (8) of that Act, *post*, § 3–131c.

As to sections 56 and 58, see *post*, §§ 15–199 and 15–206 respectively.

See also paragraph 15 of the Code of Practice for the Detention, Treatment and Questioning of Persons by Police Officers (Appendix A–85).

Where a person is detained in custody without charge for a period exceeding 24 hours but less than 36 hours, following an authorisation of continued detention for a further three hours under section 42(1), it is permissible for a second authorisation of continued detention for a further period expiring not more than 36 hours after the detention began to be made during the period of the first authorised extension even if the original 24-hour time limit had by then expired: *R. v. Taylor (Leroy)* [1991] Crim.L.R. 541, CA.

Police and Criminal Evidence Act 1984, s.43

Warrants of further detention

43.—(1) Where, on an application on oath made by a constable and supported by an information, a magistrates' court is satisfied that there are reasonable grounds for believing that the further detention of the person to whom the application relates is justified, it may issue a warrant of further detention authorising the keeping of that person in police detention. **3–117**

(2) A court may not hear an application for a warrant of further detention unless the person to whom the application relates—

(a) has been furnished with a copy of the information; and

(b) has been brought before the court for the hearing.

(3) The person to whom the application relates shall be entitled to be legally represented at the hearing and, if he is not so represented but wishes to be so represented—

(a) the court shall adjourn the hearing to enable him to obtain representation; and

(b) he may be kept in police detention during the adjournment.

(4) A person's further detention is only justified for the purposes of this section or section 44 below if—

(a) his detention without charge is necessary to secure or preserve evidence relating to an offence for which he is under arrest or to obtain such evidence by questioning him;

(b) an offence for which he is under arrest is an indictable offence; and

(c) the investigation is being conducted diligently and expeditiously.

(5) Subject to subsection (7) below, an application for a warrant of further detention may be made— **3–118**

(a) at any time before the expiry of 36 hours after the relevant time; or

(b) in a case where—

(i) it is not practicable for the magistrates' court to which the application will be made to sit at the expiry of 36 hours after the relevant time; but

(ii) the court will sit during the 6 hours following the end of that period,

at any time before the expiry of the said 6 hours.

(6) In the case to which subsection (5)(b) above applies—

(a) the person to whom the application relates may be kept in police detention until the application is heard; and

(b) the custody officer shall make a note in that person's custody record—

(i) of the fact that he was kept in police detention for more than 36 hours after the relevant time; and

(ii) of the reason why he was so kept.

(7) If— **3–119**

(a) an application for a warrant of further detention is made after the expiry of 36 hours after the relevant time; and

(b) it appears to the magistrates' court that it would have been reasonable for the police to make it before the expiry of that period,

the court shall dismiss the application.

(8) Where on an application such as is mentioned in subsection (1) above a magistrates' court is not satisfied that there are reasonable grounds for believing that the further detention of the person to whom the application relates is justified, it shall be its duty—

(a) to refuse the application; or

(b) to adjourn the hearing of it until a time not later than 36 hours after the relevant time.

(9) The person to whom the application relates may be kept in police detention during the adjournment.

(10) A warrant of further detention shall—

(a) state the time at which it is issued;

(b) authorise the keeping in police detention of the person to whom it relates for the period stated in it.

3–120 (11) Subject to subsection (12) below, the period stated in a warrant of further detention shall be such period as the magistrates' court thinks fit, having regard to the evidence before it.

(12) The period shall be no longer than 36 hours.

(13) If it is proposed to transfer a person in police detention to a police area other than that in which he is detained when the application for a warrant of further detention is made, the court hearing the application shall have regard to the distance and the time the journey would take.

(14) Any information submitted in support of an application under this section shall state—

(a) the nature of the offence for which the person to whom the application relates has been arrested;

(b) the general nature of the evidence on which that person was arrested;

(c) what inquiries relating to the offence have been made by the police and what further inquiries are proposed by them;

(d) the reasons for believing the continued detention of that person to be necessary for the purpose of such further inquiries.

3–121 (15) Where an application under this section is refused, the person to whom the application relates shall forthwith be charged or, subject to subsection (16) below, released, either on bail or without bail.

(16) A person need not be released under subsection (15) above—

(a) before the expiry of 24 hours after the relevant time; or

(b) before the expiry of any longer period for which his continued detention is or has been authorised under section 42 above.

(17) Where an application under this section is refused, no further application shall be made under this section in respect of the person to whom the refusal relates, unless supported by evidence which has come to light since the refusal.

(18) Where a warrant of further detention is issued, the person to whom it relates shall be released from police detention either on bail or without bail, upon or before the expiry of the warrant unless he is charged.

(19) [*Identical to s.41(9),* ante, *§ 3–113, save that reference to* "subsection (18)" *replaces reference to* "subsection (7)".]

[Subs. (4) is printed as amended by the *SOCPA* 2005, s.111, and Sched. 7, para. 43(1) and (8). Subs. (19) was subject to a like amendment as that made to section 41(9): *CJPOA* 1994, s.29(1), (4)(b).]

3–122 In *R. v. Slough JJ., ex p. Stirling* [1987] Crim.L.R. 576, DC, it was held that section 43(5)(b) was not limited to a situation in which the 36-hour period expired at a time when the magistrates were not sitting at all. Where a magistrates' court was already sitting, the justices had a discretion upon being notified of the intention of a constable to make an application either to hear the application straightaway or to wait, provided they did not do so for longer than six hours after the end of the 36-hour period. However, the requirements of section 43(7) were mandatory. Here, the information to support the application was drafted eight minutes before the expiry of the 36-hour period. The clerk advised the court that it was not practicable to hear the application at that time and the application was adjourned to a time beyond the 36-hour period although within the extra six hours. The Divisional Court held that the application should have been refused as it could not be said that it would have been unreasonable for the police to draft the information earlier so as to ensure that the application was heard by the court before the expiry of the 36-hour period.

Police and Criminal Evidence Act 1984, s.44

Extension of warrants of further detention

44.—(1) On an application on oath made by a constable and supported by an information a magistrates' court may extend a warrant of further detention issued under section 43 above if it is satisfied that there are reasonable grounds for believing that the further detention of the person to whom the application relates is justified. **3–123**

(2) Subject to subsection (3) below, the period for which a warrant of further detention may be extended shall be such period as the court thinks fit, having regard to the evidence before it.

(3) The period shall not—

(a) be longer than 36 hours; or

(b) end later than 96 hours after the relevant time.

(4) Where a warrant of further detention has been extended under subsection (1) above, or further extended under this subsection, for a period ending before 96 hours after the relevant time, on an application such as is mentioned in that subsection a magistrates' court may further extend the warrant if it is satisfied as there mentioned; and subsection (2) and (3) above apply to such further extensions as they apply to extensions under subsection (1) above.

(5) A warrant of further detention shall, if extended or further extended under this section, be endorsed with a note of the period of the extension.

(6) Subsections (2), (3) and (14) of section 43 above shall apply to an application made under this section as they apply to an application made under that section.

(7) [*Identical to s.43(15),* ante, *§ 3–121, save that reference to* "subsection (8)" *replaces reference to* "subsection 16".]

(8) A person need not be released under subsection (7) above before the expiry of any period for which a warrant of further detention issued in relation to him has been extended or further extended on an earlier application made under this section.

Police and Criminal Evidence Act 1984, ss.45, 45A

Detention before charge—supplementary

45.—(1) In sections 43 and 44 of this Act "magistrates' court" means a court consisting of two or more justices of the peace sitting otherwise than in open court. **3–124**

(2) Any reference in this Part of this Act to a period of time or a time of day is to be treated as approximate only.

Use of video-conferencing facilities for decisions about detention

45A.—(1) Subject to the following provisions of this section, the Secretary of State may by regulations provide that, in the case of an arrested person who is held in a police station, some or all of the functions mentioned in subsection (2) may be performed (notwithstanding anything in the preceding provisions of this Part) by an officer who— **3–124a**

(a) is not present in that police station; but

(b) has access to the use of video-conferencing facilities that enable him to communicate with persons in that station.

(2) Those functions are—

(a) the functions in relation to an arrested person taken to a police station that is not a designated police station which, in the case of an arrested person taken to, or answering to bail at, a station that is a designated police station, are functions of a custody officer under section 37, 38 or 40 above; and

(b) the function of carrying out a review under section 40(1)(b) above (review, by an officer of at least the rank of inspector, of the detention of person arrested but not charged).

(3) Regulations under this section shall specify the use to be made in the performance of the functions mentioned in subsection (2) above of the facilities mentioned in subsection (1) above.

(4) Regulations under this section shall not authorise the performance of any of the functions mentioned in subsection (2)(a) above by such an officer as is mentioned in subsection (1) above unless he is a custody officer for a designated police station.

(5) Where any functions mentioned in subsection (2) above are performed in a manner authorised by regulations under this section—

(a) any obligation of the officer performing those functions to make a record in connection with the performance of those functions shall have effect as an obligation to cause another officer to make the record; and

(b) any requirement for the record to be made in the presence of the arrested person shall apply to the making of that record by that other officer.

(6) Where the functions mentioned in subsection (2)(b) are performed in a manner authorised by regulations under this section, the requirements under section 40(12) and (13) above for—

(a) the arrested person, or

(b) a solicitor representing him,

to be given any opportunity to make representations (whether in writing or orally) to the person performing those functions shall have effect as a requirement for that person, or such a solicitor, to be given an opportunity to make representations in a manner authorised by subsection (7) below.

(7) Representations are made in a manner authorised by this subsection—

(a) in a case where facilities exist for the immediate transmission of written representations to the officer performing the functions, if they are made either—

(i) orally to that officer by means of the video-conferencing facilities used by him for performing those functions; or

(ii) in writing to that officer by means of the facilities available for the immediate transmission of the representations; and

(b) in any other case if they are made orally to that officer by means of the video-conferencing facilities used by him for performing the functions.

(8) Regulations under this section may make different provision for different cases and may be made so as to have effect in relation only to the police stations specified or described in the regulations.

(9) Regulations under this section shall be made by statutory instrument and shall be subject to annulment in pursuance of a resolution of either House of Parliament.

(10) Any reference in this section to video-conferencing facilities, in relation to any functions, is a reference to any facilities (whether a live television link or other facilities) by means of which the functions may be performed with the officer performing them, the person in relation to whom they are performed and any legal representative of that person all able to both see and to hear each other.

[This section was inserted by the *CJPA* 2001, s.73(1), (3). It is printed as amended by the *CJA* 2003, s.12, and Sched. 1, paras 1 and 9.]

Police and Criminal Evidence Act 1984, s.46

Detention after charge

3–125 **46.**—(1) Where a person—

(a) is charged with an offence; and

(b) after being charged—

(i) is kept in police detention; or

(ii) is detained by a local authority in pursuance of arrangements made under section 38(6) above,

he shall be brought before a magistrates' court in accordance with the provisions of this section.

(2) If he is to be brought before a magistrates' court in the local justice area in which the police station at which he was charged is situated, he shall be brought before such a court as soon as is practicable and in any event not later than the first sitting after he is charged with the offence.

(3) If no magistrates' court in that area is due to sit either on the day on which he is charged or on the next day, the custody officer for the police station at which he was charged shall inform the designated officer for the area that there is a person in the area to whom subsection (2) above applies.

3–126 (4) If the person charged is to be brought before a magistrates' court in a local justice area other than that in which the police station at which he was charged is situated, he shall be removed to that area as soon as is practicable and brought before such a court as soon as is practicable after his arrival in the area and in any event not later than the first sitting of a magistrates' court in that area after his arrival in the area.

(5) If no magistrates' court in that area is due to sit either on the day on which he arrives in the area or on the next day—

(a) he shall be taken to a police station in the area; and

(b) the custody officer at that station shall inform the designated officer for the area that there is a person in the area to whom subsection (4) applies.

(6) Subject to subsection (8) below, where the designated officer for a local justice area has been informed—

(a) under subsection (3) above that there is a person in the area to whom subsection (2) above applies; or

(b) under subsection (5) above that there is a person in the area to whom subsection (4) above applies,

the designated officer shall arrange for a magistrates' court to sit not later than the day next following the relevant day.

(7) In this section "the relevant day"— **3–127**

(a) in relation to a person who is to be brought before a magistrates' court in the local justice area in which the police station at which he was charged is situated, means the day on which he was charged; and

(b) in relation to a person who is to be brought before a magistrates' court in any other local justice area, means the day on which he arrives in the area.

(8) Where the day next following the relevant day is Christmas Day, Good Friday or a Sunday, the duty of the designated officer under subsection (6) above is a duty to arrange for a magistrates' court to sit not later than the first day after the relevant day which is not one of those days.

(9) Nothing in this section requires a person who is in hospital to be brought before a court if he is not well enough.

[This section is printed as amended by the *Access to Justice Act 1999 (Transfer of Justices' Clerks' Functions) Order* 2001 (S.I. 2001 No. 618); and the *Courts Act* 2003, s.109(1), and Sched. 8, para. 282.]

Appropriate magistrates' court for first appearance

The proper construction of section 46 was considered in *R. v. Avon Magistrates' Courts Committee, ex p. Broome* [1988] 1 W.L.R. 1246, DC. The court pointed out that the primary duty of the police was to bring a person charged with an offence and not released before a magistrates' court. There were two procedures, provided by subsections (2) and (4), backed up by subsections (3) and (6)(a) and (5) and (6)(b) respectively. The court said that the initial choice between subsections (2) and (4) lay with the police but if—because no court was sitting on the day of charge (subs. (3)) or the next day, or of arrival in the area (subs. (5)) or the next day—it was necessary to inform a clerk to the justices as required by those subsections, the clerk was not bound to arrange for a court to sit—in a subsection (2) case—in the petty sessions area in which the police station at which the person was charged is situated or—in a subsection (4) case—in the petty sessions area to which he has been removed. The clerk had a discretion, which should normally be exercised so as to comply with the wishes of local justices which may be expressed either by general guidelines, capable always of being adapted to accommodate special needs, or on a case by case basis. **3–128**

Police and Criminal Evidence Act 1984, s.46ZA

[Persons granted live link bail

46ZA.—(1) This section applies in relation to bail granted under this Part subject to the duty mentioned in section 47(3)(b) ("live link bail"). **3–128a**

(2) An accused person who attends a police station to answer to live link bail is not to be treated as in police detention for the purposes of this Act.

(3) Subsection (2) does not apply in relation to an accused person if—

(a) at any time before the beginning of proceedings in relation to a live link direction under section 57C of the *Crime and Disorder Act* 1998 in relation to him, he informs a constable that he does not intend to give his consent to the direction;

(b) at any such time, a constable informs him that a live link will not be available for his use for the purposes of that section;

(c) proceedings in relation to a live link direction under that section have begun but he does not give his consent to the direction; or

(d) the court determines for any other reason not to give such a direction.

(4) If any of paragraphs (a) to (d) of subsection (3) apply in relation to a person, he is to be treated for the purposes of this Part—

(a) as if he had been arrested for and charged with the offence in connection with which he was granted bail, and

(b) as if he had been so charged at the time when that paragraph first applied in relation to him.

(5) An accused person who is arrested under section 46A for failing to attend at a police station to answer to live link bail, and who is brought to a police station in accordance with that section, is to be treated for the purposes of this Part—

(a) as if he had been arrested for and charged with the offence in connection with which he was granted bail, and

(b) as if he had been so charged at the time when he is brought to the station.

(6) Nothing in subsection (4) or (5) affects the operation of section 47(6).]

[This section was inserted as from April 1, 2007 (but only in relation to the local justice area of Lambeth and Southwark (*Police and Justice Act 2006 (Commencement No. 2, Transitional and Saving Provisions) Order* 2007 (S.I. 2007 No. 709))) by the *PJA* 2006, s.46(1) and (3).]

Police and Criminal Evidence Act 1984, s.46A

Power of arrest for failure to answer police bail

3–129 **46A.**—(1) A constable may arrest without a warrant any person who, having been released on bail under this Part of this Act subject to a duty to attend at a police station, fails to attend at that police station at the time appointed for him to do so.

[(1ZA) The reference in subsection (1) to a person who fails to attend at a police station at the time appointed for him to do so includes a reference to a person who—

(a) attends at a police station to answer to bail granted subject to the duty mentioned in section 47(3)(b), but

(b) leaves the police station at any time before the beginning of proceedings in relation to a live link direction under section 57C of the *Crime and Disorder Act* 1998 in relation to him, without informing a constable that he does not intend to give his consent to the direction.]

(1A) A person who has been released on bail under section 37, 37C(2)(b) or 37CA(2)(b) above may be arrested without warrant by a constable if the constable has reasonable grounds for suspecting that the person has broken any of the conditions of bail.

(2) A person who is arrested under this section shall be taken to the police station appointed as the place at which he is to surrender to custody as soon as practicable after the arrest.

(3) For the purposes of—

(a) section 30 above (subject to the obligation in subsection (2) above), and

(b) section 31 above,

an arrest under this section shall be treated as an arrest for an offence.

[This section was inserted by the *CJPOA* 1994, s.29(1). It is printed as amended by the *CJA* 2003, s.28, and Sched. 2, paras 1 and 5; and the *PJA* 2006, s.10, and Sched. 6, paras 1 and 7. Subs. (1ZA) was inserted as from April 1, 2007 (but only in relation to the local justice area of Lambeth and Southwark (S.I. 2007 No. 709) (*ante*, § 3–128a)) by the *PJA* 2006, s.46(1) and (4).]

Section 24B(5) of the *CJA* 2003 provides that section 46A applies to a person released on bail under section 24A(2)(b) of the 2003 Act (following arrest for failure to comply with a conditional caution) as it applies to a person released on bail under section 37 of the 1984 Act.

Police and Criminal Evidence Act 1984, s.47

Bail after arrest

3–130 **47.**—(1) Subject to the following provisions of this section, a release on bail of a person under this Part of this Act shall be a release on bail granted in accordance with sections 3, 3A, 5 and 5A of the *Bail Act* 1976 as they apply to bail granted by a constable.

(1A) The normal powers to impose conditions of bail shall be available to him where a custody officer releases a person on bail under section 37(7)(a) above or section 38(1) above (including that subsection as applied by section 40(10) above) but not in any other cases.

In this subsection, "the normal powers to impose conditions of bail" has the meaning given in section 3(6) of the *Bail Act* 1976.

(1B) No application may be made under section 5B of the *Bail Act* 1976 if a person is released on bail under section 37, 37C(2)(b) or 37CA(2)(b) above.

(1C) Subsections (1D) to (1F) below apply where a person released on bail under section 37, 37C(2)(b) or 37CA(2)(b) above is on bail subject to conditions.

(1D) The person shall not be entitled to make an application under section 43B of the *Magistrates' Courts Act* 1980.

(1E) A magistrates' court may, on an application by or on behalf of the person, vary the conditions of bail; and in this subsection "vary" has the same meaning as in the *Bail Act* 1976.

(1F) Where a magistrates' court varies the conditions of bail under subsection (1E) above, that bail shall not lapse but shall continue subject to the conditions as so varied.

(2) Nothing in the *Bail Act* 1976 shall prevent the re-arrest without warrant of a person released on bail subject to a duty to attend at a police station if new evidence justifying a further arrest has come to light since his release.

(3) Subject to subsections (3A) and (4) below, in this Part of this Act references to "bail" are references to bail subject to a duty—

(a) *to appear before a magistrates' court at such time and such place; or*

(b) *to attend at such police station at such time,*

[(a) to appear before a magistrates' court at such time and such place as the custody officer may appoint;

(b) to attend at such police station as the custody officer may appoint at such time as he may appoint for the purposes of—

(i) proceedings in relation to a live link direction under section 57C of the *Crime and Disorder Act* 1998 (use of live link direction at preliminary hearings where accused is at police station); and

(ii) any preliminary hearing in relation to which such a direction is given; or

(c) to attend at such police station as the custody officer may appoint at such time as he may appoint for purposes other than those mentioned in paragraph (b)]

as the custody officer may appoint.

(3A) Where a custody officer grants bail to a person subject to a duty to appear before a magistrates' court, he shall appoint for the appearance—

(a) a date which is not later than the first sitting of the court after the person is charged with the offence; or

(b) where he is informed by the designated officer for the relevant local justice area that the appearance cannot be accommodated until a later date, that later date.

(4) Where a custody officer has granted bail to a person subject to a duty to appear at a police station, the custody officer may give notice in writing to that person that his attendance at the police station is not required.

(5) [*Repealed by* Criminal Justice and Public Order Act *1994, s.29(1), (4)(c).*] **3–131**

(6) Where a person who has been granted bail under this Part and either has attended at the police station in accordance with the grant of bail or has been arrested under section 46A above is detained at a police station, any time during which he was in police detention prior to being granted bail shall be included as part of any period which falls to be calculated under this Part of this Act.

(7) Where a person who was released on bail under this Part subject to a duty to attend at a police station is re-arrested, the provisions of this Part of this Act shall apply to him as they apply to a person arrested for the first time; but this subsection does not apply to a person who is arrested under section 46A above or has attended a police station in accordance with the grant of bail (and who accordingly is deemed by section 34(7) above to have been arrested for an offence) [or to a person to whom section 46ZA(4) or (5) applies].

(8) [*Amends* Magistrates' Courts Act *1980.*]

[This section is printed as amended by the *CJPOA* 1994, ss.27(1)(a), (b), 29(1), (4)(c), (d), (e); the *CDA* 1998, s.46; the *Access to Justice Act* 1999, s.90(1) and Sched. 13, para. 127; the *CJA* 2003, ss.12 and 28, and Scheds 1, paras 1 and 10, and 2, paras 1 and 6; the *Courts Act* 2003, s.109(1), and Sched. 8, para. 283; and the *PJA* 2006, s.10, and Sched. 6, paras 1 and 11. The words in square brackets in subss. (3) and (7) were inserted, and the italicised words in subs. (3) were omitted, as from April 1, 2007 (but only in relation to the local justice area of Lambeth and Southwark (S.I. 2007 No. 709) (*ante*, § 3–128a)) by the *PJA* 2006, s.46(1) and (5).]

Section 24B(5) of the *CJA* 2003 provides that section 47 applies to a person released on bail under section 24A(2)(b) of the 2003 Act (following arrest for failure to comply with a conditional caution) as it applies to a person released on bail under section 37 of the 1984 Act.

As to the modification of this section in relation to a person charged with an offence in accordance with section 87(4) of the *CJA* 2003 (retrial for serious offences), see section 88 of that Act, *post*, § 3–131d.

Police and Criminal Evidence Act 1984, s.47A

Early administrative hearings conducted by justices' clerks

3–131a **47A.** Where a person has been charged with an offence at a police station, any requirement imposed under this Part for the person to appear or be brought before a magistrates' court shall be taken to be satisfied if the person appears or is brought before a justices' clerk in order for the clerk to conduct a hearing under section 50 of the *Crime and Disorder Act* 1998 (early administrative hearings).

[This section was inserted by the *CDA* 1998, s.119 and Sched. 8, para. 62. It is printed as amended by the *Courts Act* 2003, s.109(1), and Sched. 8, para. 284.]

Savings

Section 51 of the *PACE Act* 1984 provides that nothing in Part IV (ss.34– 52) affects:

(a) the powers conferred on immigration officers by section 4 of, and Schedule 2 to, the *Immigration Act* 1971;

(b) the powers conferred by, or by virtue of, section 41 of, or Schedule 7 to, the *Terrorism Act* 2000 (*post*, §§ 25–85, 25–127 *et seq.*);

(c) any duty of a police officer under section 129, 190 or 202 of either the *Army Act* 1955 or the *Air Force Act* 1955, section 107 of the *Naval Discipline Act* 1957 or paragraph 10 of Schedule 2 to the *Reserve Forces Act* 1996 [s.51(c) is repealed as from a day to be appointed: *AFA* 2006, s.378(2), and Sched. 17]; or

(d) any right of a person in police detention to apply for a writ of habeas corpus or other prerogative remedy.

Retrials for serious offences

3–131b Part 10 of the *CJA* 2003 (ss.75– 97) reforms the law relating to double jeopardy, by permitting retrials in respect of a number of serious offences, where new and compelling evidence has come to light. Sections 87(3) to (8) and 88 modify the provisions of Part IV of the 1984 Act in relation to such cases.

Criminal Justice Act 2003, ss.87(3)–(8), 88

3–131c **87.**—(1), (2) [*See* post, *§ 7–273.*]

(3) Part 4 of the 1984 Act (detention) applies as follows where a person—

(a) is arrested for an offence under a warrant issued in accordance with subsection (1)(a), or

(b) having been so arrested, is subsequently treated under section 34(7) of that Act as arrested for that offence.

(4) For the purposes of that Part there is sufficient evidence to charge the person with the offence for which he has been arrested if, and only if, an officer of the rank of superintendent or above (who has not been directly involved in the investigation) is of the opinion that the evidence available or known to him is sufficient for the case to be referred to a prosecutor to consider whether consent should be sought for an application in respect of that person under section 76.

(5) For the purposes of that Part it is the duty of the custody officer at each police station where the person is detained to make available or known to an officer at that police station of the rank of superintendent or above any evidence which it appears to him may be relevant to an application under section 76(1) or (2) in respect of the offence for which the person has been arrested, and to do so as soon as practicable—

(a) after the evidence becomes available or known to him, or

(b) if later, after he forms that view.

(6) Section 37 of that Act (including any provision of that section as applied by section 40(8) of that Act) has effect subject to the following modifications—

(a) in subsection (1)—

(i) for "determine whether he has before him" there is substituted "request an officer of the rank of superintendent or above (who has not been directly involved in the investigation) to determine, in accordance with section 87(4) of the *Criminal Justice Act* 2003, whether there is";

(ii) for "him to do so" there is substituted "that determination to be made";

(b) in subsection (2)—

(i) for the words from "custody officer determines" to "before him" there is substituted "officer determines that there is not such sufficient evidence";

(ii) the word "custody" is omitted from the second place where it occurs;

(c) in subsection (3)—

(i) the word "custody" is omitted;

(ii) after "may" there is inserted "direct the custody officer to";

(d) in subsection (7) for the words from "the custody officer" to the end of that subsection there is substituted "an officer of the rank of superintendent or above (who has not been directly involved in the investigation) determines, in accordance with section 87(4) of the *Criminal Justice Act* 2003, that there is sufficient evidence to charge the person arrested with the offence for which he was arrested, the person arrested shall be charged.";

(e) subsections (7A), (7B) and (8) do not apply;

(f) after subsection (10) there is inserted—

"(10A) The officer who is requested by the custody officer to make a determination under subsection (1) above shall make that determination as soon as practicable after the request is made.".

(7) Section 40 of that Act has effect as if in subsections (8) and (9) of that section after "(6)" there were inserted "and (10A)".

(8) Section 42 of that Act has effect as if in subsection (1) of that section for the words from "who" to "detained" there were substituted "(who has not been directly involved in the investigation)".

Bail and custody before application

88.—(1) In relation to a person charged in accordance with section 87(4)— **3–131d**

(a) section 38 of the 1984 Act (including any provision of that section as applied by section 40(10) of that Act) has effect as if, in subsection (1), for "either on bail or without bail" there were substituted "on bail",

(b) section 47(3) of that Act does not apply and references in section 38 of that Act to bail are references to bail subject to a duty to appear before the Crown Court at such place as the custody officer may appoint and at such time, not later than 24 hours after the person is released, as that officer may appoint, and

(c) section 43B of the *Magistrates' Courts Act* 1980 does not apply.

(2) Where such a person is, after being charged—

(a) kept in police detention, or

(b) detained by a local authority in pursuance of arrangements made under section 38(6) of the 1984 Act,

he must be brought before the Crown Court as soon as practicable and, in any event, not more than 24 hours after he is charged, and section 46 of the 1984 Act does not apply.

(3) For the purpose of calculating the period referred to in subsection (1) or (2), the following are to be disregarded—

(za) Saturday,

(a) Sunday,

(b) Christmas Day,

(c) Good Friday, and

(d) any day which is a bank holiday under the *Banking and Financial Dealings Act* 1971 in the part of the United Kingdom where the person is to appear before the Crown Court as mentioned in subsection (1) or, where subsection (2) applies, is for the time being detained.

(4) Where a person appears or is brought before the Crown Court in accordance with subsection (1) or (2), the Crown Court may either—

(a) grant bail for the person to appear, if notice of an application is served on him under section 80(2), before the Court of Appeal at the hearing of that application, or

(b) remand the person in custody to be brought before the Crown Court under section 89(2).

(5) If the Crown Court grants bail under subsection (4), it may revoke bail and remand the person in custody as referred to in subsection (4)(b).

(6) In subsection (7) the "relevant period", in relation to a person granted bail or remanded in custody under subsection (4), means—

(a) the period of 42 days beginning with the day on which he is granted bail or remanded in custody under that subsection, or

(b) that period as extended or further extended under subsection (8).

(7) If at the end of the relevant period no notice of an application under section 76(1) or (2) in relation to the person has been given under section 80(1), the person—

(a) if on bail subject to a duty to appear as mentioned in subsection (4)(a), ceases to be subject to that duty and to any conditions of that bail, and

(b) if in custody on remand under subsection (4)(b) or (5), must be released immediately without bail.

(8) The Crown Court may, on the application of a prosecutor, extend or further extend the period mentioned in subsection (6)(a) until a specified date, but only if satisfied that—

(a) the need for the extension is due to some good and sufficient cause, and

(b) the prosecutor has acted with all due diligence and expedition.

[This section is printed as amended by the *CJIA* 2008, s.148(1), and Sched. 26, paras 59 and 63.]

(b) *The Children and Young Persons Act 1969*

Children and Young Persons Act 1969, s.29

Recognizance on release of arrested child or young person

3–132 **29.**—(1) A child or young person arrested in pursuance of a warrant shall not be released unless … his parent or guardian (with or without sureties) enters into a recognizance for such amount as the custody officer at the police station where he is detained considers will secure his attendance at the hearing of the charge; and the recognizance entered into in pursuance of this section may, if the custody officer thinks fit, be conditioned for the attendance of the parent or guardian at the hearing in addition to the child or young person.

(2) In this section "young person" means a person who has attained the age of fourteen and is under the age of eighteen years.

[This section is printed as amended by the *PACE Act* 1984, Sched. 6; and the *CJA* 1991, s.68 and Sched. 8, para. 4(1); and as repealed in part by the *CJA* 1988, s.170(1), (2) and Scheds 15, para. 36, and 16.]

(2) Magistrates' courts

(a) *The Magistrates' Courts Act 1980*

Jurisdiction

Magistrates' Courts Act 1980, s.6(3), (4)

Discharge or committal for trial

3–133 **6.**—(3) *Subject to section 4 of the* Bail Act *1976 and section 41 below, the court may commit a person for trial—*

(a) *in custody, that is to say, by committing him to custody there to be safely kept until delivered in due course of law, or*

(b) *on bail in accordance with the* Bail Act *1976, that is to say, by directing him to appear before the Crown Court for trial;*

and where his release on bail is conditional on his providing one or more surety or sureties and, in accordance with section 8(3) of the Bail Act *1976, the court fixes the amount in which the surety is to be bound with a view to his entering into his recognizance subsequently in accordance with subsections (4) and (5) or (6) of that section the court shall in the meantime commit the accused to custody in accordance with paragraph (a) of this subsection.*

3–134 (4) *Where the court has committed a person to custody in accordance with paragraph (a) of subsection (3) above, then, if that person is in custody for no other cause, the court may, at any time before his first appearance before the Crown Court, grant him bail in accordance with the* Bail Act *1976 subject to a duty to appear before the Crown Court for trial.*

[This section is repealed as from a day to be appointed by the *CJA* 2003, s.332, and Sched. 37, Pt 4.]

For sections 4 and 8 of the *Bail Act* 1976, see *ante*, §§ 3–14 and 3–40 respectively. Section 41 of this Act relates to bail in cases of treason.

Where a magistrates' court commits a person for trial on bail, the bail ceases (whatever form of words is used in the magistrates' order) when the defendant surrenders to the Crown Court: *R. v. Kent Crown Court, ex p. Jodka*, *ante*, § 3–13.

Remand for medical examination after summary trial

See the *MCA* 1980, s.30, and the *Criminal Procedure Rules* 2005 (S.I. 2005 No. 384), r.49.1.

Committal to Crown Court for sentence

Committal for sentence under sections 3, 4 or 6 of the *PCC(S)A* 2000 (*post*, §§ 5–24, 5–25, 5–27 respectively) may be in custody or on bail. **3–135**

Upon committal for sentence, the usual practice should be to commit the offender in custody only if he had been in custody prior to the hearing at which he is committed for sentence: *R. v. Rafferty* [1999] 1 Cr.App.R. 235, CA. In relation to a committal for sentence under section 3 of the 2000 Act, this conflicts with what was said in *R. v. Coe*, 53 Cr.App.R. 66, CA ("cases must be rare when magistrates can properly commit for [sentence] on bail because the whole purpose of the committal is to have the offender sent to prison and have him sent to prison for a longer period than the magistrates could impose" (at pp. 69–70)). It also overlooks the fact that section 4 of the 1976 Act (general right to bail, *ante*, § 3–14) does not apply to a convicted defendant. For this reason alone it would seem difficult to justify a practice according to which conviction should have no effect on bail.

Treason

A person charged with treason shall not be granted bail except by order of a judge of the High Court or the Secretary of State: *MCA* 1980, s.41.

Restriction on justices sitting after dealing with bail

A justice shall not participate in trying the issue of an accused's guilt on the summary trial of an information if in the course of the same proceedings, for the purpose of determining whether the accused should have bail, he has been informed of any previous convictions of his: *MCA* 1980, s.42 (repealed, as from a day to be appointed, by the *CJA* 2003, s.332, and Sched. 37, Pt 4). *Cf. R. v. McElligott, ex p. Gallagher and Seal* [1972] Crim.L.R. 332, DC. **3–136**

Magistrates' Courts Act 1980, s.43

Bail on arrest

43.—(1) Where a person has been granted bail under Part IV of the *Police and Criminal Evidence Act* 1984 subject to a duty to appear before a magistrates' court, the court before which he is to appear may appoint a later time as the time at which he is to appear and may enlarge the recognizances of any sureties for him at that time. **3–136a**

(2) The recognizance of any surety for any person granted bail subject to a duty to attend at a police station may be enforced as if it were conditioned for his appearance before a magistrates' court acting in the local justice area in which the police station named in the recognizance is situated.

[This section is printed as substituted by the *PACE Act* 1984, s.47(8); and as amended by the *CJPOA* 1994, s.168(2) and Sched. 10, para. 43; and the *Courts Act* 2003, s.109(1), and Sched. 8, para. 206.]

Magistrates' Courts Act 1980, s.43A

Function of magistrates' court where a person in custody is brought before it with a view to his appearance before the Crown Court

3–137 **43A.**—(1) Where a person in custody in pursuance of a warrant issued by the Crown Court with a view to his appearance before the Crown Court is brought before a magistrates' court in pursuance of section 81(5) of the *Supreme Court Act* 1981—

(a) the magistrates' court shall commit him in custody or release him on bail until he can be brought or appear before the Crown Court at the time and place appointed by the Crown Court;

(b) if the warrant is endorsed for bail, but the person in custody is unable to satisfy the conditions endorsed, the magistrates' court may vary those conditions, if satisfied that it is proper to do so.

(2) A magistrates' court shall have jurisdiction under subsection (1) whether or not the offence was committed, or the arrest was made, within the court's area.

[This section was inserted by the *Supreme Court Act* 1981, Sched. 5.]

For section 81(5) of the 1981 Act, see *post*, § 3–177.

Magistrates' Courts Act 1980, s.43B

Power to grant bail where police bail has been granted

3–137a **43B.**—(1) Where a custody officer—

(a) grants bail to any person under Part IV of the *Police and Criminal Evidence Act* 1984 in criminal proceedings and imposes conditions, or

(b) varies, in relation to any person, conditions of bail in criminal proceedings under section 3(8) of the *Bail Act* 1976,

a magistrates' court may, on application by or on behalf of that person, grant bail or vary the conditions.

(2) On an application under subsection (1) the court, if it grants bail and imposes conditions or if it varies the conditions, may impose more onerous conditions.

(3) On determining an application under subsection (1) the court shall remand the applicant, in custody or on bail in accordance with the determination, and, where the court withholds bail or grants bail the grant of bail made by the custody officer shall lapse.

(4) In this section "bail in criminal proceedings" and "vary" have the same meanings as they have in the *Bail Act* 1976.

[This section was inserted by the *CJPOA* 1994, s.27(4) and Sched. 3, para. 3.]

As to the disapplication of this section in relation to a person charged with an offence in accordance with section 87(4) of the *CJA* 2003 (retrial for serious offences), see section 88 of that Act, *ante*, § 3–131d.

As to the procedure on an application under this section, see *post*, § 3–159a.

Magistrates' Courts Act 1980, s.113

Bail on appeal to the Crown Court or the High Court on a case stated

3–138 **113.**—(1) Where a person has given notice of appeal to the Crown Court against the decision of a magistrates' court or has applied to a magistrates' court to state a case for the opinion of the High Court, then, if he is in custody, the magistrates' court may, subject to section 25 of the *Criminal Justice and Public Order Act* 1994, grant him bail.

(2) If a person is granted bail under subsection (1) above, the time and place at which he is to appear (except in the event of the determination in respect of which the case is stated being reversed by the High Court) shall be—

(a) if he has given notice of appeal, the Crown Court at the time appointed for the hearing of the appeal;

(b) if he has applied for the statement of a case, the magistrates' court at such time within 10 days after the judgment of the High Court has been given as may be specified by the magistrates' court;

and any recognizance that may be taken from him or from any surety for him shall be conditioned accordingly.

(3) Subsection (1) above shall not apply where the accused has been committed to the Crown Court for sentence under section 37 above or section 3 of the *Powers of Criminal Courts (Sentencing) Act* 2000.

(4) Section 37(6) of the *Criminal Justice Act* 1948 (which relates to the currency of a sentence while a person is released on bail by the High Court) shall apply to a person released

on bail by a magistrates' court under this section pending the hearing of a case stated as it applies to a person released on bail by the High Court under section 22 of the *Criminal Justice Act* 1967.

[This section is printed as amended by the *CJPOA* 1994, s.168(2) and Sched. 10, para. 44; and the *PCC(S)A* 2000, s.165(1) and Sched. 9, para. 72.]

For section 22 of the *CJA* 1967, see *post*, § 3–186; for section 37 of the 1948 Act, see *post*, § 3–187.

Recognizances

Magistrates' Courts Act 1980, s.117

Warrants endorsed for bail

117.—(1) A justice of the peace on issuing a warrant for the arrest of any person may grant him bail by endorsing the warrant for bail, that is to say, by endorsing the warrant with a direction in accordance with subsection (2) below. **3–139**

(2) A direction for bail endorsed on a warrant under subsection (1) above shall—

(a) in the case of bail in criminal proceedings, state that the person arrested is to be released on bail subject to a duty to appear before such magistrates' court and at such time as may be specified in the endorsement;

(b) in the case of bail otherwise than in criminal proceedings, state that the person arrested is to be released on bail on his entering into such a recognizance (with or without sureties) conditioned for his appearance before a magistrates' court as may be specified in the endorsement;

and the endorsement shall fix the amounts in which any sureties and, in a case falling within paragraph (b) above, that person is or are to be bound.

(3) [*Not applicable to criminal proceedings.*]

Magistrates' Courts Act 1980, s.119

Recognizances: postponement of taking

119.—(1) Where a magistrates' court has power to take any recognizance, the court may, instead of taking it, fix the amount in which the principal and his sureties, if any, are to be bound; and thereafter the recognizance may be taken by any such person as may be prescribed. **3–140**

(2) Where, in pursuance of this section, a recognizance is entered into otherwise than before the court that fixed the amount of it, the same consequences shall follow as if it had been entered into before that court; and references in this or any other Act to the court before which a recognizance was entered into shall be construed accordingly.

(3) Nothing in this section shall enable a magistrates' court to alter the amount of a recognizance fixed by the High Court or the Crown Court.

[This section is printed as amended by the *CJA* 1982, Sched. 14.]

Magistrates' Courts Act 1980, s.120

Forfeiture of recognizance

120.—(1) This section applies where— **3–141**

(a) a recognizance to keep the peace or to be of good behaviour has been entered into before a magistrates' court; or

(b) any recognizance is conditioned for the appearance of a person before a magistrates' court, or for his doing any other thing connected with a proceeding before a magistrates' court.

(1A) If, in the case of a recognizance which is conditioned for the appearance of an accused before a magistrates' court, the accused fails to appear in accordance with the condition, the court shall—

(a) declare the recognizance to be forfeited;

(b) issue a summons directed to each person bound by the recognizance as surety, requiring him to appear before the court on a date specified in the summons to show cause why he should not be adjudged to pay the sum in which he is bound;

and on that date the court may proceed in the absence of any surety if it is satisfied that he has been served with the summons.

(2) If, in any other case falling within subsection (1) above, the recognizance appears to the magistrates' court to be forfeited, the court may—

(a) declare the recognizance to be forfeited; and

(b) adjudge each person bound by it, whether as principal or surety, to pay the sum in which he is bound;

but in a case falling within subsection (1)(a) above, the court shall not declare the recognizance to be forfeited except by order made on complaint.

(3) The court which declares the recognizance to be forfeited may, instead of adjudging any person to pay the whole sum in which he is bound, adjudge him to pay part only of the sum or remit the sum.

(4) Payment of any sum adjudged to be paid under this section, including any costs awarded against the defendant, may be enforced, and any such sum shall be applied, as if it were a fine and as if the adjudication were a summary conviction of an offence not punishable with imprisonment and so much of section 85(1) above as empowers a court to remit fines shall not apply to the sum but so much thereof as relates to remission after a term of imprisonment has been imposed shall so apply; but at any time before the issue of a warrant of commitment to enforce payment of the sum, or before the sale of goods under a warrant of *distress* [control] to satisfy the sum, the court may remit the whole or any part of the sum either absolutely or on such conditions as the court thinks just.

(5) A recognizance such as is mentioned in this section shall not be enforced otherwise than in accordance with this section, and accordingly shall not be transmitted to the Crown Court nor shall its forfeiture be certified to that Court.

[This section is printed as amended by the *CDA* 1998, s.55. The italicised word in subs. (4) is replaced by the word in square brackets, as from a day to be appointed: *Tribunals, Courts and Enforcement Act* 2007, s.62(3), and Sched. 13, para. 56.]

3–142 As to the nature of a recognizance, see *R. v. Southampton JJ., ex p. Green* [1976] Q.B. 11, *ante*, § 3–44.

The power to declare a recognizance to be forfeited is strictly dependent on there being a breach of the condition of the recognizance; a mere breach of a condition of bail by the defendant provides no basis for declaring his surety's recognizance to be forfeited: *R. (Hart) v. Bow Street Magistrates' Court* [2002] 1 W.L.R. 1242, DC.

As to the standard of proof which is appropriate where a complaint is made alleging a breach of a recognizance to keep the peace or to be of good behaviour, see *R. v. Marlow JJ., ex p. O'Sullivan* [1984] Q.B. 381, DC.

As to procedure in the Crown Court, see, in particular, the *Criminal Procedure Rules* 2005 (S.I. 2005 No. 384), r.19.23 (*post*, § 3–184). As to making an application under section 139 of the *PCC(S)A* 2000 to discharge or reduce the amount due under a recognizance after an order for forfeiture thereof made by the Crown Court, see *post*, § 3–185a.

3–143 The principles which govern the forfeiture of a recognizance were reviewed by the Court of Appeal (Civil Division) in *R. v. Maidstone Crown Court, ex p. Lever and Connell* [1996] 1 Cr.App.R. 524:–

> "The general principle is that the purpose of a recognizance is to bring the defendant to court for trial. The basis of estreatment is not as a matter of punishment of the surety, but because he has failed to fulfil the obligation which he undertook. The starting point on the failure to bring a defendant to court is the forfeiture of the full recognizance. The right to estreat is triggered by the non-attendance of the defendant at court. It is for the surety to establish to the satisfaction of the trial court that there are grounds upon which the court may remit from forfeiture part or, wholly exceptionally, the whole recognizance. The presence or absence of culpability is a factor but the absence of culpability, as found in this case by the judge, is not in itself a reason to reduce or set aside the obligation entered into by the surety to pay in the event of a failure to bring the defendant to court. The court may, in the exercise of a wide discretion, decide it would be fair and just to estreat some or all of the recognizance" (*per* Butler-Sloss L.J., at p.526)

Her Ladyship went on to say that reducing the financial obligation of a surety must be the exception not the rule and be granted only in really deserving cases.

The court was of the view that dicta of Lord Denning M.R. in *R. v. Southampton JJ., ex p. Green* [1976] Q.B. 11, and Lawton L.J. in *R. v. Bow Street Magistrates' Court, ex p. Hall, The Times*, October 27, 1986, CA (Civ. Div.), were misleading in that they gave the impression that the surety's degree of culpability was the guiding principle in the exercise of the discretion. The observation of Lord Widgery C.J. in *R. v.*

Southampton JJ., ex p. Corker (1976) 120 S.J. 214, DC, was said to be particularly significant: "The real pull of bail ... is that it may cause the offender to attend his trial rather than subject his nearest and dearest who has given surety for him to endure pain and discomfort."

In *R. v. Horseferry Road Stipendiary Magistrate, ex p. Pearson* [1976] 1 W.L.R. 511, DC, it was said that the question of forfeiture should be approached "on the footing that the surety has seriously entered into a serious obligation and ought to pay the amount which he or she has promised unless there are circumstances in the case, relating either to means or to culpability, which make it fair and just to pay a smaller sum". In *R. v. Crown Court at Wood Green, ex p. Howe*, 93 Cr.App.R. 213, DC, it was held that reference in the authorities to consideration of means implied that the court should have some regard to ability to pay and to the consequences for the surety of ordering payment in an amount which would inevitably lead to a term of imprisonment in default. In *ex p. Hall, ante*, Lawton L.J. observed, however, that a surety who misled the court as to his means (when entering his recognizance) acted in a way which caused the court to do that which it would not otherwise have done and struck at the roots of the surety system. **3–143a**

In *R. v. Reading Crown Court, ex p. Bello*, 92 Cr.App.R. 303, CA (Civ. Div.), it was said that a court should always notify sureties when a hearing date was fixed and, if no date was fixed, notify them as to the dates between which the case was likely to be listed. Such a warning should be given as far in advance as possible. A surety undertook to ensure the appearance of the accused at court when required. Ignorance of the date, however, would not always be an answer to proceedings for forfeiture. Each case would depend upon its own facts. In *R. v. Inner London Crown Court, ex p. Springall*, 85 Cr.App.R. 214, DC, the court described as premature an order for forfeiture where the question had been considered in advance of a fixed date for trial. The defendant had gone abroad in breach of his bail conditions. The matter should have been considered once it was known that he would not appear to stand trial. **3–144**

In *R. v. Wells Street Magistrates' Court, ex p. Albanese*, 74 Cr.App.R. 180, DC, it was held that in entering into a recognizance, a surety had a duty to keep in touch with the bailed prisoner and to keep himself informed of the conditions of bail so as to ensure that the prisoner surrendered to his bail. Where bail was made continuous, the court had no obligation to inform a surety that it was proposing to vary the conditions of bail or to obtain his consent to a variation. Accordingly, the order varying the conditions was valid and did not affect the recognizance entered into by the applicant. However, the fact that the surety had no knowledge of a variation might be relevant to the exercise of the discretion to order forfeiture. It was for the justices to determine the degree of fault attributable to a surety in not knowing of the variation and to decide whether the surety would have acted differently if he had known of it. See also *ex p. Springall* and *ex p. Lever and Connell*, *ante*, and *Choudhry v. Birmingham Crown Court and H.M. Revenue & Customs*; *Hanson v. Same, ante*, § 3–11a.

In *R. v. Uxbridge JJ., ex p. Heward-Mills* [1983] 1 W.L.R. 56, DC, it was said that when a surety was unrepresented, the court should assist him by explaining the relevant principles in ordinary language and giving him an opportunity to call evidence and advance argument in relation to them. As to the particular duty to inquire into all the circumstances in the case of an unrepresented surety, see *ex p. Bello, ante*. Representation by the Criminal Defence Service or the Community Legal Service is not available to enable a surety to be represented in connection with forfeiture proceedings: see the definition of "criminal proceedings" in section 12(2) of the *Access to Justice Act* 1999 (*post*, § 6–135), and section 6 of, and Schedule 2 to, that Act (specifying the proceedings for which advocacy services may be funded by the Community Legal Service), and *R. v. The Chief Clerk Maidstone Crown Court, ex p. Clark* [1995] 2 Cr.App.R. 617, DC (considering the corresponding definition of "criminal proceedings" in the *Legal Aid Act* 1988). **3–144a**

In deciding whether to exercise the power under subsection (4) to remit the whole or any part of a sum adjudged to be paid, it is relevant to take account of the potential impact of making payment on the surety and others: *R. v. Leicestershire Stipendiary Magistrate, ex p. Kaur*, 164 J.P. 127, DC. **3–144b**

3–145 As to the power to make recognizances continuous, see *Choudhry v. Birmingham Crown Court and H.M. Revenue & Customs*; *Hanson v. Same*, *ante*, § 3–11a, and, as to magistrates' courts, the *MCA* 1980, s.128(4) (*post*, § 3–150).

The decision of a judge in the Crown Court to forfeit a recognizance is amenable to challenge only by judicial review, in which the High Court has a merely supervisory jurisdiction; the test that must be met in order for the decision to be overturned is therefore a high one: *Choudhry v. Birmingham Crown Court and H.M. Revenue & Customs*; *Hanson v. Same*, 172 J.P. 33, DC.

Remand

Magistrates' Courts Act 1980, s.128

Remand in custody or on bail

3–146 **128.**—(1) Where a magistrates' court has power to remand any person, then, subject to section 4 of the *Bail Act* 1976 and to any other enactment modifying that power, the court may—

(a) remand him in custody, that is to say, commit him to custody to be brought before the court subject to subsection (3A) below at the end of the period of remand or at such earlier time as the court may require; or

(b) where it is *inquiring into or* trying an offence alleged to have been committed by that person or has convicted him of an offence, remand him on bail in accordance with the *Bail Act* 1976, that is to say, by directing him to appear as provided in subsection (4) below; or

(c) except in a case falling within paragraph (b) above, remand him on bail by taking from him a recognizance (with or without sureties) conditioned as provided in that subsection;

and may, in a case falling within paragraph (c) above, instead of taking recognizances in accordance with that paragraph, fix the amount of the recognizances with a view to their being taken subsequently in accordance with section 119 above.

3–147 (1A) Where—

(a) on adjourning a case under section 5, 10(1), 17C *or 18(4)* [, 18(4) or 24C] above the court proposes to remand or further remand a person in custody; and

(b) he is before the court; and …

(d) he is legally represented in that court,

it shall be the duty of the court—

(i) to explain the effect of subsections (3A) and (3B) below to him in ordinary language; and

(ii) to inform him in ordinary language that, notwithstanding the procedure for a remand without his being brought before a court, he would be brought before a court for the hearing and determination of at least every fourth application for his remand, and of every application for his remand heard at a time when it appeared to the court that he had no legal representative acting for him in the case.

(1B) For the purposes of subsection (1A) above a person is to be treated as legally represented in a court if, but only if, he has the assistance of a legal representative to represent him in the proceedings in that court.

(1C) After explaining to an accused as provided by subsection (1A) above the court shall ask him whether he consents to the hearing and determination of such applications in his absence.

3–148 (2) Where the court fixes the amount of a recognizance under subsection (1) above or section 8(3) of the *Bail Act* 1976 with a view to its being taken subsequently the court shall in the meantime commit the person so remanded to custody in accordance with paragraph (a) of the said subsection (1).

(3) Where a person is brought before the court after remand, the court may further remand him.

(3A) Subject to subsection (3B) below, where a person has been remanded in custody and the remand was not a remand under section 128A below for a period exceeding 8 clear days, the court may further remand him (otherwise than in the exercise of the power conferred by that section) on an adjournment under section 5, 10(1), 17C *or 18(4)* [, 18(4) or 24C] above without his being brought before it if it is satisfied—

(a) that he gave his consent, either in response to a question under subsection (1C) above or otherwise, to the hearing and determination in his absence of any application for his remand on an adjournment of the case under any of those provisions; and

(b) that he has not by virtue of this subsection been remanded without being brought before the court on more than two such applications immediately preceding the application which the court is hearing; and ...

(d) that he has not withdrawn his consent to their being so heard and determined.

(3B) The court may not exercise the power conferred by subsection (3A) above if it appears to the court, on an application for a further remand being made to it, that the person to whom the application relates has no legal representative acting for him in the case (whether present in court or not). **3–149**

(3C) Where—

(a) a person has been remanded in custody on an adjournment of a case under section *5*, 10(1), 17C *or 18(4)* [, 18(4) or 24C] above; and

(b) an application is subsequently made for his further remand on such an adjournment; and

(c) he is not brought before the court which hears and determines the application; and

(d) that court is not satisfied as mentioned in subsection (3A) above,

the court shall adjourn the case and remand him in custody for the period for which it stands adjourned.

(3D) An adjournment under subsection (3C) above shall be for the shortest period that appears to the court to make it possible for the accused to be brought before it.

(3E) Where—

(a) on an adjournment of a case under section *5*, 10(1), 17C *or 18(4)* [18(4) or 24C] above a person has been remanded in custody without being brought before the court; and

(b) it subsequently appears—

(i) to the court which remanded him in custody; or

(ii) to an alternate magistrates' court to which he is remanded under section 130 below,

that he ought not to have been remanded in custody in his absence, the court shall require him to be brought before it at the earliest time that appears to the court to be possible.

(4) Where a person is remanded on bail under subsection (1) above the court may, where it remands him on bail in accordance with the *Bail Act* 1976 direct him to appear or, in any other case, direct that his recognizance be conditioned for his appearance— **3–150**

(a) before that court at the end of the period of remand; or

(b) at every time and place to which during the course of the proceedings the hearing may be from time to time adjourned;

and, where it remands him on bail conditionally on his providing a surety during an inquiry into an offence alleged to have been committed by him, may direct that the recognizance of the surety be conditioned to secure that the person so bailed appears—

(c) at every time and place to which during the course of the proceedings the hearing may be from time to time adjourned and also before the Crown Court in the event of the person so bailed being committed for trial there.

(5) Where a person is directed to appear or a recognizance is conditioned for a person's appearance in accordance with paragraph (b) or (c) of subsection (4) above, the fixing at any time of the time for him next to appear shall be deemed to be a remand; but nothing in this subsection or subsection (4) above shall deprive the court of power at any subsequent hearing to remand him afresh. **3–151**

(6) Subject to the provisions of sections 128A and 129 below, a magistrates' court shall not remand a person for a period exceeding 8 clear days, except that—

(a) if the court remands him on bail, it may remand him for a longer period if he and the other party consent;

(b) where the court adjourns a trial under section 10(3) above or section 11 of the *Powers of Criminal Courts (Sentencing) Act* 2000, the court may remand him for the period of the adjournment;

(c) where a person is charged with an offence triable either way, then, if it falls to the court to try the case summarily but the court is not at the time so constituted, and sitting in such a place, as will enable it to proceed with the trial, the court may remand him until the next occasion on which it will be practicable for the court to be so constituted, and to sit in such a place, as aforesaid, notwithstanding that the remand is for a period exceeding 8 clear days.

(7) A magistrates' court having power to remand a person in custody may, if the remand is for a period not exceeding 3 clear days, commit him to detention at a police station. **3–152**

(8) Where a person is committed to detention at a police station under subsection (7) above—

(a) he shall not be kept in such detention unless there is a need for him to be so detained for the purposes of inquiries into other offences;

(b) if kept in such detention, he shall be brought back before the magistrates' court which committed him as soon as that need ceases;

(c) he shall be treated as a person in police detention to whom the duties under section 39 of the *Police and Criminal Evidence Act* 1984 (responsibilities in relation to persons detained) relate;

(d) his detention shall be subject to periodic review at the times set out in section 40 of that Act (review of police detention).

[This section is printed as amended by the *CJA* 1982, Sched. 9; the *PACE Act* 1984, s.48; the *CJA* 1988, Sched. 15, para. 69; the *Courts and Legal Services Act* 1990, Sched. 18, para. 25; the *CPIA* 1996, ss.49(5) and 52(1) (omission of subss. (1A)(c) and (3A)(c)); and the *PCC(S)A* 2000, s.165(1) and Sched. 9, para. 75. It is further amended, as from a date to be appointed, by the *CJA* 2003, s.41, and Sched. 3, para. 51(1) and (7) (repeal of italicised words in subs. (1)(b), repeal of "5," and substitution of words in square brackets for italicised words in subss. (1A)(a), (3A), (3C)(a) and (3E)(a)).]

3–153 As to the *Bail Act* 1976, ss.4 and 8, see *ante*, §§ 3–14 and 3–40 respectively; as to section 119 of the *MCA* 1980, see *ante*, § 3–140; and as to section 39 of the *PACE Act* 1984, see *ante*, § 3–105.

Where a magistrates' court remands a person on bail but thereafter another magistrates' court remands him in custody on other charges, neither the Home Secretary nor the prison governor is under an unconditional duty to produce him at the court which remanded him on bail. Their duty is merely to consider, in accordance with paragraph 3 of Schedule 1 to the *C(S)A* 1997 (*post*, § 8–15), whether it is desirable in the interests of justice that such a person should be so produced and, if so satisfied, then not unreasonably to refuse to produce him: *Walsh v. Governor of Brixton Prison* [1985] A.C. 154, HL.

Magistrates' Courts Act 1980, s.128A

Remands in custody for more than eight days

3–154 **128A.**—(1) The Secretary of State may by order made by statutory instrument provide that this section shall have effect—

(a) in an area specified in the order; or

(b) in proceedings of a description so specified,

in relation to any accused person ("the accused") ...

(2) A magistrates' court may remand the accused in custody for a period exceeding eight clear days if—

(a) it has previously remanded him in custody for the same offence; and

(b) he is before the court,

but only if, after affording the parties an opportunity to make representations, it has set a date on which it expects that it will be possible for the next stage in the proceedings, other than a hearing relating to a further remand in custody or on bail, to take place, and only—

(i) for a period ending not later than that date; or

(ii) for a period of 28 clear days,

whichever is the less.

(3) Nothing in this section affects the right of the accused to apply for bail during the period of the remand.

(4) [*Procedure for making orders under this section.*]

[This section was inserted by the *CJA* 1988, s.155(1). It is printed as repealed in part by the *CPIA* 1996, s.52(2).]

This section applies in every petty sessions area and to any accused person: *Magistrates' Courts (Remands in Custody) Order* 1989 (S.I. 1989 No. 970); and *Magistrates' Courts (Remands in Custody) Order* 1991 (S.I. 1991 No. 2667); both as amended by the *Magistrates' Courts (Remands in Custody) (Amendment) Order* 1997 (S.I. 1997 No. 35).

and if it appears that it will be before 28 clear days have expired, he shall not be remanded in custody for more than 8 clear days or (if longer) a period ending with that date.

(2A) Where the accused person is serving a sentence of imprisonment to which an intermittent custody order under section 183 of the *Criminal Justice Act* 2003 relates, the reference in subsection (2) to the expected date of his release is to be read as a reference to the expected date of his next release on licence.

(3) [*Repealed by* Criminal Justice Act *1982, Sched. 9, para. 6*.]

[Subs. (2A) was inserted by the *CJA* 2003, s.304, and Sched. 32, paras 25 and 29.]

(b) *The Criminal Procedure Rules 2005 (S.I. 2005 No. 384)*

Criminal Procedure Rules 2005 (S.I. 2005 No. 384), rr.19.1–19.8

Application to a magistrates' court to vary conditions of police bail

3–159 **19.1.**—(1) An application under section 43B(1) of the *Magistrates' Courts Act* 1980 or section 47(1E) of the *Police and Criminal Evidence Act* 1984 shall—

(a) be made in writing;
(b) contain a statement of the grounds upon which it is made;
(c) where the applicant has been bailed following charge, specify the offence with which he was charged and, in any other case, specify the offence under investigation;
(d) specify, or be accompanied by a copy of the note of, the reasons given by the custody officer for imposing or varying the conditions of bail; and
(e) specify the name and address of any surety provided by the applicant before his release on bail to secure his surrender to custody.

(2) Any such application shall be sent to the court officer for—

(a) the magistrates' court ... appointed by the custody officer as the court before which the applicant has a duty to appear; or
(b) if no such court has been appointed, a magistrates' court acting for the local justice area in which the police station at which the applicant was granted bail or at which the conditions of his bail were varied, as the case may be, is situated ... .

(3) The court officer to whom an application is sent under paragraph (2) above shall serve notice in writing of the date, time and place fixed for the hearing of the application on—

(a) the applicant;
(b) the prosecutor or, if the applicant has not been charged, the chief officer of police or other investigator, together with a copy of the application; and
(c) any surety in connection with bail in criminal proceedings granted to, or the conditions of which were varied by a custody officer in relation to, the applicant.

(4) The time fixed for the hearing shall be not later than 72 hours after receipt of the application. In reckoning for the purposes of this paragraph any period of 72 hours, no account shall be taken of Christmas Day, Boxing Day, Good Friday, any bank holiday, or any Saturday or Sunday.

(6) If the magistrates' court hearing an application under section 43B(1) of the 1980 Act or section 47(1E) of the 1984 Act discharges or enlarges any recognizance entered into by any surety or increases or reduces the amount in which that person is bound, the court officer shall forthwith give notice thereof to the applicant and to any such surety.

(7) In this rule, "the applicant" means the person making an application under section 43B(1) of the 1980 Act or section 47(1E) of the 1984 Act.

[This rule is printed as amended, and revoked in part, by the *Criminal Procedure (Amendment) Rules* 2007 (S.I. 2007 No. 699), rr.10 and 38, and Sched. 4.]

3–160 **19.2.** [*Application to a magistrates' court to reconsider grant of police bail (amended and revoked in part by S.I. 2007 No. 699* (ante, § 3–159)).]

3–161 **19.3.** [*Notice of change of time for appearance before magistrates' court.*]

Directions by a magistrates' court as to security, etc.

3–162 **19.4.** Where a magistrates' court, under section 3(5) or (6) of the *Bail Act* 1976, imposes any requirement to be complied with before a person's release on bail, the court may give directions as to the manner in which and the person or persons before whom the requirement may be complied with.

Further remand

The *MCA* 1980, s.129 makes provision for a further remand in the absence of the person remanded where the court is satisfied that he is unable to appear or be brought before the court at the expiration of the time for which he was remanded by reason of illness or accident. In *Re Jenkins* [1997] C.O.D. 38, DC, it was held that "accident" included the situation where prison authorities could not produce a defendant because he had been remanded in custody on the same day by another court in respect of other charges. Section 129(4) (amended, as from a day to be appointed, by the *CJA* 2003) provides that where a magistrates' court commits [or sends] a person for trial on bail and the recognizance of any surety has been conditioned in accordance with section 128(4)(a) (*ante*, § 3–150) the court may, in the absence of the surety, enlarge his recognizance so that he is bound to secure that the person in respect of whom the proceedings have been transferred appears also before the Crown Court. **3–155**

As to the enlargement of recognizances, see the *Criminal Procedure Rules* 2005 (S.I. 2005 No. 384), r.19.8, *post*, § 3–166.

Magistrates' Courts Act 1980, s.130

Transfer of remand hearings

130.—(1) A magistrates' court adjourning a case under section *5*, 10, 17C *or 18(4)* [, 18(4) or 24C] above, and remanding the accused in custody, may, if he has attained the age of 17, order that he be brought up for any subsequent remands before an alternate magistrates' court nearer to the prison where he is to be confined while on remand. **3–156**

(2) The order shall require the accused to be brought before the alternate court at the end of the period of remand or at such earlier time as the alternate court may require.

(3) While the order is in force, the alternate court shall, to the exclusion of the court which made the order, have all the powers in relation to further remand (whether in custody or on bail) and the grant of a right to representation funded by the Legal Services Commission as part of the Criminal Defence Service which that court would have had but for the order.

(4) The alternate court may, on remanding the accused in custody, require him to be brought before the court which made the order at the end of the period of remand or at such earlier time as the court may require; and, if the alternate court does so, or the accused is released on bail, the order under subsection (1) above shall cease to be in force.

(4A) Where a magistrates' court is satisfied as mentioned in section 128(3A) above— **3–157**

(a) subsection (1) above shall have effect as if for the words "he be brought up for any subsequent remands before" there were substituted the words "applications for any subsequent remands be made to";

(b) subsection (2) above shall have effect as if for the words "the accused to be brought before" there were substituted the words "an application for a further remand to be made to"; and

(c) subsection (4) above shall have effect as if for the words "him to be brought before" there were substituted the words "an application for a further remand to be made to".

(5) Schedule 5 to this Act shall have effect to supplement this section.

[This section is printed as amended by the *CJA* 1982, Sched. 6; the *CPIA* 1996, s.49(5); the *Access to Justice Act* 1999, s.24 and Sched. 4, para. 18; and, as from a day to be appointed, by the *CJA* 2003, s.41, and Sched. 3, para. 51(1) and (9) (repeal of "5," and substitution of words in square brackets for italicised words in subs. (1)).]

As to subsection (1), see further the *Criminal Procedure Rules* 2005 (S.I. 2005 No. 384), r.19.13, which is not printed in this work. For sections 17C and 18(4), see *ante*, §§ 1–69, 1–73. Schedule 5 is not printed in this work.

Magistrates' Courts Act 1980, s.131

Remand of accused already in custody

131.—(1) When a magistrates' court remands an accused person in custody and he is already detained under a custodial sentence, the period for which he is remanded may be up to 28 clear days. **3–158**

(2) But the court shall inquire as to the expected date of his release from that detention;

Requirements to be complied with before release on bail granted by a magistrates' court

19.5.—(1) Where a magistrates' court has fixed the amount in which a person (including any surety) is to be bound by a recognizance, the recognizance may be entered into— **3–163**

(a) in the case of a surety where the accused is in a prison or other place of detention, before the governor or keeper of the prison or place as well as before the persons mentioned in section 8(4)(a) of the *Bail Act* 1976;

(b) in any other case, before a justice of the peace, a justices' clerk, a magistrates' court officer, a police officer who either is of the rank of inspector or above or is in charge of a police station or, if the person to be bound is in a prison or other place of detention, before the governor or keeper of the prison or place; or

(c) where a person other than a police officer is authorised under section 125A or 125B of the *Magistrates' Courts Act* 1980 to execute a warrant of arrest providing for a recognizance to be entered into by the person arrested (but not by any other person), before the person executing the warrant.

(2) The court officer for a magistrates' court which has fixed the amount in which a person (including any surety) is to be bound by a recognizance or, under section 3(5), (6) or (6A) of the 1976 Act imposed any requirement to be complied with before a person's release on bail or any condition of bail shall issue a certificate showing the amount and conditions, if any, of the recognizance, or as the case may be, containing a statement of the requirement or condition of bail; and a person authorised to take the recognizance or do anything in relation to the compliance with such requirement or condition of bail shall not be required to take or do it without production of such a certificate as aforesaid.

(3) If any person proposed as a surety for a person committed to custody by a magistrates' court produces to the governor or keeper of the prison or other place of detention in which the person so committed is detained a certificate to the effect that he is acceptable as a surety, signed by any of the justices composing the court or the clerk of the court and signed in the margin by the person proposed as surety, the governor or keeper shall take the recognizance of the person so proposed.

(4) Where the recognizance of any person committed to custody by a magistrates' court or of any surety of such a person is taken by any person other than the court which committed the first-mentioned person to custody, the person taking the recognizance shall send it to the court officer for that court:

Provided that, in the case of a surety, if the person committed has been committed to the Crown Court for trial or under any of the enactments mentioned in rule 43.1(1), the person taking the recognizance shall send it to the Crown Court officer.

Notice to governor of prison, etc, where release from custody is ordered by a magistrates' court

19.6. Where a magistrates' court has, with a view to the release on bail of a person in custody, fixed the amount in which he or any surety of such a person shall be bound or, under section 3(5), (6) or (6A) of the *Bail Act* 1976, imposed any requirement to be complied with before his release or any condition of bail— **3–164**

(a) the magistrates' court officer shall give notice thereof to the governor or keeper of the prison or place where that person is detained by sending him such a certificate as is mentioned in rule 19.5(2); and

(b) any person authorised to take the recognizance of a surety or do anything in relation to the compliance with such requirement shall, on taking or doing it, send notice thereof by post to the said governor or keeper and, in the case of a recognizance of a surety, shall give a copy of the notice to the surety.

Release when notice received by governor of prison that recognizances have been taken or requirements complied with

19.7. Where a magistrates' court has, with a view to the release on bail of a person in custody, fixed the amount in which he or any surety of such a person shall be bound or, under section 3(5) or (6) of the *Bail Act* 1976, imposed any requirement to be complied with before his release and given notice thereof in accordance with this Part to the governor or keeper of the prison or place where that person is detained, the governor or keeper shall, when satisfied that the recognizances of all sureties required have been taken and that all such requirements have been complied with, and unless he is in custody for some other cause, release him. **3–165**

Notice from a magistrates' court of enlargement of recognizances

19.8.—(1) If a magistrates' court before which any person is bound by a recognizance to appear enlarges the recognizance to a later time under section 129 of the *Magistrates' Courts Act* 1980 in his absence, it shall give him and his sureties, if any, notice thereof. **3–166**

(2) If a magistrates' court, under section 129(4) of the 1980 Act, enlarges the recognizance of a surety for a person committed for trial on bail, it shall give the surety notice thereof.

Criminal Procedure Rules 2005 (S.I. 2005 No. 384), rr.19.12, 19.21

Notification of bail decision by magistrate after arrest while on bail

3–166a **19.12.** Where a person who has been released on bail and is under a duty to surrender into the custody of a court is brought under section 7(4)(a) of the *Bail Act* 1976 before a justice of the peace, the justice shall cause a copy of the record made in pursuance of section 5 of that Act relating to his decision under section 7(5) of that Act in respect of that person to be sent to the court officer for that court:

Provided that this rule shall not apply where the court is a magistrates' court acting for the same local justice area as that for which the justice acts.

Variation of arrangements for bail on committal to Crown Court

3–166b **19.21.** Where a magistrates' court has committed or sent a person on bail to the Crown Court for trial or under any of the enactments mentioned in rule 43.1(1) and subsequently varies any conditions of the bail or imposes any conditions in respect of the bail, the magistrates' court officer shall send to the Crown Court officer a copy of the record made in pursuance of section 5 of the *Bail Act* 1976 relating to such variation or imposition of conditions.

(3) The Crown Court

(a) *Preliminaries*

Right to representation

3–167 See the definition of "representation" in section 26 of the *Access to Justice Act* 1999, *post*, § 6–146.

Procedure, etc.

3–168 See generally the *Criminal Procedure Rules* 2005 (S.I. 2005 No. 384), r.19.17 (*ante*, § 3–90), r.19.18 (*post*, § 3–182), and rr.19.22 to 19.24 (*post*, §§ 3–183 *et seq.*).

Rule 16.11(1), (2)(a) of the *Criminal Procedure Rules* 2005 (S.I. 2005 No. 384), *ante*, § 2–153, provides that the jurisdiction of the Crown Court relating to the hearing of bail applications may be exercised by a judge of the Crown Court in chambers.

The prosecution should be allowed to reply on bail applications in the Crown Court, particularly where there are, in the view of the prosecution, misstatements of fact in the application which require correction: *R. v. Isleworth Crown Court and D., ex p. Commrs of Customs and Excise* [1991] C.O.D. 1, DC.

Continuous bail

3–169 Where a person is remanded on bail the court may, where it remands him on bail in criminal proceedings (within the meaning of the *Bail Act* 1976) direct him to appear at every time and place to which during the course of the proceedings the hearing may be from time to time adjourned, without prejudice however to the power of the court to vary the order at any subsequent hearing: *Criminal Justice Administration Act* 1914, s.19. (In so far as this section related to bail granted by magistrates the section was repealed by the *MCA* 1952: see now s.128(4) of the *MCA* 1980, *ante*, § 3–150.)

Bail during trial

3–170 Paragraph III.25 of the consolidated criminal practice direction was originally issued by Lord Widgery on June 4, 1974. Paragraph III.25.1 was added to take account of the subsequent enactment of the *Bail Act* 1976.

Practice Direction (Criminal Proceedings: Consolidation), para. III.25
[2002] 1 W.L.R. 2870

Bail during trial

III.25.1 Paragraphs 25.2 to 25.5 are to be read subject to the *Bail Act* 1976, especially section 4.

III.25.2 Once a trial has begun, the further grant of bail, whether during the short adjournment or overnight, is in the discretion of the trial judge. It may be a proper exercise of this discretion to refuse bail during the short adjournment if the accused cannot otherwise be segregated from witnesses and jurors.

III.25.3 An accused who was on bail while on remand should not be refused overnight bail during the trial, unless in the opinion of the judge there are positive reasons to justify this refusal. Such reasons are likely to be: (a) that a point has been reached where there is a real danger that the accused will abscond, either because the case is going badly for him or for any other reason; (b) that there is a real danger that he may interfere with witnesses or jurors.

III.25.4 There is no universal rule of practice that bail shall not be renewed when the summing-up has begun. Each case must be decided in the light of its own circumstances and having regard to the judge's assessment from time to time of the risks involved.

III.25.5 Once the jury has returned a verdict, a further renewal of bail should be decided in the light of the gravity of the offence and the likely sentence to be passed in all the circumstances of the case.

Bail pending appeal

The Crown Court in certain circumstances has power to grant bail for the purpose of an appeal to the Court of Appeal: see *post*, §§ 7–128, 7–186. **3–171**

The appropriate forms are obtainable from the Crown Court or from the staff at the place where the defendant is in custody.

(b) *Jurisdiction in respect of cases before magistrates*

The *CJA* 1982 amended the *Bail Act* 1976, s.5 (*ante*, § 3–20) and the *Supreme Court [Senior Courts] Act*, s.81 (*post*, § 3–175) (as to the renaming of this Act, see *ante*, § 3–8) so as to permit applications for bail to be made to the Crown Court in respect of proceedings of which a magistrates' court was still seized. **3–172**

Practice Direction (Criminal Proceedings: Consolidation), para. V.53 [2002] 1 W.L.R. 2870

Bail before committal for trial

V.53.1 Rules 19 and 20 of the *Crown Court Rules* 1982 [*post*, *§§ 3–181, 3–183*] apply to these applications.

V.53.2 Before the Crown Court can deal with an application it must be satisfied that the magistrates' court has issued a certificate under section 5(6A) of the *Bail Act* 1976 that it heard full argument on the application for bail before it refused the application. A copy of the certificate will be issued to the applicant and not sent directly to the Crown Court. It will therefore be necessary for the applicant's solicitors to attach a copy of the certificate to the bail application form. If the certificate is not enclosed with the application form it will be difficult to avoid some delay in listing.

Venue

V.53.3 Applications should be made to the court to which the defendant will be or would have been committed for trial. In the event of an application in a purely summary case, it should be made to the Crown Court centre which normally receives class 4 work. The hearing will be listed as a chambers matter unless a judge has directed otherwise. **3–173**

(c) *Jurisdiction in respect of cases of which the Crown Court is then seised*

Supreme Court [Senior Courts] Act 1981, s.80

Process to compel appearance

80.—(1) Any direction to appear and any condition of a recognizance to appear before the Crown Court, and any summons or order to appear before that court, may be so framed as to require appearance at such time and place as may be directed by the Crown Court, and if a time or place is specified in the direction, condition, summons or order it may be varied by any subsequent direction of the Crown Court. **3–174**

(2) Where an indictment has been signed although the person charged has not been *committed* [sent] for trial, the Crown Court may issue a summons requiring that person to appear before the Crown Court, or may issue a warrant for his arrest.

(3) Section 4 of the *Summary Jurisdiction (Process) Act* 1881 (execution of process of English courts in Scotland) shall apply to process issued under this section as it applies to process issued under the *Magistrates' Courts Act* 1980 by a magistrates' court.

[As to the renaming of this Act, see *ante*, § 3–8. This section is printed as amended by the *CJA* 2003, s.41, and Sched. 3, para. 54(1) and (4) (substitution of words in square brackets for italicised word in subs. (2)). This amendment came into force on May 9, 2005, in relation to cases sent for trial under section 51 or 51A(3)(d) of the *CDA* 1998: *Criminal Justice Act 2003 (Commencement No. 9) Order* 2005 (S.I. 2005 No. 1267). Otherwise it comes into force on a day to be appointed.]

Supreme Court [Senior Courts] Act 1981, s.81

Bail

3–175 **81.**—(1) The Crown Court may, subject to section 25 of the *Criminal Justice and Public Order Act* 1994, grant bail to any person—

(a) *who has been committed in custody for appearance before the Crown Court or in relation to whose case a notice of transfer has been given under a relevant transfer provision or* who has been sent in custody to the Crown Court for trial under section 51 [or 51A] of the *Crime and Disorder Act* 1998; or

(b) who is in custody pursuant to a sentence imposed by a magistrates' court, and who has appealed to the Crown Court against his conviction or sentence; or

(c) who is in the custody of the Crown Court pending the disposal of his case by that court; or

(d) who, after the decision of his case by the Crown Court, has applied to that court for the statement of a case for the High Court on that decision; or

(e) who has applied to the High Court for a quashing order to remove proceedings in the Crown Court in his case into the High Court, or has applied to the High Court for leave to make such an application; or

(f) [*relates to appeals: see* post, *§ 7–191*]; or

(g) who has been remanded in custody by a magistrates' court on adjourning a case under section 11 of the *Powers of Criminal Courts (Sentencing) Act* 2000 (remand for medical examination) [, section 52(5) of the *Crime and Disorder Act* 1998 (adjournment of proceedings under section 51 etc.)] or—

(i) *section 5 (adjournment of inquiry into offence);*

(ii) section 10 (adjournment of trial); *or*

[(iia) section 17C (intention as to plea: adjournment);]

(iii) section 18 (initial procedure on information against adult for offences triable either way); [or

(iiia) section 24C (intention as to plea by child or young person: adjournment);]

of the *Magistrates' Courts Act* 1980;

and the time during which a person is released on bail under any provision of this subsection shall not count as part of any term of imprisonment or detention under his sentence.

(1A)—(1G) [*Relate to appeals,* post, *§ 7–186.*]

3–176 (1H) Where the Crown Court grants a person bail under subsection (1)(g) it may direct him to appear at a time and place which the magistrates' court could have directed and the recognizance of any surety shall be conditioned accordingly.

(1J) The Crown Court may only grant bail to a person under subsection (1)(g) if the magistrates' court which remanded him in custody has certified under section 5(6A) of the *Bail Act* 1976 that it heard full argument on his application for bail before it refused the application.

(2) [*Provision which may be made by rules of court.*]

3–177 (3) Any reference in any enactment to a recognizance shall include, unless the context otherwise requires, a reference to any other description of security given instead of a recognizance, whether in pursuance of subsection (2)(a) or otherwise.

(4) The Crown Court, on issuing a warrant for the arrest of any person, may endorse the warrant for bail, and in any such case—

(a) the person arrested under the warrant shall, unless the Crown Court otherwise directs, be taken to a police station; and

(b) the officer in charge of the station shall release him from custody if he, and any sureties required by the endorsement and approved by the officer, enter into recognizances of such amount as may be fixed by the endorsement:

Provided that in the case of criminal proceedings (within the meaning of the *Bail Act* 1976) the person arrested shall not be required to enter into a recognizance.

(5) A person in custody in pursuance of a warrant issued by the Crown Court with a view to his appearance before that court shall be brought forthwith before either the Crown Court or a magistrates' court.

(6) A magistrates' court shall have jurisdiction, and a justice of the peace may act, under or in pursuance of rules under subsection (2) whether or not the offence was committed, or the arrest was made, within the court's area, or the area for which he was appointed.

(7) *In subsection (1) above "relevant transfer provision" means—*

(a) *section 4 of the* Criminal Justice Act *1987, or*

(b) *section 53 of the* Criminal Justice Act *1991.*

[This section is printed as amended, and repealed in part, by the *CJA* 1982, ss.29 and 60; the *CJA* 1987, s.15 and Sched. 2, para. 12; the *CJPOA* 1994, s.168(1), (2), and Sched. 9, para. 19, and Sched. 10, para. 48; the *CDA* 1998, s.119 and Sched. 8, para. 48; the *PCC(S)A* 2000, s.165(1), and Sched. 9, para. 87; the *CJA* 2003, s.332, and Sched. 37, Pt 2; the *Civil Procedure (Modification of Supreme Court Act 1981) Order* 2004 (S.I. 2004 No. 1033); and the *Courts Act 2003 (Consequential Amendments) Order* 2004 (S.I. 2004 No. 2035); and, as from a day to be appointed, by the *CJA* 2003, ss.41, 331 and 332, Sched. 3, para. 54(1) and (5) (omission of italicised words and insertion of words in square brackets in subs. (1)(a), omission of subs. 1(g)(i) and subs. (7)), and Sched. 36, para. 4 (insertion of words in square brackets in subs. (1)(g), omission of "or" at the end of subs. (1)(g)(ii), insertion of subs. (1)(g)(iia) and (iiia)). The insertion of "or 51A" in subs. 1(a) took effect on May 9, 2005, in relation to cases sent for trial under section 51A(3)(d) of the *CDA* 1998: *Criminal Justice Act 2003 (Commencement No. 9) Order* 2005 (S.I. 2005 No. 1267).]

As to the disapplication of subsection (5) in the case of a person arrested on a warrant under section 89(3)(b) of the *CJA* 2003 (bail and custody before hearing of application for order for retrial of person acquitted of serious offence), see subsection (6) of that section, *post*, § 7–275.

Section 81(5) should be read in conjunction with section 43A of the *MCA* 1980, *ante*, § 3–137. As to rules of court made under this section, see the *Criminal Procedure Rules* 2005 (S.I. 2005 No. 384), rr.19.18, 19.22, 19.23 (*post*, §§ 3–182 *et seq.*). **3–178**

Applications for bail should be listed where possible before the judge by whom the case is expected to be tried: see paragraph IV.33.6 of the *Practice Direction (Criminal Proceedings: Consolidation)* [2002] 1 W.L.R. 2870. This paragraph also prescribes listing arrangements if the trial judge is unavailable.

In order to avoid unnecessary delay in releasing a prisoner who has been granted bail subject to sureties being found, the arrangements described below for notifying the prison governor when a surety's recognizance has been taken should be followed. **3–179**

When a surety enters into a recognizance before any person specified in rule 19.5(1) or 19.22(1) of the *Criminal Procedure Rules* 2005 (S.I. 2005 No. 384) (*ante*, § 3–163; *post*, § 3–183 respectively), the person taking the recognizance is required to give notice thereof to the prison governor in the prescribed form. The governor may, however, release the prisoner before receiving the written notice, provided he is satisfied (*e.g.* by oral confirmation from the person who has taken the recognizance) that the surety has in fact entered into a recognizance.

In future, when a duly authorised person has taken a surety's recognizance, he should immediately notify the prison governor by telephone that this has been done in cases where it would be impracticable (*e.g.* because of the distance involved) for the surety's copy of the notice that recognizances have been taken to be presented at the prison in time to secure the prisoner's release that day. The governor should be advised that written confirmation in the prescribed form is being despatched by first class post to the prison. When he is satisfied that the information is authentic, the governor will arrange for the immediate release of the prisoner on bail without awaiting the written notification. There should be no delay in despatching the written notification to the prison: see Home Office Circular No. 104/1972.

See further *ante*, §§ 3–40 *et seq.*

(d) *Jurisdiction in respect of cases in which an appeal is pending to the Court of Appeal*

3–180 See *post*, §§ 7–128, 7–186.

(e) *Criminal Procedure Rules 2005 (S.I. 2005 No. 384)*

Criminal Procedure Rules 2005 (S.I. 2005 No. 384), rr.19.17, 19.18, 19.22–19.24

3–181 **19.17.** [*See* ante, *§ 3–90.*]

Applications to Crown Court relating to bail

3–182 **19.18.**—(1) This rule applies where an application to the Crown Court relating to bail is made otherwise than during the hearing of proceedings in the Crown Court.

(2) Subject to paragraph (7) below, notice in writing of intention to make such an application to the Crown Court shall, at least 24 hours before it is made, be given to the prosecutor and if the prosecution is being carried on by the Crown Prosecution Service, to the appropriate Crown Prosecutor or, if the application is to be made by the prosecutor or a constable under section 3(8) of the *Bail Act* 1976, to the person to whom bail was granted.

(3) On receiving notice under paragraph (2), the prosecutor or appropriate Crown Public Prosecutor or, as the case may be, the person to whom bail was granted shall—

(a) notify the Crown Court officer and the applicant that he wishes to be represented at the hearing of the application;

(b) notify the Crown Court officer and the applicant that he does not oppose the application; or

(c) give to the Crown Court officer, for the consideration of the Crown Court, a written statement of his reasons for opposing the application, at the same time sending a copy of the statement to the applicant.

(4) A notice under paragraph (2) shall be in the form set out in the Practice Direction or a form to the like effect, and the applicant shall give a copy of the notice to the Crown Court officer.

(5) Except in the case of an application made by the prosecutor or a constable under section 3(8) of the 1976 Act, the applicant shall not be entitled to be present on the hearing of his application unless the Crown Court gives him leave to be present.

(6) Where a person who is in custody or has been released on bail desires to make an application relating to bail and has not been able to instruct a solicitor to apply on his behalf under the preceding paragraphs of this rule, he may give notice in writing to the Crown Court of his desire to make an application relating to bail, requesting that the Official Solicitor shall act for him in the application, and the Court may, if it thinks fit, assign the Official Solicitor to act for the applicant accordingly.

(7) Where the Official Solicitor has been so assigned the Crown Court may, if it thinks fit, dispense with the requirements of paragraph (2) and deal with the application in a summary manner.

(8) Any record required by section 5 of the 1976 Act (together with any note of reasons required by section 5(4) to be included) shall be made by way of an entry in the file relating to the case in question and the record shall include the following particulars, namely—

(a) the effect of the decision;

(b) a statement of any condition imposed in respect of bail, indicating whether it is to be complied with before or after release on bail;

(c) where conditions of bail are varied, a statement of the conditions as varied; and

(d) where bail is withheld, a statement of the relevant exception to the right to bail (as provided in Schedule 1 to the 1976 Act) on which the decision is based.

(9) Every person who makes an application to the Crown Court relating to bail shall inform the Court of any earlier application to the High Court or the Crown Court relating to bail in the course of the same proceedings.

As to procedure in connection with bail applications, see *ante*, § 3–16.

Conditions attached to bail granted by the Crown Court

3–183 **19.22.**—(1) Where the Crown Court grants bail, the recognizance of any surety required as a condition of bail may be entered into before an officer of the Crown Court or, where the person who has been granted bail is in a prison or other place of detention, before the governor or keeper of the prison or place as well as before the persons specified in section 8(4) of the *Bail Act* 1976.

(2) Where the Crown Court under section 3(5) or (6) of the 1976 Act imposes a requirement to be complied with before a person's release on bail, the Court may give directions as to the manner in which and the person or persons before whom the requirement may be complied with.

(3) A person who, in pursuance of an order made by the Crown Court for the grant of bail, proposes to enter into a recognizance or give security must, unless the Crown Court otherwise directs, give notice to the prosecutor at least 24 hours before he enters into the recognizance or gives security as aforesaid.

(4) Where, in pursuance of an order of the Crown Court, a recognizance is entered into or any requirement imposed under section 3(5) or (6) of the 1976 Act is complied with (being a requirement to be complied with before a person's release on bail) before any person, it shall be his duty to cause the recognizance or, as the case may be, a statement of the requirement to be transmitted forthwith to the court officer; and a copy of the recognizance or statement shall at the same time be sent to the governor or keeper of the prison or other place of detention in which the person named in the order is detained, unless the recognizance was entered into or the requirement was complied with before such governor or keeper.

(5) Where, in pursuance of section 3(5) of the 1976 Act, security has been given in respect of a person granted bail with a duty to surrender to the custody of the Crown Court and either—

(a) that person surrenders to the custody of the Court; or

(b) that person having failed to surrender to the custody of the Court, the Court decides not to order the forfeiture of the security,

the court officer shall as soon as practicable give notice of the surrender to custody or, as the case may be, of the decision not to forfeit the security to the person before whom the security was given.

Estreat of recognizances in respect of person bailed to appear before the Crown Court

19.23.—(1) Where a recognizance has been entered into in respect of a person granted bail to appear before the Crown Court and it appears to the Court that a default has been made in performing the conditions of the recognizance, other than by failing to appear before the Court in accordance with any such condition, the Court may order the recognizance to be estreated. **3–184**

(2) Where the Crown Court is to consider making an order under paragraph (1) for a recognizance to be estreated, the court officer shall give notice to that effect to the person by whom the recognizance was entered into indicating the time and place at which the matter will be considered; and no such order shall be made before the expiry of 7 days after the notice required by this paragraph has been given.

Forfeiture of recognizances in respect of person bailed to appear before the Crown Court

19.24.—(1) Where a recognizance is conditioned for the appearance of an accused before the Crown Court and the accused fails to appear in accordance with the condition, the Court shall declare the recognizance to be forfeited. **3–185**

(2) Where the Crown Court declares a recognizance to be forfeited under paragraph (1), the court officer shall issue a summons to the person by whom the recognizance was entered into requiring him to appear before the Court at a time and place specified in the summons to show cause why the Court should not order the recognizance to be estreated.

(3) At the time specified in the summons the Court may proceed in the absence of the person by whom the recognizance was entered into if it is satisfied that he has been served with the summons.

"Default" in rule 19.23 means "failure" and, therefore, the rule is to be construed as giving the Crown Court jurisdiction to estreat a recognizance on the failure of the person who entered the recognizance to fulfil his obligation thereunder to ensure that the person granted bail surrenders to his bail: if there has been such a failure, the court will then consider the merits and decide as a matter of discretion whether or not to estreat the recognizance: *R. v. Warwick Crown Court, ex p. Smalley*, 84 Cr.App.R. 51, DC. **3–185a**

As to how the discretion should be exercised, see *ante*, §§ 3–143 *et seq.*

As to the possibility of making an application under section 139 of the *PCC(S)A* 2000 (*post*, § 5–396) for an order discharging a recognizance or reducing the amount due thereunder after the Crown Court has forfeited it, see *R. v. Central Criminal Court, ex p. Naraghi and Binji*, 2 Cr.App.R.(S.) 104, DC, and *R. v. Wood Green Crown Court, ex p. Howe*, 93 Cr.App.R. 213, DC.

(4) The High Court

(a) *Abolition of inherent jurisdiction*

Criminal Justice Act 2003, s.17

Appeals to High Court

3–186 **17.**—(1) [*Amends* Criminal Justice Act *1967, s.22(1).*]

(2) The inherent power of the High Court to entertain an application in relation to bail where a magistrates' court—

(a) has granted or withheld bail, or
(b) has varied the conditions of bail,

is abolished.

(3) The inherent power of the High Court to entertain an application in relation to bail where the Crown Court has determined—

(a) an application under section 3(8) of the 1976 Act, or
(b) an application under section 81(1)(a), (b), (c) or (g) of the *Supreme Court Act* 1981,

is abolished.

(4) The High Court is to have no power to entertain an application in relation to bail where the Crown Court has determined an appeal under section 16 of this Act.

(5) The High Court is to have no power to entertain an application in relation to bail where the Crown Court has granted or withheld bail under section 88 or 89 of this Act.

(6) Nothing in this section affects—

(a) any other power of the High Court to grant or withhold bail or to vary the conditions of bail, or
(b) any right of a person to apply for a writ of habeas corpus or any other prerogative remedy.

(7) Any reference in this section to an application in relation to bail is to be read as including—

(a) an application for bail to be granted,
(b) an application for bail to be withheld,
(c) an application for the conditions of bail to be varied.

(8) Any reference in this section to the withholding of bail is to be read as including a reference to the revocation of bail.

The "1976 Act" is the *Bail Act* 1976: s.21 of the 2003 Act.

In *R. (M.) v. Isleworth Crown Court and H.M. Customs and Excise*, unreported, March 2, 2005, DC ([2005] EWHC 363 (Admin.)), it was held that judicial review lies in respect of a refusal of bail in the Crown Court; and that decisions as to bail do not fall within the exclusion of judicial review in respect of "matters relating to trial on indictment" under section 29(3) of the *Supreme Court [Senior Courts] Act* 1981 (*post*, § 7–4) (as to the renaming of this Act, see *ante*, § 3–8). It was said that the rationale behind the decision in *R. v. Croydon Crown Court, ex p. Cox* [1997] 1 Cr.App.R. 20, DC, that refusal of bail was not susceptible to judicial review was the availability of an alternative remedy, *viz.* the possibility which then existed of an application to a High Court judge; though section 17(3) of the 2003 Act abolished the right to apply to the High Court for bail, section 17(6)(b) allowed the High Court to subject a Crown Court bail decision to judicial review; but that jurisdiction should be exercised sparingly; such applications should be decided on robustly applied *Wednesbury* principles, and it should always be kept in mind that Parliament has understandably vested the decision in judges in the Crown Court who have everyday experience of, and feel for, bail applications; where, therefore, a decision as to bail could not be classified as perverse, notwithstanding that the High Court would have granted bail on the facts, it was held that the application should be dismissed.

In *R. (Thompson) v. Central Criminal Court* [2006] A.C.D. 9, QBD, Collins J. said, in relation to the suggested "super-*Wednesbury*" approach, that it was not necessarily helpful to put a gloss on the rationality test, and that a better test was whether the decision was within the bounds of what could be regarded as reasonable. His Lordship added that the proper approach of the High Court to an application for judicial review of a refusal of bail is to direct a speedy oral hearing of the permission application with a view to disposing of the whole matter then and there (*i.e.* (a) if there is merit, to grant permission and to direct immediately that the Crown Court reconsider the matter based on the judgment given, which may effectively direct that bail be granted, (b) to refuse permission if there is no arguable case, or (c) to grant permission and refuse the claim).

(b) *Bail on appeal, case stated or application for quashing order*

Criminal Justice Act 1948, s.37

37.—(1) Without prejudice to the powers vested before the commencement of this Act in any court to admit or direct the admission of a person to bail— **3–187**

(b) the High Court may, subject to section 25 of the *Criminal Justice and Public Order Act* 1994, grant bail to a person—

(i) who, after the decision of his case by the Crown Court, has applied to the Crown Court for the statement of a case for the High Court on that decision, or

(ii) who has applied to the High Court for an order of *certiorari* to remove proceedings in the Crown Court in his case into the High Court, or has applied to the High Court for leave to make such an application;

(d) the High Court may, subject to section 25 of the *Criminal Justice and Public Order Act* 1994, grant bail to a person who has been convicted or sentenced by a magistrates' court and has applied to the High Court for an order of certiorari to remove the proceedings into the High Court or has applied to the High Court for leave to make such an application.

(1A) Where the court grants bail to a person under paragraph (d) of subsection (1) above— **3–188**

(a) the time at which he is to appear in the event of the conviction or sentence not being quashed by the High Court shall be such time within ten days after the judgment of the High Court has been given as may be specified by the High Court; and

(b) the place at which he is to appear in that event shall be a magistrates' court acting for the same petty sessions area as the court which convicted or sentenced him.

(4) [*Rules of court.*]

(6) [*Computation of custodial sentences; time on bail not to count, etc.*]

[This section is printed as amended and repealed in part by the *CJA* 1967, s.103(2), and Sched. 7; the *Courts Act* 1971, Scheds 8 and 11; the *Bail Act* 1976, Scheds 2 and 3; the *Supreme Court Act* 1981, Scheds 5 and 7; the *CJA* 1988, Sched. 8, para. 1; and the *CJPOA* 1994, s.168(2), and Sched. 10, para. 6.]

(c) *Estreat of recognizances*

Civil Procedure Rules 1998 (S.I. 1998 No. 3132), Sched. 1 (RSC, Ord. 79, r.8)

8.—(1) No recognizance acknowledged in or removed into the Queen's Bench Division shall be estreated without the order of a judge. **3–189**

(2) Every application to estreat a recognizance in the Queen's Bench Division must be made by claim form and will be heard by a judge sitting in private and must be supported by a witness statement or affidavit showing in what manner the breach has been committed and proving that the claim form was duly served.

(2A) When it issues the claim form the court will fix a date for hearing of the application.

(3) A claim form under this rule must be served at least 2 clear days before the day named therein for the hearing.

(4) On the hearing of the application the judge may, and if requested by any party shall, direct any issue of fact in dispute to be tried by a jury.

(5) If it appears to the judge that a default has been made in performing the conditions of the recognizance, the judge may order the recognizance to be estreated.

See *R. v. Warwick Crown Court, ex p. Smalley*, 84 Cr.App.R. 51, DC (surety who consents to a variation of conditions of bail does not thereby "acknowledge" his recognizance).

(d) *Application to judge in chambers*

Civil Procedure Rules 1998 (S.I. 1998 No. 3132), Sched. 1 (RSC, Ord. 79, r.9)

3–190 **9.**—(1) Subject to the provisions of this rule, every application to the High Court in respect of bail in any criminal proceeding—

(a) where the defendant is in custody, must be made by claim form to a judge sitting in private to show cause why the defendant should not be granted bail;

(b) where the defendant has been admitted to bail, must be made by claim form to a judge sitting in private to show cause why the variation in the arrangements for bail proposed by the applicant should not be made.

(2) Subject to paragraph (5), the summons (in Form No. 97 or 97A in the relevant practice direction) must, at least 24 hours before the day named therein for the hearing, be served—

(a) where the application was made by the defendant, on the prosecutor and on the Director of Public Prosecutions, if the prosecution is being carried on by him;

(b) where the application was made by the prosecutor or a constable under section 3(8) of the *Bail Act* 1976, on the defendant.

(3) Subject to paragraph (5), every application must be supported by witness statement or affidavit.

(4) Where a defendant in custody who desires to apply for bail is unable through lack of means to instruct a solicitor, he may give notice in writing to the judge sitting in private stating his desire to apply for bail and requesting that the official solicitor shall act for him in the application, and the judge may, if he thinks fit, assign the official solicitor to act for the applicant accordingly.

3–191 (5) Where the official solicitor has been so assigned the judge may, if he thinks fit, dispense with the requirements of paragraphs (1) to (3) and deal with the application in a summary manner.

(6) Where the judge sitting in private by whom an application for bail in criminal proceedings is heard grants the defendant bail, the order must be in Form No. 98 in the relevant Practice Direction and a copy of the order shall be transmitted forthwith—

(a) where the proceedings in respect of the defendant have been transferred to the Crown Court for trial or where the defendant has been committed to the Crown Court to be sentenced or otherwise dealt with, to the appropriate officer of the Crown Court;

(b) in any other case, to the clerk of the court which committed the defendant.

(6A) The recognizance of any surety required as a condition of bail granted as aforesaid may, where the defendant is in a prison or other place of detention, be entered into before the governor or keeper of the prison or place as well as before the persons specified in section 8(4) of the *Bail Act* 1976.

(6B) Where under section 3(5) or (6) of the *Bail Act* 1976 a judge sitting in private imposes a requirement to be complied with before a person's release on bail, the judge may give directions as to the manner in which and the person or persons before whom the requirement may be complied with.

3–192 (7) A person who in pursuance of an order for the grant of bail made by a judge under this rule proposes to enter into a recognizance or give security must, unless the judge otherwise directs, give notice (in Form No. 100 in the relevant Practice Direction) to the prosecutor at least 24 hours before he enters into the recognizance or complies with the requirement as aforesaid.

(8) Where in pursuance of such an order as aforesaid a recognizance is entered into or requirement complied with before any person, it shall be the duty of that person to cause the recognizance or, as the case may be, a statement of the requirement complied with to be transmitted forthwith—

(a), (b) [*identical to para. (6)(a), (b),* ante];

and a copy of such recognizance or statement shall at the same time be sent to the governor or keeper of the prison or other place of detention in which the defendant is detained, unless the recognizance was entered into or the requirement complied with before such governor or keeper.

(10) An order by the judge sitting in private varying the arrangements under which the

defendant has been granted bail shall be in Form 98A in the relevant practice direction and a copy of the order shall be transmitted forthwith—

(a), (b) [*identical to para. (6)(a), (b),* ante].

(11) Where in pursuance of an order of a judge sitting in private or of the Crown Court a person is released on bail in any criminal proceeding pending the determination of an appeal to the High Court or House of Lords or an application for an order of *certiorari*, then, upon the abandonment of the appeal or application, or upon the decision of the High Court or House of Lords being given, any justice (being a justice acting for the same petty sessions area as the magistrates' court by which that person was convicted or sentenced) may issue process for enforcing the decision in respect of which such appeal or application was brought or, as the case may be, the decision of the High Court or House of Lords. **3–193**

(12) If an applicant to the High Court in any criminal proceedings is refused bail by a judge sitting in private, the applicant shall not be entitled to make a fresh application for bail to any other judge or to a Divisional Court.

(13) The record required by section 5 of the *Bail Act* 1976 to be made by the High Court shall be made by including in the file relating to the case in question a copy of the relevant order of the Court and shall contain the particulars set out in Form No. 98 or 98A in the relevant Practice Direction, whichever is appropriate, except that in the case of a decision to withhold bail the record shall be made by inserting a statement of the decision on the Court's copy of the relevant claim form and including it in the file relating to the case in question. **3–194**

(14) [*Extradition cases.*]

An appeal from the refusal of bail in criminal proceedings by a judge in chambers or from an order varying or refusing to vary conditions of bail, is precluded by the *Supreme Court [Senior Courts] Act* 1981, s.18(1)(a) (*post*, § 7–20) (as to the renaming of this Act, see *ante*, § 3–8).

(5) The Court of Appeal

The powers of the Court of Appeal to grant bail are set out in the *CAA* 1968. For bail pending (a) appeal to the court, see section 19, (b) retrial where conviction quashed, see section 8(2)(a), (c) trial where finding of disability quashed, see section 16(3), (d) appeal to the House of Lords, see sections 36 and 37(2). For the powers of the "single judge", see sections 31, 44 and 45(2). See also, Part 5 (forms) (*ante*, § 2–207), and rules 68.8 to 68.10, of the *Criminal Procedure Rules* 2005 (S.I. 2005 No. 384). The subject is discussed more fully in Chapter 7. See, in particular, §§ 7–113, 7–128, 7–152, 7–185 to 7–192, 7–231, 7–327 to 7–331 and 7–336. **3–195**

II. PROCESS TO COMPEL APPEARANCE OF THE ACCUSED

A. PROCESS TO COMPEL APPEARANCE BEFORE THE CROWN COURT

See the *Supreme Court [Senior Courts] Act* 1981, ss.80, 81, *ante*, §§ 3–174, 3–175 (as to the renaming of this Act, see *ante*, § 3–8). **3–196**

If a person against whom an indictment has been preferred and signed is present in court, or is in the custody of the court, he may at once be arraigned, upon the indictment, without any previous process: 2 Hawk. c. 27.

Criminal Law Amendment Act 1867, s.10

10. Where a person who has been granted bail in criminal proceedings is, while awaiting trial for the offence before the Crown Court, in prison, under warrant of commitment, or under sentence for some other offence, it shall be lawful for the court, by order in writing, to direct the governor of the said prison to bring up the body of such person, in order that he may be arraigned upon such indictment without writ of habeas corpus, and the said governor shall thereupon obey such order. **3–196a**

[This section is printed as amended by the *Bail Act* 1976, s.12 and Sched. 2, para. 3.]

An accused person's attendance can also be obtained by a Secretary of State's order: see the *C(S)A* 1997, Sched. 1, para. 3.

B. SERVICE OF UNITED KINGDOM PROCESS OVERSEAS

See sections 3 and 4 of the *Crime (International Co-operation) Act* 2003, *post*, §§ 8–17, 8–18. **3–196b**

III. PRESENCE OF THE ACCUSED IN COURT DURING THE TRIAL

A. GENERAL RULE

3–197 In *R. v. Jones (Anthony)* [2003] 1 A.C. 1, HL, it was held that a judge had a discretion to start or continue a trial in a defendant's absence, though it was to be exercised with great caution and with close regard to the overall fairness of the proceedings; a defendant afflicted by involuntary illness or incapacity would have much stronger grounds for resisting the continuance of the trial than one who had voluntarily chosen to abscond. If the absence of the defendant was attributable to involuntary illness or incapacity it would rarely, if ever, be right to exercise the discretion in favour of continuing the trial, at any rate until the defendant was represented and asked that the trial should begin. It was generally desirable that a defendant should be represented, even if he had voluntarily absconded. (For relevant provisions of the eighth edition of the *Code of Conduct for the Bar of England and Wales*, see Appendix C–10 and C–38.)

3–198 The House of Lords approved, with one exception, the checklist of matters relevant to the exercise of the discretion which had been drawn up by the Court of Appeal (see *R. v. Hayward; R. v. Jones; R. v. Purvis* [2001] Q.B. 862). Whilst the list was not exhaustive, it provided an invaluable guide. The Court of Appeal had said that in exercising the discretion, fairness to the defendant was of prime importance, but fairness to the prosecution should also be taken into account. The judge should have regard to all the circumstances, including:

(a) the nature and circumstances of the defendant's behaviour in absenting himself from the trial or disrupting it, and in particular whether the behaviour was voluntary and so plainly waived the right to be present;
(b) whether an adjournment would resolve the matter;
(c) the likely length of such an adjournment;
(d) whether the defendant, though absent, wished to be represented or had waived his right to representation;
(e) whether the defendant's representatives were able to receive instructions from him and the extent to which they could present his defence;
(f) the extent of the disadvantage to the defendant in not being able to present his account of events;
(g) the risk of the jury reaching an improper conclusion about the absence of the defendant;
(h) the general public interest that a trial should take place within a reasonable time;
(i) the effect of the delay on the memories of witnesses;
(j) where there was more than one defendant, and not all had absconded, the undesirability of having separate trials.

3–199 The Court of Appeal had said that the seriousness of the offence should be considered. However, the House of Lords said that the objects of ensuring that any trial would be as fair as circumstances permitted and that it should lead to a just outcome were equally important, whether the offence charged was serious or relatively minor.

For an accused to be taken to have waived his right to be present at his trial, it must be proved that he knew of, or was indifferent to, the consequences of being tried in his absence and without legal representation; a direction from the court upon the grant of bail, explaining the consequences of non-attendance at trial, and the provision to the accused of a written statement to the same effect would, therefore, generally provide an incontrovertible means of proof: *R. v. O'Hare* [2006] Crim.L.R. 950, CA.

In *R. v. Amrouchi*, unreported, November 22, 2007, CA ([2007] EWCA Crim. 3019), it was held that if the judge is sure that the defendant has deliberately absented himself and that there are no reasonable steps that can be taken to get him to court, then he is permitted to proceed in his absence. Following *R. v. Jones (Anthony)*, however, such a decision is to be made with "great caution and close regard to the overall fairness of the proceedings", and is a step which ought normally to be taken only if it is unavoidable. Where, therefore, the appellant was not produced from custody on the day of his trial, and where the judge had purported to rely on the principles in *R. v. Jones (Anthony)*, he had taken the wrong approach by, *inter alia*, (i) failing, when considering the prejudice to the defendant's case that would be caused by his absence, to consider the fact that the potential defence was self-defence and that, as in many such cases, establishment of the defence would depend entirely upon the defendant's own evidence, (ii) referring, when considering the consequences for the defendant of not being able to testify, to the potential benefit to the defendant (*viz.* neither "making a fool of himself" in the witness box nor having adverse inferences drawn from his failure to testify), but not to the possibility that he would lose the chance to give convincing evidence that would support his case, (iii) failing, upon being informed that the defendant had refused to be taken to court and had said that he could not be bothered, to consider the possibility that the defendant was unaware that this was the day of his trial, (iv) concluding that it was for the defendant to make himself aware of the nature of the proceedings, and (v) as a consequence, deciding that a 24-hour adjournment would make no difference because there was no reason to think the defendant would change his mind, without considering the possibility of directing that a specific warning be given to him informing him that his trial would take place in his absence were he not to attend.

In *R. v. Kepple* [2007] 7 *Archbold News* 3, CA ([2007] EWCA Crim. 1339), it was held that a defendant may, by absenting himself, waive his right to be arraigned according to precisely the same principle as applies to waiver of the right to be present at a trial as set out in *R. v. Jones (Anthony)*, *viz.* that he knew of, or was indifferent to, the consequences of absenting himself; a defendant could thus be taken to have waived his right to be arraigned where he absented himself after being informed by his counsel that the prosecution were intending to apply for leave to amend the indictment to add a more serious alternative offence; the possibility that he might have pleaded guilty to the less serious offence was not a bar to proceeding to trial of the more serious offence. **3–199a**

Where a magistrates' court, having been informed that an absent defendant had been arrested and detained in respect of an unrelated matter, formed the view that he had brought the arrest upon himself and should therefore be regarded as having excluded himself deliberately, it misdirected itself in fact; the direction to proceed in the accused's absence should not have been exercised on the basis that he was absent for any reason over which he had control: *R. (R.) v. Thames Youth Court*, 166 J.P. 711, QBD (Pitchford J.).

B. LIMITATIONS

(1) Preliminary and sentencing hearings

Crime and Disorder Act 1998, ss.57A–57E

PART 3A

LIVE LINKS FOR ACCUSED'S ATTENDANCE AT CERTAIN PRELIMINARY AND SENTENCING HEARINGS

Introductory

57A.—(1) This Part— **3–200**

(a) applies to preliminary hearings and sentencing hearings in the course of proceedings for an offence; and

(b) enables the court in the circumstances provided for in sections 57B, 57C and 57E to direct the use of a live link for securing the accused's attendance at a hearing to which this Part applies.

(2) The accused is to be treated as present in court when, by virtue of a live link direction under this Part, he attends a hearing through a live link.

(3) In this Part—

"custody"—

(a) includes local authority accommodation to which a person is remanded or committed by virtue of section 23 of the *Children and Young Persons Act* 1969; but

(b) does not include police detention;

"live link" means an arrangement by which a person (when not in the place where the hearing is being held) is able to see and hear, and to be seen and heard by, the court during a hearing (and for this purpose any impairment of eyesight or hearing is to be disregarded);

"police detention" has the meaning given by section 118(2) of the *Police and Criminal Evidence Act* 1984;

"preliminary hearing" means a hearing in the proceedings held before the start of the trial (within the meaning of subsection (11A) or (11B) of section 22 of the 1985 Act) including, in the case of proceedings in the Crown Court, a preparatory hearing held under—

(a) section 7 of the *Criminal Justice Act* 1987 (cases of serious or complex fraud); or

(b) section 29 of the *Criminal Procedure and Investigations Act* 1996 (other serious, complex or lengthy cases);

"sentencing hearing" means any hearing following conviction which is held for the purpose of—

(a) proceedings relating to the giving or rescinding of a direction under section 57E;

(b) proceedings (in a magistrates' court) relating to committal to the Crown Court for sentencing; or

(c) sentencing the offender or determining how the court should deal with him in respect of the offence.

Use of live link at preliminary hearings where accused is in custody

3–201 **57B.**—(1) This section applies in relation to a preliminary hearing in a magistrates' court or the Crown Court.

(2) Where it appears to the court before which the preliminary hearing is to take place that the accused is likely to be held in custody during the hearing, the court may give a live link direction under this section in relation to the attendance of the accused at the hearing.

(3) A live link direction under this section is a direction requiring the accused, if he is being held in custody during the hearing, to attend it through a live link from the place at which he is being held.

(4) If a hearing takes place in relation to the giving or rescinding of such a direction, the court may require or permit a person attending the hearing to do so through a live link.

(5) The court shall not give or rescind such a direction (whether at a hearing or otherwise) unless the parties to the proceedings have been given the opportunity to make representations.

(6) If in a case where it has power to do so a magistrates' court decides not to give a live link direction under this section, it must—

(a) state in open court its reasons for not doing so; and

(b) cause those reasons to be entered in the register of its proceedings.

Use of live link at preliminary hearings where accused is at police station

3–202 **57C.**—(1) This section applies in relation to a preliminary hearing in a magistrates' court.

(2) Where subsection (3) or (4) applies to the accused, the court may give a live link direction in relation to his attendance at the preliminary hearing.

(3) This subsection applies to the accused if—

(a) he is in police detention at a police station in connection with the offence; and

(b) it appears to the court that he is likely to remain at that station in police detention until the beginning of the preliminary hearing.

(4) This subsection applies to the accused if he is at a police station in answer to live link bail in connection with the offence.

(5) A live link direction under this section is a direction requiring the accused to attend the preliminary hearing through a live link from the police station.

(6) But a direction given in relation to an accused to whom subsection (3) applies has no effect if he does not remain in police detention at the police station until the beginning of the preliminary hearing.

(7) A live link direction under this section may not be given unless the accused has given his consent to the court.

(8) A magistrates' court may rescind a live link direction under this section at any time before or during a hearing to which it relates.

(9) A magistrates' court may require or permit—

(a) the accused to give or withhold consent under subsection (7) through a live link; and

(b) any party to the proceedings who wishes to make representations in relation to the giving or rescission of a live link direction under this section to do so through a live link.

(10) Where a live link direction under this section is given in relation to an accused person who is answering to live link bail he is to be treated as having surrendered to the custody of the court (as from the time when the direction is given).

(11) In this section, "live link bail" means bail granted under Part 4 of the *Police and Criminal Evidence Act* 1984 subject to the duty mentioned in section 47(3)(b) of that Act.

Continued use of live link for sentencing hearing following a preliminary hearing

57D.—(1) Subsection (2) applies where— **3–203**

(a) a live link direction under section 57B or 57C is in force;

(b) the accused is attending a preliminary hearing through a live link by virtue of the direction;

(c) the court convicts him of the offence in the course of that hearing (whether by virtue of a guilty plea or an indication of an intention to plead guilty); and

(d) the court proposes to continue the hearing as a sentencing hearing in relation to the offence.

(2) The accused may continue to attend through the live link by virtue of the direction if—

(a) the hearing is continued as a sentencing hearing in relation to the offence;

(b) the accused consents to his continuing to attend through the live link; and

(c) the court is satisfied that it is not contrary to the interests of justice for him to do so.

(3) But the accused may not give oral evidence through the live link during a continued hearing under subsection (2) unless–

(a) he consents to give evidence in that way; and

(b) the court is satisfied that it is not contrary to the interests of justice for him to give it in that way.

Use of live link in sentencing hearings

57E.—(1) This section applies where the accused is convicted of the offence. **3–204**

(2) If it appears to the court by or before which the accused is convicted that it is likely that he will be held in custody during any sentencing hearing for the offence, the court may give a live link direction under this section in relation to that hearing.

(3) A live link direction under this section is a direction requiring the accused, if he is being held in custody during the hearing, to attend it through a live link from the place at which he is being held.

(4) Such a direction—

(a) may be given by the court of its own motion or on an application by a party; and

(b) may be given in relation to all subsequent sentencing hearings before the court or to such hearing or hearings as may be specified or described in the direction.

(5) The court may not give such a direction unless—

(a) the offender has given his consent to the direction; and

(b) the court is satisfied that it is not contrary to the interests of justice to give the direction.

(6) The court may rescind such a direction at any time before or during a hearing to which it relates if it appears to the court to be in the interests of justice to do so (but this does not affect the court's power to give a further live link direction in relation to the offender).

The court may exercise this power of its own motion or on an application by a party.

(7) The offender may not give oral evidence while attending a hearing through a live link by virtue of this section unless—

(a) he consents to give evidence in that way; and

(b) the court is satisfied that it is not contrary to the interests of justice for him to give it in that way.

(8) The court must—

(a) state in open court its reasons for refusing an application for, or for the rescission of, a live link direction under this section; and

(b) if it is a magistrates' court, cause those reasons to be entered in the register of its proceedings.

[Ss.57A to 57E were substituted for section 57 by the *PJA* 2006, s.45. Save to the extent that it inserted section 57C, section 45 came into force on January 15, 2007: *Police and Justice Act 2006 (Commencement No. 1, Transitional and Saving Provisions) Order* 2006 (S.I. 2006 No. 3364). Article 4 of S.I. 2006 No. 3364 contains transitional provisions: (i) any direction given under section 57 before that date continues to have effect; (ii) where a preliminary hearing commenced before that date, the court may nevertheless give a direction under section 57B on or after that date; and (iii) where a direction under section 57 continues to have effect, section 57D shall have effect as if subsection (1)(a) included a reference to section 57. The insertion of section 57C took effect on April 1, 2007: *Police and Justice Act 2006 (Commencement No. 2, Transitional and Saving Provisions) Order* 2007 (S.I. 2007 No. 709).]

As to the legislation referred to in section 57A(3), for section 23 of the 1969 Act, see *ante*, § 3–69; for section 118 of the 1984 Act, see *post*, § 15–27; for section 22 of the 1985 Act, see *ante*, § 1–266; for section 7 of the 1987 Act, see *post*, § 4–84m; and for section 29 of the 1996 Act, see *post*, § 4–84t.

(2) Defendant unruly, obstructive, etc.

3–205 Unless there is a danger of violence or escape, a defendant ought not to be handcuffed or otherwise restrained in the dock: *R. v. Vratsides* [1988] Crim.L.R. 251, CA; *R. v. Mullen* [2000] 6 *Archbold News* 2, CA (the method of countering any risk should be such as to create the least risk of prejudice). Any application that the defendant should be restrained should be heard *inter partes*: *R. v. Rollinson*, 161 J.P. 107, CA. A judge is entitled to take account of hearsay when exercising his discretion; and an appropriate warning should be given to the jury to minimise the risk of prejudice: *R. v. Mullen*, *ante*. In a magistrates'court, it is for the court, not the police, to decide whether it is necessary for a defendant to be handcuffed: *R. v. Cambridgeshire JJ., ex p. Peacock*, 161 J.P. 113, DC.

For sufficient reason (such as that his presence may intimidate a witness) the defendant may be removed out of sight, though remaining within hearing distance: *R. v. Smellie*, 14 Cr.App.R. 128, CCA. As to the use of screens, see *post*, §§ 8–55e, 8–55f.

If a defendant in custody refuses to come into court, he should not be compelled to do so either by the use of force or the threat of force, even though he may be in the course of giving evidence. The only remedy is for the judge to punish him for contempt and to continue the trial in his absence: *R. v. O'Boyle*, 92 Cr.App.R. 202, CA.

In an extreme case, a trial may proceed in the absence of the accused and without him being represented; such a case arose where the accused had dispensed with the services of his solicitors and counsel, where his repeated requests for the representation order to be transferred to fresh representatives were refused on the basis that the criteria in regulation 16 of the *Criminal Defence Service (General) (No. 2) Regulations* 2001 (S.I. 2001 No. 1437) (*post*, § 6–169) were not fulfilled, and where (on account of those refusals) the accused failed to co-operate at the trial and stayed in his cell; there had been no requirement that the judge should have adjourned the trial in order to obtain representation for the appellant (in relation to which the judge was entitled to have regard to the effect of delay on the prosecution and their witnesses), since the trial would not otherwise have been unfair had it continued with the appellant present but unrepresented; and, other than giving in to the accused's attempts at blackmailing the court, the judge had had no option other than to have proceeded in the way that he had: *R. v. Smith (Henry Lee)* [2007] Crim.L.R. 325, CA.

(3) Defendant unfit

3–206 As to unfitness to plead, see *post*, §§ 4–166a *et seq.* As to the making of a hospital order in relation to a detained person who is unfit even to be brought to court, see *ante*, §§ 3–81 *et seq.*

In *Romanov v. Russia* (2007) 44 E.H.R.R. 23, ECtHR, it was said that although a court may derogate from the general entitlement of an accused to be present and to participate effectively in his trial where, *inter alia*, he is suffering from illness, if the proceedings involve an assessment of his personality and character and of his state of mind at the time of the offence, and their outcome might be of major detriment to him, it would be essential to the fairness of the proceedings that he be present at the hearing and afforded the opportunity to participate in it together with his counsel.

(4) Discharge of jury

If the jury, for any reason are discharged without giving a verdict, it is not necessary, in order to constitute a valid discharge, that the defendant should be present: *R. v. Richardson* (1913) 29 T.L.R. 228. **3–207**

(5) Proceedings in camera

In general, it is unacceptable for any part of the proceedings to take place *in camera* in the absence of the defendant: see *R. v. Agar*, 90 Cr.App.R. 318, CA, and *R. v. Preston* [1994] 2 A.C. 130, HL (*post*, § 4–77). As to the available *ex parte* procedure when the prosecution wish to rely on public interest immunity to justify non-disclosure of unused material, see *post*, §§ 12–50, 12–77 *et seq.* **3–208**

(6) Proceedings in chambers

See the *Criminal Procedure Rules* 2005 (S.I. 2005 No. 384), r.16.11 (*ante*, § 2–153). **3–209**

(7) Judgment

In the case of treason, the defendant had to be present when judgment was given: 1 Ld Raym. 48, 267. As to the variation of sentence under the *PCC(S)A* 2000, s.155(1), see *post*, § 5–945. As to clarification of a doubt or ambiguity in a sentence, see *R. v. Dowling*, 88 Cr.App.R. 88, CA, *post*, § 5–48. Apart from the foregoing, no special rules apply. **3–210**

IV. ATTENDANCE AT COURT OF PARENT OR GUARDIAN

Children and Young Persons Act 1933, s.34A

Attendance at court of parent or guardian

34A.—(1) Where a child or young person is charged with an offence or is for any other reason brought before a court, the court— **3–211**

(a) may in any case; and

(b) shall in the case of a child or a young person who is under the age of sixteen years,

require a person who is a parent or guardian of his to attend at the court during all the stages of the proceedings, unless and to the extent that the court is satisfied that it would be unreasonable to require such attendance, having regard to the circumstances of the case.

(2) In relation to a child or young person for whom a local authority have parental responsibility and who—

(a) is in their care; or

(b) is provided with accommodation by them in the exercise of any functions (in particular those under the *Children Act* 1989) which are social services functions within the meaning of the *Local Authority Social Services Act* 1970,

the reference in subsection (1) above to a person who is a parent or guardian of his shall be construed as a reference to that authority or, where he is allowed to live with such a person, as including such a reference.

In this subsection "local authority" and "parental responsibility" have the same meanings as in the *Children Act* 1989.

[This section was inserted by the *CJA* 1991, s.56; and is printed as amended by the *Local Government Act* 2000, s.107(1), and Sched. 5, para. 1.]

V. DEATH OF THE ACCUSED

Where the accused dies either before or after his trial has commenced, formal evidence of death should be given. A police officer, usually the officer in charge of the case, **3–212** will give evidence to the effect that he has seen the dead body of XY and that XY was the defendant named in the relevant indictment. The indictment should be marked accordingly. The following form of endorsement was directed by Chapman J. in a case in the Crown Court at St Albans in December 1978.

> "Inspector —— having given evidence that on the —— 20— he identified, in the mortuary of Brixton Prison, the dead body of a man alleged to have committed suicide there on ——, as being the man arrested by him on —— on the charge mentioned in this indictment and as being the man subsequently charged and committed for trial to this court on this charge; it was ordered that the indictment be endorsed as aforesaid and be declared now of no legal effect and that the file be closed unless and until the court, on cause being shown, otherwise orders."

In practice, it commonly occurs that there is nobody available who has seen the body and can identify it as being that of the person to whom the indictment relates. It is submitted that there is no legal requirement for such strict proof: all that is necessary is evidence to satisfy the court of the fact of death. The endorsement on the indictment can follow the above precedent, suitably amended to take account of the nature of the evidence and the precise terms of the judge's order.

Chapter 4

TRIAL

I. PRELIMINARIES

A. COMMENCEMENT DATE

Supreme Court [Senior Courts] Act 1981, s.77

Committal [Sending] for trial: date of trial

77.—(1) Criminal Procedure Rules shall prescribe the minimum *and the maximum* period which may elapse between a person's *committal for trial or the giving of a notice of transfer under a relevant transfer provision* [being sent for trial] and the beginning of the trial; and such rules may make different provision for different places of trial and for other different circumstances. **4–1**

(2) The trial of a person *committed by a magistrates' court or in respect of whom a notice of transfer under a relevant transfer provision has been given* [sent for trial]—

(a) shall not begin until the prescribed minimum period has expired except with his consent and the consent of the prosecutor; *and*

(b) *shall not begin later than the expiry of the prescribed maximum period unless a judge of the Crown Court otherwise orders.*

(3) For the purposes of this section the prescribed minimum *and maximum periods* [period] shall begin with the date *of committal for trial or of a notice of transfer* [when the defendant is sent for trial] and the trial shall be taken to begin when the defendant is arraigned.

(4) *In this section "relevant transfer provision" means—*

(a) *section 4 of the* Criminal Justice Act *1987, or*

(b) *section 53 of the* Criminal Justice Act *1991.*

[As from a day to be appointed, this Act may be cited as the *Senior Courts Act* 1981: *Constitutional Reform Act* 2005, s.59(5) and Sched. 11, para. 1(1). This section is printed as amended by the *CJA* 1987, s.15, Sched. 2, para. 11; the *CJPOA* 1994, s.168(1) and Sched. 9, para. 18; and the *Courts Act 2003 (Consequential Amendments) Order* 2004 (S.I. 2004 No. 2035). The words "and the maximum" in subs. (1), subs. (2)(b), and the words "and maximum periods" in subs. (3) are omitted, and the word "period" in subs. (3) is inserted, as from a day to be appointed, by the *Prosecution of Offences Act* 1985, s.31(5) and (6), and Scheds 1, Pt III, and 2. Otherwise, the words in italics are omitted, and the words in square brackets are inserted, by the *CJA* 2003, s.41, and Sched. 3, para. 54(1) and (3). Of these amendments, that relating to subsection (1) came into force on May 9, 2005, in relation to cases sent for trial under section 51 or 51A(3)(d) of the *CDA* 1998 (*Criminal Justice Act 2003 (Commencement No. 9) Order* 2005 (S.I. 2005 No. 1267)); otherwise, they come into force on a day to be appointed.]

Criminal Procedure Rules 2005 (S.I. 2005 No. 384), r.39.1

TRIAL ON INDICTMENT

Time limits for beginning of trials

4–2 **39.1.** The periods set out for the purposes of section 77(2)(a) and (b) of the *Supreme Court [Senior Courts] Act* 1981 shall be 14 days and 8 weeks respectively and accordingly the trial of a person committed by a magistrates'court—

(a) shall not begin until the expiration of 14 days beginning with the date of his committal, except with his consent and the consent of the prosecution; and

(b) shall, unless the Crown Court has otherwise ordered, begin not later than the expiration of 8 weeks beginning with the date of his committal.

Rule 39.1 reproduces, in identical terms, rule 24 of the *Crown Court Rules* 1982 (S.I. 1982 No. 1109) (the reference to the "*Senior Courts Act*" is substituted, as from a day to be appointed, by the *Constitutional Reform Act* 2005, s.59(5), and Sched. 11, para. 1(2)). It is directory and not mandatory: *R. v. Governor of Spring Hill Prison, ex p. Sohi and Dhillon*, 86 Cr.App.R. 382, DC, but see *ante*, § 1–195 *et seq.*, as to the significance of this.

Section 77 and rule 39.1 have no application where the indictment has been preferred in accordance with the voluntary bill procedure: *R. v. Coleville-Scott* [1990] Crim.L.R. 871, CA. Nor do they refer to a matter that is sent for trial pursuant to section 51 of the *CDA* 1998.

As to the requirements under Articles 5(3) and 6(1) of the ECHR for trial within a reasonable time, see *post*, §§ 16–43, 16–54, 16–57 and 16–73. As to time limits, including overall time limits, see *ante*, §§ 1–266 *et seq.*

B. HEARING IN OPEN COURT

(1) European Convention on Human Rights and common law

General principles

4–3 The openness of judicial proceedings is a fundamental principle enshrined in Article 6(1) of the ECHR, which protects individuals from secret justice administered without public control and constitutes a means of preserving confidence in the courts; making the administration of justice transparent helps to achieve the aim of Article 6(1), namely a fair trial, the guarantee of which is one of the most fundamental principles of a democratic society: *Stefanelli v. San Marino* (2001) 33 E.H.R.R. 16, ECtHR. To a similar effect, but drawing a distinction between first instance and appellate proceedings, see *Tierce v. San Marino* (2002) 34 E.H.R.R. 25, ECtHR. See further *post*, §§ 16–57, 16–68 and 16–71 as to the right to a fair trial, and the qualifications to that right, under the European Convention. See also *Werner v. Austria*; *Szücs v. Austria*, 26 E.H.R.R. 310, ECtHR, and *Riepan v. Austria* [2001] Crim.L.R. 230, ECtHR.

At common law, a trial on indictment must be held in a public court with open doors. For observations on the meaning of "open court", see *McPherson v. McPherson* [1936] A.C. 177, PC. The same principle applies to proceedings in magistrates' courts: see the *MCA* 1980, s.121(4). Nevertheless, at common law, there is inherent jurisdiction to sit *in camera* if the administration of justice so requires: *Scott v. Scott* [1913] A.C. 417, HL. The jurisdiction does not rest on the discretion of the individual judge; it depends on principle, which overrides the fixed principle requiring the administration of justice to take place in open court, and defines the extent of the exception: *ibid.*, *per* Viscount Haldane at p. 435. The question is whether a sitting in private is necessary for the administration of justice, as where there is tumult or disorder in court or the just apprehension of it: *ibid.*, *per* Lord Loreburn at pp. 445, 446. Similarly, "objectionable characters or youth of tender years" may be excluded if necessary to facilitate the proper conduct of a trial: *R. v. Denbigh JJ., ex p. Williams and Evans* [1974] Q.B. 759, DC. (As to persons under the age of 14, see *post*, §§ 4–12, 4–13.)

The risk of financial damage, or damage to reputation or goodwill, resulting from the institution of proceedings concerning a person's business, is not a valid reason for departing from the "open court" principle: *R. v. Dover JJ., ex p. Dover DC* [1992] Crim.L.R. 371, DC. Similarly, the "necessity" principle does not justify a sitting in private simply because of the embarrassing nature of the evidence, or to deny or prevent an opportunity to show interest: *Scott v. Scott*, *ante*, and *R. v. Chancellor of Chichester Consistory Court, ex p. News Group Newspapers Ltd* [1992] C.O.D. 48, DC. However, such matters may be a relevant consideration if they would result in a witness being unable or unwilling to give evidence: *ibid*. Any exception to the principle of open justice should be based on the yet more fundamental principle that the principal object of the courts is to secure that justice is done; where, therefore, a judge was satisfied that an important prosecution witness would refuse to give evidence unless the public gallery was cleared, he had been entitled to close the court to the general public, but with members of the press remaining; Article 6 of the ECHR permits departure from the general requirement for a public hearing where "publicity would prejudice the interests of justice": *R. v. Richards*, 163 J.P. 246, CA. As to the practical application of these principles, and as to the drawing of distinctions between the press and the general public, see further, *post*, § 4–4.

As to inroads that may be necessary in respect of the "open court" principle, by reason of the right to life protected by Article 2 of the European Convention (*post*, § 16–36), where there is an unacceptable risk to the life of a witness, see *R. v. Lord Saville of Newdigate, ex p. A* [2000] 1 W.L.R. 1855, CA (Civ. Div.), and *R. (A.) v. Lord Saville of Newdigate* [2002] 1 W.L.R. 1249, CA (Civ. Div.), and see *post*, § 4–5 (the facts of these cases concerned a tribunal of enquiry; in a criminal case it would also be necessary to take account of any conflicting interests of a defendant).

For further observations on the reasons for the general "open court" principle and on the courts' powers to depart from that general principle, see also *Att.-Gen. v. Leveller Magazine Ltd* [1979] A.C. 440, HL, *post*, §§ 25–321 *et seq.*; *R. v. Governor of Lewes Prison, ex p. Doyle* [1917] 2 K.B. 254; *R. v. Registrar of Building Societies, ex p. a Building Society* [1960] 1 W.L.R. 669 at 679, 687; *R. v. Malvern JJ., ex p. Evans*; *R. v. Evesham JJ., ex p. McDonagh* [1988] Q.B. 553, 87 Cr.App.R. 19, DC; *X. v. Z. Ltd, The Times*, April 18, 1997, CA (Civ. Div.); *R. v. Legal Aid Board, ex p. Kaim Todner (a firm)* [1999] Q.B. 966, CA (Civ. Div.); *Ex p. Guardian Newspapers Ltd* [1999] 1 Cr.App.R. 284, CA; *Trustor v. Smallbone* [2000] 1 All E.R. 811, Ch D (Rimer J.); and *Clibbery v. Allan* [2002] Fam. 261, CA (Civ. Div.).

As to the reception of information relating to mitigation of sentence otherwise than in open court, see *post*, § 5–92.

Practical application

The practical application of the "open court" principle was considered in *R. v. Denbigh JJ., ex p. Williams and Evans* [1974] Q.B. 759, DC: **4–4**

> "... the injunction to the presiding judge or magistrate is: do your best to enable the public to come in and see what is happening, having a proper common sense regard for the facilities available and the facility for keeping order, security and the like ... the presence or absence of the press is a vital factor in deciding whether a particular hearing was or was not in open court. I find it difficult to imagine a case which can be said to be held publicly if the press have been actively excluded. On the other hand, the fact that the press is present is not conclusive the other way ... " (*per* Lord Widgery C.J. at p. 765).

His Lordship further observed (at p. 765):

> "... the method by which this duty is to be performed in a particular case is primarily for determination by the presiding judge ... on the spot. If he has shown himself conscious of his duty in this regard and has reached a conclusion which a reasonable [judge] might reach, then I do not think it is for us in this court to substitute our own views [as to] whether the facilities offered to the public were or were not sufficient."

When considering the need to depart from the "open court" principle, a distinction **4–5** is to be drawn between matters which should never meet the public gaze and matters where the concern ends with the conclusion of the trial, or related proceedings; in the latter situation the risk of prejudice to the administration of justice can often be dealt with by an order under section 4(2) of the *Contempt of Court Act* 1981 (*post*, §§ 28–78 *et seq.*), postponing any press report: *Re Crook*, 93 Cr.App.R. 17, CA. Further, as a general rule, no distinction should be drawn between the presence of the press and the presence of the general public (*ibid.*), but there are exceptional situations where such a distinction may be necessary to ensure that justice can be done without a completely closed hearing; this was the situation in *R. v. Richards* (*ante*, § 4–3), and in *R. v. Waterfield*, 60 Cr.App.R. 296, CA (public have no right to see exhibits, particularly if exhibit is allegedly obscene film, but might want to know what kind of films are involved; therefore, if judge excludes general public when such films are shown, press should normally be permitted to remain so that they can provide public with information upon which to base opinions). See also *post*, § 16–71 as to the importance of access by the press to proceedings. A further distinction between the presence of the press and of the general public is drawn by section 37 of the *CYPA* 1933 (*post*, § 4–13).

In some situations a practical means of resolving a tension between the "open court" principle and the necessity to ensure that justice is done may be to avoid the identification of an individual by, for example, the use of letters of the alphabet rather than names, whether or not the parties to the case are made aware of the relevant name (see *post*, §§ 8–70, 8–71 and 16–68, and see *R. v. Lord Saville of Newdigate, ex p. A.*, *ante*, § 4–3), or by the use of screens (see *post*, §§ 8–67, 16–68 and 16–71), or by some combination of these devices (see *R. v. Shayler (Michael David)* [2003] A.C.D. 79, CA, in which the screening and non-identification of the witnesses was held to be in the overall interests of justice where the case against the defendant could not proceed without their evidence, where general disclosure of their identity would give rise to a real risk to their safety, where the defendant was aware of their identities, and where some of the well-recognised advantages of open justice, such as increased pressure on witnesses to tell the truth and the possibility that someone hearing the case would know something relevant to the defence, were not significant factors). However, specific statutory provision apart, a court has power to order the name of a party or witness to be withheld from the public only where failure to make such order would frustrate or render impracticable the administration of justice; the welfare interests of the person involved are not the only consideration: *R. v. Newtownabbey Magistrates' Court, ex p. Belfast Telegraph Newspapers Ltd*, *The Times*, August 27, 1997, QBD (N.I.) (fear for safety of accused if his identity disclosed, not sufficient justification). See also *R. v. Bedfordshire Coroner, ex p. Local Sunday Newspapers Ltd*, 164 J.P. 283, QBD (anonymity of witness with genuine fear appropriate, on the facts, in proceedings before coroner, but different considerations in criminal trial).

Applications to sit in camera, in chambers, or in private

4–6 As to the meanings of the expressions "in chambers", "*in camera*" and "in private", see *Clibbery v. Allan* [2002] Fam. 261, CA (Civ. Div.)

In *Re Crook*, *ante*, Lord Lane C.J. also gave the following guidance about applications to sit in private. (a) It is right to assume that when a judge agrees to sit in chambers he will have been informed by the clerk of the court of the general nature of the application. (b) Until the application and the facts on which it is based are known to him, the judge will not be in a position to decide whether the administration of justice could be prejudiced by the reasons being stated in open court. (c) Once it is clear that justice will not be prejudiced, the judge can adjourn into open court and state what has occurred. (d) A judge should not adjourn into chambers as a matter of course, but only if he believes that something might be said which makes the determination of a preliminary question in chambers appropriate. (e) If a judge does sit in chambers he should be alert to the importance of adjourning to open court if, and as soon as, it emerges that it is plainly not necessary to exclude the public. See also *R. v. Tower Bridge JJ., ex p. Osborne*, 88 Cr.App.R. 28, DC (application for proceedings to be heard *in camera* should itself be heard *in camera*) and rule 16.10 of the *Criminal Procedure Rules* 2005 (S.I. 2005 No. 384), *post*, reproducing in identical terms rule 24A of the *Crown Court Rules* 1982.

Criminal Procedure Rules 2005 (S.I. 2005 No. 384), r.16.10

Application to hold a Crown Court trial in camera

4–7 **16.10.**—(1) Where a prosecutor or a defendant intends to apply for an order that all or part of a trial be held in camera for reasons of national security or for the protection of the identity of a witness or any other person, he shall not less than 7 days before the date on which the trial is expected to begin serve a notice in writing to that effect on the Crown Court officer and the prosecutor or the defendant as the case may be.

(2) On receiving such notice, the court officer shall forthwith cause a copy thereof to be displayed in a prominent place within the precincts of the Court.

(3) An application by a prosecutor or a defendant who has served such a notice for an order that all or part of a trial be heard in camera shall, unless the Court orders otherwise, be made in camera, after the defendant has been arraigned but before the jury has been sworn and, if such an order is made, the trial shall be adjourned until whichever of the following shall be appropriate—

(a) 24 hours after the making of the order, where no application for leave to appeal from the order is made; or

(b) after the determination of an application for leave to appeal, where the application is dismissed; or

(c) after the determination of the appeal, where leave to appeal is granted.

For the statutory power to hear evidence *in camera* on grounds of national safety, see *post*, §§ 25–319, 25–337.

Rule 16.10 has no relevance where the application for a hearing *in camera* is not based on factors specified in that rule. Nor does the rule have any relevance to applications "relating to procedural matters preliminary or incidental to proceedings in the Crown Court" or any of the other matters that may be dealt with in chambers pursuant to rule 16.11 (*ante*, § 2–153): *Re Crook*, *ante*. However, in *Ex p. Guardian Newspapers Ltd* [1999] 1 Cr.App.R. 284, CA, it was held that the words "all or part of a trial" in rule 16.10 mean "all or part of the trial process", and thus (adopting the principles explained in *Re Ashton* [1994] 1 A.C. 9, HL, *post*, § 4–75), include a pre-trial application to stay the trial as an abuse of process. Accordingly, the word "trial" in "the date on which the trial is expected to begin" (rule 16.10(1)) and in "trial shall be adjourned" (rule 16.10(3)) mean "the relevant part of the trial process".

The notice of application required by rule 16.10 must specify the ground of application, must be dated and must be displayed for seven days; where it is a defence application based on national security, it is incumbent on the judge to ensure that he receives evidence from those who are the guardians of national security, so as to enable him to balance the potential risks to national security and justice: *Ex p. Guardian Newspapers Ltd*, *ante*. However, a notice which failed expressly to identify which grounds under rule 16.10(1) were relied upon was sufficient when, in context, no one could have been in any doubt as to what they were: *Re A.* [2006] 1 W.L.R. 1361, CA.

Where rule 16.10 applies and there has been ample opportunity, but no effort, to **4–8** comply with it, the trial judge is not entitled to side-step it by invoking any inherent powers which he might have, but should some matter arise suddenly in a way which precludes the possibility of compliance with rule 16.10, then it might be that the court would have the inherent powers described in *Scott* and *Leveller* (*ante*, § 4–3) to direct that evidence be given *in camera* even though no prior notice had been given: *Re Godwin* [1991] Crim.L.R. 302, CA (although notice under rule 16.10 had not been given at least seven days before the date originally fixed for the commencement of trial, commencement date had varied as matters had proceeded; what ultimately had to be determined was whether the expected date of trial was at least seven days ahead of the time when the application under rule 16.10 was made). It is submitted that if at the time of the service of the notice under rule 16.10 the then expected commencement date of the trial is less than seven days away and the commencement date of the trial is then postponed, the safe course is to serve a fresh notice. See also the final paragraph at § 1–197, *ante*.

Conduct of hearing in camera

It is unacceptable for a defendant and his solicitor to be excluded from a hearing *in* **4–9** *camera* and for restrictions to be placed on counsel as to what he may disclose to his instructing solicitor and client: *R. v. Preston* [1994] 2 A.C. 130, HL. See also *post*, §§ 4–76, 4–77.

As to the available *ex parte* procedure when the prosecution wish to rely on public interest immunity to justify non-disclosure of unused matter, see *post*, §§ 12–79 *et seq.*

Publicity

4–10 See the *Administration of Justice Act* 1960, s.12 (publication of information relating to proceedings in private), *post*, § 28–56.

Appeal

4–11 See the *CJA* 1988, s.159 (*post*, § 7–308), which provides, *inter alia*, that the Court of Appeal shall have the power to stay any proceedings in any other court until after the appeal is disposed of.

(2) Statutory exceptions

(a) *Children and young persons*

Children and Young Persons Act 1933, ss.36, 37

Prohibition against children being present in court during the trial of other persons

4–12 **36.** No child (other than an infant in arms) shall be permitted to be present in court during the trial of any other person charged with an offence, or during any proceedings preliminary thereto, except during such time as his presence is required as a witness or otherwise for the purposes of justice or while the court consents to his presence; and any child present in court when under this section he is not to be permitted to be so shall be ordered to be removed: …

[This section is printed as amended and repealed in part by the *Access to Justice Act* 1999, ss.73(1) and 106, and Sched. 15, Pt III.]

Power to clear court while child or young person is giving evidence in certain cases

4–13 **37.**—(1) Where, in any proceedings in relation to an offence against, or any conduct contrary to, decency or morality, a person who, in the opinion of the court is a child or young person is called as a witness, the court may direct that all or any persons not being members or officers of the court or parties to the case, their counsel or solicitors, or persons otherwise directly concerned with the case, be excluded from the court during the taking of the evidence of that witness:

Provided that nothing in this section shall authorise the exclusion of bona fide representatives of a *newspaper or news agency* [news gathering or reporting organisation].

(2) The powers conferred on a court by this section shall be in addition and without prejudice to any other powers of the court to hear proceedings *in camera*.

[The words in square brackets are substituted for the italicised words as from a day to be appointed: *YJCEA* 1999, s.67(1) and Sched. 4, para. 2(2).]

"Child" means a person under the age of 14; "young person" means a person who has attained the age of 14 and is under the age of 18 years: s.107 of the 1933 Act. For youth courts, see *ibid.* s.47. See also *R. v. Southwark Juvenile Court, ex p. N.J.* [1973] 1 W.L.R. 1300, DC, and *R. v. Willesden JJ., ex p. Brent London Borough* [1988] 2 F.L.R. 95, DC.

(b) *Official secrets*

4–14 See the *Official Secrets Act* 1920, s.8(4) (*post*, § 25–319) and the *Official Secrets Act* 1989, s.11(4) (*post*, § 25–337).

See rule 16.10 of the *Criminal Procedure Rules* 2005 (*ante*, § 4–7) for the procedure to be followed in relation to an application for an order that a trial or part of a trial be held *in camera* for reasons of national security.

(c) *Rules of court*

4–15 See the *Criminal Procedure Rules* 2005, rr.16.11 and 32.4 (*ante*, §§ 2–153 and 2–155 respectively), as to the business of the Crown Court which may be conducted in chambers. See also the *Indictments (Procedure) Rules* 1971, r.10 (*ante*, § 1–230), in respect of applications for leave to prefer "voluntary" bills of indictment.

(d) *Challenge for cause to jury*

4–16 See the *CJA* 1988, s.118(2), *post*, § 4–239.

C. PUBLICITY

(1) General right to publish reports

As to the general right to publish fair and accurate reports of proceedings held in public, see the *Contempt of Court Act* 1981, s.4(1), *post*, § 28–78. For the power to restrict the publication of reports where it is necessary to do so to avoid a substantial risk of prejudice to the administration of justice, see section 4(2); and for the power to prohibit the publication of a name or other matter withheld from the public in the proceedings, see section 11, *post*, § 28–96. As to the absence of any power, apart from specific statutory powers, to restrict or postpone a report of public proceedings in court, see *R. v. Newtownabbey Magistrates' Court, ex p. Belfast Telegraph Newspapers Ltd*, *The Times*, August 27, 1997, QBD (N.I.), and *Re Trinity Mirror Plc* [2008] 2 Cr.App.R. 1, CA (no jurisdiction to prevent identification of defendant in order to protect his children, who were neither defendants nor victims). **4–17**

The High Court, including a judge of the Family Division, possesses jurisdiction to restrain publicity, derived from rights under the ECHR: *Re S. (a child) (identification: restriction on publication)* [2005] 1 A.C. 593, HL. An order had been sought to restrain publication, in respect of the criminal trial of a woman who was charged with having murdered one of her two children, of any matter that might lead to the identification of the surviving child, there being no jurisdiction to make such an order under section 39 of the *CYPA* 1933 (*post*, § 4–27) as none of the charges related to him. It was held that an intense focus on the comparative importance of the specific rights being claimed under Articles 8 and 10 respectively was necessary, with neither article having precedence as such over the other, with account being taken of the justification for interfering with or restricting each right, and the proportionality test being applied to each. On the facts, the importance of open reporting of criminal proceedings outweighed the rights of the child under Article 8; such was the importance attached to the former that it is submitted that it would be rare for the rights under Article 8 of a person not directly concerned in the criminal proceedings, on whom the impact of publication will therefore be indirect, to prevail. For the need for exceptional circumstances before such an order can begin to be contemplated, see *Re Trinity Mirror Plc*, *ante*; and for the only reported case where the balance lay in favour of an injunction restraining publicity, see *A Local Authority v. W., L., W., T. and R. (by the children's guardian)* [2006] 1 F.L.R. 1, Fam D (Sir Mark Potter P.). In *Re X. Children* [2008] 1 F.L.R. 589, Fam D (Munby J.), it was held, applying *Re S. (a child) (identification: restriction on publication), ante*, that the case was not one where the interests of the children could justify the anonymisation of the defendant, their father, in criminal proceedings, who was accused of the attempted murder of a social worker, but an order was made prohibiting the publication of the names of the children, their address or other identifying information. **4–18**

See also generally, *post*, § 16–110a.

(2) Restrictions

(a) *Hearings before trial*

For restrictions on reporting: (i) committal proceedings, see *post*, §§ 4–20 *et seq.*; (ii) dismissal applications and preparatory hearings in serious fraud cases, see the *CJA* 1987, s.11, *post*, §§ 4–89 *et seq.*; (iii) dismissal applications in notice of transfer children cases, see the *CJA* 1991, Sched. 6, para. 6, *ante*, § 1–57; (iv) dismissal applications in indictable-only cases sent for trial, see the *CDA* 1998, Sched. 3, para. 3, *ante*, § 1–29; (v) preparatory hearings in long, complex or serious cases, see the *CPIA* 1996, s.37, *post*, § 4–89; and (vi) statutory pre-trial hearings, see the *CPIA* 1996, s.41, *post*, § 4–91b. **4–19**

Magistrates' Courts Act 1980, s.8

Restrictions on reports of committal proceedings

8.—(1) *Except as provided by subsections (2), (3) and (8) below, it shall not be lawful to publish in Great Britain a written report, or to include in a relevant programme for reception in Great Britain a report, of any committal proceedings in England and Wales containing any matter other than that permitted by subsection (4) below.* **4–20**

(2) *Subject to subsection (2A) below a magistrates' court shall, on an application for the purpose made with reference to any committal proceedings by the accused or one of the accused, as the case may be, order that subsection (1) above shall not apply to reports of those proceedings.*

(2A) *Where in the case of two or more accused one of them objects to the making of an order under subsection (2) above, the court shall make the order if, and only if, it is satisfied, after hearing the representations of the accused, that it is in the interests of justice to do so.*

(2B) *An order under subsection (2) above shall not apply to reports of proceedings under subsection (2A) above, but any decision of the court to make or not to make such an order may be contained in reports published, or included in a relevant programme before the time authorised by subsection (3) below.*

(3) *It shall not be unlawful under this section to publish, or include in a relevant programme a report of committal proceedings containing any matter other than that permitted by subsection (4) below—*

(a) *where the magistrates' court determines not to commit the accused, or determines to commit none of the accused, for trial, after it so determines;*

(b) *where the court commits the accused or any of the accused for trial, after the conclusion of his trial or, as the case may be, the trial of the last to be tried;*

and where at any time during the inquiry the court proceeds to try summarily the case of one or more of the accused under section 25(3) or (7) below, while committing the other accused or one or more of the other accused for trial, it shall not be unlawful under this section to publish, or include in a relevant programme as part of a report of the summary trial, after the court determines to proceed as aforesaid, a report of so much of the committal proceedings containing any such matter as takes place before the determination.

4–21 (4) *The following matters may be contained in a report of committal proceedings published, or included in a relevant programme without an order under subsection (2) above before the time authorised by subsection (3) above, that is to say—*

(a) *the identity of the court and the names of the examining justices;*

(b) *the names, addresses and occupations of the parties and witnesses and the ages of the accused and witnesses;*

(c) *the offences, or a summary of them, with which the accused is or are charged;*

(d) *the names of the legal representatives engaged in the proceedings;*

(e) *any decision of the court to commit the accused or any of the accused for trial, and any decision of the court on the disposal of the case of any accused not committed;*

(f) *where the court commits the accused or any of the accused for trial, the charge or charges, or a summary of them, on which he is committed and the court to which he is committed;*

(g) *where the committal proceedings are adjourned, the date and place to which they are adjourned;*

(h) *any arrangements as to bail on committal or adjournment;*

(i) *whether a right to representation funded by the Legal Services Commission as part of the Criminal Defence Service was granted to the accused or any of the accused.*

4–22 (5) *If a report is published, or included in a relevant programme in contravention of this section, the following persons, that is to say—*

(a) *in the case of a publication of a written report as part of a newspaper or periodical, any proprietor, editor or publisher of the newspaper or periodical;*

(b) *in the case of a publication of a written report otherwise than as part of a newspaper or periodical, the person who publishes it;*

(c) *in the case of the inclusion of a report in a relevant programme, any body corporate which provides the service in which the programme is included and any person having functions in relation to the programme corresponding to those of an editor of a newspaper,*

shall be liable on summary conviction to a fine, not exceeding level 5 on the standard scale.

(6) *Proceedings for an offence under this section shall not, in England and Wales, be instituted otherwise than by or with the consent of the Attorney-General.*

(7) *Subsection (1) above shall be in addition to, and not in derogation from, the provisions of any other enactment with respect to the publication of reports and proceedings of magistrates' and other courts.*

(8) *For the purposes of this section committal proceedings shall, in relation to an information charging an indictable offence, be deemed to include any proceedings in the magistrates' court before the court proceeds to inquire into the information as examining justices; but*

where a magistrates' court which has begun to try an information summarily discontinues the summary trial in pursuance of section 25(2) or (6) below and proceeds to inquire into the information as examining justices, that circumstance shall not make it unlawful under this section for a report of any proceedings on the information which was published or broadcast before the court determined to proceed as aforesaid to have been so published, or included in a relevant programme.

(9) [*Repealed by* Contempt of Court Act *1981, s.4(4).*]

(10) *In this section—*

"publish", in relation to a report, means publish the report, either by itself or as part of a newspaper or periodical, for distribution to the public;

"relevant programme" means a programme included in a programme service (within the meaning of the Broadcasting Act *1990).*

[This section is printed as amended and repealed in part by the *Criminal Justice (Amendment) Act* 1981, s.1; the *CJA* 1982, ss.38 and 46; the *Cable and Broadcasting Act* 1984, Sched. 5; the *Courts and Legal Services Act* 1990, Sched. 18, para. 25(5); the *Broadcasting Act* 1990, Sched. 20, para. 25, and Sched. 21; and the *Access to Justice Act* 1999, s.24 and Sched. 4, para. 16. The whole section is repealed as from a day to be appointed: *CJA* 2003, s.332, and Sched. 37, Pt 4.]

For the meaning of "programme service", see the *Broadcasting Act* 1990, s.201.

Before a magistrates' court makes an order for the lifting of reporting restrictions at committal proceedings, under section 8(2), all the defendants must be present and be given an opportunity to make representations: *R. v. Wirral District Magistrates' Court, ex p. Meikle* [1991] C.O.D. 2, DC. **4–23**

When there is a division of opinion among co-accused whether committal proceedings should be reported, section 8(2A) places on the accused who wishes to have the proceedings reported the burden of satisfying the magistrates that it is in "the interests of justice" to lift the restrictions. The magistrates must balance the conflicting views, and have regard to the rule in section 8(1) that, prima facie, committal proceedings should not be reported and to the fact that the "interests of justice" require, as a paramount consideration, that all the accused should have a fair trial: *R. v. Leeds JJ., ex p. Sykes*, 76 Cr.App.R. 129, DC.

An application for, and grant of, an order for lifting publicity restrictions may be made before the committal proceedings proper begin: *R. v. Bow Street Magistrate, ex p. Kray* [1969] 1 Q.B. 473—see now section 8(8) of the 1980 Act. When an order has been made lifting the restrictions, the particular committal proceedings to which it relates have to be ascertained in the light of the circumstances prevailing when the order was made: *ex p. Kray*, *ante*. **4–24**

Criminal Procedure Rules 2005 (S.I. 2005 No. 384), r.10.1

COMMITTAL FOR TRIAL

Restrictions on reports of committal proceedings

10.1.—(1) Except in a case where evidence is, with the consent of the accused, to be tendered in his absence under section 4(4)(b) of the *Magistrates' Courts Act* 1980 (absence caused by ill health), a magistrates' court acting as examining justices shall before admitting any evidence explain to the accused the restrictions on reports of committal proceedings imposed by section 8 of that Act and inform him of his right to apply to the court for an order removing those restrictions. **4–25**

(2) [*Where order removing restriction made, the order is to be entered in the register.*]

(3) [*At the beginning of each adjourned hearing the court must state that an order removing the restriction has been made.*]

Relationship of section 8 to section 4(2) of Contempt of Court Act 1981

The fact that section 8 provides a restriction on reporting in particular circumstances (committal proceedings) does not prevent section 4(2) of the 1981 Act (*post*, §§ 28–78 *et seq.*) from applying to such proceedings. Section 8 and section 4(2) impose restrictions in different situations and for different purposes, *i.e.* where the publication of committal **4–26** proceedings was prejudicial to the defendant's interests (s.8) and where publication of proceedings, whether or not prejudicial to the defendant, would be a contempt (s.4(2)). The words "any other proceedings pending or imminent" in section 4(2) include potential proceedings in the Crown Court: *R. v. Horsham JJ., ex p. Farquharson* [1982] Q.B. 762, 76 Cr.App.R. 87, CA (Civ. Div.). See also the wording of section 8(7) of the 1980 Act, *ante*, § 4–22.

(b) *Child or young person as victim, witness or defendant*

Children and Young Persons Act 1933, s.39

Power to prohibit publication

4–27 **39.**—(1) In relation to any proceedings in any court ... the court may direct that—

(a) no newspaper report of the proceedings shall reveal the name, address, or school, or include any particulars calculated to lead to the identification, of any child or young person concerned in the proceedings, either, as being the person by or against, or in respect of whom the proceedings are taken, or as being a witness therein;

(b) no picture shall be published in any newspaper as being or including a picture of any child or young person so concerned in the proceedings as aforesaid;

except in so far (if at all) as may be permitted by the court.

(2) [*Creates summary offence of breach of section 39(1) direction.*]

[(3) In this section "proceedings" means proceedings other than criminal proceedings.]

[This section is printed as amended and repealed in part by the *CYPA* 1963, ss.57(1) and 64(3) and Sched. 5. Subs. (3) is inserted as from a day to be appointed by the *YJCEA* 1999, s.48 and Sched. 2, para. 2(1).]

As from the commencement of subsection (3), this section will have no further application to criminal proceedings, save that its commencement will not affect the continued operation of the section in relation to any proceedings instituted before that time: *YJCEA* 1999, s.24, and Sched. 2, para. 2(2). As to when proceedings are "instituted" for this purpose, see Schedule 7, para. 1(2), to the 1999 Act, *post*, § 8–55z. For the replacement provision, see section 45 of the 1999 Act, *post*, § 4–29b.

For the definitions of "child" and "young person", see section 107(1) of the 1933 Act, *ante*, § 4–13.

Section 39 has been extended by the *CYPA* 1963, s.57(3) (to Scotland) and (4) (to sound and television broadcasts) (repealed, as from a day to be appointed, but with retrospective effect, by a combination of the *CJPOA* 1994, Sched. 11, and the *YJCEA* 1999, s.67(1) and Sched. 4, para. 24), and by the *Broadcasting Act* 1990, s.203 and Sched. 20, para. 3(2) (to reports or matters included in a "programme service", *i.e.* the television and other broadcasting services identified in s.201 of the 1990 Act).

A court has a complete discretion to hear anybody in support of, or in opposition to, an application under section 39: *R. v. Central Criminal Court, ex p. Crook* [1995] 2 Cr.App.R. 212, DC (where the judge heard representations on behalf of the press and the relevant children).

Where the alleged victim is a ward of court it is for the judge in the criminal proceedings, and not for the wardship judge, to make any necessary order restraining reporting of the criminal trial. In such a case the simplest and most economical course will be for the guardian *ad litem* to supply the prosecutor with any necessary material and for the prosecutor to make the application. Alternatively, and although the courts will generally be astute to prevent persons not involved in a trial from making statements and applications, counsel for the guardian may make an application. The defendant himself might also apply for an order on the ground that he might feel inhibited in presenting his defence if he apprehended that it would lead to publicity harmful to his child and perhaps weaken his position in the wardship proceedings: *Re R. (a Minor) (Wardship: Restrictions on Publication)* [1994] 2 F.L.R. 637, CA (Civ. Div.).

In *ex p. Crook, ante*, the court suggested the following procedure in respect of the making of orders under section 39: (a) the judge should make clear what the terms of the order are; if there is possible doubt as to the identity of the child or children to whom the order relates, the judge must identify the relevant children with clarity; (b) a written copy of the order should be drawn up as soon as possible after the order has been made orally; the written *pro forma* that should be available in every court may be amended as necessary to meet an unusual case; the order, or a copy of it, should then be available in the court office for representatives of the press to inspect; (c) the fact that an order has been made should be communicated to those who were not present when it was made, perhaps by a short notice included in the daily list; some such words as "Order made under *C. & Y.P. Act* 1933, s.39" appended to the name of the case should suffice.

An order under section 39 must be in the terms of the section or in words to a like effect. There is no power to prohibit, in terms, the publication of the name of a defendant who is not a child or young person. Such prohibition may, however, be the practical effect of an order in the correct form; judges may think it helpful in such cases to invite discussion about the identification of particular details: *Ex p. Godwin* [1992] Q.B. 190, 94 Cr.App.R. 34, CA; and see *Ex p. Gazette Media Company Ltd* [2005] E.M.L.R. 34, CA (confirming that *Ex p. Godwin* had survived the *Human Rights Act* 1998). The terms of the order should be clear and precise; merely to order that reporting restrictions under section 39 apply to a particular child or young person is too vague to found a prosecution for contravening such an order under section 39(2): *Briffett and Bradshaw v. DPP*, 166 J.P. 66, DC.

An order under section 39 need not be made during the course of the proceedings to which it relates; it may be made at any time: *R. v. Harrow Crown Court, ex p. Perkins*; *R. v. Cardiff Crown Court, ex p. M. (a Minor)*, (1998) 162 J.P. 527, DC.

Although there is a right of appeal to the Court of Appeal against the making of an order under section 39 (*post*, §§ 7–308 *et seq.*), the Court of Appeal has no jurisdiction under section 39 to make an order imposing restrictions: *R. v. Lee (a Minor)*, 96 Cr.App.R. 188, DC and CA. If there is a change of circumstances a further application may be made to the Crown Court: *ibid*.

There are conflicting decisions as to whether (or when) a decision of the Crown Court in respect of section 39 is an exercise of "its jurisdiction in matters relating to trial on indictment", within the meaning of section 29(3) of the *Supreme Court [Senior Courts] Act* 1981 (renamed as from a day to be appointed: *Constitutional Reform Act* 2005, s.59(5), and Sched. 11, para. 1) (*post*, § 7–4), and so immune from challenge by way of judicial review. Judicial review was held to be available in *R. v. Lee* (*ante*) and in *R. v. Harrow Crown Court ex p. Perkins*; *R. v. Cardiff Crown Court, ex p. M. (a Minor)* (*ante*), but in *R. v. Winchester Crown Court, ex p. B.* [2000] 1 Cr.App.R. 11, DC, the court concluded that on a proper analysis of the law and the relevant authorities a decision in respect of section 39 was not, as a matter of jurisdiction, susceptible to judicial review. Subsequently, in *R. v. Manchester Crown Court, ex p. H. and D.* [2000] 1 Cr.App.R. 262, DC, it was held that a decision in respect of section 39 is susceptible to judicial review, at least after conviction and sentence. See further *post*, §§ 7–8 *et seq*.

In *R. v. Tyne Tees Television Ltd*, *The Times*, October 20, 1997, the Court of Appeal expressed the view that where there has been an alleged breach of an order under section 39(1), the better course is to report the matter for consideration as to whether there should be a prosecution for the specific summary offence under subsection (2) of contravening such an order, rather than deal with the matter as an alleged contempt. The court declined to rule as to whether contempt proceedings would ever be appropriate in view of the specific statutory offence.

When considering an application under section 39 in respect of a child or young **4–28**
person who is the accused, considerable weight should be given to the age of the offender and to the potential damage to any young person of public identification as a criminal before having the benefit or burden of adulthood: *R. v. Inner London Crown Court, ex p. B.* [1996] C.O.D. 17, DC. There must be good reason for making an order under section 39 in such a case; the age of the accused is a matter to which considerable weight ought to be given; but to suggest (as had been done in *R. v. Leicester Crown Court, ex p. S. (a Minor)*, 94 Cr.App.R. 143, DC) that it would only be in "rare and exceptional" cases that such an order would not be made, or, once made, would be lifted, was to put an unwarranted gloss on the statute; in considering whether to lift an

order, the welfare of the child must be taken into account, but the weight to be given to that interest changes where there has been a conviction, particularly in a serious case; on the other side of the equation is the legitimate public interest in knowing the outcome of proceedings in court, and there is a potential deterrent effect in respect of the conduct of others in the disgrace accompanying the identification of those guilty of serious crimes; in deciding whether to lift an order after conviction, the judge should take account of the possibility of a successful appeal against conviction: *R. v. Central Criminal Court, ex p. S.* [1999] 1 F.L.R. 480, DC (adopting and expanding upon, the view expressed by Lloyd L.J. in *R. v. Lee* (*ante*), where the point was also made that the onus on an applicant under section 39 is to show grounds for restricting publicity, whereas in proceedings in a youth court, section 49 of the 1933 Act (*post*) requires good reason for lifting the otherwise automatic restriction on publicity; if the discretion under section 39 is too narrowly confined there is the danger of blurring this distinction drawn by statute between the youth court and the Crown Court). In *R. v. Manchester Crown Court, ex p. H. and D.* (*ante*), the fact that non-frivolous grounds of appeal had been settled in respect of 15-year-olds convicted of murder, with the possibility of a retrial in the event of success on appeal, was held to be a matter of the greatest importance in exercising the discretion as to whether or not a section 39 reporting restriction should be maintained.

In *R. v. Central Criminal Court, ex p. W., B. and C.* [2001] 1 Cr.App.R. 2, DC, the court emphasised that under section 39 the onus is on the applicant to show cause for restricting publicity. Further, there is nothing in section 39 to support an approach whereby a direction is given to protect a young defendant's identity in all but "rare and exceptional cases". Where, therefore, a trial judge had, after the applicants had been convicted of offences including murder and robbery, lifted an order previously made under section 39, having balanced the appropriate interests and considerations (the strong public interest in open justice as against the welfare of the applicants, and taking account of deterrence, the fact that the applicants would be likely to be in custody for a long period before release and that two of them were appealing against conviction) there was no basis for interfering with the order. The judge had distinguished deterrence from "naming and shaming". A further relevant consideration, which the judge might have taken into account, was that there were adult co-defendants. The court stressed that what was said in *McKerry v. Teesdale and Wear Valley JJ.*, 164 J.P. 355, DC (*post*, § 4–29) was said in relation to youth courts.

Youth courts

4–29 Section 49 of the *CYPA* 1933 (as substituted by the *CJPOA* 1994, s.49, and as subsequently amended, or prospectively amended, by the *C(S)A* 1997, s.45, the *CDA* 1998, s.119, and Sched. 8, para. 1, the *YJCEA* 1999, s.48, and Sched. 2, para. 3, the *PCC(S)A* 2000, s.165(1) and Sched. 9, para. 2, the *CJCSA* 2000, s.74 and Sched. 7, para. 5, the *CJA* 2003, s.304, and Sched. 32, para. 2, the *Legal Services Act* 2007, s.208(1), and Sched. 21, paras 15 and 19, and the *CJIA* 2008, ss.6(2) and (3) and 149, Sched. 4, paras 3 and 100, and Sched. 28, Pt 1) automatically imposes restrictions similar to those contained in section 39(1) (as extended, *ante*), in relation to proceedings in youth courts and to proceedings under Schedule 7 [2] to the *PCC(S)A* 2000 [*CJIA* 2008] (variation or revocation of supervision orders [youth rehabilitation orders]), or on appeal from any such proceedings. However, in any proceedings under either of those sections before a magistrates' court other than a youth court, or on appeal from such a court, it is the duty of the magistrates' court or the appellate court to announce that the section applies to the proceedings; failure to do so has the effect of disapplying the section (subs. (10)). The court may dispense with the restrictions if it is satisfied: (a) that it is appropriate to do so to avoid injustice to the child or young person; (b) that, as respects a child or young person charged with or convicted of a violent or sexual offence or an offence punishable in the case of a person aged 21 [18] or over with imprisonment for 14 years or more who is unlawfully at large, it is necessary for the purpose of apprehending him and bringing him before a court or returning him to the place in which he was in custody; or (c) where the child or young person has been convicted of an offence, that it is in the public interest to do so. The restrictions may not be lifted on ground (b) save on an application being made by or on behalf of the Director of Public Prosecutions and unless notice of such application has been given by the applicant to any legal representative of the child or young person; and, before making an order on ground (c), the parties must be afforded an opportunity to make representations.

The various statutory provisions in respect of the reporting of information relating to juveniles are now to be read against the background of international law and practice that draws attention to the need carefully to protect the privacy of juveniles in legal proceedings, with great weight being given to their welfare; those interests of the juvenile come into collision with, and fall to be balanced against, the right to freedom of expression and the hallowed principle that justice is administered in public, open to full and fair reporting so that the public might be informed about the justice administered in their name; in relation to section 49, the jurisdiction to dispense with reporting restrictions should be exercised with great care, caution and circumspection; it would be wholly wrong to invoke the power by way of additional punishment, and it is difficult to see any place for "naming and shaming"; it will only be very rarely that the statutory criteria are met; as to procedure, it is open to the court to allow a representative of the press to address it directly or in writing on the question whether reporting should be permitted: *McKerry v. Teesdale and Wear Valley JJ.*, 164 J.P. 355, DC.

Youth Justice and Criminal Evidence Act 1999, ss.44, 45

[Restrictions on reporting alleged offences involving persons under 18

44.—(1) This section applies (subject to subsection (3)) where a criminal investigation has begun in respect of— **4–29a**

(a) an alleged offence against the law of—

(i) England and Wales, or

(ii) Northern Ireland; or

(b) an alleged civil offence (other than an offence falling within paragraph (a)) committed (whether or not in the United Kingdom) by a person subject to service law.

(2) No matter relating to any person involved in the offence shall while he is under the age of 18 be included in any publication if it is likely to lead members of the public to identify him as a person involved in the offence.

(3) The restrictions imposed by subsection (2) cease to apply once there are proceedings in a court (whether a court in England and Wales, a service court or a court in Northern Ireland) in respect of the offence.

(4) For the purposes of subsection (2) any reference to a person involved in the offence is to—

(a) a person by whom the offence is alleged to have been committed; or

(b) if this paragraph applies to the publication in question by virtue of subsection (5)—

(i) a person against or in respect of whom the offence is alleged to have been committed, or

(ii) a person who is alleged to have been a witness to the commission of the offence;

except that paragraph (b)(i) does not include a person in relation to whom section 1 of the *Sexual Offences (Amendment) Act* 1992 (anonymity of victims of certain sexual offences) applies in connection with the offence.

(5) Subsection (4)(b) applies to a publication if—

(a) where it is a relevant programme, it is transmitted, or

(b) in the case of any other publication, it is published,

on or after such date as may be specified in an order made by the Secretary of State.

(6) The matters relating to a person in relation to which the restrictions imposed by subsection (2) apply (if their inclusion in any publication is likely to have the result mentioned in that subsection) include in particular—

(a) his name,

(b) his address,

(c) the identity of any school or other educational establishment attended by him,

(d) the identity of any place of work, and

(e) any still or moving picture of him.

(7) Any appropriate criminal court may by order dispense, to any extent specified in the order, with the restrictions imposed by subsection (2) in relation to a person if it is satisfied that it is necessary in the interests of justice to do so.

(8) However, when deciding whether to make such an order dispensing (to any extent) with the restrictions imposed by subsection (2) in relation to a person, the court shall have regard to the welfare of that person.

(9) In subsection (7) "appropriate criminal court" means—

(a) in a case where this section applies by virtue of subsection (1)(a)(i) or (ii), any court in England and Wales or (as the case may be) in Northern Ireland which has any jurisdiction in, or in relation to, any criminal proceedings (but not a service court unless the offence is alleged to have been committed by a person subject to service law);

(b) in a case where this section applies by virtue of subsection (1)(b), any court falling within paragraph (a) or a service court.

(10) The power under subsection (7) of a magistrates' court in England and Wales may be exercised by a single justice.

(11) In the case of a decision of a magistrates' court in England and Wales, or a court of summary jurisdiction in Northern Ireland, to make or refuse to make an order under subsection (7), the following persons, namely—

(a) any person who was a party to the proceedings on the application for the order, and

(b) with the leave of the Crown Court, any other person,

may, in accordance with Criminal Procedure Rules in England and Wales, or rules of court in Northern Ireland, appeal to the Crown Court against that decision or appear or be represented at the hearing of such an appeal.

(12) On such an appeal the Crown Court—

(a) may make such order as is necessary to give effect to its determination of the appeal; and

(b) may also make such incidental or consequential orders as appear to it to be just.

(13) In this section—

(a) "civil offence" means an act or omission which, if committed in England and Wales, would be an offence against the law of England and Wales;

(b) any reference to a criminal investigation, in relation to an alleged offence, is to an investigation conducted by police officers, or other persons charged with the duty of investigating offences, with a view to it being ascertained whether a person should be charged with the offence;

(c) any reference to a person subject to service law is to—

(i) a person subject to *military law, air-force law or the* Naval Discipline Act *1957,* [service law within the meaning of the *Armed Forces Act* 2006;] or

(ii) *any other person to whom provisions of Part II of the* Army Act *1955, Part II of the* Air Force Act *1955 or Parts I and II of the* Naval Discipline Act *1957 apply (whether with or without any modifications)* [a civilian subject to service discipline within the meaning of that Act].]

[Power to restrict reporting of criminal proceedings involving persons under 18

4–29b **45.**—(1) This section applies (subject to subsection (2)) in relation to—

(a) any criminal proceedings in any court (other than a service court) in England and Wales or Northern Ireland; and

(b) any proceedings (whether in the United Kingdom or elsewhere) in any service court.

(2) This section does not apply in relation to any proceedings to which section 49 of the *Children and Young Persons Act* 1933 applies.

(3) The court may direct that no matter relating to any person concerned in the proceedings shall while he is under the age of 18 be included in any publication if it is likely to lead members of the public to identify him as a person concerned in the proceedings.

(4) The court or an appellate court may by direction ("an excepting direction") dispense, to any extent specified in the excepting direction, with the restrictions imposed by a direction under subsection (3) if it is satisfied that it is necessary in the interests of justice to do so.

(5) The court or an appellate court may also by direction ("an excepting direction") dispense, to any extent specified in the excepting direction, with the restrictions imposed by a direction under subsection (3) if it is satisfied—

(a) that their effect is to impose a substantial and unreasonable restriction on the reporting of the proceedings, and

(b) that it is in the public interest to remove or relax that restriction;

but no excepting direction shall be given under this subsection by reason only of the fact that the proceedings have been determined in any way or have been abandoned.

(6) When deciding whether to make—

(a) a direction under subsection (3) in relation to a person, or

(b) an excepting direction under subsection (4) or (5) by virtue of which the restrictions imposed by a direction under subsection (3) would be dispensed with (to any extent) in relation to a person,

the court or (as the case may be) the appellate court shall have regard to the welfare of that person.

(7) For the purposes of subsection (3) any reference to a person concerned in the proceedings is to a person—

(a) against or in respect of whom the proceedings are taken, or

(b) who is a witness in the proceedings.

(8) The matters relating to a person in relation to which the restrictions imposed by a direction under subsection (3) apply (if their inclusion in any publication is likely to have the result mentioned in that subsection) include in particular—

(a)–(e) [*identical to s.44(6)(a)–(e),* ante, *§ 4–29a*].

(9) A direction under subsection (3) may be revoked by the court or an appellate court.

(10) An excepting direction—

(a) may be given at the time the direction under subsection (3) is given or subsequently; and

(b) may be varied or revoked by the court or an appellate court.

(11) In this section "appellate court", in relation to any proceedings in a court, means a court dealing with an appeal (including an appeal by way of case stated) arising out of the proceedings or with any further appeal.]

[Ss.44 and 45 come into force on a day to be appointed. S.44(11) is printed as amended by the *Courts Act* 2003, s.109(1), and Sched. 8, para. 386; and s.44(13) is printed as amended, as from a day to be appointed, by the *AFA* 2006, s.378(1), and Sched. 16, para. 158 (substitution of words in square brackets for words in italics).]

For the transitional provisions, see *post*, § 4–29i.

As to the exercise of the power to restrict reporting in respect of persons under the age of 18, see section 52 (*post*, § 4–29f), and note the international law implications outlined in *McKerry v. Teesdale and Wear Valley JJ.*, 164 J.P. 355, DC (*ante*, § 4–29).

(c) *Certain adult witnesses and victims*

For the restriction on the identification of complainants in certain sexual offences, see the *Sexual Offences (Amendment) Act* 1992, *post*, §§ 20–257 *et seq.* **4–29ba**

Youth Justice and Criminal Evidence Act 1999, s.46

Reports relating to adult witnesses

Power to restrict reports about certain adult witnesses in criminal proceedings

46.—(1) This section applies where— **4–29c**

(a) in any criminal proceedings in any court (other than a service court) in England and Wales or Northern Ireland, or

(b) in any proceedings (whether in the United Kingdom or elsewhere) in any service court,

a party to the proceedings makes an application for the court to give a reporting direction in relation to a witness in the proceedings (other than the accused) who has attained the age of 18.

In this section "reporting direction" has the meaning given by subsection (6).

(2) If the court determines—

(a) that the witness is eligible for protection, and

(b) that giving a reporting direction in relation to the witness is likely to improve—

(i) the quality of evidence given by the witness, or

(ii) the level of co-operation given by the witness to any party to the proceedings in connection with that party's preparation of its case,

the court may give a reporting direction in relation to the witness.

(3) For the purposes of this section a witness is eligible for protection if the court is satisfied—

(a) that the quality of evidence given by the witness, or

(b) the level of co-opeation given by the witness to any party to the proceedings in connection with that party's preparation of its case,

is likely to be diminished by reason of fear or distress on the part of the witness in connection with being identified by members of the public as a witness in the proceedings.

(4) In determining whether a witness is eligible for protection the court must take into account, in particular—

(a) the nature and alleged circumstances of the offence to which the proceedings relate;

(b) the age of the witness;

(c) such of the following matters as appear to the court to be relevant, namely—

(i) the social and cultural background and ethnic origins of the witness,

(ii) the domestic and employment circumstances of the witness, and

(iii) any religious beliefs or political opinions of the witness;

(d) any behaviour towards the witness on the part of—

(i) the accused,

(ii) members of the family or associates of the accused, or

(iii) any other person who is likely to be an accused or a witness in the proceedings.

(5) In determining that question the court must in addition consider any views expressed by the witness.

(6) For the purposes of this section a reporting direction in relation to a witness is a direction that no matter relating to the witness shall during the witness's lifetime be included in any publication if it is likely to lead members of the public to identify him as being a witness in the proceedings.

(7) The matters relating to a witness in relation to which the restrictions imposed by a reporting direction apply (if their inclusion in any publication is likely to have the result mentioned in subsection (6)) include in particular—

(a) the witness's name,

(b) the witness's address,

(c) the identity of any educational establishment attended by the witness,

(d) the identity of any place of work, and

(e) any still or moving picture of the witness.

(8) In determining whether to give a reporting direction the court shall consider—

(a) whether it would be in the interests of justice to do so, and

(b) the public interest in avoiding the imposition of a substantial and unreasonable restriction on the reporting of the proceedings.

(9) The court or an appellate court may by direction ("an excepting direction") dispense, to any extent specified in the excepting direction, with the restrictions imposed by a reporting direction if—

(a) it is satisfied that it is necessary in the interests of justice to do so, or

(b) it is satisfied—

(i) that the effect of those restrictions is to impose a substantial and unreasonable restriction on the reporting of the proceedings, and

(ii) that it is in the public interest to remove or relax that restriction;

but no excepting direction shall be given under paragraph (b) by reason only of the fact that the proceedings have been determined in any way or have been abandoned.

(10) A reporting direction may be revoked by the court or an appellate court.

(11) An excepting direction—

(a) may be given at the time the reporting direction is given or subsequently; and

(b) may be varied or revoked by the court or an appellate court.

(12) In this section—

(a) "appellate court", in relation to any proceedings in a court, means a court dealing with an appeal (including an appeal by way of case stated) arising out of the proceedings or with any further appeal;

(b) references to the quality of a witness's evidence are to its quality in terms of completeness, coherence and accuracy (and for this purpose "coherence" refers to a witness's ability in giving evidence to give answers which address the questions put to the witness and can be understood both individually and collectively);

(c) references to the preparation of the case of a party to any proceedings include, where the party is the prosecution, the carrying out of investigations into any offence at any time charged in the proceedings.

This section came into force on October 7, 2004: *Youth Justice and Criminal Evidence Act 1999 (Commencement No. 10) (England and Wales) Order* 2004 (S.I. 2004 No. 2428).

For the transitional provisions, see *post*, 4–29i.

See *R. v. Davis (Iain)*; *R. v. Ellis* [2006] 2 Cr.App.R. 32, CA, as to this section (and other statutory provisions) adding to, and not detracting from, the common law. The reversal by the House of Lords of the Court of Appeal's decision in the case of *Davis* (see *R. v. Davis* [2008] 3 W.L.R. 125, HL) does not affect what was said by the Court of Appeal on this point.

Rules of court

Part 16 of the *Criminal Procedure Rules* 2005 (S.I. 2005 No. 384) sets out the procedure to be followed in respect of applications under section 46. **4–29ca**

Criminal Procedure Rules 2005 (S.I. 2005 No. 384), rr.16.1–16.9

RESTRICTIONS ON REPORTING AND PUBLIC ACCESS

Application for a reporting direction under section 46(6) of the Youth Justice and Criminal Evidence Act 1999

16.1.—(1) An application for a reporting direction made by a party to any criminal proceedings, in relation to a witness in those proceedings, must be made in the form set out in the Practice Direction or orally under rule 16.3. **4–29cb**

(2) If an application for a reporting direction is made in writing, the applicant shall send that application to the court officer and copies shall be sent at the same time to every other party to those proceedings.

Opposing an application for a reporting direction under section 46(6) of the Youth Justice and Criminal Evidence Act 1999

16.2.—(1) If an application for a reporting direction is made in writing, any party to the proceedings who wishes to oppose that application must notify the applicant and the court officer in writing of his opposition and give reasons for it. **4–29cc**

(2) A person opposing an application must state in the written notification whether he disputes that the—

(a) witness is eligible for protection under section 46 of the *Youth Justice and Criminal Evidence Act* 1999; or

(b) granting of protection would be likely to improve the quality of the evidence given by the witness or the level of co-operation given by the witness to any party to the proceedings in connection with that party's preparation of its case.

(3) The notification under paragraph (1) must be given within five business days of the date the application was served on him unless an extension of time is granted under rule 16.6.

Urgent action on an application under section 46(6) of the Youth Justice and Criminal Evidence Act 1999

16.3.—(1) The court may give a reporting direction under section 46 of the *Youth Justice and Criminal Evidence Act* 1999 in relation to a witness in those proceedings, notwithstanding that the five business days specified in rule 16.2(3) have not expired if— **4–29cd**

(a) an application is made to it for the purposes of this rule; and

(b) it is satisfied that, due to exceptional circumstances, it is appropriate to do so.

(2) Any party to the proceedings may make the application under paragraph (1) whether or not an application has already been made under rule 16.1.

(3) An application under paragraph (1) may be made orally or in writing.

(4) If an application is made orally, the court may hear and take into account representations made to it by any person who in the court's view has a legitimate interest in the application before it.

(5) The application must specify the exceptional circumstances on which the applicant relies.

Excepting direction under section 46(9) of the Youth Justice and Criminal Evidence Act 1999

4–29ce **16.4.**—(1) An application for an excepting direction under section 46(9) of the *Youth Justice and Criminal Evidence Act* 1999 (a direction dispensing with restrictions imposed by a reporting direction) may be made by—

(a) any party to those proceedings; or

(b) any person who, although not a party to the proceedings, is directly affected by a reporting direction given in relation to a witness in those proceedings.

(2) If an application for an excepting direction is made, the applicant must state why—

(a) the effect of a reporting direction imposed places a substantial and unreasonable restriction on the reporting of the proceedings; and

(b) it is in the public interest to remove or relax those restrictions.

(3) An application for an excepting direction may be made in writing, pursuant to paragraph (4), at any time after the commencement of the proceedings in the court or orally at a hearing of an application for a reporting direction.

(4) If the application for an excepting direction is made in writing it must be in the form set out in the Practice Direction and the applicant shall send that application to the court officer and copies shall be sent at the same time to every party to those proceedings.

(5) Any person served with a copy of an application for an excepting direction who wishes to oppose it, must notify the applicant and the court officer in writing of his opposition and give reasons for it.

(6) The notification under paragraph (5) must be given within five business days of the date the application was served on him unless an extension of time is granted under rule 16.6.

Variation or revocation of a reporting or excepting direction under section 46 of the Youth Justice and Criminal Evidence Act 1999

4–29cf **16.5.**—(1) An application for the court to—

(a) revoke a reporting direction; or

(b) vary or revoke an excepting direction,

may be made to the court at any time after the commencement of the proceedings in the court.

(2) An application under paragraph (1) may be made by a party to the proceedings in which the direction was issued, or by a person who, although not a party to those proceedings, is in the opinion of the court directly affected by the direction.

(3) An application under paragraph (1) must be made in writing and the applicant shall send that application to the officer of the court in which the proceedings commenced, and at the same time copies of the application shall be sent to every party or, as the case may be, every party to the proceedings.

(4) The applicant must set out in his application the reasons why he seeks to have the direction varied or, as the case may be, revoked.

(5) Any person served with a copy of an application who wishes to oppose it, must notify the applicant and the court officer in writing of his opposition and give reasons for it.

(6) [*Identical to r.16.4(6),* ante, *§ 4–29ce.*]

Application for an extension of time in proceedings under section 46 of the Youth Justice and Criminal Evidence Act 1999

4–29cg **16.6.**—(1) An application may be made in writing to extend the period of time for notification under rule 16.2(3), rule 16.4(6) or rule 16.5(6) before that period has expired.

(2) An application must be accompanied by a statement setting out the reasons why the applicant is unable to give notification within that period.

(3) An application must be sent to the court officer and a copy of the application must be sent at the same time to the applicant.

Decision of the court on an application under section 46 of the Youth Justice and Criminal Evidence Act 1999

4–29ch **16.7.**—(1) The court may—

(a) determine any application made under rules 16.1 and rules 16.3 to 16.6 without a hearing; or

(b) direct a hearing of any application.

(2) The court officer shall notify all the parties of the court's decision as soon as reasonably practicable.

(3) If a hearing of an application is to take place, the court officer shall notify each party to the proceedings of the time and place of the hearing.

(4) A court may hear and take into account representations made to it by any person who in the court's view has a legitimate interest in the application before it.

Proceedings sent or transferred to the Crown Court with direction under section 46 of the Youth Justice and Criminal Evidence Act 1999 in force

16.8. Where proceedings in which reporting directions or excepting directions have been ordered are sent or transferred from a magistrates' court to the Crown Court, the magistrates' court officer shall forward copies of all relevant directions to the Crown Court officer at the place to which the proceedings are sent or transferred. **4–29ci**

Hearings in camera and applications under section 46 of the Youth Justice and Criminal Evidence Act 1999

16.9. If in any proceedings, a prosecutor or defendant has served notice under rule 16.10 of his intention to apply for an order that all or part of a trial be held in camera, any application under this Part relating to a witness in those proceedings need not identify the witness by name and date of birth. **4–29cj**

The forms referred to in rules 16.1(1) and 16.4(4) are to be found in *Practice Direction (Criminal Proceedings: Forms)* [2005] 1 W.L.R. 1479, although the forms prescribed by the *Crown Court (Reports Relating to Adult Witnesses) Rules* 2004 (S.I. 2004 No. 2420) may still be used. For rule 16.10 (applications for trials to be heard in camera), see *ante*, § 4–7; for rule 16.11 (Crown Court hearings in chambers), see *ante*, § 2–153.

Youth Justice and Criminal Evidence Act 1999, s.47

Reports relating to directions under Chapter 1, 1A or 2

Restrictions on reporting directions under Chapter 1, 1A or 2

47.—(1) Except as provided by this section, no publication shall include a report of a matter falling within subsection (2). **4–29d**

(2) The matters falling within this subsection are—

(a) a direction under section 19, 33A or 36 or an order discharging, or (in the case of a direction under section 19) varying, such a direction;

(b) proceedings—

(i) on an application for such a direction or order, or

(ii) where the court acts of its own motion to determine whether to give or make any such direction or order.

(3) The court dealing with a matter falling within subsection (2) may order that subsection (1) is not to apply, or is not to apply to a specified extent, to a report of that matter.

(4) Where—

(a) there is only one accused in the relevant proceedings, and

(b) he objects to the making of an order under subsection (3),

the court shall make the order if (and only if) satisfied after hearing the representations of the accused that it is in the interests of justice to do so; and if the order is made it shall not apply to the extent that a report deals with any such objections or representations.

(5) Where—

(a) there are two or more accused in the relevant proceedings, and

(b) one or more of them object to the making of an order under subsection (3),

the court shall make the order if (and only if) satisfied after hearing the representations of each of the accused that it is in the interests of justice to do so; and if the order is made it shall not apply to the extent that a report deals with any such objections or representations.

(6) Subsection (1) does not apply to the inclusion in a publication of a report of matters after the relevant proceedings are either—

(a) determined (by acquittal, conviction or otherwise), or

(b) abandoned,

in relation to the accused or (if there is more than one) in relation to each of the accused.

(7) In this section "the relevant proceedings" means the proceedings to which any such direction as is mentioned in subsection (2) relates or would relate.

(8) Nothing in this section affects any prohibition or restriction by virtue of any other enactment on the inclusion of matter in a publication.

[This section is printed as amended by the *PJA* 2006, s.52, and Sched. 14, para. 37.]

For Chapters I and 1A of Part II (ss.16– 33C), see *post*, §§ 8–53 *et seq*. For Chapter II of Part II (ss.34– 40), see *post*, §§ 8–123b *et seq*.

Offences and defences

4–29e Section 49 of the 1999 Act makes various people guilty of a summary offence in the event of a breach of the restrictions in sections 44 to 47. The maximum penalty is a fine not exceeding level 5 on the standard scale. Section 50 provides for various defences to allegations contrary to section 49. Section 51 is a standard provision for the liability of the officers of a corporation guilty of an offence under section 49. Sections 49 to 51 came into force on October 7, 2004, so far as they have effect for the purposes of sections 46 and 47: S.I. 2004 No. 2428 (*ante*, § 4–29c).

Youth Justice and Criminal Evidence Act 1999, s.52

Supplementary

Decisions as to public interest for purposes of Chapter IV

4–29f **52.**—(1) Where for the purposes of any provision of this Chapter it falls to a court to determine whether anything is (or, as the case may be, was) in the public interest, the court must have regard, in particular, to the matters referred to in subsection (2) (so far as relevant).

(2) Those matters are—

(a) the interest in each of the following—

(i) the open reporting of crime,

(ii) the open reporting of matters relating to human health or safety, and

(iii) the prevention and exposure of miscarriages of justice;

(b) the welfare of any person in relation to whom the relevant restrictions imposed by or under this Chapter apply or would apply (or, as the case may be, applied); and

(c) any views expressed—

(i) by an appropriate person on behalf of a person within paragraph (b) who is under the age of 16 ("the protected person"), or

(ii) by a person within that paragraph who has attained that age.

(3) In subsection (2) "an appropriate person", in relation to the protected person, has the same meaning as it has for the purposes of section 50.

This section came into force on October 7, 2004, so far as it has effect for the purposes of sections 46 and 47: S.I. 2004 No. 2428 (*ante*, § 4–29c).

Interpretation

4–29g For the interpretation of Part II, see sections 62 and 63, *post*, §§ 8–55v, 8–55w.

Determination of age

4–29h The age of a person for the purposes of the 1999 Act is to be taken to be that which it appears to the court to be after considering any available evidence: s.65(3).

Transitional

Youth Justice and Criminal Evidence Act 1999, Sched. 7, para. 6

Reporting restrictions

4–29i 6.—(1) Section 44 applies in relation to an alleged offence whether the criminal investigation into it is begun before or after the coming into force of that section.

(2) The restrictions imposed by subsection (2) of section 44 do not apply to the inclusion of matter in a publication if—

(a) where the publication is a relevant programme, it is transmitted, or
(b) in the case of any other publication, it is published,
before the coming into force of that section.

(3) Nothing in section 45 or 46 applies in relation to proceedings instituted before the commencement date for that section.

(4) In sub-paragraph (3) the reference to the institution of proceedings shall be construed—

(a) in the case of proceedings in England in [*sic*] Wales (other than proceedings before a service court), in accordance with paragraph 1(2);
(b) in the case of proceedings in Northern Ireland (other than proceedings before a service court), in accordance with sub-paragraph (5);
(c) in the case of proceedings before a service court (wherever held) in accordance with sub-paragraph (6).

(5) [*Northern Ireland.*]

(6) [*Service courts (amended, as from a day to be appointed, by the* Armed Forces Act *2006, s.378(1), and Sched. 16, para. 161).*]

This paragraph came into force on October 7, 2004, so far as it relates to section 46: S.I. 2004 No. 2428 (*ante*, § 4–29c).

For paragraph 1 of the Schedule, see *post*, § 8–55x.

(d) *Photographs*

See, generally, the *CJA* 1925, s.41 (prohibition on taking photographs, etc., in court). **4–30**
The covert filming of a defendant in the cell area of a magistrates' court for the purpose of having the film compared with pictures taken by a closed circuit television camera of a person committing a robbery was held to be unlawful as being in breach of this prohibition in *R. v. Loveridge, Lee and Loveridge* [2001] 2 Cr.App.R. 29, CA.

(e) *Sentencing hearings*

For the power to restrict publication of proceedings relating to the review of a **4–30a**
sentence passed on a person who has offered to give assistance to the prosecution under the *SOCPA* 2005, see section 74 of that Act, *post*, § 5–94c.

Criminal Procedure and Investigations Act 1996, ss.58–61

Derogatory assertions

Orders in respect of certain assertions

58.—(1) This section applies where a person has been convicted of an offence and a speech **4–30b**
in mitigation is made by him or on his behalf before—

(a) a court determining what sentence should be passed on him in respect of the offence, or
(b) a magistrates' court determining whether he should be committed to the Crown Court for sentence.

(2) This section also applies where a sentence has been passed on a person in respect of an offence and a submission relating to the sentence is made by him or on his behalf before—

(a) a court hearing an appeal against or reviewing the sentence, or
(b) a court determining whether to grant leave to appeal against the sentence.

(3) Where it appears to the court that there is a real possibility that an order under subsection (8) will be made in relation to the assertion, the court may make an order under subsection (7) in relation to the assertion.

(4) Where there are substantial grounds for believing—

(a) that an assertion forming part of the speech or submission is derogatory to a person's character (for instance, because it suggests that his conduct is or has been criminal, immoral or improper), and
(b) that the assertion is false or that the facts asserted are irrelevant to the sentence,

the court may make an order under subsection (8) in relation to the assertion.

(5) An order under subsection (7) or (8) must not be made in relation to an assertion if it appears to the court that the assertion was previously made—

(a) at the trial at which the person was convicted of the offence, or

(b) during any other proceedings relating to the offence.

(6) Section 59 has effect where a court makes an order under subsection (7) or (8).

(7) An order under this subsection—

(a) may be made at any time before the court has made a determination with regard to sentencing;

(b) may be revoked at any time by the court;

(c) subject to paragraph (b), shall cease to have effect when the court makes a determination with regard to sentencing.

(8) An order under this subsection—

(a) may be made after the court has made a determination with regard to sentencing, but only if it is made as soon as is reasonably practicable after the making of the determination;

(b) may be revoked at any time by the court;

(c) subject to paragraph (b), shall cease to have effect at the end of the period of 12 months beginning with the day on which it is made;

(d) may be made whether or not an order has been made under subsection (7) with regard to the case concerned.

(9) For the purposes of subsections (7) and (8) the court makes a determination with regard to sentencing—

(a) when it determines what sentence should be passed (where this section applies by virtue of subsection (1)(a));

(b) when it determines whether the person should be committed to the Crown Court for sentence (where this section applies by virtue of subsection (1)(b));

(c) when it determines what the sentence should be (where this section applies by virtue of subsection (2)(a));

(d) when it determines whether to grant leave to appeal (where this section applies by virtue of subsection (2)(b)).

Restriction on reporting of assertions

4–30c **59.**—(1) Where a court makes an order under section 58(7) or (8) in relation to any assertion, at any time when the order has effect the assertion must not—

(a) be published in Great Britain in a written publication available to the public, or

(b) be included in a relevant programme for reception in Great Britain.

(2) In this section—

"relevant programme" means a programme included in a programme service, within the meaning of the *Broadcasting Act* 1990;

"written publication" includes a film, a soundtrack and any other record in permanent form but does not include an indictment or other document prepared for use in particular legal proceedings.

(3) For the purposes of this section an assertion is published or included in a programme if the material published or included—

(a) names the person about whom the assertion is made or, without naming him, contains enough to make it likely that members of the public will identify him as the person about whom it is made, and

(b) reproduces the actual wording of the matter asserted or contains its substance.

Reporting of assertions: offences

4–30d **60.** [*Contravention of section 59 a summary offence; level 5 on standard scale.*]

Reporting of assertions: commencement and supplementary

4–30e **61.**—(1) Section 58 applies where the offence mentioned in subsection (1) or (2) of that section is committed on or after the appointed day.

(2) The reference in subsection (1) to the appointed day is to such day as is appointed for the purposes of this section by the Secretary of State by order.

(3) Nothing in section 58 or 59 affects any prohibition or restriction imposed by virtue of any other enactment on a publication or on matter included in a programme.

(4) Nothing in section 58 or 59 affects section 3 of the *Law of Libel Amendment Act* 1888 (privilege of newspaper reports of court proceedings).

(5) Section 8 of the *Law of Libel Amendment Act* 1888 (order of judge required for prosecution for libel published in a newspaper) does not apply to a prosecution for an offence under section 60.

(6) [*Amends* Criminal Justice Act *1988, s.159,* post, *§ 7–244 (appeals).*]

The appointed day for the purposes of section 61(1) and (2) is April 1, 1997: *Criminal Procedure Investigations Act 1996 (Appointed Day No. 3) Order* 1997 (S.I. 1997 No. 682).

For the purposes of subsection (1), where an offence is committed over a period of more than one day, or at some time during a period of more than one day, it must be taken to be committed on the last of the days in the period: *CPIA* 1996, s.75(2), (3).

(3) Publicity prejudicing fair trial

As to the possibility of adverse publicity giving rise to a breach of the right to a fair trial under Article 6(1) of the ECHR and as constituting grounds for a stay of the proceedings, see *post*, § 4–72a; and as to the European jurisprudence, see *post*, §§ 16–65 and 16–79. As to adverse publicity as a ground of appeal, see *post*, § 7–84. As to the relevance of adverse post-trial publicity to the question whether to order a retrial following the quashing of a conviction, see *R. v. Stone* [2001] Crim.L.R. 465, CA. **4–31**

The potential prejudice and appearance of bias that can be created by a judge making public comment about a case that he is trying were highlighted in *R. v. Batth* [1990] Crim.L.R. 727, CA, and in *R. v. Earnshaw* [1990] Crim.L.R. 53, CA. *Cf. R. v. Browne, The Times*, August 23, 1997, CA, *post*, § 4–32.

D. IDENTITY AND IMPARTIALITY OF JUDGE

Identity

A judge should not normally be changed in the course of a trial: see *R. v. Crown Court at Southwark, ex p. Customs and Excise Commrs*, *post*, § 4–85d. This did not, however, preclude a second judge from taking a jury's verdict: *R. v. El-Ghaidouni* [2006] 5 *Archbold News* 3, CA; though if the stand-in judge were unable to answer a question from the jury which related directly to an issue in the trial, the failure to answer it may have a significant adverse effect on the outcome of the trial and the safety of any conviction: *ibid*. **4–31a**

Impartiality

Where partiality or prejudice is actually shown in respect of the tribunal in a particular case, a litigant has irresistible grounds for objecting to the trial of his case by that tribunal (whether a judge, lay justice or juror); where a judge is shown to have an interest in the outcome of a case, bias is effectively presumed and gives rise to automatic disqualification, but this is subject to an exception where the effect of the judge's personal interest is so small as to be incapable of affecting his decision one way or the other, but any doubt should be resolved in favour of disqualification; where the interest of the judge is said to derive from the interest of a spouse, partner or other family member, any link such as to necessitate disqualification must be so close and direct as to render the interest of that other person for all practical purposes indistinguishable from an interest of the judge; the automatic disqualification rule extends to a limited class of non-financial interests, such as an interest in the subject-matter arising from the judge's promotion of some particular cause; a party with an irresistible right to object to a particular judge might waive his right to do so but any waiver must be clear and unequivocal and made with knowledge of all facts relevant to the decision whether to waive; in practice, the most effective guarantee of the right to an impartial tribunal is afforded by the rule that provides for the judge's disqualification and the setting aside of a decision if on examination of all the relevant circumstances there was a real danger or possibility of bias; when applying this test it will often be appropriate to inquire whether the judge knew of the matter relied upon as appearing to undermine his impartiality; if he did not, there was no danger of him having been influenced and the appearance of bias would be dispelled; while a court of review might receive a written statement from a judge specifying what he knew at the material time, that court is not necessarily bound to accept that at face value; much will depend on the nature of the fact of which ignorance is asserted, the source of the statement, the effect of any corroborative or contradictory statement, the inherent possibilities and all the circumstances; but the **4–32** reviewing court will pay no attention to a statement made by a judge as to the impact of any knowledge that he may have had; the insidious nature of bias makes any such statement of little value; in any case giving rise to automatic disqualification the judge should recuse himself before any objection is raised, and the same course should follow if, for solid reasons, the judge feels personally embarrassed in hearing the case; if, in any other case, the judge becomes aware of any matter which could arguably be said to give rise to a real danger of bias, it is generally desirable that disclosure be made to the parties in advance of the hearing; if objection is then made, it will be the judge's duty to consider it and exercise his judgment on it, but it would be as wrong to yield to a tenuous or frivolous objection as it would be to ignore an objection of substance; in most cases the answer will be obvious, but if there is real ground for doubt, that doubt should be resolved in favour of recusal; if appropriate disclosure is made and no objection taken, there can be no valid complaint thereafter; what disclosure is appropriate depends in large part on the stage of the proceedings; if, before he begins, the judge is alerted to some matter that might, depending on the full facts, throw doubt on his fitness to sit, he should inquire into the full facts, so fas as they are ascertainable, and make appropriate disclosure; if the matter only emerges during the hearing, he is obliged to disclose what he then knows; he is not bound to fill gaps in his knowledge, which, if filled, might provide stronger grounds for objection, but if he does make further inquiry and discovers further relevant facts, he is bound to disclose them; however, it is generally undesirable that hearings be aborted unless the reality or appearance of justice require such a step: *Locabail (U.K.) Ltd v. Bayfield Properties Ltd*; *Locabail (U.K.) Ltd v. Waldorf Investment Corporation*; *Timmins v. Gormley*; *Williams v. H.M. Inspector of Taxes*; *R. v. Bristol Betting and Gaming Licensing Committee, ex p. O'Callaghan* [2000] Q.B. 451, CA (Civ. Div.). Disqualification for apparent bias is not discretionary; either there is a real possibility of bias, in which case the judge is disqualified, or there is not: *AWG Group Ltd v. Morrison* [2006] 1 W.L.R. 1163, CA (Civ. Div.).

Where bias or apparent bias is raised as a ground of appeal, the leading authority as to the test to be applied was until recently the decision of the House of Lords in *R. v. Gough* [1996] A.C. 646. The Court of Appeal in *Re Medicaments and Related Classes of Goods (No. 2)* [2001] 1 W.L.R. 700 had to consider the compatibility of that test with the jurisprudence of the European Court of Human Rights (*post*). The conclusion was that *Gough* required modest adjustment. The relevant principles were summarised as follows [para. 83]: (1) if a judge is shown to have been influenced by actual bias, his decision must be set aside; (2) where actual bias has not been established the personal impartiality of the judge is to be presumed; (3) the court then has to decide whether, on an objective appraisal, the material facts give rise to a legitimate fear that the judge might not have been impartial; if they do, the decision of the judge must be set aside; (4) the material facts are not limited to those which were apparent to the appellant; they are those which are ascertained upon investigation by the court; (5) an important consideration in making an objective appraisal of the facts is the desirability that the public should remain confident in the administration of justice; whether or not there was a "legitimate fear that the judge might not have been impartial" will depend on whether a fair-minded and informed observer would conclude that there was a real possibility, or real danger, the two being the same, that the judge was biased; the material circumstances will include any explanation given by the judge under review as to his knowledge of those circumstances; where that explanation is accepted by the appellant it can be treated as accurate; where it is not accepted, it becomes one further matter to be considered from the viewpoint of the fair-minded observer; the court does not have to rule whether the explanation should be accepted or rejected; rather it has to decide whether a fair-minded observer would consider that there was a real danger, or real possibility (the two being the same thing) of bias, notwithstanding the explanation advanced. The correctness of these principles was confirmed by the House of Lords in *Porter v. Magill*; *Weeks v. Magill* [2002] 2 A.C. 357. See also *post*, § 4–256.

A useful summary of the Convention jurisprudence in this regard is to be found in *Incal v. Turkey*, 29 E.H.R.R. 449, where the European Court of Human Rights held that in order to establish whether a tribunal is "independent", regard must be had, *inter alia*, to the manner of appointment of its members and their terms of office, the existence of safeguards against outside pressures and the question whether it presents an appearance of impartiality; as to the condition of "impartiality", two tests are to be applied, the first of which consists of trying to determine the personal conviction of a particular judge in a given case (the subjective approach) and the second in ascertaining whether the judge offered guarantees sufficient to exclude any legitimate doubt in this respect (the objective approach); appearances may be of certain importance; what is at stake is the confidence which the courts in a democratic society must inspire in the public and, above all, as far as criminal proceedings are concerned, in the accused; in deciding whether there is a legitimate reason to fear that a particular court lacks independence or impartiality, the standpoint of the accused is important without being decisive; what is decisive is whether his doubts are objectively justified. To the same effect, see *Çiraklar v. Turkey* (2001) 32 E.H.R.R. 23, ECtHR. See also *post*, §§ 16–57, 16–73a and 16–74.

As to the personal impartiality of the judge being presumed, until there is proof to the contrary, see *Castillo Algar v. Spain*, 30 E.H.R.R. 826, ECtHR.

It has been held that a judge does not disqualify himself from trying a case because he expresses his personal views (before the start of the case) touching upon issues of law and practice that then arise in the case (that the right to silence, as it was exercised in practice, was a charter for the dishonest and never helped the innocent): *R. v. Browne*, *The Times*, August 23, 1997, CA. More recently, in *Hoekstra v. H.M. Advocate*, *The Times*, April 14, 2000, the High Court of Justiciary in Scotland has held that judges are entitled to criticise developments in the law, but that they cannot with impunity publish either criticism or praise of such a nature or in such language as to give rise to a legitimate apprehension that, when called upon in the course of their judicial duties to apply that particular branch of the law, they would not be able to do so impartially; where, therefore, a judge published in a national newspaper, shortly after hearing a criminal appeal in which issues relating to the ECHR were raised, an article that was highly critical of the Convention and its importation into national law, he might be seen as having failed to meet the test of objective impartiality that applied to judges both under Article 6 and under the common law of Scotland. See also *R. v. Batth*, and *R. v. Earnshaw*, *ante*, § 4–31.

While it is futile to attempt to define the factors which might give rise to a real danger of bias, it is inconceivable that circumstances exist in which any objection could be soundly made on the basis of the religion, ethnic or national origin, gender, age, class, means or sexual orientation of the judge hearing a case: *Seer Technologies Ltd v. Abbas*, *The Times*, March 16, 2000, Ch D (Pumfrey J.); and it is self-evident that there could be no entitlement to discharge of the jury and a retrial before a new tribunal where a defendant escaped from the dock and attacked the judge during the course of the summing up; no fair minded observer would conclude that continuing the trial was unfair or could be perceived to be so, and there would, therefore, be no need for inquiry either as to the effect of the defendant's actions on the jury or as to whether they were explicable on the basis that he was not trying to abort the trial but was merely protesting about perceived unfairness; any unfairness in the trial was remediable by way of an appeal: *R. v. Russell* [2006] Crim.L.R. 862, CA.

Judges are entitled to hold views (including strong views) on matters affecting society; but there would be a risk that a fair-minded and informed observer would see a real possibility of bias where a judge had been active in campaigning against a cause supported by the defendant (including seven years before and whilst the judge was at the Bar); in such a case, the judge should disclose the matter giving rise to the possibility of bias to the parties so that an informed decision could be made; but where the issue of bias was raised on an appeal against sentence, the appropriateness of the sentence passed was before the court and the appeal would be considered on its merits: *R. v. Harris (Joseph)* [2007] 2 Cr.App.R.(S.) 37, CA. There may be exceptional cases where a judge, having recently been the victim of a like offence to the one with which he is dealing, in circumstances capable of giving rise to a bias, should disclose this to the parties; suggestion of such a situation must be exceptional and it is one clearly for the judge to determine; but the mere fact that the judge has been the victim of a similar crime in the comparatively recent past is not a matter that disqualifies him from passing sentence or something which, in the ordinary way, ought to be disclosed: *R. v. Comer* [2001] 1 Cr.App.R.(S.) 34, CA. A judge who, upon discovering that the chief constable of a local police force was to be a witness in a trial before him, in relation to the giving of authority for a covert surveillance operation, informed the parties that he knew the officer "in a formal, civic capacity in the main" had acted correctly by disclosing the relationship, but a "fair minded and informed observer" would be conscious that the relationship was a formal one and not a personal friendship or close acquaintance of the type referred to in *Locabail, ante*; thus, the nature of the relationship had not been such as to require the judge to recuse himself, particularly where it was clear that there was to be no issue as to the credibility of the officer: *R. v. Mason* [2002] 2 Cr.App.R. 38, CA.

The mere fact that a trial judge has detailed knowledge of a case, by virtue of having been involved in a series of preliminary hearings in respect of it, does not mean that he is prejudiced in such a way that he cannot be regarded as impartial when the case comes to trial, but the position might be different if the matters dealt with in the preliminary proceedings were comparable to those upon which he had to adjudicate at trial: *Morel v. France* (2001) 33 E.H.R.R. 47, ECtHR. It is undesirable for a judge who has made findings of fact in care proceedings to preside over a criminal trial relating to the same facts: *R. v. A., The Times*, April 13, 1998, CA.

As to communications between a judge of the Court of Appeal and the trial judge about the conduct of a case currently being tried forming the basis of an application for the appeal judge to recuse himself from hearing a subsequent appeal against conviction, see *R. v. Khyam, Amin, Akbar, Garcia and Mahmood* [2008] L.S. Gazette, August 7, 20, CA ([2008] EWCA Crim. 1612).

As to retrials, see *post*, § 4–45.

Where, on an application for judicial review, an allegation of bias is made against a judge of the Crown Court, it is appropriate for both the judge and counsel for the prosecution to make affidavits: *R. v. Southwark Crown Court, ex p. Colman* [1998] 7 *Archbold News* 2, DC.

E. Proceedings Ordinarily Conducted in English

4–33 For observations upon the history of the use of English as the language in which proceedings ought ordinarily to be conducted, see Roxburgh J. in *Re Trepca Mines* [1960] 1 W.L.R. 24. For the rules relating to the use of interpreters in criminal proceedings, see *post*, §§ 4–34 *et seq*.

If a defendant in a court in England asks to give or call evidence in the Welsh language the case should not be transferred to Wales. In ordinary circumstances, interpreters can be provided on request: *Practice Direction (Criminal Proceedings: Consolidation)* [2002] 1 W.L.R. 2870, para. III.22.

For legal proceedings in Wales or Monmouthshire, see *post*, § 4–40.

F. Interpreters

(1) General

4–34 As to the rights of an accused under the ECHR, see Article 6(3)(a) and (e), *post*, §§ 16–57 *et seq.*, and § 16–94 (reviewed in *R. v. West London Youth Court, ex p. N.* [2000] 1 W.L.R. 2368, DC, *post*, § 4–37).

In 1998, the Lord Chancellor's Department announced (press release 80/98) new procedures for arranging interpreters. The police or investigating agency will arrange for interpreters for any part of an investigation, and for the requirements of the suspect, or person charged, while in custody; the court will be responsible for arranging the interpreter for the defendant at court, except where the first court appearance is within two days of the charge when the police or prosecuting agency will make the arrangements on behalf of the court. Normally a separate interpreter will be arranged for each defendant. Interpretation should take place throughout the court proceedings. The prosecution and defence will be responsible for arranging interpreters for their own witnesses. Interpreters will be expected to have knowledge of police and court procedures; ideally they will be selected from the National Register of Public Service

As to the power to give a "special measures direction", pursuant to the *YJCEA* 1999, in respect of a witness who has a physical disability or who is suffering from a physical disorder, see *post*, §§ 8–52 *et seq.*

(6) Interpreter's oath

"I swear by Almighty God that I will well and faithfully interpret and true explanation make of all such matters and things as shall be required of me according to the best of my skill and understanding." For the form of the oath in Welsh, see S.R. & O. 1943 No. 683, *post*, § 4–40. **4–39**

(7) Courts in Wales and Monmouthshire

In any legal proceeding in Wales or Monmouthshire, the Welsh language may be spoken by any party, witness or other person who desires to use it, subject in the case of proceedings in a court other than a magistrates' court to such prior notice as may be required by rules of court; and any necessary provision for interpretation shall be made accordingly: *Welsh Language Act* 1993, ss.22, 24. See too, the *Welsh Courts (Oaths and Interpreters) Rules* 1943 (S.R. & O. 1943 No. 683), as amended by the *Welsh Courts (Interpreters) Rules* 1959 and 1972 (S.I. 1959 No. 1507; S.I. 1972 No. 97). These rules were made under the *Welsh Courts Act* 1942. That Act was repealed by the 1993 Act, but by virtue of the *Interpretation Act* 1978, s.17(2)(b) (Appendix B–17), the rules now have effect as if made under section 23 of the 1993 Act. **4–40**

It is the responsibility of the legal representatives in every case in which the Welsh language might be used by any person, or in any document which might be placed before the court, to inform the court of that fact as soon as possible after this possibility becomes known so that appropriate listing arrangements can be made; an advocate in such a case must raise the matter at the plea and case management hearing; such cases should wherever possible be listed in front of a Welsh speaking judge and in a court with simultaneous translation facilities; the court manager should ensure that any interpreter employed for the translation of evidence should be from the list of approved court interpreters; jurors and witnesses should be informed that they may take the oath or affirm in either language; and unless not reasonably practicable to do so, the opening and closing of the court should be done in both languages: *Practice Direction (Criminal Procedings: Consolidation)* [2002] 1 W.L.R. 2870, para. III.23. **4–40a**

G. REPRESENTATION OF THE DEFENDANT

(1) Legal representation

As to the right of a defendant to defend himself in person or through legal assistance of his own choosing or, if he has not sufficient means to pay for legal assistance, to be given it free when the interests of justice so require, see Article 6(3)(c) of the ECHR (*post*, § 16–57) and the authorities cited at §§ 16–86 *et seq.*, *post*. In *Hinds v. Att.-Gen. of Barbados* [2002] 1 A.C. 854, PC, it was held that many criminal cases might be the subject of a fair trial without legal representation of the defendant, but the more serious the charge, the more complex the case and the greater the potential penalty, the more likely it is that representation will be needed to ensure a fair trial for a defendant who wishes to have such representation. **4–41**

An accused must not be deprived of a right to legal representation merely on account of not attending a court hearing; although the legislature must be able to discourage unjustified absences, it cannot penalise them by creating exceptions to the right to representation, even on an appeal where the point that counsel would have argued was considered by the court; counsel's assistance is indispensable for resolving conflicts and for the rights of defence to be exercised; the legitimate requirement for defendants to attend hearings can be satisfied by means other than the deprivation of the right to be defended: *Van Geyseghem v. Belgium* (2001) 32 E.H.R.R. 24, ECtHR. As to a judge's discretion to proceed with a trial where a defendant absconds either before or during a trial, see *R. v. Jones* [2003] 1 A.C. 1, HL (*ante*, § 3–197).

As to a wrongful denial of an accused's right to legal representation as a ground of appeal, see *post*, § 7–86.

As to the public funding of legal representation, see *post*, §§ 6–129 *et seq*. Given the rights conferred by Article 6(3)(c) of the Convention, and in particular the right of a defendant to free legal assistance if he does not have sufficient means to pay for representation and the interests of justice so require, it follows that a defence application for an adjournment of criminal proceedings should normally be granted where the defendant has not had a proper opportunity to apply for free legal representation; in such circumstances his right to free representation (or to a proper opportunity to apply for it) will normally outweigh other considerations, such as the convenience of other parties and use of court resources: *Berry Trade Ltd v. Moussavi* [2002] 1 W.L.R. 1910, CA (Civ. Div.).

A defendant is entitled to be represented by counsel of his choice if that is reasonably practicable; whether it is reasonably practicable will depend not only on the availability of counsel but also on such matters as the availability of a suitably equipped court, the availability of witnesses and the timescale appropriate to the case. The overriding consideration must be the requirements of justice, for the prosecution and for the defence, in the circumstances of the particular case: *R. v. De Oliveira* [1997] Crim.L.R. 600, CA. The principle of equality of arms does not require that a defendant should be represented by leading counsel merely because the prosecution are so represented; what is required is that the defendant should be represented by an advocate who can ensure that the defence case is properly and adequately placed before the court: *Att.-Gen.'s Reference (No. 82a of 2000)*; *R. v. Lea*; *R. v. Shatwell* [2002] 2 Cr.App.R. 24, CA.

If counsel decides that, consistent with his obligations to his client and the court, and the rules of his profession, he is so professionally embarrassed that he cannot continue with the case, he should provide the judge with such explanation as he can without contravening his client's legal professional privilege: *R. v. Ulcay* [2008] 1 Cr.App.R. 27, in which the Court of Appeal found it difficult to imagine cases in which it would be appropriate for the trial judge to direct counsel to continue with a case, or to refuse permission to withdraw on the grounds of professional embarrassment if, after such explanation, counsel, who would be likely to be aware of considerations which he could not reveal, remained unpersuaded that he could properly continue to act.

It would rarely be right for the trial judge, midway through a trial, to engage in a personal discussion with a defendant about his defence, and whether it was changing, or the state of the professional relationship with his lawyers, and certainly not if the judge were satisfied that the defendant was attempting to manipulate the process of the court: *ibid*.

Where counsel representing a defendant under a representation order has withdrawn, or been dismissed, the judge has a discretion whether to permit the instruction of new counsel (see *post*, § 6–169); if a defendant chooses to terminate his lawyer's retainer for improper motives, the court is not bound to agree to an application for a change of representation: *R. v. Ulcay*, *ante*; and see *R. v. Kempster*, 68 J.C.L. 201, CA (where the application was made after all the prosecution evidence in a case "of some gravity and complexity", and the judge had formed the view that the introduction of fresh counsel and solicitors would inevitably lead to the discharge of the jury); *R. v Mills* [1997] 2 Cr.App.R. 206, CA (in which the judge was entitled to take the view that it was highly probable, if not inevitable, that if new counsel and new solicitors were appointed, they too would either be discharged by the defendant or be compelled themselves to withdraw from the case); and *R. v. Smith (Henry Lee)* [2007] Crim. L.R. 325, CA (*ante*, § 3–205, and *post*, § 6–169).

On the other hand, the judge ought to have permitted new counsel to be instructed in *R. v. Al-Zubeidi* [1999] Crim.L.R. 906, CA, where the defence which the defendant wished to advance was complex and he needed clear advice as to the necessity for him to give evidence and to call any witnesses that might be available to him if his defence was to have any prospect of carrying weight with the jury; and in *R. v. Jisl, Konalki, Tekin and Mus*, unreported, July 14, 2000, CA, where the judge should also have had regard to the effect on the length of the trial and on the co-defendants, especially with the prospect of cut-throat defences.

The length of any adjournment to permit the instruction of new counsel is also a matter for the discretion of the judge; where there were co-defendants and it would either have effectively derailed the trial or resulted in a separate subsequent trial of the defendant on his own which would have been contrary to the interests of justice overall, the judge was entitled to exercise his discretion to refuse a lengthy adjournment: *R. v. Ulcay*, *ante*. The fact that new counsel and solicitors considered that the short adjournment which the judge did grant would present insuperable difficulties in the preparation and conduct of the defence did not entitle them to withdraw; their professional duty was to "soldier on" and do the best they could (*ibid.*, at [41], considering the eighth edition of the Code of Conduct for the Bar of England and Wales, paras. 602 and 701(b)(ii) (Appendix C–9 and C–11), and the Law Society Rules).

If the trial proceeds with the defendant unrepresented, it is not appropriate to appoint an *amicus curiae*: *R. v. Mills*, *ante*.

Where the legal representatives of a defendant withdraw and the trial continues with the defendant representing himself after a failure by the judge to explain the options open to him, the case is likely to be treated as one involving a wrongful denial of legal representation; *a fortiori*, if the judge misrepresents the options: *Mitchell (John) v. R.* [1999] 1 W.L.R. 1679, PC. However, where a defendant refused to plead and, having been found to be mute of malice, his counsel obtained leave to withdraw (having no instructions), the judge had a discretion to continue with the trial, without an adjournment to allow the defendant to seek alternative representation, where an adjournment had not been sought and was unlikely to be productive: *Ricketts v. R.* [1998] 1 W.L.R. 1017, PC.

As to a defendant being put in a position where he would only have legal representation if he pleaded guilty, see *R. v. Smith and Beaney* (*post*, § 7–355).

As to the rights of audience of persons other than counsel, see *ante*, §§ 2–22 *et seq.*

(2) Right to conduct own defence

Subject to certain statutory restrictions on cross examination by defendants in person (*post*, §§ 8–123a *et seq.*), a defendant has the right to conduct his own defence, with or without the services of a solicitor: *R. v. Woodward* [1944] K.B. 118, 29 Cr.App.R. 159, CCA (and see *R. v. De Courcy*, 48 Cr.App.R. 323, CCA). See also Article 6(3) of the ECHR, as to the right of a defendant "to defend himself in person ..." (*post*, §§ 16–57 and 16–86). However, the exercise of that right may bring advantages and disadvantages; a person who chooses to exercise the right cannot pray in aid the ordinary and anticipated disadvantages of his choice (lack of knowledge of the law, lack of experience of the trial process and lack of forensic skills) in support of an argument that there was such inequality of arms at trial as to render his conviction unsafe; where such a defendant, being one of several defendants in a long trial, made an application for the jury to be discharged in his case or, alternatively, for a prolonged adjournment on the ground that his mental state was such that he was no longer able to defend himself properly, the judge had been entitled to have regard to his own observation of the manner in which the defendant had conducted his case to that point; further, to the extent that various errors or omissions in the conduct of the defence were relied on as indicating that he had not in fact been in a fit state, the court was entitled to take the view that this illustrated not disability as a result of ill health, but the normal disadvantages associated with being unrepresented: *R. v. Walton* [2001] 8 *Archbold News* 2, CA. **4–42**

Where counsel does not withdraw, but the accused makes an application to dispense with his services so that he may conduct his own defence, the judge has a discretion whether to allow such application: *R. v. Lyons*, 68 Cr.App.R. 104, CA. Further, it is in his discretion whether to permit the defendant to state his reasons for making such application, although in most cases reasons will be heard and/or the application will be allowed: *ibid.* The further advanced the trial, however, the less likely an application to dispense with counsel's services is to be successful: see *Woodward*, *ante*. However, these decisions may need to be reconsidered in the light of Article 6(3)(c) of the European Convention. See also *R. v. Mills*, *ante*, § 4–41, as to the correct approach in such situations, and as to the need for a judge to caution a defendant against taking a course that, in the view of the judge, may be against his best interests.

As to the withdrawal of a representation order, see the *Criminal Defence Service (General) (No. 2) Regulations* 2001 (S.I. 2001 No. 1437), reg. 17, *post*, § 6–170.

See *R. v. De Oliveira* [1997] Crim.L.R. 600, CA, *post*, § 4–377, as to the desirability, at the outset of a trial, of explaining to the jury certain matters concerning a decision by a defendant to defend himself.

H. RECORD OF TRIAL PROCEEDINGS

4–43 See the *CAA* 1968, s.32 (*post*, § 7–237), and the *Criminal Procedure Rules* 2005 (S.I. 2005 No. 384), rr.68.12 (*post*, § 7–238) and 68.13 (*post*, § 7–240).

I. ADJOURNMENT OF TRIAL

4–44 If the trial is not concluded on the same day on which it began, the judge has authority to adjourn it from day to day without the defendant's consent: *R. v. Castro* (1880) L.R. 9 Q.B. 350 at 356. The adjournments should be stated in the record: see *O'Brien v. R.* (1890) 26 L.R.Ir. 451.

As to the specific power to postpone a trial on amendment of the indictment or severance of the counts in the indictment, see section 5(4) of the *Indictments Act* 1915, *ante*, § 1–147.

The power to grant an adjournment should not be exercised in a manner which undermines the statute under which the proceedings are brought or in a way which deprives a litigant of rights conferred by that statute: *R. v. Dudley Magistrates' Court, ex p. Hollis*; *Hollis v. Dudley M.B.C.*; *Probert v. Dudley M.B.C.* [1998] 1 All E.R. 759, DC. See also *Re Godwin* [1991] Crim.L.R. 302, CA.

As to the propriety of adjourning proceedings on indictment pending the outcome of an application for the extradition of the defendant to a foreign state, see *Re Gilligan*; *R. v. Crown Court at Woolwich, ex p. Gilligan* [1998] 2 All E.R. 1, DC (*ante*, § 1–275).

A court should not usually refuse an adjournment where a defence witness is unavailable if his evidence is plainly material (*R. v. Bradford JJ., ex p. Wilkinson*, 91 Cr.App.R. 390, DC); caution should be exercised where the witness might have "significant" evidence to give (*R. v. Ealing JJ., ex p. Avondale* [1999] Crim.L.R. 840, DC); "critical" is too strict a test (*R. v. Guildford Crown Court, ex p. Flanighan* [2000] 3 *Archbold News* 2, DC).

A court confronted by an application to adjourn proceedings so that an expert can be instructed is entitled to weigh against the general desirability of the applicant having the advantage of expert opinion, the reason for his failure to have such evidence already: *R. (Lappin) v. H.M. Customs and Excise* [2004] A.C.D. 48, QBD (Goldring J.) (persistent failure to instruct expert, notwithstanding timetable for doing so, justified refusal of application to adjourn two-day appeal to the Crown Court which had been set down months in advance).

For general considerations in respect of applications for adjournments, see also *CPS v. Picton*, 170 J.P. 567, DC; and, for other decisions in relation to the adjournment of summary trials, see *S. v. DPP*, 170 J.P. 707, DC; *R. (Costello) v. North East Essex Magistrates*, 171 J.P. 153, QBD (Collins J.); *Robinson v. Abergavenny Magistrates' Court*; *Fine v. Same*, 171 J.P. 683, DC; and *R. (DPP) v. North East Hertfordshire JJ. and Simpole*, 172 J.P. 193, DC.

A refusal to adjourn a trial is capable of constituting a terminating ruling liable to appeal by the prosecution under *CJA* 2003, s.58 (*post*, § 7–244): *R. v. Clarke* [2008] 1 Cr.App.R. 33, CA.

J. RETRIAL

4–45 A variety of circumstances may result in the defendant being retried. For example, an irregularity in the former proceedings which resulted in the jury being discharged; the failure of the jury to agree upon a verdict (see *post*, § 4–440); a retrial being ordered by the Court of Appeal (see *post*, § 7–112). See *post*, §§ 7–117, 10–56, as to certain rules of evidence which apply in a retrial ordered by the Court of Appeal, and as to sentence in the event of conviction in such a case.

In *R. v. Henworth* [2001] 2 Cr.App.R. 4, CA, it was said that the question whether there has been an abuse of process has always to be related to the facts of the particular case; and what was said by Lord Slynn in *Charles v. The State* [2000] 1 W.L.R. 384, PC (*post*, § 4–67), to the effect that it may be "contrary to due process and unacceptable ... that the prosecution having failed twice should continue to try to secure a conviction" was *obiter* and was not to be elevated into a proposition of law. On the facts, it was held that there had been no abuse where the appellant had been convicted at his fourth trial, the first having resulted in a conviction which was quashed with a retrial being ordered, the second resulting in a disagreement and the third being aborted on account of difficulties in the conduct of the defence. As to abuse of process generally, see *post*, §§ 4–48 *et seq*. Where two juries have been unable to agree, it is in the first instance for the prosecutor to judge whether, taking account of all relevant considerations, the public interest is better served by offering no evidence or by seeking a second retrial; there is no rule of law against doing so, the practice of offering no evidence in such circumstances being no more than a convention; but there may be cases in which, on the facts, a second retrial would be oppressive or unjust; whether a second retrial should be permitted depends on an informed and dispassionate assessment of how the interests of justice in the widest sense are best served; full account must be taken of the defendant's interests, particularly if there has been a long delay or if his defence may be prejudiced in any significant way, but account must also be taken of the public interest in convicting the guilty, deterring violent crime and maintaining confidence in the efficacy of the criminal justice system: *Bowe v. R.* [2001] 6 *Archbold News* 3, PC. The convention against a third trial after two jury disagreements does not apply to a third trial after a jury disagreement on a second trial ordered by the Court of Appeal when quashing a conviction returned at the first trial: *R. v. Byrne* [2002] 2 Cr.App.R. 21, CA.

As to the desirability of a retrial taking place before a different judge, see *R. v. Quinn and Bloom* [1962] 2 Q.B. 245, 45 Cr.App.R. 279, CCA. There is, however, no rule of law to this effect. It is a matter for the court's discretion (*R. v. Bogle* [1974] Crim.L.R. 424, CA) and the good sense of the judges (*R. v. Mullen* [2000] 6 *Archbold News* 2, CA).

Reference to previous trial

The mere fact that there has been a previous trial is usually irrelevant and, therefore, **4–46**
inadmissible on a retrial; but this does not mean that it is never permissible to refer to an earlier trial, for it may well be necessary to do so to establish some relevant fact as, for example, in identifying the occasion on which some particular statement or admission was made: *per* Lord MacDermott in *Sambasivam v. Public Prosecutor, Federation of Malaya* [1950] A.C. 458 at 471, PC. In *R. v. Binham* [1991] Crim.L.R. 774, CA, it was held that the prosecution had rightly been permitted to adduce evidence on a retrial of what had been said on oath by the defendant at the original trial, for the purpose of establishing that he had lied.

A transcript of evidence given at the first trial may be admissible at the retrial: see *post*, §§ 10–56, 10–57.

K. LIMITED DISCRETIONARY POWER TO PREVENT PROSECUTION PROCEEDING

(1) General principles

Once an indictment is before the court the accused must be arraigned and tried un- **4–47**
less: (a) on a motion to quash it is held defective in substance or form; (b) matter in bar is pleaded and the plea is tried or confirmed in favour of the accused; (c) a *nolle prosequi* is entered by the Attorney-General, which cannot be done before the indictment is found; or (d) the indictment discloses an offence which a particular court has no jurisdiction to try: *per* Lord Goddard C.J. in *R. v. Chairman of London County Sessions, ex p. Downes* [1954] 1 Q.B. 1, 37 Cr.App.R. 148. (See *ante*, §§ 1–190 *et seq*. for consideration of legitimate objections to an indictment.)

Where a prosecution is properly brought, a judge has no power to prevent the prosecution from presenting their evidence on the basis that he considers it unlikely there will be a convicton: *Att.-Gen.'s Reference (No. 2 of 2000)* [2001] 1 Cr.App.R. 36, CA (and see *R. v. N. Ltd*, *post*, § 4–292).

The whole of this paragraph was approved in *R. v. Plant* [2008] 2 Cr.App.R. 27, CA (at [20]).

(2) Abuse of process

(a) *Jurisdiction*

General

4–48 In *Connelly v. DPP* [1964] A.C. 1254, HL, at pp. 1354–1355, Lord Devlin added a fifth ground to the list set out in *ex p. Downes*, *ante*, *viz.* where particular criminal proceedings constitute an abuse of the court's process. See also Lord Pearce at pp. 1361, 1364 and Lord Reid at p. 1296, but *cf.* Lord Morris at pp. 1300–1302 and Lord Hodson at pp. 1335–1338. What all their Lordships do seem to agree upon is that the court has a general and inherent power to protect its process from abuse. This power must include a power to safeguard an accused person from oppression or prejudice: Lord Morris, *ante*; Lord Devlin at p. 1347; Lord Pearce, *ante*.

4–49 The views expressed in *Connelly*, *ante*, were considered, *obiter*, in *DPP v. Humphrys* [1977] A.C. 1, HL. Only Lords Dilhorne, Salmon and Edmund-Davies considered the point. Lord Salmon and Lord Edmund-Davies concurred with the views expressed by Lord Devlin and Lord Pearce in *Connelly*, while Lord Dilhorne supported the narrower approach adopted by Lord Morris and Lord Hodson.

> "I respectfully agree with [*Lord Dilhorne*] that a judge has not and should not appear to have any responsibility for the institution of prosecutions; nor has he any power to refuse to allow a prosecution to proceed merely because he considers that, as a matter of policy, it ought not to have been brought. It is only if the prosecution amounts to an abuse of the process of the court and is oppressive and vexatious that the judge has the power to intervene. Fortunately, such prosecutions are hardly ever brought but the power of the court to prevent them is, in my view, of great constitutional importance and should be jealously preserved. For a man to be harassed and be put to the expense of perhaps a long trial and then given an absolute discharge is hardly from any point of view an effective substitute for the exercise by the court of the power to which I have referred" (*per* Lord Salmon at p. 46C–F).

Lord Edmund-Davies agreed that where a charge has been properly laid and there is evidence fit to go to the jury, the judge has no power to stay the proceedings simply because he thinks a conviction is unlikely (at p. 53B–E). His Lordship reviewed the authorities and concluded (at p. 55E–G):

> "While judges should pause long before staying proceedings which on their face are perfectly regular, it would indeed be bad for justice if in such fortunately rare cases as *R. v. Riebold* [1967] 1 W.L.R. 674 their hands were tied and they were obliged to allow the further trial to proceed. In my judgment, *Connelly* ... established that they are vested with the power to do what the justice of the case clearly demands and in *R. v. Thomson Holidays Ltd* [1974] Q.B. 592 the Court of Appeal proceeded on that basis ... (see the judgment of Lawton L.J. at 597–598)."

See also the analysis of one aspect of *Connelly* in *R. v. Beedie* [1997] 2 Cr.App.R. 167, CA, *post*, §§ 4–58, 4–118, and in *R. v. Z.* [2000] 2 A.C. 483, HL.

Magistrates' courts

4–50 In *R. v. Horseferry Road Magistrates' Court, ex p. Bennett* [1994] 1 A.C. 42, the House of Lords confirmed that justices have the power to stay criminal proceedings for abuse of process, but held that such power should be strictly confined to matters directly affecting the fairness of the trial of the particular accused with whom they are dealing, such as delay or unfair manipulation of court procedures. The wider supervisory responsibility for upholding the rule of law is vested in the High Court; where, therefore, a question arises as to the deliberate abuse of extradition procedures, justices should exercise their discretion to grant an adjournment to facilitate an application to the High Court (applied in *R. v. Bow Street Magistrates' Court, ex p. Finch and Bossino* [1999] 10 *Archbold News* 1, DC).

The precise extent of the narrow category of abuse of process cases, involving alleged infractions of the rule of law outside the confines of the trial process, in respect of which a magistrates' court has no jurisdiction, remains undetermined; however, even in cases concerning complaints directed to the fairness or propriety of the trial process itself it is always open to a magistrates' court to decline jurisdiction and leave the matter to be pursued in the High Court, whether on account of the complexity or novelty of the point, or of the length of the investigation that would be required: *R. v. Belmarsh Magistrates' Court, ex p. Watts* [1999] 2 Cr.App.R. 188, DC. Remarks to the same effect were made in *R. v. Horseferry Road Magistrates' Court, ex p. DPP* [1999] C.O.D. 441, DC (*post*, § 4–62), where the court also suggested that in the sort of situation there under consideration an abuse of process application might be better addressed to the court of trial than to the committal court. An application to the High Court would, presumably, be by way of judicial review, seeking prohibition of continuation of the proceedings, rather than seeking to quash the decision to institute the proceedings, and would constitute an exception to the general rule explained in *R. v. DPP, ex p. Kebilene* [2000] 2 A.C. 326, HL, *ante*, § 1–263.

The question of the extent of the jurisdiction of magistrates in respect of abuse of process was considered again in *R. (P. (A.)) v. Leeds Youth Court*, 165 J.P. 684, DC, where it was held that whatever the exact limits may be, there is no jurisdiction to stay proceedings on the basis of a failure by the prosecution to comply with the rules requiring the giving of advance information (*post*, §§ 12–124 *et seq.*); the proper remedy is provided for by those rules, namely to adjourn the proceedings.

It should be appreciated by magistrates that the power to stay a summary trial, or committal proceedings, on the ground of abuse of process is a power to be most sparingly exercised: see *per* Lord Lane C.J. in *R. v. Oxford City JJ., ex p. Smith*, 75 Cr.App.R. 200 at 204, DC; *per* Ackner L.J. in *R. v. Horsham JJ., ex p. Reeves*, 75 Cr.App.R. 236 at 241, DC; *King v. Kucharz* [1989] C.O.D. 469, DC; *R. v. Telford JJ., ex p. Badhan* [1991] 2 Q.B. 78, 93 Cr.App.R. 171, DC; Lord Griffiths in *ex p. Bennett*, *ante*, at 63H; *R. v. Barry Magistrates' Court, ex p. Malpas* [1998] C.O.D. 90, DC, *post*, § 4–74; and *Wei Hai Restaurant Ltd v. Kingston upon Hull City Council*, 166 J.P. 185, DC.

As to the discretion to refuse to issue a summons because of delay, see *post*, § 4–72.

(b) *Procedure*

Time for application and general procedure

An application to stay proceedings as an abuse of process is, in effect, a plea in bar **4–50a**
and should be considered as a preliminary issue before plea, although there is nothing to prevent the issue being raised at a later stage: *R. v. Aldershot Youth Court, ex p. A.* [1997] 3 *Archbold News* 2, DC (CO/1911/96); and see also *R. v. Smolinski* (*post*, § 4–70); and *R. (T.P.) v. West London Youth Court* (*post*, § 4–73).

Practice Direction (Criminal Proceedings: Consolidation), para. IV.36 [2002] 1 W.L.R. 2870

Abuse of process stay applications

IV.36.1 In all cases where a defendant in the Crown Court proposes to make an application to stay an indictment on the ground of abuse of process, written notice of such application must be given to the prosecuting authority and to any co-defendant not later than 14 days before the date fixed or warned for trial ("the relevant date"). Such notice must (a) give the name of the case and the indictment number; (b) state the fixed date or the warned date as appropriate; (c) specify the nature of the application; (d) set out in numbered sub-paragraphs the grounds on which the application is to be made; (e) be copied to the chief listing officer at the court centre where the case is due to be heard.

IV.36.2 Any co-defendant who wishes to make a like application must give a like notice not later than seven days before the relevant date, setting out any additional grounds relied upon.

IV.36.3 In relation to such applications, the following automatic directions shall apply. (a) The advocate for the applicant(s) must lodge with the court and serve on all other parties a skeleton argument in support of the application at least five clear working days before the relevant date. If reference is to be made to any document not in the existing trial documents, a paginated and indexed bundle of such documents is to be provided with the skeleton argument. (b) The advocate for the prosecution must lodge with the court and serve on all other parties a responsive skeleton argument at least two clear working days before the relevant date, together with a supplementary bundle if appropriate.

IV.36.4 All skeleton arguments must specify any propositions of law to be advanced (together with the authorities relied on in support, with page references to passages relied upon), and, where appropriate, include a chronology of events and a list of *dramatis personae*. In all instances where reference is made to a document, the reference in the trial documents or supplementary bundle is to be given.

IV.36.5 The above time limits are minimum time limits. In appropriate cases the court will order longer lead times. To this end in all cases where defence advocates are, at the time of the plea and directions hearing, considering the possibility of an abuse of process application, this must be raised with the judge dealing with the matter, who will order a different timetable if appropriate, and may wish in any event to give additional directions about the conduct of the application.

In the protocol issued by the Lord Woolf C.J. on the control and management of heavy fraud and other complex criminal cases (Appendix N–20), judges are encouraged to direct full written submissions in such cases, rather than skeleton arguments, and to aim normally to conclude the hearing within an absolute maximum limit of one day, if necessary with a timetable. Nevertheless, criminal proceedings remain essentially proceedings conducted by way of oral submissions, and a party's failure to serve a skeleton argument would rarely entitle a court to shut that party out from making such submissions: *DPP v. Ayers* [2006] Crim.L.R. 62, DC.

Burden of proof

4–51 The burden of establishing that the pursuit of particular proceedings would amount to an abuse of process is on the accused and the standard of proof is the balance of probabilities: *R. v. Telford JJ., ex p. Badhan*, *ante*; *R. v. Crown Court at Norwich, ex p. Belsham*, 94 Cr.App.R. 382, DC; and *R. v. Great Yarmouth Magistrates, ex p. Thomas* [1992] Crim.L.R. 116, DC. How the accused is to discharge the onus upon him must depend on all the circumstances of the case: *ex p. Badhan*. However, the language of burden and standard of proof has been said to be potentially misleading in the context of the decision whether or not to grant a stay because of delay, which is an exercise in judicial assessment dependent on judgment rather than on any conclusion as to fact based on evidence: *R. v. S.*, 170 J.P. 434, CA (*post*, § 4–66).

Evidence

4–52 A judge must determine an application to stay proceedings for abuse of process on the material provided by the prosecution and the defence. He has no power to order discovery of documents, and a witness summons to produce documents is not appropriate, because the procedure under the *Criminal Procedure (Attendance of Witnesses) Act* 1965 relates to the requirements of the trial and is not applicable outside the confines of the trial itself: *R. v. Manchester Crown Court, ex p. Cunningham* [1992] C.O.D. 23, DC (CO/0372/91) (*Cf.* the approach adopted, in a different context, in *Ex p. Guardian Newspapers* [1999] 1 Cr.App.R. 284, CA, and see *post*, §§ 4–75 and 4–93.) There is a right, however, to call evidence: *R. v. Clerkenwell Magistrates' Court, ex p. Bell* [1991] Crim.L.R. 468, DC. Further, the prosecution must give proper disclosure of unused material that is relevant to the issue: *R. v. DPP, ex p. Lee* [1999] 2 Cr.App.R. 304, DC, *R. v. Early* [2003] 1 Cr.App.R. 19, CA, and *R. v. Grant*, 67 J.C.L. 286, CA ([2003] EWCA Crim. 123).

In *Att.-Gen. v. Morgan*; *Att.-Gen. v. News Group Newspapers Ltd*, *The Independent*, July 17, 1997, DC, it was held that where an application for a stay had been based on allegedly prejudicial publicity, it was irregular to have permitted the author of the article complained of (who was expecting to be a prosecution witness in the substantive trial) to be called as a witness on the application for a stay and subjected to lengthy cross-examination as to his entire conduct in relation to the article; he should have been offered the opportunity of legal advice and, once giving evidence he should have been warned as to his privilege against self-incrimination.

Miscellaneous

In *R. v. Crawley JJ., ex p. DPP* [1991] C.O.D. 365, DC, a decision to dismiss a prosecution on the grounds of delay was quashed because of the failure of the justices to enquire fully into the cause of the delay that had occurred and the question of whether a fair trial could take place notwithstanding that delay. **4–53**

As to the desirability of the same justices hearing an abuse argument and then conducting any ensuing committal proceedings, see *R. v. Worcester Magistrates' Court, ex p. Bell*, 157 J.P. 921, DC, *ante*, § 1–51.

When giving judgment on an application to stay proceedings, a few sentences showing the judge's command of the law on the topic will usually suffice, followed by a summary of the reasons for rejecting or granting the application: *ex p. Cunningham*, *ante*. See also *R. v. Dutton* [1994] Crim.L.R. 910, CA, as to the desirability of some explanation of reasons being given; and *R. (Ebrahim) v. Feltham Magistrates' Court*; *Mouat v. DPP* [2001] 2 Cr.App.R. 23, DC, as to it being the professional duty of the advocates to take a note of such reasons. As to the giving of reasons generally, see also *ante*, §§ 1–272, 2–202, and *post*, § 16–75.

As to the form of the order that should be sought and made if proceedings amount to an abuse of process, see *ante*, §§ 1–192, 1–193.

(c) *Principles governing exercise of jurisdiction*

The power to stay proceedings for abuse of process has been said to include a power to safeguard an accused person from oppression or prejudice (*Connelly v. DPP*, *ante*, § 4–48), and has been described as a formidable safeguard, developed by the common law, to protect persons from being prosecuted in circumstances where it would be seriously unjust to do so (*Att.-Gen. of Trinidad and Tobago v. Phillip* [1995] 1 A.C. 396, PC). An abuse of process was defined, in *Hui Chi-Ming v. R.* [1992] 1 A.C. 34, PC, as "something so unfair and wrong that the court should not allow a prosecutor to proceed with what is in all other respects a regular proceeding." **4–54**

In *Re Barings plc (No. 2)*; *Secretary of State for Trade and Industry v. Baker* [1999] 1 All E.R. 311, CA (Civ. Div.), it was said (in the context of proceedings under section 6 of the *CDDA* 1986) that a court may stay proceedings where to allow them to continue would bring the administration of justice into disrepute among right thinking people and that this would be the case if the court was allowing its process to be used as an instrument of oppression, injustice or unfairness.

The jurisdiction to stay for abuse of process can be exercised in many different circumstances; nevertheless two main strands have been identified by the Court of Appeal in the authorities, namely (a) where the defendant would not receive a fair trial, and/or (b) where it would be unfair for the defendant to be tried: *R. v. Beckford* [1996] 1 Cr.App.R. 94. The latter will include cases where the prosecution have manipulated or misused the process of the court so as to deprive the defendant of a protection provided by the law or to take unfair advantage of a technicality (*R. v. Derby Crown Court, ex p. Brooks*, 80 Cr.App.R. 164, DC) and where it would be contrary to the public interest in the integrity of the criminal justice system that a trial should take place: *R. v. Mullen* [1999] 2 Cr.App.R. 143, CA, and *R. v. Horseferry Road Magistrates' Court, ex p. Bennett* [1994] 1 A.C. 42, HL, in which the accused had been brought to this country as a result of collaboration between authorities here and abroad and in disregard of extradition procedures. The doctrine was held to apply in such a situation, even though the matters complained of would not prevent a fair trial and even though it would not be unfair to try the accused if he had been returned to this country through lawful extradition procedures. Lord Griffiths said that the court had the power to interfere with the prosecution because the judiciary accepted a responsibility for the maintenance of the rule of law that embraced a willingness to oversee executive action and to refuse to countenance behaviour that threatened either basic human rights or the rule of law. It was the function of the High Court to ensure that executive action was exercised **4–55** responsibly and as Parliament intended. If, therefore, it came to the attention of the High Court that there had been a serious abuse of power it should express its disapproval by refusing to act on it. Lord Bridge said that there is no principle more basic to any proper system of law than the maintenance of the rule of law itself.

See also the analysis of *Connelly* (*ante*, § 4–48) in *R. v. Beedie* [1997] 2 Cr.App.R. 167, CA, *post*, §§ 4–58, 4–118, for further express acknowledgement that there are situations where proceedings should be stayed although a fair trial could be conducted. Such a case was *R. v. Grant* [2005] 2 Cr.App.R. 28, CA, where it was held that where the court is faced with illegal conduct by police or prosecutors which is so grave as to threaten or undermine the rule of law itself, the court may readily conclude that it will not tolerate, far less endorse, such a state of affairs and so hold that its duty is to stop the case (the deliberate interference with a detained suspect's right to the confidence of privileged communications with his solicitor, by eavesdropping, seriously undermined the rule of law and justified a stay on grounds of abuse of process, notwithstanding the absence of prejudice); and see *R. v. Early* [2003] 1 Cr.App.R. 19, CA, and various of the authorities at §§ 4–62, 4–63, *post*.

Whilst serious failings on the part of the police or the prosecution (which, in the case under consideration, were late disclosure of matter that there was a duty to disclose, and wrongful destruction of items taken from the scene of the crime) may make it unfair to try a defendant in a particular case, that will be a rare occurrence in the absence of serious misbehaviour; if it is not such a case, then the only issue is whether it remains possible for the defendant to have a fair trial: *R. v. Sadler*, 166 J.P. 481, CA.

4–56 The question of whether the defendant would receive a fair trial overlaps with the guarantee of the right to a fair trial under Article 6 of the ECHR, *post*, § 16–57. For examples of situations which have been held to be incompatible with that right, the remedy for some of which may be a stay of proceedings, see *post*, §§ 16–58 *et seq.*, and, for consideration of the right to be tried "within a reasonable time" in the context of the doctrine of abuse of process, see *post*, § 4–67.

A stay will not be granted where the trial process is itself equipped to deal with the matters complained of: *R. (Ebrahim) v. Feltham Magistrates' Court*; *Mouat v. DPP* [2001] 2 Cr.App.R. 23, DC (*post*, § 4–65), and *Att.-Gen.'s Reference (No. 1 of 1990)* [1992] Q.B. 630, 95 Cr.App.R. 296, CA, adopting the point made in *R. v. Heston-Francois* [1984] Q.B. 278, 78 Cr.App.R. 209, CA, in which it was held that the court's jurisdiction to order a stay does not include an obligation upon the judge to hold a pre-trial inquiry into allegations such as improper obtaining of evidence, tampering with evidence or seizure of a defendant's documents prepared for his defence. Such conduct is not ordinarily an abuse of the court's process. It is conduct which falls to be dealt with at the trial itself by judicial control on admissibility of evidence, the judicial power to direct a verdict of not guilty (usually at the close of the prosecution's case), or by the jury taking account of it in evaluating the evidence before them. In *DPP v. Hussain*, *The Times*, June 1, 1994, the Divisional Court reiterated the exceptional nature of an order staying proceedings on the ground of abuse of process and stated that such an order should never be made where there were other ways of achieving a fair hearing of the case, still less where there was no evidence of prejudice to the defendant. Abuse of process arguments distort the trial process where they are not warranted; they should not be put forward as mere embroidery of a case that could be advanced equally well without them, and if they are advanced without justification the court should make it clear that such conduct is inappropriate and take appropriate steps where court time has been wasted: *R. v. Childs*, *The Times*, November 30, 2002, CA.

(d) *Application of the principles*

Misuse, manipulation, etc., of process of court

4–57 Each case will depend on its own facts; the following authorities are merely examples of the way in which the general principles (*ante*) have been refined and applied in particular circumstances. The further sub-headings are to be taken as no more than pointers to the areas with which this topic is concerned.

Decisions as to the institution/continuation of prosecutions

4–58 The jurisdiction to stay proceedings on the basis of abuse of process is to be exercised with the greatest caution; the fact that a prosecution is ill-advised or unwise is no basis for its exercise; the question whether to prosecute or not is for the prosecutor; if a conviction is obtained in circumstances where the court, on reasonable grounds, feels that the prosecution should not have been brought, this can be reflected in the penalty: *Environment Agency v. Stanford* [1998] C.O.D. 373, DC. See also *DPP v. Humphrys*, *ante*, § 4–49, and *cf. Postermobile plc v. Brent LBC*, *The Times*, December 8, 1997, DC, *post*, § 4–62.

The fact that a law had not been published and could not reasonably have been known to exist may be a ground for staying a prosecution for contravention of that law as an abuse of process: *Christian v. The Queen* [2007] 2 W.L.R. 120, PC.

In *Hui Chi-Ming v. R.* [1992] 1 A.C. 34, PC, it was held not to be oppressive or an abuse of the process of the court to prosecute a secondary party for murder when the principal had been convicted of manslaughter and when pleas of guilty to manslaughter had been accepted from other secondary parties. It was noted that: (a) the acquittal of the principal on the charge of murder appeared perverse; (b) there had been abundant evidence of murder against the appellant; and (c) he had chosen to run a defence which would have resulted in his complete acquittal if it had succeeded, rather than accept an offer that had been made to accept a plea of guilty to manslaughter. *Cf. R. v. Richards and Stober*, 96 Cr.App.R. 258, CA (*post*, § 19–87), in which the unsuccessful argument on behalf of the appellants would appear to amount to an allegation of a species of abuse of process, although not advanced as such. See also *R. v. Forsyth* [1997] 2 Cr.App.R. 299, CA, where it was held not to be an abuse of process for the Serious Fraud Office to continue with the prosecution of one defendant, who was involved in an isolated transaction, after the principal defendant had fled the jurisdiction and proceedings against other persons more centrally involved had been abandoned on the ground that they could not be dealt with fairly in his absence.

In *Connelly v. DPP* [1964] A.C. 1254, the House of Lords approved the general rule explained by Lord Cockburn C.J. in *R. v. Elrington* (1861) 1 B. & S. 688, to the effect that no man should be punished twice for an offence arising out of the same or substantially the same set of facts and that to do so would offend the established principle that there should be no sequential trials for offences on an ascending scale of gravity. In *R. v. Beedie* [1997] 2 Cr.App.R. 167, the Court of Appeal confirmed that this general rule is not part of the doctrine of *autrefois* (*post*, §§ 4–116 *et seq.*), but should, in the absence of special circumstances, give rise to the exercise of the wider discretionary power to stay proceedings which constitute an abuse of the process of the court. In the case under consideration, a charge of manslaughter should have been stayed where the accused had already been dealt with for a summary offence relating to the defective state of a gas installation which had resulted in the relevant death; the public interest in a prosecution for manslaughter and the understandable concern of the victim's family did not give rise to special circumstances; the carrying out of a balancing exercise and consideration of the question of whether there could be a fair trial were inappropriate. This principle will not prevent a trial for murder or manslaughter where the victim has died after proceedings for assault: the offences will not arise out of substantially the same set of facts because of the additional fact of the death and/or special circumstances will exist.

It is not necessarily an abuse of process to prosecute a person for an offence which could have been included in a previous indictment on which he was acquitted; it is important to scrutinise the true nature of the second set of proceedings; where the first trial would have been significantly delayed if the second matter had been joined, and the evidential overlap was not great, no principle of fairness or propriety had been flouted: *R. v. South East Hampshire Magistrates' Court, ex p. CPS* [1998] Crim.L.R. 422, DC.

It was not an abuse of process to prosecute a charge of dangerous driving where the defendant had pleaded guilty in the magistrates' court to a charge of driving with excess alcohol arising out of the same course of driving and where the prosecution intended to prove that conviction as part of their case on the charge of dangerous driving; if there was any unfairness involved in what had occurred the judge could have excluded the evidence of the conviction under section 78 of the *PACE Act* 1984: *R. v. Hartnett* [2003] Crim.L.R. 719, CA. *R. v. Forest of Dean JJ., ex p. Farley* [1990] R.T.R. 228, DC (in which it was held to be an abuse of process to pursue a charge of driving with excess alcohol before a trial of a charge of causing death by reckless driving based entirely on the allegation of excess alcohol in order to take advantage in the trial on the more serious charge of a reversed burden of proof in the trial on the lesser charge) was distinguished on its facts. *Hartnett* and *ex p. Farley* were considered in *R. v. Arnold* [2008] R.T.R. 25, Ct-MAC (*post*, § 32–29).

As to the pursuit of charges in respect of offences taken into consideration, see *post*, § 4–129.

4–59 In *R. v. Horsham JJ., ex p. Reeves*, 75 Cr.App.R. 236, DC, it was held that it would be vexatious and oppressive to permit the prosecution to pursue charges which were basically the same as those on which the justices had found there to be no case to answer in previous committal proceedings against the same defendant. This was so even though the previous finding could not give rise to a plea of *autrefois acquit*. *Cf. R. v. Manchester City Magistrates, ex p. Snelson* [1977] 1 W.L.R. 911, DC (matter of degree whether repeated committal proceedings amount to abuse of process), and see *ante*, § 1–217. See also *Brooks v. DPP* [1994] 1 A.C. 568, PC (*ante*, § 1–213), where Ackner L.J.'s observation in *ex p. Reeves* that there have to be exceptional circumstances to warrant prosecuting a defendant after committal proceedings have concluded with a ruling that there is no case to answer, was adopted.

As to the application of the doctrine of abuse of process where fresh proceedings are instituted after the dismissal of an information under section 15 of the *MCA* 1980 (non-attendance of prosecutor), see *Holmes v. Campbell*, 162 J.P. 655, DC (*post*, 4–143).

In *R. v. Faversham JJ., ex p. Stickings, The Times*, May 9, 1996, DC, magistrates who had given a considered ruling in favour of the defence, as to the admissibility of certain evidence, subsequently changed that ruling, following inappropriate communication between their clerk and the prosecutor. They had then directed a retrial before a different bench. The Divisional Court prohibited the retrial on the basis that, in the circumstances, it would be unjust to permit the prosecution to proceed. *Per contra*, *R. (Hussain) v. Peterborough Magistrates' Court*, 171 J.P. 339, DC, where a change in legal adviser between hearings (resulting, unintentionally, from a complaint made out of court by the prosecution as to the conduct of the legal adviser at the first hearing) did not have any impact on any previous ruling or decision.

In *R. v. Lincoln Magistrates' Court, ex p. Wickes Building Supplies Ltd, The Times*, August 6, 1993, DC, it was held that the laying of a multiplicity of charges in respect of each Sunday trading breach under section 47 of the *Shops Act* 1950, when the lawfulness of that section was being challenged in the European Court of Justice, was not an abuse of process. However, where an application for a declaration of lawfulness was made to the High Court, the court could make an order restraining the prosecuting authority from taking any enforcement action based on the view that the conduct was unlawful pending determination of the application, and the likelihood was that the prosecuting authority, acting reasonably, would not prosecute subsequently for acts done during the continuance of the order: *R. (O.S.S. Group Ltd) v. Environment Agency* [2007] A.C.D. 8, QBD (Sir Michael Harrison).

Before criminal proceedings are instituted by a local authority they must consider with care the terms of their own prosecution policy; consequently a prosecution brought by a local authority in circumstances where there was no material to suggest that their criteria for prosecution were met should have been stayed as an abuse of process: *R. v. Adaway*, 168 J.P. 645, CA.

For examples of applications to stay private prosecutions for abuse of process, see *R. v. Moxon-Tritsch* [1988] Crim.L.R. 46, Crown Court (H.H.Judge Faulks) (stay of private prosecution for causing death by reckless driving instituted after defendant had been dealt with for careless driving and excess alcohol offences); *R. v. Grays JJ., ex p. Low*, 88 Cr.App.R. 291, DC (abuse of process where earlier summons for same matter had been withdrawn by the CPS after the defendant had agreed to be bound over); *Hayter v. L.* [1998] 1 W.L.R. 854, DC (prosecution of a person who had been cautioned in respect of the offence but had been told at the time that the caution did not bar a private prosecution not an abuse of process), the correctness of which was left open in *Jones v. Whalley* [2007] 1 A.C. 63, HL (private prosecution an abuse where defendant had been formally cautioned by a police officer in terms which represented that he would not be prosecuted, and without reference to the possibility of a private prosecution); *R. v. Horseferry Road Magistrates' Court, ex p. Stephenson* [1989] C.O.D. 470, DC (private prosecution launched as a device to disrupt a conference an abuse of process); *R. v. Belmarsh Magistrates' Court, ex p. Watts* [1999] 2 Cr.App.R. 188, DC (private prosecution for libel and misfeasance in a public office brought by a convicted drug trafficker against an investigator who had prepared a report referring to him as a cocaine dealer should have been stayed in that it was an affront to the court's sense of justice and propriety to entertain proceedings that were admittedly brought with a view to clearing the prosecutor's name, rather than prosecuting alleged criminals to conviction; and the delay of four-and-a-half years in commencing the prosecution amounted to an abuse where civil proceedings for the same alleged libel had been brought, but not prosecuted with due diligence); and *R. (Dacre and Associated Newspapers) v. City of Westminster Magistrates' Court* [2008] 8 *Archbold News* 2, DC ([2008] EWHC 1667 (Admin.)) (fact that a private prosecution is brought with mixed motives, some indirect or improper, will in many cases be inevitable and will not necessarily vitiate it; the court should consider whether there is a primary motive which is so unrelated to the proceedings that it renders the prosecution a misuse of the process).

A declaration as to lawfulness by the civil courts is not, in itself, a bar to a criminal prosecution: *Imperial Tobacco Ltd v. Att.-Gen.* [1981] A.C. 718, HL; followed in *R. v. L.* [2007] 1 Cr.App.R. 1, CA (prosecution for murder not barred by contrary decision in care proceedings). However, in *R. v. Bingley Magistrates' Court, ex p. Morrow*, *The Times*, April 28, 1994, the Divisional Court upheld a refusal by justices to issue a summons on an information for murder in a situation where the relevant death followed the discontinuation by doctors of life sustaining treatment, which discontinuation had been implemented following a declaration by the civil courts (*Airedale N.H.S. Trust v. Bland* [1993] A.C. 789, HL) to the effect that such discontinuance would be lawful. As to the making of declarations in relation to lawfulness, see also *R. v. Environment Agency, ex p. Dockgrange Ltd*, *The Times*, June 21, 1997, QBD (Carnwath J.), *R. v. Medicines Control Agency, ex p. Pharma Nord Ltd* [1998] C.O.D. 315, CA (Civ. Div.), *R. v. DPP, ex p. Camelot Group plc* [1998] C.O.D. 54, DC, *R. v. DPP, ex p. Merton LBC* [1999] C.O.D. 161, QBD (Tucker J.), and [1999] C.O.D. 358, DC, *Blackland Park Exploration Ltd v. Environment Agency* (2004) 148 S.J. 26, CA (Civ. Div.); as to the grant of an injunction pending the hearing of an application for a declaration, see *R. (O.S.S. Group Ltd) v. Environment Agency*, *ante*; and, for applications for declarations of incompatibility under section 4 of the *Human Rights Act* 1998 (*post*, § 16–18), see *R. (Pretty) v. DPP* [2002] 1 A.C. 800, HL, and *R. (Rusbridger) v. Att.-Gen.* [2004] 1 A.C. 357, HL.

As to the charging of a particular offence in order to deny the defendant the benefit of a statutory provision that applies only to certain other offences, see *R. v. Asfaw (United Nations High Commr for Refugees intervening)* [2008] 2 W.L.R. 1178, HL, *post*, § 25–228e, and *R. v. J.* [2005] 1 A.C. 562, HL (§ 20–1 in the supplement).

See also *ante*, § 1–263 as to the means by which, and the circumstances in which, a decision to commence or continue a prosecution may be challenged.

Manipulation of particular procedures

In *R. v. Brentford JJ., ex p. Wong*, 73 Cr.App.R. 65, DC, it was held to be an abuse **4–60**
of process where the prosecutor, without having then reached a final decision to prosecute the defendant, laid an information just within the time limit for commencing a prosecution, so as to keep his options open, and did not serve the summons for some months thereafter. See also *R. v. Newcastle upon Tyne JJ., ex p. Hindle* [1984] 1 All E.R. 770, DC.

In *R. v. Rotherham JJ., ex p. Brough* [1991] C.O.D. 89, DC, the CPS had deliberately taken steps to ensure that a defendant who was charged with an offence that would be triable only on indictment in the case of an adult did not appear before the court until he had reached the age where the justices ceased to have a discretion whether or not to deal with him themselves. Although the court viewed the procedure as incorrect, it was held not to amount to an abuse of process because, on the facts, the conduct of the prosecution showed, at most, a lack of judgment rather than misconduct or *mala fides*. Furthermore, there was no prejudice to the defendant because the delay involved had been minimal, the justices would probably have committed the case to the Crown Court anyway, and in the event of conviction the judge would undoubtedly take account of the defendant's age at the time of the offence and the circumstances of his committal.

See *ante*, §§ 1–75f, 1–75g as to the propriety of substituting summary only charges for charges triable either way, or of adding charges triable only on indictment, so as to ensure that the trial takes place at a particular level of court.

In *R. v. Simpson* [1998] Crim.L.R. 481, CA, the original trial of the appellant had been aborted when he and a number of witnesses were arrested for conspiracy to pervert the course of justice in respect of the defence case at that trial. The prosecution had known of the likelihood of such a situation arising and in an *ex parte* hearing prior to the commencement of the trial had obtained a ruling from the trial judge that the situation need not be disclosed to the defence. Following his conviction on the subsequent retrial, the appellant appealed on the basis that it had been an abuse of process to embark on a trial with no intention or, at least, little likelihood of reaching a verdict. It was held that there had been no improper manipulation of the process of the court, that it had been fair to re-try the appellant, and that the trial which had resulted in his conviction had been fair.

4–61 Where a summary trial is adjourned part-heard before the conclusion of the case for the prosecution and, at the adjourned hearing, the prosecution propose to call a witness whom they had not intended to call at the original hearing but of whose existence they had always been aware, any objection based on an assertion that unfair advantage had been taken of the adjournment should be dealt with by reference to section 78 of the *PACE Act* 1984, and not by reference to the power to stay the proceedings as an abuse of process; as a matter of general principle, there is nothing improper about the taking of further statements during an adjournment and thereafter calling the makers as witnesses; on the contrary, the interests of justice may demand such a course: *DPP v. Jimale* [2001] Crim.L.R. 138, DC. However, it is submitted that it may be appropriate to exclude such new evidence, or order a retrial, if the defence case already put might have been put differently in the event that advance notice of the evidence had been given and if the defence case has, thereby, been improperly prejudiced.

It was an abuse of process for the prosecution, upon realising, after the magistrates had retired to consider sentence, that the charge was punishable only by way of a fine, to invite the magistrates back into court and then invite them to substitute a charge in respect of the same facts which carried the possibility of a custodial sentence: *R. v. Harlow Magistrates' Court, ex p. O'Farrell* [2000] Crim.L.R. 589, DC.

In *R. v. Piggott and Litwin* [1999] 2 Cr.App.R. 230, CA, it was held to be an abuse of process to prosecute an indictment that had been amended at a previous trial so as to substitute a charge that could not be tried fairly at the time of its substitution. See further *ante*, § 1–153.

Where one magistrates' court has refused to issue a summons in respect of an information alleging an offence, it is an abuse of process to apply for a summons to a second magistrates' court in respect of an identical information without disclosing the fact of the first court's refusal to issue a summons: *Gleaves v. Insall*; *Dore v. Insall*; *Bolton v. Insall*; *Gleaves v. Insall* [1999] 2 Cr.App.R. 466, DC.

It is not in the public interest to pursue criminal proceedings if both the police and the individual are prepared to proceed by way of caution, but the individual is entitled to informed legal advice as to whether to accept a caution; where, therefore the police refused to disclose the terms of an interview to the individual's solicitors, with the result that the solicitor felt unable to advise acceptance of the caution that was offered, it had been open to the magistrates' court to stay the subsequent prosecution as an abuse: *DPP v. Ara* [2002] 1 Cr.App.R. 16, DC.

As to the application of the doctrine of abuse of process in circumstances where a new charge is brought for the purpose of avoiding the effect of the expiration of a custody time limit, see *R. (Wardle) v. Crown Court at Leeds* [2002] 1 A.C. 754, HL, *ante*, § 1–270.

As to abuse of process in the context of the re-institution of proceedings against a young person following the expiry of an overall time limit, see *R. (DPP) v. Croydon Youth Court*, 165 J.P. 181, DC.

As to abuse of process and retrials, see *ante*, § 4–45.

Prosecution going back on promise, etc.

Where a defendant has been induced to believe that he will not be prosecuted, this is capable of founding a stay for abuse; however, it is not likely to do so unless (i) there has been an unequivocal representation by those with the conduct of the investigation or prosecution of a case that the defendant will not be prosecuted and (ii) the defendant has acted on that representation to his detriment; even then, if facts come to light which were not known when the representation was made, these may justify proceeding with the prosecution despite the representation: *R. v. Abu Hamza* [2007] 1 Cr.App.R. 27, CA, rejecting the common law principle of legitimate expectation as a test, and considering *R. v. Croydon JJ., ex p. Dean*, 98 Cr.App.R. 76, DC (abuse to prosecute a 17-year-old for destroying evidence after a murder when he had given evidence in the murder trial on the assurance that he would not be prosecuted), *R. v. Townsend* [1997] 2 Cr.App.R. 540, CA (the longer a person is left to believe that he will not be prosecuted, the more unjust it becomes for the prosecution to renege on their promise, and any manifest prejudice to him resulting from his co-operation will make it inherently unfair to proceed) and *R. v. Bloomfield* [1997] 1 Cr.App.R. 135, CA (abuse to prosecute after an unequivocal statement by prosecution counsel to the court that the prosecution would tender no evidence, where there had been no change of circumstances that might have justified departing from that statement). See also *R. v. Horseferry Road Magistrates' Court, ex p. DPP* [1999] C.O.D. 441, DC, in which it was held that a stipendiary magistrate had wrongly concluded that a breach of an assurance not to prosecute justified a stay *per se*, and the matter was remitted for the court to investigate what prejudice to the defendant would result from pursuit of the proceedings and whether there were special circumstances present (such as, in *ex p. Dean*, the defendant's youthfulness and the assistance he had given subsequent to the assurance, or, in *Bloomfield*, the fact that the assurance given to the court would already have been acted upon but for an adjournment to suit the convenience of the prosecution); *H. v. Guildford Youth Court* [2008] 4 *Archbold News* 1, QBD (Silber J.) (prosecution should have been stayed where it had been indicated at the police station to the defendant and his solicitor by a police officer that the offence would be dealt with by way of a final warning; but no reference was made to *R. v. Abu Hamza*, *ante*); and *D. and B. v. Commr of Police for the Metropolis, CPS and Croydon JJ.* [2008] A.C.D. 47, DC (an expression of willingness on the part of a crown prosecutor to recommend that a final warning should be administered did not give rise to a legitimate expectation that such a warning would in fact be given, so as to make continuance of the prosecution an abuse). **4–62**

There had been no abuse of process where the prosecution had indicated to the judge before whom a case of causing death by dangerous driving was listed for trial that they had decided to accept a plea of guilty to careless driving, but when invited by the judge to reconsider that decision had decided by the same afternoon to pursue the original charge; the appellant had been aware from the outset, having heard the exchange with the judge, that the judge was not happy with the original decision, and thereafter, it was only a short time before the change of decision, and there had been no prejudice to the appellant: *R. v. Mulla* [2004] 1 Cr.App.R. 6, CA. And in *DPP v. B.* [2008] Crim.L.R. 707, DC, where the judge in the Crown Court had suggested that the single charge which the defendant faced did not adequately represent his admitted criminality, as a result of which he had been charged with a series of further similar offences, the justices had been in error to stay the further proceedings as an abuse. There was nothing unjust about the additional charges, as the defendant would not be at risk of any sentence other than one that reflected his criminality.

Further, there is no rule to the effect that an early decision in a magistrates' court not to proceed on one of several charges cannot, in the absence of fresh evidence, be re-visited by counsel prosecuting in the Crown Court: *R. v. Murphy* [2003] Crim.L.R. 471, CA (prosecution withdrew at magistrates' court a charge of indecent assault, another such charge in respect of a different child being transferred to the Crown Court, where the withdrawn charge was reinstated despite the absence of any new evidence; held, that where the decision to reinstate was taken in a different court at a significantly different stage in the process, and no objection had been taken by the defence at the time, the course taken did not bring the administration of justice into disrepute).

Where there was an agreement between the prosecution and the defence that the defendant would plead guilty to two out of three charges and the prosecution would withdraw the third charge, which then happened, it was open to justices to adjudge it an abuse of process for the prosecution to seek to reinstate the third charge before the conclusion of the proceedings, but after the justices had retired to consider sentence, upon realising that what had been thought to be a legal impediment to a successful prosecution of the third charge was in fact no impediment: *DPP v. Edgar*, 164 J.P. 471, DC.

Decisions of prosecutors in foreign jurisdictions will not of themselves render a prosecution in England and Wales an abuse of process; the test will be whether the defendant can have a fair trial or whether it would be unfair for him to be tried, as set out in *Beckford*, *ante*, § 4–55: *R. v. Cheong* [2006] Crim.L.R. 1088, CA.

Where a citizen engaged in certain conduct, in reliance on the (mistaken) opinion of a public official that such conduct would be lawful and without any long term effects, it was held to be an abuse of process to permit the continuance of a prosecution in respect of that conduct: *Postermobile plc v. Brent LBC*, *The Times*, December 8, 1997, DC.

Prosecution/investigators contributing to commission of offence

4–63 In *R. v. Looseley*; *Att.-Gen.'s Reference (No. 3 of 2000)* [2002] 1 Cr.App.R. 29, the House of Lords reviewed the law relating to the topic of entrapment. In this regard it was held, in effect, as had been previously acknowledged in *R. v. Latif and Shahzad* [1996] 2 Cr.App.R. 92, HL, that the end does not always justify the means. In giving guidance their Lordships took account of the jurisprudence on the topic that has emanated from the European Court of Human Rights in *Teixeira de Castro v. Portugal*, 28 E.H.R.R. 101 (*post*, § 16–68a). The conclusions of their Lordships, in summary, were as follows—

(i) It is not acceptable that the state through its agents should lure its citizens into committing acts forbidden by the law and then seek to prosecute them for doing so. Such conduct would be entrapment, a misuse of state power, and an abuse of the process of the courts.

(ii) By recourse to the principle that every court has an inherent power and duty to prevent abuse of its process the courts can ensure that executive agents of the state do not so misuse the coercive law enforcement functions of the courts and thereby oppress citizens of the state.

(iii) As to where the boundary lies in respect of acceptable police behaviour, each case must depend on its own facts, but a useful guide to identifying the limits of the type of police conduct which is acceptable is to consider whether, in the particular circumstances, the police did no more than present the defendant with an unexceptional opportunity to commit a crime. The yardstick is, in general, whether the conduct of the police preceding the commission of the offence was no more than might have been expected from others in the circumstances; if not, then the police were not to be regarded as having instigated or incited the crime; if they did no more than others might be expected to do, they were not creating crime artificially. However, the investigatory technique of providing an opportunity to commit crime should not be applied in a random fashion or be used for wholesale virtue-testing without good reason. The greater the degree of intrusiveness, the closer will the court scrutinise the reason for using it. The ultimate consideration is whether the conduct of the law enforcement agency is so seriously improper as to bring the administration of justice into disrepute. The use of pro-active techniques is needed more, and is hence more appropriate, in some circumstances than others; the secrecy and difficulty of detection and the manner in which the particular criminal activity is carried on being relevant considerations. The police must act in good faith, and having reasonable suspicion is one way such good faith might be established, but reasonable suspicion of a particular individual will not always be necessary. In deciding what is acceptable, regard is also to be had to the defendant's circumstances, including his vulnerability.

(iv) The remedy where entrapment has occurred is not a substantive defence. It had at one time been held that the existence of entrapment could amount to no more than mitigation (as to which, see *post*, § 15–514). However, the enactment of section 78 of the *PACE Act* 1984 (*post*, § 15–452) and the development of the doctrine of abuse of process, reinforced by the *Human Rights Act* 1998, have allowed for a change of approach. Section 78 provides the power to exclude prosecution evidence if, having regard to all of the circumstances, the court considers that the admission of the evidence would have such an adverse effect on the fairness of the proceedings that the court ought not to admit it. The phrase "fairness of the proceedings" in section 78 is directed primarily at matters going to fairness in the actual conduct of proceedings, but the scope of this wide and comprehensive discretion should not be limited strictly to procedural unfairness and can justify the exclusion of evidence in entrapment cases. The doctrine of abuse of process enables a court to stay proceedings when it would not be fair to try a defendant; one such situation would be when the proceedings result from executive action that threatens either basic human rights or the rule of law. A stay will usually be the more appropriate remedy in an entrapment case. However, sometimes an application will be made for a stay and/or for exclusion of evidence under section 78. Different tests are applicable – a decision to grant a stay on the basis that it is unfair to try the defendant is distinct from a determination of the forensic fairness of admitting evidence. In such cases the court will need to reach a separate decision on each ground.

For a case in which it was held that these principles (which are not exhaustive, and no one of which is determinative: see *Re Saluja (Reference of decision by General Medical Council in disciplinary proceedings)*; *Council for the Regulation of Health Care Professionals v. General Medical Council* [2007] 2 All E.R. 905, QBD (Goldring J.)) should have led to a stay, see *R. v. Moon*, 70 J.C.L. 194, CA ([2004] EWCA Crim. 2872) (addict persuaded to sell small quantity of drugs to undercover officer pressing her with a bad luck story); and for a case in which it was held that the judge had been correct to refuse a stay, notwithstanding that an undercover police operation had not been properly authorised under the *RIPA* 2000 and the code of practice for the use of human intelligence sources, and that the undercover officers had committed criminal acts, see *R. v. Harmes and Crane* [2006] 7 *Archbold News* 1, CA (mere fact of the breaches did not dispose of the issue whether the prosecution should have been stayed, but importance of compliance with the Act of 2000 and the code should not be underestimated, in that, absent careful compliance, the purpose of the Act would be frustrated, because a lack of a careful record of that which was proposed and approved would deprive a court of the opportunity of assessing whether the undercover activities of the officers were necessary and proportionate).

As to the need for full and proper disclosure of the role of any prosecution witness as a participating informant, see *R. v. Patel* [2002] Crim.L.R. 304, CA, *R. v. Early* [2003] 1 Cr.App.R. 19, CA, and *R. v. Grant*, 67 J.C.L. 286, CA ([2003] EWCA Crim. 123).

Where a prosecution under the *Dangerous Dogs Act* 1991 was not proceeded with (because of the non-availability of a witness) and the dog was returned to the defendant in anticipation that he would take the dog out of police custody and into a public place unmuzzled, which he did, and it had already been decided that if he did so his conduct would form the basis of a further charge, the new proceedings should have been stayed because the prosecution's conduct in contributing to the commission of the offence could not be taken into account in mitigation of sentence (as would be the case with almost any other offence) as the penalty under the law at the time was mandatory destruction of the dog: *R. v. Liverpool Magistrates' Court, ex p. Slade* [1998] 1 W.L.R. 531, DC.

The position in relation to misconduct by non-state agents is different; the rationale of the doctrine of abuse is absent, but the authorities leave open the possibility of a stay on grounds related to misconduct by non-state agents, in that given sufficiently gross misconduct, it would be an abuse of the court's process for the state to seek to rely on the resulting evidence; reliance upon it would compromise the court's integrity: *Re Saluja, ante*, in which it was held that for a journalist to pose as a patient (with a view to exposing a doctor) was not akin to an abuse of power by a state agent.

A private prosecution may be considered an abuse of process if the crime which is the subject of the prosecution is one that has been encouraged by the private prosecutor or if, in some other way, the private prosecutor has essentially created the same mischief as that about which he complains: *R. (Dacre and Associated Newspapers) v. City of Westminster Magistrates' Court, ante*, § 4–59.

Matters relating to complainant or witnesses

4–63a An abuse of process exists where the plaintiff in civil proceedings is in effective control of criminal proceedings against the same defendant to the extent that the prosecution are unable to exercise independently their prosecutorial duties: *R. v. Leominster Magistrates' Court, ex p. Aston Manor Brewery Co., The Times*, January 8, 1997, DC. *Cf. R. v. Milton Keynes Magistrates' Court, ex p. Roberts* [1995] Crim.L.R. 224, DC (no evidence of control sufficient to justify a stay).

If a bank is the ultimate complainant and "prosecutor", there is a heavy burden on that bank to make available to the prosecution, for onward disclosure to the defence, documents (including privileged documents) relevant to the issues, and failure to do so might well compromise the "integrity of the proceedings"; where necessary, the prosecution can produce documents that have been suitably sanitised so as to preserve customer confidentiality: *R. v. Skingly and Burrett*, unreported, December 19, 1999, CA.

A complainant's unreliability as a witness and his obsession about his cause do not justify a decision to stay proceedings on the basis of abuse of process: *R. v. Durham Stipendiary Magistrate, ex p. Davies, The Times*, May 25, 1993, DC.

Any potential unfairness resulting from the calling by the prosecution of a witness who stands to gain by giving false evidence can be negated by suitable directions to the jury: *Chan Wei-keung* [1995] 2 Cr.App.R. 194, PC.

Machinations on the part of the prosecuting authority to prevent potential defence witnesses from giving evidence would be highly likely to result in a stay on the ground of abuse of process: *R. v. Schlesinger* [1995] Crim.L.R. 137, CA. In *R. v. Rodenhurst, The Independent (C.S.)*, July 23, 2001, CA, the defendant's alibi witnesses in respect of the primary charge had been charged (together with him) with perverting the course of justice in respect of the alibi and that matter had been joined in the same indictment as the primary charge. It was held that the potential unfairness arising from the fact that the alibi witnesses were, therefore, no longer compellable, and from the fact that if they did give evidence they would come from the dock to do so, had been cured by the judge quashing the counts against the alibi witnesses and the prosecution undertaking not to take further proceedings against them, save, possibly, for perjury if they gave false evidence.

As to the power to grant a stay on the basis of the absence of a prosecution witness whose presence is required by the defence, see *post*, §§ 4–276, 4–278.

Abuse of executive power

See generally *R. v. Horseferry Road Magistrates' Court, ex p. Bennett* [1994] 1 A.C. 42, HL (*ante*, § 4–55). The principles explained in that decision were applied in *R. v. Mullen* [1999] 2 Cr.App.R. 143, where the Court of Appeal, on the basis of information that had not been disclosed prior to the proceedings in the Crown Court, concluded that (i) the British authorities had initiated and subsequently assisted in and procured the deportation of the appellant by unlawful means from Zimbabwe to England in circumstances where specific extradition facilities existed and, in so acting, had not only encouraged unlawful conduct in Zimbabwe, but had also acted in breach of public international law, (ii) in the particular circumstances, the conduct of the British authorities had been so unworthy or shameful that it was an affront to the public conscience to allow the prosecution to succeed, and (iii) accordingly, in the exercise of the discretionary power of the court, the proceedings should have been stayed as an abuse of process. In arriving at its conclusions the court emphasised that nothing in the judgment should be taken to suggest that there may not be cases, such as *R. v. Latif and Shahzad* [1996] 2 Cr.App.R. 92, HL (as to which, see *ante*, § 4–63), in which the seriousness of the crime is so great, relative to the nature of a particular abuse of process, that it would be a proper exercise of the judicial discretion to permit a prosecution to proceed. See also *R. v. Hardwicke and Thwaites* [2001] Crim.L.R. 220, CA, *post*, § 15–523, as to the distinction between malpractice by the executive or law enforcement agencies and similar behaviour by other agencies. **4–64**

As to the judicial discretion to permit a prosecution to proceed despite an abuse of power, see also *R. v. MacDonald* [1998] Crim.L.R. 808, CA, *post*, § 4–65.

In *R. v. Staines Magistrates' Court, ex p. Westfallen*; *R. v. Same, ex p. Soper*; *R. v. Swindon Magistrates' Court, ex p. Nangle* [1998] 1 W.L.R. 652, DC, it was held that whilst there would be grounds for objection to the jurisdiction of the courts of this country if the domestic authorities had knowingly connived at or procured an authorised deportation of the accused from a foreign country for some ulterior or wrongful purpose, there were no such grounds where those authorities had not procured, influenced or colluded in either the decision of the authorities in a foreign country to deport the accused to this country or to a third country via this country or in the arrangements for carrying out the decision, and there had been no illegality, abuse of power or violation of international law or of the domestic law of the foreign country concerned.

Where a vessel flying a foreign flag was boarded by officers of Customs and Excise outside British territorial waters and brought into British waters in mistaken reliance on one provision of an international convention, but where the same action would have been justified under another provision of the same convention, the failure to adopt the correct procedure, being a technical mistake made in good faith, there had been no abuse of process in pursuing a prosecution for an offence contrary to section 19(2) of the *Criminal Justice (International Co-operation) Act* 1990 (*post*, § 25–498): *R. v. Dean and Bolden* [1998] 2 Cr.App.R. 171, CA.

Evidential matters and the impossibility of a fair trial

In *R. v. Mid-Sussex JJ., ex p. Adams*, *The Independent*, February 17, 1992, DC, the fact that a letter covered by legal professional privilege had been passed inadvertently to the prosecutor by the clerk to the justices was held not to give rise to any abuse of process because, on the facts, the defendant had not been prejudiced. **4–65**

In *R. (Ebrahim) v. Feltham Magistrates' Court*; *Mouat v. DPP* [2001] 2 Cr.App.R. 23, DC, guidance was given as to the approach that should be followed when an application to stay proceedings as an abuse of process is founded on the non-availability of a video recording that would, allegedly, contain relevant material. The first issue in such cases is the nature and extent, in the particular circumstances of the case, of the duty, if any, of the investigating authority and/or of the prosecutor to obtain and/or retain the material in question. In this context, recourse should be had to the code of practice issued under section 25 of the *CPIA* 1996 (Appendix A–232 *et seq.*) and the Attorney General's guidelines on disclosure (Appendix A–243). If, in the circumstances, there was no duty to obtain and/or retain that material before the defence first sought its retention, then there can be no question of the subsequent trial being unfair on that ground.

If there has been a breach of the obligation to obtain or retain the relevant material it
4–64 will be necessary to decide whether the defence have shown, on a balance of probabilities, that owing to the absence of the relevant material the defendant would suffer serious prejudice to the extent that a fair trial could not take place (*i.e.* that continuance would amount to a misuse of the process of the court), and in ruling on that question the court should also bear in mind that the trial process itself is equipped to deal with the bulk of the complaints on which applications for a stay are founded. A stay should also be granted if the behaviour of the prosecution has been so bad that it is not fair that the defendant should be tried, and in this regard a useful test is that there should be either an element of bad faith or at least some serious fault. This guidance was given following a detailed review of the previous authorities on this topic.

The above principles were applied in *DPP v. S.*, 67 J.C.L. 87, DC ([2002] EWHC 2982 (Admin.)), where the police had failed to obtain a video recording from a supermarket, but where it was held that the magistrates had, on the particular facts, erred in staying proceedings on the basis that there could not be a fair trial. There was no suggestion that the recording would have shown anything of the commission of the alleged offences (attempted kidnapping and indecent assault of a teenage girl by trying to drag her into a van). At best, from the defence point of view, the recording might have shown the girl in the store with others earlier in the evening, which would have gone some way to confirming the defendant's case that he had spoken to the girl in the vicinity of the store as an explanation for her identification of him. The trial process was adequate to deal with the matters that were raised, it being commonplace that there are gaps in the prosecution case, which can be exploited by the defence. In the absence of bad faith or serious default on the part of the investigative and/or prosecuting authorities, and where the missing recording went only to a side issue, rather than to the heart of the case, there were no such exceptional circumstances as to justify the grant of a stay. See also *R. v. Sadler*, *ante*, § 4–55, and *R. v. Brooks* (2004) 148 S.J. 1031, CA (judge correct to refuse a stay where satisfied that a fair trial was possible notwithstanding eight-minute gap in prosecution video evidence).

Where the issue in a case of arson was the question of whether the fire (which had as its source the defendant's bed in a guest house) had been started deliberately or accidentally, the judge had been correct to refuse an application to stay the proceedings made on the basis of a failure to preserve the bed and bedding; although it was conceded that the photographs that were available were inadequate for the purpose of enabling an independent assessment of the cause of the fire, and a literal reading of the code of practice on the retention of material, made under the *CPIA* 1996 (Appendix A–231), might have been apt to impose a duty to retain the material, a measure of flexibility had to be allowed as to the practicalities of retaining a bulky burnt-out item; whilst the police could be criticised for not having taken more detailed photographs, there had been no bad faith and the failure had to be judged against the likelihood of a challenge as to the cause of the fire, the fact that no request for preservation had been made and the fact that the defence expert said no more than that preservation might have assisted on the issue, but without giving any specifics: *R. v. Parker* [2003] 3 *Archbold News* 1, CA.

4–65 In *R. v. Boyd* [2004] R.T.R. 2, CA, in respect of a charge of causing death by careless driving whilst unfit through drugs, it was held that where, following a fatal accident, a blood sample had been taken from the defendant, but (i) the sample was was not kept properly refrigerated after it had been examined by the prosecution, with the consequence that it was impossible for the defence to carry out their own analysis, (ii) the defence called expert evidence on a *voir dire* to the effect that the prosecution interpretation of their test of the sample was open to challenge, that what was revealed by the test was no more than a borderline positive, and that had the defence had the opportunity to carry out their own analysis it might have shown that the defendant had not been materially affected by the relevant drug, the judge should not only have excluded the prosecution evidence as to the blood sample (which he had done), but should have stayed the prosecution as an abuse of the process as the defence had been deprived of an opportunity to establish a defence that might have been open to them (considering *R. (Ebrahim) v. Feltham Magistrates' Court*; *Mouat v. DPP*, *ante*).

The trial process is the normal forum for the investigation of challenges to the prosecution case; where there is an allegation of gross misconduct on the part of someone connected to the prosecution and in connection with the subject matter of the trial (defendants arrested during attempt to rob post office van; substantial amount of money subsequently found to be missing from that van, but no suggestion that it had been taken by defendants), an abuse of process application should only succeed if the defence satisfy the judge that they have suffered prejudice as a result of a failure by the authorities properly to investigate the matter; as to whether it would be fair to try defendants in such circumstances, regardless of lack of prejudice, it is for the trial judge to balance the countervailing interests of prosecuting criminals charged with serious offences and discouraging abuse of power: *R. v. MacDonald* [1998] Crim.L.R. 808, CA.

In *Sofri v. Italy* [2004] Crim.L.R. 846, ECtHR, it was said that the destruction of evidence, for which the state authorities were responsible, did not of itself give rise to a violation of the right to a fair trial under Article 6 of the European Convention (*post*, § 16–57); it was necessary to establish that the loss of the evidence put the defendant at a disadvantage compared with the prosection.

No basis for the grant of a stay of a retrial was found to exist where, following the disagreement of the original jury, a document was disclosed to the defence which should have been disclosed prior to the original trial but which had not been disclosed at that time because it could not then be found: *R. v. Jackson* [1998] Crim.L.R. 835, CA (it had been argued that it was unfair to retry the defendant because the relevant document would have made an acquittal more likely at the original trial).

When fresh evidence becomes available between a trial and a retrial, it is appropriate for the prosecution to take it into account; and if, as a result, the case against the defendant is put on a different basis at the retrial, that is not an abuse of process: *R. v. Mercer* [2001] 4 *Archbold News* 1, CA.

In *R. v. Aujla* [1998] 2 Cr.App.R. 16, CA, it was held not to be an abuse of process to pursue a trial in which reliance was placed on evidence that had been obtained abroad, under judicial authority, by means of interception of a telephone conversation and which had not been excluded under section 78 of the *PACE Act* 1984. The court commented that there is no authority for the proposition that the principles of abuse of process may be used to exclude evidence.

As to the possibility of staying a trial as an abuse of process on the basis of the inadmissibility and/or insufficiency of the committal evidence, see *R. v. Bedwellty JJ. ex p. Williams* [1997] A.C. 225, HL, *ante*, § 1–212.

Delay and the right to trial "within a reasonable time"

Common law principles

On an application for a stay on the ground of delay, a court should bear in mind the following principles: (i) even where delay is unjustifiable, a permanent stay should be the exception rather than the rule; (ii) where there is no fault on the part of the complainant or the prosecution, it will be very rare for a stay to be granted; (iii) no stay should be granted in the absence of serious prejudice to the defence so that no fair trial can be held; and (iv) on the issue of possible serious prejudice, there is a power to regulate the admissibility of evidence and the trial process itself should ensure that all relevant factual issues arising from the delay will be placed before the jury for their consideration in accordance with appropriate directions. If, having considered all these factors, a judge's assessment is that a fair trial will be possible, a stay should not be granted: *R. v. S.*, 170 J.P. 434, CA, restating the principles set out in *Att.-Gen.'s Reference (No. 1 of 1990)* [1992] Q.B. 630, 95 Cr.App.R. 296, CA, in the light of subsequent authorities, and doubting whether they would today have been expressed in terms of a burden on the defendant to show on a balance of probabilities that no fair trial could be held (*ante*, § 4–51). **4–66**

Impact of Article 6 of the European Convention on Human Rights

Article 6 of the ECHR (*post*, § 16–57) entitles a person charged with a criminal offence to a "fair and public hearing within a reasonable time by an independent and impartial tribunal". The right to a determination within a reasonable time is a separate **4–67** guarantee, to be distinguished from the right to a fair trial and not to be seen as part of the overriding right to a fair trial: *Porter v. Magill*; *Weeks v. Magill* [2002] 2 A.C. 357, HL. However, it does not follow that the appropriate remedy for a breach of the right to a trial within a reasonable time is necessarily for the proceedings to be stayed. Such a breach should result in a stay of the proceedings only if (i) a fair trial is no longer possible, or (ii) it would for some other compelling reason be unfair to try the defendant; cases where it might be unfair to try a defendant would include cases of bad faith, executive manipulation and abuse of process, and also cases where the delay was of such an order, or where the prosecutor's breach was such, as to make it unfair that the proceedings should continue, but such cases will be exceptional and a stay will never be an appropriate remedy if any lesser remedy will adequately vindicate the defendant's Convention right. The appropriate remedy will depend on the nature of the breach and all the circumstances including, particularly, the stage at which the breach is established; if established before the hearing, the appropriate remedy might be a public acknowledgement of the breach, action to expedite the hearing to the greatest extent practicable, and, perhaps, if the defendant is in custody, release on bail; neither the prosecutor nor the court will act incompatibly with the defendant's right under Article 6, within section 6(1) of the *Human Rights Act* 1998 (*post*, § 16–21), by continuing with the prosecution, since the breach consists in the delay that has accrued, and not in the prospective hearing: *Att-Gen.'s Reference (No. 2 of 2001)* [2004] 2 A.C. 72, HL, reviewing, *inter alia*, *Darmalingum v. The State* [2000] 2 Cr.App.R. 445, PC; *Flowers v. R.* [2000] 1 W.L.R. 2396, PC; *Dyer v. Watson*; *K. v. H.M. Advocate* [2004] 1 A.C. 379, PC; and *Mills v. H.M. Advocate* [2004] 1 A.C. 441, PC (unreasonable delay in hearing appeal against conviction could be recognised perfectly well by some reduction in sentence); and followed, in relation to Scotland, in *Spiers (Procurator Fiscal) v. Ruddy* [2008] 2 W.L.R. 608, PC (departing from *H.M. Advocate v. R.* [2004] 1 A.C. 462, PC, in the light of subsequent decisions of the European Court of Human Rights).

Thus, the requirements for a stay of the proceedings due to delay are similar whether the court is being asked to consider common law principles or Article 6. For the circumstances in which there will have been a breach of Article 6, see *post*, § 16–73.

Application of principles

4–67a In *R. v. Derby Crown Court, ex p. Brooks*, 80 Cr.App.R. 164, DC it was held that the delay which had occurred had not prejudiced the defendant in the preparation or conduct of his defence because he had always admitted his guilt and would, the court thought, inevitably plead guilty at his trial. The hardship which the defendant had suffered by reason of the delay could and should form part of an effective plea in mitigation of sentence. The older cases of *R. v. Oxford City JJ., ex p. Smith*, 75 Cr.App.R. 200, DC (delay caused by inefficiency on the part of the prosecution), and *R. v. Watford JJ., ex p. Outrim* [1983] R.T.R. 26, DC (where there was a clear inference that something had gone wrong with the process serving system) were explained as cases where the defendant had been or might be prejudiced in preparing and presenting his defence by reason of the delay. See also *R. v. Bow Street Magistrates' Court, ex p. Van der Holst*, 83 Cr.App.R. 114, DC; *R. v. Bow Street Metropolitan Stipendiary Magistrate, ex p. DPP*, 95 Cr.App.R. 9, DC; *R. v. Liverpool Deputy Stipendiary Magistrate, ex p. Devereux* [1991] C.O.D. 236, DC; and *R. v. Chief Constable of Devon and Cornwall, ex p. Hay*; *R. v. Chief Constable of Devon and Cornwall, ex p. Police Complaints Authority* [1996] 2 All E.R. 711 (Sedley J.), for situations where delay was held not to be such as to amount to an abuse of process.

Delay resulting from failure to comply with the rules as to advance information in the magistrates' court can amount to an abuse of process but only in exceptional cases and within the general principles already explained: *King v. Kucharz* [1989] C.O.D. 469, DC, *post*, § 12–128. See also *R. v. Willesden JJ., ex p. Clemmings*, 87 Cr.App.R. 280, DC. However a stay should not be ordered simply as a form of disciplinary disapproval of the CPS: *R. v. Crown Court at Norwich, ex p. Belsham*, 94 Cr.App.R. 382, DC.

In some cases, even a long delay will not justify a stay of the proceedings. In *R.*

v. Central Criminal Court, ex p. Randle and Pottle, 92 Cr.App.R. 323, DC, a delay of 20 years in bringing a prosecution was, on the exceptional facts, held not to amount to an abuse of process. Similarly, in *R. v. Sawoniuk* [2000] 2 Cr.App.R. 220, CA, where the case turned on the eye-witness evidence of two witnesses whose evidence was subject to cross-examination, and the jury had been afforded a view of the *locus in quo*, it was held that a fair trial had not been impossible, despite a delay of 56 years. The trial judge had highlighted the difficulties resulting from the lapse in time and directed the jury in that regard. The European Court of Human Rights subsequently found no violation of Article 6 in relation to this case: see *Sawoniuk v. U.K.* [2001] Crim.L.R. 918. However, in certain circumstances, there may come a time when delay is so great that, even having regard to the public interest in convicting the guilty, a continuance of the proceedings will be unacceptable and an abuse; such circumstances existed where the prosecution sought to proceed on a charge of murder nine years after the event, where the defendant had been in custody throughout and had already been tried twice, the first trial resulting in a conviction that was quashed on appeal and the second resulting in a failure of the jury to agree: *Charles v. The State* [2000] 1 W.L.R. 384, PC. *Cf. R. v. Henworth* [2001] 2 Cr.App.R. 4, CA (retrial not an abuse; whilst the overall length of the proceedings was found to have violated the reasonable time requirement in Article 6 of the ECHR in *Henworth v. U.K.* (2005) 40 E.H.R.R. 33, there was no criticism of the decision of the Court of Appeal), *Bowe v. R.* [2001] 6 *Archbold News* 3, PC, and *R. v. Byrne* [2002] 2 Cr.App.R. 21, CA, *ante*, § 4–45.

The particular need for expedition in prosecuting proceedings against juveniles may justify a court in coming to different conclusions in relation to applications for a stay made by co-defendents where there is nothing to distinguish their cases save that one is a juvenile and the other an adult: *R. (Knight) v. West Dorset Magistrates' Court*, 166 J.P. 705, QBD.

Where the prosecution allege that the delay has been caused by the defendant's own conduct, which itself is an issue in the trial (*e.g.* where the prosecution allege that the defendant has contributed to the delay by committing further offences to conceal his principal offence thereby delaying its discovery), the correct approach is for the judge to bear in mind the nature of the prosecution case as part of the factual background against which the alleged delay has to be considered and not as necessarily being a bar to the success of the application for a stay. However, it would not be proper for a trial to proceed merely to establish whether the defendant's criminal conduct had contributed to the delay, since unless and until his guilt or innocence were to be established at trial it would not be known whether he was responsible for any delay, while at the same time he would be deprived of the protection of not having to stand trial when to do so would amount to an abuse of process: *Att.-Gen. of Hong Kong v. Wai-bun* [1994] 1 A.C. 1, PC. See also *R. v. Wilkinson* [1996] 1 Cr.App.R. 81, CA, *post*, § 4–71a.

Where substantial delay has occurred which can be attributed in part to, for example, inefficiency on the part of the prosecution and in part to the conduct of the defendant, the court must consider to what extent the delay is attributable to prosecution inefficiency. If the delay, so attributable, is substantial and if the court considers that the defendant has been or must have been prejudiced thereby, so that the continuance of the prosecution can be regarded as an abuse of process, the jurisdiction may be exercised in the defendant's favour: *R. v. West London Magistrate, ex p. Anderson*, 80 Cr.App.R. 143, DC.

As to the need for a judge, in a case which is allowed to proceed despite substantial delay, to exercise careful scrutiny to see whether the case is safe to be left to the jury, and, if it is, to give careful directions as to any difficulties that such delay may have occasioned to the defence, see *post*, §§ 4–300a and 4–71a, respectively.

Delay in complex fraud cases

It may be more difficult to show that a fair trial would not be possible in a case wholly dependent on contemporary documents than in a case that is wholly dependent upon a late complaint and oral testimony; although it may be inferred from a **4–68** long delay that a fair trial would not be possible, such an inference may not be readily drawn where the prosecution is wholly dependent on available documents: *R. v. Telford JJ., ex p. Badhan* [1991] 2 Q.B. 78, 93 Cr.App.R. 171, DC. See also *Att.-Gen.'s Reference (No. 1 of 1990)* [1992] Q.B. 630, 95 Cr.App.R. 296, CA, *ante*, § 4–66 (delay due merely to the complexity of the case should never be the foundation of a stay), and *R. v. Buzalek and Schiffer* [1991] Crim.L.R. 115, CA (a distinction must be drawn between cases which turn largely on documentation and those which do not). *Cf. R. v. Cohen, The Independent*, July 29, 1992, CA, where the topic of abuse of process is discussed in the context of a trial which had become unmanageable by reason of various factors, including its length and complexity.

However, in a case in which 8,000 documents which had been sought by the defence for about a year and had still not been disclosed as unused material a few days before the day on which the trial, which had already been adjourned twice, was due to start, the judge, who considered that they fell to be disclosed, had been entitled to take the view that it was not possible for the defendant to have a fair trial without an adjournment, but that a further adjournment was inappropriate, and, accordingly, that the proper course was to stay the proceedings: *R. v. Olivier*, unreported, September 27, 2007, CA ([2007] EWCA Crim. 3483).

Delay by victim in reporting offence

4–69 The test to be applied in such cases is not whether the delay is justified (which would be directly relevant to the issue for the jury as to the credibility of the witness) but whether a fair trial is possible; see, *e.g.*, *R. v. J.A.K.* [1992] Crim.L.R. 30, Crown Court, in which Ognall J. decided that a fair trial would not be possible in circumstances that included the fact that any exploration by the defence, in front of the jury, of the reasons for the delay in the making of the complaint would probably have exposed the fact that the defendant had also faced charges of committing sexual offences against his daughter, albeit he had been tried and acquitted of those charges.

4–70 The Court of Appeal indicated in *R. v. Smolinski* [2004] 2 Cr.App.R. 40, that normally an application for a stay based on the delay should not be made at the outset of the trial, since unless the case is exceptional any such application will fail and will have taken up time unnecessarily; it would be preferable for such an application to be made after the evidence of the complainant(s), particularly if there is a danger of inconsistencies between witnesses, and for the judge then to scrutinise the evidence with particular care and come to a conclusion whether or not it is safe for the matter to be left to the jury. Such an application made at the outset was held to have been rightly rejected by the judge in *R. v. B.* [2003] 2 Cr.App.R. 13, where the Court of Appeal nevertheless quashed a conviction in a case where there had been a delay of approximately 30 years in the making of complaints of various alleged sexual offences. The court took this course on the basis of the importance of ensuring that an injustice was not done to the defendant who had been in an "impossible position to defend himself" by reason of the delay, which meant that he had no material to "put to the complainant to suggest that she had said something had happened on one occasion which could be established to be incorrect", nor any "material in the form of notes that were given to ... doctors which showed she had changed her account". As to this, see also *post*, § 7–48.

4–71 For a rare example of the Court of Appeal saying that a prosecution should have been stayed on the ground of delay, see *R. v. Jenkins* [1998] Crim.L.R. 411. Apart from the long delay (at least 28 years) before the first of two complainants (sisters) purported to remember the incidents, the court had regard to evidence of contamination of the second sister, inconsistencies in their evidence, their extreme youth at the time of the alleged offences (five- or six-years-old), the lack of any adequate explanation of the delay, and, in particular, the fact that it was not a case where the accused had shared a home with the complainants.

As to the significance of vagueness as to essential details concerning time and place in respect of allegations of sexual offences, in the context of the right to a fair trial under the ECHR, see *Mattocia v. Italy* (2003) 36 E.H.R.R. 47, ECtHR, *ante*, § 1–132d.

Directing the jury

Although the Court of Appeal has rarely ruled that a particular prosecution should have been stayed on account of delay, it has been readier to quash a conviction as unsafe by virtue of the judge's failure to direct the jury adequately in relation to the effect of the delay. In *R. v. H. (Henry)* [1998] 2 Cr.App.R. 161, the court reviewed and summarised the previous authorities on the topic. The court concluded that whilst a summing up is to be tailored to the facts and issues arising in the particular case, it would be unusual for a conviction to be held to be safe where there had been no direction on the difficulties faced by the defence in consequence of delay in making allegations of sexual offences and bringing the case to trial; but such a direction is not an invariable requirement except where some significant difficulty or aspect of prejudice is aired or otherwise becomes apparent to the judge during the trial; in some cases, the requirement of even-handedness as between prosecution and defence might itself demand such a direction. **4–71a**

In *R. v. Percival*, *The Times*, July 20, 1998, where there had been a delay of at least 28 years between the alleged offences and the making of the complaints, the Court of Appeal said that it was not the case that a judge was bound to stay the proceedings; but such delay must threaten the fairness of any trial (especially where the prosecution depends on late complaint and oral testimony). Before a conviction could appear safe, the court would have to be satisfied that the judge had confronted the jury with the fact of delay, and its potential impact on the formulation and conduct of the defence and on the prosecution's discharge of the burden of proof; whilst there is a place in the summing up for a reminder as to the potential unfairness to complainants in being censorious about failures to recall minutiae, it was inappropriate to do this by way of something to be balanced against the potential prejudice to the appellant; nor is it appropriate for the judge simply to recite the submissions of counsel (on both sides) on delay; there must be a clear expression from the judge (*qua* judge) on the issue of delay; it was incumbent on him to make clear that the only way of ensuring a fair trial and countering the potential prejudice to the defendant was by a conscientious concern for the burden and standard of proof. Nevertheless, each case must be considered on its own facts and there may be cases where there has been a long delay, but a warning of the sort recommended in *R. v. Percival* is not necessary: *R. v. M. (Brian)* [2000] 1 Cr.App.R. 49, CA; *R. v. W. (Graham)* [1999] 2 Cr.App.R. 201, CA; and *R. v. J.K.* [1999] Crim.L.R. 740, CA. For guidance on how to sum up the evidence where there are a number of counts relating to different events and a number of witnesses, see *R. v. R.* [2007] Crim.L.R. 478, CA, *post*, § 4–368.

Refusal to issue summons on ground of delay

See *R. v. Clerk to the Medway JJ., ex p. Department of Health and Social Security* [1986] Crim.L.R. 686, DC, where the refusal of a clerk to the justices to issue a summons although the information was laid in time (on the last permissible day), was upheld. The clerk had made extensive inquiries of the prosecutor as to the reason for the delay in laying the information and had received no response. The court said that generally it was preferable for issues of delay to be considered in open court by the justices. See also *R. v. Highbury Corner Magistrates' Court, ex p. Health and Safety Executive* [1991] C.O.D. 156, DC. **4–72**

Adverse publicity

Another basis upon which a stay may be ordered is that there has been such publicity in relation to the matter that a fair trial is not possible. In *R. v. Reade*, unreported, CCC, October 15, 1993, Garland J. stayed a prosecution for this reason. His Lordship commented that the phrase "abuse of process" was something of a misnomer in circumstances where no blame could be attached to the prosecution. **4–72a**

The issue was considered in the context of the right to a fair trial by an "independent and impartial tribunal" as guaranteed by Article 6 of the ECHR (*post*, § 16–57) by the Privy Council in *Montgomery v. H.M. Advocate*; *Coulter v. H.M. Advocate* [2003] 1 A.C. 641. It was said that the principal safeguards of the objective impartiality of a jury lie in the trial process itself and the conduct of the trial by the judge; first, there is the discipline of listening to and thinking about the evidence, which might be expected to have a far greater impact on their minds than such residual recollections as might exist about reports about the case in the media; secondly, that impact might be expected to be reinforced by such warnings and directions as the judge might think it appropriate to give; the system of trial by jury was based upon the assumption that the jury would follow the instructions which they received from the judge; and such considerations had to be borne in mind in applying the appropriate test where it was contended that a fair trial was impossible on account of adverse pre-trial publicity. The test was whether the risk of prejudice was so grave that whatever measures were adopted, the trial process could not reasonably be expected to remove it; but if that test was satisfied, there was no question of a balancing exercise.

Montgomery was considered in *R. v. Abu Hamza* [2007] 1 Cr.App.R. 27, in which the Court of Appeal held that the fact that adverse publicity may have risked prejudicing a fair trial is no reason for not proceeding with the trial if the judge concludes that, with his assistance, it will be possible to have a fair trial. In considering that question, it was right for the judge to have regard to his own experience and that of his fellow judges (as set out in *Montgomery*, *ante*, and *R. v. B.* [2007] H.R.L.R. 1, CA, *post*, § 28–83) as to the manner in which juries normally perform their duties.

For cases in which the Court of Appeal has considered the effect of adverse publicity, see *post*, § 7–84.

Miscellaneous situations

4–73 In *R. v. Munro*, 97 Cr.App.R. 183, the Court of Appeal said that there is a power to order a stay of proceedings, which exists in order to enable the court to regulate the efficient and fair disposal of criminal cases and that the ambit thereof is limited only by the purpose for which it exists. This is a power that is occasionally used where a defendant is too ill to be tried (or for his trial to continue): the prosecution must have been unwilling to offer no evidence under section 17 of the *CJA* 1967 (*post*, § 4–127), or the defendant may have been too ill to attend court to be arraigned (a pre-requisite to an order under that section) and the defence may have been unwilling to seek a *nolle prosequi*, or the Attorney-General may have refused their request.

Where a stay is sought on the ground of the youthfulness or limited intellectual capacity of the defendant, the court should consider whether it could adapt its procedures so as to allow the defendant to participate effectively; but a court has a continuing jurisdiction to grant a stay, and if it became apparent during the course of the hearing that the defendant was incapable of effective participation, a stay could be granted at that point: *R. (T.P.) v. West London Youth Court* [2006] 1 Cr.App.R. 25, DC (observing that a youth court was a specialist court designed and adapted for hearing cases where young people were charged with criminal offences). Only exceptionally should the jurisdiction to stay proceedings on such a ground be exercised before any evidence is heard in the trial; if medical evidence is adduced in support of the application, it should almost always be set in the context of other evidence relating to the child, such as what the child is said to have done, how the child reacted when arrested and how he behaved and what he said when interviewed, and his responses to direct exchanges designed to ensure that he understands each stage of the process: *DPP v. P.* [2008] 1 W.L.R. 1005, DC. It is the court's opinion of the child's level of understanding which must determine whether a criminal trial proceeds: *ibid*. If the court decides that it should halt a trial on the ground that the child cannot take an effective part in the proceedings, it should then consider whether to switch to a consideration of whether the child had done the acts alleged (under the *Criminal Procedure (Insanity) Act* 1964, s.4A (*post*, § 4–168), or, in summary proceedings, following the procedure in *R. (P.) v. Barking Youth Court* (*post*, § 4–167)): *ibid*.

(e) *Appeal and review*

4–74 A decision made in a magistrates' court may be challenged in the High Court by either side, using the case stated or judicial review procedure as may be appropriate in the particular circumstances. On an application for judicial review, the Divisional Court would expect to see a note of the lower court's reasons before deciding whether to grant permission for the application to proceed, and, if any oral evidence was given, an agreed note should be prepared, summarising its effect: *R. (Ebrahim) v. Feltham Magistrates' Court*; *Mouat v. DPP* [2001] 2 Cr.App.R. 23, DC. The matter may also be re-considered in the Crown Court on any appeal to that court after the conclusion of any summary proceedings before the justices. Where it is raised in the Crown Court, it is inappropriate to seek a stay in that court: what should be sought is an order quashing the conviction on the ground that the original trial was unfair and the unfairness was of such a nature that it cannot be remedied on appeal: *ibid*.

Where examining magistrates reject an application to stay proceedings an order can be obtained from the Divisional Court in judicial review proceedings prohibiting the justices from further proceeding with the committal proceedings: *R. v. Telford JJ., ex p. Badhan* [1991] 2 Q.B. 78, 93 Cr.App.R. 171, DC.

If the magistrates have already committed the defendant to the Crown Court for trial, that committal can be quashed in judicial review proceedings if the justices should have acceded to the abuse of process argument, but in the ordinary way, particularly if an indictment has been signed, such a situation should be dealt with by way of an application to the Crown Court. In the exercise of its discretion, the High Court may, exceptionally, deal with a matter by way of judicial review in such circumstances, if it can be decided on undisputed facts, together with any other facts that the court feels bound to accept as true: *R. v. Croydon JJ., ex p. Dean*, 98 Cr.App.R. 76, DC.

Where justices refuse an application to stay committal proceedings on the ground of delay, the High Court will only intervene if the decision was one which no bench properly directing itself could have reached; justices having been discouraged from staying proceedings as an abuse and enjoined only to do so in exceptional circumstances, it would be difficult to overrule their decision as a wrong exercise of their discretion; the refusal of relief was without prejudice to any application to be made to the Crown Court where the matter would be considered *de novo*: *R. v. Barry Magistrates' Court, ex p. Malpas* [1998] C.O.D. 90, DC. The mere existence of facts or considerations which might have led the tribunal to exercise its discretion in a different way does not begin to satisfy the test for intervention: *R. v. Liverpool City JJ. and the CPS, ex p. Price*, 162 J.P. 766, DC.

An order of the Crown Court that the whole or part of an indictment should be **4–75** stayed as an abuse of process is a decision "relating to trial on indictment" within section 29(3) of the *Supreme Court [Senior Courts] Act* 1981 (as to the renaming of which, see *ante*, § 4–1) (*post*, § 7–4) and is therefore not amenable to judicial review: *Re Ashton* [1994] 1 A.C. 9, HL. *Quaere* whether, in respect of cases committed, transferred or sent for trial on or after April 4, 2005, an appeal against a stay will lie under section 58 of *CJA* 2003 (*post*, §§ 7–244).

Where there is an unsuccessful application for a stay, and there is a conviction, the grounds for requesting the stay may be relied upon on appeal in alleging that the conviction is unsafe (see s.2(1)(a) of the *CAA* 1968, *post*, § 7–43): *Att.-Gen.'s Reference (No. 1 of 1990)* [1992] Q.B. 630, 95 Cr.App.R. 296, CA. As to the consequences, on such an appeal, of a conclusion that the application for a stay was wrongly refused, see *post*, § 7–46a.

L. ACCESS TO THE JUDGE

(1) General

A first principle of criminal law is that justice is done in public, for all to see and hear. **4–76** On the other hand, there must be freedom of access between counsel and judge when there are matters to be communicated or discussed of such a nature that counsel cannot in the interests of his client mention them in open court. A list of the situations where an approach to the judge is permissible would mislead. Such communications must never take place unless there is no alternative. There are various risks involved. The need to solve an immediate practical problem might combine with the more relaxed atmosphere of the private room to blur the formal outlines of the trial. If the object of the discussion is to maintain a degree of confidence, there is room for misunderstanding as to how far such confidence should extend. There is a risk that counsel (or solicitors) for the other party might hear something said to the judge that they would rather not hear, putting them in a state of conflict between duty to their own clients and the obligation of confidentiality relating to the private room. The absence of the defendant means he has to learn second-hand what the judge said; and that he cannot hear (or correct if necessary) what is said by counsel on his behalf: *R. v. Harper-Taylor* [1991] R.T.R. 76, CA (and reiterated "for the attention of courts up and down the country" in *R. v. Pitman* [1991] 1 All E.R. 468 at 470–471, CA). As to the need for freedom of access between an advocate and the judge in connection with sentence, see also paragraph IV.45.3 of the consolidated criminal practice direction, *post*, § 4–79.

4–77 There can be no bar on defence counsel revealing to his instructing solicitors and client what has taken place in his presence but their absence, since otherwise his relationship with his client would be wholly undermined: *R. v. Davis, Johnson and Rowe*, 97 Cr.App.R. 110, CA, endorsed in *R. v. Preston* [1994] 2 A.C. 130 at 171, HL.

For the procedure to be adopted in respect of *ex parte* applications by the prosecution for non-disclosure of sensitive material, see rule 25 of the *Criminal Procedure Rules* 2005 (S.I. 2005 No. 384), *post*, § 12–78.

(2) Pleas and sentence

4–78 A five-judge Court of Appeal in *R. v. Goodyear* [2005] 2 Cr.App.R. 20, *post*, § 5–79b, saw no clash between the principle that the defendant's plea must always be made voluntarily and free from any improper pressure, and a process by which a defendant personally may instruct his counsel to seek an indication from the judge of his current view of the maximum sentence which would be imposed on the defendant in the event of a guilty plea. Guidelines were laid down for indications from the judge as to sentence, relaxing (within a detailed framework) the practice in *R. v. Turner (F.R.)* [1970] 2 Q.B. 321, 54 Cr.App.R. 352 which was reflected in the *Practice Direction (Criminal Proceedings: Consolidation)* [2002] 1 W.L.R. 2870, para. IV.45.4.

The hearing should normally take place in open court, and in the defendant's presence, with notice to the prosecution, in cases of any complexity or difficulty, that a sentence indication will be sought; any reference to the request for a sentence indication would be inadmissible in any subsequent trial.

4–79 Whilst a request for an advance indication of sentence, pursuant to *Goodyear*, will take place in open court, paragraph IV.45.3 of *Practice Direction (Criminal Proceedings: Consolidation)* (*ante*) recognises that freedom of access between an advocate and the judge was important because there may be matters calling for communication or discussion of such a nature that the advocate cannot, in his client's interest, mention them in open court, *e.g.* the advocate, by way of mitigation, may wish to tell the judge that the accused has not long to live because he is suffering from an illness of which he is and should remain ignorant. The practice direction underlines that any such discussion in private should take place with the advocates for both sides present, and that if counsel is instructed by a solicitor who is in court, he too should be allowed to attend.

[The next paragraph is § 4–82.]

(3) Record of discussions

4–82 It is highly desirable for the shorthand writer to be present in the judge's room for any meetings with counsel, as much for counsel's protection as for protection of the judge: see *R. v. Smith (T. C.)*, 90 Cr.App.R. 413, CA (discussions on sentence should never take place in the absence of a shorthand writer or recording device); *R. v. Johnson and Lorraine*, 12 Cr.App.R.(S.) 219; and *R. v. Cullen*, 81 Cr.App.R. 17, CA (judge should ensure someone present takes a note); and paragraph IV.45.5 of *Practice Direction (Criminal Procedings: Consolidation)* (*ante*).

M. VIEW OF LOCUS IN QUO

4–83 The judge may permit the jury to view the *locus in quo* at any time during the trial

(*R. v. Whalley* (1847) 2 C. & K. 376), but he should take precautions not to allow improper communications being made to them at the view: *R. v. Martin* (1872) L.R. 1 C.C.R. 388. The judge must be present at any view, even where no witnesses are present, to control the proceedings and ensure that the correct procedure is followed: *R. v. Hunter*, 81 Cr.App.R. 40, CA.

A view is part of a criminal trial and, in the absence of exceptional circumstances, the presence of the accused at a view is as necessary as at any other part of his trial. His presence is important because he might be able to point out some matter of which his legal advisers were unaware or about which others on the view were mistaken: *R. v. Ely JJ., ex p. Burgess* [1992] Crim.L.R. 888, DC.

No view of the *locus in quo* or inspection of any object referred to in the evidence, but not exhibited, may take place after the retirement of the jury: see *post*, §§ 4–417 *et seq*.

It is no objection to a witness attending and taking part in a view that he has already given evidence at the trial. So long as the witnesses taking part are recalled to be cross-examined, if desired, the defendant will not be prejudiced in any way. It is, however, essential that every effort should be made to see that witnesses make no communication to the jury except to give a demonstration. If the defendant has declined to attend the view and has been allowed by the judge to be absent, he cannot afterwards raise the objection that his absence constituted a ground for questioning the conviction, though he could object if any evidence were given outside the scope of the view as ordered: *Karamat v. R.* [1956] A.C. 256, PC. **4–84**

For one juror to attend a view and then "report back" to the other jurors constitutes a contravention of the principle that the jury should remain together at all times when evidence is being received: *R. v. Gurney* [1976] Crim.L.R. 567, CA; and see *R. v. Smythe*, *The Times*, September 16, 1998, CA (visit of juror to scene of crime during summing up was irregularity, but in particular circumstances had not rendered conviction unsafe).

See also the *Juries Act* 1974, s.14, *post*, § 4–264.

As to the practice to be followed by justices who intend to visit the scene of an alleged offence, see *Parry v. Boyle*, 83 Cr.App.R. 310, DC.

N. PRE-TRIAL HEARINGS

(1) The court's case management powers and duties

The court's duty of active case management, both pre-trial and throughout the trial itself, emphasised by the Court of Appeal in *R. v. Jisl and Tekin*, *The Times*, April 19, 2004, has been codified in the *Criminal Procedure Rules* 2005 (S.I. 2005 No. 384). **4–84a**

In *R. v. K. (Note)* [2006] 2 All E.R. 552, CA, it was said that a judge's case management powers entitle him to deal with issues preliminary to a trial exclusively by way of written submissions, the length of which he may limit; to achieve the public element necessary in any hearing, those written submissions should be supplied to representatives of the media.

In *R. (Robinson) v. Sutton Coldfield Magistrates' Court* [2006] 2 Cr.App.R. 13, DC, it was said that compliance with the requirement in rule 1.1(2)(e) of the 2005 rules (*post*) that a case should be dealt with "efficiently and expeditiously", as an aspect of the overriding objective in rule 1.1(1) that criminal cases be dealt with "justly", depends upon adherence to timetables set out in the rules; where, however, a rule contains a discretion to shorten a time-limit or to extend it even after it has expired (*e.g.* r.35.8 (*post*, § 13–118)), the exercise of that discretion requires that the court should take into account all relevant considerations (including the furtherance of the overriding objective), and the exercise of the discretion is not to be fettered by a rule that it should only be exercised in exceptional circumstances; but any application for an extension (in this case of the time for service of a bad character notice) should be closely scrutinised and the party seeking it cannot expect indulgence unless he clearly sets out his reasons for the application.

The requirement in rule 1.1(2)(e) that all criminal cases be dealt with "efficiently and expeditiously" applies to criminal appeals, including those by way of reference by the

Criminal Cases Review Commission: *R. v. Siddall and Brooke*, *The Times*, July 26, 2006, CA.

Notwithstanding the terms of rules 3.5(1) and 3.10 (*post*, §§ 4–84d, 4–84e), an unconditional order for the disclosure of the names, addresses and dates of birth of potential defence witnesses infringes litigation privilege and legal professional privilege; and the authority under which the rules were made conferred no power to override such a fundamental right: *R. (Kelly) v. Warley Magistrates' Court* [2008] 1 Cr.App.R. 14, DC. Whilst the distinction is a fine one, an order imposing procedural sanctions if advanced disclosure of such matters is not made would not infringe either privilege; but an absolute bar on calling the witnesses concerned would not be such a procedural sanction: *ibid*. It appears that the amendment of rule 3.5 in 2008, by the addition of paragraph (6), was intended to cater for what was said in this judgment about the imposition of procedural sanctions for non-compliance with a direction such as the one under challenge in this case.

Criminal Procedure Rules 2005 (S.I. 2005 No. 384), Pt 1

THE OVERRIDING OBJECTIVE

The overriding objective

4–84b **1.1.**—(1) The overriding objective of this new code is that criminal cases be dealt with justly.

(2) Dealing with a criminal case justly includes—

(a) acquitting the innocent and convicting the guilty;

(b) dealing with the prosecution and the defence fairly;

(c) recognising the rights of a defendant, particularly those under Article 6 of the European Convention on Human Rights;

(d) respecting the interests of witnesses, victims and jurors and keeping them informed of the progress of the case;

(e) dealing with the case efficiently and expeditiously;

(f) ensuring that appropriate information is available to the court when bail and sentence are considered; and

(g) dealing with the case in ways that take into account—

(i) the gravity of the offence alleged,

(ii) the complexity of what is in issue,

(iii) the severity of the consequences for the defendant and others affected, and

(iv) the needs of other cases.

As to the overriding objective, see *ante*, § 4–84a.

The duty of the participants in a criminal case

1.2.—(1) Each participant, in the conduct of each case, must—

(a) prepare and conduct the case in accordance with the overriding objective;

(b) comply with these Rules, practice directions and directions made by the court; and

(c) at once inform the court and all parties of any significant failure (whether or not that participant is responsible for that failure) to take any procedural step required by these Rules, any practice direction or any direction of the court. A failure is significant if it might hinder the court in furthering the overriding objective.

(2) Anyone involved in any way with a criminal case is a participant in its conduct for the purposes of this rule.

The application by the court of the overriding objective

1.3. The court must further the overriding objective in particular when—

(a) exercising any power given to it by legislation (including these Rules);

(b) applying any practice direction; or

(c) interpreting any rule or practice direction.

Criminal Procedure Rules 2005 (S.I. 2005 No. 384), Pt 3

CASE MANAGEMENT

The scope of this Part

4–84c **3.1.** This Part applies to the management of each case in a magistrates' court and in the Crown Court (including an appeal to the Crown Court) until the conclusion of that case.

The duty of the court

3.2.—(1) The court must further the overriding objective by actively managing the case.

(2) Active case management includes—

(a) the early identification of the real issues;

(b) the early identification of the needs of witnesses;

(c) achieving certainty as to what must be done, by whom, and when, in particular by the early setting of a timetable for the progress of the case;

(d) monitoring the progress of the case and compliance with directions;

(e) ensuring that evidence, whether disputed or not, is presented in the shortest and clearest way;

(f) discouraging delay, dealing with as many aspects of the case as possible on the same occasion, and avoiding unnecessary hearings;

(g) encouraging the participants to co-operate in the progression of the case; and

(h) making use of technology.

(3) The court must actively manage the case by giving any direction appropriate to the needs of that case as early as possible.

The duty of the parties

3.3. Each party must—

(a) actively assist the court in fulfilling its duty under rule 3.2, without or if necessary with a direction; and

(b) apply for a direction if needed to further the overriding objective.

Case progression officers and their duties

3.4.—(1) At the beginning of the case each party must, unless the court otherwise directs—

(a) nominate an individual responsible for progressing that case; and

(b) tell other parties and the court who he is and how to contact him.

(2) In fulfilling its duty under rule 3.2, the court must where appropriate—

(a) nominate a court officer responsible for progressing the case; and

(b) make sure the parties know who he is and how to contact him.

(3) In this Part a person nominated under this rule is called a case progression officer.

(4) A case progression officer must—

(a) monitor compliance with directions;

(b) make sure that the court is kept informed of events that may affect the progress of that case;

(c) make sure that he can be contacted promptly about the case during ordinary business hours;

(d) act promptly and reasonably in response to communications about the case; and

(e) if he will be unavailable, appoint a substitute to fulfil his duties and inform the other case progression officers.

The court's case management powers

3.5.—(1) In fulfilling its duty under rule 3.2 the court may give any direction and take any step actively to manage a case unless that direction or step would be inconsistent with legislation, including these Rules. **4–84d**

(2) In particular, the court may—

(a) nominate a judge, magistrate, justices' clerk or assistant to a justices' clerk to manage the case;

(b) give a direction on its own initiative or on application by a party;

(c) ask or allow a party to propose a direction;

(d) for the purpose of giving directions, receive applications and representations by letter, by telephone or by any other means of electronic communication, and conduct a hearing by such means;

(e) give a direction without a hearing;

(f) fix, postpone, bring forward, extend or cancel a hearing;

(g) shorten or extend (even after it has expired) a time limit fixed by a direction;

(h) require that issues in the case should be determined separately, and decide in what order they will be determined; and

(i) specify the consequences of failing to comply with a direction.

(3) A magistrates' court may give a direction that will apply in the Crown Court if the case is to continue there.

(4) The Crown Court may give a direction that will apply in a magistrates' court if the case is to continue there.

(5) Any power to give a direction under this Part includes a power to vary or revoke that direction.

(6) If a party fails to comply with a rule or a direction, the court may—

(a) fix, postpone, bring forward, extend, cancel or adjourn a hearing;
(b) exercise its powers to make a costs order; and
(c) impose such other sanction as may be appropriate.

[This rule is printed as amended by the *Criminal Procedure (Amendment No. 3) Rules* 2007 (S.I. 2007 No. 3662), r.7.]

Application to vary a direction

3.6.—(1) A party may apply to vary a direction if—

(a) the court gave it without a hearing;
(b) the court gave it at a hearing in his absence; or
(c) circumstances have changed.

(2) A party who applies to vary a direction must—

(a) apply as soon as practicable after he becomes aware of the grounds for doing so; and
(b) give as much notice to the other parties as the nature and urgency of his application permits.

Agreement to vary a time limit fixed by a direction

3.7.—(1) The parties may agree to vary a time limit fixed by a direction, but only if—

(a) the variation will not—
 (i) affect the date of any hearing that has been fixed, or
 (ii) significantly affect the progress of the case in any other way;
(b) the court has not prohibited variation by agreement; and
(c) the court's case progression officer is promptly informed.

(2) The court's case progression officer must refer the agreement to the court if he doubts the condition in paragraph (1)(a) is satisfied.

Case preparation and progression

4–84e **3.8.**—(1) At every hearing, if a case cannot be concluded there and then the court must give directions so that it can be concluded at the next hearing or as soon as possible after that.

(2) At every hearing the court must, where relevant—

(a) if the defendant is absent, decide whether to proceed nonetheless;
(b) take the defendant's plea (unless already done) or if no plea can be taken then find out whether the defendant is likely to plead guilty or not guilty;
(c) set, follow or revise a timetable for the progress of the case, which may include a timetable for any hearing including the trial or (in the Crown Court) the appeal;
(d) in giving directions, ensure continuity in relation to the court and to the parties' representatives where that is appropriate and practicable; and
(e) where a direction has not been complied with, find out why, identify who was responsible, and take appropriate action.

(3) In order to prepare for a trial in the Crown Court, the court must conduct a plea and case management hearing unless the circumstances make that unnecessary.

[This rule is printed as amended by S.I. 2007 No. 3662 (*ante*, § 4–84d), r.9.]

Readiness for trial or appeal

3.9.—(1) This rule applies to a party's preparation for trial or (in the Crown Court) appeal, and in this rule and rule 3.10 trial includes any hearing at which evidence will be introduced.

(2) In fulfilling his duty under rule 3.3, each party must—

(a) comply with directions given by the court;
(b) take every reasonable step to make sure his witnesses will attend when they are needed;
(c) make appropriate arrangements to present any written or other material; and
(d) promptly inform the court and the other parties of anything that may—
 (i) affect the date or duration of the trial or appeal, or
 (ii) significantly affect the progress of the case in any other way.

(3) The court may require a party to give a certificate of readiness.

Conduct of a trial or an appeal

3.10. In order to manage a trial or (in the Crown Court) an appeal—

(a) the court must establish, with the active assistance of the parties, what disputed issues they intend to explore; and

(b) the court may require a party to identify—

(i) which witnesses that party wants to give oral evidence,

(ii) the order in which that party wants those witnesses to give their evidence,

(iii) whether that party requires an order compelling the attendance of a witness,

(iv) what arrangements are desirable to facilitate the giving of evidence by a witness,

(v) what arrangements are desirable to facilitate the participation of any other person, including the defendant,

(vi) what written evidence that party intends to introduce,

(vii) what other material, if any, that person intends to make available to the court in the presentation of the case,

(viii) whether that party intends to raise any point of law that could affect the conduct of the trial or appeal, and

(ix) what timetable that party proposes and expects to follow.

[This rule is printed as substituted by S.I. 2007 No. 3662 (*ante*, § 4–84d), r.10.]

Case management forms and records

3.11.—(1) The case management forms set out in the Practice Direction must be used, and where there is no form then no specific formality is required.

(2) The court must make available to the parties a record of directions given.

For the Practice Direction, see *post*, § 4–84g; for the case management forms, see Appendix D.

As to rules 3.5 and 3.10, see *R. (Kelly) v. Warley Magistrates' Court*, *ante*, § 4–84a.

The *Criminal Procedure Rules* 2005 are supplemented, in respect of heavy fraud and other complex criminal cases, by guidance set out in a protocol issued by Lord Woolf C.J. on March 22, 2005 (see Appendix N).

Pre-trial hearings fall into four categories: preliminary hearings in respect of cases sent to the Crown Court under the *CDA* 1998, s.51, where the magistrates' court considered that such a hearing was necessary and directed that there be one (see the *Criminal Procedure Rules* 2005, r.12.2, *ante*, § 1–36); plea and case management hearings, which are obligatory in all cases (*post*, §§ 4–84g *et seq.*); preparatory hearings under either the *CJA* 1987 for serious or complex fraud cases or Part III of the *CPIA* 1996 for cases of such complexity or of such a length, or, where they came within Crown Court's jurisdiction on or after April 4, 2005, of such seriousness, that substantial benefits are likely to accrue from such a hearing (*post*, §§ 4–84m *et seq.*); and statutory pre-trial hearings under Part IV of the 1996 Act applicable to any trial on indictment (*post*, §§ 4–90 *et seq.*). **4–84f**

(2) Plea and case management hearings

Practice Direction (Criminal Proceedings: Consolidation), para. IV.41 (as substituted by Practice Direction (Criminal Proceedings: Further Directions) [2007] 1 W.L.R. 1790)

Management of cases to be heard in the Crown Court

IV.41.1 This section of the practice direction supplements the rules in Part 3 of the *Criminal Procedure Rules* 2005 as they apply to the management of cases to be heard in the Crown Court. Where time limits or other directions in the consolidated criminal practice direction appear inconsistent with this section, the directions in this section take precedence. **4–84g**

IV.41.2 The case details form set out in Annex E should be completed by the Crown Court case progression officer in all cases to be tried on indictment.

Cases sent for trial

IV.41.3 A preliminary hearing ("PH") is not required in every case sent for trial under section 51 of the *Crime and Disorder Act* 1998: see rule 12.2 .... A PH should normally only be ordered by the magistrates' court or by the Crown Court where:

(i) there are case management issues which call for such a hearing;

(ii) the case is likely to last for more than four weeks;

(iii) it would be desirable to set an early trial date;

(iv) the defendant is a child or young person;

(v) there is likely to be a guilty plea and the defendant could be sentenced at the preliminary hearing; or

(vi) it seems to the court that it is a case suitable for a preparatory hearing in the Crown Court (see sections 7 and 9 of the *Criminal Justice Act* 1987 and sections 29 to 32 of the *Criminal Procedure and Investigations Act* 1996).

A PH, if there is one, should be held about 14 days after sending.

IV.41.4 The case progression form to be used in the magistrates' court and the PH form to be used in the Crown Court are set out in Annex E with guidance notes. The forms provide a detailed timetable to enable the subsequent plea and case management hearing ("PCMH") to be effective.

IV.41.5 Where the magistrates' court does not order a PH it should order a PCMH to be held within about 14 weeks after sending for trial where a defendant is in custody and within about 17 weeks after sending for trial where a defendant is on bail. Those periods accommodate the periods fixed by the relevant rules for the service of the prosecution case papers and for making all potential preparatory applications. Where the parties realistically expect to have completed their preparation for the PCMH in less time than that then the magistrates' court should order it to be held earlier. But it will not normally be appropriate to order that the PCMH be held on a date before the expiry of at least four weeks from the date on which the prosecutor expects to serve the prosecution case papers, to allow the defence a proper opportunity to consider them. To order that a PCMH be held before the parties have had a reasonable opportunity to complete their preparation in accordance with the *Criminal Procedure Rules* risks compromising the effectiveness of this most important pre-trial hearing and risks wasting their time and that of the court.

Cases committed for trial

IV.41.6 For cases committed to the Crown Court for trial under section 6 of the *Magistrates' Courts Act* 1980 the case progression form to be used in the magistrates' court is set out in Annex E with guidance notes. A PCMH should be ordered by the magistrates' court in every case, to be held within about seven weeks after committal. That period accommodates the periods fixed by the relevant rules for making all potential preparatory applications. Where the parties realistically expect to have completed their preparation for the PCMH in less time than that then the magistrates' court should order it to be held earlier. However, to order that a PCMH be held before the parties have had a reasonable opportunity to complete their preparation in accordance with the *Criminal Procedure Rules* risks compromising the effectiveness of this most important pre-trial hearing and risks wasting their time and that of the court.

Cases transferred for trial

IV.41.7 In a case transferred to the Crown Court for trial under section 4(1) of the *Criminal Justice Act* 1987 or under section 53(1) of the *Criminal Justice Act* 1991 the directions contained in the case progression form used in cases for committal for trial apply as if the case had been committed on the date of the notice of transfer. A PCMH should be listed by the Crown Court to be held within about seven weeks after transfer. That period accommodates the periods fixed by the relevant rules for making all potential preparatory applications. Where the parties realistically expect [*as last two sentences of para. IV.41.6*].

Plea and case management hearing

4–84h **IV.41.8** Active case management at the PCMH is essential to reduce the number of ineffective and cracked trials and delays during the trial to resolve legal issues. The effectiveness of a PCMH hearing in a contested case depends in large measure upon preparation by all concerned and upon the presence of the trial advocate or an advocate who is able to make decisions and give the court the assistance which the trial advocate could be expected to give. Resident judges in setting the listing policy should ensure that list officers fix cases as far as possible to enable the trial advocate to conduct the PCMH and the trial.

IV.41.9 In Class 1 and Class 2 cases, and in all cases involving a serious sexual offence against a child, the PCMH must be conducted by a High Court judge; by a circuit judge or by a recorder to whom the case has been assigned in accordance with section IV.33 (allocation of business within the Crown Court); or by a judge authorised by the presiding judges to conduct such hearings. In the event of a guilty plea before such an authorised judge, the case will be adjourned for sentencing by a High Court judge or by a circuit judge or recorder to whom the case has been assigned.

Use of the PCMH form

IV.41.10 The PCMH form as set out in Annex E must be used in accordance with the guidance notes. **4–84i**

Further pre-trial hearings after the PCMH

IV.41.11 Additional pre-trial hearings should be held only if needed for some compelling reason. Such hearings—often described informally as "mentions"—are expensive and should actively be discouraged. Where necessary the power to give, vary or revoke a direction without a hearing should be used. Rule 3.9(3) of the *Criminal Procedure Rules* enables the court to require the parties' case progression officers to inform the Crown Court case progression officer that the case is ready for trial, that it will proceed as a trial on the date fixed and will take no more or less time than that previously ordered. **4–84j**

The case progression form and the PCMH form are copied at Appendix D. For rule 12.2 (of the *Criminal Procedure Rules* 2005), see *ante*, § 1–36. As to particular obligations in Welsh language cases, see *ante*, § 4–40. **4–84k**

As to the use of a live television link at a pre-trial hearing where the defendant is in custody, see the *CDA* 1998, s.57, *ante*, § 3–200.

In addition to the many matters listed on the PCMH form for consideration at the hearing, that hearing was envisaged by the Court of Appeal as the normal time for any indication as to sentence to be sought: see *R. v. Goodyear* (*ante*, § 4–78).

The principle established in respect of the precursors to plea and case management hearings and the PCMH form, that what is said therein is not expected to form part of the material used at trial, and that it will rarely be appropriate to refer to it, would appear to apply equally to the new procedures (see *R. v. Diedrich and Aldridge* [1997] 1 Cr.App.R. 361, CA, in respect of a plea and directions questionnaire, and *R. v. Hutchinson*, 82 Cr.App.R. 51, CA, in respect of things said or done at a pre-trial review). **4–84l**

(3) Preparatory hearings

(a) *Serious or complex fraud cases*

Criminal Justice Act 1987, ss.7–10

Power to order preparatory hearing

7.—(1) Where it appears to a judge of the Crown Court that the evidence on an indictment reveals a case of fraud of such seriousness or complexity that substantial benefits are likely to accrue from a hearing (in this Act referred to as a "preparatory hearing") before the time when the jury are sworn, for the purpose of— **4–84m**

(a) identifying issues which are likely to be material to the determinations and findings which are likely to be required during the trial,

(b) if there is to be a jury, assisting their comprehension of those issues and expediting the proceedings before them,

(c) determining an application to which section 45 of the *Criminal Justice Act* 2003 applies,

(d) assisting the judge's management of the trial, or

(e) considering questions as to the severance or joinder of charges,

he may order that such a hearing shall be held.

(2) A judge may make an order under subsection (1) above on the application either of the prosecution or of the person indicted or, if the indictment charges a number of persons, any of them, or of his own motion.

(2A) The reference in subsection (1) above to the time when the jury are sworn includes the time when the jury would be sworn but for the making of an order under Part 7 of the *Criminal Justice Act* 2003.

(3)–(5) [*Repealed by* CPIA *1996, Sched. 3, para. 2.*]

[This section is printed as amended by the *CJPOA* 1994, Sched. 9, para. 30; and the *CJA* 2003, ss.45(4), 310(1) and 331, and Sched. 36, paras 52 and 53.]

Commencement of trial and arraignment

4–84n **8.**—(1) If a judge orders a preparatory hearing, the trial shall begin with that hearing.

(2) Arraignment shall accordingly take place at the start of the preparatory hearing.

The preparatory hearing

4–84o **9.**—(1) At the preparatory hearing the judge may exercise any of the powers specified in this section.

(2) The judge may adjourn a preparatory hearing from time to time.

(3) He may determine—

(a) [*repealed by* Criminal Justice Act *1988, s.170(2), (5) and Sched. 16*];

(aa) a question arising under section 6 of the *Criminal Justice Act* 1993 (relevance of external law to certain charges of conspiracy, attempt and incitement);

(b) any question as to the admissibility of evidence; and

(c) any other question of law relating to the case; and

(d) any question as to the severance or joinder of charges.

(4) He may order the prosecution—

(a) to supply the court and the defendant or, if there is more than one, each of them with a statement (a "case statement") of the following—

(i) the principal facts of the prosecution case;

(ii) the witnesses who will speak to those facts;

(iii) any exhibits relevant to those facts;

(iv) any proposition of law on which the prosecution proposes to rely; and

(v) the consequences in relation to any of the counts in the indictment that appear to the prosecution to flow from the matters stated in pursuance of sub-paragraphs (i) to (iv) above;

(b) to prepare their evidence and other explanatory material in such a form as appears to him to be likely to aid comprehension by a jury and to supply it in that form to the court and to the defendant or, if there is more than one, to each of them;

(c) to give the court and the defendant or, if there is more than one, each of them notice of documents the truth of the contents of which ought in the prosecution's view to be admitted and of any other matters which in their view ought to be agreed;

(d) to make any amendments of any case statement supplied in pursuance of an order under paragraph (a) above that appear to the court to be appropriate, having regard to objections made by the defendant or, if there is more than one, by any of them.

4–84p (5) Where—

(a) a judge has ordered the prosecution to supply a case statement; and

(b) the prosecution have complied with the order,

he may order the defendant or, if there is more than one, each of them—

(ii) to give the court and the prosecution notice of any objections that he has to the case statement;

(iv) to give the court and the prosecution a notice stating the extent to which he agrees with the prosecution as to documents and other matters to which a notice under subsection (4)(c) above relates and the reason for any disagreement.

(6) Criminal Procedure Rules may provide that except to the extent that disclosure is required—

(a) by section 5(7) of the *Criminal Procedure and Investigations Act* 1996 (alibi); or

(b) by such rules made by virtue of section 81 of the *Police and Criminal Evidence Act* 1984 (expert evidence),

a summary required by virtue of subsection (5) above need not disclose who will give evidence.

(7) A judge making an order under subsection (5) above shall warn the defendant or, if there is more than one, all of them of the possible consequence under section 10 below of not complying with it.

(8) If it appears to a judge that reasons given in pursuance of subsection (5)(iv) above are inadequate, he shall so inform the person giving them, and may require him to give further or better reasons.

(9) An order under this section may specify the time within which any specified requirement contained in it is to be complied with, but Criminal Procedure Rules may make provision as to the minimum or maximum time that may be specified for compliance.

(10) An order or ruling made under this section shall have effect during the trial, unless it appears to the judge, on application made to him during the trial, that the interests of justice require him to vary or discharge it.

(11) [*Interlocutory appeals: see* post, *§ 7–285*.]

(12) [*Subject to rules of court, jurisdiction under subs. (11) to be exercised by criminal division; and reference to Court of Appeal to be construed as reference to that division.*]

(13) The judge may continue a preparatory hearing notwithstanding that leave to appeal has been granted under subsection (11) above, but the preparatory hearing shall not be concluded until after the appeal has been determined or abandoned.

(14) On the termination of the hearing of an appeal, the Court of Appeal may confirm, reverse or vary the decision appealed against.

[This section is printed as amended and repealed in part by the *CJA* 1988, Sched. 16; the *CJA* 1993, s.6(8); the *CPIA* 1996, s.72, and Sched. 3, para. 3, and s.74(1) and (4); the *CJA* 2003, ss.310(2) and 331, and Sched. 36, paras 18, 52 and 54; and the *Courts Act 2003 (Consequential Amendments) Order* 2004 (S.I. 2004 No. 2035).]

Orders before preparatory hearing

9A.—(1) Subsection (2) below applies where— **4–84q**

(a) a judge orders a preparatory hearing, and

(b) he decides that any order which could be made under section 9(4) or (5) above at the hearing should be made before the hearing.

(2) In such a case—

(a) he may make any such order before the hearing (or at the hearing), and

(b) subsections (4) to (10) of section 9 above shall apply accordingly.

[This section was inserted by the *CPIA* 1996, s.72, and Sched. 3, para. 4.]

Later stages of trial

10.—(1) Any party may depart from the case he disclosed in pursuance of a requirement imposed under section 9 above. **4–84r**

(2) Where—

(a) a party departs from the case he disclosed in pursuance of a requirement imposed under section 9 above, or

(b) a party fails to comply with such a requirement,

the judge or, with the leave of the judge, any other party may make such comment as appears to the judge or the other party (as the case may be) to be appropriate and the jury or, in the case of a trial without a jury, the judge may draw such inference as appears proper.

(3) In doing anything under subsection (2) above or in deciding whether to do anything under it the judge shall have regard—

(a) to the extent of the departure or failure, and

(b) to whether there is any justification for it.

(4) Except as provided by this section, in the case of a trial with a jury no part—

(a) of a statement given under section 9(5) above, or

(b) of any other information relating to the case for the accused or, if there is more than one, the case for any of them, which was given in pursuance of a requirement imposed under section 9 above,

may be disclosed at a stage in the trial after the jury have been sworn without the consent of the accused concerned.

[This section was substituted by the *CPIA* 1996, s.72, and Sched. 3, para. 5. It is printed as amended by the *CJA* 2003, s.331, and Sched. 36, paras 52 and 55.]

(b) *Long, complex or serious cases*

Criminal Procedure and Investigations Act 1996, s.28

PART III

PREPARATORY HEARINGS

Introduction

Introduction

28.—(1) This Part applies in relation to an offence if— **4–84s**

(a) on or after the appointed day the accused is *committed for trial, or* sent for trial *under section 51 of the* Crime and Disorder Act *1998*, for the offence concerned,

(b) *proceedings for the trial on the charge concerned are transferred to the Crown Court on or after the appointed day,* or

(c) a bill of indictment relating to the offence is preferred on or after the appointed day under the authority of section 2(2)(b) of the *Administration of Justice (Miscellaneous Provisions) Act* 1933 (bill preferred by direction of Court of Appeal, or by direction or with consent of a judge).

(2) References in subsection (1) to the appointed day are to such day as is appointed for the purposes of this section by the Secretary of State by order.

(3) If an order under this section so provides, this Part applies only in relation to the Crown Court sitting at a place or places specified in the order.

(4) References in this Part to the prosecutor are to any person acting as prosecutor, whether an individual or a body.

[This section is printed as amended by the *CDA* 1998, s.119 and Sched. 8, para. 128. The words "committed for trial" and from "under" to "1998" in subs. (1)(a) and the whole of subs. (1)(b) are repealed by the *CJA* 2003, s.41, and Sched. 3, para. 66(1) and (6) (and see also s.332, and Sched. 37, Pt 4). The repeal in subs. (1)(a) came into effect on May 9, 2005, in relation to cases sent for trial under section 51 or 51A(3)(d) of the *CDA* 1998 (*Criminal Justice Act 2003 (Commencement No. 9) Order* 2005 (S.I. 2005 No. 1267)); otherwise, these repeals come into force on a day to be appointed.]

The appointed day for the purposes of this section was April 15, 1997: *CPIA 1996 (Appointed Day No. 4) Order* 1997 (S.I. 1997 No. 1019).

Criminal Procedure and Investigations Act 1996, ss.29–34

Preparatory hearings

Power to order preparatory hearing

4–84t **29.**—(1) Where it appears to a judge of the Crown Court that an indictment reveals a case of such complexity, a case of such seriousness or a case whose trial is likely to be of such length, that substantial benefits are likely to accrue from a hearing—

(a) before the time when the jury are sworn, and

(b) for any of the purposes mentioned in subsection (2),

he may order that such a hearing (in this Part referred to as a preparatory hearing) shall be held.

(1A) A judge of the Crown Court may also order that a preparatory hearing shall be held if an application to which section 45 of the *Criminal Justice Act* 2003 applies (application for trial without jury) is made.

(1B) An order that a preparatory hearing shall be held must be made by a judge of the Crown Court in every case which (whether or not it falls within subsection (1) or (1A)) is a case in which at least one of the offences charged by the indictment against at least one of the persons charged is a terrorism offence.

(1C) An order that a preparatory hearing shall be held must also be made by a judge of the Crown Court in every case which (whether or not it falls within subsection (1) or (1A)) is a case in which—

(a) at least one of the offences charged by the indictment against at least one of the persons charged is an offence carrying a maximum of at least 10 years' imprisonment; and

(b) it appears to the judge that evidence on the indictment reveals that conduct in respect of which that offence is charged had a terrorist connection.

(2) The purposes are those of—

(a) identifying issues which are likely to be material to the determinations and findings which are likely to be required during the trial,

(b) if there is to be a jury, assisting their comprehension of those issues and expediting the proceedings before them,

(c) determining an application to which section 45 of the *Criminal Justice Act* 2003 applies,

(d) assisting the judge's management of the trial,

(e) considering questions as to the severance or joinder of charges.

(3) In a case in which it appears to a judge of the Crown Court that evidence on an

indictment reveals a case of fraud of such seriousness or complexity as is mentioned in section 7 of the *Criminal Justice Act* 1987 (preparatory hearings in cases of serious or complex fraud)—

(a) the judge may make an order for a preparatory hearing under this section only if he is required to do so by subsection (1B) or (1C);

(b) before making an order in pursuance of either of those subsections, he must determine whether to make an order for a preparatory hearing under that section; and

(c) he is not required by either of those subsections to make an order for a preparatory hearing under this section if he determines that an order should be made for a preparatory hearing under that section;

and, in a case in which an order is made for a preparatory hearing under that section, requirements imposed by those subsections apply only if that order ceases to have effect.

(4) An order that a preparatory hearing shall be held may be made—

(a) on the application of the prosecutor,

(b) on the application of the accused or, if there is more than one, any of them, or

(c) of the judge's own motion.

(5) The reference in subsection (1)(a) to the time when the jury are sworn includes the time when the jury would be sworn but for the making of an order under Part 7 of the *Criminal Justice Act* 2003.

(6) In this section "terrorism offence" means—

(a) an offence under section 11 or 12 of the *Terrorism Act* 2000 (offences relating to proscribed organisations);

(b) an offence under any of sections 15 to 18 of that Act (offences relating to terrorist property);

(c) an offence under section 38B of that Act (failure to disclose information about acts of terrorism);

(d) an offence under section 54 of that Act (weapons training);

(e) an offence under any of sections 56 to 59 of that Act (directing terrorism, possessing things and collecting information for the purposes of terrorism and inciting terrorism outside the United Kingdom);

(f) an offence in respect of which there is jurisdiction by virtue of section 62 of that Act (extra-territorial jurisdiction in respect of certain offences committed outside the United Kingdom for the purposes of terrorism etc.);

(g) an offence under Part 1 of the *Terrorism Act* 2006 (miscellaneous terrorist related offences);

(h) conspiring or attempting to commit a terrorism offence;

(i) incitement to commit a terrorism offence.

(7) For the purposes of this section an offence carries a maximum of at least 10 years' imprisonment if—

(a) it is punishable, on conviction on indictment, with imprisonment; and

(b) the maximum term of imprisonment that may be imposed on conviction on indictment of that offence is 10 years or more or is imprisonment for life.

(8) For the purposes of this section conduct has a terrorist connection if it is or takes place in the course of an act of terrorism or is for the purposes of terrorism.

(9) In subsection (8) "terrorism" has the same meaning as in the *Terrorism Act* 2000 (see section 1 of that Act).

[This section is printed as amended by the *CJA* 2003, ss.45(6) and (7), 309, 310(4) and 331, and Sched. 36, paras 65 and 66; and the *Terrorism Act* 2006, s.16. In connection with the amendments made by sections 309 and 310 of the 2003 Act, see the saving provision in paragraph 3 of Schedule 2 to S.I. 2005 No. 950, *ante*, § 3–87b. The reference to the common law offence of incitement in subs. (6)(i) has effect as a reference to the offences under the *SCA* 2007, Pt 2: 2007 Act, s.63(1), and Sched. 6, para. 29.]

Start of trial and arraignment

30. If a judge orders a preparatory hearing— **4–84u**

(a) the trial shall start with that hearing, and

(b) arraignment shall take place at the start of that hearing, unless it has taken place before then.

The preparatory hearing

31.—(1) At the preparatory hearing the judge may exercise any of the powers specified in **4–84v**
this section.

(2) The judge may adjourn a preparatory hearing from time to time.

(3) He may make a ruling as to—

(a) any question as to the admissibility of evidence;

(b) any other question of law relating to the case;

(c) any question as to the severance or joinder of charges.

(4) He may order the prosecutor—

(a) to give the court and the accused or, if there is more than one, each of them a written statement (a case statement) of the matters falling within subsection (5);

(b) to prepare the prosecution evidence and any explanatory material in such a form as appears to the judge to be likely to aid comprehension by a jury and to give it in that form to the court and to the accused or, if there is more than one, to each of them;

(c) to give the court and the accused or, if there is more than one, each of them written notice of documents the truth of the contents of which ought in the prosecutor's view to be admitted and of any other matters which in his view ought to be agreed;

(d) to make any amendments of any case statement given in pursuance of an order under paragraph (a) that appear to the judge to be appropriate, having regard to objections made by the accused or, if there is more than one, by any of them.

(5) The matters referred to in subsection (4)(a) are—

(a) the principal facts of the case for the prosecution;

(b) the witnesses who will speak to those facts;

(c) any exhibits relevant to those facts;

(d) any proposition of law on which the prosecutor proposes to rely;

(e) the consequences in relation to any of the counts in the indictment that appear to the prosecutor to flow from the matters falling within paragraphs (a) to (d).

(6) Where a judge has ordered the prosecutor to give a case statement and the prosecutor has complied with the order, the judge may order the accused or, if there is more than one, each of them—

(b) to give the court and the prosecutor written notice of any objections that he has to the case statement; ...

(7) Where a judge has ordered the prosecutor to give notice under subsection (4)(c) and the prosecutor has complied with the order, the judge may order the accused or, if there is more than one, each of them to give the court and the prosecutor a written notice stating—

(a) the extent to which he agrees with the prosecutor as to documents and other matters to which the notice under subsection (4)(c) relates, and

(b) the reason for any disagreement.

(8) A judge making an order under subsection (6) or (7) shall warn the accused or, if there is more than one, each of them of the possible consequence under section 34 of not complying with it.

(9) If it appears to a judge that reasons given in pursuance of subsection (7) are inadequate, he shall so inform the person giving them and may require him to give further or better reasons.

(10) An order under this section may specify the time within which any specified requirement contained in it is to be complied with.

(11) An order or ruling made under this section shall have effect throughout the trial, unless it appears to the judge on application made to him that the interests of justice require him to vary or discharge it.

[This section is printed as amended and repealed in part by the *CJA* 2003, ss.310(5), 331 and 332, Sched. 36, paras 65 and 67, and Sched. 37, Pt 3. In connection with the amendment made by section 310 of the 2003 Act, see the saving provision in paragraph 3 of Schedule 2 to S.I. 2005 No. 950, *ante*, § 3–87b.]

Orders before preparatory hearing

4–84w **32.**—(1) This section applies where—

(a) a judge orders a preparatory hearing, and

(b) he decides that any order which could be made under section 31(4) to (7) at the hearing should be made before the hearing.

(2) In such a case—

(a) he may make any such order before the hearing (or at the hearing), and
(b) section 31(4) to (11) shall apply accordingly.

Criminal Procedure Rules

33.—(1) Criminal Procedure Rules may provide that except to the extent that disclosure is required— **4–84x**

(a) by rules under section 81 of the *Police and Criminal Evidence Act* 1984 (expert evidence), or
(b) by section 5(7) of this Act,

anything required to be given by an accused in pursuance of a requirement imposed under section 31 need not disclose who will give evidence.

(2) Criminal Procedure Rules may make provision as to the minimum or maximum time that may be specified under section 31(10).

[This section is printed as amended by the *Courts Act* 2003, s.109(1), and Sched. 8, para. 379.]

Later stages of trial

34. [*Identical to the substituted section 10 of the* CJA *1987 (as amended by the* CJA *2003, s.331, and Sched. 36, paras 52 and 55)* ante, *§ 4–84r, save that the references to* "section 9" *(subs. (1)),* "section 9 above" *(subs. (2)),* "section 9(5)" *(subs. (4)(a)) and* "section 9 above" *(subs. (4)(b)) are replaced by references to* "section 31", "section 31", "section 31(6)(a)" *and* "section 31" *respectively.*] **4–84y**

Criminal Procedure and Investigations Act 1996, ss.35, 36

Appeals to Court of Appeal

35.—(1) An appeal shall lie to the Court of Appeal from any ruling of a judge under section 31(3), from the refusal by a judge of an application to which section 45 of the *Criminal Justice Act* 2003 applies or from an order of a judge under section [43 or] 44 of that Act which is made on the determination of such an application, but only with the leave of the judge or of the Court of Appeal. **4–84z**

(2) The judge may continue a preparatory hearing notwithstanding that leave to appeal has been granted under subsection (1), but the preparatory hearing shall not be concluded until after the appeal has been determined or abandoned.

(3) On the termination of the hearing of an appeal, the Court of Appeal may confirm, reverse or vary the decision appealed against.

(4) [*Subject to rules of court, appeals to be heard by criminal division; and reference in this Part to Court of Appeal to be construed as reference to that division.*]

[This section is printed as amended by the *CJA* 2003, ss.45(9) and 331, and Sched. 36, paras 65 and 69; and as amended, as from a day to be appointed, by *ibid.*, s.45(9) (insertion of words in square brackets).]

Appeals to the House of Lords [Supreme Court]

36.—(1) [*Amends* Criminal Appeal Act *1968 ss.33 and 36.*] **4–84za**

(2) The judge may continue a preparatory hearing notwithstanding that leave to appeal has been granted under Part II of the *Criminal Appeal Act* 1968, but the preparatory hearing shall not be concluded until after the appeal has been determined or abandoned.

[This section is printed as amended by the *CJA* 2003, s.331, and Sched. 36, paras 65 and 70.]

(c) *Rules of court (all cases)*

Criminal Procedure Rules 2005 (S.I. 2005 No. 384), Pt 15 (as substituted by the Criminal Procedure (Amendment) Rules 2006 (S.I. 2006 No. 353))

PREPARATORY HEARINGS IN CASES OF SERIOUS FRAUD AND OTHER COMPLEX, SERIOUS OR LENGTHY CASES IN THE CROWN COURT

Application for a preparatory hearing

15.1.—(1) A party who wants the court to order a preparatory hearing under section 7(2) of the *Criminal Justice Act* 1987 or under section 29(4) of the *Criminal Procedure and Investigations Act* 1996 must— **4–85**

(a) apply in the form set out in the Practice Direction;
(b) include a short explanation of the reasons for applying; and
(c) serve the application on the court officer and all other parties.

(2) A prosecutor who wants the court to order that—
(a) the trial will be conducted without a jury under section 43 or section 44 of the *Criminal Justice Act* 2003; or
(b) the trial of some of the counts included in the indictment will be conducted without a jury under section 17 of the *Domestic Violence, Crime and Victims Act* 2004,

must apply under this rule for a preparatory hearing, whether or not the defendant has applied for one.

Time for applying for a preparatory hearing

15.2.—(1) A party who applies under rule 15.1 must do so not more than 28 days after—
(a) the committal of the defendant;
(b) the consent to the preferment of a bill of indictment in relation to the case;
(c) the service of a notice of transfer; or
(d) where a person is sent for trial, the service of copies of the documents containing the evidence on which the charge or charges are based.

(2) A prosecutor who applies under rule 15.1 because he wants the court to order a trial without a jury under section 44 of the *Criminal Justice Act* 2003 (jury tampering) must do so as soon as reasonably practicable where the reasons do not arise until after that time limit has expired.

(3) The court may extend the time limit, even after it has expired.

Representations concerning an application

4–85a **15.3.**—(1) A party who wants to make written representations concerning an application made under rule 15.1 must—
(a) do so within 7 days of receiving a copy of that application; and
(b) serve those representations on the court officer and all other parties.

A defendant who wants to oppose an application for an order that the trial will be conducted without a jury under section 43 or section 44 of the *Criminal Justice Act* 2003 must serve written representations under this rule, including a short explanation of the reasons for opposing that application.

Determination of an application

15.4.—(1) Where an application has been made under rule 15.1(2), the court must hold a preparatory hearing.

(2) Other applications made under rule 15.1 should normally be determined without a hearing.

(3) The court officer must serve on the parties in the case, in the form set out in the Practice Direction—
(a) notice of the determination of an application made under rule 15.1; and
(b) an order for a preparatory hearing made by the court of its own initiative, including one that the court is required to make.

Orders for disclosure by prosecution or defence

4–85b **15.5.**—(1) Any disclosure order under section 9 of the *Criminal Justice Act* 1987, or section 31 of the *Criminal Procedure and Investigations Act* 1996, must identify any documents that are required to be prepared and served by the prosecutor under that order.

(2) A disclosure order under either of those sections does not require a defendant to disclose who will give evidence, except to the extent that disclosure is required—
(a) by section 6A(2) of the 1996 Act (disclosure of alibi); or
(b) by Part 24 of these Rules (disclosure of expert evidence).

(3) The court officer must serve notice of the order, in the relevant form set out in the Practice Direction, on the parties.

[Pt 15 is printed as amended by the *Criminal Procedure (Amendment No. 2) Rules* 2006 (S.I. 2006 No. 2636), r.13; and the *Criminal Procedure (Amendment) Rules* 2007 (S.I. 2007 No. 699), r.38, and Sched. 4.]

The forms referred to in rules 15.1, 15.4 and 15.5 are to be found in *Practice Direction (Criminal Proceedings: Forms)* [2005] 1 W.L.R. 1479, with new forms having been substituted for making an application for a preparatory hearing or for an extension of time (rr.15.1(1) and 15.2(3)), and for making an order for a preparatory hearing (r.15.4(3)): *Practice Direction (Criminal Proceedings: Updated Forms)* [2006] 1 W.L.R. 1152; and *Consolidated Criminal Practice Direction (Amendment No. 14) (Forms for use in Criminal Proceedings)* [2007] 1 Cr.App.R. 22. As to the service of documents, see Part 4 of the 2005 rules (*ante*, §§ 2–207 *et seq.*). **4–85c**

(d) *Authorities (all cases)*

Preparatory hearing as the start of the trial

The trial begins with the preparatory hearing (*CJA* 1987, s.8, *ante*, § 4–84n; *CPIA* 1996, s.30, *ante*, § 4–84u). The judge presiding at a preparatory hearing must, save in exceptional circumstances, be the judge who is to conduct the trial. What amounts to exceptional circumstances will have to be resolved on a case by case basis. Clearly, death or illness of the judge would qualify as an exceptional circumstance; administrative convenience would not: *R. v. Southwark Crown Court, ex p. Customs and Excise Commrs*, 97 Cr.App.R. 266, DC. In *R. v. Lord Chancellor, ex p. Maxwell* [1997] 1 W.L.R. 104, DC, the court did not accept that exceptional circumstances were necessarily the test where an indictment had been severed. But if it were the test, the threshold would be lower in a severed trial where there had been no preparatory hearing relating to the severed counts, than in an unsevered trial where the preparatory hearing was focussed on that trial. In any event, the legal incapacity of the judge to continue to act as the trial judge for the remaining counts was capable of constituting exceptional circumstances. **4–85d**

In ordering a preparatory hearing, a judge should have particular regard to the purpose and effect of the custody time limit provisions in deciding on the date for the commencement of the hearing, which, as the start of the trial, brings to an end the operation of the custody time limit provisions: *Re Kanaris* [2003] 2 Cr.App.R. 1, HL. Whilst it was not appropriate to state as an inflexible rule that a judge should not start a preparatory hearing until he was certain that he was in a position to proceed expeditiously with the hearing, a judge who was minded to order such a hearing should be careful not to deprive a defendant in custody of the protection of the statutory time limit until it had become necessary to do so; to that end, a judge who orders a preparatory hearing should bear in mind the power to make orders in advance of the hearing (under section 9A of the 1987 Act and section 32(2) of the 1996 Act).

Separate preparatory hearings for separate defendants

In the case of an indictment that charges two or more defendants, it is open to the judge to order separate preparatory hearings in respect of separate defendants; whilst it would in most cases be appropriate for there to be a single preparatory hearing in respect of all defendants, this was not a legal requirement: *Re Kanaris*, *ante*. **4–85e**

The purpose and ambit of preparatory hearings

Each Act sets out criteria for its application (such complexity, seriousness, or, under the 1996 Act, likely trial length, that substantial benefits are likely to accrue from a preparatory hearing), the purposes for which a preparatory hearing may be held (in identical terms in section 7(1) of the 1987 Act, and section 29(2) of the 1996 Act) and, in almost identical terms in each Act, the powers which the judge may exercise (section 9 of the 1987 Act and section 31 of the 1996 Act). **4–85f**

The House of Lords considered the provisions of sections 7 and 9 of the 1987 Act afresh in *R. v. H.* [2007] 2 A.C. 270 (overruling many of the earlier authorities). The principles apply equally to the equivalent provisions of the 1996 Act. Their Lordships stated that:—

(i) the question for a judge considering whether to hold a preparatory hearing is, in practice, whether exercising any of the powers set out in section 9 at such a hearing, rather than at the trial when the jury have been sworn, is likely to result in substantial benefits; the mere fact that the reason why a question falling within section 9(3) has been raised is not in order to further one of the purposes for which a preparatory hearing can be held is irrelevant; what matters is whether, by deciding the question at a preparatory hearing rather than at a later stage, the judge is likely to achieve a substantial benefit in respect of one or more of those purposes (*per* Lord Rodger (at [52], [54]));

(ii) (by a majority) only the powers set out in section 9 can be exercised at a preparatory hearing; however, there is nothing to prevent a judge from exercising—in parallel with, though technically outside the ambit of, any such preparatory hearing—any other powers which he might, prior to the trial proper, have either at common law or under statute;

(iii) section 9 enables the judge to determine as part of the preparatory hearing, and to the extent that it involves the determination of "any question of law relating to the case" (s.9(3)(c), *ante*, § 4–84o), any other application, whether or not it might be aimed at precluding trial of the whole indictment or of any particular count, including therefore any challenge going to the validity of all or part of the proceedings or indictment (*per* Lord Mance (at [99]), overruling cases such as *R. v. Hedworth* [1997] 1 Cr.App.R. 421, CA); and

(iv) (unanimously) only orders or rulings made as part of the preparatory hearing and which fall within section 9(11) (*post*, § 7–285) are susceptible to interlocutory appeal.

Whether a ruling was made as part of a preparatory hearing thus depended on whether the court was exercising one of its powers under section 9, and not on whether the dominant purpose was the furtherance of one of the purposes set out in section 7 (overruling *R. v. Gunawardena*, 91 Cr.App.R. 55, CA, and cases which followed it); one example would be a ruling as to the admissibility of evidence under the *PACE Act* 1984, s.78, since the preparatory hearing would otherwise be unable to cover issues of a kind likely to occupy much time at trial in the absence of the jury (approving *R. v. Claydon* [2004] 1 Cr.App.R. 36, CA, on this point). The ruling in *R. v. H.* itself, on an application for disclosure under the *CPIA* 1996, s.8 (*post*, § 12–59), did not involve the determination of a question of law relating to the case, and so was outside the ambit of the preparatory hearing: the nature of the question being determined was what was important (in the instant case, consideration of factual issues and the application of the proper statutory test), not whether the process of determining it involved questions of law (as would any application to a judge, whether under statute or at common law) (*per* Lord Scott (at [41]), and *per* Lord Rodger (at [59])).

The jurisdiction to order a preparatory hearing cannot be conferred by agreement; for the purpose of making a decision, the judge should not confine his inquiry to the indictment alone; he is entitled to consider the evidence that is likely to be called: *Att.-Gen.'s Reference (No. 1 of 2004)*; *R. v. Edwards*; *R. v. Denton*; *R. v. Hendley*; *R. v. Crowley* [2004] 1 W.L.R. 2111, CA.

In *R. v. Ward* [2003] 2 Cr.App.R. 20, CA, it was said that a case involving allegations of making, possession and distribution of indecent photographs that was estimated to last up to five days was nothing out of the ordinary in terms of length; nor was it rendered "complex" for these purposes merely because there were novel issues as to how the photographs were to be shown to the jury and the defence wished to obtain preliminary rulings as to the effect of a genuine mistake on the part of the defendants as to the age of the children shown in the photographs. It was held that where a judge had mistakenly purported to conduct a preparatory hearing when he had had no jurisdiction to do so, the solution was to treat the hearing as a pre-trial hearing under Part IV of the Act (*post*, §§ 4–90 *et seq.*), from which there is no interlocutory right of appeal.

Where the criteria are met, the procedure can be highly beneficial; the marshalling of evidence can be done with direct reference to the live issues in the case; if there is an issue as to the proper interpretation of legislation or as to a direction to be given to a jury, it may be better to resolve the question sooner rather than later; such a hearing in a case under the *Official Secrets Act* 1989 was amply justified where the legal issues were complex and where the length of the trial largely depended on the rulings on the legal issues; but it is important to stress that the power at such a hearing to make rulings on questions of law is confined to questions of law "relating to the case" (see s.31(3)(b), *ante*, § 4–84v): *R. v. Shayler* [2003] 1 A.C. 247, HL (where the defendant's case had not raised any question of necessity or duress of circumstances and such issues therefore did not relate to the case, but where other issues of what defences were open to the defendant did relate to the case and could be ruled upon under section 31(3)(b)).

Orders made in the preparatory hearing

It is of prime importance that a case statement is served on the court and the defence at least seven days before the preparatory hearing: *Re Case Statements made under section 9 of the Criminal Justice Act 1987*, 97 Cr.App.R. 417, CA. **4–86**

It is also of first importance that any order made under section 9(5) of the 1987 Act (or equally section 31(6) of the 1996 Act) is clarity itself, spelling out, perhaps in the form of a schedule, specific short questions which identify the documents or the evidence upon which the prosecution seek agreement. Where there are a number of defendants, it is too onerous and wrong to expect each of them to wade through a case statement and endeavour to extract matters of evidence and documents relevant to him upon which he has to make up his mind as to whether he would agree them or otherwise provide some reasons for not agreeing. The appropriate course is for the judge to ensure that each defendant is the subject of a special order affecting him alone, which should contain, in itemised form, the precise description of the document or evidential matters upon which evidential agreement is expected to be reached: *Re Case Statements*, *ante*. The judge has no power to direct a defendant to serve a copy of his defence statement upon another defendant: *Re Tariq*, 92 Cr.App.R. 276, CA.

Judges are encouraged to use, *inter alia*, their powers under section 9 of the 1987 Act and section 31 of the 1996 Act to ensure that realistic defence statements are provided, in order to identify what is common ground and what are the real issues (see the protocol issued on March 22, 2005, Appendix N–13).

Status of prosecution and defence case statements

Neither the case statement nor the defence statement is a document of any evidential value. It does not limit the party whose document it is, in the evidence he calls; and it can only be used for comment subject to the restrictions set out in section 10 of the 1987 Act (s.34 of the 1996 Act), which apply equally to the prosecution statement as to the defence statement: *R. v. Mayhew*, unreported, November 18, 1991, CA, where Taylor L.J., in giving the judgment of the court, stated: **4–87**

> "(I)t would be undesirable for case statements to be put as a matter of course before juries as if they were projections of the indictment or particulars thereof. The object of ordering a case statement is to inform the opposing party of the case that it is intended to be put forward so as to facilitate preparation for trial and avoid surprise. If there is a significant departure, then subject to the judge's discretion under section 10, the jury may be apprised of it. But to provide the jury with pleadings and to raise pleadings arguments would tend to confusion and diversion from the factual issues."

A judge cannot forbid the prosecuting authority from re-interviewing witnesses or impose conditions under which witnesses can be re-interviewed after the defence statement has been served. Any evidence regarded by the trial judge as having an adverse effect on the fairness of the trial can instead be excluded under section 78 or 82(3) of the *PACE Act* 1984: *R. v. Nadir and Turner*, 98 Cr.App.R. 163, CA.

Interlocutory appeals

See *post*, §§ 7–284 *et seq*. **4–88**

Under section 35(3) of the 1996 Act (§ 4–84z, *ante*), the Court of Appeal may confirm, reverse or vary the decision appealed against; however, a decision so reversed or varied may be reinstated by the judge in the Crown Court, if the interests of justice so require, under section 31(11) (*ante*, § 4–84v): *R. v. M.* [2007] 3 All E.R. 53, CA (where the original decision of the Court of Appeal (to reverse the ruling of the Crown Court) had subsequently been held to have been made *per incuriam*).

(e) *Reporting restrictions*

Criminal Justice Act 1987, s.11

Restrictions on reporting

4–89 **11.**—(1) Except as provided by this section—

(a) no written report of proceedings falling within subsection (2) below shall be published in the United Kingdom;

(b) no report of proceedings falling within subsection (2) below shall be included in a relevant programme for reception in the United Kingdom.

(2) The following proceedings fall within this subsection—

(a) *an application under section 6(1) above;*

(b) a preparatory hearing;

(c) an application for leave to appeal in relation to such a hearing;

(d) an appeal in relation to such a hearing.

(3) *The judge dealing with an application under section 6(1) above may order that subsection (1) above shall not apply, or shall not apply to a specified extent, to a report of the application.*

(4) The judge dealing with a preparatory hearing may order that subsection (1) above shall not apply, or shall not apply to a specified extent, to a report of—

(a) the preparatory hearing, or

(b) an application to the judge for leave to appeal to the Court of Appeal under section 9(11) above in relation to the preparatory hearing.

(5) The Court of Appeal may order that subsection (1) above shall not apply, or shall not apply to a specified extent, to a report of—

(a) an appeal to the Court of Appeal under section 9(11) above in relation to a preparatory hearing,

(b) an application to that Court for leave to appeal to it under section 9(11) above in relation to a preparatory hearing, or

(c) an application to that Court for leave to appeal to the House of Lords under Part II of the *Criminal Appeal Act* 1968 in relation to a preparatory hearing.

(6) The *House of Lords* [Supreme Court] may order that subsection (1) above shall not apply, or shall not apply to a specified extent, to a report of—

(a) an appeal to *that House* [the Supreme Court] under Part II of the *Criminal Appeal Act* 1968 in relation to a preparatory hearing, or

(b) an application to *that House* [the Supreme Court] for leave to appeal to it under Part II of the *Criminal Appeal Act* 1968 in relation to a preparatory hearing.

(7) Where there is only one accused and he objects to the making of an order under subsection *(3)*, (4), (5) or (6) above the judge or the Court of Appeal or the House of Lords shall make the order if (and only if) satisfied after hearing the representations of the accused that it is in the interests of justice to do so; and if the order is made it shall not apply to the extent that a report deals with any such objection or representations.

(8) Where there are two or more accused and one or more of them objects to the making of an order under subsection *(3)*, (4), (5) or (6) above the judge or the Court of Appeal or the House of Lords shall make the order if (and only if) satisfied after hearing the representations of each of the accused that it is in the interests of justice to do so; and if the order is made it shall not apply to the extent that a report deals with any such objection or representations.

(9) *Subsection (1) above does not apply to—*

(a) *the publication of a report of an application under section 6(1) above, or*

(b) *the inclusion in a relevant programme of a report of an application under section 6(1) above,*

where the application is successful.

(10) *Where—*

(a) *two or more persons are jointly charged, and*

(b) *applications under section 6(1) above are made by more than one of them,*

subsection (9) above shall have effect as if for the words "the application is" there were substituted "all the applications are".

(11) Subsection (1) above does not apply to—

(a) *the publication of a report of an unsuccessful application made under section 6(1) above,*

(b) the publication of a report of a preparatory hearing,

(c) the publication of a report of an appeal in relation to a preparatory hearing or of an application for leave to appeal in relation to such a hearing,

(d) *the inclusion in a relevant programme of a report of an unsuccessful application made under section 6(1) above,*

(e) the inclusion in a relevant programme of a report of a preparatory hearing, or
(f) the inclusion in a relevant programme of a report of an appeal in relation to a preparatory hearing or of an application for leave to appeal in relation to such a hearing.

at the conclusion of the trial of the accused or of the last of the accused to be tried.

(12) Subsection (1) above does not apply to a report which contains only one or more of the following matters—

(a) the identity of the court and the name of the judge;
(b) the names, ages, home addresses and occupations of the accused and witnesses;
(c) any relevant business information;
(d) the offence or offences, or a summary of them, with which the accused is or are charged;
(e) the names of counsel and solicitors in the proceedings;
(f) where the proceedings are adjourned, the date and place to which they are adjourned;
(g) any arrangements as to bail;
(h) whether a right to representation funded by the Legal Services Commission as part of the Criminal Defence Service was granted to the accused or any of the accused.

(13) The addresses that may be published or included in a relevant programme under subsection (12) above are addresses—

(a) at any relevant time, and
(b) at the time of their publication or inclusion in a relevant programme;

and "relevant time" here means a time when events giving rise to the charges to which the proceedings relate occurred.

(14) The following is relevant business information for the purposes of subsection (12) above—

(a) any address used by the accused for carrying on a business on his own account;
(b) the name of any business which he was carrying on on his own account at any relevant time;
(c) the name of any firm in which he was a partner at any relevant time or by which he was engaged at any such time;
(d) the address of any such firm;
(e) the name of any company of which he was a director at any relevant time or by which he was otherwise engaged at any such time;
(f) the address of the registered or principal office of any such company; and
(g) any working address of the accused in his capacity as a person engaged by any such company;

and here "engaged" means engaged under a contract of service or a contract for services, and "relevant time" has the same meaning as in subsection (13) above.

(15) Nothing in this section affects any prohibition or restriction imposed by virtue of any other enactment on a publication or on matter included in a programme.

(16) In this section—

(a) "publish", in relation to a report, means publish the report, either by itself or as part of a newspaper or periodical, for distribution to the public;
(b) expressions cognate with "publish" shall be construed accordingly;
(c) "relevant programme" means a programme included in a programme service (within the meaning of the *Broadcasting Act* 1990).

[This section is printed as substituted by the *CPIA* 1996, Sched. 3, para. 8. It is printed as subsequently amended by the *Access to Justice Act* 1999, s.24 and Sched. 4, para. 40; and the *CJA* 2003, s.311(1) and (2); and as amended, as from a day to be appointed, by *ibid.*, ss.41 and 332, Sched. 3, para. 58(1) and (3), and Sched. 37, Pt 4 (omission of words in italics save for those in subs. (6)); and the *Constitutional Reform Act* 2005, s.40(4), and Sched. 9, para. 46 (omission of words in italics in subs. (6) and insertion of words in square brackets).]

Section 37 of the 1996 Act imposes restrictions on the reporting of preparatory hearings under that Act in identical terms, *mutatis mutandis*, save only that it does not include any equivalent to subss. (12)(c) or (14) (reporting of relevant business information).

4–89a A new section 11A was inserted into the 1987 Act by the 1996 Act, Sched. 3, para. 8. This creates a summary offence of publishing a report, or including one in a relevant programme, in breach of section 11; a parallel offence in respect of a breach of section 37 of the 1996 Act is created by section 38 thereof. In each case, no proceedings may be instituted for such an offence without the consent of the Attorney-General.

(4) Statutory pre-trial hearings

Introduction and general

4–90 Part IV of the *CPIA* 1996 (ss.39– 43) gives judges power to make binding rulings on points of law before the start of a trial (as to which, see s.39(3), *post*). The judge will be able to discharge or vary any such ruling if he considers it in the interests of justice to do so.

The pre-trial hearing provisions of the 1996 Act are concerned with the power to make binding rulings, not with the use that may be made subsequently of things said or done by or on behalf of a defendant at such hearings. It is therefore submitted that the position as to the use which may be made of such things should be the same as that in respect of non-statutory pre-trial hearings (as to which, see *ante*, § 4–84l).

A judge should not hear legal argument and then rule upon agreed facts before arraignment. Misunderstandings are less likely to arise and mistakes are more easily avoided if argument is taken after a plea of not guilty, a plea which reflects the true attitude of the accused to the indictment. If a ruling is later given, which in the view of the accused and his advisers is fatal to his defence, he can then change his plea. Taking such a course means that the judge is unlikely to usurp the function of the jury and there can be no difficulty about an appeal: *R. v. Vickers*, 61 Cr.App.R. 48, CA; *R. v. Marshall, Coombes and Eren* [1998] 2 Cr.App.R. 282, CA.

As to whether it is necessary to swear in a jury before a trial-within-a-trial, see *post*, § 4–93.

Where a judge is invited at such a hearing to make a ruling in law as to whether or not the facts support a particular charge, it is always desirable, if not essential, that the facts upon which such ruling is sought are committed to writing, so that on any subsequent appeal, the Court of Appeal will know the exact factual basis upon which the ruling was made: *R. v. Marshall, Coombes and Eren*, *ante*.

A pre-trial ruling made under section 40 (*post*) is not binding for the purposes of a retrial; further, a judge may discharge or vary such a ruling of his own motion if that appears to be in the interests of justice, pursuant to section 40(4)(b), even though the matter only comes to his attention on an application made by a party where there is no material change of circumstances, as required by section 40(5), to justify that application: *R. v. Clayton* [1998] 8 *Archbold News* 3, CA.

As to the use of live television links at pre-trial hearings when the defendant is in custody, see the *CDA* 1998, s.57, *ante*, § 3–200.

Where a judge purports to conduct a preparatory hearing under Part III of the 1996 Act (*ante*, §§ 4–84s *et seq.*) where there is no jurisdiction to do so, the hearing may take effect as a pre-trial hearing under Part IV: *R. v. Ward* [2003] 2 Cr.App.R. 20, CA.

Criminal Procedure and Investigations Act 1996, ss.39–42

PART IV

Meaning of pre-trial hearing

4–91 **39.**—(1) For the purposes of this Part a hearing is a pre-trial hearing if it relates to a trial on indictment and it takes place—

(a) after the accused has been *committed* [sent] for trial for the offence *concerned, after the accused has been sent for trial for the offence under section 51 of the* Crime and Disorder Act *1998, or after the proceedings for the trial have been transferred to the Crown Court,* and

(b) before the start of the trial.

(2) For the purposes of this Part a hearing is also a pre-trial hearing if—

(a) it relates to a trial on indictment to be held in pursuance of a bill of indictment preferred under the authority of section 2(2)(b) of the *Administration of Justice (Miscellaneous Provisions) Act* 1933 (bill preferred by direction of Court of Appeal, or by direction or with consent of a judge), and

(b) it takes place after the bill of indictment has been preferred and before the start of the trial.

(3) For the purposes of this section the start of a trial on indictment occurs at the time when a jury is sworn to consider the issue of guilt or fitness to plead or, if the court accepts a plea of guilty before the time when a jury is sworn, when that plea is accepted; but this is subject to section 8 of the *Criminal Justice Act* 1987 and section 30 of this Act (preparatory hearings).

(4) The references in subsection (3) to the time when a jury is sworn include the time when that jury would be sworn but for the making of an order under Part 7 of the *Criminal Justice Act* 2003.

[This section is printed as amended by the *CDA* 1998, s.119, and Sched. 8, para. 129; and the *CJA* 2003, s.331, and Sched. 36, paras 65 and 71. In subs. (1), the word in square brackets is inserted, and the italicised words are repealed, by the *CJA* 2003, s.41, and Sched. 3, para. 66(1) and (7). This amendment came into force on May 9, 2005, in relation to cases sent for trial under s.51 or s.51A(3)(d) of the *CDA* 1998: *Criminal Justice Act (Commencement No. 9) Order* 2005 (S.I. 2005 No. 1267). Otherwise it comes into force on a day to be appointed.]

Power to make rulings

40.—(1) A judge may make at a pre-trial hearing a ruling as to— **4–91a**

(a) any question as to the admissibility of evidence;

(b) any other question of law relating to the case concerned.

(2) A ruling may be made under this section—

(a) on an application by a party to the case, or

(b) of the judge's own motion.

(3) Subject to subsection (4), a ruling made under this section has binding effect from the time it is made until the case against the accused or, if there is more than one, against each of them is disposed of; and the case against an accused is disposed of if—

(a) he is acquitted or convicted, or

(b) the prosecutor decides not to proceed with the case against him.

(4) A judge may discharge or vary (or further vary) a ruling made under this section if it appears to him that it is in the interests of justice to do so; and a judge may act under this subsection—

(a) on an application by a party to the case, or

(b) of the judge's own motion.

(5) No application may be made under subsection (4)(a) unless there has been a material change of circumstances since the ruling was made or, if a previous application has been made, since the application (or last application) was made.

(6) The judge referred to in subsection (4) need not be the judge who made the ruling or, if it has been varied, the judge (or any of the judges) who varied it.

(7) For the purposes of this section the prosecutor is any person acting as prosecutor, whether an individual or a body.

Restrictions on reporting

41.—(1) [*Identical to* CJA *1987, s.11(1),* ante, *§ 4–89, apart from* "matters" *replacing* "proceedings".] **4–91b**

(2) The following matters fall within this subsection—

(a) a ruling made under section 40;

(b) proceedings on an application for a ruling to be made under section 40;

(c) an order that a ruling made under section 40 be discharged or varied or further varied;

(d) proceedings on an application for a ruling made under section 40 to be discharged or varied or further varied.

(3) The judge dealing with any matter falling within subsection (2) may order that subsection (1) shall not apply, or shall not apply to a specified extent, to a report of the matter.

(4) Where there is only one accused and he objects to the making of an order under

subsection (3) the judge shall make the order if (and only if) satisfied after hearing the representations of the accused that it is in the interests of justice to do so; and if the order is made it shall not apply to the extent that a report deals with any such objection or representations.

(5) Where there are two or more accused and one or more of them objects to the making of an order under subsection (3) the judge shall make the order if (and only if) satisfied after hearing the representations of each of the accused that it is in the interests of justice to do so; and if the order is made it shall not apply to the extent that a report deals with any such objection or representations.

(6) Subsection (1) does not apply to—

(a) the publication of a report of matters, or

(b) the inclusion in a relevant programme of a report of matters,

at the conclusion of the trial of the accused or of the last of the accused to be tried.

(7) [*Identical to* CJA *1987, s.11(15),* ante, *§ 4–89.*]

(8) [*Identical to* CJA *1987, s.11(16),* ante, *§ 4–89.*]

Offences in connection with reporting

4–91c **42.** [*Identical to s.38,* ante, *§ 4–89a, apart from appropriate references to section 41 replacing corresponding references to section 37.*]

O. PROSECUTION IN THE CROWN COURT TO BE CONDUCTED BY COUNSEL

4–92 See Halsbury's *Laws of England*, 4th ed., Vol. 3, para. 1160; *R. v. Morgan* (1852) 6 Cox 107; and *R. v. George Maxwell (Developments) Ltd*, 71 Cr.App.R. 83, Crown Court (H.H.J. David Q.C.). However, see now the *Courts and Legal Services Act* 1990, and *ante*, §§ 1–256 *et seq.* and §§ 2–22 *et seq.*

P. WHEN DOES THE TRIAL BEGIN?

4–93 In *Ex p. Guardian Newspapers* [1999] 1 Cr.App.R. 284, CA, it was said to be well settled that a trial does not start on arraignment, unless there is a statutory provision creating this effect; it starts when a jury is sworn and the defendant is put into the charge of the jury (*R. v. Tonner*, 80 Cr.App.R. 170, CA—considering a statutory provision that did not apply to a trial which "began" before the commencement date), and that the entering of a plea of "not guilty" does not mark the commencement of a trial, but merely establishes the need for a trial (*Quazi v. DPP*, 152 J.P. 414, DC); but *cf. R. v. Hammersmith Juvenile Court, ex p. O.*, 86 Cr.App.R. 343, DC, *ante*, § 1–75w. *Tonner* was referred to, with apparent approval, in *R. v. Jones (Anthony)* [2003] 1 A.C. 1 (at [5]), HL.

If a judge orders a preparatory hearing under section 7 of the *CJA* 1987 (or section 29 of the *CPIA* 1996), the trial "shall begin with that hearing": *CJA* 1987, s.8(1) (*ante*, § 4–84n); 1996 Act, s.30 (*ante*, § 4–84u). *Cf.* section 39(3) of the 1996 Act (*ante*, § 4–91).

As to when a trial on indictment starts for the purposes of custody time limits, see section 22(11A) of the *Prosecution of Offences Act* 1985, *ante*, § 1–268.

Q. THE ROLE OF PROSECUTING ADVOCATE

4–94 In 1986 the chairman of the Bar appointed a committee under Mr Justice Farquharson to consider and report on the duties and obligations of counsel when conducting a prosecution. The full text of the committee's report was set out in the 1995 edition of this work. In particular, the committee set out guidelines in respect of the relationship between prosecuting counsel and the Crown Prosecution Service and the relationship and respective responsibilities of prosecuting advocate and judge. A revised version of those guidelines has now been promulgated by the Attorney-General and Director of Public Prosecutions, with effect from February 11, 2002. In a foreword to the revised guidelines (which are set out at Appendix E–15 *et seq.*), Lord Woolf C.J. welcomes and commends them and points out that although they are not legally binding unless expressly approved by the Court of Appeal they, nonetheless, provide important practical guidance for practitioners involved in the prosecution process. The revised guidelines are stated to be subject to the *Code of Conduct* of the Bar, and to the Law Society's *Guide to the Professional Conduct of Solicitors*. They also require adherence to the

Attorney-General's Guidelines on the Acceptance of Pleas (set out at Appendix A–258 *et seq.* and cited at § 4–108, *post*). Further reference should be made to the *Code for Crown Prosecutors* and Charging Standards (set out in Appendix E, and discussed at §§ 1–262 *et seq.*, *ante*).

It should be noted that much of the original report of the Farquharson Committee is reflected in the Written Standards for the Conduct of Professional Work that accompanied the eighth edition of the *Code of Conduct* adopted by the Bar Council in 2000 (see Appendix C). See, in particular, paragraphs 9 to 16 (Standards Applicable to Criminal Cases), of which paragraph 10 relates particularly to the responsibilities of prosecution counsel. The service standards on returned briefs, agreed with the Crown Prosecution Service, should also be noted (see Appendix C–48b *et seq.*).

As to the duties of the prosecutor in relation to the presentation of the evidence and the calling of witnesses, see *post*, §§ 4–273 *et seq.*, and see Appendix C–47 *et seq.* as to certain other miscellaneous duties of prosecuting advocates. **4–95**

The Farquharson Committee Report was referred to by the Court of Appeal in *R. v. Renshaw* [1989] Crim.L.R. 811. The court stressed the importance of the judge listening to the reasons given by the prosecution for proposing to offer no evidence. The judge should keep in mind that there will be information known to the prosecution which will not be apparent to him. If the judge fails to heed what the prosecution have to say he will deprive himself of a proper basis for deciding to approve or disapprove the prosecution's proposed course of action. **4–96**

In *R. v. Grafton*, 96 Cr.App.R. 156, the Court of Appeal confirmed the correctness of the view expressed in the report as to the respective roles of the trial judge and prosecutor in deciding, at any time before the completion of the prosecution case, whether or not the charge should be pursued further. The ultimate decision rests with the prosecutor, even when the trial judge takes the view that the evidence discloses a prima facie case. The view expressed in the report as to the role of the prosecutor once the case for the Crown has been completed was also approved, namely that at this stage the prosecution cannot be discontinued nor pleas of guilty to lesser charges be accepted without the consent of the judge, although it would not be the duty of the prosecuting advocate to cross-examine defence witnesses or address the jury if he was of the view that it would not be proper to convict. Many of these points were reiterated in *R. v. O.* [1999] 1 *Archbold News* 2, CA (98 02154 Z5), in which it was also said that where, after the commencement of a trial, the prosecution take the view that the evidence is such that they would not resist a submission of no case, it is open to them to allow the proceedings to continue and to leave it to the judge to decide whether or not there is a case to answer; but, it being their responsibility to take decisions as to the conduct of the prosecution case, the better course for them to take, when they are of the view that the case is too weak to proceed, is to abandon the prosecution. See also *ante*, § 4–47.

As to the committee's view of the role of prosecuting counsel in the Court of Appeal, see *R v. McIlkenny*, 93 Cr.App.R. 287, CA, *post*, § 7–206.

R. VULNERABLE DEFENDANTS: SPECIAL ARRANGEMENTS

Provisions introduced in 2000 in response to the decision of the European Court of Human Rights in *T. v. U.K.*; *V. v. U.K.*, 30 E.H.R.R. 121, in respect of young defendants have been expanded so that they also cover adults suffering from a mental disorder or some other significant impairment of intelligence or social function. **4–96a**

Practice Direction (Criminal Proceedings: Consolidation), para. III.30 (as inserted by Practice Direction (Criminal Proceedings: Further Directions) [2007] 1 W.L.R. 1790)

Treatment of vulnerable defendants

III.30.1 This direction applies to proceedings in the Crown Court and in magistrates' courts on the trial, sentencing or (in the Crown Court) appeal of (a) children and young persons under 18 or (b) adults who suffer from a mental disorder within the meaning of the *Mental Health Act* 1983 or who have any other significant impairment of intelligence and **4–96b**

social function. In this direction such defendants are referred to collectively as "vulnerable defendants". The purpose of this direction is to extend to proceedings in relation to such persons in the adult courts procedures analogous to those in use in youth courts.

III.30.2 The steps which should be taken to comply with paragraphs III.30.3 to III.30.17 should be judged, in any given case, taking account of the age, maturity and development (intellectual, social and emotional) of the defendant concerned and all other circumstances of the case.

The overriding principle

4–96c **III.30.3** A defendant may be young and immature or may have a mental disorder within the meaning of the *Mental Health Act* 1983 or some other significant impairment of intelligence and social function such as to inhibit his understanding of and participation in the proceedings. The purpose of criminal proceedings is to determine guilt, if that is in issue, and decide on the appropriate sentence if the defendant pleads guilty or is convicted. All possible steps should be taken to assist a vulnerable defendant to understand and participate in those proceedings. The ordinary trial process should, so far as necessary, be adapted to meet those ends. Regard should be had to the welfare of a young defendant as required by section 44 of the *Children and Young Persons Act* 1933, and generally to Parts 1 and 3 of the *Criminal Procedure Rules* (the overriding objective and the court's powers of case management).

Before the trial, sentencing or appeal

4–96d **III.30.4** If a vulnerable defendant, especially one who is young, is to be tried jointly with one who is not, the court should consider at the plea and case management hearing, or at a case management hearing in a magistrates' court, whether the vulnerable defendant should be tried on his own and should so order unless of the opinion that a joint trial would be in accordance with Part 1 of the *Criminal Procedure Rules* (the overriding objective) and in the interests of justice. If a vulnerable defendant is tried jointly with one who is not, the court should consider whether any of the modifications set out in this direction should apply in the circumstances of the joint trial and so far as practicable make orders to give effect to any such modifications.

III.30.5 At the plea and case management hearing, or at a case management hearing in a magistrates' court, the court should consider and so far as practicable give directions on the matters covered in paragraphs III.30.9 to III.30.17.

III.30.6 It may be appropriate to arrange that a vulnerable defendant should visit, out of court hours and before the trial, sentencing or appeal hearing, the courtroom in which that hearing is to take place so that he can familiarise himself with it.

III.30.7 If any case against a vulnerable defendant has attracted or may attract widespread public or media interest, the assistance of the police should be enlisted to try and ensure that the defendant is not, when attending the court, exposed to intimidation, vilification or abuse. Section 41 of the *Criminal Justice Act* 1925 prohibits the taking of photographs of defendants and witnesses (among others) in the court building or in its precincts, or when entering or leaving those precincts. A direction informing media representatives that the prohibition will be enforced may be appropriate.

III.30.8 The court should be ready at this stage, if it has not already done so, where relevant to make a reporting restriction under section 39 of the *Children and Young Persons Act* 1933 or, on an appeal to the Crown Court from a youth court, to remind media representatives of the application of section 49 of that Act. Any such order, once made, should be reduced to writing and copies should on request be made available to anyone affected or potentially affected by it.

The trial, sentencing or appeal hearing

4–96e **III.30.9** Subject to the need for appropriate security arrangements the proceedings should, if practicable, be held in a courtroom in which all the participants are on the same or almost the same level.

III.30.10 A vulnerable defendant, especially if he is young, should normally, if he wishes, be free to sit with members of his family or others in a like relationship, and with some other suitable supporting adult such as a social worker, and in a place which permits easy, informal communication with his legal representatives. The court should ensure that a suitable supporting adult is available throughout the course of the proceedings.

III.30.11 At the beginning of the proceedings the court should ensure that what is to take place has been explained to a vulnerable defendant in terms he can understand, and at trial in the Crown Court it should ensure in particular that the role of the jury has been explained. It should remind those representing the vulnerable defendant and the supporting adult of their responsibility to explain each step as it takes place, and at trial to explain the possible consequences of a guilty verdict. Throughout the trial the court should continue to ensure, by any appropriate means, that the defendant understands what is happening and what has been said by those on the bench, the advocates and witnesses.

III.30.12 A trial should be conducted according to a timetable which takes full account of a vulnerable defendant's ability to concentrate. Frequent and regular breaks will often be appropriate. The court should ensure, so far as practicable, that the trial is conducted in simple, clear language that the defendant can understand and that cross-examination is conducted by questions that are short and clear.

III.30.13 A vulnerable defendant who wishes to give evidence by live link in accordance with section 33A of the *Youth Justice and Criminal Evidence Act* 1999 may apply for a direction to that effect. Before making such a direction the court must be satisfied that it is in the interests of justice to do so, and that the use of a live link would enable the defendant to participate more effectively as a witness in the proceedings. The direction will need to deal with the practical arrangements to be made, including the room from which the defendant will give evidence, the identity of the person or persons who will accompany him, and how it will be arranged for him to be seen and heard by the court.

III.30.14 In the Crown Court robes and wigs should not be worn unless the court for good reason orders that they should. It may be appropriate for the court to be robed for sentencing in a grave case even though it has sat without robes for trial. It is generally desirable that those responsible for the security of a vulnerable defendant who is in custody, especially if he is young, should not be in uniform, and that there should be no recognisable police presence in the courtroom save for good reason.

III.30.15 The court should be prepared to restrict attendance by members of the public in the court room to a small number, perhaps limited to those with an immediate and direct interest in the outcome. The court should rule on any challenged claim to attend.

III.30.16 Facilities for reporting the proceedings (subject to any restrictions under section 39 or 49 of the *Children and Young Persons Act* 1933) must be provided. But the court may restrict the number of reporters attending in the courtroom to such number as is judged practicable and desirable. In ruling on any challenged claim to attend in the court room for the purpose of reporting the court should be mindful of the public's general right to be informed about the administration of justice.

III.30.17 Where it has been decided to limit access to the courtroom, whether by reporters or generally, arrangements should be made for the proceedings to be relayed, audibly and if possible visually, to another room in the same court complex to which the media and the public have access if it appears that there will be a need for such additional facilities. Those making use of such a facility should be reminded that it is to be treated as an extension of the court room and that they are required to conduct themselves accordingly.

III.30.18 Where the court is called upon to exercise its discretion in relation to any procedural matter falling within the scope of this practice direction but not the subject of specific reference, such discretion should be exercised having regard to the principles in paragraph III.30.3.

In *R. v. H.* (2006) 150 S.J. 571, CA, it was said, in relation to what was then paragraph IV.39, the precursor to paragraph III.30, that there was a need for a court to observe this practice direction, whether or not the representatives of the defendant raise concerns about the trial process; and it was the duty of both counsel to assist the court to do so. The court added that whilst practical considerations cannot be ignored, Article 6 of the ECHR (*post*, § 16–57) does not settle for an inadequate best effort; but a failure or failures to comply with the requirements of the practice direction will not automatically render a trial unfair. **4–96f**

In *S.C. v. U.K.* (2005) 40 E.H.R.R. 10, ECtHR, it was said that whilst Article 6 does not require that a child on trial for a criminal offence should understand or be capable of understanding every point of law or evidential detail, "effective participation" presupposes that the accused has a broad understanding of the nature of the trial process and of what is at stake, including the significance of any penalty which may be imposed; if necessary with the assistance of, for example, an interpreter, lawyer, social worker or friend, the accused should be able to follow what is said by the prosecution witnesses and, if represented, to explain to his own lawyers his version of events, to point out any statements with which he disagrees and make them aware of any facts which should be put forward in his defence; and when a decision is taken to deal with a child, who risks not being able to participate effectively because of his youth and limited intellectual capacity, by way of criminal proceedings, rather than some other form of disposal directed primarily at determining the child's best interests and those of the community, it is essential that he be tried in a specialist tribunal which is able to give full consideration to, and make proper allowance for, the handicaps under which he labours, and to adapt its procedures accordingly. *Cf. R. (T.P.) v. West London Youth Court* [2006] 1 Cr.App.R. 25, DC (*ante*, § 4–73).

II. ARRAIGNMENT AND PLEA

A. ARRAIGNMENT

(1) Cases where a preparatory hearing is held

4–97 For the special provisions relating to arraignment where a preparatory hearing is held in cases of serious fraud, or other complex, lengthy or serious cases, see the *CJA* 1987, s.8(2), *ante*, § 4–84n, and the *CPIA* 1996, s.30, *ante*, § 4–84u, respectively.

(2) Method of arraignment

4–98 The arraignment of defendants, against whom bills of indictment have been preferred and signed, consists of three parts: (1) calling the defendant to the bar by name; (2) reading the indictment to him; (3) asking him whether he is guilty or not (see *R. v. Central Criminal Court, ex p. Guney* [1996] A.C. 616, HL). Where an indictment contains several counts, each count should be put to the defendant separately, and he should be asked to plead to each count as it is read to him. Where the counts are for alternative offences, the first count should be first put to the defendant separately. If he pleads guilty to that, there is no need to put the second and alternative count, but if he pleads not guilty to the first count, the second and alternative count should be put to him separately and his plea taken on it: *R. v. Boyle* [1954] Q.B. 292, 38 Cr.App.R. 111, CCA. Except in a few special cases (*e.g.* where the defendant is a deaf mute, or refuses to plead) the initial arraignment must be conducted between the clerk of the court and the defendant. The defendant must plead personally—the plea cannot be made through counsel or any other person on his behalf: *R. v. Ellis (J.)*, 57 Cr.App.R. 571, CA (*venire de novo* where plea of guilty made on the defendant's behalf by his counsel). *Cf. R. v. Boyle* where B, unlike E, was given an opportunity to plead but pleaded to the whole indictment instead of entering a plea to each count in turn, and the appeal was dismissed. *Ellis* was distinguished in *R. v. Williams*, 64 Cr.App.R. 106, CA, in which it was held that a defendant could waive his right to be arraigned; and that a waiver could be implied where the defendant was present and legally represented, was aware of the charge and proceeded to trial as if he had been arraigned. *Williams* was followed in *R. v. Kepple* [2007] 7 *Archbold News* 3, CA ([2007] EWCA Crim. 1339) (*ante*, § 3–199), where a waiver was inferred from the defendant having voluntarily absconded.

When a defendant who has not previously surrendered to custody is arraigned he thereby surrenders to the custody of the court: the defendant need not be in any particular place (*e.g.* the dock) for the purpose of arraignment: *ex p. Guney, ante*.

See also *R. v. Bristol Crown Court, ex p. Commrs of Customs and Excise* [1990] C.O.D. 11, DC (informal indication by counsel of plea to be tendered does not constitute arraignment).

(3) Re-arraignment upon amendment of indictment

4–99 See *R. v. Radley*, 58 Cr.App.R. 394, CA, and *R. v. Fyffe* [1992] Crim.L.R. 442, CA, *ante*, § 1–148.

B. PLEA

(1) Introduction

4–100 As soon as a count on the indictment has been read to the defendant, the officer of the court demands of him—"How say you, are you guilty or not guilty?" The defendant then either confesses the charge in the count or some other charge of which he can lawfully be convicted on that count (*post*, §§ 4–104 *et seq.*), or stands mute, or does not answer directly to the charge (see *CLA* 1967, s.6(1)(c), *post*, §§ 4–164 *et seq.*), or pleads to the jurisdiction—or demurs (*post*, § 4–113), or pleads specially in bar (*post*, § 4–114), or pleads the general issue, *i.e.* that he is "not guilty". The defendant may make a plea of not guilty in addition to any demurrer or special plea: *CLA* 1967, s.6(1)(a), *post*, § 4–115. This procedure is gone through in respect of each count in the indictment in turn, save where the defendant pleads guilty to the first of alternative charges: *ante*, § 4–98.

(2) Corporations and other bodies

Criminal Justice Act 1925, s.33

33.—(1), (2) [*Repealed by* Magistrates' Courts Act *1952, Sched. 6.*] **4–101**

(3) On arraignment of a corporation, the corporation may enter in writing by its representative a plea of guilty or not guilty, and if either the corporation does not appear by a representative or, though it does so appear, fails to enter as aforesaid any plea, the court shall order a plea of not guilty to be entered, and the trial shall proceed as though the corporation had duly entered a plea of not guilty.

(4) [*Provision for making of rules.*]

(5) [*Repealed by* Magistrates' Courts Act *1952, Sched. 6.*]

(6) In this section the expression "representative" in relation to a corporation means a person duly appointed by the corporation to represent it for the purpose of doing any act or thing which the representative of a corporation is by this section authorised to do, but the person so appointed shall not by virtue only of being so appointed be qualified to act on behalf of the corporation before any court for any other purpose.

A representative for the purposes of this section need not be appointed under the seal of the corporation and a statement in writing purporting to be signed by a managing director of the corporation, or by any person (by whatever name called) having, or being one of the persons having, the management of the affairs of the corporation, to the effect that the person named in the statement has been appointed as the representative of the corporation for the purposes of this section shall be admissible without further proof as prima facie evidence that that person has been so appointed.

[This section is printed as amended by the *Courts Act* 1971, s.56 and Sched. 8.]

This section and Schedule 3 to the *MCA* 1980 (*ante*, § 1–242) are frequently applied to prosecutions for particular offences against unincorporated bodies: see, *e.g.* the *SCA* 2007, ss.31(6) (partnerships) and 32(5) (unincorporated associations) (*post*, §§ 5–876d, 5–876e), and the *Companies Act* 2006, s.1130 (*post*, § 30–107).

In connection with these provisions, see rule 2.5(1) of the *Criminal Procedure Rules* 2005 (S.I. 2005 No. 384) (*ante*, § 2–206).

The form of plea by a corporation is as follows: **4–102**

R. v. X Y Z Company, Ltd

I appoint [name of solicitor], *solicitor, to represent the company in the above case.*

(Signed) *A B, Director* [or Secretary]

I enter a plea of

(Signed)
[representative appointed above]

(3) Ambiguity in plea

It is important that there should be no ambiguity in the plea, and that where the defendant makes some other answer than not guilty or guilty, care should be taken to make sure that he understands the charge and to ascertain to what the plea amounts. As to the powers of the Court of Appeal, where the Crown Court has wrongly held an imperfect or unfinished plea to be a plea of guilty, see *post*, §§ 7–102 *et seq.*, 7–355. In the case of an undefended defendant who pleads guilty, care should always be taken to see that he understands the elements of the offence, especially if the evidence suggests that he has a defence: *R. v. Griffiths*, 23 Cr.App.R. 153, CCA, and see *R. v. Blandford Justices, ex p. G. (an Infant)* [1967] 1 Q.B. 82, DC. See also *ante*, §§ 4–34 *et seq.* as to the comprehension of a defendant who does not understand English. **4–103**

(4) Plea of guilty

(a) *General*

The responsibility of pleading guilty or not guilty is that of the defendant himself (see **4–104** *ante*, § 4–98), but it is the clear duty of defending counsel to assist the defendant to make up his mind by putting forward the pros and cons of a plea, if need be in forceful language, so as to impress on the defendant what the result of a particular course of conduct is likely to be: *R. v. Hall*, 52 Cr.App.R. 528, CA; *R. v. Turner (F.R.)* [1970] 2 Q.B. 321, 54 Cr.App.R. 352, CA; *R. v. Inns*, 60 Cr.App.R. 231, CA; *R. v. Goodyear* [2005] 2 Cr.App.R. 20, CA; and *Practice Direction (Criminal Proceedings: Consolidation)*, para. IV.45.1. For the relevant provisions of the eighth edition of the *Code of Conduct for the Bar of England and Wales*, see Appendix C.

As to pleas entered under threat of deprivation of legal representation, see *R. v. Smith and Beaney* (*post*, § 7–355).

4–105 Where a judge, halfway through the prosecution case and in the absence of the jury, stated in effect that the defendant was plainly guilty and that the time of the court was being wasted, the Court of Appeal described his conduct as "wholly improper" because, *inter alia*, it was putting extreme pressure on the defendant to plead guilty, whereas after advice from his counsel the choice of plea was his: *R. v. Barnes*, 55 Cr.App.R. 100. For other examples of a defendant being held not to have had a free choice of plea, see *R. v. Brook* [1970] Crim.L.R. 600, CA; and *R. v. Inns*, *ante*.

An indication by the prosecution that pleas of guilty to lesser offences than those charged or to certain only of the charges, or by certain only of the defendants, would satisfy the public interest does not put improper pressure on a defendant who is able to make his own choice; it would, however, be wholly improper for charges to be brought against one person where, on the evidence, no such charge should properly have been contemplated, and where the purpose is to use that person as a catalyst to secure a plea of guilty from the prime suspect: *R. v. Herbert*, 94 Cr.App.R. 230, CA (no improper pressure on appellant, charged together with his wife, who pleaded guilty after being told that if he did so, proceedings would not be pursued against her); see also *R. v. Richards and Stober*, 96 Cr.App.R. 258, CA, *post*, § 19–87.

4–106 On December 7, 2000, the Attorney-General issued guidelines on the acceptance of pleas; and in October, 2005, he issued revised guidelines (see Appendix A–259). Paragraph B1 points out that justice, including the acceptance of pleas and sentencing, should, absent exceptional circumstances, be done in public. Paragraph B2 refers to the Code for Crown Prosecutors (Appendix E) for the circumstances in which pleas to reduced or a lesser number of charges may properly be accepted before trial. Paragraph B3 emphasises the need, where a case is listed for trial, but the view is taken that it is appropriate to accept a plea to a lesser offence, or a reduced number of offences, or to offer no evidence, to speak with the victim and the victim's family so that the position can be explained and their views taken into account in the decision making process. They should be kept informed, and any decisions taken should be explained to them. Sections C and D of the guidelines deal with the responsibilities of the prosecution advocate in relation to the basis of any plea and the giving of sentence indications respectively.

For the procedure to be followed when an indication as to sentence is sought, see *ante*, § 4–78.

(b) *To lesser offence*

4–107 By section 6(1)(b) of the *CLA* 1967 (*post*, § 4–115), where a defendant is arraigned on an indictment he may plead not guilty of the offence specifically charged in the indictment but guilty of another offence of which he might be found guilty on that indictment. By subsection (7), this applies to an indictment containing more than one count as if each count were a separate indictment. For a consideration of the available common law and statutory alternatives, see *post*, §§ 4–453 *et seq.* For the effect on the offence charged of the acceptance of a plea of guilty to a lesser offence, pursuant to section 6(1)(b) of the 1967 Act, see *post*, § 4–126.

4–108 As to counsel for the prosecution's responsibility and the role of the judge in relation to such matters, see *ante*, §§ 4–94 *et seq.*, the Attorney-General's guidelines to prosecutors as to the acceptance of pleas ([2001] 1 Cr.App.R. 425) (Appendix A–259), and the Code for Crown Prosecutors (Appendix E). See also *R. v. Richards and Stober*, *post*, § 19–87, and *R. v. Herbert*, *ante*, § 4–105.

Where a judge approves the acceptance of a plea of guilty to a lesser charge and the plea is entered, there is no material irregularity if the judge, upon hearing the background to the charges during the opening, changes his mind and directs the trial to proceed: *R. v. Emmanuel*, 74 Cr.App.R. 135, CA; *Richards v. R.* [1993] A.C. 217, PC.

There can only be one plea to a count in respect of which a defendant is put in charge of a jury. Thus, if a defendant pleads "not guilty" to the offence charged, but "guilty" to a lesser offence that is not specifically charged, and the prosecution are unwilling to accept that plea, the plea to the count is entered as one of not guilty and the plea of guilty to the lesser offence must be treated as having been withdrawn and as a nullity: *R. v. Hazeltine* [1967] 2 Q.B. 857, 51 Cr.App.R. 351, CA; *R. v. McGregor-Read* [1999] Crim.L.R. 860, CA; and *R. v. Yeardley* [2000] 2 Cr.App.R. 141, DC and CA (a practical approach to the situation where the proffered plea is not accepted, but a verdict on that basis is not "out of the question", would be to add a count charging the lesser offence). (See also *R. v. Notman* [1994] Crim.L.R. 518, CA: judge cannot direct conviction on basis of rejected plea of guilty to lesser offence.)

The same applies if the prosecution decline to accept a plea of guilty to part only of a count: see, for example, *R. v. Kelly* [1965] 2 Q.B. 409, 49 Cr.App.R. 352, CCA (plea of guilty to damaging one only of several articles not accepted; put in charge of jury on whole count; plea impliedly withdrawn).

As to the possibility of the prosecution adducing evidence of the guilty plea in such circumstances, or cross-examining upon it, see *R. v. Hazeltine*, *ante*.

Where offences are alleged in the alternative, in separate counts, a different proce- **4–109**
dure must be followed: *R. v. Cole* [1965] 2 Q.B. 388, 49 Cr.App.R. 199, CCA; and see *R. v. Hazeltine*, *ante*. In *Cole*, where the defendant had pleaded not guilty to a count alleging conspiracy to rob, not guilty to count two, robbery with violence, and guilty to count three, receiving, the court gave guidance as to the proper practice:

> "... in the ordinary case, a judge should allow the plea of guilty to stand. In those circumstances the defendant will be put in charge of the jury only on the serious charge, in this case the armed robbery. If he is acquitted of the armed robbery, then he can be sentenced on the count to which he has pleaded guilty. If on the other hand he is convicted of the armed robbery, then the proper course for the judge is to allow the count to which he pleaded guilty to remain on the file and not to proceed to sentence him" (*per* Lord Parker C.J. at pp. 394–395, 204).

A plea of guilty ranks as a conviction not when it is recorded but when the defendant is sentenced: *ibid*.

R. v. Cole was applied in *R. v. Bebbington*, 67 Cr.App.R. 285, CA (no separate sentence should be passed in respect of lesser offence to which guilty plea entered).

(5) Plea to the general issue

The general issue is pleaded by the defendant *ore tenus* at the bar, in the words "not **4–110**
guilty"; by which plea, without further form, every person, upon being arraigned upon any indictment, is deemed to have put himself upon the country for trial. As to the course to be taken if the defendant, when called upon to plead, either stands mute or will not answer directly, see *post*, §§ 4–164 *et seq.* If the defendant says that he declines to plead, a plea of not guilty is entered: *R. v. Bernard* (1858) 8 St.Tr.(n.s.) 887 at 889. See also *post*, § 4–115.

(6) Plea to the jurisdiction

Availability

Where an indictment is taken before a court which has no cognisance of the offence, **4–111**
the defendant may plead to the jurisdiction without answering at all to the crime alleged (2 Hale 268); as if a man had been indicted for treason at the quarter sessions or the like (*ibid.*); or if another court have exclusive jurisdiction of the offence (4 Bl.Com. 333), but it is seldom necessary to have recourse to this plea, for it is bad unless it shows a court or jurisdiction in which the defendant could lawfully be tried. If the offence was committed out of the jurisdiction of the English courts, the defendant may take advantage of this

matter under a plea to the general issue: *R. v. Johnson* (1805) 6 East 583. See also *R. v. Millar* [1970] 2 Q.B. 54, CA; *Treacey v. DPP* [1971] A.C. 537, HL; *R. v. Baxter* [1972] Q.B. 1, 55 Cr.App.R. 214, CA; *DPP v. Doot* [1973] A.C. 807, HL; see too *R. v. Borro and Abdullah* [1973] Crim.L.R. 513, CA. If the defect of jurisdiction appears upon the face of the record, the defendant may demur (*post*, § 4–113) or (it would seem) move in arrest of judgment (*post*, § 5–14), and, if convicted, may appeal. In *R. v. Jameson* [1896] 2 Q.B. 425, objections on the ground of want of jurisdiction were taken: (a) on motion to quash the indictment (*ante*, §§ 1–190 *et seq.*, §§ 1–236 *et seq.*); and (b) when this failed, under the plea of not guilty. As to jurisdiction generally, see *ante*, §§ 1–82 *et seq.* and 2–30 *et seq.*

Form

4–112 By the *Indictments Act* 1915, s.8(3), *ante*, § 1–198, the provisions of that Act are applied to any plea, replication, or other criminal pleading. The form of a plea to the jurisdiction is as follows:

The Queen v. A B
Central Criminal Court

A B says that the court ought not to take cognisance of the indictment against him because [state in ordinary language the matter of the plea].

The form of the replication to this plea is—

The Queen v. A B
Central Criminal Court

J N, the appropriate officer of the Crown Court, joins issue on behalf of the Queen.

(7) Demurrer

4–113 A demurrer, which must be made in writing, is an objection to the form or substance of the indictment apparent on the face of the indictment: *R. v. Inner London Quarter Sessions, ex p. Metropolitan Police Commr* [1970] 2 Q.B. 80, 54 Cr.App.R. 49, DC. The defendant is in all cases entitled to plead not guilty in addition to pleading the demurrer—see *post*, § 4–115. In view of the wide powers of amendment of defective indictments under section 5(1) of the *Indictments Act* 1915 (*ante*, §§ 1–147 *et seq.*), and the more convenient procedure of motions to quash the indictment (*ante*, §§ 1–190 *et seq.*, §§ 1–236 *et seq.*), demurrers were, in practice, for many years regarded as obsolete, but there have been instances of resort to demurrer, often based on a misunderstanding with regard to its scope. In *R. v. Inner London Q.S., ex p. Metropolitan Police Commr*, *ante*, Lord Parker C.J. said that he hoped demurrer in criminal cases would be allowed to die naturally.

(8) Special pleas in bar

4–114 There are four special pleas in bar to an indictment:

(a) *autrefois acquit* (*post*, §§ 4–116 *et seq.*);
(b) *autrefois convict* (*post*, §§ 4–116 *et seq.*);
(c) pardon (*post*, §§ 4–161 *et seq.*);
(d) special liability of another to repair a road, bridge, etc. (now only of historical interest).

Criminal Law Act 1967, s.6(1), (7)

4–115 **6.**—(1) Where a person is arraigned on an indictment—

(a) he shall in all cases be entitled to make a plea of not guilty in addition to any demurrer or special plea;
(b) he may plead not guilty to the offence specifically charged in the indictment but guilty of another offence of which he might be found guilty on that indictment;
(c) if he stands mute of malice or will not answer directly to the indictment, the court may order a plea of not guilty to be entered on his behalf, and he shall then be treated as having pleaded not guilty.

(7) Subsections (1) to (3) shall apply to an indictment containing more than one count as if each count were a separate indictment.

(9) Autrefois acquit and autrefois convict

(a) *Scope*

In *Connelly v. DPP* [1964] A.C. 1254, HL, C faced two indictments, one for murder, the second, arising from the same incident, for robbery. Two indictments were necessary in view of the practice laid down in *R. v. Jones* [1918] 1 K.B. 416 (disapproved of by the House of Lords in *Connelly*). He was convicted upon the first indictment, his defence having been: (a) alibi, or (b) if the jury were to find that he was present, the required intent had not been proved. He successfully appealed against that conviction and, accordingly, in law stood acquitted of murder and manslaughter, though the jury had not been directed to consider manslaughter as an alternative. The Crown then proceeded, with the leave of the Court of Criminal Appeal, upon the second indictment. C filed a plea of *autrefois acquit* which was rejected and he was subsequently convicted of robbery. The grounds of appeal were, in effect: (a) he was entitled to rely upon the plea of *autrefois acquit*; (b) if that plea was not available, the doctrine of issue estoppel operated in his favour (*post*, § 4–157); (c) the judge had a discretion to stop the trial of the second indictment if he held that further process would be unjust or oppressive (*ante*, §§ 4–48 *et seq.*); and (d) it was not open to the Crown in the second trial to adduce, for the purpose of establishing robbery, evidence of admissions (verbal statements admitting "going thieving" but denying having the gun or doing the murder) alleged to have been made by the appellant which were relied upon at the first trial for the purposes of establishing murder. The Court of Criminal Appeal and the House of Lords dismissed his appeals on all grounds. **4–116**

The following propositions are based upon the nine "governing principles" identified by Lord Morris in *Connelly* at pp. 1305–1306. **4–117**

1. A man may not be tried for a crime: (a) in respect of which he has previously been acquitted or convicted (1st principle) (*post*, §§ 4–119 *et seq.*); (b) in respect of which he could on some previous indictment have been lawfully convicted (2nd principle) (*post*, § 4–131).
2. For the rule to apply, the offence charged in the second indictment must have been committed at the time of the first charge, *e.g.* a conviction or acquittal for assault will not bar a charge of murder if the assaulted person later dies (5th principle). **4–118**
3. That the facts under examination, or the witnesses being called in the later proceedings, are the same as those in some earlier proceedings is immaterial (7th principle): and see *DPP v. Humphrys* [1977] A.C. 1, HL. Note, however, the authorities cited *post*, §§ 4–159 *et seq.*, §§ 4–331 *et seq.*
4. In all cases, the earlier adjudication must have been upon guilt or innocence (*post*, §§ 4–129 *et seq.*, §§ 4–140 *et seq.*), resulting from valid process (*post*, §§ 4–146 *et seq.*) and by a court of competent jurisdiction (*post*, §§ 4–130; §§ 4–148 *et seq.*).
5. Quite apart from cases where indictments are preferred and where pleas in bar may therefore be entered, the fundamental principle always applies that a man is not to be prosecuted twice for the same offence (9th principle). This is the, so-called, "double jeopardy" rule. Thus, where the later proceedings are summary, and the rules set out below can be successfully applied, the later proceedings will be barred "on the well established common law principle that where a person has been convicted and punished for an offence by a court of competent jurisdiction … the conviction shall be a bar to all further proceedings for the same offence, and he shall not be punished again for the same matter": *per* Blackburn J. in *Wemyss v. Hopkins* (1875) L.R. 10 Q.B. 378 at 381; *Flatman v. Light* [1946] K.B. 414 at 419; *R. v. Miles* (1890) 24 Q.B.D. 423 at 430, 436; and see generally *Connelly v. DPP*. See also *Williams v. DPP*, 93 Cr.App.R. 319, DC, and *post*, §§ 4–142 *et seq.*, as to the application of the rules to summary proceedings, and see section 27 of the *MCA* 1980, *post*, § 4–124.

The third principle identified by Lord Morris suggested that the doctrine of *autrefois* extends to situations where the crime charged is in effect the same or substantially the same as one in respect of which the person charged has previously been acquitted or convicted, or in respect of which he could on some previous indictment have been convicted. The fourth principle set out the test of whether the evidence necessary to support the second indictment, or whether the facts which constitute the second offence, would have been sufficient to procure a legal conviction upon the first indictment either as to the offence charged or as to an offence of which, on the indictment, the accused could have been found guilty. However, others of their Lordships took the view that the situations encompassed by these two principles fell not within the doctrine of *autrefois*, which gives the accused an absolute right to relief, but relate to the wider, distinct and separate, discretionary power of the court to prevent abuse of its process (see Lord Devlin at pp. 1340 and 1358 and Lord Pearce at p. 1364). In *R. v. Beedie* [1997] 2 Cr.App.R. 167, the Court of Appeal confirmed that the third and fourth principles identified by Lord Morris relate to the doctrine of abuse of process and not to the doctrine of *autrefois* (see further *ante*, § 4–58).

As to the sixth principle identified by Lord Morris, see *post*, § 4–156. As to the eighth principle (*res judicata*), his Lordship's remarks have been overtaken by the subsequent decision of the House of Lords in *DPP v. Humphreys* [1977] A.C. 1, *post*, § 4–157.

(b) *A man may not be tried for a crime in respect of which he has previously been acquitted or convicted*

4–119 Either plea will succeed where the later proceedings are for an offence which is identical to that involved in the earlier proceedings; see generally Coke, 3 *Institutes* 213–214; Blackstone, *Commentaries*, Bk IV (1775 ed.), pp. 335–336; Hale, *Pleas of the Crown* (1778 ed.), Vol. 2, pp. 240 *et seq.*; Hawkins, *Pleas of the Crown* (1824 ed.), Bk II, pp. 515 *et seq.*; Chitty, *Criminal Law* (1826 ed.), Vol. 1, pp. 451–463; and *Connelly v. DPP*, *ante*, § 4–116. What constitutes a "conviction" for the purposes of the plea of *autrefois convict* was considered by the Privy Council in *Richards v. R.* [1993] A.C. 217, *post* § 4–141.

An acquittal of a particular offence will found the basis of a successful plea of *autrefois acquit* in respect of any subsequent allegation of a more serious offence which includes within its compass the offence in respect of which there was an acquittal: *R. v. G.* [2001] 2 Cr.App.R. 31, CA (not following *R. v. Brookes* [1995] Crim.L.R. 630, CA). As to whether a conviction will preclude prosecution for a more serious offence, see *ante*, § 4–58.

Although a statutory warning or reprimand given to a child or young person under section 65 of the *CDA* 1998 may be cited in criminal proceedings like a conviction, it does not have the status of a conviction: *Jones v. Whalley* [2007] 1 A.C. 63, HL.

Relevant statutory provisions

Treason Felony Act 1848, s.7

4–120 See *post*, § 25–34 and *R. v. Mitchel* (1848) 6 St.Tr.(n.s.) 599.

Offences against the Person Act 1861, ss.44, 45

4–121 **44.** If the justices, upon the hearing of any case of assault or battery upon the merits, where the complaint was preferred by or on behalf of the party aggrieved, shall deem the offence not to be proved, or shall find the assault or battery to have been justified, or so trifling as not to merit any punishment, and shall accordingly dismiss the complaint, they shall forthwith make out a certificate ... stating the fact of such dismissal, and shall deliver such certificate to the party against whom the complaint was preferred.

4–121a **45.** If any person against whom any such complaint as is mentioned in section 44 of this Act shall have been preferred by or on behalf of the party aggrieved, shall have obtained such certificate, or, having been convicted, shall have paid the whole amount adjudged to be paid, or shall have suffered the imprisonment with hard labour awarded, in every such case he shall be released from all further or other proceedings, civil or criminal, for the same cause.

[These sections are printed as amended and repealed in part by the *CJA* 1988, Scheds 15 and 16; and the *Courts Act* 2003, s.109(1), and Sched. 8, para. 41.]

Section 45 has effect subject to section 54(4) of the *CPIA* 1996, *post*, § 4–128a.

"Forthwith" means as soon as it is applied for by the defendant, who has a right to it *ex debito justitiae*: *Hancock v. Somes* (1859) 1 E. & E. 795; *Costar v. Hetherington* (1859) 1 E. & E. 802. Such certificate of dismissal can only be granted when there has been a full hearing "upon the merits". If the certificate is granted on the withdrawal of the charge before hearing, it will be no bar to subsequent proceedings in respect of the same assault: *Reed v. Nutt* (1890) 24 Q.B.D. 669. The certificate should state on which of the three grounds the charge is dismissed: *Skuse v. Davis* (1839) 10 Ad. & El. 635. Where, following a plea of guilty and an outline of the facts, justices dismissed an information charging assault on the ground that it was "so trifling as not to merit any punishment" (see s.44), it was held that the justices had no jurisdiction to do so as there had been no hearing "upon the merits" within the meaning of the section: *Ellis v. Burton* [1975] 1 W.L.R. 386, DC. **4–122**

The conviction of a servant or agent does not operate as a release of the employer: *Dyer v. Munday* [1895] 1 Q.B. 742.

The production of the certificate is of itself sufficient evidence of the dismissal by the justices, without proof of their signature or official character: *Evidence Act* 1845, s.1 (*post*, § 9–25). If the defendant appeared before the justices, the recital in the certificate of the fact of a complaint having been made, and of a summons having been issued, is sufficient evidence of those facts, without producing the complaint or summons: *R. v. Westley* (1868) 11 Cox 139.

Sections 44 and 45 of the 1861 Act do not prevent the pursuit of a charge of murder or manslaughter where the alleged victim has died after the conclusion of proceedings for assault: *R. v. Morris* (1867) L.R. 1 C.C.R. 90; *R. v. Friel* (1890) 17 Cox 325; and *R. v. Miles* (1890) 24 Q.B.D. 423. See also *ante*, § 4–58.

Duplicated offences

Section 18 of the *Interpretation Act* 1978 (Appendix B–18) (which replaced s.33 of the *Interpretation Act* 1889) "adds nothing to, and it detracts nothing from the common law": Humphreys J. in *R. v. Thomas* [1950] 1 K.B. 26 at 31, 33 Cr.App.R. 200 at 204, CCA. The words "same offence" at the conclusion of the provision do not mean same "act" or same "cause". It is not the law that a person shall not be punished twice for the same act: *R. v. Thomas*, *ante*; see also, *Williams v. Hallam* (1943) 112 L.J.K.B. 353 and *R. v. Thomson Holidays Ltd*, *ante*, § 4–58. **4–123**

Magistrates' Courts Act 1980, s.27

Effect of dismissal of information for offence triable either way

27. Where on the summary trial of an information for an offence triable either way the court dismisses the information, the dismissal shall have the same effect as an acquittal on indictment. **4–124**

This does not preclude an appeal by case stated on a point of law under section 111 of the 1980 Act.

Army Act 1955, s.133(1)

133.—(1) *Where a person subject to military law*— **4–125**

(a) *has been tried for an offence by a court-martial or has had an offence committed by him taken into consideration by a court-martial in sentencing him, or*

(b) *has been charged with an offence under this Act and has had the charge dealt with summarily by his commanding officer or the appropriate superior authority,*

a civil court shall be debarred from trying him subsequently for the same or substantially the same offence; but except as aforesaid nothing in this Act shall be construed as restricting the jurisdiction of any civil court to try a person subject to this Act for an offence.

[This subs. is printed as substituted by the *AFA* 1966, s.25; and as amended by the *AFA* 1991, s.26 and Sched. 2, para. 5(1). It is repealed, as from a day to be appointed, by the *AFA* 2006, s.378(2), and Sched. 17.]

By Schedule 3, para. 16, to the *AFA* 1976, section 133 "shall have effect, with any necessary modifications, as if any reference to a court-martial included a reference to a Standing Civilian Court". See also, *Air Force Act* 1955, s.133, and the *Naval Discipline Act* 1957, s.129 (both likewise repealed as from a day to be appointed); and the *Visiting Forces Act* 1952, s.3; and *R. v. Aughet*, 13 Cr.App.R. 101, CCA (foreign court-martial).

Armed Forces Act 2006, s.64

[Service proceedings barring subsequent civilian proceedings

4–125a **64.**—(1) This section applies where a person—

(a) has been convicted or acquitted of an offence under section 42 (criminal conduct); or

(b) has had such an offence taken into consideration when being sentenced.

(2) A civilian court in a relevant territory may not try that person for any offence for which, under the law of that territory, it would be debarred from trying him if he had been convicted or (as the case may be) acquitted by a court in England and Wales of the relevant offence.

(3) "The relevant offence" means the offence under the law of England and Wales which the act (or alleged act) constituting the offence under section 42 amounted to.

(4) Where that act (or alleged act) would amount to an offence under the law of England and Wales if it had been done in England or Wales, for the purposes of subsection (3) it shall be assumed to amount to that offence.

(5) In this section "relevant territory" means—

(a) England and Wales;

(b) Scotland;

(c) Northern Ireland; or

(d) the Isle of Man.

(6) In this section "act" includes an omission and references to the doing of an act are to be read accordingly.]

[This section comes into force on a day to be appointed.]

4–125b Section 127(2) of the 2006 Act provides for the making of a direction by the Director of Service Prosecutions that for the purposes of sections 63 (service proceedings barring subsequent service proceedings) and 64 the person specified in the direction is to be treated as acquitted of the service offence so specified. Section 65(1) provides that if a direction under section 127(2) has been made in relation to an offence, the person to whom the direction relates shall be treated, for the purposes of section 64, as if he had been acquitted of the offence. Section 65(3) stipulates that, for the purposes of sections 63 and 64, a person shall not be taken to have had an offence taken into consideration when being sentenced if the sentence has been quashed.

Criminal Law Act 1967, s.6(5)

4–126 **6.**—(5) Where a person arraigned on an indictment pleads not guilty of an offence charged in the indictment but guilty of some other offence of which he might be found guilty on that charge and he is convicted on that plea of guilty without trial for the offence of which he has pleaded not guilty, then (whether or not the two offences are separately charged in distinct counts) his conviction of the one offence shall be an acquittal of the other.

See further *ante*, §§ 4–107 *et seq.*

Criminal Justice Act 1967, s.17

4–127 **17.** Where a defendant arraigned on an indictment or inquisition pleads not guilty and the prosecutor proposes to offer no evidence against him, the court before which the defendant is arraigned may, if it thinks fit, order that a verdict of not guilty shall be recorded without any further steps being taken in the proceedings, and the verdict shall have the same effect as if the defendant had been tried and acquitted on the verdict of a jury or a court.

[This section is printed as amended by the *CJA* 2003, s.331, and Sched. 36, para. 42.]

The entering of verdicts of not guilty upon the direction of the judge can only be done in accordance with this section. Where, therefore, a judge purported to direct that such verdicts be entered but the provisions of section 17 were not observed, the direction was a nullity and pleas of *autrefois acquit* were not available: *R. v. Griffiths*, 72 Cr.App.R. 307, CA.

Section 17 does not give the judge a discretion to order a permanent stay of the proceedings instead of entering a verdict of not guilty: *R. v. Central Criminal Court, ex p. Spens*, *The Times*, December 31, 1992, DC.

As to a new administrative procedure for offering no evidence in the absence of the defendant and with the parties unrepresented, see *post*, § 4–189.

Conviction quashed on appeal

See the *CAA* 1968, s.2(3) (*post*, § 7–43). When a conviction has been quashed in the Court of Appeal, without any order for a retrial, the appellant "is in the same position for all purposes as if he had actually been acquitted": *per* Lord Reading C.J. in *R. v. Barron*, 10 Cr.App.R. 81 at 88, CCA. See also observations in *Connelly v. DPP* [1964] A.C. 1254 at 1270–1272, HL, and see *Sambasivam v. Public Prosecutor, Federation of Malaya* [1950] A.C. 458 at 479, PC. **4–128**

Tainted acquittals

Criminal Procedure and Investigations Act 1996, ss.54–56

Acquittals tainted by intimidation, etc.

54.—(1) This section applies where— **4–128a**

(a) a person has been acquitted of an offence, and

(b) a person has been convicted of an administration of justice offence involving interference with or intimidation of a juror or a witness (or potential witness) in any proceedings which led to the acquittal.

(2) Where it appears to the court before which the person was convicted that—

(a) there is a real possibility that, but for the interference or intimidation, the acquitted person would not have been acquitted, and

(b) subsection (5) does not apply,

the court shall certify that it so appears.

(3) Where a court certifies under subsection (2) an application may be made to the High Court for an order quashing the acquittal, and the Court shall make the order if (but shall not do so unless) the four conditions in section 55 are satisfied.

(4) Where an order is made under subsection (3) proceedings may be taken against the acquitted person for the offence of which he was acquitted.

(5) This subsection applies if, because of lapse of time or for any other reason, it would be contrary to the interests of justice to take proceedings against the acquitted person for the offence of which he was acquitted.

(6) For the purposes of this section the following offences are administration of justice offences—

(a) the offence of perverting the course of justice;

(b) the offence under section 51(1) of the *Criminal Justice and Public Order Act* 1994 (intimidation etc. of witnesses, jurors and others);

(c) an offence of aiding, abetting, counselling, procuring, suborning or inciting another person to commit an offence under section 1 of the *Perjury Act* 1911.

(7) This section applies in relation to acquittals in respect of offences alleged to be committed on or after the appointed day.

(8) The reference in subsection (7) to the appointed day is to such day as is appointed for the purposes of this section by the Secretary of State by order.

[The appointed day for the purposes of section 54(8) was April 15, 1997: *CPIA 1996 (Appointed Day No. 4) Order* 1997 (S.I. 1997 No. 1019).]

For the purposes of subsection (7), where an offence is alleged to be committed over a period of more than one day, or at some time during a period of more than one day, it must be taken to be alleged to be committed on the last of the days in the period: 1996 Act, s.75(1), (2).

As to the procedure for obtaining the quashing of an acquittal under section 54(3), see the *Civil Procedure Rules* 1998 (S.I. 1998 No. 3132), Sched. 1, *RSC*, Ord. 116.

Conditions for making order

55.—(1) The first condition is that it appears to the High Court likely that, but for the interference or intimidation, the acquitted person would not have been acquitted. **4–128b**

(2) The second condition is that it does not appear to the Court that, because of lapse of time or for any other reason, it would be contrary to the interests of justice to take proceedings against the acquitted person for the offence of which he was acquitted.

(3) The third condition is that it appears to the Court that the acquitted person has been given a reasonable opportunity to make written representations to the Court.

(4) The fourth condition is that it appears to the Court that the conviction for the administration of justice offence will stand.

(5) In applying subsection (4) the Court shall—

(a) take into account all the information before it, but

(b) ignore the possibility of new factors coming to light.

(6) Accordingly, the fourth condition has the effect that the Court shall not make an order under section 54(3) if (for instance) it appears to the Court that any time allowed for giving notice of appeal has not expired or that an appeal is pending.

Time limits for proceedings

4–128c **56.**—(1) Where—

(a) an order is made under section 54(3) quashing an acquittal,

(b) by virtue of section 54(4) it is proposed to take proceedings against the acquitted person for the offence of which he was acquitted, and

(c) apart from this subsection, the effect of an enactment would be that the proceedings must be commenced before a specified period calculated by reference to the commission of the offence,

in relation to the proceedings the enactment shall have effect as if the period were instead one calculated by reference to the time the order is made under section 54(3).

(2) Subsection (1)(c) applies however the enactment is expressed so that (for instance) it applies in the case of—

(a) paragraph 10 of Schedule 2 to the *Sexual Offences Act* 1956 (prosecution for certain offences may not be commenced more than 12 months after offence);

(b) section 127(1) of the *Magistrates' Courts Act*1980 (magistrates' court not to try information unless it is laid within 6 months from time when offence committed);

(c) an enactment that imposes a time limit only in certain circumstances (as where proceedings are not instituted by or with the consent of the Director of Public Prosecutions).

Rules of court

4–128d Part 40 of the *Criminal Procedure Rules* 2005 (S.I. 2005 No. 384) effectively reproduces the *Crown Court (Criminal Procedure and Investigations Act 1996) (Tainted Acquittals) Rules* 1997 (S.I. 1997 No. 1054) and the corresponding rules in respect of magistrates' courts.

Criminal Procedure Rules 2005 (S.I. 2005 No. 384), Pt 40

Tainted Acquittals

Time of certification

4–128e **40.1.** Where a person is convicted of an offence as referred to in section 54(1)(b) of the *Criminal Procedure and Investigations Act* 1996 and it appears to the court before which the conviction has taken place that the provisions of section 54(2) are satisfied, the court shall make the certification referred to in section 54(2) at any time following conviction but no later than—

(a) immediately after the court sentences or otherwise deals with that person in respect of the offence; or

(b) where the court, being a magistrates' court, commits that person to the Crown Court, or remits him to another magistrates' court, to be dealt with in respect of the offence, immediately after he is so committed or remitted, as the case may be; or

(c) where that person is a child or young person and the court, being the Crown Court, remits him to a youth court to be dealt with in respect of the offence, immediately after he is so remitted.

Form of certification in the Crown Court

40.2. A certification referred to in section 54(2) of the *Criminal Procedure and Investigations Act* 1996 by the Crown Court shall be drawn up in the form set out in the Practice Direction.

Service of a copy of the certification

4–128f **40.3.**—(1) Where a magistrates' court or the Crown Court makes a certification as referred to in section 54(2) of the *Criminal Procedure and Investigations Act* 1996, the court officer shall, as soon as practicable after the drawing up of the form, serve a copy on the acquitted person referred to in the certification, on the prosecutor in the proceedings which led to the acquittal, and, where the acquittal has taken place before a court other than, or at a different place to, the court where the certification has been made, on—

(a) the clerk of the magistrates' court before which the acquittal has taken place; or

(b) the Crown Court officer at the place where the acquittal has taken place.

Rule 40.3(2) to (4), which dealt with service, have been revoked (*Criminal Procedure (Amendment) Rules* 2007 (S.I. 2007 No. 699), r.38, and Sched. 4) and replaced by the provisions in Part 4 of the 2005 rules (*ante*, §§ 2–207 *et seq.*). Rules 40.4 to 40.8 set out requirements for the entry of the details of certification in the register or records of the court where the certification was made and, if different, where the relevant acquittal and conviction occurred, and for the display of copies of the certification form in prominent places in the respective courts for at least 28 days. The certification form is to be found in *Practice Direction (Criminal Proceedings: Forms)* [2005] 1 W.L.R. 1479, although the form TAC 1 prescribed by the 1997 rules, *ante*, may still be used.

Retrial for serious offences

Part 10 of the *CJA* 2003 makes provision for the quashing of an acquittal and an order for a retrial in respect of certain serious offences where there is new and compelling evidence: see *post*, §§ 7–260 *et seq.* **4–129**

Offences taken into consideration

Where on the conviction of a defendant an outstanding offence has been taken into consideration by the court at his request (see *post*, §§ 5–107 *et seq.*), there is not a conviction in respect of the outstanding offence and if on appeal the conviction for the main offence should be quashed, the defendant cannot establish a plea of *autrefois convict* should he be subsequently prosecuted in respect of the outstanding offence: *R. v. Nicholson*, 32 Cr.App.R. 98, 127, CCA. It is, however, undesirable that a person should be tried for any offences which have been taken into consideration as there would be a danger of being punished twice for the same offence; therefore the practice is not to proceed on any of them: *ibid*. An attempt to proceed may well amount to an abuse of process (*ante*, §§ 4–48 *et seq.*). See also, *R. v. Howard*, 92 Cr.App.R. 223, CA, as to the status of an offence taken into consideration. **4–130**

(c) *A man may not be tried for a crime in respect of which he could on some previous indictment have been lawfully convicted*

Implied alternatives

This category relates to an offence which in the earlier proceedings constituted a common law or statutory alternative to the offence of which the defendant was convicted or acquitted. (See *ante*, § 4–107 and *post*, §§ 4–453 *et seq.* as to common law and statutory alternatives generally.) The offence would have been alternative in that, although it was not expressly charged, the jury could lawfully have convicted the defendant of it had that been appropriate. The jury must have returned no express verdict on the alternative nor expressed themselves as being unable to agree upon a verdict in respect of it. Where the jury acquit of the offence charged but are unable to agree upon a verdict in respect of the statutory or common law alternative, the plea of *autrefois acquit* will fail on a retrial of that alternative charge: *DPP v. Nasralla* [1967] 2 A.C. 238, PC; *R. v. Hearn* [1970] Crim.L.R. 175, CA (disagreement on attempt); and see *Re Shipton*, 40 Cr.App.R. 197, DC. In such a case, the correct procedure is for the prosecution to obtain a voluntary bill of indictment if it is desired to proceed on the charge upon which the jury disagreed: *DPP v. Nasralla*, *ante*, and *R. v. Hearn*, *ante*. If no verdict is asked for upon the statutory or common law alternative, an acquittal on the primary charge constitutes an acquittal on the alternative: *Connelly v. DPP* [1964] A.C. 1254; Hale, *Pleas of the Crown* (1778 ed.), Vol. 2, p. 246; but see *R. v. Carter and Canavan* [1964] 2 Q.B. 1, *post*, § 4–449. **4–131**

It should be borne in mind that magistrates' courts have no common law power to convict of a lesser offence than the one charged: *Lawrence v. Same* [1968] 2 Q.B. 93, DC; and see *Martin v. Pridgeon*, 23 J.P. 630; and *R. v. Brickill*, 28 J.P. 359. **4–132**

In the following cases the plea of *autrefois* failed where the accused was subsequently charged with an offence of which he could not have been convicted on the earlier indictment: *R. v. Serné* (1887) 16 Cox 311 (acquittal of murder no bar to subsequent indictment for arson); *R. v. Gilmore* (1882) 15 Cox 85 (sections 32 and 34 of the *Offences against the Person Act* 1861 and sections 35 and 36 of the *Malicious Damage Act* 1861, *post*, §§ 19–245, 23–58); *R. v. Norton*, 5 Cr.App.R. 65, CCA (unlawful carnal knowledge/wounding); *R. v. Kupferberg*, 13 Cr.App.R. 166, CCA (conspiracy/aiding and abetting).

4–133 In *Connelly v. DPP*, *ante*, an acquittal of murder and manslaughter was held to be no bar to a second indictment, based on the same facts, alleging robbery. The defence submission, that as the killing occurred at the time when four people were joining in a robbery the appellant's conviction of robbery would involve him also being guilty of manslaughter, failed. On the trial for murder, the accused could not have been convicted of robbery. Furthermore, the evidence necessary to support the charge of robbery would not have been sufficient to procure a conviction of murder or manslaughter.

When considering such situations, the power to stay proceedings for abuse of process (*ante*, §§ 4–48 *et seq.*) and the principles to be gathered from the authorities cited *post*, §§ 4–157 *et seq.*, and §§ 4–331 *et seq.*, should also be kept in mind.

Express alternatives

4–134 Additional considerations may arise where charges expressly averred in the indictment are alternative to each other, *e.g.* theft and handling. Where the jury return verdicts on both counts, *viz.* not guilty on both or guilty of one and not guilty on the other, in principle the ordinary rules relating to *autrefois* will apply. Furthermore, where the jury convict on the wrong count (*e.g.* handling where the evidence clearly points to theft) and acquit on the other, it has been held on appeal that the court had no power under section 5(2) of the *CAA* 1907 (*rep.*) (see now *CAA* 1968, s.3, *post*, § 7–106, in virtually identical terms) to substitute a verdict of theft. To substitute the alternative verdict in such circumstances would be to substitute a verdict which the jury not only refused to find but on which they acquitted: *R. v. Melvin and Eden* [1953] 1 Q.B. 481, 37 Cr.App.R. 1; *cf. R. v. Smith*, 17 Cr.App.R. 133 (same circumstances, verdict substituted *semble* because the jury did not give verdicts on both counts). In *R. v. Seymour*, 38 Cr.App.R. 68 at 72, CCA, the court stated that if, for example, the jury convict on the theft count, they should be discharged from giving a verdict on the handling count. Such a course enables the Court of Appeal, where it is appropriate, to substitute for the verdict of theft a verdict of handling.

In *R. v. Velasquez* [1996] 1 Cr.App.R. 155, CA, the defendant had been charged with rape and attempted rape, in the alternative. The jury had acquitted him of the attempt, but had then gone on to convict him of the substantive offence. The Court of Appeal was minded to accept the proposition that if a defendant has been convicted or acquitted of attempt he cannot thereafter be charged with the full offence on a later indictment (see the *CLA* 1967, s.6(3), *post*, § 4–455), but nevertheless held that, depending on the circumstances, where the two offences are charged as alternatives in the same indictment a defendant may be guilty of the full offence and at the same time not guilty of the attempt. On the evidence, the verdicts correctly reflected the fact that the defendant was either guilty of the full offence or nothing. Without expressing a concluded view, the court was also inclined to the view that a guilty verdict on an attempt charge precludes any verdict other than not guilty in respect of the substantive offence, even where no necessary inconsistency arises on the facts.

4–135 In *R. v. Lester*, 27 Cr.App.R. 8, CCA, the defendant was indicted for larceny and receiving in the alternative. The case proceeded on the basis that the larceny count was the realistic one for the jury to consider and indeed the judge only directed the jury upon that count. The jury acquitted of larceny and convicted of receiving. The judge accepted the verdict of not guilty, refused to accept the verdict of guilty and ordered that a fresh trial should take place. At that trial, *autrefois convict* was successfully pleaded but the judge who accepted that plea then proceeded to pass sentence in respect of the guilty verdict upon which it was based. Subsequently, when quashing the original conviction on the basis that the trial judge had not directed the jury on the charge of receiving, the court observed that there had been no power to refuse to accept the verdict of guilty. The merits of the *autrefois* plea were not in point but the court appears to have been of the view that on the facts it was appropriate: *cf.* the cases cited *post*, §§ 4–140 *et seq.*

[The next paragraph is § 4–140.]

(d) *Adjudication upon guilt or innocence*

Indictment

On indictment (see generally *DPP v. Nasralla* [1967] 2 A.C. 238, PC), this will ordinarily take one of the following forms: **4–140**

(a) a jury's express verdict on a specific charge and/or upon a common law or statutory alternative;
(b) a jury's implied verdict upon any common law or statutory alternatives to the specific charge or alternative upon which a verdict was returned;
(c) a plea of guilty being entered and accepted in respect of a specific charge or under the *CLA* 1967, s.6(1)(b), *ante*, §§ 4–107, 4–115 (see in this connection, s.6(5), *ante*, § 4–126); or
(d) a verdict of not guilty being directed under section 17 of the *CJA* 1967, *ante*, § 4–127.

The fact that a count or indictment has been marked "not to be proceeded with without the leave of this court or the Court of Appeal" will not *per se* bar subsequent proceedings upon that count or indictment: *Connelly v. DPP* [1964] A.C. 1254, HL. See also *R. v. Central Criminal Court, ex p. Randle and Pottle*, 92 Cr.App.R. 323, DC.

Where a jury announced that they had reached a verdict on only one of seven counts and the judge discharged them from returning any verdict, the Court of Appeal, in upholding a decision to reject pleas of *autrefois acquit* and *convict*, held that to sustain a plea of *autrefois* there must have been a verdict given to the court. A conviction or acquittal arises at the proper conclusion of the matter and there is no conclusion of the matter until the verdict is given to the court: *R. v. Robinson* [1975] Q.B. 508, 60 Cr.App.R. 108. *Cf. R. v. Lester*, *ante*, § 4–135.

A conviction in respect of which the defendant has not been sentenced is not sufficient to found a plea of *autrefois convict*: *Richards v. R.* [1993] A.C. 217, PC (disapproving *R. v. Sheridan*, 26 Cr.App.R. 1, CCA). The underlying rationale of *autrefois convict* is to prevent duplication of punishment; if the plea could be supported by a finding of guilt alone, a defendant might escape punishment altogether. See also, *ante*, § 4–130. **4–141**

As to offences taken into consideration, see *ante*, § 4–130.

Summary proceedings

Where a complainant was not at court when a trial was called on, and the prosecution, having failed in an application for an adjournment, offered no evidence and the justices dismissed the charge, it was not open to the justices, when the witness subsequently appeared, to rescind their dismissal of the charge and rehear the case; the court in such circumstances would be acting *functus officio* and any further hearing against the defendant in relation to the matter would inevitably give rise to a plea of *autrefois acquit*: *R. (O.) v. Stratford Youth Court*, 168 J.P. 469, DC. **4–142**

A decision by justices to dismiss an information in the absence of the prosecutor, purporting to rely on section 15 of the *MCA* 1980 (absence of prosecutor), where the absence was the result of misinformation from the court and where the court had been informed that the prosecutor was on his way to court, was so unreasonable as to be outwith the statutory power. The decision was a nullity and could not have sustained a plea of *autrefois* because there had not been a lawful acquittal: *R. v. Hendon JJ., ex p. DPP*, 96 Cr.App.R. 227, DC. See further, *post*, § 4–147.

4–143 Further, where magistrates after a submission of "no case" pronounce that they find the case proved, the court is not *functus officio*. The court retains full jurisdiction over all matters until sentence. The proper course in such circumstances is for the case to be reheard by a differently constituted bench: *R. v. Midhurst JJ., ex p. Thompson* [1974] Q.B. 137, DC.

The following circumstances will not *per se* bar subsequent proceedings for the same offence, but may give rise, in an appropriate case, to a claim of abuse of process (see *ante*, §§ 4–48 *et seq.*):

(a) the withdrawal of a summons: *Brooks v. Bagshaw*, 68 J.P. 514; *R. v. Grays JJ., ex p. Low* [1990] 1 Q.B. 54, DC; and *London Borough of Islington v. Michaelides* [2001] Crim.L.R. 843, DC; and see *Davis v. Morton* [1913] 2 K.B. 479; *Foster v. Hull*, 33 J.P. 629;

(b) the issue of a certificate under section 44 of the *Offences against the Person Act* 1861 after the dismissal of the case for want of prosecution: *Reed v. Nutt* (1890) 24 Q.B.D. 669, see *ante*, § 4–122;

(c) the dismissal of an information under section 15 of the *MCA* 1980 (non-appearance of the prosecutor): *R. v. Bennett and Bond*, 72 J.P. 362; *R. v. Hendon JJ., ex p. DPP, ante*; *Holmes v. Campbell*, 162 J.P. 655, DC (fresh proceedings could not constitute an abuse of process where there was no suggestion that the prosecution were seeking to go behind a reasonable decision of an earlier court on the merits and there was no prejudice to the accused); or *semble*, section 16 (non-appearance of both parties);

(d) the dismissal of the summons before the defendant has pleaded: *Williams v. DPP*, 93 Cr.App.R. 319, DC (the defendant had never been at risk of conviction where: (i) the summons was dismissed without him being required to enter a plea (the temporal point), and (ii) the proceedings which led to the dismissal were so imperfect that he could never validly have been convicted in those proceedings (the qualitative point));

4–144 (e) the dismissal of an information, upon which the prosecution have offered no evidence, if the information is so faulty in form and content that the defendant could never have been in jeopardy on it: *DPP v. Porthouse*, 89 Cr.App.R. 21, DC; if, moreover, the context in which a charge was summarily dismissed was a rationalisation or reorganisation of the prosecution's case, so that, no doubt in recognition of the difficulties that might lie ahead in the successful prosecution of the original charge, it was decided to substitute a new charge which was regarded as more appropriate to the facts, then the consensual dismissal of the original charge, upon the substitution of the new one, would not give rise to the application of the doctrine of *autrefois acquit*: *R. v. Dabhade*, 96 Cr.App.R. 146, CA (following *Broadbent v. High* [1985] R.T.R. 359);

(f) the fact that a "summary only" charge has been adjourned *sine die* in the magistrates' court does not prevent the inclusion of an identical charge in an indictment, pursuant to section 40 of the *CJA* 1988: *R. v. King* [1992] Crim.L.R. 47, CA (see also *ante*, § 1–75aj);

(g) a decision on an information reached by magistrates without hearing such evidence as the parties wish to and are able to put before them: *R. v. Dorking Justices, ex p. Harrington* [1984] A.C. 743, HL (any such decision is a nullity because the magistrates have not discharged their duty under the *MCA* 1980, s.9(2) to hear the evidence before adjudicating);

(h) a ruling that there is no case to answer in committal proceedings under section 6(1) of the *MCA* 1980: *R. v. Manchester City Stipendiary Magistrate, ex p. Snelson* [1977] 1 W.L.R. 911, DC (an application for a voluntary bill might be the appropriate procedure in nine out of 10 such cases); *cf. R. v. Horsham JJ., ex p. Reeves*, 75 Cr.App.R. 236, DC (the High Court will intervene if the prosecution's conduct is vexatious and oppressive—prohibition granted—see *ante*, §§ 4–48 *et seq.* as to abuse of process); and

(i) the prosecution "offering no evidence" in a magistrates' court in respect of an either way offence without mode of trial procedure having been gone through as required by section 18 of the 1980 Act; for an acquittal of an either way offence in a magistrates' court to be effective for such purpose, it must follow the acceptance of jurisdiction by the court in accordance with the relevant statutory procedures; otherwise the defendant cannot be said to have been in peril of conviction: *R. v. Bradford Magistrates' Court, ex p. Daniel, The Independent (C.S.)*, June 16, 1997, DC.

As to the power of a magistrates' court to re-open a case to rectify mistakes, etc., see the *MCA* 1980, s.142. Justices only have the power to re-open a case for the purpose of rectifying their own mistake where the defendant was convicted: *R. v. Gravesend JJ., ex p. Dexter* [1977] Crim.L.R. 298, DC; *Coles v. Camborne JJ., The Times*, July 27, 1998, DC; and *R. (Green and Green Scaffolding Ltd) v. Staines Magistrates' Court*, 172 J.P. 353, DC. As to section 142 being correctly regarded as a slip rule which is not to be extended to cover situations beyond those akin to mistake, see *R. (D.) v. Sheffield Youth Court*, unreported, March 6, 2008, DC ([2008] EWHC 601 (Admin.)). **4–145**

Decisions of foreign courts

An acquittal by a court of competent jurisdiction outside England has been held to be a bar to an indictment for the same offence before any tribunal in England: *R. v. Roche* (1775) 1 Leach 134; *R. v. Aughet*, 13 Cr.App.R. 101, CCA. The defendant should produce an exemplification of the record of his acquittal under the public seal of the state where he has been tried and acquitted: *R. v. Roche, ante*. See also *R. v. Lavercombe and Murray* [1988] Crim.L.R. 435, CA, in which it was apparently assumed that the doctrine of *autrefois convict* applies to convictions in a foreign jurisdiction. **4–145a**

Before a plea of *autrefois* based upon a decision of a foreign court can be sustained, it must be clear that the defendant currently stands for a second time "in jeopardy". For the purposes of the "double jeopardy" principle it seems that "jeopardy" means simply a real risk or danger of punishment following conviction. Accordingly, in *R. v. Thomas (K. W.)*, 79 Cr.App.R. 200, CA, it was held that where T had been tried, convicted and sentenced to imprisonment, in his absence (he could not be extradited), by an Italian court for fraud, the plea was not available when he was charged with substantially the same offences in England.

(e) *Validity of process resulting in adjudication*

An acquittal (or judgment for the defendant on demurrer: *R. v. Richmond* (1843) 1 C. & K. 240) upon an insufficient indictment is no bar to another indictment for the same offence: *R. v. Coogan* (1787) 1 Leach 448; *R. v. Taylor* (1824–25) 3 B. & C. 502. And generally it may be laid down that whenever, by reason of some defect in the record—either in the indictment, the place of trial, the process or the like—the prisoner was not lawfully liable to suffer judgment for the offences charged against him in the first indictment as it stood at the time of its finding, he has not been in jeopardy in the sense which entitles him to plead the former acquittal (or conviction) in bar of a subsequent indictment: *R. v. Drury* (1849) 3 C. & K. 193; *R. v. Green* (1856) Dears. & B. 113. In *R. v. Randall* [1960] Crim.L.R. 435, CCA, the jury returned a verdict of not guilty, but then stated that this was a majority verdict. The judge discharged the jury; the accused was tried again and convicted. *Held*, the plea of *autrefois acquit* had rightly failed. The original trial judge had a discretion either to discharge the jury or send them back: *cf. R. v. Lester*, 27 Cr.App.R. 8, *ante*, § 4–135. See also *R. v. Griffiths* (*ante*, § 4–127); *Williams v. DPP* (*ante*, § 4–143) and *DPP v. Porthouse* (*ante*, § 4–144); and *post*, § 4–149, and see the principle behind the issue of a writ of *venire de novo* (*post*, §§ 7–353 *et seq.*). **4–146**

There is a clear distinction in principle between the Crown Court allowing an appeal against conviction after proceedings in which all the available evidence, so far as admissible, had been heard, and allowing it after the proceedings had been prematurely aborted without all the available and admissible evidence having been heard: such a decision is liable to be quashed on an application for *certiorari*. The objection to such a course being taken, that it puts the defendant in peril of being convicted twice, is groundless. The defendant would remain convicted as a result of the first and only **4–147** occasion on which he had been put in peril: *R. v. Bournemouth Crown Court, ex p. Weight*, 79 Cr.App.R. 324, HL.

Where magistrates dismiss a case in circumstances rendering their decision a nullity, *certiorari* is available to quash that decision and it is no objection to such a course that as a consequence the defendant will be "in jeopardy" a second time. "Jeopardy", in the relevant sense, arises only after a lawful acquittal or a lawful conviction: *R. v. Dorking Justices, ex p. Harrington* [1984] A.C. 743, HL (*ante*, § 4–144). Although the magistrates' action amounted to a breach of natural justice, "the test is not breach of the rules of natural justice but whether the decision of the justices to dismiss an information is a decision which they had no jurisdiction to take, because they were declining to adjudicate on a matter on which it was their duty to adjudicate, and thus was a nullity," *per* Lord Roskill at p. 753H.

(f) *Adjudication by court of competent jurisdiction*

Courts exercising a civil jurisdiction

4–147a Only prior criminal proceedings before a court of competent jurisdiction will suffice: *R. v. K., B. and A.*, [2007] 2 Cr.App.R. 15, CA (Special Immigration Appeal Commission not competent to conduct such proceedings).

A plea of *autrefois* does not lie on the basis that the incident alleged is one that has been the subject of contempt proceedings in the civil courts; although a plea of double jeopardy is available in civil proceedings, as in criminal proceedings, such a plea cannot jump the boundary between those different types of proceedings: *R. v. Green (B.)* [1993] Crim.L.R. 46, CA. As to the inter-relationship between parallel jurisdictions and remedies (including criminal) in cases of domestic violence, see *Lomas v. Parle (Practice Note)* [2004] 1 W.L.R. 1642, CA (Civ. Div.); as to the making and status of declarations as to lawfulness by the civil courts, see *ante*, § 4–59.

Findings by tribunals other than courts of law

4–148 In *Lewis v. Mogan* [1943] K.B. 376, DC, it was held that the master of a ship who had held an inquiry and as a result had made an entry in the log book that the defendant was to forfeit pay for neglect of duty, was not acting on that occasion as a court of competent jurisdiction but only as a domestic tribunal, and that a plea of *autrefois convict* based upon the master's action could not be established. In *R. v. Hogan and Tompkins* [1960] 2 Q.B. 513, 44 Cr.App.R. 255, CCA, the defendants, prison escapees, had been punished under the *Prison Rules* 1949 by the visiting justices. They were subsequently tried for offences arising out of the escape, including prison breach (escaping by force) and simple escape. The second of the charges was struck out by the trial judge after he had been informed of the justices' visit to the prison. *Held*, the principle in *R. v. Elrington, ante*, § 4–58, could not be applied as the justices dealt with the matter as an offence against discipline, and did not deal with the common law offence of simple escape. Accordingly, the judge need not have struck out the count alleging simple escape. There had been no prior conviction by a court of competent jurisdiction. As to prior decisions by foreign courts, see *ante*, § 4–130.

Courts of law acting without jurisdiction

4–149 In *R. v. Kent JJ., ex p. Machin* [1952] 2 Q.B. 355, 36 Cr.App.R. 23, DC, the defendant consented to summary trial of an offence triable either way, but he was not warned of the possibility of committal for sentence as required by statute. *Held*, the summary trial and committal were bad, and, as he had never been in peril, he could be tried again. Thus, a court having acted without jurisdiction is still perfectly competent to exercise the same jurisdiction but to exercise it properly: *R. v. Marsham, ex p. Pethick Lawrence* [1912] 2 K.B. 362, DC (defendant convicted of assault after summary trial, retried same day before same magistrate after it was discovered that a witness had not given his evidence on oath in the first trial; it was held that the proceedings were unobjectionable "the defendant was never in peril [on the first hearing] and therefore was not in the position on the second hearing to take any exception to the jurisdiction of the magistrate": *per* Avory J. at p. 366). See also *Davis v. Morton* [1913] 2 K.B. 479, DC; and *cf. R. v. Norfolk Q.S., ex p. Brunson* [1953] 1 Q.B. 503, 37 Cr.App.R. 6, DC, *ante*, § 1–211.

A court is equally competent to exercise a different jurisdiction to the one it purported to exercise on the first occasion: *Bannister v. Clarke* [1920] 3 K.B. 598, DC (defendant erroneously committed for trial on summary offence. *Held*, by unlawfully committing the defendant for trial the justices had not exhausted their jurisdiction and were not therefore precluded from subsequent adjudication upon the information); and see *R. v. West* [1964] 1 Q.B. 15, 46 Cr.App.R. 296, CCA (justices purporting to deal summarily with a charge which could only be tried on indictment, acquitted W. Subsequently, substantially the same charge was preferred and the justices committed him for trial. He was convicted. *Held*, as the initial proceedings were a nullity, the committal and trial were unobjectionable). In *R. v. Cronin*, 27 Cr.App.R. 179, CCA, C was convicted before a deputy recorder who was later discovered to be disqualified from sitting. *Held*, the proceedings were void *ab initio*; *venire de novo* ordered. *Cf. R. v. Simpson* [1914] 1 K.B. 66, DC (court refused to quash acquittal by magistrates when one member of the court was disqualified by statute from sitting). **4–150**

(g) *Procedure, form, evidence*

Procedure

Under section 6(1) of the *CLA* 1967 (*ante*, § 4–115), when a person is arraigned on indictment he shall, in all cases, be entitled to make a plea of not guilty in addition to any special plea; see also *Flatman v. Light* [1946] K.B. 414, DC. But the plea may be raised at any stage in the proceedings: *per* Lord Hodson in *Connelly v. DPP* [1964] A.C. 1254, 1331, HL, and see *R. v. Tonks* [1916] 1 K.B. 443, 11 Cr.App.R. 284. In *Connelly*, the plea of *autrefois acquit* was pleaded at the commencement of the second trial (not upon the Crown's application to the Court of Criminal Appeal for leave to proceed on the second indictment) "and it is accepted that that was the right time to raise the plea": *per* Lord Morris at p. 1303, and see Lord Devlin at p. 1341. **4–151**

The rule that no person should be put in peril twice for the same offence is so fundamental that the Crown Court, on hearing an appeal against conviction from a magistrates' court, must consider any plea of *autrefois acquit* or *convict* that may be raised, notwithstanding that the defendant entered an unequivocal plea of guilty before the justices: *Cooper v. New Forest District Council* [1992] Crim.L.R. 877, DC.

Where the plea is made on arraignment (see *post*, §§ 4–154, 4–155) the Crown will either admit it, in which case the defendant will be discharged, or answer it by way of replication.

As to the burden of proof, see *post*, § 4–156.

Judge to decide issue

Criminal Justice Act 1988, s.122

122. When an accused pleads *autrefois acquit* or *autrefois convict* it shall be for the judge, without the presence of a jury, to decide the issue. **4–152**

Forms of pleas

Section 28 of the *Criminal Procedure Act* 1851 (*rep.*) provided that in any plea of *autrefois convict* or *autrefois acquit* it shall be sufficient for any defendant to state that he has been lawfully convicted or acquitted as the case may be of the said offence charged in the indictment. The plea may be made *ore tenus*, but should be reduced to writing: *R. v. Walker*, 2 M. & Rob. 446; *Indictments Act* 1915, s.8(3) (*ante*, § 1–198); and see *Flatman v. Light*, *ante*, at p. 419. Any demurrer to the plea should, likewise, be written or printed. **4–153**

Autrefois acquit

4–154 (a) *Plea*. The following is the customary form of plea of *autrefois acquit*:

The Queen v. A B

Central Criminal Court

A B says that the Queen ought not further to prosecute the indictment against him, because he has been lawfully acquitted of the offence charged therein.

(b) *Replication*. In the case of a plea of *autrefois acquit*, issue is joined on behalf of the Crown by means of a written replication: *R. v. Scott* (1785) 1 Leach 401; and see *R. v. Sheen* (1827) 2 C. & P. 634 and *Flatman v. Light, ante*.

The customary form of replication is as follows:

The Queen v. A B

Central Criminal Court

J N (the appropriate officer of the Crown Court) joins issue on behalf of the Queen.

Autrefois convict

4–155 (a) *Plea*. The following is the customary form of plea of *autrefois convict*:

The Queen v. A B

Central Criminal Court

A B says that the Queen ought not further to prosecute the indictment against him, because he has been lawfully convicted of the offence charged therein. [If the indictment is for treason add *"and as to the charge in the said indictment he says he is not guilty."*]

(b) *Replication*. As for the plea of *autrefois acquit*.

Evidence

4–156 The proof of the issues lies on the defendant; he must prove what he asserts on the balance of probabilities: *R. v. Coughlan and Young*, 63 Cr.App.R. 33, CA.

"The defendant is not restricted to a comparison between the later indictment and some previous indictment or to the records of the court. He may prove by evidence all such questions as to the identity of persons, dates and facts as may be necessary": Lord Morris's sixth principle (*Connelly v. DPP* [1964] A.C. 1254 at 1305–1306, *ante*, § 4–117). Thus, it can be shown what evidence was given at the earlier trial and there can be parol evidence to show what the charge in the previous indictment really was: *R. v. Bird* (1851) 2 Den. 74; and see *Connelly v. DPP*, *ante*, 1313–1315 (Lord Morris), 1331, 1332 (Lord Hodson), and 1366 (Lord Pearce).

Similarly, the later court is entitled to inquire into the validity of the earlier court's jurisdiction: *R. v. West* [1964] 1 Q.B. 15, 46 Cr.App.R. 296, CA, *ante*, § 4–150.

As to the proof of the acquittal or conviction, see also sections 73, 74(3) and 75 of the *PACE Act* 1984, *post*, §§ 9–79 *et seq*.

(10) Issue estoppel

Principle

4–157 (a) The civil doctrine of issue estoppel, as distinct from that of *res judicata*, has no application to the criminal law: *DPP v. Humphrys* [1977] A.C. 1, HL, not following certain dicta in *Connelly v. DPP* [1964] A.C. 1254, HL.

(b) The doctrine of *res judicta* does apply to the criminal law in the form of the maxim *nemo debet bis vexari pro eadem causa*, or *nemo debet bis puniri pro uno delicto*—"no-one should be twice put in jeopardy of being convicted and punished for the same offence" (the rule against "double jeopardy"). The pleas of *autrefois convict* and *acquit* are founded on these maxims.

(c) In certain cases, an attempt to raise again an issue that has, in effect, been decided in a previous criminal trial will amount to an abuse of process and may be stayed, even though it does not come within principle (b): *ibid.*, *per* Lords Hailsham at p. 41, Salmon at p. 46, and Edmund-Davies at pp. 52, 53. Lord Dilhorne, at pp. 22, 23, dissented on this point but said that one remedy would be for the DPP to take over the prosecution and (by implication) to offer no evidence. Lord Fraser expressed no opinion on the point as it had not been argued. (See *ante*, §§ 4–48 *et seq.* as to abuse of process generally.)

In *DPP v. Humphrys*, H had been acquitted of driving whilst disqualified; the only issue being whether a constable was correct in identifying H as the driver on a particular day. At a subsequent trial for perjury in respect of his evidence that he had not driven at all during the year in question, the constable was allowed to give the same evidence, and further evidence was called from other witnesses who had seen H driving on various occasions during that year. *Held*, the facts disclosed neither a breach of the double jeopardy rule, nor an abuse of process. **4–158**

Other authorities

In *Sambasivam v. Public Prosecutor of Malaya, Federation of Malaya* [1950] A.C. 458, PC, Lord MacDermott, delivering the opinion of the Judicial Committee, said (at p. 479): **4–159**

> "The effect of a verdict of acquittal pronounced by a competent court on a lawful charge and after a lawful trial is not completely stated by saying that the person acquitted cannot be tried again for the same offence. To that it must be added that the verdict is binding and conclusive in all subsequent proceedings between the parties to the adjudication."

The prosecution relied on a statement, purporting to be S's, but which S denied making, which contained an admission of the offence for which he was being tried (carrying a firearm) and an admission of an offence of which he had, in different proceedings, been acquitted (possessing ammunition). The conviction was quashed because the assessors who tried the case had not been told that the prosecution could not ask the court to accept a substantial and important part of what it said, namely that the defendant had committed the offence of which he had previously been acquitted.

This area of the law was reconsidered by the House of Lords in *R. v. Z.* [2000] 2 A.C. 483. Their Lordships concluded that the second sentence quoted, *ante*, from the judgment of Lord McDermott in *Sambasivam* requires qualification in order to confine its application to its proper context. The principle of double jeopardy prevents a man, in the absence of special circumstances, from being prosecuted a second time on the same or substantially the same facts as have given rise to an earlier prosecution that has resulted in his acquittal or conviction. An attempt to pursue a prosecution in breach of this principle of double jeopardy will justify a plea of *autrefois acquit* or *autrefois convict*, or an application to stay the proceedings as an abuse of process. However, provided that a defendant is not placed in double jeopardy in this sense, evidence that is relevant to a particular charge is not rendered inadmissible simply because it shows that the defendant was, in fact, guilty of an offence of which he had previously been acquitted. The court nevertheless retains the power to exclude such evidence pursuant to section 78 of the *PACE Act* 1984 if its prejudicial effect would outweigh its probative value in the circumstances of a particular case. **4–160**

Applying these principles to the facts of the case before them, where the defendant was charged with rape and the defence was that the complainant had consented to sexual intercourse or, alternatively, the defendant believed she had so consented, their Lordships held that evidence from other complainants in respect of earlier incidents in which the fact of sexual intercourse between the defendant and the relevant complainant had not been in issue was admissible on the basis of similar fact principles, notwithstanding the defendant's acquittal of charges of rape in respect of those earlier incidents. The admission of such evidence would not infringe the rule against double jeopardy because it would not put the defendant in peril of conviction in respect of the charges of which he had been acquitted, its purpose being to establish that he was guilty of an offence in respect of a different complainant at a different time, even though it might show that he was in fact guilty of earlier rapes. In so holding, their Lordships approved the decision in *R. v. Ollis* [1900] 2 Q.B. 758, CCCR, and disapproved the way in which that decision had been distinguished in *G. (an Infant) v. Coltart* [1967] 1 Q.B. 432, DC.

Lord Hutton (in a speech approved by the rest of their Lordships) expressed the view that, despite the need to qualify the statement of principle expressed in *Sambasivam*, the quashing of the conviction in that case had been appropriate on the grounds that a man should not be prosecuted a second time where the two offences are in fact founded on one and the same incident, and that a man ought not to be tried for a second offence that is manifestly inconsistent on the facts with a previous acquittal. For the related topic as to the evidential use that may be made of a prior acquittal by a defendant, see *post*, §§ 4–331 *et seq*.

In *R. v. Carroll* (2002) 194 A.L.R. 1, the High Court of Australia held that, where the defendant had given evidence at his trial for murder denying the killing and his conviction had been quashed on appeal, his subsequent prosecution for perjury at his murder trial (the false evidence alleged being his denial of the killing) should have been stayed as an abuse because the prosecution inevitably sought to controvert the earlier acquittal; there was manifest inconsistency between the charge of perjury and the acquittal of murder, the inconsistency arising because the prosecution based the perjury charge solely upon the defendant's sworn denial of guilt; the laying of the charge of perjury, solely on the basis of the defendant's sworn denial of guilt, for the evident purpose of establishing his guilt of murder, was an abuse of process regardless of the cogency and weight of any new evidence that the prosecution had available.

(11) Pardon

Plea of pardon

4–161 A pardon may be pleaded in bar to the indictment; or, after verdict, in arrest of judgment; or, after judgment, in bar of execution. But it is necessary to plead it at the first opportunity; for if, for instance, the defendant has obtained a pardon before arraignment, and instead of pleading it in bar, he pleads the general issue, he shall be deemed to have waived the benefit of it, and cannot afterwards avail himself of it in arrest of judgment: 1 Rolle 297; 2 Hawk. c.37, s.59. This relates to the Royal Pardon only; for a pardon under statute need not be pleaded: Fost. 43; 3 Inst. 234; Plowd. 83, 84, unless there be exceptions in it: 2 Hale 252; 3 Inst. 234, nor can the defendant lose the benefit of it by his own *laches* or negligence.

Form of plea

4–162 In pleading a pardon under the Great Seal, the letters patent were set out with *profert* and the plea concluded thus: "By reason of which said letters patent, the said A B prays that by the court here he may be dismissed and discharged from the said premises in the said indictment specified."

Any variance between the statement in the indictment and in the pardon could be made good, in the plea, by averments of identity.

Effect of plea

4–162a Where a pardon has been granted to forestall any criminal proceedings a successful plea of pardon will result in the discharge of the defendant.

Although the initial validity of a pardon must be judged by reference to the time of its grant it may not confer protection until any conditions to which it is subject have been met. The question of whether or not a pardon has been granted is to be judged objectively. A power to pardon cannot be used to dispense with criminal responsibility for an offence not yet committed at the time of its grant and if it purports to do so it will not be valid. A pardon will be construed in a purposive way so as to seek to uphold its validity and, if possible, any conditions to which it is subject will be construed so as not to trespass in an unacceptable way on the principle that it cannot dispense with responsibility for offences in advance of the commission of such offences: *Att.-Gen. of Trinidad and Tobago v. Phillip* [1995] 1 A.C. 396, PC. The Board also considered, but did not decide, whether a pardon could be set aside if granted under duress and considered whether a stay could be granted where the conditions of an invalid pardon have been complied with (*ante*, § 4–62).

4–163 The Crown no longer has a prerogative of justice, but only a prerogative of mercy. A

Royal Pardon does not, therefore, remove any existing conviction for the offence pardoned, it merely pardons the effects of such conviction: *R. v. Foster*, 79 Cr.App.R. 61, CA.

As to the distinction between a full pardon and other more restricted forms of pardon, see *R. v. Secretary of State for the Home Dept, ex p. Bentley* [1994] Q.B. 349, DC.

Some doubt exists as to the extent to which a pardoned conviction will render the offender liable to increased penalties in the event of his conviction of a subsequent offence for which the penalty is affected by previous convictions. In *R. v. Bolton JJ., ex p. Scally* [1991] 1 Q.B. 537 at 546, DC, certain important differences between the effect of an acquittal and a pardon, in relation to drink-driving matters, were highlighted.

(12) Defendant standing mute

Where the defendant stands mute, the court cannot itself determine whether he is mute of malice or by the visitation of God: *R. v. Schleter* (1866) 10 Cox 409; but must direct a jury to be forthwith impanelled and sworn to try this issue, and such jury may consist of any 12 persons who may happen to be present. The jury will be charged in the following manner: "Members of the jury, the defendant XY is charged upon indictment for that he, etc. ... The defendant will not answer directly to this indictment and it is your charge to say, having heard the evidence, whether he stands mute of malice or by visitation of God." **4–164**

There is no right of challenge: see *post*, § 4–234.

It has been held at assizes that the onus is on the prosecution to prove malice, and that the standard of proof is that normally resting on the prosecution in a criminal case and not the mere balance of probabilities: *R. v. Sharp*, 41 Cr.App.R. 197 (Salmon J.). **4–165**

Counsel may call witnesses for the defendant on the trial of the issue and may address the jury: *R. v. Roberts* (1816) Carr.C.L. 57.

The verdict is taken in the ordinary way, *viz.*: (a) "Have you reached a verdict upon which you are all agreed?" (b) "Do you find the defendant XY mute of malice or mute by visitation of God?" (c) "You find, etc., and that is the verdict of you all." As the verdict is "the verdict of a jury in proceedings in the Crown Court" it falls within section 17 of the *Juries Act* 1974 (majority verdicts), *post*, § 4–433. Where the jury return a verdict of mute of malice, the court will direct that a plea of not guilty be entered: *CLA* 1967, s.6(1)(c) (*ante*, § 4–115). If the verdict is "mute by visitation of God," the court must then determine whether or not the defendant is under a disability so that he cannot be tried: see *R. v. Steel* (1787) 1 Leach 451; *R. v. Governor of Stafford Prison, ex p. Emery* [1909] 2 K.B. 81, DC, and *post*, §§ 4–167 *et seq.* **4–166**

A person is mute by the visitation of God who is deaf and dumb: *R. v. Pritchard* (1836) 7 C. & P. 303; *ex p. Emery*, *ante*; or so deaf that he cannot hear the indictment when read: *R. v. Halton* (1824) Ry. & M. 78.

An accused person who is deaf and dumb may, it is submitted, plead on arraignment through an interpreter: see *ante*, § 4–37.

(13) Defendant unfit to plead or take his trial

(a) *Procedure, evidence and burden of proof*

The tribunal by which the question of disability is determined was changed by the *Domestic Violence, Crime and Victims Act* 2004 from a jury to a court. **4–166a**

Criminal Procedure (Insanity) Act 1964, ss.4, 4A

Finding of unfitness to plead

4.—(1) This section applies where on the trial of a person the question arises (at the instance of the defence or otherwise) whether the accused is under a disability, that is to say, under any disability such that apart from this Act it would constitute a bar to his being tried. **4–167**

(2) If, having regard to the nature of the supposed disability, the court are of opinion that it is expedient to do so and in the interests of the accused, they may postpone consideration of the question of fitness to be tried until any time up to the opening of the case for the defence.

(3) If, before the question of fitness to be tried falls to be determined, the jury return a

verdict of acquittal on the count or each of the counts on which the accused is being tried, that question shall not be determined.

(4) Subject to subsections (2) and (3) above, the question of fitness to be tried shall be determined as soon as it arises.

(5) The question of fitness to be tried shall be determined by the court without a jury.

(6) The court shall not make a determination under subsection (5) above except on the written or oral evidence of two or more registered medical practitioners at least one of whom is duly approved.

[This section is printed as substituted by the *Criminal Procedure (Insanity and Unfitness to Plead) Act* 1991, s.2; and as subsequently amended by the *Domestic Violence, Crime and Victims Act* 2004, s.22(1) to (3).]

The provisions of the 1964 Act have no application to summary proceedings; where there is an issue as to the mental fitness of a defendant to participate in the summary trial of an offence punishable by imprisonment, the court should first determine the issue of whether the defendant did the act or made the omission charged against him; if so satisfied, the court may then act under either or both of section 11(1) of the *PCC(S)A* 2000 (adjournment for inquiry into mental condition before method of dealing with him determined) or section 37(3) of the *MHA* 1983 (power of magistrates' court to make hospital or guardianship order without convicting defendant (*post*, § 5–894)): *R. (P.) v. Barking Youth Court* [2002] 2 Cr.App.R. 19, DC.

Finding that the accused did the act or made the omission charged against him

4–168 **4A.**—(1) This section applies where in accordance with section 4(5) above it is determined by a court that the accused is under a disability.

(2) The trial shall not proceed or further proceed but it shall be determined by a jury—

(a) on the evidence (if any) already given in the trial; and

(b) on such evidence as may be adduced or further adduced by the prosecution, or adduced by a person appointed by the court under this section to put the case for the defence,

whether they are satisfied, as respects the count or each of the counts on which the accused was to be or was being tried, that he did the act or made the omission charged against him as the offence.

(3) If as respects that count or any of those counts the jury are satisfied as mentioned in subsection (2) above, they shall make a finding that the accused did the act or made the omission charged against him.

(4) If as respects that count or any of those counts the jury are not so satisfied, they shall return a verdict of acquittal as if on the count in question the trial had proceeded to a conclusion.

(5) Where the question of disability was determined after arraignment of the accused, the determination under subsection (2) is to be made by the jury by whom he was being tried.

[This section is printed as substituted by the *Criminal Procedure (Insanity and Unfitness to Plead) Act* 1991, s.2; and as subsequently amended by the *Domestic Violence, Crime and Victims Act* 2004, s.22(1), (4) and (5).]

By section 8 of the 1964 Act (as amended by the *Medical Act 1983 (Amendment) Order* 2002 (S.I. 2002 No. 3155); and the *Domestic Violence, Crime and Victims Act* 2004, s.58(1), and Sched. 10, para. 3):

" 'duly approved' in relation to a registered medical practitioner, means approved for the purposes of section 12 of the *Mental Health Act* 1983 by the Secretary of State as having special experience in the diagnosis or treatment of mental disorder;

'local probation board' means a local probation board established under section 4 of the *Criminal Justice and Court Services Act* 2000;

'registered medical practitioner' means a fully registered person within the meaning of the *Medical Act* 1983 who holds a licence to practise;".

Section 8 also has the effect of applying to section 4(6) the evidential provisions in the *MHA* 1983, s.54(2), (3), *post*, § 5–888.

Proceedings under sections 4 and 4A of the 1964 Act do not involve the determination of a criminal charge, within the meaning of Article 6 of the ECHR (*post*, § 16–57) as they cannot result in a conviction or in any punishment or order that could be seen as retributive or deterrent; provided that the procedure was properly conducted, with scrupulous regard for the interests of the defendant, it was fair and compatible with his rights under Article 6: *R. v. H.* [2003] 2 Cr.App.R. 2, HL; but they are "criminal proceedings" within the *CJA* 2003, s.134(1) (*post*, § 11–6), to which the hearsay provisions of that Act apply: *R. v. Chal* [2008] 1 Cr.App.R. 18, CA. See also *R. (Grant) v. DPP*; *R. v. Grant* [2002] 1 Cr.App.R. 38, DC and CA.

When issue arises

The question as to fitness arises whenever before arraignment the prosecution or defence inform the judge that there is a preliminary issue as to the defendant's fitness, or, so far as the judge is concerned, he decides that he should raise the question: *R. v. McCarthy* [1967] 1 Q.B. 68, 50 Cr.App.R. 109, CCA. Once it is clear that there is an issue, careful case management is needed to ensure that full information is provided to the court without delay: *R. v. Norman*, *The Times*, August 21, 2008, CA. **4–169**

When issue is to be determined

When full information is available, the court will need carefully to consider whether to postpone trial of the issue of fitness to plead under section 4(2), given the consequences that a finding of unfitness has for the defendant: *R. v. Norman*, *ante*; if there is a reasonable chance of the evidence for the prosecution being successfully challenged so that the defence will not be called on, the issue of fitness should be postponed until some time before the defence is opened: *R. v. Webb* [1969] 2 Q.B. 278, 53 Cr.App.R. 360, CA; and see *R. v. Burles* [1970] 2 Q.B. 191, 54 Cr.App.R. 196, CA. **4–170**

Disability

Section 4(1) applies to *any* disability (including inability to communicate with legal advisers) such that, apart from the Act, it would constitute a bar to the defendant being tried: *R. v. Burles*, *ante*. The test always referred to is to be found in *R. v. Pritchard* (1836) 7 C. & P. 303, where a defendant, arraigned on an indictment, appeared to be deaf, dumb, and also of non-sane mind. Alderson B. put three distinct issues to the jury, directing the jury to be sworn separately on each: (a) whether the defendant was mute of malice or by the visitation of God; (b) whether he was able to plead; and (c) whether he was sane or not. On the last issue they were directed to inquire whether the defendant was of sufficient intellect to comprehend the course of the proceedings of the trial, so as to make a proper defence, to challenge a juror to whom he might wish to object, and to understand the details of the evidence; and he directed the jury that if there was no certain mode of communicating to the defendant the details of the evidence so that he could clearly understand them and be able properly to make his defence to the charge against him, the jury ought to find that he was not of sane mind. This direction was approved in *R. v. Berry* (1876) 1 Q.B.D. 447; *R. v. Governor of Stafford Prison, ex p. Emery* [1909] 2 K.B. 81, DC; and *R. v. Robertson*, 52 Cr.App.R. 690, CA. The issue "whether the defendant is capable of pleading to and of taking his trial on indictment" is one issue only; if the court finds that the defendant is unable to communicate with his legal advisers, he should be found unfit: *R. v. Sharp*, *ante*. **4–171**

The questions put to witnesses called to give evidence upon this issue are based upon the test enunciated in *R. v. Pritchard*, and deal with whether the defendant has sufficient intellect to instruct his solicitor and counsel, to plead to the indictment, to challenge jurors, to understand the evidence and to give evidence. The mere fact that the court may think that the accused is not capable of acting in his best interest is insufficient to entitle the court to decide that he is unfit to stand his trial: *R. v. Robertson*, *ante*. A court may conclude that a defendant is highly abnormal, but a high degree of abnormality does not mean that he is incapable of following a trial, or giving evidence or instructing counsel, etc.: *R. v. Berry*, 66 Cr.App.R. 156, CA. **4–172**

Amnesia causing the disappearance of all memory of the events surrounding the alleged crime cannot of itself render the accused unfit to plead or be tried: *R. v. Podola*, **4–173**

43 Cr.App.R. 220, CCA. In *R. v. Harris*, 61 J.P. 792, the defendant was unable to read or write, and owing to an unhealed wound in his throat could not speak. A jury impanelled to try whether he was sane and able to plead found that he was both, but that at present he was unable to give instructions for his defence, and that his condition was due to his own act, attempted suicide. He was then called on to plead, pleaded not guilty, and his trial was adjourned: *cf. R. v. Whitfield* (1850) 3 C. & K. 121. As to feigned madness, see *R. v. Davies* (1853) 6 Cox 326; *R. v. Berry* (1897) 104 L.T.J. 110.

Burden of proof, verdict and subsequent procedure

4–174 If the contention that the defendant is under a disability is put forward by the defence, the onus of proof is upon the defence and is discharged if the court is satisfied on the balance of probabilities that the contention is right. If the Crown makes the allegation and the defence disputes the issue, the burden rests upon the Crown: *R. v. Podola, ante*. Where the burden falls upon the Crown the standard of proof is proof beyond a reasonable doubt: *R. v. Robertson, ante. Quaere* as to the situation when the issue is raised by the judge.

If it is determined that the accused is under a disability, the procedure set out in section 4A of the 1964 Act (*ante*, § 4–168) must then be followed; the court must consider carefully who is the best person to be appointed to put the case for the defence (see subs. (2)(b)), since the responsibility placed on the person so appointed by the court is quite different to that placed on an advocate who can take instructions from a client: *R. v. Norman, ante*, § 4–169 (observing that the circumstances may call for an advocate experienced in mental health issues).

If it is then determined that the accused did the act or made the omission charged against him the court must make an order in accordance with section 5 (*post*).

In *R. v. O'Donnell* [1996] 1 Cr.App.R. 286, CA, where the defendant had been found unfit to be tried, the procedure required by section 4A of the 1964 Act had not been followed, a purported verdict of guilty had been returned and the trial judge had purported to make orders other than those provided for by section 5. In directing a *venire de novo*, the Court of Appeal gave detailed guidance as to the correct procedures.

Where a defendant is found to be unfit to plead, but becomes fit to plead before he is dealt with under section 4A or 5, the court should proceed to conduct a second hearing under section 4, whereupon a finding of fitness to plead would obviate the need to continue with the procedures under section 4A or 5: *R. (Hasani) v. Crown Court at Blackfriars* [2006] 1 Cr.App.R. 27, DC.

"did the act or made the omission charged"

4–174a On the trial of an issue under section 4A(2) of the 1964 Act as to whether the accused "did the act or made the omission charged as the offence", "the act" for this purpose refers to the *actus reus* of the offence and not to the *mens rea*; thus, where a defendant charged with murder is found unfit to plead, it is not open to the person appointed by the court to put the case for the defence to raise the issue of diminished responsibility for the purpose of the issue under section 4A(2); further, on the trial of such issue it would seldom, if ever, be appropriate for the accused to give evidence (a jury having found him unfit to be tried), but if there is objective evidence which raises the issue of mistake or accident or self-defence, then the jury should not find that the defendant did the "act" unless satisfied beyond reasonable doubt on all the evidence that the prosecution have negatived that possibility; what the defence cannot do, in the absence of evidence to raise the issue, is to suggest to the jury that the defendant may have acted under a mistake, or by accident, or in self-defence, and to submit that the jury should acquit unless satisfied by the prosecution that there is no reasonable possibility that that suggestion is correct: *R. v. Antoine* [2001] 1 A.C. 340, HL (overruling *R. v. Egan* [1998] 1 Cr.App.R. 121, CA, and approving *Att.-Gen.'s Reference (No. 3 of 1998)* [1999] 2 Cr.App.R. 214, CA, *post*, § 4–468). Similarly, it is not open to a defendant charged with murder to raise lack of specific intent or provocation on the trial of an issue under section 4A(2), as any consideration of such issues inevitably requires examination of his state of mind: *R. (Grant) v. DPP*; *R. v. Grant* [2002] 1 Cr.App.R. 38, DC and CA.

For the purposes of the offence contrary to section 47(1)(a) of the *Financial Services Act* 1986 (see now the *FSMA* 2000, s.397, *post*, § 30–215d) of dishonest concealment of a material fact for the purpose of inducing a person to enter into an investment agreement, etc., a person's present intention is a "fact"; where, therefore, an indictment alleged that the fact concealed was the defendant's present intention, and the defendant was found unfit to plead, the "act or … omission charged against him" for the purposes of section 4A was the concealment of his present intention; accordingly, it fell to the jury to decide in the section 4A proceedings whether he had the intention alleged against him and whether he concealed it; but neither dishonesty nor the purpose of the defendant fell for decision in such proceedings: *R. (Young) v. Central Criminal Court* [2002] 2 Cr.App.R. 12, DC.

In *R. v. M. (K.J.)* [2003] 2 Cr.App.R. 21, CA, it was said that where it is alleged that the defendant was guilty of the offence otherwise than as the principal offender, the judge must direct the jury as to the minimum facts that would establish the "act" required to be proved against the defendant; if, by reason of the definition of the particular crime, or the level of participation required to establish liability, it was necessary for the jury to be satisfied that the defendant had a particular level of knowledge as to the activities of the principal offender and/or the surrounding circumstances, the judge should so direct; in such a case, as with issues such as mistake (*ante*), the determination will fall to be made as a matter of inference from the independent evidence of witnesses and not from the evidence of the defendant or the suggestions of counsel. Accordingly, where the defendant was charged with murder, it was for the jury to decide whether there had been a common purpose, the nature of it (if any) and whether the act of the principal went outside its scope. To that extent, the jury were bound to investigate the state of the defendant's knowledge. It should be noted, however, that what was said on this issue was *obiter*, the finding being quashed on unrelated grounds.

As to the procedure for appealing in respect of determinations under sections 4 and 4A of the 1964 Act, see *post*, § 7–151.

(b) *Order to be made where accused unfit to stand trial, but found to have done act or made omission charged against him*

The powers of the court to deal with persons not guilty by reason of insanity or unfit to plead were amended by the *Domestic Violence, Crime and Victims Act* 2004. For the former powers, reference should be made to the 2005 edition of this work at § 4–175. **4–175**

Criminal Procedure (Insanity) Act 1964, ss.5, 5A

Powers to deal with persons not guilty by reason of insanity or unfit to plead etc.

5.—(1) This section applies where— **4–175a**

(a) a special verdict is returned that the accused is not guilty by reason of insanity; or

(b) findings are recorded that the accused is under a disability and that he did the act or made the omission charged against him.

(2) The court shall make in respect of the accused—

(a) a hospital order (with or without a restriction order);

(b) a supervision order; or

(c) an order for his absolute discharge.

(3) Where—

(a) the offence to which the special verdict or the findings relate is an offence the sentence for which is fixed by law, and

(b) the court have power to make a hospital order,

the court shall make a hospital order with a restriction order (whether or not they would have power to make a restriction order apart from this subsection).

(4) In this section—

"hospital order" has the meaning given in section 37 of the *Mental Health Act* 1983;

"restriction order" has the meaning given to it by section 41 of that Act;

"supervision order" has the meaning given in Part 1 of Schedule 1A to this Act.

Orders made under or by virtue of section 5

4–175b **5A.**—(1) In relation to the making of an order by virtue of subsection (2)(a) of section 5 above, section 37 (hospital orders etc) of the *Mental Health Act* 1983 ("the 1983 Act") shall have effect as if—

(a) the reference in subsection (1) to a person being convicted before the Crown Court included a reference to the case where section 5 above applies;

(b) the words after "punishable with imprisonment" and before "or is convicted" were omitted; and

(c) for subsections (4) and (5) there were substituted—

"(4) Where an order is made under this section requiring a person to be admitted to a hospital ("a hospital order"), it shall be the duty of the managers of the hospital specified in the order to admit him in accordance with it."

(2) In relation to a case where section 5 above applies but the court have not yet made one of the disposals mentioned in subsection (2) of that section—

(a) section 35 of the 1983 Act (remand to hospital for report on accused's mental condition) shall have effect with the omission of the words after paragraph (b) in subsection (3);

(b) section 36 of that Act (remand of accused person to hospital for treatment) shall have effect with the omission of the words "(other than an offence the sentence for which is fixed by law)" in subsection (2);

(c) references in sections 35 and 36 of that Act to an accused person shall be construed as including a person in whose case this subsection applies; and

(d) section 38 of that Act (interim hospital orders) shall have effect as if—

(i) the reference in subsection (1) to a person being convicted before the Crown Court included a reference to the case where section 5 above applies; and

(ii) the words "(other than an offence the sentence for which is fixed by law)" in that subsection were omitted.

(3) In relation to the making of any order under the 1983 Act by virtue of this Act, references in the 1983 Act to an offender shall be construed as including references to a person in whose case section 5 above applies, and references to an offence shall be construed accordingly.

(4) Where—

(a) a person is detained in pursuance of a hospital order which the court had power to make by virtue of section 5(1)(b) above, and

(b) the court also made a restriction order, and that order has not ceased to have effect,

the Secretary of State, if satisfied after consultation with the responsible clinician that the person can properly be tried, may remit the person for trial, either to the court of trial or to a prison.

On the person's arrival at the court or prison, the hospital order and the restriction order shall cease to have effect.

(5) Schedule 1A to this Act (supervision orders) has effect with respect to the making of supervision orders under subsection (2)(b) of section 5 above, and with respect to the revocation and amendment of such orders.

(6) In relation to the making of an order under subsection (2)(c) of section 5 above, section 12(1) of the *Powers of Criminal Courts (Sentencing) Act* 2000 (absolute and conditional discharge) shall have effect as if—

(a) the reference to a person being convicted by or before a court of such an offence as is there mentioned included a reference to the case where section 5 above applies; and

(b) the reference to the court being of opinion that it is inexpedient to inflict punishment included a reference to it thinking that an order for absolute discharge would be most suitable in all the circumstances of the case.

[S.5 is printed as substituted, and s.5A as inserted, by the *Domestic Violence, Crime and Victims Act* 2004, s.24(1). S.5A is printed as subsequently amended by the *MHA* 2007, s.15(4).]

For Schedule 1A to this Act, see *post*, § 4–176; for hospital orders and section 37 of the *MHA* 1983, see *post*, § 5–894; for restriction orders and section 41 of the 1983 Act, see *post*, § 5–898. As to the special verdict of not guilty by reason of insanity, see *post*, §§ 4–468 *et seq*.

There is a right of appeal to the Court of Appeal, with leave, against a hospital order, interim hospital order, or supervision order made under section 5 or 5A (see *post*, § 7–153a).

In *R (Grant) v. DPP*; *R. v. Grant* [2002] 1 Cr.App.R. 38, DC and CA, it was held that, on the facts under consideration in that case, the order made under the precursor to section 5(2)(a) of the 1964 Act did not violate the rights of the defendant under Article 5 of the ECHR (*post*, § 16–43), because Article 5(1)(e) specifically allows for the detention of those of unsound mind, and there was ample evidence that the defendant was suffering from mental impairment that was treatable. However, the possibility of a violation of Article 5 by reason of the making of an order under section 5 of the 1964 Act in other circumstances was left open.

Where a person charged on an indictment which includes a summary offence (*CJA* 1988, s.40 (*ante*, § 1–75ai)) is found unfit to plead and is acquitted of all offences other than the summary offence, but is found to have done the act constituting the summary offence, the court has power to act under section 5, notwithstanding section 40(3) of the 1988 Act (summary offence to be tried in same manner as if it were an indictable offence but "Crown Court may only deal with the offender in respect of it in a manner in which a magistrates' court could have dealt with him"); a finding that the accused did the act charged is not a finding of guilt and the court, when acting under section 5, is not dealing with "an offender": *R. v. Southwark Crown Court ex p. Koncar* [1998] 1 Cr.App.R. 321, DC.

Criminal Procedure (Insanity) Act 1964, Sched. 1A

SCHEDULE 1A

SUPERVISION ORDERS

PART 1

Preliminary

1.—(1) In this Schedule "supervision order" means an order which requires the person in respect of whom it is made ("the supervised person") to be under the supervision of a social worker, an officer of a local probation board or an officer of a provider of probation services ("the supervising officer") for a period specified in the order of not more than two years. **4–176**

(2) A supervision order may, in accordance with paragraph 4 or 5 below, require the supervised person to submit, during the whole of that period or such part of it as may be specified in the order, to treatment by or under the direction of a registered medical practitioner.

(3) The Secretary of State may by order direct that sub-paragraph (1) above shall be amended by substituting, for the period for the time being specified there, such period as may be specified in the order.

(4) An order under sub-paragraph (3) above may make in paragraph 11(2) below any amendment which the Secretary of State thinks necessary in consequence of any substitution made by the order.

(5) The power of the Secretary of State to make orders under sub-paragraph (3) above shall be exercisable by statutory instrument which shall be subject to annulment in pursuance of a resolution of either House of Parliament.

PART 2

Making and Effect of Orders

Circumstances in which orders may be made

2.—(1) The court shall not make a supervision order unless it is satisfied that, having regard to all the circumstances of the case, the making of such an order is the most suitable means of dealing with the accused or appellant. **4–177**

(2) The court shall not make a supervision order unless it is also satisfied—

(a) that the supervising officer intended to be specified in the order is willing to undertake the supervision; and

(b) that arrangements have been made for the treatment intended to be specified in the order.

Making of orders and general requirements

4–178 3.—(1) A supervision order shall either—

(a) specify the local social services authority area in which the supervised person resides or will reside, and require him to be under the supervision of a social worker of the local social services authority for that area; or

(b) specify the local justice area in which that person resides or will reside, and require him to be under the supervision of an officer of a local probation board appointed for or assigned to that area, or (as the case may be) an officer of a provider of probation services acting in that area.

(2) Before making such an order, the court shall explain to the supervised person in ordinary language—

(a) the effect of the order (including any requirements proposed to be included in the order in accordance with paragraph 4, 5 or 8 below); and

(b) that a magistrates' court has power under paragraphs 9 to 11 below to review the order on the application either of the supervised person or of the supervising officer.

(3) After making such an order, the court shall forthwith give copies of the order to an officer of a local probation board assigned to the court or an officer of a provider of probation services acting at the court, and he shall give a copy—

(a) to the supervised person; and

(b) to the supervising officer.

(4) After making such an order, the court shall also send to the designated officer for the local justice area in which the supervised person resides or will reside ("the local justice area concerned")—

(a) a copy of the order; and

(b) such documents and information relating to the case as it considers likely to be of assistance to a court acting for that area in the exercise of its functions in relation to the order.

(5) Where such an order is made, the supervised person shall keep in touch with the supervising officer in accordance with such instructions as he may from time to time be given by that officer and shall notify him of any change of address.

Requirements as to medical treatment

4–179 4.—(1) A supervision order may, if the court is satisfied as mentioned in sub-paragraph (2) below, include a requirement that the supervised person shall submit, during the whole of the period specified in the order or during such part of that period as may be so specified, to treatment by or under the direction of a registered medical practitioner with a view to the improvement of his mental condition.

(2) The court may impose such a requirement only if satisfied on the written or oral evidence of two or more registered medical practitioners, at least one of whom is duly registered, that the mental condition of the supervised person—

(a) is such as requires and may be susceptible to treatment; but

(b) is not such as to warrant the making of a hospital order within the meaning of the *Mental Health Act* 1983.

(3) The treatment required under this paragraph by any such order shall be such one of the following kinds of treatment as may be specified in the order, that is to say—

(a) treatment as a non-resident patient at such institution or place as may be specified in the order; and

(b) treatment by or under the direction of such registered medical practitioner as may be so specified;

but the nature of the treatment shall not be specified in the order except as mentioned in paragraph (a) or (b) above.

5.—(1) This paragraph applies where the court is satisfied on the written or oral evidence of two or more registered medical practitioners that—

(a) because of his medical condition, other than his mental condition, the supervised person is likely to pose a risk to himself or others; and

(b) the condition may be susceptible to treatment.

(2) The supervision order may (whether or not it includes a requirement under paragraph 4 above) include a requirement that the supervised person shall submit, during

the whole of the period specified in the order or during such part of that period as may be so specified, to treatment by or under the direction of a registered medical practitioner with a view to the improvement of the condition.

(3) The treatment required under this paragraph by any such order shall be such one of the following kinds of treatment as may be specified in the order, that is to say—

(a) treatment as a non-resident patient at such institution or place as may be specified in the order; and

(b) treatment by or under the direction of such registered medical practitioner as may be so specified;

but the nature of the treatment shall not be specified in the order except as mentioned in paragraph (a) or (b) above.

6.—(1) Where the medical practitioner by whom or under whose direction the supervised person is being treated in pursuance of a requirement under paragraph 4 or 5 above is of the opinion that part of the treatment can be better or more conveniently given in or at an institution or place which—

(a) is not specified in the order, and

(b) is one in or at which the treatment of the supervised person will be given by or under the direction of a registered medical practitioner,

he may, with the consent of the supervised person, make arrangements for him to be treated accordingly.

(2) Such arrangements may provide for the supervised person to receive part of his treatment as a resident patient in an institution or place of any description.

(3) Where any such arrangements are made for the treatment of a supervised person—

(a) the medical practitioner by whom the arrangements are made shall give notice in writing to the supervising officer, specifying the institution or place in or at which the treatment is to be carried out; and

(b) the treatment provided for by the arrangements shall be deemed to be treatment to which he is required to submit in pursuance of the supervision order.

7. While the supervised person is under treatment as a resident patient in pursuance of arrangements under paragraph 6 above, the supervising officer shall carry out the supervision to such extent only as may be necessary for the purpose of the revocation or amendment of the order.

Requirements as to residence

8.—(1) Subject to sub-paragraph (2) below, a supervision order may include requirements as to the residence of the supervised person. **4–180**

(2) Before making such an order containing any such requirement, the court shall consider the home surroundings of the supervised person.

PART 3

Revocation and Amendment of Orders

Revocation of order

9.—(1) Where a supervision order is in force in respect of any person and, on the application of the supervised person or the supervising officer, it appears to a magistrates' court acting for the local justice area concerned that, having regard to circumstances which have arisen since the order was made, it would be in the interests of the health or welfare of the supervised person that the order should be revoked, the court may revoke the order. **4–181**

(2) The court by which a supervision order was made may of its own motion revoke the order if, having regard to circumstances which have arisen since the order was made, it considers that it would be inappropriate for the order to continue.

Amendment of order by reason of change of residence

10.—(1) This paragraph applies where, at any time while a supervision order is in force in respect of any person, a magistrates' court acting for the local justice area concerned is satisfied that the supervised person proposes to change, or has changed, his residence from the area specified in the order to another local social services authority area or local justice area. **4–182**

(2) Subject to sub-paragraph (3) below, the court may, and on the application of the supervising officer shall, amend the supervision order by substituting the other area for the area specified in the order.

(3) The court shall not amend under this paragraph a supervision order which contains

requirements which, in the opinion of the court, cannot be complied with unless the supervised person continues to reside in the area specified in the order unless, in accordance with paragraph 11 below, it either—

(a) cancels those requirements; or

(b) substitutes for those requirements other requirements which can be complied with if the supervised person ceases to reside in that area.

Amendment of requirements of order

4–183 11.—(1) Without prejudice to the provisions of paragraph 10 above, but subject to sub-paragraph (2) below, a magistrates' court for the local justice area concerned may, on the application of the supervised person or the supervising officer, by order amend a supervision order—

(a) by cancelling any of the requirements of the order; or

(b) by inserting in the order (either in addition to or in substitution for any such requirement) any requirement which the court could include if it were the court by which the order was made and were then making it.

(2) The power of a magistrates' court under sub-paragraph (1) above shall not include power to amend an order by extending the period specified in it beyond the end of two years from the day of the original order.

Amendment of requirements in pursuance of medical report

4–184 12.—(1) Where the medical practitioner by whom or under whose direction the supervised person is being treated for his mental condition in pursuance of any requirement of a supervision order—

(a) is of the opinion mentioned in sub-paragraph (2) below, or

(b) is for any reason unwilling to continue to treat or direct the treatment of the supervised person,

he shall make a report in writing to that effect to the supervising officer and that officer shall apply under paragraph 11 above to a magistrates' court for the local justice area concerned for the variation or cancellation of the requirement.

(2) The opinion referred to in sub-paragraph (1) above is—

(a) that the treatment of the supervised person should be continued beyond the period specified in the supervision order;

(b) that the supervised person needs different treatment, being treatment of a kind to which he could be required to submit in pursuance of such an order;

(c) that the supervised person is not susceptible to treatment; or

(d) that the supervised person does not require further treatment.

Supplemental

4–185 13.—(1) On the making under paragraph 9 above of an order revoking a supervision order, the designated officer for the local justice area concerned, or (as the case may be) the Crown Court, shall forthwith give copies of the revoking order to the supervising officer.

(2) A supervising officer to whom in accordance with sub-paragraph (1) above copies of a revoking order are given shall give a copy to the supervised person and to the person in charge of any institution in which the supervised person is residing.

14.—(1) On the making under paragraph 10 or 11 above of any order amending a supervision order, the designated officer for the local justice area concerned shall forthwith—

(a) if the order amends the supervision order otherwise than by substituting a new area or a new place for the one specified in the supervision order, give copies of the amending order to the supervising officer;

(b) if the order amends the supervision order in the manner excepted by paragraph (a) above, send to the designated officer for the new local justice area concerned—

(i) copies of the amending order; and

(ii) such documents and information relating to the case as he considers likely to be of assistance to a court acting for that area in exercising its functions in relation to the order;

and in a case falling within paragraph (b) above, the designated officer for that area shall give copies of the amending order to the supervising officer.

(2) Where the designated officer for the court making the order is also the designated officer for the new local justice area—

(a) sub-paragraph (1)(b) above does not apply; but

(b) the designated officers [*sic*] shall give copies of the amending order to the supervising officer.

(3) Where in accordance with sub-paragraph (1) or (2) above copies of an order are given to the supervising officer, he shall give a copy to the supervised person and to the person in charge of any institution in which the supervised person is or was residing.

[This schedule was inserted by the *Domestic Violence, Crime and Victims Act* 2004, s.24(2), and Sched. 2. It is printed as amended by the *Offender Management Act 2007 (Consequential Amendments) Order* 2008 (S.I. 2008 No. 912), art. 3, and Sched. 1, para. 2.]

C. CHANGE OF PLEA

The arraignment is not complete till the defendant has pleaded: *R. v. Duffy* (1848) 7 St.Tr.(n.s.) 795 at 799. If the defendant pleads "not guilty" his plea is recorded by the officer of the court; either by writing on the indictment the words "not guilty" or, "*po. se*" (an abbreviation of the words *ponit se super patriam*), or, as at the Central Criminal Court, the word "puts", and by an entry in the minute book of the court: see *R. v. Newman* (1852) 2 Den. 390. A plea of not guilty may, by leave of the judge, be withdrawn during the trial, and a plea of guilty substituted. The procedure is for the relevant count to be put to the defendant again, and the new plea should be tendered by the defendant and not by someone (*e.g.* counsel) on his behalf: *R. v. Ellis (J.)*, 57 Cr.App.R. 571 at 574–575, CA. Although it is permissible to discharge the jury once the guilty plea has been tendered (*R. v. Poole* [2002] 2 Cr.App.R. 13, CA), the normal practice is for the verdict then to be taken from the jury, as the defendant is in their charge; as to how this should be done, see *post*, § 4–412. An alternative to re-arraigning the accused in front of the jury, and then taking a verdict from them, is to discharge the jury first (as in *R. v. McCarthy* [1998] 2 *Archbold News* 1, CA (96 8158 Y5) (*post*, § 9–92)); but there is a risk of a manipulative defendant wrecking a trial by indicating an intention to change plea and then failing to do so. **4–186**

Ordinarily, a plea of guilty may be changed right up to the moment that sentence is passed: *R. v. Plummer* [1902] 2 K.B. 339; *S. (an Infant) v. Manchester City Recorder* [1971] A.C. 481, HL; *R. v. Dodd*, 74 Cr.App.R. 50, CA; and *Richards v. R.* [1993] A.C. 217, PC. Only rarely, however, would it be appropriate for a judge to exercise this discretion, particularly where the accused has been represented by experienced counsel and, after full consultation with counsel, had already changed his plea from not guilty to guilty at an earlier stage in the proceedings: *R. v. Drew*, 81 Cr.App.R. 190, CA; *aliter*, where the defendant had been erroneously advised that his factual case provided him with no defence: *R. v. Sorhaindo* [2006] 7 *Archbold News* 2, CA. As to the procedure to be followed when making an application to change a plea of guilty, see *post*, § 4–187a. **4–187**

The discretion of magistrates to permit the withdrawal of an unequivocal plea of guilty was considered in *R. v. South Tameside Magistrates' Court, ex p. Rowland* [1983] 3 All E.R. 689, DC. As to how the discretion should be exercised, see *ante*, § 2–200, and *R. v. Bow Street Stipendiary Magistrate, ex p. Roche*, *The Times*, February 5, 1987, DC (proper exercise of discretion to reject an application to withdraw a plea of guilty, made without the benefit of legal advice, when the magistrate believed the application was made through fear of the imposition of a custodial sentence).

When a defendant has been committed to the Crown Court for sentence, the court has no jurisdiction to remit the matter to the magistrates' court upon it appearing that the defendant pleaded guilty on the basis of a material mistake of fact, but it does have the discretion to allow an application for a change of plea, and, if such an application is granted the court must then remit the matter to the magistrates with a direction to enter a plea of not guilty: *R. v. Isleworth Crown Court and Uxbridge Magistrates' Court, ex p. Buda* [2000] 1 Cr.App.R.(S.) 538, DC. See generally *ante*, § 2–200, as to remitting matters to the magistrates on the basis of a change of plea.

An application to change plea that is made before sentence is passed should be allowed if the court is satisfied that it is made on the ground that it is arguable that the prosecution evidence would not establish the essential ingredients of the offence; and this is so even though the plea of guilty was originally entered as part of an agreement whereunder the prosecution agreed to a not guilty verdict in respect of another offence of at least equal gravity: *R. v. Bournemouth JJ., ex p. Maguire* [1997] C.O.D. 21, DC. *Quaere* the status of the charge on which the not guilty verdict had been entered. In this regard, certain of the authorities cited at § 4–144 may be of relevance. No question of *autrefois acquit* would arise in such a case if the alternative charges had been discontinued or adjourned *sine die*, or, in the Crown Court, left on the file (*post*, § 4–190).

A court has no power to allow a plea of guilty to be withdrawn after sentence: *R. v. McNally*, 38 Cr.App.R. 90, CCA, but see *post*, § 7–46b.

As to the possible consequences of a change of plea by one of a number of defendants, see *post*, § 9–92.

Criminal Procedure Rules 2005 (S.I. 2005 No. 384), r.39.3

Application to change a plea of guilty

4–187a **39.3.**—(1) The defendant must apply as soon as practicable after becoming aware of the grounds for making an application to change a plea of guilty, and may only do so before the final disposal of the case, by sentence or otherwise.

(2) Unless the court otherwise directs, the application must be in writing and it must—

(a) set out the reasons why it would be unjust for the guilty plea to remain unchanged;
(b) indicate what, if any, evidence the defendant wishes to call;
(c) identify any proposed witness; and
(d) indicate whether legal professional privilege is waived, specifying any material name and date.

(3) The defendant must serve the written application on—

(a) the court officer; and
(b) the prosecutor.

[This rule was inserted by the *Criminal Procedure (Amendment No. 2) Rules* 2007 (S.I. 2007 No. 2317).]

Part 39 of the 2005 rules relates to trial on indictment; where a defendant has been committed to the Crown Court for sentence, identical provisions in rule 37.6, relating to summary trial, will apply.

III. PROSECUTION NOT PROCEEDING

A. ALTERNATIVE CHARGES

4–188 Where a charge is an alternative of equal gravity to a charge to which the defendant has pleaded guilty (*e.g.* where a plea of guilty is entered on a charge of theft or burglary and dishonest handling is averred as an alternative), it is usual for the alternative charge not to be put to the defendant (*ante*, § 4–98). Where a plea of guilty is to be entered to the alternative charge alleged in the second count (or in the subsequent counts), it is desirable for that count (or those counts) to be put first. Where the alternatives are of differing gravity, such a course may not be appropriate. For example, where the accused is charged, in the alternative, with contraventions of sections 18 and 20 of the *Offences against the Person Act* 1861, the proper course, if a plea of guilty is to be entered (and accepted) to the lesser charge (s.20), is for pleas to be taken upon each count and thereafter (following the Crown's acceptance of the plea to the lesser charge), for the judge to direct that a verdict of "not guilty" be entered in respect of the graver charge (s.18) under section 17 of the *CJA* 1967, *ante*, § 4–127; but see *post*, § 4–190. If, on the other hand, a plea of guilty is entered to the graver charge (s.18) the lesser charge should not be put.

B. OFFERING NO EVIDENCE

4–189 Where the Crown proposes to offer no evidence upon a particular charge, the usual practice is for the judge to direct that a verdict of not guilty be recorded under section

17 of the *CJA* 1967 (*ante*, § 4–127). If the Crown takes this course after a jury has been sworn and the defendant given in charge, the jury will be directed to return a verdict of not guilty: see *ante*, § 4–186. As to the desirability of discussions with any alleged victims before and after a decision is taken to offer no evidence, see the Attorney-General's guidelines on the acceptance of pleas (Appendix A–259); and as to the role of the judge in the decision to offer no evidence, see *ante*, §§ 4–96 *et seq.*

Under a new administrative procedure, the prosecution, if the defence and court agree, may offer no evidence without the need for the defendant to be present or for the parties to be represented. The procedure is available if the defendant has already been arraigned and as a result of new information or a change of circumstances, the prosecution decide not to proceed.

The first step will be for the prosecution to telephone the defence solicitors to explain why they do not intend to proceed and to suggest that the new procedure be used. If the defence is content for the case to be disposed of in this way, the prosecution will write in confirmation and will copy the letter to the court and to any co-defendant's solicitor. Once the judge has agreed to the procedure, the case will be listed as soon as possible. If the judge decides that the parties should be represented, or the defence subsequently withdraws consent, the case will be listed in the normal way with the parties attending. Where there is agreement, the case will be listed "For mention—parties not required to attend." At the hearing, a formal verdict of not guilty will be recorded by the court clerk following a pronouncement in open court by the judge. Steps will be taken to secure the immediate release of any defendant in custody.

Orders for costs from central funds, or in connection with legal aid contributions can be made in the absence of the parties, although the defence will need to inform the court if it wishes to apply for such an order. A full court hearing will be required if the court is not willing to make the order sought and if the defence wishes to pursue it. Wasted costs orders will also require a full hearing.

C. LEAVING COUNT OR INDICTMENT ON FILE

Where the plea (or pleas) of guilty entered by the defendant is regarded by the Crown (and by the judge if his approval is sought—see *ante*, §§ 4–96 *et seq.*) as an adequate plea to the indictment as a whole—for example, where a defendant pleads guilty to one or more serious offences alleged in an indictment and pleads not guilty to one or more relatively less serious offences—a direction under section 17 of the *CJA* 1967 (*ante*, § 4–127) may be wholly inappropriate and it is the practice for the judge to order that the particular count or counts be left on the file marked: "Not to be proceeded with without the leave of the court or the Court of Appeal." The consent of the judge is required for this order, but as a matter of practice the judge usually does consent, provided that the defence agree. See *R. v. Moorhead* [1973] Crim.L.R. 36, CA. **4–190**

For observations upon the significance of this order: see *Connelly v. DPP* [1964] A.C. 1254, HL. See also *R. v. Riebold* [1967] 1 W.L.R. 674, Assizes (Barry J.) (leave to proceed on substantive counts refused after conspiracy conviction quashed), and *R. v. Central Criminal Court, ex p. Randle and Pottle*, 92 Cr.App.R. 323, DC.

Where the accused has pleaded guilty to, or been found guilty upon, one indictment, it is common for a second indictment to which he has pleaded "not guilty" to be left on the file on the same terms with the consent of both sides.

Leave to proceed upon an indictment or counts left on the file may be given by the Court of Appeal when counts on which he was convicted are quashed on appeal: see, for example, *Connelly v. DPP*, *ante*.

Defendant's consent

It is impossible to challenge such order in the Court of Appeal (*R. v. Mackell*, 74 Cr.App.R. 27, CA), or by way of judicial review (*R. v. Central Criminal Court, ex p. Raymond*, 83 Cr.App.R. 94, DC). The court should, therefore, proceed with caution if the agreement of a defendant to such an order is not forthcoming. In *ex p. Raymond*, it was said that such an order is akin to an adjournment over which the trial judge has the final say. It should be confined to the circumstances contemplated, *ante* (*i.e.* sufficient **4–191** pleas of guilty or findings of guilt taking the indictment(s) as a whole). It should never be made where the defendant pleads not guilty and the prosecution are disinclined to proceed, but are unwilling to offer no evidence; in such circumstances, the defendant's consent is insufficient reason for ordering a whole indictment to lie on the file (*cf. R. v. Central Criminal Court, ex p. Spens, The Times*, December 31, 1992, DC, *ante*, § 4–127). *Aliter*, if there are grounds for a stay other than mere convenience (which is no ground): see *ante*, §§ 4–48 *et seq.*, for the grounds on which a stay may be granted.

IV. SENTENCING ACCOMPLICES

A. ACCOMPLICES WHO ARE NOT TO BE CALLED

4–192 The proper course is to postpone sentence on the defendant who has pleaded guilty until the other or others have been tried. By that time, the court will be in possession of the facts relating to all of them and will be able to assess properly the degree of guilt among them: *R. v. Payne*, 34 Cr.App.R. 43, CCA. Where, however, the judge is of the opinion at any stage during the proceedings that he is in possession of the material facts and is able to assess properly the degree of guilt as between the particular defendant and the other accused, it is submitted that it is within his discretion to deal with the defendant at that stage if it is desirable that he should do so.

B. ACCOMPLICES WHO ARE TO BE CALLED

The calling of an accomplice or co-defendant by the Crown

4–193 Where it is proposed to call an accomplice for the Crown, it is the practice to: (a) omit him from the indictment; or (b) take his plea of guilty on arraignment: *Winsor v. R.* (1866) L.R. 1 Q.B. 289 at 390, or during the trial, if he withdraws his plea of not guilty: *R. v. Tomey*, 2 Cr.App.R. 329, CCA; or before calling him either (c) offer no evidence and permit his acquittal: *R. v. Owen* (1839) 9 C. & P. 83; or (d) enter a *nolle prosequi*: *R. v. O'Connor (F.)* (1843) 4 St.Tr.(n.s.) 935. This statement of the practice was approved by the Court of Appeal in *R. v. Pipe*, 51 Cr.App.R. 17, CA (accomplice witness still to be tried).

In *R. v. Turner (B.J.)*, 61 Cr.App.R. 67, CA, it was contended for the defence that there had been for some time past a practice for judges not to admit the evidence of accomplices who could still be influenced by continuing inducements and that the court in *Pipe*, *ante*, had adjudged this practice to have become a rule of law. The court in rejecting the submission reviewed the origins of the practice, and concluded:

> "There is nothing either in the arguments or the judgment itself to indicate that the Court thought it was changing a rule of law as to the competency of accomplices to give evidence which had been followed ever since the 17th century .... Its *ratio decidendi* is confined to a case in which an accomplice, who has been charged, but not tried, is required to give evidence of his own offence in order to secure the conviction of another accused. *Pipe* on its facts was clearly a correct decision. The same result could have been achieved by adjudging that the trial judge should have exercised his discretion to exclude [the accomplice's] evidence on the ground that there was an obvious and powerful inducement for him to ingratiate himself with the prosecution and the Court and that the existence of this inducement made it desirable in the interests of justice to exclude it" (*per* Lawton L.J. at p. 78).

Although Lord Parker C.J., in giving the judgment in *Pipe*, had described what had occurred as being "wholly irregular":

> "it does not follow that in all cases calling a witness who can benefit from giving evidence is 'wholly irregular'. To hold so would be absurd. Examples are provided by the prosecution witness who hopes to get a reward which has been offered 'for information leading to a conviction' or even an order for compensation, or whose claim for damages may be helped by a conviction. ... If the inducement is very powerful, the judge may decide to exercise his discretion; but when doing so he must take into consideration all factors, including those affecting the public. It is in the interests of the public that criminals should be brought to justice; and the more serious the crimes the greater is the need for justice to be done" (*ibid.*, at pp. 78–79).

The line of authorities culminating in *Turner (B.J.)* was reviewed in *R. v. Governor of Pentonville Prison, ex p. Schneider*, 73 Cr.App.R. 200, DC. See also *R. v. Palmer*, *post*, § 4–195, and *Chan Wai-keung v. R.* [1995] 2 Cr.App.R. 194, PC.

In *R. v. Sinclair*, *The Times*, April 18, 1989, CA, O'Connor L.J. said that whilst it was undesirable to try to say what must be done in every case, because circumstances are so infinitely variable, in principle the prosecution must be careful before deciding to call as a witness an accomplice who is a participator in the crime of which the defendant is accused. Ordinarily, this should not be done without a clear indication from the accomplice that he is willing to give evidence in favour of the Crown. In *Sinclair*, accomplices who had incriminated the appellant in the course of interviews with the police and in pleas in mitigation entered on their behalves, but who had not made witness statements, were called as prosecution witnesses and were treated as "hostile" when they gave evidence that contradicted what they had said in their interviews. The court hoped that this sort of situation would not arise again. **4–194**

Sentencing defendant who is to give evidence for the Crown

Where a man pleads guilty and it is the prosecutor's intention to call him against a co-defendant, the decision as to whether the trial judge sentences him before or after he has given evidence for the prosecution is a matter within the discretion of the judge: *R. v. Palmer*, 99 Cr.App.R. 83, CA. The modern practice, however, is generally not to sentence an accomplice until the conclusion of all the proceedings in the case; this would enable the judge to get the flavour of the case and to view it in the round at the conclusion of all the evidence: *ibid.*, and *R. v. Weekes*, 74 Cr.App.R. 161, 166, CA. This practice is based on the risk of disparity in sentence; different considerations apply in respect of sentence on an offender who is to give evidence for the prosecution in a case that is unrelated to his own, so as to mitigate his own sentence: *Chan Wai-keung v. R.*, *ante*, § 4–193. **4–195**

The object of sentencing in advance a co-defendant who is to give evidence for the prosecution is that there should be no suggestion that he is under any inducement to give evidence which will result in his getting a shorter sentence than otherwise. Equally, a judge should never bring back an accused person in order to increase his sentence where, in giving evidence against a co-accused after being sentenced originally, he fails to adhere to the account put forward on his behalf by way of mitigation and in effect changes his evidence: *R. v. Stone*, 54 Cr.App.R. 364, CA.

For the procedure introduced by the *SOCPA* 2005, s.73, where a defendant has assisted or offered to assist the prosecution pursuant to a written agreement, see *post*, § 5–94a.

Sentencing defendant who is to give evidence for a co-defendant

Ordinarily a person falling into this category should be sentenced at the end of the case: *R. v. Coffey*, 74 Cr.App.R. 168, CA. **4–196**

Undertaking of immunity from prosecution

Such undertakings may on occasions have to be given in the public interest. They should never be given by the police: *R. v. Turner (B.J.)*, 61 Cr.App.R. 67 at 80. The further observations made by Lawton L.J. in *Turner (B.J.)* (at p. 80), which were apparently intended (at least to some extent) to regulate the conduct of the Director of Public Prosecutions, should circumstances of a similar nature arise again, were disapproved by Lord Salmon and Lord Dilhorne on the application to the House of Lords for leave to appeal. The application (unreported) was refused. As to the propriety of giving such an undertaking, the procedure to be followed, and the effect thereof, see the observations in *McDonald v. R.*, 77 Cr.App.R. 196, PC. See also *R. v. Mathias*, *The Times*, August 24, 1989, CA; *R. v. Croydon JJ., ex p. Dean*, 98 Cr.App.R. 76, DC; and *R. v. Townsend* [1997] 2 Cr.App.R. 540, CA, *ante*, § 4–62. **4–197**

For immunity notices given under the *SOCPA* 2005, s.71, see *ante*, § 1–94.

V. SEPARATE TRIALS

Where two indictments are tried together, the trial is a nullity: *Crane v. DPP* [1921] **4–198**

A.C. 299, HL, and *R. v. Olivo*, 28 Cr.App.R. 173, CCA. Consent is immaterial: *R. v. Dennis and Parker*, 18 Cr.App.R. 39, CCA.

For separate trials of persons jointly indicted, and for separate trials of counts in the same indictment, see *ante*, §§ 1–166 *et seq.*

VI. THE JURY

A. INTRODUCTION

4–199 As to the requirement under Article 6(1) of the ECHR for trial by an independent and impartial tribunal, see *post*, §§ 16–57 and 16–74.

Subject to the provisions of the *Juries Act* 1974, all enactments and rules of law relating to trials by jury, juries and jurors shall continue in force and, in criminal cases, continue to apply to proceedings in the Crown Court as they applied to proceedings before a court of oyer and terminer or gaol delivery: s.21(5).

The provisions making large groups of persons (such as those concerned with the administration of justice) ineligible for jury service, and allowing others to be excused as of right, were repealed by the *CJA* 2003, s.321, and Sched. 33. Police officers, members of the CPS, or other persons involved in the administration of justice, including judges, are not to be regarded as being disqualified from a jury by reason of their occupation: *R. v. Abdroikov*; *R. v. Green*; *R. v. Williamson* [2008] 1 Cr.App.R. 21, HL. As to whether police officers or CPS lawyers ought to sit as jurors in particular cases, see, *post*, § 4–233a. For guidance where those involved in the administration of justice apply for excusal or deferral on grounds that they may be known to a party or parties involved in the trial, see *post*, § 4–229b.

For provisions in the 2003 Act for trials on indictment without a jury in certain fraud cases and where there is a danger of, or has been, jury tampering, see *post*, §§ 4–267a *et seq.*

B. QUALIFICATION

Juries Act 1974, s.1

4–200 **1.**—(1) Subject to the provisions of this Act, every person shall be qualified to serve as a juror in the Crown Court, the High Court and county courts and be liable accordingly to attend for jury service when summoned under this Act if—

(a) he is for the time being registered as a parliamentary or local government elector and is not less than eighteen nor more than seventy years of age;

(b) he has been ordinarily resident in the United Kingdom, the Channel Islands or the Isle of Man for any period of at least five years since attaining the age of thirteen;

(c) he is not a mentally disordered person; and

(d) he is not disqualified for jury service.

(2) In subsection (1) above "mentally disordered person" means any person listed in Part 1 of Schedule 1 to this Act.

(3) The persons who are disqualified for jury service are those listed in Part 2 of that Schedule.

[This section is printed as amended by the *CJA* 2003, s.321, and Sched. 33, paras 1 and 2.]

See *post*, §§ 4–224 *et seq.* as to excusal from, and deferral of, jury service.

Juries Act 1974, Sched. 1

SCHEDULE 1

MENTALLY DISORDERED PERSONS AND PERSONS DISQUALIFIED FOR JURY SERVICE

PART 1

Mentally Disordered Persons

4–201 1. A person who suffers or has suffered from mental disorder within the meaning of the *Mental Health Act* 1983 and on account of that condition either—

(a) is resident in a hospital or similar institution; or
(b) regularly attends for treatment by a medical practitioner.

2. A person for the time being under guardianship under section 7 of the *Mental Health Act* 1983 or subject to a community treatment order under section 17A of that Act.

3. A person who, under Part 7 of that Act, has been determined by a judge to be incapable, by reason of mental disorder, of managing and administering his property and affairs.

4.—(2) For the purposes of this Part a person is to be treated as being under guardianship under section 7 of the *Mental Health Act* 1983 at any time while he is subject to guardianship pursuant to an order under section 116A(2)(b) of the *Army Act* 1955, section 116A(2)(b) of the *Air Force Act* 1955 or section 63A(2)(b) of the *Naval Discipline Act* 1957.

PART 2

Persons Disqualified

5. A person who is on bail in criminal proceedings (within the meaning of the *Bail Act* 1976). **4–202**

6. A person who has at any time been sentenced in the United Kingdom, the Channel Islands or the Isle of Man—

(a) to imprisonment for life, detention for life or custody for life,
(b) to detention during her Majesty's pleasure or during the pleasure of the Secretary of State,
(c) to imprisonment for public protection or detention for public protection,
(d) to an extended sentence under section 227 or 228 of the *Criminal Justice Act* 2003 or section 210A of the *Criminal Procedure (Scotland) Act* 1995, or
(e) to a term of imprisonment of five years or more or a term of detention of five years or more.

7. A person who at any time in the last ten years has—

(a) in the United Kingdom, the Channel Islands or the Isle of Man—
  (i) served any part of a sentence of imprisonment or a sentence of detention, or
  (ii) had passed on him a suspended sentence of imprisonment or had made in respect of him a suspended order for detention,
(b) in England and Wales, had made in respect of him a community order under section 177 of the *Criminal Justice Act* 2003, a community rehabilitation order, a community punishment order, a community punishment and rehabilitation order, a drug treatment and testing order or a drug abstinence order, or
(c) had made in respect of him any corresponding order under the law of Scotland, Northern Ireland, the Isle of Man or any of the Channel Islands [or a service community order or overseas community order under the *Armed Forces Act* 2006].

8. For the purposes of this Part of this Schedule—

(a) a sentence passed *by a court-martial* [(anywhere) in respect of a service offence within the meaning of the *Armed Forces Act* 2006] is to be treated as having been passed in the United Kingdom, and
(b) a person is sentenced to a term of detention if, but only if—
  (i) a court passes on him, or makes in respect of him on conviction, any sentence or order which requires him to be detained in custody for any period, and
  (ii) the sentence or order is available only in respect of offenders below a certain age,

and any reference to serving a sentence of detention is to be construed accordingly.

[This Schedule is printed as substituted by *CJA* 2003, s.321, and Sched. 33, paras 1 and 15. Pt 1 is printed as amended, and repealed in part, by the *MHA* 2007, ss.1(4), 32(4) and 55, Sched. 1, para. 18, Sched. 4, para. 4, and Sched. 11, Pt 1. Pt 2 is printed as amended, as from a day to be appointed, by the *AFA* 2006, s.378(1), and Sched. 16, para. 62 (omission of words in italics, insertion of words in square brackets).]

[The next paragraph is § 4–206.]

Electoral register as basis of jury selection

4–206 Section 3 of the *Juries Act* 1974 (amended, as from a day to be appointed, in relation to anonymous entries in the register, by the *Electoral Administration Act* 2006, Sched. 1, para. 1) provides for the marking of copies of electoral registers to indicate those persons whom the electoral registration officer has ascertained to be outside the age limits for jury service at a given date, and for delivery of those marked copies of the registers to such officers as the Lord Chancellor may designate. It was formerly held that it was no ground of challenge to the array (*post*, § 4–240) that justices had failed in their duty with regard to marking up the jury book, and the jury had been summoned from a book improperly made: *O'Connell v. R.* (1844) 4 St.Tr.(n.s.) 69 at 78.

Validation of verdict where juror not qualified

4–207 See the *Juries Act* 1974, s.18, *post*, § 4–222.

C. SUMMONING AND PANELS

Juries Act 1974, s.2

Summoning

4–208 **2.**—(1) Subject to the provisions of this Act, the Lord Chancellor shall be responsible for the summoning of jurors to attend for service in the Crown Court, the High Court and county courts and for determining the occasions on which they are to attend when so summoned, and the number to be summoned.

(2) In making arrangements to discharge his duty under subsection (1) above, the Lord Chancellor shall have regard to the convenience of the persons summoned and to their respective places of residence, and in particular to the desirability of selecting jurors within reasonable daily travelling distance of the place where they are to attend.

(3) Subject to subsection (2) above, there shall be no restriction on the places in England and Wales at which a person may be required to attend or serve on a jury under this Act.

(4) Subject to the provisions of this Act, jurors shall be so summoned by notice in writing sent by post, or delivered by hand.

For the purposes of section 26 of the *Interpretation Act* 1889 (presumption as to receipt of letter properly addressed and sent by post) the notice shall be regarded as properly addressed if the address is that shown in the electoral register, and a notice so addressed, and delivered by hand to that address, shall be deemed to have been delivered personally to the person to whom it is addressed unless the contrary is proved.

4–209 (5) A written summons sent or delivered to any person under subsection (4) above shall be accompanied by a notice informing him—

(a) of the effect of sections 1, … 10 and 20 (5) of this Act; and

(b) that he may make representations to the appropriate officer with a view to obtaining the withdrawal of the summons, if for any reason he is not qualified for jury service, or wishes or is entitled to be excused;

and where a person is summoned under subsection (4) above or under section 6 of this Act, the appropriate officer may at any time put or cause to be put to him such questions as the officer thinks fit in order to establish whether or not the person is qualified for jury service.

(6) A certificate signed by the appropriate officer and stating that a written summons under this Act, properly addressed and prepaid, was posted by him shall be admissible as evidence in any proceedings, and shall be so admissible without proof of his signature or official character.

[This section is printed as amended by the *Administration of Justice Act* 1982, s.61; and the *CJA* 2003, s.332, and Sched. 37, Pt 10.]

Section 26 of the *Interpretation Act* 1889 has been replaced by section 7 of the *Interpretation Act* 1978 (Appendix B–7), and see Appendix B–17.

The summoning of jurors is an administrative function of the Lord Chancellor's department, in respect of which the trial judge has no power to interfere: *R. v. Ford* [1989] Q.B. 868, 89 Cr.App.R. 278, CA; *R. v. Tarrant* [1998] Crim.L.R. 342, CA. As to this, see further *post*, § 4–233b.

The Lord Chancellor may authorise another person, or that person's employees, to perform his functions under section 2 of the 1974 Act, in so far as those functions involve the production and posting of jury summonses and the signing of certificates of posting under section 2(6): *Contracting Out (Jury Summoning Functions) Order* 1999 (S.I. 1999 No. 2128).

Juries Act 1974, ss.4, 5

Withdrawal or alteration of summons

4. If it appears to the appropriate officer, at any time before the day on which any person summoned under section 2 of this Act is first to attend, that his attendance is unnecessary, or can be dispensed with on any particular day or days, the appropriate officer may withdraw or alter the summons by notice served in the same way as a notice of summons. **4–210**

Panels

5.—(1) The arrangements to be made by the Lord Chancellor under this Act shall include the preparation of lists (called panels) of persons summoned as jurors, and the information to be included in panels, the court sittings for which they are prepared, their division into parts or sets (whether according to the day of first attendance or otherwise), their enlargement or amendment, and all other matters relating to the contents and form of the panels shall be such as the Lord Chancellor may from time to time direct. **4–211**

(2) A party to proceedings in which jurors are or may be called on to try an issue, and any person acting on behalf of a party to such proceedings, shall be entitled to reasonable facilities for inspecting the panel from which the jurors are or will be drawn.

(3) The right conferred by subsection (2) above shall not be exercisable after the close of the trial by jury (or after the time when it is no longer possible for there to be a trial by jury).

(4) The court may, if it thinks fit, at any time afford to any person facilities for inspecting the panel, although not given the right by subsection (2) above.

(5) The Lord Chancellor must consult the Lord Chief Justice before giving any direction under subsection (1).

(6) The Lord Chief Justice may nominate a judicial office holder (as defined in section 109(4) of the *Constitutional Reform Act* 2005) to exercise his functions under this section.

[Subss. (5) and (6) were inserted by the *Constitutional Reform Act* 2005, s.15(1), and Sched. 4, paras 77 and 78.]

In 1973 the Lord Chancellor issued a directive stating that information contained in jury panels should no longer include the particulars of prospective jurors' occupations.

Jury vetting

In *R. v. McCann*, 92 Cr.App.R. 239, CA, it was argued on behalf of the appellants that the vetting of a jury panel at the instigation of the Attorney-General, in order to enable him to exercise his right of stand by (*post*, § 4–250), was contrary to the principle of random selection, was unconstitutional and gave the Crown an unfair advantage. These arguments were rejected. The court held that jury vetting in accordance with the Attorney-General's Guidelines (Appendix A–265) and the exercise by the Attorney-General of his right to stand by were constitutional and properly conducted in the instant case. (Dicta of the Court of Appeal in *R. v. Sheffield Crown Court, ex p. Brownlow* [1980] Q.B. 530, 71 Cr.App.R. 19, doubting the constitutionality of jury vetting, not followed.) **4–212**

In *R. v. Mason* [1981] Q.B. 881, 71 Cr.App.R. 157, the Court of Appeal said that it was lawful for inquiries to be made as to whether potential jurors were disqualified by reason of previous convictions. There was no reason why information as to any convictions discovered (not just those amounting to disqualifications) should not be given to prosecuting counsel. Defence counsel are not entitled to the information as of right, but cases might occur when it would be fair for prosecuting counsel to disclose the information to the defence. What should be done should be left to the discretion of prosecuting counsel. The principle discussed *post*, § 16–64 may now fall to be considered. **4–213**

The court in *Mason* also pointed out that the then current statement of the Attorney-General, "Checks on Potential Jurors," issued in October 1978, constituted advice and did not have the force of law. In the light of *Mason*, in August 1980, the then Attorney-

General made a statement to Parliament and issued revised guidelines: see, 72 Cr.App.R. 14. These were amended in 1986 and again in 1989 to coincide with the implementation of section 118 of the *CJA* 1988, abolishing the right of peremptory challenge. In *R. v. McCann, ante*, the court referred to the fact that since the statement to Parliament, Parliament had not sought by legislation to place any further restraint on the use by the Attorney-General of his right of stand by.

[The next paragraph is § 4–219.]

Juries Act 1974, s.6

Summoning in exceptional circumstances

4–219 **6.**—(1) If it appears to the court that a jury to try any issue before the court will be, or probably will be, incomplete, the court may, if the court thinks fit, require any persons who are in, or in the vicinity of, the court, to be summoned (without any written notice) for jury service up to the number needed (after allowing for any who may not be qualified under section 1 of this Act, and for excusals and challenges) to make up a full jury.

(2) The names of the persons so summoned shall be added to the panel and the court shall proceed as if those so summoned had been included in the panel in the first instance.

[This section is printed as amended by the *CJA* 1988, Sched. 15, para. 45.]

The section does not exclude the right to postpone the trial and order the immediate summoning of a fresh panel of jurors. In *R. v. Solomon* [1958] 1 Q.B. 203, 42 Cr.App.R. 9, CCA, it held that a jury composed entirely of "talesmen" is no jury at all. It would appear that in view of the terms "incomplete" jury and "making up a full jury" in section 6, the jury must still include at least one person summoned under the ordinary arrangements. See also *post*, § 4–233.

Records of persons summoned and included in panels

4–220 The *Juries Act* 1974, s.8(3) provides that such records shall be kept in such manner as the Lord Chancellor may direct, and the Lord Chancellor may, if he thinks fit, make arrangements for allowing inspection of the records so kept by members of the public in such circumstances and subject to such conditions as he may prescribe.

Offences and penalties

4–221 The *Juries Act* 1974, s.20, creates various offences: see *post*, § 28–46 for subsections (1) to (4). Section 20(5), as amended, creates summary offences of making false representations for the purposes of evading jury service or enabling another to do so, of failure, without reasonable excuse, to answer questions under section 2(5) or deliberately or recklessly giving false answers, and of serving on a jury when disqualified. The offence of serving when disqualified carries a fine not exceeding level 5 on the standard scale; all the other offences carry a fine not exceeding level 3 on the standard scale.

Effect of non compliance on verdict

Juries Act 1974, s.18

Judgments: stay or reversal

4–222 **18.**—(1) No judgment after verdict in any trial by jury in any court shall be stayed or reversed by reason—

(a) that the provisions of this Act about the summoning or impanelling of jurors, or the selection of jurors by ballot, have not been complied with or,

(b) that a juror was not qualified in accordance with section 1 of this Act, or

(c) that any juror was misnamed or misdescribed, or

(d) that any juror was unfit to serve.

(2) Subsection (1)(a) above shall not apply to any irregularity if objection is taken at, or as soon as practicable after, the time it occurs, and the irregularity is not corrected.

(3) Nothing in subsection (1) above shall apply to any objection to a verdict on the ground of personation.

In *R. v. Mulkerrings and Sansom* [1997] 8 *Archbold News* 2, CA, the jury had been selected in breach of the balloting procedure prescribed by section 11 of the 1974 Act (*post*, § 4–233). It was held that since no objection had been taken at the time, or as soon as practicable thereafter, section 18(1)(a) and (2) precluded the raising of this irregularity on appeal, and it made no difference that the defendant had been unrepresented (and therefore ignorant of the law's requirements) at the relevant time.

Section 18 does not preclude an appeal on the ground that the conviction was rendered unsafe (*CAA* 1968, s.2(1), *post*, § 7–43), by the presence on the jury of a juror who was unfit or disqualified: see *R. v. Chapman and Lauday*, 63 Cr.App.R. 75 (juror deaf); *R. v. Bliss*, 84 Cr.App.R. 1 (juror assumed to have been disqualified); *R. v. Raviraj*, 85 Cr.App.R. 93 (juror ineligible); and *R. v. Salt, The Times*, February 1, 1996, CA (95/5859/Y2) (the use of the son of an usher at the Crown Court concerned as a juror to make up numbers exceeded anything which could reasonably be described as random, or random so far as possible, and was within the spirit of the provision which at the time rendered those concerned with the administration of justice ineligible).

As to personation, see *R. v. Kelly* [1950] 2 K.B. 164, 34 Cr.App.R. 95, CCA.

D. Attendance, Service, Excusals, Deferral

Juries Act 1974, ss.7–9

Attendance and service

7. Subject to the provisions of this Act, a person summoned under this Act shall attend for so many days as may be directed by the summons or by the appropriate officer, and shall be liable to serve on any jury (in the Crown Court or the High Court or any county court) at the place to which he is summoned, or in the vicinity. **4–223**

Excusal for previous jury service

8.—(1) If a person summoned under this Act shows to the satisfaction of the appropriate officer, or of the court (or any of the courts) to which he is summoned— **4–224**

(a) that he has served on a jury, or duly attended to serve on a jury, in the prescribed period ending with the service of the summons on him, or

(b) that the Crown Court or any other court has excused him from jury service for a period which has not terminated,

the officer or court shall excuse him from attending, or further attending, in pursuance of the summons.

(2) In subsection (1) above "the prescribed period" means two years or such longer period as the Lord Chancellor may prescribe by order made by statutory instrument subject to annulment in pursuance of a resolution of either House of Parliament, and any such order may be varied or revoked by a subsequent order under this subsection.

(3) [*See* ante, *§ 4–220.*]

(4) [*Entitlement to certificate of attendance.*]

(5) In subsection (1) above the words "served on a jury" refer to service on a jury in any court, including any court of assize or other court abolished by the *Courts Act* 1971, but excluding service on a jury in a coroner's court.

Excusal for certain persons and discretionary excusal

9.—(1) [*Repealed by* CJA *2003, s.332, and Sched. 37, Pt 10.*] **4–225**

(2) If any person summoned under this Act shows to the satisfaction of the appropriate officer that there is good reason why he should be excused from attending in pursuance of the summons, the appropriate officer may, subject to section 9A(1A) of this Act, excuse him from so attending.

(2A) Without prejudice to subsection (2) above, the appropriate officer shall excuse a full-time serving member of Her Majesty's naval, military or air forces from attending in pursuance of a summons if—

(a) that member's commanding officer certifies to the appropriate officer that it would be prejudicial to the efficiency of the service if that member were to be required to be absent from duty, and

(b) subsection (2A) or (2B) of section 9A of this Act applies.

(2B) Subsection (2A) above does not affect the application of subsection (2) above to a full-time serving member of Her Majesty's naval, military or air forces in a case where he is not entitled to be excused under subsection (2A).

(3) Criminal Procedure Rules shall provide a right of appeal to the court (or one of the courts) before which the person is summoned to attend against any refusal of the appropriate officer to excuse him under subsection (2) above or any failure by the appropriate officer to excuse him as required by subsection (2A) above.

(4) Without prejudice to the preceding provisions of this section, the court (or any of the courts) before which a person is summoned to attend under this Act may excuse that person from so attending.

[This section is printed as amended and repealed in part by the *AFA* 1981, s.28(2), Sched. 5, Pt I; the *CJA* 2003, s.321, and Sched. 33, paras 1 and 3 to 6; and the *Courts Act* 2003, s.109(1), and Sched. 8, para. 172.]

For the right of appeal, see the *Criminal Procedure Rules* 2005, r.39.2, *post*, § 4–230.

4–226 In *R. v. Crown Court at Guildford, ex p. Siderfin* [1990] 2 Q.B. 683, 90 Cr.App.R. 192, DC, it was held that although an applicant for excusal from jury service was not entitled, as of right, to be legally represented on an appeal from a refusal of his application, a conscientious objection should be considered carefully and sympathetically as it involved questions of a personal and sensitive nature; when time permitted and proper notice had been given, there would rarely be a valid reason for refusing an adjournment to enable an applicant to be legally represented. The question was whether the relevant belief was such as to stand in the way of the applicant fulfilling the duties of a juror properly, honestly and responsibly. That involved a willingness to enter into discussions with other members of the jury and to perform the duties of a juror in conjunction with them. Finally, the court pointed out that in relation to the initial application for excusal, the decision is for the appropriate officer of the court alone to take. The judge is not intended to be involved at that stage and the matter should not be referred to him. See also *post*, § 4–230.

Juries Act 1974, s.9A

Discretionary deferral

4–227 **9A.**—(1) If any person summoned under this Act shows to the satisfaction of the appropriate officer that there is good reason why his attendance in pursuance of the summons should be deferred, the appropriate officer may, subject to subsection (2) below, defer his attendance, and, if he does so, he shall vary the days on which that person is summoned to attend and the summons shall have effect accordingly.

(1A) Without prejudice to subsection (1) above and subject to subsection (2) below, the appropriate officer—

(a) shall defer the attendance of a full-time serving member of Her Majesty's naval, military or air forces in pursuance of a summons if subsection (1B) below applies, and

(b) for this purpose, shall vary the dates upon which that member is summoned to attend and the summons shall have effect accordingly.

(1B) This subsection applies if that member's commanding officer certifies to the appropriate officer that it would be prejudicial to the efficiency of the service if that member were to be required to be absent from duty.

(1C) Nothing in subsection (1A) or (1B) above shall affect the application of subsection (1) above to a full-time serving member of Her Majesty's naval, military or air forces in a case where subsection (1B) does not apply.

(2) The attendance of a person in pursuance of a summons shall not be deferred under subsection (1) or (1A) above if subsection (2A) or (2B) below applies.

(2A) This subsection applies where a deferral of the attendance of the person in pursuance of the summons has previously been made or refused under subsection (1) above or has previously been made under subsection (1A) above.

(2B) This subsection applies where—

(a) the person is a full-time serving member of Her Majesty's naval, military or air forces, and

(b) in addition to certifying to the appropriate officer that it would be prejudicial to the efficiency of the service if that member were to be required to be absent from duty, that member's commanding officer certifies that this position is likely to remain for any period specified for the purpose of this subsection in guidance issued under section 9AA of this Act.

(3) Criminal Procedure Rules shall provide a right of appeal to the court (or one of the courts) before which the person is summoned to attend against any refusal of the appropriate officer to defer his attendance under subsection (1) above or any failure by the appropriate officer to defer his attendance as required by subsection (1A) above.

(4) Without prejudice to the preceding provisions of this section, the court (or any of the courts) before which a person is summoned to attend under this Act may defer his attendance.

[This section was inserted by the *CJA* 1988, s.120. It is printed as amended by the *CJA* 2003, s.321, and Sched. 33, paras 1 and 7 to 11; and the *Courts Act* 2003, s.109(1), and Sched. 8, para. 172.]

For the right of appeal, see the *Criminal Procedure Rules* 2005, r.39.2, *post*, § 4–230. See *R. v. Crown Court at Guildford, ex p. Siderfin, ante*, as to legal representation.

Section 9AA of the 1974 Act (inserted by the *CJA* 2003, s.321, and Sched. 33, para. 12, and amended by the *Constitutional Reform Act* 2005, s.15(1), and Sched. 4, paras 77 and 78) requires the Lord Chancellor (or a judicial office holder nominated by him for the purpose) to issue guidance as to the manner in which the functions of the appropriate officer under sections 9 and 9A are to be exercised. The following guidance was issued on April 5, 2004.

Guidance for summoning officers when considering deferral and excusal applications

1. Applications to be deferred or excused from jury service must be considered carefully, sympathetically and with regard to the individual circumstances of the applicant. It is important that officers dealing with such applications should adopt a policy that is both fair to the individual and consistent with the needs of the court, *i.e.* providing a representative jury. Officers should therefore not hesitate to refuse a request if no "good reason" is given. **4–228**

2. If good reason is shown why the person should not sit on the date they have been summoned, deferral should always be considered in the first instance. Excusal from jury service should be reserved only for those cases where the jury summoning officer is satisfied that it would be unreasonable to require the person to serve at any time within the following twelve months.

3. When deferring jury service, the summoning officer must specify a new date of attendance, which should normally be within one year of the date of the summons. In deciding on the new date the times identified by the potential juror as being particularly inconvenient should be avoided wherever possible.

Summoning officer's discretion

4. The normal expectation is that everyone summoned for jury service will serve at the time for which they are summoned. It is recognised that there will be occasions where it is not reasonable for a person summoned to serve at the time for which they are summoned, in such circumstances, the summoning officer should use his/ her discretion to defer the individual to a time more appropriate. Only in extreme circumstances, should a person be excused from jury service. **4–229**

The summoning officer in exercising his or her discretion should observe the following principles

5. Section 8(1) of the *Juries Act* 1974 provides that a person summoned who shows to the satisfaction of the appropriate officer that they have already served, or duly attended to serve, within the prescribed period (which is two years), shall be excused from service. When a person claims to have served within the prescribed period their statement should normally be accepted, subject to subsequent checking against records where this can easily be done. **4–229a**

6. An application for excusal on the grounds of insufficient understanding of English should normally be granted. If in doubt, the juror may be brought before the judge as prescribed by section 10 of the 1974 Act.

7. When considering applications for excusal on the grounds of care responsibilities deferral should be considered in the first instance. Paragraph 4 (above) applies.

8. Applications for excusal from members of enclosed religious orders, from practising members of religious societies and orders, and from members of generic or secular organisations, whose ideology, or beliefs are incompatible with jury service, should be granted. If evidence for either situation is not provided, it should be requested before the application is further considered. Where jury service conflicts with an applicant's religious festival they should be deferred.

9. Those applying for excusal because the court to which they have been summoned is difficult for them to reach should be offered an alternative court to attend.

10. Deferral, rather than excusal, should be granted for holidays. Paragraph 4 (above) applies.

11. Jurors may be excused for valid business reasons. Applications of this type should, however, be looked at closely and granted only if there would be unusual hardship. A small business is an example of a case where such hardship might be suffered, although each case must be considered on its individual merits. Paragraph 4 (above) applies.

12. Applications for excusal by shift workers and night workers should be dealt with sympathetically. A shift worker should be deferred to a period where they do not have to attend on a rest day.

13. Cases of hardship may occasionally arise where a student, who depends on obtaining employment during the vacation in order to meet financial or vocational commitments, is summoned for jury service before taking up such employment and is subsequently refused payment for loss of earnings, because no actual loss of earnings has occurred. Where an application for excusal or deferral is made by a student on these grounds it should be treated sympathetically, otherwise genuine financial hardship may be caused.

14. Applications for excusal from teachers or students during term time, and particularly during exam periods, should be deferred in the first instance. Paragraph 4 (above) applies.

15. Those who apply for excusal on grounds that jury service would conflict with important public duties should normally be deferred. Paragraph 4 (above) applies.

16. Members of parliament who seek excusal of jury service on the grounds of parliamentary duties should be offered deferral in the first instance. If an MP feels that it would be inappropriate to do jury service in his/ her constituency, they should be allowed to do it elsewhere. Paragraph 4 (above) applies.

17. The Speaker of the House of Commons and his deputies, because of the difficulties their absence from the House would cause, should in the first instance be deferred to a time when parliament is not sitting. Paragraph 4 (above) applies.

18. Members of the judiciary or those involved in the administration of justice who apply for excusal or deferral on grounds that they may be known to a party or parties involved in the trial should normally be deferred or moved to an alternative court where the excusal grounds may not exist. If this is not possible, then they should be excused. Paragraph 4 (above) applies.

19. Full-time serving members of the Armed Forces will be deferred or excused jury service in cases where their commanding officer certifies that their absence would be prejudicial to the efficiency of the service in question (see [*ss.9A(2A) and (2B) of the* Juries Act *1974*]).

20. Applications for excusal on the grounds that jury service will conflict with work commitments should be deferred in the first instance unless excusal is clearly necessary. Each case will of course need to be considered on its own merits. Applications for excusal or deferral cannot be accepted from third parties, *e.g.* employers. Paragraph 4 (above) applies.

21. Applications for excusal on the grounds of a physical disability which would make jury service difficult to undertake should be considered sympathetically; such applications should normally be considered without the necessity for a medical certificate to be produced. However, a certificate should be requested if the summoning officer feels that that one is necessary to support an application for excusal on the grounds of illness or physical disability (for example, where there is uncertainty as to the illness/ disability), or where one is required for an appeal against non-excusal.

Practice Direction (Crown Court: Jury Service) [2005] 1 W.L.R. 1361 (substituting new paras IV.42.1 to IV.42.3 of Practice Direction (Criminal Proceedings: Consolidation) [2002] 1 W.L.R. 2870)

4–229b **IV.42.1** The effect of section 321 of the *Criminal Justice Act* 2003 was to remove certain categories of persons from those previously ineligible for jury service (the judiciary and others concerned with the administration of justice) and certain other categories ceased to be eligible for excusal as of right (such as Members of Parliament and medical professionals). Jury service is an important public duty which individual members of the public are chosen at random to undertake. The normal presumption is that everyone, unless mentally disordered or disqualified, will be required to serve when summoned to do so. This legislative change has, however, meant an increase in the number of jurors with professional and public service commitments.

One of the results of this change is that trial judges must continue to be alert to the need to exercise their discretion to adjourn a trial, excuse or discharge a juror should the need arise. Whether or not an application has already been made to the jury summoning officer for deferral or excusal it is also open to the person summoned to apply to the court to be excused. Such applications must be considered with common sense and according to the interests of justice. An explanation should be required for an application being much later than necessary.

IV.42.2 Where a juror appears on a jury panel, it may be appropriate for a judge to excuse the juror from that particular case where the potential juror is personally concerned with the facts of the particular case or is closely connected with a prospective witness. Where the length of the trial is estimated to be significantly longer than the normal period of jury service, it is good practice for the trial judge to enquire whether the potential jurors on the jury panel foresee any difficulties with the length and if the judge is satisfied that the jurors' concerns are justified he may say that they are not required for that particular jury. This does not mean that the judge must excuse the juror from sitting at that court altogether as it may well be possible for the juror to sit on a shorter trial at the same court.

IV.42.3 Where a juror unexpectedly finds him or herself in difficult professional or personal circumstances during the course of the trial, jurors should be encouraged to raise such problems with the trial judge. This might apply, for example, to a parent whose childcare arrangements unexpectedly fail or a worker who is engaged in the provision of services the need for which can be critical or Member of Parliament who has deferred their jury service to an apparently more convenient time, but is unexpectedly called back to work for a very important reason. Such difficulties would normally be raised through a jury note in the normal manner. In such circumstances, the judge must exercise his or her discretion according to the interests of justice and the requirements of each individual case. The judge must decide for himself whether the juror has presented a sufficient reason to interfere with the course of the trial. If the juror has presented a sufficient reason, in longer trials it may well be possible to adjourn for a short period in order to allow the juror to overcome the difficulty. In shorter cases it may be more appropriate to discharge the juror and to continue the trial with a reduced number of jurors. The power to do this is implicit in section 16(1) of the *Juries Act* 1974. In unusual cases (such as an unexpected emergency arising overnight) a juror need not be discharged in open court. The good administration of justice depends on the cooperation of jurors who perform an essential public service. All applications for excusal should be dealt with sensitively and sympathetically and the trial judge should always seek to meet the interests of justice without unduly inconveniencing any juror.

Criminal Procedure Rules 2005 (S.I. 2005 No. 384), r.39.2

Appeal against refusal to excuse from jury service or to defer attendance

39.2.—(1) A person summoned under the *Juries Act* 1974 for jury service may appeal in accordance with the provisions of this rule against any refusal of the appropriate court officer to excuse him under section 9(2), or to defer his attendance under section 9A(1), of that Act. **4–230**

(2) Subject to paragraph (3), an appeal under this rule shall be heard by the Crown Court.

(3) Where the appellant is summoned under the 1974 Act to attend before the High Court in Greater London the appeal shall be heard by a judge of the High Court and where the appellant is summoned under that Act to attend before the High Court outside Greater London or before a county court and the appeal has not been decided by the Crown Court before the day on which the appellant is required by the summons to attend, the appeal shall be heard by the court before which he is summoned to attend.

(4) An appeal under this rule shall be commenced by the appellant's giving notice of appeal to the appropriate officer of the Crown Court or the High Court in Greater London, as the case may be, and such notice shall be in writing and shall specify the matters upon which the appellant relies as providing good reason why he should be excused from attending in pursuance of the summons or why his attendance should be deferred.

(5) The court shall not dismiss an appeal under this rule unless the appellant has been given an opportunity of making representations.

(6) Where an appeal under this rule is decided in the absence of the appellant, the appropriate officer of the Crown Court or the High Court in Greater London, as the case may be, shall notify him of the decision without delay.

[This rule was inserted by the *Criminal Procedure (Amendment) Rules* 2006 (S.I. 2006 No. 353).]

See *R. v. Crown Court at Guildford, ex p. Siderfin*, *ante*, § 4–227.

Juries Act 1974, s.9B

Discharge of summonses to disabled persons only if incapable of acting effectively as a juror

4–231 **9B.**—(1) Where it appears to the appropriate officer, in the case of a person attending in pursuance of a summons under this Act, that on account of physical disability there is doubt as to his capacity to act effectively as a juror, the person may be brought before the judge.

(2) The judge shall determine whether or not the person should act as a juror; but he shall affirm the summons unless he is of the opinion that the person will not, on account of his disability, be capable of acting effectively as a juror, in which case he shall discharge the summons.

(3) In this section *"the judge" means any judge of the High Court or any Circuit judge or Recorder* [and section 10, "the judge" means—

(a) a judge of the High Court;

(b) a Circuit judge;

(c) a District Judge (Magistrates' Courts);

(d) a Recorder].

[This section was inserted by the *CJPOA* 1994, s.41. It is printed as amended, as from a day to be appointed, by the *Courts Act* 2003, s.65, and Sched. 4, para. 3 (omission of italicised words, insertion of words in square brackets).]

A person who is profoundly deaf and unable to follow the proceedings in court, or the deliberations in the jury room, without the assistance of an interpreter in sign language should be discharged from jury service pursuant to section 9B because such a person could not act effectively as a juror and it would be an incurable irregularity in the proceedings for the interpreter to retire with the jury to the jury room: *Re Osman* [1996] 1 Cr.App.R. 126, CCC (Sir Lawrence Verney, Recorder of London).

Juries Act 1974, s.10

Discharge of summonses in cases of doubt as to capacity to act effectively as a juror

4–232 **10.** Where it appears to the appropriate officer, in the case of a person attending in pursuance of a summons under this Act, that on account of ... insufficient understanding of English there is doubt as to his capacity to act effectively as a juror, the person may be brought before the judge, who shall determine whether or not he should act as a juror and, if not, shall discharge the summons; *and for this purpose "the judge" means any judge of the High Court or any Circuit judge or Recorder*.

[This section is printed as repealed in part by the *CJPOA* 1994, s.168(3) and Sched. 11; and, as from a day to be appointed, by the *Courts Act* 2003, s.65, and Sched. 4, para. 4 (omission of italicised words).]

E. THE BALLOT AND SWEARING OF JURORS

Juries Act 1974, s.11

4–233 **11.**—(1) The jury to try an issue before a court shall be selected by ballot in open court from the panel, or part of the panel, of jurors summoned to attend at the time and place in question.

(2) The power of summoning jurors under section 6 of this Act may be exercised after balloting has begun, as well as earlier, and if exercised after balloting has begun the court may dispense with balloting for persons summoned under that section.

(3) No two or more members of the jury to try an issue in a court shall be sworn together.

(4) Subject to subsection (5) below, the jury selected by any one ballot shall try only one issue (but any juror shall be liable to be selected on more than one ballot).

(5) Subsection (4) above shall not prevent—

(a) the trial of two or more issues by the same jury if the trial of the second or last issue begins within 24 hours from the time when the jury is constituted, or

(b) ...

(c) in a criminal case beginning with a special plea, the trial of the accused on the general issue by the jury trying the special plea.

(6) In the cases within subsection (5)(a), ... and (c) above the court may, on the trial of the second or any subsequent issue, instead of proceeding with the same jury in its entirety, order any juror to withdraw, if the court considers he could be justly challenged or excused, or if the parties to the proceedings consent, and the juror to replace him shall, subject to subsection (2) above, be selected by ballot in open court.

[This section is printed as repealed in part by the *Domestic Violence, Crime and Victims Act* 2004, s.58(1), and Sched. 10, para. 8.]

For section 6 of this Act, see *ante*, § 4–219.

See *R. v. Mulkerrings and Sansom* [1997] 8 *Archbold News* 2, CA, *ante*, § 4–222, as to the consequences of a breach of the balloting provisions.

In exceptional circumstances, where a judge is satisfied that there is a danger of an attempt to interfere with a jury, he would be justified not only in ordering jury protection but also in ordering that the names of the jurors be withheld and that they be balloted by number; such procedure will not render a trial a nullity provided that the accused's rights of challenge are preserved: *R. v. Comerford* [1998] 1 Cr.App.R. 235, CA. Further, such orders may be made on the basis of information imparted to the judge on an *ex parte* public interest immunity application: *ibid.* As to balloting by number, it should be borne in mind that a party is entitled to inspect the panel from which the jurors are to be drawn: see section 5(2) of the 1974 Act, *ante*, § 4–211.

F. The Judge's Discretion to Stand Jurors Down

In order to avoid any apprehension of jury bias leading to appeals and, where successful, the quashing of convictions and the ordering of retrials, any risk of jury bias or of unfairness as a result of partiality to witnesses should be identified before the trial begins, and where such a risk arises the juror should be stood down: *R. v. Khan* [2008] 3 All E.R. 502, CA. To this end, it has become common practice in appropriate cases for the jury panel to be provided in advance with the names of the defendants and some or all of the witnesses, and to be asked to indicate any connection with any of them, and other questions designed to identify any risk of a perception of bias, such as whether they are employed by the company which was the victim of the alleged offence. **4–233a**

Now that those concerned in the administration of justice are eligible for jury service, it is also necessary to ascertain whether any juror in waiting is or has been a member of the prosecuting authority, or (depending on the facts of the case) a police officer or a prison officer (*Khan, ante*). Awareness of adverse press reporting, however, should not be the subject of enquiries of the jury panel; such enquiries might produce the result sought to be avoided by reminding the jury of the adverse publicity: *R. v. Andrews* [1999] Crim.L.R. 156, CA.

Where a question of possible bias of a potential juror arises, the test is that approved in *Porter v. Magill*; *Weeks v. Magill* (*ante*, § 4–32), *viz.* whether a fair-minded and informed observer, having considered the facts, would conclude that there was a real possibility that the tribunal was biased: *R. v. Abdroikov*; *R. v. Green*; *R. v. Williamson* [2008] 1 Cr.App.R. 21, HL. Thus, a CPS lawyer ought not to be a juror in a case in which the CPS is the prosecuting authority, and, whilst the mere fact that a police officer's evidence is in dispute in the trial is not itself enough to bar another police officer from the jury, a police officer should not have been on the jury where the court was one to which cases from his police station were committed and he came from the same local service background as a police officer whose evidence was in dispute, even though the two officers were not known to each other: *ibid.* However, a CPS lawyer could be a juror in a case prosecuted by the another government department: *Khan, ante*.

Where a juror does personally know a witness or witnesses, an enquiry has to take place, albeit a brief one, and the juror should normally be asked to stand down unless it can be said with certainty that any such witness who is to be called will play no contested part in the determination of the issues: *R. v. I.* [2008] 1 *Archbold News* 2, CA (in which a juror knew four police officers called as witnesses whose evidence, although not vigorously challenged, had a relevant part to play in the determination of the issues, giving rise to a real possibility that he would be likely to accept the words of his colleagues, irrespective of the dispute between the parties).

The judge has a duty to discharge the jury summons in respect of a juror who has insufficient understanding of English (*Juries Act* 1974, s.10, *ante*, § 4–232), and a discretion to stand down individual jurors who are otherwise not competent to serve on the jury, such as through blindness, or who are not likely to be willing or able properly **4–233b** to perform their duties; however, this discretion cannot be invoked to discharge a competent juror or jurors in an attempt to secure a jury drawn from particular sections of the community, or otherwise to influence the overall composition of the jury; for this latter purpose, the law provides that "fairness" is achieved by the principle of random selection: *R. v. Ford* [1989] Q.B. 868, 89 Cr.App.R. 278, CA. See also *R. v. Tarrant* [1998] Crim.L.R. 342, CA; and *R. v. Smith (Lance Percival)* [2003] 1 W.L.R. 2229, CA; and see *Seer Technologies Ltd v. Abbas, The Times*, March 16, 2000, Ch D (Pumfrey J.), *ante*, § 4–32, as to the likely futility of any complaint in respect of the composition of a tribunal where the complaint is based on fear of bias arising merely from the national origin, gender, age, class, means or sexual orientation of the tribunal.

G. CHALLENGE

(1) Statute

Juries Act 1974, s.12

4–234 **12.**—(1) In proceedings for the trial of any person for an offence on indictment—

(a) that person may challenge all or any of the jurors for cause, and

(b) any challenge for cause shall be tried by the judge before whom that person is to be tried.

(2) [*County courts.*]

(3) A challenge to a juror in any court shall be made after his name has been drawn by ballot (unless the court, pursuant to section 11(2) of this Act, has dispensed with balloting for him) and before he is sworn.

(4) The fact that a person summoned to serve on a jury is not qualified to serve shall be a ground of challenge for cause; but subject to that, and to the foregoing provisions of this section, nothing in this Act affects the law relating to challenge of jurors.

(5) [*Continues amendment to* Juries Act *1825, s.29.*]

(6) Without prejudice to subsection (4) above, the right of challenge to the array, that is to say the right of challenge on the ground that the person responsible for summoning the jurors in question is biased or has acted improperly, shall continue to be unaffected by the fact that, since the coming into operation of section 31 of the *Courts Act* 1971 (which is replaced by this Act) the responsibility for summoning jurors for service in the Crown Court, the High Court and county courts has lain with the Lord Chancellor.

[This section is printed as amended by the *CJA* 1988, Sched. 16.]

For section 29 of the *Juries Act* 1825, see *post*, § 4–239.

In practice, the procedure followed is that set out, *post*, §§ 4–235 *et seq*.

An accused has no right of challenge when a jury is empanelled to determine whether he is mute of malice. Section 12 postulates that the trial has already begun to the extent that the accused has been arraigned and has pleaded to the indictment: *R. v. Paling*, 67 Cr.App.R. 299, CA.

(2) Timing

4–235 The defendant having pleaded not guilty, the next proceeding is to call the jurors into the jury box.

The clerk of the court first calls 12 jurors from the panel in the following manner: "Members of the jury in waiting, please answer to your names and step into the jury box as you are called." He then calls each juror by name (but see *R. v. Comerford*, *ante*, § 4–233, as to balloting by numbers in exceptional circumstances).

He then tells the defendant: "The names that you are about to hear called are the names of the jurors who are to try you. If therefore you wish to object to them, or to any of them, you must do so as they come to the book to be sworn, and before they are sworn, and your objection shall be heard." If the defendant is represented, any challenge will be made by his counsel.

Challenges may be either to the *array*, when exception is taken to the whole number impanelled, or to the *polls*, when individual jurors are objected to. No challenge can be taken either to the *array* or to the *polls* until a full jury has appeared: *R. v. Edmonds* (1821) 1 St.Tr.(n.s.) 785 at 916. Probably, a challenge to the *array* should be made before any juror is sworn (see *R. v. Frost* (1839) 9 C. & P. 129 at 122), but in the case of a challenge to the *polls* it is time enough to challenge before the swearing of the juror objected to begins: *R. v. Brandreth* (1817) 32 St.Tr. 755 at 777.

A challenge may properly be allowed, as a matter of discretion, after the commencement of the oath: *R. v. Harrington*, 64 Cr.App.R. 1, CA. **4–236**

There is no requirement in law to have in front of the accused 12 selected jurors each time a challenge is made. Practices vary—at some courts the gap created by a challenged juror is filled at once (that is the practice favoured by the Court of Appeal), but at others the gap is filled either at the end of the swearing of the original jurors or at a convenient moment in between (*e.g.* when the end of one row of jurors is reached): *R. v. Bhogal*, 81 Cr.App.R. 45, CA.

(3) Form

Challenges were formerly of two kinds: **4–237**

(a) *peremptory challenges*, made to the polls without reason assigned, and

(b) *challenges for cause*, made to the array or the polls for some definite reason assigned and proved.

(a) *Peremptory challenge*

The right to challenge jurors without cause was abolished by the *CJA* 1988, s.118(1). As to the right of the prosecution to ask jurors to "stand by for the Crown", see *post*, §§ 4–249 *et seq.* **4–238**

(b) *Challenge for cause*

Challenges *for cause* may be made either by the prosecutor (*Juries Act* 1825, s.29) or by the defendant (*Juries Act* 1974, s.12(1), (4), *ante*, § 4–234). They are either to the *array* (*post*, §§ 4–240 *et seq.*) or to the *polls*, *i.e.* to individual jurors (*post*, §§ 4–243 *et seq.*). **4–239**

The mere fact that a juror could have been successfully challenged for cause is no ground for interfering with the conviction of a person tried by such a juror: see *R. v. Healey* (1965) 109 S.J. 700, and *ante*, § 4–222.

A judge of the Crown Court may order that the hearing of a challenge for cause shall be *in camera* or in chambers: *CJA* 1988, s.118(2).

To the array

Although the right of challenge to the array, on the basis that the person responsible for summoning the jurors in question is biased or has acted improperly, has been expressly retained by the *Juries Act* 1974, s.12(6) (*ante*, § 4–234), notwithstanding that since 1971 the responsibility for summoning jurors has lain with the Lord Chancellor, it is submitted that it is now of historical significance only. The right cannot be used as a means of objecting to the racial composition of a particular panel or part panel (*ante*, § 4–233b), nor to the vetting of the jury panel by the Attorney-General (*R. v. McCann*, 92 Cr.App.R. 239, CA, *ante*, § 4–212). A review of the historical cases on the exercise of the right can be found in the 2008 and earlier editions of this work. **4–240**

To the polls

The challenge must be made after the juror's name (but see *R. v. Comerford*, *ante*, § 4–233, as to balloting by numbers in exceptional circumstances) has been drawn by ballot from the panel in open court, and before he is sworn (*Juries Act* 1974, s.12(3), *ante*, §§ 4–234 *et seq.*), but see *ante*, § 4–236. These challenges are generally made orally, although, in strictness, if any question is raised upon the validity of such a challenge, it must be entered in due form on the record. **4–241**

A juror can be challenged on the basis that he is not qualified (as to which see *ante*, § 4–200). Where a disqualified juror is on the panel, and no challenge is made, the presence of the juror does not invalidate the trial; see *ante*, §§ 4–222, 4–239. A juror may challenge himself, by stating that he is not qualified, and he may be examined upon oath: *R. v. Cook* (1696) 13 St.Tr. 311 at 316, 317. **4–242**

4–243 A juror can also be challenged on the ground of some presumed or actual partiality. However, such is the extent of the judge's discretion to avoid the apprehension of bias by standing down jurors with a connection to those involved in the proceedings (*ante*, § 4–233a) that in modern times a formal challenge for cause is seldom if ever made. For historical cases, see the 2008 and earlier editions of this work.

(4) Trial of challenge

4–244 See the *Juries Act* 1974, s.12(1), *ante*, § 4–234 (judge alone decides), and the *CJA* 1988, s.118(2), *ante*, § 4–239 (hearing *in camera* or chambers).

The burden of proof of a challenge for cause is on the person who makes it: *R. v. Savage* (1824) 1 Mood. 51.

Before any right to cross-examine a juror arises, there must be laid a foundation of fact, such as to create a *prima facie* case in support of the ground of challenge: *R. v. Chandler* [1964] 2 Q.B. 322 at 338, 48 Cr.App.R. 143 at 154, CCA; *R. v. Kray*, *ante*; *R. v. Broderick* [1970] Crim.L.R. 155, CA. See also *R. v. Andrews*, *ante*, § 4–233a.

When the challenge has been made, the trial proceeds by witnesses called to support or defeat the challenge; provided sufficient foundation is laid (*ante*), the juror objected to may also be examined on the *voire dire*, as to his qualification, or the leaning of his affection: *R. v. Dowling* (1848) 7 St.Tr.(n.s.) 381. But he cannot be interrogated as to matters which tend to his own discredit, as whether he has been convicted, nor, as it seems, whether he has expressed a hostile opinion as to the guilt of the prisoner: *R. v. Cook* (1696) 13 St.Tr. 311 at 334; *R. v. Edmonds* (1821) 1 St.Tr.(n.s.) 785; *R. v. Martin* (1848) 6 St.Tr.(n.s.) 925; and see 2 Hawk. c. 43, s.28.

[The next paragraph is § 4–249.]

H. Right of Prosecution to Ask Jurors to Stand By

4–249 The constitutionality of the right of the prosecution to require a juror or jurors to "stand by for the Crown" was confirmed in *R. v. McCann*, 92 Cr.App.R. 239, CA. The defendant is bound to show his causes of objection before the prosecutor can be called upon to justify standing by a juror: 2 Hawk. c. 43, s.3; 14 Bl. Com. 353.

In *R. v. Chandler* [1964] 2 Q.B. 322, 48 Cr.App.R. 143, CCA, the history of this right was investigated and it was held that the accused has no such right. As to the nature of the right, see also *R. v. Mason* [1981] Q.B. 881, 71 Cr.App.R. 157, CA and *R. v. McCann*, *ante*.

Attorney-General's guidelines on the use of stand by

4–250 The Attorney-General announced on November 29, 1988, that he had issued a new set of guidelines on the use by the prosecution of the right of stand by, following the abolition of peremptory challenges on January 5, 1989, by the *CJA* 1988, s.118. The guidelines represent an important restriction of the scope of stand by. The existing guidelines on jury checks were also amended as a consequence of the new guidelines and reissued: see *ante*, §§ 4–212, 4–413 and Appendix A–265.

4–251 For the full text of the guidelines, see Appendix A–265.

I. Swearing

4–252 See the *Juries Act* 1974, s.11(3) *ante*, § 4–233, and *post*, §§ 8–26 *et seq.*, as to the law and practice relating to oaths and affirmations generally.

The wording of the oath to be taken by jurors is: "I swear by Almighty God that I will faithfully try the defendant and give a true verdict according to the evidence." Any person who objects to being sworn shall be permitted to make his solemn affirmation instead (see *post*, § 8–31). The wording of the affirmation is: "I do solemnly, sincerely and truly declare and affirm that I will faithfully try the defendant and give a true verdict according to the evidence.": *Practice Direction (Criminal Proceedings: Consolidation)* [2002] 1 W.L.R. 2870, para. IV.42.4.

For the administration of oaths and affirmations in Welsh, see the *Welsh Language Act* 1993, ss.22, 23 and S.R. & O. 1943 No. 683, *ante*, § 4–40.

J. DISCHARGE OF JUROR OR JURY

(1) Where a necessity arises

It is established law that a jury sworn and charged in respect of a defendant may be discharged by the judge at the trial, without giving a verdict, if a "necessity", that is, a high degree of need, for such discharge is made evident to his mind: 4 Bl.Com. 360; *Winsor v. R.* (1866) L.R. 1 Q.B. 289 at 390. The existence of such a power is implicit in section 16(1) of the *Juries Act* 1974, *post*, § 4–255. It was open to the judge to exercise the power whichever party might invite him to do so or though no party invited him to do so, or even where both parties opposed the discharge of the jury: *R. v. Azam* [2006] Crim.L.R. 776, CA. **4–253**

A capricious exercise of the discretion to discharge a juror may render a conviction unsafe where, pursuant to section 16, the trial has continued: *R. v. Hambery* [1977] Q.B. 924, 65 Cr.App.R. 233, CA. Relevant considerations to the exercise of the discretion are that trial by jury depends upon the willing co-operation of the public. Those summoned to serve are entitled to such consideration as it is within the power of the courts to give them. If the administration of justice can be carried on without unduly inconveniencing jurors, it should be. Furthermore, an aggrieved and inconvenienced juror is not likely to be a good one: *ibid*.

A judge is entitled, if he has good reason, to discharge a juror otherwise than in open court, since a juror in difficulty who seeks a discharge should not have to go to court to apply for it: *R. v. Richardson* [1979] 1 W.L.R. 1316, CA (juror discharged after notifying court that her husband had died the night before).

The discretion may be exercised so as to discharge a juror on account of illness after retirement: *R. v. Hornsey* [1990] Crim.L.R. 731, CA. A juror may also be discharged after one or more verdicts have been returned and the remaining jurors may then return further valid verdicts: *R. v. Wood and Furey* [1997] Crim.L.R. 229, CA (the verdicts returned before the discharge of the juror were also upheld, the juror's discharge not having been the result of any misconduct).

As to the steps to be taken, after the commencement of Part 7 of the *CJA* 2003, before the judge discharges the jury because jury tampering appears to have taken place, see section 46(2), *post*, § 4–267d.

(2) Investigation

Practice Direction (Crown Court: Guidance to Jurors) [2004] 1 W.L.R. 665 (amending Practice Direction (Criminal Proceedings: Consolidation) [2002] 1 W.L.R. 2870)

IV.42.6 Trial judges should ensure that the jury is alerted to the need to bring any concerns about fellow jurors to the attention of the judge at the time, and not to wait until the case is concluded. At the same time, it is undesirable to encourage inappropriate criticism of fellow jurors, or to threaten jurors with contempt of court. **4–254**

IV.42.7 Judges should therefore take the opportunity, when warning the jury of the importance of not discussing the case with anyone outside the jury, to add a further warning. It is for the trial judge to tailor the further warning to the case, and to the phraseology used in the usual warning. The effect of the further warning should be that it is the duty of jurors to bring to the judge's attention, promptly, any behaviour among the jurors or by others affecting the jurors, that causes concern. The point should be made that, unless that is done while the case is continuing, it may be impossible to put matters right.

IV.42.8 The judge should consider, particularly in a longer trial, whether a reminder on the lines of the further warning is appropriate prior to the retirement of the jury.

IV.42.9 In the event that such an incident does occur, trial judges should have regard to the remarks of Lord Hope … in *R. v. Mirza* [2004] 1 A.C. 1118 (at [127]–[128]), and consider the desirability of preparing a statement that could be used in connection with any appeal arising from the incident to the Court of Appeal … . Members of the Court of Appeal … should also remind themselves of the power to request the judge to furnish them with any information or assistance under rule 22 of the *Criminal Appeal Rules* 1968 (S.I. 1968 No. 1262) and section 87(4) of the *Supreme Court Act* 1981.

Rule 22 of the 1968 rules has been replaced by rule 68.23 of the *Criminal Procedure Rules* 2005 (S.I. 2005 No. 384) (*post*, § 7–197).

The jurors' duty to inform the court of anything untoward includes any irregularity which occurs while they are deliberating. The judge must take appropriate steps to investigate any such matter that arises at any stage before verdict and deal with the allegations as the situation requires; section 8(1) of the *Contempt of Court Act* 1981 (*post*, § 28–90, enforcing the confidentiality of the jury's deliberations) applies to third parties but not to the court itself: *R. v. Mirza, ante*; nor to a juror's communications to the court: *Att.-Gen. v. Scotcher* [2005] 1 W.L.R. 1867, HL; but the common law prevents any investigation from extending into matters connected with the subject matter of the jury's deliberations: *R. v. Smith and Mercieca* [2005] 1 W.L.R. 704, HL. If a juror makes an unsupported allegation of serious misconduct against other jurors, the judge should not discharge the jury just because the allegation has been made; he is required to address the question of whether impropriety has in fact occurred, and if it has, whether it can be cured, and if so, how, or whether it is irremediable: *R. v. Momodou and Limani* [2005] 2 Cr.App.R. 6, CA.

4–254a Where it is apparent that there is friction between members of a jury, so that the inference could be drawn that certain members of the jury might not be able to perform their duty, the whole jury should be questioned in open court as to their capacity, as a body, to continue. Circumstances that gave rise to such a situation would be internal to the jury and are to be distinguished from external circumstances that might make it appropriate to question an individual juror, *e.g.* a suggestion that there had been an improper approach to that juror: *R. v. Orgles and Orgles*, 98 Cr.App.R. 185, CA.

If there is any realistic suspicion of an improper approach having been made, it is the duty of the judge to investigate the matter and probably, depending on the circumstances, the investigation will include questioning of individual jurors or even the jury as a whole. Any such questioning must be directed to the possibility of the jury's independence having been compromised and not to the jury's deliberations on the issues in the case. The judge will then be in a position to make an informed exercise of his discretion as to whether or not any or all of the jurors should be discharged: *R. v. Blackwell* [1995] 2 Cr.App.R. 625, CA. See also *R. v. Putnam*, 93 Cr.App.R. 281, CA; and *R. v. Appiah* [1998] Crim.L.R. 134, CA (having discharged one juror, proper for judge to ask others in turn whether they felt able to continue, having pointed out that if they were unable to do so, trial would be stopped). The assent of the defendant to the continuation of the trial is a relevant but not determining factor in the exercise of that discretion: *R. v. Smith and Mercieca, ante*.

See also *R. v. Thorpe, The Times*, November 2, 2000, CA (after retirement jury indicated that verdict agreed but unwilling to appoint foreman to deliver it because they felt intimidated by persons in public gallery; defence sought discharge of jury; judge investigated and reassured jury that no connection between defendant and persons in gallery; conviction returned; clear duty on court to establish factual basis as accurately as possible before exercising discretion as to discharge and should have asked whether any of jury felt that their decision had been affected in any way by their original concerns).

The duty to investigate is triggered only when there is some indication of something untoward having occurred: *R. v. Oke* [1997] Crim.L.R. 898, CA (ruling that the mere presence in court of a relative or friend of a juror during part of the proceedings did not trigger this duty).

As to the importance of a proper investigation by the trial judge, see also *post*, § 4–263.

(3) Continuation of trial

Juries Act 1974, s.16

Continuation of criminal trial on death or discharge of juror

4–255 **16.**—(1) Where in the course of a trial of any person for an offence on indictment any member of the jury dies or is discharged by the court whether as being through illness incapable of continuing to act or for any other reason, but the number of its members is not reduced below nine, the jury shall nevertheless (subject to subsections (2) and (3) below) be considered as remaining for all the purposes of that trial properly constituted, and the trial shall proceed and a verdict may be given accordingly.

(2) On a trial ... for any offence punishable with death subsection (1) shall not apply on the death or discharge of any member of the jury unless assent to its then applying is given in writing by or on behalf of both the prosecution and the accused or each of the accused.

(3) Notwithstanding subsection (1) above, on the death or discharge of a member of the jury in the course of a trial of any person for an offence on indictment the court may discharge the jury in any case where the court sees fit to do so.

[This section is printed as repealed in part by the *CJA* 1988, s.121.]

(4) Misconduct or bias

As to the test of bias, see *Re Medicaments and Related Classes of Goods (No. 2)* [2001] 1 W.L.R. 700, CA (Civ. Div.), *ante*, § 4–32. In the authorities referred to in the ensuing paragraphs, references to the question a court should ask itself being whether or not there was a real danger or risk of bias or unfairness should be suitably adapted to one in which the court should ask itself whether a fair-minded and informed observer would conclude that there was a real possibility, or real danger, the two being the same, that the jury were or would be biased. **4–256**

In *Gregory v. U.K.*, 25 E.H.R.R. 577, ECtHR, it was held that there had been no violation of Article 6, despite a suspicion of racial bias on the part of one juror having emerged after the retirement of the jury. Sufficient guarantees as to impartiality had, in the particular circumstances, existed by reason of the judge's subsequent re-direction of the jury (having consulted both counsel) in a forceful and detailed manner and with particular emphasis on the duty of the jury to try the case on the evidence, excluding thoughts of prejudice of any kind. *Gregory* was distinguished in *Sander v. U.K.* (2001) 31 E.H.R.R. 44, ECtHR, where a juror in a case concerning Asian defendants sent a note to the judge complaining that at least two of the other jurors were making openly racist remarks and jokes, and expressing concern that they would convict on account of their racism. The Court acknowledged that the personal impartiality of a judge or jury must be presumed until there is proof to the contrary, but held that in the circumstances the applicant and any reasonable observer would be justified in doubting the impartiality of the jury, and that, in the light of the particular circumstances, the steps taken by the judge to deal with the matter (re-directing the jury in strong terms to put all prejudice aside and decide the case on the evidence, and asking them to examine their consciences as to whether they could try the case fairly) provided insufficient guarantees to dispel such doubts and the jury should have been discharged (reference should be made to the case report for details of the circumstances which distinguished it from *Gregory*). The court emphasised that discharge of the jury in a case where doubts exist as to the impartiality of the tribunal will not always be the only way to achieve a fair trial; what is necessary in that regard will depend on the particular facts.

In *Crummock (Scotland Ltd) v. H.M. Advocate*, *The Times*, May 9, 2000, the High Court of Justiciary concluded that the trial of a defendant charged with contaminating a public water supply (which was not alleged to have affected the health and safety of any individual) would not violate Article 6 by virtue only of the fact that the jury would be drawn by ballot from persons residing in an area that included the area affected; there was no basis to suppose that any inconvenience that might have been occasioned to a juror would cause him to nurture such a continuing sense of grievance that he would fail to perform his duty; in any event, it would be possible to take practical steps to safeguard not only the reality but also the appearance of independence and impartiality (access by defence to addresses of jurors; notification to jury of nature of allegations, coupled with query as to whether they knew of any reason why they should not serve; and direction to put aside any prejudice).

In *R. v. Kellard* [1995] 2 Cr.App.R. 134, CA, the trial judge had refused an application to discharge a juror who, it was said, had made certain hostile remarks and/or grimaces during the cross-examination of a defendant. In rejecting a ground of appeal based on that refusal, the Court of Appeal said that it could not improve upon the judge's reasons. He had said: **4–257**

> "... it may often be the case that it becomes apparent to a defendant that some of his evidence is not being well received by a particular juror or jurors and I do not consider that what I have heard takes the position anywhere near the point where I need, in the interests of justice, discharge a juror who there is no reason whatever to suppose will not be true to her oath and decide the question of his guilt or innocence according to the overall weight of the evidence once properly directed by me as to the law. [The defendant] will, I am sure, appreciate that for a juror to have apparently formed a provisionally adverse view on some aspects of his evidence is not the same as demonstrating that he is not receiving a fair trial on the issues which are before the jury."

It should not be open to a defendant to obtain the discharge of a jury by deliberately creating some ground of aggravation between himself and them, whether inside or outside court, and whether directly or indirectly, but in order to rely on the defendant's responsibility for the situation as a ground for not discharging a jury, the circumstances giving rise to such responsibility must either be agreed, or ascertained by the judge, to exist; they cannot be assumed simply because there is a prima facie case to that effect; if there is no agreement and the judge does not establish the fact, he must apply the test of bias as set out in *Re Medicaments* (*ante*) to the circumstances, so far as they are known, but without any presumption against the defendant; if the judge deems it appropriate to ask the jury as a whole whether, having regard to what they have seen or heard, they feel able to give dispassionate consideration to the evidence, it would be advisable to require them to reflect on the matter privately before answering and, further, to bear in mind that bias, being insidious, a person may unconsciously be affected though he may in good faith believe himself to be impartial; in exercising the discretion whether to discharge the jury in such a case, a judge may also have regard to factors such as convenience of witnesses and cost; whilst such matters cannot be determinative, they are part of the background to any consideration of whether there is a sufficiently real risk of lack of impartiality as to justify discharge: *R. v. Brown (Robert Clifford)* [2002] Crim.L.R. 409, CA.

4–258 Knowledge of a defendant's previous convictions or character by a member of the jury is not an automatic disqualification which prevents him from sitting as a juror; it will be necessary to consider whether, in the particular circumstances, the knowledge creates a real danger or risk of bias or unfairness: *R. v. Barraclough* [2000] Crim.L.R. 324, CA. Any juror who knows the defendant or knows from hearsay of his bad character ought not, however, to sit and should himself ask to be excused: *R. v. Box and Box* [1964] 1 Q.B. 430, 47 Cr.App.R. 284, CCA; see also *R. v. Hood*, 52 Cr.App.R. 265, CA, and *R. v. Rashbrook* [1969] Crim.L.R. 602, CA. In *R. v. Wilson and Sprason*, *The Times*, February 24, 1995, CA, it was held that there was a real danger of bias when the wife of a prison officer employed at the prison where the defendants were on remand served on the jury. In *R. v. Prime*, 57 Cr.App.R. 632, CA, it was said that mere close contact between a juror and a member of the public or even a witness (*e.g.* sitting next to each other at lunch) does not affect the validity of the trial. *Aliter*, if it were established that somebody had tried to tamper with a juror in the sense that he had tried to pass information which should not be passed. Such an allegation would have to be established by acceptable evidence and is not to be inferred nowadays merely because by force of circumstances a juror and an outsider have been put in close company one with the other. In this connection, see *R. v. Putnam*, 93 Cr.App.R. 281, where the Court of Appeal (at p. 285) described the courses open to the judge if it emerges at trial that an improper approach has been, or may have been, made to a juror.

In *R. v. Thorpe* [1996] 1 Cr.App.R. 269, CA, it was held, following the guidance given in *R. v. Putnam*, that in the particular circumstances of the case there had been no danger of prejudice, and that the trial judge had been entitled to refuse to discharge the jury, where various improper attempts to influence jurors had been rebuffed and reported immediately by the jurors and where, following appropriate explanation and inquiry by the judge, the jurors had given an assurance that the improper attempts to influence them would not affect their decision. It will always be necessary to give careful consideration to the particular circumstances of each case.

4–259 As to the position where one juror alleges improper pressure is being applied by the other jurors, see *R. v. Smith and Mercieca* [2005] 1 W.L.R. 704, HL, in which the trial judge's remedial directions to the jury were found to have been insufficiently stern, and

R. v. Momodou and Limani [2005] 2 Cr.App.R. 6, CA, in which it was held that the judge had been right not to discharge the jury where their response to his investigation had shown that they appreciated the seriousness of the issue, and were taking a responsible view of their obligation to reach an impartial verdict. As to these cases, see also *ante*, § 4–254.

In *R. v. Knott, The Times*, February 6, 1992, CA, the trial judge had refused an application to discharge the jury in circumstances where one of the jurors, who had been drinking, caused criminal damage at the hotel where the jury were sent overnight during their retirement. In the circumstances, the Court of Appeal declined to interfere with the way in which the trial judge had exercised his discretion, but expressed the view that the wiser course for a judge to take in such circumstances would be to discharge the individual juror concerned.

Where a juror falls asleep, it is for the judge to deal with the matter on the individual facts at the time it arises: *R. v. Tomar* [1997] Crim.L.R. 682, CA (refusing to interfere where a single juror had fallen asleep for a short period during the summing up and no application had been made at the time).

(5) Miscellaneous

Where inadmissible, prejudicial material is inadvertently disclosed to the jury, the ultimate question for the judge, in determining whether the jury should be discharged, is whether to continue with the trial would or could, by reason of the disclosure, result in an unsafe conviction: *R. v. Lawson* [2007] 1 Cr.App.R. 20, CA. Where the material is capable of more than one reasonable interpretation, the test should be applied on the basis of the most prejudicial interpretation (following *R. v. Docherty* [1999] 1 Cr.App.R. 274, CA); the factors to be taken into consideration include (a) the important issues in the case, (b) the nature and impact of improperly disclosed material on those issues, having regard, *inter alia*, to the respective strengths of the prosecution and defence cases, (c) the manner and circumstances of its disclosure and whether and to what extent it is potentially unfairly prejudicial to the defendant, and (d) the extent to which, and manner in which, it is remediable by judicial direction or otherwise, so as to permit the trial to proceed: *ibid*. **4–260**

For cases where the judge was right not to discharge the jury, see *R. v. Tufail* [2007] 1 *Archbold News* 1, CA (judge directed jury in trenchant terms so as to minimise the impact of his having mentioned inadmissible material in his summing up, and there was no danger of the jury attaching any significance to it in the light of the strength of the admissible evidence which made the defendant's case doomed to failure), and *R. v. Wilson* [2008] 2 Cr.App.R. 3, CA (there was no real danger of the jury being biased by knowledge that the defendant had another case in the court's list for later in the week since they knew of his bad character; however, the judge ought to have addressed the jury directly on the issue notwithstanding defence submissions that this would draw too much attention to it).

Where no application is made on behalf of the defendant, the question of the discharge of the jury is one for the discretion of the judge: see *R. v. Wright*, 25 Cr.App.R. 35, CCA; *R. v. Wattam*, 28 Cr.App.R. 80, CCA. Where such an irregularity occurs during the trial of a defendant who is unrepresented, it is the duty of the judge to inform him that he has the right to apply that the jury should be discharged and the trial started afresh and that, if he desires to make such an application, he should make it forthwith: *R. v. Featherstone*, 28 Cr.App.R. 176, CCA; *R. v. Fripp*, 29 Cr.App.R. 6, CCA.

The jury should have been discharged where the defendant was charged with two counts of unlawful sexual intercourse with a girl under 13 and the issue was whether the complainant was to be believed, and the officer in charge of the case from whom defence counsel was trying to elicit the defendant's lack of previous convictions gave evidence that the defendant had previously been arrested and charged for a similar offence, which had no probative value but was calculated to undermine the propensity limb of the good character direction, and with it a major plank of the defence case; had good character not been so critical to the defence, any prejudice in the disclosure (particularly of alleged offending of a different character) might have been adequately addressed by an appropriate direction to the jury; sexual offending, however, is a type of offending where propensity reasoning may be significant, and it was asking too much to expect that a jury could give fair consideration to an affirmative good character propensity direction when told of a suspicion of similar offending: *Arthurton v. R.* [2005] 1 W.L.R. 949, PC.

In some circumstances, public discussion and debate may be so pointed and so prejudicial that it will be necessary to discharge a jury if a risk of injustice to the accused is to be avoided: *R. v. McCann*, 92 Cr.App.R. 239, CA (radio and television broadcasts about the proposed abolition of the right to silence during a trial in which the defendants had exercised that right, including by the minister whom the defendants were charged with conspiring to murder); however, the fact that adverse publicity may have risked prejudicing a fair trial is no reason for not proceeding with the trial if the judge concludes that, with his assistance, it will be possible to have a fair trial: *R. v. Abu Hamza* (*ante*, § 4–72a).

Where strangers (the jury bailiffs) retire with a jury, albeit they take no part, it is an irregularity which is hard to cure: *R. v. McNeil*, *The Times*, June 24, 1967, CA.

However, where the clerk of the court goes to the jury room at the request of the judge, it matters not whether he be accompanied by the bailiff or not or, *semble*, whether he be accompanied by a person other than a bailiff under oath so long as neither takes any part in the deliberations: *R. v. Glen* [1966] Crim.L.R. 112, CCA, distinguishing *Goby v. Wetherill* [1915] 2 K.B. 674; *cf. R. v. Brandon*, 53 Cr.App.R. 466, CA, where a conviction was quashed as a result of prejudicial remarks made by the jury bailiff when escorting a juror to the lavatory. See also *ante*, § 4–222, and *post*, § 4–430.

As to the necessity for discharge where, after their retirement, the jury come into possession of new information or an item that has not been exhibited, see *post*, § 4–419.

4–261 A jury should not be discharged in order to allow the prosecution to present a stronger case on another trial: *R. v. Lewis*, 2 Cr.App.R. 180, CCA (prosecution witnesses not ready).

As to discharge of the jury where the judge permits evidence to be adduced but later decides that it is inadmissible, see *R. v. Sat-Bhambra*, 88 Cr.App.R. 55, CA, *post*, § 15–450. Where that evidence is evidence of bad character which the judge later decides is contaminated, see the *CJA* 2003 , s.107, *post*, § 13–105.

In *R. v. Genese and Kaye* [1998] Crim.L.R. 679, CA, one defendant had absconded during the trial, but the trial had continued against him and other defendants despite applications for the discharge of the jury. The jury had been directed not to speculate or draw an inference against the absent defendant in respect of his absence. In dismissing appeals by other defendants, the Court of Appeal regarded the situation as analogous to that where one of a number of defendants changes his plea during a trial (as to which, see *post*, § 9–92) in that the disappearance of the one defendant might be taken as being a tacit admission of guilt; in such circumstances the judge has a discretion as to whether or not to discharge the jury; it will be a compelling reason not to discharge if the conviction of the missing defendant would be admissible against the others, but the converse will not necessarily be the case; the individual facts of the particular case must be considered; it had been relevant that one defendant had wished the trial to continue, however, it would have been better if the judge had directed the jury clearly that the absence of one defendant was not only no evidence against him, but also not evidence against the other defendants. The discretion as to whether to continue the trial in such cases must be exercised having regard to the due administration of justice, rather than anyone's convenience; where "cut-throat" defences are being run, the disappearance of one accused could be of advantage to the others, but no general rule could be laid down: *R. v. Panayis (Charalambous)* [1999] Crim.L.R. 84, CA.

In *R. v. Ricketts* [1991] Crim.L.R. 915, CA, the trial judge had permitted the prosecution to read the statement of a material witness, pursuant to the precursor to section 116(2)(e) of the *CJA* 2003 (*post*, § 11–15). The conviction was quashed upon the Court of Appeal having heard that during the retirement of the jury the missing witness had arrived at court and given an explanation for his late arrival that was inconsistent with the finding that had been made under the relevant section. The judge should have discharged the jury once the explanation for the late arrival of the witness had been made known to him. In the event, the trial had proceeded on a false basis. The appellant had been prejudiced in that his counsel had not been able to cross-examine the witness and, moreover, the jury had (apparently) been made aware of the reason why the judge had permitted the statement to be read.

Juries are sometimes discharged on the ground of the ill-health of the defendant. In *R. v. Rasool and Choudhary* [1997] 2 Cr.App.R. 190, the Court of Appeal held that a jury should have been discharged where the defendant was unable to do himself justice (including giving evidence) on account of the receipt of tragic news concerning his son. The judge should not have been influenced by considerations relating to the difficulty of organising a retrial.

As to the situation where the defendant physically attacked the judge during the summing up, see *R. v. Russell* [2006] Crim.L.R. 862, CA (*ante*, § 4–32).

(6) Effect of discharge and practical considerations

The discharge of the jury is not equivalent to a verdict of acquittal and the defendant can be remanded either on bail or in custody for a fresh trial: *R. v. Davison* (1860) 2 F. & F. 250; and see *R. v. Randall* [1960] Crim.L.R. 435, *ante*, § 4–146, and *R. v. Robinson* [1975] Q.B. 508, 60 Cr.App.R. 108, CA, *ante*, § 4–140. **4–262**

In *R. v. Russell* [1984] Crim.L.R. 425, CA, it was said that once a judge has discharged a jury, that jury are *functus officio* and cannot be recalled for the purpose of continuing the trial. But this is not an absolute rule: see *R. v. Aylott* [1996] 2 Cr.App.R. 169, CA (conviction upheld where the judge, having initially discharged the jury as a result of a fundamental mistake, subsequently took the verdict having established that the jury had in fact reached the verdict at the time of the order for discharge and that there had been no contact with anyone outside their number in the interim); *R. v. Maloney* [1996] 2 Cr.App.R. 303, CA (*post*, § 4–437); and *R. v. S.* [2006] Crim.L.R. 247, CA (where, immediately after telling a jury who had failed to reach a majority verdict that they were discharged and whilst they were still assembled, the judge acceded to a request to ask them whether there was a reasonable prospect of their reaching a verdict, and, upon being told that there was, changed his mind and asked them to deliberate further, there had been no effective discharge, and, in any event, as the integrity of the jury and their deliberations had not been compromised, the judge would have been entitled to set a discharge aside; *R. v. Follen* [1994] Crim.L.R. 225, CA, distinguished).

Where it is necessary to discharge a jury because they have heard something they should not have heard and which is prejudicial to the defence, it may sometimes be necessary, in order to obviate the risk contamination, to discharge the members of that jury from further attendance or to order a postponement of the retrial until a new panel has been summoned; such a course is more likely to be necessary at a small court centre; in a large court centre the risk of contamination where the judge has warned the discharged jury not to talk about the case will normally be outweighed by the advantages of an immediate retrial, but there are no hard and fast rules; if, however, counsel makes no application at the time of discharge, any subsequent complaint on appeal is unlikely to carry much weight: *R. v. Barraclough* [2000] Crim.L.R. 324, CA.

As to the position where, after the commencement of Part 7 of the *CJA* 2003, the judge has discharged the jury because jury tampering appears to have taken place, see *post*, § 4–267d.

(7) Approach of Court of Appeal

The decision of a judge to discharge a jury is not subject to review or appeal: *Winsor v. R.* (1866) L.R. 1 Q.B. 289 at 390; *R. v. Lewis*, 2 Cr.App.R. 180, CCA. **4–263**

A refusal to discharge the jury or a decision either way in relation to an individual juror can be reviewed in the Court of Appeal. Such refusals involve the exercise of judicial discretion, capricious exercise of which may render the conviction unsafe: *R. v. Hambery*, *ante*, § 4–253. In *R. v. Dubarry*, 64 Cr.App.R. 7, CA, one reason for quashing the conviction was that the trial judge did not exercise his discretion, and in *R. v. Hutton* [1990] Crim.L.R. 875, CA, one reason for quashing a conviction was that the judge had taken into account immaterial considerations.

It is submitted that too much should not be read into *Dubarry* and *Hutton*. The correct approach is to say that failure to exercise a discretion, failure to take account of a material consideration or taking into account an immaterial consideration are grounds which justify the appellate court reviewing the decision, but they are not in themselves grounds for overturning the decision to be reviewed. In such circumstances the Court of Appeal will itself consider how the discretion should have been exercised, and, according to the result, uphold or quash the decision. If the facts have only emerged since conviction, the Court of Appeal will simply apply the test to the facts as they are known to be at the time of the appeal: see *R. v. Quinn* [1996] Crim.L.R. 516, CA (and *post*, § 7–100).

The Court of Appeal will not lightly disturb the exercise of discretion by the trial judge as to whether to discharge either individual jurors or the whole jury, provided that the judge has properly investigated the matter (as to which, see *ante*, § 4–254), has satisfied himself that there is no possibility of individual jurors or the jury as a whole having been improperly influenced, and, where appropriate, has warned the jury to put the matter out of their minds: see *R. v. Panayis (Charalambous)* [1999] Crim.L.R. 84, CA; and *R. v. Azam* [2006] Crim.L.R. 776, CA. Where there has been no application at the trial to discharge individual jurors or the jury, the Court of Appeal is not as a matter of principle precluded from investigating the safety of a conviction, although, where there has been no prior investigation of the matter, the Court of Appeal may be too handicapped by ignorance to conclude that the conviction is unsafe: *R. v. Shuker and Shuker* [1998] Crim.L.R. 906, CA.

It is important that there should be a proper investigation by the trial judge of any complaint concerning the jury (uninhibited by the *Contempt of Court Act* 1981, s.8(1): *R. v. Mirza*, *ante*, § 4–254, and *post*) because the Court of Appeal has, traditionally, been reluctant to admit fresh evidence in this regard: see the cases cited at § 7–215, many of which were reviewed in *R. v. Mirza*; *R. v. Connor and Rollock* [2004] 1 A.C. 1118, HL, in which the majority found the rule of common law that, after trial, evidence of things said by jurors during their deliberations is inadmissible, to be compatible with the right to a fair trial under Article 6 of the ECHR (*post*, § 16–57); however, the powers of the Court of Appeal are wide enough to enable it to call for a report, if need be, from the trial judge if an irregularity at trial is alleged, so as to ensure that the allegations are subjected to the high degree of scrutiny needed to comply with the defendant's Article 6 rights, and the common law rule does not prevent the admission of evidence as to (i) comments made extrinsic to the deliberations of the jury, (ii) events that have taken place outside the jury room (such as in *R. v. Young (S.)* [1995] 2 Cr.App.R. 379, CA, in which evidence was admitted of the behaviour of jurors in an hotel room after their retirement), (iii) irregularities which might have led to the jury being provided with information which they should not have had, (iv) the possession by a juror of knowledge or characteristics which made it inappropriate for that person to serve on a jury (as, for example, in *R. v. Hood*, 52 Cr.App.R. 265, CA, where affidavit evidence was admitted as to the circumstances in which a juror knew of the defendant, and, similarly, *R. v. Gough* [1993] A.C. 646, HL), or, possibly (*R v. Mirza*, *ante*, *per* Lord Hope (at [123]), and *R. v. Smith and Mercieca* [2005] 1 W.L.R. 704, HL), (v) the failure by a jury to deliberate at all, such as if they were to decide the case by drawing lots or tossing a coin, amounting to a complete repudiation of their function.

K. VIEWS

Juries Act 1974, s.14

Views

4–264 **14.** Criminal Procedure Rules and Civil Procedure Rules may make provision as respects views by jurors, and the places to which a juror may be called on to go to view shall not be restricted to any particular county or other area.

[This section is printed as amended by the *Courts Act* 2003, s.109(1), and Sched. 8, para. 173.]

No rules have been made pursuant to section 14.

See further *ante*, §§ 4–83 *et seq.* as to the practice concerning views.

L. MISCELLANEOUS

(1) Jury protection

Occasionally, a trial judge will direct that while away from the court each member of the jury should be afforded police protection. The extent of the protection afforded will vary. In *R. v. Dodd*, 74 Cr.App.R. 50, CA, it was submitted: (a) that such a direction is improperly prejudicial if the real issue in the case is the honesty of the police officers giving evidence at the trial; and (b) that such a direction should only be made if there is evidence that one or more of the defendants had, in a previous trial, sought to interfere with the jury or if there is proper evidence in the current trial that such an attempt is to be made. *Held*, it is entirely a matter for the judge's discretion. **4–264a**

The trial judge has a discretion as to whether the prosecution should be required to call evidence in support of an application for jury protection; if he does require evidence, it is open to the defence to cross-examine the witnesses: *R. v. Ling* [1987] Crim.L.R. 495, CA. As to the making of an order for jury protection on the basis of information imparted on an *ex parte* public interest immunity application, see *R. v. Comerford* [1998] 1 Cr.App.R. 235, CA, *ante*, § 4–233.

Although jurors are informed that protection is to be extended to them, it is possible to do this by using language which is calculated to nullify any possible prejudice to the defendants which may be occasioned by the decision. In the event of an improper approach or threat being made to jurors, it is important for the trial judge to make it clear that they should not hold the defendants responsible: *R. v. Putnam*, 93 Cr.App.R. 281, CA.

(2) Direction to jury as to how to approach their role

The direction given to the jury at the outset of the trial should be given in a form which (a) reminds them of the general rule that they must try the case on the evidence alone which is what they hear in court and nothing else, (b) explains the application of the general rule so far as it relates to discussion of the case with family, friends or anybody else (as to which, see also *post*), and (c) reminds them that private research, whether in a library or on the internet, should be abjured: *R. v. Marshall and Crump* [2007] Crim.L.R. 562, CA. **4–264b**

(3) Separation

It is of critical importance that the judge should, on the first occasion when the jury separate, warn them not to talk about the case to anybody who is not one of their number: *R. v. Prime*, 57 Cr.App.R. 632, CA; and *R. v. Burley* [2001] 5 *Archbold News* 3, CA. As to this, see also *ante*, § 4–264b. **4–265**

As to the statutory provision for separation, see the *Juries Act* 1974, s.13, *post*, § 4–425.

(4) Notes received from jury before retirement

Where the jury send a communication to the judge on a matter affecting the trial, the fact and, exceptional cases (*e.g.* voting figures) apart, the content of the communication should be made known to the parties; where the communication relates to "domestic management", the same principle applies and it is desirable that the fact and general nature of the communication should be made known to the parties, but if the judge decides in a particular case that this is unnecessary, he could not be faulted (no harm being done to the integrity of the trial process); a communication prima facie relating to domestic management (inconvenient to have to come back on Monday) but having potential consequences for the conduct of the trial (timing of the retirement of the jury) should be treated as falling within the first category; where, therefore, a judge decided in consequence of receiving such a note to send the jury out at 3.15 p.m. on a Friday, counsel should have been informed of the communication and should have been given an opportunity to make submissions, although the decision as to the course to be taken **4–265a** remained a matter for the judge; in all the circumstances (short trial, short speeches/narrow issue/retirement in fact lasted only 45 minutes) there was no basis for saying that the verdicts had been rendered unsafe by virtue of undue pressure: *R. v. Brown and Stratton* [1998] Crim.L.R. 505, CA.

In *R. v. Andriamampandry* (2003) 147 S.J. 871, CA, it was said that where a judge receives a note from the jury, it may be dealt with without reference to counsel if it concerns an administrative matter unconnected with the trial; but in almost every other case, the judge should state in open court the nature and content of the communication and, if he considers it helpful to do so, seek the assistance of counsel; if counsel ask to see the note, normal practice would be to permit this; where, during the course of a trial, the jury had asked 17 questions in a series of notes, all of which were handed to the judge in open court in full view of all parties, the failure of the judge to read out the whole of two of the notes constituted an irregularity; if the judge did not think it appropriate to read out the whole note, he should have showed it to counsel, so that counsel could have decided whether to make submissions in relation to that which had not been read out or to pursue it in the evidence; but in the context of the case as a whole, the omissions were trivial; and as to a third note, which amounted to comment on the evidence, there had been no irregularity in the judge not reading it out, but rather referring it back to the jury with a request for clarification (which was never forthcoming); again, however, if counsel asks to see such a note, it should normally be shown; the failure to read out in full three of the 17 notes had not, therefore, deprived the defendant of a significant line of evidence or argument and had had no effect on the safety of the verdict.

As to notes relating to the conduct of the trial, see also *R. v. Dempsey*, *The Times*, January 9, 1991, CA; as to notes relating to domestic management, see also *R. v. Conroy and Glover* [1997] 2 Cr.App.R. 285, CA.

What a judge has to say about a matter appertaining to the trial arising from a juror's note (touching on the subject matter of the trial) must be said to all jurors in open court: *R. v. Woods*, 87 Cr.App.R. 60, CA.

See *Berry v. R.* [1992] 2 A.C. 364, PC, *post*, § 4–431, as to the entitlement of a jury at any stage to help from the judge on the facts as well as on the law. The judge has a discretion not to respond immediately, but to incorporate his answer into his summing up if satisfied that this would clarify the point: *R. v. Falls*, *The Times*, January 15, 1998, Ct–MAC.

See also, *post*, §§ 4–427 and 4–431 *et seq.*, as to notes received after retirement and as to notes that indicate a personal knowledge or expertise on the part of a juror as to a relevant matter.

VII. GIVING THE DEFENDANT IN CHARGE TO THE JURY

4–266 When a full jury have been sworn (or made solemn affirmation where entitled to do so; as to which see *post*, § 8–31) the clerk of the court addresses the jury as follows: "Members of the jury, are you all sworn? The prisoner [or defendant] stands indicted for that he, on the [*stating the substance of the offences charged in the indictment*]. To this indictment he has pleaded not guilty and it is your charge to say, having heard the evidence, whether he be guilty or not." Although this is a traditional part of the procedure, it is not essential and failure to follow it does not render the trial a nullity: *R. v. Desai* [1973] Crim.L.R. 36, CA: *R. v. Olivo*, 28 Cr.App.R. 173, CCA.

No reference should be made to any count to which the defendant has pleaded guilty: *R. v. Darke*, 26 Cr.App.R. 85, CCA, and see *R. v. Lashbrooke*, 43 Cr.App.R. 86, CCA.

4–267 As to whether it is necessary to take a verdict from the jury following a change of plea after the defendant has been put in their charge, see *post*, § 7–358, and note the alternative procedure explained at § 4–186, *ante*.

As to the giving in charge of a defendant who has pleaded guilty to only part of a count, where the prosecution have refused to accept the plea, see *R. v. Kelly*, *ante*, § 4–108.

VIII. TRIAL ON INDICTMENT WITHOUT A JURY

A. FRAUD CASES AND JURY TAMPERING

Criminal Justice Act 2003, ss.43–49

[Applications by prosecution for certain fraud cases to be conducted without a jury

43.—(1) This section applies where— **4–267a**

(a) one or more defendants are to be tried on indictment for one or more offences, and

(b) notice has been given under section 51B of the *Crime and Disorder Act* 1998 (notices in serious or complex fraud cases) in respect of that offence or those offences.

(2) The prosecution may apply to a judge of the Crown Court for the trial to be conducted without a jury.

(3) If an application under subsection (2) is made and the judge is satisfied that the condition in subsection (5) is fulfilled, he may make an order that the trial is to be conducted without a jury; but if he is not so satisfied he must refuse the application.

(4) The judge may not make such an order without the approval of the Lord Chief Justice or a judge nominated by him.

(5) The condition is that the complexity of the trial or the length of the trial (or both) is likely to make the trial so burdensome to the members of a jury hearing the trial that the interests of justice require that serious consideration should be given to the question of whether the trial should be conducted without a jury.

(6) In deciding whether or not he is satisfied that that condition is fulfilled, the judge must have regard to any steps which might reasonably be taken to reduce the complexity or length of the trial.

(7) But a step is not to be regarded as reasonable if it would significantly disadvantage the prosecution.]

[This section comes into force on a day to be appointed.]

Application by prosecution for trial to be conducted without a jury where danger of jury tampering

44.—(1) This section applies where one or more defendants are to be tried on indictment for one or more offences. **4–267b**

(2) [*Identical to s.43(2),* ante, *§ 4–267a.*]

(3) If an application under subsection (2) is made and the judge is satisfied that both of the following two conditions are fulfilled, he must make an order that the trial is to be conducted without a jury; but if he is not so satisfied he must refuse the application.

(4) The first condition is that there is evidence of a real and present danger that jury tampering would take place.

(5) The second condition is that, notwithstanding any steps (including the provision of police protection) which might reasonably be taken to prevent jury tampering, the likelihood that it would take place would be so substantial as to make it necessary in the interests of justice for the trial to be conducted without a jury.

(6) The following are examples of cases where there may be evidence of a real and present danger that jury tampering would take place—

(a) a case where the trial is a retrial and the jury in the previous trial was discharged because jury tampering had taken place,

(b) a case where jury tampering has taken place in previous criminal proceedings involving the defendant or any of the defendants,

(c) a case where there has been intimidation, or attempted intimidation, of any person who is likely to be a witness in the trial.

Procedure for applications under sections 43 and 44

45.—(1) This section applies— **4–267c**

[(a) to an application under section 43, and]

(b) to an application under section 44.

(2) An application to which this section applies must be determined at a preparatory hearing (within the meaning of the 1987 Act or Part 3 of the 1996 Act).

(3) The parties to a preparatory hearing at which an application to which this section applies is to be determined must be given an opportunity to make representations with respect to the application.

(4), (5) [*Amend* CJA *1987, ss.7(1) and 9(11).*]

(6)–(9) [*Amend* CPIA *1996, ss.29 and 35.*]

(10) In this section—

"the 1987 Act" means the *Criminal Justice Act* 1987,

"the 1996 Act" means the *Criminal Procedure and Investigations Act* 1996.

Discharge of jury because of jury tampering

4–267d **46.**—(1) This section applies where—

(a) a judge is minded during a trial on indictment to discharge the jury, and

(b) he is so minded because jury tampering appears to have taken place.

(2) Before taking any steps to discharge the jury, the judge must—

(a) inform the parties that he is minded to discharge the jury,

(b) inform the parties of the grounds on which he is so minded, and

(c) allow the parties an opportunity to make representations.

(3) Where the judge, after considering any such representations, discharges the jury, he may make an order that the trial is to continue without a jury if, but only if, he is satisfied—

(a) that jury tampering has taken place, and

(b) that to continue the trial without a jury would be fair to the defendant or defendants;

but this is subject to subsection (4).

(4) If the judge considers that it is necessary in the interests of justice for the trial to be terminated, he must terminate the trial.

(5) Where the judge terminates the trial under subsection (4), he may make an order that any new trial which is to take place must be conducted without a jury if he is satisfied in respect of the new trial that both of the conditions set out in section 44 are likely to be fulfilled.

(6) Subsection (5) is without prejudice to any other power that the judge may have on terminating the trial.

(7) Subject to subsection (5), nothing in this section affects the application of section 43 or 44 in relation to any new trial which takes place following the termination of the trial.

Appeals

4–267e **47.**—(1) An appeal shall lie to the Court of Appeal from an order under section 46(3) or (5).

(2) Such an appeal may be brought only with the leave of the judge or the Court of Appeal.

(3) An order from which an appeal under this section lies is not to take effect—

(a) before the expiration of the period for bringing an appeal under this section, or

(b) if such an appeal is brought, before the appeal is finally disposed of or abandoned.

(4) On the termination of the hearing of an appeal under this section, the Court of Appeal may confirm or revoke the order.

(5) [*Subject to rules of court, jurisdiction of Court of Appeal under this section to be exercised by criminal division.*]

(6), (7) [*Amend the* Criminal Appeal Act *1968, ss.33(1) and 36.*]

(8) [*Secretary of State's power to make provision in relation to proceedings before the Court of Appeal under this section.*]

Further provision about trials without a jury

4–267f **48.**—(1) The effect of an order under section [43,] 44 or 46(5) is that the trial to which the order relates is to be conducted without a jury.

(2) The effect of an order under section 46(3) is that the trial to which the order relates is to be continued without a jury.

(3) Where a trial is conducted or continued without a jury, the court is to have all the powers, authorities and jurisdiction which the court would have had if the trial had been conducted or continued with a jury (including power to determine any question and to make any finding which would be required to be determined or made by a jury).

(4) Except where the context otherwise requires, any reference in an enactment to a jury, the verdict of a jury or the finding of a jury is to be read, in relation to a trial conducted or continued without a jury, as a reference to the court, the verdict of the court or the finding of the court.

(5) Where a trial is conducted or continued without a jury and the court convicts a defendant—

(a) the court must give a judgment which states the reasons for the conviction at, or as soon as reasonably practicable after, the time of the conviction, and

(b) the reference in section 18(2) of the *Criminal Appeal Act* 1968 (notice of appeal or of application for leave to appeal to be given within 28 days from date of conviction etc) to the date of the conviction is to be read as a reference to the date of the judgment mentioned in paragraph (a).

(6) Nothing in this Part affects the requirement under section 4A of the *Criminal Procedure (Insanity) Act* 1964 that any question, finding or verdict mentioned in that section be determined, made or returned by a jury.

Rules of court

49.—(1) Rules of court may make such provision as appears to the authority making them to be necessary or expedient for the purposes of this Part. **4–267g**

(2) Without limiting subsection (1), rules of court may in particular make provision for time limits within which applications under this Part must be made or within which other things in connection with this Part must be done.

(3) Nothing in this section is to be taken as affecting the generality of any enactment conferring powers to make rules of court.

Sections 44 to 48 came into force on July 24, 2006, but section 45 only so far as it relates to applications under section 44, and section 48 only so far as it relates to retrials ordered under section 44 or 46: *Criminal Justice Act 2003 (Commencement No. 13 and Transitional Provisions) Order* 2006 (S.I. 2006 No. 1835).

As to the provision of police protection for a jury, see *ante*, § 4–264a.

B. SAMPLE COUNTS

Domestic Violence, Crime and Victims Act 2004, ss.17–20

Application by prosecution for certain counts to be tried without a jury

17.—(1) The prosecution may apply to a judge of the Crown Court for a trial on indictment to take place on the basis that the trial of some, but not all, of the counts included in the indictment may be conducted without a jury. **4–267h**

(2) If such an application is made and the judge is satisfied that the following three conditions are fulfilled, he may make an order for the trial to take place on the basis that the trial of some, but not all, of the counts included in the indictment may be conducted without a jury.

(3) The first condition is that the number of counts included in the indictment is likely to mean that a trial by jury involving all of those counts would be impracticable.

(4) The second condition is that, if an order under subsection (2) were made, each count or group of counts which would accordingly be tried with a jury can be regarded as a sample of counts which could accordingly be tried without a jury.

(5) The third condition is that it is in the interests of justice for an order under subsection (2) to be made.

(6) In deciding whether or not to make an order under subsection (2), the judge must have regard to any steps which might reasonably be taken to facilitate a trial by jury.

(7) But a step is not to be regarded as reasonable if it could lead to the possibility of a defendant in the trial receiving a lesser sentence than would be the case if that step were not taken.

(8) An order under subsection (2) must specify the counts which may be tried without a jury.

(9) For the purposes of this section and sections 18 to 20, a count may not be regarded as a sample of other counts unless the defendant in respect of each count is the same person.

Procedure for applications under section 17

18.—(1) An application under section 17 must be determined at a preparatory hearing. **4–267i**

(2) Section 7(1) of the 1987 Act and section 29(2) of the 1996 Act are to have effect as if the purposes there mentioned included the purpose of determining an application under section 17.

(3) Section 29(1) of the 1996 Act is to have effect as if the grounds on which a judge of

the Crown Court may make an order under that provision included the ground that an application under section 17 has been made.

(4) The parties to a preparatory hearing at which an application under section 17 is to be determined must be given an opportunity to make representations with respect to the application.

(5) Section 9(11) of the 1987 Act and section 35(1) of the 1996 Act are to have effect as if they also provided for an appeal to the Court of Appeal to lie from the determination by a judge of an application under section 17.

(6) In this section—

"preparatory hearing" means a preparatory hearing within the meaning of the 1987 Act or Part 3 of the 1996 Act;

"the 1987 Act" means the *Criminal Justice Act* 1987;

"the 1996 Act" means the *Criminal Procedure and Investigations Act* 1996.

Effect of order under section 17(2)

4–267j **19.**—(1) The effect of an order under section 17(2) is that where, in the course of the proceedings to which the order relates, a defendant is found guilty by a jury on a count which can be regarded as a sample of other counts to be tried in those proceedings, those other counts may be tried without a jury in those proceedings.

(2) Where the trial of a count is conducted without a jury because of an order under section 17(2), the court is to have all the powers, authorities and jurisdiction which the court would have had if the trial of that count had been conducted with a jury (including power to determine any question and to make any finding which would be required to be determined or made by a jury).

(3) Except where the context otherwise requires, any reference in an enactment to a jury, the verdict of a jury or the finding of a jury is to be read, in relation to the trial of a count conducted without a jury because of an order under section 17(2), as a reference to the court, the verdict of the court or the finding of the court.

(4) Where the trial of a count is conducted without a jury because of an order under section 17(2) and the court convicts the defendant of that count—

(a) the court must give a judgment which states the reasons for the conviction at, or as soon as reasonably practicable after, the time of the conviction, and

(b) the reference in section 18(2) of the *Criminal Appeal Act* 1968 (notice of appeal or of application for leave to appeal to be given within 28 days from date of conviction etc) to the date of the conviction is to be read as a reference to the date of the judgment mentioned in paragraph (a).

(5) Where, in the case of proceedings in respect of which an order under section 17(2) has been made, a jury convicts a defendant of a count, time does not begin to run under section 18(2) of the *Criminal Appeal Act* 1968 in relation to an appeal against that conviction until the date on which the proceedings end.

(6) In determining for the purposes of subsection (5) the date on which proceedings end, any part of those proceedings which takes place after the time when matters relating to sentencing begin to be dealt with is to be disregarded.

(7) Nothing in this section or section 17, 18 or 20 affects the requirement under section 4A of the *Criminal Procedure (Insanity) Act* 1964 that any question, finding or verdict mentioned in that section be determined, made or returned by a jury.

Rules of court

4–267k **20.**—(1) Rules of court may make such provision as appears to the authority making them to be necessary or expedient for the purposes of sections 17 to 19.

(2) Without limiting subsection (1), rules of court may in particular make provision for time limits within which applications under section 17 must be made or within which other things in connection with that section or section 18 or 19 must be done.

(3) Nothing in this section is to be taken as affecting the generality of any enactment conferring powers to make rules of court.

Sections 17 to 20 of the 2004 Act came into force on January 8, 2007, but have no effect in relation to cases where the defendant was committed, or the case was the subject of a notice of transfer under the *CJA* 1987, s.4, or the *CJA* 1991, s.53, or prosecution evidence was served in a case sent for trial under the *CDA* 1998, s.51, before that date: *Domestic Violence, Crime and Victims Act 2004 (Commencement No. 7 and*

Transitional Provision) Order 2006 (S.I. 2006 No. 3423). For the form of the indictment where an order is made under section 17(2), see, *ante*, § 1–120. As to when an order under section 17(2) may be appropriate and how arraignment should take place thereafter, see paragraphs IV.34.4 to IV.34.7 of the consolidated criminal practice direction, as substituted by *Consolidated Criminal Practice Direction (Amendment No. 17) (Arraignment in Two Stage Trials)* [2008] 1 Cr.App.R. 32 (*ante*, § 1–120a), and the discussion in relation thereto at § 1–120b, *ante*.

IX. PURPOSE AND CONTENT OF PROSECUTION OPENING

When the defendant is given in charge to the jury, counsel for the prosecution opens the case to the jury, outlining the evidence upon which the prosecution rely and explaining the nature of the charge(s) to the jury. Apart perhaps from reminding the jury of the burden and standard of proof, the presumption should be that the prosecution opening should not address the law, save in cases of real complication and difficulty where counsel believes and the trial judge agrees that the jury may be assisted by a brief and well-focussed submission: *R. v. Lashley* [2006] Crim.L.R. 83, CA. **4–268**

The mere mention by counsel of some evidence which he proposes to lead and which would be inadmissible if called is not *per se* a ground for quashing the conviction: *R. v. Jackson*, 37 Cr.App.R. 43, CCA. Where inadmissible material is opened it is within the judge's discretion to discharge the jury should the circumstances warrant it.

A defendant is not entitled to have his statement, that has been drafted by counsel upon instructions, not only submitted to the police officer in charge of his case but signed by that officer as a witness and thereafter employed, obligatorily, by counsel for the prosecution as part of the material which he would open to the jury: *R. v. Hedges*, 53 Cr.App.R. 206, CA.

Where two people are indicted together and one pleads guilty, a question which sometimes arises is whether the jury can properly be told, in the absence of defence consent, that the other defendant has pleaded guilty. If the fact that the co-defendant committed the offence is admissible against the defendant, then this may be established by proving his conviction under section 74 of the *PACE Act* 1984 (*post*, § 9–82); but if the conviction is not so admissible for that purpose, then in the absence of consent, there should be no reference to it. Any argument to the effect that the jury should be told of the co-defendant's plea merely for the purpose of clearing up the mystery as to what had happened to him is disingenuous and should be resisted: see *R. v. Moore*, 40 Cr.App.R. 50, CCA; and *R. v. Hall* [1993] Crim.L.R. 527, CA (approving observations to like effect in previous editions of this work). **4–269**

Where objection is to be taken by counsel for the defence to the admissibility of a piece of evidence, he should inform counsel for the prosecution beforehand, and the latter should refrain from mentioning that piece of evidence to the jury in his opening speech. As a general rule, a judge should not hear in advance arguments as to the admissibility of evidence, though there may be cases in which such practice is convenient and unobjectionable: *R. v. Cole*, 28 Cr.App.R. 43, CCA; *R. v. Hammond*, 28 Cr.App.R. 84, CCA; *R. v. Patel*, 35 Cr.App.R. 62, CCA; *R. v. Howard*, 42 Cr.App.R. 23, CCA. When any additional evidence, not mentioned in the opening speech of counsel, is discovered in the course of a trial, counsel is not allowed to make a second address to the jury: *R. v. Courvoisier* (1840) 9 C. & P. 362. Counsel may read to the jury the observations of a judge in a former case on the nature and effect of circumstantial evidence, provided that he adopts them and makes them part of his address to the jury: *ibid*. In *R. v. Dowling* (1848) 7 St.Tr.(n.s.) 381 at 390, the Attorney-General having, in his opening address to the jury, made references to disturbances in Ireland, it was held, that such reference was not irregular, it being laid down in books on evidence that allusion might be made in courts of justice to notorious matters, even of contemporaneous history. See also *R. v. Duffy* (1848) 7 St.Tr.(n.s.) 795 at 917. **4–270**

As to the opening of the facts in cases where the defendant pleads guilty, see *Practice Direction (Criminal Proceedings: Consolidation)* [2002] 1 W.L.R. 2870, para. III.26. **4–271**

See *post*, § 5–77a, as to how the alleged effect of an offence on any victim should be dealt with on a plea of guilty.

It is counsel's duty to outline the facts upon which the Crown intends to rely. It is **4–272** highly undesirable for prosecuting counsel in so doing to use unnecessarily emotive language which on any view can only excite sympathy for the victim or prejudice against the accused in the minds of the jury. Indeed, in cases where the facts themselves may have that tendency, it is desirable for prosecuting counsel to warn the jury that neither sympathy nor prejudice should be allowed to influence their approach to the evidence or their assessment of the witnesses. The jury's approach to all the evidence should be one of clinical objectivity. "Counsel for the prosecution throughout a case ought not to struggle for the verdict against the prisoner, but they ought to bear themselves rather in the character of ministers of justice assisting in the administration of justice," *per* Avory J., in *R. v. Banks* [1916] 2 K.B. 621 at 623, 12 Cr.App.R. 74 at 76, CCA.

X. DUTIES OF THE PROSECUTION RELATING TO THE PRESENTATION OF THE EVIDENCE AND THE CALLING OF WITNESSES

A. DISCLOSURE TO THE DEFENCE

4–273 One of the most important of the duties of the prosecution relates to the disclosure of matter in their possession to the defence. This is an area of law which has developed rapidly in recent years. It is also notoriously difficult. It is closely linked to the law relating to public interest immunity, as one ground for not disclosing matter to the defence is that it is immune from disclosure on the ground of public interest. Although there is a clear distinction between the two topics, in practice points about disclosure are so frequently related to a possible claim to public interest immunity that both topics are dealt with together in Chapter 12, *post*.

B. EXTENT OF PROSECUTION OBLIGATION TO CALL WITNESSES

4–274 The *CPIA* 1996 created a new scheme in respect of the calling of witnesses. The legislation provides that a witness statement or deposition that has been admitted as evidence before the examining justices may be read as evidence at the trial unless a party to the proceedings objects, although the objection may be overridden by the court of trial if that is in the interests of justice: 1996 Act, Sched. 2, *post*, §§ 10–41 *et seq.* Such objection must be made in accordance with rule 27.2 of the *Criminal Procedure Rules* 2005 (*post*, § 10–37). If an objection is made by the defence it will be necessary for the prosecution to decide whether to try to call the relevant witness to give oral evidence and/or whether to invite the court of trial to override the objection.

The issues considered below arise in respect of a witness whose evidence has been relied upon by the prosecution for the purposes of the committal proceedings and who the defence wish to be called to give oral evidence, notwithstanding the fact that the prosecution are prepared (or wish) to proceed without placing any evidence from that witness before the court of trial. Many of the authorities that are cited pre-date the implementation of the new scheme described above and concern cases where committal proceedings had taken place. In some of the cases the witnesses upon whose evidence the prosecution have relied at committal are described as witnesses named on the back of the indictment, which was a practice followed before the abolition of grand juries and the repeal of rule 1(5) of Schedule 1 to the *Indictments Act* 1915, and in some of the cases witnesses are referred to as having been fully or conditionally bound at committal, the practice before the implementation of the new scheme. However, it is submitted that the principles expounded in these authorities are equally applicable to the new scheme and also to the situation in respect of witnesses upon whose evidence the prosecution have relied in obtaining a voluntary bill of indictment or a transfer for trial without committal.

Subject to what is said below, the question of who should be called to give evidence for the prosecution is for prosecuting counsel to resolve. Where counsel is reluctant to call a witness, it is wrong for the trial judge to insist on the witness being called by the prosecution: *R. v. Baldwin*, *The Times*, May 3, 1978, CA; *R. v. Grafton*, 96 Cr.App.R. 156, CA, *post*, § 4–345. See also *post*, § 4–276.

Witnesses the prosecution choose not to call

In *R. v. Russell-Jones* [1995] 1 Cr.App.R. 538, the Court of Appeal set out the following principles, which emerge from the previous authorities and from rules of practice. **4–275**

1. Generally speaking the prosecution must have at court all the witnesses whose statements have been served as witnesses on whom the prosecution intend to rely, if the defence want those witnesses to attend. In deciding which statements to serve, the prosecution have an unfettered discretion, but must normally disclose material statements not served.
2. The prosecution enjoy a discretion whether to call, or tender, any witness they require to attend, but the discretion is not unfettered.
3. The first principle which limits this discretion is that it must be exercised in the interests of justice, so as to promote a fair trial. The dictum of Lord Thankerton in *Adel Muhammed El Dabbah v. Att.-Gen. for Palestine* [1944] A.C. 156, PC (court will only interfere if prosecutor has been influenced by some oblique motive), does not mean that the court will only interfere if the prosecutor has acted out of malice; it means that the prosecutor must direct his mind to his overall duty of fairness, as a minister of justice. Were he not to do so, he would have been moved by a consideration not relevant to his proper task—in that sense, an oblique motive.
4. The prosecution ought normally to call or offer to call all the witnesses who give direct evidence of the primary facts of the case, unless for good reason, in any instance, they regard the witnesses's evidence as unworthy of belief. In most cases, the jury should have available all of that evidence as to what actually happened, which the prosecution, when serving statements, considered to be material, even if there are inconsistencies between one witness and another. The defence cannot always be expected to call for themselves witnesses of the primary facts whom the prosecution have discarded. For example, the evidence they may give, albeit at variance with other evidence called by the Crown, may well be detrimental to the defence case. If what a witness of the primary facts has to say is properly regarded by the prosecution as being incapable of belief, or as some of the authorities say "incredible", then his evidence cannot help the jury assess the overall picture of the crucial events; hence, it is not unfair that he should not be called.
5. It is for the prosecution to decide which witnesses give direct evidence of the primary facts of the case. A prosecutor may reasonably take the view that what a witness has to say is at best marginal.
6. The prosecutor is also the primary judge of whether or not a witness to the material events is incredible, or unworthy of belief. It goes without saying that he could not properly condemn a witness as incredible merely because, for example, he gives an account at variance with that of a larger number of witnesses, and one that is less favourable to the prosecution case than that of the others.
7. A prosecutor properly exercising his discretion will not therefore be obliged to proffer a witness merely in order to give the defence material with which to attack the credit of other witnesses on whom the prosecution rely. To hold otherwise would, in truth, be to assert that the prosecution are obliged to call a witness for no purpose other than to assist the defence in their endeavour to destroy the Crown's own case. No sensible rule of justice could require such a stance to be taken.

The court added that these principles should not be regarded as a lexicon or rule book to cover all cases. There may be special situations that have not been adverted to, and in every case, it is important to emphasise, the judgment to be made is primarily that of the prosecutor, and, in general, the court will only interfere with it if he has gone wrong in principle.

For examples of the application of the principles set out above, see *R. v. Thompson* (1876) 13 Cox 181; *R. v. Oliva*, 49 Cr.App.R. 298, CCA; *R. v. Sterk* [1972] Crim.L.R. 391, CA; *R. v. Witts and Witts* [1991] Crim.L.R. 562, CA; *R. v. Balmforth* [1992] **4–276**

Crim.L.R. 825, CA; *R. v. Armstrong*, *The Times*, May 9, 1995, CA; and *R. v. Brown (D.) and Brown (M.)* [1997] 1 Cr.App.R. 112, CA. In certain of these authorities it is suggested that the trial judge has the power to order the prosecution to call a witness (*cf.* observations to the contrary in *R. v. Baldwin*, *ante*, § 4–274, and in *R. v. Oliva*, *ante*, and, *post*, § 4–345). However, the judge may, in his discretion, call a witness who has been "named on the back of the indictment" in the event that the prosecution are reluctant to do so and if the defence wish to have him called: *R. v. Thompson* and *R. v. Oliva*, *ante*. The staying of the proceedings in such circumstances as an abuse of process (*ante*, §§ 4–48 *et seq.*) would appear to be another possibility, although such an application was said to have been totally ill founded, and one that should never have been made, in *R. v. Bradish and Hall* [2004] 6 *Archbold News* 3, CA. In the alternative, failure by the prosecution to call a witness in such circumstances may lead to a successful appeal. These various possibilities, and the application of the general principles, were considered in *R. v. Haringey JJ., ex p. DPP* [1996] Q.B. 351, DC, where a police officer was a direct witness as to the central issue, but the prosecution had chosen not to call him because of an unrelated suspension from duty. The defence wished to question the officer and, in the particular circumstances, it was held (i) not to be reasonable to expect the defence to call him, and (ii) wrong for the prosecution not to call him. However, the court below had erred in staying the proceedings; there was another option; although the court could not have directed the prosecution to call the witness it could, exceptionally, have called the witness itself if the prosecution still declined to call the witness after a ruling that it was unfair to the defence for the witness not to be called. This approach was approved in *R. v. Bradish and Hall*, *ante*, although not applied since, in that case, the purpose for which the defence wished the witness to be called was to enable cross-examination to be used as a substitute for evidence.

4–277 There is no rule of law inhibiting the prosecution from calling a particular witness if they do not regard the whole of his evidence as reliable; if they consider that part of his evidence is capable of belief then, even though they might not rely on other parts of his evidence, it is a proper exercise of their discretion to call the witness; as part of the evidence might be of assistance to the court in performing its task, it would be contrary to the interests of justice to deprive the court of that assistance; but a jury should be directed as to the special need for caution in respect of the reliability of the witness: *R. v. Cairns, Zaidi and Chaudhary* [2003] 1 Cr.App.R. 38, CA.

Where witness statements have simply been served on the defence as unused material, the prosecution are not under any duty to call the makers of those statements as witnesses. For a judge to press the prosecution to do so would, in effect, be to require the Crown to act as both prosecution and defence: *R. v. Richardson*, 98 Cr.App.R. 174, CA.

Witnesses the prosecution are unable to call

4–278 Where the prosecution are anxious to call a witness whom they regard as reliable and are prevented from doing so by circumstances outside their control the principles set out at § 4–275, *ante*, do not apply: *R. v. Cavanagh*, 56 Cr.App.R. 407, CA. In such a case the prosecution should take all reasonable steps to secure the attendance of a witness required by the defence (*R. v. Woodhead* (1847) 2 C. & P. 520), but if it is impossible to have the witness present, the court might, in its discretion, permit the trial to proceed provided that no injustice would be done thereby. The considerations affecting the exercise of the court's discretion would vary greatly from case to case, *e.g.* (a) whether the defence would wish to call the witness if the prosecution did not; (b) the chances of securing the attendance of the witness in a reasonable time; (c) the extent to which the evidence of the absent witness would have been likely to assist the defendant; (d) whether other witnesses would have become unavailable by the time the attendance of the absent witness could be procured: *R. v. Cavanagh*, *ante*. The matter must be looked at in the round and even if the prosecution have not taken all reasonable steps to ensure the attendance of the witness it is for the judge to decide whether or not, in justice, the trial should proceed: *R. v. Gundem* [1997] Crim.L.R. 903, CA.

These principles were applied in *R. v. Ondhia* [1998] 2 Cr.App.R. 150, CA, and see

DPP v. Chalmers [2000] C.O.D. 2, DC, and *R. v. Martello* [2000] 8 *Archbold News* 1, CA.

C. Notices of Further Evidence

4–279 Witnesses who were not relied on in any magistrates' court's proceedings may nonetheless be called at the trial by the prosecution: see *R. v. Ward* (1848) 2 C. & K. 759. But notice of intention to call such witnesses, together with a written account of the evidence which it is proposed that they should give (usually their witness statements), ought to be served. In *R. v. Hawkins*, unreported, 1896, QBD, Lord Russell C.J. required proof of notice of new evidence. See also *R. v. Sinclair, ante*, § 4–194. If a defendant is taken by surprise by additional evidence, notice of which has not been served upon him, he may apply for an adjournment of the trial: *R. v. Wright*, 25 Cr.App.R. 35, CCA. In certain cases it may be that a retrial will be necessary if the evidence is to be admitted. The power to exclude evidence on the basis of fairness (*post*, § 15–452) should also be kept in mind.

As to the significance of Article 6(3) of the ECHR (*post*, § 16–57) in respect of the rights of the defendant when new material is relied upon against him, see *Mattocia v. Italy* (2003) 36 E.H.R.R. 47, ECtHR (*ante*, § 1–132d).

As to the prosecution not being limited, in their examination-in-chief, by the precise wording of a witness's statement, see *Filmer v. DPP* [2007] R.T.R. 28, DC (*post*, § 12–122).

D. "Editing" of Defendant's Oral and Written Statements

4–280 According to current practice, a statement made by a defendant may be "edited" to avoid prejudicing him and an effort may be made to eliminate matters which are part of the evidence, but which it is thought best the jury should not know. The best way for this to be done is for the evidence to appear unvarnished in the committal or transfer papers; then, at the trial, counsel can confer and the judge can, if necessary, take his part in the matter to ensure that any "editing" is done in the right way and to the right degree: *R. v. Weaver and Weaver* [1968] 1 Q.B. 353, 51 Cr.App.R. 77, CA. For the application of these principles to the editing of taped interviews, see *Practice Direction (Criminal Proceedings: Consolidation)* [2002] 1 W.L.R. 2870, para. IV.43, *post*, §§ 15–246 *et seq*.

4–281 Where a defendant has made a statement amounting to a confession both of the offence charged in the indictment and of other offences, the portion of the statement relating to the other offences should not be put in evidence by the prosecution unless it is, or becomes, admissible under a particular rule of evidence: *R. v. Knight and Thompson*, 31 Cr.App.R. 52, CCA.

4–282 A defendant, in making a statement, though admitting his guilt up to a certain extent, may put greater blame upon a co-defendant, or assert that certain of his actions were really innocent and it was the conduct of the co-defendant that gave them a sinister appearance or led to the belief that the defendant making the statement was implicated in the crime. That defendant would have a right to have the whole statement read and could, with good reason, complain if the prosecution picked out certain passages and left out others; although counsel often do refrain from reading passages which implicate another defendant and have no real bearing on the case against the maker of the statement: *R. v. Gunewardene* [1951] 2 K.B. 600, 35 Cr.App.R. 80, CCA; and see *Lobban v. R.* [1995] 2 Cr.App.R. 573, PC.

Various steps have been taken to protect the position of a defendant incriminated by his co-defendant's statement. One possibility is to order severance, but such a course is unlikely to be adopted for this reason alone. In *R. v. Rogers and Tarran* [1971] Crim.L.R. 413, Assizes, Crichton J. ruled that the prejudicial effect against the co-defendant outweighed the probative value against the maker of the statement and excluded it in the exercise of his discretion. Such a course is unusual; it also does not seem to do justice as between the prosecution and the maker of the statement. The course adopted in *R. v. Rice* [1963] 1 Q.B. 857, 47 Cr.App.R. 79, CA (*post*, § 15–386), is unlikely to be approved of today, and, it is submitted, should not be adopted, except, possibly, with the express assent of all parties and the judge.

See also the devices adopted in *R. v. Silcott* [1987] Crim.L.R. 765, CCC (Hodgson J.) and *R. v. Mathias* [1989] Crim.L.R. 64, Crown Court (H.H.J. Pearlman). The Privy Council in *Lobban v. R.*, *ante*, doubted that a trial judge had any power to adopt these solutions in the face of opposition from the maker of the statement.

E. "EDITING" OF WITNESS'S STATEMENT

Practice Direction (Criminal Proceedings: Consolidation), para. III.24 [2002] 1 W.L.R. 2870

Evidence by written statement

4–283 **III.24.1** Where the prosecution proposes to tender written statements in evidence either under sections 5A and 5B of the *Magistrates' Courts Act* 1980 or section 9 of the *Criminal Justice Act* 1967 it will frequently be not only proper, but also necessary for the orderly presentation of the evidence, for certain statements to be edited. This will occur either because a witness has made more than one statement whose contents should conveniently be reduced into a single, comprehensive statement or where a statement contains inadmissible, prejudicial or irrelevant material. Editing of statements should in all circumstances be done by a Crown prosecutor (or by a legal representative, if any, of the prosecutor if the case is not being conducted by the Crown Prosecution Service) and not by a police officer.

Composite statements

III.24.2 A composite statement giving the combined effect of two or more earlier statements or settled by a person referred to in paragraph 24.1 must be prepared in compliance with the requirements of sections 5A and 5B of the 1980 Act or section 9 of the 1967 Act as appropriate and must then be signed by the witness.

Editing single statements

4–284 **III.24.3** There are two acceptable methods of editing single statements. (a) By marking *copies* of the statement in a way which indicates the passages on which the prosecution will not rely. This merely indicates that the prosecution will not seek to adduce the evidence so marked. The *original signed statement* to be tendered to the court is not marked in any way. The marking on the copy statement is done by lightly striking out the passages to be edited so that what appears beneath can still be read, or by bracketing, or by a combination of both. It is not permissible to produce a photocopy with the deleted material obliterated, since this would be contrary to the requirement that the defence and the court should be served with copies of the signed original statement. Whenever the striking out/bracketing method is used, it will assist if the following words appear at the foot of the frontispiece or index to any bundle of copy statements to be tendered:

> "The prosecution does not propose to adduce evidence of those passages of the attached copy statements which have been struck out and/or bracketed (nor will it seek to do so at the trial unless a notice of further evidence is served)."

(b) By obtaining a fresh statement, signed by the witness, which omits the offending material, applying the procedure in paragraph 24.2.

4–285 **III.24.4** In most cases where a single statement is to be edited, the striking out/bracketing method will be the more appropriate, but the taking of a fresh statement is preferable in the following circumstances. (a) When a police (or other investigating) officer's statement contains details of interviews with more suspects than are eventually charged, a fresh statement should be prepared and signed omitting all details of interview with those not charged except, in so far as it is relevant, for the bald fact that a certain named person was interviewed at a particular time, date and place. (b) When a suspect is interviewed about more offences than are eventually made the subject of committal charges, a fresh statement should be prepared and signed omitting all questions and answers about the uncharged offences unless either they might appropriately be taken into consideration or evidence about those offences is admissible on the charges preferred, such as evidence of system. It may however be desirable to replace the omitted questions and answers with a phrase such as: "After referring to some other matters, I then said ... ", so as to make it clear that part of the interview has been omitted. (c) A fresh statement should normally be prepared and signed if the only part of the original on which the prosecution is relying is only a small proportion of the whole, although it remains desirable to use the alternative method if there is reason to believe that the defence might itself wish to rely, in mitigation or for any other purpose, on at least some of those parts which the prosecution does not propose to adduce. (d) When the passages contain material which the prosecution is entitled to withhold from disclosure to the defence.

III.24.5 Prosecutors should also be aware that, where statements are to be tendered under section 9 of the 1967 Act in the course of *summary* proceedings, there will be a greater need to prepare fresh statements excluding inadmissible or prejudicial material rather than using the striking out or bracketing method.

III.24.6 None of the above principles applies, in respect of committal proceedings, to documents which are exhibited (including statements under caution and signed contemporaneous notes). Nor do they apply to oral statements of a defendant which are recorded in the witness statements of interviewing police officers, except in the circumstances referred to in paragraph 24.4(b). All this material should remain in its original state in the committal bundles, any editing being left to prosecuting counsel at the Crown Court (after discussion with defence counsel and, if appropriate, the trial judge). **4–286**

III.24.7 Whenever a fresh statement is taken from a witness, a copy of the earlier, unedited statement(s) of that witness will be given to the defence in accordance with the Attorney-General's guidelines on the disclosure of unused material (*Practice Note (Criminal Evidence: Unused Material)* [1982] 1 All E.R. 734) unless there are grounds under paragraph 6 of the guidelines for withholding such disclosure.

The Attorney-General's guidelines dealt with disclosure. They have long since been superseded by the provisions of Parts I and II of the *CPIA* 1996 (*post*, §§ 12–45 *et seq.*), the code of practice issued under Part II (Appendix A–231 *et seq.*), and the guidelines issued by the Attorney-General in April, 2005 (Appendix A–242 *et seq.*).

XI. EVIDENCE USUALLY TENDERED IN PRESENCE OF JURY

A. GENERAL RULE

The general rule in trials on indictment is that evidence given in the course of the trial and before verdict must be tendered in the presence of the jury: *R. v. Reynolds* [1950] 1 K.B. 606 at 611, 34 Cr.App.R. 60 at 64, CCA. Where, however, there is an issue as to the admissibility of evidence, it may be necessary to hear evidence in the absence of the jury on the *voire dire*. The determining principle should be that stated in *R. v. Bonython* (1984) 38 S.A.S.R. 45 (*post*, § 10–65), *viz.*, where the admissibility of any piece of evidence depends on the existence of a fact or state of facts, the judge must determine the existence of the fact or state of facts in order to rule on the admissibility of the evidence. This, however, is a principle which the English courts have not adopted whole-heartedly. Whilst there are various situations (*post*) in which it has been recognised as proper to conduct a *voire dire*, there has been considerable vacillation on the issue (*e.g.* in relation to the admissibility of a previous plea of guilty, *post*, § 4–289, and as to identification evidence, *post*, § 14–80). **4–287**

Where an issue arises as to the admissibility of evidence, there should be no discussion of the matter in front of the jury; at the appropriate time, counsel should ask the judge to request the jury to withdraw so that a matter may be raised on which a ruling is sought, and the judge should simply tell the jury that a matter has arisen on which his ruling is sought and ask them to retire for the time being; at the conclusion of the *voire dire*, the judge should say nothing to the jury as to his decision or the reasons for it; to do so is to run the risk that the jury may be influenced by their knowledge or belief that some of the issues of fact have been canvassed in front of the judge and that he has formed a particular view as to where the truth lies: *Mitchell v. R.* [1998] A.C. 695, PC.

The following "exceptions" should not be taken to be exhaustive. Statutory provisions apart, they are merely a list of situations where the courts have accepted that it may be appropriate to hear evidence in the absence of the jury.

B. EXCEPTIONS

(1) Determining competence of witness

See the *YJCEA* 1999, s.54(4), *post*, § 8–36a. **4–288**

(2) Determining admissibility of defendant's previous plea of guilty

There is a conflict of authority. In *R. v. Rimmer*, 56 Cr.App.R. 196, CA, it was said **4–289**
that the circumstances of the earlier plea of guilty should be investigated in a trial-

within-a-trial. In *R. v. Hetherington* [1972] Crim.L.R. 703, however, the Court of Appeal was unable to accept as applicable to all cases the observation in *Rimmer* that the question of admissibility should be determined in a trial-within-a-trial. As to the admissibility of an earlier plea of guilty, see *post*, § 15–442.

(3) Determining admissibility of tape recordings

4–290 Tape recordings are admissible as evidence provided that they are shown to be both original and authentic. Copies are inadmissible in the absence of: (a) proper explanation as to why the originals are not available, and (b) proof of the complete accuracy of the copies: *R. v. Robson and Harris* [1972] 1 W.L.R. 651, CCC (Shaw J.), where the prosecution sought to tender in evidence tape recordings of alleged conversations between the defendants and a prosecution witness. The evidence and argument on the question of the admissibility of the tapes was heard in the absence of the jury. Shaw J. held that in considering the question of admissibility the court is required to do no more than satisfy itself that what the prosecution alleges to be original tapes are shown, prima facie, to be original by evidence which defines and describes the provenance and history of the recordings up to the moment of production in court. If that evidence appears to remain intact after cross-examination it is not incumbent on the judge to hear and weigh other evidence which might controvert the prima facie case. To embark on such an inquiry is to trespass on the ultimate function of the jury. Shaw J.'s ruling was upheld by the Court of Appeal (unreported). Ordinarily the larger issue of authenticity is manifestly a matter for the jury's consideration on admissible evidence. See also *R. v. Ali and Hussain* [1966] 1 Q.B. 688, 49 Cr.App.R. 230, CCA, in which it was acknowledged that issues of weight and admissibility may overlay each other, and *R. v. Stevenson*, 55 Cr.App.R. 171, Assizes (Kilner Brown J.).

(4) Miscellaneous

4–291 The issue also arises in respect of the admissibility of confessions (*post*, §§ 15–380 *et seq.*), the admissibility of identification evidence (*post*, § 14–35), the admissibility of *res gestae* statements (*post*, §§ 11–74 *et seq.*), questioning by the judge of a hostile or unwilling witness (*post*, §§ 8–94a, 28–122), and whether the jury should be directed that they may draw inferences against a defendant who fails to give evidence (*post*, § 4–305a).

XII. SUBMISSION OF INSUFFICIENT EVIDENCE

A. PRACTICE

4–292 It is not open to a judge to rule that there is no case to answer before the close of the prosecution case without the express agreement of the parties, as may perhaps be the case where the whole of the evidence is agreed or the remaining prosecution evidence is known with certainty: *R. v. N. Ltd*, *The Times*, August 25, 2008, CA. The proper time for such a submission is at the close of the case for the prosecution (save for the exceptional case created by the *Domestic Violence, Crime and Victims Act* 2004, s.6(4), *post*, §§ 4–298, 19–118f). Attempts have occasionally been made to renew such a submission during the course of the defence case. The Court of Appeal has said that whilst such a submission ought normally to be made at the close of the prosecution case, it may be made at the end of the defence case: *R. v. Anderson*, *The Independent (C.S.)*, July 13, 1998. Similarly, in *R. v. Ramsey* [2000] 6 *Archbold News* 3, CA, it was said that where, in a borderline case, the judge properly rules that there is a case to answer, he may be under a duty to re-visit the issue at the end of the evidence, taking account of the evidence called on behalf of the defence. In *R. v. Brown (Davina)* [2002] 1 Cr.App.R. 5, CA, reference having been made to these authorities and to other unreported decisions, it was confirmed that if, at any time after the conclusion of the prosecution case, the judge is satisfied that no jury, if properly directed, could convict, he has the power to withdraw the case from the jury, but that this is a power to be sparingly exercised. It is submitted that it would not be a proper exercise of this power for the trial judge to purport to assess the credibility of any evidence adduced on behalf of a defendant, thereby usurping the function of the jury.

Submissions of no case should be made in the absence of the jury: *R. v. Falconer-Atlee*, 58 Cr.App.R. 348, CA. One possible qualification to this principle is if the defence ask that the jury remain, in which case the judge should hear submissions in the absence of the jury as to why there should be a departure from normal procedure: *Crosdale v. R.* [1995] 2 All E.R. 500, PC. It is difficult to envisage a legitimate reason; an attempt by the defence to make an extra speech would not provide such a reason: *ibid*.

If the submission of no case is rejected, there should be no comment to the jury: *R. v. Smith and Doe*, 85 Cr.App.R. 197, CA. However, it being generally desirable, and especially so in long cases, that the judge keeps the jury informed as to what is happening, it is proper for him to give a brief explanation for upholding one or more submissions of no case, so long as he says nothing which might be construed as indicating a belief on his part that any remaining counts are well-founded: *R. v. Thirunavvkkarasu* [1998] 7 *Archbold News* 3, CA (97 03289 Y5).

As to whether the trial judge is obliged, or even entitled to stop a case where he is of the opinion (subject to inviting and considering submissions) that no prima facie case has been made out, but where no contention to that effect has been put forward by the defence advocate, see *post*, § 7–79.

See *post*, § 4–303, as to the right of a jury to acquit at any time after the close of the prosecution case.

B. PRINCIPLE

A submission of no case should be allowed when there is no evidence upon which, if the evidence adduced were accepted, a reasonable jury, properly directed, could convict. In such a case, a directed verdict must be taken from the jury. **4–293**

C. R. v. GALBRAITH

In *R. v. Galbraith*, 73 Cr.App.R. 124, CA, the earlier authorities were reviewed and guidance given as to the proper approach: **4–294**

> "(1) If there is no evidence that the crime alleged has been committed by the defendant there is no difficulty—the judge will stop the case. (2) The difficulty arises where there is some evidence but it is of a tenuous character, for example, because of inherent weakness or vagueness or because it is inconsistent with other evidence. (a) Where the judge concludes that the prosecution evidence, taken at its highest, is such that a jury properly directed could not properly convict on it, it is his duty, on a submission being made, to stop the case. (b) Where however the prosecution evidence is such that its strength or weakness depends on the view to be taken of a witness's reliability, or other matters which are generally speaking within the province of the jury and where on one possible view of the facts there *is* evidence on which the jury could properly come to the conclusion that the defendant is guilty, then the judge should allow the matter to be tried by the jury" (*per* Lord Lane C.J. at p. 127).

The Lord Chief Justice then observed that borderline cases could be left to the discretion of the judge. For an example of the approach of the Court of Appeal to the exercise of this discretion, see *R. v. Lesley* [1996] 1 Cr.App.R. 39, CA.

In *R. v. Shippey* [1988] Crim.L.R. 767, Crown Court (a decision on its facts, laying down no new principle of law: *R. v. Pryer, Sparkes and Walker*, unreported, April 7, 2004, CA ([2004] EWCA Crim. 1163)), Turner J. held that the requirement to take the prosecution evidence at its highest did not mean "picking out all the plums and leaving the duff behind". The judge should assess the evidence and if the evidence of the witness upon whom the prosecution case depended was self-contradictory and out of reason and all common sense then such evidence was tenuous and suffered from inherent weakness. His Lordship did not interpret *Galbraith* as meaning that if there are parts of the evidence which go to support the charge then that is enough to leave the matter to the jury, no matter what the state of the rest of the evidence is. It was, he said, necessary to make an assessment of the evidence as a whole and it was not simply a matter of the credibility of individual witnesses or of evidential inconsistencies between witnesses, although those matters may play a subordinate role. In *Brooks v. DPP* [1994] 1 A.C. 568 at 581, PC, it was said (in the context of committal proceedings) that questions of credibility, except in the clearest of cases, do not normally result in a finding that there is no prima facie case. **4–295**

Where the prosecution case depends entirely on circumstantial evidence, the correct approach is to look at the evidence in the round, and ask whether, looking at all the evidence and treating it with appropriate care and scrutiny, there is a case on which a properly directed jury could convict: *R. v. P.* [2008] 2 Cr.App.R. 6, CA. To similar effect, see *R. v. Jabber* [2006] 10 *Archbold News* 3, CA (where case depends on drawing a particular inference, inference does not have to be one that only an unreasonable person would fail to draw from the facts proved).

As to the evidential value of the defendant's statements for the purposes of a submission of no case, see *post*, § 15–408; and for reliance upon a co-defendant's confession where there is a case for the co-defendant to answer and the co-defendant's guilt would be probative in the case against the defendant, see *R. v. Hayter* [2005] 2 Cr.App.R. 3, HL, *post* § 9–85.

D. MAGISTRATES' COURTS

4–296 In their summary jurisdiction magistrates are judges both of facts and law. It is therefore submitted that even where at the close of the prosecution case, or later, there is some evidence which, *if accepted*, would entitle a reasonable tribunal to convict, they nevertheless have the same right as a jury to acquit if they do not accept the evidence, whether because it is conflicting, or has been contradicted or for any other reason.

4–297 It is submitted that in committal proceedings the question to be determined by the magistrates, in the event of a submission of no case being made, is the same question which a judge has to ask himself in like circumstances during a trial on indictment.

Magistrates are not obliged to give reasons for rejecting a submission of no case: *Harrison v. Department of Social Security* [1997] C.O.D. 220, DC.

E. PARTICULAR APPLICATIONS

Evidence equivocal as to which of two people, jointly indicted, committed the offence

4–298 If two people are jointly charged and the evidence does not point to one rather than the other, and there is no evidence that they were acting in concert, a verdict of not guilty is appropriate in the case of both: *R. v. Abbott* [1955] 2 Q.B. 497, 39 Cr.App.R. 141, CCA; *Collins and Fox v. Chief Constable of Merseyside* [1988] Crim.L.R. 247, DC (*post*, § 21–169); and *Swallow v. DPP* [1991] Crim.L.R. 610, DC.

The principle has been considered on a number of occasions in the context of acts of violence committed by one or both parents on a child in the home: see *R. v. Gibson and Gibson*, 80 Cr.App.R. 24, CA (convictions under section 20 of the *Offences against the Person Act* 1861 quashed, but court, *obiter*, expounded basis upon which prima facie case against each in respect of an offence contrary to section 1 of the *CYPA* 1933 could have been founded); *R. v. Lane and Lane*, 82 Cr.App.R. 5, CA (manslaughter convictions quashed, no evidence to establish presence of either at time child injured, or participation); *R. v. Russell and Russell*, 85 Cr.App.R. 388, CA; *R. v. Beard*, 85 Cr.App.R. 395, CA; *R. v. Aston and Mason*, 94 Cr.App.R. 180, CA; *R. v. Strudwick and Merry*, 99 Cr.App.R. 326, CA (see further *post*, § 4–301a); and *post*, §§ 19–24, 19–296a. Where, however, the defendant is charged in the same proceedings with murder or manslaughter and also with an offence under section 5 of the *Domestic Violence, Crime and Victims Act* 2004 in respect of the same death, the question of whether there is a case to answer on the charge of murder or manslaughter is not to be considered before the close of the evidence or such earlier time as he ceases to be charged with the section 5 offence: s.6 of the 2004 Act, *post*, § 19–118f.

As to the proper approach to a submission of no case in respect of a charge of possession of controlled drugs, where the drugs have been found in premises occupied by a number of people, see *R. v. McNamara and McNamara* [1998] Crim.L.R. 272, CA (and the commentary thereto). See also *post*, § 27–63.

Mutually inconsistent counts

4–299 See *R. v. Bellman* [1989] A.C. 836, HL, *post*, §§ 21–289 *et seq.*

Identification cases

See *post*, §§ 14–12 *et seq.* 4–300

Cases involving delay in reporting offences

Where evidence is given after many years the court should exercise careful scrutiny at the end of the evidence to see whether or not the case is safe to be left to the jury: *R. v. Smolinski* [2004] 2 Cr.App.R. 40, CA. It is not sufficient for the judge merely to leave the case to the jury on the basis that it is for them to consider what they make of any discrepancies and differences in the evidence of the witnesses; the judge must assess the significance of the discrepancies himself and rule on whether their impact upon the quality of the evidence is such that no jury could safely convict on the counts to which they relate: *R. v. R.* [2007] Crim.L.R. 478, CA. 4–300a

Confessions

As to the application of the *Galbraith* guidance to a case depending on the confession of a defendant suffering from mental disorder, see *R. v. Mackenzie*, 96 Cr.App.R. 98, CA, *post*, § 15–369. 4–301

Lies as evidence of guilt

In *R. v. Strudwick and Merry*, *ante*, it was held that lies, if they are proved to have been told through a consciousness of guilt, may support a prosecution case, but on their own they do not make a case. See also *post*, § 4–402. 4–301a

Statutory alternative offences

As to the position where the judge allows a submission of no case to answer in respect of the offence charged, but finds a case to answer in respect of a statutory alternative summary offence, see *post*, § 4–462. 4–301b

F. APPEAL

Where a submission of no case is wrongly rejected, an appeal against conviction should be allowed (*post*, § 7–79). 4–302

G. RIGHT OF JURY TO STOP CASE

The right of the jury to acquit an accused at any time after the close of the case for the Crown, either upon the whole indictment or upon one or more counts, is well established at common law. Judges may remind juries of their rights in this respect at or after the close of the case for the Crown, pointing out that they can only acquit at that stage and must wait till the whole case is over before they can convict. The Court of Appeal in *R. v. Falconer-Atlee*, 58 Cr.App.R. 348 at 357, discouraged judges from issuing such a reminder, saying that if a judge was not prepared to take the responsibility upon himself, he should not seek to cast it upon the jury. This was reiterated in *R. v. Kemp* [1995] 1 Cr.App.R. 151, CA, where it was said that a judge should not go beyond a mere intimation of the right of the jury to stop a case, in *R. v. Speechley*, *The Times*, December 1, 2004, CA, where it was said that in almost every case, in order to do justice, the jury needed to listen to all of the evidence, the submissions of counsel and the directions in law of the judge, and in *R. v. Collins* [2007] 5 *Archbold News* 3, in which the Court of Appeal described the practice of inviting the jury to exercise the right as having been comprehensively disapproved, listed the specific dangers involved in doing so, and found it difficult to envisage any circumstances when it would be appropriate for it to be adopted. 4–303

The right should only be exercised at the invitation of the judge; if a jury are invited by counsel, or seek of their own motion, to return a verdict before being asked by the judge to do so, the judge should direct them that it is his duty to ensure that justice is done, and that it is not open to them to return a verdict until he invites them to do so: *Speechley*, *ante*.

XIII. THE DEFENCE CASE

A. TABLE OF ORDER OF SPEECHES

4–304 I. *When the defendant is not defended by counsel and calls no witnesses to the facts except himself, or calls no evidence*

(1) Counsel for the prosecution opens his case.
(2) Witnesses for the prosecution.
(3) Defendant gives evidence (if he wishes).
(4) Witnesses, if any, as to defendant's good character.
(5) Defendant addresses the jury in his defence.

II. *When the defendant is not defended by counsel, but calls witnesses as to the facts, whether or not he gives evidence himself*

(1) and (2) As in I, *ante*.
(3) Defendant may open his case.
(4) Defendant gives evidence (if he wishes: whether he does or not, the order of speeches remains the same).
(5) Witnesses for the defence (including witnesses, if any, as to defendant's good character).
(6) Counsel for the prosecution may sum up his case.
(7) Defendant addresses the jury in his defence.

III. *When the defendant is defended by counsel who calls no witnesses to the facts except the defendant*

(1) and (2) As in I, *ante*.
(3) Defendant gives evidence (if he wishes: whether he does or not, the order of speeches remains the same).
(4) Witnesses, if any, as to defendant's good character.
(5) Counsel for the prosecution sums up his case (if he thinks proper).
(6) Counsel for the defence sums up the case for the defence.

IV. *When the defendant is defended by counsel who calls witnesses to the facts, whether or not he calls the defendant*

(1) and (2) As in I, *ante*.
(3) Counsel for the defence may open his case.
(4) Defendant gives evidence (if he wishes: whether he does or not, the order of speeches remains the same).
(5) Witnesses for the defence (including witnesses, if any, as to defendant's good character).
(6) Counsel for the prosecution sums up his case.
(7) Counsel for the defence sums up the case for the defence.

See also *post*, §§ 4–357 *et seq.*

B. WARNING AS TO GIVING OF EVIDENCE BY DEFENDANT

Criminal Justice and Public Order Act 1994, s.35

Effect of accused's silence at trial

4–305 **35.**—(1) At the trial of any person … for an offence, subsections (2) and (3) below apply unless—

(a) the accused's guilt is not in issue; or
(b) it appears to the court that the physical or mental condition of the accused makes it undesirable for him to give evidence;

but subsection (2) below does not apply if, at the conclusion of the evidence for the prosecution, his legal representative informs the court that the accused will give evidence or, where he is unrepresented, the court ascertains from him that he will give evidence.

(2) Where this subsection applies, the court shall, at the conclusion of the evidence for the prosecution, satisfy itself (in the case of proceedings on indictment with a jury, in the presence of the jury) that the accused is aware that the stage has been reached at which evidence can be given for the defence and that he can, if he wishes, give evidence and that, if he chooses not to give evidence, or having been sworn, without good cause refuses to answer any question, it will be permissible for the court or jury to draw such inferences as

appear proper from his failure to give evidence or his refusal, without good cause, to answer any question.

(3) Where this subsection applies, the court or jury, in determining whether the accused is guilty of the offence charged, may draw such inferences as appear proper from the failure of the accused to give evidence or his refusal, without good cause, to answer any question.

(4) This section does not render the accused compellable to give evidence on his own behalf, and he shall accordingly not be guilty of contempt of court by reason of a failure to do so.

(5) For the purposes of this section a person who, having been sworn, refuses to answer any question shall be taken to do so without good cause unless—

(a) he is entitled to refuse to answer the question by virtue of any enactment, whenever passed or made, or on the ground of privilege; or

(b) the court in the exercise of its general discretion excuses him from answering it.

(7) This section applies—

(a) in relation to proceedings on indictment for an offence, only if the person charged with the offence is arraigned on or after the commencement of this section;

(b) in relation to proceedings in a magistrates' court, only if the time when the court begins to receive evidence in the proceedings falls after the commencement of this section.

[This section is printed as amended, and repealed in part, by the *CDA* 1998, s.120(2), and Sched. 10; and the *CJA* 2003, s.331, and Sched. 36, paras 62 and 63.]

When considering the effect of section 35 of the 1994 Act, reference should also be made to section 38 of that Act (*post*, § 15–438), which provides—

(a) that a person shall not be convicted of an offence solely on an inference drawn from such a failure or refusal as is mentioned in section 35(3);

(b) that the reference in section 35(3) to an offence charged includes a reference to any other offence of which the accused could lawfully be convicted on that charge;

(c) a definition of the term "legal representative" in the context of section 35;

(d) that nothing in section 35 prejudices (a) the operation of any enactment which provides for any answer or evidence given by a person in specified circumstances not to be admissible in evidence, or (b) any power of the court to exclude evidence at is discretion.

Section 39 of the 1994 Act enables the Secretary of State to direct by statutory instrument that section 35, subject to such modifications as he may specify, applies to the various forms of military proceedings listed in section 39 (as from a day to be appointed, the *AFA* 2006, s.378(1), and Sched. 16, para. 130, amend s.39 to read "applies to any proceedings before an officer or court in respect of a service offence (other than proceedings before a civilian court)") (see *post*, § 15–439).

Where the defence seek to rely on subsection (1)(b), they must adduce evidence on this issue; if a ruling is sought, then such evidence must be adduced on the *voire dire*; if the judge declines to make an advance ruling that the case comes within this provision, it is then incumbent on the defence to adduce the evidence before the jury, otherwise the judge will be under no duty to direct the jury in relation to it: *R. v. A.* [1997] Crim.L.R. 883, CA. On such a *voire dire*, the judge may take account not only of any expert evidence, but also of the conduct of the accused before and after the offence, though not of the offence itself. A physical or mental condition which may merely cause some difficulty in giving evidence is insufficient to satisfy subsection (1)(b); such difficulties should be taken into account in assessing the weight of the defendant's evidence but would not justify a comprehensive failure to give evidence: *R. (DPP) v. Kavanagh* [2006] Crim.L.R. 370, QBD (Stanley Burnton J.). **4–305a**

It is a matter for the judge whether he hears evidence on the *voire dire* if it is submitted to him that no inference should be drawn against the accused on the basis that his failure to give evidence results from fear or duress, but there is no obligation on the judge to do so: *R. v. Chadwick* [1998] 7 *Archbold News* 3, CA (96 02755 Y2). See also *ante*, § 4–287.

As to directing the jury in relation to section 35, see *post*, §§ 4–398 *et seq.*

Practice Direction (Criminal Proceedings: Consolidation), para. IV.44 [2002] 1 W.L.R. 2870

Defendant's right to give or not to give evidence

4–306 **IV.44.1** At the conclusion of the evidence for the prosecution, section 35(2) of the *Criminal Justice and Public Order Act* 1994 requires the court to satisfy itself that the accused is aware that the stage has been reached at which evidence can be given for the defence and that he can, if he wishes, give evidence and that, if he chooses not to give evidence, or having been sworn, without good cause refuses to answer any question, it will be permissible for the jury to draw such inferences as appear proper from his failure to give evidence or his refusal, without good cause, to answer any question.

If the accused is legally represented

IV.44.2 Section 35(1) provides that section 35(2) does not apply if at the conclusion of the evidence for the prosecution the accused's legal representative informs the court that the accused will give evidence. This should be done in the presence of the jury. If the representative indicates that the accused will give evidence the case should proceed in the usual way.

IV.44.3 If the court is not so informed, or if the court is informed that the accused does not intend to give evidence, the judge should in the presence of the jury inquire of the representative in these terms:

"Have you advised your client that the stage has now been reached at which he may give evidence and, if he chooses not to do so or, having been sworn, without good cause refuses to answer any question, the jury may draw such inferences as appear proper from his failure to do so?"

IV.44.4 If the representative replies to the judge that the accused has been so advised, then the case shall proceed. If counsel replies that the accused has not been so advised, then the judge shall direct the representative to advise his client of the consequences set out in paragraph 44.3 and should adjourn briefly for this purpose before proceeding further.

If the accused is not legally represented

IV.44.5 If the accused is not represented, the judge shall at the conclusion of the evidence for the prosecution and in the presence of the jury say to the accused:

"You have heard the evidence against you. Now is the time for you to make your defence. You may give evidence on oath, and be cross-examined like any other witness. If you do not give evidence or, having been sworn, without good cause refuse to answer any question the jury may draw such inferences as appear proper. That means they may hold it against you. You may also call any witness or witnesses whom you have arranged to attend court. Afterwards you may also, if you wish, address the jury by arguing your case from the dock. But you cannot at that stage give evidence. Do you now intend to give evidence?"

It is not a breach of professional privilege to require a defence advocate to provide information in accordance with paragraph IV.44.3 of this practice direction: *R. v. Cowan*; *R. v. Gayle*; *R. v. Ricciardi* [1996] 1 Cr.App.R. 1, CA. Furthermore, the words of that paragraph should not be replaced by a simple inquiry of the defence advocate as to whether the defendant has been made aware of the provisions of section 35 of the Act: *ibid.*

A failure to give the defendant the warning required by subsection (2) is of no consequence where no adverse inference is in fact drawn: *Radford v. Kent County Council*, 162 J.P. 697, DC.

C. Defence Counsel's Duty

4–307 The following statement of principles which govern the conduct of defence counsel was made by the Chairman of the Bar following the rejection of complaints about defence counsel's conduct in the trial of *R. v. McFadden*, 62 Cr.App.R. 187 at 193, CA:

"It is the duty of counsel when defending an accused on a criminal charge to present to the court, fearlessly and without regard to his personal interests, the defence of that accused. It is not his function to determine the truth or falsity of that defence, nor should he permit his personal opinion of that defence to influence his conduct of it. No counsel may refuse to defend because of his opinion of the character of the accused nor of the crime charged. That is a cardinal rule of the Bar. ... Counsel also has a duty to the court and to the public. This duty includes the clear presentation of the issues and the avoidance of waste of time, repetition and prolixity. In the conduct of every case counsel must be mindful of this public responsibility.

Where the defence of the accused is that a fingerprint on an article, although his, was not put on the article by him, or that he never had in his possession an article which the prosecution claim was found on him (in other words that such evidence had been 'planted'), it is the duty of counsel to present that defence to the jury. Where the accused's defence leads to the conclusion from the evidence as a whole, that one or more identifiable persons were responsible for the 'planting', then it is counsel's duty, not only to the accused but also to the court, to pursue that defence and to put this allegation in cross-examination. Where, because of the instructions of the accused, a number of persons, whom the accused cannot identify, could have been responsible for the 'planting' then it is counsel's duty to test and probe the evidence for the prosecution in order to demonstrate the opportunity open to someone to have done the alleged 'planting'. In the absence of a basis for accusing a witness of responsibility for the 'planting' of evidence, counsel should not put in cross-examination that that witness is responsible. But he must put the allegation of opportunity and the general allegation that 'planting' has taken place, not necessarily to all the prosecution witnesses, but to that witness or witnesses whom counsel thinks most appropriate so that the prosecution have a proper opportunity to deal with the allegation by the accused. To do anything less would be to deny the prosecution the opportunity to rebut that defence and would deny to an accused the right to have his defence considered by the jury."

As to counsel's discretion in conducting the defence, see *R. v. Denoel*, 12 Cr.App.R. 49, CCA. **4–308**

As to counsel's duty in relation to cross-examination, see, more particularly, *post*, §§ 8–118 *et seq*.

As to counsel's duty when the defendant absconds, see Appendix C–10 and C–38 for the relevant provisions of the eighth edition of the *Code of Conduct for the Bar of England and Wales*.

As to counsel's duty in relation to the giving of advice on the appropriate plea, see *ante*, § 4–104.

As to the duty to check the accuracy of any summary of a police interview, see *R. v. Clinton*, 97 Cr.App.R. 320, CA.

As to the duty, in an appropriate case, to advise, if necessary, in strong terms, as to the desirability of giving evidence, see *ibid.* at p. 324, and see now *ante*, §§ 4–305 *et seq.* The practice described in *R. v. Bevan*, 98 Cr.App.R. 354, CA, of counsel making a record (with a brief summary of the reasons for the decision: see *Ebanks (Kurt) v. The Queen* [2006] 1 W.L.R. 1827, PC), signed by the defendant, in respect of any decision not to give evidence (as to which, see *post*, § 7–215 and Appendix C–54) should be the invariable practice, not only where the decision is contrary to advice that has been given but also where it follows such advice: *R. v. Chatroodi* [2001] 3 *Archbold News* 3, CA.

As to the need in an identification case to check that full disclosure (*e.g.* of police photographs and crime reports) has been made, see *R. v. Fergus*, 98 Cr.App.R. 313, CA.

As to the procedure to be followed when defence counsel feels that he is unable any longer properly to represent the defendant, see *R. v. Sansom*, 92 Cr.App.R. 115 at 124, CA, and *R. v. Ulcay*, *ante*, § 4–41.

Generally as to the duties of counsel, see also Appendix C, especially C–35, C–40 *et seq.*, and C–48 *et seq.*

D. DEFENDANT UNREPRESENTED

See paragraph IV.44.5 of the consolidated criminal practice direction, *ante*, § 4–306. **4–309**

It is essential that an unrepresented defendant should be asked by the judge whether he wishes to call any witnesses in his defence: *R. v. Carter*, 44 Cr.App.R. 225, CCA. The judge should endeavour to assist an unrepresented defendant in the conduct of his defence, in particular when he is examining or cross-examining witnesses, or giving evidence himself. But there is a duty to restrain unnecessary cross-examination: see *R. v. Brown (Milton)* [1998] 2 Cr.App.R. 364, CA, *post*, § 8–113.

As to the restrictions on cross-examination by a defendant in person in certain cases, see *post*, §§ 8–123a *et seq.*

A defendant's right under the *Criminal Procedure Act* 1865, s.2 (*post*, § 4–357), to call witnesses, and address the jury, is to be construed in the context of the judge's obligation to ensure the proper conduct of the trial. The right cannot be used to frustrate the trial by behaving improperly or calling unnecessary witnesses and is conditional upon its proper use for the advancement of the course of justice and the proper conduct of the trial. Although the court has an inherent power to prevent its process being abused by a defendant, that power is to be exercised exceedingly sparingly and only in an obvious case and, in relation to withholding the right to make a closing address to the jury, only if there is no alternative: *R. v. Morley* [1988] Q.B. 601, 87 Cr.App.R. 218, CA. See also *post*, § 4–313.

E. Opening Speech by Defence Counsel

4–310 The general right to make an opening speech for the defence is given by the *Criminal Procedure Act* 1865, s.2 (*post*, § 4–357). However, the generality of that right, which was given at a time when a defendant was not entitled to give evidence on his own behalf, is now subject to the *Criminal Evidence Act* 1898, s.2 (*post*, § 4–311a), which has the effect of preventing an opening speech being made for the defence where the only witness to the facts who is called by the defence is the person charged. See *R. v. Hill*, 7 Cr.App.R. 1, CCA, for confirmation of the existence of the qualified right of the defence to make an opening speech. Where the right exists, counsel for the defendant is entitled to open his case fully to the jury. This includes not only outlining the defence case, but also criticising the prosecution evidence: *R. v. Randall*, *The Times*, July 11, 1973, CA. But:

> "In the opinion of the judges it is contrary to the administration and practice of the criminal law as hitherto allowed, that counsel for prisoners should state to the jury as alleged existing facts matters which they have been told in their instructions, on the authority of the prisoner, but which they do not propose to prove in evidence": (resolution of the judges, November 26, 1881: *R. v. Shimmin* (1882) 15 Cox 122).

F. Sequence of Defence Evidence

Police and Criminal Evidence Act 1984, s.79

4–311 **79.** If at the trial of any person for an offence—

(a) the defence intends to call two or more witnesses to the facts of the case; and

(b) those witnesses include the accused,

the accused shall be called before the other witness or witnesses unless the court in its discretion otherwise directs.

This confirms the previous practice: see *R. v. Smith (Joan)*, 52 Cr.App.R. 224, CA, in which the rationale was explained and it was said that, in special circumstances, it would be proper for a formal or uncontroversial witness to be called before the defendant.

Criminal Evidence Act 1898, s.2

4–311a **2.** Where the only witness to the facts of the case called by the defence is the person charged, he shall be called as a witness immediately after the close of the evidence for the prosecution.

The effect of this section is that there is no right to make an opening speech when the only defence witness as to fact is the defendant: see *R. v. Gardner* [1899] 1 Q.B. 150.

G. Evidence from Witness Box

4–312 See section 1(4) of the *Criminal Evidence Act* 1898 (*post*, § 8–49). The intention of this provision is that a defendant shall have an opportunity of giving evidence on his own behalf in the same way and from the same place as the witnesses for the prosecution; it is not right to deprive him of the benefit of the statute without sufficient cause, *e.g.* where he exhibits violence which may be more easily quelled in the dock than in the witness box: *R. v. Symonds*, 18 Cr.App.R. 100, CCA.

See also *R. v. Farnham JJ., ex p. Gibson* [1991] Crim.L.R. 642, DC (to ask defendant whether he would prefer to give his evidence from the witness box or the dock would be a negation of right to give evidence from the witness box).

H. Duty to Stop Irrelevant Evidence

It is the duty of a judge to stop irrelevant evidence. In deciding whether evidence is irrelevant a judge may have a difficult decision to make; but, in considering the interests of justice, the interests of the prosecution have to be taken into account as well as those of the defence. A defence which is so confusing that no jury can follow it is just as much an injustice as any other kind of difficulty in a trial: *R. v. Gebreel*, *The Times*, June 8, 1974, CA. See also *ante*, § 4–309; and *R. v. Brown (Milton)* [1998] 2 Cr.App.R. 364, CA, *post*, § 8–113. **4–313**

In *R. v. King*, 57 Cr.App.R. 696, the Court of Appeal stressed that courts are not sounding boards for political views. Such views constitute wholly irrelevant matter. Counsel asked to air such views should refuse to do so and if the accused makes the pursuit of such a course the condition upon which he will accept counsel's advice, it is counsel's duty to withdraw.

I. Abolition of Right of Accused to Make Unsworn Statement

Criminal Justice Act 1982, s.72(1), (2)

72.—(1) Subject to subsections (2) and (3) below, in any criminal proceedings the accused shall not be entitled to make a statement without being sworn, and accordingly, if he gives evidence, he shall do so (subject to sections 55 and 56 of the *Youth Justice and Criminal Evidence Act* 1999) on oath and be liable to cross-examination; but this section shall not affect the right of the accused, if not represented by counsel or a solicitor, to address the court or jury otherwise than on oath on any matter on which, if he were so represented, counsel or a solicitor could address the court or jury on his behalf. **4–314**

(2) Nothing in subsection (1) above shall prevent the accused making a statement without being sworn—

(a) if it is one which he is required by law to make personally; or

(b) if he makes it by way of mitigation before the court passes sentence upon him.

[This section is printed as amended by the *YJCEA* 1999, s.67(1), and Sched. 4, para. 10.]

J. Rebuttal of Co-defendant's Evidence

Authority appears to be lacking as to when defendant A can, after closing his case, call evidence to rebut evidence adversely affecting him given by or on behalf of defendant B after A had closed his case. It is submitted that the same principles should apply as regulate the calling of evidence in rebuttal by the Crown: see *post*, §§ 4–335 *et seq.* In practice, it sometimes happens that B gives evidence adversely affecting A which has not been put to A in cross-examination on behalf of B, so that A has had no opportunity of dealing with it. In such cases it is usual, and it is submitted correct, for the judge to allow A to be recalled to deal with the matter. It would seem right for the judge to allow A to call other evidence upon the point in rebuttal if he could not reasonably have anticipated the evidence given by B. (As to counsel's duty when cross-examining a co-defendant, see *R. v. Fenlon*, 71 Cr.App.R. 307, CA, *post*, § 8–164.) **4–315**

K. Notice of Defence Case and Alibi

General

Section 11 of the *CJA* 1967, which made provision in respect of the service of alibi notices, was repealed by section 74(1) and (5) of the *CPIA* 1996. The 1996 Act provides for a scheme of more general disclosure of the defence case. For full details of this scheme, and for details of commencement and transitional provisions, see *post*, §§ 12–45 *et seq.* For details of the old law, see the 1997 edition of this work, at §§ 4–316 *et seq.* Section 6A(2) of the 1996 Act (*post*, § 12–57a) provides that if the defence statement discloses an alibi the accused must give particulars of the alibi in the statement, including the name, address and date of birth (if known) of any supporting witness and any **4–316** information which might be of assistance in finding any such witness if those details are not known to the accused. See *post*, § 4–317, as to what amounts to an alibi. By reason of section 5(5C), the defence statement, including particulars of any alibi, must be given during the period specified in regulations made by virtue of section 12 (*post*, §§ 12–56, 12–63). The relevant regulations are set out *post*, §§ 12–94 *et seq*.

The potential consequences of an accused either adducing evidence in support of an alibi without having provided particulars in accordance with the provisions of the 1996 Act, or calling witnesses in support of an alibi without having given advance information of such witnesses in accordance with the provisions of that Act, are set out in section 11 (*post*, § 12–62). See further *post*, § 4–319.

Circumstances in which particulars of alibi required

4–317 Section 6A(3) of the 1996 Act (*post*, § 12–57a) defines the term "evidence in support of an alibi", for the purposes of that Act, in terms that are, in effect, identical to the definition of the same term in the now repealed section 11(8) of the 1967 Act. In the context of the 1967 Act, it was held that the term envisages the commission of an offence which necessarily involved the defendant being at a particular place at a particular time: *R. v. Hassan*, 54 Cr.App.R. 56, CA. An alibi notice is not, therefore, required where the offence charged is a continuing one and it is intended to contradict part of the prosecution evidence by evidence that the defendant was elsewhere at the material time, albeit the time lies within the period covered by the charge: *ibid*. It would be different, it is submitted, if it were sought to prove that the defendant was out of the country throughout the entire period covered.

Evidence which merely indicates that the defendant was not present at the scene of the crime, with no positive assertion as to where he was, is not evidence in support of an alibi within the now repealed section 11(8) of the 1967 Act: *R. v. Johnson (A.)* [1995] 2 Cr.App.R. 1, CA.

Where, say, a robbery of a shop occurs at 6 p.m. and a witness says that he saw the robbery and recognised the robber as having been loitering outside the shop at 3 p.m., defence evidence to the effect that the defendant was at a different place at 3 p.m. is evidence in support of an alibi, even though he could have been at that place at 3 p.m., and at the place of the robbery at 6 p.m. (*i.e.* because the two places are only a few miles from each other): *R. v. Fields and Adams* [1991] Crim.L.R. 38, CA. (For a criticism of this decision, see the commentary in the *Criminal Law Review*.)

4–318 It is not apparent whether the court in *R. v. Fields and Adams* considered *R. v. Lewis* [1969] 2 Q.B. 1, 53 Cr.App.R. 76, CA, in which it was said that evidence relative to the defendant's whereabouts on an occasion other than the occasion of the commission of the crime is not subject to the restrictions of the alibi requirements, however significant that evidence may be to the issues in the case. The court gave as an example (pp. 6, 81) a man charged with a robbery committed on a Monday, with part of the evidence against him being that he was seen the next day driving a van containing the stolen goods. Evidence of "alibi" in relation to the Tuesday would not be subject to the alibi requirements. Similarly, where an offence was alleged to have been committed on "a day" between two dates a year apart and the statement of the alleged victim suggested that it would have been on a Wednesday, the defendant's evidence that it was his invariable practice on Wednesdays to go to a particular gym at the material time of the day was not "evidence in support of an alibi" within section 11 of the 1967 Act: *Re Beynon (Wasted Costs Order)* [1999] 8 *Archbold News* 1, CA. However, the more extensive obligation that now rests on a defendant (see *ante*, § 4–316) to set out in general terms, in a defence statement, the nature of his defence, must now be borne in mind whether or not the defence is, technically, one of alibi.

If a question arises with regard to the place or date at which the offence is alleged to have been committed, for the purpose of the giving of notice, the question must be resolved by reference to the committal charge and committal evidence: *R. v. Lewis*, *ante*.

Disproof of alibi

4–319 Under the alibi notice scheme created by section 11 of the *CJA* 1967 (*rep.*), it was held that it was proper to prove an alibi notice as part of the prosecution case: see *R. v. Brigden* [1973] Crim.L.R. 579, CA; *R. v. Rossborough*, 81 Cr.App.R. 139, CA; and *R. v. Fields and Adams*, *ante*. Under the 1996 Act, a trial judge may direct that the jury be given a copy of any defence statement (and hence any particulars of alibi therein), but only if of the opinion that seeing it would help the jury to understand the case or to resolve any issue in the case (s.6E(4) and (5) *post*, § 12–57e). There appears to be no reason why this should not happen, in appropriate circumstances, as part of the prosecution case.

As to the use which may be made of a defence statement at trial, see section 11 of the 1996 Act, *post*, § 12–62; for guidance issued by the Bar Council on the drafting of defence statements, see *post*, § 12–99a; and as to the desirability of a defendant signing his defence statement, see *post*, § 12–57a.

In *R. v. Rossborough, ante*, it was held that where persons named in an alibi notice served under the provisions of the 1967 Act had failed to attend appointments with the police, that was evidence that could be tendered to disprove the alibi. Evidence of such failure cannot, it is submitted, be admitted unless and until evidence of the service of the relevant alibi notice, or evidence in support of the alibi, has been adduced.

As to the adducing of evidence in rebuttal once evidence has been adduced in support of an alibi, see *post*, §§ 4–338 *et seq*.

In *R. v. Williams (M.)*, unreported, April 15, 1994 (92/6329/W5), the Court of Appeal rejected a submission that where the prosecution have evidence available to contradict an alibi notice, such evidence ought always to be called as part of the prosecution case. It acknowledged that the judge had a discretion, but appeared to incline to the view that this ought to be the norm. This would be consistent with the current climate which encourages maximum openness by the prosecution and is opposed to any notion of the prosecution being able to keep material back with a view to "ambushing" the defence: *aliter*, if the material goes only to the credibility of a proposed defence witness (see *R. v. Brown (Winston)* [1998] A.C. 367, HL). **4–320**

Miscellaneous

As to the propriety of continuing a trial where an alibi witness, whose evidence has been anticipated in the defence opening speech, does not appear: see *R. v. Lydon*, 85 Cr.App.R. 221, CA. **4–321**

As to the duty to consult the accused in respect of any decision not to call alibi witnesses, see *R. v. Irwin*, 85 Cr.App.R. 294, CA (in the unusual circumstances of a retrial after a disagreement when the witnesses had been called, the obtaining of clear, preferably written instructions was demanded before not calling them).

As to the appropriate direction on the burden of proof in relation to alibi evidence, see *post*, § 4–383. See *post*, §§ 4–402 *et seq.* as to the need for a careful direction in respect of the significance of lies and false alibis where rejection of an alibi would involve the conclusion that the defendant has lied. See also *R. v. Duncan*, *The Times*, July 24, 1992, CA, *post*, § 4–404, as to the need for a careful direction on the significance of the rejection of an alibi in a case where identification is in issue.

[The next paragraph is § 4–326.]

L. EXPERT EVIDENCE AS TO DEFENDANT'S MENTAL STATE, I.Q., ETC.

Principle

An expert's opinion is admissible to furnish the court with scientific information which is likely to be outside the experience and knowledge of a judge or jury. If, on the proven facts, a judge or jury can form their own conclusions without help, the opinion of an expert is unnecessary: *R. v. Turner (T.)* [1975] Q.B. 834, 60 Cr.App.R. 80, CA. See generally, *post*, §§ 10–61 *et seq*. **4–326**

It follows that a psychiatrist's evidence is inadmissible where its purpose is, in effect, to tell a jury how an ordinary person, who is not suffering from mental illness, is likely to react to the strains and stresses of life: see *R. v. Weightman*, 92 Cr.App.R. 291, CA (evidence from a psychiatrist that the defendant was histrionic, theatrical and likely to say things to draw attention to herself, the purpose being to impugn the reliability of her confession was properly excluded). Nor, save in exceptional circumstances (*e.g. Lowery v. R.* [1974] A.C. 85, PC, *post*, § 13–72), can psychiatric evidence be admitted to prove the probability of the accused's veracity. As to the related topic of medical evidence being called for the purpose of impugning the reliability of the opposite party's witnesses, see *post*, §§ 8–154 *et seq*.

Application

4–327 The principle set out in *Turner* is clear, but its application continues to cause difficulty. In *R. v. Strudwick and Merry*, 99 Cr.App.R. 326, the Court of Appeal accepted that the law is in a state of development in this area and that there may well be mental conditions other than mental illness about which a jury might require expert assistance in order to understand and evaluate their effect. In many of the reported cases on the topic the preliminary question of the relevance to the issues in the case of the matter to which the expert evidence relates has been an important factor in the refusal to admit such evidence.

The admissibility, and relevance, of psychiatric evidence, to the effect that the defendant suffered from a personality disorder, was considered in *R. v. Wood* [1990] Crim.L.R. 264, CA, in the context of a charge of murder where the defence was based on the alleged existence of a suicide pact.

In *R. v. Masih* [1986] Crim.L.R. 395, the Court of Appeal expressed the view that if a defendant came into the class of mental defective, with an I.Q. of 69 or below, then in so far as that fact was relevant to the particular case it might be that expert evidence should be admitted about it. That was in order to enlighten the jury about a matter that was abnormal, and therefore, *ex hypothesi*, presumably outside their experience. If admitted, such evidence should be confined to an assessment of the defendant's I.Q. and to an explanation of relevant abnormal characteristics which such an assessment involved. The court also expressed the view that when the defendant was within the scale of normality, albeit at the lower end, expert evidence is not as a rule necessary and should be excluded.

In *R. v. Toner*, 93 Cr.App.R. 382, CA, while acknowledging that medical evidence is entirely inappropriate where the task of the jury is to determine the intent of an ordinary man who is not afflicted by any medical condition, physical or mental, permanent or transient, the court held that evidence as to the effect of a medical abnormality (a mild attack of hypoglycaemia) on the mental processes of a person suffering such an attack was admissible.

Masih and *Toner* were considered in *R. v. Henry* [2006] 1 Cr.App.R. 6, CA. There had been no relaxation of the rule in *Masih* that expert evidence as to the effect of a defendant's intellectual impairment on his formation of *mens rea* was admissible only where the defendant was in the class of mental defective, *i.e.* having an I.Q. of 69 or below; the cut-off point of 69 had been criticised as arbitrary, but it had psychological significance and it had the advantage of being a clean rule, even if a stringent one. *Toner* was concerned with a medical matter outside the ordinary experience of a jury, and therefore *Masih* and *Toner* were on different sides of an identified line and consistent with each other. The court conceded that there had, however, been an increased willingness to admit expert evidence as to intellectual impairment in relation to the reliability of confession evidence (as in *R. v. Silcott*, *post*).

In *R. v. Silcott*, *The Times*, December 9, 1991, CA, it was held that: (a) the circumstances to be considered by a trial judge when hearing submissions under section 76(2)(b) of the *PACE Act* 1984 as to the admissibility of a confession (see *post*, § 15–352) include the mental condition of the defendant; and (b) the decision is to be taken on medical evidence rather than the trial judge's own assessment of the defendant in interview. The court was not attracted to the concept that the judicial approach to submissions under section 76(2)(b) should be governed by which side of an arbitrary line, whether at 69 or 70, or elsewhere, the I.Q. of the defendant fell. It drew attention to the definition of "mentally handicapped" in section 77 of the 1984 Act, which includes "significant impairment of intelligence and social functioning" (see *post*, § 15–370). The court also rejected a suggestion that whereas psychiatric or psychological evidence might be admissible for the purposes of a *voire dire* being conducted by a judge alone, it would not be admissible before the jury if the judge admitted the challenged evidence. *Silcott* was followed in *R. v. Ward*, 96 Cr.App.R. 1, CA. See also *R. v. Omar* [1997] 10 *Archbold News* 2, CA (depressive illness is an abnormal mental condition and its effects are relevant to the reliability of a confession).

However, for expert evidence as to some abnormality to be admissible in respect of the reliability of a defendant's confession it is neither necessary nor sufficient that the abnormality should fit into some recognised category; what is necessary is that the disorder must be of a type which might render a confession or evidence unreliable and it must represent a significant deviation from the norm; further, there must be history pre-dating the confession or evidence being impugned which is not based solely on a history given by the subject, and which points to or explains the abnormalities; if such evidence is admitted, the jury should be directed that they are not obliged to accept it; they should consider it, if they think it right to do so, as throwing light on the personality of the defendant and as bringing to their attention aspects of his personality of which they might otherwise have been unaware: *R. v. O'Brien* [2000] Crim.L.R. 676, CA (the reference to the calling of expert evidence for the purpose of impugning the reliability of a defendant's evidence, as opposed to his out-of-court confession, is, presumably, a reference to the calling of such evidence by a co-accused who has been incriminated by the evidence of the defendant). The absence of an examination of the defendant by the expert goes to the weight to be attached to the expert's opinion and not to the admissibility of that opinion: *R. v. Pinfold and Mackenny* [2004] 2 Cr.App.R. 5, CA.

Silcott was distinguished in *R. v. Coles* [1995] 1 Cr.App.R. 157, CA, where the appellant had been convicted of an offence of arson, being reckless as to whether life would be endangered. The court rejected an argument to the effect that a lack of appreciation of the relevant risks on the part of the appellant was a relevant consideration and, accordingly, held that evidence from a psychologist as to the capacity of the appellant to foresee the risks involved in his actions had been rightly excluded as irrelevant. Furthermore, the excluded evidence of the psychologist was not evidence of any abnormality of the mind of the appellant but related to characteristics which could be competently evaluated by a jury without expert assistance. Adolescents of varying stages of maturity and brightness are all within the common experience of jurors. The court pointed out that in *Silcott* the question was whether evidence of certain mental characteristics was admissible in respect of the admissibility of, or weight to be attached to, a confession and the decision did not purport to bear on the admissibility of such evidence on any issue of a defendant's *mens rea*. Unless some facet of the mental health or psychiatric state of the defendant is raised, such evidence is inadmissible in that context. **4–328**

Where the defence of a 15-year-old male to a charge of rape was that there had been an attempt at intercourse but no penetration, it was held to be impermissible to call psychiatric evidence of a pathological anxiety at the prospect of intercourse, such anxiety being founded on a physical condition (development of prominent breasts); psychiatric evidence that did not suggest any organic or psychiatric connection between the defendant's mental condition and his claimed inability to commit the offence was inadmissible since it went only to the probability of the accused's veracity, as opposed to furnishing the court with relevant information outside its experience; the jury would have been as well able as the expert to form an opinion as to the anxiety that might have resulted from the relevant medical condition: *R. v. Loughran* [1999] Crim.L.R. 404, CA.

As to the calling of expert evidence in support of a defence of duress, see *R. v. Hurst* [1995] 1 Cr.App.R. 82, CA, and *R. v. Bowen* [1996] 2 Cr.App.R. 157, CA, *post*, § 17–125.

As to medical evidence going to the issue of *mens rea*, see also *post*, §§ 17–99 *et seq.*; and see *post*, § 19–76 as to medical evidence in support of a defence of diminished responsibility.

M. TRUTH DRUG EVIDENCE

4–329 As to the inadmissibility of evidence of the results of "truth drug" tests, see *post*, § 10–70.

N. INFORMATION OR "EVIDENCE" THAT ANOTHER COMMITTED, OR MAY HAVE COMMITTED, THE OFFENCE CHARGED

4–330 See *R. v. Greenwood* [2005] 1 Cr.App.R. 7, CA, *post*, § 10–8.

O. ADDUCING EVIDENCE OF RELEVANT PREVIOUS ACQUITTAL

4–331 In the absence of some exceptional feature, such as the effect of an acquittal on the credibility of a confession or the evidence of a prosecution witness, evidence of the outcome of an earlier trial arising out of the same events is irrelevant, and therefore inadmissible, since it amounts to no more than evidence of the opinion of the jury in the earlier trial: *Hui Chi-Ming v. R.* [1992] 1 A.C.34, PC. *A fortiori*, if the earlier trial related to different events. The Privy Council referred to two English authorities in support of the limited exception set out above, namely *R. v. Hay*, 77 Cr.App.R. 70, CA, and *R. v. Cooke*, 84 Cr.App.R. 286, CA.

In *R. v. Hay*, H was alleged to have made a statement to the police admitting two unrelated offences—burglary and arson. He was tried first on the arson charge and acquitted, having asserted that the admissions were fabricated and having called alibi witnesses. The details of the burglary admission were "edited out" at the trial. At his trial for burglary, at the defence request, the whole statement under caution was put before the jury as the defendant was going to assert that the burglary admission was also fabricated and rely upon the previous acquittal in support of that defence. The trial judge however refused to admit evidence of the acquittal. The conviction was quashed on the basis that the jury should have been told of the acquittal and, applying *Sambasivam v. Public Prosecutor, Federation of Malaya* [1950] A.C. 458, PC (*ante*, § 4–159), told that it was conclusive evidence that he was not guilty of arson and that his confession to that offence was untrue. However, in *R. v. Terry* [2005] 2 Cr.App.R. 7, CA, it was held that in the latter respect *Hay* went further than was necessary and was inconsistent with the reasoning of the House of Lords in *R. v. Z.* [2000] 2 A.C. 483 (*ante*, § 4–160) which had qualified the principle expounded in *Sambasivam*. It was held that where a defendant's guilt or innocence of an offence for which he was not on trial had potential relevance to his guilt or innocence of the offence for which he was on trial, the fact that he had been acquitted of the other offence was not conclusive evidence of his innocence of it; and his acquittal did not mean that all relevant issues had been resolved in his favour.

4–332 The principle to be derived from *Cooke*, *ante*, seems to be that where there is a clear inference from a verdict that the jury has rejected a witness's testimony, on the basis that they do not believe him (as opposed to thinking he might have been mistaken), and that witness's credibility is directly in issue in a subsequent trial, evidence of the outcome of the first trial is relevant. For further refinement of this principle, see *R. v. Edwards* [1991] 1 W.L.R. 207, CA, *post*, § 13–17.

4–333 In *R. v. Doosti*, 82 Cr.App.R. 181, CA, a previous acquittal was held to be relevant in re-examination after the defendant had been cross-examined about a previous conviction which had occurred on the same occasion as the acquittal. He had been acquitted of the more serious charge. It was one which in nature and circumstance was akin to the one for which he was then being tried—indeed the officers in each case were the same. Clearly it was only fair that if the Crown chose to elicit that part of the picture of the accused's credibility favourable to them, the defendant was entitled to reveal the rest of the picture favourable to him—his and the officer's credibility being a central issue in the case.

4–334 The facts in *Cooke* and *Doosti* were distinguished in *R. v. H. (J.R.)*, 90 Cr.App.R. 440, in which there had been many possible reasons for the previous acquittal apart from a rejection of the complainant's evidence. Lord Lane C.J. said that fairness to both sides, rather than any remote, abstruse legal principle, was the matter which had to actuate a judge's reasoning. Coupled with fairness, was the necessity for the judge to ensure that the jury whom he was assisting did not have their minds clouded by issues which were not the true issues they had to determine. The danger was that the jury would have been spending their time not in determining what they believed to be true from the evidence they had heard, but that they would be deflected from that course by consideration of what had actually actuated the first jury to reach the conclusions it did. *R. v. H.* was followed in *R. v. Y.* [1992] Crim.L.R. 436, CA, and in *Terry*, *ante*, Lord Lane C.J.'s observations on fairness were said to have been echoed by Lord Hobhouse in *R. v. Z*, *ante*, at p. 510A–E.

XIV. EXTENT TO WHICH EVIDENCE OTHER THAN DEFENCE EVIDENCE MAY BE ADDUCED AFTER THE PROSECUTION HAVE CLOSED THEIR CASE

A. General Principle

The general rule that matters probative of the defendant's guilt should be adduced as part of the prosecution's case applies (a) to matters put in cross-examination to a defendant (see *post*), and (b) to the calling of evidence. **4–335**

In *R. v. Rice* [1963] 1 Q.B. 857, 47 Cr.App.R. 79, CCA, it was said that there is a general principle of practice, though no rule of law, which requires that all evidentiary matter the prosecution intend to rely upon as probative of the defendant's guilt should be adduced before the close of the prosecution case if it be available then. Whether evidence subsequently available to the prosecution should be introduced at a later stage is a matter for the trial judge's discretion, which must be exercised within the limits imposed by the authorities and in such a way and subject to such safeguards as seem to him best suited to achieve justice between the Crown and the defendants and between defendants.

This general principle was considered in *R. v. Kane*, 65 Cr.App.R. 270, CA. The court said that even where evidence which could have been led as part of the case for the Crown became available for the first time to the Crown after the close of the Crown's case, the subsequent introduction of that evidence or its exclusion were matters to be referred to and decided by the trial judge. The court was careful to point out that its observations only applied to matters put in cross-examination to a defendant which could and should have been proved as part of the case for the Crown.

The same principle was applied in *R. v. Phillipson*, 91 Cr.App.R. 226, CA, and *R. v. Sansom*, 92 Cr.App.R. 115, CA, in both of which material which could and should have been part of the prosecution case was introduced for the first time in cross-examination. In the latter case, it was circumstantial evidence of guilt; in the former case it was material which directly undermined the defence (duress) revealed on the face of the papers. In *Phillipson*, the court said that it was not ruling out, in an appropriate case, the "time-hallowed practice" of introducing material for the first time in cross-examination. No clue was given as to when this would be appropriate and it is submitted that it would be unwise to rely on this dictum; it certainly should not be relied upon as justification for not disclosing the matter in the normal way. What is permissible (and is frequently done) is for prosecution counsel to inform the defence that it is not the intention of the prosecution to adduce a particular matter in evidence, but to specify that should the defence take a particular line, then the right is reserved to introduce it. If the defence response is such as to make it apparent that the matter is relevant then the normal rule should apply. What is not permitted is the laying of an ambush. **4–336**

In *R. v. Hill*, 96 Cr.App.R. 456 at 463, CA, it was said that prosecution counsel is not limited in cross-examination to matters that have previously been established in evidence, provided that the questions are properly formulated without the use of language or other means to invest them with illegitimate weight. See *R. v. Tuegel* [2000] 2 Cr.App.R. 361, CA, for an example of cross-examination that offended this principle.

As to certain problems that may arise in the context of an alibi defence, see *ante*, §§ 4–319 *et seq.*

The principle in *Rice* does not extend to evidence of matter which goes only to the **4–337** credit of the defendant: *R. v. Halford*, 67 Cr.App.R. 318, CA. (This is *not* a justification for not disclosing such matter.)

Where an agreed summary of a defendant's tape-recorded interviews has been put before the jury as part of the prosecution case, it may, in certain circumstances, be proper to permit counsel to play the tapes to the jury at a later stage if such a course is necessary to resolve an issue that has arisen. Matters can arise which are not anticipated when summaries are agreed and it is wrong that counsel should have their hands tied: *R. v. Sinclair and Peters*, *The Times*, September 21, 1992, CA. However, where the only purpose of playing the tape would be to establish that nothing had been said about a particular matter, it will usually be possible for counsel to agree a formal admission of that fact to avoid the necessity of playing the tape: *ibid*. (This account of the case is based on the transcript (no. 92/1733/X3) in respect of certain details that are not reported accurately in *The Times*.) See also *R. v. Aitken*, *post*, § 4–346

In *R. v. M. (J.)* [1996] 2 Cr.App.R. 56, CA, a video film of a child complainant's evidence in chief had been replayed at the close of the defence case on the application of the prosecution. It was held that, generally speaking, a video of a complainant's evidence should only be played for a second time as the result of a request from the jury, as to which see *post*, § 4–423. The replaying of such film in other circumstances should be discouraged because it is a departure from the normal way in which evidence at a criminal trial is heard and, generally speaking, any departure should only be made if there are exceptional reasons. However, in some circumstances it might be necessary to replay a short part of a video film to enable the jury and witnesses to understand the nature of questions being put on a particular point: *ibid*.

B. EVIDENCE IN REBUTTAL

(1) General

4–338 "Evidence in rebuttal" is capable of embracing various categories of evidence. The category headings used hereafter are not authoritative propositions of law but are merely guides to the authorities set out beneath.

The *ex improviso* principle has to be applied by the court with a recognition that the prosecution are expected to react reasonably to what may be suggested as pre-trial warnings of evidence likely to be given which calls for denial beforehand, and also to suggestions put in cross-examination of their witnesses. They are not expected to take notice of fanciful and unreal statements no matter from what source they emanate: *R. v. Hutchinson*, 82 Cr.App.R. 51 at 59, CA.

(2) Evidence available to the prosecution ab initio, the relevance of which does not arise ex improviso, is inadmissible

4–339 See *R. v. Day*, 27 Cr.App.R. 168, CCA (conviction quashed where expert evidence, the necessity for which was obvious and did not arise *ex improviso*, called after defence case so as to remedy obvious defect in prosecution case). See also *R. v. Cleghorn* [1967] 2 Q.B. 584, 51 Cr.App.R. 291, CA, and *R. v. Joseph*, 56 Cr.App.R. 60, CA. *Cf. post*, § 4–347.

(3) Evidence falling within the ex improviso principle—admissible subject to trial judge's discretion

4–340 In *R. v. Frost* (1839) 9 C. & P. 129, Tindal C.J. said:

> "... if any matter arises *ex improviso*, which the Crown could not foresee, supposing it to be entirely new matter, which they may be able to answer only by contradictory evidence, they may give evidence in reply" (p. 159).

In *R. v. Blick*, 50 Cr.App.R. 280, CCA, during his trial for robbery, B said that his presence where he had been arrested was due to a visit to a public lavatory. A juror who knew the area passed a note to the judge informing him that the lavatory was closed at the material time. The prosecution later obtained leave to call rebutting evidence to that effect. It was held that the evidence was properly admitted. See also *R. v. Anderson (M.)*, 87 Cr.App.R. 349, CA, *post*, § 13–60.

(4) Evidence available to the prosecution ab initio, the relevance of which though not arising ex improviso was marginal, is admissible subject to trial judge's discretion

That a judge has a discretion to admit evidence in rebuttal in situations other than that contemplated in *R. v. Frost*, *ante*, has been stated by the appellate courts on many occasions: see, in particular, *R. v. Crippen* [1911] 1 K.B. 149, 5 Cr.App.R. 255, CCA; *R. v. Owen* [1952] 2 Q.B. 362, 36 Cr.App.R. 16, CCA; and *R. v. Milliken*, 53 Cr.App.R. 330, CA (evidence in rebuttal to contradict allegations of conspiracy to pervert the course of justice made against police officers). **4–341**

The formulation of a test to be applied by judges confronted with applications to admit rebuttal evidence has varied. In *R. v. Levy and Tait*, 50 Cr.App.R. 198, CCA, it was said that the field in which the discretion can be exercised is limited by the principle that evidence which is clearly relevant, not marginally, minimally or doubtfully relevant, to the issues and within the possession of the Crown should be adduced by the prosecution as part of their case.

More recently, in *R. v. Scott (A.S.)*, 79 Cr.App.R. 49, the Court of Appeal said that the principle was that if the prosecution could reasonably have foreseen that a particular piece of evidence was necessary to prove their case, they should have put it before the court as part of their case. **4–342**

(5) Character

Evidence in rebuttal may be called to meet evidence of good character given for the defence: *R. v. Rowton* (1865) L. & C. 520; *R. v. Butterwasser* [1948] 1 K.B. 4, 32 Cr.App.R. 81, CCA. As to the meaning of evidence of "bad character", see *post*, §§ 13–5 *et seq*. As to proof of a person's bad character by means of evidence as to his reputation, see section 118(1) of the *CJA* 2003 (*post*, § 11–70). **4–343**

C. FRESH EVIDENCE NOT OF A STRICTLY REBUTTING CHARACTER AND NOT PREVIOUSLY AVAILABLE

In *R. v. Doran*, 56 Cr.App.R. 429, during the course of the defence case, the prosecution obtained leave to call two witnesses of whose existence they had just learnt (members of the public present at the trial who realised that they could give material evidence). It was held that a judge is not limited in the exercise of his discretion to allow fresh evidence to cases where it is strictly of a rebutting character. Such cases, however, are rare and the court must be vigilant in the exercise of its discretion lest injustice is done to the defendant. It would have to consider, *inter alia*, the desirability of granting an adjournment. There was no suggestion of belated attempts to repair omissions in the prosecution case and the judge had properly exercised his discretion. **4–344**

In *James v. South Glamorgan County Council*, 99 Cr.App.R. 321, the Divisional Court declined to interfere with the exceptional course taken by justices to permit the prosecution to re-open their case to call an essential witness who had arrived late because he had been unable to find the building.

D. POWER OF JUDGE TO CALL A WITNESS

This is a power which should be most sparingly and rarely exercised: *R. v. Baldwin*, *The Times*, May 3, 1978, CA; *R. v. Roberts (J.M.)*, 80 Cr.App.R. 89, CA. If, prior to the close of the prosecution case, counsel for the Crown decides that it is not proper to pursue the prosecution and, accordingly, declines to call further prosecution witnesses, the trial judge should not take over the role of prosecutor and call such witnesses: *R. v. Grafton*, 96 Cr.App.R. 156, CA, and see *ante*, § 4–96. **4–345**

The judge has the right to call a witness not called either by the prosecution or the defence and without the consent of either if in his opinion this course is necessary in the interests of justice: *R. v. Chapman* (1838) 8 C. & P. 558; *R. v. Holden* (1838) 8 C. & P. 606; *R. v. Wallwork*, 42 Cr.App.R. 153, CCA. For example, where the prosecution decline the judge's invitation to call a witness whose name "appears on the back of the indictment": see *R. v. Oliva*, *ante*, § 4–276; and *R. v. Tregear* [1967] 2 Q.B. 574,

51 Cr.App.R. 280, CA. In order that injustice should not be done to a defendant, the calling of such a witness after the close of the case for the defence should generally be limited to cases where something has arisen on the part of the defendant *ex improviso*, which no human ingenuity could foresee: *R. v. Harris* [1927] 2 K.B. 587, 20 Cr.App.R. 86, CCA (applying *R. v. Frost, ante*, § 4–340). In *R. v. Harris*, the court made it clear that it was not laying down that in no circumstances could an additional witness be called by the judge after the close of defence: see *R. v. Tregear, ante*.

Where a witness is called by the judge, neither the prosecution nor the defence are entitled to examine or cross-examine him without the leave of the judge (*Coulson v. Disborough* [1894] 2 Q.B. 316; *R. v. Cliburn*, 62 J.P. 232), but if the evidence is adverse to either party, such leave should be given: *ibid*.

4–346 In *R. v. Aitken*, 94 Cr.App.R. 85, CA, the trial had proceeded on the basis of agreed summaries of police interviews of the defendant and the tape recordings of those interviews were not formally produced in evidence. During the course of the defence closing speech the jury indicated that they would like to hear one of the tape recordings. The judge, having listened to the recording in the absence of the jury, permitted the jury to hear the recording. He then gave defence counsel the opportunity to have the interviewing officer re-called and to make a further address to the jury. The Court of Appeal concluded that the situation could be approached either as one in which the judge on his own initiative had re-called a witness or caused further evidence to be put before the jury, or alternatively, one in which the prosecution's case was re-opened after the end of the defence's closing speech. There was in principle no relevant distinction between the two situations and in the circumstances the judge had exercised his discretion correctly. The jury had, no doubt, wished to hear the atmosphere and tone of the interview and the judge had taken proper steps to satisfy himself that no injustice would be caused to the defendant by permitting this. The court made clear that it was not purporting to deal with the situation that would arise if the jury's request to hear the tape recording was made for the first time after they had retired to consider their verdict. (See also *R. v. Sinclair and Peters*, and *R. v. M.(J.), ante*, § 4–337.) As to the general discretion to permit the prosecution to re-open their case, see *post*. As to the recalling of witnesses, see *post*, §§ 8–251 *et seq*.

As to the entitlement of the defence to address the jury further in the event of additional evidence being admitted after speeches, see *R. v. Ludwick, post*, § 4–364.

E. EVIDENCE INADVERTENTLY OMITTED FROM CROWN'S CASE

(1) General

4–347 From time to time evidence of a formal nature, or clearly not capable of being the subject of dispute, which should have been adduced before the prosecution closed their case, is overlooked and submissions of no case to answer are accordingly made. The extent of the judge's discretion to allow the prosecution to repair the omission was examined in *R. v. Francis*, 91 Cr.App.R. 271, CA. The discretion is not limited to the two well-established exceptions of: (a) evidence arising *ex improviso*, and (b) cases where what has been omitted is a mere formality as distinct from a central issue in the case (see *Royal v. Prescott-Clarke, post*, § 4–351). There is a wider discretion, which is to be exercised judicially; it is more likely to be exercised in the prosecution's favour the earlier any application is made. It is a discretion which should be exercised outside the two established exceptions only on the rarest of occasions (at p. 275). For the facts in *Francis*, see *post*, § 4–354.

In *R. v. Munnery*, 94 Cr.App.R. 164, CA, at the close of the case for the Crown, counsel for the appellant outlined the nature of the submission that he then proposed to make and the matter was adjourned to the next day. By the next morning the Crown had obtained evidence rectifying the alleged *lacuna*. Leave was given to re-open the prosecution case and adduce this evidence. Having reviewed the authorities, the Court of Appeal confirmed the existence of the general discretion to permit the Crown to re-open its case. A trial judge must be left with some degree of freedom to meet problems which might arise during a trial; but unless justice demands it, to depart substantially from the normal order of events is liable to cause confusion and hardship—the jurisdiction must be exercised with great caution; but it is justice that matters, both to the public as represented by the prosecution, as well as to the defence. As in *Francis*, the court pointed out that a defendant may be prejudiced if his advisers have identified a gap in the prosecution's evidence, and have drawn attention to it by a submission of no case, only to find that the judge gives leave to put it right; whereas if they had kept silent until the time to address the jury, the prosecution would have been too late, but the court held that no error could be detected in the way in which the judge had exercised the discretion.

The relevant principles were summarised in *Jolly v. DPP* [2000] Crim.L.R. 471, DC; there is a general discretion to permit the calling by the prosecution of evidence after the closure of their case; such discretion should be exercised sparingly, but it is doubtful whether it assists to speak in terms of "exceptional circumstances"; each case must be considered on its own facts, with consideration being given to the interests of justice overall, and particular attention being paid to the risk of any (unfair) prejudice whatsoever to the defendant (on the particular facts, court not in error to allow prosecution evidence as to correct working of computer to be adduced after submission of no case based on omission of such evidence). See also *Cook v. DPP* [2001] Crim.L.R. 321, DC, and *R. v. Hinchcliffe* [2002] 4 *Archbold News* 1, CA, to similar effect.

For examples of other cases where it was held that the prosecution had been rightly permitted to re-open their case in order to call essential (but non-controversial) evidence which had been omitted through oversight or forgetfulness, see *R. v. McKenna*, 40 Cr.App.R. 65, CCA, *Pigott v. Sims* [1973] R.T.R. 15, DC, and *Matthews v. Morris* [1981] Crim.L.R. 495, DC. **4–348**

In *Derbyshire County Council v. Kwik Save Group* [1997] C.O.D. 19, DC, it was held that an application by the Crown to re-open its case should have been allowed after a submission of no case to answer was made in circumstances where, on a prosecution under the *Fire Precautions Act* 1971, liability depended upon the number of persons at work at the relevant premises and the need to adduce evidence of that matter had been overlooked after a defence of "due diligence" had been indicated and the whole of the prosecution evidence had been admitted under the *CJA* 1967, s.9. In *R. v. Johnson* [2002] 1 *Archbold News* 1, CA, the prosecution omitted to adduce evidence of identification, being under the impression that identity was not in issue (a defence statement having indicated a defence of duress), but were allowed to re-open their case to deal with this; the paramount consideration was held to be the avoidance of prejudice to the defendant, but the judge had been entitled to have regard to the defence statement when considering that matter.

The discretion that exists (in this case exercisable by justices) to allow the prosecution to adduce evidence after the conclusion of their case may exceptionally be exercised even after the closure of the defence case and in consequence of an issue raised for the first time during the closing speech for the defence; but the hallmarks for the exercise of this discretion at such a late stage are that the omission was purely technical, the prosecution are in a position to correct it then and there, its correction causes the defence no prejudice, and the defence have previously neither said nor done anything to alert the prosecution to the issue; whilst there is no obligation on the defence to remind the prosecution of all the matters that need to be proved, they can hardly complain if, in the result, the tribunal exercises its discretion so as to secure justice rather than allow an unmeritorious acquittal: *Leeson v. DPP* [2000] R.T.R. 385, DC (prosecution permitted to adduce late evidence of calibration readings of breath testing device). In deciding how to exercise the discretion, account should be taken of the overriding objective in rule 1.1 of the *Criminal Procedure Rules* 2005 (*ante*, § 4–84b) and the duty of the defence implicit in rule 3.3 (*ante*, § 4–84c) to make the real issues clear, at the latest, before the prosecution close their case: *Malcolm v. DPP* [2007] 2 Cr.App.R. 1, DC.

In the following two cases the discretion was held to have been wrongly exercised. In **4–349**
R. v. Gainsborough JJ., ex p. Green, 78 Cr.App.R. 9, DC, the evidence led to support two allegations of breach of a community service order revealed no breach whatsoever. Instead of acceding to the submission of "no case", the justices allowed further evidence to be called which did establish the breaches. In *R. v. Central Criminal Court, ex p. Garnier* [1988] R.T.R. 42, DC, evidence of a formal nature was omitted on an appeal

against conviction to the Crown Court but the prosecution had had ample notice of the omission by virtue of the identical point being taken in the magistrates' court.

(2) Statutory instruments

4–350 Every Act is a public Act to be judicially noticed as such unless the contrary is expressly provided by the Act: *Interpretation Act* 1978, s.3 (Appendix B–3). There is no general provision for judicial notice of statutory instruments and it is therefore necessary for a statutory instrument, where material, to be proved during the course of the prosecution's evidence, by the formal production of a Queen's Printer copy of the instrument: see *Tyrrell v. Cole* (1918) 120 L.T. 156; *R. v. Ashley*, 52 Cr.App.R. 42, CA. As to the method of proof, see also *post*, § 9–29.

4–351 Where this is overlooked, the court, in the exercise of its discretion, should allow proof at a later stage and, if necessary, adjourn for a copy to be obtained: see *Palastanga v. Solman* [1962] Crim.L.R. 334, DC (where the court reserved the question whether the *Construction and Use Regulations* were so notorious that the court could take judicial notice of them); *Duffin v. Markham* (1918) 88 L.J.K.B. 581, DC; and *Royal v. Prescott-Clarke* [1966] 1 W.L.R. 788, DC. The principles to be applied are the same as those to be applied in the case of an omission to prove any other essential matter: *Hammond v. Wilkinson*, 165 J.P. 786, DC. As to the principles themselves, see *ante*, §§ 4–347, 4–348.

(3) Consent to the institution of proceedings

4–352 See *ante*, §§ 1–244, 1–279 *et seq.* as to the relevant law and practice.

Where a statutory provision requires the consent of either the Attorney-General or the Director of Public Prosecutions before proceedings may be instituted, that consent must be given, otherwise the proceedings will be a nullity: *R. v. Angel*, 52 Cr.App.R. 280, CA. The consent need not be proved: if objection is taken, it will be for the court to determine what evidence is required to satisfy it that the requisite consent had been given: *R. v. Waller* [1910] 1 K.B. 364, 3 Cr.App.R. 213, CCA; and *Price v. Humphries* [1958] 2 Q.B. 353, DC (it is the duty of a clerk to justices on application being made for issue of a summons to see that the statutory requirements have been complied with and, unless objection is taken by the accused before the prosecution closed their case, justices should act on the presumption that the duty has been discharged).

(4) Identity

4–353 Unlike formal evidence which does not touch the substance of the matter, establishing identity is invariably a most material step in establishing the case against a defendant. In *Middleton v. Rowlett* [1954] 1 W.L.R. 831, DC, the court upheld the magistrates' refusal to allow the prosecution to re-open their case in order to prove the identity of the driver in proceedings for dangerous driving. The court described it as "a borderline case" but affirmed that the magistrates had a discretion which they were not bound to exercise in favour of the prosecution. In *Saunders v. Johns* [1965] Crim.L.R. 49, DC, the defendant was charged with exceeding the speed limit and his solicitor stated at the beginning of the hearing that the issue was one of identity. No evidence was given which identified the defendant as the driver. A submission of "no case" was overruled and the defence called no evidence. The justices then recalled the police officer who said that the name and address in the driver's driving licence were those of the defendant. It was held that no prima facie case had been made out at the close of the prosecution and the recall of the officer after the defence case had been closed was wrong. As soon as the submission of no case was made the prosecution, or the court of its own motion, should have recalled the officer and obtained the evidence about the driving licence. This decision was explained in *Brake v. Taylor*, unreported, June 1, 1967, where the court said that it was only in the event of a technical omission (see *ante*, §§ 4–347 *et seq.*) that the magistrates were under any obligation to permit the calling of further evidence.

4–354 In *R. v. Francis*, *ante*, § 4–347, there was no evidence to prove that the defendant had been the person picked out at an identification parade. This resulted from prosecution counsel's mistaken assumption that the point was not in dispute. The defendant submitted that there was no case to answer, but the judge granted the prosecution's application to recall the inspector in charge of the parade. The Court of Appeal held that this was one of the rare cases which fell outside the two established exceptions.

XV. ARGUMENT AS TO THE RELEVANT LAW

Timing

It is incumbent on counsel and on the judge to consider, before speeches, whether there is, or may be, any doubt about the issues of fact to be left to the jury or the appropriate legal directions, and, if there is, to raise the matter so that submissions may be made with a view to the elimination of misunderstanding, if not disagreement: *R. v. N.*, *The Times*, July 15, 1998, CA. When a case calls for directions of any complexity, the judge should discuss the appropriate directions with counsel before speeches; he will then have the benefit of the submissions of counsel and counsel will be able to address the jury knowing how they are to be directed: *R. v. Wright* [2000] Crim.L.R. 510, CA. Other authorities in which these points have been made by the Court of Appeal are *R. v. Day*, *The Times*, October 3, 1991; *R. v. Miles* [1992] Crim.L.R. 657; *R. v. Wren*, *The Times*, July 13, 1993; *R. v. Redman*, *The Times*, April 25, 1994; *R. v. Rowland*, *The Times*, January 12, 2004, CA (where provocation was an issue); and *R. v. Taylor (Julie Anne)* [2004] Crim.L.R. 72, CA (it was a pity that counsel had not been invited to consider and comment on a proposed draft direction dealing with both provocation and diminished responsibility). **4–355**

As to the particular duty of the judge to raise the possibility of leaving the case to the jury on a basis different from that upon which it has been conducted by the parties, see, *inter alia*, *R. v. Feeny*, 94 Cr.App.R. 1, CA; *R. v. Goldman* [1997] Crim.L.R. 894, CA; *R. v. Gray and Evans* [1998] Crim.L.R. 570, CA; and *R. v. Ramzan* [1998] 2 Cr.App.R. 328, CA. See also *post*, § 4–378.

Where a judge, in advance of the summing up, indicates to counsel that he intends to give a certain direction, but then changes his mind, he should normally inform counsel and give them a further opportunity to address him; if nothing is said, counsel should raise the matter at the conclusion of the summing up, in the absence of the jury, in case the omission was an oversight: *R. v. Middleton*, *The Times*, April 12, 2000, CA.

To avoid the discussion being inhibited, it is clearly preferable for the jury to be out of court during discussions about the content of a summing up (see *post*, § 8–92).

Draft directions provided by judge to jury

It is sometimes useful in a complicated case for a judge to supplement his summing up by a written list of directions or questions to a jury. Where the judge considers such questions necessary he should submit them to counsel for consideration in good time before they begin their closing speeches (for the reasons explained in *R. v. Wright*, *ante*); the judge should then use those written directions as an integral part of the summing up, referring the jury to them, one by one, as he deals with the points orally: *R. v. McKechnie*, 94 Cr.App.R. 51, CA; see also *R. v. Green* (2005) 149 S.J. 1350, CA (not giving the jury such a document in a complex case where it was known that there would be two days' interruption to their deliberations was regrettable). Putting such documents before the jury without first discussing the contents with counsel is to court disaster: *R. v. McCredie* [2000] B.C.C. 617, CA. **4–356**

A judge is entitled to decline a jury's request that he give written directions on the law: *R. v. Lawson* [1998] Crim.L.R. 883, CA.

Failure by counsel to comment on draft directions when given the opportunity to do so will not be fatal to an appeal based on alleged misdirection, but the absence of any comment is likely to affect the assessment of the significance of the alleged deficiency: *R. v. Gammans and Jarman* [1999] 2 *Archbold News* 1, CA (98 00002 Z5).

The practice of providing the jury with a photocopy of a relevant statute was deplored in *R. v. C.* [1991] 2 F.L.R. 252, CA.

XVI. CLOSING SPEECHES

A. PROSECUTION

(1) Entitlement and timing

4–357 See generally the table of speeches set out at § 4–304, *ante*.

As to the inappropriateness of counsel providing the jury with a written summary of his closing speech, see *post*, § 4–364.

Criminal Procedure Act 1865 (Denman's Act), s.2

4–357a **2.** If any prisoner or prisoners, defendant or defendants, shall be defended by counsel, but not otherwise, it shall be the duty of the presiding judge, at the close of the case for the prosecution, to ask the counsel for each prisoner or defendant so defended by counsel whether he or they intend to adduce evidence; and in the event of none of them thereupon announcing his intention to adduce evidence, the counsel for the prosecution shall be allowed to address the jury a second time in support of his case, for the purpose of summing up the evidence against such prisoner or prisoners, or defendant or defendants; and upon every trial ... whether the prisoners or defendants, or any of them, shall be defended by counsel or not, each and every such prisoner or defendant, or his or their counsel respectively, shall be allowed, if he or they shall think fit, to open his or their case or cases respectively; and after the conclusion of such opening or of all such openings, if more than one, such prisoner or prisoners, or defendant or defendants, or their counsel, shall be entitled to examine such witnesses as he or they may think fit, and when all the evidence is concluded to sum up the evidence respectively; and the right of reply, and practice and course of proceedings, save as hereby altered, shall be as at present.

[This section is printed as repealed in part by the *CLA* 1967, s.10(2), Sched. 3, Pt III.]

Criminal Procedure (Right of Reply) Act 1964, s.1

4–358 **1.** Upon the trial of any person on indictment—

(a) the prosecution shall not be entitled to the right of reply on the ground only that the Attorney-General or the Solicitor-General appears for the Crown at the trial; and

(b) the time at which the prosecution is entitled to exercise that right shall, notwithstanding anything in section 2 of the *Criminal Procedure Act* 1865, be after the close of the evidence for the defence and before the closing speech (if any) by or on behalf of the accused.

Section 1 of the 1964 Act makes clear that any right of the prosecution to make a closing speech shall be exercised after the close of the evidence for the defence and before the closing speech of the defence. As to the relationship between section 2 of the 1865 Act and sections 1 and 2 of the *Criminal Evidence Act* 1898 (giving the accused the right to give evidence on his own behalf), see *R. v. Gardner* [1899] 1 Q.B. 150, and *R. v. Bryant and Oxley* [1979] Q.B. 108, 67 Cr.App.R. 157, CA.

4–359 The right to make a closing speech pursuant to section 2 of the 1865 Act, where no defence evidence is called (which is conditional upon at least one defendant being legally represented), should only rarely be exercised: *R. v. Bryant and Oxley*, *ante*; *R. v. Francis* [1988] Crim.L.R. 250, CA.

Where none of a number of defendants who are all represented by counsel gives evidence, but evidence is called on behalf of one of those defendants which is relevant to, and possibly beneficial to, one or more of the other defendants, prosecuting counsel is entitled, in his closing speech, to refer to the cases of the defendants who did not call evidence: see *R. v. Bryant and Oxley*, *ante*, applying *R. v. Trevelli* (1883) 15 Cox 289.

Where one of two defendants is unrepresented, prosecution counsel retains the right to make a closing speech, even though the nature of the case is such that comment on the evidence against the represented defendant will inevitably impinge on the case of the unrepresented defendant; any such speech should, however, be focused on the case against the represented defendant: *R. v. Tahir and Simpkins* [1997] Crim.L.R. 837, CA.

The right of prosecuting counsel to make a closing speech is also restricted by the following statutory provisions.

Criminal Evidence Act 1898, s.3

3. ... the fact that the person charged has been called as a witness shall not of itself confer on the prosecution the right of reply. **4–360**

[This section is printed as repealed in part by the *Criminal Procedure (Right of Reply) Act* 1964, s.1(2).]

Criminal Justice Act 1948, s.42(1)

42.—(1) Notwithstanding anything in section two of the *Criminal Procedure Act* 1865, as amended by section three of the *Criminal Evidence Act* 1898, the prosecution shall not be entitled to the right of reply upon the trial of any person on indictment on the ground only that documents have been put in evidence for the defence. **4–360a**

The rules which restrict prosecuting counsel's right to make a closing speech ought to be carefully observed: *R. v. Baggott*, 20 Cr.App.R. 92, CCA; *R. v. Mondon*, 52 Cr.App.R. 695, CA; *cf. R. v. Pink* [1971] 1 Q.B. 508, 55 Cr.App.R. 16, CA; and *R. v. Stovell* [2006] Crim.L.R. 760, CA (defendant represented for large part of trial, but not when it came to the time for speeches; doubt expressed as to whether a prosecution closing speech is necessarily inappropriate in all such cases). As to the effect of a failure to follow the rules, see *post*, § 7–91. **4–361**

(2) Restrictions on comment

Police and Criminal Evidence Act 1984, s.80A

Rule where accused's spouse or civil partner not compellable

80A. The failure of the spouse or civil partner of a person charged in any proceedings to give evidence in the proceedings shall not be made the subject of any comment by the prosecution. **4–362**

[This section was inserted by the *YJCEA* 1999, s.67(1), and Sched. 4, para. 14. It is printed as amended by the *Civil Partnership Act* 2004, s.261(1), and Sched. 27, para. 98.]

Section 80A replaces section 80(8) of the 1984 Act, which was in materially identical terms.

In *R. v. Naudeer*, 80 Cr.App.R. 9, CA, it was said that where prosecution counsel comments on the failure of the defence to call the spouse of the defendant in breach of this provision, it was incumbent on the judge to correct the error in his summing up and make plain what the position is. In *R. v. Whitton* [1998] Crim.L.R. 492, however, the Court of Appeal held that where the judge himself commented on such failure (as he was entitled to do), the error of counsel for the prosecution had been subsumed in the summing up, and did not render the conviction unsafe.

The former prohibition on the making of any comment on the failure of a defendant to give evidence was abolished by the *CJPOA* 1994, s.168(2), (3), and Scheds 10, para. 2, and 11.

It is not open to the prosecution to abandon the sole prosecution witness and invite inferences contrary to his evidence: *R. v. Pacey*, *The Times*, March 3, 1994, CA; but they may nevertheless point to inconsistencies, if they exist, between the evidence of the relevant prosecution witness and other prosecution evidence, or point to matters upon which the evidence of the relevant prosecution witness might be unreliable; *R. v. Cairns, Zaidi and Chaudhary* [2003] 1 Cr.App.R. 38, CA. A party may not, however, attack the credit of its own witness unless it has had permission to treat the witness as hostile: *ibid*. **4–363**

It is open to counsel to comment in a disciplined manner about a defendant's motives for denying an allegation, provided that such comment is properly founded upon the evidence or the demeanour of the witnesses, including the defendant himself: *R. v. Hill*, 96 Cr.App.R. 456 at 463, CA.

As to comment on the consequences of the evidence of police officers being disbelieved, see *R. v. Gale*, *post*, § 7–67.

There should be no reference to what occurred at an *ex parte* public interest immunity application; nor should it be asserted that the material which had not been disclosed would have been of no assistance to the defence: *R. v. Menga and Marshalleck* [1998] Crim.L.R. 58, CA.

As to the propriety of inviting the jury to reject the evidence of a witness when that evidence has not been expressly challenged in cross-examination, see *post*, § 8–116. See also *post*, § 4–366.

As to the desirability of a record being made of any important exchanges during the course of closing speeches, see *post*, § 7–89.

Reading passages from law reports is likely to confuse rather than to help the jury. The practice should stop: *R. v. Chandler*, 63 Cr.App.R. 1 at 3, CA.

B. DEFENCE

(1) Entitlement and timing

4–364 See generally the table of speeches set out at § 4–304, *ante*.

The right of counsel for the defendant, or the defendant himself, to make a speech at the conclusion of the evidence is given by section 2 of the *Criminal Procedure Act* 1865 (*ante*, § 4–357).

The right of the defence to make a closing speech will fall to be exercised after the conclusion of any closing speech for the prosecution or, if there is no closing speech for the prosecution, at the conclusion of the evidence: see *ante*, §§ 4–357 *et seq.*

Where two defendants are indicted together, and one of them only is defended by counsel, it seems to be in the discretion of the judge whether he will allow the defendant who is undefended to make his statement to the jury before or after the address of counsel. A defendant cannot have the assistance of counsel to examine witnesses and reserve to himself the right of addressing the jury: *R. v. White* (1811) 3 Camp. 98. It is not permissible for both the defendant and his counsel to address the jury: *R. v. Boucher* (1837) 8 C. & P. 141; *R. v. Taylor* (1859) 1 F. & F. 511.

Where further evidence is called after the conclusion of speeches, defence counsel should (at least) be given a further opportunity to address the jury: *R. v. Ludwick* [1977] Crim.L.R. 210, CA.

In *R. v. Berry*, *The Times*, May 20, 1992, CA, concern was expressed that, after a nine-day trial, defending counsel had been required to begin his closing speech as late in the day as 4.30 p.m.

In *R. v. Randall* [1998] 6 *Archbold News* 3, CA (97 05960 X4), it was doubted whether it would ever be proper for the jury to be provided with a document prepared by one party if not assented to by the other parties and the judge, and it was held that the judge had not erred in refusing to allow counsel to provide the jury with a summary of that part of his closing speech which had been delivered on an earlier day; the opportunity for jurors to study such a document individually would undermine the collective nature of the deliberations of the jury.

(2) Content

4–365 Defence counsel is not to be restricted to remarks on the evidence of his witnesses, but if anything occurs to him as desirable to say on the whole case, he is at liberty to say it: *R. v. Wainwright* (1895) 13 Cox 171. So in *R. v. Bateson*, *The Times*, April 10, 1991, CA, it was held that the judge was wrong to interrupt defence counsel's speech where counsel was suggesting explanations for his client's lies which went beyond the accused's version of the case, there being other evidence in the case to support such suggestions.

The judge has no discretion to prevent counsel commenting on the failure of a co-defendant to give evidence. If counsel's comments are unfair, the judge can deal with them in his summing up and draw the jury's attention to the defendant's right not to give evidence: *R. v. Wickham*, 55 Cr.App.R. 199, CA, although see now *ante*, § 4–305.

4–366 If counsel refers to the consequences of a verdict, the judge should instruct the jury that such matters are not their concern and are irrelevant to any issue they have to determine: *Att.-Gen. for South Australia v. Brown* [1960] A.C. 432, PC.

No reference should be made by counsel, either obliquely or expressly, to the privilege of the jury to add a recommendation to mercy to their verdict: *R. v. Black*, 48 Cr.App.R. 52, CCA (capital murder).

For observations upon the propriety of making allegations (or appearing to) against either co-defendants or witnesses during the course of a closing speech when such allegations were not put to the person in question when he gave evidence, see *R. v. Bircham* [1972] Crim.L.R. 430, CA. Counsel who makes such allegations when his lay client has given evidence runs the risk of the lay client being recalled for cross-examination as to character: *R. v. Seigley*, 6 Cr.App.R. 106, CCA, *post*, § 8–252. See also *ante*, § 4–307.

As to the propriety of inviting the jury to reject the evidence of a witness when that evidence has not been expressly challenged in cross-examination, see *post*, § 8–116.

Where a judge has ruled that a particular line of questioning is inadmissible, it is improper for an advocate against whom the ruling has been made to refer in a closing speech to the matter in respect of which exploration was prohibited, and it makes no difference that the reference is dressed up with acknowledgements as to the binding nature of the ruling and disclaimers of any intention of seeking to go behind that ruling: *R. v. Fahy* [2002] Crim.L.R. 596, CA.

Where co-defendants are defended by different counsel, one of whom establishes in **4–367** cross-examination the bad character of a prosecution witness (his client being of previous good character), it is submitted that it is not improper for counsel for the other defendant (having previous convictions), although he does not cross-examine the same witness, to comment in his speech to the jury on the witness's bad character and to invite them to ignore his evidence. *Quaere*, however, whether counsel would be wise to make such comment if his client has given evidence, bearing in mind the provisions of section 101(1)(g) of the *CJA* 2003 (*post*, § 13–25) and the risk of the client being recalled for cross-examination as to character (*post*, § 8–252).

Counsel should not address the jury in relation to the old law of corroboration and what was said to be its justification: *R. v. A.* [1997] Crim.L.R. 883, CA.

Where a video recording of an interview with a complainant has been shown to the jury in the context of allegations of inconsistency between what is said during the interview and the evidence-in-chief of the complainant, rather than as the evidence-in-chief of the complainant, the judge has a discretion to permit the recording to be played again during the speech of defence counsel; the guidance in *R. v. Rawlings*; *R. v. Broadbent* [1995] 2 Cr.App.R. 222, CA (*post*, § 4–423), deals with a different situation: *R. v. Eldridge and Salmon* [1999] Crim.L.R. 166, CA.

Although it might exceptionally be necessary for a judge to interrupt a speech by counsel in the presence of the jury, it is generally preferable for him not do so; such interventions might disrupt the speaker's train of thought or inappropriately divert the attention of the jury; ideally, interventions for the purpose of clarifying or correcting something said, either by judge or counsel, should be made in the first instance in the absence of the jury and at a break in the proceedings: *R. v. Tuegel* [2000] 2 Cr.App.R. 361, CA.

As to the desirability of a record being made of any important exchanges during the course of closing speeches, see *post*, § 7–89.

As to reading passages from law reports, see *ante*, § 4–363.

XVII. SUMMING UP

A. OVERALL STRUCTURE

> "It has been said before but obviously requires to be said again. The purpose of a direction to a jury is not best achieved by a disquisition on jurisprudence or philosophy or a universally applicable circular tour round the area of law affected by the case. The search for universally applicable definitions is often productive of more obscurity than light. A direction is seldom improved and may be considerably damaged by copious recitations from the total content of a judge's notebook. A direction to a jury should be custom-built to make the jury understand their task in relation to a particular case. Of course it must include references to the burden of proof and the respective roles of jury and judge. But it should also include a succinct but accurate summary of the issues of fact as to which a decision is required, a correct but concise summary of the evidence and arguments on both sides and a correct statement of the inferences which the jury are entitled to draw from their particular conclusions about the primary facts," (*per* Lord Hailsham L.C., in *R. v. Lawrence* [1982] A.C. 510 at 519, HL). **4–368**

In summarising the evidence it is often helpful to present it in chapters arranged in chronological order, each chapter drawing together all of the evidence in relation to a particular aspect of the history before moving on, rather than adopting a straightforward witness by witness presentation: *R. v. Green* (2005) 149 S.J. 1350, CA. Where there are a number of counts relating to different events and more than one witness, it is necessary to summarise the evidence which goes to each count and the significant disputes which arise upon that evidence, rather than reminding the jury of the evidence of each witness sequentially; only in that way will the jury be properly directed as to the issues of fact which they must resolve: *R. v. R.* [2007] Crim.L.R. 478, CA.

Those who try criminal cases should consider the guidelines laid down in the specimen directions drawn up by the Judicial Studies Board. Those guidelines often require adaptation and are not intended to offer solutions to vexed questions of law which might arise: *R. v. Jackson* [1992] Crim.L.R. 214, CA. Where the circumstances or issues in the case require some adaptation of the specimen direction, care must be taken to adapt it appropriately. Specimen directions drafted for one purpose should not be used for a different purpose: *R. v. Taylor (A.), The Times*, June 15, 1993, CA.

B. WHEN TO START

4–369 The Court of Appeal has discouraged starting a summing up, or starting a particularly important part thereof (*e.g.* the defence case) at a late hour or late on a Friday. The more serious and complex the case, the greater the need to ensure that the directions to the jury are given when they are likely to be fresh and attentive: see *R. v. Rimmer and Beech* [1983] Crim.L.R. 250, CA, and *R. v. Day, The Times*, October 3, 1991, CA (not reported on this point—judge summed up whole of defence case at 3 p.m. on a Friday at the end of a 22-day trial and after summing up all day; it would have been preferable to postpone this part until the Monday).

C. MISCELLANEOUS

(1) Taking verdicts on some defendants or charges before summing up others

4–370 The overriding consideration in deciding whether to deliver a divided summing up is fairness. Where a judge, after making some general observations about the case, sums up the case of each defendant separately and takes the verdict on that defendant before starting to sum up against the next defendant, such a course is inappropriate and likely to lead to unfairness when the jury's verdicts against the earlier defendants in the indictment may—despite the most careful direction—make it difficult for the jury fairly to review the evidence of a witness who has already been believed when considered against that of a later defendant who has alleged that the witness should not be believed. The possibility of this kind of unfairness is likely in nearly all cases where a number of defendants are charged with the same offence and there is a divided summing up: *R. v. Wooding*, 70 Cr.App.R. 256, CA; *cf. R. v. Simmonds* [1969] 1 Q.B. 685, 51 Cr.App.R. 316, CA, and *R. v. Newland* [1954] 1 Q.B. 158, 37 Cr.App.R. 154, CCA (practice of splitting upheld in each case). In the case of a single defendant, such a course should not be taken unless the judge is satisfied that the case really demands it: *R. v. Houssein*, 70 Cr.App.R. 267, CA.

(2) Assistance on the law from counsel

4–371 Prosecuting counsel is under a positive duty to draw to the judge's attention any failure to give adequate and proper directions on the law (*R. v. Lang-Hall, The Times*, March 24, 1989, CA) and must make sure that the essential ingredients of a summing up are put before the jury—the judge is entitled to rely on that assistance being available to him: *R. v. McVey* [1988] Crim.L.R. 127, CA. This duty is set out at paragraph 10.7 of the Written Standards for the Conduct of Professional Work that accompanied the eighth edition of the Code of Conduct for the Bar of England and Wales (Appendix C–33).

The importance of counsel's duty to draw the judge's attention to any omission to direct the jury on any essential matter of law was re-emphasised in *R. v. Roberts* [1992]

Crim.L.R. 375, CA. See also *R. v. Donoghue*, 86 Cr.App.R. 267, CA (helpful for prosecution counsel to make check-list of necessary directions on law).

The extent to which defence counsel is under the same duty is not clear. In *R. v. Cocks*, 63 Cr.App.R. 79, CA, James L.J. said, *obiter*, at p. 82: "... defending counsel owes a duty to his client and it is not his duty to correct the judge if a judge has gone wrong." In *R. v. Edwards (N.W.)*, 77 Cr.App.R. 5, CA, the court, without expressly deciding the point, proceeded upon the basis that the dictum in *Cocks* applies where the judge failed to direct the jury upon the standard of proof. However, Robert Goff L.J. said that it was inconceivable that defence counsel, acting in the best interests of their clients, could have failed to draw the judge's serious omission to his attention if they had not formed a view as to the overwhelming nature of the evidence in the case: "... if in future counsel ever find themselves placed as counsel for the defence were placed at the trial of this appellant, they may find the judgment in the present case of assistance." See also *R. v. Southgate*, 47 Cr.App.R. 252, CCA (defence counsel's action in drawing attention to misdirection on provocation "commendable and desirable"); *R. v. Holden* [1991] Crim.L.R. 478, CA (Court of Appeal will measure weight of the evidence against importance of the misdirection/non-direction—explaining dictum of Robert Goff L.J. in *Edwards*); and *R. v. L.*, *The Times*, February 9, 2001, CA (duty of defence counsel as much as of prosecution counsel, to seek to have any alleged error corrected, rather than stay silent with a view to raising the matter on appeal, but no authorities were referred to). Whatever the precise ambit of the duty, it is submitted that a failure to comply with it cannot of itself justify the dismissal of an appeal if there was an error or omission such as to render the conviction unsafe; but the failure of the defence advocate to draw the attention of the judge to the error may give rise to scepticism as to whether a correct direction would have made any difference. **4–372**

The *Code of Conduct* does not specifically deal with this matter. Paragraph 708(c) (Appendix C–17) sets out counsel's general duty to inform the court of relevant decisions and legislative provisions whether favourable or unfavourable to the contention for which he argues, and to inform the court of any procedural irregularity, rather than reserving it to raise on appeal. The applicability of this duty to defects in a summing up is unclear. **4–373**

It is submitted that the dictum in *Cocks* should be taken to represent the law until such time as it is expressly disapproved by the Court of Appeal.

As to the necessity for discussion with counsel prior to speeches, see *ante*, § 4–355.

(3) Written directions

See *ante*, § 4–356. **4–373a**

(4) Making corrections

A judge should be slow to reject the submissions of responsible counsel who are agreed that an error has been made in his summing up: *R. v. Wright* [2000] Crim.L.R. 510, CA. See *R. v. Tuegel* [2000] 2 Cr.App.R. 361, CA, *ante*, § 4–367, as to how any suggested need for a correction should be drawn to the attention of the judge. **4–374**

Where a judge, upon reflection, wishes to correct a direction he gave to the jury in the course of summing up and the jury have already retired, the judge should have the jury recalled into court for him to correct the error and give an accurate direction. He should then ask the jury to consider their verdict in the light of the correct direction: *R. v. Plimmer*, 61 Cr.App.R. 264, CA. See also *post*, § 4–431.

Where a judge misdirects a jury upon the burden of proof, the mistake must be corrected in the plainest possible terms. "It would be necessary for the [judge] to repeat the direction which he had given, to acknowledge that that direction was quite wrong, to tell the jury to put out of their minds all that they had heard from him ... up to that moment about the burden of proof and then in clear terms, which would be incapable of being misunderstood, tell them very plainly and simply what the law is": *R. v. Moon* [1969] 1 W.L.R. 1705, CA; see also, *R. v. Johnson* [1972] Crim.L.R. 180, CA.

(5) Counsel taking a note of the summing up

In *R. v. Campbell* [1976] Crim.L.R. 508, CA, the court expressed the hope that in a **4–375** case where, in the event of a conviction, the sentence was likely to be short, counsel on both sides would take a full note of the summing up in order that any application for leave to appeal could be expedited.

(6) Scope of judge's task

4–376 Generally, see the extract from the speech of Lord Hailsham L.C. in *R. v. Lawrence* [1982] A.C. 510, HL, quoted at § 4–368, *ante*.

A good starting point is that a judge should never be compelled to give meaningless or absurd directions: *R. v. Aziz* [1996] 1 A.C. 41, HL.

It is usually necessary for the judge to direct the jury as to the ingredients of the offence: see *R. v. James* [1997] Crim.L.R. 598, CA, and the cases cited at § 7–60, *post*.

It is generally desirable to give directions on the law at the beginning of the summing up, including a direction as to the respective functions of the judge and jury. It is also almost invariable nowadays to give a direction to the effect that the jury should reject any comments made by the judge with which they do not agree; the Judicial Studies Board Specimen Directions provide such a direction. However, it is pedantic to suggest that a failure to give this part of the direction at the beginning of the summing up cannot be cured by appropriate words at the end unless, possibly, the summing up contained strong adverse comments or the judge had not already directed the jury that they are the sole judges of the facts: *R. v. Everett* [1995] Crim.L.R. 76, CA, distinguishing *R. v. Jackson* [1992] Crim.L.R. 214, CA.

Where the judge considers that some reference to the evidence is appropriate, as is invariably the case, he should remind the jury of the evidence for the defence: *R. v. Tillman* [1962] Crim.L.R. 261, CCA, and *R. v. Weiner, The Times*, November 3, 1989, CA, whether or not the defendant gives evidence: *R. v. Jarman* (1962) 106 S.J. 838.

Brevity in summing up is a virtue, not a vice; there is no obligation to rehearse all the evidence or all the arguments; generally speaking, however, the longer a trial has lasted, the greater will be the jury's need for assistance in relation to the evidence; in a trial lasting several days or more it will generally be of assistance if the judge summarises those factual matters that are not in dispute and, where there is a significant dispute as to material facts, identifies succinctly those pieces of evidence that are in conflict; but the summing up should never be a mere rehearsal of the evidence and appeals based merely on the failure of the judge to refer to a particular piece of evidence or a particular argument will find little favour in the Court of Appeal: *R. v. Farr*, 163 J.P. 193, CA. Nevertheless, a judge cannot abandon his responsibility to marshall and arrange the facts, issue by issue, to counsel and their speeches, or to the jury and their notes: *R. v. Amado-Taylor* [2000] 2 Cr.App.R. 189, CA. In a case of violence, where 19 witnesses had given contradictory evidence, an appeal was allowed because the judge had omitted to make detailed reference to the evidence of any witness other than the victim and the defendant; the jury should have had assistance in relating the evidence to the issues: *R. v. Marashi* [2002] 1 *Archbold News* 3, CA. See also *R. v. A., Heppenstall and Potter* [2007] 10 *Archbold News* 3, CA (where there is a risk that the length of a trial will deprive the jury of a fair opportunity to assess the evidence, that risk must be allayed by the clarity of the directions, which should provide the jury with the basis for reaching a rational conclusion; the longer the case, the more important is a short and careful analysis of the issues).

It is the duty of the judge to identify the defence; how this is done will depend on all the circumstances of the case; where the judge had invited the jury to read the whole of the summary of an interview with a defendant who had not given evidence, and had then referred them to the salient parts in relation to each count, he had done all that he could reasonably be expected to do in placing before the jury what was being advanced as giving rise to a defence: *R. v. Soames-Waring, The Times*, July 20, 1998, CA. Where the defendant neither gives nor calls evidence, but has been extensively interviewed, it is of particular importance that the summing up should at least summarise the main points made by the defendant in the interview; only rarely, if ever, would a conviction be judged safe notwithstanding a failure to sum up the defence: *R. v. Akhtar* [2000] 1 *Archbold News* 2, CA. Where, however, there is no evidence from the defence and the defendant said nothing in interview, it has been said that the judge is under no obligation to remind the jury of the defence case: see *R. v. Briley* [1991] Crim.L.R. 444, CA; and *R. v. Hillier and Farrar*, 97 Cr.App.R. 349, CA (no part of a judge's duty to build up the defence of someone who has chosen not to give the jury the benefit of seeing him in the witness box, although he should remind them in summary form of any version of events given by the accused prior to the trial and of any assistance provided to the accused by the Crown's witnesses). See also *post*, §§ 4–397 *et seq*.

For other cases stressing the importance of the defence being adequately put to the jury, see *R. v. Waters* [1954] Crim.L.R. 147, CCA; *R. v. Olliffe* [1955] Crim.L.R. 570, CCA; *R. v. Hamilton* [1972] Crim.L.R. 266, CA; and *R. v. Badjan*, 50 Cr.App.R. 141, CCA (*post*, § 7–65).

Provided that the judge fairly reviews the essential features of the evidence, the structure of his summing up cannot be impugned simply because the defence would have preferred a different format: *R. v. Richardson*, 98 Cr.App.R. 174 at 178, CA. However, in certain cases it is preferable to summarise in one passage the defence argument and the evidence relied on to support it, rather than summarise all the evidence chronologically, taking in the defence points *en passant*: see *R. v. Goodway*, 98 Cr.App.R. 11 at 14, CA.

As to the necessity to strike a fair balance as between the prosecution case and the defence case, see *R. v. Bentley (Deceased)* [2001] 1 Cr.App.R. 21, CA. Where the case against a defendant is strong and his defence correspondingly weak, a trial judge must be scupulous to ensure that the defence is presented to the jury in an even-handed and impartial manner; justice is not served by a one-sided account given to the jury shortly before they retire to consider their verdict: *R. v. Reid, The Times*, August 17, 1999, CA.

The full transcript of *R. v. Nelson* [1997] Crim.L.R. 234, CA, contains the following guidance from Simon Brown L.J.:

> "Every defendant, we repeat, has the right to have his defence, whatever it may be, faithfully and accurately placed before the jury. But that is not to say that he is entitled to have it rehearsed blandly and uncritically in the summing up. No defendant has the right to demand that the judge shall conceal from the jury such difficulties and deficiencies as are apparent in his case. Of course, the judge must remain impartial. But if common sense and reason demonstrate that a given defence is riddled with implausibilities, inconsistencies and illogicalities ... there is no reason for the judge to withhold from the jury the benefit of his own powers of logic and analysis. Why should pointing out those matters be thought to smack of partiality? To play a case straight down the middle requires only that a judge gives full and fair weight to the evidence and arguments of each side. The judge is not required to top up the case for one side so as to correct any substantial imbalance. He has no duty to cloud the merits either by obscuring the strengths of one side or the weaknesses of the other. Impartiality means no more and no less than that the judge shall fairly state and analyse the case for both sides. Justice moreover requires that he assists the jury to reach a logical and reasoned conclusion on the evidence."

Further, the entitlement of a judge to comment on the evidence extends to the use of robust language; and if there is an imbalance in the evidence, the summing up will reflect that imbalance, but it is preferable for a judge who merely echoes an argument of an advocate to remind the jury of the point as one made by the advocate concerned: *R. v. Butler* [1999] Crim.L.R. 595, CA. What is wholly impermissible is for the judge to leave the jury with the impression that he favours the prosecution case against that of the defendant: *R. v. Bryant* [2005] 9 *Archbold News* 3, CA. See also *post*, § 4–394 as to comment and fairness.

The judge should leave to the jury every count on which there is sufficient evidence: **4–377**
R. v. Lincoln, 29 Cr.App.R. 191, CCA. It is, however, quite usual for a judge (usually with counsel's agreement) to leave only one of two counts covering much the same facts to the jury, on the understanding that if they acquit on the first they will be directed to acquit on the second. If they convict on the first, the second would be left on the file.

The jury should be directed to give separate consideration to each count (*R. v. Fisher*, 49 Cr.App.R. 116, CCA; *R. v. Lovesey and Peterson* [1970] 1 Q.B. 352, 53 Cr.App.R. 461, CA), to each defendant (*R. v. Smith and Smith*, 25 Cr.App.R. 119, CCA, and (which is the same thing as saying that each count requires separate consideration) to each complainant (where there is more than one, and there is no question of cross-admissibility) (*R. v. D.* [2004] 1 Cr.App.R. 19, CA).

Passages from statements should not be read out as if they were evidence given at the trial: *R. v. Blewitt* [1967] Crim.L.R. 61, CA.

In certain types of case it is desirable for the judge to give the jury a warning that they should not allow themselves to be swayed by emotion: see *R. v. Bowditch* [1991] Crim.L.R. 831, CA.

Where a defendant is unrepresented it is generally desirable to tell the jury that it is always open to a defendant to represent himself and that they should bear in mind the difficulty of properly presenting a defence. In appropriate cases, it might be desirable to give, in the barest outline, the relevant history as to why a defendant is unrepresented. It will usually be sensible also to explain some or all of these matters to the jury at the outset of the trial: *R. v. De Oliveira* [1997] Crim.L.R. 600, CA.

It will often be helpful for the judge expressly to direct the jury in his summing up that suggestions made by counsel in cross-examination and closing speeches do not amount to evidence: *R. v. Hill*, 96 Cr.App.R. 456 at 463, CA.

See *post*, §§ 7–52 *et seq.* for further examples of appeals based on complaints arising from a summing up.

D. PUTTING PROSECUTION OR DEFENCE CASE ON BASIS OTHER THAN THAT RELIED ON BY ADVOCATES

4–378 The judge is not confined to the arguments which have been propounded by the parties and is entitled to comment on any matters which have been given in evidence: *R. v. Evans (D.J.)*, 91 Cr.App.R. 173, CA. However, if judges plan—

> "to introduce an issue into the summing up which has not been actively canvassed in the course of the hearing [they] should at least give ample warning of their intention to do so to counsel in the absence of the jury before addresses are begun, so that there can be discussion between the judge and counsel as to the rightness of the course to be adopted by the judge, and an opportunity given to counsel to deal with the issue in their addresses to the jury" (*per* Watkins L.J. in *R. v. Cristini* [1987] Crim.L.R. 504 at 506, C.A.).

See also *R. v. White* [1987] Crim.L.R. 505, CA; *R. v. Newington*, 91 Cr.App.R. 247, CA; *R. v. Feeny*, 94 Cr.App.R. 1, CA; *R. v. Fallon* [1993] Crim.L.R. 591, CA; *R. v. Harding* [1997] Crim.L.R. 815, CA; *R. v. Goldman* [1997] Crim.L.R. 894, CA; *R. v. Gray and Evans* [1998] Crim.L.R. 570, CA; *R. v. Ramzan* [1998] 2 Cr.App.R. 328, CA; *R. v. Taylor* [1998] Crim.L.R. 582, CA; and *ante*, § 4–355, and *post*, §§ 4–382, 4–395, 4–431, 4–464 and 7–83. Whether a conviction will be rendered unsafe by the judge taking such a course will depend on the nature and circumstances of the individual case, including such matters as the stage at which notice is given to the parties and the degree of variation from the way in which the prosecution case has been put.

A change in the basis on which the case is put may infringe the right to a fair trial under Article 6 of the ECHR where such a possibility has not been properly raised in advance: see *Pelissier and Sassi v. France*, 30 E.H.R.R. 715, ECtHR, *post*, § 4–464; and *Mattocia v. Italy* (2003) 36 E.H.R.R. 47, ECtHR (*ante*, § 1–132d).

Where the defence is duress and prosecuting counsel cross-examines the defendant only in relation to the issue of whether or not the alleged duress ever occurred, it is nonetheless incumbent on the trial judge to direct the jury fully as to all ingredients of the defence, and by so doing he does not introduce a new issue into the case or change the basis of the case against the defendant: *R. v. Ward* [1998] 8 *Archbold News* 3, CA (97 05223 X5).

4–379 The judge should look for any possible defence to the charge arising from the evidence and refer to it even though the defence has not been relied on by the defending advocate: see the cases cited at §§ 7–61, 7–62 (general) and 19–53 (provocation), *post*, and *R. v. Courtnell* [1990] Crim.L.R. 115, CA (identification).

In *R. v. Williams (W. A.)*, 99 Cr.App.R. 163, CA, the defence to a charge of murder was suicide. The judge introduced the possibility of an alternative verdict of manslaughter. Neill L.J. said that in the majority of cases a judge would be guided by the way in which the case had been put by the prosecution and defence. The issues of fact which the jury had to decide would be the issues which had been identified by the parties. There are, however, cases where the judge's role is more complex. Where the courses adopted by the prosecution and defence present the jury with an incomplete picture of the range of options open to them, a judge might be under a duty to direct the jury on a version of the facts which neither the prosecution nor the defence had advanced.

For tactical reasons counsel for a defendant might not wish to enlarge upon, or even to mention, a possible conclusion which the jury would be entitled on the evidence to reach, in fear that what he might see as a compromise conclusion would detract from a more stark choice between a conviction on a serious charge and an acquittal; but if there is evidence to support such a middle ground it is the duty of the judge to explain it to the jury and leave the choice to them; if there is evidence upon which a jury could reasonably come to a particular conclusion there can be few circumstances, if any, in which a judge has no duty to put the possibility before the jury; however, if the evidence in respect of a particular matter is wholly incredible, or so tenuous or uncertain that no reasonable jury could accept it, the judge is entitled to put it aside, the threshold in that context being a low one: *Von Starck v. R.* [2000] 1 W.L.R. 1270, PC. For an example of a situation where the evidence was not such as to require the judge to leave the matter to the jury in a way that had not been relied upon by counsel, see *R. v. Elliott (Denrick)* [2000] Crim.L.R. 51, CA (identity in dispute on charge of murder; no sufficient evidence to necessitate leaving alternative of self defence).

E. Burden and Standard of Proof

The judge must always direct the jury upon the burden and standard of proof. No formula has to be followed slavishly, but two points must be made clearly: (a) the burden of proof is upon the prosecution—it is for the prosecution to establish the defendant's guilt; (b) before the jury can convict they must be satisfied beyond a reasonable doubt (*or* be sure) of the defendant's guilt. These points were reiterated in *R. v. Bentley (Deceased)* [2001] 1 Cr.App.R. 21, CA. See further *post*, §§ 4–384 *et seq.* as to the appropriate form of words. **4–380**

The direction should be given at the outset of the summing up: *R. v. Ching*, 63 Cr.App.R. 7, CA; *R. v. Milligan*, *The Times*, March 11, 1989, CA. If the jury ask for further guidance, their question should be answered as shortly as possible, using, if the judge can do so, the same language as he has used before, in order to avoid the risk of confusion: *ibid*.

Repetition of the direction, absent any request by the jury, is usually wholly unnecessary: but see *R. v. Gibson*, 77 Cr.App.R. 151, for circumstances in which the Court of Appeal thought repetition would have been appropriate (jury sent note after over two hours' deliberations indicating they were having difficulty deciding). See also *post*, § 4–432.

The importance of a clear direction on the burden of proof in child cruelty cases, so as to counteract the jury's emotional feelings about the child's injuries, was emphasised in *R. v. Bowditch* [1991] Crim.L.R. 831, CA.

Legal burden (or persuasive burden)

The law on the topic of where the burden lies was reviewed by the House of Lords in *R. v. Hunt* [1987] A.C. 352, in which it was held that the burden of proving the guilt of an accused is on the prosecution (and remains there throughout the trial: *Woolmington v. DPP* [1935] A.C. 462 at 481, HL), save in the case of the defence of insanity (*post*, §§ 17–74 *et seq.*) and subject to any statutory exception; that such exception might be express or implied and the burden of proof might be placed on the accused whether the exception appeared in the same clause of the instrument in question as that creating the offence or in a subsequent proviso and whether the offence was triable summarily or on indictment, and would be discharged on a balance of probabilities; and that where a linguistic construction did not indicate clearly on whom the burden of proof should lie, the court might look to other considerations to determine the intention of Parliament, such as the mischief at which the provision was aimed and practical considerations such **4–381** as, in particular, the ease or difficulty for the respective parties of discharging the burden of proof.

As to the implications of Article 6 of the ECHR in respect of the placing of a burden of proof on an accused, see *post*, §§ 16–77 *et seq*.

Evidential burden (the burden of adducing evidence fit for consideration by the jury)

4–382 This is a topic much canvassed in decisions upon the civil law. For the purpose of trials upon indictment it is sufficient to state that:

(a) the burden is upon the prosecution of adducing evidence upon which, if it is accepted and not contradicted, a reasonable jury may convict.

(b) The judge should only leave an issue to a jury which upon the evidence in the case is an issue fit to be left to them: *Walker v. R.* [1974] 1 W.L.R. 1090 at 1096A, PC, followed in *R. v. Bonnick*, 66 Cr.App.R. 266, CA.

(c) In practice, this question only arises where the issue, if determined in favour of the accused, would excuse him from liability to conviction of the crime charged, *e.g.* self-defence, automatism, duress, provocation (in murder), drunkenness, etc. It is sometimes said that on such issues the evidential burden is upon the defence to adduce evidence, by cross-examining witnesses or calling witnesses, upon which a reasonable jury might determine the issue in the accused's favour. This is too restrictive, because the evidence may come from a prosecution witness or a co-defendant in chief or in other ways: see *Bullard v. R.* [1957] A.C. 635, PC.

(d) Where such an issue does arise upon the evidence called by any party to the case, the judge must leave it to the jury, whether it has been mentioned by the defence or not: *Palmer v. R.* [1971] A.C. 814, PC. In *R. v. Bonnick*, *ante*, the court observed that the question of whether there was sufficient evidence to raise an issue fit to be left to a jury was one for the trial judge to answer by applying common sense to the evidence. The issue should be left to the jury when there was evidence sufficient to raise a prima facie case, if accepted. Further, it is clear that there might be evidence of self-defence or provocation even though a defendant asserted that he was not present: *ibid.*; see also § 19–53, *post*, and *R. v. Williams (W. A.)*, *ante*, § 4–379.

4–383 (e) The judge must make it plain to the jury that upon such issues, once they are left to the jury, the legal burden of proof remains throughout upon the prosecution (with the exceptions mentioned, *ante*, § 4–381): see *R. v. Wheeler*, 52 Cr.App.R. 28, CA, and *R. v. Abraham*, 57 Cr.App.R. 799 at 803, CA (*post*, §§ 19–44, 19–45). It is better to avoid referring to the "defence" of duress, self-defence, etc., being raised, as this may lead the jury to think that the legal burden of proof has shifted to the defence. Although there is no rule of law that in every case where the defendant relies on an alibi the judge must direct that it is for the prosecution to negative the alibi (*Anderson*, *post*, where no such direction was given and the appeal against conviction was dismissed), such a direction is necessary if the jury seem in danger of supposing that, because an alibi has been put forward by the defence, the burden must be on the defence to prove it: *R. v. Wood*, 52 Cr.App.R. 74, CA. In any event, even where such a direction is not strictly necessary, it is nonetheless desirable: *R. v. Anderson* [1991] Crim.L.R. 361, CA; *R. v. Preece*, 96 Cr.App.R. 264, CA. See also *post*, § 4–402.

If the question of whether a defendant has discharged an evidential burden is not agreed and the judge decides to leave it to the jury, his directions must provide, at a minimum, an understandable explanation of the difference between an evidential burden and a legal burden and the respective standards of proof: *R. v. Malinina*, unreported, December 20, 2007, CA ([2007] EWCA Crim. 3228). *Sed quaere* that the question is for the jury to determine, rather than the judge: see the commentary in *Criminal Law Week* 2008/32/7.

Standard of proof if legal burden lies on prosecution

4–384 (a) While the prosecution do not have to make the jury feel certain of the accused's guilt (*Miller v. Minister of Pensions* [1947] 2 All E.R. 372, *per* Denning J. at pp. 373, 374; *R. v. Bracewell*, 68 Cr.App.R. 44, CA), they must satisfy the jury, upon the whole of the evidence called by all parties, of the accused's guilt beyond all reasonable doubt (sometimes expressed as "a" or "any" reasonable doubt): *Woolmington v. DPP* [1935] A.C. 462, HL.

> "Throughout the web of the English criminal law one golden thread is always to be seen, that it is the duty of the prosecution to prove the prisoner's guilt, subject [*to the qualification involving the defence of insanity and to any statutory exception*]. If at the end of and on the whole of the case, there is a reasonable doubt, created by the evidence given either by the prosecution or the prisoner, as to whether [*the offence was committed by him*], the prosecution has not made out the case and the prisoner is entitled to an acquittal. No matter what the charge or where the trial, the principle that the prosecution must prove the guilt of the prisoner is part of the common law of England and no attempt to whittle it down can be entertained" (*ibid., per* Viscount Sankey L.C. at pp. 481–482).

This standard has been applied by the Court of Appeal, and by the House of Lords and Privy Council, on numerous occasions: see *R. v. Angeli*, 68 Cr.App.R. 32 at 36, CA; *Ferguson v. R.* [1979] 1 W.L.R. 94 at 99A, PC; *R. v. Sang* [1980] A.C. 402 at 436H, 445A, HL; and *R. v. Lawrence* [1982] A.C. 510 at 525G, HL.

(b) In *R. v. Kritz*, 33 Cr.App.R. 169 at 177, CCA, and in *R. v. Summers*, 36 Cr.App.R. 14 at 15, CCA, in observations which were clearly *obiter*, Lord Goddard C.J. expressed the view that it was better to tell the jury that before they convict they must be "satisfied so that they are sure" of the guilt of the accused. This form of direction on the standard of proof has frequently been used by judges since then, and was approved by the Privy Council in *Walters v. R.* [1969] 2 A.C. 26 at 30.

(c) The reason for Lord Goddard's dicta was clearly that some judges had found difficulty in explaining what was meant by "reasonable doubt." It is however submitted that this is a difficulty which very rarely arises and can easily be dealt with (see (f), *post*). In any event, there is a wealth of recent authority of the House of Lords, long after Lord Goddard's dicta were uttered, in favour of the "reasonable doubt" direction. **4–385**

(d) Apart from this, it is well established that the standard of proof is less than certainty (see (a), *ante*). As in ordinary English "sure" and "certain" are virtually indistinguishable, it savours of what the late Sir Rupert Cross might have described as "gobbledegook" to tell the jury that while they must be "sure" they need not be "certain". (Expressions such as "pretty certain," "reasonably sure" and "pretty sure" were disapproved by the Court of Criminal Appeal: *R. v. Law* [1961] Crim.L.R. 52; *R. v. Head and Warrener*, 45 Cr.App.R. 225; and *R. v. Woods* [1961] Crim.L.R. 324.) In *R. v. Stephens, The Times*, June 27, 2002, CA, it was said to be unhelpful for judges to seek to draw a distinction between being certain of guilt and being sure of guilt, as something less than certain, but see the approval in *R. v. Bracewell*, *ante*, § 4–384, of a distinction drawn between "scientific certainty" or "absolute certainty", on the one hand, and "being sure" or "legal proof" on the other.

(e) It is, therefore, submitted that it is better to give the "reasonable doubt" direction, as set out in (a), *ante*. In *R. v. Bentley (Deceased)* [2001] 1 Cr.App.R. 21, the Court of Appeal said, as to standard of proof, that a jury should be instructed that if, on reviewing all the evidence, they are unsure or left in any reasonable doubt as to the accused's guilt, that doubt must be resolved in the accused's favour.

(f) It is submitted that the judge should not volunteer an explanation of the expression "reasonable doubt." If, however, the jury ask for an explanation, they should be told that a reasonable doubt is the sort of doubt that might affect the mind of a person in dealing with matters of importance in his own affairs: *Walters v. R.* ((b), *ante*); *R. v. Gray*, 58 Cr.App.R. 177 at 183, CA. Explanations such as "a doubt for which you could give reasons if asked," and "the sort of doubt that might affect you in the conduct of your everyday affairs" have been disapproved: *R. v. Stafford and Luvaglio*, 53 Cr.App.R. 1 at 2, CA; *R. v. Gray*, *ante*.

Standard of proof if legal burden lies upon the defence

In these circumstances the standard of proof is only that required for civil proceedings, *i.e.* a preponderance (or balance) of probability: *R. v. Carr-Briant* [1943] K.B. 607, 29 Cr.App.R. 76, CCA. It is usual to tell the jury that the defence will have proved **4–386** a fact if the jury conclude that it is "more probable than not" or "more likely than not" that the fact existed.

Standard of proof if the judge decides the issue

4–387 The standard of proof wherever the judge has to decide an issue of fact in a criminal trial, where the burden of proof is on the prosecution, is proof beyond reasonable doubt: *R. v. Ewing*, 77 Cr.App.R. 47, CA (pointing out that *R. v. Angeli*, 68 Cr.App.R. 32, CA had been decided *per incuriam* on this point).

Statutory exceptions, provisos, etc.

4–388 In *R. v. Edwards* [1975] Q.B. 27, 59 Cr.App.R. 213, the Court of Appeal held that there was an exception to the fundamental rule that the prosecution must prove every element of the offence charged. The exception was "limited to offences arising under enactments which prohibit the doing of an act save in specified circumstances or by persons of specified classes or with specified qualifications or with the licence or permission of specified authorities" (at pp. 39–40, 221). The court rejected the view that merely the evidential burden, and not the legal burden, shifts to the accused.

4–389 *Edwards* was considered by the House of Lords in *R. v. Hunt* [1987] A.C. 352. It was held that there is no rule of law that the burden of proving a statutory defence lies on the defendant only where the statute specifically so provides. A statute can place the burden of proof on the defendant by necessary implication. Each case turns on the construction of the particular legislation, but a court should be slow to infer that Parliament intended to impose an onerous duty on the defendant to prove his innocence in a criminal case. Lord Griffiths (with Lord Keith and Lord Mackay concurring) said:

> "I have little doubt that the occasions on which a statute will be construed as imposing a burden of proof upon a defendant which do not fall into this formulation [*i.e.* the formulation of the principle in *Edwards*, *ante*] are likely to be exceedingly rare. But I would find it difficult to fit *Nimmo v. Alexander Cowan & Sons Ltd* [1968] A.C. 107 into this formula, and I would prefer to adopt the formula as an excellent guide to construction rather than as an exception to a rule. In the final analysis each case must turn on the construction of the particular piece of legislation to determine whether the defence is an exception within the meaning of section 101 of the Act of 1980 which the Court of Appeal rightly decided reflects the rule for trials on indictment. With this one qualification I regard *R. v. Edwards* as rightly decided" (pp. 375–376).

See also *ante*, § 4–381, and *post*, § 16–78. As to the facts in *Hunt*, see *post*, §§ 27–20 *et seq*.

Magistrates' Courts Act 1980, s.101

4–390 **101.** Where the defendant to an information relies for his defence on any exception, exemption, proviso, excuse or qualification, whether or not it accompanies the description of the offence or matter of complaint in the enactment creating the offence or on which the complaint is founded, the burden of proving the exception, exemption, proviso, excuse or qualification shall be on him; and this notwithstanding that the information or complaint contains an allegation negativing the exception, exemption, proviso, excuse or qualification.

F. What Degree of Unanimity is Required of a Jury?

4–391 It is a fundamental principle that in arriving at their verdict the jury must be agreed that every ingredient necessary to constitute the offence has been established: *R. v. Brown (K.)*, 79 Cr.App.R. 115, CA. B was charged with contravening section 13(1)(a) of the *Prevention of Fraud (Investments) Act* 1958. Each count in the indictment contained particulars of a number of different statements relied upon by the prosecution as constituting fraudulent inducements. It was held that in such a case the following principles apply: (a) each ingredient of the offence must be proved to the satisfaction of each and every member of the jury (subject to the majority direction); (b) however, where a number of matters (the different statements) are specified in the charge as together constituting one ingredient in the offence, and any one of them is capable of doing so, then it is enough to establish the ingredient that any one of them is proved;

but (c) (because of principle (a), *ante*) any such matter must be proved to the satisfaction of the whole jury.

This principle does not require each juror to follow the same evidential route in order to arrive at a unanimous decision as to the existence of the same false statement. For example, some jurors may base their conclusion on the accuracy of an alleged confession, while others may prefer to rely on evidence from the person to whom the false statement was made. **4–392**

A direction as to (c), *ante*, will be necessary only in comparatively rare cases, in which there is a realistic danger that the jury might not appreciate that they must all be agreed on the particular matter (constituting the particular ingredient) on which they rely to find their verdict of guilty, and might return a verdict of guilty on the basis that some of them found one matter proved and others found another proved (*R. v. Mitchell* [1994] Crim.L.R. 66, CA; *R. v. Keeton* [1995] 2 Cr.App.R. 241, CA). Such a direction may also be required where two distinct incidents are alleged, either of which might constitute the offence charged, particularly where they give rise to different defences (*R. v. Carr* [2000] 2 Cr.App.R. 149, CA, where death was caused either by a kick or by a punch; *R. v. Boreman* [2000] 2 Cr.App.R. 17, CA, in which death was caused either by injuries or by fire).

However, unanimity is only required in respect of ingredients of the offence: thus where the different available factual findings do not amount to different ingredients no *Brown* direction is required, *e.g.* in respect of an intent to supply controlled drugs (*R. v. Ibrahima* [2005] Crim.L.R. 887, CA, where the jury could convict on the basis of either social supply to a named friend, or commercial supply in a nightclub, without having to agree on which it was); intent to pervert the course of justice (*R. v. Sinha* [1995] Crim.L.R. 68, CA, where the defendant's intention might have been to pervert criminal, or civil, proceedings, or an inquest); and an agreement to act dishonestly to the prejudice of a defined group of people (*R. v. Hancock* [1996] 2 Cr.App.R. 241, CA, an allegation of conspiracy to defraud in which the particulars specified the nature of the prosecution case and the principal overt acts relied on rather than alternative ingredients of the offence, and which was followed in *R. v. K.* [2005] 1 Cr.App.R. 25, CA). **4–393**

Where alternative allegations do concern one of the ingredients of the offence, no *Brown* direction is necessary if they merely represent fine factual differences (*per* Lord Bingham C.J. in *R. v. Carr*, *ante*), or they form part of a continuing course of conduct (such as cruelty to a child by neglect: *R. v. Young*, 97 Cr.App.R. 280, CA; and criminal damage involving hurling missiles and ramming: *R. v. Asquith*; *R. v. Warwick* [1995] 1 Cr.App.R. 492, CA), unless that course of conduct falls into separate sequences (*R. v. Smith* [1997] 1 Cr.App.R. 14, CA, in which an affray might have been either committed inside a house on one victim, or outside on another) or is founded on acts which are disparate in time and nature (*R. v. Mitchell*, *ante*, where a *Brown* direction was required in respect of the particulars of a charge of unlawful harassment of an occupier which set out a number of acts each amounting to the offence).

A middle course tailored to the facts of the case was approved in *R. v. Cox* [1998] Crim.L.R. 810, CA, where an allegation of assault occasioning actual bodily harm in the form of anxiety, depression and other psychological conditions by "stalking" involved several types of behaviour and many instances of each over a long period. The judge was held to have struck the right level of particularity in directing the jury that they should consider each type of allegation and only find it proved if they were unanimous about it, and then should decide overall whether there were sufficient acts within a type and sufficient types to have been responsible for the actual bodily harm; it was not necessary or appropriate for him to direct the jury as to the need for unanimity on each of the possibly hundreds of incidents which had emerged in the evidence.

Where, of two alternatives, the jury are unanimous that if it was not one then it was the other, there is no requirement that they should be unanimous as to which alternative it was (such as where the defendant either committed the offence himself, or procured its commission: *R. v. Morton* [2004] Crim.L.R. 73, CA; *R. v. Strudwick and Merry*, 99 Cr.App.R. 326, CA; *R. v. Giannetto* [1997] 1 Cr.App.R. 1, CA, declining to follow *R. v. Fitzgerald* [1992] Crim.L.R. 660, CA, in which a contrary view had been expressed without extensive citation of authority; and *R. v. Tirnaveanu* [2007] 2 Cr.App.R. 23, CA).

G. COMMENT

(1) On the merits

4-394 The facts must be left to the jury to decide and the judge must not usurp their function: *R. v. West*, 4 Cr.App.R. 179, CCA; *R. v. Frampton*, 12 Cr.App.R. 202, CCA. But the judge is entitled to express his opinion strongly in a proper case, provided he leaves the issues to the jury: *R. v. Cohen and Bateman*, 2 Cr.App.R. 197, CCA (*post*, § 7-67). See also *ante*, § 4-376. However, it is an inherent principle of the system of trial in England that no matter how distasteful the offence, however repulsive the defendant, however laughable his defence, he is entitled to have his case fairly presented to the jury both by counsel and the trial judge: *R. v. Marr*, 90 Cr.App.R. 154, CA.

For an example of a summing up in which the judge was held to have gone beyond the proper bounds of judicial comment and made it very difficult, if not practically impossible, for the jury to do other than that which he was plainly suggesting, see *Mears v. R.*, 97 Cr.App.R. 239, PC. The summing up was not saved by warnings given by the judge to the jury that they were not bound by his views. This point was repeated in *R. v. Wood* [1996] 1 Cr.App.R. 207, CA, where certain passages of the summing up were criticised as being "the stuff of advocacy". To a similar effect, see *R. v. Bentley (Deceased)* [2001] 1 Cr.App.R. 21, CA, and *R. v. Farr*, 163 J.P. 193, CA. In *R. v. Berrada*, 91 Cr.App.R. 131, CA, Waterhouse J., giving the judgment of the court on an appeal against conviction for attempted rape, referred to the fact that the appellant's evidence had conflicted directly with that of both the complainant and of certain police officers.

> "It is, of course, part of the duty of the judge in a case of this kind to indicate the nature of the conflict that has arisen in the evidence and the logical consequences of the conflict. An example of such a direction, in impeccable terms, by Boreham J., is to be found in *R. v. Malcherek*; *R. v. Steel*, 73 Cr.App.R. 173, the relevant passage being quoted ... at page 188. What is inappropriate, however, is to inflate the conflict and to describe it in sarcastic or extravagant language" (at p. 135).

4-395 A judge is not confined to the arguments propounded by the prosecution on the one hand or the defence on the other: *R. v. Evans (D.J.)*, (*ante*, § 4-378).

(2) Commending witnesses and reference to occupation

4-396 Judges who wish to commend witnesses for their actions in connection with the offence being tried should do so in the absence of the jury: *R. v. Newman* [1990] Crim.L.R. 203, CA.

In *R. v. Wilson* [1991] Crim.L.R. 838, CA, the appellant had been charged with indecent assault upon a young girl. When she had concluded her evidence the judge told her, in the presence of the jury, that she had done very well. At the close of the appellant's own evidence the judge asked him, "So this 12-year-old girl has made wicked lies about you?" The Court of Appeal said that: (a) there was nothing wrong in the judge issuing a word of comfort to such a witness who has gone through what must have been an unpleasant ordeal, but (b) the judge's question to the appellant was one that should not have been asked.

Although it is impermissible to call evidence for the purpose of bolstering the credibility of a prosecution witness (see *post*, § 8-138), the standard practice of asking a witness to state his occupation is unobjectionable; nor is it objectionable for the judge to direct the jury that they may have regard to the witness's occupation (clergyman) in assessing his reliability, provided that the direction is given in such a way as to avoid any risk that they might accept the evidence merely because of the occupation of the witness: *R. v. D.S.* [1999] Crim.L.R. 911, CA.

(3) On defendant's failure to disclose his defence, etc.

4-397 This topic is now governed by the *CJPOA* 1994, ss.34, 36 and 37, as to which, see *post*, §§ 15-414 *et seq*. As to the common law in respect of silence in the face of an accusation, see *post*, §§ 15-409 *et seq*.

As to faults in defence disclosure statements and departures from such statements, see *post*, § 12–62. As to departures from the case disclosed pursuant to preparatory hearing directions, see *ante*, §§ 4–84r, 4–84y and 4–87.

(4) On defendant's failure to testify

This topic is now governed by the *CJPOA* 1994, s.35, *ante*, § 4–305. By way of guidance, a specimen direction to take account of section 35 has been suggested by the Judicial Studies Board in the following terms (see www.jsboard.co.uk): **4–398**

1. The defendant has not given evidence. That is his right. He is entitled to remain silent and to require the prosecution to make you sure of his guilt. You must not assume he is guilty because he has not given evidence. But two matters arise from his silence.

2. In the first place, you try this case according to the evidence, and you will appreciate that the defendant has not given evidence at this trial to undermine, contradict or explain the evidence put before you by the prosecution.

(If appropriate, add:) However, he did answer questions in interview, and he now seeks to rely on those answers. [The direction here advises how to deal with wholly or partly self-serving statements.]

3. In the second place, his silence at this trial may count against him. This is because you may draw the conclusion that he has not given evidence because he has no answer to the prosecution's case, or none that would bear examination. If you do draw that conclusion, you must not convict him wholly or mainly on the strength of it, but you may treat it as some additional support for the prosecution's case.

4. However, you may draw such a conclusion against him only if you think it is a fair and proper conclusion, and you are satisfied about two things: first, that the prosecution's case is so strong that it clearly calls for an answer by him; and second, that the only sensible explanation for his silence is that he has no answer, or none that would bear examination.

5. (If appropriate, add:) The defence invite you not to draw any conclusion from the defendant's silence, on the basis of the following evidence (here set out the evidence). If you [accept the evidence and] think this amounts to a reason why you should not draw any conclusion from his silence, do not do so. Otherwise, subject to what I have said, you may do so.

It should be borne in mind that this specimen direction is accompanied by various "notes" which are not set out here.

In *R. v. Cowan*; *R. v. Gayle*; *R. v. Ricciardi* [1996] 1 Cr.App.R. 1, CA, it was held that: (a) the plain words of section 35 do not justify confining its operation to exceptional cases; (b) apart from the mandatory exceptions in section 35(1), it will be open to a court to decline to draw an adverse inference from silence at trial and for a judge to direct or advise a jury against drawing such inference if the circumstances of the case justify such a course, but there would need either to be some evidential basis for doing so (as to which, see also *ante*, § 4–305a) or some exceptional factors in the case making that the fair course to take (the possibility that the defendant could be cross-examined on his previous criminal record if he gave evidence being held not to provide a justification for such a course—followed in *R. v. Taylor* [1999] Crim.L.R. 77, CA). Otherwise, it is for the jury to decide whether in fact an inference should properly be drawn; the court said that the specimen direction suggested by the Judicial Studies Board (*ante*) is, in general terms, a sound guide as to how to direct the jury, although it may be necessary to adapt or add to it in the particular circumstances of an individual case. The court went on to highlight certain essential elements, namely that: **4–399**

(a) the burden of proof remains on the prosecution throughout;
(b) a defendant is entitled to remain silent, that being his right and his choice;
(c) an inference from failure to give evidence cannot on its own prove guilt and, therefore;
(d) the jury must be satisfied that the prosecution have established a case to (sufficiently compelling as to call for an) answer before drawing any inferences from the defendant's silence (the words in brackets have been added to take account of *R. v. Birchall* [1999] Crim.L.R. 311, CA, where this point was emphasised);
(e) if, despite any evidence relied on to explain his silence or in the absence of any

such evidence, the jury concluded the silence could only sensibly be attributed to the defendant's having no answer, or none that would stand up to cross-examination, they could then draw an adverse inference.

Having said this, the court emphasised that it is impossible to anticipate all possible circumstances in which a judge might think it right to direct or advise a jury against drawing an adverse inference, or to anticipate the nature, extent and degree of inferences that might properly be drawn in a particular case. The court also emphasised that in the absence of evidence to support reasons for silence at trial by the defendant it cannot be proper for his advocate to give such reasons dressed up as submission.

In *R. v. Whitehead* [2006] 8 *Archbold News* 3, CA, it was said that the "fourth essential" is a necessary and logical conclusion from the "third essential" and it amplifies and spells out what is inherent in it; where, therefore, the prosecution case rested solely on the evidence of a single witness containing no fundamental defect, and where the jury had been directed (a) as to the burden and standard proof, (b) that they had to be sure that the witness was telling the truth, and (c) that the defendant's failure to give evidence could not prove guilt by itself, it was held that the possibility that they had relied on the defendant's silence, before first deciding that there was sufficient evidence to call for an answer from him, was a fanciful one; there was no doubt that the threshold had been crossed so as to permit consideration of the defendant's silence (but this was not to be taken as encouragement to judges not to state the "fourth essential").

The strength or weakness of the prosecution case is not, of itself, a general ground for requiring the judge to advise or direct the jury that they ought not to draw any adverse inference from the failure of the defendant to give evidence: *R. v. Byrne*, unreported, November 21, 1995, CA (95/4159/W4).

In *R. v. Napper*, 161 J.P. 16, CA, it was held that the failure of the police to question the appellant about seven of the matters that gave rise to eight similar charges did not disentitle the trial judge from giving the standard direction as to the drawing of inferences. It had been argued that this failure by the police had deprived the appellant of the opportunity of giving his account of relevant matters when they were fresher in his mind than they would have been at trial but, as the court pointed out, there had been nothing to prevent him from making a statement to his own solicitors from which he could have refreshed his recollection at trial. The defence argument was viewed as an attempt to minimalise or marginalise the operation of section 35 and as contrary to the spirit of that legislation.

A direction under section 35 is inappropriate where there is no dispute as to the central facts, the only issue being whether those facts amount to the offence charged: *R. v. McManus and Cross* [2002] 1 *Archbold News* 2, CA.

Where the judge has not excluded the operation of section 35, the jury should simply be directed to take account of all the evidence in deciding what, if any, inferences should be drawn from the failure to give evidence; there is no special test or special direction for special cases (*e.g.* a mentally handicapped defendant): *R. v. Friend* [1997] 2 Cr.App.R. 231, CA.

As to the entitlement of a judge to comment adversely on the quality of the exculpatory parts of a pre-trial statement made by a defendant who has not testified, see *R. v. Aziz* [1996] 1 A.C. 41, HL.

(5) On failure to call a particular witness

4-400 Whilst the authorities are not entirely consistent, they would seem to support the following propositions. In limited circumstances, the judge may comment on the failure of the defence to call a particular witness, but this should be confined to cases where the prosecution would have had no means of knowing that the witness had any relevant evidence to give until after the commencement of the defence case (*R. v. Gallagher*, 59 Cr.App.R. 239, CA), or where the witness in question could only have been called by the defence, as in the case of the solicitor of the defendant who might have been called to rebut a suggestion of recent fabrication (*R. v. Wilmot*, 89 Cr.App.R. 341, CA). But in *Gallagher* it was said that the judge must avoid leaving the jury with the impression that failure to call a particular witness is something of importance when there may be a valid reason for not calling him; and in *Wilmot*, it was said that such comment should only be made where there was a strong case for alleging recent fabrication. Furthermore, the danger that comment by the judge about "failure" of the defence to call a particular person as a witness will detract from what is said about the burden of proof should be borne in mind: see *R. v. Wright* [2000] Crim.L.R. 510, CA.

The authorities were reviewed in *R. v. Khan (Shakeel)* [2001] Crim.L.R. 673, CA. **4–401**
Apart from *Gallagher* and *Wilmot*, these included *R. v. Bryant and Dickson*, 31 Cr.App.R. 146, CCA (failure to call a particular witness may be a matter for the jury to take into account), and *R. v. Wheeler*, 52 Cr.App.R. 28, CA (there should be no comment). Having acknowledged the inconsistencies, the court reached no firm conclusion, but made certain general observations. A universal requirement to direct the jury not to speculate about the absence of a particular witness might, as between prosecution and defence, work unfairness; whereas a lack of any direction may be to invite speculation and thereby to work injustice because there may be a good reason, but one which it would be unfair to disclose to the jury, why the witness has not been called; and there may be an issue as between the parties as to whether a witness was equally available to both, and a judge cannot be expected to try such issue before deciding whether it is appropriate to make any comment. Much, therefore, will depend on the judge's sense of fairness in the particular situation, but the dangers of adverse comments and of failing to warn a jury not to speculate will usually be the paramount consideration; the case for permitting comment on the failure to call an available and obviously relevant witness may, however, be stronger now that it is permissible to comment on the defendant's own failure to mention facts relied on in his defence or to give evidence; and a complete embargo on comment would encourage the dishonest naming of persons as potential witnesses where there is no intention to call them; submissions should be invited from counsel before any adverse comment is made.

See also *R. v. G. (R.)* [2003] Crim.L.R. 43, CA, where criticisms of a comment on the failure of the defence to call a witness were held to have been justified in that (i) either side could have called the relevant person, (ii) the jury might have been given the impression that the absence of evidence from that person was something that could be held against the defendant, and (iii) the matter had not been discussed with counsel.

As to questions from the jury on this topic, see *post*, § 4–432.

(6) On a defendant's lies and/or an untrue alibi

In *R. v. Goodway*, 98 Cr.App.R. 11, CA, it was held that whenever lies are relied on **4–402**
by the prosecution, or might be used by the jury, to support evidence of guilt as opposed to merely reflecting on the defendant's credibility, a judge should give a full direction in accordance with *R. v. Lucas (R.)* [1981] Q.B. 720, 73 Cr.App.R. 159, CA, to the effect that a lie told by a defendant can only strengthen or support evidence against that defendant if the jury are satisfied that (a) the lie was deliberate, (b) it relates to a material issue, and (c) there is no innocent explanation for it. The jury should be reminded that people sometimes lie, for example, in an attempt to bolster up a just cause, or out of shame, or out of a wish to conceal disgraceful behaviour. A similar direction as to false alibis should routinely be given: *R. v. Lesley* [1996] 1 Cr.App.R. 39, CA, and *R. v. Drake* [1996] Crim.L.R. 109, CA. See also *R. v. Duncan* and *R. v. Pemberton*, *post*, § 4–404.

In *R. v. Strudwick and Merry*, *ante*, § 4–301a, it was emphasised that although lies may, if told through a consciousness of guilt, support other evidence, they cannot on their own make a prosecution case.

In the light of the number of appeals on this point that followed *Goodway* (for a list, see the 1998 edition to this work), the Court of Appeal gave the following further guidance in *R. v. Burge and Pegg* [1996] 1 Cr.App.R. 163. A *Lucas* direction is not required in every case where a defendant gives evidence, even if he gives evidence on a number of matters, and the jury may conclude in relation to some matters at least that he has been telling lies. It is only required if there is a danger that they may regard that conclusion as probative of his guilt of the offence which they are considering. How far a direction is necessary will depend on the circumstances. The direction will usually be required (a) where the defence has raised an alibi; or (b) where the judge considers it desirable or necessary to suggest that the jury should look for support or corroboration of one piece of evidence from other evidence in the case, and amongst that evidence draws attention to lies told, or allegedly told, by the defendant; or (c) where the prosecution seek to show that something said, either in or out of court, in relation to a separate or distinct issue was a lie, and to rely on that lie as evidence of guilt in relation to the charge which is sought to be proved; or (d) where, although the prosecution have not adopted the approach in (c) above, the judge reasonably envisages that there is a real danger that the jury may do so. It will often be wise for the judge, particularly in relation to the last category, to canvass the matter with counsel before speeches and summing up. The direction should, if given, so far as possible be tailored to the circumstances of the case, but it will normally be sufficient if it makes two basic points—first, that the lie must be admitted or proved beyond reasonable doubt; secondly, that the mere fact that the defendant lied is not of itself evidence of guilt since defendants may lie for innocent reasons, so that only if the jury are sure that the defendant did not lie for an innocent reason can a lie support the prosecution case.

4–402a Additional guidance was given in *R. v. Harron* [1996] Crim.L.R. 581, CA, where it was said that a *Lucas* direction is not required if there is no distinction between the issue of guilt and the issue of lies, *i.e.* in a case where evidence of witnesses for the Crown, on essential matters which must be established as true in order to justify a finding of guilt, is in direct and irreconcilable conflict with the evidence for the defence. In such a case the jury, as a matter of logic and common sense, must decide whether the witnesses for the Crown are telling the truth, and a conclusion that they are will necessarily involve a conclusion that the accused is lying. The issue as to lies will, thus, not be a matter which the jury have to take into account separately from the central issue in the case. A *Lucas* direction is only required where on some collateral matter, and due to some change in evidence or account by the defendant, there is scope for drawing an inference of guilt from the fact that the defendant had, on an earlier occasion, told lies, or, on some other matter, told lies at trial.

This point was further explained in *R. v. Middleton* [2001] Crim.L.R. 251, CA, where the court (emphasising that it was not purporting to re-formulate principle or to undermine existing authority) said that since the purpose of a *Lucas* direction is to guard against the forbidden line of reasoning that the telling of lies equals guilt, it follows that where there is no risk that the jury may follow such a line of reasoning there is no need for such a direction; in practice it is inherently unlikely that such a direction will be appropriate in relation to lies which the jury conclude that the defendant must have told them in his evidence, for the consequence of the jury rejecting the defendant's evidence is usually covered by the general directions of law on the burden and standard of proof; if a *Lucas* direction about lies told in evidence by the defendant is given it will often be circular and therefore confusing in its effect; in deciding whether such a direction is appropriate in any given case it will usually be more useful to analyse the question in the context of the individual case by examining the principles rather than by laboriously trawling through hosts of reported and unreported cases and learned commentaries (direction not required on particular facts where defence was one of alibi but where the issues of guilt and lies were so intricately related that it could fairly be said they stood or fell together).

In *R. v. Barnett* [2002] 2 Cr.App.R. 11, CA, it was held that in a case of handling stolen goods, where there was no issue of alibi, corroboration or identification, and where the prosecution were not relying on any specific lies as evidence of guilt, the judge had been correct not to give a *Lucas* direction in respect of three different accounts that the defendant had given for his possession of the stolen property, although the prosecution had relied upon the changing accounts as evidence that the defendant was trying to escape from the obvious inference that he must have realised that the goods were stolen. The court said that in almost every handling case the defendant denies knowing or believing that the relevant property was stolen, and the prosecution assert that such denial is a lie, but it would be absurd to suggest that a *Lucas* direction is required in each such case.

Where there is no basis for rejecting an alibi save by virtue of acceptance of the evidence of prosecution witnesses identifying the defendant as the perpetrator of the crime, there is no necessity to give a *Lucas* direction: *R. v. Patrick* [1999] 6 *Archbold News* 4, CA (98 03626 W5).

In *R. v. Peacock* [1998] Crim.L.R. 681, CA, it was held that where the defendant had given one alibi in an interview, but at trial had said that this alibi had been the result of a mistake and had proceeded to rely on a different alibi, a *Lucas* direction should have been given in respect of each matter alleged by the prosecution to be untrue.

As to directions about lies where the question is whether the offence committed by the defendant was murder or manslaughter on the ground of provocation, see *R. v. Richens*, 98 Cr.App.R. 43, CA, and *R. v. Taylor* [1998] Crim.L.R. 822, CA, *post*, § 19–64.

A direction under section 34 of the *CJPOA* 1994 (*post*, § 15–427) may be combined with a *Lucas* direction as to lies: *R. v. O. (A.)* [2000] Crim.L.R. 617, CA (in interview defendant denied ever having had sex with rape complainant, but at trial gave evidence that there had been consensual sex on one occasion).

Where a lie is told by another in the defendant's presence in response to a question from a police officer and is not corrected by the defendant, the jury should first be directed to consider the question as to whether, in all the circumstances, the question called for some response from the defendant, and secondly whether by his reaction the defendant adopted the answer made: *R. v. Collins* [2004] 1 W.L.R. 1705, CA.

(7) On the consequences of conviction

Judges would be wise to avoid saying anything about the possible consequences of conviction, although it does not necessarily follow that any mention thereof will be fatal to a conviction: *R. v. Peart*, *The Times*, November 12, 1992, CA (judge told jury not to trouble about the consequences of a conviction because that was a matter for him and he might well consider probation—appeal dismissed). **4–403**

See also *post*, §§ 7–67, 7–68.

H. ISSUE OF IDENTIFICATION

See generally, Chapter 14, *post*. **4–404**

Where the issue is one of identity, the judge must be careful in directing the jury on any alibi evidence because a jury which rejects an alibi might otherwise think that this fact supports the identification evidence: *R. v. Duncan*, *The Times*, July 24, 1992, CA; *R. v. Pemberton*, 99 Cr.App.R. 228, CA. As to the appropriate direction, see *ante*, § 4–402.

It is usually desirable in summing up to deal with the points telling against a correct identification together; if they are simply dealt with individually in a general narration of the evidence there is a risk of their combined force being dissipated; nor should they be belittled by reference to them as defence submissions: *R. v. Elliot* [1998] 1 *Archbold News* 2, CA (97/2718/W3).

In a case of purported voice identification, the jury should be directed in accordance with the directions for visual identifications, suitably adapted, *i.e.* the risk of mistake, the reasons why a witness may be mistaken, the fact that an honest witness may be mistaken and the strengths and weaknesses of the identification must all be spelt out: *R. v. Hersey* [1998] Crim.L.R. 281, CA.

I. CORROBORATION

(1) Common law

General rule

At common law, one witness is sufficient in all cases (with the exception of perjury) at the trial: 2 Hawk. c. 46, ss.2, 10; Fost. 233; and see *DPP v. Hester* [1973] A.C. 296, HL, *per* Lord Diplock at p. 324. **4–404a**

Development of special rules for special cases

With the development of the common law, there evolved certain categories of case **4–404b** where, by reason either of the nature of the allegation, or of the witness falling into a particular class, corroboration was said to be required. The corroboration requirement applied to the evidence of a complainant in any allegation of a sexual offence, to the evidence of an accomplice of the defendant when called by the prosecution and to the evidence of children. Reference to a "requirement" for corroboration was misleading as a judge was only obliged to warn a jury that it would be dangerous to convict on evidence coming from one of these sources if uncorroborated; he was entitled to go on to tell them that they could convict on such evidence, despite it being uncorroborated, if, having paid due heed to the warning, they were convinced about the guilt of the accused.

4–404c The law relating to corroboration became increasingly technical. The detailed rules related, *inter alia*, to the meaning of "corroboration", to who was an accomplice, to what evidence was capable of constituting corroboration, to the respective functions of judge and jury and to the nature of the direction to be given by the judge to the jury. The rules came to be criticised on a number of grounds. First, they were inflexible with an absolute obligation to give the warning if the witness came within one of the three categories; in particular cases, the warning would, on any sensible appraisal, be inappropriate. Secondly, the rules were so complex that it was widely believed that a typical corroboration direction bordered on the unintelligible to the ordinary person (*per* Lord Diplock in *Hester*, *ante*, at p. 328). Thirdly, the rules produced anomalies. An accomplice of a defendant who was tried with him and who gave evidence against him was not subject to the rule (although he was subject to a requirement to give a warning short of the full corroboration direction, *post*, § 4–404n). Fourthly, there was a significant change of perception as to the reliability of evidence given by children. Fifthly, the corroboration direction in sexual cases was seen as being particularly offensive to women.

4–404d In consequence of these criticisms, legislation has abolished any requirement for the court to give the jury a warning about convicting the accused on the uncorroborated evidence of a child, or of an accomplice of the accused or of the complainant in a sexual offence. These changes were effected in two stages; the change in relation to children was effected by the *CJA* 1988, s.34 (*post*, § 8–33), and the change in relation to the other two categories was brought about by the *CJPOA* 1994, s.32 (*post*, § 4–404j).

4–404e Apart from the three established categories where the common law required a full corroboration direction, there had developed certain other categories where the courts had held that justice demanded that the judge should give some warning as to a special need for caution. These categories were not well defined (see *post*, §§ 4–404m *et seq.*). If the case was held to come within one of these categories, the attitude of the Court of Appeal was that it was a matter for the judge to decide exactly what to say in the light of the evidence and the issues in the particular case; there was, however, no obligation on him to use the word "corroboration".

(2) Statute

Perjury

4–404f See the *Perjury Act* 1911, s.13, *post*, § 28–164.

Confessions by mentally handicapped persons

4–404g See the *PACE Act* 1984, s.77, *post*, § 15–370.

Children

4–404h See the *CJA* 1988, s.34, *post*, § 8–33.

As to the evidence of children generally, see *post*, § 8–41.

Sexual offences and accomplices

Criminal Justice and Public Order Act 1994, s.32

4–404i **32.**—(1) Any requirement whereby at a trial on indictment it is obligatory for the court to give the jury a warning about convicting the accused on the uncorroborated evidence of a person merely because that person is—

(a) an alleged accomplice of the accused, or

(b) where the offence charged is a sexual offence, the person in respect of whom it is alleged to have been committed,

is hereby abrogated.

(2) [*Part repeal of section 34(2) of* Criminal Justice Act *1988*, post, *§ 8–32.*]

(3) Any requirement that—

(a) is applicable at the summary trial of a person for an offence, and

(b) corresponds to the requirement mentioned in subsection (1) above or that mentioned in section 34(2) of the *Criminal Justice Act* 1988,

is hereby abrogated.

(4) [*Transitional.*]

Section 32 came into force on February 3, 1995. Its effect was considered in *R. v. Makanjuola*; *R. v. Easton* [1995] 2 Cr.App.R. 469, CA. Both cases involved applications for leave to appeal against convictions for indecent assault. It was argued on behalf of the applicants that the judge should in his discretion have given the full corroboration warning notwithstanding the abolition of any requirement to do so; the basis of the argument was that the underlying rationale of the common law rules could not disappear overnight. That argument was roundly dismissed by the court; any attempt to reimpose the "straitjacket" of the old common law rules was to be deprecated. It was held, however, that the judge does have a discretion to warn the jury if he thinks it necessary, but the use of the word "merely" in subsection (1) shows that Parliament did not envisage such a warning being given just because a witness complains of a sexual offence or is an alleged accomplice. **4–404j**

Lord Taylor C.J., giving the judgment of the court, said that they had been invited to give guidance as to the circumstances in which, as a matter of discretion, a judge, in summing up, ought to urge caution in regard to a particular witness and the terms in which that should be done. His Lordship continued: **4–404k**

> "The circumstances and evidence in criminal cases are infinitely variable and it is impossible to categorise how a judge should deal with them. But it is clear that to carry on giving 'discretionary' warnings generally and in the same terms as were previously obligatory would be contrary to the policy and purpose of the 1994 Act. Whether, as a matter of discretion, a judge should give any warning and if so its strength and terms must depend upon the content and manner of the witness's evidence, the circumstances of the case and the issues raised. The judge will often consider that no special warning is required at all. Where, however, the witness has been shown to be unreliable, he or she may consider it necessary to urge caution. In a more extreme case, if the witness is shown to have lied, to have made previous false complaints, or to bear the defendant some grudge, a stronger warning may be thought appropriate and the judge may suggest it would be wise to look for some supporting material before acting on the impugned witness's evidence. We stress that these observations are merely illustrative of some, not all, of the factors which judges may take into account in measuring where a witness stands in the scale of reliability and what response they should make at that level in their directions to the jury. We also stress that judges are not required to conform to any formula and this court would be slow to interfere with the exercise of discretion by a trial judge who has the advantage of assessing the manner of a witness's evidence as well as its content" (at p. 472).

The conclusions of the court were then summarised. First, section 32(1) abrogates the requirement to give a corroboration direction in respect of an alleged accomplice or a complainant of a sexual offence simply because a witness falls into one of those categories. Secondly, it is a matter for the judge's discretion what, if any warning is appropriate in respect of such a witness, as indeed in respect of any other witness in whatever type of case. **4–404l**

Thirdly, in some cases it might be appropriate for the judge to warn the jury to exercise caution before acting on the unsupported evidence of a witness. That would not be so simply because the witness was a complainant of a sexual offence or an alleged accomplice. There would need to be an evidential basis for suggesting that the evidence of the witness might be unreliable. Such a basis did not include mere suggestions in cross-examination by counsel.

Fourthly, if any question arises as to whether the judge should give a special warning, it is desirable that the question be resolved by a discussion with counsel in the jury's absence before final speeches.

Fifthly, where the judge does decide to give some warning in respect of a witness, it would be appropriate to do so as part of the review of the evidence and his comments as to how the jury should evaluate it, rather than as a set-piece legal direction.

Sixthly, where some warning is required, it is for the judge to decide the strength and terms of the warning. It does not have to be invested with the whole florid regime of the old corroboration rules.

The court said that they would be disinclined to interfere with the judge's exercise of his discretion save in a case where that exercise was *Wednesbury* unreasonable (*Associated Provincial Picture Houses v. Wednesbury Corporation* [1948] 1 K.B. 223).

(3) Practice

(a) *Introduction*

4–404m Prior to the abolition of the rules relating to the corroboration of the evidence of children, accomplices and complainants in sexual offences (*ante*), the courts had said that in certain other cases some form of warning as to a special need for caution should be given to a jury. These cases came to be known as the "analogous cases" (see *R. v. Spencer* [1987] A.C. 128, HL, *post*, § 4–404p).

In *R. v. Muncaster* [1999] Crim.L.R. 409, CA, it was held that the guidance of the Court of Appeal in *R. v. Makanjuola*; *R. v. Easton*, *ante* (that it is a matter for the judge's discretion what, if any, warning is appropriate), is relevant not just to accomplices, in the strict sense, and to complainants in sexual cases, but also to witnesses in the analogous categories; but it has no application to particular types of evidence (*e.g.* identification) where particular rules have been developed as to how a jury should be directed.

(b) *The "analogous" cases*

Co-defendants

4–404n Prior to the *CJPOA* 1994, a series of cases in the Court of Appeal considered what warning, if any, needed to be given by the judge to the jury where one defendant gave evidence incriminating a co-defendant. The first of these was *R. v. Prater* [1960] 2 Q.B. 464, 44 Cr.App.R. 83, CCA, which was not only the starting point, but also the high point in terms of any court saying that in such cases, as well as cases where the accomplice was called by the prosecution, a full corroboration warning was desirable. The subsequent decisions evidenced a retreat from that position. The leading case is now to be taken to be *R. v. Knowlden and Knowlden*, 77 Cr.App.R. 94, CA: in exercising his discretion as to what to say to the jury, the judge is at least expected to give a clear warning to a jury where defendants have given evidence against one another to examine the evidence of each with care because each has or may have an interest of his own to serve. This approach was confirmed in *R. v. Cheema*, 98 Cr.App.R. 195, in which the Court of Appeal reviewed the authorities at length; and in *R. v. Jones (Wayne) and Jenkins* [2004] 1 Cr.App.R. 5, CA, which treated *R. v. Burrows* [2000] Crim.L.R. 48, CA (in which each of two defendants blamed the other for having put cocaine inside a capsule within an Easter egg, and it was held that a warning in respect of each defendant would have been inappropriate) as restricted to its own particular facts. The danger which the judge should have in mind, when tailoring the warning as to how to regard the evidence of each defendant in as much as it incriminated the other to the circumstances of the particular case, is that of devaluing the evidence of both defendants in the eyes of the jury: *R. v. Petkar and Farquhar* [2004] 1 Cr.App.R. 22, CA.

Witnesses tainted by improper motive

4–404o In *R. v. Beck*, 74 Cr.App.R. 221, Ackner L.J., giving the judgment of the Court of Appeal, referred to "the obligation upon a judge to advise a jury to proceed with caution where there is material to suggest that a witness's evidence may be tainted by an improper motive ... the strength of that advice" varying according to the facts of the case (at p. 228). What is not clear is whether this obligation extended to a witness with an improper motive other than one deriving from the witness's own involvement in the offence being tried, or some related offence, and his desire to avoid liability, or the incrimination of himself or others he might naturally wish to protect, or to shift the blame elsewhere. Did it extend to motives such as jealousy, spite, levelling of an old score, hope of financial advantage? It seems the answer is probably "yes"; persons falling into such a category were referred to by the court in rejecting an argument that a full corroboration warning was necessary wherever a witness gave evidence who had a substantial interest to serve. Thus, they were clearly present to the court's mind and there is nothing in the language used by the court to restrict it to persons whose motive is tied to the particular offence. This part of the judgment of Ackner L.J. in *Beck* was quoted with apparent approval by the House of Lords in *R. v. Spencer* [1987] A.C. 128 at 140.

R. v. Beck was applied in *R. v. Witts and Witts* [1991] Crim.L.R. 562, CA. The prosecution called as witnesses persons who had attacked one of the defendants in revenge for the assault which was the subject of the count against the defendants. Those witnesses were to be sentenced for that later attack, which was the subject of a separate count in the same indictment, at the end of the trial. No warning was given to treat their evidence with caution. This was said by the court to be a classic instance of the sort of case where a warning ought to have been given as the witnesses, though not accomplices, had a strong incentive to give false evidence against the defendants.

In *Benedetto v. R.*; *Labrador v. R.* [2003] 1 W.L.R. 1545, PC, it was held that whilst it was undesirable to restrict the circumstances in which a judge might, as a matter of discretion, urge caution in regard to a particular witness in summing up to a jury, and the terms in which any warning should be given if the judge thought that that was appropriate, by laying down rules as to when warnings of that kind must be given, evidence of an untried prisoner claiming that a fellow prisoner had confessed to him that he was guilty of the crime for which he was then being held in custody, raised an acute problem which would always call for special attention in view of the danger that it might lead to a miscarriage of justice; in the case of a cell confession, the danger was not that of an honest mistake of a sincere and convincing witness giving identification evidence, but that the evidence of a prison informer was inherently unreliable in view of the personal advantage which such witness thought he might obtain by providing information to the authorities; witnesses who fall into that category tended to have no interest whatsoever in the proper course of justice; they would almost always have strong reasons of self-interest for ingratiating themselves with those who might be in a position to reward them for volunteering confession evidence; the prisoner against whom that evidence was given was at a disadvantage, in that he was afforded none of the usual protections against the inaccurate recording or invention of words used by him when interviewed by the police; and it might be difficult for him to obtain all the information needed to expose fully the informer's bad character; a judge must always be alert to the possibility that such evidence was tainted by an improper motive and the possibility that that might be so had to be regarded with particular care where a prisoner who had yet to be tried gave evidence that the other prisoner confessed to the very crime for which he was being held in custody; where there were indications that the evidence might be tainted by an improper motive, the judge should draw the attention of the jury to those indications and their possible significance, and he should then advise the jury to be cautious before acting on the evidence; thus, there were two steps for the judge to follow and they were equally important. Not every case requires such a warning, however: see *R. v. Stone* [2005] Crim.L.R. 569, CA, where the confession would not have been easy to invent, and there had been neither any evidence nor any suggestion of a motive to lie.

See also *Chan Wei-keung v. R.* [1995] 2 Cr.App.R. 194, PC (where prosecution witness has potential ulterior motives, as the hope of obtaining a discount in proceedings against himself, important that the potential fallibility and ulterior motives should be put squarely before the jury); and *R. v. Cairns, Zaidi and Chaudhary, post*, § 4–404q.

Witnesses of bad character

In *R. v. Spencer, ante*, it was held that in a case where the evidence for the Crown is **4–404p** solely that of a witness who is not in one of the accepted categories of suspect witnesses, but who by reason of his particular mental condition and criminal connection, fulfils analogous criteria, the judge must make the jury fully aware of the dangers of convicting on such evidence, there being no obligation to use either the word "danger" or the word "dangerous". In the Court of Appeal in *Spencer* ([1985] Q.B. 771), the court referred (at p. 784) to the fact that judges always warn juries about the evidence of witnesses of "admittedly bad character", "in whatever terms they think appropriate to the case". In the House of Lords, Lord Hailsham said (at 134):

> "The other point on which I would wish to comment is the Court of Appeal's view on my reference in *R. v. Kilbourne* [1973] A.C. 729, 740 when I added witnesses 'of admittedly bad character' to the number of cases where a warning of some kind was required as to the danger of convicting without corroboration. I was, of course, using the phrase in the technical sense of witnesses who have been shown to be not of a character to make them worthy to be believed on their oath. In this connexion I must say that even if there were not authority to support this view (and I believe there is plenty), I would regard it as a matter of sheer common sense that if a judge did not warn the jury of the possible danger of convicting an innocent man if they convicted solely on the disputed but uncorroborated testimony of such a person, his failure to do so would ... make a verdict unsafe and unsatisfactory in the extreme."

(c) *Form of warning*

4–404q It is clear from *Makanjuola*, *ante*, § 4–404k, and *Muncaster*, *ante*, § 4–404m, and from the authorities preceding the 1994 Act in the "analogous criteria" cases, that the content of any warning given by the judge is a matter for his discretion to be decided upon by him in the light of the evidence, the issues and the nature of the particular taint upon the evidence of the impugned witness. See also *R. v. L.* [1999] Crim.L.R. 489, CA, to the same effect. Where a judge does choose to give a warning of some description, he may wish to bear in mind that in what is now the best established category of case where a warning of some description is required (*viz.* identification cases), it was said (*R. v. Turnbull* [1977] Q.B. 224, 63 Cr.App.R. 132, CA, *post*, § 14–2) that the judge should warn the jury of "the special need for caution" before acting on the disputed evidence, and he should explain the reason for the need for the warning. In delivering the judgment of the Court of Appeal in *R. v. Spencer* [1985] Q.B. 771, May L.J. said:

> "Indeed we also agree that the attitude of our courts over recent years has in fact been to refuse to increase the number of categories in which the full warning, with all the complications it involves, has to be given, but to emphasise the duty of a trial judge in appropriate cases to warn the jury of a 'special need for caution' in relation to the evidence of certain witnesses, in terms appropriate to the particular case under consideration: see *R. v. Allen* [1965] 2 Q.B. 295; *R. v. Long* (1973) 57 Cr.App.R. 871 and *R. v. Turnbull* ..." (at p. 784).

This formula appears to have received the stamp of Parliamentary approval in section 77 of the *PACE Act* 1984 (confessions by mentally handicapped persons, *post*, § 15–370), which requires the judge to warn the jury that there is "special need for caution" before convicting an accused person who is mentally handicapped on a confession made in the absence of an independent person when the confession forms the whole, or substantially the whole, of the case against him. In addition, section 77 requires the judge to explain the reason for the special need for caution.

It should be emphasised that it is not being suggested that this form of words should be adopted formulaically wherever some warning is thought appropriate. That would be directly contrary to the opinion of the court in *Makanjuola* and in *Muncaster*. It is put forward simply as a possible starting point which seems to have the approval of Parliament. That the judge should give some explanation as to the reason for any warning he gives is advanced with more confidence; but the extent of the obligation will vary. As Lord Ackner said in delivering the principal speech in the House of Lords in *R. v. Spencer* [1987] A.C. 128 at 141–142, in some cases the potential unreliability of the sole or principal witness for the prosecution is obvious for all to see, whereas in others the potential unreliability of the witness may well not be apparent to the jury. The extent of the obligation to explain the need for caution will vary according to the extent to which the danger of relying on a particular witness is apparent.

Where the prosecution case depended in part on the evidence of serving prisoners, there was no basis for saying that the conviction was unsafe where the judge had warned the jury to exercise caution before acting on the unsupported evidence of any of them, and it must have been obvious to the jury that they were witnesses to be treated with caution; *R. v. Spencer* (*ante*) does not require any particular form of warning in relation to witnesses of bad character and there is no inconsistency between that case and the cases of *Makanjoula* and *Muncaster* (*ante*): *R. v. Causley* [1999] Crim.L.R. 572, CA.

In *R. v. Cairns, Zaidi and Chaudhary* [2003] 1 Cr.App.R. 38, CA, where a witness had been called by the prosecution although part of his evidence was not regarded by them as reliable, and where the witness had been a party to the crime alleged, was of bad character and an admitted liar in the past, the judge had correctly given a strong warning as to his reliability and potential motives, such warning being carefully tailored to the circumstances of the case, as suggested in *Makanjuola*, *ante*.

Where a judge gives some form of corroboration warning it is incumbent on him to identify what evidence is capable of lending support to the evidence in need of support, and, if there is no such evidence, to direct the jury to that effect: *R. v. B. (M.T.)* [2000] Crim.L.R. 181, CA. See further, *post*, § 4–404r.

(d) *Supporting evidence*

The old rules as to what evidence was capable of constituting corroboration were extremely complex; what constitutes supporting evidence for the purposes of any warning that the judge may in his discretion choose to give is subject to no technical rules; all that is required of it is that it makes the tribunal of fact sure that the suspect evidence is in fact accurate (see that part of the judgment of Lord Widgery C.J. in *R. v. Turnbull* quoted at § 14–2, *post*). **4–404r**

Such evidence will still be adduced, and the judge will still have to direct the jury as to its significance. As to this, see *R. v. Islam* [1999] 1 Cr.App.R. 22, CA, in which it was confirmed that section 32 of the 1994 Act (*ante*, § 4–404j) did not affect the legal effect of recent complaint evidence: such evidence could never constitute corroboration (in the technical sense) because it did not come from an independent source, and it remained the case that it cannot constitute independent confirmation of the complainant's testimony; and the jury should be directed as to its limited significance. See also *R. v. Churchill* [1999] Crim.L.R. 664, CA. As to such evidence generally, see *post*, §§ 8–105, 11–34, 11–40; as to the possibility that such evidence will be held to carry enhanced significance under the changes effected by the *CJA* 2003, see *post*, § 20–12; as to lies told by the accused, see *ante*, § 4–402; as to evidence of a complainant's distress, see *post*, § 20–32.

J. Evidential Value of Defendant's Statements and Evidence

(1) As against a co-defendant

See generally, *post*, §§ 15–388 *et seq.* **4–405**

For the appropriate direction where a defendant has given evidence implicating a co-defendant, see *ante*, § 4–404m.

Where an out-of-court statement or confession of one defendant incriminates one or more co-defendants, it will often be sensible for the judge to adopt the practice of advising the jury to consider the case of the defendant who is alleged to have made that statement or confession after considering the case of the co-defendants; this will minimise the risk of inappropriate use of material that is inadmissible against the co-defendants: *R. v. Hickey and Robinson* [1997] 8 *Archbold News* 3, CA.

(2) Evidential value of self-serving elements in statement made to the police

See *post*, §§ 15–400 *et seq.* **4–405a**

K. Defendant's Character

(1) Good character

It is up to defence counsel and the defendant to ensure that the judge is aware that **4–406** the defendant is relying on his good character; and, since the fact that a defendant has no previous convictions does not inevitably mean that he is of good character, it is good practice for the judge, where there is any doubt as to the position, to raise the matter with counsel: *Gilbert v. The Queen (Practice Note)* [2006] 1 W.L.R. 2108, PC. In *R. v. Vye*; *R. v. Wise*; *R. v. Stephenson*, 97 Cr.App.R. 134, the Court of Appeal issued fresh guidelines as to the directions that should be given where reliance is being placed on the defendant's good character.

(a) Where a defendant has given evidence a direction should be given as to the relevance of his good character to his credibility.

(b) Where a defendant does not give evidence at his trial but relies on exculpatory statements or answers given by him to the police or others, the judge should direct the jury to have regard to the defendant's good character when considering the credibility of those statements. Where the jury is considering the truthfulness of any such statements it would be logical for them to take good character into account, just as they would in regard to a defendant's evidence. The judge will be entitled, however, to make observations about the way the jury should approach such exculpatory statements in contrast to evidence given on oath.

(c) If a defendant of good character has neither given evidence nor made pre-trial answers or statements, no issue as to his credibility arises and no direction relating his good character to such issue is required.

4–407 (d) A direction as to the relevance of a defendant's good character to the likelihood of his having committed the offence charged should be given, whether or not he has testified or made pre-trial answers or statements. It must be for the trial judge in each case to decide how he tailors his direction to the particular circumstances. For example, he will probably wish to indicate that good character cannot amount to a defence, and in cases of a long-serving employee he might wish to emphasise the direction as to the relevance of good character to propensity to commit crime more than he would in the average case.

(e) A defendant who is of good character is entitled to have the judge direct the jury as to its relevance even if he is jointly tried with a defendant of bad character (applied in *R. v. Houlden*, 99 Cr.App.R. 244, CA). The judge will have to decide what, if anything, to say about the character of the defendant who is not of good character. He might think it best to grasp the nettle, and tell the jury that they have to try the case on the evidence; there having been no evidence about the character of the particular defendant, they must not speculate and must not take the absence of any information as to his character as any evidence against him. On the other hand a judge might think it best to say nothing about the absence of evidence as to character. What course he takes must depend on the circumstances of the individual case, for example, how great an issue has been made of character during the trial. The possibility of separate trials is a matter for the judge and is to be decided in accordance with well established principles. Generally, those jointly indicted should be jointly tried. (Where the co-defendant's bad character is in evidence, a full direction on its significance must be given: *R. v. Cain*, 99 Cr.App.R. 208, CA. As to the nature of the direction, see *post*, § 4–410.)

The court added that provided a judge indicates to a jury the two respects in which good character might be relevant, in accordance with the guidelines set out above, it will be slow to criticise any qualifying remarks he might make based on the facts of an individual case.

4–408 These guidelines were approved by the House of Lords in *R. v. Aziz* [1996] 1 A.C. 41, after explaining that the references to out of court statements relate only to mixed statements (*i.e.* those that contain an admission of fact which is capable of adding some degree of weight to the prosecution case on an issue relevant to guilt: *R. v. Garrod* [1997] Crim.L.R. 445, CA) and not to statements that are wholly exculpatory. See also *post*, §§ 15–400 *et seq.*

Their Lordships in *Aziz* went on to address the question whether a defendant who has no previous convictions but has admitted other criminal behaviour is entitled to the benefit of directions as to good character in accordance with the guidelines. *Held*, that prima facie the directions are required in such a case, although the judge has a residual discretion to add words of qualification concerning other proved or possible criminal conduct of the defendant that has emerged during the trial, so as to place a fair and balanced picture before the jury. Furthermore, in a limited class of case where the defendant's claim to good character, other than in respect of a lack of previous convictions, is so spurious that it would make no sense to give the general character direction, the judge may dispense with the direction in its entirety. To similar effect, see *R. v. Durbin* [1995] 2 Cr.App.R. 84, CA; *R. v. Gray* [2004] 2 Cr.App.R. 30, CA; and *Shaw v. R.* [2001] 1 W.L.R. 1519, PC.

Where, in the case of a defendant without previous convictions, evidence of bad character is admitted under the *CJA* 2003, s.101 (*post*, § 13–25), as being relevant to both propensity and credibility, it would make no sense to give a good character direction, the effect of which would be the exact opposite of the direction on bad character: *R. v. Doncaster*, 172 J.P. 202, CA. For the court's suggestion as to how a jury should be directed in such a case, see *post*, § 13–68.

Once a person has pleaded guilty to an offence, he ceases to be a person of good **4–409** character and the full character direction is inappropriate unless the offence to which he has pleaded guilty is an alternative to that on which he is being tried and the facts are such that if his conviction on the greater offence is secured then his guilty plea on the lesser offence would be vacated so that there is no conviction: *R. v. Teasdale*, 99 Cr.App.R. 80, CA; *R. v. Challenger* [1994] Crim.L.R. 202, CA. In the latter case, the court said that where there had been a plea of guilty (other than to a lesser alternative) there might be circumstances where some form of direction as to character was required. For example, the defence might give evidence of the plea and argue that the fact that the defendant had pleaded guilty to the one offence and was previously of good character supported his credibility. The judge, in putting the defence to the jury, should remind them of that argument if he thought it proper to do so.

It is submitted that care should be taken against reading too much into the requirement in *R. v. Teasdale* that a full direction be given where the plea of guilty was to a lesser alternative offence. First, the court seems to have acknowledged that the direction would have had to be tailored to take account of the plea of guilty (see p. 82). Secondly, if the plea of guilty is to a lesser offence which is a step on the way to proving the greater offence (*e.g.* wounding/wounding with intent, theft/robbery), and the plea is not accepted, it would be open to the prosecution to prove the plea should the defence be conducted along the lines that the defendant was not guilty of anything: see *R. v. Hazeltine* [1967] 2 Q.B. 857, 51 Cr.App.R. 351, CA. If, as is more likely, the defence is conducted on the simple basis that the defendant is guilty of the lesser offence but not of the greater, a "good character" direction without any tailoring at all would seem to be entirely inappropriate.

A person of previous good character who admits having lied to the police is entitled to a full character direction: *R. v. Kabariti*, 92 Cr.App.R. 362, CA, cited, with apparent approval, in *R. v. Vye*; *R. v. Wise*; *R. v. Stephenson*, *ante*.

As to when a person whose convictions are "spent" may be presented as a person of good character, see *R. v. Nye*, 75 Cr.App.R. 247, CA, and *R. v. M. (Ian)* [1999] 6 *Archbold News* 3, CA (98 07990 Y4), *post*, § 13–77.

Where a defendant has no previous convictions but has been formally cautioned on one or more occasions, a judge is entitled to decline to give the "propensity" limb of the standard good character direction: *R. v. Martin (David Paul)* [2000] 2 Cr.App.R. 42, CA.

Where counsel for the prosecution agreed not to seek to adduce evidence which might have been admissible under the similar fact principle unless the defendant's evidence was such as to justify its admission in rebuttal, and no such application was in fact made, a defendant with no previous convictions was entitled to a full good character direction: *R. v. Bowen* [1999] 8 *Archbold News* 3, CA.

Where a judge regards the defendant's previous convictions, disclosed in evidence, as lacking in significance to the extent that he should be regarded as a man of good character, the judge should give a full character direction: *R. v. Heath*, *The Times*,

February 10, 1994, CA. It is a matter for the discretion of the judge whether to direct the jury to treat as irrelevant the previous conviction(s) of a defendant whose character is not absolutely good: *R. v. H.* [1994] Crim.L.R. 205, CA (seemingly approved in *R. v. Aziz, ante*); where, however, the conviction(s) could only be regarded as irrelevant or of no significance in relation to the offence charged, the judge's discretion ought to be exercised in favour of treating the defendant as of good character: *R. v. Gray* [2004] 2 Cr.App.R. 30, CA.

Where, on a charge of possession of cannabis with intent to supply, the issue was as to the intent, where evidence had been given that the defendant had twice been cautioned and twice been convicted (on guilty pleas) for possession of cannabis, and where his credibility was very much in issue, it had been insufficient for the judge to direct the jury not to hold those matters against him; having decided that the defendant was, for the purposes of the trial, of good character, the judge should have conferred on him the benefit of a good character direction; whilst there is, in such a situation, a discretion as to how full the direction needs to be, here the appellant had been entitled at least to a direction to the effect that his credibility was intact and undamaged by the convictions and cautions, and that the jury should take that into account in assessing the credibility of his evidence: *R. v. Payton* (2006) 150 S.J. 741, CA.

Where a judge directed a jury that they could take into account in favour of an accused when considering his propensity to commit the offence with which he was charged (murder) the fact that he had but one minor conviction, he was under no obligation to direct them further that they were precluded from taking it into account against the accused on that issue: *R. v. Aziz and Pereira* [1999] 3 *Archbold News* 2, CA (97 07499 X5).

In *R. v. Fulcher* [1995] 2 Cr.App.R. 251, it was accepted by the Court of Appeal that a proper direction as to character has some value, and is therefore capable of having some effect, in every case in which it is appropriate for such a direction to be given. See also *R. v. Kamar*, *The Times*, May 14, 1999, CA, and *R. v. M. (Ian)*, *ante*. A failure to give the credibility limb of the standard good character direction is of particular significance in a matter where the defendant carries the burden of proof: *R. v. Soukala-Cacace*, unreported, October 18, 1999 CA.

It is a misdirection to link the standard good character direction with a comment that might be thought to suggest that good character is of less significance to propensity where the allegation is that the offence (of violence) was "spontaneous", rather than planned: *R. v. Fitton* [2001] 3 *Archbold News* 2, CA.

If the issue of good character is not raised by the defence, whether by calling evidence or by putting questions to witnesses for the prosecution, it is no part of the judge's duty to raise it: *Thompson v. R.* [1998] A.C. 811, PC; *Barrow v. The State* [1998] A.C. 846, PC.

A good character direction should not take the form of rhetorical questions, even if posed in a form suggestive of an answer favourable to the defendant; a defendant is entitled to an affirmative direction to the effect that his good character is something that should be taken into account: *R. v. Lloyd* [2000] 2 Cr.App.R. 355, CA.

(2) Bad character

4–410 See *post*, Chapter 13, and, in particular, §§ 13–68, 13–72a.

L. DIRECTION TO CONVICT

4–411 There are no circumstances in which a judge is entitled to direct a jury to return a verdict of guilty: *R. v. Wang* [2005] 1 W.L.R. 661, HL, rejecting for these purposes the distinction drawn by the Court of Appeal between cases in which a burden lies on the defence and those in which the burden lies solely on the Crown, and disapproving *R. v. Hill*; *R. v. Hall*, 89 Cr.App.R. 74 (*post*, § 23–49). *Wang* was followed by the Supreme Court of Canada in *R. v. Krieger* [2006] 2 S.C.R. 501 (juries not entitled as a matter of right to refuse to apply the law, but have the power to do so when their consciences permit of no other course). Where, as a matter of law, there is no evidence to raise an issue in relation to which there is an evidential burden on the defendant, a judge may withdraw that issue from the jury, but even so should not direct them to convict: *R. v. Kelleher* (2003) 147 S.J. 1395, CA, approved in *Wang*. Where, however, the jury were nonetheless left to make a decision of their own, the fact that the judge erred in directing them to convict may not render a conviction unsafe: *Kelleher*, *ante*, which was distinguished but approved in *R. v. Caley-Knowles*; *R. v. Jones (Iorwerth)* [2007] 1 Cr.App.R. 13, CA (where the juries were given no opportunity to retire and consider the matter for themselves). For a more robust approach, see *R. v. Krieger*, *ante* (made no difference that the jury had been allowed to retire where it was clear that they were being directed to convict).

Where there has been a change of plea from not guilty to guilty to a count on the indictment and that has occurred in the presence of the jury, the correct and usual practice is for the judge to invite someone to act as foreman, explain what has happened, say that what they have listened to may seem to them to be the strongest possible evidence of guilt, invite consultation without retirement and then to take a verdict, without a direction to convict (*R. v. Kelleher*, *ante*). **4–412**

If the judge takes the view that the defendant has, in the course of his evidence, admitted his guilt, then he may give the defendant an opportunity, in the absence of the jury, to change his plea, but if he maintains his plea, the defendant is entitled to the verdict of a jury, even though in the view of the judge an acquittal would be perverse: *R. v. Gent*, 89 Cr.App.R. 247, CA. **4–413**

M. DIRECTION AS TO UNANIMITY

Practice Direction (Criminal Proceedings: Consolidation), para. IV.46.1 [2002] 1 W.L.R. 2870

Majority verdicts

IV.46.1 It is important that all those trying indictable offences should so far as possible adopt a uniform practice when complying with section 17 of the *Juries Act* 1974, both in directing the jury in summing-up and also in receiving the verdict or giving further directions after retirement. So far as the summing-up is concerned, it is inadvisable for the judge and indeed for advocates, to attempt an explanation of the section for fear that the jury will be confused. Before the jury retire, however, the judge should direct the jury in some such words as the following: **4–414**

"As you may know, the law permits me in certain circumstances to accept a verdict which is not the verdict of you all. Those circumstances have not as yet arisen so that when you retire I must ask you to reach a verdict upon which each one of you is agreed. Should, however, the time come when it is possible for me to accept a majority verdict, I will give you a further direction."

IV.46.2–IV.46.8 [See *post*, § 4–434.]

It is undesirable to specify to the jury how long it is likely to be before a majority direction will be given: *R. v. Thomas (I.J.)*, *The Times*, August 4, 1983, CA; *R. v. Guthrie*, *post*, § 4–445.

As to the "majority direction" and the taking of verdicts, see *post*, §§ 4–433 *et seq*. As to the consequences of non-direction, see *post*, § 7–60.

The direction to the jury should follow with particularity the practice direction: *R. v. Georgiou*, 53 Cr.App.R. 428, CA; see too *R. v. Kalinski*, 51 Cr.App.R. 343, CA (omission to direct jury that verdict must be unanimous does not constitute a non-direction).

N. DIRECTION CONCERNING NECESSARY "GIVE AND TAKE"

In *R. v. Watson* [1988] Q.B. 690, 87 Cr.App.R. 1, CA, the court said that it is a matter for the judge's discretion as to whether he gives the following direction at all and if so at what stage. There will usually be no need to do so. Individual variations which alter the sense of the direction are often dangerous and should if possible be avoided. Where the words are thought to be necessary or desirable they are probably best included as part of the summing up, or given or repeated after the jury have had time to consider any majority direction. **4–415**

"Each of you has taken an oath to return a true verdict according to the evidence. No one must be false to that oath, but you have a duty not only as individuals but collectively. That is the strength of the jury system. Each of you takes into the jury box with you your individual experience and wisdom. Your task is to pool that experience and wisdom. You do that by giving your views and listening to the views of the others. There must necessarily be discussion, argument and give and take within the scope of your oath. That is the way in which agreement is reached. If unhappily, [*10 of*] you cannot reach agreement you must say so."

After the jurors' retirement, a "*Watson*" direction should not be given before it becomes possible to give a majority verdict direction and such a direction has in fact been given: *R. v. Atlan* [2005] Crim.L.R. 62, CA. It should never be combined with the majority direction: *R. v. Buono*, 95 Cr.App.R. 338, CA. Moreover, judges should confine themselves to the precise wording set out in *Watson* and not add anything to it: *ibid.*; nor should any part be omitted (particularly the reference to any give and take being "within the scope of your oath"): *R. v. Atlan, ante*. A departure from that wording will not necessarily be fatal to any conviction that follows, but the danger in not following it is that words may be used that can be construed as imposing upon the jury improper pressure to reach a verdict, which may render any conviction unsafe: *R. v. Morgan* [1997] Crim.L.R. 593, CA.

As to the practice to be followed where the judge receives a note from the jury indicating possible deadlock, see *post*, § 4–438.

O. RECOMMENDATION TO MERCY

4–416 It is undesirable that a judge in his summing up should make any reference to the right of the jury to add a recommendation of mercy to their verdict: *R. v. Black*, 48 Cr.App.R. 52, CCA. See also *R. v. Sahota, post*, § 4–432.

XVIII. RETIREMENT OF JURY UNTIL VERDICT

A. NO FURTHER EVIDENCE AFTER ENCLOSURE

4–417 The general principle was summed up as follows by Lord Widgery C.J. in *R. v. Davis*, 62 Cr.App.R. 194, CA:

"... The jury may not when they have once retired to consider their verdict be given any additional evidence, any additional matter or material to assist them. They can come back and ask the judge to repeat for their benefit evidence which has been given, but they cannot come back and ask for anything new and the judge must not allow them to have anything new" (at p. 201).

4–418 The objection to admitting further evidence is not confined to the calling or recalling of witnesses (as to which see *R. v. Owen* [1952] 2 Q.B. 362, 36 Cr.App.R. 16, CCA, and *R. v. Wilson*, 41 Cr.App.R. 226, CCA). *R. v. Davis, ante*, concerned the provision to the jury of prosecution witness statements which had not been exhibited. In *R. v. Gearing*, 50 Cr.App.R. 18, CCA, the jury stated they would like to see a co-defendant who had pleaded guilty. The co-defendant was thereupon brought into the dock: the conviction was quashed. In *R. v. Corless*, 56 Cr.App.R. 341, CA, the jury said that they would like further information on the distance between various points. Defence counsel made a statement which was treated as an admission under section 10(1) of the *CJA* 1967: the conviction was quashed. In *R. v. Lawrence*, 52 Cr.App.R. 163, CA, the jury asked to see a vehicle which had been referred to during the evidence and were allowed to inspect a Vauxhall Viva on the basis that this would not constitute the introduction of fresh evidence but a mere inspection of the *locus in quo*. No evidence in relation to the identity of the vehicle inspected was given: the conviction was quashed. *Cf. R. v. Nixon*, 52 Cr.App.R. 218, CA, where a car was shown to the jury in similar circumstances; the appeal was dismissed. The inspection was suggested by defence counsel in his closing speech and took place at the stage it did with his express consent. Identification of the vehicle presented no difficulty since the index number was referred to in the indictment.

4–419 In *R. v. Devichand* [1991] Crim.L.R. 446, CA, the jury asked to see some tins of paint that were exhibits in the case. It was then noticed for the first time that the price labels on them were potentially inconsistent with the defence case. The judge directed the jury to ignore the labels. The conviction was quashed because it was possible that the jury would not have been able to put out of their minds the new information which had emerged at a time when it could not be dealt with by the defence. However, the discharge of a jury is not inevitable where, after their retirement, they discover that an exhibit is not what it is supposed to be: *R. v. Abrar*, *The Times*, May 26, 2000, CA (item exhibited as remains of a landing card was in fact remains of two such cards; it was not (strictly) new evidence introduced after retirement; it was not inconsistent with the defence case, and the judge had dealt with the matter appropriately by a careful direction: conviction upheld). See also *R. v. Haque* [2005] 9 *Archbold News* 2, CA (no prejudice to the defendant when, after the summing up, a material detail was noticed in a video recording which was then replayed to the jury at their request, since it did not alter the nature of his defence; nor did it thereby become fresh evidence).

As to the inadvertent provision to the jury of an item which has not been exhibited, see *R. v. Kaul* [1998] Crim.L.R. 135, CA (item relevant, but inconsistent with, or unexplained by, defence case—conviction quashed), and *R. v. Gilder* [1997] Crim.L.R. 668, CA (item in fact innocuous but could have been thought significant—conviction quashed).

Where the jury ask for exhibits, the request should be dealt with in open court and counsel should be given the opportunity to ensure, as per their duty, that the exhibits in question are ones that might properly be seen by the jury. Where such a request is dealt with informally, and the jury see documents that they should not see, the only proper course is to discharge them and order a retrial: *R. v. Ellis and Ellis*, *The Times*, June 13, 1991, CA. See also *R. v. Callan*, 98 Cr.App.R. 467, CA, and *ante*, § 4–260.

Equipment

It is impermissible to give the jury equipment with which to conduct their own experiments in their room: *R. v. Maggs*, 91 Cr.App.R. 243 at 245, CA, explaining *R. v. Stewart and Sappleton*, 89 Cr.App.R. 273, CA (jury asking for scales with which to weigh drugs; judge acceding to request: conviction quashed). See also *R. v. Thomas (H. G.)*, *The Times*, February 9, 1987, CA (judge allowed map, not adduced in evidence, to go into the jury room without counsel's knowledge: conviction quashed), and *R. v. Higgins*, *The Times*, February 16, 1989, CA (judge acceded to request for butterfly knife in order to carry out experiment in jury room: conviction quashed). **4–420**

An important qualification to this rule is that the jury are entitled to ask for equipment (such as a tape measure, ruler, or magnifying glass) which any person might normally have in his pocket when called to serve on a jury, and which would not normally raise even the possibility of carrying out experiments: *R. v. Maggs*, *ante*. There is no need for a judge when faced with such a request to ask the jury why they want the ruler or whatever: *ibid.* not following *dicta* to the contrary in *Stewart and Sappleton*, *ante*.

Once the jury have retired, is an experiment permissible in open court with all (including the defendant) present? It might be thought that this would contravene the principle summarised at § 4–417, *ante*, but an *obiter dictum* in *Higgins*, *ante*, suggests that such a practice is acceptable.

Tape-recordings

The Court of Appeal considered the question of jury entitlement to tape recordings of interviews in *R. v. Emmerson*, 92 Cr.App.R. 284. A tape recording, when produced as an exhibit in court, is evidence and there is no reason why the jury should not take it with them on retirement in the same way as any other exhibit. The court laid down four guidelines. **4–421**

(a) If all of the tape had been played in open court there was no reason why the jury should not have the tape if either side or the jury wished, as well as any transcript. It was the tape which was the evidence. However, not to waste time, the jury should be directed to the relevant sections of the tape.

(b) If only part of the tape had been played in open court, and the jury had a transcript of the whole, there was no reason why the jury should not take the whole tape.

(c) If only part had been played in open court and the jury had no transcript, the tape should be edited so that the jury did not take any evidence that had not been given.

(d) There was no advantage and some disadvantage in re-assembling the court to enable the jury to re-hear a passage of tape which they had already heard in open court. It would not serve any useful purpose and could only cause inconvenience.

As to where any replaying of the tape should take place, see, however, *R. v. Riaz*; *R. v. Burke*, 94 Cr.App.R. 339, CA (within discretion of judge, but best done in open court), and *R. v. Tonge, The Times*, April 16, 1993, CA (transcript of tape of 999 call indicated certain passages indecipherable—replaying of tape after jury retirement should usually be done in open court).

Where the prosecution had agreed to rely on a transcript of a 999 call that had been prepared by a forensic phoneticist, with certain disputed words deleted, and the tape recording of the call had not been played to the jury, the judge should not have granted a request by the jury to hear the tape after retirement. In the circumstances the jury had been permitted to speculate. The situation was analagous to that where the prosecution decide not to rely on parts of a tape recorded interview. Had it been appropriate to play the tape, it should have been done in open court: *R. v. Hagan* [1997] 1 Cr.App.R. 464, CA.

4–422 In *R. v. Riaz*; *R. v. Burke*, *ante*, it was held that, subject to any necessary editing, it is permissible to accede to a request made by a jury, after it has retired, to hear a tape recording of a police interview with the defendant that has been made an exhibit but which has not previously been played to the jury. They may wish to hear, for example, the tone of voice which has been used.

It would be prudent to warn a jury not to go behind any transcript: *R. v. Tonge*, *ante*.

Video recording of evidence of child complainant

4–423 A video recording constituting a child complainant's evidence in chief may, at the discretion of the trial judge, be replayed to the jury after they have retired to consider their verdict if the jury wish to be reminded of how, rather than what, words were said. It would be prudent, where the reason for the request is not stated or obvious, for the judge to ask whether the jury wish to be reminded of something said, which he may be able to give them from his note, or whether they wish to be reminded of how the words were said. If the video is replayed, (a) the recording should be replayed in court with the judge, counsel and defendant present, (b) the judge should warn the jury that because they are hearing the complainant's evidence in chief a second time, after all the other evidence, they should guard against the risk of giving it disproportionate weight simply for that reason and should bear well in mind the other evidence in the case, and (c) to assist in maintaining a fair balance the judge should, after the tape has been replayed, remind the jury of the cross-examination and re-examination of the complainant, whether the jury ask him to do so or not: *R. v. Rawlings*; *R. v. Broadbent* [1995] 2 Cr.App.R. 222, CA. See also *R. v. M. (J.)*, *ante*, § 4–337; and *R. v. Mullen* [2004] 2 Cr.App.R. 18, CA (same principles apply to child witness other than the complainant; how the discretion should be exercised will depend on the nature and content of the evidence; if it goes no further than as to "recent complaint" and "opportunity", then it should normally be sufficient for the judge to remind the jury of the content of the evidence without replaying it).

In *R. v. Atkinson* [1995] Crim.L.R. 490, CA, it was held to have been permissible for the jury to have seen a video recording of an interview with the child complainant that had not been adduced as the evidence of the child, it having been shown at the request of the prosecution (and despite opposition by the defence) following admissions by the child in cross-examination of some inconsistency between what she had said in interview and her evidence-in-chief, and admissions by the interviewing officer as to the asking of leading questions during the interview. The court held that if it is legitimate for the jury to know what has been said by a witness during the recorded interview, it should not be out of bounds to see the witness actually saying it, so as to see inflection, etc. Further, the judge had been entitled to comply with the request of the jury to see the recording again after their retirement, but in such cases it is important to make clear to the jury that the recording is not the evidence of the witness. As to the replaying during closing speeches of recordings that have been admitted in the context of allegations of inconsistency, rather than as evidence-in-chief, see *R. v. Eldridge and Salmon* [1999] Crim.L.R. 166, CA, *ante*, § 4–367.

Where, following their retirement, the jury asked to be provided with a statement of the evidence of a child witness whose evidence-in-chief had been given by way of video recording, the judge had been entitled to decline to replay the video, and to deal with the request by reminding them of the essential parts of the evidence of the witness and of the cross-examination in detail; failure to follow the course approved in *R. v. Rawlings; R. v. Broadbent* (*ante*) does not automatically render a conviction unsafe: *R. v. Horley* [1999] Crim.L.R. 488, CA.

Where a judge refuses a jury request for the replaying of a video recording of a child's evidence-in-chief, but instead reminds them of the evidence by reference to a transcript, it is none the less incumbent on the judge to warn the jury not to give disproportionate weight to the evidence because it is repeated after all the other evidence and to consider it in the context of all the evidence; further, the judge should remind the jury of the cross-examination, any pertinent re-examination and of any relevant part of the defence evidence: *R. v. McQuiston* [1998] 1 Cr.App.R. 139, CA.

A jury should not usually be permitted to take a transcript of the video evidence of a complainant with them when they retire to consider their verdict unless it is with the agreement of both defence and prosecution and the jury are reminded of the other evidence and of the status of the transcript: *R. v. Coshall*, *The Times*, February 17, 1995, CA; and *R. v. Morris* [1998] Crim.L.R. 416, CA. *Cf.* the practice that may be followed when the recording is first played in evidence: *R. v. Welstead*, *post*, § 8–55n.

Video surveillance films

Where the jury ask to see again an exhibited video surveillance film, the best practice is for the film to be shown in open court; where, however, the film is silent and there is no scope for the jury to misuse it, the situation is distinguishable from the cases on experimentation with equipment (*ante*, § 4–420), and from those relating to the replaying of a video recording of a child's evidence (*ante*): *R. v. Imran and Hussain* [1997] Crim.L.R. 754, CA. Further, it may be a factor to bear in mind, depending on the precise circumstances, that there are problems associated with the practice of replaying of video evidence in open court, in that the jury are unable to discuss that evidence as it is played: *R. v. Briggs* [2002] 4 *Archbold News* 3, CA. **4–423a**

B. RETIREMENT OF JURY

If the jury are unable to agree upon their verdict without retiring from their box, they withdraw to a convenient place appointed for that purpose; an officer being sworn to keep them, and to suffer none to speak to them without leave of the court, nor to speak to them himself, except only to ask them whether they are agreed upon their verdict: 2 Hale 297. In *R. v. Rankine* [1997] Crim.L.R. 757, CA, the court expressed the view that it is not unlawful for a judge to ask the jury if they wish to consider their verdict without retiring, but doubted the wisdom of such a course as any undue pressure on a jury is liable to render a conviction unsafe. **4–424**

In a serious or complex case, it is undesirable that a jury should be sent out after 3 p.m unless there are exceptional circumstances: *R. v. Birch*, *The Times*, March 27, 1992, CA. The judge should make the decision himself as to when to send the jury out: *R. v. Hawkins*, 98 Cr.App.R. 228, CA. As to the timing of the retirement of the jury, see also *ante*, § 4–265a, and *post*, § 4–445.

They may be allowed reasonable refreshment at their own expense: *Juries Act* 1974, s.15.

Juries Act 1974, s.13

Separation

4–425 **13.** If, on the trial of any person for an offence on indictment, the court thinks fit, it may at any time (whether before or after the jury have been directed to consider their verdict) permit the jury to separate.

[This section is printed as substituted by the *CJPOA* 1994, s.43(1).]

In *R. v. Oliver* [1996] 2 Cr.App.R. 514, the Court of Appeal gave guidance on the direction to be given to a jury if they are allowed to separate during consideration of their verdict. They should be told:

(a) that they must decide the case on the evidence and the arguments that they have seen and heard in court and not on anything that they may have seen or heard or may see or hear outside the court;

(b) that the evidence has been completed and that it would be wrong for any juror to seek for or receive further evidence or information of any sort about the case;

(c) that they must not talk to anyone about the case save to other members of the jury and then only when they are [all] deliberating in the jury room; and that they must not allow anyone to talk to them about the case unless that person is a juror and he or she is in the jury room deliberating about the case;

(d) that when they leave court they should try to set the case they are trying on one side until they return to court and retire to their jury room to continue the process of deliberating about their verdict or verdicts.

The judge need not use any precise form of words provided that the above matters are properly covered. It is desirable that the direction be given in full on the first dispersal of the jury and that a brief reminder be given at each subsequent dispersal. The guidance in *Oliver* was reiterated in *R. v. Hastings*, *The Times*, December 12, 2003, CA, and would be improved by the insertion of the word "all" in (c) above, since it is of the greatest importance that it is made clear to the jury (by the judge, not the usher) that they should only deliberate after the bailiffs have been sworn and when they are all together: *ibid.*

In *R. v. Sheehan*, unreported, February 2, 1996, CA (95/3256/X5), it was said that the whole purpose of the amendment of section 13 was to give the judge a complete and unfettered discretion to allow the jury to separate at any time. The old cases on the subject are, to that extent, irrelevant.

Most of the authorities referred to, *post*, were decided before the substitution of the new section 13 which permitted separation after retirement for the first time. Where possible the propositions for which they are authority have been adapted to take account of the change.

Where separation without permission does occur after retirement, the judge has a discretion to discharge the jury: see *R. v. Ketteridge*, 11 Cr.App.R. 54, CCA; *R. v. Goodson*, 60 Cr.App.R. 266, CA (separation of one juror to make telephone call went to root of trial); *R. v. Chandler*, *The Times*, April 16, 1992, CA (judge conducted investigation and determined that the integrity of the process of deliberation by the jury as a whole had not been threatened). See also *R. v. McCluskey*, 98 Cr.App.R. 216, CA (use of mobile phone to make business call).

In any such case, the normal procedure would be for the court to be reconvened, the relevant facts stated in open court so that the defendants knew what had happened, and counsel given the opportunity to ask for further clarification. It is inadequate for counsel to be told informally what is known and for the judge to take no further steps on being informed that counsel were satisfied. It is for the judge to take a decision after the court has been reconvened and the normal procedure followed: *R. v. Farooq and Ramzan*, *The Times*, May 13, 1994, CA (two telephone calls made from hotel).

It has long been recognised that an overnight rest is preferable to a continuous sitting well into an evening, when the jury might reach a verdict which they would not have reached if they had approached it with fresh minds. A decision should be taken no later than 5 p.m. A retirement into late evening after a long day's deliberation might give cause for concern: *R. v. Akano and Amure*, *The Times*, April 3, 1992, CA.

As to misconduct by jurors after retirement, see *R. v. Mirza*; *R. v. Connor and Rollock* [2004] 1 A.C. 1118, HL, *ante*, § 4–254, and *R. v. Knott*, *ante*, § 4–259.

As to the procedure to be followed if it is thought that circumstances may exist which would make it impossible for a juror or jurors to comply with their oath, see *ante*, § 4–254; and see *ante*, § 4–256, as to the situation if a suspicion of racial bias arises during the retirement. **4–426**

A juror may, by leave of the court, have medical attention during retirement: *R. v. Newton* (1849) 13 Q.B.D. 716 at 735.

No officer of the court may enter into any discussion with the jury about the case or answer questions by the jury relating thereto: see *R. v. Brandon*, 53 Cr.App.R. 466, CA. See also *ante*, § 4–260, and *post*, § 4–430.

Where an abstract or other piece of paper containing a summary of the indictment is given to the jury, care should be taken to see that it is free from any inaccuracy, miscopying or false propositions, and it should first be shown to counsel: *R. v. Comerford and Healey*, 49 Cr.App.R. 77, CCA.

As to the need to check any items that are supplied to the jury, see *ante*, § 4–419.

C. Communication between Judge and Jury and Third Parties

(1) General duty of assistance

The judge's duty to provide appropriate assistance to the jury is one which continues throughout the period of their retirement; in the exercise of that duty he is not confined to responding to requests from the jury, but is entitled to act on his own initiative; where, therefore, in a multi-handed case, which had lasted several weeks, the jury had been in retirement for eight days and it was apparent that they were working their way through the indictment systematically, the judge had been entitled to ask (in open court) if they would like to be provided with a brief summary of some of the salient features of the case in respect of the remaining defendants, and, upon the jury indicating that they would like such assistance, to provide it; the summary lacked the volume but not the balance of the original summing up, and gave the jury a helpful and accurate synopsis of the case: *R. v. Sharif*, *The Times*, June 8, 1999, CA. **4–427**

(2) Procedure for dealing with notes

In *R. v. Connor*, *The Times*, June 26, 1985, CA, the court said that if a trial judge received a note from the jury after its retirement and the note was connected with the case, counsel had to be consulted and the jury, if necessary, brought back into court. If the note was nothing to do with the case and was purely domestic, then the judge would be wise to inform defending counsel about it simply to obviate complaints. *Connor* was referred to with approval in *R. v. Gorman*, 85 Cr.App.R. 121, CA, where Lord Lane C.J. said that a communication which raised something unconnected with the trial could be dealt with without reference to counsel and without bringing the jury back into court. In almost every other case the judge should state in open court the nature and content of the communication which he had received from the jury and should, if he considered it useful so to do, seek the assistance of counsel. That assistance would normally be sought before the jury was asked to return to court. **4–427a**

His Lordship said that if the communication contained information which the jury should not have revealed, such as details of the voting figures, then so far as possible the communication should be dealt with in the normal way, save that the judge should not disclose the detailed information which the jury ought not to have revealed. The object of the procedures was: (a) to ensure that there was no suspicion of private or secret communication between the court and the jury, and (b) to enable the judge to give proper and accurate assistance to the jury on any matter of law or fact which was troubling them. The importance of following the guidance given in *Gorman* was reaffirmed in *Ramstead v. R.* [1999] 2 A.C. 92, PC.

For a suggestion that *Gorman* does not go far enough and that what is required is complete candour, see *R. v. Black, Watts and Black*, unreported, April 5, 2007, Court of Appeal of Victoria ([2007] VCSA 61).

See also *R. v. Green (B. R.)* [1992] Crim.L.R. 292, CA (note should be read out in open court, although, presumably, following *R. v. Gorman*, *ante*, any details of voting figures should not be read out), and *post*, §§ 4–431 *et seq.* **4–428**

In *R. v. Kachikwu*, 52 Cr.App.R. 538, CA, it was said that a note from the jury should be shown to counsel, as well as read out, to guard against any mis-hearing, misunderstanding, or error in transcription, of its terms.

4–429 As to the manner in which notes from the jury should be dealt with when received during the course of the trial, see *ante*, § 4–265a.

(3) Duty of jury bailiffs

4–430 Paragraph 4(29)(i) of the *Court Manual* (published by the Lord Chancellor's Office upon the establishment of the Crown Court) provides:

> "In no circumstances should the bailiff enter the jury room once he has escorted the jury there, unless he is expressly ordered by the Court to make a communication to, or inquiry of, the jury and except in special circumstances and at the express order of the Court no other persons should have any communication with the jury."

Although this direction has no statutory authority, its terms were approved in *R. v. Lamb*, 59 Cr.App.R. 196 at 198, CA, and *R. v. Dempster*, 71 Cr.App.R. 302, CA. In *Dempster*, it was held that there had been no irregularity where, in a case involving the playing of tape recordings, the jury, after retiring, were able to hear such parts of the tapes as they wished played again via a loudspeaker placed in their room. It was connected to playing apparatus which remained in court. The jury foreman was able to communicate the jury's wishes to the technician operating the apparatus, who had been sworn in as a jury bailiff, via a two-way radio. These arrangements were adopted with the consent of both sides. Counsel were at liberty to observe in the court room and could hear what the technician said, but not what the foreman said.

Once a jury has retired to consider their verdict, the jury bailiffs are strictly limited in the communication they can make with the jury. Their fundamental duty is to prevent approaches by outsiders and to preserve the integrity of the deliberative process. However, when a juror indicated to the bailiff that he and his fellow jurors were intimidated by the atmosphere in court, that bailiff did nothing improper in asking "why" and reporting the answer to the trial judge: *R. v. Brown and Slaughter*, *The Times*, October 25, 1989, CA.

See also various of the authorities cited at § 4–426, *ante*.

(4) How to reply

4–431 If it be the fact, the judge must tell the jury that no evidence on a queried point has been given and that they must take it that there is no evidence on the point; but if the question relates to a point on which evidence has been given, it is proper for the judge to remind the jury of such evidence and to instruct them accordingly: *R. v. Owen* [1952] 2 Q.B. 362, 36 Cr.App.R. 16, CCA.

In *Berry v. R.* [1992] 2 A.C. 364, PC, the jury indicated that they had a problem. In giving the judgment of the Board, Lord Lowry stated that the jury are entitled at any stage to the judge's help on the facts as well as on the law. To withhold that assistance constitutes an irregularity, since, if the jury return a guilty verdict, one cannot tell whether some misconception or irrelevance has played a part. If the judge fears that the foreman may unwittingly say something harmful, he should obtain the query from him in writing, read it, let counsel see it and then openly give such direction as he sees fit. If he decides not to read out the query, he must ensure that it becomes part of the record. Failure to clear up a problem which is or may be legal will usually be fatal unless the facts admit of only one answer, because it will mean that the jury may not have understood their legal duty. The effect of failure to resolve a factual problem will vary with the circumstances.

Occasions will be few when it will be proper for a judge to open up a matter, to which no reference had earlier been made, after the jury have retired. In the case of an accidental omission to give a direction on a matter which has been canvassed during the trial, it may be appropriate to correct the matter by a supplementary direction, but if such a course is to be taken, it must be taken with the utmost caution. It is difficult to envisage any occasion on which an entirely new basis upon which a conviction might be founded, which had never been opened to the jury, should be volunteered at such a late stage. The more so where a defendant has chosen not to give evidence on the basis of the case as presented by the prosecution. If, in a very exceptional case, such a direction is to be volunteered, this should never happen without counsel being given a full opportunity to address themselves to the question: *R. v. Gascoigne* [1988] Crim.L.R. 317, CA. See also *ante*, §§ 4–355, 4–378.

If the form of the question shows that the jury appear to be assuming facts or drawing inferences for which there is no supporting evidence, further direction is called for and they should be reminded how far the relevant evidence went: *R. v. Adair*, 42 Cr.App.R. 227, CCA. The judge should redirect the jury upon the burden of proof if it is apparent from their inquiry that they have overlooked it or misunderstood it: *R. v. Bell* [1967] Crim.L.R. 545, CA, and see also *R. v. Rafique* [1973] Crim.L.R. 777, CA, which was applied in *R. v. Gibson*, *ante*, § 4–380. **4–432**

Where the jury ask a question which suggests a possible basis for conviction which has never been advanced, the precise words used by the judge by way of reply do not matter so long as the jury are left in no doubt as to how they should be approaching the matter: *R. v. Tarmohammed* [1997] Crim.L.R. 458, CA.

If the jury send a note that is indicative of them having forgotten or failed to appreciate the significance of the direction on the standard of proof ("in a case of one to one, what weight should we give to our feelings as to the guilt of the defendant in the absence of hard evidence"), it is incumbent on the judge to remind them in forcible terms that they are to put feelings on one side, and not merely that they are to try the case on the evidence but also that they should only convict if they are sure of guilt: *R. v. Wickramaratne* [1998] Crim.L.R. 565, CA.

If a jury question relates to the failure of a potential witness for the defence to have given evidence, it is incumbent on the judge to remind the jury as to the burden of proof (but the precise answer will depend on the particular question and the facts of the particular case): *R. v. Whitton* [1998] 7 *Archbold News* 3, CA (97 07281 W4). See also *ante*, §§ 4–400, 4–401.

Where a note from a jury raises a question as to possible sentence, the proper response is to tell them simply that questions of sentence are not for them: *R. v. Sahota* [1979] Crim.L.R. 678, CA ("Are we allowed to make a recommendation of leniency?").

Where, after retirement, the jury send a note indicating that one of their number, having a particular expertise, is in effect able to give material evidence to the other jurors on a relevant matter, the jury should be discharged or, possibly, recalled for a direction to concentrate on the evidence as presented by the parties: *R. v. Fricker*, *The Times*, July 13, 1999, CA. If such expertise on the part of a juror is communicated to the court before the conclusion of the evidence, it is open to the judge to allow evidence to be called on the relevant matter: *R. v. Blick*, 50 Cr.App.R. 280, CCA.

As to the appropriate response where a juror complains of pressure from other jurors, see *post*, § 4–446.

D. MAJORITY VERDICTS

Juries Act 1974, s.17

17.—(1) Subject to subsections (3) and (4), the verdict of a jury in proceedings in the Crown Court or the High Court need not be unanimous if— **4–433**

(a) in a case where there are not less than eleven jurors, ten of them agree on the verdict; and

(b) in a case where there are ten jurors, nine of them agree on the verdict.

(2) [*County courts.*]

(3) The Crown Court shall not accept a verdict of guilty by virtue of subsection (1) above unless the foreman of the jury has stated in open court the number of jurors who respectively agreed to and dissented from the verdict.

(4) No court shall accept a verdict by virtue of subsection (1) or (2) above unless it appears to the court that the jury have had such period of time for deliberation as the court thinks reasonable having regard to the nature and complexity of the case; and the Crown Court shall in any event not accept such a verdict unless it appears to the court that the jury have had at least two hours for deliberation.

Practice Direction (Criminal Proceedings: Consolidation), para. IV.46.2–46.8 [2002] 1 W.L.R. 2870

Majority verdicts

4–434 **IV.46.1** [See *ante*, § 4–414.]

IV.46.2 Thereafter the practice should be as follows. Should the jury return *before* two hours and ten minutes since the last member of the jury left the jury box to go to the jury room (or such longer time as the judge thinks reasonable) has elapsed (see section 17(4)), they should be asked: (a) "Have you reached a verdict upon which you are all agreed? Please answer Yes or No"; (b) (i) if unanimous, "What is your verdict?"; (ii) if not unanimous, the jury should be sent out again for further deliberation with a further direction to arrive if possible at an unanimous verdict.

IV.46.3 Should the jury return (whether for the first time or subsequently) or be sent for *after* the two hours and ten minutes (or the longer period) has elapsed, questions (a) and (b)(i) in paragraph 46.2 should be put to them and, if it appears that they are not unanimous, they should be asked to retire once more and told that they should continue to endeavour to reach an unanimous verdict but that, if they cannot, the judge will accept a majority verdict as in section 17(1).

IV.46.4 When the jury finally return they should be asked: (a) "Have at least ten (or nine as the case may be) of you agreed upon your verdict?"; (b) if "Yes", "What is your verdict? Please answer only Guilty or Not Guilty"; (c) (i) if "Not Guilty", accept the verdict without more ado; (ii) if "Guilty", "Is that the verdict of you all or by a majority?"; (d) if "Guilty" by a majority, "How many of you agreed to the verdict and how many dissented?"

IV.46.5 At whatever stage the jury return, before question (a) is asked, the senior officer of the court present shall state in open court, for each period when the jury was out of court for the purpose of considering their verdict(s), the time at which the last member of the jury left the jury box to go to the jury room and the time of their return to the jury box and will additionally state in open court the total of such periods.

IV.46.6 The reason why section 17(3) is confined to a majority verdict of guilty and for the somewhat complicated procedure set out in paragraph 46.3 and paragraph 46.4 is to prevent it being known that a verdict of "Not Guilty" is a majority verdict. If the final direction in paragraph 46.3 continues to require the jury to arrive, if possible, at an unanimous verdict and the verdict is received as in paragraph 46.4, it will not be known for certain that the acquittal is not unanimous.

IV.46.7 Where there are several counts (or alternative verdicts) left to the jury the above practice will, of course, need to be adapted to the circumstances. The procedure will have to be repeated in respect of each count (or alternative verdict), the verdict being accepted in those cases where the jury are unanimous and the further direction in paragraph 46.3 being given in cases in which they are not unanimous. Should the jury in the end be unable to agree on a verdict by the required majority (*i.e.* if the answer to the question in paragraph 46.4(a) be in the negative) the judge in his discretion will either ask them to deliberate further or discharge them.

IV.46.8 Section 17 will, of course, apply also to verdicts other than "Guilty" or "Not Guilty", *e.g.* to special verdicts under the *Criminal Procedure (Insanity) Act* 1964, verdicts under that Act as to fitness to be tried, and special verdicts on findings of fact. Accordingly in such cases the questions to jurors will have to be suitably adjusted.

4–435 As to the importance of complying with this practice direction, see *R. v. Georgiou*, 53 Cr.App.R. 428, CA; *R. v. Barry*, 61 Cr.App.R. 172, CA; and *R. v. Paley*, 63 Cr.App.R. 172, CA. Where there is more than one count or defendant, unless the judge has clear reasons for acting differently, the jury should be asked whether they have reached a unanimous verdict in respect of any count or defendant, and if so any such verdict should be taken, before the majority direction is given; the general rule is that verdicts should be taken as and when the jury are known to be ready to deliver them: *R. v. Nash* [2005] Crim.L.R. 232, CA.

Timing of majority direction

4–436 As to the propriety of telling the jury, at some stage after they have retired, how long it will be before they can be given a majority direction, see *R. v. Guthrie*, *post*, § 4–445. As to the propriety of, and the time for, a direction as to "give and take", see *ante*, § 4–415.

The statutory requirement of "not less than two hours" is mandatory: see *R. v. Barry*, *ante*. Once a jury has deliberated for two hours and 10 minutes, the question whether to, and when to, give a majority direction is entirely one for the judge's discretion. What verdicts have already been given, the order in which the jury are apparently considering the counts, whether, if it is known, they have considered the case against an individual defendant, are all relevant matters which the judge should take into account: *R. v. Thornton*, 89 Cr.App.R. 54, CA (court rejected submission that s.17(4) required jury to have at least two hours for a consideration of any one verdict).

Where, through inadvertence, a majority direction is given early, the judge has a discretion to discharge the jury or to correct the error and, if need be, at an appropriate time, repeat the direction: *R. v. Shields* [1997] Crim.L.R. 758, CA.

In a simple case where the jury, after being recalled after the "two-hour" retirement, tell the judge that there is no further assistance which he can give them, and the judge, instead of taking the course recommended in paragraph 2, *ante*, tells them that he will take a majority verdict and invites them to retire for a short time and consider the matter, the judge cannot be said to be exercising unreasonable pressure on the jury to bring in a majority verdict—see the statutory discretion conferred by section 17(4): *R. v. Wright*, 58 Cr.App.R. 444, CA.

In *R. v. Trickett and Trickett* [1991] Crim.L.R. 59, CA, the jury sent the judge a note three hours after they had retired indicating that 11 of them were agreed on a guilty verdict. The judge recalled them and gave them the majority direction. He asked them whether they wished to retire again. They indicated that they did not and responded affirmatively to his suggestion that they discuss the matter amongst themselves in the jury-box. The clerk then took their verdict. *Held*, there was no irregularity: the practice direction was directory and not mandatory (as to which, see also *R. v. Bateson*, 54 Cr.App.R. 11, CA).

Taking the verdict

A majority direction is not complete or valid until there has been compliance with section 17(3) of the 1974 Act (see *R. v. Austin* [2003] Crim.L.R. 426, CA), but the discharge of the jury is not a bar to reconvening that jury and rectifying an omission in this regard, nor, since the amendment of section 13 of that Act (so as to permit a jury to separate after having been directed to consider their verdict), is the fact that the jury has separated in the meantime: *R. v. Maloney* [1996] 2 Cr.App.R. 303, CA. In reaching this conclusion the court considered the previous authorities in respect of incomplete verdicts and rectification of verdicts (*ante*, § 4–262, and *post*, §§ 4–447, 4–450) and in that regard expressed the view that the position would be different if the jury had to deliberate further or, perhaps, if the verdict was being altered from not guilty to guilty. To the same effect, see *R. v. Alowi* [1999] 5 *Archbold News* 2, CA (97 08493 W3). **4–437**

The precise form of words used by the clerk when asking the foreman the number who agreed and dissented, and by the foreman when replying, does not constitute an essential part of that requirement. All that is necessary is that the words used by each make it clear to an ordinary person how the jury was divided: *R. v. Pigg*, 76 Cr.App.R. 79, HL.

The reluctance of the Court of Appeal to investigate whether what were, prima facie, unambiguous unanimous verdicts, returned in accordance with the proper procedures, were in fact majority verdicts returned without compliance with the procedural requirements of section 17 (see *R. v. Hart* [1998] Crim.L.R. 417; *R. v. Millward* [1999] 1 Cr.App.R. 61; and *R. v. Atkinson* [2000] 8 *Archbold News* 3) has abated following *R. v. Mirza*; *R. v. Connor and Rollock* [2004] 1 A.C. 1118, HL (*ante*, § 4–254): see *R. v. Adams* [2007] 1 Cr.App.R. 34; and *R. v. Charnley* [2007] 2 Cr.App.R. 33, CA (*post*, § 7–209). In *Charnley*, the court observed that where unanimous verdicts of guilty appear inconsistent with a prior note from the jury, the judge would be wise to ensure that the foreman had properly understood what he had been asked and that his answers accurately reflected the position.

E. DISAGREEMENT OF JURY

"... Where it appears from the length of their retirement and the circumstances of the case, **4–438** even after a majority direction has been given to them, the jury may be unable to agree on a verdict and therefore further deliberation by them may be simply a waste of time, the judge should reassemble the court, send for the jury and in open court ask the jury, through their foreman, whether there is any chance of their reaching an agreement, emphasising, needless to say, that he is not inquiring as to how they are divided. According to the answer which the judge gets from the jury, he will then decide whether to discharge the jury there and then, or whether he should ask the jury to retire once again to make a further effort to reach agreement between them" (*per* Lord Lane C.J. in *R. v. Rose*, 75 Cr.App.R. 322 at 329, CA).

In *R. v. Wharton* [1990] Crim.L.R. 877, CA, subsequent to a majority direction, the jury sent a note indicating that they were divided 9:3. The judge, with counsel's concurrence, sent them a message asking them to continue their deliberations. They returned a 10:2 verdict of guilty. An appeal against conviction was allowed: even though the judge had imposed no time-limit, his failure to ascertain in open court the prospect of the jury reaching a verdict was a material irregularity. However, in *R. v. Payne* [2001] 3 *Archbold News* 3, the Court of Appeal said that *Wharton* was not to be taken as deciding that where, following a majority direction, a judge receives a note from the jury indicating possible deadlock, it is his duty to re-assemble the court immediately for the purpose of ascertaining whether, given more time, there is any prospect of a verdict, and in order to point out that there is no pressure of time, and, if thought appropriate, to give a "give and take" direction (*ante*, § 4–415). The judge has a discretion whether to have the jury back immediately, such discretion to be exercised in the light of all the circumstances, including the length of the case, the directions already given, and the length of the retirement, bearing in mind the need to avoid the risk of any juror being subjected to inappropriate pressure.

4–439 The provisions of the practice direction, *ante*, § 4–434, should be followed in the great majority of cases, but if a jury have retired and before two hours have elapsed they return to court and inform the judge that they are hopelessly and helplessly divided, the judge may, in the exercise of his discretion, discharge them forthwith: *R. v. Elia*, 52 Cr.App.R. 342, CA; *R. v. Adams and Hogan*, 52 Cr.App.R. 588, CA.

4–440 If the jury are discharged from giving a verdict, the defendant may be, and generally is, tried upon the indictment by a second jury; in the event of the second jury disagreeing, it is a common practice for the prosecution formally to offer no evidence. If the jury agree on a verdict on some counts of an indictment, but disagree on others, the defendant can be retried on the counts on which the disagreement has taken place, even after judgment on the counts on which he has been convicted or acquitted, as each count is a separate indictment: *Latham v. R.* (1864) 5 B. & S. 635.

As to the limited discretion to decline to take a verdict (before it is known what it is, only that there is one) and discharge the jury, see *R. v. Robinson*, *ante*, § 4–140.

As to the possibility of setting aside an order discharging a jury, see *ante*, §§ 4–262, 4–433.

XIX. VERDICT

A. GENERAL

4–441 The jurors must deliver their verdict in open court. The presence of the defendant is not essential at the return of the verdict: Co.Litt. 227b, 3 Co.Inst. 110; but in practice he usually is present, see *ante*, §§ 3–197 *et seq*. The verdict is delivered by the foreman; and the assent of all jurors to a verdict pronounced by the foreman in the presence and hearing of the rest, without their express dissent, is to be conclusively presumed: *R. v. Wooler* (1817) 2 Stark.N.P. 111; and see *Lalchan Nanan v. The State* [1986] A.C. 860, PC (affidavits from four jurors to the effect that the verdict of guilty was not unanimous held to be inadmissible); *R. v. Hart* [1998] Crim.L.R. 417, CA; *R. v. Millward*, *ante*, § 4–437; and *R. v. Austin* [2003] Crim.L.R. 426, CA.

4–442 The verdict in a criminal case is either: (a) general, on the whole charge (which the jury are at liberty to find in all cases, both upon the law and facts of the case; Co.Litt. 228; 4 Bl.Com. 361); or (b) partial, as to a part of the charge; as where the jury find the defendant guilty on one or more counts of the indictment, and acquit him of the residue; or find him guilty on one part of a divisible count, and acquit him as to the residue; or find him guilty of an offence other than the full offence charged; or (c) special, where the facts of the case alone are found by the jury, the legal inference to be derived from them being referred to the court; see *post*, §§ 4–465 *et seq.*

Where an indictment contains alternative counts, a verdict should be taken first on the more serious alternative and if the verdict is guilty the jury should be discharged from returning a verdict on the less serious alternative: *R. v. Hill*, 96 Cr.App.R. 456 at 459, CA. This practice was considered in *R. v. Velasquez*, *ante*, § 4–134, where it had not been followed. If the alternatives are of equal gravity, the jury should be asked whether they find the defendant guilty on either count; the count should be identified, the verdict taken and no verdict taken on the alternative: *R. v. Seymour*, 38 Cr.App.R. 68, CCA. In this way, in either case, the power of the Court of Appeal to substitute a verdict of the lesser alternative, or the alternative of equal gravity is preserved. Where two charges arising out of the same incident have been preferred and one of them has merged, as it were, into the other, it is not proper that it should be left open to the jury to convict on both charges: *R. v. Harris*, 53 Cr.App.R. 376, CA; see also *R. v. Roma* [1956] Crim.L.R. 46, CCA. For examples, see *post*, § 21–289 (theft/handling). **4–443**

As to the power to discharge a juror after some verdicts have been returned and take further verdicts thereafter, see *R. v. Wood and Furey* [1997] Crim.L.R. 229, CA, *ante*, § 4–253.

B. Premature Verdict

It is the duty of the jury, unless they are going to return a verdict of not guilty, to keep an open mind until the end of the summing up: see *R. v. Young*, 48 Cr.App.R. 292, CCA. **4–444**

C. Verdict Obtained by Threat or Pressure

Where the judge issues an ultimatum or stipulates a deadline, a conviction is liable to be set aside: see *R. v. McKenna* [1960] 1 Q.B. 411, 44 Cr.App.R. 63, CCA; *R. v. Rose* [1982] A.C. 822, HL. **4–445**

The jury must be free to deliberate without any form of pressure, whether by way of promise or threat or otherwise. They must not be made to feel that it is incumbent on them to concur with a view they do not truly hold simply because it might be inconvenient or tiresome or expensive for the prosecution, the defendant, the victim or the public in general if they do not do so: *R. v. Watson*, 87 Cr.App.R. 1, CA, and see *ante*, § 4–415. See also *de Four v. The State* [1999] 1 W.L.R. 1731, PC (after deliberations of three-and-a-half hours, jury indicated that given time they would be able to reach a verdict; judge stated that they could have a further 30 minutes; failed to remind them that in the event of irreconcilable disagreement it was their duty to say so; held to be appreciable risk of improper pressure).

Where, in a short case (jury sworn–10.40 a.m., retired–2.48 p.m.) with a single issue, the judge said to the jury when they retired (on a Friday, their last scheduled day of sitting) that they would have to reach a verdict that day as he was not sitting the following week, this did not constitute undue pressure (having regard to fact that verdict in fact returned in 45 minutes), but it might have done had the jury been out for several hours before agreeing: *R. v. Baker (Adrian)* [1998] Crim.L.R. 351, CA (rejecting a suggestion that there should be a practice of not listing a trial in front of a judge on his last sitting day). For a case in which an argument that the judge's suggestion that the jury might have to come back on the Monday (after their scheduled period of jury service) had created undue pressure was rejected, see *R. v. Buttle* [2006] Crim.L.R. 840, CA (the court observing that had it been the case that one or more of the jurors had been unable to return on the Monday, it was to have been expected that some sort of indication would have been given, and ruling that evidence from a witness as to the jury's reaction to being told of the possibility of returning on the Monday was akin to inquiring into what had gone on in the jury room, which was impermissible). As to pressure of time, see also *ante*, §§ 4–265a, 4–424 and 4–425.

Where a judge in a civil trial, having given a majority direction to the jury, and having been informed by the foreman that there was no prospect of them reaching a majority verdict, told them that there would have to be another trial, which was not desirable, but that if there was no prospect of a verdict, he would have to discharge them, whereupon the foreman asked for further instructions on the majority direction and the other jurors indicated that they required more time, it could not be said that the verdicts that were delivered after a further retirement of approximately 15 minutes had been reached as a result of undue pressure; it was important to note that it was not the judge who had invited the jury to retire the final time; he had said no more than that they might do so if they wished, and it was the jurors themselves who indicated that they did wish to do so: *Morrison v. Chief Constable of West Midlands Police*, *The Independent*, February 28, 2003, CA (Civ. Div.).

While it is conventional not to mention to the jury the time at which a majority direction might be given, it is not necessarily wrong to do so if the effect is to alleviate any anxiety or uncertainty that the jury might entertain: *R. v. Guthrie*, *The Times*, February 23, 1994, CA. In *R. v. Court*, *The Times*, May 25, 1994, CA, it was said that whilst the jury should be kept fully informed of the proposed timetable, a judge was entitled to expect that if a juror had a personal difficulty, he would raise it.

4–446 In *R. v. Lucas* [1991] Crim.L.R. 844, CA, after the jury had been given a majority direction and a *Watson* direction (*ante*, § 4–415), the judge received a note from one of the jurors complaining of pressure from other jurors. The judge, with the concurrence of counsel, recalled the jury and they were asked in respect of each count in turn whether they had reached a verdict. A majority verdict was returned on count 2, but it was stated that no verdict had been reached on other counts. The judge then discharged the jury on other counts. It was contended on appeal against conviction on count 2 that the jury should have been discharged without any verdicts being taken. *Held*, there had been a number of options open to the judge and that in all the circumstances there was no reason to think that the appellant had suffered injustice by the judge exercising his discretion in the way that he had. The court emphasised that the complaining juror's note made it clear that he was prepared to adhere to his views, that the verdict was by a majority and was to be contrasted with the failure to reach even a majority verdict on the other counts, that the jury had received a *Watson* direction and that no juror had dissented from the verdict when it was announced. See also *R. v. Smith and Mercieca* [2005] 1 W.L.R. 704, HL (where the judge had been right not to discharge the jury after a letter from a juror showing that other jurors were disregarding his directions on the law and were engaging in horse-trading over verdicts, but had then failed to give sufficiently emphatic or detailed directions, in that in particular he failed to refer to the need for the jurors to reach verdicts on their own conscientious judgment without bargaining over them and did not remind them that they had to follow his directions on the law, which in the circumstances had required clear and strong emphasis).

Where remarks made by the jury in the jury-room were overheard by the jury bailiff, evidence of the remarks was not admissible to show that the jury were under pressure: *R. v. Bean* [1991] Crim.L.R. 843, CA.

D. RECEIVING THE VERDICT

4–447 Once a jury has formally returned a verdict which is not ambiguous and which is open to them on the indictment, the judge has no discretion to refuse to accept it: *R. v. Robinson* [1975] Q.B. 508, 60 Cr.App.R. 108, CA (see further *ante*, § 4–140). See also *R. v. Lester*, *ante*, § 4–135.

The jury may, before the verdict is recorded (or even promptly after the verdict is recorded, *R. v. Parkin* (1824) 1 Mood. 45), rectify their verdict, and it will stand as amended. This may be done even after the defendant has been discharged out of the dock (in pursuance of a supposed verdict of acquittal), if it is done before the jury have left the box: *R. v. Vodden* (1853) Dears. 229; *R. v. Froud* [1990] Crim.L.R. 197. See further *post*, §§ 4–449, 4–450; and *R. v. Alowi* [1999] 5 *Archbold News* 2, CA (97 08493 W3).

In *R. v. Williams (A.G.)*, 84 Cr.App.R. 274, CA, initial dissent between the foreman and other jurors when asked if the jury had agreed upon verdicts did not invalidate the verdicts that were properly taken after a further retirement.

Upon the delivery of the verdict, if the defendant is thereby acquitted on the merits, he is entitled to be immediately set at liberty unless there is some other legal ground for his detention (*post*, § 4–470). As to other indictments against the defendant, see *R. v. Hart*, 23 Cr.App.R. 202 at 207, CCA.

Since it is the jury's view of the facts that matters, a trial judge should not express any opinion about a verdict (including, privately, to counsel in his room): *R. v. Blackburn* [1999] 8 *Archbold News* 3, CA.

As to the rectification of verdicts, see *R. v. Maloney* and *R. v. Charnley*, *ante*, § 4–437, and see *post*, §§ 4–449, 4–450.

E. MAJORITY VERDICT

As to the taking of majority verdicts, see *ante*, §§ 4–433 *et seq.* **4–448**

F. INCOMPLETE VERDICT

A verdict is not completed until a jury has dealt with all possible alternative verdicts **4–449** open to them on the indictment. If a judge discharges a defendant before the jury have completed their verdict, the discharge is a nullity: *R. v. Carter and Canavan* [1964] 2 Q.B. 1, 48 Cr.App.R. 122, CCA.

In *R. v. Andrews (P.)*, 82 Cr.App.R. 148, CA, the court said that as a matter of gen- **4–450** eral principle, where the jury seeks to alter a verdict pronounced by the foreman, the judge has a discretion whether to allow the alteration to be made. Important considerations would be: the length of time which had elapsed between the original verdict and the moment the jury expressed their wish to alter it (in *Andrews* the period was about 10 minutes); the probable reason for the initial mistake; the necessity to ensure that justice was done, not only to the defendant, but also to the prosecution. The fact that the defendant had been discharged from custody was also a factor, but not a fatal factor. If the jury had been discharged and *a fortiori* if they had dispersed, it might well be impossible for the judge to allow the alteration to be made: see also *ante*, §§ 4–262, 4–437, and 4–447. Further, if there was any question of the verdict being altered as a result of anything that the jury saw or heard after returning the initial verdict, there could be no question of allowing a fresh verdict to be entered. An unexplained change of verdict after hearing of the defendant's previous convictions was, therefore, quashed in *R. v. Bills* [1995] 2 Cr.App.R. 643, CA. See also *R. v. Alowi* [1999] 5 *Archbold News* 2, CA; *Igwemma v. Chief Constable of Greater Manchester Police* [2002] Q.B. 1012, CA (Civ. Div.); and *R. v. Tantrum* [2001] Crim.L.R. 824, CA (rectification should not have been permitted where possibility of change of mind rather than mistake in original verdict).

G. AMBIGUOUS VERDICT

Where a single verdict is ambiguous, or two verdicts are inconsistent (*post*, § 7–70), or **4–451** the verdict is one which cannot on the indictment or in the circumstances be lawfully returned, the judge is entitled, unless the jury insist, to refuse to accept the first verdict and ask the jury to reconsider the matter and, if they change their verdict, to record only the second verdict: *R. v. Harris* [1964] Crim.L.R. 54, CCA. The judge ought to take steps to clear up any ambiguity in the verdict (*R. v. Hawkes*, 22 Cr.App.R. 172, CCA; *R. v. Moore*, 23 Cr.App.R. 138, CCA), and may in a proper case, after taking such steps, give the jury a further direction in law (*R. v. Sweetland*, 42 Cr.App.R. 62, CCA), and he is within his rights in questioning the jury as to the meaning of the words and so obtaining an unambiguous verdict: *R. v. White*, 45 Cr.App.R. 34, CCA. Where the verdict is plain and unambiguous, it is most undesirable that the judge should ask the jury any further question about it: *R. v. Larkin* [1943] K.B. 174, 29 Cr.App.R. 18, CCA.

Where the words of a verdict are not clear, but the intention of the jury is plain, the **4–452** Court of Appeal will give effect to that intention: see (on this point only) *R. v. Howell*, 27 Cr.App.R. 5, CCA.

In *R. v. Mendy* [1992] Crim.L.R. 313, CA, a verdict of guilty had been returned following a majority direction. In answer to the question whether the verdict was "of you all, or by a majority" the foreman of the jury answered "By a majority of us all". The ambiguity in this answer went unnoticed at the time. The Court of Appeal concluded that the ambiguity had to be resolved in favour of the appellant. It, therefore, had to be assumed that the verdict was that of a majority, in which case the mandatory provisions of section 17(3) of the *Juries Act* 1974 (*ante*, § 4–433) had not been complied with and the conviction had to be quashed.

H. VERDICT FOR LESSER OFFENCE THAN THAT CHARGED IN THE INDICTMENT

(1) General rule at common law

4–453 At common law conviction of a lesser offence than that charged was permissible provided that the definition of the greater offence necessarily included the definition of the lesser offence, and that both offences were of the same degree, *i.e.* felony or misdemeanour: see *R. v. Hollingberry* (1825) 4 B. & C. 329; *R. v. Woodhall and Wilkes* (1872) 12 Cox 240; *R. v. O'Brien*, 6 Cr.App.R. 108, CCA; and *R. v. Kelly* [1964] 1 Q.B. 173, 48 Cr.App.R. 1, CCA. It is important, now that distinctions between felonies and misdemeanours have been abolished, to bear in mind the significance of the second proviso, in considering the effect of the older authorities.

4–454 On an indictment for an offence contrary to section 4 of the *Libel Act* 1843, the jury may convict of the offence contrary to section 5: *Boaler v. R.* (1888) 21 Q.B.D. 284, *post*, § 29–76. Upon an indictment for perjury, it is sufficient if any one of the assignments of perjury be proved, see *R. v. Rhodes* (1703) 2 Ld.Raym. 886.

Where several persons are indicted for an aggravated offence, one may be found guilty of the aggravated offence and the others of the lesser offence without the circumstances of aggravation: *R. v. Butterworth* (1823) R. & R. 520.

The common law principles have largely been superseded by section 6(2) and (3) of the *CLA* 1967, *post*, but in *R. v. Saunders* [1988] A.C. 148, HL, the common law was relied on to justify a conviction for manslaughter where the jury were unable to reach agreement on a charge of murder.

(2) General statutory provision

Criminal Law Act 1967, s.6(3)–(4)

4–455 **6.**—(3) Where, on a person's trial on indictment for any offence except treason or murder, the jury find him not guilty of the offence specifically charged in the indictment, but the allegations in the indictment amount to or include (expressly or by implication) an allegation of another offence falling within the jurisdiction of the court of trial, the jury may find him guilty of that other offence or of an offence of which he could be found guilty on an indictment specifically charging that other offence.

(3A) For the purposes of subsection (3) above an offence falls within the jurisdiction of the court of trial if it is an offence to which section 40 of the *Criminal Justice Act* 1988 applies (power to join in indictment count for common assault etc.), even if a count charging the offence is not included in the indictment.

(3B) A person convicted of an offence by virtue of subsection (3A) may only be dealt with for it in a manner in which a magistrates' court could have dealt with him.

(4) For purposes of subsection (3) above any allegation of an offence shall be taken as including an allegation of attempting to commit that offence; and where a person is charged on indictment with attempting to commit an offence or with any assault or other act preliminary to an offence, but not with the completed offence, then (subject to the discretion of the court to discharge the jury or otherwise act with a view to the preferment of an indictment for the completed offence) he may be convicted of the offence charged notwithstanding that he is shown to be guilty of the completed offence.

[Subss. (3A) and (3B) were inserted by the *Domestic Violence, Crime and Victims Act* 2004, s.11; subs. (4) is printed as amended by the *CJA* 2003, s.331, and Sched. 36, para. 41.]

By section 6(7) (*ante*, § 4–115), subsection (3) applies to an indictment containing more than one count as if each count were a separate indictment.

For section 6(2) of the 1967 Act, which deals with alternative verdicts on a charge of murder, see *post*, § 4–459. For section 6(1)(b) and (5) (plea of guilty to lesser offence), see *ante*, §§ 4–107, 4–115, 4–126.

As to attempts, see generally *post*, §§ 33–119 *et seq.*

A verdict of guilty cannot be returned under section 6(3) of the 1967 Act unless the jury have found the defendant not guilty of the offence specifically charged: *R. v. Collison*, 71 Cr.App.R. 249, CA; and see *R. v. Griffiths* [1998] Crim.L.R. 348, CA (a decision to like effect in relation to the similarly worded provision in section 24 of the *RTOA* 1988 (*post*, § 32–165)). Where this gives rise to difficulty, because the jury are unable to agree in respect of the offence charged, an alternative count may be added to the indictment if it causes no injustice to the defendant: *Collison, ante*. See also *R. v. Saunders, post*, § 4–460.

In determining for the purposes of section 6(3) whether the allegations in the indictment "amount to or include (expressly or by implication) an allegation of another offence", the words "amount to or include" are to be read disjunctively. Section 6(3) therefore envisages that the allegations in the indictment may: (a) expressly amount to, or (b) expressly include, or (c) impliedly amount to, or (d) impliedly include, an allegation of another offence: *R. v. Wilson (C.)*; *R. v. Jenkins (E.J.)* [1984] A.C. 242, HL. **4–456**

If the allegations in the indictment are capable of including (either expressly or impliedly) an allegation of another offence, the accused can be convicted of that other offence—in other words, the allegations in the particular indictment need not necessarily involve a specific allegation of the other offence; it suffices that the allegations are capable of including such an allegation: *Wilson*; *Jenkins, ante*. It follows that if the accused is charged with inflicting grievous bodily harm contrary to section 20 of the *Offences against the Person Act* 1861, or with burglary contrary to section 9(1)(b) of the *Theft Act* 1968 (the particulars alleging that the accused inflicted grievous bodily harm), the accused may be found not guilty as charged, but guilty of assault occasioning actual bodily harm, since the inflicting of grievous bodily harm will often (though not always) involve an assault, and grievous bodily harm will necessarily include the less serious injuries involved in actual bodily harm. It being accepted that there can be an infliction of grievous bodily harm without an assault being committed, it was held that the allegation at least impliedly includes "inflicting by assault": *ibid*.

Where it is proposed to leave to the jury the possibility of a conviction for a lesser offence, it is preferable to add a separate count, rather than for the judge to give an oral direction as to their powers under section 6(3): *R. v. Mandair* [1995] 1 A.C. 208, HL. For observations to the effect that it is desirable to have a separate count alleging the lesser alternative from the outset, see *R. v. Lahaye* [2006] 1 Cr.App.R. 11, CA (*post*, § 19–203).

As to when the possibility of an alternative verdict should be left to a jury, see *post*, §§ 4–463 *et seq*.

Where a defendant is convicted of two summary offences, one by virtue of section 6(3) and (3A) and one by virtue of a count having been included in the indictment pursuant to the *CJA* 1988, s.40 (*ante*, § 1–75ai), the effect of section 6(3B) and of section 40(2), taken together, is to limit the Crown Court's sentencing powers to the maximum total sentence that could have been imposed by a magistrates' court (*i.e.* six months: *MCA* 1980, s.133(1) (*ante*, § 5–270)): *R. v. James* [2008] 1 Cr.App.R.(S.) 44, CA.

Further examples of alternatives

See *R. v. Morrison* [2003] 1 W.L.R. 1859, CA (attempting to inflict grievous bodily harm with intent is alternative to attempted murder); and *R. v. Burke* [2000] Crim.L.R. 413, CA (on prosecution for attempting to obtain property (£235,000) by deception (paying forged cheque drawn on account of X into own account), it would have been open to the jury to convict of theft of a chose in action (namely, the debt owned by X's bank to him in that amount) by virtue of section 6(3), and thus, by virtue of section 6(4), a conviction of attempted theft would also have been available). **4–457**

As to whether a person can be convicted of conspiracy to steal if charged with conspiracy to rob, see *R. v. Barnard*, 70 Cr.App.R. 28, CA, *post*, §§ 21–96, 33–76.

(3) Murder

Criminal Law Act 1967, s.6(2)

4–458 **6.**—(2) On an indictment for murder a person found not guilty of murder may be found guilty—

(a) of manslaughter, or of causing grievous bodily harm with intent to do so; or

(b) of any offence of which he may be found guilty under an enactment specifically so providing, or under section 4(2) of this Act; or

(c) of an attempt to commit murder, or of an attempt to commit any other offence of which he might be found guilty;

but may not be found guilty of any offence not included above.

4–459 For section 6(1)(b) and (5) (plea of guilty to lesser offence), see *ante*, §§ 4–107, 4–115, 4–126.

As to section 6(2)(b), see the *Infant Life (Preservation) Act* 1929, s.2(2) (*post*, § 19–131), the *Infanticide Act* 1938, s.1(2) (*post*, § 19–137) and the *Suicide Act* 1961, s.2 (*post*, § 18–6).

For section 4, see *post*, § 18–34.

By section 6(7) (*ante*, § 4–115), subsection (2) applies to an indictment containing more than one count as if each count were a separate indictment.

As to when the possibility of an alternative verdict should be left to a jury, see *post*, §§ 4–463 *et seq.*

Conviction of manslaughter where disagreement on murder

4–460 In *R. v. Saunders* [1988] A.C. 148, HL, S was charged with murder. The jury eventually made it clear that, although they were agreed upon manslaughter, a majority of them could not agree upon murder. They were permitted to return a verdict of guilty of manslaughter and were discharged from returning a verdict on murder. The suggestion that section 6(2) applied to these circumstances, and that therefore the manslaughter verdict could only follow an acquittal on the murder charge, was rejected by the House of Lords. Section 6(2) had no application to a situation where the jury had never been able to reach a verdict of not guilty of murder because they could not agree on such a verdict. That position was provided for by the common law. In a trial on an indictment for murder, where manslaughter is a possible verdict, the jury's task is first to consider whether or not they are satisfied that the accused is guilty of murder. It is only when they make the positive determination that the accused is not guilty of murder that they should proceed to consider the lesser offence of manslaughter. However, there is no legal principle which prevents that impediment to considering the lesser offence being removed by judicial intervention—namely, by discharging the jury from the obligation of returning a verdict on the major offence, if the justice of the case so requires. Such was the instant case. It is not desirable to abandon the long-established practice of indicting only for murder in cases where manslaughter would, or may, be left to the jury: *ibid.*

It is submitted that, as a matter of practice, a judge should not follow the course adopted in *Saunders*, which precludes a retrial, unless the prosecution are content to accept a conviction for manslaughter in satisfaction of the charge of murder. As to the entitlement of the prosecution to a verdict on the charge in the indictment, see the decision of the High Court of Australia in *Stanton v. R.* (2003) 198 A.L.R. 41.

See *R. v. Collison*, *ante*, § 4–455, as to the possibility of amending the indictment if the jury are unable to reach agreement on the offence specifically charged.

(4) Other statutory provisions

Assisting offenders

4–461 As to the power to return an alternative verdict of guilty of intentionally impeding the apprehension or prosecution of another, see the *CLA* 1967, s.4(2), *post*, §§ 18–34 *et seq.*

Miscellaneous

4–462 Various statutes which create particular offences contain provisions that permit conviction of the alternative offences there specified. For details of the same, reference should be made to the parts of this work which deal with specific offences.

Where a statute permits conviction of a summary offence as an alternative to an offence on the indictment and the judge upholds a submission of no case to answer on the indictable offence, he need not take a verdict at that stage and may leave the count for the jury to consider for the purpose only of considering the alternative offence: *R. v. Livesey* [2007] 1 Cr.App.R. 35, CA, following *R. v. Carson*, 92 Cr.App.R. 236, CA (*post*, § 29–37).

(5) When to leave alternative verdict to jury

In *R. v. Coutts* [2006] 1 W.L.R. 2154, HL, it was held that the public interest in the administration of justice will be best served by a judge in any trial on indictment leaving to the jury any obvious alternative offence to the offence charged, which there is evidence to support; "obvious alternative" in this context means such alternatives as suggest themselves to the mind of any ordinarily knowledgeable and alert criminal judge, but not alternatives which ingenious counsel may identify through diligent research after the trial; and the public interest being the prevailing consideration, the tactical wishes of trial counsel on either side are immaterial; by omitting to mention an alternative in a case where it might be appropriate on a reasonable view of the facts, the judge would misrepresent the position by making the law seem more rigid and less nuanced than it actually was; the only qualification to the duty would be that the defendant's right to a fair trial must not be infringed; there would ordinarily be no such infringement where a defendant who, resisting conviction of a more serious offence, succeeded in throwing doubt on an ingredient of that offence and was, as a result, convicted of a lesser offence lacking that ingredient; but it might well be the case that there would be such an infringement if the jury were first to learn of the alternative during the summing-up if counsel had not had the opportunity to address the issue in their closing speeches; to guard against this risk, the proposed direction should be indicated to counsel before closing speeches. **4–463**

However, this does not mean that every alternative verdict must always be left to the jury; the judge must examine whether the absence of a direction about a lesser alternative verdict would oblige the jury to make an unrealistic choice between the serious charge and complete acquittal which would unfairly disadvantage the defendant; a lesser alternative verdict should not be left to the jury if that verdict can properly be described in its legal and factual context as trivial, or insubstantial, or where any possible compromise verdict would not reflect the real issues in the case, although a decision not to leave a lesser alternative must be reconsidered in the light of any question which the jury may see fit to ask: *R. v. Foster*; *R. v. Newman*; *R. v. Kempster*; *R. v. Birmingham* [2008] 1 Cr.App.R. 38, CA. Furthermore, the principles in *Coutts* extend only to the application of section 6(3) of the 1967 Act (*ante*, § 4–455), and do not impose any obligation upon a judge to amend the indictment to include other offences upon which a properly directed jury might convict, the purpose of the indictment being to specify the charges upon which the prosecution, not the court, are seeking a conviction: *ibid*. **4–464**

As to the basis on which the Court of Appeal will intervene where an alternative has not been left to the jury, see *post*, § 7–97.

Where an alternative charge is to be put to the jury, that should be done as early as possible. It will be appropriate only if it will cause no improper prejudice to the defendant and he has full opportunity to deal with it: *R. v. Wilson*; *R. v. Jenkins*, *ante*, § 4–456; and generally *ante*, § 4–378. Where it was not until after the close of the defendant's evidence that the alternative of an attempt was raised for the first time, and it was impossible for the defendant's counsel to say with any confidence that he would not have conducted his examination differently, the conviction for attempt was quashed: *R. v. Harris*, *The Times*, March 22, 1993, CA.

I. SPECIAL VERDICT

The jury have a right in all criminal cases to find a special verdict: 2 Hawk. c. 47, s.3; and see *Libel Act* 1792, ss.1, 3; but the judge has no power to compel them to find a special verdict: *R. v. Allday* (1837) 8 C. & P. 136 (see forms of special verdict in *R. v. Dudley* (1884) 14 Q.B.D. 273; *R. v. Staines Local Board*, 52 J.P. 215). Such verdict **4–465** must state positively the facts themselves, and not merely the evidence adduced to prove them, and all the facts necessary to enable the court to give judgment must be found; for the court cannot supply by intendment or implication any defect in the statement: 2 Hawk. c. 47, s.9; 2 East P.C. 708, 784: see *R. v. Plummer* (1701) Kel.(J.) 109; *R. v. Royce* (1767) 4 Burr. 2073. But if the jury find all the substantial requisites of the charge, they are not bound to follow in terms the technical language of the indictment.

4–466 The jury, after stating the facts, need not, and indeed ought not, to draw any legal conclusion, for that is the matter referred to the court; and if they do so, and the inference drawn by them is erroneous, the court will reject it as superfluous, and pronounce the judgment warranted by the facts stated. A special verdict may not be amended as to matters of fact; but a mere error of form may be amended in order to fulfil the evident intention of the jury, where there is any note or minute by which to amend: 2 Hawk. c. 47, s.9; *R. v. Hazel* (1785) 1 Leach 368 at 382.

Where words are added to a verdict, the judge is entitled to take the necessary steps to secure a clear verdict of guilty or not guilty: *ante*, §§ 4–451 *et seq.* A verdict is not vitiated by surplusage: 2 Hawk. c. 47, s.10.

4–467 Special verdicts should be obtained only in the most exceptional cases: *R. v. Bourne*, 36 Cr.App.R. 125, CCA.

See further *post*, § 5–71, on questioning a jury as to the basis of their verdict.

Special verdict of insanity

Trial of Lunatics Act 1883, s.2

4–468 **2.**—(1) Where in any indictment or information any act or omission is charged against any person as an offence, and it is given in evidence on the trial of such person for that offence that he was insane, so as not to be responsible, according to law, for his action at the time when the act was done or omission made, then, if it appears to the jury before whom such person is tried that he did the act or made the omission charged, but was insane as aforesaid at the time when he did or made the same, the jury shall return a special verdict that the accused is not guilty by reason of insanity.

(2)–(4) [*Repealed.*]

[Subs. (1) is printed as amended by the *Criminal Procedure (Insanity) Act* 1964, s.1. Subss. (2) and (4) were repealed by the *Criminal Procedure (Insanity) Act* 1964, s.8(5)(a), and subs. (3) was repealed by the *Criminal Lunatics Act* 1884, s.17 and Sched. 2 (*rep.*).]

As to what constitutes insanity, see *post*, §§ 17–74 *et seq.*, and see *post* § 4–469, as to the form of the evidence required before such a special verdict may be returned. The *Trial of Lunatics Act* 1883 is concerned with responsibility rather than any definition of insanity.

The requirement in section 2 that it should appear to the jury that the defendant "did the act or made the omission charged" before he can be found not guilty by reason of insanity refers only to the *actus reus* of the crime: *Att.-Gen.'s Reference (No. 3 of 1998)* [1999] 2 Cr.App.R. 214, CA, which decision has also been approved (*per curiam*) in *R. v. Antoine* [2001] 1 A.C. 340, HL (*ante*, § 4–174a).

A verdict under this section must be taken from a jury. It is not possible for the prosecution to "accept" a plea of not guilty by reason of insanity: *R. v. Crown Court at Maidstone, ex p. Harrow LBC* [2000] 1 Cr.App.R. 117, DC.

As to appeals against special verdicts, see *post*, § 7–146.

Criminal Procedure (Insanity and Unfitness to Plead) Act 1991, s.1

Acquittals on grounds of insanity

4–469 **1.**—(1) A jury shall not return a special verdict under section 2 of the *Trial of Lunatics Act* 1883 (acquittal on ground of insanity) except on the written or oral evidence of two or more registered medical practitioners at least one of whom is duly approved.

(2) Subsections (2) and (3) of section 54 of the *Mental Health Act* 1983 ("the 1983 Act") shall have effect with respect to proof of the accused's mental condition for the purposes of the said section 2 as they have effect with respect to proof of an offender's mental condition for the purposes of section 37(2)(a) of that Act.

For the definition of the expression "duly approved" in relation to a registered medical practitioner, see section 6(1) of the Act. It is in identical terms to the definition of the same expression in section 8 of the *Criminal Procedure (Insanity) Act* 1964 (*ante*, § 4–168).

See section 5 of the 1964 Act (*ante*, § 4–175a), as to the consequences of a special verdict of not guilty by reason of insanity.

For section 54 of the 1983 Act, see *post*, § 5–888.

XX. PROCEDURE AND EVIDENCE AFTER VERDICT

The following are matters which may require consideration in a particular case after verdict: **4–470**

(a) The continued detention of an acquitted defendant is illegal, unless he is lawfully held in connection with some other matter: *Mee v. Cruickshank* (1902) 20 Cox 210.

(b) Moving in arrest of judgment: see *post*, § 5–14.

(c) The giving of evidence in respect of the defendant's previous convictions and general antecedents: see *post*, §§ 5–55 *et seq.*

(d) The determination of facts by the judge for sentencing purposes: see *post*, §§ 5–64 *et seq.*

(e) Taking outstanding matters into consideration: see *post*, §§ 5–107 *et seq.*

(f) Applications for mitigation to be heard *in camera*: see *post*, § 5–92.

(g) Mitigation on pleas of guilty: see *post*, §§ 5–78 *et seq.*

(h) The holding of a *Newton* hearing (*R. v. Newton*, 77 Cr.App.R. 13, CA): see *post*, §§ 5–74 *et seq.*

(i) Making a confiscation order, or postponing confiscation proceedings: see *post*, §§ 5–527 *et seq.*

(j) Postponement of sentence: see *post*, §§ 5–15 *et seq.*

CHAPTER 5

SENTENCES AND ORDERS ON CONVICTION

I. GENERAL INTERPRETATION

(1) Introduction

(a) *Legislative framework*

5–1 The *PCC(S)A* 2000 received Royal Assent on May 25, 2000, and, with the exception of sections 87 and 88, came into force on August 25, 2000: s.168(1), (2). It was a consolidation statute, repealing and re-enacting all of the principal statutory provisions governing the sentencing powers of the courts. Sections 161, 163 and 164 are general interpretative provisions in relation to words, phrases and other expressions that occur throughout the chapter. For convenience, they are set out here.

The *CJA* 2003 received Royal Assent on November 20, 2003. Part 12 (ss.142– 305) is exclusively concerned with sentencing. It is divided into nine chapters: general provisions about sentencing (Chap. 1 (ss.142– 176)); community orders in the case of offenders aged 16 or over (Chap. 2 (ss.177– 180)); prison sentences of less than 12 months (Chap. 3 (ss.181– 195)); further provisions about orders under Chapters 2 and 3 (Chap. 4 (ss.196– 223)); dangerous offenders (Chap. 5 (ss.224– 236)); release on licence (Chap. 6 (ss.237– 268)); effect of life sentence (Chap. 7 (ss.269– 277)); other provisions about sentencing (Chap. 8 (ss.278– 301)); and supplementary (Chap. 9 (ss.302– 305)). As at October 1, 2008, the vast majority of these provisions were in force (many of them having come into force on April 4, 2005: *Criminal Justice Act 2003 (Commencement No. 8 and Transitional and Saving Provisions) Order* 2005 (S.I. 2005 No. 950)). Their effect is to a large extent to replace the provisions of the Act of 2000. For a considerable period of time, however, offenders will continue to come before the courts in respect of offences committed before, and in relation to sentences imposed before, the commencement of the 2003 legislation. The saving provisions in relation to Chapters 1 to 5 of Part 12 are set out at §§ 5–1a, 5–1b, *post*. The transitional provisions in relation to section 156 (pre-sentence reports and other requirements) are set out at § 5–19, *post*. The transitional and saving provisions in relation to release on licence are set out at §§ 5–364b *et seq.*, *post*. For the transitional and saving provisions consequential upon the delayed commencement of sections 177, 179 and 180, and of Schedules 8 and 9 (community orders) in the case of 16- and 17-year-olds, see §§ 5–131a *et seq.* in the supplement.

The Acts of 2000 and of 2003 were subject to further substantial amendment by the *CJIA* 2008, particularly in relation to the sentencing of young offenders and of dangerous offenders and the release of offenders from custodial sentences. In particular, Part 1 (ss.1– 6, together with Schedules 1 and 2) introduces the youth rehabilitation order. The provisions of the Act of 2000 relating to curfew orders, exclusion orders, attendance centre orders, supervision orders and action plan orders are repealed. Part 1 is not anticipated to come into force before the second half of 2009. Space prohibits the inclusion in the main work of both the former provisions and the new provisions. Accordingly, the details of Part 1 of the 2008 Act will be found in the second and/or third supplements to this edition.

Section 6(1) of the 2008 Act repeals sections 33 to 40C and 60 to 72 of, and Schedules 3 and 5 to 7 to, the 2000 Act. Section 6(2) gives effect to the amendments in Part 1 (paras 1– 99) of Schedule 4, and section 6(3) gives effect to those in Part 2 (paras 100– 109) of that schedule. Section 148(2) of the 2008 Act gives effect to the transitional and saving provisions in Schedule 27, paragraph 1(1) of which provides that these repeals, any further repeals and revocations in Part 1 of Schedule 28 and the amendments in Part 1 of Schedule 4 are of no effect in relation to any offence committed before they come into force or any failure to comply with an order made in respect of such an offence, and paragraph 1(2) of which provides that so far as any amendment in Part 2 of Schedule 4 relates to a referral or reparation order under the 2000 Act or a community order under section 177 of the 2003 Act, the amendment has effect in relation to orders made before, as well as after, it comes into force.

(b) *Transitional and saving provisions (2003 Act)*

Criminal Justice Act 2003 (Commencement No. 8 and Transitional and Saving Provisions) Order 2005 (S.I. 2005 No. 950), Sched. 2, paras 5 and 6

Saving provisions relating to Chapters 1 to 5 of Part 12

5.—(1) The coming into force of the provisions mentioned in paragraph (2) is of no effect in relation to an offence committed before 4th April 2005. **5–1a**

(2) The provisions to which this paragraph applies are—

(a) sections 146 to 150, 152, 153, 166, 177, 179, 180, and 189 to 194 of and Schedules 8, 9, 12, 13 and 14 to the 2003 Act;

(b) in Schedule 32 (amendments relating to sentencing), paragraphs 2, 5 and 6(a), 8 and 9, 12(4) and (5), 13 to 15, 18(1) and (3), 20 to 23, 26, 31, 32, 35, 36, 38, 47, 54, 59 to 61, 64, 67, 68(1), (3) and (4), 69 to 81, 88, 89, 91, 92, 94 to 97(2) and (3), 98, 99, 100(2) and (3), 101, 102(1) and (2)(a), 103, 104(2) and (3), 105, 106(2), 107, 110, 122, 123, and 125 to 129, 130 to 132, 134, 135, 138, 141 and 144;

(c) in Part 7 of Schedule 37 (repeals)—

(i) the entry relating to section 18 of the *Crime and Disorder Act* 1998;

(ii) the entry relating to section 104(1) of the *Criminal Justice Act* 1967;

(iii) the entry relating to section 11(4) of the *Criminal Appeal Act* 1968;

(iv) the entry relating to the *Social Work (Scotland) Act* 1968;

(v) the entry relating to the *Bail Act* 1976;

(vi) the entry relating to Schedule 6A of the *Magistrates' Courts Act* 1980;

(vii) the entry relating to the *Road Traffic Offenders Act* 1988;

(viii) the entry relating to section 7(9) of the *Football Spectators Act* 1989;

(ix) the entry relating to the *Children Act* 1989;

(x) the entry relating to the *Criminal Justice and Public Order Act* 1994;

(xi) the entry relating to the *Criminal Procedure (Scotland) Act* 1995;

(xii) the entry relating to sections 34 to 36A, 36B, 37(9), 40A(4) and (9), 41 to 59, 62, 79 and 80, 85, 109, 118 to 125, 151 to 153, 158 to 161(2) to (4) and 163 of and Schedules 2, 4, 7 and 8 to the *Sentencing Act*;

(xiii) the entry relating to section 47 to 51, 53 to 55, 63 and 78(1) of and Schedule 7 to the *Criminal Justice and Court Services Act* 2000.

(3) Where an offence is found to have been committed over a period of two or more days, or at some time during a period of two or more days, it shall be taken for the purposes of paragraph (1) to have been committed on the last of those days.

6. The coming into force of— **5–1b**

(a) paragraphs 37, 38, 46, 93, 117, 120 and 124 of Schedule 32 to the 2003 Act; and

(b) Part 7 of Schedule 37 to the 2003 Act in so far as it relates to—

(i) section 37(1B) of the *Mental Health Act* 1983;

(ii) sections 112 to 115, and 127 of the *Sentencing Act*,

is of no effect in a case in which a court is dealing with a person whose sentence falls to be imposed under section 109 of the *Sentencing Act*.

(2) Legislation

Powers of Criminal Courts (Sentencing) Act 2000, ss.161, 163, 164

Interpretation

Meaning of "associated offence", "sexual offence", "violent offence" and "protecting the public from serious harm"

161.—(1) For the purposes of this Act, an offence is associated with another if— **5–2**

(a) the offender is convicted of it in the proceedings in which he is convicted of the other offence, or (although convicted of it in earlier proceedings) is sentenced for it at the same time as he is sentenced for that offence; or

(b) the offender admits the commission of it in the proceedings in which he is sentenced for the other offence and requests the court to take it into consideration in sentencing him for that offence.

(2)–(4) [*Repealed by* CJA *2003, s.332, and Sched. 7, Pt 7.*]

General definitions

5–3 **163.**—[(1)] In this Act, except where the contrary intention appears—

"action plan order" means an order under section 69(1) above ;

"affected person" —

(a) *in relation to an exclusion order, has the meaning given by section 40A(13) above;*

"associated", in relation to offences, shall be construed in accordance with section 161(1) above;

"attendance centre" has the meaning given by section 221(2) of the Criminal Justice Act *2003 ;*

"attendance centre order" means an order under section 60(1) above (and, except where the contrary intention is shown by paragraph 8 of Schedule 3 or paragraph 4 of Schedule 7 or 8 to this Act, includes orders made under section 60(1) by virtue of paragraph 4(1)(c) or 5(1)(c) *[4(1C)(c) or* 5(1C)(c)*] [[4(2)(b) or 5(2)(b)]] of Schedule 3 or paragraph 2(2)(a) of Schedule 7 or 8);*

"child" means a person under the age of 14;

"community order" has the meaning given by section 177(1) of the *Criminal Justice Act* 2003;

"community sentence" has the meaning given by section 33(2) above;

"compensation order" has the meaning given by section 130(1) above;

"court" does not include *a court-martial* [the Court Martial];

"curfew order" means an order under section 37(1) above (and, except where the contrary intention is shown by [paragraph 7 of Schedule 3 or] paragraph 3 of Schedule 7 or 8, includes orders made under section 37(1) by virtue of [paragraph 4(2)(a) or 5(2)(a) of Schedule 3 or] paragraph 2(2)(a) of Schedule 7 or 8);

"custodial sentence" has the meaning given by section 76 above; [and in relation to sentences passed before the coming into force of section 61 of the *Criminal Justice and Court Services Act* 2000, includes a sentence of custody for life and a sentence of custody for life and a sentence of detention in a young offender institution;]

"detention and training order" has the meaning given by section 100(3) above;

" *exclusion order" means an order under section 40A(1) above;*

"guardian" has the same meaning as in the *Children and Young Persons Act* 1933;

"local authority accommodation" means accommodation provided by or on behalf of a local authority, and "accommodation provided by or on behalf of a local authority" here has the same meaning as it has in the *Children Act* 1989 by virtue of section 105 of that Act;

"local probation board" means a local probation board established under section 4 of the *Criminal Justice and Court Services Act* 2000;

"offence punishable with imprisonment" shall be construed in accordance with section 164(2) below;

"operational period", in relation to a suspended sentence, has the meaning given by section 189(1)(b)(ii) of the *Criminal Justice Act* 2003;

"order for conditional discharge" has the meaning given by section 12(3) above;

"period of conditional discharge" has the meaning given by section 12(3) above;

"probation order" means an order under section 41(1) above;

"probation period" means the period for which a person subject to a probation or combination order is placed under supervision by the order;

"referral order" means an order under section 16(2) or (3) above;

"the register" means the register of proceedings before a magistrates' court required by Criminal Procedure Rules to be kept by the clerk of the court;

"reparation order" means an order under section 73(1) above;

"responsible officer" —

(a) *in relation to a curfew order, has the meaning given by section 37(12) above;*

(aa) *in relation to an exclusion order, has the meaning given by section 40A(14) above;*

(f) *in relation to an action plan order, has the meaning given by section 69(4) above; and*

(g) in relation to a reparation order, has the meaning given by section 74(5) above;

"sentence of imprisonment" does not include a committal—

(a) in default of payment of any sum of money;

(b) for want of sufficient distress to satisfy any sum of money; or

(c) for failure to do or abstain from doing anything required to be done or left undone;

and references to sentencing an offender to imprisonment shall be construed accordingly;

"supervision order" means an order under section 63(1) above ;

"supervisor", in relation to a supervision order, has the meaning given by section 63(3) above;

"suspended sentence" has the meaning given by section 189(7) of the *Criminal Justice Act* 2003;

"young person" means a person aged at least 14 but under 18;

"youth offending team" means a team established under section 39 of the *Crime and Disorder Act* 1998;

"youth community order" has the meaning given by section 33(1) above[;

"youth rehabilitation order" has the meaning given by section 1(1) of the *Criminal Justice and Immigration Act* 2008].

[(2) In the definition of "sentence of imprisonment" in subsection (1) the reference to want of sufficient distress to satisfy a sum includes a reference to circumstances where—

(a) there is power to use the procedure in Schedule 12 to the *Tribunals, Courts and Enforcement Act* 2007 to recover the sum from a person, but

(b) it appears, after an attempt has been made to exercise the power, that the person's goods are insufficient to pay the amount outstanding (as defined by paragraph 50(3) of that Schedule).]

[This section is printed as amended, and repealed in part, by the *CJCSA* 2000, ss.43 to 45, 70(4), 74 and 75, and Sched. 7, paras 1 and 197, and Sched. 8; the *CJA* 2003, ss.304 and 332, Sched. 32, para. 123(1), (2) and (4) to (8) and Sched. 37, Pt 7; and the *Courts Act 2003 (Consequential Amendments) Order* 2004 (S.I. 2004 No. 2035). It is printed as further amended, as from a day to be appointed, by the *CJCSA* 2000, s.74, and Sched. 7, para. 197(a) (substitution of words in single square brackets for romanised words that precede them in definition of "attendance centre order") and (e) (insertion of words in square brackets in definition of "custodial sentence"); the *AFA* 2006, s.378(1), and Sched. 16, para. 168 (substitution of words in square brackets for italicised words in definition of "court"); the *Tribunals, Courts and Enforcement Act* 2007, s.62(3), and Sched. 13, paras 131 and 133 (insertion of subs. (2) and of "(1)" at the beginning); and the *CJIA* 2008, ss.6(2) and 149, Sched. 4, paras 51 and 61, and Sched. 28, Pt 1 (omission of italicised definitions, and paras (a), (aa) and (f) in definition of "responsible officer", insertion of definition of "youth rehabilitation order"); and, as from April 4, 2009 (*Criminal Justice Act 2003 (Commencement No. 8 and Transitional and Saving Provisions) Order* 2005 (S.I. 2005 No. 950), art. 4 (as amended by the *Criminal Justice Act 2003 (Commencement No. 8 and Transitional and Saving Provisions) (Amendment) Order* 2007 (S.I. 2007 No. 391))), the *CJA* 2003, s.304, and Sched. 32, para. 123(1) and (3) (substitution of words in double square brackets in definition of "attendance centre order" for words in single square brackets or italicised words, depending on which amendment comes into force first) and (5) (insertion of words in square brackets in definition of "curfew order"). For the transitional provisions in relation to the 2008 Act amendments, see *ante*, § 5–1.]

For the saving provisions in relation to this section, see *ante*, § 5–1a.

As to the meaning of "community order", for section 177 of the 2003 Act, see *post*, § 5–130. Section 33(1) of the 2000 Act defined it as a curfew order, exclusion order,- **5–4** community rehabilitation order, community punishment order, community punishment and rehabilitation order, drug treatment and testing order, drug abstinence order, attendance centre order, supervision order or action plan order, and section 33(2) defined "community sentence" as "a sentence which consists of or includes one or more community orders". Section 33 has been substituted by a new section 33 (*CJA* 2003, s.304, and Sched. 32, para. 95). The new subsection (1) defines "youth community order", for the purposes of that Act, as a curfew order, exclusion order, attendance centre order, supervision order or action plan order, and the new subsection (2) defines "community sentence" as meaning a sentence which consists of, or includes, a community order under section 177 of the 2003 Act, or one or more youth community orders.

For section 76 (meaning of "custodial sentence"), see *post*, § 5–262.

Further interpretative provisions

5–5 **164.**—(1) For the purposes of any provision of this Act which requires the determination of the age of a person by the court or the Secretary of State, his age shall be deemed to be that which it appears to the court or (as the case may be) the Secretary of State to be after considering any available evidence.

(2) Any reference in this Act to an offence punishable with imprisonment shall be construed without regard to any prohibition or restriction imposed by or under this or any Act on the imprisonment of young offenders.

(3) References in this Act to a sentence falling to be imposed—

(a) under section 110(2) or 111(2) above,

(b) under section 51A(2) of the *Firearms Act* 1968,

(c) under section 225(2) or 226(2) of the *Criminal Justice Act* 2003, or

(d) under section 29(4) or (6) of the *Violent Crime Reduction Act* 2006,

are to be read in accordance with section 305(4) of the *Criminal Justice Act* 2003.

[This section is printed as amended by the *CJA* 2003, s.304, and Sched. 32, para. 124; the *VCRA* 2006, ss.49 and 65, Sched. 1, para. 8, and Sched. 5; and the *CJIA* 2008, s.148(1), and Sched. 26, paras 40 and 48.]

For section 305 of the 2003 Act, see *post*, § 5–7.

Criminal Justice Act 2003, ss.176, 305

Interpretation of Chapter 1

5–6 **176.** In this Chapter—

"allocation guidelines" has the meaning given by section 170(1)(b);

"the Council" means the Sentencing Guidelines Council;

"the Panel" means the Sentencing Advisory Panel;

"sentence" and "sentencing" are to be read in accordance with section 142(3);

"sentencing guidelines" has the meaning given by section 170(1)(a);

"youth community order" has the meaning given by section 147(2)[;

"youth rehabilitation order" has the meaning given by section 1(1) of the *Criminal Justice and Immigration Act* 2008;

"youth rehabilitation order with fostering" has the meaning given by paragraph 4 of Schedule 1 to that Act;

"youth rehabilitation order with intensive supervision and surveillance" has the meaning given by paragraph 3 of Schedule 1 to that Act].

[The words in square brackets are substituted for the italicised words, as from a day to be appointed (as to which, see *ante*, § 5–1), by the *CJIA* 2008, s.6(2), and Sched. 4, paras 71 and 81.]

Chapter 1 of Part 12 of the 2003 Act comprises sections 142 to 176.

Interpretation of Part 12

5–7 **305.**—(1) In this Part, except where the contrary intention appears—

"accredited programme" has the meaning given by section 202(2);

"activity requirement", in relation to a community order, custody plus order, intermittent custody order or suspended sentence order, has the meaning given by section 201;

"alcohol treatment requirement", in relation to a community order or suspended sentence order, has the meaning given by section 212;

"the appropriate officer of the court" means , in relation to a magistrates' court, the clerk of the court;

"associated", in relation to offences, is to be read in accordance with section 161(1) of the *Sentencing Act*;

"attendance centre" has the meaning given by section 221(2);

"attendance centre requirement", in relation to a community order, custody plus order, intermittent custody order or suspended sentence order, has the meaning given by section 214;

"community order" has the meaning given by section 177(1);

"community requirement", in relation to a suspended sentence order, has the meaning given by section 189(7);

"community sentence" has the meaning given by section 147(1);

["compensation order" has the meaning given by section 130(1) of the *Sentencing Act*;]

"court" (without more), except in Chapter 7, does not include a service court[, but this does not apply where a contrary intention appears from any provision of the *Armed Forces Act* 2006];

"curfew requirement", in relation to a community order, custody plus order, intermittent custody order or suspended sentence order, has the meaning given by section 204;

"custodial sentence" has the meaning given by section 76 of the *Sentencing Act*;

"custody plus order" has the meaning given by section 181(4);

"default order" has the meaning given by section 300(3);

"drug rehabilitation requirement", in relation to a community order or suspended sentence order, has the meaning given by section 209;

"electronic monitoring requirement", in relation to a community order, custody plus order, intermittent custody order or suspended sentence order, has the meaning given by section 215;

"exclusion requirement", in relation to a community order, custody plus order, intermittent custody order or suspended sentence order, has the meaning given by section 205;

"guardian" has the same meaning as in the *Children and Young Persons Act* 1933;

"intermittent custody order" has the meaning given by section 183(2);

"licence" means a licence under Chapter 6;

"local probation board" means a local probation board established under section 4 of the *Criminal Justice and Court Services Act* 2000;

"mental health treatment requirement", in relation to a community order or suspended sentence order, has the meaning given by section 207;

"pre-sentence report" has the meaning given by section 158(1);

"programme requirement", in relation to a community order, custody plus order, intermittent custody order or suspended sentence order, has the meaning given by section 202;

"prohibited activity requirement", in relation to a community order, custody plus order, intermittent custody order or suspended sentence order, has the meaning given by section 203;

"residence requirement", in relation to a community order or suspended sentence order, has the meaning given by section 206;

"responsible officer", in relation to an offender to whom a community order, a custody plus order, an intermittent custody order or a suspended sentence order relates, has the meaning given by section 197;

"sentence of imprisonment" does not include a committal—

(a) in default of payment of any sum of money,

(b) for want of sufficient distress to satisfy any sum of money, or

(c) for failure to do or abstain from doing anything required to be done or left undone [(including contempt of court or any kindred offence)],

and references to sentencing an offender to imprisonment are to be read accordingly ;

"the *Sentencing Act*" means the *Powers of Criminal Courts (Sentencing) Act* 2000;

"service court" means —

(a) *a court-martial constituted under the* Army Act *1955 , the* Air Force Act *1955 or the* Naval Discipline Act *1957*;

(b) *a summary appeal court constituted under section 83ZA of the* Army Act *1955*, *section 83ZA of the* Air Force Act *1955 or section 52FF of the* Naval Discipline Act *1957*;

(c) *the Courts-Martial Appeal Court; or*

(d) *a Standing Civilian Court;*

"service disciplinary proceedings" means —

(a) *any proceedings under the* Army Act *1955 , the* Air Force Act *1955 or the* Naval Discipline Act *1957 (whether before a court-martial or any other court or person authorised under any of those Acts to award a punishment in respect of any offence), and*

(b) *any proceedings before a Standing Civilian Court;*

["service court" means —

(a) the Court Martial;

(b) the Summary Appeal Court;

(c) the Service Civilian Court;

(d) the Court Martial Appeal Court; or

(e) the Supreme Court on an appeal brought from the Court Martial Appeal Court;]

"supervision requirement", in relation to a community order, custody plus order, intermittent custody order or suspended sentence order, has the meaning given by section 213;

"suspended sentence" and "suspended sentence order" have the meaning given by section 189(7);

"unpaid work requirement", in relation to a community order, custody plus order, intermittent custody order or suspended sentence order, has the meaning given by section 199;

"youth offending team" means a team established under section 39 of the *Crime and Disorder Act* 1998.

[(1A) [*Identical to s.163(2) of the* PCC(S)A *2000*, ante, § 5–3.]]

(2) For the purposes of any provision of this Part which requires the determination of the age of a person by the court or the Secretary of State, his age is to be taken to be that which it appears to the court or (as the case may be) the Secretary of State to be after considering any available evidence.

(3) Any reference in this Part to an offence punishable with imprisonment is to be read without regard to any prohibition or restriction imposed by or under any Act on the imprisonment of young offenders.

(4) For the purposes of this Part—

(a) a sentence falls to be imposed under subsection (2) of section 51A of the *Firearms Act* 1968 if it is required by that subsection and the court is not of the opinion there mentioned,

(b) a sentence falls to be imposed under section 110(2) or 111(2) of the *Sentencing Act* if it is required by that provision and the court is not of the opinion there mentioned,

(ba) a sentence falls to be imposed under section 29(4) or (6) of the *Violent Crime Reduction Act* 2006 if it is required by that provision and the court is not of the opinion there mentioned,

(c) a sentence falls to be imposed under subsection (2) of section 225 if the court is obliged to pass a sentence of imprisonment for life under that subsection,

(d) a sentence falls to be imposed under subsection (2) of section 226 if the court is obliged to pass a sentence of detention for life under that subsection.

[This section is printed as amended by the *VCRA* 2006, s.49, and Sched. 1, para. 9(1) and (8); and the *CJIA* 2008, ss.148(1) and 149, Sched. 26, paras 59 and 72, and Sched. 28, Pt 2; and as amended, as from a day to be appointed, by the *Domestic Violence, Crime and Victims Act* 2004, s.58(1), and Sched. 10, para. 64 (insertion of definition of "compensation order"); the *AFA* 2006, s.378(1), and Sched. 16, para. 231 (insertion of words in square bracket in the definition of "court", and substitution of definition of "service court" in square brackets for italicised definitions of "service court" and "service disciplinary proceedings"); the *PJA* 2006, s.34(1) and (6) (insertion of words in square brackets in definition of "sentence of imprisonment"); and the *Tribunals, Courts and Enforcement Act* 2007, s.62(3), and Sched. 13, paras 153 and 155 (insertion of subs. (1A)).]

Part 12 of the 2003 Act comprises sections 142 to 305.

The *Criminal Justice and Immigration Act 2008 (Transitory Provisions) Order* 2008 (S.I. 2008 No. 1587) modifies section 305(4)(c) (in relation to any time before the coming into force of section 61 of the *CJCSA* 2000 (abolition of sentences of detention in a young offender institution, custody for life, etc.)) by inserting the words "or, in the case of a person aged at least 18 but under 21, a sentence of custody for life" after the words "a sentence of imprisonment for life".

(3) Authorities

"Associated offences" (s.161(1) of the Act of 2000; s.305(1) of the 2003 Act)

An offence for which a suspended sentence has been passed is not an "associated offence" of a later offence committed during the operational period of the suspended sentence: *R. v. Cawley*, 15 Cr.App.R.(S.) 25, CA. An offence which has been dealt with by means of a conditional discharge may be an associated offence of another offence for which the offender is sentenced after the conditional discharge has been made, but only if the sentencing court passes a sentence for the original offence on the same occasion: *R. v. Godfrey*, 14 Cr.App.R.(S.) 804, CA. **5–8**

[The next paragraph is § 5–11.]

Determination of age (s.164(1) of the Act of 2000; s.305(2) of the 2003 Act)

If the age of an offender is disputed, the best course is to adjourn to allow evidence to be called to clarify the matter (see *R. v. Steed*, 12 Cr.App.R.(S.) 230, CA); if the sentencer is alerted to the fact that the offender's age may not be what he claims it to be, section 164(1) will not necessarily apply (see *R. v. Harris*, 12 Cr.App.R.(S.) 318, CA). **5–11**

II. PRELIMINARIES

(1) Legal representation

Powers of Criminal Courts (Sentencing) Act 2000, s.83

Restriction on imposing custodial sentences on persons not legally represented

83.—(1) A magistrates' court on summary conviction, or the Crown Court on committal for sentence or on conviction on indictment, shall not pass a sentence of imprisonment on a person who— **5–12**

(a) is not legally represented in that court, and

(b) has not been previously sentenced to that punishment by a court in any part of the United Kingdom,

unless he is a person to whom subsection (3) below applies.

(2) A magistrates' court on summary conviction, or the Crown Court on committal for sentence or on conviction on indictment, shall not—

(a) pass a sentence of detention under section 90 or 91 below,

[(aa) pass a sentence of imprisonment on a person who, when convicted, was aged at least 18 but under 21,]

(b) *pass a sentence of custody for life under section 93 or 94 below,*

(c) *pass a sentence of detention in a young offender institution, or*

(d) make a detention and training order,

on or in respect of a person who is not legally represented in that court unless he is a person to whom subsection (3) below applies.

(3) This subsection applies to a person if either—

(a) he was granted a right to representation funded by the Legal Services Commission as part of the Criminal Defence Service but the right was withdrawn because of his conduct [or because it appeared that his financial resources were such that he was not eligible to be granted such a right;

(aa) he applied for such representation and the application was refused because it appeared that his financial resources were such that he was not eligible to be granted a right to it; or

(b) having been informed of his right to apply for such representation and having had the opportunity to do so, he refused or failed to apply.

(4) For the purposes of this section a person is to be treated as legally represented in a court if, but only if, he has the assistance of counsel or a solicitor to represent him in the proceedings in that court at some time after he is found guilty and before he is sentenced.

(5) For the purposes of subsection (1)(b) above a previous sentence of imprisonment which has been suspended and which has not taken effect under section 119 below or under section 19 of the *Treatment of Offenders Act (Northern Ireland)* 1968 shall be disregarded.

(6) In this section "sentence of imprisonment" does not include a committal for contempt of court or any kindred offence.

[This section is printed as amended by the *Criminal Defence Service Act* 2006, s.4(2) and (3); and, as amended, as from a day to be appointed, by the *CJCSA* 2000, s.74 and Sched. 7, para. 178 (insertion of words in square brackets, repeal of italicised words in subs. (2)).]

5–13 Non-compliance with section 83 renders the sentence unlawful (see *R. v. Birmingham JJ., ex p. Wyatt*, 61 Cr.App.R. 306, DC; *McC. v. Mullan* [1985] A.C. 528 at 552, HL), but in the case of a sentence passed by the Crown Court the defect can be cured by the Court of Appeal: *R. v. McGinlay and Ballantyne*, 62 Cr.App.R. 156, CA; and as to the options open to that court, see *R. v. Howden* [2007] 1 Cr.App.R.(S.) 31, *post*, § 7–130.

In *R. v. Hollywood*, 12 Cr.App.R.(S.) 325, CA, the appellant, who had not previously been sentenced to imprisonment, was represented by counsel and solicitor when he pleaded guilty, but when he was sentenced two days later, neither was present. *Held*, the sentence of imprisonment was invalid because he had not been represented "at some time after he is found guilty and before he is sentenced" within section 83(4).

In *R. v. Wilson*, 16 Cr.App.R.(S.) 997, CA, the appellant was granted legal aid but dismissed her solicitors and a second firm of solicitors assigned under an amended legal aid order. The judge declined to adjourn for a further firm to be instructed. It was held that section 83(4) would have been complied with if at some time after conviction the appellant received advice from her lawyers, albeit that she rejected that advice, and dismissed them. The legal aid order had not, however, been withdrawn, and it entitled her to legal representation, and it was, therefore, unlawful to have sentenced her without the benefit of the representation to which she had been entitled.

(2) Arrest of judgment

5–14 At any time between conviction and sentence, the defendant may move the court in arrest of judgment. The motion must be based on some objection arising on the face of the record, such as a fundamental defect in the indictment which cannot be cured by the verdict. The court may of its own motion arrest judgment (see *R. v. Waddington* (1800) 1 East 143 at 146). If judgment is arrested, the proceedings are set aside, but this is no bar to a fresh indictment (see *Vaux's case* (1590) 4 Co.Rep. 44a). In practice, the motion in arrest of judgment has been superseded by the provision of appeals under the *CAA* 1968 (see *R. v. Laming*, 90 Cr.App.R. 450, CA, *post*, § 7–41).

(3) Adjournment after conviction and before sentence

Common law

5–15 The Crown Court has jurisdiction at common law to postpone the passing of a sentence or part thereof. Although it is generally desirable to deal with all matters relating to sentence on the same occasion, it may occasionally be necessary to pass the substantive sentence at once and postpone what has to be done in addition (*e.g.* an order for disqualification) rather than postpone the whole sentence until all the material is available: *R. v. Annesley*, 62 Cr.App.R. 113, CA. The postponement may be for more than the 28 days referred to in section 155(2) of the *PCC(S)A* 2000 (*post*, § 5–940):

ibid. If the court proposes to postpone passing part of the sentence, it must state expressly at the time that it is doing so; otherwise the normal statutory time limit for variation of sentence under section 155 of the 2000 Act will apply: see *R. v. Dorrian* [2001] 1 Cr.App.R.(S.) 135, CA; and *R. v. Jones* [2004] 1 Cr.App.R.(S.) 23, CA.

See *R. v. Reynolds*, *post*, §§ 5–309d, 5–940, as to the power of the Crown Court to adjourn where it rescinds its original sentence within 28 days, under section 155 of the 2000 Act, having failed to appreciate at the original sentencing hearing that the dangerous offender provisions of sections 224 to 229 of the *CJA* 2003 applied.

Raising expectations of non-custodial sentence

When a judge purposely postpones sentence so that an alternative to prison can be examined and that alternative is found to be a satisfactory one in all respects, the court ought to adopt the alternative. A feeling of injustice is otherwise aroused: *R. v. Gillam*, 2 Cr.App.R.(S.) 267, CA. This principle was extended in *R. v. Rennes*, 7 Cr.App.R.(S.) 343, CA, to an adjournment by a magistrates' court, which was followed by a committal to the Crown Court for sentence, where a custodial sentence was imposed (*post*, § 5–30). Similar reasoning was adopted by the Divisional Court in *Gutteridge v. DPP*, 9 Cr.App.R.(S.) 280, where it was held that the principle applies to the Crown Court deciding an appeal from a magistrates' court. **5–16**

The principle in *Gillam* has no application if the circumstances in which the case was adjourned were such that nobody present in court could have had an expectation that there would be a non-custodial penalty even if the reports were favourable: *R. v. Horton and Alexander*, 7 Cr.App.R.(S.) 299, CA. The question is whether the circumstances created an expectation of a non-custodial penalty which it would be unjust to disappoint: *R. v. Norton and Claxton*, 11 Cr.App.R.(S.) 143, CA.

The *PCC(S)A* 2000, s.81(1), required a court to obtain and consider a pre-sentence report before imposing a custodial sentence unless it was unnecessary to do so (and see now the *CJA* 2003, s.156(3)(a), (4), *post*, § 5–19). In *R. v. Woodin*, 15 Cr.App.R.(S.) 307, CA, it was held that an appellant who had been released on bail pending the preparation of a pre-sentence report, without a warning that the adjournment and release were without prejudice to the possibility that a custodial sentence might be passed, was not entitled to believe that a community order would be imposed. The sentencer had adjourned because the statute required him to do so; given its mandatory requirements and the purpose for which the report was required, the sentencer was not obliged to indicate to the appellant that he was still liable to be sentenced to imprisonment. See also *R. v. Renan*, *ibid.* at 722, CA: in the light of the statutory obligation to obtain a report before imposing a custodial sentence, silence by the judge should never be taken as an indication that a non-custodial sentence would be considered appropriate, although it was better practice for a judge, when adjourning for a pre-sentence report and granting bail, to indicate that this did not mean that a non-custodial sentence was likely.

In *R. v. Chamberlain*, 16 Cr.App.R.(S.) 473, the Court of Appeal stressed the duty of sentencers to explain what the position was when they ordered adjournments for investigation and assessment of defendants over and above those called for by the *PCC(S)A* 2000, ss.36 (see now s.156(3)(b) of the 2003 Act) and 81. The defendant should invariably be told in clear terms that he must not assume from the fact that the court was ordering an adjournment for the purposes of further assessment and investigation, that he was likely to receive any particular form of sentence or that a custodial sentence was ruled out.

Adjournment to allow use of sentencing power restricted to offenders of particular age group

It is an abuse of the power of adjournment to exercise it solely so as to wait for the offender to attain a particular age before the attainment of which a particular form of sentence could not be imposed: *Arthur v. Stringer*, 84 Cr.App.R. 361, DC (considering the *MCA* 1980, s.10(3) (power of adjournment after conviction for purpose of making inquiries as to most suitable disposal, but limited to 28 days at a time, or 21 days if in **5–17** custody)). If a statute provides that a person of a particular age who is convicted of an offence is liable to a particular penalty, the date of conviction is generally to be taken to be the date of the finding of guilt or plea of guilty, not the date sentence is passed, if different: *R. v. Danga* [1992] Q.B. 476, 94 Cr.App.R. 252, CA.

Statutory restriction

5–18 There is no provision equivalent to section 10(3) of the 1980 Act (*ante*) which applies to the Crown Court in its original jurisdiction, but this provision must be observed by the Crown Court when dealing with appeals from magistrates' courts (see *Arthur v. Stringer*, *ante*), and presumably also when dealing with an offender who has been committed for sentence under a provision to which the *PCC(S)A* 2000, s.6 applies.

(4) Pre-sentence reports

Criminal Justice Act 2003, ss.156–158

Procedural requirements for imposing community sentences and discretionary custodial sentences

5–19 **156.**—(1) In forming any such opinion as is mentioned in section *148(1), (2)(b) or (3)(b)* [148(1) or (2)(b)], section 152(2) or section 153(2), [or in section 1(4)(b) or (c) of the *Criminal Justice and Immigration Act* 2008 (youth rehabilitation orders with intensive supervision and surveillance or fostering)] a court must take into account all such information as is available to it about the circumstances of the offence or (as the case may be) of the offence and the offence or offences associated with it, including any aggravating or mitigating factors.

(2) In forming any such opinion as is mentioned in section 148(2)(a) *or (3)(a)*, the court may take into account any information about the offender which is before it.

(3) Subject to subsection (4), a court must obtain and consider a pre-sentence report before—

(a) in the case of a custodial sentence, forming any such opinion as is mentioned in section 152(2), section 153(2), section 225(1)(b), section 226(1)(b), section 227(1)(b) or section 228(1)(b)(i), or

(b) in the case of a community sentence, forming any such opinion as is mentioned in section 148(1), *(2)(b) or (3)(b)* [or (2)(b), or in section 1(4)(b) or (c) of the *Criminal Justice and Immigration Act* 2008,] or any opinion as to the suitability for the offender of the particular requirement or requirements to be imposed by the community order [or youth rehabilitation order].

(4) Subsection (3) does not apply if, in the circumstances of the case, the court is of the opinion that it is unnecessary to obtain a pre-sentence report.

(5) In a case where the offender is aged under 18, the court must not form the opinion mentioned in subsection (4) unless—

(a) there exists a previous pre-sentence report obtained in respect of the offender, and

(b) the court has had regard to the information contained in that report, or, if there is more than one such report, the most recent report.

(6) No custodial sentence or community sentence is invalidated by the failure of a court to obtain and consider a pre-sentence report before forming an opinion referred to in subsection (3), but any court on an appeal against such a sentence—

(a) must, subject to subsection (7), obtain a pre-sentence report if none was obtained by the court below, and

(b) must consider any such report obtained by it or by that court.

(7) Subsection (6)(a) does not apply if the court is of the opinion—

(a) that the court below was justified in forming an opinion that it was unnecessary to obtain a pre-sentence report, or

(b) that, although the court below was not justified in forming that opinion, in the circumstances of the case at the time it is before the court, it is unnecessary to obtain a pre-sentence report.

(8) In a case where the offender is aged under 18, the court must not form the opinion mentioned in subsection (7) unless—

(a) there exists a previous pre-sentence report obtained in respect of the offender, and

(b) the court has had regard to the information contained in that report, or, if there is more than one such report, the most recent report.

[This section is printed as amended, as from a day to be appointed (as to which, see *ante*, § 5–1), by the *CJIA* 2008, ss.6(2) and 149, Sched. 4, paras 71 and 77, and Sched. 28, Pt 1 (omission of italicised words, insertion of words in square brackets).]

The *Criminal Justice Act 2003 (Commencement No. 8 and Transitional Provisions and Savings) Order* 2005 (S.I. 2005 No. 950), arts 2 and 4, and Sched. 2, para. 4, modify section 156 where a court is dealing with an offence committed before April 4, 2005, by treating the references in subsection (1) to section 148(1), (2)(b) or (3)(b), section 152(2) and section 153(2) of the 2003 Act as if they were references to sections 35(1) and (3)(b), 79(2)(a) and 80(2)(a) of the *PCC(S)A* 2000; the references in subsection (2) to section 148(2)(a) and (3)(a) as if they were references to section 35(3)(a) of the 2000 Act; the references in subsection 3(a) to sections 152(2), 153(2), 225(1)(b), 226(1)(b), 227(1)(b) and 228(1)(b)(i) of the 2003 Act as if they were references to section 79(2) or 80(2) of the 2000 Act; and the references in subsection (3)(b) to sections 148(1), (2)(b) and (3)(b) as if they were references to section 35(1) and (3)(b) of the 2000 Act.

Additional requirements in case of mentally disordered offender

157.—(1) Subject to subsection (2), in any case where the offender is or appears to be mentally disordered, the court must obtain and consider a medical report before passing a custodial sentence other than one fixed by law. **5–20**

(2) Subsection (1) does not apply if, in the circumstances of the case, the court is of the opinion that it is unnecessary to obtain a medical report.

(3) Before passing a custodial sentence other than one fixed by law on an offender who is or appears to be mentally disordered, a court must consider—

(a) any information before it which relates to his mental condition (whether given in a medical report, a pre-sentence report or otherwise), and

(b) the likely effect of such a sentence on that condition and on any treatment which may be available for it.

(4) No custodial sentence which is passed in a case to which subsection (1) applies is invalidated by the failure of a court to comply with that subsection, but any court on an appeal against such a sentence—

(a) must obtain a medical report if none was obtained by the court below, and

(b) must consider any such report obtained by it or by that court.

(5) In this section "mentally disordered", in relation to any person, means suffering from a mental disorder within the meaning of the *Mental Health Act* 1983.

(6) In this section "medical report" means a report as to an offender's mental condition made or submitted orally or in writing by a registered medical practitioner who is approved for the purposes of section 12 of the *Mental Health Act* 1983 by the Secretary of State as having special experience in the diagnosis or treatment of mental disorder.

(7) Nothing in this section is to be taken to limit the generality of section 156.

Meaning of "pre-sentence report"

158.—(1) In this Part "pre-sentence report" means a report which— **5–21**

(a) with a view to assisting the court in determining the most suitable method of dealing with an offender, is made or submitted by an appropriate officer; and

(b) contains information as to such matters, presented in such manner, as may be prescribed by rules made by the Secretary of State.

(1A) Subject to any rules made under subsection (1)(b) and to subsection (1B), the court may accept a pre-sentence report given orally in open court.

(1B) But a pre-sentence report that—

(a) relates to an offender aged under 18, and

(b) is required to be obtained and considered before the court forms an opinion mentioned in section 156(3)(a),

must be in writing.

(2) In subsection (1) "an appropriate officer" means—

(a) where the offender is aged 18 or over, an officer of a local probation board or an officer of a provider of probation services, and

(b) where the offender is aged under 18, an officer of a local probation board, an officer of a provider of probation services, a social worker of a local authority social services department or a member of a youth offending team.

[This section is printed as amended by the *Offender Management Act 2007 (Consequential Amendments) Order* 2008 (S.I. 2008 No. 912), art. 3, and Sched. 1, para.19(1) and (2); and the *CJIA* 2008, s.12.]

Section 156 corresponds broadly to the combined effect of sections 36 and 81 of the *PCC(S)A* 2000 (as to which, see *ante*, § 5–16, and *post*, § 5–274); and section 157 corresponds almost exactly to section 82 of the 2000 Act.

Disclosure of pre-sentence reports

5–22 Section 159 of the *CJA* 2003 applies where a court obtains a pre-sentence report, other than one given orally in open court. Copies must be given to the offender, or his counsel or solicitor [reference to "legal representative" substituted, as from a day to be appointed, for the words "counsel or solicitor" by the *Legal Services Act* 2007, s.208(1), and Sched. 21, paras 145 and 147], to any parent or guardian of his who is present at court if he is under 18, and to the prosecutor. If, however, it appears to the court that disclosure to the offender or to his parent or guardian of any information contained in the report would be likely to create a risk of significant harm to the offender, a complete copy need not be given; and, if the prosecutor is not of a prescribed description, a copy need not be given to him, if the court considers it would be inappropriate to do so (subs. (4)). There is a restriction on the disclosure or use of information obtained by the prosecutor by virtue of this section, otherwise than for the purpose of determining whether representations as to matters contained in the report need to be made to the court, or of making representations to the court (subs. (5)). In relation to an offender under 18 for whom a local authority have parental responsibility, and who is in their care, or is provided with accommodation by them in the exercise of any social services functions, references to the child's parents or guardian are to be taken as references to the local authority.

Section 160 contains like provisions [with corresponding prospective amendment] in relation to reports (not being pre-sentence reports) of local probation boards, providers of probation services or youth offending teams which are made to any court, other than a youth court, with a view to assisting the court in determining the most suitable method of disposal, but there is no provision in this case for disclosure to the prosecutor.

The *Pre-sentence Report Disclosure (Prescription of Prosecutors) Order* 1998 (S.I. 1998 No. 191) has effect as if made under section 159(4) of the 2003 Act. It prescribes the following descriptions of prosecutors for the purposes of these provisions: a crown prosecutor, any other person acting on behalf of the Crown Prosecution Service, or a person acting on behalf of the Commissioners for Customs and Revenue, the Secretary of State for Social Security or the Director of the Serious Fraud Office.

(5) Pre-sentence drug testing

Criminal Justice Act 2003, s.161

[Pre-sentence drug testing

5–23 **161.**—(1) Where a person *aged 14 or over* is convicted of an offence and the court is considering passing a community sentence or a suspended sentence, it may make an order under subsection (2) for the purpose of ascertaining whether the offender has any specified Class A drug in his body.

(2) The order requires the offender to provide, in accordance with the order, samples of any description specified in the order.

(3) Where the offender has not attained the age of 17, the order must provide for the samples to be provided in the presence of an appropriate adult.

(4) If it is proved to the satisfaction of the court that the offender has, without reasonable excuse, failed to comply with the order it may impose on him a fine of an amount not exceeding level 4.

(5) In subsection (4) "level 4" means the amount which, in relation to a fine for a summary offence, is level 4 on the standard scale.

(6) The court may not make an order under subsection (2) unless it has been notified

by the Secretary of State that the power to make such orders is exercisable by the court and the notice has not been withdrawn.

(7) *The Secretary of State may by order amend subsection (1) by substituting for the age for the time being specified there a different age specified in the order.*

(8) In this section—

"appropriate adult", in relation to a person under the age of 17, means —

(a) his parent or guardian or, if he is in the care of a local authority or voluntary organisation, a person representing that authority or organisation,

(b) a social worker of a local authority social services department, or

(c) if no person falling within paragraph (a) or (b) is available, any responsible person aged 18 or over who is not a police officer or a person employed by the police;

"specified Class A drug" has the same meaning as in Part 3 of the *Criminal Justice and Court Services Act* 2000.]

This section comes into force on a day to be appointed. The italicised words in subsection (4), together with subsection (7), are repealed, as from a day to be appointed (as to which, see *ante*, § 5–1), by the *CJIA* 2008, ss.6(2) and 149, Sched. 4, paras 71 and 78, and Sched. 28, Pt 1. Its predecessor provision was section 36A of the *PCC(S)A* 2000 (inserted therein by the *CJCSA* 2000, s.48), but that provision applied only in the case of persons aged 18 or over at the time of conviction.

(6) Committal for sentence

Powers of Criminal Courts (Sentencing) Act 2000, ss.3–7

Committal to Crown Court for sentence

Committal for sentence on summary trial of offence triable either way

3.—(1) Subject to subsection (4) below, this section applies where on the summary trial of an offence triable either way a person aged 18 or over is convicted of the offence. **5–24**

(2) If the court is of the opinion—

(a) that the offence or the combination of the offence and one or more offences associated with it was so serious that *greater punishment should be inflicted for the offence than the court has power to impose* [the Crown Court should, in the court's opinion, have the power to deal with the offender in any way it could deal with him if he had been convicted on indictment], *or*

(b) *in the case of a violent or sexual offence, that a custodial sentence for a term longer than the court has power to impose is necessary to protect the public from serious harm from him,*

the court may commit the offender in custody or on bail to the Crown Court for sentence in accordance with section 5(1) below.

(3) Where the court commits a person under subsection (2) above, section 6 below (which enables a magistrates' court, where it commits a person under this section in respect of an offence, also to commit him to the Crown Court to be dealt with in respect of certain other offences) shall apply accordingly.

(4) This section does not apply in relation to an offence as regards which this section is excluded by section [17D or] 33 of the *Magistrates' Courts Act* 1980 (certain offences where value involved is small).

(5) The preceding provisions of this section shall apply in relation to a corporation as if—

(a) the corporation were an individual aged 18 or over; and

(b) in subsection (2) above, *paragraph (b) and* the words "in custody or on bail" were omitted.

[This section is printed as amended, as from a day to be appointed, by the *CJA* 2003, Sched. 3, para. 22A (omission of italicised words, insertion of words in square brackets).]

[Committal for sentence of dangerous adult offenders

3A.—(1) This section applies where on the summary trial of a specified offence triable either way a person aged 18 or over is convicted of the offence. **5–24a**

(2) If, in relation to the offence, it appears to the court that the criteria for the imposition of a sentence under section 225(3) or 227(2) of the *Criminal Justice Act* 2003 would be met, the court must commit the offender in custody or on bail to the Crown Court for sentence in accordance with section 5(1) below.

(3) Where the court commits a person under subsection (2) above, section 6 below (which enables a magistrates' court, where it commits a person under this section in respect of an offence, also to commit him to the Crown Court to be dealt with in respect of certain other offences) shall apply accordingly.

(4) In reaching any decision under or taking any step contemplated by this section—

(a) the court shall not be bound by any indication of sentence given in respect of the offence under section 20 of the *Magistrates' Courts Act* 1980 (procedure where summary trial appears more suitable); and

(b) nothing the court does under this section may be challenged or be the subject of any appeal in any court on the ground that it is not consistent with an indication of sentence.

(5) Nothing in this section shall prevent the court from committing an offender convicted of a specified offence to the Crown Court for sentence under section 3 above if the provisions of that section are satisfied.

(6) In this section, references to a specified offence are to a specified offence within the meaning of section 224 of the *Criminal Justice Act* 2003.]

[Committal for sentence on indication of guilty plea by child or young person

5–24b **3B.**—(1) This section applies where—

(a) a person aged under 18 appears or is brought before a magistrates' court ("the court") on an information charging him with an offence mentioned in subsection (1) of section 91 below ("the offence");

(b) he or his representative indicates under section 24A or (as the case may be) 24B of the *Magistrates' Courts Act* 1980 (child or young person to indicate intention as to plea in certain cases) that he would plead guilty if the offence were to proceed to trial; and

(c) proceeding as if section 9(1) of that Act were complied with and he pleaded guilty under it, the court convicts him of the offence.

(2) If the court is of the opinion that—

(a) the offence; or

(b) the combination of the offence and one or more offences associated with it,

was such that the Crown Court should, in the court's opinion, have power to deal with the offender as if the provisions of section 91(3) below applied, the court may commit him in custody or on bail to the Crown Court for sentence in accordance with section 5A(1) below.

(3) Where the court commits a person under subsection (2) above, section 6 below (which enables a magistrates' court, where it commits a person under this section in respect of an offence, also to commit him to the Crown Court to be dealt with in respect of certain other offences) shall apply accordingly.]

Committal for sentence of dangerous young offenders

5–24c **3C.**—(1) This section applies where on the summary trial of a specified offence a person aged under 18 is convicted of the offence.

(2) If, in relation to the offence, it appears to the court that the criteria for the imposition of a sentence under section 226(3) or 228(2) of the *Criminal Justice Act* 2003 would be met, the court must commit the offender in custody or on bail to the Crown Court for sentence in accordance with section 5A(1) below.

(3) Where the court commits a person under subsection (2) above, section 6 below (which enables a magistrates' court, where it commits a person under this section in respect of an offence, also to commit him to the Crown Court to be dealt with in respect of certain other offences) shall apply accordingly.

(4) Nothing in this section shall prevent the court from committing a specified offence to the Crown Court for sentence under section 3B above if the provisions of that section are satisfied.

(5) In this section, references to a specified offence are to a specified offence within the meaning of section 224 of the *Criminal Justice Act* 2003.

[Ss.3A to 3C are inserted by the *CJA* 2003, s.41, and Sched. 3, paras 21 and 23. The insertion of s.3C took effect on April 4, 2005: *Criminal Justice Act 2003 (Commencement No. 8 and Transitional and Saving Provisions) Order* 2005 (S.I. 2005 No. 950). Otherwise, these insertions take effect on a day to be appointed. S.3A is printed as amended by the *CJIA* 2008, s.53, and Sched. 13, paras 1 and 9.]

Committal for sentence on indication of guilty plea to offence triable either way

4.—(1) This section applies where— 5–25

(a) a person aged 18 or over appears or is brought before a magistrates' court ("the court") on an information charging him with an offence triable either way ("the offence");

(b) he or [(where applicable)] his representative indicates [under section 17A, 17B or 20(7) of the *Magistrates' Courts Act* 1980] that he would plead guilty if the offence were to proceed to trial; and

(c) proceeding as if section 9(1) of *the* Magistrates' Courts Act *1980* [that Act] were complied with and he pleaded guilty under it, the court convicts him of the offence.

[(1A) But this section does not apply to an offence as regards which this section is excluded by section 17D of that Act (certain offences where value involved is small).]

(2) If the court has *committed* [sent] the offender to the Crown Court for trial for one or more related offences, that is to say, one or more offences which, in its opinion, are related to the offence, it may commit him in custody or on bail to the Crown Court to be dealt with in respect of the offence in accordance with section 5(1) below.

(3) *If the power conferred by subsection (2) above is not exercisable but the court is still to inquire, as examining justices, into one or more related offences—*

(a) *it shall adjourn the proceedings relating to the offence until after the conclusion of its inquiries; and*

(b) *if it commits the offender to the Crown Court for trial for one or more related offences, it may then exercise that power.*

[(3) If the power conferred by subsection (2) above is not exercisable but the court is still to determine to, or determine whether to, send the offender to the Crown Court for trial under section 51 or 51A of the *Crime and Disorder Act* 1998 for one or more related offences—

(a) it shall adjourn the proceedings relating to the offence until after it has made those determinations; and

(b) if it sends the offender to the Crown Court for trial for one or more related offences, it may then exercise that power.]

(4) Where the court—

(a) under subsection (2) above commits the offender to the Crown Court to be dealt with in respect of the offence, and

(b) does not state that, in its opinion, it also has power so to commit him under section 3(2) [or, as the case may be, section 3A(2)] above,

section 5(1) below shall not apply unless he is convicted before the Crown Court of one or more of the related offences.

(5) Where section 5(1) below does not apply, the Crown Court may deal with the offender in respect of the offence in any way in which the magistrates' court could deal with him if it had just convicted him of the offence.

(6) Where the court commits a person under subsection (2) above, section 6 below (which enables a magistrates' court, where it commits a person under this section in respect of an offence, also to commit him to the Crown Court to be dealt with in respect of certain other offences) shall apply accordingly.

(7) For the purposes of this section one offence is related to another if, were they both to be prosecuted on indictment, the charges for them could be joined in the same indictment.

[(8) In reaching any decision under or taking any step contemplated by this section—

(a) the court shall not be bound by any indication of sentence given in respect of the offence under section 20 of the *Magistrates' Courts Act* 1980 (procedure where summary trial appears more suitable); and

(b) nothing the court does under this section may be challenged or be the subject of any appeal in any court on the ground that it is not consistent with an indication of sentence.]

[This section is printed as amended, as from a day to be appointed, by the *CJA* 2003, s.41, and Sched. 3, paras 21 and 24 (as itself amended by the *CJIA* 2008, s.53, and Sched. 13, paras 1 and 10) (omission of italicised words, insertion of words in square brackets).]

[Committal for sentence on indication of guilty plea by child or young person with related offences

4A.—(1) This section applies where— 5–25a

(a) a person aged under 18 appears or brought before a magistrates' court ("the court") on an information charging him with an offence mentioned in subsection (1) of section 91 below ("the offence");

(b) he or his representative indicates under section 24A or (as the case may be) 24B of the *Magistrates' Courts Act* 1980 (child or young person to indicate intention as to plea in certain cases) that he would plead guilty if the offence were to proceed to trial; and

(c) proceeding as if section 9(1) of that Act were complied with and he pleaded guilty under it, the court convicts him of the offence.

(2) If the court has sent the offender to the Crown Court for trial for one or more related offences, that is to say one or more offences which, in its opinion, are related to the offence, it may commit him in custody or on bail to the Crown Court to be dealt with in respect of the offence in accordance with section 5A(1) below.

(3) If the power conferred by subsection (2) above is not exercisable but the court is still to determine to, or to determine whether to, send the offender to the Crown Court for trial under section 51 or 51A of the *Crime and Disorder Act* 1998 for one or more related offences—

(a) it shall adjourn the proceedings relating to the offence until after it has made those determinations; and

(b) if it sends the offender to the Crown Court for trial for one or more related offences, it may then exercise that power.

(4) Where the court—

(a) under subsection (2) above commits the offender to the Crown Court to be dealt with in respect of the offence; and

(b) does not state that, in its opinion, it also has power so to commit him under section 3B(2) or, as the case may be, section 3C(2) above, section 5A(1) below shall not apply unless he is convicted before the Crown Court of one or more of the related offences.

(5) Where section 5A(1) below does not apply, the Crown Court may deal with the offender in respect of the offence in any way in which the magistrates' court could deal with him if it had just convicted him of the offence.

(6) Where the court commits a person under subsection (2) above, section 6 below (which enables a magistrates' court, where it commits a person under this section in respect of an offence, also to commit him to the Crown Court to be dealt with in respect of certain other offences) shall apply accordingly.

(7) Section 4(7) above applies for the purposes of this section as it applies for the purposes of that section.]

[This section is inserted, as from a day to be appointed, by the *CJA* 2003, s.41, and Sched. 3, paras 21 and 25.]

Power of Crown Court on committal for sentence under sections 3 and 4

5–26 **5.**—(1) *Where an offender is committed by a magistrates' court for sentence under section 3 or 4 above, the Crown Court shall inquire into the circumstances of the case and may deal with the offender in any way in which it could deal with him if he had just been convicted of the offence on indictment before the court.*

(2) *In relation to committals under section 4 above, subsection (1) above has effect subject to section 4(4) and (5) above.*

[Power of Crown Court on committal for sentence under sections 3, 3A and 4

5.—(1) Where an offender is committed by a magistrates' court for sentence under section 3, 3A or 4 above, the Crown Court shall inquire into the circumstances of the case and may deal with the offender in any way in which it could deal with him if he had just been convicted of the offence on indictment before the court.

(2) In relation to committals under section 4 above, subsection (1) above has effect subject to section 4(4) and (5) above.

(3) Section 20A(1) of the *Magistrates' Courts Act* 1980 (which relates to the effect of an indication of sentence under section 20 of that Act) shall not apply in respect of any specified offence (within the meaning of section 224 of the *Criminal Justice Act* 2003)—

(a) in respect of which the offender is committed under section 3A(2) above; or

(b) in respect of which—

(i) the offender is committed under section 4(2) above; and

(ii) the court states under section 4(4) above that, in its opinion, it also has power to commit the offender under section 3A(2) above.]

[S.5 (printed in square brackets) is substituted for the original s.5 (in italics) as from a day to be appointed: *CJA* 2003, s.41, and Sched. 3, paras 21 and 26.]

[Power of Crown Court on committal for sentence under sections 3B, 3C and 4A

5A.—(1) Where an offender is committed by a magistrates' court for sentence under section 3B, 3C or 4A above, the Crown Court shall inquire into the circumstances of the case and may deal with the offender in any way in which it could deal with him if he had just been convicted of the offence on indictment before the court. **5–26a**

(2) In relation to committals under section 4A above, subsection (1) above has effect subject to section 4A(4) and (5) above.]

[S.5A is inserted by the *CJA* 2003, s.41, and Sched. 3, paras 21 and 27. It came into force on April 4, 2005, in relation to cases committed under s.3C: S.I. 2005 No. 950 (*ante*, § 5–24c); otherwise, it comes into force on a day to be appointed.]

Committal for sentence in certain cases where offender committed in respect of another offence

6.—(1) This section applies where a magistrates' court ("the committing court") commits a person in custody or on bail to the Crown Court under any enactment mentioned in subsection (4) below to be sentenced or otherwise dealt with in respect of an offence ("the relevant offence"). **5–27**

(2) Where this section applies and the relevant offence is an indictable offence, the committing court may also commit the offender, in custody or on bail as the case may require, to the Crown Court to be dealt with in respect of any other offence whatsoever in respect of which the committing court has power to deal with him (being an offence of which he has been convicted by that or any other court).

(3) Where this section applies and the relevant offence is a summary offence, the committing court may commit the offender, in custody or on bail as the case may require, to the Crown Court to be dealt with in respect of—

(a) any other offence of which the committing court has convicted him, being either—

(i) an offence punishable with imprisonment; or

(ii) an offence in respect of which the committing court has a power or duty to order him to be disqualified under section 34, 35 or 36 of the *Road Traffic Offenders Act* 1988 (disqualification for certain motoring offences); or

(b) any suspended sentence in respect of which the committing court has under paragraph 11(1) of Schedule 12 to the *Criminal Justice Act* 2003 power to deal with him.

(4) The enactments referred to in subsection (1) above are—

(a) the *Vagrancy Act* 1824 (incorrigible rogues);

(b) sections *3 and 4* [3 to 4A] above (committal for sentence for offences triable either way);

(c) section 13(5) below (conditionally discharged person convicted of further offence);

(d) …; and

(e) paragraph 11(2) of Schedule 12 to the *Criminal Justice Act* 2003 (committal to Crown Court where offender convicted during operational period of suspended sentence).

[This section is printed as amended, and repealed in part, by the *CJA* 2003, ss.304 and 332, and Sched. 32, paras 90 and 91, and Sched. 37, Pt 7 (for the relevant saving provisions, see *ante*, § 5–1a). The words in square brackets in subs. (4)(b) are substituted for the italicised words by *ibid.*, s.41, and Sched. 3, paras 21 and 28. This amendment came into force on April 4, 2005, in relation to cases committed under s.3C: S.I. 2005 No. 950 (*ante*, § 5–24c); otherwise, it comes into force on a day to be appointed.]

Power of Crown Court on committal for sentence under section 6

7.—(1) Where under section 6 above a magistrates' court commits a person to be dealt with by the Crown Court in respect of an offence, the Crown Court may after inquiring into the circumstances of the case deal with him in any way in which the magistrates' court could deal with him if it had just convicted him of the offence. **5–28**

(2) Subsection (1) above does not apply where under section 6 above a magistrates' court commits a person to be dealt with by the Crown Court in respect of a suspended

sentence, but in such a case the powers under paragraphs 8 and 9 of Schedule 12 to the *Criminal Justice Act* 2003 (power of court to deal with suspended sentence) shall be exercisable by the Crown Court.

(3) Without prejudice to subsections (1) and (2) above, where under section 6 above or any enactment mentioned in subsection (4) of that section a magistrates' court commits a person to be dealt with by the Crown Court, any duty or power which, apart from this subsection, would fall to be discharged or exercised by the magistrates' court shall not be discharged or exercised by that court but shall instead be discharged or may instead be exercisable by the Crown Court.

(4) Where under section 6 above a magistrates' court commits a person to be dealt with by the Crown Court in respect of an offence triable only on indictment in the case of an adult (being an offence which was tried summarily because of the offender's being under 18 years of age), the Crown Court's powers under subsection (1) above in respect of the offender after he attains the age of 18 shall be powers to do either or both of the following—

(a) to impose a fine not exceeding £5,000;

(b) to deal with the offender in respect of the offence in any way in which the magistrates' court could deal with him if it had just convicted him of an offence punishable with imprisonment for a term not exceeding six months.

[This section is printed as amended by the *CJA* 2003, s.304, and Sched. 32, paras 90 and 92.]

For the saving provisions in relation to this section, see *ante*, § 5–1a.

5–29 The power of a magistrates' court to commit for sentence under section 3 is not confined to cases where information showing the offence to be more serious than it was originally thought to be was received after the decision as to mode of trial under section 19 of the 1980 Act (*ante*, § 1–74). Magistrates have a discretion unfettered by that decision: *R. v. North Sefton Magistrates' Court, ex p Marsh*, 16 Cr.App.R.(S.) 401, DC, following *R. v. Dover Magistrates' Court, ex p. Pamment*, 15 Cr.App.R.(S.) 778, DC, and disapproving *R. v. Manchester Magistrates' Court, ex p. Kaymanesh*, 15 Cr.App.R.(S.) 838, DC. The power of committal under section 3 may be exercised where a magistrates' court considers that the appropriate sentence is a financial penalty greater than it has power to impose: *R. v. North Essex JJ., ex p. Lloyd* [2001] 2 Cr.App.R.(S.) 15, DC.

Where, under the "plea before venue" procedure (*MCA* 1980, s.17A, *ante*, § 1–67), the accused indicates an intention to plead guilty, the court should only commit for sentence under section 3 if of the opinion specified in subsection (2) ("greater punishment should be inflicted than the court has power to impose"); there is no room for a committal for sentence on the ground that the offence is one which under the former procedure, or under the current procedure in relation to cases other than indicated guilty pleas, would have been deemed suitable for trial on indictment; in deciding whether their powers of sentence would be adequate, appropriate allowance should be made for the guilty plea, but it would be helpful if the court were to say so if it were only by virtue of the discount for the plea that it had been decided that their powers of sentence were adequate; in a clear case, the court should be prepared to commit for sentence without hearing mitigation or obtaining a pre-sentence report; in such a case, the accused should be given an opportunity to address the court on the matter and if they are minded to change their mind, the prosecution should be given a right of reply; each offence is to be considered separately; if the decision as to adequacy of sentencing powers depends on the resolution of a *Newton* hearing (*post*, § 5–74), the court should conduct such a hearing: *R. v. Warley Magistrates' Court, ex p. DPP*; *R. v. Staines Magistrates' Court, ex p. Same*; *R. v. North East Suffolk Magistrates' Court, ex p. Same* [1998] 2 Cr.App.R. 307, DC.

Where a magistrates' court deals with an offender who is in breach of a community order by revoking the order, the power of the court to deal with the offender does not include the power to commit him to the Crown Court for sentence for the offence in respect of which the order was made: *R. v. Jordan* [1998] 2 Cr.App.R.(S.) 83, DC and CA (following *R. v. Worcester Crown Court, ex p. Lamb*, 7 Cr.App.R.(S.) 44, DC, and *R. v. Daniels*, 8 Cr.App.R.(S.) 257, CA); and *R. v Andrews* [2007] 1 Cr.App.R.(S.) 81, DC and CA.

Effect of adjournment for reports before decision to commit

A magistrates' court does not disable itself from committing for sentence by adjourning for the purpose of obtaining a pre-sentence report before doing so (see *R. v. Southwark Crown Court, ex p. Commr of Police for the Metropolis*, 6 Cr.App.R.(S.) 304, DC), but may inhibit the Crown Court from imposing a custodial sentence if it has adjourned in such a way as to create expectations of a non-custodial sentence on the part of the offender: *R. v. Rennes*, 7 Cr.App.R.(S.) 343, CA (*ante*, § 5–16). **5–30**

In *R. v. Nottingham Magistrates' Court, ex p. Davidson* [2000] 1 Cr.App.R.(S.) 167, DC, the applicant indicated an intention to plead guilty before the magistrates' court under the plea before venue procedure. The case was adjourned for the preparation of a pre-sentence report, the court having given an indication that the applicant would not be committed for sentence. The applicant subsequently appeared before a differently constituted bench, and was committed for sentence. It was held that if a court at a preliminary stage of the sentencing process gave an indication as to the sentence which would or would not thereafter be passed on him, in terms sufficiently unqualified to found a legitimate expectation in the mind of the defendant that any court which later passed sentence on him would act in accordance with the indication given, and if on a later occasion a court, without reasons which justified departure from the earlier indication, and whether or not it was aware of that indication, passed a sentence which was inconsistent with and more severe than the sentence indicated, an appellate court would ordinarily feel obliged to adjust the sentence to bring it into line with that indicated. This principle was applied in *R. v. Horseferry Road Magistrates' Court, ex p. Rugless* [2000] 1 Cr.App.R.(S.) 484, DC; and *R. (Harrington) v. Bromley Magistrates' Court*, unreported, November 13, 2007, QBD (Mitting J.) ([2007] EWHC 2896 (Admin.)) (on an application for judicial review, whilst it is strictly correct that it is the rationality and lawfulness of the decision to commit that is under review, it will be the lawfulness and rationality of the indication that decides the issue, as it is impossible to conceive of circumstances where a decision to go back on a rationally and lawfully given indication would not itself be unlawful and irrational). It will be necessary to show that the statement made by the court amounted to something in the nature of a promise that the defendant would not be committed for sentence: it is not sufficient to show that the defendant formed the view that he would not be committed for sentence (see *R. v. Southampton Magistrates' Court, ex p. Sansome* [1999] 1 Cr.App.R.(S.) 112, DC). See also *R. v. Sheffield Magistrates' Court, ex p. Ojo*, 164 J.P. 659, DC, *R. v. Wirral Magistrates' Court, ex p. Jermyn* [2001] 1 Cr.App.R.(S.) 137, and *R. v. Feltham JJ., ex p. Rees* [2001] 2 Cr.App.R.(S.) 1, DC. A defendant may not, however, rely on the fact that his own representative has formed the impression that he will not be committed for sentence, and has advised him accordingly: *R. v. McHoul* [2003] 1 Cr.App.R.(S.) 76, CA.

Ancillary sentences and orders

Where an offender is committed for sentence under a provision to which the *PCC(S)A* 2000, s.6(1) (*ante*, § 5–27) applies, all powers and duties in relation to sentence fall to be exercised by the Crown Court, although the magistrates' court may disqualify from driving (see the *RTOA* 1988, s.26, *post*, § 32–197). The magistrates' court should make no other order (*e.g.* for compensation): *R. v. Brogan*, 60 Cr.App.R. 279, CA. **5–31**

Effect of unlawful committal

Where the committal to the Crown Court is clearly invalid, the Crown Court should not pass sentence, but the offender may be brought back before the magistrates' court and sentenced by that court (see *R. v. Norfolk JJ., ex p. DPP* [1950] 2 K.B. 558, 34 Cr.App.R. 120, DC). The Crown Court dealing with a committal for sentence has no power to go behind the order of a magistrates' court, if it is on its face a valid order; if the order is to be challenged, it can only properly be challenged in the Divisional Court: *R. v. Sheffield Crown Court, ex p. DPP*, 15 Cr.App.R.(S.) 768, DC. **5–32**

Upon a committal for sentence under section 3, the Crown Court has no jurisdiction to remit the matter to the magistrates' court upon it appearing that the defendant pleaded guilty upon a material mistake of fact; but it does have a discretion to allow an application for a change of plea; and, if such an application is made and granted, may remit the case to the magistrates' court: *R. v. Isleworth Crown Court and Uxbridge Magistrates' Court, ex p. Buda* [2000] 1 Cr.App.R.(S.) 538, DC.

As to a judge of the Crown Court reconstituting himself as a magistrates' court in order to remedy a defect in the committal, see *R. v. Ashton*; *R. v. Draz*; *R. v. O'Reilly* [2006] 2 Cr.App.R. 15, CA (*ante*, § 2–8).

Procedure in the Crown Court

5–33 In the case of an offender who has passed from one relevant age group to another between committal and his appearance before the Crown Court, the Crown Court should ensure that he is sentenced as a member of the appropriate age group; and it is age at the date of conviction that matters for this purpose: *R. v. Robson* [2007] 1 Cr.App.R.(S.) 54 (not following *R. v. Robinson*, unreported, November 20, 1962, CCA (decided on the *CJA* 1948, s.29(3))). Whatever the word "just" in section 5A(1) of the *PCC(S)A* 2000 added, it was not to be taken to have the effect of deeming the date of conviction to be the date of appearance before the Crown Court: *ibid*.

It was suggested in *R. v. Jeffries* [1963] Crim.L.R. 559, CCA, that formal evidence of the conviction and committal should be given other than by the offender's own admission. The court should ensure that it is aware of any limitations on its powers, particularly where it is limited to the powers of the magistrates' court (committals under the *PCC(S)A* 2000, s.6 or under the *MHA* 1983, s.43, where a hospital order is not made, or under the *PCC(S)A* 2000, s.4, where subs. (4) applies). Limitations on the powers of magistrates' courts to impose aggregate terms of consecutive sentences must also be observed where they apply (see *post*, §§ 5–270, 5–287).

As to the duties of counsel to inform themselves of the sentencing powers of the court and to correct any error, see Appendix C–51.

As to taking offences into consideration, see, in particular, *R. v. Davies (M.G.)*, 72 Cr.App.R. 262, CA (*post*, § 5–109).

As to committal for sentence after deferment thereof, and as to deferment of sentence after committal for sentence, see the *PCC(S)A* 2000, s.1D(2) (*post*, § 5–41).

The question whether a *Newton* hearing (*post*, § 5–74) should be held in the Crown Court where such a hearing was conducted in the magistrates' court before the decision was made to commit the offender for sentence under the *PCC(S)A* 2000, s.3(2) (*ante*, § 5–24) was considered in *Gillan v. DPP*; *R. (Gillan) v. DPP* [2007] 2 Cr.App.R. 12, DC. The court said that it was clear from the express terms of section 5(1) (*ante*, § 5–26) that the Crown Court had jurisdiction (or power) to hold a further *Newton* hearing if it was in the interests of justice to do so; whether a further hearing should be held was an exercise of discretion, which would depend on the facts and circumstances of the particular case; but, without laying down any strict or absolute formula, it was to be expected that the discretion would not be exercised in favour of holding a further hearing unless the offender could point to some significant development or matter such as (but not confined to) the discovery of important further evidence (approving observations of Kennedy L.J. to similar effect in *R. v. Warley Magistrates' Court* (*ante*, § 5–29)).

Appellate jurisdiction of Crown Court

5–34 Before the Crown Court deals with an offender who has been committed for sentence, it should ascertain whether he is appealing against the conviction on which the committal is based: if he intends to appeal, the question of sentence should be adjourned until the appeal has been determined (see *R. v. Faithful*, 34 Cr.App.R. 220, CCA). If the Crown Court has dealt with the committal and passed sentence, this does not prevent it from hearing an appeal against the conviction: *R. v. Croydon Crown Court, ex p. Bernard*, 72 Cr.App.R. 29, DC. The Crown Court upon hearing an appeal against a conviction or sentence passed by a magistrates' court may not in the purported exercise of its power under the *Supreme Court [Senior Courts] Act* 1981, s.48 (*ante*, § 2–178) (renamed as from a day to be appointed: *Constitutional Reform Act* 2005, s.59(5), and

Sched. 11, para. 1), commit the appellant for sentence to itself under section 3, in order to obtain enlarged powers of sentence (see *R. v. Bullock*, 47 Cr.App.R. 288, CCA (distinguished in *R. v. Ashton*; *R. v. Draz*; *R. v. O'Reilly* [2006] 2 Cr.App.R. 15, CA (*ante*, § 2–8))).

(7) Remission for sentence of young offenders

Powers of Criminal Courts (Sentencing) Act 2000, s.8

Power and duty to remit young offenders to youth courts for sentence

8.—(1) Subsection (2) below applies where a child or young person (that is to say, any person aged under 18) is convicted by or before any court of an offence other than homicide. **5–35**

(2) The court may and, if it is not a youth court, shall unless satisfied that it would be undesirable to do so, remit the case—

(a) if the offender was *committed for trial or* sent to the Crown Court for trial under section 51 [or 51A] of the *Crime and Disorder Act* 1998, to a youth court acting for the place where he was *committed for trial or* sent to the Crown Court for trial;

(b) in any other case, to a youth court acting either for the same place as the remitting court or for the place where the offender habitually resides;

but in relation to a magistrates' court other than a youth court this subsection has effect subject to subsection (6) below.

(3) Where a case is remitted under subsection (2) above, the offender shall be brought before a youth court accordingly, and that court may deal with him in any way in which it might have dealt with him if he had been tried and convicted by that court.

(4) A court by which an order remitting a case to a youth court is made under subsection (2) above—

(a) may, subject to section 25 of the *Criminal Justice and Public Order Act* 1994 (restrictions on granting bail), give such directions as appear to be necessary with respect to the custody of the offender or for his release on bail until he can be brought before the youth court; and

(b) shall cause to be transmitted to the justices' chief executive for the youth court a certificate setting out the nature of the offence and stating—

(i) that the offender has been convicted of the offence; and

(ii) that the case has been remitted for the purpose of being dealt with under the preceding provisions of this section.

(5) Where a case is remitted under subsection (2) above, the offender shall have no right of appeal against the order of remission, but shall have the same right of appeal against any order of the court to which the case is remitted as if he had been convicted by that court.

(6) Without prejudice to the power to remit any case to a youth court which is conferred on a magistrates' court other than a youth court by subsections (1) and (2) above, where such a magistrates' court convicts a child or young person of an offence it must exercise that power unless the case falls within subsection (7) or (8) below.

(7) The case falls within this subsection if the court would, were it not so to remit the case, be required by section 16(2) below to refer the offender to a youth offender panel (in which event the court may, but need not, so remit the case).

(8) The case falls within this subsection if it does not fall within subsection (7) above but the court is of the opinion that the case is one which can properly be dealt with by means of—

(a) an order discharging the offender absolutely or conditionally, or

(b) an order for the payment of a fine, or

(c) an order (under section 150 below) requiring the offender's parent or guardian to enter into a recognizance to take proper care of him and exercise proper control over him,

with or without any other order that the court has power to make when absolutely or conditionally discharging an offender.

(9) In subsection (8) above "care" and "control" shall be construed in accordance with section 150(11) below.

(10) A document purporting to be a copy of an order made by a court under this section shall, if it purports to be certified as a true copy by the justices' chief executive for the court, be evidence of the order.

[This section is printed as amended by the *CJA* 2003, s.41, and Sched. 3, para. 74(1) and (2) (insertion of words in square brackets, omission of italicised words). This amendment came into force on May 9, 2005, in relation to cases sent for trial under section 51 or 51A(3)(d) of the *CDA* 1998: *Criminal Justice Act (Commencement No. 9) Order* 2005 (S.I. 2005 No. 1267). Otherwise, it comes into force on a day to be appointed.]

Grounds for refraining from exercise of power to remit

5–36 In *R. v. Lewis*, 6 Cr.App.R.(S.) 44, CA, Lord Lane C.J. said that there had been an alignment of the powers of the Crown Court and of magistrates' courts in respect of juveniles, and that the concept of the youth court as the sole proper forum in which to deal with juveniles now seemed to be out of place. Possible reasons for not exercising the power to remit would include the fact that the judge who presided over the trial would be better informed as to the facts and circumstances of the matter, or that the exercise of the power would create a risk of disparity between co-defendants sentenced on different occasions by different courts, lead to delay or unnecessary duplication of proceedings, or confuse the position in the event of an appeal; it may be desirable to remit where the trial judge will be unable to sit and a report is to be obtained.

This statement was made in 1984, and may not be fully applicable to the current position, given the differences in the powers of the Crown Court and the youth court (in particular, the availability of referral orders to the youth court).

(8) Deferment of sentence

Power of Criminal Courts (Sentencing) Act 2000, ss.1–1D

Deferment of sentence

5–37 **1.**—(1) The Crown Court or a magistrates' court may defer passing sentence on an offender for the purpose of enabling the court, or any other court to which it falls to deal with him, to have regard in dealing with him to—

(a) his conduct after conviction (including, where appropriate, the making by him of reparation for his offence); or

(b) any change in his circumstances;

but this is subject to subsections (3) and (4) below.

(2) Without prejudice to the generality of subsection (1) above, the matters to which the court to which it falls to deal with the offender may have regard by virtue of paragraph (a) of that subsection include the extent to which the offender has complied with any requirements imposed under subsection (3)(b) below.

(3) The power conferred by subsection (1) above shall be exercisable only if—

(a) the offender consents;

(b) the offender undertakes to comply with any requirements as to his conduct during the period of the deferment that the court considers it appropriate to impose; and

(c) the court is satisfied, having regard to the nature of the offence and the character and circumstances of the offender, that it would be in the interests of justice to exercise the power.

(4) Any deferment under this section shall be until such date as may be specified by the court, not being more than six months after the date on which the deferment is announced by the court; and, subject to section 1D(3) below, where the passing of sentence has been deferred under this section it shall not be further so deferred.

(5) Where a court has under this section deferred passing sentence on an offender, it shall forthwith give a copy of the order deferring the passing of sentence and setting out any requirements imposed under subsection (3)(b) above—

(a) to the offender,

(b) where an officer of a local probation board has been appointed to act as a supervisor in relation to him, to that board,

(ba) where an officer of a provider of probation services has been appointed to act as a supervisor in relation to him, to that provider, and

(c) where a person has been appointed under section 1A(2)(b) below to act as a supervisor in relation to him, to that person.

(6) Notwithstanding any enactment, a court which under this section defers passing sentence on an offender shall not on the same occasion remand him.

(7) Where—

(a) a court which under this section has deferred passing sentence on an offender proposes to deal with him on the date originally specified by the court, or

(b) the offender does not appear on the day so specified,

the court may issue a summons requiring him to appear before the court at a time and place specified in the summons, or may issue a warrant to arrest him and bring him before the court at a time and place specified in the warrant.

(8) Nothing in this section or sections 1A to 1D below shall affect—

(a) the power of the Crown Court to bind over an offender to come up for judgment when called upon; or

(b) the power of any court to defer passing sentence for any purpose for which it may lawfully do so apart from this section.

[This section is printed as substituted, together with sections 1A to 1D, *post*, for the original sections 1 and 2 by the *CJA* 2003, s.278, and Sched. 23, para. 1. It is printed as amended by the *Offender Management Act 2007 (Consequential Amendments) Order* 2008 (S.I. 2008 No. 912), art. 3, and Sched. 1, para. 14(1) and (2).]

For the original sections 1 and 2 of the *PCC(S)A* 2000, see the 2004 edition of this work.

Further provision about undertakings

1A.—(1) Without prejudice to the generality of paragraph (b) of section 1(3) above, the requirements that may be imposed by virtue of that paragraph include requirements as to the residence of the offender during the whole or any part of the period of deferment. **5–38**

(2) Where an offender has undertaken to comply with any requirements imposed under section 1(3)(b) above the court may appoint—

(a) an officer of a local probation board or an officer of a provider of probation services, or

(b) any other person whom the court thinks appropriate,

to act as a supervisor in relation to him.

(3) A person shall not be appointed under subsection (2)(b) above without his consent.

(4) It shall be the duty of a supervisor appointed under subsection (2) above—

(a) to monitor the offender's compliance with the requirements; and

(b) to provide the court to which it falls to deal with the offender in respect of the offence in question with such information as the court may require relating to the offender's compliance with the requirements.

[This section is printed as substituted (see the note to s.1, *ante*), by the *CJA* 2003, s.278, and Sched. 23, para. 1. It is printed as amended by S.I. 2008 No. 912 (*ante*, § 5–37), art. 3, and Sched. 1, para. 14(1) and (3).]

Breach of undertakings

1B.—(1) A court which under section 1 above has deferred passing sentence on an offender may deal with him before the end of the period of deferment if— **5–39**

(a) he appears or is brought before the court under subsection (3) below; and

(b) the court is satisfied that he has failed to comply with one or more requirements imposed under section 1(3)(b) above in connection with the deferment.

(2) Subsection (3) below applies where—

(a) a court has under section 1 above deferred passing sentence on an offender;

(b) the offender undertook to comply with one or more requirements imposed under section 1(3)(b) above in connection with the deferment; and

(c) a person appointed under section 1A(2) above to act as a supervisor in relation to the offender has reported to the court that the offender has failed to comply with one or more of those requirements.

(3) Where this subsection applies, the court may issue—

(a) a summons requiring the offender to appear before the court at a time and place specified in the summons; or

(b) a warrant to arrest him and bring him before the court at a time and place specified in the warrant.

[This section is printed as substituted (see the note to s.1, *ante*), by the *CJA* 2003, s.278, and Sched. 23, para. 1.]

Conviction of offence during period of deferment

5–40 **1C.**—(1) A court which under section 1 above has deferred passing sentence on an offender may deal with him before the end of the period of deferment if during that period he is convicted in Great Britain of any offence.

(2) Subsection (3) below applies where a court has under section 1 above deferred passing sentence on an offender in respect of one or more offences and during the period of deferment the offender is convicted in England and Wales of any offence ("the later offence").

(3) Where this subsection applies, then (without prejudice to subsection (1) above and whether or not the offender is sentenced for the later offence during the period of deferment), the court which passes sentence on him for the later offence may also, if this has not already been done, deal with him for the offence or offences for which passing of sentence has been deferred, except that—

(a) the power conferred by this subsection shall not be exercised by a magistrates' court if the court which deferred passing sentence was the Crown Court; and

(b) the Crown Court, in exercising that power in a case in which the court which deferred passing sentence was a magistrates' court, shall not pass any sentence which could not have been passed by a magistrates' court in exercising that power.

(4) Where a court which under section 1 above has deferred passing sentence on an offender proposes to deal with him by virtue of subsection (1) above before the end of the period of deferment, the court may issue—

(a) a summons requiring him to appear before the court at a time and place specified in the summons; or

(b) a warrant to arrest him and bring him before the court at a time and place specified in the warrant.

[This section is printed as substituted (see the note to s.1, *ante*), by the *CJA* 2003, s.278, and Sched. 23, para. 1.]

Deferment of sentence: supplementary

5–41 **1D.**—(1) In deferring the passing of sentence under section 1 above a magistrates' court shall be regarded as exercising the power of adjourning the trial conferred by section 10(1) of the *Magistrates' Courts Act* 1980, and accordingly sections 11(1) and 13(1) to (3A) and (5) of that Act (non-appearance of the accused) apply (without prejudice to section 1(7) above) if the offender does not appear on the date specified under section 1(4) above.

(2) Where the passing of sentence on an offender has been deferred by a court ("the original court") under section 1 above, the power of that court under that section to deal with the offender at the end of the period of deferment and any power of that court under section 1B(1) or 1C(1) above, or of any court under section 1C(3) above, to deal with the offender—

(a) is power to deal with him, in respect of the offence for which passing of sentence has been deferred, in any way in which the original court could have dealt with him if it had not deferred passing sentence; and

(b) without prejudice to the generality of paragraph (a) above, in the case of a magistrates' court, includes the power conferred by section 3 below to commit him to the Crown Court for sentence.

(3) Where—

(a) the passing of sentence on an offender in respect of one or more offences has been deferred under section 1 above, and

(b) a magistrates' court deals with him in respect of the offence or any of the offences by committing him to the Crown Court under section 3 below,

the power of the Crown Court to deal with him includes the same power to defer passing sentence on him as if he had just been convicted of the offence or offences on indictment before the court.

(4) Subsection (5) below applies where—

(a) the passing of sentence on an offender in respect of one or more offences has been deferred under section 1 above;

(b) it falls to a magistrates' court to determine a relevant matter; and

(c) a justice of the peace is satisfied—

(i) that a person appointed under section 1A(2)(b) above to act as a supervisor in relation to the offender is likely to be able to give evidence that may assist the court in determining that matter; and

(ii) that that person will not voluntarily attend as a witness.

(5) The justice may issue a summons directed to that person requiring him to attend before the court at the time and place appointed in the summons to give evidence.

(6) For the purposes of subsection (4) above a court determines a relevant matter if it—

(a) deals with the offender in respect of the offence, or any of the offences, for which the passing of sentence has been deferred; or

(b) determines, for the purposes of section 1B(1)(b) above, whether the offender has failed to comply with any requirements imposed under section 1(3)(b) above.

[This section is printed as substituted (see the note to s.1, *ante*), by the *CJA* 2003, s.278, and Sched. 23, para. 1.]

When to exercise the power

Note: all of the cases referred to below were decided in relation to the legislation prior to its substitution by the *CJA* 2003. Some modification of their effect has been made to take account of the new legislation, but they may need to be reconsidered further in the light of those provisions. The explanatory notes to the Act provide some indication of the nature of the substantive changes: **5–42**

> "Currently a court can defer passing a sentence pending the good behaviour of the offender, as long as the offender consents and the court believes that deferring the sentence is in the interests of justice. If the offender commits another offence during the deferment period the court will deal with both sentences at once. This Act will require more of the offender on a deferred sentence. The power to defer ... is only exercisable if the offender undertakes to comply with any requirements as to his conduct that the court considers it appropriate to impose. He may have to complete undertakings in the community as set by the court. These can be activities such as reparation to the community. The probation service or other responsible body will monitor the offender's compliance with the requirements and will prepare a report for the court at the point of sentence. Failure to comply with a requirement will result in the offender being brought back to court early for sentence. As now, if the offender commits another offence during the deferment period the court will deal with both sentences [*sic*] at once."

According to guidance issued by the Sentencing Guidelines Council (*post*, § 5–79a and Appendix K–46), sentence should be deferred in a small group of cases at either the custody threshold or the community sentence threshold where the court may be prepared to impose a lesser sentence provided the defendant is prepared to adapt his behaviour in a way clearly specified by the court. In passing sentence, the court should indicate the type of sentence it would be minded to impose if the defendant does not comply. Whilst this guidance was given in relation to adults, it is relevant also to young offenders: *Att.-Gen.'s Reference (No. 101 of 2006) (R. v. P.)*, unreported, December 8, 2006, CA ([2006] EWCA Crim. 3335). Since any deferment clearly involves the message that compliance with whatever is required of the offender during the period of deferment will lead to a lesser category of sentence, deferment will only be appropriate if the lesser category of sentence is a proper and realistic possibility on the facts of the case; where it is not, a decision to defer is liable to be categorised as "unduly lenient": *ibid*.

In *R. v. George*, 79 Cr.App.R. 26, the Court of Appeal said that the power to defer sentence should not be used as an easy way out for a court which is unable to make up its mind, or for the purpose of obtaining information which could be provided by an adjournment for a report. In obtaining the consent of the defendant, the court should make clear the purposes of the deferment and the conduct expected of him. Deferment should not be employed without careful consideration of whether the sentencer's intentions could not best be achieved by other means.

In *R. v. Skelton* [1983] Crim.L.R. 686, the Court of Appeal criticised the action of the Crown Court in deferring sentence for six months on the basis of the offender's undertaking to reside at a mental hospital as a voluntary patient and undergo medical treatment.

Procedure

A court intending to exercise the statutory power of deferment should make clear that it is exercising the statutory power and not simply adjourning sentence: *R. v. Fair-* **5–43** *head*, 61 Cr.App.R. 102, CA. The consent of the offender to deferment should be obtained directly from him rather than through his counsel, although a consent expressed in the form of an invitation by his counsel to defer sentence may be sufficient: *ibid*. Where a court purports to defer sentence without obtaining the consent of the offender, any sentence of imprisonment passed at the end of the period of deferment will be invalid, but the Court of Appeal will have power to deal with the matter as if a valid sentence had been passed: *R. v. McQuaide*, 60 Cr.App.R. 239, CA. Once sentence has been deferred, the offender may not be sentenced for the offence unless the court exercises its power to vary the order for deferment under the *PCC(S)A* 2000, s.155 (*post*, § 5–940), or the offender is convicted of another offence, when the power to pass sentence arises under the *PCC(S)A* 2000, s.1C (see *McQuaide*, *ante*).

Section 1D(3) does not provide for a cumulative exercise of powers; it is there to ensure that the court, in addition to acquiring the new powers, still retains all the previous powers that it has always had regarding postponement of sentence or binding over to keep the peace, or to come up for judgment when called upon to do so: *R. v. Dwyer*, 60 Cr.App.R. 39, CA.

As to other orders which may be made when exercising the power to defer sentence, see the *PCC(S)A* 2000, s.148(2) (*post*, § 5–431) and the *RTOA* 1988, s.26(2) (*post*, § 32–197).

As to the possibility of a deferment of sentence being referred to the Court of Appeal under the *CJA* 1988, s.36 (*post*, § 7–368) as being "unduly lenient", see *post*, § 7–122.

Appearance of defendant at conclusion of period of deferment

5–44 Since the combined effect of sections 1(7) and 1C(4) is to preclude the court from dealing with the offender before the date to which sentence has been deferred, other than in section 1C(1) cases, and since the statute could not have been intended to require that the matter be dealt with on that date and no other, the offender should be brought back on that date or as soon as possible thereafter: *R. v. Ingle*, 59 Cr.App.R. 306, CA; *R. v. Anderson*, 78 Cr.App.R. 251, CA. When the offender appears before the court at the end of the period of deferment, the court may exercise its normal powers of adjournment, but should not do so unless there are strong reasons for doing so: *R. v. Ingle*, *ante*. Counsel who appeared for the defendant on his original appearance should regard himself as being bound to appear when the defendant appears at the conclusion of the period of deferment, "if it is at all possible to do so" (see *R. v. Ryan*, unreported, March 9, 1976).

Sentence following deferment

5–45 The court should ascertain the purpose of the deferment and determine whether the defendant has substantially conformed or attempted to conform with the proper expectations of the deferring court; if he has he may legitimately expect that an immediate custodial sentence will not be passed: *R. v. George*, *ante*. The Court of Appeal has, on a number of occasions, set aside custodial sentences imposed on offenders who have substantially complied with the expectations expressed by the court which deferred sentence, while accepting that the sentences would not have been open to objection if they had been imposed on the occasion of the offender's original appearance (*e.g. R. v. Smith (Joseph Thomas)*, 1 Cr.App.R.(S.) 339, CA; *R. v. Glossop*, 3 Cr.App.R.(S.) 347, CA; and *R. v. Fletcher*, 4 Cr.App.R.(S.) 118, CA). A custodial sentence may properly be passed where the offender has made no significant effort to comply with the clearly expressed expectations of the court which deferred sentence, even though he has not committed any further offence (see *R. v. Smith (Michael Stuart)*, 64 Cr.App.R. 116, CA), or where the offender has committed a further offence (albeit of a different kind) during the period of deferment (see *R. v. Hope*, 2 Cr.App.R.(S.) 6, CA).

A court dealing with an offender at the conclusion of the period of deferment should disregard any unresolved matters: *R. v. Benstead*, 1 Cr.App.R.(S.) 32, CA (failure to attend police interview); *R. v. Aquilina*, 11 Cr.App.R.(S.) 431, CA (proceedings pending).

(9) Function of prosecution in relation to sentence

5–46 In *Att.-Gen.'s Reference (No. 7 of 1997) (R. v. Fearon)* [1998] 1 Cr.App.R.(S.)

268, CA, Lord Bingham C.J. said that the practice of reticence by prosecuting counsel in matters of sentencing began before the Attorney-General had power to refer unduly lenient sentences to the Court of Appeal, when sentencing provisions were less complex, and before sentencing decisions were as fully reported as they are now. Judges should not be slow to invite assistance from prosecuting counsel in these matters and counsel should be ready to offer assistance if asked. The court hoped that judges would not be affronted if prosecuting counsel did offer to give guidance on the relevant provisions and appropriate authorities. To similar effect, see *R. v. Beglin* [2003] 1 Cr.App.R.(S.) 21, CA (it is the obligation of counsel for the prosecution to bring to the attention of the court any matters of law relevant to sentence); and *Att.-Gen.'s Reference (No. 52 of 2003) (R. v. Webb)* [2004] Crim.L.R. 306, CA (it is the duty of counsel for the prosecution, in a case where there were guideline sentencing cases, to indicate, before sentencing, to the judge that there were such authorities, and that copies were available should the judge wish to see them; this practice should be meticulously followed, and counsel who failed to do so could expect a frosty reception in the Court of Appeal).

As to the duty to open the facts on a plea of guilty, even where the sentence is fixed by law, see *post*, § 5–79. As to the prosecution's function and duty in relation to disputed issues of fact (*Newton* hearings, etc.), see *R. v. Tolera* [1999] 1 Cr.App.R. 29, CA, and *R. v. Beswick* [1996] 1 Cr.App.R.(S.) 343, CA, *post*, §§ 5–72 *et seq*. As to the role of the prosecution where an advance indication of sentence is sought by the defence, see *R. v. Goodyear* [2005] 2 Cr.App.R. 20, CA, *post*, §§ 5–79b, 5–79c.

As to the duty of prosecution counsel to familiarise himself with the maximum **5–47** sentence available for any given offence with which the judge has to deal, and to correct the judge if he errs, see Appendix C–33, C–51; and the comments of Lord Woolf C.J. in *R. (Inner London Probation Service) v. Tower Bridge Magistrates' Court* [2002] 1 Cr.App.R.(S.) 43 (at [27]), DC.

As to the disclosure of pre-sentence reports to the prosecution, see *ante*, § 5–22.

For the Attorney-General's guidelines on the responsibility of prosecuting counsel in connection with the acceptance of pleas and sentencing, see Appendix A–258.

(10) Imposition of sentence

Pronouncement in open court

The sentence of the court is pronounced orally by the presiding judge, normally in **5–48** the presence of the defendant. As to the sentence being that which is pronounced by the judge, as opposed to that which is recorded on the record sheet or other document recording the decision of the court, see *R. v. Venison*, 15 Cr.App.R.(S.) 624, CA; *R. v. Wilkins*, 16 Cr.App.R.(S.) 49, CA; and *Re Katchis* [2001] A.C.D. 70, DC.

Where the defendant has been convicted on more than one count of an indictment, or on more than one indictment, a separate sentence should be passed in respect of each count on which the defendant has been convicted: a sentence should not be passed generally on the indictment as a whole (see *Re Hastings*, 42 Cr.App.R. 132, DC).

Even the clarification of a doubt or ambiguity in respect of a sentence should be done in open court; only thus would all concerned hear the final decision of the judge himself in his own terms and only thus would a shorthand note be available: *R. v. Dowling*, 88 Cr.App.R. 88, CA.

As to making a sentence consecutive to a sentence currently being served, see *Practice Direction (Criminal Proceedings: Consolidation)* [2002] 1 W.L.R. 2870, para. I.8.2 (*post*, § 5–336).

Non-compliance with an obligation to state reasons does not invalidate a sentence: *R. v. Poyner*, 11 Cr.App.R.(S.) 173, CA; *R. v. Baverstock* [1993] 1 W.L.R. 202, CA.

As to the pronouncement of sentence when the Crown Court consists of a judge sitting with justices, see *R. v. Newby*, 6 Cr.App.R.(S.) 148, CA (*ante*, § 2–4).

Duty to warn of unexpected sentence

There is a general duty on a sentencer who intends to impose a sentence or order **5–49** which had not been in counsel's mind when he mitigated, to indicate to counsel what he intends to do and invite counsel to make submissions on the matter: *R. v. Scott*, 11 Cr.App.R.(S.) 249, CA. See also *R. v. Powell and Carvell*, 6 Cr.App.R.(S.) 354, CA, *R. v. Lake*, 8 Cr.App.R.(S.) 69, CA, and *R. v. Morgan*, 9 Cr.App.R.(S.) 201, CA. There is no general obligation on a judge to warn counsel that he proposes to impose a custodial sentence, but it has been held that a warning should have been given before a longer than normal sentence was imposed under the *PCC(S)A* 2000, s.80(2)(b): *R. v. Baverstock*, *ante*; or, an extended sentence under section 85: *R. v. Nelson* [2002] 1 Cr.App.R.(S.) 134, CA.

Explanation of effect of sentences

5–50 As to the duty to explain the effect of a sentence, see *post*, § 5–111.

(11) Commencement of sentence

Powers of Criminal Courts (Sentencing) Act 2000, s.154

Commencement of Crown Court sentence

5–51 **154.**—(1) A sentence imposed, or other order made, by the Crown Court when dealing with an offender shall take effect from the beginning of the day on which it is imposed, unless the court otherwise directs.

(2) The power to give a direction under subsection (1) above has effect subject to section 265 of the *Criminal Justice Act* 2003 (restriction on consecutive sentences for released prisoners).

(3) In this section "sentence" and "order" shall be construed in accordance with section 155(8) below.

[This section is printed as amended by the *CJA* 2003, s.304, and Sched. 32, para. 121.]

For section 265 of the 2003 Act, see *post*, § 5–388. For section 155, see *post*, § 5–940.

5–52 This section does not allow the court to ante-date a sentence: *R. v. Gilbert*, 60 Cr.App.R. 220, CA; and *R. v. Whitfield* [2002] 2 Cr.App.R.(S.) 44, CA. The court may direct the sentence to begin at the expiration of some other period of custody to which the offender is already subject or to which he is sentenced at the same time. This applies to a period for which the offender has been committed by a civil court for contempt: *R. v. Anomo* [1998] 2 Cr.App.R.(S.) 269, CA.

A sentence should not be ordered to run partly concurrently with, and partly consecutive to, an existing sentence: *R. v. Salmon* [2003] 1 Cr.App.R.(S.) 85, CA.

III. GENERAL PRINCIPLES

A. PURPOSES OF SENTENCING

(1) Offenders generally

Criminal Justice Act 2003, s.142

PART 12

SENTENCING

CHAPTER 1

GENERAL PROVISIONS ABOUT SENTENCING

Matters to be taken into account in sentencing

Purposes of sentencing[: offenders aged 18 or over]

5–53 **142.**—(1) Any court dealing with an offender in respect of his offence must have regard to the following purposes of sentencing—

(a) the punishment of offenders,

(b) the reduction of crime (including its reduction by deterrence),
(c) the reform and rehabilitation of offenders,
(d) the protection of the public, and
(e) the making of reparation by offenders to persons affected by their offences.

(2) Subsection (1) does not apply—

(a) in relation to an offender who is aged under 18 *at the time of conviction*,
(b) to an offence the sentence for which is fixed by law,
(c) to an offence the sentencefor which falls to be imposed under section 51A(2) of the *Firearms Act* 1968 (minimum sentence for certain firearms offences), under subsection (2) of section 110 or 111 of the *Sentencing Act* (required custodial sentences), under section 29(4) or (6) of the *Violent Crime Reduction Act* 2006 (minimum sentences in certain cases of using someone to mind a weapon) or under section 225(2) or 226(2) of this Act (dangerous offenders), or
(d) in relation to the making under Part 3 of the *Mental Health Act* 1983 of a hospital order (with or without a restriction order), an interim hospital order, a hospital direction or a limitation direction.

(3) In this Chapter "sentence", in relation to an offence, includes any order made by a court when dealing with the offender in respect of his offence; and "sentencing" is to be construed accordingly.

[This section is printed as amended by the *VCRA* 2006, s.49, and Sched. 1, para. 9(1) and (2); and the *CJIA* 2008, s.148(1), and Sched. 26, paras 59 and 64; and as amended, as from a day to be appointed, by *ibid.*, ss.9(2) and 149, and Sched. 28, Pt 2 (insertion of words in square brackets in the heading, omission of italicised words in subs. (2)(a)).]

As to deterrence, see *R. v. Oosthuizen* [2006] 1 Cr.App.R.(S.) 73, CA, *post*, § 5–275. As to the approach to this section at times of prison overcrowding, see *R. v. Seed*; *R. v. Stark* [2007] 2 Cr.App.R.(S.) 69, CA, *post*, § 5–276, in which the court said that sentencers should bear in mind that association with seasoned criminals may make re-offending more likely rather than deter it, particularly where the offender is young.

(2) Children and young persons

Crime and Disorder Act 1998, s.37

Aim of the youth justice system

37.—(1) It shall be the principal aim of the youth justice system to prevent offending by children and young persons. **5–53a**

(2) In addition to any other duty to which they are subject, it shall be the duty of all persons and bodies carrying out functions in relation to the youth justice system to have regard to that aim.

The "youth justice system" means "the system of criminal justice in so far as it relates to children and young persons": s.42(1).

Children and Young Persons Act 1933, s.44

General considerations

44.—(1) Every court in dealing with a child or young person who is brought before it, either as an offender or otherwise, shall have regard to the welfare of the child or young person and shall in a proper case take steps for removing him from undesirable surroundings, and for securing that proper provision is made for his education and training. **5–53b**

[(1A) Subsection (1) is to be read with paragraphs (a) and (c) of section 142A(2) of the *Criminal Justice Act* 2003 (which require a court dealing with an offender aged under 18 also to have regard to the principal aim of the youth justice system and the specified purposes of sentencing).

(1B) Accordingly, in determining in the case of an offender whether it should take steps as mentioned in subsection (1), the court shall also have regard to the matters mentioned in those paragraphs.]

[This section is printed as amended by the *CYPA* 1969, s.72(4), and Sched. 6. Subss. (1A) and (1B) are inserted, as from a day to be appointed, by the *CJIA* 2008, s.9(3).]

"Child" means a person under the age of 14 years; "young person" means a person who has attained the age of 14 and is under the age of 18 years: *CYPA* 1933, s.107(1) (*post*, § 19–328).

As to the determination of age, see the *PCC(S)A* 2000, s.164(1), *ante*, § 5–5, the *CJA* 2003, s.305(2), *ante*, § 5–7, and the *CYPA* 1933, s.99, *post*, § 19–326.

Criminal Justice Act 2003, s.142A

[Purposes etc. of sentencing: offenders under 18

5–53c **142A.**—(1) This section applies where a court is dealing with an offender aged under 18 in respect of an offence.

(2) The court must have regard to—

(a) the principal aim of the youth justice system (which is to prevent offending (or re-offending) by persons aged under 18: see section 37(1) of the *Crime and Disorder Act* 1998),

(b) in accordance with section 44 of the *Children and Young Persons Act* 1933, the welfare of the offender, and

(c) the purposes of sentencing mentioned in subsection (3) (so far as it is not required to do so by paragraph (a)).

(3) Those purposes of sentencing are—

(a) the punishment of offenders,

(b) the reform and rehabilitation of offenders,

(c) the protection of the public, and

(d) the making of reparation by offenders to persons affected by their offences.

(4) This section does not apply—

(a) to an offence the sentence for which is fixed by law,

(b) to an offence the sentence for which falls to be imposed under—

(i) section 51A(2) of the *Firearms Act* 1968 (minimum sentence for certain firearms offences),

(ii) section 29(6) of the *Violent Crime Reduction Act* 2006 (minimum sentences in certain cases of using someone to mind a weapon), or

(iii) section 226(2) of this Act (detention for life for certain dangerous offenders), or

(c) in relation to the making under Part 3 of the *Mental Health Act* 1983 of a hospital order (with or without a restriction order), an interim hospital order, a hospital direction or a limitation direction.]

[S.142A is inserted, as from a day to be appointed, by the *CJIA* 2008, s.9(1).]

For section 37 of the 1998 Act and section 44 of the 1933 Act, see *ante*. The one significant difference in the purposes of sentencing, as compared with those for adults (as to which, see *ante*, § 5–53) is the omission of "the reduction of crime (including its reduction by deterrence)".

B. DETERMINING THE SERIOUSNESS OF AN OFFENCE

(1) Statute

Criminal Justice Act 2003, s.143

Determining the seriousness of an offence

5–54 **143.**—(1) In considering the seriousness of any offence, the court must consider the offender's culpability in committing the offence and any harm which the offence caused, was intended to cause or might forseeably have caused.

(2) In considering the seriousness of an offence ("the current offence") committed by an offender who has one or more previous convictions, the court must treat each previous conviction as an aggravating factor if (in the case of that conviction) the court considers that it can reasonably be so treated having regard, in particular, to—

(a) the nature of the offence to which the conviction relates and its relevance to the current offence, and

(b) the time that has elapsed since the conviction.

(3) In considering the seriousness of any offence committed while the offender was on bail, the court must treat the fact that it was committed in those circumstances as an aggravating factor.

(4) Any reference in subsection (2) to a previous conviction is to be read as a reference to—

(a) a previous conviction by a court in the United Kingdom, or

(b) a previous *finding of guilt in service disciplinary proceedings* [conviction of a service offence within the meaning of the *Armed Forces Act* 2006 ("conviction" here including anything that under section 376(1) and (2) of that Act is to be treated as a conviction)].

(5) Subsections (2) and (4) do not prevent the court from treating a previous conviction by a court outside the United Kingdom as an aggravating factor in any case where the court considers it appropriate to do so.

[This section is printed as amended, as from a day to be appointed, by the *AFA* 2006, s.378(1), and Sched. 16, para. 216 (substitution of words in square brackets for italicised words).]

Sentencing guideline

The Sentencing Guidelines Council has issued a guideline on the assessment of the seriousness of any given offence: see Appendix K–13 *et seq.* Following a request by the council, this is currently (September, 2008) subject to a review by the Sentencing Advisory Panel. **5–54a**

Previous convictions

Relevance

The defendant's previous convictions and sentences (commonly referred to as his "antecedents") are relevant to the sentencing exercise in a variety of ways. First, they may go to the seriousness of the instant offence (s.143(2), (4) and (5), *ante*). Secondly, they may be indicative of the dangerousness of the offender, and of the need for the public to be protected from him. Thirdly, they may provide evidence of the effectiveness of a particular method of disposal adopted previously in the case of the offender; or, alternatively, that a particular measure was unsuccessful. Fourthly, they may provide an insight into the individual's criminal career, and, in particular, that he has made a real effort over a period of years to put a previous pattern of offending behind him. **5–55**

Practice

Paragraph 27 of the consolidated criminal practice direction (*post*) was originally issued by Lord Bingham C.J. on October 7, 1997. As to the importance of practitioners being aware of its contents, see *Re a Barrister (Wasted costs order) (No. 9 of 1999), The Times,* April 18, 2000, CA. **5–56**

Practice Direction (Criminal Proceedings: Consolidation), para.III.27 [2002] 1 W.L.R. 2870

Antecedents

Standard for the provision of information of antecedents in the Crown Court and magistrates' courts

III.27.1 In the Crown Court the police will provide brief details of the circumstances of the last three similar convictions and/or of convictions likely to be of interest to the court, the latter being judged on a case by case basis. This information should be provided separately and attached to the antecedents as set out below. **5–57**

III.27.2 Where the current alleged offence could constitute a breach of an existing community order, *e.g.* community rehabilitation order, and it is known that that order is still in force then, to enable the court to consider the possibility of revoking that order, details of the circumstances of the offence leading to the community order should be included in the antecedents as set out below.

Preparation of antecedents and standard formats to be used

5–58 **III.27.3** In magistrates' courts and the Crown Court: personal details and summary of convictions and cautions—Police National Computer ("PNC") court/defence/probation summary sheet; previous convictions—PNC court/defence/probation printout, supplemented by Form MG16 if the police force holds convictions not shown on PNC; recorded cautions—PNC court/defence/probation printout, supplemented by Form MG17 if the police force holds cautions not shown on PNC. In addition, in the Crown Court: circumstances of the last three similar convictions; circumstances of offence leading to a community order still in force; Form MG(c). The detail should be brief and include the date of the offence.

Provision of antecedents to the court and parties

Crown Court

5–59 **III.27.4** The Crown Court antecedents will be prepared by the police immediately following committal proceedings, including committals for sentence, transfers under section 4 of the *Criminal Justice Act* 1987 or section 53 of the *Criminal Justice Act* 1991 or upon receipt of a notice of appeal, excluding non-imprisonable motoring offences.

III.27.5 Seven copies of the antecedents will be prepared in respect of each defendant. Two copies are to be provided to the Crown Prosecution Service ("CPS") direct, the remaining five to be sent to the Crown Court. The court will send one copy to the defence and one to the Probation Service. The remaining copies are for the court's use. Where following conviction a custodial order is made one copy is to be attached to the order sent to the prison.

III.27.6 The antecedents must be provided, as above, within 21 days of committal or transfer in each case. Any points arising from them are to be raised with the police by the defence solicitor as soon as possible and, where there is time, at least seven days before the hearing date so that the matter can be resolved prior to that hearing.

III.27.7 Seven days before the hearing date the police will check the record of convictions. Details of any additional convictions will be provided using the standard format above. These will be provided as above and attached to the documents already supplied. Details of any additional outstanding cases will also be provided at this stage.

Magistrates' courts

5–60 **III.27.8** The magistrates' court antecedents will be prepared by the police and submitted to the CPS with the case file.

III.27.9 Five copies of the antecedents will be prepared in respect of each defendant and provided to the CPS who will be responsible for distributing them to others at the sentencing hearing. Normally two copies will be provided to the court, one to the defence and one to the Probation Service when appropriate. Where following conviction a custodial order is made, one of the court's copies is to be attached to the order sent to the prison.

III.27.10 In instances where antecedents have been provided to the court some time before the hearing the police will, if requested to do so by the CPS, check the record of convictions. Details of any additional convictions will be provided using the standard format above. These will be provided as above and attached to the documents already supplied. Details of any additional outstanding cases will also be provided at this stage.

III.27.11 The above arrangements whereby the police provide the antecedents to the CPS for passing on to others will apply unless there is a local agreement between the CPS and the court that alters the arrangement.

Content

5–61 In *R. v. Egan (Paul)*, *The Times*, March 9, 2004, CA, it was said that an offender's antecedent history should include dates of release from prior sentences and sentence expiry dates.

Disputed issues

5–62 The proper procedure where there is material in the antecedent report which is disputed by the defence is set out in *R. v. Van Pelz* [1943] K.B. 157, 29 Cr.App.R. 10, CCA; *R. v. Robinson*, 53 Cr.App.R. 314, CA; and *R. v. Sargeant*, 60 Cr.App.R. 74 (and see para. III.27.6 of the consolidated criminal practice direction, *ante*, 5–59). The disputed material should either be omitted, or proved by admissible evidence.

Offence committed whilst on bail

5–63 The fact that an offence was committed whilst on bail must be treated as an aggravating factor (s.143(3), *ante*). If the offence of which the offender is convicted is of a like nature to the offence for which he was on bail, the courts are likely to treat this as a seriously aggravating factor: see, for example, *R. v. Jeffrey* [2004] 1 Cr.App.R.(S.) 25, CA.

Where the offender falls to be sentenced both for the offence committed whilst on bail and for the offence in respect of which he was on bail, if custodial sentences are to be passed, they should normally be consecutive: see, for example, *R. v. Stevens* [1997] 2 Cr.App.R.(S.) 180, CA; *R. v. Whittaker* [1998] 1 Cr.App.R.(S.) 172, CA; *Att.-Gen.'s References (Nos 48 and 49 of 1997) (R. v. Drady and Day)* [1998] 2 Cr.App.R.(S.) 392, CA; *R. v. Watts* [2000] 1 Cr.App.R.(S.) 460, CA; *R. v. Onabanjo* [2001] 1 Cr.App.R.(S.) 7, CA; and *R. v. Middleton* [2005] 1 Cr.App.R.(S.) 42, CA.

(2) Factual basis of sentence

(a) *On conviction following plea of not guilty*

Relevance of other offences apparently committed by the offender disclosed by the evidence against him

An offender must be sentenced only for the offences of which he has been convicted, **5–64**
or which he has admitted either by his plea or by asking for the offences to be taken into consideration: *R. v. Wishart*, 1 Cr.App.R.(S.) 322, CA; *R. v. Chadderton*, 2 Cr.App.R.(S.) 272, CA; *R. v. Lawrence*, 5 Cr.App.R.(S.) 220, CA; *R. v. Reeves*, *ibid.* at 292, CA; *R. v. O'Prey* [1999] 2 Cr.App.R.(S.) 83, CA. In *R. v. Nottingham Crown Court, ex p. DPP* [1996] 1 Cr.App.R.(S.) 283, DC it was held that if a defendant is convicted of common assault, the sentencing court is not precluded from considering injuries resulting from the assault simply because the defendant could have been charged with assault occasioning actual bodily harm. However, in *R. v. Davies* [1998] 1 Cr.App.R.(S.) 380, the Court of Appeal held that it was wrong in principle to sentence a man convicted of buggery of a girl under the age of 16 on the basis that she had not consented. It was inappropriate for the appellant to be sentenced for rape when he had not been convicted of rape and the question of consent was not decided by the jury. It was not permissible for a man convicted of a lesser offence to be sentenced as if he had been convicted of a more serious one.

As to an allegation that an offender was in possession of a firearm at the time of commission of a robbery, see *post*, § 24–49.

Relevance of other offences apparently committed by the offender disclosed by statements which are not evidence against him

The same principle applies where there is evidence of offences with which the of- **5–65**
fender has not been charged in material which is not part of the case against him: *R. v. Craine*, 3 Cr.App.R.(S.) 198, CA; *R. v. Connor*, *ibid.* at 225, CA (offender not to be sentenced for offences which he admitted in statement to police, when statement was subsequently withdrawn). But a court is not required to blind itself to the obvious; where an offender, charged in a single count, claims that this was an isolated transaction, this may be rejected where the evidence establishes that this was not the case, and, accordingly, the offender should be given the appropriate sentence for a single offence, but without the credit he would receive if it really were an isolated incident: *R. v. Twisse* [2001] 2 Cr.App.R.(S.) 9, CA (supply of drugs); approved in *Tyack v. The State*, unreported, March 29, 2006, PC ([2006] UKPC 18) (fraud).

Relevance of other offences of which the offender has been acquitted by verdict of the jury

Where a defendant has been tried for a number of offences, and has been acquitted **5–66**
of some and convicted of others, or has been convicted of a lesser offence than that charged in the indictment, the sentencer must accept the implications of the verdict in determining the factual basis of the sentence: see *R. v. Ajit Singh*, 3 Cr.App.R.(S.) 180, CA (wrong to sentence defendant acquitted of wounding with intent on the basis that the wounding was "deliberate"); *R. v. Hazelwood*, 6 Cr.App.R.(S.) 52, CA (wrong to

sentence offender convicted of common assault on basis that the assault was with intent to resist arrest); *R. v. Keles*, 10 Cr.App.R.(S.) 78, CA; and *R. v. Baldwin*, 11 Cr.App.R.(S.) 139, CA.

Relevance of other offences included in the indictment in respect of which the prosecution have not proceeded

5–67 Where the prosecution does not proceed on counts to which the defendant has pleaded not guilty, the sentencer must sentence on the basis that he is not guilty of those offences: see *R. v. Booker*, 4 Cr.App.R.(S.) 53, CA; *R. v. Clutterham*, *ibid.* at 40, CA; *R. v. Ayensu and Ayensu*, *ibid.* at 248, CA; *R. v. Johnson (W.C.)*, 6 Cr.App.R.(S.) 277, CA; and *R. v. Stubbs*, 10 Cr.App.R.(S) 97, CA.

Sample counts and specimen charges

5–68 Where a case has been contested, the defendant cannot be sentenced for conduct which has not formed, expressly or by necessary implication, the subject of charges laid and proved against him (*R. v. Canavan*; *R. v. Kidd*; *R. v. Shaw* [1998] 1 Cr.App.R. 79, CA); where the defendant intends to plead guilty to a whole catalogue of offences and they can be sufficiently specified, they should be so specified in the indictment or the defendant should ask for them to be taken into consideration; where this is impracticable because the other offences are extremely numerous or cannot be precisely specified, there should be a clear agreement between the parties and this should be stated in open court and preferably recorded in written form; if this practice has not been followed with the proper precision, but the case has been so plainly approached by defence counsel on the basis of accepting the defendant's guilt as a whole, it would be wrong to limit the sentence only to that appropriate in respect of the counts on the indictment (approving to that extent *Att.-Gen.'s Reference (No. 82 of 2002)* [2003] 2 Cr.App.R.(S.) 115, CA): *Tyack v. The State*, *ante*, § 5–65. Subject to this, and to *R. v. Twisse*, *ante*, § 5–65, a defendant cannot lawfully be punished for offences for which he has not been indicted and which he has denied or declined to admit: *ibid.*; *R. v. Clark* [1996] 2 Cr.App.R.(S.) 351, CA; and *R. v. Canavan*, *ante*.

R. v. Canavan, *ante*, was followed and applied in *R. v. T.* [1999] 1 Cr.App.R.(S.) 419, CA; *R. v. Rosenburg* [1999] 1 Cr.App.R.(S.) 365, CA; *R. v. Evans* [2000] 1 Cr.App.R.(S.) 144, CA; *R. v. B.T.* [2002] 2 Cr.App.R.(S.) 2, CA; *R. v. Pardue* [2004] 1 Cr.App.R.(S.) 13, CA (indecent photographs); and *R. v. Graham*; *R. v. Whatley* [2005] 1 Cr.App.R.(S.) 115, CA (benefit fraud); but the applicability of this approach to the assessment of dangerousness under section 229 of the *CJA* 2003 (*post*, § 5–297) was doubted in *R. v. Considine*; *R. v. Davis* [2008] 1 W.L.R. 414, CA (*post*, § 5–306). As to the practice to be followed in cases involving large quantities of indecent photographs, see now *R. v. Thompson (Richard)* [2004] 2 Cr.App.R. 16, CA (*post*, § 31–117).

Matters of aggravation which are constituent elements of other offences of equivalent gravity not included in the indictment

5–69 Problems may arise where the defendant is charged with an offence and a factor alleged as part of the case against him, which aggravates the offence, is itself an element in some other offence, of equivalent gravity, which has not been charged in the indictment. A defendant charged with evading the prohibition on the importation of a controlled drug and alleged to have imported the drug with a view to sale, may claim that his importation was solely for personal use. In *R. v. Ribas*, 63 Cr.App.R. 147, the Court of Appeal rejected a submission that in such a case the sentencer was not entitled to proceed on the basis that the importation was with a view to sale in the absence of a conviction for possession with intent to supply. Importation had been treated in the legislation as "a category of offence on its own which is separate and distinct from the categories of possessing a drug once it has got into this country." A similar approach was adopted in the context of common law affray in *R. v. Cooke*, 9 Cr.App.R.(S.) 116, CA.

Where the aggravating factor is made the basis of a count in the indictment, on which the prosecution elect not to proceed, it may be that the court should disregard that factor in assessing the sentence on the count on which the defendant is convicted. In *R. v. Lawrence*, 3 Cr.App.R.(S.) 49, CA, the appellant pleaded guilty to cultivating cannabis: a count for possessing cannabis with intent to supply was not proceeded with. The sentencer referred to the "very strong suspicion that you were growing cannabis so that some of it might get into other people's hands". An appeal against sentence was allowed on the basis that the sentencer had difficulty in "banishing from his mind" the matter covered in the count not proceeded with. *Lawrence* was considered in *R. v. Rubinstein and Grandison*, 4 Cr.App.R.(S.) 202, CA, where Lord Lane C.J. said that in so far as it was inconsistent with *Ribas*, *Ribas* was to be preferred, but the cases appear to be distinguishable on the basis that in *Lawrence* the prosecution had put forward a count charging the offence of which the relevant factor was an element, and had accepted a plea of not guilty to that charge: in *Ribas*, no allegation had been made in the indictment, and the prosecution could not be taken to have accepted, by a decision not to proceed with a count, that the allegation could not be sustained.

As to where it is alleged that a defendant was in possession of a firearm or imitation firearm at the time of an offence, see *post*, § 24–49.

Interpreting the verdict of the jury

Problems of interpreting the verdict of the jury for the purpose of sentence most commonly arise where the jury has found the defendant not guilty on one count and guilty on another, often a lesser included offence. If the verdict of the jury can be explained only on one view of the facts, that view must be adopted as the basis of the sentence, but if more than one view of the facts would be consistent with the verdict, the sentencer may form his own view in the light of the evidence, and pass sentence on that basis: see *R. v. Boyer*, 3 Cr.App.R.(S.) 35; *R. v. Solomon and Triumph*, 6 Cr.App.R.(S.) 120, CA (authorities reviewed); *R. v. McGlade*, 12 Cr.App.R.(S.) 105, CA (if the verdict of the jury left open some important issue which might affect the sentence, then the sentencer, having heard all the evidence himself in the course of the trial, was free to decide where the truth lay, and was obliged to do so); and *R. v. Martin* [2002] 2 Cr.App.R.(S.) 34 (paras [28] *et seq.*), CA (extent of involvement in conspiracy). The sentencer must give the defendant the benefit of any doubt: see *R. v. Tovey*, 14 Cr.App.R.(S.) 766, CA; *R. v. Wilcox*, 6 Cr.App.R.(S.) 276, CA. He should give a short explanation of the reasons for reaching his conclusion on the facts, but it is not necessary to review the whole of the evidence: *R. v. Byrne* [2003] 1 Cr.App.R.(S.) 68, CA. The Court of Appeal will not interfere with a finding of fact made by the judge in such circumstances if the judge has properly directed himself, unless the court considers that no reasonable jury could have reached the judge's conclusion: *R. v. Wood*, 13 Cr.App.R.(S.) 207, CA; *R. v. Gore* [1998] 1 Cr.App.R.(S.) 413, CA. 5–70

If the verdict is consistent with two views of the facts and it would have been possible to amend the indictment so as to obtain the jury's view, then the judge must adopt the more favourable view: *R. v. Efionayi*, 16 Cr.App.R.(S.) 380, CA. It is not, however, permissible to obtain the view of the jury on a question which, while critical to sentence, does not reflect a distinction in the substantive law, by adding a count to the indictment containing particulars which are not necessary to substantiate the charge in law: *R. v. Young*, 12 Cr.App.R.(S.) 279, CA (defendant willing to plead guilty to buggery of female on the basis that she consented; lack of consent was not an essential ingredient of the offence; count added with particulars alleging lack of consent; held, such course was understandable but unjustified as it involved leaving to the jury an issue which it was not for them to determine; if the issue required resolution, it was a matter for the judge); and *R. v. Dowdall and Smith*, 13 Cr.App.R.(S.) 441, CA (*post*, § 21–11). See also *R. v. Cranston*, 14 Cr.App.R.(S.) 103, CA.

Where a note from the jury suggests that they are considering alternative bases for a conviction, but the verdict does not make clear the basis of the conviction, the judge is not bound to pass sentence on the more favourable basis. He must decide the basis on which to pass sentence, applying the criminal standard: *R. v. Cloud* [2001] 2 Cr.App.R.(S.) 97, CA.

Where the jury express a view on a question of fact which is not relevant to their decision, the judge is not bound to accept their view, and may reach his own conclusion on the evidence: *R. v. Mills* [2004] 1 Cr.App.R.(S.) 57, CA.

In most cases, the question in issue will be decided on the basis of evidence called in the course of the trial, but if no evidence has been called touching on the issue, it is open to the court to hold a *Newton* hearing (see *post*, § 5–74) to determine the matter: see *R. v. Finch*, 14 Cr.App.R.(S.) 226, CA.

Questioning the jury as to the basis of the verdict

5–71 The extent to which it is permissible or desirable for a sentencer to question a jury about the basis on which they have arrived at a particular verdict was considered in *R. v. Solomon and Triumph*, 6 Cr.App.R.(S.) 120. The Court of Appeal said that it was generally undesirable to ask a jury to explain an otherwise unambiguous verdict: to invite them to refine their decision could only lead to confusion. The only instance in which it might be said to be common practice to go behind the general verdict and to inquire from the jury the basis on which they had reached it was in a case of manslaughter where the jury may have reached their decision on alternative grounds (see *R. v. Matheson*, 42 Cr.App.R. 145, CCA, *post*, § 19–20). The authorities showed that the jury were not bound to answer any such questions, and that if they did the judge could reach his own view of the facts, as in *R. v. Ekwuyasi* [1981] Crim.L.R. 574, CA. See also *R. v. Frankum*, 5 Cr.App.R.(S.) 259, CA, and *R. v. Cawthorne* [1996] 2 Cr.App.R.(S.) 445, CA. Where it is proposed to attempt to elicit the basis of the jury's verdict, the necessary questions should preferably be left with the jury when they retire: the foreman should not be asked to indicate the basis on which the verdict has been reached after the verdict has been returned.

Strict liability offences

5–71a Given the potential for manifestly unjust results to arise where an offender has been convicted of an offence of strict liability, the court should, either by way of a *Newton* hearing (*post*, § 5–74) or by some other means, determine the offender's level of culpability to the criminal standard of proof; the offender who knowingly or recklessly committed the offence may expect a higher sentence than the offender who committed the offence through negligence; and if there was no knowledge, recklessness or negligence then the appropriate sentence may be an absolute discharge: *R. v. Jackson* [2007] 1 Cr.App.R. 28, Ct-MAC. For a criticism of this decision, see *Criminal Law Week* 2006/39/4.

(b) *Following plea of guilty*

The "Crown case"

5–72 In *R. v. Tolera* [1999] 1 Cr.App.R. 29, CA, Lord Bingham C.J. considered the procedure to be adopted on a plea of guilty. Ordinarily, sentence would be passed on the basis of the facts disclosed in the witness statements of the prosecution and the facts opened on behalf of the prosecution, which together could be called the "Crown case", unless the plea was the subject of a written statement of the basis of the plea which the Crown accepted. The Crown should consider such a written basis carefully, taking account of the position of any other relevant defendant and with a reasonable measure of scepticism. As to this, see also the Attorney-General's guidelines on the acceptance of pleas and the prosecutor's role in the sentencing exercise (Appendix A–258 *et seq.*).

The defence case

5–73 In *Tolera*, *ante*, Lord Bingham continued by saying that if the defendant wished to ask the court to pass sentence on any other basis than that disclosed in the Crown case, it was necessary for the defendant to make that clear. If the Crown did not accept the defence account, and if the discrepancy between the two accounts was such as to have a potentially significant effect on the level of sentence, then consideration must be given to the holding of a *Newton* hearing (*post*, § 5–74) to resolve the issue. The initiative rested with the defence which was asking the court to sentence on a basis other than that disclosed by the Crown case.

His Lordship said that it often happened that when a defendant described the facts of an offence to a probation officer for purposes of a pre-sentence report, he gave an account which differed from that which emerged from the Crown case, usually by glossing over, omitting or misdescribing the more incriminating features of the offence. While the sentencing judge would read this part of the pre-sentence report, he would not in the ordinary way pay attention for purposes of sentence to any account of the crime given by the defendent to the probation officer where it conflicted with the Crown case. If the defendant wanted to rely on such an account by asking the court to treat it as the basis of sentence, it was necessary that the defence should expressly draw the relevant paragraphs to the attention of the court and ask that it be treated as the basis of sentence. The prosecution should be forewarned of this request, even though they would now ordinarily see the report. The issue could then be resolved, if necessary by calling evidence.

If the defendant, having pleaded guilty, advanced an account of the offence which the prosecution did not, or felt they could not, challenge, but which the court felt unable to accept, whether because it conflicted with the facts disclosed in the Crown case or because it was inherently incredible and defied common sense, it was desirable that the court should make it clear that it did not accept the defence account and why. There was an obvious risk of injustice if the defendent did not learn until sentence was passed that his version of the facts was rejected, because he could not then seek to persuade the court to adopt a different view. The court should therefore make its views known and, failing any other resolution, a hearing could be held, and evidence called, to resolve the matter. That would usually involve calling the defendant, and the prosecutor should ask appropriate questions to test the defendant's evidence, adopting for this purpose the role of an *amicus*, exploring matters which the court wished to be explored. It was not generally desirable that the prosecutor, on the ground that he had no evidence to contradict that of the defendant, should leave the questioning to the judge.

In *R. v. Myers* [1996] 1 Cr.App.R.(S.) 187, the Court of Appeal commended the practice of writing down the basis on which the plea was accepted. But in *R. v. Beswick* [1996] 1 Cr.App.R.(S.) 343, CA, it was held that the sentencer is not bound by a version of the facts agreed between the parties. He is entitled to direct that a *Newton* hearing (*post*) takes place. If he does so, this does not provide a basis for withdrawing a plea of guilty, providing it was clear that the accused was admitting guilt of the offence charged. If the judge directs a *Newton* hearing, it is the duty of the prosecution to assist the court by calling evidence and testing any evidence called on behalf of the defence. The issues to be tried should be clearly identified and there should be agreement as to which prosecution witnesses were to be called and which to be read. See also *R. v. Lester*, 63 Cr.App.R. 144, CA.

In *Att.-Gen's Reference (No. 81 of 2000) (R. v. Jacobs)* [2001] 2 Cr.App.R.(S.) 16, CA, and in *Att.-Gen's Reference (No. 58 of 2000) (R. v. Wynne)* [2001] 2 Cr.App.R.(S.) 19, CA, the court commented on the undesirability of accepting a basis of plea which did not reflect the evidence and which restricted the sentencing options of the judge. In *R. v. Robotham* [2001] 2 Cr.App.R.(S.) 69, CA, it was held that the decision of a judge to adjourn a case for sentence did not give rise to a legitimate expectation on the part of the defendant that the court had accepted the basis of plea (which had not been challenged by the prosecution), and that a judge dealing with the case subsequently was entitled to insist on a *Newton* hearing before passing sentence.

In *R. v. Underwood* [2005] 1 Cr.App.R.(S.) 13, the Court of Appeal re-emphasised the following points: (i) the responsibility for taking the initiative and alerting the prosecution to the fact that their case is disputed rests with the defence; (ii) areas of dispute should be identified so as to focus the court's attention on the matters in issue; (iii) the court was not bound by any agreement as to plea, and was at liberty to ignore any document that had not been signed by both parties; (iv) where the prosecution have no evidence to dispute the defendant's account then, particularly if the facts relied on arose from his own personal knowledge and depended on his own personal account, they should not normally agree that account unless supported by other material.

The undesirability of pleas being accepted on an artificial basis was reiterated in *R. v. George* [2006] 1 Cr.App.R.(S.) 119, CA, where a complaint that the appellant had been deprived of his right to trial by an independent and impartial tribunal was rejected. It was in the public interest that an offender was properly sentenced for what he had done, and, accordingly, if a judge, on reading the papers, came to the view that a basis of plea appeared artificial, he was bound to say so; this could not give rise to a perception of bias in the fair-minded and informed observer; the judge was saying no more than that the written evidence suggested that what had happened was different from what the defendant was asserting; and, by requiring a *Newton* hearing, he was saying no more than that a hearing was required to resolve those differences. As to the use by the judge of robust language in rejecting the basis of plea, and reserving the hearing to himself, the complaint of bias was bound to fail where, thereafter, the judge had conducted the hearing with scrupulous fairness.

As a matter of good practice, the prosecution, when responding to a basis of plea in a case where confiscation proceedings might follow, ought to bear in mind the question of whether it will be asking for a confiscation inquiry to be made and, if so, what if any admission is being made (in relation to the basis of plea) which would apply to that inquiry; it is generally undesirable that a defendant should not know from the outset how far the prosecution are prepared to go; in some cases, the prosecution may be in a position to make the kind of express acknowledgment that was made in *R. v. Lunnon (Keith)* [2005] 1 Cr.App.R.(S.) 24, CA, that the indicted offence is the defendant's first involvement in relevant crime, and to do so knowing that the acknowledgment will be carried forward into confiscation proceedings; in other cases, likely to be the majority, they may be able to say no more than that for the purpose of sentence they do not and cannot dispute a particular assertion made by a defendant, but they cannot say what information may arise in any subsequent confiscation proceedings; where, therefore, the prosecution accepted as a basis of plea that the defendant had been involved in the supply of Class A drugs for a period of about six months prior to his arrest (the indictment apparently being amended to reflect this), such acceptance left wholly open the question of whether there had been any benefit from drug trafficking before that period; and it was not right to say that the acceptance of that admission carried with it the further assertion "and we agree he had never done it before"; and this was particularly so where there was no express concession by the prosecution that the defendant had never previously been involved in drugs, and detailed financial reports put forward by the prosecution shortly after the acceptance of plea made it clear that they were seeking to rely on unexplained credits to the defendant's bank statements over a six year period for the purposes of the statutory assumptions arising under section 4 of the *DTA* 1994: *R. v. Lazarus* [2005] 1 Cr.App.R.(S.) 98, CA.

Where a plea of guilty is accepted on a particular basis, but a subsequent pre-sentence report discloses information suggesting that the true view of the facts is more serious, the contents of the report should be canvassed, so that the basis on which the sentencer is to proceed is clear: *R. v. Cunnah* [1996] 1 Cr.App.R.(S.) 393, CA.

Resolution of disputed issues

5–74 The procedure to be followed where conflicting versions of the facts of the offence are put forward was considered in *R. v. Newton*, 77 Cr.App.R. 13, CA. Lord Lane C.J. said that in some cases it was possible to obtain an answer from a jury, where the different versions could be reflected in different charges in the indictment. The second method was for the judge himself to hear the evidence on one side and another, and come to his own conclusion, acting so to speak as his own jury. The third possibility was for the judge to hear no evidence, but to listen to the submissions of counsel; but if this course is adopted, "if there is a substantial conflict between the two sides ... the version of the defendant must so far as possible be accepted."

In *Underwood, ante*, the court said that where it was necessary, relevant evidence should be called by the prosecution and the defence (see also *R. v. McGrath and Casey*, 5 Cr.App.R.(S.) 460, CA), particularly where the issue arose from facts which were within the exclusive knowledge of the defendant. If the defendant did not give evidence, then, subject to any explanation offered, the judge might draw such inference as he saw fit. The judge could reject the evidence of the defendant and his witnesses, even if the prosecution had called no contradictory evidence, but reasons for doing so should be explained in a judgment. The court said that the judge could not make findings of fact and pass sentence on a basis that was inconsistent with pleas to counts already approved by the court; and particular care was needed in relation to a multi-count indictment involving one defendant, or an indictment involving a number of defendants; where there was a joint enterprise the judge, while reflecting on the individual basis of pleas, should bear in mind the seriousness of the joint enterprise on which all were involved. As to matters of mitigation, the court said that these are not normally dealt with by way of a *Newton* hearing but it was always open to the court to allow a defendant to give evidence in mitigation of sentence. If the factual issues were resolved entirely in a defendant's favour, credit for the guilty plea should not be reduced; if, however, the defendant was disbelieved, or required a prosecution witness to be called, or if the defendant showed no insight into the consequences of his offence and no genuine remorse, the court held that the discount might be reduced; and that there may be exceptional circumstances in which the entitlement to credit would be wholly dissipated by the *Newton* hearing. In such cases, the judge should explain his reasons. As to withholding the discount, or part thereof, see also *R. v. Stevens*, 8 Cr.App.R.(S.) 297, CA; *R. v. Jauncey*, *ibid.*, 401, CA; *R. v. Williams*, 12 Cr.App.R.(S.) 415, CA; and *R. v. Hassell* [2000] 1 Cr.App.R.(S.) 67, CA. As to full credit being given where a *Newton* hearing had been scheduled (necessitating case preparation), following early guilty pleas, but before the differences between the parties were resolved by agreement, see *Att.-Gen.'s References (Nos 117 and 118 of 2006) (R. v. Jesus and De Oliviera)*, *post*, § 5–82.

At a *Newton* hearing, the judge should not put questions until counsel have completed their examination (see *R. v. Myers*, *ante*). He should direct himself in accordance with the normal criminal standard of proof (see *R. v. McGrath and Casey*, *ante*, and *R. v. Nabil Ahmed*, 6 Cr.App.R.(S.) 391, CA) and in announcing his decision, should indicate that he has done so (*R. v. Kerrigan*, 14 Cr.App.R.(S.) 179, CA). If the case involves an issue of identification, the sentencer should approach the matter as if he were a jury and direct himself in accordance with the guidelines in *R. v. Turnbull* (*post*, § 14–2) (see *R. v. Gandy*, 11 Cr.App.R.(S.) 564, CA). The prosecution must not put forward a version of the facts in the course of a "*Newton* hearing" which would be consistent with a more serious offence than the offence to which the offender has pleaded guilty (see *R. v. Druce*, 14 Cr.App.R.(S.) 691, CA). It is submitted that in so far as *R. v. Nottingham Crown Court, ex p. DPP* [1966] 1 Cr.App.R.(S.) 283, DC, implies that the prosecution may allege facts in a *Newton* hearing which show that the defendant is guilty of a more serious offence than the offence of which he has been convicted, it is inconsistent with authority and principle.

If the Crown Court rejects the version put forward by the accused after hearing evidence, an appeal to the Court of Appeal on the basis that the factual question was wrongly determined will "only succeed in clear cases" which will be "rare indeed" when the accused has given evidence himself: see *R. v. Nabil Ahmed*, *ante*; and *R. v. Parker*, *ibid.* at 444.

As to the inappropriateness of a judge embarking upon a *Newton* hearing to decide whether or not the defendant had committed a discrete, but similar, offence to that (those) already before the court, when making an assessment of dangerousness under section 229 of the *CJA* 2003 (*post*, § 5–297), see *R. v. Considine*; *R. v. Davis* [2008] 1 W.L.R. 414, CA (*post*, § 5–306).

Matters of dispute not requiring resolution

The cases establish three situations where although there is a dispute as to the facts of **5–75**
the case, the court is not obliged to hear evidence under the principles laid down in *Newton*. The first is where the difference in the two versions of the facts is immaterial to the sentence (see *R. v. Hall*, 6 Cr.App.R.(S.) 321, CA; *R. v. Bent*, 8 Cr.App.R.(S.) 19, CA). If the sentencer does not hear evidence, he should specifically proceed on the defendant's version: *R. v. Hall*, *ante*; see also *R. v. Sweeting*, 9 Cr.App.R.(S.) 372, CA.

The second exception is where the defence version can be described as "manifestly false" or "wholly implausible" (see *R. v. Hawkins*, 7 Cr.App.R.(S.) 351, CA; *R. v. Bilinski*, 9 Cr.App.R.(S.) 360, CA; *R. v. Walton, ibid.* at 107, CA; and *R. v. Mudd*, 10 Cr.App.R.(S.) 22, CA). See also *R. v. Palmer*, 15 Cr.App.R.(S.) 123, CA and *R. v. Broderick, ibid.* at 476, CA (couriers claiming to believe that they were carrying cannabis as opposed to a Class A drug). A judge may form such a view of the defence basis of plea where, for example, he had presided over a trial of co-defendants; but he should only do so after hearing full submissions and giving a reasoned decision so that the basis on which subsequent mitigation would take place was entirely clear to all concerned: *R. v. Taylor* [2007] 2 Cr.App.R.(S.) 24, CA.

The third exception is the case where the matters put forward by the defendant do not amount to a contradiction of the prosecution case, but rather to extraneous mitigation explaining the background of the offence or other circumstances which may lessen the sentence. These matters are likely to be outside the knowledge of the prosecution: see *R. v. Broderick, ante*. Where the facts put forward by the defence do not contradict the prosecution evidence, the cases justify the following propositions.

(a) The defendant may seek to establish his mitigation through counsel or by calling evidence. The decision whether to call evidence is his responsibility, and there is no entitlement to an indication from the court that the mitigation is not accepted (*Gross v. O'Toole*, 4 Cr.App.R.(S.) 283, DC); but such an indication is desirable (*R. v. Tolera* [1999] 1 Cr.App.R. 29, CA).

(b) The prosecution are not bound to challenge the matter put forward by the defendant, by cross-examination or otherwise (*R. v. Kerr*, 2 Cr.App.R.(S.) 54, CA), but may do so (*R. v. Ghandi*, 8 Cr.App.R.(S.) 391, CA; *R. v. Tolera, ante*).

(c) The court is not bound to accept the truth of the matters put forward by the defendant, whether or not they are challenged by the prosecution (*Kerr, ante*): see *R. v. Broderick, ante*.

(d) In relation to extraneous matters of mitigation raised by the defendant, a civil burden of proof rests on the defendant, although in the general run of cases the court would accept the accuracy of counsel's statement: *R. v. Guppy*, 16 Cr.App.R.(S.) 25, CA.

Evidence given in trial of co-defendant(s)

5–76 A judge, in sentencing a defendant who has pleaded guilty, may take into account evidence given during the trial of a co-defendant who pleaded not guilty; he must, however, bear in mind that self-serving statements are likely to be untrue, and that the evidence given during the trial was not tested by cross-examination on behalf of the defendant who pleaded guilty; such a defendant should be given the opportunity to give evidence of his version of the facts: *R. v. Smith (Patrick)*, 10 Cr.App.R.(S.) 271, CA (preferring *R. v. Taggart*, 1 Cr.App.R.(S.) 144, CA, and *R. v. Depledge, ibid.*, at 183, CA, to *R. v. Michaels and Skoblo*, 3 Cr.App.R.(S.) 188, CA); and *R. v. Winter, Colk and Wilson* [1997] 1 Cr.App.R.(S.) 331, CA.

(c) *Following change of plea*

5–77 Where a defendant changes his plea to guilty during the course of his trial, but his plea is tendered on a basis different from that put forward by the prosecution, it is wrong for the sentencer to sentence the offender on the basis of the version of the facts put forward by the prosecution without hearing evidence from the defendant (see *R. v. Mottram*, 3 Cr.App.R.(S.) 123, CA; *R. v. Archer*, 15 Cr.App.R.(S.) 387, CA).

(3) Information about the effect of the offence on the victim

Practice Direction (Criminal Proceedings: Consolidation), para. III.28
[2002] 1 W.L.R. 2870

Personal statements of victims

5–77a **III.28.1** This section draws attention to a scheme, which started on 1 October 2001, to give victims a more formal opportunity to say how a crime has affected them. It may help to identify whether they have a particular need for information, support and protection. It will also enable the court to take the statement into account when determining sentence.

III.28.2 When a police officer takes a statement from a victim the victim will be told about the scheme and given the chance to make a victim personal statement. A victim personal statement may be made or updated at any time prior to the disposal of the case. The decision about whether or not to make a victim personal statement is entirely for the victim. If the court is presented with a victim personal statement the following approach should be adopted. (a) The victim personal statement and any evidence in support should be considered and taken into account by the court prior to passing sentence. (b) Evidence of the effects of the offence on the victim contained in the victim personal statement or other statement, must be in proper form, that is a witness statement made under section 9 of the *Criminal Justice Act* 1967 or an expert's report, and served upon the defendant's solicitor or the defendant, if he is not represented, prior to sentence. Except where inferences can properly be drawn from the nature of or circumstances surrounding the offence, a sentencer must not make assumptions unsupported by evidence about the effects of an offence on the victim. (c) The court must pass what it judges to be the appropriate sentence having regard to the circumstances of the offence and of the offender, taking into account, so far as the court considers it appropriate, the consequences to the victim. The opinions of the victim or the victim's close relatives as to what the sentence should be are therefore not relevant, unlike the consequence of the offence on them. Victims should be advised of this. If, despite the advice, opinions as to sentence are included in the statement, the court should pay no attention to them. (d) The court should consider whether it is desirable in its sentencing remarks to refer to the evidence provided on behalf of the victim.

The practice direction reflects what was said in a number of earlier authorities. See, in particular, *R. v. Perks* [2001] 1 Cr.App.R.(S.) 19, CA (if an offence had had an especially damaging or distressing effect on the victim, this should be taken into account by the court; but evidence of the victim alone should be approached with care, especially if it related to matters that the defence could not realistically be expected to investigate; and an appropriate sentence might be moderated to some degree where the victim's forgiveness or unwillingness to press charges suggested that any suffering was significantly less than might have been expected); *Att.-Gen.'s Reference (No. 2 of 1995) (R. v. S.)* [1996] 1 Cr.App.R.(S.) 274, CA; *R. v. Doe*, 16 Cr.App.R.(S.) 718, CA; *R. v. Hobstaff*, 14 Cr.App.R.(S.) 605, CA; and *R. v. O'S*, *ibid.* at 632, CA. **5–77b**

(4) Family impact statements

On May 3, 2006, Sir Igor Judge P., issued a "protocol" describing a voluntary pilot scheme (applicable in the Crown Court sitting at the Central Criminal Court, Birmingham, Cardiff, Manchester and Winchester), which allows the family of the victim of an offence of murder or manslaughter in respect of which the offender was charged on or after April 24, 2006, an opportunity to put a "family impact statement" (which describes the effect of the offence on the family) before the court after conviction and before sentence. The statement may be put before the court in written or oral form, and the family may be assisted by the crown prosecutor, an independent advocate, or a "lay friend". The defendant must be made aware of the contents of the statement in advance, and any issue between family members as to whether to make a statement about a single death, or who should make it, must be resolved by the judge. **5–77c**

The protocol envisages that effect will be given to the scheme in four stages. At stage one, the family liaison officer is to obtain an indication of the contents of the statement and the family's preferred means for it to be delivered. At stage two, the trial judge will consider the initial statement and the chosen means for it to be delivered (both having been disclosed to the court and the defendant in advance) at the plea and case management hearing, and will resolve any issues between family members. At stage three, an adjournment ("likely to be for a short period only") may be granted following a plea or conviction to allow the family to consult their representative and for the statement to be reviewed and updated. Stage four concerns the actual presentation of the statement to the court. Where it is presented in written form, the judge needs only to confirm that he has received and read it. Where it is to be presented orally by a family member, the normal process of evidence-in-chief followed by cross-examination applies. Applications for special measures may be considered in the normal way, and if the advocate strays outside the effect of the offence on the family, then the judge is to intervene. Where the statement is presented orally by the prosecutor, independent advocate or "lay friend", it will merely be read to the court.

Paragraph III.28 of the consolidated criminal practice direction (*ante*, § 5–77a) is unaffected, and is to guide the judge when considering a family impact statement.

C. REDUCTION IN SENTENCE FOR GUILTY PLEA

Criminal Justice Act 2003, s.144

Reduction in sentences for guily pleas

5–78 **144.**—(1) In determining what sentence to pass on an offender who has pleaded guilty to an offence in proceedings before that or another court, a court must take into account—

(a) the stage in the proceedings for the offence at which the offender indicated his intention to plead guilty, and

(b) the circumstances in which this indication was given.

(2) In the case of an offence the sentence for which falls to be imposed under subsection (2) of section 110 or 111 of the *Sentencing Act*, nothing in that subsection prevents the court, after taking into account any matter referred to in subsection (1) of this section, from imposing any sentence which is not less than 80 per cent of that specified in that subsection.

Subsections (1) and (2) replicate the provisions of subsections (1) and (3) of section 152 of the *PCC(S)A* 2000. Subsection (2) of that section is effectively reproduced in subsection (2)(d) of section 174 of the 2003 Act (*post*, § 5–111): this imposes a duty on the court, where it imposes a lesser sentence by reason of taking into account any matter referred to in section 144(1), to state that fact.

Facts to be stated

5–79 To enable the press and the public to know the circumstances of each offence to which an accused has pleaded guilty, the prosecution shall state the facts in open court before sentence is imposed: see *Practice Direction (Criminal Proceedings: Consolidation)* [2002] 1 W.L.R. 2870 (para. III.26).

Sentencing guidelines

5–79a In July 2007, the Sentencing Guidelines Council issued a revised guideline in accordance with section 170(9) of the *CJA* 2003 in relation to reductions in sentence for a guilty plea. By virtue of section 172 of that Act (*post*, § 5–100), every court must have regard to this guideline.

The full text of the guidelines is set out in Appendix K. It applies to offences for which sentence is passed on or after July 23, 2007. It deals with the purpose of a reduction, its application and how to determine the level of reduction (depending on the stage at which the guilty plea is entered) and when a reduction should be withheld. It applies to all offences where a determinate sentence is imposed or where a minimum term is fixed after imposing life imprisonment for an offence other than murder. Discounting the minimum term in cases of murder is dealt with separately in Part F of the guideline (Appendix K–8).

Advance indication of sentence

5–79b In *R. v. Goodyear* [2005] 2 Cr.App.R. 20, CA, it was said that any advance indication of sentence should normally be confined to the maximum sentence if a plea of guilty were tendered at the stage at which the indication was sought. As to the role of the judge, the court said that such an indication should only be given if sought by the defendant, but a judge was entitled to remind the defence advocate of the defendant's entitlement to seek such an indication; further, a judge had an unfettered discretion to refuse to give an indication or to reserve his position until he felt able to give such an indication. The court said that an indication should not be sought on the basis of hypothetical facts; where appropriate, there should be an agreed, written basis of plea, without which the judge should decline to give an indication; the judge might or might not give reasons, but once an indication was given, the court was bound by it, but the indication would cease to have effect, if, after a reasonable opportunity had been given to consider it, the defendant declined to plead guilty. As to the role of the defence advocate, the court said that no indication should be sought without written and signed authority, and the advocate remained responsible for ensuring that the defendant should not plead guilty unless he was guilty, that he understood (in an appropriate case) that the sentence might be the subject of a reference to the Court of Appeal, that if a plea did not follow on the indication, the indication would cease to have effect, and that it would relate only to the matters as to which an indication had been sought; no indication should be sought while there was any uncertainty as between the parties as to an acceptable basis of plea, and any agreed basis should be reduced to writing so that the judge could make up his own mind; the judge should not be asked to give an indication on the basis of what would be, or what would appear to be a plea bargain, and should not be asked to indicate levels of sentence on the basis of possible alternative pleas; in the case of an unrepresented defendant, he would be entitled to ask for an indication, but for the judge or the prosecution to inform him of that right might appear to be undue pressure. As to the role of the prosecution, the court said that, if necessary, the prosecution advocate should remind the defence advocate that no indication should be sought until the basis of plea had been agreed or the judge had concluded that the matter could be dealt with without resort to a *Newton* hearing; where an indication was sought, the prosecution should inquire as to whether the judge was in possession of all the relevant information, including any victim impact statement; the prosecution advocate should also draw the judge's attention to any minimum or mandatory sentencing requirements, to any relevant guidelines and to the fact that, in appropriate cases, there was a power to refer a sentence to the Court of Appeal, and in any event, should say nothing to suggest that the indicated sentence had the support or approval of the prosecution.

In relation to procedure, the court said that an indication would normally be made at the plea and case management hearing, but could be made later, including even during the trial; in complicated cases, the judge was most unlikely to be able to give an indication unless the issues between the parties had been addressed and resolved; in such cases, therefore at least seven days' notice should be given of an intention to seek an indication, and failure to give such notice, where it resulted in an adjournment, would lead to a reduced discount for any plea that eventuated; the hearing would normally take place in open court, and any reference to a sentence request would be inadmissible in a subsequent trial; reporting restrictions should normally be imposed, but they should be lifted once a plea had been entered or the defendant had been found guilty. The court added that, pending the settling in of these arrangements, they should be confined to the Crown Court. **5–79c**

As to the giving of a *Goodyear* indication in cases to which the dangerous offender provisions of the *CJA* 2003 apply, see *R. v. Kulah*, *post*, § 5–308a, in which the Court of Appeal said that where one judge has declined to give an indication, a practice of seeking an indication from another judge without reference to the earlier application, its outcome and the judge's reasoning was to be deprecated. As to *Goodyear*, see also *ante*, § 4–78b.

General entitlement to discount

As a general principle, an offender who pleads guilty may expect some credit, in the form of a reduction in the sentence which would have been imposed if he had been convicted by the jury on a plea of not guilty. Section 144 does not confer a statutory right to a discount, which remains a matter for the court's discretion, as is indicated by section 174(2)(d) (*post*, § 5–111), but it remains the policy of the Court of Appeal (and of the Sentencing Guidelines Council) to encourage pleas of guilty. Such pleas give rise to significant benefits, including a saving of court time and public money and the sparing of witnesses from having to attend trial to give evidence. A plea might also be indicative of some remorse: *R. v. Hussain* [2002] 2 Cr.App.R.(S.) 59, CA; *R. v. Boyd*, **5–80**

2 Cr.App.R.(S.) 234, CA; although in *R. v. Oosthuizen* [2006] 1 Cr.App.R.(S.) 73, CA, it was said that remorse was a separate matter from a plea of guilty and was to be taken into account at an earlier stage (and see *post*, § 5–83a).

This practice is distinguished sharply from that of imposing a sentence which is disproportionate to the offence, to reflect the manner in which the defence has been conducted. For examples of sentences quashed on this basis, see *R. v. Spinks*, 2 Cr.App.R.(S.) 335, CA; *R. v. Scott*, 5 Cr.App.R.(S.) 90, CA; *R. v. Evans*, 8 Cr.App.R.(S.) 197, CA; and *R. v. Hercules*, 9 Cr.App.R.(S.) 291, CA.

Where a judge takes a plea of guilty into account, it is important that he says that he has done so: *R. v. Fearon* [1996] 2 Cr.App.R.(S.) 25, CA (and see s.174(2)(d) of the *CJA* 2003, *post*, § 5–111). The fact that the sentencer did not specifically mention in his sentencing remarks that credit was being given for a guilty plea does not mean that the Court of Appeal will necessarily reduce the sentence; if it is clear from the nature of the sentence in relation to the offence that credit was in fact given, there will be no reduction: *R. v. Bishop* [2000] 1 Cr.App.R.(S.) 432, CA; *R. v. Wharton*, *The Times*, March 27, 2001, CA. It is, however, desirable that sentencers should indicate that credit has been given: *R. v. Araoride* [1999] 2 Cr.App.R.(S.) 406, CA.

Extent of discount

5–81 In *R. v. Buffrey*, 14 Cr.App.R.(S.) 511, CA, Lord Taylor C.J. said that there was no absolute rule as to what the discount should be, but as general guidance, the court believed that something of the order of one-third would be an appropriate discount. This coincides with the guidance of the Sentencing Guidelines Council: see paragraph 4 of the guideline (Appendix K–6).

In *Att.-Gen.'s References (Nos 14 and 15 of 2006) (R. v. French and Webster)* [2007] 1 Cr.App.R.(S.) 40, CA, it was held that there was no basis for withholding the full discount where a heavy sentence is imposed for a serious offence on the basis that the discount would be disproportionate.

First reasonable opportunity

5–81a See Annex 1 to the Sentencing Guidelines Council's guideline in relation to the reduction of sentence for a guilty plea (Appendix K–11). In *R. v. Hall* [2007] 2 Cr.App.R.(S.) 42, CA, it was held that where an offender tendered at a plea and case management hearing an oral basis of plea which was not accepted by the prosecution, before tendering a written basis of plea moving closer to the prosecution case which was also not accepted, and then finally caving in when trial of an issue loomed and agreeing to all but one minor aspect of the prosecution case, he could not be said to have pleaded guilty at the first reasonable opportunity.

A defendant cannot wait until the prosecution have served all their material and decided how to put their case before pleading guilty and expect a substantial discount, since some defendants plead guilty at the initial hearing or even make full admissions in interview to the police: *R. v. Ali and Mahmood* [2008] 1 Cr.App.R.(S.) 69, CA.

Withholding the discount

5–82 See paragraph 5 of the guidance of the Sentencing Guidelines Council (Appendix K–7), as to the limited circumstances in which the discount may be withheld or reduced on grounds (including the overwhelming nature of the prosecution case) other than the timing of the plea.

As to withholding the discount where the defendant's version of the facts is rejected after a *Newton* hearing, see *ante*, § 5–74. Full credit was, however, appropriate where the offenders had entered their pleas at the first available opportunity, but initially contested the factual basis of the prosecution case such that a *Newton* hearing was scheduled (necessitating case preparation and commissioning of experts), before the differences between the parties were resolved by agreement: *Att.-Gen.'s References (Nos 117 and 118 of 2006) (R. v. Jesus and De Oliviera)* (2007) 151 S.J. 128, CA.

Minimum sentence cases

5–83 For sections 110 and 111 of the *PCC(S)A* 2000, see *post*, §§ 5–252, 5–253.

Where a court reduces sentence in such a case under section 144(2) of the 2003 Act (*ante*), it should indicate how the final sentence was calculated: *R. v. Brown* [2000] 2 Cr.App.R.(S.) 435, CA.

Where a judge's starting point was above the minimum sentence, he was not required to apply a maximum discount of 20 per cent to the minimum sentence period and then apply a standard discount to the excess; all that was necessary was to ensure that the whole sentence was at least 80 per cent of the minimum: *R. v. Gray* [2007] 2 Cr.App.R.(S.) 78, CA.

Remorse

The foreword to the Sentencing Guidelines Council's guidance on reductions in sentence for guilty pleas (Appendix K–2 *et seq.*) is explicit about the rationale underlying the reduction being that it is in the nature of a reward for keeping the machinery of justice moving and the cost of administering the criminal justice system down. Unlike the former position, it has nothing to do with matching severity of sentence to overall culpability. Thus, the cynical and defiant career criminal is to be rewarded with the same discount as the genuinely contrite and remorseful, and the defendant who was caught red-handed and who pleads guilty only because he had no alternative receives the same discount as the person who confesses to a crime in circumstances where there would have been no prospect of a prosecution without the confession. **5–83a**

The guideline says (and see *R. v. Oosthuizen*, *ante*, §§ 5–80, 5–82) that the remorse of the offender, or other factors, such as assistance given to the investigating or prosecuting authorities, will be taken into account at an earlier stage, as mitigation. This appeared to open up the possibility that an offender who not only pleads guilty at the earliest opportunity, but also exhibits genuine contrition, may receive a discount from the appropriate sentence on conviction of significantly more than one-third. The Court of Appeal considered this suggestion in *R. v. Barney and Barney* [2008] 2 Cr.App.R.(S.) 37, but would go no further than to concede the possibility that in some circumstances clear remorse may be taken into account as an additional factor. However, this was said in the context of a case where the appellants pleaded guilty at the last minute, having done their best to evade liability, and then claimed that they were remorseful and that this should be taken into account in their favour separately from their guilty pleas. The court said that the question of remorse could not be divorced entirely from the question of plea.

D. Increase in Sentences for Racial or Religious Aggravation or Aggravation Related to Disability or Sexual Orientation

Crime and Disorder Act 1998, s.28

Meaning of "racially or religiously aggravated"

28.—(1) An offence is racially or religiously aggravated for the purposes of sections 29 to 32 below if— **5–84**

(a) at the time of committing the offence, or immediately before or after doing so, the offender demonstrates towards the victim of the offence hostility based on the victim's membership (or presumed membership) of a racial or religious group; or

(b) the offence is motivated (wholly or partly) by hostility towards members of a racial or religious group based on their membership of that group.

(2) In subsection (1)(a) above—

"membership", in relation to a racial or religious group, includes association with members of that group;

"presumed" means presumed by the offender.

(3) It is immaterial for the purposes of paragraph (a) or (b) of subsection (1) above whether or not the offender's hostility is also based, to any extent, on any other factor not mentioned in that paragraph.

(4) In this section "racial group" means a group of persons defined by reference to race, colour, nationality (including citizenship) or ethnic or national origins.

(5) In this section "religious group" means a group of persons defined by reference to religious belief or lack of religious belief.

[This section is printed as amended by the *Anti-terrorism, Crime and Security Act* 2001, s.39(1)–(5) (extension of section to religious aggravation).]

For sections 29 to 32, see *post*, §§ 19–214a, 23–31a, 29–38a and 19–277j respectively.

Criminal Justice Act 2003, ss.145, 146

Increase in sentences for racial or religious aggravation

5–85 **145.**—(1) This section applies where a court is considering the seriousness of an offence other than one under sections 29 to 32 of the *Crime and Disorder Act* 1998 (racially or religiously aggravated assaults, criminal damage, public order offences and harassment etc).

(2) If the offence was racially or religiously aggravated, the court—

(a) must treat that fact as an aggravating factor, and

(b) must state in open court that the offence was so aggravated.

(3) Section 28 of the *Crime and Disorder Act* 1998 (meaning of "racially or religiously aggravated") applies for the purposes of this section as it applies for the purposes of sections 29 to 32 of that Act.

Increase in sentences for aggravation related to disability or sexual orientation

5–86 **146.**—(1) This section applies where the court is considering the seriousness of an offence committed in any of the circumstances mentioned in subsection (2).

(2) Those circumstances are—

(a) that, at the time of committing the offence, or immediately before or after doing so, the offender demonstrated towards the victim of the offence hostility based on—

(i) the sexual orientation (or presumed sexual orientation) of the victim, or

(ii) a disability (or presumed disability) of the victim, or

(b) that the offence is motivated (wholly or partly)—

(i) by hostility towards persons who are of a particular sexual orientation, or

(ii) by hostility towards persons who have a disability or a particular disability.

(3) The court—

(a) must treat the fact that the offence was committed in any of those circumstances as an aggravating factor, and

(b) must state in open court that the offence was committed in such circumstances.

(4) It is immaterial for the purposes of paragraph (a) or (b) of subsection (2) whether or not the offender's hostility is also based, to any extent, on any other factor not mentioned in that paragraph.

(5) In this section "disability" means any physical or mental impairment.

Section 145 is identical to section 153 of the *PCC(S)A* 2000 (repealed with effect from April 4, 2005, but only in relation to offences committed on or after that day (see *ante*, § 5–1a)), save that "must" replaces "shall" at the beginning of paragraphs (a) and (b) of subsection (2).

Procedure

5–87 No procedure is laid down by which the court is to determine whether or not an offence was aggravated by any of the matters mentioned in sections 145 and 146. It is not necessary or permissible to include an allegation of racial or religious aggravation in a count charging an offence other than an offence under sections 29 to 32. Evidence tending to show a racial, etc., motivation will not necessarily be admissible at the trial, if it does not prove an element of the offence charged.

If the defendant is convicted of an offence to which section 145 or 146 applies, and evidence tending to show that the offence was racially, etc., aggravated has not been adduced during the trial, the prosecution should seek to establish the aggravating feature in a *Newton* hearing (*ante*, § 5–74) after the verdict has been returned. A *Newton* hearing may take place after conviction by a jury (see *R. v. Finch*, 14 Cr.App.R.(S.) 226, CA); the prosecution may call evidence, after conviction, to establish the existence of an aggravating factor which has not been in issue in the trial, so long as the evidence is properly particularised: see *R. v. Robinson*, 53 Cr.App.R. 314, CA. The sentencer should not draw an inference that an offence was racially, etc., aggravated and pass sentence on that basis without putting the defendant on notice and allowing him to challenge the inference: see *R. v. Lester*, 63 Cr.App.R. 144, CA.

Where a group of men were concerned in an attack on another, and the judge was satisfied that the attack was not racially motivated, but that one unidentified member of the group had used words of racial abuse at the time of the offence, it was inappropriate to sentence those who were convicted in respect thereof on the basis that the offence was racially aggravated: *R. v. Davies and Ely* [2004] 2 Cr.App.R.(S.) 29, CA.

Meaning of "racially or religiously aggravated"

The definition of "racial group" in section 28(4) of the 1998 Act clearly went beyond groups defined by their colour, race or ethnic origin, and encompassed both nationality, including citizenship, and national origins; it followed that "foreigners" were a racial group within the section; such was the result of a broad, non-technical construction of the statute; the mischiefs at which the section was aimed were racism and xenophobia, and the harmful effects of such conduct applied whether the racial group was defined exclusively or inclusively; fine distinctions depending upon the particular words used would bring the law into disrepute: *R. v. Rogers* [2007] 2 A.C. 62, HL. See also *DPP v. M.* [2004] 1 W.L.R. 2758, DC ("bloody foreigners"); and *Att.-Gen.'s Reference (No. 4 of 2004)* [2005] 2 Cr.App.R. 26, CA ("immigrant doctor"). **5–88**

In *R. v. Babbs*, unreported, October 25, 2007, CA ([2007] EWCA Crim. 2737), the court stated that whereas it was held in *Parry v. DPP* [2005] A.C.D. 64, DC, that, to bring an offence within section 28(1)(a), the conduct relied on must be in the immediate context of the substantive offence, the word "immediately" qualifying both the words "before" and "after", the important point of the provision is that it is directed not so much to words but to the hostility which is demonstrated towards a victim with the relevant racist (or religious) connotation. Where, therefore, the appellant had described the victim and his companion as "foreign fuckers" during a confrontation, and had then physically assaulted the victim during a second confrontation that occurred between five and 15 minutes later, the words used by the defendant at the initial confrontation were capable of colouring the behaviour of the defendant throughout the subsequent events. Accordingly, the jury had been entitled to conclude, from what had been said earlier, that the hostility shown later was based upon the victim being foreign.

An offence will fall within section 28 where it is motivated by hostility towards one particular member of the relevant group (the *Interpretation Act* 1978, s.6 (Appendix B–6) providing that "words in the plural include the singular"), and that hostility is based on that person's membership of that group; furthermore, that person need not be the victim of the base offence, as where the victim is singled out because of his association with that person: *Taylor v. DPP*, 170 J.P. 485, DC.

Where an Asian defendant assaulted an Asian caretaker at a community centre, having been asked by him to leave, and at the time of the assault called the victim "white man's arse licker" and "a brown Englishman", the offence was not racially aggravated as it did not fall within either section 28(1)(a) or (b) of the 1998 Act; the offence was not "motivated (wholly or partly) by hostility towards members of a racial group" (white people) "based on their membership of that group" (s.28(a)); and nor was the hostility demonstrated towards the victim "based on the victim's membership ... of a racial group" (s.28(1)(a)); whilst the victim being Asian was a *sine qua non*, that was not a sufficient basis to conclude that the hostility was in any material sense based on the victim's membership of the Asian race; what was being demonstrated was not hostility towards Asians, but towards the victim's conduct in asking him to leave, *i.e.* resentment, not racism; furthermore, the extended definition of "membership" of a racial group in section 28(2) to include "association with members of that group" could not be applied to the facts so as to make the victim for this purpose a white man: *DPP v. Pal* [2000] Crim.L.R. 756, DC. Doubt was expressed about this decision in *Rogers*, *ante*, especially in relation to the possible significance of the reference to "association" with members of a group. It was said that this would undoubtedly cover the case of a white woman who was targeted because she was married to a black man.

The fact that a person directed one foul-mouthed comment at another member of her own ethnic group in no way weakened the case against her in respect of an allegation of racially aggravated behaviour towards an Asian police officer during her arrest for other matters; the justices had been wrong to conclude that the evidence pointed to hostility towards the police generally, rather than racial hostility; section 28(1)(a) was not intended to be confined to those cases where the offender's hostility is based solely on racial malevolence; and as to the inebriation of the defendant, all that needed to be proved was that sober, or drunk, or between the two, the accused demonstrated racial hostility; the legislation was intended to deal with the offender who, sober, has no racist thoughts but, drink-fuelled, articulates them: *DPP v. Green*, *The Times*, July 7, 2004, DC. As to it being sufficient that the accused's hostility towards the victim was only partly based on the victim's membership of a particular racial group, see also*Johnson v. DPP* [2008] 4 *Archbold News* 3, DC (hostility partly based on victim being a traffic warden and partly on his colour).

Where the accused's racial hostility was not in any way the motivation for his offence, the offence could not be brought within section 28(1)(b): *DPP v. Howard* [2008] 4 *Archbold News* 3, DC (offender, apparently white, abusing his neighbours, who were off-duty policemen, by chanting, "I'd rather be a Paki, I'd rather be a Paki, I'd rather be a Paki than a cop").

Extent of uplift

5–89 Where an offender falls to be sentenced in a case to which section 145 of the 2003 Act applies, the extent to which the sentence may be increased by reference to the aggravating effect of racial aggravation is not necessarily limited to two years; the appropriate amount will depend on the circumstances of the case: see *R. v. Morrison* [2001] 1 Cr.App.R.(S.) 5, CA.

In a case of racially aggravated assault or wounding, the court should first identify the sentence which would have been appropriate in the absence of racial aggravation, and then add an appropriate amount to reflect the element of racial aggravation. The sentencer should indicate by how much the sentence has been enhanced to reflect the racial aggravation: see *R. v. Kelly and Donnelly* [2001] 2 Cr.App.R.(S.) 73, CA, considering *R. v. Saunders* [2000] 1 Cr.App.R.(S.) 71, CA. The court in *Kelly and Donnelly* identifies factors which will affect the assessment of the aggravating effect of racial aggravation in particular cases. In *R. v. Pells*; *Att.-Gen.'s Reference (No. 92 of 2003)*, *The Times*, April 21, 2004, CA, it was said that the observation in *Saunders* that, following a trial, a period of up to two years should be added to the term of imprisonment otherwise appropriate for the offence had it not been racially aggravated, remained valid, but it needed to be read in light of the Sentencing Advisory Panel's advice to the effect that the differential increase in the maximum penalties provided for by the *CDA* 1998 carried no special significance and it would be wrong for courts to determine the sentencing range for the aggravated offences primarily by reference to the maximum sentences available.

Notwithstanding what was said in *R. v. Saunders*, *ante*, there may be cases where a two-stage approach would lead to a sentence which is not necessarily appropriate, because the entire nature of the offence is changed by reason of racial or religious aggravation: see *R. v. O'Brien* [2003] 2 Cr.App.R.(S.) 66, CA (a case of criminal damage); and *R. v. Fitzgerald* [2003] 1 Cr.App.R.(S.) 74, CA (harassment).

Where an offence crossed the custody threshold by reason only of the element of racial aggravation, the approach should be to treat the appropriate sentence for the assault itself as nominal (a few days), and then to calculate the uplift for the element of racial aggravation: *R. v. Slater* [2006] 1 Cr.App.R.(S.) 129, CA (a case of racially aggravated common assault).

E. MITIGATION

(1) Statute

Criminal Justice Act 2003, s.166

Savings for power to mitigate etc

Savings for powers to mitigate sentences and deal appropriately with mentally disordered offenders

166.—(1) Nothing in— 5–90

(a) section 148 [or 151(2)] [or (2B)] (imposing community sentences),

(b) section 152, 153 or 157 (imposing custodial sentences),

(c) section 156 (pre-sentence reports and other requirements),

(d) section 164 (fixing of fines),

[(e) paragraph 3 of Schedule 1 to the *Criminal Justice and Immigration Act* 2008 (youth rehabilitation order with intensive supervision and surveillance), or

(f) paragraph 4 of Schedule 1 to that Act (youth rehabilitation order with fostering),]

prevents a court from mitigating an offender's sentence by taking into account any such matters as, in the opinion of the court, are relevant in mitigation of sentence.

(2) Section 152(2) does not prevent a court, after taking into account such matters, from passing a community sentence even though it is of the opinion that the offence, or the combination of the offence and one or more offences associated with it, was so serious that a community sentence could not normally be justified for the offence.

(3) Nothing in the sections mentioned in subsection (1)(a) to *(d)* [(f)] prevents a court—

(a) from mitigating any penalty included in an offender's sentence by taking into account any other penalty included in that sentence, and

(b) in the case of an offender who is convicted of one or more other offences, from mitigating his sentence by applying any rule of law as to the totality of sentences.

(4) Subsections (2) and (3) are without prejudice to the generality of subsection (1).

(5) Nothing in the sections mentioned in subsection (1)(a) to *(d)* [(f)] is to be taken—

(a) as requiring a court to pass a custodial sentence, or any particular custodial sentence, on a mentally disordered offender, or

(b) as restricting any power (whether under the *Mental Health Act* 1983 or otherwise) which enables a court to deal with such an offender in the manner it considers to be most appropriate in all the circumstances.

(6) In subsection (5) "mentally disordered", in relation to a person, means suffering from a mental disorder within the meaning of the *Mental Health Act* 1983.

[This section is printed as amended, as from a day to be appointed, by the *CJIA* 2008, ss.6(2) and 11(8), and Sched. 4, paras 71, 76(7) and 79 (omission of "(d)" and insertion of material in square brackets). In relation to the amendments made by Schedule 4 (all save the insertion of "or 151(2)"), see *ante*, § 5–1.]

This section corresponds closely to section 158 of the *PCC(S)A* 2000 (repealed with effect from April 4, 2005, but only in relation to offences committed on or after that day (see *ante*, § 5–1a)), but subsection (2) is new.

As to section 148, see *post*, § 5–126; as to sections 152 and 153, see *post*, §§ 5–265, 5–266; as to sections 156 and 157, see *ante*, §§ 5–19, 5–20; as to section 164, see *post*, 5–394. 5–91

(2) Procedure

When appropriate to allow speech to be made in absence of public

Any application to hear mitigation in private made by counsel or solicitor should itself be heard in private; having listened to the application in private, the court should then announce its decision in public and proceed to hear the mitigation: *R. v. Ealing JJ., ex p. Weafer*, 3 Cr.App.R.(S.) 296, DC. The power to exclude the public during mitigation should be exercised only when strictly necessary on the ground that proceeding in open court would frustrate or render impracticable the administration of justice: *R. v. Reigate JJ., ex p. Argus Newspapers*, 5 Cr.App.R.(S.) 181, DC. (As to sittings in camera generally, see *ante*, §§ 4–3 *et seq.*) 5–92

Both decisions accept that it is proper for documents relating to sentence to be put before the court without being read aloud, so long as counsel are fully informed and have the opportunity of dealing with them.

The *CPIA* 1996, s.58 (*ante*, § 4–30b), empowers a court to make an order prohibiting the publication of derogatory assertions made in the course of a speech in mitigation.

(3) Selected mitigating factors

Plea of guilty

5–93 See the *CJA* 2003, s.144 (*ante*, §§ 5–78 *et seq.*).

Age

5–94 Youthfulness is probably the best-known of all matters of mitigation. The younger the offender at the time of the offence, the greater its effect by way of mitigation. This is recognised in a host of statutory provisions that apply only to young offenders, and in countless decisions of the courts.

Old age is also a matter of potential mitigation: see *R. v. W. (Sentencing: Age of Defendant)*, *The Times*, October 26, 2000, CA (where the appropriate sentence would result in the release of the offender when well over the age of 80, there should be some reduction on this account even where the offending, or some of it, was relatively recent); and *R. v. Suckley* [2001] 2 Cr.App.R.(S.) 66, CA (any attempt at an actuarial basis for a discount is inappropriate).

Assistance to law enforcement agencies

Serious Organised Crime and Police Act 2005, ss.73–75A

Assistance by defendant: reduction in sentence

5–94a **73.**—(1) This section applies if a defendant—

(a) following a plea of guilty is either convicted of an offence in proceedings in the Crown Court or is committed to the Crown Court for sentence, and

(b) has, pursuant to a written agreement made with a specified prosecutor, assisted or offered to assist the investigator or prosecutor in relation to that or any other offence.

(2) In determining what sentence to pass on the defendant the court may take into account the extent and nature of the assistance given or offered.

(3) If the court passes a sentence which is less than it would have passed but for the assistance given or offered, it must state in open court—

(a) that it has passed a lesser sentence than it would otherwise have passed, and

(b) what the greater sentence would have been.

(4) Subsection (3) does not apply if the court thinks that it would not be in the public interest to disclose that the sentence has been discounted; but in such a case the court must give written notice of the matters specified in paragraphs (a) and (b) of subsection (3) to both the prosecutor and the defendant.

(5) Nothing in any enactment which—

(a) requires that a minimum sentence is passed in respect of any offence or an offence of any description or by reference to the circumstances of any offender (whether or not the enactment also permits the court to pass a lesser sentence in particular circumstances), or

(b) in the case of a sentence which is fixed by law, requires the court to take into account certain matters for the purposes of making an order which determines or has the effect of determining the minimum period of imprisonment which the offender must serve (whether or not the enactment also permits the court to fix a lesser period in particular circumstances),

affects the power of a court to act under subsection (2).

(6) If, in determining what sentence to pass on the defendant, the court takes into account the extent and nature of the assistance given or offered as mentioned in subsection (2), that does not prevent the court from also taking account of any other matter which it is entitled by virtue of any other enactment to take account of for the purposes of determining—

(a) the sentence, or

(b) in the case of a sentence which is fixed by law, any minimum period of imprisonment which an offender must serve.

(7) If subsection (3) above does not apply by virtue of subsection (4) above, sections 174(1)(a) and 270 of the *Criminal Justice Act* 2003 (requirement to explain reasons for sentence or other order) do not apply to the extent that the explanation will disclose that a sentence has been discounted in pursuance of this section.

(8) In this section—

(a) a reference to a sentence includes, in the case of a sentence which is fixed by law, a reference to the minimum period an offender is required to serve, and a reference to a lesser sentence must be construed accordingly;

(b) a reference to imprisonment includes a reference to any other custodial sentence within the meaning of section 76 of the *Powers of Criminal Courts (Sentencing) Act* 2000 or Article 2 of the *Criminal Justice (Northern Ireland) Order* 1996 (S.I. 1996/3160).

(9) An agreement with a specified prosecutor may provide for assistance to be given to that prosecutor or to any other prosecutor.

(10) References to a specified prosecutor must be construed in accordance with section 71.

Assistance by defendant: review of sentence

74.—(1) This section applies if— **5–94b**

(a) the Crown Court has passed a sentence on a person in respect of an offence, and

(b) the person falls within subsection (2).

(2) A person falls within this subsection if—

(a) he receives a discounted sentence in consequence of his having offered in pursuance of a written agreement to give assistance to the prosecutor or investigator of an offence but he knowingly fails to any extent to give assistance in accordance with the agreement;

(b) he receives a discounted sentence in consequence of his having offered in pursuance of a written agreement to give assistance to the prosecutor or investigator of an offence and, having given the assistance in accordance with the agreement, in pursuance of another written agreement gives or offers to give further assistance;

(c) he receives a sentence which is not discounted but in pursuance of a written agreement he subsequently gives or offers to give assistance to the prosecutor or investigator of an offence.

(3) A specified prosecutor may at any time refer the case back to the court by which the sentence was passed if—

(a) the person is still serving his sentence, and

(b) the specified prosecutor thinks it is in the interests of justice to do so.

(4) A case so referred must, if possible, be heard by the judge who passed the sentence to which the referral relates.

(5) If the court is satisfied that a person who falls within subsection (2)(a) knowingly failed to give the assistance it may substitute for the sentence to which the referral relates such greater sentence (not exceeding that which it would have passed but for the agreement to give assistance) as it thinks appropriate.

(6) In a case of a person who falls within subsection (2)(b) or (c) the court may—

(a) take into account the extent and nature of the assistance given or offered;

(b) substitute for the sentence to which the referral relates such lesser sentence as it thinks appropriate.

(7) Any part of the sentence to which the referral relates which the person has already served must be taken into account in determining when a greater or lesser sentence imposed by subsection (5) or (6) has been served.

(8) A person in respect of whom a reference is made under this section and the specified prosecutor may with the leave of the Court of Appeal appeal to the Court of Appeal against the decision of the Crown Court.

(9) Section 33(3) of the *Criminal Appeal Act* 1968 (limitation on appeal from the criminal division of the Court of Appeal) does not prevent an appeal to the Supreme Court under this section.

(10) A discounted sentence is a sentence passed in pursuance of section 73 or subsection (6) above.

(11) References—

(a) to a written agreement are to an agreement made in writing with a specified prosecutor;

(b) to a specified prosecutor must be construed in accordance with section 71.

(12) In relation to any proceedings under this section, the Secretary of State may make an order containing provision corresponding to any provision in—

(a) the *Criminal Appeal Act* 1968 (subject to any specified modifications), or

(b) the *Criminal Appeal (Northern Ireland) Act* 1980 (subject to any specified modifications).

(13) A person does not fall within subsection (2) if—

(a) he was convicted of an offence for which the sentence is fixed by law, and

(b) he did not plead guilty to the offence for which he was sentenced.

(14) Section 174(1)(a) or 270 of the *Criminal Justice Act* 2003 (as the case may be) applies to a sentence substituted under subsection (5) above unless the court thinks that it is not in the public interest to disclose that the person falls within subsection (2)(a) above.

(15) Subsections (3) to (9) of section 73 apply for the purposes of this section as they apply for the purposes of that section and any reference in those subsections to subsection (2) of that section must be construed as a reference to subsection (6) of this section.

In connection with this section, see the *Serious Organised Crime and Police Act 2005 (Appeals under Section 74) Order* 2006 (S.I. 2006 No. 2135) (*post*, § 7–312a).

Proceedings under section 74: exclusion of public

5–94c **75.**—(1) This section applies to—

(a) any proceedings relating to a reference made under section 74(3), and

(b) any other proceedings arising in consequence of such proceedings.

(2) The court in which the proceedings will be or are being heard may make such order as it thinks appropriate—

(a) to exclude from the proceedings any person who does not fall within subsection (4);

(b) to give such directions as it thinks appropriate prohibiting the publication of any matter relating to the proceedings (including the fact that the reference has been made).

(3) An order under subsection (2) may be made only to the extent that the court thinks—

(a) that it is necessary to do so to protect the safety of any person, and

(b) that it is in the interests of justice.

(4) The following persons fall within this subsection—

(a) a member or officer of the court;

(b) a party to the proceedings;

(c) counsel or a solicitor for a party to the proceedings;

(d) a person otherwise directly concerned with the proceedings.

(5) This section does not affect any other power which the court has by virtue of any rule of law or other enactment—

(a) to exclude any person from proceedings, or

(b) to restrict the publication of any matter relating to proceedings.

Proceedings under section 74: use of live link

5–94d **75A.** Section 57E of the *Crime and Disorder Act* 1998 (use of live link in sentencing hearings) applies to hearings in proceedings relating to a reference under section 74(3) as it applies to sentencing hearings.

[This section was inserted by the *PJA* 2006, s.52, and Sched. 14, para. 62.]

Assistance given in accordance with the 2005 Act

5–94e In *R. v. P.; R. v. Blackburn* [2008] 2 Cr.App.R.(S.) 5, CA, the court made various observations on the provisions of sections 73 to 75. Apart from the obvious and that which was mere restatement of the content of those sections, these included: (i) sentences imposed before their commencement fall within their ambit; (ii) where, on a review, the court is satisfied that the defendant knowingly failed to give the assistance offered, it will normally be appropriate to substitute the sentence that had been indicated as the appropriate sentence but for the assistance (see s.74(5)); (iii) the provisions do not abolish the existing system of written agreements and the "text" system (as to which, see *post*), which may still be used when appropriate, as the investigative process should not be deprived of the assistance of those who are, for whatever reason, unable to enter into the formalised process created by these provisions, but any discount in sentence under such less formal agreements is likely to be reduced, because the value of any assistance provided in this form is likely to be less and the process is not subject to the safeguards against manipulation contained in these provisions; (iv) as reviews produce a decision of the court relating to sentence, unless absolutely necessary, the normal principle that sentences should not be imposed, reduced or altered after private hearings should so far as possible be applied to them; (v) the power in section 75 to exclude the media from the review should be used with great caution, and if any practicable alternatives are available, they should, if possible, be adopted; (vi) a discount for a guilty plea is separate from and additional to any reduction under these provisions; the correct approach should be to assess the appropriate discount for assistance, against all other relevant considerations, with the notional resulting sentence so achieved then being further discounted for the guilty plea; (vii) the totality principle is, however, fundamental, a mathematical approach being liable to produce an inappropriate answer; (viii) where the defendant admits and pleads guilty to offences which would otherwise never have been attributed to him and which may indeed have been unknown to the police, this should be taken into account when sentencing for any such disclosed offences; and such sentences should normally be concurrent with the sentence for the index offence(s); and (ix) the principles governing the appropriate level of discount as set out in the previous case law are still applicable; only in the most exceptional case would the appropriate level of reduction exceed three-quarters of the total sentence which would otherwise have been passed and the normal level should continue to be a reduction of between one half and two-thirds of that sentence.

Assistance given otherwise than in accordance with the 2005 Act

As to the survival of the less formal arrangements that existed prior to the 2005 Act, see *R. v. P.*; *R. v. Blackburn*, *ante* (point (iii)). An offender who assists the police by giving information which leads to the apprehension and prosecution of his associates or of other offenders may expect a discount, possibly substantial, from his sentence: see *R. v. Sinfield*, 3 Cr.App.R.(S.) 258, CA. The extent of the discount depends on the individual circumstances: *ibid.*; *R. v. Rose and Sapiano*, 2 Cr.App.R.(S.) 239, CA. The discount is greater than the normal discount for pleading guilty: *R. v. Wood* [1997] 1 Cr.App.R.(S.) 347, CA, but the sentencer should determine the final sentence by calculating a single discount taking into account all the relevant factors, including the plea of guilty and the assistance given to the authorities: *R. v. Sehitoglu and Ozakan* [1998] 1 Cr.App.R.(S.) 89, CA. **5–95**

The court should first assess the starting figure on the basis of the gravity of the offences committed by the defendant and their number. The extent to which that figure would be reduced will depend on the quality, quantity and accuracy of the information disclosed by the offender; his willingness to give evidence if required; and the extent to which he had put himself or his family at risk of reprisal. The amount of the reduction will vary from about one-half to about two-thirds according to the circumstances: *R. v. King*, 7 Cr.App.R.(S.) 227, CA; but the maximum discount should only be given where it enables serious criminal activity to be stopped and serious criminals brought to book; this is not only because of the value of such information but also because it will place the offender at the highest risk: *R. v. Z.* [2008] 1 Cr.App.R.(S.) 60, CA. The sentence must be tailored so as to punish the defendant, but at the same time reward him as far as possible for the help he had given, in order to demonstrate to offenders that it was worth their while to disclose the criminal activities of others: *R. v. Sivan*, 10 Cr.App.R.(S.) 282, CA. As to whether the amount of any reduction under these informal procedures should be scaled back so as to allow the maximum discounts to be given to those who engage in the formalised processes under the 2005 Act, see *ante*, § 5–94e.

In *R. v. Sivan*, Lord Lane C.J. said that it was not always easy to discover the true facts, and the defendant himself would not be anxious for his activities to be aired in public, so that any information which he did impart would often have to be conveyed to the court in writing, or in private. In important cases it might be desirable for the court to have a letter from a senior officer of the investigating agency, unconnected with the case, who had examined all the facts and was able to certify that the facts were as reported by the officers conducting the investigation. There should be a statement in writing from the officer in charge of the investigation setting out those facts which would be certified by the senior officer; in the more important cases the officer in charge of the investigation should be available to give evidence if necessary, whether in court or in the judge's chambers as the situation might demand. The shorthand writer should be present to take a note of what transpired in the judge's room. Information would be equally acceptable, whether it was information relating to the crime in respect of which the defendant had been convicted, or whether it related to some other criminal activity which had nothing directly to do with that crime.

Some earlier decisions of the court (in particular *R. v. Davies and Gorman*, 68 Cr.App.R. 319, CA) suggest that this principle is limited to cases where the offender is guilty of a serious crime, but more recent decisions confirm that it is applicable to all levels of criminality (see, in particular, *R. v. Thomas*, 7 Cr.App.R.(S.) 95, CA; see also *R. v. Wood*, 9 Cr.App.R.(S.) 238, CA).

5–96 It was said in *R. v. Wood* that where credit had been given to an offender for his assistance to the authorities, that fact should be stated by the sentencer in open court, but this observation must be limited to cases where (as in *Wood*) the fact that he has given information is well known. Where one of several defendants is entitled to a reduction in sentence for reasons which cannot be made public, a judge is not entitled to reduce the sentences of the other defendants merely to avoid putting at risk the confidentiality of the information: *Att.-Gen.'s References (Nos 83 and 85 of 2004) (R. v. Gardner and Afzal)* (2005) 149 S.J. 770, CA.

Credit should be given only if assistance is offered early enough for it to be potentially useful: *R. v. Debbag and Izett*, 12 Cr.App.R.(S.) 733, CA. The purpose of the credit is to reflect the offender's own attitude and acceptance of guilt and remorse, and to assist in the arrest of others. There was no true remorse if the offender fought his corner and volunteered information only when sentenced. Where an offender gives information after conviction and sentence, the Court of Appeal will not (normally, see *post*) reduce the sentence on this account: *ibid.*; *R. v. X.*, 15 Cr.App.R.(S.) 750, CA; and *R. v. A. and B.* [1999] 1 Cr.App.R.(S.) 52, CA (where the authorities were reviewed and the relevant principles restated). And it should be noted that the procedures under sections 73 and 74 of the 2005 Act will not be available to a defendant who contested his guilt.

Although what was said in *R. v. A and B*, *ante*, represents the general rule, the Court of Appeal is not precluded, in exceptional cases, from taking into account material which has arisen subsequent to conviction and sentence following a trial: *R. v. A.* [2007] 1 Cr.App.R.(S.) 60, CA. See also *R. v. R. (Informer: Reduction of sentence)*, *The Times*, February 18, 2002, CA (where a sentence was reduced following the giving of further information after the sentence was passed).

In *R. v. X* [1999] 2 Cr.App.R. 125, the Court of Appeal considered the course to be taken if the defendant disputed the account given by the police of his assistance and its value. The court issued the following guidance, and emphasised that there should normally be no question of evidence being heard or of an issue being tried on the extent of any assistance given. A sentencing judge would be unlikely to make any adjustment to the sentence unless the defendant's assertion of having given assistance was supported by the police; the greatest care had, therefore, to be taken to ensure the accuracy of a confidential report for the judge; such a document should not usually contain such material as would require a public interest immunity application; if it did, then the usual rules about the conduct of such an application would apply; absent any such consideration, the document should be shown to counsel for the defendant, not for the purpose of debating its contents but so that the defendant might be satisfied that there was nothing unfavourable therein; expeditions to the judge's chambers should usually be unnecessary; if the defendant did not accept the contents, the remedy was not to cross-examine the officer who prepared it, who was not to be regarded as a prosecution witness for this purpose; the remedy was either to seek an adjournment for further consideration to be given to the contents of the document, or not to rely on it, and the judge should pay no heed to it if asked not to do so by the defendant; if it was taken into account, the judge should say no more than was the current practice (*i.e.* that he had taken into account all the information about the defendant with which he had been provided).

Entrapment

If a court takes the view that an offence would not have been committed but for the activities of an informer, it may, if it thinks it right to do so, mitigate the penalty: *R. v. Underhill*, 1 Cr.App.R.(S.) 270, CA. In *R. v. Beaumont*, 9 Cr.App.R.(S.) 342, CA (applied in *R. v. Chapman and Denton*, 11 Cr.App.R.(S.) 222, CA), entrapment was said to be a substantial mitigating factor (*Underhill* was not apparently cited). For further illustrations of the effect of entrapment as mitigation, see *R. v. Mackey and Shaw*, 14 Cr.App.R.(S.) 53, CA; and, as to journalistic "stings", see *R. v. Tonnessen* [1998] 2 Cr.App.R.(S.) 328, CA; and *R. v. Barnett* [2008] 1 Cr.App.R.(S.) 61, CA (both of which make the point that if the "sting" was accompanied by adverse publicity leading to public humiliation or other adverse consequences, this will add to the mitigating effect). The use of test letters to establish the guilt of a post office employee suspected of stealing mail is not a mitigating factor: *R. v. Ramen*, 10 Cr.App.R.(S.) 334, CA. It has been said that the same applies to test purchases made by undercover police officers attempting to gather evidence of dealing in drugs (see *R. v. Springer* [1999] 1 Cr.App.R.(S.) 217, CA; *R. v. Mayeri* [1999] 1 Cr.App.R.(S.) 304, CA); but this now needs to be seen in the context of decisions such as *R. v. Afonso*; *R. v. Sajid*; *R. v. Andrews* [2005] 1 Cr.App.R(S.) 99, CA (*post*, § 27–113). **5–97**

Particular meritorious conduct unrelated to offence

In *R. v. Alexander* [1997] 2 Cr.App.R.(S.) 74, CA, it was said that where a man who had shown "great courage" in assisting in the apprehension of armed robbers and who had subsequently given evidence against them, subsequently finds himself in trouble with the law, he is entitled to expect particular credit for such conduct. See also *R. v. Wenman* [2005] 2 Cr.App.R.(S.) 3, CA. **5–98**

Attitude of offender's family

In *R. v. Ferrett* [1998] 2 Cr.App.R.(S.) 384, CA, it was deemed appropriate to reduce a sentence of five years' imprisonment for drugs offences by six months on account of the fact that the defendant's mother had reported her suspicions to the police; such attitude was indicative of a supportive and responsible family that would continue to support the offender in the future. **5–99**

F. SENTENCING GUIDELINES

Criminal Justice Act 2003, s.172

Duty of court to have regard to sentencing guidelines

172.—(1) Every court must— **5–100**

(a) in sentencing an offender, have regard to any guidelines which are relevant to the offender's case, and

(b) in exercising any other function relating to the sentencing of offenders, have regard to any guidelines which are relevant to the exercise of the function.

(2) In subsection (1) "guidelines" means sentencing guidelines issued by the Council under section 170(9) as definitive guidelines, as revised by subsequent guidelines so issued.

The guidelines (on guilty pleas, the assessment of seriousness, "new" sentences, manslaughter by reason of provocation, some forms of robbery, breach of a protective order, domestic violence, sexual offences, breach of bail, non-fatal offences against the person, assaults on, and cruelty to, children, sentencing in magistrates' courts and causing death by driving) are set out in full, or summarised, in Appendix K.

A judge is obliged to have regard to relevant sentencing guidelines if they apply at the date of sentence, even if they did not apply at the time the defendant pleaded guilty and the defendant would have received a more lenient sentence under pre-guideline sentencing authorities: *R. v. Bao* [2008] 2 Cr.App.R.(S.) 10, CA. Whilst it is not the case that a guideline issued by the Sentencing Guidelines Council will always be followed, it is not open to a court to disregard such a guideline: see *R. v. Oosthuizen* [2006] 1 Cr.App.R.(S.) 73, CA; *R. v. Bowering* [2006] 2 Cr.App.R.(S.) 10, CA (duty to give reasons when not following guidelines); *Att.-Gen.'s References (Nos 14 and 15 of 2006) (R. v. French and Webster)* [2007] 1 Cr.App.R.(S.) 1, CA; and *R. v. Wilson (Daniel Rushton)* [2008] 1 Cr.App.R. 90, CA (judge not obliged slavishly to follow guidelines; and entitled to depart therefrom when satisfied that there is good reason). Where there is good reason to depart significantly from a guideline (as, for example, where the facts of the case diminish its seriousness in comparison to the norm or where there is particularly powerful personal mitigation), it would be quite wrong for a judge to refrain from imposing the sentence he thought appropriate for fear of the sentence being referred to the Court of Appeal as being unduly lenient: *Att.-Gen.'s Reference (No. 8 of 2007) (R. v. Krivec)* [2008] 1 Cr.App.R.(S.) 1, CA.

As to a sentencing decision neither representing a mathematical exercise nor resulting from an arithmetical calculation, see *R. v. Martin (Selina)* [2007] 1 Cr.App.R.(S.) 3, CA, where it was said that a judge must balance all the ingredients of the case in order to produce the appropriate sentence, there being no grid plan or points system giving rise to a notional length of sentence; and that, whilst consistency of approach is undoubtedly to be encouraged, guidelines remain guidelines.

Draft or consultation guidance should be approached with extreme caution, with preference being give to current guidance of the Court of Appeal: *R. v. Lloyd (Brian Paul)*, *The Times*, March 26, 2007, CA.

G. PARITY OF SENTENCE

Different forms of sentence

5–101 Where one of two co-defendants is amenable to a particular form of sentence, but the other is not, it is not wrong in principle to impose the particular form of sentence on the offender who is amenable to it and a term of imprisonment on the other: *R. v. Berry*, 7 Cr.App.R.(S.) 392, CA; *R. v. Whitehead*, 16 Cr.App.R.(S.) 395, CA.

Differences in responsibility

5–102 A difference in the sentences imposed on co-defendants may be justified by their different roles in the offence (see *R. v. Belton and Petrow* [1997] 1 Cr.App.R.(S.) 215, CA), or if the offence by one of them represents a breach of trust (see *R. v. Warton*, unreported, November 24, 1975).

Relevant difference in personal circumstances

5–103 It is appropriate for a court to distinguish between offenders on the ground that one is significantly younger than the other (see *R. v. Turner*, unreported, October 6, 1976), that one has a significantly less serious criminal record (see *R. v. Walsh*, 2 Cr.App.R.(S.) 224, CA), or that some other mitigating circumstance is available to one defendant which is not available to the other (see *R. v. Tremarco*, 1 Cr.App.R.(S.) 286, CA; *R. v. Strutt*, 14 Cr.App.R.(S.) 56, CA). Where the sentence on one defendant is reduced on account of mitigating circumstances which apply only to that defendant, the sentences of the other defendants should not be reduced: *Att.-Gen.'s References (Nos 62, 63 and 64 of 1995) (R. v. O'Halloran)* [1996] 2 Cr.App.R.(S.) 223, CA; and see also *Att.-Gen.'s Ref. (No. 73 of 1999) (R. v. Charles)* [2000] 2 Cr.App.R.(S.) 210, CA. The fact that one defendant is a woman is not in itself a ground for discrimination: see *R. v. Okuya and Nwaobi*, 6 Cr.App.R.(S.) 253, CA.

Where the power of the court to sentence one accomplice is restricted by reason of his age, there is no disparity if a longer sentence is passed on another accomplice to whom such restrictions do not apply: *R. v. Harper*, 16 Cr.App.R.(S.) 639, CA. Where an offender was properly sentenced to four years' imprisonment, and his co-defendant to a lesser term, the fact that the first offender was a "long term prisoner" and may have served a greater proportion of the sentence in custody did not give rise to unjustified disparity: *R. v. Ensley* [1996] 1 Cr.App.R.(S.) 294, CA. Where one offender was properly sentenced to a longer than commensurate sentence under the *PCC(S)A* 2000, s.80(2)(b), and his accomplice to a commensurate sentence under section 80(2)(a), there was no disparity: *R. v. Bestwick and Huddlestone*, 16 Cr.App.R.(S.) 168, CA.

Suspension of sentence

The fact that one defendant's sentence was to be suspended and the other's immediate did not in itself justify any difference in the lengths of the respective sentences: see *R. v. Pitblado and Kelly* [1975] Crim.L.R. 471, CA (not reported on this point). Where there are distinct grounds for distinguishing in favour of one co-defendant, both in relation to the length of the sentence and the question of suspension, it may be appropriate to impose a shorter, suspended sentence on one and a longer immediate sentence on the other: see *R. v. Gianitto*, 2 Cr.App.R.(S.) 221, CA, and *R. v. Fowler*, 6 Cr.App.R.(S.) 301, CA. **5–104**

Accomplice already dealt with by a different judge

Wherever practicable, all offenders involved in a particular offence should be sentenced by the same judge (see *R. v. Broadbridge*, 5 Cr.App.R.(S.) 269, CA), but this may not always be possible. Where a judge has to deal with an offender whose accomplice has been dealt with by another judge, the second judge should pass the sentence which he considers appropriate and leave the Court of Appeal to correct any disparity. See *R. v. Broadbridge*, *ante*, where the court indicated that the second judge should not adjourn to obtain information about the sentence imposed by the first judge, *R. v. Butcher*, 11 Cr.App.R.(S.) 104, CA, and *R. v. Rugg* [1997] 2 Cr.App.R.(S.) 350, CA. **5–105**

Disparity of sentence as a ground of appeal

Disparity of sentence may occur in a number of different forms. The most obvious is where one co-defendant receives a more severe sentence than the other, when there is no good reason for the difference (see, for example, *R. v. Church*, 7 Cr.App.R.(S.) 370, CA). There may equally be disparity when the defendants receive identical sentences, despite relevant differences in their culpability or personal circumstances (see *R. v. Sykes*, 2 Cr.App.R.(S.) 173, CA; and *R. v. Goodacre* [1996] 1 Cr.App.R.(S.) 424, CA). **5–106**

A failure to distinguish in favour of a defendant who has pleaded guilty will normally amount to disparity (see *R. v. Quirke*, 4 Cr.App.R.(S.) 187, CA). There may equally be disparity where the difference between the sentences imposed on two defendants either exaggerates the difference in their culpability or personal circumstances (see *R. v. Frankson* [1996] 2 Cr.App.R.(S.) 366, CA), or is insufficient to mark the difference (see *R. v. Tilley*, 5 Cr.App.R.(S.) 235, CA; *R. v. Griffiths* [1996] 1 Cr.App.R.(S.) 444, CA).

Where an offender has received a sentence which is not open to criticism when considered in isolation, but which is significantly more severe than has been imposed on his accomplice, and there is no reason for the differentiation, the Court of Appeal may reduce the sentence, but only if the disparity is serious. It has been said that the court would interfere where "right-thinking members of the public, with full knowledge of the relevant facts and circumstances [would] consider that something had gone wrong with the administration of justice" (*per* Lawton L.J. in *R. v. Fawcett*, 5 Cr.App.R.(S.) 158, CA); but this was rejected, as providing little guidance as to those cases in which the court's sense of injustice would be so offended that it would interfere, in *R. v. Coleman and Petch*, unreported, October 10, 2007, CA ([2007] EWCA Crim. 2318), where it was said that there was no identifiable principle on which the court would intervene on this ground. Certainly, there are cases where the court has refused to interfere with proper sentences by reference to the good fortune of another offender, where that other offender has received a lenient sentence for no apparent reason (*R. v. Tate* (2006) 150 S.J. 1192, CA) or, despite having been alleged to have been more deeply involved than the appellant, has been convicted of a lesser offence for lack of evidence (*Coleman and Petch*, *ante*).

The court will not make comparisons with sentences passed in the Crown Court in cases unconnected with that of the appellant (see *R. v. Large*, 3 Cr.App.R.(S.) 80, CA). There is some authority for the view that disparity will be entertained as a ground of appeal only in relation to sentences passed on different offenders on the same occasion: see *R. v. Stroud*, 65 Cr.App.R. 150, CA. It appears to have been ignored in more recent decisions, such as *R. v. Wood*, 5 Cr.App.R.(S.) 381, CA, *Fawcett*, *ante*, and *Broadbridge*, *ante*. The present position seems to be that the court will entertain submissions based on disparity of sentence between offenders involved in the same case, irrespective of whether they were sentenced on the same occasion or by the same judge, so long as the test stated in *Fawcett* is satisfied.

As to disparity arising from the application of the provisions of Schedule 21 to the *CJA* 2003 relating to the fixing of the minimum term to be served by persons convicted of murder, see *post*, § 5–239h.

H. TAKING OFFENCES INTO CONSIDERATION

Practice

5–107 The practice of taking offences into consideration has no statutory foundation, although it has been recognised in a number of statutory provisions. It was described by Lord Goddard C.J. in *R. v. Batchelor*, 36 Cr.App.R. 64, CCA, as:

> "simply a convention under which if a court is informed that there are outstanding charges against a prisoner who is before it for a particular offence, the court can, if the prisoner admits the offences and asks that they should be taken into account, take them into account, which means that the court can give a longer sentence than it would if it were dealing with him only on the charge mentioned in the indictment" (at pp. 67–68).

The sentence passed by the court is passed only for the offences in the indictment, and there is no conviction in respect of the offences taken into consideration. A plea of autrefois convict is not available, but it is the practice not to proceed on an offence previously taken into consideration (*ante*, § 4–129). If, in error, the practice is not observed, the court should ensure that no additional punishment is imposed on account of such offence: *R. v. North*, unreported, July 9, 1971, CA (CSP, L3–1B01).

Matters which should not be taken into consideration

5–108 A charge should not be taken into consideration if the public interest requires that it should be the subject of a separate trial (see *R. v. McClean*, 6 Cr.App.R. 26, CCA). A court should not take into consideration an offence which it is not empowered to try; in particular, the Crown Court should not take into consideration a summary offence: *R. v. Simons*, 37 Cr.App.R. 120, CCA. An offence should not be taken into consideration if it is one where a court is required to disqualify the offender from driving or endorse his driving licence in the event of conviction (such steps not being possible where the offence is taken into consideration): *ibid*. A court should not take into consideration an offence in respect of which an order of conditional discharge has been made, when sentencing the offender for a further offence committed while the order is in effect: *R. v. Webb* [1953] 2 Q.B. 390, 37 Cr.App.R. 82, CCA. A civil offence committed by a soldier may properly be taken into consideration, notwithstanding that it would otherwise be dealt with by court-martial: *R. v. Anderson*, 42 Cr.App.R. 91, CCA.

Procedure

5–109 In *R. v. Walsh*, unreported, March 8, 1973, CA, Scarman L.J. made the following observations on the procedure to be followed:

> "Since the matter is essentially one of tacit agreement between the Court and the accused person, it is essential that those administering justice, both the police in the pre-trial stage and the Court at the trial stage, should ensure that the accused man understands what is being done, admits the offences and wishes to have each and every one of them taken into consideration ... (I)t may be of some value to see what are the safeguards that both police and courts can adopt ...
>
> First of all, the police have to prepare the list or the schedule which has to be served upon an accused person. If it is known that he intends to plead guilty, this schedule can be served

before arraignment, perhaps some days before the day of the trial. If he is going to plead not guilty, then it may be that such a list should not be served until after he has been found guilty. All that one can say of the standards to be observed by the police in the preparation and service of the list is that they should exercise meticulous care in the preparation of the list and they should ensure that when the list is given to him, his signature is obtained, and in so far as it is within the power of the police to ensure it, they should ensure that he gets an opportunity of studying the list before he signs it, and certainly, of course, before he has to deal with it in court.

... When the matter is dealt with in court, it would seem to be the best practice that the police officer responsible for serving the list should be called to say that it was served, and that he had the document signed by the accused man. But in any event, it is the court's responsibility at this stage to ensure that the accused man, who after all in this matter is acting in concert and agreement with the court, understands the document that he has received, and has a proper opportunity, which means time, to consider the document; if necessary, time can be given by adjournment. Before proceeding to sentence, the court must be clear not only that he understands the document that he has received and has had time to study it, but that he accepts that the listed offences are offences which he has committed and that he desires them to be taken into consideration. If this conventional practice is to continue to the benefit of the administration of justice and to the benefit of the accused person, the burden is on the court, and to a lesser extent on the police, to ensure that the man has a full opportunity of understanding what he is being asked to accept. If that is done, then the practice is of benefit to all concerned."

If there is any doubt as to which offences in a list the defendant wishes to have taken into consideration, the doubt should be resolved in open court; and if there is any doubt about his admission of a particular offence, it should not be taken into consideration: *R. v. Urbas*, unreported, June 24, 1963, CCA. The offender should be asked to admit the offences personally and not through counsel (see *R. v. Mortimer*, unreported, March 10, 1970).

Where an offender has been committed for sentence after asking for offences to be taken into consideration by the magistrates' court, the Crown Court must follow the usual procedure and ascertain whether he wishes the offences to be taken into consideration by the Crown Court. He may decide that he no longer wishes them to be taken into account: *R. v. Davies (M.G.)*, 72 Cr.App.R. 262, CA.

Significance

When assessing the significance of offences being taken into consideration, the court is likely to attach weight to the demonstrable fact that the offender has assisted the police (particularly if they are enabled to clear up offences which might not otherwise have been brought to justice), but the way in which the court deals with them should depend on context; in some cases, the offences may add little or nothing to the sentence which the court would otherwise impose, whereas in other cases, they may aggravate the sentence and lead to a substantial increase (*e.g.* where they show a pattern of criminal activity involving careful planning or a deliberate rather than casual involvement in crime, where they show an offence or offences committed on bail, or where they show a return to crime immediately after the offender has been before a court and given a chance to redeem himself, which he has immediately rejected): *R. v. Miles*, *The Times*, April 10, 2006, CA. **5–109a**

Statutory references

A number of statutory provisions make reference to offences taken into consideration: see, in particular, the *PCC(S)A* 2000, ss.130(1) (compensation orders), 148(1) (restitution orders) and 161(1) ("associated offences"). It was held in *Anderson v. DPP* [1978] A.C. 964, HL, that such a reference in the *PCCA* 1973, s.39(1) (*rep.*) (criminal bankruptcy orders) was to an offence taken into consideration in accordance with the conventional procedure and that offences which were mentioned to the court on the basis that the offences charged in the indictment were sample counts, but which were not admitted by the offender, were not "offences ... which the court takes into consideration in determining his sentence" for this purpose. See also *R. v. Crutchley and Tonks*, 15 Cr.App.R. 627, CA, and *R. v. Hose*, 16 Cr.App.R. 682, CA. **5–110**

I. DUTY OF COURT TO GIVE REASONS FOR, AND EXPLAIN EFFECT OF, SENTENCE

Criminal Justice Act 2003, s.174

Duty to give reasons for, and explain effect of, sentence

5–111 **174.**—(1) Subject to subsections (3) and (4), any court passing sentence on an offender—

(a) must state in open court, in ordinary language and in general terms, its reasons for deciding on the sentence passed, and

(b) must explain to the offender in ordinary language—

(i) the effect of the sentence,

(ii) where the offender is required to comply with any order of the court forming part of the sentence, the effects of non-compliance with the order,

(iii) any power of the court, on the application of the offender or any other person, to vary or review any order of the court forming part of the sentence, and

(iv) where the sentence consists of or includes a fine, the effects of failure to pay the fine.

(2) In complying with subsection (1)(a), the court must—

(a) where guidelines indicate that a sentence of a particular kind, or within a particular range, would normally be appropriate for the offence and the sentence is of a different kind, or is outside that range, state the court's reasons for deciding on a sentence of a different kind or outside that range,

(b) where the sentence is a custodial sentence and the duty in subsection (2) of section 152 is not excluded by subsection (1)(a) or (b) or (3) of that section [or any other statutory provision], state that it is of the opinion referred to in section 152(2) and why it is of that opinion,

(c) where the sentence is a community sentence[, other than one consisting of or including a youth rehabilitation order with intensive supervision and surveillance or fostering,] and the case does not fall within section 151(2), state that it is of the opinion that section 148(1) applies and why it is of that opinion,

[(ca) where the sentence consists of or includes a youth rehabilitation order with intensive supervision and surveillance and the case does not fall within paragraph 5(2) of Schedule 1 to the *Criminal Justice and Immigration Act* 2008, state that it is of the opinion that section 1(4)(a) to (c) of that Act and section 148(1) of this Act apply and why it is of that opinion,

(cb) where the sentence consists of or includes a youth rehabilitation order with fostering, state that it is of the opinion that section 1(4)(a) to (c) of the *Criminal Justice and Immigration Act* 2008 and section 148(1) of this Act apply and why it is of that opinion,]

(d) where as a result of taking into account any matter referred to in section 144(1), the court imposes a punishment on the offender which is less severe than the punishment it would otherwise have imposed, state that fact, and

(e) in any case, mention any aggravating or mitigating factors which the court has regarded as being of particular importance.

(3) Subsection (1)(a) does not apply—

(a) to an offence the sentence for which is fixed by law (provision relating to sentencing for such an offence being made by section 270), or

(b) to an offence the sentence for which falls to be imposed under section 51A(2) of the *Firearms Act* 1968, under subsection (2) of section 110 or 111 of the *Sentencing Act* or under section 29(4) or (6) of the *Violent Crime Reduction Act* 2006 (required custodial sentences).

(4) The Secretary of State may by order—

(a) prescribe cases in which subsection (1)(a) or (b) does not apply, and

(b) prescribe cases in which the statement referred to in subsection (1)(a) or the explanation referred to in subsection (1)(b) may be made in the absence of the offender, or may be provided in written form.

[(4A) Subsection (4B) applies where—

(a) a court passes a custodial sentence in respect of an offence on an offender who is aged under 18, and

(b) the circumstances are such that the court must, in complying with subsection (1)(a), make the statement referred to in subsection (2)(b).

(4B) That statement must include—

(a) a statement by the court that it is of the opinion that a sentence consisting of or including a youth rehabilitation order with intensive supervision and surveillance or fostering cannot be justified for the offence, and

(b) a statement by the court why it is of that opinion.]

(5) Where a magistrates' court passes a custodial sentence, it must cause any reason stated by virtue of subsection (2)(b) to be specified in the warrant of commitment and entered on the register.

(6) In this section—

"guidelines" has the same meaning as in section 172;

"the register" has the meaning given by section 163 of the *Sentencing Act*.

[This section is printed as amended by the *VCRA* 2006, s.49, and Sched. 1, para. 9(1) and (6); and as amended, as from a day to be appointed (as to which, see *ante*, § 5–1), by the *CJIA* 2008, s.6(2), and Sched. 4, paras 71 and 80.]

The requirement to explain the reasons for a sentence or other order does not apply to the extent that the explanation will disclose that a sentence has been discounted in pursuance of section 73(3) of the *SOCPA* 2005 (*ante*, § 5–94a), but not made public in accordance with section 73(4): see s.73(7).

Practice Direction (Criminal Proceedings: Consolidation), para. I.7
[2002] 1 W.L.R. 2870

Explanations for the imposition of custodial sentences

I.7.1 The practical effect of custodial sentences imposed by the courts is almost entirely governed by statutory provisions. Those statutory provisions, changed by Parliament from time to time, are not widely understood by the general public. It is desirable that when sentence is passed the practical effect of the sentence should be understood by the defendant, any victim and any member of the public who is present in court or reads a full report of the proceedings. **5–111a**

I.7.2 Whenever a custodial sentence is imposed on an offender the court should explain the practical effect of the sentence in addition to complying with existing statutory requirements. This will be no more than an explanation; the sentence will be that pronounced by the court.

I.7.3 Sentencers should give the explanation in terms of their own choosing, taking care to ensure that the explanation is clear and accurate. No form of words is prescribed. Annexed to this Practice Direction are short statements which may, adapted as necessary, be of value as models (see Annex C). These statements are based on the statutory provisions in force on 1 January 1998 and will, of course, require modification if those provisions are materially amended.

I.7.4 Sentencers will continue to give such explanation as they judge necessary of ancillary orders relating to matters such as disqualification, compensation, confiscation, costs and so on.

I.7.5 The power of the Secretary of State to release a prisoner early under supervision is not part of the sentence. The judge is therefore not required in his sentencing remarks to provide an explanation of this power. However, in explaining the effect of custodial sentences the judge should not say anything which conflicts with the existence of this power.

Apart from the general obligation in section 174, there are specific statutory provisions requiring a court to give reasons for making or, more commonly, not making a particular order; see, for example, the *PCC(S)A* 2000, s.130(3) (*post*, § 5–411) (not ordering compensation where there is a power to do so); and the *RTOA* 1988, s.47(1) (*post*, § 32–217) (not ordering disqualification or endorsement on account of special reasons or hardship). **5–112**

As to the duty of a court, in certain circumstances, to warn an offender made the subject of a community order of the possible loss of social security benefits in the event of non-compliance, see *post*, § 5–179a.

Where a judge, when passing sentence, had told the defendant that the period he would spend in custody would be less than the time he would actually spend in custody before being entitled to automatic release (having made a mistake as to the applicable release regime), this did not give rise to a ground of appeal; while there may be cases where judges could be seen to have had particular regard to the sentencing regime in force at the time and to have tailored their sentences by reference to the effect which they understood that regime would have on the period which the defendant could expect to spend in custody, there was nothing to suggest that in determining the correct sentence the judge had directed his mind primarily, or indeed at all, to that question; the fundamental principle was that the judge's task was to determine the overall length of sentence, not how long the defendant would actually spend in custody; he was then required to explain the effect of his sentence, but it did not make the sentence unfair if he simply made an error in carrying out that function: *R. v. Giga* [2008] Crim.L.R. 579, CA.

In *R. v. Oshingbure and Odewale* [2005] 2 Cr.App.R.(S.) 102, CA, it was said that whilst it was desirable for a judge, when passing sentence, to express his view in relation to evidence given by a defendant, as it may explain to those involved and to the wider public why a particular sentence had been passed, and it might be of material assistance to the Court of Appeal, if and when the sentence came to be reviewed, and to express those views in trenchant terms, a judge who knew that he was himself likely to have to conduct fact-finding exercises in subsequent confiscation proceedings in relation to the same defendant, must not express himself at sentence, or at any earlier stage in the proceedings, in a way which might sensibly be perceived to show that he was biased against the defendant and was therefore unlikely to believe anything the defendant might tell him in future.

IV. DISCHARGE AND BINDING OVER

(1) Discharge

Powers of Criminal Courts (Sentencing) Act 2000, s.12

Absolute and conditional discharge

5–113 **12.**—(1) Where a court by or before which a person is convicted of an offence (not being an offence the sentence for which is fixed by law or falls to be imposed under section 110(2) or 111(2) below, section 51A(2) of the *Firearms Act* 1968, section 225(2) or 226(2) of the *Criminal Justice Act* 2003 or section 29(4) or (6) of the *Violent Crime Reduction Act* 2006) is of the opinion, having regard to the circumstances including the nature of the offence and the character of the offender, that it is inexpedient to inflict punishment, the court may make an order either—

(a) discharging him absolutely; or

(b) if the court thinks fit, discharging him subject to the condition that he commits no offence during such period, not exceeding three years from the date of the order, as may be specified in the order.

(2) Subsection (1)(b) above has effect subject to section 66(4) of the *Crime and Disorder Act* 1998 (effect of reprimands and warnings).

(3) An order discharging a person subject to such a condition as is mentioned in subsection (1)(b) above is in this Act referred to as an "order for conditional discharge"; and the period specified in any such order is in this Act referred to as "the period of conditional discharge".

(5) If (by virtue of section 13 below) a person conditionally discharged under this section is sentenced for the offence in respect of which the order for conditional discharge was made, that order shall cease to have effect.

(6) On making an order for conditional discharge, the court may, if it thinks it expedient for the purpose of the offender's reformation, allow any person who consents to do so to give security for the good behaviour of the offender.

(7) Nothing in this section shall be construed as preventing a court, on discharging an offender absolutely or conditionally in respect of any offence, from making an order for costs against the offender or imposing any disqualification on him or from making in respect of the offence an order under section 130, 143 or 148 below (compensation orders, deprivation orders and restitution orders).

[This section is printed as amended, and repealed in part, by the *CJA* 2003, s.304, and Sched. 32, paras 90 and 93; the *VCRA* 2006, s.49, and Sched. 1, para. 6; and the *CJIA* 2008, s.148(1), and Sched. 26, paras 40 and 41.]

As to the interpretation of the reference in subsection (1) to a sentence falling to be imposed under any of the specified statutory provisions, see section 164(3), *ante*, § 5–5.

Powers of Criminal Courts (Sentencing) Act 2000, ss.13, 14

Commission of further offence by person conditionally discharged

13.—(1) If it appears to the Crown Court, where that court has jurisdiction in accordance with subsection (2) below, or to a justice of the peace having jurisdiction in accordance with that subsection, that a person in whose case an order for conditional discharge has been made— **5–114**

(a) has been convicted by a court in Great Britain of an offence committed during the period of conditional discharge, and

(b) has been dealt with in respect of that offence,

that court or justice may, subject to subsection (3) below, issue a summons requiring that person to appear at the place and time specified in it or a warrant for his arrest.

(2) Jurisdiction for the purposes of subsection (1) above may be exercised—

(a) if the order for conditional discharge was made by the Crown Court, by that court;

(b) if the order was made by a magistrates' court, by a justice acting for the petty sessions area for which that court acts.

(3) A justice of the peace shall not issue a summons under this section except on information and shall not issue a warrant under this section except on information in writing and on oath.

(4) A summons or warrant issued under this section shall direct the person to whom it relates to appear or to be brought before the court by which the order for conditional discharge was made.

(5) If a person in whose case an order for conditional discharge has been made by the Crown Court is convicted by a magistrates' court of an offence committed during the period of conditional discharge, the magistrates' court—

(a) may commit him to custody or release him on bail until he can be brought or appear before the Crown Court; and

(b) if it does so, shall send to the Crown Court a copy of the minute or memorandum of the conviction entered in the register, signed by the justices' chief executive by whom the register is kept.

(6) Where it is proved to the satisfaction of the court by which an order for conditional discharge was made that the person in whose case the order was made has been convicted of an offence committed during the period of conditional discharge, the court may deal with him, for the offence for which the order was made, in any way in which it could deal with him if he had just been convicted by or before that court of that offence.

(7) If a person in whose case an order for conditional discharge has been made by a magistrates' court—

(a) is convicted before the Crown Court of an offence committed during the period of conditional discharge, or

(b) is dealt with by the Crown Court for any such offence in respect of which he was committed for sentence to the Crown Court,

the Crown Court may deal with him, for the offence for which the order was made, in any way in which the magistrates' court could deal with him if it had just convicted him of that offence.

(8) If a person in whose case an order for conditional discharge has been made by a magistrates' court is convicted by another magistrates' court of any offence committed during the period of conditional discharge, that other court may, with the consent of the court which made the order, deal with him, for the offence for which the order was made, in any way in which the court could deal with him if it had just convicted him of that offence.

(9) Where an order for conditional discharge has been made by a magistrates' court in the case of an offender under 18 years of age in respect of an offence triable only on indictment in the case of an adult, any powers exercisable under subsection (6), (7) or (8) above by that or any other court in respect of the offender after he attains the age of 18 shall be powers to do either or both of the following—

(a) to impose a fine not exceeding £5,000 for the offence in respect of which the order was made;

(b) to deal with the offender for that offence in any way in which a magistrates' court could deal with him if it had just convicted him of an offence punishable with imprisonment for a term not exceeding six months.

(10) The reference in subsection (6) above to a person's having been convicted of an

offence committed during the period of conditional discharge is a reference to his having been so convicted by a court in Great Britain.

Effect of discharge

5–115 **14.**—(1) Subject to subsection (2) below, a conviction of an offence for which an order is made under section 12 above discharging the offender absolutely or conditionally shall be deemed not to be a conviction for any purpose other than the purposes of the proceedings in which the order is made and of any subsequent proceedings which may be taken against the offender under section 13 above.

(2) Where the offender was aged 18 or over at the time of his conviction of the offence in question and is subsequently sentenced (under section 13 above) for that offence, subsection (1) above shall cease to apply to the conviction.

(3) Without prejudice to subsections (1) and (2) above, the conviction of an offender who is discharged absolutely or conditionally under section 12 above shall in any event be disregarded for the purposes of any enactment or instrument which—

(a) imposes any disqualification or disability upon convicted persons; or

(b) authorises or requires the imposition of any such disqualification or disability.

(4) Subsections (1) to (3) above shall not affect—

(a) any right of an offender discharged absolutely or conditionally under section 12 above to rely on his conviction in bar of any subsequent proceedings for the same offence;

(b) the restoration of any property in consequence of the conviction of any such offender; or

(c) the operation, in relation to any such offender, of any enactment or instrument in force on 1st July 1974 which is expressed to extend to persons dealt with under section 1(1) of the *Probation of Offenders Act* 1907 as well as to convicted persons.

(5) In subsections (3) and (4) above—

"enactment" includes an enactment contained in a local Act; and

"instrument" means an instrument having effect by virtue of an Act.

(6) Subsection (1) above has effect subject to section 50(1A) of the *Criminal Appeal Act* 1968 and section 108(1A) of the *Magistrates' Courts Act* 1980 (rights of appeal); and this subsection shall not be taken to prejudice any other enactment that excludes the effect of subsection (1) or (3) above for particular purposes.

(7) Without prejudice to paragraph 1(3) of Schedule 11 to this Act (references to provisions of this Act to be construed as including references to corresponding old enactments), in this section—

(a) any reference to an order made under section 12 above discharging an offender absolutely or conditionally includes a reference to an order which was made under any provision of Part I of the *Powers of Criminal Courts Act* 1973 (whether or not reproduced in this Act) discharging the offender absolutely or conditionally;

(b) any reference to an offender who is discharged absolutely or conditionally under section 12 includes a reference to an offender who was discharged absolutely or conditionally under any such provision.

Powers of Criminal Courts (Sentencing) Act 2000, s.15

Discharge: supplementary

5–116 **15.**—(1) [*Amendment of s.12(1) by order of Secretary of State.*]

(2) Where an order for conditional discharge has been made on appeal, for the purposes of section 13 above it shall be deemed—

(a) if it was made on an appeal brought from a magistrates' court, to have been made by that magistrates' court;

(b) if it was made on an appeal brought from the Crown Court or from the criminal division of the Court of Appeal, to have been made by the Crown Court.

(3) In proceedings before the Crown Court under section 13 above, any question whether any person in whose case an order for conditional discharge has been made has been convicted of an offence committed during the period of conditional discharge shall be determined by the court and not by the verdict of a jury.

Effect of discharge

5–116a The effect of section 14(1) (*ante*) is that a person who has been discharged does not make a false representation if he answers "No" when asked if he has ever been "convicted" of an offence: *R. v. Patel (Rupal)* [2007] 1 Cr.App.R. 12, CA. The court observed *obiter* that the position would be different if a person were asked whether he had ever been "found guilty" of an offence. This, however, must remain open to argument; a conclusion so completely at odds with the purpose and intent of the provision could hardly be justified on the basis of such semantics. And as to the effect of the *Rehabilitation of Offenders Act* 1974, see *post*, §§ 13–120 *et seq.*

Combined with other orders

A discharge may not be combined with a fine for the same offence: *R. v. Sanck*, 12 Cr.App.R.(S.) 155, CA. A conditional discharge may be combined with a compensation order, a restitution order, an order to pay the costs of the prosecution, or an order depriving the offender of his rights in property under section 143 of the 2000 Act (*post*, § 5–439): see s.12(7) (*ante*, § 5–113), or a recommendation for deportation (*post*, § 5–923). A court which makes an order of discharge may exercise any power arising out of the *RTOA* 1988, ss.34, 35, 36 or 44 (disqualification from driving, etc.), and must comply with any mandatory requirement of those sections: *ibid.* s.46 (*post*, § 32–216). **5–117**

Following remand in custody

Where an offender had served on remand the maximum sentence allowed for the offence for which he fell to be sentenced, a conditional discharge had been inappropriate as it exposed him to the risk of yet further punishment: *R. v. Lynch*, unreported, October 17, 2007, CA ([2007] EWCA Crim. 2624) (substituting an absolute discharge). **5–117a**

(2) Binding over

(a) *To come up for judgment*

The power to bind over an offender to come up for judgment when called upon is in effect a means of postponing sentence on conditions. It is a power that is recognised by the *PCC(S)A* 2000, s.1(8)(a) (*ante*, § 5–37), and by the *Supreme Court [Senior Courts] Act* 1981, s.79(2)(b) (*ante*, § 2–32) (renamed as from a day to be appointed: *Constitutional Reform Act* 2005, s.59(5), and Sched. 11, para. 1). The power may not be exercised where the court passes sentence for the offence (see *R. v. Ayu*, 43 Cr.App.R. 31, CCA). The offender must consent to the order and acknowledge himself to be bound by its terms. The order may include a condition (such as that the offender leaves the United Kingdom and returns to his own country for a period of time), but this power should be used sparingly and only to ensure that the offender goes to a country of which he is a citizen or where he is habitually resident, unless there are special circumstances (see *R. v. Williams (Carl)*, 75 Cr.App.R. 378, CA). **5–118**

Where it is proposed to call an offender to come up for judgment, notice must be given to him (see *R. v. David*, 27 Cr.App.R. 50, CCA). No specific provision is made for the issue of process where the offender fails to attend. When the offender appears before the court, the order and its terms must be proved (see *R. v. Philbert*, unreported, October 2, 1972), and the facts of the alleged breach of the conditions of the order proved in the same manner as the commission of a crime (see *R. v. David*, *ante*; *R. v. McGarry*, 30 Cr.App.R. 187, CCA). **5–119**

(b) *To keep the peace*

Justices of the Peace Act 1361

First, that in every county of England shall be assigned for the keeping of the peace, one lord, and with him three or four of the most worthy in the county, with some learned in the law, and they shall have power to restrain the offenders, rioters, and all other barators and to pursue, arrest, take, and chastise them according their trespass or offence; and to cause them to be imprisoned and duly punished according to the law and customs of the realm, and according to that which to them shall seem best to do by their discretions and good advisement; ... and to take of all them that they may find by indictment, or by suspicion, and put them in prison; and to take of all them that be [not] of good fame, where they shall be found, sufficient surety and mainprise **5–120** of their good behaviour towards the King and his people, and the other duly to punish; to the intent that the people be not by such rioters or rebels troubled nor endamaged, nor the peace blemished, nor merchants nor other passing by the highways of the realm disturbed, nor [put in the peril which may happen] of such offenders …

[This statute is printed as repealed in part by the *Statute Law Revision Act* 1948; and the *CLA* 1967, s.10(2), Sched. 3.]

Justices of the Peace Act 1968, s.1(7)

5–121 **1.**—(7) It is hereby declared that any court of record having a criminal jurisdiction has, as ancillary to that jurisdiction, the power to bind over to keep the peace, and power to bind over to be of good behaviour a person who or whose case is before the court, by requiring him to enter into his own recognisances or to find sureties or both, and committing him to prison if he does not comply.

[This subsection is printed as repealed in part by the *Administration of Justice Act* 1973, Sched. 5.]

The Crown Court is a superior court of record: *Supreme Court [Senior Courts] Act* 1981, s.45 (renamed as from a day to be appointed: *Constitutional Reform Act* 2005, s.59(5), and Sched. 11, para. 1).

Use of the power

5–121a The use of the power to bind over to keep the peace does not depend on a conviction: it may be used against a person who has been acquitted by a jury or on appeal (see *R. v. Sharp*, 41 Cr.App.R. 86; *R. v. Biffen* [1966] Crim.L.R. 111: cases in which a successful appellant against conviction was bound over by the Court of Criminal Appeal); or against a witness who has given evidence (see *Sheldon v. Bromfield JJ.* [1964] 2 Q.B. 573, DC), but a person who has given a witness statement in a case in which the Crown has offered no evidence is not "a person who or whose case is before the court" and may not be bound over (*R. v. Swindon Crown Court, ex p. Pawittar Singh* [1984] 1 W.L.R. 449, DC). Binding over a witness is "a serious step" which should be taken only "where facts are proved by evidence before the court which indicate the likelihood that the peace will not be kept. Such cases … will be exceedingly rare" (*per* Stephen Brown L.J. in *ex p. Pawittar Singh, ante*). It is not possible to include specific conditions in an order binding a person over to keep the peace (*R. v. Randall*, 8 Cr.App.R.(S.) 433, CA).

Procedure

5–121b If the court intends to bind over a person who has appeared as a witness, it must give him an opportunity to be heard (see *Sheldon v. Bromfield JJ., ante*; *R. v. Hendon JJ., ex p. Gorchein* [1973] 1 W.L.R. 1502, DC). It is not necessarily a rule of natural justice that a defendant who has been acquitted should be warned before being bound over, but Lord Widgery C.J. said in *R. v. Woking JJ., ex p. Gossage* [1973] 1 Q.B. 448, DC, that it would be "courteous and perhaps wise" to do so. Where a person shows by his behaviour in the face of the court that a breach of the peace is imminent, natural justice does not entitle him to a warning or the opportunity to make representations before being bound over (see *R. v. North London Magistrate, ex p. Haywood* [1973] 1 W.L.R. 965, DC).

Where it is proposed to bind a person over in a substantial sum, the court should inquire into the person's means and circumstances, and allow him to make representations in respect of them: failure to do so will amount to a breach of the rules of natural justice (see *R. v. Central Criminal Court, ex. p. Boulding*, 79 Cr.App.R. 100, DC; *R. v. Atkinson*, 10 Cr.App.R.(S.) 470, CA).

Refusal to be bound over

5–121c A magistrates' court has power to commit to prison a person whom it orders to enter a recognizance to keep the peace and who refuses to do so (*MCA* 1980, s.115(3)); no specific provision is made in the case of a person who refuses to enter a recognizance on the order of the Crown Court, but it may be that the matter should be dealt with as a contempt. A person under 21 and over 18 who refuses to be bound over by a magistrates' court may be detained under the *PCC(S)A* 2000, s.108 (see *Howley v. Oxford*, 81 Cr.App.R. 246, DC, *post*, § 5–947), but there is no power to order the detention of an offender under the age of 18 who refuses to be bound over (see *Veater v. Glennon* [1981] 1 W.L.R. 567, DC). An offender under the age of 18 who refuses to be bound over by a magistrates' court may be ordered to attend at an attendance centre (see the *PCC(S)A* 2000, s.60(1)(b), *post*, § 5–162). The fact that there is no power to commit an offender under the age of 18 to custody for refusing to be bound over does not prevent the court from binding over such an offender who consents to be bound (see *Conlan v. Oxford*, 79 Cr.App.R. 157, DC).

Procedure when breach of recognizance is alleged

Where a person who has been bound over to keep the peace is proved to have broken the terms of the recognizance, the court has power to estreat the recognizance by ordering the person to pay the amount of the recognizance, but there is no power to impose a sentence of imprisonment or otherwise for the offence itself (see *R. v. Gilbert*, unreported, April 4, 1974). The standard of proof is the civil standard: *R. v. Marlow JJ., ex p. O'Sullivan* [1984] Q.B. 381, 78 Cr.App.R. 13, DC). **5–121d**

V. COMMUNITY SENTENCES

A. INTRODUCTION

Criminal Justice Act 2003

The *CJA* 2003 introduced a largely new regime of community sentences. The principal provisions are to be found in sections 147 to 151 (general restrictions on community sentences, *post*, §§ 5–125 *et seq.*), sections 156 to 158 (procedural requirements, *ante*, §§ 5–19 *et seq.*), sections 177 to 180 (community orders for offenders aged 16 or over, *post*, §§ 5–130 *et seq.*), sections 196 to 198 (definitions) (*post*, §§ 5–132 *et seq.*), and sections 199 to 220 (requirements that may be included in community orders, and associated provisions, *post*, §§ 5–135 *et seq.*). **5–121e**

Section 147, *post*, defines "community sentence" as a community order (as defined by s.177) or one or more youth community orders, and "youth community order" is defined as a curfew order, an exclusion order, an attendance centre order, a supervision order or an action plan order. These youth community orders will still be made under the sections of the *PCC(S)A* 2000 that provided for them before the enactment of the 2003 Act, although all those provisions have been amended so as to make them available only in the case of offenders under 16 years of age. The provisions of the 2000 Act that provided for community rehabilitation orders, community punishment orders, community punishment and rehabilitation orders, drug treatment and testing orders and drug abstinence orders are all repealed.

As to enforcement, it should be noted that Schedule 3 to the 2000 Act, which was the principal schedule governing breach, revocation and amendment of community orders has been substituted by a new Schedule 3 . This, however, only relates to breach, revocation and amendment of curfew and exclusion orders. The new principal provision in relation to "community orders" under the 2003 Act (*i.e.* not including youth community orders, which have their own provisions, including the substituted Schedule 3 to the 2000 Act, *ante*) is Schedule 8 to the 2003 Act (*post*, §§ 5–180 *et seq.*).

To the extent that the provisions referred to above had not previously been brought into force, almost all of them were brought into force on April 4, 2005, by the *Criminal Justice Act 2003 (Commencement No. 8 and Transitional and Saving Provisions) Order* 2005 (S.I. 2005 No. 950). Notable exceptions are section 151 of the 2003 Act (*post*, § 5–129, in relation to which no commencement date has been set) and the substitution of Schedule 3 to the 2000 Act, which is due to take effect on April 4, 2009 (but see *post*, § 5–122): *ibid.*, as amended by the *Criminal Justice Act 2003 (Commencement No. 8 and Transitional and Saving Provisions) (Amendment) Order* 2007 (S.I. 2007 No. 391). In addition, insofar as they apply where a person aged 16 or

17 is convicted of an offence, sections 177, 179 and 180 and Schedules 8 and 9 are due to come into force on April 4, 2009 (but see *post*, § 5–122): *ibid*. For the saving of the former statutory provisions in relation to offences committed before April 4, 2005, see *ante*, § 5–1a. For the transitional and saving provisions consequential upon the delayed commencement of sections 177, 179 and 180 in the case of 16- and 17-year-olds, see §§ 5–131a *et seq.* in the supplement.

Because the former statutory provisions continue to apply to offences committed before April 4, 2005, and, in modified form, apply to offences committed by persons aged 16 or 17 on conviction until April 4, 2009, they are set out in the supplement (§§ 5–122a *et seq.*).

Criminal Justice and Immigration Act 2008

5–122 Section 1 of the 2008 Act creates a new type of order, termed a youth rehabilitation order, which a court may make where a person aged under 18 is convicted of an offence. Such an order may impose one or more of various requirements (set out in Schedule 1). If (a) the court is dealing with the offender for an imprisonable offence, (b) the court is of the opinion that the offence, or the combination of the offence and one or more offences associated with it, was so serious that, but for these provisions, a custodial sentence would be appropriate (or would be appropriate if the offender were not aged under 12), and (c) (if the offender was aged under 15 at the time of conviction) the court is of the opinion that the offender is a persistent offender, it may make a more intensive form of a youth rehabilitation order, termed a youth rehabilitation order with intensive supervision and surveillance (consisting of at least an activity requirement between 90 and 180 days, a supervision requirement and a curfew requirement) or a youth rehabilitation order with fostering (consisting of at least a fostering requirement and a supervision requirement). Schedule 2 (s.2) makes provision regarding breach, revocation and amendment of such orders. The provisions of the Act of 2000 dealing with curfew orders, exclusion orders, attendance centre orders, supervision orders and action plan orders are repealed (s.6(1)).

As at October 1, 2008, none of these provisions were in force and it was not anticipated that they would be brought into force before the second half of 2009. In addition, it is not known how the commencement of these provisions is intended to be related to the delayed commencement of the substitution of Schedule 3 to the *PCC(S)A* 2000 and of sections 177, 179 and 180 of, and Schedules 8 and 9 to, the 2003 Act, so far as they relate to 16- and 17-year-olds. It is understood, however, that it is no longer intended to bring that substitution or those sections and schedules into force at all, and that the provisions currently prescribing April 4, 2009, as their commencement date will be amended so as to avoid their coming into force before they are eventually superseded by the provisions of the 2008 Act.

Whatever the commencement date for the 2008 Act provisions, they will not apply in relation to offences committed before that date: 2008 Act, s.148(2), and Sched. 27, para. 1(1). Accordingly, it is likely to be at least September, 2009, before any cases involving offences committed on or after the commencement date will appear before the Crown Court. Space prohibits the inclusion of the current statutory provisions and the 2008 Act provisions. Because of the uncertainty as to the commencement date, and the likelihood that it will be the current provisions that are the governing provisions throughout at least half the life-cycle of this edition, those provisions have been retained in the main work, with the 2008 Act provisions being contained in the second and/or third supplements.

[The next paragraph is § 5–125.]

B. GENERAL RESTRICTIONS

Criminal Justice Act 2003, ss.147–151

General restrictions on community sentences

Meaning of "community sentence" etc.

5–125 **147.**—(1) In this Part "community sentence" means a sentence which consists of or includes—

(a) a community order (as defined by section 177), or

(b) *one or more youth community orders*

[(c) a youth rehabilitation order].

(2) *In this Chapter "youth community order" means—*

(a) *a curfew order as defined by section 163 of the* Sentencing Act,

(b) *an exclusion order under section 40A(1) of that Act,*

(c) *an attendance centre order as defined by section 163 of that Act,*

(d) *a supervision order under section 63(1) of that Act, or*

(e) *an action plan order under section 69(1) of that Act.*

[This section is printed as amended, as from a day to be appointed (as to which, see *ante*, § 5–1), by the *CJIA* 2008, ss.6(2) and 149, Sched. 4, paras 71 and 72, and Sched. 28, Pt. 1 (omission of italicised words, insertion of words in square brackets).]

This section, together with sections 148 to 150, came into force on April 4, 2005: S.I. 2005 No. 950 (*ante*, § 5–122).

For section 177, see *post*, § 5–130.

Restrictions on imposing community sentences

148.—(1) A court must not pass a community sentence on an offender unless it is of the opinion that the offence, or the combination of the offence and one or more offences associated with it, was serious enough to warrant such a sentence. **5–126**

(2) Where a court passes a community sentence *which consists of or includes a community order*—

(a) the particular requirement or requirements forming part of the community order[, or, as the case may be, youth rehabilitation order, comprised in the sentence] must be such as, in the opinion of the court, is, or taken together are, the most suitable for the offender, and

(b) the restrictions on liberty imposed by the order must be such as in the opinion of the court are commensurate with the seriousness of the offence, or the combination of the offence and one or more offences associated with it.

[(2A) Subsection (2) is subject to paragraph 3(4) of Schedule 1 to the *Criminal Justice and Immigration Act* 2008 (youth rehabilitation order with intensive supervision and surveillance).]

(3) *Where a court passes a community sentence which consists of or includes one or more youth community orders—*

(a) *the particular order or orders forming part of the sentence must be such as, in the opinion of the court, is, or taken together are, the most suitable for the offender, and*

(b) *the restrictions on liberty imposed by the order or orders must be such as in the opinion of the court are commensurate with the seriousness of the offence, or the combination of the offence and one or more offences associated with it.*

(4) Subsections (1) and (2)(b) have effect subject to section 151(2).

(5) The fact that by virtue of any provision of this section—

(a) a community sentence may be passed in relation to an offence; or

(b) particular restrictions on liberty may be imposed by a community order or youth rehabilitation order,

does not require a court to pass such a sentence or to impose those restrictions.

[This section is printed as amended by the *CJIA* 2008, s.10; and as amended, as from a day to be appointed (as to which, see *ante*, § 5–1), by the *CJIA* 2008, ss.6(2) and 149, Sched. 4, paras 71 and 73, and Sched. 28, Pt. 1 (omission of italicised words, insertion of words in square brackets).]

As to the commencement of this section, see *ante*, § 5–121e.

Passing of community sentence on offender remanded in custody

149.—(1) In determining the restrictions on liberty to be imposed by a community order or youth *community* [rehabilitation] order in respect of an offence, the court may have regard to any period for which the offender has been remanded in custody in connection with the offence or any other offence the charge for which was founded on the same facts or evidence. **5–127**

(2) In subsection (1) "remanded in custody" has the meaning given by section 242(2).

[This section is printed as amended, as from a day to be appointed (as to which, see *ante*, § 5–1), by the *CJIA* 2008, s.6(2), and Sched. 4, paras 71 and 74 (substitution of "rehabilitation" for "community").]

As to the commencement of this section, see *ante*, § 5–121e.

Community sentence not available where sentence fixed by law etc.

5–128 **150.** The power to make a community order or youth *community* [rehabilitation] order is not exercisable in respect of an offence for which the sentence—

(a) is fixed by law,

(b) falls to be imposed under section 51A(2) of the *Firearms Act* 1968 (required custodial sentence for certain firearms offences),

(c) falls to be imposed under section 110(2) or 111(2) of the *Sentencing Act* (requirement to impose custodial sentences for certain repeated offences committed by offenders aged 18 or over),

(ca) falls to be imposed under section 29(4) or (6) of the *Violent Crime Reduction Act* 2006 (required custodial sentence in certain cases of using someone to mind a weapon), or

(d) falls to be imposed under any of sections 225 to 228 of this Act (requirement to impose custodial sentences for certain offences committed by offenders posing risk to public).

[This section is printed as amended by the *VCRA* 2006, ss.49 and 65, Sched. 1, para. 9(1) and (3), and Sched. 5; and as amended, as from a day to be appointed (as to which, see *ante*, § 5–1), by the *CJIA* 2008, s.6(2), and Sched. 4, paras 71 and 75 (substitution of "rehabilitation" for "community").]

As to the commencement of this section, see *ante*, § 5–121e.

Community order available only for offences punishable with imprisonment or for persistent offenders previously fined

5–128a **150A.**—(1) The power to make a community order is only exercisable in respect of an offence if—

(a) the offence is punishable with imprisonment; or

(b) in any other case, section 151(2) confers power to make such an order.

(2) For the purposes of this section and section 151 an offence triable either way that was tried summarily is to be regarded as punishable with imprisonment only if it is so punishable by the sentencing court (and for this purpose section 148(1) is to be disregarded).

[This section was inserted by the *CJIA* 2008, s.11(1).]

[Community order [[or youth rehabilitation order]] for persistent offender previously fined

5–129 **151.**—[(A1) Subsection (2) provides for the making of a community order by the court in respect of an offence ("the current offence") committed by a person to whom subsection (1) or (1A) applies.]

(1) *Subsection (2) applies where* [This subsection applies to the offender if—

(za) the current offence is punishable with imprisonment;]

(a) *a person aged 16 or over is convicted of an offence ("the current offence")* [the offender was aged 16 [[18]] or over when he was convicted],

(b) on three or more previous occasions *he* [the offender] has, on conviction by a court in the United Kingdom of any offence committed by him after attaining the age of 16, had passed on him a sentence consisting only of a fine, and

(c) despite the effect of section 143(2), the court would not (apart from this section) regard the current offence, or the combination of the current offence and one or more offences associated with it, as being serious enough to warrant a community sentence.

[(1A) This subsection applies to the offender if—

(a) the current offence is not punishable with imprisonment;

(b) the offender was aged 16 [[18]] or over when he was convicted; and

(c) on three or more previous occasions the offender has, on conviction by a court in the United Kingdom of any offence committed by him after attaining the age of 16, had passed on him a sentence consisting only of a fine.]

(2) The court may make a community order in respect of the current offence instead of imposing a fine if it considers that, having regard to all the circumstances including the matters mentioned in subsection (3), it would be in the interests of justice to make such an order.

[[(2A) Subsection (2B) applies where—

(a) a person aged 16 or 17 is convicted of an offence ("the current offence");

(b) on three or more previous occasions the offender has, on conviction by a court in the United Kingdom of any offence committed by him after attaining the age of 16, had passed on him a sentence consisting only of a fine; and

(c) despite the effect of section 143(2), the court would not (apart from this section) regard the current offence, or the combination of the current offence and one or more offences associated with it, as being serious enough to warrant a youth rehabilitation order.

(2B) The court may make a youth rehabilitation order in respect of the current offence instead of imposing a fine if it considers that, having regard to all the circumstances including the matters mentioned in subsection (3), it would be in the interests of justice to make such an order.]]

(3) The matters referred to in subsection (2) [[and (2B)]] are—

(a) the nature of the offences to which the previous convictions mentioned in subsection (1)(b) [*or (1A)(b)* [[(1A)(b) or (2A)(b)]] (as the case may be)] relate and their relevance to the current offence, and

(b) the time that has elapsed since the offender's conviction of each of those offences.

(4) In *subsection (1)(b)* [subsections (1)(b) *and (1A)(b)* [[(1A)(b) and (2A)(b)]]], the reference to conviction by a court in the United Kingdom includes a reference to *the finding of guilt in service disciplinary proceedings; and, in relation to any such finding of guilt, the reference to the sentence passed is a reference to the punishment awarded* [conviction in service disciplinary proceedings].

(5) For the purposes of *subsection (1)(b)* [subsections (1)(b) *and (1A)(b)* [[(1A)(b) and (2A)(b)]]], a compensation order[, or a service compensation order awarded in service disciplinary proceedings,] or a surcharge under section 161A does not form part of an offender's sentence.

(6) For the purposes of *subsection (1)(b)* [subsections (1)(b) *and (1A)(b)* [[(1A)(b) and (2A)(b)]]], it is immaterial whether on other previous occasions a court has passed on the offender a sentence not consisting only of a fine.

(7) This section does not limit the extent to which a court may, in accordance with section 143(2), treat any previous convictions of the offender as increasing the seriousness of an offence.

[(8) In this section—

(a) "service disciplinary proceedings" means proceedings (whether or not before a court) in respect of a service offence within the meaning of the *Armed Forces Act* 2006; and

(b) any reference to conviction or sentence, in the context of service disciplinary proceedings, includes anything that under section 376(1) to (3) of that Act is to be treated as a conviction or sentence.]]

[This section was not in force as at October 1, 2008. It is printed as amended by the *Domestic Violence, Crime and Victims Act* 2004, s.59(1), and Sched. 10, para. 63; and as amended, as from a day to be appointed, by the *AFA* 2006, s.378(1), and Sched. 16, para. 217 (omission of the words "the finding of guilt" to "punishment awarded" in subs. (4), insertion of words in square brackets that follow those words, insertion of words in square brackets in subs. (5) that begin ", or a service compensation order ...", insertion of subs. (8)); the *CJIA* 2008, s.11(2)–(7) (insertion of subs. (A1), substitution of words in single square brackets for italicised words in subs. (1), insertion of subs. (1A), insertion of words in single square brackets in subs. (3), substitution of words in single square brackets for the italicised words that precede them at the beginning of subss. (4), (5) and (6)); and *ibid.*, s.6(2), and Sched. 4, paras 71 and 76(1)–(7) (insertion of words in double square brackets in title, substitution of "18" for "16" in subss. (1)(a) and (1A)(b), insertion of subss. (2A) and (2B), insertion of words in double square brackets in subs. (3), omission of italicised words in single square brackets in subs. (3), insertion of words in double square brackets, omission of italicised words that precede them, in subss. (4), (5) and (6)). As to the amendments made by Sched. 4 to the 2008 Act, see *ante*, § 5–1.]

C. COMMUNITY ORDERS

(1) General

Criminal Justice Act 2003, s.177

CHAPTER 2

COMMUNITY ORDERS: OFFENDERS AGED 16 OR OVER

Community orders

5–130 **177.**—(1) Where a person aged *16* [18] or over is convicted of an offence, the court by or before which he is convicted may make an order (in this Part referred to as a "community order") imposing on him any one or more of the following requirements—

(a) an unpaid work requirement (as defined by section 199),
(b) an activity requirement (as defined by section 201),
(c) a programme requirement (as defined by section 202),
(d) a prohibited activity requirement (as defined by section 203),
(e) a curfew requirement (as defined by section 204),
(f) an exclusion requirement (as defined by section 205),
(g) a residence requirement (as defined by section 206),
(h) a mental health treatment requirement (as defined by section 207),
(i) a drug rehabilitation requirement (as defined by section 209),
(j) an alcohol treatment requirement (as defined by section 212),
(k) a supervision requirement (as defined by section 213), and
(l) in a case where the offender is aged under 25, an attendance centre requirement (as defined by section 214).

(2) Subsection (1) has effect subject to sections 150 and 218 and to the following provisions of Chapter 4 relating to particular requirements—

(a) section 199(3) (unpaid work requirement),
(b) section 201(3) and (4) (activity requirement),
(c) section 202(4) and (5) (programme requirement),
(d) section 203(2) (prohibited activity requirement),
(e) section 207(3) (mental health treatment requirement),
(f) section 209(2) (drug rehabilitation requirement), and
(g) section 212(2) and (3) (alcohol treatment requirement).

(3) Where the court makes a community order imposing a curfew requirement or an exclusion requirement, the court must also impose an electronic monitoring requirement (as defined by section 215) unless—

(a) it is prevented from doing so by section 215(2) or 218(4), or
(b) in the particular circumstances of the case, it considers it inappropriate to do so.

(4) Where the court makes a community order imposing an unpaid work requirement, an activity requirement, a programme requirement, a prohibited activity requirement, a residence requirement, a mental health treatment requirement, a drug rehabilitation requirement, an alcohol treatment requirement, a supervision requirement or an attendance centre requirement, the court may also impose an electronic monitoring requirement unless prevented from doing so by section 215(2) or 218(4).

(5) A community order must specify a date, not more than three years after the date of the order, by which all the requirements in it must have been complied with; and a community order which imposes two or more different requirements falling within subsection (1) may also specify an earlier date or dates in relation to compliance with any one or more of them.

(6) Before making a community order imposing two or more different requirements falling within subsection (1), the court must consider whether, in the circumstances of the case, the requirements are compatible with each other.

[This section is printed as amended, as from a day to be appointed (as to which, see *ante*, § 5–1), by the *CJIA* 2008, s.6(2), and Sched. 4, paras 71 and 82 (substitution of "18" for "16").]

As from a day to be appointed, the *AFA* 2006, s.178(3), provides that the expression "community order" in subsections (3) to (6) includes a service community order under the 2006 Act; and the *AFA* 2006, s.182(4), provides that the expression "community order" in subsections (5) and (6) includes an "overseas community order" within the meaning of section 182 of the 2006 Act. In the application of those subsections to an overseas community order, "court" includes a relevant service court: s.182(5).

Section 178 of the 2003 Act empowers the Secretary of State to make an order to enable community orders to be reviewed periodically by the court and, in particular, to make provision as to the powers of the court on review. In exercise of this power, the Secretary of State has made the *Community Order (Review by Specified Courts) Order* 2007 (S.I. 2007 No. 2162), article 2(1) of which confers powers on specified magistrates' courts to make community orders containing provisions for periodic review by the court that makes the order or by another specified court, and to amend a community order so as to contain such a provision. Section 179 gives effect to Schedule 8 (breach, revocation and amendment (*post*, §§ 5–180 *et seq.*)). Section 180 gives effect to Schedule 9 (transfer of community orders to Scotland or Northern Ireland (not set out in this work)). **5–131**

Section 178 came into force on March 7, 2005: *Criminal Justice Act 2003 (Commencement No. 7) Order* 2005 (S.I. 2005 No. 373). Sections 177, 179 and 180, and Schedules 8 and 9 came into force on April 4, 2005, save that insofar as they apply where a person aged 16 or 17 is convicted of an offence, they come into force on April 4, 2009: S.I. 2005 No. 950, as amended by S.I. 2007 No. 391 (*ante*, § 5–121e). As to the saving of the former legislation in relation to offences committed before April 4, 2005, see *ante*, § 5–1a. As to the transitional and saving provisions consequent on the delayed commencement of sections 177, 179 and 180, and Schedules 8 and 9, in the case of 16- and 17-year-olds, see paragraphs 7 to 13 of Schedule 2 to S.I. 2005 No. 950 (§§ 5–131a *et seq.* in the supplement). As to the impact of the *CJIA* 2008, see *ante*, § 5–122.

(2) Definitions

Criminal Justice Act 2003, s.196

Chapter 4

Further Provisions about Orders under Chapters 2 and 3

Introductory

Meaning of "relevant order"

196.—(1) In this Chapter "relevant order" means— **5–132**

(a) a community order,

(b) a custody plus order,

(c) a suspended sentence order, or

(d) an intermittent custody order.

(2) In this Chapter any reference to a requirement being imposed by, or included in, a relevant order is, in relation to a custody plus order or an intermittent custody order, a reference to compliance with the requirement being required by the order to be a condition of a licence.

Chapters 2, 3 and 4 of Part 12 of the 2003 Act comprise sections 177 to 180 (*ante*, §§ 5–130, 5–131), 181 to 195 (*post*, §§ 5–314 *et seq.*) and 196 to 223 respectively. The following provisions of Chapter 4 were brought into force on January 26, 2004, for the purposes of the passing of a sentence of imprisonment to which an intermittent custody order relates and the release on licence of a person serving such a sentence (*Criminal Justice Act 2003 (Commencement No. 1) Order* 2003 (S.I. 2003 No. 3282)): sections 196(1)(d) and (2), 197 to 199, 200(1), 201 to 203, 204(1), (2), (5) and (6), 205(1), (3) and (4), 213(1), (2) and (3)(c), 214, 215, 216(2)(b), 217, 218, 219(1)(a), (b) and (d), (2) and (3), 221, 222 and 223(1), (2), (3)(a) and (b), together with Schedule 14.

Sections 197(3) and (4), 202(3)(b), 215(3), 217(3), 222 and 223 were brought into force on March 7, 2005, to the extent that they were not already in force by S.I. 2005 No. 373 (*ante*, § 5–131).

Section 196(1)(a) and (c) came into force on April 4, 2005, as did sections 197 to 203, 204(1) to (3) and (6), 205 to 212, 213(1) to (3)(a) and (d), 214, 215, 216(1) and 217 to 221, to the extent that they were not already in force: S.I. 2005 No. 950 (*ante*, § 5–122).

As at October 1, 2008, all of the provisions of Chapter 4 were, therefore, in force, save for sections 196(1)(b), 204(4) and (5), 213(3)(b) and (c), and 216(2).

For the saving of the former legislation in relation to offences committed prior to April 4, 2005, see *ante*, § 5–1a.

As from a day to be appointed, the *AFA* 2006, s.178(3), provides that the expression "community order" in Chapter 4 of Part 12 of the 2003 Act includes a service community order under the 2006 Act; and section 182(4) of that Act provides that, subject to the modifications set out in section 183, the expression "community order" also includes an overseas community order under that Act. In the application of that chapter to an overseas community order, "court" includes a relevant service court: s.182(5).

Meaning of "responsible officer"

5–133 Section 197(1) of the *CJA* 2003 makes provision as to the meaning of "the responsible officer" for the purposes of Part 12 of the Act. Where the order imposes a curfew or exclusion requirement but no other requirement mentioned in section 177(1) or, as the case requires, section 182(1) or 190(1), and an electronic requirement, it will be the person who under section 215(3) is responsible for the electronic monitoring required by the order; where the offender is aged 18 plus and the only requirement of the order is attendance at an attendance centre, it will be the officer in charge of the attendance centre; and, in any other case, it will be the qualifying officer who, as respects the offender, is for the time being responsible for discharging the functions conferred by Part 12 on the responsible officer. A "qualifying officer" will be either an officer of a local probation board or a member of a youth offending team (s.197(2)).

Duties of responsible officer

5–134 It is the duty of the responsible officer to make any arrangements that are necessary in connection with a relevant order, to promote the offender's compliance with its requirements and, where appropriate, to take steps to enforce them (s.198(1)).

(3) Requirements available in the case of all offenders

Criminal Justice Act 2003, ss.199–213

Requirements available in case of all offenders

Unpaid work requirement

5–135 **199.**—(1) In this Part "unpaid work requirement", in relation to a relevant order, means a requirement that the offender must perform unpaid work in accordance with section 200.

(2) The number of hours which a person may be required to work under an unpaid work requirement must be specified in the relevant order and must be in the aggregate—

(a) not less than 40, and

(b) not more than 300.

(3) A court may not impose an unpaid work requirement in respect of an offender unless after hearing (if the courts thinks necessary) an *appropriate officer* [officer of a local probation board or an officer of a provider of probation services], the court is satisfied that the offender is a suitable person to perform work under such a requirement.

(4) *In subsection (3) "an appropriate officer" means—*

(a) *in the case of an offender aged 18 or over, an officer of a local probation board or an officer of a provider of probation services, and*

(b) *in the case of an offender aged under 18, an officer of a local probation board, an officer of a provider of probation services, a social worker of a local authority social services department or a member of a youth offending team.*

(5) Where the court makes relevant orders in respect of two or more offences of which the offender has been convicted on the same occasion and includes unpaid work requirements in each of them, the court may direct that the hours of work specified in any of those requirements is to be concurrent with or additional to those specified in any other of those orders, but so that the total number of hours which are not concurrent does not exceed the maximum specified in subsection (2)(b).

[This section is printed as amended by the *Offender Management Act 2007 (Consequential Amendments) Order* 2008 (S.I. 2008 No. 912), art. 3, and Sched. 1, para. 19(1) and (6); and as amended, as from a day to be appointed (as to which, see *ante*, § 5–1), by the *CJIA* 2008, ss.6(2) and 149, Sched. 4, paras 71 and 84, and Sched. 28, Pt 1 (omission of italicised words, insertion of words in square brackets).]

As to commencement, see *ante*, § 5–132.

Obligations of person subject to unpaid work requirement

200.—(1) An offender in respect of whom an unpaid work requirement of a relevant order is in force must perform for the number of hours specified in the order such work at such times as he may be instructed by the responsible officer. **5–136**

(2) Subject to paragraph 20 of Schedule 8 and paragraph 18 of Schedule 12 (power to extend order), the work required to be performed under an unpaid work requirement of a community order or a suspended sentence order must be performed during a period of twelve months.

(3) Unless revoked, a community order imposing an unpaid work requirement remains in force until the offender has worked under it for the number of hours specified in it.

(4) Where an unpaid work requirement is imposed by a suspended sentence order, the supervision period as defined by section 189(1)(a) continues until the offender has worked under the order for the number of hours specified in the order, but does not continue beyond the end of the operational period as defined by section 189(1)(b)(ii).

As to commencement, see *ante*, § 5–132.

Activity requirement

201.—(1) In this Part "activity requirement", in relation to a relevant order, means a requirement that the offender must do either or both of the following— **5–137**

(a) present himself to a person or persons specified in the relevant order at a place or places so specified on such number of days as may be so specified;

(b) participate in activities specified in the order on such number of days as may be so specified.

(2) The specified activities may consist of or include activities whose purpose is that of reparation, such as activities involving contact between offenders and persons affected by their offences.

(3) A court may not include an activity requirement in a relevant order unless—

(a) it has consulted [an officer of a local probation board or an officer of a provider of probation services, and]—

(i) *in the case of an offender aged 18 or over, an officer of a local probation board or an officer of a provider of probation services,*

(ii) *in the case of an offender aged under 18, an officer of a local probation board, an officer of a provider of probation services or a member of a youth offending team, and*

(b) it is satisfied that it is feasible to secure compliance with the requirement.

(4) A court may not include an activity requirement in a relevant order if compliance with that requirement would involve the co-operation of a person other than the offender and the offender's responsible officer, unless that other person consents to its inclusion.

(5) The aggregate of the number of days specified under subsection (1)(a) and (b) must not exceed 60.

(6) A requirement such as is mentioned in subsection (1)(a) operates to require the offender—

(a) in accordance with instructions given by his responsible officer, to present himself at a place or places on the number of days specified in the order, and

(b) while at any place, to comply with instructions given by, or under the authority of, the person in charge of that place.

(7) A place specified under subsection (1)(a) must be—

(a) a community rehabilitation centre, or

(b) a place that has been approved as providing facilities suitable for persons subject to activity requirements—

(i) where the premises are situated in the area of a local probation board, by that board, or

(ii) in any other case, by a provider of probation services authorised to do so by arrangements under section 3 of the *Offender Management Act* 2007.

(8) Where the place specified under subsection (1)(a) is a community rehabilitation centre, the reference in subsection (6)(a) to the offender presenting himself at the specified place includes a reference to him presenting himself elsewhere than at the centre for the purpose of participating in activities in accordance with instructions given by, or under the authority of, the person in charge of the centre.

(9) A requirement to participate in activities operates to require the offender—

(a) in accordance with instructions given by his responsible officer, to participate in activities on the number of days specified in the order, and

(b) while participating, to comply with instructions given by, or under the authority of, the person in charge of the activities.

(10) In this section "community rehabilitation centre" means premises—

(a) at which non-residential facilities are provided for use in connection with the rehabilitation of offenders, and

(b) which are for the time being approved by the Secretary of State as providing facilities suitable for persons subject to relevant orders.

[This section is printed as amended by S.I. 2008 No. 912 (*ante*, § 5–135), art. 3, and Sched. 1, para. 19(1) and (7); and as amended, as from a day to be appointed (as to which, see *ante*, § 5–1), by the *CJIA* 2008, s.6(2), and Sched. 4, paras 71 and 85 (omission of italicised words, insertion of words in square brackets).]

As to commencement, see *ante*, § 5–132.

Programme requirement

5–138 **202.**—(1) In this Part "programme requirement", in relation to a relevant order, means a requirement that the offender must participate in an accredited programme specified in the order at a place so specified on such number of days as may be so specified.

(2) In this Part "accredited programme" means a programme that is for the time being accredited by the Secretary of State for the purposes of this section.

(3) In this section—

(a) "programme" means a systematic set of activities, and … .

(4) A court may not include a programme requirement in a relevant order unless—

(a) the accredited programme which the court proposes to specify in the order has been recommended to the court as being suitable for the offender [by an officer of a local probation board or an officer of a provider of probation services, and]—

(i) *in the case of an offender aged 18 or over, by an officer of a local probation board or an officer of a provider of probation services, or*

(ii) *in the case of an offender aged under 18, by an officer of a local probation board, an officer of a provider of probation services or by a member of a youth offending team, and*

(b) the court is satisfied that the programme is (or, where the relevant order is a custody plus order or an intermittent custody order, will be) available at the place proposed to be specified.

(5) A court may not include a programme requirement in a relevant order if compliance with that requirement would involve the co-operation of a person other than the offender and the offender's responsible officer, unless that other person consents to its inclusion.

(6) A requirement to attend an accredited programme operates to require the offender—

(a) in accordance with instructions given by the responsible officer, to participate in the accredited programme at the place specified in the order on the number of days specified in the order, and

(b) while at that place, to comply with instructions given by, or under the authority of, the person in charge of the programme.

(7) A place specified in an order must be a place that has been approved as providing facilities suitable for persons subject to programme requirements—

(a) where the premises are situated in the area of a local probation board, by that board, or

(b) in any other case, by a provider of probation services authorised to do so by arrangements under section 3 of the *Offender Management Act* 2007.

[This section is printed as amended by the *Offender Management Act* 2007, ss.31(1) and 39, and Sched. 5, Pt 3; and S.I. 2008 No. 912 (*ante*, § 5–135), art. 3, and Sched. 1, para. 19(1) and (8); and as amended, as from a day to be appointed (as to which, see *ante*, § 5–1), by the *CJIA* 2008, s.6(2), and Sched. 4, paras 71 and 86 (omission of italicised words, insertion of words in square brackets).]

As to commencement, see *ante*, § 5–132.

Prohibited activity requirement

203.—(1) In this Part "prohibited activity requirement", in relation to a relevant order, means a requirement that the offender must refrain from participating in activities specified in the order— **5–139**

(a) on a day or days so specified, or

(b) during a period so specified.

(2) A court may not include a prohibited activity requirement in a relevant order unless it has consulted [an officer of a local probation board or an officer of a provider of probation services]—

(a) *in the case of an offender aged 18 or over, an officer of a local probation board or an officer of a provider of probation services;*

(b) *in the case of an offender aged under 18, an officer of a local probation board, an officer of a provider of probation services or a member of a youth offending team.*

(3) The requirements that may by virtue of this section be included in a relevant order include a requirement that the offender does not possess, use or carry a firearm within the meaning of the *Firearms Act* 1968.

[This section is printed as amended by S.I. 2008 No. 912 (*ante*, § 5–135), art. 3, and Sched. 1, para. 19(1) and (9); and as amended, as from a day to be appointed (as to which, see *ante*, § 5–1), by the *CJIA* 2008, s.6(2), and Sched. 4, paras 71 and 87 (omission of italicised words, insertion of words in square brackets).]

As to commencement, see *ante*, § 5–132.

Curfew requirement

204.—(1) In this Part "curfew requirement", in relation to a relevant order, means a requirement that the offender must remain, for periods specified in the relevant order, at a place so specified. **5–140**

(2) A relevant order imposing a curfew requirement may specify different places or different periods for different days, but may not specify periods which amount to less than two hours or more than twelve hours in any day.

(3) A community order or suspended sentence order which imposes a curfew requirement may not specify periods which fall outside the period of six months beginning with the day on which it is made.

(4) A custody plus order which imposes a curfew requirement may not specify a period which falls outside the period of six months beginning with the first day of the licence period as defined by section 181(3)(b).

(5) An intermittent custody order which imposes a curfew requirement must not specify a period if to do so would cause the aggregate number of days on which the offender is subject to the requirement for any part of the day to exceed 182.

(6) Before making a relevant order imposing a curfew requirement, the court must obtain and consider information about the place proposed to be specified in the order (including information as to the attitude of persons likely to be affected by the enforced presence there of the offender).

As to commencement, see *ante*, § 5–132.

Exclusion requirement

205.—(1) In this Part "exclusion requirement", in relation to a relevant order, means a provision prohibiting the offender from entering a place specified in the order for a period so specified. **5–141**

(2) Where the relevant order is a community order, the period specified must not be more than two years.

(3) An exclusion requirement—

(a) may provide for the prohibition to operate only during the periods specified in the order, and

(b) may specify different places for different periods or days.

(4) In this section "place" includes an area.

As to commencement, see *ante*, § 5–132.

Residence requirement

206.—(1) In this Part, "residence requirement", in relation to a community order or a **5–142**

suspended sentence order, means a requirement that, during a period specified in the relevant order, the offender must reside at a place specified in the order.

(2) If the order so provides, a residence requirement does not prohibit the offender from residing, with the prior approval of the responsible officer, at a place other than that specified in the order.

(3) Before making a community order or suspended sentence order containing a residence requirement, the court must consider the home surroundings of the offender.

(4) A court may not specify a hostel or other institution as the place where an offender must reside, except on the recommendation of an officer of a local probation board or an officer of a provider of probation services.

[This section is printed as amended by S.I. 2008 No. 912 (*ante*, § 5–135), art. 3, and Sched. 1, para. 19(1) and (10).]

As to commencement, see *ante*, § 5–132.

Mental health treatment requirement

5–143 **207.**—(1) In this Part, "mental health treatment requirement", in relation to a community order or suspended sentence order, means a requirement that the offender must submit, during a period or periods specified in the order, to treatment by or under the direction of a registered medical practitioner or a chartered psychologist (or both, for different periods) with a view to the improvement of the offender's mental condition.

(2) The treatment required must be such one of the following kinds of treatment as may be specified in the relevant order—

(a) treatment as a resident patient in an independent hospital or care home within the meaning of the *Care Standards Act* 2000 or a hospital within the meaning of the *Mental Health Act* 1983, but not in hospital premises where high security psychiatric services within the meaning of that Act are provided;

(b) treatment as a non-resident patient at such institution or place as may be specified in the order;

(c) treatment by or under the direction of such registered medical practitioner or chartered psychologist (or both) as may be so specified;

but the nature of the treatment is not to be specified in the order except as mentioned in paragraph (a), (b) or (c).

(3) A court may not by virtue of this section include a mental health treatment requirement in a relevant order unless—

(a) the court is satisfied, on the evidence of a registered medical practitioner approved for the purposes of section 12 of the *Mental Health Act* 1983, that the mental condition of the offender—

(i) is such as requires and may be susceptible to treatment, but

(ii) is not such as to warrant the making of a hospital order or guardianship order within the meaning of that Act;

(b) the court is also satisfied that arrangements have been or can be made for the treatment intended to be specified in the order (including arrangements for the reception of the offender where he is to be required to submit to treatment as a resident patient); and

(c) the offender has expressed his willingness to comply with such a requirement.

(4) While the offender is under treatment as a resident patient in pursuance of a mental health requirement of a relevant order, his responsible officer shall carry out the supervision of the offender to such extent only as may be necessary for the purpose of the revocation or amendment of the order.

(5) Subsections (2) and (3) of section 54 of the *Mental Health Act* 1983 have effect with respect to proof for the purposes of subsection (3)(a) of an offender's mental condition as they have effect with respect to proof of an offender's mental condition for the purposes of section 37(2)(a) of that Act.

(6) In this section and section 208, "chartered psychologist" means a person for the time being listed in the British Psychological Society's Register of Chartered Psychologists.

As to commencement, see *ante*, § 5–132.

Mental health treatment at place other than that specified in order

5–144 **208.**—(1) Where the medical practitioner or chartered psychologist by whom or under whose direction an offender is being treated for his mental condition in pursuance of a mental health treatment requirement is of the opinion that part of the treatment can be better or more conveniently given in or at an institution or place which—

(a) is not specified in the relevant order, and

(b) is one in or at which the treatment of the offender will be given by or under the direction of a registered medical practitioner or chartered psychologist,

he may, with the consent of the offender, make arrangements for him to be treated accordingly.

(2) Such arrangements as are mentioned in subsection (1) may provide for the offender to receive part of his treatment as a resident patient in an institution or place notwithstanding that the institution or place is not one which could have been specified for that purpose in the relevant order.

(3) Where any such arrangements as are mentioned in subsection (1) are made for the treatment of an offender—

(a) the medical practitioner or chartered psychologist by whom the arrangements are made shall give notice in writing to the offender's responsible officer, specifying the institution or place in or at which the treatment is to be carried out; and

(b) the treatment provided for by the arrangements shall be deemed to be treatment to which he is required to submit in pursuance of the relevant order.

As to commencement, see *ante*, § 5–132.

Drug rehabilitation requirement

209.—(1) In this Part "drug rehabilitation requirement", in relation to a community order or suspended sentence order, means a requirement that during a period specified in the order ("the treatment and testing period") the offender— **5–145**

(a) must submit to treatment by or under the direction of a specified person having the necessary qualifications or experience with a view to the reduction or elimination of the offender's dependency on or propensity to misuse drugs, and

(b) for the purpose of ascertaining whether he has any drug in his body during that period, must provide samples of such description as may be so determined, at such times or in such circumstances as may (subject to the provisions of the order) be determined by the responsible officer or by the person specified as the person by or under whose direction the treatment is to be provided.

(2) A court may not impose a drug rehabilitation requirement unless—

(a) it is satisfied—

(i) that the offender is dependent on, or has a propensity to misuse, drugs, and

(ii) that his dependency or propensity is such as requires and may be susceptible to treatment,

(b) it is also satisfied that arrangements have been or can be made for the treatment intended to be specified in the order (including arrangements for the reception of the offender where he is to be required to submit to treatment as a resident),

(c) the requirement has been recommended to the court as being suitable or the offender [by an officer of a local probation board or an officer of a provider of probation services, and]—

(i) *in the case of an offender aged 18 or over, by an officer of a local probation board or an officer of a provider of probation services, or*

(ii) *in the case of an offender aged under 18, by an officer of a local probation board, an officer of a provider of probation services or by a member of a youth offending team, and*

(d) the offender expresses his willingness to comply with the requirement.

(3) The treatment and testing period must be at least six months.

(4) The required treatment for any particular period must be—

(a) treatment as a resident in such institution or place as may be specified in the order, or

(b) treatment as a non-resident in or at such institution or place, and at such intervals, as may be so specified;

but the nature of the treatment is not to be specified in the order except as mentioned in paragraph (a) or (b) above.

(5) The function of making a determination as to the provision of samples under provision included in the community order or suspended sentence order by virtue of subsection (1)(b) is to be exercised in accordance with guidance given from time to time by the Secretary of State.

(6) A community order or suspended sentence order imposing a drug rehabilitation requirement must provide that the results of tests carried out on any samples provided by

the offender in pursuance of the requirement to a person other than the responsible officer are to be communicated to the responsible officer.

(7) In this section "drug" means a controlled drug as defined by section 2 of the *Misuse of Drugs Act* 1971.

[This section is printed as amended by S.I. 2008 No. 912 (*ante*, § 5–135), art. 3, and Sched. 1, para. 19(1) and (11); and as amended, as from a day to be appointed (as to which, see *ante*, § 5–1), by the *CJIA* 2008, s.6(2), and Sched. 4, paras 71 and 88 (omission of italicised words, insertion of words in square brackets).]

As to commencement, see *ante*, § 5–132.

For a useful review of the considerations which may apply when determining whether a drug rehabilitation requirement should be imposed, see *R. v. Woods and Collins* [2006] 1 Cr.App.R.(S.) 83, CA (although relating to drug treatment and testing orders under the *PCC(S)A* 2000 (see § 5–123j in the supplement)).

In *Att.-Gen.'s Reference (No. 82 of 2005) (R. v. Toulson)* [2006] 1 Cr.App.R.(S.) 118, CA, it was said that whilst the general principle in *Att.-Gen.'s Reference (No. 28 of 2001) (R. v. McCollins)* [2002] 1 Cr.App.R.(S.) 59, CA, and *Att.-Gen.'s Reference (No. 64 of 2003)* [2004] 2 Cr.App.R.(S.) 22, CA, was that a drug treatment and testing order (under the 2000 Act) would be inappropriate in cases of serious offending (particularly where significant violence or threats were involved), no straitjacket had been imposed on sentencers in cases where they considered that in the public interest some course other than a deterrent sentence should at least be tried.

Drug rehabilitation requirement: provision for review by court

5–146 **210.**—(1) A community order or suspended sentence order imposing a drug rehabilitation requirement may (and must if the treatment and testing period is more than 12 months)—

(a) provide for the requirement to be reviewed periodically at intervals of not less than one month,

(b) provide for each review of the requirement to be made, subject to section 211(6), at a hearing held for the purpose by the court responsible for the order (a "review hearing"),

(c) require the offender to attend each review hearing,

(d) provide for the responsible officer to make to the court responsible for the order, before each review, a report in writing on the offender's progress under the requirement, and

(e) provide for each such report to include the test results communicated to the responsible officer under section 209(6) or otherwise and the views of the treatment provider as to the treatment and testing of the offender.

(2) In this section references to the court responsible for a community order or suspended sentence order imposing a drug rehabilitation requirement are references—

(a) where a court is specified in the order in accordance with subsection (3), to that court;

(b) in any other case, to the court by which the order is made.

(3) Where the area specified in a community order or suspended sentence order which is made by a magistrates' court and imposes a drug rehabilitation requirement is not the area for which the court acts, the court may, if it thinks fit, include in the order provision specifying for the purposes of subsection (2) a magistrates' court which acts for the area specified in the order.

(4) Where a community order or suspended sentence order imposing a drug rehabilitation requirement has been made on an appeal brought from the Crown Court or from the criminal division of the Court of Appeal, for the purposes of subsection (2)(b) it shall be taken to have been made by the Crown Court.

As to commencement, see *ante*, § 5–132.

The *AFA* 2006, ss.179(1) and 203(2) (into force as from a day to be appointed) provide that in section 210, as it respectively applies to a service community order under the 2006 Act and a suspended sentence order with community requirements made by a relevant service court, the expression "the court responsible for the order" means the Crown Court and subsections (2) to (4) shall be treated as omitted.

Periodic review of drug rehabilitation requirement

5–147 **211.**—(1) At a review hearing (within the meaning given by subsection (1) of section 210) the court may, after considering the responsible officer's report referred to in that subsection, amend the community order or suspended sentence order, so far as it relates to the drug rehabilitation requirement.

(2) The court—

(a) may not amend the drug rehabilitation requirement unless the offender expresses his willingness to comply with the requirement as amended,

(b) may not amend any provision of the order so as to reduce the period for which the drug rehabilitation requirement has effect below the minimum specified in section 209(3), and

(c) except with the consent of the offender, may not amend any requirement or provision of the order while an appeal against the order is pending.

(3) If the offender fails to express his willingness to comply with the drug rehabilitation requirement as proposed to be amended by the court, the court may—

(a) revoke the community order, or the suspended sentence order and the suspended sentence to which it relates, and

(b) deal with him, for the offence in respect of which the order was made, in any way in which he could have been dealt with for that offence by the court which made the order if the order had not been made.

(4) In dealing with the offender under subsection (3)(b), the court—

(a) shall take into account the extent to which the offender has complied with the requirements of the order, and

(b) may impose a custodial sentence (where the order was made in respect of an offence punishable with such a sentence) notwithstanding anything in section 152(2).

(5) *Where the order is a community order made by a magistrates' court in the case of an offender under 18 years of age in respect of an offence triable only on indictment in the case of an adult, any powers exercisable under subsection (3)(b) in respect of the offender after he attains the age of 18 are powers to do either or both of the following—*

(a) *to impose a fine not exceeding £5,000 for the offence in respect of which the order was made;*

(b) *to deal with the offender for that offence in any way in which the court could deal with him if it had just convicted him of an offence punishable with imprisonment for a term not exceeding twelve months.*

(6) If at a review hearing (as defined by section 210(1)(b)) the court, after considering the responsible officer's report, is of the opinion that the offender's progress under the requirement is satisfactory, the court may so amend the order as to provide for each subsequent review to be made by the court without a hearing.

(7) If at a review without a hearing the court, after considering the responsible officer's report, is of the opinion that the offender's progress under the requirement is no longer satisfactory, the court may require the offender to attend a hearing of the court at a specified time and place.

(8) At that hearing the court, after considering that report, may—

(a) exercise the powers conferred by this section as if the hearing were a review hearing, and

(b) so amend the order as to provide for each subsequent review to be made at a review hearing.

(9) In this section any reference to the court, in relation to a review without a hearing, is to be read—

(a) in the case of the Crown Court, as a reference to a judge of the court;

(b) in the case of a magistrates' court, as a reference to a justice of the peace acting for the commission area for which the court acts.

[Subs. (5) is repealed as from a day to be appointed (as to which, see *ante*, § 5–1) by the *CJIA* 2008, ss.6(2) and 149, Sched. 4, paras 71 and 89, and Sched. 28, Pt.1.]

As to commencement, see *ante*, § 5–132.

The *AFA* 2006, s.179(2) (into force as from a day to be appointed) provides that section 211 has effect in its application to a service community order under the 2006 Act as if there were substituted for subsections (3) to (5), new subsections (3A) to (3C). These deal with the revocation of such orders where the offender fails to indicate his willingness to comply with a proposed amendment of the order, and with re-sentencing the offender for the original offence. Where sentence is passed under section 211(3A) (as so substituted), the *CAA* 1968, s.9 (*post*, § 7–118) applies as if the offender had been convicted on indictment of the offence for which the sentence was passed: s.179(3) of the 2006 Act.

Section 203(3) of the 2006 Act (into force as from a day to be appointed) provides that section 211 has effect in its application to a suspended sentence order with community requirements made by a relevant service court, as if, (i) in subsection (3)(b), for the words from "he could have been dealt with" to the end there were substituted the words "it could deal with him as if he had just been convicted before the court of any offence punishable with imprisonment", (ii) in subsection (4)(b), the words in brackets were omitted, and (iii) a new subsection (4A) were inserted, providing that a term of imprisonment or a fine under subsection (3)(b) must not exceed the maximum permitted for the offence in respect of which the order was made, and, where the order was made by the Service Civilian Court, must not exceed 12 months' imprisonment or a fine equal to the prescribed sum. Where a sentence is passed under section 211(3)(b) (as so modified), section 9 of the 1968 Act (*ante*) applies as if the offender had been convicted on indictment of the offence for which the sentence was passed: s.203(4) of the 2006 Act.

Alcohol treatment requirement

5–148 **212.**—(1) In this Part "alcohol treatment requirement", in relation to a community order or suspended sentence order, means a requirement that the offender must submit during a period specified in the order to treatment by or under the direction of a specified person having the necessary qualifications or experience with a view to the reduction or elimination of the offender's dependency on alcohol.

(2) A court may not impose an alcohol treatment requirement in respect of an offender unless it is satisfied—

(a) that he is dependent on alcohol,

(b) that his dependency is such as requires and may be susceptible to treatment, and

(c) that arrangements have been or can be made for the treatment intended to be specified in the order (including arrangements for the reception of the offender where he is to be required to submit to treatment as a resident).

(3) A court may not impose an alcohol treatment requirement unless the offender expresses his willingness to comply with its requirements.

(4) The period for which the alcohol treatment requirement has effect must be not less than six months.

(5) The treatment required by an alcohol treatment requirement for any particular period must be—

(a) treatment as a resident in such institution or place as may be specified in the order,

(b) treatment as a non-resident in or at such institution or place, and at such intervals, as may be so specified, or

(c) treatment by or under the direction of such person having the necessary qualification or experience as may be so specified;

but the nature of the treatment shall not be specified in the order except as mentioned in paragraph (a), (b) or (c) above.

As to commencement, see *ante*, § 5–132.

Supervision requirement

5–149 **213.**—(1) In this Part "supervision requirement", in relation to a relevant order, means a requirement that, during the relevant period, the offender must attend appointments with the responsible officer or another person determined by the responsible officer, at such time and place as may be determined by the officer.

(2) The purpose for which a supervision requirement may be imposed is that of promoting the offender's rehabilitation.

(3) In subsection (1) "the relevant period" means—

(a) in relation to a community order, the period for which the community order remains in force,

(b) in relation to a custody plus order, the licence period as defined by section 181(3)(b),

(c) in relation to an intermittent custody order, the licence periods as defined by section 183(3), and

(d) in relation to a suspended sentence order, the supervision period as defined by section 189(1)(a).

As to commencement, see *ante*, § 5–132.

(4) Requirements available only in case of offenders aged under 25

Criminal Justice Act 2003, s.214

Requirements available only in case of offenders aged under 25

Attendance centre requirement

214.—(1) In this Part "attendance centre requirement", in relation to a relevant order, means a requirement that the offender must attend at an attendance centre specified in the relevant order for such number of hours as may be so specified. **5–150**

(2) The aggregate number of hours for which the offender may be required to attend at an attendance centre must not be less than 12 or more than 36.

(3) The court may not impose an attendance centre requirement unless the court is satisfied that the attendance centre to be specified in it is reasonably accessible to the offender concerned, having regard to the means of access available to him and any other circumstances.

(4) The first time at which the offender is required to attend at the attendance centre is a time notified to the offender by the responsible officer.

(5) The subsequent hours are to be fixed by the officer in charge of the centre, having regard to the offender's circumstances.

(6) An offender may not be required under this section to attend at an attendance centre on more than one occasion on any day, or for more than three hours on any occasion.

[(7) A requirement to attend at an attendance centre for any period on any occasion operates as a requirement, during that period, to engage in occupation, or receive instruction, under the supervision of and in accordance with instructions given by, or under the authority of, the officer in charge of the centre, whether at the centre or elsewhere.]

[This section is printed as amended, as from a day to be appointed (as to which, see *ante*, § 5–1) by the *CJIA* 2008, s.6(2), and Sched. 4, paras 71 and 90 (insertion of subs. (7)).]

As to commencement, see *ante*, § 5–132.

(5) Electronic monitoring

Criminal Justice Act 2003, s.215

Electronic monitoring

Electronic monitoring requirement

215.—(1) In this Part "electronic monitoring requirement", in relation to a relevant order, means a requirement for securing the electronic monitoring of the offender's compliance with other requirements imposed by the order during a period specified in the order, or determined by the responsible officer in accordance with the relevant order. **5–151**

(2) Where—

(a) it is proposed to include in a relevant order a requirement for securing electronic monitoring in accordance with this section, but

(b) there is a person (other than the offender) without whose co-operation it will not be practicable to secure the monitoring,

the requirement may not be included in the order without that person's consent.

(3) A relevant order which includes an electronic monitoring requirement must include provision for making a person responsible for the monitoring; and a person who is made so responsible must be of a description specified in an order made by the Secretary of State.

(4) Where an electronic monitoring requirement is required to take effect during a period determined by the responsible officer in accordance with the relevant order, the responsible officer must, before the beginning of that period, notify—

(a) the offender,

(b) the person responsible for the monitoring, and

(c) any person falling within subsection (2)(b),

of the time when the period is to begin.

As to commencement, see *ante*, § 5–132.

(6) Provisions applying to relevant orders generally

Criminal Justice Act 2003, ss.216–220

5–152 **216.** [*Petty sessions area to be specified in relevant order.*]

Requirement to avoid conflict with religious beliefs, etc

5–153 **217.**—(1) The court must ensure, as far as practicable, that any requirement imposed by a relevant order is such as to avoid—

(a) any conflict with the offender's religious beliefs or with the requirements of any other relevant order to which he may be subject; and

(b) any interference with the times, if any, at which he normally works or attends *school or* any *other* educational establishment.

(2) The responsible officer in relation to an offender to whom a relevant order relates must ensure, as far as practicable, that any instruction given or requirement imposed by him in pursuance of the order is such as to avoid the conflict or interference mentioned in subsection (1).

(3) The Secretary of State may by order provide that subsection (1) or (2) is to have effect with such additional restrictions as may be specified in the order.

[This section is printed as amended, as from a day to be appointed (as to which, see *ante*, § 5–1), by the *CJIA* 2008, s.6(2), and Sched. 4, paras 71 and 91 (omission of italicised words).]

As to commencement, see *ante*, § 5–132.

Availability of arrangements in local area

5–154 **218.**—(1) A court may not include an unpaid work requirement in a relevant order unless the court is satisfied that provision for the offender to work under such a requirement can be made under the arrangements for persons to perform work under such a requirement which exist in the petty sessions area in which he resides or will reside.

(2) A court may not include an activity requirement in a relevant order unless the court is satisfied that provision for the offender to participate in the activities proposed to be specified in the order can be made under the arrangements for persons to participate in such activities which exist in the petty sessions area in which he resides or will reside.

(3) A court may not include an attendance centre requirement in a relevant order in respect of an offender unless the court has been notified by the Secretary of State that an attendance centre is available for persons of his description.

(4) A court may not include an electronic monitoring requirement in a relevant order in respect of an offender unless the court—

(a) has been notified by the Secretary of State that electronic monitoring arrangements are available in the relevant areas mentioned in subsections (5) to (7), and

(b) is satisfied that the necessary provision can be made under those arrangements.

(5) In the case of a relevant order containing a curfew requirement or an exclusion requirement, the relevant area for the purposes of subsection (4) is the area in which the place proposed to be specified in the order is situated.

(6) In the case of a relevant order containing an attendance centre requirement, the relevant area for the purposes of subsection (4) is the area in which the attendance centre proposed to be specified in the order is situated.

(7) In the case of any other relevant order, the relevant area for the purposes of subsection (4) is the petty sessions area proposed to be specified in the order.

(8) In subsection (5) "place", in relation to an exclusion requirement, has the same meaning as in section 205.

As to commencement, see *ante*, § 5–132.

5–155 **219.** [*Provision of copies of relevant orders.*]

5–156 **220.** [*Duty of offender to keep in touch with responsible officer, and to notify him of any change of address, such duties being enforceable as if requirements of the order.*]

(7) Guidelines

The Sentencing Guidelines Council has issued a guideline in relation to community orders under the *CJA* 2003 (Appendix K–28 *et seq.*). Misleadingly, it refers throughout to "community sentence". Under the 2003 Act, "community sentence" means a "community order" or a "youth community order". The guideline has no application to youth community orders. **5–156a**

(8) Authorities

A community order, and in particular one coupled with requirements which have a real impact on an offender's liberty, is a form of punishment and it is not right that an offender should receive substantial further punishment in the form of such an order where he has already served (on remand) what is in practice the maximum punishment by way of imprisonment which the law could have imposed; on appeal, the appropriate course to take was to set aside the community penalty, and substitute a conditional discharge for a period such that it would terminate at or before the date of appeal (so as to avoid the risk of further punishment for the original offence in the event of a breach): *R. v. Hemmings* [2008] 1 Cr.App.R.(S.) 106, CA. **5–156b**

Whereas section 220 provides that an offender must keep in touch with the responsible officer in accordance with such instructions as he may from time to time be given by that officer, and that this obligation is enforceable as if it were a requirement imposed by the order, a responsible officer, when setting conditions, is entitled to require an offender to inform him in advance if he knows he cannot keep an appointment and why, and to require that information to be in writing and to be supported by third-party evidence; however, it would not be permissible to impose an independent requirement to provide evidence after an apparent breach, as that could not be viewed as a requirement to stay in touch; standing on its own, it is merely an obligation to provide evidence, and so it is not within the range of conditions that may be set: *Richards v. National Probation Service*, 172 J.P. 100, DC.

D. YOUTH COMMUNITY ORDERS

(1) Curfew orders

Powers of Criminal Courts (Sentencing) Act 2000, s.37

Curfew orders

37.—(1) *Where a person [aged under 16] is convicted of an offence, the court by or before which he is convicted may (subject to sections 148 , 150 and 156 of the* Criminal Justice Act *2003) make an order requiring him to remain, for periods specified in the order, at a place so specified.* **5–157**

(2) *An order under subsection (1) above is in this Act referred to as a "curfew order".*

(3) *A curfew order may specify different places or different periods for different days, but shall not specify—*

(a) *periods which fall outside the period of six months beginning with the day on which it is made; or*

(b) *periods which amount to less than two hours or more than twelve hours in any one day.*

(4) In relation to an offender aged under 16 on conviction, subsection (3)(a) above shall have effect as if the reference to six months were a reference to three months.

(5) *The requirements in a curfew order shall, as far as practicable, be such as to avoid—*

(a) *any conflict with the offender's religious beliefs or with the requirements of any other [youth] community order to which he may be subject; and*

(b) *any interference with the times, if any, at which he normally works or attends school or any other educational establishment.*

(6) *A curfew order shall include provision for making a person responsible for monitoring the offender's whereabouts during the curfew periods specified in the order; and a person who is made so responsible shall be of a description specified in an order made by the Secretary of State.*

(7) *A court shall not make a curfew order unless the court has been notified by the Secretary of State that arrangements for monitoring the offender's whereabouts are available in*

the area in which the place proposed to be specified in the order is situated and the notice has not been withdrawn.

(8) *Before making a curfew order, the court shall obtain and consider information about the place proposed to be specified in the order (including information as to the attitude of persons likely to be affected by the enforced presence there of the offender).*

(9) *Before making a curfew order in respect of an offender who on conviction is under 16, the court shall obtain and consider information about his family circumstances and the likely effect of such an order on those circumstances.*

(11) *The court by which a curfew order is made shall give a copy of the order to the offender and to the responsible officer.*

(12) *In this Act, "responsible officer", in relation to an offender subject to a curfew order, means—*

(a) *where the offender is also subject to a supervision order, the person who is the supervisor in relation to the supervision order;*

(b) *in any other case, the person who is responsible for monitoring the offender's whereabouts during the curfew periods specified in the order.*

[This section is printed as amended, and repealed in part, by the *CJCSA* 2000, s.74, and Sched. 7, para. 162; the *Anti-Social Behaviour Act* 2003, s.88, and Sched. 2, para. 2(1) and (3); and the *CJA* 2003, s.302, and Sched. 32, paras 90 and 97(1), (2)(b) and (4). As to the words in square brackets in subss. (1) and (5)(a), these were inserted as from April 4, 2005 (S.I. 2005 No. 950, *ante*, § 5–121e) by *ibid.*, paras 90 and 97(1), (2)(a) and (3), but these insertions are of no effect in the case of 16- and 17-year-olds convicted of an offence prior to April 4, 2009 (as to which, see *ante*, §§ 5–121e, 5–122, 5–131): S.I. 2005 No. 950, Sched. 2, paras 12 and 13 (§§ 5–131f, 5–131g in the supplement). Subs. (4) is repealed by the *Anti-social Behaviour Act* 2003, s.88, and Sched. 2, para. 2(1) and (2). This repeal came into force on September 30, 2004, in the areas of 33 specified local authorities: *Anti-social Behaviour Act (Commencement No. 4) Order* 2004 (S.I. 2004 No. 2168). For the local authorities concerned, see art. 3(2) of that order. Otherwise, it comes into force on a day to be appointed. The whole of this section is repealed as from a day to be appointed (as to which, see *ante*, §§ 5–1, 5–122) by the *CJIA* 2008, ss.6(1) and 149, and Sched. 28, Pt 1.]

5–158 As to the requirements to be complied with before imposing a curfew order, see sections 35 and 36 of the *PCC(S)A* 2000 (§§ 5–122c, 5–122d in the supplement) (it being a "community order" within that Act), and section 148 of the *CJA* 2003 (*ante*, § 5–126) (it being a "community sentence" within that Act).

5–159 As to the making of a curfew order with an electronic monitoring requirement, see section 36B, *post*, § 5–179. Rule 48.1 of the *Criminal Procedure Rules* 2005 (S.I. 2005 No. 384) (as amended by the *Offender Management Act 2007 (Consequential Amendments) Order* 2008 (S.I. 2008 No. 912)) makes provision as to the service of notice of the curfew order on the defendant and on the person responsible for electronically monitoring compliance, and where any community order additional to the curfew order has been made, as to service of a copy of the notice served on the person responsible for electronically monitoring compliance on the local probation board, provider of probation services or youth offending team responsible for the offender.

As to breach, revocation and amendment, see the substituted Schedule 3 to the 2000 Act, *post*, §§ 5–201 *et seq.*; and, in relation to any period prior to the substitution taking effect, see the original Schedule 3 (§§ 5–123p *et seq.* in the supplement).

(2) Exclusion orders

Powers of Criminal Courts (Sentencing) Act 2000, s.40A

Exclusion orders

5–160 **40A.**—(1) *Where a person [aged under 16] is convicted of an offence, the court by or before which he is convicted may (subject to sections 148 , 150 and 156 of the* Criminal Justice Act *2003) make an order prohibiting him from entering a place specified in the order for a period so specified of not more than* two years *[three months].*

(2) *An order under subsection (1) above is in this Act referred to as an "exclusion order".*

(3) *An exclusion order—*

(a) *may provide for the prohibition to operate only during the periods specified in the order;*

(b) *may specify different places for different periods or days.*

(5) *The requirements in an exclusion order shall, as far as practicable, be such as to avoid—*

(a) *any conflict with the offender's religious beliefs or with the requirements of any other [youth] community order to which he may be subject; and*

(b) *any interference with the times, if any, at which he normally works or attends school or any other educational establishment.*

(6) *An exclusion order shall include provision for making a person responsible for monitoring the offender's whereabouts during the periods when the prohibition operates; and a person who is made so responsible shall be of a description specified in an order made by the Secretary of State.*

(7) *An exclusion order shall specify the petty sessions area in which the offender resides or will reside.*

(8) *A court shall not make an exclusion order unless the court has been notified by the Secretary of State that arrangements for monitoring the offender's whereabouts are available in the area in which the place proposed to be specified in the order is situated and the notice has not been withdrawn.*

(9) *Before making an exclusion order in respect of an offender, the court shall obtain and consider information about his family circumstances and the likely effect of such an order on those circumstances.*

(11) *The court by which an exclusion order is made shall—*

(a) *give a copy of the order to the offender and the responsible officer; and*

(b) *give to any affected person any information relating to the order which the court considers it appropriate for him to have.*

(12) *In this section, "place" includes an area.*

(13) *For the purposes of this Act, a person is an affected person in relation to an exclusion order if—*

(a) *a requirement under section 36B(1) above is included in the order by virtue of his consent; or*

(b) *a prohibition is included in the order for the purpose (or partly for the purpose) of protecting him from being approached by the offender.*

(14) *In this Act, "responsible officer", in relation to an offender subject to an exclusion order, means the person who is responsible for monitoring the offender's whereabouts during the periods when the prohibition operates.*

[This section is inserted by the *CJCSA* 2000, s.46. It is printed as amended, and repealed in part, by the *CJA* 2003, ss.304 and 332, and Sched. 32, paras 90 and 100(1), (2)(b) and (4), and Sched. 37, Pt 7. As to the words in square brackets in subss. (1) and (5)(a), these were inserted, and the romanised words were omitted, as from April 4, 2005 (S.I. 2005 No. 950, *ante*, § 5–121e) by the 2003 Act, s.304, and Sched. 32, paras 90 and 100(1), (2)(a) and (c), and (3), but these insertions are of no effect in the case of 16- and 17-year-olds convicted of an offence prior to April 4, 2009 (as to which, see *ante*, §§ 5–121e, 5–122, 5–131): S.I. 2005 No. 950, Sched. 2, paras 12 and 13 (§§ 5–131f, 5–131g in the supplement). The whole of this section is repealed as from a day to be appointed (as to which, see *ante*, §§ 5–1, 5–122) by the *CJIA* 2008, ss.6(1) and 149, and Sched. 28, Pt 1.]

Section 40B (inserted by the *CJCSA* 2000, s.46) gives effect to Schedule 3 to the Act **5–161**
(breach, revocation and amendment of youth community orders) so far as relating to exclusion orders: see *post*, §§ 5–201 *et seq.* For the original Schedule 3 to the 2000 Act (breach, revocation and amendment of certain community orders), see §§ 5–123p *et seq.* in the supplement.

(3) Attendance centre orders

Powers of Criminal Courts (Sentencing) Act 2000, s.60

Attendance centre orders

60.—(1) *Where—* **5–162**

(a) *(subject to sections* 34 to 36 above *[148 , 150 and 156 of the* Criminal Justice Act

2003]) a person aged under 21 [16] is convicted by or before a court of an offence punishable with imprisonment, or

(b) *a court [has power or] would have power, but for section 89 below (restrictions on imprisonment of young offenders and defaulters), to commit a person aged under 21 [16] to prison in default of payment of any sum of money or for failing to do or abstain from doing anything required to be done or left undone*, or

(c) a court has power to commit a person aged at least 21 but under 25 to prison in default of payment of any sum of money,

the court may, if it has been notified by the Secretary of State that an attendance centre is available for the reception of persons of his description, order him to attend at such a centre, to be specified in the order, for such number of hours as may be so specified.

(2) *An order under subsection (1) above is in this Act referred to as an "attendance centre order".*

(3) *The aggregate number of hours for which an attendance centre order may require a person to attend at an attendance centre shall not be less than 12 except where—*

(a) *he is aged under 14; and*

(b) *the court is of the opinion that 12 hours would be excessive, having regard to his age or any other circumstances.*

(4) *The aggregate number of hours shall not exceed 12 except where the court is of the opinion, having regard to all the circumstances, that 12 hours would be inadequate, and in that case [shall not exceed 24]—*

(a) shall not exceed 24 where the person is aged under 16; and

(b) shall not exceed 36 where the person is aged 16 or over but under 21 or (where subsection (1)(c) above applies) under 25.

(5) *A court may make an attendance centre order in respect of a person before a previous attendance centre order made in respect of him has ceased to have effect, and may determine the number of hours to be specified in the order without regard—*

(a) *to the number specified in the previous order; or*

(b) *to the fact that order is still in effect.*

(6) *An attendance centre order shall not be made unless the court is satisfied that the attendance centre to be specified in it is reasonably accessible to the person concerned, having regard to his age, the means of access available to him and any other circumstances.*

(7) *The times at which a person is required to attend at an attendance centre shall, as for as practicable, be such as to avoid—*

(a) *any conflict with his religious beliefs or with the requirements of any other [youth] community order to which he may be subject; and*

(b) *any interference with the times, if any, at which he normally works or attends school or any other educational establishment.*

(8) *The first time at which the person is required to attend at an attendance centre shall be a time at which the centre is available for his attendance in accordance with the notification of the Secretary of State, and shall be specified in the order.*

(9) *The subsequent times shall be fixed by the officer in charge of the centre, having regard to the person's circumstances.*

(10) *A person shall not be required under this section to attend at an attendance centre on more than one occasion on any day, or for more than three hours on any occasion.*

(11) *Where a court makes an attendance centre order, the clerk of the court shall—*

(a) *deliver or send a copy of the order to the officer in charge of the attendance centre specified in it; and*

(b) *deliver a copy of the order to the person in respect of whom it is made or send a copy by registered post or the recorded delivery service addressed to his last or usual place of abode.*

(12) *Where a person ("the defaulter") has been ordered to attend at an attendance centre in default of the payment of any sum of money—*

(a) *on payment of the whole sum to any person authorised to receive it, the attendance centre order shall cease to have effect;*

(b) *on payment of a part of the sum to any such person, the total number of hours for which the defaulter is required to attend at the centre shall be reduced proportionately, that is to say by such number of complete hours as bears to the total number the proportion most nearly approximating to, without exceeding, the proportion which the part bears to the whole sum.*

[This section is printed as amended, as from a day to be appointed, by the *CJCSA*

2000, s.74 and Sched. 7, para. 173 (insertion of words in first set of square brackets in subs. (1)(b)); and the *CJA* 2003, s.304, and Sched. 32, paras 90 and 102 (omission of italicised words and insertion of other words printed in square brackets). The amendments to subss. (1)(a) and (7) came into force on April 4, 2005: S.I. 2005 No. 950 (*ante*, § 5–121e), save that, in the case of persons aged 16 or 17 upon conviction, they come into force on April 4, 2009 (as to which, see *ante*, §§ 5–121e, 5–122, 5–131): *ibid.*, Sched. 2, paras 12 and 13 (§§ 5–131f, 5–131g in the supplement). The whole of this section is repealed as from a day to be appointed (as to which, see *ante*, §§ 5–1, 5–122) by the *CJIA* 2008, ss.6(1) and 149, and Sched. 28, Pt 1.]

As to the requirements to be complied with before imposing an attendance centre order, see sections 35 and 36 of the *PCC(S)A* 2000 (§§ 5–122c, 5–122d in the supplement) (it being a "community order" within that Act), and section 148 of the *CJA* 2003 (*ante*, § 5–126) (it being a "community sentence" within that Act). **5–163**

It is not entirely clear whether a court may make attendance centre orders on the same occasion in respect of a number of offences with an aggregate in excess of the limits in subsection (4). It is submitted that the better view is that it cannot; section 60(1) appears to be concerned with defining an *occasion* when an attendance centre order may be made. On any such occasion *one* order may be made. Subsection (5) appears to confirm the correctness of this approach: if it were incorrect, subsection (5) would not be needed.

Section 61 gives effect to Schedule 5 (*post*, §§ 5–211 *et seq.*).

(4) Supervision orders

Powers of Criminal Courts (Sentencing) Act 2000, ss.63, 64

Supervision orders

63.—(1) *Where a child or young person (that is to say, any person aged under 18) is convicted of an offence, the court by or before which he is convicted may (subject to sections 148 , 150 and 156 of the* Criminal Justice Act *2003) make an order placing him under the supervision of—* **5–164**

(a) *a local authority designated by the order;*

(b) *an officer of a local probation board or an officer of a provider of probation services (as the case may be); or*

(c) *a member of a youth offending team.*

(2) *An order under subsection (1) above is in this Act referred to as a "supervision order".*

(3) *In this Act "supervisor", in relation to a supervision order, means the person under whose supervision the offender is placed or to be placed by the order.*

(4) *Schedule 6 to this Act (which specifies requirements that may be included in supervision orders) shall have effect.*

(5) *A court shall not make a supervision order unless it is satisfied that the offender resides or will reside in the area of a local authority; and a court shall be entitled to be satisfied that the offender will so reside if he is to be required so to reside by a provision to be included in the order in pursuance of paragraph 1 of Schedule 6 to this Act.*

(6) *A supervision order—*

(a) *shall name the area of the local authority and the petty sessions area in which it appears to the court making the order (or to the court amending under Schedule 7 to this Act any provision included in the order in pursuance of this paragraph) that the offender resides or will reside; and*

(b) *may contain such prescribed provisions as the court making the order (or amending it under that Schedule) considers appropriate for facilitating the performance by the supervisor of his functions under section 64(4) below, including any prescribed provisions for requiring visits to be made by the offender to the supervisor;*

and in paragraph (b) above "prescribed" means prescribed by Criminal Procedure Rules.

(7) *A supervision order shall, unless it has previously been revoked, cease to have effect at the end of the period of three years, or such shorter period as may be specified in the order, beginning with the date on which the order was originally made.*

(8) *A court which makes a supervision order shall forthwith send a copy of its order—*

(a) *to the offender and, if the offender is aged under 14, to his parent or guardian;*

(b) *to the supervisor;*

(c) *to any local authority who are not entitled by virtue of paragraph (b) above to such a copy and whose area is named in the supervision order in pursuance of subsection (6) above;*

(d) *where the offender is required by the order to reside with an individual or to undergo treatment by or under the direction of an individual or at any place, to the individual or the person in charge of that place; and*

(e) *where a petty sessions area named in the order in pursuance of subsection (6) above is not that for which the court acts, to the justices' chief executive for the petty sessions area so named;*

and, in a case falling within paragraph (e) above, shall also send to the justices' chief executive in question such documents and information relating to the case as the court considers likely to be of assistance to them.

(9) *If a court makes a supervision order while another such order made by any court is in force in respect of the offender, the court making the new order may revoke the earlier order (and paragraph 10 of Schedule 7 to this Act (supplementary provision) shall apply to the revocation).*

[This section is printed as amended by the *CJCSA* 2000, s.74, and Sched. 7, para. 4; the *CJA* 2003, s.304, and Sched. 32, paras 90 and 103; the *Courts Act 2003 (Consequential Amendments) Order* 2004 (S.I. 2004 No. 2035); and the *Offender Management Act 2007 (Consequential Amendments) Order* 2008 (S.I. 2008 No. 912), art. 3, and Sched. 1, para. 14(1) and (9). The whole section is repealed as from a day to be appointed (as to which, see *ante*, §§ 5–1, 5–122) by the *CJIA* 2008, ss.6(1) and 149, and Sched. 28, Pt 1.]

As to the requirements to be complied with before imposing a supervision order, see sections 35 and 36 of the *PCC(S)A* 2000 (§§ 5–122c, 5–122d in the supplement) (it being a "community order" within that Act), and section 148 of the *CJA* 2003 (*ante*, § 5–126) (it being a "community sentence" within that Act).

For Schedule 6, see *post*, §§ 5–168 *et seq*.

Selection and duty of supervisor and certain expenditure of his

5–165 **64.**—(1) *A court shall not designate a local authority as the supervisor by a provision of a supervision order unless—*

(a) *the authority agree; or*

(b) *it appears to the court that the offender resides or will reside in the area of the authority.*

(2) *Where a provision of a supervision order places the offender under the supervision of an officer of a local probation board, the supervisor shall be an officer of a local probation board appointed for or assigned to the petty sessions area named in the order in pursuance of section 63(6) above.*

(2A) *Where a provision of a supervision order places the offender under the supervision of an officer of a provider of probation services, the supervisor shall be an officer of a provider of probation services acting in the local justice area named in the order in pursuance of section 63(6) above.*

(3) *Where a provision of a supervision order places the offender under the supervision of a member of a youth offending team, the supervisor shall be a member of a team established by the local authority within whose area it appears to the court that the offender resides or will reside.*

(4) *While a supervision order is in force, the supervisor shall advise, assist and befriend the offender.*

(5) [Defrayment of expenditure.]

[This section is printed as amended and repealed in part by the *CJCSA* 2000, s.74, and Sched. 7, paras 4 and 174; and S.I. 2008 No. 912 (*ante*, § 5–164), art. 3, and Sched. 1, para. 14(1) and (10). The whole section is repealed as from a day to be appointed (as to which, see *ante*, §§ 5–1, 5–122) by the *CJIA* 2008, ss.6(1) and 149, and Sched. 28, Pt 1.]

5–166 Section 64A (inserted by the *Anti-social Behaviour Act* 2003, s.88, and Sched. 2, para. 3) provides that nothing in Chapter V of Part IV of the Act prevents a court which makes a supervision order in respect of an offender from also making a curfew order in respect of him. Section 65 gives effect to Schedule 7 (*post*, §§ 5–217 *et seq.*). This makes provision for dealing with failures to comply with supervision orders and for revoking and amending such orders. Section 66 makes provision for facilities for implementing supervision orders. All these provisions are repealed as from a day to be appointed (as to which, see *ante*, §§ 5–1, 5–122) by the *CJIA* 2008, ss.6(1) and 149, and Sched. 28, Pt 1.

Powers of Criminal Courts (Sentencing) Act 2000, s.67

Meaning of "local authority", "reside" and "parent"

67.—(1) *Unless the contrary intention appears, in sections 63 to 66 above and Schedules 6 and 7 to this Act—* **5–167**

"local authority" means the council of a county or of a county borough, metropolitan district or London borough or the Common Council of the City of London ;

"reside" means habitually reside, and cognate expressions shall be construed accordingly except in paragraph 6(2) and (3) of Schedule 6.

(2) *In the case of a child or young person—*

(a) *whose father and mother were not married to each other at the time of his birth, and*

(b) *with respect to whom a residence order is in force in favour of the father,*

any reference in sections 63 to 66 and Schedules 6 and 7 to the parent of the child or young person includes a reference to the father.

(3) *In subsection (2) above "residence order" has the meaning given by section 8(1) of the* Children Act *1989, and subsection (2) above is without prejudice to the operation of section 1(1) of the* Family Law Reform Act *1987 (construction of references to relationships) in relation to the provisions of this Act other than those mentioned in subsection (2).*

[This section is repealed as from a day to be appointed (as to which, see *ante*, §§ 5–1, 5–122) by the *CJIA* 2008, ss.6(1) and 149, and Sched. 28, Pt 1.]

Section 63

SCHEDULE 6

REQUIREMENTS WHICH MAY BE INCLUDED IN SUPERVISION ORDERS

Requirement to reside with named individual

1. *A supervision order may require the offender to reside with an individual named in the order who agrees to the requirement, but a requirement imposed by a supervision order in pursuance of this paragraph shall be subject to any such requirement of the order as is authorised by paragraph 2 , 3 , 6 [, 6A] or 7 below.* **5–168**

[Para. 1 is printed as amended, as from a day to be appointed, by the *CJA* 2003, s.279, and Sched. 24, para. 2(1) and (2) (insertion of reference to para. 6A). The whole of Schedule 6 is repealed as from a day to be appointed (as to which, see *ante*, §§ 5–1, 5–122) by the *CJIA* 2008, ss.6(1) and 149, and Sched. 28, Pt 1.]

Requirement to comply with directions of supervisor

2.—(1) *Subject to sub-paragraph (2) below, a supervision order may require the offender to comply with any directions given from time to time by the supervisor and requiring him to do all or any of the following things—* **5–169**

(a) *to live at a place or places specified in the directions for a period or periods so specified;*

(b) *to present himself to a person or persons specified in the directions at a place or places and on a day or days so specified;*

(c) *to participate in activities specified in the directions on a day or days so specified.*

(2) *A supervision order shall not require compliance with directions given by virtue of sub-paragraph (1) above unless the court making it is satisfied that a scheme under section 66 of this Act (local authority schemes) is in force for the area where the offender resides or will reside; and no such directions may involve the use of facilities which are not for the time being specified in a scheme in force under that section for that area.*

(3) *A requirement imposed by a supervision order in pursuance of sub-paragraph (1) above shall be subject to any such requirement of the order as is authorised by paragraph 6 below (treatment for offender's mental condition).*

(4) *It shall be for the supervisor to decide—*

(a) *whether and to what extent he exercises any power to give directions conferred on him by virtue of sub-paragraph (1) above; and*

(b) *the form of any directions.*

(5) *The total number of days in respect of which an offender may be required to comply with directions given by virtue of paragraph (a), (b) or (c) of sub-paragraph (1) above shall not exceed 180 or such lesser number, if any, as the order may specify for the purposes of this sub-paragraph.*

(6) *For the purpose of calculating the total number of days in respect of which such directions may be given, the supervisor shall be entitled to disregard any day in respect of which directions were previously given in pursuance of the order and on which the directions were not complied with.*

(7) *Directions given by the supervisor by virtue of sub-paragraph (1)(b) or (c) above shall, as far as practicable, be such as to avoid—*

(a) *any conflict with the offender's religious beliefs or with the requirements of any other youth community order or any community order to which he may be subject; and*

(b) *any interference with the times, if any, at which he normally works or attends school or any other educational establishment.*

[Para. 2 is printed as amended by the *Anti-social Behaviour Act* 2003, s.88, and Sched. 2, para. 4(1) and (2); and the *CJA* 2003, s.304, and Sched. 32, para. 127(a). As to the prospective repeal of the whole of Schedule 6, see *ante*, § 5–168.]

Requirements as to activities, reparation, night restrictions etc.

5–170 3.—(1) *This paragraph applies to a supervision order unless the order requires the offender to comply with directions given by the supervisor under paragraph 2(1) above.*

(2) *Subject to the following provisions of this paragraph …, a supervision order to which this paragraph applies may require the offender—*

(a) *to live at a place or places specified in the order for a period or periods so specified;*

(b) *to present himself to a person or persons specified in the order at a place or places and on a day or days so specified;*

(c) *to participate in activities specified in the order on a day or days so specified;*

(d) *to make reparation specified in the order to a person or persons so specified or to the community at large;*

(e) [repealed by *Anti-social Behaviour Act* 2003, s.88, and Sched. 2, para. 4(1) and (3)(a)];

(f) *to refrain from participating in activities specified in the order—*

(i) *on a specified day or days during the period for which the supervision order is in force; or*

(ii) *during the whole of that period or a specified portion of it;*

and in this paragraph "make reparation" means make reparation for the offence otherwise than by the payment of compensation.

(3) *The total number of days in respect of which an offender may be subject to requirements imposed by virtue of paragraph (a), (b), (c) or (d) of sub-paragraph (2) above shall not exceed 180.*

(4) *The court may not include requirements under sub-paragraph (2) above in a supervision order unless—*

(a) *it has first consulted the supervisor as to—*

(i) *the offender's circumstances, and*

(ii) *the feasibility of securing compliance with the requirements,*

and is satisfied, having regard to the supervisor's report, that it is feasible to secure compliance with them;

(b) *having regard to the circumstances of the case, it considers the requirements necessary for securing the good conduct of the offender or for preventing a repetition by him of the same offence or the commission of other offences; and*

(c) *if the offender is aged under 16, it has obtained and considered information about his family circumstances and the likely effect of the requirements on those circumstances.*

(5) *The court shall not by virtue of sub-paragraph (2) above include in a supervision order—*

(a) *any requirement that would involve the co-operation of a person other than the supervisor and the offender, unless that other person consents to its inclusion;*

(b) *any requirement to make reparation to any person unless that person—*

(i) *is identified by the court as a victim of the offence or a person otherwise affected by it; and*

(ii) *consents to the inclusion of the requirement;*

(c) *any requirement requiring the offender to reside with a specified individual; or*

(d) *any such requirement as is mentioned in paragraph 6(2) below (treatment for offender's mental condition).*

(6) *Requirements included in a supervision order by virtue of sub-paragraph (2)(b) or (c) above shall, as far as practicable, be such as to avoid—*

(a) *any conflict with the offender's religious beliefs or with the requirements of any other youth community order to which he may be subject; and*

(b) *any interference with the times, if any, at which he normally works or attends school or any other educational establishment;*

and sub-paragraphs (7) and (8) below are without prejudice to this sub-paragraph.

(7) *Subject to sub-paragraph (8) below, a supervision order may not by virtue of sub-paragraph (2) above include—*

(a) *any requirement that would involve the offender in absence from home—*

(i) *for more than two consecutive nights, or*

(ii) *for more than two nights in any one week, or*

(b) *if the offender is of compulsory school age, any requirement to participate in activities during normal school hours,*

unless the court making the order is satisfied that the facilities whose use would be involved are for the time being specified in a scheme in force under section 66 of this Act for the area in which the offender resides or will reside.

(8) *Sub-paragraph (7)(b) above does not apply to activities carried out in accordance with arrangements made or approved by the local education authority in whose area the offender resides or will reside.*

(9) *Expressions used in sub-paragraphs (7) and (8) above and in the Education Act 1996 have the same meaning in those sub-paragraphs as in that Act.*

[Para. 3 is printed as amended and repealed in part by the *Anti-social Behaviour Act* 2003, ss.88 and 92, and Scheds 2, para. 4(1) and (3), and 3; and the *CJA* 2003, s.304, and Sched. 32, para. 127(b). As to the prospective repeal of the whole of Schedule 6, see *ante*, § 5–168.]

4. [*Repealed by* Anti-social Behaviour Act *2003, s.92, and Sched. 3.*]

Requirement to live for specified period in local authority accommodation

5.—(1) *Where the conditions mentioned in sub-paragraph (2) below are satisfied, a supervision order may impose a requirement ("a local authority residence requirement") that the offender shall live for a specified period in local authority accommodation (as defined by section 163 of this Act).* **5–171**

(2) *The conditions are that—*

(a) *a supervision order has previously been made in respect of the offender;*

(b) *that order imposed—*

(i) *a requirement under paragraph 1 , 2 , 3 or 7 of this Schedule; or*

(ii) *a local authority residence requirement;*

(c) *the offender fails to comply with that requirement, or is convicted of an offence committed while that order was in force; and*

(d) *the court is satisfied that—*

(i) *the failure to comply with the requirement, or the behaviour which constituted the offence, was due to a significant extent to the circumstances in which the offender was living; and*

(ii) *the imposition of a local authority residence requirement will assist in his rehabilitation;*

except that sub-paragraph (i) of paragraph (d) above does not apply where the condition in paragraph (b)(ii) above is satisfied.

(3) *A local authority residence requirement shall designate the local authority who are to receive the offender, and that authority shall be the authority in whose area the offender resides.*

(4) *The court shall not impose a local authority residence requirement without first consulting the designated authority.*

(5) *A local authority residence requirement may stipulate that the offender shall not live with a named person.*

(6) *The maximum period which may be specified in a local authority residence requirement is six months.*

(7) *A court shall not impose a local authority residence requirement in respect of an offender who is not legally represented at the relevant time in that court unless—*

(a) *he was granted a right to representation funded by the Legal Services Commission as part of the Criminal Defence Service for the purposes of the proceedings but the right was withdrawn because of his conduct [or because it appeared that his financial resources were such that he was not eligible to be granted such a right;*

(aa) *he applied for such representation and the application was refused because it appeared that his financial resources were such that he was not eligible to be granted a right to it; or*

(b) *he has been informed of his right to apply for such representation for the purposes of the proceedings and has had the opportunity to do so, but nevertheless refused or failed to apply.*

(8) *In sub-paragraph (7) above—*

(a) *"the relevant time" means the time when the court is considering whether or not to impose the requirement; and*

(b) *"the proceedings" means—*

(i) *the whole proceedings; or*

(ii) *the part of the proceedings relating to the imposition of the requirement.*

(9) *A supervision order imposing a local authority residence requirement may also impose any of the requirements mentioned in paragraphs 2 , 3 , 6 and 7 of this Schedule.*

[Para. 5(7) is printed as amended by the *Criminal Defence Service Act* 2006, s.4(2) and (3). As to the prospective repeal of the whole of Schedule 6, see *ante*, § 5–168.]

Requirement to live for specified period with local authority foster parent

5–171a 5A.—(1) *Where the conditions mentioned in sub-paragraph (2) below are satisfied, a supervision order may impose a requirement ("a foster parent residence requirement") that the offender shall live for a specified period with a local authority foster parent.*

(2) *The conditions are that—*

(a) *the offence is punishable with imprisonment in the case of an offender aged 18 or over;*

(b) *the offence, or the combination of the offence and one or more offences associated with it, was so serious that a custodial sentence would normally be appropriate (or, where the offender is aged 10 or 11, would normally be appropriate if the offender were aged 12 or over); and*

(c) *the court is satisfied that—*

(i) *the behaviour which constituted the offence was due to a significant extent to the circumstances in which the offender was living, and*

(ii) *the imposition of a foster parent residence requirement will assist in his rehabilitation.*

(3) *A foster parent residence requirement shall designate the local authority who are to place the offender with a local authority foster parent under section 23(2)(a) of the* Children Act *1989, and that authority shall be the authority in whose area the offender resides.*

(4) *A court shall not impose a foster parent residence requirement unless—*

(a) *the court has been notified by the Secretary of State that arrangements for implementing such a requirement are available in the area of the designated authority;*

(b) *the notice has not been withdrawn; and*

(c) *the court has consulted the designated authority.*

(5) *Subject to paragraph 5(2A) of Schedule 7 to this Act, the maximum period which may be specified in a foster parent residence requirement is twelve months.*

(6) *A court shall not impose a foster parent residence requirement* [otherwise identical to para. 5(7), *ante*].

(7) *In sub-paragraph (6)* [otherwise identical to para. 5(8), *ante*.]

(8) *A supervision order imposing a foster parent residence requirement may also impose any of the requirements mentioned in paragraphs 2 , 3 , 6 and 7 of this Schedule.*

(9) *If at any time while a supervision order imposing a foster parent residence requirement is in force, the supervisor notifies the offender—*

(a) *that no suitable local authority foster parent is available, and*

(b) *that the supervisor has applied or proposes to apply under paragraph 5 of Schedule 7 for the variation or revocation of the order,*

the foster parent residence requirement shall, until the determination of the application, be taken to require the offender to live in local authority accommodation (as defined by section 163 of this Act).

(10) *This paragraph does not affect the power of a local authority to place with a local authority foster parent an offender to whom a local authority residence requirement under paragraph 5 above relates.*

(11) *In this paragraph "local authority foster parent" has the same meaning as in the* Children Act *1989.*

[Para. 5A is inserted by the *Anti-social Behaviour Act* 2003, s.88, and Sched. 2, para. 4(1) and (5). The *Criminal Defence Service Act* 2006, s.4(2) and (3), effected an identical amendment to sub-para. (6), as that made to para. 5(7), *ante*. As to the prospective repeal of the whole of Schedule 6, see *ante*, § 5–168.]

Requirements as to treatment for mental condition

6.—(1) *This paragraph applies where a court which proposes to make a supervision order is satisfied, on the evidence of a registered medical practitioner approved for the purposes of section 12 of the* Mental Health Act *1983, that the mental condition of the offender—* **5–172**

(a) *is such as requires and may be susceptible to treatment; but*

(b) *is not such as to warrant the making of a hospital order or guardianship order within the meaning of that Act.*

(2) *Where this paragraph applies, the court may include in the supervision order a requirement that the offender shall, for a period specified in the order, submit to treatment of one of the following descriptions so specified, that is to say—*

(a) *treatment as a resident patient in an independent hospital or care home within the meaning of the* Care Standards Act *2000 or a hospital within the meaning of the* Mental Health Act *1983, but not a hospital at which high security psychiatric services within the meaning of that Act are provided;*

(b) *treatment as a non-resident patient at an institution or place specified in the order;*

(c) *treatment by or under the direction of a registered medical practitioner specified in the order; or*

(d) *treatment by or under the direction of a chartered psychologist specified in the order.*

(3) *A requirement shall not be included in a supervision order by virtue of sub-paragraph (2) above—*

(a) *in any case, unless the court is satisfied that arrangements have been or can be made for the treatment in question and, in the case of treatment as a resident patient, for the reception of the patient;*

(b) *in the case of an order made or to be made in respect of a person aged 14 or over, unless he consents to its inclusion;*

and a requirement so included shall not in any case continue in force after the offender attains the age of 18.

(4) *Subsections (2) and (3) of section 54 of the* Mental Health Act *1983 shall have effect with respect to proof for the purposes of sub-paragraph (1) above of an offender's mental condition as they have effect with respect to proof of an offender's mental condition for the purposes of section 37(2)(a) of that Act.*

(5) *In sub-paragraph (2) above "chartered psychologist" means a person for the time being listed in the British Psychological Society's Register of Chartered Psychologists.*

[Para. 6 is printed as amended by the *Care Standards Act* 2000, s.116, and Sched. 4, para. 28(3). As to the prospective repeal of the whole of Schedule 6, see *ante*, § 5–168.]

[Requirements as to drug treatment and testing

6A.—(1) *This paragraph applies where a court proposing to make a supervision order is satisfied—* **5–172a**

(a) *that the offender is dependent on, or has a propensity to misuse, drugs, and*

(b) *that his dependency or propensity is such as requires and may be susceptible to treatment.*

(2) *Where this paragraph applies, the court may include in the supervision order a requirement that the offender shall, for a period specified in the order ("the treatment period"), submit to treatment by or under the direction of a specified person having the necessary qualifications and experience ("the treatment provider") with a view to the reduction or elimination of the offender's dependency on or propensity to misuse drugs.*

(3) *The required treatment shall be—*

(a) *treatment as a resident in such institution or place as may be specified in the order, or*

(b) *treatment as a non-resident at such institution or place, and at such intervals, as may be so specified;*

but the nature of the treatment shall not be specified in the order except as mentioned in paragraph (a) or (b) above.

(4) *A requirement shall not be included in a supervision order by virtue of sub-paragraph (2) above—*

(a) *in any case, unless—*

(i) *the court is satisfied that arrangements have been or can be made for the treatment intended to be specified in the order (including arrangements for the reception of the offender where he is to be required to submit to treatment as a resident), and*

(ii) *the requirement has been recommended to the court as suitable for the offender by an officer of a local probation board, by an officer of a provider of probation services or by a member of a youth offending team; and*

(b) *in the case of an order made or to be made in respect of a person aged 14 or over, unless he consents to its inclusion.*

(5) *Subject to sub-paragraph (6), a supervision order which includes a treatment requirement may also include a requirement ("a testing requirement") that, for the purpose of ascertaining whether he has any drug in his body during the treatment period, the offender shall during that period, at such times or in such circumstances as may (subject to the provisions of the order) be determined by the supervisor or the treatment provider, provide samples of such description as may be so determined.*

(6) *A testing requirement shall not be included in a supervision order by virtue of sub-paragraph (5) above unless—*

(a) *the offender is aged 14 or over and consents to its inclusion, and*

(b) *the court has been notified by the Secretary of State that arrangements for implementing such requirements are in force in the area proposed to be specified in the order.*

(7) *A testing requirement shall specify for each month the minimum number of occasions on which samples are to be provided.*

(8) *A supervision order including a testing requirement shall provide for the results of tests carried out on any samples provided by the offender in pursuance of the requirement to a person other than the supervisor to be communicated to the supervisor.]*

[Para. 6A is inserted by the *CJA* 2003, s.279, and Sched. 24, para. 2(1) and (3). For the purpose of sentencing persons resident in Bradford, Calderdale, Keighley, Manchester, Newham and the part of the Teesside petty sessions area that is coterminous with the borough of Middlesborough, this insertion took effect on December 1, 2004, but not in relation to offences committed before that date (and where an offence is found to have been committed over a period of two or more days or at some time during that period, it shall be taken to have been committed on the last of those days): *Criminal Justice Act 2003 (Commencement No. 6 and Transitional Provisions) Order* 2004 (S.I. 2004 No. 3033). Otherwise, it was not in force as at October 1, 2008. It is printed as amended by S.I. 2008 No. 912 (*ante*, § 5–164), art. 3, and Sched. 1, para. 14(1) and (17). As to the prospective repeal of the whole of Schedule 6, see *ante*, § 5–168.]

Requirements as to education

5–173 7.—(1) *This paragraph applies to a supervision order unless the order requires the offender to comply with directions given by the supervisor under paragraph 2(1) above.*

(2) *Subject to the following provisions of this paragraph, a supervision order to which this paragraph applies may require the offender, if he is of compulsory school age, to comply,*

for as long as he is of that age and the order remains in force, with such arrangements for his education as may from time to time be made by his parent, being arrangements for the time being approved by the local education authority.

(3) *The court shall not include such a requirement in a supervision order unless—*

(a) *it has consulted the local education authority with regard to its proposal to include the requirement; and*

(b) *it is satisfied that in the view of the local education authority arrangements exist for the offender to receive efficient full-time education suitable to his age, ability and aptitude and to any special educational need he may have.*

(4) *Expressions used in sub-paragraphs (2) and (3) above and in the* Education Act *1996 have the same meaning in those sub-paragraphs as in that Act.*

(5) *The court may not include a requirement under sub-paragraph (2) above unless it has first consulted the supervisor as to the offender's circumstances and, having regard to the circumstances of the case, it considers the requirement necessary for securing the good conduct of the offender or for preventing a repetition by him of the same offence or the commission of other offences.*

[As to the prospective repeal of the whole of Schedule 6, see *ante*, § 5–168.]

Exercise of powers under paragraphs 3, 6 and 7

8.—(1) *Any power to include a requirement in a supervision order which is exercisable in relation to a person by virtue of paragraph 3 , 6 or 7 above may be exercised in relation to him whether or not any other such power is exercised.* **5–174**

(2) *Sub-paragraph (1) above is without prejudice to the power to include in a supervision order any other combination of requirements under different paragraphs of this Schedule that is authorised by this Schedule.*

[As to the prospective repeal of the whole of Schedule 6, see *ante*, § 5–168.]

(5) Action plan orders

Powers of Criminal Courts (Sentencing) Act 2000, ss.69–72

Action plan orders

69.—(1) *Where a child or young person (that is to say, any person aged under 18) is convicted of an offence and the court by or before which he is convicted is of the opinion mentioned in subsection (3) below, the court may (subject to sections 148 , 150 and 156 of the* Criminal Justice Act *2003) make an order which—* **5–175**

(a) *requires the offender, for a period of three months beginning with the date of the order, to comply with an action plan, that is to say, a series of requirements with respect to his actions and whereabouts during that period;*

(b) *places the offender for that period under the supervision of the responsible officer; and*

(c) *requires the offender to comply with any directions given by the responsible officer with a view to the implementation of that plan;*

and the requirements included in the order, and any directions given by the responsible officer, may include requirements authorised by section 70 below.

(2) *An order under subsection (1) above is in this Act referred to as an "action plan order".*

(3) *The opinion referred to in subsection (1) above is that the making of an action plan order is desirable in the interests of—*

(a) *securing the rehabilitation of the offender; or*

(b) *preventing the commission by him of further offences.*

(4) *In this Act "responsible officer", in relation to an offender subject to an action plan order, means one of the following who is specified in the order, namely—*

(a) *an officer of a local probation board or an officer of a provider of probation services (as the case may be);*

(b) *a social worker of a local authority social services department;*

(c) *a member of a youth offending team.*

(5) *The court shall not make an action plan order in respect of the offender if—*

(a) *he is already the subject of such an order; or*

(b) *the court proposes to pass on him a custodial sentence or to make in respect of him a* community rehabilitation order, a community punishment order, a community punishment and rehabilitation order *[community order under section 177 of the* Criminal Justice Act *2003], an attendance centre order, a supervision order or a referral order.*

(6) *Before making an action plan order, the court shall obtain and consider—*

(a) *a written report by an officer of a local probation board, an officer of a provider of probation services, a social worker of a local authority social services department or a member of a youth offending team indicating—*

(i) *the requirements proposed by that person to be included in the order;*

(ii) *the benefits to the offender that the proposed requirements are designed to achieve; and*

(iii) *the attitude of a parent or guardian of the offender to the proposed requirements; and*

(b) *where the offender is aged under 16, information about the offender's family circumstances and the likely effect of the order on those circumstances.*

(7) *The court shall not make an action plan order unless it has been notified by the Secretary of State that arrangements for implementing such orders are available in the area proposed to be named in the order under subsection (8) below and the notice has not been withdrawn.*

(8) *An action plan order shall name the petty sessions area in which it appears to the court making the order (or to the court amending under Schedule 8 to this Act any provision included in the order in pursuance of this subsection) that the offender resides or will reside.*

(9) *Where an action plan order specifies an officer of a local probation board under subsection (4) above, the officer specified must be an officer appointed for or assigned to the petty sessions area named in the order.*

(9A) *Where an action plan order specifies an officer of a provider of probation services under subsection (4) above, the officer specified must be an officer acting in the local justice area named in the order.*

(10) *Where an action plan order specifies under that subsection—*

(a) *a social worker of a local authority social services department, or*

(b) *a member of a youth offending team,*

the social worker or member specified must be a social worker of, or a member of a youth offending team established by, the local authority within whose area it appears to the court that the offender resides or will reside.

[This section is printed as amended by the *CJCSA* 2000, s.74 and Sched. 7, paras 1–4; the *CJA* 2003, s.304, and Sched. 32, paras 90 and 104(1), (2) and (4); and S.I. 2008 No. 912 (*ante*, § 5–164), art. 3, and Sched. 1, para. 14(1) and (12). The words in square brackets in subs. (5)(b) were substituted for the romanised words as from April 4, 2005 (S.I. 2005 No. 950, *ante*, § 5-121e): *CJA* 2003, s.304, and Sched. 32, paras 90 and 104(1) and (3); but, in the case of persons aged 16 or 17 upon conviction, this amendment only comes into force on April 4, 2009 (as to which, see *ante*, §§ 5–121e, 5–122, 5–131): S.I. 2005 No. 950, Sched. 2, paras 12 and 13 (§§ 5–131f, 5–131g in the supplement). The whole section is repealed as from a day to be appointed (as to which, see *ante*, §§ 5–1, 5–122) by the *CJIA* 2008, ss.6(1) and 149, and Sched. 28, Pt 1.]

Requirements which may be included in action plan orders and directions

5–176 **70.**—(1) *Requirements included in an action plan order, or directions given by a responsible officer, may require the offender to do all or any of the following things, namely—*

(a) *to participate in activities specified in the requirements or directions at a time or times so specified;*

(b) *to present himself to a person or persons specified in the requirements or directions at a place or places and at a time or times so specified;*

(c) *subject to subsection (2) below, to attend at an attendance centre specified in the requirements or directions for a number of hours so specified;*

(d) *to stay away from a place or places specified in the requirements or directions;*

(e) *to comply with any arrangements for his education specified in the requirements or directions;*

(f) *to make reparation specified in the requirements or directions to a person or persons so specified or to the community at large; and*

(g) *to attend any hearing fixed by the court under section 71 below.*

(2) *Subsection (1)(c) above applies only where the offence committed by the offender is an offence punishable with imprisonment.*

(3) *In subsection (1)(f) above "make reparation", in relation to an offender, means make reparation for the offence otherwise than by the payment of compensation.*

(4) *A person shall not be specified in requirements or directions under subsection (1)(f) above unless—*

(a) *he is identified by the court or (as the case may be) the responsible officer as a victim of the offence or a person otherwise affected by it; and*

(b) *he consents to the reparation being made.*

[(4A) *Subsection (4B) below applies where a court proposing to make an action plan order is satisfied—*

(a) *that the offender is dependent on, or has a propensity to misuse, drugs, and*

(b) *that his dependency or propensity is such as requires and may be susceptible to treatment.*

(4B) *Where this subsection applies, requirements included in an action plan order may require the offender for a period specified in the order ("the treatment period") to submit to treatment by or under the direction of a specified person having the necessary qualifications and experience ("the treatment provider") with a view to the reduction or elimination of the offender's dependency on or propensity to misuse drugs.*

(4C) *The required treatment shall be—*

(a) *treatment as a resident in such institution or place as may be specified in the order, or*

(b) *treatment as a non-resident at such institution or place, and at such intervals, as may be so specified;*

but the nature of the treatment shall not be specified in the order except as mentioned in paragraph (a) or (b) above.

(4D) *A requirement shall not be included in an action plan order by virtue of subsection (4B) above—*

(a) *in any case, unless—*

(i) *the court is satisfied that arrangements have been or can be made for the treatment intended to be specified in the order (including arrangements for the reception of the offender where he is to be required to submit to treatment as a resident), and*

(ii) *the requirement has been recommended to the court as suitable for the offender by an officer of a local probation board, by an officer of a provider of probation services or by a member of a youth offending team; and*

(b) *in the case of an order made or to be made in respect of a person aged 14 or over, unless he consents to its inclusion.*

(4E) *Subject to subsection (4F), an action plan order which includes a requirement by virtue of subsection (4B) above may, if the offender is aged 14 or over, also include a requirement ("a testing requirement") that, for the purpose of ascertaining whether he has any drug in his body during the treatment period, the offender shall during that period, at such times or in such circumstances as may (subject to the provisions of the order) be determined by the responsible officer or the treatment provider, provide samples of such description as may be so determined.*

(4F) *A testing requirement shall not be included in an action plan order by virtue of subsection (4E) above unless—*

(a) *the offender is aged 14 or over and consents to its inclusion, and*

(b) *the court has been notified by the Secretary of State that arrangements for implementing such requirements are in force in the area proposed to be specified in the order.*

(4G) *A testing requirement shall specify for each month the minimum number of occasions on which samples are to be provided.*

(4H) *An action plan order including a testing requirement shall provide for the results of tests carried out on any samples provided by the offender in pursuance of the requirement to a person other than the responsible officer to be communicated to the responsible officer.]*

(5) *Requirements included in an action plan order and directions given by a responsible officer shall, as far as practicable, be such as to avoid—*

(a) *any conflict with the offender's religious beliefs or with the requirements of any other youth community order or any community order to which he may be subject; and*

(b) *any interference with the times, if any, at which he normally works or attends school or any other educational establishment.*

[This section is printed as amended by the *CJA* 2003, s.302, and Sched. 32, paras 90 and 105; and S.I. 2008 No. 912 (*ante*, § 5–164), art. 3, and Sched. 1, para. 14(1) and (13); and as amended, as from a day to be appointed, by *ibid.*, s.279 and Sched. 24, para. 1 (insertion of subss. (4A) to (4H)). As to the commencement of section 279 and Schedule 24 in certain areas on December 1, 2004, see *ante*, § 5–172a. The whole section is repealed as from a day to be appointed (as to which, see *ante*, §§ 5–1, 5–122) by the *CJIA* 2008, ss.6(1) and 149, and Sched. 28, Pt 1.]

Action plan orders: power to fix further hearings

5–177 **71.**—(1) *Immediately after making an action plan order, a court may—*

(a) *fix a further hearing for a date not more than 21 days after the making of the order; and*

(b) *direct the responsible officer to make, at that hearing, a report as to the effectiveness of the order and the extent to which it has been implemented.*

(2) *At a hearing fixed under subsection (1) above, the court—*

(a) *shall consider the responsible officer's report; and*

(b) *may, on the application of the responsible officer or the offender, amend the order—*

(i) *by cancelling any provision included in it; or*

(ii) *by inserting in it (either in addition to or in substitution for any of its provisions) any provision that the court could originally have included in it.*

[This section is repealed as from a day to be appointed (as to which, see *ante*, §§ 5–1, 5–122) by the *CJIA* 2008, ss.6(1) and 149, and Sched. 28, Pt 1.]

Breach, revocation and amendment

5–178 As to breach, revocation, and amendment, see Schedule 8 to the 2000 Act, *post*, §§ 5–227 *et seq.*

(6) Electronic monitoring

Powers of Criminal Courts (Sentencing) Act 2000, s.36B

Electronic monitoring of requirements in [youth] community orders

5–178a **36B.**—(1) *Subject to subsections (2) to (4) [and (3)] below, a [youth] community order may include requirements for securing the electronic monitoring of the offender's compliance with any other requirements imposed by the order.*

(2) *A court shall not include in a [youth] community order a requirement under subsection (1) above unless the court—*

(a) *has been notified by the Secretary of State that electronic monitoring arrangements are available in the relevant areas specified in subsections (7) to (10) below; and*

(b) *is satisfied that the necessary provisions can be made under those arrangements.*

(3) *Where—*

(a) *it is proposed to include in an exclusion order a requirement for securing electronic monitoring in accordance with this section; but*

(b) *there is a person (other than the offender) without whose co-operation it will not be practicable to secure the monitoring,*

the requirement shall not be included in the order without that person's consent.

(4) Where—

(a) it is proposed to include in a community rehabilitation order or a community punishment and rehabilitation order a requirement for securing the electronic monitoring of the offender's compliance with a requirement such as is mentioned in paragraph 8(1) of Schedule 2 to this Act; but

(b) there is a person (other than the offender) without whose co-operation it will not be practicable to secure the monitoring,

the requirement shall not be included in the order without that person's consent.

(5) *An order which includes requirements under subsection (1) above shall include provision for making a person responsible for the monitoring; and a person who is made so responsible shall be of a description specified in an order made by the Secretary of State.*

(6) *The Secretary of State may make rules for regulating—*

(a) *the electronic monitoring of compliance with requirements included in a [youth] community order; and*

(b) *without prejudice to the generality of paragraph (a) above, the functions of persons made responsible for securing the electronic monitoring of compliance with requirements included in the order.*

(7) *In the case of a curfew order or an exclusion order, the relevant area is the area in which the place proposed to be specified in the order is situated.*

In this subsection, "place", in relation to an exclusion order, has the same meaning as in section 40A below.

(8) In the case of a community rehabilitation order or a community punishment and rehabilitation order, the relevant areas are each of the following—

(a) where it is proposed to include in the order a requirement for securing compliance with a requirement such as is mentioned in sub-paragraph (1) of paragraph 7 of Schedule 2 to this Act, the area mentioned in sub-paragraph (5) of that paragraph;

(b) where it is proposed to include in the order a requirement for securing compliance with a requirement such as is mentioned in sub-paragraph (1) of paragraph 8 of that Schedule, the area mentioned in sub-paragraph (5) of that paragraph;

(c) where it is proposed to include in the order a requirement for securing compliance with any other requirement, the area prposed to be specified under section 41(3) below.

(9) *In the case of* a community punishment order, a drug treatment and testing order, a drug abstinence order, *a supervision order or an action plan order, the relevant area is the petty sessions area proposed to be specified in the order.*

(10) *In the case of an attendance centre order, the relevant area is the petty sessions area in which the attendance centre proposed to be specified in the order is situated.*

[This section was inserted by the *CJCSA* 2000, s.52, as from July 2, 2001 (except to the extent that it relates to exclusion requirements); and from September 2, 2004 (to the extent that it does relate to such requirements): *Criminal Justice and Court Services Act 2000 (Commencemenet No. 13) Order* 2004 (S.I. 2004 No. 2171). It is printed as amended and repealed in part by the *CJA* 2003, ss.304 and 332, Sched. 32, paras 90 and 96, and Sched. 37, Pt 7 (omission of romanised words, insertion of words in square brackets). These amendments came into force on April 4, 2005 (S.I. 2005 No. 950, *ante*, § 5–121e), save that in the case of persons aged 16 or 17 at the time of conviction, they only come into force on April 4, 2009 (as to which, see *ante*, §§ 5–121e, 5–122, 5–131): *ibid.*, Sched. 2, paras 12 and 13 (§§ 5–131f, 5–131g in the supplement). The whole section is repealed as from a day to be appointed (as to which, see *ante*, §§ 5–1, 5–122) by the *CJIA* 2008, ss.6(1) and 149, and Sched. 28, Pt 1.]

E. YOUTH REHABILITATION ORDERS

As to the creation of these orders by the *CJIA* 2008, s.1, and as to the commencement and transitional arrangements and saving provisions, see *ante*, §§ 5–1, 5–121e, 5–122. The new statutory provisions (which are anticipated to come into force in the second half of 2009) will be set out in the second and/or third supplements. **5–179**

F. ENFORCEMENT, ETC.

(1) Of community orders

(a) *Loss of benefit*

Part III (ss.62– 73) of the *Child Support, Pensions and Social Security Act* 2000 relates to social security. Section 62 makes provision for the Secretary of State to withdraw or reduce benefit where a person fails to comply with a designated community sentence. The sanction is to be for a fixed period (to be prescribed in regulations) and will commence after a court has determined that a relevant community order (*i.e.* a community order made under section 177 of the *CJA* 2003, or falling to be treated as if so made) has been breached. Section 63 makes provision for the case where one of a couple entitled to joint-claim jobseeker's allowance is in breach of a community order. Section 64 obliges a court, before making a relevant community order in relation to any person, to explain to that person in ordinary language the consequences by virtue of sections 62 and 63 of a failure to comply. **5–179a**

Part III comes into force on a day or days to be appointed. The *Child Support, Pensions and Social Security Act 2000 (Commencement No. 10) Order* 2001 (S.I. 2001 No. 2619) brought sections 62 to 66 fully into force on October 15, 2001, for the purposes of their application to persons in relation to whom relevant community orders are made, and who fall to be supervised in the probation areas of Derbyshire, Hertfordshire, Teesside or the West Midlands.

(b) *Amendment, revocation and re-sentencing*

Criminal Justice Act 2003, Sched. 8

Section 179 SCHEDULE 8

BREACH, REVOCATION OR AMENDMENT OF COMMUNITY ORDER

PART 1

Preliminary

Interpretation

5–180 1. In this Schedule—

"the offender", in relation to a community order, means the person in respect of whom the order is made;

"the petty sessions area concerned", in relation to a community order, means the petty sessions area for the time being specified in the order;

"the responsible officer" has the meaning given by section 197.

2. In this Schedule—

(a) references to a drug rehabilitation requirement of a community order being subject to review are references to that requirement being subject to review in accordance with section 210(1)(b);

(b) references to the court responsible for a community order imposing a drug rehabilitation requirement which is subject to review are to be construed in accordance with section 210(2).

3. For the purposes of this Schedule—

(a) a requirement falling within any paragraph of section 177(1) is of the same kind as any other requirement falling within that paragraph, and

(b) an electronic monitoring requirement is a requirement of the same kind as any requirement falling within section 177(1) to which it relates.

Orders made on appeal

5–181 4. Where a community order has been made on appeal, it is to be taken for the purposes of this Schedule to have been made by the Crown Court.

PART 2

Breach of Requirement of Order

Duty to give warning

5–182 5.—(1) If the responsible officer is of the opinion that the offender has failed without reasonable excuse to comply with any of the requirements of a community order, the officer must give him a warning under this paragraph unless—

(a) the offender has within the previous twelve months been given a warning under this paragraph in relation to a failure to comply with any of the requirements of the order, or

(b) the officer causes an information to be laid before a justice of the peace in respect of the failure.

(2) A warning under this paragraph must—

(a) describe the circumstances of the failure,

(b) state that the failure is unacceptable, and

(c) inform the offender that, if within the next twelve months he again fails to comply with any requirement of the order, he will be liable to be brought before a court.

(3) The responsible officer must, as soon as practicable after the warning has been given, record that fact.

(4) In relation to any community order which was made by the Crown Court and does not include a direction that any failure to comply with the requirements of the order is to be dealt with by a magistrates' court, the reference in sub-paragraph (1)(b) to a justice of the peace is to be read as a reference to the Crown Court.

Breach of order after warning

6.—(1) If— **5–183**

(a) the responsible officer has given a warning under paragraph 5 to the offender in respect of a community order, and

(b) at any time within the twelve months beginning with the date on which the warning was given, the responsible officer is of the opinion that the offender has since that date failed without reasonable excuse to comply with any of the requirements of the order,

the officer must cause an information to be laid before a justice of the peace in respect of the failure in question.

(2) In relation to any community order which was made by the Crown Court and does not include a direction that any failure to comply with the requirements of the order is to be dealt with by a magistrates' court, the reference in sub-paragraph (1) to a justice of the peace is to be read as a reference to the Crown Court.

Issue of summons or warrant by justice of the peace

7.—(1) This paragraph applies to— **5–184**

(a) a community order made by a magistrates' court, or

(b) any community order which was made by the Crown Court and includes a direction that any failure to comply with the requirements of the order is to be dealt with by a magistrates' court.

(2) If at any time while a community order to which this paragraph applies is in force it appears on information to a justice of the peace that the offender has failed to comply with any of the requirements of the order, the justice may—

(a) issue a summons requiring the offender to appear at the place and time specified in it, or

(b) if the information is in writing and on oath, issue a warrant for his arrest.

(3) Any summons or warrant issued under this paragraph must direct the offender to appear or be brought—

(a) in the case of a community order imposing a drug rehabilitation requirement which is subject to review, before the magistrates' court responsible for the order, or

(b) in any other case, before a magistrates' court acting for the petty sessions area in which the offender resides or, if it is not known where he resides, before a magistrates' court acting for the petty sessions area concerned.

(4) Where a summons issued under sub-paragraph (2)(a) requires the offender to appear before a magistrates' court and the offender does not appear in answer to the summons, the magistrates' court may issue a warrant for the arrest of the offender.

Issue of summons or warrant by Crown Court

8.—(1) This paragraph applies to a community order made by the Crown Court which does not include a direction that any failure to comply with the requirements of the order is to be dealt with by a magistrates' court. **5–185**

(2) If at any time while a community order to which this paragraph applies is in force it appears on information to the Crown Court that the offender has failed to comply with any of the requirements of the order, the Crown Court may—

(a) issue a summons requiring the offender to appear at the place and time specified in it, or

(b) if the information is in writing and on oath, issue a warrant for his arrest.

(3) Any summons or warrant issued under this paragraph must direct the offender to appear or be brought before the Crown Court.

(4) Where a summons issued under sub-paragraph (2)(a) requires the offender to appear before the Crown Court and the offender does not appear in answer to the summons, the Crown Court may issue a warrant for the arrest of the offender.

Powers of magistrates' court

9.—(1) If it is proved to the satisfaction of a magistrates' court before which an offender appears or is brought under paragraph 7 that he has failed without reasonable excuse to comply with any of the requirements of the community order, the court must deal with him in respect of the failure in any one of the following ways— **5–186**

(a) by amending the terms of the community order so as to impose more onerous requirements which the court could include if it were then making the order;

(b) where the community order was made by a magistrates' court, by dealing with him, for the offence in respect of which the order was made, in any way in which the court could deal with him if he had just been convicted by it of the offence;

(c) where—

(i) the community order was made by a magistrates' court,

(ii) the offence in respect of which the order was made was not an offence punishable by imprisonment,

(iii) the offender is aged 18 or over, and

(iv) the offender has wilfully and persistently failed to comply with the requirements of the order,

by dealing with him, in respect of that offence, by imposing a sentence of imprisonment for a term not exceeding 51 weeks.

(2) In dealing with an offender under sub-paragraph (1), a magistrates' court must take into account the extent to which the offender has complied with the requirements of the community order.

(3) In dealing with an offender under sub-paragraph (1)(a), the court may extend the duration of particular requirements (subject to any limit imposed by Chapter 4 of Part 12 of this Act) but may not extend the period specified under section 177(5).

(3A) Where—

(a) the court is dealing with the offender under sub-paragraph (1)(a), and

(b) the community order does not contain an unpaid work requirement,

section 199(2)(a) applies in relation to the inclusion of such a requirement as if for "40" there were substituted "20".

(4) In dealing with an offender under sub-paragraph (1)(b), the court may, in the case of an offender who has wilfully and persistently failed to comply with the requirements of the community order, impose a custodial sentence (where the order was made in respect of an offence punishable with such a sentence) notwithstanding anything in section 152(2).

(5) Where a magistrates' court deals with an offender under sub-paragraph (1)(b) or (c), it must revoke the community order if it is still in force.

(5A) Where a magistrates' court dealing with an offender under sub-paragraph (1)(a) would not otherwise have the power to amend the community order under paragraph 16 (amendment by reason of change of residence), that paragraph has effect as if the references to the appropriate court were references to the court dealing with the offender.

(6) Where a community order was made by the Crown Court and a magistrates' court would (apart from this sub-paragraph) be required to deal with the offender under sub-paragraph (1)(a), (b) or (c), it may instead commit him to custody or release him on bail until he can be brought or appear before the Crown Court.

(7) A magistrates' court which deals with an offender's case under subparagraph (6) must send to the Crown Court—

(a) a certificate signed by a justice of the peace certifying that the offender has failed to comply with the requirements of the community order in the respect specified in the certificate, and

(b) such other particulars of the case as may be desirable;

and a certificate purporting to be so signed is admissible as evidence of the failure before the Crown Court.

(8) A person sentenced under sub-paragraph (1)(b) or (c) for an offence may appeal to the Crown Court against the sentence.

Powers of Crown Court

5–187 10.—(1) Where under paragraph 8 or by virtue of paragraph 9(6) an offender appears or is brought before the Crown Court and it is proved to the satisfaction of that court that he has failed without reasonable excuse to comply with any of the requirements of the community order, the Crown Court must deal with him in respect of the failure in any one of the following ways—

(a) by amending the terms of the community order so as to impose more onerous requirements which the Crown Court could impose if it were then making the order;

(b) by dealing with him, for the offence in respect of which the order was made, in any way in which he could have been dealt with for that offence by the court which made the order if the order had not been made;

(c) where—

(i) the offence in respect of which the order was made was not an offence punishable by imprisonment,

(ii) the offender is aged 18 or over,

(iii) the offender has wilfully and persistently failed to comply with the requirements of the order,

by dealing with him, in respect of that offence, by imposing a sentence of imprisonment for a term not exceeding 51 weeks.

(2) In dealing with an offender under sub-paragraph (1), the Crown Court must take into account the extent to which the offender has complied with the requirements of the community order.

(3) In dealing with an offender under sub-paragraph (1)(a), the court may extend the duration of particular requirements (subject to any limit imposed by Chapter 4 of Part 12 of this Act) but may not extend the period specified under section 177(5).

(3A) [*Identical to para. 9(3A),* ante, *§ 5–186.*]

(4) In dealing with an offender under sub-paragraph (1)(b), the Crown Court may, in the case of an offender who has wilfully and persistently failed to comply with the requirements of the community order, impose a custodial sentence (where the order was made in respect of an offence punishable with such a sentence) notwithstanding anything in section 152(2).

(5) Where the Crown Court deals with an offender under sub-paragraph (1)(b) or (c), it must revoke the community order if it is still in force.

(6) In proceedings before the Crown Court under this paragraph any question whether the offender has failed to comply with the requirements of the community order is to be determined by the court and not by the verdict of a jury.

Restriction of powers in paragraphs 9 and 10 where treatment required

11.—(1) An offender who is required by any of the following requirements of a community order— **5–188**

(a) a mental health treatment requirement,

(b) a drug rehabilitation requirement, or

(c) an alcohol treatment requirement,

to submit to treatment for his mental condition, or his dependency on or propensity to misuse drugs or alcohol, is not to be treated for the purposes of paragraph 9 or 10 as having failed to comply with that requirement on the ground only that he had refused to undergo any surgical, electrical or other treatment if, in the opinion of the court, his refusal was reasonable having regard to all the circumstances.

(2) A court may not under paragraph 9(1)(a) or 10(1)(a) amend a mental health treatment requirement, a drug rehabilitation requirement or an alcohol treatment requirement unless the offender expresses his willingness to comply with the requirement as amended.

Supplementary

12. *Where a community order was made by a magistrates' court in the case of an offender under 18 years of age in respect of an offence triable only on indictment in the case of an adult, any powers exercisable under paragraph 9(1)(b) in respect of the offender after he attains the age of 18 are powers to do either or both of the following—* **5–189**

(a) *to impose a fine not exceeding £5,000 for the offence in respect of which the order was made;*

(b) *to deal with the offender for that offence in any way in which a magistrates' court could deal with him if it had just convicted him of an offence punishable with imprisonment for a term not exceeding 51 weeks.*

PART 3

Revocation of Order

Revocation of order with or without re-sentencing: powers of magistrates' court

13.—(1) This paragraph applies where a community order, other than an order made by the Crown Court and falling within paragraph 14(1)(a), is in force and on the application of the offender or the responsible officer it appears to the appropriate magistrates' court that, having regard to circumstances which have arisen since the order was made, it would be in the interests of justice— **5–190**

(a) for the order to be revoked, or

(b) for the offender to be dealt with in some other way for the offence in respect of which the order was made.

(2) The appropriate magistrates' court may—

(a) revoke the order, or

(b) both—

(i) revoke the order, and

(ii) deal with the offender, for the offence in respect of which the order was made, in any way in which it could deal with him if he had just been convicted by the court of the offence.

(3) The circumstances in which a community order may be revoked under subparagraph (2) include the offender's making good progress or his responding satisfactorily to supervision or treatment (as the case requires).

(4) In dealing with an offender under sub-paragraph (2)(b), a magistrates' court must take into account the extent to which the offender has complied with the requirements of the community order.

(5) A person sentenced under sub-paragraph (2)(b) for an offence may appeal to the Crown Court against the sentence.

(6) Where a magistrates' court proposes to exercise its powers under this paragraph otherwise than on the application of the offender, it must summon him to appear before the court and, if he does not appear in answer to the summons, may issue a warrant for his arrest.

(7) In this paragraph "the appropriate magistrates' court" means—

(a) in the case of an order imposing a drug rehabilitation requirement which is subject to review, the magistrates' court responsible for the order, and

(b) in the case of any other community order, a magistrates' court acting for the petty sessions area concerned.

Revocation of order with or without re-sentencing: powers of Crown Court

5–191 14.—(1) This paragraph applies where—

(a) there is in force a community order made by the Crown Court which does not include a direction that any failure to comply with the requirements of the order is to be dealt with by a magistrates' court, and

(b) the offender or the responsible officer applies to the Crown Court for the order to be revoked or for the offender to be dealt with in some other way for the offence in respect of which the order was made.

(2) If it appears to the Crown Court to be in the interests of justice to do so, having regard to circumstances which have arisen since the order was made, the Crown Court may—

(a) revoke the order, or

(b) both—

(i) revoke the order, and

(ii) deal with the offender, for the offence in respect of which the order was made, in any way in which he could have been dealt with for that offence by the court which made the order if the order had not been made.

(3) The circumstances in which a community order may be revoked under subparagraph (2) include the offender's making good progress or his responding satisfactorily to supervision or treatment (as the case requires).

(4) In dealing with an offender under sub-paragraph (2)(b), the Crown Court must take into account the extent to which the offender has complied with the requirements of the order.

(5) Where the Crown Court proposes to exercise its powers under this paragraph otherwise than on the application of the offender, it must summon him to appear before the court and, if he does not appear in answer to the summons, may issue a warrant for his arrest.

Supplementary

5–192 15. *Paragraph 12 applies for the purposes of paragraphs 13 and 14 as it applies for the purposes of paragraph 9 above, but as if for the words "paragraph 9(1)(b)" there were substituted "paragraph 13(2)(b)(ii) or 14(2)(b)(ii)".*

PART 4

Amendment of Order

Amendment by reason of change of residence

5–193 16.—(1) This paragraph applies where, at any time while a community order is in force in respect of an offender, the appropriate court is satisfied that the offender proposes to change, or has changed, his residence from the petty sessions area concerned to another petty sessions area.

(2) Subject to sub-paragraphs (3) and (4), the appropriate court may, and on the application of the responsible officer must, amend the community order by substituting the other petty sessions area for the area specified in the order.

(3) The court may not under this paragraph amend a community order which contains requirements which, in the opinion of the court, cannot be complied with unless the offender continues to reside in the petty sessions area concerned unless, in accordance with paragraph 17, it either—

(a) cancels those requirements, or

(b) substitutes for those requirements other requirements which can be complied with if the offender ceases to reside in that area.

(4) The court may not amend under this paragraph a community order imposing a programme requirement unless it appears to the court that the accredited programme specified in the requirement is available in the other petty sessions area.

(5) In this paragraph "the appropriate court" means—

(a) in relation to any community order imposing a drug rehabilitation requirement which is subject to review, the court responsible for the order,

(b) in relation to any community order which was made by the Crown Court and does not include any direction that any failure to comply with the requirements of the order is to be dealt with by a magistrates' court, the Crown Court, and

(c) in relation to any other community order, a magistrates' court acting for the petty sessions area concerned.

Amendment of requirements of community order

17.—(1) The appropriate court may, on the application of the offender or the responsible officer, by order amend a community order— **5–194**

(a) by cancelling any of the requirements of the order, or

(b) by replacing any of those requirements with a requirement of the same kind, which the court could include if it were then making the order.

(2) The court may not under this paragraph amend a mental health treatment requirement, a drug rehabilitation requirement or an alcohol treatment requirement unless the offender expresses his willingness to comply with the requirement as amended.

(3) If the offender fails to express his willingness to comply with a mental health treatment requirement, drug rehabilitation requirement or alcohol treatment requirement as proposed to be amended by the court under this paragraph, the court may—

(a) revoke the community order, and

(b) deal with him, for the offence in respect of which the order was made, in any way in which he could have been dealt with for that offence by the court which made the order if the order had not been made.

(4) In dealing with the offender under sub-paragraph (3)(b), the court—

(a) must take into account the extent to which the offender has complied with the requirements of the order, and

(b) may impose a custodial sentence (where the order was made in respect of an offence punishable with such a sentence) notwithstanding anything in section 152(2).

(5) *Paragraph 12 applies for the purposes of this paragraph as it applies for the purposes of paragraph 9, but as if for the words "paragraph 9(1)(b)" there were substituted "paragraph 17(3)(b)".*

(6) In this paragraph "the appropriate court" has the same meaning as in paragraph 16.

Amendment of treatment requirements of community order on report of practitioner

18.—(1) Where the medical practitioner or other person by whom or under whose direction an offender is, in pursuance of any requirement to which this subparagraph applies, being treated for his mental condition or his dependency on or propensity to misuse drugs or alcohol— **5–195**

(a) is of the opinion mentioned in sub-paragraph (3), or

(b) is for any reason unwilling to continue to treat or direct the treatment of the offender, he must make a report in writing to that effect to the responsible officer and that officer must apply under paragraph 17 to the appropriate court for the variation or cancellation of the requirement.

(2) The requirements to which sub-paragraph (1) applies are—

(a) a mental health treatment requirement,

(b) a drug rehabilitation requirement, and

(c) an alcohol treatment requirement.

(3) The opinion referred to in sub-paragraph (1) is—

(a) that the treatment of the offender should be continued beyond the period specified in that behalf in the order,

(b) that the offender needs different treatment,

(c) that the offender is not susceptible to treatment, or

(d) that the offender does not require further treatment.

(4) In this paragraph "the appropriate court" has the same meaning as in paragraph 16.

Amendment in relation to review of drug rehabilitation requirement

5–196 19. Where the responsible officer is of the opinion that a community order imposing a drug rehabilitation requirement which is subject to review should be so amended as to provide for each subsequent periodic review (required by section 211) to be made without a hearing instead of at a review hearing, or vice versa, he must apply under paragraph 17 to the court responsible for the order for the variation of the order.

Extension of unpaid work requirement

5–197 20.—(1) Where—

(a) a community order imposing an unpaid work requirement is in force in respect of any offender, and

(b) on the application of the offender or the responsible officer, it appears to the appropriate court that it would be in the interests of justice to do so having regard to circumstances which have arisen since the order was made,

the court may, in relation to the order, extend the period of twelve months specified in section 200(2).

(2) In this paragraph "the appropriate court" has the same meaning as in paragraph 16.

PART 5

Powers of Court in Relation to Order Following Subsequent Conviction

Powers of magistrates' court following subsequent conviction

5–198 21.—(1) This paragraph applies where—

(a) an offender in respect of whom a community order made by a magistrates' court is in force is convicted of an offence by a magistrates' court, and

(b) it appears to the court that it would be in the interests of justice to exercise its powers under this paragraph, having regard to circumstances which have arisen since the community order was made.

(2) The magistrates' court may—

(a), (b) [*identical to para. 14(2)(a), (b)*, ante, *§ 5–191*].

(3) In dealing with an offender under sub-paragraph (2)(b), a magistrates' court must take into account the extent to which the offender has complied with the requirements of the community order.

(4) A person sentenced under sub-paragraph (2)(b) for an offence may appeal to the Crown Court against the sentence.

22.—(1) Where an offender in respect of whom a community order made by the Crown Court is in force is convicted of an offence by a magistrates' court, the magistrates' court may commit the offender in custody or release him on bail until he can be brought before the Crown Court.

(2) Where the magistrates' court deals with an offender's case under sub-paragraph (1), it must send to the Crown Court such particulars of the case as may be desirable.

Powers of Crown Court following subsequent conviction

5–199 23.—(1) This paragraph applies where—

(a) an offender in respect of whom a community order is in force—

(i) is convicted of an offence by the Crown Court, or

(ii) is brought or appears before the Crown Court by virtue of paragraph 22 or having been committed by the magistrates' court to the Crown Court for sentence, and

(b) it appears to the Crown Court that it would be in the interests of justice to exercise its powers under this paragraph, having regard to circumstances which have arisen since the community order was made.

(2) The Crown Court may—

(a), (b) [*identical to para. 14(2)(a), (b)*, ante, *§ 5–191*].

(3) In dealing with an offender under sub-paragraph (2)(b), the Crown Court must take into account the extent to which the offender has complied with the requirements of the community order.

PART 6

Supplementary

24.—(1) No order may be made under paragraph 16, and no application may be made under paragraph 13, 17 or 20, while an appeal against the community order is pending. **5–200**

(2) Sub-paragraph (1) does not apply to an application under paragraph 17 which—

(a) relates to a mental health treatment requirement, a drug rehabilitation requirement or an alcohol treatment requirement, and

(b) is made by the responsible officer with the consent of the offender.

25.—(1) Subject to sub-paragraph (2), where a court proposes to exercise its powers under Part 4 or 5 of this Schedule, otherwise than on the application of the offender, the court—

(a) must summon him to appear before the court, and

(b) if he does not appear in answer to the summons, may issue a warrant for his arrest.

(2) This paragraph does not apply to an order cancelling a requirement of a community order or reducing the period of any requirement, or substituting a new petty sessions area or a new place for the one specified in the order.

[25A.—(1) This paragraph applies to any hearing relating to an offender held by a magistrates' court in any proceedings under this Schedule.

(2) The court may adjourn the hearing, and, where it does so, may—

(a) direct that the offender be released forthwith, or

(b) remand the offender.

(3) Where the court remands the offender under sub-paragraph (2)—

(a) it must fix the time and place at which the hearing is to be resumed, and

(b) that time and place must be the time and place at which the offender is required to appear or be brought before the court by virtue of the remand.

(4) Where the court adjourns the hearing under sub-paragraph (2) but does not remand the offender—

(a) it may fix the time and place at which the hearing is to be resumed, but

(b) if it does not do so, it must not resume the hearing unless it is satisfied that the offender and the responsible officer have had adequate notice of the time and place for the resumed hearing.

(5) The powers of a magistrates' court under this paragraph may be exercised by a single justice of the peace, notwithstanding anything in the *Magistrates' Courts Act* 1980.

(6) This paragraph—

(a) applies to any hearing in any proceedings under this Schedule in place of section 10 of the *Magistrates' Courts Act* 1980 (adjournment of trial) where that section would otherwise apply, but

(b) is not to be taken to affect the application of that section to hearings of any other description.]

26. Paragraphs 9(1)(a), 10(1)(a) and 17(1)(b) have effect subject to the provisions mentioned in subsection (2) of section 177, and to subsections (3) and (6) of that section.

27.—(1) On the making under this Schedule of an order revoking or amending a community order, the proper officer of the court must—

(a) provide copies of the revoking or amending order to the offender and the responsible officer,

(b) in the case of an amending order which substitutes a new petty sessions area, provide a copy of the amending order to—

(i) the local probation board acting for that area, or (as the case may be) a provider of probation services operating in that area, and

(ii) the magistrates' court acting for that area, and

(c) in the case of an amending order which imposes or amends a requirement specified in the first column of Schedule 14, provide a copy of so much of the amending order as relates to that requirement to the person specified in relation to that requirement in the second column of that Schedule, and

(d) where the court acts for a petty sessions area other than the one specified in the order prior to the revocation or amendment, provide a copy of the revoking or amending order to a magistrates' court acting for the area so specified.

(2) Where under sub-paragraph (1)(b) the proper officer of the court provides a copy of an amending order to a magistrates' court acting for a different area, the officer must also provide to that court such documents and information relating to the case as it considers likely to be of assistance to a court acting for that area in the exercise of its functions in relation to the order.

(3) In this paragraph "proper officer" means—

(a) in relation to a magistrates' court, the justices' chief executive for the court; and

(b) in relation to the Crown Court, the appropriate officer.

[Schedule 8 is printed as amended by the *Domestic Violence, Crime and Victims Act* 2004, s.29, and Sched. 5, para. 7; S.I. 2008 No. 912 (*ante*, § 5–164), art. 3, and Sched. 1, para. 14(1) and (17); and the *CJIA* 2008, s.38; and as amended, as from a day to be appointed (as to which, see *ante*, § 5–1), by *ibid.*, ss.6(2) and (3) and 149, Sched. 4, Pt 1, paras 71 and 96 (omission of paras 12, 15 and 17(5)), and Pt 2, paras 106 and 109 (insertion of para. 25A).]

The *Criminal Justice Act 2003 (Sentencing) (Transitory Provisions) Order* 2005 (S.I. 2005 No. 643) modifies Schedule 8 (in relation to any time before the commencement of the repeal of section 78 of the *PCC(S)A* 2000 (*post*, § 5–267)) by substituting the words "6 months" for "51 weeks" in paragraphs 9(1)(c), 10(1)(c) and 12(b). Further, in relation to any time before the coming into force of section 61 of the *CJCSA* 2000, the words "or, in the case of a person aged at least 18 but under 21, detention in a young offender institution" are inserted after "sentence of imprisonment" in paragraphs 9(1)(c), 10(1)(c).

As from a day to be appointed, "community order" in Schedule 8 includes a "service community order" under the *AFA* 2006: 2006 Act, s.181, and Sched. 5, para 1(1). In its application to such an order, Schedule 8 has effect as if paragraphs 2(b), 4, 5(4), 6(2), 7, 9, 12, 13, 15, 16(5), 17(5) and (6), 18(4), 20(2), 21 and 27(1)(b)(ii) and (d), (2) and (3)(a), were omitted: *ibid.*, para. 1(2). Paragraphs 5(1)(b) and 6(1) have effect in relation to a service community order as if the references to a justice of the peace were to the Crown Court: *ibid.*, para. 2. Paragraph 8 applies to such an order as it applies to an order mentioned in sub-paragraph (1) of that paragraph: *ibid.*, para. 3. Paragraph 14 has effect as if the reference in sub-paragraph (1)(a) to a community order as there mentioned included a service community order: *ibid.*, para. 4. In Part 4, as it applies to a service community order, "the appropriate court" means the Crown Court: *ibid.*, para. 5. In paragraph 19, as it applies to such an order, "the court responsible for the order" means the Crown Court: *ibid.*, para. 6. Paragraph 22 has effect as if the reference in sub-paragraph (1)(a) to a community order made by the Crown Court included a service community order: *ibid.*, para. 7. Paragraph 8 of Schedule 5 to the 2006 Act modifies the re-sentencing powers of the Crown Court under paragraphs 10(1)(b), 14(2)(b)(ii), 17(3)(b) and 23(2)(ii) in relation to a service community order. In essence, the Crown Court may deal with the offender as if he had just been convicted before it of the offence for which the order was made, but if the order was made by the Service Civilian Court, any term of imprisonment must not exceed 12 months and any fine must not exceed the prescribed sum. Where sentence is passed by virtue of paragraph 8, the *CAA* 1968, s.9 (*post*, § 7–118) applies as if the offender had been convicted on indictment of the offence for which the sentence was passed: *ibid.*, para. 9.

Reasonable excuse (paras 9 and 10)

5–200a The mere fact that a person who is the subject of a community order has lodged an appeal against the making of the order or against the conviction on which it is founded cannot amount to a "reasonable excuse" for non-compliance with the order: *West Midlands Probation Board v. Sadler* [2008] 1 W.L.R. 918, DC.

Sentencing guidelines

For the guidelines issued by the Sentencing Guidelines Council on breach of community sentences under the *CJA* 2003, see Appendix K–44. **5–200b**

Crediting time on remand in custody

As to the need to give credit for time on remand in custody when re-sentencing to a custodial sentence, see *R. v. Stickley*, *post*, § 5–368d. **5–200c**

(2) Of youth community orders

(a) *Curfew and exclusion orders*

Powers of Criminal Courts (Sentencing) Act 2000, Sched. 3

SCHEDULE 3

BREACH, REVOCATION AND AMENDMENT OF CURFEW ORDERS AND EXCLUSION ORDERS

PART 1

Preliminary

[Definitions

1. *In this Schedule—* **5–201**

"the petty sessions area concerned" means—

(a) *in relation to a curfew order, the petty sessions area in which the place for the time being specified in the order is situated; and*

(b) *in relation to an exclusion order, the petty sessions area for the time being specified in the order;*

"relevant order" means a curfew order or an exclusion order.

Orders made on appeal

2. *Where a relevant order has been made on appeal, for the purposes of this Schedule it shall be deemed—*

(a) *if it was made on an appeal brought from a magistrates' court, to have been made by a magistrates' court;*

(b) *if it was made on an appeal brought from the Crown Court or from the criminal division of the Court of Appeal, to have been made by the Crown Court.*

PART 2

Breach of Requirement of Order

Issue of summons or warrant

3.—(1) *If at any time while a relevant order is in force in respect of an offender it appears on information to a justice of the peace that the offender has failed to comply with any of the requirements of the order, the justice may—* **5–202**

(a) *issue a summons requiring the offender to appear at the place and time specified in it; or*

(b) *if the information is in writing and on oath, issue a warrant for his arrest.*

(2) *Any summons or warrant issued under this paragraph shall direct the offender to appear or be brought—*

(a) *in the case of any relevant order which was made by the Crown Court and included a direction that any failure to comply with any of the requirements of the order be dealt with by the Crown Court, before the Crown Court; and*

(b) *in the case of a relevant order which is not an order to which paragraph (a) above applies, before a magistrates' court acting for the petty sessions area in which the offendcr resides or, if it is not known where he resides, before a magistrates' court acting for the petty sessions area concerned.*

(3) *Where a summons issued under sub-paragraph (1)(a) above requires an offender to appear before the Crown Court and the offender does not appear in answer to the summons, the Crown Court may issue a further summons requiring the offender to appear at the place and time specified in it.*

(4) *Where a summons issued under sub-paragraph (1)(a) above or a further summons issued under sub-paragraph (3) above requires an offender to appear before the Crown Court and the offender does not appear in answer to the summons, the Crown Court may issue a warrant for the arrest of the offender.*

Powers of magistrates' court

5–203 4.—(1) *This paragraph applies if it is proved to the satisfaction of a magistrates' court before which an offender appears or is brought under paragraph 3 above that he has failed without reasonable excuse to comply with any of the requirements of the relevant order.*

(2) *The magistrates' court may deal with the offender in respect of the failure in one of the following ways (and must deal with him in one of those ways if the relevant order is in force)—*

(a) *by making a curfew order in respect of him (subject to paragraph 7 below);*

(b) *by making an attendance centre order in respect of him (subject to paragraph 8 below); or*

(c) *where the relevant order was made by a magistrates' court, by dealing with him, for the offence in respect of which the order was made, in any way in which he could have been dealt with for that offence by the court which made the order if the order had not been made.*

(3) *In dealing with an offender under sub-paragraph (2)(c) above, a magistrates' court—*

(a) *shall take into account the extent to which the offender has complied with the requirements of the relevant order; and*

(b) *in the case of an offender who has wilfully and persistently failed to comply with those requirements, may impose a custodial sentence (where the relevant order was made in respect of an offence punishable with such a sentence) notwithstanding anything in section 152(2) of the* Criminal Justice Act *2003.*

(4) *Where a magistrates' court deals with an offender under sub-paragraph (2)(c) above, it shall revoke the relevant order if it is still in force.*

(4A) *Where a magistrates' court dealing with an offender under sub-paragraph (2)(a) or (b) above would not otherwise have the power to amend the relevant order under paragraph 15 below (amendment by reason of change or residence), that paragraph has effect as if the reference to a magistrates' court acting for the petty sessions area concerned were a reference to the court dealing with the offender.*

(5) *Where a relevant order was made by the Crown Court and a magistrates' court has power to deal with the offender under sub-paragraph (2)(a) or (b) above, it may instead commit him to custody or release him on bail until he can be brought or appear before the Crown Court.*

(6) *A magistrates' court which deals with an offender's case under sub-paragraph (5) above shall send to the Crown Court—*

(a) *a certificate signed by a justice of the peace certifying that the offender has failed to comply with the requirements of the relevant order in the respect specified in the certificate; and*

(b) *such other particulars of the case as may be desirable;*

and a certificate purporting to be so signed shall be admissible as evidence of the failure before the Crown Court.

(7) *A person sentenced under sub-paragraph (2)(c) above for an offence may appeal to the Crown Court against the sentence.*

Powers of Crown Court

5–204 5.—(1) *This paragraph applies where under paragraph 3 or by virtue of paragraph 4(5) above an offender is brought or appears before the Crown Court and it is proved to the satisfaction of that court that he has failed without reasonable excuse to comply with any of the requirements of the relevant order.*

(2) *The Crown Court may deal with the offender in respect of the failure in one of the following ways (and must deal with him in one of those ways if the relevant order is in force)—*

(a) *by making a curfew order in respect of him (subject to paragraph 7 below);*

(b) *by making an attendance centre order in respect of him (subject to paragraph 8 below); or*

(c) *by dealing with him, for the offence in respect of which the order was made, in any way in which he could have been dealt with for that offence by the court which made the order if the order had not been made.*

(3) *In dealing with an offender under sub-paragraph (2)(c) above, the Crown Court—*

(a) *shall take into account the extent to which the offender has complied with the requirements of the relevant order; and*

(b) *in the case of an offender who has wilfully and persistently failed to comply with those requirements, may impose a custodial sentence (where the relevant order was made in respect of an offence punishable with such a sentence) notwithstanding anything in section 152(2) of the* Criminal Justice Act *2003.*

(4) *Where the Crown Court deals with an offender under subparagraph (2)(c) above, it shall revoke the relevant order if it is still in force.*

(5) *In proceedings before the Crown Court under this paragraph any question whether the offender has failed to comply with the requirements of the relevant order shall be determined by the court and not by the verdict of a jury.*

Exclusions from paragraphs 4 and 5

6. *Without prejudice to paragraphs 10 and 11 below, an offender who is convicted of a further offence while a relevant order is in force in respect of him shall not on that account be liable to be dealt with under paragraph 4 or 5 in respect of a failure to comply with any requirement of the order.*

Curfew orders imposed for a breach of relevant order

7.—(1) *Section 37 of this Act (curfew orders) shall apply for the purposes of paragraphs* **5–205**
4(2)(a) and 5(2)(a) above as if for the words from the beginning to "make" there were substituted "Where a court has power to deal with an offender under Part 2 of Schedule 3 to this Act for failure to comply with any of the requirements of a relevant order, the court may make in respect of the offender".

(2) *The following provisions of this Act, namely—*

(a) *section 37(3) to (12), and*

(b) *so far as applicable, sections 36B and 40 and this Schedule so far as relating to curfew orders;*

have effect in relation to a curfew order made by virtue of paragraphs 4(2)(a) and 5(2)(a) as they have effect in relation to any other curfew order, subject to sub-paragraph (3) below.

(3) *This Schedule shall have effect in relation to such a curfew order as if—*

(a) *the power conferred on the court by each of paragraphs 4(2)(c) , 5(2)(c) and 10(3)(b) to deal with the offender for the offence in respect of which the order was made were a power to deal with the offender, for his failure to comply with the relevant order, in any way in which the appropriate court could deal with him for that failure if it had just been proved to the satisfaction of the court;*

(b) *the reference in paragraph 10(1)(b) to the offence in respect of which the order was made were a reference to the failure to comply in respect of which the curfew order was made; and*

(c) *the power conferred on the Crown Court by paragraph 11(2)(b) to deal with the offender for the offence in respect of which the order was made were a power to deal with the offender, for his failure to comply with the relevant order, in any way in which the appropriate court (if the relevant order was made by the magistrates' court) or the Crown Court (if that order was made by the Crown Court) could deal with him for that failure if it had just been proved to its satisfaction.*

(4) *For the purposes of the provisions mentioned in paragraphs (a) and (c) of sub-paragraph (3) above, as applied by that subparagraph, if the relevant order is no longer in force the appropriate court's powers shall be determined on the assumption that it is still in force.*

(5) *Sections 148 and 156 of the* Criminal Justice Act *2003 (restrictions and procedural requirements for community sentences) do not apply in relation to a curfew order made by virtue of paragraph 4(2)(a) or 5(2)(a) above.*

Attendance centre orders imposed for breach of relevant order

8.—(1) *Section 60(1) of this Act (attendance centre orders) shall apply for the purposes of paragraphs 4(2)(b) and 5(2)(b) above as if for the words from the beginning to "the court may," there were substituted "Where a court has power to deal with an offender under Part 2 of Schedule 3 to this Act for failure to comply with any of the requirements of a relevant order, the court may,".*

(2) *The following provisions of this Act, namely—*

(a) *subsections (3) to (11) of section 60, and*

(b) *so far as applicable, section 36B and Schedule 5,*

have effect in relation to an attendance centre order made by virtue of paragraph 4(2)(b) or 5(2)(b) above as they have effect in relation to any other attendance centre order, but as if there were omitted from each of paragraphs 2(1)(b) , 3(1) and 4(3) of Schedule 5 the words ", for the offence in respect of which the order was made," and "for that offence".

(3) *Sections 148 and 156 of the* Criminal Justice Act *2003 (restrictions and procedural requirements for community sentences) do not apply in relation to an attendance centre order made by virtue of paragraph 4(2)(b) or 5(2)(b) above.*

Supplementary

9. *Any exercise by a court of its powers under paragraph 4(2)(a) or (b) or 5(2)(a) or (b) above shall be without prejudice to the continuance of the relevant order.*

PART 3

Revocation of Order

Revocation of order with or without re-sentencing: powers of magistrates' court

5–206 10.—(1) *This paragraph applies where a relevant order made by a magistrates' court is in force in respect of any offender and on the application of the offender or the responsible officer it appears to the appropriate magistrates' court that, having regard to circumstances which have arisen since the order was made, it would be in the interests of justice—*

(a) *for the order to be revoked; or*

(b) *for the offender to be dealt with in some other way for the offence in respect of which the order was made.*

(2) *In this paragraph "the appropriate magistrates' court" means a magistrates' court acting for the petty sessions area concerned.*

(3) *The appropriate magistrates' court may—*

(a) *revoke the order; or*

(b) *both—*

(i) *revoke the order; and*

(ii) *deal with the offender for the offence in respect of which the order was made, in any way in which he could have been dealt with for that offence by the court which made the order if the order had not been made.*

(4) *In dealing with an offender under sub-paragraph (3)(b) above, a magistrates' court shall take into account the extent to which the offender has complied with the requirements of the relevant order.*

(5) *A person sentenced under sub-paragraph (3)(b) above for an offence may appeal to the Crown Court against the sentence.*

(6) *Where a magistrates' court proposes to exercise its powers under this paragraph otherwise than on the application of the offender, it shall summon him to appear before the court and, if he does not appear in answer to the summons, may issue a warrant for his arrest.*

(7) *No application may be made by the offender under subparagraph (1) above while an appeal against the relevant order is pending.*

Revocation of order with or without re-sentencing: powers of Crown Court on conviction etc.

5–207 11.—(1) *This paragraph applies where—*

(a) *a relevant order made by the Crown Court is in force in respect of an offender and the offender or the responsible officer applies to the Crown Court for the order to be revoked or for the offender to be dealt with in some other way for the offence in respect of which the order was made; or*

(b) *an offender in respect of whom a relevant order is in force is convicted of an offence before the Crown Court or, having been committed by a magistrates' court to the Crown Court for sentence, is brought or appears before the Crown Court.*

(2) *If it appears to the Crown Court to be in the interests of justice to do so, having regard to circumstances which have arisen since the order was made, the Crown Court may—*

(a), (b) [identical to para. 10(3)(a), (b), *ante*, § 5–206].

(3) *In dealing with an offender under sub-paragraph (2)(b) above, the Crown Court shall take into account the extent to which the offender has complied with the requirements of the relevant order.*

Revocation following custodial sentence by magistrates' court unconnected with order

12.—(1) *This paragraph applies where—* **5–208**

(a) *an offender in respect of whom a relevant order is in force is convicted of an offence by a magistrates' court unconnected with the order;*

(b) *the court imposes a custodial sentence on the offender; and*

(c) *it appears to the court, on the application of the offender or the responsible officer, that it would be in the interests of justice to exercise its powers under this paragraph having regard to circumstances which have arisen since the order was made.*

(2) *In sub-paragraph (1) above "a magistrates' court unconnected with the order" means a magistrates' court not acting for the petty sessions area concerned.*

(3) *The court may—*

(a) *if the order was made by a magistrates' court, revoke it;*

(b) *if the order was made by the Crown Court, commit the offender in custody or release him on bail until he can be brought or appear before the Crown Court.*

(4) *Where the court deals with an offender's case under subparagraph (3)(b) above, it shall send to the Crown Court such particulars of the case as may be desirable.*

13. *Where by virtue of paragraph 12(3)(b) above an offender is brought or appears before the Crown Court and it appears to the Crown Court to be in the interests of justice to do so, having regard to circumstances which have arisen since the relevant order was made, the Crown Court may revoke the order.*

Supplementary

14.—(1) *On the making under this Part of this Schedule of an order revoking a relevant order, the proper officer of the court shall forthwith give copies of the revoking order to the responsible officer.*

(2) *In sub-paragraph (1) above "proper officer" means—*

(a) *in relation to a magistrates' court, the justices' chief executive for the court; and*

(b) *in relation to the Crown Court, the appropriate officer.*

(3) *A responsible officer to whom in accordance with sub-paragraph (1) above copies of a revoking order are given shall give a copy to the offender and to the person in charge of any institution in which the offender was required by the order to reside.*

PART 4

Amendment of Order

Amendment by reason of change of residence

15.—(1) *This paragraph applies where, at any time while a relevant order is in force in respect of an offender, a magistrates' court acting for the petty sessions area concerned is satisfied that the offender proposes to change, or has changed, his residence from that petty sessions area to another petty sessions area.* **5–209**

(2) *Subject to sub-paragraph (3) below, the court may, and on the application of the responsible officer shall, amend the relevant order by substituting the other petty sessions area for the area specified in the order or, in the case of a curfew order, a place in that other area for the place so specified.*

(3) *The court shall not amend under this paragraph a curfew order which contains requirements which, in the opinion of the court, cannot be complied with unless the offender continues to reside in the petty sessions area concerned unless, in accordance with paragraph 16 below, it either—*

(a) *cancels those requirements; or*

(b) *substitutes for those requirements other requirements which can be complied with if the offender ceases to reside in that area.*

Amendment of requirements of order

16.—(1) *Without prejudice to the provisions of paragraph 15 above but subject to the following provisions of this paragraph, a magistrates' court acting for the petty sessions area concerned may, on the application of an eligible person, by order amend a relevant order—*

(a) *by cancelling any of the requirements of the order; or*

(b) *by inserting in the order (either in addition to or in substitution for any of its requirements) any requirement which the court could include if it were then making the order.*

(2) *A magistrates' court shall not under sub-paragraph (1) above amend a curfew order by extending the curfew periods beyond the end of six months from the date of the original order.*

(3) *A magistrates' court shall not under sub-paragraph (1) above amend an exclusion order by extending the period for which the offender is prohibited from entering the place in question beyond the end of three months from the date of the original order.*

(4) *For the purposes of this paragraph the eligible persons are—*

(a) *the offender;*

(b) *the responsible officer; and*

(c) *in relation to an exclusion order, any affected person.*

But an application under sub-paragraph (1) by a person such as is mentioned in paragraph (c) above must be for the cancellation of a requirement which was included in the order by virtue of his consent or for the purpose (or partly for the purpose) of protecting him from being approached by the offender, or for the insertion of a requirement which will, if inserted, be such a requirement.

Supplementary

5–210 17. *No order may be made under paragraph 15 above, and no application may be made under paragraph 16 above, while an appeal against the relevant order is pending.*

18.—(1) *Subject to sub-paragraph (2) below, where a court proposes to exercise its powers under this Part of this Schedule, otherwise than on the application of the offender, the court—*

(a) *shall summon him to appear before the court; and*

(b) *if he does not appear in answer to the summons, may issue a warrant for his arrest.*

(2) *This paragraph shall not apply to an order cancelling a requirement of a relevant order or reducing the period of any requirement, or to an order under paragraph 15 above substituting a new petty sessions area or a new place for the one specified in a relevant order.*

19.—(1) *On the making under this Part of this Schedule of an order amending a relevant order, the justices' chief executive for the court shall forthwith—*

(a) *if the order amends the relevant order otherwise than by substituting, by virtue of paragraph 15 above, a new petty session area or a new place for the one specified in the relevant order, give copies of the amending order to the responsible officer;*

(b) *if the order amends the relevant order in the manner excepted by paragraph (a) above, send to the chief executive to the justices for the new petty sessions area or, as the case may be, for the petty sessions area in which the new place is situated—*

(i) *copies of the amending order; and*

(ii) *such documents and information relating to the case as he considers likely to be of assistance to a court acting for that area in the exercise of its functions in relation to the order;*

and in a case falling within paragraph (b) above the chief executive of the justices for that area shall give copies of the amending order to the responsible officer.

(2) *A responsible officer to whom in accordance with sub-paragraph (1) above copies of an order are given shall give a copy to the offender and to the person in charge of any institution in which the offender is or was required by the order to reside.]*

[Schedule 3 is printed as substituted, as from April 4, 2009 (S.I. 2005 No. 950 (as amended by S.I. 2007 No. 391), *ante*, § 5–121e), by the *CJA* 2003, s.304, and Sched. 32, para. 125. It is printed as amended by the *Domestic Violence, Crime and Victims Act* 2004, s.29, and Sched. 5, para. 5. The whole of the substituted Schedule 3 is repealed as from a day to be appointed (as to which, see *ante*, §§ 5–1, 5–121e, 5–122) by the *CJIA* 2008, ss.6(1) and 149, and Sched. 28, Pt 1. For the original Schedule 3, see §§ 5–123p *et seq.* in the supplement.]

(b) *Attendance centre orders*

Powers of Criminal Courts (Sentencing) Act 2000, Sched. 5

Section 61 SCHEDULE 5

BREACH, REVOCATION AND AMENDMENT OF ATTENDANCE CENTRE ORDERS

Breach of order or attendance centre rules

5–211 1.—(1) *Where an attendance centre order is in force and it appears on information to a justice that the offender—*

(a) *has failed to attend in accordance with the order, or*

(b) *while attending has committed a breach of rules made under section 222(1)(d) or (e) of the* Criminal Justice Act *2003 which cannot be adequately dealt with under those rules,*

the justice may issue a summons requiring the offender to appear at the place and time specified in the summons or, if the information is in writing and on oath, may issue a warrant for the offender's arrest.

(2) *Any summons or warrant issued under this paragraph shall direct the offender to appear or be brought—*

(a) *before a magistrates' court acting for the petty sessions area in which the offender resides; or*

(b) *if it is not known where the offender resides, before a magistrates' court acting for the petty sessions area in which is situated the attendance centre which the offender is required to attend by the order or by virtue of an order under paragraph 5(1)(b) below.*

2.—(1) *If it is proved to the satisfaction of the magistrates' court before which an offender appears or is brought under paragraph 1 above that he has failed without reasonable excuse to attend as mentioned in sub-paragraph (1)(a) of that paragraph or has committed such a breach of rules as is mentioned in sub-paragraph (1)(b) of that paragraph, that court may deal with him in any one of the following ways—*

(a) *it may impose on him a fine not exceeding £1,000;*

(b) *where the attendance centre order was made by a magistrates' court, it may deal with him, for the offence in respect of which the order was made, in any way in which he could have been dealt with for that offence by the court which made the order if the order had not been made; or*

(c) *where the order was made by the Crown Court, it may commit him to custody or release him on bail until he can be brought or appear before the Crown Court.*

(2) *Any exercise by the court of its power under sub-paragraph (1)(a) above shall be without prejudice to the continuation of the order.*

(3) *A fine imposed under sub-paragraph (1)(a) above shall be deemed, for the purposes of any enactment, to be a sum adjudged to be paid by a conviction.*

(4) *Where a magistrates' court deals with an offender under sub-paragraph (1)(b) above, it shall revoke the attendance centre order if it is still in force.*

(5) *In dealing with an offender under sub-paragraph (1)(b) above, a magistrates' court—*

(a) *shall take into account the extent to which the offender has complied with the requirements of the attendance centre order; and*

(b) *in the case of an offender who has wilfully and persistently failed to comply with those requirements, may impose a custodial sentence notwithstanding anything in section 152(2) of the* Criminal Justice Act *2003.*

(5A) *Where a magistrates' court dealing with an offender under sub-paragraph (1)(a) above would not otherwise have the power to amend the order under paragraph 5(1)(b) below (substitution of different attendance centre), that paragraph has effect as if references to an appropriate magistrates' court were references to the court dealing with an offender.*

(6) *A person sentenced under sub-paragraph (1)(b) above for an offence may appeal to the Crown Court against the sentence.*

(7) *A magistrates' court which deals with an offender's case under sub-paragraph (1)(c) above shall send to the Crown Court—*

(a) *a certificate signed by a justice of the peace giving particulars of the offender's failure to attend or, as the case may be, the breach of the rules which he has committed; and*

(b) *such other particulars of the case as may be desirable;*

and a certificate purporting to be so signed shall be admissible as evidence of the failure or the breach before the Crown Court.

3.—(1) *Where by virtue of paragraph 2(1)(c) above the offender is brought or appears before the Crown Court and it is proved to the satisfaction of the court—*

(a) *that he has failed without reasonable excuse to attend as mentioned in paragraph 1(1)(a) above, or*

(b) *that he has committed such a breach of rules as is mentioned in paragraph 1(1)(b) above,*

that court may deal with him, for the offence in respect of which the order was made, in any way in which it could have dealt with him for that offence if it had not made the order.

(2) *Where the Crown Court deals with an offender under sub-paragraph (1) above, it shall revoke the attendance centre order if it is still in force.*

(3) *In dealing with an offender under sub-paragraph (1) above, the Crown Court—*

(a) *shall take into account the extent to which the offender has complied with the requirements of the attendance centre order; and*

(b) *in the case of an offender who has willfully and persistently failed to comply with those requirements, may impose a custodial sentence notwithstanding anything in section 152(2) of the* Criminal Justice Act *2003.*

(4) *In proceedings before the Crown Court under this paragraph any question whether there has been a failure to attend or a breach of the rules shall be determined by the court and not by the verdict of a jury.*

Revocation of order with or without re-sentencing

5–212 4.—(1) *Where an attendance centre order is in force in respect of an offender, an appropriate court may, on an application made by the offender or by the officer in charge of the relevant attendance centre, revoke the order.*

(2) *In sub-paragraph (1) above "an appropriate court" means—*

(a) *where the court which made the order was the Crown Court and there is included in the order a direction that the power to revoke the order is reserved to that court, the Crown Court;*

(b) *in any other case, either of the following—*

(i) *a magistrates' court acting for the petty sessions area in which the relevant attendance centre is situated;*

(ii) *the court which made the order.*

(3) *Any power conferred by this paragraph—*

(a) *on a magistrates' court to revoke an attendance centre order made by such a court, or*

(b) *on the Crown Court to revoke an attendance centre order made by the Crown Court,*

includes power to deal with the offender, for the offence in respect of which the order was made, in any way in which he could have been dealt with for that offence by the court which made the order if the order had not been made.

(4) *A person sentenced by a magistrates' court under sub-paragraph (3) above for an offence may appeal to the Crown Court against the sentence.*

(5) *The proper officer of a court which makes an order under this paragraph revoking an attendance centre order shall—*

(a) *deliver a copy of the revoking order to the offender or send a copy by registered post or the recorded delivery service addressed to the offender's last or usual place of abode; and*

(b) *deliver or send a copy to the officer in charge of the relevant attendance centre.*

(6) *In this paragraph "the relevant attendance centre", in relation to an attendance centre order, means the attendance centre specified in the order or substituted for the attendance centre so specified by an order made by virtue of paragraph 5(1)(b) below.*

(7) *In this paragraph "proper officer" means—*

(a) *in relation to a magistrates' court, the justices' chief executive for the court; and*

(b) *in relation to the Crown Court, the appropriate officer.*

Amendment of order

5–213 5.—(1) *Where an attendance centre order is in force in respect of an offender, an appropriate magistrates' court may, on application made by the offender or by the officer in charge of the relevant attendance centre, by order—*

(a) *vary the day or hour specified in the order for the offender's first attendance at the relevant attendance centre; or*

(b) *substitute for the relevant attendance centre an attendance centre which the court is satisfied is reasonably accessible to the offender, having regard to his age, the means of access available to him and any other circumstances.*

(2) *In sub-paragraph (1) above "an appropriate magistrates' court" means—*

(a) *a magistrates' court acting for the petty sessions area in which the relevant attendance centre is situated; or*

(b) *(except where the attendance centre order was made by the Crown Court) the magistrates' court which made the order.*

(3) *The justices' chief executive for a court which makes an order under this paragraph shall—*

(a) *deliver a copy to the offender or send a copy by registered post or the recorded delivery service addressed to the offender's last or usual place of abode; and*

(b) *deliver or send a copy—*

(i) *if the order is made by virtue of sub-paragraph (1)(a) above, to the officer in charge of the relevant attendance centre; and*

(ii) *if it is made by virtue of sub-paragraph (1)(b) above, to the officer in charge of the attendance centre which the order as amended will require the offender to attend.*

(4) *In this paragraph "the relevant attendance centre" has the meaning given by paragraph 4(6) above.*

Orders made on appeal

6.—(1) *Where an attendance centre order has been made on appeal, for the purposes of this Schedule it shall be deemed—* **5–214**

(a) *if it was made on an appeal brought from a magistrates' court, to have been made by that magistrates' court;*

(b) *if it was made on an appeal brought from the Crown Court or from the criminal division of the Court of Appeal, to have been made by the Crown Court.*

(2) *In relation to an attendance centre order made on appeal, paragraphs 2(1)(b) and 4(3) above shall each have effect as if the words "if the order had not been made" were omitted and paragraph 3(1) above shall have effect as if the words "if it had not made the order" were omitted.*

Orders for defaulters

7.—(1) *References in this Schedule to an "offender" include a person who has been ordered to attend at an attendance centre for such a default or failure as is mentioned in section 60(1)(b) or (c) of this Act.* **5–215**

(2) *Where a person has been ordered to attend at an attendance centre for such a default or failure—*

(a) *paragraphs 2(1)(b) , 3(1) and 4(3) above shall each have effect in relation to the order as if the words ", for the offence in respect of which the order was made," and "for that offence" were omitted; and*

(b) *paragraphs 2(5)(b) and 3(3)(b) above (which relate to custodial sentences for offences) do not apply.*

[This Schedule is printed as amended by the *CJA* 2003, s.304, and Sched. 32, paras 90 and 126; and the *Domestic Violence, Crime and Victims Act* 2004, s.29, and Sched. 5, para. 6. The whole schedule is repealed as from a day to be appointed (as to which, see *ante*, §§ 5–1, 5–121e, 5–122) by the *CJIA* 2008, ss.6(1) and 149, and Sched. 28, Pt 1.]

When dealing with an offender under paragraph 3(1), the court must observe any limitations related to his age which applied at the time when he was sentenced: he must be sentenced on the basis of his age when he was originally convicted of the offence for which the attendance centre order was made. **5–216**

In a case coming within paragraph 4, the failure to attend the attendance centre, or breach of the rules, must be proved to the satisfaction of the Crown Court: the certificate of the magistrates' court is merely evidence.

(c) *Supervision orders*

Powers of Criminal Courts (Sentencing) Act 2000, Sched. 7

Section 65 SCHEDULE 7

BREACH, REVOCATION AND AMENDMENT OF SUPERVISION ORDERS

Meaning of "relevant court", etc.

1.—(1) *In this Schedule, "relevant court", in relation to a supervision order, means—* **5–217**

(a) *where the offender is under the age of 18, a youth court acting for the petty sessions area for the time being named in the order in pursuance of section 63(6) of this Act;*

(b) *where the offender has attained that age, a magistrates' court other than a youth court, being a magistrates' court acting for the petty sessions area for the time being so named.*

(2) *If an application to a youth court is made in pursuance of this Schedule and while it is pending the offender to whom it relates attains the age of 18, the youth court shall deal with the application as if he had not attained that age.*

Breach of requirement of supervision order

5–218 2.—(1) *This paragraph applies if while a supervision order is in force in respect of an offender it is proved to the satisfaction of a relevant court, on the application of the supervisor, that the offender has failed to comply with any requirement included in the supervision order in pursuance of paragraph 1 , 2 , 3 , 5 , 5A [, 6A] or 7 of Schedule 6 to this Act or section 63(6)(b) of this Act.*

(2) *Where this paragraph applies, the court—*

(a) *whether or not it also makes an order under paragraph 5(1) below (revocation or amendment of supervision order)—*

  (i) *may order the offender to pay a fine of an amount not exceeding £1,000; or*

  (ii) *subject to sub-paragraph (2A) below and paragraph 3 below, may make a curfew order in respect of him; or*

  (iii) *subject to paragraph 4 below, may make an attendance centre order in respect of him; or*

(b) *if the supervision order was made by a magistrates' court, may revoke the supervision order and deal with the offender, for the offence in respect of which the order was made, in any way in which he could have been dealt with for that offence by the court which made the order if the order had not been made; or*

(c) *if the supervision order was made by the Crown Court, may commit him in custody or release him on bail until he can be brought or appear before the Crown Court.*

(2A) *The court may not make a curfew order under sub-paragraph (2)(a)(ii) above in respect of an offender who is already subject to a curfew order.*

(3) *Where a court deals with an offender under sub-paragraph (2)(c) above, it shall send to the Crown Court a certificate signed by a justice of the peace giving—*

(a) *particulars of the offender's failure to comply with the requirement in question; and*

(b) *such other particulars of the case as may be desirable;*

and a certificate purporting to be so signed shall be admissible as evidence of the failure before the Crown Court.

(4) *Where—*

(a) *by virtue of sub-paragraph (2)(c) above the offender is brought or appears before the Crown Court, and*

(b) *it is proved to the satisfaction of the court that he has failed to comply with the requirement in question,*

that court may deal with him, for the offence in respect of which the supervision order was made, in any way in which it could have dealt with him for that offence if it had not made the order.

(5) *Where the Crown Court deals with an offender under sub-paragraph (4) above, it shall revoke the supervision order if it is still in force.*

(6) *A fine imposed under this paragraph shall be deemed, for the purposes of any enactment, to be a sum adjudged to be paid by a conviction.*

(7) *In dealing with an offender under this paragraph, a court shall take into account the extent to which he has complied with the requirements of the supervision order.*

(8) *Where a supervision order has been made on appeal, for the purposes of this paragraph it shall be deemed—*

(a) *if it was made on an appeal brought from a magistrates' court, to have been made by that magistrates' court;*

(b) *if it was made on an appeal brought from the Crown Court or from the criminal division of the Court of Appeal, to have been made by the Crown Court;*

and, in relation to a supervision order made on appeal, sub-paragraph (2)(b) above shall have effect as if the words "if the order had not been made" were omitted and sub-paragraph (4) above shall have effect as if the words "if it had not made the order" were omitted.

(9) *This paragraph has effect subject to paragraph 7 below.*

Curfew orders imposed for breach of supervision order

3.—(1) *Section 37(1) of this Act (curfew orders) shall apply for the purposes of paragraph 2(2)(a)(ii) above as if for the words from the beginning to "make" there were substituted "Where a court considers it appropriate to make an order in respect of any person in pursuance of paragraph 2(2)(a)(ii) of Schedule 7 to this Act, it may make".* **5–219**

(2) *The following provisions of this Act, namely—*

(a) *section 37(3) to (12), and*

(b) *so far as applicable, sections 36B and 40 and Schedule 3 so far as relating to curfew orders,*

have effect in relation to a curfew order made by virtue of paragraph 2(2)(a)(ii) above as they have effect in relation to any other curfew order, subject to sub-paragraph (5) below.

(3) *Sections 148 and 156 of the* Criminal Justice Act *2003 (restrictions and procedural requirements for community sentences) do not apply in relation to a curfew order made by virtue of paragraph 2(2)(a)(ii) above.*

(5) *Schedule 3 to this Act (breach, revocation and amendment of orders) shall have effect in relation to such a curfew order as if—*

(a) *the power conferred on the court by each of paragraphs 4(2)(c) and 10(3)(b) to deal with the offender for the offence in respect of which the order was made were a power to deal with the offender, for his failure to comply with the supervision order, in any way in which a relevant court could deal with him for that failure if it had just been proved to the satisfaction of that court;*

(b) *the reference in paragraph 10(1)(b) to the offence in respect of which the order was made were a reference to the failure to comply in respect of which the curfew order was made; and*

(c) *the power conferred on the Crown Court by paragraph 11(2)(b) to deal with the offender for the offence in respect of which the order was made were a power to deal with the offender, for his failure to comply with the supervision order, in any way in which a relevant court (if the supervision order was made by a magistrates' court) or the Crown Court (if the supervision order was made by the Crown Court) could deal with him for that failure if it had just been proved to its satisfaction.*

(6) *For the purposes of the provisions mentioned in paragraphs (a) and (c) of sub-paragraph (5) above, as applied by that sub-paragraph, if the supervision order is no longer in force the relevant court's powers shall be determined on the assumption that it is still in force.*

Attendance centre orders imposed for breach of supervision order

4.—(1) *Section 60(1) of this Act (attendance centre orders) shall apply for the purposes of paragraph 2(2)(a)(iii) above as if for the words from the beginning to "the court may," there were substituted "Where a court considers it appropriate to make an order in respect of any person in pursuance of paragraph 2(2)(a)(iii) of Schedule 7 to this Act, the court may,".* **5–220**

(2) *The following provisions of this Act, namely—*

(a) *subsections (3) to (11) of section 60, and*

(b) *so far as applicable, Schedule 5,*

have effect in relation to an attendance centre order made by virtue of paragraph 2(2)(a)(iii) above as they have effect in relation to any other attendance centre order, subject to sub-paragraph (4) below.

(3) *Sections 148 and 156 of the* Criminal Justice Act *2003 (restrictions and procedural requirements for community sentences) do not apply in relation to an attendance centre order made by virtue of paragraph 2(2)(a)(iii) above.*

(4) *Schedule 5 to this Act (breach, revocation and amendment of attendance centre orders) shall have effect in relation to such an attendance centre order as if there were omitted—*

(a) *from each of paragraphs 2(1)(b) and 4(3) the words ", for the offence in respect of which the order was made," and "for that offence"; and*

(b) *from paragraphs 2(6) and 4(4) the words "for an offence".*

Revocation and amendment of supervision order

5.—(1) *If while a supervision order is in force in respect of an offender it appears to a* **5–221** *relevant court, on the application of the supervisor or the offender, that it is appropriate to make an order under this sub-paragraph, the court may—*

(a) *make an order revoking the supervision order; or*

(b) *make an order amending it—*

(i) *by cancelling any requirement included in it in pursuance of Schedule 6 to, or section 63(6)(b) of, this Act; or*

(ii) *by inserting in it (either in addition to or in substitution for any of its provisions) any provision which could have been included in the order if the court had then had power to make it and were exercising the power.*

(2) *Sub-paragraph (1) above has effect subject to paragraphs 7 to 9 below.*

(2A) *In relation to a supervision order imposing a foster parent residence requirement under paragraph 5A of Schedule 6 to this Act, the power conferred by sub-paragraph (1)(b)(ii) above includes power to extend the period specified in the requirement to a period of not more than 18 months beginning with the day on which the requirement first had effect.*

(3) *The powers of amendment conferred by sub-paragraph (1) above do not include power—*

(a) *to insert in the supervision order, after the end of three months beginning with the date when the order was originally made, a requirement in pursuance of paragraph 6 of Schedule 6 to this Act (treatment for mental condition), unless it is in substitution for such a requirement already included in the order;*

(b) [repealed by *Anti-social Behaviour Act* 2003, s.88, and Sched. 2, para. 6(3)(b)].

(4) *Where an application under sub-paragraph (1) above for the revocation of a supervision order is dismissed, no further application for its revocation shall be made under that sub-paragraph by any person during the period of three months beginning with the date of the dismissal except with the consent of a court having jurisdiction to entertain such an application.*

Amendment of order on report of medical practitioner

5–222 6.—(1) *If a medical practitioner by whom or under whose direction an offender is being treated for his mental condition in pursuance of a requirement included in a supervision order by virtue of paragraph 6 of Schedule 6 to this Act—*

(a) *is unwilling to continue to treat or direct the treatment of the offender, or*

(b) *is of the opinion mentioned in sub-paragraph (2) below,*

the practitioner shall make a report in writing to that effect to the supervisor.

(2) *The opinion referred to in sub-paragraph (1) above is—*

(a) *that the treatment of the offender should be continued beyond the period specified in that behalf in the order;*

(b) *that the offender needs different treatment;*

(c) *that the offender is not susceptible to treatment; or*

(d) *that the offender does not require further treatment.*

(3) *On receiving a report under sub-paragraph (1) above the supervisor shall refer it to a relevant court; and on such a reference the court may make an order cancelling or varying the requirement.*

(4) *Sub-paragraph (3) above has effect subject to paragraphs 7 to 9 below.*

Presence of offender in court, remands etc.

5–223 7.—(1) *Where the supervisor makes an application or reference under paragraph 2(1), 5(1) or 6(3) above to a court he may bring the offender before the court; and, subject to sub-paragraph (9) below, a court shall not make an order under paragraph 2, 5(1) or 6(3) above unless the offender is present before the court.*

(2) *Without prejudice to any power to issue a summons or warrant apart from this sub-paragraph, a justice may issue a summons or warrant for the purpose of securing the attendance of an offender before the court to which any application or reference in respect of him is made under paragraph 2(1), 5(1) or 6(3) above.*

(3) *Subsections (3) and (4) of section 55 of the* Magistrates' Courts Act *1980 (which among other things restrict the circumstances in which a warrant may be issued) shall apply with the necessary modifications to a warrant under sub-paragraph (2) above as they apply to a warrant under that section, but as if in subsection (3) after the word "summons" there were inserted the words "cannot be served or".*

(4) *Where the offender is arrested in pursuance of a warrant issued by virtue of sub-*

paragraph (2) above and cannot be brought immediately before the court referred to in that sub-paragraph, the person in whose custody he is—

(a) *may make arrangements for his detention in a place of safety for a period of not more than 72 hours from the time of the arrest (and it shall be lawful for him to be detained in pursuance of the arrangements); and*

(b) *shall within that period, unless within it the offender is brought before the court referred to in sub-paragraph (2) above, bring him before a justice;*

and in paragraph (a) above "place of safety" has the same meaning as in the Children and Young Persons Act *1933.*

(5) *Where an offender is brought before a justice under sub-paragraph (4)(b) above, the justice may—*

(a) *direct that he be released forthwith; or*

(b) *subject to sub-paragraph (7) below, remand him to local authority accommodation.*

(6) *Subject to sub-paragraph (7) below, where an application is made to a youth court under paragraph 5(1) above, the court may remand (or further remand) the offender to local authority accommodation if—*

(a) *a warrant has been issued under sub-paragraph (2) above for the purpose of securing the attendance of the offender before the court; or*

(b) *the court considers that remanding (or further remanding) him will enable information to be obtained which is likely to assist the court in deciding whether and, if so, how to exercise its powers under paragraph 5(1) above.*

(7) *Where the offender is aged 18 or over at the time when he is brought before a justice under sub-paragraph (4)(b) above, or is aged 18 or over at a time when (apart from this sub-paragraph) a youth court could exercise its powers under sub-paragraph (6) above in respect of him, he shall not be remanded to local authority accommodation but may instead be remanded—*

(a) to a remand centre, if the justice or youth court has been notified that such a centre is available for the reception of persons under this sub-paragraph; or

(b) *to a prison,* if the justice or youth court has not been so notified.

(8) *A justice or court remanding a person to local authority accommodation under this paragraph shall designate, as the authority who are to receive him, the authority named in the supervision order.*

(9) *A court may make an order under paragraph 5(1) or 6(3) above in the absence of the offender if the effect of the order is confined to one or more of the following, that is to say—*

(a) *revoking the supervision order;*

(b) *cancelling a provision included in the supervision order in pursuance of Schedule 6 to, or section 63(6)(b) of, this Act;*

(c) *reducing the duration of the supervision order or any provision included in it in pursuance of that Schedule;*

(d) *altering in the supervision order the name of any area;*

(e) *changing the supervisor.*

Restrictions on court's powers to revoke or amend order

8.—(1) *A youth court shall not—* **5-224**

(a) *exercise its powers under paragraph 5(1) above to make an order—*

(i) *revoking a supervision order, or*

(ii) *inserting in it a requirement authorised by Schedule 6 to this Act, or*

(iii) *varying or cancelling such a requirement,*

except in a case where the court is satisfied that the offender either is unlikely to receive the care or control he needs unless the court makes the order or is likely to receive it notwithstanding the order;

(b) *exercise its powers to make an order under paragraph 6(3) above except in such a case as is mentioned in paragraph (a) above;*

(c) *exercise its powers under paragraph 5(1) above to make an order inserting a requirement authorised by paragraph 6 of Schedule 6 to this Act in a supervision order which does not already contain such a requirement, unless the court is satisfied as mentioned in paragraph 6(1) of that Schedule on such evidence as is there mentioned.*

(2) *For the purposes of this paragraph "care" includes protection and guidance and "control" includes discipline.*

9. *Where the offender has attained the age of 14, then except with his consent a court shall not make an order under paragraph 5(1) or 6(3) above containing provisions—*

(a) *which insert in the supervision order a requirement authorised by paragraph 6 of Schedule 6 to this Act; or*

(b) *which alter such a requirement already included in the supervision order otherwise than by removing it or reducing its duration.*

10. [Copies of revoking or amending orders.]

Appeals

5–225 11. *The offender may appeal to the Crown Court against—*

(a) *any order made under paragraph 2(2) , 5(1) or 6(3) above by a relevant court, except—*

(i) *an order made or which could have been made in the absence of the offender (by virtue of paragraph 7(9) above); and*

(ii) *an order containing only provisions to which the offender consented in pursuance of paragraph 9 above;*

(b) *the dismissal of an application under paragraph 5(1) above to revoke a supervision order.*

Power of parent or guardian to make application on behalf of young person

5–226 12.—(1) *Without prejudice to any power apart from this sub-paragraph to bring proceedings on behalf of another person, any power to make an application which is exercisable by a child or young person by virtue of paragraph 5(1) above shall also be exercisable on his behalf by his parent or guardian.*

(2) *In this paragraph "guardian" includes any person who was a guardian of the child or young person in question at the time when any supervision order to which the application relates was originally made.*

[This Schedule is printed as amended by the *CJCSA* 2000, s.74, and Sched. 7, para. 201(1) and (2)(a); the *Anti-social Behaviour Act* 2003, s.88, and Sched. 2, para. 6; and the *CJA* 2003, s.302, and Sched. 32, para. 128. The romanised words in para. 7(7) are omitted as from a day to be appointed: *CJCSA* 2000, s.74, and Sched. 7, para. 201(1) and (3). The paragraph number in square brackets in para. 2(1) was inserted by the *CJA* 2003, s.279, and Sched. 24, para. 7. As to the commencement of section 279 and Schedule 24 in certain areas on December 1, 2004, see *ante*, § 5–172a. The whole schedule is repealed as from a day to be appointed (as to which, see *ante*, §§ 5–1, 5–121e, 5–122) by the *CJIA* 2008, ss.6(1) and 149, and Sched. 28, Pt 1.]

(d) *Action plan and reparation orders*

Powers of Criminal Courts (Sentencing) Act 2000, Sched. 8

SCHEDULE 8

BREACH, REVOCATION AND AMENDMENT OF ACTION PLAN ORDERS AND REPARATION ORDERS

Meaning of "the appropriate court"

5–227 1. *In this Schedule, "the appropriate court", in relation to an action plan order or reparation order, means a youth court acting in a local justice area for the time being named in the order in pursuance of section 69(8) or, as the case may be, 74(4) of this Act.*

Breach of requirement of action plan order or reparation order

5–228 2.—(1) This paragraph applies if while an action plan order or reparation order is in force in respect of an offender it is proved to the satisfaction of *the appropriate court,*

[(a) a youth court acting in the local justice area in which the offender resides, or

(b) if it is not known where the offender resides, a youth court acting in the local justice area for the time being named in the order in pursuance of section 74(4) of this Act,]

on the application of the responsible officer, that the offender has failed to comply with any requirement included in the order.

(2) Where this paragraph applies, the court—

(a) whether or not it also makes an order under paragraph 5(1) below (revocation or amendment of order)—

(i) may order the offender to pay a fine of an amount not exceeding £1,000; or

(ii) *subject to paragraph 3 below, may make a curfew order in respect of him; or*

(iii) *subject to paragraph 4 below, may make an attendance centre order in respect of him; or*

(b) if the *action plan order or* reparation order was made by a magistrates' court, may revoke the order and deal with the offender, for the offence in respect of which the order was made, in any way in which he could have been dealt with for that offence by the court which made the order if the order had not been made; or

(c) if the *action plan order or* reparation order was made by the Crown Court, may commit him in custody or release him on bail until he can be brought or appear before the Crown Court.

(3) Where a court deals with an offender under sub-paragraph (2)(c) above, it shall send to the Crown Court a certificate signed by a justice of the peace giving—

(a) particulars of the offender's failure to comply with the requirement in question; and

(b) such other particulars of the case as may be desirable;

and a certificate purporting to be so signed shall be admissible as evidence of the failure before the Crown Court.

(4) Where—

(a) by virtue of sub-paragraph (2)(c) above the offender is brought or appears before the Crown Court, and

(b) it is proved to the satisfaction of the court that he has failed to comply with the requirement in question,

that court may deal with him, for the offence in respect of which the order was made, in any way in which it could have dealt with him for that offence if it had not made the order.

(5) Where the Crown Court deals with an offender under sub-paragraph (4) above, it shall revoke the *action plan order or* reparation order if it is still in force.

(6) A fine imposed under this paragraph shall be deemed, for the purposes of any enactment, to be a sum adjudged to be paid by a conviction.

(7) In dealing with an offender under this paragraph, a court shall take into account the extent to which he has complied with the requirements of the *action plan order or* reparation order.

(8) Where a reparation order or action plan order has been made on appeal, for the purposes of this paragraph it shall be deemed—

(a) if it was made on an appeal brought from a magistrates' court, to have been made by that magistrates' court;

(b) if it was made on an appeal brought from the Crown Court or from the criminal division of the Court of Appeal, to have been made by the Crown Court;

and, in relation to a reparation order or action plan order made on appeal, sub-paragraph (2)(b) above shall have effect as if the words "if the order had not been made" were omitted and sub-paragraph (4) above shall have effect as if the words "if it had not made the order" were omitted.

(9) This paragraph has effect subject to paragraph 6 below.

Curfew orders imposed for breach of action plan order or reparation order

3.—(1) *Section 37(1) of this Act (curfew orders) shall apply for the purposes of paragraph 2(2)(a)(ii) above as if for the words from the beginning to "make" there were substituted "Where a court considers it appropriate to make an order in respect of any person in pursuance of paragraph 2(2)(a)(ii) of Schedule 8 to this Act, it may make".* **5–229**

(2) *The following provisions of this Act, namely—*

(a) *section 37(3) to (12), and*

(b) *so far as applicable, sections 36B and 40 and Schedule 3 so far as relating to curfew orders,*

have effect in relation to a curfew order made by virtue of paragraph 2(2)(a)(ii) above as they have effect in relation to any other curfew order, subject to sub-paragraph (5) below.

(3) *Sections 148 and 156 of the* Criminal Justice Act *2003 (restrictions and procedural requirements for community sentences) do not apply in relation to a curfew order made by virtue of paragraph 2(2)(a)(ii) above.*

(5) *Schedule 3 to this Act (breach, revocation and amendment of orders) shall have effect in relation to such a curfew order as if—*

(a) *the power conferred on the court by each of paragraphs 4(2)(c) and 10(3)(b) to deal with the offender for the offence in respect of which the order was made were a power to deal with the offender, for his failure to comply with the action plan order or reparation order, in any way in which the appropriate court could deal with him for that failure if it had just been proved to the satisfaction of that court;*

(b) *the reference in paragraph 10(1)(b) to the offence in respect of which the order was made were a reference to the failure to comply in respect of which the curfew order was made; and*

(c) *the power conferred on the Crown Court by paragraph 11(2)(b) to deal with the offender for the offence in respect of which the order was made were a power to deal with the offender, for his failure to comply with the action plan order or reparation order, in any way in which the appropriate court (if the action plan order or reparation order was made by a magistrates' court) or the Crown Court (if that order was made by the Crown Court) could deal with him for that failure if it had just been proved to its satisfaction.*

(6) *For the purposes of the provisions mentioned in paragraphs (a) and (c) of sub-paragraph (5) above, as applied by that sub-paragraph, if the action plan order or reparation order is no longer in force the appropriate court's powers shall be determined on the assumption that it is still in force.*

Attendance centre orders imposed for breach of action plan or reparation order

5–230 4.—(1) *Section 60(1) of this Act (attendance centre orders) shall apply for the purposes of paragraph 2(2)(a)(iii) above as if for the words from the beginning to "the court may," there were substituted "Where a court considers it appropriate to make an order in respect of any person in pursuance of paragraph 2(2)(a)(iii) of Schedule 8 to this Act, the court may,".*

(2) *The following provisions of this Act, namely—*

(a) *subsections (3) to (11) of section 60, and*

(b) *so far as applicable, Schedule 5,*

have effect in relation to an attendance centre order made by virtue of paragraph 2(2)(a)(iii) above as they have effect in relation to any other attendance centre order, subject to sub-paragraph (4) below.

(3) *Sections 148 and 156 of the* Criminal Justice Act *2003 (restrictions and procedural requirements for community sentences) do not apply in relation to an attendance centre order made by virtue of paragraph 2(2)(a)(iii) above.*

(4) *Schedule 5 to this Act (breach, revocation and amendment of attendance centre orders) shall have effect in relation to such an attendance centre order as if there were omitted—*

(a) *from each of paragraphs 2(1)(b) and 4(3) the words ", for the offence in respect of which the order was made," and "for that offence"; and*

(b) *from paragraphs 2(6) and 4(4) the words "for an offence".*

Revocation and amendment of action plan order or reparation order

5–231 5.—(1) If while an action plan order or reparation order is in force in respect of an offender it appears to the *appropriate* [relevant] court, on the application of the responsible officer or the offender, that it is appropriate to make an order under this sub-paragraph, the court may—

(a) make an order revoking the *action plan order* or reparation order; or

(b) make an order amending it—

(i) by cancelling any provision included in it; or

(ii) by inserting in it (either in addition to or in substitution for any of its provisions) any provision which could have been included in the order if the court had then had power to make it and were exercising the power.

(2) Sub-paragraph (1) above has effect subject to paragraph 6 below.

(3) Where an application under sub-paragraph (1) above for the revocation of an action plan order or reparation order is dismissed, no further application for its revocation shall be made under that sub-paragraph by any person except with the consent of the *appropriate* [relevant] court.

[(4) In this paragraph, "the relevant court" means—

(a) a youth court acting in the local justice area for the time being named in the order in pursuance of section 74(4) of this Act, or

(b) in the case of an application made both under this paragraph and under paragraph 2(1), the court mentioned in paragraph 2(1).]

Presence of offender in court, remands etc.

6.—(1) Where the responsible officer makes an application under paragraph 2(1) or 5(1) above to *the appropriate* [a] court he may bring the offender before the court; and, subject to sub-paragraph (9) below, a court shall not make an order under paragraph 2 or 5(1) above unless the offender is present before the court. **5–232**

(2) Without prejudice to any power to issue a summons or warrant apart from this sub-paragraph, the court to which an application under paragraph 2(1) or 5(1) above is made may issue a summons or warrant for the purpose of securing the attendance of the offender before it.

(3) [*Identical to Sched. 7, para. 7(3),* ante, *§ 5–223.*]

(4) Where the offender is arrested in pursuance of a warrant issued by virtue of sub-paragraph (2) above and cannot be brought immediately before the *appropriate* court [before which the warrant directs the offender to be brought ("the relevant court")], the person in whose custody he is—

(a) may make arrangements for his detention in a place of safety for a period of not more than 72 hours from the time of the arrest (and it shall be lawful for him to be detained in pursuance of the arrangements); and

(b) shall within that period bring him before a youth court;

and in paragraph (a) above "place of safety" has the same meaning as in the *Children and Young Persons Act* 1933.

(5) Where an offender is under sub-paragraph (4)(b) above brought before a youth court other than the *appropriate* [relevant] court, the youth court may—

(a) direct that he be released forthwith; or

(b) subject to sub-paragraph (7) below, remand him to local authority accommodation.

(6) [*Identical to Sched. 7, para. 7(6),* ante, *§ 5–223.*]

(7) Where the offender is aged 18 or over at the time when he is brought before a youth court other than the *appropriate* [relevant] court under sub-paragraph (4)(b) above, or is aged 18 or over at a time when (apart from this sub-paragraph) the *appropriate* [relevant] court could exercise its powers under sub-paragraph (6) above in respect of him, he shall not be remanded to local authority accommodation but may instead be remanded—

(a) *to a remand centre, if the court has been notified that such a centre is available for the reception of persons under this sub-paragraph; or*

(b) to a prison, *if it has not been so notified.*

(8) A court remanding an offender to local authority accommodation under this paragraph shall designate, as the authority who are to receive him, the local authority for the area in which the offender resides or, where it appears to the court that he does not reside in the area of a local authority, the local authority—

(a) specified by the court; and

(b) in whose area the offence or an offence associated with it was committed.

(9) A court may make an order under paragraph 5(1) above in the absence of the offender if the effect of the order is confined to one or more of the following, that is to say—

(a) revoking the *action plan order or* reparation order;

(b) cancelling a requirement included in the *action plan order or* reparation order;

(c) altering in the *action plan order or* reparation order the name of any area;

(d) changing the responsible officer.

[Power to adjourn hearing and remand offender

6A.—(1) This paragraph applies to any hearing relating to an offender held by a youth court in any proceedings under this Schedule. **5–232a**

(2), (3) [*Identical to* CJA *2003, Sched. 8, para. 25A(2), (3),* ante, *§ 5–200.*]

(4) Where the court adjourns the hearing under sub-paragraph (2) but does not remand the offender—

(a) it may fix the time and place at which the hearing is to be resumed, but

(b) if it does not do so, it must not resume the hearing unless it is satisfied that the persons mentioned in sub-paragraph (5) have had adequate notice of the time and place for the resumed hearing.

(5) The persons referred to in sub-paragraph (4)(b) are—

(a) the offender,

(b) if the offender is aged under 14, a parent or guardian of the offender, and

(c) the responsible officer.

(6) If a local authority has parental responsibility for an offender who is in its care or provided with accommodation by it in the exercise of any social services functions, the reference in sub-paragraph (5)(b) to a parent or guardian of the offender is to be read as a reference to that authority.

(7) In sub-paragraph (6)—

"local authority" has the same meaning as it has in Part 1 of the *Criminal Justice and Immigration Act* 2008 by virtue of section 7 of that Act,

"parental responsibility" has the same meaning as it has in the *Children Act* 1989 by virtue of section 3 of that Act, and

"social services functions" has the same meaning as it has in the *Local Authority Social Services Act* 1970 by virtue of section 1A of that Act.

(8) The powers of a youth court under this paragraph may be exercised by a single justice of the peace, notwithstanding anything in the *Magistrates' Courts Act* 1980.

(9) [*Identical to* CJA *2003, Sched. 8, para. 25A(6),* ante, *§ 5–200.*]]

Appeals

5–232b 7. The offender may appeal to the Crown Court against—

(a) any order made under paragraph 2(2) or 5(1) above except an order made or which could have been made in his absence (by virtue of paragraph 6(9) above);

(b) the dismissal of an application under paragraph 5(1) above to revoke an action plan order or reparation order.

[This Schedule is printed as amended by the *CJCSA* 2000, s.74, and Sched. 7, para. 202(1) and (2)(a); the *CJA* 2003, s.302, and Sched. 32, paras 90 and 129; and the *Courts Act 2003 (Consequential Provisions) Order* 2005 (S.I. 2005 No. 886). The italicised words in para. 6(7)(a) and (b) are omitted as from a day to be appointed: *CJCSA* 2000, s.74, and Sched. 7, para. 202(1) and (3). Paras 1, 3 and 4 and the italicised words in paras 2, 5 and 6 (other than those in para. 6(7)(a) and (b), as to which, see *ante*) are omitted, and para. 6A and the words in square brackets in paras 2, 5 and 6 are inserted, as from a day to be appointed (as to which, see *ante*, § 5–1), by the *CJIA* 2008, ss.6(3) and 149, Sched. 4, paras 106 and 108, and Sched. 28, Pt 1.]

Reparation orders

5–232c A reparation order is not a community sentence. As to the power to make such an order, see section 73 of the 2000 Act, *post*, § 5–435.

(3) Of youth rehabilitation orders

5–233 As to the introduction of youth rehabilitation orders by the *CJIA* 2008, and as to the commencement and transitional arrangements and saving provisions, see *ante*, §§ 5–1, 5–121e, 5–122. The provisions of that Act (which are anticipated to come into force in the second half of 2009) governing the making of such orders and the requirements that may be included in them will be set out in the second and/or third supplements. Their enforcement is governed by Schedule 2 to that Act, the provisions of which will also be set out in the second and/or third supplements (at §§ 5–233a *et seq.*)

[The next paragraph is § 5–235.]

VI. CUSTODIAL SENTENCES

A. MANDATORY LIFE SENTENCE

(1) Introduction

5–235 Where a court imposes a life sentence in circumstances where the sentence is fixed by law, section 269 of the *CJA* 2003 requires the court to order that the early release provisions in section 28(5) to (8) of the *C(S)A* 1997 are to apply to the offender after he has served such part of the sentence as the court specifies. This exercise has become known as fixing the "minimum term". The requirement to fix a minimum term does not apply where the court orders, under section 269(4), that the early release provisions are not to apply to the particular offender (a "whole life order": see Sched. 21, para. 1, *post*, § 5–245).

Section 277 of the 2003 Act defines "life sentence" as a sentence of imprisonment for life, a sentence of detention during Her Majesty's pleasure, and a sentence of custody for life. The only offence for which any such sentence is "fixed by law" is murder.

(2) Legislation

Murder (Abolition of Death Penalty) Act 1965, s.1(1)

Abolition of death penalty for murder

1.—(1) No person shall suffer death for murder, and a person convicted of murder shall, subject to subsection (5) below, be sentenced to imprisonment for life. **5–236**

Powers of Criminal Courts (Sentencing) Act 2000, ss.90, 93

Offenders who commit murder when under 18: duty to detain at Her Majesty's pleasure

90. Where a person convicted of murder appears to the court to have been aged under 18 at the time the offence was committed, the court shall (notwithstanding anything in this or any other Act) sentence him to be detained during Her Majesty's pleasure. **5–237**

Duty to impose custody for life in certain cases where offender under 21

93. Where a person aged under 21 is convicted of murder or any other offence the sentence for which is fixed by law as imprisonment for life, the court shall sentence him to custody for life unless he is liable to be detained under section 90 above. **5–238**

Criminal Justice Act 2003, ss.269, 270, 276, 277

Determination of minimum term in relation to mandatory life sentence

269.—(1) This section applies where after the commencement of this section a court passes a life sentence in circumstances where the sentence is fixed by law. **5–239**

(2) The court must, unless it makes an order under subsection (4), order that the provisions of section 28(5) to (8) of the *Crime (Sentences) Act* 1997 (referred to in this Chapter as "the early release provisions") are to apply to the offender as soon as he has served the part of his sentence which is specified in the order.

(3) The part of his sentence is to be such as the court considers appropriate taking into account—

(a) the seriousness of the offence, or of the combination of the offence and any one or more offences associated with it, and

(b) the effect of any direction which it would have given under section 240 (crediting periods of remand in custody) [[or under section 240A (crediting periods of remand on bail spent subject to certain types of condition]] [or under section 246 of the *Armed Forces Act* 2006 (equivalent provision for service courts)] if it had sentenced him to a term of imprisonment.

(4) If the offender was 21 or over when he committed the offence and the court is of the opinion that, because of the seriousness of the offence, or of the combination of the offence and one or more offences associated with it, no order should be made under subsection (2), the court must order that the early release provisions are not to apply to the offender.

(5) In considering under subsection (3) or (4) the seriousness of an offence (or of the combination of an offence and one or more offences associated with it), the court must have regard to—

(a) the general principles set out in Schedule 21, and

(b) any guidelines relating to offences in general which are relevant to the case and are not incompatible with the provisions of Schedule 21.

(6), (7) [*Power of Secretary of State to amend Sched. 21 by order; duty to consult Sentencing Guidelines Council before doing so.*]

[This section is printed as amended, as from a day to be appointed, by the *AFA* 2006, s.378(1), and Sched. 16, para. 228 (insertion of words in single square brackets); and the *CJIA* 2008, s.22(1) and (3) (insertion of words in double square brackets).]

For section 240 of the 2003 Act, see *post*, § 5–368.

Fixing the minimum term

5–239a It was said in *R. v. Jones* [2006] 2 Cr.App.R.(S.) 19, CA, that the guidance in Schedule 21 (*post*, § 5–245) was provided to assist a court to determine the appropriate sentence, that although the court must have regard to the guidance, each case will depend critically on its particular facts; and that where the court concludes that it is appropriate to follow a course that does not appear to reflect the guidance, it should explain its reasons. Having made these general observations, the court proceeded to make the following comments (edited to take account of more recent decisions) on the particular provisions of Schedule 21.

The three starting points

5–239b There are huge gaps between the three starting points; they are so far apart that it will often be impossible to divorce the choice of starting point from the application of aggravating and mitigating factors, and where aggravating factors have led the court to adopt the higher of two potential starting points, or the mitigation has led it to adopt the lower, it must be careful not to apply those factors a second time when adjusting that starting point to reflect the other material facts; the starting points give guidance as to the range within which the appropriate sentence is likely to fall having regard to the more salient features of the offence, but, even then, detailed consideration of aggravating or mitigating factors may result in a minimum term of any length (whatever the starting point), or in the making of a whole life order; the starting points must not be used mechanistically so as to produce, in effect, three different categories of murder and full regard must be had to the features of the individual case so that the sentence truly reflects the seriousness of the particular offence. Further, section 143 of the *CJA* 2003 (*ante*, § 5–54) is of relevance, and in the context of culpability, the mental state of the offender is of obvious importance; and all but one of the mitigating factors in paragraph 11 relate to culpability. A killing for which there is no rational explanation may reflect a mental disorder or disability in the offender, and although such murders are sometimes more horrifying than killings that are motivated, it is important to bear in mind that in the case of such a murder it is the task of the Parole Board to ensure that the offender is not released unless this presents no danger to the public (protection of the public not being relevant to the minimum term). As to it not generally being helpful or desirable to attach particular figures to any particular element in what is an overall assessment, see *R. v. Tucker*, *post*, § 5–239h. As to the wording of paragraphs 4 (whole-life starting point) and 5 (30-year starting point), not being prescriptive, see *R. v. Duncan*, *post*, § 5–239j.

The whole life starting point

5–239c In relation to the whole life starting point, application of the scheme of Schedule 21 is manifestly impossible; a whole life order should be imposed where the seriousness of the offending is so exceptionally high that just punishment requires the offender to be kept in prison for the rest of his life; and often where such an order is called for, the case will not be on the borderline (having considered the facts as a whole), leaving the court in no doubt that the offender must be kept in prison for the rest of his life; where there is any doubt, this may well be an indication that a finite minimum term which leaves open the possibility that the offender may be released for the final years of his life is the appropriate disposal (to be imprisoned for a finite period of thirty years or more is a severe penalty); if the case includes one or more of the factors set out in paragraph 4(2), it is likely to be one that calls for a whole life order, but the court must consider all the material facts before concluding that a lengthy finite term will not suffice. (As to whether a whole life order is compatible with Article 3 of the ECHR (*post*, § 16–39), see *R. v. Bieber*, *The Times*, August 11, 2008, CA, *De Boucherville v. Mauritius* [2008] 8 *Archbold News* 4, PC, and *Kafkaris v. Cyprus*, *post*, § 16–40.)

In *R. v. Mullen* [2008] 2 Cr.App.R.(S.) 88, CA, where the judge had taken a 30-year starting point for a case which fell four-square within paragraph 4 of Schedule 21 (whole-life order) on account of an early guilty plea (as to which, see also *post*, § 5–239d) and the fact that the offender had only just attained the age of 21, and had then inflated that figure to reflect the matters of aggravation, he had not been obliged then to reduce it on account of those same matters of mitigation.

A guilty plea

Appropriate credit should be given for a guilty plea; in relation to whole life terms, the court should consider the fact that the defendant has pleaded guilty to murder when deciding whether it is appropriate to make such an order (see, for example, *R. v. Mullen*, *ante*); but since a case which calls for the imposition of a whole life term is unlikely to be a borderline case, where it is not, there may be no need for a court to spell out why, although it has had regard to the plea, this has not affected the sentence. **5–239d**

The 30-year starting point and the use of a firearm

In relation to the 30-year starting point and the use of a firearm, whereas paragraph 5(2)(b) provides that "a murder involving the use of a firearm" will normally have a starting point of 30 years, there was no doubt that the reason why the seriousness of such an offence is normally considered to be particularly high is that it results from the unlawful carrying of a loaded firearm and the fact that the usual purpose of carrying such a firearm is to be able to kill or to cause really serious injury; it is possible to imagine such circumstances where this is not the case, but they will be rare. Therefore, where a firearm is carried for the purpose of being used as an offensive weapon, it is hard to envisage what reason there could be for not following the guidance and adopting 30 years as the starting point. **5–239e**

The 30-year starting point and deliberate arson

In relation to the 30-year starting point and deliberate arson, setting fire to a person's home with the intention of causing death or really serious injury is peculiarly horrifying and in such cases questions as to the different states of mind are immaterial; deliberately to cause really serious injury by fire is likely to involve agony for the victim and the possibility of permanent injury or disfigurement, and such conduct carries with it the obvious risk of causing death; although causing death by arson does not feature in the list of examples of cases where the seriousness is likely to be particularly high, using petrol to set fire to a victim's home should be taken to fall within that category. **5–239f**

Lack of intent to kill/ plea of guilty

Further assistance as to the significance of a lack of intent to kill and of a guilty plea may be derived from *R. v. Peters*; *R. v. Palmer*; *R. v. Campbell* [2005] 2 Cr.App.R.(S.) 101, CA. Although lack of intent to kill is specified as a mitigating factor in paragraph 11(a) of Schedule 21 (*post*, § 5–247), the court pointed out that there is no specific or special starting point for such cases; lack of intention "may" provide relevant mitigation, but will not necessarily do so; there may be cases where there was an intent to kill but which nevertheless attract greater mitigation (*e.g.* mercy killing); and where conduct is likely to, or may possibly, cause death, notwithstanding that such a consequence is unintended, mitigation is likely to be minimal (see also *Att.-Gen.'s References (Nos 98 and 99 of 2006) (R. v. McGarry and Wells)* [2007] 2 Cr.App.R.(S.) 19, CA: when a high level of violence has been inflicted, the difference in intention will be less significant; and *R. v. Connor* [2008] 1 Cr.App.R.(S.) 89, CA: absent a larger number of deaths, nearly impossible to imagine a worse case of murder by arson); but in many cases, particularly where violence resulting in death has erupted suddenly and unexpectedly, lack of intent to kill will provide mitigation, and the level of mitigation may be greater still where the fatal injuries were not inflicted with a weapon. **5–239g**

In some cases, particularly where the defendant is young or suffers from mental or emotional problems, the court said that the first reasonable opportunity firmly and finally to indicate an intention to plead guilty may not arise until after the defendant has seen leading counsel; a defendant may accept responsibility for the fatal injuries, or a contribution to them, but he will often need expert legal advice as to whether the case should properly be contested on the basis of absence of intent, self-defence, provocation, or diminished responsibility; but generally, even if there is delay in obtaining the advice of leading counsel, the defendant should not expect to receive the maximum discount unless an early indication is given that as a matter of fact he accepts responsibility for the fatal injuries, or involvement in the death; once he has seen leading counsel and received advice, if he is then to benefit from the maximum discount, it is necessary for the plea to be indicated as soon as is reasonably practicable thereafter.

Youthfulness/ the prescribed starting points/ disparity

5–239h In *R. v. Peters*; *R. v. Palmer*; *R. v. Campbell*, *ante*, it was said that it should be borne in mind that although eighteenth and twenty-first birthdays represent significant moments in the life of an individual, they are not necessarily indicative of the individual's true level of maturity, insight and understanding; that such characteristics are not postponed or suddenly accelerated by those birthdays; and that the first stage in the process is to select the prescribed statutory starting point; then to allow, where the offender's age, as it affects his culpability and the seriousness of the crime justifies it, a substantial discount from the starting point. The court added that there is no mathematical scale (as to which, see also *post*), but one way in which a judge may check that the discount is proportionate would be to consider it in the context of the overall statutory framework, as if Schedule 21 envisaged a flexible starting point for offenders between 18 and 21 years old; that has the advantage of linking the mitigation which would normally arise from the offender's relative youth with the statutory provisions which apply to an offender a year or two older, or younger, and would contribute to a desirable level of sentencing consistency. To similar effect, see *R. v. Matthew* [2006] 1 Cr.App.R.(S.) 88, CA (there should be no sudden postponement or acceleration of sentence levels due to age; there is a need for flexibility in that there are no sudden step changes in growth to maturity). The youthfulness of the offender does not, however, require that there should be a specific quantified adjustment to the starting point before consideration of the aggravating and mitigating factors: *R. v. Tucker* [2008] 2 Cr.App.R.(S.) 27, CA (considering *R. v. Jones* (*ante*) and *R. v. Peters*; *R. v. Palmer*; *R. v. Campbell*).

In *Att.-Gen.'s Reference (No. 126 of 2006) (R. v. H.)* [2007] 2 Cr.App.R.(S.) 59, CA, it was said that whilst the starting point specified for an offender under the age of 18 at the time of the offence is 12 years (see para. 7), it is clear that the appropriate minimum term remains fact specific and may be well above or well below the starting point; that nothing precludes the court from reflecting on all the express features identified in the starting points for adult offenders in paragraphs 4 (whole life starting point) and 5 (30-year starting point) and, when they are found to be present, treating them as features which aggravate an offence to which the 12-year starting point applies; and that whilst the schedule underlines the long established sentencing principle that the level of ultimate criminality of an offender, who is young, is likely to be (but may not necessarily be) lower than the criminality of an older offender, there is no mathematical table for this purpose and no list can provide an accurate reflection of the way in which a young offender may or may not have learned from, or been damaged by, the experiences to which he has been exposed.

In *R. v. Taylor* [2007] 1 Cr.App.R.(S.) 59, CA, it was said that where two offenders fell to be sentenced in respect of the same murder, which was of a type falling within the categories of case which would attract the 30-year starting point in the case of an offender aged 18 or over, save in exceptional cases, any disparity arising by virtue only of the fact that one offender was aged under 18, and was thus to be sentenced by reference to the 12-year starting point, was consequent on the statutory scheme and could not provide a proper basis for a successful appeal against sentence on the part of the other. However, in *R. v. Taylor* [2008] 1 Cr.App.R.(S.) 4, CA, the court observed, *obiter*, that where two offenders of equal culpability kill in circumstances which would, in the case of an 18-year-old, attract the 30-year starting point, it would be neither just nor rational for significantly divergent minimum terms to be imposed because one offender was just below the age of 18 (and so liable to the 12-year starting point under paragraph 7) and the other just above it. This approach was followed by the Court of Appeal in *Att.-Gen.'s References (Nos 143 and 144) (R. v. Brown and Carty)* [2008] 1 Cr.App.R.(S.) 28 (making no reference to *R. v. Taylor, ante*) where it was said that it would be wrong for the sentencer to determine the sentences for each offender in such a situation independently of the other. The proper approach would be to move from each starting point to a position where any disparity was no more than a fair reflection of the age difference.

Dangerousness

A judge should only have regard to the seriousness of the offence in fixing the minimum term. The dangerousness of the offender is catered for by the indeterminate nature of the sentence, and is thus not a justification for making a "whole life order": *R. v. Leigers* [2005] 2 Cr.App.R.(S.) 104, CA. But a judge could express a view that, in the absence of some wholly unexpected change, the offender should not be released once the tariff term had expired, nor for a considerable time thereafter, if at all, and then direct that a transcript of his remarks was to remain with the appropriate authorities so that it could be drawn to the attention of the Parole Board when determining an application for early release: *R. v. Duncan* [2007] 1 Cr.App.R.(S.) 26, CA. **5–239i**

As to the likelihood that the dangerousness criterion will be satisfied where an offender falls to be sentenced for a terrorist offence where he is in such a grip of idealistic extremism that, over a prolonged period, he has been plotting to commit murder of innocent citizens, see *R. v. Barot* [2008] 1 Cr.App.R.(S.) 31, CA.

Starting points generally

As to the importance of identifying the right starting point so as to fit a case into the correct place in the hierarchy, see *R. v. Randall* [2008] 1 Cr.App.R.(S.) 93, CA (sentencer should be left in no doubt that a whole life order was necessary before making such an order). But the wording of paragraph 5 is not prescriptive: *R. v. Duncan, ante*, where it was said that the categorisation in sub-paragraph (2) of cases that would normally attract the 30-year starting point does not exclude other categories of case. **5–239j**

An intention to kill is assumed within the relevant starting point, but the ferocity of an attack may properly be taken into account as an aggravating factor: *R. v. Ainsworth, The Times*, September 13, 2006, CA.

As to whether a killing involved "sexual conduct", contrast *Att.-Gen.'s Reference (No. 149 of 2006) (R. v. Pollard)* [2007] 2 Cr.App.R.(S.) 96, CA (in absence of any material which could properly disassociate the killing of the 13-year-old daughter of the offender's partner from the sexual activity with the victim in which he had indulged at the time of, or immediately before, the killing, case fell with para. 5(2)(e)), with *R. v. Walker* [2008] 2 Cr.App.R.(S.) 6, CA (offender had intercourse with victim shortly before the murder, but case not within para. 5(2)(e), which was intended to cover circumstances where the acts which resulted in the death were sexual in nature or accompanied by sexual activity that increased the ordeal of the victim or the depravity of the murder).

As to whether a killing involved "sadistic conduct", it was said in *R. v. Bonellie, Hughes and Miller, The Times*, July 15, 2008, CA, that whilst it is often the case that those who attack others derive pleasure from so doing, this is not enough to constitute "sadistic conduct". What is contemplated is a significantly greater degree of awareness of pleasure in the infliction of pain, suffering or humiliation. But the word "sadistic" does not import a sexual element: *Att.-Gen.'s References (Nos 108 and 109 of 2005) (R. v. Swindon and Peart)* [2006] 2 Cr.App.R.(S.) 80, CA.

In *R. v. Bouhaddou* [2007] 2 Cr.App.R.(S.) 23, CA, it was held that where a burglar, upon being confronted by the householder, attacked him and killed him in order to make good his escape, his offence fell within paragraph 5(2)(c), so as normally to attract the 30-year starting point as much as if the killing had been committed in order to facilitate the gain. To similar effect, see *R. v. Cullen* [2007] 2 Cr.App.R.(S.) 65, CA (robbery); but for a somewhat different approach, see *Att.-Gen.'s References (Nos 7 and 8 of 2006) (R. v. Ellis and McAfee)* [2006] 2 Cr.App.R.(S.) 112, CA.

In *R. v. Tailor* [2008] 1 Cr.App.R.(S.) 37, CA, it was said, in relation to paragraph 5(2)(c), that cases in a domestic context, where a husband murders his wife not only in the expectation of substantial financial gain but also in the expectation that he will achieve other ends, such as satisfying lust and selfishness, should be distinguished from those where professional criminals kill for gain or where they do so in the course of executing a serious offence; cases involving mixed motives will ordinarily require a shorter minimum term.

Aggravating factors

5–239k The standard of proof that the court should apply when deciding whether aggravating factors exist to lift the starting point for the minimum term from 15 years to 30 years is the same standard as that to be applied by the jury when reaching their verdict: *R. v. Davies* [2008] Crim.L.R. 733, CA.

An attack which occurred within the victim's home amounts to an aggravating factor, see *R. v. Ainsworth*, *ante*.

In *R. v. King* [2006] 1 Cr.App.R.(S.) 121, CA, it was said, (i) that the fact that the deceased had been hospitalised for six weeks following his injuries was "mental or physical suffering inflicted on the victim before his death" and, therefore, an aggravating factor under paragraph 10(c); and (ii) that the fact that the offender had armed himself with a knife as a preliminary to the altercation in which it was used was an aggravating factor, albeit not one which was expressly listed (for a criticism of this decision, see *Criminal Law Week* 2006/20/40). See also *R. v. Wynne* [2007] 1 Cr.App.R.(S.) 68, CA (judge had been entitled to treat the use of a meat cleaver as an aggravating factor, on the basis that it was more dangerous than an ordinary knife and it had not been a case of something immediately to hand being grabbed, it having been kept in case of trouble).

In *R. v. Pile and Rossiter* [2006] 1 Cr.App.R.(S.) 131, CA, it was said that a killing which took place in public, so as inevitably to cause public concern, amounts to an aggravating factor, albeit not specifically mentioned in Schedule 21; and see *R. v. Allardyce, Turner and Porter* [2006] 1 Cr.App.R.(S.) 98, CA, where it was said that the fact that the defendant was a member of a pack who had hunted down and killed the deceased was an aggravating factor, albeit not one which was expressly listed as such.

Being under the influence of a Class A drug at the time of the offence is not an aggravating factor: *R. v. McDonald* (2007) 151 S.J. 436, CA (and see paragraph IV.49.20 of the consolidated criminal practice direction (§ 5–251a in the supplement)).

A previous conviction for manslaughter must weigh heavily as an aggravating factor; whilst such a conviction would be material to the assessment of dangerousness by the Parole Board at the end of the minimum term, the fact that an offender has already taken a life is also highly relevant to the assessment of seriousness: *R. v. Brady and Paton* [2007] 1 Cr.App.R.(S.) 117, CA.

As to the vulnerability of the deceased, in *R. v. Latham* [2006] 2 Cr.App.R.(S.) 64, CA, it was said that a judge can make an assessment of whether the deceased was vulnerable by reason of disability for the purposes of determining the existence of the aggravating factor expressly listed in paragraph 10(b) without referring to particular medical evidence and, likewise, the degree of physical suffering inflicted on the deceased before death need not be proved to the criminal standard for the purposes of paragraph 10(c). In *R. v. Arshad* [2006] 1 Cr.App.R.(S.) 65, CA, it was said that a 56-year-old victim could not be described as "particularly vulnerable because of age" within the meaning of paragraph 10(b) of Schedule 21 where she was fit and well, in good health and lively for her age. But in *R. v. Duncan*, *ante*, § 5–239i, it was said that even if a victim could not properly be described as vulnerable by reason of age or disability within paragraph 10(b), since the court was not confined to the provisions of the statute in identifying aggravating factors, the judge could treat other vulnerability as an aggravating factor (here, that the diminutive victim was in the offender's flat alone with him, and at his mercy).

Mitigating factors

5–239l As to mitigating factors, mere drunkenness leading to extreme violence cannot

The requirement for a court to state in open court its reasons for deciding on an order made under section 269 does not apply to the extent that the explanation will disclose that a sentence has been discounted in pursuance of section 73(3) of the *SOCPA* 2005 (*ante*, § 5–94a) but not made public in accordance with section 73(4) of that Act: see s.73(7).

Mandatory life sentences: transitional cases

5–241 **276.** Schedule 22 (which relates to the effect in transitional cases of mandatory life sentences) shall have effect.

Interpretation of Chapter 7

5–242 **277.** In this Chapter—

"court" includes *a court-martial* [the Court Martial];

"guidelines" has the same meaning as in section 172(1);

"life sentence" means —

(a) a sentence of imprisonment for life,

(b) a sentence of detention during Her Majesty's pleasure, or

(c) a sentence of custody for life passed before the commencement of section 61(1) of the *Criminal Justice and Court Services Act* 2000 (which abolishes that sentence).

[This section is printed as amended, as from a day to be appointed, by the *AFA* 2006, s.378(1), and Sched. 16, para. 230 (omission of italicised words, insertion of words in square brackets).]

Crime (Sentences) Act 1997, s.28

Duty to release certain life prisoners

5–243 **28.**—(1A) This section applies to a life prisoner in respect of whom a minimum term order has been made; and any reference in this section to the relevant part of such a prisoner's sentence is a reference to the part of the sentence specified in the order.

(1B) But if a life prisoner is serving two or more life sentences—

(a) this section does not apply to him unless a minimum term order has been made in respect of each of those sentences; and

(b) the provisions of subsections (5) to (8) below do not apply in relation to him until he has served the relevant part of each of them.

(5) As soon as—

(a) a life prisoner to whom this section applies has served the relevant part of his sentence, and

(b) the Parole Board has directed his release under this section,

it shall be the duty of the Secretary of State to release him on licence.

(6) The Parole Board shall not give a direction under subsection (5) above with respect to a life prisoner to whom this section applies unless—

(a) the Secretary of State has referred the prisoner's case to the Board; and

(b) the Board is satisfied that it is no longer necessary for the protection of the public that the prisoner should be confined.

(7) A life prisoner to whom this section applies may require the Secretary of State to refer his case to the Parole Board at any time—

(a) after he has served the relevant part of his sentence; and

(b) where there has been a previous reference of his case to the Board, after the end of the period of two years beginning with the disposal of that reference; and

(c) where he is also serving a sentence of imprisonment or detention for a term, after he has served one-half of that sentence;

and in this subsection "previous reference" means a reference under subsection (6) above or section 32(4) below.

(8) In determining for the purpose of subsection (5) or (7) above whether a life prisoner to whom this section applies has served the relevant part of his sentence, no account shall be taken of any time during which he was unlawfully at large within the meaning of section 49 of the *Prison Act* 1952.

(8A) In this section"minimum term order" means an order under—

(a) subsection (2) of section 82A of the *Powers of Criminal Courts (Sentencing) Act* 2000 (determination of minimum term in respect of life sentence that is not fixed by law), or amount to a mitigating factor: *Re Waters* [2006] 3 All E.R. 1251, QBD (Mitting J.). The calling of the emergency services may properly be regarded as a mitigation: *R. v. King, ante*.

In *Re Brown (reference under paragraph 6 of Schedule 22 to the Criminal Justice Act 2003), The Independent*, March 21, 2006, QBD (Pitchers J.), it was said that although there was no express provision for such a course, the court should, as a matter of justice, give credit to an offender for time served for an offence where the victim subsequently died and the offender was re-sentenced for murder arising out of the same facts.

Other than in cases where a whole life order is made under paragraph 4 of Schedule 21 (*post*, § 5–246), the risk of an offender dying in prison (either due to a particular health problem or simply by reason of general life expectancy) falls within the mitigating factor expressly referred to in paragraph 11(g) (age of offender); there should be some light at the end of the tunnel: *R. v. Archer* [2007] 2 Cr.App.R.(S.) 71, CA.

As to the character of the offender, although it had omitted previous good character from the list of mitigating factors in paragraph 11, Parliament is not to be taken to have intended that good character is irrelevant to all offences of murder and is to be ignored: *R. v. Simmons* [2007] 1 Cr.App.R.(S.) 27, CA.

Terrorism cases

As to the likelihood that the dangerousness criterion will be satisfied in a case of conspiracy to commit mass murder, see *R. v. Barot, ante*, § 5–239i. The court said that where mass murder is committed, a whole life term under Schedule 21 would be appropriate, and that it was accordingly impossible to adopt an arithmetical approach so as to derive from the schedule the proper level of sentence for a conspiracy or attempt to commit mass murder; but the increased level of sentencing for completed offences of murder and the current public emergency posed by terrorism support an increase in the level of sentences for inchoate offences as compared to previous authorities. A minimum term of 40 years should (on conviction after trial), save in quite exceptional circumstances, represent the maximum sentence for a viable attempted mass murder which causes no physical harm and minimum terms in conspiracy cases should be significantly lower (unless the conspiracy was likely to lead to an attempt and the attempt was likely to succeed) and should depend on the nature of the conspiracy and the offender's involvement in it. **5–239m**

Conspiracy and attempt

As to sentencing for attempted murder or conspiracy to murder where there is a terrorist context, see *ante*, § 5–239m. **5–239n**

In a case of conspiracy, where the substantive offence was completed and the offender's culpability was high, it was legitimate for the sentencer to have regard to the starting points in Schedule 21, when determining the appropriate sentence: *R. v. McNee, Gunn and Russell* [2008] 1 Cr.App.R.(S.) 24, CA.

As to sentencing in cases of attempted murder by analogy to the principles set out in Schedule 21 not necessarily being appropriate to every case, but the sentencing exercise needing to bear a proper relationship to the sentence for the completed offence (particularly in a case of cold-blooded attempted execution in a public place), see *R. v. Szypusz and Gaynor* [2007] 1 Cr.App.R.(S.) 49, CA. And see also *post*, § 33–138.

Duty to give reasons

270.—(1) Any court making an order under subsection (2) or (4) of section 269 must state in open court, in ordinary language, its reasons for deciding on the order made. **5–240**

(2) In stating its reasons the court must, in particular—

(a) state which of the starting points in Schedule 21 it has chosen and its reasons for doing so, and

(b) state its reasons for any departure from that starting point.

(b) subsection (2) of section 269 of the *Criminal Justice Act* 2003 (determination of minimum term in respect of mandatory life sentence).

[This section is printed as amended, and repealed in part, by the *CDA* 1998, s.119 and Sched. 8, para. 130; the *PCC(S)A* 2000, s.165(1), Sched. 9, para. 182; the *CJCSA* 2000, s.74 and Sched. 7, para. 136; and the *CJA* 2003, s.275.]

Crime (Sentences) Act 1997, s.34

34.—(1) In this Chapter "life prisoner" means a person serving one or more life sentences; and includes a transferred life prisoner as defined by section 273 of the *Criminal Justice Act* 2003. **5–244**

(2) In this section "life sentence" means any of the following imposed for an offence, whether committed before or after the commencement of this Chapter, namely—

(a) a sentence of imprisonment for life;

(b) a sentence of detention during Her Majesty's pleasure or for life under section 90 or 91 of the *Powers of Criminal Courts (Sentencing) Act* 2000; and

(c) a sentence of custody for life under section 93 or 94 of that Act;

(d) a sentence of imprisonment for public protection under section 225 of the *Criminal Justice Act* 2003 [(including one passed as a result of section 219 of the *Armed Forces Act* 2006)]; *and*

(e) a sentence of detention for public protection under section 226 of that Act [(including one passed as a result of section 221 of the *Armed Forces Act* 2006)];.

[(f) a sentence of detention for life under section 209 of the *Armed Forces Act* 2006;

(g) a sentence under section 218 of that Act (detention at Her Majesty's pleasure)].

(3) ... *in subsection (2) above—*

(a) *the reference to section 90 or 91 of the* Powers of Criminal Courts (Sentencing) Act *2000 includes a reference to subsections (3) and (4) of section 71A of the* Army Act *1955 and the* Air Force Act *1955 and section 43A of the* Naval Discipline Act *1957; and*

(b) *the reference to section 93 or 94 of that Act of 2000 includes a reference to subsections (1A) and (1B) of section 71A of the* Army Act *1955 and the* Air Force Act *1955 and section 43A of the* Naval Discipline Act *1957*.

(4) Where a person has been sentenced to one or more life sentences and to one or more terms of imprisonment, nothing in this Chapter shall require the Secretary of State to release the person in respect of any of the life sentences unless and until the Secretary of State is required to release him in respect of each of the terms.

[This section is printed as amended, and repealed in part, by the *CDA* 1998, s.101(2); the *PCC(S)A* 2000, s.165(1), and Sched. 9, para. 183; the *CJCSA* 2000, s.74, and Sched. 7, para. 138; and the *CJA* 2003, ss.230, 273(4) and 332, Sched. 7, Pt 8, and Sched. 18, para. 3; and as amended, as from a day to be appointed, by the *AFA* 2006, s.378(1) and (2), Sched. 16, para. 142, and Sched. 17 (omission of italicised words, insertion of words in square brackets). As to transitional provision in relation to a "transferred life prisoner", see the *CJA* 2003, s.276, and Sched. 22, para. 17.]

The *Criminal Justice Act 2003 (Sentencing) (Transitory Provisions) Order* 2005 (S.I. 2005 No. 643) modifies section 34(2)(d) (in relation to any time before the coming force of the *CJCSA* 2000, s.61) (abolition of sentences of detention in a young offender institution, custody for life etc.) by inserting the words "or detention in a young offender institution" after "sentence of imprisonment".

Criminal Justice Act 2003, Sched. 21

Section 269(5) SCHEDULE 21

DETERMINATION OF MINIMUM TERM IN RELATION TO MANDATORY LIFE SENTENCE

Interpretation

1. In this Schedule— **5–245**

"child" means a person under 18 years;

"mandatory life sentence" means a life sentence passed in circumstances where the sentence is fixed by law;

"minimum term", in relation to a mandatory life sentence, means the part of the sentence to be specified in an order under section 269(2);

"whole life order" means an order under subsection (4) of section 269.

2. Section 28 of the *Crime and Disorder Act* 1998 (meaning of "racially or religiously aggravated") applies for the purposes of this Schedule as it applies for the purposes of sections 29 to 32 of that Act.

3. For the purposes of this Schedule an offence is aggravated by sexual orientation if it is committed in circumstances falling within subsection (2)(a)(i) or (b)(i) of section 146.

Starting points

5–246 4.—(1) If—

(a) the court considers that the seriousness of the offence (or the combination of the offence and one or more offences associated with it) is exceptionally high, and

(b) the offender was aged 21 or over when he committed the offence,

the appropriate starting point is a whole life order.

(2) Cases that would normally fall within sub-paragraph (1)(a) include—

(a) the murder of two or more persons, where each murder involves any of the following—

(i) a substantial degree of premeditation or planning,

(ii) the abduction of the victim, or

(iii) sexual or sadistic conduct,

(b) the murder of a child if involving the abduction of the child or sexual or sadistic motivation,

(c) a murder done for the purpose of advancing a political, religious or ideological cause, or

(d) a murder by an offender previously convicted of murder.

5.—(1) If—

(a) the case does not fall within paragraph 4(1) but the court considers that the seriousness of the offence (or the combination of the offence and one or more offences associated with it) is particularly high, and

(b) the offender was aged 18 or over when he committed the offence,

the appropriate starting point, in determining the minimum term, is 30 years.

(2) Cases that (if not falling within paragraph 4(1)) would normally fall within sub-paragraph (1)(a) include—

(a) the murder of a police officer or prison officer in the course of his duty,

(b) a murder involving the use of a firearm or explosive,

(c) a murder done for gain (such as a murder done in the course or furtherance of robbery or burglary, done for payment or done in the expectation of gain as a result of the death),

(d) a murder intended to obstruct or interfere with the course of justice,

(e) a murder involving sexual or sadistic conduct,

(f) the murder of two or more persons,

(g) a murder that is racially or religiously aggravated or aggravated by sexual orientation, or

(h) a murder falling within paragraph 4(2) committed by an offender who was aged under 21 when he committed the offence.

6. If the offender was aged 18 or over when he committed the offence and the case does not fall within paragraph 4(1) or 5(1), the appropriate starting point, in determining the minimum term, is 15 years.

7. If the offender was aged under 18 when he committed the offence, the appropriate starting point, in determining the minimum term, is 12 years.

Aggravating and mitigating factors

5–247 8. Having chosen a starting point, the court should take into account any aggravating or mitigating factors, to the extent that it has not allowed for them in its choice of starting point.

9. Detailed consideration of aggravating or mitigating factors may result in a minimum term of any length (whatever the starting point), or in the making of a whole life order.

10. Aggravating factors (additional to those mentioned in paragraph 4(2) and 5(2)) that may be relevant to the offence of murder include—

(a) a significant degree of planning or premeditation,
(b) the fact that the victim was particularly vulnerable because of age or disability,
(c) mental or physical suffering inflicted on the victim before death,
(d) the abuse of a position of trust,
(e) the use of duress or threats against another person to facilitate the commission of the offence,
(f) the fact that the victim was providing a public service or performing a public duty, and
(g) concealment, destruction or dismemberment of the body.

11. Mitigating factors that may be relevant to the offence of murder include—
(a) an intention to cause serious bodily harm rather than to kill,
(b) lack of premeditation,
(c) the fact that the offender suffered from any mental disorder or mental disability which (although not falling within section 2(1) of the *Homicide Act* 1957), lowered his degree of culpability,
(d) the fact that the offender was provoked (for example, by prolonged stress) in a way not amounting to a defence of provocation,
(e) the fact that the offender acted to any extent in self-defence,
(f) a belief by the offender that the murder was an act of mercy, and
(g) the age of the offender.

12. Nothing in this Schedule restricts the application of—
(a) section 143(2) (previous convictions),
(b) section 143(3) (bail), or
(c) section 144 (guilty plea)[,
or of section 238(1)(b) or (c) or 239 of the *Armed Forces Act* 2006].

[Schedule 21 is printed as amended, as from a day to be appointed, by the *AFA* 2006, s.378(1), and Sched. 16, para. 236 (insertion of words in square brackets in para. 12).]

As to the terms of Schedule 21, see *ante*, §§ 5–239a *et seq.*

Offences committed before December 18, 2003

Section 269 of the 2003 Act came into force on December 18, 2003. The setting of **5–248** the minimum term for offences committed before that day is governed by a combination of that section, Schedule 21 to the 2003 Act, Schedule 22, paras 1, 2, 9 and 10, to the 2003 Act (given effect by s.276) and paragraphs IV.49.14 *et seq.* of the consolidated criminal practice direction. For the details, see the supplement.

[The next paragraph is § 5–251.]

(3) Practice

Practice Direction (Criminal Proceedings: Consolidation), para. IV.49 (as substituted by Practice Direction (Crime: Mandatory Life Sentences) (No. 2) [2004] 1 W.L.R. 2551

Life sentences

IV.49.1 This direction replaces amendment number 6 to the consolidated criminal **5–251** practice direction handed down on 18 May 2004 (previously inserted at paragraphs IV.49.1 to IV.49.25 ...). Its purpose is to give practical guidance as to the procedure for passing a mandatory life sentence under section 269 and Schedule 21 of [*sic*] the *Criminal Justice Act* 2003 ("the Act"). This direction also gives guidance as to the transitional arrangements under section 276 and Schedule 22 ... . It clarifies the correct approach to looking at the practice of the Secretary of State prior to December 2002 for the purposes of Schedule 22 of [*sic*] the Act, in the light of the judgment in *R. v. Sullivan, Gibbs, Elener and Elener* [2004] EWCA Crim. 1762 ("*Sullivan*").

IV.49.2 Section 269 of the Act came into force on 18 December 2003. Under section 269 all courts passing a mandatory life sentence must either announce in open court the minimum term the prisoner must serve before the Parole Board can consider release on licence under the provisions of section 28 of the *Crime (Sentences) Act* 1997 (as amended by section 275 of the Act) or announce that the seriousness of the offence is so exceptionally high that the early release provisions should not apply at all (a "whole life order").

IV.49.3 In setting the minimum term the court must set the term it considers appropriate taking into account the seriousness of the offence. In considering the seriousness of the offence the court must have regard to the general principles set out in Schedule 21 … and any other guidelines issued by the Sentencing Guidelines Council which are relevant to the case and not incompatible with the provisions of Schedule 21. Although it is necessary to have regard to the guidance, it is always permissible not to apply the guidance if a judge considers there are reasons for not following it. It is always necessary to have regard to the need to do justice in the particular case. However, if a court departs from any of the starting points given in Schedule 21 the court is under a duty to state its reasons for doing so.

IV.49.4 The guidance states that where the offender is 21 or over, the first step is to choose one of three starting points: "whole life", 30 years or 15 years. Where the 15 year starting point has been chosen, judges should have in mind that this starting point encompasses a very broad range of murders. At para. 35 of *Sullivan* the court found that it should not be assumed that Parliament intended to raise all minimum terms that would previously have had a lower starting point to 15 years.

IV.49.5 Where the offender was 21 or over at the time of the offence, and the court takes the view that the murder is so grave that the offender ought to spend the rest of his life in prison, the appropriate starting point is a "whole life order". The effect of such an order is that the early release provisions in section 28 of the *Crime (Sentences) Act* 1997 will not apply. Such an order should only be specified where the court considers that the seriousness of the offence (or the combination of the offence and one or more other offences associated with it) is exceptionally high. …

IV.49.6 Where the offender is aged 18 to 20 and commits a murder that is so serious that it would require a whole life order if committed by an offender aged 21 or over, the appropriate starting point will be 30 years.

IV.49.7 Where a case is not so serious as to require a "whole life order" but where the seriousness of the offence is particularly high and the offender was aged 18 or over when he committed the offence the appropriate starting point, is 30 years. …

IV.49.8 Where the offender was aged 18 or over when he committed the offence and the case does not fall within paragraph 4(1) or 5(1) of Schedule 21 the appropriate starting point is 15 years.

IV.49.9 18 to 20 year olds are only the subject of the 30 year and 15 year starting points.

IV.49.10 The appropriate starting point when setting a sentence of detention during Her Majesty's pleasure for offenders aged under 18 when they committed the offence is always 12 years.

IV.49.11 The second step after choosing a starting point is to take account of any aggravating or mitigating factors which would justify a departure from the starting point. Additional aggravating factors (other than those specified in paragraphs 4(1) and 5(1)) are listed at paragraph 10 of Schedule 21. Examples of mitigating factors are listed in paragraph 11 of Schedule 21. Taking into account the aggravating and mitigating features the court may add to or subtract from the starting point to arrive at the appropriate punitive period.

IV.49.12 The third step is that the court should consider the effect of … section 143(2) of the Act in relation to previous convictions and … section 143(3) … where the offence was committed whilst the offender was on bail. The court should also consider the effect of … section 144 … where the offender has pleaded guilty. The court should then take into account what credit the offender would have received for a remand in custody under section 240 of the Act, but for the fact that the mandatory sentence is one of life imprisonment. Where the offender has been remanded in custody in connection with the offence or a related offence, the court should have in mind that no credit will otherwise be given for this time when the prisoner is considered for early release. The appropriate time to take it into account is when setting the minimum term. The court should normally subtract the time for which the offender was remanded in custody in connection with the offence or a related offence from the punitive period it would otherwise impose in order to reach the minimum term.

IV.49.13 Following these calculations the court should have arrived at the appropriate minimum term to be announced in open court. As paragraph 9 … makes clear, the judge retains ultimate discretion and the court may arrive at any minimum term from any starting point. …

Transitional arrangements for new sentences where the offence was committed before 18 December 2003

IV.49.14 Where the court is passing a sentence of mandatory life imprisonment for an offence committed before 18 December 2003, the court should take a fourth step in determining the minimum term in accordance with section 276 and Schedule 22 .... **5–251a**

IV.49.15–IV.49.37 [*See the supplement.*]

As to the authority referred to in IV.49.1, see *R. v. Sullivan*; *R. v. Gibbs*; *R. v. Elener (Barry) and Elener (Derek)* [2005] 1 Cr.App.R. 3, CA.

[The next paragraph is § 5–251h.]

Sentencing guidelines

See Appendix K for the application of the "Reduction in Sentence for a Guilty Plea" guidelines to sentencing for murder. **5–251h**

B. Automatic Life Sentences

Section 109 of the *PCC(S)A* 2000 provided for an automatic life sentence where a person was convicted of a serious offence committed after September 30, 1997, and at the time when that offence was committed, he was 18 or over and had been convicted in any part of the United Kingdom of another serious offence. The court was absolved of this obligation if of the opinion that there were exceptional circumstances to justify it not passing such a sentence. What was a "serious offence" was prescribed by subsections (5) to (7) of section 109. The repeal of section 109 is provided for by the *CJA* 2003, s.332, and Sched. 37, Pt 7. It took effect on April 4, 2005 (S.I. 2005 No. 950, *ante*, § 5–121e), but has no application in relation to offences committed before that date: see the saving provisions in paragraphs 5 and 6 of Schedule 2 to S.I. 2005 No. 950, *ante*, §§ 5–1a, 5–1b. For the text of section 109, and the authorities in relation thereto, see §§ 5–251j *et seq.* in the supplement. **5–251i**

C. Minimum Fixed Term Sentences

(1) Legislation

Powers of Criminal Courts (Sentencing) Act 2000, ss.110, 111

Minimum of seven years for third class A drug trafficking offence

110.—(1) This section applies where— **5–252**

(a) a person is convicted of a class A drug trafficking offence committed after 30th September 1997;

(b) at the time when that offence was committed, he was 18 or over and had been convicted in any part of the United Kingdom of two other class A drug trafficking offences; and

(c) one of those other offences was committed after he had been convicted of the other.

(2) The court shall impose *an appropriate custodial sentence* [a term of imprisonment] for a term of at least seven years except where the court is of the opinion that there are particular circumstances which—

(a) relate to any of the offences or to the offender; and

(b) would make it unjust to do so in all the circumstances.

(3) [*Repealed by* CJA *2003, s.332, and Sched. 7, Pt 7.*]

(4) Where—

(a) a person is charged with a class A drug trafficking offence (which, apart from this subsection, would be triable either way), and

(b) the circumstances are such that, if he were convicted of the offence, he could be sentenced for it under subsection (2) above,

the offence shall be triable only on indictment.

(5) In this section "class A drug trafficking offence" means a drug trafficking offence committed in respect of a class A drug; and for this purpose—

"class A drug" has the same meaning as in the *Misuse of Drugs Act* 1971;

"drug trafficking offence" means any offence which is specified in—

(a) paragraph 1 of Schedule 2 to the *Proceeds of Crime Act* 2002 (drug trafficking offences), or

(b) so far as it relates to that paragraph, paragraph 10 of that Schedule.

(6) *In this section "an appropriate custodial sentence" means*—

(a) *in relation to a person who is 21 or over when convicted of the offence mentioned in subsection (1)(a) above, a sentence of imprisonment;*

(b) *in relation to a person who is under 21 at that time, a sentence of detention in a young offender institution.*

[This section is printed as amended by the *PCA* 2002, s.456, and Sched. 11, para. 37(1) and (2); and as amended, as from a day to be appointed, by the *CJCSA* 2000, s.74, and Sched. 7, para. 190 (omission of italicised words, insertion of words in square brackets).]

Minimum of three years for third domestic burglary

5–253 **111.**—(1) This section applies where—

(a) a person is convicted of a domestic burglary committed after 30th November 1999;

(b) at the time when that burglary was committed, he was 18 or over and had been convicted in England and Wales of two other domestic burglaries; and

(c) one of those other burglaries was committed after he had been convicted of the other, and both of them were committed after 30th November 1999.

(2) The court shall impose *an appropriate custodial sentence* [a sentence of imprisonment] for a term of at least three years except where the court is of the opinion that there are particular circumstances which—

(a) relate to any of the offences or to the offender; and

(b) would make it unjust to do so in all the circumstances.

(3) [*Repealed by* CJA *2003, s.332, and Sched. 7, Pt 7.*]

(4) Where—

(a) a person is charged with a domestic burglary which, apart from this subsection, would be triable either way, and

(b) the circumstances are such that, if he were convicted of the burglary, he could be sentenced for it under subsection (2) above,

the burglary shall be triable only on indictment.

(5) In this section "domestic burglary" means a burglary committed in respect of a building or part of a building which is a dwelling.

(6) [*Identical to s.110(6)*, ante, *and subject to like prospective repeal.*]

[This section is printed as amended, as from a day to be appointed, by the *CJCSA* 2000, s.74, and Sched. 7, para. 191 (omission of italicised words, insertion of words in square brackets).]

Powers of Criminal Courts (Sentencing) Act 2000, ss.112–115

Appeals where previous convictions set aside

5–254 **112.**—(1) This section applies where—

(a) a sentence has been imposed on any person under subsection (2) of section … 110 or 111 above; and

(b) any previous conviction of his without which that section would not have applied has been subsequently set aside on appeal.

(2) Notwithstanding anything in section 18 of the *Criminal Appeal Act* 1968, notice of appeal against the sentence may be given at any time within 28 days from the date on which the previous conviction was set aside.

[The words omitted from subs. (1) were repealed by the *CJA* 2003, s.332, and Sched. 37, Pt 7. For the saving provisions in relation to this repeal, see *ante*, § 5–1b.]

Certificates of convictions for purposes of Chapter III

5–255 **113.**—(1) Where—

(a) on any date after 30th September 1997 a person is convicted in England and Wales of … a class A drug trafficking offence, or on any date after 30th November 1999 a person is convicted in England and Wales of a domestic burglary, and

(b) the court by or before which he is so convicted states in open court that he has been convicted of such an offence on that date, and

(c) that court subsequently certifies that fact,

the certificate shall be evidence, for the purposes of the relevant section of this Chapter, that he was convicted of such an offence on that date.

(2) Where—

(a) after 30th September 1997 a person is convicted in England and Wales of a class A drug trafficking offence or after 30th November 1999 a person is convicted in England and Wales of a domestic burglary, and

(b) the court by or before which he is so convicted states in open court that the offence was committed on a particular day or over, or at some time during, a particular period, and

(c) that court subsequently certifies that fact,

the certificate shall be evidence, for the purposes of the relevant section of this Chapter, that the offence was committed on that day or over, or at some time during, that period.

(3) In this section—

..., "class A drug trafficking offence" and "domestic burglary" have the same meanings as in sections ..., 110 and 111 respectively; and

"the relevant section of this Chapter", in relation to any such offence, shall be construed accordingly.

[The words omitted were repealed by the *CJA* 2003, s.332, and Sched. 37, Pt 7. For the saving provision in relation to this repeal, see *ante*, § 5–1b.]

Offences under service law

114.—(1) Where— **5–256**

(a) a person has at any time been convicted of an offence under section *70 of the* Army Act *1955, section 70 of the* Air Force Act *1955 or section 42 of the* Naval Discipline Act *1957* [42 of the *Armed Forces Act* 2006], and

(b) the corresponding *civil offence (within the meaning of that Act) was* ... [offence under the law of England and Wales (within the meaning given by that section) was] a class A drug trafficking offence or a domestic burglary,

the relevant section of this Chapter shall have effect as if he had at that time been convicted in England and Wales of *the* [that] corresponding *civil* offence.

(2) Subsection (3) of section 113 above applies for the purposes of this section as it applies for the purposes of that section.

[(3) Section 48 of the *Armed Forces Act* 2006 (attempts, conspiracy, encouragement and assistance and aiding and abetting outside England and Wales) applies for the purposes of this section as if the reference in subsection (3)(b) of that section to any of the following provisions of the Act were a reference to this section.]

[As to the words omitted from subs. (1)(b), see the note to s.113, *ante*. As from a day to be appointed, the words in square brackets are inserted and the italicised words are omitted by the *AFA* 2006, s.378(1), and Sched. 16, para. 166. Subs. (3) is printed as itself amended by the *SCA* 2007, s.60, and Sched. 5, para. 3.]

As to the limited effect of this section, see *R. v. Sanders* [2007] 1 Cr.App.R.(S.) 74, CA. For further details, see the supplement, as the decision bites only in relation to section 109 of the Act of 2000 (as to which, see § 5–251j in the supplement).

Determination of day when offence committed

115. Where an offence is found to have been committed over a period of two or more days, or at some time during a period of two or more days, it shall be taken for the purposes of sections ... 110 and 111 above to have been committed on the last of those days. **5–257**

[See the note to s.113, *ante*.]

Firearms Act 1968, s.51A

Minimum sentence for certain offences under s.5

51A.—(1) This section applies where— **5–258**

(a) an individual is convicted of—

(i) an offence under section 5(1)(a), (ab), (aba), (ac), (ad), (ae), (af) or (c) of this Act,

(ii) an offence under section 5(1A)(a) of this Act, or
(iii) an offence under any of the provisions of this Act listed in subsection (1A) in respect of a firearm or ammunition specified in section 5(1)(a), (ab), (aba), (ac), (ad), (ae), (af) or (c) or section 5(1A)(a) of this Act, and

(b) the offence was committed after the commencement of this section and at a time when he was aged 16 or over.

(1A) The provisions are—
(a) section 16 (possession of firearm with intent to injure);
(b) section 16A (possession of firearm with intent to cause fear of violence);
(c) section 17 (use of firearm to resist arrest);
(d) section 18 (carrying firearm with criminal intent);
(e) section 19 (carrying a firearm in a public place);
(f) section 20(1) (trespassing in a building with firearm).

(2) The court shall impose an appropriate custodial sentence (or order for detention) for a term of at least the required minimum term (with or without a fine) unless the court is of the opinion that there are exceptional circumstances relating to the offence or to the offender which justify its not doing so.

(3) [*Effectively identical to s.115 of the 2000 Act*, ante, *§ 5–257*.]

(4) In this section "appropriate custodial sentence (or order for detention)" means—
(a) in relation to England and Wales—
(i) in the case of an offender who is aged 18 or over when convicted, a sentence of imprisonment, and
(ii) in the case of an offender who is aged under 18 at that time, a sentence of detention under section 91 of the *Powers of Criminal Courts (Sentencing) Act* 2000;
(b) [*Scotland*].

(5) In this section "the required minimum term" means—
(a) in relation to England and Wales—
(i) in the case of an offender who was aged 18 or over when he committed the offence, five years, and
(ii) in the case of an offender who was under 18 at that time, three years, and
(b) [*Scotland*].

[This section was inserted by the *CJA* 2003, s.287, as from January 22, 2004 (*Criminal Justice Act 2003 (Commencement No. 2 and Saving Provisions) Order* 2004 (S.I. 2004 No. 81)). It is printed as amended, and repealed in part, by the *VCRA* 2006, ss.30(1) to (3), and 65, and Sched. 5. The amendments (insertion of subss. (1)(a)(iii) and (1A)) apply only in relation to offences committed on or after April 6, 2007: see s.30(5), and the *Violent Crime Reduction Act 2006 (Commencement No. 2) Order* 2007 (S.I. 2007 No. 858).]

The *Firearms (Sentencing) (Transitory Provisions) Order* 2007 (S.I. 2007 No. 1324) provides that in relation to any time before the commencement of the *CJCSA* 2000, s.61 (abolition of sentences of detention in young offender institution, custody for life, *etc.*), section 51A(4) of the 1968 Act has effect as if (a) the reference, in sub-paragraph (a)(i), to an offender aged 18 or over were a reference to an offender aged 21 or over, and (b) there were inserted a new sub-paragraph (ia) after sub-paragraph (a), providing that in the case of an offender who is aged at least 18 but who is under 21 when convicted "appropriate custodial sentence" means a sentence of detention under the *PCC(S)A* 2000, s.96. The order, which remedies the lacuna identified in *R. v. Campbell* [2006] 2 Cr.App.R.(S.) 96, CA, does not apply to offences committed before it came into force (May 28, 2007).

(2) Practice

Burglary

5–259 Attempted burglary is not "burglary" for the purposes of section 111: *R. v. Maguire* [2003] 2 Cr.App.R.(S.) 10, CA.

In *R. v. Webster* [2004] 2 Cr.App.R.(S.) 25, CA, it was held that an offender who had indicated an intention to plead guilty to an offence of burglary and had been committed for sentence to the Crown Court had been "convicted" of the offence for the purposes of section 111 even though he had not been sentenced for it. The court's attention does not appear to have been drawn to *S. (an Infant) v. Manchester City Recorder* [1971] A.C. 481, HL (*ante*, §§ 2–200, 4–186). In *R. v. Hoare* [2004] 2 Cr.App.R.(S.) 50, CA, it was held that the offences and convictions must occur in the right sequence, *viz.* (i) commission of the first offence; (ii) conviction of the first offence; (iii) commission of the second offence; (iv) conviction of the second offence; (v) commission of the third offence; and (vi) the conviction of the third offence.

"unjust"

A minimum sentence prescribed by section 110 is not to be regarded as "unjust" within subsection (2) merely because it would be regarded as "manifestly excessive" for the offence in question; the purpose of the section is to oblige the court, absent circumstances making it unjust to do so, to impose the minimum sentence in circumstances where, otherwise, a sentence of such length would be inappropriate; if that were not the intention, it was difficult to see what the intention was: *R. v. Harvey* [2000] 1 Cr.App.R.(S.) 368, CA. **5–260**

The recommendation in the Sentencing Guidelines Council's "New sentences: *Criminal Justice Act* 2003" guideline (Appendix K–49) recommending that custodial sentences of 12 months or more imposed under the framework of the 2003 Act be reduced by 15 per cent does not apply to a sentence imposed under section 110; the terms of section 110 require the imposition of the minimum sentence except in prescribed circumstances, and whilst section 170 of the 2003 Act (*ante*, § 5–100) requires the court to have regard to any guideline issued by the council, the guideline itself did not expressly purport to refer to sentences under section 110 and it could not be said that the existence of the guideline fell within the prescribed circumstances justifying the non-imposition of the minimum sentence: *Att.-Gen.'s Reference (No. 6 of 2006)* (*R. v. Farish*) [2007] 1 Cr.App.R.(S.) 12, CA.

Where sentence was adjourned for an assessment of the offender's suitability for a drug treatment and testing order, in circumstances giving rise to a legitimate expectation that such a sentence would be imposed if the report were favourable, it was unjust to impose sentence under section 111 where the report was favourable: *R. v. Gibson* [2004] 2 Cr.App.R.(S.) 84, CA.

For other examples of the Court of Appeal finding that there were "particular circumstances" that made it unjust to impose the minimum sentence required by section 110 on conviction of a third drug trafficking offence, see *R. v. Turner* [2006] 1 Cr.App.R.(S.) 95, and *R. v. McDonagh* [2006] 1 Cr.App.R.(S.) 111. In the latter case, the court emphasised that the test of "particular circumstances" under sections 110 and 111 is not the same as the "exceptional circumstances" test in section 109 (see § 5–251l in the supplement).

"exceptional circumstances" (1968 Act, s.51A(2))

In *R. v. Rehman*; *R. v. Wood* [2006] 1 Cr.App.R.(S.) 77, CA, it was held that when section 51A(2) of the 1968 Act was read in its context, it became clear that circumstances were to be regarded as "exceptional" where to impose the minimum term would result in an arbitrary and disproportionate sentence; the provision was capable of resulting in such a sentence because of the requirement that, for deterrent purposes, the minimum sentence was to be passed irrespective of the circumstances of the offence or the offender, unless they passed the exceptional threshold, and the possibility was increased by virtue of the fact that an offence under section 5 could be committed without *mens rea*; the deterrent purpose of the provision could have no effect in relation to a person who was not aware that he might be committing an offence under the section; accordingly, the reference in that section to the circumstances of the offender was most important; and it followed that the fact that an offender was unfit to serve a five-year sentence might be relevant, as was the fact that he was of advanced years; however, it was important not to divide the circumstances into those that were capable of being **5–260a** exceptional and those which were not; moreover, the section made it clear that it was the opinion of the court that was critical as to what exceptional circumstances were; unless, therefore, the judge was clearly wrong in identifying exceptional circumstances when they did not exist, or in not identifying them when they did exist, the Court of Appeal would not readily interfere.

In *R. v. Harrison* [2006] 2 Cr.App.R.(S.) 56, CA, it was held that when a judge is considering whether there were exceptional circumstances where an offender was intent on disposing of a weapon for another, it was wrong to focus only on the nature of the weapon, without taking an overall view of all the relevant aspects of the case, including the way in which the offender initially came into possession of the weapon, how long he had had it, what he did with it, and what he intended to do with it. There may be circumstances where a person who unwillingly and unexpectedly found himself with a prohibited weapon foisted upon him may feel impelled to dispose of it so that it could never again be used, rather than involve himself in the upheaval and disturbance of a police inquiry; but anyone who chose such a course had to be prepared to justify himself, should his involvement with the weapon come to light.

In *R. v. Edwards (Michelle Marie)* [2007] 1 Cr.App.R.(S.) 111, CA, the court quashed a minimum sentence imposed on an offender who had acted as a custodian of an automatic firearm for a period of two months and adopted the "holistic approach" recommended in *R. v. Rehman*; *R. v. Wood* (*ante*), to the mitigating factors (none of which was decisive by itself), namely that she had been unable to resist the pressure of apparently seasoned criminal acquaintances, those who had commissioned the offences were probably those who caused her detection, her immediate reaction when police officers attended her house was to admit the offence and to name those who had given her the gun, she had pleaded guilty, the weapon was in a poor state of repair, she presented a low risk of re-offending and she was a single mother of three young children.

Where exceptional circumstances are found, the minimum term should be kept as a starting point: *R. v. Bowler*, unreported, July 27, 2007, CA ([2007] EWCA Crim. 2068); and *R. v. Beard* [2008] 2 Cr.App.R.(S.) 41, CA (there being a clear obligation on those who possess prohibited weapons/ammunition to ensure that they comply with the law).

In *R. v. Barber (David Stuart)* [2006] 1 Cr.App.R.(S.) 90, CA, it was said that the regime under section 51A was not comparable to the automatic life sentence regime under section 109 of the 2000 Act, since its rationale was the inherent danger of unlawful possession of certain firearms and their availability, rather than the dangerousness of the offender (distinguishing *R. v. Offen* [2001] 1 W.L.R. 253, CA (§ 5–251l in the supplement)); the rights of the offender under the ECHR are safeguarded by the possibility of the imposition of a lesser sentence in exceptional circumstances, and compatibility with the Convention should therefore be determined on a case-by-case basis.

Plea of guilty

5–261 As to the permissible reduction of a minimum sentence under section 110 or 111 of the 2000 Act (but not s.51A of the 1968 Act) where there is a plea of guilty, see section 144(2) of the *CJA* 2003, *ante*, § 5–78.

The meaning of section 51A(2) is "plain and unambiguous" and does not allow for a reduction of the required minimum term on account of a guilty plea: *R. v. Jordan*; *R. v. Alleyne*; *R. v. Redfern* [2005] 2 Cr.App.R.(S.) 44, CA.

D. DISCRETIONARY CUSTODIAL SENTENCES

(1) General restrictions

(a) *Legislation*

Powers of Criminal Courts (Sentencing) Act 2000, s.76

Meaning of "custodial sentence"

5–262 **76.**—(1) In this Act "custodial sentence" means—

(a) a sentence of imprisonment (as to which, see section 89(1)(a) below);

(b) a sentence of detention under section 90 or 91 below;
(c) *a sentence of custody for life under section 93 or 94 below*;
(d) *a sentence of detention in a young offender institution (under section 96 below or otherwise)*; or
(e) a detention and training order (under section 100 below).

(2) In subsection (1) above "sentence of imprisonment" does not include a committal for contempt of court or any kindred offence.

[The words italicised are repealed as from a day to be appointed by the *CJCSA* 2000, Sched. 8.]

[The next paragraph is § 5–265.]

Criminal Justice Act 2003, ss.152, 153

General restrictions on discretionary custodial sentences

General restrictions on imposing discretionary custodial sentences

152.—(1) This section applies where a person is convicted of an offence punishable with a custodial sentence other than one— **5–265**
(a) fixed by law, or
(b) falling to be imposed under section 51A(2) of the *Firearms Act* 1968, under section 110(2) or 111(2) of the *Sentencing Act*, under section 29(4) or (6) of the *Violent Crime Reduction Act* 2006 or under section 225(2) or 226(2) of this Act.

(2) The court must not pass a custodial sentence unless it is of the opinion that the offence, or the combination of the offence and one or more offences associated with it, was so serious that neither a fine alone nor a community sentence can be justified for the offence.

(3) Nothing in subsection (2) prevents the court from passing a custodial sentence on the offender if—
(a) he fails to express his willingness to comply with a requirement which is proposed by the court to be included in a community order and which requires an expression of such willingness, or
(b) he fails to comply with an order under section 161(2) (pre-sentence drug testing).

[This section is printed as amended by the *VCRA* 2006, s.49, and Sched. 1, para. 9(1) and (4); and the *CJIA* 2008, s.148(1), and Sched. 26, paras 59 and 66.]

Length of discretionary custodial sentences: general provision

153.—(1) This section applies where a court passes a custodial sentence other than one fixed by law or ... imposed under section 225 or 226. **5–266**

(2) Subject to section 51A(2) of the *Firearms Act* 1968, sections 110(2) and 111(2) of the *Sentencing Act*, section 29(4) or (6) of the *Violent Crime Reduction Act* 2006 and sections 227(2) and 228(2) of this Act, the custodial sentence must be for the shortest term (not exceeding the permitted maximum) that in the opinion of the court is commensurate with the seriousness of the offence, or the combination of the offence and one or more offences associated with it.

[This section is printed as amended by the *VCRA* 2006, s.49, and Sched. 1, para. 9(1) and (5); and the *CJIA* 2008, ss.148(1) and 149, Sched. 26, paras 59 and 67, and Sched. 28, Pt 2.]

Sections 152 and 153 came into force on April 4, 2005 (S.I. 2005 No. 950, *ante*, § 5–122). For the saving of the former legislation (*PCC(S)A* 2000, ss.79 and 80) and the disapplication of these provisions in relation to offences committed before that date, see paragraph 5 of Schedule 2 to S.I. 2005 No. 950, *ante*, § 5–1a. For the text of the former provisions, see §§ 5–275a *et seq.* in the supplement.

Powers of Criminal Courts (Sentencing) Act 2000, s.78

General limit on magistrates' courts' powers

General limit on magistrates' court's power to impose imprisonment or detention in a young offender institution

78.—(1) *A magistrates' court shall not have power to impose imprisonment,* or detention in a young offender institution, *for more than six months in respect of any one offence.* **5–267**

(2) *Unless expressly excluded, subsection (1) above shall apply even if the offence in question is one for which a person would otherwise be liable on summary conviction to imprisonment* or detention in a young offender institution *for more than six months.*

(3) *Subsection (1) above is without prejudice to section 133 of the* Magistrates' Courts Act *1980 (consecutive terms of imprisonment).*

(4) *Any power of a magistrates' court to impose a term of imprisonment for non-payment of a fine, or for want of sufficient* distress [goods] *to satisfy a fine, shall not be limited by virtue of subsection (1) above.*

[(4A) *In subsection (4) the reference to want of sufficient goods to satisfy a fine is a reference to circumstances where—*

(a) *there is power to use the procedure in Schedule 12 to the* Tribunals, Courts and Enforcement Act *2007 to recover the fine from a person, but*

(b) *it appears, after an attempt has been made to exercise the power, that the person's goods are insufficient to pay the amount outstanding (as defined by paragraph 50(3) of that Schedule).*]

(5) *In subsection (4) above "fine" includes a pecuniary penalty but does not include a pecuniary forfeiture or pecuniary compensation.*

(6) *In this section "impose imprisonment" means pass a sentence of imprisonment or fix a term of imprisonment for failure to pay any sum of money, or for want of sufficient distress to satisfy any sum of money, or for failure to do or abstain from doing anything required to be done or left undone.*

(7) *Section 132 of the* Magistrates' Courts Act *1980 contains provision about the minimum term of imprisonment which may be imposed by a magistrates' court.*

[This section is printed as amended, as from a day to be appointed, by the *Tribunals, Courts and Enforcement Act* 2007, s.62(3), and Sched. 13, paras 131 and 132 (substitution of "goods" for "distress" in subs. (4), insertion of subs. (4A)). It is repealed in part, as from a day to be appointed, by the *CJCSA* 2000, s.74 and Sched. 7, para. 177 (omission of "or detention in a young offender institution" in side note and in subss. (1) and (2)); and is repealed as a whole, as from a day to be appointed, by the *CJA* 2003, s.334, and Sched. 37, Pt 7.]

Criminal Justice Act 2003, s.154

General limit on magistrates' court's power to impose imprisonment

[General limit on magistrates' court's power to impose imprisonment

5–268 **154.**—(1) A magistrates' court does not have power to impose imprisonment for more than 12 months in respect of any one offence.

(2) Unless expressly excluded, subsection (1) applies even if the offence in question is one for which a person would otherwise be liable on summary conviction to imprisonment for more than 12 months.

(3)–(5) [*Identical to s.78(3)–(5) of the* PCC(S)A *2000*, ante, *§ 5–267, save for the omission from each subsection of the word* "above".]

(6) [*Identical to s.78(6) of the* PCC(S)A *2000*, ante, *§ 5–267*.]

(7) Section 132 of the *Magistrates' Courts Act* 1980 contains provisions about the minimum term of imprisonment which may be imposed by a magistrates' court.

[(8) In this section references to want of sufficient goods to satisfy a fine or other sum of money have the meaning given by section 79(4) of the *Magistrates' Courts Act* 1980.]]

[This section comes into force on a day to be appointed. As from a day to be appointed, in subss. (4) and (6), the word "goods" is substituted for the word "distress", and subs. (8) is inserted, by the *Tribunals, Courts and Enforcement Act* 2007, s.62(3), and Sched. 13, paras 153 and 154.]

Magistrates' Courts Act 1980, ss.132, 133

Minimum term

5–269 **132.** A magistrates' court shall not impose imprisonment for less than 5 days.

Consecutive terms of imprisonment

5–270 **133.**—(1) Subject to section 265 of the *Criminal Justice Act* 2003, a magistrates' court imposing imprisonment *or youth custody* on any person may order that the term of imprisonment *or youth custody* shall commence on the expiration of any other term of imprisonment or youth custody imposed by that or any other court; but where a magistrates' court imposes two or more terms of imprisonment *or youth custody* to run consecutively the aggregate of such terms shall not, subject to the provisions of this section, exceed *6 months* [65 weeks].

(2) *If two or more of the terms imposed by the court are imposed in respect of an offence triable either way which was tried summarily otherwise than in pursuance of section 22(2) above, the aggregate of the terms so imposed and any other terms imposed by the court may exceed 6 months but shall not, subject to the following provisions of this section, exceed 12 months.*

(2A) *In relation to the imposition of terms of detention in a young offender institution subsection (2) above shall have effect as if the reference to an offence triable either way were a reference to such an offence or an offence triable only on indictment.*

(3) The limitations imposed by *the preceding subsections* [subsection (1) above] shall not operate to reduce the aggregate of the terms that the court may impose in respect of any offences below the term which the court has power to impose in respect of any one of these offences.

(4) Where a person has been sentenced by a magistrates' court to imprisonment and a fine for the same offence, a period of imprisonment imposed for non-payment of the fine, or for want of sufficient *distress* [goods] to satisfy the fine, shall not be subject to the limitations imposed by the preceding subsections.

(5) For the purposes of this section a term of imprisonment shall be deemed to be imposed in respect of an offence if it is imposed as a sentence or in default of payment of a sum adjudged to be paid by the conviction or for want of sufficient *distress* [goods] to satisfy such a sum.

[This section is printed as amended by the *CJA* 1982, Sched. 14; the *CJA* 1988, Sched. 15; the *CDA* 1998, s.119, and Sched. 8, para. 46; the *PCC(S)A* 2000, s.165(1), and Sched. 9, para. 76; and the *CJA* 2003, s.304, and Sched. 32, paras 25 and 30. The references to "youth custody" in subs. (1) should be read as references to "detention in a young offender institution" by virtue of the *CJA* 1988, s.123, and Sched. 8, para. 2. The first, second and fourth of those references are repealed, together with subs. (2A), as from a day to be appointed by the *CJCSA* 2000, s.74, and Sched. 7, para. 66. The words in square brackets in subss. (1) and (3) are substituted, as from a day to be appointed, for the italicised words that precede them, by the *CJA* 2003, s.155(1), (2) and (4). Subs. (2) is repealed, as from a day to be appointed, by *ibid.*, s.155(1) and (3). In subss. (4) and (5), the word in square brackets is substituted for the italicised word, as from a day to be appointed, by the *Tribunals, Courts and Enforcement Act* 2007, s.62(3), and Sched. 13, paras 45 and 62.]

(b) *Authorities*

"Associated offences" (see ss.152(2) and 153(2))

See section 161(1) of the *PCC(S)A* 2000 (*ante*, § 5–2); and the authorities referred to **5–271** at § 5–8, *ante*.

The criterion of seriousness

The starting point under the 2003 legislation must be section 143 (*ante*, § 5–54), **5–272** which focuses attention on culpability, harm caused or intended or which ought to have been foreseen, previous convictions and whether or not the offence was committed whilst on bail. There was no corresponding provision in the legislation of 2000, but section 79(2)(a) of the *PCC(S)A* 2000 did stipulate that a court should not pass a custodial sentence unless of the opinion "that the offence, or the combination of the offence and one or more offences associated with it, was so serious that only such a sentence can be justified" for it (*cf.* s.152(2) of the 2003 Act, *ante*). The meaning of this provision was considered in *R. v. Howells* [1999] 1 Cr.App.R. 98, CA. Lord Bingham C.J. said that it would be dangerous and wrong for the Court of Appeal to lay down prescriptive rules, and any guidance given, however general, would be subject to exceptions and qualifications. In approaching cases which were on or near the custody threshold, courts would usually find it helpful to begin by considering the nature and extent of the defendant's criminal intention and the nature and extent of any injury or damage caused to the victim. Other things being equal, an offence which was deliberate and pre-meditated would usually be more serious than one which was spontaneous or which involved an excessive response to provocation; an offence which inflicted personal injury or mental trauma, particularly if permanent, would usually be more serious than one which inflicted financial loss only.

In deciding whether to impose a custodial sentence in borderline cases the sentencing court would ordinarily take account of matters relating to the offender, such as an admission of responsibility for the offence, particularly if reflected in a plea of guilty tendered at the earliest opportunity and accompanied by hard evidence of genuine remorse, as shown (for example) by an expression of regret to the victim and an offer of compensation.

Where offending has been fuelled by addiction to drink or drugs, the court would be inclined to look more favourably on an offender who has already demonstrated (by taking practical steps to that end) a genuine, self-motivated determination to address his addiction. Youth and immaturity will often justify a less rigorous penalty than would be appropriate for an adult.

Some measure of leniency would ordinarily be extended to offenders of previous good character, the more so if there is evidence of positive good character (such as a solid employment record or faithful discharge of family duties) as opposed to a mere absence of previous convictions. It will sometimes be appropriate to take account of family responsibilities, or physical or mental disability.

While the court would never impose a custodial sentence unless satisfied that it was necessary to do so, there would be even greater reluctance to impose a custodial sentence on an offender who had never before served such a sentence.

Courts should always bear in mind that criminal sentences are in almost every case intended to protect the public, whether by punishing the offender or reforming him, or deterring him and others, or all of these things. Courts could not and should not be unmindful of the important public dimension of criminal sentencing and the importance of maintaining public confidence in the sentencing system.

5–273 Where the court was of the opinion that an offence, or the combination of an offence and one or more offences associated with it, was so serious that only a custodial sentence could be justified and that such a sentence should be passed, the sentence imposed should be no longer than was necessary to meet the penal purpose which the court has in mind (see *R. v. Ollerenshaw* [1999] 1 Cr.App.R.(S.) 65, CA).

Sentences commensurate with the seriousness of the offence

5–274 In deciding what term of custody is commensurate with an offence or group of offences, the court may take account of all the offences for which the offender is to be sentenced on the same occasion provided that they are "associated offences." Where a defendant has been indicted on a small number of charges representing a greater number of offences as sample counts or specimen charges, the offences which are not included in the indictment are not "associated offences", as section 161(1) (*ante*, § 5–2) limits the expression to offences of which the offender has been convicted, or which he has asked the court to take into consideration. The charges which are represented by the specimen charges cannot be treated as offences taken into consideration unless they are identified and admitted in the usual way; see *Anderson v. DPP* [1978] A.C. 964, HL; *R. v. Crutchley and Tonks*, 15 Cr.App.R.(S.) 627, CA; and *R. v. Hose*, 16 Cr.App.R.(S.) 682, CA (*ante*, § 5–110). Section 156(1) and (2) of the *CJA* 2003 requires the court, when assessing the seriousness of an offence or group of offences for the purpose of section 152(2) or section 153(2), to "take into account all such information as is available to it about the circumstances of the offence or (as the case may be) of the offence and the offence or offences associated with it, including any aggravating or mitigating factors."

Deterrence/ prevalence

5–275 In *R. v. Oosthuizen* [2006] 1 Cr.App.R.(S.) 73, CA, it was said that, having regard to the "Overarching principles: Seriousness" guideline issued by the Sentencing Guidelines Council (Appendix K–27), a judge should not, in the absence of statistics or other evidence demonstrating a prevalence greater than that nationally of a particular type of offence (which evidence could and should be made available to the court by the CPS, the local Criminal Justice Board or otherwise), assume that prevalence of that offence was more marked in the locality of the court than it was nationally; to do so would be particularly hazardous where a guideline (whether in the form of a decision of the Court of Appeal or issued by the Sentencing Guidelines Council) or specific guidance in relation to particular offences was intended to be of national application.

Prison overcrowding

In *Att.-Gen.'s Reference (No. 11 of 2006) (R. v. Scarth)* [2006] 2 Cr.App.R.(S.) 108, CA, it was said that prison overcrowding may be a relevant factor where a case falls on the borderline between a non-custodial and a custodial disposal, as it might hinder or obstruct the process of reformation and rehabilitation, whereas a court should have regard to the importance of imposing a sentence that promotes those objectives. Furthermore, prison overcrowding made it particularly important that courts should abide by sections 152 and 153 of the 2003 Act (*ante*, §§ 5–265, 5–266), and not impose a custodial sentence unless of the opinion that the offence was so serious that neither a fine nor a community sentence could be justified, and limit any custodial sentence to the shortest term commensurate with the seriousness of the offence. **5–276**

See also *R. v. Seed*; *R. v. Stark* [2007] 2 Cr.App.R.(S.) 69, CA, as to the importance of courts paying close regard to the requirements of sections 152 and 153 and as to the need, when considering the length of a custodial sentence, to bear in mind that the prison regime is likely to be more punitive at times of overcrowding.

[The next paragraph is § 5–278.]

(2) Imprisonment

(a) *Age*

Powers of Criminal Courts (Sentencing) Act 2000, s.89

Restriction on imposing imprisonment on persons under 21

89.—(1) Subject to subsection (2) below, no court shall— **5–278**

(a) pass a sentence of imprisonment on a person for an offence if he is aged under *21* [18] when convicted of the offence; or

(b) commit a person aged under *21* [18] to prison for any reason.

(2) Nothing in subsection (1) above shall prevent the committal to prison of a person aged under *21* [18] who is—

(a) remanded in custody;

(b) committed in custody for *trial or* sentence; or

(c) sent in custody for trial under section 51 [or 51A] of the *Crime and Disorder Act* 1998.

[This section is printed as amended as from a day to be appointed by the *CJCSA* 2000, s.74 and Sched. 7, para. 180 (substitution of "18" for "21"); and the *CJA* 2003, s.41, and Sched. 3, para. 74(1) and (3) (omission of the words "trial or", insertion of "or 51A"). The first of the amendments made by the 2003 Act came into force on May 9, 2005 (*Criminal Justice Act 2003 (Commencement No. 9) Order* 2005 (S.I. 2005 No. 1267)) in relation to cases sent for trial under section 51A(3)(d) of the *CDA* 1998. Otherwise they come into force on a day to be appointed.]

As to the determination of age, see section 164(1) of the 2000 Act, *ante*, § 5–5; and section 305(2) of the *CJA* 2003 (*ante*, § 5–7). **5–279**

Where a court imposes a sentence on the basis of an assumption that the offender is of a particular age, the sentence will not be unlawful if it is subsequently discovered that he is of a different age: see *R. v. Brown*, 11 Cr.App.R.(S.) 263, CA.

Where an offender has crossed a relevant age threshold between the date of the offence and the date of conviction, culpability was to be judged by reference to the offender's age at the time of committing the offence, and it was fair and just to take as the starting point the sentence that the offender would be likely to have received if he had been sentenced at the date of the offence; but there was scope for flexibility in that the sentence which would have been imposed at the time of the offence was not a sole or determining factor, though a powerful one: *R. v. Bowker* [2008] 1 Cr.App.R.(S.) 72, CA; and, where the court was dealing with an 18-year-old at the date of conviction, it was bound to have regard to the purposes of sentencing as set out in section 142 of the *CJA* 2003 (*ante*, § 5–53), whereas a court that is dealing with an offender under that age, should generally focus more on the requirements of the offender and his rehabilitation (*CDA* 1998, s.37 (*ante*, § 5–53a)): *ibid*. In an earlier decision (*R. v. Ghafoor* [2003] 1 Cr.App.R.(S.) 84), the court had said that it would rarely be necessary for a court even to consider passing a sentence that is more severe than the maximum that it would have had jurisdiction to pass at the date of the offence. Whilst, as the court emphasised in *Bowker*, this allowed for a measure of flexibility, it was applied with excessive rigidity in a series of subsequent decisions: see *R. v. L.M.* [2003] 2 Cr.App.R.(S.) 26, CA, *R. v. Jones* [2004] 1 Cr.App.R.(S.) 18, CA, *R. v. R.* (2006) 150 S.J. 1607, CA, and *R. v. Britton* [2007] 1 Cr.App.R.(S.) 121, CA.

In *R. v. A.H.*, 167 J.P. 30, the Court of Appeal appears to have proceeded on the basis that, provided that there had been no undue delay in the prosecution of the offence, no issue arose as to the appropriateness of sentencing the offender in accordance with the regime applicable at the date of conviction.

As to there being no issue under Article 7 of the ECHR (*post*, § 16–97) where an offender is sentenced by reference to the regime applicable at the date of conviction, see the *obiter* observation of the court in *Bowker*, *ante* (at [27]), and the 2006 edition of this work where it was also suggested that the *Ghafoor* approach was too inflexible; that the starting point should be that Parliament has decreed that the regime to be applied is that applicable at the date of conviction and that, therefore, the sentence that would have been applied at the date of the offence should be no more than one consideration—the weight to be accorded to it varying according to all the circumstances.

(b) *Maximum*

Powers of Criminal Courts (Sentencing) Act 2000, s.77

Liability to imprisonment on conviction on indictment

5–280 **77.** Where a person is convicted on indictment of an offence against any enactment and is for that offence liable to be sentenced to imprisonment, but the sentence is not by any enactment either limited to a specified term or expressed to extend to imprisonment for life, the person so convicted shall be liable to imprisonment for not more than two years.

Common law offences

5–281 For a common law offence (for which no maximum has been provided by statute), there is no limit to the term of imprisonment that may be imposed, provided it is not inordinate: *Castro v. R.* (1880) 5 Q.B.D. 490 at 508, 509. A sentence of life imprisonment may therefore be imposed, if the criteria for such a sentence are satisfied: *R. v. Szczerba* [2002] 2 Cr.App.R.(S.) 86, CA.

Most serious example of the offence

5–282 The maximum sentence provided by law for an offence should normally be reserved for the most serious examples of the offence: *R. v. Byrne*, 62 Cr.App.R. 159, CA; and *R. v. Pinto* [2006] 2 Cr.App.R.(S.) 87, CA (maximum should be passed only in the most truly exceptional cases, which are so serious that it is difficult to imagine a yet more serious example of the offence). Judges should not use their imaginations to conjure up unlikely worst possible kinds of case. What they should consider is the worst type of offence which comes before the court and ask themselves whether the particular case they are dealing with comes within the broad band of that type. When the maximum sentence is low, the band may be wide: *R. v. Ambler and Hargreaves* [1976] Crim.L.R. 266, CA (approved in *R. v. Butt (Sohail)* [2006] 2 Cr.App.R.(S.) 59, CA, and *R. v. Bright* [2008] Crim.L.R. 482, CA). Where a statute provides that an offence can be committed in more than one way, and one way of committing it is clearly more serious than the other, it will normally be wrong to impose the maximum term for the less serious mode of committing the offence.

The fact that the sentencer considers that Parliament has set the maximum sentence for a particular offence too low is not a ground for imposing the maximum sentence when there are relevant mitigating factors such as a plea of guilty (see *R. v. Carroll*, 16 Cr.App.R.(S.) 488, CA). The maximum sentence for any offence should be reserved for the most serious offences of that kind, while any appropriate discount (for example, for a plea of guilty, the recovery of stolen property or subsequent co-operation with the police) should be made from a level of sentence which is commensurate with the seriousness of that offence within the range established by the relevant statute.

Where the offender is convicted of an offence of a general nature on facts which would fall within a more narrowly defined offence for which a lower maximum sentence is provided, the sentencer should have regard to the lower maximum sentence, notwithstanding that it is not strictly applicable. In *R. v. Quayle*, 14 Cr.App.R.(S.) 726, CA, where the charge was of indecent assault consisting of sexual intercourse with a girl under 16, it was held that the sentencer should not have imposed a sentence of more than two years, the maximum sentence for unlawful sexual intercourse with a girl of that age. See also *R. v. Hinton*, 16 Cr.App.R.(S.) 523, CA; *R. v. Blair* [1996] 1 Cr.App.R.(S.) 336, CA (a case of indecent assault on a defective); and *R. v. J.* [2003] 1 W.L.R. 1590, CA. *Per contra*, *R. v. Figg* [2004] 1 Cr.App.R.(S.) 68, CA, where it was said that there was no general principle to the effect that the sentencer was limited to the lower maximum sentence, and observing that the fact of an anomaly in sentencing powers is not in itself decisive.

Cases with substantial mitigation

It will seldom be appropriate to impose the maximum sentence in a case where there are substantial mitigating factors: see *R. v. Markus* [1974] 3 W.L.R. 645, CA; *R. v. Thompson*, 2 Cr.App.R.(S.) 244, CA; and *R. v. Cade*, 6 Cr.App.R.(S.) 28, CA. **5–283**

Plea of guilty

As an offender who pleads guilty to a charge may normally expect some recognition in the form of a reduction in the sentence which would have been appropriate on a conviction by the jury, it will seldom be appropriate to impose the maximum sentence on an offender who has pleaded guilty, if the case is one to which the normal practice of recognising guilty pleas applies (*ante*, § 5–80): see *R. v. Barnes*, 5 Cr.App.R.(S.) 368, CA; and *R. v. Green*, 14 Cr.App.R.(S.) 682, CA. **5–284**

Consecutive maximum terms

It is not necessarily wrong in principle to impose consecutive maximum sentences, provided that each individual offence is of the most serious kind that can reasonably be contemplated, and the normal principles relating to consecutive terms are observed. For examples, see *R. v. Hunter*, 1 Cr.App.R.(S.) 7, CA; *R. v. Prime*, 5 Cr.App.R.(S.) 127, CA. **5–285**

Effect of change in maximum sentence

Where a statute increases a penalty for an existing offence, or introduces a new sentencing power, it is the usual (although not invariable) practice to include in the statute itself or in the commencement order which brings the relevant provision into force a provision to the effect that the new penalty or sentencing power will apply only to offences committed on or after the commencement date of the provision concerned. Where no such express provision is made, the statute must, by virtue of the *Human Rights Act* 1998, s.3, be interpreted consistently with Article 7 of the ECHR (*post*, § 16–97), which provides that no heavier penalty shall be imposed for an offence than the one that was applicable at the time the offence was committed. This gives statutory effect to the established principle of English law that a statute will not be interpreted so as to create a retrospective increase in penalty in the absence of express statutory language to **5–286** that effect (see *Att.-Gen.'s Reference (No. 48 of 1994) (R. v. Jeffrey)*, 16 Cr.App.R.(S.) 980, CA, *R. v. Penwith JJ., ex p. Casey*, 1 Cr.App.R.(S.) 265, DC, and *Re Barretto* [1994] Q.B. 392, CA (Civ. Div.). A statute which expressly provides for an increased or new penalty to have retrospective effect is likely to be found incompatible with a Convention right under the *Human Rights Act* 1998, s.4 (see *Welch v. U.K.*, 20 E.H.R.R. 247).

Where an offence of indecent assault was charged as having been committed on a day unknown between days before and after the increased penalty under the *SOA* 1985 took effect, the maximum was the pre-increase penalty, this being an Act with express provision against retroactivity (see s.5(5)): *R. v. S.*, 13 Cr.App.R.(S.) 306, CA. *Aliter*, where, notwithstanding the dates in the indictment, the case was conducted throughout on the basis that the offence, if committed at all, was committed after the date of the increase: *R. v. B.*, 14 Cr.App.R.(S.) 744, CA.

Where a count alleged a conspiracy to facilitate the illegal entry of immigrants between January 1, 2000, and March 9, 2000, and the maximum sentence for the offence was increased by legislation taking effect on February 14, 2000, it was held that the maximum sentence for the offence was the pre-increase maximum, notwithstanding that the largest number of immigrants was landed on February 24, 2000: *R. v. Hobbs* [2002] 2 Cr.App.R.(S.) 22, CA. In *Ecer and Zeyrek v. Turkey* (2002) 35 E.H.R.R. 26, however, the European Court of Human Rights implied that, in the case of a continuing offence the maximum penalty for which was increased during the continuation of the offence, there would be no violation of the principle against retroactivity if sentence were passed by reference to the increased maximum, provided, first, that the charge alleges the continuation of the offence to a date after the date of increase, and, secondly, that the court is satisfied that the criminal activity did in fact continue after the date of increase.

Where there is doubt as to whether an offence was committed before or after the date of an increase in penalty, the solution is to have two counts, appropriately worded: see *R. v. Cairns* [1998] 1 Cr.App.R.(S.) 434, CA.

Where the maximum penalty is reduced between the date of offence and the date of sentence, the reduced maximum will normally apply: see *R. v. Shaw* [1996] 2 Cr.App.R.(S.) 278, CA. The decision of the Court of Appeal in *Att.-Gen.'s Reference (No. 48 of 1994), ante*, does not constitute an exception to this principle. The defendant was convicted of non-consensual buggery; at the time of the offence the maximum was 10 years. By the time of conviction, Parliament had re-defined rape so as to include non-consensual buggery, the maximum penalty remaining life imprisonment; the offence of which the defendant had been convicted no longer existed as such and the new offence of buggery contrary to section 12 of the *SOA* 1956 was a different offence. It was held that there was no question of the maximum penalty for the offence committed having been lowered; Parliament had plainly intended to increase the penalty for such conduct. The court could have relied on section 16(1)(d) of the *Interpretation Act* 1978 (Appendix B–16), to reach the same result.

Powers of magistrates' courts

5–287 Where an offender is committed for sentence for either way offences under the *PCC(S)A* 2000, s.3 and for summary offences under section 6 of that Act, the Crown Court must observe all the limitations which would apply in the magistrates' court in passing sentence for the summary offences, including the limitation in section 133 of the *MCA* 1980, *ante*, § 5–270, on the permissible aggregate terms: *R. v. Cattell*, 8 Cr.App.R.(S.) 268, CA; *R. v. Whitlock*, 13 Cr.App.R.(S.) 157, CA. The activation of a suspended sentence is not subject to the restrictions imposed on aggregate sentences by section 133: *R. v. Chamberlain*, 13 Cr.App.R.(S.) 535, CA.

(c) *Life sentences, sentences for public protection and extended sentences for dangerous offenders*

Introduction

5–288 The *CJA* 2003 introduced a new scheme of custodial sentences for dangerous offenders. This consists of two new sentences, *viz.* imprisonment for public protection, and an extended sentence, and the making of express provision as to when a sentence of life imprisonment or of detention for life under section 91 of the *PCC(S)A* 2000 (*post*, § 5–358) is to be imposed. The new scheme applies only to offences committed on or after April 4, 2005. Offenders being sentenced after the commencement date in respect of offences committed before that date will continue to be subject to the former regime, *i.e.* imprisonment or detention for life (the appropriateness of which was governed principally by *Att.-Gen.'s Reference (No. 32 of 1996) (R. v. Whittaker)* [1997] 1 Cr.App.R.(S.) 261, CA, and *R. v. Chapman* [2000] 1 Cr.App.R. 77, CA), longer than commensurate sentences under section 80(2)(b) of the *PCC(S)A* 2000 (§ 5–275b in the supplement), extended sentences under section 85 of that Act (§ 5–288b in the supplement), and automatic life sentences under section 109 of the Act of 2000 (*ante*, § 5–251i). As to the saving of these provisions, see paragraphs 5 and 6 of Schedule 2 to S.I. 2005 No. 950, *ante*, §§ 5–1a, 5–1b. It should be noted that despite the similarity in their names, the sentences under the old and the new schemes are different, and, in particular, that extended sentences under sections 227 and 228 of the 2003 Act are fundamentally different from those under section 85 of the 2000 Act.

The criteria for the imposition of a sentence of life imprisonment or detention for life, as specified in sections 225 and 226, are more restrictive than those which previously governed the imposition of a discretionary life sentence (see *R. v. Kehoe*, *post*, § 5–304), and it may be that the life sentence will be replaced in practice by the new sentence of imprisonment for public protection. This is an indefinite sentence which may be imposed on a person convicted of a "serious offence", as defined by section 224. A court which imposes a sentence of imprisonment for public protection must fix a minimum term to be served in accordance with section 82A of the *PCC(S)A* 2000 (*post*, § 5–310). Once the offender has served the minimum term, he may require his case to be referred to the Parole Board, who may direct his release under the *C(S)A* 1997, s.28 (*ante*, § 5–243), if they are satisfied that it is no longer necessary for the protection of the public that he should be confined. If they are not so satisfied, the prisoner will remain in custody even though he has served a period which is longer than the maximum term permitted for the offence of which he has been convicted. The only substantial difference between a sentence of imprisonment for public protection and a life sentence is that, in the case of the former, the Parole Board may, under the *C(S)A* 1997, s.31A (inserted by the *CJA* 2003, Sched. 18, para. 2), direct the Secretary of State to order that a prisoner's licence shall cease to have effect, but no such direction may be given until at least 10 years after the prisoner's release from custody.

Extended sentences under the *CJA* 2003 may be imposed on adult offenders only on conviction of a "specified violent offence" or "specified sexual offence" whether or not it is a "serious offence"; and only where the court considers that there is a significant risk to the public of serious harm occasioned by the commission by the offender of further "specified offences", whether or not they are "serious offences". This is a much higher threshold than applied under section 85 of the 2000 Act. When released, the offender will be on licence until the conclusion of the whole term of the sentence (*i.e.* custodial term plus extension period): *R. v. S.*; *R. v. Burt* [2006] 2 Cr.App.R.(S.) 35, CA.

The *CJIA* 2008 amended these provisions, so as substantially to reduce their potency by making most of the powers discretionary rather than mandatory, introducing new conditions to be met and removing the presumption of dangerousness that applied in certain cases. The amendments came into force on July 14, 2008, but have no effect in relation to anybody sentenced before that date (*Criminal Justice and Immigration Act 2008 (Commencement No. 2 and Transitional and Saving Provisions) Order* 2008 (S.I. 2008 No. 1586)).

Powers of Criminal Courts (Sentencing) Act 2000, s.86

Sexual offences committed before 30th September 1998

86.—(1) Where, in the case of a long-term or short-term prisoner— **5–289**

(a) the whole or any part of his sentence was imposed for a sexual offence committed before 30th September 1998, and

(b) the court by which he was sentenced for that offence, having had regard to the matters mentioned in section 32(6)(a) and (b) of the *Criminal Justice Act* 1991, ordered that this section should apply,

sections 33(3) and 37(1) of that Act shall each have effect as if for the reference to three-quarters of his sentence there were substituted a reference to the whole of that sentence.

(2) Expressions used in this section shall be construed as if they were contained in Part II of the *Criminal Justice Act* 1991.

(3) The reference in subsection (1) above to section 33(3) of the *Criminal Justice Act* 1991 is to section 33(3) as it has effect without the amendment made by section 104(1) of the *Crime and Disorder Act* 1998 (which substituted the words "on licence" for the word "unconditionally" and does not apply in relation to a prisoner whose sentence or any part of whose sentence was imposed for an offence committed before 30th September 1998).

5–290 The matters mentioned in section 32(6)(a) and (b) are "the need to protect the public from serious harm from offenders" and "the desirability of preventing the commission by them of further offences and of securing their rehabilitation".

The provision from which section 86 is derived, the *CJA* 1991, s.44, came into force on October 1, 1992. Before that date the longest period which an offender could serve under any determinate sentence was two-thirds of the term of the sentence pronounced by the court. There is a conflict of authority as to whether an order under this section may be made in relation to an offence committed before that date. In *R. v. Massie* [2003] 1 Cr.App.R.(S.) 80, CA, and *R. v. T.* [2003] 4 All E.R. 877, CA, it was held that this was not permissible. On the other hand, in *R. v. R.* [2004] 1 W.L.R. 490, CA, the court came to the opposite conclusion. The decision of the civil division of the Court of Appeal in *R. (Uttley) v. Secretary of State for the Home Department* [2003] 1 W.L.R. 2590 lends support to the view that an order may not be made in relation to an offence committed before that date. The decision was reversed in the House of Lords ([2004] 1 W.L.R. 2278), but the point in issue was not the same, and it does not follow from their Lordships' reversal of the Court of Appeal that the decision in *R. v. R.* was correct (see the commentary to the latter case in *Criminal Law Week* 2003/31/12).

5–291 In *Att.-Gen.'s Reference (No. 7 of 1996) (R. v. Hodgeon)* [1997] 1 Cr.App.R.(S.) 399, the Court of Appeal commended section 86 to the attention of those passing sentence for sexual offences; making an order under the section gives the court additional control over the offender, in that it affects both the period of supervision after release and the period to be served if recalled to prison.

Criminal Justice Act 2003, ss.224–229

CHAPTER 5

DANGEROUS OFFENDERS

Meaning of "specified offence" etc.

5–292 **224.**—(1) An offence is a "specified offence" for the purposes of this Chapter if it is a specified violent offence or a specified sexual offence.

(2) An offence is a "serious offence" for the purposes of this Chapter if and only if—

(a) it is a specified offence, and

(b) it is, apart from section 225, punishable in the case of a person aged 18 or over by—

(i) imprisonment for life, or

(ii) imprisonment for a determinate period of ten years or more.

(3) In this Chapter—

"serious harm" means death or serious personal injury, whether physical or psychological;

"specified violent offence" means an offence specified in Part 1 of Schedule 15;

"specified sexual offence" means an offence specified in Part 2 of that Schedule.

[This section is printed as repealed in part by the *CJIA* 2008, ss.148(1) and 149, Sched. 26, paras 59 and 69, and Sched. 28, Pt 2.]

The *Criminal Justice Act 2003 (Sentencing) (Transitory Provisions) Order* 2005 (S.I. 2005 No. 643) modifies section 224(2) (in relation to any time before the coming force of the *CJCSA* 2000, s.61) (abolition of sentences of detention in a young offender institution, custody for life, etc.) by inserting the words "or in the case of a person aged at least 18 but under 21, custody for life" after "imprisonment for life" in paragraph (b)(i) and the words "or, in the case of a person aged at least 18 but under 21, detention in a young offender institution" after "imprisonment" in paragraph b(ii).

An offence contrary to the *SOA* 2003, s.9 (*post*, § 20–79) is not a "serious" specified offence: *R. v. B.* [2008] Crim.L.R. 730, CA.

For guidance on the meaning of "serious harm, see *R. v. Lang* [2006] 2 Cr.App.R.(S.) 3, CA, *post*, §§ 5–302 *et seq*.

Life sentence or imprisonment for public protection for serious offences

225.—(1) This section applies where— **5–293**

(a) a person aged 18 or over is convicted of a serious offence committed after the commencement of this section, and

(b) the court is of the opinion that there is a significant risk to members of the public of serious harm occasioned by the commission by him of further specified offences.

(2) If—

(a) the offence is one in respect of which the offender would apart from this section be liable to imprisonment for life, and

(b) the court considers that the seriousness of the offence, or of the offence and one or more offences associated with it, is such as to justify the imposition of a sentence of imprisonment for life,

the court must impose a sentence of imprisonment for life.

(3) In a case not falling within subsection (2), the court may impose a sentence of imprisonment for public protection if the condition in subsection (3A) or the condition in subsection (3B) is met.

(3A) The condition in this subsection is that, at the time the offence was committed, the offender had been convicted of an offence specified in Schedule 15A.

(3B) The condition in this subsection is that the notional minimum term is at least two years.

(3C) The notional minimum term is the part of the sentence that the court would specify under section 82A(2) of the *Sentencing Act* (determination of tariff) if it imposed a sentence of imprisonment for public protection but was required to disregard the matter mentioned in section 82A(3)(b) of that Act (crediting periods of remand).

(4) A sentence of imprisonment for public protection is a sentence of imprisonment for an indeterminate period, subject to the provisions of Chapter 2 of Part 2 of the *Crime (Sentences) Act* 1997 as to the release of prisoners and duration of licences.

(5) An offence the sentence for which is imposed under this section is not to be regarded as an offence the sentence for which is fixed by law.

[This section is printed as amended by the *CJIA* 2008, s.13(1).]

S.I. 2005 No. 643 (*ante*, § 5–293) modifies section 225 (in relation to any time before the coming force of the *CJCSA* 2000, s.61) (abolition of sentences of detention in a young offender institution, custody for life etc.) by inserting the words "or in the case of a person aged at least 18 but under 21, a sentence of custody for life" at the end of subsection (2); and by inserting the words "or a sentence of detention in a young offender institution for public protection" after "imprisonment for public protection"; and substituting the words "imprisonment or detention for an indeterminate period" for "imprisonment for an indeterminate period" in subsection (4).

The *Criminal Justice and Immigration Act 2008 (Transitory Provisions) Order* 2008 (S.I. 2008 No. 1587) further modifies section 225 (in relation to any time before the coming into force of section 61 of the Act of 2000) by inserting the words "or, in the case of a person aged at least 18 but under 21, a sentence of detention in a young offender institution for public protection" after the words "public protection" in subsections (3) and (3C).

Detention for life or detention for public protection for serious offences committed by those under 18

226.—(1) This section applies where— **5–294**

(a) a person aged under 18 is convicted of a serious offence committed after the commencement of this section, and

(b) the court is of the opinion that there is a significant risk to members of the public of serious harm occasioned by the commission by him of further specified offences.

(2) If—

(a) the offence is one in respect of which the offender would apart from this section be liable to a sentence of detention for life under section 91 of the *Sentencing Act*, and

(b) the court considers that the seriousness of the offence, or of the offence and one or more offences associated with it, is such as to justify the imposition of a sentence of detention for life,

the court must impose a sentence of detention for life under that section.

(3) In a case not falling within subsection (2), the court may impose a sentence of detention for public protection if the notional minimum term is at least two years.

(3A) The notional minimum term is the part of the sentence that the court would specify under section 82A(2) of the *Sentencing Act* (determination of tariff) if it imposed a sentence of detention for public protection but was required to disregard the matter mentioned in section 82A(3)(b) of that Act (crediting periods of remand).

(4) A sentence of detention for public protection is a sentence of detention for an indeterminate period, subject to the provisions of Chapter 2 of Part 2 of the *Crime (Sentences) Act* 1997 as to the release of prisoners and duration of licences.

(5) An offence the sentence for which is imposed under this section is not to be regarded as an offence the sentence for which is fixed by law.

[This section is printed as amended by the *CJIA* 2008, s.14.]

Extended sentence for certain violent or sexual offences: persons 18 or over

5–295 **227.**—(1) This section applies where—

(a) a person aged 18 or over is convicted of a specified offence committed after the commencement of this section, and

(b) the court considers that there is a significant risk to members of the public of serious harm occasioned by the commission by the offender of further specified offences, but

(c) the court is not required by section 225(2) to impose a sentence of imprisonment for life.

(2) The court may impose on the offender an extended sentence of imprisonment, if the condition in subsection (2A) or the condition in subsection (2B) is met.

(2A) The condition in this subsection is that, at the time the offence was committed, the offender had been convicted of an offence specified in Schedule 15A.

(2B) The condition in this subsection is that, if the court were to impose an extended sentence of imprisonment, the term that it would specify as the appropriate custodial term would be at least 4 years.

(2C) An extended sentence of imprisonment is a sentence of imprisonment the term of which is equal to the aggregate of—

(a) the appropriate custodial term, and

(b) a further period ("the extension period") for which the offender is to be subject to a licence and which is of such length as the court considers necessary for the purpose of protecting members of the public from serious harm occasioned by the commission by him of further specified offences.

(3) In subsections (2B) and (2C) "the appropriate custodial term" means a term of imprisonment (not exceeding the maximum term permitted for the offence) which—

(a) is the term that would (apart from this section) be imposed in compliance with section 153(2), or

(b) where the term that would be so imposed is a term of less than 12 months, is a term of 12 months.

(4) The extension period must not exceed—

(a) five years in the case of a specified violent offence, and

(b) eight years in the case of a specified sexual offence.

(5) The term of an extended sentence of imprisonment passed under this section in respect of an offence must not exceed the maximum term permitted for the offence.

(6) The Secretary of State may by order amend subsection (2B) so as to substitute a different period for the period for the time being specified in that subsection.

[This section is printed as amended and repealed in part by the *CJIA* 2008, ss.15 and 149, and Sched. 28, Pt 2.]

S.I. 2005 No. 643 (*ante*, § 5–293) modifies section 227 (in relation to any time before the coming force of the *CJCSA* 2000, s.61) (abolition of sentences of detention in a young offender institution, custody for life etc.) by inserting the words "or, in the case of a person aged at least 18 but under 21, an extended sentence of detention in a young offender institution" after "extended sentence of imprisonment" in subsection (2); and by inserting the words "or detention in a young offender institution" after the words "a term of imprisonment" in subsection (3) and "sentence of imprisonment" in subsection (5).

S.I. 2008 No. 1587 (*ante*, § 5–293) further modifies section 227 (in relation to any time before the coming into force of section 61 of the Act of 2000) by inserting the words "or, in the case of a person aged at least 18 but under 21, a sentence of custody for life" after the words "a sentence of imprisonment for life" in subsection (1)(c), the words "or, in the case of an offender aged at least 18 but under 21, an extended sentence of detention in a young offender institution" after the words "extended sentence of imprisonment" in subsections (2B) and (2C), and the words "or detention in a young offender institution" after the words "a sentence of imprisonment" in subsection (2C).

Extended sentence for certain violent or sexual offences: persons under 18

228.—(1) This section applies where— **5–296**

(a) a person aged under 18 is convicted of a specified offence committed after the commencement of this section, and

(b) the court considers—

(i) that there is a significant risk to members of the public of serious harm occasioned by the commission by the offender of further specified offences, and

(ii) where the specified offence is a serious offence, that the case is not one in which the court is required by section 226(2) to impose a sentence of detention for life under section 91 of the *Sentencing Act*.

(2) The court may impose on the offender an extended sentence of detention, if the condition in subsection (2A) is met.

(2A) The condition in this subsection is that, if the court were to impose an extended sentence of detention, the term that it would specify as the appropriate custodial term would be at least 4 years.

(2B) An extended sentence of detention is a sentence of detention the term of which is equal to the aggregate of—

(a) the appropriate custodial term, and

(b) a further period ("the extension period") for which the offender is to be subject to a licence and which is of such length as the court considers necessary for the purpose of protecting members of the public from serious harm occasioned by the commission by him of further specified offences.

(3) In subsections (2A) and (2B) "the appropriate custodial term" means such term as the court considers appropriate, which—

(b) must not exceed the maximum term of imprisonment permitted for the offence.

(4) The extension period must not exceed—

(a) five years in the case of a specified violent offence, and

(b) eight years in the case of a specified sexual offence.

(5) The term of an extended sentence of detention passed under this section in respect of an offence must not exceed the maximum term of imprisonment permitted for the offence.

(6) Any reference in this section to the maximum term of imprisonment permitted for an offence is a reference to the maximum term of imprisonment that is, apart from section 225, permitted for the offence in the case of a person aged 18 or over.

(7) The Secretary of State may by order amend subsection (2A) so as to substitute a different period for the period for the time being specified in that subsection.

[This section is printed as amended and repealed in part by the *CJIA* 2008, ss.16 and 149, and Sched. 28, Pt 2.]

The assessment of dangerousness

5–297 **229.**—(1) This section applies where—

(a) a person has been convicted of a specified offence, and

(b) it falls to a court to assess under any of sections 225 to 228 whether there is a significant risk to members of the public of serious harm occasioned by the commission by him of further such offences.

(2) … the court in making the assessment referred to in subsection (1)(b)—

(a) must take into account all such information as is available to it about the nature and circumstances of the offence,

(aa) may take into account all such information as is available to it about the nature and circumstances of any other offences of which the offender has been convicted by a court anywhere in the world,

(b) may take into account any information which is before it about any pattern of behaviour of which any of the offences mentioned in paragraph (a) or (aa) forms part, and

(c) may take into account any information about the offender which is before it.

(2A) The reference in subsection (2)(aa) to a conviction by a court includes a reference to—

(a) a finding of guilt in service disciplinary proceedings, and

(b) a conviction of a service offence within the meaning of the *Armed Forces Act* 2006 ("conviction" here including anything that under section 376(1) and (2) of that Act is to be treated as a conviction).

[This section is printed as amended and repealed in part by the *CJIA* 2008, ss.17(1)–(3) and 149, and Sched. 28, Pt 2.]

As at October 1, 2008, section 376 of the *AFA* 2006 was not in force.

Criminal Justice Act 2003, ss.231, 232

Appeals where previous convictions set aside

5–297a **231.**—(1) This section applies where—

(a) a sentence has been imposed on any person under section 225(3) or 227(2),

(b) the condition in section 225(3A) or (as the case may be) 227(2A) was met but the condition in section 225(3B) or (as the case may be) 227(2B) was not, and

(c) any previous conviction of his without which the condition in section 225(3A) or (as the case may be) 227(2A) would not have been met has been subsequently set aside on appeal.

(2) [*Identical to* PCC(S)A *2000, s.112(2)*, ante, *§ 5–254*.]

[This section is printed as amended by the *CJIA* 2008, s.18(1).]

Certificates of convictions for purposes of sections 225 and 227

5–298 **232.** Where—

(a) on any date after the commencement of Schedule 15A a person is convicted in England and Wales of an offence specified in that Schedule, and

(b) the court by or before which he is so convicted states in open court that he has been convicted of such an offence on that date, and

(c) that court subsequently certifies that fact,

that certificate shall be evidence, for the purposes of sections 225(3A) and 227(2A), that he was convicted of such an offence on that date.

[This section is printed as amended by the *CJIA* 2008, s.18(2).]

Specified violent and sexual offences

5–299 Specified violent offences are listed in Part 1 of Schedule 15 to the 2003 Act. They are manslaughter, kidnapping, false imprisonment, an offence under section 4, 16, 18, 20, 21, 22, 23, 27, 28, 29, 30, 31, 32, 35, 37, 38 or 47 of the *Offences against the Person Act* 1861, an offence under section 2 or 3 of the *Explosive Substances Act* 1883, under the *Infant Life (Preservation) Act* 1929, s.1, under the *CYPA* 1933, s.1, under the *Infanticide Act* 1938, s.1, under section 16, 16A, 17(1) 17(2) or 18 of the *Firearms Act* 1968, under section 8 of the *Theft Act* 1968, an offence of burglary under section 9 of that Act if committed with intent to inflict grievous bodily harm on a person, or to do unlawful damage to a building or anything in it, an offence under section 10 of that Act, an offence of aggravated vehicle-taking under section 12A of that Act involving an accident which caused the death of any person, an offence of arson under section 1 of the *Criminal Damage Act* 1971, an offence under section 1(2) of that Act, an offence under the *Taking of Hostages Act* 1982, s.1, under section 1 to 4 of the *Aviation Security Act* 1982, under the *MHA* 1983, s.127, under the *Prohibition of Female Circumcision Act* 1985, s.1, under section 1 to 3 of the *Public Order Act* 1986, under the *CJA* 1988, s.134, under section 1 or 3A of the *RTA* 1988, under section 1, 9, 10, 12, or 13 of the *Aviation and Maritime Security Act* 1990, under Part II of the *Channel Tunnel (Security) Order* 1994 (S.I. 1994 No. 570), under the *Protection from Harassment Act* 1997, s.4, under section 29 of the *CDA* 1998, or falling within section 31(1)(a) or (b) of that Act, under section 51 or 52 of the *International Criminal Court Act* 2001, under section 1 to 3 of the *Female Genital Mutilation Act* 2003, under the *Domestic Violence, Crime and Victims Act* 2005, s.5, an offence of aiding, abetting, counselling procuring or inciting the commission of an offence specified in Part 1 of the Schedule, an offence of conspiring or attempting to commit an offence so specified and an offence of conspiracy or attempt to commit murder.

Specified sexual offences are listed in Part 2 of Schedule 15. They are offences under the *SOA* 1956, sections 1 to 7, 9 to 11, 14 to 17, 19 to 29, 32 and 33, under the *MHA* 1959, s.128, under the *Indecency with Children Act* 1960, s.1, under section 4, 5 or 9 of the *SOA* 1967, under section 9 of the *Theft Act* 1968 (where the offence takes the form of burglary with intent to commit rape), under section 54 of the *CLA* 1977, under the *Protection of Children Act* 1978, s.1, an offence under section 170 of the *CEMA* 1979, in relation to goods prohibited to be imported under the *Customs Consolidation Act* 1876, s.42, under the *CJA* 1988, s.160, under sections 1 to 19, 25, 26, 30 to 41, 47 to 50, 52, 53, 57 to 59, 61 to 67, 69 or 70 of the *SOA* 2003, and an offence of aiding, abetting, counselling procuring or inciting the commission of an offence specified in Part 1 of the Schedule, or of conspiring or attempting to commit an offence so specified.

The references to the common law offence of incitement in Schedule 15 take effect as references to the offences under the *SCA* 2007, Pt 2: 2007 Act, s.63(1), and Sched. 6, para. 48.

Schedule 15A offences (ss.225(3A), 227(2A))

There are five parts to the schedule. Part 1 lists offences under the law of England **5–300**
and Wales. They are (1) murder; (2) manslaughter; (3) an offence contrary to section 4 or 18 of the *Offences against the Person Act* 1861; (4) an offence contrary to section 1 or 5 of the *SOA* 1956; (5) an offence contrary to section 16, 17(1) or 18 of the *Firearms Act* 1968; (6) an offence contrary to section 8 of the *Theft Act* 1968, where at some time during the commission of the offence, the offender had in his possession a firearm or an imitation firearm within the meaning of the *Firearms Act* 1968; (7) an offence contrary to section 1, 2, 5 or 6 of the *SOA* 2003; (8) an offence contrary to section 4, 8, 30, 31, 34, 35, 47 or 62 of that Act, if the offender was liable on conviction on indictment to imprisonment for life; or (9) an offence of aiding, abetting, counselling, procuring, inciting or attempting to commit any any such offence or conspiring to commit any such offence or committing an offence under the *SCA* 2007, Pt 2, in relation to any such offence.

Part 2 lists offences under the law of Scotland. They are (10) murder; (11) culpable **5–301**
homicide; (12) rape; (13) assault where the assault (a) is aggravated because it caused severe injury or endangered the victim's life, or (b) was carried out with intent to rape or ravish the victim; (14) non-consensual sodomy; (15) lewd, indecent or libidinous behaviour or practices; (16) robbery, subject to the same condition as in (6), *ante*; (17) as (5), *ante*; (18) an offence under section 5(1) of the *Criminal Law (Consolidation) (Scotland) Act* 1995; and (19) as (9), but without the reference to the 2007 Act.

Part 3 lists offences under the law of Northern Ireland. They are (20) to (22), as (1) to (3), *ante*; (23) an offence under the *Criminal Law Amendment Act* 1885, s.4; (24) offences under the Northern Ireland legislation that directly correspond to the offences in

(5) and (6), *ante*; (25) an offence under the *SOA* 2003, s.47, if the offender was liable on conviction on indictment to imprisonment for life; and (26) as (9), *ante*. As from a day to be appointed, there will be added references to the offences contrary to the *Sexual Offences (Northern Ireland) Order* 2008 (S.I. 2008 No. 1769) that correspond to the offences under the 2003 Act that are listed in Part 1: *Sexual Offences (Northern Ireland Consequential Amendments) Order* 2008 (S.I. 2008 No. 1779).

Part 4 lists offences under service law. They are offences under the *Army Act* 1955, s.70, the *Air Force Act* 1955, s.70, the *Naval Discipline Act* 1957, s.42, or the *AFA* 2006, s.42, as respects which the corresponding civil offence is one listed in Part 1.

Part 5 provides that in the schedule, "imprisonment for life" includes custody for life and detention for life.

Age

5–301a The material date for the purposes of determining which sentencing regime (ss.225 and 227 or ss.226 and 228) applies to an offender is the date of conviction: *R. v. Robson* [2007] 1 Cr.App.R.(S.) 54, CA.

Information

5–301b It was held in *R. v. Bryan and Bryan* [2007] 1 Cr.App.R.(S.) 53, CA that it is incumbent upon the prosecution in cases where a sentence under sections 225 to 228 is a possibility, to furnish the court with the fullest information in relation to the offender's previous offences and it is not proper for a sentencer who has not been provided with sufficient information to impose a sentence under these provisions notwithstanding the inadequacy of the information. A judge should adjourn sentence until that information is forthcoming. However, this should now be regarded as subject to what was said in *R. v. Johnson*, *post*, § 5–306, to the effect that whilst this is desirable, it is not always practicable and an adjournment is not always obligatory. In any such case, the court said that counsel for the defendant should be in a position to explain the circumstances of previous offences, on the basis of his instructions.

As to the meaning of "information" (in s.229(2)(a)), see *R. v. Considine*; *R. v. Davis*, *post*, § 5–306.

Life sentences, sentences for public protection, extended sentences

5–302 In *R. v. Lang* [2006] 2 Cr.App.R.(S.) 3, the Court of Appeal offered the following guidance as to the application of sections 225 to 229. This has been modified to take account of the amendments effected by the *CJIA* 2008 (the general effect of which is described at § 5–288, *ante*) and of subsequent, more specific decisions of the court.

(i) *General matters*

5–303 Where a defendant is being sentenced for offences committed before and after April 4, 2005, it would generally be preferable to pass sentence by reference to the new regime for the later offences, imposing no separate penalties for the earlier offences (but this might not be possible if the later offences were less serious than the earlier ones (and as to offences that overlap that date, see *post*, § 5–309b)). The risk to be assessed is to "members of the public" and there was no reason to construe this as excluding any particular group, and in some cases, particular members of the public (such as the cohabitee of a violent offender, or the children of the cohabitee of a sex offender) may be at more risk than members of the public generally. Where an offender is sentenced for several offences, only some of which are specified, a court which imposes an indeterminate sentence or extended sentence under sections 225 to 228 should generally impose a shorter concurrent sentence for the other offences (as to which, see also *post*, § 5–307a). It will not usually be appropriate to impose consecutive extended sentences. Care should be taken to ensure that a continuing offence which, as initially indicted, straddled April 4, 2005, is indicted, if necessary by amendment, so that sentence can properly be passed by reference to the new and/or old regime as appropriate. Where, in relation to a dangerous offender, the provisions of the *MHA* 1983 are satisfied, the court can dispose of the case under section 37 thereof (*post*, § 5–894).

(ii) *Imposition of life imprisonment or detention for life*

What was said on this issue in *Lang* has been overtaken by the decision in *R. v. Kehoe* [2008] Crim.L.R. 728, CA, to the effect that considerations of public protection are irrelevant to a decision to impose life imprisonment rather than imprisonment for public protection; and that life imprisonment should now be reserved for those cases where the culpability of the offender is particularly high or the offence itself particularly grave. **5–304**

(iii) *Fixing the minimum term*

For all practical purposes, sentences of imprisonment and detention for public protection are the same as sentences of imprisonment or detention for life; the only differences are, first, that in the case of imprisonment or detention for public protection, the Parole Board may on application 10 years after release, direct the Secretary of State to order that a licence shall cease to have effect; and secondly, in the case of such sentences, no order can be made under section 82A(4) of the *PCC(S)A* 2000 (*post*, § 5–310) that the early release provisions are not to apply at all. The procedure for fixing a minimum term in relation to all such sentences should be as before the Act in relation to discretionary and automatic life sentences. This must now be read subject to the amendments made to section 82A by the *CJIA* 2008, which modify the process of fixing the minimum term in two cases (one of which has no application to sentences of imprisonment or detention for public protection), and provide for allowance to be made for time spent on bail subject to certain conditions. **5–305**

(iv) *Assessment of significant risk*

Before a sentence of life imprisonment or imprisonment for public protection can be imposed under section 225 (or the equivalents thereof in relation to young offenders under section 226), a significant risk must be shown in relation to two matters; first, the commission of further specified (but not necessarily serious) offences, and secondly, the causing thereby of serious harm to members of the public; in assessing significant risk, the following matters are to be borne in mind, (i) "significant" is a higher threshold than mere possibility of occurrence, and it can be taken to mean "noteworthy, of considerable ... importance"; (ii) as to assessing the risk of further offences being committed, the court should take into account the nature and circumstances of the current offence, the offender's history of offending (including kind of offence, its circumstances, sentence passed, whether offending demonstrates any pattern), social and economic factors in relation to the offender (including accommodation, employability, education, associates, relationships and drug and alcohol abuse), and the offender's thinking/attitude towards offending and supervision and emotional state; such information most readily, though not exclusively, should come from antecedents (the detail of which must be provided by the prosecution) and pre-sentence probation and medical reports; in relation to such reports, the court will be guided, but not bound, by any assessment of risk, but if departure from any such assessment is contemplated, both counsel should be given the opportunity of addressing the point; (iii) as to assessing the risk of serious harm, courts must guard against assuming there to be a significant risk of serious harm merely because the foreseen specified offence is serious; a pre-sentence report (and in the small number of cases where the circumstances of the current offence or the history of the offender suggest mental abnormality, a medical report) should usually be obtained before any sentence is passed which is based on significant risk of serious harm; (iv) where the foreseen specified offence is not serious, there will be comparatively few cases in which a risk of serious harm will properly be regarded as significant; repetitive violent or sexual offending at a relatively low level without serious harm does not of itself give rise to a significant risk of serious harm in the future (there may, in such cases, be some risk of future victims being more adversely affected than past victims but this, of itself, does not give rise to significant risk of serious harm); (v) in relation to young offenders, it is necessary to bear in mind that, within a shorter time than adults, they may change and develop (which might, together with their level of maturity, be highly pertinent when assessing what their **5–306** future conduct may be and whether it may give rise to a significant risk of serious harm); (vi) as to a particularly young offender, an indeterminate sentence may be inappropriate even where a serious offence has been committed and there is a significant risk of serious harm from further offences; (vii) in accordance with section 174(1)(a) of the 2003 Act (*ante*, § 5–111), sentencers should usually give reasons (briefly identifying the information which they have taken into account) for all their conclusions, particularly as to whether there is or is not a significant risk of further offences or serious harm, and also for not imposing an extended sentence under section 227 or 228 where this is available.

Further guidance was given in *R. v. Johnson* [2007] 1 Cr.App.R.(S.) 112, CA, in relation to the criteria of dangerousness when imposing a sentence for public protection (although the principles undoubtedly apply equally to the assessment of dangerousness in relation to life sentences and extended sentences). The court said that it is important to remember that whilst the judgment in *Lang* (*ante*), was given in clear and trenchant terms, it should not be treated as a statute. It is plain that an indeterminate sentence is concerned with future risk and the future protection of the public and, although punitive in effect, with far reaching consequences for the offender on whom it is imposed, it does not strictly speaking, represent punishment for past offending.

As to the significance of previous convictions, the court said that it is not a prerequisite to a finding of dangerousness that the offender should be an individual with previous convictions. However, just as the absence of previous convictions does not preclude a finding of dangerousness, the existence of convictions for specified offences does not compel such a finding. The court added that if a finding of dangerousness can be made against an offender without previous convictions, it followed that previous offences, not in fact specified for the purposes of section 229, are not disqualified from consideration. Thus, for example, a pattern of minor previous offences of gradually escalating seriousness may be significant. As to the significance of the offender not having caused any harm when committing the index, or any prior, offence, this, the court said, may be advantageous to the offender, but it may be entirely fortuitous. The court may wish to reflect on the likely response of the offender, if his victim, instead of surrendering, resolutely defended himself. It does not, therefore, follow from the absence of actual harm caused by the offender to date, that the risk that he will cause serious harm in the future is negligible (as to this, see also *R. v. Islam* [2007] 1 Cr.App.R.(S.) 43, CA).

The court said that characteristics of the offender such as inadequacy, suggestibility or vulnerability may serve to mitigate his culpability; but they may also serve to produce or reinforce the conclusion that he is dangerous. The court should be alert to risks of aberrant moments in the future, and their consequences.

As to the giving of reasons for an indeterminate sentence, the court said that it is not obligatory for a judge to spell out all the details of all the earlier specified offences. To the extent that a judge is minded to rely upon a disputed fact in reaching a finding of dangerousness, he should not rely on that fact unless the dispute can fairly be resolved adversely to the defendant. In the end, the requirement is that the sentencing remarks should explain the reasons which have led the court to its conclusion. The Court of Appeal will not normally interfere with the conclusions reached by a sentencer who has accurately identified the relevant principles, and applied his mind to the relevant facts. As to the giving of reasons for rejecting an expert's opinion, see *R. v. Rocha*, *post*, § 5–306a.

In *R. v. Considine*; *R. v. Davis* [2008] 1 W.L.R. 414, CA, it was said (explaining *R. v. Farrar* [2007] 2 Cr.App.R.(S.) 35, CA) that the critical word in section 229 is "information", which is neither restricted to "evidence", nor limited to the offender's previous convictions or a pattern of behaviour established by them. What is prohibited is the introduction of a hybrid arrangement in which an offender is effectively convicted of a serious criminal offence by a judge alone in the course of a sentencing hearing. It is, therefore, inappropriate to embark on a *Newton* hearing (*ante*, § 5–74), to decide whether or not the defendant had committed a discrete, but similar, offence to the one already before the court, solely for the purpose of making an assessment of dangerousness.

Whereas section 227(3) (*ante*, § 5–295) of the Act requires that where an extended sentence is imposed in respect of an offender convicted of a specified offence (other than a serious offence) for which the custodial sentence commensurate with the seriousness of the offence would have been less than 12 months' duration, the "appropriate custodial term" is to be one of 12 months, the fact that the court is of the view that the appropriate non-extended custodial sentence would otherwise have been of less than 12 months' duration does not, as a matter of principle, or common sense, lead to the conclusion that the offender does not pose a significant risk of serious harm by the commission of further specified offences so that the criteria for the imposition of an extended sentence are not met: *R. v. Smith* [2007] 1 Cr.App.R.(S.) 98, CA.

In *R. v. Hillman* [2006] 2 Cr.App.R.(S.) 85, CA, it was held to have been legitimate for the court to take account of material that had led a court on a previous occasion to make an anti-social behaviour order against the offender, for the purposes of deciding on the risk he presented. This was so notwithstanding that the distinct allegations had not been the subject of distinct adjudications.

Use of reports. Whilst it may be obvious where a case fell at an extreme of the spectrum of sexual offending that the offender posed or did not pose a significant risk to members of the public of serious harm occasioned by the commission of further specified offences, in most cases the answer would not be obvious and it would be necessary to obtain assistance from the probation service in the form of a pre-sentence report: *R. v. Carter*; *Att.-Gen.'s Reference (No. 145 of 2006)*, *The Times*, March 20, 2007, CA (observing that under s.156(3) and (4) of the 2003 Act (*ante*, § 5–19), there is a duty to obtain such a report before forming an opinion as to risk that is adverse to the defendant, unless the court "is of the opinion that it is unnecessary to obtain" such a report); and see *ante*, § 5–306 (point (iii)). **5–306a**

In *R. v. Boswell*, unreported, June 26, 2007 ([2007] EWCA Crim. 1587), the Court of Appeal rejected criticism of a probation report which had assessed the appellant as presenting "a high risk of harm to the public", where the author had referred to the fact that he had applied "probation tools", "actuarial assessment tools" and "research"; those tools were no doubt the product of a good deal of research and provided a satisfactory basis for reaching conclusions of the kind that were reached. As to the use of such tools by probation officers being necessary, see also *R. v. Griffin* [2008] 2 Cr.App.R.(S.) 61, CA.

A sentencer will be entitled to reject a suitably qualified expert's report tending towards a conclusion that the defendant is not dangerous, but he must explain his reasons for doing so: *R. v. Rocha*, unreported, June 11, 2007, CA ([2007] EWCA Crim. 1505).

Where there were conflicting psychiatric reports, and the judge indicated that it was unnecessary to hear evidence from the psychiatrists, the offender was entitled to expect that the evidence of the defence psychiatrist would be accepted: *R. v. Strachan* [2008] 1 Cr.App.R.(S.) 43, CA.

Availability of other sentences and orders. In *Att.-Gen.'s Reference (No. 134 of 2006) (R. v. Bennett)* [2007] 2 Cr.App.R.(S.) 54, CA, a judge was held to have been in error in concluding that the offender was not dangerous because he was a suitable candidate for a sex offender treatment programme and was willing to take part in such a programme, since this would be to speculate that he would successfully complete the programme. This must now be read subject to *R. v. Terrell* [2008] 2 Cr.App.R.(S.) 49, CA, where the court was particularly concerned with sexual offences prevention orders and the assessment of dangerousness (as to which, see *post*, § 20–324a), but made the all-important point of general application that, in assessing future dangerousness, a sentencer should consider all the other available sentencing options and ask whether the imposition of any of them would sufficiently address the risk presented by the offender as to mean that the criteria for dangerousness are not met. **5–306b**

Application of principles

In the context of sexual offending, reference may be made to *R. v. Isa* [2006] 2 Cr.App.R.(S.) 29, CA (repetitive minor offending did not of itself provide a basis for **5–307** inferring a future significant risk of serious harm and that was particularly so where there was no evidence that any of the victims, albeit young, had suffered any harm of a serious nature); *R. v. Swinscoe* (2006) S.J. 1332, CA (it is important to have regard to the fact that not all harm is sufficiently grave to fall within the definition of "serious harm"; important also to consider whether, even if there is a risk of further offending, the type of offending which can be foreseen, is likely to cause "serious harm"); *R. v. Xhelollari* (2007) 151 S.J. 1265, CA (finding of dangerousness should not automatically be made on first conviction of rape where there is only speculation or mere apprehension, rather than actual evidence, of some risk of harm from future offending); and *R. v. Terrell, post*, § 20–324a (indecent photographs).

As to robbery, see, for example, *R. v. Bryan and Bryan, ante*, § 5–301b (imprisonment for public protection upheld where offenders had not actually caused serious harm but where there was a serious risk of further robberies and a significant risk of serious harm if anyone got in their way); *Att-Gen.'s Reference (No. 56 of 2006) (R. v. Sharrock)* [2007] 1 Cr.App.R.(S.) 96, CA (decision not to impose sentence for public protection unduly lenient where offender had previous convictions for robbery and possession of firearm and had entered guilty pleas to three armed robberies; although no harm had in fact been caused to victims, the provisions required the court to look to the future, particularly where the offender had a pattern of offending which was plainly becoming more serious); *R. v. Logan* [2007] 2 Cr.App.R.(S.) 7, CA ("classic case" for imprisonment for public protection where there was no evidence of serious harm to victims from the index or previous offences but use of syringe as a threat gave rise to risk of such harm in the future); *R. v. Ings* [2007] 2 Cr.App.R.(S.) 2, CA (indeterminate sentence upheld where it was not possible on information available to be confident that within the finite, custodial element of an extended sentence, there would be a sufficient change in maturity of 17-year old offender to present a manageable risk on licence); and *R. v. McGrady* [2007] 1 Cr.App.R.(S.) 45, CA (handbag snatch; indeterminate sentence quashed).

As to offences of violence, see *Att.-Gen.'s Reference (No. 35 of 2006) (R. v. Green)* [2007] 1 Cr.App.R.(S.) 36, CA; and *R. v. Bailey (Timothy)* [2006] 2 Cr.App.R.(S.) 50, CA; and see *R. v. Porter* [2007] 1 Cr.App.R.(S.) 115, CA, and *R. v. Hogan* [2007] 1 Cr.App.R.(S.) 110, CA, for two different approaches to manslaughter. As to the significance of the offender having been drunk at the time of committing a serious offence of violence, see *R. v. Chapman* [2008] 1 Cr.App.R.(S.) 103, CA (there is an obvious public risk from a person who gets himself so drunk that he does not realise the potential consequences of his actions).

Consecutive/ concurrent sentences

5–307a Whilst it is not unlawful to impose consecutive indeterminate sentences, or to impose an indeterminate sentence consecutive to another period of imprisonment, such a course is undesirable; where a judge seeks to make the period before which an offender would become eligible for parole consecutive to an existing sentence or to an order for return to custody under section 116 of the *PCC(S)A* 2000 (§ 5–364t in the supplement), he may legitimately do so by increasing the notional determinate sentence; and where a judge sought to impose concurrent indeterminate sentences for two or more offences with corresponding minimum terms where he would otherwise have passed consecutive determinate sentences, he may legitimately reflect the totality of the offending in the notional determinate sentences either by choosing the same notional determinate sentence for all of the offences, or by setting an increased notional determinate sentence for the most serious offence: *R. v. O'Brien* [2007] 1 Cr.App.R.(S.) 75, CA (followed in *R. v. O'Halloran*, unreported, November 14, 2006, CA ([2006] EWCA Crim. 3148), as to inflating minimum term to reflect overall criminality where concurrent sentences were being imposed); and, to similar effect, see *R. v. Edwards (Frederick)* [2007] 1 Cr.App.R.(S.) 106, CA (judge entitled to impose specified minimum terms for serious offences which reflect the totality of the whole offending where offender is to be sentenced for a number of specified offences, of which some only are serious offences, whilst imposing concurrent extended sentences for the specified non-serious offences), and *R. v. Meade* [2007] 1 Cr.App.R.(S.) 123, CA.

In *R. v. Ashes* [2008] 1 Cr.App.R.(S.) 86, CA, the court considered *R. v. O'Brien* (*ante*) and held that when imposing a sentence of imprisonment for public protection in the case of an offender who is serving a determinate sentence, the sentence should be concurrent and the minimum term should, subject to considerations as to totality, be calculated by taking the period remaining to be served under the determinate sentence (*i.e.* half the original sentence less time already served) and then adding half the notional determinate sentence for the fresh offence.

The fixing of the minimum term is governed by section 82A of the *PCC(S)A* 2000 (*post*, § 5–310). One of the amendments to that section effected by the *CJIA* 2008 was intended to provide for a modified process of fixing the minimum term in a situation where the court is of the opinion that the term it would otherwise specify would have little or no effect on time spent in custody (see new subss. (3B) and (3C)). It remains to be seen whether the Court of Appeal takes the view that this modified statutory process is to be adopted to the exclusion of the solutions suggested in *O'Brien* and *Ashes*. It is submitted, however, that, Parliament having considered the problem and having provided a remedy, which is limited to reducing the discount from the notional determinate term to one-third (instead of the usual one-half), it would be wrong, as a matter of principle, to avoid the effect of this limited remedy by increasing the notional determinate term (*O'Brien*) or lengthening the minimum term (*Ashes*).

In *R. v. Brown and Butterworth* [2007] 1 Cr.App.R.(S.) 77, CA, it was said that, whilst not expressly prohibited, it will not generally be appropriate to impose, consecutive to an extended sentence under section 227 or 228, another extended sentence, or non-extended determinate sentence; otherwise, sections 244 (*post*, § 5–372) and 247 (*post*, § 5–375) of the 2003 Act may give rise to considerable difficulties in calculating release dates and licence periods (but see now *R. v. Hills*; *R. v. Pomfret*; *R. v. Davies*, *post*); difficulties should not arise, however, where an extended sentence is made consecutive to a non-extended determinate sentence; and as to concurrent extended and non-extended determinate sentences, the court said it would be sensible to avoid imposing, concurrent with an extended sentence, a non-extended determinate sentence which was longer than the custodial element of the extended sentence; otherwise the extension period may be subsumed in the longer determinate sentence (thereby defeating the purpose of the extension period).

In *R. v. C.* [2007] 3 All E.R. 735, CA, it was said: (i) there is nothing unlawful about the imposition of consecutive extended sentences under either the legislative regime that preceded the 2003 Act or under the 2003 Act, nor is it unlawful to make an extended sentence consecutive to a non-extended determinate sentence or a non-extended determinate sentence consecutive to an extended sentence; and the Court of Appeal will not interfere unless the practical result in any given case is manifestly excessive or gives rise to real administrative problems; but (ii) judges should try to avoid consecutive sentences if that is at all possible, and should adjust the custodial term within concurrent sentences to reflect the overall criminality if that is possible within other sentencing restraints; (iii) if consecutive sentences are considered appropriate or necessary, and if one or more of the sentences is a non-extended determinate term, then that term should be ordered to run first, with the extended sentence or sentences to follow; and (iv) in shaping the overall sentence, judges should remember that there is no obligation for the order of the sentences to correspond to the chronological order of the offences.

R. v. Brown and Butterworth and *R. v. C.* should now be read in light of *R. v. Hills*; *R. v. Pomfret*; *R. v. Davies*, *The Times*, August 7, 2008, CA. It was held that there was no reason why a judge should not direct that a determinate sentence should commence on the date on which a minimum term currently being served would expire (which date could be calculated with precision). Giving such a direction would be appropriate where the current offence fully justified a significant sentence of imprisonment, and where imposition of a concurrent sentence would have no practical effect on the time to be spent in custody. Having regard to the amendment of section 247 of the *CJA* 2003 by the *CJIA* 2008, one effect of which is to make calculation of the date of release from an extended sentence significantly more straightforward, it is submitted, by parity of reasoning, that a judge may direct that a determinate sentence should commence on the anticipated release date from an extended sentence.

As to the general desirability of avoiding consecutive sentences in this context, see also *R. v. Lang*, *ante*, § 5–303.

Extended sentences (licence period)

5–308 As to the period for which an offender sentenced to an extended sentence will be on licence, see *R. v. S.*; *R. v. Burt*, *ante*, § 5–288.

Advance indications as to sentence

5–308a The fact that an offender has been charged with a "specified offence" such that sections 225 to 228 apply does not of itself make it inappropriate to seek, or to give, a *Goodyear* indication (see *ante*, §§ 5–79b, 5–79c); if an indication is sought, and the risk assessment in accordance with section 229 remains to be made, any direction given must be qualified by stating that the offence is a specified offence and that the dangerous offender provisions will be brought into operation, that the risk assessment necessitated by those provisions would be carried out in spite of the indication, that if the offender is subsequently assessed as dangerous, the indication given would relate only to the notional determinate term of any indeterminate sentence under section 225 or 226 or the appropriate custodial term of any extended sentence under section 227 or 228, and that accordingly, if an indeterminate or extended sentence is to be imposed, the actual amount of time spent in custody would not be in the control of the sentencing judge, only its minimum; where a qualified *Goodyear* indication has been given, the assessment of dangerousness should normally be made by the judge who gave the indication, and if this is not possible, the second judge should be provided with a transcript of the indication given: *R. v. Kulah* [2008] 1 Cr.App.R.(S.) 85, CA

In *R. v. McDonald* [2008] 1 Cr.App.R.(S.) 36, CA, it was held that if an unqualified indication was given, then it was binding on the judge. This was disapproved in *R. v. Seddon* [2008] 2 Cr.App.R.(S.) 30, CA, on the basis that the provisions of the Act were mandatory. As amended by the *CJIA* 2008, however, the court has a discretion (life imprisonment cases apart) whether to impose an indeterminate sentence even where a finding of dangerousness is made. In light of this, it would seem likely that it will be *McDonald* and not *Seddon* that holds sway in the future.

Inter-relationship with hospital orders

5–309 As to the considerations to which the court should have regard when deciding whether to impose a discretionary life sentence or a hospital order under the *MHA* 1983, s.37, see *post*, § 5–897a.

Inter-relationship with sexual offences prevention orders

5–309a As to the relationship between the conditions for an indeterminate sentence and the criteria for making a sexual offences prevention order, see *post*, § 20–324a.

Inter-relationship with recommendation for deportation

5–309b See *R. v. Abdi*, *post*, § 5–920.

Transitional cases

5–309c Whereas sentences under sections 225 to 228 may only be imposed in relation to offences committed on or after the commencement date of the sections (see subs. (1) of each section), the presumption as to the date of commission of an offence committed over two or more days or alleged to have been committed at some time during a period of two or more days in paragraph 5(3) of Schedule 2 to the *Criminal Justice Act 2003 (Commencement No. 8 and Transitional and Saving Provisions) Order* 2005 (S.I. 2005 No. 950) (*ante*, § 5–1a) has no express application to sections 225 to 228 and cannot be construed as if it was intended to have such application; accordingly, where a count in an indictment alleges the commission of an offence between dates spanning April 4, 2005, the court must not impose a sentence under sections 225 to 228 unless it is satisfied that at least one offence was committed on or after that date; once the court is so satisfied, then the mere fact that the count was framed as spanning the commencement date will not preclude the imposition of the sentence under the relevant section: *R. v. Harries* [2008] 1 Cr.App.R.(S.) 47, CA. That S.I. 2005 No. 950 was not intended to deal with such cases is wide open to doubt, however: see the commentary to *Harries* in *Criminal Law Week* 2007/27/8, and see the commentary of David Thomas Q.C. to *R. v. Pressdee* [2008] 1 Cr.App.R.(S.) 25, CA, as to the consequences of this approach where it is impossible for a judge to be sure that the offence was committed either before or after commencement of the new regime.

Correction of errors

The power to vary a sentence within 28 days under the *PCC(S)A* 2000, s.155 (*post*, § 5–940), may properly be exercised to increase a sentence where the sentencer had failed to realise that an offence was a "specified" offence (such that the Chapter 5 provisions had in fact been triggered) or had failed to realise that a "specified" offence was a "serious" offence; and, provided that the original sentence was rescinded within 28 days, nothing prevented the sentencer from then exercising his common law power to adjourn (*e.g.* for the preparation of reports in relation to the issue of dangerousness), including beyond 28 days after the rescinded sentence was imposed: *R. v. Reynolds* [2007] 2 Cr.App.R.(S.) 87, CA. **5–309d**

Fixing the minimum term (life sentences not fixed by law)

Powers of Criminal Courts (Sentencing) Act 2000, s.82A

Determination of tariffs

82A.—(1) This section applies if a court passes a life sentence in circumstances where the sentence is not fixed by law. **5–310**

(2) The court shall, unless it makes an order under subsection (4) below, order that the provisions of section 28(5) to (8) of the *Crime (Sentences) Act* 1997 (referred to in this section as the "early release provisions") shall apply to the offender as soon as he has served the part of his sentence which is specified in the order.

(3) The part of his sentence shall be such as the court considers appropriate taking into account—

(a) the seriousness of the offence, or the combination of the offence and one or more offences associated with it;

(b) the effect of any direction which it would have given under section 240 of the *Criminal Justice Act* 2003 *below (crediting periods of remand in custody)* [(crediting periods of remand in custody) or under section 246 of the *Armed Forces Act* 2006 (equivalent provision for service courts)] [[or under section 240A of that Act of 2003 (crediting periods of remand on bail subject to certain types of condition)]] if it had sentenced him to a term of imprisonment; and

(c) the early release provisions as compared with section 244(1) of the *Criminal Justice Act* 2003.

In Case A or Case B below, this subsection has effect subject to, and in accordance with, subsection (3C) below.

(3A) Case A is where the offender was aged 18 or over when he committed the offence and the court is of the opinion that the seriousness of the offence, or of the combination of the offence and one or more other offences associated with it,—

(a) is exceptional (but not such that the court proposes to make an order under subsection (4) below), and

(b) would not be adequately reflected by the period which the court would otherwise specify under subsection (2) above.

(3B) Case B is where the court is of the opinion that the period which it would otherwise specify under subsection (2) above would have little or no effect on time spent in custody, taking into account all the circumstances of the particular offender.

(3C) In Case A or Case B above, in deciding the effect which the comparison required by subsection (3)(c) above is to have on reducing the period which the court determines for the purposes of subsection (3)(a) (and before giving effect to subsection (3)(b) above), the court may, instead of reducing that period by one-half,—

(a) in Case A above, reduce it by such lesser amount (including nil) as the court may consider appropriate according to the seriousness of the offence, or

(b) in Case B above, reduce it by such lesser amount (but not by less than one-third) as the court may consider appropriate in the circumstances.

(4) If the offender was aged 21 or over when he committed the offence and the court is of the opinion that, because of the seriousness of the offence or of the combination of the offence and one or more offences associated with it, no order should be made under subsection (2) above, the court shall order that ... the early release provisions shall not apply to the offender.

(4A) No order under subsection (4) above may be made, and Case A above does not apply, where the life sentence is—

(a) a sentence of imprisonment for public protection under section 225 of the *Criminal Justice Act* 2003, or

(b) a sentence of detention for public protection under section 226 of that Act.

(7) In this section—

"court" includes *a court-martial* [the Court Martial];

"life sentence" has the same meaning as in Chapter II of Part II of the *Crime (Sentences) Act* 1997.

(8) So far as this section relates to sentences passed by *a court-martial* [the Court Martial], section 167(1) below does not apply.

[This section was inserted as from November 30, 2000, by the *CJCSA* 2000, s.60(1). It has effect in relation to sentences passed on or after that date: *ibid.*, s.60(3). It is printed as amended, and repealed in part, by the *CJA* 2003, ss.230, 304 and 332, Sched. 18, para. 4, Sched. 32, para. 109, and Sched. 37, Pt 8; and the *CJIA* 2008, s.19; and as amended, as from a day to be appointed, by the *AFA* 2006, s.378(1), and Sched. 16, para. 163 (omission of italicised words, insertion of words in single square brackets); and the *CJIA* 2008, s.22(5) (insertion of words in double square brackets).]

The *Criminal Justice Act 2003 (Sentencing) (Transitory Provisions) Order* 2005 (S.I. 2005 No. 643) modifies section 82A(4A) (in relation to any time before the coming force of the *CJCSA* 2000, s.61) (abolition of sentences of detention in a young offender institution, custody for life etc) by inserting the words "or detention in a young offender institution" after the words "a sentence of imprisonment".

For the meaning of "life sentence" in Chapter II of Part II of the *C(S)A* 1997, see section 34(2) of that Act, *ante*, § 5–244.

Practice Direction (Criminal Proceedings: Consolidation), para. IV.47
[2002] 1 W.L.R. 2870

Imposition of discretionary life sentences

5–311 **IV.47.1** Section 82A of the *Powers of Criminal Courts (Sentencing) Act* 2000 empowers a judge when passing a sentence of life imprisonment, where such a sentence is not fixed by law, to specify by order such part of the sentence ('the relevant part') as shall be served before the prisoner may require the Secretary of State to refer his case to the Parole Board.

IV.47.2 Thus the discretionary life sentence falls into two parts: (a) the relevant part, which consists of the period of detention imposed for punishment and deterrence, taking into account the seriousness of the offence, and (b) the remaining part of the sentence, during which the prisoner's detention will be governed by considerations of risk to the public.

IV.47.3 The judge is not obliged by statute to make use of the provisions of section 82A when passing a discretionary life sentence. However, the judge should do so, save in the very exceptional case where the judge considers that the offence is so serious that detention for life is justified by the seriousness of the offence alone, irrespective of the risk to the public. In such a case, the judge should state this in open court when passing sentence.

IV.47.4 In cases where the judge is to specify the relevant part of the sentence under section 82A, the judge should permit the advocate for the defendant to address the court as to the appropriate length of the relevant part. Where no relevant part is to be specified, the advocate for the defendant should be permitted to address the court as to the appropriateness of this course of action.

IV.47.5 In specifying the relevant part of the sentence, the judge should have regard to the specific terms of section 82A and should indicate the reasons for reaching his decision as to the length of the relevant part.

IV.47.6 Whether or not the court orders that section 82A should apply, the judge shall not, following the imposition of a discretionary life sentence, make a written report to the Secretary of State through the Lord Chief Justice as was the practice until 8 February 1993.

In *R. v. M. (Discretionary Life Sentence)*; *R. v. L.* [1999] 1 W.L.R. 485, CA, it was held that the practice, when imposing a discretionary life sentence, should be to fix what would have been the appropriate determinate sentence had an indeterminate sentence not been necessary, and then to specify a proportion of the sentence being between one-half and two-thirds, although in the case of young offenders sentenced to an indeterminate period of detention, the general rule should be to fix the period at one-half (see *R. v. Secretary of State for the Home Department, ex p. Furber* [1998] 1 All E.R. 23, DC); in the case of adult offenders, this should be the starting point and, in many cases, would be the appropriate period, but the judge had a discretion to fix a period up to two-thirds of the appropriate determinate sentence. Both the notional determinate sentence and the specified part should be made plain in passing sentence. In *R. v. Szczerba* [2002] 2 Cr.App.R.(S.) 86, CA, it was said that the specified period should be fixed at half the notional determinate term unless there were particular grounds for taking a greater proportion; and that the grounds for doing so should be stated by the court. As amended by the *CJIA* 2008, section 82A now allows (in the case of a discretionary or automatic life sentence) for the possibility of the specified period being fixed at anything between one-half and the full term of the notional determinate term (see subss. (3A) and (3C)(a)). **5–312**

As to the requirement on the court, in fixing the specified period, to take account of any direction that it would have given under section 240 (*post*, § 5–368), the court in *R. v. M. (Discretionary Life Sentence)*; *R. v. L.z*, *ante*, said (in relation to the previous similar, but not identical provision) that in the usual case, the judge should give credit for remand time in fixing the appropriate period, but he had a discretion in the matter and there might well be circumstances where it would not be appropriate to do so. Detailed information should be available to the court (whether from the prosecution or the prison service) as to time spent in custody (or, once the amendment to subs. (3)(b) effected by the *CJIA* 2008, s.22(5) is in force, time on bail subject to specified conditions) before a discretionary life sentence was imposed.

A period must be specified under section 82A unless section 82A(4) applies: see *R. v. Hollies*, 16 Cr.App.R.(S.) 463, CA. The scheme of the original Act was that the judiciary should specify a period appropriate to the punishment or retribution required and needed to deter the prisoner and others from committing similar grave offences. The Parole Board would decide whether he still represented a danger to the public. Save in cases of exceptional gravity, where the judge thought that a prisoner should remain a prisoner for the rest of his life, he should specify a period under the Act: *ibid*.

In deciding on the part of the sentence to be specified, the need to protect the public from danger posed by the defendant should not be taken into account in arriving at a notional determinate term for the offence (the first step in the process); otherwise, there was a risk of double sentencing; the elements of dangerousness and risk to the public are covered by the passing of the discretionary life sentence and so should not feature in fixing the notional determinate term; and this was particularly so when fixing a term by reference to any guidelines which had factored into them an element for the protection of the public: *R. v. Wheaton* [2005] 1 Cr.App.R.(S.) 82, CA.

In *R. v. Mills*, *The Times*, December 3, 2004, CA, it was said that the principle that where a court declares a principle of the common law, it is as if it had always been the law, has no application to matters of practice in tariff sentencing; it followed that it was not open to an appellant sentenced to a discretionary life sentence to attack the part of that sentence specified under section 34 of the *CJA* 1991 (replaced by the *C(S)A* 1997, s.28, and with the relevant provisions now being in the *PCC(S)A* 2000, s.82A) on the ground that it had been fixed at 60 per cent of the notional determinate sentence, as against what had now become the standard practice of fixing the specified part at one-half of the notional determinate term (*R. v. Royal* [2004] 1 Cr.App.R.(S.) 2, CA); at the time the sentence was passed (1995), there was no such settled practice and it had been accepted as being proper to fix the specified part within the range of one-half to two-thirds.

In fixing the notional determinate sentence, allowance should be made for a plea of guilty: *R. v. Meek*, 16 Cr.App.R.(S.) 1003, CA. Where an offender is convicted of a number of offences, and is sentenced to life imprisonment for some of them and to determinate sentences for the others, the period specified should take account of the offences for which determinate sentences have been passed: *R. v. Lundberg*, 16 Cr.App.R.(S.) 948, CA; *R. v. Hann* [1966] 1 Cr.App.R.(S.) 267, CA; and *R. v. Edwards (Frederick)*, *ante*, § 5–307a.

As to fixing a period under section 82A in the case of an automatic life sentence under section 109 of the *PCC(S)A* 2000 (as to which, see *ante*, § 5–251i) where the offender is already serving a determinate sentence, see *R. v. Haywood* [2000] 2 Cr.App.R.(S). 418, CA (subject now to the provisions of subss. (3B) and (3C)(b), as to which, see the discussion at § 5–307a, *ante*).

Where a life sentence is passed for conspiracy to murder, the court should make an order under section 82A, and should not follow the practice adopted in cases of persons convicted of murder: *R. v. Mason and Sellars* [2002] 2 Cr.App.R.(S.) 128, CA.

An order under section 82A is a "sentence" for the purposes of the *CAA* 1968, s.9: *R. v. Dalton* [1995] 2 Cr.App.R. 340, CA; *R. v. McBean* [2002] 1 Cr.App.R.(S.) 98, CA.

(d) *Suspended sentences ("old style")*

5–312a The *CJA* 2003 repealed the provisions of the *PCC(S)A* 2000 which allowed for the suspension of a prison sentence of not more than two years (ss.118– 125). The 2003 Act introduced an entirely new form of suspended sentence (commonly referred to as "custody minus" although that expression appears nowhere in the Act). For the details of the new-style suspended sentence, see *post*, §§ 5–313b and 5–321 *et seq.*

The repeal of the former provisions and the commencement of the "custody minus" provisions took effect on April 4, 2005: S.I. 2005 No. 950 (*ante*, § 5–293), but only in relation to offences committed on or after that date. As to the saving of the former legislation in relation to offences committed before that date, see paragraphs 5 and 6 of Schedule 2 to S.I. 2005 No. 950, *ante*, §§ 5–1a, 5–1b. Sections 118 to 225 of the 2000 Act are set out in the 2004 edition of this work.

(e) *Prison sentences of less than 12 months*

Introduction

Custody plus

5–313 Section 181 of the *CJA* 2003 (not in force as at October 1, 2008) provides for a new system for dealing with sentences of imprisonment for a term of less than 12 months. The term of the sentence must be expressed in weeks, must not be less than 28 weeks, and must not be more than 51 weeks in respect of any one offence. When passing such a sentence, the court must specify a period (the "custodial period") at the end of which the offender is to be released on licence, and by order (to be known as a "custody plus order") require the licence to be granted on condition that the offender complies during the remainder of the term or any part of it with such requirements as the court may specify. The requirements that may be a specified are listed in section 182 and are substantially similar to the requirements that may be made in connection with a community order, although some of the requirements that may be made under a community order may not be made by virtue of an order under this section (*viz.* a residence requirement, a mental health requirement, a drug rehabilitation requirement and an alcohol treatment requirement). When making a custody plus order, the court will be required to give the explanations required by section 174 (*ante*, § 5–111).

Intermittent custody

5–313a Section 183 provided for a new power under which a court passing a sentence of imprisonment for a term of at least 28 weeks, and not more than 51 weeks in respect of any one offence may make an order (an "intermittent custody order") that the offender be released temporarily on licence before he has served the whole number of days which he is required to serve in custody.

A sentence of imprisonment passed in conjunction with an intermittent custody order will require the court first to identify the term of the sentence in accordance with subsection (4), then to specify the number of custodial days in accordance with subsection (5) (at least 14, not more than 90), and then to specify the periods during which the offender is to be released temporarily on licence during that period. The court may also require that the offender's licence (both during the periods of intermediate release, and after final release) be granted subject to conditions requiring compliance with one or more of the requirements falling within section 182(1). The court may not make an intermittent custody order unless the offender has expressed his willingness to serve the custodial part of the sentence intermittently.

Section 183 came into force in January, 2004, and remains in force, but a court may not make an intermittent custody order unless it has been notified that arrangements for implementing such orders are available in the area concerned. In November, 2006, the Home Office effectively suspended section 183 as a result of all relevant notifications being withdrawn.

Suspended sentences

Section 189 provides that a court which passes a sentence, for a term of at least 28 weeks but not more than 51 weeks, may order the offender to comply during a specified "supervision period" with one or more requirements (s.189(1)), and order that the sentence of imprisonment is not to take effect unless either the offender fails to comply with any requirement, or the offender commits another offence (whether or not punishable with imprisonment) during the "operational period" (to be specified by the court). Where two or more sentences are imposed consecutively there is no power to suspend the sentence unless the aggregate is less than 65 weeks (s.189(2)). The "supervision period" and the "operational period" must each be a period of not less than 6 months and not more than two years beginning with the date of the order (s.189(3)), and the former must not end later than the latter (s.189(4)). A court may not impose a community sentence as well as a suspended sentence (s.189(5)). Section 190 lists the requirements which may be imposed by a suspended sentence order (identical to s.177(1), including as to electronic monitoring), and the various restrictions that apply. Section 191 states that a suspended sentence order may provide for its periodic review. Section 192 makes procedural provision in relation to periodic reviews, and authorises the making of amendments. Section 193 gives effect to Schedule 12 (breach, revocation or amendment of community requirements of suspended sentence orders, and effect of any further conviction). **5–313b**

Statutory provisions

In the absence of any apparent intention on the part of the government to bring section 181 (custody plus) into force or to revoke the effective suspension of section 183 (intermittent custody), the following provisions of the 2003 Act are to be found in the supplement (§§ 5–314 *et seq.*, 5–327b *et seq.*): sections 181 (prison sentences of less than 12 months), 182 (licence conditions), 183 (intermittent custody), 184 (restrictions on power to make intermittent custody order) and 185 (intermittent custody: licence conditions) and Schedule 10 (revocation or amendment of custody plus orders and amendment of intermittent custody orders). **5–313c**

[The next paragraph is § 5–321.]

Criminal Justice Act 2003, ss.189–192

Suspended sentences

Suspended sentences of imprisonment

189.—(1) A court which passes a sentence of imprisonment for a term of at least 28 weeks but not more than 51 weeks in accordance with section 181 may— **5–321**

(a) order the offender to comply during a period specified for the purposes of this paragraph in the order (in this Chapter referred to as "the supervision period") with one or more requirements falling within section 190(1) and specified in the order, and

(b) order that the sentence of imprisonment is not to take effect unless either—

(i) during the supervision period the offender fails to comply with a requirement imposed under paragraph (a), or

(ii) during a period specified in the order for the purposes of this sub-paragraph (in this Chapter referred to as "the operational period") the offender commits in the United Kingdom another offence (whether or not punishable with imprisonment),

and (in either case) a court having power to do so subsequently orders under paragraph 8 of Schedule 12 that the original sentence is to take effect.

(2) Where two or more sentences imposed on the same occasion are to be served consecutively, the power conferred by subsection (1) is not exercisable in relation to any of them unless the aggregate of the terms of the sentences does not exceed 65 weeks.

(3) The supervision period and the operational period must each be a period of not less than six months and not more than two years beginning with the date of the order.

(4) The supervision period must not end later than the operational period.

(5) A court which passes a suspended sentence on any person for an offence may not impose a community sentence in his case in respect of that offence or any other offence of which he is convicted by or before the court or for which he is dealt with by the court.

(6) Subject to any provision to the contrary contained in the *Criminal Justice Act* 1967, the *Sentencing Act* or any other enactment passed or instrument made under any enactment after 31st December 1967, a suspended sentence which has not taken effect under paragraph 8 of Schedule 12 is to be treated as a sentence of imprisonment for the purposes of all enactments and instruments made under enactments.

(7) In this Part—

(a) "suspended sentence order" means an order under subsection (1),

(b) "suspended sentence" means a sentence to which a suspended sentence order relates, and

(c) "community requirement", in relation to a suspended sentence order, means a requirement imposed under subsection (1)(a).

Section 189 came into force on April 4, 2005, but only in relation to offences committed on or after that day: *Criminal Justice Act 2003 (Commencement No. 8 and Transitional and Saving Provisions) Order* 2005 (S.I. 2005 No. 950). For the relevant saving provisions, see *ante*, § 5–1a.

The *Criminal Justice Act 2003 (Sentencing) (Transitory Provisions) Order* 2005 (S.I. 2005 No. 643) modifies section 189 (in relation to any time before the commencement of the repeal of statute

Imposition of requirements by suspended sentence order

5–322 **190.**—(1) The requirements falling within this subsection are—

(a) an unpaid work requirement (as defined by section 199),

(b) an activity requirement (as defined by section 201),

(c) a programme requirement (as defined by section 202),

(d) a prohibited activity requirement (as defined by section 203),

(e) a curfew requirement (as defined by section 204),

(f) an exclusion requirement (as defined by section 205),

(g) a residence requirement (as defined by section 206),

(h) a mental health treatment requirement (as defined by section 207),

(i) a drug rehabilitation requirement (as defined by section 209),

(j) an alcohol treatment requirement (as defined by section 212),

(k) a supervision requirement (as defined by section 213), and

(l) in a case where the offender is aged under 25, an attendance centre requirement (as defined by section 214).

(2) Section 189(1)(a) has effect subject to section 218 and to the following provisions of Chapter 4 relating to particular requirements—

(a) section 199(3) (unpaid work requirement),

(b) section 201(3) and (4) (activity requirement),

(c) section 202(4) and (5) (programme requirement),
(d) section 203(2) (prohibited activity requirement),
(e) section 207(3) (mental health treatment requirement),
(f) section 209(2) (drug rehabilitation requirement), and
(g) section 212(2) and (3) (alcohol treatment requirement).

(3) Where the court makes a suspended sentence order imposing a curfew requirement or an exclusion requirement, it must also impose an electronic monitoring requirement (as defined by section 215) unless—

(a) the court is prevented from doing so by section 215(2) or 218(4), or
(b) in the particular circumstances of the case, it considers it inappropriate to do so.

(4) Where the court makes a suspended sentence order imposing an unpaid work requirement, an activity requirement, a programme requirement, a prohibited activity requirement, a residence requirement, a mental health treatment requirement, a drug rehabilitation requirement, an alcohol treatment requirement, a supervision requirement or an attendance centre requirement, the court may also impose an electronic monitoring requirement unless the court is prevented from doing so by section 215(2) or 218(4).

(5) Before making a suspended sentence order imposing two or more different requirements falling within subsection (1), the court must consider whether, in the circumstances of the case, the requirements are compatible with each other.

Section 190 came into force on April 4, 2005: S.I. 2005 No. 950 (*ante*, § 5–321). As to the word "court", see *ante*, § 5–321.

Power to provide for review of suspended sentence order

191.—(1) A suspended sentence order may— **5–323**

(a) provide for the order to be reviewed periodically at specified intervals,
(b) provide for each review to be made, subject to section 192(4), at a hearing held for the purpose by the court responsible for the order (a "review hearing"),
(c) require the offender to attend each review hearing, and
(d) provide for the responsible officer to make to the court responsible for the order, before each review, a report on the offender's progress in complying with the community requirements of the order.

(2) Subsection (1) does not apply in the case of an order imposing a drug rehabilitation requirement (provision for such a requirement to be subject to review being made by section 210).

(3) In this section references to the court responsible for a suspended sentence order are references—

(a) where a court is specified in the order in accordance with subsection (4), to that court;
(b) in any other case, to the court by which the order is made.

(4) Where the area specified in a suspended sentence order made by a magistrates' court is not the area for which the court acts, the court may, if it thinks fit, include in the order provision specifying for the purpose of subsection (3) a magistrates' court which acts for the area specified in the order.

(5) Where a suspended sentence order has been made on an appeal brought from the Crown Court or from the criminal division of the Court of Appeal, it is to be taken for the purposes of subsection (3)(b) to have been made by the Crown Court.

Section 191 came into force on April 4, 2005: S.I. 2005 No. 950 (*ante*, § 5–321). As from a day to be appointed, the *AFA* 2006, s.203(1), provides that in section 191, as it applies to a suspended sentence order with community requirements made by a relevant service court, the "court responsible for the order" means the Crown Court, and that subsections (3) to (5) shall be treated as omitted.

Periodic reviews of suspended sentence order

192.—(1) At a review hearing (within the meaning of subsection (1) of section 191) the court may, after considering the responsible officer's report referred to in that subsection, amend the community requirements of the suspended sentence order, or any provision of the order which relates to those requirements. **5–324**

(2) The court—

(a) may not amend the community requirements of the order so as to impose a requirement of a different kind unless the offender expresses his willingness to comply with that requirement,

(b) may not amend a mental health treatment requirement, a drug rehabilitation requirement or an alcohol treatment requirement unless the offender expresses his willingness to comply with the requirement as amended,

(c) may amend the supervision period only if the period as amended complies with section 189(3) and (4),

(d) may not amend the operational period of the suspended sentence, and

(e) except with the consent of the offender, may not amend the order while an appeal against the order is pending.

(3) For the purposes of subsection (2)(a)—

(a) a community requirement falling within any paragraph of section 190(1) is of the same kind as any other community requirement falling within that paragraph, and

(b) an electronic monitoring requirement is a community requirement of the same kind as any requirement falling within section 190(1) to which it relates.

(4) If before a review hearing is held at any review the court, after considering the responsible officer's report, is of the opinion that the offender's progress in complying with the community requirements of the order is satisfactory, it may order that no review hearing is to be held at that review; and if before a review hearing is held at any review, or at a review hearing, the court, after considering that report, is of that opinion, it may amend the suspended sentence order so as to provide for each subsequent review to be held without a hearing.

(5) If at a review held without a hearing the court, after considering the responsible officer's report, is of the opinion that the offender's progress under the order is no longer satisfactory, the court may require the offender to attend a hearing of the court at a specified time and place.

(6) If at a review hearing the court is of the opinion that the offender has without reasonable excuse failed to comply with any of the community requirements of the order, the court may adjourn the hearing for the purpose of dealing with the case under paragraph 8 of Schedule 12.

(7) At a review hearing the court may amend the suspended sentence order so as to vary the intervals specified under section 191(1).

(8) In this section any reference to the court, in relation to a review without a hearing, is to be read—

(a) in the case of the Crown Court, as a reference to a judge of the court, and

(b) in the case of a magistrates' court, as a reference to a justice of the peace acting for the commission area for which the court acts.

Section 192 came into force on April 4, 2005: S.I. 2005 No. 950 (*ante*, § 5–321).

Revocation or amendment

5–325 Section 193 gives effect to Schedule 12 (*post*, §§ 5–328 *et seq.*), which contains provisions relating to breach, revocation or amendment of the community requirements of suspended sentence orders, and to the effect of any further conviction.

Transfer of orders

5–326 Section 194 gives effect to Schedule 13 (not set out in this work), which makes provision for the transfer of suspended sentence orders to Scotland or Northern Ireland.

Criminal Justice Act 2003, s.195

Interpretation of Chapter 3

5–327 **195.** In this Chapter—

"custodial period", in relation to a term of imprisonment imposed in accordance with section 181, has the meaning given by subsection (3)(a) of that section;

"licence period"—

(a) in relation to a term of imprisonment imposed in accordance with section 181, has the meaning given by subsection (3)(b) of that section, and

(b) in relation to a term of imprisonment to which an intermittent custody order relates, has the meaning given by section 183(3);

"the number of custodial days", in relation to a term of imprisonment to which an intermittent custody order relates, has the meaning given by section 183(3);

"operational period" and "supervision period", in relation to a suspended sentence, are to be read in accordance with section 189(1);

"sentence of imprisonment" does not include *a committal for contempt of court* [a sentence of imprisonment passed in respect of a summary conviction for an offence under section 6(1) or (2) of the *Bail Act* 1976].

[This section is printed as amended, as from a day to be appointed, by the *PJA* 2006, s.34(1) and (2) (omission of italicised words, insertion of words in square brackets).]

Chapter 3 comprises sections 181 to 195.

Further provisions

Chapter 4 of Part 12 (ss.196– 223) contains further provisions in relation to Chapters 2 and 3: see *ante*, §§ 5–132 *et seq*. **5–327a**

Criminal Justice Act 2003, Sched. 12

Section 193 SCHEDULE 12

BREACH OR AMENDMENT OF SUSPENDED SENTENCE ORDER, AND EFFECT OF FURTHER CONVICTION

PART 1

Preliminary

Interpretation

1. In this Schedule— **5–328**

"the offender", in relation to a suspended sentence order, means the person in respect of whom the order is made;

"the petty sessions area concerned", in relation to a suspended sentence order, means the petty sessions area for the time being specified in the order;

"the responsible officer" has the meaning given by section 197.

2. In this Schedule—

(a) any reference to a suspended sentence order being subject to review is a reference to such an order being subject to review in accordance with section 191(1)(b) or to a drug rehabilitation requirement of such an order being subject to review in accordance with section 210(1)(b);

(b) any reference to the court responsible for a suspended sentence order which is subject to review is to be construed in accordance with section 191(3) or, as the case may be, 210(2).

Orders made on appeal

3. Where a suspended sentence order is made on appeal it is to be taken for the purposes of this Schedule to have been made by the Crown Court.

PART 2

Breach of Community Requirement or Conviction of Further Offence

Duty to give warning in relation to community requirement

4.—(1) If the responsible officer is of the opinion that the offender has failed without reasonable excuse to comply with any of the community requirements of a suspended sentence order, the officer must give him a warning under this paragraph unless— **5–329**

(a) the offender has within the previous twelve months been given a warning under this paragraph in relation to a failure to comply with any of the community requirements of the order, or

(b) the officer causes an information to be laid before a justice of the peace in respect of the failure.

(2) A warning under this paragraph must—

(a) describe the circumstances of the failure,

(b) state that the failure is unacceptable, and

(c) inform the offender that if within the next twelve months he again fails to comply with any requirement of the order, he will be liable to be brought before a court.

(3) The responsible officer must, as soon as practicable after the warning has been given, record that fact.

(4) In relation to any suspended sentence order which is made by the Crown Court and does not include a direction that any failure to comply with the community requirements of the order is to be dealt with by a magistrates' court, the reference in sub-paragraph (1)(b) to a justice of the peace is to be read as a reference to the Crown Court.

Breach of order after warning

5–330 5.—(1) If—

(a) the responsible officer has given a warning under paragraph 4 to the offender in respect of a suspended sentence order, and

(b) at any time within the twelve months beginning with the date on which the warning was given, the responsible officer is of the opinion that the offender has since that date failed without reasonable excuse to comply with any of the community requirements of the order,

the officer must cause an information to be laid before a justice of the peace in respect of the failure in question.

(2) In relation to any suspended sentence order which is made by the Crown Court and does not include a direction that any failure to comply with the community requirements of the order is to be dealt with by a magistrates' court, the reference in sub-paragraph (1) to a justice of the peace is to be read as a reference to the Crown Court.

Issue of summons or warrant by justice of the peace

5–331 6.—(1) This paragraph applies to—

(a) a suspended sentence order made by a magistrates' court, or

(b) any suspended sentence order which was made by the Crown Court and includes a direction that any failure to comply with the community requirements of the order is to be dealt with by a magistrates' court.

(2) If at any time while a suspended sentence order to which this paragraph applies is in force it appears on information to a justice of the peace that the offender has failed to comply with any of the community requirements of the order, the justice may—

(a) issue a summons requiring the offender to appear at the place and time specified in it, or

(b) if the information is in writing and on oath, issue a warrant for his arrest.

(3) Any summons or warrant issued under this paragraph must direct the offender to appear or be brought—

(a) in the case of a suspended sentence order which is subject to review, before the court responsible for the order,

(b) in any other case, before a magistrates' court acting for the petty sessions area in which the offender resides or, if it is not known where he resides, before a magistrates' court acting for the petty sessions area concerned.

(4) Where a summons issued under sub-paragraph (2)(a) requires the offender to appear before a magistrates' court and the offender does not appear in answer to the summons, the magistrates' court may issue a warrant for the arrest of the offender.

Issue of summons or warrant by Crown Court

5–332 7.—(1) This paragraph applies to a suspended sentence order made by the Crown Court which does not include a direction that any failure to comply with the community requirements of the order is to be dealt with by a magistrates' court.

(2) If at any time while a suspended sentence order to which this paragraph applies is in force it appears on information to the Crown Court that the offender has failed to comply with any of the community requirements of the order, the Crown Court may—

(a) issue a summons requiring the offender to appear at the place and time specified in it, or

(b) if the information is in writing and on oath, issue a warrant for his arrest.

(3) Any summons or warrant issued under this paragraph must direct the offender to appear or be brought before the Crown Court.

(4) Where a summons issued under sub-paragraph (1)(a) requires the offender to appear before the Crown Court and the offender does not appear in answer to the summons, the Crown Court may issue a warrant for the arrest of the offender.

Powers of court on breach of community requirement or conviction of further offence

5–333 8.—(1) This paragraph applies where—

(a) it is proved to the satisfaction of a court before which an offender appears or is brought under paragraph 6 or 7 or by virtue of section 192(6) that he has failed without reasonable excuse to comply with any of the community requirements of the suspended sentence order, or

(b) an offender is convicted of an offence committed during the operational period of a suspended sentence (other than one which has already taken effect) and either—

(i) he is so convicted by or before a court having power under paragraph 11 to deal with him in respect of the suspended sentence, or

(ii) he subsequently appears or is brought before such a court.

(2) The court must consider his case and deal with him in one of the following ways—

(a) the court may order that the suspended sentence is to take effect with its original term and custodial period unaltered,

(b) the court may order that the sentence is to take effect with either or both of the following modifications—

(i) the substitution for the original term of a lesser term complying with section 181(2), and

(ii) the substitution for the original custodial period of a lesser custodial period complying with section 181(5) and (6),

(c) the court may amend the order by doing any one or more of the following—

(i) imposing more onerous community requirements which the court could include if it were then making the order,

(ii) subject to subsections (3) and (4) of section 189, extending the supervision period, or

(iii) subject to subsection (3) of that section, extending the operational period.

(3) The court must make an order under sub-paragraph (2)(a) or (b) unless it is of the opinion that it would be unjust to do so in view of all the circumstances, including the matters mentioned in sub-paragraph (4); and where it is of that opinion the court must state its reasons.

(4) The matters referred to in sub-paragraph (3) are—

(a) the extent to which the offender has complied with the community requirements of the suspended sentence order, and

(b) in a case falling within sub-paragraph (1)(b), the facts of the subsequent offence.

(4A) Where a magistrates' court dealing with an offender under sub-paragraph (2)(c) would not otherwise have the power to amend the suspended sentence order under paragraph 14 (amendment by reason of change of residence), that paragraph has effect as if the references to the appropriate court were references to the court dealing with the offender.

(5) Where a court deals with an offender under sub-paragraph (2) in respect of a suspended sentence, the appropriate officer of the court must notify the appropriate officer of the court which passed the sentence of the method adopted.

(6) Where a suspended sentence order was made by the Crown Court and a magistrates' court would (apart from this sub-paragraph) be required to deal with the offender under sub-paragraph (2)(a), (b) or (c) it may instead commit him to custody or release him on bail until he can be brought or appear before the Crown Court.

(7) A magistrates' court which deals with an offender's case under subparagraph (6) must send to the Crown Court—

(a) a certificate signed by a justice of the peace certifying that the offender has failed to comply with the community requirements of the suspended sentence order in the respect specified in the certificate, and

(b) such other particulars of the case as may be desirable;

and a certificate purporting to be so signed is admissible as evidence of the failure before the Crown Court.

(8) In proceedings before the Crown Court under this paragraph any question whether the offender has failed to comply with the community requirements of the suspended sentence order and any question whether the offender has been convicted of an offence committed during the operational period of the suspended sentence is to be determined by the court and not by the verdict of a jury.

Further provisions as to order that suspended sentence is to take effect

9.—(1) When making an order under paragraph 8(2)(a) or (b) that a sentence is to take effect (with or without any variation of the original term and custodial period), the court— **5–334**

(a) must also make a custody plus order, and

(b) may order that the sentence is to take effect immediately or that the term of that sentence is to commence on the expiry of another term of imprisonment passed on the offender by that or another court.

(2) The power to make an order under sub-paragraph (1)(b) has effect subject to section 265 (restriction on consecutive sentences for released prisoners).

(3) For the purpose of any enactment conferring rights of appeal in criminal cases, any order made by the court under paragraph 8(2)(a) or (b) is to be treated as a sentence passed on the offender by that court for the offence for which the suspended sentence was passed.

Restriction of powers in paragraph 8 where treatment required

5–334a 10.—(1) An offender who is required by any of the following community requirements of a suspended sentence order—

(a) a mental health treatment requirement,

(b) a drug rehabilitation requirement, or

(c) an alcohol treatment requirement,

to submit to treatment for his mental condition, or his dependency on or propensity to misuse drugs or alcohol, is not to be treated for the purposes of paragraph 8(1)(a) as having failed to comply with that requirement on the ground only that he had refused to undergo any surgical, electrical or other treatment if, in the opinion of the court, his refusal was reasonable having regard to all the circumstances.

(2) A court may not under paragraph 8(2)(c)(i) amend a mental health treatment requirement, a drug rehabilitation requirement or an alcohol treatment requirement unless the offender expresses his willingness to comply with the requirement as amended.

Court by which suspended sentence may be dealt with under paragraph 8(1)(b)

5–334b 11.—(1) An offender may be dealt with under paragraph 8(1)(b) in respect of a suspended sentence by the Crown Court or, where the sentence was passed by a magistrates' court, by any magistrates' court before which he appears or is brought.

(2) Where an offender is convicted by a magistrates' court of any offence and the court is satisfied that the offence was committed during the operational period of a suspended sentence passed by the Crown Court—

(a) the court may, if it thinks fit, commit him in custody or on bail to the Crown Court, and

(b) if it does not, must give written notice of the conviction to the appropriate officer of the Crown Court.

Procedure where court convicting of further offence does not deal with suspended sentence

5–334c 12.—(1) If it appears to the Crown Court, where that court has jurisdiction in accordance with sub-paragraph (2), or to a justice of the peace having jurisdiction in accordance with that sub-paragraph—

(a) that an offender has been convicted in the United Kingdom of an offence committed during the operational period of a suspended sentence, and

(b) that he has not been dealt with in respect of the suspended sentence,

that court or justice may, subject to the following provisions of this paragraph, issue a summons requiring the offender to appear at the place and time specified in it, or a warrant for his arrest.

(2) Jurisdiction for the purposes of sub-paragraph (1) may be exercised—

(a) if the suspended sentence was passed by the Crown Court, by that court;

(b) if it was passed by a magistrates' court, by a justice acting for the petty sessions area for which that court acted.

(3) Where—

(a) an offender is convicted in Scotland or Northern Ireland of an offence, and

(b) the court is informed that the offence was committed during the operational period of a suspended sentence passed in England or Wales,

the court must give written notice of the conviction to the appropriate officer of the court by which the suspended sentence was passed.

(4) Unless he is acting in consequence of a notice under sub-paragraph (3), a justice of the peace may not issue a summons under this paragraph except on information and may not issue a warrant under this paragraph except on information in writing and on oath.

(5) A summons or warrant issued under this paragraph must direct the offender to appear or be brought before the court by which the suspended sentence was passed.

PART 3

Amendment of Suspended Sentence Order

Cancellation of community requirements of suspended sentence order

13.—(1) Where at any time while a suspended sentence order is in force, it appears to the appropriate court on the application of the offender or the responsible officer that, having regard to the circumstances which have arisen since the order was made, it would be in the interests of justice to do so, the court may cancel the community requirements of the suspended sentence order. **5–334d**

(2) The circumstances in which the appropriate court may exercise its power under sub-paragraph (1) include the offender's making good progress or his responding satisfactorily to supervision.

(3) In this paragraph "the appropriate court" means—

(a) in the case of a suspended sentence order which is subject to review, the court responsible for the order,

(b) in the case of a suspended sentence order which was made by the Crown Court and does not include any direction that any failure to comply with the community requirements of the order is to be dealt with by a magistrates' court, the Crown Court, and

(c) in any other case, a magistrates' court acting for the petty sessions area concerned.

Amendment by reason of change of residence

14.—(1) This paragraph applies where, at any time while a suspended sentence order is in force, the appropriate court is satisfied that the offender proposes to change, or has changed, his residence from the petty sessions area concerned to another petty sessions area. **5–334e**

(2) Subject to sub-paragraphs (3) and (4), the appropriate court may, and on the application of the responsible officer must, amend the suspended sentence order by substituting the other petty sessions area for the area specified in the order.

(3) The court may not amend under this paragraph a suspended sentence order which contains requirements which, in the opinion of the court, cannot be complied with unless the offender resides in the petty sessions area concerned unless, in accordance with paragraph 15 it either—

(a) cancels those requirements, or

(b) substitutes for those requirements other requirements which can be complied with if the offender does not reside in that area.

(4) The court may not amend under this paragraph any suspended sentence order imposing a programme requirement unless it appears to the court that the accredited programme specified in the requirement is available in the other petty sessions area.

(5) In this paragraph "the appropriate court" has the same meaning as in paragraph 13.

Amendment of community requirements of suspended sentence order

15.—(1) At any time during the supervision period, the appropriate court may, on the application of the offender or the responsible officer, by order amend any community requirement of a suspended sentence order— **5–334f**

(a) by cancelling the requirement, or

(b) by replacing it with a requirement of the same kind, which the court could include if it were then making the order.

(2) For the purposes of sub-paragraph (1)—

(a) a requirement falling within any paragraph of section 190(1) is of the same kind as any other requirement falling within that paragraph, and

(b) an electronic monitoring requirement is a requirement of the same kind as any requirement falling within section 190(1) to which it relates.

(3) The court may not under this paragraph amend a mental health treatment requirement, a drug rehabilitation requirement or an alcohol treatment requirement unless the offender expresses his willingness to comply with the requirement as amended.

(4) If the offender fails to express his willingness to comply with a mental health treatment requirement, drug rehabilitation requirement or alcohol treatment requirement as proposed to be amended by the court under this paragraph, the court may—

(a) revoke the suspended sentence order and the suspended sentence to which it relates, and

(b) deal with him, for the offence in respect of which the suspended sentence was imposed, in any way in which it could deal with him if he had just been convicted by or before the court of the offence.

(5) In dealing with the offender under sub-paragraph (4)(b), the court must take into account the extent to which the offender has complied with the requirements of the order.

(6) In this paragraph "the appropriate court" has the same meaning as in paragraph 13.

Amendment of treatment requirements on report of practitioner

5–334g 16.—(1) Where the medical practitioner or other person by whom or under whose direction an offender is, in pursuance of any requirement to which this sub-paragraph applies, being treated for his mental condition or his dependency on or propensity to misuse drugs or alcohol—

(a) is of the opinion mentioned in sub-paragraph (3), or

(b) is for any reason unwilling to continue to treat or direct the treatment of the offender,

he must make a report in writing to that effect to the responsible officer and that officer must apply under paragraph 15 to the appropriate court for the variation or cancellation of the requirement.

(2) The requirements to which sub-paragraph (1) applies are—

(a) a mental health treatment requirement,

(b) a drug rehabilitation requirement, and

(c) an alcohol treatment requirement.

(3) The opinion referred to in sub-paragraph (1) is—

(a) that the treatment of the offender should be continued beyond the period specified in that behalf in the order,

(b) that the offender needs different treatment,

(c) that the offender is not susceptible to treatment, or

(d) that the offender does not require further treatment.

(4) In this paragraph "the appropriate court" has the same meaning as in paragraph 13.

Amendment in relation to review of drug rehabilitation requirement

5–334h 17. Where the responsible officer is of the opinion that a suspended sentence order imposing a drug rehabilitation requirement which is subject to review should be so amended as to provide for each periodic review (required by section 211) to be made without a hearing instead of at a review hearing, or vice versa, he must apply under paragraph 15 to the court responsible for the order for the variation of the order.

Extension of unpaid work requirement

5–334i 18.—(1) Where—

(a) a suspended sentence order imposing an unpaid work requirement is in force in respect of the offender, and

(b) on the application of the offender or the responsible officer, it appears to the appropriate court that it would be in the interests of justice to do so having regard to circumstances which have arisen since the order was made,

the court may, in relation to the order, extend the period of twelve months specified in section 200(2).

(2) In this paragraph "the appropriate court" has the same meaning as in paragraph 13.

Supplementary

5–334j 19.—(1) No application may be made under paragraph 13, 15 or 18, and no order may be made under paragraph 14, while an appeal against the suspended sentence is pending.

(2) Sub-paragraph (1) does not apply to an application under paragraph 15 which—

(a) relates to a mental health treatment requirement, a drug rehabilitation requirement or an alcohol treatment requirement, and

(b) is made by the responsible officer with the consent of the offender.

20.—(1) Subject to sub-paragraph (2), where a court proposes to exercise its powers under paragraph 15, otherwise than on the application of the offender, the court—

(a) must summon him to appear before the court, and

(b) if he does not appear in answer to the summons, may issue a warrant for his arrest.

(2) This paragraph does not apply to an order cancelling any community requirement of a suspended sentence order.

21. Paragraphs 8(2)(c) and 15(1)(b) have effect subject to the provisions mentioned in subsection (2) of section 190, and to subsections (3) and (5) of that section.

22.—(1) On the making under this Schedule of an order amending a suspended sentence order, the proper officer of the court must—

(a) provide copies of the amending order to the offender and the responsible officer,

(b) in the case of an amending order which substitutes a new petty sessions area, provide a copy of the amending order to—

(i) the local probation board acting for that area, or (as the case may be) a provider of probation services operating in that area, and

(ii) the magistrates' court acting for that area, and

(c) in the case of an amending order which imposes or amends a requirement specified in the first column of Schedule 14, provide a copy of so much of the amending order as relates to that requirement to the person specified in relation to that requirement in the second column of that Schedule, and

(d) where the court acts for a petty sessions area other than the one specified in the order prior to the revocation or amendment, provide a copy of the revoking or amending order to a magistrates' court acting for the area so specified.

(2) Where under sub-paragraph (1)(b) the proper officer of the court provides a copy of an amending order to a magistrates' court acting for a different area, the officer must also provide to that court such documents and information relating to the case as it considers likely to be of assistance to a court acting for that area in the exercise of its functions in relation to the order.

(3) In this paragraph "proper officer" means—

(a) in relation to a magistrates' court, the justices' chief executive for the court; and

(b) in relation to the Crown Court, the appropriate officer.

[Sched. 12 is printed as amended by the *Domestic Violence, Crime and Victims Act* 2004, s.29, and Sched. 5, para. 8; and the *Offender Management Act 2007 (Consequential Amendments) Order* 2008 (S.I. 2008 No. 912), art. 3, and Sched. 1, para.19(1) and (20).]

The *Criminal Justice Act 2003 (Sentencing) (Transitory Provisions) Order* 2005 (S.I. 2005 No. 643) modifies Schedule 12 (in relation to any time before the commencement of the repeal of the *PCC(S)A* 2000, s.78 (*ante*, § 5–267)), by omitting the words "and custodial period" in paragraph 8(2)(a) and substituting the words "subject to the substitution for the original term of a lesser term" for "with either or both of" onwards in paragraph 8(2)(b) and omitting the words "and custodial period" and sub-paragraph (a) in paragraph 9(1).

As from a day to be appointed, the *AFA* 2006, s.205(1) provides that in Part 3 of Schedule 12, as it applies to a suspended sentence order with community requirements made by a relevant service court, "the appropriate court" means the Crown Court, the reference in paragraph 17 to the court responsible for the order is to be read as a reference to the Crown Court and paragraphs 13(3), 14(5), 15(6), 16(4), 18(2) and 22(1)(b)(ii) and (d) and (2) shall be treated as omitted. Paragraph 15 has effect in its application to such an order as if, in sub-paragraph (4)(b), for the words "of the offence" there were substituted "of an offence punishable with imprisonment" and a new sub-paragraph (5A) is inserted which states that a term of imprisonment or fine must not exceed the maximum permitted for the offence in respect of which the order was made, nor exceed a term of 12 months' imprisonment or the prescribed sum where the order was made by the Service Civilian Court: s.205(2). Paragraphs 2(b) and 3 shall be treated as omitted for the purposes of Part 3 as it applies to such an order: s.205(3). Where a sentence is passed under paragraph 15(4)(b), as modified by subsection (2), section 9 of the *CAA* 1968 (*post*, § 7–118) applies as if the offender had been convicted on indictment of the offence for which he was sentenced: s.205(4). Section 206 gives effect to Schedule 7 to the 2006 Act, which contains further modifications to Schedule 12 in relation to suspended sentences passed by relevant service courts.

Authorities

A defendant who has partially complied with the terms of a suspended sentence **5–334k** order is not automatically entitled to credit for that compliance when the suspended sentence is activated following a breach; paragraph 8(2) (*ante*, § 5–333), taken together with the accompanying guideline of the Sentencing Guidelines Council (Appendix K–60), envisages a two-stage test; first, the court must order the sentence to take effect either in whole or in part unless it would be unjust to do so, the extent of compliance with the original order being relevant to that decision; secondly, if it is not unjust to activate the sentence, then the court must decide whether or not to impose the original sentence or to modify the term, partial compliance again being relevant at this stage; it is clear from the language of Schedule 12 that, at the second stage, either option is available where there has been partial compliance; whilst, therefore, partial compliance is a factor to be taken into account in the exercise of the court's discretion, it will not always be appropriate to reduce a suspended sentence in such circumstances, and particularly not where compliance has been dilatory, spasmodic and grudging and where breach of the original order has been repeated: *R. v. Sheppard* [2008] 2 Cr.App.R.(S.) 93, CA.

(f) *Consecutive sentences*

Authority to impose

5–335 As to the statutory restriction on consecutive sentences for released prisoners, see the *CJA* 2003, s.265, *post*, § 5–388.

Where an offender is convicted on two or more counts of an indictment, or on two or more indictments, the court should normally impose a separate sentence on each count of each indictment. The sentences imposed may be ordered to run concurrently with each other, or consecutively, or there may be a mixture of concurrent and consecutive sentences. The court should indicate which sentences are imposed in relation to which counts.

For cases establishing the authority of a court to impose consecutive sentences, on different counts, or different indictments, see *R. v. Cutbush* (1867) L.R. 2 Q.B. 379; *R. v. Morriss*, 19 Cr.App.R. 75, CCA; and *R. v. Greenberg (No. 2)* [1943] K.B. 381, CCA. See also *R. v. Wilkes* (1770) 19 St.Tr. 1075, at 1132. A sentence of imprisonment for an offence may be ordered to run consecutively to a term of imprisonment for which the offender has been committed for contempt: *R. v. Anomo* [1998] 2 Cr.App.R.(S.) 269, CA.

Section 153(2) of the *CJA* 2003 (*ante*, § 5–266) provides that a discretionary custodial sentence "must be for the shortest term (not exceeding the permitted maximum) that in the opinion of the court is commensurate with the seriousness of the offence, or the combination of the offence and one or more offences associated with it". It was held in *R. v. A.M.* [1998] 2 Cr.App.R. 57, CA, that section 80(2)(a) of the *PCC(S)A* 2000 (in broadly similar terms to s.153(2)) permitted a court dealing with an offender under the age of 18 for a variety of offences to impose a single sentence of detention under section 91 of the 2000 Act, in respect of one of the offences, and to make the length of that sentence commensurate with the gravity of all the offences, passing no separate penalty for the other offences.

Form of words

Practice Direction (Criminal Proceedings: Consolidation), para. I.8 [2002] 1 W.L.R. 2870

Words to be used when passing sentence

5–336 **I.8.1** Where a court passes on a defendant more than one term of imprisonment the court should state in the presence of the defendant whether the terms are to be concurrent or consecutive. Should this not be done the court clerk should ask the court, before the defendant leaves the court, to do so.

I.8.2 If a prisoner is, at the time of sentence, already serving two or more consecutive terms of imprisonment and the court intends to increase the total period of imprisonment, it should use the expression "consecutive to the total period of imprisonment to which you are already subject" rather than "at the expiration of the term of imprisonment you are now serving", lest the prisoner be not then serving the last of the terms to which he is already subject.

Offenders serving existing sentences

As to the treatment of prisoners serving concurrent or consecutive sentences under the *CJA* 2003, see sections 263 and 264 (*post*, §§ 5–386, 5–387). **5–337**

As to the form of words to be used where the defendant is, at the time of sentence, serving two or more consecutive sentences, see *Practice Direction (Criminal Proceedings: Consolidation)*, para. I.8.2 (*ante*, § 5–336).

Offences arising out of same transaction

As a general principle, consecutive terms should not be imposed for offences which arise out of the same transaction or incident, whether or not they arise out of precisely the same facts, but much is left to the discretion of the court: see *R. v. Lawrence*, 11 Cr.App.R.(S.) 580, CA; and *R. v. Noble* [2003] 1 Cr.App.R.(S.) 65, CA (consecutive sentences for causing death by dangerous driving quashed; exceptional cases justifying departure from the normal principle tend to involve different offences). As to *Lawrence*, and the application of this principle to road traffic offences, see also *post*, § 32–180. **5–338**

A court may depart from the principle requiring concurrent sentences for offences forming part of one transaction if there are exceptional circumstances: *R. v. Wheatley*, 5 Cr.App.R.(S.) 417, CA; and *R. v. Dillon*, *ibid.* at 439, CA. See also *R. v. Jordan* [1996] 1 Cr.App.R.(S.) 181, CA; and *R. v. Fletcher* [2002] 2 Cr.App.R.(S.) 127, CA (consecutive offences for indecent assault and threats to kill arising from the same incident justified, the gravamen of the offences being different).

Where an offender attempts to interfere with the course of justice in relation to the trial of charges against him, any sentence for the offence of attempting to pervert the course of justice should normally be consecutive to the sentence for the principal offence: *Att.-Gen.'s Reference (No. 1 of 1990) (R. v. Atkinson)*, 12 Cr.App.R.(S.) 245, CA.

Use of violence to resist arrest

Where an offender uses violence to avoid apprehension for another offence, the use of violence is not part of the same incident as the original offence: *R. v. Kastercum*, 56 Cr.App.R. 298, CA; *R. v. Hill*, 5 Cr.App.R.(S.) 214, CA; and *R. v. Fitter*, *ibid.* at 168, CA. **5–339**

Possession of firearm at time of commission of offence

See *post*, § 24–49. **5–340**

Breaches of non-custodial sentences, etc.

Where an offender commits a further offence during the currency of a community order or conditional discharge, and is sentenced to a term of imprisonment for that offence, it will normally be appropriate for any sentence of imprisonment imposed for the earlier offence to be ordered to run consecutively (see *R. v. Webb*, 37 Cr.App.R. 82, CCA). **5–341**

Totality of sentences

A court which passes a number of consecutive sentences should review the aggregate of the sentences, and consider whether the aggregate sentence is just and appropriate taking the offences as a whole. This principle, known as the "totality principle", has been expressly recognised by statute: see the *CJA* 2003, s.166(3)(b) (*ante*, § 5–90). **5–342**

The duty of the court to review the totality of the sentence applies in any case where consecutive sentences are imposed: see *R. v. Reeves*, 2 Cr.App.R.(S.) 35, CA; *R. v. Jones* [1996] 1 Cr.App.R.(S.) 153, CA (different indictments); *R. v. Millen*, 2 Cr.App.R.(S.) 357, CA; *R. v. Jones* [1996] 1 Cr.App.R.(S.) 153, CA; *R. v. Stevens* [1997] 2 Cr.App.R.(S.) 180, CA (different judges); and *R. v. Bocskei*, 54 Cr.App.R. 519, CA (activation of suspended sentence).

The principle appears to be recognised in three situations in particular—where the offender has committed a series of offences of moderate gravity and has received an aggregate sentence equivalent to the sentence which would have been imposed for an offence of a much more serious nature (see *R. v. Holderness*, unreported, July 15, 1974); where the offender is relatively young and has not previously served a custodial sentence (see *R. v. Koyce*, 1 Cr.App.R.(S.) 21, CA); and where an offender who is sentenced to a long term of imprisonment for a grave crime is also liable to be sentenced to a much shorter term for some other matter (*e.g.* where he is subject to a short suspended sentence). See also *R. v. Smith (Arthur)*, 3 Cr.App.R.(S.) 201, CA; and *R. v. Christie*, 1 Cr.App.R.(S.) 84, CA.

Where a court decides to adjust a series of sentences because the aggregate is too high, it is generally preferable to do so by ordering sentences to run concurrently rather than by passing a series of short consecutive sentences (see *R. v. Simpson*, unreported, February 1, 1972), but where concurrent sentences are imposed for a series of offences of varying gravity, the individual sentences should not be out of proportion to the individual offences for which they are imposed (see *R. v. Smith*, unreported, February 13, 1975).

Other forms of sentence

5–343 A sentence of imprisonment may not be imposed consecutively to a sentence of life imprisonment: *R. v. Foy*, 46 Cr.App.R. 290, CCA, and a sentence of life imprisonment should not be imposed to run consecutively to an existing determinate sentence (see *R. v. Jones*, 46 Cr.App.R. 129 at 149, CCA). As to indeterminate sentences under the *CJA* 2003, see *ante*, §§ 5–303, 5–307a.

Sentences of detention in a young offender institution (abolished, as from a day to be appointed by the *CJCSA* 2000, s.61) may be imposed consecutively one to another (*PCC(S)A* 2000, s.97(4), *post*, § 5–345); where an offender over 21 who is serving a sentence of detention in a young offender institution is liable to be sentenced for some further offence, the court may pass a sentence of imprisonment to run consecutively to the sentence of detention in a young offender institution (*ibid.*, s.97(5)).

(3) Detention in young offender institution

Powers of Criminal Courts (Sentencing) Act 2000, ss.96, 97

Detention in a young offender institution for other cases where offender at least 18 but under 21

5–344 **96.** *Subject to sections 90 , 93 and 94 above, where—*

(a) *a person aged at least 18 but under 21 is convicted of an offence which is punishable with imprisonment in the case of a person aged 21 or over, and*

(b) *the court is of the opinion that either or both of paragraphs (a) and (b) of section 79(2) above apply or the case falls within section 79(3),*

the sentence that the court is to pass is a sentence of detention in a young offender institution.

Term of detention in a young offender institution, and consecutive sentences

5–345 **97.**—(1) *The maximum term of detention in a young offender institution that a court may impose for an offence is the same as the maximum term of imprisonment that it may impose for that offence.*

(2) *Subject to subsection (3) below, a court shall not pass a sentence for an offender's detention in a young offender institution for less than 21 days.*

(3) *A court may pass a sentence of detention in a young offender institution for less than 21 days for an offence under section 65(6) of the* Criminal Justice Act *1991 (breach of requirement imposed on young offender on his release from detention).*

(4) *Where—*

(a) *an offender is convicted of more than one offence for which he is liable to a sentence of detention in a young offender institution, or*

(b) *an offender who is serving a sentence of detention in a young offender institution is convicted of one or more further offences for which he is liable to such a sentence,*

the court shall have the same power to pass consecutive sentences of detention in a young offender institution as if they were sentences of imprisonment.

(5) *Subject to section 84 above (restriction on consecutive sentences for released prisoners), where an offender who—*

(a) *is serving a sentence of detention in a young offender institution, and*

(b) *is aged 21 or over,*

is convicted of one or more further offences for which he is liable to imprisonment, the court shall have the power to pass one or more sentences of imprisonment to run consecutively upon the sentence of detention in a young offender institution.

[Ss.96 and 97 are repealed, as from a day to be appointed: *CJCSA* 2000, s.75, and Sched. 8.]

As to offenders sentenced before April 1, 2000, see the transitional provision in Schedule 11, para. 6. **5–346**

Minimum term

The requirement that sentences of detention in a young offender institution should be for a minimum term applies to individual terms of detention: see *R. v. Dover Youth Court, ex p. K. (a Minor)* [1999] 1 W.L.R. 27, DC. **5–347**

(4) Detention and training orders

Powers of Criminal Courts (Sentencing) Act 2000, s.100

Offenders under 18: detention and training orders

100.—(1) Subject to sections 90 and 91 above, sections 226 to 228 of the *Criminal Justice Act* 2003, and subsection (2) below, where— **5–348**

(a) a child or young person (that is to say, any person aged under 18) is convicted of an offence which is punishable with imprisonment in the case of a person aged *21* [18] or over, and

(b) the court is of the opinion that subsection (2) of section 152 of the *Criminal Justice Act* 2003 applies or the case falls within subsection (3) of that section,

the sentence that the court is to pass is a detention and training order.

(2) A court shall not make a detention and training order—

(a) in the case of an offender under the age of 15 at the time of the conviction, unless it is of the opinion that he is a persistent offender;

(b) in the case of an offender under the age of 12 at that time, unless—

(i) it is of the opinion that only a custodial sentence would be adequate to protect the public from further offending by him; and

(ii) the offence was committed on or after such date as the Secretary of State may by order appoint.

(3) A detention and training order is an order that the offender in respect of whom it is made shall be subject, for the term specified in the order, to a period of detention and training followed by a period of supervision.

[This section is printed as amended by the *CJA* 2003, s.304, and Sched. 32, paras 90 and 111; and as amended, as from a day to be appointed, by the *CJCSA* 2000, s.74, and Sched. 7, para. 184 (substitution of "18" for "21" in subs. (1)(a)).]

As at September 20, 2006, no order had been made under section 100(2)(b)(ii).

Powers of Criminal Courts (Sentencing) Act 2000, ss.101, 102

Term of order, consecutive terms and taking account of remands

101.—(1) Subject to *subsection (2)* [subsections (2) and (2A)] below, the term of a detention and training order made in respect of an offence (whether by a magistrates' court or otherwise) shall be 4, 6, 8, 10, 12, 18 or 24 months. **5–349**

(2) The term of a detention and training order may not exceed the maximum term of imprisonment that the Crown Court could (in the case of an offender aged *21* [18] or over) impose for the offence.

[(2A) Where—

(a) the offence is a summary offence,

(b) the maximum term of imprisonment that a court could (in the case of an offender aged 18 or over) impose for the offence is 51 weeks,

the term of a detention and training order may not exceed 6 months.]

(3) Subject to subsections (4) and (6) below, a court making a detention and training order may order that its term shall commence on the expiry of the term of any other detention and training order made by that or any other court.

(4) A court shall not make in respect of an offender a detention and training order the effect of which would be that he would be subject to detention and training orders for a term which exceeds 24 months.

(5) Where the term of the detention and training orders to which an offender would otherwise be subject exceeds 24 months, the excess shall be treated as remitted.

(6) A court making a detention and training order shall not order that its term shall commence on the expiry of the term of a detention and training order under which the period of supervision has already begun (under section 103(1) below).

(7) Where a detention and training order ("the new order") is made in respect of an offender who is subject to a detention and training order under which the period of supervision has begun ("the old order"), the old order shall be disregarded in determining—

(a) for the purposes of subsection (4) above whether the effect of the new order would be that the offender would be subject to detention and training orders for a term which exceeds 24 months; and

(b) for the purposes of subsection (5) above whether the term of the detention and training orders to which the offender would (apart from that subsection) be subject exceeds 24 months.

(8) In determining the term of a detention and training order for an offence, the court shall take account of any period for which the offender has been remanded *in custody* [—

(a) in custody, or

(b) on bail subject to a qualifying curfew condition and an electronic monitoring condition (within the meaning of section 240A of the *Criminal Justice Act* 2003),]

in connection with the offence, or any other offence the charge for which was founded on the same facts or evidence.

(9) Where a court proposes to make detention and training orders in respect of an offender for two or more offences—

(a) subsection (8) above shall not apply; but

(b) in determining the total term of the detention and training orders it proposes to make in respect of the offender, the court shall take account of the total period (if any) for which he has been remanded *in custody* [as mentioned in that subsection] in connection with any of those offences, or any other offence the charge for which was founded on the same facts or evidence.

(10) Once a period of remand has, under subsection (8) or (9) above, been taken account of in relation to a detention and training order made in respect of an offender for any offence or offences, it shall not subsequently be taken account of (under either of those subsections) in relation to such an order made in respect of the offender for any other offence or offences.

(11) Any reference in subsection (8) or (9) above to an offender's being remanded in custody is a reference to his being—

(a) held in police detention;

(b) remanded in or committed to custody by an order of a court;

(c) remanded or committed to local authority accommodation under section 23 of the *Children and Young Persons Act* 1969 and placed and kept in secure accommodation or detained in a secure training centre pursuant to arrangements under subsection (7A) of that section; or

(d) remanded, admitted or removed to hospital under section 35, 36, 38 or 48 of the *Mental Health Act* 1983.

(12) A person is in police detention for the purposes of subsection (11) above—

(a) at any time when he is in police detention for the purposes of the *Police and Criminal Evidence Act* 1984; and

(b) at any time when he is detained under section 41 of the *Terrorism Act* 2000;

and in that subsection "secure accommodation" has the same meaning as in section 23 of the *Children and Young Persons Act* 1969.

(12A) Section 243 of the *Criminal Justice Act* 2003 (persons extradited to the United Kingdom) applies in relation to a person sentenced to a detention and training order as it applies in relation to a fixed-term prisoner, with the reference in subsection (2) of that section to section 240 being read as a reference to subsection (8) above.

(13) For the purpose of any reference in sections 102 to 105 below to the term of a

detention and training order, consecutive terms of such orders and terms of such orders which are wholly or partly concurrent shall be treated as a single term if—

(a) the orders were made on the same occasion; or

(b) where they were made on different occasions, the offender has not been released (by virtue of subsection (2), (3), (4) or (5) of section 102 below) at any time during the period beginning with the first and ending with the last of those occasions.

[This section is printed as amended by the *Terrorism Act* 2000, s.125(1), and Sched. 15, para. 20(1) and (3); the *CJPA* 2001, s.133(3); and the *PJA* 2006, s.42, and Sched. 13, para. 32; and as amended, as from a day to be appointed, by the *CJCSA* 2000, s.74, and Sched. 7, para. 185 (substitution of "18" for "21" in subs. (2)); the *CJA* 2003, s.298 (substitution of words in square brackets for italicised words in subs. (1), and insertion of subs. (2A)); and the *CJIA* 2008, s.22(6) (omission of italicised words, insertion of words in square brackets, in subss. (8) and (9)).]

As from a day to be appointed, in sections 101(3) to (10) and (13) and sections 102 to 105, 106A and 107 of the 2000 Act (*post*), references to a detention and training order include a detention and training order imposed by the Court Martial or the Service Civilian Court under the *AFA* 2006, s.211: *AFA* 2006, s.213(1); in sections 101(3) to (10) and (13) and 106A, "court" includes a relevant service court (within the meaning given by the *AFA* 2006, s.196(2)): *AFA* 2006, s.213(2); and, in section 101(8) and (9), in their application to an order under section 211 of the 2006 Act, any reference to an offender's being "remanded in custody" is a reference to his being kept in service custody, and section 101(11) and (12) of the 2000 Act do not apply to such an order: *AFA* 2006, s.213(3).

The period of detention and training

102.—(1) An offender shall serve the period of detention and training under a detention and training order in such youth detention accommodation as may be determined by the Secretary of State. **5–350**

(2) Subject to subsections (3) to (5) below, the period of detention and training under a detention and training order shall be one-half of the term of the order.

(3) The Secretary of State may at any time release the offender if he is satisfied that exceptional circumstances exist which justify the offender's release on compassionate grounds.

(4) The Secretary of State may release the offender—

(a) in the case of an order for a term of 8 months or more but less than 18 months, at any time during the period of one month ending with the half-way point of the term of the order; and

(b) in the case of an order for a term of 18 months or more, at any time during the period of two months ending with that point.

(5) If a youth court so orders on an application made by the Secretary of State for the purpose, the Secretary of State shall release the offender—

(a) in the case of an order for a term of 8 months or more but less than 18 months, one month after the half-way point of the term of the order; and

(b) in the case of an order for a term of 18 months or more, one month or two months after that point.

(6) An offender detained in pursuance of a detention and training order shall be deemed to be in legal custody.

[This section is printed as amended by the *Offender Management Act* 2007, ss.33(1), 34(1) and (2), and 39, and Sched. 5, Pt 3.]

Powers of Criminal Courts (Sentencing) Act 2000, ss.103, 104

The period of supervision

103.—(1) The period of supervision of an offender who is subject to a detention and training order— **5–351**

(a) shall begin with the offender's release, whether at the half-way point of the term of the order or otherwise; and

(b) subject to subsection (2) below, shall end when the term of the order ends.

(2) The Secretary of State may by order provide that the period of supervision shall end at such point during the term of a detention and training order as may be specified in the order under this subsection.

(3) During the period of supervision, the offender shall be under the supervision of—

(a) an officer of a local probation board or an officer of a provider of probation services;

(b) a social worker of a local authority social services department; or

(c) a member of a youth offending team;

and the category of person to supervise the offender shall be determined from time to time by the Secretary of State.

(4) Where the supervision is to be provided by an officer of a local probation board, the officer of a local probation board shall be an officer appointed for or assigned to the petty sessions area within which the offender resides for the time being.

(4A) Where the supervision is to be provided by an officer of a provider of probation services, the officer of a provider of probation services shall be an officer acting in the local justice area within which the offender resides for the time being.

(5) Where the supervision is to be provided by—

(a) a social worker of a local authority social services department, or

(b) a member of a youth offending team,

the social worker or member shall be a social worker of, or a member of a youth offending team established by, the local authority within whose area the offender resides for the time being.

(6) The offender shall be given a notice from the Secretary of State specifying—

(a) the category of person for the time being responsible for his supervision; and

(b) any requirements with which he must for the time being comply.

(7) A notice under subsection (6) above shall be given to the offender—

(a) before the commencement of the period of supervision; and

(b) before any alteration in the matters specified in subsection (6)(a) or (b) above comes into effect.

[This section is printed as amended by the *CJCSA* 2000, s.74 and Sched. 7, para. 4; and S.I. 2008 No. 912 (*ante*, § 5–334j), art. 3, and Sched. 1, para. 14(1) and (16).]

Breach of supervision requirements

5–352 **104.**—(1) Where a detention and training order is in force in respect of an offender and it appears on information to a justice of the peace that the offender has failed to comply with requirements under section 103(6)(b) above, the justice—

(a) may issue a summons requiring the offender to appear at the place and time specified in the summons; or

(b) if the information is in writing and on oath, may issue a warrant for the offender's arrest.

(2) Any summons or warrant issued under this section shall direct the offender to appear or be brought—

(a) before a youth court acting for the petty sessions area in which the offender resides;

(b) if it is not known where the offender resides, before a youth court acting for the same petty sessions area as the justice who issued the summons or warrant.

(3) If it is proved to the satisfaction of the youth court before which an offender appears or is brought under this section that he has failed to comply with requirements under section 103(6)(b) above, that court may—

(a) order the offender to be detained, in such youth detention accommodation as the Secretary of State may determine, for such period, not exceeding the shorter of three months or the remainder of the term of the detention and training order, as the court may specify; or

(b) impose on the offender a fine not exceeding level 3 on the standard scale.

(4) An offender detained in pursuance of an order under subsection (3)(a) above shall be deemed to be in legal custody.

(5) A fine imposed under subsection (3)(b) above shall be deemed, for the purposes of any enactment, to be a sum adjudged to be paid by a conviction.

(6) An offender may appeal to the Crown Court against any order made under subsection (3)(a) or (b) above.

[This section is printed as amended by the *Domestic Violence, Crime and Victims*

Act 2004, s.29, and Sched. 5, para. 2; and the *Offender Management Act* 2007, s.34(1) and (3).]

Powers of Criminal Courts (Sentencing) Act 2000, ss.105–107

Offences during currency of order

105.—(1) This section applies to a person subject to a detention and training order if— **5–353**

(a) after his release and before the date on which the term of the order ends, he commits an offence punishable with imprisonment in the case of a person aged *21* [18] or over ("the new offence"); and

(b) whether before or after that date, he is convicted of the new offence.

(2) Subject to section 8(6) above (duty of adult magistrates' court to remit young offenders to youth court for sentence), the court by or before which a person to whom this section applies is convicted of the new offence may, whether or not it passes any other sentence on him, order him to be detained in such youth detention accommodation as the Secretary of State may determine for the whole or any part of the period which—

(a) begins with the date of the court's order; and

(b) is equal in length to the period between the date on which the new offence was committed and the date mentioned in subsection (1) above.

(3) The period for which a person to whom this section applies is ordered under subsection (2) above to be detained in youth detention accommodation—

(a) shall, as the court may direct, either be served before and be followed by, or be served concurrently with, any sentence imposed for the new offence; and

(b) in either case, shall be disregarded in determining the appropriate length of that sentence.

(4) Where the new offence is found to have been committed over a period of two or more days, or at some time during a period of two or more days, it shall be taken for the purposes of this section to have been committed on the last of those days.

(5) A person detained in pursuance of an order under subsection (2) above shall be deemed to be in legal custody.

[This section is printed as amended by the *Offender Management Act* 2007, s.34(1) and (4); and as amended, as from a day to be appointed, by the *CJCSA* 2000, s.74, and Sched. 7, para. 186 (substitution of "18" for "21" in subs. (1)).]

Interaction with sentences of detention in a young offender institution

106.—(1) *Where a court passes a sentence of detention in a young offender institution in the case of an offender who is subject to a detention and training order, the sentence shall take effect as follows—* **5–354**

(a) *if the offender has been released by virtue of subsection (2), (3), (4) or (5) of section 102 above, at the beginning of the day on which it is passed;*

(b) *if not, either as mentioned in paragraph (a) above or, if the court so orders, at the time when the offender would otherwise be released by virtue of subsection (2), (3), (4) or (5) of section 102.*

(2), (3) [*Repealed by* CJA *2003, s.304, and Sched. 32, paras 90 and 112.*]

(4) Subject to subsection (5) below, where at any time an offender is subject concurrently—

(a) to a detention and training order, and

(b) to a sentence of detention in a young offender institution,

he shall be treated for the purposes of sections 102 to 105 above and of section *98 above* [61 of the *Criminal Justice and Court Services Act* 2000] (place of detention), Chapter IV of this Part (return to detention) and Part II of the *Criminal Justice Act* 1991 (early release) as if he were subject only to the one of them that was imposed on the later occasion.

(5) Nothing in subsection (4) above shall require the offender to be released in respect of either the order or the sentence unless and until he is required to be released in respect of each of them.

(6) Where, by virtue of any enactment giving a court power to deal with a person in a way in which a court on a previous occasion could have dealt with him, a detention and training order for any term is made in the case of a person who has attained the age of 18, the person shall be treated as if he had been sentenced to *detention in a young offender institution* [imprisonment] for the same term.

[This section is printed as amended, as from a day to be appointed, by the *CJCSA*

2000, s.74, and Sched. 7, para. 187 (omission of subs. (1) and of italicised words in subss. (4) and (6), and insertion of words in square brackets).]

Interaction with sentences of detention

5–354a **106A.**—(1) In this section—

"the 2003 Act" means the *Criminal Justice Act* 2003;

"sentence of detention" means—

(a) a sentence of detention under section 91 above [or section 209 of the *Armed Forces Act* 2006], or

(b) a sentence of detention under section 228 of the 2003 Act (extended sentence for certain violent or sexual offences: persons under 18)

[and references in this section to a sentence of detention under section 228 of the 2003 Act include such a sentence passed as a result of section 222 of the *Armed Forces Act* 2006].

(2) Where a court passes a sentence of detention in the case of an offender who is subject to a detention and training order, the sentence shall take effect as follows—

(a) if the offender has at any time been released by virtue of subsection (2), (3), (4) or (5) of section 102 above, at the beginning of the day on which the sentence is passed, and

(b) if not, either as mentioned in paragraph (a) above or, if the court so orders, at the time when the offender would otherwise be released by virtue of subsection (2), (3), (4) or (5) of section 102.

(3) Where a court makes a detention and training order in the case of an offender who is subject to a sentence of detention, the order shall take effect as follows—

(a) if the offender has at any time been released under Chapter 6 of Part 12 of the 2003 Act (release on licence of fixed-term prisoners), at the beginning of the day on which the order is made, and

(b) if not, either as mentioned in paragraph (a) above or, if the court so orders, at the time when the offender would otherwise be released under that Chapter.

(4) Where an order under section 102(5) above is made in the case of a person in respect of whom a sentence of detention is to take effect as mentioned in subsection (2)(b) above, the order is to be expressed as an order that the period of detention attributable to the detention and training order is to end at the time determined under section 102(5)(a) or (b) above.

(5) In determining for the purposes of subsection (3)(b) the time when an offender would otherwise be released under Chapter 6 of Part 12 of the 2003 Act, section 246 of that Act (power of Secretary of State to release prisoners on licence before he is required to do so) is to be disregarded.

(6) Where by virtue of subsection (3)(b) above a detention and training order made in the case of a person who is subject to a sentence of detention under section 228 of the 2003 Act is to take effect at the time when he would otherwise be released under Chapter 6 of Part 12 of that Act, any direction by the Parole Board under subsection (2)(b) of section 247 of that Act in respect of him is to be expressed as a direction that the Board would, but for the detention and training order, have directed his release under that section.

(7) Subject to subsection (9) below, where at any time an offender is subject concurrently—

(a) to a detention and training order, and

(b) to a sentence of detention,

he shall be treated for the purposes of the provisions specified in subsection (8) below as if he were subject only to the sentence of detention.

(8) Those provisions are—

(a) sections 102 to 105 above,

(b) section 92 above *and*[,] section 235 of the 2003 Act [and section 210 of the *Armed Forces Act* 2006] (place of detention etc.), *and*

(c) Chapter 6 of Part 12 of the 2003 Act[, and

(d) section 214 of the *Armed Forces Act* 2006 (offences committed during a detention and training order under that Act)].

(9) Nothing in subsection (7) above shall require the offender to be released in respect of either the order or the sentence unless and until he is required to be released in respect of each of them.

[This section is inserted by the *CJA* 2003, s.304, and Sched. 32, paras 90 and 113. It is printed as amended, as from a day to be appointed, by the *AFA* 2006, s.378(1), and Sched. 16, para. 165 (omission of italicised words, insertion of words in square brackets).]

Meaning of "secure [youth detention] accommodation" and references to terms

107.—(1) In sections 102, 104 and 105 above " youth detention accommodation" means— **5–355**

(a) a secure training centre;

(b) a young offender institution;

(c) accommodation provided by or on behalf of a local authority for the purpose of restricting the liberty of children and young persons;

(d) accommodation provided for that purpose under section 82 of the *Children Act* 1989 (financial support by the Secretary of State); or

(e) such other accommodation or descriptions of accommodation as the Secretary of State may by order specify.

(2) In sections 102 to 105 above references to the term of a detention and training order shall be construed in accordance with section 101(13) above.

[This section is printed as amended by the *Offender Management Act* 2007, s.34(1), (5) and (6).]

Before making a detention and training order, the court must be satisfied that the criteria for the imposition of a custodial sentence in the *PCC(S)A* 2000, s.79 (*ante*, § 5–263) or the *CJA* 2003, s.152(2) (*ante*, § 5–265) are satisfied. If the offender is under 15, the court must also be of the opinion that the offender is a "persistent offender", and in the case of an offender under the age of 12, the court must be of the opinion, in addition, that only a custodial sentence would be adequate to protect the public from further offending by the offender. These conditions appear to be cumulative, and in the case of an offender under the age of 12, all three conditions must be satisfied. **5–356**

The effect of section 29(1) of the *CYPA* 1963 ("Where proceedings in respect of a young person are begun ... for an offence and he attains the age of eighteen before the conclusion of the proceedings, the court may ... deal with the case and make any order which it could have made if he had not attained that age.") is that the court may make a detention and training order notwithstanding that the offender had attained the age of 18 by the time of conviction and that section 100(1) is expressed to apply only to persons under 18 at the time of conviction: *Aldis v. DPP* [2002] 2 Cr.App.R.(S.) 88, DC.

The maximum term of a detention and training order is two years, or whatever sentence the Crown Court might impose on an adult, if less. The powers of a youth court to impose detention and training orders are not restricted, as were the powers of magistrates' courts, in respect of all other custodial sentences, to a term of six months (at the time of this decision) for a single offence: see *R. v. Medway Youth Court, ex p. A.* [2000] 1 Cr.App.R.(S.) 191, DC.

A detention and training order may be for any of the periods specified in s.101(1). Consecutive detention and training orders may be passed, if the defendant is convicted of more than one offence, or is convicted of offences while he is subject to an existing detention and training order: s.101(3). Consecutive orders, each for one of the terms specified in section 101(1), may be passed, notwithstanding that the aggregate of the terms is not one of the specified terms: *R. v. Norris* [2001] 1 Cr.App.R.(S.) 116, CA.

A court passing detention and training orders for a number of summary offences may pass orders which in aggregate exceed a total of six months; the *MCA* 1980, s.133 (*ante*, § 5–270) does not apply so as to restrict the maximum aggegate to the maximum aggregate term of imprisonment available in respect of older offenders: *C. v. DPP* [2001] 1 Cr.App.R.(S.) 45, DC.

It has been held that a detention and training order may not be imposed to run consecutively to a term of detention under the *PCC(S)A* 2000, s.91: *R. v. Hayward and Hayward* [2001] 2 Cr.App.R.(S.) 31, CA; and a term of detention under section 91 may not be ordered to run consecutively to a detention and training order: *R. v. Lang* [2001] 2 Cr.App.R.(S.) 39, CA. These decisions must now be seen in the light of section 106A.

There is no power to impose a detention and training order together with an extended sentence under the *PCC(S)A* 2000, s.85(1): *R. v. B.* [2005] 2 Cr.App.R.(S.) 87, CA.

It was held in *R. v. D.* [2001] 1 Cr.App.R.(S.) 59, CA, that in determining whether an offender under the age of 15 could be considered a "persistent offender", the court could take account of offences in respect of which he had been cautioned. The decision would clearly apply to offences in respect of which an offender had been reprimanded or warned under the *CDA* 1998, s.65. It is not necessary for the offender to have committed a series of offences of a similar character, or that he should have failed to respond to a previous order of the court: *R. v. B.* [2001] 1 Cr.App.R.(S.) 113, CA. An offender with no previous conviction who is convicted on the same occasion of a number of offences committed within a short space of time may be a persistent offender: *R. v. S.(A.)* [2001] 1 Cr.App.R.(S.) 18, CA.

5–357 The treatment of time spent in custody on remand has been considered in particular in *R. v. Inner London Crown Court, ex p. N. and S.* [2001] 1 Cr.App.R.(S.) 99, DC, *R. v. Fieldhouse and Watts* [2001] 1 Cr.App.R.(S.) 104, CA, and *R. v. Eagles* [2007] 1 Cr.App.R.(S.) 99, CA. The decisions indicate that whilst it is not appropriate or desirable that any precise reflection should be given for a day or two spent in custody, the normal approach would be to double the period spent on remand and to subtract that from the otherwise appropriate period. Where the resulting figure does not match one of the prescribed periods, the court should not always settle on the next permissible lower period, but should generally do so. A court should take all the circumstances into account, including the apparent impact of any period spent on remand in custody, but where the otherwise appropriate sentence was 18 or 24 months, a court might well conclude that no reduction could properly be made for periods on remand of up to two months (equivalent to four months).

Where an offender is not liable to a term of detention under the *PCC(S)A* 2000, s.91 (*post*, § 5–358), a court which imposes a detention and training order should reduce the term of the order to a point below the maximum available term to reflect a plea of guilty, unless there are proper grounds for not granting a discount: *R. v. Kelly* [2002] 1 Cr.App.R.(S.) 11, CA. Where the offender is liable to a term of detention under section 91, a discount for a plea of guilty might properly be reflected by the imposition of a detention and training order for the maximum period: *R. v. March* [2002] 2 Cr.App.R.(S.) 98, CA; but a judge is not entitled to withhold the normal discount on account of his view that the pleas accepted by the prosecution did not reflect the true criminality involved; accordingly, where the defendant pleaded guilty to various offences for which the only custodial option was a detention and training order, some discount should have been given notwithstanding the judge's view that the prosecution had improperly accepted pleas of not guilty to charges which would have allowed of a sentence of detention under section 91 of the 2000 Act: *ibid*.

As to whether it is permissible to impose a detention and training order on a defendant who was 14 at the time of commission of the offence, and in respect of whom a custodial sentence would not have been available had he been convicted before his fifteenth birthday, see *ante*, § 5–279.

Release on compassionate grounds

5–357a As to the proper construction of section 102(3), see *R. (A.) v. Governor of Huntercombe Young Offenders Institute and the Secretary of State for the Home Department*, 171 J.P. 65, QBD. (Stanley Burnton J.).

(5) Detention of offenders under 18 convicted of certain serious offences

Powers of Criminal Courts (Sentencing) Act 2000, s.91

Offenders under 18 convicted of certain serious offences: power to detain for specified period

5–358 **91.**—(1) Subsection (3) below applies where a person aged under 18 is convicted on indictment of—

(a) an offence punishable in the case of a person aged *21* [18] or over with imprisonment for 14 years or more, not being an offence the sentence for which is fixed by law; or

(b) an offence under section 3 of the *Sexual Offences Act* 2003 (in this section, "the 2003 Act") (sexual assault); or

(c) an offence under section 13 of the 2003 Act (child sex offences committed by children or young persons); or

(d) an offence under section 25 of the 2003 Act (sexual activity with a child family member); or

(e) an offence under section 26 of the 2003 Act (inciting a child family member to engage in sexual activitiy).

(1A) Subsection (3) below also applies where—

(a) a person aged under 18 is convicted on indictment of an offence—

(i) under subsection (1)(a), (ab), (aba), (ac), (ad), (ae), (af) or (c) of section 5 of the *Firearms Act* 1968 (prohibited weapons), or

(ii) under subsection (1A)(a) of that section.

(b) the offence was committed after the commencement of section 51A of that Act and for the purposes of subsection (3) of that section at a time when he was aged 16 or over, and

(c) the court is of the opinion mentioned in section 51A(2) of that Act (exceptional circumstances which justify its not imposing required custodial sentence).

(1B) Subsection (3) below also applies where—

(a) a person aged under 18 is convicted on indictment of an offence under the *Firearms Act* 1968 that is listed in section 51A(1A)(b), (e) or (f) of that Act and was committed in respect of a firearm or ammunition specified in section 5(1)(a), (ab), (aba), (ac), (ad), (ae), (af) or (c) or section 5(1A)(a) of that Act;

(b) the offence was committed after the commencement of section 30 of the *Violent Crime Reduction Act* 2006 and for the purposes of section 51A(3) of the *Firearms Act* 1968 at a time when he was aged 16 or over; and

(c) the court is of the opinion mentioned in section 51A(2) of the *Firearms Act* 1968.

(1C) Subsection (3) below also applies where—

(a) a person aged under 18 is convicted of an offence under section 28 of the *Violent Crime Reduction Act* 2006 (using someone to mind a weapon);

(b) section 29(3) of that Act applies (minimum sentences in certain cases); and

(c) the court is of the opinion mentioned in section 29(6) of that Act (exceptional circumstances which justify not imposing the minimum sentence).

(2) [*Repealed by* CJA *2003, s.332, and Sched. 37, Pt* 7.]

(3) If the court is of the opinion that neither a *community sentence* [youth rehabilitation order] nor a detention and training order is suitable, the court may sentence the offender to be detained for such period, not exceeding the maximum term of imprisonment with which the offence is punishable in the case of a person aged 21 or over, as may be specified in the sentence.

(4) Subsection (3) above is subject to (in particular) section 152 and 153 of the *Criminal Justice Act* 2003.

(5) Where—

(a) subsection (2) of section 51A of the *Firearms Act* 1968, or

(b) subsection (6) of section 29 of the *Violent Crime Reduction Act* 2006,

requires the imposition of a sentence of detention under this section for a term of at least the term provided for in that section, the court shall sentence the offender to be detained for such period, of at least the term so provided for but not exceeding the maximum term of imprisonment with which the offence is punishable in the case of a person aged 18 or over, as may be specified in the sentence.

[This section is printed as amended by the *SOA* 2003, s.139, and Sched. 6, para. 43 (substitution of new paras (b) to (e) in subs. (1) for original paras (b) and (c), which referred to offences contrary to the *SOA* 1956, ss.14 and 15); the *CJA* 2003, ss.289 and 304, and Sched. 32, paras 90 and 110; and the *VCRA* 2006, s.49, and Sched. 1, para. 7; and as amended, as from a day to be appointed, by the *CJCSA* 2000, s.74, and Sched. 7, para. 181 (substitution of "18" for "21" in subs. (1)(a)); and the *CJIA* 2008, s.6(2), and Sched. 4, paras 51 and 56 (omission of italicised words, insertion of words in square brackets in subs. (3)). As to the transitional and saving arrangements in relation to the latter amendment, see *ante*, § 5–1.]

As to the circumstances in which a magistrates' court should commit a defendant for trial so as to allow for the possibility of sentence being imposed under this section, see *ante*, §§ 1–75m *et seq*.

The date for the determination of an offender's age for the purposes of section 91 is the date of conviction: *R. v. Robinson*, 96 Cr.App.R. 418, CA.

Availability

Detention under section 91 is a custodial sentence for the purposes of the 2000 Act **5–359** (see s.76(1), *ante*, § 5–262), and its use is subject to the principles in sections 152, 153, 156 and 157 of the *CJA* 2003. For sections 152 and 153 of the 2003 Act, see *ante*, §§ 5–263 *et seq.* For sections 156 and 157 of the 2003 Act, see *ante*, §§ 5–19, 5–20.

The power may be used where the offence is a common law offence for which the maximum sentence is at large (see *R. v. Bosomworth*, 57 Cr.App.R. 708, CA).

Where an offender is to be sentenced for a number of offences, for some of which the power to order detention is available and for some of which it is not, the proper course is to order the offender to be detained for those offences in respect of which the power under section 91 is available, but to impose a term of detention which is commensurate with the seriousness of all the offences: see *R. v. A.M.* [1998] 1 W.L.R. 363, CA.

As to making a sentence of detention under section 91 consecutive to a detention and training order, see section 106A of the 2000 Act (*ante*, § 5–354a), and *R. v. Lang* [2001] 2 Cr.App.R.(S.) 39, CA (*ante*, § 5–356).

Use of the power in cases of dangerous young offenders

5–360 With the commencement of Chapter 5 of Part 12 of the *CJA* 2003 (dangerous offenders, *ante*, §§ 5–292 *et seq.*), any sentence of detention for the purposes of protecting the public from harm from the offender will either be a sentence of detention for life or for public protection under section 91 and section 226 of the 2003 Act, or an extended sentence under section 228. The appropriateness of any such sentence will be governed by the criteria specified in those sections (as to which, see *R. v. Lang*, *ante*, §§ 5–302 *et seq.*).

A court which passes a sentence of detention for life, or for public protection, must specify a period to be served in accordance with the *PCC(S)A* 2000, s.82A(2), unless it makes an order under section 82A(4) (*ante*, § 5–310). As to this process, see *ante*, § 5–312.

Length of sentence

5–361 The guidelines governing the use of the power to order detention under section 91 laid down in *R. v. Fairhurst*, 84 Cr.App.R. 19, CA, were reconsidered in *R. v. A.M.* [1998] 1 W.L.R. 363, CA. Lord Bingham C.J. said that while a court should not pass a sentence involving detention of an offender under the age of 18 for a period more than 24 months without much careful thought, the rule that a court should not pass a term of detention of less than three years should no longer be followed. If the court concluded that a sentence longer than two years, even if not much longer, was called for, then the court should impose whatever it considered the appropriate period of detention under section 91.

The term of the sentence should not be longer than would have been appropriate as a term of imprisonment or detention in a young offender institution in the case of an older offender (*R. v. Burrowes*, 7 Cr.App.R.(S.) 106, CA). In *R. v. Storey*, 6 Cr.App.R.(S.) 104, CA, it was stated that, "it is important, when using the powers under the Act, that the court should not impose a sentence which, the far end of it, would to young men ... seem completely out of sight. ... The court must take care to select a duration for the order upon which the offender can fix his eye." These observations have been adopted in a number of subsequent decisions (*R. v. Conway*, 7 Cr.App.R.(S.) 303, CA; *R. v. Evans*, 8 Cr.App.R.(S.) 253, CA; *R. v. Roberts*, 11 Cr.App.R.(S.) 34, CA).

In *R. v. J.-R. and G.* [2001] 1 Cr.App.R.(S.) 109, CA, it was held that a court may impose a term of detention under section 91 of an offender under the age of 15 who is not a "persistent offender" and who would not qualify for a detention and training order. This was not, however, followed in *R. (M.) v. Waltham Forest Youth Court and DPP*; *R. (W.) v. Thetford Youth Court and DPP*, 166 J.P. 453, DC, where Gage J., said that in general, unless after considering any potential mitigating factors, not least the youth of the offender, the offence merits a sentence longer than two years and the criteria for section 91 are satisfied, a court ought to deal with an offender under 18 by means of a detention and training order, and if such is prohibited, in general a custodial sentence ought not to be considered; and Sedley L.J. said that detention under section

91 cannot as a matter of law be used in any case where, if a detention and training order either is or were available, it would be used. This decision was followed in *R. (W.) v. Southampton Youth Court*; *R. (K.) v. Wirral Borough Magistrates' Court* [2003] 1 Cr.App.R.(S.) 87, DC.

(6) Custody for life

Powers of Criminal Courts (Sentencing) Act 2000, ss.93, 94

Duty to impose custody for life in certain cases where offender under 21

93. [*See* ante, *§ 5–238*.] **5–362**

Power to impose custody for life in certain other cases where offender at least 18 but under 21

94.—(1) *Where a person aged at least 18 but under 21 is convicted of an offence—*

(a) *for which the sentence is not fixed by law, but*

(b) *for which a person aged 21 or over would be liable to imprisonment for life,*

the court shall, if it considers that a sentence for life would be appropriate, sentence him to custody for life.

(2) *Subsection (1) above is subject to (in particular) sections 79 and 80 above, but this subsection does not apply in relation to a sentence which falls to be imposed under section 109(2) below.*

[This section is repealed, as from a day to be appointed, by the *CJCSA* 2000, s.75, and Sched. 8.]

Before passing a discretionary sentence of custody for life, the court must comply with the general criteria for custodial sentences in sections 152, 153, 156 and 157 of the *CJA* 2003. For sections 152 and 153 of the 2003 Act, see *ante*, §§ 5–263 *et seq*. For sections 156 and 157 of the 2003 Act, see *ante*, §§ 5–19, 5–20. When a court passes such a sentence, it must also heed section 82A of the *PCC(S)A* 2000 (*ante*, § 5–310), which applies to persons sentenced to custody for life: see the *C(S)A* 1997, s.34(1), (2), *ante*, § 5–244. **5–363**

For decisions on the use of custody for life, where it is a discretionary sentence, see *R. v. Turton*, 8 Cr.App.R.(S.) 174, CA; *R. v. Hall*, *ibid.* at 458, CA; *R. v. Kelly*, 9 Cr.App.R.(S.) 181, CA; *R. v. Powell*, 11 Cr.App.R.(S.) 113, CA; *R. v. Busby*, 13 Cr.App.R.(S.) 291, CA; and *R. v. Lynas*, *ibid.* at 363, CA. These cases indicate that the general criteria for the use of life imprisonment in the case of adults (*ante*, §§ 5–302 *et seq.*) should be observed.

E. RELEASE ON LICENCE

Introduction

Chapter 6 of Part 12 of the *CJA* 2003 (ss.237– 268) established a new system governing the release on licence of persons serving determinate terms of imprisonment or detention. Offenders other than those sentenced to special forms of sentence for dangerous offenders, will serve half of the term imposed by the court and then become entitled to be released on licence. A court imposing a determinate sentence of 12 months or more is empowered to make a recommendation as to the conditions to be included in any licence granted to an offender on his release. The Secretary of State is not bound to act on such a recommendation, but must take it into account. **5–364**

A defendant who has been released on licence may have his licence revoked and be required to return to custody to continue serving the sentence. The power of a court to order a defendant to serve a part of an earlier sentence, when he is convicted of an offence committed after his release from that sentence, previously contained in the *PCC(S)A* 2000, s.116, is not reproduced.

Commencement

The *Criminal Justice Act 2003 (Commencement No. 1) Order* 2003 (S.I. 2003 No. 3282) brought into force on January 26, 2004, for the purposes of passing a sentence of imprisonment to which an intermittent custody order relates and the release on licence **5–364a** of a person serving such a sentence, sections 237, 239 (and Schedule 19), 241, 244(1), (2) and (3)(c) and (d), 245, 246(1)(b), (3), (4)(b) to (i), (5) and (6), 248(1), 249, 250(1) to (3) and (5) to (8), 251 to 253, 254 to 256, 257, 259, 263 to 265 and 268.

The *Criminal Justice Act 2003 (Commencement No. 8 and Transitional and Saving Provisions) Order* 2005 (S.I. 2005 No. 950) brought sections 237 to 244(1), (2) and (3)(a) and (d), 246 to 250(1) and (4) to (7), 252 to 257 (other than subs. (2)(c)), 258 to 261, 263, 264(1) to (3), (6) and (7), 265 and 268 into force on April 4, 2005, to the extent that they were not already in force. The commencement of these provisions is subject to the saving and transitional provisions in paragraphs 14 to 34 of Schedule 2 to the order.

Saving and transitional provisions

S.I. 2005 No. 950, Sched. 2, paras 14–31

Saving and transitional provisions relating to Chapter 6 of Part 12

Saving for prisoners serving sentences of imprisonment of less than 12 months

5–364b 14. The coming into force of sections 244 to 264 and 266 to 268 of, and paragraph 30 of Schedule 32 to the 2003 Act, and the repeal of sections 33 to 51 of the 1991 Act, is of no effect in relation to any sentence of imprisonment of less than twelve months (whether or not such a sentence is imposed to run concurrently or consecutively with another such sentence).

[This paragraph is printed as amended by the *CJIA* 2008, s.148(1), and Sched. 26, para. 78.]

As to the effect of this provision where an offender was sentenced on or after April 4, 2005, to consecutive sentences of imprisonment totalling 12 months or more, with one of the sentences being for a term of less than 12 months, see *R. (Noone) v. Governor of H.M.P. Drake Hall* [2008] A.C.D. 43, QBD (Mitting J.).

Power of court to recommend licence conditions for certain prisoners

5–364c 15. The coming into force of section 238 of the 2003 Act (power of court to recommend licence conditions) is of no effect in a case in which a court sentences an offender in respect of an offence committed before 4th April 2005.

16. [*The Parole Board.*]

Remand time

5–364d 17. The coming into force of section 243 of the 2003 Act (persons extradited to the United Kingdom) is of no effect in the case of an extradited prisoner where the offence referred to in subsection (1) of section 243 was committed before 4th April 2005.

18. The coming into force of paragraph 10 of Schedule 32 to the 2003 Act is of no effect in a case where a court has imposed a sentence on conviction on retrial in respect of an offence committed before 4th April 2005.

Savings for prisoners convicted of offences committed before 4th April 2005

5–364e 19. The coming into force of—

(a) sections 244 (duty to release prisoners), 246 (power to release prisoners before required to do so), 248 (power to release on compassionate grounds), 249 (duration of licence) and 250 (licence conditions);

(b) paragraph 8(2)(b) of Schedule 32 (*Criminal Appeal Act* 1968);

(c) the repeal of sections 33, 33A to 38A, 40A to 44, and 46 to 47 and 51 of the 1991 Act; and

(d) the repeal of sections 59 and 60, 99 and 100, 101, 103 to 105 and 121 of the *Crime and Disorder Act* 1998,

is of no effect in relation to a prisoner serving a sentence of imprisonment imposed in respect of an offence committed before 4th April 2005.

The *CJIA* 2008, s.27, provides that section 46(1) and part of section 50(2) of the 1991 Act shall cease to have effect even in relation to persons serving sentences for offences committed before April 4, 2005; and section 32(2) of the 2008 Act provides that the savings made by paragraph 19 in respect of sections 249 and 250 of the 2003 Act do not apply in relation to a licence granted under Chapter 6 of Part 12 of that Act, or under section 36 of the 1991 Act, to a person to whom section 50A of the 1991 Act (inserted therein by s.32(1) of the 2008 Act) applies.

20. The coming into force of the repeal of sections 49 and 50 of the 1991 Act does not affect the power of the Secretary of State to make orders under those provisions relating to prisoners serving sentences of imprisonment in respect of offences committed before 4th April 2005. **5–364f**

21. The coming into force of the repeal of section 38 of the *Crime and Disorder Act* 1998 is of no effect in relation to a child or young person whose post-release supervision relates to a sentence in respect of an offence committed before 4th April 2005. **5–364g**

22. Until the repeal of section 34A of the 1991 Act comes fully into force, subsection (2)(g) of that section shall be treated as if at the end there were added the words "or section 254 of the *Criminal Justice Act* 2003". **5–364h**

Transitional arrangements for recall after release

23.—(1) Subject to sub-paragraphs (2) and (3), in relation to a prisoner who falls to be released under the provisions of Part 2 of the 1991 Act after 4th April 2005— **5–364i**

(a) the reference to release on licence in section 254(1) of the 2003 Act (recall of prisoners while on licence) shall be taken to include release on licence under those provisions; and

(b) the reference in sections 37(1) and 44(3) and (4) of the 1991 Act to revocation under section 39 of that Act shall be treated as a reference to revocation under section 254 of the 2003 Act.

(2) Paragraph 12(1) and (2) of Schedule 9 to the *Crime and Disorder Act* 1988 shall continue to apply to the recall of prisoners whose sentence [*sic*] was committed before the commencement of section 103 of that Act.

(3) The repeal of section 39 of the 1991 Act is of no effect in a case in which the Secretary of State has received a request for the recall of an offender from an officer of a local Probation Board before 4th April 2005.

For the avoidance of doubt, in paragraph 23(1), the reference to a prisoner who falls to be released under the provisions of Part 2 of the *CJA* 1991 is to be read as including a prisoner who was released before April 4, 2005, and the words "after 4th April 2005" are to be read only as indicating the date from which sub-paragraphs (a) and (b) take effect: *Criminal Justice Act 2003 (Commencement No. 8 and Transitional and Saving Provisions) Order 2005 (Supplementary Provisions) Order* 2005 (S.I. 2005 No. 2122). That this was the effect of the transitional provision even without the supplementary order was confirmed in *Buddington v. Secretary of State for the Home Department* [2006] Crim.L.R. 765, CA (Civ. Div.). As to the purpose and effect of the transitional provisions, see also *R. (Stellato) v. Secretary of State for the Home Department* [2007] 2 A.C. 70, HL (an offender, who had been released on licence under Part II of the 1991 Act and had then been recalled to prison, after the commencement date, under section 254 of the 2003 Act, remained subject to the provisions of the 1991 Act).

Fine defaulters and contemnors

24. The coming into force of section 258 of the 2003 Act, and the repeal of section 45 of the 1991 Act (early release of fine defaulters and contemnors) is of no effect in relation to a person committed to prison in the circumstances set out in subsection (1)(a) or (b) of section 258 before 4th April 2005. **5–364j**

Consecutive or concurrent terms

25. The coming into force of— **5–364k**

(a) sections 263 and 264 of the 2003 Act (consecutive or concurrent terms);

(b) paragraphs 4 and 6(b) of Schedule 32 (*Criminal Justice Act* 1967);

(c) in Schedule 37, the entry relating to section 104(2) of the *Criminal Justice Act* 1967,

does not affect the date on which the Secretary of State is required to release an offender from a sentence of imprisonment passed in respect of an offence committed before 4th April 2005, whether or not that sentence of imprisonment is to run concurrently or consecutively with one passed in respect of an offence committed after that date.

26. [*The* Repatriation of Prisoners Act *1984*.] **5–364l**

Crime (Sentences) Act 1997

27. The coming into force of paragraph 85 of Schedule 32 to the 2003 Act is of no effect in the case of a person who falls under Part 1 of Schedule 1 to the 1997 Act where the remand in custody or sentence of imprisonment referred to in that Part is in respect of an offence committed before 4th April 2005. **5–364m**

28. The coming into force of paragraph 86 of Schedule 32 to the 2003 Act and the entry in Part 7 of Schedule 37 to that Act relating to Schedule 2 of the 1997 Act does not affect the continuing application of paragraphs 2 and 3 to Schedule 2 to the 1997 Act to persons to whom they applied immediately before 4th April 2005.

Powers of Criminal Courts (Sentencing) Act 2000

5–364n 29. The coming into force of paragraph 116 of Schedule 32 to the 2003 Act and the repeal of sections 6(4)(d), 116 and 117 of the *Sentencing Act* is of no effect in relation to a person in a case in which the sentence of imprisonment referred to in section 116(1)(a) of the *Powers of Criminal Courts (Sentencing) Act* 2000—

(a) is imposed in respect of an offence committed before 4th April 2005; or

(b) is for a term of less than twelve months.

30. [*Revoked by* CJIA *2008, ss.20(5) and 149, and Sched. 28, Pt 2.*]

The Criminal Justice and Court Services Act 2000

5–364o 31. The commencement of paragraph 136(2) of Schedule 32 to the 2003 Act is of no effect in relation to a person released under section 34A of the 1991 Act, whether or not that release takes place after 4th April 2005.

Order for return to prison (offences committed before April 4, 2005/short sentences)

5–364p For sections 116 and 117 of the *PCC(S)A* 2000 (as to which, see para. 29 of Sched. 2 to S.I. 2005 No. 950, *ante*, § 5–364n), see the supplement.

Criminal Justice Act 2003, s.237

RELEASE ON LICENCE

Preliminary

Meaning of "fixed-term prisoner" [etc.]

5–365 **237.**—(1) In this Chapter "fixed-term prisoner" means—

(a) a person serving a sentence of imprisonment for a determinate term, or

(b) a person serving a determinate sentence of detention under section 91 of the *Sentencing Act* or under section 228 of this Act.

[(1A) In this Chapter—

(a) references to a sentence of imprisonment include such a sentence passed by a service court;

(b) references to a sentence of detention under section 91 of the *Sentencing Act* include a sentence of detention under section 209 of the *Armed Forces Act* 2006;

(c) references to a sentence under section 227 of this Act include a sentence under that section passed as a result of section 220 of the *Armed Forces Act* 2006; and

(d) references to a sentence under section 228 of this Act include a sentence under that section passed as a result of section 222 of that Act.]

[[(1A) In subsection (1)(a) "sentence of imprisonment" does not include a sentence of imprisonment passed in respect of a summary conviction for an offence under section 6(1) or (2) of the *Bail Act* 1976.]]

[(1B) Nothing in subsection (1A) has the effect that section 240 or 265 (provision equivalent to which is made by the *Armed Forces Act* 2006) [[[or section 240A]]] applies to a service court.]

(2) In this Chapter, unless the context otherwise requires, "prisoner" includes a person serving a sentence falling within subsection (1)(b); and "prison" includes any place where a person serving such a sentence is liable to be detained.

[This section is printed as amended, as from a day to be appointed, by the *AFA* 2006, s.378(1), and Sched. 16, para. 219 (insertion of words in single square brackets); the *PJA* 2006, s.34(1) and (3) (insertion of words in double square brackets); and the *CJIA* 2008, s.21(1) and (2) (insertion of words in triple square brackets).]

As to commencement, see *ante*, § 5–364a.

The *Criminal Justice Act 2003 (Sentencing) (Transitory Provisions) Order* 2005 (S.I. 2005 No. 643) modifies section 237 in relation to any time before the coming force of the *CJCSA* 2000, s.61 (abolition of sentences of detention in a young offender institution, custody for life etc.) by inserting at the end the words "or a determinate sentence of detention in a young offender institution under section 96 of the *Sentencing Act* or section 227 of this Act".

Criminal Justice Act 2003, ss.238, 239

Power of court to recommend licence conditions

Power of court to recommend licence conditions for certain prisoners

238.—(1) A court which sentences an offender to a term of imprisonment of twelve months or more in respect of any offence may, when passing sentence, recommend to the Secretary of State particular conditions which in its view should be included in any licence granted to the offender under this Chapter on his release from prison. **5–366**

(2) In exercising his powers under section 250(4)(b) in respect of an offender, the Secretary of State must have regard to any recommendation under subsection (1).

As to commencement, see *ante*, § 5–364a. As to the transitional provision in relation to this section, see *ante*, § 5–364c.

S.I. 2005 No. 643 (*ante*, § 5–365) modifies section 238 in relation to any time before the coming force of the *CJCSA* 2000, s.61 (abolition of sentences of detention in a young offender institution, custody for life etc.) by inserting the words "or detention in a young offender institution" after "a term of imprisonment" in subsection (1).

239. [*The Parole Board.*] **5–367**

Criminal Justice Act 2003, ss.240–243

Effect of remand in custody or on bail subject to certain types of condition

Crediting of periods of remand in custody: terms of imprisonment and detention

240.—(1) This section applies where— **5–368**

(a) a court sentences an offender to imprisonment for a term in respect of an offence committed after the commencement of this section, and

(b) the offender has been remanded in custody (within the meaning given by section 242) in connection with the offence or a related offence, that is to say, any other offence the charge for which was founded on the same facts or evidence.

(2) It is immaterial for that purpose whether the offender—

(a) has also been remanded in custody in connection with other offences; or

(b) has also been detained in connection with other matters.

(3) Subject to subsection (4), the court must direct that the number of days for which the offender was remanded in custody in connection with the offence or a related offence is to count as time served by him as part of the sentence.

(4) Subsection (3) does not apply if and to the extent that—

(a) rules made by the Secretary of State so provide in the case of—

(i) a remand in custody which is wholly or partly concurrent with a sentence of imprisonment, or

(ii) sentences of imprisonment for consecutive terms or for terms which are wholly or partly concurrent, or

(b) it is in the opinion of the court just in all the circumstances not to give a direction under that subsection.

(5) Where the court gives a direction under subsection (3), it shall state in open court—

(a) the number of days for which the offender was remanded in custody, and

(b) the number of days in relation to which the direction is given.

(6) Where the court does not give a direction under subsection (3), or gives such a direction in relation to a number of days less than that for which the offender was remanded in custody, it shall state in open court—

(a) that its decision is in accordance with rules made under paragraph (a) of subsection (4), or

(b) that it is of the opinion mentioned in paragraph (b) of that subsection and what the circumstances are.

(7) For the purposes of this section a suspended sentence—

(a) is to be treated as a sentence of imprisonment when it takes effect under paragraph 8(2)(a) or (b) of Schedule 12, and

(b) is to be treated as being imposed by the order under which it takes effect.

(8) For the purposes of the reference in subsection (3) to the term of imprisonment to which a person has been sentenced (that is to say, the reference to his "sentence"), consecutive terms and terms which are wholly or partly concurrent are to be treated as a single term if—

(a) the sentences were passed on the same occasion, or

(b) where they were passed on different occasions, the person has not been released under this Chapter at any time during the period beginning with the first and ending with the last of those occasions.

(9) Where an offence is found to have been committed over a period of two or more days, or at some time during a period of two or more days, it shall be taken for the purposes of subsection (1) to have been committed on the last of those days.

(10) This section applies to a determinate sentence of detention under section 91 of the *Sentencing Act* or section 228 of this Act as it applies to an equivalent sentence of imprisonment.

As to commencement, see *ante*, § 5–364a; and *R. v. Frank* [2006] 2 Cr.App.R.(S.) 37, CA.

S.I. 2005 No. 643 (*ante*, § 5–365) modifies section 240 in relation to any time before the coming force of the *CJCSA* 2000, s.61 (abolition of sentences of detention in a young offender institution, custody for life etc.) by inserting the words "or a sentence of detention in a young offender institution under section 96 of the *Sentencing Act* or section 227 of this Act" after "of this Act" in subsection (10).

Section 240(3) does not apply in relation to a day for which an offender was remanded in custody if on that day he was serving a sentence of imprisonment (and it was not a day on which he was on licence under Chapter 6 of Part 12 of the 2003 Act or Part 2 of the *CJA* 1991) or where the term of imprisonment referred to in subsection (1) is ordered to be served consecutively to another term of imprisonment, if the length of that other term falls to be reduced by the same day by virtue of section 67 of the *CJA* 1967: *Remand in Custody (Effect of Concurrent and Consecutive Sentences of Imprisonment) Rules* 2005 (S.I. 2005 No. 2054).

Home Office Circular 37/2005 further explains the effect of these rules.

Criminal Justice Act 2003, s.240A

[Crediting periods of remand on bail: terms of imprisonment and detention

5–368a **240A.**—(1) This section applies where—

(a) a court sentences an offender to imprisonment for a term in respect of an offence committed on or after 4th April 2005,

(b) the offender was remanded on bail by a court in course of or in connection with proceedings for the offence, or any related offence, after the coming into force of section 21 of the *Criminal Justice and Immigration Act* 2008, and

(c) the offender's bail was subject to a qualifying curfew condition and an electronic monitoring condition ("the relevant conditions").

(2) Subject to subsection (4), the court must direct that the credit period is to count as time served by the offender as part of the sentence.

(3) The "credit period" is the number of days represented by half of the sum of—

(a) the day on which the offender's bail was first subject to conditions that, had they applied throughout the day in question, would have been relevant conditions, and

(b) the number of other days on which the offender's bail was subject to those conditions (excluding the last day on which it was so subject),

rounded up to the nearest whole number.

(4) Subsection (2) does not apply if and to the extent that—

(a) rules made by the Secretary of State so provide, or

(b) it is in the opinion of the court just in all the circumstances not to give a direction under that subsection.

(5) Where as a result of paragraph (a) or (b) of subsection (4) the court does not give a direction under subsection (2), it may give a direction in accordance with either of those paragraphs to the effect that a period of days which is less than the credit period is to count as time served by the offender as part of the sentence.

(6) Rules made under subsection (4)(a) may, in particular, make provision in relation to—

(a) sentences of imprisonment for consecutive terms;
(b) sentences of imprisonment for terms which are wholly or partly concurrent;
(c) periods during which a person granted bail subject to the relevant conditions is also subject to electronic monitoring required by an order made by a court or the Secretary of State.

(7) In considering whether it is of the opinion mentioned in subsection (4)(b) the court must, in particular, take into account whether or not the offender has, at any time whilst on bail subject to the relevant conditions, broken either or both of them.

(8) Where the court gives a direction under subsection (2) or (5) it shall state in open court—
(a) the number of days on which the offender was subject to the relevant conditions, and
(b) the number of days in relation to which the direction is given.

(9) Subsection (10) applies where the court—
(a) does not give a direction under subsection (2) but gives a direction under subsection (5), or
(b) decides not to give a direction under this section.

(10) The court shall state in open court—
(a) that its decision is in accordance with rules made under paragraph (a) of subsection (4), or
(b) that it is of the opinion mentioned in paragraph (b) of that subsection and what the circumstances are.

(11) Subsections (7) to (10) of section 240 apply for the purposes of this section as they apply for the purposes of that section but as if—
(a) in subsection (7)—
(i) the reference to a suspended sentence is to be read as including a reference to a sentence to which an order under section 118(1) of the *Sentencing Act* relates;
(ii) in paragraph (a) after "Schedule 12" there were inserted "or section 119(1)(a) or (b) of the *Sentencing Act*"; and
(b) in subsection (8) the reference to subsection (3) of section 240 is to be read as a reference to subsection (2) of this section and, in paragraph (b), after "Chapter" there were inserted "or Part 2 of the *Criminal Justice Act* 1991.

(12) In this section—
"electronic monitoring condition" means any electronic monitoring requirements imposed under section 3(6ZAA) of the *Bail Act* 1976 for the purpose of securing the electronic monitoring of a person's compliance with a qualifying curfew condition;
"qualifying curfew condition" means a condition of bail which requires the person granted bail to remain at one or more specified places for a total of not less than 9 hours in any given day; and
"related offence" means an offence, other than the offence for which the sentence is imposed ("offence A"), with which the offender was charged and the charge for which was founded on the same facts or evidence as offence A.

[This section is inserted, as from a day to be appointed, by the *CJIA* 2008, s.21(1) and (4).]

Offences committed before April 4, 2005

As from a day to be appointed, section 23 of the *CJIA* 2008 gives effect to Schedule 6, which makes provision for the crediting of periods on bail subject to certain conditions to count in the calculation of the time to be served under a custodial sentence imposed for an offence committed before April 4, 2005. It corresponds in all material respects to the provision made by section 240A of the 2003 Act (*ante*) in relation to custodial sentences imposed for offences committed on or after that date. Thus, paragraph 1 specifies that a period specified under paragraph 2 is to be treated as being a relevant period within the meaning of the *CJA* 1967 (saved in relation to offences committed prior to that date: *Crime (Sentences) Act 1997 (Commencement No. 4) Order* 2005 (S.I. 2005 No. 932)), and thus is to count towards service of the offender's sentence. Paragraph 2(1) is effectively identical to section 240(1), but is expressed to apply to offences committed before April 4, 2005. Sub-paragraph (2) provides that, subject **5–368b** to sub-paragraph (4), the court must by order specify the credit period. Sub-paragraphs (3) to (10) are identical to, or effectively identical to subsections (3) to (10), and sub-paragraph (11) is identical to subsection (12) of section 240. There is nothing that corresponds to subsection (11).

Guidance

5–368c In *R. v. Gordon* [2007] 2 Cr.App.R.(S.) 66, the Court of Appeal issued guidance (to supplement that previously given in *R. v. Norman, post*) in relation to the operation of section 240. The court said that the imperative is that no prisoner should serve a day longer than the period justified by the sentence of the court; save in cases specifically identified for express reasons, credit should be given under section 240 unless to do so would contravene some other statutory provision or result in double counting.

As to differences between the current and predecessor regimes, section 240, which replaced the *CJA* 1967, s.67, as from April 4, 2005 ("the commencement date"), no longer permits treatment of time spent in police detention as a "relevant period" for the purposes of calculating time spent on remand; and the deduction under section 240 does not follow automatically and must be ordered positively by the court; but, despite the fact that the deduction is not automatic, it remains essential, if the court is exercising the power under section 240(4) (*i.e.* positively to withhold the allowance), to announce its decision in open court and explain its reasons.

As to offences which straddle the commencement date, the 2003 Act regime applies (see s.240(9)).

As to "mixed cases" where an offender is sentenced for offences committed before and after the commencement date, where the sentences for the post-commencement date offences are ordered to run consecutively to those for the pre-commencement date offences, then any period of remand in custody for the pre-commencement date offences will be credited under the 1967 Act in respect of those offences and section 240(3) will not apply in respect of any days on remand in custody for the post-commencement date offences if those days counted under the 1967 Act in relation to the pre-commencement date offences (S.I. 2005 No. 2054, *ante*); in such a case, either no direction should be given for the remand days for the post-commencement days to count or the direction should be limited to that number of days that do not count under section 67, and the court should so announce, as required by subsection (6); where, however, a sentence for a post-commencement date offence is ordered to be served concurrently with a sentence for a pre-commencement date offence, the deduction under section 67 of the 1967 Act would be automatic, but in relation to the post-commencement date offence, section 240(3) applies, and the court must consider whether to make a direction; time on remand will not be credited without a direction, but the court may consider that to grant credit would in effect produce a double credit, and accordingly may disallow it by making a direction under subsection (4)(b) (but as to this, see *Criminal Law Week* 2007/07/18).

As to cases where an offender is subject to administrative recall to prison (either under the *CJA* 1991, s.39(6), or the 2003 Act, s.254(6)) time spent in custody in connection with a fresh offence while serving a sentence of imprisonment following recall after release on licence does not form part of the "relevant period" for the purposes of section 67 of the 1967 Act (*R. v. Stocker* [2003] 2 Cr.App.R.(S.) 54, CA) and the same applies in relation to section 240 (see S.I. 2005 No. 2054, *ante*).

As to cases where the court orders an offender's return to prison, the effect of S.I. 2005 No. 950, Sched. 2, paras 29 and 30 (*ante*, § 5–364n) is to preserve the power of a court under section 116 of the *PCC(S)A* 2000 (§ 5–364r in the supplement) to order the return of an offender to prison in respect of a pre-commencement date offence (*R. v. Howell* [2006] 2 Cr.App.R.(S.) 115, CA), provided that the "new" offence was committed before the date on which the original sentence would have been completed; the court could both order a return to prison and make an order that the sentence for the new offence was to begin at the end of the "return date"; but an order under section 116 would not be available if the "new" offence was committed before release on licence.

As to consecutive sentences for released prisoners, section 265 of the 2003 Act (*post*,

§ 5–388) prevents a court from ordering a sentence to begin on the expiry of another sentence from which the defendant has been released and in respect of which he has been recalled to prison. Where the offence giving rise to the original sentence was committed before April 4, 2005, there is the possibility of an order for return to prison under section 116 of the Act of 2000 with the fresh sentence to run consecutively to it. Otherwise, the sentence for the fresh offence will of necessity be concurrent to the existing sentence; in this situation, any element of double credit should be a reason for exercising the power under section 240(4) to order that remand days should not count towards the new sentence.

As to discretionary life sentences and imprisonment for public protection (and their equivalents in respect of young offenders), when fixing a tariff in accordance with section 82A of the 2000 Act (*ante*, § 5–310) the court must apply the section 240 regime.

Re-sentencing following breach of suspended sentence or community order

When the Crown Court re-sentences a defendant who has breached a community order to a custodial sentence, it is required by section 240(3) to make an order that time in custody on remand prior to the imposition of the community sentence should count towards the sentence, unless subsection (4) applies, and the mere fact that the time spent on remand had been a factor that had led to the making of the community sentence was not sufficient to trigger that subsection: *R. v. Stickley* [2008] 2 Cr.App.R.(S.) 33, CA. Similarly, time in custody on remand prior to the imposition of a suspended sentence for an offence committed on or after April 4, 2005, falls to be taken into account when the sentence is activated: *R. v. Fairbrother* [2008] 2 Cr.App.R.(S.) 43, CA. **5–368d**

Warning to defence advocate

In *R. v. Barber* [2006] 2 Cr.App.R.(S.) 81, CA, it was held that before a judge forms an opinion pursuant to section 240(4)(b) that it would be just in all the circumstances not to direct under subsection (3) that the number of days for which the offender had been remanded in custody should count towards the sentence, it was plainly good practice to warn the defence advocate that he was considering whether to make no direction and to give the advocate an opportunity of addressing the issue and seeking to persuade him otherwise; if this were not done, mitigation might proceed with defence and judge at cross purposes as to the effect of the period spent on remand; furthermore, if there were any reason to suppose that the judge might be considering making no (or a limited) direction, the defence advocate should seek clarification. **5–368e**

Errors and omissions

In *R. v. Gordon*, *ante*, it was said that whilst section 155 of the *PCC(S)A* 2000 (*post*, § 5–940) (and the corresponding provision in the *MCA* 1980, s.142) is a route whereby an error or omission in relation to section 240 may be corrected, once the 28-day period has expired the power to correct the sentence expires; but (applying *R. v. Annesley* (*ante*, § 5–15)), a court could state that credit is to be given to the offender (for however many days he has been on remand) and then adjourn for accurate information to be provided; where this approach is taken, the final calculation should be made promptly (exceptional cases apart, within 28 days); a further short oral hearing may be ordered if necessary, and the final order must, in any event, be listed and announced in open court; where a court takes this course, it would not be varying or rescinding the sentence but would merely be concluding an adjourned part of the sentencing process (and thus the 28-day time limit would have no application); and whenever a sentencer makes a direction as to the number of days that are to count towards the sentence, he may do so on the basis that, on the information currently available, the number of days is X, but that, should it subsequently emerge that the information is incorrect, the order would be corrected; such an order could be regarded as a temporary, rather than a final order, and hence not subject to section 155; again the corrected order should be pronounced in open court. **5–368f**

In the earlier case of *R. v. Norman* [2007] 1 Cr.App.R.(S.) 82, CA, it was said that where inaccurate information has been given, and the 28 days under section 155 have expired, (i) the court may amend the record where the judge's order identified the period in question, but the order as drafted miscalculated the number of days (*i.e.* where the amendment has no effect on the sentence or other orders made, but merely corrects an error (*R. v. Saville*, 70 Cr.App.R. 204, CA)); (ii) where both parties agree that the period specified in the direction was wrong, this should be stated in the application for leave to appeal; on receipt of such an agreement, the matter will be remitted by the Registrar of Criminal Appeals direct to the Court of Appeal; a representation order will not normally be made and the court will hear the application as an appeal; where the mistake has been to the detriment of the appellant, he will be informed that no purpose would be served by his attendance and it will be assumed that he does not intend to attend unless he informs the court otherwise within 28 days; (iii) since the period spent on remand could be a significant proportion of the sentence, failure to identify (correctly or at all) the period which should be treated as served renders the sentence wrong in principle; the offender is entitled (subs. (4) cases apart) to a direction and an appeal is the only route available (in relation to which the procedure in (ii) may also apply) where a direction under section 155 or an administrative correction (as in (i)) is not available (not following *R. v. Oosthuizen* [2006] 1 Cr.App.R.(S.) 73, CA, on this point).

Effect of direction under section 240 [or 240A] on release on licence

5–369 **241.**—(1) In determining for the purposes of this Chapter or Chapter 3 (prison sentences of less than twelve months) whether a person to whom a direction under section 240 [or 240A] relates—

(a) has served, or would (but for his release) have served, a particular proportion of his sentence, or

(b) has served a particular period,

the number of days specified in the direction are to be treated as having been served by him as part of that sentence or period.

[(1A) In subsection (1) the reference to a direction under section 240 [or 240A] includes a direction under section 246 of the *Armed Forces Act* 2006.]

(2) In determining for the purposes of section 183 (intermittent custody) whether any part of a sentence to which an intermittent custody order relates is a licence period, the number of custodial days, as defined by subsection (3) of that section, is to be taken to be reduced by the number of days specified in a direction under section 240 [or 240A].

[This section is printed as amended, as from a day to be appointed, by the *AFA* 2006, s.378(1), and Sched. 16, para. 220 (insertion of subs. (1A)); and the *CJIA* 2008, s.21(1) and (5) (insertion of references to s.240A) .]

As to commencement, see *ante*, § 5–364a.

Interpretation of sections 240 [, 204A] and 241

5–370 **242.**—(1) For the purposes of sections 240[, 240A] and 241, the definition of "sentence of imprisonment" in section 305 applies as if for the words from the beginning of the definition to the end of paragraph (a) there were substituted—

" 'sentence of imprisonment' does not include a committal—

(a) in default of payment of any sum of money, other than one adjudged to be paid on a conviction,";

and references in those sections to sentencing an offender to imprisonment, and to an offender's sentence, are to be read accordingly.

(2) References in sections 240 and 241 to an offender's being remanded in custody are references to his being—

(a) remanded in or committed to custody by order of a court,

(b) remanded or committed to local authority accommodation under section 23 of the *Children and Young Persons Act* 1969 and kept in secure accommodation or detained in a secure training centre pursuant to arrangements under subsection (7A) of that section, or

(c) remanded, admitted or removed to hospital under section 35, 36, 38 or 48 of the *Mental Health Act* 1983.

(3) In subsection (2), "secure accommodation" has the same meaning as in section 23 of the *Children and Young Persons Act* 1969.

[This section is printed as amended, as from a day to be appointed, by the *CJIA* 2008, s.21(1) and (6) (insertion of references to s.240A).]

As to commencement, see *ante*, § 5–364a.

Persons extradited to the United Kingdom

243.—(1) A fixed-term prisoner is an extradited prisoner for the purposes of this section if— **5–371**

(a) he was tried for the offence in respect of which his sentence was imposed or he received that sentence—

(i) after having been extradited to the United Kingdom, and

(ii) without having first been restored or had an opportunity of leaving the United Kingdom, and

(b) he was for any period kept in custody while awaiting his extradition to the United Kingdom as mentioned in paragraph (a).

(2) In the case of an extradited prisoner, section 240 has effect as if the days for which he was kept in custody while awaiting extradition were days for which he was remanded in custody in connection with the offence, or any other offence the charge for which was founded on the same facts or evidence.

(3) [*Repealed by* Extradition Act 2003 (Repeals) Order *2004 (S.I. 2004 No. 1897)*.]

[This section is printed as amended by the *PJA* 2006, s.42, and Sched. 13, para. 31.]

As to commencement, see *ante*, § 5–364a. As to the transitional provision in relation to this section, see *ante*, § 5–364d.

Criminal Justice Act 2003, ss.244–253

Release on licence

Duty to release prisoners

244.—(1) As soon as a fixed-term prisoner, other than a prisoner to whom section 247 applies, has served the requisite custodial period, it is the duty of the Secretary of State to release him on licence under this section. **5–372**

(2) Subsection (1) is subject to section 245.

(3) In this section "the requisite custodial period" means—

(a) in relation to a person serving a sentence of imprisonment for a term of twelve months or more or any determinate sentence of detention under section 91 of the *Sentencing Act*, one-half of his sentence,

(b) in relation to a person serving a sentence of imprisonment for a term of less than twelve months (other than one to which an intermittent custody order relates), the custodial period within the meaning of section 181,

(c) in relation to a person serving a sentence of imprisonment to which an intermittent custody order relates, any part of the term which for the purposes of section 183 (as read with section 263(2) or 264A(2) in the case of concurrent or consecutive sentences) is not a licence period, and

(d) in relation to a person serving two or more concurrent or consecutive sentences none of which falls within paragraph (c), the period determined under sections 263(2) and 264(2).

[This section is printed as amended by the *Domestic Violence, Crime and Victims Act* 2004, s.31, and Sched. 6, paras 1 and 2.]

As to commencement, see *ante*, § 5–364a. As to the transitional and saving provisions in relation to this section, see *ante*, §§ 5–364b *et seq.*

S.I. 2005 No. 643 (*ante*, § 5–365) modifies section 244(3) in relation to any time before the coming force of the *CJCSA* 2000, s.61 (abolition of sentences of detention in a young offender institution, custody for life etc) by inserting the words "or 96" after the words "section 91".

Intermittent custody prisoners

For section 245, which restricts the operation of section 244(1) in relation to intermittent custody prisoners (as to which, see *ante*, §§ 5–313a, 5–313c), see the supplement. **5–373**

Power to release prisoners on licence before required to do so

5–374 **246.**—(1) Subject to subsections (2) to (4), the Secretary of State may—

(a) release on licence under this section a fixed-term prisoner, other than an intermittent custody prisoner, at any time during the period of 135 days ending with the day on which the prisoner will have served the requisite custodial period, and

(b) release on licence under this section an intermittent custody prisoner when 135 or less of the required custodial days remain to be served.

(2) Subsection (1)(a) does not apply in relation to a prisoner unless—

(a) the length of the requisite custodial period is at least 6 weeks, [and]

(b) he has served—

(i) at least 4 weeks of *his sentence* [that period], and

(ii) at least one-half of the *requisite custodial period* [that period].

(3) Subsection (1)(b) does not apply in relation to a prisoner unless—

(a) the number of required custodial days is at least 42, and

(b) the prisoner has served—

(i) at least 28 of those days, and

(ii) at least one-half of the total number of those days.

(4) Subsection (1) does not apply where—

(a) the sentence is imposed under section 227 or 228,

(b) the sentence is for an offence under section 1 of the *Prisoners (Return to Custody) Act* 1995,

(c) the prisoner is subject to a hospital order, hospital direction or transfer direction under section 37, 45A or 47 of the *Mental Health Act* 1983,

(d) the sentence was imposed by virtue of paragraph 9(1)(b) or (c) or 10(1)(b) or (c) of Schedule 8 in a case where the prisoner has failed to comply with a curfew requirement of a community order,

(e) the prisoner is subject to the notification requirements of Part 2 of the *Sexual Offences Act* 2003,

(f) the prisoner is liable to removal from the United Kingdom,

(g) the prisoner has been released on licence under this section during the currency of the sentence, and has been recalled to prison under section 255(1)(a),

(h) the prisoner has been released on licence under section 248 during the currency of the sentence, and has been recalled to prison under section 254, or

(i) in the case of a prisoner to whom a direction under section 240 [or 240A] relates, the interval between the date on which the sentence was passed and the date on which the prisoner will have served the requisite custodial period is less than 14 days or, where the sentence is one of intermittent custody, the number of the required custodial days remaining to be served is less than 14.

[(4A) In subsection (4)—

(a) the reference in paragraph (d) to a community order includes a service community order or overseas community order under the *Armed Forces Act* 2006; and

(b) the reference in paragraph (i) to a direction under section 240 includes a direction under section 246 of that Act.]

(5) The Secretary of State may by order—

(a) amend the number of days for the time being specified in subsection (1)(a) or (b), (3) or (4)(i),

(b) amend the number of weeks for the time being specified in subsection (2)(a) or (b)(i), and

(c) amend the fraction for the time being specified in subsection (2)(b)(ii) or (3)(b)(ii).

(6) In this section—

"the required custodial days", in relation to an intermittent custody prisoner, means—

(a) the number of custodial days specified under section 183, *or*

(b) in the case of two or more sentences of intermittent custody which are consecutive, the aggregate of the numbers so specified; or,

(c) in the case of two or more sentences of intermittent custody which are wholly or partly concurrent, the aggregate of the numbers so specified less the number of days that are to be served concurrently;

"the requisite custodial period" in relation to a person serving any sentence other than a sentence of intermittent custody, has the meaning given by paragraph (a), (b) or (d) of section 244(3);

"sentence of intermittent custody" means a sentence to which an intermittent custody order relates.

[This section is printed as amended by the *Domestic Violence, Crime and Victims Act* 2004, s.31, and Sched. 6, paras 1 and 3. The word "or" immediately preceding para. (b) in the definition of "the required custodial days" is repealed as from a day to be appointed: *ibid.*, s.58(2), and Sched. 11. Subs. (4A) is inserted, as from a day to be appointed, by the *AFA* 2006, s.378(1), and Sched. 16, para. 221. In subs. (2), the italicised words are omitted, and the words in square brackets are inserted, as from a day to be appointed, by the *CJIA* 2008, s.24. In subs. (4)(i), the reference to s.240A is inserted, as from a day to be appointed, by *ibid.*, s.22(1) and (2).]

As to commencement, see *ante*, § 5–364a. As to the transitional and saving provisions in relation to this section, see *ante*, §§ 5–364b *et seq.*

It was held in relation to the corresponding provision of the *CJA* 1991 (s.34A), that sentencing courts should ignore the possibility of release under that provision in deciding upon the length of a custodial sentence: see *R. v. Al-Buhairi* [2004] 1 Cr.App.R.(S.) 83, CA; *R. v. Alkazraji* [2004] 2 Cr.App.R.(S.) 55, CA; and *R. v. Dale* [2004] 2 Cr.App.R.(S.) 58, CA.

Release on licence of prisoner serving extended sentence under section 227 or 228

247.—(1) This section applies to a prisoner who is serving an extended sentence imposed under section 227 or 228. **5–375**

(2) As soon as—

(a) a prisoner to whom this section applies has served one-half of the appropriate custodial term, …

it is the duty of the Secretary of State to release him on licence.

(7) In this section "the appropriate custodial term" means the period determined by the court as the appropriate custodial term under section 227 or 228.

[This section is printed as repealed in part by the *CJIA* 2008, ss.25 and 149, and Sched. 28, Pt 2.]

As to commencement, see *ante*, § 5–364a. As to the saving of the former legislation, see *ante*, § 5–364b.

248. [*Power to release prisoners on compassionate grounds.*] **5–376**

Duration of licence

249.—(1) Subject to subsections (2) and (3), where a fixed-term prisoner is released on licence, the licence shall, subject to any revocation under section 254 or 255, remain in force for the remainder of his sentence. **5–377**

(2) Where an intermittent custody prisoner is released on licence under section 244, the licence shall, subject to any revocation under section 254, remain in force—

(a) until the time when he is required to return to prison at the beginning of the next custodial period of the sentence, or

(b) where it is granted at the end of the last custodial period, for the remainder of his sentence.

(3) Subsection (1) has effect subject to sections 263(2) (concurrent terms) and 264(3) and (4) (consecutive terms) and subsection (2) has effect subject to section 264A(3) (consecutive terms: intermittent custody).

(4) In subsection (2) "custodial period", in relation to a sentence to which an intermittent custody order relates, means any period which is not a licence period as defined by 183(3).

[This section is printed as amended by the *Domestic Violence, Crime and Victims Act* 2004, s.31, and Sched. 6, paras 1 and 4.]

As to commencement, see *ante*, § 5–364a. As to the transitional and saving provisions in relation to this section, see *ante*, §§ 5–364b *et seq.*

Licence conditions

250.—(1) In this section— **5–378**

(a) "the standard conditions" means such conditions as may be prescribed for the purposes of this section as standard conditions, and

(b) "prescribed" means prescribed by the Secretary of State by order.

(2) Subject to subsection (6) and section 251, any licence under this Chapter in respect of a prisoner serving one or more sentences of imprisonment of less than twelve months and no sentence of twelve months or more—

(a) must include—

(i) the conditions required by the relevant court order, and

(ii) so far as not inconsistent with them, the standard conditions, and

(b) may also include—

(i) any condition which is authorised by section 62 of the *Criminal Justice and Court Services Act* 2000 (electronic monitoring) or section 64 of that Act (drug testing requirements) and which is compatible with the conditions required by the relevant court order, and

(ii) such other conditions of a kind prescribed for the purposes of this paragraph as the Secretary of State may for the time being consider to be necessary for the protection of the public and specify in the licence.

[(2A) If the sentence (or, if more than one, each sentence) that the prisoner is serving is one in relation to which no custody plus or intermittent custody order is in force, subsection (2) has effect as if there were omitted—

(a) paragraph (a)(i);

(b) the words "so far as not inconsistent with them," in paragraph (a)(ii); and

(c) the words from "and which" in paragraph (b)(i).]

(3) For the purposes of subsection (2)(a)(i), any reference in the relevant court order to the licence period specified in the order is, in relation to a prohibited activity requirement, exclusion requirement, residence requirement or supervision requirement, to be taken to include a reference to any other period during which the prisoner is released on licence under section 246 or 248.

(4) Any licence under this Chapter in respect of a prisoner serving a sentence of imprisonment for a term of twelve months or more (including such a sentence imposed under section 227) or any sentence of detention under section 91 of the *Sentencing Act* or section 228 of this Act—

(a) must include the standard conditions, and

(b) may include—

(i) any condition authorised by section 62 or 64 of the *Criminal Justice and Court Services Act* 2000, and

(ii) such other conditions of a kind prescribed by the Secretary of State for the purposes of this paragraph as the Secretary of State may for the time being specify in the licence.

(5) A licence under section 246 must also include a curfew condition complying with section 253.

(6) Where—

(a) a licence under section 246 is granted to a prisoner serving one or more sentences of imprisonment of less than 12 months and no sentence of 12 months or more, and

(b) the relevant court order requires the licence to be granted subject to a condition requiring his compliance with a curfew requirement (as defined by section 204),

that condition is not to be included in the licence at any time while a curfew condition required by section 253 is in force.

(7) The preceding provisions of this section have effect subject to section 263(3) (concurrent terms), section 264(3) and (4) (consecutive terms) and section 264(A)(3) (consecutive terms: intermittent custody).

(8) In exercising his powers to prescribe standard conditions or the other conditions referred to in subsection (4)(b)(ii), the Secretary of State must have regard to the following purposes of the supervision of offenders while on licence under this Chapter—

(a) the protection of the public,

(b) the prevention of re-offending, and

(c) securing the successful re-integration of the prisoner into the community.

[This section is printed as amended by the *Domestic Violence, Crime and Victims Act* 2004, s.31, and Sched. 6, paras 1 and 5; and as amended, as from a day to be appointed, by the *AFA* 2006, s.378(1), and Sched. 16, para. 222 (insertion of subs. (2A)).]

As to commencement, see *ante*, § 5–364a. As to the transitional and saving provisions in relation to this section, see *ante*, § 5–364b *et seq.*

S.I. 2005 No. 643 (*ante*, § 5–365) modifies section 250(4) in relation to any time before the coming force of the *CJCSA* 2000, s.61 (abolition of sentences of detention in a young offender institution, custody for life etc) by inserting the words "or detention in a young offender institution" after the words "sentence of imprisonment".

The *Criminal Justice (Sentencing) (Licence Conditions) Order* 2005 (S.I. 2005 No. 648) came into force on April 4, 2005. Article 2 sets out the standard conditions of a licence under section 250. These require that the prisoner must keep in touch, receive visits from and permanently reside at an address approved by the responsible officer; undertake work only with the approval of the responsible officer; not travel outside the United Kingdom without prior permission and be of good behaviour and not commit any offence. Article 3 prescribes the conditions for the purposes of section 250(2)(b)(ii) and (4)(b)(ii). These may require that the prisoner resides at a certain place; impose a restriction or requirement relating to his making or maintaining contact with a person; impose a restriction on his participation in an activity or a requirement that he participate in, or co-operate with, a programme or set of activities; a requirement that he comply with a curfew arrangement; impose a restriction on his freedom of movement and a requirement relating to his supervision in the community by a responsible officer.

Licence conditions on re-release of prisoner serving sentence of less than 12 months

251.—(1) In relation to any licence under this Chapter which is granted to a prisoner serving one or more sentences of imprisonment of less than twelve months and no sentence of twelve months or more on his release in pursuance of a decision of the Board under section 254 or 256, subsections (2) and (3) apply instead of section 250(2). **5–379**

(2) The licence—

(a) must include the standard conditions, and

(b) may include—

(i) any condition authorised by section 62 or 64 of the *Criminal Justice and Court Services Act* 2000, and

(ii) such other conditions of a kind prescribed by the Secretary of State for the purposes of section 250(4)(b)(ii) as the Secretary of State may for the time being specify in the licence.

(3) In exercising his powers under subsection (2)(b)(ii), the Secretary of State must have regard to the terms of the relevant court order [(if any)].

(4) In this section "the standard conditions" has the same meaning as in section 250.

[This section is printed as amended, as from a day to be appointed, by the *AFA* 2006, s.378(1), and Sched. 16, para. 223 (insertion of words in square brackets).]

This section came into force on January 26, 2004, for the purposes of intermittent custody only: S.I. 2003 No. 3282 (*ante*, § 5–364a).

252. [*Duty to comply with licence conditions (amended, as from a day to be appointed, by* AFA *2006, s.378(1), and Sched. 16, para. 224).*] **5–380**

Curfew condition to be included in licence under section 246

253.—(1) For the purposes of this Chapter, a curfew condition is a condition which— **5–381**

(a) requires the released person to remain, for periods for the time being specified in the condition, at a place for the time being so specified (which may be premises approved by the Secretary of State under section 13 of the *Offender Management Act* 2007), and

(b) includes requirements for securing the electronic monitoring of his whereabouts during the periods for the time being so specified.

(2) The curfew condition may specify different places or different periods for different days, but may not specify periods which amount to less than 9 hours in any one day (excluding for this purpose the first and last days of the period for which the condition is in force).

(3) The curfew condition is to remain in force until the date when the released person would (but for his release) fall to be released on licence under section 244.

(4) Subsection (3) does not apply in relation to a released person to whom an intermittent custody order relates; and in relation to such a person the curfew condition is to

remain in force until the number of days during which it has been in force is equal to the number of the required custodial days, as defined in section 246(6), that remained to be served at the time when he was released under section 246.

(5) The curfew condition must include provision for making a person responsible for monitoring the released person's whereabouts during the periods for the time being specified in the condition; and a person who is made so responsible shall be of a description specified in an order made by the Secretary of State.

(6) Nothing in this section is to be taken to require the Secretary of State to ensure that arrangements are made for the electronic monitoring of released persons' whereabouts in any particular part of England and Wales.

[This section is printed as amended by the *Offender Management Act 2007 (Consequential Amendments) Order* 2008 (S.I. 2008 No. 912), art. 3, and Sched. 1, para.19(1) and (14).]

As to commencement, see *ante*, § 5–364a. As to the saving of the former legislation, see *ante*, § 5–364b.

Recall after release

5–382 Sections 254 to 256 (as substantially amended by the *CJIA* 2008, including by way of the insertion of new sections 255A to 255D) deal with recall after release and with re-release after recall.

[The next paragraph is § 5–386.]

Criminal Justice Act 2003, ss.263, 264, 264A

Consecutive or concurrent terms

Concurrent terms

5–386 **263.**—(1) This section applies where—

(a) a person ("the offender") has been sentenced *by any court* to two or more terms of imprisonment which are wholly or partly concurrent, and

(b) the sentences were passed on the same occasion or, where they were passed on different occasions, the person has not been released under this Chapter at any time during the period beginning with the first and ending with the last of those occasions.

(2) Where this section applies—

(a) nothing in this Chapter requires the Secretary of State to release the offender in respect of any of the terms unless and until he is required to release him in respect of each of the others,

(b) section 244 does not authorise the Secretary of State to release him on licence under that section in respect of any of the terms unless and until that section authorises the Secretary of State to do so in respect of each of the others,

(c) on and after his release under this Chapter the offender is to be on licence for so long, and subject to such conditions, as is required by this Chapter in respect of any of the sentences.

(3) Where the sentences include one or more sentences of twelve months or more and one or more sentences of less than twelve months, the terms of the licence may be determined by the Secretary of State in accordance with section 250(4)(b), without regard to the requirements of any custody plus order or intermittent custody order.

(4) In this section "term of imprisonment" includes a determinate sentence of detention under section 91 of the *Sentencing Act* or under section 228 of this Act.

[The italicised words in subs. (1)(a) are omitted as from a day to be appointed: *AFA* 2006, s.378(1) and (2), Sched. 16, para. 226, and Sched. 17.]

As to commencement, see *ante*, § 5–364a. As to the transitional and saving provisions in relation to this section, see *ante*, §§ 5–364b *et seq*.

S.I. 2005 No. 643 (*ante*, § 5–365) modifies section 263(4) in relation to any time before the coming force of the *CJCSA* 2000, s.61 (abolition of sentences of detention in a young offender institution, custody for life etc) by inserting at the end the words "or a sentence of detention in a young offender institution under section 96 of the *Sentencing Act* or section 227 of this Act".

Consecutive terms

264.—(1) This section applies where— 5–387

(a) a person ("the offender") has been sentenced to two or more terms of imprisonment which are to be served consecutively on each other, *and*

(b) the sentences were passed on the same occasion or, where they were passed on different occasions, the person has not been released under this Chapter at any time during the period beginning with the first and ending with the last of those occasions, and

(c) none of those terms is a term to which an intermittent custody order relates.

(2) Nothing in this Chapter requires the Secretary of State to release the offender on licence until he has served a period equal in length to the aggregate of the length of the custodial periods in relation to each of the terms of imprisonment.

(3) Where any of the terms of imprisonment is a term of twelve months or more, the offender is, on and after his release under this Chapter, to be on licence—

(a) until he would, but for his release, have served a term equal in length to the aggregate length of the terms of imprisonment, and

(b) subject to such conditions as are required by this Chapter in respect of each of those terms of imprisonment.

(4) Where each of the terms of imprisonment is a term of less than twelve months, the offender is, on and after his release under this Chapter, to be on licence until the relevant time, and subject to such conditions as are required by this Chapter in respect of any of the terms of imprisonment, and none of the terms is to be regarded for any purpose as continuing after the relevant time.

(5) In subsection (4) "the relevant time" means the time when the offender would, but for his release, have served a term equal in length to the aggregate of—

(a) all the custodial periods in relation to the terms of imprisonment, and

(b) the longest of the licence periods in relation to those terms.

(6) In this section—

(a) "custodial period"—

(i) in relation to an extended sentence imposed under section 227 or 228, means one-half of the appropriate custodial term determined under that section,

(ii) in relation to a term of twelve months or more, means one—half of the term, and

(iii) in relation to a term of less than twelve months complying with section 181, means the custodial period as defined by subsection (3)(a) of that section;

(b) "licence period", in relation to a term of less than twelve months complying with section 181, has the meaning given by subsection (3)(b) of that section.

(7) This section applies to a determinate sentence of detention under section 91 of the *Sentencing Act* or under section 228 of this Act as it applies to a term of imprisonment of 12 months or more.

[This section is printed as amended by the *Domestic Violence, Crime and Victims Act* 2004, s.31, and Sched. 6, paras 1 and 6; and the *CJIA* 2008, s.148(1), and Sched. 26, paras 59 and 71. The word "and" immediately preceding subs. (1)(b) is repealed as from a day to be appointed: 2004 Act, s.58(2), and Sched. 11.]

As to commencement, see *ante*, § 5–364a (subss. (4) and (5) are in force for certain purposes only). As to the transitional and saving provisions in relation to this section, see *ante*, §§ 5–364b *et seq.*

S.I. 2005 No. 643 (*ante*, § 5–365) modifies section 264(7) in relation to any time before the coming force of the *CJCSA* 2000, s.61 (abolition of sentences of detention in a young offender institution, custody for life etc) by inserting the words "or a sentence of detention in a young offender institution under section 96 of the *Sentencing Act* or section 227 of this Act" after "of this Act".

Consecutive terms: intermittent custody

264A.—(1) This section applies where— 5–387a

(a) a person ("the offender") has been sentenced to two or more terms of imprisonment which are to be served consecutively on each other,

(b) the sentences were passed on the same occasion or, where they were passed on different occasions, the person has not been released under this Chapter at any time during the period beginning with the first and ending with the last of those occasions, and

(c) each of the terms is a term to which an intermittent custody order relates.

(2) The offender is not to be treated as having served all the required custodial days in relation to any of the terms of imprisonment until he has served the aggregate of all the required custodial days in relation to each of them.

(3) After the number of days served by the offender in prison is equal to the aggregate of the required custodial days in relation to each of the terms of imprisonment, the offender is to be on licence until the relevant time and subject to such conditions as are required by this Chapter in respect of any of the terms of imprisonment, ...

(4) In subsection (3) "the relevant time" means the time when the offender would, but for his release, have served a term equal in length to the aggregate of—

(a) all the required custodial days in relation to the terms of imprisonment, and

(b) all the periods in relation to those terms.

(5) In this section—

"licence period" has the same meaning as in section 183(3);

"the required custodial days", in relation to such a term, means the number of days specified under that section.

[This section was inserted by the *Domestic Violence, Crime and Victims Act* 2004, s.31, and Sched. 6, paras 1 and 7; and the *CJIA* 2008, s.20(1) and (3).]

Criminal Justice Act 2003, s.265

Restriction on consecutive sentences for released prisoners

Restriction on consecutive sentences for released prisoners

5–388 **265.**—(1) A court sentencing a person to a term of imprisonment may not order or direct that the term is to commence on the expiry of any other sentence of imprisonment from which he has been released—

(a) under this Chapter; or

(b) under Part 2 of the *Criminal Justice Act* 1991.

(1A) Subsection (1) applies to a court sentencing a person to—

(a) a term of imprisonment for an offence committed before 4 April 2005, or

(b) a term of imprisonment of less than 12 months for an offence committed on or after that date, as it applies to the imposition of any other term of imprisonment.

(1B) Where an intermittent custody order applies to the other sentence, the reference in subsection (1) to release under this Chapter does not include release by virtue of section 183(1)(b)(i) (periods of temporary release on licence before the custodial days specified under section 183(1)(a) have been served).

(2) In this section "sentence of imprisonment" includes a sentence of detention under section 91 of the *Sentencing Act* or section 228 of this Act, and "term of imprisonment" is to be read accordingly.

[This section is printed as amended by the *CJIA* 2008, s.20(1) and (4).]

As to commencement, see *ante*, § 5–364a.

S.I. 2005 No. 643 (*ante*, § 5–365) modifies section 265(2) in relation to any time before the coming force of the *CJCSA* 2000, s.61 (abolition of sentences of detention in a young offender institution, custody for life etc) by inserting the words "or a sentence of detention in a young offender institution under section 96 of the *Sentencing Act* or under section 227 of this Act" after "of this Act".

5–389 Section 265 corresponds to section 84 of the *PCC(S)A* 2000 (*rep.*). As to the effect of this provision see *R. v. Lowe*; *R. v. Leask* [1999] 2 Cr.App.R.(S.) 316, CA; *R. v. Laurent* [2001] 1 Cr.App.R.(S.) 65, CA; and *R. v. Cawthorn* [2001] 1 Cr.App.R.(S.) 136, CA.

Criminal Justice Act 2003, s.268

Interpretation of Chapter 6

268. In this Chapter— 5–390

"the 1997 Act" means the *Crime (Sentences) Act* 1997;

"the Board" means the Parole Board;

"fixed-term prisoner" has the meaning given by section 237(1) [(as extended by section 237(1A))];

"intermittent custody prisoner" means a prisoner serving a sentence of imprisonment to which an intermittent custody order relates;

"prison" and "prisoner" are to be read in accordance with section 237(2);

"release", in relation to a prisoner serving a sentence of imprisonment to which an intermittent custody order relates, includes temporary release;

"relevant court order", in relation to a person serving a sentence of imprisonment to which a custody plus order or intermittent custody order relates, means that order.

[This section is printed as amended, as from a day to be appointed, by the *AFA* 2006, s.378(1), and Sched. 16, para. 227 (insertion of words in square brackets).]

As to commencement, see *ante*, § 5–364a.

VII. FINES

Criminal Law Act 1977, s.32(1)

32.—(1) Where a person convicted on indictment of any offence (whether triable only on indictment or either way) would, apart from this subsection, be liable to a fine not exceeding a specified amount, he shall by virtue of this subsection be liable to a fine of any amount. 5–391

Criminal Justice Act 2003, s.162

Powers to order statement as to offender's financial circumstances

162.—(1) Where an individual has been convicted of an offence, the court may, before sentencing him, make a financial circumstances order with respect to him. 5–392

(2) Where a magistrates' court has been notified in accordance with section 12(4) of the *Magistrates' Courts Act* 1980 that an individual desires to plead guilty without appearing before the court, the court may make a financial circumstances order with respect to him.

(3) In this section "a financial circumstances order" means, in relation to any individual, an order requiring him to give to the court, within such period as may be specified in the order, such a statement of his financial circumstances as the court may require.

(4) An individual who without reasonable excuse fails to comply with a financial circumstances order is liable on summary conviction to a fine not exceeding level 3 on the standard scale.

(5) If an individual, in furnishing any statement in pursuance of a financial circumstances order—

(a) makes a statement which he knows to be false in a material particular,

(b) recklessly furnishes a statement which is false in a material particular, or

(c) knowingly fails to disclose any material fact,

he is liable on summary conviction to a fine not exceeding level 4 on the standard scale.

(6) Proceedings in respect of an offence under subsection (5) above may, notwithstanding anything in section 127(1) of the *Magistrates' Courts Act* 1980 (limitation of time), be commenced at any time within two years from the date of the commission of the offence or within six months from its first discovery by the prosecutor, whichever period expires the earlier.

Criminal Justice Act 2003, ss.163–165

Fines: general

General power of Crown Court to fine offender convicted on indictment

163. Where a person is convicted on indictment of any offence, other than an offence for which the sentence is fixed by law or falls to be imposed under section 110(2) or 111(2) of the *Sentencing Act* or under section 225(2) or 226(2) of this Act, the court, if not precluded from sentencing an offender by its exercise of some other power, may impose a fine instead of or in addition to dealing with him in any other way in which the court has power to deal with him, subject however to any enactment requiring the offender to be dealt with in a particular way. 5–393

[This section is printed as amended by the *CJIA* 2008, s.148(1), and Sched. 26, paras 59 and 68.]

Fixing of fines

5–394 **164.**—(1) Before fixing the amount of any fine to be imposed on an offender who is an individual, a court must inquire into his financial circumstances.

(2) The amount of any fine fixed by a court must be such as, in the opinion of the court, reflects the seriousness of the offence.

(3) In fixing the amount of any fine to be imposed on an offender (whether an individual or other person), a court must take into account the circumstances of the case including, among other things, the financial circumstances of the offender so far as they are known, or appear, to the court.

(4) Subsection (3) above applies whether taking into account the financial circumstances of the offender has the effect of increasing or reducing the amount of the fine.

(4A) In applying subsection (3), a court must not reduce the amount of a fine on account of any surcharge it orders the offender to pay under section 161A, except to the extent that he has insufficient means to pay both.

(5) Where—

(a) an offender has been convicted in his absence in pursuance of section 11 or 12 of the *Magistrates' Courts Act* 1980 (non-appearance of accused), or

(b) an offender—

(i) has failed to furnish a statement of his financial circumstances in response to a request which is an official request for the purposes of section 20A of the *Criminal Justice Act* 1991 (offence of making false statement as to financial circumstances),

(ii) has failed to comply with an order under section 162(1) above, or

(iii) has otherwise failed to co-operate with the court in its inquiry into his financial circumstances,

and the court considers that it has insufficient information to make a proper determination of the financial circumstances of the offender, it may make such determination as it thinks fit.

[This section is printed as amended by the *Domestic Violence, Crime and Victims Act* 2004, s.14(2).]

As to section 161A, see *post*, § 5–948.

Remission of fines

5–395 **165.**—(1) This section applies where a court has, in fixing the amount of a fine, determined the offender's financial circumstances under section 164(5) above.

(2) If, on subsequently inquiring into the offender's financial circumstances, the court is satisfied that had it had the results of that inquiry when sentencing the offender it would—

(a) have fixed a smaller amount, or

(b) not have fined him,

it may remit the whole or part of the fine.

(3) Where under this section the court remits the whole or part of a fine after a term of imprisonment has been fixed under section 139 of the *Sentencing Act* (powers of Crown Court in relation to fines) or section 82(5) of the *Magistrates' Courts Act* 1980 (magistrates' powers in relation to default), it must reduce the term by the corresponding proportion.

(4) In calculating any reduction required by subsection (3), any fraction of a day is to be ignored.

Powers of Criminal Courts (Sentencing) Act 2000, ss.139, 140, 142

Miscellaneous powers and duties of Crown Court in relation to fines etc.

Powers and duties of Crown Court in relation to fines and forfeited recognizances

5–396 **139.**—(1) Subject to the provisions of this section, if the Crown Court imposes a fine on any person or forfeits his recognizance, the court may make an order—

(a) allowing time for the payment of the amount of the fine or the amount due under the recognizance;

(b) directing payment of that amount by instalments of such amounts and on such dates as may be specified in the order;

(c) in the case of a recognizance, discharging the recognizance or reducing the amount due under it.

(2) Subject to the provisions of this section, if the Crown Court imposes a fine on any person or forfeits his recognizance, the court shall make an order fixing a term of imprisonment *or of detention under section 108 above (detention of persons aged 18 to 20 for default)* which he is to undergo if any sum which he is liable to pay is not duly paid or recovered.

(3) No person shall on the occasion when a fine is imposed on him or his recognizance

is forfeited by the Crown Court be committed to prison *or detained* in pursuance of an order under subsection (2) above unless—

(a) in the case of an offence punishable with imprisonment, he appears to the court to have sufficient means to pay the sum forthwith;

(b) it appears to the court that he is unlikely to remain long enough at a place of abode in the United Kingdom to enable payment of the sum to be enforced by other methods; or

(c) on the occasion when the order is made the court sentences him to immediate imprisonment, *custody for life or detention in a young offender institution* for that or another offence, or so sentences him for an offence in addition to forfeiting his recognizance, or he is already serving a sentence of custody for life or a term—

(i) of imprisonment;

(ii) of detention in a young offender institution; or

(iii) of detention under section 108 above.

(4) The periods set out in the second column of the following Table shall be the maximum periods of imprisonment *or detention* under subsection (2) above applicable respectively to the amounts set out opposite them.

TABLE

An amount not exceeding £200	7 days
An amount exceeding £200 but not exceeding £500	14 days
An amount exceeding £500 but not exceeding £1,000	28 days
An amount exceeding £1,000 but not exceeding £2,500	45 days
An amount exceeding £2,500 but not exceeding £5,000	3 months
An amount exceeding £5,000 but not exceeding £10,000	6 months
An amount exceeding £10,000 but not exceeding £20,000	12 months
An amount exceeding £20,000 but not exceeding £50,000	18 months
An amount exceeding £50,000 but not exceeding £100,000	2 years
An amount exceeding £100,000 but not exceeding £250,000	3 years
An amount exceeding £250,000 but not exceeding £1 million	5 years
An amount exceeding £1 million	10 years

(5) Where any person liable for the payment of a fine or a sum due under a recognizance to which this section applies is sentenced by the court to, or is serving or otherwise liable to serve, a term of imprisonment or detention in a young offender institution or a term of detention under section 108 above, the court may order that any term of imprisonment *or detention* under subsection (2) above shall not being to run until after the end of the first-mentioned term.

(6) The power conferred by this section to discharge a recognizance or reduce the amount due under it shall be in addition to the powers conferred by any other Act relating to the discharge, cancellation, mitigation or reduction of recognizances or sums forfeited under recognizances.

(7) Subject to subsection (8) below, the powers conferred by this section shall not be taken as restricted by any enactment which authorises the Crown Court to deal with an offender in any way in which a magistrates' court might have dealt with him or could deal with him.

(8) Any term fixed under subsection (2) above as respects a fine imposed in pursuance of such an enactment, that is to say a fine which the magistrates' court could have imposed, shall not exceed the period applicable to that fine (if imposed by the magistrates' court) under section 149(1) of the *Customs and Excise Management Act* 1979 (maximum periods of imprisonment in default of payment of certain fines).

(9) This section shall not apply to a fine imposed by the Crown Court on appeal against a decision of a magistrates' court, but subsections (2) to (4) above shall apply in relation to a fine imposed or recognizance forfeited by the criminal division of the Court of Appeal, or by the *House of Lords* [Supreme Court] on appeal from that division, as they apply in relation to a fine imposed or recognizance forfeited by the Crown Court, and the references to the Crown Court in subsections (2) and (3) above shall be construed accordingly.

(10) For the purposes of any reference in this section, however expressed, to the term of imprisonment or other detention to which a person has been sentenced or which, or

part of which, he has served, consecutive terms and terms which are wholly or partly concurrent shall, unless the context otherwise requires, be treated as a single term.

(11) Any reference in this section, however expressed, to a previous sentence shall be construed as a reference to a previous sentence passed by a court in Great Britain.

[This section is printed as amended, as from a day to be appointed, by the *CJCSA* 2000, s.74 and Sched. 7, para. 193 (omission of italicised words in subss. (2) to (5)); and the *Constitutional Reform Act* 2005, s.40(4), and Sched. 9, para. 69 (substitution of reference to "Supreme Court" for reference to "House of Lords").]

Enforcement of fines imposed and recognizances forfeited by Crown Court

5–397 **140.**—(1) Subject to subsection (5) below, a fine imposed or a recognizance forfeited by the Crown Court shall be treated for the purposes of collection, enforcement and remission of the fine or other sum as having been imposed or forfeited—

(a) by a magistrates' court specified in an order made by the Crown Court, or

(b) if no such order is made, by the magistrates' court by which the offender *was committed to the Crown Court to be tried or dealt with or by which he* was sent to the Crown Court for trial under section 51 [or 51A] of the *Crime and Disorder Act* 1998,

and, in the case of a fine, as having been so imposed on conviction by the magistrates' court in question.

(2) Subsection (3) below applies where a magistrates' court issues a warrant of commitment on a default in the payment of—

(a) a fine imposed by the Crown Court; or

(b) a sum due under a recognizance forfeited by the Crown Court.

(3) In such a case, the term of imprisonment *or detention under section 108 above* specified in the warrant of commitment as the term which the offender is liable to serve shall be—

(a) the term fixed by the Crown Court under section 139(2) above, or

(b) if that term has been reduced under section 79(2) of the *Magistrates' Courts Act* 1980 (part payment) or section 85(2) of that Act (remission), that term as so reduced,

notwithstanding that that term exceeds the period applicable to the case under section 149(1) of the *Customs and Excise Management Act* 1979 (maximum periods of imprisonment in default of payment of certain fines).

(4) Subsections (1) to (3) above shall apply in relation to a fine imposed or recognizance forfeited by the criminal division of the Court of Appeal, or by the *House of Lords* [Supreme Court] on appeal from that division, as they apply in relation to a fine imposed or recognizance forfeited by the Crown Court; and references in those subsections to the Crown Court (except the references in subsection (1)(b)) shall be construed accordingly.

(5) A magistrates' court shall not, under section 85(1) or 120 of the *Magistrates' Courts Act* 1980 as applied by subsection (1) above, remit the whole or any part of a fine imposed by, or sum due under a recognizance forfeited by—

(a) the Crown Court,

(b) the criminal division of the Court of Appeal, or

(c) the *House of Lords* [Supreme Court] on appeal from that division,

without the consent of the Crown Court.

(6) Any fine or other sum the payment of which is enforceable by a magistrates' court by virtue of this section shall be treated for the purposes of the *Justices of the Peace Act* 1997 and, in particular, section 60 of that Act (application of fines and fees) as having been imposed by a magistrates' court, or as being due under a recognizance forfeited by such a court.

[This section is printed as amended, as from a day to be appointed, by the *CJCSA* 2000, s.74 and Sched. 7, para. 194 (omission of italicised words in subs. (3)); the *CJA* 2003, s.41, and Sched. 3, para. 74(1) and (4) (omission of italicised words in subs. (1) and insertion of words in square brackets); and the *Constitutional Reform Act* 2005, s.40(4), and Sched. 9, para. 69 (substitution of references to "Supreme Court" for references to "House of Lords").]

Power of Crown Court to order search of persons before it

5–398 **142.**—(1) Where—

(za) the Crown Court orders a person to pay a surcharge under section 161A of the *Criminal Justice Act* 2003,

(a) the Crown Court imposes a fine on a person or forfeits his recognizance,

(b) the Crown Court makes against a person any such order as is mentioned in paragraph 3, 4 or 9 of Schedule 9 to the *Administration of Justice Act* 1970 (orders for the payment of costs),

(c) the Crown Court makes a compensation order against a person,

(d) the Crown Court makes against a person an order under section 137 above (order for parent or guardian to pay fine, costs, compensation or surcharge), or

(e) on the determination of an appeal brought by a person under section 108 of the *Magistrates' Courts Act* 1980 a sum is payable by him, whether by virtue of an order of the Crown Court or by virtue of a conviction or order of the magistrates' court against whose decision the appeal was brought,

then, if that person is before it, the Crown Court may order him to be searched.

(2) Any money found on a person in a search under this section may be applied, unless the court otherwise directs, towards payment of the fine or other sum payable by him; and the balance, if any, shall be returned to him.

[This section is printed as amended by the *Domestic Violence, Crime and Victims Act* 2004, s.58(1), and Sched. 10, para. 53.]

As to section 161A of the 2003 Act, see *post*, § 5–948.

Magistrates' Courts Act 1980, s.32

Penalties on summary conviction for offences triable either way

32. [*See* ante, *§ 1–75aa.*] **5–399**

Magistrates' Courts Act 1980, ss.36, 75, 82(1)

Restriction on fines in respect of young persons

36.—(1) Where a person under 18 years of age is found guilty by a magistrates' court of an offence for which, apart from this section, the court would have power to impose a fine of an amount exceeding £1,000, the amount of any fine imposed by the court shall not exceed £1,000. **5–400**

(2) In relation to a person under the age of 14 subsection (1) shall have effect as if for the words "£1,000", in both the places where they occur, there were substituted the words "£250".

[This section is printed as amended and repealed in part by the *CJA* 1991, s.17(2) and Sched. 13.]

Power to dispense with immediate payment

75.—(1) A magistrates' court by whose conviction or order a sum is adjudged to be paid may, instead of requiring immediate payment, allow time for payment, or order payment by instalments. **5–401**

(2) Where a magistrates' court has allowed time for payment, the court may, on application by or on behalf of the person liable to make the payment, allow further time or order payment by instalments.

(2A), (2B), (2C) [*Inserted by* Maintenance Enforcement Act *1991: relate to maintenance orders.*]

(3) Where a court has ordered payment by instalments and default is made in the payment of any one instalment, proceedings may be taken as if the default had been made in the payment of all the instalments then unpaid.

Restriction on power to impose imprisonment for default

82.—(1) A magistrates' court shall not on the occasion of convicting an offender of an offence issue a warrant of commitment for a default in paying any sum adjudged to be paid by the conviction unless— **5–402**

(a) in the case of an offence punishable with imprisonment, he appears to the court to have sufficient means to pay the sum forthwith;

(b) it appears to the court that he is unlikely to remain long enough at a place of abode in the United Kingdom to enable payment of the sum to be enforced by other methods; or

(c) on the occasion of that conviction the court sentences him to immediate imprisonment, *or detention in a young offender institution* for that or another offence or he is already serving a sentence of custody for life, or a term of imprisonment, ..., detention under *section 9 of the* Criminal Justice Act *1982* [section 108 of the *Powers of Criminal Courts (Sentencing) Act* 2000] or detention in a young offender institution.

[The words "or detention in a young offender institution" were substituted for the words "youth custody or detention in a detention centre" by the *CJA* 1988, s.123(6) and Sched. 8, para. 2. The *CJCSA* 2000, s.74 and Sched. 7, para. 63(a) makes provision for the repeal, as from a day to be appointed, of the original words. It is submitted that this provision should be construed as applying to the substituted words, for otherwise the amendment is to be deprived of all meaning. The words in square brackets in para. (c) are inserted instead of the italicised words preceding them as from a day to be appointed by the *CJCSA* 2000, s.74 and Sched. 7, para. 63(b).]

Criminal Justice Act 1982, s.37

The standard scale of fines for summary offences

5–403 **37.**—(1) There shall be a standard scale of fines for summary offences, which shall be known as "the standard scale".

(2) The standard scale is shown below—

Level on the scale	*Amount of fine*
1	£200
2	£500
3	£1,000
4	£2,500
5	£5,000

(3) Where any enactment (whether contained in an Act passed before or after this Act) provides—

(a) that a person convicted of a summary offence shall be liable on conviction to a fine or a maximum fine by reference to a specified level on the standard scale; or

(b) confers power by subordinate instrument to make a person liable on conviction of a summary offence (whether or not created by the instrument) to a fine or maximum fine by reference to a specified level on the standard scale,

it is to be construed as referring to the standard scale for which this section provides as that standard scale has effect from time to time by virtue either of this section or of an order under section 143 of the *Magistrates' Courts Act* 1980.

[Subs. (2) was substituted by the *CJA* 1991, s.17(2).]

Inappropriate where the offence requires a custodial sentence

5–404 The Court of Appeal has on occasion criticised the imposition of a fine where the gravity of the offence is such that the only proper penalty is an immediate custodial sentence: see *R. v. Sisodia*, 1 Cr.App.R.(S.) 291, CA. For observations on the danger of allowing affluent offenders to escape custodial sentences by the payment of fines, see *R. v. Markwick*, 37 Cr.App.R. 125, CCA; *R. v. Lewis* [1965] Crim.L.R. 121, CCA.

Determining the amount of the fine

5–405 For the application of the principles relating to the imposition of a financial penalty to a case involving a series of like offences, see *R. v. Chelmsford Crown Court, ex p. Birchall*, 11 Cr.App.R.(S.) 510, DC (a rigid formula should not be adopted to a single offence, let alone to a series where the result is a total fine out of all proportion to the ability of the individual to pay).

It is wrong in principle to impose a fine on the assumption that it will be paid by some other person, such as the instigator of the offence who has not been apprehended: *R. v. Curtis*, 6 Cr.App.R.(S.) 250, CA; or the defendant's spouse: *R. v. Charalambous*, *ibid.* at 389, CA.

Where an offender's means are such that it is unrealistic to expect him to pay a fine, it is wrong in principle to impose a custodial sentence instead: *R. v. Reeves*, 56 Cr.App.R. 366, CA; *R. v. Ball*, 3 Cr.App.R.(S.) 283, CA.

In the case of a corporate defendant, there is no principle that, regardless of the offence, it is necessary for the court to have detailed particulars of the financial position of a company where those acting for it make it plain to the court that the means of the company are substantial: *R. v. Transco plc* [2006] 2 Cr.App.R.(S.) 111, CA.

In *R. v. Balfour Beatty Infrastructure Ltd* [2007] 1 Cr.App.R.(S.) 65, CA, it was said that knowledge that breach of the duty under the *Health and Safety at Work etc. Act* 1974, s.3, to take positive steps to ensure that the company's activities involve the minimum risk to employees and to third parties would result in a fine of sufficient size to impact on shareholders provides a powerful incentive for management to comply with the duty; whilst this was not to say that a fine should always be large enough to affect dividends or share prices, a fine should reflect both the degree of fault and its consequences so as to raise appropriate concern on the part of shareholders as to what had occurred; such an approach, the court said, would satisfy the requirement that the sentence should act as a deterrent, and also the requirement that a company should be punished for culpable failure to pay due regard for safety, and for the consequences of that failure (see the purposes of sentencing in the *CJA* 2003, s.142 (*ante*, § 5–53)).

As to taking account of the fact that the public might suffer as a result of the imposition of a substantial financial penalty, see *R. v. Southampton University N.H.S. Trust* [2007] 2 Cr.App.R.(S.) 9, CA.

Payment by instalments

There is nothing wrong in principle with the period of payment being longer than one year, provided that it is not an undue burden and too severe a punishment, having regard to the nature of the offence and the offender: *R. v. Olliver and Olliver*, 11 Cr.App.R.(S.) 10, CA (a two-year period would seldom be too long, and in an appropriate case three years would be unassailable). **5–406**

Where payment by instalments is ordered, the term of imprisonment or detention which the court is obliged to fix should be expressed to be in default of the fine, and not of any one instalment (see *R. v. Aitchison and Bentley*, 4 Cr.App.R.(S.) 404, CA; *R. v. Power*, 8 Cr.App.R.(S.) 8, CA).

As to the payment of fines imposed on corporate defendants, see *R. v. Rollco Screw and Rivet Co. Ltd* [1999] 2 Cr.App.R.(S.) 436, CA, and *R. v. B. & Q. plc*, *The Times*, November 3, 2005, CA (*post*, § 6–29).

Combined with custodial sentence

A fine may properly be combined with a sentence of imprisonment, particularly where the offender has made a substantial profit from the offence. A fine should not be imposed for the purpose of depriving the offender of the proceeds of supposed offences of which he has not been convicted and which are not admitted: see *R. v. Ayensu and Ayensu*, 4 Cr.App.R.(S.) 248, CA; *R. v. Johnson*, 6 Cr.App.R.(S.) 227, CA. **5–407**

Where the offender has made no substantial profit from the offence, it will be inappropriate to impose substantial fines in addition to a substantial custodial sentence, particularly if the effect will be to deprive the offender of any assets he has obtained lawfully or to make it inevitable that he will serve an additional period in custody in default of payment, after he has served the sentence of imprisonment: see *R. v. Forsythe*, 2 Cr.App.R.(S.) 15, CA; *R. v. Maund*, 2 Cr.App.R.(S.) 289, CA. It is also inappropriate to impose a fine which will place an undue financial burden on an offender on his release from custody, particularly if his prospects of employment are uncertain (see *R. v. McCormack*, unreported, January 16, 1976).

In a number of cases the Court of Appeal has considered the approach to be adopted in dealing with an offender who can reasonably be supposed to have derived substantial gains from his offences, but whose precise means are unknown. In *R. v. Benmore*, 5 Cr.App.R.(S.) 468, *R. v. Chatt*, 6 Cr.App.R.(S.) 75, *R. v. Green and Green*, *ibid.* at 329, and *R. v. Michel*, *ibid.* at 379, the court adopted the principle that in such cases the court may impose a substantial fine, but should ensure that the aggregate of the sentence of imprisonment imposed for the offence, and the default term which the offender will have to serve if the fine is not paid, does not constitute an excessive sentence when considered as a whole. The obligation to discount the sentence of imprisonment was doubted in *R. v. Garner*, 7 Cr.App.R.(S.) 285, CA, where the earlier decisions were reviewed. In practice, it seems that in situations such as these, the court would now make use of its powers to make a confiscation order and the problem would seldom arise in the same form.

Combined with sentences not involving immediate custody

5–408 Section 163 of the 2003 Act (*ante*, § 5–393) is explicit as to the lawfulness of combining a fine with any other form of sentence, unless a court is precluded from doing so by virtue of the exercise of some other power. Thus, a fine may not be combined with a discharge of the offender: see the *PCC(S)A* 2000, s.12(1) (*ante*, § 5–113). It was held in relation to "old-style" suspended sentences that there was no objection to the imposition of a fine at the same time (*R. v. Lang*, 54 Cr.App.R. 169, CA; *R. v. Genese*, 63 Cr.App.R. 152, CA), but that it was wrong to do so where a fine standing alone would have been an adequate penalty (*R. v. Ankers*, 61 Cr.App.R. 170, CA). As to the need to take particular care to ensure that the offender has the means to pay the fine, when imposed in conjunction with a suspended sentence, see *R. v. King*, 54 Cr.App.R. 362, CA; and *R. v. Whybrew*, 1 Cr.App.R.(S.) 121, CA.

Terms of imprisonment in default

5–409 In *R. v. Szrajber*, 15 Cr.App.R.(S.) 821, CA, it was held that the default terms set out in section 139(4), were maximum terms. The court had a discretion to fix a period below the maximum. Normally the court was likely to determine that the appropriate period in default would fall between the maximum for the band immediately below the band that was being considered, and the maximum for the band itself. In determining the right term in default, the court had to consider the circumstances of the case and the overall seriousness of the matter, and in particular that the purpose of the imposition of a period of imprisonment in default was to secure payment of the amount which the court had ordered to be confiscated. It was not necessarily appropriate to approach the case on a simple arithmetical basis.

Time spent in custody on remand

5–410 Where an offender has spent time in custody on remand before a fine is imposed, it will usually be appropriate to make an allowance for that time in fixing the amount of the fine: *R. v. Warden* [1996] 2 Cr.App.R.(S.) 269, CA.

VIII. COMPENSATION, RESTITUTION AND REPARATION

A. COMPENSATION ORDERS

Powers of Criminal Courts (Sentencing) Act 2000, ss.130–132

Compensation orders

Compensation orders against convicted persons

5–411 **130.**—(1) A court by or before which a person is convicted of an offence, instead of or in addition to dealing with him in any other way, may, on application or otherwise, make an order (in this Act referred to as a "compensation order") requiring him—

(a) to pay compensation for any personal injury, loss or damage resulting from that offence or any other offence which is taken into consideration by the court in determining sentence; or

(b) to make payments for funeral expenses or bereavement in respect of a death resulting from any such offence, other than a death due to an accident arising out of the presence of a motor vehicle on a road;

but this is subject to the following provisions of this section and to section 131 below.

(2) Where the person is convicted of an offence the sentence for which is fixed by law or falls to be imposed under section 110(2) or 111(2) above, section 51A(2) of the *Firearms Act* 1968, section 225(2) or 226(2) of the *Criminal Justice Act* 2003 or section 29(4) or (6) of the *Violent Crime Reduction Act* 2006, subsection (1) above shall have effect as if the words "instead of or" were omitted.

(3) A court shall give reasons, on passing sentence, if it does not make a compensation order in a case where this section empowers it to do so.

(4) Compensation under subsection (1) above shall be of such amount as the court considers appropriate, having regard to any evidence and to any representations that are made by or on behalf of the accused or the prosecutor.

(5) In the case of an offence under the *Theft Act* 1968 or *Fraud Act* 2006, where the property in question is recovered, any damage to the property occurring while it was out of the owner's possession shall be treated for the purposes of subsection (1) above as having resulted from the offence, however and by whomever the damage was caused.

(6) A compensation order may only be made in respect of injury, loss or damage (other than loss suffered by a person's dependants in consequence of his death) which was due to an accident arising out of the presence of a motor vehicle on a road, if—

(a) it is in respect of damage which is treated by subsection (5) above as resulting from an offence under the *Theft Act* 1968 or *Fraud Act* 2006; or

(b) it is in respect of injury, loss or damage as respects which—

(i) the offender is uninsured in relation to the use of the vehicle; and

(ii) compensation is not payable under any arrangements to which the Secretary of State is a party.

(7) Where a compensation order is made in respect of injury, loss or damage due to an accident arising out of the presence of a motor vehicle on a road, the amount to be paid may include an amount representing the whole or part of any loss of or reduction in preferential rates of insurance attributable to the accident.

(8) A vehicle the use of which is exempted from insurance by section 144 of the *Road Traffic Act* 1988 is not uninsured for the purposes of subsection (6) above.

(9) A compensation order in respect of funeral expenses may be made for the benefit of any one who incurred the expenses.

(10) A compensation order in respect of bereavement may be made only for the benefit of a person for whose benefit a claim for damages for bereavement could be made under section 1A of the *Fatal Accidents Act* 1976; and the amount of compensation in respect of bereavement shall not exceed the amount for the time being specified in section 1A(3) of that Act.

(11) In determining whether to make a compensation order against any person, and in determining the amount to be paid by any person under such an order, the court shall have regard to his means so far as they appear or are known to the court.

(12) Where the court considers—

(a) that it would be appropriate both to impose a fine and to make a compensation order, but

(b) that the offender has insufficient means to pay both an appropriate fine and appropriate compensation,

the court shall give preference to compensation (though it may impose a fine as well).

[This section is printed as amended by the *CJA* 2003, s.304, and Sched. 32, paras 90 and 117; the *Fraud Act* 2006, s.14(1), and Sched. 1, para. 29; the *VCRA* 2006, s.49, and Sched. 1, para. 6; and the *CJIA* 2008, s.148(1), and Sched. 26, paras 40 and 46. As to the saving provision in relation to the 2003 Act amendment, see *ante*, § 5–1b.]

The amount specified in section 1A(3) of the *Fatal Accidents Act* 1976 is £10,000 (S.I. 2002 No. 644).

As to ordering compensation to be paid by an offender's parent or guardian, see *post*, § 5–928.

Limit on amount payable under compensation order of magistrates' court

131.—(1) The compensation to be paid under a compensation order made by a magistrates' court in respect of any offence of which the court has convicted the offender shall not exceed £5,000. **5–412**

(2) The compensation or total compensation to be paid under a compensation order or compensation orders made by a magistrates' court in respect of any offence or offence taken into consideration in determining sentence shall not exceed the difference (if any) between—

(a) the amount or total amount which under subsection (1) above is the maximum for the offence or offences of which the offender has been convicted; and

(b) the amount or total amounts (if any) which are in fact ordered to be paid in respect of that offence or those offences.

Enforcement and appeals

132.—(1) [*Payee not entitled to payment until possibility of appeal exhausted.*] **5–413**

(2) [*Rules of court to make provision for dealing with compensation whilst entitlement thereto suspended.*]

(3) The Court of Appeal may by order annul or vary any compensation order made by the court of trial, although the conviction is not quashed; and the order, if annulled, shall not take effect and, if varied, shall take effect as varied.

(4) Where the *House of Lords* [Supreme Court] restores a conviction, it may make any compensation order which the court of trial could have made.

(4A) Where an order is made in respect of a person under subsection (3) or (4) above, the Court of Appeal or House of Lords shall make such order for the payment of a surcharge under section 161A of the *Criminal Justice Act* 2003, or such variation of the order of the Crown Court under that section, as is necessary to secure that the person's liability under that section is the same as it would be if he were being dealt with by the Crown Court.

(5) Where a compensation order has been made against any person in respect of an offence taken into consideration in determining his sentence—

(a) the order shall cease to have effect if he successfully appeals against his conviction of the offence or, if more than one, all the offences, of which he was convicted in the proceedings in which the order was made;

(b) he may appeal against the order as if it were part of the sentence imposed in respect of the offence or, if more than one, any of the offences, of which he was so convicted.

[This section is printed as amended by the *Domestic Violence, Crime and Victims Act* 2004, s.58(1), and Sched. 10, para. 49; and, as amended, as from a day to be appointed, by the *Constitutional Reform Act* 2005, s.40(4), and Sched. 9, para. 69 (substitution of reference to "Supreme Court" for reference to "House of Lords").]

As to the power of the Crown Court to allow time for payment or payment by instalments, see the *PCC(S)A* 2000, s.141, *post*, § 6–117.

As to the enforcement of orders for costs and compensation, see the *Administration of Justice Act* 1970, s.41 and Sched. 9, *post*, §§ 6–119 *et seq.*

Review of compensation orders

5–414 Section 133 of the 2000 Act authorises a magistrates' court to discharge a compensation order or reduce the amount that remains to be paid in various circumstances, including the fact that the offender has "suffered a substantial reduction in his means which was unexpected at the time when the compensation order was made." If the compensation order was made by the Crown Court, the magistrates' court must obtain the consent of the Crown Court before exercising this power on this ground, or on the ground that the offender's means are insufficient to satisfy the compensation order and a confiscation order made under the *CJA* 1988 in the same proceedings.

Review of failure to make order

5–414a Judicial review does not lie in respect of a failure of the Crown Court to make a compensation order: *R. (Faithfull) v. Crown Court at Ipswich* [2008] 1 W.L.R. 1636, DC (*post*, § 7–12).

"Personal injury, loss or damage"

5–415 A compensation order may be made only in respect of personal injury, loss or damage which results from an offence of which the offender is convicted, or an offence which is taken into consideration (*ante*, § 5–110). If property is stolen and recovered undamaged, it is not open to the court to make a compensation order in respect of the value of the goods (see *R. v. Hier*, 62 Cr.App.R. 233, CA; *R. v. Boardman*, 9 Cr.App.R.(S.) 74, CA; *R. v. Tyce*, 15 Cr.App.R.(S.) 415, CA). Similarly, if the offender is acquitted of an offence out of which loss, damage or injury is said to have arisen, but convicted of some other offence related to the same subject matter, a compensation order cannot be made (see *R. v. Halliwell*, 12 Cr.App.R.(S.) 692, CA; *R. v. Graves*, 14 Cr.App.R.(S.) 790, CA). The question is not whether the loss results solely from the offence, but whether it can "fairly be said to result from the offence": *Rowlston v. Kenny*, 4 Cr.App.R.(S.) 85, CA.

Questions relating to the power to make a compensation order in cases of violent disorder or affray, where loss, damage or personal injury has been caused by persons other than the offender, were considered in *R. v. Derby*, 12 Cr.App.R.(S.) 502, CA; *R. v. Taylor*, 14 Cr.App.R.(S.) 276, CA; *R. v. Geurtjens*, 14 Cr.App.R.(S.) 280, CA; and *R. v. Deary*, 14 Cr.App.R.(S.) 648, CA. The effect of these decisions appears to be that if the offender has instigated the incident by an initial act of violence or abuse, or joined in after the incident has started but before the loss, damage or personal injury has been caused, the loss, damage or personal injury can be said to have resulted from the offence of which he has been convicted. If the actions which cause the injuries go beyond the expected scope of the fracas, the offender will not be responsible for the injuries so inflicted. See also *R. v. Denness* [1996] 1 Cr.App.R.(S.) 159, CA.

Where an offender is indicted on a limited number of specimen charges which are representative of a larger number of offences, but none of the other offences are taken into consideration, the compensation order must be limited to the loss or damage resulting from the specimen charges and may not include an amount reflecting the other offences: *R. v. Crutchley and Tonks*, 15 Cr.App.R.(S.) 627, CA, followed in *R. v. Hose*, 16 Cr.App.R.(S.) 682, CA; but distinguished in *Revenue and Customs Prosecutions Office v. Duffy* [2008] Crim.L.R. 734, DC (where a single offence, under the *Tax Credits Act* 2002, s.35, led to a series of payments).

It is not necessary that the loss, damage or personal injury should be inflicted intentionally (see *R. v. Corbett*, 14 Cr.App.R.(S.) 101, CA).

The fact that the person who suffered the loss has died does not necessarily mean that it is inappropriate to order compensation: *Holt v. DPP* [1996] 2 Cr.App.R.(S.) 314, DC.

Non-actionable loss

It is not necessary that the loss, damage or personal injury should be actionable: *R. v. Chappell*, 6 Cr.App.R.(S.) 214, CA. **5–416**

Traffic accidents

Section 130(6) has been interpreted strictly. In *Quigley v. Stokes*, 64 Cr.App.R. 198, **5–417** DC, the appellant took a car without permission, and while driving it collided with two other cars: all three were damaged. It was held that a compensation order was properly made in respect of the damage to the vehicle which had been taken, by virtue of section 130(5), but that there was no power to make a compensation order in respect of the damage to the other vehicles. In *Mayor v. Oxford*, 2 Cr.App.R.(S.) 280, DC, the appellants took a lorry without consent and drove it into a wall, which was damaged as a result. They were convicted of recklessly causing damage to the wall. A compensation order made in respect of the damage to the wall was quashed, on the basis that the incident was "plainly an accident" and a compensation order was precluded by section 130(6).

The power to award compensation under section 130(5) is limited to damage to property which is recovered; it does not apply to property which is not returned to the owner (see *R. v. Ahmad (Asif)*, 13 Cr.App.R.(S.) 212, CA).

Compensation orders in these cases might now be possible under section 130(6)(b) (introduced by way of amendment to the previous legislation). This requires that the offender is uninsured in respect of the use of the vehicle, and that compensation is not payable under any arrangements to which the Secretary of State is a party. This is a reference to the Motor Insurers' Bureau agreement, which was revised with effect from December 31, 1988: see *Scott v. DPP*, 16 Cr.App.R.(S.) 292, DC (in which it was held that "payable" in section 130(6)(b) means payable at some future time, as opposed to being payable under an existing judgment which the MIB were obliged to satisfy). *Scott v. DPP* was followed in *R. v. Austin* [1996] 2 Cr.App.R.(S.) 191, CA. Under the current agreement, the MIB will satisfy unpaid judgments obtained against uninsured drivers; but there are certain exclusions, namely—

(a) the first £300 worth of any damage to property;

(b) any property damage in excess of £250,000;

(c) any loss or damage suffered by the driver of another vehicle who was not himself insured to the extent required by law at the time of the accident;

(d) any loss or damage suffered by a person being carried in a vehicle driven by the uninsured person, who at the time of the accident either knew or ought to have known that the vehicle had been stolen or unlawfully taken, or that the required insurance policy was not in force;

(e) the judgment was obtained by a person exercising a right of subrogation.

The net effect of section 130(6)(b) seems to be in normal circumstances that compensation may be awarded for injury, loss or damage which was due to an accident arising out of the presence of a motor vehicle on a road if the offender was uninsured and there was damage to property up to a value of £300, there was loss in respect of property damage in excess of £250,000 or the injury, loss or damage was suffered by another driver who was not himself insured to the extent required by the law at the time of the accident. It appears that a compensation order may also be made in favour of a person exercising a right of subrogation (*i.e.* the insurer of the damaged vehicle).

Crown vehicles are exempt from the requirement of insurance, and hence no compensation order can be made in respect of damage resulting from an accident involving a vehicle belonging to the Crown by virtue of section 130(6).

Determination of amount of loss

5–418 In *R. v. Vivian*, 68 Cr.App.R. 53, the Court of Appeal stated that "no order for compensation should be made unless the sum claimed by way of compensation is either agreed or proved." In *R. v. Swann and Webster*, 6 Cr.App.R.(S.) 22, CA, it was said that the effect of the amendments of the original provisions by the *CJA* 1982 was "slightly to reduce the obligation which was laid down by this court in *Vivian's* case," but that "there is nothing in these new statutory provisions which indicates that a trial judge, when considering compensation, should simply pluck a figure out of the air." In *R. v. Horsham JJ., ex p. Richards*, 82 Cr.App.R. 254, DC, Neill L.J. said that the court had no jurisdiction to make a compensation order without receiving any evidence where there were real issues raised as to whether the claimants had suffered any, and if so what, loss. Section 130(4) seemed to contemplate that the court could make assessments and approximations where the evidence was scanty or incomplete; but where there were plain issues as to liability, it was for the prosecution to place evidence before the court. Plainly, any award should not exceed the sum that would be awarded by a court in civil proceedings: *R. v. Flinton* [2008] 1 Cr.App.R.(S.) 96, CA.

The principle that a compensation order should not be made unless the fact that a loss has been incurred, and the extent of the loss, are either proved or admitted, was applied in *R. v. Watson*, 12 Cr.App.R.(S.) 508, CA; and *R. v. Clelland*, *ibid.*, at 697, CA.

Avoiding difficult or complex issues as to liability

5–419 Although it is open to the court to hear evidence in order to determine questions as to the fact or the amount of loss, the Court of Appeal has discouraged criminal courts from embarking on complicated investigations: see *R. v. Kneeshaw*, 58 Cr.App.R. 439; *Hyde v. Emery*, 6 Cr.App.R.(S.) 206; *R. v. Briscoe*, 15 Cr.App.R.(S.) 699; *R. v. White* [1996] 2 Cr.App.R.(S.) 58; and *R. v. Bewick* [2008] 2 Cr.App.R.(S.) 31 (since sentencer may hear submissions only from prosecution and defence, third or non-parties (including victims) being expressly excluded, policy demands that complex issues should not be dealt with in criminal courts).

Personal injury cases

5–420 There should be detailed information about the precise injuries suffered: *R. v. Cooper*, 4 Cr.App.R.(S.) 55, CA; *R. v. Welch*, 6 Cr.App.R.(S.) 13, CA.

Where the victim was involved in unlawful conduct that contributed to the occurrence of the offence, the court is entitled to make a reduction to any award: *R. v. Flinton*, *ante*.

Duty of counsel

5–425 If counsel puts before the court information relating to the means of the offender, with a view to the making of a compensation order, particularly where the making of a compensation order is expected to affect the decision whether to impose a custodial sentence on the offender, or the length of the sentence, it is the responsibility of counsel to satisfy himself of the accuracy of the information; it is not sufficient to rely on instructions without further inquiry or supporting documentation: *R. v. Coughlin*, 6 Cr.App.R.(S.) 102, CA; *R. v. Huish*, 7 Cr.App.R.(S.) 272, CA; *R. v. Bond*, 8 Cr.App.R.(S.) 11, CA; and *R. v. Roberts*, 9 Cr.App.R.(S.) 275, CA, when the attention of counsel and solicitors was drawn to "the need to ensure ... that the information placed before the court is not merely believed to be accurate but is accurate as well." In these cases the compensation order was quashed, but in *R. v. Slack*, 9 Cr.App.R.(S.) 65, where counsel took instructions from his client in court, the Court of Appeal declined to quash a compensation order, although the appellant was unable to pay the amount ordered. See also *R. v. Hayes*, 13 Cr.App.R.(S.) 454, CA; and *R. v. Dando* [1996] 1 Cr.App.R.(S.) 155, CA.

Period of payment

5–426 For general statements of the need to avoid excessively long periods of payment by instalments, see *R. v. Bradburn*, 57 Cr.App.R. 948, CA; *R. v. Daly*, 58 Cr.App.R. 333, CA; *R. v. McCulloch*, 4 Cr.App.R.(S.) 98, CA; *R. v. Makin*, *ibid.* at 180, CA. In appropriate cases a period of two years, or three years in exceptional cases, would not be open to criticism: *R. v. Olliver and Olliver*, 11 Cr.App.R.(S.) 10, CA; *R. v. Yehou* [1997] 2 Cr.App.R.(S.) 48, CA.

Sale of assets to raise funds

5–427 Where it is proposed to make a compensation order against an offender on the assumption that he will raise the necessary funds by selling an asset, it is essential that the court should have a proper valuation of the article concerned before making the order. In *R. v. Chambers*, 3 Cr.App.R.(S.) 318, CA, Lord Lane C.J. stated that it was for the trial court to ascertain the value of the article concerned; if it could not be properly valued, no compensation order should be made. In *R. v. Heads and Redfern*, *ibid.* at 322, CA, one appellant put forward evidence of his means based on a draft balance sheet of his business, showing substantial assets. The Court of Appeal observed that the estimates of the appellant's assets had been put forward by an expert and the judge had had ample evidence on which to make the order.

5–428 The Court of Appeal has generally discouraged the making of compensation orders on the basis that the offender will raise the funds by the sale of the matrimonial home, especially if the consequence is that his family will become homeless: see *R. v. Butt*, 8 Cr.App.R.(S.) 216, CA; *R. v. Hackett*, 10 Cr.App.R.(S.) 388, CA; and *R. v. Holah*, 11 Cr.App.R.(S.) 282, CA. But this is not an absolute rule: see *R. v. McGuire*, 13 Cr.App.R.(S.) 332, CA (compensation order upheld as the appellant had enough left over to buy less expensive house).

Offenders receiving custodial sentence

5–429 A compensation order should not be made if its effect would be to subject the offender on his discharge from custody to a financial burden which he would not be able to meet from his available resources and which might encourage him to commit further crime to obtain the means to meet the requirements of the order: *R. v. Panayioutou*, 11 Cr.App.R.(S.) 535, CA: see also *R. v. Clarke*, 12 Cr.App.R.(S.) 10, CA. Where the offender has assets, it is not necessarily wrong to make a compensation order in conjunction with a custodial sentence: *R. v. Martin*, 11 Cr.App.R.(S.) 424, CA. See also *R. v. Jorge* [1999] 2 Cr.App.R.(S.) 1, CA; and *R. v. Love and Tompkins* [1999] 1 Cr.App.R.(S.) 484, CA.

Inability to pay compensation is not a matter which should affect the length of his sentence. The significance of an offer to pay compensation is that it might be taken as

For guidance on the amount of compensation to be awarded in particular cases, reference may be made to the Judicial Studies Board, *Guidelines for the Assessment of General Damages in Personal Injury Cases*.

Emotional distress, etc.

Compensation orders in modest amounts for emotional distress and related matters have been upheld: see *R. v. Thomson Holidays Ltd* [1974] Q.B. 592, 58 Cr.App.R. 429, CA (£50 against a holiday company convicted of recklessly making a false statement as to the amenities available at a particular hotel), and *Bond v. Chief Constable of Kent*, 4 Cr.App.R.(S.) 324, DC (£25 in respect of terror experienced by a householder as a result of a stone being thrown through the window of the house). **5–421**

There must be some evidence that the person concerned did experience distress or shock; the court is not necessarily justified in inferring from the facts of the offence that a witness was distressed: see *R. v. Vaughan*, 12 Cr.App.R.(S.) 46, CA.

Interest

A compensation order may properly include an amount in respect of interest, particularly where the amounts are large and the relevant period a long one, provided that the amount can be calculated without complication: *R. v. Schofield*, 67 Cr.App.R. 282, CA. **5–422**

The means of the offender (s.130(11))

A compensation order should not be made unless it is "realistic" in the sense that the court is satisfied that the offender either has the means available, or will have the means to pay the compensation within a reasonable time. These principles were not affected by the enactment of a presumption in favour of compensation: see *R. v. Bagga*, 11 Cr.App.R.(S.) 497, CA, and *R. v. Stanley*, *ibid.* at 446, CA, where it was held that it was the duty of a judge who had a compensation order in mind to raise the matter so that it could be properly and fairly ventilated, if it had not been raised by counsel. See also *R. v. Hewitt*, 12 Cr.App.R.(S.) 466, CA (if a sentencer makes a substantial compensation order without a proper inquiry into the defendant's means, it is the duty of counsel to point out that such an order should not be coupled with an immediate custodial sentence without an inquiry). **5–423**

The court is not limited to funds which are themselves the proceeds of crime (see *R. v. Copley*, 1 Cr.App.R.(S.) 55, CA), nor is it necessary that the offender should have derived any profit from the offence (see *R. v. Ford*, unreported, June 22, 1976).

Compensation orders have frequently been set aside for lack of sufficient inquiry as to means: see *R. v. Phillips*, 10 Cr.App.R.(S.) 419, CA, in which it was said that problems could be avoided if the sentencing judge indicated a provisional amount by way of compensation: he was then fully entitled to turn to defence counsel to ask him to provide information about the means of the defendant. If the defendant was obdurate and insisted on keeping silent, that might in some cases afford a basis for the court to draw inferences as to his financial position. Where there is material before the court which suggests that the offender is in possession of substantial resources, a compensation order may properly be made even though no precise evidence of the offender's means is available to the court: see *R. v. Bolden*, 9 Cr.App.R.(S.) 83, CA, and *R. v. Owen*, 12 Cr.App.R.(S.) 561, CA.

There appears to be no reason why a financial circumstances order under section 162 of the *CJA* 2003 (*ante*, § 5–392) should not be made when a court is considering whether to make a compensation order.

The means of third parties

As a general rule, the court should not make a compensation order against an offender without means on the assumption that the order will be paid by other persons, such as relatives or friends: see *R. v. Mortimer* [1977] Crim.L.R. 624, CA, applying *R. v. Inwood*, 60 Cr.App.R. 70, CA. **5–424** some token of remorse on the defendant's behalf as well as redressing the victim's loss. To that extent and no further it features in the sentencing exercise; compensation orders are otherwise wholly independent of that exercise: see *R. v. Barney*, 11 Cr.App.R.(S.) 448, CA.

Where a compensation order is made against an offender who at the same time receives a suspended sentence or is made the subject of a community order, a court which subsequently activates the suspended sentence or, upon revocation of the community order, re-sentences for the original offence to custody, has no power to review the compensation order, even though the result of the court's action will be to prevent the offender from earning the funds with which to pay the compensation. The magistrates' court responsible for enforcing the order may consider the matter under section 133 (*ante*, § 5–414); see *R. v. Jama*, 13 Cr.App.R.(S.) 63, CA, applying *R. v. Wallis*, 1 Cr.App.R.(S.) 168, CA and *R. v. Mathieson*, 9 Cr.App.R.(S.) 54, CA.

Change in offender's circumstances

Where there is a material change in financial circumstances after an order is made, the appropriate course is to apply to the magistrates' court under section 133 (*ante*, § 5–414), rather than to appeal to the Court of Appeal: *R. v. Palmer*, 15 Cr.App.R.(S.) 550, CA. **5–430**

B. RESTITUTION ORDERS

Powers of Criminal Courts (Sentencing) Act 2000, ss.148, 149

Restitution orders

148.—(1) This section applies where goods have been stolen, and either— **5–431**

(a) a person is convicted of any offence with reference to the theft (whether or not the stealing is the gist of his offence); or

(b) a person is convicted of any other offence, but such an offence as is mentioned in paragraph (a) above is taken into consideration in determining his sentence.

(2) Where this section applies, the court by or before which the offender is convicted may on the conviction (whether or not the passing of sentence is in other respects deferred) exercise any of the following powers—

(a) the court may order anyone having possession or control of the stolen goods to restore them to any person entitled to recover them from him; or

(b) on the application of a person entitled to recover from the person convicted any other goods directly or indirectly representing the stolen goods (as being the proceeds of any disposal or realisation of the whole or part of them or of goods so representing them), the court may order those other goods to be delivered or transferred to the applicant; or

(c) the court may order that a sum not exceeding the value of the stolen goods shall be paid, out of any money of the person convicted which was taken out of his possession on his apprehension, to any person who, if those goods were in the possession of the person convicted, would be entitled to recover them from him;

and in this subsection "the stolen goods" means the goods referred to in subsection (1) above;

(3) Where the court has power on a person's conviction to make an order against him both under paragraph (b) and under paragraph (c) of subsection (2) above with reference to the stealing of the same goods, the court may make orders under both paragraphs provided that the person in whose favour the orders are made does not thereby recover more than the value of those goods.

(4) Where the court on a person's conviction makes an order under subsection (2)(a) above for the restoration of any goods, and it appears to the court that the person convicted—

(a) has sold the goods to a person acting in good faith, or

(b) has borrowed money on the security of them from a person so acting,

the court may order that there shall be paid to the purchaser or lender, out of any money of the person convicted which was taken out of his possession on his apprehension, a sum not exceeding the amount paid for the purchase by the purchaser or, as the case may be, the amount owed to the lender in respect of the loan.

(5) The court shall not exercise the powers conferred by this section unless in the

opinion of the court the relevant facts sufficiently appear from evidence given at the trial or the available documents, together with admissions made by or on behalf of any person in connection with any proposed exercise of the powers.

(6) In subsection (5) above "the available documents" means—

(a) any written statements or admissions which were made for use, and would have been admissible, as evidence at the trial; and

(b) *such written statements, depositions and other documents as were tendered by or on behalf of the prosecutor at any committal proceedings* [such documents as were served on the offender in pursuance of regulations made under paragraph 1 of Schedule 3 to the *Crime and Disorder Act* 1998].

(7) Any order under this section shall be treated as an order for the restitution of property within the meaning of section 30 of the *Criminal Appeal Act* 1968 (which relates to the effect on such orders of appeals).

(8) Subject to subsection (9) below, references in this section to stealing shall be construed in accordance with section 1(1) of the *Theft Act* 1968 (read with the provisions of that Act relating to the construction of section 1(1)).

(9) Subsections (1) and (4) of section 24 of that Act (interpretation of certain provisions) shall also apply in relation to this section as they apply in relation to the provisions of that Act relating to goods which have been stolen.

(10) In this section and section 149 below, "goods", except in so far as the context otherwise requires, includes money and every other description of property (within the meaning of the *Theft Act* 1968) except land, and includes things severed from the land by stealing.

(11) An order may be made under this section in respect of money owed by the Crown.

[The words in square brackets in subs. (6)(b) are substituted for the italicised words by the *CJA* 2003, s.41, and Sched. 3, para. 74(1) and (5). This amendment came into force on May 9, 2005 (*Criminal Justice Act 2003 (Commencement No. 9) Order* 2005 (S.I. 2005 No. 1267), in relation to cases sent for trial under section 51 or 51A(3)(d) of the 1998 Act; otherwise it comes into force on a day to be appointed.]

In relation to an offence into which a criminal investigation began before April 1, 1997, see the transitional provision in Sched. 11, para. 9 (repealed, as from a day to be appointed, by the *CJA* 2003, s.332, and Sched. 37, Pt 4).

Restitution orders: supplementary

5–432 **149.**—(1) The following provisions of this section shall have effect with respect to section 148 above.

(2) The powers conferred by subsections (2)(c) and (4) of that section shall be exercisable without any application being made in that behalf or on the application of any person appearing to the court to be interested in the property concerned.

(3) Where an order is made under that section against any person in respect of an offence taken into consideration in determining his sentence—

(a) the order shall cease to have effect if he successfully appeals against his conviction of the offence or, if more than one, all the offences, of which he was convicted in the proceedings in which the order was made;

(b) he may appeal against the order as if it were part of the sentence imposed in respect of the offence or, if more than one, any of the offences, of which he was so convicted.

(4) Any order under that section made by a magistrates' court shall be suspended—

(a) in any case until the end of the period for the time being prescribed by law for the giving of notice of appeal against a decision of a magistrates' court;

(b) where notice of appeal is given within the period so prescribed, until the determination of the appeal;

but this subsection shall not apply where the order is made under section 148(2)(a) or (b) and the court so directs, being of the opinion that the title to the goods to be restored or, as the case may be, delivered or transferred under the order is not in dispute.

Evidence and procedure

5–433 The court has no power to receive evidence after the conclusion of the trial to establish the basis for making a restitution order: *R. v. Church*, 55 Cr.App.R. 65, CA. Restitution orders should be made "only in the plainest cases" where there is no doubt about the rights of the parties; where there is an issue, the matter should be left to be decided in the civil courts: *R. v. Ferguson*, 54 Cr.App.R. 410, CA; *R. v. Calcutt and Varty*, 7 Cr.App.R.(S.) 385, CA.

Money seized from offender on his apprehension

Money seized before an offender is arrested may not be the subject of a restitution order under section 148(2)(c) or (4) (see *R. v. Hinde*, 64 Cr.App.R. 213, CA, decided on similar wording in what is now section 143 of the 2000 Act, *post*), but it was held in *R. v. Ferguson*, *ante*, that where money was seized by police officers from a safe deposit box in the offender's name several days after his arrest, the money was taken out of his possession on his apprehension. An offender may not complain on the ground that the order is for a greater sum than he received as his share of the proceeds of the crime, so long as it is not larger than the total amount stolen (see *R. v. Lewis*, unreported, January 31, 1975), or on the ground that there is objectionable disparity in making such an order against him but not against his accomplices: *ibid*. An order of this kind should not be made when another offender is ordered to make restitution of the stolen goods themselves (see *R. v. Parsons and Haley*, unreported, October 14, 1976, where one appellant bought stolen goods from the other, and both the stolen goods and the price paid for them were seized). Where all of the goods in respect of which the offender has been convicted have been recovered, it will be an incorrect exercise of discretion to make a restitution order out of money taken out of his possession in relation to goods in respect of which he has not been convicted of any offence (see *R. v. Parker*, 54 Cr.App.R. 339, CA). **5-434**

Voluntary restitution and confiscation proceedings

As to the institution of confiscation proceedings where an offender has made or is willing to make voluntary restitution, see, *post*, § 5-767a. **5-434a**

C. REPARATION ORDERS

Power of Criminal Courts (Sentencing) Act 2000, s.73-75

Reparation orders

73.—(1) Where a child or young person (that is to say, any person aged under 18) is convicted of an offence other than one for which the sentence is fixed by law, the court by or before which he is convicted may make an order requiring him to make reparation specified in the order— **5-435**

(a) to a person or persons so specified; or

(b) to the community at large;

and any person so specified must be a person identified by the court as a victim of the offence or a person otherwise affected by it.

(2) An order under subsection (1) above is in this Act referred to as a "reparation order".

(3) In this section and section 74 below "make reparation", in relation to an offender, means make reparation for the offence otherwise than by the payment of compensation; and the requirements that may be specified in a reparation order are subject to section 74(1) to (3).

(4) The court shall not make a reparation order in respect of the offender if it proposes—

(a) to pass on him a custodial sentence; or

(b) to make in respect of him a *community order under section 177 of the* Criminal Justice Act *2003, a supervision order which includes requirements authorised by Schedule 6 to this Act, an action plan order* [youth rehabilitation order] or a referral order.

[(4A) The court shall not make a reparation order in respect of the offender at a time when a youth rehabilitation order is in force in respect of him unless when it makes the reparation order it revokes the youth rehabilitation order.

(4B) Where a youth rehabilitation order is revoked under subsection (4A), paragraph 24 of Schedule 2 to the *Criminal Justice and Immigration Act* 2008 (breach, revocation or amendment of youth rehabilitation order) applies to the revocation.]

(5) Before making a reparation order, a court shall obtain and consider a written report

by an officer of a local probation board, an officer of a provider of probation services, a social worker of a local authority social services department or a member of a youth offending team indicating—

(a) the type of work that is suitable for the offender; and

(b) the attitude of the victim or victims to the requirements proposed to be included in the order.

(6) The court shall not make a reparation order unless it has been notified by the Secretary of State that arrangements for implementing such orders are available in the area proposed to be named in the order under section 74(4) below and the notice has not been withdrawn.

(7) [*Repealed by* CJA *2003, s.304, and Sched. 32, paras 90 and 106.*]

(8) The court shall give reasons if it does not make a reparation order in a case where it has power to do so.

[This section is printed as amended by the *CJCSA* 2000, s.74, and Sched. 7, para. 4; the *CJA* 2003, s.304, and Sched. 32, paras 90 and 106; and the *Offender Management Act 2007 (Consequential Amendments) Order* 2008 (S.I. 2008 No. 912), art. 3, and Sched. 1, para.14(1) and (14); and as amended, as from a day to be appointed (as to which, see *ante*, § 5–1), by the *CJIA* 2008, s.6(2), and Sched. 4, paras 51 and 53 (omission of italicised words, insertion of words in square brackets) .]

Requirements and provisions of reparation order, and obligations of person subject to it

5–436 **74.**—(1) A reparation order shall not require the offender—

(a) to work for more than 24 hours in aggregate; or

(b) to make reparation to any person without the consent of that person.

(2) Subject to subsection (1) above, requirements specified in a reparation order shall be such as in the opinion of the court are commensurate with the seriousness of the offence, or the combination of the offence and one or more offences associated with it.

(3) Requirements so specified shall, as far as practicable, be such as to avoid—

(a) any conflict with the offender's religious beliefs *or with the requirements of any community order or any youth community order to which he may be subject*; and

(b) any interference with the times, if any, at which he normally works or attends school or any other educational establishment.

(4) A reparation order shall name the petty sessions area in which it appears to the court making the order (or to the court amending under Schedule 8 to this Act any provision included in the order in pursuance of this subsection) that the offender resides or will reside.

(5) In this Act "responsible officer", in relation to an offender subject to a reparation order, means one of the following who is specified in the order, namely—

(a) an officer of a local probation board or an officer of a provider of probation services;

(b) a social worker of a local authority social services department;

(c) a member of a youth offending team.

(6A) Where a reparation order specifies an officer of a provider of probation services under subsection (5) above, the officer specified must be an officer acting in the local justice area named in the order.

(6) Where a reparation order specifies an officer of a local probation board under subsection (5) above, the officer specified must be an officer appointed for or assigned to the petty sessions area named in the order.

(7) Where a reparation order specifies under that subsection—

(a) a social worker of a local authority social services department, or

(b) a member of a youth offending team,

the social worker or member specified must be a social worker of, or a member of a youth offending team established by, the local authority within whose area it appears to the court that the offender resides or will reside.

(8) Any reparation required by a reparation order—

(a) shall be made under the supervision of the responsible officer; and

(b) shall be made within a period of three months from the date of the making of the order.

[This section is printed as amended by the *CJCSA* 2000, s.74, and Sched. 7, para. 4; the *CJA* 2003, s.304, and Sched. 32, paras 90 and 107; and S.I. 2008 No. 912 (*ante*,

§ 5–435)), art. 3, and Sched. 1, para.14(1) and (15); and as amended, as from a day to be appointed (as to which, see *ante*, § 5–1), by the *CJIA* 2008, ss.6(2) and 149, Sched. 4, paras 51 and 54, and Sched. 28, Pt 1 (omission of italicised words).]

Breach, revocation and amendment of reparation orders

75. [*Gives effect to Sched. 8*, ante, *§§ 5–227 et seq.*] **5–437**

A reparation order may be made in respect of an offender under the age of 18 by a court which has been notified that arrangements for implementing such orders have been made. A reparation order may not be made if the court proposes to pass a custodial sentence or make any of the orders specified in section 73(4)(b). A reparation order may not require the offender to work for more than 24 hours in all, or to make reparation to any person without the consent of that person. The requirements of the order must so far as possible avoid conflict with the offender's religious beliefs, with any community order or youth community order to which he is subject, and with the times at which he normally works or attends school. The reparation must be made within three months of the making of the order. **5–438**

IX. DEPRIVATION AND CONFISCATION

A. DEPRIVATION

Powers of Criminal Courts (Sentencing) Act 2000, ss.143–145

Powers to deprive offender of property used etc. for purposes of crime

143.—(1) Where a person is convicted of an offence and the court by or before which he is convicted is satisfied that any property which has been lawfully seized from him, or which was in his possession or under his control at the time when he was apprehended for the offence or when a summons in respect of it was issued— **5–439**

(a) has been used for the purpose of committing, or facilitating the commission of, any offence, or

(b) was intended by him to be used for that purpose,

the court may (subject to subsection (5) below) make an order under this section in respect of that property.

(2) Where a person is convicted of an offence and the offence, or an offence which the court has taken into consideration in determining his sentence, consists of unlawful possession of property which—

(a) has been lawfully seized from him, or

(b) was in his possession or under his control at the time when he was apprehended for the offence of which he has been convicted or when a summons in respect of that offence was issued,

the court may (subject to subsection (5) below) make an order under this section in respect of that property.

(3) An order under this section shall operate to deprive the offender of his rights, if any, in the property to which it relates, and the property shall (if not already in their possession) be taken into the possession of the police.

(4) Any power conferred on a court by subsection (1) or (2) above may be exercised—

(a) whether or not the court also deals with the offender in any other way in respect of the offence of which he has been convicted; and

(b) without regard to any restrictions on forfeiture in any enactment contained in an Act passed before 29th July 1988.

(5) In considering whether to make an order under this section in respect of any property, a court shall have regard—

(a) to the value of the property; and

(b) to the likely financial and other effects on the offender of the making of the order (taken together with any other order that the court contemplates making).

(6) Where a person commits an offence to which this subsection applies by—

(a) driving, attempting to drive, or being in charge of a vehicle, or

(b) failing to comply with a requirement made under section 7 or 7A of the *Road Traffic Act* 1988 (failure to provide specimen for analysis or laboratory test or to give permission for such a test) in the course of an investigation into whether the offender had committed an offence while driving, attempting to drive or being in charge of a vehicle, or

(c) failing, as the driver of a vehicle, to comply with subsection (2) or (3) of section 170 of the *Road Traffic Act* 1988 (duty to stop and give information or report accident),

the vehicle shall be regarded for the purposes of subsection (1) above (and section 144(1)(b) below) as used for the purpose of committing the offence (and for the purpose of committing any offence of aiding, abetting, counselling or procuring the commission of the offence).

(7) Subsection (6) above applies to—

(a) an offence under the *Road Traffic Act* 1988 which is punishable with imprisonment;

(b) an offence of manslaughter; and

(c) an offence under section 35 of the *Offences Against the Person Act* 1861 (wanton and furious driving).

(8) Facilitating the commission of an offence shall be taken for the purposes of subsection (1) above to include the taking of any steps after it has been committed for the purpose of disposing of any property to which it relates or of avoiding apprehension or detection.

[This section is printed as amended by the *Police Reform Act* 2002, s.56(6).]

A court making a forfeiture order under section 143 may order that the property be taken into the possession of the Secretary of State (and not of the police) where the court thinks that the offence in connection with which the order is made either related to immigration or asylum or was committed for a purpose connected with immigration or asylum: *UK Borders Act* 2007, s.25(1).

Property which is in possession of police by virtue of section 143

5–440 **144.**—(1) The *Police (Property) Act* 1897 shall apply, with the following modifications, to property which is in the possession of the police by virtue of section 143 above—

(a) no application shall be made under section 1(1) of that Act by any claimant of the property after the end of six months from the date on which the order in respect of the property was made under section 143 above; and

(b) no such application shall succeed unless the claimant satisfies the court either—

(i) that he had not consented to the offender having possession of the property; or

(ii) where an order is made under subsection (1) of section 143 above, that he did not know, and had no reason to suspect, that the property was likely to be used for the purpose mentioned in that subsection.

(2) In relation to property which is in the possession of the police by virtue of section 143 above, the power to make regulations under section 2 of the *Police (Property) Act* 1897 (disposal of property in cases where the owner of the property has not been ascertained and no order of a competent court has been made with respect to it) shall, subject to subsection (3) below, include power to make regulations for disposal (including disposal by vesting in the relevant authority) in cases where no application by a claimant of the property has been made within the period specified in subsection (1)(a) above or no such application has succeeded.

(3) The regulations may not provide for the vesting in the relevant authority of property in relation to which an order has been made under section 145 below (court order as to application of proceeds of forfeited property).

(4) Nothing in subsection (2A)(a) or (3) of section 2 of the *Police (Property) Act* 1897 limits the power to make regulations under that section by virtue of subsection (2) above.

(5) In this section "relevant authority" has the meaning given by section 2(2B) of the *Police (Property) Act* 1897.

Application of proceeds of forfeited property

5–441 **145.**—(1) Where a court makes an order under section 143 above in a case where—

(a) the offender has been convicted of an offence which has resulted in a person suffering personal injury, loss or damage, or

(b) any such offence is taken into consideration by the court in determining sentence,

the court may also make an order that any proceeds which arise from the disposal of the property and which do not exceed a sum specified by the court shall be paid to that person.

(2) The court may make an order under this section only if it is satisfied that but for the inadequacy of the offender's means it would have made a compensation order under which the offender would have been required to pay compensation of an amount not less than the specified amount.

(3) An order under this section has no effect—

(a) before the end of the period specified in section 144(1)(a) above; or

(b) if a successful application under section 1(1) of the *Police (Property) Act* 1897 has been made.

Scope of power

The power does not extend to real property: *R. v. Khan (Sultan Ashraf)* [1984] 1 W.L.R. 1405, CA. As to the time of apprehension, and the concepts of "possession" and "control", see *R. v. Hinde*, 64 Cr.App.R. 213, CA. **5–442**

Relation of property to offence

Section 143 requires that the property concerned should have been used, or intended to be used, to commit or facilitate the commission of any offence (not necessarily the offence of which the offender has been convicted); facilitation includes taking steps to dispose of stolen property or avoid conviction. Orders have been upheld in respect of vehicles used to transport stolen property by persons convicted of handling (see *R. v. Lidster* [1976] R.T.R. 240, and *R. v. Brown*, unreported, February 28, 1974), but an order was quashed in a case where a girl who was given a lift in a car was indecently assaulted, apparently on the basis that the offence was not shown to have been intended when the girl got into the car (*R. v. Lucas*, unreported, July 4, 1975). Money found in the possession of a person, convicted of supplying a controlled drug, and found to be his working capital for future purchases of drugs was held to be within the scope of the section in *R. v. Farrell*, 10 Cr.App.R.(S.) 74, CA. The power is not available in respect of property which has been used by persons other than the offender to commit offences: *R. v. Slater*, 8 Cr.App.R.(S.) 217, CA; *R. v. Neville*, 9 Cr.App.R.(S.) 222, CA. *Aliter*, if the property was used by another to facilitate the commission of an offence by the offender: *R. v. Coleville-Scott*, 12 Cr.App.R.(S.) 238, CA. **5–443**

An order depriving the offender of his rights in a motor vehicle may be made on his conviction for driving while disqualified, provided that the other requirements of section 143 are satisfied: *R. v. Highbury Corner Stipendiary Magistrates' Court, ex p. Di Matteo*, 92 Cr.App.R. 263, DC. (See now section 143(6) and (7), which may restrict the power in relation to offences under the *RTA* 1988 to those punishable with imprisonment.)

The court should not make an order unless there is adequate supporting evidence: *R. v. Pemberton*, 4 Cr.App.R.(S.) 328, CA.

Relationship of deprivation order to other sentences

An order under section 143 is to be viewed as part of the total penalty imposed for the offence; if a deprivation order is made in conjunction with a sentence of imprisonment or a substantial fine, there is a risk of "overdoing the punishment" (*per* Park J. in *R. v. Buddo*, 4 Cr.App.R.(S.) 268, DC). See also *R. v. Scully*, 7 Cr.App.R.(S.) 119, CA; *R. v. Joyce*, 11 Cr.App.R.(S.) 253, CA; *R. v. Thompson*, 66 Cr.App.R. 130, CA; and *R. v. Priestley* [1996] 2 Cr.App.R.(S.) 144, CA. **5–444**

In *ex p. Di Matteo, ante*, Watkins L.J. said that a court considering whether to make an order under section 143 should have regard to the totality principle and the two matters specifically set out in subsection (5)—the value of the property concerned and the likely financial and other effects on the offender of making the order, taken together with any other order which the court contemplated making.

Hardship to offender

An order under section 143 may be inappropriate where it would result in unusual hardship, *e.g.* vehicles adapted for the use of disabled drivers: see *R. v. Tavernor*, unreported, April 4, 1974; *R. v. Bucholz*, unreported, May 10, 1974. **5–445**

Disparity of sentence

Where co-defendants are equally culpable and receive the same custodial sentence, an order under section 143 against one of them only will constitute an additional **5–446** penalty and may give rise to legitimate complaint on the ground of disparity: *R. v. Ottey*, 6 Cr.App.R.(S.) 163, CA; but this principle should not be taken too far: see *R. v. Burgess* [2001] 2 Cr.App.R.(S.) 2, CA.

Property subject to multiple ownership

5–447 In *R. v. Troth*, 1 Cr.App.R.(S.) 341, CA, Wien J. observed that "forfeiture orders ought not to be made except in simple uncomplicated cases." Difficulties would arise where the property was subject to encumbrances, and it might be appropriate to impose "an increased financial penalty ... in lieu of making a forfeiture order". The case concerned partnership property.

Value of the property and the likely financial effects of the order on the offender (s.143(5))

5–448 In *ex p. Di Matteo*, *ante*, the Divisional Court quashed an order on the grounds that the court did not have sufficient information before it to comply with the obligation under subsection (5)(a). The effect of this decision appears to be that in any case where an item of substantial value is to be the subject of an order under section 143, the sentencer must have some information about its value, unless the property is such that the sentencer can form a fair estimate of its value without evidence.

B. CONFISCATION UNDER THE DRUG TRAFFICKING ACT 1994

5–449 The confiscation provisions of the *DTA* 1994 have been repealed and replaced by Part 2 of the *PCA* 2002. Part 2 came into force on March 24, 2003: *Proceeds of Crime Act 2002 (Commencement No. 5, Transitional Provisions, Savings and Amendment) Order* 2003 (S.I. 2003 No. 333) (§§ 5–663 *et seq.* in the supplement). Article 3 of this order provides, however, that section 6 (confiscation orders) shall not have effect where the offence, or any of the offences, mentioned in section 6(2) of the Act was committed before March 24, 2003; that section 27 (defendant convicted or committed absconds) shall not have effect where the offence, or any of the offences, mentioned in section 27(2) was committed before that date; and that section 28 (defendant neither convicted nor acquitted absconds) shall not have effect where the offence, or any of the offences, in respect of which proceedings have been started but not concluded was committed before that date. Article 5 provides that sections 41 (restraint orders) and 74 (enforcement abroad) shall not have effect where the powers in those sections would otherwise be exercisable by virtue of a condition in section 40(2) or (3) of the Act being satisfied, and the offence mentioned in section 40(2)(a) or 40(3)(a), as the case may be, was committed before that date. Article 10 provides that where under article 3 or 5 a provision of the Act does not have effect, various provisions of the former law shall continue to have effect. Among the listed provisions are sections 1 to 36 and 41 of the 1994 Act.

It follows that the confiscation provisions of the 1994 Act will continue to operate for an indefinite period. Space prohibits the inclusion of the whole of the old law and the new law in this work. Those needing to refer to the former legislation will find it in the 2003 edition of this work, and in the supplements to the 2004 edition. New case law will be noted in the supplements.

C. CONFISCATION UNDER THE CRIMINAL JUSTICE ACT 1988

5–450 The confiscation provisions of Part VI of the *CJA* 1988 have been repealed and replaced by Part 2 of the *PCA* 2002. As to the commencement, transitional and saving provisions, see *ante*, § 5–449. Sections 71 to 89 and 102 of the 1988 Act are, however, among the provisions listed in article 10 of S.I. 2003 No. 333 as continuing to have effect where the provisions of the 2002 Act mentioned in articles 3 and 5 do not have effect. It follows that the provisions of the 1988 Act will continue to operate for an indefinite period. As in the case of the drug trafficking provisions (*ante*, § 5–449), space prohibits inclusion of the old law and the new law in this work. As with the drug trafficking legislation, those needing to refer to the 1988 legislation will find it in the 2003 edition of this work, and in the supplements to the 2004 edition. As with the 1994 legislation (*ante*), new case law will continue to be collected in the supplement.

[The next paragraph is § 5–527.]

D. CONFISCATION UNDER THE PROCEEDS OF CRIME ACT 2002

(1) Summary

Royal Assent, commencement, etc.

The *PCA* 2002 received Royal Assent on July 24, 2002. The confiscation provisions were brought into force on March 24, 2003, by the *Proceeds of Crime Act 2002 (Commencement No. 5, Transitional Provisions, Savings and Amendment) Order* 2003 (S.I. 2003 No. 333). For the details of this order, see §§ 5–663 *et seq.* in the supplement. In essence, the new regime applies only in respect of offences committed on or after that date. As to the limited application of the Act to investigations of offences committed before the commencement date, see *Re Hill (Restraint order), post*, § 5–602. As to the continued application of the former legislation where the new regime does not have effect, see *ante*, §§ 5–449, 5–450. **5–527**

As to the relationship of the new legislation to that which it replaces, see *post*, § 5–766. **5–528**

Outline of Act

The Act is divided into 12 parts consisting of 462 sections and 12 schedules. Part 2 (ss.6– 91) is concerned with confiscation orders in criminal proceedings (see *post*, §§ 5–566 *et seq.*). Parts 3 and 4 relate to Scotland and Northern Ireland respectively. Part 5 (ss.240– 316) makes provision for the recovery of the proceeds of unlawful conduct in civil proceedings. Part 6 (ss.317– 326) makes provison in relation to the functions of the Inland Revenue. Part 7 (ss.327– 340) creates the new money laundering offences: see Chapter 26, *post*. Part 8 (ss.341– 416) makes provision in relation to investigations. These provisions, other than sections 380 to 412 which relate to Scotland, are set out in Chapter 15, *post*, §§ 15–271 *et seq*. The provisions of Parts 10 (ss.435– 442 (information)), 11 (ss.443– 447 (co-operation)) and 12 (ss.448– 462 (miscellaneous and general)) are dealt with to the extent necessary, as and where it is appropriate. **5–529**

Key provisions

Confiscation orders (s.6)

To be liable to confiscation proceedings under the legislation as originally enacted, the defendant must either have been convicted of an offence in proceedings before the Crown Court, committed to the Crown Court for sentence under the *PCC(S)A* 2000, ss.3, 4 or 6, or committed to the Crown Court under section 70 of this Act (*post*, § 5–631). So far as confiscation is concerned, the power under which the defendant has been committed for sentence appears to make no difference, but it will affect the powers of the Crown Court in respect of the principal sentence for the offence. **5–530**

If the defendant is liable to confiscation proceedings, the court must proceed with a view to a confiscation order if it is asked to do so either by the prosecutor, or if the court believes "it is appropriate for it to do so". If the defendant absconds, there is no power to proceed under section 6 (see s.6(8)), but the court may proceed under section 27. The Act is unclear as to the procedure to be followed where a defendant absconds after the court has embarked on confiscation proceedings under section 6.

The mandatory requirements of section 6 are qualified by subsection (6), which permits the Crown Court not to make the decisions required by subsection (5) if it believes that any victim of the offence has initiated, or intends to initiate, civil proceedings against the defendant.

Section 97 of the *SOCPA* 2005 empowers the Secretary of State to make such provision as he considers appropriate for, or in connection with, enabling confiscation orders under Part 2 of the 2002 Act to be made by magistrates' courts in England and Wales and Northern Ireland; but no such order may be made in a sum in excess of £10,000.

Criminal lifestyle (s.6(4)(a), (b))

5–531 Where the Crown Court embarks on confiscation proceedings, it must first decide whether the defendant has a "criminal lifestyle" within section 75 (*post*, § 5–636). A person has a "criminal lifestyle" if either he is convicted of one of the offences specified in Schedule 2, or the offence constitutes "conduct forming part of a course of criminal activity", or was committed over a period of at least six months and the defendant has benefited from the conduct. Important transitional provisions in this connection are contained in article 7 of S.I. 2003 No. 333 (§ 5–663 in the supplement).

If the court decides that the defendant has a "criminal lifestyle", it must decide whether he has benefited from his "general criminal conduct". "General criminal conduct" is defined as "all his criminal conduct", whether occurring before or after the passing of the Act or whether property constituting a benefit from conduct was obtained before or after the passing of the Act (s.76(2)).

For the purpose of deciding whether a defendant with a criminal lifestyle has benefited from his general criminal conduct and, if he has, the extent of his benefit, the court is required to make various assumptions by section 10, unless the assumption is "shown to be incorrect" or there would be a "serious risk of injustice" if the assumption were made. If the court decides that the defendant has a criminal lifestyle and has benefited from his general criminal conduct, it must determine the "recoverable amount" for the purposes of section 7 by taking the benefit from the general criminal conduct as the starting point for calculation, and then making any reduction required by section 7(2) where the available amount is less than the benefit.

5–532 **Offence constituting "conduct forming part of a course of criminal activity".** Conduct forms part of a course of criminal activity in two cases only. The first is that the defendant has benefited from the conduct and in the proceedings in which he was convicted he was convicted of three or more other offences and each of three or more of them constituted conduct from which he has benefited. The second is that the defendant has benefited from the conduct and in the period of six years ending with the day when the proceedings in which he was convicted were started he was convicted on at least two separate occasions of an offence constituting conduct from which he has benefited.

In neither case will the test be satisfied, however, unless the relevant benefit is at least £5,000 (s.75(4)). In essence, "relevant benefit" is any benefit from the conduct constituting the offence, any benefit from conduct constituting an offence to be taken into consideration, and any benefit from conduct forming part of the course of criminal activity and constituting an offence of which the defendant has been convicted (s.75(5)).

5–533 As to whether offences committed before March 24, 2003, may be taken into account for these purposes, see article 7 of the *Proceeds of Crime Act 2002 (Commencement No. 5, Transitional Provisions, Savings and Amendment) Order* 2003 (S.I. 2003 No. 333) (§ 5–667 in the supplement).

5–534 **Offence committed over a period of six months.** A defendant will have a criminal lifestyle if he has been convicted of an offence committed over a period of at least six months, and from which he has benefited. Again, the relevant benefit must be at least £5,000. The "relevant benefit" is any benefit from the conduct constituting the offence, together with any benefit from conduct constituting an offence to be taken into consideration (s.75(6)); but excluding offences taken into consideration which were committed before March 24, 2003 (see art. 7(6) of S.I. 2003 No. 333, *ante*).

The assumptions (s.10)

5–535 If the court decides that the defendant has a criminal lifestyle, it must make four assumptions for the purpose of deciding whether he has benefited from his "general criminal conduct" (*i.e.* "all his criminal conduct" before or after the passing of the Act—see s.76(2)), and the amount of his benefit. The court has no discretion as to whether or not to make an assumption, but it must not make an assumption if it is shown to be incorrect or there would be a serious risk of injustice if it were made (s.10(6)). It seems clear that the burden of showing that an assumption is incorrect falls on the defendant. In respect of the second exception, no burden of proof being provided for, it is submitted that it is a matter for the court to determine in the exercise of its discretion whether there is a serious risk of injustice.

The substance of the four assumptions is closely based on the earlier legislation. The first is that any property transferred to the defendant within the period of six years ending on the day on which proceedings were started was obtained by him as a result of his general criminal conduct. The second is that any property held by him at any time after the date of conviction was obtained by him as a result of his general criminal conduct, and at the earliest time at which he appears to have held it. The third is that any expenditure incurred by him within a period of six years ending with the date on which the proceedings were started against him was met from property obtained by him as a result of his general criminal conduct. The fourth is that any property obtained or assumed to have been obtained by the defendant was free of any other interest in the property. Where the defendant has been subject to an earlier confiscation order made under the "general criminal conduct" provisions or their equivalent, the relevant period begins on the day the previous calculation of benefit was made, if that order was made within the six year period.

Non-criminal lifestyle (s.6(4)(c))

If the court decides that the defendant does not have a criminal lifestyle, it must then decide whether the defendant has benefited from his "particular criminal conduct". This is defined as "all his criminal conduct" which constitutes "the offence or offences concerned", or "offences of which he was convicted in the same proceedings as those in which he was convicted of the offence or offences concerned", or "offences which the court will be taking into consideration in deciding his sentence for the offence or offences concerned." This definition does not include uncharged offences which are represented by specimen counts in an indictment, unless they are specifically listed and the court is asked to take them into consideration under the conventional procedure for doing so. As to conduct occurring prior to March 24, 2003, see S.I. 2003 No. 333 (§ 5–668 in the supplement). **5–536**

In determining whether the defendant has benefited from his "particular criminal conduct" the court may not make any of assumptions under section 10, but it may order the defendant to give the court "information specified in the order" (s.18). If the defendant fails to comply, the court may "draw such inference as it believes is appropriate" (s.18(4)).

Standard of proof (s.6(7))

Any question arising in connection with whether the defendant has a criminal lifestyle or has benefited from his criminal conduct must be decided on a "balance of probabilities" (s.6(7)). **5–537**

Statements of information (s.16)

If the Crown Court is acting on the application of the prosecutor, the prosecutor must give the court a statement of information within a period specified by the court. If the court is acting on its own initiative, it may order the prosecutor to give such a statement within a specified period. **5–538**

If the prosecutor believes that the defendant has a criminal lifestyle, the statement must include matters which the prosecutor believes are relevant in connection with deciding whether the defendant has a criminal lifestyle, whether he has benefited from his general criminal conduct, and his benefit from the conduct. The statement must include information relevant to the making of the required assumptions. This will normally consist of information relating to the defendant's assets or his expenditure and receipts during the six-year period specified in section 10(8).

In other cases, the statement is limited to information relating to whether the defendant has benefited from his particular criminal conduct, and the amount of his benefit.

Further statements of information may be given, and the court may direct a further statement to be given.

Defendant's response (s.17)

5–539 Where a statement of information has been given to the court and a copy served on the defendant, the court may order the defendant to indicate to what extent he accepts the allegations made therein, and in so far as he does not accept an allegation, "to give particulars of any matters he proposes to rely on." If the defendant accepts any allegation, the court may treat that as conclusive. If he fails to comply with an order, he may be treated as accepting every allegation in the statement of information other than an allegation in respect of which he has complied with the requirement, or an allegation that he has benefited from his criminal conduct.

No acceptance of an allegation by the defendant that he has benefited from conduct is admissible in evidence in proceedings for an offence.

Orders requiring the defendant to provide information (s.18)

5–540 Where the Crown Court is proceeding with a view to a confiscation order, or is considering whether to proceed on its own initiative, it may order the defendant to give it "information specified in the order". There is no restriction on the kind of information that may be specified. If the defendant fails "without reasonable excuse" to comply with an order, the court "may draw such inference as it believes is appropriate" from the failure.

No information given in response to an order under the section which amounts to an admission by the defendant that he has benefited from criminal conduct is admissible in evidence in proceedings for an offence. This provision, which is new, may well affect the matters which may be put forward by the defendant as a "reasonable excuse" under subsection (4) for failing to comply with the court's order.

Postponement (s.14)

5–541 The postponement powers in the former legislation (*DTA* 1994, s.3, *CJA* 1988 s.72A) led to many difficulties. This provision, which must be read in conjunction with section 15, is derived from those sections, although with substantial changes. It makes no assumption that the court will deal with confiscation matters before sentence. The court is given the option to deal with confiscation matters before it sentences the defendant, or to postpone them for a specified period. The assumption of the earlier legislation that confiscation would come first is not repeated, but it is clear that the court must address the question of confiscation before sentencing the defendant and either proceed with the confiscation hearing under subsection (1)(a) prior to sentence, or postpone confiscation under subsection (1)(b), and proceed to sentence. The court may not sentence the defendant without making any reference to confiscation, and then deal with confiscation matters on a subsequent occasion, but a confiscation order must not be quashed only on the ground that there was a defect or omission in the procedure connected with the application for or granting of a postponement (s.14(11), *post*).

The permissible postponement period is increased from six months to two years from conviction. In "exceptional circumstances" a longer period may be specified (s.14(4)). Section 14(6) makes provision for the extension of the permitted period where there is an appeal against conviction.

Postponement, or an extension thereof, may be ordered on the application of either party or by the court of its own motion. An application for an extension made during an existing period of postponement may be granted after the period of postponement has ended. It is not clear whether the court acting of its own motion may extend a period of postponement, where no application has been made within an existing period, after that period has ended.

A confiscation order must not be quashed on the ground that there was a defect or omission in the procedure connected with the application for or granting of a postponement (s.14(11)).

The recoverable amount (s.7)

The "recoverable amount" for the purposes of section 6 is an amount equal to the defendant's benefit from the conduct concerned (s.7(1)), and the court must make an order for that amount, unless either it exercises the discretion given by section 6(6) (*ante*, § 5–530), or the defendant shows that the "available amount" is less than the benefit. Section 9 provides that the "available amount" is the total value of all "free property" (see s.82) held by the defendant at the time the confiscation order is made, and of all "tainted gifts" (see s.77). **5–542**

Where the court exercises its discretion under section 6(6), the recoverable amount is such amount "as the court believes is just", but it must not exceed the amount of the defendant's benefit. If the defendant shows that the available amount is less than his benefit, the recoverable amount is either the available amount, or a nominal amount if the available amount is nil.

If the court decides the available amount, it must include in the confiscation order a statement of its findings as to the matters relevant to its decision. This statement will be of particular importance if an application is subsequently made under section 22 or 23 for reconsideration of the amount.

The available amount (s.9)

The "available amount" is the sum of two calculations. The first is the total value at the time the confiscation order is made of all the "free property" held by the defendant (see s.82), minus the total amount payable in pursuance of "obligations which then have priority". Obligations having priority are obligations to pay orders made by criminal courts upon conviction and obligations to pay any sum which would be included among the preferential debts of the defendant if he had been made bankrupt on the date on which the confiscation order was made (s.9(2)). Other general debts of the defendant are not "obligations which then have priority". Where, however, another person holds an interest in property held by the defendant, the value of the property in relation to the defendant is the market value of his interest at the time (ignoring charging orders under specified statutory provisions) (s.79), so that the practical effect is much the same. **5–543**

The second calculation is the value of all "tainted gifts" (see s.77). If a court has decided that the defendant has a criminal lifestyle, or if no court has made a decision as to that, a gift is "tainted" if it was made by the defendant at any time after the "relevant day", *i.e.* the first day of the period of six years ending on the day when the proceedings for the offence concerned were started. If the gift was made outside that period, it is "tainted" if it was a gift of property which was obtained by the defendant as a result of or in connection with his general criminal conduct, or which directly or indirectly represented in his hands property so obtained by him.

If a court has decided that the defendant does not have a criminal lifestyle, a gift is tainted if it was made by the defendant at any time after the date on which the offence (or the earliest of the offences, including any offences taken into consideration) which constitutes his particular criminal conduct was committed. If the offence was a continuing offence, the offence is treated as having been committed on the first occasion when it was committed.

A "gift" includes any transfer of property for a consideration of significantly less value than the value of the property transferred at the time of the transfer (s.78(1)). In such a case, the "gift" is that share of the property transferred as is determined in accordance with the formula in section 78(2). In simple terms, if the property is transferred for half its value, the gift is a half share in the property. Having identified any tainted gifts, they then need to be valued under section 82.

Property and its valuation (ss.79–84)

"Realisable property" is any "free property" held by the defendant or by the **5–544** recipient of a tainted gift (s.83). There is therefore no requirement that the property has any connection with the offence or the tainted gift. Property is "free" unless it is subject to one of the orders mentioned in section 82 (forfeiture, deprivation, *etc.*).

"Property" is all property wherever situated (s.84(1)). The value of property held by a person at any time is the market value of his interest in it at that time (but ignoring charging orders under specified statutory provisions) (s.79).

The provisions of section 79 as to the valuation of property are subject to section 80 which applies for the purpose of deciding the value of property obtained by a person as a result of or in connection with his criminal conduct. The value of such property at the time the court makes its decision is the greater of (a) the value of the property at the time the person obtained it, adjusted to take account of changes in the value of money, or (b) the value at the time the court makes its decision of the property "found" under subsection (3). Property "found" under subsection (3) is the property obtained or any part of it which is still held by the person who obtained it, or property in the hands of that person which directly or indirectly represents that property.

If the defendant has obtained cash as a result of or in connection with his criminal conduct, the normal procedure will be to take the cash obtained as the basis of the determination and adjust it to take account of later changes in the value of money. If shares have been obtained and are still held by the defendant, the court must value the shares at the time they were obtained, adjust that figure to take account of changes in the value of money and adopt that as the value of the property obtained where it is greater than the current value of the shares.

If a defendant has obtained real property as a result of or in connection with criminal conduct, and still holds that property, the value of the property is its value at the time the confiscation order is made, notwithstanding that this figure represents a large increase over the value at the time it was obtained, and that the figure represents a greater increase than would be produced by adjusting the original value of the property to take account of changes in the value of money. The same would apply where the original property has been sold and the proceeds applied to the purchase of another property. Where, however, the defendant has mortgaged the property, so as to reduce his equity to a figure below the value at the time he obtained it, adjusted for inflation, the latter figure will be taken as the value of the property he obtained.

There is some uncertainty as to the correct approach where the defendant obtains cash as a result of or in connection with his criminal conduct, and uses the cash to purchase property, which then increases in value faster than the rate of inflation. There are three possible solutions. The first is take the cash figure and adjust it for inflation. The second is to say that the property purchased was obtained "as a result of or in connection with" the defendant's criminal conduct, and then apply the rule in section 80(2). The third is to say that whilst the property purchased was not itself obtained as a result of or in connection with the defendant's criminal conduct, it nevertheless represents such property in his hands. In this case, the value would be the greater of the cash adjusted for inflation or the current value of the defendant's interest in the property. Whether property has been obtained as a result of or in connection with the defendant's criminal conduct is a question of fact, but it would seem likely that where stolen cash or cash obtained from the unlawful supply of drugs is used to finance the purchase of property, the court would conclude that the property had been so obtained. Such conclusion is certainly consistent with the assumptions in section 10 (albeit they only apply to criminal lifestyle cases).

Sentencing the defendant for the offence (ss.13–15, 71)

5–545 If the court postpones the confiscation proceedings under section 14, it may sentence the defendant in the normal way, but must not make any of the orders specified in subsection (2) (fine, compensation, forfeiture, etc.). Where the defendant has been sentenced during the postponement period, the sentence may be varied by the addition of one of the prohibited orders within 28 days starting with the last day of the period of postponement (s.14(3), (4)). The 28-day time limit may cause difficulty where the period of postponement ends on the day upon which the confiscation proceedings begin, but those proceedings last longer than 28 days.

Where a sentence is varied under section 14, the sentence is to be regarded as having been imposed on the date of the variation, for the purpose of time limits relating to appeal. This provision effectively gives the defendant a right to a second appeal against sentence.

If the Crown Court makes a confiscation order before sentencing the defendant, it must, when sentencing the defendant, take account of the order before imposing a fine, making any order involving payment by the defendant other than a compensation order, or any of the other orders of forfeiture or deprivation specified in section 13(3): s.13(2). A confiscation order may, however, be left out of account in deciding whether to make a compensation order, and in deciding its amount. It is open to the Crown Court to make a confiscation order and a compensation order in respect of the same offence, even though this means that the defendant will be required to pay twice the amount involved in the offence.

Subject to this, in deciding the appropriate sentence for the offence, the confiscation order must be left out of account. The defendant cannot claim that his sentence should be mitigated because a confiscation order has been made.

If the defendant has been committed for sentence under section 70 for an either way offence, the powers of the Crown Court to deal with the offender for the offence depend on whether the magistrates' court at the time of committal stated in accordance with section 70(5) that it would have committed the defendant for sentence under the *PCC(S)A* 2000, s.3 (*ante*, § 5–24). If it did, the Crown Court may deal with the defendant in any way in which it could deal with him if he had just been convicted of the offence on indictment.

If the magistrates' court did not make a statement under section 70(5) in respect of an either way offence, or the offence is not an either way offence, the Crown Court, having inquired into the circumstances of the case, may deal with the defendant in any way in which the magistrates' court could deal with him if it had just convicted him of the offence. The Crown Court must observe all the restrictions on the powers of magistrates' courts, including, in particular, those in the *MCA* 1980, s.133 (consecutive terms of imprisonment (*ante*, § 5–270)).

Committal under section 70

Section 70, which supplements the *PCC(S)A* 2000, s.3, appears to have two distinct **5–546**
purposes. In respect of cases where a magistrates' court would be entitled, in its discretion, to commit a defendant for sentence under section 3, this section obliges the magistrates' court to commit the defendant if the prosecutor asks the court to commit the defendant with a view to a confiscation order being considered.

The second objective is to provide for the committal for sentence of defendants who have been convicted of summary offences and who are not eligible for committal for sentence. Where a magistrates' court commits a defendant under this section in respect of an offence or offences, it may commit him in respect of other offences of which he has been convicted and in respect of which the magistrates' court has power to deal with him, whether or not any question of confiscation arises in respect of those offences.

If the case is one in which the magistrates' court would have had power to commit the defendant for sentence under section 3 of the Act of 2000, the court must state whether it would have done so. The Crown Court's powers vary according to whether or not such statement is made (*ante*, § 5–545).

[The next paragraph is § 5–566.]

(2) Legislation

(a) *Statute*

Proceeds of Crime Act 2002, ss.6–91

PART 2

CONFISCATION: ENGLAND AND WALES

Confiscation orders

Making of order

5–566 **6.**—(1) The Crown Court must proceed under this section if the following two conditions are satisfied.

(2) The first condition is that a defendant falls within any of the following paragraphs—

(a) he is convicted of an offence or offences in proceedings before the Crown Court;

(b) he is committed to the Crown Court for sentence in respect of an offence or offences under *section 3, 4, or 6* [section 3, 3A, 3B, 3C, 4, 4A or 6] of the *Sentencing Act*;

(c) he is committed to the Crown Court in respect of an offence or offences under section 70 below (committal with a view to a confiscation order being considered).

(3) The second condition is that—

(a) the prosecutor asks the court to proceed under this section, or

(b) the court believes it is appropriate for it to do so.

(4) The court must proceed as follows—

(a) it must decide whether the defendant has a criminal lifestyle;

(b) if it decides that he has a criminal lifestyle it must decide whether he has benefited from his general criminal conduct;

(c) if it decides that he does not have a criminal lifestyle it must decide whether he has benefited from his particular criminal conduct.

(5) If the court decides under subsection (4)(b) or (c) that the defendant has benefited from the conduct referred to it must—

(a) decide the recoverable amount, and

(b) make an order (a confiscation order) requiring him to pay that amount.

(6) But the court must treat the duty in subsection (5) as a power if it believes that any victim of the conduct has at any time started or intends to start proceedings against the defendant in respect of loss, injury or damage sustained in connection with the conduct.

(7) The court must decide any question arising under subsection (4) or (5) on a balance of probabilities.

(8) The first condition is not satisfied if the defendant absconds (but section 27 may apply).

(9) References in this Part to the offence (or offences) concerned are to the offence (or offences) mentioned in subsection (2).

[This section is printed as amended by the *SCA* 2007, ss.74(2) and 92, Sched. 8, paras 1 and 2, and Sched. 14; and as amended, as from a day to be appointed, by the *CJA* 2003, s.41, and Sched. 3, para. 75(1) and (2) (substitution of words in square brackets for italicised words that precede them).]

As to the lack of discretion under this section, see *post*, § 5–767a. As to the duty of a prosecutor/victim who intends to take civil action against the defendant to make full disclosure of this fact to the court, see *Revenue and Customs Commrs v. Crossman* [2008] 1 All E.R. 483, Ch D (Rimer J.).

Recoverable amount

5–567 **7.**—(1) The recoverable amount for the purposes of section 6 is an amount equal to the defendant's benefit from the conduct concerned.

(2) But if the defendant shows that the available amount is less than that benefit the recoverable amount is—

(a) the available amount, or

(b) a nominal amount, if the available amount is nil.

(3) But if section 6(6) applies the recoverable amount is such amount as—

(a) the court believes is just, but

(b) does not exceed the amount found under subsection (1) or (2) (as the case may be).

(4) In calculating the defendant's benefit from the conduct concerned for the purposes of subsection (1), any property in respect of which—

(a) a recovery order is in force under section 266, or

(b) a forfeiture order is in force under section 298(2),

must be ignored.

(5) If the court decides the available amount, it must include in the confiscation order a statement of its findings as to the matters relevant for deciding that amount.

Defendant's benefit

8.—(1) If the court is proceeding under section 6 this section applies for the purpose of— **5–568**

(a) deciding whether the defendant has benefited from conduct, and

(b) deciding his benefit from the conduct.

(2) The court must—

(a) take account of conduct occurring up to the time it makes its decision;

(b) take account of property obtained up to that time.

(3) Subsection (4) applies if—

(a) the conduct concerned is general criminal conduct,

(b) a confiscation order mentioned in subsection (5) has at an earlier time been made against the defendant, and

(c) his benefit for the purposes of that order was benefit from his general criminal conduct.

(4) His benefit found at the time the last confiscation order mentioned in subsection (3)(c) was made against him must be taken for the purposes of this section to be his benefit from his general criminal conduct at that time.

(5) If the conduct concerned is general criminal conduct the court must deduct the aggregate of the following amounts—

(a) the amount ordered to be paid under each confiscation order previously made against the defendant;

(b) the amount ordered to be paid under each confiscation order previously made against him under any of the provisions listed in subsection (7).

(6) But subsection (5) does not apply to an amount which has been taken into account for the purposes of a deduction under that subsection on any earlier occasion.

(7) These are the provisions—

(a) the *Drug Trafficking Offences Act* 1986;

(b) Part 1 of the *Criminal Justice (Scotland) Act* 1987;

(c) Part 6 of the *Criminal Justice Act* 1988;

(d) the *Criminal Justice (Confiscation) (Northern Ireland) Order* 1990 (S.I. 1990 No. 2588 (N.I. 17));

(e) Part 1 of the *Drug Trafficking Act* 1994;

(f) Part 1 of the *Proceeds of Crime (Scotland) Act* 1995;

(g) the *Proceeds of Crime (Northern Ireland) Order* 1996 (S.I. 1996 No. 1299 (N.I. 9));

(h) Part 3 or 4 of this Act.

(8) The reference to general criminal conduct in the case of a confiscation order made under any of the provisions listed in subsection (7) is a reference to conduct in respect of which a court is required or entitled to make one or more assumptions for the purpose of assessing a person's benefit from the conduct.

Available amount

9.—(1) For the purposes of deciding the recoverable amount, the available amount is the aggregate of— **5–569**

(a) the total of the values (at the time the confiscation order is made) of all the free property then held by the defendant minus the total amount payable in pursuance of obligations which then have priority, and

(b) the total of the values (at that time) of all tainted gifts.

(2) An obligation has priority if it is an obligation of the defendant—

(a) to pay an amount due in respect of a fine or other order of a court which was imposed or made on conviction of an offence and at any time before the time the confiscation order is made, or

(b) to pay a sum which would be included among the preferential debts if the defendant's bankruptcy had commenced on the date of the confiscation order or his winding up had been ordered on that date.

(3) "Preferential debts" has the meaning given by section 386 of the *Insolvency Act* 1986.

Assumptions to be made in case of criminal lifestyle

5–570 **10.**—(1) If the court decides under section 6 that the defendant has a criminal lifestyle it must make the following four assumptions for the purpose of—

(a) deciding whether he has benefited from his general criminal conduct, and

(b) deciding his benefit from the conduct.

(2) The first assumption is that any property transferred to the defendant at any time after the relevant day was obtained by him—

(a) as a result of his general criminal conduct, and

(b) at the earliest time he appears to have held it.

(3) The second assumption is that any property held by the defendant at any time after the date of conviction was obtained by him—

(a) as a result of his general criminal conduct, and

(b) at the earliest time he appears to have held it.

(4) The third assumption is that any expenditure incurred by the defendant at any time after the relevant day was met from property obtained by him as a result of his general criminal conduct.

(5) The fourth assumption is that, for the purpose of valuing any property obtained (or assumed to have been obtained) by the defendant, he obtained it free of any other interests in it.

(6) But the court must not make a required assumption in relation to particular property or expenditure if—

(a) the assumption is shown to be incorrect, or

(b) there would be a serious risk of injustice if the assumption were made.

(7) If the court does not make one or more of the required assumptions it must state its reasons.

(8) The relevant day is the first day of the period of six years ending with—

(a) the day when proceedings for the offence concerned were started against the defendant, or

(b) if there are two or more offences and proceedings for them were started on different days, the earliest of those days.

(9) But if a confiscation order mentioned in section 8(3)(c) has been made against the defendant at any time during the period mentioned in subsection (8)—

(a) the relevant day is the day when the defendant's benefit was calculated for the purposes of the last such confiscation order;

(b) the second assumption does not apply to any property which was held by him on or before the relevant day.

(10) The date of conviction is—

(a) the date on which the defendant was convicted of the offence concerned, or

(b) if there are two or more offences and the convictions were on different dates, the date of the latest.

Time for payment

5–571 **11.**—(1) The amount ordered to be paid under a confiscation order must be paid on the making of the order; but this is subject to the following provisions of this section.

(2) If the defendant shows that he needs time to pay the amount ordered to be paid, the court making the confiscation order may make an order allowing payment to be made in a specified period.

(3) The specified period—

(a) must start with the day on which the confiscation order is made, and

(b) must not exceed six months.

(4) If within the specified period the defendant applies to the Crown Court for the period to be extended and the court believes there are exceptional circumstances, it may make an order extending the period.

(5) The extended period—

(a) must start with the day on which the confiscation order is made, and

(b) must not exceed 12 months.

(6) An order under subsection (4)—

(a) may be made after the end of the specified period, but

(b) must not be made after the end of the period of 12 months starting with the day on which the confiscation order is made.

(7) The court must not make an order under subsection (2) or (4) unless it gives—

(a) the prosecutor, …

an opportunity to make representations.

[This section is printed as amended by the *SCA* 2007, ss.74(2) and 92, Sched. 8, paras 1 and 3, and Sched. 14.]

Interest on unpaid sums

12.—(1) If the amount required to be paid by a person under a confiscation order is not paid when it is required to be paid, he must pay interest on the amount for the period for which it remains unpaid. **5–572**

(2) The rate of interest is the same rate as that for the time being specified in section 17 of the *Judgments Act* 1838 (interest on civil judgment debts).

(3) For the purposes of this section no amount is required to be paid under a confiscation order if—

(a) an application has been made under section 11(4),

(b) the application has not been determined by the court, and

(c) the period of 12 months starting with the day on which the confiscation order was made has not ended.

(4) In applying this Part the amount of the interest must be treated as part of the amount to be paid under the confiscation order.

Effect of order on court's other powers

13.—(1) If the court makes a confiscation order it must proceed as mentioned in subsections (2) and (4) in respect of the offence or offences concerned. **5–573**

(2) The court must take account of the confiscation order before—

(a) it imposes a fine on the defendant, or

(b) it makes an order falling within subsection (3).

(3) These orders fall within this subsection—

(a) an order involving payment by the defendant, other than an order under section 130 of the *Sentencing Act* (compensation orders);

(b) an order under section 27 of the *Misuse of Drugs Act* 1971 (forfeiture orders);

(c) an order under section 143 of the *Sentencing Act* (deprivation orders);

(d) an order under section 23 of the *Terrorism Act* 2000 (forfeiture orders).

(4) Subject to subsection (2), the court must leave the confiscation order out of account in deciding the appropriate sentence for the defendant.

(5) Subsection (6) applies if—

(a) the Crown Court makes both a confiscation order and an order for the payment of compensation under section 130 of the *Sentencing Act* against the same person in the same proceedings, and

(b) the court believes he will not have sufficient means to satisfy both the orders in full.

(6) In such a case the court must direct that so much of the compensation as it specifies is to be paid out of any sums recovered under the confiscation order; and the amount it specifies must be the amount it believes will not be recoverable because of the insufficiency of the person's means.

Procedural matters

Postponement

14.—(1) The court may— **5–574**

(a) proceed under section 6 before it sentences the defendant for the offence (or any of the offences) concerned, or

(b) postpone proceedings under section 6 for a specified period.

(2) A period of postponement may be extended.

(3) A period of postponement (including one as extended) must not end after the permitted period ends.

(4) But subsection (3) does not apply if there are exceptional circumstances.

(5) The permitted period is the period of two years starting with the date of conviction.

(6) But if—

(a) the defendant appeals against his conviction for the offence (or any of the offences) concerned, and

(b) the period of three months (starting with the day when the appeal is determined or otherwise disposed of) ends after the period found under subsection (5),

the permitted period is that period of three months.

(7) A postponement or extension may be made—

(a) on application by the defendant;

(b) on application by the prosecutor;

(c) by the court of its own motion.

(8) If—

(a) proceedings are postponed for a period, and

(b) an application to extend the period is made before it ends,

the application may be granted even after the period ends.

(9) The date of conviction is—

(a) the date on which the defendant was convicted of the offence concerned, or

(b) if there are two or more offences and the convictions were on different dates, the date of the latest.

(10) References to appealing include references to applying under section 111 of the *Magistrates' Courts Act* 1980 (statement of case).

(11) A confiscation order must not be quashed only on the ground that there was a defect or omission in the procedure connected with the application for or the granting of a postponement.

(12) But subsection (11) does not apply if before it made the confiscation order the court—

(a) imposed a fine on the defendant;

(b) made an order falling within section 13(3);

(c) made an order under section 130 of the *Sentencing Act* (compensation orders).

[This section is printed as amended by the *SCA* 2007, ss.74(2) and 92, Sched. 8, paras 1 and 4, and Sched. 14.]

Effect of postponement

5–575 **15.**—(1) If the court postpones proceedings under section 6 it may proceed to sentence the defendant for the offence (or any of the offences) concerned.

(2) In sentencing the defendant for the offence (or any of the offences) concerned in the postponement period the court must not—

(a) impose a fine on him,

(b) make an order falling within section 13(3), or

(c) make an order for the payment of compensation under section 130 of the *Sentencing Act*.

(3) If the court sentences the defendant for the offence (or any of the offences) concerned in the postponement period, after that period ends it may vary the sentence by—

(a) imposing a fine on him,

(b) making an order falling within section 13(3), or

(c) making an order for the payment of compensation under section 130 of the *Sentencing Act*.

(4) But the court may proceed under subsection (3) only within the period of 28 days which starts with the last day of the postponement period.

(5) For the purposes of—

(a) section 18(2) of the *Criminal Appeal Act* 1968 (time limit for notice of appeal or of application for leave to appeal), and

(b) paragraph 1 of Schedule 3 to the *Criminal Justice Act* 1988 (time limit for notice of application for leave to refer a case under section 36 of that Act),

the sentence must be regarded as imposed or made on the day on which it is varied under subsection (3).

(6) If the court proceeds to sentence the defendant under subsection (1), section 6 has effect as if the defendant's particular criminal conduct included conduct which constitutes offences which the court has taken into consideration in deciding his sentence for the offence or offences concerned.

(7) The postponement period is the period for which proceedings under section 6 are postponed.

In connection with this section, see *R. v. Donohoe*, *post*, § 5–767.

Statement of information

16.—(1) If the court is proceeding under section 6 in a case where section 6(3)(a) applies, the prosecutor must give the court a statement of information within the period the court orders. **5–576**

(2) If the court is proceeding under section 6 in a case where section 6(3)(b) applies and it orders the prosecutor to give it a statement of information, the prosecutor must give it such a statement within the period the court orders.

(3) If the prosecutor believes the defendant has a criminal lifestyle the statement of information is a statement of matters the prosecutor believes are relevant in connection with deciding these issues—

(a) whether the defendant has a criminal lifestyle;

(b) whether he has benefited from his general criminal conduct;

(c) his benefit from the conduct.

(4) A statement under subsection (3) must include information the prosecutor believes is relevant—

(a) in connection with the making by the court of a required assumption under section 10;

(b) for the purpose of enabling the court to decide if the circumstances are such that it must not make such an assumption.

(5) If the prosecutor does not believe the defendant has a criminal lifestyle the statement of information is a statement of matters the prosecutor believes are relevant in connection with deciding these issues—

(a) whether the defendant has benefited from his particular criminal conduct;

(b) his benefit from the conduct.

(6) If the prosecutor gives the court a statement of information—

(a) he may at any time give the court a further statement of information;

(b) he must give the court a further statement of information if it orders him to do so, and he must give it within the period the court orders.

(7) If the court makes an order under this section it may at any time vary it by making another one.

[This section is printed as amended by the *SCA* 2007, ss.74(2) and 92, Sched. 8, paras 1 and 5, and Sched. 14.]

Defendant's response to statement of information

17.—(1) If the prosecutor gives the court a statement of information and a copy is served on the defendant, the court may order the defendant— **5–577**

(a) to indicate (within the period it orders) the extent to which he accepts each allegation in the statement, and

(b) so far as he does not accept such an allegation, to give particulars of any matters he proposes to rely on.

(2) If the defendant accepts to any extent an allegation in a statement of information the court may treat his acceptance as conclusive of the matters to which it relates for the purpose of deciding the issues referred to in section 16(3) or (5) (as the case may be).

(3) If the defendant fails in any respect to comply with an order under subsection (1) he may be treated for the purposes of subsection (2) as accepting every allegation in the statement of information apart from—

(a) any allegation in respect of which he has complied with the requirement;

(b) any allegation that he has benefited from his general or particular criminal conduct.

(4) For the purposes of this section an allegation may be accepted or particulars may be given in a manner ordered by the court.

(5) If the court makes an order under this section it may at any time vary it by making another one.

(6) No acceptance under this section that the defendant has benefited from conduct is admissible in evidence in proceedings for an offence.

[This section is printed as amended by the *SCA* 2007, ss.74(2) and 92, Sched. 8, paras 1 and 6, and Sched. 14.]

[The next paragraph is § 5–579.]

Provision of information by defendant

5–579 **18.**—(1) This section applies if—

(a) the court is proceeding under section 6 in a case where section 6(3)(a) applies, or

(b) it is proceeding under section 6 in a case where section 6(3)(b) applies or it is considering whether to proceed.

(2) For the purpose of obtaining information to help it in carrying out its functions the court may at any time order the defendant to give it information specified in the order.

(3) An order under this section may require all or a specified part of the information to be given in a specified manner and before a specified date.

(4) If the defendant fails without reasonable excuse to comply with an order under this section the court may draw such inference as it believes is appropriate.

(5) Subsection (4) does not affect any power of the court to deal with the defendant in respect of a failure to comply with an order under this section.

(6) If the prosecutor accepts to any extent an allegation made by the defendant—

(a) in giving information required by an order under this section, or

(b) in any other statement given to the court in relation to any matter relevant to deciding the available amount under section 9,

the court may treat the acceptance as conclusive of the matters to which it relates.

(7), (8) [*Identical to s.16(4), (5),* ante.]

(9) No information given under this section which amounts to an admission by the defendant that he has benefited from criminal conduct is admissible in evidence in proceedings for an offence.

[This section is printed as amended by the *SCA* 2007, ss.74(2) and 92, Sched. 8, paras 1 and 7, and Sched. 14.]

Reconsideration

No order made: reconsideration of case

5–580 **19.**—(1) This section applies if—

(a) the first condition in section 6 is satisfied but no court has proceeded under that section,

(b) there is evidence which was not available to the prosecutor on the relevant date,

(c) before the end of the period of six years starting with the date of conviction the prosecutor applies to the Crown Court to consider the evidence, and

(d) after considering the evidence the court believes it is appropriate for it to proceed under section 6.

(2) If this section applies the court must proceed under section 6, and when it does so subsections (3) to (8) below apply.

(3) If the court has already sentenced the defendant for the offence (or any of the offences) concerned, section 6 has effect as if his particular criminal conduct included conduct which constitutes offences which the court has taken into consideration in deciding his sentence for the offence or offences concerned.

(4) Section 8(2) does not apply, and the rules applying instead are that the court must—

(a) take account of conduct occurring before the relevant date;

(b) take account of property obtained before that date;

(c) take account of property obtained on or after that date if it was obtained as a result of or in connection with conduct occurring before that date.

(5) In section 10—

(a) the first and second assumptions do not apply with regard to property first held by the defendant on or after the relevant date;

(b) the third assumption does not apply with regard to expenditure incurred by him on or after that date;

(c) the fourth assumption does not apply with regard to property obtained (or assumed to have been obtained) by him on or after that date.

(6) The recoverable amount for the purposes of section 6 is such amount as—

(a) the court believes is just, but

(b) does not exceed the amount found under section 7.

(7) In arriving at the just amount the court must have regard in particular to—

(a) the amount found under section 7;

(b) any fine imposed on the defendant in respect of the offence (or any of the offences) concerned;

(c) any order which falls within section 13(3) and has been made against him in respect of the offence (or any of the offences) concerned and has not already been taken into account by the court in deciding what is the free property held by him for the purposes of section 9;

(d) any order which has been made against him in respect of the offence (or any of the offences) concerned under section 130 of the *Sentencing Act* (compensation orders).

(8) If an order for the payment of compensation under section 130 of the *Sentencing Act* has been made against the defendant in respect of the offence or offences concerned, section 13(5) and (6) above do not apply.

(9) The relevant date is—

(a) if the court made a decision not to proceed under section 6, the date of the decision;

(b) if the court did not make such a decision, the date of conviction.

(10) The date of conviction is—

(a) the date on which the defendant was convicted of the offence concerned, or

(b) if there are two or more offences and the convictions were on different dates, the date of the latest.

[This section is printed as amended by the *SCA* 2007, ss.74(2) and 92, Sched. 8, paras 1 and 8, and Sched. 14.]

No order made: reconsideration of benefit

20.—(1) This section applies if the following two conditions are satisfied. **5–581**

(2) The first condition is that in proceeding under section 6 the court has decided that—

(a) the defendant has a criminal lifestyle but has not benefited from his general criminal conduct, or

(b) the defendant does not have a criminal lifestyle and has not benefited from his particular criminal conduct.

(4) ... the second condition is that—

(a) there is evidence which was not available to the prosecutor when the court decided that the defendant had not benefited from his general or particular criminal conduct, ... and

(c) after considering the evidence the court concludes that it would have decided that the defendant had benefited from his general or particular criminal conduct (as the case may be) if the evidence had been available to it.

(5) If this section applies the court—

(a) must make a fresh decision under section 6(4)(b) or (c) whether the defendant has benefited from his general or particular criminal conduct (as the case may be);

(b) may make a confiscation order under that section.

(6) Subsections (7) to (12) below apply if the court proceeds under section 6 in pursuance of this section.

(7) If the court has already sentenced the defendant for the offence (or any of the offences) concerned, section 6 has effect as if his particular criminal conduct included conduct which constitutes offences which the court has taken into consideration in deciding his sentence for the offence or offences concerned.

(8) Section 8(2) does not apply, and the rules applying instead are that the court must—

(a) take account of conduct occurring before the date of the original decision that the defendant had not benefited from his general or particular criminal conduct;

(b) take account of property obtained before that date;

(c) take account of property obtained on or after that date if it was obtained as a result of or in connection with conduct occurring before that date.

(9) In section 10—

(a) the first and second assumptions do not apply with regard to property first held by the defendant on or after the date of the original decision that the defendant had not benefited from his general or particular criminal conduct;

(b) the third assumption does not apply with regard to expenditure incurred by him on or after that date;

(c) the fourth assumption does not apply with regard to property obtained (or assumed to have been obtained) by him on or after that date.

(10) The recoverable amount for the purposes of section 6 is such amount as—
(a) the court believes is just, but
(b) does not exceed the amount found under section 7.

(11) In arriving at the just amount the court must have regard in particular to—
(a) the amount found under section 7;
(b) any fine imposed on the defendant in respect of the offence (or any of the offences) concerned;
(c) any order which falls within section 13(3) and has been made against him in respect of the offence (or any of the offences) concerned and has not already been taken into account by the court in deciding what is the free property held by him for the purposes of section 9;
(d) any order which has been made against him in respect of the offence (or any of the offences) concerned under section 130 of the *Sentencing Act* (compensation orders).

(12) If an order for the payment of compensation under section 130 of the *Sentencing Act* has been made against the defendant in respect of the offence or offences concerned, section 13(5) and (6) above do not apply.

(13) The date of conviction is the date found by applying section 19(10).

[This section is printed as amended by the *SCA* 2007, ss.74(2) and 92, Sched. 8, paras 1 and 9, and Sched. 14.]

Order made: reconsideration of benefit

5–582 **21.**—(1) This section applies if—
(a) a court has made a confiscation order,
(b) there is evidence which was not available to the prosecutor at the relevant time,
(c) the prosecutor believes that if the court were to find the amount of the defendant's benefit in pursuance of this section it would exceed the relevant amount,
(d) before the end of the period of six years starting with the date of conviction the prosecutor applies to the Crown Court to consider the evidence, and
(e) after considering the evidence the court believes it is appropriate for it to proceed under this section.

(2) The court must make a new calculation of the defendant's benefit from the conduct concerned, and when it does so subsections (3) to (6) below apply.

(3) If a court has already sentenced the defendant for the offence (or any of the offences) concerned section 6 has effect as if his particular criminal conduct included conduct which constitutes offences which the court has taken into consideration in deciding his sentence for the offence or offences concerned.

(4) Section 8(2) does not apply, and the rules applying instead are that the court must—
(a) take account of conduct occurring up to the time it decided the defendant's benefit for the purposes of the confiscation order;
(b) take account of property obtained up to that time;
(c) take account of property obtained after that time if it was obtained as a result of or in connection with conduct occurring before that time.

(5) In applying section 8(5) the confiscation order must be ignored.

(6) In section 10—
(a) the first and second assumptions do not apply with regard to property first held by the defendant after the time the court decided his benefit for the purposes of the confiscation order;
(b) the third assumption does not apply with regard to expenditure incurred by him after that time;
(c) the fourth assumption does not apply with regard to property obtained (or assumed to have been obtained) by him after that time.

(7) If the amount found under the new calculation of the defendant's benefit exceeds the relevant amount the court—
(a) must make a new calculation of the recoverable amount for the purposes of section 6, and
(b) if it exceeds the amount required to be paid under the confiscation order, may vary the order by substituting for the amount required to be paid such amount as it believes is just.

(8) In applying subsection (7)(a) the court must—

(a) take the new calculation of the defendant's benefit;

(b) apply section 9 as if references to the time the confiscation order is made were to the time of the new calculation of the recoverable amount and as if references to the date of the confiscation order were to the date of that new calculation.

(9) In applying subsection (7)(b) the court must have regard in particular to—

(a) any fine imposed on the defendant for the offence (or any of the offences) concerned;

(b) any order which falls within section 13(3) and has been made against him in respect of the offence (or any of the offences) concerned and has not already been taken into account by the court in deciding what is the free property held by him for the purposes of section 9;

(c) any order which has been made against him in respect of the offence (or any of the offences) concerned under section 130 of the *Sentencing Act* (compensation orders).

(10) But in applying subsection (7)(b) the court must not have regard to an order falling within subsection (9)(c) if a court has made a direction under section 13(6).

(11) In deciding under this section whether one amount exceeds another the court must take account of any change in the value of money.

(12) The relevant time is—

(a) when the court calculated the defendant's benefit for the purposes of the confiscation order, if this section has not applied previously;

(b) when the court last calculated the defendant's benefit in pursuance of this section, if this section has applied previously.

(13) The relevant amount is—

(a) the amount found as the defendant's benefit for the purposes of the confiscation order, if this section has not applied previously;

(b) the amount last found as the defendant's benefit in pursuance of this section, if this section has applied previously.

(14) The date of conviction is the date found by applying section 19(10).

[This section is printed as amended by the *SCA* 2007, ss.74(2) and 92, Sched. 8, paras 1 and 10, and Sched. 14.]

Order made: reconsideration of available amount

22.—(1) This section applies if— **5-583**

(a) a court has made a confiscation order,

(b) the amount required to be paid was the amount found under section 7(2), and

(c) an applicant falling within subsection (2) applies to the Crown Court to make a new calculation of the available amount.

(2) These applicants fall within this subsection—

(a) the prosecutor; ...

(c) a receiver appointed under section 50.

(3) In a case where this section applies the court must make the new calculation, and in doing, so it must apply section 9 as if references to the time the confiscation order is made were to the time of the new calculation and as if references to the date of the confiscation order were to the date of the new calculation.

(4) If the amount found under the new calculation exceeds the relevant amount the court may vary the order by substituting for the amount required to be paid such amount as—

(a) it believes is just, but

(b) does not exceed the amount found as the defendant's benefit from the conduct concerned.

(5) In deciding what is just the court must have regard in particular to—

(a) any fine imposed on the defendant for the offence (or any of the offences) concerned;

(b) any order which falls within section 13(3) and has been made against him in respect of the offence (or any of the offences) concerned and has not already been taken into account by the court in deciding what is the free property held by him for the purposes of section 9;

(c) any order which has been made against him in respect of the offence (or any of the offences) concerned under section 130 of the *Sentencing Act* (compensation orders).

(6) But in deciding what is just the court must not have regard to an order falling within subsection (5)(c) if a court has made a direction under section 13(6).

(7) In deciding under this section whether one amount exceeds another the court must take account of any change in the value of money.

(8) The relevant amount is—

(a) the amount found as the available amount for the purposes of the confiscation order, if this section has not applied previously;

(b) the amount last found as the available amount in pursuance of this section, if this section has applied previously.

(9) The amount found as the defendant's benefit from the conduct concerned is—

(a) the amount so found when the confiscation order was made, or

(b) if one or more new calculations of the defendant's benefit have been made under section 21 the amount found on the occasion of the last such calculation.

[This section is printed as amended by the *SCA* 2007, ss.74(2) and 92, Sched. 8, paras 1 and 11, and Sched. 14.]

Inadequacy of available amount: variation of order

5–584 **23.**—(1) This section applies if—

(a) a court has made a confiscation order, and

(b) the defendant, or a receiver appointed under section 50, applies to the Crown Court to vary the order under this section.

(2) In such a case the court must calculate the available amount, and in doing so it must apply section 9 as if references to the time the confiscation order is made were to the time of the calculation and as if references to the date of the confiscation order were to the date of the calculation.

(3) If the court finds that the available amount (as so calculated) is inadequate for the payment of any amount remaining to be paid under the confiscation order it may vary the order by substituting for the amount required to be paid such smaller amount as the court believes is just.

(4) If a person has been adjudged bankrupt or his estate has been sequestrated, or if an order for the winding up of a company has been made, the court must take into account the extent to which realisable property held by that person or that company may be distributed among creditors.

(5) The court may disregard any inadequacy which it believes is attributable (wholly or partly) to anything done by the defendant for the purpose of preserving property held by the recipient of a tainted gift from any risk of realisation under this Part.

(6) In subsection (4) "company" means any company which may be wound up under the *Insolvency Act* 1986 or the *Insolvency (Northern Ireland) Order* 1989 (S.I. 1989 No. 2405 (N.I. 19)).

[This section is printed as amended by the *SCA* 2007, ss.74(2) and 92, Sched. 8, paras 1 and 12, and Sched. 14.]

Inadequacy of available amount: discharge of order

5–585 **24.**—(1) This section applies if—

(a) a court has made a confiscation order,

(b) the designated officer for a magistrates' court applies to the Crown Court for the discharge of the order, and

(c) the amount remaining to be paid under the order is less than £1,000.

(2) In such a case the court must calculate the available amount, and in doing so it must apply section 9 as if references to the time the confiscation order is made were to the time of the calculation and as if references to the date of the confiscation order were to the date of the calculation.

(3) If the court—

(a) finds that the available amount (as so calculated) is inadequate to meet the amount remaining to be paid, and

(b) is satisfied that the inadequacy is due wholly to a specified reason or a combination of specified reasons,

it may discharge the confiscation order.

(4) The specified reasons are—

(a) in a case where any of the realisable property consists of money in a currency other than sterling, that fluctuations in currency exchange rates have occurred;

(b) any reason specified by the Secretary of State by order.

(5) The Secretary of State may by order vary the amount for the time being specified in subsection (1)(c).

[This section is printed as amended by the *Courts Act* 2003, s.109(1), and Sched. 8, para. 406.]

The Crown Court will not be able to make a finding under subsection (3) if some of the defendant's property is unidentified: see *Telli v. Revenue and Customs Prosecutions Office* (*post*, § 5–775).

Small amount outstanding: discharge of order

25.—(1) This section applies if— **5–586**

(a) a court has made a confiscation order,

(b) the designated officer for a magistrates' court applies to the Crown Court for the discharge of the order, and

(c) the amount remaining to be paid under the order is £50 or less.

(2) In such a case the court may discharge the order.

(3) The Secretary of State may by order vary the amount for the time being specified in subsection (1)(c).

[This section is printed as amended by the *Courts Act* 2003, s.109(1), and Sched. 8, para. 406.]

Information

26.—(1) This section applies if— **5–587**

(a) the court proceeds under section 6 in pursuance of section 19 or 20, or

(b) the prosecutor applies under section 21.

(2) In such a case—

(a) the prosecutor must give the court a statement of information within the period the court orders;

(b) section 16 applies accordingly (with appropriate modifications where the prosecutor applies under section 21);

(c) section 17 applies accordingly;

(d) section 18 applies as it applies in the circumstances mentioned in section 18(1).

[This section is printed as amended by the *SCA* 2007, ss.74(2) and 92, Sched. 8, paras 1 and 13, and Sched. 14.]

Defendant absconds

Defendant convicted or committed

27.—(1) This section applies if the following two conditions are satisfied. **5–588**

(2) The first condition is that a defendant absconds after—

(a) he is convicted of an offence or offences in proceedings before the Crown Court,

(b) he is committed to the Crown Court for sentence in respect of an offence or offences under section *3, 4 or 6* [3, 3A, 3B, 3C, 4, 4A or 6] of the *Sentencing Act*, or

(c) he is committed to the Crown Court in respect of an offence or offences under section 70 below (committal with a view to a confiscation order being considered).

(3) The second condition is that—

(a) the prosecutor applies to the Crown Court to proceed under this section, and

(b) the court believes it is appropriate for it to do so.

(4) If this section applies the court must proceed under section 6 in the same way as it must proceed if the two conditions there mentioned are satisfied; but this is subject to subsection (5).

(5) If the court proceeds under section 6 as applied by this section, this Part has effect with these modifications—

(a) any person the court believes is likely to be affected by an order under section 6 is entitled to appear before the court and make representations;

(b) the court must not make an order under section 6 unless the prosecutor has taken reasonable steps to contact the defendant;

(c) section 6(9) applies as if the reference to subsection (2) were to subsection (2) of this section;

(d) sections 10, 16(4), 17 and 18 must be ignored;

(e) sections 19, 20 and 21 must be ignored while the defendant is still an absconder.

(6) Once the defendant ceases to be an absconder section 19 has effect as if subsection (1)(a) read—

"(a) at a time when the first condition in section 27 was satisfied the court did not proceed under section 6,".

(7) If the court does not believe it is appropriate for it to proceed under this section, once the defendant ceases to be an absconder section 19 has effect as if subsection (1)(b) read—

"(b) there is evidence which was not available to the prosecutor on the relevant date,".

[This section is printed as amended by the *SCA* 2007, ss.74(2) and 92, Sched. 8, paras 1 and 14, and Sched. 14; and as amended, as from a day to be appointed, by the *CJA* 2003, s.41, and Sched. 3, para. 75(1) and (3) (substitution of words in square brackets for italicised words that precede them).]

Defendant neither convicted nor acquitted

5–589 **28.**—(1) This section applies if the following two conditions are satisfied.

(2) The first condition is that—

(a) proceedings for an offence or offences are started against a defendant but are not concluded,

(b) he absconds, and

(c) the period of two years (starting with the day the court believes he absconded) has ended.

(3) The second condition is that—

(a) the prosecutor applies to the Crown Court to proceed under this section, and

(b) the court believes it is appropriate for it to do so.

(4) [*Identical to s.27(4),* ante.]

(5) If the court proceeds under section 6 as applied by this section, this Part has effect with these modifications—

(a)–(c) [*identical to s.27(5)(a)-(c),* ante, *§ 5–588*];

(d) sections 10, 16(4) and 17 to 20 must be ignored;

(e) section 21 must be ignored while the defendant is still an absconder.

(6) Once the defendant has ceased to be an absconder section 21 has effect as if references to the date of conviction were to—

(a) the day when proceedings for the offence concerned were started against the defendant, or

(b) if there are two or more offences and proceedings for them were started on different days, the earliest of those days.

(7) If—

(a) the court makes an order under section 6 as applied by this section, and

(b) the defendant is later convicted in proceedings before the Crown Court of the offence (or any of the offences) concerned,

section 6 does not apply so far as that conviction is concerned.

[This section is printed as amended by the *SCA* 2007, ss.74(2) and 92, Sched. 8, paras 1 and 15, and Sched. 14.]

Variation of order

5–590 **29.**—(1) This section applies if—

(a) the court makes a confiscation order under section 6 as applied by section 28,

(b) the defendant ceases to be an absconder,

(c) he is convicted of an offence (or any of the offences) mentioned in section 28(2)(a),

(d) he believes that the amount required to be paid was too large (taking the circumstances prevailing when the amount was found for the purposes of the order), and

(e) before the end of the relevant period he applies to the Crown Court to consider the evidence on which his belief is based.

(2) If (after considering the evidence) the court concludes that the defendant's belief is well founded—

(a) it must find the amount which should have been the amount required to be paid (taking the circumstances prevailing when the amount was found for the purposes of the order), and

(b) it may vary the order by substituting for the amount required to be paid such amount as it believes is just.

(3) The relevant period is the period of 28 days starting with—

(a) the date on which the defendant was convicted of the offence mentioned in section 28(2)(a), or

(b) if there are two or more offences and the convictions were on different dates, the date of the latest.

(4) But in a case where section 28(2)(a) applies to more than one offence the court must not make an order under this section unless it is satisfied that there is no possibility of any further proceedings being taken or continued in relation to any such offence in respect of which the defendant has not been convicted.

Discharge of order

30.—(1) Subsection (2) applies if— **5–591**

(a) the court makes a confiscation order under section 6 as applied by section 28,

(b) the defendant is later tried for the offence or offences concerned and acquitted on all counts, and

(c) he applies to the Crown Court to discharge the order.

(2) In such a case the court must discharge the order.

(3) Subsection (4) applies if—

(a) the court makes a confiscation order under section 6 as applied by section 28,

(b) the defendant ceases to be an absconder,

(c) subsection (1)(b) does not apply, and

(d) he applies to the Crown Court to discharge the order.

(4) In such a case the court may discharge the order if it finds that—

(a) there has been undue delay in continuing the proceedings mentioned in section 28(2), or

(b) the prosecutor does not intend to proceed with the prosecution.

(5) If the court discharges a confiscation order under this section it may make such a consequential or incidental order as it believes is appropriate.

Appeals

Appeal by prosecutor

31.—(1) If the Crown Court makes a confiscation order the prosecutor may appeal to the Court of Appeal in respect of the order. **5–592**

(2) If the Crown Court decides not to make a confiscation order the prosecutor may appeal to the Court of Appeal against the decision.

(3) Subsections (1) and (2) do not apply to an order or decision made by virtue of section 19, 20, 27 or 28.

[This section is printed as amended by the *SCA* 2007, ss.74(2) and 92, Sched. 8, paras 1 and 16, and Sched. 14.]

A decision to adjourn a confiscation application *sine die* is a decision "not to make a confiscation order" within subsection (2), and is thus subject to appeal by the prosecution: *R. v. Hockey* [2008] 1 Cr.App.R.(S.) 50, CA.

Court's powers on appeal

32.—(1) On an appeal under section 31(1) the Court of Appeal may confirm, quash or vary the confiscation order. **5–593**

(2) On an appeal under section 31(2) the Court of Appeal may confirm the decision, or if it believes the decision was wrong it may—

(a) itself proceed under section 6 (ignoring subsections (1) to (3)), or

(b) direct the Crown Court to proceed afresh under section 6.

(3) In proceeding afresh in pursuance of this section the Crown Court must comply with any directions the Court of Appeal may make.

(4) If a court makes or varies a confiscation order under this section or in pursuance of a direction under this section it must—

(a) have regard to any fine imposed on the defendant in respect of the offence (or any of the offences) concerned;

(b) have regard to any order which falls within section 13(3) and has been made against him in respect of the offence (or any of the offences) concerned, unless the order has already been taken into account by a court in deciding what is the free property held by the defendant for the purposes of section 9.

(5) If the Court of Appeal proceeds under section 6 or the Crown Court proceeds afresh under that section in pursuance of a direction under this section subsections (6) to (10) apply.

(6) If a court has already sentenced the defendant for the offence (or any of the offences) concerned, section 6 has effect as if his particular criminal conduct included conduct which constitutes offences which the court has taken into consideration in deciding his sentence for the offence or offences concerned.

(7) If an order has been made against the defendant in respect of the offence (or any of the offences) concerned under section 130 of the *Sentencing Act* (compensation orders)—

(a) the court must have regard to it, and

(b) section 13(5) and (6) above do not apply.

(8) Section 8(2) does not apply, and the rules applying instead are that the court must—

(a) take account of conduct occurring before the relevant date;

(b) take account of property obtained before that date;

(c) take account of property obtained on or after that date if it was obtained as a result of or in connection with conduct occurring before that date.

(9) In section 10—

(a) the first and second assumptions do not apply with regard to property first held by the defendant on or after the relevant date;

(b) the third assumption does not apply with regard to expenditure incurred by him on or after that date;

(c) the fourth assumption does not apply with regard to property obtained (or assumed to have been obtained) by him on or after that date.

(10) Section 26 applies as it applies in the circumstances mentioned in subsection (1) of that section.

(11) The relevant date is the date on which the Crown Court decided not to make a confiscation order.

Appeal to House of Lords [Supreme Court]

5–594 **33.**—(1) An appeal lies to the *House of Lords* [Supreme Court] from a decision of the Court of Appeal on an appeal under section 31.

(2) An appeal under this section lies at the instance of—

(a) the defendant or the prosecutor; … .

(3) On an appeal from a decision of the Court of Appeal to confirm, vary or make a confiscation order the *House of Lords* [Supreme Court] may confirm, quash or vary the order.

(4) On an appeal from a decision of the Court of Appeal to confirm the decision of the Crown Court not to make a confiscation order or from a decision of the Court of Appeal to quash a confiscation order the *House of Lords* [Supreme Court] may—

(a) confirm the decision, or

(b) direct the Crown Court to proceed afresh under section 6 if it believes the decision was wrong.

(5) In proceeding afresh in pursuance of this section the Crown Court must comply with any directions the *House of Lords* [Supreme Court] may make.

(6) If a court varies a confiscation order under this section or makes a confiscation order in pursuance of a direction under this section it must—

(a) have regard to any fine imposed on the defendant in respect of the offence (or any of the offences) concerned;

(b) have regard to any order which falls within section 13(3) and has been made against him in respect of the offence (or any of the offences) concerned, unless the order has already been taken into account by a court in deciding what is the free property held by the defendant for the purposes of section 9.

(7) If the Crown Court proceeds afresh under section 6 in pursuance of a direction under this section subsections (8) to (12) apply.

(8)–(12) [*Identical to s.32(6)–(10),* ante.]

(13) The relevant date is—

(a) in a case where the Crown Court made a confiscation order which was quashed by the Court of Appeal, the date on which the Crown Court made the order;

(b) in any other case, the date on which the Crown Court decided not to make a confiscation order.

[This section is printed as amended by the *SCA* 2007, ss.74(2) and 92, Sched. 8, paras 1 and 17, and Sched. 14; and as amended, as from a day to be appointed, by the *Constitutional Reform Act* 2005, s.40(4), and Sched. 9, para. 77(1) and (2) (substitution of references to "Supreme Court" for references to "House of Lords").]

Enforcement authority

34. [*Repealed by* SCA *2007, ss.74(2) and 92, Sched. 8, paras 1 and 18, and Sched. 14.*] **5–595**

Enforcement as fines etc.

Enforcement as fines

35.—(1) This section applies if a court— **5–596**

(a) makes a confiscation order, … .

(2) Sections 139(2) to (4) and (9) and 140(1) to (4) of the *Sentencing Act* (functions of court as to fines and enforcing fines) apply as if the amount ordered to be paid were a fine imposed on the defendant by the court making the confiscation order.

(3) In the application of Part 3 of the *Magistrates' Courts Act* 1980 to an amount payable under a confiscation order—

(a) ignore section 75 of that Act (power to dispense with immediate payment);

(b) such an amount is not a sum adjudged to be paid by a conviction for the purposes of section 81 (enforcement of fines imposed on young offenders) or a fine for the purposes of section 85 (remission of fines) of that Act;

(c) in section 87 of that Act ignore subsection (3) (inquiry into means).

[This section is printed as amended by the *SCA* 2007, ss.74(2) and 92, Sched. 8, paras 1 and 19, and Sched. 14.]

Director appointed as enforcement authority

36. [*Repealed by* SCA *2007, ss.74(2) and 92, Sched. 8, paras 1 and 20, and Sched. 14.*] **5–597**

Director's application for enforcement

37. [*Repealed by* SCA *2007, ss.74(2) and 92, Sched. 8, paras 1 and 20, and Sched. 14.*] **5–598**

Provisions about imprisonment or detention

38.—(1) Subsection (2) applies if— **5–599**

(a) a warrant committing the defendant to prison or detention is issued for a default in payment of an amount ordered to be paid under a confiscation order in respect of an offence or offences, and

(b) at the time the warrant is issued the defendant is liable to serve a term of custody in respect of the offence (or any of the offences).

(2) In such a case the term of imprisonment or of detention under section 108 of the *Sentencing Act* (detention of persons aged 18 to 20 for default) to be served in default of payment of the amount does not begin to run until after the term mentioned in subsection (1)(b) above.

(3) The reference in subsection (1)(b) to the term of custody the defendant is liable to serve in respect of the offence (or any of the offences) is a reference to the term of imprisonment, or detention in a young offender institution, which he is liable to serve in respect of the offence (or any of the offences).

(4) For the purposes of subsection (3) consecutive terms and terms which are wholly or partly concurrent must be treated as a single term and the following must be ignored—

(a) any sentence suspended under section 189(1) of the *Criminal Justice Act* 2003 which has not taken effect at the time the warrant is issued;

(b) in the case of a sentence of imprisonment passed with an order under section 47(1) of the *Criminal Law Act* 1977 (sentences of imprisonment partly served and partly suspended) any part of the sentence which the defendant has not at that time been required to serve in prison;

(c) any term of imprisonment or detention fixed under section 139(2) of the *Sentencing Act* (term to be served in default of payment of fine etc) for which a warrant committing the defendant to prison or detention has not been issued at that time.

(5) If the defendant serves a term of imprisonment or detention in default of paying any amount due under a confiscation order, his serving that term does not prevent the confiscation order from continuing to have effect so far as any other method of enforcement is concerned.

[This section is printed as amended by the *CJA* 2003, s.304, and Sched. 32, paras 90 and 141.]

Reconsideration etc: variation of prison term

5–600 **39.**—(1) Subsection (2) applies if—

(a) a court varies a confiscation order under section 21, 22, 23, 29, 32 or 33,

(b) the effect of the variation is to vary the maximum period applicable in relation to the order under section 139(4) of the *Sentencing Act*, and

(c) the result is that that maximum period is less than the term of imprisonment or detention fixed in respect of the order under section 139(2) of the *Sentencing Act*.

(2) In such a case the court must fix a reduced term of imprisonment or detention in respect of the confiscation order under section 139(2) of the *Sentencing Act* in place of the term previously fixed.

(3) Subsection (4) applies if paragraphs (a) and (b) of subsection (1) apply but paragraph (c) does not.

(4) In such a case the court may amend the term of imprisonment or detention fixed in respect of the confiscation order under section 139(2) of the *Sentencing Act*.

(5) If the effect of section 12 is to increase the maximum period applicable in relation to a confiscation order under section 139(4) of the *Sentencing Act*, on the application of the prosecutor the Crown Court may amend the term of imprisonment or detention fixed in respect of the order under section 139(2) of that Act.

[This section is printed as amended by the *SCA* 2007, ss.74(2) and 92, Sched. 8, paras 1 and 21, and Sched. 14.]

Restraint orders

Conditions for exercise of powers

5–601 **40.**—(1) The Crown Court may exercise the powers conferred by section 41 if any of the following conditions is satisfied.

(2) The first condition is that—

(a) a criminal investigation has been started in England and Wales with regard to an offence, and

(b) there is reasonable cause to believe that the alleged offender has benefited from his criminal conduct.

(3) The second condition is that—

(a) proceedings for an offence have been started in England and Wales and not concluded, and

(b) there is reasonable cause to believe that the defendant has benefited from his criminal conduct.

(4) The third condition is that—

(a) an application by the prosecutor has been made under section 19, 20, 27 or 28 and not concluded, or the court believes that such an application is to be made, and

(b) there is reasonable cause to believe that the defendant has benefited from his criminal conduct.

(5) The fourth condition is that—

(a) an application by the prosecutor has been made under section 21 and not concluded, or the court believes that such an application is to be made, and

(b) there is reasonable cause to believe that the court will decide under that section that the amount found under the new calculation of the defendant's benefit exceeds the relevant amount (as defined in that section).

(6) The fifth condition is that—

(a) an application by the prosecutor has been made under section 22 and not concluded, or the court believes that such an application is to be made, and

(b) there is reasonable cause to believe that the court will decide under that section that the amount found under the new calculation of the available amount exceeds the relevant amount (as defined in that section).

(7) The second condition is not satisfied if the court believes that—

(a) there has been undue delay in continuing the proceedings, or

(b) the prosecutor does not intend to proceed.

(8) If an application mentioned in the third, fourth or fifth condition has been made the condition is not satisfied if the court believes that—

(a) there has been undue delay in continuing the application, or

(b) the prosecutor does not intend to proceed.

(9) If the first condition is satisfied—

(a) references in this Part to the defendant are to the alleged offender;

(b) references in this Part to the prosecutor are to the person the court believes is to have conduct of any proceedings for the offence;

(c) section 77(9) has effect as if proceedings for the offence had been started against the defendant when the investigation was started.

[This section is printed as amended by the *SCA* 2007, ss.74(2) and 92, Sched. 8, paras 1 and 22, and Sched. 14.]

Restraint orders

41.—(1) If any condition set out in section 40 is satisfied the Crown Court may make an order (a restraint order) prohibiting any specified person from dealing with any realisable property held by him. **5–602**

(2) A restraint order may provide that it applies—

(a) to all realisable property held by the specified person whether or not the property is described in the order;

(b) to realisable property transferred to the specified person after the order is made.

(3) A restraint order may be made subject to exceptions, and an exception may in particular—

(a) make provision for reasonable living expenses and reasonable legal expenses;

(b) make provision for the purpose of enabling any person to carry on any trade, business, profession or occupation;

(c) be made subject to conditions.

(4) But an exception to a restraint order must not make provision for any legal expenses which—

(a) relate to an offence which falls within subsection (5), and

(b) are incurred by the defendant or by a recipient of a tainted gift.

(5) These offences fall within this subsection—

(a) the offence mentioned in section 40(2) or (3), if the first or second condition (as the case may be) is satisfied;

(b) the offence (or any of the offences) concerned, if the third, fourth or fifth condition is satisfied.

(6) Subsection (7) applies if—

(a) a court makes a restraint order, and

(b) the applicant for the order applies to the court to proceed under subsection (7) (whether as part of the application for the restraint order or at any time afterwards).

(7) The court may make such order as it believes is appropriate for the purpose of ensuring that the restraint order is effective.

(8) A restraint order does not affect property for the time being subject to a charge under any of these provisions—

(a) section 9 of the *Drug Trafficking Offences Act* 1986;

(b) section 78 of the *Criminal Justice Act* 1988;

(c) Article 14 of the *Criminal Justice (Confiscation) (Northern Ireland) Order* 1990 (S.I. 1990 No. 2588 (N.I. 17));

(d) section 27 of the *Drug Trafficking Act* 1994;

(e) Article 32 of the *Proceeds of Crime (Northern Ireland) Order* 1996 (S.I. 1996 No. 1299 (N.I. 9)).

(9) Dealing with property includes removing it from England and Wales.

Whereas the combined effect of sections 40 and 41 is that the Crown Court may make a restraint order if satisfied that a criminal investigation has been started with regard to an offence and there is reasonable cause to believe that the alleged offender has benefited from his criminal conduct, the effect of the transitional provisions in the *Proceeds of Crime Act 2002 (Commencement No. 5, Transitional Provisions, Savings and Amendment) Order* 2003 (S.I. 2003 No. 333), arts 3 and 5 (*post*, §§ 5–665, 5–667), was that the investigation must be into an offence that occurred on or after the commencement date (March 24, 2003); but it mattered not that the investigating authority was also investigating one or more offences which had occurred before that date (at least not where the authority had given an undertaking to the court that any charges would relate to offences after that date), nor that the criminal conduct that underlay the post March 24, 2003 (money-laundering) offences had occurred before that date; and the time at which the test was to be applied was the time when the application was made, not when the investigation had begun: *Re Hill (Restraint order)*, *The Times*, December 27, 2005, CA.

In *Director of Serious Fraud Office v. A.* (2007) 151 S.J. 1058, CA, the court observed, *obiter*, that whilst the legislative "steer" of the 2002 Act, as divined from section 69 (*post*, § 5–630), reflected the legitimate public interest justifying the making of a restraint order (*viz.* to prevent a person from dissipating or hiding his assets once he knows a criminal investigation is under way), it did not follow that if the conditions for making an order were satisfied, an order would inevitably be made.

On an application under this section for a pre-proceedings restraint order, (i) a judge is entitled, in deciding on the ambit of the order, to have regard to the likelihood that the defendant would in due course be found to have a "criminal lifestyle" within section 75, and to have benefited from his general criminal conduct within section 10, and to the assumptions as to property held by him that would flow from such findings under that section; and (ii) where there was strong evidence that the appellants and the companies controlled by them were engaged in a smuggling operation, the proceeds of which were being concealed behind the façade of the companies, the judge had been entitled to make a restraint order unlimited in amount; it would have been artificial to conclude that the realisable assets were to be treated as limited to the ill-gotten gains that were expressly demonstrated: *R. v. K.* [2006] B.C.C. 362, CA.

In *Re S. (Restraint Order)* [2005] 1 W.L.R. 1338, CA, it was held that the court has no jurisdiction to release assets, which have been frozen by a restraint order under this section, in order to fund legal advice and representation in relation to the restraint order; while section 41(3) allowed for exceptions to be made to a restraint order (including for "reasonable legal expenses"), section 41(4) prevented an exception being made for legal expenses for proceedings in connection with a restraint order; such proceedings "related to" the underlying offence; the fact that reference was made to recipients of tainted gifts was strong support for the conclusion that the legislation was not directed simply at excluding legal expenses in connection with the defendant's criminal proceedings themselves; and the fact that it was clearly intended that public funding should be available for proceedings in relation to a restraint order was further support for that interpretation.

Re S. (Restraint Order) was applied in *R. v. A.P.*; *R. v. U. Ltd* [2008] 1 Cr.App.R. 39, CA, in which it was held that section 41(4) is not incompatible with the defendant's right to peaceful enjoyment of his possessions under Article 1 of the First Protocol to the ECHR. Although section 41(4) produced harsh results in some cases, that fact in itself did not justify the conclusion that it was incompatible, as that would only be the case if there was such a significant number of people unable to obtain representation that there was a clear systemic failure to provide the alternative which Parliament had considered appropriate. Where problems did arise, it was held that they would fall to be addressed when the proceedings were heard, in the light of the defendant's right to a fair trial under Article 6 (*post*, § 16–57), by considering whether the proceedings should be stayed due to potential unfairness.

Application, discharge and variation

42.—(1) A restraint order— **5–603**

(a) may be made only on an application by an applicant falling within subsection (2);

(b) may be made on an *ex parte* application to a judge in chambers.

(2) [*Repealed by* SCA *2007, ss.74(2) and 92, Sched. 8, paras 1 and 23, and Sched. 14.*]

(3) An application to discharge or vary a restraint order or an order under section 41(7) may be made to the Crown Court by—

(a) the person who applied for the order;

(b) any person affected by the order.

(4) Subsections (5) to (7) apply to an application under subsection (3).

(5) The court—

(a) may discharge the order;

(b) may vary the order.

(6) If the condition in section 40 which was satisfied was that proceedings were started or an application was made, the court must discharge the order on the conclusion of the proceedings or of the application (as the case may be).

(7) If the condition in section 40 which was satisfied was that an investigation was started or an application was to be made, the court must discharge the order if within a reasonable time proceedings for the offence are not started or the application is not made (as the case may be).

On an application to discharge a restraint order on the basis of non-disclosure by the authority that obtained the order, the Crown Court should determine whether the non-disclosure was material to the making of the order and, if so, whether the public interest required the order to remain in place nonetheless (for which purpose the question of whether the non-disclosure was deliberate or accidental would be material but not necessarily determinative): *Director of Serious Fraud Office v. A., ante*.

In connection with this section, see also section 69, *post*, § 5–630.

Appeal to Court of Appeal

43.—(1) If on an application for a restraint order the court decides not to make one, the person who applied for the order may appeal to the Court of Appeal against the decision. **5–604**

(2) If an application is made under section 42(3) in relation to a restraint order or an order under section 41(7) the following persons may appeal to the Court of Appeal in respect of the Crown Court's decision on the application—

(a) the person who applied for the order;

(b) any person affected by the order.

(3) On an appeal under subsection (1) or (2) the Court of Appeal may—

(a) confirm the decision, or

(b) make such order as it believes is appropriate.

Appeal to House of Lords [Supreme Court]

44.—(1) An appeal lies to the *House of Lords* [Supreme Court] from a decision of the Court of Appeal on an appeal under section 43. **5–605**

(2) An appeal under this section lies at the instance of any person who was a party to the proceedings before the Court of Appeal.

(3) On an appeal under this section the *House of Lords* [Supreme Court] may—

(a) confirm the decision of the Court of Appeal, or

(b) make such order as it believes is appropriate.

[This section is printed as amended, as from a day to be appointed, by the the *Constitutional Reform Act* 2005, s.40(4), and Sched. 9, para. 77(1) and (3) (substitution of references to "Supreme Court" for references to "House of Lords").]

Seizure

45.—(1) If a restraint order is in force a constable, an accredited financial investigator or a customs officer may seize any realisable property to which it applies to prevent its removal from England and Wales. **5–606**

(2) Property seized under subsection (1) must be dealt with in accordance with the directions of the court which made the order.

(3) The reference in subsection (1) to an accredited financial investigator is a reference to an accredited financial investigator who falls within a description specified in an order made for the purposes of that subsection by the Secretary of State under section 453.

[This section is printed as amended by the *SCA* 2007, s.78(1) and (2).]

Hearsay evidence

5–607 **46.**—(1) Evidence must not be excluded in restraint proceedings on the ground that it is hearsay (of whatever degree).

(2) Sections 2 to 4 of the *Civil Evidence Act* 1995 apply in relation to restraint proceedings as those sections apply in relation to civil proceedings.

(3) Restraint proceedings are proceedings—

(a) for a restraint order;

(b) for the discharge or variation of a restraint order;

(c) on an appeal under section 43 or 44.

(4) Hearsay is a statement which is made otherwise than by a person while giving oral evidence in the proceedings and which is tendered as evidence of the matters stated.

(5) Nothing in this section affects the admissibility of evidence which is admissible apart from this section.

Supplementary

5–608 **47.**—(1) The registration Acts—

(a) apply in relation to restraint orders as they apply in relation to orders which affect land and are made by the court for the purpose of enforcing judgments or recognisances;

(b) apply in relation to applications for restraint orders as they apply in relation to other pending land actions.

(2) The registration Acts are—

(a) the *Land Registration Act* 1925;

(b) the *Land Charges Act* 1972;

(c) the *Land Registration Act* 2002.

(3) But no notice may be entered in the register of title under the *Land Registration Act* 2002 in respect of a restraint order.

(4) The person applying for a restraint order must be treated for the purposes of section 57 of the *Land Registration Act* 1925 (inhibitions) as a person interested in relation to any registered land to which—

(a) the application relates, or

(b) a restraint order made in pursuance of the application relates.

Management receivers

Appointment

5–609 **48.**—(1) Subsection (2) applies if—

(a) the Crown Court makes a restraint order, and

(b) the applicant for the restraint order applies to the court to proceed under subsection (2) (whether as part of the application for the restraint order or at any time afterwards).

(2) The Crown Court may by order appoint a receiver in respect of any realisable property to which the restraint order applies.

Powers

5–610 **49.**—(1) If the court appoints a receiver under section 48 it may act under this section on the application of the person who applied for the restraint order.

(2) The court may by order confer on the receiver the following powers in relation to any realisable property to which the restraint order applies—

(a) power to take possession of the property;

(b) power to manage or otherwise deal with the property;

(c) power to start, carry on or defend any legal proceedings in respect of the property;

(d) power to realise so much of the property as is necessary to meet the receiver's remuneration and expenses.

(3) The court may by order confer on the receiver power to enter any premises in England and Wales and to do any of the following—

(a) search for or inspect anything authorised by the court;

(b) make or obtain a copy, photograph or other record of anything so authorised;

(c) remove anything which the receiver is required or authorised to take possession of in pursuance of an order of the court.

(4) The court may by order authorise the receiver to do any of the following for the purpose of the exercise of his functions—

(a) hold property;

(b) enter into contracts;

(c) sue and be sued;

(d) employ agents;

(e) execute powers of attorney, deeds or other instruments;

(f) take any other steps the court thinks appropriate.

(5) The court may order any person who has possession of realisable property to which the restraint order applies to give possession of it to the receiver.

(6) The court—

(a) may order a person holding an interest in realisable property to which the restraint order applies to make to the receiver such payment as the court specifies in respect of a beneficial interest held by the defendant or the recipient of a tainted gift;

(b) may (on the payment being made) by order transfer, grant or extinguish any interest in the property.

(7) Subsections (2), (5) and (6) do not apply to property for the time being subject to a charge under any of these provisions—

(a) section 9 of the *Drug Trafficking Offences Act* 1986;

(b) section 78 of the *Criminal Justice Act* 1988;

(c) Article 14 of the *Criminal Justice (Confiscation) (Northern Ireland) Order* 1990 (S.I. 1990 No. 2588 (N.I. 17));

(d) section 27 of the *Drug Trafficking Act* 1994;

(e) Article 32 of the *Proceeds of Crime (Northern Ireland) Order* 1996 (S.I. 1996 No. 1299 (N.I. 9)).

(8) The court must not—

(a) confer the power mentioned in subsection (2)(b) or (d) in respect of property, or

(b) exercise the power conferred on it by subsection (6) in respect of property,

unless it gives persons holding interests in the property a reasonable opportunity to make representations to it.

(8A) Subsection (8), so far as relating to the power mentioned in subsection (2)(b), does not apply to property which—

(a) is perishable; or

(b) ought to be disposed of before its value diminishes.

(9) The court may order that a power conferred by an order under this section is subject to such conditions and exceptions as it specifies.

(10) Managing or otherwise dealing with property includes—

(a) selling the property or any part of it or interest in it;

(b) carrying on or arranging for another person to carry on any trade or business the assets of which are or are part of the property;

(c) incurring capital expenditure in respect of the property.

[This section is printed as amended by the *SCA* 2007, s.82(1).]

Enforcement receivers

Appointment

50.—(1) This section applies if— **5–611**

(a) a confiscation order is made,

(b) it is not satisfied, and

(c) it is not subject to appeal.

(2) On the application of the prosecutor the Crown Court may by order appoint a receiver in respect of realisable property.

Powers

51.—(1) If the court appoints a receiver under section 50 it may act under this section on the application of the prosecutor. **5–612**

(2) The court may by order confer on the receiver the following powers in relation to the realisable property—

(a) power to take possession of the property;

(b) power to manage or otherwise deal with the property;

(c) power to realise the property, in such manner as the court may specify;

(d) power to start, carry on or defend any legal proceedings in respect of the property.

(3), (4) [*Identical to s.49(3), (4),* ante.]

(5) The court may order any person who has possession of realisable property to give possession of it to the receiver.

(6) The court—

(a) may order a person holding an interest in realisable property to make to the receiver such payment as the court specifies in respect of a beneficial interest held by the defendant or the recipient of a tainted gift;

(b) may (on the payment being made) by order transfer, grant or extinguish any interest in the property.

(7) [*Identical to s.49(7),* ante.]

(8) The court must not—

(a) confer the power mentioned in subsection (2)(b) or (c) in respect of property, or

(b) exercise the power conferred on it by subsection (6) in respect of property,

unless it gives persons holding interests in the property a reasonable opportunity to make representations to it.

(8A), (9), (10) [*Identical to s.49(8A), (9), (10),* ante.]

[Subs. (8A) was inserted by the *SCA* 2007, s.82(2).]

Director's receivers

Appointment

5–613 **52.** [*Repealed by* SCA *2007, ss.74(2) and 92, Sched. 8, paras 1 and 24, and Sched. 14.*]

Powers

5–614 **53.** [*Repealed by* SCA *2007, ss.74(2) and 92, Sched. 8, paras 1 and 24, and Sched. 14.*]

Application of sums

Enforcement receivers

5–615 **54.**—(1) This section applies to sums which are in the hands of a receiver appointed under section 50 if they are—

(a) the proceeds of the realisation of property under section 51;

(b) sums (other than those mentioned in paragraph (a)) in which the defendant holds an interest.

(2) The sums must be applied as follows—

(a) first, they must be applied in payment of such expenses incurred by a person acting as an insolvency practitioner as are payable under this subsection by virtue of section 432;

(b) second, they must be applied in making any payments directed by the Crown Court;

(c) third, they must be applied on the defendant's behalf towards satisfaction of the confiscation order.

(3) If the amount payable under the confiscation order has been fully paid and any sums remain in the receiver's hands he must distribute them—

(a) among such persons who held (or hold) interests in the property concerned as the Crown Court directs, and

(b) in such proportions as it directs.

(4) Before making a direction under subsection (3) the court must give persons who held (or hold) interests in the property concerned a reasonable opportunity to make representations to it.

(5) For the purposes of subsections (3) and (4) the property concerned is—

(a) the property represented by the proceeds mentioned in subsection (1)(a);

(b) the sums mentioned in subsection (1)(b).

(6) The receiver applies sums as mentioned in subsection (2)(c) by paying them to the appropriate designated officer on account of the amount payable under the order.

(7) The appropriate designated officer is the one for the magistrates' court responsible for enforcing the confiscation order as if the amount ordered to be paid were a fine.

[This section is printed as amended by the *Courts Act* 2003, s.109(1), and Sched. 8, para. 407.]

Sums received by justices' chief executive

55.—(1) This section applies if a designated officer receives sums on account of the amount payable under a confiscation order (whether the sums are received under section 54 or otherwise). **5–616**

(2) The designated officer's receipt of the sums reduces the amount payable under the order, but he must apply the sums received as follows.

(3) First he must apply them in payment of such expenses incurred by a person acting as an insolvency practitioner as—

(a) are payable under this subsection by virtue of section 432, but

(b) are not already paid under section 54(2)(a).

(4) If the designated officer received the sums under section 54 he must next apply them—

(a) first, in payment of the remuneration and expenses of a receiver appointed under section 48, to the extent that they have not been met by virtue of the exercise by that receiver of a power conferred under section 49(2)(d);

(b) second, in payment of the remuneration and expenses of the receiver appointed under section 50.

(5) If a direction was made under section 13(6) for an amount of compensation to be paid out of sums recovered under the confiscation order, the designated officer must next apply the sums in payment of that amount.

(6) If any amount remains after the designated officer makes any payments required by the preceding provisions of this section, the amount must be treated for the purposes of section 38 of the *Courts Act* 2003 (application of fines etc) as if it were a fine imposed by a magistrates' court.

(7) Subsection (4) does not apply if the receiver is a member of the staff of the Crown Prosecution Service or of the Commissioners of Customs and Excise; and it is immaterial whether he is a permanent or temporary member or he is on secondment from elsewhere.

[This section is printed as amended by the *Courts Act* 2003, s.109(1), and Sched. 8, para. 408.]

Director's receivers

56. [*Repealed by* SCA *2007, ss.74(2) and 92, Sched. 8, paras 1 and 25, and Sched. 14.*] **5–617**

Sums received by Director

57. [*Repealed by* SCA *2007, ss.74(2) and 92, Sched. 8, paras 1 and 25, and Sched. 14.*] **5–618**

Restrictions

Restraint orders

58.—(1) Subsections (2) to (4) apply if a court makes a restraint order. **5–619**

(2) No distress may be levied[, and no power to use the procedure in Schedule 12 to the *Tribunals, Courts and Enforcement Act* 2007 (taking control of goods) may be exercised,] against any realisable property to which the order applies except with the leave of the Crown Court and subject to any terms the Crown Court may impose.

(3) If the order applies to a tenancy of any premises, no landlord or other person to whom rent is payable may exercise a right within subsection (4) except with the leave of the Crown Court and subject to any terms the Crown Court may impose.

(4) A right is within this subsection if it is a right of forfeiture by peaceable re-entry in relation to the premises in respect of any failure by the tenant to comply with any term or condition of the tenancy.

(5) If a court in which proceedings are pending in respect of any property is satisfied that a restraint order has been applied for or made in respect of the property, the court may either stay the proceedings or allow them to continue on any terms it thinks fit.

(6) Before exercising any power conferred by subsection (5), the court must give an opportunity to be heard to—

(a) the applicant for the restraint order, and

(b) any receiver appointed in respect of the property under section 48 or 50.

[This section is printed as amended by the *SCA* 2007, s.74(2), and Sched. 8, paras 1 and 26; and as amended, as from a day to be appointed, by the *Tribunals, Courts and Enforcement Act* 2007, s.62(3), and Sched. 13, paras 142 and 143 (insertion of words in square brackets).]

Enforcement receivers

5–620 **59.**—(1) Subsections (2) to (4) apply if a court makes an order under section 50 appointing a receiver in respect of any realisable property.

(2) No distress may be levied[, and no power to use the procedure in Schedule 12 to the *Tribunals, Courts and Enforcement Act* 2007 (taking control of goods) may be exercised,] against the property except with the leave of the Crown Court and subject to any terms the Crown Court may impose.

(3) If the receiver is appointed in respect of a tenancy of any premises, no landlord or other person to whom rent is payable may exercise a right within subsection (4) except with the leave of the Crown Court and subject to any terms the Crown Court may impose.

(4) [*Identical to s.58(4),* ante.]

(5) If a court in which proceedings are pending in respect of any property is satisfied that an order under section 50 appointing a receiver in respect of the property has been applied for or made, the court may either stay the proceedings or allow them to continue on any terms it thinks fit.

(6) Before exercising any power conferred by subsection (5), the court must give an opportunity to be heard to—

(a) the prosecutor, and

(b) the receiver (if the order under section 50 has been made).

[This section is printed as amended, as from a day to be appointed, by the *Tribunals, Courts and Enforcement Act* 2007, s.62(3), and Sched. 13, paras 142 and 144 (insertion of words in square brackets).]

Director's receivers

5–621 **60.** [*Repealed by* SCA *2007, ss.74(2) and 92, Sched. 8, paras 1 and 27, and Sched. 14.*]

Receivers: further provisions

Protection

5–622 **61.** If a receiver appointed under section 48 or 50—

(a) takes action in relation to property which is not realisable property,

(b) would be entitled to take the action if it were realisable property, and

(c) believes on reasonable grounds that he is entitled to take the action,

he is not liable to any person in respect of any loss or damage resulting from the action, except so far as the loss or damage is caused by his negligence.

[This section is printed as amended by the *SCA* 2007, s.74(2), and Sched. 8, paras 1 and 28.]

Further applications

5–623 **62.**—(1) This section applies to a receiver appointed under section 48 or 50.

(2) The receiver may apply to the Crown Court for an order giving directions as to the exercise of his powers.

(3) The following persons may apply to the Crown Court—

(a) any person affected by action taken by the receiver;

(b) any person who may be affected by action the receiver proposes to take.

(4) On an application under this section the court may make such order as it believes is appropriate.

[This section is printed as amended by the *SCA* 2007, s.74(2), and Sched. 8, paras 1 and 29.]

Discharge and variation

5–624 **63.**—(1) The following persons may apply to the Crown Court to vary or discharge an order made under any of sections 48 to 51—

(a) the receiver;
(b) the person who applied for the order;
(c) any person affected by the order.

(2) On an application under this section the court—
(a) may discharge the order;
(b) may vary the order.

(3) But in the case of an order under section 48 or 49—
(a) if the condition in section 40 which was satisfied was that proceedings were started or an application was made, the court must discharge the order on the conclusion of the proceedings or of the application (as the case may be);
(b) if the condition which was satisfied was that an investigation was started or an application was to be made, the court must discharge the order if within a reasonable time proceedings for the offence are not started or the application is not made (as the case may be).

[This section is printed as amended by the *SCA* 2007, ss.74(2) and 92, Sched. 8, paras 1 and 30, and Sched. 14.]

Management receivers: discharge

64.—(1) This section applies if— 5–625
(a) a receiver stands appointed under section 48 in respect of realisable property (the management receiver), and
(b) the court appoints a receiver under section 50.

(2) The court must order the management receiver to transfer to the other receiver all property held by the management receiver by virtue of the powers conferred on him by section 49.

(4) Subsection (2) does not apply to property which the management receiver holds by virtue of the exercise by him of his power under section 49(2)(d).

(5) If the management receiver complies with an order under subsection (2) he is discharged—
(a) from his appointment under section 48;
(b) from any obligation under this Act arising from his appointment.

(6) If this section applies the court may make such a consequential or incidental order as it believes is appropriate.

[This section is printed as amended by the *SCA* 2007, ss.74(2) and 92, Sched. 8, paras 1 and 31, and Sched. 14.]

Appeal to Court of Appeal

65.—(1) If on an application for an order under any of sections 48 to 51 the court decides not to make one, the person who applied for the order may appeal to the Court of Appeal against the decision. 5–626

(2) If the court makes an order under any of sections 48 to 51, the following persons may appeal to the Court of Appeal in respect of the court's decision—
(a) the person who applied for the order;
(b) any person affected by the order.

(3) If on an application for an order under section 62 the court decides not to make one, the person who applied for the order may appeal to the Court of Appeal against the decision.

(4) If the court makes an order under section 62, the following persons may appeal to the Court of Appeal in respect of the court's decision—
(a) the person who applied for the order;
(b) any person affected by the order;
(c) the receiver.

(5) The following persons may appeal to the Court of Appeal against a decision of the court on an application under section 63—
(a) the person who applied for the order in respect of which the application was made;
(b) any person affected by the court's decision;
(c) the receiver.

(6) On an appeal under this section the Court of Appeal may—
(a) confirm the decision, or
(b) make such order as it believes is appropriate.

[This section is printed as amended by the *SCA* 2007, ss.74(2) and 92, Sched. 8, paras 1 and 32, and Sched. 14.]

Appeal to House of Lords [Supreme Court]

5–627 **66.**—(1) An appeal lies to the *House of Lords* [Supreme Court] from a decision of the Court of Appeal on an appeal under section 65.

(2) An appeal under this section lies at the instance of any person who was a party to the proceedings before the Court of Appeal.

(3) On an appeal under this section the *House of Lords* [Supreme Court] may—

(a) confirm the decision of the Court of Appeal, or

(b) make such order as it believes is appropriate.

[This section is printed as amended, as from a day to be appointed, by the *Constitutional Reform Act* 2005, s.40(4), and Sched. 9, para. 77(1) and (3) (substitution of references to "Supreme Court" for references to "House of Lords").]

Seized money

Seized money

5–628 **67.**—(1) This section applies to money which—

(a) is held by a person, and

(b) is held in an account maintained by him with a bank or a building society.

(2) This section also applies to money which is held by a person and which—

(a) has been seized by a constable under section 19 of the *Police and Criminal Evidence Act* 1984 (general power of seizure etc), and

(b) is held in an account maintained by a police force with a bank or a building society.

(3) This section also applies to money which is held by a person and which—

(a) has been seized by a customs officer under section 19 of the 1984 Act as applied by order made under section 114(2) of that Act, and

(b) is held in an account maintained by the Commissioners of Customs and Excise with a bank or a building society.

(4) This section applies if the following conditions are satisfied—

(a) a restraint order has effect in relation to money to which this section applies;

(b) a confiscation order is made against the person by whom the money is held; ...

(d) a receiver has not been appointed under section 50 in relation to the money;

(e) any period allowed under section 11 for payment of the amount ordered to be paid under the confiscation order has ended.

(5) In such a case a magistrates' court may order the bank or building society to pay the money to the designated officer for the court on account of the amount payable under the confiscation order.

(6) If a bank or building society fails to comply with an order under subsection (5)—

(a) the magistrates' court may order it to pay an amount not exceeding £5,000, and

(b) for the purposes of the *Magistrates' Courts Act* 1980 the sum is to be treated as adjudged to be paid by a conviction of the court.

(7) [*Power of Secretary of State, by order, to substitute different sum in subs. (6)(a).*]

(8) For the purposes of this section—

(a) a bank is a deposit-taking business within the meaning of the *Banking Act* 1987;

(b) "building society" has the same meaning as in the *Building Societies Act* 1986.

[This section is printed as amended by the *Courts Act* 2003, s.109(1), and Sched. 8, para. 409; and the *SCA* 2007, ss.74(2) and 92, Sched. 8, paras 1 and 33, and Sched. 14.]

Financial investigators

Applications and appeals

5–629 **68.**—(1) Subsections (2) and (3) apply to—

(a) an application under section 41, 42, 48, 49 or 63;

(b) an appeal under section 43, 44, 65 or 66.

(2) An accredited financial investigator must not make such an application or bring such an appeal unless he falls within subsection (3).

(3) An accredited financial investigator falls within this subsection if he is one of the following or is authorised for the purposes of this section by one of the following—

(a) a police officer who is not below the rank of superintendent,

(b) a customs officer who is not below such grade as is designated by the Commissioners of Customs and Excise as equivalent to that rank,

(c) an accredited financial investigator who falls within a description specified in an order made for the purposes of this paragraph by the Secretary of State under section 453.

(4) If such an application is made or appeal brought by an accredited financial investigator any subsequent step in the application or appeal or any further application or appeal relating to the same matter may be taken, made or brought by a different accredited financial investigator who falls within subsection (3).

(5) If—

(a) an application for a restraint order is made by an accredited financial investigator, and

(b) a court is required under section 58(6) to give the applicant for the order an opportunity to be heard,

the court may give the opportunity to a different accredited financial investigator who falls within subsection (3).

Exercise of powers

Powers of court and receiver

69.—(1) This section applies to— 5–630

(a) the powers conferred on a court by sections 41 to 59 and sections 62 to 67;

(b) the powers of a receiver appointed under section 48 or 50.

(2) The powers—

(a) must be exercised with a view to the value for the time being of realisable property being made available (by the property's realisation) for satisfying any confiscation order that has been or may be made against the defendant;

(b) must be exercised, in a case where a confiscation order has not been made, with a view to securing that there is no diminution in the value of realisable property;

(c) must be exercised without taking account of any obligation of the defendant or a recipient of a tainted gift if the obligation conflicts with the object of satisfying any confiscation order that has been or may be made against the defendant;

(d) may be exercised in respect of a debt owed by the Crown.

(3) Subsection (2) has effect subject to the following rules—

(a) the powers must be exercised with a view to allowing a person other than the defendant or a recipient of a tainted gift to retain or recover the value of any interest held by him;

(b) in the case of realisable property held by a recipient of a tainted gift, the powers must be exercised with a view to realising no more than the value for the time being of the gift;

(c) in a case where a confiscation order has not been made against the defendant, property must not be sold if the court so orders under subsection (4).

(4) If on an application by the defendant, or by the recipient of a tainted gift, the court decides that property cannot be replaced it may order that it must not be sold.

(5) An order under subsection (4) may be revoked or varied.

[This section is printed as amended by the *SCA* 2007, ss.74(2) and 92, Sched. 8, paras 1 and 34, and Sched. 14.]

Having regard to subsection (3)(a), a restraint order may be varied in favour of a third party who establishes a proprietary equitable interest in assets which are subject to the restraint order, but, having regard to subsection (2)(c), it may not be varied so as to permit the payment off of an unsecured creditor: *Serious Fraud Office v. Lexi Holdings plc (in administration)*, *The Times*, August 18, 2008, CA.

Committal

Committal by magistrates' court

70.—(1) This section applies if— 5–631

(a) a defendant is convicted of an offence by a magistrates' court, and

(b) the prosecutor asks the court to commit the defendant to the Crown Court with a view to a confiscation order being considered under section 6.

(2) In such a case the magistrates' court—

(a) must commit the defendant to the Crown Court in respect of the offence, and

(b) may commit him to the Crown Court in respect of any other offence falling within subsection (3).

(3) An offence falls within this subsection if—

(a) the defendant has been convicted of it by the magistrates' court or any other court, and

(b) the magistrates' court has power to deal with him in respect of it.

(4) If a committal is made under this section in respect of an offence or offences—

(a) section 6 applies accordingly, and

(b) the committal operates as a committal of the defendant to be dealt with by the Crown Court in accordance with section 71.

(5) If a committal is made under this section in respect of an offence for which (apart from this section) the magistrates' court could have committed the defendant for sentence under section 3(2) of the *Sentencing Act* (offences triable either way) [or under section 3B(2) of that Act (committal of child or young person)] the court must state whether it would have done so.

(6) A committal under this section may be in custody or on bail.

[The words in square brackets in section 70(5) are inserted, as from a day to be appointed, by the *CJA* 2003, s.41, and Sched. 3, para. 75(1) and (3).]

Sentencing by Crown Court

5–632 **71.**—(1) If a defendant is committed to the Crown Court under section 70 in respect of an offence or offences, this section applies (whether or not the court proceeds under section 6).

(2) In the case of an offence in respect of which the magistrates' court has stated under section 70(5) that it would have committed the defendant for sentence, the Crown Court—

(a) must inquire into the circumstances of the case, and

(b) may deal with the defendant in any way in which it could deal with him if he had just been convicted of the offence on indictment before it.

(3) In the case of any other offence the Crown Court—

(a) must inquire into the circumstances of the case, and

(b) may deal with the defendant in any way in which the magistrates' court could deal with him if it had just convicted him of the offence.

Compensation

Serious default

5–633 **72.**—(1) If the following three conditions are satisfied the Crown Court may order the payment of such compensation as it believes is just.

(2) The first condition is satisfied if a criminal investigation has been started with regard to an offence and proceedings are not started for the offence.

(3) The first condition is also satisfied if proceedings for an offence are started against a person and—

(a) they do not result in his conviction for the offence, or

(b) he is convicted of the offence but the conviction is quashed or he is pardoned in respect of it.

(4) If subsection (2) applies the second condition is that—

(a) in the criminal investigation there has been a serious default by a person mentioned in subsection (9), and

(b) the investigation would not have continued if the default had not occurred.

(5) If subsection (3) applies the second condition is that—

(a) in the criminal investigation with regard to the offence or in its prosecution there has been a serious default by a person who is mentioned in subsection (9), and

(b) the proceedings would not have been started or continued if the default had not occurred.

(6) The third condition is that an application is made under this section by a person who held realisable property and has suffered loss in consequence of anything done in relation to it by or in pursuance of an order under this Part.

(7) The offence referred to in subsection (2) may be one of a number of offences with regard to which the investigation is started.

(8) The offence referred to in subsection (3) may be one of a number of offences for which the proceedings are started.

(9) Compensation under this section is payable to the applicant and—

(a) if the person in default was or was acting as a member of a police force, the compensation is payable out of the police fund from which the expenses of that force are met;

(b) if the person in default was a member of the Crown Prosecution Service or was acting on its behalf, the compensation is payable by the Director of Public Prosecutions;

(c) if the person in default was a member of the Serious Fraud Office, the compensation is payable by the Director of that Office;

(d) if the person in default was a member of or acting on behalf of the Revenue and Customs Prosecutions Office, the compensation is payable by the Director of Revenue and Customs Prosecutions;

(e) if the person in default was an officer of Revenue and Customs, the compensation is payable by the Commissioners for Her Majesty's Revenue and Customs.

[This section is printed as amended by the *Commissioners for Revenue and Customs Act* 2005, s.50(1), (2) and (6), and Sched. 4, para. 97.]

Order varied or discharged

73.—(1) This section applies if— **5–634**

(a) the court varies a confiscation order under section 29 or discharges one under section 30, and

(b) an application is made to the Crown Court by a person who held realisable property and has suffered loss as a result of the making of the order.

(2) The court may order the payment of such compensation as it believes is just.

(3) Compensation under this section is payable—

(a) to the applicant;

(b) by the Lord Chancellor.

74. [*Enforcement abroad*.] **5–635**

Interpretation

Criminal lifestyle

75.—(1) A defendant has a criminal lifestyle if (and only if) the following condition is satisfied. **5–636**

(2) The condition is that the offence (or any of the offences) concerned satisfies any of these tests—

(a) it is specified in Schedule 2;

(b) it constitutes conduct forming part of a course of criminal activity;

(c) it is an offence committed over a period of at least six months and the defendant has benefited from the conduct which constitutes the offence.

(3) Conduct forms part of a course of criminal activity if the defendant has benefited from the conduct and—

(a) in the proceedings in which he was convicted he was convicted of three or more other offences, each of three or more of them constituting conduct from which he has benefited, or

(b) in the period of six years ending with the day when those proceedings were started (or, if there is more than one such day, the earliest day) he was convicted on at least two separate occasions of an offence constituting conduct from which he has benefited.

(4) But an offence does not satisfy the test in subsection (2)(b) or (c) unless the defendant obtains relevant benefit of not less than £5000.

(5) Relevant benefit for the purposes of subsection (2)(b) is—

(a) benefit from conduct which constitutes the offence;

(b) benefit from any other conduct which forms part of the course of criminal activity and which constitutes an offence of which the defendant has been convicted;

(c) benefit from conduct which constitutes an offence which has been or will be taken into consideration by the court in sentencing the defendant for an offence mentioned in paragraph (a) or (b).

(6) Relevant benefit for the purposes of subsection (2)(c) is—

(a) benefit from conduct which constitutes the offence;

(b) benefit from conduct which constitutes an offence which has been or will be taken into consideration by the court in sentencing the defendant for the offence mentioned in paragraph (a).

(7) The Secretary of State may by order amend Schedule 2.

(8) The Secretary of State may by order vary the amount for the time being specified in subsection (4).

Conduct and benefit

5–637 **76.**—(1) Criminal conduct is conduct which—

(a) constitutes an offence in England and Wales, or

(b) would constitute such an offence if it occurred in England and Wales.

(2) General criminal conduct of the defendant is all his criminal conduct, and it is immaterial—

(a) whether conduct occurred before or after the passing of this Act;

(b) whether property constituting a benefit from conduct was obtained before or after the passing of this Act.

(3) Particular criminal conduct of the defendant is all his criminal conduct which falls within the following paragraphs—

(a) conduct which constitutes the offence or offences concerned;

(b) conduct which constitutes offences of which he was convicted in the same proceedings as those in which he was convicted of the offence or offences concerned;

(c) conduct which constitutes offences which the court will be taking into consideration in deciding his sentence for the offence or offences concerned.

(4) A person benefits from conduct if he obtains property as a result of or in connection with the conduct.

(5) If a person obtains a pecuniary advantage as a result of or in connection with conduct, he is to be taken to obtain as a result of or in connection with the conduct a sum of money equal to the value of the pecuniary advantage.

(6) References to property or a pecuniary advantage obtained in connection with conduct include references to property or a pecuniary advantage obtained both in that connection and some other.

(7) If a person benefits from conduct his benefit is the value of the property obtained.

In connection with this section, see *post*, § 5–768 *et seq*.

Tainted gifts

5–638 **77.**—(1) Subsections (2) and (3) apply if—

(a) no court has made a decision as to whether the defendant has a criminal lifestyle, or

(b) a court has decided that the defendant has a criminal lifestyle.

(2) A gift is tainted if it was made by the defendant at any time after the relevant day.

(3) A gift is also tainted if it was made by the defendant at any time and was of property—

(a) which was obtained by the defendant as a result of or in connection with his general criminal conduct, or

(b) which (in whole or part and whether directly or indirectly) represented in the defendant's hands property obtained by him as a result of or in connection with his general criminal conduct.

(4) Subsection (5) applies if a court has decided that the defendant does not have a criminal lifestyle.

(5) A gift is tainted if it was made by the defendant at any time after—

(a) the date on which the offence concerned was committed, or

(b) if his particular criminal conduct consists of two or more offences and they were committed on different dates, the date of the earliest.

(6) For the purposes of subsection (5) an offence which is a continuing offence is committed on the first occasion when it is committed.

(7) For the purposes of subsection (5) the defendant's particular criminal conduct includes any conduct which constitutes offences which the court has taken into consideration in deciding his sentence for the offence or offences concerned.

(8) A gift may be a tainted gift whether it was made before or after the passing of this Act.

(9) The relevant day is the first day of the period of six years ending with—

(a) the day when proceedings for the offence concerned were started against the defendant, or

(b) if there are two or more offences and proceedings for them were started on different days, the earliest of those days.

Gifts and their recipients

78.—(1) If the defendant transfers property to another person for a consideration whose value is significantly less than the value of the property at the time of the transfer, he is to be treated as making a gift. **5–639**

(2) If subsection (1) applies the property given is to be treated as such share in the property transferred as is represented by the fraction—

(a) whose numerator is the difference between the two values mentioned in subsection (1), and

(b) whose denominator is the value of the property at the time of the transfer.

(3) References to a recipient of a tainted gift are to a person to whom the defendant has made the gift.

In connection with this provision, see *Gibson v. Revenue and Customs Prosecution Office*, *post*, § 5–775 (decided in relation to the similarly worded s.8 of the *DTA* 1994).

Value: the basic rule

79.—(1) This section applies for the purpose of deciding the value at any time of property then held by a person. **5–640**

(2) Its value is the market value of the property at that time.

(3) But if at that time another person holds an interest in the property its value, in relation to the person mentioned in subsection (1), is the market value of his interest at that time, ignoring any charging order under a provision listed in subsection (4).

(4) The provisions are—

(a) section 9 of the *Drug Trafficking Offences Act* 1986;

(b) section 78 of the *Criminal Justice Act* 1988;

(c) Article 14 of the *Criminal Justice (Confiscation) (Northern Ireland) Order* 1990 (S.I. 1990 No. 2588 (N.I. 17));

(d) section 27 of the *Drug Trafficking Act* 1994;

(e) Article 32 of the *Proceeds of Crime (Northern Ireland) Order* 1996 (S.I. 1996 No. 1299 (N.I. 9)).

(5) This section has effect subject to sections 80 and 81.

As to this section, see *post*, § 5–774.

Value of property obtained from conduct

80.—(1) This section applies for the purpose of deciding the value of property obtained by a person as a result of or in connection with his criminal conduct; and the material time is the time the court makes its decision. **5–641**

(2) The value of the property at the material time is the greater of the following—

(a) the value of the property (at the time the person obtained it) adjusted to take account of later changes in the value of money;

(b) the value (at the material time) of the property found under subsection (3).

(3) The property found under this subsection is as follows—

(a) if the person holds the property obtained, the property found under this subsection is that property;

(b) if he holds no part of the property obtained, the property found under this subsection is any property which directly or indirectly represents it in his hands;

(c) if he holds part of the property obtained, the property found under this subsection is that part and any property which directly or indirectly represents the other part in his hands.

(4) The references in subsection (2)(a) and (b) to the value are to the value found in accordance with section 79.

Value of tainted gifts

81.—(1) The value at any time (the material time) of a tainted gift is the greater of the following— **5–642**

(a) the value (at the time of the gift) of the property given, adjusted to take account of later changes in the value of money;

(b) the value (at the material time) of the property found under subsection (2).

(2) The property found under this subsection is as follows—

(a) if the recipient holds the property given, the property found under this subsection is that property;

(b) if the recipient holds no part of the property given, the property found under this subsection is any property which directly or indirectly represents it in his hands;

(c) if the recipient holds part of the property given, the property found under this subsection is that part and any property which directly or indirectly represents the other part in his hands.

(3) The references in subsection (1)(a) and (b) to the value are to the value found in accordance with section 79.

Free property

5–643 **82.** Property is free unless an order is in force in respect of it under any of these provisions—

(a) section 27 of the *Misuse of Drugs Act* 1971 (forfeiture orders);

(b) Article 11 of the *Criminal Justice (Northern Ireland) Order* 1994 (S.I. 1994 No. 2795 (N.I. 15)) (deprivation orders);

(c) Part 2 of the *Proceeds of Crime (Scotland) Act* 1995 (forfeiture of property used in crime);

(d) section 143 of the *Sentencing Act* (deprivation orders);

(e) section 23 or 111 of the *Terrorism Act* 2000 (forfeiture orders);

(f) section 245A, 246, 255A, 256, 266, 295(2) or 298(2) of this Act.

[This section is printed as amended by the *SOCPA* 2005, s.109, and Sched. 6, para. 5.]

Realisable property

5–644 **83.** Realisable property is—

(a) any free property held by the defendant;

(b) any free property held by the recipient of a tainted gift.

As to this section and section 84, see *post*, § 5–775.

Property: general provisions

5–645 **84.**—(1) Property is all property wherever situated and includes—

(a) money;

(b) all forms of real or personal property;

(c) things in action and other intangible or incorporeal property.

(2) The following rules apply in relation to property—

(a) property is held by a person if he holds an interest in it;

(b) property is obtained by a person if he obtains an interest in it;

(c) property is transferred by one person to another if the first one transfers or grants an interest in it to the second;

(d) references to property held by a person include references to property vested in his trustee in bankruptcy, permanent or interim trustee (within the meaning of the *Bankruptcy (Scotland) Act* 1985) or liquidator;

(e) references to an interest held by a person beneficially in property include references to an interest which would be held by him beneficially if the property were not so vested;

(f) references to an interest, in relation to land in England and Wales or Northern Ireland, are to any legal estate or equitable interest or power;

(g) references to an interest, in relation to land in Scotland, are to any estate, interest, servitude or other heritable right in or over land, including a heritable security;

(h) references to an interest, in relation to property other than land, include references to a right (including a right to possession).

Proceedings

5–646 **85.**—(1) Proceedings for an offence are started—

(a) when a justice of the peace issues a summons or warrant under section 1 of the *Magistrates' Courts Act* 1980 in respect of the offence;

(aa) when a public prosecutor issues a written charge and requisition in respect of the offence;

(b) when a person is charged with the offence after being taken into custody without a warrant;

(c) when a bill of indictment is preferred under section 2 of the *Administration of Justice (Miscellaneous Provisions) Act* 1933 in a case falling within subsection (2)(b) of that section (preferment by Court of Appeal or High Court judge).

(2) If more than one time is found under subsection (1) in relation to proceedings they are started at the earliest of them.

(3) If the defendant is acquitted on all counts in proceedings for an offence, the proceedings are concluded when he is acquitted.

(4) If the defendant is convicted in proceedings for an offence and the conviction is quashed or the defendant is pardoned before a confiscation order is made, the proceedings are concluded when the conviction is quashed or the defendant is pardoned.

(5) If a confiscation order is made against the defendant in proceedings for an offence (whether the order is made by the Crown Court or the Court of Appeal) the proceedings are concluded—

(a) when the order is satisfied or discharged, or

(b) when the order is quashed and there is no further possibility of an appeal against the decision to quash the order.

(6) If the defendant is convicted in proceedings for an offence but the Crown Court decides not to make a confiscation order against him, the following rules apply—

(a) if an application for leave to appeal under section 31(2) is refused, the proceedings are concluded when the decision to refuse is made;

(b) if the time for applying for leave to appeal under section 31(2) expires without an application being made, the proceedings are concluded when the time expires;

(c) if on appeal under section 31(2) the Court of Appeal confirms the Crown Court's decision, and an application for leave to appeal under section 33 is refused, the proceedings are concluded when the decision to refuse is made;

(d) if on appeal under section 31(2) the Court of Appeal confirms the Crown Court's decision, and the time for applying for leave to appeal under section 33 expires without an application being made, the proceedings are concluded when the time expires;

(e) if on appeal under section 31(2) the Court of Appeal confirms the Crown Court's decision, and on appeal under section 33 the *House of Lords* [Supreme Court] confirms the Court of Appeal's decision, the proceedings are concluded when the *House of Lords* [Supreme Court] confirms the decision;

(f) if on appeal under section 31(2) the Court of Appeal directs the Crown Court to reconsider the case, and on reconsideration the Crown Court decides not to make a confiscation order against the defendant, the proceedings are concluded when the Crown Court makes that decision;

(g) if on appeal under section 33 the *House of Lords* [Supreme Court] directs the Crown Court to reconsider the case, and on reconsideration the Crown Court decides not to make a confiscation order against the defendant, the proceedings are concluded when the Crown Court makes that decision.

(7) In applying subsection (6) any power to extend the time for making an application for leave to appeal must be ignored.

(8) In applying subsection (6) the fact that a court may decide on a later occasion to make a confiscation order against the defendant must be ignored.

(9) In this section "public prosecutor", "requisition" and "written charge" have the same meaning as in section 29 of the *Criminal Justice Act* 2003.

[This section is printed as amended by the *CJA* 2003, s.331, and Sched. 36, para. 15; and as amended, as from a day to be appointed, by the *Constitutional Reform Act* 2005, s.40(4), and Sched. 9, para. 77(1) and (4) (substitution of references to "Supreme Court" for references to "House of Lords").]

Applications

86.—(1) An application under section 19, 20, 27 or 28 is concluded— **5–647**

(a) in a case where the court decides not to make a confiscation order against the defendant, when it makes the decision;

(b) in a case where a confiscation order is made against him as a result of the application, when the order is satisfied or discharged, or when the order is quashed and there is no further possibility of an appeal against the decision to quash the order;

(c) in a case where the application is withdrawn, when the person who made the application notifies the withdrawal to the court to which the application was made.

(2) An application under section 21 or 22 is concluded—

(a) in a case where the court decides not to vary the confiscation order concerned, when it makes the decision;

(b) in a case where the court varies the confiscation order as a result of the application, when the order is satisfied or discharged, or when the order is quashed and there is no further possibility of an appeal against the decision to quash the order;

(c) in a case where the application is withdrawn, when the person who made the application notifies the withdrawal to the court to which the application was made.

Confiscation orders

5–648 **87.**—(1) A confiscation order is satisfied when no amount is due under it.

(2) A confiscation order is subject to appeal until there is no further possibility of an appeal on which the order could be varied or quashed; and for this purpose any power to grant leave to appeal out of time must be ignored.

Other interpretative provisions

5–649 **88.**—(1) A reference to the offence (or offences) concerned must be construed in accordance with section 6(9).

(2) A criminal investigation is an investigation which police officers or other persons have a duty to conduct with a view to it being ascertained whether a person should be charged with an offence.

(3) A defendant is a person against whom proceedings for an offence have been started (whether or not he has been convicted).

(4) A reference to sentencing the defendant for an offence includes a reference to dealing with him otherwise in respect of the offence.

(5) The *Sentencing Act* is the *Powers of Criminal Courts (Sentencing) Act* 2000.

(6) The following paragraphs apply to references to orders—

(a) a confiscation order is an order under section 6;

(b) a restraint order is an order under section 41.

(7) Sections 75 to 87 and this section apply for the purposes of this Part.

General

Procedure on appeal to the Court of Appeal

5–650 **89.**—(1) An appeal to the Court of Appeal under this Part lies only with the leave of that Court.

(2) Subject to rules of court made under section 53(1) of the *Supreme Court Act* 1981 (distribution of business between civil and criminal divisions) the criminal division of the Court of Appeal is the division—

(a) to which an appeal to that Court under this Part is to lie, and

(b) which is to exercise that Court's jurisdiction under this Part.

(3) In relation to appeals to the Court of Appeal under this Part, the Secretary of State may make an order containing provision corresponding to any provision in the *Criminal Appeal Act* 1968 (subject to any specified modifications).

(4) Subject to any rules made under section 91, the costs of and incidental to all proceedings on an appeal to the criminal division of the Court of Appeal under—

(a) section 43(1) or (2) (appeals against orders made in restraint proceedings), or

(b) section 65 (appeals against, or relating to, the making of receivership orders) are in the discretion of the court.

(5) Such rules may in particular make provision for regulating matters relating to the costs of those proceedings, including prescribing scales of costs to be paid to legal or other representatives.

(6) The court shall have full power to determine by whom and to what extent the costs are to be paid.

(7) In any proceedings mentioned in subsection (4), the court may—

(a) disallow, or

(b) (as the case may be) order the legal or other representative concerned to meet, the whole of any wasted costs or such part of them as may be determined in accordance with rules under section 91.

(8) In subsection (7) "wasted costs" means any costs incurred by a party—

(a) as a result of any improper, unreasonable or negligent act or omission on the part of any legal or other representative or any employee of such a representative, or

(b) which, in the light of any such act or omission occurring after they were incurred, the court considers it is unreasonable to expect that party to pay.

(9) "Legal or other representative", in relation to a party to proceedings means any person exercising a right of audience or right to conduct litigation on his behalf.

[Subss. (4)–(9) were inserted by the *Courts Act* 2003, s.94(1) and (2). They apply in relation to proceedings on appeals in respect of offences committed or alleged to have been committed on or after March 24, 2003.]

Procedure on appeal to the House of Lords

90.—(1) Section 33(3) of the *Criminal Appeal Act* 1968 (limitation on appeal from criminal division of the Court of Appeal) does not prevent an appeal to the *House of Lords* [Supreme Court] under this Part. **5–651**

(2) In relation to appeals to the *House of Lords* [Supreme Court] under this Part, the Secretary of State may make an order containing provision corresponding to any provision in the *Criminal Appeal Act* 1968 (subject to any specified modifications).

[This section is printed as amended, as from a day to be appointed, by the *Constitutional Reform Act* 2005, s.40(4), and Sched. 9, para. 77(1) and (5) (substitution of references to "Supreme Court" for references to "House of Lords").]

Crown Court Rules

91. In relation to— **5–652**

(a) proceedings under this Part, or

(b) receivers appointed under this Part,

Criminal Procedure Rules may make provision corresponding to provision in Civil Procedure Rules.

[This section is printed as amended by the *Courts Act* 2003, ss.94(1) and (4), and 109(1), and Sched. 8, para. 410.]

Proceeds of Crime Act 2002, Sched. 2

Section 75

SCHEDULE 2

LIFESTYLE OFFENCES: ENGLAND AND WALES

Drug trafficking

1.—(1) An offence under any of the following provisions of the *Misuse of Drugs Act* 1971— **5–653**

(a) section 4(2) or (3) (unlawful production or supply of controlled drugs);

(b) section 5(3) (possession of controlled drug with intent to supply);

(c) section 8 (permitting certain activities relating to controlled drugs);

(d) section 20 (assisting in or inducing the commission outside the UK of an offence punishable under a corresponding law).

(2) An offence under any of the following provisions of the *Customs and Excise Management Act* 1979 if it is committed in connection with a prohibition or restriction on importation or exportation which has effect by virtue of section 3 of the *Misuse of Drugs Act* 1971—

(a) section 50(2) or (3) (improper importation of goods);

(b) section 68(2) (exploration of prohibited or restricted goods);

(c) section 170 (fraudulent evasion).

(3) An offence under either of the following provisions of the *Criminal Justice (International Co-operation) Act* 1990—

(a) section 12 (manufacture or supply of a substance for the time being specified in Schedule 2 to that Act);

(b) section 19 (using a ship for illicit traffic in controlled drugs).

Money laundering

5–654 2. An offence under either of the following provisions of this Act—

(a) section 327 (concealing etc criminal property);

(b) section 328 (assisting another to retain criminal property).

Directing terrorism

5–655 3. An offence under section 56 of the *Terrorism Act* 2000 (directing the activities of a terrorist organisation).

People trafficking

5–656 4.—(1) An offence under section 25, 25A or 25B of the *Immigration Act* 1971 (assisting unlawful immigration, etc.).

(2) An offence under any of sections 57 to 59 of the *Sexual Offences Act* 2003 (trafficking for sexual exploitation).

[Para. 4 is printed as substituted by the *Nationality, Immigration and Asylum Act* 2002, s.114, and Sched. 7, para. 31; and as subsequently amended by the *SOA* 2003, s.139, and Sched. 6, para. 46(2).]

Arms trafficking

5–657 5.—(1) An offence under either of the following provisions of the *Customs and Excise Management Act* 1979 if it is committed in connection with a firearm or ammunition—

(a) section 68(2) (exportation of prohibited goods);

(b) section 170 (fraudulent evasion).

(2) An offence under section 3(1) of the *Firearms Act* 1968 (dealing in firearms or ammunition by way of trade or business).

(3) In this paragraph "firearm" and "ammunition" have the same meanings as in section 57 of the *Firearms Act* 1968.

Counterfeiting

5–658 6. An offence under any of the following provisions of the *Forgery and Counterfeiting Act* 1981—

(a) section 14 (making counterfeit notes or coins);

(b) section 15 (passing etc counterfeit notes or coins);

(c) section 16 (having counterfeit notes or coins);

(d) section 17 (making or possessing materials or equipment for counterfeiting).

Intellectual property

5–659 7.—(1) An offence under any of the following provisions of the *Copyright, Designs and Patents Act* 1988—

(a) section 107(1) (making or dealing in an article which infringes copyright);

(b) section 107(2) (making or possessing an article designed or adapted for making a copy of a copyright work);

(c) section 198(1) (making or dealing in an illicit recording);

(d) section 297A (making or dealing in unauthorised decoders).

(2) An offence under section 92(1), (2) or (3) of the *Trade Marks Act* 1994 (unauthorised use etc of trade mark).

Prostitution and child sex

5–660 8.—(1) An offence under section 33 or 34 of the *Sexual Offences Act* 1956 (keeping or letting premises for use as a brothel).

(2) An offence under any of the following provisions of the *Sexual Offences Act* 2003—

(a) section 14 (arranging or facilitating commission of a child sex offence);

(b) section 48 (causing or inciting child prostitution or pornography);

(c) section 49 (controlling a child prostitute or a child involved in pornography);

(d) section 50 (arranging or facilitating child prostitution or pornography);

(e) section 52 (causing or inciting prostitution for gain);

(f) section 53 (controlling prostitution for gain).

[Para. 8 is printed as substituted by the *SOA* 2003, s.139, and Sched. 6, para. 46(3).]

Blackmail

5–661 9. An offence under section 21 of the *Theft Act* 1968 (blackmail).

9A. An offence under section 12(1) or (2) of the *Gangmasters (Licensing) Act* 2004 (acting as a gangmaster other than under the authority of a licence, possession of false documents etc). **5–661a**

[Para. 9A was inserted by the *Gangmasters (Licensing) Act* 2004, s.14(4).]

Inchoate offences

10.—(1) An offence of attempting, conspiring or inciting the commission of an offence specified in this Schedule. **5–662**

[(1A) An offence under section 44 of the *Serious Crime Act* 2007 of doing an act capable of encouraging or assisting the commission of an offence specified in this Schedule.]

(2) An offence of aiding, abetting, counselling or procuring the commission of such an offence.

[Para. 10 is printed as amended, as from a day to be appointed, by the *SCA* 2007, s.63(2), and Sched. 6, para. 62 (insertion of sub-para. (1A)).]

Financial reporting orders

Where a person is convicted of a "lifestyle offence", the sentencing court may make a financial reporting order under section 76 of the *SOCPA* 2005, if the court is satisfied that the risk of the person committing another offence is sufficiently high to justify making such an order. For the details of these provisions, see *post*, §§ 5–886 *et seq.* **5–662a**

(b) *Subordinate legislation*

Commencement

Part 2 of the 2002 Act (along with other provisions) was brought into force on March 24, 2003 by the *Proceeds of Crime Act 2002 (Commencement No. 5, Transitional Provisions, Savings and Amendment) Order* 2003 (S.I. 2003 No. 333). This contains important transitional and saving provisions, the most significant of which is that section 6 has no effect where the offence, or any of the offences mentioned in section 6(2), was committed before that date, with the consequence that the former confiscation provisions in the *CJA* 1988 and the *DTA* 1994 continue to apply in relation to such cases. For the full text of this commencement order, see the supplement. **5–662b**

[The next paragraph is § 5–671.]

Rules of court relating to confiscation, restraint and receivership proceedings

Criminal Procedure Rules 2005 (S.I. 2005 No. 384), Pt 57

Interpretation

57.1. In this Part and in Parts 58, 59, 60 and 61: **5–671**

"business day" means any day other than a Saturday, Sunday, Christmas Day or Good Friday, or a bank holiday under the *Banking and Financial Dealings Act* 1971, in England and Wales;

"document" means anything in which information of any description is recorded;

"hearsay evidence" means evidence consisting of hearsay within the meaning of section 1(2) of the *Civil Evidence Act* 1995;

"restraint proceedings" means proceedings under sections 42 and 58(2) and (3) of the *Proceeds of Crime Act* 2002;

"receivership proceedings" means proceedings under sections 48, 49, 50, 51, 54(4), 59(2) and (3), 62 and 63 of the 2002 Act;

"witness statement" means a written statement signed by a person which contains the evidence, and only that evidence, which that person would be allowed to give orally; and

words and expressions used have the same meaning as in Part 2 of the 2002 Act.

Calculation of time

57.2.—(1) This rule shows how to calculate any period of time for doing any act which is specified by this Part and Parts 58, 59, 60 and 61 for the purposes of any proceedings under **5–672**

Part 2 of the *Proceeds of Crime Act* 2002 or by an order of the Crown Court in restraint proceedings or receivership proceedings.

(2) A period of time expressed as a number of days shall be computed as clear days.

(3) In this rule "clear days" means that in computing the number of days—

(a) the day on which the period begins; and

(b) if the end of the period is defined by reference to an event, the day on which that event occurs are not included.

(4) Where the specified period is five days or less and includes a day which is not a business day that day does not count.

Court office closed

5–673 **57.3.** When the period specified by this Part or Parts 58, 59, 60 and 61, or by an order of the Crown Court under Part 2 of the *Proceeds of Crime Act* 2002, for doing any act at the court office falls on a day on which the office is closed, that act shall be in time if done on the next day on which the court office is open.

Application for registration of Scottish or Northern Ireland Order

5–674 **57.4.**—(1) This rule applies to an application for registration of an order under article 6 of the *Proceeds of Crime Act 2002 (Enforcement in different parts of the United Kingdom) Order* 2002 (S.I. 2002 No. 3133).

(2) The application may be made without notice.

(3) The application must be in writing and may be supported by a witness statement which must—

(a) exhibit the order or a certified copy of the order; and

(b) to the best of the witness's ability, give full details of the realisable property located in England and Wales in respect of which the order was made and specify the person holding that realisable property.

(4) If the court registers the order, the applicant must serve notice of the registration on—

(a) any person who holds realisable property to which the order applies; and

(b) any other person whom the applicant knows to be affected by the order.

(5) The permission of the Crown Court under rule 57.13 is not required to serve the notice outside England and Wales.

Application to vary or set aside registration

5–675 **57.5.**—(1) An application to vary or set aside registration of an order under article 6 of the *Proceeds of Crime Act 2002 (Enforcement in different parts of the United Kingdom) Order* 2002 (S.I. 2002 No. 3133) may be made to the Crown Court by—

(a) any person who holds realisable property to which the order applies; and

(b) any other person affected by the order.

(2) The application must be in writing and may be supported by a witness statement.

(3) The application and any witness statement must be lodged with the Crown Court.

(4) The application must be served on the person who applied for registration at least seven days before the date fixed by the court for hearing the application, unless the Crown Court specifies a shorter period.

(5) No property in England and Wales may be realised in pursuance of the order before the Crown Court has decided the application.

Register of orders

5–676 **57.6.**—(1) The Crown Court must keep, under the direction of the Lord Chancellor, a register of the orders registered under article 6 of the *Proceeds of Crime Act 2002 (Enforcement in different parts of the United Kingdom) Order* 2002 (S.I. 2002 No. 3133).

(2) The register must include details of any variation or setting aside of a registration under rule 57.5 and of any execution issued on a registered order.

(3) If the person who applied for registration of an order which is subsequently registered notifies the Crown Court that the court which made the order has varied or discharged the order, details of the variation or discharge, as the case may be, must be entered in the register.

Statements of truth

5–677 **57.7.**—(1) Any witness statement required to be served by this Part or by Parts 58, 59, 60 or 61 must be verified by a statement of truth contained in the witness statement.

(2) A statement of truth is a declaration by the person making the witness statement to the effect that the witness statement is true to the best of his knowledge and belief and that he made the statement knowing that, if it were tendered in evidence, he would be liable to prosecution if he wilfully stated in it anything which he knew to be false or did not believe to be true.

(3) The statement of truth must be signed by the person making the witness statement.

(4) If the person making the witness statement fails to verify the witness statement by a statement of truth, the Crown Court may direct that it shall not be admissible as evidence.

Use of witness statements for other purposes

57.8.—(1) Except as provided by this rule, a witness statement served in proceedings under Part 2 of the *Proceeds of Crime Act* 2002 may be used only for the purpose of the proceedings in which it is served. **5–678**

(2) Paragraph (1) does not apply if and to the extent that—

(a) the witness gives consent in writing to some other use of it;

(b) the Crown Court gives permission for some other use; or

(c) the witness statement has been put in evidence at a hearing held in public.

Expert evidence

57.9.—(1) A party to proceedings under Part 2 of the *Proceeds of Crime Act* 2002 who wishes to adduce expert evidence (whether of fact or opinion) in the proceedings must, as soon as practicable— **5–679**

(a) serve on the other parties a statement in writing of any finding or opinion which he proposes to adduce by way of such evidence; and

(b) serve on any party who requests it in writing, a copy of (or if it appears to the party proposing to adduce the evidence to be more practicable, a reasonable opportunity to examine)—

(i) the record of any observation, test, calculation or other procedure on which the finding or opinion is based, and

(ii) any document or other thing or substance in respect of which the observation, test, calculation or other procedure mentioned in paragraph (1)(b)(i) has been carried out.

(c) A party may serve notice in writing waiving his right to be served with any of the matters mentioned in paragraph (1) [*sic*] and, in particular, may agree that the statement mentioned in paragraph (1)(a) may be given to him orally and not served in writing.

(d) If a party who wishes to adduce expert evidence in proceedings under Part 2 of the 2002 Act fails to comply with this rule he may not adduce that evidence in those proceedings without the leave of the court, except where rule 57.10 applies.

Exceptions to procedure for expert evidence

57.10.—(1) If a party has reasonable grounds for believing that the disclosure of any evidence in compliance with rule 57.9 might lead to the intimidation, or attempted intimidation, of any person on whose evidence he intends to rely in the proceedings, or otherwise to the course of justice being interfered with, he shall not be obliged to comply with those requirements in relation to that evidence, unless the Crown Court orders otherwise. **5–680**

(2) Where, in accordance with paragraph (1), a party considers that he is not obliged to comply with the requirements imposed by rule 57.9 with regard to any evidence in relation to any other party, he must serve notice in writing on that party stating—

(a) that the evidence is being withheld; and

(b) the reasons for withholding the evidence.

Service of documents

57.11.—(1) Part 4 and rule 32.1 (notice required to accompany process served outside the United Kingdom and translations) shall not apply in restraint proceedings and receivership proceedings. **5–681**

(2) Where this Part or Parts 58, 59, 60 or 61 requires service of a document, then, unless the Crown Court directs otherwise, the document may be served by any of the following methods—

(a) in all cases, by delivering the document personally to the party to be served;

(b) if no solicitor is acting for the party to be served by delivering the document at, or by sending it by first class post to, his residence or his last-known residence; or

(c) if a solicitor is acting for the party to be served—

(i) by delivering the document at, or sending it by first class post to, the solicitor's business address, or

(ii) where the solicitor's business address includes a numbered box at a document exchange, by leaving the document at that document exchange or at a document exchange which transmits documents on every business day to that document exchange, or

(iii) if the solicitor has indicated that he is willing to accept service by facsimile transmission, by sending a legible copy of the document by facsimile transmission to the solicitor's office.

(3) A document shall, unless the contrary is proved, be deemed to have been served—

(a) in the case of service by first class post, on the second business day after posting;

(b) in the case of service in accordance with paragraph (2)(c)(ii), on the second business day after the day on which it is left at the document exchange; and

(c) in the case of service in accordance with paragraph (2)(c)(iii), where it is transmitted on a business day before 4 p.m., on that day and in any other case, on the next business day.

(4) An order made in restraint proceedings or receivership proceedings may be enforced against the defendant or any other person affected by it notwithstanding that service of a copy of the order has not been effected in accordance with this rule if the Crown Court is satisfied that the person had notice of the order by being present when the order was made.

Service by an alternative method

5–682 **57.12.**—(1) Where it appears to the Crown Court that there is a good reason to authorise service by a method not otherwise permitted by rule 57.11, the court may make an order permitting service by an alternative method.

(2) An application for an order permitting service by an alternative method—

(a) must be supported by evidence; and

(b) may be made without notice.

(3) An order permitting service by an alternative method must specify—

(a) the method of service; and

(b) the date when the document will be deemed to be served.

Service outside the jurisdiction

5–683 **57.13.**—(1) Where this Part requires a document to be served on someone who is outside England and Wales, it may be served outside England and Wales with the permission of the Crown Court.

(2) Where a document is to be served outside England and Wales it may be served by any method permitted by the law of the country in which it is to be served.

(3) Nothing in this rule or in any court order shall authorise or require any person to do anything in the country where the document is to be served which is against the law of that country.

(4) Where this Part requires a document to be served a certain period of time before the date of a hearing and the recipient does not appear at the hearing, the hearing must not take place unless the Crown Court is satisfied that the document has been duly served.

Certificates of service

5–684 **57.14.**—(1) Where this Part requires that the applicant for an order in restraint proceedings or receivership proceedings serve a document on another person, the applicant must lodge a certificate of service with the Crown Court within seven days of service of the document.

(2) The certificate must state—

(a) the method of service;

(b) the date of service; and

(c) if the document is served under rule 57.12, such other information as the court may require when making the order permitting service by an alternative method.

(3) Where a document is to be served by the Crown Court in restraint proceedings and receivership proceedings and the court is unable to serve it, the court must send a notice of non-service stating the method attempted to the party who requested service.

External requests and orders

57.15.—(1) The rules in this Part and in Parts 59 to 61 and 71 apply with the necessary modifications to proceedings under the *Proceeds of Crime Act 2002 (External Requests and Orders) Order* 2005 (S.I. 2005 No. 3181) in the same way that they apply to corresponding proceedings under Part 2 of the *Proceeds of Crime Act* 2002.

(2) [*Contains a table showing how provisions of the 2005 order correspond with provisions of the 2002 Act.*]

[Pt 57 is printed as amended by the *Criminal Procedure (Amendment) Rules* 2006 (S.I. 2006 No. 353); the *Criminal Procedure (Amendment) Rules* 2007 (S.I. 2007 No. 699); and the *Criminal Procedure (Amendment No. 3) Rules* 2007 (S.I. 2007 No. 3662).]

Criminal Procedure Rules 2005 (S.I. 2005 No. 384), Pt 58 (as substituted by the Criminal Procedure (Amendment No. 3) Rules 2007 (S.I. 2007 No. 3662), r.17)

Statements in connection with confiscation orders

58.1.—(1) When the prosecutor is required, under section 16 of the *Proceeds of Crime Act* 2002, to give a statement to the Crown Court, the prosecutor must also, as soon as practicable, serve a copy of the statement on the defendant. **5–685**

(2) Any statement given to the Crown Court by the prosecutor under section 16 of the 2002 Act must, in addition to the information required by the 2002 Act, include the following information—

(a) the name of the defendant;

(b) the name of the person by whom the statement is made and the date on which it is made; and

(c) where the statement is not given to the Crown Court immediately after the defendant has been convicted, the date on which and the place where the relevant conviction occurred.

(3) Where, under section 17 of the 2002 Act, the Crown Court orders the defendant to indicate the extent to which he accepts each allegation in a statement given by the prosecutor, the defendant must indicate this in writing to the prosecutor and must give a copy to the Crown Court.

(4) Where the Crown Court orders the defendant to give to it any information under section 18 of the 2002 Act, the defendant must provide the information in writing and must, as soon as practicable, serve a copy of it on the prosecutor.

Postponement of confiscation proceedings

58.2. The Crown Court may grant a postponement under section 14(1)(b) of the *Proceeds of Crime Act* 2002 without a hearing. **5–686**

Application for reconsideration

58.3.—(1) This rule applies where the prosecutor makes an application under section 19, 20 or 21 of the *Proceeds of Crime Act* 2002. **5–687**

(2) The application must be in writing and give details of—

(a) the name of the defendant;

(b) the date on which and the place where any relevant conviction occurred;

(c) the date on which and the place where any relevant confiscation order was made or varied;

(d) the grounds for the application; and

(e) an indication of the evidence available to support the application.

(3) The application must be lodged with the Crown Court.

(4) The application must be served on the defendant at least seven days before the date fixed by the court for hearing the application, unless the Crown Court specifies a shorter period.

Application for new calculation of available amount

58.4.—(1) This rule applies where the prosecutor or a receiver makes an application under section 22 of the *Proceeds of Crime Act* 2002 for a new calculation of the available amount. **5–688**

(2) The application must be in writing and may be supported by a witness statement.

(3) The application and any witness statement must be lodged with the Crown Court.

(4) The application and any witness statement must be served on—

(a) the defendant;

(b) the receiver, if the prosecutor is making the application and a receiver has been appointed under section 50 of the 2002 Act; and

(c) the prosecutor, if the receiver is making the application,

at least seven days before the date fixed by the court for hearing the application, unless the Crown Court specifies a shorter period.

Variation of confiscation order due to inadequacy of available amount

5–689 **58.5.**—(1) This rule applies where the defendant or a receiver makes an application under section 23 of the *Proceeds of Crime Act* 2002 for the variation of a confiscation order.

(2), (3) [*Identical to r.58.4(2), (3),* ante, *§ 5–688.*]

(4) The application and any witness statement must be served on—

(a) the prosecutor;

(b) the defendant, if the receiver is making the application; and

(c) the receiver, if the defendant is making the application and a receiver has been appointed under section 50 of the 2002 Act,

at least seven days before the date fixed by the court for hearing the application, unless the Crown Court specifies a shorter period.

Application by magistrates' court officer to discharge confiscation order

5–690 **58.6.**—(1) This rule applies where a magistrates' court officer makes an application under section 24 or 25 of the *Proceeds of Crime Act* 2002 for the discharge of a confiscation order.

(2) The application must be in writing and give details of—

(a) the confiscation order;

(b) the amount outstanding under the order; and

(c) the grounds for the application.

(3) The application must be served on—

(a) the defendant;

(b) the prosecutor; and

(c) any receiver appointed under section 50 of the 2002 Act.

(4) The Crown Court may determine the application without a hearing unless a person listed in paragraph (3) indicates, within seven days after the application was served on him, that he would like to make representations.

(5) If the Crown Court makes an order discharging the confiscation order, the court must, at once, send a copy of the order to—

(a) the magistrates' court officer who applied for the order;

(b) the defendant;

(c) the prosecutor; and

(d) any receiver appointed under section 50 of the 2002 Act.

Application for variation of confiscation order made against an absconder

5–691 **58.7.**—(1) This rule applies where the defendant makes an application under section 29 of the *Proceeds of Crime Act* 2002 for the variation of a confiscation order made against an absconder.

(2) The application must be in writing and supported by a witness statement which must give details of—

(a) the confiscation order made against an absconder under section 6 of the 2002 Act as applied by section 28 of the 2002 Act;

(b) the circumstances in which the defendant ceased to be an absconder;

(c) the defendant's conviction of the offence or offences concerned; and

(d) the reason why he believes the amount required to be paid under the confiscation order was too large.

(3) The application and witness statement must be lodged with the Crown Court.

(4) The application and witness statement must be served on the prosecutor at least seven days before the date fixed by the court for hearing the application, unless the Crown Court specifies a shorter period.

Application for discharge of confiscation order made against an absconder

5–692 **58.8.**—(1) This rule applies if the defendant makes an application under section 30 of the *Proceeds of Crime Act* 2002 for the discharge of a confiscation order.

(2) The application must be in writing and supported by a witness statement which must give details of—

(a) the confiscation order made under section 28 of the 2002 Act;

(b) the date on which the defendant ceased to be an absconder;

(c) the acquittal of the defendant if he has been acquitted of the offence concerned; and

(d) if the defendant has not been acquitted of the offence concerned—

(i) the date on which the defendant ceased to be an absconder,

(ii) the date on which the proceedings taken against the defendant were instituted and a summary of steps taken in the proceedings since then, and

(iii) any indication given by the prosecutor that he does not intend to proceed against the defendant.

(3), (4) [*Identical to r.58.7(3), (4),* ante, *§ 5–691*.]

(5) If the Crown Court orders the discharge of the confiscation order, the court must serve notice on the magistrates' court responsible for enforcing the order.

Application for increase in term of imprisonment in default

58.9.—(1) This rule applies where the prosecutor makes an application under section 39(5) of the *Proceeds of Crime Act* 2002 to increase the term of imprisonment in default of payment of a confiscation order. **5–693**

(2) The application must be made in writing and give details of—

(a) the name and address of the defendant;

(b) the confiscation order;

(c) the grounds for the application; and

(d) the enforcement measures taken, if any.

(3) On receipt of the application, the court must—

(a) at once, send to the defendant and the magistrates' court responsible for enforcing the order, a copy of the application; and

(b) fix a time, date and place for the hearing and notify the applicant and the defendant of that time, date and place.

(4) If the Crown Court makes an order increasing the term of imprisonment in default, the court must, at once, send a copy of the order to—

(a) the applicant;

(b) the defendant;

(c) where the defendant is in custody at the time of the making of the order, the person having custody of the defendant; and

(d) the magistrates' court responsible for enforcing the order.

Compensation—general

58.10.—(1) This rule applies to an application for compensation under section 72 of the *Proceeds of Crime Act* 2002. **5–694**

(2) The application must be in writing and may be supported by a witness statement.

(3) The application and any witness statement must be lodged with the Crown Court.

(4) The application and any witness statement must be served on—

(a) the person alleged to be in default; and

(b) the person by whom the compensation would be payable under section 72(9) of the 2002 Act (or if the compensation is payable out of a police fund under section 72(9)(a), the chief officer of the police force concerned),

at least seven days before the date fixed by the court for hearing the application, unless the Crown Court directs otherwise.

Compensation—confiscation order made against absconder

58.11.—(1) This rule applies to an application for compensation under section 73 of the *Proceeds of Crime Act* 2002. **5–695**

(2) The application must be in writing and supported by a witness statement which must give details of—

(a) the confiscation order made under section 28 of the 2002 Act;

(b) the variation or discharge of the confiscation order under section 29 or 30 of the 2002 Act;

(c) the realisable property to which the application relates; and

(d) the loss suffered by the applicant as a result of the confiscation order.

(3), (4) [*Identical to r.58.7(3), (4),* ante, *§ 5–691*.]

Payment of money in bank or building society account in satisfaction of confiscation order

5–696 **58.12.**—(1) An order under section 67 of the *Proceeds of Crime Act* 2002 requiring a bank or building society to pay money to a magistrates' court officer ("a payment order") shall—

(a) be directed to the bank or building society in respect of which the payment order is made;

(b) name the person against whom the confiscation order has been made;

(c) state the amount which remains to be paid under the confiscation order;

(d) state the name and address of the branch at which the account in which the money ordered to be paid is held and the sort code of that branch, if the sort code is known;

(e) state the name in which the account in which the money ordered to be paid is held and the account number of that account, if the account number is known;

(f) state the amount which the bank or building society is required to pay to the court officer under the payment order;

(g) give the name and address of the court officer to whom payment is to be made; and

(h) require the bank or building society to make payment within a period of seven days beginning on the day on which the payment order is made, unless it appears to the court that a longer or shorter period would be appropriate in the particular circumstances.

(2) The payment order shall be served on the bank or building society in respect of which it is made by leaving it at, or sending it by first class post to, the principal office of the bank or building society.

(3) A payment order which is served by first class post shall, unless the contrary is proved, be deemed to have been served on the second business day after posting.

(4) In this rule "confiscation order" has the meaning given to it by section 88(6) of the *Proceeds of Crime Act* 2002.

Criminal Procedure Rules 2005 (S.I. 2005 No. 384), Pt 59

Application for restraint order

5–697 **59.1.**—(1) This rule applies where the prosecutor, or an accredited financial investigator makes an application for a restraint order under section 42 of the *Proceeds of Crime Act* 2002.

(2) The application may be made without notice.

(3) The application must be in writing and supported by a witness statement which must—

(a) give the grounds for the application;

(b) to the best of the witness's ability, give full details of the realisable property in respect of which the applicant is seeking the order and specify the person holding that realisable property;

(c) give the grounds for, and full details of, any application for an ancillary order under section 41(7) of the 2002 Act for the purposes of ensuring that the restraint order is effective; and

(d) where the application is made by an accredited financial investigator, include a statement that he has been authorised to make the application under section 68 of the 2002 Act.

Restraint orders

5–698 **59.2.**—(1) The Crown Court may make a restraint order subject to exceptions, including, but not limited to, exceptions for reasonable living expenses and reasonable legal expenses, and for the purpose of enabling any person to carry on any trade, business or occupation.

(2) But the Crown Court must not make an exception for legal expenses where this is prohibited by section 41(4) of the *Proceeds of Crime Act* 2002.

(3) An exception to a restraint order may be made subject to conditions.

(4) The Crown Court must not require the applicant for a restraint order to give any undertaking relating to damages sustained as a result of the restraint order by a person who is prohibited from dealing with realisable property by the restraint order.

(5) The Crown Court may require the applicant for a restraint order to give an undertaking to pay the reasonable expenses of any person, other than a person who is prohibited from dealing with realisable property by the restraint order, which are incurred in complying with the restraint order.

(6) A restraint order must include a statement that disobedience of the order, either by

a person to whom the order is addressed, or by another person, may be contempt of court and the order must include details of the possible consequences of being held in contempt of court.

(7) Unless the Crown Court directs otherwise, a restraint order made without notice has effect until the court makes an order varying or discharging the restraint order.

(8) The applicant for a restraint order must—

(a) serve copies of the restraint order and of the witness statement made in support of the application on the defendant and any person who is prohibited from dealing with realisable property by the restraint order; and

(b) notify any person whom the applicant knows to be affected by the restraint order of the terms of the restraint order.

Application for discharge or variation of restraint order by person affected by order

59.3.—(1) This rule applies where a person affected by a restraint order makes an application to the Crown Court under section 42(3) of the *Proceeds of Crime Act* 2002 to discharge or vary the restraint order or any ancillary order made under section 41(7) of the Act. **5–699**

(2), (3) [*Identical to r.58.4(2), (3),* ante, *§ 5–688.*]

(4) The application and any witness statement must be served on the person who applied for the restraint order and any person who is prohibited from dealing with realisable property by the restraint order (if he is not the person making the application) at least two days before the date fixed by the court for hearing the application, unless the Crown Court specifies a shorter period.

Application for variation of restraint order by the person who applied for the order

59.4.—(1) This rule applies where the applicant for a restraint order makes an application under section 42(3) of the *Proceeds of Crime Act* 2002 to the Crown Court to vary the restraint order or any ancillary order made under section 41(7) of the 2002 Act (including where the court has already made a restraint order and the applicant is seeking to vary the order in order to restrain further realisable property). **5–700**

(2) The application may be made without notice if the application is urgent or if there are reasonable grounds for believing that giving notice would cause the dissipation of realisable property which is the subject of the application.

(3) The application must be in writing and must be supported by a witness statement which must—

(a) give the grounds for the application;

(b) where the application is for the inclusion of further realisable property in the order give full details, to the best of the witness's ability, of the realisable property in respect of which the applicant is seeking the order and specify the person holding that realisable property; and

(c) where the application is made by an accredited financial investigator, include a statement that he has been authorised to make the application under section 68 of the 2002 Act.

(4) The application and witness statement must be lodged with the Crown Court.

(5) Except where, under paragraph (2), notice of the application is not required to be served, the application and witness statement must be served on any person who is prohibited from dealing with realisable property by the restraint order at least 2 days before the date fixed by the court for hearing the application, unless the Crown Court specifies a shorter period.

(6) If the court makes an order for the variation of a restraint order, the applicant must serve copies of the order and of the witness statement made in support of the application on—

(a) the defendant;

(b) any person who is prohibited from dealing with realisable property by the restraint order (whether before or after the variation); and

(c) any other person whom the applicant knows to be affected by the order.

Application for discharge of a restraint order by the person who applied for the order

59.5.—(1) This rule applies where the applicant for a restraint order makes an application under section 42(3) of the *Proceeds of Crime Act* 2002 to discharge the order or any ancillary order made under section 41(7) of the 2002 Act. **5–701**

(2) The application may be made without notice.

(3) The application must be in writing and must state the grounds for the application.

(4) If the court makes an order for the discharge of a restraint order, the applicant must serve copies of the order on—

(a) the defendant;

(b) any person who is prohibited from dealing with realisable property by the restraint order (whether before or after the discharge); and

(c) any other person whom the applicant knows to be affected by the order.

[Pt 59 is printed as amended by the *Criminal Procedure (Amendment No. 3) Rules* 2007 (S.I. 2007 No. 3662).]

Criminal Procedure Rules 2005 (S.I. 2005 No. 384), Pt 60 (as substituted by the Criminal Procedure (Amendment No. 3) Rules 2007 (S.I. 2007 No. 3662), r.20)

Application for appointment of a management or an enforcement receiver

5–702 **60.1.**—(1) This rule applies to an application for the appointment of a management receiver under section 48(1) of the *Proceeds of Crime Act* 2002 and an application for the appointment of an enforcement receiver under section 50(1) of the 2002 Act.

(2) The application may be made without notice if—

(a) the application is joined with an application for a restraint order under rule 59.1;

(b) the application is urgent; or

(c) there are reasonable grounds for believing that giving notice would cause the dissipation of realisable property which is the subject of the application.

(3) The application must be in writing and must be supported by a witness statement which must—

(a) give the grounds for the application;

(b) give full details of the proposed receiver;

(c) to the best of the witness' [*sic*] ability, give full details of the realisable property in respect of which the applicant is seeking the order and specify the person holding that realisable property;

(d) where the application is made by an accredited financial investigator, include a statement that he has been authorised to make the application under section 68 of the 2002 Act; and

(e) if the proposed receiver is not a member of staff of the Crown Prosecution Service or the Revenue and Customs Prosecutions Office and the applicant is asking the court to allow the receiver to act—

(i) without giving security, or

(ii) before he has given security or satisfied the court that he has security in place,

explain the reasons why that is necessary.

(4) Where the application is for the appointment of an enforcement receiver, the applicant must provide the Crown Court with a copy of the confiscation order made against the defendant.

(5) The application and witness statement must be lodged with the Crown Court.

(6) Except where, under paragraph (2), notice of the application is not required to be served, the application and witness statement must be lodged with the Crown Court and served on—

(a) the defendant;

(b) any person who holds realisable property to which the application relates; and

(c) any other person whom the applicant knows to be affected by the application,

at least seven days before the date fixed by the court for hearing the application, unless the Crown Court specifies a shorter period.

(7) If the court makes an order for the appointment of a receiver, the applicant must serve copies of the order and of the witness statement made in support of the application on—

(a) the defendant;

(b) any person who holds realisable property to which the order applies; and

(c) any other person whom the applicant knows to be affected by the order.

Application for conferral of powers on management receiver or enforcement receiver

5–703 **60.2.**—(1) This rule applies to an application for the conferral of powers on a management receiver under section 49(1) of the *Proceeds of Crime Act* 2002 or an enforcement receiver under section 51(1) of the 2002 Act.

(2) The application may be made without notice if the application is to give the receiver power to take possession of property and—

(a)-(c) [*identical to r.60.1(2)(a)-(c),* ante, *§ 5–702*].

(3) The application must be made in writing and supported by a witness statement which must—

(a) give the grounds for the application;

(b) give full details of the realisable property in respect of which the applicant is seeking the order and specify the person holding that realisable property; and

(c) where the application is made by an accredited financial investigator, include a statement that he has been authorised to make the application under section 68 of the 2002 Act.

(4) Where the application is for the conferral of powers on an enforcement receiver, the applicant must provide the Crown Court with a copy of the confiscation order made against the defendant.

(5) The application and witness statement must be lodged with the Crown Court.

(6) Except where, under paragraph (2), notice of the application is not required to be served, the application and witness statement must be served on—

(a) the defendant;

(b) any person who holds realisable property in respect of which a receiver has been appointed or in respect of which an application for a receiver has been made;

(c) any other person whom the applicant knows to be affected by the application; and

(d) the receiver (if one has already been appointed),

at least seven days before the date fixed by the court for hearing the application, unless the Crown Court specifies a shorter period.

(7) If the court makes an order for the conferral of powers on a receiver, the applicant must serve copies of the order on—

(a) the defendant;

(b) any person who holds realisable property in respect of which the receiver has been appointed; and

(c) any other person whom the applicant knows to be affected by the order.

Applications for discharge or variation of receivership orders and applications for other orders

60.3.—(1) This rule applies to applications under section 62(3) of the *Proceeds of Crime Act* 2002 for orders (by persons affected by the action of receivers) and applications under section 63(1) of the 2002 Act for the discharge or variation of orders relating to receivers. **5–704**

(2) The application must be made in writing and lodged with the Crown Court.

(3) The application must be served on the following persons (except where they are the person making the application)—

(a) the person who applied for appointment of the receiver;

(b) the defendant;

(c) any person who holds realisable property in respect of which the receiver has been appointed;

(d) the receiver; and

(e) any other person whom the applicant knows to be affected by the application,

at least seven days before the date fixed by the court for hearing the application, unless the Crown Court specifies a shorter period.

(4) If the court makes an order for the discharge or variation of an order relating to a receiver under section 63(2) of the 2002 Act, the applicant must serve copies of the order on any persons whom he knows to be affected by the order.

Sums in the hands of receivers

60.4.—(1) This rule applies where the amount payable under a confiscation order has been fully paid and any sums remain in the hands of an enforcement receiver. **5–705**

(2) The receiver must make an application to the Crown Court for directions as to the distribution of the sums in his hands.

(3) The application and any evidence which the receiver intends to rely on in support of the application must be served on—

(a) the defendant; and

(b) any other person who held (or holds) interests in any property realised by the receiver,

at least seven days before the date fixed by the court for hearing the application, unless the Crown Court specifies a shorter period.

(4) If any of the provisions listed in paragraph (5) (provisions as to the vesting of funds in a trustee in bankruptcy) apply, then the Crown Court must make a declaration to that effect.

(5) These are the provisions—

(a) section 31B of the *Bankruptcy (Scotland) Act* 1985;

(b) section 306B of the *Insolvency Act* 1986; and

(c) article 279B of the *Insolvency (Northern Ireland) Order* 1989.

Security

5–706 **60.5.**—(1) This rule applies where the Crown Court appoints a receiver under section 48 or 50 of the *Proceeds of Crime Act* 2002 and the receiver is not a member of staff of the Crown Prosecution Service or the Revenue and Customs Prosecutions Office (and it is immaterial whether the receiver is a permanent or temporary member or he is on secondment from elsewhere).

(2) The Crown Court may direct that before the receiver begins to act, or within a specified time, he must either—

(a) give such security as the Crown Court may determine; or

(b) file with the Crown Court and serve on all parties to any receivership proceedings evidence that he already has in force sufficient security,

to cover his liability for his acts and omissions as a receiver.

(3) The Crown Court may terminate the appointment of a receiver if he fails to—

(a) give the security; or

(b) satisfy the court as to the security he has in force,

by the date specified.

Remuneration

5–707 **60.6.**—(1) This rule applies where the Crown Court appoints a receiver under section 48 or 50 of the *Proceeds of Crime Act* 2002 and the receiver is not a member of staff of the Crown Prosecution Service or of the Revenue and Customs Prosecutions Office (and it is immaterial whether the receiver is a permanent or temporary member or he is on secondment from elsewhere).

(2) The receiver may only charge for his services if the Crown Court—

(a) so directs; and

(b) specifies the basis on which the receiver is to be remunerated.

(3) Unless the Crown Court orders otherwise, in determining the remuneration of the receiver, the Crown Court shall award such sum as is reasonable and proportionate in all the circumstances and which takes into account—

(a) the time properly given by him and his staff to the receivership;

(b) the complexity of the receivership;

(c) any responsibility of an exceptional kind or degree which falls on the receiver in consequence of the receivership;

(d) the effectiveness with which the receiver appears to be carrying out, or to have carried out, his duties; and

(e) the value and nature of the subject matter of the receivership.

(4) The Crown Court may refer the determination of a receiver's remuneration to be ascertained by the taxing authority of the Crown Court and rules 78.4 to 78.7 shall have effect as if the taxing authority was ascertaining costs.

(5) A receiver appointed under section 48 of the 2002 Act is to receive his remuneration by realising property in respect of which he is appointed, in accordance with section 49(2)(d) of the 2002 Act.

(6) A receiver appointed under section 50 of the 2002 Act is to receive his remuneration by applying to the magistrates' court officer for payment under section 55(4)(b) of the 2002 Act.

Accounts

5–708 **60.7.**—(1) The Crown Court may order a receiver appointed under section 48 or 50 of the *Proceeds of Crime Act* 2002 to prepare and serve accounts.

(2) A party to receivership proceedings served with such accounts may apply for an order permitting him to inspect any document in the possession of the receiver relevant to those accounts.

(3) Any party to receivership proceedings may, within 14 days of being served with the accounts, serve notice on the receiver—

(a) specifying any item in the accounts to which he objects;

(b) giving the reason for such objection; and

(c) requiring the receiver within 14 days of receipt of the notice, either—

(i) to notify all the parties who were served with the accounts that he accepts the objection, or

(ii) if he does not accept the objection, to apply for an examination of the accounts in relation to the contested item.

(4) When the receiver applies for the examination of the accounts he must at the same time lodge with the Crown Court—

(a) the accounts; and

(b) a copy of the notice served on him under this section of the rule.

(5) If the receiver fails to comply with paragraph (3)(c) of this rule, any party to receivership proceedings may apply to the Crown Court for an examination of the accounts in relation to the contested item.

(6) At the conclusion of its examination of the accounts the court will certify the result.

Non-compliance by receiver

60.8.—(1) If a receiver appointed under section 48 or 50 of the *Proceeds of Crime Act* 2002 fails to comply with any rule, practice direction or direction of the Crown Court, the Crown Court may order him to attend a hearing to explain his non-compliance. **5–709**

(2) At the hearing, the Crown Court may make any order it considers appropriate, including—

(a) terminating the appointment of the receiver;

(b) reducing the receiver's remuneration or disallowing it altogether; and

(c) ordering the receiver to pay the costs of any party.

Criminal Procedure Rules (S.I. 2005 No. 384), Pt 61

Distress and forfeiture

61.1.—(1) This rule applies to applications under sections 58(2) and (3) and 59(2) and (3) of the *Proceeds of Crime Act* 2002 for leave of the Crown Court to levy distress against property or exercise a right of forfeiture by peaceable re-entry in relation to a tenancy, in circumstances where the property or tenancy is the subject of a restraint order or a receiver has been appointed in respect of the property or tenancy. **5–710**

(2) The application must be made in writing to the Crown Court.

(3) The application must be served on—

(a) the person who applied for the restraint order or the order appointing the receiver; and

(b) any receiver appointed in respect of the property or tenancy,

at least seven days before the date fixed by the court for hearing the application, unless the Crown Court specifies a shorter period.

Joining of applications

61.2. An application for the appointment of a management receiver or enforcement receiver under rule 60.1 may be joined with— **5–711**

(a) an application for a restraint order under rule 59.1; and

(b) an application for the conferral of powers on the receiver under rule 60.2.

Applications to be dealt with in writing

61.3. Applications in restraint proceedings and receivership proceedings are to be dealt with without a hearing, unless the Crown Court orders otherwise. **5–712**

Business in chambers

61.4. Restraint proceedings and receivership proceedings may be heard in chambers. **5–713**

Power of court to control evidence

61.5.—(1) When hearing restraint proceedings and receivership proceedings, the Crown Court may control the evidence by giving directions as to— **5–714**

(a) the issues on which it requires evidence;

(b) the nature of the evidence which it requires to decide those issues; and

(c) the way in which the evidence is to be placed before the court.

(2) The court may use its power under this rule to exclude evidence that would otherwise be admissible.

(3) The court may limit cross-examination in restraint proceedings and receivership proceedings.

Evidence of witnesses

5–715 **61.6.**—(1) The general rule is that, unless the Crown Court orders otherwise, any fact which needs to be proved in restraint proceedings or receivership proceedings by the evidence of a witness is to be proved by their evidence in writing.

(2) Where evidence is to be given in writing under this rule, any party may apply to the Crown Court for permission to cross-examine the person giving the evidence.

(3) If the Crown Court gives permission under paragraph (2) but the person in question does not attend as required by the order, his evidence may not be used unless the court gives permission.

Witness summons

5–716 **61.7.**—(1) Any party to restraint proceedings or receivership proceedings may apply to the Crown Court to issue a witness summons requiring a witness to—

(a) attend court to give evidence; or

(b) produce documents to the court.

(2) Rule 28.3 applies to an application under this rule as it applies to an application under section 2 of the *Criminal Procedure (Attendance of Witnesses) Act* 1965.

Hearsay evidence

5–717 **61.8.** Section 2(1) of the *Civil Evidence Act* 1995 (duty to give notice of intention to rely on hearsay evidence) does not apply to evidence in restraint proceedings and receivership proceedings.

Disclosure and inspection of documents

5–718 **61.9.**—(1) This rule applies where, in the course of restraint proceedings or receivership proceedings, an issue arises as to whether property is realisable property.

(2) The Crown Court may make an order for disclosure of documents.

(3) Part 31 of the *Civil Procedure Rules* 1998 (S.I. 1998 No. 3132) as amended from time to time shall have effect as if the proceedings were proceedings in the High Court.

Court documents

5–719 **61.10.**—(1) Any order which the Crown Court issues in restraint proceedings or receivership proceedings must—

(a) state the name and judicial title of the person who made it;

(b) bear the date on which it is made; and

(c) be sealed by the Crown Court.

(2) The Crown Court may place the seal on the order—

(a) by hand; or

(b) by printing a facsimile of the seal on the order whether electronically or otherwise.

(3) A document purporting to bear the court's seal shall be admissible in evidence without further proof.

Consent orders

5–720 **61.11.**—(1) This rule applies where all the parties to restraint proceedings or receivership proceedings agree the terms in which an order should be made.

(2) Any party may apply for a judgment or order in the terms agreed.

(3) The Crown Court may deal with an application under paragraph (2) without a hearing.

(4) Where this rule applies—

(a) the order which is agreed by the parties must be drawn up in the terms agreed;

(b) it must be expressed as being "By Consent"; and

(c) it must be signed by the legal representative acting for each of the parties to whom the order relates or by the party if he is a litigant in person.

(5) Where an application is made under this rule, then the requirements of any other rule as to the procedure for making an application do not apply.

Slips and omissions

61.12.—(1) The Crown Court may at any time correct an accidental slip or omission in an order made in restraint proceedings or receivership proceedings. **5–721**

(2) A party may apply for a correction without notice.

Supply of documents from court records

61.13.—(1) No document relating to restraint proceedings or receivership proceedings may be supplied from the records of the Crown Court for any person to inspect or copy unless the Crown Court grants permission. **5–722**

(2) An application for permission under paragraph (1) must be made on notice to the parties to the proceedings.

Disclosure of documents in criminal proceedings

61.14.—(1) This rule applies where— **5–723**

(a) proceedings for an offence have been started in the Crown Court and the defendant has not been either convicted or acquitted on all counts; and

(b) an application for a restraint order under section 42(1) of the *Proceeds of Crime Act* 2002 has been made.

(2) The judge presiding at the proceedings for the offence may be supplied from the records of the Crown Court with documents relating to restraint proceedings and any receivership proceedings.

(3) Such documents must not otherwise be disclosed in the proceedings for the offence.

Preparation of documents

61.15.—(1) Every order in restraint proceedings or receivership proceedings will be drawn up by the Crown Court unless— **5–724**

(a) the Crown Court orders a party to draw it up;

(b) a party, with the permission of the Crown Court, agrees to draw it up; or

(c) the order is made by consent under rule 61.10.

(2) The Crown Court may direct that—

(a) an order drawn up by a party must be checked by the Crown Court before it is sealed; or

(b) before an order is drawn up by the Crown Court, the parties must lodge an agreed statement of its terms.

(3) Where an order is to be drawn up by a party—

(a) he must lodge it with the Crown Court no later than seven days after the date on which the court ordered or permitted him to draw it up so that it can be sealed by the Crown Court; and

(b) if he fails to lodge it within that period, any other party may draw it up and lodge it.

(4) Nothing in this rule shall require the Crown Court to accept a document which is illegible, has not been duly authorised, or is unsatisfactory for some other similar reason.

Change of solicitor

61.16.—(1) This rule applies where— **5–725**

(a) a party for whom a solicitor is acting in restraint proceedings or receivership proceedings wants to change his solicitor;

(b) a party, after having represented himself in such proceedings, appoints a solicitor to act on his behalf (except where the solicitor is appointed only to act as an advocate for a hearing); or

(c) a party, after having been represented by a solicitor in such proceedings, intends to act in person.

(2) Where this rule applies, the party or his solicitor (where one is acting) must—

(a) lodge notice of the change at the Crown Court; and

(b) serve notice of the change on every other party and, where paragraph (1)(a) or (c) applies, on the former solicitor.

(3) The notice lodged at the Crown Court must state that notice has been served as required by paragraph (2)(b).

(4) Subject to paragraph (5), where a party has changed his solicitor or intends to act in person, the former solicitor will be considered to be the party's solicitor unless and until—

(a) notice is served in accordance with paragraph (2); or

(b) the Crown Court makes an order under rule 61.17 and the order is served as required by paragraph (3) of that rule.

(5) Where the certificate of a LSC funded client is revoked or discharged—

(a) the solicitor who acted for that person will cease to be the solicitor acting in the proceedings as soon as his retainer is determined under regulation 4 of the *Community Legal Service (Costs) Regulations* 2000 (S.I. 2000 No. 441); and

(b) if that person wishes to continue, where he appoints a solicitor to act on his behalf paragraph (2) will apply as if he had previously represented himself in the proceedings.

(6) "Certificate" in paragraph (5) means a certificate issued under the Funding Code (approved under section 9 of the *Access to Justice Act* 1999) and "LSC funded client" means an individual who receives services funded by the Legal Services Commission as part of the Community Legal Service within the meaning of Part I of the 1999 Act.

Application by solicitor for declaration that solicitor has ceased to act

5–726 **61.17.**—(1) A solicitor may apply to the Crown Court for an order declaring that he has ceased to be the solicitor acting for a party to restraint proceedings or receivership proceedings.

(2) Where an application is made under this rule—

(a) notice of the application must be given to the party for whom the solicitor is acting, unless the Crown Court directs otherwise; and

(b) the application must be supported by evidence.

(3) Where the Crown Court makes an order that a solicitor has ceased to act, the solicitor must serve a copy of the order on every party to the proceedings.

Application by other party for declaration that solicitor has ceased to act

5–727 **61.18.**—(1) Where—

(a) a solicitor who has acted for a party to restraint proceedings or receivership proceedings—

(i) has died,

(ii) has become bankrupt,

(iii) has ceased to practise, or

(iv) cannot be found, and

(b) the party has not given notice of a change of solicitor or notice of intention to act in person as required by rule 61.16,

any other party may apply to the Crown Court for an order declaring that the solicitor has ceased to be the solicitor acting for the other party in the proceedings.

(2) Where an application is made under this rule, notice of the application must be given to the party to whose solicitor the application relates unless the Crown Court directs otherwise.

(3) Where the Crown Court makes an order under this rule, the applicant must serve a copy of the order on every other party to the proceedings.

Order for costs

5–728 **61.19.**—(1) This rule applies where the Crown Court is deciding whether to make an order for costs under rule 78.1 in restraint proceedings or receivership proceedings.

(2) The court has discretion as to—

(a) whether costs are payable by one party to another;

(b) the amount of those costs; and

(c) when they are to be paid.

(3) If the court decides to make an order about costs—

(a) the general rule is that the unsuccessful party will be ordered to pay the costs of the successful party; but

(b) the court may make a different order.

(4) In deciding what order (if any) to make about costs, the court must have regard to all of the circumstances, including—

(a) the conduct of all the parties; and

(b) whether a party has succeeded on part of an application, even if he has not been wholly successful.

(5) The orders which the court may make under rule 78.1 include an order that a party must pay—

(a) a proportion of another party's costs;

(b) a stated amount in respect of another party's costs;

(c) costs from or until a certain date only;

(d) costs incurred before proceedings have begun;

(e) costs relating to particular steps taken in the proceedings;

(f) costs relating only to a distinct part of the proceedings; and

(g) interest on costs from or until a certain date, including a date before the making of an order.

(6) Where the court would otherwise consider making an order under paragraph (5)(f), it must instead, if practicable, make an order under paragraph (5)(a) or (c).

(7) Where the court has ordered a party to pay costs, it may order an amount to be paid on account before the costs are assessed.

Assessment of costs

61.20.—(1) Where the Crown Court has made an order for costs in restraint proceedings or receivership proceedings it may either— **5–729**

(a) make an assessment of the costs itself; or

(b) order assessment of the costs under rule 78.3.

(2) In either case, the Crown Court or the taxing authority, as the case may be, must—

(a) only allow costs which are proportionate to the matters in issue; and

(b) resolve any doubt which it may have as to whether the costs were reasonably incurred or reasonable and proportionate in favour of the paying party.

(3) The Crown Court or the taxing authority, as the case may be, is to have regard to all the circumstances in deciding whether costs were proportionately or reasonably incurred or proportionate and reasonable in amount.

(4) In particular, the Crown Court or the taxing authority must give effect to any orders which have already been made.

(5) The Crown Court or the taxing authority must also have regard to—

(a) the conduct of all the parties, including in particular, conduct before, as well as during, the proceedings;

(b) the amount or value of the property involved;

(c) the importance of the matter to all the parties;

(d) the particular complexity of the matter or the difficulty or novelty of the questions raised;

(e) the skill, effort, specialised knowledge and responsibility involved;

(f) the time spent on the application; and

(g) the place where and the circumstances in which work or any part of it was done.

Time for complying with an order for costs

61.21.—(1) A party to restraint proceedings or receivership proceedings must comply with an order for the payment of costs within 14 days of— **5–729a**

(a) the date of the order if it states the amount of those costs;

(b) if the amount of those costs is decided later under rule 78.3, the date of the taxing authority's decision; or

(c) in either case, such later date as the Crown Court may specify.

Application of costs rules

61.22. Rules 61.19, 61.20 and 61.21 do not apply to the assessment of costs in proceedings to the extent that section 11 of the *Access to Justice Act* 1999 applies and provisions made under that Act make different provision. **5–729b**

[Pt 61 is printed as amended by the *Criminal Procedure (Amendment No. 3) Rules* 2007 (S.I. 2007 No. 3662).]

Appeals

Proceeds of Crime Act 2002 (Appeals under Part 2) Order 2003 (S.I. 2003 No. 82)

PART 1

INTRODUCTION

Citation and commencement

5–730 **1.** This Order may be cited as the *Proceeds of Crime Act 2002 (Appeals under Part 2) Order* 2003 and shall come into force on 24th March 2003.

Interpretation

5–731 **2.** In this Order—

"the Act" means the *Proceeds of Crime Act* 2002;

"the registrar" means the registrar of criminal appeals of the Court of Appeal;

references to the Court of Appeal are to the criminal division of the Court of Appeal;

references to a single judge are to any judge of the Court of Appeal or of the High Court.

PART 2

APPEALS TO COURT OF APPEAL

Initiating procedure

5–732 **3.**—(1) A person who wishes to obtain the leave of the Court of Appeal to appeal to the Court of Appeal under Part 2 of the Act shall give notice of application for leave to appeal, in such manner as may be directed by rules of court.

(2) Notice of application for leave to appeal shall be given within—

(a) 28 days from the date of the decision appealed against, in the case of an appeal under section 31 of the Act; or

(b) 14 days from the date of the decision appealed against, in the case of an appeal under section 43 or 65 of the Act.

(3) The time for giving notice under this article may be extended by the Court of Appeal.

4. [*Disposal of groundless appeal or application for leave to appeal: corresponds to* Criminal Appeal Act *1968, s.20*, post, *§ 7–193*.]

Preparation of case for hearing

5–733 **5.**—(1) The registrar shall—

(a) take all necessary steps for obtaining a hearing of any application for leave to appeal to the Court of Appeal under Part 2 of the Act of which notice is given to him and which is not referred and dismissed summarily under article 4;

(b) where an application for leave to appeal to the Court of Appeal under Part 2 of the Act is granted, take all necessary steps for obtaining a hearing of an appeal; and

(c) obtain and lay before the Court of Appeal in proper form all documents, exhibits and other things which appear necessary for the proper determination of the application for leave to appeal under Part 2 of the Act or the appeal under Part 2 of the Act.

(2) A party to an appeal under Part 2 of the Act may obtain from the registrar any documents or things, including copies or reproductions of documents, required for his appeal, in accordance with rules of court.

(3) The registrar may make charges in accordance with such rules of court and with scales and rates fixed from time to time by the Treasury.

6. [*Right of defendant to be present: corresponds to* Criminal Appeal Act *1968, s.22*, post, *§ 7–201*.]

Evidence

5–734 **7.**—(1) For the purposes of an appeal under Part 2 of the Act, the Court of Appeal may, if they think it necessary or expedient in the interests of justice—

(a) order the production of any document, exhibit or other thing connected with the proceedings, the production of which appears to them necessary for the determination of the appeal;

(b) order any witness to attend for examination and be examined before the Court of Appeal; and

(c) receive any evidence which was not adduced in the proceedings from which the appeal lies.

(2), (3) [*Correspond to* Criminal Appeal Act *1968, s.23(2), (4)*, post, *§ 7-208*.]

Powers of Court of Appeal which are exercisable by single judge

8.—(1) There may be exercised by a single judge in the same manner as by the Court of Appeal and subject to the same provisions the powers— **5-735**

(a) to give leave to appeal to the Court of Appeal under Part 2 of the Act;

(b) to extend the time within which notice of application for leave to appeal may be given under article 3(3);

(c) to allow, under article 6, the defendant to be present at any proceedings which he would not otherwise be entitled to attend; and

(d) to order a witness to attend for examination under article 7.

(2) If the single judge refuses an application on the part of any party to exercise in his favour any of the powers specified in paragraph (1), the party shall be entitled to have his application determined by the Court of Appeal.

Powers of Court of Appeal which are exercisable by registrar

9.—(1) The following powers of the Court of Appeal under this Order may be exercised by the registrar— **5-736**

(a) the power to extend the time within which notice of application for leave to appeal may be given under article 3(3); and

(b) the power to order a witness to attend for examination under article 7.

(2) If the registrar refuses an application on the part of any party to exercise in his favour any of the powers specified in paragraph (1), the party shall be entitled to have his application determined by a single judge.

10. [*Transcripts: corresponds to* Criminal Appeal Act *1968, s.32*, post, *§ 7-237*.] **5-737**

PART 3

APPEAL TO HOUSE OF LORDS

Leave to appeal to House of Lords

11. An appeal to the House of Lords under section 33, 44 or 66 of the Act lies only with the leave of the Court of Appeal or the House of Lords; and leave shall not be granted unless it is certified by the Court of Appeal that a point of law of general public importance is involved in the decision and it appears to the Court of Appeal or the House of Lords (as the case may be) that the point is one which ought to be considered by that House. **5-738**

Application for leave to appeal

12.—(1) [*Application for leave to appeal: corresponds to* Criminal Appeal Act *1968, s.34(1)*, post, *§ 7-257*.] **5-739**

(2) The House of Lords or the Court of Appeal may, upon application made at any time by the appellant, extend the time within which an application may be made by him to that House or the Court under paragraph (1).

(3) [*Corresponds to* Criminal Appeal Act *1968, s.34(3)*, post, *§ 7-257*.]

13. [*Hearing and disposal of appeal: corresponds to* Criminal Appeal Act *1968, s.35(1), (2)*, post, *§ 7-260*.]

Presence of defendant at hearing

14. A defendant who is in custody shall not be entitled to be present on the hearing of an appeal to the House of Lords under section 33, 44 or 66 of the Act or of any proceedings preliminary or incidental thereto, except where an order of the House of Lords authorises him to be present, or where the House or the Court of Appeal, as the case may be, give him leave to be present. **5-740**

Powers of Court of Appeal under Part 3 which are exercisable by single judge

15. There may be exercised by a single judge the powers of the Court of Appeal— **5-741**

(a) to extend the time for making an application for leave to appeal under article 12(2); and

(b) to give leave for a person to be present at the hearing of any proceedings preliminary or incidental to an appeal under article 14,

but where the judge refuses an application to exercise any of the said powers the applicant shall be entitled to have the application determined by the Court of Appeal.

Criminal Procedure Rules 2005 (S.I. 2005 No. 384), Pt 71 (as substituted by the Criminal Procedure (Amendment No. 3) Rules 2007 (S.I. 2007 No. 3662), r.32)

Extension of time

5–742 **71.1.**—(1) An application to extend the time limit for giving notice of application for leave to appeal under Part 2 of the *Proceeds of Crime Act* 2002 must—

(a) be included in the notice of appeal; and

(b) state the grounds for the application.

(2) The parties may not agree to extend any date or time limit set by this Part, Part 72 or Part 73, or by the *Proceeds of Crime Act 2002 (Appeals under Part 2) Order* 2003.

Other applications

5–743 **71.2.** Rule 68.3(2)(h) (form of appeal notice) applies in relation to an application—

(a) by a party to an appeal under Part 2 of the *Proceeds of Crime Act* 2002 that, under article 7 of the *Proceeds of Crime Act 2002 (Appeals under Part 2) Order* 2003, a witness be ordered to attend or that the evidence of a witness be received by the Court of Appeal; or

(b) by the defendant to be given leave by the court to be present at proceedings for which leave is required under article 6 of the 2003 Order,

as it applies in relation to applications under Part I of the *Criminal Appeal Act* 1968 and the form in which rule 68.3 requires notice to be given may be modified as necessary.

Examination of witness by court

5–744 **71.3.** Rule 65.7 (notice of hearings and decisions) applies in relation to an order of the court under article 7 of the *Proceeds of Crime Act 2002 (Appeals under Part 2) Order* 2003 to require a person to attend for examination as it applies in relation to such an order of the court under Part I of the *Criminal Appeal Act* 1968.

Supply of documentary and other exhibits

5–745 **71.4.** Rule 65.11 (Registrar's duty to provide copy documents for appeal or reference) applies in relation to an appellant or respondent under Part 2 of the *Proceeds of Crime Act* 2002 as it applies in relation to an appellant and respondent under Part I of the *Criminal Appeal Act* 1968.

Registrar's power to require information from court of trial

5–746 **71.5.** The Registrar may require the Crown Court to provide the Court of Appeal with any assistance or information which they may require for the purposes of exercising their jurisdiction under Part 2 of the *Proceeds of Crime Act* 2002, the *Proceeds of Crime Act 2002 (Appeals under Part 2) Order* 2003, this Part or Parts 72 and 73.

Hearing by single judge

5–747 **71.6.** Rule 65.6(4) (hearings) applies in relation to a judge exercising any of the powers referred to in article 8 of the *Proceeds of Crime Act 2002 (Appeals under Part 2) Order* 2003 or the powers in rules 72.2(3) and (4) (respondent's notice), 73.2(2) (notice of appeal) and 73.3(6) (respondent's notice), as it applies in relation to a judge exercising the powers referred to in section 31(2) of the *Criminal Appeal Act* 1968.

Determination by full court

5–748 **71.7.** Rule 65.5 (renewing an application refused by a judge or the registrar) shall apply where a single judge has refused an application by a party to exercise in his favour any of the powers listed in article 8 of the *Proceeds of Crime Act 2002 (Appeals under Part 2) Order* 2003, or the power in rule 72.2(3) or (4) as it applies where the judge has refused to exercise the powers referred to in section 31(2) of the *Criminal Appeal Act* 1968.

Notice of determination

5–749 **71.8.**—(1) This rule applies where a single judge or the Court of Appeal has determined an application or appeal under the *Proceeds of Crime Act 2002 (Appeals under Part 2) Order* 2003 or under Part 2 of the *Proceeds of Crime Act* 2002.

(2) The Registrar must, as soon as practicable, serve notice of the determination on all of the parties to the proceedings.

(3) Where a single judge or the Court of Appeal has disposed of an application for leave to appeal or an appeal under section 31 of the 2002 Act, the registrar must also, as soon as practicable, serve the order on a court officer of the court of trial and any magistrates' court responsible for enforcing any confiscation order which the Crown Court has made.

Record of proceedings and transcripts

71.9. Rule 65.8(2)(a) and (b) (duty of Crown Court officer—arranging recording of proceed- **5–750** ings in Crown Court and arranging transcription) and rule 65.9 (duty of person transcribing proceedings in the Crown Court) apply in relation to proceedings in respect of which an appeal lies to the Court of Appeal under Part 2 of the *Proceeds of Crime Act* 2002 as they apply in relation to proceedings in respect of which an appeal lies to the Court of Appeal under Part I of the *Criminal Appeal Act* 1968.

Appeal to House of Lords

71.10.—(1) An application to the Court of Appeal for leave to appeal to the House of Lords **5–751** under Part 2 of the *Proceeds of Crime Act* 2002 must be made—

(a) orally after the decision of the Court of Appeal from which an appeal lies to the House of Lords; or

(b) in the form set out in the Practice Direction, in accordance with article 12 of the *Proceeds of Crime Act 2002 (Appeals under Part 2) Order* 2003 and served on the Registrar.

(2) The application may be abandoned at any time before it is heard by the Court of Appeal by serving notice in writing on the Registrar.

(3) Rule 65.6(5) (hearings) applies in relation to a single judge exercising any of the powers referred to in article 15 of the 2003 Order, as it applies in relation to a single judge exercising the powers referred to in section 31(2) of the *Criminal Appeal Act* 1968.

(4) Rule 65.5 (renewing an application refused by a judge or the Registrar) applies where a single judge has refused an application by a party to exercise in his favour any of the powers listed in article 15 of the 2003 Order as they apply where the judge has refused to exercise the powers referred to in section 31(2) of the 1968 Act.

(5) The form in which rule 65.5(2) requires an application to be made may be modified as necessary.

[The next paragraph is § 5–753.]

Criminal Procedure Rules 2005 (S.I. 2005 No. 384), Pt 72

Notice of appeal

72.1.—(1) Where an appellant wishes to apply to the Court of Appeal for leave to appeal **5–753** under section 31 of the *Proceeds of Crime Act* 2002, he must serve a notice of appeal in the form set out in the Practice Direction on—

(a) the Crown Court officer; and

(b) the defendant.

(2) When the notice of the appeal is served on the defendant, it must be accompanied by a respondent's notice in the form set out in the Practice Direction for the defendant to complete and a notice which—

(a) informs the defendant that the result of an appeal could be that the Court of Appeal would increase a confiscation order already imposed on him, make a confiscation order itself or direct the Crown Court to hold another confiscation hearing;

(b) informs the defendant of any right he has under article 6 of the *Proceeds of Crime Act 2002 (Appeals under Part 2) Order* 2003 (S.I. 2003 No. 82) to be present at the hearing of the appeal, although he may be in custody;

(c) invites the defendant to serve notice on the registrar if he wishes—

(i) to apply to the Court of Appeal for leave to be present at proceedings for which leave is required under article 6 of the 2003 Order, or

(ii) to present any argument to the Court of Appeal on the hearing of the application or, if leave is given, the appeal, and whether he wishes to present it in person or by means of a legal representative;

(d) draws to the defendant's attention the effect of rule 71.4 (supply of documentary and other exhibits); and

(e) advises the defendant to consult a solicitor as soon as possible.

(3) The appellant must provide a Crown Court officer with a certificate of service stating that he has served the notice of appeal on the defendant in accordance with paragraph (1) or explaining why he has been unable to effect service.

Respondent's notice

5–754 **72.2.**—(1) This rule applies where a defendant is served with a notice of appeal under rule 72.1.

(2) If the defendant wishes to oppose the application for leave to appeal, he must, not later than 14 days after the date on which he received the notice of appeal, serve on the Registrar and on the appellant a notice in the form set out in the Practice Direction—

(a) stating the date on which he received the notice of appeal;

(b) summarising his response to the arguments of the appellant; and

(c) specifying the authorities which he intends to cite.

(3) The time for giving notice under this rule may be extended by the Registrar, a single judge or by the Court of Appeal.

(4) Where the Registrar refuses an application under paragraph (3) for the extension of time, the defendant shall be entitled to have his application determined by a single judge.

(5) Where a single judge refuses an application under paragraph (3) or (4) for the extension of time, the defendant shall be entitled to have his application determined by the Court of Appeal.

Amendment and abandonment of appeal

5–755 **72.3.**—(1) The appellant may amend a notice of appeal served under rule 72.1 or abandon an appeal under section 31 of the *Proceeds of Crime Act* 2002—

(a) without the permission of the Court at any time before the Court of Appeal have begun hearing the appeal; and

(b) with the permission of the Court after the Court of Appeal have begun hearing the appeal,

by serving notice in writing on the Registrar.

(2) Where the appellant serves a notice abandoning an appeal under paragraph (1), he must send a copy of it to—

(a) the defendant;

(b) a court officer of the court of trial; and

(c) the magistrates' court responsible for enforcing any confiscation order which the Crown Court has made.

(3) Where the appellant serves a notice amending a notice of appeal under paragraph (1), he must send a copy of it to the defendant.

(4) Where an appeal is abandoned under paragraph (1), the application for leave to appeal or appeal shall be treated, for the purposes of section 85 of the 2002 Act (conclusion of proceedings), as having been refused or dismissed by the Court of Appeal.

Criminal Procedure Rules 2005 (S.I. 2005 No. 384), Pt 73

Leave to appeal

5–756 **73.1.**—(1) Leave to appeal to the Court of Appeal under section 43 or section 65 of the *Proceeds of Crime Act* 2002 will only be given where—

(a) the Court of Appeal considers that the appeal would have a real prospect of success; or

(b) there is some other compelling reason why the appeal should be heard.

(2) An order giving leave may limit the issues to be heard and be made subject to conditions.

Notice of appeal

5–757 **73.2.**—(1) Where an appellant wishes to apply to the Court of Appeal for leave to appeal under section 43 or 65 of the *Proceeds of Crime Act* 2002 Act, he must serve a notice of appeal in the form set out in the Practice Direction on the Crown Court officer.

(2) Unless the Registrar, a single judge or the Court of Appeal directs otherwise, the appellant must serve the notice of appeal, accompanied by a respondent's notice in the form set out in the Practice Direction for the respondent to complete, on—

(a) each respondent;

(b) any person who holds realisable property to which the appeal relates; and

(c) any other person affected by the appeal,

as soon as practicable and in any event not later than 7 days after the notice of appeal is served on a Crown Court officer.

(3) The appellant must serve the following documents with his notice of appeal—

(a) four additional copies of the notice of appeal for the Court of Appeal;

(b) four copies of any skeleton argument;

(c) one sealed copy and four unsealed copies of any order being appealed;

(d) four copies of any witness statement or affidavit in support of the application for leave to appeal;

(e) four copies of a suitable record of the reasons for judgment of the Crown Court; and

(f) four copies of the bundle of documents used in the Crown Court proceedings from which the appeal lies.

(4) Where it is not possible to serve all of the documents referred to in paragraph (3), the appellant must indicate which documents have not yet been served and the reasons why they are not currently available.

(5) The appellant must provide a Crown Court officer with a certificate of service stating that he has served the notice of appeal on each respondent in accordance with paragraph (2) and including full details of each respondent or explaining why he has been unable to effect service.

Respondent's notice

73.3.—(1) This rule applies to an appeal under section 43 or 65 of the *Proceeds of Crime Act* 2002. **5–758**

(2) A respondent may serve a respondent's notice on the Registrar.

(3) A respondent who—

(a) is seeking leave to appeal from the Court of Appeal; or

(b) wishes to ask the Court of Appeal to uphold the decision of the Crown Court for reasons different from or additional to those given by the Crown Court,

must serve a respondent's notice on the Registrar.

(4) A respondent's notice must be in the form set out in the Practice Direction and where the respondent seeks leave to appeal to the Court of Appeal it must be requested in the respondent's notice.

(5) A respondent's notice must be served on the Registrar not later than 14 days after—

(a) the date the respondent is served with notification that the Court of Appeal has given the appellant leave to appeal; or

(b) the date the respondent is served with notification that the application for leave to appeal and the appeal itself are to be heard together.

(6) Unless the Registrar, a single judge or the Court of Appeal directs otherwise, the respondent serving a respondent's notice must serve the notice on the appellant and any other respondent—

(a) as soon as practicable; and

(b) in any event not later than seven days,

after it is served on the Registrar.

Amendment and abandonment of appeal

73.4.—(1) The appellant may amend a notice of appeal served under rule 73.2 or abandon an appeal under section 43 or 65 of the *Proceeds of Crime Act* 2002— **5–759**

(a) without the permission of the Court at any time before the Court of Appeal have begun hearing the appeal; and

(b) with the permission of the Court after the Court of Appeal have begun hearing the appeal,

by serving notice in writing on the Registrar.

(2) Where the appellant serves a notice under paragraph (1), he must send a copy of it to each respondent.

Stay

73.5. Unless the Court of Appeal or the Crown Court orders otherwise, an appeal under section 43 or 65 of the *Proceeds of Crime Act* 2002 shall not operate as a stay of any order or decision of the Crown Court. **5–760**

Striking out appeal notices and setting aside or imposing conditions on leave to appeal

5–761 **73.6.**—(1) The Court of Appeal may—

(a) strike out the whole or part of a notice of appeal served under rule 73.2; or

(b) impose or vary conditions upon which an appeal under section 43 or 65 of the *Proceeds of Crime Act* 2002 may be brought.

(2) The Court of Appeal will only exercise its powers under paragraph (1) where there is a compelling reason for doing so.

(3) Where a party is present at the hearing at which leave to appeal was given, he may not subsequently apply for an order that the Court of Appeal exercise its powers under paragraph (1)(b).

Hearing of appeals

5–762 **73.7.**—(1) This rule applies to appeals under section 43 or 65 of the *Proceeds of Crime Act* 2002.

(2) Every appeal will be limited to a review of the decision of the Crown Court unless the Court of Appeal considers that in the circumstances of an individual appeal it would be in the interests of justice to hold a re-hearing.

(3) The Court of Appeal will allow an appeal where the decision of the Crown Court was—

(a) wrong; or

(b) unjust because of a serious procedural or other irregularity in the proceedings in the Crown Court.

(4) The Court of Appeal may draw any inference of fact which it considers justified on the evidence.

(5) At the hearing of the appeal a party may not rely on a matter not contained in his notice of appeal unless the Court of Appeal gives permission.

[The next paragraph is § 5–765.]

Forms

5–765 The forms (or forms to like effect) set out in Annex D to the consolidated criminal practice direction are to be used in criminal courts as from April 4, 2005; almost all are identical to those in use previously, and accordingly a form in use before that date which corresponds with one in Annex D may still be used in connection with the rule to which it applies: *Practice Direction (Criminal Proceedings: Forms)* [2005] 1 W.L.R. 1479. The forms may be found on the website of the Department of Constitutional Affairs (www.dca.gov.uk). From the home page, follow the links "Procedure Rules", "Criminal Procedure Rules", "Forms".

(3) Authorities

Relationship to former law

5–766 Whilst many of the basic concepts of the new Act are borrowed from the earlier legislation, different terminology is frequently used. It will be for the courts to decide the extent to which earlier case law is relevant to this statute. It is, however, possible to be confident that certain decisions under the repealed legislation will carry over to the new law.

Effect of postponement

5–767 In *R. v. Donohoe* [2007] 1 Cr.App.R.(S.) 88, CA, it was held that the Crown Court will not be deprived of jurisdiction to make a confiscation order under section 6 of the *PCA* 2002 (*ante*, § 5–566) if it has breached the express prohibition in section 15(2) (*ante*, § 5–575) by imposing a fine, forfeiture order, deprivation order, or compensation order, when sentencing an offender after having postponed the confiscation hearing to a later date; there is nothing in the remaining provisions of the Act to oust the jurisdiction of the Crown Court in such a situation; whilst section 14(11) (*ante*, § 5–574) provides that a confiscation order "must not be quashed" only on the ground of a procedural defect connected with an application for postponement, and whilst subsection (12) provides that subsection (11) does not apply if, before the Crown Court makes the confiscation order, it breaches the section 15(2) prohibition, this does not oust the jurisdiction of the Crown Court by implication; rather, it is intended to preserve the jurisdiction of the Court of Appeal to quash or vary a confiscation order in circumstances such as where there is a danger of double counting or double penalty; if the effect of breaching the prohibition under section 15(2) by the imposition of a fine or by the forfeiture of drug paraphernalia were to render any subsequent confiscation order a nullity, this would frustrate the operation of the Act.

Lack of discretion/abuse of process

Where the conditions in section 6(2) and (3) of the *PCA* 2002 (*ante*, § 5–566) are **5–767a**
met, the court has no discretion not to make a confiscation order if it concludes that the defendant has benefited from his criminal conduct and has realisable assets. The only exception is provided for by subsection (6), where the court believes that the victim has taken, or intends to take, civil action against the accused, in which case the court is not under a duty to make a confiscation order; instead, it has a power to do so: *R. v. Hockey* [2008] 1 Cr.App.R.(S.) 50, CA. Where there is nothing to suggest that the victim intends to take civil action, it is not open to the Crown Court to adjourn the application for a confiscation order *sine die* in order to preserve the victim's position, on the basis that making a confiscation order might prejudice the victim's chances of obtaining full recovery if the defendant were to default on agreed repayments and civil proceedings were subsequently to become necessary: *ibid*.

That there is no discretion has been reiterated in *R. v. Farquhar* [2008] Crim.L.R. 645, CA, and *R. v. Morgan*; *R. v. Bygrave* [2008] Crim.L.R. 805, CA. In the latter case, it was said that this was so even in the limited class of cases where demonstrably (i) the offender's criminality is limited to offences causing loss to one or more identifiable losers, (ii) his benefit is limited to those offences, (iii) the losers have neither brought nor intend to bring any civil proceedings to recover the loss, and (iv) the offender either has repaid the losers, or stands ready, willing and able immediately to repay them, the full amount of the loss; and this is despite the high public interest in encouraging voluntary repayment, despite the provisions of section 71(1C) of the 1988 Act and section 6(6) of the 2002 Act, which provide such a discretion where a loser has, or intends to, bring a civil claim to recover his loss, and despite the anomaly this creates whereby the court has a discretion whether to make a confiscation order, and as to the amount in which to make it, in the case of an offender who waits to be sued, but no such discretion for someone who voluntarily makes a repayment. The court added, however, that the mandatory nature of the confiscation process makes the prosecution's decision to invoke it, and continue it, critical, and there must be an individual exercise of judgment involved in each case (a point reiterated in *R. v. Shabir*, *post*); moreover, in the limited class of cases set out *ante*, the court retains jurisdiction, before or during a confiscation hearing, to stay an application for confiscation where it amounts to an abuse of the court's process (*R. v. Mahmood and Shahin* [2006] 1 Cr.App.R.(S.) 96, CA, and *R. v. Farquhar* (*ante*)), for instance, where it would be oppressive to seek confiscation. For this purpose, oppression must be considered individually on the facts of each case; it is not sufficient to establish that the effect of a confiscation order would be to extract from a defendant a sum greater than his profit from the crime, since confiscation orders are not intended to be restitutionary measures; additionally, where a defendant has obtained through his crime a benefit beyond the loss inflicted, or where repayment is offered in full but it is uncertain that it will be accomplished, a finding of oppression will not be appropriate; but where the prosecution are simply attempting to inflict an additional financial penalty on an offender, especially if it is apparent that this is the sole reason underlying the application for the confiscation order, this may constitute oppression; the confiscation jurisdiction should not operate as a fine (see *R. v. May*, *post*, § 5–768).

In *R. v. Shabir*, unreported, July 31, 2008, CA ([2008] EWCA Crim. 1809), where a pharmacist had inflated his monthly claims to the Prescription Pricing Authority, it was held that it had been oppressive, first, to trigger the criminal lifestyle provisions when they could not have been applied if the charges had reflected the fact that the defendant's crimes involved fraud to an extent very much less than the threshold of £5,000 (see s.75(1)-(4), *ante*, § 5–636), and, secondly, to advance the contention that the defendant had benefited to the tune of £179,000 when in any ordinary language his benefit was a few hundred pounds. The court said that the enormous disparity between the amount of the defendant's illicit gain (£464) and that of the confiscation order (£212,464) raised the real possibility that the order was oppressive, but that disparity between the sum gained and the sum claimed would not constitute oppression in every case, especially where the lifestyle provisions applied.

General approach

5–768 In *R. v. May* [2008] 2 W.L.R. 1131, HL, their Lordships issued general guidance on the power to make confiscation orders and set out the following broad principles: (a) the legislation is intended to deprive defendants of the benefit they have gained from relevant criminal conduct, whether or not they have retained such benefit, within the limits of their available means, and it does not provide for confiscation in the sense understood by schoolchildren and others, but nor does it operate by way of fine; the benefit gained is the total value of the property or advantage obtained, not the defendant's net profit after deduction of expenses or any amounts payable to co-conspirators; (b) the court should proceed by asking (i) if the defendant has benefited from relevant criminal conduct, (ii) if so, what the value of the benefit he has so obtained is, and (iii) what sum is recoverable from him; these are separate questions calling for separate answers, and the questions and answers must not be elided, although the questions must be modified where issues of criminal lifestyle arise; (c) in addressing these questions, the court should, first, establish the facts as best it can on the material available, relying as appropriate on the statutory assumptions, and in many cases the factual findings made will be decisive; and should, secondly, focus closely on the language of the statutory provision in question in the context of the statute and in the light of any statutory definition, viewing any judicial gloss or exegesis with caution, and ordinarily seeking guidance in the statutory language rather than in the proliferating case law; (e) in determining whether the defendant has obtained property or a pecuniary advantage and, if so, the value of any property or advantage so obtained, the court should (subject to any relevant statutory definition) apply ordinary common law principles to the facts as found, and should not depart from familiar rules governing entitlement and ownership; while the answering of the third question calls for inquiry into the defendant's financial resources at the date of the determination, the answering of the first two questions plainly calls for an historical inquiry into past transactions; (f) the defendant ordinarily obtains property if in law he owns it, whether alone or jointly, which will ordinarily connote a power of disposition or control, as where a person directs a payment or conveyance of property to someone else; he ordinarily obtains a pecuniary advantage if (amongst other things) he evades a liability for which he is personally subject; mere couriers or custodians or other minor contributors to an offence, rewarded by a specific fee and having no interest in the property or the proceeds of sale, are unlikely to be found to have obtained that property, although it may be otherwise with money launderers.

In light of these observations, due caution will be required when assessing the value of earlier decisions of the Court of Appeal. Examples are *R. v. Stanley* [2008] 2 Cr.App.R.(S.) 19, which now would almost certainly be decided differently, and *R. v. Newman* [2008] Crim.L.R. 653, CA, which must be wide open to question: see the commentaries in *Criminal Law Week* 2008/08/16 & 28/15 respectively. An example of a case having been decided adversely to the defendant in the Crown Court prior to the decisions of the House of Lords and then having been reversed on appeal in light of those decisions is *R. v. Sivaraman* [2008] 8 *Archbold News* 3, CA, where it was said that a person who, when acting purely in the capacity of an employee, receives property or a pecuniary advantage on behalf of his employer, but who, as a reward for doing so, receives himself only an enhanced wage or cash payment, must not necessarily be taken to profit to the same extent as his employer, since the court is concerned with the benefit not to an abstract entity called "a conspiracy", but to the benefit gained by each conspirator, whether individually or jointly, which again is a question of fact. Where, therefore, the appellant had received a pecuniary advantage in his capacity as such, and not as a joint trader, his benefit was accordingly his enhanced wage, and not the full pecuniary advantage received on behalf of his employer.

Benefit

Property

Section 76(4) and (7) (taken together) effectively correspond to section 71(4) of the *CJA* 1988 (save that the new provision refers to "conduct" whereas the former provision referred to "the commission of an offence"). The leading authorities on these provisions are now *R. v. May*, *ante* (where several defendants jointly held property that had been obtained as a result of a fraud for which they were jointly responsible, each had benefited in the amount jointly held, and there was no requirement to apportion the amount between them); *R. v. Green* [2008] 2 W.L.R. 1154, HL (to similar effect); and *Jennings v. CPS* [2008] 2 W.L.R. 1148, HL, in which it was held that, for the purposes of section 71(4) of the 1988 Act, a person does not obtain property unless he obtains it so as to own it, whether alone or jointly, which will ordinarily connote a power of disposition or control, as where a person directs a payment or conveyance of property to someone else. Their Lordships said that the rationale of the confiscation regime is to deprive the defendant of what he has gained or its equivalent, not to operate by way of fine, and he cannot and should not be deprived of what he has never gained or its equivalent, because that is a fine; in particular, it is not sufficient that a person is instrumental in the property being obtained, as his acts may contribute significantly to property being obtained without his obtaining it. **5–769**

In *R. v. Patel* [2000] 2 Cr.App.R.(S.) 10, CA, it was held that where an offender received the whole proceeds of a fraudulent scheme, and passed half to his accomplice, his benefit was the whole of the proceeds. This was followed in *R. v. Sharma* [2006] 2 Cr.App.R.(S.) 63, CA, in which it was held that where a member of a criminal enterprise had fraudulently received money into a bank account on which he was the sole signatory, his "benefit" was the whole of that money, notwithstanding that money from the account had been paid after receipt to other members of the enterprise. The court said that it followed that the total amount which might be recovered from all members of the enterprise was not limited by the amount of the victim's loss. *Patel* and *Sharma* were approved by the House of Lords in *R. v. May*, *ante*, although they were both treated under the second question, *viz.* that relating to the valuation of the offender's benefit. **5–770**

In *R. v. Omar* [2005] 1 Cr.App.R.(S.) 86, CA, the appellant was convicted (having been recruited by a co-defendant) of cheating the Public Revenue following a VAT fraud conducted through what was originally a legitimate company, owned by the offender and his wife, and which owned several properties which had been purchased whilst operating as a legitimate business. It was held that the judge had been entitled to lift the corporate veil and to treat the benefit accruing during the period of the company's involvement in the fraud as a benefit of the offender (whether or not it was set up as a sham or was an existing legitimate company); the important point was that the company was used by the appellant for the purposes of fraud and it was his *alter ego*, with him running it and making all the decisions, including as to the purchase of the (pre-fraud) properties. Once the corporate veil was lifted, there was no unfairness in treating the company's realisable assets as those of the offender. In relation to the division of benefit between participants in the fraud, it was said that the suggestion in *R. v. Gibbons*, *post*, § 5–774, that the total benefit should be equally divided between conspirators was a good starting point, but was not a rule and therefore where the combined amount of any confiscation orders made against the other two participants in respect of the relevant count would be significantly less than two-thirds of the total benefit (by virtue of their limited realisable assets), it had been appropriate to make an order for more than one-third of the total benefit against the appellant, the judge having been satisfied that there would be no unfairness in doing so and, in particular, that there would be no possibility of "double recovery".

The principle in *R. v. Dore* [1997] 2 Cr.App.(S.) 152, CA (controlled drugs in the possession of an offender could not be sold lawfully and had no market value for the purposes of determining realisable assets under the *DTA* 1994, s.7) applies to the assessment of whether an offender had benefited from his general or particular criminal conduct under section 6(4) of the 2002 Act (*ante*, § 5–566): *R. v. Ajibade* [2006] 2 Cr.App.R.(S.) 70, CA.

In *R. v. Olubitan* [2004] 2 Cr.App.R.(S.) 14, CA, the appellant joined a conspiracy to defraud after an initial consignment of goods had been obtained; an attempt to obtain a second consignment was unsuccessful. It was held that he had not benefited from the offence. *Olubitan* was specifically approved in *R. v. May*, *ante*; and to similar effect, see *R. v. Byatt* [2006] 2 Cr.App.R.(S.) 116, CA (conspirator withdrawing from conspiracy to rob before any robbery took place); and *R. v. Davy* [2003] 2 Cr.App.R.(S.) 101, CA (conspirator arranging for purchase of a consignment of drugs subsequently seized by the police whilst in transit, but never being in possession of them).

In *R. v. Davis* [2004] 2 Cr.App.R.(S.) 12, CA, it was held that a confiscation order could be made in respect of offences of having possession, custody or control in the course of a business, and with a view to gain, of goods bearing a sign identical to, or likely to be mistaken for, a registered trade mark; the question was whether the items that bore the false trademarks were property, and whether they were obtained in connection with the commission of the offences charged; there was no reason to gloss the wording of section 71(4), and, accordingly, they were to be regarded as property obtained in connection with the commission of those offences.

In *R. v. Wilkes* [2003] 2 Cr.App.R.(S.) 105, CA, the appellant was arrested whilst in the course of burglary. Goods had been removed with a view to theft, but they were recovered immediately. It was held that the appellant had benefited. In *R. v. Alagobola* [2004] 2 Cr.App.R.(S.) 48, CA, it was held that a person "obtains" property "in connection with" the commission of an offence of being concerned in an arrangement whereby the retention or control of another's proceeds of criminal conduct was facilitated (s.93A(1) of the *CJA* 1988) when, the proceeds having been paid into his bank account without his knowledge, he disposed of them with guilty knowledge to the instructions of the criminal; he obtained them at the point that he decided to retain them and deal with them as owner. In *R. v. McKinnon* [2004] 2 Cr.App.R.(S.) 46, CA, it was held that where a person obtains property abroad as a result of, or in connection with, an offence committed by him within the jurisdiction, he thereby benefits from the offence notwithstanding that no offence was committed in the overseas jurisdiction, by virtue of the conduct in question not being criminal in that jurisdiction.

5–771 In *R. v. Neuberg* [2007] 1 Cr.App.R.(S.) 84, CA, it was held (i) that, on conviction of an offence of trading under a prohibited name without leave of the court, contrary to the *Insolvency Act* 1986, s.216, an offender would be liable to the making of a confiscation order assessed according to a "benefit" figure derived from the turnover of the business during the period of the unlawful trading; the authorities clearly established that when calculating "benefit", it was right to look at the turnover of the business and not simply the profit; and (ii) as to the application of Article 1 of the First Protocol to the ECHR (right to peaceful enjoyment of possessions), the requirement of proportionality was satisfied by the fact that any order actually made was limited to the realisable assets of the offender.

In *R. v. Waller* [2008] L.S. Gazette, September 25, 24, CA ([2008] EWCA Crim. 2037), where the defendant pleaded guilty to being knowingly concerned in the fraudulent evasion of the duty payable on the importation of tobacco which he had bought for £14,000 in France, it was held that his benefit was to be regarded as the tobacco itself plus the value of the duty evaded (£27,505) in that he obtained the tobacco "in connection with" his offence (see s.76(4)). Whilst the court purported to rely on *R. v. May*, *ante*, see the commentary in *Criminal Law Week* 2008/35/30, where it is suggested that the decision misapplies *May* and is out of line with *R. v. Smith (David)*, *post*, § 5–772, where, on effectively identical facts, it was never suggested that the offenders' benefit included the fraudulently imported goods themselves.

For a case involving a number of counts under the *Trade Descriptions Act* 1968, s.1(a) and (b) in respect of a series of motor vehicles which had been "clocked" and then sold, see *R. v. Raphael*, *The Daily Telegraph*, March 27, 2003, CA ([2003] EWCA

Crim. 698), in which the court accepted that what was "obtained" was at least the difference between the true value of the vehicle and its enhanced value (as indicated by Glass's Guide), but hinted that it might well have concluded that what was obtained was the whole of the price at which the offender sold the clocked vehicles, had the prosecution sought to argue the point.

For a case under the *FSMA* 2000, s.397(1) (causing a false or misleading trading statement to be issued to the market (*post*, § 30–215d)), see *R. v. Rigby and Bailey* [2007] 1 Cr.App.R.(S.) 73, CA, *post*, § 30–215f.

Pecuniary advantage

Section 76(5) (*ante*, § 5–637) is in materially identical terms to section 71(5) of the *CJA* 1988 (save that the new provision refers to the pecuniary advantage being obtained as a result of or in connection with "conduct" whereas the former provision referred to "the commission of an offence"). In *R. v. Dimsey and Allen* [2000] 1 Cr.App.R.(S.) 497, CA, it was held that where a fraudulent scheme to cheat the Revenue results in the evasion of tax, the unpaid tax was a "pecuniary advantage" within section 71(5). And in *R. v. Smith (David)* [2002] 1 W.L.R. 54, HL, it was held that where a person is knowingly concerned in the fraudulent evasion of excise duty on goods which he imports, but those goods are seized from him after the moment of importation but before being sold or otherwise dealt with by him, he obtains a pecuniary advantage as a result of or in connection with the commission of the offence within section 71(5), the value of the advantage being the amount of duty evaded. **5–772**

R. v. Bakewell [2006] 2 Cr.App.R.(S.) 42, CA and *R. v. Rowbotham* [2006] 2 Cr.App.R.(S.) 99, CA, were both cases of evasion of duty in which the defendant had acted as a courier or minder of the contraband, and in both of which it was held that his benefit was the full amount of the duty evaded. In light of the observations of the House of Lords in *R. v. May*, *ante*, about couriers and minders, it must be open to question whether these decisions can survive their Lordships' decision (*cf. R. v. Sivaraman*, *ante*, § 5–768). *R. v. Houareau* [2006] 1 Cr.App.R.(S.) 89, CA, was similar. Unlike the other two cases, however, it was specifically mentioned in the opinion of their Lordships in *May* (at [33]). It seems that their Lordships were prepared to approve the judge's assessment of the appellant's benefit as one-third of the duty evaded on the basis that he had found as a fact (making a "robust" inference that the Court of Appeal had held he had been entitled to make) that the appellant did in fact have a beneficial interest in the contraband itself. And as to the controversial suggestion that the benefit of a person who fraudulently imports goods is not confined to the duty evaded but extends to the goods themselves, see *R. v. Waller*, *ante*, § 5–771.

Assumptions to be made in case of a criminal lifestyle

In *R. v. Jones* [2007] 1 Cr.App.R.(S.) 71, CA, it was held that where, following conviction for an offence, the court has decided under section 6 (*ante*, § 5–566) that the offender has a criminal lifestyle, section 10(6) (required assumption not to be made if there would be a serious risk of injustice if the assumption were made (*ante*, § 5–570)) does not refer to hardship that would be sustained by the offender by virtue of the making of a confiscation order, and it does not operate so as to confer a discretion on the court to determine whether it is fair to make a confiscation order at all; Parliament's plain intention was that a confiscation order should be made in every case where the court concludes that the offender has benefited from his general criminal conduct, the purpose of section 10(6) being to ensure that the assumptions under section 10, which are to be made in relation to particular property or expenditure when deciding questions as to benefit from general criminal conduct, were not so unreasonable or unjust that they should not be made (*e.g.* they should not be made if they gave rise to double counting or were inconsistent with an agreed factual basis of sentence). **5–773**

Where (in a case concerned with the *DTA* 1994, ss.4(1) and (3), which correspond broadly to the *PCA* 2002, ss.8 and 10, *ante*, §§ 5–568, 5–570) it was clear that the defendant had purchased and sold drugs continuously over a period of time, with the proceeds of sale being recycled into the next purchase and so on, it was inappropriate to assume, pursuant to section 4(3), that the drugs purchased had been bought out of payments received in connection with drug trafficking and then to aggregate the sale proceeds; to do so would be to treat the defendant as having received two sums of money when in fact he had received only one; such a case was to be determined by reference to section 4(1), which required the court to identify payments and rewards received by the defendant in connection with drug trafficking, not by reference to section 4(3), which merely provides a tool that can be used for that purpose; and it was to be noted that, although section 4(3) requires the court to assume that money used to finance expenditure was derived from drug trafficking, it does not require the court to assume that such money was derived from sources other than those to which the evidence naturally points: *R. v. Green* [2007] 3 All E.R. 751, CA (this aspect of the decision not being affected by the decision of the House of Lords (*ante*, § 5–769)).

Valuation of benefit

5–774 In *R. v. Pattison* [2008] 1 Cr.App.R.(S.) 51, CA, it was held that, when valuing property obtained by an offender as a result of his criminal conduct, the combined effect of sections 79 and 80 of the 2002 Act (*ante*, §§ 5–640, 5–641) is clear; the value, where he still holds the property, is the greater of the market value when he obtained the property adjusted for changes in the value of money and the market value at the time the court makes its decision (less the value of any third party interest). No allowance is to be made for the cost to the defendant of acquiring the property in the first place. Accordingly, the judge had been correct not to deduct the value of an unsecured loan which the defendant had used to help fund the purchase of a house from a drug dealer at an undervalue, and correct also not to deduct expenses associated with its acquisition or (potential) sale or sums spent on its improvement. Whilst it may be permissible to take into account the costs inherently involved in the realisation of an asset when determining a defendant's realisable assets, the cost involved in their potential realisation has no relevance to the assessment of the benefit received. However, any argument that, where a defendant acquires property through criminal conduct, and subsequently deals with that property (as by mortgaging it or selling it), any proceeds of that dealing are additional benefits from the original offending and are therefore to be aggregated with the original value of the property, overlooks the provisions of section 80 and offends common sense. Section 80 addresses this situation and provides that, if, at the material time, a person holds no part of the property obtained, the value of his benefit is the greater of the value of the property obtained at the time it was obtained and adjusted for the value of money and the value of any property in his hands that represents that property; and similarly, where part only of the property obtained has been disposed of in the meantime. The court further held that section 80 does not address the situation where a defendant generates an income from his criminal property without his interest in the property itself being diminished (*e.g.* rent or interest) and such proceeds should be regarded as property obtained as a result of the criminal conduct.

In *R. v. Rose*; *R. v. Whitwam* [2008] 2 Cr.App.R. 15, CA, it was held that whereas section 76(7) of the 2002 Act (*ante*, § 5–637) provides that a person's benefit is "the value of the property obtained", whereas section 80 is expressed without qualification to apply "for the purpose of deciding the value of property obtained ..." and whereas section 79 (value: the basic rule) is brought into play by the express words of section 80(4), it is plain that both sections 79 and 80 apply not only to the determination of the realisable amount but also to the calculation of benefit. However, it was further held that the "market value", within section 79(2) of property obtained by a thief or a handler is the amount it would have cost the defendant to obtain the property legitimately, or the economic value to the loser, rather than what the defendant could get for the property if he sold it. That the property has been restored to its true owner is irrelevant when calculating the benefit to the defendant. For criticism of this decision, see *Criminal Law Week* 2008/09/2, and see also the observations of the House of Lords in *R. v. May* and *Jennings v. CPS*, *ante*, §§ 5–768, 5–769, as to a person ordinarily obtaining property if in law he owns it. See also *R. v. Ascroft* [2004] 1 Cr.App.R.(S.) 56, CA (where offender stole large quantity of goods in transit, they were to be valued at their normal wholesale price, not at the amount he had received on their sale).

Where it was possible to quantify the total value of the property obtained by the parties to a conspiracy to defraud, but impossible to quantify the value of the property received by individual conspirators, it was permissible to divide the total by the number of identified conspirators and say that the resulting figure was the amount obtained by each individual: *R. v. Gibbons* [2003] 2 Cr.App.R.(S.) 34, CA (approved by the House of Lords in *R. v. May*). *Gibbons* was distinguished in *R. v. Omar, ante*, § 5–770.

"Realisable property" (s.83) and "property" (s.84)

A defendant will not be able to avoid an order for the full value of his proceeds of crime unless he has identified all the realisable property held by him; if he refuses to do that, then the Crown Court has no option but to order the full amount to be recovered: *Telli v. Revenue and Customs Prosecutions Office* [2008] Crim.L.R. 400, CA (Civ. Div.) (a decision on the *DTA* 1994). **5–775**

In *Re Maye* [2008] 1 W.L.R. 315, the House of Lords considered the definition of "property" in article 3(1) of the *Proceeds of Crime (Northern Ireland) Order* 1996 (N.I. 9). Whilst the definition is not identical to the definition of "property" in section 84 of the 2002 Act (*ante*, § 5–645), it is submitted that the court's conclusions will carry across to the 2002 Act. It was held: (i) that an interest in an unadministered estate at the time a confiscation order is made falls within the definition and can therefore form part of the realisable amount, which, if less than the amount of the defendant's benefit, will be the amount that he will be required to pay under the confiscation order; whilst it is true that until the administration of an estate is complete, the defendant would have no proprietary interest in any particular asset of the estate, his interest in the estate would nonetheless be a proprietary interest; and (ii) "things in action" include a "personal" action for damages for false imprisonment, defamation or tortious injury to the person causing pain and suffering or loss of amenities, and this is so even if the action is still pending when the confiscation order is made.

In *R. v. Cornfield* [2007] 1 Cr.App.R.(S.) 124, CA, it was held that although realisable property may extend to a contingent beneficial interest under a will (*R. v. Wallbrook and Glasgow*, 15 Cr.App.R.(S.) 783, CA), it does not extend to the putative possible future receipt of a lump sum pension payment which could not be used as security for a loan and which (if it were paid) would go to a trustee in bankruptcy. In *R. v. Ford* [2008] Crim.L.R. 648, CA, however, it was held that, where an offender held pension funds, due to mature in five years, with a fund value of £80,000 but a surrender value of only £17,500 and a market value (*i.e.* the value at which the funds could pass between a willing seller and a willing buyer) of nil (since the funds could not be assigned to another person, whether by sale or otherwise), the value to be assigned to those funds for the purposes of calculating the realisable value of the offender's assets in accordance with section 74(3)(a) of the 1988 Act was £80,000.

Where an offender's home had been purchased in joint names with his wife before the offences of which he stood convicted were committed, his wife's share was not realisable property, notwithstanding that mortgage payments had been met out of the proceeds of his offending and that she knew that the money had not been legitimately earned; the payments were not tainted gifts as she had given consideration by bringing up the children and looking after the home; and there was no legal principle under which a person could be deprived of the benefit of illegally obtained property on grounds of public policy: *Gibson v. Revenue and Customs Prosecution Office, The Times*, July 14, 2008, CA (Civ. Div.) (a decision on the *DTA* 1994). Where, however, an offender transferred his share in the matrimonial home to his wife for no consideration after the commission of an offence in respect of which a confiscation order was subsequently made, half the equity in the property was "realisable property", as it had been the subject of a gift made by the offender following the commission of his offence. Neither the fact that it had not been made with a view to defeating the confiscation order, but with a view to getting the family's finances in order (in that it facilitated a re-mortgage in his wife's name), nor the fact that the 50 per cent interest that the law regarded him as having in the house may not have reflected what he actually contributed over the 16 years that he and his wife had lived there made a difference; whilst the wife had been the principal breadwinner, there was no reason to suppose that the offender, who had been in receipt of incapacity benefit, had not contributed directly or indirectly to the mortgage payments: *Re. B. (confiscation order)* [2008] 2 F.L.R. 1, QBD (Cranston J.) (a decision under the *CJA* 1988).

As to controlled drugs having no market value for the purposes of determining realisable assets, see *R. v. Dore, ante*, § 5–770.

Third party interests

5–776 In *Webber v. Webber (CPS intervening)* [2007] 1 W.L.R. 1052, Fam D, Sir Mark Potter P. observed *obiter* that (i) the Crown Court, when making a confiscation order, must disregard what a former wife may obtain in other proceedings over and above any interest which she holds at the time the order is made; the mere right of a spouse to apply for relief under the *Matrimonial Causes Act* 1973 does not amount to "an interest" falling within the terms of section 69(3)(a) of the 2002 Act (*ante*, § 5–630) (which requires a court to exercise its powers so as to allow a third party to recover the value of any interest held by him) (see s.84(2)(f), *ante*, § 5–645, as to "references to an interest"); accordingly, when a confiscation order is made, the Crown Court should have no regard to, and make no allowance for, any possible adverse consequences for a former spouse and her child when deciding the amount to be confiscated (applying *R. v. Ahmed* [2005] 1 All E.R. 128, CA (§ 5–452 in the supplement)); but (ii) sections 42(3), 49(8) and 53(8) (*ante*, §§ 5–603, 5–610, 5–614) provide rights to affected third parties to make representations in relation to the making and variation, etc., of restraint orders and the enforcement of confiscation orders; and (iii) if a property adjustment order is made under the 1973 Act in favour of a third party, the Crown Court must have regard to it when determining the "available amount" under the 2002 Act; and similarly, where a property adjustment order is made after the confiscation order, but before enforcement, the Crown Court must on the application of the prosecuting authority or the defendant have regard to it in adjusting "the available amount" under section 23 of the 2002 Act (*ante*, § 5–584).

[The next paragraph is § 5–822.]

X. DISQUALIFICATION, RESTRICTION, EXCLUSION, ETC., ORDERS

A. BANNING ORDERS UNDER THE FOOTBALL SPECTATORS ACT 1989

(1) Summary

Football (Disorder) Act 2000

5–822 Where a person is convicted of a "relevant offence" (*i.e.* one listed in Schedule 1 to the 1989 Act), the court must make a banning order if satisfied that there are reasonable grounds to believe that it would help to prevent violence or disorder at or in connection with any regulated football matches (s.14A(1)). If the court is not so satisfied, it must state its reasons in open court (s.14A(2)). Banning orders may also be made on a complaint made by the chief officer of police for the area in which the respondent resides or appears to reside. The court must make an order if satisfied that the respondent has at any time caused or contributed to any violence or disorder in the United Kingdom or elsewhere and that there are reasonable grounds to believe that it would help to prevent violence or disorder at or in connection with any regulated football matches (s.14B). Section 14C provides for the interpretation of "violence" and "disorder", and makes clear that they are not limited to violence or disorder in connection with football. It also makes provision as to what a magistrates' court may take into account in deciding whether to make an order under section 14B. Section 14D provides for appeals to the Crown Court. Section 14E requires a court to explain the effect of a banning order. This must require the subject of the order to report initially to a police station specified in the order within five days. It must also, unless it appears to the court that there are exceptional circumstances, impose a requirement as to the surrender, in connection with regulated football matches outside the United Kingdom, of the person's passport. Section 14F provides for the period of an order. Where it is made together with a sentence of immediate imprisonment, it must be for not less than six nor more than 10 years. Other orders under section 14A must be for between three to five years, and an order under section 14B must be for two to three years. Section 14G allows the court to impose additional requirements. Section 14J makes non-compliance with any requirement of a banning order, or imposed by the enforcing authority under section 19(2B) or (2C), a summary offence.

Section 21A confers a summary power of detention of up to six hours. Section 21B provides for reference of a person detained to a court. This has effect as a complaint under section 14B, and there is a power of arrest where the constable believes it is necessary to secure the person's attendance. **5–823**

(2) Legislation

Football Spectators Act 1989, s.14

PART II

REGULATED FOOTBALL MATCHES

Preliminary

Main definitions

14.—(1) This section applies for the purposes of this Part. **5–824**

(2) "Regulated football match" means an association football match (whether in England and Wales or elsewhere) which is a prescribed match or a match of a prescribed description.

(3) "External tournament" means a football competition which includes regulated football matches outside England and Wales.

(4) "Banning order" means an order made by the court under this Part which—

(a) in relation to regulated football matches in England and Wales, prohibits the person who is subject to the order from entering any premises for the purpose of attending such matches, and

(b) in relation to regulated football matches outside England and Wales, requires that person to report at a police station in accordance with this Part.

(5) "Control period", in relation to a regulated football match outside England and Wales, means the period—

(a) beginning five days before the day of the match, and

(b) ending when the match is finished or cancelled.

(6) "Control period", in relation to an external tournament, means any period described in an order made by the Secretary of State—

(a) beginning five days before the day of the first football match outside England and Wales which is included in the tournament, and

(b) ending when the last football match outside England and Wales which is included in the tournament is finished or cancelled,

but, for the purposes of paragraph (a), any football match included in the qualifying or prequalifying stages of the tournament is to be left out of account.

(7) Reference to football matches are to football matches played or intended to be played.

(8) "Relevant offence" means an offence to which Schedule 1 to this Act applies.

[This section was substituted by the *Football (Disorder) Act* 2000, s.1(1), and Sched. 1, para. 2.]

The *Football Spectators (Prescription) Order* 2004 (S.I. 2004 No. 2409) (as amended by the *Football Spectators (Prescription) (Amendment) Order* 2006 (S.I. 2006 No. 761)) describes the football matches in England and Wales and outside England and Wales which are regulated football matches for the purposes of Part II of the 1989 Act. In England and Wales, a regulated match is any match in which either team is a member of the Football League, the Premier League, the Football Conference or the League of

Wales, represents a club from outside England and Wales or represents a country or territory. Outside England and Wales, a regulated match is one involving a national team representing England or Wales or a team representing a Football League, Premier League, Football Conference or League of Wales club, or one involving a country or territory whose football association is a member of the Fédération Internationale de Football Associations, and being part of a competition or tournament organised by or under the authority of the federation or of the Union des Associations Européennes de Football, and where the competition or tournament is one in which the England or Wales national team is eligible to participate or has participated.

Football Spectators Act 1989, ss.14A–14H

Banning orders

Banning orders made on conviction of an offence

5–825 **14A.**—(1) This section applies where a person (the "offender") is convicted of a relevant offence.

(2) If the court is satisfied that there are reasonable grounds to believe that making a banning order would help to prevent violence or disorder at or in connection with any regulated football matches, it must make such an order in respect of the offender.

(3) If the court is not satisfied, it must in open court state that fact and give its reasons.

(3A) For the purpose of deciding whether to make an order under this section the court may consider evidence led by the prosecution and the defence.

(3B) It is immaterial whether evidence led in pursuance of subsection (3A) would have been admissible in the proceedings in which the offender was convicted.

(4) A banning order may only be made under this section—

- (a) in addition to a sentence imposed in respect of the relevant offence, or
- (b) in addition to an order discharging him conditionally.

(4A) The court may adjourn any proceedings in relation to an order under this section even after sentencing the offender.

(4B) If the offender does not appear for any adjourned proceedings, the court may further adjourn the proceedings or may issue a warrant for his arrest.

(4BA) If the court adjourns or further adjourns any proceedings under subsection (4A) or (4B), the court may remand the offender.

(4BB) A person who, by virtue of subsection (4BA), is remanded on bail may be required by the conditions of his bail—

- (a) not to leave England and Wales before his appearance before the court, and
- (b) if the control period relates to a regulated football match outside the United Kingdom or to an external tournament which includes such matches, to surrender his passport to a police constable, if he has not already done so.

(4C) ... the court may not issue a warrant under subsection (4B) above for the offender's arrest unless it is satisfied that he has had adequate notice of the time and place of the adjourned proceedings.

(5) A banning order may be made as mentioned in subsection (4)(b) above in spite of anything in section 12 and 14 of the *Powers of the Criminal Courts (Sentencing) Act* 2000 (which relate to orders discharging a person absolutely or conditionally and their effect).

(5A) The prosecution has a right of appeal against a failure by the court to make a banning order under this section—

- (a) where the failure is by a magistrates' court, to the Crown Court; and
- (b) where it is by the Crown Court, to the Court of Appeal.

(5B) An appeal under subsection (5A)(b) may be brought only if the Court of Appeal gives permission or the judge who decided not to make an order grants a certificate that his decision is fit for appeal

(5C) An order made on appeal under this section (other than one directing that an application be re-heard by the court from which the appeal was brought) is to be treated for the purposes of this Part as if it were an order of the court from which the appeal was brought.

(6) In this section, "the court" in relation to an offender means—

- (a) the court by or before which he is convicted of the relevant offence, or
- (b) if he is committed to the Crown Court to be dealt with for that offence, the Crown Court.

[This section was inserted by the *Football Disorder Act* 2000, s.1(1), and Sched. 1, para. 2. It is printed as amended by the *Anti-social Behaviour Act* 2003, s.86(4); the *SOCPA* 2005, s.139(10); and the *VCRA* 2006, ss.52(2) and 65, Sched. 3, paras 1, 2(1) and (2), and 3(1), and Sched. 5.]

A banning order does not constitute a "penalty" within Article 7 of the ECHR (*post*, § 16–97); accordingly, where an individual was convicted after the date of commencement of the amendments to the 1989 Act effected by the *Football (Disorder) Act* 2000 (*ante*, § 5–821) of an offence falling within Schedule 1 to the 1989 Act committed before that date, Article 7 did not preclude the making of a banning order for a period longer than would have been permissible had he been convicted before that date: *Gough v. Chief Constable of Derbyshire Constabulary*; *R. (Miller) v. Leeds Magistrates' Court*; *Lilley v. DPP* [2002] Q.B. 459, DC. The appeal to the civil division of the Court of Appeal of the first two appellants (*post*, § 5–826) was not directly concerned with orders made under section 14A.

In *R. v. Hughes* [2006] 1 Cr.App.R.(S.) 107, CA, it was held that where an offender is convicted of a "relevant offence", it is apparent from section 14A(2) and (3), that Parliament expected, in a normal case, that the conviction itself would be sufficient to satisfy the court under subsection (2); there is no requirement for repetition or propensity. *Hughes* was followed in *R. (White) v. Crown Court at Blackfriars*, 172 J.P. 321, DC, in which it was held that section 14A(2) entitles a court to take into account, and to give great weight to, deterrence and that there are clear benefits in it being widely known that a person who assaults an official at a football match is liable to be made the subject of a football banning order even if the incident was, for the person, an isolated one.

14B. [*Banning orders made on complaint.*] **5–826**

Banning orders: supplementary

14C.—(1) In this Part, "violence" means violence against persons or property and includes threatening violence and doing anything which endangers the life of any person. **5–827**

(2) In this Part, "disorder" includes—

(a) stirring up hatred against a group of persons defined by reference to colour, race, nationality (including citizenship) or ethnic or national origins, or against an individual as a member of such a group,

(b) using threatening, abusive or insulting words or behaviour or disorderly behaviour,

(c) displaying any writing or other thing which is threatening, abusive or insulting.

(3) In this Part, "violence" and "disorder" are not limited to violence or disorder in connection with football.

(4) The magistrates' court may take into account the following matters (among others), so far as they consider it appropriate to do so, in determining whether to make an order under section 14B above—

(a) any decision of a court or tribunal outside the United Kingdom,

(b) deportation or exclusion from a country outside the United Kingdom,

(c) removal or exclusion from premises used for playing football matches, whether in the United Kingdom or elsewhere,

(d) conduct recorded on video or by any other means.

(5) In determining whether to make such an order—

(a) the magistrates' court may not take into acocunt anything done by the respondent before the beginning of the period of ten years ending with the application under section 14B(1) above, except circumstances ancillary to a conviction,

(b) before taking into account any conviction for a relevant offence, where a court made a statement under section 14A(3) above (or section 15(2A) below or section 30(3) of the *Public Order Act* 1986), the magistrates' court must consider the reasons given in the statement,

and in this subsection "circumstances ancillary to a conviction" has the same meaning as it has for the purposes of section 4 of the *Rehabilitation of Offenders Act* 1974 (effect of rehabilitation).

(6) Subsection (5) does not prejudice anything in *Rehabilitation of Offenders Act* 1974.

[This section was inserted by the *Football Disorder Act* 2000, s.1(1), and Sched. 1, para. 2.]

5–828 **14D.** [*Banning orders made on complaint: appeals.*]

Banning orders: general

5–829 **14E.**—(1) On making a banning order, a court must in ordinary language explain its effect to the person subject to the order.

(2) A banning order must require the person subject to the order to report initially at a police station in England and Wales specified in the order within the period of five days beginning with the day on which the order is made.

(2A) A banning order must require the person subject to the order to give notification of the events mentioned in subsection (2B) to the enforcing authority.

(2B) The events are—

(a) a change of any of his names;

(b) the first use by him after the making of the order of a name for himself that was not disclosed by him at the time of the making of the order;

(c) a change of his home address;

(d) his acquisition of a temporary address;

(e) a change of his temporary address or his ceasing to have one;

(f) his becoming aware of the loss of his travel authorisation;

(g) receipt by him of a new travel authorisation;

(h) an appeal made by him in relation to the order;

(i) an application made by him under section 14H(2) for termination of the order;

(j) an appeal made by him under section 23(3) against the making of a declaration of relevance in respect of an offence of which he has been convicted.

(2C) A notification required by a banning order by virtue of subsection (2A) must be given before the end of the period of seven days beginning with the day on which the event in question occurs and—

(a) in the case of a change of a name or address or the acquisition of a temporary address, must specify the new name or address;

(b) in the case of a first use of a previously undisclosed name, must specify that name; and

(c) in the case of a receipt of a new travel authorisation, must give details of that travel authorisation.

(3) A banning order must ... impose a requirement as to the surrender in accordance with this Part, in connection with regulated football matches outside the United Kingdom, of the *passport* [travel authorisation] of the person subject to the order.

(4) [*Repealed by the* VCRA *2006, s.65 and Sched. 5.*]

(5) In the case of a person detained in legal custody—

(a) the requirement under this section to report at a police station, and

(b) any requirement imposed under section 19 below, is suspended until his release from custody.

(6) If—

(a) he is released from custody more than five days before the expiry of the period for which the order has effect, and

(b) he was precluded by his being in custody from reporting initially,

the order is to have effect as if it required him to report initially at the police station specified in the order within the period of five days beginning with the date of his release.

(7) A person serving a sentence of imprisonment to which an intermittent custody order under section 183 of the *Criminal Justice Act* 2003 relates is to be treated for the purposes of this section as having been detained in legal custody until his final release; and accordingly any reference in this section to release is, in relation to a person serving such a sentence, a reference to his final release.

(8) In this section—

"declaration of relevance" has the same meaning as in section 23;

"home address", in relation to any person, means the address of his sole or main residence;

"loss" includes theft or destruction;

"new" includes replacement;

"temporary address", in relation to any person, means the address (other than his home address) of a place at which he intends to reside, or has resided, for a period of at least four weeks.

[This section was inserted by the *Football Disorder Act* 2000, s.1(1), and Sched. 1, para. 2. It is printed as amended, and repealed in part, by the *CJA* 2003, s.304, and Sched. 32, paras 55 and 57; and the *VCRA* 2006, ss.52(2) and 65, Sched. 3, paras 1 and 5(1) to (5), and Sched. 5; and as amended, as from a day to be appointed, by the *Identity Cards Act* 2006, s.39(1) (omission of italicised words and insertion of words in square brackets in subs. (3)). In relation to times before the commencement of section 39(2) of the latter Act, the references to a travel authorisation in subss. (2B) and (2C) shall have effect as references to a passport: *VCRA* 2006, s.52(2), and Sched. 3, para. 5(6). The repeals of subs. (4), and of the omitted words in subs. (3), only apply to a banning order made on or after April 6, 2007, and for the purposes of any appeal falling to be determined on or after that date: *ibid.*, para. 5(7), and the *Violent Crime Reduction Act 2006 (Commencement No. 2) Order* 2007 (S.I. 2007 No. 858).]

Whilst an issue may arise as to the compatibility of subsection (3) with Directive 2004/38/EC of the European Parliament and of the Council (freedom of movement), this does not provide a basis for challenging a banning order or the decision to impose it; it could, at most, relate to the validity of the requirement relating to surrender of the offender's passport: *R. (White) v. Crown Court at Blackfriars*, 172 J.P. 321, DC.

Period of banning orders

14F.—(1) Subject to the following provisions of this Part, a banning order has effect for a period beginning with the day on which the order is made. **5–830**

(2) The period must not be longer than the maximum or shorter than the minimum.

(3) Where the order is made under section 14A above in addition to a sentence of imprisonment taking immediate effect, the maximum is ten years and the minimum is six years: and in this subsection "imprisonment" includes any form of detention.

(4) In any other case where the order is made under section 14A above, the maximum is five years and the minimum is three years.

(5) Where the order is made under section 14B above, the maximum is five years and the minimum is three years.

[This section was inserted by the *Football Disorder Act* 2000, s.1(1), and Sched. 1, para. 2. It is printed as amended by the *VCRA* 2006, s.52(2), and Sched. 3, paras 1 and 6.]

Additional requirements of orders

14G.—(1) A banning order may, if the court making the order thinks fit, impose additional requirements on the person subject to the order in relation to any regulated football matches. **5–831**

(2) The court by which a banning order was made may, on an application made by—

(a) the person subject to the order, or

(b) the person who applied for the order or who was the prosecutor in relation to the order,

vary the order so as to impose, replace or omit any such requirements.

(3) In the case of a banning order made by a magistrates' court, the reference in subsection (2) above to the court by which it was made includes a reference to any magistrates' court acting in the same local justice area as that court.

[This section was inserted by the *Football Disorder Act* 2000, s.1(1), and Sched. 1, para. 2. It is printed as amended by the *Courts Act* 2003, s.109(1), and Sched. 8, para. 332.]

Termination of orders

14H.—(1) If a banning order has had effect for at least two-thirds of the period determined under section 14F above, the person subject to the order may apply to the court by which it was made to terminate it. **5–832**

(2) On the application, the court may by order terminate the banning order as from a specified date or refuse the application.

(3) In exercising its powers under subsection (2) above, the court must have regard to the person's character, his conduct since the banning order was made, the nature of the offence or conduct which led to it and any other circumstances which appear to it to be relevant.

(4) Where an application under subsection (1) above in respect of a banning order is

refused, no further application in respect of the order may be made within the period of six months beginning with the day of the refusal.

(5) The court may order the applicant to pay all or any part of the costs of an application under this section.

(6) In the case of a banning order made by a magistrates' court, the reference in subsection (1) above to the court by which it was made includes a reference to any magistrates' court acting in the same local justice area as that court.

[This section was inserted by the *Football Disorder Act* 2000, s.1(1), and Sched. 1, para. 2. It is printed as amended by the *Courts Act* 2003, s.109(1), and Sched. 8, para. 332.]

Football Spectators Act 1989, s.14J

Offences

5–833 **14J.**—(1) A person subject to a banning order who fails to comply with—

(a) any requirement imposed by the order, or

(b) any requirement imposed under section 19(2B) or(2C) below,

is guilty of an offence.

(2) A person guilty of an offence under this section is liable on summary conviction to imprisonment for a term not exceeding six months, or a fine not exceeding level 5 on the standard scale, or both.

[This section was inserted by the *Football (Disorder) Act* 2000, s.1(1), and Sched. 1, para. 2.]

Football Spectators Act 1989, s.18

Information

5–834 **18.**—(1) Where a court makes a banning order, the designated officer for the court (in the case of a magistrates' court) or the appropriate officer (in the case of the Crown Court)—

(a) shall give a copy of it to the person to whom it relates;

(b) shall (as soon as reasonably practicable) send a copy of it to the enforcing authority and to any prescribed person;

(c) shall (as soon as reasonably practicable) send a copy of it to the police station (addressed to the officer responsible for the police station) at which the person subject to the order is to report initially; and

(d) in a case where the person subject to the order is detained in legal custody, shall (as soon as reasonably practicable) send a copy of it to the person in whose custody he is detained.

(2) Where a court terminates a banning order under section 14H above, the designated officer of the court (in the case of a magistrates' court) or the appropriate officer (in the case of the Crown Court)—

(a) shall give a copy of the terminating order to the person to whom the banning order relates;

(b) shall (as soon as reasonably practicable) send a copy of it to the enforcing authority and to any prescribed person; and

(c) in a case where the person subject to the banning order is detained in legal custody, shall (as soon as reasonably practicable) send a copy of the terminating order to the person in whose custody he is detained.

(3) Where a person subject to a banning order is released from custody and, in the case of a person who has not reported initially to a police station, is released more than five days before the expiry of the banning order, the person in whose custody he is shall (as soon as reasonably practicable) give notice of his release to the enforcing authority.

(5) In relation to a person serving a sentence of imprisonment to which an intermittent custody order under section 183 of the *Criminal Justice Act* 2003 relates, any reference in this section to his detention or to his release shall be construed in accordance with section 14E(7).

[This section is printed as amended, and repealed in part, by the *Football (Offences and Disorder) Act* 1999, ss.1(2)(a) and (d); the *Access to Justice Act* 1999, s.90(1) and Sched. 13, para. 158; the *Football (Disorder) Act* 2000, s.1(2), and Sched. 2, paras 10 and 14; the *CJA* 2003, s.304, and Sched. 32, paras 50 and 58; and the *Courts Act* 2003, s.109(1), and Sched. 8, para. 333.]

Article 5 of S.I. 2004 No. 2409 (*ante*, § 5–824) prescribes the Football Banning Orders Authority (established under the *Police Act* 1996, s.57) as the enforcing authority for the purposes of Part II of the 1989 Act, and the Chief Executive of the Football Association for the purposes of section 18(1) and (2) of that Act.

Banning orders arising out of offences outside England and Wales

See section 22 of the 1989 Act (as amended by the *Football (Offences and Disorder) Act* 1999, and the *Football (Disorder) Act* 2000, s.1(2) and Sched. 2, paras 9– 11 and 17) and a series of orders made thereunder, the most recent of which was the *Football Spectators (Corresponding Offences in the Netherlands) Order* 2000 (S.I. 2000 No. 1109). **5–835**

Football Spectators Act 1989, s.22A

Other interpretation, etc.

22A.—(1) In this Part— **5–836**

"British citizen" has the same meaning as in the *British Nationality Act* 1981,

"country" includes territory,

"enforcing authority" means a prescribed organisation established by the Secretary of State under section 57 of the *Police Act* 1996 (central police organisations),

"passport" means a United Kingdom passport within the meaning of the *Immigration Act* 1971,

"prescribed" means prescribed by an order made by the Secretary of State[,

"travel authorisation", in relation to a person, means one or both of the following—

(a) any UK passport (within the meaning of the *Immigration Act* 1971) that has been issued to him;

(b) any ID card issued to him under the *Identity Cards Act* 2006 which records that he is a British citizen].

(2) The Secretary of State may, if he considers it necessary or expedient to do so in order to secure the effective enforcement of this Part, by order provide for section 14(5) and (6) above to have effect in relation to any, or any description of, regulated football match or external tournament as if, for any reference to five days, there were substituted a reference to the number of days (not exceeding ten) specified in the order.

(3), (4) [*Order making procedure.*]

[This section was inserted by the *Football (Disorder) Act* 2000, s.1(2), and Sched. 2, para. 18. It is printed as repealed in part by the *VCRA* 2006, s.65, and Sched. 5 (definition of "declaration of relevance"); and as amended, as from a day to be appointed, by the *Identity Cards Act* 2006, s.39(2) (insertion of words in square brackets).]

Football Spectators Act 1989, s.23

Further provision about, and appeals against, declarations of relevance

23.—(1) Subject to subsection (2) below, a court may not make a declaration of relevance as respects any offence unless it is satisfied that the prosecutor gave notice to the defendant, at least five days before the first day of the trial, that it was proposed to show that the offence related to football matches, to a particular football match or to particular football matches (as the case may be). **5–837**

(2) A court may, in any particular case, make a declaration of relevance notwithstanding that notice to the defendant as required by subsection (1) above has not been given if he consents to waive the giving of full notice or the court is satisfied that the interests of justice do not require more notice to be given.

(3) A person convicted of an offence as respects which the court makes a declaration of relevance may appeal against the making of the declaration of relevance as if the declaration were included in any sentence passed on him for the offence and, accordingly—(a) …, (b) …, (c) … .

(4) A banning order made upon a person's conviction of a relevant offence shall be quashed if the making of a declaration of relevance as respects that offence is reversed on appeal.

(5) In this section "declaration of relevance" means a declaration by a court for the purposes of Schedule 1 to this Act that an offence related to football matches, or that it related to one or more particular football matches.

[Subss. (1) and (4) are printed as amended by the *Football (Offences and Disorder)*

Act 1999, s.1(2)(b) and 2(6); and the *Football (Disorder) Act* 2000, s.1(2) and Sched. 2, para. 10. Subs. (5) was inserted by the *VCRA* 2006, s.52(2), and Sched. 3, para. 12. Paras (a)–(c) of subsection (3) amend the *CAA* 1968, ss.10 and 50, and the *MCA* 1980, s.108.]

5–838 Where a court proposes to make a "declaration of relevance" in respect of which no notice has been given by the prosecution, it is submitted that the court should warn the offender or his counsel of its intentions, and invite submissions on the matter, before making the declaration (see *R. v. Scott*, 11 Cr.App.R.(S.) 249, CA, *ante*, § 5–55). It may be that if the offender has been given notice that the prosecution intend to show that "the offence related to football matches", the offender should be asked whether he agrees that the offences do relate to football matches, in which case the court should make the "declaration of relevance"; if the offender disputes this allegation, it appears to be necessary for the court to conduct a hearing, analogous to a *Newton* hearing, to determine the matter.

Football Spectators Act 1989, Sched. 1

Offences

5–839 1. This Schedule applies to the following offences:

(a) any offence under section … 14J(1) or 21C(2) of this Act,

(b) any offence under section 2 or 2A of the *Sporting Events (Control of Alcohol etc.) Act* 1985 (alcohol, containers and fireworks) committed by the accused at any football match to which this Schedule applies or while entering or trying to enter the ground,

(c) any offence under section 4A or 5 of the *Public Order Act* 1986 (harassment, alarm or distress) or any provision of Part *III* [3 or 3A] of that Act (*racial* hatred [by reference to race *etc.*]) committed during a period relevant to a football match to which this Schedule applies at any premises while the accused was at, or was entering or leaving or trying to enter or leave, the premises,

(d) any offence involving the use or threat of violence by the accused towards another person committed during a period relevant to a football match to which this Schedule applies at any premises while the accused was at, or was entering or leaving or trying to enter or leave, the premises,

(e) any offence involving the use or threat of violence towards property committed during a period relevant to a football match to which this Schedule applies at any premises while the accused was at, or was entering or leaving or trying to enter or leave, the premises,

(f) any offence involving the use, carrying or possession of an offensive weapon or a firearm committed during a period relevant to a football match to which this Schedule applies at any premises while the accused was at, or was entering or leaving or trying to enter or leave, the premises,

(g) any offence under section 12 of the *Licensing Act* 1872 (persons found drunk in public places, etc.) of being found drunk in a highway or other public place committed while the accused was on a journey to or from a football match to which this Schedule applies being an offence as respects which the court makes a declaration that the offence related to football matches,

(h) any offence under section 91(1) of the *Criminal Justice Act* 1967 (disorderly behaviour while drunk in a public place) committed in a highway or other public place while [*continues as para. (g)*]

(j) any offence under section 1 of the *Sporting Events (Control of Alcohol etc.) Act* 1985 (alcohol on coaches or trains to or from sporting events) committed while [*continues as para. (g)*]

(k) any offence under section 4A or 5 of the *Public Order Act* 1986 (harassment, alarm or distress) or any provision of Part *III* [3 or 3A] of that Act (*racial* hatred [by reference to race *etc.*]) committed while [*continues as para. (g)*]

(l) any offence under section 4 or 5 of the *Road Traffic Act* 1988 (driving etc. when under the influence of drink or drugs or with an alcohol concentration above the prescribed limit) committed while [*continues as para. (g)*]

(m) any offence involving the use or threat of violence by the accused towards another person committed while one or each of them was on a journey to or from a football match to which this Schedule applies being an offence as respects which the court makes a declaration that the offence related to football matches,

(n) any offence involving the use or threat of violence towards property committed while [*continues as para. (g)*]

(o) any offence involving the use, carrying or possession of an offensive weapon or a firearm committed while [*continues as para. (g)*]

(p) any offence under the *Football (Offences) Act* 1991,

(q) any offence under section 4A or 5 of the *Public Order Act* 1986 (harassment, alarm or distress) or any provision of Part *III* [3 or 3A] of that Act (*racial* hatred [by reference to race *etc*.])—

(i) which does not fall within paragraph (c) or (k) above,

(ii) which was committed during a period relevant to a football match to which this Schedule applies, and

(iii) as respects which the court makes a declaration that the offence related to that match or to that match and any other football match which took place during that period,

(r) any offence involving the use or threat of violence by the accused towards another person—

(i) which does not fall within paragraph (d) or (m) above,

(ii), (iii) [*identical to para. (q)(ii), (iii),* ante],

(s) any offence involving the use or threat of violence towards property—

(i) which does not fall within paragraph (e) or (n) above,

(ii), (iii) [*identical to para. (q)(ii), (iii),* ante],

(t) any offence involving the use, carrying or possession of an offensive weapon or a firearm—

(i) which does not fall within paragraph (f) or (o) above,

(ii), (iii) [*identical to para. (q)(ii), (iii),* ante],

(u) any offence under section 166 of the *Criminal Justice and Public Order Act* 1994 (sale of tickets by unauthorised persons) which relates to tickets for a football match.

2. Any reference to an offence in paragraph 1 above includes—

(a) a reference to any attempt, conspiracy or incitement to commit that offence, and

(b) a reference to aiding and abetting, counselling or procuring the commission of that offence.

3. For the purposes of paragraphs 1(g) to (o) above—

(a) a person may be regarded as having been on a journey to or from a football match to which this Schedule applies whether or not he attended or intended to attend the match, and

(b) a person's journey includes breaks (including overnight breaks).

4. In this Schedule, "football match" means a match which is a regulated football match for the purposes of Part II of this Act.

(2) For the purposes of this Schedule each of the following periods is "relevant to" a football match to which this Schedule applies—

(a) in the case of a match which takes place on the day on which it is advertised to take place, the period—

(i) beginning 24 hours before whichever is the earlier of the start of the match and the time at which it was advertised to start; and

(ii) ending 24 hours after it ends;

(b) in the case of a match which does not take place on the day on which it was advertised to take place, the period—

(i) beginning 24 hours before the time at which it was advertised to start on that day; and

(ii) ending 24 hours after that time.

[This schedule was substituted by the *Football (Disorder) Act* 2000, s.1(1), and Sched. 1, para. 5. It is printed as amended, and repealed in part, by the *VCRA* 2006, ss.52(2) and 65, Sched. 3, paras 1, 9(1) and 13, and Sched. 5. An offence is not a relevant offence by virtue of the insertion of the references to section 4A of the 1986 Act in para. 1(c), (k) and (q) if it was committed before April 6, 2007: *ibid*., Sched. 3, para. 9(2), and S.I. 2007 No. 858 (*ante*, § 5–829). The words in italics in para. 1(c), (k) and (q) are omitted, and the words in square brackets are inserted, as from a day to be appointed, by the *CJIA* 2008, s.148(1), and Sched. 26, para. 26. The reference to the common law offence of incitement in para. 2(a) has effect as a reference to the offences under the *SCA* 2007, Pt 2: 2007 Act, s.63(1), and Sched. 6, para. 16.]

Any offence contrary to section 4(1)(a) of the *Public Order Act* 1986 falls within Schedule 1; the specific reference to section 5 of the 1986 Act makes it plain beyond argument that Parliament had taken the view that the more serious offences under section 4(1)(a) would be caught by the general words "any offence involving the use or threat of violence": *R. v. O'Keefe* [2004] 1 Cr.App.R.(S.) 67, CA.

Whether an offence was committed during a period "relevant to" a football match is to be determined by reference to paragraph 4(2), and not by reference to the definition of that term in section 1(8) which applies only for the purposes of Part I: *DPP v. Beaumont*; *DPP v. Dowling*, 172 J.P. 283, DC.

Where a football supporter, who had gathered together with other supporters at a place away from a football ground for reasons relating to a designated football match (that was where fans of the particular team traditionally congregated after away matches in London), committed an offence of violence during a period relevant to the match by attacking a person for a reason wholly unconnected with the match, it would not be open to a sentencer to make a declaration of relevance (see s.23(5), *ante* § 5–837); whilst the offence was sparked by the presence of the football supporters, if the spark had nothing to do with the match itself, the statutory requirement would not be satisfied: *R. v. Elliott* [2007] 2 Cr.App.R.(S.) 68, CA (observing, *obiter*, that where supporters were violent on their way to or from a match (and even where they had failed to get to the match), it may well be open to a court to declare that the offence related to a football match even if the spark for the violence was not itself football related; the fact that the spark was not intrinsically football-related does not mean that the offence is not related to a football match (doubting to that extent *R. v. Smith (Paul Roger)* [2004] 1 Cr.App.R.(S.) 341(58), CA)). *Elliott* was followed in *R. v. Mabee* [2008] 2 Cr.App.R.(S.) 25, CA.

Public Order Act 1986, s.35

Photographs

5–840 **35.**—(1) The court by which a banning order is made may make an order which—

(a) requires a constable to take a photograph of the person to whom the banning order relates or to cause such a photograph to be taken, and

(b) requires that person to go to a specified police station not later than 7 clear days after the day on which the order under this section is made, and at a specified time of day or between specified times of day, in order to have his photograph taken.

(2) In subsection (1) "specified" means specified in the order made under this section and "banning order" has the same meaning as in Part II of the *Football Spectators Act* 1989.

(3) No order may be made under this section unless an application to make it is made to the court by or on behalf of the person who is the prosecutor in respect of the offence leading to the banning order or (in the case of a banning order made under section 14B of the *Football Spectators Act* 1989) the complainant.

(4) If the person to whom the exclusion order relates fails to comply with an order under this section a constable may arrest him without warrant in order that his photograph may be taken.

[This section is printed as amended by the *Football (Offences and Disorder) Act* 1999, s.6(2)(a) and (b); and the *Football (Disorder) Act* 2000, s.1(2), and Sched. 2, para. 5.]

B. EXCLUSION FROM LICENSED PREMISES

Licensed Premises (Exclusion of Certain Persons) Act 1980, s.1

Exclusion orders

5–841 **1.**—(1) *Where a court by or before which a person is convicted of an offence committed on licensed premises is satisfied that in committing that offence he resorted to violence or offered or threatened to resort to violence, the court may, subject to subsection (2) below, make an order (in this Act referred to as an "exclusion order") prohibiting him from entering those premises or any other specified premises, without the express consent of the licensee of the premises or his servant or agent.*

(2) *An exclusion order may be made either—*

(a) *in addition to any sentence which is imposed in respect of the offence of which the person is convicted; or*

(b) *where the offence was committed in England and Wales notwithstanding the provisions of sections 12 and 14 of the* Powers of Criminal Courts (Sentencing) Act *2000 (cases in which absolute and conditional discharges may be made, and their effect), in addition to an order discharging him absolutely or conditionally;*

(c) [Scotland];

but not otherwise.

(3) *An exclusion order shall have effect for such period, not less than three months or more than two years, as is specified in the order, unless it is terminated under section 2(2) below.*

[This section is printed as amended by the *CJA* 1991, s.101(1), Sched. 11, para. 23; and the *PCC(S)A* 2000, s.165(1) and Sched. 9, para. 60. It is repealed, as from a day to be appointed, by the *VCRA* 2006, s.65, and Sched. 5.]

Section 2 creates a summary offence of non-compliance with an exclusion order: it is punishable by means of a fine not exceeding level 3 on the standard scale or imprisonment for one month. The convicting court may terminate the order, or may vary it by deleting the name of any specified premises, but otherwise the conviction does not affect the order.

Licensed Premises (Exclusion of Certain Persons) Act 1980, s.4

Definitions

4.—(1) *In this Act* 5–842

"licensed premises", in relation to England and Wales, means premises in respect of which there is in force a justices' on-licence (within the meaning of section 1 of the Licensing Act *1964) and, in relation to Scotland, means premises in respect of which a licence under the* Licensing (Scotland) Act *1976, other than an off-sales licence or a licence under Part III of that Act (licences for seamen's canteens), is in force; and*

"licensee", in relation to any licensed premises means the holder of the licence granted in respect of those premises; and

"specified premises", in relation to an exclusion order, means any licensed premises which the court may specify by name and address in the order.

(2) [Scotland.]

(3) *Where a court makes an exclusion order or an order terminating or varying an exclusion order, the proper officer of the court shall send a copy of the order to the licensee of the premises to which the order relates.*

(4) *For the purposes of subsection (3) above—*

(a) *the proper officer of a magistrates' court in England and Wales is the designated officer for the court;*

(b) *the proper officer of the Crown Court is the appropriate officer; and*

(c) *the proper officer of a court in Scotland is the clerk of the court.*

[This section is printed as amended by the *Access to Justice Act* 1999, s.90(1), and Sched. 13, para. 94; and the *Courts Act* 2003, s.109(1), and Sched. 8 (unnumbered para. following para. 200). It is repealed, as from a day to be appointed, by the *VCRA* 2006, s.65, and Sched. 5.]

Orders excluding persons from entering licensed premises were designed for those who might shortly be described as making a nuisance of themselves in public houses and as therefore qualifying to be debarred from going in to the annoyance of other customers and the possible danger to the licensee: *R. v. Grady*, 12 Cr.App.R.(S.) 152, CA. An order may specify all licensed premises in a particular area (any one of which the offender could readily visit) where the court is satisfied that the offender is prone to the commission of offences of violence on licensed premises generally; but the order would have to identify the premises to which it related individually as the Act requires that a copy should be sent to the licensee of the premises to which it relates: *R. v. Arrowsmith* [2003] 2 Cr.App.R.(S.) 46, CA. 5–843

An exclusion order may be made by the court of its own motion: *R. v. Penn* [1996]

2 Cr.App.R.(S.) 214, CA. It is undesirable for an application to be made by a third party who is not a victim or a party to the proceedings; the proper course for an interested third party to take is to make representations to the prosecuting authority: *ibid.*

C. DRINKING BANNING ORDERS

(1) Summary

5–843a Chapter 1 (ss.1– 14) of the *VCRA* 2006 provides for a court to make a "drinking banning order" either on an application to a magistrates' court (s.3) or the county court (s.4) by a relevant authority or on conviction in criminal proceedings (s.6) where the court is satisfied that the conditions in section 3(2) are satisfied in relation to the offender. The conditions "are (a) that the individual has, after the commencement of [section 3] engaged in criminal or disorderly conduct while under the influence of alcohol and (b) that such an order is necessary to protect other persons from further conduct by him of that kind while he is under the influence of alcohol." Such an order may impose any prohibition on the subject which is necessary for the purpose of protecting other persons from criminal or disorderly conduct by the offender when he is under the influence of alcohol (s.1(2)). The length of the order must be not less than two months and not more than two years (s.2(1)), although different prohibitions contained in the order may have effect for different periods (s.2(2)). For the purpose of deciding whether to make a drinking banning order under section 6, the court may consider evidence led by the prosecution and defence and it is immaterial whether the evidence would have been admissible in the proceedings in which the offender was convicted: s.7(1), (2). A drinking banning order under section 6 must not be made except in addition to a sentence imposed in respect of the offender or in addition to the imposition of a conditional discharge: s.7(3). Section 9 provides for the imposition of an interim drinking banning order. The subject of the order or the relevant authority may make an application to discharge the order (ss.5 and 8). Breach of a drinking banning order is a summary offence, punishable with a fine not exceeding level 4 on the standard scale (s.11). These sections of the Act come into force on a day to be appointed.

(2) Legislation

Violent Crime Reduction Act 2006, ss.1, 2

[Drinking banning orders

5–843b **1.**—(1) A drinking banning order is an order that prohibits the individual against whom it is made ("the subject") from doing the things described in the order.

(2) Such an order may impose any prohibition on the subject which is necessary for the purpose of protecting other persons from criminal or disorderly conduct by the subject while he is under the influence of alcohol.

(3) The prohibitions imposed by such an order must include such prohibition as the court making it considers necessary, for that purpose, on the subject's entering—

(a) premises in respect of which there is a premises licence authorising the use of the premises for the sale of alcohol by retail; and

(b) premises in respect of which there is a club premises certificate authorising the use of the premises for the supply of alcohol to members or guests.

(4) A drinking banning order may not impose a prohibition on the subject that prevents him—

(a) from having access to a place where he resides;

(b) from attending at any place which he is required to attend for the purposes of any employment of his or of any contract of services to which he is a party;

(c) from attending at any place which he is expected to attend during the period for which the order has effect for the purposes of education or training or for the purpose of receiving medical treatment; or

(d) from attending at any place which he is required to attend by any obligation imposed on him by or under an enactment or by the order of a court or tribunal.

(5) Expressions used in subsection (3) and in the *Licensing Act* 2003 or in a Part of that Act have the same meanings in that subsection as in that Act or Part.]

[Duration of drinking banning orders

5–843c **2.**—(1) A drinking banning order has effect for a period specified in the order ("the specified period"), which must be not less than two months and not more than two years.

(2) A drinking banning order may provide that different prohibitions contained in the order have effect for different periods; but, in each case, the period ("the prohibition period") must be not less than two months and not more than two years.

(3) A drinking banning order may include provision for—

(a) the order, or

(b) a prohibition contained in it,

to cease to have effect before the end of the specified period or the prohibition period if the subject satisfactorily completes the approved course specified in the order.

(4) Provision under subsection (3) must fix the time at which the order or the prohibition will cease to have effect if the subject satisfactorily completes the specified approved course as whichever is the later of—

(a) the time specified in the order in accordance with subsection (5); and

(b) the time when he does satisfactorily complete that course.

(5) The time specified for the purposes of subsection (4)(a) must be a time after the expiry of at least half the specified period or (as the case may be) the prohibition period.

(6) Provision under subsection (3) may be included in a drinking banning order only if—

(a) the court making the order is satisfied that a place on the specified approved course will be available for the subject; and

(b) the subject has agreed to the inclusion of the provision in question in the order.

(7) Before making provision under subsection (3), the court must inform the subject in ordinary language (whether in writing or otherwise) about—

(a) the effect of including the provision in the order;

(b) what, in general terms, attendance on the course will involve if he undertakes it;

(c) any fees he will be required to pay for the course if he undertakes it; and

(d) when he will have to pay any such fees.

(8) Where a court makes a drinking banning order which does not include provision under subsection (3), it must give its reasons for not including such provision in open court.

(9) [*Power of Secretary of State to make regulations to amend subs. (5) to modify the earlierst time that a drinking banning order may cease to have effect.*]]

Violent Crime Reduction Act 2006, ss.6–9

[Orders on conviction in criminal proceedings

6.—(1) This section applies where— **5–843d**

(a) an individual aged 16 or over is convicted of an offence (the "offender"); and

(b) at the time he committed the offence, he was under the influence of alcohol.

(2) The court must consider whether the conditions in section 3(2) are satisfied in relation to the offender.

(3) If the court decides that the conditions are satisfied in relation to the offender, it may make a drinking banning order against him.

(4) If the court—

(a) decides that the conditions are satisfied in relation to the offender, but

(b) does not make a drinking banning order,

it must give its reasons for not doing so in open court.

(5) If the court decides that the conditions are not satisfied in relation to the offender, it must state that fact in open court and give its reasons.]

As to the conditions in section 3(2), see *ante*, § 5–843a.

[Supplementary provision about orders on conviction

7.—(1) For the purpose of deciding whether to make a drinking banning order under section 6 the court may consider evidence led by the prosecution and evidence led by the defence. **5–843e**

(2) It is immaterial whether the evidence would have been admissible in the proceedings in which the offender was convicted.

(3) A drinking banning order under section 6 must not be made except—

(a) in addition to a sentence imposed in respect of the offence; or

(b) in addition to an order discharging the offender conditionally.

(4) The court may adjourn any proceedings in relation to a drinking banning order under section 6 even after sentencing the offender.

(5) If the offender does not appear for any adjourned proceedings, the court may further adjourn the proceedings or may issue a warrant for his arrest.

(6) But the court may not issue a warrant for the offender's arrest unless it is satisfied that he has had adequate notice of the time and place of the adjourned proceedings.

(7) A drinking banning order under section 6 takes effect on—

(a) the day on which it is made; or

(b) if on that day the offender is detained in legal custody, the day on which he is released from that custody.

(8) Subsection (9) applies in relation to proceedings in which a drinking banning order is made under section 6 against a young person.

(9) In so far as the proceedings relate to the making of the order—

(a) section 49 of the *Children and Young Persons Act* 1933 (restrictions on reports of proceedings in which children and young persons are concerned) does not apply in respect of the young person against whom the order is made; and

(b) section 39 of that Act (power to prohibit publication of certain matters) does so apply.

(10) [*Amends the* Prosecution of Offences Act *1985, s.3*, ante, *§ 1–253*.]

(11) In this section and section 6 "the court" in relation to an offender means—

(a) the court by or before which he is convicted of the offence; or

(b) if he is committed to the Crown Court to be dealt with for the offence, the Crown Court.]

[Variation or discharge of orders under s. 6

5–843f **8.**—(1) The following persons may apply to the court which made a drinking banning order under section 6 for the order to be varied or discharged by a further order—

(a) the subject;

(b) the Director of Public Prosecutions; or

(c) a relevant authority.

(2) If the subject makes an application under subsection (1), he must also send notice of his application to the Director of Public Prosecutions.

(3) If the Director of Public Prosecutions or a relevant authority makes an application under subsection (1), he or it must also send notice of the application to the subject.

(4) In the case of an order under section 6 made by a magistrates' court, the reference in subsection (1) to the court which made the order includes a reference to a relevant local court.

(5) An order under section 6 may not be varied so as to extend the specified period to more than two years.

(6) No order under section 6 is to be discharged on an application under subsection (1)(a) unless—

(a) it is discharged from a time after the end of the period that is half the duration of the specified period; or

(b) the Director of Public Prosecutions has consented to its earlier discharge.

(7) [*Amends the* Prosecution of Offences Act *1985, s.3*, ante, *§ 1–253*.]]

[Interim orders

5–843g **9.**—(1) This section applies in each of the following cases—

(a) where an application is made for a drinking banning order;

(b) where the court is required under section 6 to consider whether the conditions for making a drinking banning order are satisfied.

(2) Before—

(a) determining the application, or

(b) considering whether the conditions are satisfied,

the court may make an order under this section ("an interim order") if it considers that it is just to do so.

(3) Where this section applies by virtue of subsection (1)(a), an application for an interim order against an individual—

(a) may be made without notice being given to that individual; and

(b) may be heard in the absence of that individual.

(4) The following permission is required for the making or hearing of an application in accordance with subsection (3)—

(a) in the case of proceedings in the county court, the permission of the court; and

(b) in the case of an application to a magistrates' court, the permission of the proper officer.

(5) Permission may only be given under subsection (4) if the court or proper officer is satisfied—

(a) that it is necessary for the application to be made without notice being given to the individual in question; and

(b) that it is not necessary for the application to be heard in the presence of the individual.

(6) An interim order—

(a) may contain any provision that may be contained in a drinking banning order; but

(b) has effect, unless renewed, only for such fixed period of not more than four weeks as may be specified in the order.

(7) An interim order—

(a) may be renewed (on one or more occasions) for a period of not more than four weeks from the end of the period when it would otherwise cease to have effect;

(b) must cease to have effect (if it has not previously done so) on the determination of the application mentioned in subsection (1)(a) or on the court's making its decision whether to make a drinking banning order under section 6.

(8) Section 5 applies in relation to an interim order made in a case falling within subsection (1)(a) as it applies in relation to a drinking banning order made under section 3 or 4, but with the omission of section 5(5) and (6).

(9) Section 8 applies in relation to an interim order made in a case falling within subsection (1)(b) as it applies in relation to a drinking banning order made under section 6, but with the omission of section 8(5) and (6).]

Section 5 relates to the variation or discharge of orders made under section 3 or 4.

Breach of drinking banning orders

If a person does, without reasonable excuse, anything he is prohibited from doing by a drinking banning order or an interim order he is guilty of an offence (s.11(1)) and is liable on summary conviction to a fine not exceeding level 4 on the standard scale (s.11(2)). A conditional discharge is not available as a means of disposal (s.11(3)). A local authority may bring proceedings for an offence under subsection (1) (s.11(4)); and the Secretary of State may by order provide that a person of a description specified in the order may bring proceedings for an offence under subsection (1) in such cases and in such circumstances as may be prescribed by the order. **5–843h**

Approved courses

The Secretary of State must decide whether to grant or refuse an application for the approval of a course for the purposes of section 2 (s.12(1)). An approval may be subject to conditions specified by the Secretary of State (s.12(3)) and it may be for a period not exceeding seven years. The Secretary of State may issue guidance about the conduct of approved courses and must have regard to the guidance that is for the time being in force in exercising the powers and duties conferred on him under subsections (1) to (5) (s.12(6)). A court must have regard to that guidance in determining for the purposes of section 13 what constitutes reasonable instructions or reasonable requirements by a person providing an approved course (s.12(7)). **5–843i**

Violent Crime Reduction Act 2006, ss.13, 14

[Certificates of completion of approved courses

13.—(1) For the purposes of section 2— **5–843j**

(a) the subject of a drinking banning order is to be regarded as having completed an approved course satisfactorily if, and only if, the person providing the course has given a certificate that the subject has done so; and

(b) the time at which the subject is to be regarded as having satisfactorily completed the course is the time when that certificate is received by the proper officer of the court that made the order.

(2) For the purposes of this section a certificate that a person has satisfactorily completed a course—

(a) has to be in such form, and

(b) has to contain such particulars,

as may be specified in, or determined under, regulations made by the Secretary of State.

(3) The person providing an approved course must give the subject of a drinking banning order in which that course is specified a certificate for the purposes of this section unless that subject—

(a) has failed to make due payment of fees for the course;

(b) has failed to attend the course in accordance with the reasonable instructions of the person providing the course; or

(c) has failed to comply with any other reasonable requirement of that person.

(4) Where a person providing an approved course decides not to give the subject of a drinking banning order a certificate under subsection (1), he must give the subject written notice of the decision, setting out the grounds of the decision.

(5) The obligation of the person providing an approved course to give, in the case of the subject of a drinking banning order in which that course is specified, either—

(a) a certificate for the purposes of this section, or

(b) a notice under subsection (4),

must be discharged before the end of 14 days beginning with the day on which any request to do so is made by that subject.

(6) The subject of a drinking banning order who is given a notice under subsection (4) or who claims that a request for the purposes of subsection (5) has not been complied with may, within such period as may be prescribed by rules of court, apply to—

(a) the court which made the order, or

(b) if that court is not the Crown Court or a relevant local court, to either the court which made the order or a relevant local court,

for a declaration that there has been a contravention of subsection (3).

(7) If the court grants the application, the applicant is to be treated for the purposes of section 2 as having satisfactorily completed the course at the time of the making of the declaration.

(8) The Secretary of State may by regulations make provision as to—

(a) the form of a notice under subsection (4); and

(b) the manner in which such a notice is given and the time to be taken as the time of the giving of such a notice.]

[Interpretation of Chapter 1

5–843k **14.**—(1) In this Chapter—

"appropriate persons", in relation to an application for a drinking banning order or an application referred to in section 4(6)(b) or (c), means such of the following as is not a party to the application—

(a) the chief officer of police of the police force for the police area where the conduct to which the application relates occurred;

(b) the chief officer of police of the police force for the police area in which the individual to whose conduct the application relates normally resides;

(c) every local authority in whose area the place where that individual normally resides is situated; and

(d) the Chief Constable of the British Transport Police Force;

"approved course" means a course approved by the Secretary of State for the purposes of section 2;

"drinking banning order" means an order under section 3, 4 or 6;

"interim order" means an order under section 9;

"local authority" means—

(a) a county council in England;

(b) a district council in England;

(c) a London borough council;

(d) the Common Council of the City of London;

(e) the Council of the Isles of Scilly;

(f) a county council or a county borough council in Wales;

"proper officer"—

(a) in relation to a magistrates' court, means the justices' clerk; and

(b) in relation to any other court, means the clerk of the court;

"relevant authority" means—

(a) the chief officer of police of a police force for a police area;
(b) the Chief Constable of the British Transport Police Force;
(c) a local authority;

"relevant local court", in relation to a drinking banning order, means a magistrates' court acting for the local justice area in which the subject normally resides;

"specified period", in relation to a drinking banning order, means the period specified in the order for the purposes of section 2(1) as the period for which the order is to have effect;

"subject", in relation to an order, means the individual against whom it is made;

"young person" has the same meaning as in the *Children and Young Persons Act* 1933 (see section 107(1) of that Act).

(2) References in this Chapter to protecting persons from criminal or disorderly conduct include references to protecting their property from unlawful loss or damage.

(3) The Secretary of State may by order provide that a person of a description specified in the order is to be regarded as a relevant authority for such purposes of the provisions of this Chapter as are specified in the order.

(4)–(8) [*Procedure for making orders or regulations under this chapter.*]]

D. DISQUALIFICATION FROM DRIVING

(1) Legislation

Powers of Criminal Courts (Sentencing) Act 2000, ss.146, 147

Driving disqualification for any offence

146.—(1) The court by or before which a person is convicted of an offence committed after 31st December 1997 may, instead of or in addition to dealing with him in any other way, order him to be disqualified, for such period as it thinks fit, for holding or obtaining a driving licence. **5–844**

(2) Where the person is convicted of an offence the sentence for which is fixed by law or falls to be imposed under section 110(2) or 111(2) above, section 51A(2) of the *Firearms Act* 1968, section 225(2) or 226(2) of the *Criminal Justice Act* 2003 or section 29(4) or (6) of the *Violent Crime Reduction Act* 2006 subsection (1) above shall have effect as if the words "instead of or" were omitted.

(3) A court shall not make an order under subsection (1) above unless the court has been notified by the Secretary of State that the power to make such orders is exercisable by the court and the notice has not been withdrawn.

(4) A court which makes an order under this section disqualifying a person for holding or obtaining a driving licence shall require him to produce—

(a) any such licence held by him *together with its counterpart*;
(aa) in the case where he holds a Northern Ireland licence (within the meaning of Part 3 of the *Road Traffic Act* 1988), his Northern Ireland licence *and its counterpart (if any)*; or
(b) in the case where he holds a Community licence (within the meaning of Part III of the *Road Traffic Act* 1988), his Community licence *and its counterpart (if any)*.

(5) In this section—

"driving licence" means a licence to drive a motor vehicle granted under Part III of the *Road Traffic Act* 1988;

"counterpart"—

(a) *in relation to a driving licence, has the meaning given in relation to such a licence by section 108(1) of that Act;*
(aa) *in relation to a Northern Ireland licence, has the meaning given by section 109A of that Act ; and*
(b) *in relation to a Community licence, has the meaning given by section 99B of that Act.*

[This section is printed as amended by the *CJA* 2003, s.304, and Sched. 32, para. 120; the *Crime (International Co-operation) Act* 2003, s.91(1), and Sched. 5, paras 72 and 73; the *VCRA* 2006, s.49, and Sched. 1, para. 6; and the *CJIA* 2008, s.148(1), and Sched. 26, paras 40 and 47; and as amended, as from a day to be appointed, by the *RSA* 2006, ss.10(12) and 59, Sched. 3, paras 71 and 72, and Sched. 7(4) (omission of italicised words in subss. (4) and (5)). For the saving provision in relation to the amendments made by the *CJA* 2003, see *ante*, § 5–1b.]

As to subsection (2), see section 164(3), *ante*, § 5–5.

For section 108 of the 1988 Act, see *post*, § 32–111.

The power to make orders for disqualification under this section is now available to all courts: see Home Office Circular 59/2003.

Driving disqualification where vehicle used for purposes of crime

5–845 **147.**—(1) This section applies where a person—

(a) is convicted before the Crown Court of an offence punishable on indictment with imprisonment for a term of two years or more; or

(b) having been convicted by a magistrates' court of such an offence, is committed under section 3 above to the Crown Court for sentence.

(2) This section also applies where a person is convicted by or before any court of common assault or of any other offence involving an assault (including an offence of aiding, abetting, counselling or procuring, or inciting to the commission of, an offence).

(3) If, in a case to which this section applies by virtue of subsection (1) above, the Crown Court is satisfied that a motor vehicle was used (by the person convicted or by anyone else) for the purpose of committing, or facilitating the commission of, the offence in question, the court may order the person convicted to be disqualified, for such period as the court thinks fit, for holding or obtaining a driving licence.

(4) If, in a case to which this section applies by virtue of subsection (2) above, the court is satisfied that the assault was committed by driving a motor vehicle, the court may order the person convicted to be disqualified, for such period as the court thinks fit, for holding or obtaining a driving licence.

(5) [*Identical to s.146(4),* ante, *§ 5–844 (including the prospective omissions).*]

(6) Facilitating the commission of an offence shall be taken for the purposes of this section to include the taking of any steps after it has been committed for the purpose of disposing of any property to which it relates or of avoiding apprehension or detection.

(7) In this section "driving licence" *and "counterpart" have the meanings* [has the meaning] given by section 146(5) above.

[This section is printed as amended by the *Crime (International Co-operation) Act* 2003, s.91(1), and Sched. 5, paras 72 and 74; and as amended, as from a day to be appointed, by the *RSA* 2006, ss.10(12) and 59, Sched. 3, paras 71 and 73, and Sched. 7(4) (omission of italicised words, insertion of words in square brackets). The reference to the common law offence of incitement in subs. (2) has effect as a reference to the offences under the *SCA* 2007, Pt 2: 2007 Act, s.63(1), and Sched. 6, para. 39.]

(2) Notes on disqualification from driving (s.146)

5–846 Section 146 derives from section 39 of the *C(S)A* 1997. It is significantly wider than the power under section 147 (derived from the *PCCA* 1973, s.44) in that it is available to both the Crown Court and to magistrates' courts; it is not limited to any particular offence; and it is not necessary that the offence should be connected in any way with the use of a motor vehicle.

In *R. v. Cliff* [2005] R.T.R. 11, CA, it was held that, for the purposes of section 146, it was not necessary that the offence should be connected in any way with the use of a motor vehicle. Accordingly, it was not wrong in principle for a judge to exercise his discretion to disqualify the defendant on his conviction for affray, where he had admitted that during the course of the incident that led to the conviction he had been driving (albeit not on a public road) whilst under the influence of drink or drugs.

In *R. v. Waring* [2006] 1 Cr.App.R.(S.) 9, CA, the appellant, having been arrested after a positive roadside breath test for alcohol, ran off when the police officer had to stop the vehicle in which he was driving the appellant to the police station, in order to handcuff a co-arrestee. The appellant was re-arrested the following day, by which time he had avoided the possibility of providing an evidential specimen of breath, and thereby being prosecuted for driving with excess alcohol. An order for 18 months' disqualification under section 146 was upheld, on a plea of guilty to escaping lawful custody; the judge had been right to ensure that no benefit had been gained by escaping. Although the offender would be disadvantaged in the labour market, the disqualification was entirely merited.

In *R. v. Bye* [2006] 1 Cr.App.R.(S.) 27, CA, the facts were that in a "road rage" incident, the 46-year-old defendant, who had numerous convictions, including recent "road rage" conduct, approached the victim's vehicle, swore at him, opened his car door, punched him in the face and chest and kicked him. An order that he should be disqualified under section 146 for 12 months, in addition to a sentence of eight months' imprisonment on conviction for affray, was upheld. The offender, having shown himself to be lacking in tolerance when on the road, and being a danger on the road by virtue of the risk of such conduct leading to an accident, such an order was necessary to mark the gravity of the offence notwithstanding that it would have a serious impact on his ability to earn a living as a self-employed trader.

Now that the power under section 146 is available to all courts (*ante*), it is likely to make section 147 and section 34(2) of the *RTOA* 1988 (*post*, § 32–181) effectively redundant.

(3) Notes on disqualification from driving (s.147)

Relevance to offence

The court must be satisfied that a vehicle was used in the commission, or to facilitate the commission, of the offence of which the offender is convicted: see *R. v. Parrington*, 7 Cr.App.R.(S.) 18, CA. It is not necessary that the vehicle should have been used in the immediate commission of the offence: see *R. v. Mathews*, unreported, July 29, 1974 (plea of guilty to handling stolen cheques by offender who had been driven from bank to bank for the purpose of encashing them); and *R. v. Rajesh Patel*, 16 Cr.App.R.(S.) 756, CA (appellant pursued another car, prior to assaulting its driver; car was used to "facilitate" offence). **5–847**

Conspiracy

The power is not available on conviction of conspiracy: *R. v. Riley*, 5 Cr.App.R.(S.) 335, CA. *R. v. Riley* was, however, distinguished in *R. v. Devine*, 12 Cr.App.R.(S.) 236, CA, where the appellant pleaded guilty to conspiracy to rob. Police officers interrupted an intended robbery and the appellant tried to escape by driving away from the scene. The court upheld a disqualification under section 147: facilitating the commission of an offence included taking any steps after its commission for the purpose of avoiding apprehension or deception (s.147(6)). **5–848**

Effect of disqualification on offender after release from prison

It is the policy of the law that once a person has served any custodial sentence passed on him, he should not have any additional handicap hanging over him and inhibiting any effort to rehabilitate himself: *R. v. Wright*, 1 Cr.App.R.(S.) 82, CA. Accordingly, where the offender depends on the ability to drive for his livelihood and the circumstances of the case do not disclose anything adverse as to his capacity to drive or his judgment when driving, the court may temper the period of disqualification so that it should not inhibit the offender from rehabilitating himself: *R. v. Davegun*, 7 Cr.App.R.(S.) 110, CA. But there is no absolute principle that a period of disqualification should always come to an end before the offender's release from custody: *R. v. Arif*, *ibid.* at 92, CA. **5–849**

As *R. v. Davegun* indicates, a different approach may be appropriate in cases of disqualification imposed for persistent or dangerous road traffic offences under the *RTOA* 1988: see in particular *R. v. Gibbons*, 9 Cr.App.R.(S.) 21, CA, and *R. v. Mathews*, 9 Cr.App.R.(S.) 1, CA, for decisions in such cases.

Duty of court to warn counsel of intention to disqualify

Where a sentencer has it in mind to impose a disqualification under this infrequently used section, he should indicate his intention to counsel and invite submissions on the matter: *R. v. Lake*, 8 Cr.App.R.(S.) 69, CA; *R. v. Powell and Carvell*, 6 Cr.App.R.(S.) 354, CA. **5–850**

E. DISQUALIFICATION OF COMPANY DIRECTORS

(1) Legislation

Company Directors Disqualification Act 1986, ss.1, 2

Disqualification orders: general

5–851 **1.**—(1) In the circumstances specified below in this Act a court may, and under section 6 shall, make against a person a disqualification order, that is to say an order that for a period specified in the order—

(a) he shall not be a director of a company, act as a receiver of a company's property, or in any way, whether directly or indirectly, be concerned or take part in the promotion, formation or management of a company unless (in each case) he has the leave of the court, and

(b) he shall not act as an insolvency practitioner.

(2) In each section of this Act which gives to a court power or, as the case may be, imposes on it the duty to make a disqualification order there is specified the maximum (and, in section 6, the minimum) period of disqualification which may or (as the case may be) must be imposed by means of the order and, unless the court otherwise orders, the period of disqualification so imposed shall begin at the end of the period of 21 days beginning with the date of the order.

(3) Where a disqualification order is made against a person who is already subject to such an order or to a disqualification undertaking, the periods specified in those orders or, as the case may be, in the order and the undertaking shall run concurrently.

(4) A disqualification order may be made on grounds which are or include matters other than criminal convictions, notwithstanding that the person in respect of whom it is to be made may be criminally liable in respect of those matters.

[This section is printed as amended by the *Insolvency Act* 2000, ss.5 and 8, and Sched. 4, para. 2.]

1A. [*Disqualification undertakings: general.*]

Disqualification on conviction of indictable offence

5–852 **2.**—(1) The court may make a disqualification order against a person where he is convicted of an indictable offence (whether on indictment or summarily) in connection with the promotion, formation, management or liquidation of a company, with the receivership of a company's property or with his being an administrative receiver of a company.

(2) "The court" for this purpose means—

(a) any court having jurisdiction to wind up the company in relation to which the offence was committed, or

(b) the court by or before which the person is convicted of the offence, or

(c) in the case of a summary conviction in England and Wales, any other magistrates' court acting in the same local justice area;

and for the purposes of this section the definition of "indictable offence" in Schedule 1 to the *Interpretation Act* 1978 applies for Scotland as it does for England and Wales.

(3) The maximum period of disqualification under this section is—

(a) where the disqualification order is made by a court of summary jurisdiction, five years, and

(b) in any other case, 15 years.

[This section is printed as amended by the *Insolvency Act* 2000, s.8, and Sched. 4, para. 3; and the *Courts Act* 2003, s.109(1), and Sched. 8, para. 300.]

For disqualification on summary conviction, see section 5.

As to acting in contravention of a disqualification order, see section 13 (*post*, § 30–197a).

For general interpretation provisions, see section 22 (*post*, § 30–200).

For the application of the Act to building societies and friendly societies as it applies to companies, see sections 22A and 22B respectively (*post*, § 30–201).

(2) Notes on disqualification of company directors

5–853 The expression "management" of a company is not limited to the internal affairs of the company; disqualification orders have been upheld in cases of obtaining by deception and similar offences committed in the course of the trading activities of the company (see *R. v. Corbin*, 6 Cr.App.R.(S.) 17, DC; *R. v. Austen*, 7 Cr.App.R.(S.) 214, CA; and *R. v. Georgiou*, 87 Cr.App.R. 207, CA; and see also *Att.-Gen.'s References (Nos 88, etc., of 2006) (R. v. Meehan)* [2007] 2 Cr.App.R.(S.) 28, CA (wrong not to have made disqualification orders on offenders who had involved their companies in significant dishonest activity by allowing them to be used as "buffer" companies in a missing trader fraud)). A person convicted of "insider dealing" may be disqualified from acting as the director of a company: *R. v. Goodman*, 97 Cr.App.R. 210, CA (the correct test is whether the offence had some relevant factual connection with the company).

The power to disqualify a director under section 6 of the 1986 Act, which is exercised by the judges of the Chancery Division, requires an express finding that the person concerned is guilty of conduct which makes him unfit to be concerned in the management of a company, but section 2 is concerned with a different situation and gives the sentencer a completely general and unfettered discretion: *R. v. Young (S.K.)*, 12 Cr.App.R.(S.) 262, CA. An order for disqualification is however a punishment and it is inappropriate for a punishment to be linked with a conditional discharge: *ibid.*

It is inappropriate to combine an order for disqualification with a compensation order, if the effect of the disqualification would be to deprive the offender of the means to earn money with which to pay compensation: *R. v. Holmes*, 13 Cr.App.R.(S.) 29, CA.

The upper bracket of disqualifications, above 10 years, should be reserved for particularly serious cases, including those where the director concerned had been disqualified previously; the middle bracket of six to 10 years should be imposed for serious cases which did not merit the top bracket: *R. v. Millard*, 15 Cr.App.R.(S.) 445, CA. See also *R. v. Cobbey*, 14 Cr.App.R.(S.) 82, CA.

A court which disqualifies an offender under section 2 may not specify the functions from which the offender is disqualified under section 1; section 1 envisages a single disqualification with a number of different consequences: *R. v. Cole, Lees and Birch* [1998] B.C.C. 87, CA.

F. Disqualification or Being Barred from Working with Children or Vulnerable Adults

(1) Summary

The *CJCSA* 2000, Part II introduced a new power to make a disqualification order by which a person convicted of an "offence against a child" may (and in some cases must) be disqualified indefinitely from working with children. "Offence against a child" is defined in section 26 and Schedule 4. A child for this purpose is a person under the age of 18. The conditions for making a disqualification order are set out in sections 28 and 29. The relevant provisions came into force on January 11, 2001. They are significantly amended by provisions of the *CJA* 2003. **5–854**

The provisions of the 2000 Act are due to be repealed by the *Safeguarding Vulnerable Groups Act* 2006, which introduces a barring scheme in relation to working with children or vulnerable adults. There will be a limited role for a criminal court as inclusion in the scheme will be automatic in certain circumstances and in no circumstances will it depend on an order of a court. It is anticipated (as at September, 2007) that these provisions will come into force in the second half of 2008. The new scheme is summarised at § 5–865a, *post*.

In *R. v. Field*; *R. v. Young* [2003] 1 W.L.R. 882, CA, it was held that a disqualification order was not a "penalty" for the purposes of Article 7 of the ECHR (*post*, § 16–97). The effect of an order was entirely prospective, because it only affected future conduct. In such circumstances, the statute did not offend against the presumption against retrospective effect merely because it depended for its future application upon events that might have occurred before it came into force. The purpose of section 28 was plainly to protect children. That purpose would be severely undermined if a disqualification order could be imposed only in relation to offences committed after it came into force.

In *R. v. G.* [2006] 1 Cr.App.R.(S.) 30, CA, it was held that there was nothing in the Strasbourg jurisprudence to suggest that a disqualification order engaged Article 8 of the European Convention (right to respect for private and family life (*post*, § 16–101)), but, even if it did, such an inference was plainly in accordance with domestic law, pursued a legitimate purpose, and, in the circumstances, was proportionate (within Article 8(2)).

(2) Legislation

Criminal Justice and Court Services Act 2000, ss.26–31

Meaning of "offence against a child"

5–855 **26.**—(1) *For the purposes of this Part, an individual commits an offence against a child if—*

(a) *he commits any offence mentioned in paragraph 1 of Schedule 4,*

(b) *he commits against a child any offence mentioned in paragraph 2 of that Schedule, or*

(c) *he falls within paragraph 3 of that Schedule,*

and references to being convicted of, or charged with, an offence against a child are to be read accordingly.

(2) *The Secretary of State may by order amend Schedule 4 so as to add, modify or omit any entry.*

[As from a day to be appointed, this section is repealed by the *Safeguarding Vulnerable Groups Act* 2006, s.63(2), and Sched. 10.]

Equivalent armed forces offences

5–856 **27.**—(1) *For the purposes of this Part, an individual is treated as being convicted of or (as the case may be) charged with an offence against a child if he is convicted of or charged with an equivalent armed forces offence.*

(2) *In subsection (1), "equivalent armed forces offence" means* an armed forces offence [*an offence under section 42 of the* Armed Forces Act *2006*] *constituted by an act or omission which—*

(a) *is an offence against a child, or*

(b) *would, if committed in England or Wales, be an offence against a child.*

(3) In that subsection, "equivalent armed forces offence" also includes a civil offence of attempting to commit—

(a) an offence against a child, or

(b) an act that would, if committed in England or Wales, be an offence against a child.

(4) For the purpose of determining whether an offence is an equivalent armed forces offence, Schedule 4 shall have effect as if the words "or attempting" were omitted from paragraph 3(t).

(5) In this section, "civil offence" has the same meaning as in the *Army Act* 1955.

[(3) *Section 48 of the* Armed Forces Act *2006 (attempts, conspiracy, incitement and aiding and abetting outside England and Wales) applies for the purposes of subsection (2) of this section as if the reference in subsection (3)(b) of that section to any of the following provisions of that Act were a reference to subsection (2) of this section.*]

[This section is printed as amended, as from a day to be appointed, by the *AFA* 2006, s.378(1), and Sched. 16, para. 179 (omission of romanised words, insertion of words in square brackets). It is repealed, as from a day to be appointed, by the *Safeguarding Vulnerable Groups Act* 2006, s.63(2), and Sched. 10.]

Disqualification from working with children: adults

5–857 **28.**—(1) *This section applies where either of the conditions set out below is satisfied in the case of an individual.*

(2) *The first condition is that—*

(a) *the individual is convicted of an offence against a child committed when he was aged 18 or over, and*

(b) *a qualifying sentence is imposed by a* senior [*superior*] *court in respect of the conviction.*

(3) *The second condition is that—*

(a) *the individual is charged with an offence against a child committed when he was aged 18 or over, and*

(b) *a relevant order is made by a* senior [*superior*] *court in respect of the act or omission charged against him as the offence.*

(4) *Subject to subsection (5), the court must order the individual to be disqualified from working with children.*

(5) *An order shall not be made under this section if the court is satisfied, having regard to all the circumstances, that it is unlikely that the individual will commit any further offence against a child.*

(6) *If the court does not make an order under this section, it must state its reasons for not doing so and cause those reasons to be included in the record of the proceedings.*

[This section is printed as amended, as from a day to be appointed, by the *Constitutional Reform Act* 2005, s.59(5), and Sched. 11, para. 35 (substitution of references to "superior" for references to "senior"). It is repealed, as from a day to be appointed, by the *Safeguarding Vulnerable Groups Act* 2006, s.63(2), and Sched. 10.]

Disqualification from working with children: juveniles

29.—(1) *This section applies where either of the conditions set out below is satisfied in the case of an individual.* **5–858**

(2) *The first condition is that—*

(a) *the individual is convicted of an offence against a chld committed at a time when the individual was under the age of 18, and*

(b) *a qualifying sentence is imposed by a* senior [*superior*] *court in respect of the conviction.*

(3) *The second condition is that—*

(a) *the individual is charged with an offence against a child committed at a time when the individual was under the age of 18, and*

(b) *a relevant order is made by a* senior [*superior*] *court in respect of the act or omission charged against him as the offence.*

(4) *If the court is satisfied, having regard to all the circumstances, that it is likely that the individual will commit a further offence against a child it must order the individual to be disqualified from working with children.*

(5) *If the court makes an order under this section, it must state its reasons for doing so and cause those reasons to be included in the record of the proceedings.*

[See the note to s.28, *ante*.]

Disqualification at discretion of court: adults and juveniles

29A.—(1) *This section applies where—* **5–859**

(a) *an individual is convicted of an offence against a child (whether or not committed when he was aged 18 or over),*

(b) *the individual is sentenced by a* senior [*superior*] *court, and*

(c) *no qualifying sentence is imposed in respect of the conviction.*

(2) *If the court is satisfied, having regard to all the circumstances, that it is likely that the individual will commit a further offence against a child, it may order the individual to be disqualified from working with children.*

(3) [Identical to s.29(5), *ante*, § 5–858.]

[This section was inserted by the *CJA* 2003, s.299, and Sched. 30, paras 1 and 2. As to its prospective amendment by the *Constitutional Reform Act* 2005, see the note to s.28, *ante*. It is repealed, as from a day to be appointed, by the *Safeguarding Vulnerable Groups Act* 2006, s.63(2), and Sched. 10.]

Subsequent application for order under section 28 or 29

29B.—(1) *Where—* **5–860**

(a) *section 28 applies but the court has neither made an order under that section nor complied with subsection (6) of that section, or*

(b) *section 29 applies but the court has not made an order under that section, and it appears to the prosecutor that the court has not considered the making of an order under that section,*

the prosecutor may at any time apply to that court for an order under section 28 or 29.

(2) *Subject to subsection (3), on an application under subsection (1)—*

(a) *in a case falling within subsection (1)(a), the court—*

(i) *must make an order under section 28 unless it is satisfied as mentioned in subsection (5) of that section, and*

(ii) *if it does not make an order under that section, must comply with subsection (6) of that section,*

(b) *in a case falling within subsection (1)(b), the court—*

(i) *must make an order under section 29 if it is satisfied as mentioned in subsection (4) of that section, and*

(ii) *if it does so, must comply with subsection (5) of that section.*

(3) *Subsection (2) does not enable or require an order under section 28 or 29 to be made where the court is satisfied that it had considered the making of an order under that section at the time when it imposed the qualifying sentence or made the relevant order.*

[This section was inserted by the *CJA* 2003, s.299, and Sched. 30, paras 1 and 2. It is repealed, as from a day to be appointed, by the *Safeguarding Vulnerable Groups Act* 2006, s.63(2), and Sched. 10.]

Sections 28 to 29B: supplemental

5–861 **30.**—(1) *In sections 28 to 29B and this section—*

"guardianship order" means a guardianship order within the meaning of the Army Act *1955, the* Air Force Act *1955, the* Naval Discipline Act *1957 or the* Mental Health Act *1983,*

"qualifying sentence" means—

(a) *a sentence of imprisonment for a term of 12 months of more,*

(b) *a sentence of detention in a young offender institution for a term of 12 months or more,*

(c) *a sentence of detention during Her Majesty's pleasure,*

(d) *a sentence of detention for a period of 12 months or more under section 91 of the* Powers of Criminal Courts (Sentencing) Act *2000* [*or section 209 of the* Armed Forces Act *2006*] *(offenders under 18 convicted of certain serious offences),*

(dd) *a sentence of detention under section 226 or 228 of the* Criminal Justice Act *2003,*

(e) *a detention and training order for a term of 12 months or more* [*under section 100 of the* Powers of Criminal Courts (Sentencing) Act *2000 or section 211 of the* Armed Forces Act *2006*],

(f) a sentence of detention for a term of 12 months or more imposed by a court-martial or the Courts-Martial Appeal Court,

(g) *a hospital order within the meaning of the* Mental Health Act *1983, or*

(h) *a guardianship order,*

"relevant order" means—

(a) *an order made by the Crown Court, the Court of Appeal,* a court-martial or the Courts-Martial Appeal Court [*the Court Martial or the Court Martial Appeal Court*] *that the individual in question be admitted to hospital, or*

(b) *a guardianship order,*

" senior [*superior*] *court" means the Crown Court, the Court of Appeal,* a court-martial or the Courts-Martial Appeal Court [*the Court Martial or the Court Martial Appeal Court*].

(2) The reference to detention in paragraph (f) of the above definition of "qualifying sentence" includes a reference to detention by virtue of a custodial order under—

(a) section 71AA of, or paragraph 10 of Schedule 5A to, the *Army Act* 1955,

(b) section 71AA of, or paragraph 10 of Schedule 5A to, the *Air Force Act* 1955,

(c) section 43AA of, or paragraph 10 of Schedule 4A to, the *Naval Discipline Act* 1957.

(3) *In this Part, references to a sentence of imprisonment,* or to a sentence of detention imposed by a court-martial or the Courts-Martial Appeal Court, *include references to a suspended sentence.*

(4) *If, for the purpose of making an order under section 28 or 29, the court determines, after considering any available evidence, that an individual was, or was not, under the age of 18 at the time when the offence in question was committed, his age at that time shall be taken, for the purposes of that sections [sic] (and in particular for the purpose of determining any question as to the validity of the order), to be that which the court determined it to be.*

(5) *Below in this Part—*

(a) *references to a disqualification order are to an order under section 28, 29 or 29A,*

(b) *in relation to an individual on whom a sentence has been passed, or in relation to whom an order has been made, as mentioned in subsection (2) or (3) of section 28 or 29, references to his sentence are to that sentence or order,*

(c) *in relation to an individual to whom section 29A applies and on whom a sentence has been passed, references to his sentence are to that sentence.*

[This section is printed as amended by the *CJA* 2003, s.299, and Sched. 30, paras 1 and 3. It is printed as amended, as from a day to be appointed, by the *Constitutional Reform Act* 2005, s.59(5), and Sched. 11, para. 35 (substitution of reference to "superior" for reference to "senior"); and the *AFA* 2006, s.378(1), and Sched. 16, para. 180 (omission of words from "Army" to "1957" in definition of "guardianship order", insertion of words in square brackets in paras (d) and (e) of definition of "qualifying offence", omission of para. (f) in that definition, substitution of words in square brackets for romanised words in definition of "relevant order", substitution of words at the end of subs. (1) for romanised words that precede them, omission of subs. (2) and of romanised words in subs. (3)). The whole section is repealed, as from a day to be appointed, by the *Safeguarding Vulnerable Groups Act* 2006, s.63(2), and Sched. 10.]

Appeals

31.—(1) *An individual may appeal against a disqualification order*— **5–862**

(a) *where the first condition mentioned in section 28 or 29 is satisfied in his case, as if the order were a sentence passed on him for the offence of which he has been convicted,*

(b) *where the second condition mentioned in section 28 or 29 is satisfied in his case as if he had been convicted on indictment and the order were a sentence passed on him for that offence,*

(c) *where an order is made under section 29A, as if the order were a sentence passed on him for the offence of which he has been convicted.*

(2) *In relation to a disqualification order made by* a court-martial [*the Court Martial*], *subsection (1)(b) has effect as if the reference to conviction on indictment were a reference to a conviction by* a court-martial [*the Court Martial*].

[This section is printed as amended by the *CJA* 2003, s.299, and Sched. 30, paras 1 and 4; and as amended, as from a day to be appointed, by the *AFA* 2006, s.378(1), and Sched. 16, para. 181 (omission of romanised words, insertion of words in square brackets). It is repealed, as from a day to be appointed, by the *Safeguarding Vulnerable Groups Act* 2006, s.63(2), and Sched. 10.]

Criminal Justice and Court Services Act 2000, s.42

Interpretation of Part II

42.—(1) In this Part— **5–863**

"armed forces offence" means an offence under section 70 of the Army Act *1955, section 70 of the* Air Force Act *1955 or section 42 of the* Naval Discipline Act *1957,*

"care home" has the same meaning as in the *Care Standards Act* 2000,

"charity" and "charity trustee" have the same meanings as in the *Charities Act* 1993,

"child" means a person under the age of 18,

"children's home" has—

(a) in relation to England and Wales, the same meaning as in the *Care Standards Act* 2000,

(b) in relation to Northern Ireland, the meaning which would be given by Article 90(1) of the *Children (Northern Ireland) Order* 1995 if, in Article 91(2) of that *Order*, sub-paragraphs (a), (f) and (g) and the words after sub-paragraph (h) were omitted,

"Class A drug" has the same meaning as in the *Misuse of Drugs Act* 1971,

"day care premises" means—

(a) in relation to England, premises in respect of which a person is registered, otherwise than as a childminder, under Part 3 of the *Childcare Act* 2006,

(b) in relation to Wales, premises in respect of which a person is registered under Part 10A of the *Children Act* 1989 for providing day care,

"disqualification order" has the meaning given by section 30,

"educational institution" means an institution which is exclusively or mainly for the provision of full-time education to children, "employment" means paid employment, whether under a contract of service or apprenticeship or under a contract for services,

"hospital" has—

(a) in relation to England and Wales, the meaning given by section 128(1) of the *National Health Service Act* 2006 or the *National Health Service (Wales) Act* 2006,

(b) in relation to Northern Ireland, the meaning given by Article 2(2) of the *Health and Personal Social Services (Northern Ireland) Order* 1972,

"local authority" has the same meaning as in the *Education Act* 1996,

"nursing home" has the meaning given by Article 16 of the *Registered Homes (Northern Ireland) Order* 1992,

"private hospital" has the meaning given by Article 90(2) of the *Mental Health (Northern Ireland) Order* 1986,

"residential care home" has the meaning given by Article 3 of the *Registered Homes (Northern Ireland) Order* 1992,

"the Tribunal" means the tribunal established by section 9 of the *Protection of Children Act* 1999,

"voluntary home" has the meaning given by Article 74(1) of the *Children (Northern Ireland) Order* 1995,

"work" includes—

(a) work of any kind, whether paid or unpaid and whether under a contract of service or apprenticeship, under a contract for services, or otherwise than under a contract, and

(b) an office established by or by virtue of an enactment,and "working" is to be read accordingly.

(2) *In this Part references, in relation to a suspended sentence, to taking effect are to taking effect by virtue of—*

(a) *an order or direction under section 91 of the* Naval Discipline Act *1957 or paragraph 8(2)(a) or (b) of Schedule 11 to the* Criminal Justice Act *2003, or*

(b) *the determination of the suspension under section 120 of the* Army Act *1955 or section 120 of the* Air Force Act *1955.*

[This section is printed as amended by the *CJA* 2003, s.304, and Sched. 32, paras 133 and 135; the *National Health Service (Consequential Provisions) Act* 2006, s.2, and Sched. 1, paras 212 and 213; and the *Childcare Act* 2006, s.103(1), and Sched. 2, para. 40; and as amended, as from a day to be appointed, by the *AFA* 2006, s.378(1), and Sched. 16, para. 181 (omission of definition of "armed forces offence" in subs. (1), and subs. (2)); and the *Safeguarding Vulnerable Groups Act* 2006, s.63(2), and Sched. 10 (repeal of definition of "disqualification order").]

Meaning of "offence against a child"

5–864 Schedule 4 to the *CJCSA* 2000 (as amended by the *Nationality, Immigration and Asylum Act* 2002, s.146(4), the *SOA* 2003, s.139, and Sched. 6, para. 44(1) and (5), and the *Domestic Violence, Crime and Victims Act* 2004, s.58(1), and Sched. 10, para. 56) lists the offences referred to in section 26. Schedule 4 is repealed, as from a day to be appointed, by the *Safeguarding Vulnerable Groups Act* 2006, s.63(2), and Sched. 10. Pending commencement of the repeal, the offences mentioned in section 26(1)(a) are those under the *CYPA* 1933, s.1, the *Infanticide Act* 1938, s.1, the *SOA* 1956, ss.5, 6, 19, 20, 25, 26 and 28, the *Indecency with Children Act* 1960, s.1, the *CLA* 1977, s.54, the *Protection of Children Act* 1978, s.1, the *Child Abduction Act* 1984, s.1, the *CJA* 1988, s.160, and the *SOA* 2003, ss.5 to 26 and 47 to 50.

The offences mentioned in section 26(1)(b) are murder, manslaughter, kidnapping, false imprisonment, an offence under the *Offences against the Person Act* 1861, ss.18, 20 and 47, under the *SOA* 1956, ss.1 to 4, 14 to 17 and 24 and under the *SOA* 2003, ss.1 to 4, 30 to 41, 52, 53, 57 to 61, 66 and 67.

A person falls within paragraph 3 of Schedule 4 (see s.26(1)(c)) if he or she commits an offence, (a) under the *Offences Against the Person Act* 1861, s.16, by making a threat to kill a child; (b) under the *SOA* 1956, s.7, by having sexual intercourse with a child; (c) under the 1956 Act, s.9, by procuring a child to have sexual intercourse; (d) under the 1956 Act, s.10, by having sexual intercourse with a child; (e) being a woman, under the 1956 Act, s.11, by allowing a child to have sexual intercourse with her; (f) under the 1956 Act, s.12, by committing buggery with a child under 16; (g) under the 1956 Act, s.13, by committing an act of gross indecency with a child; (h) under the 1956 Act, s.21, by taking a child out of the possession of his parent or guardian; (i) under the 1956 Act, s.22, in relation to a child; (j) under the 1956 Act, s.23, by procuring a child to have sexual intercourse with a third person; (k) under the 1956 Act, s.27, by inducing or suffering a child to resort to or to be on premises for the purpose of having sexual intercourse; (l) under the 1956 Act, s.29, by causing or encouraging the prostitution of a child; (m) under the 1956 Act, s.30, in a case where the prostitute is a child; (n) under the 1956 Act, s.31, in a case where the prostitute is a child; (o) under the *MHA* 1983, s.128, by having sexual intercourse with a child; (p) under the *SOA* 1967, s.4, by procuring a child to commit an act of buggery with any person or procuring any person to commit an act of buggery with a child; (q) under the 1967 Act, s.5, by living on the earnings of a child prostitute; (r) under the *Theft Act* 1968, s.9(1)(a) by entering a building (or part thereof) with intent to rape a child; (s) under the *Misuse of Drugs Act* 1971, s.4(3), by supplying or offering to supply a Class A drug to a child, or being concerned in the supplying of such a drug to a child, or being concerned in making to a child of an offer to supply such drug; (sa) under the *SOA* 2003, ss.62 or 63, in a case where the intended offence was an offence against a child; (sb) under the *Domestic Violence, Crime and Victims Act* 2004, s.5, in respect of a child; or (t) of aiding, abetting, counselling, procuring or inciting (to be construed as a reference to the offences under the *SCA* 2007, Pt 2: 2007 Act, s.63(1), and Sched. 6, para. 40) the commission of "an offence against a child" or of conspiring or attempting to commit such an offence. Whilst there is an obvious element of circularity about paragraph (t), it is submitted that the intended meaning is clear, *viz.* aiding and abetting, etc., the commission of any of the specific offences listed in any of the preceding paragraphs and sub-paragraphs of the schedule.

(3) Notes on disqualification from working with children

In *R. v. M.G.* [2002] 2 Cr.App.R.(S.) 1, CA, it was held that the test to be applied by a court considering whether it was satisfied that it was unlikely that the individual would commit further offences against a child was not the criminal standard; where the judge found that the offender would probably not commit further offences against a child, but was not "satisfied" to this effect, a disqualification order was quashed. **5–865**

In considering whether an extended sentence imposed under the *PCC(S)A* 2000, s.85, is a "qualifying sentence" for the purposes of section 28, the relevant period is the whole length of the sentence, not the custodial term alone: *R. v. Wiles* [2004] 2 Cr.App.R.(S.) 88, CA.

(4) Bars on working with children or vulnerable adults

The *Safeguarding Vulnerable Groups Act* 2006 introduces an "Independent Barring Board" which must establish and maintain the "children's barred list" and the "adults' barred list" (s.2). Section 2 also gives effect to Parts 1 and 2 of Schedule 3 which apply for the purpose of determining whether an individual is included in the children's barred list or the adults' barred list respectively. Part 1 (paras 1-6) deals with the children's list and Part 2 (paras 7-12) deals with the adults' list, the two parts essentially mirroring each other, with Part 3 (paras 13-25) making general provision common (and essential) to both parts. Thus, paragraphs 1 and 7 respectively make provision for automatic inclusion on the children's barred list or the adults' barred list without the possibility of the person concerned making any representations. Inclusion occurs when it appears to the Secretary of State that one of the criteria to be prescribed under paragraph 24(1) (*post*) is fulfilled, and he has referred the matter to the board. Paragraphs 2 and 8 operate in a similar way, save that once the matter has been referred to the board, the person concerned is automatically to be included in the list but must then be given an opportunity to make representations as to his removal from it. Which of the mechanisms under paragraphs 1 and 7 or 2 and 8 applies will depend on what **5–865a** criteria are prescribed under paragraph 24(1) (*i.e.* it will depend on provisions to be contained in a statutory instrument). Paragraphs 3 and 9 apply where it appears to the board that the person concerned has engaged in "relevant conduct" (defined in paras 4 and 10) and the board proposes to include him in the relevant list. The person concerned must be given an opportunity to make representations, but he must be included in the relevant list if the board is satisfied that he engaged in relevant conduct and it appears to be appropriate to include him in the list. In the case of the children's barred list only, the mechanism for inclusion does not apply to conduct occurring before the commencement of section 2 where a court decided not to make a disqualification order (under the 2000 Act, *ante*) against the person concerned: para. 3(4), (5). Paragraphs 4 and 10 set out lengthy definitions of the term "relevant conduct". In essence, they encompass conduct which would, or would be likely to, endanger a child or vulnerable person, conduct which involves sexual material relating to children, conduct which involves sexually explicit images depicting violence against human beings (including possession of such images), and conduct of an inappropriate sexual nature involving a child or vulnerable person. Both paragraphs provide that a person does not engage in relevant conduct merely by committing an offence of a type to be prescribed. Paragraphs 5 and 11 mirror the mechanism of paragraphs 3 and 9, but make provision instead for a person to be included in the relevant list if it appears to the board that he poses a risk of harm to a child or vulnerable adult.

5–865b Paragraph 24(1) provides that the criteria which may be prescribed for the purposes of paragraphs 1, 2, 7 and 8 are: (a) that the person concerned has been convicted of, or cautioned in relation to, an offence of a specified description, (b) that an order of a specified description has been made against him, (c) that he has been included in a specified list maintained outside the United Kingdom, or (d) that an order or direction of a specified description has been made against him outside the United Kingdom. Offences committed before the person concerned attained the age of 18 are to be ignored, as are orders or directions made before that time: para. 24(4). The criteria which may be prescribed under paragraph 1 or 2 must not consist only of circumstances in which the person has committed an offence against a child before the commencement of section 2 if the court had considered whether to make a disqualification order under the 2000 Act and had decided not to do so: para. 24(5). Where an offender is convicted of an offence of a specified description for the purposes of paragraph 24(1)(a), or where an order of a specified description under paragraph 24(1)(b) is made against him, paragraph 25 requires the court to inform the offender that the board will include him in the list concerned: para. 25.

5–865c The Act comes into force on a day or days to be appointed. As at October 1, 2008, there had been two commencement orders for England and Wales, which brought various provisions into force for limited purposes (rule-making powers, transitional arrangements, *etc.*) on a range of different dates between December 31, 2007, and May 19, 2008.

G. RESTRAINING ORDERS AND SEXUAL OFFENCES PREVENTION ORDERS

5–866 For restraining orders under the *Protection from Harassment Act* 1997, see section 5 thereof, *post*, § 19–277f. Restraining orders under section 5A of the *Sex Offenders Act* 1997 have been replaced by sexual offences prevention orders under the *SOA* 2003. As to these see *post*, §§ 20–323 *et seq.*

H. TRAVEL RESTRICTION ORDERS

(1) Introduction

5–867 Chapter 3 (ss.33– 49) of the *CJPA* 2001 is headed "Other Provisions for Combatting Crime and Disorder". The first group of sections (ss.33– 37) provide for travel restrictions on drug trafficking offenders. The power to make a travel restriction order is contained in section 33. It is one that may be exercised by the convicting court where the term of imprisonment considered appropriate is four years or more. The court is bound to consider making such an order, and is under an obligation to give reasons for not making such order where otherwise it would be appropriate. The order should restrict the travel of the offender for at least two years from the date of his release. Section 34 defines "drug trafficking offence" for these purposes. Section 35 provides for the revocation and suspension of such order. Section 36 creates various offences in relation to contraventions of such orders, with the more serious ones being triable either way and carrying imprisonment of up to five years. Section 37 saves various powers of removal of persons from the United Kingdom.

Sections 33 to 37 came into force on April 1, 2002: *Criminal Justice and Police Act 2001 (Commencement No. 4 and Transitional Provisions) Order* 2002 (S.I. 2002 No. 344).

(2) Legislation

Criminal Justice and Police Act 2001, ss.33–37

Travel restrictions on drug trafficking offenders

Power to make travel restriction orders

33.—(1) This section applies where— **5–868**

(a) a person ("the offender") has been convicted by any court of a post-commencement drug trafficking offence;

(b) the court has determined that it would be appropriate to impose a sentence of imprisonment for that offence; and

(c) the term of imprisonment which the court considers appropriate is a term of four years or more.

(2) It shall be the duty of the court, on sentencing the offender—

(a) to consider whether it would be appropriate for the sentence for the offence to include the making of a travel restriction order in relation to the offender;

(b) if the court determines that it is so appropriate, to make such travel restriction order in relation to the offender as the court thinks suitable in all the circumstances (including any other convictions of the offender for post-commencement drug trafficking offences in respect of which the court is also passing sentence); and

(c) if the court determines that it is not so appropriate, to state its reasons for not making a travel restriction order.

(3) A travel restriction order is an order that prohibits the offender from leaving the United Kingdom at any time in the period which—

(a) begins with the offender's release from custody; and

(b) continues after that time for such period of not less than two years as may be specified in the order.

(4) A travel restriction order may contain a direction to the offender to deliver up, or cause to be delivered up, to the court any UK *passport* [travel authorisation] held by him; and where such a direction is given, the court shall send any *passport* [travel authorisation] delivered up in pursuance of the direction to the Secretary of State at such address as the Secretary of State may determine.

(5) Where the offender's *passport* [travel authorisation] is held by the Secretary of State by reason of the making of any direction contained in a travel restriction order, the Secretary of State (without prejudice to any other power or duty of his to retain the *passport* [travel authorisation])—

(a) may retain it for so long as the prohibition imposed by the order applies to the offender, and is not for the time being suspended; and

(b) shall not return the *passport* [travel authorisation] after the prohibition has ceased to apply, or when it is suspended, except where the *passport* [travel authorisation] has not expired and an application for its return is made to him by the offender.

(6) In this section "post-commencement"—

(a) except in relation to an offence that is a drug trafficking offence by virtue of an order under section 34(1)(c), means committed after the coming into force of this section; and

(b) in relation to an offence that is a drug trafficking offence by virtue of such an order, means committed after the coming into force of that order.

(7) References in this section to the offender's release from custody are references to his first release from custody after the imposition of the travel restriction order which is neither—

(a) a release on bail; nor
(b) a temporary release for a fixed period.

(8) *In this section "UK passport" means a United Kingdom passport within the meaning of the* Immigration Act *1971*.

[(8) In this section "UK travel authorisation", in relation to a person, means one or both of the following—

(a) any UK passport (within the meaning of the *Immigration Act* 1971) that has been issued to him;
(b) any ID card issued to him under the *Identity Cards Act* 2006 which records that he is a British Citizen.]

[This section is printed as amended, as from a day to be appointed, by the *Identity Cards Act* 2006, s.39(3) and (4) (omission of italicised words, insertion of words in square brackets).]

Meaning of "drug trafficking offence"

5–869 **34.**—(1) In section 33 "drug trafficking offence" means any of the following offences (including one committed by aiding, abetting, counselling or procuring)—

(a) an offence under section 4(2) or (3) of the *Misuse of Drugs Act* 1971 (production and supply of controlled drugs);
(b) an offence under section 20 of that Act (assisting in or inducing commission outside United Kingdom of an offence punishable under a corresponding law);
(c) any such other offence under that Act as may be designated by order made by the Secretary of State;
(d) an offence under—
  (i) section 50(2) or (3) of the *Customs and Excise Management Act* 1979 (improper importation),
  (ii) section 68(2) of that Act (exportation), or
  (iii) section 170 of that Act (fraudulent evasion),

  in connection with a prohibition or restriction on importation or exportation having effect by virtue of section 3 of the *Misuse of Drugs Act* 1971;
(e) an offence under section 1 of the *Criminal Law Act* 1977 or Article 9 of the *Criminal Attempts and Conspiracy (Northern Ireland) Order* 1983 (S.I. 1983 No. 1120 (N.I. 13)), or in Scotland at common law, of conspiracy to commit any of the offences in paragraphs (a) to (d) above;
(f) an offence under section 1 of the *Criminal Attempts Act* 1981 or Article 3 of the *Criminal Attempts and Conspiracy (Northern Ireland) Order* 1983, or in Scotland at common law, of attempting to commit any of those offences; and
(g) an offence under section 19 of the *Misuse of Drugs Act* 1971 or at common law of inciting another person to commit any of those offences.

(2) [*Procedure for making order under subs. (1)(c).*]

(3) An order under subsection (1)(c) may provide, in relation to any offence designated by such an order, that it is to be treated as so designated only—

(a) for such purposes, and
(b) in cases where it was committed in such manner or in such circumstances,

as may be described in the order.

The reference to the common law offence of incitement in subsection (1)(g) has effect as a reference to the offences under the *SCA* 2007, Pt 2: 2007 Act, s.63(1), and Sched. 6, para. 41.

Revocation and suspension of a travel restriction order

5–870 **35.**—(1) Subject to the following provisions of this section, the court by which a travel restriction order has been made in relation to any person under section 33 may—

(a) on an application made by that person at any time which is—
  (i) after the end of the minimum period, and
  (ii) is not within three months after the making of any previous application for the revocation of the prohibition,

  revoke the prohibition imposed by the order with effect from such date as the court may determine; or
(b) on an application made by that person at any time after the making of the order, suspend the prohibition imposed by the order for such period as the court may determine.

(2) A court to which an application for the revocation of the prohibition imposed on any person by a travel restriction order is made shall not revoke that prohibition unless it considers that it is appropriate to do so in all the circumstances of the case and having regard, in particular, to—

(a) that person's character;

(b) his conduct since the making of the order; and

(c) the offences of which he was convicted on the occasion on which the order was made.

(3) A court shall not suspend the prohibition imposed on any person by a travel restriction order for any period unless it is satisfied that there are exceptional circumstances, in that person's case, that justify the suspension on compassionate grounds of that prohibition for that period.

(4) In making any determination on an application for the suspension of the prohibition imposed on any person by a travel restriction order, a court (in addition to considering the matters mentioned in subsection (3)) shall have regard to—

(a) that person's character;

(b) his conduct since the making of the order;

(c) the offences of which he was convicted on the occasion on which the order was made; and

(d) any other circumstances of the case that the court considers relevant.

(5) Where the prohibition imposed on any person by a travel restriction order is suspended, it shall be the duty of that person—

(a) to be in the United Kingdom when the period of the suspension ends; and

(b) if the order contains a direction under section 33(4), to surrender, before the end of that period, any *passport* [travel authorisation] returned or issued to that person, in respect of the suspension, by the Secretary of State;

and a *passport* [travel authorisation] that is required to be surrendered under paragraph (b) shall be surrendered to the Secretary of State in such manner or by being sent to such address as the Secretary of State may direct at the time when he returns or issues it.

(6) Where the prohibition imposed on any person by a travel restriction order is suspended for any period under this section, the end of the period of the prohibition imposed by the order shall be treated (except for the purposes of subsection (7)) as postponed (or, if there has been one or more previous suspensions, further postponed) by the length of the period of suspension.

(7) In this section "the minimum period"—

(a) in the case of a travel restriction order imposing a prohibition for a period of four years or less, means the period of two years beginning at the time when the period of the prohibition began;

(b) in the case of a travel restriction order imposing a prohibition of more than four years but less than ten years, means the period of four years beginning at that time; and

(c) in any other case, means the period of five years beginning at that time.

[This section is printed as amended, as from a day to be appointed, by the *Identity Cards Act* 2006, s.39(3) (omission of italicised words, insertion of words in square brackets).]

Offences of contravening orders

36.—(1) A person who leaves the United Kingdom at a time when he is prohibited from leaving it by a travel restriction order is guilty of an offence and liable— **5–871**

(a) on summary conviction to imprisonment for a term not exceeding *six* [12] months or to a fine not exceeding the statutory maximum, or to both;

(b) on conviction on indictment, to imprisonment for a term not exceeding five years or to a fine, or to both.

(2) A person who is not in the United Kingdom at the end of a period during which a prohibition imposed on him by a travel restriction order has been suspended shall be guilty of an offence and liable—

(a), (b) [*identical to subs. (1)(a), (b),* ante].

(3) A person who fails to comply with—

(a) a direction contained in a travel restriction order to deliver up a *passport* [travel authorisation] to a court, or to cause such a *passport* [travel authorisation] to be delivered up, or

(b) any duty imposed on him by section 35(5)(b) to surrender a *passport* [travel authorisation] to the Secretary of State,

shall be guilty of an offence and liable, on summary conviction, to imprisonment for a term not exceeding *six months* [51 weeks] or to a fine not exceeding level 5 on the standard scale, or to both.

(4) This section has effect subject to section 37(3).

[In subss. (1)(a) and (2)(a), "12" is substituted for "6", and in subs. (3), "51 weeks" is substituted for "six months", as from a day to be appointed, by the *CJA* 2003, ss.281(4) and (5), and 282(2) and (3). The increases have no application to offences committed before the substitutions take effect: ss.281(6) and 282(4). In subs. (3), the words in square brackets are substituted for the italicised words, as from a day to be appointed, by the *Identity Cards Act* 2006, s.39(3).]

Saving for powers to remove a person from the United Kingdom

5–872 **37.**—(1) A travel restriction order made in relation to any person shall not prevent the exercise in relation to that person of any prescribed removal power.

(2) A travel restriction order made in relation to any person shall remain in force, notwithstanding the exercise of any prescribed removal power in relation to that person, except in so far as either—

(a) the Secretary of State by order otherwise provides; or

(b) the travel restriction order is suspended or revoked under section 35.

(3) No person shall be guilty of an offence under section 36 in respect of any act or omission required of him by an obligation imposed in the exercise of a prescribed removal power.

(4) In this section "a prescribed removal power" means any such power conferred by or under any enactment as—

(a) consists in a power to order or direct the removal of a person from the United Kingdom; and

(b) is designated for the purposes of this section by an order made by the Secretary of State.

(5) An order under subsection (2)(a) or (4) shall be made by statutory instrument subject to annulment in pursuance of a resolution of either House of Parliament.

(6) An order under subsection (2)(a)—

(a) may make different provision for different cases; and

(b) may contain such incidental, supplemental, consequential and transitional provision as the Secretary of State thinks fit.

(7) References in this section to a person's removal from the United Kingdom include references to his deportation, extradition, repatriation, delivery up or other transfer to a place outside the United Kingdom.

(3) Notes on travel restriction orders

5–873 In *R. v. Mee* [2004] 2 Cr.App.R.(S.) 81, CA, it was said that section 33 of the 2001 Act conferred a discretion in broad terms; the discretion had to be exercised for the purpose granted (reduction of risk of re-offending after release), and had to be proportionate; whilst the power to make such an order was not confined to importation cases, it was most likely to be appropriate in such cases; it was the duty of the sentencer to consider the making of such an order and to give reasons for doing so (including as to the chosen length); the mere fact that the offender had been convicted of an offence of importation did not give rise to an inference that he would do it again on release; if, on an assessment of all the circumstances, a risk did arise such as to require an order, proportionality was required as to length; in restricting a person's freedom to travel (a significant aspect of modern life), there was a need for balance; the length of any order should be restricted to that which was necessary to protect the public; but, the drug trade being truly international, the provisions of the Act did not contemplate an order being made in relation to certain parts of the world only. For an example of a travel restriction being quashed, see *R. v. Onung* [2007] 2 Cr.App.R.(S.) 3, CA (one-off importation by person who had not become criminally involved until late stage).

As to the need for a court to have regard to the effect of a travel restriction order on the offender's children, see *R. v. Fuller* [2006] 1 Cr.App.R.(S.) 8, CA.

I. SERIOUS CRIME PREVENTION ORDERS

(1) Summary

Serious Crime Act 2007, Pt 1

Part 1 of the *SCA* 2007 (ss.1– 43) introduced the concept of the "serious crime prevention order". Sections 1 to 5 contain general provisions. Section 1 confers power on the High Court to make such an order in prescribed circumstances and defines the term for the purposes of this part of the Act. Sections 2 and 4 elaborate on when a person is to be regarded as having been involved in serious crime and section 5 specifies the type of provision that may be made by an order. **5–873a**

Sections 6 to 10 contain general safeguards in relation to the making of such orders. Thus there are restrictions on who may be the subject of an order (ss.6, 7), who may apply for an order (s.8) and on the making of an order which may affect a third party without that party being given an opportunity to be heard (s.9). Section 10 provides that a person is only bound by an order (or a variation of an order) if he is represented at the proceedings at which the order (or the variation) is made or if notice setting out the terms of the order has been served on him.

Sections 11 to 15 contain restrictions on the information that may be required under the terms of an order and limit the use to which information that is obtained under an order may be put. In particular, there is an embargo, subject to limited exceptions, on the use of a statement made by a person in response to a requirement imposed by an order in evidence against him in any criminal proceedings (s.15).

An order must specify when it comes into force and when it ceases, and may specify different dates of commencement and cessation for different provisions, but the order as a whole may not be in force for more than five years; however, the court may make a new order to the same or similar effect, either after an order (or any of its provisions) has expired or in anticipation of an earlier order (or provision) ceasing to be in force (s.16). Sections 17 and 18 provide for applications to the High Court for the variation or discharge of an order.

The Crown Court is given the power, on the same basis as the High Court under section 1, to make an order in relation to a person convicted of a serious offence (whether convicted in the Crown Court or committed for sentence there), in addition to sentencing the person in relation to the offence or conditionally discharging him, but such an order is also subject to the safeguards in sections 6 to 15 (s.19). It is also given power, on application, to vary a pre-existing order in like circumstances (s.20); and section 21 gives it a similar power of variation when it is dealing with a person convicted of an offence under section 25 (failing to comply with an order). The Crown Court may vary an order made or varied by the High Court, the High Court may vary or discharge an order made or varied by the Crown Court, and a decision by the Crown Court not to make or vary an order under section 19, 20 or 21 does not prevent the High Court subsequently making or varying an order in relation to the same offence (s.22).

In addition to the normal rights of appeal, a decision of the High Court to make, to vary, not to vary or not to discharge an order may be appealed by any person who was given an opportunity to make representations in the proceedings (s.23). Such a person also has a corresponding right of appeal against a decision of the Crown Court to make, to vary or not to vary an order, and any decision of the Crown Court in relation to an order may be appealed by the subject of the order or the relevant applicant authority (s.24(1), (2)). Appeals from the Crown Court may only be made with the leave of the Court of Appeal (unless the judge in the Crown Court grants a certificate that the decision is fit for appeal) (s.24(3), (4)), and they are to be heard by the criminal division of the Court of Appeal (s.24(5)).

Section 25 makes it an either-way offence to fail, without reasonable excuse, to comply with an order. The court before which a person is convicted of this offence is given the power (subject to the duty to allow representations to be made by anyone who claims ownership or any other interest) to make an order for the forfeiture of anything in the defendant's possession at the time of the offence which the court considers to have been involved in the offence (s.26). Where a company, etc., has been convicted of this offence, the DPP, the Director of Revenue and Customs Prosecutions or the Director of the Serious Fraud Office may, if they consider it to be in the public interest, petition for the winding up of the company, etc., under the *Insolvency Act* 1986, and the court may order such a winding up if it considers it just and equitable to do so (s.27).

Sections 30 to 34 make provision in regard to: bodies corporate, including limited liability partnerships (s.30); other partnerships (s.31); unincorporated associations (s.32); overseas bodies (s.33); and providers of information society services (s.34). They relate, in particular, to notice and service requirements, the liability of officers, partners, members, etc., and limitations on the restrictions that an order may make on the freedom of a service provider who is established in an EEA state other than the United Kingdom to provide information society services in relation to an EEA state.

Proceedings in the High Court concerning orders are civil proceedings, subject to the civil standard of proof (s.35), and such proceedings in the Crown Court are also civil proceedings, subject to the same standard of proof, and, as a consequence, the court may consider evidence that would not have been admissible in the criminal proceedings and may adjourn the proceedings concerning the order even after sentence, but the Crown Court in such circumstances is still a criminal court for the purposes of rules of procedure and practice directions (s.36). Section 38 provides protection for those disclosing information in accordance with an order, sections 39 and 40 provide for authorised monitors to be appointed to provide monitoring services in relation to orders made against corporations, partnerships and unincorporated associations, and section 41 provides for the retention of documents by law enforcement officers.

Commencement

5–873b The whole of Part 1 was in force by April 6, 2008, with all but specified subsections in sections 24 and 40 coming into force on that day: see the *Serious Crime Act 2007 (Commencement No. 1) Order* 2008 (S.I. 2008 No. 219) and the *Serious Crime Act 2007 (Commencement No. 2 and Transitional and Transitory Provisions and Savings) Order* 2008 (S.I. 2008 No. 755).

Procedure

5–873c The *Civil Procedure (Amendment No. 2) Rules* 2007 (S.I. 2007 No. 3543) insert a new Part 77 into the *Civil Procedure Rules* 1998 (S.I. 1998 No. 3132). This makes provision for applications to the High Court for or relating to serious crime prevention orders under the 2007 Act.

As to the procedure in the Crown Court, see Part 50 of the *Criminal Procedure Rules* 2005 (S.I. 2005 No. 384), *post*, §§ 5–886g *et seq.*

(2) Legislation

Serious Crime Act 2007, ss.1, 2, 4, 5

PART 1

SERIOUS CRIME PREVENTION ORDERS

General

Serious crime prevention orders

5–873d **1.**—(1)-(4) [*High Court Power to make order.*]

(5) In this Part "serious crime prevention order" means—

(a) an order under this section; or

(b) an order under section 19 (corresponding order of the Crown Court on conviction).

(6) For the purposes of this Part references to the person who is the subject of a serious crime prevention order are references to the person against whom the public are to be protected.

Involvement in serious crime: England and Wales orders

2.—(1) For the purposes of this Part, a person has been involved in serious crime in England and Wales if he— **5–873e**

(a) has committed a serious offence in England and Wales;

(b) has facilitated the commission by another person of a serious offence in England and Wales; or

(c) has conducted himself in a way that was likely to facilitate the commission by himself or another person of a serious offence in England and Wales (whether or not such an offence was committed).

(2) In this Part "a serious offence in England and Wales" means an offence under the law of England and Wales which, at the time when the court is considering the application or matter in question—

(a) is specified, or falls within a description specified, in Part 1 of Schedule 1; or

(b) is one which, in the particular circumstances of the case, the court considers to be sufficiently serious to be treated for the purposes of the application or matter as if it were so specified.

(3) For the purposes of this Part, involvement in serious crime in England and Wales is any one or more of the following—

(a) the commission of a serious offence in England and Wales;

(b) conduct which facilitates the commission by another person of a serious offence in England and Wales;

(c) conduct which is likely to facilitate the commission, by the person whose conduct it is or another person, of a serious offence in England and Wales (whether or not such an offence is committed).

(4) For the purposes of section 1(1)(a), a person has been involved in serious crime elsewhere than in England and Wales if he—

(a) has committed a serious offence in a country outside England and Wales;

(b) has facilitated the commission by another person of a serious offence in a country outside England and Wales; or

(c) has conducted himself in a way that was likely to facilitate the commission by himself or another person of a serious offence in a country outside England and Wales (whether or not such an offence was committed).

(5) In subsection (4) "a serious offence in a country outside England and Wales" means an offence under the law of a country outside England and Wales which, at the time when the court is considering the application or matter in question—

(a) would be an offence under the law of England and Wales if committed in or as regards England and Wales; and

(b) either—

(i) would be an offence which is specified, or falls within a description specified, in Part 1 of Schedule 1 if committed in or as regards England and Wales; or

(ii) is conduct which, in the particular circumstances of the case, the court considers to be sufficiently serious to be treated for the purposes of the application or matter as if it meets the test in sub-paragraph (i).

(6) [*Northern Ireland.*]

(7) An act punishable under the law of a country outside the United Kingdom constitutes an offence under that law for the purposes of subsection (5), however it is described in that law.

Involvement in serious crime: supplementary

4.—(1) In considering for the purposes of this Part whether a person has committed a serious offence— **5–873f**

(a) the court must decide that the person has committed the offence if—

(i) he has been convicted of the offence; and

(ii) the conviction has not been quashed on appeal nor has the person been pardoned of the offence; but

(b) the court must not otherwise decide that the person has committed the offence.

(2) In deciding for the purposes of this Part whether a person ("the respondent") facilitates the commission by another person of a serious offence, the court must ignore—

(a) any act that the respondent can show to be reasonable in the circumstances; and

(b) subject to this, his intentions, or any other aspect of his mental state, at the time.

(3) In deciding for the purposes of this Part whether a person ("the respondent") conducts himself in a way that is likely to facilitate the commission by himself or another person of a serious offence (whether or not such an offence is committed), the court must ignore—

(a) any act that the respondent can show to be reasonable in the circumstances; and

(b) subject to this, his intentions, or any other aspect of his mental state, at the time.

(4) The Secretary of State may by order amend Schedule 1.

Type of provision that may be made by orders

5–873g **5.**—(1) This section contains examples of the type of provision that may be made by a serious crime prevention order but it does not limit the type of provision that may be made by such an order.

(2) Examples of prohibitions, restrictions or requirements that may be imposed by serious crime prevention orders in England and Wales or Northern Ireland include prohibitions, restrictions or requirements in relation to places other than England and Wales or (as the case may be) Northern Ireland.

(3) Examples of prohibitions, restrictions or requirements that may be imposed on individuals (including partners in a partnership) by serious crime prevention orders include prohibitions or restrictions on, or requirements in relation to—

(a) an individual's financial, property or business dealings or holdings;

(b) an individual's working arrangements;

(c) the means by which an individual communicates or associates with others, or the persons with whom he communicates or associates;

(d) the premises to which an individual has access;

(e) the use of any premises or item by an individual;

(f) an individual's travel (whether within the United Kingdom, between the United Kingdom and other places or otherwise).

(4) Examples of prohibitions, restrictions or requirements that may be imposed on bodies corporate, partnerships and unincorporated associations by serious crime prevention orders include prohibitions or restrictions on, or requirements in relation to—

(a) financial, property or business dealings or holdings of such persons;

(b) the types of agreements to which such persons may be a party;

(c) the provision of goods or services by such persons;

(d) the premises to which such persons have access;

(e) the use of any premises or item by such persons;

(f) the employment of staff by such persons.

(5) Examples of requirements that may be imposed on any persons by serious crime prevention orders include—

(a) a requirement on a person to answer questions, or provide information, specified or described in an order—

(i) at a time, within a period or at a frequency;

(ii) at a place;

(iii) in a form and manner; and

(iv) to a law enforcement officer or description of law enforcement officer;

notified to the person by a law enforcement officer specified or described in the order;

(b) a requirement on a person to produce documents specified or described in an order—

(i) at a time, within a period or at a frequency;

(ii) at a place;

(iii) in a manner; and

(iv) to a law enforcement officer or description of law enforcement officer;

notified to the person by a law enforcement officer specified or described in the order.

(6) The prohibitions, restrictions or requirements that may be imposed on individuals by serious crime prevention orders include prohibitions, restrictions or requirements in relation to an individual's private dwelling (including, for example, prohibitions or restrictions on, or requirements in relation to, where an individual may reside).

(7) In this Part—

"document" means anything in which information of any description is recorded (whether or not in legible form);

"a law enforcement officer" means —

(a) a constable;

(b) a member of the staff of the Serious Organised Crime Agency who is for the time being designated under section 43 of the *Serious Organised Crime and Police Act* 2005;

(c) an officer of Revenue and Customs; or

(d) a member of the Serious Fraud Office; and

"premises" includes any land, vehicle, vessel, aircraft or hovercraft.

(8) Any reference in this Part to the production of documents is, in the case of a document which contains information recorded otherwise than in legible form, a reference to the production of a copy of the information in legible form.

Serious Crime Act 2007, ss.6–10

General safeguards in relation to orders

Any individual must be 18 or over

6. An individual under the age of 18 may not be the subject of a serious crime prevention order. **5–874**

Other exceptions

7. A person may not be the subject of a serious crime prevention order if the person falls within a description specified by order of the Secretary of State. **5–874a**

Limited class of applicants for making of orders

8. A serious crime prevention order may be made only on an application by— **5–874b**

(a) in the case of an order in England and Wales—

(i) the Director of Public Prosecutions;

(ii) the Director of Revenue and Customs Prosecutions; or

(iii) the Director of the Serious Fraud Office; and

(b) in the case of an order in Northern Ireland, the Director of Public Prosecutions for Northern Ireland.

Right of third parties to make representations

9.—(1)-(3) [*Proceedings in High Court.*] **5–874c**

(4) The Crown Court must, on an application by a person, give the person an opportunity to make representations in proceedings before it arising by virtue of section 19, 20 or 21 if it considers that the making or variation of the serious crime prevention order concerned (or a decision not to vary it) would be likely to have a significant adverse effect on that person.

(5) A court which is considering an appeal in relation to a serious crime prevention order must, on an application by a person, give the person an opportunity to make representations in the proceedings if that person was given an opportunity to make representations in the proceedings which are the subject of the appeal.

Notice requirements in relation to orders

10.—(1) The subject of a serious crime prevention order is bound by it or a variation of it only if— **5–874d**

(a) he is represented (whether in person or otherwise) at the proceedings at which the order or (as the case may be) variation is made; or

(b) a notice setting out the terms of the order or (as the case may be) variation has been served on him.

(2) The notice may be served on him by—

(a) delivering it to him in person; or

(b) sending it by recorded delivery to him at his last-known address (whether residential or otherwise).

(3) For the purposes of delivering such a notice to him in person, a constable or a person authorised for the purpose by the relevant applicant authority may (if necessary by force)—

(a) enter any premises where he has reasonable grounds for believing the person to be; and

(b) search those premises for him.

(4) In this Part "the relevant applicant authority" means—

(a) in relation to a serious crime prevention order in England and Wales—

(i) where the order was applied for by the Director of Public Prosecutions, the Director of Public Prosecutions;

(ii) where the order was applied for by the Director of Revenue and Customs Prosecutions, the Director of Revenue and Customs Prosecutions; and

(iii) where the order was applied for by the Director of the Serious Fraud Office, the Director of the Serious Fraud Office; and

(b) in relation to a serious crime prevention order in Northern Ireland, the Director of Public Prosecutions for Northern Ireland.

Serious Crime Act 2007, ss.11–15

Information safeguards

Restrictions on oral answers

5–874e **11.** A serious crime prevention order may not require a person to answer questions, or provide information, orally.

Restrictions for legal professional privilege

5–874f **12.**—(1) A serious crime prevention order may not require a person—

(a) to answer any privileged question;

(b) to provide any privileged information; or

(c) to produce any privileged document.

(2) A "privileged question" is a question which the person would be entitled to refuse to answer on grounds of legal professional privilege in proceedings in the High Court.

(3) "Privileged information" is information which the person would be entitled to refuse to provide on grounds of legal professional privilege in such proceedings.

(4) A "privileged document" is a document which the person would be entitled to refuse to produce on grounds of legal professional privilege in such proceedings.

(5) But subsection (1) does not prevent an order from requiring a lawyer to provide the name and address of a client of his.

Restrictions on excluded material and banking information

5–874g **13.**—(1) A serious crime prevention order may not require a person to produce—

(a) in the case of an order in England and Wales, any excluded material as defined by section 11 of the *Police and Criminal Evidence Act* 1984; and

(b) [*Northern Ireland*].

(2) A serious crime prevention order may not require a person to disclose any information or produce any document in respect of which he owes an obligation of confidence by virtue of carrying on a banking business unless condition A or B is met.

(3) Condition A is that the person to whom the obligation of confidence is owed consents to the disclosure or production.

(4) Condition B is that the order contains a requirement—

(a) to disclose information, or produce documents, of this kind; or

(b) to disclose specified information which is of this kind or to produce specified documents which are of this kind.

Restrictions relating to other enactments

5–874h **14.**—(1) A serious crime prevention order may not require a person—

(a) to answer any question;

(b) to provide any information; or

(c) to produce any document;

if the disclosure concerned is prohibited under any other enactment.

(2) In this section—

"enactment" includes an Act of the Scottish Parliament, Northern Ireland legislation and an enactment comprised in subordinate legislation, and includes an enactment whenever passed or made; and

"subordinate legislation" has the same meaning as in the *Interpretation Act* 1978 and also includes an instrument made under—

(a) an Act of the Scottish Parliament; or
(b) Northern Ireland legislation.

Restrictions on use of information obtained

15.—(1) A statement made by a person in response to a requirement imposed by a serious crime prevention order may not be used in evidence against him in any criminal proceedings unless condition A or B is met. **5–874i**

(2) Condition A is that the criminal proceedings relate to an offence under section 25.

(3) Condition B is that—

(a) the criminal proceedings relate to another offence;
(b) the person who made the statement gives evidence in the criminal proceedings;
(c) in the course of that evidence, the person makes a statement which is inconsistent with the statement made in response to the requirement imposed by the order; and
(d) in the criminal proceedings evidence relating to the statement made in response to the requirement imposed by the order is adduced, or a question about it is asked, by the person or on his behalf.

Serious Crime Act 2007, ss.16–18

Duration, variation and discharge of orders

Duration of orders

16.—(1) A serious crime prevention order must specify when it is to come into force and when it is to cease to be in force. **5–875**

(2) An order is not to be in force for more than 5 years beginning with the coming into force of the order.

(3) An order can specify different times for the coming into force, or ceasing to be in force, of different provisions of the order.

(4) Where it specifies different times in accordance with subsection (3), the order—

(a) must specify when each provision is to come into force and cease to be in force; and
(b) is not to be in force for more than 5 years beginning with the coming into force of the first provision of the order to come into force.

(5) The fact that an order, or any provision of an order, ceases to be in force does not prevent the court from making a new order to the same or similar effect.

(6) A new order may be made in anticipation of an earlier order or provision ceasing to be in force.

17. [*Application to High Court for variation of order.*] **5–875a**

18. [*Application to High Court for discharge of order.*] **5–875b**

Serious Crime Act 2007, ss.19–22

Extension of jurisdiction to Crown Court

Orders by Crown Court on conviction

19.—(1) Subsection (2) applies where the Crown Court in England and Wales is dealing with a person who— **5–875c**

(a) has been convicted by or before a magistrates' court of having committed a serious offence in England and Wales and has been committed to the Crown Court to be dealt with; or
(b) has been convicted by or before the Crown Court of having committed a serious offence in England and Wales.

(2) The Crown Court may, in addition to dealing with the person in relation to the offence, make an order if it has reasonable grounds to believe that the order would protect the public by preventing, restricting or disrupting involvement by the person in serious crime in England and Wales.

(3), (4) [*Northern Ireland.*]

(5) An order under this section may contain—

(a) such prohibitions, restrictions or requirements; and
(b) such other terms;

as the court considers appropriate for the purpose of protecting the public by preventing, restricting or disrupting involvement by the person concerned in serious crime in England and Wales or (as the case may be) Northern Ireland.

(6) The powers of the court in respect of an order under this section are subject to sections 6 to 15 (safeguards).

(7) An order must not be made under this section except—

(a) in addition to a sentence imposed in respect of the offence concerned; or

(b) in addition to an order discharging the person conditionally.

(8) An order under this section is also called a serious crime prevention order.

Powers of Crown Court to vary orders on conviction

5–875d **20.**—(1) Subsection (2) applies where the Crown Court in England and Wales is dealing with a person who—

(a) has been convicted by or before a magistrates' court of having committed a serious offence in England and Wales and has been committed to the Crown Court to be dealt with; or

(b) has been convicted by or before the Crown Court of having committed a serious offence in England and Wales.

(2) The Crown Court may—

(a) in the case of a person who is the subject of a serious crime prevention order in England and Wales; and

(b) in addition to dealing with the person in relation to the offence;

vary the order if the court has reasonable grounds to believe that the terms of the order as varied would protect the public by preventing, restricting or disrupting involvement by the person in serious crime in England and Wales.

(3), (4) [*Northern Ireland.*]

(5) A variation under this section may be made only on an application by the relevant applicant authority.

(6) A variation must not be made except—

(a) in addition to a sentence imposed in respect of the offence concerned; or

(b) in addition to an order discharging the person conditionally.

(7) A variation may include an extension of the period during which the order, or any provision of it, is in force (subject to the original limits imposed on the order by section 16(2) and (4)(b)).

Powers of Crown Court to vary orders on breach

5–875e **21.**—(1) Subsection (2) applies where the Crown Court in England and Wales is dealing with a person who—

(a) has been convicted by or before a magistrates' court of having committed an offence under section 25 in relation to a serious crime prevention order and has been committed to the Crown Court to be dealt with; or

(b) has been convicted by or before the Crown Court of having committed an offence under section 25 in relation to a serious crime prevention order.

(2) The Crown Court may—

(a) in the case of an order in England and Wales; and

(b) in addition to dealing with the person in relation to the offence;

vary the order if it has reasonable grounds to believe that the terms of the order as varied would protect the public by preventing, restricting or disrupting involvement by the person in serious crime in England and Wales.

(3), (4) [*Northern Ireland.*]

(5)–(7) [*Identical to s.20(5)-(7)*, ante, *§ 5–879a.*]

Inter-relationship between different types of orders

5–875f **22.**—(1) The fact that a serious crime prevention order has been made or varied by the High Court does not prevent it from being varied by the Crown Court in accordance with this Part.

(2) The fact that a serious crime prevention order has been made or varied by the Crown Court does not prevent it from being varied or discharged by the High Court in accordance with this Part.

(3) A decision by the Crown Court not to make an order under section 19 does not prevent a subsequent application to the High Court for an order under section 1 in consequence of the same offence.

(4) A decision by the Crown Court not to vary a serious crime prevention order under section 20 or 21 does not prevent a subsequent application to the High Court for a variation of the order in consequence of the same offence.

Serious Crime Act 2007, ss.23, 24

Appeals

23. [*Additional right of appeal from High Court.*] **5–875g**

Appeals from Crown Court

24.—(1) An appeal against a decision of the Crown Court in relation to a serious crime prevention order may be made to the Court of Appeal by— **5–875h**

(a) the person who is the subject of the order; or

(b) the relevant applicant authority.

(2) In addition, an appeal may be made to the Court of Appeal in relation to a decision of the Crown Court—

(a) to make a serious crime prevention order; or

(b) to vary, or not to vary, such an order;

by any person who was given an opportunity to make representations in the proceedings concerned by virtue of section 9(4).

(3) Subject to subsection (4), an appeal under subsection (1) or (2) lies only with the leave of the Court of Appeal.

(4) An appeal under subsection (1) or (2) lies without the leave of the Court of Appeal if the judge who made the decision grants a certificate that the decision is fit for appeal under this section.

(5) Subject to any rules of court made under section 53(1) of the *Senior Courts Act* 1981 (distribution of business between civil and criminal divisions), the criminal division of the Court of Appeal is the division which is to exercise jurisdiction in relation to an appeal under subsection (1) or (2) from a decision of the Crown Court in the exercise of its jurisdiction in England and Wales under this Part.

(6) An appeal against a decision of the Court of Appeal on an appeal to that court under subsection (1) or (2) may be made to the Supreme Court by any person who was a party to the proceedings before the Court of Appeal.

(7) An appeal under subsection (6) lies only with the leave of the Court of Appeal or the Supreme Court.

(8) Such leave must not be granted unless—

(a) it is certified by the Court of Appeal that a point of law of general public importance is involved in the decision; and

(b) it appears to the Court of Appeal or (as the case may be) the Supreme Court that the point is one which ought to be considered by the Supreme Court.

(9) The Secretary of State may for the purposes of this section by order make provision corresponding (subject to any specified modifications) to that made by or under an enactment and relating to—

(a) appeals to the Court of Appeal under Part 1 of—

(i) the *Criminal Appeal Act* 1968; or

(ii) the *Criminal Appeal (Northern Ireland) Act* 1980;

(b) appeals from any decision of the Court of Appeal on appeals falling within paragraph (a); or

(c) any matter connected with or arising out of appeals falling within paragraph (a) or (b).

(10) An order under subsection (9) may, in particular, make provision about the payment of costs.

(11) The power to make an appeal to the Court of Appeal under subsection (1)(a) operates instead of any power for the person who is the subject of the order to make an appeal against a decision of the Crown Court in relation to a serious crime prevention order by virtue of—

(a) section 9 or 10 of the *Criminal Appeal Act* 1968; or

(b) section 8 of the *Criminal Appeal (Northern Ireland) Act* 1980.

(12) Section 33(3) of the *Criminal Appeal Act* 1968 (limitation on appeal from criminal division of the Court of Appeal: England and Wales) does not prevent an appeal to the Supreme Court under subsection (6) above.

For the current order under subsections (9) and (10), see *post*, §§ 7–312d *et seq.*

Serious Crime Act 2007, ss.25–29

Enforcement

Offence of failing to comply with order

25.—(1) A person who, without reasonable excuse, fails to comply with a serious crime prevention order commits an offence. **5–876**

(2) A person who commits an offence under this section is liable—

(a) on summary conviction, to imprisonment for a term not exceeding 12 months or to a fine not exceeding the statutory maximum or to both;

(b) on conviction on indictment, to imprisonment for a term not exceeding 5 years or to a fine or to both.

(3) [*Northern Ireland.*]

(4) In proceedings for an offence under this section, a copy of the original order or any variation of it, certified as such by the proper officer of the court which made it, is admissible as evidence of its having been made and of its contents to the same extent that oral evidence of those things is admissible in those proceedings.

Powers of forfeiture in respect of offence

5–876a **26.**—(1) The court before which a person is convicted of an offence under section 25 may order the forfeiture of anything in his possession at the time of the offence which the court considers to have been involved in the offence.

(2) Before making an order under subsection (1) in relation to anything the court must give an opportunity to make representations to any person (in addition to the convicted person) who claims to be the owner of that thing or otherwise to have an interest in it.

(3) An order under subsection (1) may not be made so as to come into force at any time before there is no further possibility (ignoring any power to appeal out of time) of the order being varied or set aside on appeal.

(4) Where the court makes an order under subsection (1), it may also make such other provision as it considers to be necessary for giving effect to the forfeiture.

(5) That provision may, in particular, include provision relating to the retention, handling, destruction or other disposal of what is forfeited.

(6) Provision made by virtue of this section may be varied at any time by the court that made it.

5–876b **27.-29.** [*Powers to wind up companies etc.*]

Serious Crime Act 2007, ss.30–34

Particular types of persons

Bodies corporate including limited liability partnerships

5–876c **30.**—(1) For the purposes of section 10 in its application to a serious crime prevention order against a body corporate or to the variation of such an order—

(a) a notice setting out the terms of the order or variation—

(i) is delivered to the body corporate in person if it is delivered to an officer of the body corporate in person; and

(ii) is sent by recorded delivery to the body corporate at its last known address if it is so sent to an officer of the body corporate at the address of the registered office of that body or at the address of its principal office in the United Kingdom; and

(b) the power conferred by subsection (3) of that section is a power to enter any premises where the person exercising the power has reasonable grounds for believing an officer of the body corporate to be and to search those premises for the officer.

(2) If an offence under section 25 committed by a body corporate is proved to have been committed with the consent or connivance of—

(a) an officer of the body corporate; or

(b) a person who was purporting to act in any such capacity;

he (as well as the body corporate) is guilty of the offence and liable to be proceeded against and punished accordingly.

(3) Nothing in this section prevents a serious crime prevention order from being made against an officer or employee of a body corporate or against any other person associated with a body corporate.

(4) In this section—

"body corporate" includes a limited liability partnership;

"director", in relation to a body corporate whose affairs are managed by its members, means a member of the body corporate; and

"officer of a body corporate" means any director, manager, secretary or other similar officer of the body corporate.

Other partnerships

31.—(1) A serious crime prevention order against a partnership must be made in the name of the partnership (and not in that of any of the partners). **5–876d**

(2) An order made in the name of the partnership continues to have effect despite a change of partners provided that at least one of the persons who was a partner before the change remains a partner after it.

(3) For the purposes of this Part, a partnership is involved in serious crime in England and Wales, Northern Ireland or elsewhere if the partnership, or any of the partners, is so involved; and involvement in serious crime in England and Wales or Northern Ireland is to be read accordingly.

(4) For the purposes of section 10 in its application to a serious crime prevention order against a partnership or to the variation of such an order—

(a) a notice setting out the terms of the order or variation—

(i) is delivered to the partnership in person if it is delivered to any of the partners in person or to a senior officer of the partnership in person; and

(ii) is sent by recorded delivery to the partnership at its last-known address if it is so sent to any of the partners or to a senior officer of the partnership at the address of the principal office of the partnership in the United Kingdom; and

(b) the power conferred by subsection (3) of that section is a power to enter any premises where the person exercising the power has reasonable grounds for believing a partner or senior officer of the partnership to be and to search those premises for the partner or senior officer.

(5) Proceedings for an offence under section 25 alleged to have been committed by a partnership must be brought in the name of the partnership (and not in that of any of the partners).

(6) For the purposes of such proceedings—

(a) rules of court relating to the service of documents have effect as if the partnership were a body corporate; and

(b) the following provisions apply as they apply in relation to a body corporate—

(i) section 33 of the *Criminal Justice Act* 1925 and Schedule 3 to the *Magistrates' Courts Act* 1980;

(ii), (iii) [*Scotland and Northern Ireland*].

(7) A fine imposed on the partnership on its conviction for an offence under section 25 is to be paid out of the partnership assets.

(8) If an offence under section 25 committed by a partnership is proved to have been committed with the consent or connivance of a partner or a senior officer of the partnership, he (as well as the partnership) is guilty of the offence and liable to be proceeded against and punished accordingly.

(9) For the purposes of subsection (8)—

(a) references to a partner or to a senior officer of a partnership include references to any person purporting to act in such a capacity; and

(b) subsection (5) is not to be read as prejudicing any liability of a partner under subsection (8).

(10) Nothing in this section prevents a serious crime prevention order from being made against—

(a) a particular partner; or

(b) a senior officer or employee of a partnership or any other person associated with a partnership.

(11) In this section—

"senior officer of a partnership" means any person who has the control or management of the business carried on by the partnership at the principal place where it is carried on; and

"partnership" does not include a limited liability partnership.

Unincorporated associations

32.—(1) A serious crime prevention order against an unincorporated association must be made in the name of the association (and not in that of any of its members). **5–876e**

(2) An order made in the name of the association continues to have effect despite a change in the membership of the association provided that at least one of the persons who was a member of the association before the change remains a member after it.

(3) For the purposes of section 10 in its application to a serious crime prevention order against an unincorporated association or to the variation of such an order—

(a) a notice setting out the terms of the order or variation—

(i) is delivered to the association in person if it is delivered to an officer of the association in person; and

(ii) is sent by recorded delivery to the association at its last-known address if it is so sent to an officer of the association at the address of the principal office of the association in the United Kingdom; and

(b) the power conferred by subsection (3) of that section is a power to enter any premises where the person exercising the power has reasonable grounds for believing an officer of the association to be and to search those premises for the officer.

(4) Proceedings for an offence under section 25 alleged to have been committed by an unincorporated association must be brought in the name of the association (and not in that of any of its members).

(5) For the purposes of such proceedings—

(a) rules of court relating to the service of documents have effect as if the association were a body corporate; and

(b) [*identical to s.31(6)(b)*, ante, *§ 5–880h*].

(6) A fine imposed on the association on its conviction for an offence under section 25 is to be paid out of the funds of the association.

(7) If an offence under section 25 committed by an unincorporated association is proved to have been committed with the consent or connivance of an officer of the association, he (as well as the association) is guilty of the offence and liable to be proceeded against and punished accordingly.

(8) For the purposes of subsection (7)—

(a) references to an officer of an unincorporated association include references to any person purporting to act in such a capacity; and

(b) subsection (4) is not to be read as prejudicing any liability of an officer of an unincorporated association under subsection (7).

(9) Nothing in this section prevents a serious crime prevention order from being made against—

(a) a member, officer or employee of an unincorporated association; or

(b) any other person associated with an unincorporated association.

(10) In this section—

"officer of an unincorporated association" means any officer of an unincorporated association or any member of its governing body; and

"unincorporated association" means any body of persons unincorporate but does not include a partnership.

Overseas bodies

5–876f **33.** The Secretary of State may by order modify section 30, 31 or 32 in its application to a body of persons formed under law having effect outside the United Kingdom.

Providers of information society services

5–876g **34.**—(1) A serious crime prevention order may not include terms which restrict the freedom of a service provider who is established in an EEA state other than the United Kingdom to provide information society services in relation to an EEA state unless the conditions in subsections (2) and (3) are met.

(2) The condition in this subsection is that the court concerned considers that the terms—

(a) are necessary for the objective of protecting the public by preventing, restricting or disrupting involvement in—

(i) in the case of an order in England and Wales, serious crime in England and Wales; and

(ii) in the case of an order in Northern Ireland, serious crime in Northern Ireland;

(b) relate to an information society service which prejudices that objective or presents a serious and grave risk of prejudice to it; and

(c) are proportionate to that objective.

(3) The conditions in this subsection are that—

(a) a law enforcement officer has requested the EEA state in which the service provider is established to take measures which the law enforcement officer considers to be of equivalent effect under the law of the EEA state to the terms and the EEA state has failed to take the measures; and

(b) a law enforcement officer has notified the Commission of the European Communities and the EEA state of—

(i) the intention to seek an order containing the terms; and

(ii) the terms.

(4) It does not matter for the purposes of subsection (3) whether the request or notification is made before or after the making of the application for the order.

(5) A serious crime prevention order may not include terms which impose liabilities on service providers of intermediary services so far as the imposition of those liabilities would result in a contravention of Article 12, 13 or 14 of the E-Commerce Directive (various protections for service providers of intermediary services).

(6) A serious crime prevention order may not include terms which impose a general obligation on service providers of intermediary services covered by Articles 12, 13 and 14 of the E-Commerce Directive—

(a) to monitor the information which they transmit or store when providing those services; or

(b) actively to seek facts or circumstances indicating illegal activity when providing those services.

(7) For the purposes of this section—

(a) a service provider is established in a particular EEA state if he effectively pursues an economic activity using a fixed establishment in that EEA state for an indefinite period and he is a national of an EEA state or a company or firm mentioned in Article 48 of the EEC Treaty;

(b) the presence or use in a particular place of equipment or other technical means of providing an information society service does not, of itself, constitute the establishment of a service provider;

(c) where it cannot be determined from which of a number of establishments a given information society service is provided, that service is to be regarded as provided from the establishment where the service provider has the centre of his activities relating to the service;

and references to a person being established in an EEA state are to be read accordingly.

(8) In this section—

"the E-Commerce Directive" means Directive 2000/31/EC of the European Parliament and of the Council of 8 June 2000 on certain legal aspects of information society services, in particular electronic commerce, in the Internal Market (Directive on electronic commerce);

"information society services" —

(a) has the meaning given in Article 2(a) of the E-Commerce Directive (which refers to Article 1(2) of Directive 98/34/EC of the European Parliament and of the Council of 22 June 1998 laying down a procedure for the provision of information in the field of technical standards and regulations); and

(b) is summarised in recital 17 of the E-Commerce Directive as covering "any service normally provided for remuneration, at a distance, by means of electronic equipment for the processing (including digital compression) and storage of data, and at the individual request of a recipient of a service";

"intermediary services" means an information society service which—

(a) consists in the provision of access to a communication network or the transmission in a communication network of information provided by a recipient of the service;

(b) consists in the transmission in a communication network of information which—

(i) is provided by a recipient of the service; and

(ii) is the subject of automatic, intermediate and temporary storage which is solely for the purpose of making the onward transmission of the information to other recipients of the service at their request more efficient; or

(c) consists in the storage of information provided by a recipient of the service;

"recipient", in relation to a service, means any person who, for professional ends or otherwise, uses an information society service, in particular for the purposes of seeking information or making it accessible; and

"service provider" means a person providing an information society service.

(9) For the purposes of paragraph (a) of the definition of "intermediary services", the provision of access to a communication network and the transmission of information in a communication network includes the automatic, intermediate and transient storage of the information transmitted so far as the storage is for the sole purpose of carrying out the transmission in the network.

(10) Subsection (9) does not apply if the information is stored for longer than is reasonably necessary for the transmission.

Serious Crime Act 2007, ss.35–41

Supplementary

5–877 **35.** [*High Court proceedings are civil.*]

Proceedings in the Crown Court

5–877a **36.**—(1) Proceedings before the Crown Court arising by virtue of section 19, 20 or 21 are civil proceedings.

(2) One consequence of this is that the standard of proof to be applied by the court in such proceedings is the civil standard of proof.

(3) Two other consequences of this are that the court—

(a) is not restricted to considering evidence that would have been admissible in the criminal proceedings in which the person concerned was convicted; and

(b) may adjourn any proceedings in relation to a serious crime prevention order even after sentencing the person concerned.

(4) The Crown Court, when exercising its jurisdiction in England and Wales under this Part, is a criminal court for the purposes of Part 7 of the *Courts Act* 2003 (procedure rules and practice directions).

(5) A serious crime prevention order may be made as mentioned in section 19(7)(b) in spite of anything in sections 12 and 14 of the *Powers of Criminal Courts (Sentencing) Act* 2000 or (as the case may be) Articles 4 and 6 of the *Criminal Justice (Northern Ireland) Order* 1996 (S.I. 1996/3160 (N.I. 24)) (which relate to orders discharging a person absolutely or conditionally and their effect).

(6) A variation of a serious crime prevention order may be made as mentioned in section 20(6)(b) or 21(6)(b) in spite of anything in sections 12 and 14 of the Act of 2000 or (as the case may be) Articles 4 and 6 of the Order of 1996.

Functions of applicant authorities

5–877b **37.** Schedule 2 (functions of applicant authorities under this Part) has effect.

Disclosure of information in accordance with orders

5–877c **38.**—(1) A person who complies with a requirement imposed by a serious crime prevention order to answer questions, provide information or produce documents does not breach—

(a) any obligation of confidence; or

(b) any other restriction on making the disclosure concerned (however imposed).

(2) But see sections 11 to 14 (which limit the requirements that may be imposed by serious crime prevention orders in connection with answering questions, providing information or producing documents).

Compliance with orders: authorised monitors

5–877d **39.**—(1) A serious crime prevention order against a body corporate, partnership or unincorporated association may authorise a law enforcement agency to enter into arrangements with—

(a) a specified person; or

(b) any person who falls within a specified description of persons;

to perform specified monitoring services or monitoring services of a specified description.

(2) A person with whom the agency has entered into arrangements in accordance with such an authorisation is known for the purposes of this section as an authorised monitor.

(3) A serious crime prevention order which provides for an authorised monitor may, for the purpose of enabling the performance of monitoring services, impose requirements

of the type mentioned in section 5(5) as if the references in paragraph (a)(iv) and (b)(iv) of that provision to a law enforcement officer included references to an authorised monitor.

(4) A serious crime prevention order which provides for an authorised monitor may require any body corporate, partnership or unincorporated association which is the subject of the order to pay to the law enforcement agency concerned some or all of the costs incurred by the agency under the arrangements with the authorised monitor.

(5) Any such order—

(a) must specify the period, or periods, within which payments are to be made;

(b) may require the making of payments on account;

(c) may include other terms about the calculation or payment of costs.

(6) The tests for making or varying a serious crime prevention order in sections 1(1)(b), (2)(b) and (3), 17(1) and (2), 19(2), (4) and (5), 20(2) and (4) and 21(2) and (4) do not operate in relation to an order so far as the order contains terms of the kind envisaged by subsections (4) and (5) above (or by subsection (1) above for the purposes of those subsections).

(7) But a court must not include in a serious crime prevention order (whether initially or on a variation) terms of the kind envisaged by subsection (4) or (5) unless it considers that it is appropriate to do so having regard to all the circumstances including, in particular—

(a) the means of the body corporate, partnership or unincorporated association concerned;

(b) the expected size of the costs; and

(c) the effect of the terms on the ability of any body corporate, partnership or unincorporated association which is carrying on business to continue to do so.

(8) A law enforcement agency must inform the subject of a serious crime prevention order which provides for an authorised monitor of the name of, and an address for, any person with whom the agency has entered into arrangements in accordance with the authorisation in the order.

(9) Nothing in this section affects the ability of law enforcement agencies to enter into arrangements otherwise than in accordance with an authorisation under this section.

(10) In this section—

"law enforcement agency" means —

(a) a police authority or the Northern Ireland Policing Board;

(b) the Serious Organised Crime Agency;

(c) the Commissioners for Her Majesty's Revenue and Customs; or

(d) the Director of the Serious Fraud Office;

"monitoring services" means —

(a) analysing some or all information received in accordance with a serious crime prevention order;

(b) reporting to a law enforcement officer as to whether, on the basis of the information and any other information analysed for this purpose, the subject of the order appears to be complying with the order or any part of it; and

(c) any related services; and

"specified", in relation to a serious crime prevention order, means specified in the order.

Costs in relation to authorised monitors

40.—(1) The Secretary of State may by order make provision about the practice and procedure for determining the amount of— **5–877e**

(a) any costs payable by virtue of section 39(4) and (5); and

(b) any interest payable in respect of those costs.

(2) Such provision may, in particular, include provision about appeals.

(3) Where any amounts required to be paid by virtue of section 39(4) and (5) have not been paid within a required period, the law enforcement agency concerned must take reasonable steps to recover them and any interest payable in respect of them.

(4) The Secretary of State must by order provide for what are reasonable steps for the purposes of subsection (3).

(5) Any amounts which have not been recovered despite the taking of the reasonable steps are recoverable as if due to the law enforcement agency concerned by virtue of a civil order or judgment.

(6) Where any amounts required to be paid by virtue of section 39(4) and (5) are, in the

case of an order of the Crown Court, not paid within a required period, the unpaid balance from time to time carries interest at the rate for the time being specified in section 17 of the *Judgments Act* 1838 (interest on civil judgment debts).

(7) For the purposes of section 25, a failure to comply with a requirement imposed by virtue of section 39(4) and (5) to make payments occurs when the amounts become recoverable as mentioned in subsection (5) above (and not before).

(8) In this section "law enforcement agency" has the same meaning as in section 39.

Powers of law enforcement officers to retain documents

5-877f **41.**—(1) A law enforcement officer—

(a) may take and retain copies of, or extracts from, any document produced to a law enforcement officer in pursuance of a serious crime prevention order; and

(b) may retain any document so produced for as long as he considers that it is necessary to retain it (rather than any copy of it) for the purposes for which the document was obtained.

(2) A law enforcement officer may retain any document produced to a law enforcement officer in pursuance of a serious crime prevention order until the conclusion of any legal proceedings if he has reasonable grounds for believing that the document—

(a) may have to be produced for the purposes of those proceedings; and

(b) might be unavailable unless retained.

Serious Crime Act 2007, ss.42, 43

Interpretation: Part 1

Interpretation: Part 1

5-877g **42.** In this Part—

"act" and "conduct" include omissions and statements;

"country" includes territory;

"modifications" includes additions and omissions (and "modify" is to be read accordingly);

"the public" includes a section of the public or a particular member of the public.

Index of defined expressions: Part 1

5-877h **43.** In this Part, the expressions listed in the left-hand column have the meaning given by, or are to be interpreted in accordance with, the provisions listed in the right-hand column.

Expression	*Provision*
act	section 42
committed a serious offence	section 4(1)
conduct	section 42
conducts oneself in a way likely to facilitate the commission by oneself or another person of a serious offence	section 4(3)
country	section 42
Director of Public Prosecutions, Director of Revenue and Customs Prosecutions, Director of the Serious Fraud Office and Director of Public Prosecutions for Northern Ireland	Paragraphs 2(2), 7(2), 13(2) and 17 of Schedule 2
document	section 5(7)
facilitates the commission by another person of a serious offence	section 4(2)
involvement in serious crime: England and Wales orders	sections 2, 4 and 31(3)
involvement in serious crime: Northern Ireland orders	sections 3, 4 and 31(3)
law enforcement officer	section 5(7)
modifications (and modify)	section 42
person who is the subject of a serious crime prevention order	section 1(6)
premises	section 5(7)
production of documents	section 5(8)
the public	section 42

Expression	*Provision*
relevant applicant authority	section 10(4)
serious crime prevention order	section 1(5)
serious offence in England and Wales	section 2(2)
serious offence in Northern Ireland	section 3(2)

Serious offences

Part 1 of Schedule 1 to the 2007 Act lists serious offences in England and Wales in 16 paragraphs. **5–878**

(i) *Drug trafficking*: an offence under the *Misuse of Drugs Act* 1971, s.4(2) or (3), 5(3), 8 or 20; under the *CEMA* 1979, s.50(2), 68(2) or 170, if it is committed in connection with a prohibition or restriction on importation which has effect by virtue of the 1971 Act, s.3; or under the *Criminal Justice (International Co-operation) Act* 1990, s.12 or 19.

(ii) *People trafficking*: an offence under the *Immigration Act* 1971, s.25, 25A or 25B; under the *SOA* 2003, s.57, 58 or 59; or under the *Asylum and Immigration (Treatment of Claimants, etc.) Act* 2004, s.4.

(iii) *Arms trafficking*: an offence under the *CEMA* 1979, s.68(2) or 170(2), if it is committed in connection with a firearm or ammunition; or under the *Firearms Act* 1968, s.3(1) ("firearm" and "ammunition" having the same meanings in this paragraph as in the 1968 Act, s.57).

(iv) *Prostitution and child sex*: an offence under the *SOA* 1956, s.33; or under the *SOA* 2003, s.14, 48, 49, 50, 52 or 53.

(v) *Armed robbery, etc.*: an offence of assault with intent to rob or under the *Theft Act* 1968, s.8(1), where the assault or, as the case may be, the use or threat of force involves a firearm, an imitation firearm or an offensive weapon ("firearm" and "imitation firearm" having the same meanings as in the 1968 Act, s.57(1) and (4), and "offensive weapon" meaning any weapon to which the *CJA* 1988, s.141, applies).

(vi) *Money laundering*: an offence under the *PCA* 2002, s.327, 328 or 329.

(vii) *Fraud*: an offence of conspiracy to defraud; an offence under the *Theft Act* 1968, s.17; or an offence under the *Fraud Act* 2006, s.1, 6, 7, 9 or 11.

(viii) *Offences in relation to public revenue*: an offence under the *CEMA* 1979, s.170 (so far as not falling within (i) or (iii) *ante*); under the *Value Added Tax Act* 1994, s.72; under the *Finance Act* 2000, s.144; under the *Tax Credits Act* 2002, s.35; or an offence of cheating the public revenue.

(ix) *Corruption and bribery*: an offence under the *Public Bodies Corrupt Practices Act* 1889, s.1; an offence which is the first or second offence under the *Prevention of Corruption Act* 1906, s.1(1); or an offence of bribery at common law.

(x) *Counterfeiting*: an offence under the *Forgery and Counterfeiting Act* 1981, s.14, 15, 16 or 17.

(xi) *Blackmail*: an offence under the *Theft Act* 1968, s.21; or under the *Gangmasters (Licensing) Act* 2004, s.12(1) or (2).

(xii) *Intellectual property*: an offence under the *Copyright, Designs and Patents Act* 1988, s.107(1)(a), (b), (d)(iv) or (e), 198(1)(a), (b) or (d)(iii) or 297A; or under the *Trade Marks Act* 1994, s.92(1), (2) or (3).

(xiii) *Environment*: an offence under the *Salmon and Freshwater Fisheries Act* 1975, s.1; under the *Wildlife and Countryside Act* 1981, s.14; under the *Environmental Protection Act* 1990, s.33; or under the *Control of Trade in Endangered Species (Enforcement) Regulations* 1997 (S.I. 1997/1372), reg. 8.

(xiv) *Inchoate offences*: an offence of attempting or conspiring to commit an offence specified or described in this part of this schedule; an offence under Part 2 of this Act (as to which, see *post*, §§ 33–92 *et seq.*) where the offence (or one of the offences) which the person in question intends or believes would be committed is an offence specified or described in this part of this schedule; an offence of aiding, abetting, counselling or procuring the commission of an offence specified or described in this part of this schedule (but the references to offences specified or described in this part of this schedule do not include the offence at common law of conspiracy to defraud).

(xv) *Earlier offences*: this part of this schedule (apart from the reference to offences under Pt 2 of this Act) has effect, in its application to conduct before the passing of this Act, as if the offences specified or described in this part included any corresponding offences under the law in force at the time of the conduct; and paragraph 14(2) (the reference to offences under Pt 2 of this Act) has effect, in its application to conduct before the passing of this Act or before the coming into force of section 59 of this Act (abolition of common law replaced by Pt 2), as if the offence specified or described in that provision were an offence of inciting the commission of an offence specified or described in this part of this schedule.

(xvi) *Scope of offences*: where this part of this schedule refers to offences which are offences under the law of England and Wales and another country, the reference is to be read as limited to the offences so far as they are offences under the law of England and Wales.

Serious Crime Act 2007, Sched. 2

Section 37

SCHEDULE 2

FUNCTIONS OF APPLICANT AUTHORITIES UNDER PART 1

Director of Public Prosecutions

5–879 1. The functions of the Director of Public Prosecutions under this Part are—

(a) to have the conduct of applications for serious crime prevention orders in England and Wales or for their variation or discharge;

(b) to appear on any application made under section 17 or 18 by another person for the variation or discharge of a serious crime prevention order in England and Wales;

(c) to have the conduct of, or (as the case may be) appear in, any other proceedings in connection with serious crime prevention orders (whether proceedings on appeal, by virtue of section 27 or otherwise);

(d) to give advice in connection with any proceedings or possible proceedings in connection with serious crime prevention orders; and

(e) to do anything for the purposes of, or in connection with, the functions in paragraphs (a) to (d).

2.—(1) The Director may, to such extent as he may decide, delegate the exercise of his functions under this Part to a Crown Prosecutor.

(2) References in this Part to the Director are accordingly to be read, so far as necessary for the purposes of sub-paragraph (1), as references to the Director or any Crown Prosecutor.

3. The functions of the Director under this Part are exercisable under the superintendence of the Attorney General.

4.—(1) The Code for Crown Prosecutors issued under section 10 of the *Prosecution of Offences Act* 1985 (guidelines for Crown Prosecutors) may include guidance by the Director on general principles to be applied by Crown Prosecutors in determining in any case—

(a) whether to make an application for a serious crime prevention order in England and Wales or for the variation or discharge of such an order;

(b) whether to present a petition by virtue of section 27 of this Act; or

(c) where such an application has been made or petition presented, whether the proceedings concerned should be discontinued.

(2) Section 10(2) and (3) of that Act (power to make alterations in the Code and duty to set out alterations in Director's report) are to be read accordingly.

5. Section 14 of that Act (power of Attorney General to make regulations about fees of legal representatives and costs and expenses of witnesses) applies in relation to proceedings in connection with serious crime prevention orders and attendance for the purposes of such cases as it applies in relation to criminal proceedings and attendance for the purposes of such cases.

5–879a 6–11. [*Director of Revenue and Customs Prosecutions.*]

5–879b 12–15. [*Director of Serious Fraud Office.*]

5–879c 16–20. [*Director of Public Prosecutions for Northern Ireland.*]

Interpretation

21. In this Schedule references to having the conduct of proceedings include references to starting or discontinuing proceedings. **5–879d**

J. ANTI-SOCIAL BEHAVIOUR ORDERS

Crime and Disorder Act 1998, s.1C

Orders on conviction in criminal proceedings

1C.—(1) This section applies where a person (the "offender") is convicted of a relevant offence. **5–880**

(2) If the court considers—

(a) that the offender has acted, at any time since the commencement date, in an anti-social manner, that is to say in a manner that caused or was likely to cause harassment, alarm or distress to one or more persons not of the same household as himself, and

(b) that an order under this section is necessary to protect persons in any place in England and Wales from further anti-social acts by him,

it may make an order which prohibits the offender from doing anything described in the order.

(3) The court may make an order under this section—

(a) if the prosecutor asks it to do so, or

(b) if the court thinks it is appropriate to do so.

(3A) For the purpose of deciding whether to make an order under this section the court may consider evidence led by the prosecution and the defence.

(3B) It is immaterial whether evidence led in pursuance of subsection (3A) would have been admissible in the proceedings in which the offender was convicted.

(4) An order under this section shall not be made except—

(a) in addition to a sentence imposed in respect of the relevant offence; or

(b) in addition to an order discharging him conditionally.

(4A) The court may adjourn any proceedings in relation to an order under this section even after sentencing the offender.

(4B) If the offender does not appear for any adjourned proceedings, the court may further adjourn the proceedings or may issue a warrant for his arrest.

(4C) But the court may not issue a warrant for the offender's arrest unless it is satisfied that he has had adequate notice of the time and place of the adjourned proceedings.

(5) An order under this section takes effect on the day on which it is made, but the court may provide in any such order that such requirements of the order as it may specify shall, during any period when the offender is detained in legal custody, be suspended until his release from that custody.

(9) Subsections (7), (10), (10C), (10D), (10E) and (11) of section 1 apply for the purposes of the making and effect of orders made by virtue of this section as they apply for the purposes of the making and effect of anti-social behaviour orders.

[(9ZA) An order under this section made in respect of a person under the age of 17, or an order varying such an order, may specify a relevant authority (other than the chief officer of police mentioned in section 1K(2)(a)) as being responsible for carrying out a review under section 1J of the operation of the order.]

(9A) The council for the local government area in which a person in respect of whom an anti-social behaviour order has been made resides or appears to reside may bring proceedings under section 1(10) (as applied by subsection (9) above) for breach of an order under subsection (2).

[(9AA) Sections 1AA and 1AB apply in relation to orders under this section, with any necessary modifications, as they apply in relation to anti-social behaviour orders.

(9AB) In their application by virtue of subsection (9AA), sections 1AA(1A)(b) and 1AB(6) have effect as if the words "by complaint" were omitted.

(9AC) In its application by virtue of subsection (9AA), section 1AA(1A)(b) has effect as if the reference to the relevant authority which applied for the anti-social behaviour order were a reference to the chief officer of police, or other relevant authority, responsible under section 1K(2)(a) or (b) for carrying out a review of the order under this section.]

(9B) Subsection (9C) applies in relation to proceedings in which an order under subsection (2) is made against a child or young person who is convicted of an offence.

(9C) In so far as the proceedings relate to the making of the order—

(a) section 49 of the *Children and Young Persons Act* 1933 (restrictions on reports of proceedings in which children and young persons are concerned) does not apply in respect of the child or young person against whom the order is made;

(b) section 39 of that Act (power to prohibit publication of certain matter) does so apply.

(10) In this section—

"the commencement date" has the same meaning as in section 1 above;

"child" and "young person" have the same meaning as in the *Children and Young Persons Act* 1933;

"the court" in relation to an offender means—

(a) the court by or before which he is convicted of the relevant offence; or

(b) if he is committed to the Crown Court to be dealt with for that offence, the Crown Court; and

"relevant offence" means an offence committed after the coming into force of section 64 of the *Police Reform Act* 2002.

[This section was inserted by the *Police Reform Act* 2002, s.64. It is printed as amended, and repealed in part, by the *Anti-social Behaviour Act* 2003, s.86; and the *SOCPA* 2005, ss.139(1) and (4), 140(1) and (3), 141(1) and (3), and 174(2), and Sched. 17, Pt 2; and as amended, as from a day to be appointed, by the *CJIA* 2008, ss.123(3) and 124(7) (insertion of subss. (9ZA) and (9AA) to (9AC)). These prospective amendments have no application to an order under this section made more than nine months before the amendment came into force unless the order has been varied by a further order made no more than nine months before that day: 2008 Act, s.148(2), and Sched. 27, paras 33 and 34.]

Section 64 of the 2002 Act came into force on December 2, 2002: *Police Reform Act 2002 (Commencement No. 3) Order* 2002 (S.I. 2002 No. 2750). The power given by section 1C applies to offences committed on or after that date (see the definition of "relevant offence"). As to "the commencement date", see *post*, § 5–885.

One consequence of the amendments to section 1C made by the 2008 Act is that criminal courts will need to consider making an individual support order under section 1AA (*post*, § 5–882) when making an order under section 1C against a child or young person.

Crime and Disorder Act 1998, s.1(5A), (7), (10), (10A), (10B), (10C), (10D), (10E), (11), (12)

5–881 **1.**—[(5A) Nothing in this section affects the operation of section 127 of the *Magistrates' Courts Act* 1980 (limitation of time in respect of informations laid or complaints made in magistrates' court).]

(7) An anti-social behaviour order shall have effect for a period (not less than two years) specified in the order or until further order.

(10) If without reasonable excuse a person does anything which he is prohibited from doing by an anti-social behaviour order, he shall be liable—

(a) on summary conviction, to imprisonment for a term not exceeding six months or to a fine not exceeding the statutory maximum, or to both; or

(b) on conviction on indictment, to imprisonment for a term not exceeding five years or to a fine, or to both.

(10A) The following may bring proceedings for an offence under subsection (10)—

(a) a council which is a relevant authority;

(b) the council for the local government area in which a person in respect of whom an anti-social behaviour order has been made resides or appears to reside.

(10B) If proceedings for an offence under subsection (10) are brought in a youth court section 47(2) of the *Children and Young Persons Act* 1933 has effect as if the persons entitled to be present at a sitting for the purposes of those proceedings include one person authorised to be present by a relevant authority.

(10C) In proceedings for an offence under subsection (10), a copy of the original anti-social behaviour order, certified as such by the proper officer of the court which made it, is admissible as evidence of its having been made and of its contents to the same extent that oral evidence of those things is admissible in those proceedings.

(10D) In relation to proceedings brought against a child or a young person for an offence under subsection (10)—

(a) section 49 of the *Children and Young Persons Act* 1933 (restrictions on reports of proceedings in which children and young persons are concerned) does not apply in respect of the child or young person against whom the proceedings are brought;

(b) section 45 of the *Youth Justice and Criminal Evidence Act* 1999 (power to restrict reporting of criminal proceedings involving persons under 18) does so apply.

(10E) If, in relation to any such proceedings, the court does exercise its power to give a direction under section 45 of the *Youth Justice and Criminal Evidence Act* 1999, it shall give its reasons for doing so.

(11) Where a person is convicted of an offence under subsection (10) above, it shall not be open to the court by or before which he is so convicted to make an order under subsection (1)(b) (conditional discharge) of section 12 of the *Powers of Criminal Courts (Sentencing) Act* 2000 in respect of the offence.

(12) In this section—

"child" and "young person" shall have the same meaning as in the *Children and Young Persons Act* 1933;

"the commencement date" means the date of the commencement of this section;

"local government area" means—

(a) in relation to England, a district or London borough, the City of London, the Isle of Wight and the Isles of Scilly;

(b) in relation to Wales, a county or county borough.

[Subs. (5A) is inserted, as from a day to be appointed, by the *VCRA* 2006, s.59(1). Subss. (10A) and (10B) were inserted by the *Anti-social Behaviour Act* 2003, s.85(1) and (4). Subss. (10C) to (10E) were inserted by the *SOCPA* 2005, ss.139(1) and (2), and 141(1) and (2)(a). Subs. (11) is printed as amended by the *PCC(S)A* 2000, s.165, and Sched. 9, para. 192. Subs. (12) is printed as amended by the *SOCPA* 2005, s.141(1) and (2)(b).]

Section 1 of the 1998 Act came into force on April 1, 1999: *Crime and Disorder Act 1998 (Commencement No. 3 and Appointed Day) Order* 1998 (S.I. 1998 No. 3263).

Section 141(4) of the *SOCPA* 2005 provides that, subject to paragraph 2(2) of Schedule 2 to the *YJCEA* 1999, until section 45 of that Act comes into force, the references to it in section 1(10D)(b) and (10E) shall be read as references to section 39 of the *CYPA* 1933.

Crime and Disorder Act 1998, ss.1AA, 1AB

Individual support orders

1AA.—(1) *Where a court makes an anti-social behaviour order in respect of a defendant who is a child or young person when that order is made, it must consider whether the individual support conditions are fulfilled.* **5–882**

[(1) This section applies where a court makes an anti-social behaviour order in respect of a defendant who is a child or young person when that order is made.]

[(1A) This section also applies where —

(a) an anti-social behaviour order has previously been made in respect of such a defendant;

(b) an application is made by complaint to the court which made that order, by the relevant authority which applied for it, for an order under this section; and

(c) at the time of the hearing of the application —

(i) the defendant is still a child or young person, and

(ii) the anti-social behaviour order is still in force.

(1B) The court must consider whether the individual support conditions are fulfilled and, if satisfied that they are, must make an individual support order.]

(2) *If it is satisfied that those conditions are fulfilled, the court must make an order under this section ("an individual support order") which* [An individual support order is an order which] —

(a) requires the defendant to comply, for a period not exceeding six months, with such requirements as are specified in the order; and

(b) requires the defendant to comply with any directions given by the responsible officer with a view to the implementation of the requirements under paragraph (a) above.

(3) The individual support conditions are —

(a) that an individual support order would be desirable in the interests of preventing any repetition of the kind of behaviour which led to the *making of the anti-social behaviour order* [the making of —
  (i) the anti-social behaviour order, or
  (ii) an order varying that order (in a case where the variation is made as a result of further anti-social behaviour by the defendant)];
(b) that the defendant is not already subject to an individual support order; and
(c) that the court has been notified by the Secretary of State that arrangements for implementing individual support orders are available in the area in which it appears to it that the defendant resides or will reside and the notice has not been withdrawn.

(4) If the court is not satisfied that the individual support conditions are fulfilled, it shall state in open court that it is not so satisfied and why it is not.

(5) The requirements that may be specified under subsection (2)(a) above are those that the court considers desirable in the interests of preventing any repetition of the kind of behaviour *which led to the making of the anti-social behaviour order* [mentioned in subsection (3)(a) above].

(6) Requirements included in an individual support order, or directions given under such an order by a responsible officer, may require the defendant to do all or any of the following things —
(a) to participate in activities specified in the requirements or directions at a time or times so specified;
(b) to present himself to a person or persons so specified at a place or places and at a time or times so specified;
(c) to comply with any arrangements for his education so specified.

(7) But requirements included in, or directions given under, such an order may not require the defendant to attend (whether at the same place or at different places) on more than two days in any week; and "week" here means a period of seven days beginning with a Sunday.

(8) Requirements included in, and directions given under, an individual support order shall, as far as practicable, be such as to avoid —
(a) any conflict with the defendant's religious beliefs; and
(b) any interference with the times, if any, at which he normally works or attends school or any other educational establishment.

(9) Before making an individual support order, the court shall obtain from a social worker of a local authority or a member of a youth offending team any information which it considers necessary in order —
(a) to determine whether the individual support conditions are fulfilled, or
(b) to determine what requirements should be imposed by an individual support order if made,

and shall consider that information.

(10) In this section and section 1AB below "responsible officer", in relation to an individual support order, means one of the following who is specified in the order, namely —
(a) a social worker of a local authority;
(b) a person nominated by a person appointed as director of children's services under section 18 of the *Children Act* 2004 or by a person appointed as chief education officer under section 532 of the *Education Act* 1996;
(c) a member of a youth offending team.

[This section was inserted by the *CJA* 2003, s.322. It is printed as amended, and repealed in part, by the *Children Act* 2004, ss.18(9) and 64, Sched. 2, para. 8, and Sched. 5, Pt 4; and as amended, as from a day to be appointed, by the *CJIA* 2008, s.124(1)–(3) (omission of italicised words, insertion of words in square brackets). In connection with the amendments made by the 2008 Act, see that Act, s.148(2), and Sched. 27, para. 34 (*ante*, § 5–880).]

Individual support orders: explanation, breach, amendment etc.

5–883 **1AB.**—(1) Before making an individual support order, the court shall explain to the defendant in ordinary language —
(a) the effect of the order and of the requirements proposed to be included in it;
(b) the consequences which may follow (under subsection (3) below) if he fails to comply with any of those requirements; and

(c) that the court has power (under subsection (6) below) to review the order on the application either of the defendant or of the responsible officer.

(2) The power of the Secretary of State under section 174(4) of the *Criminal Justice Act* 2003 includes power by order to —

(a) prescribe cases in which subsection (1) above does not apply; and

(b) prescribe cases in which the explanation referred to in that subsection may be made in the absence of the defendant, or may be provided in written form.

(3) If the person in respect of whom an individual support order is made fails without reasonable excuse to comply with any requirement included in the order, he is guilty of an offence and liable on summary conviction to a fine not exceeding —

(a) if he is aged 14 or over at the date of his conviction, £1,000;

(b) if he is aged under 14 then, £250.

(4) No referral order under section 16(2) or (3) of the *Powers of Criminal Courts (Sentencing) Act* 2000 (referral of young offenders to youth offender panels) may be made in respect of an offence under subsection (3) above.

(5) If the anti-social behaviour order as a result of which an individual support order was made ceases to have effect, the individual support order (if it has not previously ceased to have effect) ceases to have effect when the anti-social behaviour order does.

[(5A) The period specified as the term of an individual support order made on an application under section 1AA(1A) above must not be longer than the remaining part of the term of the anti-social behaviour order as a result of which it is made.]

(6) On an application made by complaint by —

(a) the person subject to an individual support order, or

(b) the responsible officer,

the court which made the individual support order may vary or discharge it by a further order.

(7) If the anti-social behaviour order as a result of which an individual support order was made is varied, the court varying the anti-social behaviour order may by a further order vary or discharge the individual support order.

[This section was inserted by the *CJA* 2003, s.322. It is printed as amended, as from a day to be appointed, by the *CJIA* 2008, s.124(5) (insertion of subs. (5A)). In connection with this amendment, see that Act, s.148(2), and Sched. 27, para. 34 (*ante*, § 5–880).]

Authorities

Evidence and procedure

In *C. v. Sunderland Youth Court* [2004] 1 Cr.App.R.(S.) 76, the Divisional Court was concerned with an order under the *CDA* 1998, s.1C, made by a youth court. The court held that a court must act fairly and have regard to all relevant considerations. What fairness required and what considerations were relevant would depend on the circumstances of each particular case. In addition to the requirement to act fairly, there was an elementary requirement that there should be clarity as to the basis for, and the scope of, any order, particularly as breach of the order exposed a person to potential criminal penalties. Elementary fairness required a court, if it proposed to make an order of its own motion, to indicate the basis on which it provisionally considered an order to be appropriate, and the material on which it proposed to rely, so that the person potentially liable could make meaningful submissions as to why the order should not be made at all, or should not be made in the form provisionally proposed by the court. It was vital that the terms of an order were clearly and correctly explained to the defendant in open court. **5–884**

In *R. v. P. (Shane Tony)* [2004] 2 Cr.App.R.(S.) 63, CA, it was said that the whole of the procedure should take place in the presence of the defendant; the terms of any order must be precise and capable of being understood by the defendant, to whom it must be explained; the findings of fact giving rise to the making of the order must be recorded; the exact terms of the order must be pronounced in open court; and the written order must accurately reflect the order as pronounced.

In *R. (W.) v. Acton Youth Court*, 170 J.P. 31, DC, it was held that proceedings in relation to the making of an order under section 1C are civil and accordingly the rules relating to the admissibility of hearsay in civil proceedings apply. From this, it was held to follow in *R. v. W. and F.* [2006] 2 Cr.App.R.(S.) 110, CA, that since section 11 of the *Civil Evidence Act* 1995 provides that civil proceedings are civil proceedings "before any tribunal", hearsay evidence is capable of being adduced in support of a section 1C application under section 1(1) and (2)(a) and (b) of that Act (in civil proceedings, "evidence shall not be excluded on the grounds that it is hearsay"); but, so as scrupulously to observe the requirements of procedural fairness, a defendant must have the opportunity to consider the evidence to be adduced by the prosecution in support of the application, especially where the material relied on goes far beyond the offence of which the defendant has been convicted; and for this purpose, the relevant principles in the *Magistrates' Courts (Hearsay Evidence in Civil Proceedings) Rules* 1999 (S.I. 1999 No. 681) should be taken to apply by analogy (in particular their requirements for adequate notice of an intention to rely on hearsay, for identification of the hearsay evidence and for a statement as to why the maker of the hearsay statement is not to be called). The court observed that, in future cases, the prosecution should identify the particular facts (as opposed to evidence) said to constitute anti-social behaviour; that if those facts are accepted, they should be put in writing; and that if they are disputed, then they must be proved to the criminal standard before they can be acted upon, following which the judge should state his findings of fact expressly and record them in writing in the order.

It is submitted that the introduction of the rules of evidence applicable to civil proceedings is unhelpful and calculated to confuse. The substance is that proceedings under section 1C are part of the criminal process, and should be regarded as such. The admissibility of hearsay should be governed by the hearsay rules applicable to criminal proceedings, *i.e.* sections 114 *et seq.* of the *CJA* 2003 (*post*, §§ 11–3 *et seq.*). It is understood (as at September, 2007) that the Criminal Procedure Rule Committee are proposing to add rules governing section 1C applications to the *Criminal Procedure Rules* 2005 (S.I. 2005 No. 384). This presupposes that the committee are of the view that such applications are in a "criminal cause or matter" (see the *Courts Act* 2003, s.69 as to the *vires* of the committee). If such rules are adopted, then, it is submitted, that the courts will be compelled to abandon the fiction that section 1C proceedings are civil.

In *M. v. DPP*, 171 J.P. 457, DC, the court expressly left open the "extremely important" point as to whether it would be lawful to make an anti-social behaviour order where the evidence in support thereof consisted entirely of the hearsay evidence of anonymous witnesses.

Necessity for, and ambit of, order

5–884a Whereas one of the criteria to be satisfied, before an anti-social behaviour order may be made is, "(a) that the person has acted ... in a manner that caused or was likely to cause harassment, alarm or distress to one or more persons not of the same household as himself" (see s.1C(2)), this criterion could not be satisfied where there was no potential victim present at the time of the past events relied on: *R. (Gosport B.C.) v. Fareham Magistrates' Court* [2007] 1 W.L.R. 634, QBD (Bean J.). And it was clear from this provision that it had never been intended that an anti-social behaviour order could be made so as to prohibit contact between co-habitees: *R. v. Gowan* [2008] 1 Cr.App.R.(S.) 12, CA.

In *R. v. P. (Shane Tony)*, *ante*, it was said that where a custodial sentence of more than a few months was passed and the offender was liable to be released on licence and therefore subject to recall, the circumstances in which there would be a demonstrable necessity to make a suspended anti-social behaviour order, to take effect on release, would be limited, although there would be cases in which geographical restraints could properly supplement licence conditions.

In *R. v. Boness* [2006] 1 Cr.App.R.(S.) 120, CA, it was said that the test for making an order prohibiting the offender from doing something being one of necessity, each separate prohibition must be necessary to protect persons from further anti-social acts by him and be tailor-made for the individual offender, not designed on a word processor for use in every case. A court should not allow itself to be diverted into making an order as an alternative to prison or other sanction, and it may be better to decide the appropriate sentence and then move on to consider whether an anti-social behaviour order should be made. The court added that it also followed from the requirement of necessity that an order should not be made which prohibits an offender from committing a specified criminal offence if the sentence which could be passed following conviction for the offence should be a sufficient deterrent; if the offender is not going to be deterred from committing the offence by a sentence of imprisonment for that offence, the anti-social behaviour order is not likely (it may be thought) further to deter and would not therefore be necessary. Accordingly, another reason why a court should be reluctant to make an order prohibiting an offender from committing a specified criminal offence is that the aim of the order is to prevent anti-social behaviour, and thus the order should be drafted in terms that enable the police or other authorities to take action before the anti-social behaviour takes place. The terms of the order must be proportionate in the sense that they must be commensurate with the risk to be guarded against and this, the court said, is particularly important where an order may interfere with an offender's rights under the ECHR.

In *Hills v. Chief Constable of Essex*, 171 J.P. 14, QBD (Keith J.), it was held that *R. v. Boness*, *ante*, does not constitute an absolute bar on making anti-social behaviour orders containing prohibitions on specific acts which are, in any event, made offences by the criminal law; what matters is whether the particular prohibition is really necessary in order to protect members of the public from anti-social behaviour by the person who is the subject of the order (upholding order preventing a teenager from carrying any knife or bladed article in a public place (the *CJA* 1988, s.139, *post*, § 24–125, not applying to folding pocket knifes with cutting edges of less than three inches) where it was necessary to protect the public from the use of knives by him, and where the knives to which he was likely to have ready access were, by reason of his age, likely to be those with blades less than three inches).

An order should not, however, be made so as to prohibit particular conduct which itself constitutes an offence (*e.g.* driving whilst disqualified), where the purpose of the order is to provide for an increased penalty in the event of repetition in breach of the order: *R. v. Kirby* [2006] 1 Cr.App.R.(S.) 26, CA; *R. v. Williams* [2006] 1 Cr.App.R.(S.) 56, CA; *R. v. Lawson* [2006] 1 Cr.App.R.(S.) 59; *R. v. Morrison* [2006] 1 Cr.App.R.(S.) 85, CA; and *R. v. Boness*, *ante* (disapproving *R. v. Hall* [2005] 1 Cr.App.R.(S.) 118, CA).

In *R. (W.) v. DPP*, 169 J.P. 435, DC, a clause in an order which prohibited the offender from committing any criminal offence was held to be invalid and unlawful. The prohibitions contained in such orders had to be sufficiently specific and clear to enable the restricted party to comply without difficulty. See also *N. v. DPP*, 171 J.P. 393, DC (terms of order were disproportionate where they could have led to inadvertent breach); and *M. v. DPP*, *ante*, § 5–885a (prohibition in order insufficiently "precise, clear and certain" where it effectively required defendant to be in a position to make an instant decision as to whether those with whom he was associating had got to the point of conspiring or attempting to commit an offence).

As to there being no requirement that the acts prohibited by the order should, by themselves, give rise to alarm, harassment or distress, see *R. v. McGrath* [2005] 2 Cr.App.R.(S.) 85, CA; and *R. v. Boness*, *ante*.

There is nothing objectionable about drafting an order so that its subject is prohibited from associating with another named person, where there is no corresponding order in place preventing that other person from associating with the subject; if the other person were to try to associate with the subject, the subject may have a defence of reasonable excuse if it were alleged that he had breached the order: *Hills v. Chief Constable of Essex*, *ante*.

Breach

In order to judge whether a breach of an anti-social behaviour order had occurred, the tribunal of fact had to consider the specific terms of the order; whether the person subject to the order had breached it was a question of fact: *R. v. Doughan*, 171 J.P. 397, CA. **5–884b**

Questions as to the validity of an anti-social behaviour order (such as a submission that it was too widely drawn) cannot found a defence in subsequent breach proceedings; but the court could consider whether the order lacked sufficient clarity to warrant a finding that the defendant's behaviour amounted to a breach, whether the lack of clarity amounted to a reasonable excuse for non-compliance and whether, if a breach was established, it would be appropriate in the circumstances to impose a penalty: *DPP v. T.* [2006] 3 All E.R. 471, DC.

Ignorance, forgetfulness or misunderstanding of the terms of an anti-social behaviour order (whether arising from an error as to its terms, or a lack of knowledge on the part of the defendant as to where he was at the time of the alleged breach) are capable of amounting to a reasonable excuse for the purposes of section 1(10) of the 1998 Act and should be left to the jury as an issue of fact and value judgment: *R. v. Nicholson* [2006] 2 Cr.App.R. 30, CA.

In *R. v. Tripp*, unreported, August 17, 2005, CA ([2005] EWCA Crim. 2253), it was said that where an anti-social behaviour order was breached by conduct consisting of a criminal offence (here, effectively being drunk and disorderly), the potential sentence may be far longer than the maximum for that basic offence (following *R. v. Braxton* [2005] 1 Cr.App.R.(S.) 36, CA).

In *R. v. Lamb* [2006] 2 Cr.App.R.(S.) 11, CA, it was said that the offender neither having committed a crime other than the breach, nor having harassed nor caused distress to any member of the public, the only justification for imposing punishment was his persistent and deliberate failure to comply with the order of the court. The court said that there was a vital distinction between such cases having little social impact and those in which the breach involved harassment, alarm or distress to the public of the type that the legislation was designed to prevent (as to which, where the breach was also the commission of another offence, the approach in *R. v. Tripp* and *R. v. Braxton*, *ante*, was to be preferred to that in *R. v. Morrison*, *ante* (tariff should be dictated by reference to maximum for base offence)); where the breach did not involve harassment, alarm or distress, community penalties should be considered in order to help the offender live within the terms of the order; and where there was no available community penalty (such as here, given the offender's refusal to engage with agencies prepared to help him, and the frequency of the breaches), any custodial sentence necessary to maintain the order of the court could be kept as short as possible.

In *R. v. H., Stevens and Lovegrove* [2006] 2 Cr.App.R.(S.) 68, CA, it was said that where the conduct constituting the breach also amounts to a distinct criminal offence for which the maximum sentence is prescribed by statute, whilst this should be borne in mind in the interests of proportionality, the sentencer is not limited to that maximum and should impose a sentence commensurate with the breach.

Crime and Disorder Act 1998, ss.1CA, 1I

Variation and discharge of orders under section 1C

5–885 **1CA.**—(1) An offender subject to an order under section 1C may apply to the court which made it for it to be varied or discharged.

(2) If he does so, he must also send written notice of his application to the Director of Public Prosecutions.

(3) The Director of Public Prosecutions may apply to the court which made an order under section 1C for it to be varied or discharged.

(4) A relevant authority may also apply to the court which made an order under section 1C for it to be varied or discharged if it appears to it that—

(a) in the case of variation, the protection of relevant persons from anti-social acts by the person subject to the order would be more appropriately effected by a variation of the order;

(b) in the case of discharge, that it is no longer necessary to protect relevant persons from anti-social acts by him by means of such an order.

(5) If the Director of Public Prosecutions or a relevant authority applies for the variation or discharge of an order under section 1C, he or it must also send written notice of the application to the person subject to the order.

(6) In the case of an order under section 1C made by a magistrates' court, the references in subsections (1), (3) and (4) to the court by which the order was made include a reference to any magistrates' court acting in the same local justice area as that court.

(7) No order under section 1C shall be discharged on an application under this section before the end of the period of two years beginning with the day on which the order takes effect, unless—

(a) in the case of an application under subsection (1), the Director of Public Prosecutions consents, or

(b) in the case of an application under subsection (3) or (4), the offender consents.

[This section is inserted by the *SOCPA* 2005, s.140(1) and (4).]

An order made on complaint under section 1 of the 1998 Act may be "varied", within the meaning of subsection (8), by extending its duration: *Leeds City Council v. G.* [2007] 1 W.L.R. 3025, DC (applying *DPP v. Hall*, *post*, § 19–277f). There would appear to be no reason why the word "varied" in section 1CA should not bear the same meaning.

Special measures for witnesses

11.—(1) This section applies to the following proceedings— **5–885a**

(a) any proceedings in a magistrates' court on an application for an anti-social behaviour order,

(b) any proceedings in a magistrates' court or the Crown Court so far as relating to the issue whether to make an order under section 1C, and

(c) any proceedings in a magistrates' court so far as relating to the issue whether to make an order under section 1D.

(2) Chapter 1 of Part 2 of the *Youth Justice and Criminal Evidence Act* 1999 (special measures directions in the case of vulnerable and intimidated witnesses) shall apply in relation to any such proceedings as it applies in relation to criminal proceedings, but with—

(a) the omission of the provisions of that Act mentioned in subsection (3) (which make provision appropriate only in the context of criminal proceedings), and

(b) any other necessary modifications.

(3) The provisions are—

(a) section 17(4),

(b) section 21(1)(b) and (5) to (7),

(c) section 22(1)(b) and (2)(b) and (c),

(d) section 27(10), and

(e) section 32.

(4) Any rules of court made under or for the purposes of Chapter 1 of Part 2 of that Act shall apply in relation to proceedings to which this section applies—

(a) to such extent as may be provided by rules of court, and

(b) subject to such modifications as may be so provided.

(5) Section 47 of that Act (restrictions on reporting special measures directions etc.) applies, with any necessary modifications, in relation to—

(a) a direction under section 19 of the Act as applied by this section, or

(b) a direction discharging or varying such a direction,

and sections 49 and 51 of that Act (offences) apply accordingly.

[This section was inserted by the *SOCPA* 2005, s.143.]

Review of anti-social behaviour orders

Section 123 of the *CJIA* 2008 (in force as from a day to be appointed) provides for **5–885b** yearly reviews of an anti-social behaviour order made in respect of a person aged under 17, by inserting into the *CDA* 1998 new sections 1J and 1K. Section 1J provides that a review of the operation of such an order (made under the *CDA* 1998, s.1, 1B or 1C) is to take place not more than 12 months after the order (or a varying order or an individual support order) was made and again not more than 12 months after each review, the review including consideration of the subject's compliance, the adequacy of the support provided to assist with compliance, and whether the order should be varied or discharged. Section 1K sets out who is responsible for carrying out such a review, essentially providing that, in the case of an order under section 1C (*ante*, § 5–880), the authority specified under section 1C(9ZA) or chief officer of police is so responsible, acting in co-operation with certain other persons and bodies.

K. FINANCIAL REPORTING ORDERS

(1) Summary

5–886 Section 76(1) and (2) of the *SOCPA* 2005 provide for a "financial reporting order" to be made when a court is sentencing or otherwise dealing with a person convicted of an offence specified in subsection (3), where it is satisfied that the risk of a person committing another such offence is sufficiently high to justify making such an order. The specified offences are those under the *Theft Act* 1968, ss.15, 15A, 16 and 20(2), under the *Theft Act* 1978, ss.1 and 2, and "lifestyle offences" under the *PCA* 2002. Section 76(5) to (7) make provision as to the length of such orders. Section 79 provides for the effect of the order. A person subject to such an order must: make a report in respect of the period of a specified length beginning with the date on which the order comes into force, and subsequent periods of specified lengths, each period beginning immediately after the end of the previous one (s.79(2)); set out in each report, in the specified manner, such particulars of his financial affairs relating to the period in question as may be specified (s.79(3)); include any specified documents within each report (s.79(4)); make each report within the specified number of days after the end of the period in question (s.79(5)); and make each report to the specified person (s.79(6)). A summary offence is committed where a person, without reasonable excuse, includes false or misleading information in a report, or otherwise fails to comply with any requirement of the section (51 weeks' imprisonment, level 5, or both): s.79(10). Section 80 provides for the variation and revocation of financial reporting orders, and the procedure in relation thereto. Section 81 provides that the person to whom the reports are made may disclose the contents of the report to any person he reasonably believes may be able to assist in checking the accuracy of the report or of any other report made pursuant to the same order, or discovering the true position (s.81(4)), or may disclose it for the purposes of the prevention, detection, etc., of criminal offences, or other conduct for which non-criminal penalties are prescribed, here or abroad (s.81(5)), but nothing authorises a disclosure, in contravention of any provisions of the *Data Protection Act* 1998, of personal data which are not exempt from these provisions (s.81(7)).

(2) Legislation

Serious Organised Crime and Police Act 2005, ss.76–81

Financial reporting orders: making

5–886a **76.**—(1) A court sentencing or otherwise dealing with a person convicted of an offence mentioned in subsection (3) may also make a financial reporting order in respect of him.

(2) But it may do so only if it is satisfied that the risk of the person's committing another offence mentioned in subsection (3) is sufficiently high to justify the making of a financial reporting order.

(3) The offences are—

(aa) an offence under either of the following provisions of the *Fraud Act* 2006—

(i) section 1 (fraud)

(ii) section 11 (obtaining services dishonestly),

(ab) a common law offence of conspiracy to defraud,

(ac) an offence under section 17 of the *Theft Act* 1968 (false accounting),

(c) any offence specified in Schedule 2 to the *Proceeds of Crime Act* 2002 ("lifestyle offences"),

(d) a common law offence of bribery,

(e) an offence under section 1 of the *Public Bodies Corrupt Practices Act* 1889 (corruption in office),

(f) the first two offences under section 1 of the *Prevention of Corruption Act* 1906 (bribes obtained by or given to agents),

(g) an offence under any of the following provisions of the *Criminal Justice Act* 1988—

section 93A (assisting another to retain the benefit of criminal conduct),

section 93B (acquisition, possession or use of proceeds of criminal conduct),

section 93C (concealing or transferring proceeds of criminal conduct),

(h) an offence under any of the following provisions of the *Drug Trafficking Act* 1994—
section 49 (concealing or transferring proceeds of drug trafficking),
section 50 (assisting another person to retain the benefit of drug trafficking),
section 51 (acquisition, possession or use of proceeds of drug trafficking),

(i) an offence under any of the following provisions of the *Terrorism Act* 2000—
section 15 (fund-raising for purposes of terrorism),
section 16 (use and possession of money etc. for purposes of terrorism),
section 17 (funding arrangements for purposes of terrorism),
section 18 (money laundering in connection with terrorism),

(j) an offence under section 329 of the *Proceeds of Crime Act* 2002 (acquisition, use and possession of criminal property),

(k) a common law offence of cheating in relation to the public revenue,

(l) an offence under section 170 of the *Customs and Excise Management Act* 1979 (fraudulent evasion of duty),

(m) an offence under section 72 of the *Value Added Tax Act* 1994 (offences relating to VAT),

(n) an offence under section 144 of the *Finance Act* 2000 (fraudulent evasion of income tax),

(o) an offence under section 35 of the *Tax Credits Act* 2002 (tax credit fraud),

(p) an offence of attempting, conspiring or inciting the commission of an offence mentioned in paragraphs (aa), (ac) or (d) to (o),

(q) an offence of aiding, abetting, counselling or procuring the commission of an offence mentioned in paragraphs (aa), (ac) or (d) to (o).

(4) The Secretary of State may by order amend subsection (3) so as to remove an offence from it or add an offence to it.

(5) A financial reporting order—

(a) comes into force when it is made, and

(b) has effect for the period specified in the order, beginning with the date on which it is made.

(6) If the order is made by a magistrates' court, the period referred to in subsection (5)(b) must not exceed 5 years.

(7) Otherwise, that period must not exceed—

(a) if the person is sentenced to imprisonment for life, 20 years,

(b) otherwise, 15 years.

[This section is printed as amended by the *Fraud Act* 2006, s.14(1), and Sched. 1, para. 36; and the *Serious Organised Crime and Police Act 2005 (Amendment of Section 76(3)) Order* 2007 (S.I. 2007 No. 1392). The reference to the common law offence of incitement in subs. (3)(p) has effect as a reference to the offences under the *SCA* 2007, Pt 2: 2007 Act, s.63(1), and Sched. 6, para. 51.]

77. [*Financial reporting orders: making in Scotland*] **5–886b**

78. [*Financial reporting orders: making in Northern Ireland*] **5–886c**

Financial reporting orders: effect

79.—(1) A person in relation to whom a financial reporting order has effect must do the following. **5–886d**

(2) He must make a report, in respect of—

(a) the period of a specified length beginning with the date on which the order comes into force, and

(b) subsequent periods of specified lengths, each period beginning immediately after the end of the previous one.

(3) He must set out in each report, in the specified manner, such particulars of his financial affairs relating to the period in question as may be specified.

(4) He must include any specified documents with each report.

(5) He must make each report within the specified number of days after the end of the period in question.

(6) He must make each report to the specified person.

(7) Rules of court may provide for the maximum length of the periods which may be specified under subsection (2).

(8) In this section, "specified" means specified by the court in the order.

(9) [*Scotland.*]

(10) A person who without reasonable excuse includes false or misleading information in a report, or otherwise fails to comply with any requirement of this section, is guilty of an offence and is liable on summary conviction to—

(a) imprisonment for a term not exceeding—

(i) in England and Wales, 51 weeks,

(ii) in Scotland, 12 months,

(iii) in Northern Ireland, 6 months, or

(b) a fine not exceeding level 5 on the standard scale,

or to both.

Financial reporting orders: variation and revocation

5–886e **80.**—(1) An application for variation or revocation of a financial reporting order may be made by—

(a) the person in respect of whom it has been made,

(b) the person to whom reports are to be made under it (see section 79(6)).

(2) The application must be made to the court which made the order.

(3) But if the order was made on appeal, the application must be made to the court which originally sentenced the person in respect of whom the order was made.

(4) If (in either case) that court was a magistrates' court, the application may be made to any magistrates' court acting in the same local justice area (or in Northern Ireland for the same county court division) as that court.

(5) Subsections (3) and (4) do not apply to Scotland.

Financial reporting orders: verification and disclosure

5–886f **81.**—(1) In this section, "the specified person" means the person to whom reports under a financial reporting order are to be made.

(2) The specified person may, for the purpose of doing either of the things mentioned in subsection (4), disclose a report to any person who he reasonably believes may be able to contribute to doing either of those things.

(3) Any other person may disclose information to—

(a) the specified person, or

(b) a person to whom the specified person has disclosed a report,

for the purpose of contributing to doing either of the things mentioned in subsection (4).

(4) The things mentioned in subsections (2) and (3) are—

(a) checking the accuracy of the report or of any other report made pursuant to the same order,

(b) discovering the true position.

(5) The specified person may also disclose a report for the purposes of—

(a) the prevention, detection, investigation or prosecution of criminal offences, whether in the United Kingdom or elsewhere,

(b) the prevention, detection or investigation of conduct for which penalties other than criminal penalties are provided under the law of any part of the United Kingdom or of any country or territory outside the United Kingdom.

(6) A disclosure under this section does not breach—

(a) any obligation of confidence owed by the person making the disclosure, or

(b) any other restriction on the disclosure of information (however imposed).

(7) But nothing in this section authorises a disclosure, in contravention of any provisions of the *Data Protection Act* 1998, of personal data which are not exempt from those provisions.

(8) In this section, references to a report include any of its contents, any document included with the report, or any of the contents of such a document.

L. PROCEDURE

Introduction

5–886g With effect from April 7, 2008, the *Criminal Procedure (Amendment No. 3) Rules* 2007 (S.I. 2007 No. 3662), r.12, substitutes a new Part 50 in the *Criminal Procedure Rules* 2005 (S.I. 2005 No. 384) (*post*, §§ 5–886k *et seq.*). This is headed "Civil behaviour orders after verdict or hearing". The new part does not define "a civil order". It merely declares that it applies where a magistrates' court or the Crown Court has power to make a civil order that requires someone to do, or not to do, something. It is important to note that this is not a definition: the rules themselves are silent as to what might be a "civil order", but the note to rule 50.1 suggests that the Criminal Procedure Rule Committee had in mind football banning orders, restraining orders, anti-social behaviour orders (including interim orders), parenting orders, sexual offences prevention orders and serious crime prevention orders. This, however, begs the question. Any such order (and there are others such as financial reporting orders, drinking banning orders, disqualifications from driving or from being a company director), when made on conviction, is part of the sentence of the criminal court, and is part of the overall penalty imposed for the offence. To describe such orders as civil orders is a fiction which has its roots in the efforts of the courts to avoid (a) the retrospective penalty provisions of Article 7 of the ECHR (*post*, § 16–97) (see *R. v. Field*; *R. v. Young* [2003] 1 W.L.R. 882, CA (*ante*, § 5–854) and *Gough v. Chief Constable of Derbyshire*; *R. (Miller) v. Leeds Magistrates' Court*; *Lilley v. DPP* [2002] Q.B. 459, DC) (*ante*, § 5–825)), and (b) the criminal hearsay rules (see *R. (W.) v. Acton Youth Court*, 170 J.P. 31, DC). A second difficulty with Part 50 is that it purports to relate to civil proceedings, but the Criminal Procedure Rule Committee has no power to make rules other than in relation to a "criminal cause or matter". If proceedings in relation to such orders are civil, then it is submitted that Part 50 is *ultra vires*. The true position, it is submitted, is that such proceedings are part of the criminal process, that they are criminal in form and substance, and that, therefore, the committee does indeed have power to make rules in relation to them, but that it does not have power to apply civil evidence rules to them.

There is one *caveat* in relation to the foregoing and that concerns serious crime prevention orders. Parliament has declared (*SCA* 2007, s.36(1), *ante*, § 5–877a) that proceedings in the Crown Court on an application for such an order are civil, but that they are to be regarded as criminal for the purposes of the power to make rules of court. So far then as Part 50 concerns such orders, it is *intra vires*, but it is submitted it takes nothing less than an Act of Parliament to turn criminal proceedings into civil proceedings.

Criminal Procedure Rules 2005 (S.I. 2005 No. 384), Pt 50 (as substituted by the Criminal Procedure (Amendment No. 3) Rules 2007 (S.I. 2007 No. 3662), r.12)

When this Part applies

50.1.—(1) This Part applies in magistrates' courts and in the Crown Court where the court could decide to make, vary or revoke a civil order— **5–886h**

(a) under a power that the court can exercise after reaching a verdict or making a finding, and

(b) that requires someone to do, or not do, something.

(2) A reference to a "behaviour order" in this Part is a reference to any such order.

(3) A reference to "hearsay evidence" in this Part is a reference to evidence consisting of hearsay within the meaning of section 1(2) of the *Civil Evidence Act* 1995.

Behaviour orders: general rules

50.2.—(1) The court must not make a behaviour order unless the person to whom it is directed has had an opportunity— **5–886i**

(a) to consider what order is proposed and why; and

(b) to make representations at a hearing (whether or not that person in fact attends).

(2) That restriction does not apply to making an interim behaviour order.

(3) But an interim behaviour order has no effect unless the person to whom it is directed—

(a) is present when it is made; or

(b) is handed a document recording the order not more than 7 days after it is made.

Application for behaviour order: special rules

50.3.—(1) This rule applies where a prosecutor wants the court to make— **5–886j**

(a) an anti-social behaviour order; or

(b) a serious crime prevention order,

if the defendant is convicted.

(2) The prosecutor must serve a notice of intention to apply for such an order on—

(a) the court officer;

(b) the defendant against whom the prosecutor wants the court to make the order; and

(c) any person on whom the order would be likely to have a significant adverse effect,

as soon as practicable (without waiting for the verdict).

(3) The notice must be in the form set out in the Practice Direction and must—

(a) summarise the relevant facts;

(b) identify the evidence on which the prosecutor relies in support;

(c) attach any written statement that the prosecutor has not already served; and

(d) specify the order that the prosecutor wants the court to make.

(4) The defendant must then—

(a) serve written notice of any evidence on which the defendant relies on—

(i) the court officer, and

(ii) the prosecutor,

as soon as practicable (without waiting for the verdict); and

(b) in the notice, identify that evidence and attach any written statement that has not already been served.

(5) This rule does not apply to an application for an interim anti-social behaviour order.

Evidence to assist the court: special rules

5–886k **50.4.**—(1) This rule applies where the court indicates that it may make on its own initiative—

(a) a football banning order;

(b) a restraining order;

(c) an anti-social behaviour order; or

(d) a drinking banning order.

(2) A party who wants the court to take account of any particular evidence before making that decision must—

(a) serve notice in writing on—

(i) the court officer, and

(ii) every other party,

as soon as practicable (without waiting for the verdict); and

(b) in that notice identify that evidence and attach any written statement that has not already been served.

Application to vary or revoke behaviour order

5–886l **50.5.**—(1) The court may vary or revoke a behaviour order if—

(a) the legislation under which it is made allows the court to do so; and

(b) one of the following applies—

(i) the prosecutor,

(ii) the person to whom the order is directed,

(iii) any other person mentioned in the order,

(iv) the relevant authority or responsible officer,

(v) the relevant Chief Officer of Police, or

(vi) the Director of Public Prosecutions.

(2) A person applying under this rule must—

(a) apply in writing as soon as practicable after becoming aware of the grounds for doing so, explaining why the order should be varied or revoked; and

(b) serve the application, and any notice under paragraph (3), on the court officer and, as appropriate, anyone listed in paragraph (1)(b).

(3) A party who wants the court to take account of any particular evidence before making its decision must, as soon as practicable—

(a) serve notice in writing on—

(i) the court officer, and

(ii) as appropriate, anyone listed in paragraph (1)(b); and

(b) in that notice identify the evidence and attach any written statement that has not already been served.

(4) The court may decide an application under this rule with or without a hearing.

(5) But the court must not—

(a) dismiss an application under this rule unless the applicant has had an opportunity to make representations at a hearing (whether or not the applicant in fact attends); or

(b) allow an application under this rule unless everyone served with the application has had at least 14 days in which to make representations, including representations about whether there should be a hearing.

(6) Where a person applies under this rule to a magistrates' court—

(a) the application must be by complaint; and

(b) the court officer must give notice by summons of any hearing.

Notice of hearsay evidence

50.6.—(1) A party who wants to introduce hearsay evidence must— **5–886m**

(a) serve notice in writing on—

(i) the court officer, and

(ii) every other party directly affected; and

(b) in that notice—

(i) explain that it is a notice of hearsay evidence,

(ii) identify that evidence,

(iii) identify the person who made the statement which is hearsay, or explain why if that person is not identified, and

(iv) explain why that person will not be called to give oral evidence.

(2) A party may serve one notice under this rule in respect of more than one statement and more than one witness.

Cross-examination of maker of hearsay statement

50.7.—(1) This rule applies where a party wants the court's permission to cross-examine a person who made a statement which another party wants to introduce as hearsay. **5–886n**

(2) The party who wants to cross-examine that person must—

(a) apply in writing, with reasons, not more than 7 days after service of the notice of hearsay evidence; and

(b) serve the application on—

(i) the court officer,

(ii) the party who served the hearsay evidence notice, and

(iii) every party on whom the hearsay evidence notice was served.

(3) The court may decide an application under this rule with or without a hearing.

(4) But the court must not—

(a) dismiss an application under this rule unless the applicant has had an opportunity to make representations at a hearing (whether or not the applicant in fact attends); or

(b) allow an application under this rule unless everyone served with the application has had at least 7 days in which to make representations, including representations about whether there should be a hearing.

Credibility and consistency of maker of hearsay statement

50.8.—(1) This rule applies where a party wants to challenge the credibility or consistency of a person who made a statement which another party wants to introduce as hearsay. **5–886o**

(2) The party who wants to challenge the credibility or consistency of that person must—

(a) serve a written notice of intention to do so on—

(i) the court officer, and

(ii) the party who served the notice of hearsay evidence

not more than 7 days after service of that hearsay evidence notice; and

(b) in the notice, identify any statement or other material on which that party relies.

(3) The party who served the hearsay notice—

(a) may call that person to give oral evidence instead; and

(b) if so, must serve a notice of intention to do so on—

(i) the court officer, and

(ii) every party on whom he served the hearsay notice

not more than 7 days after service of the notice under paragraph (2).

Court's power to vary requirements under this Part

5–886p **50.9.** The court may—

(a) shorten a time limit or extend it (even after it has expired);

(b) allow a notice or application to be given in a different form, or presented orally.

XI. ORDERS UNDER THE MENTAL HEALTH ACT 1983

(1) Hospital and guardianship orders

Mental Health Act 1983, s.1

Application of Act: "mental disorder"

5–887 **1.**—(1) The provisions of this Act shall have effect with respect to the reception, care and treatment of mentally disordered patients, the management of their property and other related matters.

(2) In this Act—

"mental disorder" means any disorder or disability of the mind and "mentally disordered" shall be construed accordingly;

and other expressions shall have the meanings assigned to them in section 145 below.

(2A) But a person with learning disability shall not be considered by reason of that disability to be—

(a) suffering from mental disorder for the purposes of the provisions mentioned in subsection (2B) below; or

(b) requiring treatment in hospital for mental disorder for the purposes of sections 17E and 50 to 53 below,

unless that disability is associated with abnormally aggressive or seriously irresponsible conduct on his part.

(2B) The provisions are—

(a) sections 3, 7, 17A, 20 and 20A below;

(b) sections 35 to 38, 45A, 47, 48 and 51 below; and

(c) section 72(1)(b) and (c) and (4) below.

(3) Nothing in subsection (2) above shall be construed as implying that a person may be dealt with under this Act as suffering from mental disorder, or from any form of mental disorder described in this section, by reason only of promiscuity or other immoral conduct, sexual deviancy or dependence on alcohol or drugs.

[(3) Dependence on alcohol or drugs is not considered to be a disorder or disability of the mind for the purposes of subsection (2) above.

(4) In subsection (2A) above, "learning disability" means a state of arrested or incomplete development of the mind which includes significant impairment of intelligence and social functioning.]

[This section is printed as amended by the *MHA* 2007, ss.1(1)–(3), 2, 3 and 55, and Sched. 11, Pt 1.]

Mental Health Act 1983, s.54

Requirements as to medical evidence

5–888 **54.**—(1) The registered medical practitioner whose evidence is taken into account under section 35(3)(a) above and at least one of the registered medical practitioners, whose evidence is taken into account under sections 36(1), 37(2)(a), 38(1), 45A(2) and 51(6)(a) above and whose reports are taken into account under sections 47(1) and 48(1) above shall be a practitioner approved for the purposes of section 12 above by the Secretary of State as having special experience in the diagnosis or treatment of mental disorder.

(2) For the purposes of any provision of this Part of this Act under which a court may act on the written evidence of any person, a report in writing purporting to be signed by that person may, subject to the provisions of this section, be received in evidence without proof of the following—

(a) the signature of the person; or

(b) his having the requisite qualifications or approval or authority or being of the requisite description to give the report.

(2A) But the court may require the signatory of any such report to be called to give oral evidence.

(3) Where, in pursuance of a direction of the court, any such report is tendered in evidence otherwise than by or on behalf of the person who is the subject of the report, then—

(a) if that person is represented by *counsel or a solicitor* [an authorised person], a copy of the report shall be given to *his counsel or solicitor* [that authorised person];

(b) if that person is not so represented, the substance of the report shall be disclosed to him or, where he is a child or young person, to his parent or guardian if present in court; and

(c) except where the report relates only to arrangements for his admission to a hospital, that person may require the signatory of the report to be called to give oral evidence, and evidence to rebut the evidence contained in the report may be called by or on behalf of that person.

[This section is printed as amended by the *C(S)A* 1997, s.55, and Sched. 4, para. 12(6); and the *MHA* 2007, s.11(1) and (6); and as amended, as from a day to be appointed, by the *Legal Services Act* 2007, s.208(1), and Sched. 21, paras 53 and 58 (omission of italicised words, insertion of words in square brackets).]

Mental Health Act 1983, ss.39, 39A

Information as to hospitals

39.—(1) Where a court is minded to make a hospital order or interim hospital order in respect of any person it may request— **5–889**

(a) the Health Authority for the area in which that person resides or last resided; or

(b) any other Health Authority that appears to the court to be appropriate,

to furnish the court with such information as that Health Authority have or can reasonably obtain with respect to the hospital or hospitals (if any) in their area or elsewhere at which arrangements could be made for the admission of that person in pursuance of the order, and that Health Authority shall comply with any such request.

(1A) In relation to a person who has not attained the age of 18 years, subsection (1) above shall have effect as if the reference to the making of a hospital order included a reference to a remand under section 35 or 36 above or the making of an order under section 44 below.

(1B) Where the person concerned has not attained the age of 18 years, the information which may be requested under subsection (1) above includes, in particular, information about the availability of accommodation or facilities designed so as to be specially suitable for patients who have not attained the age of 18 years.

[This section is printed as amended, and repealed in part, by the *Health Authorities Act* 1995, s.2(1), and Sched. 1, para. 107(1) and (5); and the *MHA* 2007, s.31(1) and (2).]

Paragraph 173 of the *Mental Health Act* 1983 Memorandum (published by the Department of Health and the Welsh Office) provides that a court requesting information under this section should get in touch with the Regional Mental Health Lead [*sic*] at the respective regional office of the NHS Executive for details of the relevant Health Authority contact. Courts have a list of these contacts.

Information to facilitate guardianship orders

39A. Where a court is minded to make a guardianship order in respect of any offender, it may request the local social services authority for the area in which the offender resides or last resided, or any other local social services authority that appears to the court to be appropriate— **5–890**

(a) to inform the court whether it or any other person approved by it is willing to receive the offender into guardianship; and

(b) if so, to give such information as it reasonably can about how it or the other person could be expected to exercise in relation to the offender the powers conferred by section 40(2) below;

and that authority shall comply with any such request.

[This section was inserted by the *CJA* 1991, s.27(1).]

Mental Health Act 1983, s.35

Remand to hospital for report on accused's mental condition

35.—(1) Subject to the provisions of this section, the Crown Court or a magistrates' court may remand an accused person to a hospital specified by the court for a report on his mental condition. **5–891**

(2) For the purposes of this section an accused person is—

(a) in relation to the Crown Court, any person who is awaiting trial before the court for an offence punishable with imprisonment or who has been arraigned before the court for such an offence and has not yet been sentenced or otherwise dealt with for the offence on which he has been arraigned;

(b) in relation to a magistrates' court, any person who has been convicted by the court of an offence punishable on summary conviction with imprisonment and any person charged with such an offence if the court is satisfied that he did the act or made the omission charged or he has consented to the exercise by the court of the powers conferred by this section.

(3) Subject to subsection (4) below, the powers conferred by this section may be exercised if—

(a) the court is satisfied, on the written or oral evidence of a registered medical practitioner that there is reason to suspect that the accused person is suffering from mental disorder; and

(b) the court is of the opinion that it would be impracticable for a report on his mental condition to be made if he were remanded on bail;

but those powers shall not be exercised by the Crown Court in respect of a person who has been convicted before the court if the sentence for the offence of which he has been convicted is fixed by law.

(4) The court shall not remand an accused person to a hospital under this section unless satisfied, on the written or oral evidence of the approved clinician who would be responsible for making the report or of some other person representing the managers of the hospital, that arrangements have been made for his admission to that hospital and for his admission to it within the period of seven days beginning with the date of the remand; and if the court is so satisfied it may, pending his admission, give directions for his conveyance to and detention in a place of safety.

(5) Where a court has remanded an accused person under this section it may further remand him if it appears to the court, on the written or oral evidence of the approved clinician responsible for making the report, that a further remand is necessary for completing the assessment of the accused person's mental condition.

(6) The power of further remanding an accused person under this section may be exercised by the court without his being brought before the court if he is represented by *counsel or a solicitor and his counsel or solicitor* [an authorised person who] is given an opportunity of being heard.

(7) An accused person shall not be remanded or further remanded under this section for more than 28 days at a time or for more than 12 weeks in all; and the court may at any time terminate the remand if it appears to the court that it is appropriate to do so.

(8) An accused person remanded to hospital under this section shall be entitled to obtain at his own expense an independent report on his mental condition from a registered medical practitioner or approved clinician chosen by him and to apply to the court on the basis of it for his remand to be terminated under subsection (7) above.

(9) Where an accused person is remanded under this section—

(a) a constable or any other person directed to do so by the court shall convey the accused person to the hospital specified by the court within the period mentioned in subsection (4) above; and

(b) the managers of the hospital shall admit him within that period and thereafter detain him in accordance with the provisions of this section.

(10) If an accused person absconds from a hospital to which he has been remanded under this section, or while being conveyed to or from that hospital, he may be arrested without warrant by any constable and shall, after being arrested, be brought as soon as practicable before the court that remanded him: and the court may thereupon terminate the remand and deal with him in any way in which it could have dealt with him if he had not been remanded under this section.

[This section is printed as amended by the *MHA* 2007, ss.1(4) and 10(1) and (2), and Sched. 1, paras 1 and 5; and as amended, as from a day to be appointed, by the *Legal Services Act* 2007, s.208(1), and Sched. 21, paras 53 and 54 (omission of italicised words, insertion of words in square brackets).]

As to remands under this section, see *R. (Bitcon) v. West Allerdale Magistrates' Court* (2003) 147 S.J. 1028, QBD (Collins J.).

Mental Health Act 1983, s.36

Remand of accused person to hospital for treatment

36.—(1) Subject to the provisions of this section, the Crown Court may, instead of remanding an accused person in custody remand him to a hospital specified by the court if satisfied, on the written or oral evidence of two registered medical practitioners, that— **5–892**

(a) he is suffering from mental disorder of a nature or degree which makes it appropriate for him to be detained in a hospital for medical treatment;

(b) appropriate medical treatment is available for him.

(2) For the purposes of this section an accused person is any person who is in custody awaiting trial before the Crown Court for an offence punishable with imprisonment (other than an offence the sentence for which is fixed by law) or who at any time before sentence is in custody in the course of a trial before that court for such an offence.

(3) The court shall not remand an accused person under this section to a hospital unless it is satisfied, on the written or oral evidence of the approved clinician who would have overall responsibility for his case or of some other person representing the managers of the hospital, that arrangements have been made for his admission to that hospital and for his admission to it within the period of seven days beginning with the date of the remand; and if the court is so satisfied it may, pending his admission, give directions for his conveyance to and detention in a place of safety.

(4) Where a court has remanded an accused person under this section it may further remand him if it appears to the court, on the written or oral evidence of the responsible clinician, that a further remand is warranted.

(5), (6) [*Identical to s.35(6), (7),* ante.]

(7) [*Identical to s.35(8),* ante, *save for reference to* "subsection (6)" *(and subject to a like prospective amendment).*]

(8) Subsections (9) and (10) of section 35 above shall have effect in relation to a remand under this section as they have effect in relation to a remand under that section.

[This section is printed as amended by the *MHA* 2007, ss.1(4), 5(1) and (2) and 10(1) and (3), and Sched. 1, paras 1 and 6. Subs. (6) is subject to an identical prospective amendment as that for s.35(6): 2007 Act, s.208(1), and Sched. 21, paras 53 and 55.]

Mental Health Act 1983, s.38

Interim hospital orders

38.—(1) Where a person is convicted before the Crown Court of an offence punishable with imprisonment (other than an offence the sentence for which is fixed by law) or is convicted by a magistrates' court of an offence punishable on summary conviction with imprisonment and the court before or by which he is convicted is satisfied, on the written or oral evidence of two registered medical practitioners— **5–893**

(a) that the offender is suffering from mental disorder; and

(b) that there is reason to suppose that the mental disorder from which the offender is suffering is such that it may be appropriate for a hospital order to be made in his case,

the court may, before making a hospital order or dealing with him in some other way, make an order (in this Act referred to as "an interim hospital order") authorising his admission to such hospital as may be specified in the order and his detention there in accordance with this section.

(2) In the case of an offender who is subject to an interim hospital order the court may make a hospital order without his being brought before the court if he is represented by *counsel or a solicitor and his counsel or solicitor* [an authorised person who] is given an opportunity of being heard.

(3) At least one of the registered medical practitioners whose evidence is taken into account under subsection (1) above shall be employed at the hospital which is to be specified in the order.

(4) An interim hospital order shall not be made for the admission of an offender to a hospital unless the court is satisfied, on the written or oral evidence of the approved clinician who would have overall responsibility for his case or of some other person representing the managers of the hospital, that arrangements have been made for his admission to that hospital and for his admission to it within the period of 28 days beginning with the date of the order; and if the court is so satisfied the court may, pending his admission, give directions for his conveyance to and detention in a place of safety.

(5) An interim hospital order—

(a) shall be in force for such period, not exceeding 12 weeks, as the court may specify when making the order; but

(b) may be renewed for further periods of not more than 28 days at a time if it appears to the court, on the written or oral evidence of the responsible clinician, that the continuation of the order is warranted;

but no such order shall continue in force for more than twelve months in all and the court shall terminate the order if it makes a hospital order in respect of the offender or decides after considering the written or oral evidence of the responsible clinician to deal with the offender in some other way.

(6) The power of renewing an interim hospital order may be exercised without the offender being brought before the court if he is represented by counsel or a solicitor and his counsel or solicitor is given an opportunity of being heard.

(7) If an offender absconds from a hospital in which he is detained in pursuance of an interim hospital order, or while being conveyed to or from such a hospital, he may be arrested without warrant by a constable and shall, after being arrested, be brought as soon as practicable before the court that made the order; and the court may thereupon terminate the order and deal with him in any way in which it could have dealt with him if no such order had been made.

[This section is printed as amended by the *C(S)A* 1997, s.49(1); and the *MHA* 2007, ss.1(4) and 10(1) and (5), and Sched. 1, paras 1 and 8; and as amended, as from a day to be appointed, by the *Legal Services Act* 2007, s.208(1), and Sched. 21, paras 53 and 56 (omission of italicised words, insertion of words in square brackets).]

At least one of the medical practitioners whose evidence is taken into account must be approved for the purposes of section 12: see s.54, *ante*, § 5–888.

Mental Health Act 1983, s.37

Powers of courts to order hospital admission or guardianship

5–894 **37.**—(1) Where a person is convicted before the Crown Court of an offence punishable with imprisonment other than an offence the sentence for which is fixed by law, or is convicted by a magistrates' court of an offence punishable on summary conviction with imprisonment, and the conditions mentioned in subsection (2) below are satisfied, the court may by order authorise his admission to and detention in such hospital as may be specified in the order or, as the case may be, place him under the guardianship of a local social services authority or of such other person approved by a local social services authority as may be so specified.

(1A) In the case of an offence the sentence for which would otherwise fall to be imposed—

(a) under section 51A(2) of the *Firearms Act* 1968,

(b) under section 110(2) or 111(2) of the *Powers of Criminal Courts (Sentencing) Act* 2000,

(c) under any of section 225(2) or 226(2) of the *Criminal Justice Act* 2003, or

(d) under section 29(4) or (6) of the *Violent Crime Reduction Act* 2006 (minimum sentences in certain cases of using someone to mind a weapon),

nothing in those provisions shall prevent a court from making an order under subsection (1) above for the admission of the offender to a hospital.

(1B) References in subsection (1A) above to a sentence falling to be imposed under any of the provisions mentioned in that subsection are to be read in accordance with section 305(4) of the *Criminal Justice Act* 2003.

(2) The conditions referred to in subsection (1) above are that—

(a) the court is satisfied, on the written or oral evidence of two registered medical practitioners, that the offender is suffering from mental disorder and that either—

(i) the mental disorder from which the offender is suffering is of a nature or degree which makes it appropriate for him to be detained in a hospital for medical treatment and appropriate medical treatment is available for him; or

(ii) in the case of an offender who has attained the age of 16 years, the mental disorder is of a nature or degree which warrants his reception into guardianship under this Act; and

(b) the court is of the opinion, having regard to all the circumstances including the nature of the offence and the character and antecedents of the offender, and to the other available methods of dealing with him, that the most suitable method of disposing of the case is by means of an order under this section.

(3) Where a person is charged before a magistrates' court with any act or omission as an offence and the court would have power, on convicting him of that offence, to make an order under subsection (1) above in his case, then, if the court is satisfied that the accused did the act or made the omission charged, the court may, if it thinks fit, make such an order without convicting him.

(4) An order for the admission of an offender to a hospital (in this Act referred to as "a hospital order") shall not be made under this section unless the court is satisfied on the written or oral evidence of the approved clinician who would have overall responsibility for his case or of some other person representing the managers of the hospital that arrangements have been made for his admission to that hospital ... and for his admission to it within the period of 28 days beginning with the date of the making of such an order; and the court may, pending his admission within that period, give such directions as it thinks fit for his conveyance to and detention in a place of safety.

(5) If within the said period of 28 days it appears to the Secretary of State that by reason of an emergency or other special circumstances it is not practicable for the patient to be received into the hospital specified in the order, he may give directions for the admission of the patient to such other hospital as appears to be appropriate instead of the hospital so specified; and where such directions are given—

(a) the Secretary of State shall cause the person having the custody of the patient to be informed; and

(b) the hospital order shall have effect as if the hospital specified in the directions were substituted for the hospital specified in the order.

(6) An order placing an offender under the guardianship of a local social services authority or of any other person (in this Act referred to as "a guardianship order") shall not be made under this section unless the court is satisfied that that authority or person is willing to receive the offender into guardianship.

(8) Where an order is made under this section, the court shall not—

(a) pass sentence of imprisonment or impose a fine or make a community order (within the meaning of Part 12 of the *Criminal Justice Act* 2003) [or a youth rehabilitation order (within the meaning of Part 1 of the *Criminal Justice and Immigration Act* 2008)] in respect of the offence,

(b) if the order under this section is a hospital order, make a referral order (within the meaning of the *Powers of Criminal Courts (Sentencing) Act* 2000) in respect of the offence,

(c) make in respect of the offender *a supervision order (within the meaning of that Act) or* an order under section 150 of that Act (binding over of parent or guardian),

but the court may make any other order which it has power to make apart from this section; and for the purposes of this subsection "sentence of imprisonment" includes any sentence or order for detention.

[This section is printed as amended and repealed in part by the *C(S)A* 1997, ss.55 and 56(2), and Scheds 4, para. 12(1)–(3), and 6; the *YJCEA* 1999, s.67(1) and Sched. 4, para. 11; the *PCC(S)A* 2000, s.165(1) and Sched. 9, para. 90(1), (6); the *CJA* 2003, ss.304 and 332, Sched. 32, paras 37 and 38; the *VCRA* 2006, ss.49 and 65, Sched. 1, para. 2, and Sched. 5; the *MHA* 2007, ss.1(4), 4(1) and (5), 10(1) and (4), and 55, Sched. 1, paras 1 and 7, and Sched. 11, Pt 1; and the *CJIA* 2008, s.148(1), and Sched. 26, para. 8; and as amended, as from a day to be appointed (as to which, see *ante*, § 5–1), by *ibid.*, ss.6(2) and 149, Sched. 4, para. 30, and Sched. 28, Pt 1. For the saving provision in relation to the amendments made by the 2003 Act, see *ante*, § 5–1b.]

For section 305 of the *CJA* 2003, see *ante*, § 5–7. As to the meaning of "community order" for the purposes of Part 12 of that Act, see section 177 thereof, *ante*, § 5–130.

Mental Health Act 1983, s.40

Effect of hospital orders, guardianship orders and interim hospital orders

40.—(1) A hospital order shall be sufficient authority— **5–895**

(a) for a constable, an approved social worker or any other person directed to do so by the court to convey the patient to the hospital specified in the order within a period of 28 days; and

(b) for the managers of the hospital to admit him at any time within that period and thereafter detain him in accordance with the provisions of this Act.

(2) A guardianship order shall confer on the authority or person named in the order as

guardian the same powers as a guardianship application made and accepted under Part II of this Act.

(3) Where an interim hospital order is made in respect of an offender—

(a) a constable or any other person directed to do so by the court shall convey the offender to the hospital specified in the order within the period mentioned in section 38(4) above; and

(b) the managers of the hospital shall admit him within that period and thereafter detain him in accordance with the provisions of section 38 above.

(4) A patient who is admitted to a hospital in pursuance of a hospital order, or placed under guardianship by a guardianship order shall, subject to the provisions of this subsection, be treated for the purposes of the provisions of this Act mentioned in Part I of Schedule 1 to this Act as if he had been so admitted or placed on the date of the order in pursuance of an application for admission for treatment or a guardianship application, as the case may be, duly made under Part II of this Act, but subject to any modifications of those provisions specified in that Part of that Schedule.

(5) Where a patient is admitted to a hospital in pursuance of a hospital order, or placed under guardianship by a guardianship order, any previous application, hospital order or guardianship order by virtue of which he was liable to be detained in a hospital or subject to guardianship shall cease to have effect; but if the first-mentioned order, or the conviction on which it was made, is quashed on appeal, this subsection shall not apply and section 22 above shall have effect as if during any period for which the patient was liable to be detained or subject to guardianship under the order, he had been detained in custody as mentioned in that section.

Interrelationship with discretionary life sentences

5–895a Where the criteria for a discretionary life sentence were met and the criteria for a hospital order under section 37 of the 1983 Act were also met, and a hospital place was available, the court was still bound to consider "having regard to all the circumstances including the nature of the offence and the character and antecedents of the offender" whether an order under section 37 was "the most suitable method of disposing of the case" before it could make such an order; and for the purpose of deciding what was most suitable, a court could give appropriate weight to the different release regimes (with the Parole Board taking a wider view of risk in relation to a discretionary lifer than a mental heath review tribunal in the case of a restricted patient, the focus in the latter case being on the existence, or potential risk of recurrence, of any mental impairment, *etc*., making detention in hospital for appropriate medical treatment necessary for the patient's health or safety or for the protection of others); but this did not mean that it should be assumed that a hospital order, which had the advantage of guaranteeing hospital treatment, would in any particular case necessarily afford significantly less protection to the public: *R. v. I.A.* [2006] 1 Cr.App.R.(S.) 91, CA. On the one hand, the court said that the judge had to weigh the seriousness of the offending, the impact on the victims and their families, the fact (as was the case here) that the defendant could not be excused all responsibility (fit to plead and no defence of insanity) and the fact that a discretionary life sentence afforded the most clear-cut security to the public; on the other hand, the judge in this case had had to weigh the fact that the doctors were unanimous as to a hospital order being the preferred option, and the fact that if a prison sentence were passed, there was no guarantee of a transfer to hospital even where, as here, the judge expressed a strong hope and expectation that such a transfer would occur forthwith; where, however, it had not been considerations of responsibility or punishment that determined the judge's decision to order a discretionary life sentence, but considerations of public safety, his order would be quashed and substituted by a hospital order (with restriction without limit of time); on the evidence, the hospital order regime was designed and able to offer great protection, if necessary indefinitely, for the public in respect of the risks posed by the defendant; and furthermore, those risks were associated with conditions in respect of which medical treatment would be appropriate.

In *R. v. Beatty*, unreported, October 17, 2006, CA ([2006] EWCA Crim. 2359), it was held that the fact that an offender who was subject to a discretionary life sentence had been subsequently transferred to hospital by a direction under section 47 of the

1983 Act, coupled with a restriction direction under section 49, was no bar on appeal to the quashing of the life sentence and the substitution of a hospital order under section 37, coupled with a restriction order under section 41, where fresh evidence demonstrated that the criteria under section 37 had in fact been satisfied at the time of sentence (explaining the critical distinction between sections 37 and 47).

Relevance of the offence of which the offender is convicted

A hospital order may be made even though there is no causal connection between the offender's disorder and the offences he had committed: *R. v. McBride* [1972] Crim.L.R. 322, CA. In making a hospital order, the court is not concerned with the gravity of the offence of which the offender is convicted, except in so far as the offence is an indication of the need for treatment in special conditions. Hospital orders have been made in respect of offenders guilty of very minor offences, but for whom there was a clear indication of the need for treatment (see for example *R. v. Eaton* [1976] Crim.L.R. 390, CA, and *R. v. Allison*, unreported, January 31, 1977). **5–896**

The principle that a hospital order may be made even though there is no causal connection between the offender's disorder and the offences he had committed was not followed in *R. v. Nafei* [2005] 2 Cr.App.R.(S.) 24, CA. The judge's decision to impose a sentence of 12 years' imprisonment and not to follow the recommendation for a hospital order for an offender charged with the fraudulent evasion of the prohibition on the importation of Class A drugs was upheld. There was no causal connection between the offending and the mental illness, and, when dealing with this type of offence, the courts tend to focus primarily, if not solely on the offence itself, and, for reasons of policy and deterrence, personal factors ordinarily tend to count for relatively little. This approach was particularly justified given that treatment is, or at least ought to be, available to mentally ill patients when in prison, and that there are powers (under sections 47 and 49 of the 1983 Act) available for a transfer to hospital if appropriate.

In *R. v. Khelifi* [2006] 2 Cr.App.R.(S.) 100, CA, it was held that the approach taken in *R. v. Nafei* (*ante*), was not limited to serious drugs cases. The decision whether to make a hospital order, instead of imposing a sentence of imprisonment, is discretionary, and fulfilment of the conditions in section 37(2) will not give rise to a presumption that an order will be made. Whilst the welfare of the offender is an important matter to be taken into consideration, it must be assessed in the light of the seriousness of the offence. Where the offender was being sentenced with other offenders in respect of whom substantial sentences of imprisonment would be imposed, it would not be wrong in principle to take account of concerns as to parity of sentencing.

Admission to hospital

It is not necessary that the offender should be admitted to a hospital in the part of the country where he is normally resident: *R. v. Marsden*, 52 Cr.App.R. 301, CA. A hospital order may be made only if the hospital to be specified in the order is willing to admit the offender. In the case of an offender who is thought to be dangerous to himself or others if at liberty, the court may wish to specify a special hospital in the order: but if the responsible authority is not able to offer a place in a special hospital, the court is not empowered to order it to do so, and must deal with the offender in some other way (see *R. v. Parker*, unreported, March 21, 1975; and *R. v. Jones*, unreported, November 19, 1976). **5–897**

Summary proceedings

A defendant is not entitled to a trial of an issue of insanity, and a possible acquittal on that account, before the court disposes of the case (if appropriate) by making an order under section 37(3) of the 1983 Act; accordingly, in all cases where a section 37(3) order is a possibility, the court should first conduct the fact-finding exercise (whether by admissions or evidence); if it is not satisfied that the act alleged was done or the omission made, an unqualified acquittal must follow whatever anxieties there may be as to the **5–897a** defendant's mental health; if it is so satisfied, and the conditions for making a section 37(3) order are met, and the court thinks it appropriate to make such an order, the court may nevertheless, in an appropriate case (and before it makes the order), try the issue of insanity and pronounce its conclusion upon it, without convicting or acquitting the accused; if, however, it is clear that no section 37(3) order could possibly be made (*e.g.* because the defendant has since recovered), then, in the absence of some compelling factor, the case must proceed to trial and the accused must be acquitted if the insanity defence prevails: *R. (Surat Singh) v. Stratford Magistrates' Court* [2008] 1 Cr.App.R. 2, DC.

(2) Restriction orders

Mental Health Act 1983, s.41

Power of higher courts to restrict discharge from hospital

5–898 **41.**—(1) Where a hospital order is made in respect of an offender by the Crown Court, and it appears to the court, having regard to the nature of the offence, the antecedents of the offender and the risk of his committing further offences if set at large, that it is necessary for the protection of the public from serious harm so to do, the court may, subject to the provisions of this section, further order that the offender shall be subject to the special restrictions set out in this section, … ; and an order under this section shall be known as "a restriction order".

(2) A restriction order shall not be made in the case of any person unless at least one of the registered medical practitioners whose evidence is taken into account by the court under section 37(2)(a) above has given evidence orally before the court.

(3) The special restrictions applicable to a patient in respect of whom a restriction order is in force are as follows—

(a) none of the provisions of Part II of this Act relating to the duration, renewal and expiration of authority for the detention of patients shall apply, and the patient shall continue to be liable to be detained by virtue of the relevant hospital order until he is duly discharged under the said Part II or absolutely discharged under sections 42, 73, 74 or 75 below;

(aa) none of the provisions of Part II of this Act relating to community treatment orders and community patients shall apply;

(b) no application shall be made to a Mental Health Review Tribunal in respect of a patient under sections 66 or 69(1) below;

(c) the following powers shall be exercisable only with the consent of the Secretary of State, namely—

(i) power to grant leave of absence to the patient under section 17 above;

(ii) power to transfer the patient in pursuance of regulations under section 19 above or in pursuance of subsection (3) of that section; and

(iii) power to order the discharge of the patient under section 23 above;

and if leave of absence is granted under the said section 17 power to recall the patient under that section shall vest in the Secretary of State as well as the responsible clinician; and

(d) the power of the Secretary of State to recall the patient under the said section 18 above may be exercised at any time;

and in relation to any such patient section 40(4) above shall have effect as if it referred to Part II of Schedule 1 to this Act instead of Part I of that Schedule.

(4) A hospital order shall not cease to have effect under section 40(5) above if a restriction order in respect of the patient is in force at the material time.

(5) Where a restriction order in respect of a patient ceases to have effect while the relevant hospital order continues in force, the provisions of section 40 above and Part I of Schedule 1 to this Act shall apply to the patient as if he had been admitted to the hospital in pursuance of a hospital order (without a restriction order) made on the date on which the restriction order ceased to have effect.

(6) While a person is subject to a restriction order the responsible clinician shall at such intervals (not exceeding one year) as the Secretary of State may direct examine and report to the Secretary of State on that person; and every report shall contain such particulars as the Secretary of State may require.

[This section is printed as amended by the *Mental Health (Patients in the Community) Act* 1995, s.1(2), and Sched. 1, para. 5; the *C(S)A* 1997, s.49(2); and the *MHA* 2007, ss.10(1) and (6), 32(4) and 40(1), and Sched. 3, paras 1 and 17.]

Mental Health Act 1983, s.43

Power of magistrates' courts to commit for restriction order

43.—(1) If in the case of a person of or over the age of 14 years who is convicted by a magistrates' court of an offence punishable on summary conviction with imprisonment— **5–899**

(a) the conditions which under section 37(1) above are required to be satisfied for the making of a hospital order are satisfied in respect of the offender; but

(b) it appears to the court, having regard to the nature of the offence, the antecedents of the offender and the risk of his committing further offences if set at large, that if a hospital order is made a restriction order should also be made,

the court may, instead of making a hospital order or dealing with him in any other manner, commit him in custody to the Crown Court to be dealt with in respect of the offence.

(2) Where an offender is committed to the Crown Court under this section, the Crown Court shall inquire into the circumstances of the case and may—

(a) if that court would have power so to do under the foregoing provisions of this Part of this Act upon the conviction of the offender before the court of such an offence as is described in section 37(1) above, make a hospital order in his case, with or without a restriction order;

(b) if the court does not make such an order, deal with the offender in any other manner in which the magistrates' court might have dealt with him.

(3) The Crown Court shall have the same power to make orders under sections 35, 36 and 38 above in the case of a person committed to the court under this section as the Crown Court has under those sections in the case of an accused person within the meaning of section 35 or 36 above or of a person convicted before that court as mentioned in section 38 above.

(4) *The power of a magistrates' court under section 3 of the* Powers of Criminal Courts (Sentencing) Act *2000 (which enables such a court to commit an offender to the Crown Court where the court is of the opinion that greater punishment should be inflicted for the offence than the court has power to inflict) shall also be exercisable by a magistrates' court where it is of the opinion that greater punishment should be inflicted as aforesaid on the offender unless a hospital order is made in his case with a restriction order.*

[(4) The powers of a magistrates' court under section 3 or 3B of the *Powers of Criminal Courts (Sentencing) Act* 2000 (which enable such a court to commit an offender to the Crown Court where the court is of the opinion, or it appears to the court, as mentioned in the section in question) shall also be exercisable by a magistrates' court where it is of that opinion (or it so appears to it) unless a hospital order is made in the offender's case with a restriction order.]

(5) *The power of the Crown Court to make a hospital order, with or without a restriction order, in the case of a person convicted before that court of an offence may, in the same circumstances and subject to the same conditions, be exercised by such a court in the case of a person committed to the court under section 5 of the* Vagrancy Act *1824 (which provides for the committal to the Crown Court of persons who are incorrigible rogues within the meaning of that section).*

[This section is printed as amended by the *PCC(S)A* 2000, s.165(1), and Sched. 9, para. 91. Subs. (4) (printed in square brackets) is substituted for the original subs. (4) (printed in italics), as from a day to be appointed, by the *CJA* 2003, s.41, and Sched. 3, para. 55(1) and (2). Subs. (5) is repealed, as from a day to be appointed, by *ibid.*, s.332, and Sched. 37, Pt 9.]

Mental Health Act 1983, s.44

Committal to hospital under section 43

44.—(1) Where an offender is committed under section 43 (1) above and the magistrates' court by which he is committed is satisfied on written or oral evidence that arrangements have been made for the admission of the offender to a hospital in the event of an order being made under this section, the court may, instead of committing him in custody, by order direct him to be admitted to that hospital, specifying it, and to be detained there until the case is disposed of by the Crown Court, and may give such directions as it thinks fit for his production from the hospital to attend the Crown Court by which his case is to be dealt with. **5–900**

(2) The evidence required by subsection (1) above shall be given by the approved clinician who would have overall responsibility for the offender's case or by some other person representing the managers of the hospital in question.

(3) The power to give directions under section 37(4) above, section 37(5) above and section 40(1) above shall apply in relation to an order under this section as they apply in relation to a hospital order, but as if references to the period of 28 days mentioned in section 40(1) above were omitted; and subject as aforesaid an order under this section shall, until the offender's case is disposed of by the Crown Court, have the same effect as a hospital order together with a restriction order, … .

[This section is printed as amended by the *MHA* 2007, ss.10(1) and (7) and 40(3)(a).]

General considerations

5–901 If the offender qualifies for a hospital order with restriction, and a place is available in a suitable hospital, it is wrong in principle to impose a sentence of life imprisonment to prevent his premature release by order of the Mental Health Review Tribunal: *R. v. Howell*, 7 Cr.App.R.(S.) 360, CA; *R. v. Mbatha, ibid.* at 373, CA. *R. v. Fleming*, 14 Cr.App.R.(S.) 151, CA, which indicated that an exception might be made to this principle where the offender had previously been released from a hospital order, was disapproved in *R. v. Mitchell* [1997] 1 Cr.App.R.(S.) 90. See also *R. v. Moses* [1996] 2 Cr.App.R.(S.) 407, CA, and *R. v. Hutchinson* [1997] 2 Cr.App.R.(S.) 60, CA, for decisions to similar effect.

Desirability of restriction orders

5–902 If a restriction order is made, the safer course is to make it unlimited in time, unless the doctors are able to assert confidently that recovery will take place within a fixed period: *R. v. Gardiner*, 51 Cr.App.R. 187, CA (in which the consequences of making a hospital order with and without a restriction order are set out). See also *R. v. Haynes*, 3 Cr.App.R.(S.) 330 (there is no analogy between a restriction order and a determinate sentence of imprisonment); and *R. v. Nwohia* [1996] 1 Cr.App.R.(S.) 170, CA (predictions about the future in this type of case are difficult; without medical evidence to say that the patient can be cured within a particular period, it would be unwise to put a limit on the restriction order).

Necessity for evidence that offender dangerous to public

5–903 Where a court was considering whether to exercise its discretion to make a restriction order, the test to be applied was whether the offender posed a risk of serious harm to the public, not whether he posed a serious or significant risk of such harm (*R. v. Birch*, 90 Cr.App.R. 78, CA); and the court was not bound to determine that issue by reference to the nature of any past violence (*R. (Jones) v. Isleworth Crown Court*, unreported, March 2, 2005, DC ([2005] EWHC 662 (Admin.)): *R. v. Golding* [2007] 1 Cr.App.R.(S.) 79, CA. In *Birch, ante*, it was further pointed out that the responsibility for assessing the risk was that of the court, which was not bound to follow the advice of the medical witnesses, that harm was not limited to personal injury, and that a court should not impose a restriction order to mark the gravity of the offence (which is not necessarily of critical importance).

Conviction of summary offence

5–904 Where a person is tried on indictment for a summary offence by virtue of section 40 of the *CJA* 1988 (*ante*, § 1–75ai) and is convicted, the Crown Court has power to make a hospital order with a restriction order under sections 37(1) and 41(1) of the 1983 Act; although section 40(3) of the 1988 Act restricts the court to dealing with the offender in a manner in which a magistrates' court could have dealt with him, a magistrates' court has power under section 43(1) of the 1983 Act to commit with a view to the imposition of a restriction order; accordingly, the Crown Court may notionally commit the matter to itself and then exercise the power under section 41: *R. v. Avbunudje* [1999] 2 Cr.App.R.(S.) 189, CA.

Responsibility of judge

5–905 A restriction order may be made even though the medical witnesses recommend that no restriction order should be made: *R. v. Royse*, 3 Cr.App.R.(S.) 58, CA.

The *C(S)A* 1997, s.46, inserts new sections 45A and 45B into the 1983 Act. The new section 45A empowers the Crown Court to make a hospital and limitation direction in relation to an offender who has been sentenced to imprisonment. The court must be satisfied on the evidence of two medical practitioners (one of whom must give evidence orally) that the offender is suffering from a psychopathic disorder, that the disorder is of a nature or degree which makes it appropriate for him to be detained in a hospital for medical treatment, and that such treatment is likely to alleviate or prevent a deterioration in his condition. The order must direct that the offender be removed to a hospital, and be subject to the restrictions set out in section 41 of the 1983 Act (*ante*, § 5–898). It does not appear to be intended that the court should make a hospital direction without a limitation direction. The hospital must be specified in the direction, and the court must be satisfied that the offender will be admitted to the hospital within 28 days of the making of the order. An offender subject to a hospital and limitation direction will be treated for the purpose of his detention in hospital as if he had been sentenced to imprisonment and transferred to hospital by order of the Secretary of State under section 47 of the 1983 Act. **5–906**

The *C(S)A* 1997, s.47 (*post*, § 5–909), empowers a court which makes a hospital order (*MHA* 1983, s.37), or a hospital and limitation direction (*MHA* 1983, s.45A), to specify a hospital unit, as opposed to a hospital, as the place where the person subject to the order will be liable to be detained.

(3) Hospital and limitation directions

Mental Health Act 1983, ss.45A, 45B

Hospital and limitation directions

Power of higher courts to direct hospital admission

45A.—(1) This section applies where, in the case of a person convicted before the Crown Court of an offence the sentence for which is not fixed by law— **5–907**

(a) the conditions mentioned in subsection (2) below are fulfilled; and

(b) the court considers making a hospital order in respect of him before deciding to impose a sentence of imprisonment ("the relevant sentence") in respect of the offence.

(2) The conditions referred to in subsection (1) above are that the court is satisfied, on the written or oral evidence of two registered medical practitioners—

(a) that the offender is suffering from mental disorder;

(b) that the mental disorder from which the offender is suffering is of a nature or degree which makes it appropriate for him to be detained in a hospital for medical treatment; and

(c) that appropriate medical treatment is available for him.

(3) The court may give both of the following directions, namely—

(a) a direction that, instead of being removed to and detained in a prison, the offender be removed to and detained in such hospital as may be specified in the direction (in this Act referred to as a "hospital direction"); and

(b) a direction that the offender be subject to the special restrictions set out in section 41 above (in this Act referred to as a "limitation direction").

(4) A hospital direction and a limitation direction shall not be given in relation to an offender unless at least one of the medical practitioners whose evidence is taken into account by the court under subsection (2) above has given evidence orally before the court.

(5) A hospital direction and a limitation direction shall not be given in relation to an offender unless the court is satisfied on the written or oral evidence of the approved clinician who would have overall responsibility for his case, or of some other person representing the managers of the hospital that arrangements have been made—

(a) for his admission to that hospital; and

(b) for his admission to it within the period of 28 days beginning with the day of the giving of such directions;

and the court may, pending his admission within that period, give such directions as it thinks fit for his conveyance to and detention in a place of safety.

(6) If within the said period of 28 days it appears to the Secretary of State that by reason of an emergency or other special circumstances it is not practicable for the patient to be

received into the hospital specified in the hospital direction, he may give instructions for the admission of the patient to such other hospital as appears to be appropriate instead of the hospital so specified.

(7) Where such instructions are given—

(a) the Secretary of State shall cause the person having the custody of the patient to be informed, and

(b) the hospital direction shall have effect as if the hospital specified in the instructions were substituted for the hospital specified in the hospital direction.

(8) Section 38(1) and (5) and section 39 above shall have effect as if any reference to the making of a hospital order included a reference to the giving of a hospital direction and a limitation direction.

(9) A hospital direction and a limitation direction given in relation to an offender shall have effect not only as regards the relevant sentence but also (so far as applicable) as regards any other sentence of imprisonment imposed on the same or a previous occasion.

[Ss.45A and 45B were inserted by the *C(S)A* 1997, s.46. This section is printed as amended and repealed in part by the *CJA* 2003, s.332, and Sched. 37, Pt 7; and the *MHA* 2007, ss.1(4), 4(1) and (6), 10(1) and (8), and 55, Sched. 1, paras 1 and 9, and Sched. 11, Pt 1.]

In *R. v. Staines* [2006] 2 Cr.App.R.(S.) 61, CA, it was held: (i) whereas section 45A provides the court with a power to direct that a person sentenced to imprisonment who is suffering from a psychopathic disorder be removed and detained in a hospital rather than removed and detained in prison, it was not necessarily wrong in principle to make such an order in respect of an offender in whom both a psychopathic disorder and a mental illness co-existed instead of making a hospital order under section 37 (*ante*, § 5–894); section 45A applied both to offenders suffering from a psychopathic disorder alone and to offenders for whom neither imprisonment, nor a hospital order on its own, was appropriate and where the mutually exclusive operation of such disposals was unsatisfactory (see *R. v. Drew* [2003] 2 Cr.App.R. 24, HL (§ 5–251l in the supplement)); furthermore, it could not be said that the existence of the mental illness should allay a judge's fear that lack of treatability (of the psychopathic disorder) might result in release at a time when there remained a considerable risk of serious danger to the public (if a hospital order were made); (ii) whilst it had been thought that sentencers might on occasion give insufficient weight to the different conditions governing the release and recall of restricted patients as opposed to those serving sentences of imprisonment, an order made under section 45A carried with it the distinct advantage that both sets of criteria could be taken into account, *viz.* those focussing upon medical grounds and those focussing upon the safety of the public.

Effect of hospital and limitation directions

5–908 **45B.**—(1) A hospital direction and a limitation direction shall be sufficient authority—

(a) for a constable or any other person directed to do so by the court to convey the patient to the hospital specified in the hospital direction within a period of 28 days; and

(b) for the managers of the hospital to admit him at any time within that period and thereafter detain him in accordance with the provisions of this Act.

(2) With respect to any person—

(a) a hospital direction shall have effect as a transfer direction; and

(b) a limitation direction shall have effect as a restriction direction.

(3) While a person is subject to a hospital direction and a limitation direction the responsible clinician shall at such intervals (not exceeding one year) as the Secretary of State may direct examine and report to the Secretary of State on that person; and every report shall contain such particulars as the Secretary of State may require.

[As to the insertion of this section, see the note to s.45A, *ante*. It is printed as amended by the *MHA* 2007, s.10(1) and (9).]

Crime (Sentences) Act 1997, s.47

Power to specify hospital units

5–909 **47.**—(1) Subject to subsection (2) below, any power to specify a hospital which is conferred by—

(a) section 37 of the 1983 Act (hospital orders);

(b) section 45A of that Act (hospital and limitation directions);

(c) section 47 of that Act (transfer directions);

includes power to specify a hospital unit; and where such a unit is specified in relation to any person in the exercise of such a power, any reference in any enactment (including one contained in this Act) to him being, or being liable to be, detained in a hospital shall be construed accordingly.

(2) In subsection (1) above—

(a) paragraph (a) shall not apply unless the court also makes an order under section 41 of the 1983 Act (restriction orders);

(b) paragraph (c) shall not apply unless the Secretary of State also gives a direction under section 49 of that Act (restriction directions); ….

(3) In this section—

"hospital", in relation to any exercise of a power, has the same meaning as in the enactment which confers the power;

"hospital unit" means any part of a hospital which is treated as a separate unit.

(4) A reference in this section to section 37 or 41 of the 1983 Act includes a reference to that section as it applies by virtue of—

(a) section 5 of the *Criminal Procedure (Insanity) Act* 1964,

(b) section 6 or 14 of the *Criminal Appeal Act* 1968, [or]

(c) *section 116A of the* Army Act *1955 or the* Air Force Act *1955 or section 63A of the* Naval Discipline Act *1957, or*

(d) *section 16 or 23 of the* Courts-Martial (Appeals) Act *1968*

[(c) Schedule 4 to the *Armed Forces Act* 2006 (including as applied by section 16(2) of the *Court Martial Appeals Act* 1968)].

[This section is printed as amended, and repealed in part, by the *Domestic Violence, Crime and Victims Act* 2004, s.58(1) and (2), Sched. 10, para. 45, and Sched. 11; and as amended, as from a day to be appointed, by the *AFA* 2006, s.378(1), and Sched. 16, para. 143 (substitution of para. (c) (in square brackets) for paras (c) and (d) in subs. (4)).]

The substitution of a new subsection (4) by the 2004 Act does not apply in relation to proceedings before the Crown Court where the accused was arraigned before the commencement of the amendment (March 31, 2005 (*Domestic Violence, Crime and Victims Act 2004 (Commencement No. 1) Order* 2005 (S.I. 2005 No. 579))), or to proceedings before the Court of Appeal where the hearing began before that commencement: *Domestic Violence, Crime and Victims Act* 2004, s.59, and Sched. 12, para. 8.

XII. RECOMMENDATION FOR DEPORTATION

Immigration Act 1971, s.3(6), (8)

General provisions for regulation and control

3.—(6) Without prejudice to the operation of subsection (5) above, a person who is not a British citizen shall also be liable to deporation from the United Kingdom if, after he has attained the age of 17 he is convicted of an offence for which he is punishable with imprisonment and on his conviction is recommended for deportation by a court empowered by this Act to do so. **5–910**

(8) When any question arises under this Act whether or not a person is a British citizen, or is entitled to any exemption under this Act, it shall lie on the person asserting it to prove that he is.

[These subsections are printed as amended by the *British Nationality Act* 1981, Sched. 4.]

For definition of "British citizen", see the *British Nationality Act* 1981, Pt I. A person is deemed to have attained the age of 17 if he appears to have done so to the court (s.6(3)(a), *post*,§ 5–911), and persons exempted from the operation of the Act by order of the Secretary of State under section 8(2) (*post*, § 5–913). See also section 8 for provisions relating to crews of ships and aircraft, military personnel and persons with diplomatic immunity.

Immigration Act 1971, s.6

Power of court to recommend deportation

5–911 **6.**—(1) Where under section 3(6) above a person convicted of an offence is liable to deportation on the recommendation of a court, he may be recommended for deportation by any court having power to sentence him for the offence unless the court commits him to be sentence or further dealth with for that offence by another court: …

(2) A court shall not recommend a person for deporation unless he has been given not less that seven days' notice in writing stating that a person is not liable for deportation if he is a British citizen, describing the persons who are British citizens and stating (so far as material) the effect of section 3(8) and section 7 below; but the powers of adjournment conferred by section 10(3) of the *magistrates' Courts Act* 1980, section 179 or 380 of the *Criminal Procedure (Scotland) Act* 1975 or any corresponding enactment for the time being in force in Northern Ireland shall include power to adjourn, after convicting an offender, for the purpose of enabling a notice to be given to him under this subsection or, if a notice was so given to him less than seven days previously, for the purpose of enabling the necessary seven days to elapse.

(3) For the purposes of section 3(6) above—

(a) a person shall be deemed to have attained the age of seventeen at the time of his conviction if, on consideration of any available evidence, he appears to have done so to the court making or considering a recommendation for deportation; and

(b) the question whether an offence is one for which a person is punishable with imprisonment shall be determined without regard to any enactment restricting the imprisonment of young offenders or persons who have not previously been sentenced to imprisonment;

and for purposes of deportation a person who is being charged with an offence is found to have committed it shall, notwithstanding any enactment to the contrary and notwithstanding that the court does not proceed to conviction, be regarded as a person convicted of the offence, and references to conviction shall be construed accordingly.

(4) Notwithstanding any rule of practice restricting the matters which ought to be taken into account in dealing with an offender who is sentenced to imprisonment, a recommendation for deportation may be made in respect of an offender who is sentenced to imprisonment for life.

(5) Where a court recommends or purports to recommend a person for deportation, the validity of the recommendation shall not be called in question except on an appeal against the recommendation or agains the conviction on whihc it is made; but—

(a) the recommendation shall be treated as a sentence for the purpose of any enactment providing an appeal against sentence; and

(b) [*Scotland*].

(6) A deportation order shall not be made on the recommendation of a court so long as an appeal or further appeal is pending against the recommendation or against the conviction on which it was made; and for this purpose an appeal or further appeal shall be treated as pending (where one is competent but has not been brought) until the expiration of the time for bringing that appeal or, in Scotland, until the expiration of twenty-eight days from the date of the recommendation.

[This section is printed as amended by the *CJA* 1972, Sched. 5; the *Criminal Procedure (Scotland) Act* 1975, Sched. 9; the *MCA* 1980, Sched. 7; the *CJA* 1982, Sched. 15; and as repealed in part by the *Criminal Justice (Scotland) Act* 1980, Sched. 8; and the *CJA* 1982, s.16.]

In *R. v. Abdi* [2008] 1 Cr.App.R.(S.) 87, CA, it was held that where a non-British citizen who had been recommended for deportation had not been given seven days' notice of the non-liability to deportation of British citizens, as required by subsection (2), the court should not impute to Parliament an intention that this would necessarily render a recommendation for deportation invalid.

The final paragraph of subsection (3) is a reference to the *PCC(S)A* 2000, s.14(1): the effect of the provision is to allow a recommendation for deportation to be made in conjunction with a discharge.

Immigration Act 1971, s.7

Exemption from deportation for certain existing residents

5–912 **7.**—(1) Notwithstanding anything in section 3(5) or (6) above but subject to the provisions of this section, a Commonwealth citizen or citizen of the Republic of Ireland who was such a citizen at the coming into force of this Act and was then ordinarily resident in the United Kingdom—

(a) shall not be liable to deportation under section 3(5)(a) if at the time of the Secretary of State's decision he had at all times since the coming into force of this Act been ordinarily resident in the United Kingdom and Islands; and

(b) shall not be liable to deportation under section 3(5)(a) or (b) or 10 of the *Immigration and Asylum Act* 1999 if at the time of the Secretary of State's decision he had for the last five years been ordinarily resident in the United Kingdom and Islands; and

(c) shall not on conviction of an offence be recommended for deportation under section 3(6) if at the time of the conviction he had for the last five years been ordinarily resident in the United Kingdom and Islands.

(2) A person who has at any time become ordinarily resident in the United Kingdom or in any of the Islands shall not be treated for the purposes of this section as having ceased to be so by reason only of his having remained there in breach of the immigration law.

(3) The "last five years" before the material under subsection 1(b) or (c) above is to be taken as a period amounting in total to five years exclusive of any time during which the person claiming exemption under this section was undergoing imprisonment or detention by virtue of a sentence passed for an offence on a conviction in the United Kingdom and Islands, and for the period for which he was imprisoned or detained by virtue of the sentence amounted to six months or more.

(4) For purposes of subsection (3) above—

(a) "sentence" includes any order made on conviction of an offence; and

(b) two or more sentences for consecutive (or partly consecutive) terms shall be treated as a single sentence; and

(c) a person shall be deemed to be detained by virtue of a sentence—

(i) at any time when he is liable to imprisonment or detention by virtue of the sentence, but is unlawfully at large; and

(ii) (unless the sentence is passed after the material time) during any period of custody by which under any relevant enactment the term to be served under the sentence is reduced.

In paragraph (c)(ii) above "relevant enactment" means section 240 of the *Criminal Justice Act* 2003 (or, before that section operated, section 17(2) of the *Criminal Justice Administration Act* 1962) and any similar enactment which is for the time being or has (before or after the passing of this Act) been in force in any part of the United Kingdom and Islands.

(5) Nothing in this section shall be taken to exclude the operation of section 3(8) in relation to an exemption under this section.

[This section is printed as amended by the *Immigration and Asylum Act* 1999, s.169(1), and Sched. 14, para. 46; and the *CJA* 2003, s.304, and Sched. 32, para. 16.]

For the definition of a Commonwealth citizen, see the *British Nationality Act* 1981, s.37 and Sched. 3. The *Immigration Act* 1971 came into force on January 1, 1973. A period of continuous residence is not broken for the purpose of this section by an ordinary holiday abroad, but a period of 20 months' absence was held in *R. v. Hussain*, 56 Cr.App.R. 165, CA, to break the period of residence. A person cannot be ordinarily resident in the United Kingdom if his presence in the country is in breach of the immigration laws, except as provided by the Act (see s.33(2)). Section 7(2) does not apply to a person whose presence in the United Kingdom was unlawful from the beginning; it is intended to apply to a person who has entered the United Kingdom lawfully but remained after the expiry of the period for which he was allowed to enter: *R. v. Bangoo* [1976] Crim.L.R. 746, CA.

Immigration Act 1971, s.8(2), (3), (3A)

8.—(2) [*Power of Secretary of State to exempt person or class of persons from provisions of Act.*] **5–913**

(3) Subject to subsection (3A) below provisions of this Act relating to those who are not British citizens shall not apply to any person so long as he is a member of a mission (within the meaning of the *Diplomatic Privileges Act* 1964), a person who is a member of the family and forms part of the household of such a member, or a person otherwise entitled to the like immunity from jurisdiction as is conferred by that Act on a diplomatic agent.

(3A) For the purposes of subsection (3), a member of a mission other than a diplomatic agent (as defined by the 1964 Act) is not to count as a member of a mission unless—

(a) he was resident outside the United Kingdom, and was not in the United Kingdom, when he was offered a post as such a member; and

(b) he has not ceased to be such a member after having taken up the post.

[This section is printed as amended by the *British Nationality Act* 1981, Sched. 4; the *Immigration Act* 1988, s.4; and the *Immigration and Asylum Act* 1999, s.6.]

Immigration Act 1971, Sched. 3, paras 2–6

Detention or control pending deportation

5–914 2.—(1) Where a recommendation for deportation made by a court is in force in respect of any person, and that person is neither detained in pursuance of the sentence or order of any court nor for the time being released on bail by any court having power so to release him, he shall, unless the court by which the recommendation is made otherwise directs or a direction is given under sub-paragraph (1A) below, be detained pending the making of a deportation order in pursuance of the recommendation, unless the Secretary of State directs him to be released pending further consideration of his case.

(1A) Where—

(a) a recommendation for deportation made by a court on conviction of a person is in force in respect of him; and

(b) he appeals against his conviction or against that recommendation,

the powers that the court determining the appeal may exercise include power to direct him to be released without setting aside the recommendation.

(2) Where notice has been given to a person in accordance with regulations under section 18 of this Act of a decision to make a deportation order against him, and he is neither detained in pursuance of the sentence or order of a court nor for the time being released on bail by a court having power so to release him, he may be detained under the authority of the Secretary of State pending the making of the deportation order.

(3) Where a deportation order is in force against any person, he may be detained under the authority of the Secretary of State pending his removal or departure from the United Kingdom (and if already detained by virtue of sub-paragraph (1) or (2) above when the order is made, shall continue to be detained unless the Secretary of State directs otherwise).

(4) In relation to detention under sub-paragraph (2) or (3) above, paragraphs 17, 18 and 25A to 25E of Schedule 2 to this Act shall apply as they apply in relation to detention under paragraph 16 of that Schedule.

(5) A person to whom this sub-paragraph applies shall be subject to such restrictions as to residence, as to his employment or occupation and as to reporting to the police or an immigration officer as may from time to time be notified to him in writing by the Secretary of State.

(6) The persons to whom sub-paragraph (5) above applies are—

(a) a person liable to be detained under sub-paragraph (1) above, while by virtue of a direction of the Secretary of State he is not so detained; and

(b) a person liable to be detained under sub-paragraph (2) or (3) above, while he is not so detained.

Effect of appeals

5–915 3. Part II of Schedule 2 to this Act, so far as it relates to appeals under section 66 or 67 of the *Immigration and Asylum Act* 1999, shall apply for purposes of this Schedule as if the references in paragraph 29(1) to Part I of that Schedule were references to this Schedule; and paragraphs 29 to 33 shall apply in like manner in relation to appeals under section 63(1)(a) or 69(4)(a) of the *Immigration and Asylum Act* 1999.

Powers of courts pending deportation

5–916 4. Where the release of a person recommended for deportation is directed by a court, he shall be subject to such restrictions as to residence, as to his employment or occupation and as to reporting to the police as the court may direct.

5.—(1) On an application made—

(a) by or on behalf of a person recommended for deportation whose release was so directed; or

(b) by a constable; or

(c) by an immigration officer,

the appropriate court shall have the powers specified in sub-paragraph (2) below.

(2) The powers mentioned in sub-paragraph (1) above are—

(a) if the person to whom the application relates is not subject to any such restrictions imposed by a court as are mentioned in paragraph 4 above, to order that he shall be subject to such restrictions as the court may direct; and

(b) if he is subject to such restrictions imposed by a court by virtue of that paragraph or this paragraph—

(i) to direct that any of them shall be varied or shall cease to have effect; or

(ii) to give further directions as to his residence and reporting.

6.—(1) In this Schedule "the appropriate court" means, except in a case to which sub-paragraph (2) below applies, the court which directed release. **5–917**

(2) This sub-paragraph applies where the court which directed release was—

(a) the Crown Court;

(b) the Court of Appeal;

(c) the High Court of Justiciary;

(d) the Crown Court in Northern Ireland; or

(e) the Court of Appeal in Northern Ireland.

(2A) Where the Crown Court directed release, the appropriate court is that court or a magistrates' court.

(3) [*Northern Ireland*.]

(4) Where the Court of Appeal or the Court of Appeal in Northern Ireland gave the direction, the appropriate court is the Crown Court or the Crown Court in Northern Ireland, as the case may be.

(5) [*Scotland*.]

[This Schedule is printed as amended by the *CJA* 1982, s.64, Sched. 10; the *Immigration Act* 1988, Sched.; the *Asylum and Immigration Act* 1996, Sched. 2, para. 13; the *Immigration and Asylum Act* 1999, s.169(1), and Sched. 14, paras 68 and 69; and the *Courts Act* 2003, s.109(1), and Sched. 8, para. 150(1)–(3).]

Procedure

As to the giving of notice, see section 6(2), *ante*, § 5–911. A recommendation for deportation should not be added as if by an afterthought; there should be a full inquiry into all the circumstances and counsel should be invited to address the court specifically on the possibility of a recommendation being made: *R. v. Nazari*, 71 Cr.App.R. 87, CA; *R. v. Omojudi*, 13 Cr.App.R.(S.) 346, CA; *R. v. Frank*, *ibid.* at 500, CA. **5–918**

In *R. v. Bozat* [1997] 1 Cr.App.R.(S.) 270, the Court of Appeal stressed the importance of giving reasons for making a recommendation for deportation, in fairness to the defendant, and to assist the Secretary of State who would have to make the ultimate decision whether the offender would be deported. A failure by the sentencer to give reasons did not necessarily mean that the recommendation should be quashed. The Court of Appeal could give its own reasons if it considered a recommendation for deportation appropriate. The court did not endorse the decision to the contrary effect in *R. v. Rodney* [1996] 2 Cr.App.R.(S.) 230, CA.

Criteria for exercise of power to make recommendation

The *UK Borders Act* 2007 makes provision for the automatic deportation of foreign criminals. Sections 32 to 39 cover the conditions and procedure under which a foreign national prisoner will be automatically deported. The Secretary of State must make a deportation order in respect of a "foreign criminal" unless certain exceptions apply. "Foreign criminal" is defined in section 32 as a person who is not a British citizen, is convicted in the United Kingdom of an offence and who has either been sentenced to imprisonment for at least 12 months ("condition 1") or who has committed an offence specified by the Secretary of State under the *Nationality and Asylum Act* 2002, s.72(4)(a) (serious criminal) and who is subject to a period of imprisonment ("condition 2"). In respect of a "condition 1" prisoner, these provisions came into force on into August 1, 2008: *UK Borders Act 2007 (Commencement No. 3 and Transitional* **5–919**

Provisions) Order 2008 (S.I. 2008 No. 1818). Section 33 provides for certain exceptions to liability to this procedure. Whilst the current provisions relating to a recommendation for deportation by a court are neither amended nor repealed, the scope for making a recommendation will be severely curtailed in view of the breadth of the provisions for automatic deportation and to the established criteria for making a recommendation for deportation.

Where it does fall to a court to consider making a recommendation for deportation, the first matter for the court to consider is whether the accused's continued presence in this country is to its detriment, on the basis that the country has no use for criminals of other nationalities, particularly if they have committed serious crimes or have long criminal records; and the more serious the crime and the longer the record, the more obvious it is that there should be a recommendation for deportation: *R. v. Nazari*, *ante*.

In *R. v. Carmona* [2006] 2 Cr.App.R.(S.) 102, CA, it was held that notwithstanding the *Human Rights Act* 1998, there is no need for a sentencing court to consider the rights of an offender under Articles 2 (right to life), 3 (prohibition of torture) and 8 (right to respect for private and family life) of the ECHR (*post*, §§ 16–36, 16–39 and 16–101) when considering whether to make a recommendation. These, the court held, are for the Secretary of State to consider when deciding whether to act on the recommendation, as is the effect of deportation on the family of the offender. Accordingly, in the case of non-EU citizens the only question to be addressed is whether the offender's continued presence in this country is contrary to the public interest.

In the case of citizens of member states of the European Union, Article 39 (formerly Article 48) of the E.C. Treaty and Council Directive 64/221 restricted the authority of member states to exclude nationals of other member states who are workers, or spouses or dependants of workers. The European Court of Justice held in *R. v. Bouchereau* [1978] Q.B. 732, 66 Cr.App.R. 202, that a recommendation for deportation was a "measure" for the purposes of Directive 64/221, and that accordingly a recommendation could be made only in accordance with Article 48 and the Directive. Article 48 permits restrictions on the free movement of persons subject to community law on grounds of public policy, which the European Court held to presuppose "in addition to the perturbation of the social order which any infringement of the law involves ... a genuine and sufficiently serious threat to the requirements of public policy affecting one of the fundamental interests of society". The court further held that the terms of Directive 64/221 meant that "the existence of a previous conviction can only be taken into account insofar as the circumstances which gave rise to the conviction are evidence of personal conduct constituting a present threat to the requirements of public policy" and added that "although in general a finding that such a threat exists implies the existence in the individual concerned of a propensity to act in the same way in the future, it is possible that past conduct may constitute such a threat to the requirements of public policy."

Directive 64/221 has been repealed and replaced by Directive 2004/38/EC of the European Parliament and the Council. Article 28 provides that before taking an expulsion decision on grounds of public policy or public security, the host member state shall take account of considerations such as how long the individual concerned has resided on its territory, his age, state of health, family and economic situation, social and cultural integration in the host state and the extent of his links with the country of origin; that the host state may not take an expulsion decision against Union citizens or their family members, irrespective of nationality, who have the right of permanent residence on its territory, except on serious grounds of public policy or public security; and that an expulsion decision may not be taken against Union citizens, except if the decision is based on imperative grounds of public security, as defined by member states, if they (a) have resided in the host state for the previous 10 years, or (b) are a minor, except if the expulsion is necessary for the best interests of the child, as provided for in the United Nations Convention on the Rights of the Child (November 20, 1989).

These provisions are given effect in domestic law, as from April 30, 2006, by the *Immigration (European Economic Area) Regulations* 2006 (S.I. 2006 No. 1003) (which extends them to citizens of Norway, Iceland, Liechtenstein and Switzerland): see, in particular, regulations 19 and 21. Regulation 21(5) requires an expulsion decision taken on public policy or public security grounds also to comply with the following principles:

(a) proportionality, (b) it must be based exclusively on the personal conduct of the person concerned, which (c) must represent a genuine, present and sufficiently serious threat affecting one of the fundamental interests of society, (d) matters isolated from the particulars of the case or which relate to considerations of general prevention must be left out of account, and (e) a person's previous criminal convictions cannot in themselves justify the decision.

In *Carmona*, *ante*, the court acknowledged the possibility that whereas a recommendation for deportation may have been a "measure" for the purposes of the 1964 directive (*ante*), it might well not be a "decision" for the purposes of the 2004 directive (any "decision" being made by the Secretary of State), but it was of the opinion that the provisions of the Directive would have a significant effect on the exercise by courts of the power to recommend deportation, "since it would not be right to make a recommendation ... where the Directive precludes actual deportation" (at [3]). It is likely, therefore, that courts dealing with persons covered by these regulations will apply the principles in Article 28 of the Directive, as elaborated by regulation 21(5) of the 2006 regulations.

In *Bulale v. Secretary of State for the Home Department*, *The Times*, July 25, 2008, CA (Civ. Div.) it was said that the thrust of the thinking that led to Directive 2004/38/EC seemed fairly clearly to have been that it should be, at the least, difficult to expel an EU citizen on the basis of crimes of dishonesty, but that violence is a different matter; as to the necessary level of violence, no attempt having been made to lay down rules at Community level, member states must be taken to have been given a certain amount of judgment in deciding what its law-abiding citizens must put up with; accordingly, the organs of the member state, provided that they conscientiously apply the terms of the legislation, are given power to determine, with due regard to the seriousness ascribed to forms of conduct by domestic law, whether that conduct fulfils the Community criterion of seriousness.

Criterion of "potential detriment"

An isolated offence, even of a serious nature, committed by a person of previous good character whose behaviour while in the United Kingdom has been otherwise satisfactory may well not indicate that there is a potential detriment if he remains: see *R. v. David*, 2 Cr.App.R.(S.) 362, CA (theft of passport by man with previous convictions in distant past, recommendation quashed); *R. v. Tshuma*, 3 Cr.App.R.(S.) 97, CA (arson by young woman under emotional stress, recommendation quashed); and *R. v. Altawel*, 3 Cr.App.R.(S.) 281, CA (obtaining student grant by deception, recommendation quashed). These cases do not necessarily mean that it is wrong to make a recommendation against an offender with no previous convictions, particularly for a serious offence of a deliberate character: see *R. v. Nazari*, *ante*; *R. v. Kouyoumdjian*, 12 Cr.App.R.(S.) 35, CA (fraudulent trading involving debts of about £400,000); and *R. v. Ahemed* [2006] 1 Cr.App.R.(S.) 78, CA (entering marriage as part of "well thought out scheme of deception" designed to obtain an immigration advantage). **5–920**

In *R. v. Abdi* [2008] 1 Cr.App.R.(S.) 87, CA, it was held that there was no inconsistency between the judge's conclusion that the criteria for significant risk under section 229 of the *CJA* 2003 (*ante*, § 5–297) had not been satisfied and his decision to make a recommendation for deportation on the basis that there was a degree of risk of re-offending (although not sufficient to satisfy s.229) and that serious harm would undoubtedly result from any re-offending.

As to the potential effect of deportation on the offender's family, see *R. v. Carmona*, *ante*, § 5–919.

Persons in breach of immigration laws

In *R. v. Khandari*, unreported, April 24, 1979, Bridge L.J. observed that the question whether to recommend deportation should be decided "quite independently of the status of the particular offender before the court in relation to his position under the *Immigration Act*." The relevant considerations were his history, particularly his criminal history, and the gravity of the offence. See also *Miller v. Lenton*, 3 Cr.App.R.(S.) 171, DC; and *R. v. Nunu*, 12 Cr.App.R.(S.) 752, CA. **5–921**

However in *R. v. Benabbas* [2006] 1 Cr.App.R.(S.) 94, CA, it was said that there was a distinction to be drawn between the person who had entered the United Kingdom by fraudulent means and the person who was in this country unlawfully and who was convicted of an offence unconnected with his status and the circumstances in which he had entered the country. The public interest in preventing the fraudulent use of passports to gain entry or support residence was of considerable importance and deserved protection; where the essential gravamen of the offence for which the offender was being sentenced was itself an abuse of the immigration laws, the issue of detriment, when applying *R. v. Nazari* (*ante* § 5–920), was intimately bound up with the protection of public order afforded by confidence in a system of passports; therefore, the approach identified in *R. v. Khandari* was inappropriate to the offence of entering without a passport, although it might, for entirely different reasons, nevertheless be appropriate where the defendant had immediately claimed asylum upon entry (because the asylum claim would be assessed by the Secretary of State, who was best left to consider it without any possible complication arising from a recommendation for deportation).

Relevance of conditions prevailing in offender's country of origin

5–922 The courts are not concerned with the political systems which operate in other countries. They have no knowledge of such matters over and above what is common knowledge, and that may be wrong. Such matters are for the Secretary of State: *R. v. Nazari*, *ante*, § 5–918; *R. v. Antypas*, 57 Cr.App.R. 207, CA; and *R. v. Carmona*, *ante*, § 5–919.

The fact that the offender has been granted refugee status does not prevent the court from making a recommendation for deportation (see *R. v. Villa and Villa*, 14 Cr.App.R.(S.) 34, CA).

Effect of making recommendation on principal sentence

5–923 A recommendation for deportation is not part of the punishment such as to justify a reduction in the sentence properly so called: *R. v. Edgehill*, 47 Cr.App.R. 41, CCA.

There is no legal objection to making a recommendation for deportation in respect of an offender granted a conditional discharge: *R. v. Akan* [1973] 1 Q.B. 491, 56 Cr.App.R. 716, CA. In practice it is unlikely that such an offender will satisfy the criterion of "potential detriment".

The terms of paragraph 2(1) of Schedule 3 to the 1971 Act (*ante*, § 5–914) do not create a presumption that an offender who has been recommended for deportation, but who is not serving a sentence, is to be detained pending the making of a deportation order (*R. (Sedrati) v. Secretary of State for the Home Department*, unreported, May 17, 2001, QBD (Moses J.) ([2001] EWHC 418 (Admin.)); from which it follows that it is unlawful not to release a person satisfying the criteria for release from custody pending the making of a deportation order unless there has been some conscious decision authorising continued detention until that time: *R. (Vovk) v. Secretary of State for the Home Department* [2007] A.C.D. 48, QBD (Calvert Smith J.).

XIII. REFERRAL TO YOUTH OFFENDER PANEL

5–924 Referral to a youth offender panel under section 16 of the *PCC(S)A* 2000 is not available to the Crown Court sitting as a court of first instance. The Crown Court's engagement with referrals to a youth offender panel is, therefore, limited to the hearing of appeals against sentence where the offender has been re-sentenced following referral back to the youth court by a youth offender panel (which can be on any one of a number of grounds) and to dealing with offenders subject to a referral when they fall to be sentenced for some other offence. If the Crown Court does anything other than discharge the offender absolutely, the referral order and any related orders will be revoked (Sched. 1, para. 14(1) and (2)). Where the referral order and any associated orders are so revoked, it is open to the Crown Court to deal with the offender for the original offence, if it appears to the court that it would be in the interests of justice to do so. If it does so, it may deal with the offender in any way that he could have been dealt with for the offence by the court which made the order (other than by making another order under section 16) (*ibid.*, para. 14(3)). In deciding how to deal with the offender, the court shall take into account the extent of the offender's compliance with the terms of the contract entered into by the offender with the youth offender panel pursuant to section 23 (*ibid.*, para. 14(4)).

XIV. ORDERS AGAINST PARENTS OR GUARDIANS

(1) Orders for the payment of money

Powers of Criminal Courts (Sentencing) Act 2000, ss.136–138

Power to order statement as to financial circumstances of parent or guardian

136.—(1) Before exercising its powers under section 137 below (power to order parent or guardian to pay fine, costs, compensation or surcharge) against the parent or guardian of an individual who has been convicted of an offence, the court may make a financial circumstances order with respect to the parent or (as the case may be) guardian. **5–927**

(2) In this section "financial circumstances order" has the meaning given by subsection (3) of section 162 of the *Criminal Justice Act* 2003, and subsections (4) to (6) of that section shall apply in relation to a financial circumstances order made under this section as they apply in relation to such an order made under that section.

[This section is printed as amended by the *CJA* 2003, s.304, and Sched. 32, paras 90 and 118; and the *Domestic Violence, Crime and Victims Act* 2004, s.58(1), and Sched. 10, para. 50.]

Power to order parent or guardian to pay fine, costs, compensation or surcharge

137.—(1) Where— **5–928**

(a) a child or young person (that is to say, any person aged under 18) is convicted of any offence for the commission of which a fine or costs may be imposed or a compensation order may be made, and

(b) the court is of the opinion that the case would best be met by the imposition of a fine or costs or the making of such an order, whether with or without any other punishment,

the court shall order that the fine, compensation or costs awarded be paid by the parent or guardian of the child or young person instead of by the child or young person himself, unless the court is satisfied—

(i) that the parent or guardian cannot be found; or

(ii) that it would be unreasonable to make an order or payment, having regard to the circumstances of the case.

(1A) Where but for this subsection a court would order a child or young person to pay a surcharge under section 161A of the *Criminal Justice Act* 2003, the court shall order that the surcharge be paid by the parent or guardian of the child or young person instead of by the child or young person himself, unless the court is satisfied—

(a) that the parent or guardian cannot be found; or

(b) that it would be unreasonable to make an order for payment, having regard to the circumstances of the case.

(2) Where but for this subsection a court would impose a fine on a child or young person under—

[(za) paragraph 6(2)(a) or 8(2)(a) of Schedule 2 to the *Criminal Justice and Immigration Act* 2008 (breach of youth rehabilitation order),]

(a) *paragraph 4(1)(a) or 5(1)(a) of Schedule 3 to this Act (breach of curfew, probation, community service, combination or drug treatment and testing order),*

(b) *paragraph 2(1)(a) of Schedule 5 to this Act (breach of attendance centre order or attendance centre rules),*

(c) *paragraph 2(2)(a) of Schedule 7 to this Act (breach of supervision order),*

(d) paragraph 2(2)(a) of Schedule 8 to this Act (breach of *action plan order or* reparation order),

(e) section 104(3)(b) above (breach of requirements of supervision under a detention and training order), or

(f) section 4(3)(b) of the *Criminal Justice and Public Order Act* 1994 (breach of requirements of supervision under a secure training order), the court shall order that the fine be paid by the parent or guardian of the child or young person instead of by the child or young person himself, unless the court is satisfied—

(i) that the parent or guardian cannot be found; or

(ii) that it would be unreasonable to make an order for payment, having regard to the circumstances of the case.

(3) In the case of a young person aged 16 or over, subsections (1) to (2) above shall have effect as if, instead of imposing a duty, they conferred a power to make such an order as is mentioned in those subsections.

(4) Subject to subsection (5) below, no order shall be made under this section without giving the parent or guardian an opportunity of being heard.

(5) An order under this section may be made against a parent or guardian who, having been required to attend, has failed to do so.

(6) A parent or guardian may appeal to the Crown Court against an order under this section made by a magistrates' court.

(7) A parent or guardian may appeal to the Court of Appeal against an order under this section made by the Crown Court, as if he had been convicted on indictment and the order were a sentence passed on his conviction.

(8) In relation to a child or young person for whom a local authority have parental responsibility and who—

(a) is in their care, or

(b) is provided with accommodation by them in the exercise of any functions (in particular those under the *Children Act* 1989) which are social services functions within the meaning of the *Local Authority Social Services Act* 1970,

references in this section to his parent or guardian shall be construed as references to that authority.

(9) In subsection (8) above "local authority" and "parental responsibility" have the same meanings as in the *Children Act* 1989.

[This section is printed as amended by the *Local Government Act* 2000, s.107, and Sched. 5, para. 2; and the *Domestic Violence, Crime and Victims Act* 2004, s.58(1), and Sched. 10, para. 51; and as amended, as from a day to be appointed (as to which, see *ante*, § 5–1), by the *CJIA* 2008, ss.6(2) and 149, Sched. 4, paras 51 and 57, and Sched. 28, Pt 1 (insertion of subs. (2)(za), omission of subs. (2)(a)-(c) and italicised words in subs. (2)(d)). The repeal of subs. (2)(a) was already provided for (as from a day to be appointed) by the *CJCSA* 2000, s.74, and Sched. 7, para. 192 (which provision is itself prospectively repealed by the 2008 Act, s.149, and Sched. 28, Pt 1). Thus, the 2000 Act provision is still capable of biting should it be brought into force before it is itself repealed.]

Fixing of fine, compensation or surcharge to be paid by parent or guardian

5–929 **138.**—(1) For the purposes of any order under section 137 above made against the parent or guardian of a child or young person—

(za) subsection (3) of section 161A of the *Criminal Justice Act* 2003 (surcharges) and subsection (4A) of section 164 of that Act (fixing of fines) shall have effect as if any reference in those subsections to the offender's means were a reference to those of the parent or guardian;

(a) section 164 of the *Criminal Justice Act* 2003 (fixing of fines) shall have effect as if any reference in subsections (1) to (4) to the financial circumstances of the offender were a reference to the financial circumstances of the parent or guardian, and as if subsection (5) were omitted;

(b) section 130(11) above (determination of compensation order) shall have effect as if any reference to the means of the person against whom the compensation order is made were a reference to the financial circumstances of the parent or guardian; and

(c) section 130(12) above (preference to be given to compensation if insufficient means to pay both compensation and a fine) shall have effect as if the reference to the offender were a reference to the parent or guardian;

but in relation to an order under section 137 made against a local authority this subsection has effect subject to subsection (2) below.

(2) For the purposes of any order under section 137 above made against a local authority, section 164 of the *Criminal Justice Act* 2003 and section 130(11) above shall not apply.

(3) For the purposes of any order under section 137 above, where the parent or guardian of an offender who is a child or young person—

(a) has failed to comply with an order under section 136 above, or

(b) has otherwise failed to co-operate with the court in its inquiry into his financial circumstances,

and the court considers that it has insufficient information to make a proper determination of the parent's or guardian's financial circumstances, it may make such determination as it thinks fit.

(4) Where a court has, in fixing the amount of a fine, determined the financial circumstances of a parent or guardian under subsection (3) above, subsections (2) to (4) of section 165 of the *Criminal Justice Act* 2003 (remission of fines) shall (so far as applicable) have effect as they have effect in the case mentioned in section 165(1), but as if the reference in section 165(2) to the offender's financial circumstances were a reference to the financial circumstances of the parent or guardian.

(5) In this section "local authority" has the same meaning as in the *Children Act* 1989.

[This section is printed as amended by the *CJA* 2003, s.304, and Sched. 32, paras 90 and 119; and the *Domestic Violence, Crime and Victims Act* 2004, s.58(1), and Sched. 10, para. 52.]

For the meanings of "local authority" and "parental responsibility", see sections 105(1) and (3) respectively of the *Children Act* 1989.

Section 163(1) (*ante*, § 5–4) provides that in the 2000 Act "guardian" has the same meaning as in the *CYPA* 1933. Neither a local authority nor a company providing residential accommodation for "difficult to place" young people fall within the extended definition of "guardian" in section 107(1) of that Act (*post*, § 19–328): *Leeds City Council v. West Yorkshire Metropolitan Police* [1983] 1 A.C. 29, HL; accordingly, no order could be made against them under section 137: *Marlowe Child and Family Services Ltd v. DPP* [1998] 2 Cr.App.R.(S.) 438, DC (unless, in the case of a local authority, it falls within subsection (8)).

Conduct of parent or guardian

In determining whether it is unreasonable to make an order against a parent or guardian, the court should not make use of information contained in a pre-sentence report, if that information is disputed by the parent or guardian: see *Lenihan v. West Yorkshire Metropolitan Police*, 3 Cr.App.R.(S.) 42, DC (the use of reports to provide material showing that the parent or guardian has not supervised the juvenile adequately, would lead to less co-operation by parents or guardians in the preparation of reports). **5–930**

It would be "unreasonable" to make an order against the parent/ guardian, where it was impossible to identify any fault on their part or anything done by them that may have caused the defendant to commit the crime: *R. v. J.-B.* [2004] 2 Cr.App.R.(S.) 41, CA.

Where the child or young person has been living in local authority accommodation under a voluntary arrangement with a local authority, and while doing so commits an offence, it will normally be unreasonable to make an order requiring the parent or guardian to pay compensation in respect of the offence: see *T.A. v. DPP* [1997] 1 Cr.App.R.(S.) 1, DC.

An order should not be made against a local authority under section 137 if it had done everything it could reasonably and properly do to protect the public from the young offender: *D. v. DPP*; *R. v. DPP*, 16 Cr.App.R.(S.) 1040, DC. There should be a causative link between some fault on the part of the authority and the offending: *Bedfordshire County Council v. DPP* [1996] 1 Cr.App.R.(S.) 322, DC. The role of the prosecution was to be strictly neutral: *ibid*. If the court was minded to make an order, the authority should be notified in writing of its right to make representations and provided with any documents supplied to the court in support of the application for compensation. The authority should notify the court in writing whether there was any dispute about the amount of compensation, or whether an order should be made; if there was any dispute as to either matter, a hearing must be obtained with reasonable notice to the authority. The authority should supply documents relevant to the matter to the court and to the prosecution, and the hearing should be kept as simple as possible: *ibid*.

Enforcement

5–931 Where the Crown Court orders a parent or guardian to pay a fine imposed on an offender, it does not "impose" the fine on the parent or guardian, and there is accordingly no power under section 139 of the 2000 Act (*post*, § 5–396) to fix a term to be served by the parent or guardian in default of payment. The order against the parent or guardian is enforced by the magistrates' court in accordance with the *Administration of Justice Act* 1970, s.41 (*post*, § 6–119), as if it were a fine imposed following a summary conviction.

(2) Binding over orders

Power of Criminal Courts (Sentencing) Act 2000, s.150

Binding over of parent or guardian

5–932 **150.**—(1) Where a child or young person (that is to say, any person aged under 18) is convicted of an offence, the powers conferred by this section shall be exercisable by the court by which he is sentenced for that offence, and where the offender is aged under 16 when sentenced it shall be the duty of that court—

(a) to exercise those powers if it is satisfied, having regard to the circumstances of the case, that their exercise would be desirable in the interests of preventing the commission by him of further offences; and

(b) if it does not exercise them, to state in open court that it is not satisfied as mentioned in paragraph (a) above and why it is not so satisfied;

but this subsection has effect subject to section 19(5) above and paragraph 13(5) of Schedule 1 to this Act (cases where referral orders made or extended).

(2) The powers conferred by this section are as follows—

(a) with the consent of the offender's parent or guardian, to order the parent or guardian to enter into a recognizance to take proper care of him and exercise proper control over him; and

(b) if the parent or guardian refuses consent and the court considers the refusal unreasonable, to order the parent or guardian to pay a fine not exceeding £1,000;

and where the court has passed *a community sentence* on the offender [a sentence which consists of or includes a youth rehabilitation order], it may include in the recognizance a provision that the offender's parent or guardian ensure that the offender complies with the requirements of that sentence.

(3) An order under this section shall not require the parent or guardian to enter into a recognizance for an amount exceeding £1,000.

(4) An order under this section shall not require the parent or guardian to enter into a recognizance—

(a) for a period exceeding three years; or

(b) where the offender will attain the age of 18 in a period shorter than three years, for a period exceeding that shorter period.

(5) Section 120 of the *Magistrates' Courts Act* 1980 (forfeiture of recognizances) shall apply in relation to a recognizance entered into in pursuance of an order under this section as it applies in relation to a recognizance to keep the peace.

(6) A fine imposed under subsection (2)(b) above shall be deemed, for the purposes of any enactment, to be a sum adjudged to be paid by a conviction.

(7) In fixing the amount of a recognizance under this section, the court shall take into account among other things the means of the parent or guardian so far as they appear or are known to the court; and this subsection applies whether taking into account the means of the parent or guardian has the effect of increasing or reducing the amount of the recognizance.

(8) A parent or guardian may appeal to the Crown Court against an order under this section made by a magistrates' court.

(9) A parent or guardian may appeal to the Court of Appeal against an order under this section made by the Crown Court, as if he had been convicted on indictment and the order were a sentence passed on his conviction.

(10) A court may vary or revoke an order made by it under this section if, on the application of the parent or guardian, it appears to the court, having regard to any change in the circumstances since the order was made, to be in the interests of justice to do so.

(11) For the purposes of this section, taking "care" of a person includes giving him protection and guidance and "control" includes discipline.

[This section is printed as amended, as from a day to be appointed (as to which, see *ante*, § 5–1), by the *CJIA* 2008, s.6(2), and Sched. 4, paras 51 and 58.]

(3) Parenting orders

Crime and Disorder Act 1998, ss.8–10

Parenting orders

8.—(1) This section applies where, in any court proceedings— **5–933**

(a) a child safety order is made in respect of a child or the court determines on an application under section 12(6) below that a child has failed to comply with any requirement included in such an order;

(b) an anti-social behaviour order or sexual offences prevention order is made in respect of a child or young person;

(c) a child or young person is convicted of an offence; or

(d) a person is convicted of an offence under section 443 (failure to comply with school attendance order) or section 444 (failure to secure regular attendance at school of registered pupil) of the *Education Act* 1996.

(2) Subject to subsection (3) and section 9(1) below ..., if in the proceedings the court is satisfied that the relevant condition is fulfilled, it may make a parenting order in respect of a person who is a parent or guardian of the child or young person or, as the case may be, the person convicted of the offence under section 443 or 444 ("the parent").

(3) A court shall not make a parenting order unless it has been notified by the Secretary of State that arrangements for implementing such orders are available in the area in which it appears to the court that the parent resides or will reside and the notice has not been withdrawn.

(4) A parenting order is an order which requires the parent—

(a) to comply, for a period not exceeding twelve months, with such requirements as are specified in the order; and

(b) subject to subsection (5) below, to attend, for a concurrent period not exceeding three months and not more than once in any week, such counselling or guidance sessions as may be specified in directions given by the responsible officer;

and in this subsection "week" means a period of seven days beginning with a Sunday.

(5) A parenting order may, but need not, include such a requirement as is mentioned in subsection (4)(b) above in any case where such an order has been made in respect of the parent on a previous occasion.

(6) The relevant condition is that the parenting order would be desirable in the interests of preventing—

(a) in a case falling within paragraph (a) or (b) of subsection (1) above, any repetition of the kind of behaviour which led to the child safety order, anti-social behaviour order or sexual offences prevention order being made;

(b) in a case falling within paragraph (c) of that subsection, the commission of any further offence by the child or young person;

(c) in a case falling within paragraph (d) of that subsection, the commission of any further offence under section 443 or 444 of the *Education Act* 1996.

(7) The requirements that may be specified under subsection (4)(a) above are those which the court considers desirable in the interests of preventing any such repetition or, as the case may be, the commission of any such further offence.

(8) In this section and section 9 below "responsible officer", in relation to a parenting order, means one of the following who is specified in the order, namely—

(a) a probation officer or an officer of a provider of probation services;

(b) a social worker of a local authority social services department; and

(c) a member of a youth offending team.

(9) In this section "sexual offences prevention order" means an order under section 104 of the *Sexual Offences Act* 2003 (sexual offences prevention orders).

[This section is printed as amended, and repealed in part, by the *YJCEA* 1999, s.67(1), and Sched. 4, para. 26; the *PCC(S)A* 2000, s.165, and Sched. 9, para. 194; the *CJA* 2003, s.324, and Sched. 34, para. 1; the *Children Act* 2004, s.60(2); the *VCRA* 2006, s.60(1) and (2); and the *Offender Management Act 2007 (Consequential Amendments) Order* 2008 (S.I. 2008 No. 912), art. 3, and Sched. 1, para. 13(1) and (3).]

Parenting orders: supplemental

5–934 **9.**—(1) Where a person under the age of 16 is convicted of an offence, the court by or before which he is so convicted—

(a) if it is satisfied that the relevant condition is fulfilled, shall make a parenting order; and

(b) if it is not so satisfied, shall state in open court that it is not and why it is not.

(1A) The requirements of subsection (1) do not apply where the court makes a referral order in respect of the offence.

(2) Before making a parenting order—

(a) in a case falling within paragraph (a) of subsection (1) of section 8 above;

(b) in a case falling within paragraph (b) or (c) of that subsection, where the person concerned is under the age of 16; or

(c) in a case falling within paragraph (d) of that subsection, where the person to whom the offence related is under that age,

a court shall obtain and consider information about the person's family circumstances and the likely effect of the order on those circumstances.

(2A) In a case where a court proposes to make both a referral order in respect of a child or young person convicted of an offence and a parenting order, before making the parenting order the court shall obtain and consider a report by an appropriate officer—

(a) indicating the requirements proposed by that officer to be included in the parenting order;

(b) indicating the reasons why he considers those requirements would be desirable in the interests of preventing the commission of any further offence by the child or young person; and

(c) if the child or young person is aged under 16, containing the information required by subsection (2) above.

(2B) In subsection (2A) above "an appropriate officer" means—

(a) an officer of a local probation board or an officer of a provider of probation services;

(b) a social worker of a local authority social services department; or

(c) a member of a youth offending team.

(3) Before making a parenting order, a court shall explain to the parent in ordinary language—

(a) the effect of the order and of the requirements proposed to be included in it;

(b) the consequences which may follow (under subsection (7) below) if he fails to comply with any of those requirements; and

(c) that the court has power (under subsection (5) below) to review the order on the application either of the parent or of the responsible officer.

(4) Requirements specified in, and directions given under, a parenting order shall, as far as practicable, be such as to avoid—

(a) any conflict with the parent's religious beliefs; and

(b) any interference with the times, if any, at which he normally works or attends an educational establishment.

(5) If while a parenting order is in force it appears to the court which made it, on the application of the responsible officer or the parent, that it is appropriate to make an order under this subsection, the court may make an order discharging the parenting order or varying it—

(a) by cancelling any provision included in it; or

(b) by inserting in it (either in addition to or in substitution for any of its provisions) any provision that could have been included in the order if the court had then had power to make it and were exercising the power.

(6) Where an application under subsection (5) above for the discharge of a parenting order is dismissed, no further application for its discharge shall be made under that subsection by any person except with the consent of the court which made the order.

(7) If while a parenting order is in force the parent without reasonable excuse fails to comply with any requirement included in the order, or specified in directions given by the responsible officer, he shall be liable on summary conviction to a fine not exceeding level 3 on the standard scale.

(7A) In this section, "referral order" means an order under section 16(2) or (3) of the *Powers of Criminal Courts (Sentencing) Act* 2000 (referral of offender to youth offender panel).

[This section is printed as amended by the *YJCEA* 1999, s.67(1), and Sched. 4, para. 27; the *CJA* 2003, s.324, and Sched. 34, para. 2; and S.I. 2008 No. 912 (*ante*, § 5–933), art. 3, and Sched. 1, para. 13(1) and (4).]

Appeals against parenting orders

10.—(1) An appeal shall lie— **5–935**

(a) to the High Court against the making of a parenting order by virtue of paragraph (a) of subsection (1) of section 8 above; and

(b) to the Crown Court against the making of a parenting order by virtue of paragraph (b) of that subsection.

(2) On an appeal under subsection (1) above the High Court or the Crown Court—

(a) may make such orders as may be necessary to give effect to its determination of the appeal; and

(b) may also make such incidental or consequential orders as appear to it to be just.

(3) Any order of the High Court or the Crown Court made on an appeal under subsection (1) above (other than one directing that an application be re-heard by a magistrates' court) shall, for the purposes of subsections (5) to (7) of section 9 above, be treated as if it were an order of the court from which the appeal was brought and not an order of the High Court or the Crown Court.

(4) A person in respect of whom a parenting order is made by virtue of section 8(1)(c) above shall have the same right of appeal against the making of the order as if—

(a) the offence that led to the making of the order were an offence committed by him; and

(b) the order were a sentence passed on him for the offence.

(5) A person in respect of whom a parenting order is made by virtue of section 8(1)(d) above shall have the same right of appeal against the making of the order as if the order were a sentence passed on him for the offence that led to the making of the order.

(6) The Lord Chancellor may by order make provision as to the circumstances in which appeals under subsection (1)(a) above may be made against decisions taken by courts on questions arising in connection with the transfer, or proposed transfer, of proceedings by virtue of any order under paragraph 2 of Schedule 11 (jurisdiction) to the *Children Act* 1989 ("the 1989 Act").

(7) Except to the extent provided for in any order made under subsection (6) above, no appeal may be made against any decision of a kind mentioned in that subsection.

A parenting order may be made only if the court has been notified by the Secretary of State that arrangements for implementing the order are available in the relevant area, and if one of the conditions specified in section 8(6) is satisfied. **5–936**

The order must require the parent or guardian to comply, for a period not exceeding 12 months, with such requirements as the court may consider desirable in the interests of preventing repetition of the kind of behaviour which has led to the making of the order, or the commission of a further offence. The order must also include a requirement to attend for a period not exceeding three months at such counselling or guidance sessions as may be specified in directions given by the responsible officer, unless the parent has previously been the subject of a parenting order. **5–937**

XV. MISCELLANEOUS MATTERS

A. REWARDS

Criminal Law Act 1967, ss.28, 29

28. Where any person shall appear to any Crown Court, to have been active in or towards the apprehension of any person charged with an arrestable offence, every such court is hereby authorized and empowered, in any of the cases aforesaid, to order the sheriff of the county in which the offence shall have been committed to pay to the person or persons who shall appear to the court to have been active in or towards the apprehension of any person charged with that offence such sum or sums of money as to the court shall seem reasonable and sufficient to compensate such person or persons for his, her, or their expenses, exertions, and loss of time in or towards such apprehension; **5–938**

[This section is printed as amended by the *CLA* 1967, s.58, and Sched. 2, para. 3(1)(a), (b), Sched. 3, and Pt II; the *Courts Act* 1971, s.56, and Sched. 8, Pt I, para. 2; and as repealed in part by the *Statute Law (Repeals) Act* 1998, Sched. 1, Pt I.]

5–939 **29.** Every order for payment to any person in respect of such apprehension as aforesaid shall be forthwith made out and delivered by the proper officer of the court unto such person, ... ; and the sheriff of the county for the time being is hereby authorised and required, upon sight of such order, forthwith to pay to such person, or to any one duly authorised on his or her behalf, the money in such order mentioned; and every such sheriff may immediately apply for repayment of the same to the Lord Chancellor, who, upon inspecting such order, together with the acquittance of the person entitled to receive the money thereon, shall forthwith order repayment to the sheriff of the money so by him paid, without any fee or reward whatsoever.

[This section is printed as amended by the *Statute Law Revision Act* 1890; and S.I. 1976 No. 229; and as repealed in part by the *Statute Law (Repeals) Act* 1998, Pt I.]

B. ALTERATION OF SENTENCE

Power of Criminal Courts (Sentencing) Act 2000, s.155

Alteration of Crown Court sentence

5–940 **155.**—(1) Subject to the following provisions of this section, a sentence imposed, or other order made, by the Crown Court when dealing with an offender may be varied or rescinded by the Crown Court within the period of 28 days beginning with the day on which the sentence or other order was imposed or made within the time allowed by that subsection.

(4) A sentence or other order shall not be varied or rescinded under this section except by the court constituted as it was when the sentence or other order was imposed or made, or, where that court comprised one or more justices of the peace, a court so constituted except for the omission of any one or more of those justices.

(5) Subject to subsection (6) below, where a sentence or other order is varied under this section the sentence or other order, as so varied, shall take effect from the beginning of the day on which it was originally imposed or made, unless the court otherwise directs.

(6) For the purposes of—

(a) section 18(2) of the *Criminal Appeal Act* 1968 (time limit for notice of appeal or of application for leave to appeal), and

(b) paragraph 1 of Schedule 3 to the *Criminal Justice Act* 1988 (time limit for notice of an application for leave to refer a case under section 36 of that Act),

the sentence or other order shall be regarded as imposed or made on the day on which it is varied under this section.

(7) Criminal Procedure Rules—

(a) may, as respects cases where two or more persons are tried separately on the same or related facts alleged in one or more indictments, provide for extending the period fixed by subsection (1) above;

(b) may, subject to the preceding provisions of this section, prescribe the cases and circumstances in which, and the time within which, any order or other decision made by the Crown Court may be varied or rescinded by that court.

(8) In this section—

"sentence" includes a recommendation for deportation made when dealing with an offender;

"order" does not include an order under section 17(2) of the *Access to Justice Act* 1999.

[This section is printed as amended by the *Courts Act 2003 (Consequential Amendments) Order* 2004 (S.I. 2004 No. 2035); and the *CJIA* 2008, s.149, and Sched. 28, Pt 3.]

5–941 As to the power of magistrates' courts to re-open cases to rectify mistakes, etc., see the *MCA* 1980, s.142.

Scope of power

5–942 Provided that it is acting within the relevant time limit, the Crown Court may vary the original sentence by substituting a sentence or order of a different kind for the sentence originally imposed (see *R. v. Sodhi*, 66 Cr.App.R. 260, CA, hospital order with unlimited restriction order substituted for sentence of imprisonment; *R. v. Iqbal*, 7 Cr.App.R.(S.) 35, CA, order for detention under the *PCC(S)A* 2000, s.91, substituted for youth custody sentence), adding an additional order (see *R. v. Reilly* [1982] Q.B. 1208, 75 Cr.App.R. 266, CA, criminal bankruptcy order added) or varying the nature of a custodial sentence (see *R. v. Hart*, 5 Cr.App.R.(S.) 25, CA, suspended sentence to immediate sentence). There seems to be no objection to using the power to impose a custodial sentence of greater length than the sentence originally imposed, in appropriate circumstances: see *Commissioners of Customs and Excise v. Menocal* [1980] A.C. 598, 69 Cr.App.R. 148, HL, *per* Lord Edmund Davies; *R. v. Hart, ante*; *R. v. McLean*, 10 Cr.App.R.(S.) 18; *R. v. Hadley*, 16 Cr.App.R.(S.) 358, CA; and *R. v. Reynolds, ante*, § 5–309d (substitution of sentence under dangerous offender provisions of *CJA* 2003).

Variation after expiration of relevant time limit

Any variation of substance made after the expiration of the time limit will be of no effect: *Commissioners of Customs and Excise v. Menocal, ante*; *R. v. Hart, ante*; *R. v. Stillwell and Jewell*, 94 Cr.App.R. 65, CA; *R. v. Onwuka*, 13 Cr.App.R.(S.) 486, CA; but this will not apply where the original sentence is set aside within the time limit and the court then exercises its common law power to adjourn to a date beyond the time limit: see *R. v. Gordon, ante*, § 5–368f. Where a merely formal variation in the sentence is made after the expiration of the time limit, which does not alter the substance of the penalty, but merely cures an irregularity in the order of the court, the amendment will not be invalid: *R. v. Saville*, 2 Cr.App.R.(S.) 26, CA; and *R. v. Norman, ante*, § 5–368c. **5–943**

Grounds for alteration

The usual reason for altering a sentence is that further information relevant to the sentence has become available to the court (such as information relating to the offender's mental condition, as in *R. v. Sodhi, ante*, and *R. v. Crozier*, 12 Cr.App.R.(S.) 206, CA), or the court has overlooked some statutory provision limiting the exercise of its powers (as in *R. v. Iqbal, ante*), or, the sentence is found to take effect in a manner other than that expected by the sentencer (as in *R. v. Davies* [1998] 1 Cr.App.R.(S.) 252, CA). **5–944**

The exercise of the power was approved in principle in *R. v. Hart, ante*, where it was established that the offender had caused false information, which was critical to the sentence imposed, to be put before the court. See also *R. v. McLean, ante*. The judge should not decide that false information has been put before the court without a proper inquiry and allowing the offender to give evidence (see *R. v. Tout*, 15 Cr.App.R.(S.) 30, CA). It is wrong to exercise the power to substitute a more severe sentence than that originally imposed simply on the basis that on reflection the original sentence seems inadequate (see *R. v. Nodjoumi*, 7 Cr.App.R.(S.) 183, CA; and *R. v. Evans*, 13 Cr.App.R.(S.) 377, CA). Misbehaviour in the dock immediately after sentence is imposed, by shouting abuse or otherwise, is not a ground for varying a sentence: the matter should be dealt with if necessary as a contempt of court: *R. v. Powell*, 7 Cr.App.R.(S.) 247, CA.

In *R. v. Hadley* 16 Cr.App.R.(S.) 358, CA, it was held that if a sentencer found himself in the situation of having passed a sentence which was too low because of a mistake about his sentencing powers, he could usefully adopt the approach of the Court of Appeal, on a reference by the Attorney-General, and vary the sentence if it was so low as to be outside the bracket of sentences which the judge could reasonably impose. However, where a judge passed sentence under a mistaken impression as to the maximum permissible sentence, he was entitled to exercise his power to vary the sentence by way of increase where he did so within one hour of the original sentence being imposed, having been informed that the maximum sentence had in fact been increased as of a date approximately one year earlier; the alteration taking place so soon, the approach in *R. v. Hadley* was inapplicable; but the greater the interval between sentence and variation, the greater the need to proceed with caution: *R. v. Woop* [2002] 2 Cr.App.R.(S.) 65, CA.

Procedure

Variation of sentence should be in the presence of the defendant unless either **5–945** expressly or by implication (*e.g.* by absconding) he has waived the right to be present: *R. v. May*, 3 Cr.App.R.(S.) 165, CA; *R. v. Cleere*, 5 Cr.App.R.(S.) 465, CA; *R. v. McLean*, *ante*; and *R. v. Hussain* [2000] 1 Cr.App.R.(S.) 181, CA. Where, however, the court varied an unlawful sentence in the absence of the offender but in the presence of his counsel, the Court of Appeal refused to reduce the sentence on the ground that the variation was unlawful, observing that the action of the Crown Court did not give rise to any breach of natural justice, as the offender was represented by counsel who was present when the variation was made: see *R. v. Shacklady*, 9 Cr.App.R.(S.) 258, CA.

C. DETENTION IN DEFAULT OR FOR CONTEMPT

Powers of Criminal Courts (Sentencing) Act 2000, s.108

Detention of persons aged at least 18 but under 21 for default or contempt

5–946 **108.**—(1) *In any case where, but for section 89(1) above, a court would have power—*

(a) *to commit a person aged at least 18 but under 21 to prison for default in payment of a fine or any other sum of money, or*

(b) *to make an order fixing a term of imprisonment in the event of such a default by such a person, or*

(c) *to commit such a person to prison for contempt of court or any kindred offence,*

the court shall have power, subject to subsection (3) below, to commit him to be detained under this section or, as the case may be, to make an order fixing a term of detention under this section in the event of default, for a term not exceeding the term of imprisonment.

(2) *For the purposes of subsection (1) above, the power of a court to order a person to be imprisoned under section 23 of the* Attachment of Earnings Act *1971 shall be taken to be a power to commit him to prison.*

(3) *No court shall commit a person to be detained under this section unless it is of the opinion that no other method of dealing with him is appropriate; and in forming any such opinion, the court—*

(a) *shall take into account all such information about the circumstances of the default or contempt (including any aggravating or mitigating factors) as is available to it; and*

(b) *may take into account any information about that person which is before it.*

(4) *Where a magistrates' court commits a person to be detained under this section, it shall—*

(a) *state in open court the reason for its opinion that on other method of dealing with him is appropriate; and*

(b) *cause that reason to be specified in the warrant of commitment and to be entered in the register.*

(5) [Place of detention.]

[This section is repealed, as from a day to be appointed, by the *CJCSA* 2000, s.75 and Sched. 8.]

5–947 A sentence of detention under the section is not a "custodial sentence" for the purposes of s.79: see section 76(2), *ante*, § 5–262.

The power to commit an offender in default of payment under section 108 does not apply to offenders under the age of 18, whether in respect of orders to pay a sum of money (see *R. v. Basid* [1996] 1 Cr.App.R.(S.) 421, CA) or in respect of a contempt of court (see *R. v. Byas*, 16 Cr.App.R.(S.) 869, CA).

The alternative to an order under section 108 in most cases will be an attendance centre order under section 60, *ante*, § 5–162.

A refusal to enter into a recognizance to keep the peace by a person ordered to do so by a magistrates' court acting under the *MCA* 1980, s.115, is a "kindred offence" for the purposes of this section, and accordingly a person aged 18 who refuses to enter a recognizance may properly be committed to custody under this section: *Howley v. Oxford*, 81 Cr.App.R. 246, DC.

As to the release of persons ordered to be detained under section 108, see the *CJA* 2003, s.258 (replacing s.45 of the *CJA* 1991 as from a day to be appointed).

D. SURCHARGES

Criminal Justice Act 2003, ss.161A, 161B

Court's duty to order payment of surcharge

161A.—(1) A court when dealing with a person for one or more offences must also (subject to subsections (2) and (3)) order him to pay a surcharge. **5–948**

(2) Subsection (1) does not apply in such cases as may be prescribed by an order made by the Secretary of State.

(3) Where a court dealing with an offender considers—

(a) that it would be appropriate to make a compensation order, but

(b) that he has insufficient means to pay both the surcharge and appropriate compensation,

the court must reduce the surcharge accordingly (if necessary to nil).

(4) For the purposes of this section a court does not "deal with" a person if it—

(a) discharges him absolutely, or

(b) makes an order under the *Mental Health Act* 1983 in respect of him.

Amount of surcharge

161B.—(1) The surcharge payable under section 161A is such amount as the Secretary of State may specify by order. **5–949**

(2) An order under this section may provide for the amount to depend on—

(a) the offence or offences committed,

(b) how the offender is otherwise dealt with (including, where the offender is fined, the amount of the fine),

(c) the age of the offender.

This is not to be read as limiting section 330(3) (power to make different provision for different purposes etc.).

(4) In subsection (3) "the relevant time" means the time when the offender would, but for his release, have served a term equal in length to the aggregate of—

(a) all the required custodial days in relation to the terms of imprisonment, and

(b) the longest of the total licence periods in relation to those terms.

(5) In this section—

"total licence period", in relation to a term of imprisonment to which an intermittent custody order relates, means a period equal in length to the aggregate of all the licence periods as defined by section 183 in relation to that term;

"the required custodial days", in relation to such a term, means the number of days specified under that section.

[Ss.161A and 161B are inserted in Chapter 1 of Part 12 of the *CJA* 2003 by the *Domestic Violence, Crime and Victims Act* 2004, s.14. They apply only in relation to offences committed on or after April 1, 2007: 2004 Act, s.59, and Sched. 12, para. 7, and *Domestic Violence, Crime and Victims Act 2004 (Commencement No. 8) Order* 2007 (S.I. 2007 No. 602).]

The *Criminal Justice Act 2003 (Surcharge) (No. 2) Order* 2007 (S.I. 2007 No. 1079) provides (a) that section 161A(1) does not apply where a court deals with a person for one or more offences and does not impose a fine, and (b) that the amount specified as the surcharge is £15. **5–950**

CHAPTER 6

COSTS AND CRIMINAL DEFENCE SERVICE

I. COSTS

A. INTRODUCTION

Statutory framework

The award of costs in criminal proceedings is largely governed by Part II (ss.16– 21) of the *Prosecution of Offences Act* 1985. This is supplemented by the *Costs in Criminal Cases (General) Regulations* 1986 (S.I. 1986 No. 1335) made under sections 19 and 20. In addition to the 1985 Act and the 1986 regulations, there remains in force a miscellany of other statutory provisions and subordinate legislation appertaining to costs in criminal proceedings. **6–1**

Practice direction

The legislative framework is complemented by *Practice Direction (Costs: Criminal Proceedings)* [2004] 2 All E.R. 1070 (*post*, §§ 6–102 *et seq.*) which not only gives practical guidance on the operation of the legislation, but also emphasises the greater and more direct responsibility of the judge for costs in criminal cases than in civil cases (see, in particular, para. VII.1.2, *post*, § 6–114e). **6–2**

B. PROSECUTION OF OFFENCES ACT 1985

(1) Award of costs out of central funds

(a) *Defence costs*

Prosecution of Offences Act 1985, s.16

16.—(1) Where— **6–3**

(a) an information laid before a justice of the peace for any area, charging any person with an offence, is not proceeded with;

(b) *a magistrates' court inquiring into an indictable offence as examining justices determines not to commit the accused for trial;*

(c) a magistrates' court dealing summarily with an offence dismisses the information;

that court or, in a case falling within paragraph (a) above, a magistrates' court for that area, may make an order in favour of the accused for a payment to be made out of central funds in respect of his costs ("a defendant's costs order").

6–4 (2) Where—

(a) any person is not tried for an offence for which he has been indicted or *committed* [sent] for trial; or

(aa) *a notice of transfer is given under a relevant transfer provision but a person in relation to whose case it is given is not tried on a charge to which it relates; or*

(b) any person is tried on indictment and acquitted on any count in the indictment;

the Crown Court may make a defendant's costs order in favour of the accused.

(3) Where a person convicted of an offence by a magistrates' court appeals to the Crown Court under section 108 of the *Magistrates' Courts Act* 1980 (right of appeal against conviction or sentence) and, in consequence of the decision on appeal—

(a) his conviction is set aside; or

(b) a less severe punishment is awarded;

the Crown Court may make a defendant's costs order in favour of the accused.

6–5 (4) Where the Court of Appeal—

(a) allows an appeal under Part I of the *Criminal Appeal Act* 1968 against—

(i) conviction;

(ii) a verdict of not guilty by reason of insanity; or

(iii) a finding under the *Criminal Procedure (Insanity) Act* 1964 that the appellant is under a disability, or that he did the act or made the omission charged against him;

(aa) directs under section 8(1B) of the *Criminal Appeal Act* 1968 the entry of a judgment and verdict of acquittal;

(b) on an appeal under that Part against conviction—

(i) substitutes a verdict of guilty of another offence;

(ii) in a case where a special verdict has been found, orders a different conclusion on the effect of that verdict to be recorded; or

(iii) is of the opinion that the case falls within paragraph (a) or (b) of section 6(1) of that Act (cases where the court substitutes a finding of insanity or unfitness to plead);

(c) on an appeal under that Part against sentence, exercises its powers under section 11(3) of that Act (powers where the court considers that the appellant should be sentenced differently for an offence for which he was dealt with by the court below); or

(d) allows, to any extent, an appeal under section 16A of that Act (appeal against order made in cases of insanity or unfitness to plead);

the court may make a defendant's costs order in favour of the accused.

6–6 (4A) The court may also make a defendant's costs order in favour of the accused on an appeal under section 9(11) of the *Criminal Justice Act* 1987 or section 35(1) of the *Criminal Procedure and Investigations Act* 1996 (appeals against orders or rulings at preparatory hearings) or under Part 9 of the *Criminal Justice Act* 2003.

(5) Where—

(a) any proceedings in a criminal cause or matter are determined before a Divisional Court of the Queen's Bench Division;

(b) the *House of Lords* [Supreme Court] determines an appeal, or application for leave to appeal, from such a Divisional Court in a criminal cause or matter;

(c) the Court of Appeal determines an application for leave to appeal to the House of Lords under Part II of the *Criminal Appeal Act* 1968; or

(d) the *House of Lords* [Supreme Court] determines an appeal, or application for leave to appeal, under Part II of that Act;

the court may make a defendant's costs order in favour of the accused.

6–7 (6) A defendant's costs order shall, subject to the following provisions of this section, be for the payment out of central funds, to the person in whose favour the order is made, of such amount as the court considers reasonably sufficient to compensate him for any expenses properly incurred by him in the proceedings.

(7) Where a court makes a defendant's costs order but is of the opinion that there are circumstances which make it inappropriate that the person in whose favour the order is made should recover the full amount mentioned in subsection (6) above, the court shall—

(a) assess what amount would, in its opinion, be just and reasonable; and

(b) specify that amount in the order.

(8) [*Repealed by* Legal Aid Act *1988, s.45(2) and Sched. 6.*]

6–8 (9) Subject to subsection (7) above, the amount to be paid out of central funds in pursuance of a defendant's costs order shall—

(a) be specified in the order, in any case where the court considers it appropriate for the amount to be so specified and the person in whose favour the order is made agrees the amount; and

(b) in any other case, be determined in accordance with regulations made by the Lord Chancellor for the purposes of this section.

(10) Subsection (6) above shall have effect, in relation to any case falling within subsection (1)(a) or (2)(a) above, as if for the words "in the proceedings" there were substituted the words "in or about the defence".

(11) Where a person ordered to be retried is acquitted at his retrial, the costs which may be ordered to be paid out of central funds under this section shall include—

(a) any costs which, at the original trial, could have been ordered to be so paid under this section if he had been acquitted; and

(b) if no order was made under this section in respect of his expenses on appeal, any sums for the payment of which such an order could have been made.

(12) *In subsection (2)(aa) "relevant transfer provision" means—*

(a) *section 4 of the* Criminal Justice Act *1987, or*

(b) *section 53 of the* Criminal Justice Act *1991.*

[This section is printed as amended by the *CJA* 1987, s.15 and Sched. 2; the *CJA* 1988, s.170(1) and Sched. 15, para. 103; the *Criminal Procedure (Insanity and Unfitness to Plead) Act* 1991, Sched. 3, para. 7; the *CJPOA* 1994, Sched. 9, para. 25; the *CJA* 2003, ss.69(1) and (2), and 312(1) and (2); and the *Domestic Violence, Crime and Victims Act* 2004, s.58(1), and Sched. 10, para. 25; and, as from a day to be appointed, by the *CJA* 2003, s.41, and Sched. 3, para. 57(1) and (3) (substitution of the word "sent" for "committed" in subs. (2)(a), omission of subss. (1)(b), 2(aa) and (12)); and the *Constitutional Reform Act* 2005, s.40(4), and Sched. 9, para. 41(1) and (3) (substitution of words in square brackets for italicised words in subs. (5)). The substitution in subs. (2)(a) took effect on May 9, 2005, in relation to cases sent for trial under section 51 or 51A(3)(d) of the *CDA* 1998: *Criminal Justice Act 2003 (Commencement No. 9) Order* 2005 (S.I. 2005 No. 1267).] **6–9**

For the extended application of this section, see regulation 14(4) of S.I. 1986 No. 1335, *post*, § 6–71.

"information ... not proceeded with"—section 16(1)(a)

A magistrates' court is entitled to make an award of costs in favour of a defendant under section 16(1) where the court has no jurisdiction to proceed to summary trial of an information because it was laid outside the limitation period prescribed by section 127(1) of the *MCA* 1980: see *Patel v. Blakey* [1988] R.T.R. 65, DC. **6–10**

Where an information is withdrawn, an application for costs may be made on the date on which the application is withdrawn or on a later date: see *R. v. Bolton JJ., ex p. Wildish*, 147 J.P. 309, DC.

"a magistrates' court ... dismisses the information"—section 16(1)(c)

A defendant's costs order under section 16(1)(c) does not have to be made by the particular bench of magistrates who dismissed the information; nor does it have to be made timeously: *R. v. Liverpool Magistrates' Court, ex p. Abiaka*, 163 J.P. 497, DC. **6–10a**

"any person is not tried for an offence"—section 16(2)(a)

Where an indictment is not proceeded with and is ordered to lie on the file marked not to be proceeded with without the leave of the Crown Court or the Court of Appeal, an order may be made in favour of the defendant pursuant to section 16(2)(a): *R. v. Spens*, *The Independent*, March 18, 1992, Crown Court (Henry J.). **6–11**

"the accused"

A defendant's costs order may be made in favour of a parent or guardian ordered to pay a child or young person's fine, costs or compensation pursuant to the *PCC(S)A* 2000, s.137(1) (*ante*, § 5–928), where a successful application for judicial review is made **6–11a** for the purpose of quashing the order; the reference to "the accused" in section 16(5)(a) is to be construed as including a parent or guardian against whom such an order has been made: *R. v. Preston Crown Court, ex p. Lancashire C.C.*; *R. v. Burnley Crown Court, ex p. Same* [1999] 1 W.L.R. 142, DC.

"in the proceedings"—section 16(6)

6–12 Section 21(1) (*post*, § 6–49) provides that "'proceedings': includes—(a) proceedings in any court below ... ." In view of this, it is submitted that there is no need for a specific order for the defendant's costs in the court below to be paid out of central funds. Such an order was necessary under the former legislation: see *R. v. Michael* [1976] Q.B. 414, Crown Court (H.H.J. Rubin); and *R. v. Agritraders Ltd* [1983] Q.B. 464, 76 Cr.App.R. 183, CA. Under subsection (6) the proceedings in respect of which expenses have been incurred and for which the defendant is to be compensated are defined by section 21 as including proceedings in any court below. If, however, the court takes the view that it would be inappropriate for the defendant to recover the expenses incurred in the court below (*e.g.* on a successful appeal against sentence only), this could presumably be achieved by the exercise of the power contained in subsection (7).

Costs incurred for solicitor's attendances when the client had been on bail prior to charge fall within the subsection as expenses incurred "in the proceedings": *R. (Hale) v. Southport JJ.*, *The Times*, January 29, 2002, DC.

"incurred by him"—section 16(6)

6–13 In *R. v. Miller and Glennie*, 78 Cr.App.R. 71, QBD (Lloyd J.), it was held that costs were incurred by a party if he was responsible or liable for those costs, even though they were in fact paid by a third party and even though the third party was also liable for the costs. It was only if it had been agreed that the client should in no circumstances be liable for the costs that they ceased to be incurred by him. Once it was shown that the defendant was the client of the solicitor then a presumption arose that he was to be personally liable for the costs. That presumption could be rebutted if it were established that there was an express or implied agreement binding on the solicitors that the defendant would not have to pay those costs in any circumstances.

In *R. v. Jain*, *The Times*, December 10, 1987, CA, a defendant's costs order was made in favour of a named person other than the accused, who had financed the proceedings. It is not clear from this short report how the court dealt with an apparent obstacle to any such order, namely that the Act appears to contemplate by the express terms of subsections (1) to (5) that the only person in whose favour a "defendant's costs order" may be made is the accused. It is not apparent whether any argument was addressed to the court in opposition to the making of the order.

There can be more than one claim in pursuance of an order under section 16. Where, therefore, the defendant's solicitor had put in a claim, it had been open to the defendant to put in a separate claim for disbursements he had incurred in the preparation of his case: *R. v. Bedlington Magistrates' Court, ex p. Wilkinson*, 164 J.P. 163, DC; followed in *R. (Brewer) v. Supreme Court Costs Office* [2007] Costs L.R. 20, DC (where the court said that practitioners should present separate claims together in a manner which makes clear the relationship between them, and that determining officers and costs judges should ensure that assessments in such cases do not take place separately and sequentially, but are assessed by reference to each other).

Principles governing exercise of discretion

6–14 Section 16 says nothing about how the discretion should be exercised. Guidance may be derived from the *Practice Direction (Costs: Criminal Proceedings)* [2004] 2 All E.R. 1070 (*post*, §§ 6–105 *et seq.*).

The fact that the defendant has brought the prosecution on himself is a reason for not making an order: *R. v. Spens*, *The Independent*, March 18, 1992, Crown Court (Henry J.). Where a prosecution is not proceeded with in a magistrates' court, the court may conclude that the accused brought the prosecution on himself on the basis of a statement of facts provided by the prosecution; where, however, the justices were simply told that on a charge of assault the complainant had withdrawn her complaint, there was no basis for refusing a defendant's costs order in the absence of independent evidence to support the truth of the complaint: *Mooney v. Cardiff Magistrates' Court*, 164 J.P. 220, DC. Nor were justices entitled to rule that the defendant had brought a prosecution on himself, where they were told, following the withdrawal of an allegation of assault by the complainant, that he had made partial admissions in interview, but were not told what he had actually said: *R. v. South West Surrey JJ., ex p. James* [2001] Crim.L.R. 690, DC.

Where an information alleged the commission of an offence by a company, where, on any view, if any company had committed the offence it was the defendant's subsidiary (with a different, albeit similar name) and where the parent company had attended by counsel in answer to the summons, the magistrates' court had been wrong to refuse it a defendant's costs order where it had not in any way been responsible for the mistake made by the prosecuting authority: *Sainsbury's Supermarkets Ltd and J. Sainsbury plc v. H.M. Courts Service (South West Region, Devon and Cornwall area), Plymouth City Council (interested party)*, 170 J.P. 690, DC.

Where a defendant accepted a formal caution, whereupon no evidence was offered, and where his application for a defendant's costs order was refused on the basis that acceptance of a caution was equivalent to a plea of guilty and on the ground that he had unnecessarily incurred costs by not offering to accept a caution at a much earlier stage, the court had erred; a caution (whilst it constituted an admission of guilt) was not to be equated to a plea of guilty and, there being no duty on a defendant to seek resolution of proceedings by way of caution, the court had taken into account an irrelevance: *R. (Stoddard) v. Oxford Magistrates' Court*, 169 J.P. 683, DC.

On a successful appeal against conviction to the Crown Court, the court does not have an unfettered discretion as to whether or not to make a defendant's cost order; *Practice Direction (Costs: Criminal Proceedings)* (*post*, §§ 6–102 *et seq.*) applies by analogy to such appeals; accordingly, a defendant's costs order should "normally be made unless there are positive reasons for not doing so" (paras II.1.1 and II.2.1); where the prosecution does not proceed because a witness is unavailable, that is not something for which the defendant is responsible, and an application for costs should normally succeed: *R. (Barrington) v. Preston Crown Court*, unreported, July 16, 2001, QBD (Silber J.) ([2001] EWHC Admin. 599). Similarly, on a successful appeal against sentence to the Crown Court, a defendant's costs order should be made unless there are positive reasons for not doing so; if the court declined to make such order, it should give its reasons; on judicial review, however, the court would interfere with a decision for which no reasons were given only if there were no obvious reason for the decision: *Cunningham v. Exeter Crown Court*, 167 J.P. 93, DC.

A decision to refuse costs to a defendant against whom proceedings have been discontinued may raise an issue under Article 6(2) of the ECHR (*post*, § 16–57), if the supporting reasoning amounts in substance to a determination of the guilt of the former accused, particularly if he has not had an opportunity to exercise the rights of defence: *Hussain v. UK* (2006) 43 E.H.R.R. 22, ECtHR; where, however, a court refers to the state of suspicion against the accused in support of an exercise of its discretion to refuse costs, there is no violation of the presumption of innocence: *Leutscher v. Netherlands*, 24 E.H.R.R.181, ECtHR. See also the *Practice Direction (Costs: Criminal Proceedings)*, para. II.2.1 (*post*, § 6–106).

Awards by Court of Appeal

A large and arbitrary sum in the nature of a reward paid by an appellant to an informer should not be paid out of central funds. Such an item is not an expense "properly incurred ... in the proceedings": *R. v. Whitby*, 65 Cr.App.R. 257, CA. **6–15**

In *R. v. Agritraders Ltd*, *ante*, it was said, *per curiam*, that the Court of Appeal has power to vary an order for the payment of a successful appellant's costs out of central funds and has inherent jurisdiction to reconsider an order for costs so as to enlarge it in some particular way on being satisfied that an omission to make a material application was due to a genuine accidental omission on the part of counsel. *Quaere*: whether the court has jurisdiction to entertain a fresh application for costs which has arisen as a result of an afterthought.

Amount of award

6–16 The relevant provisions are section 16(6), (7) and (9), and regulation 7 of the 1986 regulations (*post*, § 6–59), supplemented by the *Practice Direction (Costs: Criminal Proceedings)* [2004] 2 All E.R. 1070 (*post*, § 6–101). It is submitted, however, that the terms of the practice direction are not entirely consistent with the contents of the Act.

Section 16(6) stipulates that once the decision has been made to make a defendant's costs order, it shall, subject to the following provisions of the section, be for the payment of such amount as the court considers reasonably sufficient to compensate the person in whose favour the order is made for any expenses properly incurred by him in the proceedings. Subsection (9) provides that, subject to subsection (7), the amount to be paid shall be specified in the order if the court considers it appropriate for it to be so specified and the person in whose favour the award is made agrees the amount. Otherwise it is to be determined in accordance with the regulations. If it is so determined, the overriding criterion is exactly the same as under subsection (6). Regulation 7(1) (*post*, § 6–59) provides for the appropriate authority allowing such costs in respect of (a) such work as appears to it to have been actually and reasonably done, and (b) such disbursements as appear to it to have been actually and reasonably incurred, as it considers reasonably sufficient to compensate the person in whose favour the award was made for any expenses properly incurred by him in the proceedings. The regulations provide an elaborate procedure for redeterminations and appeals.

On the basis of the foregoing, it is submitted that the intention behind the Act and the regulations was that the ultimate arbiter of what expenses were properly incurred and what was reasonably sufficient compensation for such expenses should be the appropriate authority under the regulations, subject to the possibility of redetermination and appeals to a costs judge and the High Court. Subject to subsection (7), the court making the defendant's costs order was not, it is submitted, intended to make any final order with which the person in whose favour the order was made did not agree. If the court sought to disallow any particular item as being improperly incurred, but nevertheless intended to specify an amount under subsection (9), the person in whose favour the order was made need only refuse his agreement to the amount. By adopting this course, he would ensure that what expenses were properly incurred would be determined in accordance with the regulations.

6–17 Subsection (7) does give the court making the order the ultimate power to determine the amount in the situation specified therein. It does not appertain to the situation where the court takes the view that some expenses may have been improperly incurred, but to the situation where, for whatever reason, the court takes the view that the person in whose favour it is making the order should not be compensated for all his expenses even though they were properly incurred. In such a case, there is no procedure under the regulations for determining the amount to be paid. The court must determine the figure. If, for example, it takes the view that it would be "just and reasonable" for the defendant to recover half of his properly incurred expenses, it seems it should determine first of all what amount would sufficiently compensate him for the whole of his properly incurred expenses. It should then halve that figure and specify it in the order. But the power under subsection (7) may only be exercised where the court has identified circumstances making it inappropriate for the full amount to be recovered: see *Galandauer v. Snaresbrook Crown Court* [2007] Costs L.R. 205, DC.

Where the amount of a defendant's costs order is to be determined in accordance with the regulations, it has been submitted that the court making the order cannot make any determination against the interests of the person in whose favour the award is made either as to what expenses were properly incurred or as to what amount would be reasonably sufficient compensation for such expenses as were properly incurred. The procedure provided for by the regulations does, however, allow for the views of the presiding judge to be ascertained at the stage of an appeal to a costs judge: see reg. 10(11), *post*, § 6–64.

The practice direction, *ante*, appears to confer on the court making a defendant's costs order a greater role than that contemplated by the legislation. Part V of the practice direction (replacing effectively identical provisions in the 1991 costs practice direction (*Practice Direction (Costs in Criminal Proceedings)*, 93 Cr.App.R. 89)) coincides almost exactly with paragraphs (5) to (8) of the *Practice Direction (Crown Court: Costs)*, 64 Cr.App.R. 113. That direction was issued at a time when the governing legislation was the *Costs in Criminal Cases Act* 1973. There were no provisions in that Act comparable to subsections (7) and (9) of section 16. Furthermore, there were no regulations comparable to regulations 5 to 8 of the 1986 regulations (*post*, §§ 6–57 *et seq.*). **6–18**

However appropriate the 1977 practice direction may have been to the law prior to the 1985 Act, it is submitted that it does not fit so easily into the current legislative framework.

In *R. v. McFadden*, 62 Cr.App.R. 187, CA, it was said by the court, considering the *Legal Aid in Criminal Proceedings (Fees and Expenses) Regulations* 1968, which were made under section 83 of the *CJA* 1967, that they contained no provision for a direction to be given by the trial judge to the taxing authority or the taxing master. **6–19**

> "The reason for this seems clear. The judge is not in a position to know many of the facts which are relevant to the taxation of costs, and is not in a position to conduct the inquiries necessary to establish the correctness or otherwise of an impression he may have formed as to the way in which the case has been prepared or conducted. The judge is limited, unless and until he is later consulted by the taxing authority, to drawing attention to specific or general matters which in his view might be relevant to the task of the taxing authority. If and when the judge is consulted it is for the purpose of enabling the person responsible for making decisions as to what should or should not be allowed on taxation to be better informed as to the course of the trial and, in particular, as to what, if anything, in the view of the judge represented work resulting in unreasonable or unnecessary expense, that is, work not 'reasonably done'. The judge makes no decision and he gives no direction. If it were otherwise, a situation might arise in which the taxing master or authority would have to override the directions of the judge" (*per* James L.J., at pp. 189–190).

Although the court in *McFadden* was considering a different statutory provision and different regulations, the rationale of what was said seems to apply equally to section 16 of the 1985 Act. There is no provision in the Act or the regulations for the court to make a direction such as is referred to in paragraph V.1.1 of the practice direction. There is, however, provision for taxation by the appropriate officer and for consultation with the presiding judge at a later stage in the process. All this is directly comparable to the position under the 1968 regulations, as is the possibility of the appropriate authority forming a different view to that of the court as to the propriety of a particular item of expenditure. These considerations suggest that the spirit of *McFadden* may be held to apply if a "direction" under paragraph V.1.1 should ever be challenged in other proceedings.

Where the defendant's solicitors were initially retained privately but were then the selected representative under a representation order and where the defendant, having been acquitted, obtained a defendant's costs order, the solicitors were not entitled to submit a bill for payment out of central funds at the private rates agreed with the defendant before the obtaining of the representation order; for the purposes of section 21(4A) of the 1985 Act (*post*, § 6–50), a person in respect of whom a representation order had been granted was a "legally assisted person", regardless of whether a claim had been made under that order, or whether, as in this case, a claim had instead been made under a private retainer; "funded" means "being funded" rather than "has been paid" and relates to the funding arrangement in place rather than to payment; accordingly, the solicitors were entitled to be paid under the *Criminal Defence Service (Funding) Order* 2001 (S.I. 2001 No. 855) in respect of the period after the grant of the representation order, and that cost was, pursuant to section 21(4A) to be excluded from the amount payable under the defendant's costs order; in any event, regulation 22 of the *Criminal Defence Service (General No. 2) Regulations* 2001 (S.I. 2001 No. 1437) (*post*, § 6–176) made it quite clear that where a representation order was in place, solicitors could not expect to recover any payment for work done other than under that order: *R. v. Hayes* [2008] Costs L.R. 186, S.C.C.O.

Appropriate test

6–20 In *R. v. Dudley Magistrates' Court, ex p. Power City Stores Ltd*, 154 J.P. 654, the Divisional Court quashed a justices' clerk's decision to disallow the costs of leading counsel when assessing costs payable to the applicants out of central funds. The appropriate question was whether the defendant acted reasonably in instructing the counsel he did and not whether more junior counsel or a solicitor could have dealt with the case.

The test of reasonable sufficiency has nothing to do with whether a legal representative of less experience would have been adequate to the task; the question was not whether a less experienced advocate would have been sufficient, but whether the instruction of the particular advocate was reasonable; for a defendant charged with common assault and battery, the instruction of a solicitor of more than four years' standing was reasonable, as was the agreement to incur costs using a flat hourly rate: *R. (Hale) v. Southport JJ.*, *The Times*, January 29, 2002, DC.

Solicitor defendant in person

6–21 In *R. v. Stafford, Stone and Eccleshall JJ., ex p. Robinson* [1988] 1 W.L.R. 369, QBD (Simon Brown J.), it was held that where a solicitor had acted on his own behalf for part of proceedings against him which were dismissed at the committal stage, and was awarded costs out of central funds, he was entitled to all his costs, including those incurred in the course of conducting his own case. His own time was properly to be regarded as an expense incurred by him. Solicitors' expenses could properly be held to include their own fees such as they would otherwise be earning on behalf of the firm.

Interest

6–22 There is no basis in statute, regulation or rule for the payment of interest on costs awarded from central funds in a criminal cause or matter. Sections 17 and 18 of the *Judgments Act* 1838 do not apply to criminal proceedings: *Westminster City Council v. Wingrove* [1991] 1 Q.B. 652, 92 Cr.App.R. 179, DC.

(b) *Prosecution costs*

Prosecution of Offences Act 1985, s.17

6–23 **17.**—(1) Subject to subsection (2) below, the court may—

(a) in any proceedings in respect of an indictable offence; and

(b) in any proceedings before a Divisional Court of the Queen's Bench Division or the *House of Lords* [Supreme Court] in respect of a summary offence;

order the payment out of central funds of such amount as the court considers reasonably sufficient to compensate the prosecutor for any expenses properly incurred by him in the proceedings.

(2) No order under this section may be made in favour of—

(a) a public authority or;

(b) a person acting—

(i) on behalf of a public authority; or

(ii) in his capacity as an official appointed by such an authority.

(3) Where a court makes an order under this section but is of the opinion that there are circumstances which make it inappropriate that the prosecution should recover the full amount mentioned in subsection (1) above, the court shall—

(a) assess what amount would, in its opinion, be just and reasonable; and

(b) specify that amount in the order.

(4) Subject to subsection (3) above, the amount to be paid out of central funds in pursuance of an order under this section shall—

(a) be specified in the order, in any case where the court considers it appropriate for the amount to be so specified and the prosecutor agrees the amount; and

(b) in any other case, be determined in accordance with regulations made by the Lord Chancellor for the purposes of this section.

6–24 (5) Where the conduct of proceedings to which subsection (1) above applies is taken over by the Crown Prosecution Service, that subsection shall have effect as if it referred to the prosecutor who had the conduct of the proceedings before the intervention of the Service and to expenses incurred by him up to the time of intervention.

(6) In this section "public authority" means—

(a) a police force within the meaning of section 3 of this Act;

(b) the Crown Prosecution Service or any other government department;

(c) a local authority or other authority or body constituted for purposes of—

(i) the public service or of local government; or

(ii) carrying on under national ownership any industry or undertaking or part of an industry or undertaking; or

(d) any other authority or body whose members are appointed by Her Majesty or by any Minister of the Crown or government department or whose revenues consist wholly or mainly of money provided by Parliament.

[This section is printed as amended, as from a day to be appointed, by the *Constitutional Reform Act* 2005, s.40(4), and Sched. 9, para. 41(1) and (3) (substitution of words in square brackets for italicised words).]

For section 3 of the Act, see *ante*, § 1–253. For the extended application of this section, see regulation 14(1) of S.I. 1986 No. 1335, *post*, § 6–70.

As to the phrase "in the proceedings" (subs. (1)), see *ante*, § 6–12.

In *R. v. Stockport Magistrates' Court, ex p. Cooper*, 148 J.P. 261, DC, the court considered the corresponding provision of the 1973 Act in relation to magistrates' courts. It was held that a private prosecutor was not entitled to be compensated for trouble or loss of time in carrying on the prosecution and was only entitled to expenses such as travel and secretarial expenses incurred. The prosecutor was only entitled to expenses, in the plural. Witnesses were entitled to compensation for expense, in the singular. Compensation for loss of time was specifically provided for only in relation to attendance by witnesses. Contrast now the wording of section 17(1) and that of section 21(4), *post*, § 6–50.

Principles governing exercise of discretion

See the *Practice Direction (Costs: Criminal Proceedings)* [2004] 2 All E.R. 1070 (*post*, § 6–101), especially paragraph III.1.1 thereof. **6–25**

Amount of award

What was said in § 6–16, *ante*, in relation to a defendant's costs order applies, *mutatis mutandis*, to an order for the payment of a private prosecutor's costs out of central funds under section 17. **6–26**

See also *R. v. Dudley Magistrates' Court, ex p. Power City Stores Ltd*, *ante*, § 6–20 (appropriate test); and *Westminster City Council v. Wingrove*, *ante*, § 6–22 (no interest on costs).

(2) Award of costs against accused

Prosecution of Offences Act 1985, s.18

18.—(1) Where— **6–27**

(a) any person is convicted of an offence before a magistrates' court;

(b) the Crown Court dismisses an appeal against such a conviction or against the sentence imposed on that conviction; or

(c) any person is convicted of an offence before the Crown Court;

the court may make such order as to the costs to be paid by the accused to the prosecutor as it considers just and reasonable.

(2) Where the Court of Appeal dismisses—

(a) an appeal or application for leave to appeal under Part I of the *Criminal Appeal Act* 1968; or

(b) an application by the accused for leave to appeal to the *House of Lords* [Supreme Court] under Part II of that Act; or

(c) an appeal or application for leave to appeal under section 9(11) of the *Criminal Justice Act* 1987; or

(d) an appeal or application for leave to appeal under section 35(1) of the *Criminal Procedure and Investigations Act* 1996;

it may make such order as to the costs to be paid by the accused, to such person as may be named in the order, as it considers just and reasonable.

(2A) Where the Court of Appeal reverses or varies a ruling on an appeal under Part 9 of the *Criminal Justice Act* 2003, it may make such order as to the costs to be paid by the accused, to such person as may be named in the order, as it considers just and reasonable.

(3) The amount to be paid by the accused in pursuance of an order under this section shall be specified in the order.

(4) Where any person is convicted of an offence before a magistrates' court and—

(a) under the conviction the court orders payment of any sum as a fine, penalty, forfeiture or compensation; and

(b) the sum so ordered to be paid does not exceed £5;

the court shall not order the accused to pay any costs under this section unless in the particular circumstances of the case it considers it right to do so.

(5) Where any person under the age of eighteen is convicted of an offence before a magistrates' court, the amount of any costs ordered to be paid by the accused under this section shall not exceed the amount of any fine imposed on him.

(6) Costs ordered to be paid under subsection (2) [or (2A)] above may include the reasonable cost of any transcript of a record of proceedings made in accordance with rules of court made for the purposes of section 32 of the Act of 1968.

[This section is printed as amended by the *CJA* 1987, s.15 and Sched. 2; the *CJPOA* 1994, Sched. 9, para. 26; and the *CJA* 2003, ss.69(1), (3) and (4), and 312(1) and (3); and as amended, as from a day to be appointed, by the *Constitutional Reform Act* 2005, s.40(4), and Sched. 9, para. 41(1) and (3) (substitution of words in square brackets for italicised words).]

For the extended application of this section, see regulation 14 of S.I. 1986 No. 1335, *post*, § 6–70.

There was no violation of section 8 of the Constitution of Gibraltar (in analogous terms to Art. 6 of the ECHR (*post*, § 16–57)) by reason of a court having a discretion following a trial on indictment to make a costs order in favour of the prosecution against a convicted defendant, but to be precluded from making such orders in favour of acquitted defendants against the prosecution: *Att.-Gen. for Gibraltar v. Shimidzu (Berllaque intervening)* [2005] 1 W.L.R. 3335, PC.

Amount to be fixed

6–28 Subsection (3) requires that the amount to be paid in pursuance of an order under the section is specified in the order. There is, therefore, no current provision for the taxation of costs orders against an accused. (See, however, s.52 of the *Supreme Court [Senior Courts] Act* 1981 (renamed as from a day to be appointed: *Constitutional Reform Act* 2005, s.59(5), and Sched. 11, para. 1), as amended by the 1985 Act, *post*, § 6–86, which allows for such a possibility in the future.)

Relevance of means

6–29 Orders for costs should not be made which are beyond the means of the defendant: *R. v. Maher* [1983] Q.B. 784, 76 Cr.App.R. 309, CA; *R. v. Mountain*, 68 Cr.App.R. 41, CA; *R. v. Nottingham JJ., ex p. Fohmann*, 84 Cr.App.R. 316, DC (wrong in principle to order a convicted person to pay prosecution costs in such a sum that, through lack of means, he was unable to pay the sum within a reasonable period of about one year). This must now be read in the light of *R. v. Olliver and Olliver*, 11 Cr.App.R.(S.) 10, CA. The court was concerned principally with fines, but there had been, in addition to the fines imposed on the appellants, substantial orders for compensation and costs. The effect was that the total sums ordered to be paid would take the appellants two-and-a-half years to pay. It was held that there was no principle requiring a financial penalty payable by instalments to run for no more than one year. There was nothing wrong in principle with the period being much longer than a year, provided that it was not an undue burden and so too severe a punishment, having regard to the nature of the offence and the offender. The judgment was directed primarily at fines and compensation, but, it is submitted that the spirit thereof plainly embraces costs orders as well. None of the orders were varied or quashed: payment of the orders for costs alone would have taken one appellant eight months to pay and the other appellant seven months to pay.

A fine imposed on a large company (here, "modest when set against the [company's] overall profitability and turnover") should, as a matter of course, be paid either immediately or in a period to be measured in single figure days, unless cogent evidence was provided that more time was needed; such a requirement can bring home the seriousness of the offending and the impact of the penalty: *R. v. B. & Q. plc*, *The Times*, November 3, 2005, CA.

In the case of a small company, it is legitimate for a fine to be payable over a significantly longer period than would be regarded as reasonable in the case of an individual, and it is not necessarily a more severe course to order a larger sum over a longer period than a smaller sum over a shorter period, since the former course might give the company a greater opportunity to control its cash flow and survive difficult trading conditions; in considering the appropriate fines on the directors of a company, the court should bear in mind, on the one hand, the need to avoid the risk of double punishment which arose where the directors of a small company were also its shareholders, and, on the other, that it was important to make clear that there is a personal responsibility on directors which could not simply be shuffled off onto the company: *R. v. Rollco Screw and Rivet Co. Ltd* [1999] 2 Cr.App.R.(S.) 436, CA.

It is for the defendant to provide evidence of his means; failure to do so would entitle the court to draw reasonable inferences as to his means from the evidence and all the circumstances of the case: *R. v. Northallerton Magistrates' Court, ex p. Dove* [2000] 1 Cr.App.R.(S.) 136, DC.

Relevance of election for trial, nature of defence

In *Mountain*, *ante*, Lawton L.J. referred to the principle that an order to pay the costs of the prosecution should not be imposed merely because a defendant has elected trial on indictment. He said that one relevant consideration was the conduct of the defence. Where that was of the type which involved allegations that everyone except the defendant was telling lies and the case against him was fabricated, an order for costs might well be appropriate. **6–30**

It is not the case that every defendant who is convicted after a plea of not guilty should be ordered to pay the costs of the prosecution, but there is a discretion which the judge can exercise if he takes into account such matters as the fact that the defendant had chosen to contest a strong case against him or the fact that the defendant must have known the real truth of the matter. If the defendant, knowing his guilt, has elected trial by jury, it is permissible, if the trial judge decides on all the facts that the costs ought to be paid, to refer to the waste of time and money when passing sentence: *R. v. Singh*, 4 Cr.App.R.(S.) 38, CA. In *R. v. Hayden*, 60 Cr.App.R. 304, CA, it was said that if it was an appropriate case in which to order costs there could be no objection to an observation that those costs will inevitably be higher in consequence of the decision to elect trial. See also *R. v. Ioannou*, 61 Cr.App.R. 257, CA, and *R. v. Bushell*, 2 Cr.App.R.(S.) 77, CA.

Several defendants

Where some only of several defendants have the means to pay costs, it is wrong to divide the total costs of the prosecution between those defendants. If it is not possible to say what part of the total costs is attributable to any given defendant, the court should divide the total costs between the total number of defendants, including any who are not in a position to pay, and to order those who do have sufficient means to pay their share only: *R. v. Ronson and Parnes*, 13 Cr.App.R.(S.) 153, CA. See also *R. v. Harrison*, 14 Cr.App.R.(S.) 419, CA. In *R. v. Davies (Ceri)* [1999] 2 Cr.App.R.(S.) 356, CA, it was held to have been appropriate to make an order for the appellant to pay his share of the whole of the costs of the prosecution, as opposed to a share of the costs incurred from the moment when he was brought in as a defendant (at a late stage). **6–31**

Plea of guilty

Where a defendant pleads guilty there is equally no rule that an order for costs **6–32** cannot be made against him; a plea of guilty is a factor to be taken into account in deciding whether to make an order, the weight to be attached to it being dependent on the nature of the case. The nature of the case may also make it proper to make substantial orders for costs against defendants upon whom long terms of imprisonment have been imposed: *R. v. Maher, ante.*

Convictions on some only of several counts

6–32a In *R. v. B. & Q. plc, ante*, § 6–29, where the appellant had been convicted at a third trial on some counts and acquitted on others, the two previous trials having been aborted because of the unsatisfactory nature of some closed circuit television evidence, it was held that the judge had erred in taking a global approach to the question of costs; the appellant should not have been required to pay costs in respect of the aborted trials, and allowance should have been made for the acquittals on some counts.

Investigation expenses

6–33 In *Neville v. Gardner Merchant Ltd*, 5 Cr.App.R.(S.) 349, DC, the court had to consider section 2(2) of the 1973 Act. That subsection was effectively in the same terms as section 18(1)(a), (4) and (5). It was held that the discretion to award costs under section 2(2) was wide enough to cover an amount in respect of the time of an investigating officer, paid out of public funds, whose job it was to investigate alleged offences: *R. v. Burt, ex p. Presburg* [1960] 1 Q.B. 625, DC, applied. Kerr L.J. added, in giving the court's judgment, that prima facie such costs ought to be awarded and, if the facts revealed that the whole of the costs of the investigation were the result of a specific complaint and not of any routine inspection, it would be right to award the whole sum. Where, however, an officer of the prosecuting authority conducted the case without legal representation, it was inappropriate to use as a guideline the scale of costs in legal aid cases; the amount to be awarded should be such sum as would reimburse the authority for those items of time and trouble which the offence committed had made necessary: *R. v. Tottenham JJ., ex p. Joshi*, 75 Cr.App.R. 72, DC.

Neville v. Gardner Merchant Ltd was followed in *R. v. Associated Octel Ltd* [1997] 1 Cr.App.R.(S.) 435, CA (an order for costs under section 18 could properly include an amount in respect of the costs of the investigation carried out by the prosecuting authority). The court said that the prosecution should serve the defence as early as possible with full details of their costs, so as to afford a proper opportunity to consider them and make representations on them; if the defendant wished to dispute them, he should, if possible, give proper notice to the prosecution of the objections which it was proposed to make; at the least, such objections should be made clear to the court. In exceptional cases, a full hearing might be necessary, as there is no provision for taxation.

Neville v. Gardner Merchant Ltd was further considered in *BPS Advertising Ltd v. London Borough of Barnet*, 171 J.P. 223, QBD (Collins J.), in which it was said that where there was a conflict between the principle that the costs ordered should not be grossly disproportionate to the level of the fine (*post*, § 6–35), and the principle that costs incurred by an investigating officer whose job it was to investigate alleged offences are recoverable as costs incurred by the prosecutor, the fact that the costs of investigating and of prosecuting a case may be significantly greater than the maximum penalty for that offence should not provide an individual with effective immunity from prosecution simply because it would be too expensive (any eventual costs order having to be proportionate to the fine); but, at the same time, care was necessary not to inflate the amount of costs by reference to an investigation where the investigating authority would have incurred costs in any event by virtue of the fact that the investigator was carrying out his duties in the normal way and would be paid for doing so, whatever he had been doing at the relevant time.

As to the amounts to be allowed in respect of time reasonably spent on an investigation by one of the prosecutor's investigators, see *Federation against Copyright Theft v. Broomhall* [2007] Costs L.R. 640, S.C.C.O.

Costs on abandonment/dismissal of appeal

6–34 Where an application for leave or an appeal is abandoned at a late stage and the

Court of Appeal is in consequence put to a great deal of trouble unnecessarily, the court would say "you put the court to a lot of expense and you ought to pay the costs of your appeal": *R. v. Howitt*, 61 Cr.App.R. 327, CA.

If the prosecution intend to make an application for costs against an unsuccessful legally-aided appellant in the Court of Appeal, they should give advance notice of such intention: *R. v. Emmett (Stephen Roy)*, *The Times*, October 15, 1999, CA.

In *Griffiths v. Pembrokeshire C.C.*, *The Times*, April 19, 2000, DC, it was held that an unsuccessful appellant to the Crown Court against conviction, having put the prosecution to avoidable expense, ought in principle to bear the whole of the prosecution's reasonable costs of resisting the appeal; and there was no reason for making any link between the penalty imposed in the lower court and the costs to be paid on appeal. If, however, the costs claimed on appeal were far in excess of those awarded in the lower court, an independent bystander might well conclude that the appellant was being punished for having chosen to exercise his statutory right to appeal; accordingly, a balance had to be struck; and for this purpose, the legal aid scale fees payable to solicitors and counsel were a useful marker as to the costs that it would be reasonable to expect an unsuccessful appellant to pay. Where the respondent instructed specialist counsel in a case that did not demand it, there was no reason why the appellant should have to reimburse them for the fees they chose to agree.

In *Johnson v. RSPCA*, 164 J.P. 345, DC, it was held that the Crown Court, on dismissing an appeal, could make an order against the appellant in respect of the costs of the proceedings in the magistrates' court, either by virtue of section 18(1)(b) of the 1985 Act, or of section 48(2)(a) of the *Supreme Court [Senior Courts] Act* 1981 (*ante*, § 2–178) (as to the renaming of this Act, see *ante*, § 6–28). The court said that in the usual case, however, the Crown Court should hesitate to modify the magistrates' costs order, the magistrates being better placed to decide how much of the costs of the proceedings before them the prosecution should recover; where the prosecution intend to invite the Crown Court to vary a costs order made by the magistrates' court in the event of the appeal being dismissed, they should provide the appellant with written details of their proposed application so that he could be informed of the possible consequence of an unsuccessful appeal; if they did not do so, the Crown Court would generally be expected not to interfere.

The relationship between sentence and costs

There is a conflict of authority on this issue. In *R. v. Whalley*, 56 Cr.App.R. 304, CA, **6–35**
it was held to be wrong in principle to impose a small fine and a heavy order for costs. See also *R. v. Firmston*, 6 Cr.App.R.(S.) 189, CA, and *R. v. Jones (N.C.J.)*, 10 Cr.App.R.(S.) 95, CA, to similar effect. In *R. v. Bushell*, *ante*, § 6–30, and *Cozens v. Hobbs* [1999] C.O.D. 24, DC, however, it was said that there is no necessary relationship between sentence and costs. All these authorities, together with *R. v. Hayward* [1975] 1 W.L.R. 852, CA, and *R. v. Nottingham JJ., ex p. Fohmann*, 84 Cr.App.R. 316, DC, were reviewed in *R. v. Northallerton Magistrates' Court, ex p. Dove* [2000] 1 Cr.App.R.(S.) 136, DC. An order for the payment of costs should not ordinarily be grossly disproportionate to a fine, although there was no requirement that the two amounts should necessarily stand in some arithmetical relationship to each other; the fine should be fixed first, and then a decision should be made as to costs; if the total sum exceeded that which the defendant could reasonably be expected to pay, it was preferable to achieve an acceptable total by reducing the costs order.

See also *BPS Advertising Ltd v. London Borough of Barnet*, *ante*, § 6–33.

Appeal against order for costs

Subject to the obtaining of leave, there is a right of appeal to the Court of Appeal **6–36**
against an order that the accused should pay the whole or any part of the costs of the prosecution: *R. v. Hayden*, 60 Cr.App.R. 304, CA (*post*, § 7–120).

Where, however, an order for costs is made against the accused by a magistrates' court there is no right of appeal against the order to the Crown Court: *MCA* 1980, s.108(3)(b), *ante*, § 2–161. An appeal to the High Court can, however, be made:

"if it can be shown that the magistrates, in purporting to exercise their discretion ... have acted on some improper principle, have taken into consideration something they ought not to have taken into account or have failed to take into consideration something which they should. ... We have to ask ourselves this question: has there been an error of law? Has there been a purported exercise of discretion based upon some wrong principle or assumption? Could any reasonable bench of magistrates have reached this decision without having misdirected themselves?"

per Lord Lane C.J. in *R. v. Tottenham JJ., ex p. Joshi, ante*, at 76 (applying *R. v. St Albans Crown Court, ex p. Cinnamond* [1981] Q.B. 480, DC).

In *R. v. Bow Street Stipendiary Magistrate, ex p. Screen Multimedia Ltd, The Times*, January 28, 1998, DC, judicial review was refused in respect of orders for costs in the sum of £7,500 made against a company and its managing director upon their conviction of 10 offences contrary to the *Copyright, Designs and Patents Act* 1988, s.107; although the profit to the defendants from the offences had been negligible, a lot of research had had to be done in order to negative various defences; in the circumstances, therefore, the orders could not be said to be "manifestly excessive".

Rules of court

6–37 See *post*, § 6–88.

(3) Provision for orders as to costs in other circumstances

Prosecution of Offences Act 1985, s.19

6–38 **19.**—(1) The Lord Chancellor may by regulations make provision empowering magistrates' courts, the Crown Court and the Court of Appeal, in any case where the court is satisfied that one party to criminal proceedings has incurred costs as a result of an unnecessary or improper act or omission by, or on behalf of, another party to the proceedings, to make an order as to the payment of those costs.

(2) Regulations made under subsection (1) above may in particular—

(a) allow the making of such an order at any time during the proceedings;

(b) make provision as to the account to be taken, in making such an order, of any other order as to costs ... which has been made in respect of the proceedings or any grant of a right to representation funded by the Legal Services Commission as part of the Criminal Defence Service;

(c) make provision as to the account to be taken of any such order in the making of any other order as to costs in respect of the proceedings; and

(d) contain provisions similar to those in section 18(4) and (5) of this Act.

6–39 (3) The Lord Chancellor may by regulations make provision for the payment out of central funds, in such circumstances and in relation to such criminal proceedings as may be specified, of such sums as appear to the court to be reasonably necessary—

(a) to compensate any witness in the proceedings, and any other person who in the opinion of the court necessarily attends for the purpose of the proceedings otherwise than to give evidence, for the expense, trouble or loss of time properly incurred in or incidental to his attendance;

(b) to cover the proper expenses of an interpreter who is required because of the accused's lack of English;

(c) to compensate a duly qualified medical practitioner who—

(i) makes a report otherwise than in writing for the purpose of section 11 of the *Powers of Criminal Courts (Sentencing) Act* 2000 (remand for medical examination); or

(ii) makes a written report to a court in pursuance of a request *to which section 32(2) of the* Criminal Justice Act *1967 (report by medical practitioner on medical condition of offender) applies* [within subsection (3B) below];

for the expenses properly incurred in or incidental to his reporting to the court;

(d) to cover the proper fee or costs of a person appointed by the Crown Court under section 4A of the *Criminal Procedure (Insanity) Act* 1964 to put the case for the defence;

(e) to cover the proper fee or costs of a legal representative appointed under section 38(4) of the *Youth Justice and Criminal Evidence Act* 1999 (defence representation for purposes of cross-examination) and any expenses properly incurred in providing such a person with evidence or other material in connection with his appointment.

(3A) In subsection (3)(a) above "attendance" means attendance at the court or elsewhere.

[(3B) A request is within this subsection if—

(a) it is a request to a registered medical practitioner to make a written or oral report on the medical condition of an offender or defendant; and

(b) it is made by a court—

(i) for the purpose of determining whether or not to include *in a community order (within the meaning of Part 12 of the* Criminal Justice Act *2003) a mental health treatment requirement under section 207 of that Act* [[a mental health treatment requirement in a community order or youth rehabilitation order]] or make an order under section 37 of the *Mental Health Act* 1983 (hospital orders and guardianship orders) or otherwise for the purpose of determining the most suitable method of dealing with an offender; or

(ii) in exercise of the powers conferred by section 11 of the *Powers of Criminal Courts (Sentencing) Act* 2000 (remand of a defendant for medical examination).]

[["(3C) For the purposes of subsection (3B)(b)(i)—

"community order" has the same meaning as in Part 12 of the *Criminal Justice Act* 2003;

"mental health treatment requirement" means—

(a) in relation to a community order, a mental health treatment requirement under section 207 of the *Criminal Justice Act* 2003, and

(b) in relation to a youth rehabilitation order, a mental health treatment requirement under paragraph 20 of Schedule 1 to the *Criminal Justice and Immigration Act* 2008;

"youth rehabilitation order" has the same meaning as in Part 1 of the *Criminal Justice and Immigration Act* 2008.]]

(4) The Court of Appeal may order the payment out of central funds of such sums as appear to it to be reasonably sufficient to compensate an appellant who is not in custody and who appears before it on, or in connection with, his appeal under Part I of the *Criminal Appeal Act* 1968.

(5) The Lord Chancellor may by regulations provide that any provision made by or under this Part which would not otherwise apply in relation to any category of proceedings in which an offender is before a magistrates' court or the Crown Court shall apply in relation to proceedings of that category, subject to any specified modifications.

[This section is printed as amended and repealed in part by the *Legal Aid Act* 1988, s.45(1), (2), Sched. 5, para. 12, and Sched. 6; the *CJA* 1988, s.166(2), (3); the *Criminal Procedure (Insanity and Unfitness to Plead) Act* 1991, Sched. 3, para. 8; the *Access to Justice Act* 1999, s.24, and Sched. 4, para. 28; the *YJCEA* 1999, s.40(1); and the *PCC(S)A* 2000, s.165(1), and Sched. 9, para. 99; and as amended, as from a day to be appointed, by the *AFA* 2006, s.378(1), and Sched. 16, para. 107 (insertion of words in square brackets and omission of italicised text in subs. (3)(c)(ii) and insertion of subs. (3B)); and the *CJIA* 2008, s.6(2), and Sched. 4, para. 32 (insertion of words in double square brackets). For the transitional and saving provisions in relation to the 2008 Act amendments, see *ante*, § 5–1.]

For regulations under this section, see S.I. 1986 No. 1335, *post*, §§ 6–52 *et seq.*

(4) Costs against legal representatives, etc.

Prosecution of Offences Act 1985, s.19A

19A.—(1) In any criminal proceedings— **6–40**

(a) the Court of Appeal;

(b) the Crown Court; or

(c) a magistrates' court,

may disallow, or (as the case may be) order the legal or other representative concerned to meet, the whole of any wasted costs or such part of them as may be determined in accordance with regulations.

(2) Regulations shall provide that a legal or other representative against whom action is taken by a magistrates' court under subsection (1) may appeal to the Crown Court and that a legal or other representative against whom action is taken by the Crown Court under subsection (1) may appeal to the Court of Appeal.

(3) In this section—

"legal or other representative", in relation to any proceedings, means a person who is exercising a right of audience, or a right to conduct litigation, on behalf of any party to the proceedings;

"regulations" means regulations made by the Lord Chancellor; and

"wasted costs" means any costs incurred by a party—

(a) as a result of any improper, unreasonable or negligent act or omission on the part of any representative or any employee of a representative; or

(b) which, in the light of any such act or omission occurring after they were incurred, the court considers it is unreasonable to expect that party to pay.

[This section was inserted by the *Courts and Legal Services Act* 1990, s.111.]

For regulations under this section, see S.I. 1986 No. 1335, *post*, §§ 6–52 *et seq.*, and, in particular, Part IIA thereof, *post*, § 6–55.

As to the inherent jurisdiction of the Crown Court, as part of the Supreme Court [Senior Courts] of England and Wales, over solicitors, see *post*, § 6–285.

A person who made an application under section 2(2) of the *Criminal Procedure (Attendance of Witnesses) Act* 1965 (as originally enacted) for a direction that a witness summons be of no effect was a "party" for the purposes of section 19A: *Re Ronald A. Prior & Co. (Solicitors)* [1996] 1 Cr.App.R. 248, CA. See now section 2C of the 1965 Act (*post*, § 8–3b).

The jurisdiction to make wasted costs orders is not restricted to the making of orders against the applicant's own legal representatives; nor, in the case of barristers, is it restricted to their conduct when exercising their right of audience in court; a barrister is liable to an order under the wasted costs legislation in relation to conduct immediately relevant to the exercise of a right of audience but not involving advocacy in open court: *Medcalf v. Mardell* [2003] 1 A.C. 120, HL.

Procedure

6–41 In *Re A Barrister (Wasted Costs Order) (No. 1 of 1991)* [1993] Q.B. 293, a wasted costs order under section 19A made against a barrister acting for the defence in a trial in the Crown Court was quashed. One reason for quashing it was that it was fatally flawed because the judge had not specified the amount of costs disallowed, as required by regulation 3B of the *Costs in Criminal Cases (General) Regulations* 1991 (*post*, § 6–55). The barrister's appeal was upheld on the merits as well: at the worst, it was said, the remark he had made which had caused the judge to discharge the jury could be described as inapt. He was not guilty of any such unreasonable act or omission as could justify a wasted costs order. The court then issued guidance (approved in *Re Mintz (Wasted Costs Order)*, *The Times*, July 16, 1999, CA) concerning the making of such orders. This is now set out in *Practice Direction (Costs: Criminal Proceedings)* [2004] 2 All E.R. 1070, at para. VIII.1.4, as sub-paras (i) to (vi) (*post*, § 6–114e). Further guidance was given in *Re P. (a Barrister) (Wasted Costs Order)* [2002] 1 Cr.App.R. 19, CA. This has also been incorporated into the practice direction (see para. VIII.1.5, *post*, § 6–114e). It deals in particular with the possibility that a judge might have to recuse himself on the ground that there might be an appearance of bias.

6–42 As to the failure to specify an amount payable being a fatal flaw in any such order, see also *Re Wiseman Lee (Solicitors) (Wasted costs order) (No. 5 of 2000)*, *The Times*, April 5, 2001, CA. And such a defect cannot be cured by amendment of the order at a later date, several months after the conclusion of the proceedings, so as to insert an amount: *Re Harry Jagdev & Co. (Wasted Costs Order) (No. 2 of 1999)*, *The Times*, August 12, 1999, CA (expressing the view that it would have been open to the judge to exercise his powers *de novo*, but not deciding the point).

The obligation under regulation 3B(2) of the 1991 regulations (*post*, § 6–55) to allow a legal representative to make representations "before" making an order against him is not satisfied by making an order and at the same time giving the legal representative against whom the order was made a fixed period thereafter within which any representations could be made as to why the order should not have been made: *Re Wiseman Lee (Solicitors) (Wasted costs order) (No. 5 of 2000)*, *ante*.

Before any wasted costs order is considered, justices should be advised of the principles to be derived from *Re A Barrister (Wasted Costs Order) (No. 1 of 1991)*, *ante*, and *S. v. M. (Wasted Costs Order)*, *post*, § 6–45, and the principles should be read out in open court; where, therefore, justices had not properly formulated the charge, had given no clear description of the nature of the conduct said to merit a wasted costs order, and the solicitor concerned had been given no proper opportunity to make representations, the order would be quashed: *R. (Osler) v. Cambridge Magistrates' Court*, *The Independent (C.S.)*, July 5, 2004, DC.

"improper", "unreasonable", "negligent"

In *Ridehalgh v. Horsefield* [1994] Ch. 205, CA (Civ.Div.), Sir Thomas Bingham M.R., giving the judgment of the court, said that a tension existed between two important public interests. The first was that lawyers should not be deterred from pursuing their clients' cases by fear of incurring a personal liability to their clients' opponents; that they should not be penalised by orders to pay costs without a fair opportunity to defend themselves; that wasted costs orders should not become a back-door means of recovering costs not otherwise recoverable against a legally aided or impoverished litigant; and that the remedy should not grow unchecked to become more damaging than the disease. The second was that litigants should not be financially prejudiced by the unjustifiable conduct of litigation by their own or their opponents' lawyers. **6–43**

His Lordship referred to the definition of "wasted costs" (in section 51(7) of the *Supreme Court [Senior Courts] Act* 1981 (in the same terms in relation to civil proceedings as that in section 19A of the 1985 Act, *ante*)) (as to the renaming of the 1981 Act, see *ante*, § 6–28), and said that "improper" covered, but was not confined to, conduct which would ordinarily be held to justify disbarment, striking off, suspension from practice or other serious professional penalty. Conduct which would be regarded as improper according to the consensus of professional, including judicial, opinion could be fairly stigmatised as such whether it violated the letter of a professional code or not.

"Unreasonable" aptly described conduct which was vexatious, designed to harass the other side rather than advance the resolution of the case and it made no difference that the conduct was the product of excessive zeal and not improper motive. Conduct could not be described as unreasonable simply because it led in the event to an unsuccessful result or because other more cautious legal representatives would have acted differently. The acid test was whether the conduct permitted of a reasonable explanation. If so, the course adopted might be regarded as optimistic and reflecting on a practitioner's judgment, but it was not unreasonable. **6–44**

"Negligent" should be understood in an untechnical way to denote failure to act with the competence reasonably expected of ordinary members of the profession. In adopting that approach, the court firmly discountenanced any suggestion that an applicant for a wasted costs order needed to prove under the negligence head anything less than he would have had to prove in an action for negligence: see *Saif Ali v. Sydney Mitchell & Co.* [1980] A.C. 198, HL.

A legal representative was not to be held to have acted improperly, unreasonably or negligently simply because he acted for a party who pursued a claim or defence which was plainly doomed to fail. It was rarely, if ever, safe for a court to assume that a hopeless case was being litigated on the advice of the lawyers involved.

However, a legal representative could not lend his assistance to proceedings which were an abuse of process and was not entitled to use litigious procedures for purposes for which they were not intended, such as issuing or pursuing proceedings for reasons unconnected with success in the litigation or pursuing a case known to be dishonest; nor was he entitled to evade rules intended to safeguard the interests of justice, such as knowingly failing to make full disclosure on an *ex parte* application or knowingly conniving at incomplete disclosure of documents.

It was not easy to distinguish by definition between the hopeless case and the case which amounted to an abuse of the process, but in practice it was not hard to say which was which, and, if there was doubt, the legal representative was entitled to the benefit of it.

His Lordship said that although the wasted costs legislation was intended to encroach on the traditional immunity of the advocate (*Rondel v. Worsley* [1969] 1 A.C. 191, HL; *Saif Ali v. Sydney Mitchell & Co., ante*), it did not follow that the public interest considerations on which the immunity was founded were to be regarded as irrelevant. Any judge must make full allowance for the fact that an advocate in court often had to make decisions quickly and under pressure. Mistakes would inevitably be made, things done which the outcome showed to be unwise. It was only when, with all allowances made, an advocate's conduct of court proceedings was quite plainly unjustifiable that it could be appropriate to make a wasted costs order against him.

Judges faced with applications for wasted costs orders should make full allowance for the possible difficulty caused by client confidentiality for the respondent lawyers in answering such an application.

As to causation, the court stressed the need to demonstrate the causal link between the conduct complained of and the waste of costs. The court then made certain further observations relating to procedure, burden of proof and discretion. These coincide with what was said in *Re A Barrister (Wasted Costs Order) (No. 1 of 1991) (ante)*.

Finally, the court alluded to the fact that the underlying proceedings were civil, but it was desirable that there should be no divergence of practice between civil and criminal proceedings. The court expressed the hope that their judgment would give guidance valuable as much in criminal proceedings as in civil proceedings.

6–45 It is important for a judge considering making a wasted costs order, which is a draconian penalty, to remember that he is removed from the demands of daily practice and to make allowances for difficulties with time estimates: *Re a Barrister (Wasted Costs Order) (No. 4 of 1993)*, *The Times*, April 21, 1995, CA (barrister over-optimistic in failing to anticipate delays, but conduct not unreasonable).

Where a wasted costs order is sought against a legal representative precluded by legal professional privilege from giving his full answer to the application, a court should not make an order unless, proceeding with extreme care, it was satisfied that there was nothing the respondent could say, if unconstrained, to resist the order, and that it was in all the circumstances fair to make the order: *Medcalf v. Mardell* [2003] 1 A.C. 120, HL.

Applications should normally be made at the end of the proceedings in question in order to prevent a party from being deprived of representation by the lawyer of his choice; and fairness requires that the respondent to any application for a wasted costs order should be told clearly what he was said to have done wrong and what was claimed: *S. v. M. (Wasted Costs Order)*, *The Times*, March 26, 1998, Ch D (Pumfrey J.).

The cure often being worse than the disease, the jurisdiction to make wasted costs orders should be restricted to clear and obvious cases; and where there has been a refusal to waive privilege by the lay client, maximum allowance must be made so far as the lawyer is concerned, with any doubt being resolved in his favour: *Re Beynon (Wasted Costs Order)* [1999] 8 *Archbold News* 1, CA.

The issue of a witness summons without reasonable cause gives rise to the risk of a wasted costs order being made; and it is not proper to issue a summons for disclosure of documents for the speculative purpose that material might come to light which could discredit a complainant: *Wasted Costs Order (No. 5 of 1997)*, *The Times*, September 7, 1999, CA.

A solicitor's decision to withdraw from a trial rather than to continue after the defendant had voluntarily absented himself would not be unreasonable where it could not be inferred that the defendant had expected his legal representatives to continue to represent him in his absence and where the solicitor genuinely believed that it would not be in the defendant's best interests to continue to represent him; the responsibility for deciding whether a trial should continue in a defendant's absence was that of the trial judge, but the judge should not assume, when making a decision to proceed, that legal representation would continue; fundamental questions of trust between lawyers and litigants arise when a defendant absents himself (as do practical questions as to the conduct of the trial), and the role of the independent professional representative in the administration of justice must be borne in mind together with the need not to undermine it by illegitimate pressures: *Re Boodhoo* [2007] 1 Cr.App.R. 32, CA.

Where counsel in the Court of Appeal asserts matters relating to the unfairness of the trial process which were shown to be quite unsustainable and to be complaints which should never have been made, the court would in future consider making a wasted costs order: *R. v. Naylor*, *The Times*, February 8, 1995, CA.

Where a case is simply listed for a particular day, with no time marking, it is irresponsible of solicitors to instruct counsel known to have a prior commitment in the afternoon of that day; where, therefore, counsel became unavailable and the solicitors failed to obtain alternative representation or to attend court to explain the problem, they were guilty of acting improperly, unreasonably or negligently; as was counsel in accepting a brief when there was a known risk that he would be unavailable, and in departing to attend to his other commitment without arranging for alternative representation or raising the matter with the judge with a view to him agreeing to arrange his list so as to accommodate counsel: *R. v. Secretary of State for the Home Department, ex p. Mahmood* [1999] C.O.D. 119, QBD (Richards J.).

In many, if not most, cases, defence counsel would be bound to check his client's antecedents; that might not be a fair view on the particular facts, however; where, therefore, a barrister and his instructing solicitors had asked for a copy of the defendant's antecedents before trial but having not been supplied with a copy, the barrister, acting on the basis of his instructions which referred to a dissimilar offence in 1981 but not to a similar offence in 1959, agreed a formula with the prosecution for dealing with the issue of character, which formula was, however, based on the two barristers apparently being at cross-purposes (as to what was being referred to by "the old offence") and led to the discharge of the jury after the defence barrister had asked the defendant whether he had ever been accused of, or convicted of any offence of a similar nature to that with which he was charged, and he had answered in the negative, the barrister's mistake was understandable and was not an error which "no reasonably well informed and competent member of [the] profession could have made" (*Ridehalgh v. Horsefield*, *ante*); practitioners should, however, be aware of the *Practice Direction (Criminal Proceedings: Consolidation)*, para. III.27 [2002] 1 W.L.R. 2870 (*ante*, § 5–57), compliance with which would have prevented the error which had occurred: *Re a Barrister (Wasted costs order) (No. 9 of 1999)*, *The Times*, April 18, 2000, CA.

It is unreasonable for a barrister in sole practice to rely wholly on instructing solicitors to notify him of the dates and times of his cases; it is his responsibility to adopt a system which enables him to keep abreast of the listing arrangements for his cases: *Re a Barrister (Wasted Costs Order) (No. 4 of 1992)*, *The Times*, March 15, 1994, CA.

Counsel is responsible for his clerk's errors; where, therefore, counsel's failure to appear at court results from an oversight by a junior clerk, a wasted costs order may be made: *R. v. Rodney (Wasted Costs Order)* [1997] 1 *Archbold News* 2, CA.

(5) Costs against third parties

Prosecution of Offences Act 1985, s.19B

Provision for award of costs against third parties

19B.—(1) The Lord Chancellor may by regulations make provision empowering magistrates' courts, the Crown Court and the Court of Appeal to make a third party costs order if the condition in subsection (3) is satisfied. **6–45a**

(2) A "third party costs order" is an order as to the payment of costs incurred by a party to criminal proceedings by a person who is not a party to those proceedings ("the third party").

(3) The condition is that—

(a) there has been serious misconduct (whether or not constituting a contempt of court) by the third party, and

(b) the court considers it appropriate, having regard to that misconduct, to make a third party costs order against him.

(4) Regulations made under this section may, in particular—

(a) specify types of misconduct in respect of which a third party costs order may not be made;

(b) allow the making of a third party costs order at any time;

(c) make provision for any other order as to costs which has been made in respect of the proceedings to be varied on, or taken account of in, the making of a third party costs order;

(d) make provision for account to be taken of any third party costs order in the making of any other order as to costs in respect of the proceedings.

(5) Regulations made under this section in relation to magistrates' courts must provide that the third party may appeal to the Crown Court against a third party costs order made by a magistrates' court.

(6) Regulations made under this section in relation to the Crown Court must provide that the third party may appeal to the Court of Appeal against a third party costs order made by the Crown Court.

[This section was inserted by the *Courts Act* 2003, s.93.]

For regulations under this section, see *post*, §§ 6–55a *et seq.*

(6) Supplemental provisions

Prosecution of Offences Act 1985, ss.20, 21

Regulations

6–46 **20.**—(1) The Lord Chancellor may make regulations for carrying this Part into effect and the regulations may, in particular, make provision as to—

(a) the scales or rates of payments of any costs payable out of central funds in pursuance of any costs order, the circumstances in which and conditions under which such costs may be allowed and paid and the expenses which may be included in such costs; and

(b) the review, as respects costs payable out of central funds in pursuance of any costs order, of any decision on taxation, or determination of the amount, of the costs;

and any provision made by or under this Part enabling any sum to be paid out of central funds shall have effect subject to any such regulations.

(2) The Lord Chancellor may by regulation make provision for the recovery of sums paid by the Legal Services Commission or out of central funds in cases where—

(a) a costs order has been made against a person; and

(b) the person in whose favour the order was made is a legally assisted person or a person in whose favour a defendant's costs order or, as the case may be, an order under section 17 of this Act has been made.

6–47 (3) Regulations made under subsection (1) above may provide that rates or scales of allowances payable out of central funds under a costs order shall be determined by the Lord Chancellor with the consent of the Treasury.

(4) Regulations made under subsection (2) above may, in particular—

(a) require the person mentioned in paragraph (a) of that subsection to pay sums due under the costs order in accordance with directions given by the Lord Chancellor (either generally or in respect of the particular case); and

(b) enable the Lord Chancellor to enforce those directions in cases to which they apply.

(5) [*Repealed by* Courts Act *2003, s.109(1), and Sched. 8, para. 288(1) and (2).*]

6–48 (6) Any regulations under this Part may contain such incidental, supplemental and transitional provisions as the Lord Chancellor considers appropriate.

(7) [*Duty to consult relevant rule committee.*]

(8) In this section "costs order" means—

(a) an order made under or by virtue of this Part for payment to be made—

(i) out of central funds; or

(ii) by any person; or

(b) an order made in a criminal case by the *House of Lords* [Supreme Court] for the payment of costs by a party to proceedings.

[This section is printed as amended by the *Legal Aid Act* 1988, s.45(1) and Sched. 5, para. 13; the *Courts and Legal Services Act* 1990, s.125(3) and Sched. 18, para. 53; the *Access to Justice Act* 1999, s.24 and Sched. 4, para. 29; and the *Courts Act* 2003, s.109(1), and Sched. 8, para. 288(1) and (3)–(5); and as amended, as from a day to be appointed, by the *Constitutional Reform Act* 2005, s.40(4), and Sched. 9, para. 41(1) and (4) (substitution of words in square brackets for italicised words).]

For regulations under this section, see *post*, §§ 6–52 *et seq.*

where they are discharging their public duty, any order in favour of a successful appellant or defendant should be for costs out of central funds: *Vehicle and Operator Services Agency v. Greenfarms Ltd* [2006] R.T.R. 20, DC.

Nolan L.J., giving the principal judgment in *DPP v. Denning, ante*, said that the word "improper" in the context of regulation 3 "does not necessarily connote some grave impropriety. Used, as it is, in conjunction with the word 'unnecessary', it is ... intended to cover an act or omission which would not have occurred if the party concerned had conducted his case properly" (at pp. 541, 280). A magistrates' court had been entitled to conclude that the institution of a private prosecution was improper where a previous prosecution instituted by the CPS for identical conduct had, to the prosecutor's knowledge, been dismissed on the same grounds, with no appeal by the CPS, and no representations made to the CPS by the private prosecutor: *Oddy v. Bug Bugs Ltd, ante*.

In *R. v. Wood Green Crown Court, ex p. DPP* [1993] 1 W.L.R. 723, DC, the court emphasised that before an order could be made under regulation 3, a causal relationship had to be established between the "unnecessary or improper act or omission" and the incurring of costs. Where, therefore, the prosecution had offered no evidence, the judge had not been entitled to assume that the whole of the defence costs since committal were a consequence of the prosecution's default.

Part IIA—Wasted costs orders (regs 3A–3D)

Application and definitions

3A. This Part of these Regulations applies to action taken by a court under section 19A of the Act and in this Part of these Regulations— **6–55**

"wasted costs order" means any action taken by a court under section 19A of the Act; and

"interested party" means the party benefiting from the wasted costs order and, where he was receiving services funded for him as part of the Criminal Defence Service, or an order for the payment of costs out of central funds was made in his favour, shall include the authority responsible for determining costs payable in respect of work done under the representation order or out of central funds as the case may be.

[This regulation is printed as amended by the *Costs in Criminal Cases (General) (Amendment) Regulations* 2004 (S.I. 2004 No. 2408).]

General

3B.—(1) A wasted costs order may provide for the whole or any part of the wasted costs to be disallowed or ordered to be paid and the court shall specify the amount of such costs.

(2) Before making a wasted costs order the court shall allow the legal or other representative and any party to the proceedings to make representations.

(3) When making a wasted costs order the court may take into account any other order as to costs in respect of the proceedings and may take the wasted costs order into account when making any other such order.

(4) Where a wasted costs order has been made the court shall notify any interested party of the order and the amount disallowed or ordered to be paid.

[This regulation is printed as amended by S.I. 2004 No. 2408, *ante*.]

As to procedure, see *ante*, §§ 6–40, 6–41.

Appeals

3C.—(1) A legal or other representative against whom the wasted costs order is made may appeal—

(a) in the case of an order made by a magistrates' court, to the Crown Court, and
(b) in the case of an order made at first instance by the Crown Court to the Court of Appeal.

(2) Subject to paragraph (4), an appeal shall be instituted within 21 days of the wasted costs order being made by the appellant's giving notice in writing to the court which made the order, stating the grounds of appeal.

(3) The appellant shall serve a copy of the notice of appeal and grounds, including any application for an extension of time in which to appeal, on any interested party.

(4) The time limit within which an appeal may be instituted may, for good reason, be extended before or after it expires—

(a) in the case of an appeal to the Crown Court, by a judge of that court;

(b) in the case of an appeal to the Court of Appeal, a judge of the High Court or Court of Appeal, or by the Registrar of Criminal Appeals,

and in each case the court to which the appeal is made shall give notice of the extension to the appellant, the court which made the wasted costs order and any interested party.

(5) The court shall give notice of the hearing date to the appellant, the court which made the wasted costs order and any interested party and shall allow the interested party to make representations which may be made orally or in writing.

(6) The court may affirm, vary or revoke the order as it thinks fit and shall notify its decision to the appellant, any interested party and the court which made the order.

[This regulation is printed as amended by S.I. 2004 No. 2408, *ante*.]

3D. [*Recovery of sums due under a wasted costs order.*]

[Part IIA was inserted by the *Costs in Criminal Cases (General) (Amendment) Regulations* 1991 (S.I. 1991 No. 789).]

See, generally, Part VIII of the costs practice direction, *post*, § 6–114e.

The House of Lords expressed the view, *obiter*, in *Holden & Co. v. CPS (No. 2)* [1994] 1 A.C. 22, that on an appeal to the Court of Appeal under regulation 3C, there is no power to award the costs of a successful appellant out of central funds. This conforms with the decision of the Court of Appeal in *Re A Barrister (Wasted Costs Order) (No. 1 of 1991)* (*ante*, § 6–41).

Part IIB—Third party costs orders (regs 3E–3I)

Application and definitions

6–55a **3E.**—(1) This Part of these Regulations applies where there are, or have been criminal proceedings in a magistrates' court, the Crown Court or the Court of Appeal.

(2) In this Part of these Regulations—

"court" means the court in which the criminal proceedings are taking, or took, place;

"interested party" means the party benefiting from the third party costs order and, where he was receiving services funded for him as part of the Criminal Defence Service or an order for the payment of costs out of central funds was made in his favour, shall include the authority responsible for determining costs payable in respect of work done under the representation order or out of central funds as the case may be;

"party" means a party to the criminal proceedings;

"third party" means a person who is not a party;

"third party costs order" means an order as to the payment, by a third party, of costs incurred by a party in accordance with regulation 3F.

[This regulation is printed as amended by S.I. 2008 No. 2448 (*ante*, § 6–54).]

General

6–55b **3F.**—(1) If—

(a) there has been serious misconduct (whether or not constituting a contempt of court) by a third party; and

(b) the court considers it appropriate, having regard to that misconduct, to make a third party costs order against him

the court may order the third party to pay all or part of the costs incurred or wasted by any party as a result of the misconduct.

(2) The court may make a third party costs order—

(a) subject to paragraph (3), at any time during or after the criminal proceedings; and

(b) on the application of any party or of its own initiative (but not otherwise).

(3) The court shall make a third party costs order during the proceedings only if it decides that there are good reasons to do so, rather than making the order after the proceedings, and it shall notify the parties and the third party of those reasons and allow any of them to make representations.

(4) Before making a third party costs order the court shall allow the third party and any party to make representations and may hear evidence.

(5) When making a third party costs order the court may take into account any other order as to costs in respect of the criminal proceedings and may take the third party costs order into account when making any other order as to costs in respect of the criminal proceedings.

(6) A third party costs order shall specify the amount of costs to be paid in pursuance of the order.

(7) When a third party costs order has been made the court shall notify the third party and any interested party of the order and the amount ordered to be paid.

[This regulation is printed as amended by S.I. 2008 No. 2448 (*ante*, § 6–54).]

Procedure for third party costs orders

3G.—(1) This regulation applies where a party ("the applicant") applies to the court for a third party costs order or the court decides that it might make a third party costs order of its own initiative. **6–55c**

(2) In this regulation—

"appropriate officer" means—

(a) in relation to a magistrates' court, a designated officer (as defined in section 37(1) of the *Courts Act* 2003);

(b) in relation to the Crown Court, an officer appointed by the Lord Chancellor; and

(c) in relation to the Court of Appeal, the Registrar of Criminal Appeals;

"serve" means serve in accordance with rules of court.

(2) [*sic*] An application for a third party costs order shall be in writing and shall contain—

(a) the name and address of the applicant;

(b) the names and addresses of the other parties;

(c) the name and address of the third party against whom the order is sought;

(d) the date of the end of the criminal proceedings;

(e) a summary of the facts upon which the applicant intends to rely in making the application, including details of the alleged misconduct of the third party.

(3) The application shall be sent to the appropriate officer and, upon receiving it, the appropriate officer shall serve copies of it on the third party and to [*sic*] the other parties.

(4) Where the court decides that it might make a third party costs order of its own initiative the appropriate officer shall serve notice in writing accordingly on the third party and the parties.

(5) At the same time as serving notice under paragraph (4) the appropriate officer shall serve a summary of the reasons why the court might make a third party costs order, including details of the alleged misconduct of the third party.

(6) When the appropriate officer serves copies of an application under paragraph (3) or serves notice under paragraph (4) he shall at the same time serve notice on the parties and the third party of the time and place fixed for the hearing.

(7) At the time notified the court may proceed in the absence of the third party and of any party if it is satisfied that they have been duly served with the notice given under paragraph (6) and the copy of the application or (as the case may be) the notices given under paragraphs (4) and (5), but the court may set aside any third party costs order if it is later shown that the third party did not receive them.

Appeals

3H.—(1) A third party against whom a third party costs order is made may appeal— **6–55d**

(a) in the case of an order made by a magistrates' court, to the Crown Court; and

(b) in the case of an order made at first instance by the Crown Court, to the Court of Appeal.

(2) Subject to paragraph (4), an appeal shall be instituted within 21 days of the third party costs order being made by the appellant giving notice in writing to the court which made the order, stating the grounds of appeal.

(3) The appellant shall serve a copy of the notice of appeal and grounds, including any application for extension of time in which to appeal, on any interested party.

(4) The time limit within which an appeal may be instituted may, for good reason, be extended before or after it expires—

(a) in the case of an appeal to the Crown Court, by a judge of that court;

(b) in the case of an appeal to the Court of Appeal, by a judge of the High Court or Court of Appeal, or by the Registrar of Criminal Appeals,

and in each case the court to which the appeal is made ("the appeal court") shall give notice of the extension to the appellant, the court which made the third party costs order and any interested party.

(5) The appeal court shall give notice of the hearing date to the appellant, the court which made the third party costs order and any interested party and shall allow the interested party to make representations which may be made orally or in writing.

(6) The appeal court may affirm, vary or revoke the order as it thinks fit and shall notify its decision to the appellant, any interested party and the court which made the order.

6–55e **3I.** [*Recovery of sums due under a third party costs order.*]

[Part IIB was inserted by the *Costs in Criminal Cases (General) (Amendment) Regulations* 2004 (S.I. 2004 No. 2408).]

Transitional

6–55f Article 2 of S.I. 2004 No. 2408 provides that a third party costs order may not be made in respect of any misconduct which occurred before October 18, 2004; and that a court making a third party costs order in respect of misconduct occurring after that date shall disregard any misconduct that occurred before that date.

Part III—Costs out of central funds (regs 4–13)

Application and definitions

6–56 **4.** This Part of these Regulations applies to costs payable out of central funds in pursuance of an order made under or by virtue of Part II of the Act and in this Part of these Regulations—

"applicant" means the person in whose favour a costs order has been made;

"appropriate authority" has the meaning assigned to it by regulation 5;

"costs judge" means a taxing master of the Supreme Court;

"costs order" means an order made under or by virtue of Part II of the Act for the payment of costs out of central funds;

"disbursements" do not include any payment made out of central funds to a witness, interpreter, intermediary or medical practitioner in accordance with Part V of these Regulations;

"expenses" means out of pocket expenses, travelling expenses and subsistence allowance;

"presiding judge" means the judge who presided at the hearing in respect of which the costs are payable; and

[This regulation is printed as amended by the *Costs in Criminal Cases (General) Regulations* 1999 (S.I. 1999 No. 2096); and S.I. 2008 No. 2448 (*ante*, § 6–54).]

The appropriate authority

6–57 **5.**—(1) Costs shall be determined by the appropriate authority in accordance with these Regulations.

(2) Subject to paragraph (3), the appropriate authority shall be—

(a) the registrar of criminal appeals in the case of proceedings in the Court of Appeal,

(b) the master of the Crown Office in the case of proceedings in a Divisional Court of the Queen's Bench Division,

(c) an officer appointed by the Lord Chancellor in the case of proceedings in the Crown Court or, subject to sub-paragraph (d), a magistrates' court,

(d) the justices' clerk in the case of proceedings in a magistrates' court, where the costs consist solely of expenses claimed by the applicant.

(3) The appropriate authority may appoint or authorise the appointment of determining officers to act on its behalf under these Regulations in accordance with directions given by it or on its behalf.

[This regulation is printed as amended by S.I. 2008 No. 2448 (*ante*, § 6–54).]

Claims for costs

6–58 **6.**—(1) Subject to regulation 12, no claim for costs shall be entertained unless it is submitted within three months of the date on which the costs order was made.

(2) Subject to paragraph (3), a claim for costs shall be submitted to the appropriate authority, in such form or manner as it may direct and shall be accompanied by receipts or other evidence of the applicant's payment of the costs claimed, and any receipts or other documents in support of any disbursements claimed.

(3) A claim shall—

(a) summarise the items of work done by a solicitor;

(b) state, where appropriate, the dates on which items of work were done, the time taken and the sums claimed,

(c) specify any disbursements claimed, including counsel's fees, the circumstances in which they were incurred and the amounts claimed in respect of them, and

(d) contain either full particulars, including the date and outcome, of any claim for payment in respect of services funded for the applicant as part of the Criminal Defence Service, or a certificate by the solicitor that he has not made, and will not make, any such claim.

(4) Where there are any special circumstances which should be drawn to the attention of the appropriate authority, the applicant shall specify them.

(5) The applicant shall supply such further particulars, information and documents as the appropriate authority may require.

[This regulation is printed as amended by S.I. 1999 No. 2096 (*ante*, § 6–56); the *Costs in Criminal Cases (General) (Amendment) Regulations* 2001 (S.I. 2001 No. 611); and S.I. 2008 No. 2448 (*ante*, § 6–54).]

Determination of costs

7.—(1) The appropriate authority shall consider the claim, any further particulars, information or documents submitted by the applicant under regulation 6 and shall allow such costs in respect of— **6–59**

(a) such work as appears to it to have been actually and reasonably done; and

(b) such disbursements as appear to it to have been actually and reasonably incurred,

as it considers reasonably sufficient to compensate the applicant for any expenses properly incurred by him in the proceedings.

(2) In determining costs under paragraph (1) the appropriate authority shall take into account all the relevant circumstances of the case including the nature, importance, complexity or difficulty of the work and the time involved.

(3) When determining costs for the purpose of this regulation, there shall be allowed a reasonable amount in respect of all costs reasonably incurred and any doubts which the appropriate authority may have as to whether the costs were reasonably incurred or were reasonable in amount shall be resolved against the applicant.

Where it was reasonable for solicitors to instruct counsel to attend a magistrates' court, counsel's fee should have been allowed on taxation: *R. v. South Devon Magistrates' Court, ex p. Hallett* [2000] C.O.D. 279, DC.

Payment of costs

8.—(1) When the appropriate authority has determined the costs payable to an applicant in accordance with these Regulations, the appropriate authority shall notify the applicant of the costs payable and authorise payment accordingly. **6–60**

(2) Where the costs payable under paragraph (1) are varied as a result of a redetermination under regulation 9, an appeal to a costs judge under regulation 10, or an appeal to the High Court under regulation 11, then—

(a) where the costs are increased, the appropriate authority shall authorise payment of the increase;

(b) where the costs are decreased, the applicant shall repay the amount of such decrease; and

(c) where the payment of the costs of an appeal is ordered under regulation 10(14) or 11(8), the appropriate authority shall authorise such payment to the applicant.

[This regulation is printed as amended by S.I. 1999 No. 2096 (*ante*, § 6–56); S.I. 2001 No. 611 (*ante*, § 6–58); and S.I. 2008 No. 2448 (*ante*, § 6–54).]

Redetermination of costs by an appropriate authority

9.—(1) An applicant who is dissatisfied with the costs determined under these Regulations by **6–61**

an appropriate authority in respect of proceedings other than proceedings before a magistrates' court may apply to the appropriate authority to redetermine them.

(2) Subject to regulation 12, the application shall be made, within 21 days of the receipt of notification of the costs payable under regulation 8(1), by giving notice in writing to the appropriate authority specifying the items in respect of which the application is made and the grounds of objection and shall be made in such form and manner as the appropriate authority may direct.

(3) The notice of application shall state whether the applicant wishes to appear or to be represented and, if the applicant so wishes, the appropriate authority shall notify the applicant of the time at which it is prepared to hear him or his representative.

(4) The notice of application shall be accompanied by any particulars, information and documents supplied under regulation 6 and the applicant shall supply such further particulars, information and documents as the appropriate authority may require.

(5) The appropriate authority shall redetermine the costs, whether by way of increase, decrease or at the level previously determined, in the light of the objections made by the applicant or on his behalf and shall notify the applicant of its decision.

(6) The applicant may request the appropriate authority to give reasons in writing for its decision and, if so requested, the appropriate authority shall comply with the request.

(7) Subject to regulation 12, any request under paragraph (6) shall be made within 21 days of receiving notification of the decision.

Appeals to a costs judge

6–62 **10.**—(1) Where the appropriate authority has given its reasons for its decision on a redetermination under regulation 9, an applicant who is dissatisfied with that decision may appeal to a costs judge.

(2) Subject to regulation 12, an appeal shall be instituted within 21 days of the receipt of the appropriate authority's reasons by giving notice in writing to the Senior Costs Judge specifying the items in respect of which the appeal is brought and the grounds of objection.

(3) The appellant shall send a copy of any notice given under paragraph (2) to the appropriate authority.

(4) The notice of appeal shall be accompanied by—

(a) a copy of the written notice given under regulation 9(2);

(b) any particulars, information and documents supplied to the appropriate authority under regulation 9, and

(c) the appropriate authority's reasons for its decision given under regulation 9(6).

(5) The notice of appeal shall state whether the appellant wishes to appear or to be represented or whether he will accept a decision given in his absence.

6–63 (6) The Senior Costs Judge may, and if so directed by the Lord Chancellor either generally or in a particular case shall, send to the Lord Chancellor a copy of the notice of appeal together with copies of such other documents as the Lord Chancellor may require.

(7) With a view to ensuring that the public interest is taken into account, the Lord Chancellor may arrange for written or oral representations to be made on his behalf and, if he intends to do so, he shall inform the Senior Costs Judge and the appellant.

(8) Any written representations made on behalf of the Lord Chancellor under paragraph (7) shall be sent to the Senior Costs Judge and to the appellant and, in the case of oral representations, the Senior Costs Judge and the appellant shall be informed of the grounds on which such representations will be made.

(9) The appellant shall be permitted a reasonable opportunity to make representations in reply.

(10) The costs judge shall inform the appellant (or his representative) and the Lord Chancellor, where representations have been or are to be made on his behalf, of the date of any hearing and, subject to the provisions of this regulation, may give directions as to the conduct of the appeal.

6–64 (11) The costs judge may consult the presiding judge, and the appropriate authority or the determining officer who redetermined the costs on its behalf as the case may be, and may require the appellant to provide any further information which he requires for the purpose of the appeal and, unless the costs judge otherwise directs, no further evidence shall be received on the hearing of the appeal and no ground of objection shall be valid which was not raised on the redetermination under regulation 9.

(12) The costs judge shall have the same powers as the appropriate authority under these Regulations and, in the exercise of such powers, may alter the redetermination of the

appropriate authority in respect of any sum allowed, whether by increase or decrease, as he thinks fit.

(13) The costs judge shall communicate his decision and the reasons for it in writing to the appellant, the Lord Chancellor, and the appropriate authority or the determining officer who redetermined the costs on its behalf as the case may be.

(14) Save where he confirms or decreases the sums redetermined under regulation 9, the costs judge may allow the appellant a sum in respect of part or all of any reasonable costs (including any fee payable in respect of an appeal) incurred by him in connection with the appeal.

[This regulation is printed as amended by S.I. 1999 No. 2096 (*ante*, § 6–56).]

As to making an order in favour of a barrister for his costs and fees where he appears on his own behalf or on behalf of another barrister, see *R. v. Boswell*; *R. v. Halliwell* [1987] 1 W.L.R. 705 (Leggatt J.).

Whereas the High Court has no jurisdiction to entertain an application for judicial review of the substantive decision of a costs judge (who acts as a delegate of the Supreme Court), it retains an inherent jurisdiction to control the exercise of the authority of the court which has been delegated to the costs judge where there has been a "real injustice" (*R. v. Supreme Court Taxing Office, ex p. Singh* [1997] 1 Costs L.R. 49, CA (Civ. Div.)); such an injustice would arise where a costs judge hearing an appeal against a decision of a determining officer under this regulation admitted the claim in principle, but then failed to carry out a detailed assessment of the claim, and instead awarded a notional sum: *R. (Brewer) v. Supreme Court Costs Office* [2007] Costs L.R. 20, DC.

Appeals to the High Court

11.—(1) An applicant who is dissatisfied with the decision of a costs judge on an appeal under regulation 10 may apply to a costs judge to certify a point of principle of general importance. **6–65**

(2) Subject to regulation 12, an application under paragraph (1) shall be made within 21 days of notification of a costs judge's decision under regulation 10(13).

(3) Where a cost judge certifies a point of principle of general importance, the applicant may appeal to the High Court against the decision of a costs judge on an appeal under regulation 10, and the Lord Chancellor shall be a respondent to the appeal.

(4) Subject to regulation 12, an appeal under paragraph (3) shall be instituted within 21 days of receiving a costs judge's certificate under paragraph (1).

(5) Where the Lord Chancellor is dissatisfied with the decision of a costs judge on an appeal under regulation 10 he may, if no appeal has been made by the applicant under paragraph (3), appeal to the High Court against that decision and the applicant shall be a respondent to the appeal.

(6) Subject to regulation 12, an appeal under paragraph (5) shall be instituted within 21 days of receiving notification of the costs judge's decision under regulation 10(13).

(7) An appeal under paragraphs (3) and (5) shall be brought in the Queen's Bench Division, follow the procedure set out in Part 52 of the *Civil Procedure Rules* 1998 and shall be heard and determined by a single judge whose decision shall be final.

(8) The judge shall have the same powers as the appropriate authority and a costs judge under these Regulations and may reverse, affirm or amend the decision appealed against or make such other order as he thinks fit.

[This regulation is printed as amended by S.I. 1999 No. 2096 (*ante*, § 6–56); and the *Costs in Criminal Cases (General) (Amendment) Regulations* 2005 (S.I. 2005 No. 2622).]

As to the limited jurisdiction of the High Court in relation to decisions of costs judges where there is no certificate under this regulation, see *R. (Brewer) v. Supreme Court Costs Office*, *ante*, § 6–64.

Time limits

12.—(1) Subject to paragraph (2), the time limit within which there must be made or instituted— **6–66**

(a) a claim for costs by an applicant under regulation 6, an application for a redetermination under regulation 9, or a request for an appropriate authority to give reasons for its decision on a redetermination under regulation 9;

(b) an appeal to a Senior Costs Judge under regulation 10 or an application for a certificate under regulation 11; or

(c) an appeal to the High Court under regulation 11;

may, for good reason, be extended by the appropriate authority, the Senior Costs Judge or the High Court, as the case may be.

(2) Where an applicant without good reason has failed (or, if an extension were not granted, would fail) to comply with a time limit, the appropriate authority, the Senior Costs Judge or the High Court, as the case may be, may, in exceptional circumstances, extend the time limit and shall consider whether it is reasonable in the circumstances to reduce the costs; provided that the costs shall not be reduced unless the representative has been allowed a reasonable opportunity to show cause orally or in writing why the costs should not be reduced.

(3) An applicant may appeal to the Senior Costs Judge against a decision made under this regulation by an appropriate authority in respect of proceedings other than proceedings before a magistrates' court and such an appeal shall be instituted within 21 days of the decision being given by giving notice in writing to the Senior Costs Judge specifying the grounds of appeal.

[This regulation is printed as amended by S.I. 1999 No. 2096 (*ante*, § 6–56); and S.I. 2005 No. 2622 (*ante*, § 6–65).]

An application to extend the time limit "for good reason" may be made both before and after the expiry of the time limit; it is only if the appropriate authority, etc., is satisfied that there is no good reason for failure to comply with the time limit, that he should consider whether there are nevertheless "exceptional circumstances" justifying an extension thereof: *R. v. Clerk to the North Kent JJ., ex p. McGoldrick & Co.*, 160 J.P. 30, QBD (Schiemann J.); and *R. (Leask) v. South Western Magistrates' Court*, 171 J.P. 489, QBD (Gibbs J.). When making a decision under this regulation, it would be legitimate for the decision-maker to take into account (*inter alia*) a general proposition that the parties, and particularly professional advisers to the parties, are responsible for ascertaining the law and would be unwise to rely on oral remarks (however helpfully intended) made by members of the court staff or officers of the court as to the existence and/or length of a time-limit: *R. (Leask) v. South Western Magistrates' Court*, *ante*.

In connection with this provision, see also *R. v. Mahmood* [2008] Costs L.R. 326 and *R. v. Roberts* [2008] Costs L.R. 323, being two decisions of costs judges on corresponding provisions in the *Criminal Defence Service (Funding) Order* 2001 (S.I. 2001 No. 855). For further details thereof, see Appendix G–269.

House of Lords

6–67 **13.**—(1) In the case of proceedings in the House of Lords, the costs payable to any person under section 16(5) or 17(1) of the Act shall be determined by such officer as may be prescribed by order of the House of Lords.

(2) Subject to paragraph (1), this Part of these Regulations shall not apply to proceedings in the House of Lords.

6–68 As to the taxation of costs in the House of Lords, see also *post*, § 7–333. As to appeals to a costs judge and to the High Court, see also Part XIII of *Practice Direction (Costs: Criminal Proceedings)* [2004] 2 All E.R. 1070 (*post*, § 6–114j).

Part IIIA—Fees of court appointees (regs 13A–13C)

6–69 **13A.** Subject to the following provisions of this Part, Part III of these Regulations shall apply, with any necessary modifications, to the determination of the proper fee or costs of a court appointee.

13B.—(1) For the purposes of this Part of the Regulations:—

(a) the reference to "solicitor" in regulation 6(3)(a) and any reference to "applicant" in Part III shall be construed as including a reference to a court appointee;

(b) any reference to "costs" in Part III shall be construed as including a reference to the proper fee or costs of a court appointee; and

(c) the words after paragraph (b) in regulation 7(1) shall be omitted.

13C. In this Part of the Regulations "court appointee" means:—

(a) a person appointed by the Crown Court under section 4A of the *Criminal Procedure (Insanity) Act* 1964 to put the case for the defence;

(b) a legal representative appointed by the court under section 38(4) of the *Youth Justice and Criminal Evidence Act* 1999 to cross-examine a witness in the interests of the accused.

[Part IIIA was inserted by the *Costs in Criminal Cases (General) (Amendment) Regulations* 1992 (S.I. 1992 No. 323). Reg. 13C is printed as subsequently substituted by the *Costs in Criminal Cases (General) (Amendment) Regulations* 2000 (S.I. 2000 No. 2094).]

The express provision for the payment of the appointee's costs in the Crown Court out of central funds should be taken to extend to the determination of his costs in the Court of Appeal: *R. v. Antoine* [1999] 2 Cr.App.R. 225, CA.

Part IV—Miscellaneous applications of the Act (reg. 14)

Application of sections 16, 17 and 18 of the Act

14.—(1) Sections 17 and 18 of the Act shall apply to proceedings in the Crown Court in respect of a person committed by a magistrates' court to that Court— **6–70**

(a) with a view to his being sentenced for an indictable offence in accordance with section [5 of the *Powers of Criminal Courts (Sentencing) Act* 2000]; or

(b) with a view to his being sentenced by the Crown Court under section 6(6) or 9(3) of the *Bail Act* 1976; or

(c) with a view to the making of a hospital order with an order restricting his discharge under Part III of the *Mental Health Act* 1983,

as they apply where a person is convicted in proceedings before the Crown Court.

(2) Section 18 of the Act shall apply to proceedings in the Crown Court—

(a) in respect of a person committed by a magistrates' court as an incorrigible rogue under section 5 of the *Vagrancy Act* 1824 as if he were committed for trial before the Crown Court and as if the committing court were examining justices; and

(b) in respect of an appeal under section 14 of the *Vagrancy Act* 1824 as if the hearing of the appeal were a trial on indictment and as if the magistrates' court from which the appeal was brought were examining justices.

(3) Section 18 of the Act shall apply to proceedings in a magistrates' court or the Crown Court for dealing with an offender— **6–71**

(a) under any of the following provisions of the *Powers of Criminal Courts (Sentencing) Act* 2000—

(i) section 13 (commission of further offence by person conditionally discharged);

(ii) section 119(1) or 123 (power of court on conviction of further offence to deal with suspended sentence and breach of requirement of suspended sentence supervision order);

(iii) paragraph 5 of Schedule 1 (power of court on referral back from panel);

(iv) Part II of Schedule 3 (breach of requirement of certain community orders);

(v) paragraphs 1 to 3 of Schedule 5 (breach etc of attendance centre order);

(vi) paragraphs 2 to 4 of Schedule 7 (breach of requirement of supervision order);

(vii) paragraphs 2 to 4 of Schedule 8 (breach of requirement of action plan order or reparation order); and

(b) under either of the following provisions of the *Criminal Justice Act* 2003—

(i) Part 2 of Schedule 8 (breach of requirement of community order);

(ii) Part 2 of Schedule 12 (breach of community requirement of suspended sentence order or conviction of further offence)

as if the offender had been tried in those proceedings for the offence for which the order was made or the sentence passed.

(4) Section 16 of the Act shall apply to proceedings in a magistrates' court or the Crown Court in which it is alleged that an offender required to enter into a recognisance to keep the peace or be of good behaviour has failed to comply with a condition of that recognisance, as if that failure were an indictable offence.

[This regulation is printed as amended by the *Costs in Criminal Cases (General) (Amendment) (No. 2) Regulations* 1992 (S.I. 1992 No. 2956); and S.I. 2008 No. 2448 (*ante*, § 6–54). The reference in square brackets in para. (1)(a) to section 5 of the *PCC(S)A* 2000 has been substituted by virtue of s.165(3) of, and Sched. 11, para. 1(4), to that Act.]

For sections 16, 17 and 18 of the Act, see *ante*, §§ 6–3, 6–23 and 6–27, respectively.

Part V—Allowances to witnesses (regs 15–25)

Definitions

6–72 **15.** In this Part of these Regulations—

"expenses" include compensation to a witness for his trouble or loss of time and out of pocket expenses;

"proceedings in a criminal cause or matter" includes any case in which—

(a) an information charging the accused with an offence is laid before a justice of the peace for any area but not proceeded with; or

(b) the accused is committed for trial but not tried;

"professional witness" means a witness practising as a member of the legal or medical profession or as a dentist, veterinary surgeon or accountant who attends to give professional evidence as to matters of fact;

"private prosecutor" means any person in whose favour an order for the payment of costs out of central funds could be made under section 17 of the Act;

"the relevant amount" has the meaning assigned to it by regulation 17;

"witness" means any person properly attending to give evidence, whether or not he gives evidence or is called at the instance of one of the parties or of the court, but does not include—

(a) a person attending as a witness to character only unless the court has certified that the interests of justice required his attendance;

(b) a member of a police force attending court in his capacity as such;

(c) a full-time officer of an institution to which the *Prison Act* 1952 applies attending court in his capacity as such; or

(d) a prisoner in respect of any occasion on which he is conveyed to court in custody.

General

6–73 **16.**—(1) Where, in any proceedings in a criminal cause or matter in a magistrates' court, the Crown Court, a Divisional Court of the Queen's Bench Division, the Court of Appeal or the House of Lords—

(a) a witness attends at the instance of the accused, a private prosecutor or the court; or

(b) an interpreter is required because of the accused's lack of English; or

(ba) a witness called by the defendant is examined through an intermediary under section 29 of the *Youth Justice and Criminal Evidence Act* 1999; or

(c) a medical practitioner makes a report otherwise than in writing,

the expenses properly incurred by a witness referred to in sub-paragraph (a) or by that interpreter, intermediary or medical practitioner shall be allowed out of central funds in accordance with this Part of these Regulations, unless the court directs that the expenses are not to be allowed out of central funds.

(2) Subject to paragraph (3), any entitlement to an allowance under this Part of these Regulations shall be the same whether the witness, interpreter, intermediary or medical practitioner attends on the same day in one case or more than one case.

(3) Paragraph (2) shall not apply to allowances under regulation 25.

[This regulation is printed as amended by S.I. 2008 No. 2448 (*ante*, § 6–54).]

6–74 **17.** [*Determination of rates or scales of allowances payable out of central funds.*]

Witnesses other than professional or expert witnesses

6–75 **18.**—(1) A witness (other than a witness to whom regulation 19 or 20 applies) may be allowed—

(a) a loss allowance not exceeding the relevant amount in respect of—

(i) any expenditure incurred (other than on travelling, lodging or subsistence) to which the witness would not otherwise be subject; or

(ii) any loss of earnings or of benefit under the enactments relating to National Insurance; and

(b) a subsistence allowance not exceeding the relevant amount.

(2) Any other person who in the opinion of the court necessarily attends for the purpose

of any proceedings otherwise than to give evidence may be allowed the same allowances under paragraph (1) as if he attended as a witness other than a professional or expert witness.

(3) Paragraph (2) shall not apply to—

(a) a member of a police force attending court in his capacity as such;

(b) a full-time officer of an institution to which the *Prison Act* 1952 applies attending court in his capacity as such, or

(c) a prisoner in respect of any occasion on which he is conveyed to court in custody.

19. [*Professional witnesses.*] **6–76**

20. [*Expert witnesses etc.*] **6–77**

21. [*Night allowances.*] **6–78**

22. [*Seamen.*] **6–79**

Prosecutors and defendants

23. A person in whose favour an order is made under section 16, 17 or 19(4) of the Act may be allowed the same subsistence allowance and travelling expenses as if he attended as a witness other than a professional or expert witness. **6–80**

24. [*Travelling expenses.*] **6–81**

Written medical reports

25.—(1) A medical practitioner who makes a written report to a court in pursuance of a request to which section 32(2) of the *Criminal Justice Act* 1967 applies may be allowed a medical report allowance not exceeding the relevant amount. **6–82**

(2) A medical practitioner who makes a report to which paragraph (1) applies and incurs travelling expenses in connection with the preparation of that report may be allowed a travelling allowance not exceeding the relevant amount.

(3) Nothing in this regulation shall apply to a report by the medical officer of an institution to which the *Prison Act* 1952 applies.

Section 32 of the 1967 Act applies to a request to a registered medical practitioner to make a written or oral report on the medical condition of an offender or defendant, being a request made by a court: (a) for the purpose of determining whether or not to make a probation order with a requirement of treatment for a mental condition, or a hospital or guardianship order or otherwise for the purpose of determining the most suitable method of dealing with an offender; or (b) in exercise of the powers conferred by section 30 of the *MCA* 1980 to remand a defendant for a medical examination after summary trial.

Part VI—Recovery of sums paid out of the legal aid fund or central funds (regs 26, 27)

Directions by the Lord Chancellor

26.—(1) The Lord Chancellor shall recover in accordance with directions given by him any sums paid out as part of the Criminal Defence Service or central funds where a costs order has been made against a person in favour of— **6–83**

(a) a person receiving services funded for him as part of the Criminal Defence Service, or

(b) a person in whose favour an order for the payment of costs out of central funds has been made.

(2) Directions given by the Lord Chancellor under this regulation may be given generally or in respect of a particular case and may require the payment of sums due under a costs order and stipulate the mode of payment and the person to whom payment is to be made.

(3) In this regulation and regulation 27 "costs order" shall include a wasted costs order as defined by regulation 3A, or a third party costs order as defined by regulation 3E, of these Regulations.

[This regulation is printed as amended by the *Costs in Criminal Cases (General) (Amendment) Regulations* 1991 (S.I. 1991 No. 789); and S.I. 2004 No. 2408, *ante*, § 6–55.]

The words "out of the legal aid fund or" in the governing provision, namely section 20(2) of the 1985 Act, were initially substituted by the words "by the Legal Aid Board or", and have subsequently been substituted by the words "by the Legal Services Commission or": see *ante*, § 6–46. No corresponding amendment has been made in regulation 26.

6–84 **27.** [*Recovery of sums due under a costs order.*]

D. Miscellaneous Enactments

(1) Supreme Court [Senior Courts] Act 1981

High Court

6–85 The Divisional Court has the power to award costs *inter partes* on an appeal by way of case stated and on an application for any of the prerogative orders and whether from or in respect of a decision of a magistrates' court or the Crown Court. Such orders are in the discretion of the court: *Supreme Court [Senior Courts] Act* 1981, ss.28A, 51 (as to the renaming of this Act, see *ante*, § 6–28). For detailed provision in relation to the exercise of the discretion and the taxation of any award of costs, see the *CPR* 1998 (S.I. 1998 No. 3132), Parts 44 and 47. No power to make orders for costs out of central funds can be implied in section 51(1) of the 1981 Act: *Holden & Co. v. CPS (No. 2)* [1994] 1 A.C. 22, HL.

The decision whether to make a costs order against the Legal Services Commission in favour of an unassisted party was expressly assigned to the costs judge or district judge under the Community Legal Service funding scheme brought in by the *Access to Justice Act* 1999; the present practice of the trial court deciding whether it was just and equitable to make a costs order against the Commission should no longer be followed; in exercising their discretion, costs judges should proceed on the premise that it is just and equitable that the Commission should stand behind its client unless it was aware of facts which rendered that result unjust and inequitable; and costs judges and district judges have power to accede to an application for costs against the Commission made by a government department: *R. (Gunn) v. Secretary of State for the Home Department*; *R. (Kelly) v. Same*; *R. (Zahid Khan) v. Same* [2001] 1 W.L.R. 1634, CA (Civ. Div.). The significance of this to criminal practitioners is that applications for judicial review or *habeas corpus* relating to criminal investigations or proceedings are to be funded as part of the Community Legal Service: see paragraph 3 of Schedule 2 to the *Access to Justice Act 1999 (Commencement No. 7, Transitional Provisions and Savings) Order* 2001 (S.I. 2001 No. 916) (*post*, § 6–132).

Failure to observe time limits for lodging skeleton arguments and paginated bundles might result in hearings being adjourned with consequent penalties in costs: see *Haggis v. DPP (Note)* [2004] 2 All E.R. 382, DC.

Where the court allowed a prosecution appeal by way of case stated, it was unjust to make an order for costs against the respondent who was neither present nor represented at the hearing and who had not been asked whether she would consent to the appeal being allowed in her absence: *Canterbury City Council v. Cook*, *The Times*, December 23, 1992, DC. Mann L.J. said that what was or was not just in the circumstances was in the last resort a matter of impression. It appears that the point upon which the respondent had succeeded in the Crown Court was not of her making, but had been raised by the Crown Court.

As to awards of costs against justices, see section 34 of the *Courts Act* 2003. This prohibits the making of an award of costs against a justice of the peace, save where it is proved that he acted in bad faith in respect of the matters giving rise to the proceedings in question. Similar protection is extended to a justices' clerk and an assistant clerk in respect of their exercise of a function of a single justice of the peace.

As to the award of costs on appeal from the High Court, see *post*, § 7–332.

Crown Court

Supreme Court [Senior Courts] Act 1981, s.52

52.—(1) Rules of court may authorise the Crown Court to award costs and may regulate any matters relating to costs of proceedings in that court, and in particular may make provision as to— **6–86**

(a) any discretion to award costs;

(b) the taxation of costs, or the fixing of a sum instead of directing a taxation, and as to the officer of the court or other person by whom costs are to be taxed;

(c) a right of appeal from any decision on the taxation of costs, whether to a Taxing Master of the *Supreme Court* [Senior Courts] or to any other officer or authority;

(d) a right of appeal to the High Court, subject to any conditions specified in the rules, from any decision on an appeal brought by virtue of paragraph (c);

(e) the enforcement of an order for costs; and

(f) the charges or expenses or other disbursements which are to be treated as costs for the purposes of the rules.

(2) The costs to be dealt with by rules made in pursuance of this section may, where an appeal is brought to the Crown Court from the decision of a magistrates' court, or from the decision of any other court or tribunal, include costs in the proceedings in that court or tribunal.

(3) Nothing in this section authorises the making of rules about the payment of costs out of central funds, whether under Part II of the *Prosecution of Offences Act* 1985 or otherwise, but rules made in pursuance of this section may make any such provision as in relation to costs of proceedings in the Crown Court, is contained in section 18 of that Act or in regulations made under section 19 of that Act (awards of party and party costs in criminal proceedings). **6–87**

(4) Rules made in pursuance of this section may amend or repeal all or any of the provisions of any enactment about costs between party and party in criminal or other proceedings in the Crown Court, being an enactment passed before, or contained in, Part II of the *Prosecution of Offences Act* 1985.

(5) Rules made in pursuance of this section shall have effect subject to the provisions of section 41 of, and Schedule 9 to, the *Administration of Justice Act* 1970 (method of enforcing orders for costs).

[This section is printed as amended by the *Prosecution of Offences Act* 1985, s.31(5) and Sched. 1, paras 9 and 10; and the *Courts Act 2003 (Consequential Amendments) Order* 2004 (S.I. 2004 No. 2035); and as amended, as from a day to be appointed, by the *Constitutional Reform Act* 2005, s.59(5), and Sched. 11, paras 1(1) (renaming of Act) and 26 (substitution of words in square brackets for italicised words).]

Part IV of the *Crown Court Rules* 1982 (S.I. 1982 No. 1109) was headed "Costs between Parties in Crown Court". It comprised rules 12 to 18, which were made in pursuance of section 52 as originally enacted. They have now been substituted by Part 78 of the *Criminal Procedure Rules* 2005 (S.I. 2005 No. 384). Because of the changes in the law effected by the *Prosecution of Offences Act* 1985, rules 12 to 18 of the 1982 rules had come to have strictly limited application to the criminal jurisdiction of the Crown Court. Thus, section 18 of the Act (*ante*, § 6–27) and regulation 3 of the *Costs in Criminal Cases (General) Regulations* 1986 (*ante*, § 6–54) provide that the amount of any *inter partes* award shall be specified in the order. In the light of these two provisions, rules 78.3 to 78.7, which relate to the taxation and review of *inter partes* awards, must be regarded as having no current practical significance, at least so far as the ordinary criminal jurisdiction of the Crown Court is concerned. They do, however, apply in relation to awards of costs in restraint proceedings or receivership proceedings under Part 2 of the *PCA* 2002, by virtue of rules 61.19 to 61.21 of the 2005 rules (*ante*, §§ 5–718 *et seq.*). **6–88**

With respect to rules 78.1 and 78.2 it is submitted that they too are almost devoid of practical effect in ordinary criminal proceedings. The position is not, however, so straightforward as with rules 78.3 to 78.7. Section 52(3) expressly provides that no rules may be made under the section about the payment of costs from central funds. It follows that rules 78.1 and 78.2 can only relate to the making of *inter partes* awards: see also the heading to Part IV of the 1982 rules, *ante* (the heading to Part 78 of the 2005 rules being "Costs orders against the parties"). Clearly, they must be read subject to the provisions of the Act and of the 1986 regulations. It is submitted that those provisions effectively cover every situation. Section 18 of the Act governs the making of orders for costs *against* the accused whether in respect of proceedings on indictment or on appeal. Furthermore, the application of section 18 is extended by regulation 14 of the 1986 regulations (*ante*, § 6–70).

A successful defendant or appellant in the Crown Court, or a defendant who is not tried, may obtain a defendant's costs order under section 16(2) or (3) of the Act. Such an order will, in the absence of an express order to the contrary, include the costs of any proceedings in the magistrates' court: see *ante*, § 6–12. A successful appellant will not need to rely on rule 78.2. There is no jurisdiction, however, under the Act to make an award of costs against the prosecution or the respondent and, it is submitted, it would be quite wrong to construe the general provision of rule 78.1(2) as conferring any such jurisdiction. There is always the possibility of an order against the prosecution/respondent under regulation 3 of the 1986 regulations, *ante*, § 6–54. That, however, is a specific jurisdiction: the scheme of the legislation is clearly that, unless the case or some aspect of the case comes within regulation 3, a successful defendant or appellant is to recover his costs, if he recovers them at all, from central funds under section 16.

One possible use of rule 78.2 would be where the Crown Court takes the view, having allowed an appeal against conviction, that the magistrates' court should have made an order against the prosecution under regulation 3 in respect of the magistrates' court proceedings. This is a situation which is unlikely to arise in practice, but if it does, the Crown Court may make the order it thinks the magistrates should have made.

Criminal Procedure Rules 2005 (S.I. 2005 No. 384), r.78.1

Crown Court's jurisdiction to award costs in appeal from magistrates' court

6–89 **78.1.**—(1) Subject to the provisions of section 109(1) of the *Magistrates' Courts Act* 1980 (power of magistrates' courts to award costs on abandonment of appeals from magistrates' courts), no party shall be entitled to recover any costs of any proceedings in the Crown Court from any other party to the proceedings except under an order of the Court.

(2) Subject to the following provisions of this rule, the Crown Court may make such order for costs as it thinks just.

(4) Without prejudice to the generality of paragraph (2), the Crown Court may make an order for costs on dismissing an appeal where the appellant has failed to proceed with the appeal or on the abandonment of an appeal.

[This rule is printed as amended by the *Criminal Procedure (Amendment) Rules* 2008 (S.I. 2008 No. 2076), r.25.]

6–90 See *ante*, § 6–88 as to whether this rule or rule 78.2 (*post*) has any current application to the criminal jurisdiction of the Crown Court, having regard to the changes in the law relating to costs effected by the *Prosecution of Offences Act* 1985.

Criminal Procedure Rules 2005 (S.I. 2005 No. 384), r.78.2

Crown Court's jurisdiction to award costs in magistrates' court proceedings from which appeal is brought

6–91 **78.2.** Where an appeal is brought to the Crown Court from the decision of a magistrates' court and the appeal is successful, the Crown Court may make any order as to the costs of the proceedings in the magistrates' court which that court had power to make.

The scope of this rule is considered *ante*, § 6–88.

Criminal Procedure Rules 2005 (S.I. 2005 No. 384), r.78.3

Taxation of Crown Court costs

6–92 **78.3.**—(1) Where under these Rules the Crown Court has made an order for the costs of any proceedings to be paid by a party and the Court has not fixed a sum, the amount of the costs to be paid shall be ascertained as soon as practicable by the Crown Court officer (hereinafter referred to as the taxing authority).

(2) On a taxation under the preceding paragraph there shall be allowed the costs reasonably incurred in or about the prosecution and conviction or the defence, as the case may be.

As to the limited application of this rule, see *ante*, § 6–88. Paragraph (2) will have no practical application. The reference to "the costs reasonably incurred in or about the prosecution and conviction or the defence" is meaningless in the context of awards in restraint proceedings or receivership proceedings under Part 2 of the *PCA* 2002.

Reviews of taxations

Any party dissatisfied with the taxation of any costs by the taxing authority under rule 78.3 may apply to the taxing authority to review his decision: r.78.4(1). The application shall be made by giving notice to the taxing authority and to any other party to the taxation within 14 days of the taxation, specifying the items in respect of which the application is made and the grounds of objection: r.78.4(2). Any party to whom notice is given under the preceding paragraph may within 14 days of the service of the notice deliver to the taxing authority answers in writing to the objections specified in that notice to the taxing authority and, if he does, shall send copies to the applicant for the review and to any other party to the taxation: r.78.4(3). The taxing authority shall reconsider his taxation in the light of the objections and answers, if any, of the parties and any oral representations made by or on their behalf and shall notify them of the result of his review: r.78.4(4). **6–92a**

Any party dissatisfied with the result of a review of taxation under rule 78.4 may, within 14 days of receiving notification thereof, request the taxing authority to supply him with reasons in writing for his decision and may within 14 days of the receipt of such reasons apply to the senior costs judge for a further review and shall, in that case, give notice of the application to the taxing authority and to any other party to the taxation, to whom he shall also give a copy of the reasons given by the taxing authority: r.78.5(1). Such application shall state whether the applicant wishes to appear or be represented, or whether he will accept a decision given in his absence and shall be accompanied by a copy of the notice given under rule 78.4, of any answer which may have been given under paragraph (3) thereof and of the reasons given by the taxing authority for his decision, together with the bill of costs and full supporting documents: r.78.5(2). A party to the taxation who receives notice of an application under this rule shall inform the senior costs judge whether he wishes to appear or be represented at a further review, or whether he will accept a decision given in his absence: r.78.5(3). The further review shall be conducted by a costs judge and, if the applicant or any other party to the taxation has given notice of his intention to appear or be represented, the costs judge shall inform the parties (or their agents) of the date on which the further review will take place: r.78.5(4). Before reaching his decision the costs judge may consult the judge who made the order for costs and the taxing authority and, unless the costs judge otherwise directs, no further evidence shall be received on the hearing of the further review; and no ground of objection shall be valid which was not raised on the review under rule 78.4: r.78.5(5). In making his review, the costs judge may alter the assessment of the taxing authority in respect of any sum allowed, whether by increase or decrease: r.78.5(6). The costs judge shall communicate the result of the further review to the parties and to the taxing authority: r.78.5(7).

Any party dissatisfied with the result of a further review under rule 78.5 may, within 14 days of receiving notification thereof, appeal by originating summons to a judge of the Queen's Bench Division of the High Court if, and only if (but see, *ante*, § 6–64), the costs judge certifies that the question to be decided involves a point of principle of general importance: r.78.6(1). On the hearing of the appeal the judge may reverse, affirm or amend the decision appealed against or make such other order as he thinks appropriate: r.78.6(2).

On a further review or an appeal to a judge of the High Court the costs judge or judge may make such order as he thinks just in respect of the costs of the hearing of the further review or the appeal, as the case may be: r.78.7(1). The time prescribed under any of the three preceding rules may be extended by the taxing authority, costs judge or judge of the High Court on such terms as he thinks just: r.78.7(2).

(2) Magistrates' Courts Act 1980

6–93 For the award of costs on the abandonment of an appeal, see section 109 of the *MCA* 1980, *ante*, § 2–177.

(3) Mental Health (Amendment) Act 1982

Mental Health (Amendment) Act 1982, s.34(5)

Medical costs relating to reports on persons accused of murder

6–94 **34.**—(5) Without prejudice to its powers under section 3 of the *Costs in Criminal Cases Act* 1973, the Crown Court may order the payment out of central funds of such sums as appear to it reasonably sufficient to compensate any medical practitioner for the expenses, trouble or loss of time properly incurred by him in preparing and making a report to the court on the mental condition of a person accused of murder.

The whole of the *Costs in Criminal Cases Act* 1973 has been repealed. This does not, however, affect the sense of this provision. "Central funds" means "money provided by Parliament": *Interpretation Act* 1978, s.5 and Sched. 1 (Appendix B–5, B–28).

(4) Police and Criminal Evidence Act 1984

6–95 Schedule 1, para. 16, to this Act (*post*, § 15–92) provides that the costs of any application under the schedule for access to excluded material or special procedure material and of anything done or to be done in pursuance of an order made thereunder shall be in the discretion of the judge.

(5) Criminal Justice Act 1972

References by Attorney-General

6–96 Section 36(5) of the *CJA* 1972, makes provision for the payment out of "central funds" (*ante*, § 6–94) of the costs of an acquitted person who appears by counsel on a point being referred to the Court of Appeal or further referred to the House of Lords under that section. Subsection (5A) provides that section 20(1) of the *Prosecution of Offences Act* 1985 (*ante*, § 6–46) shall apply in relation to section 36 as it applies in relation to Part II of that Act. Section 36 is set out in full, *post*, §§ 7–361, 7–362.

(6) Criminal Justice Act 1988

Sentencing reviews

6–97 Where a case is referred to the Court of Appeal under section 36 of the 1988 Act for the purpose of the sentence being reviewed or is further referred to the House of Lords under section 36(5) and the person whose sentencing is subject to the reference appears by counsel for the purpose of presenting argument to the Court of Appeal or the House of Lords, he is entitled to his costs. This means that he is entitled to the payment out of "central funds" (*ante*, § 6–94) of such funds as are reasonably sufficient to compensate him for the expenses properly incurred by him for the purpose of being represented on the reference. The amount recoverable under this provision is to be ascertained, as soon as practicable, by the registrar of criminal appeals or, as the case may be, such officer as may be prescribed by order of the House of Lords: Sched. 3, para. 11. Section 36 of, and Schedule 3 to, the 1988 Act are set out in full, *post*, §§ 7–368 *et seq.*

Appeals against orders restricting or preventing reporting of trial, or restricting access thereto

6–98 Section 159 (*post*, § 7–308) provides for appeals to the Court of Appeal by a person aggrieved by an order restricting or preventing reports of a trial on indictment or restricting public access thereto. On the hearing of such an appeal, the Court of Appeal has power, *inter alia*, to make such order as to costs as it thinks fit: s.159(5)(c). As to how the discretion should be exercised, see *Ex p. News Group Newspapers Ltd*, *The Times*, May 21, 1999, CA, *post*, § 7–309. The power to order costs under this provision does not include a power to order that the costs should come out of central funds: *Holden & Co. v. CPS (No. 2)* [1994] 1 A.C. 22, HL.

(7) Football Spectators Act 1989

As to the costs of applications to terminate banning orders, see section 14H(5), *ante*, § 5–832. **6–99**

(8) Bankers' Books Evidence Act 1879

As to the costs of applications under this Act, see section 8 thereof, *post*, § 11–66. **6–100**

(9) Criminal Procedure (Attendance of Witnesses) Act 1965

As to the costs of an application to set aside a witness summons, see section 2C(8) of the 1965 Act, *post*, §§ 8–3b, 8–6c. **6–100a**

(10) Serious Crime Act 2007 (Appeals under Section 24) Order 2008 (S.I. 2008 No. 1863)

This order makes provision in relation to appeals under section 24 of the 2007 Act (*ante*, § 5–875h)) concerning serious crime prevention orders. **6–100b**

Part 2 (arts 3–12) concerns appeals to the Court of Appeal, and corresponds in large part to various provisions in Part I of the *CAA* 1968, modified to take account of the nature of proceedings concerning serious crime prevention orders, in particular with regard to which parties may appeal various decisions. Article 5 provides that the court (i) has all the powers of the Crown Court, (ii) may (a) make a serious crime prevention order, (b) affirm, set aside or vary any order or judgment made or given by the Crown Court, (c) refer any issue for determination by the Crown Court, (d) order a new hearing in the Crown Court, (e) make an order for costs in accordance with Part 3, and (f) make an order for the payment of interest on those costs, and (iii) may exercise its powers in relation to the whole or part of an order of the Crown Court.

Part 3 (arts 13–38) concerns costs, and corresponds in large part to various enactments, again modified to take account of the nature of the proceedings. Article 13 concerns interpretation and makes transitional provision. Article 14 (costs out of central funds) broadly corresponds to sections 16 and 17 of the *Prosecution of Offences Act* 1985 (*ante*, §§ 6–3, 6–23). Article 15 (*inter partes* awards) broadly corresponds to section 18 of that Act (*ante*, § 6–27). Article 16 (unnecessary or improper acts or omissions) broadly corresponds to regulation 3 of the *Costs in Criminal Cases (General) Regulations* 1986 (S.I. 1986 No. 1335) (*ante*, § 6–54). Article 17 (wasted costs) broadly corresponds to section 19A of the 1985 Act (*ante*, § 6–40) and regulation 3B of those regulations (*ante*, § 6–55). Article 18 (third party costs order) broadly corresponds to regulation 3F(1) of those regulations (*ante*, § 6–55b). Article 19 provides for the payment out of central funds of such sums as appear to the court to be reasonably sufficient to compensate a party to an appeal who is not in custody and who appears before the court in connection with any proceedings before it. Articles 20, 21 to 28, 29, 30, 31, 32 to 36, 37 and 38 broadly correspond to regulations 16, 5 to 12, 3F(2) to (7), 3G, 3I, 17 to 21, 23 and 24 of those regulations respectively (*ante*, §§ 6–73, 6–57 *et seq.*, 6–55b, 6–55c, 6–55e, 6–74 *et seq.*, 6–80, 6–81).

Part 4 (arts 39–43) concerns appeals to the House of Lords [Supreme Court (as to which, see art. 43)] and costs on such appeals, and corresponds in large part to various provisions in Part II of the 1968 Act, again modified to take account of the nature of the proceedings. Article 42 corresponds to article 14 (*ante*).

As to this order, see also *post*, §§ 7–312c *et seq.*

E. PRACTICE DIRECTION

On May 18, 2004, Lord Woolf C.J. issued a new practice direction to replace the one issued by Lord Lane C.J. in May 1991 (as amended), and the practice direction relating to taxation appeals that had been issued by the chief taxing master in June, 1994. Apart from a few paragraphs which do no more than restate the text of the legislation, the practice direction is set out in full, *post*, subject only to some grammatical correction and the omission of Parts XIV (VAT) and XV (revocations) and the schedules. References to **6–101** the *Crown Court Rules* 1982 (S.I. 1982 No. 1109) and to the *Crown Court (Confiscation, Restraint and Receivership) Rules* 2003 (S.I. 2003 No. 421) have been replaced by references to the corresponding provisions of the *Criminal Procedure Rules* 2005 (S.I. 2005 No. 384). As to whether Part V is compatible with the legislation, see *ante*, §§ 6–16 *et seq.*

Practice Direction (Costs: Criminal Proceedings)
[2004] 2 All E.R. 1070

PART I: INTRODUCTION

I.1 Scope

6–102 **I.1.1** This direction shall have effect in magistrates' courts, the Crown Court, the Administrative Court and the Court of Appeal (criminal division) where the court, in the exercise of its discretion, considers an award of costs in criminal proceedings or deals with Criminal Defence Service funded work and recovery of defence costs orders. The provisions in this practice direction will take effect from 18 May 2004.

I.2 The power to award costs

6–103 **I.2.1** The powers enabling the court to award costs in criminal proceedings are primarily contained in Part II of the *Prosecution of Offences Act* 1985 (the Act) (ss.16, 17 and 18), the *Access to Justice Act* 1999 (in relation to funded clients) and in regulations made under those Acts including the *Costs in Criminal Cases (General) Regulations* 1986 (S.I. 1986 No. 1335, as amended) (the General Regulations). References in this direction are to the *Prosecution of Offences Act* and those regulations unless otherwise stated. Schedule 1 sets out details of the relevant regulations.

I.2.2 [*Summary of ss.16–19A of 1985 Act*, ante, *§§ 6–3* et seq.]

I.2.3 The Supreme Court also has the power under its inherent jurisdiction over officers of the court to order a solicitor personally to pay costs thrown away. It may also give directions relating to CDS funded costs and recovery of defence costs orders.

I.3 Extent of orders for costs from central funds

I.3.1 Where a court orders that the costs of a defendant, appellant or private prosecutor should be paid from central funds, the order will be for such amount as the court considers sufficient reasonably to compensate the party for expenses incurred by him in the proceedings. This will include the costs incurred in the proceedings in the lower courts unless for good reason the court directs that such costs are not included in the order, but it cannot include expenses incurred which do not directly relate to the proceedings themselves, such as loss of earnings. Where the party in whose favour the costs order is made is CDS funded, he will only recover his personal costs (see section 21(4A)(a)). Schedule 2 sets out the extent of availability of costs from central funds and the relevant statutory authority.

I.4 Amount of costs to be paid

6–104 **I.4.1** Except where the court has directed, in an order for costs out of central funds, that only a specified sum shall be paid, the amount of costs to be paid shall be determined by the appropriate officer of the court. The court may however order the disallowance of costs out of central funds not properly incurred or direct the determining officer to consider whether or not specific items have been properly incurred. The court may also make observations regarding CDS funded costs. The procedures to be followed when such circumstances arise are set out in this direction.

I.4.2 Where the court orders an offender to pay costs to the prosecutor, orders one party to pay costs to another party, disallows or orders a legal or other representative to meet any wasted costs, the order for costs must specify the sum to be paid or disallowed.

I.4.3 Where the court is required to specify the amount of costs to be paid it cannot delegate the decision. Wherever practicable those instructing advocates should provide the advocate with details of costs incurred at each stage in the proceedings. The court may however require the appropriate officer of the court to make enquiries to inform the court as to the costs incurred and may adjourn the proceedings for enquiries to be made if necessary. Special provisions apply in relation to recovery of defence costs orders as to which see Part XI below.

PART II: DEFENCE COSTS FROM CENTRAL FUNDS

II.1 In a magistrates' court

II.1.1 Where an information laid before a justice of the peace charging a person with an offence is not proceeded with, a magistrates' court enquiring into an indictable offence as examining justices determines not to commit the accused for trial, or a magistrates' court dealing summarily with an offence dismisses the information, the court may make a defendant's costs order. An order under section 16 of the Act may also be made in relation to breach of bind-over proceedings in a magistrates' court or the Crown Court (regulation 14(4) of the General Regulations). As is the case with the Crown Court (see below) such an order should normally be made unless there are positive reasons for not doing so. For example, where the defendant's own conduct has brought suspicion on himself and has misled the prosecution into thinking that the case against him was stronger than it was, the defendant can be left to pay his own costs. In the case of a partial acquittal the court may make a part order (details are at paragraphs II.2.1 and II.2.2 below). **6–105**

II.1.2 Whether to make such an award is a matter in the discretion of the court in the light of the circumstances of each particular case.

II.2 In the Crown Court

II.2.1 Where a person is not tried for an offence for which he has been indicted, or in respect of which proceedings against him have been sent for trial or transferred for trial, or has been acquitted on any count in the indictment, the court may make a defendant's costs order in his favour. Such an order should normally be made whether or not an order for costs between the parties is made, unless there are positive reasons for not doing so. For example, where the defendant's own conduct has brought suspicion on himself and has misled the prosecution into thinking that the case against him was stronger than it was, the defendant can be left to pay his own costs. The court when declining to make a costs order should explain, in open court, that the reason for not making an order does not involve any suggestion that the defendant is guilty of any criminal conduct but the order is refused because of the positive reason that should be identified. **6–106**

II.2.2 Where a person is convicted of some count(s) in the indictment and acquitted on other(s) the court may exercise its discretion to make a defendants costs order but may order that only part of the costs incurred be paid. The court should make whatever order seems just having regard to the relative importance of the two charges and the conduct of the parties generally. Where the court considers that it would be inappropriate that the defendant should recover all of the costs properly incurred, the amount must be specified in the order.

II.2.3 The Crown Court may make a defendant's costs order in favour of a successful appellant. (See section 16(3) of the Act.)

II.3 In the Administrative Court

II.3.1 The court may make a defendant's costs order on determining proceedings in a criminal cause or matter. **6–107**

II.4 In the Court of Appeal criminal division

II.4.1 A successful appellant under Part 1 of the *Criminal Appeal Act* 1968 may be awarded a defendant's costs order. Orders may also be made on an appeal against an order or ruling at a preparatory hearing (s.16(4A)), to cover the costs of representing an acquitted defendant in respect of whom there is an Attorney General's reference under section 36 of the *Criminal Justice Act* 1972 (see s.36(5) and (5A) of the 1972 Act) and in the case of a person whose sentence is reviewed under section 36 of the *Criminal Justice Act* 1988 (see s.36 and Sched. 3, para. 11 of the 1988 Act). **6–108**

II.4.2 On determining an application for leave to appeal to the House of Lords under Part II of the *Criminal Appeal Act* 1968, whether by prosecutor or by defendant, the court may make a defendant's costs order.

II.4.3 In considering whether to make such an order the court will have in mind the principles applied by the Crown Court in relation to acquitted defendants (see paragraph II.2.1 and II.2.2 above).

PART III: PRIVATE PROSECUTOR'S COSTS FROM CENTRAL FUNDS

III.1.1 There is no power to order the payment of costs out of central funds of any prosecutor who is a public authority, a person acting on behalf of a public authority, or acting as an official appointed by a public authority as defined in the Act. In the limited number of cases in which a prosecutor's costs may be awarded out of central funds, an application is to be made by the prosecution in each case. An order should be made save where there is **6–109**

good reason for not doing so, for example, where proceedings have been instituted or continued without good cause. This provision applies to proceedings in respect of an indictable offence or proceedings before the Administrative Court in respect of a summary offence. Regulation 14(1) of the General Regulations extends it to certain committals for sentence from a magistrates' court.

PART IV: COSTS OF WITNESS, INTERPRETER OR MEDICAL EVIDENCE

6–110 **IV.1** The costs of attendance of a witness required by the accused, a private prosecutor or the court, or of an interpreter required because of the accused's lack of English or of an oral report by a medical practitioner are allowed out of central funds unless the court directs otherwise (see s.20(3) of the Act and regulation 16(1) of the General Regulations). If, and only if, the court makes such a direction can the expense of the witness be claimed as a disbursement out of CDS funds. A witness includes any person properly attending to give evidence whether or not he gives evidence or is called, but it does not include a character witness unless the court has certified that the interests of justice require his attendance.

IV.2 The Crown Court may order the payment out of central funds of such sums as appear to be sufficient reasonably to compensate any medical practitioner for the expenses, trouble or loss of time properly incurred in preparing and making a report on the mental condition of a person accused of murder (see s.34(5) of the *Mental Health (Amendment) Act* 1982).

PART V: DISALLOWANCE OF COSTS OUT OF CENTRAL FUNDS

6–111 **V.1.1** Where the court makes an order for costs out of central funds, it must:

(a) direct the appropriate authority to disallow the costs incurred in respect of any items if it is plain that those costs were not properly incurred; such costs are not payable under sections 16(6) and 17(1) of the Act, and it may:

(b) direct the appropriate authority to consider or investigate on determination any items which may have been improperly incurred.

Costs not properly incurred include costs in respect of work unreasonably done, *e.g.*, if the case has been conducted unreasonably so as to incur unjustified expense, or costs have been wasted by failure to conduct proceedings with reasonable competence and expedition. In a plain case it will usually be more appropriate to make a wasted costs order under section 19A of the Act (see Part VIII below). The precise terms of the order for costs and of any direction must be entered in the court record.

V.1.2 Where the court has in mind that a direction in accordance with paragraph V.1.1(a) or (b) might be given it must inform any party whose costs might be affected, or his legal representative, of the precise terms thereof and give a reasonable opportunity to show cause why no direction should be given. If a direction is given under paragraph V.1.1(b) the court should inform the party concerned of his rights to make representations to the appropriate authority.

V.1.3 The appropriate authority may consult the court on any matter touching upon the allowance or disallowance of costs. It is not appropriate for the court to make a direction under paragraph V.1.1(a) when so consulted.

PART VI: AWARD OF COSTS AGAINST OFFENDERS AND APPELLANTS

6–112 **VI.1.1** [*Summary of s.18(1) of 1985 Act*, ante, *§ 6–27*.]

VI.1.2 [*Summary of s.18(2), (6) of 1985 Act*, ante, *§ 6–27*.]

VI.1.3 [*Summary of s.18(4), (5) of 1985 Act*, ante, *§ 6–27*.]

VI.1.4 An order should be made where the court is satisfied that the offender or appellant has the means and the ability to pay.

VI.1.5 The amount must be specified in the order by the court.

VI.1.6 The Administrative Court is not covered by section 18 of the Act but it has complete discretion over all costs between the parties in relation to proceedings before it.

VI.1.7 An order under section 18 of the Act includes LSC funded costs (see s.21(4A)(b) of the Act).

PART VII: AWARD OF COSTS BETWEEN THE PARTIES

VII.1 Costs incurred as a result of unnecessary or improper act or omission

6–113 **VII.1.1** A magistrates' court, the Crown Court and the Court of Appeal criminal division may order the payment of any costs incurred as a result of any unnecessary or improper act or omission by or on behalf of any party to the proceedings as distinct from his legal representative (s.19 of the Act and reg. 3 of the General Regulations).

VII.1.2 The court must hear the parties and may then order that all or part of the costs so incurred by one party shall be paid to him by the other party.

VII.1.3 Before making such an order the court must take into account any other order as to costs and the order must specify the amount of the costs to be paid. The court is entitled to take such an order into account when making any other order as to costs in the proceedings (reg. 3(2) to (4) of the General Regulations). The order can extend to LSC costs incurred on behalf of any party (s.21(4A)(b) of the Act).

VII.1.4 In a magistrates' court no order may be made which requires a convicted person under 18 to pay an amount by way of costs which exceeds the amount of any fine imposed upon him (reg. 3(5) of the General Regulations).

VII.1.5 Such an order is appropriate only where the failure is that of the defendant or of the prosecutor. Where the failure is that of the legal representative(s) Parts VIII and IX (below) apply.

VII.2 Costs in restraint, confiscation or receivership proceedings

The order for costs

VII.2.1 This part of this practice direction applies where the Crown Court is deciding whether to make an order for costs under rule 78.1 of the *Criminal Procedure Rules* 2005 in relation to restraint proceedings or receivership proceedings brought under the *Criminal Procedure Rules* 2005, Pts 57 to 61. (Confiscation proceedings are treated for costs purposes as part of the criminal trial.) The court has discretion as to: whether costs are payable by one party to another; the amount of those costs; and, when they are to be paid. The general rule is that if the court decides to make an order about costs the unsuccessful party will be ordered to pay the costs of the successful party but the court may make a different order (*Criminal Procedure Rules* 2005, r. 61.19). **6–114**

VII.2.2 Attention is drawn to the fact that in receivership proceedings the 2005 rules provide that the Crown Court may make orders in respect of security to be given by a receiver to cover his liability for his acts and omissions as a receiver (r. 60.5). The court may also make orders in relation to determining the remuneration of the receiver (r. 60.6). (Paragraph VII.2.15 below deals with determination of the remuneration of a receiver).

VII.2.3 In deciding what if any order to make about costs the court is required to have regard to all the circumstances including the conduct of all the parties and whether a party has succeeded on part of an application, even if that party has not been wholly successful.

VII.2.4 The 2005 rules set out the type of order which the court may make (the list is not exclusive):

(a) a proportion of another party's costs;
(b) a stated amount in respect of another party's costs;
(c) costs from or until a certain date only;
(d) costs incurred before proceedings have begun;
(e) costs relating to particular steps taken in the proceedings;
(f) costs relating only to a distinct part of the proceedings; and
(g) interest on costs from or until a certain date including a date before the making of an order.

VII.2.5 The court is required, where it is practicable, to award a proportion (*e.g.* a percentage) of the costs, or costs between certain dates, rather than making an order relating only to a distinct part or issue in the proceedings. The latter type of order makes it extremely difficult for the costs to be assessed.

VII.2.6 Where the court orders a party to pay costs it may, in addition, order an amount to be paid on account by one party to another before the costs are assessed. Where the court makes such an order, the order should state the amount to be paid and the date on or before which payment is to be made.

Assessment of costs

VII.2.7 Where the Crown Court makes an order for costs in restraint, or receivership proceedings it may make an assessment of the costs itself there and then (a summary assessment), or order assessment of the costs under rule 78.3 of the *Criminal Procedure Rules* 2005 (*ibid.*, r. 61.20). If the court neither makes an assessment of the costs nor orders assessment as specified above, the order for costs will be treated as an order for the amount of costs to be decided by assessment under rule 14 of the 1982 rules unless the order otherwise provides. **6–114a**

VII.2.8 Whenever the court awards costs to be assessed under rule 14 of the 1982 rules it should consider whether to exercise the power to order the paying party to pay such sum of money, as it thinks just, on account of those costs.

VII.2.9 In carrying out the assessment of costs the court or the taxing authority is required to allow only costs which are proportionate to the matters in issue, and to resolve any doubt which it may have, as to whether the costs were reasonably incurred or were reasonable and proportionate in amount, in favour of the paying party.

VII.2.10 The court or taxing authority carrying out the assessment should have regard to all the circumstances in deciding whether costs were proportionately or reasonably incurred or proportionate and reasonable in amount. Effect must be given to any orders for costs which have already been made. The court or the taxing authority should also have regard to:

(a) the conduct of all the parties, including in particular conduct before as well as during the proceedings;

(b) the amount or value of any property involved;

(c) the importance of the matter to all the parties;

(d) the particular complexity of the matter or the difficulty or novelty of the questions raised;

(e) the skill, effort, specialised knowledge and responsibility involved;

(f) the time spent on the case; and

(g) the place where and the circumstances in which work or any part of it was done.

VII.2.11 In applying the test of proportionality regard should be had to the objective of dealing with cases justly. Dealing with a case justly includes, so far as practicable, dealing with it in ways which are proportionate to:

(i) the amount of money involved;

(ii) the importance of the case;

(iii) the complexity of the issues; and

(iv) the financial position of each party.

The relationship between the total of the costs incurred and the financial value of the claim may not be a reliable guide.

VII.2.12 In any proceedings there will be costs which will inevitably be incurred and which are necessary for the successful conduct of the case. Solicitors are not required to conduct litigation at rates which are uneconomic, thus in a modest claim the proportion of costs is likely to be higher than in a large claim and may even equal or possibly exceed the amount in dispute.

VII.2.13 Where a hearing takes place, the time taken by the court in dealing with a particular issue may not be an accurate guide to the amount of time properly spent by the legal or other representatives in preparing for the trial of that issue.

VII.2.14 The 2003 rules do not apply to the assessment of costs in proceedings to the extent that section 11 of the *Access to Justice Act* 1999 (costs in funded cases) applies and statutory instruments made under that Act make different provision (in this regard attention is drawn to the guidance notes issued by the senior costs judge: Costs Orders Against an LSC Funded Client and Against the LSC under section 11(1) of the *Access to Justice Act* 1999).

Remuneration of a receiver

6–114b **VII.2.15** A receiver may only charge for his services if the Crown Court so directs and specifies the basis on which the receiver is to be remunerated (*Criminal Proceure Rules* 2005, r. 60.6). The Crown Court (unless it orders otherwise) is required to award such sum as is reasonable and proportionate in all the circumstances. In arriving at the figure for remuneration the court should take into account:

(a) the time properly given by the receiver and his staff to the receivership;

(b) the complexity of the receivership;

(c) any responsibility of an exceptional kind or degree which falls on the receiver in consequence of the receivership;

(d) the effectiveness with which the receiver appears to be carrying out or to have carried out his duties; and

(e) the value and nature of the subject matter of the receivership.

VII.2.16 The Crown Court may instead of determining the receiver's remuneration itself refer it to be ascertained by the taxing authority of the Crown Court. In these circumstances

readily available, there is a possibility of conflict between the legal representatives as to the apportionment of blame, or the legal representative concerned is unable to make full representations because of a possible conflict with the duty to the client.

VIII.1.8 A wasted costs order should normally be made regardless of the fact that the client of the legal representative concerned is CDS funded. However, where the court is minded to disallow substantial costs out of the CDS fund, it may, instead of making a wasted costs order, make observations to the determining authority that work may have been unreasonably done (see paragraph X.1.1 below). This practice should only be adopted where the extent and amount of the costs wasted is not entirely clear.

VIII.2 The Administrative Court

VIII.2.1 In the Administrative Court where the court is considering whether to make an order under section 51(6) of the *Supreme Court Act* 1981 (a wasted costs order) it will do so in accordance with *CPR* 48.7 which contains similar provisions as to giving the legal representative a reasonable opportunity to attend a hearing to give reasons why the court should not make such an order. In addition to the power to make a wasted costs order, the Administrative Court has powers in relation to misconduct under *CPR* 44.14 which enable the court to make an order against a party or his legal representative where it appears to the court that the conduct of a party or his legal representative before or during the proceedings which gave rise to the summary or detailed assessment proceedings was unreasonable or improper.

PART IX: AWARDS OF COSTS AGAINST SOLICITORS UNDER THE COURT'S INHERENT JURISDICTION

IX.1.1 In addition to the power under regulation 3 of the General Regulations to order that costs improperly incurred be paid by a party to the proceedings and the power to make wasted costs orders under section 19A of the Act, the Supreme Court (which includes the Crown Court) may, in the exercise of its inherent jurisdiction over officers of the court, order a solicitor personally to pay costs thrown away by reason of a serious dereliction on the part of the solicitor of his duty to the court. **6–114f**

IX.1.2 No such order may be made unless reasonable notice has been given to the solicitor of the matter alleged against him and he is given a reasonable opportunity of being heard in reply.

IX.1.3 This power should be used only in exceptional circumstances not covered by the statutory powers.

PART X: CDS FUNDED COSTS

X.1.1 Where it appears to any judge of the Crown Court or the Court of Appeal criminal division, sitting in proceedings for which CDS funding has been granted, that work may have been unreasonably done, *e.g.*, if the CDS funded person's case may have been conducted unreasonably so as to incur unjustifiable expense, or costs may have been wasted by failure to conduct the proceedings with reasonable competence or expedition, the judge may make observations to the that effect for the attention of the appropriate authority. The judge or the court, as the case may be, should specify as precisely as possible the item, or items, which the determining officer should consider or investigate on the determination of the costs payable pursuant to the representation order. The precise terms of the observations must be entered in the court record. **6–114g**

X.1.2 This power co-exists with the power to disallow fees when making a wasted costs order. The *Criminal Defence Service (Funding) Order* 2001 allows the determining officer to disallow the amount of the order from the amount otherwise payable to solicitors and counsel and allows for deduction of a greater amount if appropriate (Sched. 1, para. 16 to the funding order).

X.1.3 In the Crown Court, in proceedings specified in paragraph 1 of Part II of Schedule 1 [*sic*] [the reference should be to Schedule 2] of [*sic*] the *Criminal Defence Service (Funding) Order* 2001, where standard fees would otherwise be payable, where the trial judge is dissatisfied with the solicitor's conduct of the case or he considers that for exceptional reasons, the fees should be determined by the appropriate authority, he may direct that such determination shall take place.

X.1.4 Where the judge or the court has in mind that observations under paragraph X.1.1 or that a direction under paragraph X.1.3 should be made, the solicitor or counsel whose fees or expenses might be affected must be informed of the precise terms thereof and of his right to make representations to the appropriate authority and be given a reasonable opportunity to show cause why the observations or direction should not be made.

X.1.5 Where such observations or directions are made the appropriate authority must afford an opportunity to the solicitor or counsel whose fees might be affected to make representations in relation to them.

X.1.6 Whether or not observations under paragraph X.1.1 have been made the appropriate authority may consult the judge or the court on any matter touching the allowance or disallowance of fees and expenses, but if the observations then made are to the effect mentioned in paragraph X.1.1, the appropriate authority should afford an opportunity to the solicitor or counsel concerned to make representations in relation to them.

X.2 Very high cost cases

X.2.1 In proceedings which are classified as a very high cost case (vhcc) as defined by regulation 2 of the *Criminal Defence Service (General) Regulations* 2001, the judge or court should, at the earliest opportunity, ask the representative of the LSC funded person whether they have notified the LSC of the case in accordance with regulation 23. If they have not they should be warned that they may not be able to recover their costs. Further, if the vhcc is one of fraud or serious financial impropriety, the judge or court should inform the representatives that the case can only be conducted by a firm who is a member of the specialist fraud panel and non-panel firms and advocates instructed by such firms may not be able to recover their costs.

PART XI: RECOVERY OF DEFENCE COSTS ORDERS

6–114h **XI.1.1** Recovery of defence costs orders (RDCOs) are created and regulated by the *Criminal Defence Service (Recovery of Defence Costs Orders) Regulations* 2001 (as amended) made under section 17 of the *Access to Justice Act* 1999.

XI.1.2 Where an individual receives representation in respect of criminal proceedings funded as part of the Criminal Defence Service, the court before which the proceedings are heard, other than a magistrates' court, must make an order requiring him to pay some or all of the costs of any representation, except for the following:

- an RDCO may not be made against a funded defendant who has appeared in the [*sic*] magistrates' court only;
- where a funded defendant is committed for sentence to the Crown Court;
- where a funded defendant is appealing against sentence to the Crown Court; or
- where a funded defendant has been acquitted, other than in exceptional circumstances (*Criminal Defence Service (Recovery of Defence Costs Orders) Regulations* 2001, reg. 4).

XI.1.3 An RDCO may be made up to the maximum of the full costs of the representation in any court under the representation order and may provide for the payment to be made forthwith or in specified instalments (*ibid.*, reg. 5). This includes the cost of representation in the magistrates' court.

XI.1.4 Subject to the exceptions set out above, the judge must make an RDCO (*ibid.*, reg. 11).

XI.1.5 Where a funded defendant has been acquitted the judge must consider whether it is reasonable in all the circumstances to make such an order.

XI.1.6 Where a person of modest means properly brings an appeal against conviction, it should be borne in mind that it will not usually be desirable or appropriate for the court to make an RDCO for a significant amount, if to do so would inhibit an appellant from bringing an appeal. (There is no power to make an RDCO in an appeal against sentence.)

XI.1.7 The judge should consider the amount or value of every source of income and capital available to the defendant and the funded defendant's partner. Other than in exceptional circumstances, the judge shall not take into account:

- the first £3,000 of available capital,
- the first £100,000 of equity in the principal residence, or
- his income where his gross annual income is less than £25,000 (*ibid.*, reg. 9 as amended by *CDS (RDCO) (Amendment) Regulations* 2003).

These limits are prescribed and are subject to annual amendments by regulation change to the *CDS (RDCO) Regulations*.

XI.1.8 The judge may ask the defendant's solicitor to provide an estimate of the total costs which are likely to be incurred under the representation order. It should be borne in mind that whilst the solicitor may have little difficulty in producing an estimate of the costs incurred up until the point of request, this estimate may not be accurate. In a very high cost case which has been managed under contract, the solicitor will be able to provide accurate figures of all costs incurred to date and to say what costs have been agreed as reasonable for the next stage of the case. Where an RDCO is made based on this estimate the defendant's solicitor must inform the commission if it subsequently transpires that the costs incurred were lower than the amount ordered to be paid under an RDCO. In these circumstances, where the defendant has paid the amount ordered, the balance will be repaid to him (*ibid.*, reg. 14.). An RDCO for full costs may be made at the end of the proceedings. The appropriate authority will tax the costs incurred under the representation order. The defendant will be notified of the amount of the RDCO once this figure is known.

XI.1.9 Where a representation order has been made or is being considered, the appropriate officer or the court may refer the financial resources of the funded defendant to the special investigations unit (SIU) at the Legal Services Commission for a report, where:

- the defendant is being prosecuted by Customs and Excise, Serious Fraud Office, the Department of Trade and Industry or Inland Revenue;
- the information that the defendant supplies suggests that he has sufficient means to pay all of the costs incurred in his defence; or
- there is some other information that suggests that the defendant has more resources than he has disclosed; for example the type of charge he faces or his reputation.

The special investigations unit will produce a report for the judge to consider at the end of the case in the same way that the court will provide the judge with a summary of the defendant's means. This report is made to support the role of the court, and is not an application for costs.

XI.1.10 During the proceedings, the judge may refer the matter to the Legal Services Commission/special investigations unit for investigation where further information has come to light which had previously not been disclosed by the defendant to the court. The special investigations unit may investigate the financial resources of the funded defendant and require him to provide further information or evidence as required.

XI.1.11 At the end of the case where the judge is considering what order to make, he may make the order or, if further information is required, adjourn the making of the order and order that any further information which is required should be provided (*ibid.*, reg. 12). This power may be used where further information has come to light during the case about the defendant's means. Where the defendant has failed to co-operate either with the court or the special investigations unit, the judge may order that the further information should be provided.

XI.1.12 The defendant is obliged to provide details of his means or evidence as is required by the court or the Legal Services Commission (*ibid.*, reg. 6). Arrangements are in place to ensure that a summary of the means information is available for the judge at the first hearing, or details as to whether or not the defendant has provided any information. Where the funded defendant does not provide this information, the judge may order him to do so.

XI.1.13 Where information required under the regulations is not provided the judge must make an RDCO for the full cost of the representation incurred under the representation order (*ibid.*, reg. 13).

XI.1.14 Where it appears to the judge that the funded defendant has:

- directly or indirectly transferred any resources to another person;
- another person is or has been maintaining him in any proceedings;
- or any of the resources of another person are or have been made available to him,

the value of the resources of that other person may be assessed or estimated and may be treated as those of the funded defendant. In this context "person" includes a company, partnership, body of trustees and any body of persons, whether corporate or not corporate (*ibid.*, reg. 8).

XI.1.15 The judge may make an order prohibiting any individual who is required to furnish information or evidence from dealing with property where:

- information has failed to be provided in accordance with the regulations;
- he considers that there is a real risk that relevant property will be disposed of; or
- at the conclusion of the case, the assessment of costs incurred under the representation order or of the financial resources of the defendant has not yet been completed (*ibid.*, reg. 15).

PART XII: ADVICE ON APPEAL TO THE COURT OF APPEAL CRIMINAL DIVISION

XII.1.1 In all cases the procedure set out in "A Guide to Proceedings in the Court of Appeal Criminal Division" published by the Criminal Appeal Office with the approval of the Lord Chief Justice in 1997 should be followed. The reference to "Appendix 1" which follows is to the appendix to that guide. **6–114i**

XII.1.2 This procedure requires written advice to be delivered to the defendant within 21 days of conviction or sentence. In simple cases this will involve little or no expense. If the procedure is not followed and the work has not been done with due care, fees may be reduced accordingly. The advocate will have received instructions in the form of Appendix 1 from the defendant solicitor [*sic*] which will specifically refer to the guide. The advocate is required to complete Appendix 1 immediately following the conclusion of the case and the solicitor should give a copy to the defendant at that stage. Where the advocate's immediate and final view is that there are no reasonable grounds of appeal, no additional fee will normally be allowed. In any other circumstances the advocate must further advise in writing within 14 days and where it was reasonable for the advocate so to advise an allowance will be made for the advice.

XII.1.3 When both (a) the advocate or the solicitor has given positive advice to appeal; and (b) notice of application for leave to appeal or notice of appeal has been lodged with the Crown Court on the strength of that advice, the Registrar of Criminal Appeals is the appropriate authority to determine the fees in respect of the work in connection with the advice and notice of application, *etc*. The Crown Court should not determine those fees unless the solicitor confirms that the notice of application, *etc*., was not given on the solicitors' [*sic*] or the advocates' [*sic*] advice. Where no notice of application is given, either because of unfavourable advice or despite favourable advice, the appropriate authority is the appropriate officer for the Crown Court.

XII.1.4 If it appears that the defendant was never given advice, the Crown Court should direct the solicitors' [*sic*] attention to this fact and if there is no satisfactory explanation as to why no advice was sent, the determining officer should bear this in mind when determining the solicitor's costs and should draw the solicitor's attention to the above mentioned guide of 1997.

PART XIII: APPEALS TO A COSTS JUDGE AND TO THE HIGH COURT PURSUANT TO THE COSTS IN CRIMINAL CASES (GENERAL) REGULATIONS 1986, THE LEGAL AID IN CRIMINAL AND CARE PROCEEDINGS (COSTS) REGULATIONS 1989, THE CROWN COURT RULES 1982 AND THE CRIMINAL DEFENCE SERVICE (FUNDING) ORDER 2001

6–114j **XIII.1.1** Solicitors and counsel dissatisfied with the determination of costs under the above regulations may apply to the appropriate authority for a review of the determination. Appeal against a decision on such a review is made to a costs judge of the Supreme Court Costs Office. Written notice of appeal must be given to a costs judge within 21 days of receipt of the reasons given for the decision (14 days in the case of appeals under rules 78.5 and 78.7 of the *Criminal Procedure Rules*) or within such longer time as the costs judge may direct.

XIII.1.2 The notice of appeal should be in Form A set out in Schedule 3 (adapted where appropriate) setting out in separate numbered paragraphs each fee or item of costs or disbursement in respect of which the appeal is brought, showing the amount claimed for the item, the amount determined and the grounds of objection to the decision on the assessment or determination. Counsel and solicitors must provide detailed grounds of objection in respect of each item in accordance with regulation 10(2) of the General Regulations 1986, regulation 15(5) of the *Legal Aid in Criminal and Care Proceedings (Costs) Regulations* 1989, rule 78.5(1) of the *Criminal Procedure Rules* 2005 and paragraph 21(5)(b) of the *Criminal Defence Service (Funding) Order* 2001 [*sic*]. Reference to accompanying correspondence or documents is insufficient and will result in the appeal being dismissed.

XIII.1.3 The appeal must be accompanied by a cheque for the appropriate fee made payable to "H.M. Paymaster General". The notice must state whether the appellant wishes to appear or to be represented, or whether he will accept a decision given in his absence. The following documents should be forwarded with the notice of appeal:

(a) a legible copy of the bill of costs (with any supporting submissions) showing the allowance made;

(b) advocate's fee claimed, fee note, together with any note or memorandum by counsel submitted to the determining authority;

(c) a copy of the original determination of costs and a copy of the redetermination;

(d) a copy of the appellant's representations made to the determining authority on seeking redetermination;

(e) the written reasons of the determining officer;

(f) a copy of the representation order and any authorities given under regulation 54 of the *Legal Aid in Criminal and Care Proceedings (General) Regulations* 1989, or the representation order under section 26 of the *Access to Justice Act* 1999 and article 3(1) of the *Criminal Defence Service (Funding) Order* 2001.

XIII.2 Supporting papers

XIII.2.1 Appellants who do not intend to appear at the hearing of their appeal should lodge all relevant supporting papers with the documents listed above. Appellants who do wish to attend the hearing of their appeal should not lodge their supporting papers until directed to do so by the Supreme Court Costs Office. **6–114k**

XIII.2.2 Appellants are reminded that it is their responsibility to procure the lodgment of the relevant papers, even if they are in the possession of the Crown Court or other persons. Appeals may be listed for dismissal if the relevant papers are not lodged when required.

XIII.2.3 Delays frequently arise in dealing with appeals by counsel because the relevant papers have been returned by the court to the solicitor whose file may not be readily available or who may have destroyed the papers. These problems would be avoided if counsel's clerk were, immediately on lodging with the court a request for redetermination, to ask instructing solicitors to retain safely the relevant papers.

XIII.2.4 In complex or multi-handed appeals guidance should be sought from the clerk of appeals before lodging large volumes of papers to avoid duplication and unnecessary reading by the costs judge.

XIII.3 Time limits

XIII.3.1 Appellants who are likely to be unable to lodge an appeal within the time limits should make an application prior to the expiry of the time limit seeking a reasonable extension with brief reasons for the request. **6–114l**

XIII.3.2 Appellants who have not been able to lodge an appeal within the time limits, and who have failed to make application before those time limits have expired, should make application to the costs judge for leave to appeal out of time in writing setting out in full the circumstances relied upon. If the application is refused on the papers it can be renewed to a costs judge at an oral hearing. Such oral hearings should not be necessary if a full explanation is given in writing in the initial request for extension of time. Appeals should not be delayed because certain relevant documents are not available, an accompanying note setting out the missing documents and undertaking to lodge within a specified period, normally not exceeding 28 days, should be sent with the notice of appeal.

XIII.4 Appeals to the High Court

XIII.4.1 An appellant desiring to appeal to a judge from a decision of the costs judge should, within 21 days of the costs judge's decision, request him to certify that a point of principle of general importance (specifying the same) is involved. The appeal can proceed only if such a certificate is granted. Such an appeal is instituted by claim form under *CPR*, Part 8 in the Queen's Bench Division within 21 days of the receipt of the costs judge's certificate. The times may be extended by a costs judge or the High Court as the case may be. **6–115**

XIII.4.2 The claim form by which an appeal is to be instituted must contain full particulars of the item or items, or the amount allowed in respect of which the appeal is brought. After issue of the claim form the appellant must forthwith lodge with the clerk of appeals at the Supreme Court Costs Office, all the documents used on the appeal to the costs judge.

XIII.4.3 The claim form is to be served in accordance with the provisions of *CPR*, Part 6 and the practice direction thereto. It is no longer necessary to endorse an estimate of the length of hearing on the claim form, the clerk to the senior costs judge will obtain from the judge a date for hearing and will notify the parties.

XIII.4.4 The appeal, which is final, will be heard by a judge of the Queen's Bench Division who will normally sit with two assessors, one of whom will be a costs judge and the other a practising solicitor or barrister.

XIII.4.5 After the appeal has been heard and determined the clerk will obtain the documents together with a sealed copy of any order of the judge which may have been drawn up and will notify the court concerned of the result of the appeal.

Parts XIV (VAT) (since amended by *Practice Direction (Criminal Proceedings: Costs)* [2008] 1 W.L.R. 152) and XV (revocations) and the schedules are not set out in this work. **6–116**

For the *Costs in Criminal Cases (General) Regulations* 1986 (S.I. 1986 No. 1335), referred to in paragraph I.2.1, see *ante*, §§ 6–52 *et seq*. For section 34(5) of the *Mental Health (Amendment) Act* 1982, referred to in paragraph IV.2, see *ante*, § 6–94. For the *Criminal Procedure Rules* 2005 (S.I. 2005 No. 384), Pts 57 to 61 and 78, referred to in paragraph VII.2.1 *et seq*., see *ante*, §§ 5–671 *et seq*. and §§ 6–88 *et seq*. For section 89(8) of the *PCA* 2002, referred to in paragraph VIII.1.1, see *ante*, § 5–650. For the *Criminal Defence Service (Funding) Order* 2001 (S.I. 2001 No. 855), referred to in paragraph X.1.2, see *post*, §§ 6–191 *et seq*. For the *Criminal Defence Service (General) (No. 2) Regulations* 2001 (S.I. 2001 No. 1437), referred to by the wrong title in paragraph X.2.1, see *post*, §§ 6–152 *et seq*. For the *Criminal Defence Service (Recovery of Defence Costs Orders) Regulations* 2001 (S.I. 2001 No. 1856), referred to in paragraph XI.1.1, see *post*, §§ 6–266 *et seq*. For the 2008 version of the *Guide to Commencing Proceedings in the Court of Appeal (Criminal Division)*, referred to in paragraph XII.1.1, see Appendix J.

F. ENFORCING ORDERS AS TO COSTS (AND COMPENSATION)

(1) Statute

Powers of Criminal Courts (Sentencing) Act 2000, ss.141, 142

Power of Crown Court to allow time for payment, or payment by instalments, of costs and compensation

6–117 **141.** Where the Crown Court makes any such order as is mentioned in Part I of Schedule 9 to the *Administration of Justice Act* 1970 (orders against accused for the payment of costs or compensation), the court may—

(a) allow time for the payment of the sum due under the order;

(b) direct payment of that sum by instalments of such amounts and on such dates as the court may specify.

Power of Crown Court to order search of persons before it

6–118 **142.**—(1) Where—

(a) the Crown Court imposes a fine on a person or forfeits his recognizance,

(b) the Crown Court makes against a person any such order as is mentioned in paragraph 3, 4 or 9 of Schedule 9 to the *Administration of Justice Act* 1970 (orders for the payment of costs),

(c) the Crown Court makes a compensation order against a person,

(d) the Crown Court makes against a person an order under section 137 above (order for parent or guardian to pay fine, costs or compensation), or

(e) on the determination of an appeal brought by a person under section 108 of the *Magistrates' Courts Act* 1980 a sum is payable by him, whether by virtue of an order of the Crown Court or by virtue of a conviction or order of the magistrates' court against whose decision the appeal was brought,

then, if that person is before it, the Crown Court may order him to be searched.

(2) Any money found on a person in a search under this section may be applied, unless the court otherwise directs, towards payment of the fine or other sum payable by him; and the balance, if any, shall be returned to him.

It is the duty of a prisoner custody officer acting in pursuance of prisoner escort arrangements who is on any premises in which the Crown Court is sitting to give effect to any order of that court under section 34A: *CJA* 1991, s.82(4). Where necessary, he may use reasonable force to perform that duty: *ibid*. s.82(5).

Administration of Justice Act 1970, s.41

6–119 **41.**—(1) In the cases specified in Part I of Schedule 9 to this Act (being cases where, in criminal proceedings, a court makes an order against the accused for the payment of costs, compensation, etc.) any sum required to be paid by such an order as is there mentioned shall be treated, for the purposes of collection and enforcement, as if it had been adjudged to be paid on a conviction by a magistrates' court, being—

(a) where the order is made by a magistrates' court, that court; and

(b) in any other case, such magistrates' court as may be specified in the order.

(2) In the cases specified in Part II of the said Schedule (being cases where a court makes an order against the prosecutor in criminal proceedings, and certain cases where an order for costs arises out of an appeal to the Crown Court in proceedings which are not

criminal) any sum required to be paid by such an order as is there mentioned shall be enforceable as if the order were for the payment of money recoverable summarily as a civil debt.

(3) Without prejudice to the foregoing subsections, but subject to subsection (4) below, in the cases specified in Schedule 9 to this Act any sum required to be paid by such an order as is there mentioned shall be enforceable by the High Court or a county court (otherwise than by issue of a writ of *fieri facias* or other process against goods or by imprisonment or attachment of earnings) as if the sum were due in pursuance of a judgment or order of the High Court or county court as the case may be.

(4), (4A) [*Repealed by* High Court and County Courts Jurisdiction Order *1991 (S.I. 1991 No. 724).*]

(5) [*Transitional provisions.*]

(6) [*Repealed by* Magistrates' Courts Act *1980.*]

(7) [*Amends* Courts- Martial (Appeals) Act *1968 , s.32(2).*]

(8) Subject to subsection (8A) below, where in the case specified in paragraph 10 of Schedule 9 to this Act the Crown Court thinks that the period for which the person subject to the order is liable apart from this subsection to be committed to prison for default under the order is insufficient, it may specify a longer period for that purpose; and then, in the case of default— **6–120**

(a) the specified period shall be substituted as the maximum for which the person may be imprisoned under section 76 of the *Magistrates' Courts Act* 1980; and

(b) paragraph 2 of Schedule 4 to that Act shall apply, with any necessary modifications, for the reduction of the specified period where, at the time of the person's imprisonment, he has made part payment under the order.

(8A) The Crown Court may not specify under subsection (8) above a period of imprisonment longer than that which it could order a person to undergo on imposing on him a fine equal in amount to the sum required to be paid by the order.

(9) Where a magistrates' court has power to commit a person to prison for default in paying a sum due under an order enforceable as mentioned in this section, the court shall not exercise the power unless it is satisfied that all other methods of enforcing payment have been tried or considered and either have proved unsuccessful or are likely to do so.

[This section is printed as amended or repealed in part by the *CLA* 1977, Sched. 13; the *MCA* 1980, Scheds 7 and 9; the *County Courts Act* 1984, Sched. 2; the *CJA* 1988, s.106; and the *High Court and County Courts Jurisdiction Order* 1991 (S.I. 1991 No. 724).]

Administration of Justice Act 1970, Sched. 9

SCHEDULE 9

PART I

Cases where Payment Enforceable as on Summary Conviction

Costs awarded by magistrates

1. Where a magistrates' court, on the summary trial of an information, makes an order as to costs to be paid by the accused to the prosecutor. **6–121**

1A. Where a magistrates' court makes an order as to costs to be paid by the accused in exercise of any power in that behalf conferred by regulations made under section 19(1) of the *Prosecution Offences Act* 1985.

2. Where an appellant to the Crown Court against conviction or sentence by a magistrates' court abandons his appeal and the magistrates' court orders him to pay costs to the other party to the appeal.

Costs awarded by the Crown Court

3. Where a person appeals to the Crown Court against conviction or sentence by a magistrates' court, and the Crown Court makes an order as to costs to be paid by him.

4. Where a person is prosecuted or tried on indictment before the Crown Court and is convicted, and the court makes an order as to costs to be paid by him.

4A. Where the Crown Court makes an order as to costs to be paid by the accused in exercise of any power in that behalf conferred by regulations made under section 19(1) of the *Prosecution of Offences Act* 1985.

5. [*Repealed by* Costs in Criminal Cases Act *1973, Sched. 1.*]

Costs awarded by the Court of Appeal (criminal division) or House of Lords

6–122 6. Where the criminal division of the Court of Appeal makes an order as to costs to be paid by—

(a) an appellant;

(b) an applicant for leave to appeal to that court; or

(c) in the case of an application for leave to appeal to the *House of Lords* [Supreme Court], an applicant who was the appellant before the criminal division.

7. [*Repealed by* Prosecution of Offences Act *1985, Sched. 1.*]

8. [*Repealed by* Courts Act *1971, Sched. 11, Pt IV.*]

Miscellaneous orders for costs, compensation, etc.

6–123 9. Where a court makes an order by virtue of regulations made under section 19(5) of the *Prosecution of Offences Act* 1985 for the payment of costs by an offender.

9A. [*Repealed, see* Criminal Justice Act *1972, Sched. 6 and* Powers of Criminal Courts Act *1973, Sched. 5.*]

10. Where under section 130 of the *Powers of Criminal Courts (Sentencing) Act* 2000 a court orders the payment of compensation.

11. [*Repealed, see entry against paragraph 9A,* ante.]

12. Where under section 137 of the *Powers of Criminal Courts (Sentencing) Act* 2000 a court orders any fine ... compensation or costs, or any sum awarded by way of satisfaction or compensation to be paid by the parent or guardian of a child or young person.

13. Where under section 161A of the *Criminal Justice Act* 2003 a court orders the payment of a surcharge.

PART II

Cases where Costs Enforceable Summarily as Civil Debt

Costs awarded by magistrates

6–124 13. Where a magistrates' court makes an order as to costs to be paid by the prosecutor in exercise of any power in that behalf conferred by regulations made under section 19(1) of the *Prosecution of Offences Act* 1985.

14. Where an appellant to the Crown Court from a magistrates' court (otherwise than against conviction or sentence) abandons his appeal and the magistrates' court orders him to pay costs to the other party to the appeal.

15. [*Repealed by* Prosecution of Offences Act *1985, Sched. 1.*]

Costs awarded by the Crown Court

16. Any order for the payment of costs made by the Crown Court, other than an order falling within Part I above, or an order for costs to be paid out of money provided by Parliament.

Costs awarded by the Court of Appeal (criminal division)

16A. Where the criminal division of the Court of Appeal makes an order as to costs to be paid by the respondent or, in the case of an application for leave to appeal to the *House of Lords* [Supreme Court], an applicant who was the respondent before the criminal division, and does so in exercise of any power in that behalf conferred by regulations made under section 19(1) of the *Prosecution of Offences Act* 1985.

21. [*Repealed by* Courts Act *1971, Sched. 11, Pt IV.*]

[Schedule 9 is printed as amended or repealed in part by the *Courts Act* 1971, s.56(1) and Sched. 8, para. 60 (which, *inter alia*, substituted para. 16 for the original paras 16– 20) and s.56(4) and Sched. 11; the *CJA* 1972, Sched. 6; the *Costs in Criminal Cases Act* 1973, Sched. 1; the *PCCA* 1973, Sched. 5; the *CLA* 1977, Sched. 13; the *Prosecution of Offences Act* 1985, Scheds 1 and 2 (which, *inter alia*, inserted new paras 1A, 4A and 16A and substituted new paras 6 and 13); the *PCC(S)A* 2000, s.165(1), and Sched. 9, para. 43; and the *Domestic Violence, Crime and Victims Act* 2004, s.14(3); and as amended, as from a day to be appointed, by the *Constitutional Reform Act*

2005, s.40(4), and Sched. 9, para. 22 (substitution of references to "Supreme Court" for references to "House of Lords").]

Magistrates' Courts Act 1980, s.76

Enforcement of sums adjudged to be paid

76.—(1) Subject to the following provisions of this Part of this Act, and to section 132 below …, where default is made in paying a sum adjudged to be paid by a conviction or order of a magistrates' court, the court may issue a warrant of *distress* [control] for the purpose of *levying* [recovering] the sum or issue a warrant committing the defaulter to prison. **6–125**

(2) A warrant of commitment may be issued as aforesaid either—

(a) where it appears on the return to a warrant of *distress* [control] that the money and goods of the defaulter are insufficient to *satisfy the sum with the costs and charges of levying the sum* [pay the amount outstanding, as defined by paragraph 50(3) of Schedule 12 to the *Tribunals, Courts and Enforcement Act* 2007]; or

(b) instead of a warrant of *distress* [control].

(3) The period for which a person may be committed to prison under such a warrant as aforesaid shall not, subject to the provisions of any enactment passed after 31st December 1879, exceed the period applicable to the case under Schedule 4 to this Act.

(4)–(6) [*Not printed.*]

[This section is printed as repealed in part by the *CJA* 1982, s.78 and Sched. 16. In subss. (1) and (2), the words in square brackets are substituted for the italicised words, as from a day to be appointed, by the *Tribunals, Courts and Enforcement Act* 2007, s.62(3), Sched. 13, para. 46.]

Magistrates' Courts Act 1980, Sched. 4

SCHEDULE 4

MAXIMUM PERIODS OF IMPRISONMENT IN DEFAULT OF PAYMENT

1. Subject to the following provisions of this Schedule, the periods set out in the second column of the following Table shall be the maximum periods applicable respectively to the amounts set out opposite thereto, being amounts due at the time the imprisonment or detention is imposed. **6–126**

An amount not exceeding £200	7 days
An amount exceeding £200 but not exceeding £500	14 days
An amount exceeding £500 but not exceeding £1,000	28 days
An amount exceeding £1,000 but not exceeding £2,500	45 days
An amount exceeding £2,500 but not exceeding £5,000	3 months
An amount exceeding £5,000 but not exceeding £10,000	6 months
An amount exceeding £10,000	12 months

2.—(1) Where the amount due at the time imprisonment or detention is imposed is so much of a sum adjudged to be paid by a summary conviction as remains due after part payment, then, subject to sub-paragraph (2) below, the maximum period applicable to the amount shall be the period applicable to the whole sum reduced by such number of days as bears to the total number of days therein the same proportion as the part paid bears to the whole sum.

(2) In calculating the reduction required under sub-paragraph (1) above, any fraction of a day shall be left out of account and the maximum period shall not be reduced to less than seven days.

[Paragraph 2(2) is printed as amended by the *CJA* 1991, Sched. 11, para. 28.]

(2) Summary of provisions

The following summary of the relevant provisions is based upon the judgment of the Court of Appeal in *R. v. Bunce*, 66 Cr.App.R. 109. It takes account, however, of the provisions of the new subsections (8) and (8A) of section 41 (*ante*, § 6–120) introduced by the *CJA* 1988, s.106. **6–127**

1. The Crown Court may allow, in respect of orders for costs or compensation, time for payment or payment by instalments (see s.141 of the *PCC(S)A* 2000). Magistrates have a like power (see s.75 of the *MCA* 1980).

2. An order for costs or compensation made by the Crown Court is enforceable as a sum adjudged to be paid on conviction by a magistrates' court (*Administration of Justice Act* 1970, s.41(1) and Sched. 9).

3. In the case of a compensation order, if the Crown Court thinks that the period of imprisonment for which the person subject to the order is liable in default of payment is insufficient, it may specify a longer period, but the longer period may not exceed the period of imprisonment which it could order a person to undergo in default of paying a fine equal in amount to the amount of the compensation order. This power is only of practical significance where compensation in excess of £20,000 is ordered. In such cases, the normal maximum alternative of 12 months' imprisonment may be increased in accordance with the table in section 139(4) of the *PCC(S)A* 2000 (*ante*, § 5–396). If an increased period is specified, then that period is treated as the maximum for which the defaulter may be imprisoned under section 76 of the *MCA* 1980 (see s.41(8) of the 1970 Act).

6–128 4. Default: (a) on default the court may issue (i) a warrant of distress or (ii) a warrant committing the defaulter to prison. A warrant of commitment may be issued where it appears on the return to a warrant of distress that the property of the defaulter is insufficient to satisfy the sum due and the charges of levying the sum or instead of a warrant of distress (s.76 of the 1980 Act).

(b) The minimum period of imprisonment is five days (s.132 of the 1980 Act). There is no power to imprison persons under 21 years of age, but, for those aged 18 to 20 years, detention is substituted for imprisonment: see section 108(1) of the *PCC(S)A* 2000, *ante*, § 5–946. As from a day to be appointed the minimum age for imprisonment is reduced to 18, and section 108 of the 2000 Act is repealed: *CJCSA* 2000, ss.74 and 75, and Scheds 7, para. 180, and 8.

(c) For the maximum periods of imprisonment in default, see Schedule 4 to the *MCA* 1980 (*ante*, § 6–126). The only circumstance in which a Crown Court judge is required to say anything about serving a period of imprisonment in default is if under section 41(8) he wishes to extend for the purposes of the case in question the period of time under the *MCA* 1980 which would otherwise be the maximum for committal for failure to pay: *R. v. O'Donoghue and Dallas-Cope*, 66 Cr.App.R. 116, CA.

II. CRIMINAL DEFENCE SERVICE

A. INTRODUCTION

Right to legal representation

6–129 As to the right to legal representation generally, see *ante*, § 4–41, and *post*, §§ 16–86 *et seq*. As to a defendant's right to conduct his own defence, see *ante*, § 4–42. As to an alleged wrongful denial of legal representation as a ground of appeal, see *post*, § 7–86. As to the alleged incompetence or misconduct of the defendant's legal representatives as a ground of appeal, see *post*, § 7–82.

Replacement of "legal aid"

6–130 The *Legal Aid Act* 1988, the Legal Aid Board and "legal aid" were replaced by the *Access to Justice Act* 1999, the Legal Services Commission and, in the case of criminal proceedings, a "right to representation" funded by the Criminal Defence Service, to be established, maintained and developed by the Legal Services Commission. The effect of the *Access to Justice Act 1999 (Commencement No. 3, Transitional Provisions and Savings) Order* 2000 (S.I. 2000 No. 774) was to bring into force, *inter alia*, section 1 of the 1999 Act, which established the Legal Services Commission, on April 1, 2000. Schedule 14, para. 2, to the 1999 Act provides for the transfer from the Legal Aid Board to the Legal Services Commission of all its functions, property, rights and liabilities, such transfer to take effect on the commencement of section 1. Schedule 14, para. 3(3), provides for references in any enactment to the Legal Aid Board to be construed as references to the Legal Services Commission.

Article 5(1)(b) of S.I. 2000 No. 774 stipulates that nothing in the provisions commenced by the order was to take effect in relation to representation, advice and assistance by way of representation under any part of the 1988 Act relating to actual or contemplated criminal investigations or proceedings. Article 1(2) gave "criminal proceedings" a broad definition. The combined effect of this order and the transitional and saving provisions of Schedule 14 to the 1999 Act was, therefore, that the *Legal Aid Act* 1988 and the regulations made thereunder continued to apply to criminal proceedings, but with the functions of the Legal Aid Board being transferred to the Legal Services Commission and with various words and expressions in the regulations being substituted by different words and expressions (see article 5(2) of S.I. 2000 No. 774).

The *Access to Justice Act 1999 (Commencement No. 7, Transitional Provisions and Savings) Order* 2001 (S.I. 2001 No. 916) brought into force on April 2, 2001, sections 12 to 18 and 24 and Schedules 3 and 4 (to the extent that they were not already in force), together with the repeals and revocations in Part I of Schedule 15. It is sections 12 to 18, together with Schedule 3, that make provision for funded representation in criminal proceedings. They are set out *in extenso*, *post*, §§ 6–135 *et seq.*

Transitional provisions and savings

The repeal of the 1988 legislation was subject to important transitional provisions (*post*, § 6–131). For those needing to refer to the 1988 Act and the regulations made thereunder reference should be made to the 2001 edition of the work and to the supplements to both the 2001 and 2002 editions for details of further amendments to the two principal sets of regulations, namely the *Legal Aid in Criminal and Care Proceedings (General) Regulations* 1989 (S.I. 1989 No. 344), and the *Legal Aid in Criminal and Care Proceedings (Costs) Regulations* 1989 (S.I. 1989 No. 343). **6–130a**

Access to Justice Act 1999 (Commencement No. 7, Transitional Provisions and Savings) Order 2001 (S.I. 2001 No. 916), art. 4 and Sched. 2

Transitional provisions and savings

4. The transitional provisions and savings in Schedules 1 and 2 to this Order have effect. **6–131**

Article 4 SCHEDULE 2

CRIMINAL DEFENCE SERVICE: TRANSITIONAL PROVISIONS AND SAVINGS

1. In this Schedule: **6–132**

"the 1988 Act" means the *Legal Aid Act* 1988;

"authorised" means authorised under regulation 15 of the *Legal Advice and Assistance Regulations* 1989 (clients resident abroad);

"the Commission" means the Legal Services Commission established under section 1 of the Act;

"funded services" means services funded by the Commission under sections 4 to 11 of the Act as part of the Community Legal Service;

"solicitor" includes a firm of solicitors.

2. Nothing in the provisions commenced by this Order or in the transitional provisions of this Order shall have effect:

(a) for the purposes of the application to funded services, by virtue of the *Community Legal Service (Funding) Orders* 2000, of the following regulations made under the 1988 Act:
  (i) the *Civil Legal Aid (General) Regulations* 1989;
  (ii) the *Legal Advice and Assistance Regulations* 1989;
  (iii) the *Legal Aid in Family Proceedings (Remuneration) Regulations* 1991; or
  (iv) the *Legal Aid in Civil Proceedings (Remuneration) Regulations* 1994

(b) subject to paragraph 4 of this Schedule, and to the provisions of any contract, in relation to any work carried out under a legal aid order or legal aid certificate dated prior to 2nd April 2001;

(c) in relation to assistance by way of representation under Part III of the 1988 Act:
  (i) where the application is signed prior to 2nd April 2001 and received by the Commission prior to 10th April 2001; or
  (ii) which is granted by a solicitor prior to 2nd April 2001 and notified to the Commission prior to 10th April 2001;

(d) in relation to advice and assistance under Part III of the 1988 Act (other than assistance by way of representation) where the application is signed or is authorised prior to 2nd April 2001;

(e) for the purposes of assessment for payment, where both a legal aid order under the 1988 Act and a representation order under the Act exist, in proceedings which form part of a single case in that they relate to one or more charges or informations which are preferred or laid at the same time, or which are founded on the same facts, or which form or are part of a series of offences;

(f) in relation to any work carried out before 2nd April 2001 and paid for by the Lord Chancellor other than under the terms of any contract; or

(g) for the application of paragraphs 10(3)(b), 33, 34 and 36 of Schedule 4 to the Act to work carried out under the provisions of the 1988 Act.

3. Notwithstanding the provisions of article 1(2)(a) of the *Access to Justice Act 1999 (Commencement No. 3, Transitional Provisions and Savings) Order* 2000 the Commission shall fund applications for judicial review or *habeas corpus* relating to criminal investigations or proceedings as part of the Community Legal Service.

4.—(1) Subject to the provisions of any contract, any claim for payment for work carried out under the provisions of the 1988 Act shall be submitted so as to be received by the Commission no later than five months after the completion of the work for which payment is claimed.

(2) Subject to sub-paragraph (3), the Commission may refuse any claim for payment mentioned in sub-paragraph (1) which is received late without good reason.

(3) No claim for payment shall be refused unless the solicitor has been given a reasonable opportunity to show why it should not be refused.

5. Where an application for a legal aid order under the 1988 Act is considered on or after 2nd April 2001, it shall be treated as an application for a representation order under section 14 of the Act.

B. PRIMARY LEGISLATION

Access to Justice Act 1999

6–133 Section 1 establishes the Legal Services Commission, which is to have the functions relating to the Community Legal Service and the Criminal Defence Service which are conferred on it by this or any other enactment. Section 2 authorises the Lord Chancellor to make an order establishing, in place of the Commission, two bodies, one having the functions relating to the Community Legal Service and one the functions relating to the Criminal Defence Service. Section 3 provides for the powers of the Commission.

6–134 Sections 4 to 11 contain general provisions in relation to the Community Legal Service; and sections 12 to 18 contain corresponding provisions in relation to the Criminal Defence Service. Sections 19 to 26 are supplementary provisions for the purposes of Part I of the Act. Of these, only sections 20 (restriction of disclosure of information), 22 (position of service providers and other parties, etc.) and 26 (interpretation) are set out in full here.

Access to Justice Act 1999, ss.12–18

Criminal Defence Service

6–135 **12.**—(1) The Commission shall establish, maintain and develop a service known as the Criminal Defence Service for the purpose of securing that individuals involved in criminal investigations or criminal proceedings have access to such advice, assistance and representation as the interests of justice require.

(2) In this Part "criminal proceedings" means—

(a) proceedings before any court for dealing with an individual accused of an offence,

(b) proceedings before any court for dealing with an individual convicted of an offence (including proceedings in respect of a sentence or order),

(c) proceedings for dealing with an individual under the *Extradition Act* 2003,

(d) proceedings for binding an individual over to keep the peace or to be of good behaviour under section 115 of the *Magistrates' Courts Act* 1980 and for dealing with an individual who fails to comply with an order under that section,

(e) proceedings on an appeal brought by an individual under section 44A of the *Criminal Appeal Act* 1968,

(f) proceedings for contempt committed, or alleged to have been committed, by an individual in the face of a court, and

(g) such other proceedings concerning an individual, before any such court or other body, as may be prescribed.

(3) The Commission shall fund services as part of the Criminal Defence Service in accordance with sections 13 to 15.

(4) The Commission may accredit, or authorise others to accredit, persons or bodies providing services which may be funded by the Commission as part of the Criminal Defence Service; and any system of accreditation shall include provision for the monitoring of the services provided by accredited persons and bodies and for the withdrawal of accreditation from any providing services of unsatisfactory quality.

(5) The Commission may charge—

(a) for accreditation,

(b) for monitoring the services provided by accredited persons and bodies, and

(c) for authorising accreditation by others;

and persons or bodies authorised to accredit may charge for accreditation, and for such monitoring, in accordance with the terms of their authorisation.

(6) The Lord Chancellor may by order require the Commission to discharge the functions in subsections (4) and (5) in accordance with the order.

[This section is printed as amended by the *Extradition Act* 2003, s.182.]

"criminal proceedings"

For regulations made under section 12(2)(g), see the *Criminal Defence Service (General) (No. 2) Regulations* 2001 (S.I. 2001 No. 1437), reg. 3(2), *post*, § 6–154. **6–136**

Section 19(5) of the *Legal Aid Act* 1988 defined "criminal proceedings" as including "proceedings for dealing with an offender for an offence or in respect of a sentence". In *R. v. Recorder of Liverpool, ex p. McCann*, *The Times*, May 4, 1994, DC, it was held that this definition covered an application for the removal of a driving disqualification under the *RTOA* 1988, s.42 (*post*, § 32–207). Applications under section 42(2) or 43(1) of the *DTA* 1994 (repealed and replaced by the *PCA* 2002, ss.295 and 298) for the continued detention of cash seized under section 42(1), or for the forfeiture thereof, did not fall within the definition: *R. v. Crawley JJ., ex p. Ohakwe*, *The Times*, May 26, 1994, DC; and nor did proceedings in relation to the proposed forfeiture of a surety's recognizance: *R. v. Chief Clerk of Maidstone Crown Court, ex p. Clark* [1995] 2 Cr.App.R. 617, DC.

Advice and assistance

13.—(1) The Commission shall fund such advice and assistance as it considers appropriate— **6–137**

(a) for individuals who are arrested and held in custody at a police station or other premises, and

(b) in prescribed circumstances, for individuals who—

(i) are not within paragraph (a) but are involved in investigations which may lead to criminal proceedings,

(ii) are before a court or other body in such proceedings, or

(iii) have been the subject of such proceedings;

and the assistance which the Commission may consider appropriate includes assistance in the form of advocacy.

(2) The Commission may comply with the duty imposed by subsection (1) by—

(a) entering into contracts with persons or bodies for the provision of advice or assistance by them,

(b) making payments to persons or bodies in respect of the provision of advice or assistance by them,

(c) making grants or loans to persons or bodies to enable them to provide, or facilitate the provision of, advice or assistance,

(d) establishing and maintaining bodies to provide, or facilitate the provision of, advice or assistance,

(e) making grants to individuals to enable them to obtain advice or assistance,

(f) employing persons to provide advice or assistance, or

(g) doing anything else which it considers appropriate for funding advice and assistance.

(3) The Lord Chancellor may by order require the Commission to discharge the function in subsection (2) in accordance with the order.

(4) The Commission may fund advice and assistance by different means—

(a) in different areas in England and Wales, and

(b) in relation to different descriptions of cases.

[This section is printed as amended by the *Criminal Defence Service (Advice and Assistance) Act* 2001, s.1(1).]

Representation

6–138 **14.**—(1) Schedule 3 (which makes provision about the grant of a right to representation in criminal proceedings and about the provisional grant of a right to representation in prescribed circumstances) has effect; and the Commission shall fund representation to which an individual has been granted, or provisionally granted, a right in accordance with that Schedule.

(2) Subject to the following provisions, the Commission may comply with the duty imposed by subsection (1) by—

(a) entering into contracts with persons or bodies for the provision of representation by them,

(b) making payments to persons or bodies in respect of the provision of representation by them,

(c) making grants or loans to persons or bodies to enable them to provide, or facilitate the provision of, representation,

(d) establishing and maintaining bodies to provide, or facilitate the provision of, representation,

(e) making grants to individuals to enable them to obtain representation,

(f) employing persons to provide representation, or

(g) doing anything else which it considers appropriate for funding representation.

(3) The Lord Chancellor—

(a) shall by order make provision about the payments which may be made by the Commission in respect of any representation provided by non-contracted private practitioners, and

(b) may by order make any other provision requiring the Commission to discharge the function in subsection (2) in accordance with the order.

(4) For the purposes of subsection (3)(a) representation is provided by a non-contracted private practitioner if it is provided, otherwise than pursuant to a contract entered into by the Commission, by a person or body which is neither—

(a) a person or body in receipt of grants or loans made by the Commission as part of the Criminal Defence Service, nor

(b) the Commission itself or a body established or maintained by the Commission.

(5) The provision which the Lord Chancellor is required to make by order under subsection (3)(a) includes provision for reviews of, or appeals against, determinations required for the purposes of the order.

(6) The Commission may fund representation by different means—

(a) in different areas in England and Wales, and

(b) in relation to different descriptions of cases.

[This section is printed as amended by the *CJIA* 2008, s.56(1) and (2).]

Selection of representative

6–139 **15.**—(1) An individual who has been granted, or provisionally granted, a right to representation in accordance with Schedule 3 may select any representative or representatives willing to act for him; and, where he does so, the Commission is to comply with the duty imposed by section 14(1) by funding representation by the selected representative or representatives.

(2) Regulations may provide that in prescribed circumstances—

(a) the right conferred by subsection (1) is not to apply in cases of prescribed descriptions,

(b) an individual who has been provided with advice or assistance funded by the Commission under section 13 by a person whom he chose to provide it for him is to be taken to have selected that person as his representative pursuant to that right,

(c) that right is not to include a right to select a representative of a prescribed description,

(d) that right is to select only a representative of a prescribed description,

(e) that right is to select not more than a prescribed number of representatives to act at any one time, and

(f) that right is not to include a right to select a representative in place of a representative previously selected.

(3) Regulations under subsection (2)(b) may prescribe circumstances in which an individual is to be taken to have chosen a person to provide advice or assistance for him.

(4) Regulations under subsection (2) may not provide that only a person employed by the Commission, or by a body established and maintained by the Commission, may be selected.

(5) Regulations may provide that in prescribed circumstances the Commission is not required to fund, or to continue to fund, representation for an individual by a particular representative (but such provision shall not prejudice any right of the individual to select another representative).

(6) The circumstances which may be prescribed by regulations under subsection (2) or (5) include that a determination has been made by a prescribed body or person.

[This section is printed as amended by the *CJIA* 2008, s.56(1) and (3).]

Code of conduct

16.—(1) The Commission shall prepare a code of conduct to be observed by employees of the Commission, and employees of any body established and maintained by the Commission, in the provision of services as part of the Criminal Defence Service. **6–140**

(2) The code shall include—

(a) duties to avoid discrimination,

(b) duties to protect the interests of the individuals for whom services are provided,

(c) duties to the court,

(d) duties to avoid conflicts of interest, and

(e) duties of confidentiality,

and duties on employees who are members of a professional body to comply with the rules of the body.

(3) The Commission may from time to time prepare a revised version of the code.

(4) Before preparing or revising the code the Commission shall consult the Law Society and the General Council of the Bar and such other bodies or persons as it considers appropriate.

(5) After preparing the code or a revised version of the code the Commission shall send a copy to the Lord Chancellor.

(6) If he approves it he shall lay it before each House of Parliament.

(7) The Commission shall publish—

(a) the code as first approved by the Lord Chancellor, and

(b) where he approves a revised version, either the revisions or the revised code as appropriate.

(8) The code, and any revised version of the code, shall not come into force until it has been approved by a resolution of each House of Parliament.

The first version of the code was published in 2001, and is available from the Stationery Office and on the government website (www.legalservices.gov.uk/docs/pds/PDS_Code_of_Conduct.pdf).

Terms of provision of funded services

17.—(1) An individual for whom services are funded by the Commission as part of the Criminal Defence Service shall not be required to make any payment in respect of the services except where subsection (2) applies or regulations under section 17A otherwise provide. **6–141**

(2) Where representation for an individual in respect of criminal proceedings in any court other than a magistrates' court is funded by the Commission as part of the Criminal Defence Service, the court may, subject to regulations under subsection (3), make an order requiring him to pay some or all of the cost of any representation so funded for him (in proceedings in that or any other court), except insofar as he has already been ordered under regulations under section 17A to pay that cost.

(3) Regulations may make provision about—

(a) the descriptions of individuals against whom an order under subsection (2) may be made,

(b) the circumstances in which such an order may be made and the principles to be applied in deciding whether to make such an order and the amount to be paid,

(c) the determination of the cost of representation for the purposes of the making of such an order,

(d) the furnishing of information and evidence to the court or the Commission for the purpose of enabling the court to decide whether to make such an order and (if so) the amount to be paid,

(e) prohibiting individuals who are required to furnish information or evidence from dealing with property until they have furnished the information or evidence or until a decision whether to make an order, or the amount to be paid, has been made,

(f) the person or body to which, and manner in which, payments required by such an order must be made and what that person or body is to do with them, and

(g) the enforcement of such an order (including provision for the imposition of charges in respect of unpaid amounts).

[This section is printed as amended by the *Criminal Defence Service Act* 2006, s.3(1) and (2).]

Contribution orders

6–141a **17A**—(1) Regulations may provide that, in prescribed circumstances, where—

(a) an individual has been granted a right to representation, and

(b) his financial resources are such as to make him liable under the regulations to do so,

the relevant authority shall order him to pay the cost of his representation or to make a contribution in respect of that cost of such amount as is fixed by or determined under the regulations.

(2) Regulations under subsection (1) may include—

(a) provision requiring the furnishing of information;

(b) provision for the determination of the cost of representation for the purposes of liability under a contribution order;

(c) provision enabling the relevant authority to require that an amount payable under a contribution order be paid by periodical payments or one or more capital sums, or both;

(d) provision for the payment by an individual of interest (on such terms as may be prescribed) in respect of—

(i) any payment in respect of the cost of representation required by a contribution order to be made by him later than the time when the representation is provided;

(ii) so much of any payment which he is required by a contribution order to make which remains unpaid after the time when it is required to be made;

(e) provision about the enforcement of any liability under a contribution order, including provision for the withdrawal of the individual's right to representation in certain circumstances;

(f) provision for the variation or revocation of contribution orders;

(g) provision for an appeal to lie to such court or other person or body as may be prescribed against a contribution order;

(h) such transitional provision as the Lord Chancellor may consider appropriate.

(3) Regulations under subsection (1) shall include provision for the repayment to an individual of any payment made by him in excess of his liability under a contribution order.

(4) Regulations under subsection (1) shall provide that an order made under the regulations may not order the payment of costs to the extent that they are already the subject of an order under section 17(2).

(5) [*Repealed by* CJIA *2008, ss.58(1) and (2), and 149, and Sched. 28, Pt 4*.]

(6) In this section, "contribution order" means an order under regulations under subsection (1).

[This section was inserted by the *Criminal Defence Service Act* 2006, s.3(1) and (3).]

Funding

6–142 **18.**—(1) The Lord Chancellor shall pay to the Commission such sums as are required to meet the costs of any advice, assistance and representation funded by the Commission as part of the Criminal Defence Service.

(2) The Lord Chancellor may—

(a) determine the manner in which and times at which the sums referred to in subsection (1) shall be paid to the Commission, and

(b) impose conditions on the payment of the sums.

(3) In funding services as part of the Criminal Defence Service the Commission shall aim to obtain the best possible value for money.

Pilot schemes

Section 58 of the *CJIA* 2008 provides for secondary legislation concerning the Criminal Defence Service to be made to apply for certain periods only to specified areas or localities, descriptions of court, offences or descriptions of offence or classes of person, or only to persons selected by reference to specified criteria or on a sampling basis, so as to allow for pilot schemes, by inserting a new section 18A into the 1999 Act and by amending, *inter alia*, section 17A (*ante*). **6–142a**

Access to Justice Act 1999, s.20

Restriction of disclosure of information

20.—(1) Subject to the following provisions of this section, information which is furnished— **6–143**

(a) to the Commission or any court, tribunal or other person or body on whom functions are imposed or conferred by or under this Part, and

(b) in connection with the case of an individual seeking or receiving services funded by the Commission as part of the Community Legal Service or Criminal Defence Service,

shall not be disclosed except as permitted by subsection (2).

(2) Such information may be disclosed—

(a) for the purpose of enabling or assisting the Commission to discharge any functions imposed or conferred on it by or under this Part,

(b) for the purpose of enabling or assisting the Lord Chancellor to discharge any functions imposed or conferred on him by or under this Part,

(c) for the purpose of enabling or assisting any court, tribunal or other person or body to discharge any functions imposed or conferred on it by or under this Part,

(d) except where regulations otherwise provide, for the purpose of the investigation or prosecution of any offence (or suspected offence) under the law of England and Wales or any other jurisdiction,

(e) in connection with any proceedings relating to the Community Legal Service or Criminal Defence Service, or

(f) for the purpose of facilitating the proper performance by any tribunal of disciplinary functions.

(3) Subsection (1) does not limit the disclosure of—

(a) information in the form of a summary or collection of information so framed as not to enable information relating to any individual to be ascertained from it, or

(b) information about the amount of any grant, loan or other payment made to any person or body by the Commission.

(4) Subsection (1) does not prevent the disclosure of information for any purpose with the consent of the individual in connection with whose case it was furnished and, where he did not furnish it himself, with that of the person or body who did.

(4A) Subsection (1) does not prevent the disclosure of information after the end of the restricted period, if—

(a) the disclosure is by a person who is, or is acting on behalf of a person who is, a public authority for the purposes of the *Freedom of Information Act* 2000, and

(b) the information is not held by the authority on behalf of another person.

(4B) The restricted period is the period of one hundred years starting at the end of the calendar year in which a record containing the information was first created.

(5) A person who discloses any information in contravention of this section shall be guilty of an offence and liable on summary conviction to a fine not exceeding level 4 on the standard scale.

(6) Proceedings for an offence under this section shall not be brought without the consent of the Director of Public Prosecutions.

(7) Nothing in this section applies to information furnished to a person providing services funded as part of the Community Legal Service or the Criminal Defence Service by or on behalf of an individual seeking or receiving such services.

[This section is printed as amended by the *Freedom of Information (Removal and Relaxation of Statutory Prohibitions on Disclosure of Information) Order* 2004 (S.I. 2004 No. 3363), art. 9.]

Misrepresentation

6–144 Section 21 penalises the intentional non-compliance with any requirement of Part I as to the furnishing of information, and also the furnishing of information known or believed to be false. Such offences are summary only, with a maximum penalty of three months' imprisonment (increased to 51 weeks, as from a day to be appointed, by the *CJA* 2003, s.280(2), and Sched. 26, para. 51) or a fine not exceeding level 4 on the standard scale, or both.

Access to Justice Act 1999, ss.22, 26

Position of service providers and other parties

6–145 **22.**—(1) Except as expressly provided by regulations, the fact that services provided for an individual are or could be funded by the Commission as part of the Community Legal Service or Criminal Defence Service shall not affect—

(a) the relationship between that individual and the person by whom they are provided or any privilege arising out of that relationship, or

(b) any right which that individual may have to be indemnified in respect of expenses incurred by him by any other person.

(2) A person who provides services funded by the Commission as part of the Community Legal Service or Criminal Defence Service shall not take any payment in respect of the services apart from—

(a) that made by way of that funding, and

(b) any authorised by the Commission to be taken.

(3) The withdrawal of a right to representation previously granted to an individual shall not affect the right of any person who has provided to him services funded by the Commission as part of the Criminal Defence Service to remuneration for work done before the date of the withdrawal.

(4) Except as expressly provided by regulations, any rights conferred by or by virtue of this Part on an individual for whom services are funded by the Commission as part of the Community Legal Service or Criminal Defence Service in relation to any proceedings shall not affect—

(a) the rights or liabilities of other parties to the proceedings, or

(b) the principles on which the discretion of any court or tribunal is normally exercised.

(5) Regulations may make provision about the procedure of any court or tribunal in relation to services funded by the Commission as part of the Community Legal Service or Criminal Defence Service.

(6) Regulations made under subsection (5) may in particular authorise the exercise of the functions of any court or tribunal by any member or officer of that or any other court or tribunal.

Interpretation

6–146 **26.** In this Part—

"the Commission" means the Legal Services Commission,

"the Community Legal Service Fund" has the meaning given by section 5(1),

"criminal proceedings" has the meaning given in section 12(2),

"prescribed" means prescribed by regulations and "prescribe" shall be construed accordingly,

"regulations" means regulations made by the Lord Chancellor,

"relevant authority" means any such person or body as may be prescribed, and

"representation" means representation for the purposes of proceedings and includes the assistance which is usually given by a representative in the steps preliminary or incidental to any proceedings and, subject to any time limits which may be prescribed, advice and assistance as to any appeal,

and, for the purposes of the definition of "representation", "proceedings" includes, in the context of a provisional grant of a right to representation, proceedings that may result from the investigation concerned.

[This section is printed as amended by the *Criminal Defence Service Act* 2006, s.2(1) and (6); and the *CJIA* 2008, s.56(1) and (5).]

Access to Justice Act 1999, Sched. 3

Section 14

SCHEDULE 3

CRIMINAL DEFENCE SERVICE: RIGHT TO REPRESENTATION

Individuals to whom right may be granted

1.—(1) A right to representation for the purposes of any kind of criminal proceedings before a court may be granted to an individual such as is mentioned in relation to that kind of proceedings in section 12(2). **6–147**

(2) A right to representation for the purposes of criminal proceedings may also be granted to an individual to enable him to resist an appeal to the Crown Court otherwise than in an official capacity.

(3) In this Schedule "court" includes any body before which criminal proceedings take place.

Individuals to whom right may be provisionally granted

1A.—(1) Regulations may provide that, in prescribed circumstances, and subject to any prescribed conditions, a right to representation may be provisionally granted to an individual where—

(a) the individual is involved in an investigation which may result in criminal proceedings, and

(b) the right is so granted for the purposes of criminal proceedings that may result from the investigation.

(2) Regulations under sub-paragraph (1) may, in particular, make provision about—

(a) the stage in an investigation at which a right to representation may be provisionally granted;

(b) the circumstances in which a right which has been so granted—

(i) is to become, or be treated as if it were, a right to representation under paragraph 1, or

(ii) is to be, or may be, withdrawn.

Grant of right by court

2.—(1) A court before which any criminal proceedings take place, or are to take place, has power to grant a right to representation in respect of those proceedings subject to sub-paragraph (1A).

(1A) The power under sub-paragraph (1) shall not be exercisable—

(a) in relation to proceedings in respect of which the Commission has power to grant a right to representation under paragraph 2A, unless regulations otherwise provide, or

(b) in such other circumstances as may be prescribed.

(2) Where a right to representation is granted for the purposes of criminal proceedings it includes the right to representation for the purposes of any related bail proceedings and any preliminary or incidental proceedings; and regulations may make provision specifying whether any proceedings are or are not to be regarded as preliminary or incidental.

(3) A court also has power to grant a right to representation for the purposes of criminal proceedings before another court in such circumstances as may be prescribed.

(4) The form of the application for a grant of a right to representation under this paragraph, and the form of the grant of such a right, shall be such as may be prescribed.

(5) Subject to sub-paragraph (1A), a right to representation in respect of proceedings may be withdrawn by any court before which the proceedings take place; and a court must consider whether to withdraw a right to representation in such circumstances as may be prescribed.

(5A) Sub-paragraph (5) does not apply where the Commission has power to withdraw the right to representation in respect of the proceedings.

(6) The powers of a magistrates' court for any area under this paragraph may be exercised by a single justice of the peace for the area.

(7) [*Repealed by* Courts Act 2003 (Consequential Amendments) Order *2004 (S.I. 2004 No. 2035)*.]

Grant of right by commission

2A.—(1) Regulations may—

(a) provide that the Commission shall have power to grant rights to representation in respect of criminal proceedings of a prescribed description;

(b) provide that the Commission shall, except in such circumstances as may be prescribed, have power to withdraw any rights to representation granted in respect of proceedings of a description prescribed under paragraph (a);

(c) provide that any provisional grant of a right to representation, or any withdrawal of a right so granted, in accordance with regulations under paragraph 1A is to be made by the Commission.

(2) In sub-paragraph (1)(a), the reference to criminal proceedings does not include proceedings prescribed under section 12(2)(g).

(3) Regulations under sub-paragraph (1) may make such consequential amendment or repeal of any enactment, including an enactment contained in subordinate legislation (within the meaning of the *Interpretation Act* 1978), as the Lord Chancellor may consider appropriate.

3.—(1) Regulations may provide that the Commission shall have power to grant rights to representation in respect of any one or more of the descriptions of proceedings prescribed under section 12(2)(g), and to withdraw any rights to representation granted by it.

3A.—(1) The form of the grant, or provisional grant, of a right to representation under paragraph 2A or 3 shall be such as may be prescribed.

(2) Regulations under paragraph 2A or 3 may make such transitional provision as the Lord Chancellor may consider appropriate.

Financial eligibility

3B.—(1) Power under this Schedule to grant, or provisionally grant, a right to representation may only be exercised in relation to an individual whose financial resources appear to the relevant authority to be such that, under regulations, he is eligible to be granted, or provisionally granted, such a right.

(2) Power under this Schedule to withdraw a right to representation shall be exercised in relation to an individual if it appears to the relevant authority—

(a) that his financial resources are not such that, under regulations, he is eligible to be granted, or provisionally granted, such a right, or

(b) that he has failed, in relation to the right, to comply with regulations under this paragraph about the furnishing of information.

(3) Regulations may make provision for exceptions from sub-paragraph (1) or (2).

(4) Regulations under this paragraph may include—

(a) provision requiring the furnishing of information;

(b) provision for the notification of decisions about the application of—

(i) sub-paragraph (1) or (2), or

(ii) regulations under sub-paragraph (3);

(c) provision for the review of such decisions;

(d) such transitional provision as the Lord Chancellor may consider appropriate.

(5) The provision which may be made under sub-paragraph (4)(c) includes provision prescribing circumstances in which the person or body reviewing a decision may refer a question to the High Court for its decision.

(6) Section 16 of the *Supreme Court Act* 1981 (appeals from the High Court) shall not apply to decisions of the High Court on a reference under regulations under this paragraph.

Appeals

4. Except where regulations otherwise provide, an appeal shall lie to such court or other person or body as may be prescribed against a decision to refuse to grant a right to representation or to withdraw a right to representation.

This paragraph does not apply in relation to any right to representation granted in accordance with paragraph 1A.

Criteria for grant of right

5.—(1) Any question as to whether power to grant, or provisionally grant, a right to representation should be exercised shall be determined according to the interests of justice.

(2) In deciding what the interests of justice consist of in relation to any individual, the following factors must be taken into account—

(a) whether the individual would, if any matter arising in the proceedings is decided against him, be likely to lose his liberty or livelihood or suffer serious damage to his reputation,

(b) whether the determination of any matter arising in the proceedings may involve consideration of a substantial question of law,

(c) whether the individual may be unable to understand the proceedings or to state his own case,

(d) whether the proceedings may involve the tracing, interviewing or expert cross-examination of witnesses on behalf of the individual, and

(e) whether it is in the interests of another person that the individual be represented.

(2A) For the purposes of sub-paragraph (2), "proceedings" includes, in the context of a provisional grant of a right to representation, proceedings that may result from the investigation in which the individual is involved.

(3) The Lord Chancellor may by order amend sub-paragraph (2) by adding new factors or varying any factor.

(4) Regulations may prescribe circumstances in which the grant, or provisional grant, of a right to representation shall be taken to be in the interests of justice.

Information requests

6.—(1) The relevant authority may make an information request to—

(a) the Secretary of State, or

(b) the Commissioners,

for the purpose of facilitating the making of a decision by the authority about the application of paragraph 3B(1) or (2), or regulations under paragraph 3B(3), in relation to an individual.

(2) An information request made to the Secretary of State is a request for the disclosure of some or all of the following information—

(a) the individual's full name;

(b) the individual's address;

(c) the individual's date of birth;

(d) the individual's national insurance number;

(e) the individual's benefit status;

(f) information of any description specified in regulations.

(3) An information request made to the Commissioners is a request for the disclosure of some or all of the following information—

(a) whether or not the individual is employed;

(b) the name and address of the employer (if the individual is employed);

(c) the individual's national insurance number;

(d) information of any description specified in regulations made with the agreement of the Commissioners.

(4) The information that may be specified under subsection (3)(d) includes, in particular, information relating to the individual's income (as defined in the regulations) for a period so specified.

(5) On receiving an information request, the Secretary of State or (as the case may be) the Commissioners may disclose the information requested to the relevant authority.

Restrictions on disclosure

7.—(1) A person to whom information is disclosed under paragraph 6(5), or this sub-paragraph, may disclose the information to any person to whom its disclosure is necessary or expedient in connection with facilitating the making of a decision by the relevant authority about the application of paragraph 3B(1) or (2), or regulations under paragraph 3B(3), in relation to an individual.

(2) A person to whom such information is disclosed commits an offence if the person—

(a) discloses or uses the information, and

(b) the disclosure is not authorised by sub-paragraph (1) or (as the case may be) the use is not for the purpose of facilitating the making of such a decision as is mentioned in that sub-paragraph.

(3) But it is not an offence under sub-paragraph (2)—

(a) to disclose any information in accordance with any enactment or order of a court or for the purposes of any proceedings before a court; or

(b) to disclose any information which has previously been lawfully disclosed to the public.

(4) It is a defence for a person charged with an offence under sub-paragraph (2) to prove that the person reasonably believed that the disclosure or use was lawful.

(5) A person guilty of an offence under sub-paragraph (2) is liable—

(a) on conviction on indictment, to imprisonment for a term not exceeding 2 years or a fine or both;

(b) on summary conviction, to imprisonment for a term not exceeding 12 months or a fine not exceeding the statutory maximum or both.

(6) In sub-paragraph (5)(b) the reference to 12 months is to be read as a reference to 6 months in relation to an offence committed before the commencement of section 154(1) of the *Criminal Justice Act* 2003.

(7) Nothing in section 20 applies in relation to the disclosure of information to which sub-paragraph (1) applies.

Paragraphs 6 and 7: supplementary

8.—(1) This paragraph applies for the purposes of paragraphs 6 and 7.

(2) "Benefit status", in relation to an individual, means whether or not the individual is in direct or indirect receipt of any prescribed benefit or benefits and, if so (in the case of each benefit)—

(a) which benefit the individual is so receiving, and

(b) (in prescribed cases) the amount the individual is so receiving by way of the benefit.

(3) "The Commissioners" means the Commissioners for Her Majesty's Revenue and Customs.

(4) "Information" means information held in any form.

(5) Nothing in paragraph 6 or 7 authorises the making of a disclosure which contravenes the *Data Protection Act* 1998.

[Schedule 3 is printed as amended by the *Criminal Defence Service Act* 2006, ss.1(1) to (7), and 2(1) to (4); and the *CJIA* 2008, ss.56(1) and (6) to (11), and 57(1) and (3)]

Individuals to whom right may be granted

6–148 In connection with paragraph 1(2), see *R. v. Inner London Crown Court, ex p. Bentham* [1989] 1 W.L.R. 408, DC.

Grant of right by court

6–149 For regulations made under paragraph 2(2), see the *Criminal Defence Service (General) (No. 2) Regulations* 2001 (S.I. 2001 No. 1437), reg. 3(3) and (4), *post*, § 6–154.

Financial eligibility

6–149a For regulations made under paragraph 3B, see the *Criminal Defence Service (Financial Eligibility) Regulations* 2006 (S.I. 2006 No. 2492), *post*, §§ 6–192 *et seq.*

Appeals

6–150 See the *Criminal Defence Service (Representation Orders: Appeals etc.) Regulations* 2006 (S.I. 2006 No. 2494), *post*, §§ 6–183 *et seq.*

Criteria for grant of right

6–151 Where an application for a representation order is made at the conclusion of proceedings in a magistrates' court, the interests of justice test should be applied on the basis of the facts as at the time when the solicitor would first have been consulted, and not on the basis of hindsight; where, therefore, the accused was charged with an imprisonable offence, in relation to which there was "a real and practical (as opposed to theoretical risk) of imprisonment" (*R. (Sonn & Co. (a firm)) v. West London Magistrates'*

Court, unreported, October 30, 2000, DC), an application made at the end of the proceedings should have been granted; it had not been open to the appropriate officer to refuse it on the basis that there was, in the end, no risk of imprisonment because the prosecution had substituted a charge of a non-imprisonable offence to which the accused had pleaded guilty: *R. (Punatar & Co.) v. Horseferry Road Magistrates' Court*, unreported, May 24, 2002, DC ([2002] EWHC 1196 (Admin.)).

In *R. (Matara) v. Brent Magistrates' Court*, 169 J.P. 576, DC, it was held that where a person was due to be tried for failing to provide a specimen for analysis, contrary to the *RTA* 1988, s.7 (*post*, § 32–93), and where his defence of reasonable excuse was to be advanced on the basis that, because of his poor language skills, he had not understood what was required of him, at least one of the "interests of justice" criteria in paragraph 5(2) was met (*viz.* sub-para. (c)); that an interpreter would be available at the trial did not meet the point that the defendant was unable to understand what was being said at the time the requirement for a specimen was made; that was a point going to the heart of the defence and it was, therefore, a point going to his ability to state his own case and to the overall fairness of the trial.

The following cases were decided in relation to section 22(2) of the *Legal Aid Act* 1988, the provisions of which were in similar terms of those of paragraph 5(2).

Where a defendant intends to raise as a special reason for non-disqualification from driving, on conviction of driving with access alcohol, the suggestion that his drink had been laced, it is in the interests of justice that he is granted legal aid and that it should extend to the instruction of an expert witness: *R. v. Gravesend Magistrates' Court, ex p. Baker*, 161 J.P. 765, DC.

In *R. v. Scunthorpe JJ., ex p. S.*, *The Times*, March 5, 1998, DC, a refusal to grant legal aid to a 16-year-old charged with obstruction of a police officer in the execution of his duty was quashed as irrational, where there was an issue as to whether the officer was acting in the execution of his duty; the expertise required for the purpose of cross-examination and for proofing defence witnesses was beyond that of a 16-year-old (see s.22(2)(d)); further, conviction would have damaged a young man of good character on the threshold of his life (s.22(2)(a)); if justices feel that they have insufficient information about alleged defence witnesses, they should adjourn the matter, rather than simply refuse the application. See also *R. v. Chester Magistrates' Court, ex p. Ball*, 163 J.P. 757, DC (refusal of legal aid quashed where justices had considered only the likelihood of a loss of liberty in the event of conviction and had failed to have regard to whether a conviction was likely to lead to serious damage to the reputation of the accused, as required by s.22(2)(a)).

C. SECONDARY LEGISLATION

Criminal Defence Service (General) (No. 2) Regulations 2001 (S.I. 2001 No. 1437)

PART I

GENERAL

1. [*Citation and commencement.*] **6–152**

Interpretation

2. In these Regulations: **6–153**

"the Act" means the *Access to Justice Act* 1999;

"advocacy assistance" means assistance in the form of advocacy;

"advocate" means:

a barrister; or

a solicitor who has obtained a higher courts advocacy qualification in accordance with regulations and rules of conduct of the Law Society; or

a solicitor who is exercising automatic rights of audience in the Crown Court;

"assisted person" means a person in receipt of funded services;

"appropriate officer" means:

in the case of the High Court or the Crown Court, the court manager;

in the case of a magistrates' court, the justices' clerk or designated officer; and in the case of the Court of Appeal, the Courts-Martial Appeal Court or the House of Lords, the registrar of criminal appeals or the head of the Civil Appeals Office,

and, in any case, includes an officer designated by him to act on his behalf in that regard;

"the Commission" means the Legal Services Commission established under section 1 of the Act;

"the Costs Committee" means a committee appointed under arrangements made by the Commission to deal with, *inter alia*, applications for appeal against, or review of assessments of costs;

"the Financial Services and Markets Tribunal" means the Tribunal established under section 132 of the *Financial Services and Markets Act*;

"funded services" means services which are provided directly for an individual and funded for that individual as part of the Criminal Defence Service established under sections 12 to 18 of the Act;

"income-related employment and support allowance" means an income-related allowance under Part 1 of the *Welfare Reform Act* 2007 (employment and support allowance);

"judge of the court" means, in relation to a magistrates' court, a single justice;

"litigator" means the person named on the representation order as representing an assisted person, being a solicitor, firm of solicitors or other appropriately qualified person;

"representation order" means a document granting a right to representation under section 14 of the Act;

"representative" means a litigator or advocate;

"tax credit" means a tax credit under the *Tax Credits Act* 2002 and "working tax credit" and "child tax credit" shall be construed in accordance with section 1(1) and (2) of that Act;

"Very High Cost Case" means a case in which a representation order has been granted and which the Commission classifies as a Very High Cost Case on the grounds that—

(a) if the case were to proceed to trial, the trial would in the opinion of the Commission be likely to last for more than 40 days, and the Commission considers that there are no exceptional circumstances which make it unsuitable to be dealt with under its contractual arrangements for Very High Cost Cases; or

(b) if the case were to proceed to trial, the trial would in the opinion of the Commission be likely to last no fewer than 25 and no more than 40 days, and the Commission considers that there are circumstances which make it suitable to be dealt with under its contractual arrangements for Very High Cost Cases;

"Very High Cost Case (Crime) Panel" means a panel set up by the Commission from which representatives may be chosen to provide representation in Very High Cost Cases; and

"volunteer" means a person who, for the purpose of assisting with an investigation, attends voluntarily at a police station or a customs office, or at any other place where a constable or customs officer is present, or accompanies a constable or customs officer to a police station or a customs office or any other such place, without having been arrested.

[This regulation is printed as amended by the *Criminal Defence Service (General) (No. 2) (Amendment) Regulations* 2002 (S.I. 2002 No. 712); the *Criminal Defence Service (General) (No. 2) (Amendment) Regulations* 2003 (S.I. 2003 No. 644); the *Criminal Defence Service (General) (No. 2) (Amendment No. 2) Regulations* 2004 (S.I. 2004 No. 2046); the *Criminal Defence Service (General) (No. 2) (Amendment) Regulations* 2006 (S.I. 2006 No. 2490); the *Criminal Defence Service (General) (No. 2) (Amendment No. 2) Regulations* 2007 (S.I. 2007 No. 2936); the *Employment and Support Allowance (Consequential Provisions) (No. 3) Regulations* 2008 (S.I. 2008 No. 1879); and, in relation only to proceedings in which a representation order was granted on or after January 14, 2008, the *Criminal Defence Service (General) (No. 2) (Amendment No. 3) Regulations* 2007 (S.I. 2007 No. 3550) (substitution of definition of "Very High Cost Case" and insertion of next following definition).]

PART II

SCOPE

Criminal proceedings

3.—(1) For the purposes of this regulations, "the 1998 Act" means the *Crime and Disorder Act* 1998. **6–154**

(2) The following proceedings are criminal proceedings for the purposes of section 12(2)(g) of the Act:

(a) civil proceedings in a magistrates' court arising from failure to pay a sum due or to obey an order of that court where such failure carries the risk of imprisonment;

(b) proceedings under sections 1, 1D and 4 of the 1998 Act relating to anti-social behaviour orders;

(ba) proceedings under sections 1G and 1H of the 1998 Act relating to intervention orders, in which an application for an anti-social behaviour order has been made;

(c) proceedings under section 8(1)(b) of the 1998 Act relating to parenting orders made where an anti-social behaviour order or a sex offender order is made in respect of a child;

(d) proceedings under section 8(1)(c) of the 1998 Act relating to parenting orders made on the conviction of a child;

(e) proceedings under section 9(5) of the 1998 Act to discharge or vary a parenting order made as mentioned in sub-paragraph (c) or (d);

(f) proceedings under section 10 of the 1998 Act to appeal against a parenting order made as mentioned in sub-paragraph (c) or (d); and

(g) proceedings under sections 14B, 14D, 14G, 14H, 21B and 21D of the *Football Spectators Act* 1989 (banning orders and references to a court); and

(h) proceedings under section 137 of the *Financial Services and Markets Act* 2000 to appeal against a decision of the Financial Services and Markets Tribunal;

(i) proceedings under sections 2, 5 and 6 of the *Anti-social Behaviour Act* 2003 relating to closure orders;

(j) proceedings under sections 20, 22, 26 and 28 of the *Anti-Social Behaviour Act* 2003 relating to parenting orders in cases of exclusion from school and parenting orders in respect of criminal conduct and anti-social behaviour;

(k) proceedings under sections 97, 100 and 101 of the *Sexual Offences Act* 2003 relating to notification orders and interim notification orders;

(l) proceedings under sections 104, 108, 109 and 110 of the *Sexual Offences Act* 2003 relating to sexual offences prevention orders and interim sexual offences prevention orders;

(m) proceedings under sections 114, 118 and 119 of the *Sexual Offences Act* 2003 relating to foreign travel orders;

(n) proceedings under sections 123 , 125, 126 and 127 of the *Sexual Offences Act* 2003 relating to risk of sexual harm orders and interim risk of sexual harm orders;

(o) proceedings under Part 1A of Schedule 1 to the *Powers of Criminal Courts (Sentencing) Act* 2000 relating to parenting orders for failure to comply with orders under section 20 of that Act;

[(p) proceedings under section 5A of the *Protection from Harassment Act* 1997 relating to restraining orders on acquittal];

(q) proceedings before the Crown Court or the Court of Appeal relating to serious crime prevention orders and arising by virtue of section 19, 20, 21 or 24 of the *Serious Crime Act* 2007.

(3) Proceedings:

(a) in the Crown Court, following committal for sentence by a magistrates' court;

(b) to quash an acquittal under the *Criminal Procedure and Investigations Act* 1996; and

(c) for confiscation and forfeiture in connection with criminal proceedings under *RSC* Order 115 in Schedule 1 to the *Civil Procedure Rules* 1998,

are to be regarded as incidental to the criminal proceedings from which they arise.

(4) Applications for judicial review or *habeas corpus* relating to any criminal investigations

or proceedings are not to be regarded as incidental to such criminal investigations or proceedings.

(5) Proceedings in a magistrates' court in which the court sends an assisted person for trial in the Crown Court under section 51 of the *Crime and Disorder Act* 1998 are to be regarded as preliminary to the proceedings in the Crown Court.

[This regulation is printed as amended by S.I. 2002 No. 712 (*ante*, § 6–153); the *Criminal Defence Service (General) (No. 2) (Amendment No. 2) Regulations* 2002 (S.I. 2002 No. 2785); the *Criminal Defence Service (General) (No. 2) (Amendment) Regulations* 2004 (S.I. 2004 No. 1196); the *Criminal Defence Service (General) (No. 2) (Amendment) Regulations* 2005 (S.I. 2005 No. 2784); S.I. 2007 No. 2936 (*ante*, § 6–153); and the *Criminal Defence Service (General) (No. 2) (Amendment) Regulations* 2008 (S.I. 2008 No. 725); and as amended, as from the date on which section 12(5) of the *Domestic Violence, Crime and Victims Act* 2004 comes into force (insertion of para. (2)(p)), by S.I. 2005 No. 2784 (*ante*).]

Advice and assistance—scope

6–155 **4.** The Commission shall fund such advice and assistance, including advocacy assistance, as it considers appropriate in relation to any individual who:

(a) is the subject of an investigation which may lead to criminal proceedings;
(b) is the subject of criminal proceedings;
(c) requires advice and assistance regarding his appeal or potential appeal against the outcome of any criminal proceedings or an application to vary a sentence;
(d) requires advice and assistance regarding his sentence;
(e) requires advice and assistance regarding his application or potential application to the Criminal Cases Review Commission;
(f) requires advice and assistance regarding his treatment or discipline in prison (other than in respect of actual or contemplated proceedings regarding personal injury, death or damage to property);
(g) is the subject of proceedings before the Parole Board;
(h) requires advice and assistance regarding representations to the Home Office in relation to a mandatory life sentence or other parole review;
(i) is a witness in criminal proceedings and requires advice regarding self-incrimination; or
(j) is a volunteer; or
(k) is detained under Schedule 7 to the *Terrorism Act* 2000.

[This regulation is printed as amended by S.I. 2002 No. 712 (*ante*, § 6–153).]

Advice prior to the grant of a representation order

6–155a **4A.** Advice given prior to the grant of a representation order in the Crown Court shall be deemed to have been given under that order where:

(a) the interests of justice required that the advice was provided as a matter of urgency;
(b) there was no undue delay in making the application for a representation order; and
(c) the advice was given by the represenative who was subsequently assigned under the representation order.

[This regulation was inserted by S.I. 2004 No. 1196, *ante*, § 6–154.]

Advice and assistance—financial eligibility

6–156 **5.**—(1) The following advice and assistance may be granted without reference to the financial resources of the individual:

(a) all advice and assistance provided to an individual who is arrested and held in custody at a police station or other premises;
(b) all advocacy assistance before a magistrates' court or the Crown Court;
(c) all advice and assistance provided by a court duty solicitor in accordance with his contract with the Commission;
(d) all advice and assistance provided to a volunteer during his period of voluntary attendance;
(e) all advice and assistance provided to an individual being interviewed in connection with a serious service offence; and

(f) all advice and assistance provided in respect of an individual who is the subject of an identification procedure carried out by means of video recordings in connection with that procedure, notwithstanding the indvidual's non-attendance at a police station at the time the procedure is carried out.

(2) For the purposes of paragraph (1), a serious service offence is an offence under the *Army Act* 1955, the *Air Force Act* 1955 or the *Navy Discipline Act* 1957 which cannot be dealt with summarily.

(3) Advocacy assistance may be granted to an individual regarding his treatment or discipline in prison (other than in respect of actual or contemplated proceedings regarding personal injury, death or damage to property), or where he is the subject of proceedings before the Parole Board, if his weekly disposable income does not exceed £209 and his disposable capital does not exceed £3,000.

(4) Except where paragraph (1) applies, the Commission, or a person acting on behalf of the Commission where such function has been delegated in accordance with section 3(4) of the Act, shall determine the financial eligibility of the individual in accordance with the following paragraphs.

(5) Except where paragraph (1) or (3) applies, an individual is eligible for advice and assistance if his weekly disposable income does not exceed £99 and his disposable capital does not exceed £1,000.

(6) The Commission shall assess the disposable income and disposable capital of the individual and, where appropriate, of any person whose financial resources may be treated as those of the individual, in accordance with Schedule 1 to these *Regulations*.

(7) Where the Commission is satisfied that any person whose disposable income is to be assessed under paragraph (6) is directly or indirectly in receipt of any qualifying benefit, it shall take that person's disposable income as not exceeding the sum for the time being specified in paragraph (3) or (5), as appropriate.

(8) The following are qualifying benefits for the purposes of paragraph (7):

(a) income support;

(b) income-based jobseeker's allowance;

(c) working tax credit claimed together with child tax credit where the gross annual income is not more than £14,213;

(d) working tax credit with a disability element or severe disability element (or both) where the gross annual income is not more than £14,213;

(e) guarantee … credit under section 1(3)(a) of the *State Pension Credit Act* 2002; and

(f) income-related employment and support allowance payable under Part 1 of the *Welfare Reform Act* 2007.

(9) Where the Commission is satisfied that any person whose disposable capital is to be assessed in accordance with paragraph (3) is directly or indirectly in receipt of income support, income-based jobseeker's allowance, guarantee state pension credit or income-related employment and support allowance, it shall take that person's disposable capital as not exceeding the capital sum for the time being specified in paragraph (3).

[This regulation is printed as amended by S.I. 2002 No. 712 (*ante*, § 6–153); S.I. 2002 No. 2785 (*ante*, § 6–154); S.I. 2003 No. 644 (*ante*, § 6–153) (substituting new sub-paras (c) and (d) in para. (8); but it is provided that a person who is directly or indirectly in receipt of working families' tax credit or disabled persons' tax credit at any time on or after April 6, 2003, shall be treated as if the amendment to para. (8) had not come into force); the *Criminal Defence Service (General) (No. 2) (Amendment No. 2) Regulations* 2003 (S.I. 2003 No. 2378); S.I. 2005 No. 2784 (*ante*, § 6–154); S.I. 2006 No. 2490 (*ante*, § 6–153); the *Criminal Defence Service (General) (No. 2) (Amendment) Regulations* 2007 (S.I. 2007 No. 780); S.I. 2008 No. 725 (*ante*, § 6–154); and S.I. 2008 No. 1879 (*ante*, § 6–153).]

PART III

APPLICATIONS FOR REPRESENTATION ORDERS

Representation order

6.—(1) The date of any representation order is the date on which the application for the grant of such an order is received in accordance with these Regulations. **6–157**

(2) Any application for the grant of a representation order in respect of proceedings in the Crown Court or the Court of Appeal which are mentioned in section 12(2)(a) to (f) of the Act and in regulation 3(2)(h), shall be made in accordance with regulations 9 and 10.

(3) Any application for the grant of a representation order in respect of the proceedings mentioned in regulation 3(2) (criminal proceedings for the purposes of section 12(2)(g) of Act), except those mentioned in regulation 3(2)(h):

(a) shall be made to the Commission; and

(b) may be granted only by the Commission or a person acting on behalf of the Commission where such function has been delegated in accordance with section 3(4) of the Act.

(4) Where an application under paragraph (3) is refused, the Commission shall provide to the applicant:

(a) written reasons for the refusal; and

(b) details of the appeal process.

(5) Where the person who requires representation is aged less than 18, the application for the grant of representation order may be made by his parent or guardian on his behalf.

(6) The appropriate officer of each court shall keep a record of every application to that court for a representation order, and of its outcome.

(7) The appropriate officer shall send to the Lord Chancellor such information from the record mentioned in paragraph (6) as the Lord Chancellor may request.

[This regulation is printed as amended by S.I. 2002 No. 712 (*ante*, § 6–153); and S.I. 2006 No. 2490 (*ante*, § 6–153).]

General power to grant representation

6–158 **7.** The court, a judge of the court, the head of the Civil Appeals Office, or the registrar of criminal appeals may grant a representation order at any stage of criminal proceedings (other than criminal proceedings in a magistrates' court) in the circumstances set out in these Regulations whether or not an application has been made for such an order.

[This regulation is printed as amended by S.I. 2002 No. 712 (*ante*, § 6–153); and S.I. 2006 No. 2490 (*ante*, § 6–153).]

Proceedings in a magistrates' court

6–159 **8.** [*Revoked by S.I. 2006 No. 2490*, ante, *§ 6–153*.]

Proceedings in the Crown Court

6–160 **9.**—(1) Other than where regulation 6(3) applies, an application for a representation order in respect of proceedings in the Crown Court may be made, where an application for such an order in respect of the proceedings in a magistrates' court has not been made or has been refused:

(a) orally or in writing to the Crown Court;

(b) in writing to the appropriate officer of that court;

(c) ... in writing to a magistrates' court at the conclusion of any proceedings in that magistrates' court;

(d) ... in writing to a magistrates' court inquiring into the offence as examining justices or sending for trial under section 51 of the *Crime and Disorder Act* 1998;

(e) where a magistrates' court has been given a notice of transfer under section 4 of the *Criminal Justice Act* 1987 (serious fraud cases), in writing to the appropriate officer of that magistrates' court;

(f) in the case of an appeal to the Crown Court from a magistrates' court, in writing to the appropriate officer of that magistrates' court;

(g) where the applicant ... was committed for trial in the Crown Court under section 6(2) of the *Magistrates' Courts Act* 1980, in writing to the appropriate officer of the magistrates' court ordering the committal; ... .

(1A) Where a representation order has been granted in respect of proceedings in a magistrates' court, an application for a representation order in respect of an appeal to the Crown Court in those proceedings may be made—

(a) orally to that magistrates' court;

(b) in writing to the appropriate officer of that magistrates' court;

(c) orally or in writing to the Crown Court; or

(d) in writing to the appropriate officer of the Crown Court.

(1B) An application for a representation order in respect of a retrial ordered under section 7 of the *Criminal Appeal Act* 1968 may be made—

(a) orally or in writing to the court ordering the retrial; or

(b) orally or in writing to the Crown Court or in writing to the appropriate officer of the Crown Court.

(2) An application for a representation order in respect of representations to the High Court against a voluntary bill of indictment may be made:

(a) in writing to the appropriate officer of the Crown Court; or

(b) orally to the judge considering the voluntary bill

and where any such order is granted it shall also apply to any proceedings to which the applicant in indicted.

(3) Where an application is made to the court, it may refer it to the appropriate officer for determination.

(4) Where an application is refused, the appropriate officer shall provide to the applicant:

(a) written reasons for the refusal; and

(b) details of the appeal process.

[This regulation is printed as amended by S.I. 2006 No. 2490 (*ante*, § 6–153); and S.I. 2007 No. 2936 (*ante*, § 6–153).]

Proceedings in the High Court

9A.—(1) Except where regulation 6(3) applies, an application for a representation order in respect of proceedings in the High Court may be made— **6–160a**

(a) in the case of an appeal by way of case stated from a decision of a magistrates' court, orally to that court or in writing to the appropriate officer of that court;

(b) in the case of an appeal by way of case stated from a decision of the Crown Court, orally or in writing to that Court or in writing to the appropriate officer at that court; or

(c) orally or in writing to a judge of the High Court or in writing to the appropriate officer of that court.

(2) Where an application is made to a court or a judge, the court or judge may refer it to the appropriate officer.

(3) The appropriate officer may grant the application or refer it to the court or a judge of the court.

[This regulation was inserted by S.I. 2007 No. 2936 (*ante*, § 6–153).]

As to the funding of applications for judicial review, see the *Access to Justice Act 1999 (Commencement No. 7, Transitional Provisions and Savings) Order* 2001 (S.I. 2001 No. 916), Sched. 2, para. 3 (*ante*, § 6–132). It may be noted that prior to the insertion of this regulation in 2007, the 2001 regulations made no provision at all for representation orders in the High Court.

Proceedings in the Court of Appeal and the House of Lords

10.—(1) An application for a representation order in respect of proceedings in the Court of Appeal or the House of Lords may be made: **6–161**

(a) orally to the Court of Appeal, or a judge of the court; or

(b) in writing to the Court of Appeal, a judge of the court, or the appropriate officer of the court.

(2) Where an application is made to the court, it may refer it to a judge or the appropriate officer for determination.

(3) Where an application is made to a judge, he may refer it to the appropriate officer for determination.

(4) The appropriate officer may:

(a) grant the application; or

(b) refer it to the court or a judge of the court.

(5) A representation order shall not be granted until notice of leave to appeal has been given in respect of the proceedings which are the subject of the application.

(6) Where a representation order is granted in respect of proceedings in the Court of Appeal, a judge or the appropriate officer may specify the stage of the proceedings at which the representation order shall take effect.

(7) The House of Lords may not grant a representation order in respect of any proceedings.

[This regulation is printed as amended by S.I. 2002 No. 712 (*ante*, § 6–153).]

The Court of Appeal may grant a representation order before leave to appeal has been given. Whereas regulation 10(5) provides that "a representation order shall not be granted until notice of leave to appeal has been given…", it was clear from the history of the relevant legislation that the wording of this provision was a result of a conflation by the draftsman of the terms "notice of appeal" and "notice of application for leave to appeal". Though it was unfortunate when a court was obliged to read words into a legislative provision, there was no choice in this instance but to read "notice of leave to appeal" in regulation 10(5) as "notice of appeal or application for leave to appeal": *Revenue and Customs Prosecution Office v. Stokoe Partnership (M., J. and P. and Ministry of Justice, interveners)* [2007] A.C.D. 84, DC.

In *R. v. K., G. and M.*, *The Times*, February 15, 2005, Thomas L.J. (sitting apparently as a single judge) said that a representation order for an appeal only covered work on and attendance or appearance at the hearing in respect of grounds upon which the court had granted leave to appeal; it was therefore essential in every case where there was a failure of a renewed application for leave to appeal made at the same time as an appeal and the court did not specifically and exceptionally order that the advocates or solicitors representing the applicant were entitled to a representation order for the costs of the failed application, that the fee notes submitted by the advocates or solicitors showed a detailed account of the work done for the appeal and a detailed account of the work done for the renewed application for leave to appeal, so as to ensure that no amount was paid under the representation order in respect of the renewed application.

As to the practice to be followed where it is sought to extend a representation order for an appeal to cover the cost of an expert witness, see *R. v. Bowman* [2007] Costs L.R. 1, CA, *post*, § 7–215b.

PART IV

SELECTION OF REPRESENTATIVE

Representation in magistrates' courts and some Crown Court proceedings

6–162 **11.**—(1) The right conferred by section 15(1) of the Act, as regards representation in respect of any proceedings to which this regulation applies, shall be exercisable only in relation to those representatives who are:

(a) employed by the Commission to provide such representation; or

(b) authorised to provide such representation under a crime franchise contract with the Commission which commences on or after April 2, 2001 and specifies the rate of remuneration for such representation.

(2) This regulation applies to:

(a) any criminal proceedings in a magistrates' court;

(b) any proceedings in the Crown Court mentioned in regulation 3(2);

(c) any appeal by way of case stated from a magistrates' court; and

(d) any proceedings which are preliminary or incidental to proceedings mentioned in sub-paragraphs (a) to (c).

(3) This regulation does not apply to proceedings referred to in section 12(2)(f) of the Act (proceedings for contempt in the face of a court).

Advocates in magistrates' courts

6–163 **12.**—(1) A representation order for the purposes of proceedings before a magistrates' court may only include representation by an advocate in the case of:

(a) any indictable offence, including an offence which is triable either way; or

(b) extradition hearings under the *Extradition Act* 2003

where the court is of the opinion that, because of circumstances which make the proceedings unusually grave or difficult, representation by both a litigator and an advocate would be desirable.

(2) A representation order for the purposes of proceedings before a magistrates' court may not include representation by an advocate other than as provided in paragraph (1).

(3) A representation order for the purposes of proceedings before a magistrates' court may provide for the services of a Queen's Counsel or of more than one advocate only—

(a) in extradition hearings under the *Extradition Act* 2003; and

(b) where the court is of the opinion that the assisted person could not be adequately represented except by a Queen's Counsel or by more than one advocate.

[This regulation is printed as amended by S.I. 2007 No. 2936 (*ante*, § 6–153).]

The following authorities were decided in relation to provisions of earlier legislation corresponding to regulation 12(1), namely the *CJA* 1967, s.74(2), and the *Legal Aid in Criminal and Care Proceedings (General) Regulations* 1989 (S.I. 1989 No. 344), reg. 44(3). **6–164**

In the case of committal proceedings for murder, it should be recognised as a rule of practice that legal aid should include representation by counsel: *R. v. Derby JJ., ex p. Kooner* [1971] 1 Q.B. 147, 54 Cr.App.R. 455, DC.

Before justices can properly exercise their discretion to assign counsel in a case other than a charge of murder, the applicant must show not only that the case is of unusual gravity or difficulty but also that that circumstance leads to the conclusion that such representation is desirable in the particular proceedings—whether summary trial or committal proceedings. The justices' approach should be for them to recognise that, in a large number of cases which might in themselves be grave or difficult, it was nevertheless possible at an early stage for any competent solicitor to realise that no useful purpose would be likely to be served in the interests of his client by opposing a simple committal for trial under section 6(2) of the *MCA* 1980. Where there is no conceivable reason for opposing such a committal, no matter how grave or difficult the case might be, it is difficult to see how there can be any reason for assigning counsel at that stage. Certainly, the mere multiplicity of simple, straightforward charges could not make it desirable for counsel to be instructed. However, the facts in relation to a single charge might be so complex that it is desirable that counsel should at least advise whether there were good grounds for opposing a committal under section 6(2). Justices might well be persuaded that both unusual gravity or difficulty and also a good reason why counsel should be assigned at committal stage existed if the case was of some weight and there were affirmative reasons for supposing that counsel might discover a basis for a sensible submission of no case to answer: *R. v. Guildford JJ., ex p. Scott* [1975] Crim.L.R. 286, DC.

Representation in the Crown Court, Court of Appeal and House of Lords

13.—(1) Subject to paragraph (2) and regulation 11, the right conferred by section 15(1) of the Act, as regards representation in respect of any proceedings in the Crown Court (other than proceedings mentioned in regulation 3(2)), Court of Appeal or House of Lords, shall be exercisable only in relation to those representatives who are: **6–165**

(a) employed by the Commission to provide such representation; or

(b) authorised to provide such representation under a crime franchise contract with the Commission; or

(c) in respect of an appeal from the Financial Services and Markets Tribunal, the representatives of the assisted person before the Court of Appeal.

(2) In a case which is, or is likely to be classified as, a Very High Cost Case, the right conferred by section 15(1) of the Act is to select only a member of a Very High Cost Case (Crime) Panel.

(4) This regulation does not apply to any proceedings referred to in section 12(2)(f) of the Act.

[This regulation is printed as amended by S.I. 2002 No. 712 (*ante*, § 6–153); and, in relation only to proceedings in which a representation order was granted on or after January 14, 2008, S.I. 2007 No. 3550 (*ante*, § 6–153) (substitution of para. (2), omission of para. (3)).]

Advocates in the Crown Court and above

14.—(1) A representation order for the purposes of proceedings in the Crown Court (including a representation order which extends to that court by virtue of regulation 4 of the *Criminal Defence Service (Representation Orders and Consequential Amendments) Regulations* 2006), High Court, Court of Appeal or House of Lords— **6–166**

(a) includes representation by one junior advocate; and

(b) may include representation by a Queen's Counsel or by more than one advocate in respect of the whole or any specified part of the proceedings only in the cases specified and in the manner provided for by this regulation.

(1A) In this regulation "junior advocate" means any advocate who is not a Queen's Counsel.

(2) Subject to paragraphs (3) to (9), a representation order may provide for the services of a Queen's Counsel or of more than one advocate in any of the following terms:

(a) a Queen's Counsel alone;

(b) where two advocates are required:

(i) a Queen's Counsel with a junior counsel;

(ii) a Queen's Counsel with a noting junior counsel;

(iii) two junior counsel; or

(iv) a junior counsel with a noting junior counsel;

(c) where three advocates are required:

(i) in any of the terms provided for in sub-paragraph (b) plus an extra junior counsel; or

(ii) in any of the terms provided for in sub-paragraph (b) plus an extra noting junior counsel.

(3) A representation order relating to proceedings in the Crown Court may be made in the terms of paragraph 2(a) if and only if:

(a) in the opinion of the court the case for the assisted person involves substantial novel or complex issues of law or fact which could not be adequately presented except by a Queen's Counsel; and

(b) either:

(i) a Queen's Counsel or senior Treasury counsel has been instructed on behalf of the prosecution; or

(ii) the case for the assisted person is exceptional compared with the generality of cases involving similar offences.

(4) A representation order relating to proceedings in the Crown Court may be made in the terms of paragraph (2)(b)(iii) or (iv) if and only if:

(a) in the opinion of the court the case for the assisted person involves substantial novel or complex issues of law or fact which could not be adequately presented by a single advocate; and

(b) either:

(i) two or more advocates have been instructed on behalf of the prosecution;

(ii) the case for the assisted person is exceptional compared with the generality of cases involving similar offences;

(iii) the number of prosecution witnesses exceeds 80; or

(iv) the number of pages of prosecution evidence exceeds 1,000;

and for this purpose the number of pages of prosecution evidence shall include all witness statements, documentary and pictorial exhibits and records of interview with the assisted person and with other defendants forming part of the committal documents or included in any notice of additional evidence.

(5) A representation order relating to proceedings in the Crown Court may be made in the terms of paragraph 2(b)(i) or (ii) if and only if:

(a) in the opinion of the court the case for the assisted person involves substantial novel or complex issues of law or fact which could not be adequately presented except by a Queen's Counsel assisted by junior counsel; and

(b) either—

(i) the case for the assisted person is exceptional compare with the generality of cases involving similar offences; or

(ii) a Queen's Counsel or senior Treasury counsel has been instructed on behalf of the prosecution and one of the conditions in paragraph (4)(b)(i), (iii) or (iv) is satisfied.

(6) A representation order may be made in the terms of paragraph (2)(c) if and only if:

(a) the proceedings arise from a prosecution brought by the Serious Fraud Office;

(b) the court making the order considers that three advocates are required; and

(c) in the case of proceedings in the Crown Court, the conditions in paragraph (4) or (5) are satisfied.

(7) The fact that a Queen's Counsel has been or is proposed to be assigned under this regulation shall not by itself be a reason for making an order in any of the terms provided for by paragraph (2)(b) or (c).

(8) Where a Queen's Counsel has been or is proposed to be assigned under this regulation, no order in any of the terms provided for by paragraph (2)(b) or (c) shall be made where the case relates to an appeal to the Court of Appeal or to the House of Lords and it appears to the court at the time of making the order that representation can properly be undertaken by a Queen's Counsel alone.

(9) No order shall be made or amended so as to provide for representation:

(a) in the terms of paragraph (2)(b) unless the court making the order is of the opinion that the assisted person could not be adequately represented under an order in the terms of paragraph (2)(a);

(b) in the terms of paragraph (2)(b)(i) unless the court making the order is of the opinion that the assisted person could not be adequately represented under an order in the terms of paragraph (2)(b)(ii), (iii) or (iv);

(c) in the terms of paragraph (2)(b)(ii) unless the court making the order is of the opinion that the assisted person could not be adequately represented under an order in the terms of paragraph (2)(b)(iii) or (iv);

(d) in the terms of paragraph (2)(b)(iii) unless the court making the order is of the opinion that the assisted person could not be adequately represented under an order in the terms of paragraph (2)(b)(iv);

(e) in any of the terms provided for by paragraph (2)(c)(i) unless the court making the order is of the opinion that the assisted person could not be adequately represented under the corresponding order under paragraph (2)(c)(ii).

(10) Every application for a representation order in any of the terms provided for by paragraph (2), or for an amendment under paragraph (15), shall be in writing specifying:

(a) the terms of the order sought and the grounds of the application; and

(b) which of the conditions in paragraphs (3), (4), (5), (6) and (9) is relied upon in support of the order sought, and on what grounds it is contended that each such condition is fulfilled.

(11) A court may, before making a representation order in the terms provided for by paragraph (2) or amending the order under paragraph (15), require written advice from any advocate already assigned to the applicant on the question of what representation is needed in the proceedings.

(12) A court making a decision whether to make an order under paragraph (2) or to amend an order under paragraph (15) shall make annotations to the written application under paragraph (10), stating whether each of the conditions relied upon in support of the order made or sought is fulfilled.

(13) Subject to paragraph (14), a decision to make or amend a representation order so as to provide for the services of a Queen's Counsel or of more than one advocate may only be made:

(a) in the course of a trial or of a preliminary hearing, pre-trial review or pleas and directions hearing, by the judge presiding at that trial or hearing;

(b) where the proceedings are in the Crown Court, by a High Court judge, the resident judge of the Crown Court or (in the absence of the resident judge) a judge nominated for that purpose by the presiding judge of the circuit; or

(c) where the proceedings are in the Court of Appeal, by the registrar, a High Court judge or a judge of the Court of Appeal.

(14) A magistrates' court which may grant a representation order as respects any proceedings in the Crown Court by virtue of these Regulations may make:

(a) a representation order providing for the services of a Queen's Counsel without a junior counsel where the proceedings are a trial for murder and the order is made upon committal, transfer or sending for trial; or

(b) a representation order providing for the services of a Queen's Counsel with one junior counsel where the prosecution is brought by the Serious Fraud Office and the order is made upon receiving a notice of transfer under section 4 of the *Criminal Justice Act* 1987,

but shall have no other power to make an order under this regulation.

(15) In proceedings to which paragraph (3), (4), (5) or (6) applies, a representation order may be amended:

(a) in any terms provided for by paragraph (2) in accordance with the provisions of this regulation; or

(b) to provide for representation by one junior counsel only.

(16) In every case in which a representation order is made under this regulation for the provision of funded services in terms provided for by paragraph (2)(b) or (c), it shall be the duty of:

(a) each representative:

(i) to keep under review the need for more than one advocate to be present in court or otherwise providing services; and

(ii) to consider whether the representation order should be amended as providing for in paragraph (15);

(b) Queen's Counsel, where the services of a Queen's Counsel are provided, to keep under review the question whether he could act alone.

(17) It shall be the duty of each representative, if of the opinion that the representation order should be amended as provided for in paragraph (15), to notify that opinion in writing:

(a) to the other representatives for the assisted person; and

(b) to the court

and the court shall, after considering the opinion and any representations made by any other representatives for the assisted person, determine whether and in what manner the representation order should be amended.

[This regulation is printed as amended by S.I. 2007 No. 2936 (*ante*, § 6–153).]

As to regulation 4 of the 2006 regulations, see *post*, § 6–182d.

6–167 The principle of equality of arms does not require that a defendant should be represented by leading counsel merely because the prosecution were so represented; what was required was that the defendant should be represented by an advocate who could ensure that the defendant's case was properly and adequately placed before the court: *Att.-Gen.'s Reference (No. 82a of 2000)*; *R. v. Lea*; *R. v. Shatwell* [2002] 2 Cr.App.R. 24, CA.

As to the importance of ensuring that the representation coincides with the grant, see *R. v. Liverpool Crown Court, ex p. The Lord Chancellor*, *The Times*, April 22, 1993, DC.

For observations of the Court of Appeal as to the need to avoid wasteful representation orders, whether by way of two-counsel orders or by way of separate representation for each of two or more defendants, between whom there is no conflict and no possibility of forensic embarrassment, see *R. v. Azam* [2006] Crim.L.R. 776, CA.

6–168 **15.** The court may grant a representation order for representation by an advocate alone:

(a) in any proceedings referred to in section 12(2)(f) of the Act;

(b) in respect of an appeal to the Court of Appeal or the Courts-Martial Appeal Court; or

(c) in cases of urgency where it appears to the court that there is no time to instruct a litigator:

(i) in respect of an appeal to the Crown Court; or

(ii) in proceedings in which a person is committed to or appears before the Crown Court for trial or sentence, or appears or is brought before that court to be dealt with.

[This regulation is printed as amended by S.I. 2007 No. 2936 (*ante*, § 6–153).]

Change of representative

6–169 **16.**—(1) Where a representation order has been granted an application may be made to the court before which the proceedings are heard to select a litigator in place of a litigator previously selected, and any such application shall state the grounds on which it is made.

(2) The court may:

(a) grant the application where:

(i) the litigator considers himself to be under a duty to withdraw from the case in accordance with his professional rules of conduct and, in such a case, the litigator shall provide details of the nature of such duty;

(ii) there is a breakdown in the relationship between the assisted person and the litigator such that effective representation can no longer be provided and, in such a case, the litigator shall provide details of the nature of such breakdown;

(iii) through circumstances beyond his control, the litigator is no longer able to represent the assisted person; or

(iv) some other substantial compelling reason exists; or

(b) refuse the application.

[This regulation is printed as amended by S.I. 2007 No. 2936 (*ante*, § 6–153).]

In *R. v. Smith (Henry Lee)* [2007] Crim.L.R. 325, CA, it was said that there was no evidence of a "breakdown in the relationship between the assisted person and the representative" where the defendant had invented a spurious reason for dispensing with the services of his legal representatives. A better view, it is submitted, is that whilst there was a breakdown in the relationship, the fact that the defendant had no good reason for his behaviour would be a ground for refusing the application: see the commentary in *Criminal Law Week* 2007/13/5. In connection with the provisions of this regulation, see also the authorities cited at § 7–86, *post*.

Selection of a representative by two or more co-defendants

16A. Where an individual who is granted a right to representation is one of two or more co-defendants whose cases are to be heard together, that individual must select the same litigator as a co-defendant unless there is, or is likely to be, a conflict of interest. **6–169a**

[This regulation was inserted by S.I. 2004 No. 1196, *ante*, § 6–154. It is printed as amended by S.I. 2007 No. 2936 (*ante*, § 6–153).]

PART V

WITHDRAWAL OF REPRESENTATION

17.—(1) Where any charge or proceedings against the assisted person are varied, the court before which the proceedings are heard or, in respect of any proceedings mentioned in regulation 3(2)(a) to (g), the Commission, must— **6–170**

(a) consider whether the interests of justice continue to require that he be represented in respect of the varied charge or proceedings; and

(b) withdraw the representation order if the interests of justice do not so require.

(1A) The court before which the proceedings are heard or, in respect of any proceedings mentioned in regulation 3(2)(a) to (g), the Commission, must consider whether to withdraw the representation order in any of the following circumstances—

(a) where the assisted person declines to accept the order in the terms which are offered;

(b) otherwise at the request of the assisted person; or

(c) where the litigator named in the representation order declines to continue to represent the assisted person.

(2) Where representation is withdrawn, the appropriate officer or the Commission, as appropriate, shall provide written notificiation to the assisted person and to the litigator (or, where there was no litigator assigned, to the advocate), who shall inform any assigned advocate (or, where notification is given to the advocate, any other assigned advocate).

(3) On any subsequent application by the assisted person for a representation order in respect of the same proceedings—

(a) he must declare the withdrawal of the previous representation order and the reason for it; and

(b) where the representation order was withdrawn in the circumstances set out in paragraph (1) or paragraph (1A)(a) or (b) and a representation order is subsequently granted, the court or the Commission, as appropriate, must select the same litigator, unless it considers that there are good reasons why it should select a different litigator.

[This regulation is printed as amended by S.I. 2002 No. 712 (*ante*, § 6–153); S.I. 2006 No. 2490 (*ante*, § 6–153); and S.I. 2007 No. 2936 (*ante*, § 6–153).].]

In connection with the provisions of this regulation, see the authorities cited at § 7–86, *post*.

PART VI

MISCELLANEOUS

Transfer of documents

6–171 **18.** Where an individual is committed or sent for trial by a lower court to a higher court, or appeals or applies for leave to appeal from a lower court to a higher court, the appropriate officer of the lower court shall send to the appropriate officer of the higher court the following documents:

(a) a copy of any representation order previously made in respect of the same proceedings; and

(b) a copy of any application for a representation order which has been refused.

Authorisation of expenditure

6–172 **19.**—(1) Where it appears to the litigator necessary for the proper conduct of proceedings in the Crown Court for costs to be incurred under the representation order by taking any of the following steps:

(a) obtaining a written report or opinion of one or more experts;

(b) employing a person to provide a written report or opinion (otherwise than as an expert);

(c) obtaining any transcripts or recordings; or

(d) performing an act which is either unusual in its nature or involves unusually large expenditure,

he may apply to the Costs Committee for prior authority to do so.

(2) The Commission may authorise a person acting on behalf of the Costs Committee to grant prior authority in respect of any application made under paragraph (1).

(3) Where the Costs Committee or a person acting on its behalf authorises the taking of any step specified in paragraph (1), it shall also authorise the maximum to be paid in respect of that step.

[This regulation is printed as amended by S.I. 2007 No. 2936 (*ante*, § 6–153).]

6–173 The following authorities were decided under the corresponding provisions in the legal aid legislation: see, in particular, regulation 54 of the *Legal Aid in Criminal and Care Proceedings (General) Regulations* 1989 (S.I. 1989 No. 344).

In *R. v. Silcott, Braithwaite and Raghip, The Times*, December 9, 1991, the Court of Appeal said that all members of the legal profession were under a duty not to involve the legal aid fund in unnecessary expenditure. If an expert consulted by the defence was hostile to the accused's case or his solicitor considered the opinion to be wrong or defective it was most unlikely that legal aid authority would be given on application by the solicitor to consult more than one expert and certainly no more than two. In the instant case, the opinions of two experts had been obtained on behalf of one defendant. They were adverse to the defendant. Neither expert was called, but both changed their views in the light of the opinion of a third expert, who had been consulted after the trial's conclusion. This demonstrated that a third opinion had been necessary in the interests of justice. "Expert shopping" was to be discouraged, but there were exceptional cases where the need for a further expert opinion could be demonstrated. In such cases counsel should be asked to advise on evidence in support of an extension of the legal aid certificate, if he thought it right to do so. The courts and those responsible for the legal aid fund must rely on the proper professional standards being observed by all the lawyers concerned.

A judge has no power to authorise the incurring of costs under a legal aid order for an expert witness, although he may express his opinion as to the desirability of legal aid being so extended: *R. v. Donnelly* [1998] Crim.L.R. 131, CA.

6–174 **20.** A representative assigned to an assisted person in any proceedings in the Crown Court may apply to the court for prior authority for the incurring of travelling and accommodation expenses in order to attend at the trial or other main hearing in those proceedings.

6–175 **21.**—(1) No question as to the propriety of any step, or as to the amount of the payment within the maximum authorised, with regard to which prior authority has been given under regulation 19 or 20 or under any contract, shall be raised on any determination of costs unless the representative knew or should reasonably have known that the purpose for which it was given had become unnecessary.

(2) Payment may be allowed on a determination of costs in respect of any step with regard to which prior authority may be given, notwithstanding that no such authority was given or that the maximum authorised was exceeded.

Restriction on payment

22. Where a representation order has been made, the assisted person's solicitor or advocate, whether acting under a representation order or otherwise, shall not receive or be a party to the making of any payment for work done in connection with the proceedings in respect of which the representation order was made except such payments as may be made: **6–176**

(a) by the Lord Chancellor or the Commission; or

(b) in respect of any expenses or fees incurred in:

(i) preparing, obtaining or considering any report, opinion or further evidence, whether provided by an expert witness or otherwise; or

(ii) obtaining any transcripts or recordings

where an application for an authority to incur such fees or expenses has been refused by the Costs Committee.

[This regulation is printed as amended by S.I. 2004 No. 1196, *ante*, § 6–154.]

In connection with this regulation, see *R. v. Hayes*, *ante*, § 6–19.

Notification of very high cost cases

23.—(1) Any litigator who has conduct of a case which is, or is likely to be classified as, a Very High Cost Case must notify the Commission accordingly, in writing, as soon as is practicable. **6–177**

(3) Where a solicitor fails to comply with the provisions of this regulation without good reason, and as a result there is a loss to public funds, the court or Costs Committee, as appropriate, may refuse payment of his costs up to the extent of such loss.

(4) No payment under paragraph (3) shall be refused unless the solicitor has been given a reasonable opportunity to show why it should not be refused.

[This regulation is printed, in relation only to proceedings in which a representation order was granted on or after January 14, 2008, as amended by S.I. 2007 No. 3550 (*ante*, § 6–153) (substitution of para. (1), omission of para. (2)).]

Duty to report abuse

24. Notwithstanding the relationship between or rights of a representative and client or any privilege arising out of such relationship, where the representative for an applicant or assisted person knows or suspects that that person: **6–178**

(a) has intentionally failed to comply with any provision of regulations made under the Act concerning the information to be furnished by him; or

(b) in furnishing such information has knowingly made a false statement or false representation,

the representative shall immediately report the circumstances to the Commission.

Schedule

The schedule to the regulations relates to the assessment of resources. It is not set out in this work. **6–179**

Choice in very high cost cases

The *Criminal Defence Service (Very High Cost Cases) Regulations* 2008 (S.I. 2008 No. 40) revoked the *Criminal Defence Service (Choice in Very High Cost Cases) Regulations* 2001 (S.I. 2001 No. 1169) and provided that where a representative, at the date a case is classified as a very high cost case (defined as in the *Criminal Defence Service (General) (No. 2) Regulations* 2001 (S.I. 2001 No. 1437), as amended by the *Criminal Defence Service (General) (No. 2) (Amendment No. 3) Regulations* 2007 (S.I. 2007 No. 3550) (*ante*, § 6–153)) is not a member of a very high cost case (crime) panel (as similarly defined), the Legal Services Commission is no longer required to fund representation by that representative. The individual in whose favour the representation order was granted may select a different representative from such a panel in **6–180** accordance with the 2001 regulations. These regulations came into force on January 12, 2008, and apply to proceedings which the commission classifies as a very high cost case on or after that date.

Criminal Defence Service (Representation Orders and Consequential Amendments) Regulations 2006 (S.I. 2006 No. 2493), regs 1-6

6–181 **1.** [*Citation and commencement (October 2, 2006).*]

Interpretation

6–182 **2.** In these Regulations—

"the Act" means the *Access to Justice Act* 1999;

"the Commission" means the Legal Services Commission established under section 1 of the Act;

"relevant proceedings" means criminal proceedings which—

(a) are mentioned in section 12(2)(a) to (f) of the Act; and

(b) are in a magistrates' court;

"representation authority" means the Commission or a court officer or other person to whom the Commission, in accordance with section 3(4) of the Act, has delegated its functions under paragraph 2A of Schedule 3 to the Act;

"representation order" means a document granting a right to representation under section 14 of the Act.

Proceedings in which representation order may be granted

6–182a **3.** The Commission may, at any stage of the proceedings, grant to an individual a representation order in respect of relevant proceedings.

Extension of representation order

6–182b **4.** A representation order granted to an individual extends to—

(a) the Crown Court, if the proceedings continue there; and

(b) any proceedings incidental to the proceedings,

but does not extend to an appeal.

Withdrawal of representation order

6–182c **5.**—(1) Where any charge or proceedings against the individual are varied, the representation authority must—

(a) consider whether the interests of justice require that he be represented in respect of the varied charge or proceedings; and

(b) withdraw the representation order if the interests of justice do not so require.

(2) The representation authority must consider whether to withdraw the representation order in any of the following circumstances—

(a) where the individual declines to accept the order in the terms on which it is granted;

(b) otherwise at the request of the individual; or

(c) where the representative named in the representation order declines to continue to represent the individual.

Transitional provisions

6–182d **6.** An application for a representation order which is received before 2nd October 2006 is to be dealt with as if these Regulations had not been made.

Criminal Defence Service (Representation Orders: Appeals etc.) Regulations 2006 (S.I. 2006 No. 2494)

6–183 **1.** [*Citation and commencement (October 2, 2006).*]

Interpretation

6–184 **2.** In these Regulations—

"the Act" means the *Access to Justice Act* 1999;

"appropriate officer" means —

in a magistrates' court, the justices' clerk or the designated officer;

in the Crown Court, a court manager or a court officer designated by him to act on his behalf for the purposes of these Regulations;

in the Court of Appeal—

the Registrar of Criminal Appeals or the Head of the Civil Appeals Office, as appropriate; or

in either case, a court officer designated by him to act on his behalf for the purposes of these Regulations;

"the Commission" means the Legal Services Commission established under section 1 of the Act;

"representation authority" has the same meaning as in the *Criminal Defence Service (Representation Orders and Consequential Amendments) Regulations* 2006;

"representation order" means a document granting a right to representation under section 14 of the Act.

As to the definition of "representation authority", see *ante*, § 6–182b.

General provisions

3.—(1) An appeal or a renewed application under these Regulations must be made on such form as is from time to time specified— **6–185**

(a) in the case of appeals, and renewed applications under regulation 8, by the Commission; and

(b) in the case of renewed applications under regulations 6 and 7, by the Lord Chancellor.

(2) The individual must provide such further particulars and documents as the person or body determining the appeal or renewed application may require in relation to his appeal or application.

(3) An appeal or a renewed application will be determined without a hearing unless the person or body determining the appeal or application directs otherwise.

(4) Where an application is referred under regulation 6(2)(b), 7(2)(b) or 9(3)(b), it is to be treated thereafter as if it were an appeal.

(5) Written reasons must be given for any decision on an appeal or a renewed application.

(6) The date of any representation order granted on an appeal or a renewed application under these Regulations—

(a) in proceedings in the Court of Appeal, is the date on which the original application for the order was received, subject to regulation 10(6) of the *Criminal Defence Service (General) (No. 2) Regulations* 2001; and

(b) in other proceedings, is the date on which the original application was received.

For regulation 10(6) of the 2001 regulations, see *ante*, § 6–161.

Appeals: magistrates' courts

4.—(1) In this regulation "court" means the magistrates' court in which the proceedings in respect of which the individual is seeking a representation order are being or are to be heard and includes a single justice. **6–186**

(2) An individual may appeal to the court against a decision to refuse to grant a representation order made on the grounds that the interests of justice do not require such an order to be granted.

(3) The court must either—

(a) uphold the decision; or

(b) decide that it would be in the interests of justice for a representation order to be granted.

(4) Where the court makes a decision under paragraph (3)(b), the individual may apply to the representation authority for a representation order; and—

(a) if the individual states in writing, verified by a statement of truth, that his financial resources have not changed since the date of his original application so as to make him financially ineligible for a representation order, the representation authority must grant the order; or

(b) if his financial resources may have so changed, the representation authority—

(i) must determine whether the individual is financially eligible to be granted a representation order in accordance with the *Criminal Defence Service (Financial Eligibility) Regulations* 2006; and

(ii) if he is so eligible, must grant the order.

For the *Criminal Defence Service (Financial Eligibility) Regulations* 2006 (S.I. 2006 No. 2492), see *post*, §§ 6–192 *et seq*.

6–187 **5.** An appeal does not lie against a decision to refuse to grant a representation order in respect of proceedings in a magistrates' court made on the grounds that the individual is not financially eligible to be granted such an order.

Renewals of application where representation order refused: Crown Court

6–188 **6.**—(1) An individual whose application for the grant of a representation order in respect of proceedings in the Crown Court has been refused on the grounds that the interests of justice do not require such an order to be granted may make a renewed application to the appropriate officer who, or court which, refused the application.

(2) Where a renewed application is made to the appropriate officer, he may—

(a) grant the order; or

(b) refer the application—

(i) in the Crown Court, to a judge of the Crown Court; or

(ii) in a magistrates' court, to the court or a District Judge (Magistrates' Court),

who may grant the order or refuse the application.

Renewals of application where representation order refused: Court of Appeal

6–189 **7.**—(1) An individual whose application for the grant of a representation order in respect of proceedings in the Court of Appeal has been refused by the court or the appropriate officer on the grounds that the interests of justice do not require such an order to be granted may make a renewed application to the court or the appropriate officer (as the case may be).

(2) Where a renewed application is made to the appropriate officer, he may—

(a) grant the order; or

(b) refer the application to a judge of the Court of Appeal, who may grant the order or refuse the application.

Renewals of application where representation order refused: Commission

6–189a **8.** An individual whose application for the grant of a representation order in respect of proceedings, other than proceedings in a magistrates' court, has been refused by the Commission on the grounds that the interests of justice do not require such an order to be granted may make a renewed application to the Commission, which may grant the order or refuse the application.

Withdrawals of representation order

6–190 **9.**—(1) An individual whose representation order has been withdrawn may apply on one occasion to the person who, or body which, withdrew the order to set aside the withdrawal.

(2) Any application must be made on such form as is from time to time specified—

(a) by the Commission, in the case of withdrawal by the Commission or by the representation authority in proceedings in a magistrates' court; and

(b) by the Lord Chancellor, in the case of withdrawal by the appropriate officer or the court in proceedings in the Crown Court or the Court of Appeal.

(3) Where an application is made to the appropriate officer, he may—

(a) set aside the withdrawal; or

(b) refer the application—

(i) in a magistrates' court, to the court or a District Judge (Magistrates' Court);

(ii) in the Crown Court, to a judge of the Crown Court; or

(iii) in the Court of Appeal, to a judge of the Court of Appeal,

who may set aside the withdrawal or refuse the application.

Transitional provisions

6–191 **10.** A renewed application which is pending immediately before 2nd October 2006 is to be dealt with as if these Regulations had not been made.

Criminal Defence Service (Financial Eligibility) Regulations 2006 (S.I. 2006 No. 2492)

6–192 **1.** [*Citation and commencement (October 2, 2006).*]

Interpretation

6–193 **2.**—(1) In these Regulations—

"the Act" means the *Access to Justice Act* 1999;

"child care costs" means the costs of care which is provided by one or more of the following care providers—

(a) a school on school premises, out of school hours;

(b) a local authority, out of school hours—

(i) for children who are not disabled, in respect of the period beginning on their eighth birthday and ending on the day preceding the first Monday in September following their 15th birthday;

(ii) for children who are disabled, in respect of the period beginning on their eighth birthday and ending on the day preceding the first Monday in September following their 16th birthday;

(c) a child care provider approved in accordance with the *Tax Credit (New Category of Care Provider) Regulations* 1999 (S.I. 1993 No. 3110);

(d) persons registered under Part XA of the *Children Act* 1989;

(e) persons referred to in paragraph 1 or 2 of Schedule 9A to the *Children Act* 1989, in schools or establishments referred to in those paragraphs;

(f) persons prescribed in regulations made pursuant to section 12(4) of the *Tax Credits Act* 2002;

other than costs paid in respect of the child's compulsory education or by the individual to his partner (or vice versa) in respect of any child for whom either or any of them is responsible in accordance with regulation 10 of the *Council Tax Benefit Regulations* 2006 (S.I. 2006 No. 215), or in respect of care provided by a relative of the child wholly or mainly in the child's home;

"the Commission" means the Legal Services Commission established under section 1 of the Act;

"gross annual income" means total annual income, as at the date of the application for a representation order, from all sources, other than the receipt of any of the following—

(a) any of the following payments made under the *Social Security Contributions and Benefits Act* 1992—

(i) attendance allowance paid under section 64;

(ii) severe disablement allowance;

(iii) carer's allowance;

(iv) disability living allowance;

(v) constant attendance allowance paid under section 104 or paragraph 4 or 7(2) of Schedule 8 as an increase to a disablement pension;

(vi) council tax benefit;

(vii) any payment made out of the social fund;

(b) any direct payments made under the *Community Care, Services for Carers and Children's Services (Direct Payments) (England) Regulations* 2003 (S.I. 2003 No. 762) or the *Community Care, Services for Carers and Children's Services (Direct Payments) (Wales) Regulations* 2004 (S.I. 2004 No. 1748);

(c) any exceptionally severe disablement allowance paid under the *Personal Injuries (Civilians) Scheme* 1983 (S.I. 1983 No. 686);

(d) any pensions paid under the *Naval, Military and Air Forces etc (Disablement and Death) Service Pensions Order* 2006 (S.I. 2006 No. 606);

(e) any Independent Living Funds payments;

(f) any financial support paid under an agreement for the care of a foster child;

"the Independent Living Funds" means the Independent Living Fund, the Independent Living (Extension) Fund, the Independent Living Fund (1993) and the Independent Living Fund (2006);

"the Independent Living Fund" means the charitable trust established out of funds provided by the Secretary of State for the purpose of providing financial assistance to those persons incapacitated by or otherwise suffering from very severe disablement who are in need of such assistance to enable them to live independently;

"the Independent Living (Extension) Fund" means the Trust of that name established by a deed dated 25th February 1993 and made between the Secretary of State for Social Security of the one part and Robin Glover Wendt and John Fletcher Shepherd of the other part;

"the Independent Living (1993) Fund" means the Trust of that name established by a deed dated 25th February 1993 and made between the Secretary of State for Social Security of the one part and Robin Glover Wendt and John Fletcher Shepherd of the other part;

"the Independent Living Fund (2006)" means the Trust of that name established by a deed dated 10th April 2006 and made between the Secretary of State for Work and Pensions of the one part and Margaret Rosemary Cooper, Michael Beresford Boyall and Marie Theresa Martin of the other part;

"partner" means a person with whom the individual lives as a couple, and includes a person with whom the individual is not currently living but from whom he is not living separate and apart;

"period of calculation" means the period of one year ending on the date on which an application for a representation order is made;

"representation authority" means the Commission or a court officer or other person to whom the Commission, in accordance with section 3(4) of the Act, has delegated its functions under paragraph 2A of Schedule 3 to the Act;

"representation order" means a document granting a right to representation under section 14 of the Act.

(2) Subject to the proviso in regulation 7(1), in these Regulations a reference to the financial resources, income or financial circumstances of the individual includes a reference to the financial resources, income or financial circumstances of his partner.

[This regulation is printed as amended by the *Criminal Defence Service (Financial Eligibility) (Amendment No. 2) Regulations* 2007 (S.I. 2007 No. 2937).]

Scope

6–194 **3.** These Regulations apply to those criminal proceedings which—

(a) are referred to in section 12(2)(a) to (f) of the Act and in regulation 3(2) (other than sub-paragraph (h)) of the *Criminal Defence Service (General) (No. 2) Regulations* 2001 (S.I. 2001 No. 1437); and

(b) are in a magistrates' court.

Relevant authority

6–195 **4.** The representation authority is the relevant authority for the purposes of section 26 of, and paragraph 3B of Schedule 3 to, the Act.

Assessment by representation authority

6–196 **5.**—(1) The representation authority must assess whether the financial resources of the individual are such that he is eligible to be granted a representation order in accordance with this regulation and regulations 7 to 10.

(2) The representation authority must treat an individual who at the date of the application is under the age of 18 as financially eligible for a representation order, and paragraphs (3) to (5) of this regulation and regulations 7 to 14 do not apply in such a case.

(3) Where the representation authority is satisfied that the individual is directly or indirectly in receipt of a qualifying benefit, it must take his gross annual income as not exceeding the sum specified for the time being in regulation 9(2).

(4) The following are qualifying benefits for the purposes of paragraph (3)—

(a) income support;

(b) income-based jobseeker's allowance;

(c) guarantee credit under section 1(3)(a) of the *State Pension Credit Act* 2002;

(d) income-related employment and support allowance payable under Part 1 of the *Welfare Reform Act* 2007.

(5) Except where paragraph (2) or (3) applies, the representation authority must calculate the gross annual income and, if applicable, the annual disposable income of the individual in accordance with regulations 7 to 10.

[This regulation is printed as amended by S.I. 2007 No. 2937 (*ante*, § 6–193); and the *Employment and Support Allowance (Consequential Provisions) (No. 3) Regulations* 2008 (S.I. 2008 No. 1879).]

Furnishing evidence

6–197 **6.** The representation authority may at any time require the individual to provide documentary evidence in support of his application.

Resources of other persons

6–198 **7.**—(1) In calculating the income of the individual, the representation authority must treat the resources of his partner as his resources, unless the partner has a contrary interest in the proceedings in respect of which he is seeking a representation order.

(2) Where it appears to the representation authority that—

(a) another person is or has been or is likely to be substantially maintaining the individual or his partner; or

(b) any of the resources of another person have been or are likely to be made available to the individual or his partner,

the representation authority may assess or estimate the value of the resources of that other person and may treat all or any part of them as the resources of the individual.

Deprivation etc. of resources

8. If it appears to the representation authority that the individual or his partner has, with intent to reduce the amount of his resources, whether for the purpose of making the individual eligible for a representation order or otherwise— **6–199**

(a) directly or indirectly deprived himself of any resources; or

(b) transferred any resources to another person,

the resources of which he has so deprived himself, or which he has transferred, are to be treated as part of the individual's resources.

Financial eligibility

9.—(1) Where an individual applies for a representation order, the representation authority must calculate the gross annual income of the individual and, where he has a partner or has children living in his household, must divide the total according to the scale set out in the Schedule to these Regulations. **6–200**

(2) An individual is eligible for a representation order if his gross annual income, as adjusted under paragraph (1) where appropriate, is £12,475 or less.

(3) An individual is not eligible for a representation order if his gross annual income, as adjusted under paragraph (1) where appropriate, is £22,325 or more.

[This regulation is printed as amended by the *Criminal Defence Service (Financial Eligibility) (Amendment) Regulations* 2007 (S.I. 2007 No. 777); and the *Criminal Defence Service (Financial Eligibility) (Amendment) Regulations* 2008 (S.I. 2008 No. 723); but an application for a representation order which was made before April 7, 2008, is to be dealt with as if the amendments (uprating the amounts) had not been made (reg.1(2)).]

10.—(1) Where an individual's gross annual income, as adjusted under regulation 9(1) where appropriate, is more than £12,475 and less than £22,325, the representation authority must calculate the individual's annual disposable income in accordance with paragraph (2). **6–201**

(2) There are to be deducted from the individual's gross annual income—

(a) any income tax paid or payable in respect of the period of calculation;

(b) any contributions estimated to have been paid under Part 1 of the *Social Security Contributions and Benefits Act* 1992, in respect of the period of calculation;

(c) any council tax paid or payable in respect of the period of calculation;

(d) either—

(i) any annual rent or annual payment (whether of interest or capital) in respect of a mortgage debt or hereditable security, payable by him in respect of his only or main dwelling, less any housing benefit paid under the *Social Security Contributions and Benefits Act* 1992; or

(ii) the annual cost of his living accommodation;

(e) any child care costs paid or payable in respect of the period of calculation;

(f) if the individual is making bona fide payments for the maintenance of a former partner or of a child or a relative who is not (in such case) a member of his household, the amount of such payments paid or payable in respect of the period of calculation;

(g) an amount representing cost of living expenses in respect of the period of calculation, being either—

(i) £5,676; or

(ii) if the individual has a partner or has children living in his household, an amount calculated in accordance with the scale set out in the Schedule to these Regulations.

(3) An individual is eligible for a representation order if his annual disposable income, as calculated under this regulation, does not exceed £3,398.

[This regulation is printed as amended by S.I. 2007 No. 777 (*ante*, § 6–200); and S.I. 2008 No. 723 (*ante*, § 6–200); but an application for a representation order which was made before April 7, 2008, is to be dealt with as if the amendments (uprating the amounts) had not been made (reg. 1(2)).]

Duty to report change in financial circumstances

6–202 **11.**—(1) An individual who has been granted a representation order must—

(a) forthwith inform the representation authority of any change in his financial circumstances of which he is aware, which has occurred since any calculation of his resources and which might affect his eligibility for a representation order; and

(b) inform the representation authority of any change in his financial circumstances of which he should reasonably be aware, which has occurred since any calculation of his resources and which might affect his eligibility for a representation order.

(2) Where, as a result of any such change, the individual is no longer financially eligible for a representation order, the representation authority must withdraw the grant of representation.

Re-calculation of income following error etc.

6–203 **12.** Where—

(a) it appears to the representation authority that there has been some error in the calculation of the individual's income; or

(b) new information which is relevant to the application has come to light (whether under regulation 11 or otherwise),

the representation authority must re-calculate the income and, if the individual is no longer financially eligible for a representation order, must withdraw the order.

Renewal of application

6–204 **13.** An individual who has been refused a representation order on the grounds that his financial resources are not such that he is eligible for such an order may renew his application if, but only if—

(a) there is a change in his financial circumstances which might affect his eligibility for a representation order; or

(b) a decision refusing him a representation order has been quashed under regulation 14(5)(c).

[This regulation is printed as amended by S.I. 2007 No. 2937 (*ante*, § 6–193).]

Review of decision

6–205 **14.**—(1) An individual who has been refused a representation order on the grounds that his financial resources are not such that he is eligible for such an order may apply for a review of the decision—

(a) to the representation authority, on the ground that there has been a miscalculation of his income or an administrative error; or

(b) to the Commission, on the ground that he does not have sufficient means to pay for the cost of legal assistance, notwithstanding that his financial resources are such that he is not eligible for a representation order under these Regulations.

(2) An application for a review must be made on such form as the Commission may specify.

(3) Where the grounds of the application are those mentioned in paragraph (1)(b), the individual must provide full particulars of his income and expenditure and a certificate by a solicitor as to the individual's likely costs of the proceedings.

(4) Where—

(a) the grounds of the application are those mentioned in paragraph (1)(a); and

(b) the representation authority is not the Commission,

the representation authority may refer the application to the Commission for its decision.

(5) On a review the representation authority or the Commission (as the case may be) may—

(a) uphold the decision;

(b) grant the individual a representation order; or

(c) quash the decision.

(6) The Commission may, if it thinks that the application raises a question of such importance that it should be decided by the High Court, refer that question to the High Court for its decision.

[This regulation is printed as amended by S.I. 2007 No. 2937 (*ante*, § 6-193).]

Withdrawal of representation order

15. Where the individual fails to comply with a requirement under regulation 6 and a representation order has been granted, the representation authority must withdraw the order unless it is satisfied that there are good reasons why it should not do so. **6–206**

Transitional provisions

16. An application for a representation order which is received before 2nd October 2006 is to be dealt with as if these Regulations had not been made. **6–207**

SCHEDULE

Scale for the purposes of regulations 9(1) and 10(2)(g)(ii)

For the purposes of regulation 9(1), add the relevant figure below to 1.00 and divide the individual's gross annual income by the total. **6–208**

For the purpose of regulation 10(2)(g)(ii), add the relevant figure below to 1.00 and multiply £5,676 by the total.

A partner	0.64
Each child of the individual in his household, aged 0–1	0.15
Each child, as above, aged 2–4	0.30
Each child, as above, aged 5–7	0.34
Each child, as above, aged 8–10	0.38
Each child, as above, aged 11–12	0.41
Each child, as above, aged 13–15	0.44
Each child, as above, aged 16–18	0.59

[The schedule is printed as amended by S.I. 2007 No. 777 (*ante*, § 6–200); and S.I. 2008 No. 723 (*ante*, § 6–200); but an application for a representation order which was made before April 7, 2008, is to be dealt with as if the amendment (substituting "£5,676" for "£5,463") had not been made (reg. 1(2)).]

[The next paragraph is § 6–266.]

Criminal Defence Service (Recovery of Defence Costs Orders) Regulations 2001 (S.I. 2001 No. 856)

1. [*Citation and commencement.*] **6–266**

2. In these Regulations: **6–267**

"the Act" means the *Access to Justice Act* 1999;

"appropriate officer" means:

in the case of the Crown Court, the court manager; and

in the case of the Court of Appeal or the House of Lords, the registrar of criminal appeals

and, in either case, includes an officer designated by him to act on his behalf in that regard;

"the Commission" means the Legal Services Commission established under section 1 of the Act;

"the Criminal Defence Service" means the Criminal Defence Service established under section 12 of the Act;

"funded defendant" means an individual who has received representation in respect of criminal proceedings before any court which is funded by the Commission or the Lord Chancellor as part of the Criminal Defence Service; and

"representation order" means a document granting a right to representation, and includes any other representation order under which representation has been provided for the funded defendant in the same proceedings.

6–268 **3.**—(1) Where an individual receives representation in respect of criminal proceedings which is funded by the Commission or the Lord Chancellor as part of the Criminal Defence Service, the court before which the proceedings are heard, other than a magistrates' court, shall, subject to regulation 4, make an order requiring him to pay some or all of the cost of any representation so funded for him in the circumstances set out in these Regulations.

(2) An order of the type mentioned in paragraph (1) shall be known as a Recovery of Defence Costs Order (an "RDCO").

[This regulation is printed as amended by the *Criminal Defence Service (Recovery of Defence Costs Orders) (Amendment) Regulations* 2004 (S.I. 2004 No. 1195); and (in relation to representation orders granted on or after October 6, 2008) the *Criminal Defence Service (Recovery of Defence Costs Orders) (Amendment) Regulations* 2008 (S.I. 2008 No. 2430).]

6–269 **4.**—(1) The judge hearing the case shall make an RDCO against a funded defendant except as provided in paragraph (2), (3) or (4).

(2) An RDCO shall not be made against a funded defendant who—

(a) has appeared in the magistrates' court only; or

(b) is committed for sentence to the Crown Court.

(3) Subject to regulation 13, an RDCO shall not be made against a funded defendant who—

(a) has been acquitted, other than in exceptional circumstances;

(b) is directly or indirectly in receipt of—

(i) guarantee credit;

(ii) income support;

(iii) income-based jobseeker's allowance; or

(iv) income-related employment and support allowance;

(c) has none of the following assets—

(i) capital over £3,000;

(ii) equity in that defendant's principal residence over £100,000;

(iii) gross annual income over £22,235; or

(d) is under the age of 18.

(4) Subject to regulation 13, an RDCO shall not be made where the judge hearing the case is satisfied that—

(a) it would not be reasonable to make such an order, on the basis of the information and evidence available; or

(b) the payment of an RDCO would, owing to the exceptional circumstances of the case, involve undue financial hardship.

[This regulation is printed as substituted by S.I. 2008 No. 2430 (*ante*, § 6–268). As so substituted, it applies only to representation orders made on or after October 6, 2008 (other than where a representation order has previously been granted to the same individual in the same proceedings): *ibid.*, reg. 2.]

6–270 **5.**—(1) An RDCO may be made up to a maximum amount of the full cost of the representation incurred in any court under the representation order.

(2) An RDCO may provide for payment to be made forthwith, or in specified instalments.

6–271 **6.** Except in the circumstances mentioned in regulation 4(2), the funded defendant shall provide such information and evidence about their financial circumstances as the court or Commission requires.

[This regulation is printed as substituted by S.I. 2008 No. 2430 (*ante*, § 6–268). As to its application, as so substituted, see the note to reg. 4 (*ante*, § 6–269).]

6–272 **7.**—(1) Where a representation order has been made or is being considered, the court or the appropriate officer may refer the financial resources of the funded defendant to the Commission for a report, and the Commission shall produce such a report.

(2) In compiling a report under this regulation, the Commission may investigate the financial resources of the funded defendant and may subsequently require him to provide further information or evidence, and details of any change in his financial circumstances.

7A. Where further information is required in order to decide whether to make an RDCO or to decide the terms of the RDCO the judge may— **6–272a**

(a) adjourn consideration of the matter; and

(b) order that any further information which is required shall be provided.

[This regulation was inserted by S.I. 2008 No. 2430 (*ante*, § 6–268). As so to its application, see the note to reg. 4 (*ante*, § 6–269).]

8.—(1) Without prejudice to regulation 9(1)(a), where it appears to the judge, the appropriate officer or the Commission that: **6–273**

(a) the funded defendant has directly or indirectly transferred any resources to another person;

(aa) the funded defendant has directly or indirectly deprived themselves of any resources or expectations;

(b) another person is or has been maintaining him in any proceedings; or

(c) any of the resources of another person are or have been made available to him;

the judge, the appropriate officer or the Commission (as the case may be) may assess or estimate the value of the resources of that other person or the value of the resources or expectations of which the funded defendant has so deprived themself [*sic*], and may treat all or any of such resources or expectations as those of the funded defendant.

(2) In this regulation, "person" includes a company, partnership, body of trustees and any body of persons whether corporate or not corporate.

[This regulation is printed as amended by S.I. 2008 No. 2430 (*ante*, § 6–268). As to its application, as so amended, see the note to reg. 4 (*ante*, § 6–269).]

9.—(1) Except as provided in paragraph (2), for the purpose of calculating the financial resources of the funded defendant: **6–274**

(a) the amount or value of every source of income and every resource of a capital nature available to him shall be taken into account; and

(b) the amount or value of every source of income and every resource of a capital nature available to the funded defendant's partner shall be treated as the financial resources of the funded defendant, unless the partner has a contrary interest in the criminal proceedings before the court.

(2) Unless there are exceptional circumstances, the following assets of the funded defendant shall be taken into account by the judge when considering the terms of the order—

(a) capital over £3,000;

(b) equity in the funded defendant's principal residence over £100,000;

(c) gross annual income over £22,235.

(3) In this regulation, "funded defendant's partner" means a person with whom the funded defendant lives as a couple, and includes a person with whom the funded defendant is not currently living but from whom he is not living separate and apart.

[This regulation was amended by the *Criminal Defence Service (Recovery of Defence Costs Orders) (Amendment) Regulations* 2005 (S.I. 2005 No. 2783). This amendment only applied to representation orders made on or after October 31, 2005. It is printed as subsequently amended by S.I. 2008 No. 2430 (*ante*, § 6–268). As to its application, as so amended, see the note to reg. 4 (*ante*, § 6–269).]

10. Where he is requested to do so by the judge or the Commission, the litigator for the funded defendant shall provide an estimate of the total costs which are likely to be incurred under the representation order. **6–275**

[This regulation is printed as amended by S.I. 2008 No. 2430 (*ante*, § 6–268). As to its application, as so amended, see the note to reg. 4 (*ante*, § 6–269).]

11. At the conclusion of the relevant proceedings the judge shall— **6–276**

(a) subject to regulation 4, make an RDCO and give reasons for the terms of the order;

(b) where an RDCO may be made under regulation 4(3)(a), consider whether it is reasonable in all the circumstances of the case to make such an order;

(c) where an RDCO is made under regulation 4(3)(a), give reasons for the decision to make such an order;

(d) if pursuant to regulation 4(4) an RDCO is not made, give reasons for the decision not to make such an order.

[This regulation is printed as substituted by S.I. 2008 No. 2430 (*ante*, § 6–268). As to its application, as so substituted, see the note to reg. 4 (*ante*, § 6–269).]

6–277 **12.** [*Revoked by S.I. 2008 No. 2430 (*ante, *§ 6–268).*]

6–278 **13.** Where information is required under regulation 6, 7(2) or 7A(b) and such information fails to be provided, an RDCO shall ... be made for the full cost of the representation incurred under the representation order.

[This regulation is printed as amended by S.I. 2004 No. 1195 (*ante*, § 6–268); and S.I. 2008 No. 2430 (*ante*, § 6–268). As to its application as amended by the 2008 order, see the note to reg. 4 (*ante*, § 6–269).]

6–279 **14.**—(1) The litigator for the funded defendant shall inform the Commission if it subsequently transpires that the costs incurred under the representation order were lower than the amount ordered to be paid under an RDCO.

(2) In the circumstances mentioned in paragraph (1), where the funded defendant has paid the amount ordered to be paid under the RDCO, the balance shall be repaid to him.

[This regulation is printed as amended by S.I. 2008 No. 2430 (*ante*, § 6–268).]

6–280 **15.** The judge may make an order prohibiting an individual who is required to furnish information or evidence from dealing with property where:

(a) information has failed to be provided in accordance with these Regulations;
(b) he considers that there is a real risk that relevant property will be disposed of; or
(c) at the conclusion of the case, the assessment of the costs incurred under the representation order or of the financial resources of the funded defendant has not yet been completed.

6–281 **16.** Any payment required to be made under an RDCO shall be made to the Commission in accordance with the order.

6–282 **17.** The Commission may enforce an RDCO in any manner which would be applicable to a civil debt between parties, and may add any costs incurred in connection with the enforcement to the amount to be paid under the RDCO.

[This regulation is printed as amended by S.I. 2004 No. 1195, *ante*, § 6–268.]

6–283 In *R. v. K., G. and M.*, *The Times*, February 15, 2005, Thomas L.J. (sitting apparently as a single judge) said that it was important to ensure that the court had the necessary information to make, where appropriate, a recovery of defence costs order against an appellant who had failed in his appeal, rather than letting the burden fall on the taxpayer; to this end, the lodging of the statement of means form and the supplying of accurate information was an important matter and not a formality; if the requisite statement had not been lodged two weeks before the hearing, the Criminal Appeal Office should list the matter before the registrar so that the advocate could attend, without fee, and explain the failure; any appellant, who was unable to provide exceptional reasons for the failure, would be at risk of having the representation order revoked by the registrar. For the suggestion that the registrar has no power to revoke an order, and that the intended sanction for non-provision of information is the making of an order for the full cost of the appellant's representation, see *Criminal Law Week* 2005/07/13.

Funding

6–284 The *Criminal Defence Service (Funding) Order* 2007 (S.I. 2007 No. 1174) makes provision for the funding and remuneration of services provided under Part I of the *Access to Justice Act* 1999, as part of the Criminal Defence Service; and revokes, subject to transitional provisions that apply to representation orders made before April 30, 2007, the *Criminal Defence Service (Funding) Order* 2001 (S.I. 2001 No. 855). See Appendix G–6 *et seq.*, where the order is set out *in extenso*.

III. DISCIPLINARY JURISDICTION OVER SOLICITORS

6–285 If a solicitor has been guilty of neglect or misconduct as a result of which costs are needlessly incurred, the Supreme Court [Senior Courts] has [have] inherent jurisdiction to order the solicitor to pay those costs. This jurisdiction was described by Lord Wright in *Myers v. Elman* [1940] A.C. 282 at 317–319, HL. The jurisdiction is retained by judges of the Crown Court as a constituent element of the Supreme Court [Senior Courts] of England and Wales, see the *Supreme Court [Senior Courts] Act* 1981, ss.1(1) and 45(1) (as to the renaming of the 1981 Act, see *ante*, § 6–28), *Weston v. Central Criminal Court Courts Administrator* [1977] Q.B. 32, CA (Civ. Div.), and *R. v. Smith (Martin)* [1975] Q.B. 531, CA (Civ. Div.).

In *Holden & Co. v. CPS* [1990] 2 Q.B. 261, CA (Civ. Div.), it was held that the jurisdiction is not available in cases of mistake, error of judgment or mere negligence. It is only available where the conduct of the solicitor is inexcusable and such as to merit reproof: dictum of Lord Denning M.R. in *R. & T. Thew Ltd v. Reeves (No. 2) (Note)* [1982] 1 Q.B. 1283 at 1286, approved.

No order should be made against a solicitor unless fair notice is given to him of the matter alleged against him and he is given a fair opportunity of being heard in answer: see *R. v. Smith (Martin)*, *ante*.

There is a right of appeal to the Court of Appeal (Civil Division): see the *Solicitors* **6–286**
Act 1974, s.50(3), as amended by the 1981 Act (*ante*), ss.147, 152(4) and Sched. 7. In *Holden & Co. v. CPS (No. 2)* [1994] 1 A.C. 22, HL, it was held that on an appeal under section 50(3) there is no power to award a successful solicitor his costs out of central funds. Their Lordships expressed the view (*obiter*) that the same position obtained under section 19A of the *Prosecution of Offences Act* 1985 (*ante*, § 6–40) which now governs wasted costs orders made against solicitors in criminal proceedings.

With the enactment of section 19A, the inherent jurisdiction of the court is going to be of less significance.

Chapter 7

CRIMINAL APPEAL

I. INTRODUCTION

7–1 Prior to the *CJA* 1987, it was only the defendant who had any right of appeal to the Court of Appeal from the Crown Court, although both prosecution and defence had a right of appeal, subject to the grant of leave, from a decision of the Court of Appeal to the House of Lords. Prior to the *CJA* 1988, the power of the Court of Appeal to order a retrial was limited to cases where the conviction was quashed only by reason of "fresh" evidence received, or available to be received, under section 23 of the *CAA* 1968 (*post*, § 7–208), or, in those exceptional cases, where the proceedings in the Crown Court were deemed to have been a nullity, in which case a *venire de novo* could be ordered (*post*, §§ 7–351 *et seq.*).

The 1987 Act provided for interlocutory appeals by either side from rulings in preparatory hearings in cases of serious or complex fraud, and the *CPIA* 1996 introduced a set of almost identical provisions in relation to preparatory hearings in other long and complex cases. The 1988 Act amended section 7 of the 1968 Act so as to allow of the possibility of a retrial whenever a conviction was quashed. This amendment significantly reduced the importance of the court's jurisdiction to issue a writ of *venire de novo*. The 1988 Act also conferred power on the Attorney-General to refer what were considered to be unduly lenient sentences to the Court of Appeal. Unlike the power to refer a point of law to that court for its opinion following an acquittal which had existed since the *CJA* 1972, which could have no effect on the acquittal, on a sentencing reference the Court of Appeal had power to increase the sentence. In the intervening years, the range of offences, the sentence for which could be referred under this provision, has been considerably extended, and there has been much greater willingness on the part of the Attorney-General to refer cases.

The movement towards common rights of appeal for prosecution and defence, given a push by the *PCA* 2002, was taken considerably further by the *CJA* 2003. Part 9 confers rights of appeal on the prosecution from rulings of the trial judge that would effectively result in an acquittal if not reversed, and from certain rulings as to the admissibility of evidence. Part 10 further extends the jurisdiction of the Court of Appeal by conferring on it power to order a retrial following an acquittal of a "serious offence". The power to order such a retrial depends on the availability of fresh evidence; but it may be seen to mirror the original strictly limited power of the court to order a retrial following a conviction (*i.e.* where there was fresh evidence).

The defendant's rights of appeal following conviction and sentence on indictment, or following being dealt with by the Crown Court on committal for sentence or being dealt with in certain other specified proceedings are contained in the *CAA* 1968. Part I provides for rights of appeal against conviction and sentence, and its provisions are set out in the fourth section of this chapter. The prosecution's rights of appeal under Part 9 of the 2003 Act are dealt with in the fifth section of this chapter. The jurisdiction to order a retrial under Part 10 of the 2003 Act (an appeal against an acquittal in all but name) is dealt with in section VI of this chapter.

Interlocutory appeals under the Acts of 1987 and 1996 (*ante*) are dealt with in section VII, and miscellaneous rights of appeal to the Court of Appeal are set out in section VIII. Procedure and forms are dealt with in section IX. The provisions of the *CAA* 1968 relating to appeals to the House of Lords [Supreme Court] are contained in section X, and miscellaneous provisions of that Act that pertain to appeals to and from the Court of Appeal are set out in section XI. The power to order a *venire de novo* is described in section XII, and the final two sections of the chapter deal with references of points of law and of sentences to the Court of Appeal and of points of Community law to the European Court of Justice.

Apart from the foregoing, in matters not relating to trial on indictment, the High Court has jurisdiction to hear appeals by way of case stated and applications for judicial review in respect of decisions of the Crown Court. This jurisdiction is considered in the second section of the chapter. **7–2**

For appeals to the Crown Court from magistrates' courts, see *ante*, §§ 2–159 *et seq.*

II. HIGH COURT JURISDICTION IN CROWN COURT PROCEEDINGS

A. JURISDICTION

(1) Appeal by way of case stated

Supreme Court [Senior Courts] Act 1981, s.28

Appeals from Crown Court and inferior courts

28.—(1) Subject to subsection (2), any order, judgment or other decision of the Crown Court may be questioned by any party to the proceedings, on the ground that it is wrong in law or is in excess of jurisdiction, by applying to the Crown Court to have a case stated by that court for the opinion of the High Court. **7–3**

(2) Subsection (1) shall not apply to—

(a) a judgment or other decision of the Crown Court relating to trial on indictment; or

(b) any decision of that court under the *Betting, Gaming and Lotteries Act* 1963, the *Licensing Act* 1964, the *Gaming Act* 1986 or the *Local Government (Miscellaneous) Provisions Act* 1982 which, by any provision of any of those Acts is to be final.

(3) Subject to the provisions of this Act and to rules of court, the High Court shall, in accordance with section 19(2), have jurisdiction to hear and determine—

(a) any application, or any appeal (whether by way of case stated or otherwise), which it has power to hear and determine under or by virtue of this or any other Act; and

(b) all such other appeals as it had jurisdiction to hear and determine immediately before the commencement of this Act.

(4) In subsection (2)(a) the reference to a decision of the Crown Court relating to trial on indictment does not include a decision relating to an order under section 17 of the *Access to Justice Act* 1999.

[The 1981 Act is renamed the *Senior Courts Act* as from a day to be appointed and the Supreme Court of England and Wales is renamed the Senior Courts of England and Wales as from a day to be appointed: see the *Constitutional Reform Act* 2005, s.59, and Sched. 11. This section is printed as amended by the *Access to Justice Act* 1999, s.24 and Sched. 4, para. 22.]

The High Court may send a case back for amendment: *Supreme Court [Senior Courts] Act* 1981, s.28A(2). On determining the question arising on the case, it shall reverse, affirm or amend the determination in respect of which the case has been stated, or remit the matter to the lower court with its opinion, and it may make such other order in relation to the matter (including as to costs) as it thinks fit: *ibid.*, s.28A(3).

For procedural provision in relation to an appeal by way of case stated, see the *Criminal Procedure Rules* 2005 (S.I. 2005 No. 384), r.64.7 (*post*, § 7–17), and Part 52 of the *Civil Procedure Rules* 1998 (S.I. 1998 No. 3132).

As to the expression "judgment or other decision … relating to trial on indictment", see *post*, § 7–8.

"Decision" means "final decision": *Loade v. DPP* [1990] 1 Q.B. 1052, 90 Cr.App.R. 162, DC.

A finding on an issue of fact would only involve an error of law if perverse; preferring the evidence of one witness to that of another could not be perverse in this sense; where the essence of the complaint is that the Crown Court was mistaken in its findings of fact, it is futile to dress up a question of fact as a question of law ("was there any evidence on which a reasonable bench … could have concluded … ?"): *R. v. Mildenhall Magistrates' Court, ex p. Forest Heath D.C.*, 161 J.P. 401, CA (Civ. Div.).

(2) Judicial review

(a) *Statute*

Supreme Court [Senior Courts] Act 1981, ss.29, 31

Mandatory, prohibiting and quashing orders

7–4 **29.**—(1) The orders of *mandamus*, prohibition and *certiorari* shall be known instead as mandatory, prohibiting and quashing orders respectively.

(1A) The High Court shall have jurisdiction to make mandatory, prohibiting and quashing orders in those classes of case in which, immediately before 1st May 2004, it had jurisdiction to make orders of *mandamus*, prohibition and *certiorari* respectively.

(2) Every such order shall be final, subject to any right of appeal therefrom.

(3) In relation to the jurisdiction of the Crown Court, other than its jurisdiction in matters relating to trial on indictment, the High Court shall have all such jurisdiction to make mandatory, prohibiting or quashing orders as the High Court possesses in relation to the jurisdiction of an inferior court.

(3A) The High Court shall have no jurisdiction to make mandatory, prohibiting or quashing orders in relation to the jurisdiction of *a court-martial* [the Court Martial] in matters relating to—

(a) trial by *court-martial* [the Court Martial] for an offence, or

(b) appeals from *a Standing Civilian Court* [the Service Civilian Court];

and in this subsection "court-martial" means a court-martial under the Army Act *1955, the* Air Fce Act *1955 or the* Naval Discipline Act *1957.*

(4) The power of the High Court under any enactment to require justices of the peace or a judge or officer of a county court to do any act relating to the duties of their respective offices, or to require a magistrates' court to state a case for the opinion of the High Court, in any case where the High Court formerly had by virtue of any enactment jurisdiction to make a rule absolute, or an order, for any of those purposes, shall be exercisable by mandatory order.

(5) In any statutory provision—

(a) references to *mandamus* or to a writ or order of *mandamus* shall be read as references to a mandatory order;

(b) references to prohibition or to a writ or order of prohibition shall be read as references to a prohibiting order;

(c) references to *certiorari* or to a writ or order of *certiorari* shall be read as references to a quashing order; and

(d) references to the issue or award of a writ of *mandamus*, prohibition or *certiorari* shall be read as references to the making of the corresponding mandatory, prohibiting or quashing order.

(6) In subsection (3) the reference to the Crown Court's jurisdiction in matters relating to trial on indictment does not include its jurisdiction relating to orders under section 17 of the *Access to Justice Act* 1999.

[As to the renaming of the 1981 Act, see *ante*, § 7–3. This section is printed as amended by the *Access to Justice Act* 1999, s.24, and Sched. 4, para. 23; the *AFA* 2001, s.23; and the *Civil Procedure (Modification of Supreme Court Act 1981) Order* 2004 (S.I. 2004 No. 1033); and as amended, as from a day to be appointed, by the

AFA 2006, s.378(1), and Sched. 16, para. 93 (omission of italicised words in subs. (3A), insertion of words in square brackets).]

Section 29(3) confers jurisdiction where otherwise there would be none. It does not limit a general jurisdiction to review decisions of the Crown Court. Accordingly, in relation to "its jurisdiction in matters relating to trial on indictment", there is no power to grant a declaration or issue an injunction under section 31 (*post*): *R. v. Chelmsford Crown Court, ex p. Chief Constable of Essex* [1994] 1 W.L.R. 359, DC. In *R. (T.B.) v. Stafford Crown Court* [2006] 2 Cr.App.R. 34, DC, a declaration was granted, but no reference was made to this case, and no argument was addressed to the court as to its jurisdiction under section 29(3) (as to which, see *post*, § 7–12) or as to the power to grant a declaration.

Application for judicial review

31.—(1) An application to the High Court for one or more of the following forms of relief namely— **7–5**

(a) a mandatory, prohibiting or quashing order;
(b) a declaration or injunction under subsection (2); or
(c) an injunction under section 30 restraining a person not entitled to do so from acting in an office to which that section applies,

shall be made in accordance with rules of court by a procedure to be known as an application for judicial review.

(2) A declaration may be made or an injunction granted under this subsection in any case where an application for judicial review, seeking that relief, has been made and the High Court considers that, having regard to—

(a) the nature of the matters in respect of which relief may be granted by mandatory, prohibiting or quashing orders;
(b) the nature of the persons and bodies against whom relief may be granted by such orders; and
(c) all the circumstances of the case,

it would be just and convenient for the declaration to be made or the injunction to be granted, as the case may be,

(3) No application for judicial review shall be made unless the leave of the High Court has been obtained in accordance with rules of court; and the court shall not grant leave to make such an application unless it considers that the applicant has a sufficient interest in the matter to which the application relates.

(4) On an application for judicial review the High Court may award to the applicant damages, restitution or the recovery of a sum due if—

(a) the application includes a claim for such an award arising from any matter to which the application relates; and
(b) the court is satisfied that such an award would have been made if the claim had been made in an action begun by the applicant at the time of making the application.

(5) If, on an application for judicial review, the High Court quashes the decision to which the application relates, it may in addition—

(a) remit the matter to the court, tribunal or authority which made the decision, with a direction to reconsider the matter and reach a decision in accordance with the findings of the High Court, or
(b) substitute its own decision for the decision in question.

(5A) But the power conferred by subsection (5)(b) is exercisable only if—

(a) the decision in question was made by a court or tribunal,
(b) the decision is quashed on the ground that there has been an error of law, and
(c) without the error, there would have been only one decision which the court or tribunal could have reached.

(5B) Unless the High Court otherwise directs, a decision substituted by it under subsection (5)(b) has effect as if it were a decision of the relevant court or tribunal.

(6) Where the High Court considers that there has been undue delay in making an application for judicial review, the court may refuse to grant—

(a) leave for making of the application; or
(b) any relief sought on the application,

if it considers that the granting of the relief sought would be likely to cause substantial hardship to, or substantially prejudice the rights of, any person or would be detrimental to good administration.

(7) Subsection (6) is without prejudice to any enactment or rule of court which has the effect of limiting the time within which an application for judicial review may be made.

[This section is printed as amended by S.I. 2004 No. 1033 (*ante*, § 7–4); and the *Tribunals, Courts and Enforcement Act* 2007, s.141.]

For procedural provision in relation to applications for judicial review, see the *Civil Procedure Rules* 1998 (S.I. 1998 No. 3132), Pt 54.

Section 19 of the *Tribunals, Courts and Enforcement Act* 2007 inserts (as from a day to be appointed) a new section 31A in the 1981 Act, which requires the High Court to transfer to the Upper Tribunal (established under Part 1 of the 2007 Act) an application for judicial review or an application for permission to apply for judicial review if four conditions are met. The second condition is that the application does not call into question anything done by the Crown Court (s.31A(5)). It remains to be seen whether the Upper Tribunal will be accorded any jurisdiction in a "criminal cause or matter", but it would seem to be unlikely.

Supreme Court [Senior Courts] Act 1981, s.43

Power of High Court to vary sentence on application for quashing order

7–6 **43.**—(1) Where a person who has been sentenced for an offence—

(a) by a magistrates' court; or

(b) by the Crown Court after being convicted of the offence by a magistrates' court and committed to the Crown Court for sentence, or

(c) by the Crown Court on appeal against conviction or sentence,

applies to the High Court in accordance with section 31 for a quashing order to remove the proceedings of the magistrates' court or the Crown Court into the High Court, then, if the High Court determines that the magistrates' court or the Crown Court had no power to pass the sentence, the High Court may, instead of quashing the conviction, amend it by substituting for the sentence passed any sentence which the magistrates' court or, in a case within paragraph (b), the Crown Court had power to impose.

(2) Any sentence passed by the High Court by virtue of this section in substitution for the sentence passed in the proceedings of the magistrates' court or the Crown Court shall, unless the High Court otherwise directs, begin to run from the time when it would have begun to run if passed in those proceedings; but in computing the term of the sentence, any time during which the offender was released on bail in pursuance of section 37(1)(d) of the *Criminal Justice Act* 1948 shall be disregarded.

(3) Subsections (1) and (2) shall, with the necessary modifications, apply in relation to any order of a magistrates' court or the Crown Court which is made on, but does not form part of, the conviction of an offender as they apply in relation to a conviction and sentence.

[As to the renaming of the 1981 Act, see *ante*, § 7–3. This section is printed as amended by S.I. 2004 No. 1033 (*ante*, § 7–4).]

(b) *Case stated or judicial review?*

7–7 See *ante*, § 2–160.

(c) *Matters relating to trial on indictment*

General

7–8 There does not seem to be any significant difference between the expression "matters relating to trial on indictment" in section 29(3) and the expresion "judgment or other decision ... relating to trial on indictment" in section 28(2)(a) (*ante*). Most of the authorities have, however, been decided in the context of applications for judicial review, and have, therefore, been primarily concerned with the wording of section 29.

In *Re Smalley* [1985] A.C. 622, HL, it was held that these words excluded from appeal by way of case stated or judicial review the verdict given or the sentence passed at the end of a trial on indictment, including a trial of a person pleading guilty on arraignment. Without attempting to define words Parliament had chosen to leave undefined, their Lordships held that the test to be applied was whether the decision of the Crown Court was one affecting the conduct of a trial on indictment given in the course of the trial or by way of pre-trial directions. In any such case, to allow an appellate or review process might seriously delay the trial; any aggrieved defendant has his remedy by way of an appeal against conviction or sentence under the *CAA* 1968. *Re Smalley* was considered by the House of Lords in *Re Ashton* [1994] 1 A.C. 9, in which Lord Slynn stated that it was unnecessary to depart from the guidance given therein.

In determining whether a given decision fell within or without the phrase, Lord Browne-Wilkinson suggested in *R. v. Manchester Crown Court, ex p. DPP*, 98 Cr.App.R. 461, HL, that a helpful pointer was posed by the answer to the question: "Is the decision sought to be reviewed one arising in the issue between the Crown and the defendant formulated by the indictment (including the costs of such issue)? If the answer is 'yes' then to permit the decision to be challenged by judicial review may lead to delay in the trial and the matter is therefore probably excluded from review by the section. If the answer is 'no', the decision of the Crown Court is truly collateral to the indictment and judicial review of that decision will not delay the trial, therefore it may well not be excluded by the section" (at p. 467).

Where a judge makes an order which is jurisdictionally flawed, the High Court has power to intervene notwithstanding that the order relates to trial on indictment: *R. v. Crown Court at Maidstone, ex p. London Borough of Harrow* [2000] 1 Cr.App.R. 117, DC; *R. (Kenneally) v. Crown Court at Snaresbrook*; *R. (Kenneally) v. Rampton Hospital Authority* [2002] Q.B. 1169, DC.

The current interpretation of section 29(3), as represented by the decision in *Re Smalley*, and *Re Ashton*, is not incompatible with "a Convention right" within the *Human Rights Act* 1998; section 29(3) is concerned with judicial review and there is no Convention right to have decisions reviewed; the fact that some decisions that would not be subject to review by virtue of section 29(3) might involve breaches of the Convention, did not require that that subsection should be read so as to allow for review of all such decisions: *R. v. Canterbury Crown Court, ex p. Regentford Ltd*, *The Times*, February 6, 2001, DC. See also *R. (Shields) v. Liverpool Crown Court* [2001] A.C.D. 325, DC, to similar effect. *Cf. R. (Lichniak) v. Secretary of State for the Home Department*; *R. (Pyrah) v. Same*; *R. v. Lichniak*; *R. v. Pyrah* [2002] Q.B. 296, DC and CA (*post*, § 7–118).

In *R. (D.) v. Central Criminal Court* [2004] 1 Cr.App.R. 41, DC, it was said that whilst it would be inappropriate to seek judicial review of a decision to prosecute or to continue with a prosecution as a device to avoid the effect of section 29(3), leave would exceptionally be granted to challenge a decision to continue with a prosecution following a decision of the trial judge to refuse to order that there should be no disclosure of the claimant's defence statement to his co-defendants where all were agreed that disclosure would entail a significant risk to the life of the claimant and his family.

Matters not relating to trial on indictment

The following matters do not relate to trial on indictment. **7–9**

(a) An order estreating the recognizance of a surety for a defendant who failed to surrender to his trial at the Crown Court: *Re Smalley*, *ante*.

(b) A forfeiture order under section 27 of the *Misuse of Drugs Act* 1971 made against the owner of property who was not a defendant in the criminal proceedings: *R. v. Maidstone Crown Court, ex p. Gill*, 84 Cr.App.R. 96, DC.

(c) An order committing an acquitted defendant to prison unless he agrees to be bound over: *R. v. Inner London Crown Court, ex p. Benjamin*, 85 Cr.App.R. 267, DC.

(d) An order under section 39 of the *CYPA* 1933 (*ante*, § 4–27) protecting the anonymity of a child or young person who is the defendant in proceedings on indictment, or an order discharging an earlier such order, is not necessarily an order within the jurisdiction of the Crown Court "in matters relating to trial on indictment"; in deciding whether any particular order is excluded from review, the subject matter of the order is not the only consideration; the stage of the proceedings at which the order is made is also relevant: *R. v. Manchester*

Crown Court, ex p. H. and D. [2000] 1 Cr.App.R. 262, DC (preferring *R. v. Cardiff Crown Court, ex p. M (a Minor)*, 162 J.P. 527, DC, to *R. v. Winchester Crown Court, ex p. B.* [2000] 1 Cr.App.R. 11, DC, and *R. v. Central Criminal Court, ex p. Crook*, *The Times*, November 8, 1984, DC).

(e) A decision as to bail given at "an early stage" in proceedings that have been sent for trial: *R. (M.) v. Isleworth Crown Court and H.M. Customs and Excise*, unreported, March 2, 2005, DC ([2005] EWHC 363 (Admin.)). It should be noted, however, that the judgment of the court does not disclose how far proceedings had gone. The court refers to the case having been "transferred" to the Crown Court, but it is apparent that it would have been "sent" under section 51 of the *CDA* 1998. In particular, the judgment does not reveal whether an indictment was in existence at the time. It is submitted that there must be some limit to the decision, as the court itself implies by its use of the word "early". A decision as to bail given at trial would certainly be a decision relating to trial on indictment. The only sensible cut-off point would be the moment that the indictment is signed. As to the authoritative status of this decision, it was given without the benefit of full argument. The prosecution were represented, but no argument was advanced to the effect that the court did not have jurisdiction or as to the limits of that jurisdiction. As to the substantive point, see *ante*, § 3–186.

(f) A decision as to the manner in which the Crown Court deals with an application for bail (*e.g.* whether to sit in public or not): *R. (Malik) v. Central Criminal Court* [2006] 4 All E.R. 1141, DC. As with the previous case, no argument to the contrary was presented to the court.

Although the following matters have been held to be matters not relating to trial on indictment, the decisions were based either specifically or by implication on *R. v. Central Criminal Court, ex p. Randle*, 92 Cr.App.R. 323, DC, and *R. v. Crown Court at Norwich, ex p. Belsham*, 94 Cr.App.R. 382, both of which were specifically disapproved and overruled in *Re Ashton* [1994] 1 A.C. 9, HL.

7–10 (a) An order under regulation 3 of the *Costs in Criminal Cases (General) Regulations* 1986 (S.I. 1986 No. 1335) requiring the prosecution to pay defence costs incurred after committal where no evidence was offered: *R. v. Wood Green Crown Court, ex p. DPP* [1993] 1 W.L.R. 723, DC.

(b) A decision to stay a criminal trial, notwithstanding that it is made after an abortive trial: *R. v. Central Criminal Court, ex p. Spens* [1993] C.O.D. 194, DC. In *Re Ashton*, the question whether this decision could be justified on other grounds was left open.

(c) A listing decision which could affect the validity of the trial: *R. v. Southwark Crown Court, ex p. Customs and Excise Commrs*, 97 Cr.App.R. 266, DC, *ante*, § 2–116. In *Re Ashton*, the question whether this decision could be justified on other grounds was also left open.

Matters relating to trial on indictment

7–11 Matters relating to trial on indictment have been held to include the following.

(a) A refusal to award costs after acquittal: *ex p. Meredith*, 57 Cr.App.R. 451, DC; *R. v. Harrow Crown Court, ex p. Perkins*, 162 J.P. 527, DC; *R. v. Canterbury Crown Court, ex p. Regentford Ltd*, *ante*, § 7–8.

(b) An order discharging a jury: *ex p. Marlowe* [1973] Crim.L.R. 294, DC.

(c) An order in relation to the taking of steps to vet a jury panel: *R. v. Sheffield Crown Court, ex p. Brownlow* [1980] Q.B. 530, 71 Cr.App.R. 19, DC and CA (Civ. Div.).

(d) An order that an indictment lie on the file marked "not be proceeded with without leave": *R. v. Central Criminal Court, ex p. Raymond*, 83 Cr.App.R. 94, DC, approved in *Re Ashton*, *ante*.

(e) The refusal of a Crown Court judge to grant legal aid: *R. v. Chichester Crown Court, ex p. Abodunrin*, 79 Cr.App.R. 293, DC; or to amend an order so as to provide for representation by Queen's Counsel: *R. (Shields) v. Crown Court at*

Liverpool [2001] A.C.D. 325, DC; or the revocation of a legal aid certificate by a judge: *R. v. Isleworth Crown Court, ex p. Willington* [1993] 1 W.L.R. 713, DC.

(f) *Semble*, the decision of a judge to order a defence solicitor to pay the costs occasioned by the granting of a defence application for an adjournment: *R. v. Smith (M.)* [1975] Q.B. 531, CA (Civ. Div.). (But see now the *Solicitors Act* 1974, s.50(3), *ante*, § 6–286.) **7–12**

(g) A witness summons issued under section 2(1) of the *Criminal Procedure (Attendance of Witnesses) Act* 1965 (*post*, § 8–2): *ex p. Rees*, *The Times*, May 7, 1986, DC. *R. (T.B.) v. Stafford Crown Court* [2006] 2 Cr.App.R. 34, DC (see also *ante*, § 7–4) is inconsistent with this view, but no argument to the contrary was presented to the court, and there was no reference to authority. Its status as a precedent was further undermined by the reliance of the court on *ex p. Rees* in *R. (H.) v. Wood Green Crown Court*, *post*.

(h) Exercise of the power, under section 4(3) of the 1965 Act (*post*, § 8–13), to remand a witness in a trial on indictment in custody until such time as the court may appoint for receiving his evidence: *R. (H.) v. Wood Green Crown Court* [2007] 2 All E.R. 259, DC (relying on *ex p. Rees*, *ante*).

(i) A refusal to fix a date for trial until a certain event has occurred, such as the trial of another matter: *R. v. Liverpool Crown Court, ex p. Mende* [1991] C.O.D. 483, DC; *R. v. Southwark Crown Court, ex p. Ward* [1996] Crim.L.R. 123, DC.

(j) An order made following an application to stay a criminal trial on the ground of abuse of process: *Re Ashton*, *ante*.

(k) A warrant of imprisonment ordering a defendant to serve his sentence consecutively to a term he was then serving, where the judge had not said the sentence was consecutive, is not reviewable: *R. v. Lewes Crown Court, ex p. Sinclair* [1992] Crim.L.R. 886, DC.

(l) A refusal to grant a further extension of time in which to prefer a bill of indictment: *R. v. Isleworth Crown Court, ex p. King* [1992] C.O.D. 298, DC.

(m) The arraignment of a defendant, and the conduct of a plea and directions hearing generally: *R. v. Leeds Crown Court, ex p. Hussain* [1995] 1 W.L.R. 1329, DC (not following *R. v. Maidstone Crown Court, ex p. Clark* [1995] 1 W.L.R. 831, DC).

(n) An order that social service files on prosecution witnesses be seen by all legal representatives to assist the court, in the absence of an *amicus curiae*, by allowing them to reach agreement on which documents should be disclosed: *R. v. Chester Crown Court, ex p. Cheshire County Council*, *The Times*, October 23, 1995, DC.

(o) A refusal to allow a private individual to conduct a private prosecution in person: *R. v. Southwark Crown Court, ex p. Tawfick, CPS intervening*, *The Times*, December 1, 1994, DC.

(p) A decision as to whether there had been a proper extradition procedure in relation to an indictment and therefore whether the trial should proceed: *R. (Rogerson) v. Stafford Crown Court* [2002] Crim.L.R. 318, DC.

(q) A decision on a dismissal application of a charge sent for trial under section 51 of the *CDA* 1998: *R. (Snelgrove) v. Woolwich Crown Court* [2005] 1 Cr.App.R. 18, DC, in which it was said unequivocally that *R. v. Central Criminal Court and Nadir, ex p. Serious Fraud Office*, 96 Cr.App.R. 248, DC (decision on an application under the *CJA* 1987 to dismiss transfer charges did not relate to trial on indictment) should no longer be regarded as authoritative. *Snelgrove* was followed in *R. (O.) v. Central Criminal Court*, unreported, January 27, 2006, DC ([2006] EWHC 256 (Admin.)).

(r) An error made by a judge when passing sentence by failing to pass the sentence required by statute (here a sentence of life imprisonment or imprisonment for public protection under the *CJA* 2003, s.225, rather than an extended sentence under s.227): *R. (CPS) v. Guildford Crown Court*, *The Times*, July 16, 2007, DC (distinguishing the *London Borough of Harrow* and *Kenneally* decisions referred to at § 7–8, *ante*).

(s) A decision by a judge at the end of a trial on indictment not to make a compensation order: *R. (Faithfull) v. Crown Court at Ipswich* [2008] 1 W.L.R. 1636, DC.

There is a conflict of authority as to whether an order under section 39 of the *CYPA* 1933 (*ante*, § 4–27) is a matter relating to trial on indictment (see *ante*, § 7–9 at (d)). The latest authority is to the effect that such an order is, or may be, reviewable; but the better view, it is submitted, is that when the order is made in the context of trial on indictment, it falls within the prohibition in section 29(3).

(d) *Principles governing granting of relief*

7–13 The High Court will grant relief, in its discretion, on an application for judicial review where: (a) the inferior court has exceeded its jurisdiction; (b) the inferior court has acted in breach of the rules of natural justice; (c) there is an error of law on the face of the record; or (d) the decision of the inferior court is "*Wednesbury*" unreasonable (*Associated Picture Houses Ltd v. Wednesbury Corporation* [1948] 1 K.B. 223): *R. v. West Sussex Q. S., ex p. Albert and Maud Johnson Trust Ltd* [1973] 1 Q.B. 188, DC (*per* Lord Widgery C.J. at p. 194) (the decision of the Divisional Court was upheld by the Court of Appeal— [1974] Q.B. 24); *R. v. St Albans Crown Court, ex p. Cinnamond* [1981] Q.B. 480, DC. Where human rights are engaged, however, a stricter test than *Wednesbury* unreasonableness will be applied. The High Court will not simply substitute its own view, but it will subject the decision under review to a degree of scrutiny appropriate to the interest to be protected. In particular, it will need to be satisfied as to the proportionality of the decision: see *R. (Daly) v. Secretary of State for the Home Department* [2001] 2 A.C. 532, HL.

For the purposes of granting a quashing order for error on the face of the record, the "record" is not restricted to the formal order but extends to the reasons given by the judge in the official transcript of his oral judgment: *R. v. Knightsbridge Crown Court, ex p. International Sporting Club (London) Ltd* [1982] Q.B. 304, DC. In *R. v. Knightsbridge Crown Court, ex p. Aspinall Curzon Ltd*, *The Times*, December 16, 1982, Woolf J. said that the approach to what could be regarded as the record had been liberally treated in recent times. In the instant case, it was only by looking at affidavit evidence sworn by the applicant's solicitor that it was possible to understand the basis of the case. The procedures indicated in the new Order 53 of the *RSC* (see now Pt 54 of the *Civil Procedure Rules* 1998 (S.I. 1998 No. 3132)) were different from those that previously existed, and, where necessary, the court could therefore look at evidence not technically part of the record, although in the majority of cases the judgment and the reasons would be all that it was necessary to look at.

A quashing order does not lie to set aside a decision of an inferior court merely on the ground that fresh evidence has been discovered after the trial: *R. v. West Sussex Q. S., ex p. Albert and Maud Johnson Trust Ltd* [1974] Q.B. 24, CA (Civ. Div.); *R. v. Carlisle Crown Court, ex p. Marcus-Moore*, *The Times*, October 26, 1981, DC.

7–14 In *R. v. Wolverhampton Crown Court, ex p. Crofts*, 76 Cr.App.R. 8, DC, it was held that a quashing order lay in respect of a decision of the Crown Court to allow an appeal against conviction by magistrates where the decision of the Crown Court had been reached on the basis of perjured evidence. Where there is a conflict between the principle that no one should be put in peril of conviction twice for the same offence and the principle that the court should intervene to quash a decision of an inferior court obtained by fraud, the former principle should prevail. In the instant case no such conflict arose—the quashing of the Crown Court's decision on the ground that it had been obtained by fraud meant that the defendant remained convicted as a result of the first and only occasion upon which he was put in peril.

Where a conviction has been procured before justices, or before the Crown Court on appeal from justices, by fraud or perjury of a party to or a witness in the proceedings, the High Court has jurisdiction to quash the conviction. This is so even if the perjured evidence goes only to credit. Further, the assertion in evidence by a person in the role of a prosecutor (*e.g.* a store detective in a shoplifting case) of his good character and his failure to disclose his bad character amounts to a denial of natural justice entitling the court to quash the conviction so obtained: *R. v. Knightsbridge Crown Court, ex p. Goonatilleke* [1986] Q.B. 1, 81 Cr.App.R. 31, DC; and as to convictions obtained by conduct which is analogous to fraud, collusion or perjury, see *R. v. Leyland JJ., ex p. Hewthorn* [1979] Q.B. 283, 68 Cr.App.R. 269, DC; *ex p. Goonatilleke*, *ante*; *R. v. Kingston-upon-Thames JJ., ex p. Khanna* [1986] R.T.R. 364, DC (conviction secured on basis of evidence that was crucially erroneous); and *R. v. Bolton JJ., ex p. Scally* [1991] 1 Q.B. 537, DC.

Where an application for judicial review in a criminal cause or matter, coupled with an ancillary claim for damages, is made primarily with the damages claim in view, the court should, in its discretion, decline to deal with the application and allow the damages claim to proceed as if begun by writ: *R. v. Blandford JJ., ex p. Pamment* [1990] 1 W.L.R. 1490, CA (Civ. Div.).

(e) *Powers of High Court*

Where, on an application for judicial review, the High Court quashes a decision of the Crown Court to dismiss an appeal, there is no power to remit the matter to the lower court (unlike an appeal by way of case stated) and so the conviction remains extant: *R. v. Leeds Crown Court, ex p. Barlow* [1980] R.T.R. 246, DC. To quash the conviction, the applicant would have to have the appeal reinstated before the Crown Court, and it should be listed before a different bench. However, it does not follow that the conviction must be quashed: if the High Court's ruling was based upon a failure of natural justice, and the Crown determine to proceed with the appeal, then it would be for the differently constituted Crown Court to determine the matter *de novo*: *ibid*. **7–15**

(f) *Variation of sentence*

The High Court will act pursuant to section 43 of the *Supreme Court [Senior Courts] Act* 1981 (*ante*, § 7–6) (as to the renaming of this Act, see *ante*, § 7–3) where the lower court has acted in excess of jurisdiction or otherwise wrongly in law: *R. v. Crown Court at Croydon, ex p. Miller*, 85 Cr.App.R. 152, DC. In *R. v. St Albans Crown Court, ex p. Cinnamond* [1981] Q.B. 480, DC, it had been held that a discretionary sentence is "wrong in law or in excess of jurisdiction" if it is harsh and oppressive or otherwise so far outside the normal sentence imposed for the offence as to lead the court to conclude that its imposition must have involved an error of law. **7–16**

In *ex p. Miller*, it was said that the principle in *ex p. Cinnamond* would only operate in the case of a sentence, which was prima facie lawful, if it was "by any acceptable standard, truly astonishing" (*per* Watkins L.J. at p. 155). Similar observations were made in *R. v. Acton Crown Court, ex p. Bewley*, 10 Cr.App.R.(S.) 105, DC ("irrational and truly astonishing"); and *Tucker v. DPP*, 13 Cr.App.R.(S.) 495, DC. More recent authorities have suggested a slightly lesser test: see *R. v. Truro Crown Court, ex p. Adair* [1997] C.O.D. 296, DC; and *R. (Sogbesan) v. Inner London Crown Court* [2003] 1 Cr.App.R.(S.) 79, DC (sentence liable to be quashed if it falls so far outside the broad area of the lower court's discretion as to demonstrate an error of law or an excess of jurisdiction); and *R. v. Bow Street Stipendiary Magistrate, ex p. Screen Multimedia Ltd*, *The Times*, January 28, 1998, DC, where the court declined to quash orders for costs against the defendants, saying that they were not "manifestly excessive" (one of the tests applied in the Court of Appeal on an appeal against sentence (*post*, § 7–141)).

In *R. v. Swansea Crown Court, ex p. Davies*, *The Times*, May 2, 1989, DC, the decision of the Crown Court to increase sentence was quashed as being harsh and oppressive; it involved a quantum leap from the sentence imposed by the magistrates and was so far from the norm as to call for intervention (*ex p. Cinnamond* applied).

B. PRACTICE AND PROCEDURE

(1) Rules of court

Criminal Procedure Rules 2005 (S.I. 2005 No. 384), r.64.7

Application to the Crown Court to state a case

64.7.—(1) An application under section 28 of the *Supreme Court [Senior Courts] Act* 1981 **7–17**

to the Crown Court to state a case for the opinion of the High Court shall be made in writing to a court officer within 21 days after the date of the decision in respect of which the application is made.

(2) The application shall state the ground on which the decision of the Crown Court is questioned.

(3) After making the application, the applicant shall forthwith send a copy of it to the parties to the proceedings in the Crown Court.

(4) On receipt of the application, the Crown Court officer shall forthwith send it to the judge who presided at the proceedings in which the decision was made.

(5) On receipt of the application, the judge shall inform the Crown Court officer as to whether or not he has decided to state a case and that officer shall give notice in writing to the applicant of the judge's decision.

(6) If the judge considers that the application is frivolous, he may refuse to state a case and shall in that case, if the applicant so requires, cause a certificate stating the reasons for the refusal to be given to him.

(7) If the judge decides to state a case, the procedure to be followed shall, unless the judge in a particular case otherwise directs, be the procedure set out in paragraphs (8) to (12) of this rule.

(8) The applicant shall, within 21 days of receiving the notice referred to in paragraph (5), draft a case and send a copy of it to the Crown Court officer and to the parties to the proceedings in the Crown Court.

(9) Each party to the proceedings in the Crown Court shall, within 21 days of receiving a copy of the draft case under paragraph (8), either—

(a) give notice in writing to the applicant and the Crown Court officer that he does not intend to take part in the proceedings before the High Court;

(b) indicate in writing on the copy of the draft case that he agrees with it and send the copy to a court officer; or

(c) draft an alternative case and send it, together with the copy of the applicant's case, to the Crown Court officer.

7–18 (10) The judge shall consider the applicant's draft case and any alternative draft case sent to the Crown Court officer under paragraph (9)(c).

(11) If the Crown Court so orders, the applicant shall, before the case is stated and delivered to him, enter before the Crown Court officer into a recognizance, with or without sureties and in such sum as the Crown Court considers proper, having regard to the means of the applicant, conditioned to prosecute the appeal without delay.

(12) The judge shall state and sign a case within 14 days after either—

(a) the receipt of all the documents required to be sent to a court officer under paragraph (9); or

(b) the expiration of the period of 21 days referred to in that paragraph,

whichever is the sooner.

(13) A case stated by the Crown Court shall state the facts found by the Crown Court, the submissions of the parties (including any authorities relied on by the parties during the course of those submissions), the decision of the Crown Court in respect of which the application is made and the question on which the opinion of the High Court is sought.

(14) Any time limit referred to in this rule may be extended either before or after it expires by the Crown Court.

(15) If the judge decides not to state a case but the stating of a case is subsequently required by a mandatory order of the High Court, paragraphs (7) to (14) shall apply to the stating of the case save that—

(a) in paragraph (7) the words "If the judge decides to state a case" shall be omitted; and

(b) in paragraph (8) for the words "receiving the notice referred to in paragraph (5)" there shall be substituted the words "the day on which the mandatory order was made".

[The *Supreme Court Act* 1981 is renamed the *Senior Courts Act* 1981 as from a day to be appointed: *Constitutional Reform Act* 2005, s.59(5), and Sched. 11, para. 1.]

See also Parts 52 (case stated) and 54 (judicial review) of the *Civil Procedure Rules* 1998 (S.I. 1998 No. 3132).

"Frivolous" means "futile, misconceived, hopeless or academic"; where an application to state a case is considered to be frivolous, it would be helpful if the judge gave a brief indication of his reasons: *R. v. Mildenhall Magistrates' Court, ex p. Forest Heath D.C.*, 161 J.P. 401, CA (Civ. Div.).

Where a court refuses to state a case, the aggrieved party should without delay apply for permission to bring judicial review, seeking either a mandatory order to compel the statement of a case or an order quashing the challenged decision; if the court below has given a reasoned judgment containing all the necessary findings of fact and/or explained its refusal to state a case in terms which clearly raise the true point of law in issue, then the correct course would be for the single judge, assuming he thinks the point properly arguable, to grant permission for judicial review which directly challenges the decision complained of, thereby avoiding the need to state a case; if the court below has stated a case in respect of some questions only, the better course is to apply to have the case amended, unless again there exists sufficient material to enable the High Court to deal with all arguable issues; and whilst it is impossible to lay down principles which will apply in every case, the High Court needing to retain the flexibility to deal with unusual situations as they arise, the court would generally adopt whatever course involves the fewest additional steps and the least expense, delay and duplication of proceedings: *Sunworld Ltd v. Hammersmith and Fulham L.B.C.*; *R. v. Blackfriars Crown Court, ex p. Sunworld Ltd* [2000] 1 W.L.R. 2102, DC.

(2) Practice directions, etc.

See, in particular: **7–19**

(a) The practice direction relating to Part 52 of the *Civil Procedure Rules* 1998 (S.I. 1998 No. 3132), as to which, see also *Haggis v. DPP (Note)* [2004] 2 All E.R. 382, DC; and *Harvey Shopfitters Ltd v. ADI Ltd* [2004] 2 All E.R. 982, CA (Civ. Div.);

(b) *Practice Statement (Administrative Court: annual statement)* [2002] 1 W.L.R. 810, dealing, in particular, with the pre-action protocol, listing policy, the procedure to be followed for urgent cases, the revised form for renewing an application for permission (requiring claimants to set out the grounds for renewal in the light of the reasons given by the single judge for refusing permission), and email addresses for use for urgent communications; and

(c) *Practice Note (Administrative Court)* [2004] 2 All E.R. 994—a grant of permission to pursue a claim for judicial review, whether made on the papers or after oral argument, will be deemed to contain an order that costs be costs in the case; any different order made by the judge must be reflected in the court order granting permission.

C. APPEAL FROM HIGH COURT

(1) Right of appeal

An appeal lies to the House of Lords [Supreme Court], at the instance of the prosecutor or the defendant from any decision of the High Court in a criminal cause or matter; but leave of the House or the High Court is necessary and such leave shall not be granted unless the High Court certifies that a point of law of general public importance is involved in its decision and it appears to that court or to the House [Supreme Court] that the point is one which ought to be considered by the House [Supreme Court]: *Administration of Justice Act* 1960, s.1(1)(a), (2) (as amended, as from a day to be appointed, by the *Constitutional Reform Act* 2005, s.40(4), and Sched. 9, para. 13(1) and (2)). **7–20**

Section 18(1)(a) of the *Supreme Court [Senior Courts] Act* 1981 (renamed as from a day to be appointed: *Constitutional Reform Act* 2005, s.59(5), and Sched. 11, para. 1) specifically excludes any right of appeal to the Court of Appeal from any judgment of the High Court in any criminal cause or matter.

Section 1(1) of the 1960 Act and section 18(1)(a) of the 1981 Act are disapplied in relation to decisions of the High Court fixing tariffs for "transferred life prisoners" and "existing life prisoners": see the *CJA* 2003, ss.274(4) and 276, and Sched. 22, para. 14(2).

(2) Criminal cause or matter

7–21 What is, and what is not, a criminal cause or matter, has given rise to a considerable volume of litigation; it would be idle to pretend that the authorities are entirely consistent, but it is now possible to discern a line of demarcation between the main stream of cases and a smaller number of decisions, which were once thought to be irreconcilable with the main stream.

The earliest case that is normally referred to is *ex p. Woodhall* (1888) 20 Q.B.D. 832, CA, in which Lord Esher M.R. said that the result of all the decided cases is to show that these words should receive the widest possible interpretation. They apply to the judicial determination of any question raised in or with regard to proceedings the subject matter of which is criminal, at whatever stage of the proceedings the question arises.

The leading case seems still to be *Amand v. Home Secretary* [1943] A.C. 147, HL. Lord Wright, having reviewed the authorities, concluded:

> "The principle which I deduce from the authorities I have cited and the other relevant authorities which I have considered, is that if the cause or matter is one which, if carried to its conclusion, might result in the conviction of the person charged and in a sentence of some punishment, such as imprisonment or fine, it is a 'criminal cause or matter'. The person charged is thus put in jeopardy. Every order made in such a cause or matter by an English Court, is an order in a criminal cause or matter, even though the order taken by itself, is neutral in character and might equally have been made in a cause or matter which is not criminal. The order may not involve punishment by the law of this country, but if the effect of the order is to subject by means of the operation of English law the persons charged to the criminal jurisdiction of a foreign country, the order is, in the eyes of English law, for the purposes being considered, an order in a criminal cause or matter ..." (at p. 162).

Viscount Simon L.C. adumbrated the following test: "If the matter is one the direct outcome of which may be trial of the applicant and his possible punishment for an alleged offence by a court claiming jurisdiction to do so, the matter is criminal" (at p. 156).

7–22 In reliance on these principles, the following have been held to be "in a criminal cause or matter":

(a) a decision to order a prosecution: *Provisional Cinematograph Theatres Ltd v. Newcastle-upon-Tyne Profiteering Committee*, 27 Cox 63, HL;

(b) an order by a judge under the *Law of Libel (Amendment) Act* 1888 giving leave for the commencement of a prosecution for libel: *ex p. Pulbrook* [1892] 1 Q.B. 86;

(c) a recommendation for deportation: *R. v. Secretary of State for the Home Department, ex p. Dannenberg* [1984] Q.B. 766, CA (Civ. Div.);

(d) extradition proceedings: *R. v. Governor of Brixton Prison, ex p. Levin* [1997] A.C. 741, HL; and an order under the *Bankers' Books Evidence Act* 1879, s.7, made in connection with such proceedings: *Bonalumi v. Secretary of State for the Home Department* [1985] Q.B. 675, CA (Civ. Div.) (not following *R. v. Grossman*, 73 Cr.App.R. 302, CA (Civ. Div.);

(e) decisions in relation to witness summonses issued under section 2(1) of the *Criminal Procedure (Attendance of Witnesses) Act* 1965 (*post*, § 8–4);

(f) orders made by a circuit judge under section 9 of, and Schedule 1 to, the *PACE Act* 1984 (*post*, §§ 15–88 *et seq.*) for the production of various documents, notwithstanding that no proceedings had been commenced: *Carr v. Atkins* [1987] Q.B. 963, 85 Cr.App.R. 343, CA (Civ. Div.);

(g) a decision of the Home Secretary refusing to refer a case to the Court of Appeal under the *CAA* 1968, s.17 (*rep.*): *R. v. Secretary of State for the Home Department, ex p. Garner* [1990] C.O.D. 457, CA (Civ. Div.);

(h) a judgment of the High Court dismissing an application for judicial review of a decision of a police force to issue a caution; an official caution was a way of disposing of a criminal matter, and it was important to keep in mind that the words of section 18(1) were "criminal cause or matter" not "proceedings", the words "or matter" denoting a wider ambit: *R. (Aru) v. Chief Constable of Merseyside Police* [2004] 1 W.L.R. 1697, CA (Civ. Div.); and

(i) proceedings under the *Criminal Procedure (Insanity) Act* 1964 (*ante*, §§ 4–167 *et seq.*): *R. (South West Yorkshire Mental Health N.H.S. Trust) v. Crown Court at Bradford* [2004] 1 W.L.R. 1664, CA (Civ. Div.).

On the other side of the line are the following cases; where there are related proceedings which are undoubtedly criminal, the test seems to be whether the judgment sought to be appealed was made in proceedings which are so collateral to the underlying criminal proceedings that they do not themselves constitute a criminal cause or matter (see *per* Sir John Donaldson M.R. in *Carr v. Atkins, ante*, at pp. 970, 351): **7–23**

(a) a decision to estreat a recognizance entered into by a surety: *R. v. Southampton JJ., ex p. Green* [1976] Q.B. 11, CA (Civ. Div.);

(b) proceedings brought by the defendant seeking a declaration as to the nature of the responsibilities of the Director of Public Prosecutions in relation to exhibits produced during commital proceedings: *R. v. Lambeth Metropolitan Stipendiary Magistrate, ex p. McComb* [1983] Q.B. 551, CA (Civ. Div.) (a decision about which the court (Sir John Donaldson M.R. and May L.J.) clearly had reservations, reiterated by the Master of the Rolls in *Carr v. Atkins, ante*);

(c) decisions of a board of visitors upon hearing charges alleging contraventions of the *Prison Rules* 1964; *R. v. Board of Visitors of Hull Prison, ex p. St Germain* [1979] Q.B. 425, 68 Cr.App.R. 212, CA (Civ. Div.) (the offences were offences against discipline in a code of private law);

(d) garnishee proceedings taken by a magistrates' clerk to enforce payment of compensation or costs orders made on the conviction of the judgment debtor for an offence: *Gooch v. Ewing (Allied Irish Banks Ltd, garnishee)* [1986] Q.B. 791, 82 Cr.App.R. 200, CA (Civ. Div.); and

(e) an order requiring disclosure of assets made in connection with a restraint order under the *CJA* 1988; *Re O. (Restraint order: Disclosure of Assets)* [1991] 2 Q.B. 520, CA (Civ. Div.).

In *R. v. Blandford JJ. ex p. Pamment* [1990] 1 W.L.R. 1490, CA (Civ. Div.), it was held that where, on an application for judicial review, the Divisional Court determined a question in respect of criminal proceedings after such proceedings had been concluded, the court's decision was nevertheless made in a criminal cause or matter.

III. THE COURT OF APPEAL

A. CONSTITUTION

The Court of Appeal is part of the Supreme Court [Senior Courts] of England and Wales having such jurisdiction as is conferred on it by the *Supreme Court [Senior Courts] Act* 1981 or by any other Act: *Supreme Court Act* 1981, s.1(1) (as to the renaming of the Supreme Court as the Senior Courts of England and Wales, and as to the renaming of the 1981 Act as the *Senior Courts Act* 1981, as from a day to be appointed, see the *Constitutional Reform Act* 2005, s.59, and Sched. 11). Section 2 of the 1981 Act provides for the judges of the Court of Appeal and section 3 provides for there being a criminal and a civil division of the court, the former being presided over by the Lord Chief Justice. **7–24**

Section 9 (which provides for certain judges to act on request in courts other than that to which they were appointed) was amended by the *CJPOA* 1994, s.52 so as to permit a circuit judge to sit as a judge of the criminal division. A circuit judge or recorder shall not by virtue of these amendments exercise any of the powers conferred on a single judge by the *CAA* 1968, ss.31 (*post*, § 7–231), 31B (*post*, § 7–236a), 31C (*post*, § 7–236b) and 44 (*post*, § 7–336): s.9(6A).

B. JURISDICTION

Supreme Court [Senior Courts] Act 1981, s.15

General jurisdiction of Court of Appeal

15.—(1) The Court of Appeal shall be a superior court of record. **7–25**

(2) Subject to the provisions of this Act, there shall be exercisable by the Court of Appeal—

(a) all such jurisdiction (whether civil or criminal) as is conferred on it by this or any other Act; and

(b) all such other jurisdiction (whether civil or criminal) as was exercisable by it immediately before the commencement of this Act.

(3), (4) [*Appeals to civil division.*]

[As to the renaming of the 1981 Act, see *ante*, § 7–3.]

No inherent jurisdiction: interlocutory matters

7–26 In *R. v. Jefferies* [1969] 1 Q.B. 120, 52 Cr.App.R. 654, the Court of Appeal held that whatever may be the powers of courts exercising a jurisdiction which does not derive from statute, its powers in criminal appeals derived from and were confined to those given by the *CAA* 1907, which has now been repealed and replaced successively by the *Criminal Appeal Acts* 1966 and 1968 and the *Supreme Court [Senior Courts] Act* 1981. There is no inherent jurisdiction, the appeal itself being the creature of statute.

Jefferies was applied in *R. v. Collins* [1970] 1 Q.B. 710, 54 Cr.App.R. 19. It was held that the Court of Appeal (Criminal Division) having the same powers as its predecessor, the Court of Criminal Appeal, which was created by the *CAA* 1907, had no statutory jurisdiction to hear an interlocutory appeal and that, since the court was created by statute, it had no powers beyond those conferred on it by Parliament. (There is now a limited statutory right of appeal from interlocutory rulings in serious fraud and other long, complex or serious cases: see *post*, §§ 7–284 *et seq.*) See also *R. v. Grantham* [1969] 2 Q.B. 574, 53 Cr.App.R. 369, Ct-MAC; *Re Central Funds Costs Order* [1975] 1 W.L.R. 1227, CA; *R. v. Mackell*, 74 Cr.App.R. 27, CA; and *R. v. McIlkenny*, 93 Cr.App.R. 287, CA, and *post*, §§ 7–76, 7–223.

C. PRACTICE AND PROCEDURE

Supreme Court [Senior Courts] Act 1981, ss.53, 55

Distribution of business between civil and criminal divisions

7–27 **53.**—(1) Rules of court may provide for the distribution of business in the Court of Appeal between the civil and criminal divisions, but subject to any such rules business shall be distributed in accordance with the following provisions of this section.

(2) The criminal division of the Court of Appeal shall exercise—

(a) all jurisdiction of the Court of Appeal under Parts I and II of the *Criminal Appeal Act* 1968;

(b) the jurisdiction of the Court of Appeal under section 13 of the *Administration of Justice Act* 1960 (appeals in cases of contempt of court) in relation to appeals from orders and decisions of the Crown Court;

(c) all other jurisdiction expressly conferred on that division by this or any other Act; and

(d) the jurisdiction to order the issue of writs of *venire de novo*.

(3) The civil division of the Court of Appeal shall exercise the whole of the jurisdiction of that court not exercisable by the criminal division.

(4) Where any class of proceedings in the Court of Appeal is by any statutory provision assigned to the criminal division of that court, rules of court may provide for any enactment relating to—

(a) appeals to the Court of Appeal under Part I of the *Criminal Appeal Act* 1968; or

(b) any matter connected with or arising out of such appeals,

to apply in relation to proceedings of that class or, as the case may be, to any corresponding matter connected with or arising out of such proceedings, as it applies in relation to such appeals or, as the case may be, to the relevant matter within paragraph (b), with or without prescribed modifications in either case.

[As to the renaming of the 1981 Act, see *ante*, § 7–3.]

For the *Administration of Justice Act* 1960, s.13, see *post*, § 28–138.

Section 53(1) derives from the *CAA* 1966, s.1(5). No rules containing provisions made by virtue of section 1(5) of the 1966 Act or section 53(1) of the 1981 Act have been made.

Court of criminal division

55.—(1) This section relates to the criminal division of the Court of Appeal; and in this section "court" means a court of that division. **7–28**

(2) Subject to subsection (6), a court shall be duly constituted for the purpose of exercising any of its jurisdiction if it consists of any uneven number of judges not less than three.

(3) Where—

(a) part of any proceedings before a court has been heard by an uneven number of judges greater than three; and

(b) one or more members of the court are unable to continue,

the court shall remain duly constituted for the purpose of those proceedings so long as the number of members (whether even or uneven) is not reduced to less than three.

(4) Subject to subsection (6), a court shall, if it consists of two judges, be duly constituted for every purpose except—

(a) determining an appeal against—

(i) conviction; or

(ii) a verdict of not guilty by reason of insanity; or

(iii) a finding ... under section 4 of the *Criminal Procedure (Insanity) Act* 1964 (unfitness to plead) that a person is under a disability;

(aa) reviewing sentencing under Part IV of the *Criminal Justice Act* 1988;

(b) determining an application for leave to appeal to the *House of Lords* [Supreme Court]; and

(c) refusing an application for leave to appeal to the criminal division against conviction or any such verdict or finding as is mentioned in paragraph (a) (ii) or (iii), other than an application which has been refused by a single judge.

(5) Where an appeal has been heard by a court consisting of an even number of judges and the members of the court are equally divided, the case shall be re-argued before and determined by an uneven number of judges not less than three.

(6) A court shall not be duly constituted if it includes more than one Circuit judge acting as a judge of the court under section 9.

[This section is printed as amended, and repealed in part, by the *CJA* 1988, s.170(1) and Sched. 15, para. 80; the *CJPOA* 1994, s.52(1), (7); and the *Domestic Violence, Crime and Victims Act* 2004, s.58(1), and Sched. 10, para. 14; and as amended, as from a day to be appointed, by the *Constitutional Reform Act* 2005, s.40(4), and Sched. 9, para. 36(1) and (5) (omission of italicised words, insertion of words in square brackets).]

Where, following argument on an appeal against conviction or an application for leave to appeal against conviction, judgment was reserved, and before it was given, one of three judges who had heard the appeal or application was unable to continue, the terms of section 55 precluded the other two judges from continuing the proceedings even by delivering a decision upon which all three had been agreed. Where it had been left to one of the three judges to prepare a draft judgment, it was open to either of the other two to change his mind on further reflection, and none of the judges was bound by their decision until delivered in open court (but see *R v. Steele*, *post*). In such eventuality, the only course open was for the appeal or application to be reheard by a differently constituted court: *R. v. Coates and Graves*; *R. v. Terry* [2005] 1 Cr.App.R. 14, CA. The position was different where the decision of the court was announced at the conclusion of oral argument, with reasons to be given later. That amounted to a final determination, the court being unable to change its mind: *ibid*. **7–29**

In *R. v. Steele* [2007] 1 W.L.R. 222, CA, it was held that since an appeal would be "determined" for the purposes of section 55 when the judgment of the court was properly to be treated as binding on the judges themselves (*R. v. Coates and Graves*; *R. v. Terry* (*ante*)), an appeal would be so "determined" where the court, having reserved its decision, circulated its judgment to counsel in advance, but did not then reconvene, at the hearing when the judgment was formally handed down, in such a way as to consist of all members of the constitution; and since the handing down of the judgment was merely its formal promulgation, the parties would be precluded from making further submissions as to the merits of the appeal.

Where an appeal against conviction is argued before a court of three judges who are not unanimous, there used to be a practice of relisting the appeal for argument *de novo* before a differently constituted court of five judges. This practice, described by Lloyd L.J. in *R. v. Shama*, 91 Cr.App.R. 138, as "well-established" (p. 139), had fallen into disuse. The court in *Shama*, however, proceeded on the assumption that there was an alternative possibility, namely relisting before a three-judge court. This is what was done. When the case was relisted, however, the jurisdiction of the second court to hear the appeal was apparently questioned by both parties to the appeal. Accordingly, the case was simply referred back to the original court who dismissed the appeal without further argument. The jurisdictional point was not decided. The practice of relisting may have no statutory backing, but as was pointed out in the Report of the Interdepartmental Committee on the Court of Criminal Appeal (Cmnd. 2755) ("the Donovan Committee") it was a departure from the strict statutory position in favour of the appellant.

Supreme Court [Senior Courts] Act 1981, ss.56, 56B, 59

Judges not to sit on appeal from their own judgments, etc.

7–30 **56.**—(1) [*Civil division.*]

(2) No judge shall sit as a member of the criminal division of the Court of Appeal on the hearing of, or shall determine any application in proceedings incidental or preliminary to, an appeal against—

(a) a conviction before himself or a court of which he was a member; or

(b) a sentence passed by himself or such a court.

[As to the renaming of the 1981 Act, see *ante*, § 7–3.]

Allocation of cases in criminal division

7–31 **56B.**—(1) The appeals or classes of appeals suitable for allocation to a court of the criminal division of the Court of Appeal in which a Circuit judge is acting under section 9 shall be determined in accordance with directions given by or on behalf of the Lord Chief Justice *with the concurrence of* [after consulting] the Lord Chancellor.

(2) In subsection (1) "appeal" includes the hearing of, or any application in proceedings incidental or preliminary to, an appeal.

[Section 56B was inserted by the *CJPOA* 1994, s.52(6) and (9). The words in square brackets are substituted for the italicised words as from a day to be appointed: *Constitutional Reform Act* 2005, s.15(1), and Sched. 4, paras 114 and 127.]

Form of judgment of court of criminal division

7–32 **59.** Any judgment of a court of the criminal division of the Court of Appeal on any question shall, except where the judge presiding over the court states that in his opinion the question is one of law on which it is convenient that separate judgments should be pronounced by the members of the court, be pronounced by the judge presiding over the court or by such other member of the court as he directs and, except as aforesaid, no judgment shall be separately pronounced on any question by any member of the court.

D. STARE DECISIS IN THE CRIMINAL DIVISION OF THE COURT OF APPEAL

7–33 In civil matters the Court of Appeal is bound to follow its own decisions and those of courts of co-ordinate jurisdiction, and the "full" court is in the same position as a division of the court consisting of three judges. There are three exceptions to this rule: first, the court is bound to decide which of two conflicting decisions of its own it will follow; secondly, it is bound to refuse to follow a decision of its own which, although not expressly overruled, cannot, in its opinion stand with a decision of the House of Lords; and, thirdly, the court is not bound to follow a decision of its own if it is satisfied that the decision was given *per incuriam*: *Young v. Bristol Aeroplane Co. Ltd* [1944] K.B. 718. The rule of *stare decisis* is less strictly applied in criminal matters. In *R. v. Taylor* [1950] 2 K.B. 368, 34 Cr.App.R. 138, Lord Goddard C.J., delivering the judgment of a full Court of Criminal Appeal, stated the rule in civil cases and continued:

"This court however, has to deal with questions involving the liberty of the subject, and if it finds, on reconsideration, that in the opinion of a full court assembled for that purpose the law has been either misapplied or misunderstood in a decision which it has previously given, and that, on the strength of that decision, an accused person has been sentenced and imprisoned it is the bounden duty of the court to reconsider the earlier decision with a view to seeing whether that person had been properly convicted" (at pp. 371, 142–143).

In *R. v. Gould* [1968] 2 Q.B. 65, 52 Cr.App.R. 152, Diplock L.J. presided over a court of three judges. Having cited *Taylor*, his Lordship made similar observations (at pp. 68, 153), to those of Lord Goddard C.J., but his observations were not expressly confined to departure from precedent in favour of the appellant. The court was, however, contemplating such a departure and it was generally assumed that his Lordship had had no intention of extending the ambit of *Taylor*. In *R. v. Newsome*; *R. v. Browne* [1970] 2 Q.B. 711, 54 Cr.App.R. 485, CA, Widgery L.J., who had been a member of the court in *Gould*, rejected this view. A court of five judges decided that in relation to matters relating to the principles governing the exercise of the sentencing discretion, a court of five judges should have liberty to depart from an earlier view expressed by a court of three, especially where that earlier view is recent and was expressed without the benefit of full argument. "Accordingly, within that restricted sphere, ... we take the view that a court of five can, and indeed should, depart from an earlier direction on the exercise of a judge's discretion if satisfied that the earlier direction was wrong" (at pp. 717, 491). **7–34**

In *R. v. Spencer*; *R. v. Smails* [1985] Q.B. 771, 80 Cr.App.R. 264, CA, the court disagreed with the view expressed by Widgery L.J. that the dictum of Diplock L.J. in *Gould* was intended to broaden the principle in *Taylor*. The principles relating to the doctrine of *stare decisis* should be the same in the civil and criminal divisions; *Young v. Bristol Aeroplane Co. Ltd* should apply in both divisions, subject to the criminal division's freedom to depart from precedent in favour of an appellant in accordance with *Taylor*. Their Lordships did not, however, seek to impugn the actual decision in *R. v. Newsome*; *R. v. Browne* (confined as it was to matters of sentencing discretion, not points of law). **7–35**

The application of the doctrine of *stare decisis* in the criminal division has been considerably relaxed by a combination of the decisions of the court in *R. v. Sekhon* [2003] 1 Cr.App.R. 34, *R. v. Simpson* [2003] 2 Cr.App.R. 36, and *R. v. Rowe* [2007] 2 Cr.App.R. 14, CA. In the first two cases, the court was considering the correctness of its decision in *R. v. Palmer (No. 1)* [2003] 1 Cr.App.R.(S.) 112 on an issue relating to confiscation of the proceeds of crime. In *Sekhon*, it was said that it was wrong and was not to be regarded as binding at it had been decided *per incuriam*. If, however, the *per incuriam* exception was formerly limited to decisions which were "demonstrably wrong" by virtue of having been made in ignorance of a statutory rule or of binding authority (*Morelle Ltd v. Wakeling* [1955] 2 Q.B. 379 at 406, CA), then it was significantly extended by this decision, which held that it could be applied to a decision made without the benefit of a particular argument. In *Simpson*, the court again referred to the *per incuriam* doctrine, but also justified departure from precedent on the ground that the law had been "misunderstood or misapplied" in *Palmer*, thus extending that exception which was formerly limited to departures from precedent in favour of the accused to departures in favour of the prosecution. No reference was made to *R. v. Spencer*; *R. v. Smails*, *ante*. **7–35a**

In *R. v. Rowe*, *ante*, the court went yet further, in holding that a five-judge court could decline to follow a decision of a three-judge court, even on a conviction appeal, and even where the previous decision was one that favoured the defendant, where it was satisfied that the earlier decision was manifestly unsound and that it was reached *per incuriam* and in an unsatisfactory manner. As in *Sekhon*, the *per incuriam* doctrine was itself extended so as to embrace a decision given in the "absence of relevant information". For criticism of this approach, see *Criminal Law Week* 2007/13/11.

In *R. v. James*; *R. v. Karimi* [2006] 1 Cr.App.R. 29, the Court of Appeal held that whilst it was ordinarily bound to follow a decision of the House of Lords and its own decision rather than a decision of the Privy Council, in exceptional circumstances it could follow a decision of the Privy Council in preference to one of the House of Lords. Such circumstances existed where (i) a board of nine judges, although divided 6:3 on the substantive issue, were unanimous that the result reached by the majority should be taken to have clarified definitively English law on the issue in question (provocation),

(ii) the majority constituted half of the appellate committee of the House of Lords, and (iii) the result of any appeal on the issue to the House of Lords would be a foregone conclusion.

IV. APPEAL TO COURT OF APPEAL BY THE DEFENDANT

A. APPEAL AGAINST CONVICTION ON INDICTMENT

(1) The right of appeal

Criminal Appeal Act 1968, s.1

Right of appeal against conviction on indictment

7–36 **1.**—(1) Subject to subsection (3) below, a person convicted of an offence on indictment may appeal to the Court of Appeal against his conviction.

(2) An appeal under this section lies only—

(a) with the leave of the Court of Appeal; or

(b) if, within 28 days from the date of the conviction, the judge of the court of trial grants a certificate that the case is fit for appeal.

(3) Where a person is convicted before the Crown Court of a scheduled offence it shall not be open to him to appeal to the Court of Appeal against the conviction on the ground that the decision of the court which *committed him* [sent him to the Crown Court] for trial as to the value involved was mistaken.

(4) In subsection (3) above "scheduled offence" and "the value involved" have the same meanings as they have in section 22 of the *Magistrates' Courts Act* 1980 (certain offences against property to be tried summarily if value of property or damages is small).

[This section is printed as amended by the *MCA* 1980, Sched. 7; the *CAA* 1995, s.1(1); and the *CJIA* 2008, s.47, and Sched. 8, paras 1 and 2. The words in square brackets in subs. (3) are substituted for the italicised words by the *CJA* 2003, s.41, and Sched. 3, para. 44(1) and (2). This amendment came into force on May 9, 2005, in relation to cases sent for trial under section 51 or 51A(3)(d) of the *CDA* 1998: *Criminal Justice Act 2003 (Commencement No. 9) Order* 2005 (S.I. 2005 No. 1267). Otherwise it comes into force on a day to be appointed.]

References in Parts I and II of the Act to the Court of Appeal are to be construed as references to the criminal division of the court: *CAA* 1968, s.45(1), *post*, § 7–348.

Sections 1(1), 2(1) (*post*, § 7–43) and 23(1) (*post*, § 7–208) of the 1968 Act provide for only one appeal against conviction: *R. v. Pinfold* [1988] Q.B. 462, 87 Cr.App.R. 15, CA, applying *R. v. Grantham* [1969] 2 Q.B. 574, 53 Cr.App.R. 369, Ct-MAC. See also *R. v. Berry*, 92 Cr.App.R. 147, CA.

Certificate of trial judge

7–37 Where a certificate is granted, bail pending appeal may be granted by the Crown Court: *Supreme Court [Senior Courts] Act* 1981 (as to the renaming of the 1981 Act, see *ante*, § 7–3), s.81(1)(f), *post*, § 7–186.

In paragraph IV.50 of the consolidated criminal practice direction, *post*, § 7–128, it is said that a judge should not grant a certificate in regard to conviction on a ground where he considers the chance of a successful appeal as not substantial.

The granting of a certificate precludes an order being made under section 29 (*post*, § 7–225) directing that time spent in custody should not count towards the sentence.

7–38 As to the procedure for making an application for a certificate, see rule 68.4 of the *Criminal Procedure Rules* 2005 (S.I. 2005 No. 384) (*post*, § 7–313r).

A specimen certificate is set out as Appendix 3 to the Registrar of Criminal Appeals' Guide to Proceedings in the Court of Appeal Criminal Division, *post*, § 7–177.

Leave to appeal

7–39 Where leave to appeal is specifically limited to one or some only of the grounds of appeal, the Court of Appeal will not permit the other grounds to be argued without leave: *R. v. Jackson* [1999] 1 All E.R. 572, CA; *R. v. Bullock* [1998] 9 *Archbold News* 1, CA; and *R. v. Cox*; *R. v. Thomas* [1999] 2 Cr.App.R. 6, CA.

As to the considerations relevant to the grant of leave to appeal, see *post*, § 7–235.

(2) Meaning of conviction

The word "conviction" includes a verdict which is held to warrant a judgment as well as a verdict actually followed by judgment: *R. v. Ireland*, 4 Cr.App.R. 74, CCA, *R. v. Drew*, 81 Cr.App.R. 190, CA; a plea of guilty followed by judgment: *R. v. Verney*, 2 Cr.App.R. 107, CCA, *R. v. Forde* [1923] 2 K.B. 400, 17 Cr.App.R. 99, CCA, *DPP v. Shannon* [1975] A.C. 717, HL; and even a plea of guilty not followed by judgment: *R. v. Dasour* [1998] 4 *Archbold News* 1, CA. In *R. v. Drew* it was said that it would generally be inappropriate to seek to appeal before sentence had been passed and that rarely would the Court of Appeal entertain an appeal short of that stage. No reference was, however, made to section 18(2) of the *CAA* 1968 (*post*, § 7–157), which stipulates that time runs from the date of conviction; and, in the case of conviction by a jury following a plea of not guilty, this has been held to refer to the date of verdict: *R. v. Long*, 161 J.P. 769, CA. **7–40**

For an instance of an appeal against conviction being entertained before sentence was passed, see *R. v. Laming*, 90 Cr.App.R. 450, in which the court said that where, after conviction but before sentence, a point arises as to the validity of the indictment it should be investigated by the Court of Appeal and not by the Crown Court. **7–41**

A free pardon removes from the subject of the pardon all pain, penalties and punishments ensuing from the conviction but does not eliminate the conviction itself, which may, therefore, be quashed by the Court of Appeal: *R. v. Foster* [1985] Q.B. 115, 79 Cr.App.R. 61, CA. **7–42**

Conviction does not include a finding that a person arraigned was or was not fit to plead: *R. v. Larkins*, 6 Cr.App.R. 194, CCA. Nor, it is submitted, does it include a finding under section 4A of the *Criminal Procedure (Insanity) Act* 1964 (*ante*, § 4–168), that the accused did the act or made the omission complained of. If, however, at the hearing of the preliminary issue there has been a finding that the person arraigned is fit to plead and he is thereafter convicted, he may appeal against his conviction on the ground that the hearing of the preliminary issue was open to objection for error in law, so that he should never have been tried on the substantive charge at all: *R. v. Podola* [1960] 1 Q.B. 325, 43 Cr.App.R. 220, CCA. Furthermore, if there is a finding of disability upon the hearing of the preliminary issue together with a finding that the accused did the act or made the omission charged against him, there is a specific right of appeal against either or both those findings: see *CAA* 1968, s.15 (*post*, § 7–151). See also section 6 of the *CAA* 1968, *post*, § 7–110.

(3) Determination of appeals

Criminal Appeal Act 1968, s.2

Determination of appeals

2.—(1) Subject to the provisions of this Act, the Court of Appeal— **7–43**

(a) shall allow an appeal against conviction if they think that the conviction is unsafe; and

(b) shall dismiss such an appeal in any other case.

(2) In the case of an appeal against conviction the Court shall, if they allow the appeal, quash the conviction.

(3) An order of the Court of Appeal quashing a conviction shall, except when under section 7 below the appellant is ordered to be retried, operate as a direction to the court of trial to enter, instead of the record of conviction, a judgment and verdict of acquittal.

[This section is printed as amended by the *CLA* 1977, s.44; and the *CAA* 1995, s.2(1).]

For section 7 of the 1968 Act, see *post*, § 7–112. **7–44**

The provision that the Court of Appeal "shall" allow an appeal is mandatory: *R. v. Pattinson and Laws*, 58 Cr.App.R. 417, CA.

It would be outwith the function of the Court of Appeal under section 2 to determine an appeal by accepting a "deal" reached by the parties, pursuant to which the appellant would remain convicted on some counts and not others: *R. v. Owens and Owens* (2006) 150 S.J. 1188, CA.

As to the effect of an order quashing a conviction under section 2(3), see *ante*, § 4–128.

Conviction "unsafe"

Background

7–45 Prior to the substitution of a new subsection (1) of section 2 by the *CAA* 1995, the section provided that the court should allow an appeal if they thought that (a) the conviction was unsafe or unsatisfactory, (b) that the judgment of the court of trial should be set aside on the ground of a wrong decision of any question of law, or (c) that there had been a material irregularity in the course of the trial, provided that the court could dismiss the appeal, notwithstanding that they were of the opinion that the point raised might be decided in favour of the appellant, if they were satisfied that no miscarriage of justice had occurred (known as "the proviso").

In practice, the three paragraphs of section 2(1) and the proviso became substantially intertwined and it was obvious that there was considerable overlap. For example, it became widely recognised that paragraph (a) and the proviso were effectively prescribing an identical test. Sometimes the court would speak in terms of the conviction being safe and satisfactory; on other occasions, it would go straight to the proviso and say that it was satisfied that there had been no miscarriage of justice. Frequently, the court would say that there had been a material irregularity and, therefore, the conviction was unsafe.

7–46 There is now a single basis for allowing an appeal, namely that the court thinks that the conviction is unsafe. In *R. v. Graham (H.K.)*; *R. v. Kansal*; *R. v. Ali (Sajid)*; *R. v. Marsh* [1997] 1 Cr.App.R. 302, the Court of Appeal said, in relation to the new version of section 2(1) of the 1968 Act, that it was intended to concentrate attention on one question only, namely whether, in the light of any arguments raised or evidence adduced on the appeal, the court considered the conviction unsafe. If the court was satisfied despite any misdirection or any irregularity in the conduct of the trial or any fresh evidence, that the conviction was safe, the court would dismiss the appeal. But if, for whatever reason, the court concluded that the appellant was wrongly convicted of the offence charged, or was left in doubt as to whether he was rightly convicted of that offence, then it must of necessity quash the conviction. It could make no difference that the appellant might, if duly indicted, have been convicted of some other offence.

Lord Bingham C.J., giving the judgment of the court, referred to *R. v. McHugh*, 64 Cr.App.R. 92, CA (*post*, § 21–60), *R. v. Molyneux and Farmborough*, 72 Cr.App.R. 111, CA, *R. v. Ayres* [1984] A.C. 447, HL, *R. v. Pickford* [1995] 1 Cr.App.R. 420, CA, and *R. v. Power*, 66 Cr.App.R. 159, CA, and said that a conviction would not be regarded as unsafe because it was possible to point to some drafting or clerical error, or omission, or discrepancy, or departure from good or prescribed practice. If, however, it was clear that the particulars of the offence specified in the indictment could not, even if established, support a conviction of the offence of which the defendant was accused, a conviction of such offence had, in their Lordships' opinion, to be considered unsafe. If a defendant could not in law be guilty of the offence charged on the facts relied on, no conviction of that offence could be other than unsafe.

To the extent that the proviso had been relied on in *Ayres, Molyneux and Farmborough* and *Pickford* to uphold convictions where proof of the particulars specified in the indictment could not support a conviction for the offence of which the appellants had been accused, on the basis that it was clear that they were guilty of other offences which could have been charged, the Court of Appeal considered that the amendment effected by the 1995 Act did change the law. Such convictions are to be regarded as unsafe.

Where the particulars of offence alleged "knowledge or belief" as the relevant *mens rea* when the offence in question, properly understood, required proof of knowledge, the count was not to be taken to charge an offence not known to law for these purposes, so as to result in the automatic quashing of the conviction: *R. v. K.*; *R. v. S. and R.*; *R. v. X.* [2008] 1 Cr.App.R. 1, CA. As to this case, see also *post*, § 7–52.

In the vast majority of appeals against conviction, the appellant will have contested his guilt at trial, and on appeal will be contending that the conviciton should be quashed as being unsafe because there is at the least a doubt about his guilt of the offence of which he was convicted. Exceptionally, it may be conceded that there was no error at trial, but it is argued that the Court of Appeal should nevertheless review the evidence and intervene on the ground that it has a "lurking doubt" about guilt (*post*, §§ 7–47 *et seq.*). In all other cases, however, it will be alleged that the conviction is unsafe because of some error or irregularity of procedure, such that a court cannot be satisfied that had the error or irregularity not occurred, the jury would still have convicted. As to such grounds of appeal, see *post*, §§ 7–52 *et seq.*

In a small minority of cases, the appellant will be seeking to have a conviction quashed despite a plea of guilty at trial or on grounds that do not go to the issue of whether or not he in fact committed the offence of which he was convicted. Such cases have given rise to a body of case law quite distinct from the case law of the court when dealing with conventional appeals against conviction.

Grounds of appeal unrelated to the issue of guilt

Under the former law, the Court of Appeal seldom concerned itself with the distinction between "unsafe" and "unsatisfactory" because of the overriding nature of the proviso. That there was an important distinction was, however, illustrated by *R. v. Llewellyn*, 67 Cr.App.R. 149, CA, where the conviction was quashed as being "unsatisfactory" but not "unsafe", where justice had not been seen to be done. **7–46a**

In *R. v. Chalkley and Jeffries* [1998] 2 Cr.App.R. 79, the Court of Appeal accepted that the omission of the word "unsatisfactory" had changed the law, and held that a conviction would not be liable to be quashed on account only of procedural irregularity, or abuse of process or a failure of justice to be seen to be done. As to abuse of process alone being insufficient to warrant a conviction being quashed, see also *R. v. Martin (A.)* [1998] A.C. 917, HL, *per* Lord Lloyd (at pp. 928, 929). And for support for the view that the 1995 amendment to section 2(1) of the 1968 Act changed the law, see also *R. v. Callaghan* [1999] 5 *Archbold News* 2, CA (97 08628 X4), and *R. v. Clarke and Hewins* [1999] 6 *Archbold News* 2, CA (97 04882 W3).

The decision in *Chalkley and Jeffries* was not, however, followed in *R. v. Mullen* [1999] 2 Cr.App.R. 143, CA, where it was held that a conviction may be quashed as being unsafe where an application to stay the proceedings should have been upheld on the ground that it would have been unfair to try the defendant, even though he had in fact had a fair trial and there were no grounds for doubting his guilt. The conflict between the two authorities was considered in *R. v. Togher* [2001] 3 All E.R. 463, and the court preferred *Mullen*, which must now be taken to be decisive of this issue. In *Togher*, there had been pleas of guilty and the court said *obiter* that a conviction should be liable to be quashed on the ground of abuse of process even after a plea of guilty where the appellant had been unable to apply for a stay at trial because the facts constituting the abuse had not been disclosed by the prosecution, contrary to their duty of disclosure. *Mullen* and *Togher* were followed and applied in *R. v. Early* [2003] 1 Cr.App.R. 19, CA (*post*, §§ 12–34, 12–80a); and *R. v. Smith* [2004] 8 *Archbold News* 1, CA ([2004] EWCA Crim. 2212) (*post*, § 12–54). As to an appeal against conviction based on a plea of guilty following an unsuccessful application for a stay, see *R. v. Rajcoomar* [1999] Crim.L.R. 728, CA (*post*, § 7–46b).

Alternative grounds of appeal having no necessary connection with the issue of guilt or innocence are to be found in Article 6(1) of the ECHR (*post*, § 16–57). Article 6(1) guarantees the right to a fair and public hearing within a reasonable time by an independent and impartial tribunal. It is now established that these are distinct guarantees, and that establishment of a violation does not depend on proof of prejudice: see *Darmalingum v. The State* [2000] 2 Cr.App.R. 445, PC; *Porter v. Magill*; *Weeks v. Magill* [2002] 2 A.C. 357, HL (trial within reasonable time); *Montgomery v. H.M. Advocate* [2003] 1 A.C. 641, PC; and *Millar v. Dickson*; *Payne v. Heywood*;

Stewart v. Same; *Tracey v. Same* [2002] 1 W.L.R. 1615, PC (independent and impartial tribunal). It is clear that the remedy for a violation of the guarantees as to a fair trial, or as to a hearing by an independent and impartial tribunal, is to quash the conviction: see *post*, § 7–51c; *Montgomery v. H.M. Advocate, ante*; *Millar v. Dickson, ante*; and *Dyer v. Watson*; *K. v. H.M. Advocate* [2004] 1 A.C. 379, PC.

In *Att.-Gen.'s Reference (No. 2 of 2001)* [2004] 2 A.C. 72, the House of Lords held (not following *Darmalingum, ante*) that where a conviction follows a trial in breach of the reasonable time guarantee, the remedy would not be to quash the conviction unless the trial had been unfair or it had been unfair to try the appellant at all. The appropriate remedy might be a public acknowledgment, a reduction in sentence or the payment of compensation to an acquitted defendant. As to this case, see also *ante*, § 4–67. In *Mills v. H.M. Advocate* [2004] 1 A.C. 441, PC, the delay occurred between trial and appeal, and it was held that, there being no other reason for impugning the conviction, a reduction in sentence would be an adequate remedy. To similar effect, see *R. v. Ashton, Lyons and Webber*, *The Times*, December 10, 2002, CA, where sentences of 18 years' and 14 years' imprisonment were reduced by one year on account of delay in hearing the appeal, but it was pointed out that such result would not follow where there was delay due to circumstances outside the control of the court or the prosecution.

Appeals following pleas of guilty

7–46b The principle is the same as for defendants who plead not guilty. If the defendant can bring his case within section 2(1), the Court of Appeal will be bound to quash the conviction: see *R. v. Boal* [1992] 1 Q.B. 591, 95 Cr.App.R. 272, CA. In *R. v. Lee*, 79 Cr.App.R. 108, CA, the court stressed that although a plea of guilty could not deprive the court of jurisdiction to hear an appeal against conviction, it was highly relevant to the issue whether the conviction was unsafe that the appellant had been fit to plead, had known what he was doing, had intended to plead guilty and had done so without equivocation and after receiving expert advice.

By far the most common ground of appeal, where there has been a plea of guilty is that as a result of an erroneous ruling on a point of law by the trial judge, the appellant pleaded guilty or changed his plea to guilty. To succeed, however, it must be shown that the erroneous ruling left the defendant with no legal escape from a verdict of guilty; and a conviction would not normally be regarded as unsafe where the defendant was influenced to change his plea because he recognised that, as a result of a decision to admit certain evidence against him, his case on the facts was hopeless: *R. v. Chalkley and Jeffries, ante*. In *R. v. Togher, ante*, the Court of Appeal specifically disavowed any intention to call into question this aspect of the decision in *Chalkley and Jeffries*. It was followed in *R. v. Rajcoomar* [1999] Crim.L.R. 728, CA, where a change of plea followed the rejection of an application for a stay on the grounds of abuse of process. *Mullen, ante*, was distinguished on the ground that there the appellant had contested his guilt from start to finish. *Rajcoomar* was referred to without dissent in *Togher*. For other cases in which *Chalkley and Jeffries* has been followed, see *R. v. Thomas* [2000] 1 Cr.App.R. 447, CA; *R. v. Blackwood* [2000] 6 *Archbold News* 1, CA; *R. v. Llewellyn and Gray* [2001] 7 *Archbold News* 1, CA (adverse ruling as to admissibility of evidence); and *R. v. N. and P.* [1999] 6 *Archbold News* 1, CA (98 02543 X4) (refusal of an adjournment). Its continuing authority was reaffirmed in *R. v. Bailey, Brewin and Gangji* [2001] 5 *Archbold News* 1, CA. To similar effect, see *R. v. Hanson*; *R. v. Gilmore*; *R. v. P.* [2005] 2 Cr.App.R. 21, CA (if, following a ruling that evidence of bad character was admissible, a defendant pleaded guilty, it was highly unlikely that an appeal against conviction would be entertained).

The court may, however, find a conviction based on a plea of guilty unsafe on other grounds: see, for example, *R. v. Swain* [1986] Crim.L.R. 480, and *R. v. Foster* [1985] Q.B. 115, 79 Cr.App.R. 61 (*post*, § 7–215a); and *R. v. Brady* [2005] 8 *Archbold News* 1, CA, in all of which the convictions were quashed as being "unsafe and unsatisfactory" following the reception of fresh evidence under section 23 of the *CAA* 1968 (*post*, § 7–208), the court observing in *Brady* that once the fresh evidence had shown the conviction to be unsafe, it mattered not what the reason for an unequivocal plea had been. In *Boal*, *ante*, the appellant had been convicted on 10 counts alleging offences contrary to section 23 of the *Fire Precautions Act* 1971. He had pleaded guilty to some and had been found guilty of others. The Court of Appeal concluded that the evidence did not form a sufficient basis for finding an essential ingredient of all the offences proved. As a result of legal advice, this ingredient had never been in issue, even on the contested counts. All the convictions were quashed as being "unsafe and unsatisfactory". In *R. v. W. (A.G.)* [1999] Crim.L.R. 87, CA, convictions on two counts were quashed as unsafe despite pleas of guilty where the appellant had pleaded guilty, without admitting guilt, following advice from his counsel that the evidence in relation to those counts would be highly damaging on the remaining counts, but that if he pleaded guilty there would be no evidence of those matters; whereas, in fact, a successful application was made by the prosecution to admit the evidence of the guilty pleas as similar fact evidence.

For an appeal against conviction to succeed where an application to vacate a plea has been refused, it must be shown that the judge misdirected himself or took account of matters which he should not have taken account of, or failed to take account of matters to which he should have had regard, or that he exercised his discretion in a wholly unreasonable manner: *R. v. Sheikh* [2004] 2 Cr.App.R. 13, CA. See also *R. v. Sorhaindo* [2006] 7 *Archbold News* 2, CA (*ante*, § 4–187).

In *R. v. Saik* [2005] 1 *Archbold News* 1, CA, it was held that where a defendant enters a guilty plea and subsequently appeals on the basis that the plea was entered following erroneous legal advice as to likely sentence and/or the likelihood of any confiscation proceedings affecting the security of his matrimonial home, the facts must be so strong as to show that the plea of guilty was not a true acknowledgement of guilt; the advice must have gone to the heart of the plea, so as to render it a nullity as not being a free plea; and it was difficult to see how erroneous advice as to the length of sentence likely to be imposed could ever go to the heart of a plea, except perhaps where the maximum penalty for the offence was understated, for the decision as to length of sentence lies with the judge or the Court of Appeal. The appellant's conviction was quashed by the House of Lords on other grounds: see *post*, §§ 26–9, 33–4, 33–17.

As to the jurisdiction of the Court of Appeal to order the issue of a writ of *venire de novo* where there has been an irregularity in relation to the defendant's plea, see *post*, § 7–355.

Relevance of former law

Whether or not the correct view is that the amendment to section 2(1) of the 1968 Act changed the law, it is beyond argument that much of the former law will be relevant in deciding what is liable to render a conviction unsafe. The grounds for a finding that a conviction is unsafe are examined in the following paragraphs; wherever possible, the principles to be derived from the authorities have been adapted to take account of the terms of the new section 2(1). **7–46c**

The safety test

In *R. v. Cooper* [1969] 1 Q.B. 267, 53 Cr.App.R. 82, Widgery L.J., delivering the judgment of the Court of Appeal, said that it was: **7–47**

> "a case in which every issue was before the jury and in which the jury was properly instructed, and, accordingly, a case in which this Court will be very reluctant indeed to intervene. It has been said over and over again throughout the years that this Court must recognise the advantage which a jury has in seeing and hearing the witnesses, and if all the material was before the jury and the summing-up was impeccable, this Court should not lightly interfere. … (W)e are … charged to allow an appeal against conviction if we think that the verdict of the jury should be set aside on the ground that under all the circumstances of the case it is unsafe … . That means that in cases of this kind the Court must in the end ask itself a subjective question, whether we are content to let the matter stand as it is, or whether there is not some lurking doubt in our minds which makes us wonder whether an injustice has been done. This is a reaction which may not be based strictly on the evidence as such: it is a reaction which can be produced by the general feel of the case as the Court experiences it" (at pp. 271, 85–86).

See also *R. v. Pattinson and Laws*, 58 Cr.App.R. 417, CA, and *R. v. Lake*, 64 Cr.App.R. 172, in which Lord Widgery C.J. gave the Court of Appeal's judgment: **7–48**

"In this Court ... the first matter we are concerned with is to see whether the rules have been obeyed and to see whether the trial judge has followed the rules of practice appropriate to the protection of the defence. ... Once you have decided that the rules of procedure were followed and there remains the only residual question of whether there is a lurking doubt in the mind of the Court, such doubts are resolved not, as I say by rules of thumb and not by arithmetic, but they are largely by the experience of the judges concerned and the feel which the case has for them" (at pp. 175–177).

The test applied by the Court of Appeal is different to that applied by the trial judge on a submission of "no case": see *R. v. Arobieke* [1988] Crim.L.R. 314, CA.

In *R. v. B.* [2003] 2 Cr.App.R. 13, the Court of Appeal said that it has a residual discretion, to be exercised in limited circumstances and with caution, to set aside a conviction if it feels it to be unsafe or unfair; this is so even where the trial process cannot be faulted. This approach was, however, rejected in *R. v. E. (T.)* [2004] 2 Cr.App.R. 36, CA, where it was said that whether a conviction was unsafe was not a matter about which the court had any discretion. Both cases concerned stale allegations of sexual offences where there was little evidence other than a direct conflict between the complainant's allegations and the defendant's denial of any impropriety. Both seem to be in agreement that in such a case, a conviction would be quashed as being unsafe, where the court concludes that the defendant had been put in an impossible position to defend himself. In *B.* it was held that such was the case and that the conviction would be quashed, notwithstanding that the judge had been correct to reject an application for a stay, that no criticism could be made of the summing up, and that there had been an explanation for the delay. See also *R. v. R.* [2007] Crim.L.R. 478, CA (cases concerning events long ago require special consideration as to whether any verdicts based upon such distant recollections are unsafe).

7–49 In *R. v. Wallace and Short*, 67 Cr.App.R. 291, Roskill L.J. said that Lord Widgery in *Cooper*, *ante*, was not "talking about a reaction based on inadmissible evidence; he was talking about a subjective reaction which this court after appraising admissible evidence in the end felt on its own appraisal of all the circumstances of the case" (at p. 298). The court accordingly held that it would be quite wrong to overturn the verdicts of the jury on the basis of a bundle of inadmissible documents after a summing up which was not open to criticism. The appellants, who were endeavouring to rely on statements which were almost wholly inadmissible, could not be placed in a stronger position than those seeking to rely upon section 23 of the *CAA* 1968 (*post*, § 7–208), which is concerned with admissible fresh evidence. *Cf. R. v. Beckford and Daley* [1991] Crim.L.R. 833, CA, where convictions were quashed having regard to a confession of a co-defendant which was held to be inadmissible at trial. This approach is inconsistent with *Wallace and Short* (see *R. v. Thomas* [1996] Crim.L.R. 654, CA); *Beckford and Daley* should either be regarded as a decision on its unique facts (*R. v. Brown and Ciarla* [1995] Crim.L.R. 328, CA) or as being wrong.

In *R. v. Farrow (Anthony Robin)*, *The Times*, October 20, 1998, CA, it was said to be undesirable to place a gloss on the language used by Parliament, and that reference to the concept of a "lurking doubt" is inappropriate. Notwithstanding this observation, the Court of Appeal has continued to refer to this test: see, *e.g. R. v. Litchfield* [1998] Crim.L.R. 507. And in *R. v. Benton and Joseph* [2000] 7 *Archbold News* 2, Ct-MAC, it was said that the "lurking doubt" test, and an alternative formulation advanced in *R. v. Wellington* [1991] Crim.L.R. 543, CA ("whether we feel a reasoned and substantial unease about the finding of guilt"), are both acceptable and come to the same thing, "Was the conviction safe?"

As to whether it is legitimate to have regard to apparent admissions of guilt made by counsel during mitigation, in deciding whether a conviction is unsafe, see *Wu Chun-piu v. R.* [1996] 1 W.L.R. 1113, PC.

Fresh evidence cases

7–50 In *Stafford and Luvaglio v. DPP* [1974] A.C. 878, the House of Lords approved the judgment of Lord Widgery in *Cooper*, *ante*, as correctly stating the effect of section 2(1). It also decided that on an appeal where fresh evidence has been admitted the question for the appellate court was no different from that in a case such as *Cooper* where no fresh evidence has been heard: it has to decide whether the conviction was unsafe.

In *R. v. Pendleton* [2002] 1 W.L.R. 72, HL, their Lordships were unanimous in adhering to *Stafford and Luvaglio*. It was held that, where fresh evidence is admitted, the decision for the Court of Appeal is the same as in any other appeal; it has to make a judgment whether the conviction is unsafe; it is not incumbent on the court to ask itself what effect the evidence would have had on the jury; but the Court of Appeal should bear in mind, first, that it is a court of review and that it is not and should never become the primary decision-maker, and, secondly, that it can only ever have an imperfect and incomplete understanding of the processes which led the jury to convict; whilst the Court of Appeal can make its own assessment of the evidence that it has heard, it is, clear cases apart, at a disadvantage in seeking to relate that evidence to the rest of the evidence that was before the jury; accordingly, it will usually be wise for the Court of Appeal to test their own provisional view by asking whether the evidence, if given at trial, might reasonably have affected the decision of the jury to convict; if it might have done, then the conviction must be thought to be unsafe. See also *Bain v. The Queen*, 72 J.C.L. 34, PC ([2007] UKPC 33), where it was said that a substantial miscarriage of justice will occur if fresh, admissible and apparently credible evidence is admitted which the jury had no opportunity to consider but which might have led them, acting reasonably, to reach a different verdict if they had had the opportunity to consider it; and that (i) the issue of guilt is for a properly informed and directed jury, not for an appellate court, (ii) the issue is not whether there is or was evidence on which a jury could reasonably have convicted, but whether there is or was evidence on which they might reasonably have declined to do so, (iii) a fair trial ordinarily requires that the jury hear the evidence they ought to hear before returning their verdict, and that they should not act on evidence which is, or may be, false or misleading, and (iv) even a guilty defendant is entitled to a trial that conforms to these precepts; *R. (Farnell) v. Criminal Cases Review Commission*, *The Times*, June 2, 2003, DC, where it was said that the need for the court to guard against the temptation of converting itself into a jury is particularly important in fresh evidence provocation cases where Parliament has, by section 3 of the *Homicide Act* 1957 (*post*, § 19–52), given the jury not simply primacy, but an unfettered freedom of decision; and *R. v. Hakala* [2002] Crim.L.R. 578, CA, where it was said that it was integral to this process that if the fresh evidence is disputed, the Court of Appeal must decide whether and to what extent it should be accepted or rejected, and if it is to be accepted, to evaluate its importance, or otherwise, relative to the remaining material which was before the jury; hence, the jury impact test. **7–51**

Where, by its nature, the fresh evidence could not have been given at trial (*e.g.* a post-trial retraction by a prosecution witness), the court will have no alternative to making its own assessment of the evidence, and then deciding, in the light of that assessment, what effect it has on the safety of the conviction. In such a case, to ask what effect the evidence would have had on the jury's verdict would be meaningless: see *R. v. Ishtiaq Ahmed*, unreported, December 6, 2002, CA ([2002] EWCA Crim. 2781).

Views of trial judge

7–51a The views of the trial judge as to the merits of a conviction are irrelevant to the task of the Court of Appeal: *R. v. Jones (J.H.)* [1998] 2 Cr.App.R. 53, CA. See also *R. v. Brown (Jamie)* [1998] Crim.L.R. 196, CA (judge should not write to Court of Appeal expressing doubts).

Where, however, an appeal is based on alleged inconsistency of verdicts, the Court of Appeal has expressed itself willing to have regard to the views of the trial judge: *R. v. Rigby* [1997] 9 *Archbold News* 2, CA (97/4020/X3).

Ancient convictions

7–51b As to the approach of the Court of Appeal to appeals against convictions which occurred when the substantive law, the law of evidence and the rules of procedure were different to those prevailing at the time of the appeal, see *R. v. Ward*, 96 Cr.App.R. 1; *R. v. Gerald* [1999] Crim.L.R. 315; *R. v. Bentley (Deceased)* [2001] 1 Cr.App.R. 21;

R. v. King [2000] Crim.L.R. 835; *R. v. Johnson (Harold)* [2001] 1 Cr.App.R. 26; *R. v. Clark* [2001] 4 *Archbold News* 5; *R. v. Kansal (No. 2)* [2002] 2 A.C. 69; *R. v. Hussain* [2005] 3 *Archbold News* 1 ([2005] EWCA Crim. 31); and *R. v. Blackburn* [2005] 2 Cr.App.R. 30. See also *R. v. Hendy* [2006] 2 Cr.App.R. 33, CA (*post*, § 19–70); *R. v. R.*, *post*, § 7–182, in which *Hendy* was distinguished; *R. v. K.*; *R. v. S. and R.*; *R. v. X.* [2008] 1 Cr.App.R. 1; and *R. v. Cottrell*; *R. v. Fletcher* [2008] 1 Cr.App.R. 7, CA.

Where there is a reference of a conviction to the Court of Appeal by the Criminal Cases Review Commission under section 9 of the *CAA* 1995 (*post*, § 7–154) on the ground that "it appears to the Commission that there are exceptional circumstances which justify making it" (s.13(2)), notwithstanding that there has been a previous unsuccessful appeal and there are no new arguments or evidence, the court is not bound by its own previous determination on the merits; but departure from its previous determination should be similarly confined to "exceptional circumstances", *i.e.* the court would have to be convinced that had the appeal been argued in like manner before the previous court, the conviction would have been quashed: *R. v. Thomas* [2003] 1 Cr.App.R. 11, CA; but the restraint of exceptionality did not govern the court's consideration of grounds rejected by the Commission; whilst the court would treat the Commission's reasoning on making a reference with considerable respect, its discretion to consider a ground not included in the Commission's reasons for the reference or to reject or follow the Commission's reasoning one way or another on any matter considered by it was unfettered: *R. v. Mills (No. 2)* [2004] 1 Cr.App.R. 7, CA.

Right to a fair trial

7–51c Article 6 of the ECHR guarantees a person a right to a fair trial in the determination of a criminal charge. The jurisprudence in relation to this right is dealt with in detail in Chapter 16 (*post*, §§ 16–57 *et seq.*). The first question which arises in the context of criminal appeals is whether a conviction at the end of a trial which fails to match up to the requirements of Article 6 can ever be anything other than unsafe. It is submitted that the answer must be in the negative, and that section 3 of the *Human Rights Act* 1998 (*post*, § 16–15) obliges the Court of Appeal and the House of Lords to "read and [give] effect to" the word "unsafe" so as to include any conviction resulting from such a trial. Strong support for this approach is to be found in *R. v. A. (No. 2)* [2002] 1 A.C. 45, HL, where Lord Steyn observed (at [38]) that it was well-established that the right to a fair trial was absolute in the sense that a conviction obtained in breach of it cannot stand. See also *R. v. Forbes* [2001] 1 A.C. 473, HL; *R. v. Togher* [2001] 3 All E.R. 463, CA (if a defendant has been denied a fair trial, it would be almost inevitable that the conviction would be regarded as unsafe); *Randall v. R.* [2002] 1 W.L.R. 2237, PC (right to a fair trial is absolute, and there would come a point when departure from good practice was so gross, or so persistent, or so prejudicial, or so irremediable that an appellate court would be bound to condemn a trial as unfair and quash the conviction as unsafe, however strong the grounds for believing the defendant to have been guilty); and *Bernard v. State of Trinidad and Tobago* [2007] 2 Cr.App.R. 22, PC (where a trial had been vitiated by irregularity, the strength of the evidence would only be relevant to the issue of whether the trial had been fair if the irregularity was an incorrect admission of evidence; in cases of procedural irregularity, however, the approach should be to weigh the seriousness of the defects; the trial may still have been fair if they were minor, but if they were sufficiently serious, the trial would have been unfair, however strong the evidence (*Randall v. R.*, *ante*, considered)).

A second question relates to the determination of whether a trial was fair. It is submitted that it is for the Court of Appeal to conduct an independent assessment of this issue. Whilst an appellate court will always defer to the view of a tribunal of first instance in relation to live evidence which it has not had the benefit of hearing, the issue of whether or not a trial has been fair is one in respect of which no deference is due to the court of first instance (see *R. v. Davis (Iain)*; *R. v. Ellis* [2006] Cr.App.R. 32, CA (at [63], [64]) (the reversal of the decision of the Court of Appeal (in *R. v. Davis*) by the House of Lords (see [2008] 3 W.L.R. 125) does not affect this point)).

A third question concerns the issue of whether the appellate process may itself cure

Cooper [1969] 1 Q.B. 267, 53 Cr.App.R. 82, and his Lordship cited the extract from Widgery L.J.'s judgment which is set out in § 7–47, *ante*. His Lordship then referred to *Turnbull* and quoted the above extract from the judgment of Lord Widgery, now Lord Chief Justice. Lawton L.J. said that the instant case did not come within any of the three circumstances set out in *Turnbull* as being the circumstances in which the Court of Appeal will interfere: yet the conviction was quashed because the court did not feel that it was safe.

It is submitted, however, that there is no real conflict between *Cooper* and *Turnbull*, and that the true explanation of *Pope* is that despite the impeccable directions of the judge to the jury, he had, in fact, failed to follow the *Turnbull* guidelines, which, as Lord Widgery said (at pp. 231, 139) "is likely to result in a conviction being quashed." The case should have been withdrawn from the jury.

Improper withdrawal of issue of fact

7–57 If the trial judge fails to direct the jury as to some issue of fact which forms part of the ingredients of the offence this will be a misdirection: *a fortiori*, if he actually withdraws an issue of fact from the jury. As to a direction to convict, see *ante*, § 4–411.

For examples of convictions being quashed where an issue of fact, although not actually withdrawn from the jury, was not left clearly to them, see *R. v. Ptohopoulos*, 52 Cr.App.R. 47; and *R. v. Davison*, 57 Cr.App.R. 113. For examples of convictions being quashed, an issue of fact having actually been withdrawn from the jury, see *R. v. Feely* [1973] Q.B. 530, 57 Cr.App.R. 312; and *R. v. Inwood*, 57 Cr.App.R. 529.

7–58 A similar form of misdirection arises where some matter has been raised by way of defence, there being at least an evidential burden upon the defendant, and the judge wrongly rules and directs the jury that there is no evidence in relation to this matter: see *R. v. Johnson*, 89 Cr.App.R. 148 (provocation); *R. v. Burke*, 67 Cr.App.R. 220 (whether certain firearms were antiques); and *R. v. Shepherd*, 86 Cr.App.R. 47, CA (duress). In each case, the Court of Appeal held that the trial judge had been wrong to withdraw the issue from the jury and the convictions were accordingly quashed.

7–59 A slightly different form of misdirection is that which does not so much withdraw an issue from the jury's consideration as, by mis-stating the law as to the ingredients of the offence, fails to identify the correct issues. Thus, in *R. v. Smith (D.R.)* [1974] Q.B. 354, 58 Cr.App.R. 320, the Court of Appeal "applying the ordinary principles of *mens rea*" held that on a charge of criminal damage, the *actus reus* being "destroying or damaging property belonging to another", the intention and recklessness and the absence of lawful excuse required to constitute the offence have reference to property belonging to another and accordingly quashed the conviction, the trial judge having directed the jury that the defendant's honest belief that the property he damaged was his own was irrelevant. See also *R. v. Allamby and Medford*, 59 Cr.App.R. 189, and *R. v. Kimber*, 77 Cr.App.R. 225.

Non-direction

7–60 There is an overlap between this category and the previous category for in every case of an issue of fact not being left to the jury it follows that there has been no direction where there ought to have been one. However, the duties of the trial judge are more extensive than merely directing the jury as to the ingredients of the offence charged. He must, for example, give certain warnings as to how to approach certain evidence and he must consider whether the evidence raises any possible defence to the charge, regardless of whether the defendant has raised the point and, if it does, he must direct the jury on it. The conviction was quashed in each of the following cases where there was a simple failure to direct the jury fully as to the ingredients that had to be proved: *R. v. Manners-Astley*, 52 Cr.App.R. 5; *R. v. Ashley*, 52 Cr.App.R. 42; *R. v. Gambling* [1975] Q.B. 207, 60 Cr.App.R. 25; and *R. v. McVey* [1988] Crim.L.R. 127.

A failure to direct the jury on the burden and standard of proof is a serious defect in a summing up: *R. v. Edwards (N.W.)*, 77 Cr.App.R. 5, CA. In *R. v. Ching*, 63 Cr.App.R. 7, the Court of Appeal said that the best place to deal with the burden and standard of proof is at the beginning of the summing up. On appeal, however, the direction given by the judge would be considered against the whole background of the case and, in particular, the whole effect of the summing up. In *R. v. Gibson*, 77 Cr.App.R. 151, the Court of Appeal held on the particular facts that the failure of the judge to repeat his direction on the burden and standard of proof rendered the verdict unsafe and unsatisfactory. It was said that usually such a repetition "is wholly unnecessary" (at p. 156).

7–61 In *R. v. Falconer-Atlee*, 58 Cr.App.R. 348, on a charge of theft the defendant raised a claim of right. Nowhere in the summing up was there a reference to section 2(1)(a) of the *Theft Act* 1968. Roskill L.J., giving the Court of Appeal's judgment, said it was extremely important that the judge should have referred to this provision:

> "To give the jury the limited direction which the learned judge gave, impeccable so far as it went in relation to 'dishonestly,' but on the facts of this case not to go on to tell them what section 2(1)(a) expressly provided was *not* to be regarded as 'dishonest' was to omit what was an extremely important direction" (at pp. 358–359).

The extent to which reference needs to be made to section 2(1)(a) where a claim of right is raised was further considered in *R. v. Woolven*, *post*, § 21–28.

7–62

> "It is asking much of judges ... to require that they should always have in mind possible answers, possible excuses in law which have not been relied upon by defending counsel or even, as has happened ..., have been expressly disclaimed by defending counsel. Nevertheless, it is perfectly clear that this Court has always regarded it as the duty of the judge ... to ensure that he himself looks for and sees any such possible answers and refers to them in summing up to the jury and takes care to ensure that the jury's verdict rests upon their having in fact excluded any of those excusatory circumstances" (*per* Winn L.J., *R. v. Kachikwu*, 52 Cr.App.R. 538, 543).

See also *Bullard v. R.* [1957] A.C. 635 at 642, PC; *R. v. Porritt*, 45 Cr.App.R. 348, CCA; *R. v. Cascoe*, 54 Cr.App.R. 401, CA; *R. v. Rossiter*, 95 Cr.App.R. 326, CA; *Von Starck v. R.* [2000] 1 W.L.R. 1270, PC. The extensive nature of this duty is well illustrated by *R. v. Hector*, 67 Cr.App.R. 224, and *R. v. Bashir*, 77 Cr.App.R. 59, in which Watkins L.J. said–

> "There can be, and there is, no doubt firstly that a defence can be said to be raised whenever there is evidence, no matter from what source, of a kind which calls upon a judge to conclude that this defence should be left to the jury, and secondly, that his decision as to whether or not that defence should be left to the jury is open to review in this Court" (at p. 62).

7–63 In a case which depends wholly or substantially on the correctness of one or more identifications of the accused, a failure to follow the guidelines laid down by the Court of Appeal in *R. v. Turnbull*, *ante*, § 7–55 "is likely to result in a conviction being quashed" (*per* Lord Widgery C.J. at pp. 231, 139). See also *R. v. Keane*, 65 Cr.App.R. 247, and *R. v. Hunjan*, 68 Cr.App.R. 99.

Where evidence is given of previous convictions of the accused, a failure by the trial judge to identify the issues to which such evidence is relevant may result in any conviction which ensues being quashed: *R. v. Vickers* [1972] Crim.L.R. 101; *R. v. Wilkins*, 60 Cr.App.R. 300; *R. v. Inder*, 67 Cr.App.R. 143; and, since the commencement of the *CJA* 2003, *R. v. Hanson*; *R. v. Gilmore*; *R. v. P.* [2005] 2 Cr.App.R. 21.

There should be an express direction to disregard as against one defendant a statement made in his absence by a co-defendant: *R. v. Lawrence and Pomroy*, 57 Cr.App.R. 64 (*aliter* if the statement is admitted in evidence under the *CJA* 2003, s.114 (*post*, § 11–3)).

7–64 Where more than one defendant is on trial, the jury should be directed to give separate consideration to the position of each defendant: *R. v. Smith and Smith*, 25 Cr.App.R. 119. Where an indictment contains more than one count, the jury should be directed to give separate consideration to each count: *R. v. Fisher*, 49 Cr.App.R. 116; *R. v. Lovesey and Peterson* [1970] 1 Q.B. 352, 53 Cr.App.R. 461.

Where no direction is given to guide the jury in making a decision about the reliability of a confession, a conviction may be quashed: *R. v. Mushtaq* [2005] 1 W.L.R. 1513, HL.

The Court of Appeal has accepted that a proper direction as to the good character of the defendant has some value and is therefore capable of having some effect in every case in which it is appropriate for such a direction to be given: see *R. v. Fulcher*

[1995] 2 Cr.App.R. 251. It follows that a failure to give such direction when it should be given is liable to render a conviction unsafe: see *R. v. Kamar*, *The Times*, May 14, 1999, CA; and *R. v. M. (Ian)* [1999] 6 *Archbold News* 3 (it would be a rare case in which it would be possible to say that the giving of an appropriate direction would have made no difference to the outcome); but in *Jagdeo Singh v. State of Trinidad and Tobago* [2006] 1 W.L.R. 146, PC, it was said that an omission to give a good character direction on credibility is not necessarily fatal to a conviction and that much may turn on the nature of the issues in the case and the other available evidence. As to directing the jury as to character generally, see *ante*, §§ 4–406 *et seq.*

Failure to refer to defence

7–65 In *R. v. Badjan*, 50 Cr.App.R. 141, CCA, it was held that where a cardinal line of defence is placed before the jury and that finds no reflection at any stage in the summing up, it is in general impossible to say that the conviction is secure. See also *R. v. Jones (P.)* [1987] Crim.L.R. 701, CA (in a complicated and lengthy case, it is incumbent on the judge to deal with salient points arising in the evidence, and to put the essential thrust of the defence); *R. v. Bury* [1997] 10 *Archbold News* 2 (where summing up fails to put defence before jury, it will be rare for the Court of Appeal not to conclude that conviction is unsafe); *R. v. Akhtar* [2000] 1 *Archbold News* 2 (where the defendant neither gives, nor calls evidence, but has been extensively interviewed, it is of particular importance that the summing up should at least summarise the main points made by the defendant; only rarely, if ever, would a conviction be adjudged safe notwithstanding a failure to sum up the defence); and *R. v. Marashi* [2002] 1 *Archbold News* 3, CA (in a case of violence, where a total of 19 witnesses had given contradictory evidence over a period of days, the omission of the judge to make any detailed reference to the evidence of any witness other than the victim and the defendant had rendered the trial unfair; the jury should have had the judge's assistance in relating the evidence to the issues to be resolved between the protagonists).

It is, however, no part of the judge's duty to build up the defence of someone who has not given evidence, although he should remind the jury in summary form of what the defendant said about the matter prior to trial: *R. v. Hillier and Farrar*, 97 Cr.App.R. 349, CA.

Misdirection on fact

7–66 To have any effect in itself, a misstatement of the evidence or a misdirection as to the effect of the evidence must be such as to make it reasonably probable that the jury would not have returned their verdict of guilty if there had been no misstatements: *R. v. Wann*, 7 Cr.App.R. 135, CCA; *R. v. Bateson*, 54 Cr.App.R. 11, CA; *R. v. Wright*, 58 Cr.App.R. 444, CA.

Improper comment

7–67 A judge may comment on the facts and may do so in confident terms; a judge has experience of the bearing of evidence and in dealing with the relevancy of questions of fact, and it is therefore right that the jury should have his assistance: *R. v. Cohen and Bateman*, 2 Cr.App.R. 197, CCA; and see *R. v. Evans (D.J.)*, 91 Cr.App.R. 173, CA. If, however, the judge comments in such a way as to make the summing up fundamentally unbalanced, repetition of the standard direction that the facts are for the jury and that an expression of opinion by the judge is to be ignored if the jury disagree with it, would not remedy the unfairness: *Mears v. R.*, 97 Cr.App.R. 239, PC. (This was not a decision on the *CAA* 1968, but their Lordships adopted this formula from the judgment of the Court of Appeal in *R. v. Gilbey*, unreported, January 26, 1990.) In *R. v. Wood* [1996] 1 Cr.App.R. 207, CA, one ground (not sufficient on its own) for quashing a conviction was the improper comment of the judge (described as "advocacy" by the Court of Appeal). The court said that they would not act on information as to the demeanour or tone of voice of the judge unless it is agreed between the parties or supported by evidence.

In certain restricted areas the Court of Appeal has developed particular principles as to the extent to which a judge may properly comment. A summing up should not contain any words indicating that the acquittal of the defendant will or may ruin a police witness who has given evidence against him; nor should any comment be made to place police witnesses in any special category: *R. v. Culbertson*, 54 Cr.App.R. 311; *R. v. Harris, The Times*, October 16, 1985; *R. v. Beycan* [1990] Crim.L.R. 185, CA; and *cf. R. v. Wellwood-Kerr* [1978] Crim.L.R. 760, and *R. v. Keane* [1992] Crim.L.R. 306, CA, in which it was held to be reasonable to point out that anyone, police officer or otherwise, who gives deliberately false evidence runs the risk of severe punishment for perjury and perverting the course of justice, and to tell the jury that they may weigh that against any suggested motive on the part of the witness.

7–68 There should be no comment on the consequences of conviction: *R. v. Milligan, The Times*, March 11, 1989, CA (the judge could have corrected the error of counsel, who had also referred to the consequences of conviction, without falling into error himself by following the guidance of the Privy Council in *Att.-Gen. for South Australia v. Brown* [1960] A.C. 432).

Whilst strong comment in an appropriate case is permissible, the judge should never give an express indication of his own disbelief in relation to the evidence of a witness, let alone that of the defendant: *R. v. Iroegbu, The Times*, August 2, 1988.

In *R. v. Smith and Doe*, 85 Cr.App.R. 197, CA, it was said to be improper for a judge in summing up to a jury to comment that when a submission had been made at the close of the prosecution case that there was no case to answer, if he had not thought there was sufficient evidence of identification available to the jury, he would have withdrawn the case from them. Although the convictions were quashed, it was made clear that they would not have been, had this been the only ground of complaint.

As to comment by the judge generally, see also *ante*, §§ 4–394 *et seq.*

Particulars of misdirection

7–69 As to the necessity for the grounds of appeal including substantial particulars where misdirection is alleged, see *post*, § 7–179.

Inconsistent verdicts

Of same court

7–70 An appellant who seeks to obtain the quashing of a conviction on the ground that the verdict against him was inconsistent with his acquittal on another count has a burden cast upon him to show not merely that the verdicts on the two counts were inconsistent, but that they were so inconsistent as to call for interference by an appellate court. The court will interfere if it is satisfied that no reasonable jury who had applied their mind properly to the facts in the case could have arrived at the conclusion which was reached: *R. v. Durante*, 56 Cr.App.R. 708; *R. v. Malashev* [1997] Crim.L.R. 586; *R. v. Hayward* [2000] Crim.L.R. 189. In *R. v. Green* (2005) 149 S.J. 1350, CA, the same test was applied in relation to alleged inconsistency of the appellant's conviction with a co-accused's acquittal. There is no shortage of authority to support the proposition that logical inconsistency does not make the verdict complained of unsafe unless the only explanation of the inconsistency must or might be that the jury was confused or adopted the wrong approach: see *R. v. McCluskey*, 98 Cr.App.R. 216, CA; *R. v. Segal* [1976] Crim.L.R. 324, CA; *R. v. Velasquez* [1996] 1 Cr.App.R. 155, CA; and *R. v. Andrews-Weatherfoil Ltd*, 56 Cr.App.R. 31, CA (*per* Eveleigh L.J. at pp. 40–41). In *R. v. Cova Products Ltd* [2005] Crim.L.R. 667, however, the Court of Appeal said that there was much to be said for the view that once logical inconsistency was established, the onus should be on the prosecution to show that the verdicts had not resulted from confusion of, or a wrong approach by, the jury. The court doubted the approach in *R. v. Clarke and Fletcher* [1997] 9 *Archbold News* 2 (96/5638/X2), where it had been said that a conviction would not be unsafe if a legitimate train of reasoning were postulated that would explain the verdicts; "how can a legitimate train of reasoning, itself a matter of speculation, lead to logically inconsistent verdicts?" (at [29]).

The mere fact that the different counts all depended on the evidence of the same witness, whose evidence was uncorroborated, and whose credibility was in issue, could not render different verdicts on the different counts inconsistent for this purpose: *R. v. Bell* [1997] 6 *Archbold News* 2, CA (observing that *R. v. Cilgam* [1994] Crim.L.R. 861, CA, is to be regarded as an exceptional case; as should, it is submitted, *R. v. B.* (2005) 149 S.J. 1353, CA); *R. v. Van der Molen* [1997] Crim.L.R. 604, CA; *R. v. Clarke and Fletcher*, *ante*; *R. v. G.* [1998] Crim.L.R. 483, CA; and *R. v. Rogers* [2004] Crim.L.R. 747, CA. In *R. v. Rafferty and Rafferty* [2004] 4 *Archbold News* 1, CA (no logical inconsistency between conviction for affray and acquittal of assault), the court said that too little heed had been paid to the observation of the court in *G.* that when such ground was advanced, the decision in *Bell*, as well as the decision in that case should be before the court and the appellant should be in a position to explain why the approach adumbrated in *Bell* should not be followed.

For an example of a conviction being upheld, although the guilty verdict was logically inconsistent with an acquittal on another count in the light of the way the jury had been directed, see *R. v. Fielder-Beech* [1998] Crim.L.R. 503, CA, where it was said that the verdicts were not legally inconsistent and it was not the case that the only explanation of the verdict was that the jury were confused.

For examples of a conviction being quashed though there was no logical inconsistency between the verdicts, see *R. v. Eldridge and Salmon* [1999] Crim.L.R. 166; *R. v. Smolinski* [2004] 2 Cr.App.R. 40; and *R. v. McGill* (2005) 149 S.J. 638. All three cases are probably best regarded as being dependent on their own peculiar facts. It is impossible to reconcile them with the other authorities. Indeed, in *Smolinski*, it appears that counsel had not even advanced inconsistency of verdict as a ground of appeal; and the court referred to no authorities on the issue.

In *R. v. Dayle*, 58 Cr.App.R. 100, the appellant was originally charged with two offences: at the first trial the jury disagreed on the first count and acquitted on the second count. At a retrial of the first count he was convicted. His conviction was quashed because the disagreement and the verdict of acquittal at the first trial were inconsistent. See also *R. v. Batten*, *The Times*, March 16, 1990, where a conviction was quashed as being inconsistent with a disagreement in respect of a co-defendant who was jointly charged with the appellant with an offence of gross indecency and, in respect of whom, the issue which the jury had had to determine was essentially the same as the issue in the case of the appellant.

In *R. v. McKechnie, Gibbons and Dixon*, 94 Cr.App.R. 51, CA, the court was concerned with the consequences of inconsistent guilty verdicts. *Held*, it did not necessarily follow that all guilty verdicts on either side of the inconsistency would be quashed. Where one verdict is readily explicable from the way in which the prosecution put their case, from the evidence and from a proper direction by the judge on the law and facts, and where the second may well be attributable to the jury's attempt to do justice on the facts regardless of the constraints of the charges or to a failure by the judge to give adequate directions as to the consequences for the second verdict of a possible conclusion on the first, only the second verdict should be quashed. *Cf. R. v. Lawrence*, *The Times*, December 4, 1989, CA, where convictions for both burglary and handling were quashed, the counts having been put forward in the alternative. **7–71**

Where a charge against two defendants is put on the basis of a joint enterprise, the mere fact that one defendant is acquitted does not render the conviction of the other inconsistent for these purposes: *R. v. Shuker and Shuker* [1998] Crim.L.R. 906, CA.

As to the preparedness of the Court of Appeal to have regard to the views of the trial judge in relation to an alleged inconsistency of verdict, see *R. v. Rigby*, *ante*, § 7–51a.

Where a judge directs a jury that whilst they may think that various counts stand or fall together, they were nevertheless to consider each count separately, the defence are liable to be taken to have acquiesced in such direction if no submission is made to the effect that the judge should direct the jury in stronger terms: *R. v. W. (Martyn)* [1999] 6 *Archbold News* 3, CA (98 03892 W4).

Of another court

In *R. v. Ireland* [1985] Crim.L.R. 367, CA, the appellant had been convicted of driving whilst disqualified. The defence had been that he was not the driver of the vehicle. **7–72**

Subsequently, he was tried by a magistrates' court for driving with excess alcohol, the charge arising from the same incident. The prosecution evidence was the same and the issue was the same. The defence, however, called three further witnesses and the magistrates acquitted. The Court of Appeal quashed the conviction for driving whilst disqualified having regard to the affidavits before it of the three extra witnesses and the fact of acquittal by the magistrates. Taken together, they rendered the verdict unsafe.

In *R. v. Warner*, 50 Cr.App.R. 291, CCA, the appellant was tried at the same sessions, first on an indictment for taking and driving away a motor vehicle, of which he was convicted; and shortly afterwards on another indictment for driving the same vehicle when disqualified, of which he was acquitted. On each trial, the evidence for the prosecution rested on identification of the appellant as the driver by a police officer. *Held*, in view of the inconsistency of the verdicts, the conviction must be quashed. See also *R. v. Andrews*, 51 Cr.App.R. 42, CA.

Where the verdicts alleged to be inconsistent are verdicts returned by different juries in respect of different defendants, the onus cast upon an appellant will be an almost impossible one to discharge; inevitably, there will be a difference in the evidence, however similar the case may be against two persons jointly charged with an offence but separately tried: *R. v. Andrews-Weatherfoil Ltd*, *ante*. Eveleigh L.J. said (at p. 41) that if the difference in the evidence consists of additional material favourable to the accused being called at the second trial, the first accused should seek to call that evidence in the Court of Appeal and not merely rely on the inconsistent verdicts.

Andrews-Weatherfoil Ltd was followed and applied in *R. v. Burke* [2007] 1 *Archbold News* 2, CA (where the appellant sought to have his conviction for a money laundering offence quashed on account of the acquittal in separate proceedings of the individual alleged to have committed the substantive offence). In *R. v. Rowley*, 32 Cr.App.R. 147, CCA, however, R's conviction, following his plea of guilty to being an accessory after the fact, was quashed when the alleged principals were acquitted.

Wrongful admission or exclusion of evidence

7–73 Where evidence has been wrongly admitted or excluded, this will render the conviction unsafe unless the Court of Appeal is satisfied that had the error not been made, the only reasonable and proper verdict would nevertheless have been one of guilty: see *Stirland v. DPP* [1944] A.C. 315, HL; *R. v. Oyesiku*, 56 Cr.App.R. 240, CA; *R. v. Mustafa*, 65 Cr.App.R. 26, CA (the old law); and *R. v. Davis, Rowe and Johnson*, *ante*, § 7–52 (the new law). It may, of course, be that the wrongfully admitted or excluded evidence is just one of a number of factors which combine to render a conviction unsafe, as in *R. v. Tricoglus*, 65 Cr.App.R. 16, CA.

7–74 The failure of counsel to object to the admission of inadmissible evidence will not be fatal to an appeal but it may have a bearing on the question whether the accused was really prejudiced. The judge should stop inadmissible questions without waiting for objection to be taken: *Stirland v. DPP*, *ante*. In *R. v. Moghal*, 65 Cr.App.R. 56, the Court of Appeal made clear that in determining whether a verdict was unsafe it would consider material which was admissible but upon which no final ruling had in fact been obtained because of an earlier "indication" given by the trial judge as to the probable nature of any ruling he might give, *i.e.* that it was likely to be excluded.

An error as to the competence or compellability of a witness which leads to evidence being either wrongly admitted or excluded is in the same category as a ruling about specific evidence: see *R. v. Deacon*, 57 Cr.App.R. 688, CA; *R. v. Conti*, 58 Cr.App.R. 387, CA; *Hoskyn v. Metropolitan Police Commr* [1979] A.C. 474, HL; and *R. v. Yacoob*, 72 Cr.App.R. 313, CA.

As to an alleged erroneous exercise of a discretion in relation to the admission of evidence as a ground of appeal, see *post*, § 7–99.

Defects in the indictment

(i) *Indictment disclosing no offence known to law*

7–75 Where the facts stated in the indictment do not amount to an offence known to law, the conviction will be quashed: *DPP v. Bhagwan* [1972] A.C. 60, HL; *DPP v. Withers* [1975] A.C. 842, HL. This is so even though no point is taken at the trial and the defendant pleaded guilty: *R. v. Whitehouse* [1977] Q.B. 868, 65 Cr.App.R. 33, CA.

(ii) *Counts not properly included in the indictment*

Whether or not a count was properly included in the indictment will depend on whether the provisions of section 2(2) of the *Administration of Justice (Miscellaneous Provisions) Act* 1933 (*ante*, § 1–204) and section 40 of the *CJA* 1988 (*ante*, § 1–75ai) have been complied with. Section 2(3) of the 1933 Act provides that where the provisions of subsection (2) have not been complied with, the indictment shall be liable to be quashed subject to the proviso that where a person has been committed for trial, the indictment shall not be quashed on appeal unless application was made at the trial for it to be quashed. In *R. v. Morry* [1946] K.B. 153, 31 Cr.App.R. 19, where the defendant was unrepresented, the trial judge raised the point; the Court of Criminal Appeal clearly took the view that this was sufficient. In *R. v. Nisbet* [1972] 1 Q.B. 37, 55 Cr.App.R. 490, the Court of Appeal said, *obiter*, that it had inherent jurisdiction to prevent injustice by quashing counts in an indictment which had been substituted or added if injustice might result, even though they were founded on evidence in the committal papers and even though no application was made at the trial. (As to whether the court has any inherent jurisdiction, see *ante*, § 7–26, and *post*, § 7–223; the point is academic in this context as the court could simply categorise the conviction as unsafe, if of the view that injustice might have resulted from the addition or substitution of counts.) **7–76**

Where counts are improperly joined in breach of rule 9 of the *Indictment Rules* 1971 or of section 40 of the 1988 Act, the conviction on the count wrongly joined will be quashed: *R. v. Smith (B.P.)* [1997] 1 Cr.App.R. 390, CA; *R. v. Lockley and Sainsbury* [1997] Crim.L.R. 455, CA.

(iii) *Indictment preferred and signed without jurisdiction*

This will render the proceedings a nullity: see *R. v. Thompson and Clein*, 61 Cr.App.R. 108, CA (where the court acted under its residual powers to quash a conviction in the case of a mistrial); and *R. v. Cairns*, 87 Cr.App.R. 287, CA. As to the jurisdiction to grant a writ of *venire de novo*, see *post*, §§ 7–351 *et seq.* **7–77**

(iv) *Duplicity and other defects of form*

The validity of the form of an indictment or of a count in an indictment is a matter of law. Duplicity is a matter of form and, where an indictment is defective because of duplicity, a conviction may be quashed: *R. v. Jones (J.)*, 59 Cr.App.R. 120 (but see *ante*, §§ 1–132c, 1–141, as to the recasting of the rule against duplicity). In *R. v. Cain* [1983] Crim.L.R. 802, the Court of Appeal quashed a conviction, on the ground that the count upon which it was based was bad for "duplicity, or perhaps more properly, uncertainty." The fact that objection was not taken at the trial will not prevent the conviction being quashed: *R. v. Molloy* [1921] 2 K.B. 364, 15 Cr.App.R. 170, CCA; *R. v. Wilmot*, 24 Cr.App.R. 63, CCA. **7–78**

A conviction on a duplicitous count will not necessarily be quashed, however, the sole question being whether it is "unsafe": *R. v. Levantiz* [1999] 1 Cr.App.R. 465, CA (applying *R. v. Thompson* [1914] 2 K.B. 99, 9 Cr.App.R. 252, CCA); and *R. v. Marchese* [2008] 2 Cr.App.R. 12, CA (the principle in *R. v. Thompson* was not affected by the decision of the House of Lords in *R. v. Clarke and McDaid* [2008] 2 Cr.App.R. 2 (*ante*, § 1–196), the question on appeal being whether the duplicity resulted in injustice to the appellant). It should be noted, however, that *Levantiz* was not itself a case of duplicity in the strict sense. It was in fact a case where the indictment was regular on its face, but the evidence in support revealed two or more offences. Where the indictment is truly duplicitous, the difficulty about concluding that "the conviction" is safe may be illustrated by asking the question: of what was the defendant convicted? See *Wilmot*, *ante*, approving the observation of Avory J. in *R. v. Surrey JJ., ex p. Witherick* [1932] 1 K.B. 450 at 452: "It is an elementary principle that an information must not charge offences in the alternative, since the defendant cannot then know with precision with what he is charged and of what he is convicted and may be prevented on a future occasion from pleading *autrefois convict*."

As to defects in the indictment as a ground of appeal, see also *R. v. Graham*; *R. v. Kansal*; *R. v. Ali (Sajid)*; *R. v. Marsh*, *ante*, § 7–46.

No case to go to the jury

7–79 Whilst the test under section 2 of the *CAA* 1968 is concerned with the safety of the conviction, it is not proper, where the ground of appeal is that a rejection of a submission of no case to answer was erroneous, for the Court of Appeal to have regard to evidence subsequently given in the course of the trial during the case for the defendant or a co-defendant; an erroneous ruling must be considered to render the conviction unsafe, because it follows that, but for the ruling, the judge would have directed an acquittal and the jury's verdict would, therefore, have been different: *R. v. Broadhead*, unreported, June 23, 2006, CA ([2006] EWCA Crim. 1705), following *R. v. Smith (Patrick Joseph)* [1999] 2 Cr.App.R. 238, CA. See also *R. v. Berry* [1998] Crim.L.R. 487, CA; and *R. v. Davis, Rowe and Johnson* [2001] 1 Cr.App.R. 8, CA. *R. v. Clarke and Hewins* [1999] 6 *Archbold News* 2 (97 04882 W3), whilst consistent with the wording of section 2 of the 1968 Act (as amended), is inconsistent with this line of authority, and must now be taken to have been erroneous.

In *R. v. Juett* [1988] Crim.L.R. 113, CA, it was held that where no submission is made and evidence is thereafter forthcoming of the defendant's guilt, the Court of Appeal will not interfere on the ground that had a submission been made it ought to have been upheld: the responsibility of the judge does not require, nor entitle him to interfere with what is counsel's responsibility in the absence of improper or irregular conduct. In *Hoang Hai-veit v. R.* [1997] H.K.L.R.D. 203, the Privy Council appears to have assumed, however, that it is not only the judge's right, but his duty, to stop a case regardless of whether a submission is made if he considers that there is insufficient evidence; and in *R. v. Brown (Jamie)* [1998] Crim.L.R. 196, CA, it was said *obiter* that if, at the conclusion of the evidence, the judge is of the opinion that no reasonable jury properly directed could safely convict, he should raise the matter with the advocates, and if his view remained the same after hearing submissions, he should withdraw the case from the jury.

Miscellaneous

7–80 It is obviously impossible to draw up a definitive list of circumstances which will result in a conviction being held to be unsafe. Certain points warrant restating, however. First, where a conviction is quashed it is often on account of the combination of two or more factors. It should not be assumed that the Court of Appeal would have concluded that the conviction was unsafe had one or other factor stood alone. *Aliter*, of course, if the court expressly stated, as it sometimes does, that a particular ground of appeal has been made out and would have been enough to decide the appeal in the appellant's favour. Secondly, it is submitted that any tendency to say that in a certain situation the Court of Appeal will automatically hold the conviction to be unsafe should be resisted. Each case is different and in each case it is submitted that the ultimate test for the court to apply is the "lurking doubt" test expounded in *Cooper*, *ante*, § 7–47. This was the approach of Lord Ackner who delivered the principal judgment of the House of Lords in *R. v. Spencer*; *R. v. Smails* [1987] A.C. 128, *post*, § 7–88. Instead of having different tests for different situations, each test being no more than a rule of thumb, it is submitted that the more general approach of the House of Lords is much to be preferred.

(i) *Mistakes by, misconduct of, trial judge*

7–81 Where a judge inadvertently disclosed a matter to the jury in the course of his summing up which would not otherwise have been put before them, and where an application for the jury to be discharged had been refused, the factors to be borne in mind, on an appeal against conviction, were (a) the nature of the judge's actions to cure the error, (b) the strength of the case against the accused, and (c) the degree to which the jury might have been influenced in reaching their verdict by the disclosure: *R. v. Tufail* [2007] 1 *Archbold News* 1, CA; and, to similar effect, see *R. v. Brown* [2006] Crim.L.R. 995, CA. Where, however, the prosecution had not resisted the application to discharge the jury and do not resist the appeal, a conviction would be likely to be quashed whatever the apparent weight of the evidence against the appellant: see *R. v. Purdy* [2007] 3 *Archbold News* 1, CA.

Interventions by the judge during a trial will lead to the quashing of a conviction: (a) when they have invited the jury to disbelieve the evidence for the defence in such strong terms that the mischief cannot be cured by the common formula in the summing up that the facts are for the jury, and that they may disregard anything said on the facts by the judge with which they do not agree; (b) when they have made it impossible for defending counsel to do his duty; (c) when they have effectively prevented the defendant or a witness for the defence from telling his story in his own way: *R. v. Hulusi and Purvis*, 58 Cr.App.R. 378, CA; see also *R. v. Frixou* [1998] Crim.L.R. 352, CA, *R. v. Roncoli* [1998] Crim.L.R. 584, CA, and *C.G. v. U.K.* (2001) 34 E.H.R.R. 31, ECtHR. In *R. v. Barnes*, 55 Cr.App.R. 100, Lord Parker C.J. said: "Just as interruptions by a trial judge, making it impossible for defending counsel to do justice to the defence, will result in a conviction being quashed so also conduct producing the same impossibility must have the same result" (at p. 107). In *Barnes*, the judge had put such pressure on the defendant to plead guilty that the relationship of confidence between counsel and defendant was destroyed, thereby gravely handicapping counsel in the presentation of the defence. In *R. v. Matthews and Matthews*, 78 Cr.App.R. 23, the Court of Appeal said that in considering the effect of interventions made by the trial judge the critical aspect of the investigation was the quality of the interventions as they related to the attitude of the judge as might be observed by the jury and the effect that the interventions had either on the orderly, proper and lucid deployment of the defendant's case by his advocate or on the efficiency of the attack to be made on the defendant's behalf on vital prosecution witnesses by cross-examination administered by his advocate on his behalf. Ultimately the question was: might the case for the defendant as presented to the jury over the trial as a whole, including the adducing and testing of evidence, the submissions of counsel and the summing up of the judge, be such that the jury's verdict might be unsafe? In *Jahree v. State of Mauritius* [2005] 1 W.L.R. 1952, PC, it was said that however much hostile questioning of the accused by the judge was to be deprecated, on appeal the issue would be as to whether the questioning was of such central significance as to affect the overall fairness of the trial.

In *R. v. Bryant* [2005] 9 *Archbold News* 3, CA, it was said that it could not be right for a judge ever to give the impression that he favoured the prosecution case as against that of the defendant. In *R. v. Lashley* [2006] Crim.L.R. 83, the Court of Appeal said that whilst it expected judges to be robust, where the trial had become over-infused with repeated and unnecessary demonstrations of inappropriate personal animosity towards counsel which involved public criticism not only of his ability, but also his integrity, this interfered to a marked degree with the normal due process required at every trial and had the inevitable effect of damaging the defendant's confidence in the administration of justice; and would have had the same effect on the mind of any reasonable observer present at the trial. The overall effect was to render a conviction unsafe. In *R. v. C.* (2005) 149 S.J. 1151, CA, it was said that comments made by a judge to defence counsel in the presence of the jury suggesting that the defence was endeavouring to mislead the jury and was content with half truths were offensive and were likely to have a damaging effect on the jury, the mischief of which was unlikely to be cured by the conventional direction in the judge's summing up about rejecting any views with which the jury disagreed; further, the prejudicial effect of the remarks, coupled with the animosity to counsel implicit in them, may well have been considerable, and there was a real risk that the remarks may unfairly have prejudiced the jury against the defendant, thereby compromising the fairness of the trial; and, having regard to the entitlement to a fair trial, that the case against the defendant was a strong one was not a reason for dismissing his appeal against conviction. To similar effect as these cases, see also *R. v. Hare*; *R. v. O'Sullivan*, *The Times*, December 16, 2004, CA; and *R. v. Cordingley* [2008] Crim.L.R. 299, CA (safety of a conviction does not depend merely upon the strength of the evidence but upon the observation of due process, and every defendant is entitled to be tried fairly, *i.e.* courteously and with due regard for the presumption of innocence).

Where the judge had fallen asleep during counsel's speeches, it did not necessarily follow that the trial was unfair; it was the effect that mattered, rather than the fact of the inattention; and it was significant that the summing up was comprehensive, balanced, and accurate as to the law and as to the defence case: *R. v. Betson*; *R. v. Cockran*, *The Times*, January 28, 2004, CA. See also *Cesan and Mas Rivadavia v. DPP*, unreported, September 5, 2007, New South Wales Court of Criminal Appeal ([2007] NSWCCA 273) (an appellate court should therefore only intervene if it can be demonstrated that the judge's conduct resulted in error or deprived the accused of a fair trial in some respect).

The fact that the defendant was represented by experienced counsel who made no complaint at the time is not decisive, but it is significant: *R. v. Beckles and Montague* [1999] Crim.L.R. 148, CA; *R. v. Betson*; *R. v. Cockran*, *ante*.

See also *post*, § 8–248 as to the limits of legitimate judicial intervention.

As to the need to give full particulars where one of the grounds of appeal upon which an application for leave is made is excessive intervention by the trial judge, see *R. v. Usher* [1998] 3 *Archbold News* 1, CA (97 0997 Y2).

(ii) *Conduct of counsel*

7–82 The failings of counsel may directly or indirectly lead to the conclusion that a conviction is unsafe. What is clear, however, is that decisions made in good faith after proper consideration of the competing arguments, and, where appropriate, after due discussion with the defendant, will not without more render a conviction unsafe even though the Court of Appeal may disagree with them; particularly does this apply to a decision as to whether or not to call the defendant. Conversely, if a decision was taken either in defiance of, or without proper instruction, or when all promptings of reason and good sense pointed the other way, this may render a conviction unsafe: see *R. v. Clinton*, 97 Cr.App.R. 320, CA.

The Court of Appeal has on occasion sought to prescribe particular tests to be applied in alleged incompetence cases. Thus, in *R. v. Donnelly* [1998] Crim.L.R. 131, it was said that nothing less than flagrant incompetence would do; in *R. v. Ullah* [2000] 1 Cr.App.R. 351, it was said that a proper and convenient approach is to apply the test of reasonableness in *Associated Picture Houses Ltd v. Wednesbury Corporation* [1948] 1 K.B. 223; in *R. v. Bolivar*; *R. v. Lee* (2003) 147 S.J. 538, CA, it was said that not only must there be *Wednesbury* unreasonableness, but it must have been such as to affect the fairness of the trial; and in *R. v. Chatroodi* [2001] 3 *Archbold News* 3, it was said in relation to counsel's advice to the defendant not to give evidence, that the question was whether the advice given was within the acceptable exercise of counsel's judgment, and, if it was, whether it had been acted upon with a full understanding of the consequences. It should be noted that this was a case in which counsel had failed to heed the practice recommended by the court in *R. v. Bevan*, 98 Cr.App.R. 354 (Appendix C–54).

This approach was, however, firmly rejected in *R. v. Day* [2003] 6 *Archbold News* 1, CA ([2003] EWCA Crim. 1060), where it was said that the test is the single test of safety, and the court does not have to concern itself with any such intermediate questions; but in order to establish lack of safety in an incompetence case, the appellant has to show that the incompetence led to identifiable errors or irregularities in the trial, which themselves rendered the process unfair or unsafe. See also *R. v. Clinton*, *ante*, where it was said that since the sole issue is the safety of the conviction, a qualitative assessment of counsel's alleged ineptitude is going to be less helpful than an assessment of its effect on the verdict; and *Teeluck v. State of Trinidad and Tobago*; *John v. Same* [2005] 1 W.L.R. 2421, PC, where it was held that the focus of the appellate court ought to be on the impact which counsel's errors had had on the trial and the verdict, rather than on attempting to rate his conduct according to some scale of ineptitude.

In *Boodram v. State of Trinidad and Tobago* [2002] 1 Cr.App.R. 12, PC, it was held that whilst complaints about counsel's competence must be approached with a healthy scepticism by an appellate tribunal, if it was demonstrated that counsel's failures were of a fundamental nature, the court should proceed with great care before it concluded that, on the hypotheses that the failures did not occur, the verdict would inevitably have been the same; and if the failings were so fundamental as to have deprived the defendant of due process, the conclusion would be that the defendant had not had a fair trial and the conviction should be quashed without embarking on an inquiry as to the impact of the failings.

See also *R. v. Irwin*, 85 Cr.App.R. 294, CA; *R. v. Gautam* [1988] Crim.L.R. 109; *R. v. Ensor*, 89 Cr.App.R. 139 (if court has a lurking doubt that an injustice may have occurred as a result of incompetent advocacy, it will quash the conviction); *R. v. Scollan and Smith* [1998] 10 *Archbold News* 1, CA (the approach to an appeal based on the alleged failings of counsel should be the same after the amendment of section 2 of the 1968 Act by the 1995 Act (*ante*, §§ 7–42 *et seq.*), as it was before, *viz.* that of the court in *Clinton*); and, as to the particular importance of ensuring that a defendant, who is entitled to a good character direction, receives the benefit of such direction in a case where his credibility is in issue, see *Sealey v. The State*, *The Times*, November 5, 2002, PC; and *Teeluck v. State of Trinidad and Tobago*; *John v. Same*, *ante*.

Where counsel at trial assented to a particular course of action by the judge, this did not preclude complaint being made on appeal about the course of action taken; counsel's assent was at most a relevant factor to be taken into account in considering the justification for the judge's choice of course of action: *R. v. Smith (Patrick) and Mercieca (Joseph)* [2005] 1 W.L.R. 704, HL.

Matters which are personal to an advocate which might affect performance cannot *per se* render a conviction unsafe; the issue must always be whether they did affect performance to such an extent as to render the conviction unsafe: see *R. v. Hall*, *The Times*, August 27, 2002, CA (illness); and *R. v. Bolivar*; *R. v. Lee*, *ante* (being under investigation for serious offences throughout trial and being declared bankrupt during it).

Where a ground of appeal relates to the conduct of counsel, the guidance issued by the Bar Council (Appendix C–45) should be followed; if there is pressure of time, the Registrar of Criminal Appeals should be informed in order to avoid the waste of time and costs involved in the unnecessary listing of cases: *R. v. Nasser*, *The Times*, February 19, 1998, CA.

(iii) *Late change in nature of case*

In *R. v. Falconer-Atlee*, 58 Cr.App.R. 348, one reason for quashing the conviction **7–83** was that the judge had left it open to the jury to convict on a basis which had never been put forward by the prosecution. In *R. v. Gregory*, 77 Cr.App.R. 41, the Court of Appeal said that it was desirable that counsel should be told by the judge before speeches began of any direction that he proposed to give which would allow of a conviction on a basis of which no previous indication had been given during the trial. See also *R. v. Lamb (S.J.)*, 59 Cr.App.R. 196, and *R. v. Lunn* [1985] Crim.L.R. 797, CA, in which it was said that it was axiomatic that, if the judge thought that prosecuting counsel had made an omission, he should draw the attention of both counsel to that omission and indicate how he proposed to sum up, so that they would have an opportunity to address him, and if necessary to apply to call further evidence. This point was repeated in *R. v. Cristini* [1987] Crim.L.R. 504, in which the conviction was quashed as it was in *R. v. Utting*, 86 Cr.App.R. 164; *R. v. White* [1987] Crim.L.R. 505; *R. v. Gascoigne (K.)* [1988] Crim.L.R. 317; and *R. v. Warburton-Pitt*, 92 Cr.App.R. 136.

Where an amendment to the indictment was permitted at the end of the evidence, but before counsel's speeches, and was of such a nature as materially to alter the nature of the case the defence had to meet, it was held that the amendment, coming at so late a stage, might have caused injustice and the verdict could not be regarded as safe: *R. v. Gregory*, 56 Cr.App.R. 441, CA. In *R. v. Pacey*, *The Times*, March 3, 1994, a conviction was quashed as unsafe where the prosecution in their closing speech had invited the jury to make an inference contrary to the evidence given by the sole prosecution witness, there being no evidential foundation for such inference.

Where the prosecution and judge adopt a uniform approach but the jury appear to have departed from that approach, this itself will raise an issue as to whether the conviction is safe: *R. v. Eden*, 55 Cr.App.R. 193.

In *R. v. Cross and Channon*, 55 Cr.App.R. 540, CA, it was held that the introduction of the possibility of a conviction for an offence under section 4 of the *CLA* 1967 (*post*, § 18–34) as an alternative to the substantive charge had been erroneous when done at the conclusion of the evidence, thus leaving the defence no opportunity to deal with it; and the jury having convicted on the substantive offence, the conviction was quashed on the basis that the judge had thought there to be insufficient evidence to warrant a conviction (hence his decision to allow a verdict under section 4).

(iv) *Prejudicial publicity*

7–84 The possibility of a conviction being quashed because of adverse pre-trial publicity was acknowledged in *R. v. Malik*, 52 Cr.App.R. 140, CA, and *R. v. Savundra*, 52 Cr.App.R. 637, CA. In *R. v. Wood* [1996] 1 Cr.App.R. 207, CA, this was one of the grounds for quashing the conviction.

In *R. v. McCann*, 92 Cr.App.R. 239, CA, and *R. v. Taylor and Taylor*, 98 Cr.App.R. 361, CA, convictions were quashed where there had been adverse publicity during the trials. In *Taylor and Taylor*, the adverse publicity consisted of the "unremitting, extensive, sensational, inaccurate and misleading" press coverage of the case. This was only one ground for quashing the conviction, but it was the principal reason for not ordering a retrial.

(v) *Matters occurring at earlier trial*

7–85 In *R. v. Graham*, 61 Cr.App.R. 292, the Court of Appeal recognised that there may be circumstances outside the conduct of the trial itself which might render the verdict unsafe, but an alleged improper exercise of judicial discretion in discharging the jury at a first trial cannot of itself render the verdict at a retrial unsafe. See also *R. v. Home Office, ex. p. Graham*, 78 Cr.App.R. 124, DC (a decision to the same effect).

Where a jury are discharged and the defendant is retried and convicted, the decision to discharge the first jury is not itself open to review in the Court of Appeal: *R. v. Gorman*, 85 Cr.App.R. 121, CA.

(vi) *Wrongful denial of legal representation*

7–86 Where the defendant is wrongly denied legal representation this may result in a conviction being quashed: see *R. v. Davies (C.S.)*, *The Times*, February 11, 1987; *R. v. Harris* [1985] Crim.L.R. 244, CA (counsel and solicitors withdrew, but legal aid order not revoked; adjournment to seek fresh representation refused); *R. v. Kirk*, 76 Cr.App.R. 194, CA (where a legal aid order was discharged otherwise than in the prescribed manner); *R. v. Shaw*, 70 Cr.App.R. 313, CA (after accused had absconded, judge wrongly barred his legal representatives from taking any further part in the case); and *R. v. Al-Zubeidi* [1999] 6 *Archbold News* 2, CA (98 02435 Z3) (counsel withdrawing on account of professional embarrassment, judge wrongly refusing adjournment to permit instruction of fresh counsel). But it will not do so if the court is satisfied that but for the irregularity the outcome would have been the same: see *Kirk*, *ante*; *R. v. Dimech* [1991] Crim.L.R. 846, CA; *R. v. Seale* [1997] Crim.L.R. 898, CA; and *R. v. Stovell* [2006] Crim.L.R. 760, CA (fundamental question is whether a fair trial was possible and in fact took place).

As to the right to legal representation under Article 6 of the ECHR, see *post*, §§ 16–57, 16–86 *et seq.*

(vii) *Improper denial of rights*

7–87 See, for example, *R. v. Andrews*, 27 Cr.App.R. 12, CCA (unrepresented defendant not informed of rights); *R. v. Cunningham* [1988] Crim.L.R. 543, CA (as a result of misunderstanding of judge's ruling about the defendant, a male, not being allowed to appear in court in female clothing, defendant effectively deprived of his right to give evidence); and *R. v. Hamand*, 82 Cr.App.R. 65, CA (as a result of judge's indication as to how he would sum up if there were no further evidence, the indication being based on an incorrect view of the law, defendant deprived of free choice as to whether to give evidence or not).

(viii) *Bias*

7–88 As to the test to be applied where an appeal is based on an allegation that the appellant did not have a fair trial because one or more jurors knew of his previous convictions, or knew him or his family or a witness, or had been seen in conversation with a witness or worked for the company alleged to have been defrauded, or the like, see now *Re Medicaments and Related Classes of Goods (No. 2)* [2001] 1 W.L.R. 700, CA (Civ. Div.); and *Porter v. Magill*; *Weeks v. Magill* [2002] 2 A.C. 357, HL (*ante*, § 4–32), adapting the former test prescribed by the House of Lords in *R. v. Gough* [1993] A.C. 646, in the light of the jurisprudence of the European Court of Human Rights.

As to whether police officers, prison officers or prosecution lawyers should be allowed to sit on a jury, see *ante*, § 4–248. Where, on appeal, it is alleged that there was actual bias or an appearance of bias by reason of the presence on the jury of some such person, it is important to distinguish between partiality towards the case of one of the parties and partiality towards a particular witness or particular witnesses; each can be described as "bias" but they are different in kind and have different consequences; just because a juror feels partial to a particular witness does not mean that the juror will be partial to the case in support of which that witness is called, but it may do so if the witness is so closely associated with the prosecution that partiality to the witness is to be equated with partiality towards the party calling the witness: *R. v. Khan* [2008] 3 All E.R. 502, CA. Where an impartial juror is shown to have had reason to favour a particular witness, this will only render the trial unfair if (a) a fair minded observer would consider that the partiality of the juror to the witness may have caused the jury to accept the evidence of that witness and, if this is so, (b) the fair minded observer would consider that this may have affected the outcome of the trial: *ibid.*

A fair minded and reasonable observer would conclude that there was a real possibility that a juror was biased from the mere fact that she knew and worked with police officers giving evidence in the case; and in turn, without needing to consider the juror's role in the jury's deliberations, there was no doubt that the fair minded and reasonable observer would also conclude that there was a real possibility that the juror had influenced her fellow jurors: *R. v. Pintori* [2007] Crim.L.R. 997, CA (observing *obiter* that evidence of a juror's association with prosecution witnesses is a matter extrinsic to the jury's deliberations, and that evidence from the juror herself as to the association and what she had told other jurors would not therefore be subject to the common law rule that evidence of the jury's deliberations is inadmissible (as to which, see *post*, §§ 7–209, 7–215)).

Where a police officer was a juror and a minor evidential issue arose, during the course of the trial, over the testimony of a police officer who was known to the juror, there was apparent bias: *R. v. I.* [2008] 1 *Archbold News* 2, CA (considering *R. v. Pintori*, *ante*).

As to the unqualified nature of the right of an accused to a trial by an independent and impartial tribunal, see also *ante*, § 7–46a.

(ix) *Lack of adequate trial record*

7–89 The mere fact that there is no, or no adequate, shorthand note of the trial is not of itself a ground for saying that a conviction is unsafe. The appellant must be able to show something to suggest that there was an irregularity at the trial or a misdirection in the summing up, in which case the absence or insufficiency of a proper record may be material: *R. v. Elliott*, 2 Cr.App.R. 171, CCA; *R. v. LeCaer*, 56 Cr.App.R. 727. See also *R. v. Spillane and Payne*, 56 Cr.App.R. 9, CA; *R. v. Richards* [1997] Crim.L.R. 48, CA (conviction liable to be deemed unsafe where unclear whether jury were properly directed); and *R. v. Osborne-Odelli* [1998] Crim.L.R. 902, CA (important exchanges during final speeches should be recorded).

(x) *Prosecution failure to comply with duty of disclosure*

7–90 A failure by the prosecution to comply with their duty of disclosure will constitute a ground of appeal; whether a conviction is thereby rendered unsafe will depend on the nature of the matter not disclosed in the context of the issues in the case and the other evidence. See *R. v. Craven* [2001] 2 Cr.App.R. 12, CA (*ante*, § 7–51c); *R. v. Clark* (2003) 147 S.J. 472, CA; and *R. v. Hampton* [2006] Crim.L.R. 60, CA (material not disclosed was "double-edged"). In many cases it would suffice to show that the failure was such that it is reasonable to suppose that it might have affected the outcome of the trial: *R. v. Alibhai* [2004] 5 *Archbold News* 1, CA.

Where there has been a failure to disclose the convictions of a prosecution witness, the question for the Court of Appeal to determine is how relevant the missing information was to the defence of the appellant, with the view of the court being likely to vary according to whether the witness was the complainant or a third party witness whose evidence was not central to the issue: *R. v. Eccleston*, unreported, July 10, 2001, CA ([2001] EWCA Crim. 1626). See also *R. v. Underwood* (2003) 147 S.J. 657, CA, where the approach was almost identical.

Non-disclosure may lead to the quashing of a conviction even where there has been a plea of guilty: see *R. v. Smith* [2004] 8 *Archbold News* 1, CA ([2004] EWCA Crim. 2212) (*post*, § 12–54) (material could have had a causative impact on a tenable abuse argument).

As to the procedure to be adopted where an issue arises as to the manner in which the judge in the Crown Court dealt with an issue of public interest immunity, see *post*, § 7–200b.

As to the extent of the prosecution's duty of disclosure, see *post*, §§ 12–47 *et seq.*

(xi) *Prosecution improperly making second speech or commenting on failure to give evidence*

7–91 See *R. v. Mondon*, 52 Cr.App.R. 695, CA, *R. v. Pink* [1971] 1 Q.B. 508, 55 Cr.App.R. 16, CA and *R. v. Stovell* (*ante*, § 7–86) (prosecution improperly making second speech where defendant unrepresented will not necessarily result in quashing of conviction). As to comment by the prosecution on the failure of the spouse of the accused to give evidence, see *R. v. Naudeer*, 80 Cr.App.R. 9, CA (conviction quashed, but appears that result might well have been different had error been corrected by judge); and *R. v. Whitton* [1998] Crim.L.R. 492, CA (conviction upheld where counsel's error was subsumed in judge's own comment).

(xii) *Post-trial discoveries or events*

7–91a See *R. v. Hassan and Kotaish*, 52 Cr.App.R. 291, CA (complainant's convictions); *R. v. Cummins and Perks*, 84 Cr.App.R. 71, CA (conviction of prosecution witness for perjury in course of trial); *R. v. Williams and Smith* [1995] 1 Cr.App.R. 74, CA (discreditable conduct of police officers subsequent to trial); *R. v. Quick and Paddison* [1973] Q.B. 910, 57 Cr.App.R. 722, CA (quashing of principal's conviction introduced element of unreality into conviction of alleged aider and abettor); and *R. v. Jones (Y.)*, 67 Cr.App.R. 166, CA (quashing of two convictions led to quashing of third conviction because conviction might have been induced by mass of evidence led in support of the first two convictions).

In *R. v. Putnam*, 93 Cr.App.R. 281, CA, it emerged after the trial that one of the jurors had received an improper approach during the trial. The juror had been offered money in return for verdicts of not guilty. The source of the information was unknown. An investigation was conducted, having been authorised by the Attorney-General. The juror said that this is what happened. She said she had not mentioned the incident because she wanted to forget it. The Court of Appeal heard no evidence on the issue, but proceeded on the basis that these were the facts. It said that the test was whether there was a "real danger" of prejudice to the defendants and quashed the convictions as unsafe and unsatisfactory.

> "(W)e cannot view without grave unease verdicts reached by a jury when we know that there was a source of poison which (because its presence was unknown) could not be isolated and neutralised, when we do not know how far the poison may have spread and when we do not know what effect it may have had" (*per* Bingham L.J. at p. 286).

It is submitted that this case is likely to be unique. The Court of Appeal will be slow to countenance claims made after trials that approaches were made to jurors during the trial. To entertain such allegations, without the most cogent grounds for doing so, would place a premium on the post-trial intimidation of jurors.

As to the extent to which the Court of Appeal will entertain evidence of irregularities at trial, see *post*, § 7–215.

(xiii) *Abuse of process*

In *R. v. Heston-Francois* [1984] Q.B. 278, 78 Cr.App.R. 209, it was said (at pp. 287, 216) that "oppressive conduct savouring of abuse of process" might result in a conviction being quashed as "unsafe" or "unsatisfactory". Since the amendment of section 2(1) of the 1968 Act (*ante*, §§ 7–43 *et seq.*), it should not be enough that the abuse renders the conviction "unsatisfactory"; it should be of such a nature, whether on its own or when combined with other considerations, as to lead to the conclusion that the conviction was "unsafe". The current position is not this straightforward, however: see *ante*, §§ 7–46, 7–46a, and, in particular, *R. v. Mullen* [1999] 2 Cr.App.R. 143, CA. **7–92**

(xiv) *Offence committed beyond jurisdiction of Crown Court*

In *R. v. Cox*, 52 Cr.App.R. 106, CA, the conviction was quashed because of lack of jurisdiction, despite the fact that no objection had been taken at trial and the defendant had pleaded guilty. See also *Board of Trade v. Owen* [1957] A.C. 602, HL, and *R. v. Davies (D.W.M.)*, 76 Cr.App.R. 120, CA, where a conviction was quashed following a plea of guilty, it being held that it made no difference that the parties had purported to confer jurisdiction by agreement. Jurisdiction could not be conferred by consent. **7–93**

(xv) *Failure to follow guidelines on plea-bargaining*

Guidelines as to the extent to which there could be discussions between judge and counsel about sentence prior to plea were formerly to be found in the judgment of the Court of Appeal in *R. v. Turner (F.R.)* [1970] 2 Q.B. 321, 54 Cr.App.R. 352, CA. A conviction was liable to be quashed where there had been a total disregard of the guidelines (see *R. v. Grice*, 66 Cr.App.R. 167), or where a plea of guilty had followed an indication of a particular form of sentence, but a more severe form of sentence was in the event imposed (see *R. v. Ryan*, 67 Cr.App.R. 177), or, more generally, where there had been undue pressure on the defendant to plead guilty (see *R. v. Pitman* [1991] 1 All E.R. 468). The *Turner* guidance has now been replaced by *R. v. Goodyear* [2005] 3 All E.R. 117, CA (*ante*, § 5–79b), in which detailed guidance was laid down as to the giving of advance indications of sentence. Where a plea of guilty follows an advance indication of sentence, the safety of the conviction will in large part depend on whether or not the defendant was put under undue pressure to plead guilty. Whether or not there was compliance with the *Goodyear* guidelines will doubtless be taken to be highly significant. **7–94**

As to discussions improperly taking place in the judge's room in the absence of the accused, see *ante*, §§ 4–76 *et seq.*

(xvi) *Irregularity in relation to jury*

See *R. v. Gash*, 51 Cr.App.R. 37, CA (improper denial of challenge for cause); *R. v. Hood*, 52 Cr.App.R. 265, CA; *R. v. Brandon*, 53 Cr.App.R. 466, CA (jury discovering defendant of bad character; as to this, see also *ante*, §§ 7–81, 7–88); *R. v. Osborne-Odelli* [1998] Crim.L.R. 902, CA (grave danger that jury would have been given impression that defendant had had his bail revoked during trial on account of misconduct); *R. v. Alexander*, 58 Cr.App.R. 294, CA; *R. v. Goodson*, 60 Cr.App.R. 266, CA (improper separation after retirement); *R. v. Woods*, 87 Cr.App.R. 60, CA; *R. v. Gorman*, 85 Cr.App.R. 121, CA (improper communication with court); *R. v. Harrison*; *R. v. Matthews* [1983] Crim.L.R. 684, CA (omission to give further direction after receipt of note raising question of law); *R. v. Young (Stephen)* [1995] 2 Cr.App.R. 379, CA (consultation of ouija board by some members of jury whilst at hotel during retirement). **7–95**

As to the prohibition on further evidence after the retirement of the jury, see *ante*, §§ 4–417 *et seq.*; but a breach of this prohibition will not automatically render a conviction unsafe: *R. v. Marshall and Crump* [2007] Crim.L.R. 562, CA.

As to undue pressure being placed on a jury, see *ante*, §§ 4–445, 4–446 *et seq.*

(xvii) *Irregularity in relation to verdict*

7–96 Convictions were quashed because of irregularities in relation to the verdict in the following cases: *R. v. Hazeltine* [1967] 2 Q.B. 857, 51 Cr.App.R. 351, CA (for the facts, see *ante*, § 4–108); *R. v. Cummerson* [1968] 2 Q.B. 534, 52 Cr.App.R. 519, CA (convictions on each of two alternative counts, one conviction quashed); *R. v. Harris*, 53 Cr.App.R. 376, CA (conviction on two charges, one of which, being a lesser included offence, had merged with the other; conviction for the lesser offence quashed); *R. v. Barry*, 61 Cr.App.R. 172, CA (failure to comply with the mandatory provisions of the *Juries Act* 1974 as to the taking of majority verdicts).

In *R. v. Plimmer*, 61 Cr.App.R. 264, CA, the judge having apparently taken the view that his direction to the jury on the law was defective, waited for the jury to return with a verdict, and the verdict being one of guilty, he then questioned the jury on the basis of the verdict. The proper way to correct a slip is to have the jury back and give them a correct direction and then let them retire again to consider the case in the light of the corrected direction. See also *R. v. Russell*, *post*, § 7–358.

(xviii) *Alternative verdicts*

7–97 A failure to leave an obvious alternative verdict to the jury for their consideration will render a conviction on the offence charged unsafe: *R. v. Coutts* [2006] 1 W.L.R. 2154, HL (not following *R. v. Maxwell*, 91 Cr.App.R. 61, HL). As to what constitutes an "obvious" alternative for this purpose, see *ante*, § 4–463. Whilst *R. v. Coutts* provided clarity where previously there was confusion, the water has been muddied again by the decision of the Court of Appeal in *R. v. Foster*; *R. v. Newman*; *R. v. Kempster*; *R. v. Birmingham* [2008] 1 Cr.App.R. 38, where it was said that on appeal the issue is not whether a direction as to an alternative verdict was erroneously omitted, but whether the safety of the conviction was undermined. This, it is submitted, is circular. The omission will only be erroneous if the jury ought to have been instructed about the available alternative, which they only ought to have been if it was an "obvious" alternative. Leaving them with an "all or nothing" choice where the middle course arises on the facts is bound to render a conviction unsafe. That was the essence of the decision of the House of Lords in *R. v. Coutts*.

Where the judge erroneously decides that it is open to the jury to convict the defendant of an offence other than the offence charged in the indictment and so directs the jury, any resulting conviction will be quashed: *R. v. Woods* [1969] 1 Q.B. 447, 53 Cr.App.R. 30, CA; *R. v. Beasley*, 73 Cr.App.R. 44, CA. Similarly, if a plea of guilty is entered and accepted by the court but it is in fact a plea to an offence which it would not be open to the jury to convict of either at common law or under the *CLA* 1967, s.6(3), the conviction will be quashed: *R. v. McCready and Hurd*, 67 Cr.App.R. 345, CA.

In *R. v. Hazell* [1985] Crim.L.R. 513, CA, a conviction was quashed as being unsatisfactory and irregular where the judge had directed the jury that they could convict the defendant of a lesser offence which had not been charged and which had not been the subject of submission or argument before them.

(xix) *Other procedural irregularities*

7–98 See *R. v. Pipe*, 51 Cr.App.R. 17, CA (departure from established rules of practice as to the circumstances in which an accomplice may be called to give evidence for the Crown); *R. v. Plain*, 51 Cr.App.R. 91 (revival during the defence case of a count in respect of which there had been a successful submission of no case at the close of the prosecution case, although no verdict had been formally obtained); *R. v. Smith (M.G.)*, 52 Cr.App.R. 648 (jury allowed to compare a specimen of handwriting given by the defendant with a disputed signature without the assistance of expert evidence); *R. v. Smith (Winston)*, 61 Cr.App.R. 128 (pupil who had had access to defence papers prior to trial attended trial in wig and gown and during the greater part of it sat behind prosecuting counsel); *R. v. Hunter*, 81 Cr.App.R. 40 (failure of judge to attend a view); and *R. v. Windass*, 89 Cr.App.R. 258 (cross-examination of one defendant on document admissible only against co-defendant).

Discretionary matters

"It is well settled that this court will not interfere with the exercise of a discretion by the judge below unless he has erred in principle or there is no material on which he could properly have arrived at his decision." This passage of Devlin J.'s judgment in *R. v. Cook* [1959] 2 Q.B. 340 at 348, 43 Cr.App.R. 138 at 147, CCA, was cited with approval by Viscount Dilhorne in *Selvey v. DPP* [1970] A.C. 304 at 342, HL. **7–99**

In *R. v. Quinn* [1996] Crim.L.R. 516, the Court of Appeal approved the statement in the 1995 edition of this work (see now § 4–263, *ante*) to the effect that in relation to an exercise of discretion it would only interfere if there has been a failure to exercise any discretion, a failure to take into account a material consideration or a taking account of an immaterial consideration. In such event, the Court of Appeal would itself consider how the discretion should have been exercised (see also *R. v. Cook*, *ante*, as to the appellate court exercising its own discretion). If the result of this exercise is that a different conclusion is reached to that of the trial judge, it is submitted that it does not necessarily follow that the conviction will be quashed. The court will still have to ask itself whether the conviction is unsafe; thus, for example, if it concludes in relation to an objection to the admissibility of certain evidence made under section 78 of the *PACE Act* 1984 (*post*, § 15–452) that the judge should have excluded it, it will be faced with the same decision as faces the court in a case where legally inadmissible evidence has been admitted (*ante*, § 7–73). This was the approach of the Court of Appeal in *R. v. Docherty* [1999] 1 Cr.App.R. 274. **7–100**

For similar statements as to the limited circumstances in which the Court of Appeal will interfere with a matter within the discretion of the trial judge, see *R. v. Flack*, 53 Cr.App.R. 166, CA (*per* Salmon L.J. at p. 168); *Ludlow v. Metropolitan Police Commr* [1971] A.C. 29, HL (*per* Lord Pearson at p. 40); *R. v. Josephs and Christie*, 65 Cr.App.R. 253, CA (*per* Lord Widgery C.J. at p. 255); and *R. v. Khan, Sakkaravej and Pamarapa* [1997] Crim.L.R. 508, CA.

In *R. v. McCann*, 92 Cr.App.R. 239, however, the Court of Appeal appears to have adopted a somewhat looser approach to the issue of when it is proper to interfere with the trial judge's exercise of his discretion.

> "To reverse the judge's ruling it is not enough that the members of this court would have exercised their discretion differently. We must be clearly satisfied that the judge was wrong; but our power to review the exercise of his discretion is not limited to cases in which he has erred in principle or there is shown to have been no material on which he could properly have arrived at his decision. The court must, if necessary, examine anew the relevant facts and circumstances to exercise a discretion by way of review if it thinks that the judge's ruling may have resulted in injustice to the appellants. See *Evans v. Bartlam* [1937] A.C. 473" (*per* Beldam L.J., at p. 251).

In *R. v. Hambery* [1977] Q.B. 924, 65 Cr.App.R. 233, it was said that the Court of Appeal would interfere with the trial judge's decision in relation to the discharge of a single juror if his discretion had been exercised capriciously.

Whilst both English law and the jurisprudence of the European Court of Human Rights require a judge to give his reasons, however briefly, when exercising a discretion as to the admission of evidence, a failure to do so will not automatically render a conviction unsafe; the issue on appeal is whether it is clear that the discretion was properly exercised: *R. v. Denton* [2001] 1 Cr.App.R. 16, CA.

Investigation of irregularities

An investigation of a possible irregularity (such as the use of a mobile telephone by a juror after retirement) should only be embarked upon with the consent of the Court of Appeal; the trial court will be *functus officio* after verdict and sentence: *R. v. McCluskey*, 98 Cr.App.R. 216, CA. See also *R. v. Mickleburgh* [1995] 1 Cr.App.R. 297, where the Court of Appeal said that solicitors (or anyone else) would be well advised to seek the leave of the court before making any inquiries of jurors; this was so even where contact was first made by a juror; and *R. v. Adams* [2007] 1 Cr.App.R. 34, CA (since it was difficult to draw the line between inquiries as to the deliberations of the jury and inquiries as to extrinsic matters (*e.g.* an allegation of bias), it would be highly undesirable **7–101** for any person to seek to interview a juror without first obtaining leave from the Court of Appeal). Failure to heed this advice risked breaching section 8 of the *Contempt of Court Act* 1981 (*post*, § 28–90). *Cf. R. v. Putnam*, 93 Cr.App.R. 281 (*ante*, § 7–91), in which a police investigation of a possible approach to a juror was authorised by the Attorney-General; and *Att.-Gen. v. Scotcher* [2005] 1 W.L.R. 1867, HL, as to the non-application of section 8 of the 1981 Act to communications between the court and a juror.

As to the investigation of alleged irregularities, see also *ante*, § 4–263; and *post*, §§ 7–215, 28–91.

See also rule 65.8(1) of the *Criminal Procedure Rules* 2005 (S.I. 2005 No. 384) (*post*, §§ 7–196, 7–313h).

[The next paragraph is § 7–106.]

(5) Substitution of conviction for alternative offence

Criminal Appeal Act 1968, s.3

Power to substitute conviction of alternative offence

7–106 **3.**—(1) This section applies on an appeal against conviction, where the appellant has been convicted of an offence to which he did not plead guilty and the jury could on the indictment have found him guilty of some other offence, and on the finding of the jury it appears to the Court of Appeal that the jury must have been satisfied of facts which proved him guilty of the other offence.

(2) The Court may, instead of allowing or dismissing the appeal, substitute for the verdict found by the jury a verdict of guilty of the other offence, and pass such sentence in substitution for the sentence passed at the trial as may be authorised by law for the other offence, not being a sentence of greater severity.

[This section is printed as amended by the *CJA* 2003, s.316(1) and (2).]

7–107 There are two issues in relation to section 3; the first is whether the jury could on the indictment have found the defendant guilty of some other offence and the second is whether it appears to the court on the finding of the jury that the jury must have been satisfied of facts which proved him guilty of the other offence. In considering the first issue, *R. v. Wilson*; *R. v. Jenkins* [1984] A.C. 242, HL (*ante*, § 4–456), does not authorise the court to step outside the ingredients of the offence in the indictment and look at the underlying facts to see whether the evidential ingredients were the same as for the alternative suggested offence: *R. v. Cooke* [1997] Crim.L.R. 436, CA. In deciding the second issue, the fact that the jury did not receive a proper direction as to the suggested alternative is a highly relevant consideration, as is the question whether the conduct of the defence would have been materially affected if the appellant had been charged with that offence: *R. v. Caslin*, 45 Cr.App.R. 47, CCA; *R. v. Graham*; *R. v. Kansal*; *R. v. Ali (Sajid)*; *R. v. Marsh* [1997] 1 Cr.App.R. 302, CA.

Where a conviction is quashed on account of the reception of inadmissible evidence, it is not open to the Court of Appeal to substitute a conviction under section 3 for an alternative offence, even though it appears to the court on the finding of the jury that they must have been satisfied of facts which proved him guilty of the alternative offence, if they may have been influenced in relation to those facts by the inadmissible evidence: *R. v. Deacon*, 57 Cr.App.R. 688, CA (distinguished in *R. v. Spratt*, 71 Cr.App.R. 125, CA).

Where a conviction for conspiracy is quashed, a conviction for a substantive offence may not be substituted under this section where the prosecution had invited the jury to infer the existence of the conspiracy from evidence of the commission of substantive offences, though the Court of Appeal is satisfied that the jury must have been sure of the appellant's guilt of one or more of the substantive offences: *R. v. R.* [2007] 1 Cr.App.R. 10, CA. See also *R. v. K.*; *R. v. S. and R.*; *R. v. X.* [2008] 1 Cr.App.R. 1, CA, to similar effect. As to this case, see also *ante*, §§ 7–46, 7–52.

A conviction for manslaughter on the grounds of diminished responsibility may be substituted for a conviction for murder, despite there having been no evidence of diminished responsibility before the jury, the issue having been raised for the first time on appeal: *R. v. Weekes* [1999] 2 Cr.App.R. 520, CA.

The power to substitute a conviction for an alternative offence under section 3 is discretionary, and it is to be exercised in the light of what would be just in all the circumstances of the case: *R. v. Peterson* [1997] Crim.L.R. 339, CA.

It is important, in order to preserve the powers of the Court of Appeal under this provision, that where an indictment contains counts in the alternative, the jury should, in the event that they convict on either count, be discharged from returning a verdict on the other count: *R. v. Seymour*, 38 Cr.App.R. 68, CCA.

As to the requirement that the sentence be not of "greater severity" than the sentence passed at the trial, see *post*, §§ 7–126, 7–131, 7–132.

Criminal Appeal Act 1968, s.3A

Power to substitute conviction of alternative offence after guilty plea

3A.—(1) This subsection applies on an appeal against conviction where— **7–107a**

(a) an appellant has been convicted of an offence to which he pleaded guilty,

(b) if he had not so pleaded, he could on the indictment have pleaded, or been found, guilty of some other offence, and

(c) it appears to the Court of Appeal that the plea of guilty indicates an admission by the appellant of facts which prove him guilty of the other offence.

(2) The Court of Appeal may, instead of allowing or dismissing the appeal, substitute for the appellant's plea of guilty a plea of guilty of the other offence and pass such sentence in substitution for the sentence passed at the trial as may be authorised by law for the other offence, not being a sentence of greater severity.

[This section was inserted by the *CJA* 2003, s.316(1) and (3).]

(6) Sentence when appeal allowed on part of indictment

Criminal Appeal Act 1968, s.4

Power to re-sentence where appellant remains convicted of related offences

4.—(1) This section applies where— **7–108**

(a) two or more related sentences are passed,

(b) the Court of Appeal allow an appeal against conviction in respect of one or more of the offences for which the sentences were passed ("the related offences"), but

(c) the appellant remains convicted of one or more of those offences.

(2) Except as provided by subsection (3) below, the Court may in respect of any related offence of which the appellant remains convicted pass such sentence, in substitution for any sentence passed thereon at the trial, as they think proper and is authorised by law.

(3) The Court shall not under this section pass any sentence such that the appellant's sentence (taken as a whole) for all the related offences of which he remains convicted will, in consequence of the appeal, be of greater severity than the sentence (taken as a whole) which was passed at the trial for all the related offences.

(4) For the purposes of subsection (1)(a), two or more sentences are related if—

(a) they are passed on the same day,

(b) they are passed on different days but the court in passing any one of them states that it is treating that one together with the other or others as substantially one sentence, or

(c) they are passed on different days but in respect of counts on the same indictment.

(5) Where—

(a) two or more sentences are related to each other by virtue of subsection (4)(a) or (b), and

(b) any one or more of those sentences is related to one or more other sentences by virtue of subsection (4)(c),

all the sentences are to be treated as related for the purposes of subsection (1)(a).

[This section is printed as amended and repealed in part by the *CJIA* 2008, ss.47 and 149, Sched. 8, paras 1 and 6, and Sched. 28, Pt 3. These amendments came into force on July 14, 2008: *Criminal Justice and Immigration Act 2008 (Commencement*

No. 2 and Transitional and Saving Provisions) Order 2008 (S.I. 2008 No. 1586). They apply in relation to an appeal if the proceedings on appeal began on or after that date; and for this purpose, the proceedings begin (a) if the Criminal Cases Review Commission refer the case to the Court of Appeal, on the date the reference is made, and (b) in any other case, on the date on which notice of appeal or, as the case may be, notice of application for leave to appeal, is served on the Crown Court officer: *ibid.*, art. 2(3), and Sched. 2, para. 4(1) and (2). The reference to service on the Crown Court officer is to be read in accordance with the *Criminal Procedure Rules* 2005 (S.I. 2005 No. 384): *ibid.*, para. 4(3). For the relevant provisions of the 2005 rules, see Pt 4 thereof (*ante*, §§ 2–207 *et seq.*).]

Where there is a conviction on two counts, but no sentence passed in respect of one of them, this section allows the Court of Appeal to pass sentence on that count where it has quashed the conviction on the count in respect of which sentence was pronounced: *R. v. O'Grady*, 28 Cr.App.R. 33, CCA; *R. v. Dolan*, 62 Cr.App.R. 36, CA.

As to the requirement that the sentence be not of "greater severity" than the sentence passed at trial, see *post*, §§ 7–126, 7–131, 7–132.

(7) Appeal against conviction on special verdict

Criminal Appeal Act 1968, s.5

Disposal of appeal against conviction on special verdict

7–109 **5.**—(1) This section applies on an appeal against conviction by a person in whose case the jury have found a special verdict.

(2) If the Court of Appeal consider that a wrong conclusion has been arrived at by the court of trial on the effect of the jury's verdict they may, instead of allowing the appeal, order such conclusion to be recorded as appears to them to be in law required by the verdict, and pass such sentence in substitution for the sentence passed at the trial as may be authorised by law.

(8) Substitution of finding of insanity or findings of unfitness to plead, etc.

Criminal Appeal Act 1968, s.6

Substitution of finding of insanity or findings of unfitness to plead etc.

7–110 **6.**—(1) This section applies where, on an appeal against conviction, the Court of Appeal, on the written or oral evidence of two or more registered medical practitioners at least one of whom is duly approved, are of opinion—

(a) that the proper verdict would have been one of not guilty by reason of insanity; or

(b) that the case is not one where there should have been a verdict of acquittal, but there should have been findings that the accused was under a disability and that he did the act or made the omission charged against him.

(2) The Court of Appeal shall make in respect of the accused—

(a) a hospital order (with or without a restriction order);

(b) a supervision order; or

(c) an order for his absolute discharge.

(3) Where—

(a) the offence to which the appeal relates is an offence the sentence for which is fixed by law, and

(b) the court have power to make a hospital order,

the court shall make a hospital order with a restriction order (whether or not they would have power to make a restriction order apart from this subsection).

(4) Section 5A of the *Criminal Procedure (Insanity) Act* 1964 ("the 1964 Act") applies in relation to this section as it applies in relation to section 5 of that Act.

(6) Where the Court of Appeal make a supervision order by virtue of this section, any power of revoking or amending it shall be exercisable as if the order had been made by the court below.

(7) In this section—

"hospital order" has the meaning given in section 37 of the *Mental Health Act* 1983;

"restriction order" has the meaning given to it by section 41 of that Act;
"supervision order" has the meaning given in Part 1 of Schedule 1A to the 1964 Act.

[This section was substituted by the *Criminal Procedure (Insanity and Unfitness to Plead) Act* 1991, s.6. It is printed as subsequently amended (substitution of subss. (2) and (3) by new subss. (2) to (7)) by the *Domestic Violence, Crime and Victims Act* 2004, s.24(3); and the *CJIA* 2008, ss.47 and 149, Sched. 8, paras 1 and 7(a), and Sched. 28, Pt 3.]

For sections 5 and 5A of, and Schedule 1A to, the 1964 Act, see *ante*, §§ 4–175a *et seq.* For sections 37, 38 and 41 of the 1983 Act, see *ante*, §§ 5–893 *et seq.*

The expressions "duly approved", "registered medical practitioner" and "under disability" are defined in section 51(1) of the Act, *post*, § 7–350.

Although the 1968 Act confers no specific right of appeal against a finding of fitness to plead (*ante*, § 7–42), this section does give the Court of Appeal power upon an appeal against conviction to make a similar order to the order that would have been made had there been a finding of disability together with a finding that the appellant did the act or made the omission charged against him; see *Criminal Procedure (Insanity) Act* 1964, s.5, *ante*, § 4–175a. See also *R. v. Podola*, *ante*, § 7–42. **7–111**

(9) Retrials

Criminal Appeal Act 1968, s.7

Power to order a retrial

7.—(1) Where the Court of Appeal allow an appeal against conviction and it appears to the Court that the interests of justice so require, they may order the appellant to be retried. **7–112**

(2) A person shall not under this section be ordered to be retried for any offence other than—

(a) the offence of which he was convicted at the original trial and in respect of which his appeal is allowed as mentioned in subsection (1) above;

(b) an offence of which he could have been convicted at the original trial on an indictment for the first-mentioned offence; or

(c) an offence charged in an alternative count of the indictment in respect of which no verdict was given in consequence of his being convicted of the first-mentioned offence.

[This section is printed as repealed in part by the *CJA* 1988, ss.43(1) and 170(2), and Sched. 16; and the *CJA* 2003, s.331, and Sched. 36, para. 44.]

Where a conviction was quashed because of the defective nature of the indictment (alleging knowledge or suspicion when nothing less than knowledge was required), it was still open to the Court of Appeal to order a retrial; a count in an indictment which alleged the same offence without reference to "suspicion" was still the offence of which the appellant had been convicted within the meaning of subsection (2)(a): *R. v. K.*; *R. v. S. and R.*; *R. v. X.* [2008] 1 Cr.App.R. 1, CA. As to this case, see also *ante*, §§ 7–46, 7–52.

The decision whether to order a retrial requires an exercise of judgment, involving consideration of the public interest and the legitimate interests of the defendant. The former was generally served by the prosecution of those reasonably suspected on available evidence of serious crime, if such prosecution could be conducted without unfairness to, or oppression of, the defendant. The legitimate interests of the defendant would call for consideration of the time which had passed since the alleged offence and any penalty already paid: *R. v. Graham*; *R. v. Kansal*; *R. v. Ali (Sajid)*; *R. v. Marsh* [1997] 1 Cr.App.R. 302, CA. As to time since the offence, see also *R. v. Saunders*, 58 Cr.App.R. 248 (retrial not ordered having regard to delay of three-and-a-half years and fact that appellant had been in prison for a number of years), and *R. v. Grafton and Grafton*, *The Times*, March 6, 1992 (retrials ordered in respect of serious offences after similar lapse of time, the court pointing out that since 1973 it had become much more common for trials to take longer to come to court).

Where a defendant who had been properly brought before a criminal court had his conviction quashed on grounds of bias (actual or apparent) in the trial court, there was no reason why a retrial should not be ordered, provided it would be possible to have a fair trial before a different tribunal: *Panday v. Virgil (Senior Superintendent of Police)* [2008] 3 W.L.R. 296, PC.

Where, following the quashing of a conviction, objection was taken to the ordering of a retrial on the ground that there had been such adverse publicity following the conviction and immediately prior to the appeal, some of which was inaccurate and some of which consisted of material which could not be placed before a jury, the objection should be sustained only if the Court of Appeal was satisfied on a balance of probabilities that if at the retrial the jury returned one or more verdicts of guilty, the effect of the publicity would be such as to render any such verdict unsafe; in considering this issue, the court would take account of the likely lapse of time between the offending publicity and the retrial and the possibility of mitigating the effect of the publicity by altering the trial venue, and by addressing a few careful questions to the jury panel: *R. v. Stone* [2001] Crim.L.R. 465, CA.

If the court is satisfied that fresh evidence received or available to be received under section 23 is true and conclusive of the appeal, no retrial will be ordered: *R. v. Flower* [1966] 1 Q.B. 146, 50 Cr.App.R. 22, CCA, and *R. v. McIlkenny*, 93 Cr.App.R. 287 at 313, CA.

Criminal Appeal Act 1968, s.8

Supplementary provisions as to retrial

7–113 **8.**—(1) A person who is to be retried for an offence in pursuance of an order under section 7 of this Act shall be tried on a fresh indictment preferred by direction of the Court of Appeal but after the end of two months from the date of the order for his retrial he may not be arraigned on an indictment preferred in pursuance of such a direction unless the Court of Appeal give leave.

(1A) Where a person has been ordered to be retried but may not be arraigned without leave, he may apply to the Court of Appeal to set aside the order for retrial and to direct the court of trial to enter a judgment and verdict of acquittal of the offence for which he was ordered to be retried.

(1B) On an application under subsection (1) or (1A) above the Court of Appeal shall have power—

(a) to grant leave to arraign; or

(b) to set aside the order for retrial and direct the entry of a judgment and verdict of acquittal,

but shall not give leave to arraign unless they are satisfied—

(i) that the prosecution has acted with all due expedition; and

(ii) that there is a good and sufficient cause for a retrial in spite of the lapse of time since the order under section 7 of this Act was made.

(2) The Court of Appeal may, on ordering a retrial, make such orders as appear to them to be necessary or expedient—

(a) for the custody or, subject to section 25 of the *Criminal Justice and Public Order Act* 1994, release on bail of the person ordered to be retried pending his retrial; or

(b) for the retention pending the retrial of any property or money forfeited, restored or paid by virtue of the original conviction or any order made on that conviction.

(3) If the person ordered to be retried was, immediately before the determination of his appeal, liable to be detained in pursuance of an order or direction under Part V of the *Mental Health Act* 1959, or under Part III of the *Mental Health Act* 1983 (other than under section 35, 36 or 38 of that Act)—

(a) that order or direction shall continue in force pending the retrial as if the appeal had not been allowed; and

(b) any order made by the Court of Appeal under this section for his custody or release on bail shall have effect subject to the said order or direction.

7–114 (3A) If the person ordered to be retried was, immediately before the determination of his appeal, liable to be detained in pursuance of a remand under section 36 of the *Mental Health Act* 1983 or an interim hospital order under section 38 of that Act, the Court of Appeal may, if they think fit, order that he shall continue to be detained in a hospital or mental nursing home, and in that event Part III of that Act shall apply as if he had been ordered under this section to be kept in custody pending his retrial and were detained in pursuance of a transfer direction together with a restriction direction.

(3B) If the person ordered to be retried—

(a) was liable to be detained in pursuance of an order or direction under Part 3 of the *Mental Health Act* 1983;

(b) was then made subject to a community treatment order (within the meaning of that Act); and

(c) was subject to that community treatment order immediately before the determination of his appeal,

the order or direction under Part 3 of that Act and the community treatment order shall continue in force pending the retrial as if the appeal had not been allowed, and any order made by the Court of Appeal under this section for his release on bail shall have effect subject to the community treatment order.

(4) Schedule 2 to this Act has effect with respect to the procedure in the case of a person ordered to be retried, the sentence which may be passed if the retrial results in his conviction and the order for costs which may be made if he is acquitted.

[This section is printed as amended by the *Courts Act* 1971, s.56 and Sched. 11; the *Mental Health (Amendment) Act* 1982, s.65(1) and Sched. 3, para. 36; the *MHA* 1983, s.148 and Sched. 4, para. 23(b); the *CJA* 1988, s.43(3), (4); the *CJPOA* 1994, Sched. 10, para. 19; the *Access to Justice Act* 1999, s.58(2); and the *MHA* 2007, s.32(4), and Sched. 4, para. 2(1) and (2).]

The word "due" in the expression "all due expedition" means "reasonable" or "proper": *R. v. Coleman*, 95 Cr.App.R. 345; *R. v. Horne*, *The Times*, February 27, 1992, CA.

Provisions of the *Criminal Procedure Rules* 2005 (S.I. 2005 No. 384) relevant to an order for a retrial are rules 68.8 (application for bail pending retrial (*post* § 7–189)), 68.9 (conditions of bail (*post* § 7–190)) and 68.14 (renewal or setting aside order for retrial (*post* § 7–115)).

On ordering a retrial, the Court of Appeal has no power to direct that arraignment on the fresh indictment should take place within a specified time limit less than the two months allowed by section 8(1): *R. v. Khan* [2001] 4 *Archbold News* 3, CA.

The requirement that the prosecution should have acted "with all due expedition" is a less exacting one than that for the extension of a custody time limit ("with all due diligence and expedition"); where, therefore, the prosecution, in apparent ignorance of the fact that arraignment had not taken place at an earlier hearing, sought and obtained an adjournment from the court office of the next scheduled hearing date from a day before the expiry of the time limit to a day nine days after its expiry, the prosecution might not have been able to show "due diligence" but could show "due expedition" where the delay was unlikely to affect the hearing date of the retrial; and, whilst the primary responsibility for arraigning the defendant within time, lay with the court, both parties had a duty to ensure that effect was given to the order of the Court of Appeal; it was not open to the defence to do nothing even if that might favour their lay client: *R. v. Jones (Paul Garfield)* [2003] 1 Cr.App.R. 20, CA.

As to the amendment of an indictment preferred by direction of the court under section 8(1), see *R. v. Hemmings* [2000] 1 Cr.App.R. 360, CA (*ante*, § 1–149).

Criminal Procedure Rules 2005 (S.I. 2005 No. 384), r.68.14

Renewal or setting aside of order for retrial

68.14.—(1) This rule applies where— **7–115**

(a) a prosecutor wants a defendant to be arraigned more than 2 months after the court ordered a retrial under section 7 of the *Criminal Appeal Act* 1968; or

(b) a defendant wants such an order set aside after 2 months have passed since it was made.

(2) That party must apply in writing, with reasons, and serve the application on—

(a) the Registrar;

(b) the other party.

[Rule 68.14 is printed as substituted by the *Criminal Procedure (Amendment No. 2) Rules* 2007 (S.I. 2007 No. 2317).]

Criminal Appeal Act 1968, Sched. 2

Depositions

7–116 1. [*See* post, *§ 10–56*.]

Sentence on conviction at retrial

7–117 2.—(1) Where a person ordered to be retried is again convicted on retrial, the court before which he is convicted may pass in respect of the offence any sentence authorised by law, not being a sentence of greater severity than that passed on the original conviction.

(2) Without prejudice to its power to impose any other sentence, the court before which an offender is convicted on retrial may pass in respect of the offence any sentence passed in respect of that offence on the original conviction notwithstanding that, on the date of the conviction on retrial, the offender has ceased to be of an age at which such a sentence could otherwise be passed.

(3) Where the person convicted on retrial is sentenced to imprisonment or other detention, the sentence shall begin to run from the time when a like sentence passed at the original trial would have begun to run; but in computing the term of his sentence or the period for which he may be detained thereunder, as the case may be, there shall be disregarded—

(a) any time before his conviction on retrial which would have been disregarded in computing that term or period if the sentence had been passed at the original trial and the original conviction had not been quashed; and

(b) any time during which he was released on bail under section 8(2) of this Act.

(4) *Section* [Sections] 240 [and 240A] of the *Criminal Justice Act* 2003 (crediting of periods of remand in custody [or on bail subject to certain types of condition]: terms of imprisonment and detention), shall apply to any sentence imposed on conviction on retrial as if it had been imposed on the original conviction.

[This Schedule is printed as amended or repealed in part by the *Supreme Court Act* 1981, Sched. 5; the *Prosecution of Offences Act* 1985, s.16(11); the *CJA* 1988, s.170(1), and Sched. 15, para. 32; and the *CJA* 2003, s.304, and Sched. 32, paras 7 and 10; and as amended, as from a day to be appointed, by the *CJIA* 2008, s.22(4) (omission of italicised word, insertion of words in square brackets).]

B. APPEAL AGAINST SENTENCE

(1) Who can appeal

Criminal Appeal Act 1968, s.9

Appeal against sentence following conviction on indictment

7–118 **9.**—(1) A person who has been convicted of an offence on indictment may appeal to the Court of Appeal against any sentence (not being a sentence fixed by law) passed on him for the offence, whether passed on his conviction or in subsequent proceedings.

(1A) In subsection (1) of this section, the reference to a sentence fixed by law does not include a reference to an order made under subsection (2) or (4) of section 269 of the *Criminal Justice Act* 2003 in relation to a life sentence (as defined in section 277 of that Act) that is fixed by law.

(2) A person who on conviction on indictment has also been convicted of a summary offence under *section 41 of the* Criminal Justice Act *1988 (power of Crown Court to deal with summary offence where person committed for either way offence)* or paragraph 6 of Schedule 3 to the *Crime and Disorder Act* 1998 (power of Crown Court to deal with summary offence where person sent for trial for indictable-only offence) may appeal to the Court of Appeal against any sentence passed on him for the summary offence (whether on his conviction or in subsequent proceedings) under subsection (7) of that section or sub-paragraph (4) of that paragraph.

[This section is printed as amended by the *CJA* 1988, s.170(1) and Sched. 15, para. 21; the *CDA* 1998, s.119 and Sched. 8, para. 12; the *Access to Justice Act* 1999, s.58(3); and the *CJA* 2003, s.271(1); and as amended, as from a day to be appointed, by *ibid.*, ss.41 and 332, Sched. 3, para. 44(1) and (3), and Sched. 7, Pt 4 (omission of words from "section 41" to "either way offence)" in subs. (2)).]

Sections 179(3), 203(4) and 205(4) of the *AFA* 2006 respectively provide that where a sentence is passed under the *CJA* 2003, s.211(3A) (as substituted by s.179(2) of the 2006 Act (*ante*, § 5–147)), under section 211(3)(b) of the 2003 Act (as modified by s.203(3) of the 2006 Act) or under Schedule 12, para. 15(4)(b), to the 2003 Act (as modified by s.205(2) of the 2006 Act (*ante*, § 5–334m)), section 9 of the 1968 Act applies as if the offender had been convicted on indictment of the offence for which sentence was passed. Section 181 of the 2006 Act gives effect to Part 1 of Schedule 5 (application of Sched. 8 to the 2003 Act (*ante*, §§ 5–180 *et seq.*) to service community orders); and paragraph 9 of Schedule 5 (in Pt 1) provides that where a sentence is passed by virtue of paragraph 8 (power of Crown Court to re-sentence following imposition of service community order), section 9 of the 1968 Act applies as if the offender had been convicted on indictment of the offence for which sentence was passed.

Where different orders, each of which fall within the definition of "sentence" in section 50 of the *CAA* 1968 (*post*), are made in separate proceedings (as to which, see s.10(4) of the 1968 Act (*post*, § 7–123)), there may be two appeals against sentence under section 9; where, therefore, a defendant convicted of a drug trafficking offence was sentenced to imprisonment but the confiscation proceedings were postponed, the fact that he had already appealed against the sentence of imprisonment was no bar to a subsequent appeal against the confiscation order that was eventually made: *R. v. Neal* [1999] 2 Cr.App.R.(S.) 352, CA.

A sentence is not to be regarded as fixed by law for the purposes of section 9(1) if the statutory provision which requires the imposition of such sentence is incompatible with the ECHR: *R. (Lichniak) v. Secretary of State for the Home Department*; *R. (Pyrah) v. Same*; *R. v. Lichniak*; *R. v. Pyrah* [2002] Q. B. 296, DC and CA (the point not being considered in the House of Lords ([2003] 1 A.C. 903)).

Criminal Appeal Act 1968, s.50

Meaning of "sentence"

50.—(1) In this Act, "sentence", in relation to an offence, includes any order made by a court when dealing with an offender including, in particular— **7–119**

(a) a hospital order under Part III of the *Mental Health Act 1983*, with or without a restriction order;

(b) an interim hospital order under that Part;

(bb) a hospital direction and a limitation direction under that Part;

(ca) a confiscation order under Part 2 of the *Proceeds of Crime Act* 2002;

(cb) an order which varies a confiscation order made under Part 2 of the *Proceeds of Crime Act* 2002 if the varying order is made under section 21, 22 or 29 of that Act (but not otherwise);

(c) a recommendation for deportation;

(d) a confiscation order under the *Drug Trafficking Act* 1994 other than one made by the High Court;

(e) a confiscation order under Part VI of the *Criminal Justice Act* 1988;

(f) an order varying a confiscation order of a kind which is included by virtue of paragraph (d) or (e) above;

(g) an order made by the Crown Court varying a confiscation order which was made by the High Court by virtue of section 19 of the Act of 1994; and

(h) a declaration of relevance within the meaning of section 23 of the *Football Spectators Act* 1989; and

(i) an order under section 129(2) of the *Licensing Act* 2003 (forfeiture or suspension of personal licence).

(1A) Section 14 of the *Powers of Criminal Courts (Sentencing) Act* 2000 (under which a conviction of an offence for which … an order for conditional or absolute discharge is made is deemed not to be a conviction except for certain purposes) shall not prevent an appeal under this Act, whether against conviction or otherwise.

(2) Any power of the Criminal Division of the Court of Appeal to pass a sentence includes a power to make a recommendation for deportation in cases where the court from which the appeal lies had power to make such a recommendation.

(3) An order under section 17 of the *Access to Justice Act* 1999 is not a sentence for the purposes of this Act.

[This section is printed as amended and repealed in part by the *CJA* 1982, s.66(1); the *CJA* 1991, s.100, and Sched. 11, para. 4; the *CJA* 1993, Sched. 5, para. 1; the *DTA* 1994, Sched. 1, para. 2; the *C(S)A* 1997, s.55, and Sched. 4, para. 6(1)(a); the *Access to Justice Act* 1999, s.24, and Sched. 4, para. 3; the *PCC(S)A* 2000, s.165(1), and Sched.

9, para. 30; the *Football (Disorder) Act* 2000, s.1(3), and Sched. 3; the *PCA* 2002, s.456, and Sched. 11, para. 4(1) and (3); the *Licensing Act* 2003, s.198(1), and Sched. 6, paras 38 and 42; and the *VCRA* 2006, s.52(2), and Sched. 3, para. 14(1) and (2).]

7–120 An order that an accused should pay the whole or any part of the costs of the prosecution is a "sentence" within section 50(1) of the 1968 Act: *R. v. Hayden*, 60 Cr.App.R. 304. The key to the meaning of "sentence" within that provision is that it is an order made by a court when dealing with an offender in respect of his offence: *ibid*. Where there are two or more defendants and some order is made upon sentence which the court has power to make by virtue only of the special position of one defendant, a co-defendant will have no right to appeal against such order even though he may be prejudiced thereby: *R. v. Ioannou*, 61 Cr.App.R. 257, applying *Hayden*, *ante*.

7–121 In *R. v. Thebith*, 54 Cr.App.R. 35, it was doubted whether there was any right of appeal against a restitution order made under section 148(2) of the *PCC(S)A* 2000 (*ante*, § 5–431). This issue was considered in detail in the 1993 edition of this work. It is submitted, however, that should the matter arise for decision, such an order would be held to be within the meaning of "sentence". It satisfies the *Hayden* test, in that it is an order dependent on conviction; and see section 149(3) of the 2000 Act (*ante*, § 5–432).

7–122 A compensation order order is clearly within the definition of "sentence" in section 50: see *R. v. Thebith*, *ante*; and *R. v. Hayden*, *ante*.

In *R. v. Williams (C.)*, 75 Cr.App.R. 378, it was held that a binding over order made upon conviction was contingent upon conviction and, therefore, came within the definition of "sentence" in section 50(1). A period specified under section 82A of the *PCC(S)A* 2000 (*ante*, § 5–310) (discretionary life sentences) is a "sentence" for the purposes of section 9: *R. v. Dalton* [1995] 2 Cr.App.R. 340, CA.

In *Att.-Gen.'s Reference (No. 22 of 1992)*, 97 Cr.App.R. 275, the Court of Appeal held that deferment of sentence was a sentence within section 50. For a critique of this decision, see the 1994 supplements to this work. It was, however, confirmed in *R. v. L. (Deferred Sentence)*; *R. v. J.* [1999] 1 W.L.R. 479, CA.

Criminal Appeal Act 1968, s.10(1)–(4)

Appeal against sentence in other cases dealt with at the Crown Court

7–123 **10.**—(1) This section has effect for providing rights of appeal against sentence when a person is dealt with by the Crown Court (otherwise than on appeal from a magistrates' court) for an offence of which he was not convicted on indictment.

(2) The proceedings from which an appeal against sentence lies under this section are those where an offender convicted of an offence by a magistrates' court—

(a) is committed by the court to be dealt with for his offence before the Crown Court; or

(b) having been *the subject of an order for conditional discharge, a youth community order within the meaning of the* Powers of Criminal Courts (Sentencing) Act *2000 or a community order within the meaning of the* Criminal Justice Act *2003 … or given a suspended sentence, appears or is brought before the Crown Court to be further dealt with for his offence* [given a suspended sentence or made the subject of—

(i) an order for conditional discharge,

(ii) a youth rehabilitation order within the meaning of Part 1 of the *Criminal Justice and Immigration Act* 2008, or

(iii) a community order within the meaning of Part 12 of the *Criminal Justice Act* 2003,

appears or is brought before the Crown Court to be further dealt with for the offence]; … .

(3) An offender dealt with for an offence before the Crown Court in a proceeding to which subsection (2) of this section applies may appeal to the Court of Appeal against any sentence passed on him for the offence by the Crown Court.

(4) *For purposes of subsection (3) (a) of this section and section 11, any two or more sentences are to be treated as passed in the same proceeding if—*

(a) *they are passed on the same day; or*

(b) *they are passed on different days but the court in passing any one of them states that it is treating that one together with the other or others as substantially one sentence;*

and consecutive terms of imprisonment or detention and terms which are wholly or partly concurrent are to be treated as a single term.

[This section is printed as amended and repealed in part by the *Courts Act* 1971, Sched. 8; the *CJA* 1972, Sched. 5; the *PCCA* 1973, Sched. 5, para. 28; the *CJA* 1982, Sched. 14; the *CJA* 1988, ss.123(6) and 170(1), (2) and Sched. 8, para. 2, Sched. 15, para. 22 and Sched. 16; the *Football Spectators Act* 1989, ss.15(7) and 23(3); the *CJA 1991*, s.100 and Sched. 11, para. 3; the *CDA* 1998, s.119 and Sched. 8, para. 13; the *Football (Offences and Disorder) Act* 1999, ss.1(2)(e), 6(2)(e) and 7(2)(a); the *Access to Justice Act* 1999, s.58(4), (5) and (7); the *PCC(S)A* 2000, s.165(1), and Sched. 9, para. 28; the *Football Disorder Act* 2000, s.1(2), and Sched. 2, para. 1; and the *CJA* 2003, ss.304, 319(1) and (2), and 332, and Scheds 32, paras 7 and 8, and 37, Pt 7; and as amended, as from a day to be appointed, by *ibid.*, s.332, and Sched. 37, Pt 12 (omission of subs. (4)); and the *CJIA* 2008, s.6(2), and Sched. 4, para. 4 (substitution of words in square brackets for italicised words in subs. (2)(b)). As to the commencement of the repeal of subs. (4), see *post*, § 7–127. As to the amendment by the 2008 Act, it is of no effect in relation to any offence committed before it comes into force or any failure to comply with an order made in respect of an offence committed before it comes into force: 2008 Act, s.148(2), and Sched. 27, para. 1(1).]

The *CJA* 1982, Sched. 14, para. 23, added a new subsection (5) to section 10. This **7–124** subsection has not itself been repealed, but, having regard to the repeals of sections 4 and 14 of the 1982 Act by the 1988 Act, it has been rendered superfluous and, accordingly, is not printed here.

Criminal Appeal Act 1968, s.11

Supplementary provisions as to appeal against sentence

11.—(1) Subject to subsection (1A) below, an appeal against sentence, whether under section **7–125** 9 or under section 10 of this Act, lies only with the leave of the Court of Appeal.

(1A) If, within 28 days from the date on which the sentence was passed, the judge who passed it grants a certificate that the case is fit for appeal under section 9 or 10 of this Act, an appeal lies under this section without the leave of the Court of Appeal.

(2) Where the Crown Court in dealing with an offender either on his conviction on indictment or in a proceeding to which section 10(2) of this Act applies, has passed on him two or more sentences in the same proceeding (*which expression has the same meaning in this subsection as it has for the purposes of section 10*), being sentences against which an appeal lies under section 9(1) or section 10, an appeal or application for leave to appeal against any one of those sentences shall be treated as an appeal or application in respect of both or all of them.

(2A) Where following conviction on indictment a person has been convicted under section 41 of the *Criminal Justice Act* 1988 of a summary offence an appeal or application for leave to appeal against any sentence for the offence triable either way shall be treated also as an appeal or application in respect of any sentence for the summary offence and an appeal or application for leave to appeal against any sentence for the summary offence shall be treated also as an appeal or application in respect of the offence triable either way.

(2B) If the appellant or applicant was convicted on indictment of two or more offences triable either way, the references to the offence triable either way in subsection (2A) above are to be construed, in relation to any summary offence of which he was convicted under section 41 of the *Criminal Justice Act* 1988 following the conviction on indictment, as references to the offence triable either way specified in the notice relating to that summary offence which was given under subsection (2) of that section.

(3) On an appeal against sentence the Court of Appeal, if they consider that the appel- **7–126** lant should be sentenced differently for an offence for which he was dealt with by the court below may—

(a) quash any sentence or order which is the subject of the appeal; and
(b) in place of it pass such sentence or make such order as they think appropriate for the case and as the court below had power to pass or make when dealing with him for the offence;

but the Court shall so exercise their powers under this subsection that, taking the case as a whole, the appellant is not more severely dealt with on appeal than he was dealt with by the court below.

(4) [*Repealed by* Criminal Justice Act *2003, s.304 and Sched. 32, paras 7 and 9.*]

7–127 (5) The fact that an appeal is pending against an interim hospital order under the *Mental Health Act* 1983 shall not affect the power of the court below to renew or terminate the order or to deal with the appellant on its termination: and where the Court of Appeal quash such an order but do not pass any sentence or make any other order in its place the court may, subject to section 25 of the *Criminal Justice and Public Order Act* 1994, direct the appellant to be kept in custody or released on bail pending his being dealt with by the court below.

(7) For the purposes of this section, any two or more sentences are to be treated as passed in the same proceeding if—

(a) they are passed on the same day; or

(b) they are passed on different days but the court in passing any one of them states that it is treating that one together with the other or others as substantially one sentence.

[This section is printed as amended, and repealed in part, by the *Courts Act* 1971, s.56, and Sched. 8; the *PCCA* 1973, Sched. 3; the *Supreme Court Act* 1981, Sched. 7; the *CJA* 1982, s.29; the *Mental Health (Amendment) Act* 1982, Sched. 3; the *MHA* 1983, Sched. 4; the *CJA* 1988, ss.123(6) and 170(1), and Sched. 8, para. 3, and Sched. 15, paras 23 and 24; the *CJPOA* 1994, Sched. 10, para. 20; the *PCC(S)A* 2000, s.165(1), and Sched. 9, para. 29; the *CJA* 2003, ss.304, 319(1) and (3), and 332, and Scheds 32, paras 7 and 9, and 37, Pt 7; and the *CJIA* 2008, ss.47 and 149, Sched. 8, paras 1, 3 and 7(b), and Sched. 28, Pt 3; and as amended, as from a day to be appointed, by the *CJA* 2003, s.332, and Sched. 37, Pt 12 (omission of italicised words in subs. (2)).]

It is not apparent whether the amendment made by section 319 of the 2003 Act (insertion of subs. (7)) was commenced prematurely, or whether the failure to bring into force the repeals of section 10(4) (*ante*, § 7–123) and of the italicised words in subsection (2) of this section was an oversight.

As to the meaning of "taking the case as a whole … " in section 11(3), see *post*, § 7–131.

Certificate of sentencing judge: bail pending appeal

Practice Direction (Criminal Proceedings: Consolidation), para. IV.50 [2002] 1 W.L.R. 2870

7–128 **IV.50.1** The procedure … is described in the *Guide to Proceedings in the Court of Appeal Criminal Division* [see Appendix J]. This is available at the Crown Court.

IV.50.2 The procedure is also set out in outline on Criminal Appeal Office Form C (Crown Court judge's certificate of fitness for appeal) and Form BC (Crown Court judge's order granting bail), copies of which are held by the Crown Court. The court clerk will ensure that these forms are always available when a judge hears an application under these provisions.

IV.50.3 The judge may well think it right (a) to hear the application in chambers with a shorthand writer present; (b) to invite the defendant's advocate to submit before the hearing of the application a draft of the grounds which he will ask the judge to certify on Form C. The advocate for the Crown will be better able to assist the judge at the hearing if the draft ground is sent beforehand to him also.

IV.50.4 The first question for the judge is whether there exists a particular and cogent ground of appeal. If there is no such ground there can be no certificate, and if there is no certificate there can be no bail. A judge should not grant a certificate with regard to sentence merely in the light of mitigation to which he has, in his opinion, given due weight, nor in regard to conviction on a ground where he considers the chance of a successful appeal is not substantial. The judge should bear in mind that, where a certificate is refused, application may be made to the Court of Appeal for leave to appeal and for bail.

IV.50.5 The length of the period which might elapse before the hearing of an appeal is not relevant to the grant of a certificate, but, if the judge does decide to grant a certificate, it may be one factor in the decision whether or not to grant bail. A judge who is minded to take this factor into account may find it advisable to have the court clerk contact the Criminal Appeal Office listing co-ordinator in order that he may have an accurate and up-to-date assessment of the likely waiting time. This can be very short. The co-ordinator will require a general account of the weight and urgency of the case.

IV.50.6 Where the defendant's representative considers that bail should be applied for as a matter of urgency, the application should normally be made, in the first instance, to the trial judge, and the Court of Appeal may decline to treat such an application as urgent if there is no good reason why it has not been made to the trial judge.

As to certificates that a case is fit for appeal against conviction, see *ante*, §§ 7–37 *et seq.*; as to certificates that a case is fit for appeal on a question of law alone, see *post*, § 7–186; as to certificates that a case is fit for appeal against sentence, see *ante*, § 7–125. As to the power to grant bail, see *post*, § 7–186. **7–129**

As to the procedure for making an application for a certificate, see rule 68.4 of the *Criminal Procedure Rules* 2005 (S.I. 2005 No. 384) (*post*, § 7–313r).

The Court of Appeal has repeatedly stressed the importance of adhering to this practice direction, and, in particular, paragraph 4: see, for example, *R. v. Williams (P.D.), The Times*, October 28, 1991 (a certificate should not be issued "unless very exceptional circumstances were present"); *R. v. Bansal* [1999] Crim.L.R. 484 (exceptional reasons must exist); and *R. v. Harries, The Times*, March 26, 2007 (certificate should not be granted unless there are clear reasons for doing so, such as an unresolved issue of law or an obvious basis for considering that an appeal would be allowed).

Proper construction of section 11(3)

The opening words of section 11(3) are apt to cover the substitution of a lawful sentence (of the same length) for a sentence that was unlawful on account only of some procedural impropriety (such as failure to observe the restriction on the imposition of a custodial sentence on an unrepresented defendant in the *PCC(S)A* 2000, s.83 (*ante*, § 5–12)); the offender would be being sentenced "differently" in that the substituted sentence would be compliant with section 83: *R. v Howden* [2007] 1 Cr.App.R.(S.) 31, CA. **7–130**

The words "taking the case as a whole" in section 11(3) mean taking together the totality of the matters in respect of which an appellant against sentence was being dealt with in the court below: *R. v. Sandwell*, 80 Cr.App.R. 78, CA.

There is no basis upon which subsection (3) could be construed as applying only to discretionary sentences; accordingly, it operates so as to preclude the Court of Appeal from interfering with a sentence even if the provisions of Chapter 5 of Part 12 of the *CJA* 2003 mandated a different, *ex hypothesi*, more severe, sentence: *R. v. Reynolds* [2007] 2 Cr.App.R.(S.) 87, CA.

A sentence of life imprisonment cannot be substituted for a sentence of imprisonment for a fixed term of years: *R. v. Whitaker* [1967] Crim.L.R. 431.

In *R. v. Bennett*, 52 Cr.App.R. 514, the Court of Appeal held that a hospital order under (what is now) section 37 of the *MHA* 1983 with a restriction order under section 41 for an indefinite period was not more severe than a sentence of three years' imprisonment saying that a remedial order designed to treat and cure the appellant could not be regarded as more severe than a sentence of imprisonment. See also *R. v. Gardiner*, 51 Cr.App.R. 187. There must, however, be some limit on this principle, bearing in mind just how restrictive a restriction order is: see *Gardiner, ante*. In *R. v. Marsden*, 52 Cr.App.R. 301, a simple hospital order was substituted for a sentence of borstal training. **7–131**

In *R. v. McLaren (A.)*, 5 Cr.App.R.(S.) 332, the defendant was fined £100 and disqualified from driving for five years. On appeal, the disqualification was reduced to three years, but the fine was increased to £500. Section 11(3) does not appear to have been considered. In *R. v. Ardani*, 77 Cr.App.R. 302, it was held that there was no infringement of section 11(3) where a period of disqualification was added, a substantial reduction having been made to the period of imprisonment imposed. In *R. v. Murphy (A.J.)*, 89 Cr.App.R. 176, CA, a period of disqualification of eight years was reduced to six years on appeal, but an order under section 93(7) of the *RTA* 1972 (*rep.*) was added that at the end of the period of disqualification the appellant be not permitted to drive until he had passed a test. (See now *RTOA* 1988, s.36, *post*, § 32–198.) **7–132**

In *R. v. Williams (C.)*, 75 Cr.App.R. 378, CA, an order binding the defendant over to come up for judgment was set aside and a conditional discharge was substituted.

7–133 As to costs orders in postponed confiscation proceedings under the *CJA* 1988, see the conflicting authorities of *R. v. Threapleton* [2002] 2 Cr.App.R.(S.) 46, and *R. v. Ruddick* [2004] 1 Cr.App.R.(S.) 7.

Appeal by parent or guardian

7–134 Section 137 of the *PCC(S)A* 2000 confers powers on courts to order the parent or guardian of a child or young person to pay a fine or compensation instead of ordering the defendant to do so. Section 150 confers powers on courts to bind over a parent or guardian or, in default of agreement to enter a recognizance, to fine him. Sections 137(6) (*ante*, § 5–928) and 150(9) (*ante*, § 5–932) confer rights of appeal to the Court of Appeal.

(2) Notes on appeal against sentence

Where appeal lies

7–135 Except where the Crown Court has granted a certificate under section 11(1A), appeal lies only by leave of the Court of Appeal (s.11(1), (1A), *ante*, § 7–125): the power to give leave may, however, be exercised by a single judge (s.31, *post*, § 7–231). Where a conviction has been quashed with regard to certain counts and affirmed with regard to others, the court may reduce the sentence, although there has been an appeal against conviction only. "It … is within the power of the Court to treat his notice of appeal as if it had included an appeal against sentence" *per* Lord Hewart C.J., *R. v. Hervey and Goodwin*, 27 Cr.App.R. 146 at 148, CCA. An alternative approach would be to extend the time for making the application for leave to appeal against sentence.

The court is not obliged to pass an alternative sentence; it may, in a proper case, merely quash the sentence passed at the trial: *R. v. Bradford*, 7 Cr.App.R. 42, and *R. v. Brook* [1949] 2 K.B. 138, 33 Cr.App.R. 92.

Principles on which court acts

7–136 With the growth in the number of sentencing cases being reported it is becoming increasingly difficult to be precise about the principles upon which the Court of Appeal acts. In broad terms, it is submitted that the court will interfere when: (a) the sentence is not justified by law, in which case it will interfere not as a matter of discretion but of law; (b) where sentence has been passed on the wrong factual basis; (c) where some matter has been improperly taken into account or there is some fresh matter to be taken into account; (d) where there has been a failure to honour a legitimate expectation; or (e) where the sentence was wrong in principle or manifestly excessive.

These categories are not exhaustive and they overlap. They are considered in the following paragraphs, but the whole subject is considered in more detail in Chapter 5, *ante*, to which reference should be made especially so far as concerns the second and fourth categories.

The attitude of the Court of Appeal towards the citation of authorities has vacillated. The customary view is exemplified in *R. v. De Havilland*, 5 Cr.App.R.(S.) 109: the vast majority of decisions on sentencing are no more than examples, with no binding effect, but useful as an aid to uniformity of sentence (see *per* Dunn L.J. at p. 114).

More recently, the court has positively encouraged the citation of sentencing decisions as part of the sentencing process and counsel have been criticised for omitting to do so: see, in particular, *R. v. Ozair Ahmed*, 15 Cr.App.R.(S.) 286; *R. v. Johnson* [1994] Crim.L.R. 537; *Att.-Gen.'s Reference (No. 7 of 1997) (R. v. Fearon)* [1998] 1 Cr.App.R.(S.) 268; and *Att.-Gen.'s Reference (No. 52 of 2003) (R. v. Webb)* [2004] Crim.L.R. 306.

In the Court of Appeal itself, it is common for judgments on sentence appeals to make extensive reference to earlier sentence appeals (including some unreported cases), but the court has discouraged excessive citation, as in *R. v. Lyon*, *The Times*, May 19, 2005, in which it said that it would be reluctant to look at previous cases which were merely illustrative of the sentence appropriate to particular facts. For the future, it is likely that there will be a movement towards confining advocates, so far as level of sentence is concerned, to definitive guidelines of the Sentencing Guidelines Council (and authorities concerning those guidelines) and to cases included in the council's compendium of cases that it regards as "considered guidance". For current guidelines and the compendium, see Appendix K.

Where a judge passes sentence on the basis that the maximum available sentence is lower than the actual maximum sentence, it is open to the Court of Appeal to approach an appeal against sentence by reference to the actual maximum sentence: *R. v. Bright* [2008] Crim.L.R. 482, CA.

(i) *Where the sentence was not justified by law*

The Court of Appeal will quash any sentence if the Crown Court, in imposing it, **7–137** has exceeded the power conferred on it by Parliament and will do so even though there may be a statutory prohibition on appeals against such a "sentence": *R. v. Cain* [1985] A.C. 46, HL; *R. v. Wehner*, 65 Cr.App.R. 1. Thus, a sentence may be quashed because it exceeds the prescribed maximum, because there was no power to impose it in the particular circumstances or because some procedural requirement has not been complied with: see *R. v. Marquis*, 59 Cr.App.R. 228.

Where the Crown Court increases a sentence in purported exercise of its power to do so under section 155(1) of the *PCC(S)A* 2000 (*ante*, § 5–940), the increased sentence will be held to be a nullity if no opportunity is given to the defendant or his counsel to address the court: *R. v. Cleere*, 5 Cr.App.R.(S.) 465, *ante*, § 5–945.

As to a failure to observe the requirements of legal representation, see *ante*, §§ 5–12 *et seq.*

Non-compliance with an obligation to state reasons does not invalidate a sentence: *R. v. Poyner*, 11 Cr.App.R.(S.) 173, CA; *R. v. Baverstock* [1993] 1 W.L.R. 202, CA.

As to the scope of an appeal where sentence is passed upon a finding of a breach of a recognizance to be of good behaviour and to come up for judgment if called upon, such recognizance having been entered into on conviction, see *R. v. David*, 27 Cr.App.R. 50, CCA.

(ii) *Sentence upon wrong factual basis*

Where the evidence would justify only one view of the facts but the sentence is **7–138** passed on a basis which is mere supposition the sentence will be quashed: see, for example, *R. v. Reeves* [1983] Crim.L.R. 826. In many cases, however, a verdict or plea of guilty admits of two or more possible views of the facts. In such cases, the Court of Appeal will intervene if it concludes that the sentencer has made the wrong decision as to the proper factual basis for sentence or has adopted the wrong procedure for determining the issue: see, for example, *R. v. Ayensu and Ayensu*, 4 Cr.App.R.(S.) 248; *R. v. Newton*, 77 Cr.App.R. 13; *R. v. McGrath and Casey*, 5 Cr.App.R.(S.) 460; *R. v. Courtie* [1984] A.C. 463, HL; and *R. v. Solomon and Triumph*, 6 Cr.App.R.(S.) 120.

Where the judge does not make it plain which version of the facts he accepts in passing sentence, the Court of Appeal will regard itself as bound to approach the question of the propriety of the sentence upon the basis put forward by the defence: *R. v. Brown (W.T.)*, 3 Cr.App.R.(S.) 250. In *R. v. Kesler* [2001] 2 Cr.App.R.(S.) 126, CA, however, the court said that it would not determine an appeal against sentence on a particular factual basis unless there had either been a written basis of plea (preferably signed by counsel) or the judge had accepted it expressly. This was especially so in cases where the factual basis of the plea tendered was inherently unlikely.

The proper approach to the determination of the correct factual basis for sentencing is considered in detail in Chapter 5: see *ante*, §§ 5–64 *et seq.*

(iii) *Matters improperly taken into account or fresh matters to be taken into account*

The Court of Appeal will interfere with a sentence where there has been an error by the judge in appreciating the material laid before him relating to the **7–139** defendant's history: *e.g. R. v. Wilson*, 70 Cr.App.R. 219. It will also intervene where the sentence has been or may have been affected by inadmissible evidence relating to the defendant's character or by some irrelevant consideration, such as the nature of his defence: see *ante*, § 5–80. The proper procedure where there is material in the antecedent report which is disputed by the defence is set out in *R. v. Van Pelz* [1943] K.B. 157, 29 Cr.App.R. 10; *R. v. Robinson*, 53 Cr.App.R. 314; *R. v. Sargeant*, 60 Cr.App.R. 74 (and see para. III.27.6 of the *Practice Direction (Criminal Proceedings: Consolidation)* [2002] 1 W.L.R. 2870, *ante* § 5–59). The disputed material should either be omitted from the evidence called after conviction or be proved by admissible evidence.

7–140 The Court of Appeal is entitled to have regard to material which was not available at the time sentence was passed and also to have regard to what has happened since sentence was passed. Whereas the *CAA* 1907 provided for the quashing of a sentence where it was thought that a different sentence should "have been" passed, section 11 of the 1968 Act (*ante*, § 7–125) provides for a sentence to be quashed where the Court of Appeal considers that the appellant "should be" sentenced differently. As to the power of the Court of Appeal to consider fresh evidence, see *post*, § 7–208. It is impossible to be precise about the circumstances in which the Court of Appeal will have regard to fresh material or to events occurring subsequent to the passing of sentence. However, cases occur in which the Court of Appeal says that, having regard to a certain report, usually a prison governor's report, the court now feels able to take a lenient course, *e.g. R. v. Plows*, 5 Cr.App.R.(S.) 20, *R. v. Thomas* [1983] Crim.L.R. 493, *R. v. Bacon* [1997] 1 Cr.App.R.(S.) 335, and *R. v. Dalby and Berry* [2006] 1 Cr.App.R.(S.) 38; but there are equally cases in which the court has taken the attitude that progress in custody is a matter for the parole authorities: see, for example, *R. v. Waddingham*, 5 Cr.App.R.(S.) 66, and *R. v B.* (2003) 147 S.J. 1149. Progress in custody will not be considered relevant where a finding of significant risk is challenged on an appeal against a sentence under Chapter 5 of Part 12 of the *CJA* 2003 (*ante*, §§ 5–292 *et seq.*): *R. v. Sheehan and O'Mahoney* [2007] 1 Cr.App.R.(S.) 29, CA.

In *R. v. Ashraf*, 13 Cr.App.R.(S.) 451, the Court of Appeal said that if it is contended on an appellant's behalf that he has provided help to the authorities, it is imperative that the court is supplied with clear details of that assistance. This could be done either by providing the court with a transcript of the proceedings at the Crown Court disclosing exactly what had been put before the judge or by a letter or statement from the prosecuting authority or the police. As to assistance given to the authorities after conviction and sentence, see *ante*, § 5–96.

On an appeal against a fine on a company, the court would confine itself to the material before the Crown Court and would not investigate a submission that there had been a change in financial circumstances such that the company was less profitable than when the sentence had been imposed and thereby no longer able to meet the fine; in such a case, an application should be made to a magistrates' court to remit part of the fine under the *MCA* 1980, s.85, whereupon the financial circumstances of the company could be examined in detail: *R. v. Farrell and Hough Green Garage Ltd* (2007) 151 S.J. 1130, CA ([2007] EWCA Crim. 1896).

(iv) *Failure to honour legitimate expectation*

7–140a See *R. v. Gibson, ante*, § 5–260.

As to a mistake by a judge in explaining the effect of a sentence, see *R. v. Giga, ante*, § 5–112.

(v) *Sentence manifestly excessive or wrong in principle*

7–141 The traditional view of the proper role of the Court of Appeal in sentence appeals is that, apart from cases coming within (i) and (ii) above, it should only intervene where the sentence imposed was manifestly excessive or wrong in principle: for a restatement of this approach, see *R. v. Waddingham, ante*. These are not distinct grounds of appeal, for the court will conclude that if the sentence is manifestly excessive there must have been an error in principle. Where this approach is adopted, the court will not interfere with the discretion of the sentencing court merely on the ground that it might have passed a somewhat different sentence: *R. v. Gumbs*,

19 Cr.App.R. 74, CCA; *R. v. Ball*, 35 Cr.App.R. 164, CCA. The Court of Appeal aims not at uniformity of sentence but at uniformity of approach: see *R. v. Bibi*, 71 Cr.App.R. 360.

Where a person was sentenced in accordance with the legislation in force at the time, and with the tariff prevailing at the time, the Court of Appeal will not intervene on account of subsequent changes in the legislation, or in the tariff: *R. v. Graham* [1999] 2 Cr.App.R.(S.) 312, CA.

7–141a There being a duty on all courts to have regard to any definitive guidelines issued by the Sentencing Guidelines Council that are relevant to the particular case (see the *CJA* 2003, s.172, *ante*, § 5–100), any clear failure to follow such guidelines is likely to provide a ground of appeal; *a fortiori*, if the judge does not give a relevant reason for a departure from the guideline. As at October 1, 2008, there were thirteen definitive guidelines. These related to pleas of guilty (revised in July, 2007), the assessment of seriousness, new sentences under the 2003 Act, manslaughter by reason of provocation, certain forms of robbery, breach of a protective order, domestic violence, sexual offences, failing to surrender to bail, assaults and other offences against the person, assaults on, and cruelty to, children, sentencing in magistrates' courts and causing death by driving. They are set out in full or summarised at Appendix K. In connection with definitive guidance issued by the council, see, in particular, *R. v. Oosthuizen* [2006] 1 Cr.App.R.(S.) 73, CA (not open to a court to disregard a guideline, although it was not the case that a guideline would always be followed); *R. v. Bowering* [2006] 2 Cr.App.R.(S.) 10, CA (section 172 requires a court to have regard to, but not to follow, a guideline, but it is incumbent on a court, whenever it decides not to follow a guideline, to give an explanation why); and *Att.-Gen.'s References (Nos 14 and 15 of 2006) (R. v. French and Webster)* [2007] 1 Cr.App.R.(S.) 40, CA (section 172 cannot be said to have been complied with if the judge deliberately or inadvertently flouts the guideline).

7–142 Sentencing Guidelines Council guidance apart, some assistance is to be found in the so-called "guideline" cases (now collected together in a compendium by the council (see Appendix K–500)). These are a relatively modern development and they may relate to a type of offence, type of offender or type of penalty. Those in the first category are dealt with in detail in the sections dealing with the particular offences. Those in the second and third categories are dealt with in more detail in Chapter 5, *ante*.

In relation to all guideline cases, what was said by Lord Lane C.J., in *R. v. Nicholas*, *The Times*, April 23, 1986, should be borne in mind. His Lordship emphasised that the guidelines were only guidelines and were not meant to be applied rigidly to every case. They were for assistance only and were not to be used as rules never to be departed from. See also *R. v. Mawson*, 13 Cr.App.R.(S.) 218, CA, in which it was said that no guideline case could cover the entire field of offences arising under a particular section of an Act.

7–143 Where a person has been dealt with on one occasion and is subsequently dealt with for another matter which could have been dealt with at the same time as the first matter and it is clear that had it been so dealt with, it would not substantially have affected the overall sentence, the Court of Appeal may interfere with the sentence eventually imposed if it does, in fact, add substantially to the overall burden: see *R. v. Carey and Ames*, 26 Cr.App.R. 133, CCA; and *R. v. Watts* [2000] 1 Cr.App.R.(S.) 460, CA. As to the duty on legal representatives and the judiciary to do all within their power to see that all outstanding charges against a defendant are dealt with at the same time, see *R. v. Bennett*, 2 Cr.App.R.(S.) 96, CA.

Delay

7–143a Where there is delay between the grant of leave to appeal and the hearing of the appeal, for which the appellant is blameless, and the delay is such as to amount to a violation of the right to determination of a criminal charge within a reasonable time, as guaranteed by Article 6(1) of the ECHR (*post*, § 16–57), appropriate redress might take the form of a reduction of sentence; where, therefore, the circumstances were quite exceptional, sentences of 18 years' and 14 years' imprisonment were reduced by one year each; but such result would not follow where there was delay due to circumstances outside the control of the court or the prosecution: *R. v. Ashton, Lyons and Webber, The Times*, December 10, 2002, CA. See also *Att.-Gen.'s Reference (No. 2 of 2001)* [2004] 2 A.C. 72, HL (*post*, § 16–73), and *Yetkinsekerci v. U.K.* (2006) 43 E.H.R.R. 4, ECtHR (reduction in sentence must be measurable and expressly directed to the excessive length of the proceedings).

Contents of document not made public

7–144 On an appeal against sentence, it may be proper for the court not to refer publicly to the contents of a document or report which it has considered, provided that counsel for the appellant has been made fully aware of the contents and has had full opportunity of dealing with them: *R. v. Beckett*, 51 Cr.App.R. 180.

Dismissal of appeal against hospital order

7–145 Rule 68.13 of the *Criminal Procedure Rules* 2005 (S.I. 2005 No. 384) (*post*, § 7–150) makes consequential provision where the appellant had been released on bail pending an appeal against a hospital order which was dismissed.

C. APPEAL IN CASES OF INSANITY

Criminal Appeal Act 1968, s.12

Appeal against verdict of not guilty by reason of insanity

7–146 **12.** A person in whose case there is returned a verdict of not guilty by reason of insanity may appeal to the Court of Appeal against the verdict—

(a) with the leave of the Court of Appeal; or

(b) if, within 28 days from the date of the verdict, the judge of the court of trial grants a certificate that the case is fit for appeal.

[This section is printed as amended by the *CAA* 1995, s.1(3); and the *CJIA* 2008, s.47, and Sched. 8, paras 1 and 3.]

As to the certificate of the trial judge, see *ante*, § 7–37.

Criminal Appeal Act 1968, s.13

Disposal of appeal under section 12

7–147 **13.**—(1) Subject to the provisions of this section, the Court of Appeal—

(a) shall allow an appeal under section 12 of this Act if they think that the verdict is unsafe; and

(b) shall dismiss such an appeal in any other case.

(2) [*Effectively repealed by the* CAA *1995, s.2(3).*]

(3) Where apart from this subsection—

(a) an appeal under section 12 of this Act would fall to be allowed; and

(b) none of the grounds for allowing it relates to the question of the insanity of the accused,

the Court of Appeal may dismiss the appeal if they are of opinion that, but for the insanity of the accused, the proper verdict would have been that he was guilty of an offence other than the offence charged.

(4) Where an appeal under section 12 of this Act is allowed, the following provisions apply:—

(a) if the ground, or one of the grounds, for allowing the appeal is that the finding of the jury as to the insanity of the accused ought not to stand and the Court of Appeal are of opinion that the proper verdict would have been that he was guilty of an offence (whether the offence charged or any other offence of which the jury could have found him guilty), the Court—

(i) shall substitute for the verdict of not guilty by reason of insanity a verdict of guilty of that offence; and

(ii) shall, subject to subsection (5) below, have the like powers of punishing or otherwise dealing with the appellant, and other powers, as the court of trial would have had if the jury had come to the substituted verdict; and

(b) in any other case, the Court of Appeal shall substitute for the verdict of the jury a verdict of acquittal.

(5) The Court of Appeal shall not by virtue of subsection (4)(a) above sentence any person to death; but where under that paragraph they substitute a verdict of guilty of an offence for which apart from this subsection they would be required to sentence the appellant to death, their sentence shall (whatever the circumstances) be one of imprisonment for life.

(6) An order of the Court of Appeal allowing an appeal in accordance with this section shall operate as a direction to the court of trial to amend the record to conform with the order.

[This section is printed as amended by the *CAA* 1995, s.2(3).]

As to section 13(1), see generally, *ante*, §§ 7–45 *et seq.* In *R. v. Dickie*, 79 Cr.App.R. 213, CA, a verdict of not guilty by reason of insanity was quashed because the trial judge had raised the possibility of such a verdict when the evidence did not form a sufficient basis for such a verdict.

Criminal Appeal Act 1968, s.14

Substitution of findings of unfitness to plead etc.

14.—(1) This section applies where, on an appeal under section 12 of this Act, the Court of Appeal, on the written or oral evidence of two or more registered medical practitioners at least one of whom is duly approved, are of opinion that— **7–148**

(a) the case is not one where there should have been a verdict of acquittal; but

(b) there should have been findings that the accused was under a disability and that he did the act or made the omission charged against him.

(2)–(7) [*Identical to s.6(2)–(7),* ante, *§ 7–110.*]

[This section was substituted by the *Criminal Procedure (Insanity and Unfitness to Plead) Act* 1991, s.4(2). Subss. (2) and (3) were then substituted by new subss. (2) to (7) by the *Domestic Violence, Crime and Victims Act* 2004, s.24(3). Subs. (5) and the definition of "interim hospital order" in subs. (7) were repealed by the *CJIA* 2008, ss.47 and 149, Sched. 8, paras 1 and 7(c), and Sched. 28, Pt 3.]

The expressions "duly approved", "registered medical practitioner" and "under disability" are defined in section 51(1) of the Act, *post*, § 7–350. **7–149**

Criminal Procedure Rules 2005 (S.I. 2005 No. 384), r.68.13

Directions about re-admission to hospital on dismissal of appeal

68.13.—(1) This rule applies where— **7–150**

(a) an appellant subject to—

(i) an order under section 37(1) of the *Mental Health Act* 1983 (detention in hospital on conviction), or

(ii) an order under section 5(2) of the *Criminal Procedure (Insanity) Act* 1964 (detention in hospital on finding of insanity or disability)

has been released on bail pending appeal; and

(b) the court—

(i) refuses permission to appeal,

(ii) dismisses the appeal, or

(iii) affirms the order under appeal.

(2) The court must give appropriate directions for the appellant's—

(a) re-admission to hospital; and

(b) if necessary, temporary detention pending re-admission.

[Rule 68.13 is printed as substituted by the *Criminal Procedure (Amendment No. 2) Rules* 2007 (S.I. 2007 No. 2317).]

D. APPEAL AGAINST FINDINGS OF DISABILITY, ETC.

Criminal Appeal Act 1968, s.15

Appeal against finding of disability

15.—(1) Where there has been a determination under section 4 of the *Criminal Procedure (Insanity) Act* 1964, of the question of a person's fitness to be tried, and there have been findings that he is under a disability and that he did the act or made the omission charged against him, the person may appeal to the Court of Appeal against either or both those findings. **7–151**

(2) An appeal under this section lies only—

(a) with the leave of the Court of Appeal; or

(b) if, within 28 days from the date of the finding that the accused did the act or made the omission charged, the judge of the court of trial grants a certificate that the case is fit for appeal.

[This section is printed as amended by the *Criminal Procedure (Insanity and Unfitness to Plead) Act* 1991, Sched. 3, para. 2; the *CAA* 1995, s.1(5); the *Domestic Violence, Crime and Victims Act* 2004, s.58(1), and Sched. 10, para. 4; and the *CJIA*, s.47, and Sched. 8, paras 1 and 5.]

As to the certificate of the trial judge, see *ante*, § 7–37. For section 4 of the 1964 Act, see *ante*, § 4–167.

The expressions "duly approved", "registered medical practitioner" and "under disability" are defined in section 51(1) of the Act, *post*, § 7–350.

There is no right of appeal against a finding of fitness to plead. But see *R. v. Podola* [1960] 1 Q.B. 325, 43 Cr.App.R. 220, *ante*, § 7–42.

Criminal Appeal Act 1968, s.16

Disposal of appeal under section 15

7–152 **16.**—(1) The Court of Appeal—

(a) shall allow an appeal under section 15 of this Act against a finding if they think that the finding is unsafe; and

(b) shall dismiss such an appeal in any other case.

(2) [*Repealed by* Criminal Procedure (Insanity and Unfitness to Plead) Act *1991, Sched. 3, para. 3.*]

(3) Where the Court of Appeal allow an appeal under section 15 of this Act against a finding that the appellant is under a disability—

(a) the appellant may be tried accordingly for the offence with which he was charged; and

(b) the Court may, subject to section 25 of the *Criminal Justice and Public Order Act* 1994, make such orders as appear to them necessary or expedient pending any such trial for his custody, release on bail or continued detention under the *Mental Health Act* 1983;

and Schedule 3 to this Act has effect for applying provisions in Part III of that Act to persons in whose case an order is made by the Court under this subsection.

(4) Where, otherwise than in a case falling within subsection (3) above, the Court of Appeal allow an appeal under section 15 of this Act against a finding that the appellant did the act or made the omission charged against him, the Court shall, in addition to quashing the finding, direct a verdict of acquittal to be recorded (but not a verdict of not guilty by reason of insanity).

[This section is printed as amended and repealed in part by the *MHA* 1983, s.148 and Sched. 4, para. 23(f); the *Criminal Procedure (Insanity and Unfitness to Plead) Act* 1991, s.7 and Sched. 3, para. 3; the *CJPOA* 1994, Sched. 10, para. 21; and the *CAA* 1995, s.2(5).]

The expression "under disability" is defined in section 51(1) of the Act, *post*, § 7–350. For consequential provisions where the appeal is dismissed and the appellant has been released on bail pending appeal, see *ante*, § 7–150.

Criminal Appeal Act 1968, Sched. 3, para. 2

SCHEDULE 3

7–153 2. Where an order is made by the Court of Appeal under section 16(3) of this Act for a person's continued detention under the *Mental Health Act* 1983, Part III of that Act (patients concerned in criminal proceedings or under sentence) shall apply to him as if he had been ordered under the said section 16(3) to be kept in custody pending trial and were detained in pursuance of a transfer direction together with a restriction direction.

[Para. 1 was repealed by the *Mental Health (Amendment) Act* 1982, s.65(2) and Sched. 4; para. 2 is printed as substituted by the *MHA* 1983, s.148 and Sched. 4, para. 23(n).]

As to section 16(1), see generally, *ante*, §§ 7–45 *et seq.*

Findings of disability were quashed in *R. v. Robertson*, 52 Cr.App.R. 690 (jury misdirected as to the relevant considerations and not directed at all on the burden and standard of proof); *R. v. Berry*, 66 Cr.App.R. 156 (no direction as to the relevant considerations—judge apparently misled by fact that it had been on the application of the defence that the issue had been raised); and *R. v. Burles* [1970] 2 Q.B. 191, 54 Cr.App.R. 196 (judge erred in law in his interpretation of section 4 of the 1964 Act, ruling that it gave him no power to postpone determination of the issue).

E. Appeal Against Order Made in Cases of Insanity or Unfitness to Plead

Criminal Appeal Act 1968, ss.16A, 16B

Right of appeal against hospital order, etc.

16A.—(1) A person in whose case the Crown Court— **7–153a**

(a) makes a hospital order or interim hospital order by virtue of section 5 or 5A of the *Criminal Procedure (Insanity) Act* 1964, or

(b) makes a supervision order under section 5 of that Act,

may appeal to the Court of Appeal against the order.

(2) An appeal under this section lies only—

(a) with the leave of the Court of Appeal; or

(b) if the judge of the court of trial grants a certificate that the case is fit for appeal.

Disposal of appeal under s.16A

16B.—(1) If on an appeal under section 16A of this Act the Court of Appeal consider that the appellant should be dealt with differently from the way in which the court below dealt with him— **7–153b**

(a) they may quash any order which is the subject of the appeal; and

(b) they may make such order, whether by substitution for the original order or by variation of or addition to it, as they think appropriate for the case and as the court below had power to make.

(2) The fact that an appeal is pending against an interim hospital order under the *Mental Health Act* 1983 shall not affect the power of the court below to renew or terminate the order or deal with the appellant on its termination.

(3) [*Repealed by* CJIA *2008, ss.47 and 149, Sched. 8, paras 1 and 7(d), and Sched. 28, Pt 3.*]

(4) The fact that an appeal is pending against a supervision order under section 5 of the *Criminal Procedure (Insanity) Act* 1964 shall not affect the power of the court below to revoke the order, or of a magistrates' court to revoke or amend it.

(5) Where the Court of Appeal make a supervision order by virtue of this section, the power of revoking or amending it shall be exercisable as if the order had been made by the court below.

[Ss.16A and 16B were inserted by the *Domestic Violence, Crime and Victims Act* 2004, s.25.]

For consequential provision where an appeal under section 16A is dismissed, see *ante*, § 7–150.

F. Reference of Cases to Court of Appeal

Criminal Appeal Act 1995, s.9

Cases dealt with on indictment in England and Wales

9.—(1) Where a person has been convicted on indictment in England and Wales, the Commission— **7–154**

(a) may at any time refer the conviction to the Court of Appeal, and

(b) (whether or not they refer the conviction) may at any time refer to the Court of Appeal any sentence (not being a sentence fixed by law) imposed on, or in subsequent proceedings relating, to the conviction.

(2) A reference under subsection (1) of a person's conviction shall be treated for all purposes as an appeal by the person under section 1 of the 1968 Act against the conviction.

(3) A reference under subsection (1) of a sentence imposed on, or in subsequent proceedings relating to, a person's conviction on an indictment shall be treated for all purposes as an appeal by the person under section 9 of the 1968 Act against—

(a) the sentence, and

(b) any other sentence (not being a sentence fixed by law) imposed on, or in subsequent proceedings relating to, the conviction or any other conviction on the indictment.

(4) On a reference under subsection (1) of a person's conviction on an indictment the Commission may give notice to the Court of Appeal that any other conviction on the indictment which is specified in the notice is to be treated as referred to the Court of Appeal under subsection (1).

(5) Where a verdict of not guilty by reason of insanity has been returned in England and Wales in the case of a person, the Commission may at any time refer the verdict to the Court of Appeal; and a reference under this subsection shall be treated for all purposes as an appeal by the person under section 12 of the 1968 Act against the verdict.

(6) Where in England and Wales there have been returned findings that a person is under a disability and that he did the act or made the omission charged against him, the Commission may at any time refer either or both of those findings to the Court of Appeal; and a reference under this subsection shall be treated for all purposes as an appeal by the person under section 15 of the 1968 Act against the finding or findings referred.

[This section is printed as amended by the *Domestic Violence, Crime and Victims Act* 2004, s.58(1), and Sched. 10, para. 31.]

7–155 The reference to "the Commission" is to the Criminal Cases Review Commission established by section 8 of the *CAA* 1995, and "sentence" has the same meaning as in the 1968 Act (*ante*, § 7–119): *CAA* 1995, s.30(1). Subsection (5) is supplemented by the *Criminal Cases (Insanity) Act* 1999 which makes provision for the reference by the commission to the Court of Appeal of a verdict of "guilty but insane" (abolished by the *Criminal Procedure (Insanity) Act* 1964).

As to cases dealt with summarily, see section 11 of the 1995 Act, *ante*, § 2–173.

Section 13 specifies the conditions for making a reference under either section 9 or 11. The commission must consider that there is a "real possibility" (as to which, see *R. v. Criminal Cases Review Commission, ex p. Pearson* [2000] 1 Cr.App.R. 141, DC) that the conviction, etc., would not be upheld on account of some argument, evidence or (in the case of sentence) information not raised in the proceedings which led to it and there must have been an appeal or application for leave to appeal which has been refused. Failing these conditions, the commission may nevertheless make a reference if there appear to be "exceptional circumstances" to justify it. In *R. v. Gerald* [1999] Crim.L.R. 315, the Court of Appeal expressed surprise that it should be thought that such circumstances might exist where there was no new evidence and the point raised had never been canvassed at trial.

In *R. v. Cottrell*; *R. v. Fletcher* [2008] 1 Cr.App.R. 7, the Court of Appeal observed that where there has been a post-conviction change, correction or development in the law, the commission should, in deciding whether to refer the conviction to the court, have regard to the practice that would be applied by the court when dealing with an application for leave to appeal out of time that was founded on the change or development. As to the court's approach to applications for leave to appeal out of time, see *post*, § 7–182; and as to the court's power to dismiss an appeal where such leave would have been refused, see section 16C of the 1968 Act, *post*, § 7–156a.

As to the timetable to be followed on a reference, see *R. v. Siddall and Brooke*, *The Times*, July 26, 2006, CA. As to the approach of the Court of Appeal to appeals following references by the Commission, see *R. v. Thomas*, *ante*, § 7–51b (conviction), and *R. v. Graham*, *ante*, § 7–141 (sentence); and see section 16C of the 1968 Act, *post*, § 7–156a.

The commission may make a reference on application to them or without any such application (s.14(1)). In considering whether to make a reference, they may refer any point on which they desire the assistance of the Court of Appeal to that court for the court's opinion on it, and on such a reference the court shall consider the point referred and furnish the commission with its opinion on the point (s.14(3)). Where a reference under section 9 is treated as an appeal, grounds of appeal not related to any reason given by the commission in making the reference may not be raised other than with the leave of the court (s.14(4A), (4B), as inserted by the *CJA* 2003, s.315(1) and (2)). This restriction does not apply to a reference under section 11 (s.14(5), as amended by the 2003 Act, s.315(1) and (3)).

Rule 68.5(1) of the *Criminal Procedure Rules* 2005 (S.I. 2005 No. 384) (as amended by the *Criminal Procedure (Amendment No. 2) Rules* 2007 (S.I. 2007 No. 2317)) provides for service by the Registrar of Criminal Appeals on the appellant of a reference by the commission; and rule 68.5(2) stipulates that the court must treat the reference as the appeal notice if the appellant does not serve such a notice under rule 68.2 (*post*, § 7–313p). **7–156**

The principal supplementary powers of the commission are contained in sections 15 (investigations for the Court of Appeal pursuant to a request under section 23A of the 1968 Act (*post*, § 7–216)), 16 (assistance in connection with prerogative of mercy), 17 (power to obtain documents, etc.) and 19 (power to require appointment of investigating officers). The commission, in making its report to the court under section 15 is entitled to make evaluative judgments (*e.g.* as to whether or not a prosecution witness who had retracted his evidence had done so freely and voluntarily): *R. v. Coles and Bradley* [1999] 8 *Archbold News* 3, CA.

Paragraph 7 of Schedule 1 to the 1995 Act provides that a document purporting to be duly executed under the seal of the commission or to be signed on behalf of the commission shall be received in evidence and, unless the contrary is proved, shall be taken to be so executed or signed.

In *R. v. Conway*, 70 Cr.App.R. 4, CA, it was held in relation to section 17 of the 1968 Act that the power to receive fresh evidence was no greater on a reference than on an ordinary appeal.

Criminal Appeal Act 1968, s.16C

Power to dismiss certain appeals following references by the CCRC

16C.—(1) This section applies where there is an appeal under this Part following a reference by the Criminal Cases Review Commission under section 9(1)(a), (5) or (6) of the *Criminal Appeal Act* 1995 or section 1(1) of the *Criminal Cases Review (Insanity) Act* 1999. **7–156a**

(2) Notwithstanding anything in section 2, 13 or 16 of this Act, the Court of Appeal may dismiss the appeal if—

(a) the only ground for allowing it would be that there has been a development in the law since the date of the conviction, verdict or finding that is the subject of the appeal, and

(b) the condition in subsection (3) is met.

(3) The condition in this subsection is that if—

(a) the reference had not been made, but

(b) the appellant had made (and had been entitled to make) an application for an extension of time within which to seek leave to appeal on the ground of the development in the law,

the Court would not think it appropriate to grant the application by exercising the power conferred by section 18(3).

[This section was inserted, as from July 14, 2008 (*Criminal Justice and Immigration Act 2008 (Commencement No. 2) Order* 2008 (S.I. 2008 No. 1586)), by the *CJIA* 2008, s.42. It applies to an appeal under Pt I of the 1968 Act if it is made on or after the date on which s.42 came into force: 2008 Act, s.148(2), and Sched. 27, para. 14.]

As to the approach of the Court of Appeal to applications for leave to appeal out of time, see *post*, § 7–182; and see *R. v. Cottrell*; *R. v. Fletcher*, *ante*, § 7–155, as to not making references where leave to appeal out of time would not be given.

G. PROCEDURE FROM NOTICE OF APPEAL TO HEARING

(1) Time for appealing

Criminal Appeal Act 1968, s.18

18.—(1) A person who wishes to appeal under this Part of this Act to the Court of Appeal, or **7–157**

to obtain the leave of that court to appeal, shall give notice of appeal or, as the case may be, notice of application for leave to appeal, in such manner as may be directed by rules of court.

(2) Notice of appeal, or of application for leave to appeal, shall be given within twenty-eight days from the date of the conviction, verdict or finding appealed against, or in the case of appeal against sentence, from the date on which sentence was passed or, in the case of an order made or treated as made on conviction, from the date of the making of the order.

(3) The time for giving notice under this section may be extended, either before or after it expires, by the Court of Appeal.

This section is excepted by the *PCC(S)A* 2000, s.112(2) (*ante*, § 5–254); and the *CJA* 2003, s.231(2) (*ante*, § 5–297a). As to its application to trials without a jury, see section 48(5) of the 2003 Act (*ante*, § 4–267f).

For the purposes of an appeal against conviction, time runs from the date of conviction (*i.e.* verdict), not from the date of sentence, if later: *R. v. Long*, 161 J.P. 769, CA.

Where a sentence or other order of the Crown Court is varied under section 155 of the *PCC(S)A* 2000, for the purposes of section 18(2) of the 1968 Act and of paragraph 1 of Schedule 3 to the *CJA* 1988 (*post*, § 7–370) the sentence or other order shall be regarded as imposed or made on the day on which it is so varied: s.155(6) of the 2000 Act, *ante*, § 5–940.

Criminal Appeal Act 1968, s.18A

Appeal in cases of contempt

7–158 **18A.**—(1) A person who wishes to appeal under section 13 of the *Administration of Justice Act* 1960 from any order or decision of the Crown Court in the exercise of jurisdiction to punish for contempt of court shall give notice of appeal in such manner as may be directed by rules of court.

(2) Notice of appeal shall be given within twenty-eight days from the date of the order or decision appealed against.

(3) [*Identical to s.18(3),* ante, *save for* "its expiry" *in lieu of* "it expires".]

[Section 18A was inserted by the *CJA* 1988, s.170(1) and Sched. 15, para. 25.]

For section 13 of the *Administration of Justice Act* 1960, see *post*, § 28–138.

Notice of appeal and of an application for an extension of time

7–159 As to the form of a notice of appeal, see rule 68.3 of the *Criminal Procedure Rules* 2005 (S.I. 2005 No. 384) (*post*, § 7–313q).

As to applications for an extension of time, see rule 65.4 of the 2005 rules (*post*, § 7–313d).

Service of documents

7–160 As to service of a notice of appeal, see rule 68.2 of the *Criminal Procedure Rules* 2005 (S.I. 2005 No. 384) (*post*, § 7–313p).

7–161 Where notice of appeal is served on the Crown Court, in accordance with the 2005 rules, the Crown Court will then forward the notice to the Criminal Appeal Office together with the trial documents and any others that may be required: *Practice Direction (Criminal Proceedings: Consolidation)* [2002] 1 W.L.R. 2870, para. II.14.

(2) Right to representation

7–162 A right to representation in the Crown Court under the *Access to Justice Act* 1999, s.14, and Sched. 3, includes advice and assistance as to any appeal: see the definition of "representation" in section 26 of the 1999 Act (*ante*, § 6–146). In relation to advice and assistance, see also section 13 of the 1999 Act (*ante*, § 6–137) and regulation 4 of the *Criminal Defence Service (General) (No. 2) Regulations* 2001 (S.I. 2001 No. 1437) (*ante*, § 6–155). Applications for the grant of a representation order in respect of proceedings in the Court of Appeal are governed by regulation 10 of S.I. 2001 No. 1437 (*ante*, § 6–161). The selection of representatives is governed by section 15 of the Act, and regulations 13 to 15 of S.I. 2001 No. 1437 (*ante*, §§ 6–139, 6–165 *et seq.*).

In *R. v. Gibson*, 77 Cr.App.R. 151, the Court of Appeal held that the renewal of an application which had been refused to the full court was but a further step in the making of an application which was not finally dealt with until it was: (a) granted by the single judge; (b) refused by the single judge and not renewed; or (c) renewed to the full court and either granted or refused. Until one of those events had occurred the application was in being and attracted the provisions of section 30(7) of the *Legal Aid Act* 1974. The assistance given by counsel or solicitor in the preparation of the application for leave to appeal was covered by the original legal aid certificate. See now section 26 of the *Access to Justice Act* 1999, *ante*, § 6–146. **7–163**

In *R. v. Kearney*, 77 Cr.App.R. 187, the Court of Appeal rejected an argument based on *Gibson* that the original legal aid certificate covered the hearing of the application itself. It was further contended that the result of such a decision would be that there was no proper provision under legal aid for what might turn out to be a meritorious appeal. Lord Lane C.J. pointed out, however, that in some cases the court, having considered the papers, either of its own motion or at the invitation of the registrar, granted legal aid before the hearing. In any event, the court at the hearing might grant legal aid and proceed with the case if counsel was already present or adjourn the case to enable counsel to be instructed. That the Court of Appeal may grant a representation order before leave to appeal has been given was confirmed in *Revenue and Customs Prosecution Office v. Stokoe Partnership (M., J. and P. and Ministry of Justice, interveners)* [2007] A.C.D. 84, DC (*ante*, § 6–161).

The point at which a trial legal aid order expired was left open to question by the decision of Sachs J., sitting with assessors, in *R.M. Broudie & Co. (a Firm) v. Lord Chancellor, The Times*, July 4, 2000, QBD. His Lordship is reported as having held that it expires upon refusal of an application for leave by the single judge, and that he was not bound by anything said in *Gibson*. The report should, however, be treated with a degree of caution. First, there is no indication as to why his Lordship should have thought himself free not to follow *Gibson*. Secondly, there appears to be an element of contradiction, in that his Lordship apparently agreed with the view of the determining officer, who is quoted as having said that the registrar had always been of the opinion that the trial legal aid order ceases with the lodging of an application to renew. There is no suggestion in this report that either the determining officer or the judge thought that the registrar was wrong. The view attributed to the registrar, however, is plainly based on the decision of the court in *Gibson*.

In *R. v. Oates* [2002] 2 Cr.App.R. 39, CA, it was held that the right to free legal assistance "when the interests of justice so require", as guaranteed by Article 6(3)(c) of the ECHR (*post*, § 16–57), does not require that a defendant who renews an application for leave to appeal to the full court after refusal by the single judge should have free legal representation on the making of such application.

In connection with the obligation to give advice on the question of appeal, see also part XII of *Practice Direction (Costs: Criminal Proceedings)* [2004] 2 All E.R. 1070 (*ante*, § 6–114i).

(3) Guide to proceedings in the Court of Appeal

In October, 2008, the Registrar of Criminal Appeals published a new *Guide to Commencing Proceedings in the Court of Appeal (Criminal Division)*. This replaces the 1983 guide, as revised in 1997 and 2002. As Lord Judge C.J. points out in his foreword, the guide provides "invaluable advice as to the initial steps for commencing proceedings" in the criminal division. His Lordship then underlines the importance of well drafted grounds of appeal, which "assist the single judge when considering leave and serve to shorten any hearing before the full court", whereas "ill-prepared and prolix documents necessarily lead to wasted time spent on preparation and unnecessarily protracted hearings." **7–164**

The full text of the new guide is set out in Appendix J. It is also available on the internet (http://www.hmcourts-service.gov.uk/docs/proc_guide.pdf). Copies may be obtained free of charge from the Criminal Appeal Office and also from each location of the Crown Court.

[The next paragraph is § 7–179.]

(4) Drafting of grounds

7–179 The particulars of any alleged misdirection or non-direction should be set out in the grounds of appeal: *R. v. Fielding*, 26 Cr.App.R. 211, CCA. See also *R. v. Wyman*, 13 Cr.App.R. 163, CCA; and *Practice Direction (Criminal Procedings: Consolidation)* [2002] 1 W.L.R. 2870, para. II.15.1. And as to the need to give full particulars where one of the grounds of appeal is excessive intervention by the trial judge, see *R. v. Usher* [1998] 3 *Archbold News* 1, CA. However, counsel, in drafting grounds of appeal, should not go too far in the opposite direction. In *R. v. Pybus*, *The Times*, February 23, 1983, CA, it was said that the preparation of elaborate, detailed and lengthy grounds of appeal which, when truly analysed, demonstrated a miscarriage of justice, but also raised unsubstantiated details, not merely hampered the court in applying its mind to such points as might be valid, but also acted to cause injustice and was a breach of counsel's duty to his client not to bolster falsely his hopes of success. The need for the careful preparation of concise grounds of appeal and the time-wasting effect of "ill-prepared and prolix" grounds were stressed by Lord Judge C.J. in his foreword to *A Guide to Commencing Proceedings in the Court of Appeal (Criminal Division)*, *ante*, § 7–164.

Where complaint is made of particular passages in a summing up, amended particulars identifying the passages by references to the transcript should be given as soon as possible after the transcript has been obtained. Furthermore, it is counsel's duty to check grounds of appeal, which were drafted before a transcript was available against the transcript and to correct any inaccuracies: *R. v. Logan* [1974] Crim.L.R. 609.

It is counsel's duty when drafting grounds to see that all the material is fairly and properly put before the court. Sentences from the summing up should not be extracted out of context if within context they cannot properly be the subject of criticism: *R. v. Singh* [1973] Crim.L.R. 36. It is contrary to counsel's duty to put forward as a ground of appeal a general and sweeping attack on the summing up (*e.g.* "the summing up read as a whole was unfair in that it was a direction to the jury to convict ... ") which is wholly unjustified: *R. v. Mason*, 62 Cr.App.R. 236.

The Court of Appeal emphasised in *R. v. Haycraft*, 58 Cr.App.R. 121, and in *R. v. Kalia*, 60 Cr.App.R. 200, that proper compliance with the rules of court regarding the giving or amending of grounds of appeal is essential. A notice of appeal endorsed "grounds of appeal to follow" is not a notice of appeal within the rules: *R. v. Wilson* [1973] Crim.L.R. 572. As to the importance of complying with the *CAA* and the rules, see also *R. v. Suggett*, 81 Cr.App.R. 243, CA.

As to the variation and amplification of grounds, see *post*, § 7–183.

Grounds of appeal settled by counsel are not *per se* a protection against an order for loss of time; counsel should not settle grounds, or support them with written advice, unless he considers that the proposed appeal is properly arguable: see *R. v. Howitt*, 61 Cr.App.R. 327, CA, and *R. v. Hart*; *R. v. George*; *R. v. Clarke*; *R. v. Brown* [2007] 1 Cr.App.R. 31, CA, and *post*, § 7–227. A copy of an advocate's positive advice about the merits should be attached as part of the grounds: *Practice Direction (Criminal Proceedings: Consolidation)* [2002] 1 W.L.R. 2870, para. II.15.2.

(5) Defendant absconding before conviction

7–180 An application for leave to appeal by a defendant who absconded before the conclusion of his trial and is still at large is not to be treated as ineffective on the basis of the decision in *R. v. Jones* [1971] Q.B. 546, 55 Cr.App.R. 321, CA (*viz.* where a defendant, by absconding, puts it out of his power to give instructions at the proper time, the Court of Appeal will as a general rule take the view that his solicitors have not been duly authorised to prosecute appeal proceedings on his behalf); it was open to the court to conclude that his legal representatives did have actual or implied authority to submit the applicaiton: *R. v. Charles*; *R. v. Tucker* [2001] 2 Cr.App.R. 15, CA.

As to an applicant or appellant who escapes from custody or, being on bail, absconds prior to the determination of his case, see *post*, § 7–204.

(6) Death of applicant or appellant prior to hearing

7–181 See *post*, § 7–346.

(7) Extension of time

The relevant sections (ss.18 and 18A) and rules are set out, *ante*, §§ 7–157 *et seq.* **7–182**

Substantial grounds must be given for the delay before the court will exercise its power to extend the time allowed for giving the appropriate notice, and the longer the delay the more onerous will be this duty: see *R. v. Rigby*, 17 Cr.App.R. 111, CCA; *R. v. Lesser*, 27 Cr.App.R. 69, CCA; and *R. v. Hawkins (P.)* [1997] 1 Cr.App.R. 234, CA; but the court will take account of matters other than the reason for the delay, such as whether or not there might have been a conviction of some other offence on the facts: *R. v. Richardson* [1998] 10 *Archbold News* 1, CA. The fact that one of two persons jointly convicted has successfully appealed is not necessarily a ground for extending the time in favour of the other: *R. v. Marsh*, 25 Cr.App.R. 49, CCA; *R. v. Rigby*, *ante*. In deciding whether to grant an extension of time, the court will be influenced by the likelihood of a successful appeal if the extension is granted: *Marsh*, *ante*. Where an application for an extension is made by a defendant who absconded during the course of the trial, it will be subjected to rigorous scrutiny, and the Court of Appeal will be reluctant to grant such an application as to do so might put a premium on absconding: *R. v. Jones (No. 2)*, 56 Cr.App.R. 413; but it should not be routinely dismissed on the basis that there was no good reason for the delay; some regard should be had to the merits: *R. v. Charles*; *R. v. Tucker*, *ante*.

In exceptional circumstances, where it is apparent that there are matters worthy of consideration, an extension of time in which to appeal may be granted even where the delay is "inordinate" and unexplained; refusal merely raised the possibility of an eventual reference by the Criminal Cases Review Commission with inevitable further delay: *R. v. King* [2000] Crim.L.R. 835, CA.

In *R. v. R.* [2007] 1 Cr.App.R. 10, CA, it was said that there was a well established practice only to grant an extension of time where there had been a subsequent judicial development in the law if a substantial injustice would otherwise be done (distinguishing *R. v. Hendy* (*post*, § 19–70)). That this is indeed the practice of the court was affirmed in *R. v. Cottrell*; *R. v. Fletcher* [2008] 1 Cr.App.R. 7, CA. See also *R. v. Ramsden* [1972] Crim.L.R. 547, CA; *R. v. Mitchell*, 65 Cr.App.R. 185, CA; *R. v. Hawkins (P.)*, *ante*; *R. v. Campbell (No. 2)* [1997] Crim.L.R. 227, CA; *R. v. Jones (Beatrice)* [1999] Crim.L.R. 820, CA (extension refused where there had been delay even after the development in the law, and likely that defendant would have been convicted of other similar offences had they been included in the indictment); *R. v. Benjafield* [2003] 1 A.C. 1099, CA; and *R. v. Kansal* [2002] A.C. 69, CA. In *R. v. R.*, *ante*, the court said that in all such cases, the application for an extension should be referred by the registrar directly to the full court, so that the merits of the application may be investigated, with representation, perhaps on both sides, and a reasonable decision made as to whether or not there has been substantial injustice.

In *R. v. Ballinger* [2005] 2 Cr.App.R. 29, Ct-MAC, it was held that there was nothing incompatible with the ECHR in the imposition of time limits on the institution of appellate proceedings, provided that they were not too short or too rigorously enforced; and an applicant seeking an extension of time for leave to appeal on the ground of a violation of the provisions of Article 6 (*post*, § 16–57) had to show more than that there had been a breach of Article 6; he had also to show that he had suffered a substantial injury or injustice.

Variation and amplification of grounds

The *Criminal Procedure Rules* 2005 (S.I. 2005 No. 384), as amended by the *Criminal Procedure (Amendment No. 2) Rules* 2007 (S.I. 2007 No. 2317), unlike the original rules, contain no explicit provision for the variation or amplification of grounds of appeal, but there is a general power in rule 65.3 (*post*, § 7–313c) to vary the requirements of the rules, including by allowing a party to vary a notice that that party has served. **7–183**

Counsel ought not to assume that any ground of appeal which is not set out will be entertained by the Court of Appeal; should leave to amend be granted, it is most unlikely that further grounds will be entertained: see *Practice Direction (Criminal*

Proceedings: Consolidation) [2002] 1 W.L.R. 2870, para. II.15.1; *R. v. Haycraft*, 58 Cr.App.R. 121; *R. v. Upton* [1973] 3 All E.R. 318; and *R. v. Khan* [1991] Crim.L.R. 51.

7–184 See also *R. v. Kalia*, 60 Cr.App.R. 200 at 204. The Court of Appeal has drawn attention to the waste of time and money involved where there is a last minute application to vary or amplify grounds: see *R. v. Upton, ante*; and *R. v. Kalia, ante*.

(8) Bail pending appeal

Criminal Appeal Act 1968, s.19

7–185 **19.**—(1) The Court of Appeal may, subject to section 25 of the *Criminal Justice and Public Order Act* 1994, if they think fit,—

(a) grant an appellant bail pending the determination of his appeal; or

(b) revoke bail granted to an appellant by the Crown Court under paragraph (f) of section 81(1) of the *Supreme Court Act* 1981 or paragraph (a) above; or

(c) vary the conditions of bail granted to an appellant in the exercise of the power conferred by either of those paragraphs.

(2) The powers conferred by subsection (1) above may be exercised—

(a) on the application of an appellant; or

(b) if it appears to the registrar of criminal appeals of the Court of Appeal (hereafter referred to as "the registrar") that any of them ought to be exercised, on a reference to the court by him.

[This section is printed as substituted by the *CJA* 1982, s.29(2)(b); and as subsequently amended by the *CJA* 1988, s.170(1) and Sched. 15, para. 26; and the *CJPOA* 1994, Sched. 10, para 22.]

The effect of rule 68.7(1) of the *Criminal Procedure Rules* 2005 (S.I. 2005 No. 384) (in their original form) was that, until proper notice of application for leave to appeal had been given in accordance with section 18, it was impermissible to apply to a High Court judge, in his capacity as a judge of the Court of Appeal, for bail: see *R. v. Suggett*, 81 Cr.App.R. 243, CA. *Aliter*, if the High Court judge, in his capacity as a judge of the Crown Court, has granted a certificate that the case is fit for appeal. The replacement procedure rules (as to which, see *post*, § 7–313) contain no requirement corresponding to rule 68.7(1), but it is submitted that such a requirement flows from the terms of the 1968 Act itself, in that bail, under section 19 can only be granted to an "appellant", and a defendant will not have "appellant" status until he has served a notice of appeal, or of an application for leave to appeal, in accordance with section 18 and the rules (see the definition of "appellant" in s.51(1), *post*, § 7–350). As to the grant of certificates, see *ante*, §§ 7–37, 7–38, 7–128, 7–129.

The power to grant bail includes a power to grant bail to an appellant subject to a recommendation for deportation who is detained by virtue of paragraph 2(1) of Schedule 3 to the *Immigration Act* 1971 (*ante*, § 5–914): *R. v. Ofori and Tackie*, 99 Cr.App.R. 219, CA. (If the appeal is dismissed, the Court of Appeal may nevertheless direct his release under para. 2(1A) of Sched. 3.) A court proposing to grant bail or to direct the release of an offender subject to a recommendation for deportation might, depending on the circumstances, consider it wise to give the Secretary of State an opportunity to make representations: *ibid*.

Supreme Court [Senior Courts] Act 1981, s.81(1)–(1G)

7–186 **81.**—(1) The Crown Court may, subject to section 25 of the *Criminal Justice and Public Order Act* 1994, grant bail to any person—

(a)–(e) [ante, *§ 3–175*];

(f) to whom the Crown Court has granted a certificate under section 1(2) or 11(1A) of the *Criminal Appeal Act* 1968 or under subsection (1B) below; or

(g) [ante, *§ 3–175*];

and the time during which a person is released on bail under any provisions of this subsection shall not count as any part of any term of imprisonment or detention under his sentence.

(1A) The power conferred by subsection (1)(f) does not extend to a case to which section 12 *or 15* [, 15 or 16A] of the *Criminal Appeal Act* 1968 (appeal against verdict of not guilty by reason of insanity or against findings that the accused is under a disability and that he did the act or made the omission charged against him) applies.

(1B) A certificate under this subsection is a certificate that a case is fit for appeal on a ground which involves a question of law alone.

(1C) The power conferred by subsection (1)(f) is to be exercised—

(a) where the appeal is under section 1 or 9 of the *Criminal Appeal Act* 1968, by the judge who tried the case; and

(b) where it is under section 10 of that Act, by the judge who passed the sentence.

(1D) The power may only be exercised within twenty-eight days from the date of the conviction appealed against, or in the case of appeal against sentence, from the date on which sentence was passed or, in the case of an order made or treated as made on conviction, from the date of the making of the order.

(1E) The power may not be exercised if the appellant has made an application to the Court of Appeal for bail in respect of the offence or offences to which the appeal relates.

(1F) It shall be a condition of bail granted in the exercise of the power that, unless a notice of appeal has previously been lodged in accordance with subsection (1) of section 18 of the *Criminal Appeal Act* 1968—

(a) such a notice shall be so lodged within the period specified in subsection (2) of that section; and

(b) not later than 14 days from the end of that period, the appellant shall lodge with the Crown Court a certificate from the registrar of criminal appeals that a notice of appeal was given within that period.

(1G) If the Crown Court grants bail to a person in the exercise of the power, it may direct him to appear—

(a) if a notice of appeal is lodged within the period specified in section 18(2) of the *Criminal Appeal Act* 1968 at such time and place as the Court of Appeal may require; and

(b) if no such notice is lodged within that period, at such time and place as the Crown Court may require.

[As to the renaming of the 1981 Act, see *ante*, § 7–3. Subs. (1) is printed as amended by the *CJA* 1982, s.29(1); and the *CJPOA* 1994, Sched. 10, para. 48; subss. (1A) to (1G) were inserted by the *CJA* 1982, s.29(1); subs. (1A) is printed as subsequently amended by the *Criminal Procedure (Insanity and Unfitness to Plead) Act* 1991, s.7 and Sched. 3, para. 6. The words in square brackets in subs. (1A) are substituted for the italicised words, as from a day to be appointed, by the *Domestic Violence, Crime and Victims Act* 2004, s.58(1), and Sched. 10, para. 15. For the remainder of the section, see *ante*, §§ 3–176, 3–177.]

As to certificates under section 1 of the *CAA* 1968 and section 81(1B) of the *Supreme Court Act* 1981 (which seems to be superfluous in the light of the amendments to section 1 of the 1968 Act), see *ante*, §§ 7–37, 7–38. As to a certificate under section 11(1A) of the 1968 Act, see *ante*, § 7–125. In relation to the granting of bail generally, where a certificate has been granted, see *ante*, § 7–128. As to the procedure for making an application for a certificate, see rule 68.4 of the *Criminal Procedure Rules* 2005 (S.I. 2005 No. 384) (*post*, § 7–313r). **7–187**

"Appellant" in section 19 includes a person who has given notice of application for leave to appeal: see s.51 (1) of 1968 Act, *post*, § 7–350.

In deciding whether to grant bail pending appeal "the true question is, are there exceptional circumstances, which would drive the Court to the conclusion that justice can only be done by the granting of bail?": *R. v. Watton*, 68 Cr.App.R. 293, 297, CA. Such circumstances will exist where it appears prima facie that the appeal is likely to be successful or where there is a risk that the sentence will have been served by the time the appeal is heard: *ibid*. In *R. v. Landy*, 72 Cr.App.R. 237 (unreported on this point), the court granted an appellant bail pending appeal, having been satisfied that there was "a substantial point" to be argued on misdirection "and that it could result in the conviction being quashed". A further determining factor was that the hearing of the appeal would be delayed for some months in order for the transcript to be prepared.

There is no general principle that once an appellant has, after conviction, been released on bail there is never any question of sending him back to prison: *R. v. Cullis and Nash*, 53 Cr.App.R. 162. In *R. v. Kalia*, 60 Cr.App.R. 200, Roskill L.J. said: **7–188**

"This Court desires to say as plainly as possible that where (exceptionally), intending appellants or applicants are released on bail and delay follows in the hearing of the appeal, that delay cannot and must not be relied upon, whenever the appeal or application fails, as a reason for their not being sent back to prison to serve their sentence. That is usually made plain when bail is granted, and it must be clearly understood that this is so" (at p. 209).

See also *R. v. Callan*, 98 Cr.App.R. 467, CA.

Criminal Procedure Rules 2005 (S.I. 2005 No. 384), rr.68.8, 68.9, 68.10

Application for bail pending appeal or retrial

7–189 **68.8.**—(1) This rule applies where a party wants to make an application to the court about bail pending appeal or retrial.

(2) That party must serve an application in the form set out in the Practice Direction on—

(a) the Registrar, unless the application is with the appeal notice; and

(b) the other party.

(3) The court must not decide such an application without giving the other party an opportunity to make representations, including representations about any condition or surety proposed by the applicant.

Conditions of bail pending appeal or retrial

7–190 **68.9.**—(1) This rule applies where the court grants a party bail pending appeal or retrial subject to any condition that must be met before that party is released.

(2) The court may direct how such a condition must be met.

(3) The Registrar must serve a certificate in the form set out in the Practice Direction recording any such condition and direction on—

(a) that party;

(b) that party's custodian; and

(c) any other person directly affected by any such direction.

(4) A person directly affected by any such direction need not comply with it until the Registrar serves that person with that certificate.

(5) Unless the court otherwise directs, if any such condition or direction requires someone to enter into a recognizance it must be—

(a) in the form set out in the Practice Direction and signed before—

(i) the Registrar,

(ii) the custodian, or

(iii) someone acting with the authority of the Registrar or custodian;

(b) copied immediately to the person who enters into it; and

(c) served immediately by the Registrar on the appellant's custodian or vice versa, as appropriate.

(6) Unless the court otherwise directs, if any such condition or direction requires someone to make a payment, surrender a document or take some other step—

(a) that payment, document or step must be made, surrendered or taken to or before—

(i) the Registrar,

(ii) the custodian, or

(iii) someone acting with the authority of the Registrar or custodian;

(b) the Registrar or the custodian, as appropriate, must serve immediately on the other [*sic*] a statement that the payment, document or step has been made, surrendered or taken, as appropriate.

(7) The custodian must release the appellant where it appears that any condition ordered by the court has been met.

(8) For the purposes of section 5 of the *Bail Act* 1976 (record of decision about bail), the Registrar must keep a copy of—

(a) any certificate served under paragraph (3);

(b) a notice of hearing given under rule 65.7(1); and

(c) a notice of the court's decision served under rule 65.7(2).

(9) Where the court grants bail pending retrial the Registrar must serve on the Crown Court officer copies of the documents kept under paragraph (8).

Forfeiture of a recognizance given as a condition of bail

7–191 **68.10.**—(1) This rule applies where—

(a) the court grants a party bail pending appeal or retrial; and

(b) the bail is subject to a condition that that party provides a surety to guarantee that he will surrender to custody as required; but

(c) that party does not surrender to custody as required.

(2) The Registrar must serve notice on—

(a) the surety; and

(b) the prosecutor

of the hearing at which the court may order the forfeiture of the recognizance given by that surety.

(3) The court must not forfeit a surety's recognizance—

(a) less than 7 days after the Registrar serves notice under paragraph (2); and

(b) without giving the surety an opportunity to make representations at a hearing.

[Rules 68.8 to 68.10 are printed as substituted by the *Criminal Procedure (Amendment No. 2) Rules* 2007 (S.I. 2007 No. 2317).]

As to the forms to be used in connection with rules 68.8 and 68.9, see *post*, § 7–314b.

[The next paragraph is § 7–193.]

(9) Disposal of groundless appeal or application for leave to appeal

Criminal Appeal Act 1968, s.20

20. If it appears to the registrar that a notice of appeal or application for leave to appeal does not show any substantial ground of appeal, he may refer the appeal or application for leave to the Court for summary determination; and where the case is so referred the Court may, if they consider that the appeal or application for leave is frivolous or vexatious, and can be determined without adjourning it for a full hearing, dismiss the appeal or application for leave summarily, without calling on anyone to attend the hearing or to appear for the Crown thereon. **7–193**

[This section is printed as substituted by the *CJA* 1988, s.157.]

In relation to the exercise of the powers under section 20, see *per* Lawton L.J. in giving the judgment of the Court of Appeal in *R. v. Majewski* [1977] A.C. 443 at 451, CA and HL. (It should be noted that at the time the section was confined to grounds of appeal involving a question of law alone.) See also *R. v. Taylor* [1979] Crim.L.R. 649, CA ("frivolous" must include a ground of appeal which could not possibly succeed on argument).

(10) Preparation of the case for hearing

Criminal Appeal Act 1968, s.21

21.—(1) The registrar shall— **7–194**

(a) take all necessary steps for obtaining a hearing of any appeal or application of which notice is given to him and which is not referred and dismissed summarily under the foregoing section; and

(b) obtain and lay before the Court of Appeal in proper form all documents, exhibits and other things which appear necessary for the proper determination of the appeal or application.

(2) [*Provision for rules of court.*]

Procedural rules

Documents, exhibits, etc.

See, in particular, rules 65.10 (duty of party exhibiting a document or object) and 65.11 (registrar's duty to provide copy documents for appeal or reference) of the *Criminal Procedure Rules* 2005 (S.I. 2005 No. 384) (*post*, §§ 7–313j, 7–313k). **7–195**

The Registrar of Criminal Appeals

Rule 65.8(1) of the *Criminal Procedure Rules* 2005 (S.I. 2005 No. 384) (*post*, § 7–313h) imposes a duty on an officer of the Crown Court to provide the registrar with any document, object or information for which he asks within such period as he may require. Where, therefore, it is alleged that there was some irregularity at trial, the registrar may take advantage of this rule to investigate what happened at the Crown Court. **7–196**

7–197 As to the Registrar's functions in relation to representation orders under the *Access to Justice Act* 1999, see, *ante*, §§ 7–162, 7–169, 7–172, and regulations 7 and 10 of the *Criminal Defence Service (General) (No. 2) Regulations* 2001 (S.I. 2001 No. 1437), *ante*, §§ 6–158, 6–161.

(11) Procedural directions

7–197a As to the giving of procedural directions by the Court of Appeal, the single judge and the Registrar of Criminal Appeals, see sections 31B and 31C of the *CAA* 1968, *post*, §§ 7–236a, 7–236b.

(12) Abandonment of appeal

Criminal Procedure Rules 2005 (S.I. 2005 No. 384), rr.65.13, 65.14

Abandoning an appeal

7–198 **65.13.**—(1) This rule applies where an appellant wants to—

(a) abandon—

(i) an application to the court for permission to appeal, or

(ii) an appeal; or

(b) reinstate such an application or appeal after abandoning it.

(2) The appellant—

(a) may abandon such an application or appeal without the court's permission by serving a notice of abandonment on—

(i) the Registrar, and

(ii) any respondent

before any hearing of the application or appeal; but

(b) at any such hearing, may only abandon that application or appeal with the court's permission.

(3) A notice of abandonment must be in the form set out in the Practice Direction, signed by or on behalf of the appellant.

(4) On receiving a notice of abandonment the Registrar must—

(a) date it;

(b) serve a dated copy on—

(i) the appellant,

(ii) the appellant's custodian, if any,

(iii) the Crown Court officer, and

(iv) any other person on whom the appellant or the Registrar served the appeal notice; and

(c) treat the application or appeal as if it had been refused or dismissed by the Court of Appeal.

(5) An appellant who wants to reinstate an application or appeal after abandoning it must—

(a) apply in writing, with reasons; and

(b) serve the application on the Registrar.

As to the form to be used in connection with this rule, see *post*, § 7–314b.

Abandoning a ground of appeal or opposition

7–198a **65.14.**—(1) This rule applies where a party wants to abandon—

(a) a ground of appeal identified in an appeal notice; or

(b) a ground of opposition identified in a respondent's notice.

(2) Such a party must give written notice to—

(a) the Registrar; and

(b) every other party,

before any hearing at which that ground will be considered by the court.

[Rules 65.13 and 65.14 are printed as substituted by the *Criminal Procedure (Amendment No. 2) Rules* 2007 (S.I. 2007 No. 2317).]

As to the application of the rules in Part 65 to appeals and references under Parts 66 to 70, see rule 65.1, *post*, § 7–313a.

7–198b In *R. v. De Courcy*, 48 Cr.App.R. 323, CCA, it was held that if an appellant or his counsel does not abandon an appeal orally when it is called on, he cannot, as of right, abandon it after it has been opened, whether the appeal is against conviction or sentence; the appeal or part of it can be abandoned in such circumstances only by leave of the court. What was said in *De Courcy* was followed and approved in *R. v. Spicer*, 87 Cr.App.R. 297, CA. This was to prevent mischievous applications being made. This is reflected in rule 65.13(2) (*ante*).

Reinstatement

In *R. v. Medway* [1976] Q.B. 779, 62 Cr.App.R. 85 (a court of five judges), the Court of Appeal emphasised that alongside the jurisdiction which undoubtedly existed to give leave to withdraw an abandonment where it was shown that the circumstances were such as to enable the court to say that the abandonment should be treated as a nullity, there did *not* co-exist an inherent jurisdiction, in other special circumstances, which enabled the court to give such leave. The kernel of the "nullity test" is that the court must be satisfied that the mind of the applicant did not go with his act of abandonment. It was impossible to foresee when and how such a state of affairs might come about, and it would be wrong to make a list under headings—mistake, fraud, wrong advice and misapprehension—which purported to be exhaustive of the types of case where the jurisdiction could be exercised. *Medway* was followed and applied in *R. v. Burt* [2005] 1 *Archbold News* 1, CA. **7–199**

In *R. v. Grant* (2005) 149 S.J. 1186, CA, it was held that notice of abandonment of an application for leave to appeal could not be treated as a nullity where the applicant had instructed his solicitor by letter that he no longer wished to appeal, where the solicitor had thereafter written to him advising that a formal notice of abandonment had to be completed and proposing to serve such notice on the applicant's behalf if no reply was received in seven days, and where, as a result of various moves between different institutions, the applicant did not receive the solicitor's letter until after formal notice had been served on his behalf; at all material times, the applicant knew of the effect of his letter to his solicitors, and although he had not received the correspondence from his solicitor, he knew what the state of their instructions were and he knew that those instructions would stand unless countermanded by him; his mind having gone with the notice of abandonment, it could not be said to be a nullity; all that the applicant had lost was the opportunity afforded to him by his solicitor to change his mind; that being so, by virtue of rule 68.22(4) of the 2005 rules (in their original form), and the decision in *R. v. Medway (ante)*, the application was deemed to have been refused.

(13) Case summaries

Practice Direction (Criminal Proceedings: Consolidation), para. II.18
[2002] 1 W.L.R. 2870

Criminal Appeal Office summaries

II.18.1 To assist the court the Criminal Appeal Office prepares summaries of the cases coming before it. These are entirely objective and do not contain any advice about how the court should deal with the case or any view about its merits. They consist of two parts. **7–200**

II.18.2 Part I, which is provided to all of the advocates in the case, generally contains (a) particulars of the proceedings in the Crown Court, including representation and details of any co-accused, (b) particulars of the proceedings in the Court of Appeal (Criminal Division), (c) the facts of the case, as drawn from the transcripts, advice of the advocates, witness statements and/or the exhibits, (d) the submissions and rulings, summing up and sentencing remarks. Should an advocate not want any factual material in his advice taken into account this should be stated in the advice.

II.18.3 The contents of the summary are a matter for the professional judgment of the writer, but an advocate wishing to suggest any significant alteration to Part I should write to the Registrar of Criminal Appeals. If the registrar does not agree, the summary and the letter will be put to the court for decision. The court will not generally be willing to hear oral argument about the content of the summary.

II.18.4 Advocates may show Part I of the summary to their professional or lay clients (but to no one else) if they believe it would help to check facts or formulate arguments, but summaries are not to be copied or reproduced without the permission of the Criminal Appeal Office; permission for this will not normally be given in cases involving children or sexual offences or where the Crown Court has made an order restricting reporting.

II.18.5 Unless a judge of the High Court or the Registrar of Criminal Appeals gives a direction to the contrary in any particular case involving material of an explicitly salacious or sadistic nature, Part I will also be supplied to appellants who seek to represent themselves before the full court or who renew to the full court their applications for leave to appeal against conviction or sentence.

II.18.6 Part II, which is supplied to the court alone, contains (a) a summary of the grounds of appeal and (b) in appeals against sentence (and applications for such leave), summaries of the antecedent histories of the parties and of any relevant pre-sentence, medical or other reports.

II.18.7 All of the source material is provided to the court and advocates are able to draw attention to anything in it which may be of particular relevance.

(14) Listing practice

7–200a *As to the fixing of appeals*, hearing dates would be fixed by list officers in the Criminal Appeal Office under the superintendence of the Registrar of Criminal Appeals, who could give such directions as he deemed necessary; in fixing appeals, regard would be had to an advocate's commitments but the Court of Appeal takes precedence over all lower courts, and wherever practicable a lower court will have regard to that principle when making arrangements to release an advocate to appear in the Court of Appeal; in case of difficulty the lower court should communicate with the registrar, and in general an advocate's commitment in a lower court would not be regarded as a good reason for not accepting a date proposed by the listing officer; *as to time estimates*, the Criminal Appeal Office summary would contain an estimate for the length of the whole of the appeal, including delivery of judgment; the list officer would rely on that estimate unless one of the advocates provided a different estimate within seven days of receipt of the summary; where the estimate was considered by an advocate to be inaccurate or to be in need of alteration (*e.g.* because a ground of appeal was to be abandoned), the advocate was under a duty to inform the court promptly, in which case the registrar would reconsider the time estimate; *as to target times*, in respect of appeals received on or after March 22, 2004, the following target times would apply; in the case of sentence appeals, 14 days from receipt by listing officer to fixing a hearing date, and 14 days from fixing the date to the date of hearing; in the case of conviction appeals, the corresponding times would be 21 and 42 days respectively; and, where a witness is to attend, the times would be 28 and 52 days respectively; where legal vacations impinged on those periods, they might be extended, and where expedition was required they might be abridged; and, for these purposes, "appeal" included an application for leave to appeal which required an oral hearing: *Practice Direction (Criminal Proceedings: Consolidation)*, para. II.2 [2004] 1 W.L.R. 1285 (*sub nom. Practice Direction (Criminal Proceedings: Appeals Listing)*).

(15) Public interest immunity hearing

7–200b Where an issue arises as to the trial judge's conduct of an *ex parte* public interest immunity hearing, (i) the approach should be the same whether the hearing had been on notice or not; (ii) the Court of Appeal would have to review all the material, with the prosecution present, but a summary should be provided, for the purposes of assistance, where the material was voluminous; (iii) such review should be conducted by the same constitution of the court as would hear the appeal; (iv) enough time should be allowed for the appointment of special counsel, if the need arose; (v) in the majority of cases, where the material could be read in an hour or two, the hearing should take place in the first week in which the constitution sat, with the appeal following in the third week; (vi) where the material was unusually voluminous, special listing arrangements would have to be made: *R. v. McDonald, Rafferty and O'Farrell*, *The Times*, November 8, 2004, CA.

As to hearings about public interest rulings being in private, see rule 65.6 of the *Criminal Procedure Rules* 2005 (S.I. 2005 No. 384) (*post*, § 7–313f).

(16) Delay

As to delay in hearing an appeal and the right to trial within a reasonable time, as guaranteed by Article 6 of the ECHR, see *Massey v. U.K.*, *post*, § 16–73. **7–200c**

As to a reduction in sentence as a possible remedy for a violation of Article 6 in relation to the hearing of an appeal, see *ante*, § 7–143a.

H. THE HEARING

(1) Presence of appellant

Criminal Appeal Act 1968, s.22

22.—(1) Except as provided by this section, an appellant shall be entitled to be present, if he wishes it, on the hearing of his appeal, although he may be in custody. **7–201**

(2) A person in custody shall not be entitled to be present—

(a) where his appeal is on some ground involving a question of law alone; or

(b) on an application by him for leave to appeal; or

(c) on any proceedings preliminary or incidental to an appeal; or

(d) where he is in custody in consequence of a verdict of not guilty by reason of insanity or of a finding of disability,

unless the Court of Appeal give him leave to be present.

(3) The power of the Court of Appeal to pass sentence on a person may be exercised although he is for any reason not present.

(4) The Court of Appeal may give a live link direction in relation to a hearing at which the appellant is expected to be in custody but is entitled to be present (by virtue of subsection (1) or leave given under subsection (2)) at any time before the beginning of that hearing.

(5) For this purpose—

(a) a "live link direction" is a direction that the appellant (if he is being held in custody at the time of the hearing) is to attend the hearing through a live link from the place at which he is held; and

(b) "live link" means an arrangement by which the appellant is able to see and hear, and to be seen and heard by, the Court of Appeal (and for this purpose any impairment of eyesight or hearing is to be disregarded).

(6) The Court of Appeal—

(a) must not give a live link direction unless the parties to the appeal have had the opportunity to make representations about the giving of such a direction; and

(b) may rescind a live link direction at any time before or during any hearing to which it applies (whether of its own motion or on the application of a party).

[This section is printed as amended by the *PJA* 2006, s.48(1).]

Criminal Procedure Rules 2005 (S.I. 2005 No. 384), rr.68.11, 68.12

Right to attend hearing

68.11. A party who is in custody has a right to attend a hearing in public unless— **7–201a**

(a) it is a hearing preliminary or incidental to an appeal, including the hearing of an application for permission to appeal; or

(b) that party is in custody in consequence of—

(i) a verdict of not guilty by reason of insanity, or

(ii) a finding of disability.

Power to vary determination of appeal against sentence

68.12.—(1) This rule applies where the court decides an appeal affecting sentence in a party's absence. **7–201b**

(2) The court may vary such a decision if it did not take account of something relevant because that party was absent.

(3) A party who wants the court to vary such a decision must—

(a) apply in writing, with reasons;

(b) serve the application on the Registrar not more than 7 days after—

(i) the decision, if that party was represented at the appeal hearing, or

(ii) the Registrar serves the decision, if that party was not represented at that hearing.

[Rules 68.11 and 68.12 are printed as substituted by the *Criminal Procedure (Amendment No. 2) Rules* 2007 (S.I. 2007 No. 2317).]

7–202 There is no obligation upon an appellant who is neither in custody nor on bail to attend the hearing; the court will proceed to determine the appeal in his absence where the correct steps have been taken to give him notice of the date of the hearing: *R. v. Field*, unreported, October 13, 1975.

In *R. v. Crisp*, *The Times*, June 18, 2002, CA, it was held that an appeal against conviction could proceed in the absence of an appellant who refused to comply with a requirement imposed by the security officers responsible for transporting him to the Royal Courts of Justice that he be handcuffed whilst in transit.

In *R. v. Spruce*; *R. v. Anwar* [2006] 1 Cr.App.R.(S.) 11, CA, it was said that, given that section 22(1) conferred on a defendant the right to be to present if he wished to hear his appeal, but a defendant had no such right under section 22(2) on an application for leave, where a defendant's appeal against sentence was allowed in his absence, after a renewed application for leave to the full court, the matter could be re-listed, at the defendant's request, for reconsideration in his presence; but the court's decision would not be varied on the second hearing unless there was an entirely fresh matter to be considered which had a bearing on the sentence; otherwise the appellant or counsel would be invited to comment only on the court's earlier judgment; the court did not encourage applications for re-hearing; and it was not right to say either that (i) if a defendant was not present he had the right to re-apply for hearing of the appeal to take place before a differently constituted court; the right was not in such wide terms; or (ii) there was a risk that a freshly constituted court might uphold the original sentence; that was not a realistic risk if the case was re-listed. The court added that counsel appearing on a renewed application for leave should obtain instructions in advance to allow him to proceed, if the occasion arose, in the appellant's absence (if leave were granted); if counsel had no instructions, he could normally be expected either to obtain instructions on the day of the hearing or, if that was impossible, to communicate the result of his appeal to the appellant and his right to have the matter re-listed; the question of a representation order at a re-listed hearing would not normally be considered until the conclusion of the hearing and would not normally be made unless relevant fresh material was presented to the court.

Rule 68.12 of the 2005 rules (*ante*, § 7–201b) was intended to give legislative effect to the practice described in *R. v. Spruce*; *R. v. Anwar*. As to whether it was successful in this regard, see *Criminal Law Week* 2007/31/14.

(2) Appellant who has died

7–203 See section 44A of the *CAA* 1968, *post*, § 7–346.

(3) Appellant who has escaped or absconded

7–204 The Court of Appeal has a discretion, in exceptional circumstances to hear an appeal where an offender has escaped from custody: *R. v. Gooch* [1998] 2 Cr.App.R. 130, CA. The practice of the Court of Criminal Appeal in such circumstances was to adjourn the appeal or to dismiss it, according to the justice of the case: *R. v. Flower* [1966] 1 Q.B. 146, 50 Cr.App.R. 22 (although the court did in fact deal with the appeal in that case as it was apparent that all the points which it was sought to raise were points which had been thoroughly canvassed by counsel on behalf of two other appellants). See also *R. v. Panayi and Karte (No. 2)* [1989] 1 W.L.R. 187, CA.

Semble, the approach of the Court of Appeal will be the same where a person released on bail pending appeal fails to surrender to custody by the time his appeal is called on: see *R. v. Whiting*, 85 Cr.App.R. 78 (application adjourned, warrant issued); and *R. v. Carter*, 98 Cr.App.R. 106 (appeal dismissed). A person on bail pending appeal will be notified that he should surrender to custody prior to the court commencing its list on the day his appeal or application is to be heard.

(4) Adjournment

7–204a The Court of Appeal has power to regulate the way in which appeals are conducted before it, which power includes a discretionary power to adjourn the hearing of an appeal if practical considerations so require; and the desirable practice in appeals where leave to appeal has been given that all grounds that the appellant wishes to raise must be raised and resolved in that appeal (*R. v. Berry* [1991] 1 W.L.R. 125), applies equally to a case referred by the Criminal Cases Review Commission; such practice is desirable because it saves time and expense and avoids the risk of inconsistent views being taken of the same case: *R. v. Smith (Wallace Duncan) (No. 2)* [1999] 2 Cr.App.R. 444, CA.

(5) Skeleton argument

**Practice Direction (Criminal Proceedings: Consolidation), para. II.17
[2002] 1 W.L.R. 2870**

Skeleton arguments

II.17.1 In all appeals against conviction a skeleton argument from the advocate for the appellant is to be lodged with the Registrar of Criminal Appeals and served on the prosecuting authority within 14 days of receipt by the advocate of the notification of the grant of leave to appeal against conviction or such longer period as the registrar or the court may direct. The skeleton may refer to an advice, which should be annexed with an indication of which parts of it are relied upon, and should include any additional arguments to be advanced. **7–205**

II.17.2 The advocate for the prosecuting authority should lodge with the registrar and the advocate for the appellant his skeleton argument within 14 days of the receipt of the skeleton argument for the appellant or such longer (or, in exceptional cases, shorter) period as the registrar or the court may direct.

II.17.3 Practitioners should ensure that, where reliance is placed upon unreported cases in skeleton arguments, short headnotes are included.

II.17.4 Advocates should ensure that the correct Criminal Appeal Office number appears at the beginning of their skeleton arguments and that their names are at the end.

II.17.5 A skeleton argument should contain a numbered list of the points the advocate intends to argue, grouped under each ground of appeal, and stated in no more than one or two sentences. It should be as succinct as possible, the object being to identify each point, not to argue it or elaborate on it. Each listed point should be followed by full references to the material to which the advocate will refer in support of it, *i.e.* the relevant passages in the transcripts, authorities, *etc.* It should also contain anything the advocate would expect to be taken down by the court during the hearing, such as propositions of law, chronologies, *etc.* If more convenient, these can be annexed to the skeletons rather than included in it. For points of law, the skeleton should state the point and cite the principal authority or authorities in support with reference to the passages where the principle is enunciated. Chronologies should, if possible, be agreed with the opposing advocate before the hearing. Respondents' skeletons should follow the same principles.

(6) Attendance and role of prosecution

The role of the prosecution in the appeal process was considered in *R. v. McIlkenny*, 93 Cr.App.R. 287, CA. Where counsel has formed the view that an appeal should succeed, it is proper for him not to oppose it: *ibid*. The court, however, highlighted the difficulties to which such a stance can give rise in the adversarial system under which the Court of Appeal operates, especially in fresh evidence cases. **7–206**

Where counsel for the prosecution took the view in relation to an appeal against conviction that it could not be opposed, which view was communicated to the court and to the appellant, the prosecution were not estopped from instructing fresh counsel and seeking to uphold the conviction where the second counsel instructed took a different view; and the court was not, in any event, bound by any such views: *R. v. Hartnett* [2003] Crim.L.R. 719, CA.

The prosecution are generally represented only on an appeal against conviction. However, the court may require the attendance of counsel for the prosecution on an appeal against sentence or on an application for leave to appeal where some point of principle is involved, or the case is one of great weight or difficulty or the court is likely to require information which the prosecution might be able to supply (and see *post*, § 7–207b).

Criminal Procedure Rules 2005 (S.I. 2005 No. 384), r.68.6

Respondent's notice

7–207 **68.6.**—(1) The Registrar—

(a) may serve an appeal notice on any party directly affected by the appeal; and

(b) must do so if the Criminal Cases Review Commission refers a conviction, verdict, finding or sentence to the court.

(2) Such a party may serve a respondent's notice, and must do so if—

(a) that party wants to make representations to the court; or

(b) the court or the Registrar so directs.

(3) Such a party must serve the respondent's notice on—

(a) the appellant;

(b) the Registrar; and

(c) any other party on whom the Registrar served the appeal notice.

(4) Such a party must serve the respondent's notice not more than 14 days after the Registrar serves—

(a) the appeal notice; or

(b) a direction to do so.

(5) The respondent's notice must be in the form set out in the Practice Direction.

(6) The respondent's notice must—

(a) give the date on which the respondent was served with the appeal notice;

(b) identify each ground of opposition on which the respondent relies, numbering them consecutively (if there is more than one), concisely outlining each argument in support and identifying the ground of appeal to which each relates;

(c) identify the relevant sentencing powers of the Crown Court, if sentence is in issue;

(d) summarise any relevant facts not already summarised in the appeal notice;

(e) identify any relevant authorities;

(f) include or attach any application for the following, with reasons—

(i) an extension of time within which to serve the respondent's notice,

(ii) bail pending appeal,

(iii) a direction to attend in person a hearing that the respondent could attend by live link, if the respondent is in custody,

(iv) the introduction of evidence, including hearsay evidence and evidence of bad character,

(v) an order requiring a witness to attend court,

(vi) a direction for special measures for a witness; and

(g) identify any other document or thing that the respondent thinks the court will need to decide the appeal.

[Rule 68.6 is printed as substituted by the *Criminal Procedure (Amendment No. 2) Rules* 2007 (S.I. 2007 No. 2317).]

Practice Direction (Criminal Proceedings: Consolidation), para. II.1
[2003] 4 All E.R. 665

Appeals against sentence—the provision of notice to the prosecution

7–207a **II.1.1** The Registrar of Criminal Appeals will notify the relevant prosecution authority in the event that: (a) leave to appeal against sentence is granted by the single judge; or (b) the single judge or the Registrar refers an application for leave to appeal against sentence to the full court for determination; or (c) the Registrar becomes aware that counsel for the applicant will be appearing at a renewed application for leave to appeal against sentence.

II.1.2 The prosecution will have seven days from the grant of leave by the single judge or the referral by the Registrar to notify the Registrar if they wish to be represented at the hearing OR to request sight of the grounds of appeal and/or any comments made by the single judge when granting leave or referring the case to the full court. Upon such a request, the prosecution will have a further seven days from receipt to notify the Registrar if they wish to be represented at the hearing.

II.1.3 Occasionally, for example, where the single judge fixes a hearing date at short notice, the Registrar may have to foreshorten the period specified in II.1.2, above.

II.1.4 In relation to (c) in para II.1.1, the prosecution will have 72 hours or, if the case is listed, 48 hours, to notify the Registrar that they wish to be represented at the hearing. Should the prosecution require sight of the grounds of appeal and the single judge's comments, such a request should be made as expeditiously as possible.

II.1.5 If the prosecution wishes to be represented at any hearing, the notification should include details of counsel instructed, a time estimate and an indication whether a skeleton argument will be lodged no later than 14 days before the hearing (or such shorter period as may be necessary). If a skeleton argument is to be lodged, it must be served on the court and the applicant/appellant.

II.1.6 An application by the prosecution to remove a case from the list for counsel's convenience, or to allow further preparation time, will rarely be granted.

II.1.7 There may be occasions when the Court of Appeal Criminal Division will grant leave to appeal to an unrepresented applicant and proceed forthwith with the appeal in the absence of the appellant and counsel. In those circumstances there will be no opportunity to notify the prosecution.

II.1.8 As a court of review, the Court of Appeal Criminal Division would expect the prosecution to have raised any specific matters of relevance with the sentencing judge in the first instance.

II.1.9 When the prosecution attend a hearing as a result of this practice direction, the prosecution should not volunteer assistance in relation to any unrepresented applicant.

II.1.10 This direction will come into force as from 10 November 2003.

II.1.11 The prosecution are already invited to appear and respond, as a matter of course, in appeals against confiscation orders and where the court is considering issuing sentencing guidelines. This practice will continue without change.

II.1.12 This practice direction replaces the existing protocol whereby the prosecution were responsible for lodging a letter of interest with the Registrar of Criminal Appeals via the Crown Court.

In *R. v. Dempster*, 85 Cr.App.R. 176, Lord Lane C.J. said that as problems of sentencing became more and more complicated, so help from the Crown became more and more necessary: the court hoped for the more frequent presence of counsel for the Crown on sentence appeals. **7–207b**

Where the prosecution are to be represented, the court has emphasised the desirability of counsel who prosecuted at the trial appearing on the appeal, unless there are exceptionally impelling reasons to the contrary: *R. v. Phillips* [1973] Crim.L.R. 573.

(7) Leave to call additional evidence

Criminal Appeal Act 1968, s.23

23.—(1) For the purposes of an appeal, or an application for leave to appeal, under this Part of this Act the Court of Appeal may, if they think it necessary or expedient in the interests of justice— **7–208**

(a) order the production of any document, exhibit or other thing connected with the proceedings, the production of which appears to them necessary for the determination of the case;

(b) order any witness to attend for examination and be examined before the Court, (whether or not he was called in the proceedings from which the appeal lies); and

(c) receive any evidence which was not adduced in the proceedings from which the appeal lies.

(1A) The power conferred by subsection (1)(a) may be exercised so as to require the production of any document, exhibit or other thing mentioned in that subsection to—

(a) the Court;

(b) the appellant;

(c) the respondent.

(2) The Court of Appeal shall, in considering whether to receive any evidence, have regard in particular to—

(a) whether the evidence appears to the Court to be capable of belief;

(b) whether it appears to the Court that the evidence may afford any ground for allowing the appeal;

(c) whether the evidence would have been admissible in the proceedings from which the appeal lies on an issue which is the subject of the appeal; and

(d) whether there is a reasonable explanation for the failure to adduce the evidence in those proceedings.

(3) Subsection (1)(c) above applies to any evidence of a witness (including the appellant) who is competent but not compellable. ...

(4) For the purposes of an appeal, or an application for leave to appeal, under this Part of this Act, the Court of Appeal may, if they think it necessary or expedient in the interests of justice, order the examination of any witness whose attendance might be required under subsection (1)(b) above to be conducted, in manner provided by rules of court, before any judge or officer of the Court or other person appointed by the Court for the purpose, and allow the admission of any depositions so taken as evidence before the Court.

(5) A live link direction under section 22(4) does not apply to the giving of oral evidence by the appellant at any hearing unless that direction, or any subsequent direction of the court, provides expressly for the giving of such evidence through a live link.

(6) In this section, "respondent" includes a person who will be a respondent if leave to appeal is granted.

[This section is printed as amended and repealed in part by the *CAA* 1995, ss.4(1) and 29, and Scheds 2, para. 4(1) and (3), and 3; the *PJA* 2006, s.48(2); and the *CJIA* 2008, s.47, and Sched. 8, paras 1 and 10.]

7–209 Where there is an application for leave to call fresh evidence, it is necessary to provide the court in advance with all information relevant to the issue under subsection (2)(d); if a lengthy or complicated explanation is needed, it would usually be appropriate for the court to be provided with an affidavit or signed statement from the appellant or his solicitor setting out the matters relied on: *R. v. Trevor* [1998] Crim.L.R. 652, CA.

An application to call fresh evidence should be supported by affidavit evidence from all involved in the obtaining of the new evidence; this is particularly important where the fresh evidence is that of a witness who had previously made a statement to different effect, for the circumstances surrounding the obtaining of the new evidence are potentially highly relevant to its credibility: *R. v. Gogana*, *The Times*, July 12, 1999, CA; *R. v. James* [2000] Crim.L.R. 571, CA.

The court has power to hear evidence from the appellant but it has no jurisdiction to compel him to give evidence, either orally or by way of affidavit: *R. v. Guppy*, *The Times*, March 8, 1994, CA (93/2422/Z5).

In *R. v. Adams* [2007] 1 Cr.App.R. 34, the Court of Appeal observed *obiter*, (i) that it was implicit in *R. v. Mirza*; *R. v. Connor and Rollock* (*post*, § 7–215), that the court would be entitled to hear evidence from jurors to resolve an issue of alleged jury bias raised on an appeal; (ii) that since it was difficult to draw the line between inquiries as to the deliberations of the jury and inquiries as to extrinsic matters (*e.g.* an allegation of bias), it would be highly undesirable for any person to seek to interview a juror without first obtaining leave from the court; and (iii) that whilst hearing evidence from a juror or jurors may be the only way to resolve an issue of bias, the circumstances in which such a course would be necessary would be rare and exceptional; if the judge had directed the jury that they should report any irregularities during the course of the trial to the court, silence would almost certainly be taken as a basis for assuming that no irregularity had occurred. See also *R. v. Charnley* [2007] 2 Cr.App.R. 33 (letter from a juror was received as evidence on appeal, and questions were asked of the jury as to how their deliberations had progressed); and *R. v. Pintori*, *ante*, § 7–88.

The Court of Appeal may examine such material as it thinks fit in deciding whether to order production of documents at the hearing of the appeal; it will not in principle restrict itself to reading material relating to the trial and such documents as the parties place before it: *R. v. Callaghan*, 86 Cr.App.R. 181, CA.

In *R. v. D. and J.* [1996] 1 Cr.App.R. 455, the Court of Appeal held that whilst evidence admitted under section 23 must be admissible (*post*), the section is not confined to evidence (referring to s.23(1)(a)). Accordingly, it was held that a judgment of a Family Division judge who had considered issues which were identical or similar to the issues before the jury or which bore on those issues could be considered by the Court of Appeal. *D. and J.* was followed in *R. v. B.* [1999] 1 *Archbold News* 2, in which the court specifically rejected criticism of the decision, to the effect that it was at variance with the purpose of the Act and with authority, in the 1999 edition of this work.

Where, subsequent to conviction, material becomes available to the prosecution which they would have been under a duty to disclose prior to conviction, but in relation to which they would have made an application to the court for an order that the material should not be disclosed on the ground that it was not in the public interest to disclose it, it is open to the Court of Appeal to examine the material *ex parte*: *R. v. Botmeh and Alami* [2002] 1 Cr.App.R. 28, CA. This procedure was approved in *Botmeh and Alami v. U.K.* (2008) 46 E.H.R.R. 31, ECtHR (the fact that the Court of Appeal had been able to consider the impact of the new material on the safety of the applicants' convictions in the light of detailed argument from their counsel and the fact that the undisclosed material had been found to add nothing of significance to what had been disclosed at trial, meant that the failure to place the material before the trial judge was in the particular circumstances remedied by the subsequent procedure before the Court of Appeal).

Determination of appeals where fresh evidence admitted

See *ante*, §§ 7–50, 7–51. **7–210**

As to the proper approach, where fresh evidence is not tested by cross-examination on behalf of the Crown, see *R. v. McIlkenny*, 93 Cr.App.R. 287 at 313, CA.

Construction of section 23(1), (2)

Section 23 is concerned only with admissible evidence: see *R. v. Wallace and Short*, 67 Cr.App.R. 291, CA (*per* Roskill L.J. at p. 298), and *R. v. Lattimore*, 62 Cr.App.R. 53, CA (*per* Scarman L.J. at p. 56). This will include prosecution evidence erroneously ruled to be inadmissible at the trial: see *R. v. Gilfoyle* [1996] 1 Cr.App.R. 302, CA; and evidence which has only become available to the prosecution after the conclusion of the trial: see *R. v. Craven* [2001] 2 Cr.App.R. 12, CA; and notwithstanding that its purpose was not to evaluate or rebut fresh evidence called by the appellant, provided only that it tended to assist the court in furthering the interests of justice: *R. v. Hanratty* [2002] 3 All E.R. 534, CA; but not, however, where its purpose is to advance an entirely new basis for conviction, which had never been put before the jury: *R. v. Fitzgerald* (2006) 150 S.J. 985, CA. **7–211**

It was held in *R. v. Beresford*, 56 Cr.App.R. 143, CA, that there is a "reasonable explanation" for a failure to adduce evidence at trial if the evidence could not with reasonable diligence have been obtained for use at the trial. Reasonable diligence must include the need for the defendant himself to play a proper part in assisting in the preparation of the defence. Nowhere is that more important than in the case of an alibi (as to which, see *R. v. Hampton and Brown*, *post*, § 7–215). The words "on an issue" refer to an issue which was raised at the trial and is the subject of the appeal: *R. v. Melville*, 62 Cr.App.R. 100, CA. The existence or otherwise of a reasonable explanation for not calling the evidence at trial is, however, but one factor to be taken account of in deciding whether it is necessary or expedient in the interests of justice to receive the evidence: *R. v. Cairns* [2000] Crim.L.R. 473, CA. Evidence may be received even though none of the conditions in subsection (2) are satisfied: *R. v. Sale*, *The Times*, June 16, 2000, CA.

In *R. v. McLoughlin* [2000] 3 *Archbold News* 1, CA, it was held that if the evidence to which the application relates complies with paragraphs (a) to (d) of section 23(2), the court should then consider the evidence without hearing the witness(es), and if having considered it, it thinks the conviction unsafe, it should quash the conviction and, if appropriate, order a retrial. This, however, runs together what is a clearly defined two-stage process. The matters set out in section 23(2) are to be taken into account in deciding whether to receive the evidence. If the decision is taken that the evidence should be received, then the witnesses must be called (unless the evidence is agreed). Evidence which appears to be capable of belief (s.23(2)(a)) may lose all credibility as a result of cross-examination. *McLoughlin* was disapproved in *Sale*, *ante*, where it was said that the court would sometimes find it necessary to hear evidence *de bene esse* to determine whether it was capable of belief or whether or not it affords a ground of appeal.

Evidence of facts of which the appellant was aware at the time of trial cannot constitute "fresh" or "new" evidence, even though his legal representatives may have had no knowledge of it: *R. v. Hayes*, unreported, July 19, 2002, CA ([2002] EWCA Crim. 1945); but see *R. v. Underwood* (2003) 147 S.J. 657, CA, where the court treated evidence of a prosecution witness's convictions as "fresh" where they had not been disclosed to the defence by the prosecution, even though the appellant had himself known about them, and had so instructed his solicitor.

Practical application

7–212 In *R. v. Boal and Cordrey* [1965] 1 Q.B. 402, 48 Cr.App.R. 342, CCA, where a co-defendant who had pleaded guilty was willing to give evidence on appeal, having been unwilling to do so at trial, it was held that since he had been compellable, the evidence could not be regarded as "fresh", it being the practice of the Court of Criminal Appeal at that time to insist on this requirement. This is no longer a requirement, the current provision allowing of considerable flexibility; nevertheless, it seems likely that the Court of Appeal will be slow to entertain any application to call a co-defendant who could have been called at trial (see *R. v. Stokes* [1997] 6 *Archbold News* 1, CA).

7–213 Evidence may be received of matters which have arisen only after conviction, which, of course, is itself the explanation for the failure to adduce it at the trial: *R. v. Ditch*, 53 Cr.App.R. 627; *R. v. Conway*, 70 Cr.App.R. 4; *R. v. Williams and Smith* [1995] 1 Cr.App.R. 74; *R. v. Twitchell* [2000] 1 Cr.App.R. 373. In *Ditch*, evidence was admitted of a confession of a convicted co-defendant of the applicant made after conviction which exculpated the applicant. Although the court would be careful in acting on such evidence, it will nevertheless in a proper case, where it accepts the co-defendant's evidence as genuine, quash the conviction. In *Conway*, the evidence which it was sought to adduce was of statements made by prosecution witnesses after the conclusion of the trial which, it was said, were inconsistent with their evidence at the trial. It was held that the proper procedure in such circumstances, in accordance with section 4 of the *Criminal Procedure Act* 1865 (*post*, § 8–125), was for the witnesses themselves to be called so that the alleged statements could be put to them and, thereafter, if they denied making them, the court could hear the evidence of the witnesses that the applicant sought to call. In *Williams and Smith*, evidence of discreditable conduct of police officers subsequent to the trial of the appellants was admitted. Their integrity had been in issue; the court held that the evidence discredited their earlier testimony. See also *R. v. Edwards (M.)* [1996] 2 Cr.App.R. 345, CA (refusal of juries to accept evidence of key police witnesses in respect of like allegations in subsequent cases); and *Twitchell*, *ante*.

7–214 As to the reception of expert evidence on appeal, see *R. v. Melville*, 62 Cr.App.R. 100, CA, and *R. v. Jones (Steven)* [1997] 1 Cr.App.R. 86, in which the Court of Appeal considered the issue in the context of the amendments to section 23 effected by the 1995 Act. Such evidence is admissible on appeal, but section 23(2)(d) acknowledges the crucial obligation on a defendant to advance his whole defence before the jury. There would rarely be a reasonable explanation for failure to call such evidence at trial, for expert witnesses were interchangeable in a way in which factual witnesses were not (as to which, see also *R. v. Lomas*, 53 Cr.App.R. 256). It would subvert the trial process if a defendant were to be generally free to mount on appeal an expert case which, if sound, could and should have been advanced before the jury.

For an example of expert evidence being admitted on appeal to support a defence (diminished responsibility) not advanced at trial, see *R. v. Hobson* [1998] 1 Cr.App.R. 31 (the disease from which the appellant was said to be suffering at the time of the killing—"battered women's syndrome"—was not a condition which would readily have been considered by British psychiatrists at the time of the trial, the condition having only entered the standard British classification of mental diseases since the trial). Leave may be given where it is at least arguable that the illness of the appellant was itself the explanation of the course taken at trial: see *R. v. Borthwick* [1998] Crim.L.R. 274, CA; and *R. v. Weekes* [1999] 2 Cr.App.R. 520, CA (*ante*, § 7–107), and *R. v. Gilfillan* [1999] 3 *Archbold News* 1, CA (98 01047 54), to similar effect; but whether or not the appellant's illness prevented him from reaching a rational decision as to his defence is not the sole test for determining whether the evidence should be received: see *R. v.*

Neaven [2006] 6 *Archbold News* 1, CA (where there had been no evidence of diminished responsibility at the time of the trial). *Cf. R. v. Straw* [1995] 1 All E.R. 187, CA (where defendant fit to plead and properly advised in relation to diminished responsibility, but gave express instructions that such defence was not to be advanced, an application to call evidence on this issue will not be allowed); *R. v. Sale, ante* (it would only be in a rare case that evidence would be received in support of a defence which was completely different to the one advanced at trial, the public interest being best served when the parties presented their case at trial and not years later); *R. v. Hakala* [2002] Crim.L.R. 578, CA (opportunity for the defendant to give evidence is provided at trial, and that is where he must take it; accordingly, an appellant will only be permitted to present a factual case inconsistent with his instructions and sworn testimony at trial in the most exceptional circumstances); *R. v. Andrews (Jane Dawn Elizabeth)* [2004] Crim.L.R. 376, CA (a professional coming late into the field in support of a defence which was advanced at trial, and who may have something to say which requires the court to exercise its powers under section 23 could not be excluded as a possibility, but it should be remembered that in almost every case, there is room for only one trial); and *R. v. Latus* [2007] 1 *Archbold News* 1, CA (appellant's explanations evidenced a deliberate tactical decision not to allow diminished responsibility to be investigated because he believed that he had a good chance of acquittal based on his denial of all responsibility, *R. v. Borthwick* and *R. v. Neaven, ante*, being distinguished).

More recent examples of expert evidence being admitted on appeal are *R. v. T.S.*, unreported, January 23, 2008, CA ([2008] EWCA Crim. 6) (defence at trial to charge of rape was consent; evidence that appellant may have been suffering from Asperger's Syndrome admitted; this may have gone to his ability to determine the complainant's intentions or desires and thus to his *mens rea* and to the jury's assessment of his evidence; it also may have explained his unusual behaviour at trial); and *R. v. Holdsworth* [2008] 5 *Archbold News* 1, CA (fresh evidence as to causation in case of murder where foundation of prosecution case had been uncontradicted medical evidence and where the fresh evidence provided a credible alternative medical explanation that was consistent with the appellant's account of events; no consideration was given to the provisions of s.23(2), the court merely concluding that it was in the "interests of justice" for the evidence to be admitted).

R. v. Clark (Michael) [1999] Crim.L.R. 573, is out-of-step with the requirement that the defendant should advance his whole defence at trial. Having alleged at his trial one form of police impropriety to explain his confession, he was allowed on appeal to allege a completely different and much more serious impropriety, his explanation for not having done so at trial being that he thought no-one would believe him. The case is best explained by reference to its own facts, the Court of Appeal having apparently taken cognisance of the fact of an official investigation which had commenced since conviction into allegations of like misconduct by officers in the same police force. The legal basis for heeding such matter is unclear.

Evidence may be received of events at the trial or of matters which relate to an alleged irregularity at the trial: *R. v. Hircock* [1970] 1 Q.B. 67, 53 Cr.App.R. 51; *R. v. Smith (Winston)*, 61 Cr.App.R. 128; and *R. v. Kemble*, 91 Cr.App.R. 178 (evidence in relation to the tenets of the Muslim faith as to what formalities were required to make an oath binding). Where complaint is made in relation to the conduct of the trial judge, evidence in support thereof is a requirement (in the absence of agreement): see *R. v. Wood* [1996] 1 Cr.App.R. 207 at 214; *R. v. Tancred* [1997] 6 *Archbold News* 2; and *R. v. Moringiello* [1997] Crim.L.R. 902. The court will not inquire into what occurred in the jury room while the jury were considering their verdict: *R. v. Thompson*, 46 Cr.App.R. 72, CCA; *R. v. Bean* [1991] Crim.L.R. 843, CA; *R. v. Mickleburgh* [1995] 1 Cr.App.R. 297, CA; *R. v. Miah and Akhbar* [1997] 2 Cr.App.R. 12, CA; *R. v. Hart* [1998] Crim.L.R. 417, CA; *R. v. Millward* [1999] 1 Cr.App.R. 61, CA; and *R. v. Qureshi* [2002] 1 Cr.App.R. 33; and *R. v. Moran*, unreported, November 29, 2007, CA ([2007] EWCA Crim. 2947) (in which the court refused to countenance an investigation on the basis of letters from two jurors alleging they had been pressurised into giving a verdict, and observing that the phenomenon of a juror being present at, and **7–215** apparently assenting to, a guilty verdict, but then regretting it, is unusual but not particularly rare); and this is so even where the evidence, if admitted, would provide a prima facie case of partiality: *R. v. Mirza; R. v. Connor and Rollock* [2004] 1 A.C. 1118, HL (but see now *R. v. Adams, ante*, § 7–209). Accordingly, in *R. v. Chionye*, 89 Cr.App.R. 285, CA, it was held that where, after convicting the defendant, a jury learned of facts which were not disclosed during the trial and told the judge that the absence of such evidence had influenced their verdict, the Court of Appeal should ignore what the jury told the judge, but should admit the material which had not been disclosed during the trial under section 23 and decide the appeal in the light of the "fresh evidence".

Cf. R. v. Young (S.) [1995] 2 Cr.App.R. 379, CA, where the court caused affidavits to be taken from all 12 jurors and the bailiffs as to events whilst they were accommodated overnight at a hotel after they had retired to consider their verdict.

Where it is sought to call a witness who was not called at trial as a result of the advice or decision of the appellant's counsel and it is alleged that that advice or decision was mistaken, the Court of Appeal will not admit the evidence even if it disagreed with counsel's decision, unless the court was left with a lurking doubt that injustice had been caused by flagrantly incompetent advocacy: *R. v. Roberts* [1990] Crim.L.R. 122, CA. See also *R. v. Shields and Patrick* [1977] Crim.L.R. 281, CA, where it was said that it would seldom if ever be a "reasonable explanation" for not calling a witness that the risk of calling him was at the time considered too great and counsel advised that he should not be called; and *R. v. Hampton* [2006] Crim.L.R. 60, where it was said that the court would be most unlikely to conclude that it was "expedient in the interests of justice" for a witness to be called to give evidence of an alibi where the witness had been able and willing to give evidence at trial, albeit upset, and a deliberate and informed decision had been made not to call her. A much more lax attitude was taken in *R. v. Loughran* [1999] Crim.L.R. 404, CA, where it was said that counsel's "tactical decision" not to elicit certain facts about the appellant constituted a reasonable explanation for a failure to call the evidence at trial.

In *R. v. Bevan*, 98 Cr.App.R. 354, CA, the principal ground of appeal was an allegation that the appellant's solicitors and counsel had been negligent, particularly in relation to the question whether or not the appellant should give evidence on his own behalf. The court heard evidence from both solicitors and counsel. It was made clear that this was an exceptional course, "done so that it can never be said ... that [the appellant] has not had the opportunity of ventilating his grievance against his advisers who, he says, let him down" (see p. 357).

Section 23 applies to an appeal against sentence: see *R. v. Bennett*, 52 Cr.App.R. 514, CA, and *R. v. Guppy, The Times*, March 8, 1994, CA (93/2422/Z5), in which it was said that it was possible to conduct a *Newton* hearing (*ante*, § 5–74) on appeal.

Fresh evidence following plea of guilty

7–215a It is submitted that as with the application of section 2(1) of the 1968 Act to appeals following pleas of guilty, so with applications to admit fresh evidence in such cases, there are no special principles. It is convenient, however, to deal with such exceptional appeals under a separate heading.

In *R. v. Lee*, 79 Cr.App.R. 108 (*ante*, § 7–46b), the court said that it would be very rare that the discretion to admit fresh evidence under section 23 would be exercised where there had been an unequivocal plea of guilty. *Lee* was referred to in *R. v. Swain* [1986] Crim.L.R. 480, CA, where the appellant had changed his plea to guilty during the course of the trial. His conviction was quashed after the Court of Appeal had admitted evidence from which they concluded that there was a real risk that at the time of changing his plea the appellant was affected by delusions as a result of taking drugs. The court appears to have acted under section 2(1) of the 1968 Act, holding that the conviction was unsafe and unsatisfactory.

See also *R. v. Verney*, 2 Cr.App.R. 107, CCA, and *R. v. Foster* [1985] Q.B. 115, 79 Cr.App.R. 61, in both of which convictions, based upon pleas of guilty, were quashed as a result of the receipt of fresh evidence. In *Verney*, it established an alibi; in *Foster*, it established the guilt of another person.

Funding issues

Where an appellant funded by the Criminal Defence Service seeks to call expert evidence, it is the duty of counsel to submit an advice on evidence (identifying the expert sought to be called and the nature of the evidence to be given) to the registrar, so as to enable the registrar to decide whether or not to extend the representation order to cover the costs of the expert and any other witnesses (upon refusal, directions may be sought from the court); where the representation order is not extended, it must be made clear to the expert that whilst the court might extend the order after the hearing, it may not do so: *R. v. Bowman (Legal Aid)* [2006] 7 *Archbold News* 1, CA. **7–215b**

Criminal Appeal Act 1968, s.23A

Power to order investigations

23A.—(1) On an appeal against conviction or an application for leave to appeal the Court of Appeal may direct the Criminal Cases Review Commission to investigate and report to the Court on any matter if it appears to the Court that— **7–216**

(a) in the case of an appeal, the matter is relevant to the determination of the appeal and ought, if possible, to be resolved before the appeal is determined;

(aa) in the case of an application for leave to appeal, the matter is relevant to the determination of the application and ought, if possible, to be resolved before the application is determined;

(b) an investigation of the matter by the Commission is likely to result in the Court being able to resolve it; and

(c) the matter cannot be resolved by the Court without an investigation by the Commission.

(1A) A direction under subsection (1) above may not be given by a single judge, notwithstanding that, in the case of an application for leave to appeal, the application may be determined by a single judge as provided for by section 31 of this Act.

(2) [*Direction to be in writing*.]

(3) Copies of such a direction shall be made available to the appellant and the respondent.

(4) Where the Commission have reported to the Court of Appeal on any matter which they have been directed under subsection (1) above to investigate, the Court—

(a) shall notify the appellant and the respondent that the Commission have reported; and

(b) may make available to the appellant and the respondent the report of the Commission and any statements, opinions and reports which accompanied it.

(5) In this section "respondent" includes a person who will be a respondent if leave to appeal is granted.

[This section was inserted by the *CAA* 1995, s.5(1). It is printed as amended by the *CJA* 2003, s.313.]

Procedure

In the *Criminal Procedure Rules* 2005 (S.I. 2005 No. 384), see, in particular, rule 68.3(2) (*post*, § 7–313p) which states that an appeal notice must include any application for the introduction of evidence, including hearsay and evidence of bad character, an order requiring the attendance of a witness, a direction for special measures for a witness or a direction for special measures for the giving of evidence by the appellant, rule 68.6 (*ante*, § 7–207), which makes broadly corresponding requirements of a respondent's notice, and rule 68.7(1), which applies Parts 29 (special measures directions (*post*, §§ 8–56 *et seq.*)), 30 (use of live television link other than for vulnerable witnesses (*post*, § 8–67)), 34 (hearsay (*post*, §§ 11–52 *et seq.*)), 35 (bad character evidence (*post*, §§ 13–111 *et seq.*)) and 36 of the 2005 rules (evidence of a complainant's previous sexual behaviour (*post*, §§ 8–123h *et seq.*)) "with such adaptations as the court or registrar may direct". **7–217**

[The next paragraph is § 7–221.]

(8) Declaration of incompatibility

See rule 65.12 of the *Criminal Procedure Rules* 2005 (S.I. 2005 No. 384) (*post*, § 7–313l). **7–221**

I. NOTIFICATION OF RESULT OF APPEAL AND MATTERS DEPENDING THEREON

(1) Notifying result of appeal

7–222 See the *Criminal Procedure Rules* 2005 (S.I. 2005 No. 384), r.65.9 (*post*, § 7–313i).

As to notification of the result of applications dealt with on the papers, see *R. v. Cadnam-Smith*, *post*, § 7–223.

(2) Alteration of decision, relisting of cases

7–223 In *R. v. Cross* [1973] Q.B. 937, 57 Cr.App.R. 660, the Court of Appeal held that the criminal division has jurisdiction to withdraw and alter a decision or order until such decision or order has been recorded by the proper officer of the court of trial, pursuant to rule 68.29(2) (see now r.65.7(2)) of the *Criminal Procedure Rules* 2005 (S.I. 2005 No. 384) (but see *ante*, § 7–222) and directions appearing in the *Crown Court Manual*.

In *R. v. Daniel* [1977] Q.B. 364, 64 Cr.App.R. 50, the Court of Appeal said that the limits set in *Cross* do not apply where what has happened is a nullity, as in *R. v. Majewski* [1977] A.C. 443, CA and HL, where the court had ruled that earlier proceedings in which it had purported to dispose of an appeal under section 20 of the 1968 Act (*ante*, § 7–193) were a nullity because there had been no proper reference of the appeal to the court as required by that section. Having referred to *Majewski*, Lawton L.J., giving the court's judgment in *Daniel*, said of *Cross*:

> "But does it apply when an applicant has been deprived of his right to be represented by counsel? The Court clearly has jurisdiction within the ambit of the 1968 Act and Rules to see that no injustice is done to any applicant or appellant. If in any particular case because of a failure of the Court to follow the Rules or the well-established practice there is a likelihood that injustice may have been done, then it seems to be right, despite the generality of what was said in *Cross*, that a case should be relisted for hearing" (pp. 369–370, 53).

Daniel was considered in *R. v. Blake*, *The Times*, October 20, 1995, CA, in which it was said that where an application for leave to appeal was refused on a non-counsel basis, the court would be reluctant to relist on a counsel basis unless satisfied that before the non-counsel hearing, counsel had been prepared to appear and his non-appearance was because of a failure of communication beyond the applicant's control. See also *R. v. Dowling*, *The Times*, October 20, 1995, CA (*post*, § 7–234); *R. v. Grantham* [1969] 2 Q.B. 574, 53 Cr.App.R. 369, Ct-MAC; *R. v. Pegg* [1988] Crim.L.R. 370, CA; and *R. v. Berry*, 92 Cr.App.R. 147, CA.

In *R. v. Roberts* [1990] Crim.L.R. 122, the Court of Appeal had announced its decision at the conclusion of argument that the appeal would be dismissed, with reasons to be given later. At the adjourned hearing, counsel for the appellant had sought to re-open argument, having submitted an opinion which the court had read. The court said that it would normally regard itself as *functus officio* once it had announced its decision and would not in the instant case take the rare step of hearing further oral argument.

The Court of Appeal has inherent power to see that its orders are properly carried out. The court had quashed a conviction and set aside the judgment on the ground that the trial had been a nullity and had ordered that a *venire de novo* should issue. Owing to a mistake in the office, the order was drawn up in the form appropriate to a verdict of acquittal. The court, on its attention being directed to the error, set aside the aforementioned order and made an order in the proper form (*post*, § 7–352): *R. v. Gatenby*, 34 Cr.App.R. 255, CCA. See also *Lawrie v. Lees* (1881) 7 App.Cas. 19, *per* Lord Penzance at p. 34, approved by the Court of Appeal in *R. v. Agritraders Ltd* [1983] Q.B. 464 at 470, 76 Cr.App.R. 183 at 189. In *Agritraders Ltd*, it was said that, apart from the "slip rule" there was no reason to doubt "that the inherent jurisdiction of this court would enable us to reconsider an order for costs, so as to enlarge it in some particular way, if we were satisfied that the omission to make the material application was due to a genuine accidental omission on the part of counsel" (*per* Watkins L.J. at pp. 470–471, 190); and in *R. v. Moore* [2003] 1 W.L.R. 2170, in which the court reviewed an order for costs out of central funds which it had had no power to make, it was said that whilst the power to review its own decision was exercisable only in exceptional circumstances (*Taylor v. Lawrence* [2003] Q.B. 528, CA (Civ. Div.)), the making of an order out of public funds when the public were not represented was capable of constituting such circumstances.

In *R. v. Cadnam-Smith* [2001] Crim.L.R. 644, the Court of Appeal held that where it had considered a prosecution application for the certification of a point of general public importance and for leave to appeal to the House of Lords [Supreme Court], pursuant to section 33 of the 1968 Act (*post*, § 7–318), and the court having considered the applications on the papers had certified such a point but refused leave, but had then failed to communicate that decision to the prosecution until 24 days later, the court was not *functus officio*; to hold otherwise would be to deny the prosecution their statutory right to apply to the House of Lords [Supreme Court] for leave to appeal within 14 days of the date of refusal by the Court of Appeal; accordingly, it was open to the court to re-list the matter and to re-issue its decisions; for the future, the most obvious practice to adopt in such a situation would be for the decision to be given in open court, the parties having been notified so that they could attend; the court could then indicate whether it required oral argument; where an application was considered on the papers, the safest way of informing the parties would be by oral communication followed by fax.

As to the relisting of an appeal where the court is not unanimous, see *R. v. Shama*, 91 Cr.App.R. 138, CA, *ante*, § 7–28.

(3) Costs

See the *Prosecution of Offences Act* 1985, Pt II (ss.16–21), *ante*, Chapter 6. **7–224**

(4) Effect of appeal on sentence

Criminal Appeal Act 1968, s.29

29.—(1) The time during which an appellant is in custody pending the determination of his appeal shall, subject to any direction which the Court of Appeal may give to the contrary, be reckoned as part of the term of any sentence to which he is for the time being subject. **7–225**

(2) Where the Court of Appeal give a contrary direction under subsection (1) above, they shall state their reasons for doing so; and they shall not give any such direction where—

(a) leave to appeal has been granted; or

(b) a certificate has been given by the judge of the court of trial under—

(i) section 1 or 11(1A) of this Act; or

(ii) section 81(1B) of the *Supreme Court [Senior Courts] Act* 1981; or

(c) the case has been referred to them by the Secretary of State under section 17 of this Act.

(3) When an appellant is granted bail under section 19 of this Act, the time during which he is released on bail shall be disregarded in computing the term of any sentence to which he is for the time being subject.

(4) The term of any sentence passed by the Court of Appeal under section 3, 4, 5, 11 or 13(4) of this Act shall, unless the Court otherwise direct, begin to run from the time when it would have begun to run if passed in the proceedings from which the appeal lies.

[This section is printed as amended by the *CJA* 1988, s.170(1) and Sched. 15, para. 27; and as amended, as from a day to be appointed, by the *Constitutional Reform Act* 2005, s.59(5), and Sched. 11, para. 1(2) (renaming of 1981 Act).]

In 1980, Lord Widgery C.J. issued a practice direction to remind practitioners and prisoners of the provisions of sections 29 and 31. This has now been incorporated, with amendments, into the consolidated criminal practice direction.

Practice Direction (Criminal Proceedings: Consolidation), para. II.16 [2002] 1 W.L.R. 2870

II.16. Both the court and the single judge have power in their discretion to direct that part of the time during which an applicant is in custody after putting in his notice of application for leave to appeal should not count towards sentence. Those who contemplate putting in such a notice and their legal advisers should bear this in mind. It is important that those contemplating an appeal should seek advice and should remember that it is useless to appeal without grounds and that grounds should be substantiated and particularised and not a **7–226**

mere formula. Where an application devoid of merit has been refused by the single judge and a direction for loss of time has been made, the full court, on renewal of the application, may direct that additional time shall be lost if, once again, it thinks it right so to exercise its discretion in all the circumstances of the case.

7–227 This practice direction supplements what was said by James L.J. when giving the Court of Appeal's judgment in *R. v. Howitt*, 61 Cr.App.R. 327. His Lordship stated that the court wished to make clear:

> "that an application for leave to appeal to the single judge is not a formality. It is just as important a step as an application to the full court and it must not be considered that an application to the single judge is merely one stage of no great consequence in the ultimate application to the full court, if the matter is pursued that far. … There are cases where counsel may quite properly consider that the grounds that can be put forward in support of the appeal are ones which justify an application to find out the advice of the single judge, but, if the single judge is adverse, then not worthy to pursue further. But in so far as there is a tendency … to settle somewhat nebulous grounds of appeal merely to have the first bite of the cherry that tendency is to be discouraged" (at pp. 328–329).

7–228 In *R. v. Hart*; *R. v. George*; *R. v. Clarke*; *R. v. Brown* [2007] 1 Cr.App.R. 31, CA, it was said that despite previous exhortations, the number of unmeritorious applications for leave to appeal was so substantial that it was necessary for the court to exercise its power under section 29 to order that time in custody pending determination of an application for leave to appeal should not count towards sentence more frequently in future than it had done in the past; the fact that counsel had advised (even to the extent of drafting an advice supporting grounds of appeal) that there were grounds of appeal was not dispositive of the question whether an application was totally unmeritorious. In *R. v. Brind*, unreported, April 16, 2008, CA ([2008] EWCA Crim. 934), it was pointed out that this applied equally to applications for leave to appeal against conviction; and that the forms relating to appeals having now been amended to allow a single judge considering the matter under section 31 of the 1968 Act (*post*, § 7–231) to indicate whether in his view an appeal is one which is without merit, where that part of the form has been so completed by the single judge, an applicant who renews his application to the full court and is unsuccessful should expect that an order for loss of time will be made.

Complexity and bulk do not turn an unarguable application into one which is arguable and do not operate as some kind of unspoken barrier to an order that time in custody pending determination of an application for leave to appeal should not count towards sentence: *R. v. Greaves*, *The Times*, April 28, 2008, CA.

Where there has been a dispute as to the proper factual basis for sentencing and the trial judge has followed the correct procedure for determining that issue and has rejected the defendant's account, an order for loss of time can be expected even at the single judge stage if the version advanced by the defendant was wholly fanciful: *R. v. Ahmed (N.)*, 80 Cr.App.R. 295, CA.

European Convention on Human Rights

7–229 Neither the right to liberty under Article 5 of the ECHR (*post*, § 16–43), nor the right to a fair trial under Article 6 (*post*, § 16–57) were violated by a direction under section 29(1): *Monnell and Morris v. U.K.*, 10 E.H.R.R. 205, ECtHR.

(5) Suspension of order for restitution, etc., pending appeal

Criminal Appeal Act 1968, s.30

7–230 **30.**—(1) The operation of an order for the restitution of property to a person made by the Crown Court shall, unless the Court direct to the contrary in any case in which, in their opinion, the title to the property is not in dispute, be suspended until (disregarding any power of a court to grant leave to appeal out of time) there is no further possibility of an appeal on which the order could be varied or set aside, and provision may be made by rules of court for the custody of any property in the meantime.

(2) The Court of Appeal may by order annul or vary any order made by the court of trial for the restitution of property to any person, although the conviction is not quashed; and the order, if annulled, shall not take effect and, if varied, shall take effect as so varied.

(3) Where the *House of Lords* [Supreme Court] restores a conviction, it may make any order for the restitution of property which the court of trial could have made.

[This section is printed as substituted by the *CJA* 1988, s.170(1) and Sched. 15, para. 28. The reference to the "Supreme Court" is substituted for the reference to the "House of Lords" as from a day to be appointed: *Constitutional Reform Act* 2005, s.40(4), and Sched. 9, para. 16(1) and (2).]

Subsection (2) is in identical terms to the original subsection (4). It is doubtful whether this subsection was intended itself to confer any right of appeal: see *ante*, § 7–121.

A person in whose favour a compensation order is made shall not be entitled to receive the amount due to him until, disregarding any power of a court to grant leave to appeal out of time, there is no further possibility of an appeal on which the order could be varied or set aside: *PCC(S)A* 2000, s.132(1). Section 132(3) and (4) contain provisions which correspond to section 30(2) and (3). For section 132, see *ante*, § 5–413.

J. SUPPLEMENTARY PROVISIONS

(1) Effect of interim hospital orders

Criminal Appeal Act 1968, s.30A

Effect of interim hospital orders

30A.—(1) This section applies where the Court of Appeal— **7–230a**

(a) make an interim hospital order by virtue of any provision of this Part, or

(b) renew an interim hospital order so made.

(2) The court below shall be treated for the purposes of section 38(7) of the *Mental Health Act* 1983 (absconding offenders) as the court that made the order.

[This section was inserted by the *CJIA* 2008, s.47, and Sched. 8, paras 1 and 8, with effect from July 14, 2008 (*Criminal Justice and Immigration Act 2008 (Commencement No. 2) Order* 2008 (S.I. 2008 No. 1586)). It applies to an interim hospital order made by the court on or after that date: S.I. 2008 No. 1586, art. 2(3), and Sched. 2, para. 5.]

(2) Powers exercisable by a single judge

Criminal Appeal Act 1968, s.31

31.—(1) There may be exercised by a single judge in the same manner as by the Court of Appeal and subject to the same provisions— **7–231**

(a) the powers of the Court of Appeal under this Part of this Act specified in subsection (2) below;

(aa) the power to give leave under section 14(4B) of the *Criminal Appeal Act* 1995;

(b) the power to give directions under section *4(4)* [3(4)] of the *Sexual Offences (Amendment) Act 1976* [1992]; and

(c) the powers to make orders for the payment of costs under sections 16 to 18 of the *Prosecution of Offences Act* 1985 in proceedings under this Part of this Act.

(2) The powers mentioned in subsection (1)(a) above are the following—

(a) to give leave to appeal;

(b) to extend the time within which notice of appeal or of application for leave to appeal may be given;

(c) to allow an appellant to be present at any proceedings;

(ca) to give a direction under section 22(4);

(d) to order a witness to attend for examination;

(e) to exercise the powers conferred by section 19 of this Act;

(f) to make orders under section 8(2) of this Act and discharge or vary such orders;

(g) [*repealed*];

(h) to give directions under section 29(1) of this Act;

(i) to make orders under section 23(1)(a).

(2ZA) The power of the Court of Appeal to renew an interim hospital order made by them by virtue of any provision of this Part may be exercised by a single judge in the same manner as it may be exercised by the Court.

(2A) The power of the Court of Appeal to suspend a person's disqualification under section 40(2) of the *Road Traffic Offenders Act* 1988 may be exercised by a single judge in the same manner as it may be exercised by the Court.

(2B) The power of the Court of Appeal to grant leave to appeal under section 159 of the *Criminal Justice Act* 1988 may be exercised by a single judge in the same manner as it may be exercised by the Court.

(2C) The power of the Court of Appeal, under section 130 of the *Licensing Act* 2003, to suspend an order under section 129 of that Act may be exercised by a single judge in the same manner as it may be exercised by the Court.

(2D) The power of the Court of Appeal to grant leave to appeal under section 9(11) of the *Criminal Justice Act* 1987 may be exercised by a single judge in the same manner as it may be exercised by the Court.

(2E) The power of the Court of Appeal to grant leave to appeal under section 35(1) of the *Criminal Procedure and Investigations Act* 1996 may be exercised by a single judge in the same manner as it may be exercised by the Court.

(3) If the single judge refuses an application on the part of an appellant to exercise in his favour any of the powers above specified, the appellant shall be entitled to have the application determined by the Court of Appeal.

[This section is printed as amended, and repealed in part, by the *Costs in Criminal Cases Act* 1973, Scheds 1 and 2; the *RTA* 1974, Sched. 6; the *Bail Act* 1976, s.12, and Sched. 2; the *Sexual Offences (Amendment) Act* 1976, s.5(6); the *CJA* 1982, s.29(2)(c); the *CJA* 1988, s.170(1), and Sched. 15, paras 29 and 30; the *Road Traffic (Consequential Provisions) Act* 1988, s.4, and Sched. 3, para. 4(1); the *Courts Act* 2003, s.87(1); the *CJA* 2003, s.331, and Sched. 32, paras 86 and 87; the *Licensing Act* 2003, s.198(1), and Sched. 6, paras 38 and 40; the *PJA* 2006, s.48(3); and the *CJIA* 2008, s.47, and Sched. 8, paras 1, 9 and 11; and as amended, as from a day to be appointed, by the *YJCEA* 1999, s.67(1), and Sched. 4, para. 4(1), (3) (substitution of references in square brackets in subs. (1)(b)). The insertion of subs. (2ZA) by the 2008 Act, s.47, and Sched. 8, paras 1 and 9, applies only to an interim hospital order made by the court on or after July 14, 2008: S.I. 2008 No. 1586 (*ante*, § 7–230a), art. 2(3), and Sched. 2, para. 5.]

As to the making of directions under section 29(1) of the Act by the single judge, see *ante*, §§ 7–225 *et seq.*

The single judge may also grant an application for a representation order in respect of proceedings in the Court of Appeal or the House of Lords: *Criminal Defence Service (General) (No. 2) Regulations* 2001 (S.I 2001 No. 1437), reg. 10(1), *ante*, § 6–161. Where such an application is made to a judge, he may refer it to the registrar: *ibid.*, reg. 10(2).

The judge may refer the case to the full court: see *R. v. Munns*, 1 Cr.App.R. 4, CCA, and *A Guide to Commencing Proceedings in the Court of Appeal (Criminal Division)*, para. A.10 (Appendix J).

It is improper to ask a High Court judge to act under section 31 until the proper application for leave to appeal has been made in accordance with section 18(1): *R. v. Suggett*, 81 Cr.App.R. 243, CA, *ante*, § 7–185.

Criminal Appeal Act 1968, s.45(2)

7–232 **45.**—(2) The references in sections 23A, 31 to 31C, 44 and 44A of this Act to a single judge are to any judge of the Court of Appeal or of the High Court.

[Subs. (2) is printed as amended by the *CAA* 1995, s.29, and Sched. 2, para. 4(1) and (5)(b); the *CJA* 2003, s.331, and Sched. 32, paras 86 and 89(b); and the *Courts Act* 2003, s.109(1), and Sched. 8, para. 128.]

For section 44, see § 7–336, *post*.

7–233 In the *Criminal Procedure Rules* 2005 (S.I. 2005 No. 384), rule 65.4 (*post*, § 7–313d) provides for an application for an extension of time within which to serve a notice or make an application, and rule 65.5 provides for renewal to a judge of an application refused by the registrar and renewal to the court of an application refused by a judge. Service of the renewed application must be within 14 days of refusal or of service of the refusal if the applicant was not present, in person or by live link, when the original application was refused.

7–234 The power to extend the time limit retrospectively will rarely be exercised, the only issue being whether the applicant has an excuse for not having renewed his application within the time limit: *R. v. Doherty*, 55 Cr.App.R. 548. The power will not be exercised unless there is some good and reasonable excuse for failure to act within the prescribed period. A change of heart is not an excuse. Moreover, it is contemplated that, at the time when notice of a single judge's refusal of leave to appeal is received by the applicant, he should not require further advice, but rather should be able to make up his own mind as to whether to refer the matter to the court, and so an excuse based upon his inability to obtain advice will not be a sufficient excuse: *R. v. Sullivan*, 56 Cr.App.R. 541; *R. v. Towers*, 80 Cr.App.R. 231. On the other hand, positively misleading advice may be a sufficient excuse: *Doherty, ante*.

If counsel intends to appear on a renewed application on a *pro bono* basis, he should so inform the Criminal Appeal Office within 14 days of notification of refusal by the single judge: *R. v. Dowling*, *The Times*, October 20, 1995, CA.

As to notification of any determination by the single judge under section 31 to the applicant, see *ante*, § 7–222.

Considerations in deciding whether to grant leave

The prima facie test to be applied in deciding whether to grant leave to appeal is **7–235**
whether the court feels the need to hear the prosecution on the merits. The fact that the prosecution are represented is not conclusive. There are cases where the court finds it convenient to invite the prosecution to attend even though it is not clear whether their assistance will be required. The fact that the court chooses to deal with a legal issue although the evidential foundation is not established does not change an application into an appeal. Nor does the fact that the court contemplates the receipt of, or receives, evidence. There are cases where the court finds it convenient to investigate the possibility and strength of fresh evidence before deciding that the matter should be elevated to the status of an appeal: *R. v. Mealey and Sheridan* [1975] Crim.L.R. 154.

Where leave to appeal is specifically limited to one or some only of the grounds of appeal, the Court of Appeal will not permit the other grounds to be argued without leave: *R. v. Jackson* [1999] 1 All E.R. 572, CA; *R. v. Bullock* [1998] 9 *Archbold News* 1, CA; and *R. v. Cox*; *R. v. Thomas* [1999] 2 Cr.App.R. 6. If it is intended to renew the application in relation to a ground on which leave has been refused, notice should be given to the Criminal Appeal Office and, in the case of a conviction appeal, to the prosecution: *R. v. Cox*; *R. v. Thomas, ante*.

(3) Powers exercisable by registrar

Criminal Appeal Act 1968, s.31A

Powers exercisable by registrar

31A.—(1) The powers of the Court of Appeal under this Part of this Act which are specified **7–236**
in subsection (2) below may be exercised by the registrar.

(2) The powers mentioned in subsection (1) above are the following—

(a) to extend the time within which notice of appeal or of application for leave to appeal may be given;

(b) to order a witness to attend for examination;

(c) to vary the conditions of bail granted to an appellant by the Court of Appeal or the Crown Court;

(d) to make orders under section 23(1)(a).

(3) No variation of the conditions of bail granted to an appellant may be made by the registrar unless he is satisfied that the respondent does not object to the variation; but, subject to that, the powers specified in that subsection are to be exercised by the registrar in the same manner as by the Court of Appeal and subject to the same provisions.

(4) If the registrar refuses an application on the part of an appellant to exercise in his favour any of the powers specified in subsection (2) above, the appellant shall be entitled to have the application determined by a single judge.

(5) In this section "respondent" includes a person who will be a respondent if leave to appeal is granted.

[This section is inserted by the *CAA* 1995, s.6. It is printed as amended by the *Courts Act* 2003, s.87(2); and the *CJA* 2003, s.331, and Sched. 32, paras 86 and 88.]

(4) Procedural directions

Criminal Appeal Act 1968, ss.31B, 31C

Procedural directions: powers of single judge and registrar

7–236a **31B.**—(1) The power of the Court of Appeal to determine an application for procedural directions may be exercised by—

(a) a single judge, or
(b) the registrar.

(2) "Procedural directions" means directions for the efficient and effective preparation of—

(a) an application for leave to appeal, or
(b) an appeal,

to which this section applies.

(3) A single judge may give such procedural directions as he thinks fit—

(a) when acting under subsection (1);
(b) on a reference from the registrar;
(c) of his own motion, when he is exercising, or considering whether to exercise, any power of his in relation to the application or appeal.

(4) The registrar may give such procedural directions as he thinks fit—

(a) when acting under subsection (1);
(b) of his own motion.

(5) This section applies to an appeal, and an application to the Court of Appeal for leave to appeal, under—

(a) this Part,
(b) section 9 of the *Criminal Justice Act* 1987, or
(c) section 35 of the *Criminal Procedure and Investigations Act* 1996.

Appeals against procedural directions

7–236b **31C.**—(3) Subsection (4) applies if the registrar gives, or refuses to give, procedural directions.

(4) A single judge may, on an application to him under subsection (5)—

(a) confirm, set aside or vary any procedural directions given by the registrar, and
(b) give such procedural directions as he thinks fit.

(5) An application under this subsection may be made by—

(a) an appellant;
(b) a respondent, if the directions—
 (i) relate to an application for leave to appeal and appear to need the respondent's assistance to give effect to them,
 (ii) relate to an application for leave to appeal which is to be determined by the Court of Appeal, or
 (iii) relate to an appeal.

(6) In this section—

"appellant" includes a person who has given notice of application for leave to appeal under any of the provisions mentioned in section 31B(5);

"respondent" includes a person who will be a respondent if leave to appeal is granted.

[Ss.31B and 31C were inserted by the *Courts Act* 2003, s.87(3). Subss. (1) and (2) were repealed by the *CJIA* 2008, ss.47 and 149, Sched. 8, paras 1 and 12, and Sched. 28, Pt 3.]

(5) Record of proceedings at trial, transcripts, etc.

Criminal Appeal Act 1968, s.32

7–237 **32.**—(1) Rules of court may provide—

(a) for the making of a record (whether by means of shorthand notes, by mechanical means or otherwise) of any proceedings in respect of which an appeal lies (with or without leave) to the Court of Appeal; and
(b) for the making and verification of a transcript of any such record and for supplying the transcript (on payment of such charge, if any, as may be fixed for the time being by the Treasury) to the registrar for the use of the Court of Appeal or any judge exercising the powers of a judge of the Court, and to such other persons and in such circumstances as may be prescribed by the rules.

(2) Without prejudice to subsection (1) above, the Secretary of State may, if he thinks fit, in any case direct that a transcript shall be made of any such record made in pursuance of the rules and be supplied to him.

(3) [*Costs of records and transcripts ordered by Secretary of State or registrar to be defrayed out of moneys provided by Parliament.*]

In the *Criminal Procedure Rules* 2005 (S.I. 2005 No. 384), rule 65.8(2)(a) (*post*, § 7–313h) obliges "the Crown Court officer" to arrange for the recording of proceedings in the Crown Court from which an appeal lies to the Court of Appeal, unless the Crown Court otherwise directs. **7–238**

If there is any possibility that a fully competent shorthand writer will not be in court, it is the duty of counsel and the officers of the court to draw the attention of the judge to the position, so that he can make an order under rule 18(3) for a record of the proceedings. It is the duty of the judge in such circumstances to do everything practicable to ensure by means of his own note, and by requesting the co-operation of counsel for all parties concerned, that there will be an adequate note and one which will not be subject to dispute or challenge. When it is realised or suspected that a purported transcript of the summing up is inadequate, the matter should immediately be brought to the notice of the judge: *R. v. Payne and Spillane*, 56 Cr.App.R. 9. **7–239**

As to the inadequacy of the record of the proceedings at trial being a ground of appeal, see *ante*, § 7–89.

(6) Transcript for the purposes of appeal

In the *Criminal Procedure Rules* 2005 (S.I. 2005 No. 384), rule 65.8(2)(b) (*post*, § 7–313h) obliges "the Crown Court officer" to arrange the transcription of a recording made under paragraph (a) (as to which, see *ante*, § 7–238) if the registrar wants such a transcript or, subject to rule 65.9(2), anyone else wants such a transcript. Rule 65.9(1) (*post*, § 7–313i) stipulates that a person who transcribes a recording of proceedings in the Crown Court under arrangements made by the Crown Court officer must provide the registrar with any transcript for which the registrar asks within such period as the registrar may require. Rule 65.9(2) states that, unless the Crown Court otherwise directs, such a person must not provide anyone with a transcript of a public interest ruling or of an application for such a ruling, but must otherwise provide anyone else with any transcript for which that person asks in accordance with the transcription arrangements made by the Crown Court officer and on payment of any charge fixed by the Treasury. **7–240**

It is wrong for the trial judge to revise the draft of a transcript before it is submitted to the Court of Appeal: see *R. v. Kluczynski* [1973] 1 W.L.R. 1230, CA.

Where anything in addition to a "short transcript" (*i.e.* a transcript of the charges, pleas, summing up and evidence after verdict) is required, the only further transcript to be given without leave of the court is a transcript of such part of the evidence as is referred to in the notice of appeal or counsel's opinion as the registrar or the single judge may think proper: *R. v. Lurie*, 35 Cr.App.R. 113. Transcripts of material other than that contained in the "short transcript" are rarely necessary. Both sides should try to agree the relevant evidence. If agreement cannot be reached, counsel for the appellant should bring the matter to the attention of the registrar: *R. v. Campbell*, *The Times*, July 21, 1981. An appellant may always obtain a full transcript at his own expense. Any such order should be placed through the registrar to ensure uniformity of pagination. See also *A Guide to Commencing Proceedings in the Court of Appeal (Criminal Division)*, para. A.4 (Appendix J). **7–241**

In *R. (H.M. Customs and Excise) v. Blackfriars Crown Court* [2004] 9 *Archbold News* 1, DC, it was said that a transcript may be supplied under rule 68.13 of the original rules for purposes other than an appeal (such as another trial in the Crown Court), and that there is no limitation on the time within which this may be done. **7–242**

K. Appellants Liable To Automatic Deportation

Section 32 of the *UK Borders Act* 2007 (in force from August 1, 2008 (*UK Borders Act 2007 (Commencement No. 3 and Transitional Provisions) Order* 2008 (S.I. 2008 No. 1818)) in relation to persons sentenced to 12 months' imprisonment or more) **7–242a** provides that conviction of certain offences will render the offender liable to automatic deportation, subject to exceptions listed in section 33. Section 36(1) provides that a person who has served a period of imprisonment may be detained under the authority of the Secretary of State while he considers whether the person is a person liable to automatic deportation and, if he thinks that he is so liable, pending the making of a deportation order. Subsection (2) provides that where a deportation order is made under section 32, the Secretary of State shall exercise the power of detention under paragraph 2(3) of Schedule 3 to the *Immigration Act* 1971 (*ante*, § 5–914) unless he thinks it inappropriate in the circumstances. Subsection (3) provides that a court determining an appeal against conviction or sentence may direct release from detention under subsection (1) or (2). The provision is unrestricted, and is thus not confined to successful appeals. As to appellants subject to a recommendation for deportation, see *ante*, § 7–185.

V. APPEAL TO COURT OF APPEAL BY THE PROSECUTION

A. GENERAL

Criminal Justice Act 2003, s.57

Introduction

7–243 **57.**—(1) In relation to a trial on indictment, the prosecution is to have the rights of appeal for which provision is made by this Part.

(2) But the prosecution is to have no right of appeal under this Part in respect of—

(a) a ruling that a jury be discharged, or

(b) a ruling from which an appeal lies to the Court of Appeal by virtue of any other enactment.

(3) An appeal under this Part is to lie to the Court of Appeal.

(4) Such an appeal may be brought only with the leave of the judge or the Court of Appeal.

Sections 57 to 61, 67 to 72 and 74 of the 2003 Act came into force on April 4, 2005: *Criminal Justice Act 2003 (Commencement No. 8 and Transitional and Saving Provisions) Order* 2005 (S.I. 2005 No. 950). The coming into force of these provisions confers no additional prosecution right of appeal, however, in criminal proceedings in which the defendant was committed or sent for trial, the proceedings were transferred to the Crown Court or a bill of indictment was preferred by the direction or with the consent of a High Court judge before that date: *ibid.*, Sched. 2, para. 3.

In deciding whether to give leave, rather than ask merely whether the prosecutor's case was arguable or had some prospect of success, the court should look ahead to see what options were available under section 61(4) and (5) (*post*, § 7–247): *R. v. Al-Ali, The Times*, October 3, 2008, CA.

B. TERMINATING RULINGS

Criminal Justice Act 2003, ss.58–61

General right of appeal in respect of rulings

7–244 **58.**—(1) This section applies where a judge makes a ruling in relation to a trial on indictment at an applicable time and the ruling relates to one or more offences included in the indictment.

(2) The prosecution may appeal in respect of the ruling in accordance with this section.

(3) The ruling is to have no effect whilst the prosecution is able to take any steps under subsection (4).

(4) The prosecution may not appeal in respect of the ruling unless—

(a) following the making of the ruling, it—

(i) informs the court that it intends to appeal, or

(ii) requests an adjournment to consider whether to appeal, and

(b) if such an adjournment is granted, it informs the court following the adjournment that it intends to appeal.

(5) If the prosecution requests an adjournment under subsection (4)(a)(ii), the judge may grant such an adjournment.

(6) Where the ruling relates to two or more offences—

(a) any one or more of those offences may be the subject of the appeal, and

(b) if the prosecution informs the court in accordance with subsection (4) that it intends to appeal, it must at the same time inform the court of the offence or offences which are the subject of the appeal.

(7) Where—

(a) the ruling is a ruling that there is no case to answer, and

(b) the prosecution, at the same time that it informs the court in accordance with subsection (4) that it intends to appeal, nominates one or more other rulings which have been made by a judge in relation to the trial on indictment at an applicable time and which relate to the offence or offences which are the subject of the appeal,

that other ruling, or those other rulings, are also to be treated as the subject of the appeal.

(8) The prosecution may not inform the court in accordance with subsection (4) that it intends to appeal, unless, at or before that time, it informs the court that it agrees that, in respect of the offence or each offence which is the subject of the appeal, the defendant in relation to that offence should be acquitted of that offence if either of the conditions mentioned in subsection (9) is fulfilled.

(9) Those conditions are—

(a) that leave to appeal to the Court of Appeal is not obtained, and

(b) that the appeal is abandoned before it is determined by the Court of Appeal.

(10) If the prosecution informs the court in accordance with subsection (4) that it intends to appeal, the ruling mentioned in subsection (1) is to continue to have no effect in relation to the offence or offences which are the subject of the appeal whilst the appeal is pursued.

(11) If and to the extent that a ruling has no effect in accordance with this section—

(a) any consequences of the ruling are also to have no effect,

(b) the judge may not take any steps in consequence of the ruling, and

(c) if he does so, any such steps are also to have no effect.

(12) Where the prosecution has informed the court of its agreement under subsection (8) and either of the conditions mentioned in subsection (9) is fulfilled, the judge or the Court of Appeal must order that the defendant in relation to the offence or each offence concerned be acquitted of that offence.

(13) In this section "applicable time", in relation to a trial on indictment, means any time (whether before or after the commencement of the trial) before the time when the judge starts his summing-up to the jury.

(14) The reference in subsection (13) to the time when the judge starts his summing-up to the jury includes the time when the judge would start his summing-up to the jury but for the making of an order under Part 7.

[This section is printed as amended by the *Domestic Violence, Crime and Victims Act* 2004, s.30.]

The prosecution's right of appeal under this section does not extend to a ruling dismissing charges sent for trial under section 51 of the *CDA* 1998 (*ante*, § 1–17) upon a successful application under paragraph 2 of Schedule 3 to that Act (*ibid.*, § 1–28): *R. v. Thompson and Hanson* [2007] 1 Cr.App.R. 15, CA.

A refusal to grant a prosecution application for an adjournment is a "ruling" within this section: *R. v. Clarke* [2008] 1 Cr.App.R. 33, CA (see the definition of "ruling" in s.74(2), *post*, § 7–259).

Although the right of appeal requires the agreement of the prosecution that the defendant should be acquitted should the appeal fail (see s.58(8)), there is no requirement on the court to undertake an investigation to decide whether an "acquittal agreement" is objectively justified on the facts of the case; provided that an "acquittal agreement" is made in good faith, the prosecution are the sole judge of whether the consequence of a ruling which they wish to appeal would be the acquittal of the defendant: *R. v. R.* [2008] 3 *Archbold News* 2, CA.

The fact that a ruling is an "evidentiary ruling" under section 62(9) (*post*, § 7–248), and thus subject to the provisions, not yet in force, of sections 62 to 66, does not prevent it from being in addition a "ruling in relation to a trial on indictment" within section 58: *R. v. Y.* [2008] 1 Cr.App.R. 34, CA.

When a judge exercised his discretion or made a judgment during a trial, the very fact that he had carefully to balance conflicting circumstances would almost inevitably mean that he could reasonably have reached a different or opposite conclusion to the one he did reach. However, this did not begin to provide the prosecution with the basis for a successful appeal. Leave to appeal would not be given in such a case unless it was seriously arguable that it had been unreasonable for the judge to have decided the matter in the way that he did: *R. v. B. (Judicial discretion)*, *The Times*, May 22, 2008, CA.

Expedited and non-expedited appeals

7–245 **59.**—(1) Where the prosecution informs the court in accordance with section 58(4) that it intends to appeal, the judge must decide whether or not the appeal should be expedited.

(2) If the judge decides that the appeal should be expedited, he may order an adjournment.

(3) If the judge decides that the appeal should not be expedited, he may—

(a) order an adjournment, or

(b) discharge the jury (if one has been sworn).

(4) If he decides that the appeal should be expedited, he or the Court of Appeal may subsequently reverse that decision and, if it is reversed, the judge may act as mentioned in subsection (3)(a) or (b).

Continuation of proceedings for offences not affected by ruling

7–246 **60.**—(1) This section applies where the prosecution informs the court in accordance with section 58(4) that it intends to appeal.

(2) Proceedings may be continued in respect of any offence which is not the subject of the appeal.

Determination of appeal by Court of Appeal

7–247 **61.**—(1) On an appeal under section 58, the Court of Appeal may confirm, reverse or vary any ruling to which the appeal relates.

(2) Subsections (3) to (5) apply where the appeal relates to a single ruling.

(3) Where the Court of Appeal confirms the ruling, it must, in respect of the offence or each offence which is the subject of the appeal, order that the defendant in relation to that offence be acquitted of that offence.

(4) Where the Court of Appeal reverses or varies the ruling, it must, in respect of the offence or each offence which is the subject of the appeal, do any of the following—

(a) order that proceedings for that offence may be resumed in the Crown Court,

(b) order that a fresh trial may take place in the Crown Court for that offence,

(c) order that the defendant in relation to that offence be acquitted of that offence.

(5) But the Court of Appeal may not make an order under subsection (4)(c) in respect of an offence unless it considers that the defendant could not receive a fair trial if an order were made under subsection (4)(a) or (b).

(6) Subsections (7) and (8) apply where the appeal relates to a ruling that there is no case to answer and one or more other rulings.

(7) Where the Court of Appeal confirms the ruling that there is no case to answer, it must, in respect of the offence or each offence which is the subject of the appeal, order that the defendant in relation to that offence be acquitted of that offence.

(8) Where the Court of Appeal reverses or varies the ruling that there is no case to answer, it must in respect of the offence or each offence which is the subject of the appeal, make any of the orders mentioned in subsection (4)(a) to (c) (but subject to subsection (5)).

[This section is printed as amended by the *CJIA* 2008, s.44. The amendment applies in relation to an appeal if the proceedings on appeal began on or after July 14, 2008: 2008 Act, s.148(2), and Sched. 27, para. 16(1), and S.I. 2008 No. 1586 (*ante*, § 7–230a). As to when appeal proceedings begin for this purpose, see the 2008 Act, Sched. 27, para. 16(2).]

As to the commencement of sections 58 to 61, see *ante*, § 7–243.

As to rules of procedure in connection with an appeal under section 58, see *post*, §§ 7–259a *et seq.*

The "interests of justice" (see subs. (5)) are broad enough to allow the court to consider an issue on which the trial judge had ruled against the defence, but which was integral to the terminating ruling and to the ground of appeal upon which the prosecution were given leave; but this does not lead to the conclusion that it is open to the defence to raise issues which are neither the subject of, nor at the heart of, the ground of appeal upon which leave was given: *R. v. K. (I.)* [2007] 2 Cr.App.R. 10, CA.

C. EVIDENTIARY RULINGS

Criminal Justice Act 2003, s.62

[Right of appeal in respect of evidentiary rulings

62.—(1) The prosecution may, in accordance with this section and section 63, appeal in respect of— **7–248**

(a) a single qualifying evidentiary ruling, or

(b) two or more qualifying evidentiary rulings.

(2) A "qualifying evidentiary ruling" is an evidentiary ruling of a judge in relation to a trial on indictment which is made at any time (whether before or after the commencement of the trial) before the opening of the case for the defence.

(3) The prosecution may not appeal in respect of a single qualifying evidentiary ruling unless the ruling relates to one or more qualifying offences (whether or not it relates to any other offence).

(4) The prosecution may not appeal in respect of two or more qualifying evidentiary rulings unless each ruling relates to one or more qualifying offences (whether or not it relates to any other offence).

(5) If the prosecution intends to appeal under this section, it must before the opening of the case for the defence inform the court—

(a) of its intention to do so, and

(b) of the ruling or rulings to which the appeal relates.

(6) In respect of the ruling, or each ruling, to which the appeal relates—

(a) the qualifying offence, or at least one of the qualifying offences, to which the ruling relates must be the subject of the appeal, and

(b) any other offence to which the ruling relates may, but need not, be the subject of the appeal.

(7) The prosecution must, at the same time that it informs the court in accordance with subsection (5), inform the court of the offence or offences which are the subject of the appeal.

(8) For the purposes of this section, the case for the defence opens when, after the conclusion of the prosecution evidence, the earliest of the following events occurs—

(a) evidence begins to be adduced by or on behalf of a defendant,

(b) it is indicated to the court that no evidence will be adduced by or on behalf of a defendant,

(c) a defendant's case is opened, as permitted by section 2 of the *Criminal Procedure Act* 1865.

(9) In this section—

"evidentiary ruling" means a ruling which relates to the admissibility or exclusion of any prosecution evidence,

"qualifying offence" means an offence described in Part 1 of Schedule 4.

(10) The Secretary of State may by order amend that Part by doing any one or more of the following—

(a) adding a description of offence,

(b) removing a description of offence for the time being included,

(c) modifying a description of offence for the time being included.

(11) Nothing in this section affects the right of the prosecution to appeal in respect of an evidentiary ruling under section 58.]

This section comes into force on a day to be appointed.

As to the overlap between the provisions of this section and those of section 58, see *R. v. Y.* (*ante*, § 7–244).

Qualifying offences for purposes of section 62 (Sched. 4)

Offences against the person: murder; attempted murder (*Criminal Attempts Act* 1981, s.1); soliciting murder (*Offences Against the Person Act* 1861, s.4); manslaughter; corporate manslaughter (*Corporate Manslaughter and Corporate Homicide Act* 2007, s.1); wounding or causing grievous bodily harm with intent (1861 Act, s.18); kidnapping. **7–249**

Sexual offences: offences contrary to sections 1, 5 and 10 (where alleged to have been committed with girl under 13) of the *SOA* 1956; offences contrary to sections 1, 2, 4 (where it is alleged that the activity caused involved penetration within subs. 4(a) to (d)), 5, 6, 8 (where it is alleged that an activity involving penetration within subs. 2(a) to (d) was caused), 30 (where it is alleged that the touching involved penetration within subs. 3(a) to (d)) and 31 (where it is alleged that an activity involving penetration within subs. 3(a) to (d) was caused) of the *SOA* 2003; attempts to commit offences contrary to section 1 of either the 1956 or the 2003 Act, or section 5 of the 2003 Act (contrary to the *Criminal Attempts Act* 1981, s.1).

Drugs offences: where the offences are alleged to have been committed in respect of a Class A drug (as defined by the *Misuse of Drugs Act* 1971, s.2), offences contrary to sections 50(2), 68(2) and 170(1) or (2) of the *CEMA* 1979, and offences contrary to section 4(2) and (3) of the *Misuse of Drugs Act* 1971.

Theft offences: robbery (where it is alleged that, at or some time during the commission of the offence, the defendant had in his possession a firearm or imitation firearm (as defined by the *Firearms Act* 1968, s.57)).

Criminal damage offences: arson endangering life (*Criminal Damage Act* 1971, s.1(2)); causing explosion likely to endanger life or property (*Explosive Substances Act* 1883, s.2); intent or conspiracy to cause explosion likely to endanger life or property (*Explosive Substances Act* 1883, s.3(1)(a)).

War crimes and terrorism: offences contrary to the *International Criminal Court Act* 2001, ss.51 and 52; the *Geneva Conventions Act* 1957, s.1; the *Terrorism Act* 2000, s.56; and the *Taking of Hostages Act* 1982, s.1.

Hijacking and other offences relating to aviation, maritime and rail security: offences contrary to the *Aviation Security Act* 1982, ss.1 and 2; the *Aviation and Maritime Security Act* 1990, ss.9 to 11; and the *Channel Tunnel (Security) Order* 1994 (S.I. 1994 No. 570), arts 4 and 5.

Conspiracy: an offence under the *CLA* 1977, s.1 (conspiracy), in relation to any of the above offences.

Paragraphs 40 and 41 of Schedule 4 provide that a reference in the preceding paragraphs includes a reference to an offence of aiding, abetting, counselling or procuring the commission of the offence; and that a reference to an enactment includes a reference to the enactment as amended from time to time.

Criminal Justice Act 2003, ss.63–67

[Condition that evidentiary ruling significantly weakens prosecution case

7–250 **63.**—(1) Leave to appeal may not be given in relation to an appeal under section 62 unless the judge or, as the case may be, the Court of Appeal is satisfied that the relevant condition is fulfilled.

(2) In relation to an appeal in respect of a single qualifying evidentiary ruling, the relevant condition is that the ruling significantly weakens the prosecution's case in relation to the offence or offences which are the subject of the appeal.

(3) In relation to an appeal in respect of two or more qualifying evidentiary rulings, the relevant condition is that the rulings taken together significantly weaken the prosecution's case in relation to the offence or offences which are the subject of the appeal.]

[Expedited and non-expedited appeals

7–251 **64.**—(1) Where the prosecution informs the court in accordance with section 62(5), the judge must decide whether or not the appeal should be expedited.

(2)–(4) [*Identical to* s.59(2)–(4), ante, *§ 7–245*.]]

[Continuation of proceedings for offences not affected by ruling

7–252 **65.**—(1) This section applies where the prosecution informs the court in accordance with section 62(5).

(2) [*Identical to* s.60(2), ante, *§ 7–246*.]]

[Determination of appeal by Court of Appeal

7–253 **66.**—(1) On an appeal under section 62, the Court of Appeal may confirm, reverse or vary any ruling to which the appeal relates.

(2) In addition, the Court of Appeal must, in respect of the offence or each offence which is the subject of the appeal, do any of the following—

(a) order that proceedings for that offence be resumed in the Crown Court,
(b) order that a fresh trial may take place in the Crown Court for that offence,
(c) order that the defendant in relation to that offence be acquitted of that offence.

(3) But no order may be made under subsection (2)(c) in respect of an offence unless the prosecution has indicated that it does not intend to continue with the prosecution of that offence.]

Sections 63 to 66 come into force on a day to be appointed.

Reversal of rulings

67. The Court of Appeal may not reverse a ruling on an appeal under this Part unless it is satisfied— **7–254**

(a) that the ruling was wrong in law,
(b) that the ruling involved an error of law or principle, or
(c) that the ruling was a ruling that it was not reasonable for the judge to have made.

As to the commencement of this section, see *ante*, § 7–243.

D. MISCELLANEOUS AND SUPPLEMENTAL

Appeals to the House of Lords [Supreme Court], costs, time limits

Sections 68 to 70 amend provisions of the *CAA* 1968 and of the *Prosecution of Offences Act* 1985 that relate to appeal to the House of Lords [Supreme Court], awards of costs and time limits for preliminary stages of proceedings. These are noted in the appropriate places elsewhere in this work. **7–255**

Criminal Justice Act 2003, ss.71–74

Restrictions on reporting

71.—(1) Except as provided by this section no publication shall include a report of— **7–256**

(a) anything done under section 58, 59, 62, 63 or 64,
(b) an appeal under this Part,
(c) an appeal under Part 2 of the 1968 Act in relation to an appeal under this Part, or
(d) an application for leave to appeal in relation to an appeal mentioned in paragraph (b) or (c).

(2) The judge may order that subsection (1) is not to apply, or is not to apply to a specified extent, to a report of—

(a) anything done under section 58, 59, 62, 63 or 64, or
(b) an application to the judge for leave to appeal to the Court of Appeal under this Part.

(3) The Court of Appeal may order that subsection (1) is not to apply, or is not to apply to a specified extent, to a report of—

(a) an appeal to the Court of Appeal under this Part,
(b) an application to that Court for leave to appeal to it under this Part, or
(c) an application to that Court for leave to appeal to the *House of Lords* [Supreme Court] under Part 2 of the 1968 Act.

(4) The *House of Lords* [Supreme Court] may order that subsection (1) is not to apply, or is not to apply to a specified extent, to a report of—

(a) an appeal to *that House* [the Supreme Court] under Part 2 of the 1968 Act, or
(b) an application to *that House* [the Supreme Court] for leave to appeal to it under Part 2 of that Act.

(5) Where there is only one defendant and he objects to the making of an order under subsection (2), (3) or (4)—

(a) the judge, the Court of Appeal or the *House of Lords are* [Supreme Court is] to make the order if (and only if) satisfied, after hearing the representations of the defendant, that it is in the interests of justice to do so, and
(b) the order (if made) is not to apply to the extent that a report deals with any such objection or representations.

(6) Where there are two or more defendants and one or more of them object to the making of an order under subsection (2), (3) or (4)—

(a) the judge, the Court of Appeal or the *House of Lords are* [Supreme Court is] to make the order if (and only if) satisfied, after hearing the representations of each of the defendants, that it is in the interests of justice to do so, and

(b) the order (if made) is not to apply to the extent that a report deals with any such objection or representations.

(7) Subsection (1) does not apply to the inclusion in a publication of a report of—

(a) anything done under section 58, 59, 62, 63 or 64,

(b) an appeal under this Part,

(c) an appeal under Part 2 of the 1968 Act in relation to an appeal under this Part, or

(d) an application for leave to appeal in relation to an appeal mentioned in paragraph (b) or (c),

at the conclusion of the trial of the defendant or the last of the defendants to be tried.

(8) Subsection (1) does not apply to a report which contains only one or more of the following matters—

(a) the identity of the court and the name of the judge,

(b) the names, ages, home addresses and occupations of the defendant or defendants and witnesses,

(c) the offence or offences, or a summary of them, with which the defendant or defendants are charged,

(d) the names of counsel and solicitors in the proceedings,

(e) where the proceedings are adjourned, the date and place to which they are adjourned,

(f) any arrangements as to bail,

(g) whether a right to representation funded by the Legal Services Commission as part of the Criminal Defence Service was granted to the defendant or any of the defendants.

(9) The addresses that may be included in a report by virtue of subsection (8) are addresses—

(a) at any relevant time, and

(b) at the time of their inclusion in the publication.

(10) Nothing in this section affects any prohibition or restriction by virtue of any other enactment on the inclusion of any matter in a publication.

(11) In this section—

"programme service" has the same meaning as in the *Broadcasting Act* 1990,

"publication" includes any speech, writing, relevant programme or other communication in whatever form, which is addressed to the public at large or any section of the public (and for this purpose every relevant programme is to be taken to be so addressed), but does not include an indictment or other document prepared for use in particular legal proceedings,

"relevant time" means a time when events giving rise to the charges to which the proceedings relate are alleged to have occurred,

"relevant programme" means a programme included in a programme service.

[This section is printed as amended, as from a day to be appointed, by the *Constitutional Reform Act* 2005, s.40(4), and Sched. 9, para. 82(1) and (3) (omission of italicised words, insertion of words in square brackets).]

Offences in connection with reporting

7–257 **72.**—(1) This section applies if a publication includes a report in contravention of section 71.

(2) Where the publication is a newspaper or periodical, any proprietor, editor or publisher of the newspaper or periodical is guilty of an offence.

(3) Where the publication is a relevant programme—

(a) any body corporate or Scottish partnership engaged in providing the programme service in which the programme is included, and

(b) any person having functions in relation to the programme corresponding to those of an editor of a newspaper,

is guilty of an offence.

(4) In the case of any other publication, any person publishing it is guilty of an offence.

(5) If an offence under this section committed by a body corporate is proved—

(a) to have been committed with the consent or connivance of, or
(b) to be attributable to any neglect on the part of,

an officer, the officer as well as the body corporate is guilty of the offence and liable to be proceeded against and punished accordingly.

(6) In subsection (5), "officer" means a director, manager, secretary or other similar officer of the body, or a person purporting to act in any such capacity.

(7) If the affairs of a body corporate are managed by its members, "director" in subsection (6) means a member of that body.

(8) Where an offence under this section is committed by a Scottish partnership and is proved to have been committed with the consent or connivance of a partner, he as well as the partnership shall be guilty of the offence and shall be liable to be proceeded against and punished accordingly.

(9) A person guilty of an offence under this section is liable on summary conviction to a fine not exceeding level 5 on the standard scale.

(10) Proceedings for an offence under this section may not be instituted—

(a) in England and Wales otherwise than by or with the consent of the Attorney General, or
(b) [*Northern Ireland*.]

(11) [*Northern Ireland*.]

Rules of court

73.—(1) Rules of court may make such provision as appears to the authority making them to be necessary or expedient for the purposes of this Part. **7–258**

(2) Without limiting subsection (1), rules of court may in particular make provision—

(a) for time limits which are to apply in connection with any provisions of this Part,
(b) as to procedures to be applied in connection with this Part,
(c) enabling a single judge of the Court of Appeal to give leave to appeal under this Part or to exercise the power of the Court of Appeal under section 58(12).

(3) Nothing in this section is to be taken as affecting the generality of any enactment conferring powers to make rules of court.

For rules of procedure in connection with an appeal under section 58, see *post*, §§ 7–259a *et seq*.

Interpretation of Part 9

74.—(1) In this Part— **7–259**

"programme service" has the meaning given by section 71(11),
"publication" has the meaning given by section 71(11),
"qualifying evidentiary ruling" is to be construed in accordance with section 62(2),
"the relevant condition" is to be construed in accordance with section 63(2) and (3),
"relevant programme" has the meaning given by section 71(11),
"ruling" includes a decision, determination, direction, finding, notice, order, refusal, rejection or requirement,
"the 1968 Act" means the *Criminal Appeal Act* 1968.

(2) Any reference in this Part (other than section 73(2)(c)) to a judge is a reference to a judge of the Crown Court.

(3) There is to be no right of appeal under this Part in respect of a ruling in relation to which the prosecution has previously informed the court of its intention to appeal under either section 58(4) or 62(5).

(4) Where a ruling relates to two or more offences but not all of those offences are the subject of an appeal under this Part, nothing in this Part is to be regarded as affecting the ruling so far as it relates to any offence which is not the subject of the appeal.

(5) Where two or more defendants are charged jointly with the same offence, the provisions of this Part are to apply as if the offence, so far as relating to each defendant, were a separate offence (so that, for example, any reference in this Part to a ruling which relates to one or more offences includes a ruling which relates to one or more of those separate offences).

(6) Subject to rules of court made under section 53(1) of the *Supreme Court [Senior Courts] Act* 1981 (power by rules to distribute business of Court of Appeal between its civil and criminal divisions)—

(a) the jurisdiction of the Court of Appeal under this Part is to be exercised by the criminal division of that court, and

(b) references in this Part to the Court of Appeal are to be construed as references to that division.

[(7) In its application to a trial on indictment in respect of which an order under section 17(2) of the *Domestic Violence, Crime and Victims Act* 2004 has been made, this Part is to have effect with such modifications as the Secretary of State may by order specify.]

[The *Supreme Court Act* 1981 is renamed the *Senior Courts Act* 1981 as from a day to be appointed: see the *Constitutional Reform Act* 2005, s.59, and Sched. 11. Subs. (7) is inserted, as from a day to be appointed, by the *Domestic Violence, Crime and Victims Act* 2004, s.58(1), and Sched. 10, para. 62.]

As to the commencement of sections 71, 72 and 74, see *ante*, § 7–243.

As to the meaning of "ruling", see *R. v. Clarke* (*ante*, § 7–244).

E. RULES OF PROCEDURE

Criminal Procedure Rules 2005 (S.I. 2005 No. 384), Pt 67 (as substituted by the Criminal Procedure (Amendment No. 2) Rules 2007 (S.I. 2007 No. 2317))

When this Part applies

7–259a **67.1.**—(1) This Part applies where a prosecutor wants to appeal under section 58(2) of the *Criminal Justice Act* 2003.

(2) A reference to an "appellant" in this Part is a reference to such a prosecutor.

Decision to appeal

7–259b **67.2.**—(1) An appellant must tell the Crown Court judge of any decision to appeal—

(a) immediately after the ruling against which the appellant wants to appeal; or
(b) on the expiry of the time to decide whether to appeal allowed under paragraph (2).

(2) If an appellant wants time to decide whether to appeal—

(a) the appellant must ask the Crown Court judge immediately after the ruling; and
(b) the general rule is that the judge must not require the appellant to decide there and then but instead must allow until the next business day.

Service of appeal notice

7–259c **67.3.**—(1) An appellant must serve an appeal notice on—

(a) the Crown Court officer;
(b) the Registrar; and
(c) every defendant directly affected by the ruling against which the appellant wants to appeal.

(2) The appellant must serve the appeal notice not later than—

(a) the next business day after telling the Crown Court judge of the decision to appeal, if the judge expedites the appeal; or
(b) 5 business days after telling the Crown Court judge of that decision, if the judge does not expedite the appeal.

Form of appeal notice

7–259d **67.4.**—(1) An appeal notice must be in the form set out in the Practice Direction.

(2) The appeal notice must—

(a) specify each ruling against which the appellant wants to appeal;
(b) identify each ground of appeal on which the appellant relies, numbering them consecutively (if there is more than one) and concisely outlining each argument in support;
(c) summarise the relevant facts;
(d) identify any relevant authorities;
(e) include or attach any application for the following, with reasons—
 (i) permission to appeal, if the appellant needs the court's permission,
 (ii) an extension of time within which to serve the appeal notice,
 (iii) expedition of the appeal, or revocation of a direction expediting the appeal;

(f) include a list of those on whom the appellant has served the appeal notice;

(g) attach—

(i) a transcript or note of each ruling against which the appellant wants to appeal,

(ii) all relevant skeleton arguments considered by the Crown Court judge,

(iii) any written application for permission to appeal that the appellant made to the Crown Court judge,

(iv) a transcript or note of the decision by the Crown Court judge on any application for permission to appeal,

(v) a transcript or note of the decision by the Crown Court judge on any request to expedite the appeal, and

(vi) any other document or thing that the appellant thinks the court will need to decide the appeal; and

(h) attach a form of respondent's notice for any defendant served with the appeal notice to complete if that defendant wants to do so.

Crown Court judge's permission to appeal

67.5.—(1) An appellant who wants the Crown Court judge to give permission to appeal must— **7–259e**

(a) apply orally, with reasons, immediately after the ruling against which the appellant wants to appeal; or

(b) apply in writing and serve the application on—

(i) the Crown Court officer, and

(ii) every defendant directly affected by the ruling

on the expiry of the time allowed under rule 67.2 to decide whether to appeal.

(2) A written application must include the same information (with the necessary adaptations) as an appeal notice.

(3) The Crown Court judge must allow every defendant directly affected by the ruling an opportunity to make representations.

(4) The general rule is that the Crown Court judge must decide whether or not to give permission to appeal on the day that the application for permission is made.

Expediting an appeal

67.6.—(1) An appellant who wants the Crown Court judge to expedite an appeal must ask, giving reasons, on telling the judge of the decision to appeal. **7–259f**

(2) The Crown Court judge must allow every defendant directly affected by the ruling an opportunity to make representations.

(3) The Crown Court judge may revoke a direction expediting the appeal unless the appellant has served the appeal notice.

Respondent's notice

67.7.—(1) A defendant on whom an appellant serves an appeal notice may serve a respondent's notice, and must do so if— **7–259g**

(a) the defendant wants to make representations to the court; or

(b) the court so directs.

(2) Such a defendant must serve the respondent's notice on—

(a) the appellant;

(b) the Crown Court officer;

(c) the Registrar; and

(d) any other defendant on whom the appellant served the appeal notice.

(3) Such a defendant must serve the respondent's notice—

(a) not later than the next business day after—

(i) the appellant serves the appeal notice, or

(ii) a direction to do so

if the Crown Court judge expedites the appeal; or

(b) not more than 5 business days after—

(i) the appellant serves the appeal notice, or

(ii) a direction to do so

if the Crown Court judge does not expedite the appeal.

(4) The respondent's notice must be in the form set out in the Practice Direction.

(5) The respondent's notice must—

(a) give the date on which the respondent was served with the appeal notice;

(b) identify each ground of opposition on which the respondent relies, numbering them consecutively (if there is more than one), concisely outlining each argument in support and identifying the ground of appeal to which each relates;

(c) summarise any relevant facts not already summarised in the appeal notice;

(d) identify any relevant authorities;

(e) include or attach any application for the following, with reasons—

(i) an extension of time within which to serve the respondent's notice,

(ii) a direction to attend in person any hearing that the respondent could attend by live link, if the respondent is in custody;

(f) identify any other document or thing that the respondent thinks the court will need to decide the appeal.

Public interest ruling

7–259h **67.8.**—(1) This rule applies where the appellant wants to appeal against a public interest ruling.

(2) The appellant must not serve on any defendant directly affected by the ruling—

(a) any written application to the Crown Court judge for permission to appeal; or

(b) an appeal notice

if the appellant thinks that to do so in effect would reveal something that the appellant thinks ought not be disclosed.

(3) The appellant must not include in an appeal notice—

(a) the material that was the subject of the ruling; or

(b) any indication of what sort of material it is

if the appellant thinks that to do so in effect would reveal something that the appellant thinks ought not be disclosed.

(4) The appellant must serve on the Registrar with the appeal notice an annex—

(a) marked to show that its contents are only for the court and the Registrar;

(b) containing whatever the appellant has omitted from the appeal notice, with reasons; and

(c) if relevant, explaining why the appellant has not served the appeal notice.

(5) Rules 67.5(3) and 67.6(2) do not apply.

Powers of Court of Appeal judge

7–259i **67.9.** A judge of the Court of Appeal may—

(a) give permission to appeal;

(b) revoke a Crown Court judge's direction expediting an appeal; and

(c) where an appellant abandons an appeal, order a defendant's acquittal, his release from custody and the payment of his costs,

as well as exercising the powers given by other legislation (including these Rules).

Renewing applications

7–259j **67.10.** Rule 65.5 (renewing an application refused by a judge or the Registrar) applies with a time limit of 5 business days.

Right to attend hearing

7–259k **67.11.**—(1) A respondent who is in custody has a right to attend a hearing in public.

(2) The court or the Registrar may direct that such a respondent is to attend a hearing by live link.

As to the forms to be used in connection with rules 67.4, 67.7 and 67.10, see *post*, § 7–314b.

As to general rules which apply to appeals within this part, see Part 65 of the 2005 rules, *post*, §§ 7–313a *et seq.*

VI. RETRIAL FOR SERIOUS OFFENCES

A. Cases that may be Retried

Criminal Justice Act 2003, s.75

Cases that may be retried

75.—(1) This Part applies where a person has been acquitted of a qualifying offence in proceedings— **7–260**

(a) on indictment in England and Wales,

(b) on appeal against a conviction, verdict or finding in proceedings on indictment in England and Wales, or

(c) on appeal from a decision on such an appeal.

(2) A person acquitted of an offence in proceedings mentioned in subsection (1) is treated for the purposes of that subsection as also acquitted of any qualifying offence of which he could have been convicted in the proceedings because of the first-mentioned offence being charged in the indictment, except an offence—

(a) of which he has been convicted,

(b) of which he has been found not guilty by reason of insanity, or

(c) in respect of which, in proceedings where he has been found to be under a disability (as defined by section 4 of the *Criminal Procedure (Insanity) Act* 1964), a finding has been made that he did the act or made the omission charged against him.

(3) References in subsections (1) and (2) to a qualifying offence do not include references to an offence which, at the time of the acquittal, was the subject of an order under section 77(1) or (3).

(4) This Part also applies where a person has been acquitted, in proceedings elsewhere than in the United Kingdom, of an offence under the law of the place where the proceedings were held, if the commission of the offence as alleged would have amounted to or included the commission (in the United Kingdom or elsewhere) of a qualifying offence.

(5) Conduct punishable under the law in force elsewhere than in the United Kingdom is an offence under that law for the purposes of subsection (4), however it is described in that law.

(6) This Part applies whether the acquittal was before or after the passing of this Act.

(7) References in this Part to acquittal are to acquittal in circumstances within subsection (1) or (4).

(8) In this Part "qualifying offence" means an offence listed in Part 1 of Schedule 5.

References to "this Part" are references to Part 10 of the Act, comprising sections 75 to 97.

Qualifying offences (Sched. 5)

Offences against the person: as in Schedule 4 (*ante*, § 7–249). **7–261**

Sexual offences: as in Schedule 4 (*ante*, § 7–249).

Drugs offences: as in Schedule 4 (*ante*, § 7–249), but not an offence contrary to section 4(3) of the 1971 Act.

Criminal damage offences: as in Schedule 4 (*ante*, § 7–249).

War crimes and terrorism: as in Schedule 4 (*ante*, § 7–249).

Conspiracy: an offence under the *CLA* 1977, s.1 (conspiracy), in relation to any of the above offences.

The above offences are listed in paragraphs 1 to 29 of Schedule 5. Paragraphs 30 to 50 list Northern Ireland offences.

Paragraphs 51 and 52 correspond to paragraphs 40 and 41 of Schedule 4 (*ante*).

B. Application for Retrial

Criminal Justice Act 2003, ss.76–83

Application to Court of Appeal

76.—(1) A prosecutor may apply to the Court of Appeal for an order— **7–262**

(a) quashing a person's acquittal in proceedings within section 75(1), and

(b) ordering him to be retried for the qualifying offence.

(2) A prosecutor may apply to the Court of Appeal, in the case of a person acquitted elsewhere than in the United Kingdom, for—

(a) a determination whether the acquittal is a bar to the person being tried in England and Wales for the qualifying offence, and

(b) if it is, an order that the acquittal is not to be a bar.

(3) A prosecutor may make an application under subsection (1) or (2) only with the written consent of the Director of Public Prosecutions.

(4) The Director of Public Prosecutions may give his consent only if satisfied that—

(a) there is evidence as respects which the requirements of section 78 appear to be met,

(b) it is in the public interest for the application to proceed, and

(c) any trial pursuant to an order on the application would not be inconsistent with obligations of the United Kingdom under Article 31 or 34 of the Treaty on European Union relating to the principle of *ne bis in idem*.

(5) Not more than one application may be made under subsection (1) or (2) in relation to an acquittal.

Determination by Court of Appeal

7–263 **77.**—(1) On an application under section 76(1), the Court of Appeal—

(a) if satisfied that the requirements of sections 78 and 79 are met, must make the order applied for;

(b) otherwise, must dismiss the application

(2) Subsections (3) and (4) apply to an application under section 76(2).

(3) Where the Court of Appeal determines that the acquittal is a bar to the person being tried for the qualifying offence, the court—

(a) if satisfied that the requirements of sections 78 and 79 are met, must make the order applied for;

(b) otherwise, must make a declaration to the effect that the acquittal is a bar to the person being tried for the offence.

(4) Where the Court of Appeal determines that the acquittal is not a bar to the person being tried for the qualifying offence, it must make a declaration to that effect.

New and compelling evidence

7–264 **78.**—(1) The requirements of this section are met if there is new and compelling evidence against the acquitted person in relation to the qualifying offence.

(2) Evidence is new if it was not adduced in the proceedings in which the person was acquitted (nor, if those were appeal proceedings, in earlier proceedings to which the appeal related).

(3) Evidence is compelling if—

(a) it is reliable,

(b) it is substantial, and

(c) in the context of the outstanding issues, it appears highly probative of the case against the acquitted person.

(4) The outstanding issues are the issues in dispute in the proceedings in which the person was acquitted and, if those were appeal proceedings, any other issues remaining in dispute from earlier proceedings to which the appeal related.

(5) For the purposes of this section, it is irrelevant whether any evidence would have been admissible in earlier proceedings against the acquitted person.

In *R. v. Miell* [2008] 1 Cr.App.R. 23, CA, the court considered *R. v. Dunlop* (*post*, § 7–265) and held that, where an application under section 76 was based on the defendant's plea of guilty to perjury in respect of his evidence at the original trial in which he had denied the offence, it was for the Court of Appeal to form its own view as to whether the fresh evidence was "compelling" within section 78. The fact that, if the application were granted, the conviction for perjury would be admissible at the retrial and that, pursuant to section 74 of the *PACE Act* 1984 (*post*, § 9–82), proof of the conviction should be taken to be proof of the defendant's guilt unless he proved the contrary, did not absolve the court at the stage of an application for a retrial from making its own assessment.

Interests of justice

7–265 **79.**—(1) The requirements of this section are met if in all the circumstances it is in the interests of justice for the court to make the order under section 77.

(2) That question is to be determined having regard in particular to—

(a) whether existing circumstances make a fair trial unlikely;

(b) for the purposes of that question and otherwise, the length of time since the qualifying offence was allegedly committed;

(c) whether it is likely that the new evidence would have been adduced in the earlier proceedings against the acquitted person but for a failure by an officer or by a prosecutor to act with due diligence or expedition;

(d) whether, since those proceedings or, if later, since the commencement of this Part, any officer or prosecutor has failed to act with due diligence or expedition.

(3) In subsection (2) references to an officer or prosecutor include references to a person charged with corresponding duties under the law in force elsewhere than in England and Wales.

(4) Where the earlier prosecution was conducted by a person other than a prosecutor, subsection (2)(c) applies in relation to that person as well as in relation to a prosecutor.

Where section 78 (*ante*) was satisfied by new and compelling evidence in the form of subsequent confessions to the offence by the acquitted person (made at a time when retrial after acquittal was not permissible) and a subsequent plea of guilty by him to perjury in relation to his evidence at the original trial, the fact that it was possible that he would not so have confessed or pleaded had he believed that he might be retried did not operate in such a way as to prevent the "interests of justice" test under section 79 being satisfied; in such a situation, the public would be rightly outraged if the exception to the double jeopardy rule were not to be applied; and, to the extent that the sentence for perjury went beyond punishment for lying on oath, and also reflected the consequence of having done so (*i.e.* the acquittal), any such period should be taken into account when determining the sentence upon conviction after the retrial (if there were a conviction): *R. v. Dunlop* [2007] 1 Cr.App.R. 8, CA.

Procedure and evidence

80.—(1) A prosecutor who wishes to make an application under section 76(1) or (2) must give notice of the application to the Court of Appeal. **7–266**

(2) Within two days beginning with the day on which any such notice is given, notice of the application must be served by the prosecutor on the person to whom the application relates, charging him with the offence to which it relates or, if he has been charged with it in accordance with section 87(4), stating that he has been so charged.

(3) Subsection (2) applies whether the person to whom the application relates is in the United Kingdom or elsewhere, but the Court of Appeal may, on application by the prosecutor, extend the time for service under that subsection if it considers it necessary to do so because of that person's absence from the United Kingdom.

(4) The Court of Appeal must consider the application at a hearing.

(5) The person to whom the application relates—

(a) is entitled to be present at the hearing, although he may be in custody, unless he is in custody elsewhere than in England and Wales or Northern Ireland, and

(b) is entitled to be represented at the hearing, whether he is present or not.

(6) For the purposes of the application, the Court of Appeal may, if it thinks it necessary or expedient in the interests of justice—

(a) order the production of any document, exhibit or other thing, the production of which appears to the court to be necessary for the determination of the application, and

(b) order any witness who would be a compellable witness in proceedings pursuant to an order or declaration made on the application to attend for examination and be examined before the court.

(7) The Court of Appeal may at one hearing consider more than one application (whether or not relating to the same person), but only if the offences concerned could be tried on the same indictment.

As to the exercise of powers under this section by a single judge or the registrar, see S.I. 2005 No. 679, *post*, §§ 7–283a *et seq*.

81. [*Amends* CAA *1968, ss.33, 34 and 38.*] **7–267**

Restrictions on publication in the interests of justice

82.—(1) Where it appears to the Court of Appeal that the inclusion of any matter in a publication would give rise to a substantial risk of prejudice to the administration of justice in a retrial, the court may order that the matter is not to be included in any publication while the order has effect. **7–268**

(2) In subsection (1) "retrial" means the trial of an acquitted person for a qualifying offence pursuant to any order made or that may be made under section 77.

(3) The court may make an order under this section only if it appears to it necessary in the interests of justice to do so.

(4) An order under this section may apply to a matter which has been included in a publication published before the order takes effect, but such an order—

(a) applies only to the later inclusion of the matter in a publication (whether directly or by inclusion of the earlier publication), and

(b) does not otherwise affect the earlier publication.

(5) After notice of an application has been given under section 80(1) relating to the acquitted person and the qualifying offence, the court may make an order under this section only—

(a) of its own motion, or

(b) on the application of the Director of Public Prosecutions.

(6) Before such notice has been given, an order under this section—

(a) may be made only on the application of the Director of Public Prosecutions, and

(b) may not be made unless, since the acquittal concerned, an investigation of the commission by the acquitted person of the qualifying offence has been commenced by officers.

(7) The court may at any time, of its own motion or on an application made by the Director of Public Prosecutions or the acquitted person, vary or revoke an order under this section.

(8) Any order made under this section before notice of an application has been given under section 80(1) relating to the acquitted person and the qualifying offence must specify the time when it ceases to have effect.

(9) An order under this section which is made or has effect after such notice has been given ceases to have effect, unless it specifies an earlier time—

(a) when there is no longer any step that could be taken which would lead to the acquitted person being tried pursuant to an order made on the application, or

(b) if he is tried pursuant to such an order, at the conclusion of the trial.

(10) Nothing in this section affects any prohibition or restriction by virtue of any other enactment on the inclusion of any matter in a publication or any power, under an enactment or otherwise, to impose such a prohibition or restriction.

(11) [*Definitions of "programme service", "publication" and "relevant programme" identical to those in s.71(11)*, ante, *§ 7–256*.]

Where notice of an application under section 76(1) has been given to the Court of Appeal, the prosecutor should make an application under section 82 for an order restricting the publication of potentially prejudicial material as soon as such risk became apparent (and publicity of the fact that the Court of Appeal had concluded that there was compelling evidence for granting the application might reasonably be considered as prejudicial to a subsequent retrial); the acquitted person should be notified, and the court should be informed as to his attitude to the application; the media should be informed of the proposed application 14 days before the hearing date, so as to allow them an opportunity to be heard; representatives of the media should notify the court and the applicant not later than 48 hours in advance of the hearing of any intention to attend, and, if possible, of the nature of any submissions; if nothing was heard from the media, and the terms of any order were agreed between the applicant and the acquitted person, the attendance of counsel would only be required when an indication to that effect was given; any order would be pronounced in open court; and it would cease to have effect if the application was dismissed or at the conclusion of any retrial, subject to an order of the Court of Appeal or the judge bringing it to an end at an earlier time: *Re D. (Acquitted person: Retrial)* [2006] 2 Cr.App.R. 18, CA.

Offences in connection with publication restrictions

7–269 **83.**—(1) This section applies if—

(a) an order under section 82 is made, whether in England and Wales or Northern Ireland, and

(b) while the order has effect, any matter is included in a publication, in any part of the United Kingdom, in contravention of the order.

(2)–(11) [*Identical to* CJA *2003, s.72(2)–(11)*, ante, *§ 7–257*.]

C. RETRIAL

Criminal Justice Act 2003, s.84

Retrial

84.—(1) Where a person— 7–270

(a) is tried pursuant to an order under section 77(1), or

(b) is tried on indictment pursuant to an order under section 77(3),

the trial must be on an indictment preferred by direction of the Court of Appeal.

(2) After the end of 2 months after the date of the order, the person may not be arraigned on an indictment preferred in pursuance of such a direction unless the Court of Appeal gives leave.

(3) The Court of Appeal must not give leave unless satisfied that—

(a) the prosecutor has acted with due expedition, and

(b) there is a good and sufficient cause for trial despite the lapse of time since the order under section 77.

(4) Where the person may not be arraigned without leave, he may apply to the Court of Appeal to set aside the order and—

(a) for any direction required for restoring an earlier judgment and verdict of acquittal of the qualifying offence, or

(b) in the case of a person acquitted elsewhere than in the United Kingdom, for a declaration to the effect that the acquittal is a bar to his being tried for the qualifying offence.

(5) An indictment under subsection (1) may relate to more than one offence, or more than one person, and may relate to an offence which, or a person who, is not the subject of an order or declaration under section 77.

(6) Evidence given at a trial pursuant to an order under section 77(1) or (3) must be given orally if it was given orally at the original trial, unless—

(a) all the parties to the trial agree otherwise,

(b) section 116 applies, or

(c) the witness is unavailable to give evidence, otherwise than as mentioned in subsection (2) of that section, and section 114(1)(d) applies.

(7) At a trial pursuant to an order under section 77(1), paragraph 5 of Schedule 3 to the *Crime and Disorder Act* 1998 (use of depositions) does not apply to a deposition read as evidence at the original trial.

For sections 114 and 116 of this Act, see *post*, §§ 11–3, 11–15. For paragraph 5 of Schedule 3 to the 1998 Act, see *ante*, § 1–31.

D. INVESTIGATIONS

Criminal Justice Act 2003, ss.85, 86

Authorisation of investigations

85.—(1) This section applies to the investigation of the commission of a qualifying offence by a person— 7–271

(a) acquitted in proceedings within section 75(1) of the qualifying offence, or

(b) acquitted elsewhere than in the United Kingdom of an offence the commission of which as alleged would have amounted to or included the commission (in the United Kingdom or elsewhere) of the qualifying offence.

(2) Subject to section 86, an officer may not do anything within subsection (3) for the purposes of such an investigation unless the Director of Public Prosecutions—

(a) has certified that in his opinion the acquittal would not be a bar to the trial of the acquitted person in England and Wales for the qualifying offence, or

(b) has given his written consent to the investigation (whether before or after the start of the investigation).

(3) The officer may not, either with or without the consent of the acquitted person—

(a) arrest or question him,

(b) search him or premises owned or occupied by him,

(c) search a vehicle owned by him or anything in or on such a vehicle,

(d) seize anything in his possession, or

(e) take his fingerprints or take a sample from him.

(4) The Director of Public Prosecutions may only give his consent on a written application, and such an application may be made only by an officer who—

(a) if he is an officer of the metropolitan police force or the City of London police force, is of the rank of commander or above, or

(b) in any other case, is of the rank of assistant chief constable or above.

(5) An officer may make an application under subsection (4) only if—

(a) he is satisfied that new evidence has been obtained which would be relevant to an application under section 76(1) or (2) in respect of the qualifying offence to which the investigation relates, or

(b) he has reasonable grounds for believing that such new evidence is likely to be obtained as a result of the investigation.

(6) The Director of Public Prosecutions may not give his consent unless satisfied that—

(a) there is, or there is likely as a result of the investigation to be, sufficient new evidence to warrant the conduct of the investigation, and

(b) it is in the public interest for the investigation to proceed.

(7) In giving his consent, the Director of Public Prosecutions may recommend that the investigation be conducted otherwise than by officers of a specified police force or specified team of customs and excise officers.

Urgent investigative steps

7–272 **86.**—(1) Section 85 does not prevent an officer from taking any action for the purposes of an investigation if—

(a) the action is necessary as a matter of urgency to prevent the investigation being substantially and irrevocably prejudiced,

(b) the requirements of subsection (2) are met, and

(c) either—

(i) the action is authorised under subsection (3), or

(ii) the requirements of subsection (5) are met.

(2) The requirements of this subsection are met if—

(a) there has been no undue delay in applying for consent under section 85(2),

(b) that consent has not been refused, and

(c) taking into account the urgency of the situation, it is not reasonably practicable to obtain that consent before taking the action.

(3) An officer of the rank of superintendent or above may authorise the action if—

(a) he is satisfied that new evidence has been obtained which would be relevant to an application under section 76(1) or (2) in respect of the qualifying offence to which the investigation relates, or

(b) he has reasonable grounds for believing that such new evidence is likely to be obtained as a result of the investigation.

(4) An authorisation under subsection (3) must—

(a) if reasonably practicable, be given in writing;

(b) otherwise, be recorded in writing by the officer giving it as soon as is reasonably practicable.

(5) The requirements of this subsection are met if—

(a) there has been no undue delay in applying for authorisation under subsection (3),

(b) that authorisation has not been refused, and

(c) taking into account the urgency of the situation, it is not reasonably practicable to obtain that authorisation before taking the action.

(6) Where the requirements of subsection (5) are met, the action is nevertheless to be treated as having been unlawful unless, as soon as reasonably practicable after the action is taken, an officer of the rank of superintendent or above certifies in writing that he is satisfied that, when the action was taken—

(a) new evidence had been obtained which would be relevant to an application under section 76(1) or (2) in respect of the qualifying offence to which the investigation relates, or

(b) the officer who took the action had reasonable grounds for believing that such new evidence was likely to be obtained as a result of the investigation.

E. ARREST, CUSTODY AND BAIL

Criminal Justice Act 2003, ss.87–91

Arrest and charge

7–273 **87.**—(1) Where section 85 applies to the investigation of the commission of an offence by any person and no certification has been given under subsection (2) of that section—

(a) a justice of the peace may issue a warrant to arrest that person for that offence only if satisfied by written information that new evidence has been obtained which would be relevant to an application under section 76(1) or (2) in respect of the commission by that person of that offence, and

(b) that person may not be arrested for that offence except under a warrant so issued.

(2) Subsection (1) does not affect section 89(3)(b) or 91(3), or any other power to arrest a person, or to issue a warrant for the arrest of a person, otherwise than for an offence.

(3)–(8) [*Application of Part IV of* Police and Criminal Evidence Act *1984: see* ante, *§ 3–131c*.]

88. [*Bail and custody before application: see* ante, *§ 3–131d*.] **7–274**

Bail and custody before hearing

89.—(1) This section applies where notice of an application is given under section 80(1). **7–275**

(2) If the person to whom the application relates is in custody under section 88(4)(b) or (5), he must be brought before the Crown Court as soon as practicable and, in any event, within 48 hours after the notice is given.

(3) If that person is not in custody under section 88(4)(b) or (5), the Crown Court may, on application by the prosecutor—

(a) issue a summons requiring the person to appear before the Court of Appeal at the hearing of the application, or

(b) issue a warrant for the person's arrest,

and a warrant under paragraph (b) may be issued at any time even though a summons has previously been issued.

(4) Where a summons is issued under subsection (3)(a), the time and place at which the person must appear may be specified either—

(a) in the summons, or

(b) in a subsequent direction of the Crown Court.

(5) The time or place specified may be varied from time to time by a direction of the Crown Court.

(6) A person arrested under a warrant under subsection (3)(b) must be brought before the Crown Court as soon as practicable and in any event within 48 hours after his arrest, and section 81(5) of the *Supreme Court [Senior Courts] Act* 1981 does not apply.

(7) If a person is brought before the Crown Court under subsection (2) or (6) the court must either—

(a) remand him in custody to be brought before the Court of Appeal at the hearing of the application, or

(b) grant bail for him to appear before the Court of Appeal at the hearing.

(8) If bail is granted under subsection (7)(b), the Crown Court may revoke the bail and remand the person in custody as referred to in subsection (7)(a).

(9) For the purpose of calculating the period referred to in subsection (2) or (6), the following are to be disregarded—

(za) Saturday,

(a) Sunday,

(b) Christmas Day,

(c) Good Friday, and

(d) any day which is a bank holiday under the *Banking and Financial Dealings Act* 1971 in the part of the United Kingdom where the person is for the time being detained.

[The *Supreme Court Act* 1981 is renamed the *Senior Courts Act* 1981 as from a day to be appointed: see the *Constitutional Reform Act* 2005, s.59, and Sched. 11. Subs. (9)(za) was inserted by the *CJIA* 2008, s.148(1), and Sched. 26, paras 59 and 63.]

Bail and custody during and after hearing

90.—(1) The Court of Appeal may, at any adjournment of the hearing of an application under section 76(1) or (2)— **7–276**

(a) remand the person to whom the application relates on bail, or

(b) remand him in custody.

(2) At a hearing at which the Court of Appeal—

(a) makes an order under section 77,
(b) makes a declaration under subsection (4) of that section, or
(c) dismisses the application or makes a declaration under subsection (3) of that section, if it also gives the prosecutor leave to appeal against its decision or the prosecutor gives notice that he intends to apply for such leave,

the court may make such order as it sees fit for the custody or bail of the acquitted person pending trial pursuant to the order or declaration, or pending determination of the appeal.

(3) For the purpose of subsection (2), the determination of an appeal is pending—
(a) until any application for leave to appeal is disposed of, or the time within which it must be made expires;
(b) if leave to appeal is granted, until the appeal is disposed of.

(4) Section 4 of the *Bail Act* 1976 applies in relation to the grant of bail under this section as if in subsection (2) the reference to the Crown Court included a reference to the Court of Appeal.

(5) The court may at any time, as it sees fit—
(a) revoke bail granted under this section and remand the person in custody, or
(b) vary an order under subsection (2).

Revocation of bail

7–277 **91.**—(1) Where—
(a) a court revokes a person's bail under this Part, and
(b) that person is not before the court when his bail is revoked,

the court must order him to surrender himself forthwith to the custody of the court.

(2) Where a person surrenders himself into the custody of the court in compliance with an order under subsection (1), the court must remand him in custody.

(3) A person who has been ordered to surrender to custody under subsection (1) may be arrested without a warrant by an officer if he fails without reasonable cause to surrender to custody in accordance with the order.

(4) A person arrested under subsection (3) must be brought as soon as practicable, and, in any event, not more than 24 hours after he is arrested, before the court and the court must remand him in custody.

(5) For the purpose of calculating the period referred to in subsection (4), the following are to be disregarded—
(a)–(d) [*identical to s.89(9)(a)–(d),* ante, *§ 7–275, including the amendment*].

F. SUPPLEMENTARY

Criminal Justice Act 2003, ss.92–97

Functions of the DPP

7–278 **92.**—(1) Section 1(7) of the *Prosecution of Offences Act* 1985 (DPP's functions exercisable by Crown Prosecutor) does not apply to the provisions of this Part other than section 85(2)(a).

(2) In the absence of the Director of Public Prosecutions, his functions under those provisions may be exercised by a person authorised by him.

(3) An authorisation under subsection (2)—
(a) may relate to a specified person or to persons of a specified description, and
(b) may be general or relate to a specified function or specified circumstances.

Rules of court

7–279 **93.**—(1) Rules of court may make such provision as appears to the authority making them to be necessary or expedient for the purposes of this Part.

(2) Without limiting subsection (1), rules of court may in particular make provision as to procedures to be applied in connection with sections 76 to 82, 84 and 88 to 90.

(3) Nothing in this section is to be taken as affecting the generality of any enactment conferring power to make rules of court.

7–280 **94.** [*Armed forces (amended, as from a day to be appointed, by* Armed Forces Act *2006, s.378(1), and Sched. 16, para. 214).*]

Interpretation of Part 10

7–281 **95.**—(1) In this Part—

"the 1984 Act" means the *Police and Criminal Evidence Act* 1984, "acquittal" and related expressions are to be read in accordance with section 75(7),

"customs and excise officer" means an officer as defined by section 1(1) of the *Customs and Excise Management Act* 1979, or a person to whom section 8(2) of that Act applies,

"new evidence" is to be read in accordance with section 78(2),

"officer", except in section 83, means an officer of a police force or a customs and excise officer,

"police force" has the meaning given by section 3(3) of the *Prosecution of Offences Act* 1985,

"prosecutor" means an individual or body charged with duties to conduct criminal prosecutions,

"qualifying offence" has the meaning given by section 75(8).

(2) Subject to rules of court made under section 53(1) of the *Supreme Court [Senior Courts] Act* 1981 (power by rules to distribute business of Court of Appeal between its civil and criminal divisions)—

(a) the jurisdiction of the Court of Appeal under this Part is to be exercised by the criminal division of that court, and

(b) references in this Part to the Court of Appeal are to be construed as references to that division.

(3) References in this Part to an officer of a specified rank or above are, in the case of a customs and excise officer, references to an officer of such description as—

(a) appears to the Commissioners of Customs and Excise to comprise officers of equivalent rank or above, and

(b) is specified by the Commissioners for the purposes of the provision concerned.

[As to the renaming of the *Supreme Court Act* 1981, see the note to s.89, *ante*, § 7–275. By virtue of the *Commissioners for Revenue and Customs Act* 2005, s.50(2), references to a "customs and excise officer" are to be taken as references to an officer of Revenue and Customs.]

96. [*Northern Ireland*.] **7–282**

Application of Criminal Appeal Acts to proceedings under Part 10

97. Subject to the provisions of this Part, the Secretary of State may make an order containing provision, in relation to proceedings before the Court of Appeal under this Part, which corresponds to any provision, in relation to appeals or other proceedings before that court, which is contained in the *Criminal Appeal Act* 1968 or the *Criminal Appeal (Northern Ireland) Act* 1980 (subject to any specified modifications). **7–283**

Criminal Justice Act (Retrial for Serious Offences) Order 2005 (S.I. 2005 No. 679)

Citation, commencement and interpretation

1.—(1) [*Citation and commencement*.] **7–283a**

(2) In this Order—

(a) "the 2003 Act" means the *Criminal Justice Act* 2003;

(b) "the Registrar" means the registrar of criminal appeals.

(3) References to the Court of Appeal are to the criminal division of the Court of Appeal;

(4) References to a single judge are to any judge of the Court of Appeal.

Powers of Court of Appeal which are exercisable by single judge

2.—(1) There may be exercised by a single judge in the same manner as by the Court of Appeal, and subject to the same provisions the powers— **7–283b**

(a) to order the production of any document, exhibit or other thing under section 80(6)(a) of the 2003 Act; and

(b) to order any witness who would be a compellable witness in proceedings pursuant to an order or declaration made on the application to attend for examination and be examined before the Court of Appeal under section 80(6)(b) of the 2003 Act.

(2) If the single judge refuses an application on the part of a party to exercise in his favour the power specified in paragraph (1), the party shall be entitled to have his application determined by the Court of Appeal.

Powers of Court of Appeal which are exercisable by Registrar

7–283c **3.**—(1) The following powers of the Court of Appeal may be exercised by the Registrar—

(a) the power to order the production of any document, exhibit or other thing under section 80(6)(a) of the 2003 Act; and

(b) the power to order any witness who would be a compellable witness in proceedings pursuant to an order or declaration made on the application to attend for examination and be examined before the Court of Appeal under section 80(6)(b) of the 2003 Act.

(2) If the Registrar refuses an application on the part of a party to exercise in his favour any of the powers specified in paragraph (1), the party shall be entitled to have his application determined by a single judge.

Procedural directions: powers of single judge and Registrar

7–283d **4.**—(1) [*Identical to* CAA *1968, s.31B(1),* ante, *§ 7–236a.*]

(2) "Procedural directions" means directions for the efficient and effective preparation of an application by a prosecutor under section 76(1) or (2) of the 2003 Act.

(3), (4) [*Identical to* CAA *1968, s.31B(3) and (4),* ante, *§ 7–236a, save for substitution of "paragraph" for "subsection".*]

Appeals against procedural directions

7–283e **5.**—(1)–(4) [*Identical to* CAA *1968, s.31C(1)–(4),* ante, *§ 7–236a, save for substitution of "paragraph" for "subsection".*]

(5) An application under this article may be made by either a prosecutor or an acquitted person.

VII. INTERLOCUTORY, ETC., APPEALS

A. SERIOUS OR COMPLEX FRAUD CASES

Introduction

7–284 Section 7(1) of the *CJA* 1987 (*ante*, § 4–84m) provides that where it appears to a judge that the evidence on an indictment reveals a case of fraud of such seriousness or complexity that substantial benefits are likely to accrue from a preparatory hearing, for the purpose of—

(a) identifying issues which are likely to be material to the verdict of the jury;

(b) assisting their comprehension of any such issues;

(c) expediting the proceedings before the jury;

(d) assisting the judge's management of the trial; or

(e) considering questions as to the severance or joinder of charges,

he may order that such a hearing shall be held. Section 9(1) (*ante*, § 4–84o) provides that the judge may exercise any of the powers specified in that section at the hearing. Section 9(3) authorises him to determine "(aa) a question arising under section 6 of the *CJA* 1993 (relevance of external law to certain charges of conspiracy, attempt and incitement)", "(b) any question as to the admissibility of evidence", "(c) any other question of law relating to the case", and "(d) any questions as to the severance or joinder of charges". Paragraph (a) has been repealed. For section 6 of the 1993 Act, see *ante*, § 2–42.

Right of appeal

Criminal Justice Act 1987, s.9(11)

7–285 **9.**—(11) An appeal shall lie to the Court of Appeal from any order or ruling of a judge under subsection (3)(b), (c) or (d) above, from the refusal by a judge of an application to which section 45 of the *Criminal Justice Act* 2003 applies or from an order of a judge under section 43 or 44 of that Act which is made on the determination of such an application, but only with the leave of the judge or of the Court of Appeal.

[Subs. (11) is printed as amended by the *CJA* 2003, ss.45(5) and 310(3).]

Scope of appeals

7–286 In *R. v. H.* [2007] 2 A.C. 270, HL, it was held (i) that the purposes for which a preparatory hearing could be held, pursuant to section 7(1) of the 1987 Act, should be given a broad and generous interpretation, (ii) that the powers specified in section 9 of the Act may only be exercised for one or more of the section 7(1) purposes, (iii) that those powers do not extend to the determination of an application for disclosure under the *CPIA* 1996, s.8 (*post*, § 12–59), and (iv) that an order or ruling on such an application cannot of itself be the subject of an appeal under section 9(11). As to the scope of sections 7 and 9, their Lordships referred to a series of authorities in the Court of Appeal, and said that it was time to make a fresh start. In particular, their Lordships rejected a line of authorities (including *Re Gunawardena*, 91 Cr.App.R. 55, CA, *R. v. Moore*, unreported, February 5, 1991, CA, and *R. v. Hedworth* [1997] 1 Cr.App.R. 421, CA), in which it was held that it was not sufficient to bring a ruling within section 7 that a possible incidental effect of the ruling would fall within the section 7 purposes, and that what was required was that the dominant purpose of the ruling should fall within section 7. Whilst there was some disagreement among their Lordships (in particular, as to whether section 9 set out the entirety of a judge's powers at a preparatory hearing), it seems that Lord Mance represented the views of all of their Lordships when he said—

> "Once a preparatory hearing has validly been ordered, the power to make a ruling under section 9 is thus on any view exercisable—whatever the direct or dominant object of the application or ruling—whenever the judge reasonably considers that it would also serve a useful trial purpose within one of the heads in section 7(1) to make such a ruling. Courts do not and should not have to engage in minute and, as the authorities show, sometimes elusive arguments, about whether the direct or dominant purpose of the ruling would be one specified in section 7(1); I find it difficult to envisage any case, from now on, in which an appellate court should entertain an argument or refuse to hear an appeal from a ruling on a subject-matter falling within paragraph (b), (c) or … (d) of section 9(3) on the ground that the purpose of the ruling fell outside section 7(1)" (at [92]).

Interlocutory appeals are by their nature heard as a matter of urgency. There is accordingly a clear duty on legal advisers to scrutinise with particular care (a) whether there is jurisdiction in the court to entertain the appeal, and (b) where the appeal amounts to a challenge to the exercise of the judge's discretion, whether there is any real prospect of successfully arguing that the exercise of the discretion was fundamentally flawed: *R. v. Jennings*, 98 Cr.App.R. 308, CA.

As section 9(3) restricts appeals to rulings on questions of law, there is some doubt as to whether there can ever be an appeal in respect of matters falling within the discretion of the judge. In *Re Saunders*, *The Times*, February 8, 1990, CA, it was said that the exercise of a discretion could only involve a question of law if it could be demonstrated that the discretion had been exercised on a fundamentally flawed basis. In *Moore*, *ante*, the court said that the view expressed in *Saunders* was *obiter* and was arrived at without any detailed consideration of the intricacies of the legislation. It appears to have been the court's view in *Moore* that there could be no appeal in respect of such matters; the court in *Jennings*, *ante*, appears to have inclined to this view, but did no more than discourage attempts to mount appeals alleging that the exercise of a discretion was fundamentally flawed (*ante*).

Procedural directions

See section 31B(5) of the *CAA* 1968, *ante*, § 7–236a. **7–287**

[The next paragraph is § 7–297.]

B. COMPLEX, LENGTHY OR SERIOUS CASES

Introduction

Section 29(1) of the *CPIA* 1996 (*ante*, § 4–84t) provides that where it appears to a judge that an indictment reveals a case of such complexity, or a case whose trial is likely to be of such length, or of such seriousness, that substantial benefits are likely to accrue from a preparatory hearing for any of the purposes set out in subsection (2), he may **7–297** order such a hearing. The purposes listed in section 29(2) are identical to those listed in section 7(1) of the 1987 Act (*ante*, § 7–284). Section 31(1) and (3) correspond exactly to section 9(1) and (3)(b) to (d).

Right of appeal

7–298 Section 35(1) provides that an appeal shall lie to the Court of Appeal from any ruling of a judge under section 31(3), but only with the leave of the judge or of the Court of Appeal. As to the scope of appeals under section 35(1), see *ante*, § 7–286.

Procedural directions

7–299 See section 31B(5) of the *CAA* 1968, *ante*, § 7–236a.

C. PROCEDURE

Criminal Procedure Rules 2005 (S.I. 2005 No. 384), Pt 66 (as substituted by the Criminal Procedure (Amendment No. 2) Rules 2007 (S.I. 2007 No. 2317))

When this Part applies

7–300 **66.1.**—(1) This Part applies where a party wants to appeal under—

(a) section 9(11) of the *Criminal Justice Act* 1987 or section 35(1) of the *Criminal Procedure and Investigations Act* 1996; or

(b) section 47(1) of the *Criminal Justice Act* 2003.

(2) A reference to an "appellant" in this Part is a reference to such a party.

Section 47(1) of the 2003 Act (*ante*, § 4–267e) provides for a right of appeal against an order by a judge who has discharged a jury on the ground of jury tampering that the trial should proceed without a jury, or that there should be a retrial without a jury.

Service of appeal notice

7–301 **66.2.**—(1) An appellant must serve an appeal notice on—

(a) the Crown Court officer;

(b) the Registrar; and

(c) every party directly affected by the order or ruling against which the appellant wants to appeal.

(2) The appellant must serve the appeal notice not more than 5 business days after—

(a) the order or ruling against which the appellant wants to appeal; or

(b) the Crown Court judge gives or refuses permission to appeal.

Form of appeal notice

7–302 **66.3.**—(1) An appeal notice must be in the form set out in the Practice Direction.

(2) The appeal notice must—

(a) specify each order or ruling against which the appellant wants to appeal;

(b) identify each ground of appeal on which the appellant relies, numbering them consecutively (if there is more than one) and concisely outlining each argument in support;

(c) summarise the relevant facts;

(d) identify any relevant authorities;

(e) include or attach any application for the following, with reasons—

(i) permission to appeal, if the appellant needs the court's permission,

(ii) an extension of time within which to serve the appeal notice,

(iii) a direction to attend in person a hearing that the appellant could attend by live link, if the appellant is in custody;

(f) include a list of those on whom the appellant has served the appeal notice; and

(g) attach—

(i) a transcript or note of each order or ruling against which the appellant wants to appeal,

(ii) all relevant skeleton arguments considered by the Crown Court judge,

(iii) any written application for permission to appeal that the appellant made to the Crown Court judge,

(iv) a transcript or note of the decision by the Crown Court judge on any application for permission to appeal, and

(v) any other document or thing that the appellant thinks the court will need to decide the appeal.

Crown Court judge's permission to appeal

66.4.—(1) An appellant who wants the Crown Court judge to give permission to appeal must— **7–303**

(a) apply orally, with reasons, immediately after the order or ruling against which the appellant wants to appeal; or

(b) apply in writing and serve the application on—

(i) the Crown Court officer, and

(ii) every party directly affected by the order or ruling

not more than 2 business days after that order or ruling.

(2) A written application must include the same information (with the necessary adaptations) as an appeal notice.

Respondent's notice

66.5.—(1) A party on whom an appellant serves an appeal notice may serve a respondent's notice, and must do so if— **7–304**

(a) that party wants to make representations to the court; or

(b) the court so directs.

(2) Such a party must serve the respondent's notice on—

(a) the appellant;

(b) the Crown Court officer;

(c) the Registrar; and

(d) any other party on whom the appellant served the appeal notice.

(3) Such a party must serve the respondent's notice not more than 5 business days after—

(a) the appellant serves the appeal notice; or

(b) a direction to do so.

(4) The respondent's notice must be in the form set out in the Practice Direction.

(5) The respondent's notice must—

(a) give the date on which the respondent was served with the appeal notice;

(b) identify each ground of opposition on which the respondent relies, numbering them consecutively (if there is more than one), concisely outlining each argument in support and identifying the ground of appeal to which each relates;

(c) summarise any relevant facts not already summarised in the appeal notice;

(d) identify any relevant authorities;

(e) include or attach any application for the following, with reasons—

(i) an extension of time within which to serve the respondent's notice,

(ii) a direction to attend in person any hearing that the respondent could attend by live link, if the respondent is in custody;

(f) identify any other document or thing that the respondent thinks the court will need to decide the appeal.

Powers of Court of Appeal judge

66.6. A judge of the Court of Appeal may give permission to appeal as well as exercising the powers given by other legislation (including these Rules). **7–305**

Renewing applications

66.7. Rule 65.5 (renewing an application refused by a judge or the Registrar) applies with a time limit of 5 business days. **7–306**

Right to attend hearing

66.8.—(1) A party who is in custody has a right to attend a hearing in public. **7–307**

(2) The court or the Registrar may direct that such a party is to attend a hearing by live link.

As to the forms to be used in connection with rules 66.3, 66.5 and 66.7, see *post*, § 7–314b.

As to general rules which apply to appeals within this part, see Part 65 of the 2005 rules, *post*, §§ 7–313a *et seq.*

VIII. MISCELLANEOUS RIGHTS OF APPEAL

A. APPEAL IN RESPECT OF ORDERS RESTRICTING REPORTING OR PUBLIC ACCESS

Criminal Justice Act 1988, s.159

Crown Court proceedings—orders restricting or preventing reports or restricting public access

7–308 **159.**—(1) A person aggrieved may appeal to the Court of Appeal, if that court grants leave, against—

(a) an order under section 4 or 11 of the *Contempt of Court Act* 1981 made in relation to a trial on indictment;

(aa) an order made by the Crown Court under section 58(7) of the *Criminal Procedure and Investigations Act* 1996 in a case where the court has convicted a person on trial on indictment;

(b) any order restricting the access of the public to the whole or any part of a trial on indictment or to any proceedings ancillary to such a trial; and

(c) any order restricting the publication of any report of the whole or any part of a trial on indictment or any such ancillary proceedings;

and the decision of the Court of Appeal shall be final.

(2) [*Subject to rules of court, jurisdiction to be exercised by criminal division and references to Court of Appeal to be construed as references to that division.*]

(3) On an application for leave to appeal under this section a judge shall have power to give such directions as appear to him to be appropriate and, without prejudice to the generality of this subsection, power—

(a) to order the production in court of any transcript or note of proceedings or other document;

(b) to give directions as to persons who are to be parties to the appeal or who may be parties to it if they wish and as to service of documents on any person;

and the Court of Appeal shall have the same powers as the single judge.

7–309 (4) Subject to Rules of Court made by virtue of subsection (6) below, any party to an appeal under this section may give evidence before the Court of Appeal orally or in writing.

(5) On the hearing of an appeal under this section the Court of Appeal shall have power—

(a) to stay any proceedings in any other court until after the appeal is disposed of,

(b) to confirm, reverse or vary the order complained of; and

(c) to make such order as to costs as it thinks fit.

(6) Rules of Court may make in relation to trials satisfying specified conditions special provision as to the practice and procedure to be followed in relation to hearings *in camera* and appeals from orders for such hearings and may in particular, but without prejudice to the generality of this subsection, provide that subsection (4) above shall not have effect.

(7) [*Application to Northern Ireland.*]

[This section is printed as amended, and repealed in part, by the *CPIA* 1996, s.61(6); and the *Courts Act 2003 (Consequential Amendments) Order* 2004 (S.I. 2004 No. 2035).]

Section 159(5)(b) was enacted to provide an effective remedy against orders wrongly made under section 4(2) of the *Contempt of Court Act* 1981 (*post*, § 28–78); it would not be an effective remedy if such orders could not be reversed simply because they had ceased to operate: *Re Central Independent Television plc*, 92 Cr.App.R. 154, CA.

On an appeal against an order undersection 4(2) of the 1981 Act, it is the duty of the Court of Appeal not merely to review the judge's decision, but to come to its own independent conclusion on the matter: *Ex p. The Telegraph Group plc* [2001] 1 W.L.R. 1983, CA.

If, on an appeal under this section, an order under section 4(2) of the 1981 Act is set aside, no order for costs should be made against the prosecution provided that they had not departed from their proper role (*viz.* to assist the court, in an objective and unpartisan spirit, on the proper principles to be applied); but it should not be thought that orders for costs would not be made if a section 4(2) order was improperly sought and made: *Ex p. News Group Newspapers Ltd*, *The Times*, May 21, 1999, CA.

Section 159(5)(c) does not authorise an award of costs out of central funds: *Holden & Co. v. CPS (No. 2)* [1994] 1 A.C. 22, HL.

There is no appeal under section 159 against a refusal to order that proceedings be heard *in camera*: *R. v. S.* [1995] 2 Cr.App.R. 347, CA.

Criminal Procedure Rules 2005 (S.I. 2005 No. 384), Pt 69 (as substituted by the Criminal Procedure (Amendment No. 2) Rules 2007 (S.I. 2007 No. 2317))

When this Part applies

69.1.—(1) This Part applies where a person directly affected by an order to which section 159(1) of the *Criminal Justice Act* 1988 applies wants to appeal against that order. **7–310**

(2) A reference to an "appellant" in this Part is a reference to such a party.

Service of appeal notice

69.2.—(1) An appellant must serve an appeal notice on— **7–311**

(a) the Crown Court officer;
(b) the Registrar;
(c) the parties; and
(d) any other person directly affected by the order against which the appellant wants to appeal.

(2) The appellant must serve the appeal notice not later than—

(a) the next business day after an order restricting public access to the trial;
(b) 10 business days after an order restricting reporting of the trial.

Form of appeal notice

69.3.—(1) An appeal notice must be in the form set out in the Practice Direction. **7–311a**

(2) The appeal notice must—

(a) specify the order against which the appellant wants to appeal;
(b) identify each ground of appeal on which the appellant relies, numbering them consecutively (if there is more than one) and concisely outlining each argument in support;
(c) summarise the relevant facts;
(d) identify any relevant authorities;
(e) include or attach, with reasons—
  (i) an application for permission to appeal,
  (ii) any application for an extension of time within which to serve the appeal notice,
  (iii) any application for a direction to attend in person a hearing that the appellant could attend by live link, if the appellant is in custody,
  (iv) any application for permission to introduce evidence, and
  (v) a list of those on whom the appellant has served the appeal notice; and
(f) attach any document or thing that the appellant thinks the court will need to decide the appeal.

Advance notice of appeal against order restricting public access

69.4.—(1) This rule applies where the appellant wants to appeal against an order restricting public access to a trial. **7–311b**

(2) The appellant may serve advance written notice of intention to appeal against any such order that may be made.

(3) The appellant must serve any such advance notice—

(a) on—
  (i) the Crown Court officer,
  (ii) the Registrar,
  (iii) the parties, and
  (iv) any other person who will be directly affected by the order against which the appellant intends to appeal, if it is made; and

(b) not more than 5 business days after the Crown Court officer displays notice of the application for the order.

(4) The advance notice must include the same information (with the necessary adaptations) as an appeal notice.

(5) The court must treat that advance notice as the appeal notice if the order is made.

Duty of applicant for order restricting public access

7–311c **69.5.**—(1) This rule applies where the appellant wants to appeal against an order restricting public access to a trial.

(2) The party who applied for the order must serve on the Registrar—

(a) a transcript or note of the application for the order; and

(b) any other document or thing that that party thinks the court will need to decide the appeal.

(3) That party must serve that transcript or note and any such other document or thing as soon as practicable after—

(a) the appellant serves the appeal notice; or

(b) the order, where the appellant served advance notice of intention to appeal.

Respondent's notice on appeal against reporting restriction

7–311d **69.6.**—(1) This rule applies where the appellant wants to appeal against an order restricting the reporting of a trial.

(2) A person on whom an appellant serves an appeal notice may serve a respondent's notice, and must do so if—

(a) that person wants to make representations to the court; or

(b) the court so directs.

(3) Such a person must serve the respondent's notice on—

(a) the appellant;

(b) Crown Court officer;

(c) the Registrar;

(d) the parties; and

(e) any other person on whom the appellant served the appeal notice.

(4) Such a person must serve the respondent's notice not more than 3 business days after—

(a) the appellant serves the appeal notice; or

(b) a direction to do so.

(5) The respondent's notice must be in the form set out in the Practice Direction.

(6) The respondent's notice must—

(a) give the date on which the respondent was served with the appeal notice;

(b) identify each ground of opposition on which the respondent relies, numbering them consecutively (if there is more than one), concisely outlining each argument in support and identifying the ground of appeal to which each relates;

(c) summarise any relevant facts not already summarised in the appeal notice;

(d) identify any relevant authorities;

(e) include or attach any application for the following, with reasons

(i) an extension of time within which to serve the respondent's notice,

(ii) a direction to attend in person any hearing that the respondent could attend by live link, if the respondent is in custody,

(iii) permission to introduce evidence; and

(f) identify any other document or thing that the respondent thinks the court will need to decide the appeal.

Renewing applications

7–311e **69.7.** Rule 65.5 (renewing an application refused by a judge or the Registrar) applies with a time limit of 5 business days.

Right to introduce evidence

7–311f **69.8.** No person may introduce evidence without the court's permission.

Right to attend hearing

7–311g **69.9.**—(1) A party who is in custody has a right to attend a hearing in public of an appeal against an order restricting the reporting of a trial.

(2) The court or the Registrar may direct that such a party is to attend a hearing by live link.

As to the forms to be used in connection with rules 69.3, 69.4 and 69.7, see *post*, § 7–314b.

As to general rules which apply to appeals within this part, see Part 65 of the 2005 rules, *post*, §§ 7–313a *et seq.*

B. Appeals Under The Proceeds of Crime Act 2002

The *Proceeds of Crime Act 2002 (Appeals under Part 2) Order* 2003 (S.I. 2003 No. 82) makes provision in relation to appeals under Part 2 (confiscation orders) of the 2002 Act (*i.e.* appeals by the prosecution or an applicant for a restraint order or for the appointment of a receiver). The provisions correspond closely to provisions of the *CAA* 1968, relating to appeals by the defendant. They are complemented by Parts 71 to 73 of the *Criminal Procedure Rules* 2005 (S.I. 2005 No. 384), which make provision as to the procedure for the purposes of the new rights of appeal introduced by the 2002 Act. Because they relate exclusively to appeals under that Act, they are set out *in extenso* in Chapter 5, *ante*: see §§ 5–730 *et seq.*, and §§ 5–742 *et seq.* **7–312**

C. Appeals in Respect of Discounted Sentences

The *Serious Organised Crime and Police Act 2005 (Appeals under Section 74) Order* 2006 (S.I. 2006 No. 2135) makes provision in relation to appeals by offenders or specified prosecutors under section 74(8) of the 2005 Act (*ante*, § 5–94b) against a decision of a Crown Court judge under section 74(5) or (6) to discount a sentence where the offender has provided assistance to the prosecution or investigation, or to increase a discounted sentence where an offender has promised to give assistance but has failed to do so. The provisions correspond closely (but are modified) to their counterparts in the *CAA* 1968 concerning appeals against sentence. The order is in six parts (of which Parts 4 to 6 relate to Northern Ireland). **7–312a**

Part 1 (arts 1, 2) is introductory. Part 2 (arts 3–14) deals with appeals to the Court of Appeal. Article 3 sets out matters of general interpretation for the purposes of Parts 2 and 3. Article 4 (corresponding to s.11(3) of the 1968 Act (*ante*, § 7–125)) sets out the powers of the Court of Appeal on appeal. Article 5 (corresponding to s.18 (*ante*, § 7–157)) sets out the initiating procedure for a person seeking leave to appeal. Article 6 (corresponding to s.19 (*ante*, § 7–185)) provides for bail pending determination of the appeal. Article 7 (corresponding to s.21 (*ante*, § 7–194)) sets out the duties of the Registrar of Criminal Appeals in relation to the preparation of cases for hearing. Article 8 (corresponding to s.22 (*ante*, § 7–201)) makes provision in relation to the offender's right to be present. Article 9 (corresponding to s.23 (*ante*, § 7–208)) makes provision as to the reception of evidence on appeal. Article 10 (corresponding to s.29 (*ante*, § 7–225)) makes provision as to the effect of an appeal on the sentence imposed, including a power to make a direction for loss of time. Articles 11 and 12 (corresponding to ss.31 and 31A, respectively (*ante*, §§ 7–231, 7–236)) set out the powers of the court which are, respectively, exercisable by a single judge and the registrar. Article 13 (corresponding to s.31B (*ante*, § 7–236a)) sets out the powers of a single judge and the registrar to give procedural directions; and article 14 (corresponding to s.31C (*ante*, § 7–236b)) makes provision for appeals against such directions.

Part 3 (arts 15–22) deals with appeals from the Court of Appeal to the House of Lords. Article 15 (corresponding to s.33 (*post*, § 7–318)) sets out the rights of appeal of the defendant and prosecution. Article 16 (corresponding to s.34 (*post*, § 7–322)) deals with applications for leave to appeal. Article 17 (corresponding to s.35 (*post*, § 7–325)) makes provision for the hearing and disposal of appeals. Article 18 (corresponding to s.36 (*post*, § 7–327)) makes provision for the grant of bail by the Court of Appeal pending determination of the appeal by the House of Lords. Article 19 (corresponding to s.37 (*post*, § 7–328)) makes provision for detention of the offender pending an appeal to the House of Lords on an application by the specified prosecutor. Article 20 (corresponding to s.38 (*post*, § 7–331)) makes provision as to the presence of the defendant at the hearing. Article 21 (corresponding to s.43(1) (*post*, § 7–335)) provides that time spent on bail granted under article 18 is to be disregarded in the computation of the term of the offender's sentence; and article 22 (corresponding to s.44 (*post*, § 7–336)) sets out the powers of the Court of Appeal under Part 3 which are exercisable by a single judge.

7–312b Part 68 of the *Criminal Procedure Rules* 2005 (S.I. 2005 No. 384) (as substituted by the *Criminal Procedure (Amendment No. 2) Rules* 2007 (S.I. 2007 No. 2317)) applies to appeals under section 74(8): see rule 68.1, *post*, § 7–313o.

D. Appeals in Relation to Serious Crime Prevention Orders

7–312c Part 1 of the *SCA* 2007 makes provision for the making of serious crime prevention orders by the High Court and the Crown Court. Section 24(1) provides for an appeal to the Court of Appeal against a decision of the Crown Court in relation to such an order by a person who is the subject of the order or by the relevant applicant authority. Subsection (2) confers a right of appeal against a decision to make, vary or not to vary such an order on persons who were given an opportunity to make representations in the Crown Court. Save where the Crown Court judge has certified that the decision is fit for appeal, such an appeal lies only with leave of the Court of Appeal. The section also provides for a further appeal to the House of Lords [Supreme Court] with leave. Section 24(9) authorises the making of an order by the Secretary of State containing provisions corresponding to the provisions of the *CAA* 1968 for the purposes of an appeal under that section. For the details of Part 1 of the 2007 Act, including section 24, see *ante*, §§ 5–873a *et seq.*

Serious Crime Act 2007 (Appeals under Section 24) Order 2008 (S.I. 2008 No. 1863)

Part 1

Introduction

7–312d **1.** [*Citation, commencement and extent.*]

General interpretation

2. In this Order—

"the Act" means the *Serious Crime Act* 2007;

"party under section 24(2)" means a person who is entitled to appeal by virtue of section 24(2) of the Act;

"person who is a party to the appeal" means—

(a) the person who is the subject of a serious crime prevention order,

(b) the relevant applicant authority, or

(c) a party under section 24(2), who is a party to the appeal in question whether as an appellant or otherwise.

Part 2

Appeals to the Court of Appeal: England and Wales

Interpretation of Parts 2, 3 and 4

7–312e **3.**—(1) In this Part and Part 3 "the registrar" means the registrar of Criminal Appeals of the Court of Appeal.

(2) References in this Part and Parts 3 and 4 to a single judge are to any judge of the Court of Appeal or of the High Court.

(3) In this Part and Part 3, except in articles 26 to 28, "appeal" means an appeal under section 24(1) or (2) of the Act.

(4) In Part 4 "appeal" means an appeal under section 24(6) of the Act.

Hearing of appeal and grounds for allowing an appeal

7–312f **4.**—(1) Every appeal will be limited to a review of the decision of the Crown Court unless the Court of Appeal considers that in the circumstances of an appeal it would be in the interests of justice to hold a re-hearing.

(2) The Court of Appeal will allow an appeal where the decision of the Crown Court was—

(a) wrong; or

(b) unjust because of a serious procedural or other irregularity in the proceedings in the Crown Court.

Powers of the Court of Appeal on appeal

5.—(1) The Court of Appeal has all the powers of the Crown Court. **7–312g**

(2) The Court of Appeal may—

(a) make a serious crime prevention order;

(b) affirm, set aside or vary any order or judgment made or given by the Crown Court;

(c) refer any issue for determination by the Crown Court;

(d) order a new hearing in the Crown Court;

(e) make an order for costs in accordance with Part 3;

(f) make an order for the payment of interest on those costs.

(3) The Court of Appeal may exercise its powers in relation to the whole or part of an order of the Crown Court.

Presence and live links

6.—(1) A person has a right to attend a hearing in public unless— **7–312h**

(a) it is a hearing preliminary or incidental to an appeal, including the hearing of an application for permission to appeal; or

(b) that person is in custody in consequence of—

(i) a verdict of not guilty by reason of insanity; or

(ii) a finding of disability.

(2) At any time before the beginning of a hearing, the Court of Appeal may give a live link direction in relation to that hearing if—

(a) a person who is a party to the appeal is expected to be in custody; and

(b) that person has a right to attend the hearing in accordance with paragraph (1).

(3), (4) [*Effectively identical to s.22(5) and (6) of the 1968 Act*, ante, *§ 7–201*.]

Evidence

7.—(1) [*Effectively identical to s.23(1) of the 1968 Act*, ante, *§ 7–208, with substitution of references to* "the proceedings under section 19, 20 or 21 of the Act" *for the references to* "the proceedings from which the appeal lies".] **7–312i**

(2) [*Corresponds to s.23(2) of the 1968 Act*, ante, *§ 7–208, with substitution of reference to* "any person who is a party to the appeal" *for the references to* "the appellant" *and* "the respondent".].

(3) [*Effectively identical to s.23(3) of the 1968 Act*, ante, *§ 7–208*.]

(4) [*Effectively identical to s.23(4) of the 1968 Act*, ante, *§ 7–208*.]

Effect of appeal on serious crime prevention order

8. The coming into force of a serious crime prevention order shall not be affected by an appeal, subject to any direction which the Court of Appeal may give to the contrary. **7–312j**

Powers of the Court of Appeal under Part 2 which are exercisable by a single judge

9.—(1) There may be exercised by a single judge in the same manner as by the Court of Appeal and subject to the same provisions— **7–312k**

(a) the powers of the Court of Appeal under this Part and Part 3 specified in paragraph (2); and

(b) the power to give leave under section 24(3) of the Act.

(2) The powers referred to in sub-paragraph (1)(a) are—

(a) to extend time within which notice of appeal or notice of application for leave to appeal may be given;

(b) to order a witness to attend for examination;

(c) to give a live link direction under article 6(2);

(d) to make orders under article 7(1)(a) (production of documents etc.);

(e) to give directions under article 8 (effect of appeal on serious crime prevention order); and

(f) to make orders for the payment of costs under Part 3.

(3) [*Effectively identical to s.31(3) of the 1968 Act*, ante, *§ 7–231, but with references to* "a person who is a party to the appeal" *in lieu of the references to* "an appellant".]

Powers of the Court of Appeal under Part 2 which are exercisable by the registrar

10.—(1) [*Effectively identical to s.31A(1) of the 1968 Act*, ante, *§ 7 –236.*]

(2) (a), (b), (c) [*Directly correspond to s.31A(2)(a), (b), (d) respectively*, ante, *§ 7–236.*]

(3) [*Effectively identical to s.31A(4) of the 1968 Act*, ante, *§ 7–236.*]

Procedural directions: powers of single judge and registrar

11.—(1) [*Effectively identical to s.31B(1) of the 1968 Act*, ante, *§ 7–236a.*]

(2) [*Effectively identical to s.31B(2) of the 1968 Act*, ante, *§ 7–236a.*]

(3) [*Effectively identical to s.31B(3) of the 1968 Act*, ante, *§ 7–236a.*]

(4) [*Effectively identical to s.31B(4) of the 1968 Act*, ante, *§ 7–236a.*]

Appeals against procedural directions

12.—(1), (2) [*Directly correspond to s.31C(3), (4) of the 1968 Act*, ante, *§ 7–236b.*]

(3) An application under this article may be made by a person who is a party to the appeal.

PART 3

COSTS OF APPEALS IN THE COURT OF APPEAL: ENGLAND AND WALES

CHAPTER 1

Introduction

Interpretation and transitional provision

7–312l **13.**—(1) In this Part—

"appeal costs order" means an order under article 14;

"applicant" means—

(a) in Chapter 3, the person in whose favour an appeal costs order has been made, and

(b) in Chapter 5, the person who has applied for a third party costs order;

"costs judge" means a taxing master of the Senior Courts;

"expenses" include compensation to a witness for the witness's trouble or loss of time and out of pocket expenses;

"interested party" means—

(a) the person who is a party to the appeal benefiting from the wasted costs order or third party costs order; and

(b) where that person was receiving services funded for that person by the Legal Services Commission, or an order for the payment of costs out of central funds was made in that person's favour, shall include the authority responsible for determining costs payable in respect of those services or out of central funds as the case may be;

"legal or other representative" means a person who is exercising a right of audience, or a right to conduct litigation, on behalf of any person who is a party to an appeal;

"presiding judge" means the judge that presided at the hearing in respect of which the costs are payable under an appeal costs order;

"proceedings before the Court of Appeal" means any proceedings before the Court of Appeal including an application for leave to appeal and an appeal;

"professional witness" means a witness practising as a member of the legal or medical profession or as a dentist, veterinary surgeon or accountant who attends to give professional evidence as to matters of fact;

"relevant amount" has the meaning assigned to it by article 32;

"third party" means a person who is not a party to the proceedings before the Court of Appeal;

"third party costs order" means an order under article 18;

"wasted costs order" means an order under article 17; and

"witness" means any person properly attending to give evidence, whether or not the person gives evidence or is called at the instance of one of the persons who is a party to the appeal or of the Court of Appeal, but does not include—

(c) a person attending as a witness to character only unless the Court of Appeal has certified that the interests of justice required the witness's attendance;

(d) a member of a police force attending the Court of Appeal in the member's capacity as such;

(e) a full-time officer of an institution to which the *Prison Act* 1952 applies attending the Court of Appeal in the officer's capacity as such; or

(f) a prisoner in respect of any occasion on which the prisoner is conveyed to the Court of Appeal in custody.

(2) For the purposes of article 14, the costs of the subject of a serious crime prevention order or any party under section 24(2) shall be taken to include the expense of compensating any witness for the expenses, trouble or loss of time properly incurred in or incidental to the witness's attendance.

(3) Where any person who is a party to an appeal is in receipt of services funded for that person by the Legal Services Commission, then—

(a) for the purposes of article 14, that person's costs shall be taken not to include the cost of those services; and

(b) for the purposes of articles 15 to 20, that person's costs shall be taken to include the cost of those services.

(4) In the application of this Part before the commencement of section 59(1) of the *Constitutional Reform Act* 2005 (renaming of Supreme Courts of England and Wales), the reference to the Senior Courts is to be read as a reference to the Supreme Court.

CHAPTER 2

Orders as to costs

Award of costs in favour of subject or party under section 24(2)

14.—(1) Where the Court of Appeal— **7–312m**

(a) allows an appeal by the person who is the subject of a serious crime prevention order;

(b) dismisses an appeal by the relevant applicant authority;

(c) hears an appeal by a party under section 24(2); or

(d) determines an application for leave to appeal to the Supreme Court,

it may make an appeal costs order in favour of the person who is the subject of the serious crime prevention order.

(2) Where the Court of Appeal—

(a) allows an appeal by a party under section 24(2);

(b) dismisses an appeal by the relevant applicant authority;

(c) hears an appeal by the person who is the subject of a serious crime prevention order; or

(d) determines an application for leave to appeal to the Supreme Court,

it may make an appeal costs order in favour of a party under section 24(2).

(3) Subject to paragraphs (4) and (5), an order under this article shall be for the payment out of central funds, to the person in whose favour the order is made, of such amounts as the Court of Appeal considers reasonably sufficient to compensate that person for any expenses properly incurred by that person in the proceedings before the Court of Appeal.

(4) [*Effectively identical to s.16(7) of the* Prosecution of Offences Act *1985*, ante, *§ 6-7*.]

(5) *Effectively identical to s.16(9) of the 1985 Act*, ante, *§ 6–7, save for reference to* "Chapter 3 of this Part and article 37" *in lieu of reference to* "regulations made by the Lord Chancellor".]

Award of costs against subject or party under section 24(2)

15.—(1) Where the Court of Appeal dismisses— **7–312n**

(a) an appeal or an application for leave to appeal by the person who is the subject of a serious crime prevention order; or

(b) an application by that person for leave to appeal to the Supreme Court under section 24(7) of the Act,

it may make such order as to costs to be paid by that person, to such person as may be named in the order (including the relevant applicant authority or a party under section 24(2)), as it considers just and reasonable.

(2) Where the Court of Appeal dismisses—

(a) an appeal or an application for leave to appeal by a party under section 24(2); or

(b) an application by that person for leave to appeal to the Supreme Court under section 24(7) of the Act,

it may make such order as to costs to be paid by that person, to such person as may be named in the order (including the relevant applicant authority or the person who is the subject of a serious crime prevention order), as it considers just and reasonable.

(3) The amount to be paid in pursuance of an order under this article shall be specified in the order.

Unnecessary or improper acts and omissions

7–312o **16.**—(1) [*Directly corresponds to reg. 3(1) of S.I. 1986 No. 1335,* ante, § 6–53.]

(2) When making an order under paragraph (1) the Court of Appeal may take into account any other order as to costs which has been made in respect of the proceedings before the Court of Appeal and may take the order into account when making any other order as to costs in respect of those proceedings.

(3) The amount to be paid in pursuance of an order under this article shall be specified in the order.

(4) Before making an order under paragraph (1), the Court of Appeal shall allow any person who is a party to the appeal to make representations and may hear evidence.

Wasted costs order

7–312p **17.**—(1) If in any proceedings before the Court of Appeal, costs have been incurred by a person who is a party to the appeal—

(a) as a result of any improper, unreasonable or negligent act or omission on the part of any legal or other representative or any employee of such a representative; or

(b) which, in the light of any such act or omission occurring after they were incurred, the Court of Appeal considers it is unreasonable to expect that person to pay,

the Court of Appeal may disallow, or (as the case may be) order the legal or other representative to pay, the whole of any wasted costs or such part of them as may be determined in accordance with this article.

(2) [*Directly corresponds to reg. 3B(3) of S.I. 1986 No. 1335,* ante, § 6-55.]

(3) The amount to be paid or disallowed in pursuance of a wasted costs order shall be specified in the order.

(4) Before making a wasted costs order, the Court of Appeal shall allow the legal or other representative and any person who is a party to the appeal to make representations and may hear evidence.

(5) [*Directly corresponds to reg. 3B(4) of S.I. 1986 No. 1335,* ante, § 6–55.]

(6) Where the person required to make a payment in respect of sums due under a wasted costs order fails to do so, the payment may be recovered summarily as a sum adjudged to be paid as a civil debt by order of a magistrates' court by the person benefiting from the order, save that where that person was in receipt of services funded for that person by the Legal Services Commission or an order for the payment of costs out of central funds was made in that person's favour, the power to recover shall be exercisable by the Lord Chancellor.

Third party costs order

7–312q **18.** If—

(a) there has been serious misconduct (whether or not constituting a contempt of court) by a third party; and

(b) the Court of Appeal considers it appropriate, having regard to that misconduct, to make a third party costs order against the third party

the Court of Appeal may order the third party to pay the whole of any costs incurred or wasted by any person who is a party to the appeal as a result of the misconduct or such part of them as may be determined in accordance with Chapter 4 of this Part.

Costs of attendance at any proceedings before the Court of Appeal

19.—(1) The Court of Appeal may order the payment out of central funds of such sums as **7–312r** appear to it to be reasonably sufficient to compensate a person who is a party to an appeal who is not in custody and who appears before it on, or in connection with, any proceedings before the Court of Appeal.

(2) Article 37 will apply for the purpose of determining the amount of any subsistence allowance or travelling expenses ordered to be paid under this article.

Costs of witnesses etc.

20.—(1) [*Directly corresponds to reg. 16(1) of S.I. 1986 No. 1335,* ante, *§ 6–73, but without para. (c) and with reference to* "Chapter 5 of this Part" *in lieu of reference to* "this Part".

(2) [*Directly corresponds to reg. 16(2), but without the opening words.*]

CHAPTER 3

Appeal costs orders: procedure

Person who is to determine costs

21.—(1) Costs under an appeal costs order shall be determined by the registrar in accor- **7–312s** dance with this Chapter.

(2) [*Effectively identical to reg. 5(3) of S.I. 1986 No. 1335,* ante, *§ 6–57.*]

Claims for costs

22.—(1), (2) [*Effectively identical to reg. 6(1), (2) of S.I. 1986 No. 1335,* ante, *§ 6–58.*]

(3) [*Effectively identical to reg. 6(3), but without sub-para. (d).*]

(4), (5) [*Effectively identical to reg. 6(4), (5).*]

Determination of costs

23. [*Effectively identical to reg. 7 of S.I. 1986 No. 1335,* ante, *§ 6–59.*]

Payment of costs

24. [*Effectively identical to reg. 8 of S.I. 1986 No. 1335,* ante, *§ 6–60.*]

Re-determination of costs by the registrar

25. [*Effectively identical to reg. 9 of S.I. 1986 No. 1335,* ante, *§ 6–61.*]

Appeals to a costs judge

26. [*Effectively identical to reg. 10 of S.I. 1986 No. 1335,* ante, *§ 6–62.*]

Appeals to the High Court

27. [*Effectively identical to reg. 11 of S.I. 1986 No. 1335,* ante, *§ 6–65.*]

Time limits

28. [*Effectively identical to reg. 12 of S.I. 1986 No. 1335,* ante, *§ 6–66.*]

CHAPTER 4

Third party costs orders: procedure

Determination of a third party costs order

29.—(1)–(3) [*Effectively identical to reg. 3F(2)-(4) of S.I. 1986 No. 1335,* ante, *§ 6–* **7–312t** *55b.*]

(4) [*Effectively identical to reg. 3F(5), but without the words* "vary or".]

(5), (6) [*Effectively identical to reg. 3F(6), (7).*]

Procedure for third party costs orders

30. [*Effectively identical to reg. 3G of S.I. 1986 No. 1335,* ante, *§ 6–55c, but without the first para. (2) and with references to* "the registrar" *substituted for the references to* "the appropriate officer".]

31. [*Recovery of sums due under a third party costs order.*]

CHAPTER 5

Costs of witnesses etc: procedure

7–312u **32.** [*Determination of rates or scales of allowances payable out of central funds.*]

Witnesses other than professional or expert witnesses

33. [*Effectively identical to reg. 18 of S.I. 1986 No. 1335,* ante, *§ 6–75.*]

34. [*Professional witnesses.*]

35. [*Expert witnesses and interpreters.*]

36. [*Night allowances.*]

Expenses of subject or party under section 24(2)

37. [*Effectively identical to reg. 23 of S.I. 1986 No. 1335,* ante, *§ 6–80.*]

38. [*Travelling expenses.*]

PART 4

APPEALS TO THE SUPREME COURT: ENGLAND AND WALES

Application for leave to appeal

7–312v **39.**—(1) An application to the Supreme Court for leave to appeal shall be made in writing within 28 days beginning with the date on which the application for leave to appeal is refused by the Court of Appeal.

(2) The Supreme Court may, upon an application made at any time by a person who was a party to the appeal before the Court of Appeal, extend the time within which an application may be made by that person to the Supreme Court under paragraph (1).

Hearing and disposal of appeal

7–312w **40.** For the purposes of disposing of an appeal, the Supreme Court may exercise any powers of the Court of Appeal or may remit the case to the Court of Appeal.

Powers of Court of Appeal under Part 4 which are exercisable by a single judge

41. [*Effectively corresponds to s.44(1)(a)(i) of the 1968 Act,* post, *§ 7–336.*]

Award of costs in favour of subject or party under section 24(2)

7–312x **42.**—(1) Where the Supreme Court determines an appeal to which the person who is the subject of the serious crime prevention order was a party it may make a costs order in favour of that person.

(2) Where the Supreme Court determines an appeal to which a party under section 24(2) was a party it may make a costs order in favour of that person.

(3)–(5) [*Effectively identical to art. 14(3)-(5),* ante, *§ 7–312m, but with substitution of* "by such officer as may be prescribed by order of the Supreme Court" *in lieu of* "in accordance with Chapter 3 of this Part and article 37" *in para. (5).*]

Transitional provisions in relation to the Supreme Court

7–312y **43.**—(1) In the application of Parts 2 to 4 before the commencement of paragraph 16(3)(b) of Schedule 9 to the *Constitutional Reform Act* 2005 (amendment of section 33(2) of the *Criminal Appeal Act* 1968), references to the Supreme Court are to be read as references to the House of Lords.

(2) During the time that this Part is to be read as referring to the House of Lords in accordance with paragraph (1)—

(a) an appeal shall not be heard and determined by the House of Lords unless there are present at least three of the persons designated Lords of Appeal by section 5 of the *Appellate Jurisdiction Act* 1876; and

(b) any order of the House of Lords which provides for the hearing of applications for leave to appeal by a committee constituted in accordance with section 5 of that Act may direct that the decision of that committee shall be taken on behalf of the House.

IX. APPEAL TO THE COURT OF APPEAL: PROCEDURE AND FORMS

A. PROCEDURAL RULES

Introduction

The *Criminal Procedure (Amendment No. 2) Rules* 2007 (S.I. 2007 No. 2317) replaced Parts 65 (appeal against ruling in preparatory hearing), 66 (appeal against ruling adverse to prosecution), 67 (appeal against order restricting reporting or public access), 68 (appeal against conviction, sentence or sentence review decision), 69 (reference of point of law) and 70 (reference of sentence) with new Parts 65 (appeal to the Court of Appeal: general rules), 66 (appeal against ruling at preparatory hearing), 67 (appeal against ruling adverse to prosecution), 68 (appeal about conviction or sentence), 69 (appeal regarding reporting or public access restriction) and 70 (references of points of law and sentences). **7–313**

Part 65 (*post*, §§ 7–313a *et seq.*) applies to all the applications, appeals and references to the Court of Appeal to which Parts 66 to 70 apply. There is little change of substance in the contents thereof. Similarly, there is little change of substance in either Part 66 (*ante*, §§ 7–300 *et seq.*) or 67 (*ante*, §§ 7–259a *et seq.*), but time limits in relation to appeals against rulings in preparatory hearings are now expressed in "business days".

Part 68 applies to an appeal by a defendant under Part I of the *CAA* 1968, or Schedule 22 to the *CJA* 2003, to a reference by the Criminal Cases Review Commission under section 9 of the *CAA* 1995, to a prosecutor's appeal under section 14A(5A) of the *Football Spectators Act* 1989 (*ante*, § 5–825), to an appeal under the *SOCPA* 2005, s.74(8) (*ante*, § 5–94b), to an appeal by a person found to be in contempt, under the *Administration of Justice Act* 1960, s.13 (*post*, § 28–138) and the *CAA* 1968, s.18A (*ante*, § 7–158), to appeals in respect of serious crime prevention orders and to an appeal against a wasted costs order or a third party costs order. The substance is much the same as that of the replaced rules, but (i) explicit provision is made for the participation of the prosecution (it being a matter for the discretion of the registrar whether to invite or direct their participation) (see r.68.6), (ii) there is a prescribed procedure for making an application to the Crown Court for a certificate that a case is fit for appeal (see r.68.4) and (iii) rule 68.12 is intended to accommodate the practice of the Court of Appeal as described in *R. v. Spruce*; *R. v. Anwar* [2006] 1 Cr.App.R.(S.) 11 (*ante*, § 7–202). Parts 69 (*ante*, §§ 7–310 *et seq.*) and 70 (*post*, §§ 7–372 *et seq.*) reproduce the substance of their predecessor rules.

The rules in the new Parts 65 to 70 came into force on October 1, 2007, but they apply only where an appeal, application or reference, to which one of those parts applies, "is made" on or after October 1, 2007, and that, in other cases the rules replaced by those rules apply: rule 2.1(7) (*ante*, § 2–206).

Certain of the rules have subsequently been amended by the *Criminal Procedure (Amendment No. 3) Rules* 2007 (S.I. 2007 No. 3662), and the *Criminal Procedure (Amendment) Rules* 2008 (S.I. 2008 No. 2076).

Criminal Procedure Rules 2005 (S.I. 2005 No. 384), Pt 65
(as substituted by the Criminal Procedure (Amendment No. 2) Rules 2007 (S.I. 2007 No. 2317))

When this Part applies

65.1.—(1) This Part applies to all the applications, appeals and references to the Court of Appeal to which Parts 66, 67, 68, 69, 70 and 74 apply. **7–313a**

(2) In this Part and in those, unless the context makes it clear that something different is meant—

"court" means the Court of Appeal or any judge of that court;

"Registrar" means the Registrar of Criminal Appeals or a court officer acting with the Registrar's authority.

[This rule is printed as amended by S.I. 2007 No. 3662 (*ante*, § 7–313).]

Case management in the Court of Appeal

7–313b **65.2.**—(1) The court and the parties have the same duties and powers as under Part 3 (case management).

(2) The Registrar—

(a) must fulfil the duty of active case management under rule 3.2; and

(b) in fulfilling that duty may exercise any of the powers of case management under—

(i) rule 3.5 (the court's general powers of case management),

(ii) rule 3.9(3) (requiring a certificate of readiness), and

(iii) rule 3.10 (requiring a party to identify intentions and anticipated requirements)

subject to the directions of the court.

(3) The Registrar must nominate a case progression officer under rule 3.4.

The requirement that cases are dealt with "efficiently and expeditiously" as an aspect of the overriding objective that cases be dealt with justly (see rule 1.1(1) and (2)(e) of the 2005 rules, *ante*, § 4–84b) applies to criminal appeals: see *R. v. Siddall and Brooke*, *The Times*, July 26, 2006, CA.

Power to vary requirements

7–313c **65.3.** The court or the Registrar may—

(a) shorten a time limit or extend it (even after it has expired) unless that is inconsistent with other legislation;

(b) allow a party to vary any notice that that party has served;

(c) direct that a notice or application be served on any person;

(d) allow a notice or application to be in a different form, or presented orally.

Application for extension of time

7–313d **65.4.** A person who wants an extension of time within which to serve a notice or make an application must—

(a) apply for that extension of time when serving that notice or making that application; and

(b) give the reasons for the application for an extension of time.

Renewing an application refused by a judge or the Registrar

7–313e **65.5.**—(1) This rule applies where a party with the right to do so wants to renew—

(a) to a judge of the Court of Appeal an application refused by the Registrar; or

(b) to the Court of Appeal an application refused by a judge of that court.

(2) That party must—

(a) renew the application in the form set out in the Practice Direction, signed by or on behalf of the applicant;

(b) serve the renewed application on the Registrar not more than 14 days after—

(i) the refusal of the application that the applicant wants to renew; or

(ii) the Registrar serves that refusal on the applicant, if the applicant was not present in person or by live link when the original application was refused.

[This rule is printed as amended by S.I. 2008 No. 2076 (*ante*, § 7–313).]

As to the forms to be used in connection with this rule, see *post*, § 7–314b.

Hearings

7–313f **65.6.**—(1) The general rule is that the Court of Appeal must hear in public—

(a) an application, including an application for permission to appeal; and

(b) an appeal or reference,

but it may order any hearing to be in private.

(2) Where a hearing is about a public interest ruling that hearing must be in private unless the court otherwise directs.

(3) Where the appellant wants to appeal against an order restricting public access to a trial the court must decide without a hearing—

(a) an application, including an application for permission to appeal; and
(b) an appeal.

(4) Where the appellant wants to appeal or to refer a case to the House of Lords the court—

(a) may decide without a hearing an application—
(i) for permission to appeal or to refer a sentencing case, or
(ii) to refer a point of law; but
(b) must announce its decision on such an application at a hearing in public.

(5) A judge of the Court of Appeal and the Registrar may exercise any of their powers—

(a) at a hearing in public or in private; or
(b) without a hearing.

[This rule is printed as amended by S.I. 2007 No. 3662 (*ante*, § 7–313).]

Notice of hearings and decisions

65.7.—(1) The Registrar must give as much notice as reasonably practicable of every hearing to— **7–313g**

(a) the parties;
(b) any party's custodian;
(c) any other person whom the court requires to be notified; and
(d) the Crown Court officer, where Parts 66, 67 or 69 apply.

(2) The Registrar must serve every decision on—

(a) the parties;
(b) any other person whom the court requires to be served; and
(c) the Crown Court officer and any party's custodian, where the decision determines an appeal or application for permission to appeal.

(3) But where a hearing or decision is about a public interest ruling, the Registrar must not—

(a) give notice of that hearing to; or
(b) serve that decision on,

anyone other than the prosecutor who applied for that ruling, unless the court otherwise directs.

Duty of Crown Court officer

65.8.—(1) The Crown Court officer must provide the Registrar with any document, object or information for which the Registrar asks within such period as the Registrar may require. **7–313h**

(2) Unless the Crown Court otherwise directs, where someone may appeal to the Court of Appeal the Crown Court officer must—

(a) arrange for the recording of the proceedings in the Crown Court;
(b) arrange for the transcription of such a recording if—
(i) the Registrar wants such a transcript, or
(ii) anyone else wants such a transcript (but that is subject to the restrictions in rule 65.9(2)); and
(c) arrange for any document or object exhibited in the proceedings in the Crown Court to be kept there, or kept by some other appropriate person, until 6 weeks after the conclusion of those proceedings.

(3) Where Part 66 applies (appeal to the Court of Appeal against ruling at preparatory hearing), the Crown Court officer must as soon as practicable serve on the appellant a transcript or note of—

(a) each order or ruling against which the appellant wants to appeal; and
(b) the decision by the Crown Court judge on any application for permission to appeal.

(4) Where Part 67 applies (appeal to the Court of Appeal against ruling adverse to prosecution), the Crown Court officer must as soon as practicable serve on the appellant a transcript or note of—

(a) each ruling against which the appellant wants to appeal;
(b) the decision by the Crown Court judge on any application for permission to appeal; and
(c) the decision by the Crown Court judge on any request to expedite the appeal.

(5) Where Part 68 applies (appeal to the Court of Appeal about conviction or sentence), the Crown Court officer must as soon as practicable serve on the Registrar—

(a) the appeal notice and any accompanying application that the appellant serves on the Crown Court officer;
(b) any Crown Court judge's certificate that the case is fit for appeal;
(c) the decision on any application at the Crown Court centre for bail pending appeal;
(d) such of the Crown Court case papers as the Registrar requires; and
(e) such transcript of the Crown Court proceedings as the Registrar requires.

(6) Where Part 69 applies (appeal to the Court of Appeal regarding reporting or public access) and an order is made restricting public access to a trial, the Crown Court officer must—

(a) immediately notify the Registrar of that order, if the appellant has given advance notice of intention to appeal; and
(b) as soon as practicable provide the applicant for that order with a transcript or note of the application.

Duty of person transcribing proceedings in the Crown Court

7–313i **65.9.**—(1) A person who transcribes a recording of proceedings in the Crown Court under arrangements made by the Crown Court officer must provide the Registrar with any transcript for which the Registrar asks within such period as the Registrar may require.

(2) Unless the Crown Court otherwise directs, such a person—

(a) must not provide anyone else with a transcript of a public interest ruling or of an application for such a ruling;
(b) subject to that, must provide anyone else with any transcript for which that person asks—
  (i) in accordance with the transcription arrangements made by the Crown Court officer, and
  (ii) on payment by that person of any charge fixed by the Treasury.

Duty of person keeping exhibit

7–313j **65.10.** A person who under arrangements made by the Crown Court officer keeps a document or object exhibited in the proceedings in the Crown Court must—

(a) keep that exhibit until—
  (i) 6 weeks after the conclusion of the Crown Court proceedings, or
  (ii) the conclusion of any appeal proceedings that begin within that 6 weeks,

unless the court, the Registrar or the Crown Court otherwise directs; and

(b) provide the Registrar with any such document or object for which the Registrar asks within such period as the Registrar may require.

[This rule is printed as amended by S.I. 2007 No. 3662 (*ante*, § 7–313).]

Registrar's duty to provide copy documents for appeal or reference

7–313k **65.11.** Unless the court otherwise directs, for the purposes of an appeal or reference—

(a) the Registrar must—
  (i) provide a party with a copy of any document or transcript held by the Registrar for such purposes, or
  (ii) allow a party to inspect such a document or transcript

on payment by that party of any charge fixed by the Treasury; but

(b) the Registrar must not provide a copy or allow the inspection of—
  (i) a document provided only for the court and the Registrar, or
  (ii) a transcript of a public interest ruling or of an application for such a ruling.

[This rule is printed as amended by S.I. 2008 No. 2076 (*ante*, § 7–313).]

Declaration of incompatibility with a Convention right

7–313l **65.12.**—(1) This rule applies where a party—

(a) wants the court to make a declaration of incompatibility with a Convention right under section 4 of the *Human Rights Act* 1998; or
(b) raises an issue that the Registrar thinks may lead the court to make such a declaration.

(2) The Registrar must serve notice on—

(a) the relevant person named in the list published under section 17(1) of the *Crown Proceedings Act* 1947; or

(b) the Treasury Solicitor, if it is not clear who is the relevant person.

(3) That notice must include or attach details of—

(a) the legislation affected and the Convention right concerned;

(b) the parties to the appeal; and

(c) any other information or document that the Registrar thinks relevant.

(4) A person who has a right under the 1998 Act to become a party to the appeal must—

(a) serve notice on—

(i) the Registrar, and

(ii) the other parties,

if that person wants to exercise that right; and

(b) in that notice—

(i) indicate the conclusion that that person invites the court to reach on the question of incompatibility, and

(ii) identify each ground for that invitation, concisely outlining the arguments in support.

(5) The court must not make a declaration of incompatibility—

(a) less than 21 days after the Registrar serves notice under paragraph (2); and

(b) without giving any person who serves a notice under paragraph (4) an opportunity to make representations at a hearing.

65.13. [*Abandoning an appeal: see* ante, *§ 7–198.*] **7–313m**

65.14. [*Abandoning a ground of appeal or opposition: see* ante, *§ 7–198a.*] **7–313n**

[Pt 65 is printed as substituted by the *Criminal Procedure (Amendment (No. 2) Rules* 2007 (S.I. 2007 No. 2317).]

Criminal Procedure Rules 2005 (S.I. 2005 No. 384), Pt 68 (as substituted by the Criminal Procedure (Amendment No. 2) Rules 2007 (S.I. 2007 No. 2317))

When this Part applies

68.1.—(1) This Part applies where— **7–313o**

(a) a defendant wants to appeal under—

(i) Part 1 of the *Criminal Appeal Act* 1968, or

(ii) paragraph 14 of Schedule 22 to the *Criminal Justice Act* 2003;

(b) the Criminal Cases Review Commission refers a case to the Court of Appeal under section 9 of the *Criminal Appeal Act* 1995;

(c) a prosecutor wants to appeal to the Court of Appeal under section 14A(5A) of the *Football Spectators Act* 1989;

(d) a party wants to appeal under section 74(8) of the *Serious Organised Crime and Police Act* 2005;

(e) a person found to be in contempt of court wants to appeal under section 13 of the *Administration of Justice Act* 1960 and section 18A of the *Criminal Appeal Act* 1968; or

(f) a person wants to appeal to the Court of Appeal under—

(i) section 24 of the *Serious Crime Act* 2007, or

(ii) regulation 3C or 3H of the *Costs in Criminal Cases (General) Regulations* 1986.

(2) A reference to an "appellant" in this Part is a reference to such a party or person.

[This rule is printed as amended by S.I. 2007 No. 3662 (*ante*, § 7–313); and S.I. 2008 No. 2076 (*ante*, § 7–313).]

For regulations 3C and 3H of the 1986 regulations, see *ante*, §§ 6–55, 6–55d.

Service of appeal notice

68.2.—(1) The general rule is that an appellant must serve an appeal notice— **7–313p**

(a) on the Crown Court officer at the Crown Court centre where there occurred—

(i) the conviction, verdict, or finding,

(ii) the sentence, or

(iii) the order, or the failure to make an order
about which the appellant wants to appeal; and

(b) not more than—

(i) 28 days after that occurred, or

(ii) 21 days after the order, in a case in which the appellant appeals against a wasted or third party costs order.

(2) But an appellant must serve an appeal notice—

(a) on the Registrar instead where—

(i) the appeal is against a minimum term review decision under paragraph 14 of Schedule 22 to the *Criminal Justice Act* 2003, or

(ii) the Criminal Cases Review Commission refers the case to the court; and

(b) not more than—

(i) 28 days after such a decision, or after the Registrar serves notice that the Commission has referred a sentence, or

(ii) 56 days after the Registrar serves notice that the Commission has referred a conviction.

[This rule is printed as amended by S.I. 2008 No. 2076 (*ante*, § 7–313).]

Form of appeal notice

7–313q **68.3.**—(1) An appeal notice must be in the form set out in the Practice Direction.

(2) The appeal notice must—

(a) specify—

(i) the conviction, verdict, or finding,

(ii) the sentence, or

(iii) the order, or the failure to make an order
about which the appellant wants to appeal;

(b) identify each ground of appeal on which the appellant relies, numbering them consecutively (if there is more than one) and concisely outlining each argument in support;

(c) identify the transcript that the appellant thinks the court will need, if the appellant wants to appeal against a conviction;

(d) identify the relevant sentencing powers of the Crown Court, if sentence is in issue;

(e) where the Criminal Cases Review Commission refers a case to the court, explain how each ground of appeal relates (if it does) to the reasons for the reference;

(f) summarise the relevant facts;

(g) identify any relevant authorities;

(h) include or attach any application for the following, with reasons—

(i) permission to appeal, if the appellant needs the court's permission,

(ii) an extension of time within which to serve the appeal notice,

(iii) bail pending appeal,

(iv) a direction to attend in person a hearing that the appellant could attend by live link, if the appellant is in custody,

(v) the introduction of evidence, including hearsay evidence and evidence of bad character,

(vi) an order requiring a witness to attend court,

(vii) a direction for special measures for a witness,

(viii) a direction for special measures for the giving of evidence by the appellant;

(i) identify any other document or thing that the appellant thinks the court will need to decide the appeal.

As to the form to be used in connection with this rule, see *post*, § 7–314b.

Crown Court judge's certificate that case is fit for appeal.

7–313r **68.4.**—(1) An appellant who wants the Crown Court judge to certify that a case is fit for appeal must—

(a) apply orally, with reasons, immediately after there occurs—

(i) the conviction, verdict, or finding,

(ii) the sentence, or

(iii) the order, or the failure to make an order

about which the appellant wants to appeal; or

(b) apply in writing and serve the application on the Crown Court officer not more than 14 days after that occurred.

(2) A written application must include the same information (with the necessary adaptations) as an appeal notice.

68.5. [*Reference by Criminal Cases Review Commission: see* ante, *§ 7–156.*] 7–313s

68.6. [*Respondent's notice: see* ante, *§ 7–207.*] 7–313t

Adaptation of rules about introducing evidence

68.7.—(1) The following Parts apply with such adaptations as the court or the Registrar may direct— 7–313u

(a) Part 29 (special measures directions);

(b) Part 30 (use of live television link other than for vulnerable witnesses);

(c) Part 34 (hearsay evidence);

(d) Part 35 (evidence of bad character); and

(e) Part 36 (evidence of a complainant's previous sexual behaviour).

(2) But the general rule is that—

(a) a respondent who opposes an appellant's application to which one of those Parts applies must do so in the respondent's notice, with reasons;

(b) an appellant who opposes a respondent's application to which one of those Parts applies must serve notice, with reasons, on—

(i) the Registrar, and

(ii) the respondent

not more than 14 days after service of the respondent's notice; and

(c) the court or the Registrar may give directions with or without a hearing.

As to the form to be used in connection with this rule, see *post*, § 7–314b.

68.8. [*Application for bail pending appeal or retrial: see* ante, *§ 7–189.*] 7–313v

68.9. [*Conditions of bail pending appeal or retrial: see* ante, *§ 7–190.*] 7–313w

68.10. [*Forfeiture of a recognizance given as a condition of bail: see* ante, *§ 7–191.*] 7–313x

68.11. [*Right to attend hearing: see* ante, *§ 7–201a.*] 7–313y

68.12. [*Power to vary determination of appeal against sentence: see* ante, *§ 7–201b.*] 7–313z

68.13. [*Directions about re-admission to hospital on dismissal of appeal: see* ante, *§ 7–150.*] 7–314

68.14. [*Renewal or setting aside of order for retrial: see* ante, *§ 7–115.*] 7–314a

B. FORMS

Rule 5.1 of the *Criminal Procedure Rules* 2005 (S.I. 2005 No. 384) (*ante*, § 2–219) provides simply that the forms set out in the consolidated criminal practice direction shall be used as appropriate in connection with the rules to which they apply. 7–314b

The sixteenth amendment to that practice direction amends Annex D (prescribed forms). It sets out the forms to be substituted for various existing forms and adds three new forms. The new forms are to be used in conjunction with the new rules about appeals contained in Parts 65 to 70 of the 2005 rules (*ante*, § 7–313). They have been comprehensively revised to correspond with the new rules. A new lettering system has been added to the forms to make them more identifiable, for example, all notices and grounds of appeal are referred to with the prefix 'NG', dependent upon the type of notice of application or appeal being lodged. Likewise the respondent's notices required for each type of application or appeal are now identified as: RN (Prep), RN (Pros), RN, and RN (159). The format of the appeal forms has also been standardised where possible, including by the addition of the identifying letters to the top right hand corner. The form of notice and grounds of appeal or application for leave to appeal against conviction or sentence (Form NG) has been revised to highlight the detailed grounds and information now required under the rules when initiating appeal proceedings. This amendment took effect on October 1, 2007, when the new Parts 65 to 70 came into force. The new forms must be used where the new appeal rules apply.

The forms attached to the amendment to the practice direction for use in connection with: (a) rules 65.5(2) and 65.13(3); (b) rules 66.3(1), 66.5(4) and 66.7; (c) rules 67.4(1), 67.7(4) and 67.10; (d) rules 68.3(1), 68.7, 68.8(2), 68.9(3) and 68.9(5); and (e) rules 69.3 and 69.4 are substituted for the corresponding forms in Annex D. The forms attached to the amendment to the practice direction for use in connection with rules 65.5(2) and 69.7 are added to the forms set out in Annex D.

X. APPEAL TO THE HOUSE OF LORDS [SUPREME COURT] FROM THE COURT OF APPEAL

A. THE APPEAL

(1) Introduction—practice

Procedure directions

7–315 In November, 2000, the House of Lords issued directions as to the procedure applicable to criminal appeals to the House of Lords from courts in England and Wales and Northern Ireland. The directions will have to be consulted for the purposes of pursuing an appeal to the House of Lords: copies of the booklet containing the directions (*House of Lords—Practice Directions applicable to Criminal Appeals*, May, 1997) may be obtained from the judicial office of the House of Lords (020 7219 3111/3). The directions, which supersede all previous editions of the directions as to procedure, provide for a joint statement of facts and issues to be lodged in an appeal, and for the parties' cases to be lodged after setting down, in line with the procedure in civil appeals. The appendices contain, *inter alia*, a form of criminal petition for leave to appeal, a form of criminal petition for leave to appeal out of time and a form of petition of appeal. For subsequent amendments to the directions, see *Practice Direction (House of Lords: Criminal Appeals)* (2001) 145 S.J. (LB 130). The full text of the directions, as amended, is available on the internet (www.parliament.the-stationery-office.co.uk/pa/ld/ldjudinf.htm).

Attendance of counsel

7–315a Counsel instructed to appear before the House of Lords are expected to be present at and throughout the hearing. Hearings in the House ordinarily take precedence over hearings in lower courts, but counsel should not ordinarily take instructions to appear in the House for a hearing on a fixed date if they already have a conflicting commitment. It is, however, appreciated that unforeseen circumstances may arise making it difficult or embarrassing for counsel to appear in the House as instructed, and the proper course in such circumstances is to write to the presiding Law Lord and seek his leave to be absent, which will ordinarily be given if sufficient reason is shown. When more than one appeal is heard, whether together or in succession, the House is content that those representing a party whose case has been fully presented should withdraw at the next convenient adjournment: *Practice Statement (House of Lords: Appearance of counsel)* [2008] 1 W.L.R. 1143, HL.

Admission passes

7–316 Admission passes to the Palace of Westminster are required by counsel and all those attending the Judicial Office. Applications for passes in respect of attendance at the hearing and judgment should be made in advance by letter to the Judicial Office (House of Lords, London, SW1A 0PW), specifying the names of counsel and a maximum of two clerks and two solicitors for each party and for whom, and the number of days for which, a pass is required. The pass will be available for collection from the Pass Office on the first day on which the pass is required. Applications for passes in respect of attendance at the Judicial Office should be made on the day in person to the Pass Office, where a day-pass will be issued. The Pass Office is located at Black Rod's Garden Entrance near the Victoria Tower. In no circumstances will passes be sent by post, nor will applications by telephone be considered.

Standing Order No. 86 of the House of Lords relating to public business

Standing Order No. 86 provides that for the purposes of its appellate jurisdiction, the House shall have Appellate and Appeal Committees, of which all lords qualified under the *Appellate Jurisdiction Acts* 1876 and 1887 shall be members. These committees shall be: **7–317**

(a) two Appellate Committees, which shall hear any cause or matter referred to them and shall report thereon to the House; and

(b) two Appeal Committees, which shall consider any petition or application for leave to appeal that may be referred to them and any matter relating thereto, or to causes depending, or formerly depending, in the House, and shall report thereon to the House.

Order 86 further provides that in any criminal matter, or in any matter concerning extradition, an Appeal Committee may take decisions and give directions on behalf of the House.

For the purposes of the *Appellate Jurisdiction Act* 1876, s.8 (repealed as from a day to be appointed: *Constitutional Reform Act* 2005, s.145, and Sched. 17, para. 9), any Appellate Committee may sit and act while Parliament is prorogued.

Transfer of jurisdiction to Supreme Court

Part 3 (ss.23–60) of the *Constitutional Reform Act* 2005 makes provision in relation to the Supreme Court of the United Kingdom (established by s.23(1)). The court will consist of 12 judges. Section 40 provides for the jurisdiction of the Supreme Court, and gives effect to Schedule 9 (amendments relating to jurisdiction of the Supreme Court). One effect of these amendments is to transfer jurisdiction from the House of Lords to the Supreme Court. These provisions are to come into force on a day to be appointed. **7–317a**

(2) Right of appeal

Criminal Appeal Act 1968, s.33

33.—(1) An appeal lies to the *House of Lords* [Supreme Court], at the instance of the defendant or the prosecutor, from any decision of the Court of Appeal on an appeal to that court under Part I of this Act or Part 9 of the *Criminal Justice Act* 2003 or section 9 (preparatory hearings) of the *Criminal Justice Act* 1987 or section 35 of the *Criminal Procedure and Investigations Act* 1996 or section 47 of the *Criminal Justice Act* 2003. **7–318**

(1B) An appeal lies to the *House of Lords* [Supreme Court], at the instance of the acquitted person or the prosecutor, from any decision of the Court of Appeal on an application under section 76(1) or (2) of the *Criminal Justice Act* 2003 (retrial for serious offences).

(2) The appeal lies only with the leave of the Court of Appeal or the *House of Lords* [Supreme Court]; and leave shall not be granted unless it is certified by the Court of Appeal that a point of law of general public importance is involved in the decision and it appears to the Court of Appeal or the *House of Lords* [Supreme Court] (as the case may be) that the point is one which ought to be considered by that *House* [Supreme Court].

(3) Except as provided by this part of this Act and section 13 of the *Administration of Justice Act* 1960 (appeal in cases of contempt of court), no appeal shall lie from any decision of the criminal division of the Court of Appeal.

(4) In relation to an appeal under subsection (1B), references in this Part to a defendant are references to the acquitted person.

[This section is printed as amended by the *Supreme Court Act* 1981, Sched. 5; the *CJA* 1987, s.15, and Sched. 2, para. 3; the *CPIA* 1996, s.36(1); the *PCA* 2002, s.456, and Sched. 11, para. 4(1) and (2); the *CJA* 2003, ss.47(6), 68(1) and 81(1)–(3); and the *SCA* 2007, ss.74(2) and 92, Sched. 8, para. 144, and Sched. 14; and as amended, as from a day to be appointed, by the *Constitutional Reform Act* 2005, s.40(4), and Sched.

9, paras 16(1) and (3), and 82(1) and (4) (substitution of references to "Supreme Court" for references to "House of Lords").]

Section 33(3) is disapplied by paragraph 14(4) of Schedule 22 to the *CJA* 2003 (rights of appeal of existing life prisoners); by section 74(9) of the *SOCPA* 2005 (assistance by defendant; review of sentence) (*ante*, § 5–94b); and by the *SCA* 2007, s.24(12) (appeals relating to serious crime prevention orders) (*ante*, § 5–875h). As to appeals to the House of Lords [Supreme Court] under section 74 of the 2005 Act, see *ante*, § 7–314a.

On March 6, 1979, two practice directions were issued.

Practice Direction (House of Lords: Petitions: Leave to Appeal)
[1979] 1 W.L.R. 497

7–319 **1.** As from 1st October 1976 petitions for leave to appeal to the House of Lords will be referred to an appeal committee consisting of three Lords of Appeal, who will consider whether the petition appears to be competent to be received by the House and, if so, whether it should be referred for an oral hearing. For the purposes of this direction, petitions are incompetent if they fall under one of the following heads: (a) petitions for leave to appeal to the House of Lords against a refusal of the Court of Appeal to grant leave to appeal to that court from a judgment of a lower court; (b) …; (c) …; (d) … .

2. Petitions for leave to appeal will be referred for an oral hearing if any member of the appeal committee (i) considers that the petition is competent or expresses doubts as to whether it is incompetent and (ii) considers that it is fit for oral hearing.

3. Where a petition is not considered fit for an oral hearing, the Clerk of the Parliaments will notify the parties that the petition is dismissed.

4. This practice direction supersedes the previous practice directions on petitions for leave to appeal.

The previous directions referred to are to be found at [1976] 1 W.L.R. 549; [1976] 1 W.L.R. 638; [1977] 1 W.L.R. 1098.

Paragraph 1(b) to (d) are irrelevant to criminal proceedings.

Practice Direction (House of Lords: Petitions: Criminal)
[1979] 1 W.L.R. 498

7–320 Criminal petitions for leave to appeal to the House of Lords in respect of which no certificate has been granted by the court below under section 1(2) of the *Administration of Justice Act* 1960 or section 33(2) of the *Criminal Appeal Act* 1968 will not be received in the Judicial Office.

This accords with the decision of this House in *Gelberg v. Miller* [1961] 1 W.L.R. 459; [1961] 1 All E.R. 618 which has been held by the Appeal Committee to apply to section 33(2) of the *Criminal Appeal Act* 1968 as it applies to section 1(2) of the *Administration of Justice Act* 1960.

As to the notification of the parties of the decision of the Court of Appeal on an application for a certificate that there was a point of law of general public importance involved in their decision, and as to the right of the prosecution to apply to the House of Lords [Supreme Court] for leave to appeal following the refusal of leave by the Court of Appeal, see *R. v. Cadnam-Smith*, *ante*, § 7–223.

The certificate of the Court of Appeal should state what the point of law is that is certified: *per* Lord Reid in *Jones v. DPP* [1962] A.C. 635 at 660. When the Court of Appeal refuses an application for a certificate it is not the practice of the court to give reasons: *R. v. Cooper and MacMahon*, 61 Cr.App.R. 215; *cf. R. v. Blaue*, 61 Cr.App.R. 271 at 275.

Section 51 of the 1968 Act (*post*, § 7–350) makes an intentional distinction between proceedings which are an appeal and proceedings which are an application for leave to appeal. There is no way in which an application for leave to appeal can achieve the status of an appeal, otherwise than by order of the Court of Appeal. Before there can be an application for leave to appeal to the House of Lords [Supreme Court] there must be a decision by the court "on an appeal" (see s.33, *ante*): *R. v. Mealey and Sheridan* [1975] Crim.L.R. 154, CA.

Appeal against sentence

Where the trial judge has passed a sentence which was within his discretion, no point of law of general public importance can arise: *R. v. Ashdown*, 58 Cr.App.R. 339, CA. **7–321**

(3) Application for leave to appeal

Criminal Appeal Act 1968, s.34

34.—(1) An application to the Court of Appeal for leave to appeal to the *House of Lords* [Supreme Court] shall be made within the period of 28 days beginning with the relevant date; and an application to the *House of Lords* [Supreme Court] for leave shall be made within the period of 28 days beginning with the date on which the application for leave is refused by the Court of Appeal. **7–322**

(1A) In subsection (1), the "relevant date" means—

(a) the date of the Court of Appeal's decision; or

(b) if later, the date on which the Court [of Appeal] gives reasons for its decision.

(2) The *House of Lords* [Supreme Court] or the Court of Appeal may, upon application made at any time by the defendant or, in the case of an appeal under section 33(1B), by the prosecutor, extend the time within which an application may be made by him to *that House or the Court* [the Supreme Court or the Court of Appeal] under subsection (1) above.

(3) An appeal to the *House of Lords* [Supreme Court] shall be treated as pending until any application for leave to appeal is disposed of and, if leave to appeal is granted, until the appeal is disposed of; and for purposes of this Part of this Act an application for leave to appeal shall be treated as disposed of at the expiration of the time within which it may be made, if it is not made within that time.

[This section is printed as amended by the *Courts Act* 2003, s.88(4)–(6); and the *CJA* 2003, s.81(1) and (4); and as amended, as from a day to be appointed, by the *Constitutional Reform Act* 2005, s.40(4), and Sched. 9, paras 16(1) and (4), and 80(1) and (2) (omission of italicised words, insertion of words in square brackets).]

Once an application for leave to appeal to the House of Lords [Supreme Court] has been properly made to the Court of Appeal, considered by the court and rejected by it, the court has no jurisdiction to entertain a renewed application for leave to appeal: *R. v. Ashdown*, *ante*, applying *R. v. Grantham* [1969] 2 Q.B. 574, 53 Cr.App.R. 369, Ct-MAC.

In a case where there does not seem to be any point of law of general public importance, the Court of Appeal will deal with an application for leave to appeal to the House of Lords [Supreme Court] on the papers without granting legal aid or leave to be present: *R. v. Daines and Williams*, 45 Cr.App.R. 57, CCA. Not affording a party seeking leave to appeal an opportunity to make oral submissions would involve no violation of the right to a fair trial, as guaranteed by Article 6 of the ECHR (*post*, § 16–57); no injustice arose, and there could be no justifiable sense of grievance, where there had been the opportunity to prepare lengthier written submissions than could have been made in the time allowed for oral submissions; and the proceedings were no longer at the stage of a "trial": *R. v. Steele* [2007] 1 W.L.R. 222, CA.

There is no power, upon an application by the prosecutor, to extend the time limit of 28 days (other than in the case of an appeal under s.33(1B)): *R. v. Weir* [2001] 1 W.L.R. 421, HL.

Criminal Procedure Rules 2005 (S.I. 2005 No. 384), Pt 74
(as substituted by the Criminal Procedure (Amendment No. 3) Rules 2007
(S.I. 2007 No. 3662))

When this Part applies

74.1.—(1) This Part applies where— **7–323**

(a) a party wants to appeal to the House of Lords after—

(i) an application to the Court of Appeal to which Part 41 applies (retrial following acquittal for serious offence), or

(ii) an appeal to the Court of Appeal to which applies Part 66 (appeal to the Court of Appeal against ruling at preparatory hearing), Part 67 (appeal to the Court of Appeal against ruling adverse to prosecution), or Part 68 (appeal to the Court of Appeal about conviction or sentence); or

(b) a party wants to refer a case to the House of Lords after a reference to the Court of Appeal to which Part 70 applies (reference to the Court of Appeal of point of law or unduly lenient sentencing).

(2) A reference to an "appellant" in this Part is a reference to such a party.

Application for permission or reference

7–324 **74.2.**—(1) An appellant must—

(a) apply orally to the Court of Appeal—

(i) for permission to appeal or to refer a sentencing case, or

(ii) to refer a point of law

immediately after the court gives the reasons for its decision; or

(b) apply in writing and serve the application on the Registrar and every other party not more than—

(i) 14 days after the court gives the reasons for its decision if that decision was on a sentencing reference to which Part 70 applies (Attorney General's reference of sentencing case), or

(ii) 28 days after the court gives those reasons in any other case.

(2) An application for permission to appeal or to refer a sentencing case must—

(a) identify the point of law of general public importance that the appellant wants the court to certify is involved in the decision; and

(b) give reasons why—

(i) that point of law ought to be considered by the House of Lords, and

(ii) the court ought to give permission to appeal.

(3) An application to refer a point of law must give reasons why that point ought to be considered by the House of Lords.

(4) An application must include or attach any application for the following, with reasons—

(a) an extension of time within which to make the application for permission or for a reference,

(b) bail pending appeal,

(c) permission to attend any hearing in the House of Lords, if the appellant is in custody.

(5) A written application must be in the form set out in the Practice Direction.

Determination of detention pending appeal, etc.

7–324a **74.3.** On an application for permission to appeal the Court of Appeal must—

(a) decide whether to order the detention of a defendant who would have been liable to be detained but for the decision of the court; and

(b) determine any application for—

(i) bail pending appeal,

(ii) permission to attend any hearing in the House of Lords, or

(iii) a representation order.

Bail pending appeal

7–324b **74.4.** Rules 68.8 (application for bail pending appeal or retrial), 68.9 (conditions of bail pending appeal or retrial) and 68.10 (forfeiture of a recognizance given as a condition of bail) apply.

(4) Hearing and disposal of appeal

Criminal Appeal Act 1968, s.35

7–325 **35.**—(1) *An appeal under this Part of this Act shall not be heard and determined by the House of Lords unless there are present at least three of the persons designated Lords of Appeal by section 5 of the* Appellate Jurisdiction Act *1876.*

(2) *Any order of the House of Lords which provides for the hearing of applications for leave to appeal by a committee constituted in accordance with section 5 of the said Act of 1876 may direct that the decision of that committee shall be taken on behalf of the House.*

(3) For the purpose of disposing of an appeal, the *House of Lords* [Supreme Court] may exercise any powers of the Court of Appeal or may remit the case to the Court.

[As from a day to be appointed, subss. (1) and (2) are repealed, and the italicised words in subs. (3) are replaced by the words in square brackets: *Constitutional Reform Act* 2005, s.40(4), and Sched. 9, para. 16(1) and (5).]

In *Att.-Gen. (Northern Ireland) v. Gallagher* [1963] A.C. 349, the House of Lords held that its jurisdiction under section 1 of the *Administration of Justice Act* 1960 was not limited to determining the point of law set out in the certificate. The provisions of section 1 of the 1960 Act were repealed by, and re-enacted in, the *CAA* 1968. The extent to which matters unrelated to the question certified could be raised by the appellant was left open. Lord Tucker said that it will always be a matter for the exercise of their Lordships' discretion whether to allow a point in no way connected with the certified point of law to be argued on the appeal and it was not to be assumed from the decision in the instant case that an appellant can as a matter of right raise any such point (see p. 370). Lord Denning said: "If it were necessary to consider any other point in order to dispose of the appeal, I would certainly be prepared to do so, for I take the view that, once leave to appeal is given to your Lordships' House, all points are open as well as the point stated ..." (at p. 383). See also, *per* Lord Reid at pages 365 to 366. In *Jones v. DPP* [1962] A.C. 635, the House of Lords held that where a certificate of appeal on *conviction* has been given, argument in regard to sentence cannot be heard.

It is a common practice of the Court of Appeal to leave grounds of appeal unresolved where it has come to a clear conclusion in favour of the appellant on another ground which is conclusive of the appeal. The House of Lords in *R. v. Mandair* [1995] 1 A.C. 208, held that where this occurred, the House could, in the event of a successful appeal by the prosecution, consider any unresolved grounds itself or remit them to the Court of Appeal. The House stressed the absolute necessity when preparing an appeal to the House for the statement of facts and issues to state plainly whether any grounds of appeal had been left undetermined in the court below. The written cases of the parties should include submissions on those grounds and on how the House should dispose of them. In *R. v. Berry*, 99 Cr.App.R. 88, the Court of Appeal said that the Crown should inform the court before judgment if there was any reason to believe that it would seek to have the decisive point certified for consideration by the House of Lords. It could then decide whether the other grounds ought to be considered there and then. In view of the confirmation by the House of Lords in *Mandair* of its powers (which the Court of Appeal in *Berry* seemed to think were in doubt), it seems unlikely that the court will depart from its usual practice; as it pointed out in *Berry*, it is a practice which assists in the speedy and economic disposal of appeals. **7–326**

When a case is remitted to the Court of Appeal, its powers under Part I of the 1968 Act revive; it deals with the matter by the exercise of the powers conferred on it in relation to appeals from lower courts; its decision is not a delegated decision of the House of Lords [Supreme Court]: *R. v. Kearley (No. 2)* [1994] 2 A.C. 414, HL.

Where the Court of Appeal has dismissed an appeal and there is a further appeal to the House of Lords [Supreme Court], it will not suffice for the appellant to show that the Court of Appeal has erred in its approach. The appeal will be determined according to the criteria laid down in Part I of the *CAA* 1968: see *Stafford and Luvaglio v. DPP* [1974] A.C. 878, *per* Viscount Dilhorne at p. 894.

B. MATTERS PRELIMINARY TO HEARING

Criminal Appeal Act 1968, s.36

Bail on appeal by defendant

36. The Court of Appeal may, subject to section 25 of the *Criminal Justice and Public Order Act* 1994, if it seems fit, on the application of a person appealing or applying for leave to appeal to the *House of Lords* [Supreme Court] other than a person appealing or applying for leave to appeal from a decision on an appeal under Part 9 of the *Criminal Justice Act* 2003 or section 9(11) of the *Criminal Justice Act* 1987 or section 35 of the *Criminal Procedure and Investigations Act* 1996 (appeals against orders or rulings at preparatory hearings) [or section 47 of the *Criminal Justice Act* 2003], grant him bail pending the determination of his appeal. **7–327**

[This section is printed as amended by the *CJA* 1987, s.15 and Sched. 2, para. 4; the *CJPOA* 1994, Sched. 10, para. 23; the *CPIA* 1996, s.36(1); and the *CJA* 2003, s.68(2); and as amended, as from a day to be appointed, by *ibid.*, s.47(7) (insertion of words in second set of square brackets); and the *Constitutional Reform Act* 2005, s.40(4), and Sched. 9, para. 16(1) and (6) (substitution of reference to "Supreme Court" for reference to "House of Lords").]

See also Part 74 of the *Criminal Procedure Rules* 2005 (S.I. 2005 No. 384), *ante*, §§ 7–323 *et seq.*, and section 43, *post*, § 7–335.

Criminal Appeal Act 1968, ss.37[, 37A]

Detention of defendant on appeal by the Crown

7–328 **37.**—(1) The following provisions apply where, immediately after a decision of the Court of Appeal from which an appeal lies to the *House of Lords* [Supreme Court], the prosecutor is granted or gives notice that he intends to apply for, leave to appeal.

(2) If, but for the decision of the Court of Appeal, the defendant would be liable to be detained, the Court of Appeal shall make—

(a) an order providing for his detention, or directing that he shall not be released except on bail (which may be granted by the Court as under section 36 above), so long as the appeal is pending, or

(b) an order that he be released without bail.

(2A) The Court may make an order under subsection (2)(b) only if they think that it is in the interests of justice that the defendant should not be liable to be detained as a result of the decision of the Supreme Court on the appeal.

(3) An order under subsection (2)(a) shall (unless the appeal has previously been disposed of) cease to have effect at the expiration of the period for which the defendant would have been liable to be detained but for the decision of the Court of Appeal.

(4) Where an order is made under subsection (2)(a) in the case of a defendant who, but for the decision of the Court of Appeal, would be liable to be detained in pursuance of—

(a) an order or direction under Part III of the *Mental Health Act* 1983 (otherwise than under sections 35, 36 or 38 of that Act) (admission to hospital of persons convicted by criminal courts); or

(b) a hospital order made by virtue of section 5(2)(a) of the *Criminal Procedure (Insanity) Act* 1964 (powers to deal with persons not guilty by reason of insanity or unfit to plead, etc.)

the order under subsection (2)(a) shall be one authorising his continued detention in pursuance of the order or direction referred to in paragraph (a) or (b) of this subsection; and the provisions of the *Mental Health Act* 1983, with respect to persons liable to be detained as mentioned in this subsection (including provisions as to the renewal of authority for detention and the removal or discharge of patients) shall apply accordingly.

7–329 (4A) Where an order is made under subsection (2)(a) in the case of a defendant who, but for the decision of the Court of Appeal, would be liable to be detained in pursuance of a remand under section 36 of the *Mental Health Act* 1983 or an interim hospital order under section 38 of that Act, the order may, if the Court of Appeal thinks fit, be one authorising his continued detention in a hospital or mental nursing home and in that event—

(a) subsection (3) of this section shall not apply to the order;

(b) Part III of the said Act of 1983 shall apply to him as if he had been ordered under this section to be detained in custody so long as an appeal to the *House of Lords* [Supreme Court] is pending and were detained in pursuance of a transfer direction together with a restriction direction; and

(c) if the defendant, having been subject to an interim hospital order, is detained by virtue of this subsection and the appeal by the prosecutor succeeds, subsection (2) of the said section 38 (power of the court to make a hospital order in the absence of an offender who is subject to an interim hospital order) shall apply as if the defendant were still subject to an interim hospital order.

(5) The defendant shall not be liable to be detained again as a result of the decision of the Supreme Court on the appeal if—

(a) the Court of Appeal have made an order under subsection (2)(b), or

(b) the Court have made an order under subsection (2)(a) but the order has ceased to have effect by virtue of subsection (3) or the defendant has been released or discharged by virtue of subsection (4) or (4A).

[This section is printed as amended by the *Mental Health (Amendment) Act* 1982, s.65(1), and Sched. 3, para. 39; the *MHA* 1983, s.148, and Sched. 4, para. 23(g) and (h); the *Domestic Violence, Crime and Victims Act* 2004, s.58(1), and Sched. 10, para. 5; and the *CJIA* 2008, s.47, and Sched. 8, paras 1 and 13. References to the "Supreme Court" are substituted for the references to the "House of Lords" in subss. (1) and (4A) as from a day to be appointed by the *Constitutional Reform Act* 2005, s.40(4), and Sched. 9, para. 16(1) and (6).]

Pending the commencement of paragraph 16(6) of Schedule 9 to the 2005 Act, the references to the Supreme Court are to be read as references to the House of Lords: *Criminal Justice and Immigration Act 2008 (Transitory Provisions) Order* 2008 (S.I. 2008 No. 1587), art. 5.

Continuation of community treatment order on appeal by the Crown

37A.—(1) The following provisions apply where, immediately after a decision of the Court of Appeal from which an appeal lies to the Supreme Court, the prosecutor is granted, or gives notice that he intends to apply for, leave to appeal. **7–329a**

(2) If, but for the decision of the Court of Appeal, the defendant would be liable to recall, the Court of Appeal may make an order under this section.

(3) For the purposes of this section, a person is liable to recall if he is subject to a community treatment order (within the meaning of the *Mental Health Act* 1983) and, when that order was made, he was liable to be detained in pursuance of an order or direction under Part 3 of that Act.

(4) An order under this section is an order providing for the continuation of the community treatment order and the order or direction under Part 3 of that Act so long as an appeal to the Supreme Court is pending.

(5) Where an order is made under this section the provisions of the *Mental Health Act* 1983 with respect to persons liable to recall (including provisions as to the extension of the community treatment period, the removal or discharge of community patients, the revocation of community treatment orders and the re-detention of patients following revocation) shall apply accordingly.

(6) An order under this section shall (unless the appeal has previously been disposed of) cease to have effect at the expiration of the period for which the defendant would, but for the decision of the Court of Appeal, have been—

(a) liable to recall; or

(b) where the community treatment order is revoked, liable to be detained in pursuance of the order or direction under Part 3 of the *Mental Health Act* 1983.

(7) Where the Court of Appeal have power to make an order under this section, and either no such order is made or the defendant is discharged, by virtue of subsection (5) or (6) of this section, before the appeal is disposed of, the defendant shall not be liable to be again detained as the result of the decision of the Supreme Court on the appeal.

[This section was inserted by the *MHA* 2007, s.32(4), and Sched. 4, para. 2(1) and (3).]

In *DPP v. Merriman* [1973] A.C. 584, HL, the House emphasised the desirability of the provisions of section 37 being brought to the attention of the Court of Appeal in all cases in which the prosecution seek leave to appeal to the House of Lords from the quashing of a conviction and sentence of imprisonment. See also *Government of the United States of America v. McCaffery*, 80 Cr.App.R. 82 at 88, HL, and *R. v. Hollinshead* [1985] A.C. 975, in which the House again underlined the importance of this provision (see particularly s.37(5)): **7–330**

> "… the Court of Appeal should, unless there are strong reasons for not so doing, make such order under section 37(2) as will ensure that, if this House takes a different view of the law from that taken in the Court of Appeal and therefore restores the quashed convictions, the offenders in question do not avoid all punishment …" (*per* Lord Roskill at p. 999).

Criminal Appeal Act 1968, s.38

Presence of defendant at hearing

38. A defendant who has been convicted of an offence, or in whose case an order under section 77 of the *Criminal Justice Act* 2003 or a declaration under section 77(4) of that Act has been made, and who is detained pending an appeal to the *House of Lords* [Supreme Court] shall not be entitled to be present on the hearing of the appeal or of any proceedings preliminary or incidental thereto, except where an order of the House of Lords authorises him to be present, or where the *House* [Supreme Court] or the Court of Appeal, as the case may be, give him leave to be present. **7–331**

[This section is printed as amended by the *CJA* 1987, s.15, and Sched. 2, para. 5; and the *CJA* 2003, s.81(1) and (5); and as amended, as from a day to be appointed, by the *Constitutional Reform Act* 2005, s.40(4), and Sched. 9, para. 16(1) and (7) (omission of italicised words, insertion of words in square brackets).]

See also Part 74 of the *Criminal Procedure Rules* 2005 (S.I. 2005 No. 384), *ante*, §§ 7–323 *et seq.*

C. MATTERS DEPENDING ON RESULT OF APPEAL AND SUPPLEMENTARY PROVISIONS

(1) Costs

7–332 As to awards of costs out of central funds, see Part II (ss.16–21) of the *Prosecution of Offences Act* 1985, especially ss.16(5) and 17, *ante*, §§ 6–6, 6–23.

On appeal from the Court of Appeal (Criminal Division) under Part II of the *CAA* 1968, there is no power to make an *inter partes* order. On appeal from the High Court, such an award is possible (see the *Administration of Justice Act* 1960, s.1(4)).

As to the award of costs *inter partes* where a petition for leave to appeal is not referred for an oral hearing, see directions 6.1 and 6.2 of the *Practice Directions applicable to Criminal Appeals* (*ante*, § 7–315).

Direction 20 provides that if counsel wish to seek an order other than that costs be awarded to the successful party, submissions to that effect should be made at the conclusion of argument at the hearing of the appeal. Should this not be done, leave may be given to a party to make such submissions at the judgment in the House. Prior notice of intention to make submissions on costs at judgment must be given in writing to the Judicial Office, at least two clear days before the judgment, stating the nature of the order sought. A copy of the submissions must be sent to the agents for the other party or parties to the appeal.

Taxation

7–333 Regulation 13(1) of the *Costs in Criminal Cases (General) Regulations* 1986 (S.I. 1986 No. 1335) (*ante*, § 6–67) and article 9 of the *Criminal Defence Service (Funding) Order* 2007 (S.I. 2007 No. 1174) (Appendix G–6 *et seq.*) provide that in the case of central funds and Criminal Defence Service taxations respectively the costs payable shall be determined by such officer as may be prescribed by order of the House of Lords. Otherwise, neither the regulations nor the order has any application to proceedings in the House of Lords: reg. 13(2) and art. 9(2) respectively. By Standing Order XIII of the Standing Orders of the House of Lords regulating judicial business, made in pursuance of the *Appellate Jurisdiction Act* 1876 (repealed as from a day to be appointed: *Constitutional Reform Act* 2005, s.145, and Sched. 17, para. 9) and subsequent enactments, it is—

> "*Ordered*, that the Clerk of the Parliaments shall appoint such person as he may think fit as Taxing Officer, and in all cases in which this House shall make any order for payment of costs by any party or parties in any cause, the amount thereof to be certified by the Clerk of the Parliaments, the Taxing Officer shall tax the Bill of Costs so ordered to be paid, and ascertain the amount thereof, and report the same to the Clerk of the Parliaments or Clerk Assistant: And it is further Ordered, that the same fees shall be demanded from and paid by the party applying for such taxation for and in respect thereof as are now charged or shall be authorised from time to time by the House; and such fees shall be added at the foot of the said Bill of Costs as taxed."

The taxing officer is the Principal Clerk of the Judicial Office. In addition to the procedural directions (*ante*, § 7–315) there is a set of *Directions for the Taxation of Bills of Costs in the House of Lords* (1997): these, together with the 1997 edition of *Forms of Bills of Costs in the House of Lords*, are contained in a separate booklet which is available from the Judicial Office of the House of Lords (020–7219–3111/3). Direction 10 relates to a review of taxation in the House of Lords. An appeal lies on principle, but not on *quantum*, and such appeal must be made within 14 days of the taxation. A copy of the review procedure is available on request from the Taxing Clerk.

On July 27, 1999, the House of Lords announced amendments to the forms of bills of costs, to give effect, with respect to legal aid taxations, to the recommendations of the Report of the Appeal Committee of the House of Lords upon a reference thereto by the Clerk of the Parliaments regarding criminal legal aid taxation [1999] 1 Cr.App.R. 241 (*ante*, § 6–228). For the full text of the amendments, see [1999] 1 W.L.R. 1860.

As to time limits for the lodgment of bills for taxation, see direction 24.1 of the procedural directions (*ante*, § 7–315). Bills should be lodged within three months from the date of judgment or from the date on which a petition was before an Appeal Committee; if further time is required, an application for such extension must be made to the taxing officer of the House of Lords in writing before the expiry of the three month period. A bill presented outside the time limit, where no application for an extension has been received, will only be accepted in exceptional circumstances.

(2) Orders for the restitution of property or compensation

The relevant provisions are section 30 of the *CAA* 1968 (*ante*, § 7–230) in relation to restitution orders and section 132 of the *PCC(S)A* 2000 (*ante*, § 5–413) in relation to orders for compensation. **7–334**

(3) Sentence

Criminal Appeal Act 1968, s.43

43.—(1) Where a person subject to a sentence is granted bail under section 36 or 37 of this Act, the time during which he is released on bail shall be disregarded in computing the term of his sentence. **7–335**

(2) Subject to the foregoing subsection, any sentence passed on an appeal to the *House of Lords* [Supreme Court] in substitution for another sentence shall, unless that *House* [the Supreme Court] or the Court of Appeal otherwise direct, begin to run from the time when the other sentence would have begun to run.

[The italicised words are omitted, and the words in square brackets are inserted, as from a day to be appointed: *Constitutional Reform Act* 2005, s.40(4), and Sched. 9, para. 16(1) and (8).]

As to section 36, see *ante*, § 7–327; as to section 37, see *ante*, § 7–328.

(4) Powers exercisable by single judge

Criminal Appeal Act 1968, s.44

44.—(1) There may be exercised by a single judge— **7–336**

(a) the powers of the Court of Appeal under this Part of this Act—

(i) to extend the time for making an application for leave to appeal;

(ii) to make an order for or in relation to bail; and

(iii) to give leave for a person to be present at the hearing of any proceedings preliminary or incidental to an appeal; and

(b) their powers to make orders for the payment of costs under sections 16 and 17 of the *Prosecution of Offences Act* 1985 in proceedings under this Part of this Act,

but where the judge refuses an application to exercise any of the said powers the applicant shall be entitled to have the application determined by the Court of Appeal.

(2) The power of the Court of Appeal to suspend a person's disqualification under section 40(3) of the *Road Traffic Offenders Act* 1988 may be exercised by a single judge, but where the judge refuses an application to exercise that power the applicant shall be entitled to have the application determined by the Court of Appeal.

(3) The power of the Court of Appeal, under section 130 of the *Licensing Act* 2003, to suspend an order under section 129 of that Act may be exercised by a single judge, but where the judge refuses an application to exercise that power the applicant shall be entitled to have the application determined by the Court of Appeal.

[This section is printed as amended by the *RTA* 1974, Sched. 6; the *CJA* 1988, s.170(1), and Sched. 15, para. 31; the *Road Traffic (Consequential Provisions) Act* 1988, s.4, and Sched. 3, para. 4(2); and the *Licensing Act* 2003, s.198(1), and Sched. 6, paras 38 and 41.]

Criminal Appeal Act 1968, s.45(2)

45.—(2) [*Construction of references to "single judge": see* ante, *§ 7–232.*] **7–337**

[The next paragraph is § 7–346.]

XI. GENERAL PROVISIONS RELATING TO APPEALS TO AND FROM THE COURT OF APPEAL

A. APPEALS IN CASES OF DEATH

Criminal Appeal Act 1968, s.44A

Appeals in cases of death

7–346 **44A.**—(1) Where a person has died—

(a) any relevant appeal which might have been begun by him had he remained alive may be begun by a person approved by the Court of Appeal; and

(b) where any relevant appeal was begun by him while he was alive or is begun in relation to his case by virtue of paragraph (a) above or by a reference by the Criminal Cases Review Commission, any further step which might have been taken by him in connection with the appeal if he were alive may be taken by a person so approved.

(2) In this section "relevant appeal" means—

(a) an appeal under section 1, 9, 12 or 15 of this Act; or

(b) an appeal under section 33 of this Act from any decision of the Court of Appeal on an appeal under any of those sections.

(3) Approval for the purposes of this section may only be given to—

(a) the widow or widower or surviving civil partner of the dead person;

(b) a person who is the personal representative (within the meaning of section 55(1)(xi) of the *Administration of Estates Act* 1925) of the dead person; or

(c) any other person appearing to the Court of Appeal to have, by reason of a family or similar relationship with the dead person, a substantial financial or other interest in the determination of a relevant appeal relating to him.

(4) Except in the case of an appeal begun by a reference by the Criminal Cases Review Commission, an application for such approval may not be made after the end of the period of one year beginning with the date of death.

(5) Where this section applies, any reference in this Act to the appellant shall, where appropriate, be construed as being or including a reference to the person approved under this section.

(6) The power of the Court of Appeal to approve a person under this section may be exercised by a single judge in the same manner as by the Court of Appeal and subject to the same provisions; but if the single judge refuses the application, the applicant shall be entitled to have the application determined by the Court of Appeal.

[This section was inserted by the *CAA* 1995, s.7(1). It is printed as amended by the *Civil Partnership Act* 2004, s.261(1), and Sched. 27, para. 26.]

See *R. v. Whelan* [1997] Crim.L.R. 659, CA (a defendant's spouse should be allowed the opportunity to clear his name).

B. PREROGATIVE OF MERCY

Criminal Appeal Act 1968, s.49

7–347 **49.** Nothing in this Act is to be taken as affecting Her Majesty's prerogative of mercy.

C. INTERPRETATION

Criminal Appeal Act 1968, s.45

7–348 **45.**—(1) References in Parts I and II and sections 44A and 51 of this Act to the Court of Appeal shall be construed as references to the criminal division of the Court.

(2) [*Construction of references to "single judge": see* ante, *§ 7–232.*]

[Subs. (1) was substituted by the *Supreme Court Act* 1981, Sched. 5. It is printed as amended by the *CAA* 1995, s.29(1), and Sched. 2, para. 4(1) and (5)(a); and the *CJA* 2003, s.331, and Sched. 36, paras 86 and 89(a).]

Meaning of "sentence"

7–349 For section 50 of the 1968 Act, see *ante*, § 7–119.

Criminal Appeal Act 1968, s.51

51.—(1) In this Act, except where the context otherwise requires— 7–350

"appeal", where used in Part I or II of this Act, means appeal under that Part, and "appellant" has a corresponding meaning and in Part I includes a person who has given notice of application for leave to appeal;

"the court of trial", in relation to an appeal, means the court from which the appeal lies;

"duly approved", in relation to a registered medical practitioner, means approved for the purposes of section 12 of the *Mental Health Act* 1983 by the Secretary of State as having special experience in the diagnosis or treatment of mental disorder;

"the judge of the court of trial" means, where the Crown Court comprises justices of the peace, the judge presiding;

"registered medical practitioner" means a fully registered person within the meaning of the *Medical Act* 1983 who holds a licence to practise;

"under disability" has the meaning assigned to it by section 4 of the *Criminal Procedure (Insanity) Act* 1964 (unfitness to plead).

(1A) In Part 2 of this Act "the defendant"—

(a) in relation to an appeal under section 33(1) of this Act against a decision of the Court of Appeal on an appeal under Part 1 of this Act, means the person who was the appellant before the Court of Appeal,

(b) in relation to an appeal under section 33(1) of this Act against any other decision, means a defendant in the proceedings before the Crown Court who was a party to the proceedings before the Court of Appeal, and

(c) in relation to an appeal under section 33(1B) of this Act, shall be construed in accordance with section 33(4) of this Act; and "prosecutor" shall be construed accordingly.

(2) Any expression used in this Act which is defined in section 145(1) and (1AA) of the *Mental Health Act* 1983 has the same meaning in this Act as in that Act.

(2A) Subsections (2) and (3) of section 54 of the *Mental Health Act* 1983 shall have effect with respect to proof of the appellant's mental condition for the purposes of section 6 or 14 of this Act as they have effect with respect to proof of an offender's mental condition for the purposes of section 37(2)(a) of that Act.

[This section is printed as amended or repealed in part by the *Courts Act* 1971, s.56 and Sched. 8; the *Immigration Act* 1971, Sched. 6; the *Supreme Court Act* 1981, s.152(4) and Sched. 7; the *MHA* 1983, s.148, and Sched. 4, para. 23(j); the *Criminal Procedure (Insanity and Unfitness to Plead) Act* 1991, s.7, and Sched. 3, para. 5(1); the *Health Act 1999 (Supplementary, Consequential etc. Provisions) Order* 2000 (S.I. 2000 No. 90); the *Medical Act 1983 (Amendment) Order* 2002 (S.I. 2002 No. 3135), Sched. 1, para. 6; the *CJA* 2003, s.331, and Sched. 36, paras 86 and 90; the *Domestic Violence, Crime and Victims Act* 2004, s.58(1), and Sched. 10, para. 6; and the *SCA* 2007, ss.74(2) and 92, Sched. 8, para. 145, and Sched. 14.]

XII. *VENIRE DE NOVO*

A. GENERAL

The *CAA* 1907 did not mention the issue of writs of *venire de novo*, but in *Crane v. DPP* [1921] 2 A.C. 299, the House of Lords decided that the 1907 Act did, in fact, preserve the power that was formerly vested in the Court for Crown Cases Reserved to award a *venire de novo* and transferred it to the Court of Criminal Appeal. The *CAA* 1966 abolished the Court of Criminal Appeal and provided for two divisions of the Court of Appeal. By section 1(2) of the 1966 Act, it was provided that the criminal division should exercise all jurisdiction which was that of the Court of Criminal Appeal immediately before it ceased to exist, including the jurisdiction to order the issue of writs of *venire de novo*. The 1966 Act was repealed by the *Supreme Court Act* 1981, which provides that the criminal division of the Court of Appeal shall exercise the jurisdiction to issue writs of *venire de novo*: s.53(2)(d), *ante*, § 7–27. See also *R. v. Inns*, 60 Cr.App.R. 231, *per* Lawton L.J. at p. 234. 7–351

B. EFFECT AND FORM OF WRIT

The old form of the writ, *venire facias de novo juratores*, was a writ addressed to 7–352 the sheriff calling upon him to cause other lawful jurors to come *de novo* to try the case. By the *Courts Act* 1971, Sched. 4, para. 4, a writ or order of *venire de novo* shall no longer be addressed to the sheriff and shall be in such form as the court considers appropriate.

In *R. v. Ellis (J.)*, 57 Cr.App.R. 571, the Court of Appeal, considering *R. v. Baker*, 7 Cr.App.R. 217, CCA, ordered: "That the conviction and judgment in this case be set aside and annulled and that J.E. do appear at the next session of the … Crown Court … and plead to and answer the indictment in this case and that in the meantime the said J.E. shall be remanded in custody" (at p. 577).

Where the Court of Appeal has jurisdiction to issue a writ of *venire de novo*, there is no obligation to order a new trial; the court may simply hold that the proceedings were a nullity and quash the conviction, *e.g. R. v. Heyes* [1951] 1 K.B. 29, 34 Cr.App.R. 161, CCA; and *R. v. Gash*, 51 Cr.App.R. 37, CA.

C. When Awarded

(1) General

7–353 A writ of *venire de novo* will be awarded where a purported trial "is actually no trial at all": *Crane v. DPP* [1921] 2 A.C. 299, *per* Lord Atkinson at p. 330, and *R. v. Rose* [1982] A.C. 822, HL, *per* Lord Diplock at p. 831.

(2) Condition precedent to lawful trial not fulfilled

7–354 See *R. v. Angel*, 52 Cr.App.R. 280 (DPP's consent to institution of proceedings never obtained); *R. v. Gee* [1936] 2 K.B. 442, 25 Cr.App.R. 198 (no lawful committal for trial); *R. v. Cronin*, 27 Cr.App.R. 179 ("judge" not possessing necessary qualification to sit); and *R. v. Thompson and Clein*, 61 Cr.App.R. 108 (circuit judge purporting to give leave to prefer bill of indictment).

In connection with *Gee*, *ante*, see also *R. v. Lamb* [1968] 1 W.L.R. 1946, CA, and *R. v. Braden*, 87 Cr.App.R. 289, CA (conviction for criminal damage quashed where the magistrates' court had erred in committing the appellant for trial on a single charge of criminal damage to the value of £65 and the Crown Court had wrongfully rejected a submission of no jurisdiction as the value was below £400).

(3) Defect in relation to plea

7–355 If the defendant can establish that he pleaded guilty without understanding the nature of the charge or without intending to admit that he was guilty of what was alleged, the conviction will be quashed: *R. v. Forde* [1923] 2 K.B. 400, 17 Cr.App.R. 99, CCA; *DPP v. Shannon* [1975] A.C. 717, HL; *R. v. Phillips*, 74 Cr.App.R. 199, CA. Equally, where the plea is equivocal, the proceedings will be held to be a nullity: *R. v. Baker*, 7 Cr.App.R. 217, CCA; *R. v. Ingleson* [1915] 1 K.B. 512, 11 Cr.App.R. 21, CCA. *A fortiori*, if no plea is taken: *R. v. Brennan*, 28 Cr.App.R. 41, CCA; or a plea is entered by the defendant's counsel: *R. v. Ellis (J.)*, 57 Cr.App.R. 571, CA (*cf. R. v. Williams (R.)*, 64 Cr.App.R. 106, CA, *ante*, § 4–98).

See also *R. v. O'Reilly*, 90 Cr.App.R. 40, CA (plea of guilty to defective indictment because of misjoinder; defect cured by amendment; no re-arraignment; proceedings prior to amendment a nullity; *ante*, § 1–232).

In *R. v. Inns*, 60 Cr.App.R. 231, CA, it was held that a plea of guilty made by a defendant after pressure had been put on his counsel by the judge was not a proper plea and the proceedings which ensued were a nullity; and in *R. v. Smith and Beaney* [1999] 6 *Archbold News* 1, CA (98 01798 X5), where an illiterate defendant had been put in position where he would only have legal representation if he pleaded guilty, it was said that if the circumstances were such as effectively to deny a defendant a free choice as to his plea, a plea of guilty will be deemed a nullity.

On the other side of the line are *R. v. Peace* [1976] Crim.L.R. 119, CA; *R. v. Willcock*, *The Times*, March 31, 1982; and *R. v. Nazham and Nazham* [2004] 4 *Archbold News* 1, CA. In *Peace*, it was held that an accused who pleaded guilty following and adopting the advice of his counsel, albeit unhappily and with reluctance, could not be said to have lost his power to make a voluntary and deliberate choice and thus say that his plea amounted to a nullity. In *Willcock*, it was said that firm advice by counsel as to the consequences of being found guilty as opposed to pleading guilty did not vitiate a subsequent plea of guilty. In *Nazham and Nazham*, it was emphasised that there is a burden on the defendant to show not only that there was an irregularity, but also that it so influenced the decision to plead guilty as to render it a nullity.

(4) Defect in relation to indictment

Where two or more indictments are tried together the trial is a nullity: *Crane v. DPP, ante*; *R. v. Olivo*, 28 Cr.App.R. 173, CCA; as it is where the indictment is unsigned: *R. v. Clarke and McDaid* [2008] 2 Cr.App.R. 2, HL. **7–356**

(5) Defect in relation to jury

In *R. v. Solomon* [1958] 1 Q.B. 203, 42 Cr.App.R. 9, CCA, the proceedings were held to have been a nullity, the jury having consisted entirely of *talesmen*. Where the defendant's rights of challenge are improperly denied him this will vitiate the whole of the proceedings: *R. v. Williams (H.)*, 19 Cr.App.R. 67, CCA; *R. v. Gash*, 51 Cr.App.R. 37, CA. **7–357**

(6) Defect in relation to verdict

Where the defendant having initially pleaded not guilty subsequently changed his plea and the trial judge proceeded to sentence without taking a verdict from the jury, the proceedings were held to be a nullity: *R. v. Hancock*, 23 Cr.App.R. 16; *R. v. Heyes* [1951] 1 K.B. 29, 34 Cr.App.R. 161. *Hancock* was referred to with approval by the House of Lords in *R. v. Rose* [1982] A.C. 822 (see *per* Lord Diplock at pp. 833–834), but, despite this, the Court of Appeal declined to follow *Hancock* and *Heyes* in *R. v. Poole* [2002] 1 W.L.R. 1528, in which it was held that a conviction based upon a change of plea by a defendant was not a nullity where the defendant being in charge of the jury entered the plea of guilty in their presence, but the judge failed to take a verdict from them and simply discharged them. See also *R. v. McPeake* [2006] Crim.L.R. 376, CA. Notwithstanding *Poole*, it is submitted that in the straightforward case of a change of plea, good practice should dictate that the rule in *Hancock* and *Heyes* should be followed (for the reasons given by Lord Diplock, and in the commentaries to *Poole* in *Criminal Law Week* (2001/45/6) and in the *Criminal Law Review* ([2002] Crim.L.R. 242)). **7–358**

Where the verdict that is returned is so imperfectly worded or so ambiguous or so inconsistent that no judgment could be founded thereon, this will be tantamount to no verdict being returned at all and, accordingly, if the trial court purports to proceed to judgment, a *venire de novo* may be granted: *R. v. Murphy* (1869) L.R. 2 P.C. 535. In *R. v. Russell* [1984] Crim.L.R. 425, the jury, having failed to agree, were discharged. The jury bailiff then indicated the jury had wanted more time. The court was reconvened and the jury were asked to resume their deliberations. It was held that the proceedings subsequent to the discharge of the jury were a nullity and, accordingly, the conviction was quashed.

In *R. v. Lewis (G.)*, 87 Cr.App.R. 270, CA, convictions were quashed because it was not clear whether the verdicts had been unanimous or by a majority.

D. Trial Resulting in an Acquittal

There is no jurisdiction to order a *venire de novo* following an acquittal, however irregular the proceedings may have been: see *R. v. Middlesex Q.S., ex p. DPP* [1952] 2 Q.B. 758, 36 Cr.App.R. 114, DC; *R. v. Dorking JJ., ex p. Harrington* [1984] A.C. 743, HL. **7–359**

XIII. REFERENCES TO THE COURT OF APPEAL BY THE ATTORNEY-GENERAL

A. Of Points of Law

Criminal Justice Act 1972, s.36

36.—(1) Where a person tried on indictment has been acquitted (whether in respect of the whole or part of the indictment) the Attorney-General may, if he desires the opinion of the **7–360**

Court of Appeal on a point of law which has arisen in the case, refer that point to the court, and the court shall, in accordance with this section, consider the point and give their opinion on it.

(2) For the purpose of their consideration of a point referred to them under this section the Court of Appeal shall hear argument—

(a) by, or by counsel on behalf of, the Attorney-General; and

(b) if the acquitted person desires to present any argument to the court, by counsel on his behalf or, with the leave of the court, by the acquitted person himself.

(3) Where the Court of Appeal have given their opinion on a point referred to them under this section, the court may, of their own motion or in pursuance of an application in that behalf, refer the point to the *House of Lords* [Supreme Court] if it appears to the *court* [Court of Appeal] that the point ought to be considered by *that House* [the Supreme Court].

(4) If a point is referred to the *House of Lords* [Supreme Court] under subsection (3) of this section, the *House shall consider the point and give their opinion on it accordingly; and section 35 (1) of the* Criminal Appeal Act *1968 (composition of House for appeals) shall apply also in relation to any proceedings of the House under this section* [Supreme Court shall consider the point and give its opinion on it accordingly].

7–361 (5) Where, on a point being referred to the Court of Appeal under this section or further referred to the *House of Lords* [Supreme Court], the acquitted person appears by counsel for the purpose of presenting any argument to the *court or the House* [the Court of Appeal or the Supreme Court], he shall be entitled to his costs, that is to say to the payment out of central funds of such sums as are reasonably sufficient to compensate him for expenses properly incurred by him for the purpose of being represented on the reference or further reference; and any amount recoverable under this subsection shall be ascertained, as soon as practicable, by the registrar of criminal appeals or, as the case may be, such officer as may be prescribed by order of the *House of Lords* [Supreme Court].

(5A) Section 20(1) of the *Prosecution of Offences Act* 1985 (regulations as to rules and rates of payment of costs payable out of central funds) shall apply in relation to this section as it applies to Part II of that Act.

(6) Subject to rules of court made under section 1(5) of the *Criminal Appeal Act* 1966 (power by rules to distribute business of Court of Appeal between its civil and criminal divisions), the jurisdiction of the Court of Appeal under this section shall be exercised by the criminal division of the court; and references in this section to the Court of Appeal shall be construed accordingly as references to that division of the court.

(7) A reference under this section shall not affect the trial in relation to which the reference is made or any acquittal in that trial.

[This section is printed as amended by the *Prosecution of Offences Act* 1985, s.31(5) and Sched. 1, para. 8. The words in square brackets are substituted for the italicised words that precede them as from a day to be appointed: *Constitutional Reform Act* 2005, s.40(4), and Sched. 9, para. 23.]

7–362 As to section 35 of the *CAA* 1968, see, *ante*, § 7–325. The reference to the *CAA* 1966, s.1(5) should be construed as a reference to the *Supreme Court [Senior Courts] Act* 1981, s.53(1) (*ante*, § 7–27): *Interpretation Act* 1978, s.17(2)(a) (Appendix B–17).

Use of the provisions

7–363 "It would be a mistake to think ... that references by the Attorney-General are confined to cases where very heavy questions of law arise and that they should not be used in other cases. On the contrary, we hope to see this procedure used extensively for short but important points which require a quick ruling of this court before a potentially false decision of law has too wide a circulation in the courts": *per* Lord Widgery C.J. in *Att.-Gen's Reference (No. 1 of 1975)* [1975] Q.B. 773 at 778, 61 Cr.App.R. 118 at 120.

There is no power to refer theoretical questions of law, however interesting or difficult: *Att.-Gen's Reference (No. 4 of 1979)*, 71 Cr.App.R. 341, CA.

Procedure

7–364 See *post*, §§ 7–372 *et seq*.

[The next paragraph is § 7–366.]

B. OF SENTENCES

Criminal Justice Act 1988, s.35

Scope of Part IV

35.—(1) A case to which this Part of this Act applies may be referred to the Court of Appeal under section 36 below. **7–366**

(2) Subject to Rules of Court, the jurisdiction of the Court of Appeal under section 36 below shall be exercised by the criminal division of the Court, and references to the Court of Appeal in this Part of this Act shall be construed as references to that division.

(3) This Part of this Act applies to any case—

(a) of a description specified in an order under this section; or

(b) in which sentence is passed on a person—

(i) for an offence triable only on indictment; or

(ii) for an offence of a description specified in an order under this section.

(4) The Secretary of State may by order made by statutory instrument provide that this Part of this Act shall apply to any case of a description specified in the order or to any case in which sentence is passed on a person for an offence triable either way of a description specified in the order.

(5) [*Making of statutory instrument.*]

(6) In this Part of this Act "sentence" has the same meaning as in the *Criminal Appeal Act* 1968, except that it does not include an interim hospital order under Part III of the *Mental Health Act* 1983 and "sentencing" shall be construed accordingly.

(7) In its application to Northern Ireland, this section shall have effect subject to the modifications set out in subsections (8) to (11).

(8) Subsection (2) shall be omitted.

(9) In this section—

"offence triable only on indictment" means an offence punishable only on conviction on indictment;

"offence triable either way" means an offence punishable on conviction on indictment or on summary conviction.

(10), (11) [*Northern Ireland.*]

[This section is printed as amended by the *CJPOA* 1994, Sched. 9, para. 34.]

There appears to be a drafting error: subsection (7) expresses subsection (9) to be a subsection modifying the section in its application to Northern Ireland. Subsection (9) does not appear to be a modification subsection (unlike subsections (8), (10) and (11)): it was presumably intended to be of general application.

The *Criminal Justice Act 1988 (Reviews of Sentencing) Order* 2006 (S.I. 2006 No. 1116) provides that, to the extent that it does not apply by virtue of section 35(3)(b)(i), Part IV of the 1988 Act shall apply to any case— **7–367**

(a) tried on indictment following a notice of transfer under the *CJA* 1987, s.4, or in which one or more of the counts in respect of which sentence is passed relates to a charge which was dismissed under section 6(1) of that Act and on which further proceedings were brought by means of preferment of a voluntary bill of indictment;

(b) in which sentence is passed for an offence under the *Offences against the Person Act* 1861, s.16, the *Criminal Law Amendment Act* 1885, s.5(1), the *CYPA* 1933, s.1, the *SOA* 1956, s.6, 14 or 15, the *Indecency with Children Act* 1960, s.1, the *Misuse of Drugs Act* 1971, s.4(2) or (3) or 6(2), the *CLA* 1977, s.54, the *CEMA* 1979, s.50(2) or (3), 68(2) or 170(1) or (2) (insofar as such offence is in connection with a prohibition or restriction on importation or exportation having effect under the *Misuse of Drugs Act* 1971, s.3, or the *Customs Consolidation Act* 1876, s.42), or the *CDA* 1998, ss.29 to 32 (or their Northern Ireland equivalents, where applicable);

(c) in which sentence is passed for an offence under the *SOA* 2003, s.3, 4, 7 to 12, 14, 15, 25, 47 to 50, 52, 57 to 59 or 61; or

(d) in which sentence is passed for attempting to commit or inciting the commission of an offence in (ii) (other than offences under the 1998 Act) or (iii).

An offence which is triable only on indictment when committed by an adult (*e.g.* rape) is "an offence triable only on indictment" within section 35(3) notwithstanding that, by virtue of section 24 of the *MCA* 1980 (*ante*, § 1–75m), a person under the age of 18 years may be tried summarily: *Att.-Gen's Reference (No. 3 of 1993) (R. v. W.)*, 98 Cr.App.R. 84, CA.

Criminal Justice Act 1988, s.36

Reviews of sentencing

7–368 **36.**—(1) If it appears to the Attorney General—

(a) that the sentencing of a person in a proceeding in the Crown Court has been unduly lenient; and

(b) that the case is one to which this Part of this Act applies,

he may, with the leave of the Court of Appeal, refer the case to them for them to review the sentencing of that person; and on such a reference the Court of Appeal may—

(i) quash any sentence passed on him in the proceeding; and

(ii) in place of it pass such sentence as they think appropriate for the case and as the court below had power to pass when dealing with him.

(2) Without prejudice to the generality of subsection (1) above, the condition specified in paragraph (a) of that subsection may be satisfied if it appears to the Attorney General that the judge—

(a) erred in law as to his powers of sentencing; or

(b) failed to impose a sentence required by—

(i) section 51A(2) of the *Firearms Act* 1968;

(ii) section 110(2) or 111(2) of the *Powers of Criminal Courts (Sentencing) Act* 2000;

(iii) section 225(5) or 226(2) of the *Criminal Justice Act* 2003; or

(iv) under section 29(4) or (6) of the *Violent Crime Reduction Act* 2006.

(3) For the purposes of this Part of this Act any two or more sentences are to be treated as passed in the same proceeding if they would be so treated for the purposes of section 11 of the *Criminal Appeal Act* 1968.

(3A) Where a reference under this section relates to *an order under subsection (2) of section 269 of the* Criminal Justice Act *2003 (determination of minimum term in relation to mandatory life sentence), the Court of Appeal shall not, in deciding what order under that section is appropriate for the case, make any allowance for the fact that the person to whom it relates is being sentenced for a second time* [a case in which the judge made an order specified in subsection (3B), the Court of Appeal shall not, in deciding what sentence is appropriate for the case, make any allowance for the fact that the person to whom it relates is being sentenced for a second time].

[(3B) The orders specified in this subsection are—

(a) an order under section 269(2) of the *Criminal Justice Act* 2003 (determination of minimum term in relation to mandatory life sentence);

(b) an order under section 82A(2) of the *Powers of Criminal Courts (Sentencing) Act* 2000 (determination of minimum term in relation to discretionary life sentences and certain other sentences).]

(4) No judge shall sit as a member of the Court of Appeal on the hearing of, or shall determine any application in proceedings incidental or preliminary to, a reference under this section of a sentence passed by himself.

(5) Where the Court of Appeal have concluded their review of a case referred to them under this section the Attorney General or the person to whose sentencing the reference relates may refer a point of law involved in any sentence passed on that person in the proceeding to the *House of Lords for their opinion* [the Supreme Court for its opinion], and the *House* [Supreme Court] shall consider the point and give *their* [its] opinion on it accordingly, and either remit the case to the Court of Appeal to be dealt with or *deal with it themselves* [itself deal with the case]; and section 35(1) of the *Criminal Appeal Act* 1968 (composition of House for appeals) shall apply also in relation to any proceedings of the House under this section.

(6) A reference under subsection (5) above shall be made only with the leave of the Court of Appeal or the *House of Lords* [Supreme Court]; and leave shall not be granted unless it is certified by the Court of Appeal that the point of law is of general public importance and it appears to the Court of Appeal or the *House of Lords* [Supreme Court] (as the case may be) that the point is one which ought to be considered by *that House* [the Supreme Court].

(7) For the purpose of dealing with a case under this section the *House of Lords* [Supreme Court] may exercise any powers of the Court of Appeal.

(8) The supplementary provisions contained in Schedule 3 to this Act shall have effect.

(9) [*Application to Northern Ireland.*]

[This section is printed as amended by the *C(S)A* 1997, s.55, and Sched. 4, para. 13; the *PCC(S)A* 2000, s.165(1), and Sched. 9, para. 102; the *CJA* 2003, ss.272(1), 304 and 331, Sched. 32, paras 45 and 46, and Sched. 36, para. 96; the *VCRA* 2006, s.49, and Sched. 1, para. 3(1) and (2); and the *CJIA* 2008, s.148(1), and Sched. 26, paras 22 and 23; and as amended, as from a day to be appointed, by the *Constitutional Reform Act* 2005, s.40(4), and Sched. 9, para. 48(1) and (2) (omission of italicised words, insertion of words in square brackets, in subss. (5)–(7)); and the *CJIA* 2008, s.46(1) and (2) (omission of italicised words, insertion of words in square brackets, in subs. (3A), and insertion of subs. (3B)).]

The *Criminal Justice Act 2003 (Reviews of Sentencing) (Consequential and Supplementary Provisions) Order* 2007 (S.I. 2007 No. 1762) provides that section 36 shall apply to an order made by the High Court, on or after July 12, 2007, under section 269(2) of the 2003 Act (determination of minimum term in relation to mandatory life sentence) on a reference under paragraph 6 of Schedule 22 to that Act (*ante*, § 5–248 *et seq.*) as it applies to an order under section 269(2) (*ante*, § 5–243) made by the Crown Court. **7–369**

Duty of Attorney-General

In *Att.-Gen.'s Reference (No. 14 of 2003) (R. v. Sheppard)*, *The Times*, April 18, 2003, it was said that two of the safeguards built into the legislation were that the Attorney-General should personally consider the matter and decide for himself whether to seek leave, and that he had a discretion; where, therefore, his discretion had been exercised on a false basis, not having been put properly in the picture as to the nature of the case, leave would be refused. **7–369a**

Factual basis

The Court of Appeal will consider a reference on the basis of the facts proved or admitted; it would not constitute itself as a court of first instance inquiring into facts which had not been pursued or proved in the Crown Court: *Att.-Gen.'s Reference (No. 95 of 1998) (R. v. Highfield)*, *The Times*, April 21, 1999, CA. Nor is it the function of the court to substitute, in the light of new material which had not been available to the sentencer, its own view of what the sentence ought to be in the light of that new material; the court's task was to decide whether the sentence imposed in the light of the material before the judge could properly be characterised as being unduly lenient: *Att.-Gen.'s Reference (No. 19 of 2005) (R. v. Bowden)*, *The Times*, May 3, 2006, CA. **7–369b**

Deferred sentence

A deferment of sentence may be referred under this section: *Att.-Gen.'s Reference (No. 22 of 1992)*, 97 Cr.App.R. 275, CA; *R. v. L. (Deferred Sentence)*; *R. v. J.* [1999] 1 W.L.R. 479, CA. (As to this, see also *ante*, § 7–122.) **7–369c**

Plea of guilty following judicial indication as to sentence

In a series of cases, the Court of Appeal has considered the extent to which its approach to a reference should be influenced by the fact that a plea of guilty followed an indication as to sentence by the judge at first instance. In *Att.-Gen.'s Reference (No. 40 of 1996) (R. v. Robinson)* [1997] 1 Cr.App.R.(S.) 357 and *Att.-Gen.'s Reference (No. 17 of 1998) (R. v. Stokes)* [1999] 1 Cr.App.R.(S.) 407, this was said to be a factor to be taken into account, but it was not a barrier to the substitution of a more severe sentence. In *Att.-Gen.'s References (Nos 87 and 86 of 1999) (R. v. Webb and Simpson)* [2001] 1 Cr.App.R.(S.) 141, it was said to be a matter to be taken into account, particularly if the prosecution had acquiesced in the indication. In *Att.-Gen.'s References (Nos 80 and 81 of 1999) (R. v. Thompson and Rodgers)* [2000] 2 Cr.App.R.(S.) 138, an application to refer a sentence was regarded as "almost abusive" where a guilty **7–369d** plea had followed an indication by the judge of his view of the facts and of his view that such facts did not warrant a custodial sentence and the prosecution had taken no exception to the expressed view as to the facts. In *Att.-Gen.'s Reference (No. 44 of 2000) (R. v. Peverett)* [2001] 1 Cr.App.R.(S.) 27, it was said that if the prosecution are party to a bargain with the defence as to the basis of a plea of guilty, or acquiesce in one between the court and the defence as to sentence, it would be an abuse for the prosecution subsequently to resile from the bargain or acquiescence by seeking to refer the sentence to the Court of Appeal. And in *Att.-Gen.'s References (Nos 8, 9 and 10 of 2002) (R. v. Mohammed)* [2003] 1 Cr.App.R.(S.) 55, the court felt constrained not to interfere with an unduly lenient non-custodial sentence, where guilty pleas followed an indication by the judge that he was not thinking of a custodial sentence, and prosecution counsel had expressed no dissent either immediately or within an hour or two. Most recently, in *Att.-Gen.'s Reference (No. 48 of 2006) (R. v. Farrow)* [2007] 1 Cr.App.R.(S.) 90, the court said that where an offender pleads guilty to an offence following a *Goodyear* indication (see *ante*, § 5–79b) by the judge which is unduly lenient, the Court of Appeal will not be precluded from considering a reference merely because prosecuting counsel failed to remind the judge that the possibility of a referral of the sentence was unaffected.

Approach of Court of Appeal to reference

7–369e As to the approach of the Court of Appeal to the powers conferred by this section, see *Att.-Gen.'s Reference (No. 4 of 1989)*, 90 Cr.App.R. 366, CA, *Att.-Gen.'s Reference (No. 5 of 1989) (R. v. Hill-Trevor)*, 90 Cr.App.R. 358, and *Att.-Gen.'s Reference (No. 132 of 2001) (R. v. Johnson)* [2003] 1 Cr.App.R.(S.) 41, where it was said that the purpose of the system being the avoidance of gross error, the allaying of widespread public concern at what appears to be an unduly lenient sentence, and the preservation of public confidence in cases where a judge appears to have departed to a substantial extent from the norms of sentencing generally applied, the distinction between a lenient sentence and an "unduly" lenient sentence needs to be kept in mind, and careful consideration needs to be given to the individual circumstances before a decision is taken to make a case the subject of a reference; *R. v. Reynolds* [2007] 2 Cr.App.R.(S.) 87, CA, where it was said that it was not the function of section 36 to provide the prosecution with a general right of appeal against sentence; and *Att.-Gen.'s Reference (No. 8 of 2007) (R. v. Krivec)* [2008] 1 Cr.App.R.(S.) 1, CA, where it was said that judges should not refrain from imposing the sentence considered to be appropriate because of apprehension that the Attorney-General might seek a reference, and that whereas the test for his intervention is undue leniency, leniency, where the facts justify it, is to be commended and not condemned. Notwithstanding such observations, it has been held that it is open to the Court of Appeal to increase a sentence on a reference under this section although it is in accord with the current tariff for the offence in question: *Att.-Gen.'s Reference (No. 33 of 1996) (R. v. Latham)* [1997] 2 Cr.App.R.(S.) 10.

Double jeopardy

7–369f Where a sentence is increased, the practice of the Court of Appeal has been to allow some discount from what it considers to have been the correct sentence on account of what it commonly refers to as the "double jeopardy" principle. In *Att.-Gen.'s References (Nos 14 and 15 of 2006) (R. v. French and Webster)* [2007] 1 Cr.App.R.(S.) 40, CA, it was said that double jeopardy is but one aspect of the court's task when considering whether and how to intervene where an unduly lenient sentence has been imposed; where an offender had no responsibility for the undue leniency, justice required that some regard (the degree to which being fact-specific) should be had to the distress and anxiety experienced by the offender; these were likely to be particularly great where a custodial sentence was employed in place of a non-custodial sentence, where a custodial sentence had been completed, where the offender was young and immature or where he was about to be released, and in such cases, discounts for double jeopardy should tend to be near the upper end of the range (generally at about 30 per cent); distress and anxiety are much less significant where a lengthy period of imprisonment was still to be served, and, in such cases double jeopardy was of limited application and in some cases could properly not be taken into account (this being discretionary). See also *Att.-Gen.'s Reference (No. 82 of 2000) (R. v. Vinnicombe)* [2001] 2 Cr.App.R.(S.) 60, CA; and *Att.-Gen.'s References (Nos 41 and 42 of 2007) (R. v. Naidoo and Manton)* [2008] 1 Cr.App.R.(S.) 77, CA (the longer the original sentence, the less effect double jeopardy can have on the court's approach to the ultimate sentence).

Disparity

In *Att.-Gen.'s Reference (No. 44 of 2005) (R. v. Guirham)* (2005) 149 S.J. 988, CA, it was held that it would not be appropriate to substitute an appropriate custodial sentence for an unduly lenient non-custodial sentence where, (i) to do so would create an immediate, significant and unjust disparity as compared with the respondent's co-defendant who had received a similar sentence for his part in the incident that had given rise to the prosecution of the respondent, but who had been convicted of an offence which could not be made the subject of a sentencing reference; and (ii) the respondent had made considerable progress since the sentence had been passed and had done everything that was expected of him, such that it was not in the public interest to terminate his community sentence. **7–369g**

Delay

Where there is significant delay (not attributable to the respondent) in hearing a reference, the court may not alter the sentence even if of the opinion that it was unduly lenient; and the shorter the sentence, the more likely it is that any delay will be deemed significant: *Att.-Gen.'s References (Nos 83 and 85 of 2004) (R. v. Gardner and Afzal)* (2005) 149 S.J. 770, CA. **7–369h**

Criminal Justice Act 1988, Sched. 3

Section 36 SCHEDULE 3

REVIEWS OF SENTENCING—SUPPLEMENTARY

1. Notice of an application for leave to refer a case to the Court of Appeal under section 36 above shall be given within 28 days from the day on which the sentence, or the last of the sentences, in the case was passed. **7–370**

2. If the registrar of criminal appeals is given notice of a reference or application to the Court of Appeal under section 36 above, he shall—

(a) take all necessary steps for obtaining a hearing of the reference or application; and

(b) obtain and lay before the Court in proper form all documents, exhibits and other things which appear necessary for the proper determination of the reference or application.

3. [*Provision for rules of court.*]

4. An application to the Court of Appeal for leave to refer a case to the *House of Lords* [Supreme Court] under section 36(5) above shall be made within the period of 14 days beginning with the date on which the Court of Appeal conclude their review of the case; and an application to the *House of Lords* [Supreme Court] for leave shall be made within the period of 14 days beginning with the date on which the Court of Appeal conclude their review or refuse leave to refer the case to the *House of Lords* [Supreme Court].

5. The time during which a person whose case has been referred for review under section 36 above is in custody pending its review and pending any reference to the *House of Lords* [Supreme Court] under subsection (5) of that section shall be reckoned as part of the term of any sentence to which he is for the time being subject.

6. Except as provided by paragraphs 7 and 8 below, a person whose sentencing is the subject of a reference to the Court of Appeal under section 36 above shall be entitled to be present, if he wishes it, on the hearing of the reference, although he may be in custody.

7. A person in custody shall not be entitled to be present—

(a) on an application by the Attorney General for leave to refer a case; or

(b) on any proceedings preliminary or incidental to a reference,

unless the Court of Appeal give him leave to be present.

8. The power of the Court of Appeal to pass sentence on a person may be exercised although he is not present.

7–371 9. A person whose sentencing is the subject of a reference to the *House of Lords* [Supreme Court] under section 36(5) above and who is detained pending the hearing of that reference shall not be entitled to be present on the hearing of the reference or of any proceeding preliminary or incidental thereto except where an order of the *House* [Supreme Court] authorises him to be present, or where the *House* [Supreme Court] or the Court of Appeal, as the case may be, give him leave to be present.

10. The term of any sentence passed by the Court of Appeal or *House of Lords* [Supreme Court] under section 36 above shall, unless they otherwise direct, begin to run from the time when it would have begun to run if passed in the proceeding in relation to which the reference was made.

11. Where on a reference to the Court of Appeal under section 36 above or a reference to the *House of Lords* [Supreme Court] under subsection (5) of that section the person whose sentencing is the subject of the reference appears by counsel for the purpose of presenting any argument to the *Court or the House* [the Court of Appeal or the Supreme Court], he shall be entitled to his costs, that is to say to the payment out of central funds of such funds as are reasonably sufficient to compensate him for expenses properly incurred by him for the purpose of being represented on the reference; and any amount recoverable under this paragraph shall be ascertained, as soon as practicable, by the registrar of criminal appeals or, as the case may be, *such officer as may be prescribed by order of the House of Lords* [under Supreme Court Rules].

12. [*Application to Northern Ireland.*]

[The words in square brackets are substituted for the italicised words as from a day to be appointed: *Constitutional Reform Act* 2005, s.40(4), and Sched. 9, para. 48(1) and (3).]

Criminal Procedure Rules 2005 (S.I. 2005 No. 384), Pt 70
(as substituted by the Criminal Procedure (Amendment No. 2) Rules 2007
(S.I. 2007 No. 2317))

When this Part applies

7–372 **70.1.** This Part applies where the Attorney General wants to—

(a) refer a point of law to the Court of Appeal under section 36 of the *Criminal Justice Act* 1972; or
(b) refer a sentencing case to the Court of Appeal under section 36 of the *Criminal Justice Act* 1988.

Service of notice of reference and application for permission

7–373 **70.2.**—(1) The Attorney General must—

(a) serve on the Registrar—
  (i) any notice of reference, and
  (ii) any application for permission to refer a sentencing case; and
(b) with a notice of reference of a point of law, give the Registrar details of—
  (i) the defendant affected,
  (ii) the date and place of the relevant Crown Court decision, and
  (iii) the relevant verdict and sentencing.

(2) The Attorney General must serve an application for permission to refer a sentencing case not more than 28 days after the last of the sentences in that case.

Form of notice of reference and application for permission

7–374 **70.3.**—(1) A notice of reference and an application for permission to refer a sentencing case must be in the appropriate form set out in the Practice Direction, giving the year and number.

(2) A notice of reference of a point of law must—

(a) specify the point of law in issue and indicate the opinion that the Attorney General invites the court to give;
(b) identify each ground for that invitation, numbering them consecutively (if there is more than one) and concisely outlining each argument in support;
(c) exclude any reference to the defendant's name and any other reference that may identify the defendant;
(d) summarise the relevant facts; and
(e) identify any relevant authorities.

(3) An application for permission to refer a sentencing case must—

(a) give details of—
  (i) the defendant affected,
  (ii) the date and place of the relevant Crown Court decision, and
  (iii) the relevant verdict and sentencing;
(b) explain why that sentencing appears to the Attorney General unduly lenient, concisely outlining each argument in support; and
(c) include the application for permission to refer the case to the court.

(4) A notice of reference of a sentencing case must—
(a) include the same details and explanation as the application for permission to refer the case;
(b) summarise the relevant facts; and
(c) identify any relevant authorities.

(5) Where the court gives the Attorney General permission to refer a sentencing case, it may treat the application for permission as the notice of reference.

Registrar's notice to defendant

70.4.—(1) The Registrar must serve on the defendant— **7–375**
(a) a notice of reference;
(b) an application for permission to refer a sentencing case.

(2) Where the Attorney General refers a point of law, the Registrar must give the defendant notice that—
(a) the outcome of the reference will not make any difference to the outcome of the trial; and
(b) the defendant may serve a respondent's notice.

(3) Where the Attorney General applies for permission to refer a sentencing case, the Registrar must give the defendant notice that—
(a) the outcome of the reference may make a difference to that sentencing, and in particular may result in a more severe sentence; and
(b) the defendant may serve a respondent's notice.

Respondent's notice

70.5.—(1) A defendant on whom the Registrar serves a reference or an application for permission to refer a sentencing case may serve a respondent's notice, and must do so if— **7–376**
(a) the defendant wants to make representations to the court; or
(b) the court so directs.

(2) Such a defendant must serve the respondent's notice on—
(a) the Attorney General; and
(b) the Registrar.

(3) Such a defendant must serve the respondent's notice—
(a) where the Attorney General refers a point of law, not more than 28 days after—
  (i) the Registrar serves the reference, or
  (ii) a direction to do so;
(b) where the Attorney General applies for permission to refer a sentencing case, not more than 14 days after—
  (i) the Registrar serves the application, or
  (ii) a direction to do so.

(4) Where the Attorney General refers a point of law, the respondent's notice must—
(a) identify each ground of opposition on which the respondent relies, numbering them consecutively (if there is more than one), concisely outlining each argument in support and identifying the Attorney General's ground or reason to which each relates;
(b) summarise any relevant facts not already summarised in the reference;
(c) identify any relevant authorities; and
(d) include or attach any application for the following, with reasons—
  (i) an extension of time within which to serve the respondent's notice,
  (ii) permission to attend a hearing that the respondent does not have a right to attend,
  (iii) a direction to attend in person a hearing that the respondent could attend by live link, if the respondent is in custody.

(5) Where the Attorney General applies for permission to refer a sentencing case, the respondent's notice must—

(a) say if the respondent wants to make representations at the hearing of the application or reference; and
(b) include or attach any application for the following, with reasons—
  (i) an extension of time within which to serve the respondent's notice,
  (ii) permission to attend a hearing that the respondent does not have a right to attend,
  (iii) a direction to attend in person a hearing that the respondent could attend by live link, if the respondent is in custody.

Variation or withdrawal of notice of reference or application for permission

7–377 **70.6.**—(1) This rule applies where the Attorney General wants to vary or withdraw—
(a) a notice of reference; or
(b) an application for permission to refer a sentencing case.

(2) The Attorney General—
(a) may vary or withdraw the notice or application without the court's permission by serving notice on—
  (i) the Registrar, and
  (ii) the defendant
before any hearing of the reference or application; but
(b) at any such hearing, may only vary or withdraw that notice or application with the court's permission.

Right to attend hearing

7–378 **70.7.**—(1) A respondent who is in custody has a right to attend a hearing in public unless it is a hearing preliminary or incidental to a reference, including the hearing of an application for permission to refer a sentencing case.

(2) The court or the Registrar may direct that such a respondent is to attend a hearing by live link.

Anonymity of defendant on reference of point of law

7–378a **70.8.** Where the Attorney General refers a point of law, the court must not allow anyone to identify the defendant during the proceedings unless the defendant gives permission.

[Part 70 is printed as substituted by the *Criminal Procedure (Amendment No. 2) Rules* 2007 (S.I. 2007 No. 2317).]

XIV. THE EUROPEAN COURT

European law

7–379 European Community law is part of United Kingdom law: *European Communities Act* 1972, s.2. Any question as to the meaning or effect of any of the Treaties, or as to the validity, meaning or effect of any Community instrument, shall be treated as a question of law, and, if not referred to the European Court, be for determination as such in accordance with the principles laid down by, and any relevant decision of, the European Court: *ibid.* s.3(1). Judicial notice shall be taken of the Treaties, of the Official Journal of the Communities and of any decision of, or expression of opinion by, the European Court on any such question as aforesaid; and the Official Journal shall be admissible as evidence of any instrument or other act thereby communicated of any of the Communities or of any Community institution: *ibid.* s.3(2). For the meaning to be given to "the Communities" and "the Treaties", see *ibid.* s.1(2).

In order to determine a question of community law within section 3(1), it may be necessary for the court to hear evidence (in the absence of the jury, if there is one) and make findings of fact: see, *e.g. R. v. Goldstein* [1983] 1 W.L.R. 151, HL.

In the course of his speech in *Goldstein*, Lord Diplock (with whom the remainder of their Lordships agreed) made certain limited observations on the procedure for dealing with questions of law under section 3(1). His Lordship said that it was impossible to foresee all the circumstances in which such a question may arise in the course of legal proceedings. So far as criminal trials were concerned, it was appropriate for the criminal division of the Court of Appeal to lay down such guidelines as its experience suggests are desirable for the convenient disposal of section 3(1) questions. Where it is apparent from the outset that such a question will arise, the most appropriate time to take it is by a motion to quash the indictment before arraignment (see p. 156).

Where a question of community law is raised, and the court considers that a decision thereon is necessary to enable it to give judgment, it may, if the point is not clear, refer the point to the European Court: see *post*.

Making of references

Rules have been made which regulate the procedure of the Crown Court and the criminal division of the Court of Appeal on references to the European Court for preliminary rulings under Article 234 (formerly 177) of the E.C. Treaty, Article 150 of the Euratom Treaty, and Article 41 of the ECSC Treaty. These articles directly confer a power, and in some cases a duty, on courts to refer certain questions as to the interpretation and validity of Community law to the European Court for a preliminary ruling. Part 75 of the *Criminal Procedure Rules* 2005 (S.I. 2005 No. 384) (*ante*, § 2–220) makes procedural provision in connection with such references. Rule 75.1(2) stipulates that an order may be made by the Crown Court of its own motion or on application by a party to the proceedings; or by the Court of Appeal, on application or otherwise, at any time before the determination of an appeal or application for leave to appeal under Part I of the 1968 Act. **7–380**

Article 234 (formerly 177) of the E.C. Treaty of 1957 provides as follows:

> "The Court of Justice shall have jurisdiction to give preliminary rulings concerning: (a) the interpretation of this Treaty; (b) the validity and interpretation of acts of the institutions of the Community; (c) the interpretation of the statutes of bodies established by an act of the Council, where those statutes so provide.
>
> Where such a question is raised before any court or tribunal of a Member State, that court or tribunal may, if it considers that a decision on the question is necessary to enable it to give judgment, request the Court of Justice to give a ruling thereon.
>
> Where any such question is raised in a case pending before a court or tribunal of a Member State, against whose decisions there is no judicial remedy under national law, that court or tribunal shall bring the matter before the Court of Justice."

In *Henn and Darby v. DPP* [1981] A.C. 850, HL, Lord Diplock stated that in a criminal trial upon indictment— **7–381**

> "it can seldom be a proper exercise of the presiding judge's discretion to seek a preliminary ruling" [*i.e.* under Art. 177] "before the facts of the alleged offence have been ascertained, with the result that the proceedings will be held up for nine months or more in order that at the end of the trial he may give to the jury an accurate instruction as to the relevant law, if the evidence turns out in the event to be as was anticipated at the time the reference was made—which may not always be the case. It is generally better, as the judge himself put it, that the question be decided by him in the first instance and reviewed thereafter if necessary through the hierarchy of the national Courts" (at p. 904).

That the warning of the Advocate General in his opinion delivered in Case 9/75, *Meyer-Burckhardt v. E.C. Commission* [1975] E.C.R. 1171 at 1186, that "… national courts should exercise great caution before reaching the conclusion on any point of Community law, that the answer to it admits of no possible doubt," should always be borne in mind was underlined by Lord Diplock. Although he did not refer to this opinion, he said that the history of the instant case served "as a timely warning to English judges not to be too ready to hold that because the meaning of the English text … seems plain to them no question of interpretation can be involved" (at p. 906). His Lordship also referred to "the danger of an English court applying English canons of statutory construction to the interpretation of the Treaty or, for that matter, of Regulations or Directives" (at p. 904). See also generally, *R. v. Plymouth JJ., ex p. Rogers* [1982] Q.B. 863, 75 Cr.App.R. 64, DC.

In *S.A. Magnavision N.V. v. General Optical Council (No.2)* [1987] 2 C.M.L.R. 262, DC, it was held that when a court of final decision in a member state has come to a decision as a consequence of being clear in its mind as to the construction to be put upon relevant E.C. legislation, then it is under no obligation at all to make a reference to the European Court. Further, where a national court is the final court of appeal except by leave (of itself) and it refuses leave, it is too late, judgment having been given, to make an Article 234 reference.

Evidence

7–382 The *Evidence (European Court) Order* 1976 (S.I. 1976 No. 428) applies sections 1 to 3 of the *Evidence (Proceedings in Other Jurisdictions) Act* 1975 to the European Court of Justice thus enabling evidence for proceedings before that court to be taken in the United Kingdom.

Chapter 8

ORAL TESTIMONY OF WITNESSES

I. PRELIMINARIES

A. Securing Attendance of Witnesses, Production of Documents, etc.

(1) Witness orders in committal proceedings

Witness orders in committal proceedings (provided for by the *Criminal Procedure (Attendance of Witnesses) Act* 1965, s.1) have been abolished: section 1 of the 1965 Act was repealed by the *CPIA* 1996, ss.65(1) and 80, and Sched. 5, Pt 6. For details of the former law, which still applies in relation to offences into which a criminal investigation began before April 1, 1997, see the 1997 edition of this work. For details of the commencement and transitional provisions, see the 2007 edition. **8–1**

In cases governed by the current regime, there is no obligation on a witness, whose evidence is included in the committal evidence, to attend the Crown Court, unless the prosecution obtain a witness summons under section 2 of the 1965 Act (*post*). This was confirmed in *R. v. Wang* [2005] 4 *Archbold News* 1, CA.

(2) Summons to witness to attend Crown Court

Criminal Procedure (Attendance of Witnesses) Act 1965, s.2

Issue of witness summons on application

Issue of witness summons on application to Crown Court

2.—(1) This section applies where the Crown Court is satisfied that— **8–2**

(a) a person is likely to be able to give evidence likely to be material evidence, or produce any document or thing likely to be material evidence, for the purpose of any criminal proceedings before the Crown Court, and

(b) it is in the interests of justice to issue a summons under this section to secure the attendance of that person to give evidence or to produce the document or thing.

(2) In such a case the Crown Court shall, subject to the following provisions of this section, issue a summons (a witness summons) directed to the person concerned and requiring him to—

(a) attend before the Crown Court at the time and place stated in the summons, and

(b) give the evidence or produce the document or thing.

(3) A witness summons may only be issued under this section on an application; and the Crown Court may refuse to issue the summons if any requirement relating to the application is not fulfilled.

(4) Where a person has been *committed for trial, or sent for trial under section 51 of the* Crime and Disorder Act 1998 *for any offence to which the proceedings concerned relate, an application must be made as soon as is reasonably practicable after the committal* [sent for trial for any offence to which the proceedings relate, an application must be made as soon as is reasonably practicable after service on that person, in pursuance of regulations made under paragraph 1 of Schedule 3 to the *Crime and Disorder Act* 1998, of documents relevant to that offence].

(5) *Where the proceedings concerned have been transferred to the Crown Court, an application must be made as soon as is reasonably practicable after the transfer.*

(6) Where the proceedings concerned relate to an offence in relation to which a bill of indictment has been preferred under the authority of section 2(2)(b) of the *Administration of Justice (Miscellaneous Provisions) Act* 1933 (bill preferred by direction of Court of Appeal, or by direction or with consent of judge) an application must be made as soon as is reasonably practicable after the bill was preferred.

(7) An application must be made in accordance with Criminal Procedure Rules; and different provision may be made for different cases or descriptions of case.

(8), (9) [*Matters for which Criminal Procedure Rules may provide.*]

(10) In subsection (9) above—

(a) references to any stipulated evidence, document or thing are to any evidence, document or thing whose giving or production is proposed to be required by the witness summons;

(b) references to the directed person are to the person to whom the witness summons is proposed to be directed.

[This section, together with sections 2A to 2E (*post*) were substituted for the original section 2 in relation to any proceedings for the purpose of which no witness summons had been issued under the original section 2 before April 1, 1999: *CPIA* 1996, s.66(1), (2), (7), (8); and the *Criminal Procedure and Investigations Act 1996 (Appointed Day No. 9) Order* 1999 (S.I. 1999 No. 718). It is printed as subsequently amended by the *CDA* 1998, s.119, and Sched. 8, para. 8; the *Courts Act* 2003, s.109, and Sched. 8, para. 126; and the *SOCPA* 2005, s.169(1). The words in square brackets in subs. (4) are substituted for the italicised words that precede them, and subs. (5) is repealed, by the *CJA* 2003, ss.41 and 332, Sched. 3, para. 42, and Sched. 37, Pt 4. The amendment of subs. (4) came into force on May 9, 2005, in relation to cases sent for trial under section 51A(3)(d) of the *CDA* 1998: *Criminal Justice Act 2003 (Commencement No. 9) Order* 2005 (S.I. 2005 No. 1267). Otherwise, this amendment and the repeal of subs. (5) come into force on a day to be appointed.]

As to the making of an application for a witness summons, see rule 28.3 of the *Criminal Procedure Rules* 2005 (S.I. 2005 No. 384), *post*, § 8–7b.

A court has no jurisdiction to decline to issue a witness summons addressed to a child on account of section 44 of the *CYPA* 1933 (*ante*, § 5–53b): *R. v. Highbury Magistrates' Court, ex p. Deering*, 161 J.P. 138, DC.

Criminal Procedure (Attendance of Witnesses) Act 1965, ss.2A–2E

Power to require advance production

8–3 **2A.** A witness summons which is issued under section 2 above and which requires a person to produce a document or thing as mentioned in section 2(2) above may also require him to produce the document or thing—

(a) at a place stated in the summons, and

(b) at a time which is so stated and precedes that stated under section 2(2) above, for inspection by the person applying for the summons.

[See the note to s.2, *ante*.]

Summons no longer needed

2B.—(1) If— 8–3a

(a) a document or thing is produced in pursuance of a requirement imposed by a witness summons under section 2A above,

(b) the person applying for the summons concludes that a requirement imposed by the summons under section 2(2) above is no longer needed, and

(c) he accordingly applies to the Crown Court for a direction that the summons shall be of no further effect,

the court may direct accordingly.

(2) An application under this section must be made in accordance with Criminal Procedure Rules; and different provision may be made for different cases or descriptions of case.

(3) Criminal Procedure Rules may, in such cases as the rules may specify, require the effect of a direction under this section to be notified to the person to whom the summons is directed.

[See the note to s.2, *ante*. The section is printed as amended by the *Courts Act* 2003, s.109, and Sched. 8, para. 126.]

The *Criminal Procedure Rules* 2005 (S.I. 2005 No. 384) no longer make specific provision for an application under this section, but see rule 28.7, *post*, § 8–8c.

Application to make summons ineffective

2C.—(1) If a witness summons issued under section 2 above is directed to a person who— 8–3b

(a) applies to the Crown Court,

(b) satisfies the court that he was not served with notice of the application to issue the summons and that he was neither present nor represented at the hearing of the application, and

(c) satisfies the court that he cannot give any evidence likely to be material evidence or, as the case may be, produce any document or thing likely to be material evidence,

the court may direct that the summons shall be of no effect.

(2) For the purposes of subsection (1) above it is immaterial—

(a) whether or not Criminal Procedure Rules require the person to be served with notice of the application to issue the summons;

(b) whether or not Criminal Procedure Rules enable the person to be present or represented at the hearing of the application.

(3) In subsection (1)(b) above "served" means—

(a) served in accordance with Criminal Procedure Rules, in a case where such rules require the person to be served with notice of the application to issue the summons;

(b) served in such way as appears reasonable to the court to which the application is made under this section, in any other case.

(4) The Crown Court may refuse to make a direction under this section if any requirement relating to the application under this section is not fulfilled.

(5) An application under this section must be made in accordance with Criminal Procedure Rules; and different provision may be made for different cases or descriptions of case.

(6), (7) [*Matters for which Criminal Procedure Rules may provide*.]

(8) Where a direction is made under this section that a witness summons shall be of no effect, the person on whose application the summons was issued may be ordered to pay the whole or any part of the costs of the application under this section.

(9) [*Enforcement of order for costs*.]

[See the note to s.2, *ante*. The section is printed as amended by the *Courts Act* 2003, s.109, and Sched. 8, para. 126.]

As to applications to set aside generally, see *post*, §§ 8–4 *et seq.* The *Criminal Procedure Rules* 2005 (S.I. 2005 No. 384) no longer make specific provision for an application under this section, but see rule 28.7, *post*, § 8–8c.

Issue of summons of court's own motion

Issue of witness summons of Crown Court's own motion

2D. For the purpose of any criminal proceedings before it, the Crown Court may of its own motion issue a summons (a witness summons) directed to a person and requiring him to— 8–3c

(a) attend before the court at the time and place stated in the summons, and

(b) give evidence, or produce any document or thing specified in the summons.

[See the note to s.2, *ante*.]

Application to make summons ineffective

8–3d **2E.**—(1) If a witness summons issued under section 2D above is directed to a person who—

(a) applies to the Crown Court, and

(b) satisfies the court that he cannot give any evidence likely to be material evidence or, as the case may be, produce any document or thing likely to be material evidence,

the court may direct that the summons shall be of no effect.

(2) [*Identical to s.2C(4),* ante.]

(3) [*Identical to s.2C(5),* ante.]

(4) [*Matters for which Criminal Procedure Rules may provide.*]

[See the notes to ss.2 and 2C, *ante*.]

As to applications to set aside generally, see *post*, §§ 8–4 *et seq.* The *Criminal Procedure Rules* 2005 (S.I. 2005 No. 384) no longer make specific provision for an application under this section, but see rule 28.7, *post*, § 8–8c.

Grounds for setting aside witness summons

8–4 There is a slight difference in wording between section 2C(1)(c) and 2E(1)(b) on the one hand, and the original section 2(2) on the other, in that the original provision simply referred to the witness satisfying "the court that he cannot give any material evidence or, as the case may be, produce any document or thing likely to be material evidence". It is submitted, however, that this is not sufficient to effect any change of substance; and the fact that the previous formulation has been followed so closely would suggest that no change of substance was intended. If anything, it has slightly lowered the threshold for setting aside a summons; the court may now set it aside if satisfied that any evidence the witness can give is "unlikely" to be material, whereas previously the court would have had to be satisfied that any evidence the witness could give would not be material.

(i) *Lack of particularity*

8–5 In *R. v. Milner*, unreported, July 5, 1993, CCC (indictment no. 921602) (H.H.J. Laughland Q.C.), it was held that a summons must specify the document or thing required to be produced with reasonable particularity, and it must be admissible. It must either be individually identified or be identified by reference to a class of documents or things by which criterion the recipient can know what is the obligation which the court places on him. A summons is not a proper and effective order if it requires the recipient to make judgments, for example, of relevance or weight. It is only where there is a lawful and effective use of the limited powers under the 1965 Act that any question of the consideration of particular documents in regard to public interest immunity falls to be considered.

(ii) *Inadmissibility*

8–6 A summons requiring the production of material which is not prima facie admissible is liable to be set aside: *R. v. Cheltenham JJ., ex p. Secretary of State for Trade* [1977] 1 W.L.R. 95, DC. The court quashed a summons served on an inspector appointed under section 165 of the *Companies Act* 1948 to produce transcripts of evidence and other materials obtained during the course of the investigation. The material was not prima facie admissible since it was required only for use in cross-examination to contradict statements a witness might make by reference to what he had said previously. *Per curiam*: even if the evidence was material, it should not be produced because the public interest in maintaining sources of information in respect of an inquiry of the kind carried out under section 165 would outweigh the private disadvantage of non-disclosure of the evidence.

In *Re Barlow Clowes Gilt Managers Ltd* [1992] Ch. 208, Millett J. dealt with an application by the liquidators of a company for directions concerning a witness summons under section 2, with which they had been served requiring production of transcripts of interviews conducted on their behalf with various people, many of whom were to be called by the prosecution in the criminal proceedings. Although his Lordship reviewed the principles involved, his directions were confined to directing the liquidators to apply to the Crown Court to set aside the summons on the grounds that (a) the transcripts were not material evidence, and (b) public interest immunity attached thereto.

On the liquidators' application to the Central Criminal Court, Phillips J. ruled that the summons should not be set aside: *R. v. Clowes*, 95 Cr.App.R. 440. His Lordship did not purport to depart from any of the principles in the *Cheltenham JJ.* case, and reviewed by Millett J. However, he distinguished *Cheltenham JJ.*, (a) in relation to admissibility, on the ground that the transcripts fell within section 24 of the *CJA* 1988 (*rep.*—see now s.117 of the *CJA* 2003, *post*, § 11–26); (b) in relation to abuse of process, on the ground that he was satisfied that the transcripts were likely to contain material not disclosed in the witness statements or subsequent Department of Trade and Industry interviews of the witnesses, and that the defence was likely to want to put this material in evidence as part of their case, and, therefore, it was not just a disguised attempt at discovery for the purpose of digging up material for cross-examination; and (c) in relation to public interest immunity, his Lordship had balanced the competing considerations and concluded on the facts that the interests of justice demanded that the transcripts be disclosed.

In *R. v. Derby Magistrates' Court, ex p. B.* [1996] A.C. 487, the House of Lords was concerned with section 97(1) of the *Magistrates' Courts Act* 1980, which like sections 2C(1)(c) and 2E(1)(b) of the 1965 Act, refers to the production "of any document or thing likely to be material evidence". It was held that section 97 contemplates the production of documents which are immediately admissible *per se* and without more; it may not be used to obtain discovery of documents which might, or might not, upon examination, prove to be admissible. The law relating to the production of documents by third parties was untouched by developments in the law relating to the prosecution's duty of disclosure. See also *R. v. H.(L.)* [1997] 1 Cr.App.R. 176, Crown Court (Sedley J.) (a summons cannot be used to compel production of documents merely because they are likely to afford or assist a relevant line of inquiry or challenge).

(iii) *Immateriality*

Evidence is material if it is relevant to an issue in the case: see *R. v. Reading JJ., ex p. Berkshire County Council* [1996] 1 Cr.App.R. 239, DC. Where the recipient of a summons asserts the immateriality of the matter sought, the judge may either accept that assertion or look at the matter himself. The course to be adopted is a matter for his discretion: *R. v. W.(G.) and W.(E.)* [1997] 1 Cr.App.R. 166, CA. If the claim that the matter was immaterial was suspect or implausible, the judge would no doubt look for himself. On the other hand, he might regard an assurance from an independent competent member of the Bar as sufficient reason for drawing the conclusion that the matter was irrelevant but, at the end of the day, the judge, in his discretion, had either to accept the assurance or to look at the matter and decide for himself: *ibid.* In *R. v. H.(L.), ante*, Sedley J. (sitting at first instance) said that a person applying to set aside a summons should "weed" the documents where they are copious to remove anything which is plainly incapable of having a bearing on the issues. **8–6a**

(iv) *Public interest immunity*

The recipient of a witness summons may object to the production of the matter sought on the grounds that public interest immunity attaches thereto: see *R. v. Milner* (*ante*, § 8–5); *R. v. Cheltenham JJ., ex p. Secretary of State for Trade* (*ante*, § 8–6); *R. v. Clowes* (*ante*, § 8–6); *R. v. K. (Trevor Douglas)*, 97 Cr.App.R. 342, CA; and *R. v. W.(G.) and W.(E.), ante*. **8–6b**

Where a claim to public interest immunity is made, it will be the duty of the judge to inspect the matter: *R. v. K. (Trevor Douglas), ante*.

As to whether a claim to public interest immunity should be upheld, there are two stages. First, does public interest immunity in principle attach to the matter in question? As to this, see *post*, §§ 12–26 *et seq.* Secondly, if it does, should the claim thereto nevertheless be overridden in the interests of justice? This involves a balancing exercise (as in the case of a claim to public interest immunity made by the prosecution): as to this, see *post*, §§ 12–44d *et seq.*

As to whether there is an entitlement to make voluntary disclosure of matter to which public interest immunity attaches, or whether there is a duty to assert a claim thereto, see *post*, § 12–44a.

(v) *Confidentiality, etc., rights of witness or person to whom evidence relates*

8–6c Rule 28.7 of the *Criminal Procedure Rules* 2005 (S.I. 2005 No. 384) (*post*, § 8–8c) makes provision for a witness summons to be withdrawn on the ground that the duties or rights, including rights of confidentiality, of the witness or of any person to whom the proposed evidence relates outweigh the reasons for the issue of the summons. This does not match any ground for which the statute provides, but it, together with rules 28.5 and 28.6, gives effect to the opinion of the Divisional Court in *R. (T.B.) v. Stafford Crown Court* [2006] 2 Cr.App.R. 34, that a witness summons directed to a hospital seeking production of a patient's medical records will engage the patient's right to privacy under Article 8 of the ECHR (*post*, § 16–101). See also *Z. v. Finland*, 25 E.H.R.R. 371, ECtHR (the need to protect the confidentiality of medical records may be outweighed by the public interest in the investigation and prosecution of crime and in the publicity of court proceedings; but any measure compelling disclosure calls for the most careful scrutiny, as do the safeguards designed to secure effective protection, *e.g.* an order that will protect the anonymity of the witness).

Setting aside a witness summons—procedure, etc.

8–6d See the *Criminal Procedure Rules* 2005 (S.I. 2005 No. 384), r.28.7, *post*, § 8–8a. The following authorities were all decided under the legislation prior to the enactment of the amending provisions in the *CPIA* 1996, and the consequent amendment of the *Crown Court Rules* 1982 (from which the 2005 rules derive). They appear, however, to have at least some continuing relevance.

The prosecution should be represented on an application to set aside a summons issued on a defence application: *R. v. K. (Trevor Douglas)*, *ante*.

It should ordinarly be possible for the parties to agree that the application should be dealt with on the basis of their written representations; a hearing will only be appropriate where oral argument is clearly necessary or the judge requires it: *R. v. H.(L.)*, *ante*.

As to costs, there is specific provision in section 2C(8) of the Act (*ante*, § 8–3b) for an order for the costs of the application to be paid by the party on whose application the summons was issued, if the application to set aside is successful. Apart from this, a wasted costs order may be made in favour of the recipient of a summons who successfully applies for it to be set aside: see *Re Ronald A. Prior & Co. (Solicitors)* [1996] 1 Cr.App.R. 248, CA (*ante*, § 6–40). The issue of a purely speculative summons may well amount to an "improper, unreasonable or negligent act" capable of attracting a wasted costs order: *R. v. H.(L.)*, *ante*; and *Wasted Costs Order (No. 5 of 1997)*, *The Times*, September 7, 1999, CA.

Criminal Procedure Rules 2005 (S.I. 2005 No. 384), Pt 28
(as substituted by the Criminal Procedure (Amendment) Rules 2007
(S.I. 2007 No. 699), r.16)

When this Part applies

8–7 **28.1.**—(1) This Part applies in magistrates' courts and in the Crown Court where—

(a) a party wants the court to issue a witness summons, warrant or order under—
  (i) section 97 of the *Magistrates' Courts Act* 1980,
  (ii) section 2 of the *Criminal Procedure (Attendance of Witnesses) Act* 1965, or
  (iii) section 7 of the *Bankers' Books Evidence Act* 1879;
(b) the court considers the issue of such a summons, warrant or order on its own initiative as if a party had applied; or
(c) one of those listed in rule 28.7 wants the court to withdraw such a summons, warrant or order.

(2) A reference to a "witness" in this Part is a reference to a person to whom such a summons, warrant or order is directed.

Issue etc. of summons, warrant or order with or without a hearing

28.2.—(1) The court may issue or withdraw a witness summons, warrant or order with or without a hearing. **8–7a**

(2) A hearing under this Part must be in private unless the court otherwise directs.

Application for summons, warrant or order: general rules

28.3.—(1) A party who wants the court to issue a witness summons, warrant or order must apply as soon as practicable after becoming aware of the grounds for doing so. **8–7b**

(2) The party applying must—

(a) identify the proposed witness;

(b) explain—

(i) what evidence the proposed witness can give or produce,

(ii) why it is likely to be material evidence, and

(iii) why it would be in the interests of justice to issue a summons, order or warrant as appropriate.

(3) The application may be made orally unless—

(a) rule 28.5 applies; or

(b) the court otherwise directs.

Written application: form and service

28.4.—(1) An application in writing under rule 28.3 must be in the form set out in the Practice Direction, containing the same declaration of truth as a witness statement. **8–8**

(2) The party applying must serve the application—

(a) in every case, on the court officer and as directed by the court; and

(b) as required by rule 28.5, if that rule applies.

Application for summons to produce a document, etc.: special rules

28.5.—(1) This rule applies to an application under rule 28.3 for a witness summons requiring the proposed witness— **8–8a**

(a) to produce in evidence a document or thing; or

(b) to give evidence about information apparently held in confidence, that relates to another person.

(2) The application must be in writing in the form required by rule 28.4.

(3) The party applying must serve the application—

(a) on the proposed witness, unless the court otherwise directs; and

(b) on one or more of the following, if the court so directs—

(i) a person to whom the proposed evidence relates,

(ii) another party.

(4) The court must not issue a witness summons where this rule applies unless—

(a) everyone served with the application has had at least 14 days in which to make representations, including representations about whether there should be a hearing of the application before the summons is issued; and

(b) the court is satisfied that it has been able to take adequate account of the duties and rights, including rights of confidentiality, of the proposed witness and of any person to whom the proposed evidence relates.

(5) This rule does not apply to an application for an order to produce in evidence a copy of an entry in a banker's book.

Application for summons to produce a document, etc.: court's assessment of relevance and confidentiality

28.6.—(1) This rule applies where a person served with an application for a witness summons requiring the proposed witness to produce in evidence a document or thing objects to its production on the ground that— **8–8b**

(a) it is not likely to be material evidence; or

(b) even if it is likely to be material evidence, the duties or rights, including rights of confidentiality, of the proposed witness or of any person to whom the document or thing relates outweigh the reasons for issuing a summons.

(2) The court may require the proposed witness to make the document or thing available for the objection to be assessed.

(3) The court may invite—

(a) the proposed witness or any representative of the proposed witness; or

(b) a person to whom the document or thing relates or any representative of such a person,

to help the court assess the objection.

Application to withdraw a summons, warrant or order

8–8c **28.7.**—(1) The court may withdraw a witness summons, warrant or order if one of the following applies for it to be withdrawn—

(a) the party who applied for it, on the ground that it is no longer is needed;

(b) the witness, on the grounds that—

(i) he was not aware of any application for it, and

(ii) he cannot give or produce evidence likely to be material evidence, or

(iii) even if he can, his duties or rights, including rights of confidentiality, or those of any person to whom the evidence relates outweigh the reasons for the issue of the summons, warrant or order; or

(c) any person to whom the proposed evidence relates, on the grounds that—

(i) he was not aware of any application for it, and

(ii) that evidence is not likely to be material evidence, or

(iii) even if it is, his duties or rights, including rights of confidentiality, or those of the witness outweigh the reasons for the issue of the summons, warrant or order.

(2) A person applying under the rule must—

(a) apply in writing as soon as practicable after becoming aware of the grounds for doing so, explaining why he wants the summons, warrant or order to be withdrawn; and

(b) serve the application on the court officer and as appropriate on—

(i) the witness,

(ii) the party who applied for the summons, warrant or order, and

(iii) any other person who he knows was served with the application for the summons, warrant or order.

(3) Rule 28.6 applies to an application under this rule that concerns a document or thing to be produced in evidence.

Court's power to vary requirements under this Part

8–8d **28.8.**—(1) The court may—

(a) shorten or extend (even after it has expired) a time limit under this Part; and

(b) where a rule or direction requires an application under this Part to be in writing, allow that application to be made orally instead.

(2) Someone who wants the court to allow an application to be made orally under paragraph (1)(b) of this rule must—

(a) give as much notice as the urgency of his application permits to those on whom he would otherwise have served an application in writing; and

(b) in doing so explain the reasons for the application and for wanting the court to consider it orally.

Abolition of subpoena

Criminal Procedure (Attendance of Witnesses) Act 1965, s.8

8–9 **8.** No *subpoena ad testificandum* or *subpoena duces tecum* shall issue after the commencement of this Act in respect of any proceedings for the purpose of which a witness summons may be issued under section 2 of this Act or in respect of any proceedings for the purpose of which a summons may be issued under section 97 of the *Magistrates' Courts Act* 1980 (process for attendance of witnesses in magistrates' courts).

[This section is printed as amended by the *MCA* 1980, s.154, and Sched. 7, para. 56.]

Service of summons outside jurisdiction

8–10 By the *Writ of Subpoena Act* 1805, ss.3 and 4, the service of a writ of *subpoena* in any one part of the United Kingdom is as effectual to compel the appearance of a witness in any other part of the same, as if the *subpoena* were served in that part of the kingdom in which the person so served is required to appear; and in case of non-attendance the court from which the *subpoena* issued may transmit a certificate of such default in the manner pointed out in the statute, *i.e.* in the case of an English court to the High Court of Justiciary in Scotland; and the court to which it is so transmitted may punish the party for his default, in like manner as if he had refused to appear to a *subpoena* issuing out of that court, provided it appears that a reasonable and sufficient sum of money to defray the witness's expenses of coming, attending to give evidence, and returning, were tendered to him at the time he was served with the *subpoena*.

Where a *subpoena* is served in England, a tender of expenses does not seem to be necessary either on the part of the Crown or of the defendant: 2 Hawk. c. 46, s.173; *R. v. Cooke* (1824) 1 C. & P. 321; yet if the witness is so poor as not to be able to go to the Crown Court at his own cost, the fact of the expenses not having been tendered would probably be deemed by the court a sufficient excuse for his non-attendance. (See the terms of the 1965 Act, s.3, *post*, § 8–12.)

In sections 3 and 4 of the Act of 1805, references to a writ of *subpoena* requiring the appearance of a person to give evidence shall be construed as including references to a witness summons under section 2 of the 1965 Act: *ibid.*, Sched. 2, Pt I.

Privilege of witnesses from arrest

A person *subpoenaed* as a witness, or in respect of whom a witness order has been made, either to prosecute or give evidence, enjoys a privilege from arrest on civil process whilst attending the court, not only on the day mentioned in the *subpoena*, etc., but also on every day, until the cause is tried; he is also privileged in like manner during a reasonable time before and after the trial, while coming to or returning from a place where the court's sittings are held. See *Lightfoot v. Cameron* (1776) 2 W.Bl. 1113; *Arding v. Flower* (1800) 8 T.R. 534; *Re Freston* (1883) 11 Q.B.D. 545; Taylor, *Evid.*, 12th ed., ss.1330 *et seq.* This privilege has also been held to extend to witnesses attending voluntarily, and not *subpoenaed*: see *Meekins v. Smith* (1791) 1 H.Bl. 629 at 636. If a witness, under these circumstances, is arrested, the court out of which the *subpoena* was issued, or the judge of the court in which the cause has been or is to be tried, will, upon application, order him to be discharged. See 3 Stark.N.P. 132. The Crown Court has, in relation to the attendance and examination of witnesses, any contempt of court, the enforcement of its orders and all other matters incidental to its jurisdiction, the like powers, rights, privileges and authority as the High Court: *Supreme Court [Senior Courts] Act* 1981, s.45(8) (renamed as from a day to be appointed: *Constitutional Reform Act* 2005, s.59(5), and Sched. 11, para. 1(1)). This is subject to section 8 of the 1965 Act, *ante*, § 8–9, and to any provision contained in or having effect under the 1981 Act: *ibid.* **8–11**

(3) Disobedience to witness order or witness summons

Criminal Procedure (Attendance of Witnesses) Act 1965, s.3

3.—(1) Any person who without just excuse disobeys a … witness summons requiring him to attend before any court shall be guilty of contempt of that court and may be punished summarily by that court as if his contempt had been committed in the face of the court. **8–12**

(1A) Any person who without just excuse disobeys a requirement made by any court under section 2A above shall be guilty of contempt of that court and may be punished summarily by that court as if his contempt had been committed in the face of the court.

(2) No person shall by reason of any disobedience mentioned in subsection (1) or (1A) above be liable to imprisonment for a period exceeding three months.

(3) [*Repealed by* Courts Act *1971, s.56 and Sched. 11.*]

[This section is printed as amended by the *CPIA* 1996, ss.65(2)(a), 66(1), (3) and (4), and 80, and Sched. 5, Pt 6.]

As to the exercise of the summary power to deal with a contempt, see *post*, §§ 28–105 *et seq.*

Where a summons was issued requiring a witness to attend at the Crown Court on a particular day "and on subsequent days until the court releases you", where the witness did not attend, in consequence of which the matter was adjourned to a particular day and a warrant was issued for his arrest, where the warrant was not executed but a police officer spoke to the witness on the eve of the day to which the matter had been adjourned and told him that he was required by a witness summons to appear the next day, and where he failed to appear, he was in contempt by virtue of his failure to appear on that day; the original summons remained in force until the person to whom it was addressed obeyed it by giving the evidence he was able to give: *R. v. Popat*, *The Times*, September 10, 2008, CA. As to this case, see also *post*, § 8–14, and the commentary at *Criminal Law Week* 2008/34/7.

Liability is absolute absent "just excuse", and culpable forgetfulness can never amount to such excuse: *R. v. Lennock*, 97 Cr.App.R. 228, CA.

In *R. v. Yusuf* [2003] 2 Cr.App.R. 32, CA, a sentence of three months' imprisonment was upheld, having regard to the deliberate nature of the contempt, the seriousness of the charge (murder) and the importance of the evidence (a confession); the courts could only provide the public with protection against criminal conduct if the public co-operated with the courts; a witness who ignored a summons could expect to be punished because failure to attend was likely to disrupt, if not undermine entirely, the trial process; it was commonly the case for prosecution witnesses to be fearful of the consequences of attending court, but in most cases they did their duty; if they did not, the alternative would be anarchy.

(4) Further process to secure attendance of witness

Criminal Procedure (Attendance of Witnesses) Act 1965, s.4

8–13 **4.**—(1) If a judge of the ... Crown Court is satisfied by evidence on oath that a witness in respect of whom a ... witness summons is in force is unlikely to comply with the ... summons, the judge may issue a warrant to arrest the witness and bring him before the court before which he is required to attend.

Provided that a warrant shall not be issued under this subsection ... unless the judge is satisfied by such evidence as aforesaid that the witness is likely to be able to give evidence likely to be material evidence or produce any document or thing likely to be material evidence in the proceedings.

(2) Where a witness who is required to attend before the Crown Court by virtue of ... a witness summons fails to attend in compliance with the ... summons, that court may—

(a) in any case, cause to be served on him a notice requiring him to attend the court forthwith or at such time as may be specified in the notice;

(b) if the court is satisfied that there are reasonable grounds for believing that he has failed to attend without just excuse, or if he has failed to comply with a notice under paragraph (a) above, issue a warrant to arrest him and bring him before the court.

(3) A witness brought before a court in pursuance of a warrant under this section may be remanded by that court in custody or on bail (with or without sureties) until such time as the court may appoint for receiving his evidence or dealing with him under section 3 of this Act; and where a witness attends a court in pursuance of a notice under this section the court may direct that the notice shall have effect as if it required him to attend at any later time appointed by the court for receiving his evidence or dealing with him as aforesaid.

[This section is printed as amended, and repealed in part, by the *CPIA* 1996, ss.65(2)(b)–(d), 66(1) and (5), 67(1) and 80, and Sched. 5, Pt 6.]

8–14 As to the use of section 4(1) in the case of a person serving a sentence of imprisonment abroad, see *R. v. Sokolovics* [1981] Crim.L.R. 788, CCC (Skinner J.). (See also section 6 of the *Criminal Justice (International Co-operation) Act* 1990, *post*, § 8–19.)

The power to issue a warrant to arrest a witness is one which ought to be exercised where evidence is critical: *R. v. Bradford JJ., ex p. Wilkinson*, 91 Cr.App.R. 390, DC (a decision in relation to s.97 of the *MCA* 1980). A judge who is anxious that a witness should not be under arrest for longer than necessary could either back the warrant for bail or direct that it should not be executed if the witness accompanied the officer to court or if the officer was satisfied that the witness would attend voluntarily; but a direction that it should only be executed at the Crown Court was likely to be self-defeating: *R. v. Popat*, *ante*, § 8–12.

As to the execution of a warrant to arrest a witness in Scotland or Northern Ireland, see section 136 of the *CJPOA* 1994.

The power of a court under section 4(3) to remand a witness in custody until such time as the court may appoint for receiving his evidence does not expire merely upon the commencement of the witness's evidence, or, indeed, upon the conclusion of the ordinary process of examination-in-chief, cross-examination and re-examination; it continues for as long as there is a real possibility that the witness may be required to give evidence or further evidence; and whereas the second limb of Article 5(1)(b) of the ECHR ("No one shall be deprived of his liberty save in the following cases ... (b) the lawful ... detention of a person ... in order to secure the fulfilment of any obligation prescribed by law ...") (*post*, § 16–43) refers only to the fulfilment of "specific and concrete" obligations, this encompassed an obligation to give further evidence if so required in connection with a specific trial; and the judge's order fixing a specific date for the witness to be brought back before the court to give any further evidence that was required had given sufficient specificity and concreteness to the obligation: *R. (H.) v. Wood Green Crown Court* [2007] 2 All E.R. 259, DC.

(5) Home Office order

Crime (Sentences) Act 1997, Sched. 1, para. 3

SCHEDULE 1

TRANSFER OF PRISONERS WITHIN UNITED KINGDOM

PART I

Powers of Transfer

Transfer of prisoners for other judicial purposes

3.—(1) If the Secretary of State is satisfied, in the case of— **8–15**

(a) a person remanded in custody in any part of the United Kingdom in connection with an offence;

(b) a person serving a sentence of imprisonment in any part of the United Kingdom; or

(c) a person not falling within paragraph (a) or (b) above who is detained in a prison in any part of the United Kingdom,

that the attendance of that person at any place in that or any other part of the United Kingdom or in any of the Channel islands is desirable in the interests of justice or for the purposes of any public inquiry, the Secretary of State may direct that person to be taken to that place.

(2) [*Corresponding provision in relation to persons in custody in Channel Islands.*]

(3) Where any person is directed under this paragraph to be taken to any place he shall, unless the Secretary of State otherwise directs, be kept in custody while being so taken, while at that place, and while being taken back to the prison or other institution or place in which he is required in accordance with law to be detained.

Paragraph 20 provides that in Schedule 1 "prison", unless the context otherwise requires, includes a young offender institution, a young offenders institution and a remand centre, and that "sentence of imprisonment" includes any sentence of detention and a sentence of custody for life under section 8 of the *CJA* 1982.

As to who meets the expenses which may be involved, see *Becker v. The Home Office* [1972] 2 Q.B. 407, CA (Civ. Div.); *R. v. Secretary of State for the Home Department, ex p. Greenwood, The Times*, August 2, 1986, QBD; and *R. v. Secretary of State for the Home Department, ex p. Wynne* [1992] Q.B. 406, CA (Civ. Div.) (considering the *CJA* 1961, s.29). An appeal to the House of Lords in *ex p. Wynne* ([1993] 1 W.L.R. 115) was decided on different grounds. **8–16**

(6) Evidence from overseas

(a) *Service of process*

Crime (International Co-operation) Act 2003, s.3

General requirements for service of process

3.—(1) This section applies to any process issued or made for the purposes of criminal **8–17**

proceedings by a court in England and Wales or Northern Ireland.

(2) The process may be issued or made in spite of the fact that the person on whom it is to be served is outside the United Kingdom.

(3) Where the process is to be served outside the United Kingdom and the person at whose request it is issued or made believes that the person on whom it is to be served does not understand English, he must—

(a) inform the court of that fact, and

(b) provide the court with a copy of the process, or of so much of it as is material, translated into an appropriate language.

(4) Process served outside the United Kingdom requiring a person to appear as a party or attend as a witness—

(a) must not include notice of a penalty,

(b) must be accompanied by a notice giving any information required to be given by rules of court.

(5) If process requiring a person to appear as a party or attend as a witness is served outside the United Kingdom, no obligation to comply with the process under the law of the part of the United Kingdom in which the process is issued or made is imposed by virtue of the service.

(6) Accordingly, failure to comply with the process does not constitute contempt of court and is not a ground for issuing a warrant to secure the attendance of the person in question.

(7) But the process may subsequently be served on the person in question in the United Kingdom (with the usual consequences for non-compliance).

8–18 Section 4 of the 2003 Act supplements section 3 by making provision for service of process by post. In connection with sections 3 and 4, reference should also be made to rules 32.1 (notice required to accompany process served outside the United Kingdom and translations) and 32.2 (proof of service outside the United Kingdom) of the *Criminal Procedure Rules* 2005 (S.I. 2005 No. 384).

(b) *Overseas prisoners as witnesses in United Kingdom proceedings*

Criminal Justice (International Co-operation) Act 1990, s.6

Transport of overseas prisoner to give evidence or assist in investigation in the United Kingdom

8–19 **6.**—(1) This section has effect where—

(a) a witness order has been made or a witness summons or citation issued in criminal proceedings in the United Kingdom in respect of a person ("a prisoner") who is detained in custody in a country or territory outside the United Kingdom by virtue of a sentence or order of a court or tribunal exercising criminal jurisdiction in that country or territory; or

(b) it appears to the Secretary of State that it is desirable for a prisoner to be identified in, or otherwise by his presence to assist, such proceedings or the investigation in the United Kingdom of an offence.

(2) If the Secretary of State is satisfied that the appropriate authority in the country or territory where the prisoner is detained will make arrangements for him to come to the United Kingdom to give evidence pursuant to the witness order, witness summons or citation or, as the case may be, for the purpose mentioned in subsection (1)(b) above, he may issue a warrant under this section.

(3) No warrant shall be issued under this section in respect of any prisoner unless he has consented to being brought to the United Kingdom to give evidence as aforesaid or, as the case may be, for the purpose mentioned in subsection (1)(b) above but a consent once given shall not be capable of being withdrawn after the issue of the warrant.

(4) The effect of the warrant shall be to authorise—

(a) the bringing of the prisoner to the United Kingdom;

(b) the taking of the prisoner to, and his detention in custody at, such place or places in the United Kingdom as are specified in the warrant; and

(c) the returning of the prisoner to the country or territory from which he has come.

(5) Subsections (4) to (8) of section 5 shall have effect in relation to a warrant issued under this section as they have effect in relation to a warrant issued under that section.

(6) [*Application of* Immigration Act *1971*.]

(7) This section applies to a person detained in custody in a country or territory outside the United Kingdom in consequence of—

(b) having been transferred there, or responsibility for his detention and release having been transferred there, from the United Kingdom under the *Repatriation of Prisoners Act* 1984;

(c) having been transferred there, or responsibility for his detention and release having been transferred there, under any similar provision or arrangement from any other country or territory,

as it applies to a person detained as mentioned in subsection (1) above.

[This section is printed as amended by the *CJIA* 2008, s.148(1), and Sched. 26, para. 27.]

Section 5 of the Act, referred to in section 6(5), relates to the transfer of United Kingdom prisoners to give evidence or assist an investigation overseas. Subsections (4) to (8) thereof have effect in relation to a warrant under section 6 as they have effect in relation to a warrant issued under section 5: s.6(5).

Criminal Justice (International Co-operation) Act 1990, s.5(4)–(8)

5.—(4) Where a warrant has been issued in respect of a prisoner under this section he shall be deemed to be in legal custody at any time when, being in the United Kingdom or on board a British ship, British aircraft or British hovercraft, he is being taken under the warrant to or from any place or being kept in custody under the warrant. **8–20**

(5) A person authorised by or for the purposes of the warrant to take the prisoner to or from any place or to keep him in custody shall have all the powers, authority, protection and privileges—

(a) of a constable in the part of the United Kingdom in which that person is for the time being; or

(b) if he is outside the United Kingdom, of a constable in the part of the United Kingdom to or from which the prisoner is to be taken under the warrant.

(6) If the prisoner escapes or is unlawfully at large, he may be arrested without warrant by a constable and taken to any place to which he may be taken under the warrant issued under this section.

(7) In subsection (4) above—

"British aircraft" means a British-controlled aircraft within the meaning of section 92 of the *Civil Aviation Act* 1982 (application of criminal law to aircraft) or one of Her Majesty's aircraft;

"British hovercraft" means a British-controlled hovercraft within the meaning of that section as applied in relation to hovercraft by virtue of provisions made under the *Hovercraft Act* 1968 or one of Her Majesty's hovercraft;

"British ship" means a British ship for the purposes of the *Merchant Shipping Acts* 1894 to 1988 or one of Her Majesty's ships;

and in this subsection references to Her Majesty's aircraft, hovercraft or ships are references to aircraft, hovercraft or, as the case may be, ships belonging to or exclusively employed in the service of Her Majesty in right of the Government of the United Kingdom.

(8) In subsection (6) above "constable", in relation to any part of the United Kingdom, means any person who is a constable in that or any other part of the United Kingdom or any person who, at the place in question has, under any enactment including subsection (5) above, the powers of a constable in that or any other part of the United Kingdom.

As to the issue of a warrant under section 6 in respect of proceedings before a service court, see section 11 of the Act (not printed in this work).

(7) Evidence given in Children Act 1989, wardship or family proceedings

Necessity for leave

Rule 10.20A of the *Family Proceedings Rules* 1991 (S.I. 1991 No. 1247) restricts the disclosure of information, including documents filed with the court, and relating to family proceedings to anyone other than designated persons without the leave of the court. Furthermore, section 12 of the *Administration of Justice Act* 1960 prohibits the publi- **8–21** cation of information relating to proceedings under the *Children Act* 1989 or relating to the inherent jurisdiction of the High Court with respect to minors or otherwise relating wholly or mainly to the maintenance or upbringing of a minor. But the court has an absolute discretion to give leave to publish such information: *Re S. (Minors) (Wardship: Police Investigation)* [1987] Fam. 199, Fam D. The words "information relating to the proceedings" should not be given too narrow a construction: they include not only the evidence given, but also statements prepared by a party or a witness for the purpose of such proceedings: *ibid*.

A social worker does not require the leave of the court before disclosing to the police any potentially incriminating statements or admissions made by a child's parents. The information obtained by social workers in the course of their duties is confidential and covered by public interest immunity. It can however be disclosed to fellow members of the child protection team engaged in the investigation of the possible abuse of the child concerned: *Re G. (A Minor) (Social Worker: Disclosure)* [1996] 2 All E.R. 65, CA (Civ. Div.). To the extent that *Oxfordshire County Council v. P.* [1995] Fam. 161, Fam D, and *Cleveland County Council v. F.* [1995] 2 All E.R. 236, Fam D, appeared to equate the position of the social worker with that of a guardian *ad litem*, the Court of Appeal disagreed. The guardian had no function outside the proceedings to which he had been appointed, whereas a social worker's duties towards children in his area were far wider and were by no means confined to court proceedings.

See also *Re W. (Minors) (Social Workers: Disclosure)* [1999] 1 W.L.R. 205, CA (Civ. Div.) (documents prepared and compiled by social workers when investigating injuries sustained by a child and which had not been filed with a court as part of court proceedings could be disclosed to the police without leave).

Exercise of discretion

8–21a In deciding whether to give leave, a judge must balance the importance of confidentiality in proceedings relating to children and the frankness which it engenders in those who give evidence against the public interest in seeing that the ends of justice are properly served: *Re D. (Minors) (Wardship: Disclosure)* [1994] 1 F.L.R. 346, CA (Civ. Div.). The interests of the child must have priority, but it is in the interests of a child, as well as its parent, that the parent should have a fair trial: *Kent County Council v. K.* [1994] 1 W.L.R. 912, Fam D (Booth J.); and a fair and just sentence: *Re X. (Children)* [2008] 1 F.L.R. 589, Fam D (Munby J.).

Family judges ought not to frustrate the investigation of potential crimes, which includes the dissipation of unfounded suspicions against the innocent, without good reason, even more so when the police are working alongside the social workers on the same case; there would be cases where the evidence was peripheral and the harm of giving leave would outweigh the value of the information; but police investigations require them to put together a jigsaw of information in order to carry out their public duty: *Re W. (Minors) (Social workers: Disclosure), ante*.

In *Re X. Children, ante*, Munby J. listed the matters to be weighed in the balance as: the welfare and interests of the children concerned, the welfare and other interests of children generally, the maintenance of confidentiality in children cases, the importance of encouraging frankness in children's cases, the public interest in the administration of justice and in the prosecution of serious crime, the gravity of the alleged offence and the relevance of the evidence to it, the desirability of co-operation between various agencies concerned with the welfare of children, any other material disclosure which had already taken place, and, in a case to which the *Children Act* 1989, s.98(2) (*post*, § 8–21c) applies, the terms of the provision itself.

As to the exercise of the discretion in the context of private law proceedings, see *Re D. and M. (Disclosure: Private Law)* [2003] 1 F.L.R. 647, Fam D (Hedley J.).

Disclosure ordered to defence

8–21b For examples, see *Re D. (Minors) (Wardship: Disclosure), ante*; *Kent County Council v. K., ante*; *Re A. (Criminal Proceedings: Disclosure)* [1996] 1 F.L.R. 221, CA (Civ. Div.); and *Re Z. (Children) (Disclosure: Criminal Proceedings)*

[2003] 1 F.L.R. 1194, Fam D (Munby J.). As to the necessity to make an application to the family proceedings court, rather than rely on the prosecution's duty of disclosure, and as to how to make such an application, see *Borough Council v. A. (Chief Constable intervening)* [2007] 1 All E.R. 293, Fam D (Sumner J.) (*post*, § 12–51a).

Disclosure ordered to prosecution/police

For examples, see *Re S. (Minors) (Wardship: Police Investigation), ante*; *Re F. (Minors) (Wardship: Police Investigation)* [1989] Fam. 18, CA (Civ. Div.); *Re L. (A Minor) (Police Investigation: Privilege)* [1997] A.C. 16, HL (*post*, § 12–9); *Re C. (A Minor) (Care Proceedings: Disclosure)* [1997] Fam. 76, CA (Civ. Div.); *Re A.B. (Care Proceedings: Disclosure of Medical Evidence to Police)* [2003] 1 F.L.R. 579, Fam D (Wall J.); and *Re X. Children, ante*. **8–21c**

It should be noted that section 98 of the *Children Act* 1989 removes the privilege against self-incrimination in proceedings under Parts IV and V of the Act, but by subsection (2) it is provided that a statement or admission in such proceedings shall not be admissible in evidence against the person making it or his spouse in proceedings for an offence other than perjury. Section 98 does not apply to a police investigation into a suspected offence (*i.e.* so as to preclude disclosure of self-incriminatory statements): *Re C. (A Minor) (Care Proceedings: Disclosure), ante*; but it does apply to statements to expert witnesses: *Re A.B. (Care Proceedings: Disclosure of Medical Evidence to Police), ante*. In *Re X. Children (children) (disclosure for purposes of criminal proceedings)* [2008] 3 All E.R. 958, Fam D, Munby J. ordered disclosure of admissions made by the defendant when compelled to give evidence with a view to those admissions being used by the prosecution to rebut anticipated mitigation that the single count of incest with which he was charged was an isolated act. Whilst conceding that the actual use to which the evidence could be put would be for the trial judge, his Lordship expressed the view that so to use the material would not breach section 98(2). For the suggestion that it would, see *Criminal Law Week* 2008/08/18/5.

As to whether material disclosed to the prosecution may be disclosed by them to the defence, pursuant to their duty of disclosure, see *post*, § 12–51a.

B. ISSUES ARISING PRIOR TO ENTRY INTO WITNESS BOX

(1) Presence in court

In practice, witnesses remain out of court until called to give their evidence, so that each witness may be examined out of the hearing of the other witnesses on the same side who are to be examined after him. But there is no rule of law to this effect: see *Moore v. Lambeth County Court* [1969] 1 W.L.R. 141, CA (Civ. Div.). Experts are permitted to be in court before giving their evidence, and it is common for the police officer in charge of a case to be in court, even though he is a witness, but this is usually subject to the consent of the defence. **8–22**

Where the judge has made no ruling and a party wishes to call a witness who has remained in court, it has been held that the judge has no discretion to refuse to allow such a witness to be called: *R. v. Briggs*, 22 Cr.App.R. 68, CCA; and *R. v. Thompson* [1967] Crim.L.R. 62, CA. It is submitted, however, that these authorities must be read subject to the general discretion contained in section 78 of the *PACE* 1984, *post*, § 15–452.

As to whether a potential witness in a trial and a person who had been present in court during the proceedings would be in contempt merely because they spoke to each other before the potential witness gave evidence, see *R. v. Jales and Lawrence* (2007) 151 S.J. 194, CA (*post*, § 28–111).

(2) Right to read statement

There is no general rule (which in any event, unlike the rule as to what can be done in the witness box, would be unenforceable) that witnesses may not, before the trial, see the statements they made at some period reasonably close to the time of the event which is the subject of the trial; though obviously it would be wrong if several witnesses were **8–23** handed statements in circumstances which enabled one to compare with another what each had said: *R. v. Richardson (D.)* [1971] 2 Q.B. 484, 55 Cr.App.R. 244, CA. The court adopted the following opinion expressed by the Supreme Court of Hong Kong in *Lau Pak Ngam v. R.* [1966] Crim.L.R. 443: "Testimony in the witness box becomes more a test of memory than of truthfulness if witnesses are deprived of the opportunity of checking their recollection beforehand by reference to statements or notes made at a time closer to the events in question.... Refusal of access to statements would tend to create difficulties for honest witnesses but be likely to do little to hamper dishonest witnesses." The court also drew attention to: (a) Home Office Circular No. 82/1969 ("Supplies of Copies of Witnesses' Statements") in which it is recognised with the approval of the then Lord Chief Justice and the judges of the Queen's Bench Division, that witnesses for the prosecution in criminal cases are normally entitled, if they so request, to copies of any statements taken from them by police officers; and (b) the fact that witnesses for the defence are normally allowed to have copies of their statements and to refresh their memories from them at any time up to the moment they go into the witness box.

Where the prosecution follow this procedure, it is obviously desirable that the defence are informed of what has been done as it may be relevant to the weight which can properly be attached to the witness's evidence, see *Worley v. Bentley*, 62 Cr.App.R. 239, DC, and *R. v. Westwell*, 62 Cr.App.R. 251, CA. The relevant parts of the Home Office Circular No. 82/1969 are set out on p. 255 of the latter report.

(3) Discussion between witnesses/making further statements

8–24 In *R. v. Arif*, *The Times*, June 17, 1993, the Court of Appeal said that the fact that there had been a pre-trial discussion of evidence between potential witnesses did not necessarily make the evidence of such witnesses so unsafe that it ought to be excluded. Each case had to be dealt with on its own facts. It might emerge that such discussions could well have led to the fabrication of evidence: in such a case, the court might properly take the view that it would be unsafe to leave any of the evidence of the witnesses concerned to the jury. In other cases, it would be quite sufficient to draw to the jury's attention, in the course of summing up, the implications which such conduct might have for the reliability of the evidence of the witnesses concerned. The court said that in each case it was a matter for the trial judge, but that they did not wish to be taken as affording the slightest encouragement to the rehearsal of the evidence of witnesses either for the Crown or the defence, much less to the coaching of witnesses. Such practices were to be strongly discouraged because the risk of abuse was so great. See also *R. v. Skinner*, 99 Cr.App.R. 212, CA (*Arif* considered).

In *R. v. Roberts*, 162 J.P. 691, CA, it was held that where, after a witness has made a statement, a video recording is discovered which shows some or all of the events touched on in the statement, it is not wrong in principle for the witness to be shown the video; if, on seeing it he concludes that he had been in error in his statement, it is permissible for him to make a further statement correcting the matter; but nothing should be done by way of rehearsing a witness or to encourage him to alter his previous statement; the acid test is whether the procedure adopted in any particular case was such as to taint the subsequent evidence; furthermore, there must be equality of arms with facilities available to the prosecution being equally available to the defence.

II. SWEARING OF WITNESSES

A. INTRODUCTION

8–25 This topic has always been closely related to that of the competence and compellability of witnesses. This is particularly so in the case of children and young persons and persons of unsound mind. The competence and compellability of witnesses are dealt with more fully in the next section of this chapter. The topics have been brought yet closer together by Chapter V of Part II of the *YJCEA* 1999. This enacts a general rule to the effect that all persons are competent to give evidence in criminal proceedings, and stipulates specific exceptions. It further provides for the determination of competency, and lays down a clear rule as to whether a competent witness should give evidence sworn or unsworn.

B. GIVING OF SWORN OR UNSWORN EVIDENCE

Youth Justice and Criminal Evidence Act 1999, s.55

Determining whether witness to be sworn

55.—(1) Any question whether a witness in criminal proceedings may be sworn for the purpose of giving evidence on oath, whether raised— **8–26**

(a) by a party to the proceedings, or
(b) by the court of its own motion,

shall be determined by the court in accordance with this section.

(2) The witness may not be sworn for that purpose unless—

(a) he has attained the age of 14, and
(b) he has a sufficient appreciation of the solemnity of the occasion and of the particular responsibility to tell the truth which is involved in taking an oath.

(3) The witness shall, if he is able to give intelligible testimony, be presumed to have a sufficient appreciation of those matters if no evidence tending to show the contrary is adduced (by any party).

(4) If any such evidence is adduced, it is for the party seeking to have the witness sworn to satisfy the court that, on a balance of probabilities, the witness has attained the age of 14 and has a sufficient appreciation of the matters mentioned in subsection (2)(b).

(5) Any proceedings held for the determination of the question mentioned in subsection (1) shall take place in the absence of the jury (if there is one).

(6) Expert evidence may be received on the question.

(7) Any questioning of the witness (where the court considers that necessary) shall be conducted by the court in the presence of the parties.

(8) For the purposes of this section a person is able to give intelligible testimony if he is able to—

(a) understand questions put to him as a witness, and
(b) give answers to them which can be understood.

Where a witness is to be sworn, the swearing must take place in open court: *R. v. Tew* (1855) Dears 429.

At common law it was held that provided the witness has a sufficient appreciation of the seriousness of the occasion and a realisation that taking the oath involved something more than the duty to tell the truth in ordinary day-to-day life, and provided that the witness has no objection to being sworn, he should be sworn: *R. v. Bellamy*, 82 Cr.App.R. 222, CA.

C. OATH

(1) Form and procedure

Oaths Act 1978, s.1

Manner of administration of oath

1.—(1) Any oath may be administered and taken in England, Wales or Northern Ireland in the following form and manner— **8–27**

The person taking the oath shall hold the New Testament, or, in the case of a Jew, the Old Testament, in his uplifted hand, and shall say or repeat after the officer administering the oath the words "I swear by Almighty God that ...," followed by the words of the oath prescribed by law.

(2) The officer shall (unless the person about to take the oath voluntarily objects thereto, or is physically incapable of so taking the oath) administer the oath in the form and manner aforesaid without question.

(3) In the case of a person who is neither a Christian nor a Jew, the oath shall be administered in any lawful manner.

(4) In this section "officer" means any person duly authorised to administer oaths.

As to the validity of oaths generally, see section 4 of the 1978 Act, *post*, § 8–30. As to the directive nature of section 1 and the effect of non-compliance, see *R. v. Chapman* [1980] Crim.L.R. 42, CA, and *R. v. Kemble*, 91 Cr.App.R. 178, CA, *post*, § 8–30.

Oaths Act 1978, s.3

Swearing with uplifted hand

8–28 **3.** If any person to whom an oath is administered desires to swear with uplifted hand in the form and manner in which an oath is usually administered in Scotland, he shall be permitted so to do, and the oath shall be administered to him in such form and manner without further question.

Children and Young Persons Act 1963, s.28

Form of oath for use in youth courts and by children and young persons in other courts

8–29 **28.**—(1) Subject to subsection (2) of this section, in relation to any oath administered to and taken by any person before a youth court or administered to and taken by any child or young person before any other court, section 1 of the *Oaths Act* 1978 shall have effect as if the words "I promise before Almighty God" were set out in it instead of the words "I swear by Almighty God that".

(2) Where in any oath otherwise duly administered and taken either of the forms mentioned in this section is used instead of the other, the oath shall nevertheless be deemed to have been duly administered and taken.

[This section is printed as amended by the *Oaths Act* 1978, s.2; and the *CJA* 1991, s.100, and Sched. 11, para. 40.]

(2) Validity of oaths

Oaths Act 1978, s.4

Validity of oaths

8–30 **4.**—(1) In any case in which an oath may lawfully be and has been administered to any person, if it has been administered in a form and manner other than that prescribed by law, he is bound by it if it has been administered in such form and with such ceremonies as he may have declared to be binding.

(2) Where an oath has been duly administered and taken, the fact that the person to whom it was administered had, at the time of taking it, no religious belief, shall not for any purpose affect the validity of the oath.

The words in section 1 (*ante*, § 8–27) are directive. Accordingly, failure to comply does not necessarily invalidate the oath. The efficacy of an oath depends upon it being taken in a way binding and intended to be binding upon the conscience of the taker: *R. v. Chapman* [1980] Crim.L.R. 42, CA (witness failed to take the Testament in his hand).

In *R. v. Kemble*, 91 Cr.App.R. 178, CA, it was held that in the light of section 1(3) of the 1978 Act, the question whether the administration of an oath to a person who was neither a Christian nor a Jew was lawful concerned two matters only, namely, whether the oath appeared to the court to be binding on the conscience of the witness and, if so, whether the witness himself considered the oath to be binding on his conscience. The Court of Appeal admitted expert evidence to the effect that no oath taken by a Muslim is valid unless it is taken upon the Koran in Arabic and that there were many sub-rules relating to the validity of oaths. The court said, however, that the question whether the administration of an oath was lawful concerned only the two matters referred to above: it did not depend upon what may be the considerable intricacies of the particular religion which is adhered to by the witness.

D. AFFIRMATION

Oaths Act 1978, ss.5, 6

Affirmation

8–31 **5.**—(1) Any person who objects to being sworn shall be permitted to make his solemn affirmation instead of taking an oath.

(2) Subsection (1) above shall apply in relation to a person to whom it is not reasonably practicable without inconvenience or delay to administer an oath in the manner appropriate to his religious belief as it applies in relation to a person objecting to be sworn.

(3) A person who may be permitted under subsection (2) above to make his solemn affirmation may also be required to do so.

(4) A solemn affirmation shall be of the same force and effect as an oath.

Form of affirmation

6.—(1) Subject to subsection (2) below, every affirmation shall be as follows—

"I, do solemnly, sincerely and truly declare and affirm,"

and then proceed with the words of the oath prescribed by law, omitting any words of imprecation or calling to witness.

(2) Every affirmation in writing shall commence—

"I, of do solemnly and sincerely affirm,"

and the form in lieu of *jurat* shall be

"Affirmed at —— this —— day of —— 19—,

Before me."

E. UNSWORN EVIDENCE

Youth Justice and Criminal Evidence Act 1999, s.56

Reception of unsworn evidence

56.—(1) Subsections (2) and (3) apply to a person (of any age) who— **8–32**

(a) is competent to give evidence in criminal proceedings, but

(b) (by virtue of section 55(2)) is not permitted to be sworn for the purpose of giving evidence on oath in such proceedings.

(2) The evidence in criminal proceedings of a person to whom this subsection applies shall be given unsworn.

(3) A deposition of unsworn evidence given by a person to whom this subsection applies may be taken for the purposes of criminal proceedings as if that evidence had been given on oath.

(4) A court in criminal proceedings shall accordingly receive in evidence any evidence given unsworn in pursuance of subsection (2) or (3).

(5) Where a person ("the witness") who is competent to give evidence in criminal proceedings gives evidence in such proceedings unsworn, no conviction, verdict or finding in those proceedings shall be taken to be unsafe for the purposes of any of sections 2(1), 13(1) and 16(1) of the *Criminal Appeal Act* 1968 (grounds for allowing appeals) by reason only that it appears to the Court of Appeal that the witness was a person falling within section 55(2) (and should accordingly have given his evidence on oath).

Criminal Justice Act 1988, s.34

34.—(1) [*Repealed by* Criminal Justice Act *1991, s.101(2) and Sched. 13*.] **8–33**

(2) Any requirement whereby at a trial on indictment it is obligatory for the court to give the jury a warning about convicting the accused on the uncorroborated evidence of a child is abrogated....

(3) Unsworn evidence admitted by virtue of section 56 of the *Youth Justice and Criminal Evidence Act* 1999 may corroborate evidence (sworn or unsworn) given by any other person.

[The words omitted from subs. (2) were repealed by the *CJPOA* 1994, s.32(2). Subs. (3) is printed as amended by the *YJCEA* 1999, s.67(1), and Sched. 4, paras 15 and 17.]

Section 57 of the 1999 Act makes it an offence for a person wilfully to give false evidence in such circumstances that, had the evidence been given on oath, he would have been guilty of perjury. The offence is triable only summarily and carries a maximum penalty of six months' imprisonment or a fine of £1,000, or both. In the case of an offender aged under 14, the maximum penalty is a fine of £250. **8–34**

III. COMPETENCE AND COMPELLABILITY

(1) General

A witness is competent if he may lawfully give evidence and compellable if he may lawfully be required to give evidence. Competent witnesses are usually but not necessarily compellable. **8–35**

Section 53 of the *YJCEA* 1999 (*post*) enacted a general rule to the effect that all persons are competent to give evidence in criminal proceedings. This is subject to just two exceptions which are specified in subsections (3) and (4). Section 54 (*post*, § 8–36b) provides for the manner in which issues as to competence are to be determined.

(2) Test of competency

Youth Justice and Criminal Evidence Act 1999, s.53

Competence of witnesses to give evidence

8–36 **53.**—(1) At every stage in criminal proceedings all persons are (whatever their age) competent to give evidence.

(2) Subsection (1) has effect subject to subsections (3) and (4).

(3) A person is not competent to give evidence in criminal proceedings if it appears to the court that he is not a person who is able to—

(a) understand questions put to him as a witness, and

(b) give answers to them which can be understood.

(4) A person charged in criminal proceedings is not competent to give evidence in the proceedings for the prosecution (whether he is the only person, or is one of two or more persons, charged in the proceedings).

(5) In subsection (4) the reference to a person charged in criminal proceedings does not include a person who is not, or is no longer, liable to be convicted of any offence in the proceedings (whether as a result of pleading guilty or for any other reason).

In *R. v. MacPherson* [2006] 1 Cr.App.R. 30, CA, it was said that the test of competence in section 53(3) was one of understanding, namely whether the witness understood what was being asked, and whether the jury could understand the witness's answers; the words "put to him as a witness" meant the equivalent of "being asked of him in court", so that a young child who could speak and understand basic English with strangers would be competent; and there was no requirement that the witness should be aware of his status as a witness. The court added that questions as to reliability and credibility went to weight, not competence.

(3) Determination of competency

Youth Justice and Criminal Evidence Act 1999, s.54

Determining competence of witnesses

8–36a **54.**—(1) Any question whether a witness in criminal proceedings is competent to give evidence in the proceedings, whether raised—

(a) by a party to the proceedings, or

(b) by the court of its own motion,

shall be determined by the court in accordance with this section.

(2) It is for the party calling the witness to satisfy the court that, on a balance of probabilities, the witness is competent to give evidence in the proceedings.

(3) In determining the question mentioned in subsection (1) the court shall treat the witness as having the benefit of any directions under section 19 which the court has given, or proposes to give, in relation to the witness.

(4) Any proceedings held for the determination of the question shall take place in the absence of the jury (if there is one).

(5) Expert evidence may be received on the question.

(6) Any questioning of the witness (where the court considers that necessary) shall be conducted by the court in the presence of the parties.

As to section 19 of the 1999 Act, see *post*, § 8–55a.

Timing of

8–37 It is plainly advisable to take any objection to competency before the witness is sworn or commences to give evidence: see *Wollaston v. Hakewill* (1841) 3 Scott N.R. 593; *Bartlett v. Smith* (1843) 12 L.J.Ex. 287; *R. v. Hampshire* [1995] 2 Cr.App.R. 319, CA. In *R. v. Yacoob*, 72 Cr.App.R. 313, CA, it was said that the beginning of the trial is the appropriate time for determining the competence and compellability of a prosecution witness (and see *R. v. MacPherson*, *ante*, § 8–36, to similar effect). Whilst this may be convenient, there is plainly no rule of law to this effect; if the objection has been communicated to the prosecution, then the opening should omit all reference to the evidence to be given by the witness concerned; if it should be impossible to open the case without reference to the witness, then it would be inevitable that the matter be resolved prior to the opening.

The incompetency of a witness may become apparent, however, only after he has commenced to give evidence (see *Jacobs v. Layborn* (1843) 11 M. & W. 685); and, at common law, the objection has been allowed to be taken at any time during the trial: *Stone v. Blackburn* (1793) 1 Esp. 37; *Turner v. Pearte* (1787) 1 T.R. 717. In *R. v. Whitehead* (1866) L.R. 1 C.C.R. 33, it was said that where a judge has admitted a witness as competent to give evidence, but upon proof of facts affecting the capacity of the witness, and upon observation of his subsequent behaviour, changes his opinion with regard thereto, he may stop the examination, and direct the jury to consider the case exclusively on the evidence of the other witnesses. It would clearly be within his discretion to discharge the jury.

In *R. v. Powell* [2006] 1 Cr.App.R. 31, CA, where the competence of a child complainant had been determined for the purposes of section 53 of the 1999 Act (*ante*), on the basis of a pre-recorded video interview (admitted as her evidence-in-chief under s.27 (*post*, § 8–55k)), it was held that it was the child's competence to give evidence at the time of the trial that was relevant, and, therefore, if the position had changed when the evidence was looked at as a whole (including cross-examination), the question of competence should be reconsidered at the end of the child's evidence. It was further said that where a case depends on the evidence of an infant complainant (here a three-and-a-half-year-old) it is essential, (a) that the interview of the complainant takes place promptly after the event of which the complainant speaks, and (b) that the trial (at which the complainant has to be cross-examined) takes place soon after that; infants, the court said, simply do not have the ability to lay down memory in a manner comparable to adults, and special efforts must be made to fast-track such cases (it simply not being an option to wait weeks, for example for forensic evidence to become available).

Manner of

It is the business of the judge to determine the competency of a witness: *R. v. Whitehead*, *ante*. For this purpose, the judge should conduct an inquiry hearing evidence on the *voire dire* from the witness himself or from others: see *R. v. Wakefield* (1827) 2 Lew. 279; *R. v. Hampshire*, *ante*. Where the witness is a child, the court should watch the videotaped interview with the child and/or ask the child appropriate questions: *R. v. MacPherson*, *ante*, § 8–36. **8–38**

It has been held that once a witness has been sworn and examined, it is not open to another party to adduce other evidence to show his incompetency: see *Dewdney v. Palmer* (1839) 4 M. & W. 664; but this must be read subject to *Toohey v. Metropolitan Police Commr* [1965] A.C. 595, HL (*post*, § 8–154) (medical evidence admissible to show that a witness suffers from some disease or defect or abnormality of mind such as to affect the reliability of his evidence).

(4) Mentally handicapped persons

No witness is competent who is prevented by reason of mental illness, drunkenness and the like from giving rational testimony. Where it is contended that a witness is within such a category it is for the judge to ascertain whether he is of competent understanding to give evidence; if satisfied that he is, the judge should allow him to be examined, leaving the jury to decide the worth of his testimony: *R. v. Hill* (1851) 2 Den. 254; and see *R. v. Dunning* [1965] Crim.L.R. 372. **8–39**

(5) Deaf and dumb persons

A person who is deaf and dumb is competent if he can be made to understand the nature of an oath, and if intelligence can be conveyed to and received from him by means of signs: *R. v. Ruston* (1786) 1 Leach 408, and he may be examined through the medium of a sworn interpreter, who understands his signs: *ibid*. A dumb man, not deaf, is sworn by signs, and then the interpreter is sworn to interpret them. If a dumb witness can write, he will be allowed to write down his evidence. **8–40**

See also *R. v. O'Brien* (1845) 1 Cox. 185 (Ir.).

(6) Children and young persons

8–41 There are no longer any special rules as to the competency of a child, but a child under 14 is not permitted to give sworn evidence: see section 55(2) of the 1999 Act (*ante*, § 8–26). In order to determine the ability of a child to give intelligible testimony, the court should watch any video-taped interview with the child or ask questions of the child, or both: see *DPP v. M* [1997] 2 Cr.App.R. 70, DC, where it was held that a child should not be adjudged incompetent on the basis of age alone. See also *R. v. Powell*, *ante*, § 8–37.

As to the form of oath for use in youth courts and by young persons in other courts, see section 28 of the *CYPA* 1963 (*ante*, § 8–29). As to the reception of unsworn evidence, see section 56 of the 1999 Act (*ante*, § 8–32).

As to the issue of a witness summons addressed to a child, see *ante*, § 8–2.

Wards of court/children in care

Practice Direction (Criminal Proceedings: Consolidation), para. I.5
[2002] 1 W.L.R. 2870

Wards of court

8–42 **I.5.1** Where a child has been interviewed by the police in connection with contemplated criminal proceedings and the child subsequently becomes a ward of court, no leave of the wardship court is required for the child to be called as a witness in those proceedings. Where, however, the police desire to interview a child who is already a ward of court, application must, other than in the exceptional cases referred to in paragraph 5.3, be made to the wardship court, on summons and on notice to all parties, for leave for the police to do so. Where, however, a party may become the subject of a criminal investigation and it is considered necessary for the ward to be interviewed without that party knowing that the police are making inquiries, the application for leave may be made *ex parte* to a judge without notice to that party. Notice should, where practicable be given to the reporting officer.

I.5.2 Where leave is given the order should, unless some special reason requires the contrary, give leave for any number of interviews which may be required by the prosecution or the police. If it is desired to conduct any interview beyond what has been permitted by the order, a further application should be made.

8–43 **I.5.3** The exceptional cases are those where the police need to deal with complaints or alleged offences concerning wards and it is appropriate, if not essential, for action to be taken straight away without the prior leave of the wardship court. Typical examples may be: (a) serious offences against the ward such as rape, where medical examination and the collection of scientific evidence ought to be carried out promptly, (b) where the ward is suspected by the police of having committed a criminal act and the police wish to interview him about it, (c) where the police wish to interview the ward as a potential witness. This list is not exhaustive: there will inevitably be other instances where immediate action is appropriate. In such cases the police should notify the parent or foster parent with whom the ward is living or other "appropriate adult" within the Code of Practice for the Detention, Treatment and Questioning of Persons by Police Officers (Code C…), so that that adult has the opportunity of being present when the police interview the child. Additionally, if practicable the reporting officer (if one has been appointed) should be notified and invited to attend the police interview or to nominate a third party to attend on his behalf. A record of the interview or a copy of any statement made by the ward should be supplied to the reporting officer. Where the ward has been interviewed without the reporting officer's knowledge he should be informed at the earliest opportunity. So too, if it be the case that the police wish to conduct further interviews. The wardship court should be apprised of the situation at the earliest possible opportunity thereafter by the reporting officer, the parent, foster-parent (through the local authority) or other responsible adult.

I.5.4 No evidence or documents in the wardship proceedings or information about the proceedings should be disclosed in the criminal proceedings without leave of the wardship court.

8–44 In *Re R. (Minor) (Wardship: Criminal Proceedings)* [1991] Fam. 56, CA (Civ. Div.), it was held that in the conduct of criminal proceedings it was for the judge of the criminal court, not the wardship judge, to consider whether or not a ward of court should be called as a witness in those proceedings. Accordingly, a defendant's application for leave to call his son, a ward of court, as a defence witness was unnecessary. However, leave to interview the child was necessary and the governing procedure was similar to the practice directions relating to such applications when made by the prosecution or the police. The Court of Appeal ordered that the ward be interviewed by the father's solicitors in the presence of a representative of the Official Solicitor on condition that the father was not present and that, unless distress would be caused to the ward, no other member of his family was present. Lord Donaldson M.R. said that it would not be appropriate for a ward to be interviewed on behalf of a defendant if and so long as the child was likely to be a prosecution witness. The circumstances might dictate the need to impose special conditions such as those in this case.

As to children in care or the subject of care proceedings, see *Re M. (Care: Leave to Interview Child)* [1995] 1 F.L.R. 825, Fam D (Hale J.) (where there was a prospect of a prosecution of the father, the court had jurisdiction to allow the child, who was the alleged victim, to be interviewed by the parents' solicitors); and *Re M.* (2007) 151 S.J. 1401, CA (Civ. Div.) (where the parents were charged with serious offences against their three sons, they should be allowed to instruct an expert to interview the boys, provided that they came up with an identified expert and a coherent reason as to what this might achieve; and, it being proper for the parents to wish to interview their daughter, their solicitors should be allowed to do so (at a time and place determined by the local authority and in the presence of her social worker) to ascertain whether or not she was reliable and had something to contribute to the proceedings).

Effect of parental objection

Where the police sought a declaration from the High Court in the exercise of its inherent jurisdiction that it was lawful, and in the best interests of twin sisters aged seven, for the police to interview them as to what they knew of the circumstances of the shooting by their 17-year-old brother of their 12-year-old sister, to which they were the only witnesses, and where the mother did not consent to such interview, it was held by Ryder J. in *Chief Constable of Greater Manchester v. K.I. and K.W. (by their children's guardian, CAFCASS Legal) and N.P.* [2008] 1 F.L.R. 504, Fam D, that the question of whether or not the sisters should be interviewed was not a matter relating to their "upbringing" within section 1 of the *Children Act* 1989, and thus their welfare was not paramount in the resolution of the question; and that whilst there was no doubting that consent to an interview was an aspect of parental responsibility and that there were serious welfare considerations, it was not something that related exclusively to the rearing of the child; rather, it was a matter where the undoubted issue of the child's welfare interacted with the rights and interests of others. On the facts, his Lordship held that even if the welfare of the children were the only consideration, the balance would come down in favour of interviewing them (on the basis that offering them the opportunity to talk about what had happened would be therapeutic); and that, once the interests of others (including the public and the defendant) were factored in, the decision became clear as it was apparent that what the girls would say might be crucial to the proper determination of the criminal process. **8–44a**

(7) Accomplices

As to calling an accomplice as a witness either for the Crown or for the defence, see *ante*, §§ 4–193 *et seq.* **8–45**

(8) The spouse or civil partner of the defendant

Police and Criminal Evidence Act 1984, s.80

80.—(2) In any proceedings the spouse or civil partner of a person charged in the proceedings shall, subject to subsection (4) below, be compellable to give evidence on behalf of that person. **8–46**

(2A) In any proceedings the spouse or civil partner of a person charged in the proceedings shall, subject to subsection (4) below, be compellable—

(a) to give evidence on behalf of any other person charged in the proceedings but only in respect of any specified offence with which that other person is charged; or

(b) to give evidence for the prosecution but only in respect of any specified offence with which any person is charged in the proceedings.

(3) In relation to the spouse or civil partner of a person charged in any proceedings, an offence is a specified offence for the purposes of subsection (2A) above if—

(a) it involves an assault on, or injury or a threat of injury to, the spouse or civil partner or a person who was at the material time under the age of 16;

(b) it is a sexual offence alleged to have been committed in respect of a person who was at the material time under that age; or

(c) it consists of attempting or conspiring to commit, or of aiding, abetting, counselling, procuring or inciting the commission of, an offence falling within paragraph (a) or (b) above.

(4) No person who is charged in any proceedings shall be compellable by virtue of subsection (2) or (2A) above to give evidence in the proceedings.

(4A) References in this section to a person charged in any proceedings do not include a person who is not, or is no longer, liable to be convicted of any offence in the proceedings (whether as a result of pleading guilty or for any other reason).

(5) In any proceedings a person who has been but is no longer married to the accused shall be … compellable to give evidence as if that person and the accused had never been married.

(5A) In any proceedings a person who has been but is no longer the civil partner of the accused shall be compellable to give evidence as if that person and the accused had never been civil partners.

(6) Where in any proceedings the age of any person at any time is material for the purposes of subsection (3) above, his age at the material time shall for the purposes of that provision be deemed to be or to have been that which appears to the court to be or to have been his age at that time.

(7) In subsection (3)(b) "sexual offence" means an offence under … the *Protection of Children Act* 1978 or Part 1 of the *Sexual Offences Act* 2003.

(9) [*Repeal of* Criminal Evidence Act *1898, s.1(d) and* Matrimonial Causes Act *1965, s.43(1).*]

[This section is printed as amended and repealed in part by the *YJCEA* 1999, s.67(1) and (3), Sched. 4, para. 13, and Sched. 6; the *SOA* 2003, ss.139 and 140, Sched. 6, para. 28(2), and Sched. 7; and the *Civil Partnership Act* 2004, s.261(1), and Sched. 27, para. 97. The reference to the common law offence of incitement in subs. (3)(c) has effect as a reference to the offences under the *SCA* 2007, Pt 2: 2007 Act, s.63(1), and Sched. 6, para. 8.]

As to the meaning of "proceedings", see section 82 (interpretation), *post*, § 9–84. The phrase "in any proceedings" in subsection (5) means any proceedings taking place after the commencement of the subsection: *R. v. Cruttenden* [1991] 2 Q.B. 66, 93 Cr.App.R. 119, CA. A person within the subsection is compellable in relation to events occurring during the subsistence of the marriage and before the commencement of the subsection: *ibid.*

As to the prohibition on comment by the prosecution on the failure of the spouse or civil partner of the defendant to give evidence, see section 80A of the 1984 Act, *ante*, § 4–362.

There is no power to prevent the marriage of a prisoner on remand and a witness for the prosecution, despite the fact that their marriage would make her a non-compellable witness for the prosecution in his pending trial: *R. (CPS) v. Registrar-General of Births, Deaths and Marriages* [2003] Q.B. 1222, CA (Civ. Div.).

"spouse"

8–47 The position of a wife of a second polygamous marriage so far as her competence and compellability to give evidence are concerned is no different to a woman who had not gone through a ceremony of marriage at all or who had gone through a ceremony of marriage which was invalid: see *R. v. Yacoob*, 72 Cr.App.R. 313, CA; and *R. v. Khan (Junaid)*, 84 Cr.App.R. 44, CA.

Section 80 has no application to the defendant's unmarried partner: *R. v. Pearce* [2002] 1 Cr.App.R. 39, CA; and, to the extent that compelling one member of a family to give evidence against another member of the same family might conflict with the right to family life as guaranteed by Article 8 of the ECHR (*post*, § 16–101), the interference was justified under Article 8(2) as necessary in a democratic society for the prevention of crime: *ibid*.

Warning to non-compellable spouse or civil partner

It is desirable if a wife within this category is called as a witness for the prosecution at her husband's trial, that the judge should explain to her, in the absence of the jury, before she takes the oath that she has a right to refuse to give evidence but that if she chooses to give evidence she may be treated like any other witness (see *R. v. Acaster*, 7 Cr.App.R. 187, CCA, *per* Darling J., at p. 189): *R. v. Pitt* [1983] Q.B. 25, 75 Cr.App.R. 254, CA. The court stated that it was not a rule of law that the judge should adopt such a course—"Nor do we seek to lay down any rule of practice for the future." **8–48**

The prosecution have a duty to disclose to the defence that a wife has informed the prosecutor outside court that she did not wish to give evidence against her husband and that her statement to the police was inaccurate, and also to inform the court, so that she could be warned that she need not give evidence: *R. v. Birmingham JJ., ex p. Shields*, *The Times*, August 3, 1994, DC.

There is no requirement to tell a woman that she is not a compellable witness against her husband before interviewing her about a crime of which her husband is suspected, and section 80 does not pose a legal bar to the admission of a woman's statement to the police that implicates her husband when she is not a compellable witness and has declined to give oral evidence against him: *R. v. L. (R.)* [2008] 2 Cr.App.R. 18, CA. However, the court said that there may be circumstances in which the police would be well advised to make it plain to a woman that she need not make a statement that implicates her husband. If a question is raised at trial as to whether it is in the interests of justice to admit her statement as hearsay under the *CJA* 2003, s.114(1)(d) (*post*, § 11–3), the prosecution hand is likely to be strengthened if they can show that she made her statement voluntarily, having been expressly informed that she was under no obligation to make it. As to this case, see also *post*, § 11–3. On the essential point of principle, the court's conclusion may be contrasted with that reached by the Supreme Court of Canada in *R. v. Couture* [2007] 2 S.C.R. 517.

(9) The defendant

Criminal Evidence Act 1898, s.1

1.—(1) A person charged in criminal proceedings shall not be called as a witness in the proceedings except upon his own application. **8–49**

(2) [*See* post, *§ 8–161*.]

(3) [*Repealed by* Criminal Justice Act *2003, s.331, and Sched. 36, para. 80*.]

(4) Every person charged in criminal proceedings who is called as a witness in the proceedings shall, unless otherwise ordered by the court, give his evidence from the witness box or other place from which the other witnesses give their evidence.

[This section is printed as amended and repealed in part by the *PACE Act* 1984, Sched. 7; the *CJPOA* 1994, Sched. 10, para. 2, and Sched. 11; and the *YJCEA* 1999, s.67(1) and Sched. 4, para. 1.]

As to subs. (4), see *ante*, § 4–312.

"Person charged"

A defendant who has pleaded guilty is not a "person charged" within the meaning of section 1 of the 1898 Act, because he is not concerned in any issue before the jury. He is, therefore, both competent and compellable for a co-defendant: *R. v. Boal and Cordrey* [1965] 1 Q.B. 402, 48 Cr.App.R. 342, CCA; *R. v. Conti*, 58 Cr.App.R. 387, CA; and *R. v. Finch* [2007] 1 Cr.App.R. 33, CA. **8–50**

"Upon his own application"

This appears to mean on the application of the defendant himself or of his counsel with his consent. **8–51**

IV. RULES OF EVIDENCE AND PRACTICE RELATING TO THE QUESTIONING OF WITNESSES

A. GENERAL

(1) Special measures directions

Introduction

8–52 Chapter I of Part II of the *YJCEA* 1999 is headed "Special measures directions in case of vulnerable and intimidated witnesses". Sections 16 and 17 identify witnesses who are eligible for assistance on grounds of age (under 17 at time of hearing) or incapacity (s.16) or of fear or distress at the prospect of testifying (s.17). Section 18 authorises the making of a special measures direction which may provide for any of the measures in sections 23 to 30 in the case of a section 16 witness and for any of the measures in sections 23 to 28 in the case of a section 17 witness. Section 19 regulates the procedure for the giving of such direction. This may be the result of application by a party to the proceedings, or it may be done of the court's own motion. Section 20 supplements section 19. Section 21 makes special provision in the case of child witnesses, and extra-special provision for child witnesses "in need of special protection" (*i.e.* those giving evidence on allegations of sexual and certain other offences). The effect is to restrict such discretion as the judge has in deciding what special measures should be imposed. Measures such as the use of video-recorded evidence and live links become practically mandatory. Section 22 extends section 21 to certain witnesses who do not qualify on a strict application of the provisions (*e.g.* a witness who is 17 at the time of the hearing but who was under 17 when he made a relevant recording). It should be noted that section 65(3) provides that for the purposes of the Act, the age of a person "shall be taken to be that which it appears to the court to be after considering any available evidence".

The special measures in sections 23 to 30 relate to the use of screens (s.23), the giving of evidence by live link (s.24), the giving of evidence in private (s.25), the removal of wigs and gowns (s.26), the use of video recorded evidence-in-chief (s.27), the use of video recorded cross-examination or re-examination (s.27), the examination of a witness through an intermediary (s.29), and aids to communication (s.30). Section 31 governs the status of evidence given by virtue of the provisions in this chapter; section 32 requires the judge to give "the jury such warning (if any) as the judge considers necessary to ensure that the fact that [a special measures] direction was given in relation to the witness does not prejudice the accused"; and section 33 regulates the interpretation of Chapter I.

Sections 16 to 27 and 31 to 33 came into force on July 24, 2002: *Youth Justice and Criminal Evidence Act 1999 (Commencement No. 7) Order* 2002 (S.I. 2002 No. 1739). As to the transitional arrangements, see paragraphs 1 and 3 of Schedule 7 to the Act, *post*, §§ 8–55x, 8–55y. Sections 32 (evidence via television link) and 32A (video recordings of evidence of child witnesses) of the *CJA* 1988 are repealed as from the same date, but, in the case of section 32 (*post*, § 8–65), only to the extent that it relates to child witnesses. Some of the case law in relation to those provisions (*e.g.* as to the provision of transcripts, and as to the replaying of video recorded evidence) will continue to have persuasive authority in relation to the corresponding provisions of the new legislation. For those needing to consult the former law, reference should be made to the 2002 edition of this work.

Section 29 came into force on February 23, 2004: *Youth Justice and Criminal Evidence Act 1999 (Commencement No. 9) Order* 2004 (S.I. 2004 No. 299).

The possibility of making a special measures direction will be something to be borne in mind by a judge confronted with an application for the statement of a witness to be admitted in evidence under section 116 of the *CJA* 2003 (*post*, § 11–15) on the ground that the witness will not attend to give oral evidence through fear.

As to restrictions on the reporting of special measures directions and of proceedings relating thereto, see section 47 of the 1999 Act, *ante*, § 4–29d.

As to "best practice", see *post*, § 8–55m.

Defendants

8–52a Sections 16 and 17 apply to defence witnesses as much as they apply to prosecution witnesses, but neither applies to the defendant. As to equality of arms, the fact that the accused may need assistance to give his best evidence, which was not provided for by the 1999 Act (but see now, *post*), did not justify excluding methods by which others may give their best evidence: *R. (D.) v. Camberwell Green Youth Court*; *R. (DPP) v. Same* [2005] 2 Cr.App.R. 1, HL (see also *post*, § 8–55c).

In *R. v. H. (Special measures)*, *The Times*, April 15, 2003, the Court of Appeal expressed the *obiter* opinion that a trial judge has a discretion as to the measures to be taken to assist a defendant with learning difficulties; this would extend to (a) permitting him to have the assistance of an interpreter whilst giving evidence, (b) reading a detailed defence statement to the jury, and (c) allowing leading questions based on that statement in examination-in-chief where it was apparent that he was having difficulty recalling facts. This has now been supplemented by the *PJA* 2006, s.47, which inserted a new Chapter 1A in Part II of the 1999 Act (*post*, §§ 8–55ta *et seq.*). This makes provision for vulnerable defendants to give evidence via a live link. See also *R. v. Ukpabio* [2008] 1 Cr.App.R. 6, CA (there is no limit on a court's power when it comes to securing the accused's participation in his trial; where, therefore, an accused was unable to participate properly by being present, there was a power, exceptionally, to permit him not to be present and to stay in touch by live link or some other means).

Proceedings for anti-social behaviour orders

As to the application of the special measures regime to proceedings for an anti-social behaviour order, see the *CDA* 1998, s.1I, *ante*, § 5–886b. **8–52b**

Youth Justice and Criminal Evidence Act 1999, ss.16–18

Part II

Giving of Evidence or Information for Purposes of Criminal Proceedings

Chapter I

Special Measures Directions in Case of Vulnerable and Intimidated Witnesses

Preliminary

Witnesses eligible for assistance on grounds of age or incapacity

16.—(1) For the purposes of this Chapter a witness in criminal proceedings (other than the accused) is eligible for assistance by virtue of this section— **8–53**

(a) if under the age of 17 at the time of the hearing; or

(b) if the court considers that the quality of evidence given by the witness is likely to be diminished by reason of any circumstances falling within subsection (2).

(2) The circumstances falling within this subsection are—

(a) that the witness—

(i) suffers from mental disorder within the meaning of the *Mental Health Act* 1983, or

(ii) otherwise has a significant impairment of intelligence and social functioning;

(b) that the witness has a physical disability or is suffering from a physical disorder.

(3) In subsection (1)(a) "the time of the hearing", in relation to a witness, means the time when it falls to the court to make a determination for the purposes of section 19(2) in relation to the witness.

(4) In determining whether a witness falls within subsection (1)(b) the court must consider any views expressed by the witness.

(5) In this Chapter references to the quality of a witness's evidence are to its quality in terms of completeness, coherence and accuracy; and for this purpose "coherence" refers to a witness's ability in giving evidence to give answers which address the questions put to the witness and can be understood both individually and collectively.

Witnesses eligible for assistance on ground of fear or distress about testifying

17.—(1) For the purposes of this Chapter a witness in criminal proceedings (other than the **8–54**

accused) is eligible for assistance by virtue of this subsection if the court is satisfied that the quality of evidence given by the witness is likely to be diminished by reason of fear or distress on the part of the witness in connection with testifying in the proceedings.

(2) In determining whether a witness falls within subsection (1) the court must take into account, in particular—

(a) the nature and alleged circumstances of the offence to which the proceedings relate;

(b) the age of the witness;

(c) such of the following matters as appear to the court to be relevant, namely—

(i) the social and cultural background and ethnic origins of the witness,

(ii) the domestic and employment circumstances of the witness, and

(iii) any religious beliefs or political opinions of the witness;

(d) any behaviour towards the witness on the part of—

(i) the accused,

(ii) members of the family or associates of the accused, or

(iii) any other person who is likely to be an accused or a witness in the proceedings.

(3) In determining that question the court must in addition consider any views expressed by the witness.

(4) Where the complainant in respect of a sexual offence is a witness in proceedings relating to that offence (or to that offence and any other offences), the witness is eligible for assistance in relation to those proceedings by virtue of this subsection unless the witness has informed the court of the witness' [*sic*] wish not to be so eligible by virtue of this subsection.

In *R. v. Brown* [2004] Crim.L.R. 1034, CA, it was held that: (i) whilst section 17(2) obliged a judge to have regard to various matters for the purpose of determining whether a witness was "eligible for assistance" within subsection (1) on the ground that the quality of the witness's evidence was likely to be diminished by reason of fear or distress, it was open to the judge so to conclude by reference to paragraph (a) alone, and he could do so notwithstanding that the witness was neither young nor particularly vulnerable; and (ii) where several witnesses to an alleged offence were eligible for special measures, the fact that another witness was not, could not possibly be a reason for saying that the judge should not make a special measures direction in the case of any of the witnesses. See also *post*, §§ 8–55e, 8–59.

Special measures available to eligible witnesses

8–55 **18.**—(1) For the purposes of this Chapter—

(a) the provision which may be made by a special measures direction by virtue of each of sections 23 to 30 is a special measure available in relation to a witness eligible for assistance by virtue of section 16; and

(b) the provision which may be made by such a direction by virtue of each of sections 23 to 28 is a special measure available in relation to a witness eligible for assistance by virtue of section 17;

but this subsection has effect subject to subsection (2).

(2) Where (apart from this subsection) a special measure would, in accordance with subsection (1)(a) or (b), be available in relation to a witness in any proceedings, it shall not be taken by a court to be available in relation to the witness unless—

(a) the court has been notified by the Secretary of State that relevant arrangements may be made available in the area in which it appears to the court that the proceedings will take place, and

(b) the notice has not been withdrawn.

(3) In subsection (2) "relevant arrangements" means arrangements for implementing the measure in question which cover the witness and the proceedings in question.

(4) The withdrawal of a notice under that subsection relating to a special measure shall not affect the availability of that measure in relation to a witness if a special measures direction providing for that measure to apply to the witness's evidence has been made by the court before the notice is withdrawn.

(5) The Secretary of State may by order make such amendments of this Chapter as he considers appropriate for altering the special measures which, in accordance with subsection (1)(a) or (b), are available in relation to a witness eligible for assistance by virtue of section 16 or (as the case may be) section 17, whether—

(a) by modifying the provisions relating to any measure for the time being available in relation to such a witness,

(b) by the addition—

(i) (with or without modifications) of any measure which is for the time being available in relation to a witness eligible for assistance by virtue of the other of those sections, or

(ii) of any new measure, or

(c) by the removal of any measure.

As at October 1, 2008, the availability (see subs. (2)) of the measures under sections 23 to 30 could be summarised as follows: those under sections 23 to 26 and 30 were available generally (though section 26 has no application in magistrates' courts and section 30 has no application to section 17 witnesses). Section 28 was not available. In the Crown Court, section 27 was fully available for section 16 witnesses; for section 17 witnesses it was available for complainants in respect of alleged sexual offences (provided the investigation started after that date). In magistrates' courts, section 27 was available for child witnesses in need of special protection only (see s.21(1)(b), *post*). Section 29 (which has no application to section 17 witnesses) was available in specified pilot areas, including the Crown Court at Cardiff, Plymouth, Leicester and Derby and the related magistrates' courts.

In *R. v. R. (S.A.)* [2008] 2 Cr.App.R. 10, CA, however, it was held that evidence given in chief by means of pre-recorded video had been properly admitted under the 1999 Act notwithstanding that the Secretary of State had not given any notification to the relevant location of the Crown Court under section 18(2). That subsection was simply intended to give the court a clear means of knowledge that the necessary equipment was available and that the necessary training had taken place without the court making its own enquiries. Whilst the court's scathing indictment of the Home Office's chaotic treatment of the issue (at [21]) is completely convincing, it is submitted that no judge would be justified in ordering a special measure in face of a valid objection that it was not to be taken to be available because of a lack of notification or a withdrawn notification (see *Criminal Law Week* 2008/14/3).

Youth Justice and Criminal Evidence Act 1999, ss.19–22

Special measures directions

Special measures direction relating to eligible witness

19.—(1) This section applies where in any criminal proceedings— **8–55a**

(a) a party to the proceedings makes an application for the court to give a direction under this section in relation to a witness in the proceedings other than the accused, or

(b) the court of its own motion raises the issue whether such a direction should be given.

(2) Where the court determines that the witness is eligible for assistance by virtue of section 16 or 17, the court must then—

(a) determine whether any of the special measures available in relation to the witness (or any combination of them) would, in its opinion, be likely to improve the quality of evidence given by the witness; and

(b) if so—

(i) determine which of those measures (or combination of them) would, in its opinion, be likely to maximise so far as practicable the quality of such evidence; and

(ii) give a direction under this section providing for the measure or measures so determined to apply to evidence given by the witness.

(3) In determining for the purposes of this Chapter whether any special measure or measures would or would not be likely to improve, or to maximise so far as practicable, the quality of evidence given by the witness, the court must consider all the circumstances of the case, including in particular—

(a) any views expressed by the witness; and

(b) whether the measure or measures might tend to inhibit such evidence being effectively tested by a party to the proceedings.

(4) A special measures direction must specify particulars of the provision made by the direction in respect of each special measure which is to apply to the witness's evidence.

(5) In this Chapter "special measures direction" means a direction under this section.

(6) Nothing in this Chapter is to be regarded as affecting any power of a court to make an order or give leave of any description (in the exercise of its inherent jurisdiction or otherwise)—

(a) in relation to a witness who is not an eligible witness, or

(b) in relation to an eligible witness where (as, for example, in a case where a foreign language interpreter is to be provided) the order is made or the leave is given otherwise than by reason of the fact that the witness is an eligible witness.

Further provisions about directions: general

8–55b **20.**—(1) Subject to subsection (2) and section 21(8), a special measures direction has binding effect from the time it is made until the proceedings for the purposes of which it is made are either—

(a) determined (by acquittal, conviction or otherwise), or

(b) abandoned,

in relation to the accused or (if there is more than one) in relation to each of the accused.

(2) The court may discharge or vary (or further vary) a special measures direction if it appears to the court to be in the interests of justice to do so, and may do so either—

(a) on an application made by a party to the proceedings, if there has been a material change of circumstances since the relevant time, or

(b) of its own motion.

(3) In subsection (2) "the relevant time" means—

(a) the time when the direction was given, or

(b) if a previous application has been made under that subsection, the time when the application (or last application) was made.

(4) Nothing in section 24(2) and (3), 27(4) to (7) or 28(4) to (6) is to be regarded as affecting the power of the court to vary or discharge a special measures direction under subsection (2).

(5) The court must state in open court its reasons for—

(a) giving or varying,

(b) refusing an application for, or for the variation or discharge of, or

(c) discharging,

a special measures direction and, if it is a magistrates' court, must cause them to be entered in the register of its proceedings.

(6) Criminal Procedure Rules may make provision—

(a) for uncontested applications to be determined by the court without a hearing;

(b) for preventing the renewal of an unsuccessful application for a special measures direction except where there has been a material change of circumstances;

(c) for expert evidence to be given in connection with an application for, or for varying or discharging, such a direction;

(d) for the manner in which confidential or sensitive information is to be treated in connection with such an application and in particular as to its being disclosed to, or withheld from, a party to the proceedings.

[This section is printed as amended by the *Courts Act* 2003, s.109(1), and Sched. 8, para. 384.]

Special provisions relating to child witnesses

8–55c **21.**—(1) For the purposes of this section—

(a) a witness in criminal proceedings is a "child witness" if he is an eligible witness by reason of section 16(1)(a) (whether or not he is an eligible witness by reason of any other provision of section 16 or 17);

(b) a child witness is "in need of special protection" if the offence (or any of the offences) to which the proceedings relate is—

(i) an offence falling within section 35(3)(a) (sexual offences etc.), or

(ii) an offence falling within section 35(3)(b), (c) or (d) (kidnapping, assaults etc.); and

(c) a "relevant recording", in relation to a child witness, is a video recording of an interview of the witness made with a view to its admission as evidence in chief of the witness.

(2) Where the court, in making a determination for the purposes of section 19(2), determines that a witness in criminal proceedings is a child witness, the court must—

(a) first have regard to subsections (3) to (7) below; and

(b) then have regard to section 19(2);

and for the purposes of section 19(2), as it then applies to the witness, any special measures required to be applied in relation to him by virtue of this section shall be treated as if they were measures determined by the court, pursuant to section 19(2)(a) and (b)(i), to be ones that (whether on their own or with any other special measures) would be likely to maximise, so far as practicable, the quality of his evidence.

(3) The primary rule in the case of a child witness is that the court must give a special measures direction in relation to the witness which complies with the following requirements—

(a) it must provide for any relevant recording to be admitted under section 27 (video recorded evidence in chief); and

(b) it must provide for any evidence given by the witness in the proceedings which is not given by means of a video recording (whether in chief or otherwise) to be given by means of a live link in accordance with section 24.

(4) The primary rule is subject to the following limitations—

(a) the requirement contained in subsection (3)(a) or (b) has effect subject to the availability (within the meaning of section 18(2)) of the special measure in question in relation to the witness;

(b) the requirement contained in subsection (3)(a) also has effect subject to section 27(2); and

(c) the rule does not apply to the extent that the court is satisfied that compliance with it would not be likely to maximise the quality of the witness's evidence so far as practicable (whether because the application to that evidence of one or more other special measures available in relation to the witness would have that result or for any other reason).

(5) However, subsection (4)(c) does not apply in relation to a child witness in need of special protection.

(6) Where a child witness is in need of special protection by virtue of subsection (1)(b)(i), any special measures direction given by the court which complies with the requirement contained in subsection (3)(a) must in addition provide for the special measure available under section 28 (video recorded cross-examination or re-examination) to apply in relation to—

(a) any cross-examination of the witness otherwise than by the accused in person, and

(b) any subsequent re-examination.

(7) The requirement contained in subsection (6) has effect subject to the following limitations—

(a) it has effect subject to the availability (within the meaning of section 18(2)) of that special measure in relation to the witness; and

(b) it does not apply if the witness has informed the court that he does not want that special measure to apply in relation to him.

(8) Where a special measures direction is given in relation to a child witness who is an eligible witness by reason only of section 16(1)(a), then—

(a) subject to subsection (9) below, and

(b) except where the witness has already begun to give evidence in the proceedings,

the direction shall cease to have effect at the time when the witness attains the age of 17.

(9) Where a special measures direction is given in relation to a child witness who is an eligible witness by reason only of section 16(1)(a) and—

(a) the direction provides—

(i) for any relevant recording to be admitted under section 27 as evidence in chief of the witness, or

(ii) for the special measure available under section 28 to apply in relation to the witness, and

(b) if it provides for that special measure to so apply, the witness is still under the age of 17 when the video recording is made for the purposes of section 28,

then, so far as it provides as mentioned in paragraph (a)(i) or (ii) above, the direction shall continue to have effect in accordance with section 20(1) even though the witness subsequently attains that age.

For section 35, see *post*, § 8–123c.

In *R. (D.) v. Camberwell Green Youth Court*; *R. (DPP) v. Same* [2005] 2 Cr.App.R. 1, the House of Lords held: (i) that the special measures regime for child witnesses in need of special protection (primary rule is for video-recorded evidence in chief and otherwise evidence by live link) was subject to only limited circumstances in which it could be disapplied; it was difficult to think of reasons which might make a live link or the admission of a recording unjust which were unrelated either to the quality of the equipment on the day, to the content and quality of the video recording, or the unavailability of the recorded witness for cross-examination; the court was there to ensure justice was done on the day of trial, but the court must always start from the statutory presumption that there was nothing intrinsically unfair in children giving their evidence in this way; and (ii) the regime was compatible with the rights guaranteed to a person charged with a criminal offence by Article 6 of the ECHR (*post*, § 16–57); it afforded the accused the opportunity of challenging the witness directly at the time when the trial was taking place, and the court had the opportunity to scrutinise the video-recorded interview at the outset and exclude all or part of it; at trial, the court had the fall-back of allowing the witness to give evidence in the courtroom or to expand upon the video recording if the interests of justice required it; all that was missing was face-to-face confrontation; and the Convention did not guarantee such a right. See also *ante*, § 8–52a.

Extension of provisions of section 21 to certain witnesses over 17

8–55d **22.**—(1) For the purposes of this section—

(a) a witness in criminal proceedings (other than the accused) is a "qualifying witness" if he—
  (i) is not an eligible witness at the time of the hearing (as defined by section 16(3)), but
  (ii) was under the age of 17 when a relevant recording was made;

(b) a qualifying witness is "in need of special protection" if the offence (or any of the offences) to which the proceedings relate is—
  (i) an offence falling within section 35(3)(a) (sexual offences etc.), or
  (ii) an offence falling within section 35(3)(b), (c) or (d) (kidnapping, assaults etc.); and

(c) a "relevant recording", in relation to a witness, is a video recording of an interview of the witness made with a view to its admission as evidence in chief of the witness.

(2) Subsections (2) to (7) of section 21 shall apply as follows in relation to a qualifying witness—

(a) subsections (2) to (4), so far as relating to the giving of a direction complying with the requirement contained in subsection (3)(a), shall apply to a qualifying witness in respect of the relevant recording as they apply to a child witness (within the meaning of that section);

(b) subsection (5), so far as relating to the giving of such a direction, shall apply to a qualifying witness in need of special protection as it applied to a child witness in need of special protection (within the meaning of that section); and

(c) subsections (6) and (7) shall apply to a qualifying witness in need of special protection by virtue of subsection (1)(b)(i) above as they apply to such a child witness as is mentioned in subsection (6).

For section 35 of the 1999 Act, see *post*, § 8–123c.

Youth Justice and Criminal Evidence Act 1999, ss.23–30

Special measures

Screening witness from accused

8–55e **23.**—(1) A special measures direction may provide for the witness, while giving testimony or being sworn in court, to be prevented by means of a screen or other arrangement from seeing the accused.

(2) But the screen or other arrangement must not prevent the witness from being able to see, and to be seen by—

(a) the judge or justices (or both) and the jury (if there is one);

(b) legal representatives acting in the proceedings; and

(c) any interpreter or other person appointed (in pursuance of the direction or otherwise) to assist the witness.

(3) Where two or more legal representatives are acting for a party to the proceedings, subsection (2)(b) is to be regarded as satisfied in relation to those representatives if the witness is able at all material times to see and be seen by at least one of them.

In *R. v. X.*, 91 Cr.App.R. 36, the Court of Appeal approved the erection of a screen in a courtroom to prevent young children seeing, or being seen by, the defendants. Social workers had been permitted to sit alongside the child witnesses when they gave evidence to comfort and console them when necessary. Lord Lane C.J., giving the court's judgment, said that, plainly, to have anyone sitting alongside a witness was a course of conduct that had to be undertaken with considerable care. When it happened, the court had to be astute to see that nothing improper passed and no undue encouragement was given to the witness to say anything other than the truth. **8–55f**

In *R. v. Ghani*, unreported, October 25, 1999, CA (99 04599 Z4), it was said that it would normally be appropriate to direct the jury not to draw any adverse inference against the accused from the use of the screen This authority can be regarded as no more than persuasive, however, having regard to the broad discretion given a judge by section 32, *post*, § 8–55s.

In *R. v. Brown* [2004] Crim.L.R. 1034, CA, it was said that where a judge gave a clear direction to the jury as to the use of screens before the first witness gave evidence from behind a screen, which was entirely fair to the defendants, and expressly explained why one witness was giving evidence without a screen and others were not, there was no need for the judge to repeat the direction when summing up. See also *ante*, § 8–54; and *post*, § 8–59.

The fact that on an application to a magistrates' court for permission for use of a screen, material adverse to the defendant is placed before the court does not necessarily preclude fair-minded consideration of the case, and accordingly cannot constitute an objection in principle to the justices continuing the hearing; and where they asked for the screen to be brought into court before the application was concluded, the High Court could not go behind their statement that this was done as a precautionary measure; such precaution was sensible, and it could not reasonably be taken to suggest that they had pre-judged the issue: *K.L. and L.K. v. DPP*, 166 J.P. 369, QBD (Richards J.).

As to the use of screens to protect a witness's identity, see *post*, § 8–71a.

Evidence by live link

24.—(1) A special measures direction may provide for the witness to give evidence by means of a live link. **8–55g**

(2) Where a direction provides for the witness to give evidence by means of a live link, the witness may not give evidence in any other way without the permission of the court.

(3) The court may give permission for the purposes of subsection (2) if it appears to the court to be in the interests of justice to do so, and may do so either—

(a) on an application by a party to the proceedings, if there has been a material change of circumstances since the relevant time, or

(b) of its own motion.

(4) In subsection (3) "the relevant time" means—

(a) the time when the direction was given, or

(b) if a previous application has been made under that subsection, the time when the application (or last application) was made.

(5)–(7) [*Repealed by* Courts Act *2003*, *s.109(1)*, *and Sched. 8*, *para. 385*.]

(8) In this Chapter "live link" means a live television link or other arrangement whereby a witness, while absent from the courtroom or other place where the proceedings are being held, is able to see and hear a person there and to be seen and heard by the persons specified in section 23(2)(a) to (c).

As to a defendant giving evidence by live link, see *post*, §§ 8–55ta *et seq*.

Evidence given in private

25.—(1) A special measures direction may provide for the exclusion from the court, during the giving of the witness's evidence, of persons of any description specified in the direction. **8–55h**

(2) The persons who may be so excluded do not include—

(a) the accused,

(b) legal representatives acting in the proceedings, or

(c) any interpreter or other person appointed (in pursuance of the direction or otherwise) to assist the witness.

(3) A special measures direction providing for representatives of news gathering or reporting organisations to be so excluded shall be expressed not to apply to one named person who—

(a) is a representative of such an organisation, and

(b) has been nominated for the purpose by one or more such organisations,

unless it appears to the court that no such nomination has been made.

(4) A special measures direction may only provide for the exclusion of persons under this section where—

(a) the proceedings relate to a sexual offence; or

(b) it appears to the court that there are reasonable grounds for believing that any person other than the accused has sought, or will seek, to intimidate the witness in connection with testifying in the proceedings.

(5) Any proceedings from which persons are excluded under this section (whether or not those persons include representatives of news gathering or reporting organisations) shall nevertheless be taken to be held in public for the purposes of any privilege or exemption from liability available in respect of fair, accurate and contemporaneous reports of legal proceedings held in public.

8–55i Any limitation on the principle of open justice should be based on the yet more fundamental principle that the principal object of the courts is to secure that justice is done; where, therefore, a judge was satisfied that an important prosecution witness in respect of an allegation of a serious offence would refuse to give evidence unless the public gallery was cleared (although she made no specific allegation of fear or intimidation), he had been entitled to order that the public gallery be cleared, whilst allowing the press to remain in court; and there was no conflict with Article 6 of the ECHR (*post*, § 16–57), which permits departure from the general rule where "publicity would prejudice the interests of justice": *R. v. Richards*, 163 J.P. 246, CA (decided in relation to the common law).

Removal of wigs and gowns

8–55j **26.** A special measures direction may provide for the wearing of wigs or gowns to be dispensed with during the giving of the witness's evidence.

Video recorded evidence in chief

8–55k **27.**—(1) A special measures direction may provide for a video recording of an interview of the witness to be admitted as evidence in chief of the witness.

(2) A special measures direction may, however, not provide for a video recording, or a part of such a recording, to be admitted under this section if the court is of the opinion, having regard to all the circumstances of the case, that in the interests of justice the recording, or that part of it, should not be so admitted.

(3) In considering for the purposes subsection (2) whether any part of a recording should not be admitted under this section, the court must consider whether any prejudice to the accused which might result from that part being so admitted is outweighed by the desirability of showing the whole, or substantially the whole, of the recorded interview.

(4) Where a special measures direction provides for a recording to be admitted under this section, the court may nevertheless subsequently direct that it is not to be so admitted if—

(a) it appears to the court that—

(i) the witness will not be available for cross-examination (whether conducted in the ordinary way or in accordance with any such direction), and

(ii) the parties to the proceedings have not agreed that there is no need for the witness to be so available; or

(b) any Criminal Procedure Rules requiring disclosure of the circumstances in which the recording was made have not been complied with to the satisfaction of the court.

(5) Where a recording is admitted under this section—

(a) the witness must be called by the party tendering it in evidence, unless—

(i) a special measures direction provides for the witness's evidence on cross-examination to be given otherwise than by testimony in court, or

(ii) the parties to the proceedings have agreed as mentioned in subsection (4)(a)(ii); and

(b) the witness may not give evidence in chief otherwise than by means of the recording—

(i) as to any matter which, in the opinion of the court, has been dealt with adequately in the witness's recorded testimony, or

(ii) without the permission of the court, as to any other matter which, in the opinion of the court, is dealt with in that testimony.

(6) Where in accordance with subsection (2) a special measures direction provides for part only of a recording to be admitted under this section, references in subsections (4) and (5) to the recording or to the witness's recorded testimony are references to the part of the recording or testimony which is to be so admitted.

(7) The court may give permission for the purposes of subsection (5)(b)(ii) if it appears to the court to be in the interests of justice to do so, and may do so either—

(a) on an application by a party to the proceedings, if there has been a material change of circumstances since the relevant time, or

(b) of its own motion.

(8) In subsection (7) "the relevant time" means—

(a) the time when the direction was given, or

(b) if a previous application has been made under that subsection, the time when the application (or last application) was made.

(9) The court may, in giving permission for the purposes of subsection (5)(b)(ii), direct that the evidence in question is to be given by the witness by means of a live link; and, if the court so directs, subsections (5) to (7) of section 24 shall apply in relation to that evidence as they apply in relation to evidence which is to be given in accordance with a special measures direction.

(10) *A magistrates' court inquiring into an offence as examining justices under section 6 of the* Magistrates' Courts Act *1980 may consider any video recording in relation to which it is proposed to apply for a special measures direction providing for it to be admitted at the trial in accordance with this section.*

(11) Nothing in this section affects the admissibility of any video recording which would be admissible apart from this section.

[This section is printed as amended by the *Courts Act* 2003, s.109(1), and Sched. 8, para. 384. Subs. (10) is repealed as from a day to be appointed: *CJA* 2003, s.332, and Sched. 37, Pt 4.]

Practice Direction (Criminal proceedings: Consolidation), para. IV.40
[2002] 1 W.L.R. 2870

Video-recorded evidence in chief

IV.40.1 [*Recites the relevant provisions.*] **8–55l**

IV.40.2 Where a court, on application by a party to the proceedings or of its own motion, grants leave to admit a video recording in evidence under section 27(1) of the 1999 Act it may direct that any part of the recording be excluded (section 27(2) and (3)). When such direction is given, the party who made the application to admit the video recording must edit the recording in accordance with the judge's directions and send a copy of the edited recording to the appropriate officer of the Crown Court and to every other party to the proceedings.

IV.40.3 Where a video recording is to be adduced during proceedings before the Crown Court, it should be produced and proved by the interviewer, or any other person who was present at the interview with the witness at which the recording was made. The applicant should ensure that such a person will be available for this purpose, unless the parties have agreed to accept a written statement in lieu of attendance by that person.

IV.40.4 Once a trial has begun if, by reason of faulty or inadequate preparation or for some other cause, the procedures set out above have not been properly complied with and an application is made to edit the video recording, thereby making it necessary an adjournment for the work to be carried out, the court may make at its discretion an appropriate award of costs.

This practice direction was originally published in relation to section 32A of the *CJA* 1988 at [1992] 1 W.L.R. 839.

Good practice

8–55m The Home Office Communication Direcorate have published (January, 2002) assistance for those preparing video-recorded interviews for criminal proceedings and for those dealing with witnesses subject to special measures, *Achieving Best Evidence in Criminal Proceedings: Guidance for Vulnerable or Intimidated Witnesses, including Children*. The guidance is available from the Stationery Office and on the Crown Prosecution Service website (www.cps.gov.uk). The guidance revises, expands on and replaces the *Memorandum of Good Practice* produced by the Home Office and the Department of Health. It describes good practice in preparing for and conducting interviews with vulnerable or intimidated witnesses, both adults and children, to enable them to give their best evidence in criminal proceedings, as well as providing guidance on supporting and preparing the witnesses for court. The Home Office has advised that great care should be taken to ensure that video recordings for criminal proceedings are only made by those familiar with the guidance and suitably trained for the task.

In *G. v. DPP* [1997] 2 Cr.App.R. 78, DC, it was held that a failure to comply with the *Memorandum of Good Practice* was a matter to be taken into account by a court in deciding whether to exercise its discretion to refuse to admit the recording; but the decision as to exclusion or not should depend not so much on the nature and extent of any breaches, but more on whether the passages tainted by breaches are confirmed by other untainted passages or are corroborated by independent evidence.

In *R. v. K.* [2006] 2 Cr.App.R. 10, CA, it was said that the appropriate test when determining whether to give a special measures direction in respect of a video recorded interview in relation to which there had been a number of breaches of the 2002 guidance (*ante*) was that set out in *R. v. Hanton*, unreported, June 27, 2005, CA ([2005] EWCA Crim. 2009) (*viz.* "could a reasonable jury properly directed be sure that the witness had given a credible and accurate account on the video tape, notwithstanding any breaches?"); *G. v. DPP* (*ante*) should not be construed as determining that the existence of corroborating material is of central importance, but should be considered to indicate that the prime consideration is the reliability of the videoed evidence, which will normally be assessed by reference to the interview itself, the conditions under which it had been held, the age of the child, and the nature and extent of any breach; but that was not to say that there may not be cases in which other evidence would demonstrate that the breaches had not had the effect of undermining the credibility or accuracy of the video interview. For a critique of this approach, see, however, *Criminal Law Week* 2006/14/3.

In *R. v. D. and S.*, 166 J.P. 792, CA, it was held that a failure to comply with the memorandum (by virtue of there being present at a second such interview a 19-year-old who was supposedly acting as "appropriate adult", who had herself informally "interviewed" the complainant since the first interview and who was herself a complainant in the case in relation to one relatively minor count) did not *per se* render inadmissible the underlying material to which the complainant spoke in the interview, nor did it render that material inadmissible by use of the video; it often being the case that before there is a police interview, a child will have been questioned by others such as a parent, teacher or friend, in leading form, it could not be right that because of such questioning having taken place, such matters should not be allowed to go before the jury; as to the use of the video, the judge had been correct to start from the premise that the use of such recording was the normal way for such evidence to be given; on the facts, this resulted in fairness to both sides, in that the complainant would clearly have had great difficulty giving a coherent account if he had to do so by way of live oral evidence and it meant that his account was before the jury "warts and all"; the irregularity in the recording of the interview had been dealt with by the judge's reminders as to the inconsistencies in the evidence of the complainant and his direction as to the possible effect that the 19-year-old's involvement might have had, both by her questioning of the complainant, and by her presence at the second interview, in causing him to come out with a fuller version than he might otherwise have done.

Where the interviewer makes a comment to a child witness, such as "You're doing really well", there should be a direction by the judge to the jury that they should disregard any such comment for the purposes of their assessment of the evidence: *R. v. B. (K.)* [2002] 10 *Archbold News* 1, CA.

Transcript for jury

A judge is entitled to allow the jury to have a transcript of a video recording of a child's evidence whilst the recording is being played, provided: (a) that the transcript would be likely to assist them in following the evidence of the witness in question; (b) that the judge makes clear to the jury that the transcript is made available to them only for that limited purpose; and (c) that the judge gives the jury such directions, both at the time and in summing up, as would be likely to be effective safeguards against the risk of disproportionate weight being given to the transcript: *R. v. Welstead* [1996] 1 Cr.App.R. 59, CA (transcript withdrawn from jury before retirement). It makes no difference to this duty that the transcript was provided at the suggestion of the defence: *R. v. Morris* [1998] Crim.L.R. 416, CA. At the end of the evidence, consideration should be given to what is to happen to the transcript; only rarely should the jury be permitted to retire with it: *ibid.* **8–55n**

As to replaying video evidence, see *R. v. M. (John)* [1996] 2 Cr.App.R. 56, CA (*ante*, § 4–337) (prosecution request after suggestion by judge); *R. v. Rawlings*; *R. v. Broadbent* [1995] 2 Cr.App.R. 222, CA (*ante*, § 4–423) (jury request after retirement); and *R. v. Mullen* [2004] 2 Cr.App.R. 18, CA (*ante*, § 4–423) (discretion extends to child witnesses other than the complainant).

Where a judge refuses a jury request for a video recording of a child's evidence-in-chief to be replayed to them, but instead reminds them of the evidence by reference to a transcript, it is none the less incumbent on the judge to warn the jury not to give disproportionate weight to the evidence because it is repeated after all the other evidence and to direct them that they should consider it in the context of all the evidence; further, he should remind the jury of the cross-examination, any pertinent re-examination and of any relevant part of the defendant's evidence: *R. v. McQuiston* [1998] 1 Cr.App.R. 139, CA. See also *R. v. Horley* [1999] Crim.L.R. 488, CA, in which it is said that *McQuiston* was "not followed", but there is no indication as to in what respect it was not followed, save that the commentary suggests that the court was of the view that there could be no hard and fast rules as to what should be said to the jury, provided always that the jury's request was dealt with in a balanced manner.

As to a request by the jury, after retirement to consider their verdict, for a transcript of evidence given on video, see *R. v. Coshall*, *The Times*, February 17, 1995, CA (*ante*, § 4–423).

[Video recorded cross-examination or re-examination

28.—(1) Where a special measures direction provides for a video recording to be admitted under section 27 as evidence in chief of the witness, the direction may also provide— **8–55o**

(a) for any cross-examination of the witness, and any re-examination, to be recorded by means of a video recording; and

(b) for such a recording to be admitted, so far as it relates to any such cross-examination or re-examination, as evidence of the witness under cross-examination or on re-examination, as the case may be.

(2) Such a recording must be made in the presence of such persons as Criminal Procedure Rules or the direction may provide and in the absence of the accused, but in circumstances in which—

(a) the judge or justices (or both) and legal representatives acting in the proceedings are able to see and hear the examination of the witness and to communicate with the persons in whose presence the recording is being made, and

(b) the accused is able to see and hear any such examination and to communicate with any legal representative acting for him.

(3) Where two or more legal representatives are acting for a party to the proceedings, subsection (2)(a) and (b) are to be regarded as satisfied in relation to those representatives if at all material times they are satisfied in relation to at least one of them.

(4) Where a special measures direction provides for a recording to be admitted under

this section, the court may nevertheless subsequently direct that it is not to be so admitted if any requirement of subsection (2) or Criminal Procedure Rules or the direction has not been complied with to the satisfaction of the court.

(5) Where in pursuance of subsection (1) a recording has been made of any examination of the witness, the witness may not be subsequently cross-examined or re-examined in respect of any evidence given by the witness in the proceedings (whether in any recording admissible under section 27 or this section or otherwise than in such a recording) unless the court gives a further special measures direction making such provision as is mentioned in subsection (1)(a) and (b) in relation to any subsequent cross-examination, and re-examination, of the witness.

(6) The court may only give such a further direction if it appears to the court—

(a) that the proposed cross-examination is sought by a party to the proceedings as a result of that party having become aware, since the time when the original recording was made in pursuance of subsection (1), of a matter which that party could not with reasonable diligence have ascertained by then, or

(b) that for any other reason it is in the interests of justice to give the further direction.

(7) Nothing in this section shall be read as applying in relation to any cross-examination of the witness by the accused in person (in a case where the accused is to be able to conduct any such cross-examination).]

[This section comes into force on a day to be appointed. No day had been appointed as at October 1, 2008. It is printed as amended by the *Courts Act* 2003, s.109(1), and Sched. 8, para. 384.]

Examination of witness through intermediary

8–55p **29.**—(1) A special measures direction may provide for any examination of the witness (however and wherever conducted) to be conducted through an interpreter or other person approved by the court for the purposes of this section ("an intermediary").

(2) The function of an intermediary is to communicate—

(a) to the witness, questions put to the witness, and

(b) to any person asking such questions, the answers given by the witness in reply to them,

and to explain such questions or answers so far as necessary to enable them to be understood by the witness or person in question.

(3) Any examination of the witness in pursuance of subsection (1) must take place in the presence of such persons as rules of court or the direction may provide, but in circumstances in which—

(a) the judge or justices (or both) and legal representatives acting in the proceedings are able to see and hear the examination of the witness and to communicate with the intermediary, and

(b) (except in the case of a video recorded examination) the jury (if there is one) are able to see and hear the examination of the witness.

(4) Where two or more legal representatives are acting for a party to the proceedings, subsection (3)(a) is to be regarded as satisfied in relation to those representatives if at all material times it is satisfied in relation to at least one of them.

(5) A person may not act as an intermediary in a particular case except after making a declaration, in such form as may be prescribed by rules of court, that he will faithfully perform his function as intermediary.

(6) Subsection (1) does not apply to an interview of the witness which is recorded by means of a video recording with a view to its admission as evidence in chief of the witness; but a special measures direction may provide for such a recording to be admitted under section 27 if the interview was conducted through an intermediary and—

(a) that person complied with subsection (5) before the interview began, and

(b) the court's approval for the purposes of this section is given before the direction is given.

(7) Section 1 of the *Perjury Act* 1911 (perjury) shall apply in relation to a person acting as an intermediary as it applies in relation to a person lawfully sworn as an interpreter in a judicial proceeding; and for this purpose, where a person acts as an intermediary in any proceeding which is not a judicial proceeding for the purposes of that section, that proceeding shall be taken to be part of the judicial proceeding in which the witness's evidence is given.

Aids to communication

8–55q **30.** A special measures direction may provide for the witness, while giving evidence (whether by testimony in court or otherwise), to be provided with such device as the court considers appropriate with a view to enabling questions or answers to be communicated to or by the witness despite any disability or disorder or other impairment which the witness has or suffers from.

Youth Justice and Criminal Evidence Act 1999, ss.31–33

Supplementary

Status of evidence given under Chapter I

31.—(1) Subsections (2) to (4) apply to a statement made by a witness in criminal proceedings which, in accordance with a special measures direction, is not made by the witness in direct oral testimony in court but forms part of the witness's evidence in those proceedings. **8–55r**

(2) The statement shall be treated as if made by the witness in direct oral testimony in court; and accordingly—

(a) it is admissible evidence of any fact of which such testimony from the witness would be admissible;

(b) it is not capable of corroborating any other evidence given by the witness.

(3) Subsection (2) applies to a statement admitted under section 27 or 28 which is not made by the witness on oath even though it would have been required to be made on oath if made by the witness in direct oral testimony in court.

(4) In estimating the weight (if any) to be attached to the statement, the court must have regard to all the circumstances from which an inference can reasonably be drawn (as to the accuracy of the statement or otherwise).

(5) Nothing in this Chapter (apart from subsection (3)) affects the operation of any rule of law relating to evidence in criminal proceedings.

(6) Where any statement made by a person on oath in any proceeding which is not a judicial proceeding for the purposes of section 1 of the *Perjury Act* 1911 (perjury) is received in evidence in pursuance of a special measures direction, that proceeding shall be taken for the purposes of that section to be part of the judicial proceeding in which the statement is so received in evidence.

(7) Where in any proceeding which is not a judicial proceeding for the purposes of that Act—

(a) a person wilfully makes a false statement otherwise than on oath which is subsequently received in evidence in pursuance of a special measures direction, and

(b) the statement is made in such circumstances that had it been given on oath in any such judicial proceeding that person would have been guilty of perjury,

he shall be guilty of an offence and liable to any punishment which might be imposed on conviction of an offence under section 57(2) (giving of false unsworn evidence in criminal proceedings).

(8) In this section "statement" includes any representation of fact, whether made in words or otherwise.

Warning to jury

32. Where on a trial on indictment with a jury evidence has been given in accordance with a special measures direction, the judge must give the jury such warning (if any) as the judge considers necessary to ensure that the fact that the direction was given in relation to the witness does not prejudice the accused. **8–55s**

[This section is printed as amended by the *CJA* 2003, s.331, and Sched. 36, paras 74 and 75.]

Interpretation of Chapter I

33.—(1) In this Chapter— **8–55t**

"eligible witness" means a witness eligible for assistance by virtue of section 16 or 17;

"live link" has the meaning given by section 24(8);

"quality", in relation to the evidence of a witness, shall be construed in accordance with section 16(5);

"special measures direction" means (in accordance with section 19(5)) a direction under section 19.

(2) In this Chapter references to the special measures available in relation to a witness shall be construed in accordance with section 18.

(3) In this Chapter references to a person being able to see or hear, or be seen or heard by, another person are to be read as not applying to the extent that either of them is unable to see or hear by reason of any impairment of eyesight or hearing.

(4) In the case of any proceedings in which there is more than one accused—

(a) any reference to the accused in sections 23 to 28 may be taken by a court, in connection with the giving of a special measures direction, as a reference to all or any of the accused, as the court may determine, and

(b) any such direction may be given on the basis of any such determination.

Youth Justice and Criminal Evidence Act 1999, ss.33A–33C

CHAPTER 1A

USE OF LIVE LINK FOR EVIDENCE OF CERTAIN ACCUSED PERSONS

Live link directions

8–55ta **33A.**—(1) This section applies to any proceedings (whether in a magistrates' court or before the Crown Court) against a person for an offence.

(2) The court may, on the application of the accused, give a live link direction if it is satisfied—

(a) that the conditions in subsection (4) or, as the case may be, subsection (5) are met in relation to the accused, and

(b) that it is in the interests of justice for the accused to give evidence through a live link.

(3) A live link direction is a direction that any oral evidence to be given before the court by the accused is to be given through a live link.

(4) Where the accused is aged under 18 when the application is made, the conditions are that—

(a) his ability to participate effectively in the proceedings as a witness giving oral evidence in court is compromised by his level of intellectual ability or social functioning, and

(b) use of a live link would enable him to participate more effectively in the proceedings as a witness (whether by improving the quality of his evidence or otherwise).

(5) Where the accused has attained the age of 18 at that time, the conditions are that—

(a) he suffers from a mental disorder (within the meaning of the *Mental Health Act* 1983) or otherwise has a significant impairment of intelligence and social function,

(b) he is for that reason unable to participate effectively in the proceedings as a witness giving oral evidence in court, and

(c) use of a live link would enable him to participate more effectively in the proceedings as a witness (whether by improving the quality of his evidence or otherwise).

(6) While a live link direction has effect the accused may not give oral evidence before the court in the proceedings otherwise than through a live link.

(7) The court may discharge a live link direction at any time before or during any hearing to which it applies if it appears to the court to be in the interests of justice to do so (but this does not affect the power to give a further live link direction in relation to the accused). The court may exercise this power of its own motion or on an application by a party.

(8) The court must state in open court its reasons for—

(a) giving or discharging a live link direction, or

(b) refusing an application for or for the discharge of a live link direction,

and, if it is a magistrates' court, it must cause those reasons to be entered in the register of its proceedings.

Section 33A: meaning of "live link"

8–55tb **33B.**—(1) In section 33A "live link" means an arrangement by which the accused, while absent from the place where the proceedings are being held, is able—

(a) to see and hear a person there, and

(b) to be seen and heard by the persons mentioned in subsection (2),

and for this purpose any impairment of eyesight or hearing is to be disregarded.

(2) The persons are—

(a) the judge or justices (or both) and the jury (if there is one),

(b) where there are two or more accused in the proceedings, each of the other accused,

(c) legal representatives acting in the proceedings, and

(d) any interpreter or other person appointed by the court to assist the accused.

Saving

33C. Nothing in this Chapter affects— 8–55tc

(a) any power of a court to make an order, give directions or give leave of any description in relation to any witness (including an accused), or

(b) the operation of any rule of law relating to evidence in criminal proceedings.

[Chapter 1A of Part II of the 1999 Act was inserted by the *PJA* 2006, s.47.]

Youth Justice and Criminal Evidence Act 1999, ss.61–63

CHAPTER VII

GENERAL

61. [*Application of Part II to service courts.*] 8–55u

Meaning of "sexual offence" and other references to offences

62.—(1) In this Part "sexual offence" means any offence under Part 1 of the *Sexual Offences Act* 2003 or any relevant superseded offence. 8–55v

(1A) In subsection (1) "relevant superseded offence" means—

(a) rape or burglary with intent to rape;

(b) an offence under any of sections 2 to 12 and 14 to 17 of the *Sexual Offences Act* 1956 (unlawful intercourse, indecent assault, forcible abduction etc.);

(c) an offence under section 128 of the *Mental Health Act* 1959 (unlawful intercourse with person receiving treatment for mental disorder by member of hospital staff etc.);

(d) an offence under section 1 of the *Indecency with Children Act* 1960 (indecent conduct towards child under 14);

(e) an offence under section 54 of the *Criminal Law Act* 1977 (incitement of child under 16 to commit incest).

(2) In this Part any reference (including a reference having effect by virtue of this subsection) to an offence of any description ("the substantive offence") is to be taken to include a reference to an offence which consists of attempting or conspiring to commit, or of aiding, abetting, counselling, procuring or inciting the commission of, the substantive offence.

[Subs. (1) is printed as substituted by the *SOA* 2003, s.139, and Sched. 6, para. 41(1) and (3); and as subsequently amended (retrospectively to May 1, 2004) by the *CJIA* 2008, s.148(1), and Sched. 26, paras 35 and 37. The reference to the common law offence of incitement in subs. (2) has effect as a reference to the offences under the *SCA* 2007, Pt 2: 2007 Act, s.63(1), and Sched. 6, para. 37.]

As to the lacuna in the definition of "sexual offence" that led to its retrospective amendment by the 2008 Act, see *R. v. C.* [2008] 1 Cr.App.R. 22, CA.

General interpretation etc. of Part II

63.—(1) In this Part (except where the context otherwise requires)— 8–55w

"accused", in relation to any criminal proceedings, means any person charged with an offence to which the proceedings relate (whether or not he has been convicted);

"the complainant", in relation to any offence (or alleged offence), means a person against or in relation to whom the offence was (or is alleged to have been) committed;

"court" (except in Chapter IV or V or subsection (2)) means a magistrates' court, the Crown Court or the criminal division of the Court of Appeal;

"legal representative" means *any authorised advocate or authorised litigator (as defined by section 119(1) of the* Courts and Legal Services Act *1990)* [a person who, for the purposes of the *Legal Services Act* 2007, is an authorised person in relation to an activity which constitutes the exercise of a right of audience or the conduct of litigation (within the meaning of that Act)];

"picture" includes a likeness however produced;

"the prosecutor" means any person acting as prosecutor, whether an individual or body;

"publication" includes any speech, writing, relevant programme or other communication in whatever form, which is addressed to the public at large or any section of the public (and for this purpose every relevant programme shall be taken to be so addressed), but does not include an indictment or other document prepared for use in particular legal proceedings;

"relevant programme" means a programme included in a programme service, within the meaning of the *Broadcasting Act* 1990;

"service court" means—

(a) *a court-martial constituted under the* Army Act *1955, the* Air Force Act *1955 or the* Naval Discipline Act *1957 or a disciplinary court constituted under section 52G of the* Naval Discipline Act *1957* [the Court Martial];

(b) *the Courts-Martial Appeal Court, or* [the Service Civilian Court; or]

(c) *a Standing Civilian Court* [the Court Martial Appeal Court];

"video recording" means any recording, on any medium, from which a moving image may by any means be produced, and includes the accompanying sound-track;

"witness", in relation to any criminal proceedings, means any person called, or proposed to be called, to give evidence in the proceedings.

(2) Nothing in this Part shall affect any power of a court to exclude evidence at its discretion (whether by preventing questions being put or otherwise) which is exercisable apart from this Part.

[This section is printed as amended, as from a day to be appointed, by the *AFA* 2006, s.378(1), and Sched. 16, para. 159 (substitution of words in square brackets in definition of "service court" for the italicised words that precede them); and the *Legal Services Act* 2007, s.208(1), and Sched. 21, para. 132 (omission of italicised words, insertion of words in square brackets in definition of "legal representative").]

Youth Justice and Criminal Evidence Act 1999, Schedule 7, paras 1, 3

SCHEDULE 7

TRANSITIONAL PROVISIONS AND SAVINGS

Interpretation

8–55x 1.—(1) In this Schedule—

"the 1988 Act" means the *Criminal Justice Act* 1988;

"commencement date", in relation to any provisions of this Act and proceedings of any description, means the date on which those provisions come into force in relation to such proceedings;

"continuing proceedings" (except in paragraph 3) means proceedings instituted before the commencement date;

"existing special measures power" means any power of the court to make an order or give leave, in the exercise of its inherent jurisdiction, for the taking of measures in relation to a witness which are similar to those which could be provided for by a special measures direction.

(2) For the purposes of this Schedule—

(a) proceedings other than proceedings on appeal are to be taken to be instituted at the time when they would be taken to be instituted for the purposes of Part I of the *Prosecution of Offences Act* 1985 in accordance with section 15(2) of that Act; and

(b) proceedings on appeal are to be taken to be instituted at the time when the notice of appeal is given or (as the case may be) the reference under section 9 or 11 of the *Criminal Appeal Act* 1995 is made.

(3) Expressions used in this Schedule which are also used in Part II of this Act have the same meaning in this Schedule as in that Part.

Special measures under Chapter I of Part II

8–55y 3.—(1) A special measures direction may be given in relation to a witness in continuing proceedings unless the court has before the specified date—

(a) given leave in relation to the witness in connection with those proceedings under section 32 (evidence through television links) or section 32A (video recordings of testimony of child witnesses) of the 1988 Act, or

(b) exercised any existing special measures power in relation to the witness in connection with those proceedings.

(2) The repeals made by this Act shall not affect the continued operation in relation to a witness in continuing proceedings of section 32 or 32A of the 1988 Act where before the specified date leave was given in relation to the witness in connection with those proceedings by virtue of section 32(1)(b) or 32A, as the case may be.

(3) Nothing in this Act affects the continued operation in relation to a witness in continuing proceedings of any order made or leave given under any existing special measures power exercised by the court before the specified date in relation to the witness in connection with those proceedings.

(4) In this paragraph—

(a) "continuing proceedings" means proceedings instituted before the specified date;

(b) "the specified date", in relation to a witness in any proceedings, means such date as may be specified by the Secretary of State in a notice given to the court in question under section 18(2), where the date is expressed to apply—

(i) for the purposes of this paragraph, and

(ii) in relation to any description of witnesses and proceedings within which the witness and the proceedings fall.

Criminal Procedure Rules 2005 (S.I. 2005 No. 384), Pt 29

Application for special measures directions

29.1.—(1) An application by a party in criminal proceedings for a magistrates' court or the Crown Court to give a special measures direction under section 19 of the *Youth Justice and Criminal Evidence Act* 1999 must be made in writing in the form set out in the Practice Direction. **8–56**

(2) If the application is for a special measures direction—

(a) enabling a witness to give evidence by means of a live link, the information sought in Part B of that form must be provided;

(b) providing for any examination of a witness to be conducted through an intermediary, the information sought in Part C of that form must be provided; or

(c) enabling a video recording of an interview of a witness to be admitted as evidence in chief of the witness, the information sought in Part D of that form must be provided.

(3) The application under paragraph (1) above must be sent to the court officer and at the same time a copy thereof must be sent by the applicant to every other party to the proceedings.

(4) The court officer must receive the application—

(a) in the case of an application to a youth court, within 28 days of the date on which the defendant first appears or is brought before the court in connection with the offence;

(b) in the case of an application to a magistrates' court, within 14 days of the defendant indicating his intention to plead not guilty to any charge brought against him and in relation to which a special measures direction may be sought; and

(c) in the case of an application to the Crown Court, within 28 days of

(i) the committal of the defendant, or

(ii) the consent to the preferment of a bill of indictment in relation to the case, or

(iii) the service of a notice of transfer under section 53 of the *Criminal Justice Act* 1991, or

(iv) where a person is sent for trial under section 51 of the *Crime and Disorder Act* 1998, the service of copies of the documents containing the evidence on which the charge or charges are based under paragraph 1 of Schedule 3 to that Act, or

(v) the service of a Notice of Appeal from a decision of a youth court or a magistrates' court.

(5) A party to whom an application is sent in accordance with paragraph (3) may oppose the application for a special measures direction in respect of any, or any particular, measure available in relation to the witness, whether or not the question whether the witness is eligible for assistance by virtue of section 16 or 17 of the 1999 Act is in issue.

(6) A party who wishes to oppose the application must, within 14 days of the date the application was served on him, notify the applicant and the court officer, as the case may be, in writing of his opposition and give reasons for it.

(7) Paragraphs (5) and (6) do not apply in respect of an application for a special measures direction enabling a child witness in need of special protection to give evidence by means of a live link if the opposition is that the special measures direction is not likely to maximise the quality of the witness's evidence.

(8) In order to comply with paragraph (6)—

(a) a party must in the written notification state whether he—

(i) disputes that the witness is eligible for assistance by virtue of section 16 or 17 of the 1999 Act,

(ii) disputes that any of the special measures available would be likely to improve the quality of evidence given by the witness or that such measures (or a combination of them) would be likely to maximise the quality of that evidence, and

(iii) opposes the granting of a special measures direction; and

(b) where the application relates to the admission of a video recording, a party who receives a recording must provide the information required by rule 29.7(7) below.

(9) Except where notice is received in accordance with paragraph (6), the court (including, in the case of an application to a magistrates' court, a single justice of the peace) may—

(a) determine the application in favour of the applicant without a hearing; or

(b) direct a hearing.

(10) Where a party to the proceedings notifies the court in accordance with paragraph (6) of his opposition to the application, the justices' clerk or the Crown Court must direct a hearing of the application.

(11) Where a hearing of the application is to take place in accordance with paragraph (9) or (10) above, the court officer shall notify each party to the proceedings of the time and place of the hearing.

(12) A party notified in accordance with paragraph (11) may be present at the hearing and be heard.

(13) The court officer must, within 3 days of the decision of the court in relation to an application under paragraph (1) being made, notify all the parties of the decision, and if the application was made for a direction enabling a video recording of an interview of a witness to be admitted as evidence in chief of that witness, the notification must state whether the whole or specified parts only of the video recording or recordings disclosed are to be admitted in evidence.

(14) In this Part:

"an intermediary" has the same meaning as in section 29 of the 1999 Act; and

"child witness in need of protection" shall be construed in accordance with section 21(1) of the 1999 Act.

Application for an extension of time

8–57 **29.2.**—(1) An application may be made in writing for the period of 14 days or, as the case may be, 28 days specified in rule 29.1(4) to be extended.

(2) The application may be made either before or after that period has expired.

(3) The application must be accompanied by a statement setting out the reasons why the applicant is or was unable to make the application within that period and a copy of the application and the statement must be sent to every other party to the proceedings.

(4) An application for an extension of time under this rule shall be determined by a single justice of the peace or a judge of the Crown Court without a hearing unless the justice or the judge otherwise directs.

(5) The court officer shall notify all the parties of the court's decision.

Late applications

8–58 **29.3.**—(1) Notwithstanding the requirements of rule 29.1—

(a) an application may be made for a special measures direction orally at the trial; or

(b) a magistrates' court or the Crown Court may of its own motion raise the issue whether a special measures direction should be given.

(2) Where an application is made in accordance with paragraph (1)(a)—

(a) the applicant must state the reasons for the late application; and

(b) the court must be satisfied that the applicant was unable to make the application in accordance with rule 29.1.

(3) The court shall determine before making a special measures direction—

(a) whether to allow other parties to the proceedings to make representations on the question;

(b) the time allowed for making such representations (if any); and

(c) whether the question should be determined following a hearing at which the parties to the proceedings may be heard.

(4) Paragraphs (2) and (3) do not apply in respect of an application made orally at the trial for a special measures direction—

(a) enabling a child witness in need of special protection to give evidence by means of a live link; or

(b) enabling a video recording of such a child to be admitted as evidence in chief of the witness,

if the opposition is that the special measures direction will not maximise the quality of the witness's evidence.

In *R. v. Brown* [2004] Crim.L.R. 1034, CA, it was held that the requirement in paragraph (2)(b) was directory only; the importance of complying with paragraph (2) would vary according to the nature of the direction sought (there being obvious reasons, for example, for a prompt application for the giving of evidence by video recording); where the application was for the use of screens, the need for a prompt application was less obvious; if there was any handicap to the defence then the judge would have to take that carefully into account. **8–59**

Discharge or variation of a special measures direction

29.4.—(1) An application to a magistrates' court or the Crown Court to discharge or vary a special measures direction under section 20(2) of the *Youth Justice and Criminal Evidence Act* 1999 must be in writing and each material change of circumstances which the applicant alleges has occurred since the direction was made must be set out. **8–60**

(2) An application under paragraph (1) must be sent to the court officer as soon as reasonably practicable after the change of circumstances occurs.

(3) The applicant must also send copies of the application to each party to the proceedings at the same time as the application is sent to the court officer.

(4) A party to whom an application is sent in accordance with paragraph (3) may oppose the application on the ground that it discloses no material change of circumstances.

(5) Rule 29.1(6) to (13) shall apply to an application to discharge or vary a special measures direction as it applies to an application for a direction.

Renewal application following a material change of circumstances

29.5.—(1) Where an application for a special measures direction has been refused by a magistrates' court or the Crown Court, the application may only be renewed ("renewal application") where there has been a material change of circumstances since the court refused the application. **8–61**

(2) The applicant must—

(a) identify in the renewal application each material change of circumstances which is alleged to have occurred; and

(b) send the renewal application to the court officer as soon as reasonably practicable after the change occurs.

(3) The applicant must also send copies of the renewal application to each of the parties to the proceedings at the same time as the application is sent to the court officer.

(4) A party to whom the renewal application is sent in accordance with paragraph (3) above may oppose the application on the ground that it discloses no material change of circumstances.

(5) Rules 29.1(6) to (13), 29.6 and 29.7 apply to a renewal application as they apply to the application which was refused.

Application for special measures direction for witness to give evidence by means of a live television link

29.6.—(1) Where the application for a special measures direction is made, in accordance with rule 29.1(2)(a), for a witness to give evidence by means of a live link, the following provisions of this rule shall also apply. **8–62**

(2) A party who seeks to oppose an application for a child witness to give evidence by means of a live link must, in order to comply with rule 29.1(5), state why in his view the giving of a special measures direction would not be likely to maximise the quality of the witness's evidence.

(3) However, paragraph (2) does not apply in relation to a child witness in need of special protection.

(4) Where a special measures direction is made enabling a witness to give evidence by means of a live link, the witness shall be accompanied at the live link only by persons acceptable to the court.

(5) If the special measures directions combine provisions for a witness to give evidence by means of a live link with provision for the examination of the witness to be conducted through an intermediary, the witness shall be accompanied at the live link only by—

(a) the intermediary; and

(b) such other persons as may be acceptable to the court.

Video recording of testimony from witnesses

8–63 **29.7.**—(1) Where an application is made to a magistrates' court or the Crown Court for a special measures direction enabling a video recording of an interview of a witness to be admitted as evidence in chief of the witness, the following provisions of this rule shall also apply.

(2) The application made in accordance with rule 29.1(1) must be accompanied by the video recording which it is proposed to tender in evidence and must include—

(a) the name of the defendant and the offence to be charged;

(b) the name and date of birth of the witness in respect of whom the application is made;

(c) the date on which the video recording was made;

(d) a statement as to whether, and if so at what point in the video recording, an oath was administered to, or a solemn declaration made by, the witness;

(e) a statement that, in the opinion of the applicant, either—

(i) the witness is available for cross-examination, or

(ii) the witness is not available for cross-examination and the parties have agreed that there is no need for the witness to be so available;

(f) a statement of the circumstances in which the video recording was made which complies with paragraph (4) of this rule; and

(g) the date on which the video recording was disclosed to the other party or parties.

(3) Where it is proposed to tender part only of a video recording of an interview with the witness, the application must specify that part and be accompanied by a video recording of the entire interview, including those parts which it is not proposed to tender in evidence, and by a statement of the circumstances in which the video recording of the entire interview was made which complies with paragraph (4) of this rule.

(4) The statement of the circumstances in which the video recording was made referred to in paragraphs (2)(f) and (3) of this rule shall include the following information, except in so far as it is contained in the recording itself—

(a) the times at which the recording commenced and finished, including details of interruptions;

(b) the location at which the recording was made and the usual function of the premises;

(c) in relation to each person present at any point during, or immediately before, the recording—

(i) their name, age and occupation,

(ii) the time for which each person was present, and

(iii) the relationship, if any, of each person to the witness and to the defendant;

(d) in relation to the equipment used for the recording—

(i) a description of the equipment,

(ii) the number of cameras used,

(iii) whether the cameras were fixed or mobile,

(iv) the number and location of the microphones,

(v) the video format used; and

(vi) whether it offered single or multiple recording facilities and, if so, which were used; and

(e) the location of the mastertape if the video recording is a copy and details of when and by whom the copy was made.

(5) If the special measures directions enabling a video recording of an interview of a witness to be admitted as evidence in chief of the witness with provision for the examination of the witness to be conducted through an intermediary, the information to be provided

under paragraph (4)(c) shall be the same as that for other persons present at the recording but with the addition of details of the declaration made by the intermediary under rule 29.9.

(6) If the special measures directions enabling a video recording of an interview of a witness to be admitted as evidence in chief of the witness with provision for the witness, in accordance with section 30 of the *Youth Justice and Criminal Evidence Act* 1999, to be provided with a device as an aid to communication during the video recording of the interview the information to be included under paragraph (4)(d) shall include also details of any such device used for the purposes of recording.

(7) A party who receives a recording under paragraph (2) must within 14 days of its receipt, notify the applicant and the court officer, in writing—

(a) whether he objects to the admission under section 27 of the 1999 Act of any part of the video recording or recordings disclosed, giving his reasons why it would not be in the interests of justice for the recording or any part of it to be admitted;

(b) whether he would agree to the admission of part of the video recording or recordings and, if so, which part or parts; and

(c) whether he wishes to be represented at any hearing of the application.

(8) A party who seeks to oppose an application for a special measures direction enabling a video recording of an interview of a child witness to be admitted as evidence in chief of the witness must, in order to comply with rule 29.1(6), state why in his view the giving of a special measures direction would not be likely to maximise the quality of the witness's evidence.

(9) However, paragraph (8) does not apply if the witness is a child witness in need of special protection.

(10) Notwithstanding the provisions of rule 29.1 and this rule, any video recording which the defendant proposes to tender in evidence need not be sent to the prosecution until the close of the prosecution case at the trial.

(11) The court may determine an application by the defendant to tender in evidence a video recording even though the recording has not, in accordance with paragraph (10), been served upon the prosecution.

(12) Where a video recording which is the subject of a special measures direction is sent to the prosecution after the direction has been made, the prosecutor may apply to the court for the direction to be varied or discharged.

(13) An application under paragraph (12) may be made orally to the court.

(14) A prosecutor who makes an application under paragraph (12) must state—

(a) why he objects to the admission under section 27 of the 1999 Act of any part of the video recording or recordings disclosed, giving his reasons why it would not be in the interests of justice for the recording or any part of it to be admitted; and

(b) whether he would agree to the admission of part of the video recording or recordings and, if so, which part or parts.

(15) The court must, before determining the application—

(a) direct a hearing of the application; and

(b) allow all the parties to the proceedings to be present and be heard on the application.

(16) The court officer must notify all parties to the proceedings of the decision of the court as soon as may be reasonable after the decision is given.

(17) Any decision varying a special measures direction must state whether the whole or specified parts of the video recording or recordings subject to the application are to be admitted in evidence.

Expert evidence in connection with special measures directions

29.8. Any party to proceedings in a magistrates' court or the Crown Court who proposes to adduce expert evidence (whether of fact or opinion) in connection with an application or renewal application for, or for varying or discharging, a special measures direction must, not less than 14 days before the date set for the trial to begin— **8–64**

(a) furnish the other party or parties and the court with a statement in writing of any finding or opinion which he proposes to adduce by way of such evidence; and notify the expert of this disclosure; and

(b) where a request is made to him in that behalf by any other party to those proceedings, provide that party also with a copy of (or if it appears to the party proposing to adduce the evidence to be more practicable, a reasonable opportunity to examine) the record of any observation, test, calculation or other procedure on which such finding or opinion is based and any document or other thing or substance in respect of which any such procedure has been carried out.

[This rule is printed as amended by the *Criminal Procedure (Amendment No. 2) Rules* 2006 (S.I. 2006 No. 2636).]

Intermediaries

8–64a **29.9.** The declaration required to be made by an intermediary in accordance with section 29(5) of the *Youth Justice and Criminal Evidence Act* 1999 shall be in the following form:

"I solemnly, sincerely and truly declare that I will well and faithfully communicate questions and answers and make true explanation of all matters and things as shall be required of me according to the best of my skill and understanding."

(2) Evidence through television link where witness outside United Kingdom

Criminal Justice Act 1988, s.32

8–65 **32.**—(1) A person other than the accused may give evidence through a live television link in proceedings to which subsection (1A) below applies if—

(a) the witness is outside the United Kingdom;

but evidence may not be so given without the leave of the court.

(1A) This subsection applies—

(a) to trials on indictment, appeals to the criminal division of the Court of Appeal and hearings of references under section 9 of the *Criminal Appeal Act* 1995; and

(b) to proceedings in youth courts and appeals to the Crown Court arising out of such proceedings and hearings of references under section 11 of the *Criminal Appeal Act* 1995 so arising.

(3) A statement made on oath by a witness outside the United Kingdom and given in evidence through a link by virtue of this section shall be treated for the purposes of section 1 of the *Perjury Act* 1911 as having been made in the proceedings in which it is given in evidence.

(4) [*Provision for rules of court.*]

[This section is printed as amended, and repealed in part, by the *CJA* 1991, s.55(2)–(6); the *CJPOA* 1994, Sched. 9, para. 32; the *CAA* 1995, Sched. 2, para. 16; the *YJCEA* 1999, s.67(3), and Sched. 6; and the *Courts Act 2003 (Consequential Amendments) Order* 2004 (S.I. 2004 No. 2035).]

8–66 Section 32, except subsections (1)(a) and (3) came into force on January 5, 1989: *Criminal Justice Act 1988 (Commencement No. 4) Order* 1988 (S.I. 1988 No. 2073). The *Criminal Justice Act 1988 (Commencement No. 12) Order* 1990 (S.I. 1990 No. 2084) brought the remainder of the section into force on November 26, 1990, for the following purposes:

(a) proceedings for murder, manslaughter or any other offence consisting of the killing of any person;

(b) proceedings being conducted by the Director of the Serious Fraud Office under section 1(5) of the *CJA* 1987;

(c) proceedings (other than those falling within para. (b) above) in which a notice of transfer has been given under section 4 of that Act by any of the authorities designated by subsection (2) of that section.

The proceedings must be by way of trial on indictment, appeal to the criminal division of the Court of Appeal or the hearing of a reference under section 9 of the *CAA* 1995.

The *Criminal Justice Act 1988 (Commencement No. 14) Order* 2004 (S.I. 2004 No. 2167) brought subsections (1)(a) and (3) into force, so far as they were not already in force, on September 1, 2004, but only in so far as they relate to proceedings within subsection (1A)(a). Furthermore, this order has no application to a trial, appeal or hearing that began before that date: art.3(1); and, for this purpose, the start of a trial is to be taken to occur when the jury are sworn, or would be sworn but for the making of an order under Part 7 of the *CJA* 2003 for trial without a jury: art.3(2), (3).

For rules of court made under this section, see rules 30.1 and 68.19 of the *Criminal Procedure Rules* 2005 (S.I. 2005 No. 384), *post*, § 8–67, and *ante*, § 7–220 respectively.

Criminal Procedure Rules 2005 (S.I. 2005 No. 384), Pt 30

Evidence through television link in the Crown Court where witness is outside the United Kingdom

30.1.—(1) Any party may apply for leave under section 32(1) of the *Criminal Justice Act* 1988 for evidence to be given through a live television link by a witness who is outside the United Kingdom. **8–67**

(2) An application under paragraph (1), and any matter relating thereto which, by virtue of the following provisions of this rule, falls to be determined by the Crown Court, may be dealt with in chambers by any judge of the Crown Court.

(3) An application under paragraph (1) shall be made by giving notice in writing, which shall be in the form set out in the Practice Direction.

(4) An application under paragraph (1) shall be made within 28 days after the date of the committal of the defendant or, as the case may be, of the giving of a notice of transfer under section 4(1)(c) of the *Criminal Justice Act* 1987, or of the service of copies of the documents containing the evidence on which the charge or charges are based under paragraph 1 of Schedule 3 to the *Crime and Disorder Act* 1998, or of the preferring of a bill of indictment in relation to the case.

(5) The period of 28 days in paragraph (4) may be extended by the Crown Court, either before or after it expires, on an application made in writing, specifying the grounds of the application. The court officer shall notify all the parties of the decision of the Crown Court.

(6) The notice under paragraph (3) or any application under paragraph (5) shall be sent to the court officer and at the same time a copy thereof shall be sent by the applicant to every other party to the proceedings.

(7) A party who receives a copy of a notice under paragraph (3) shall, within 28 days of the date of the notice, notify the applicant and the court officer, in writing—

(a) whether or not he opposes the application, giving his reasons for any such opposition, and

(b) whether or not he wishes to be represented at any hearing of the application.

(8) After the expiry of the period referred to in paragraph (7), the Crown Court shall determine whether an application under paragraph (1) is to be dealt with—

(a) without a hearing, or

(b) at a hearing at which the applicant and such other party or parties as the court may direct may be represented,

(c) and the court officer shall notify the applicant and, where necessary, the other party or parties, of the time and place of any such hearing.

(9) The court officer shall notify all the parties of the decision of the Crown Court in relation to an application under paragraph (1) and, where leave is granted, the notification shall state—

(a) the country in which the witness will give evidence,

(b) if known, the place where the witness will give evidence,

(c) where the witness is to give evidence on behalf of the prosecutor, or where disclosure is required by section 5(7) of the *Criminal Procedure and Investigations Act* 1996 (alibi) or by rules under section 81 of the *Police and Criminal Evidence Act* 1984 (expert evidence), the name of the witness,

(d) the location of the Crown Court at which the trial should take place, and

(e) any conditions specified by the Crown Court in accordance with paragraph (10).

(10) The Crown Court dealing with an application under paragraph (1) may specify that as a condition of the grant of leave the witness should give the evidence in the presence of a specified person who is able and willing to answer under oath or affirmation any questions the trial judge may put as to the circumstances in which the evidence is given, including questions about any persons who are present when the evidence is given and any matters which may affect the giving of the evidence.

(3) Evidence by video recording

Criminal Justice Act 2003, ss.137, 138

[Evidence by video recording

8–67a **137.**—(1) This section applies where—

(a) a person is called as a witness in proceedings for an offence triable only on indictment, or for a prescribed offence triable either way,

(b) the person claims to have witnessed (whether visually or in any other way)—

(i) events alleged by the prosecution to include conduct constituting the offence or part of the offence, or

(ii) events closely connected with such events,

(c) he has previously given an account of the events in question (whether in response to questions asked or otherwise),

(d) the account was given at a time when those events were fresh in the person's memory (or would have been, assuming the truth of the claim mentioned in paragraph (b)),

(e) a video recording was made of the account,

(f) the court has made a direction that the recording should be admitted as evidence in chief of the witness, and the direction has not been rescinded, and

(g) the recording is played in the proceedings in accordance with the direction.

(2) If, or to the extent that, the witness in his oral evidence in the proceedings asserts the truth of the statements made by him in the recorded account, they shall be treated as if made by him in that evidence.

(3) A direction under subsection (1)(f)—

(a) may not be made in relation to a recorded account given by the defendant;

(b) may be made only if it appears to the court that—

(i) the witness's recollection of the events in question is likely to have been significantly better when he gave the recorded account than it will be when he gives oral evidence in the proceedings, and

(ii) it is in the interests of justice for the recording to be admitted, having regard in particular to the matters mentioned in subsection (4).

(4) Those matters are—

(a) the interval between the time of the events in question and the time when the recorded account was made;

(b) any other factors that might affect the reliability of what the witness said in that account;

(c) the quality of the recording;

(d) any views of the witness as to whether his evidence in chief should be given orally or by means of the recording.

(5) For the purposes of subsection (2) it does not matter if the statements in the recorded account were not made on oath.

(6) In this section "prescribed" means of a description specified in an order made by the Secretary of State.]

[Video evidence: further provisions

8–67b **138.**—(1) Where a video recording is admitted under section 137, the witness may not give evidence in chief otherwise than by means of the recording as to any matter which, in the opinion of the court, has been dealt with adequately in the recorded account.

(2) The reference in subsection (1)(f) of section 137 to the admission of a recording includes a reference to the admission of part of the recording; and references in that section and this one to the video recording or to the witness's recorded account shall, where appropriate, be read accordingly.

(3) In considering whether any part of a recording should be not admitted under section 137, the court must consider—

(a) whether admitting that part would carry a risk of prejudice to the defendant, and

(b) if so, whether the interests of justice nevertheless require it to be admitted in view of the desirability of showing the whole, or substantially the whole, of the recorded interview.

(4) A court may not make a direction under section 137(1)(f) in relation to any proceedings unless—

(a) the Secretary of State has notified the court that arrangements can be made, in the area in which it appears to the court that the proceedings will take place, for implementing directions under that section, and

(b) the notice has not been withdrawn.

(5) Nothing in section 137 affects the admissibility of any video recording which would be admissible apart from that section.]

Sections 137 and 138 come into force on a day to be appointed. Section 141 of the Act stipulates that no provision of Part 3 of the Act (*i.e.* ss.98–141) has effect in relation to criminal proceedings begun before the commencement of that provision. As to this, see *R. v. Bradley* [2005] 1 Cr.App.R. 24, CA (*post*, § 13–2). **8–67c**

Criminal Justice Act 2003, s.140

Interpretation of Chapter 3

140. In this Chapter— **8–67d**

"criminal proceedings" means criminal proceedings in relation to which the strict rules of evidence apply;

"defendant", in relation to criminal proceedings, means a person charged with an offence in those proceedings;

"document" means anything in which information of any descrption is recorded, but not including any recording of sounds or moving images;

"oral evidence" includes evidence which, by reason of any disability, disorder or other impairment, a person called as a witness gives in writing or by signs or by way of any device;

"video recording" means any recording, on any medium, from which a moving image may by any means be produced, and includes the accompanying sound-track.

Chapter 3 comprises sections 137 to 140. For section 139 (memory-refreshing), see *post*, § 8–74. As to the definition of "criminal proceedings", see *R. v. Bradley* [2005] 1 Cr.App.R. 24, CA (*post*, § 13–2).

(4) Evidence by live link

Criminal Justice Act 2003, ss.51–56

Live links in criminal proceedings

51.—(1) A witness (other than the defendant) may, if the court so directs, give evidence through a live link in the following criminal proceedings. **8–67e**

(2) They are—

(a) a summary trial,

(b) an appeal to the Crown Court arising out of such a trial,

(c) a trial on indictment,

(d) an appeal to the criminal division of the Court of Appeal,

(e) the hearing of a reference under section 9 or 11 of the *Criminal Appeal Act* 1995,

(f) a hearing before a magistrates' court or the Crown Court which is held after the defendant has entered a plea of guilty, and

(g) a hearing before the Court of Appeal under section 80 of this Act.

(3) A direction may be given under this section—

(a) on an application by a party to the proceedings, or

(b) of the court's own motion.

(4) But a direction may not be given under this section unless—

(a) the court is satisfied that it is in the interests of the efficient or effective administration of justice for the person concerned to give evidence in the proceedings through a live link,

(b) it has been notified by the Secretary of State that suitable facilities for receiving evidence through a live link are available in the area in which it appears to the court that the proceedings will take place, and

(c) that notification has not been withdrawn.

(5) The withdrawal of such a notification is not to affect a direction given under this section before that withdrawal.

(6) In deciding whether to give a direction under this section the court must consider all the circumstances of the case.

(7) Those circumstances include in particular—

(a) the availability of the witness,

(b) the need for the witness to attend in person,
(c) the importance of the witness's evidence to the proceedings,
(d) the views of the witness,
(e) the suitability of the facilities at the place where the witness would give evidence through a live link,
(f) whether a direction might tend to inhibit any party to the proceedings from effectively testing the witness's evidence.

(8) The court must state in open court its reasons for refusing an application for a direction under this section and, if it is a magistrates' court, must cause them to be entered in the register of its proceedings.

Effect of, and rescission of, direction

8–67f **52.**—(1) Subsection (2) applies where the court gives a direction under section 51 for a person to give evidence through a live link in particular proceedings.

(2) The person concerned may not give evidence in those proceedings after the direction is given otherwise than through a live link (but this is subject to the following provisions of this section).

(3) The court may rescind a direction under section 51 if it appears to the court to be in the interests of justice to do so.

(4) Where it does so, the person concerned shall cease to be able to give evidence in the proceedings through a live link, but this does not prevent the court from giving a further direction under section 51 in relation to him.

(5) A direction under section 51 may be rescinded under subsection (3)—
(a) on an application by a party to the proceedings, or
(b) of the court's own motion.

(6) But an application may not be made under subsection (5)(a) unless there has been a material change of circumstances since the direction was given.

(7) The court must state in open court its reasons—
(a) for rescinding a direction under section 51, or
(b) for refusing an application to rescind such a direction,

and, if it is a magistrates' court, must cause them to be entered in the register of its proceedings.

8–67g **53.** [*Permission to magistrates' courts to sit at other locations according to availability of suitable facilities.*]

Warning to jury

8–67h **54.**—(1) This section applies where, as a result of a direction under section 51, evidence has been given through a live link in proceedings before the Crown Court.

(2) The judge may give the jury (if there is one) such direction as he thinks necessary to ensure that the jury gives the same weight to the evidence as if it had been given by the witness in the courtroom or other place where the proceedings are held.

Rules of court

8–67i **55.**—(1) Criminal Procedure Rules may make such provision as appears to the Criminal Procedure Rule Committee to be necessary or expedient for the purposes of this Part.

(2) Criminal Procedure Rules may in particular make provision—
(a) as to the procedure to be followed in connection with applications under section 51 or 52, and
(b) as to the arrangements or safeguards to be put in place in connection with the operation of live links.

(3) The provision which may be made by virtue of subsection (2)(a) includes provision—
(a) for uncontested applications to be determined by the court without a hearing,
(b) for preventing the renewal of an unsuccessful application under section 51 unless there has been a material change of circumstances,
(c) for the manner in which confidential or sensitive information is to be treated in connection with an application under section 51 or 52 and in particular as to its being disclosed to, or withheld from, a party to the proceedings.

(4) Nothing in this section is to be taken as affecting the generality of any enactment conferring power to make Criminal Procedure Rules.

[This section is printed as amended by the *Courts Act 2003 (Consequential Amendments) Order* 2004 (S.I. 2004 No. 2035).]

Interpretation of Part 8

56.—(1) In this Part— 8–67j

"legal representative" means *an authorised advocate or authorised litigator (as defined by section 119(1) of the* Courts and Legal Services Act *1990)* [a person who, for the purposes of the *Legal Services Act* 2007, is an authorised person in relation to an activity which constitutes the exercise of a right of audience or the conduct of litigation (within the meaning of that Act)],

"local justice area" has the same meaning as in the *Courts Act* 2003,

"witness", in relation to any criminal proceedings, means a person called, or proposed to be called, to give evidence in the proceedings.

(2) In this Part "live link" means a live television link or other arrangement by which a witness, while at a place in the United Kingdom which is outside the building where the proceedings are being held, is able to see and hear a person at the place where the proceedings are being held and to be seen and heard by the following persons.

(3) They are—

(a) the defendant or defendants,

(b) the judge or justices (or both) and the jury (if there is one),

(c) legal representatives acting in the proceedings, and

(d) any interpreter or other person appointed by the court to assist the witness.

(4) The extent (if any) to which a person is unable to see or hear by reason of any impairment of eyesight or hearing is to be disregarded for the purposes of subsection (2).

(5) Nothing in this Part is to be regarded as affecting any power of a court—

(a) to make an order, give directions or give leave of any description in relation to any witness (including the defendant or defendants), or

(b) to exclude evidence at its discretion (whether by preventing questions being put or otherwise).

[This section is printed as amended, and repealed in part, by S.I. 2004 No. 2035 (*ante*, § 8–67i); and the *Courts Act 2003 (Consequential Provisions) Order* 2005 (S.I. 2005 No. 886), art. 2, and Sched., para. 100; and as amended, as from a day to be appointed, by the *Legal Services Act* 2007, s.208(1), and Sched. 21, para. 145 (omission of italicised words, insertion of words in square brackets in definition of "legal representative").]

Section 55 came into force on January 29, 2004: *Criminal Justice Act 2003 (Commencement No. 2 and Saving Provisions) Order* 2004 (S.I. 2004 No. 81).

The *Criminal Justice Act 2003 (Commencement No. 19 and Transitional Provisions) Order* 2007 (S.I. 2007 No. 3451) brought sections 51, 52, 54 and 56 of the Act into force on December 7, 2007, but only in relation to proceedings in the Crown Court for an offence specified in article 2(3) (*viz.* offences under the *SOA* 2003, Pt 1, "rape or burglary with intent to rape", offences under the *SOA* 1956, ss.2 to 12 and 14 to 17, and offences contrary to the *MHA* 1983, s.128, the *Indecency with Children Act* 1960, s.1, and the *CLA* 1977, s.54). The fact that the proceedings in question may also be for some other offence is irrelevant: art. 3. However, the provision for the giving of such a direction only applies in relation "to any proceedings that begin" on or after December 7, 2007: art. 4.

(5) Witness preparation

In *R. v. Momodou and Limani* [2005] 2 Cr.App.R. 6, CA, it was said that there is a dramatic difference between witness training or coaching, and witness familiarisation; training or coaching of witnesses in criminal proceedings is not permitted; such rule minimises the risk, inherent in witness training, that a witness may tailor his evidence in light of what someone else said, and, equally, avoids any unfounded perception that he may have done so; and that was so even where the training takes place one-to-one with someone completely remote from the facts of the case; the witness may come, even unconsciously, to appreciate which aspects of his evidence are perhaps not quite consistent with what others are saying, or indeed not quite what is required of him; but the principle does not extend to preclude pre-trial arrangements to familiarise witnesses with the layout of the court, the likely sequence of events when the witness is giving evidence, and a balanced appraisal of the different responsibilities of the various participants; such arrangements should be welcomed; and nor does the principle prohibit the training of expert and similar witnesses in, for example, the technique of giving 8–67k comprehensive evidence of a specialist kind to a jury, or development of the ability to resist the inevitable pressure of going further in evidence than matters covered by the witness's specific expertise. The court added that, if arrangements are made for familiarisation with outside agencies rather than the witness service, then the following guidance should be followed; in relation to prosecution witnesses, the CPS should be informed in advance of any proposal for familiarisation; if appropriate after obtaining police input, they should be invited to comment in advance on the proposals; if relevant information comes to the police, the police should inform the CPS; the proposals for the intended familiarisation programme should be reduced into writing, rather than left to informal conversations; if, having examined them, the CPS suggest that the programme may be breaching the permitted limits, it should be amended; if the defence engage in the process, it would be wise for counsel's advice to be sought, again in advance, and again with written information about the nature and extent of the training; in any event, it is a matter of professional duty on counsel and solicitors to ensure that the judge is informed of any familiarisation process organised by the defence using outside agencies, and it will follow that the prosecution will be made aware of what has happened; the familiarisation process should normally be supervised or conducted by a lawyer, or someone who is responsible to a lawyer with experience of the criminal justice process, and preferably by an organisation accredited for the purpose by the Bar Council and Law Society; none of those involved should have any personal knowledge of the matters in issue; records should be maintained of all those present and the identity of those responsible for the familiarisation process, whenever it takes place; the programme should be retained, together with all the written material (or appropriate copies) used during the familiarisation sessions; none of the material should bear any similarity whatever to the issues in the proceedings to be attended by the witnesses, and nothing in it should play on or trigger the witness's recollection of events; if discussion of the instant criminal proceedings begins, as it almost inevitably will, it must be stopped, and advice given about precisely why it is impermissible, with a warning against the danger of evidence contamination and the risk that the course of justice may be perverted; a note should be made if and when any such warning is given; all documents used in the process should be retained, and if relevant to prosecution witnesses, handed to the CPS as a matter of course, and in relation to defence witnesses, produced to the court; none should be destroyed. The court added that it should be a matter of professional obligation for lawyers involved in these processes, or indeed the trial itself, to see that the guidance is followed.

B. EXAMINATION-IN-CHIEF

(1) Introduction

8–68 After the witness has been sworn or has made the necessary affirmation or declaration (see *ante*, §§ 8–26 *et seq.*) counsel for the party who calls him proceeds to examine him. The purpose of examination-in-chief is to adduce by the putting of proper questions which are not in leading form, relevant and admissible evidence which supports the contentions of the party who calls the witness.

(a) *Identification of witness*

Name

8–69 Ordinarily, a witness at the beginning of his examination-in-chief, is asked to state his full name. However, the law protects witnesses from being identified at three levels. At the lowest level, there are statutory restrictions on the publication of any material that would identify the witness. In particular, there are protections for the alleged victims of sexual offences, as to which, see *post*, §§ 20–1, 20–266 *et seq.*; and for children and young persons, as to which, see §§ 4–27 *et seq.* At the second level, a judge has a discretion at common law to permit a witness, whose identity will be known to the court and to the parties, to refrain from identifying himself openly so that the press and public may hear. In such cases, the witness will usually be permitted simply to write down his name. This discretion has typically been exercised in certain types of blackmail, the rationale being that there is a keen public interest in securing the conviction of blackmailers, an interest that is likely to be thwarted unless their victims are afforded this protection: see *R. v. Socialist Worker, ex p. Att.-Gen.* [1975] Q.B. 637 at 644, DC, where the court referred, without disapproval, to the course adopted by a judge at the Central Criminal Court of allowing former prostitutes giving evidence against a woman accused of exercising control over a prostitute to be referred to throughout by letters of the alphabet. The rationale was that, unless this limited anonymity was preserved, grave difficulty may be suffered in obtaining the necessary evidence in future similar cases. See also *Shaw v. DPP* [1962] A.C. 220, HL, where a similar device had been adopted at trial. As to the giving of directions prohibiting publication of matters exempted from disclosure in court, see the *Contempt of Court Act* 1981, s.11 (*post*, § 28–96).

In considering whether or not to permit a departure from the normal practice, a judge should bear in mind, *inter alia*, that publication of a witness's name and/or address may result in further witnesses coming forward, the existence of whom may not otherwise have been known. This consideration is equally relevant to any decision as to whether to afford the witness protection at the third and highest level. This involves complete anonymity from all save the party calling the witness and the court. The Court of Appeal approved this practice in certain circumstances in *R. v. Taylor (G.)*, *The Times*, August 17, 1994, which circumstances were effectively extended by that court's decision in *R. v. Davis (Iain)*; *R. v. Ellis* [2006] 2 Cr.App.R. 32. However, on appeal to the House of Lords in the first of those cases, the decision was reversed: see *R. v. Davis* [2008] 3 W.L.R. 125. In essence, their Lordships held that no conviction should be based solely or to a decisive extent upon the statements or testimony of anonymous witnesses, and that any such conviction would result from a trial which could not be regarded as fair. This, their Lordships said, was consistent with the common law and the jurisprudence of the European Court of Human Rights. **8–70**

The immediate response of the government was to publish the bill which became the *Criminal Evidence (Witness Anonymity) Act* 2008, having been rushed through Parliament with virtually no debate. It came into force (with a measure of retrospectivity) on Royal Assent (July 21, 2008), which was just 33 days after judgment was given in *R. v. Davis*.

Criminal Evidence (Witness Anonymity) Act 2008, s.1

Introduction

New rules relating to anonymity of witnesses

1.—(1) This Act provides for the making of witness anonymity orders in relation to witnesses in criminal proceedings. **8–71**

(2) The common law rules relating to the power of a court to make an order for securing that the identity of a witness in criminal proceedings is withheld from the defendant (or, on a defence application, from other defendants) are abolished.

(3) Nothing in this Act affects the common law rules as to the withholding of information on the grounds of public interest immunity.

Criminal Evidence (Witness Anonymity) Act 2008, ss.2–8

Witness anonymity orders

Witness anonymity orders

2.—(1) In this Act a "witness anonymity order" is an order made by a court that requires such specified measures to be taken in relation to a witness in criminal proceedings as the court considers appropriate to ensure that the identity of the witness is not disclosed in or in connection with the proceedings. **8–71a**

(2) The kinds of measures that may be required to be taken in relation to a witness include measures for securing one or more of the following—

(a) that the witness's name and other identifying details may be—

(i) withheld;

(ii) removed from materials disclosed to any party to the proceedings;

(b) that the witness may use a pseudonym;

(c) that the witness is not asked questions of any specified description that might lead to the identification of the witness;

(d) that the witness is screened to any specified extent;
(e) that the witness's voice is subjected to modulation to any specified extent.

(3) Subsection (2) does not affect the generality of subsection (1).

(4) Nothing in this section authorises the court to require—
(a) the witness to be screened to such an extent that the witness cannot be seen by—
(i) the judge or other members of the court (if any);
(ii) the jury (if there is one); or
(iii) any interpreter or other person appointed by the court to assist the witness;
(b) the witness's voice to be modulated to such an extent that the witness's natural voice cannot be heard by any persons within paragraph (a)(i) to (iii).

(5) In this section "specified" means specified in the witness anonymity order concerned.

Applications

8–71b 3.—(1) An application for a witness anonymity order to be made in relation to a witness in criminal proceedings may be made to the court by the prosecutor or the defendant.

(2) Where an application is made by the prosecutor, the prosecutor—
(a) must (unless the court directs otherwise) inform the court of the identity of the witness, but
(b) is not required to disclose in connection with the application—
(i) the identity of the witness, or
(ii) any information that might enable the witness to be identified,
to any other party to the proceedings or his or her legal representatives.

(3) Where an application is made by the defendant, the defendant—
(a) must inform the court and the prosecutor of the identity of the witness, but
(b) (if there is more than one defendant) is not required to disclose in connection with the application—
(i) the identity of the witness, or
(ii) any information that might enable the witness to be identified,
to any other defendant or his or her legal representatives.

(4) Accordingly, where the prosecutor or the defendant proposes to make an application under this section in respect of a witness, any relevant material which is disclosed by or on behalf of that party before the determination of the application may be disclosed in such a way as to prevent—
(a) the identity of the witness, or
(b) any information that might enable the witness to be identified,
from being disclosed except as required by subsection (2)(a) or (3)(a).

(5) "Relevant material" means any document or other material which falls to be disclosed, or is sought to be relied on, by or on behalf of the party concerned in connection with the proceedings or proceedings preliminary to them.

(6) The court must give every party to the proceedings the opportunity to be heard on an application under this section.

(7) But subsection (6) does not prevent the court from hearing one or more parties in the absence of a defendant and his or her legal representatives, if it appears to the court to be appropriate to do so in the circumstances of the case.

(8) Nothing in this section is to be taken as restricting any power to make rules of court.

On July 21, 2008, the Attorney-General issued guidelines on the overarching principles which a prosecutor must consider when deciding whether to apply for an order under this section: see Appendix A–273 *et seq.*

Conditions for making order

8–71c 4.—(1) This section applies where an application is made for a witness anonymity order to be made in relation to a witness in criminal proceedings.

(2) The court may make such an order only if it is satisfied that Conditions A to C below are met.

(3) Condition A is that the measures to be specified in the order are necessary—
(a) in order to protect the safety of the witness or another person or to prevent any serious damage to property, or

(b) in order to prevent real harm to the public interest (whether affecting the carrying on of any activities in the public interest or the safety of a person involved in carrying on such activities, or otherwise).

(4) Condition B is that, having regard to all the circumstances, the taking of those measures would be consistent with the defendant receiving a fair trial.

(5) Condition C is that it is necessary to make the order in the interests of justice by reason of the fact that it appears to the court that—

(a) it is important that the witness should testify, and
(b) the witness would not testify if the order were not made.

(6) In determining whether the measures to be specified in the order are necessary for the purpose mentioned in subsection (3)(a), the court must have regard (in particular) to any reasonable fear on the part of the witness—

(a) that the witness or another person would suffer death or injury, or
(b) that there would be serious damage to property,

if the witness were to be identified.

Relevant considerations

5.—(1) When deciding whether Conditions A to C in section 4 are met in the case of an application for a witness anonymity order, the court must have regard to— **8–71d**

(a) the considerations mentioned in subsection (2) below, and
(b) such other matters as the court considers relevant.

(2) The considerations are—

(a) the general right of a defendant in criminal proceedings to know the identity of a witness in the proceedings;
(b) the extent to which the credibility of the witness concerned would be a relevant factor when the weight of his or her evidence comes to be assessed;
(c) whether evidence given by the witness might be the sole or decisive evidence implicating the defendant;
(d) whether the witness's evidence could be properly tested (whether on grounds of credibility or otherwise) without his or her identity being disclosed;
(e) whether there is any reason to believe that the witness—
  (i) has a tendency to be dishonest, or
  (ii) has any motive to be dishonest in the circumstances of the case,

having regard (in particular) to any previous convictions of the witness and to any relationship between the witness and the defendant or any associates of the defendant;

(f) whether it would be reasonably practicable to protect the witness's identity by any means other than by making a witness anonymity order specifying the measures that are under consideration by the court.

Discharge or variation of order

6.—(1) A court that has made a witness anonymity order in relation to any criminal proceedings may subsequently discharge or vary (or further vary) the order if it appears to the court to be appropriate to do so in view of the provisions of sections 4 and 5 that applied to the making of the order. **8–71e**

(2) The court may do so—

(a) on an application made by a party to the proceedings if there has been a material change of circumstances since the relevant time, or
(b) on its own initiative.

(3) "The relevant time" means—

(a) the time when the order was made, or
(b) if a previous application has been made under subsection (2), the time when the application (or the last application) was made.

Warning to jury

7.—(1) Subsection (2) applies where, on a trial on indictment with a jury, any evidence has been given by a witness at a time when a witness anonymity order applied to the witness. **8–71f**

(2) The judge must give the jury such warning as the judge considers appropriate to ensure that the fact that the order was made in relation to the witness does not prejudice the defendant.

8. [*Special provisions for service courts.*] **8–71g**

Criminal Evidence (Witness Anonymity) Act 2008, ss.9–11

Application of provisions etc.

Proceedings to which new rules apply

9.—(1) Sections 2 to 8 apply to criminal proceedings in cases where— **8–71h**

(a) the trial or hearing begins on or after the day on which this Act is passed, or
(b) the trial or hearing has begun, but has not ended, before that day.

(2) Section 10 applies to certain proceedings falling within subsection (1)(b).

Pre-commencement anonymity orders: existing proceedings

8–71i **10.**—(1) This section has effect in relation to criminal proceedings in cases where—

(a) the trial or hearing has begun, but has not ended, before commencement, and
(b) the court has made a pre-commencement anonymity order in relation to a witness at the trial or hearing.

(2) Subsection (3) applies if the witness has not begun to give evidence under the terms of that order before commencement.

(3) In such a case the court—

(a) must consider whether that order was one that the court could have made if this Act had been in force at the material time,
(b) if it considers that that order was one that it could have made in those circumstances, may direct that the order is to remain in place, and
(c) otherwise, must discharge the order and consider whether instead it should make a witness anonymity order in relation to the witness in accordance with sections 2 to 5.

(4) Any witness anonymity order made by virtue of subsection (3)(c) must be made so as to come into effect immediately on the discharge of the pre-commencement anonymity order.

(5) Subsections (6) and (7) apply if the witness began before commencement to give evidence under the terms of the order mentioned in subsection (1)(b) (whether or not he or she has finished doing so).

(6) In such a case the court must consider whether the effect of that order is that the defendant has been prevented from receiving a fair trial, having regard (in particular) to—

(a) whether the order was one that the court could have made if this Act had been in force at the material time, and
(b) whether the court should exercise any power to give a direction to the jury (if there is one) regarding the evidence given under the terms of the order.

(7) If the court determines that the defendant has been prevented from receiving a fair trial, it must give such directions as it considers appropriate for and in connection with bringing the trial or hearing to a conclusion.

(8) In this section—

"commencement" means the day on which this Act is passed;

"pre-commencement anonymity order" means an order made before commencement that falls within section 1(2).

Pre-commencement anonymity orders: appeals

8–71j **11.**—(1) This section applies where—

(a) an appeal court is considering an appeal against a conviction in criminal proceedings in a case where the trial ended before commencement, and
(b) the court from which the appeal lies ("the trial court") made a pre-commencement anonymity order in relation to a witness at the trial.

(2) The appeal court—

(a) may not treat the conviction as unsafe solely on the ground that the trial court had no power at common law to make the order mentioned in subsection (1)(b), but
(b) must treat the conviction as unsafe if it considers—
  (i) that the order was not one that the trial court could have made if this Act had been in force at the material time, and
  (ii) that, as a result of the order, the defendant did not receive a fair trial.

(3) In this section—

"appeal court" means—

(a) the Court of Appeal;
(b) the Court of Appeal in Northern Ireland; or
(c) the Courts-Martial Appeal Court or the Court Martial Appeal Court;

"commencement" and "pre-commencement anonymity order" have the meanings given by section 10(8).

Criminal Evidence (Witness Anonymity) Act 2008, ss.12–15

Supplementary

Interpretation

12.—(1) In this Act— **8–71k**

"court" means—

(a) in relation to England and Wales, a magistrates' court, the Crown Court or the criminal division of the Court of Appeal;

(b) [*Northern Ireland*]; or

(c) a service court;

"criminal proceedings" means—

(a) in relation to a court within paragraph (a) or (b) above, criminal proceedings consisting of a trial or other hearing at which evidence falls to be given;

(b) [*service courts*];

"the defendant", in relation to any criminal proceedings, means any person charged with an offence to which the proceedings relate (whether or not convicted);

"prosecutor" means an individual or body charged with duties to conduct criminal prosecutions;

"service court" has the meaning given by subsection (2);

"service offence" has the meaning given by subsection (3);

"witness", in relation to any criminal proceedings, means any person called, or proposed to be called, to give evidence at the trial or hearing in question;

"witness anonymity order" has the meaning given by section 2.

(2) [*Definition of "service court"*.]

(3) [*Definition of "service offence"*.]

13. [*Commencement: Royal Assent* (ante, *§ 8–70*).] **8–71l**

Expiry of power to make witness anonymity orders

14.—(1) No witness anonymity order may be made under this Act after the relevant date. **8–71m**

(2) Subject to subsection (3), the relevant date is 31 December 2009.

(3) The Secretary of State may by order provide for the relevant date to be a date specified in the order that falls not more than 12 months after—

(a) 31 December 2009, or

(b) (if an order has already been made under this subsection) the date specified in the last order.

(4) Nothing in this section affects—

(a) the continuation in effect of a witness anonymity order made before the relevant date, or

(b) the power to discharge or vary such an order under section 6.

(5) An order under subsection (3)—

(a) is to be made by statutory instrument; and

(b) may not be made unless a draft of the instrument containing the order has been laid before and approved by a resolution of each House of Parliament.

15. [*Short title and extent.*]

Practice Direction (Criminal Proceedings: Consolidation), para. I.15 (as inserted by Consolidated Criminal Practice Direction (Amendment No. 21) (Criminal Proceedings: Witness Anonymity Orders; Forms), unreported, August 29, 2008)

Witness anonymity orders

I.15.1 Pending the making by the Criminal Procedure Rule Committee of specific rules for the purpose, this direction sets out the procedure to be followed on an application for a witness anonymity order. … . **8–71n**

Case management

I.15.2 Where such an application is proposed, with the parties' active assistance the court should set a realistic timetable, in accordance with the duties imposed by rules 3.2 and 3.3. Where possible, the trial judge should determine the application, and any hearing should be attended by the parties' trial advocates. **8–71o**

Service of evidence and disclosure of prosecution material pending an application

8–71p **I.15.3** Where the prosecutor proposes an application … it is not necessary for that application to have been determined before the proposed evidence is served. In most cases an early indication of what that evidence will be if an order is made will be consistent with a party's duties under rules 1.2 and 3.3. The prosecutor should serve with the other prosecution evidence a witness statement setting out the proposed evidence, redacted in such a way as to prevent disclosure of the witness's identity, as permitted by section 3(4) … . Likewise the prosecutor should serve with other prosecution material disclosed under the *Criminal Procedure and Investigations Act* 1996 any such material appertaining to the witness, similarly redacted.

The application

8–71q **I.15.4** An application … should be made as early as possible and within any period directed by the court. It should be in writing and in two parts, one containing non-confidential information and the other confidential information. The applicant … should serve the non-confidential part on the other parties and on the court. The confidential part should be served only on the court and, where the applicant is a defendant, on the prosecutor. In accordance with rules 1.2 and 3.3, the applicant must provide the court with all available information relevant to the considerations to which the Act requires a court to have regard.

I.15.5 The non-confidential part … should contain nothing that might reveal the witness's identity. Consistently with that, it should:

(a) specify the measures proposed by the applicant;

(b) explain how the proposed order meets the conditions prescribed by section 4 …;

(c) explain why no measures other than those proposed will suffice, such as [see *post*]; and

(d) attach:

- (i) a witness statement setting out the proposed evidence, redacted in such a way as to prevent disclosure of the witness's identity,
- (ii) on a prosecutor's application, any prosecution material disclosed under the [1996 Act] appertaining to the witness, similarly redacted, and
- (iii) any defence statement that has been served, or as much information from any other source as may be available to the applicant which gives particulars of the defence.

I.15.6 The confidential part … should:

(a) be clearly marked to show that its contents are confidential; and

(b) contain the information withheld from the non-confidential part, including:

- (i) the identity of the witness, or (where a prosecutor so applies) the reasons why the applicant invites the court to exercise the power under section 3(2)(a) … to waive that requirement,
- (ii) the unredacted witness statement from which the redacted version has been prepared,
- (iii) on a prosecutor's application, the unredacted version of any prosecution material from which a redacted version has been prepared, and
- (iv) such further material as the applicant relies on to establish that the proposed order meets the conditions prescribed by section 4 … .

I.15.7 The confidential part … usually should be served at the same time as the non-confidential part. Exceptionally, and subject to any contrary direction by the court, its service may be postponed until after a hearing of the non-confidential part.

Response to the application

8–71r **I.15.8** A party upon whom an application for a witness anonymity order is served should serve a response on the other parties and on the court within 14 days. That period may be extended or shortened in the court's discretion.

I.15.9 To avoid the risk of injustice a respondent must actively assist the court. If not already done, a respondent defendant should serve a defence statement under section 5 or 6 of the [1996 Act], so that the court is fully informed of what is in issue. The prosecutor's continuing duty to disclose material under section 7A of [that Act] may be engaged by a defendant's application for a witness anonymity order. Therefore a prosecutor's response should include confirmation that that duty has been considered. Nothing disclosed under the 1996 Act by a respondent prosecutor to a respondent defendant should contain anything that might reveal the witness's identity. A respondent prosecutor should provide an applicant defendant and the court with all available information relevant to the considerations to which the Act requires a court to have regard, whether or not that information falls to be disclosed under the 1996 Act.

Determination of the application

I.15.10 ... [A] hearing may not be needed if none is sought. ... Where the court directs a hearing ... then it should allow adequate time for service of the representations in response. **8–71s**

I.15.11 The hearing ... usually should be in private. ... In the Crown Court, a recording of the proceedings will be made, in accordance with rule 65.8(2). The Crown Court officer must treat such a recording in the same way as the recording of an application for a public interest ruling. It must be kept in secure conditions, and the arrangements made by the Crown Court officer for any transcription must impose restrictions that correspond with those under rule 65.9(2)(a).

I.15.12 At a hearing the court will receive, usually in this sequence, representations by: (i) the applicant, in each respondent's presence; (ii) each respondent; (iii) the applicant in reply, in each respondent's presence; then finally (iv) the applicant in elaboration of the confidential part of the application, in a respondent defendant's absence but in the presence of a respondent prosecutor.

I.15.13 Where the confidential part of the application is served on the court before the last stage of the hearing, the court may prefer not to read the information in that part until that last stage.

I.15.14 The court may adjourn the hearing at any stage, and should do so if its duty under rule 3.2 so requires.

I.15.15 On a prosecutor's application, the court is likely to be assisted by the attendance of a senior investigator or other person of comparable authority who is familiar with the case.

I.15.16 During the last stage of the hearing it is essential that the court test thoroughly the information supplied in confidence in order to satisfy itself that the conditions prescribed by the Act are met. At that stage, if the court concludes that this is the only way in which it can satisfy itself as to a relevant condition or consideration, exceptionally it may invite the applicant to present the proposed witness to be questioned by the court. Any such questioning should be carried out at such a time, and the witness brought to the court in such a way, as to prevent disclosure of his or her identity.

I.15.17 The court may ask [in accordance with the principles in *R. v. H.*, *post*, § 12–80d] the Attorney-General to appoint special counsel to assist. ... Whether to accede to such a request is a matter for the Attorney-General, and adequate time should be allowed for the consideration of such a request.

I.15.18 Following a hearing the court should announce its decision ... in the parties' presence and in public. The court should give such reasons as it is possible to give without revealing the witness's identity. In the Crown Court, the court will be conscious that reasons given in public may be reported and reach the jury. Consequently, the court should ensure that nothing in its decision or its reasons could undermine any warning it may give jurors under section 7(2) ... . A record of the reasons must be kept. ... .

Order

I.15.19 Where the court makes [an] ... order it is essential that the measures to be taken are clearly specified in a written record of that order approved by the court and issued on its behalf. An order made in a magistrates' court must be recorded in the court register, in accordance with rule 6.1. **8–71t**

I.15.20 Self-evidently, the written record of the order must not disclose the identity of the witness to whom it applies. However, it is essential that there be maintained some means of establishing a clear correlation between witness and order, and especially where in the same proceedings witness anonymity orders are made in respect of more than one witness, specifying different measures in respect of each. Careful preservation of the application for the order, including the confidential part, ordinarily will suffice for this purpose.

Discharge or variation of the order

I.15.21 Section 6 ... allows the court to discharge or vary a witness anonymity order ... . Rule 3.6 allows the parties to apply for the variation of a pre-trial direction where circumstances have changed. **8–71u**

I.15.22 The court should keep under review the question of whether the conditions for making an order are met. In addition, consistently with the parties' duties under rules 1.2 and 3.3, it is incumbent on each, and in particular on the applicant for the order, to keep the need for it under review.

I.15.23 Where the court considers the discharge or variation of an order, the procedure that it adopts should be appropriate to the circumstances. As a general rule, that procedure should approximate to the procedure for determining an application for an order. The court may need to hear further representations by the applicant for the order in the absence of a respondent defendant and that defendant's representatives.

Retention of confidential material

8–71v **I.15.24** If retained by the court, confidential material must be stored in secure conditions by the court officer. Alternatively, subject to such directions as the court may give, such material may be committed to the safe keeping of the applicant or any other appropriate person in exercise of the powers conferred by (as the case may be) rule 3.5(1), 63.4(b) or 65.8(2)(c). If the material is released to any such person, the court should ensure that it will be available to the court at trial.

8–71w The reference to various rules are to the *Criminal Procedure Rules* 2005 (S.I. 2005 No. 384). For rules 1.1 and 1.2, see *ante*, § 4–84b; for rules 3.2 and 3.3, see *ante*, § 4–84c; for rule 3.5, see *ante*, § 4–84d; for rule 63.4, see *ante*, § 2–180c; for rule 65.8, see *ante*, § 7–313h; and for rule 65.9, see *ante*, § 7–313i.

The suggested alternative measures (see para. I.15.5(c)) are an admission, reporting restrictions or a restriction on public access (see *ante*, §§ 4–3 *et seq.*), a special measure under the *YJCEA* 1999 (*ante*, §§ 8–52 *et seq.*) or the admission of the witness's statement under the *CJA* 2003, s.116 (*post*, § 11–15).

Address

8–71x In July 1996, Lord Bingham C.J. approved the Criminal Justice Consultative Council's Trial Issues Group's Statement of National Standards of Witness Care in the Criminal Justice System (see 161 J.P.N. 353). This approval has never been published as a practice direction in any of the law reports. The statement provides that unless it is necessary for evidential purposes, witnesses should not be required to disclose their addresses in open court.

Occupation

8–71y The standard practice of asking a witness his occupation is unobjectionable: *R. v. D.S.* [1999] Crim.L.R. 911, CA.

(b) *Leading questions*

8–72 It is a general rule that, in a direct examination of a witness, he shall not be asked leading questions, or, in other words, questions framed in such a manner as to suggest to the witness the answers required of him. The answers to leading questions are not *per se* inadmissible, see *Moor v. Moor* [1954] 1 W.L.R. 927, although the weight which can properly be attached to them may be substantially reduced, see *R. v. Wilson*, 9 Cr.App.R. 124, CCA. To this general rule, however, there are a few exceptions. Where a witness swears to a certain fact, and another witness is called for the purpose of contradicting him, the latter may be asked, in direct terms, whether that fact ever took place: *Courteen v. Touse* (1807) 1 Camp. 43.

Questions which are merely introductory to others that are material or which relate to undisputed matter are in general allowed to be asked in direct terms, without objection: *R. v. Robinson*, 61 J.P. 520. Leading questions may be put where the party calling the witness is given leave to treat him as hostile, see *post*, §§ 8–94 *et seq.*

(c) *Examination-in-chief by two counsel*

8–73 When a witness is under the examination of a junior counsel, the leading counsel may interpose and finish the examination; but after one counsel has brought his examination to a close, no other counsel on the same side can put a question to the witness: *Doe v. Roe* (1809) 2 Camp. 280.

(2) Matters arising in examination-in-chief

(a) *Refreshing memory*

Criminal Justice Act 2003, s.139

Use of documents to refresh memory

139.—(1) A person giving oral evidence in criminal proceedings about any matter may, at any stage in the course of doing so, refresh his memory of it from a document made or verified by him at an earlier time if— **8–74**

(a) he states in his oral evidence that the document records his recollection of the matter at that earlier time, and

(b) his recollection of the matter is likely to have been significantly better at that time than it is at the time of his oral evidence.

(2) Where—

(a) a person giving oral evidence in criminal proceedings about any matter has previously given an oral account, of which a sound recording was made, and he states in that evidence that the account represented his recollection of the matter at that time,

(b) his recollection of the matter is likely to have been significantly better at the time of the previous account than it is at the time of his oral evidence, and

(c) a transcript has been made of the sound recording,

he may, at any stage in the course of giving his evidence, refresh his memory of the matter from that transcript.

As to the interpretation of this section, see section 140 of the Act, *ante*, § 8–67d. **8–75**

Common law

The common law rule was that a witness was allowed to refresh his memory by reference to any writing concerning the facts to which he testified, and which had been made or verified by himself at a time when his memory was clear: *Att.-Gen.'s Reference (No. 3 of 1979)*, 69 Cr.App.R. 411 at 414, CA. The 2003 Act does not expressly purport to abolish the rules of common law in relation to memory refreshing, but it is submitted that the intention behind the legislation was that the new provision should in effect supersede the common law. However, from the mass of authority that had built up at common law, certain of the authorities would appear to have continuing potential relevance. **8–76**

When a witness may be permitted to refresh his memory

Quite apart from the requirements of the rule itself being satisfied, there is frequently much preliminary (albeit unnecessary) discussion in court between judge and counsel, once counsel (usually counsel for the Crown) has applied for the witness to be allowed to refresh his memory. This situation arises not so often when police officers are giving evidence (when, if there is any argument, it is almost always confined to whether the requirements of the rule itself are satisfied), but when a private witness is giving evidence and the document in question is the "contemporaneous" statement he made to the police. If, at the stage the application is made, the witness's evidence is of importance (as it usually is), the defence often object. The basis of the objection is variously expressed. Sometimes it is said that the witness cannot refresh his memory because "he has not asked to." On other occasions, where the witness has materially departed from his statement (*e.g.*, instead of saying he cannot remember the time, he has said it was 5.00 p.m., having said 3.00 p.m. in the statement), it is said that it is too late to refresh his memory—he has given his answer. This argument is often taken further and it is asserted that what the Crown is seeking to do (the witness having given "the wrong answer"—5.00 p.m.) is to cross-examine its own witness (see, *e.g. R. v. Sutton*, 94 Cr.App.R. 70 at 73, CA). On other occasions, counsel for the Crown, as a precaution, seeks leave for the witness to refresh his memory before there has been any departure from the statement. Such an application is often met with the objection that the application is premature. In short, the only situation in which objections of this sort are forestalled is when the witness himself says "I cannot remember," and witnesses, for a variety of reasons, are reluctant to say that. Sometimes they do not appreciate the crucial importance of the evidence they are then giving; sometimes they appreciate it only too well and are reluctant to appear imprecise about what they are recollecting; **8–77** and sometimes they in fact have forgotten, but do not realise it, and give a precise answer which they then believe to be true.

8–78 In considering the answer to the question—"when may a witness be permitted to refresh his memory?" the following points should be borne in mind.

(a) That the timing of the application should depend upon the twin chances of the witness who has forgotten (i) realising it, and (ii) saying so, is as absurd as it is to suggest that the witness who has forgotten but does not realise it (and gives a mistaken answer) can never refresh his memory on the point in question (see *Sutton*, *ante*).

(b) The application in question is counsel's not the witness's.

(c) The "memory refreshing" principles apply equally to notes made by a defendant, see *R. v. Britton*, 85 Cr.App.R. 14, CA.

In *R. v. Tyagi*, *The Times*, July 21, 1986, CA, the suggestion that the witness should refresh his memory came from the judge: it appears that he was allowed to do so outside court while the court adjourned. The Court of Appeal said that the fact that the suggestion came from the judge was nothing to the point. "It is the proper function of the judge where the interests of justice demand to intervene in this way provided that the process is made plain to the jury" (*per* Ralph Gibson L.J.). The court also said that it would have been preferable for the witness to have remained in court and to have had the document in front of him in the witness box.

By whom document may be written: verification

8–79 The writing may have been made by either the witness himself or by others, provided that in the latter case it was verified by the witness: *R. v. Langton* (1876) 2 Q.B.D. 296; *R. v. Mills and Rose*, 46 Cr.App.R. 336 at 342, CCA.

8–80 A witness may, for this purpose, refer to a newspaper report read by him. "If a man at the time he has a recollection of certain facts reads a document containing a statement, which he knows to be true, of the facts, he may again refer to it to refresh his memory although, at the time he first read it, he made no memorandum": *Dyer v. Best* (1866) 4 H. & C. 189 at 192; *cf. R. v. McLean*, 52 Cr.App.R. 80, CA, where A, the victim of an attack, dictated the registration number of the get-away car some three minutes later to B who wrote it down. A did not see what B had written and could not remember at the trial what he had dictated. It was held that, for B to give evidence of what A had told him was in contravention of the hearsay rule. The fact that B could also produce the piece of paper was immaterial. See also *Jones v. Metcalfe* [1967] 1 W.L.R. 1286, DC.

8–81 In *R. v. Kelsey*, 74 Cr.App.R. 213, CA, the court held that a witness of an incident involving a motor car could refresh his memory as to the registration number from a note of it he dictated to a policeman who then read it back to him. The police officer gave evidence that the note used in court was the one he had made at the time. What has to be shown is that the witness had verified (in the sense of satisfying himself while the matters were fresh in his mind) (a) that the record had been made; and (b) that it was accurate. In cases such as this, where the witness did not see the note, it is necessary for the maker to prove that the note used in court was the one the witness saw being made and the one he heard read back.

Independent recollection

8–82 It is not essential that the witness should have any independent recollection of the facts: *R. v. Bryant and Dickson*, 31 Cr.App.R. 146, CCA.

Originals and copies

8–83 Section 139 of the 2003 Act (*ante*) is silent as to the use of a copy of the document that was made or verified by the witness. The unmistakeable intent of the Act being to relax the rule relating to the use of a document by a witness for the purpose of refreshing his memory, it seems inconceivable that the courts will not permit the use of a copy at least in those cases where a copy document could have been used prior to the commencement of the Act.

8–84 At common law, the rule was that where the original document was in existence and the witness had no recollection of the facts which was independent of what he saw recorded on the other document, a copy document could not be used and the original had to be produced: *Doe v. Perkins* (1790) 3 T.R. 749; *Tanner v. Taylor* (1790) 3 T.R. 754; and *R. v. Harvey* (1869) 11 Cox 546. However, where the copy was made or verified by the witness while the facts were fresh in his recollection it would be admissible on the footing of a duplicate or quasi-original: *Burton v. Plummer* (1834) 2 A. & E. 341; and *Horne v. Mackenzie* (1839) 6 C. & F. 628. Where the original had been lost or destroyed, a copy proved to be correct either by the witness or some third person could be used. In *Topham v. McGregor* (1844) 1 C. & K. 320, a journalist was allowed to refresh his memory by a 14-year-old newspaper, although he had no independent recollection, proof being given by the editor that the manuscript was lost and that the newspaper was a copy of it and by the witness that he had no doubt the facts stated therein were true; see also *Talbot v. Cusack* (1864) 17 Ir.C.L.R. 213. Where a copy was either not proved to be correct, see *Alcock v. Royal Exchange Assurance* (1849) 13 Q.B. 292, or consisted of an imperfect extract made by the witness, see *R. v. St. Martins* (1834) 2 A. & E. 210, it could not be used to refresh memory, whether or not the original was in existence.

In *R. v. Cheng*, 63 Cr.App.R. 20, CA, it was held that a judge should allow a witness to refresh his memory from a statement prepared from his original notes, provided that it is substantially the same as the notes, even though it does not contain all the material in them, and to that extent is not an exact copy. If the statement or transcription bears little relation to the original then a different situation arises. The judge, in the exercise of his discretion, would be entitled to refuse to allow a witness to refresh his memory from such an imperfect source of information. Similarly, where an officer, having made brief jottings of questions and answers during an interview, later compiled his notebook from these jottings at a time when the interview was still fresh in his mind he could refresh his memory from the notebook while giving evidence notwithstanding that at the time of giving evidence he could neither decipher the jottings nor recollect the full content of the questions and answers: *Att.-Gen.'s Reference (No. 3 of 1979)*, 69 Cr.App.R. 411 (notebook compiled within two hours of the interview).

Inadmissible documents may be used

See *Maugham v. Hubbard* (1828) 8 B. & C. 14; *Birchall v. Bullough* [1896] 1 Q.B. 325; and *R. v. Mann*, 49 J.P. 743. **8–85**

Exhibiting memory refreshing documents: circumstances and effect

There is a long-standing rule of the common law regulating the admissibility of memory refreshing documents. Cross-examining counsel may inspect the note in order to check its contents and he may cross-examine on it. If cross-examination is confined to those parts of the note which have already been used by the witness to refresh his memory, the document cannot by reason of the inspection and/or the cross-examination become evidence in the case. If the cross-examination strays beyond that part of the note which the witness has used, the party calling the witness may insist on it being treated as evidence in the case and it will thereupon become an exhibit (see *Gregory v. Tavernor* (1833) 6 C. & P. 280 at 281; *Senat v. Senat* [1965] 2 All E.R. 505 at 511). The distinction between looking at notes used by a witness to refresh his memory and calling for and looking at other documents should be borne well in mind. In the latter case, the party calling for and inspecting is bound to put the document(s) in evidence if he is required to do so (see *Palmer v. Maclear and M'Grath* (1858) 1 Sw. & Tr. 149 at 151 and *Senat v. Senat, ante*). **8–86**

At common law, the effect of exhibiting a memory refreshing document was simply to show consistency in the witness producing it. Such a document was not evidence of the truth of the facts stated in it: *R. v. Britton*, 85 Cr.App.R. 14, CA, and see *R. v. Sekhon*, 85 Cr.App.R. 19, CA, *post*. Usually, the document in question is used by a prosecution witness and the application to have it exhibited will be made by the Crown. As indicated in *R. v. Virgo*, 67 Cr.App.R. 323, CA, in any particular case where the judge takes the view that the interests of justice so require, he will have a discretion to refuse to allow the document to go before the jury, if this could give rise to prejudice to the defendant: *Britton*, *ante*. The *CJA* 2003, s.120 (*post*, § 11–34) does not purport to alter the common law rule as to the circumstances in which a memory refreshing document may be exhibited, but it does provide that the effect of exhibiting such a document is that it becomes evidence as to the truth of its contents.

Where a witness, before giving evidence for the prosecution has refreshed his memory from a notebook outside the court, but does not use the notebook in the witness-box, the defence is none the less entitled to examine it and cross-examine upon the relevant matters in it: *Owen v. Edwards*, 77 Cr.App.R. 191, DC.

Officers' notebooks, police observation logs and contemporaneous (unsigned) interview notes

8–87 In *R. v. Bass* [1953] 1 Q.B. 680, 37 Cr.App.R. 51, CCA, police officers had denied collaborating in making the notes in their books. The notes were in identical terms. The trial judge refused defence counsel's application for the notebooks to be exhibited. It was held that the credibility and accuracy of the two officers was vital and as they had denied collaborating in the making of their notes the jury should have been given the opportunity of examining them. See also *R. v. Benjamin*, 8 Cr.App.R. 146, CCA, and *R. v. Callum* [1975] R.T.R. 415, CA (applying *Bass*, *ante*). *Cf. R. v. Fenlon*, 71 Cr.App.R. 307, CA, and *R. v. Dillon*, 85 Cr.App.R. 27, CA. *Fenlon* and *Dillon*, however, must be read in the light of *R. v. Sekhon*, 85 Cr.App.R. 19, CA.

In *Sekhon*, the court considered the status and admissibility of an observation log maintained by one officer which was based both on what he himself observed and on what was reported to him by other officers engaged in the same activity. The entries made as a result of information supplied by other officers were verified by those officers signing the appropriate entries at the first convenient opportunity. The Court of Appeal rejected a submission that a distinction was to be drawn between notes used to refresh the memory of a witness which were made by him of matters he observed and a record such as this log. The position in relation to both categories was reasonably clear.

(a) They could both be referred to by witnesses to refresh their memory if the usual basis for that to be done was established without being put before the jury.
(b) Documents used to refresh memory must be available for inspection by the other parties who could cross-examine on the documents if it was relevant to do so. In the majority of cases the fact that there was such cross-examination would not make the record evidence in the case nor would it be necessary for a jury to inspect the document and it would not be appropriate for the record to become an exhibit.
(c) Where, however, the nature of the cross-examination involved a suggestion that the witness had subsequently made up his evidence, which would usually involve if not expressly at least by implication, the allegation that the record was concocted, the record might be admissible to show consistency, and if the nature of the record assisted as to that, to show whether it was genuine, that is to say whether or not it has the appearance of being a contemporaneous record which had not been subsequently altered.
(d) Where the record was inconsistent with the witness's evidence it could be admitted as evidence of that inconsistency.
(e) It was also appropriate for the record to be put before the jury where it was difficult for the jury to follow the cross-examination of the witness who had refreshed his memory without having the record or, in practice, copies before them.
(f) However, subject to one exception, where the record was permitted to go before the jury, it would not be placed before them as evidence of the truth of the contents of the record. Its more limited purpose was as a "tool" to assist the jury in evaluating the truth of the evidence given in the witness box.
(g) There may be cases where it was also convenient to use the record as an *aide memoire* as to the witness's evidence where that evidence was long and involved. Care should be exercised in adopting that course where the evidence and therefore the record were bitterly contested.

(h) Although normally ((f), *ante*) the document when admitted was not evidence of the truth of its contents, in those cases where it provided, because of its nature, material by which its authenticity could be judged, then in respect of that material and only for the purpose of assessing its authenticity, it could amount to evidence in the case.

With the commencement of section 120 of the 2003 Act (*ante*), the issue as to whether or not the memory-refreshing document is made an exhibit (*i.e.* is admitted in evidence) will be crucial. Once admitted, it may be used by the tribunal of fact not just in the ways identified in *Sekhon*; it will be evidence as to the truth of the matters stated/ recorded therein. **8–88**

Tape recordings

In *R. v. Mills and Rose*, 46 Cr.App.R. 336, CCA, it was held that a police officer could refresh his memory by referring to a note of a conversation between two defendants which he had made from a tape recording of the conversation. While the conversation was being recorded he could hear what was said and the note agreed with his recollection of what he had heard. **8–89**

Interpreters

Where a defendant is interviewed by the police through an interpreter only the interpreter can give evidence of the questions which he put to the defendant on behalf of the police and of the answers given to him by the defendant: *R. v. Attard*, 43 Cr.App.R. 90, CCC (Gorman J.). Accordingly, in the absence of any note made by the interpreter of the questions put and answers given, he should be asked to initial the record of the interview made in the notebook of the police officer conducting the interview so that it can be used by the interpreter to refresh his memory when giving evidence. **8–90**

(b) *Tape recordings and transcripts*

For use of a tape recording as a memory refresher, see section 139(2) of the *CJA* 2003, *ante*, § 8–74, and *R. v. Mills and Rose*, *ante*, § 8–89. **8–91**

For the relevant considerations in determining the question of admissibility in the absence of the jury, see *R. v. Robson and Harris* [1972] 1 W.L.R. 651, CCC (Shaw J.), and *R. v. Stevenson*, 55 Cr.App.R. 171, Assizes (Kilner Brown J.), *ante*, § 4–290.

The following general observations upon this category of evidence were made in *R. v. Ali and Hussain* [1966] 1 Q.B. 688, 49 Cr.App.R. 230, CCA:

> "... provided the accuracy of the recording can be proved and the voices recorded properly identified; provided also that the evidence is relevant and otherwise admissible ... a tape recording is admissible in evidence. Such evidence should always be regarded with some caution and assessed in the light of all the circumstances. ... There can be no question of laying down any exhaustive set of rules by which the admissibility of such evidence should be judged" (at pp. 701, 238).
>
> "Having a transcript of a tape recording is ... a most obvious convenience and a great aid to the jury. Provided that a jury is guided by what they hear themselves and on that they base their ultimate decision we can see no objection to a copy of a transcript, properly proved, being put before them" (at p. 702, (not included in 49 Cr.App.R.)).

In *Ali and Hussain*, the trial judge agreed to undertake an inquiry into the weight of the evidence in the absence of the jury. The court stated that although such cases must be rare as the weight to be attached to any evidence is a matter for the jury, there can be cases where the issues of admissibility and weight overlay each other and the judge was justified in doing what he did. In *R. v. Senat and Sin*, 52 Cr.App.R. 282, CA, recordings of conversations obtained through telephone tapping by private individuals were held to be admissible.

See also *Butera v. DPP (Vic.)* (1988) 76 A.L.R. 45, in which the High Court of Australia considered issues of admissibility of covert tape recordings of conversations, the translation of those conversations into the language used by the court, the making of transcripts of the translations and the use which could be made at trial of such transcripts.

(c) *Argument in absence of jury*

8–92 It is for the judge to decide whether or not a submission made during the trial is to be made in the absence of the jury: *R. v. Hendry*, 88 Cr.App.R. 187, CA.

See *ante*, §§ 4–287 *et seq.* for the circumstances in which evidence may be given in the absence of the jury for the purpose of determining admissibility.

(d) *Privilege against self-incrimination*

8–93 For the position of accused persons who have chosen to give evidence on oath, see the *Criminal Evidence Act* 1898, s.1, *post*, § 8–161.

For the position of other witnesses, see *post*, §§ 12–2 *et seq.*

(e) *Hostile witness*

8–94 Before any question arises under *Denman's Act* (*post*), counsel and judge should keep in mind the possibility of the witness being allowed to refresh his memory from his witness statement (*ante*, §§ 8–74 *et seq.*): see *R. v. Maw* [1994] Crim.L.R. 841, CA.

Denman's Act

Criminal Procedure Act 1865, s.3

How far witnesses may be discredited by the party producing

8–94a **3.** A party producing a witness shall not be allowed to impeach his credit by general evidence of bad character; but he may, in case the witness shall, in the opinion of the judge, prove adverse, contradict him by other evidence, or, by leave of the judge, prove that he has made at other times a statement inconsistent with his present testimony; but before such last-mentioned proof can be given, the circumstances of the supposed statement, sufficient to designate the particular occasion, must be mentioned to the witness, and he must be asked whether or not he has made such statement.

Section 112(3) of the *CJA* 2003 (*post*, § 13–8) provides that nothing in Chapter 1 of Part 11 of that Act (evidence of bad character) affects the exclusion of evidence under the rule in this section against a party impeaching the credit of his own witness.

The question of the hostility of a witness should be determined as a result of his answers and demeanour when being questioned in the presence of the jury: *R. v. Darby* [1989] Crim.L.R. 817, CA. *Darby* was distinguished in the case of an unwilling witness in *R. v. Jones (K.M.)* [1998] Crim.L.R. 579, CA (*post*, § 28–122); and in *R. v. Honeyghon and Sayles* [1999] Crim.L.R. 221, CA, it was said that a judge should have regard to what was likely to happen as and when the witness was confronted with his statement, to which end it was legitimate to conduct a *voire dire*. This, however, was doubted in turn by the court in *R. v. Khan, Dad and Afsar* [2003] Crim.L.R. 428, CA, where it was said that a *voire dire* would only be appropriate in exceptional circumstances, and that it was difficult to see how a judge could assess in advance what a witness would do when confronted with his statement. This, it is submitted, represents the better view, the applicable principle being that everything that the witness says that may affect the weight of his testimony should be said in front of the jury.

The word "adverse" in section 3 means "hostile," and not merely "unfavourable": *Greenhough v. Eccles* (1859) 5 C.B.(n.s.) 786, decided on section 22 of the *Common Law Procedure Act* 1854 (*rep.*). Assistance as to when a witness is to be regarded as hostile is derived from Article 147 of Stephen's *Digest of the Law of Evidence*, which was approved by the Court of Appeal in *R. v. Prefas and Pryce*, 86 Cr.App.R. 111:

8–95 "*Unfavourable and Hostile Witnesses*: If a witness called by a party to prove a particular fact in issue or relevant to the issue fails to prove such fact or proves an opposite fact the party calling him may contradict him by calling other evidence, and is not thereby precluded from relying on those parts of such witnesses's evidence as he does not contradict.

If a witness appears to the judge to be hostile to the party calling him, that is to say, not desirous of telling the truth to the Court at the instance of the party calling him, the judge may in his discretion permit his examination by such party to be conducted in the manner of a cross-examination to the extent to which the judge considers necessary for the purpose of doing justice.

> Such a witness may by leave of the judge be cross-examined as to—(1) facts in issue or relevant or deemed to be relevant to the issue; (2) matters affecting his accuracy, veracity, or credibility in the particular circumstances of the case; and as to (3) whether he has made any former statement, oral or written, relative to the subject-matter of the proceeding and inconsistent with his present testimony. …
>
> In the case of a witness who is treated as hostile, proof of former statements, oral or written, made by him inconsistent with his present testimony may by leave of the judge be given in accordance with Articles 144 and 145."

To be inconsistent within the meaning of the section, the statement need not be directly or absolutely at variance: *Jackson v. Thomason* (1861) 31 L.J.Q.B. 11. **8–96**

No distinction in principle is to be drawn between a witness who gives evidence inconsistent with a witness statement and one who is reluctant to say anything, or professes to have forgotten what happened; if the judge is satisfied that he is hostile, he has a discretion to allow cross-examination: *R. v. Honeyghon and Sayles*, *ante*.

As to the duty of prosecution counsel to cross-examine a hostile witness, see *R. v. Fraser*, 40 Cr.App.R. 160, CCA.

The discretion of the judge to give or refuse leave to cross-examine the party's own witness, however hostile he may be, is absolute: *Rice v. Howard* (1886) 16 Q.B.D. 681; *Price v. Manning* (1889) 42 Ch.D. 372, CA, and can be raised on appeal only in exceptional circumstances: *R. v. Williams (John)*, 8 Cr.App.R. 133, CCA; *R. v. Manning* [1968] Crim.L.R. 675, CA.

In *R. v. Powell* [1985] Crim.L.R. 592, CA, it was held to be permissible to treat a witness as hostile at any stage of his evidence, including re-examination. See also *R. v. Little* (1883) 15 Cox 319 (leave given to put previous statement to witness which was inconsistent with answers given in cross-examination).

Common law

In *R. v. Thompson*, 64 Cr.App.R. 96, CA, a prosecution witness, having been sworn and having answered certain preliminary questions, said that she was not going to give evidence. The judge allowed her to be treated as hostile and to be cross-examined about a statement which she had made to the police. It was argued on appeal that, (a) the witness's previous statement was not "inconsistent with her present testimony" (see s.3 of the 1865 Act), as she had given no material evidence at all; and (b) the case not coming within section 3, the judge was wrong in allowing the cross-examination. *Held*, it was unnecessary to decide whether the case came within the statute since in two cases decided at common law long before the 1865 statute or its precursor, it had been laid down that, (i) there is no fixed rule which binds counsel calling a witness to a particular way of examining him—"if a witness by his conduct in the box, shows himself decidedly adverse, it is always in the discretion of the judge to allow a cross-examination," *per* Best C.J. in *Clarke v. Saffery* (1824) Ry. & M. 126; and (ii) "in each particular case there must be some discretion in the presiding judge as to the mode in which the examination shall be conducted in order best to answer the purposes of justice," *per* Lord Abbott C.J. in *Bastin v. Carew* (1824) Ry. & M. 127; see also *Price v. Manning*, *ante*. Accordingly, the judge was right to allow counsel to ask leading questions and there is no reason to suppose that the subsequent statutory intervention into the subject in any way removed or destroyed the basic common law right of the judge in his discretion to allow cross-examination when a witness proved to be hostile. **8–97**

Hostile witness called by defence

Where a defence witness "goes" hostile he may be cross-examined under section 3 of *Denman's Act*: *R. v. Booth*, 74 Cr.App.R. 123, CA. **8–98**

Hostile witness: competent but not compellable spouse

It is desirable that a witness within the category "competent but not compellable" should be told by the judge before taking the oath and in the absence of the jury that she has the right to refuse to give evidence. If she chooses to proceed, she can be treated like any other witness and this includes, if the circumstances warrant it, being cross-examined as a hostile witness: *R. v. Pitt* [1983] Q.B. 25, 75 Cr.App.R. 254, CA. **8–99**

Evidential value of the testimony of a hostile witness

8–100 Section 119(1) of the *CJA* 2003 (*post*, § 11–33) reversed the common law rule that a previous inconsistent statement is not evidence of the truth of its contents, by providing that if a witness admits making a previous inconsistent statement or such a statement is proved under section 3 of the 1865 Act, the statement is admissible as evidence of any matter stated of which oral evidence by the witness would be admissible. This, of course, says nothing about the relative weight to be attached to the previous statement and to the evidence given orally. This will be a matter for the tribunal of fact, but it would appear to be open to it to act on the statement and to reject the oral evidence, provided it is satisfied to the requisite standard that it is the statement that represents the truthful account.

8–101 In *R. v. Ugorji* [1999] 9 *Archbold News* 3, CA (98 06131 W3) it was said that where leave is given to treat a witness as hostile, and the witness, upon being cross-examined upon a previous statement, says that its contents are true, it is incumbent on the judge to warn the jury to approach any evidence given by the witness incriminating the accused after being treated as hostile with caution, pointing out that the evidence was only elicited as a result of cross-examination by prosecution counsel.

As to the obvious need for caution when assessing the weight to be attached to the statements of a person who has said different things on different occasions, see *R. v. Maw* [1994] Crim.L.R. 841, CA. More generally, however, it would seem that under the Act of 2003, it is for the tribunal of fact to weigh the out-of-court statement of the witness and his evidence in court in the light of all the circumstances (including the circumstances in which the original statement was made, his explanation for the inconsistency, and the evidence of any other witnesses on the matter).

(f) *Previous consistent statements*

General rule

8–102 There is a "general rule of evidence that statements may be used against a witness as admissions but that you are not entitled to give evidence of statements on other occasions by the witness in confirmation of the testimony": *Jones v. S.E. and Chatham Ry.* (1918) 87 L.J.K.B. 775 at 779, and see *Gillie v. Posho* [1939] 2 All E.R. 196 at 201, PC. The law on the matter is well settled. The rule is sometimes expressed as being that a party is not permitted to make evidence for himself: *R. v. Roberts*, 28 Cr.App.R. 102, CCA. Thus a defendant is not permitted to call evidence to show that after he had been charged with an offence he told a number of persons what his defence was. The evidential value of such testimony is nil: *ibid.*, and see *R. v. Larkin* [1943] K.B. 174, 29 Cr.App.R. 18, CCA. The general rule was reaffirmed in *R. v. Oyesiku*, 56 Cr.App.R. 240 at 245–247, CA, *post*, § 8–109. But in *R. v. Evans and Caffrey* [2001] 6 *Archbold News* 2, CA, it was said that there may be circumstances where, although it is not possible to say that a prosecution witness is "adverse" to one defendant, fairness will demand that that defendant should be entitled to bring out a previous consistent statement in order to enhance the evidence of that witness for the benefit of that defendant, even though the effect of such statement was to incriminate a co-defendant. It is submitted that this is inconsistent with what is a well-established principle, and that the decision is best regarded as one depending on its own particular circumstances, including the court's view that the evidence could have been elicited by another means without infringing any rule.

Where there is no suggestion of recent fabrication (*post*), a previous statement is inadmissible if the sole purpose of seeking to put it in evidence is to support a chain of reasoning to the effect that the statement showed that the maker had knowledge of certain facts at the time of the statement (the lay-out of a particular dwelling and its condition), and that at that time he could not have had such knowledge unless, as he asserted in evidence, he had been there himself (thereby making his evidence that much more credible): *R. v. Williams (David)* [1998] Crim.L.R. 495, CA.

As to general evidence of the demeanour of the victim of an alleged offence being inadmissible for the purpose of supporting the veracity of his or her account of the offence, see *R. v. Keast* [1998] Crim.L.R. 748, CA; and *post*, § 20–13.

Exceptions

Common law

At common law, there were three well-established exceptions to the general rule, *viz.* statements constituting recent complaints in sexual cases, statements forming part of the *res gestae* and statements which tended to rebut an allegation of recent fabrication. In the first and third cases, the statement was not admissible as evidence of the truth of its contents. A recent complaint was admitted to show consistency on the part of the complainant, and as tending to negative consent: see *R. v. Lillyman* [1896] 2 Q.B. 167, CCR. A statement in the third category was admitted for the purpose of rebutting a suggestion that the witness's evidence was recent invention, this being done by showing that far from having recently made it up, the witness had said the same thing in a statement made shortly after the events in question. Statements admitted as part of the *res gestae* were true exceptions to the common law prohibition on hearsay. **8–103**

Statute

Section 120 of the *CJA* 2003 (*post*, § 11–34) does not affect the *res gestae* exception, affects the recent invention exception to the extent that it provides that a statement admitted under this exception is evidence of the truth of its contents (subs. (2)) whilst not purporting to dictate when a statement is admissible under this head, and affects the recent complaint exception, both as to the conditions of admissibility and as to the effect of a statement once admitted (*post*). **8–104**

In addition, it should be noted that subsection (3) provides that a memory-refreshing document that has been made an exhibit becomes evidence of its contents; subsection (5) (taken together with subsection (4)) provides that a statement of a witness that "identifies or describes a person, object or place" is admissible if the witness indicates that to the best of his belief he made the statement and it states the truth; and subsection (6) (taken together with subsection (4)) provides that the statement of a witness is admissible if it was made by the witness when the matters stated were fresh in his memory but he does not remember them, and cannot be reasonably expected to remember them, well enough to give oral evidence of them, and the witness indicates that to the best of his belief he made the statement and it states the truth. The second and third of these cases do not represent real exceptions to the rule against previous consistent statements, as they appear to presuppose that the witness is unable to give oral evidence of the matters stated. Had he been able to do so, there would have been no need to resort to either of these provisions for the purpose of putting in evidence his prior statement.

Statements constituting recent complaint

The *CJA* 2003, s.120(4) and (7) (*post*, § 11–34), effects two radical changes to the law relating to recent complaint evidence. First, the complaint may relate to any offence. All that is necessary is that the witness "claims to be a person against whom an offence has been committed". Secondly, the terms of the complaint (if admitted) are admissible, not merely to show consistency, but as evidence of their truth. **8–105**

Whilst the provisions of section 120 supersede the common law both as to the conditions of admissibility and as to terms of the complaint being evidence of its truth, the courts are likely to adhere to the principle underlying the decision in *R. v. Islam* [1999] 1 Cr.App.R. 22, CA, to the effect that recent complaint evidence cannot constitute independent confirmation of the complainant's evidence because it does not come from an independent source. **8–106**

Statements forming part of the res gestae

See *R. v. Roberts*, 28 Cr.App.R. 102 at 105–106, CCA; *Jones v. S.E. and Chatham Ry* (1918) 87 L.J.K.B. 775 at 778; and, *post*, § 11–74, for the *res gestae* principle (preserved by the *CJA* 2003, s.118 (*post*, § 11–70)). **8–107**

Statements rebutting an allegation of recent fabrication

Statements admissible under this exception will, of course, often be adduced in re-examination. **8–108**

> "If, in cross-examination, a witness's account of some incident or set of facts is challenged as being a recent invention, thus presenting a clear issue as to whether at some previous time he said or thought what he has been saying at the trial, he may support himself by evidence of earlier statements by him to the same effect. Plainly the rule that sets up the exception cannot be formulated with any great precision, since its application will depend on the nature of the challenge offered by the course of cross-examination and the relative cogency of the evidence tendered to repel it": *Fox v. General Medical Council* [1960] 1 W.L.R. 1017 at 1025, PC.

8–109 In *R. v. Oyesiku*, 56 Cr.App.R. 240, the Court of Appeal approved the following statement of principle (at p. 246): "If the credit of a witness is impugned as to some material fact to which he deposes upon the ground that his account is a late invention or has been lately devised or reconstructed, even though not with conscious dishonesty, that makes admissible a statement to the same effect as the account he gave as a witness, if it was made by the witness contemporaneously with the event or at a time sufficiently early to be inconsistent with the suggestion that his account is a late invention or reconstruction". The judge must exercise great care in deciding that (a) the evidence has been attacked on the ground of recent invention or reconstruction or that a foundation for such an attack has been laid, (b) the contents of the statement are to the like effect as the testimony, and (c) having regard to the time and circumstances in which the statement was made, it rationally tends to answer the attack: *ibid*. See also *R. v. Sekhon*, 85 Cr.App.R. 19, CA, *ante*, § 8–87.

8–110 *Oyesiku* was applied in *R. v. Weekes* [1988] Crim.L.R. 244, CA, and in *R. v. Beattie*, 89 Cr.App.R. 302, CA, where it was said that there were three exceptions to the rule that it was not competent for a party calling a witness to put to that witness a statement made by him to lend weight to his evidence, but there was no general fourth exception to the effect that where counsel cross-examined to show inconsistencies, the witness could be re-examined to show consistency. But a court does have a residual discretion to allow re-examination on a prior statement where such was necessary to avoid the jury being positively misled as to the existence of some fact or the terms of an earlier statement: *R. v. Ali* [2004] 1 Cr.App.R. 39, CA.

A statement may be admitted under this exception though it has been rejected as a recent complaint (*ante*, § 8–105) on the ground that it was not made at the first opportunity that reasonably offered itself: *R. v. Tyndale* [1999] Crim.L.R. 320, CA.

8–111 The purpose of admitting a previous inconsistent statement under this exception being to show consistency, and to rebut a suggestion of recent fabrication, the common law rule was that the statement would not be evidence of the truth of the facts stated: see *R. v. Benjamin*, 8 Cr.App.R. 146, CCA. As with evidence of recent complaint, however (*ante*), the *CJA* 2003, s.120(2) (*post*, § 11–34), alters this rule, so that a statement admitted to rebut a suggestion that a witness's oral evidence has been fabricated is admissible as evidence of any matter stated in it of which oral evidence by the witness would be admissible.

C. CROSS-EXAMINATION

(1) General principles

8–112 When the examination-in-chief is finished, the witness may be cross-examined by counsel for the opposite party. Or, if the party calling a witness does not think it proper to examine him after he is called and sworn, the witness may nevertheless be cross-examined by or on behalf of any other party who has a legitimate interest in putting questions to him: *Morgan v. Brydges* (1818) 2 Stark.N.P. 314; *R. v. Brooke* (1819) 2 Stark.N.P. 472; *R. v. Bingham and Cooke* [1999] 1 W.L.R. 598, HL.

Questions put in cross-examination must be either relevant and pertinent to the matter in issue, or calculated to attack the witness's title to credit.

As to a judge taking over the cross-examination of a recalcitrant prosecution witness, see *R. v. Cameron* [2001] Crim.L.R. 587, CA, *post*, § 8–249.

Judge's duty to restrain unnecessary cross-examination

8–113 A judge should do his utmost to restrain unnecessary cross-examination. Although counsel must not be deterred from doing his duty, counsel for the defence should exercise a proper discretion not to prolong the case unnecessarily. It is no part of his duty to embark on lengthy cross-examination on matters which are not really in issue: *R. v. Kalia*, 60 Cr.App.R. 200, CA (approving dicta in *R. v. Simmonds* [1969] 1 Q.B. 685, 51 Cr.App.R. 316, CA; and *Mechanical and General Inventions Co. Ltd v. Austin* [1935] A.C. 346 at 359, HL). The observations in *Kalia* were reiterated in *R. v. Maynard*, 69 Cr.App.R. 309, CA.

It is erroneous for a judge to take the view that cross-examination cannot be stopped merely because there is some tenuous legal reason for it: *R. v. Flynn* [1972] Crim.L.R. 428,CA. Counsel should not forget that a trial takes place in public and that therefore names of third parties should not be bandied about unless it is necessary for the proper conduct of the trial: *ibid*. Judges were entitled to impose time limits on cross-examination where it was repetitious and time was being wasted; such a course did not render the trial unfair: *R. v. B.* [2006] Crim.L.R. 54, CA (where transcript showed 24 pages of intense, detailed cross-examination of the complainant, during which time the judge intervened on 24 occasions with gentle pleas for counsel to close, his eventual imposition of a 10-minute limit for the cross-examination to conclude, had been justified).

In *R. v. Brown (Milton)* [1998] 2 Cr.App.R. 364, the Court of Appeal reminded judges (*obiter*) that a trial is not fair if an unrepresented defendant gains an advantage he would not otherwise have had by abusing the rules in relation to relevance and repetition when cross-examining; it would often be desirable, before cross-examination for the judge to discuss the course of proceedings with the defendant in the jury's absence; the general nature of the defence could then be elicited and specific aspects of the witness's evidence with which the defendant took issue identified; the substance of any evidence to be given by defence witnesses could be elicited with a view to obtaining the witness's observations; the defendant should be allowed to begin the questioning but it should be made clear in advance that repetition would not be permitted; if it occurred, the judge should intervene; if the defendant proved unable or unwilling to comply with the instructions, the judge should stop the questioning and take over; if the defendant sought by his dress, bearing, manner or questions to dominate, intimidate or humiliate the witness, or if it were reasonably apprehended that he would seek to do so, the judge should order the erection of a screen as well as controlling the questioning; if a judge took such steps, the Court of Appeal would be slow to intervene, in the absence of clear evidence of injustice.

As to the statutory restrictions on cross-examination by a defendant in person, see *post*, §§ 8–123a *et seq*.

As to the restraint which may properly be put on cross-examination as to credit, see *post*, §§ 8–138 *et seq*.

[The next paragraph is § 8–116.]

Form of questioning in cross-examination

In cross-examining a witness, counsel may ask leading questions; that is he may ask questions which suggest what the answer should be. **8–116**

Questions should not be put in such a manner as to be in the nature of invitations to argument rather than to elicit answers to matters of fact, which is the true purpose of cross-examination: see *R. v. Baldwin*, 18 Cr.App.R. 175, CCA; and *Randall v. R.* [2002] 2 Cr.App.R. 17, PC. In *Baldwin*, Lord Hewart C.J. deprecated questions in cross-examination such as "I suggest to you that..."; "Is your evidence to be taken as suggesting that ... ?"; "Do you ask the jury to believe that ...," (at pp. 178, 179). As his Lordship said, referring to cross-examination, "What is wanted from the witness is answers to questions of fact."

An advocate must not in the course of cross-examination state matters of fact or opinion, or say what someone else has said or is expected to say. Defending counsel on occasion break this rule by saying, *e.g.* "the defendant's recollection is" or "the defendant will say" or "my instructions are that ... ." The time to make such statements is in an opening speech, not in cross-examination. Nor is it permissible to evade this rule by putting the statement in the form of a question, *e.g.* "What would you say if the defendant were to say?" Similarly, cross-examination must not be used for making comments, which should be confined to speeches. For example, it is wrong for prosecuting counsel to say to the defendant in cross-examination "You heard what the sergeant said, is he lying?" Some flexibility may, however, be allowed where a strict insistence on the rule's observance may hinder the witness or the jury. Thus in a long or complex case, the witness or the jury may be assisted by being reminded of the evidence of another witness. So long as the golden rule is observed that the witness should not be invited to comment on, or explain any discrepancy in the evidence, there can be no objection to such inroad on the general prohibition on stating to one witness what another witness has said.

If, in a crucial part of the case, the prosecution intend to ask the jury to disbelieve the evidence of a witness for the defence it is right and proper that the witness should be challenged when in the witness-box or, at any rate, that it should be made plain while the witness is in the box that his evidence is not accepted: *R. v. Hart*, 23 Cr.App.R. 202, CCA (alibi witnesses not cross-examined at all); and *R. (Wilkinson) v. DPP*, 167 J.P. 229, QBD (Stanley Burnton J.) (defendant not cross-examined). See also, *Browne v. Dunn* (1893) 6 R. 67 at 76–77, HL, and *Flanagan v. Fahy* [1918] 2 I.R. 361 at 388–389. Counsel is, however, entitled to invite the jury to reject the evidence of a defence witness where he has adopted a "raised eyebrow" approach, but has not explicitly put to the witness that he is lying: *R. v. Lovelock* [1997] Crim.L.R. 821, CA.

It is permissible, in a case of an alleged sexual offence, for the defendant to be asked in cross-examination whether he knows of any reason why the complainant might be lying; the existence or non-existence of a motive for lying was relevant to the credibility of the complainant; and it is permissible for prosecution counsel to comment on the matter in a closing speech; the evidential effect of the answer, in the context of the burden of proof, is a matter for the summing up, with directions tailored to the circumstances of the particular case: *R. v. B.* [2003] 1 W.L.R. 2809, CA.

Order of cross-examination where more than one counsel

8–117 Where two defendants are jointly indicted, and are defended by different counsel, the established rule is that, in the absence of agreement between counsel, the court will call on them to cross-examine and address the jury in the order in which the names of the defendants whom they represent stand on the indictment: *R. v. Barber* (1844) 1 C. & K. 434; *R. v. Richards* (1844) 1 Cox 62.

(2) Counsel's duty

8–118 In deciding what counsel's duty is, regard must be had (a) to the relevant provisions of the current edition of the *Code of Conduct for the Bar of England and Wales*; (b) to relevant pronouncements to the profession made by or on behalf of the Bar Council; and (c) to relevant statements made by the higher courts.

The Code of Conduct

8–119 Those provisions of the code which are of particular significance to the barrister in independent practice are printed in Appendix C. In this context, reference should be made to paragraph 708, and in the Written Standards for the Conduct of Professional Work, to paragraph 5.10(e)–(h) of the General Standards, and to paragraphs 12.5, 15.3.1 and 15.3.2. of the Standards applicable to Criminal Cases.

Bar Council statements

8–120 After the Professional Conduct Committee of the Bar Council rejected complaints against certain defence counsel in relation to their conduct at the trial of *R. v. McFadden* (see 62 Cr.App.R. 187), the Chairman of the Bar restated the principles which govern the conduct of counsel when defending a person accused of crime. The statement is set out at the end of the report of the Court of Appeal proceedings in *R. v. McFadden*, 62 Cr.App.R. 187 at 193. It is printed in full, *ante*, § 4–307.

Judicial pronouncements (see also ante, § 8–113)

In *R. v. O'Neil*, 34 Cr.App.R. 108, CCA, Lord Goddard C.J. observed: **8–121**

"In this case a violent attack was made on the police. It was suggested that they had done improper things. ... The applicants had the opportunity of going into the box at the trial and explaining and supporting what they had instructed their counsel to say. They did not dare go into the box and therefore counsel, who knew that they were not going into the box, ought not to have made these suggestions against the police. ... It is ... entirely wrong to make such suggestions as were made in this case, namely that the police beat the prisoners until they made confessions, and then, when there is the chance for the prisoners to substantiate what has been said by going into the box, for counsel not to call them ... " (at p. 111).

These observations were endorsed in *R. v. Callaghan*, 69 Cr.App.R. 88, CA.

The pronouncements in *Callaghan* (Waller L.J., Lawson and Jupp JJ.) placed counsel in difficulties in a number of cases. They were subsequently modified by Waller L.J., following representations by the Professional Conduct Committee. Where a client requires the police evidence to be challenged in the manner considered in *Callaghan* and *O'Neil*, but he nonetheless refuses to go into the witness box because of his bad record, it is counsel's duty to warn his client that the judge will probably make a very strong comment upon his failure to support the allegations on oath. If the client persists with his instructions counsel must carry them out despite the fact that he knows that his client will not be supporting the allegations by going into the witness box; see *The Times*, February 20, 1980. **8–122**

There can be no objection to strong comment in such cases: see, for example, *R. v. Brigden* [1973] Crim.L.R. 579, CA. The scope of legitimate comment has been extended since the enactment of the *CJPOA* 1994, s.35 (*ante*, § 4–305) (which also permits comment by the prosecution).

A failure to put to a witness matter which tends to contradict the evidence of the witness does not render such matter inadmissible; the proper course is for the witness to be recalled in order that he or she has the opportunity to deal with the matter: *R. v. Cannan* [1998] Crim.L.R. 284, CA.

As to defence counsel's duty when cross-examining a co-defendant, see *R. v. Fenlon*, 71 Cr.App.R. 307, CA, *post*, § 8–164.

Relationship between the three sources

The Court of Appeal has not pronounced on the status of the *Code of Conduct*. There is no reason for supposing, however, that its approach to the code will differ materially to the approach adopted to Bar Council statements, observations upon which were made in *McFadden*, *ante*. **8–123**

"Disciplinary functions in regard to the Bar are exclusively vested in the Senate of the Inns of Court and the Bar and are exercised by the Bar Council. A judge who considers that he has cause to complain of the professional conduct of a barrister may make his complaint to the Bar Council but he has no power himself to take disciplinary action in that regard. He can of course commit to prison a barrister who is guilty of contempt of court.

The Bar Council issues statements from time to time to give guidance to the profession in matters of etiquette and procedure. A barrister who conforms to the Council's rulings knows that he cannot be committing an offence against professional discipline. But such statements, although they have strong persuasive force, do not bind the Courts. If therefore a judge requires a barrister to do, or refrain from doing, something in the course of a case, the barrister may protest and may cite any relevant ruling of the Bar Council, but since the judge is the final authority in his own Court, if counsel's protest is unavailing, he must either withdraw or comply with the ruling or look for redress in a higher Court" (*per* James L.J. at pp. 189–190).

(3) Restrictions

(a) *Where defendant acting in person*

Introduction

The provisions of Chapter II of Part II of the *YJCEA* 1999 (*post*, §§ 8–123b *et seq.*) replaced the more limited provision in section 34A of the *CJA* 1988. **8–123a**

As to the duty of a judge to restrain cross-examination by a defendant in person apart from the provisions of any statute, see *R. v. Brown (Milton)*, *ante*, § 8–113.

Youth Justice and Criminal Evidence Act 1999, ss.34, 35

CHAPTER II

PROTECTION OF WITNESSES FROM CROSS-EXAMINATION BY ACCUSED IN PERSON

General prohibitions

Complainants in proceedings for sexual offences

8–123b **34.** No person charged with a sexual offence may in any criminal proceedings cross-examine in person a witness who is the complainant, either—

(a) in connection with that offence, or

(b) in connection with any other offence (of whatever nature) with which that person is charged in the proceedings.

Child complainants and other child witnesses

8–123c **35.**—(1) No person charged with an offence to which this section applies may in any criminal proceedings cross-examine in person a protected witness, either—

(a) in connection with that offence, or

(b) in connection with any other offence (of whatever nature) with which that person is charged in the proceedings.

(2) For the purposes of subsection (1) a "protected witness" is a witness who—

(a) either is the complainant or is alleged to have been a witness to the commission of the offence to which this section applies, and

(b) either is a child or falls to be cross-examined after giving evidence in chief (whether wholly or in part)—

(i) by means of a video recording made (for the purposes of section 27) at a time when the witness was a child, or

(ii) in any other way at any such time.

(3) The offences to which this section applies are—

(a) any offence under—

(i)–(iv) [*repealed by* Sexual Offences Act *2003*, *s.140*, *and Sched*. *7*];

(iva) any of sections 33 to 36 of the *Sexual Offences Act* 1956;

(v) the *Protection of Children Act* 1978; or

(vi) Part 1 of the *Sexual Offences Act* 2003 or any relevant superseded enactment;

(b) kidnapping, false imprisonment or an offence under section 1 or 2 of the *Child Abduction Act* 1984;

(c) any offence under section 1 of the *Children and Young Persons Act* 1933;

(d) any offence (not within any of the preceding paragraphs) which involves an assault on, or injury or a threat of injury to, any person.

(3A) In subsection (3)(a)(vi) "relevant superseded enactment" means—

(a) any of sections 1 to 32 of the *Sexual Offences Act* 1956;

(b) the *Indecency with Children Act* 1960;

(c) the *Sexual Offences Act* 1967;

(d) section 54 of the *Criminal Law Act* 1977.

(4) In this section "child" means—

(a) where the offence falls within subsection (3)(a), a person under the age of 17; or

(b) where the offence falls within subsection (3)(b), (c) or (d), a person under the age of 14.

(5) For the purposes of this section "witness" includes a witness who is charged with an offence in the proceedings.

[This section is printed as amended by the *SOA* 2003, s.139, and Sched. 6, para. 41(1) and (2); and as subsequently amended (retrospectively to May 1, 2004) by the *CJIA* 2008, s.148(1), and Sched. 26, paras 35 and 36.]

For procedural provision in relation to sections 34 and 35, see rules 31.1 to 31.3 of the *Criminal Procedure Rules* 2005 (S.I. 2005 No. 384), *post*, §§ 8–123h, 8–123i.

Youth Justice and Criminal Evidence Act 1999, ss.36, 37

Prohibition imposed by court

Direction prohibiting accused from cross-examining particular witness

36.—(1) This section applies where, in a case where neither of sections 34 and 35 operates to prevent an accused in any criminal proceedings from cross-examining a witness in person— **8–123d**

(a) the prosecutor makes an application for the court to give a direction under this section in relation to the witness, or

(b) the court of its own motion raises the issue whether such a direction should be given.

(2) If it appears to the court—

(a) that the quality of evidence given by the witness on cross-examination—

(i) is likely to be diminished if the cross-examination (or further cross-examination) is conducted by the accused in person, and

(ii) would be likely to be improved if a direction were given under this section, and

(b) that it would not be contrary to the interests of justice to give such a direction,

the court may give a direction prohibiting the accused from cross-examining (or further cross-examining) the witness in person.

(3) In determining whether subsection (2)(a) applies in the case of a witness the court must have regard, in particular, to—

(a) any views expressed by the witness as to whether or not the witness is content to be cross-examined by the accused in person;

(b) the nature of the questions likely to be asked, having regard to the issues in the proceedings and the defence case advanced so far (if any);

(c) any behaviour on the part of the accused at any stage of the proceedings, both generally and in relation to the witness;

(d) any relationship (of whatever nature) between the witness and the accused;

(e) whether any person (other than the accused) is or has at any time been charged in the proceedings with a sexual offence or an offence to which section 35 applies, and (if so) whether section 34 or 35 operates or would have operated to prevent that person from cross-examining the witness in person;

(f) any direction under section 19 which the court has given, or proposes to give, in relation to the witness.

(4) For the purposes of this section—

(a) "witness", in relation to an accused, does not include any other person who is charged with an offence in the proceedings; and

(b) any reference to the quality of a witness's evidence shall be construed in accordance with section 16(5).

Further provisions about directions under section 36

37.—(1) Subject to subsection (2), a direction has binding effect from the time it is made until the witness to whom it applies is discharged. **8–123e**

In this section "direction" means a direction under section 36.

(2) The court may discharge a direction if it appears to the court to be in the interests of justice to do so, and may do so either—

(a) on an application made by a party to the proceedings, if there has been a material change of circumstances since the relevant time, or

(b) of its own motion.

(3) In subsection (2) "the relevant time" means—

(a) the time when the direction was given, or

(b) if a previous application has been made under that subsection, the time when the application (or last application) was made.

(4) The court must state in open court its reasons for—

(a) giving, or

(b) refusing an application for, or for the discharge of, or

(c) discharging,

a direction and, if it is a magistrates' court, must cause them to be entered in the register of its proceedings.

(5) Criminal Procedure Rules may make provision—

(a) for uncontested applications to be determined by the court without a hearing;
(b) for preventing the renewal of an unsuccessful application for a direction except where there has been a material change of circumstances;
(c) for expert evidence to be given in connection with an application for, or for discharging, a direction;
(d) for the manner in which confidential or sensitive information is to be treated in connection with such an application and in particular as to its being disclosed to, or, withheld from, a party to the proceedings.

[This section is printed as amended by the *Courts Act* 2003, s.109(1), and Sched. 8, para. 384.]

For procedural provision in relation to section 36, see rule 31.4 of the *Criminal Procedure Rules* 2005 (S.I. 2005 No. 384), *post*, § 8–123j.

Youth Justice and Criminal Evidence Act 1999, ss.38, 39

Cross-examination on behalf of accused

Defence representation for purposes of cross-examination

8–123f **38.**—(1) This section applies where an accused is prevented from cross-examining a witness in person by virtue of section 34, 35 or 36.

(2) Where it appears to the court that this section applies, it must—
(a) invite the accused to arrange for a legal representative to act for him for the purpose of cross-examining the witness; and
(b) require the accused to notify the court, by the end of such period as it may specify, whether a legal representative is to act for him for that purpose.

(3) If by the end of the period mentioned in subsection (2)(b) either—
(a) the accused has notified the court that no legal representative is to act for him for the purpose of cross-examining the witness, or
(b) no notification has been received by the court and it appears to the court that no legal representative is to so act,

the court must consider whether it is necessary in the interests of justice for the witness to be cross-examined by a legal representative appointed to represent the interests of the accused.

(4) If the court decides that it is necessary in the interests of justice for the witness to be so cross-examined, the court must appoint a qualified legal representative (chosen by the court) to cross-examine the witness in the interests of the accused.

(5) A person so appointed shall not be responsible to the accused.

(6) Criminal Procedure Rules may make provision—
(a) as to the time when, and the manner in which, subsection (2) is to be complied with;
(b) in connection with the appointment of a legal representative under subsection (4), and in particular for securing that a person so appointed is provided with evidence or other material relating to the proceedings.

(7) Criminal Procedure Rules made in pursuance of subsection (6)(b) may make provision for the application, with such modifications as are specified in the rules, of any of the provisions of—
(a) Part I of the *Criminal Procedure and Investigations Act* 1996 (disclosure of material in connection with criminal proceedings), or
(b) the *Sexual Offences (Protected Material) Act* 1997.

(8) For the purposes of this section—
(a) any reference to cross-examination includes (in a case where a direction is given under section 36 after the accused has begun cross-examining the witness) a reference to further cross-examination; and
(b) "qualified legal representative" means a legal representative who has a right of audience (within the meaning of the *Courts and Legal Services Act* 1990) in relation to the proceedings before the court.

[This section is printed as amended by the *Courts Act* 2003, s.109(1), and Sched. 8, para. 384.]

Warning to jury

8–123g **39.**—(1) Where on a trial on indictment with a jury an accused is prevented from cross-examining a witness in person by virtue of section 34, 35 or 36, the judge must give the jury such warning (if any) as the judge considers necessary to ensure that the accused is not prejudiced—

(a) by inferences that might be drawn from the fact that the accused has been prevented from cross-examining the witness in person;

(b) where the witness has been cross-examined by a legal representative appointed under section 38(4), by the fact that the cross-examination was carried out by such a legal representative and not by a person acting as the accused's own legal representative.

(2) Subsection (8)(a) of section 38 applies for the purposes of this section as it applies for the purposes of section 38.

[This section is printed as amended by the *CJA* 2003, s.331, and Sched. 36, paras 74 and 76.]

Criminal Procedure Rules 2005, Pt 31

Restrictions on cross-examination of witness

31.1.—(1) This rule and rules 31.2 and 31.3 apply where an accused is prevented from cross-examining a witness in person by virtue of section 34, 35 or 36 of the *Youth Justice and Criminal Evidence Act* 1999. **8–123h**

(2) The court shall explain to the accused as early in the proceedings as is reasonably practicable that he—

(a) is prevented from cross-examining a witness in person; and

(b) should arrange for a legal representative to act for him for the purpose of cross-examining the witness.

(3) The accused shall notify the court officer within 7 days of the court giving its explanation, or within such other period as the court may in any particular case allow, of the action, if any, he has taken.

(4) Where he has arranged for a legal representative to act for him, the notification shall include details of the name and address of the representative.

(5) The notification shall be in writing.

(6) The court officer shall notify all other parties to the proceedings of the name and address of the person, if any, appointed to act for the accused.

(7) Where the court gives its explanation under paragraph (2) to the accused either within 7 days of the day set for the commencement of any hearing at which a witness in respect of whom a prohibition under section 34, 35 or 36 of the 1999 Act applies may be cross-examined or after such a hearing has commenced, the period of 7 days shall be reduced in accordance with any directions issued by the court.

(8) Where at the end of the period of 7 days or such other period as the court has allowed, the court has received no notification from the accused it may grant the accused an extension of time, whether on its own motion or on the application of the accused.

(9) Before granting an extension of time, the court may hold a hearing at which all parties to the proceedings may attend and be heard.

(10) Any extension of time shall be of such period as the court considers appropriate in the circumstances of the case.

(11) The decision of the court as to whether to grant the accused an extension of time shall be notified to all parties to the proceedings by the court officer.

Appointment of legal representative

31.2.—(1) Where the court decides, in accordance with section 38(4) of the *Youth Justice and Criminal Evidence Act* 1999, to appoint a qualified legal representative, the court officer shall notify all parties to the proceedings of the name and address of the representative.

(2) An appointment made by the court under section 38(4) of the 1999 Act shall, except to such extent as the court may in any particular case determine, terminate at the conclusion of the cross-examination of the witness or witnesses in respect of whom a prohibition under section 34, 35 or 36 of the 1999 Act applies.

Appointment arranged by the accused

31.3.—(1) The accused may arrange for the qualified legal representative, appointed by the court under section 38(4) of the *Youth Justice and Criminal Evidence Act* 1999, to be appointed to act for him for the purpose of cross-examining any witness in respect of whom a prohibition under section 34, 35 or 36 of the 1999 Act applies. **8–123i**

(2) Where such an appointment is made—

(a) both the accused and the qualified legal representative appointed shall notify the court of the appointment; and

(b) the qualified legal representative shall, from the time of his appointment, act for the accused as though the arrangement had been made under section 38(2)(a) of the 1999 Act and shall cease to be the representative of the court under section 38(4).

(3) Where the court receives notification of the appointment either from the qualified legal representative or from the accused but not from both, the court shall investigate whether the appointment has been made, and if it concludes that the appointment has not been made, paragraph (2)(b) shall not apply.

(4) An accused may, notwithstanding an appointment by the court under section 38(4) of the 1999 Act, arrange for a legal representative to act for him for the purpose of cross-examining any witness in respect of whom a prohibition under section 34, 35 or 36 of the 1999 Act applies.

(5) Where the accused arranges for, or informs the court of his intention to arrange for, a legal representative to act for him, he shall notify the court, within such period as the court may allow, of the name and address of any person appointed to act for him.

(6) Where the court is notified within the time allowed that such an appointment has been made, any qualified legal representative appointed by the court in accordance with section 38(4) of the 1999 Act shall be discharged.

(7) The court officer shall, as soon as reasonably practicable after the court receives notification of an appointment under this rule or, where paragraph (3) applies, after the court is satisfied that the appointment has been made, notify all the parties to the proceedings—

(a) that the appointment has been made;

(b) where paragraph (4) applies, of the name and address of the person appointed; and

(c) that the person appointed by the court under section 38(4) of the 1999 Act has been discharged or has ceased to act for the court.

Prohibition on cross-examination of witness

8–123j **31.4.**—(1) An application by the prosecutor for the court to give a direction under section 36 of the *Youth Justice and Criminal Evidence Act* 1999 in relation to any witness must be sent to the court officer and at the same time a copy thereof must be sent by the applicant to every other party to the proceedings.

(2) In his application the prosecutor must state why, in his opinion—

(a) the evidence given by the witness is likely to be diminished if cross-examination is undertaken by the accused in person;

(b) the evidence would be improved if a direction were given under section 36(2) of the 1999 Act; and

(c) it would not be contrary to the interests of justice to give such a direction.

(3) On receipt of the application the court officer must refer it—

(a) if the trial has started, to the court of trial; or

(b) if the trial has not started when the application is received—

(i) to the judge or court designated to conduct the trial, or

(ii) if no judge or court has been designated for that purpose, to such judge or court designated for the purposes of hearing that application.

(4) Where a copy of the application is received by a party to the proceedings more than 14 days before the date set for the trial to begin, that party may make observations in writing on the application to the court officer, but any such observations must be made within 14 days of the receipt of the application and be copied to the other parties to the proceedings.

(5) A party to whom an application is sent in accordance with paragraph (1) who wishes to oppose the application must give his reasons for doing so to the court officer and the other parties to the proceedings.

(6) Those reasons must be notified—

(a) within 14 days of the date the application was served on him, if that date is more than 14 days before the date set for the trial to begin;

(b) if the trial has begun, in accordance with any directions issued by the court; or

(c) if neither paragraph (6)(a) nor (b) applies, before the date set for the trial to begin.

(7) Where the application made in accordance with paragraph (1) is made before the date set for the trial to begin and—

(a) is not contested by any party to the proceedings, the court may determine the application without a hearing;

(b) is contested by a party to the proceedings, the court must direct a hearing of the application.

(8) Where the application is made after the trial has begun—

(a) the application may be made orally; and

(b) the court may give such directions as it considers appropriate to deal with the application.

(9) Where a hearing of the application is to take place, the court officer shall notify each party to the proceedings of the time and place of the hearing.

(10) A party notified in accordance with paragraph (9) may be present at the hearing and be heard.

(11) The court officer must, as soon as possible after the determination of an application made in accordance with paragraph (1), give notice of the decision and the reasons for it to all the parties to the proceedings.

(12) A person making an oral application under paragraph (8)(a) must—

(a) give reasons why the application was not made before the trial commenced; and

(b) provide the court with the information set out in paragraph (2).

[Part 31 is printed as amended by the *Criminal Procedure (Amendment) Rules* 2007 (S.I. 2007 No. 699), rr.18, 20, 22, 23 and 25 to 28.]

(b) *In proceedings for sexual offences*

Introduction

Prior to the enactment of the *Sexual Offences (Amendment) Act* 1976, the ambit of legitimate cross-examination was governed by the common law. The 1976 Act introduced restrictions on the cross-examination of a complainant in a case of rape as to her previous sexual experience. As a result of a perception that the judiciary were not applying the provisions of the 1976 legislation in the spirit in which they were intended, the restrictions were significantly extended by the *YJCEA* 1999. First, the provisions of the 1999 legislation apply to a wide range of sexual offences. Secondly, the restrictions have themselves been tightened. The 1976 Act restrictions had no application to previous sexual experience with the defendant. This exception has been removed. Under the 1976 Act, the judge could disapply the restrictions if satisfied that it would be "unfair to the defendant" to refuse to allow the evidence to be adduced or the question to be asked. Under the 1999 Act, the judge may only give leave if satisfied that it is relevant to an issue in the case and that a refusal of leave might render the jury's conclusion "unsafe". "Unsafe" is, of course, the single ground for allowing an appeal against conviction under the *CAA* 1968. The choice of this word appears to be no accident. The judge is required, therefore, to perform the unusual exercise of putting himself in the position of an appeal court, looking back at an adverse verdict. Finally, as to relevance, the judge may not give leave at all if the issue to which the evidence is relevant is consent, unless the case can be brought within closely defined exceptions. For further consideration of the 1999 Act provisions, see *post*, § 8–123p. **8–123k**

Sections 41 to 43 of the 1999 Act, together with the transitional provision in Schedule 7, paragraph 5 (*post*, § 8–123t), came into force on December 4, 2000: *Youth Justice and Criminal Evidence Act 1999 (Commencement No. 5) Order* 2000 (S.I. 2000 No. 3075). As of that date, the 1976 Act ceased to have any further relevance (save as provided by the transitional provision), and it is submitted that the authorities decided in relation thereto will have no continuing authority. For the detail of the former legislation, see the 2001 edition of this work at §§ 8–123j *et seq.* The common law will continue to govern issues of admissibility where the 1999 Act does not apply. Furthermore, it may still be possible to derive some guidance from the common law as to what material may be regarded as relevant to consent as opposed merely to credit.

Common law

At common law, the complainant could be contradicted if she denied having previously had intercourse with the defendant. Such a fact would be relevant to consent: **8–123l**

R. v. Riley (1887) 18 Q.B.D. 481. And evidence could be given that the complainant was a common prostitute: *R. v. Clay* (1851) 5 Cox 146. The effect of a complainant being a prostitute is relevant to the issue of consent: see *R. v. Greatbanks* [1959] Crim.L.R. 450, CCC (Elwes J.); *R. v. Holmes* (1871) L.R. 1 C.C.R. 334; *R. v. Clay, ante*. After a proper foundation has been laid in cross-examination of the complainant, a defence witness may be called to say "I say she is a prostitute because of so-and-so", provided that the evidence is directed to prostitution as opposed to mere sexual intercourse: *R. v. Bashir*, 54 Cr.App.R. 1, Assizes (Veale J.).

Apart from questions directed to previous sexual experience with the defendant and those directed to the issue of prostitution, it seems that the common law regarded all other questioning of the complainant as to previous sexual experience as going only to credit, to which the answers were final: *R. v. Holmes, ante*; *R. v. Bashir, ante*. *R. v. Krausz*, 57 Cr.App.R. 466, CA, is an exception to this analysis, but it is so out of line with modern thinking as to what is permissible by way of cross-examination that it is submitted that it may now be safely ignored. For more detailed criticism of this decision, see the 1999 and earlier editions of this book.

Statutory restrictions

Youth Justice and Criminal Evidence Act 1999, ss.41–43

CHAPTER III

PROTECTION OF COMPLAINANTS IN PROCEEDINGS FOR SEXUAL OFFENCES

Restriction on evidence or questions about complainant's sexual history

8–123m **41.**—(1) If at a trial a person is charged with a sexual offence, then, except with the leave of the court—

(a) no evidence may be adduced, and

(b) no question may be asked in cross-examination,

by or on behalf of any accused at the trial, about any sexual behaviour of the complainant.

(2) The court may give leave in relation to any evidence or question only on an application made by or on behalf of an accused, and may not give such leave unless it is satisfied—

(a) that subsection (3) or (5) applies, and

(b) that a refusal of leave might have the result of rendering unsafe a conclusion of the jury or (as the case may be) the court on any relevant issue in the case.

(3) This subsection applies if the evidence or question relates to a relevant issue in the case and either—

(a) that issue is not an issue of consent; or

(b) it is an issue of consent and the sexual behaviour of the complainant to which the evidence or question relates is alleged to have taken place at or about the same time as the event which is the subject matter of the charge against the accused; or

(c) it is an issue of consent and the sexual behaviour of the complainant to which the evidence or question relates is alleged to have been, in any respect, so similar—

(i) to any sexual behaviour of the complainant which (according to evidence adduced or to be adduced by or on behalf of the accused) took place as part of the event which is the subject matter of the charge against the accused, or

(ii) to any other sexual behaviour of the complainant which (according to such evidence) took place at or about the same time as that event,

that the similarity cannot reasonably be explained as a coincidence.

(4) For the purposes of subsection (3) no evidence or question shall be regarded as relating to a relevant issue in the case if it appears to the court to be reasonable to assume that the purpose (or main purpose) for which it would be adduced or asked is to establish or elicit material for impugning the credibility of the complainant as a witness.

(5) This subsection applies if the evidence or question—

(a) relates to any evidence adduced by the prosecution about any sexual behaviour of the complainant; and

(b) in the opinion of the court, would go no further than is necessary to enable the evidence adduced by the prosecution to be rebutted or explained by or on behalf of the accused.

(6) For the purposes of subsections (3) and (5) the evidence or question must relate to a specific instance (or specific instances) of alleged sexual behaviour on the part of the complainant (and accordingly nothing in those subsections is capable of applying in relation to the evidence or question to the extent that it does not so relate).

(7) Where this section applies in relation to a trial by virtue of the fact that one or more of a number of persons charged in the proceedings is or are charged with a sexual offence—

(a) it shall cease to apply in relation to the trial if the prosecutor decides not to proceed with the case against that person or those persons in respect of that charge; but

(b) it shall not cease to do so in the event of that person or those persons pleading guilty to, or being convicted of, that charge.

(8) Nothing in this section authorises any evidence to be adduced or any question to be asked which cannot be adduced or asked apart from this section.

Interpretation and application of section 41

42.—(1) In section 41— **8–123n**

(a) "relevant issue in the case" means any issue falling to be proved by the prosecution or defence in the trial of the accused;

(b) "issue of consent" means any issue whether the complainant in fact consented to the conduct constituting the offence with which the accused is charged (and accordingly does not include any issue as to the belief of the accused that the complainant so consented);

(c) "sexual behaviour" means any sexual behaviour or other sexual experience, whether or not involving any accused or other person, but excluding (except in section 41(3)(c)(i) and (5)(a)) anything alleged to have taken place as part of the event which is the subject matter of the charge against the accused; and

(d) subject to any order made under subsection (2), "sexual offence" shall be construed in accordance with section 62.

(2) The Secretary of State may by order make such provision as he considers appropriate for adding or removing, for the purposes of section 41, any offence to or from the offences which are sexual offences for the purposes of this Act by virtue of section 62.

(3) Section 41 applies in relation to the following proceedings as it applies to a trial, namely—

(a) *proceedings before a magistrates' court inquiring into an offence as examining justices,*

(b) *the hearing of an application under paragraph 5(1) of Schedule 6 to the* Criminal Justice Act *1991 (application to dismiss charge following notice of transfer of case to Crown Court),*

(c) the hearing of an application under paragraph 2(1) of Schedule 3 to the *Crime and Disorder Act* 1998 (application to dismiss charge by person sent for trial under section 51 or [51A] of that Act),

(d) any hearing held, between conviction and sentencing, for the purpose of determining matters relevant to the court's decision as to how the accused is to be dealt with, and

(e) the hearing of an appeal,

and references (in section 41 or this section) to a person charged with an offence accordingly include a person convicted of an offence.

[Subs. (3)(a) and (b) are repealed, and the words in square brackets in subs. (3)(c) are inserted, by the *CJA* 2003, ss.41 and 332, and Sched. 3, para. 73(1) and (3), and Sched. 37, Pt 4. The amendment to subs. (3)(c) came into force on May 9, 2005, in relation to cases sent for trial under section 51A(3)(d) of the *CDA* 1998: *Criminal Justice Act 2003 (Commencement No. 9) Order* 2005 (S.I. 2005 No. 1267). Otherwise, these provisions come into force on a day to be appointed.]

Procedure on applications under section 41

43.—(1) An application for leave shall be heard in private and in the absence of the complainant. **8–123o**

In this section "leave" means leave under section 41.

(2) Where such an application has been determined, the court must state in open court (but in the absence of the jury, if there is one)—

(a) its reasons for giving, or refusing, leave, and

(b) if it gives leave, the extent to which evidence may be adduced or questions asked in pursuance of the leave,

and, if it is a magistrates' court, must cause those matters to be entered in the register of its proceedings.

(3) Criminal Procedure Rules may make provision—

(a) requiring applications for leave to specify, in relation to each item of evidence or question to which they relate, particulars of the grounds on which it is asserted that leave should be given by virtue of subsection (3) or (5) of section 41;

(b) enabling the court to request a party to the proceedings to provide the court with information which it considers would assist it in determining an application for leave;

(c) for the manner in which confidential or sensitive information is to be treated in connection with such an application, and in particular as to its being disclosed to, or withheld from, parties to the proceedings.

[This section is printed as amended by the *Courts Act* 2003, s.109(1), and Sched. 8, para. 384.]

8–123p Sections 41 to 43 came into force on December 4, 2000: see *ante*, § 8–123k. For the transitional provisions, see *post*, § 8–123t.

For the general interpretation of Part II of this Act, see sections 62 and 63, *ante*, §§ 8–55v, 8–55w.

As to the background to this legislation, see *ante*, § 8–123k.

Section 112(3) provides that nothing in Chapter 1 of Part 11 of the *CJA* 2003 (evidence of bad character (*post*, §§ 13–5 *et seq.*)) affects the exclusion of evidence under this section.

In *R. v. A. (No. 2)* [2002] 1 A.C. 45, the House of Lords held that on ordinary principles of statutory interpretation, section 41 is incompatible with the right to a fair trial as guaranteed by Article 6 of the ECHR (*post*, § 16–57), in that it renders inadmissible evidence which may be relevant to a defence of consent on a charge of rape, *viz.* evidence of a previous consensual sexual relationship between the complainant and the accused, where the limited exceptions in subsection (3)(b) and (c) would have no application; but section 3 of the *Human Rights Act* 1998 (*post*, § 16–15) requires a court to subordinate the niceties of the language of section 41(3)(c), and in particular the touchstone of coincidence, to broader considerations of relevance judged by logical and common sense criteria of time and circumstances; and it is possible, under section 3, to read section 41(3)(c) as subject to the implied provision that evidence or questioning which is required to ensure a fair trial under Article 6 should not be treated as inadmissible; whether any particular episode of previous consensual experience should be admissible is to be left to the judgment of trial judges, the test of admissibility being (at [46]) whether the evidence, and questioning in relation to it is nevertheless so relevant to the issue of consent that to exclude it would endanger the fairness of the trial.

Judges who have to deal with applications under section 41 may find the examples given by Lord Hope (at [79]) of issues which might fall within section 41(3)(a) of more practical value than the test in relation to section 41(3)(c). The four examples were: (a) honest belief in consent; (b) the complainant was biased against the accused or had a motive to fabricate the evidence; (c) there is an alternative explanation for the physical conditions on which the prosecution rely to establish that intercourse took place; and (d), especially applicable in the case of young complainants, that the detail of their account must have come from some other sexual activity which provides an explanation for their knowledge of that activity.

In *R. v. Soroya* [2007] Crim.L.R. 181, CA, it was held that an argument that section 41 is incompatible with Article 6 on account of the fact that its prohibitions apply only to the accused without embracing the prosecution, did not arise in a case of alleged rape where, as part of a formula agreed between the parties and permitted by the judge, the jury were informed that the complainant had had intercourse on one previous occasion with a boyfriend, so as to avoid them being misled by evidence she had given to the effect that, during the alleged rape, she had told the defendant that she was a virgin so as to make him desist; what the complainant had said was relevant and admissible as important evidence bearing on the issue of consent, and no complaint could be directed at the admission of the evidence of her previous sexual experience where the result was to suggest that the confidence of the jury in the complainant's credibility might be undermined by the certain knowledge that she had told an admitted lie. Where prosecution evidence as to the complainant's prior sexual behaviour is misleading (*e.g.* a false claim to having been a virgin at the material time), it is submitted that the remedy for the defence is to be found in subsection (5).

In *R. v. T.* [2004] 2 Cr.App.R. 32, CA, it was held that where it is sought to adduce evidence or ask a question in cross-examination about the sexual behaviour of the complainant in reliance on section 41(3)(c), there is probably no requirement, under sub-paragraph (ii), of a temporal link between the behaviour of which it is sought to give evidence or ask questions about, and the sexual behaviour falling within that sub-paragraph, but there is certainly no requirement of any such link in the case of sub-paragraph (i).

The phrase "evidence adduced by the prosecution" in section 41(5) does not naturally extend to evidence given by prosecution witnesses in cross-examination; however, applying *R. v. A. (No. 2)*, *ante*, there may be cases where, in order to ensure a fair trial, that phrase ought to be read in a broader sense and the defendant ought to be allowed to call evidence to explain or rebut something said about the complainant's sexual history by a prosecution witness in cross-examination which is potentially damaging to the defendant's case, but only where the thing said was not deliberately elicited by defence counsel: *R. v. Hamadi* [2008] Crim.L.R. 635, CA.

In *R. v. F.* [2005] 2 Cr.App.R. 13, CA, it was held that where it was established that the criteria for the admissibility of sexual history evidence had been fulfilled, the court had no discretion to refuse to admit it, or to limit relevant evidence which is properly admissible; if the criteria were met, all the evidence relevant to the issues could be adduced. Whilst a judge is required to ensure that a complainant is not unnecessarily humiliated or cross-examined with inappropriate aggression, that obligation does not permit him, by way of general discretion, to prevent the proper deployment of evidence which falls within the ambit permitted by the statute merely because it comes in stark, uncompromising form.

On a charge of rape of a man, the defence were properly prohibited from questioning the complainant about his sexual orientation, even where there was medical evidence to suggest past homosexual experience and the defence was consent: *R. v. B.* [2007] Crim.L.R. 910, CA. For criticism of this decision, see *Criminal Law Week* 2007/38/8.

In *R. v. R.T.*; *R. v. M.H.* [2002] 1 W.L.R. 632, CA, it was held that for the purposes of section 41, a distinction is to be drawn between questions about sexual behaviour itself and questions concerning statements about such behaviour by the complainant; even if the questions concerned the credibility of the complainant they were not automatically barred by section 41; accordingly, in the first case, the defence should have been permitted to cross-examine the complainant about a failure to mention the allegation during an earlier investigation; and, in the second case, the defence should have been allowed to cross-examine the complainant about previous alleged lies about sexual behaviour; a failure to mention the allegation on an occasion when it might reasonably have been expected to be mentioned and established lies about previous sexual behaviour would be relevant to the credibility of the complainant; and it would be for the judge to prevent abuse where there was no evidential basis for the assertion that a previous statement was made and that it was untrue, and it would be professionally improper to elicit details of previous sexual behaviour under the guise of previous false complaints.

R. v. R.T.; *R. v. M.H.* was considered in *R. v. C. and B.* [2003] 2 *Archbold News* 2, CA, where it was held that questioning a complainant about a complaint of a sexual offence made against a person other than the defendant where there is no basis for suggesting that the complaint was false is to question the complainant about his or her sexual behaviour; if evidence is adduced about complaints which cannot properly be challenged as false, then the intention must be to elicit evidence of the sexual behaviour, the subject of such complaints, and so to deploy it in one way or another to the complainant's discredit, *e.g.* by arguing that it has been transposed and attributed to the present defendant; on that basis, the judge would have a discretion whether to permit such questioning. See also *R. v. E.* [2005] Crim.L.R. 227, CA (where it is sought to cross-examine a complainant about allegations made against persons other than the defendant, there must be a proper evidential basis for asserting not only that the statement was made, but also that it was untrue; otherwise, the questions would be about sexual behaviour, which was inadmissible; where there was no such evidential basis, to permit cross-examination about other allegations would be to descend into factual inquiries, with no obvious limit, which were wholly collateral to the issue); *R. v. W.* [2005] Crim.L.R. 966, CA (where it was sought to cross-examine the complainant about statements about previous intimacy with another man, without any intention to suggest such statements were false, on the basis that such statements were relevant to a defence of "belief in consent", the proposed questions were questions about sexual behaviour, and within the section; the judge had been correct to rule against the application where the primary issue had been the stark one of consent, belief in consent having been at best a secondary issue); and *R. v. Winter* (2008) 152(2) S.J. 29, CA (prohibition on questioning about statement concerning sexual behaviour cannot be circumvented by saying that the purpose was either to show that another such statement was untrue and that therefore the complainant was a person whose word could not be relied upon or, in the case of a statement made to the defendant, that it was only the fact of the making of the statement (not its truth) that was in issue as it went to the defendant's belief in consent; there is a difference between a belief that a woman would consent and a belief that she was in fact consenting; statements made prior to the event may encourage a belief as to the former, but they are irrelevant to the latter).

In *R. v. V.*, unreported, July 27, 2006, CA ([2006] EWCA Crim. 1901) it was said, (i) that where it was sought to cross-examine a complainant about a previous sexual allegation and to suggest that the allegation had been false, it may be necessary to obtain leave under both section 41 and section 100 of the *CJA* 2003 (non-defendant's bad character (*post*, § 13–11)); in many cases, the ruling under the 1999 Act would be the more formidable obstacle; (ii) where there was a sufficient evidential basis for asserting that the previous allegation was untrue, questioning as to the incident would not be as to "sexual behaviour" for the purposes of the 1999 Act (*R. v. R.T.*; *R. v. M.H.*, *ante*), and the test for leave under the 2003 Act would be passed; and (iii) where, in cross-examination, the complainant denied having previously admitted that a prior complaint had been false, the situation would classically be one for deployment of section 4 of the *Criminal Procedure Act* 1865 (*post*, § 8–125), and it would be open to the defence to call evidence of such admission having been made; once cross-examination as to the previous complaint was permitted under the 2003 Act, the denied statement would be one "relative to the subject-matter of the indictment" (doubting *R. v. C. and B.*, *ante*, to the extent that the contrary was suggested). As to the third point, see *R. v. Nagrecha*, *post*, § 8–123s, and the commentary in *Criminal Law Week* 2006/31/2.

In *R. v. Garaxo* [2005] Crim.L.R. 883, CA, it was held that where the appellant had been charged with sexual assault and common assault on the same person, both alleged offences arising out of the same incident, and where the defence involved admission that the defendant had been with the complainant at the time and place alleged, but complete denial of the allegations of assault (and a counter-allegation that the complainant had offered sex for money, which offer had been declined), leave should have been given to the defence to cross-examine the complainant about two previous complaints she had made, which related to different occasions and different men, and in which she alleged (as here) a blow to the head following her refusal of a sexual advance; the facts surrounding the earlier complaints were such that it would have been open to the jury to conclude that they were false (in the first case, the fact that the complainant had prefaced her complaint by saying that she wanted a crime reference number "for the social" opened up the possibility of an improper motive, and in the second case her refusal to co-operate with the police was also capable of founding an inference that the complaint was not true); and, if the jury concluded that the earlier complaints were false, this might have affected their view of the current allegation. In *R. v. V., ante*, the court observed *obiter* that *Garaxo* was a case on its own facts, and that failure by a complainant to co-operate with the police in relation to a previous allegation of a sexual offence may or may not justify a conclusion that the allegation was false, depending on the circumstances.

R. v. R.T.; *R. v. M.H., ante*, was also considered in *R. v. Abdelrahman*, *The Times*, June 15, 2005, CA, where it was said that the purpose of section 41 was not simply to protect the sexual reputation of a complainant; it was to protect her from having to relive previous sexual experiences and ordeals in the witness box, save to the extent permitted by that section; where, therefore, the defence sought leave to cross-examine the complainant about a previous allegation of rape (which had not resulted in proceedings), they could not avoid section 41 by disclaiming any intention of impeaching the complainant's sexual reputation (that she was a prostitute was in evidence); the proposed question related to sexual behaviour, and, in the absence of any evidential basis for saying it had been false, the judge had correctly refused the application.

In *R. v. Singh (Gulab)*, unreported, February 27, 2003, CA ([2003] EWCA Crim. 485), the appellant was convicted of rape at a retrial following the quashing of his conviction in the previous trial on account of fresh evidence to the effect that the complainant had not been a virgin at the time of the alleged rape whereas she had said in evidence that she had been. It was held that the judge at the retrial had been correct to refuse an application under section 41 for leave to cross-examine her as to the fact that at the first trial she had given evidence to the effect that she was a virgin at the time, that such evidence had been false, and, if necessary, to call the man with whom she had previously had intercourse. Since it had not been the intention of the prosecution to elicit from the witness evidence that she was a virgin, the only purpose of such cross-examination and evidence would have been to impugn her credibility as a witness, and section 41(4) provided that questioning for such purpose was not to be regarded as "relating to a relevant issue in the case", which was a condition precedent to the giving of leave.

In *R. v. Mokrecovas* [2002] 1 Cr.App.R. 20, CA, the defence to a charge of rape of a 17-year-old girl that was alleged to have occurred during a night when both parties were at the flat of the defendant's brother was that no intercourse took place and that the complainant lied when she first complained of rape to her father and was persisting in that lie. It was held that questioning of her as to a suggestion that she had had consensual intercourse with the defendant's brother twice (approximately two hours and approximately 12 hours before the time of the alleged rape) was not permissible as being relevant to an issue in the case (motive for lying) that was not an issue of consent, where there was other material to found a basis for saying that the complainant had a motive for lying to her father (excessive drinking and that she had gone to the flat to see the brother with whom she was friendly) and where the allowing of such questioning (even assuming that the complainant admitted the truth of the suggestions) could not improve the defence; such questioning would invade her privacy and subject her to humiliating accusations and drive a coach and horses through section 41.

Where the complainant alleged that she had met the defendant in a public house, **8–123q**
and that they had gone back to her flat where he raped her, and where the defendant's case was that consensual sexual intercourse had occurred, but that the complainant had asked for money, which he had refused, and that after intercourse had taken place he had awoken to find her with his wallet, whereupon there was a struggle, following which he had left, the judge had been correct to refuse to allow evidence of, or cross-examination as to the fact that the complainant had worked for 19 years as a prostitute; the judge had been correct to rule that the issue in the case was "an issue of consent" within section 41(3); there could be no contention that the bare fact that the victim was a prostitute was relevant to the issue of consent: *R. v. White* (2004) 148 S.J. 300, CA. As to section 41(6), it could not be accepted that information contained in a list of previous convictions for prostitution was capable of fulfilling the requirements of this subsection; to decide otherwise would be tantamount to saying that any encounter could come within the provision if it could be given a time and date.

For an example of a case in which a conviction was quashed on the basis that the judge had wrongly refused to permit cross-examination as to "sexual behaviour" of the complainant, see *R. v. Mukadi* [2004] Crim.L.R. 373, CA.

For criticism of both *White* and *Mukadi*, the former for taking too restrictive a view of the legislation, the latter for failing to embrace the rationale thereof, see *Criminal Law Week* 2004/04/11/2 (*White*) and 2004/04/17/9 (*Mukadi*).

For other examples of decisions on section 41, see *R. v. Tilambala* [2006] Crim.L.R. 344, CA (complainant in case of rape, where defence was consent, said that she was faithful to her boyfriend; evidence to the effect that she had contemplated going to the flat of a male she met at a night club correctly excluded as either falling foul of section 41 or as being irrelevant); and *R. v. Miah and Uddin* (2006) 150 S.J. 702, CA (where defence had been "belief in consent", based in part on what a non-defendant had told the appellants as to the complainant having had intercourse with him at a party on an occasion prior to the date of the alleged offence, appellants should have been allowed to identify the man in question; whilst the truth of his claim was irrelevant, the question having been whether the appellants had a genuine belief in consent, they should have been allowed to identify the source of their information). For criticism of the latter decision as eliding a belief that the complainant was consenting (relevant) with a belief that she would consent (irrelevant), see *Criminal Law Week* 2006/22/7; and see *R. v. Winter*, *ante*, as to the importance of this distinction.

8–123r In applying section 41(4), proper attention needs to be paid to the distinction between sexual history evidence "the purpose (or main purpose)" of which appears to be the impugning of the credibility of the complainant, and evidence which relates directly to the weight to be attached to the complainant's or the defendant's evidence about the central allegation; where, therefore, the evidence in question, if believed, would have strengthened the defence case on the central issue, the application under section 41 should have been acceded to: *R. v. Martin* [2004] 2 Cr.App.R. 22, CA. The complainant and defendant were known to each other (not well). The latter was a friend of man who lived in a flat adjacent to the complainant, and that man was a regular visitor to her flat. The prosecution adduced evidence that two days before the alleged offence the three of them were in her flat until late in the evening. According to the complainant, the defendant did not want to go (saying it was late), and thereafter he pestered her for sex. At one point she said that she would have sex with him, but not then. Her evidence was that this was said in order to get him to desist. According to her, he turned up unannounced two days later, asking for her promise to be kept. When she said she had not meant it, he attacked her. The case which he sought leave to put to her in cross-examination was that it had been her that had been pestering him through the night on the first day, to the extent that she had performed oral sex on him, but when, thereafter, she wanted him to go further, he rejected her and made it clear to her that he was not interested in her. The defence case was that there was no second day, and this was spiteful invention.

It appears that the court thought that the case could be brought within the "bias" example given by Lord Hope in *R. v. A. (No. 2)* (*ante*). As the court said, if the defendant's case were true, it involved his rejection of the complainant immediately after her performance of a peculiarly intimate act. This might have been especially hurtful and might have engendered hostility or spite. Indeed, the defence case was that her immediate response was "I'll have you fucked". If true, there was an undoubted issue as to bias or motivation to fabricate; and not a mere issue as to the credibility of the complainant in general.

In *R. v. E.*, *ante*, § 8–123p, it was held that the prohibition in section 41 on questioning a complainant about sexual behaviour cannot be circumvented in the case of young children on the basis that they would be too young to have an understanding of sexual matters, and therefore they would not appreciate the true nature of the experience; what they experienced was, in ordinary English, sexual; whether or not it was could not depend on the perception of the complainant.

Common law authorities

8–123s The following authorities, decided under the common law, will be of persuasive authority as to whether a particular line of questioning goes to the subject-matter of the indictment, or is relevant merely to credibility. That the distinction is a fine one is beyond argument. In *R. v. Funderburk*, 90 Cr.App.R. 466, the Court of Appeal agreed with the editors of *Cross on Evidence*, 6th ed., p. 295 (11th ed., p. 358), that where the disputed issue is a sexual one between two persons in private the difference between questions going to credit and questions going to the issue is reduced to vanishing point.

In *Funderburk* itself, the evidence of the complainant, in respect of three counts of unlawful sexual intercourse with a girl under the age of 16, had been given in such a way as to suggest that she had been a virgin at the time of the first occasion. It was held that the jury, having heard a graphic account from the girl as to how she had lost her virginity might reasonably have wished to re-appraise her evidence and her credibility if they had heard that on other occasions she had spoken of experiences which, if true, would indicate that she could not have been a virgin at the time of the incident she so vividly described. And not only should the defence have been allowed to put such statements to her, they should have been allowed, if she had denied making them, to call evidence to prove them, on the basis that they were relevant to the subject-matter of the indictment, within section 4 of the *Criminal Procedure Act* 1865 (*post*, § 8–125).

In *R. v. Nagrecha* [1997] 2 Cr.App.R. 401, CA, it was held that a suggestion in cross-examination to a complainant that she had previously made a false allegation of a similar nature against a different person went not merely to credit, but to the issue of whether or not there had been an offence committed in the instant case; and the suggestion having been denied, the defence should have been permitted to call a witness to say that she had made such an allegation. It was the fact of the similar allegation having been made, not its truth or falsity, that was relevant.

Youth Justice and Criminal Evidence Act 1999, Sched. 7, para. 5

Protection of complainants in proceedings for sexual offences

5.—(1) Nothing in Chapter III of Part II applies in relation to continuing proceedings in which leave has been given before the commencement date for that Chapter— **8–123t**

(a) under section 2 of the *Sexual Offences (Amendment) Act* 1976, or

(b) (in the case of proceedings to which section 2 does not apply) in the exercise of any similar power of the court exercisable by virtue of its inherent jurisdiction.

(2) Nothing in this Act affects the continued operation of any leave so given in relation to any such proceedings.

Criminal Procedure Rules 2005 (S.I. 2005 No. 384), Pt 36
(as substituted by the Criminal Procedure (Amendment No. 2) Rules 2006
(S.I. 2006 No. 2636))

When this Part applies

36.1. This Part applies in magistrates' courts and in the Crown Court where a defendant wants to— **8–123u**

(a) introduce evidence; or

(b) cross-examine a witness

about a complainant's sexual behaviour despite the prohibition in section 41 of the *Youth Justice and Criminal Evidence Act* 1999.

Application for permission to introduce evidence or cross-examine

36.2. The defendant must apply for permission to do so— **8–123ua**

(a) in writing; and

(b) not more than 28 days after the prosecutor has complied or purported to comply with section 3 of the *Criminal Procedure and Investigations Act* 1996 (disclosure by prosecutor).

Content of application

36.3. The application must— **8–123ub**

(a) identify the issue to which the defendant says the complainant's sexual behaviour is relevant;

(b) give particulars of—

(i) any evidence that the defendant wants to introduce, and

(ii) any questions that the defendant wants to ask;

(c) identify the exception to the prohibition in section 41 of the *Youth Justice and Criminal Evidence Act* 1999 on which the defendant relies; and

(d) give the name and date of birth of any witness whose evidence about the complainant's sexual behaviour the defendant wants to introduce.

Service of application

8–123uc **36.4.** The defendant must serve the application on the court officer and all other parties.

Reply to application

8–123ud **36.5.** A party who wants to make representations about an application under rule 36.2 must—

(a) do so in writing not more than 14 days after receiving it; and

(b) serve those representations on the court officer and all other parties.

Application for special measures

8–123ue **36.6.** If the court allows an application under rule 36.2 then—

(a) a party may apply not more than 14 days later for a special measures direction or for the variation of an existing special measures direction; and

(b) the court may shorten the time for opposing that application.

Court's power to vary requirements under this Part

8–123uf **36.7.** The court may shorten or extend (even after it has expired) a time limit under this Part.

(c) *As to bad character*

8–123v As from the commencement of Chapter 1 of Part 11 of the *CJA* 2003 (*post*, §§ 13–2 *et seq.*), and of section 100 in particular (*post*, § 13–11), cross-examination of a witness as to his "bad character" (as to which, see section 98 of the 2003 Act) has been governed by those provisions.

(d) *Where defendant has absconded*

8–123w As to the ambit of permissible cross-examination by counsel where the defendant has absconded, see *R. v. Kepple* [2007] 7 *Archbold News* 3, CA (*ante*, § 3–199).

(4) Previous inconsistent statements

8–124 Sections 4 and 5 of the *Criminal Procedure Act* 1865 (commonly referred to as *Denman's Act*) (a) re-enact sections 23 and 24 of the *Common Law Procedure Act* 1854, and (b) apply to both civil and criminal proceedings (see s.1). For other aspects of cross-examination as to credit, see *post*, §§ 8–137 *et seq.*

As to the receipt of evidence, proof of which is regulated by the provisions of the 1865 Act, under section 23 of the *CAA* 1968, see *R. v. Conway*, 70 Cr.App.R. 4, *ante*, § 7–213.

Criminal Procedure Act 1865, s.4

As to proof of contradictory statements of adverse witness

8–125 **4.** If a witness, upon cross-examination as to a former statement made by him relative to the subject-matter of the indictment or proceeding, and inconsistent with his present testimony, does not distinctly admit that he has made such statement, proof may be given that he did in fact make it; but before such proof can be given the circumstances of the supposed statement, sufficient to designate the particular occasion, must be mentioned to the witness, and he must be asked whether or not he has made such statement.

As to whether a former statement is "relative to the subject-matter of the indictment", Veale J. observed in *R. v. Bashir*, 54 Cr.App.R. 1 at 5: "I have in my opinion some discretion with regard to the subject-matter of the indictment"; see also Devlin J. in *R. v. Hart*, 42 Cr.App.R. 47 at 50, CCA.

In *R. v. Derby Magistrates' Court, ex p. B.* [1996] A.C. 487, HL, it was said that section 4 applies to written statements as well as to oral statements. But it is submitted that this is not what the legislature had in mind; the rationale behind sections 4 and 5 (*post*, § 8–127) was plainly that if a party intended to contradict a witness by proving a previous inconsistent statement of the witness, he should give the witness a proper opportunity to deal with the alleged inconsistency. In the case of a written statement, there is no better way of doing this than by showing the witness the statement (the section 5 requirement); in the case of an oral statement, section 4 demands that the witness be given sufficient detail of the circumstances of the supposed statement as will designate the occasion thereof. It is submitted that it would be quite wrong and would undermine the purpose of the legislation if the cross-examiner were to be allowed to avoid the requirements of section 5 in relation to written statements, by relying on section 4.

If a witness, when examined-in-chief as to the occurrence of a fact, answers that he does not remember it, counsel on the opposite side cannot give evidence of a former declaration by the witness of the fact having occurred, unless he has in cross-examination questioned the witness as to such a declaration; for the fact may have occurred, and the witness have formerly declared his knowledge of it, and yet he may not recollect it at the time of his examination: *Queen Caroline's case* (1820) 2 B. & B. 284 at 292. **8–126**

Where the previous inconsistent statement was made during the course of a video-recorded interview with a child, which does not form part of the examination-in-chief, the judge, in dealing with any request for the video to be replayed, is not bound by cases such as *R. v. M. (J.)* [1996] 2 Cr.App.R. 56, CA (*ante*, § 4–337), and *R. v. Rawlings*; *R. v. Broadbent* [1995] 2 Cr.App.R. 222, CA (*ante*, § 4–423), which were concerned with requests for videos forming the child's examination-in-chief to be replayed: *R. v. Eldridge and Salmon* [1999] Crim.L.R. 166, CA.

As to the evidential significance of the former inconsistent statement, see *post*, § 8–130.

Criminal Procedure Act 1865, s.5

Cross-examination as to previous statements in writing

5. A witness may be cross-examined as to previous statements made by him in writing, or reduced into writing, relative to the subject-matter of the indictment or proceeding, without such writing being shown to him; but if it is intended to contradict such witness by the writing, his attention must, before such contradictory proof can be given, be called to those parts of the writing which are to be used for the purpose of so contradicting him: Provided always, that it shall be competent for the judge, at any time during the trial, to require the production of the writing for his inspection, and he may thereupon make such use of it for the purposes of the trial as he may think fit. **8–127**

As to whether a former statement is relative to the subject-matter of the indictment, see Veale J. in *R. v. Bashir*, 54 Cr.App.R. 1 at 5, and *R. v. Funderburk*, *ante*, § 8–123s.

Where a witness is cross-examined on a previous statement, this should be done selectively and with precision; it is inappropriate to read to the witness long extracts from the statement and then merely to ask one or two short questions; such method lengthens the proceedings, makes the cross-examination difficult to follow and creates the risk that the jury will muddle the evidence of the witness with what was said on the previous occasion: *R. v. Clarke and Hewins* [1999] 6 *Archbold News* 2, CA (97 04882 W3).

In *R. v. Beattie*, 89 Cr.App.R. 302, CA, a prosecution witness had been cross-examined upon a statement made by her to the police. The cross-examination was strictly confined to two particular matters dealt with in the statement, the purpose being to show that her evidence was inconsistent on these two matters with what she said in the statement. The whole of the statement was exhibited and copied for the jury. On appeal, it was held that under section 5 it was open to the judge to allow the whole of the statement to go before the jury, but, in the view of the court, he would have been well advised in the circumstances to confine that portion of the statement to be shown to the jury to the two matters the subject of cross-examination. **8–128**

Although a witness may be cross-examined about a former written statement which is inconsistent with his testimony, without being shown the document (see s.5) the cross-examiner must have the document available even if he does not intend to contradict the witness with it: *R. v. Anderson*, 21 Cr.App.R. 178, CCA (for the position at common **8–129** law, see *Queen Caroline's case*, *ante*, referred to in *R. v. Anderson*, *ante*). If such a course is adopted, *i.e.* cross-examination about the existence of the document and indeed its contents or part of its contents, the witness's answers may not be contradicted by putting the document in evidence unless and until the witness has been shown the document and he has been given an opportunity of explaining its contents. Even if the cross-examiner shows the document to the witness he is not obliged to put it in evidence. Thus, a witness may be cross-examined as to what he said before the magistrate, and the deposition may be put into his hand for that purpose without reading it as part of the evidence of the cross-examining party. The latter, however, is bound by the answer of the witness, unless the deposition is put in (*i.e.* read out) to contradict him. It is not permissible to state that the deposition does contradict him unless it is so put in: *R. v. Riley* (1866) 4 F. & F. 964; and *R. v. Wright* (1866) 4 F. & F. 967.

> "The Act allows you to put them [*the depositions*] into the hands of the witness to refresh his recollection thereby, and to enable you to cross-examine him upon them; but you must take his answers, and if with the deposition before him he denies the suggested contradiction, or adheres to a statement which you suggest is inconsistent with the deposition, then, in order to contradict him you must put the deposition in evidence that the whole may be read; and then it will appear how far the suggested contradiction exists, and the absence of a particular statement may be explained by the context; or even if there is a discrepancy on one point, it may appear that it is only one minute point, and that in all the rest of the evidence there is a perfect consistency, so that the *general* result of the comparison may be confirmation rather than contradiction" (*per* Channell B. in *Riley*, *ante*).

8–129a In *R. v. Hayes* [2005] 1 Cr.App.R. 33, CA, it was held that where a defendant was on trial in respect of an allegation of wounding with intent, with the prosecution alleging that he had kicked or stamped on the victim's head, and his solicitor had written a letter to the CPS prior to the trial indicating his willingness to accept that he had caused actual bodily harm, and to plead guilty to such a charge, which was consistent with what he had said to the police in interview, but during cross-examination he denied having injured the victim, the judge had been right to allow the prosecution to cross-examine the defendant regarding the letter; the letter was admissible to show that the defendant had said something that was inconsistent with the evidence he had given, provided that the judge concluded there was no countervailing reason not to permit it; it went to his credibility.

As to cross-examination upon documents generally, see *post*, § 8–131.

Evidential significance of former inconsistent statements

8–130 In criminal proceedings, the common law rule was that the inconsistency went to credit and the earlier statement could not be treated as evidence of the truth of its contents: see *R. v. O'Neill* [1969] Crim.L.R. 260, CA (s.4); *R. v. Golder*, 45 Cr.App.R. 5, CCA (hostile witness, s.3 of the 1865 Act); *R. v. Birch*, 18 Cr.App.R. 26, CCA, where it was held that the proviso in section 5 with regard to the judge making such use of it as he may think fit did not entitle the judge to rule that the document was evidence of the truth of its contents. "The last words of section 5 mean for example that the judge may call attention to other parts of the statement to which no reference has been made," *per* Avory J., at p. 28.

The common law rule is effectively reversed by section 119 of the *CJA* 2003 (*post*, § 11–33). This provides that where a person who gives oral evidence admits making a previous inconsistent statement, or such a statement is proved under section 3, 4 or 5 of the 1865 Act, the statement is admissible as evidence of any matter stated in it of which oral evidence would be admissible.

(5) As to documents

8–131 For cross-examination under the *Criminal Procedure Act* 1865, s.5 (prior inconsistent written statement), see *ante*, § 8–127.

For cross-examination upon memory refreshing documents, see *ante*, § 8–86.

Police officer's notebook and contemporaneous note of interview unsigned by accused

8–132 As to the question of whether such documents should be exhibited having been cross-examined upon, see *ante*, §§ 8–86 *et seq.*, and *post*, § 15–394.

As to the limits on the use which may be made of a defendant's confession in cross-examination, see *post*, §§ 15–388 *et seq.*

Police records

In *R. v. Hackney*, 74 Cr.App.R. 194, the Court of Appeal made certain observations on the use which can properly be made of police records relating to persons in custody. The court pointed out that whilst such records should be accurate, it was inevitable that they would be completed by a number of different officers; that such records were often called for at short notice; that questions based thereon were often directed at police officers who were not responsible for making the relevant entries; that they do not prove themselves; and that the prosecution do not have to produce them without notice which allows proper opportunity of proving and explaining their contents by the evidence of officers who actually made the records. The court advised that judges should control the use made of such documents with a view to ensuring that they are used only in relation to an issue in the case. **8–133**

It should be recognised, however, that law and practice have developed since the date (1981) of this decision. The *PACE Act* 1984 and Code C issued thereunder created the position of custody officer with the specific responsibility of maintaining a custody record (see Code C:2 (Appendix A–44)). Code C:2.4A confers a right to a copy of the custody record and such records are routinely disclosed by the prosecution. Moreover, there is a possibility of statements in such records being admitted in evidence under section 117 of the *CJA* 2003 (*post*, § 11–26), subject to compliance with subsection (5). Notwithstanding these developments, it remains the case that questioning based on a custody record should be directed to the proper officer and should be confined to the issues in the case. The "proper officer" will almost invariably be the custody officer, and what was said in *Hackney* about the giving of adequate notice of the need for him to attend (assuming he is not already a prosecution witness) is as valid today as it was in 1981. **8–134**

Procedure: use to be made of document, etc.

If cross-examining counsel puts a paper into the witness's hands, and puts questions on it, and anything comes of those questions, his opponent has a right to see the paper, and re-examine on it; but if the cross-examination founded on the paper entirely fails and nothing comes of it, opposing counsel cannot demand to see the paper: *R. v. Duncombe* (1838) 8 C. & P. 369; and *R. v. Ramsden* (1827) 2 C. & P. 603. **8–135**

It is improper for counsel, in cross-examining a witness, to describe to the jury the nature of a document inadmissible in evidence which he holds in his hand, while asking the witness to look at it and then say whether he still adheres to his answer: *R. v. Yousry*, 11 Cr.App.R. 13, CCA. The proper way is for counsel to put the document into the hands of the witness and, without describing it at all, simply to ask, "Look at that piece of paper, do you still adhere to your answer?": *ibid.*, *per* Lord Coleridge J., at p. 18; and see *R. v. Tompkins*, 67 Cr.App.R. 181, CA. A document which is inadmissible cannot be made admissible simply because it is put to a defendant in cross-examination: *R. v. Treacy*, 30 Cr.App.R. 93, CCA (considered *post*, § 15–386).

In *R. v. Martin and White* [1998] 2 Cr.App.R. 385, CA, it was held to have been permissible for a defendant to have been cross-examined on an affidavit he had sworn in restraint proceedings in the High Court although the affidavit would not have been admissible at the behest of the prosecution, as the judge who had ordered the affidavit had also ordered that no disclosure made in it should be used as evidence in a prosecution of the person making the disclosure. Such a practice appears to be dangerously close to that which was condemned by the European Court of Human Rights in *Saunders v. U.K.*, 23 E.H.R.R. 313 (*post*, § 16–69). The guidance to prosecutors issued by the Attorney-General on February 3, 1998 (set out in full at 148 N.L.J. 208), as to not making use of material obtained under compulsory process was expressed to apply only to material obtained by virtue of the exercise of particular statutory powers, but the spirit thereof would apear to apply to disclosures made in compliance with an order of the High Court in restraint proceedings.

If a document written by some other person is put to a defendant and the defendant accepts what the document purports to record as true, the contents of the document become evidence against him; but if the defendant refuses to accept as true what the document purports to record, the contents of the document cannot be evidence against him: *R. v. Gillespie and Simpson*, 51 Cr.App.R. 172, CA. *Gillespie and Simpson* was applied in *R. v. Cooper (W.J.)*, 82 Cr.App.R. 74, CA, and *R. v. Cross*, 91 Cr.App.R. 115: see *post*, § 9–8.

8–136 Cross-examination of one defendant on a document admissible only against a co-defendant is improper: *R. v. Windass*, 89 Cr.App.R. 258, CA. The cross-examination took the form of asking the defendant what the co-defendant meant by various entries in the document. The Court of Appeal made clear, however, that it would be proper to put genuine questions as to fact which are based on such a document, so long as they are not linked to the document. Cross-examination of one defendant on another defendant's interview is impermissible, although this is not to say that it would never be appropriate to ask a question about what appeared in a co-defendant's interview: *R. v. Gray and Evans* [1998] Crim.L.R. 570, CA; *R. v. Clarke and Hewins* [1999] 6 *Archbold News* 2, CA (97 04882 W3).

(6) As to credit

(a) *On what credibility of witness depends*

8–137 The credibility of a witness depends upon: (a) his knowledge of the facts to which he testifies; (b) his disinterestedness; (c) his integrity; (d) his veracity; and (e) his being bound to speak the truth by such an oath as he deems obligatory, or by such affirmation or declaration as may by law be substituted for an oath. The degree of credit his testimony deserves will be in proportion to the jury's assessment of these qualities.

8–138 In addition to questions concerning a witness's means of knowledge, opportunity of observation, reasons for recollection, or belief, a witness may be asked questions about his antecedents, associations or mode of life which although irrelevant to the issue would be likely to discredit his testimony. However, such cross-examination must be within the limits prescribed by the rules laid down by the Bar Council, see *ante*, § 8–119; and section 100 of the *CJA* 2003 (*post*, § 13–11). The witness can, in general, be compelled to answer questions which go to credit: *Cundell v. Pratt* (1827) M. & M. 108. The judge has a discretion to excuse an answer when the truth of the matter suggested would not in his opinion affect the credibility of the witness as to the subject matter of his testimony. In *R. v. Sweet-Escott*, 55 Cr.App.R. 316, Assizes, Lawton J. stated that the relevant principle was this: "Since the purpose of cross-examination as to credit is to show that the witness might not be believed on oath, the matters about which he is questioned must relate to his likely standing after cross-examination with the tribunal which is trying him or listening to his evidence": at p. 320. This statement of the test was approved in *R. v. Funderburk*, 90 Cr.App.R. 466, CA. Witnesses cannot be asked to draw inferences of fact discreditable to themselves, *e.g.* whether a police officer masquerading as a reporter who was attending a meeting went there "as a spy": *R. v. Bernard* (1858) 1 F. & F. 240. Nor are inquiries as to their religious belief admissible to discredit them: *Darby v. Ouseley* (1856) 1 H. & N. 1. A witness should not be told what others have said on a subject and then be asked if he contradicts them: *North Australian Co. v. Goldsborough* [1893] 2 Ch. 381, CA. See also *ante*, § 8–116.

Where particular allegations of misconduct are put to a witness, it is not open to the party calling the witness to call evidence as to the good character of the witness for the purpose of rebutting such allegations; the character of the witness not being itself in issue, such evidence is to be excluded on the ground of collaterality: *R. v. Hamilton*, *The Times*, July 25, 1998, CA; *R. v. Beard* [1998] Crim.L.R. 585, CA; and *R. v. T. (A.B.)* [2007] 1 Cr.App.R. 4, CA (mere fact that complainant's credit is in issue cannot open the door to evidence being called simply in order to support the argument that the witness is a credible witness); but the standard practice of asking a witness his occupation is unobjectionable: *R. v. D.S.* [1999] Crim.L.R. 911, CA. See *post*, § 8–153, as to the admissibility of evidence to rebut evidence of a reputation for untruthfulness. And see

R. v. Amado-Taylor [2001] 8 *Archbold News* 1, CA, and *R. v. Tobin* [2003] Crim.L.R. 408, CA (*post*, § 20–11), as to the admissibility of evidence as to a complainant's previous behaviour and as to her attitudes and belief for the purpose of rebutting a defence of consent upon an allegation of a sexual offence.

(b) *Particular topics*

Previous inconsistent statements

See the *Criminal Procedure Act* 1865, ss.4 and 5, *ante*, §§ 8–124 *et seq.* **8–139**

Credibility of informer witness

Cross-examination of a police officer as to matters said to have an adverse effect on the credibility of an informer witness for the prosecution will now be governed by section 100 of the *CJA* 2003 (*post*, § 13–11), but the common law authorities may assist in deciding what material has "probative value" when the "matter in issue" is the credibility of a prosecution witness. As to this, see, in particular, *R. v. Thorne*, 66 Cr.App.R. 6, CA, *post*, § 13–17. **8–140**

Complaints, disciplinary proceedings, acquittals, etc.

Cross-examination of police officers as to criminal offences of which they have been convicted, disciplinary charges that have been found proved, outstanding criminal or disciplinary charges, acquittals in prior cases in which they gave evidence, or as to allegedly discreditable conduct of other police officers in the same squad will also now be governed by section 100 of the *CJA* 2003 (*post*, § 13–11). As in the case of questioning a police officer as to matters going to the credibility of a prosecution witness (*ante*), so, in this case, the common law authorities are likely to have persuasive force when an assessment is made of the "probative value" of such material. As to this, see, *post*, § 13–17. **8–141**

[The next paragraph is § 8–146.]

(c) *Finality of answers*

General rule

Generally, evidence is not admissible to contradict answers given on cross-examination as to credit—*i.e.* the answer cannot be impeached by the other party calling witnesses to contradict a witness on collateral matters: *Harris v. Tippett* (1811) 2 Camp. 637, and see *Palmer v. Trower* (1852) 8 Exch. 247; *R. v. Watson* (1817) 32 St.Tr. 1; *R. v. Cracknell* (1866) 10 Cox 408; *R. v. Cargill* [1913] 2 K.B. 271, 8 Cr.App.R. 224, CCA; and *R. v. Mendy*, 64 Cr.App.R. 4, CA, *post*, § 8–149. The borderlines of cross-examination to credit are often hard to trace. One test was formulated by Pollock C.B. in *Att.-Gen. v. Hitchcock* (1847) 1 Exch. 91 at 99: "If the answer of a witness is a matter which you would be allowed on your own part to prove in evidence—if it had such a connection with the issues, that you would be allowed to give it in evidence—then it is a matter on which you may contradict him." The question whether evidence is relevant to an issue in the case or truly collateral being one for the judge, the Court of Appeal will only interfere where his decision was plainly wrong: *R. v. Somers* [1999] Crim.L.R. 744, CA (in which the court observed, however, that the rule should be applied in a flexible way). **8–146**

As to the investigation of issues of contamination where the complainant in a sexual case denies collusion, see *R. v. R. (David)* [1999] Crim.L.R. 909, CA (*post*, § 13–108).

Where contradictory matter affecting credit has come to light since the trial, leave to cross-examine the witness about it may be given on appeal even though, had it been known, witnesses could not have been called at the trial to prove it: *R. v. Hamilton*, 13 Cr.App.R. 32, CCA; and *Ladd v. Marshall* [1954] 1 W.L.R. 1489, CA. (See also *R. v. Conway*, 70 Cr.App.R. 4, CA, *ante*, § 7–213.) **8–147**

Exceptions

(i) *Bias*

Facts showing that the witness is biased in relation to the party calling him may **8–148** be elicited on cross-examination or if denied, independently proved: *Att.-Gen. v. Hitchcock* (1847) 1 Ex. 91; *R. v. Yewin* (1811) 2 Camp. 638; *Dunn v. Aslett* (1838) 2 M. & R. 122; *R. v. Shaw* (1888) 16 Cox 503, and see *R. v. Denley* [1970] Crim.L.R. 583, Assizes (Brabin J.). In *Thomas v. David* (1836) 7 C. & P. 350, a witness denied that she was the mistress of the party calling her. It was held that evidence in rebuttal was admissible. The fact that a witness has accepted a bribe to testify may, if denied, be proved: *Att.-Gen. v. Hitchcock, ante*. Where a witness denies saying previously that he had been offered a bribe, he cannot be contradicted: *ibid.* Where a witness for the prosecution denied on cross-examination that he had had a quarrel with the defendant and had threatened to be revenged on him, evidence was allowed to be given to contradict him: *R. v. Shaw* (1888) 16 Cox 503. In *R. v. Phillips and Quayle*, 26 Cr.App.R. 200, CCA, P was charged with incest with his daughter B. B and I, a younger sister, were the principal prosecution witnesses. P's defence was that the charge was a fabrication and that the children had been "schooled" by their mother into giving false evidence. Each child denied in cross-examination that she had admitted to another person that her evidence at an earlier trial in a magistrates' court, when P was charged with indecent assault on B and bound over, was false. Each child denied too, that on the occasion of the trial for incest she was repeating what her mother had told her to say. The trial judge refused to allow the defence to call two persons to whom the children's admissions in respect of the summary trial were alleged to have been made, on the ground that the questions went to credit only. It was held that the evidence was admissible. The questions went not to credibility but to the foundation of P's defence.

8–149 In *R. v. Mendy*, 64 Cr.App.R. 4, CA, the court observed that the rule had been of great practical use and had prevented the indefinite prolongation of trials which would otherwise result if there was a minute examination of the character and credit of witnesses. However, the rule was not all-embracing (see, *e.g.*, *Att.-Gen. v. Hitchcock, ante*—the words used by Pollock C.B. at p. 101 applied almost precisely to the instant case). Accordingly, where someone in the public gallery was observed taking notes, and later, speaking to a defence witness about the case, the court held that evidence was admissible to rebut the denial of the witness in cross-examination that such a communication had taken place. The court observed that it would be strange if a jury and the court were to be kept ignorant of such behaviour by a witness. The evidence in question was intended to suggest that the witness was a participant in a scheme designed to defeat the purpose of keeping prospective witnesses out of court. The jury were entitled to know that the witness was prepared to cheat in order to deceive them so as to aid the accused. *Cf. R. v. Jales and Lawrence* (2007) 151 S.J. 194, CA (*post*, § 28–111).

8–150 In *R. v. Busby*, 75 Cr.App.R. 79, CA, B alleged that certain remarks attributed to him by the police had been fabricated. The police officers concerned were cross-examined to this effect. It was also put to the same officers in cross-examination that one of them, when visiting his premises, saw a copy of a statement made by W to B's solicitors which related to B's defence and then, in the presence of the other officer, threatened W to stop him giving evidence. Each officer denied there had been any threat. *Held*, the judge had erred in refusing to allow the defence to call W on the basis that the cross-examination had gone only to credit. The point went to an issue in the case (in the light of the suggestion that they had fabricated damaging remarks), namely, whether the police were prepared to go to improper lengths in order to secure the accused's conviction. See also *R. v. Marsh*, 83 Cr.App.R. 165, CA, and *R. v. Edwards* [1991] 1 W.L.R. 207, CA (*post*, 13–17).

(ii) *Previous convictions*

Criminal Procedure Act 1865, s.6

Proof of conviction

8–151 **6.**—(1) If, upon a witness being lawfully questioned as to whether he has been convicted of any felony or misdemeanor … he either denies or does not admit the fact or refuses to answer, it shall be lawful for the cross-examining party to prove such conviction; …

[That part of this section which is set out here is printed as amended, and repealed in part, by the *CJA* 2003, s.331, and Sched. 36, para. 79. The remainder of the section was repealed in relation to criminal proceedings by the *PACE Act* 1984, Sched. 7. The *Access to Justice Act* 1999, Sched. 13, para. 4, amends that part of the section which applies only to civil proceedings, and inserts a new subs. (2). The new subs. (2) relates to that part of subs. (1) which concerns civil proceedings.]

The circumstances in which a witness other than the defendant may lawfully be questioned as to whether he has been convicted of an offence are now governed by the *CJA* 2003, s.100, and the circumstances in which a defendant may be so questioned are governed by section 101 of that Act. For sections 100 and 101, see *post*, §§ 13–11, 13–25. **8–152**

The principal provision governing the manner in which convictions may be proved is now section 73 of the *PACE Act* 1984. As to this and related statutory provisions, see *post*, §§ 9–79 *et seq.*

(iii) *Evidence of reputation for untruthfulness*

Whether a witness has or has not been convicted, witnesses may be called to speak as to his general character, although not as to any particular offence of which he may be guilty: 2 Hawk. c. 46, s.207; *R. v. Rookwood* (1696) 13 St.Tr. 139 at 211; and *R. v. Watson* (1817) 32 St.Tr. 1. In order to impeach the credit of a witness for veracity, witnesses may be called by the other side to prove that his general reputation is such that they would not believe him upon his oath: *R. v. Brown and Hedley* (1867) L.R. 1 C.C.R. 70. They need not have heard him on oath: *R. v. Bispham* (1830) 4 C. & P. 392. In practice the question usually put is "From your knowledge of [the witness] would you believe him on his oath?": *R. v. Brown and Hedley*, *ante*; *Toohey v. Metropolitan Police Commr* [1965] A.C. 595 at 606, HL. The position was summarised by Edmund-Davies L.J. in *R. v. Richardson and Longman*, 52 Cr.App.R. 317 at 323, CA: **8–153**

> "1. A witness may be asked whether he has knowledge of the impugned witness's general reputation for veracity and whether (from such knowledge) he would believe the impugned witness's sworn testimony. 2. The witness called to impeach the credibility of another witness may also express his individual opinion (based upon his personal knowledge) as to whether the latter is to be believed upon his oath, and is not confined to giving an opinion based merely on general reputation."

The impeaching witness may not, in examination-in-chief, give reasons for his belief, but he may be asked for his reasons in cross-examination, and his answers in cross-examination cannot be contradicted: *R. v. Gunewardene* [1951] 2 K.B. 600, 35 Cr.App.R. 80, CCA; *R. v. Richardson*, *ante*; *cf. Toohey v. Metropolitan Police Commr*, *post*.

A "reputation for untruthfulness" cannot be based on two allegations of making false reports of crime; if, therefore, the defence are in possession of information that a prosecution witness has made allegations of crime against persons other than the defendant (which they denied), it would be open to the defence to put it to the witness that she had previously made such allegations and that they were false; if the witness denied the falsity, however, it would not be open to the defence to call the persons against whom the allegations were made to say that they were false under the guise of this exception: *R. v. Colwill* [2002] 6 *Archbold News* 2, CA.

Where general evidence is given of the bad character of a witness, the opposite party may cross-examine the witnesses as to the grounds of their opinion, if he thinks it prudent to do so; or he may call witnesses who can speak for the general good conduct of the witness. It has been held that, where a witness refuses to answer such a question, his not answering ought not, legally, to have any effect with the jury: *R. v. Watson* (1817) 32 St.Tr. 1; *Rose v. Blakemore* (1826) Ry. & M. 382; but the soundness of this rule is questionable: see Taylor, *Evid.*, 12th ed., s.1467.

It should be noted that the combined effect of sections 99 and 118 of the *CJA* 2003 (*post*, §§ 13–1 and 11–70 respectively) is to preserve the common law rule whereunder a person's good or bad character could be proved by evidence of reputation.

As to the inadmissibility of evidence to rebut particular allegations of misconduct, see *ante*, § 8–138.

As to the right to refuse to answer incriminating questions, see *post*, § 12–2.

(iv) *Medical evidence relating to reliability of witness's evidence*

8–154 In *Toohey v. Metropolitan Police Commr* [1965] A.C. 595, HL, it was held that medical evidence (see *post*) is admissible to show that a witness suffers from some disease, defect or abnormality of mind which affects the reliability of his evidence. Such evidence is not confined to general opinion of the unreliability of the witness, but may include all the matters necessary to show not only the foundation of and reason for the diagnosis but also the extent to which the credibility of the witness is affected. To this extent, *R. v. Gunewardene*, *ante*, is overruled.

8–155 For an example of the application of the principle in *Toohey* at first instance, see *R. v. Eades* [1972] Crim.L.R. 99, Assizes, where Nield J. permitted the prosecution to call psychiatric evidence in rebuttal to show that the defendant's account of how he had suddenly recovered his memory of a fatal road accident several weeks thereafter was inconsistent with current medical knowledge.

8–156 In *R. v. Robinson (R.)*, 98 Cr.App.R. 370, the Court of Appeal referred, *inter alia*, to *Toohey*, *ante*, and to *R. v. Turner (T.)*, 60 Cr.App.R. 80, *R. v. Silcott, Braithwaite and Raghip*, *The Times*, December 9, 1991, and *R. v. Ward*, 96 Cr.App.R. 1 (*ante*, §§ 4–326 *et seq.*). It was held that the prosecution could not call a witness of fact and then, without more, call a psychologist or psychiatrist to give reasons why the jury should regard that witness as reliable; but, if the defence proposed to call an expert witness to say that a Crown witness of fact should be regarded as unreliable because of some mental abnormality outwith the jury's experience, then, depending on the precise issue, it might be open to the Crown to call an expert in rebuttal, or even, anticipating the defence expert, as part of the prosecution case. It might even be open to the Crown to rebut by expert evidence a case put only in cross-examination that a prosecution witness was unreliable in a particular respect arising from abnormality. If such evidence was admitted, great care would need to be taken to restrict the expert opinion to meeting the specific challenge and not to allow it to extend to oath-helping.

8–157 "Medical evidence" means the evidence of medically qualified persons including psychiatrists (as to psychologists, see *post*). Before it is proper for a psychiatrist to give evidence as to a witness's reliability, the mental illness need not be such as to make the witness totally incapable of giving accurate evidence, but it must substantially affect the witness's capacity to give reliable evidence. An expert may not be called to warn a jury about a witness who is capable of giving reliable evidence, but who may well choose not to do so. If the witness is mentally capable of giving reliable evidence, it is for the jury, with the warnings from counsel and the court which the law requires, to decide whether or not that witness is giving reliable evidence: *R. v. Mackenney*, 76 Cr.App.R. 271, CA.

In *R. v. H. (J.R.) (Childhood Amnesia)* [2006] 1 Cr.App.R. 10, CA, it was said that childhood amnesia usually existed until the age of seven, so that if a witness gave a detailed narrative account, particularly if it contained extraneous detail, of events occurring before that age, a judge should direct the jury to treat such evidence with caution; and whilst childhood amnesia was a proper subject of expert evidence, it would only be in most unusual circumstances where such evidence would be relevant. In *R. v. S.*; *R. v. W.* [2007] 2 All E.R. 974, CA, it was said that such evidence would only be admissible in those rare cases in which a witness provided a description of early events containing an unrealistic amount of detail; and that expert evidence would be inadmissible where it sought to analyse the accuracy or otherwise of a statement made by the witness; it was the evidence that the witness gave at the trial that mattered, and issues as to the accuracy and truthfulness of the allegations made by the witness were critically for the jury, upon careful reflection on a claimed memory of distant childhood events. The court added that save where there was evidence of mental disability or learning difficulties, attempts to persuade the court to admit such evidence should be scrutinised with great care.

Expert evidence may be given under this head by a psychologist with suitable expertise, notwithstanding that he has no medical qualifications: *R. v. Pinfold and Mackenney* [2004] 2 Cr.App.R. 5, CA. It is not necessary that the expert should have examined the witness himself: *ibid.*; and the same principles apply both to the defendant and any other witness: *ibid.*

Evidence produced by the administration of a mechanically or chemically or hypnotically induced test on a witness so as to show the veracity or otherwise of that witness is not admissible in English law: *Fennell v. Jerome Property Maintenance Ltd, The Times*, November 26, 1986, QBD. And as to the inadmissibility of evidence obtained during a polygraph session conducted as a condition of release on licence, see section 30 of the *Offender Management Act* 2007. **8–158**

As to the admissibility of expert evidence which the defence wish to call in relation to the defendant, whether to impugn his confession, to explain his conduct at the time of the alleged offence or of arrest or interview, to show that he could not have done what is alleged or could not have known what he was doing, or intended to do it, etc., see *ante*, §§ 4–326 *et seq.*

(v) *List of exceptions not closed*

In *R. v. Funderburk*, 90 Cr.App.R. 466, CA (*ante*, § 8–123s), Henry J. said (at p. 477) that the list of exceptions to the rule that answers going to credit are final may not be closed. His Lordship listed the exceptions at p. 470. In addition to the four listed above, he includes (a) matters going to an issue in the case; (b) previous inconsistent statements relating to an issue in the case; and (c) matters tending to show that the police are prepared to go to improper lengths to secure a conviction. As to (c), see *post*, §§ 13–17, 13–21. The first two are, of course, not exceptions to the rule at all: the rule relates to matters going to credit only. **8–159**

Ambit of collateral inquiry

Where evidence is admitted for the purpose of contradicting the denial of a witness in relation to a matter going to credit only, under one of the above exceptions, and the other party seeks to call evidence to rebut that evidence, it is for the judge to balance the necessity of avoiding the pursuit of collateral matters with the risk that the trial will get out of hand, and the requirements of fairness to the accused, and, in particular, that the whole picture should be before the jury; whether the collateral matter should be investigated at all is a matter for the judge who should have regard to how extensive such inquiry is likely to become: *R. v. James* [1998] 4 *Archbold News* 3, CA (97/2785/Y4) (ruling that the judge should have allowed the calling of alibi witnesses to rebut prosecution evidence admitted under the bias exception, *ante*, that a defence witness had during an overnight adjournment assaulted one of the principal prosecution witnesses). **8–160**

(7) Of the defendant

(a) *The legislation*

Criminal Evidence Act 1898, s.1

1.—(1) [*See* ante, *§ 8–49*.] **8–161**

(2) Subject to section 101 of the *Criminal Justice Act* 2003 (admissibility of evidence of defendant's bad character), a person charged in criminal proceedings who is called as a witness in the proceedings may be asked any question in cross-examination notwithstanding that it would tend to criminate him as to any offence with which he is charged in the proceedings.

(3) [*Repealed by* Criminal Justice Act *2003, s.331, and Sched. 36, para. 80(b)*.]

(4) [*See* ante, *§ 8–49*.]

[Subs. (2) is printed as amended by the *YJCEA* 1999, s.67(1), and Sched. 4, para. 1; and the *CJA* 2003, s.331, and Sched. 36, para. 80(a).]

As to section 101 of the *CJA* 2003, and cross-examination of a defendant as to his bad character, see *post*, § 13–25.

Criminal Evidence Act 1898, s.6

6.—(1) This Act shall apply to all criminal proceedings *including proceedings in courts-martial under the* Army Act *1955 and the* Air Force Act *1955, and proceedings in courts-martial and disciplinary courts under the* Naval Discipline Act *1957, and in standing civilian courts established under the* Armed Forces Act *1976*. **8–162**

[(1A) This Act applies in relation to service proceedings as it applies in relation to criminal proceedings before a court in England and Wales.

(1B) In this section "service proceedings" means proceedings before a court (other than a civilian court) in respect of a service offence; and "service offence" and "civilian court" here have the same meanings as in the *Armed Forces Act* 2006.]

[This section is printed as amended by the *Revision of the Army and Air Force Acts (Transitional Provisions) Act* 1955, Sched. 2; and the *Armed Forces Acts* 1971 and 1976; and as repealed in part by Schedule 4 to the Act of 1955; the *Statute Law (Repeals) Act* 1981; and the *PACE Act* 1984, Sched. 7, Pt V. As from a day to be appointed, the words from "including" to the end of subs. (1) are repealed, and subss. (1A) and (1B) are inserted, by the *AFA* 2006, s.378(1) and (2), Sched. 16, para. 12, and Sched. 17.]

(b) *Competence of defendant*

8–163 As to the competence of a defendant generally, see *ante*, §§ 8–49 *et seq.*

If a defendant goes into the witness-box and admits his guilt, the Crown is still entitled to elicit from him evidence which incriminates his co-defendants: *R. v. Paul and McFarlane* [1920] 2 K.B. 183, 14 Cr.App.R. 155, CCA. See also *R. v. O'Neill* [1969] Crim.L.R. 260, CA.

Counsel for one of two or more co-defendants may cross-examine a co-defendant who has given evidence whether or not such evidence is any way adverse to his client: *R. v. Hilton* [1972] 1 Q.B. 421, 55 Cr.App.R. 466, CA; *Murdoch v. Taylor* [1965] A.C. 574 at 584, 587, HL; *R. v. Bingham and Cooke* [1999] 1 W.L.R. 598, HL.

(c) *Evidential significance of defendant's evidence in the witness-box as against a co-defendant*

8–164 Although a statement made in the absence of the defendant cannot be evidence against him (see *post*, § 15–388), if a defendant goes into the witness-box and gives evidence in the course of a joint trial then what he says becomes evidence for all the purposes of the case including the purpose of being evidence against his co-defendant: *R. v. Rudd*, 32 Cr.App.R. 138, CCA.

Where counsel for one defendant intends to suggest on behalf of his client that a co-defendant has not given truthful evidence, it is his duty to cross-examine the co-defendant, making it plain that his evidence is not accepted and in what respects it is not accepted; but this need not be done in minute detail: *R. v. Fenlon*, 71 Cr.App.R. 307, CA.

As to the issue of how to direct the jury where the evidence of one defendant incriminates another, see *ante*, §§ 4–404n, 4–404q.

(d) *Upon psychiatrists' reports*

8–165 In *R. v. Smith (S.I.)*, 69 Cr.App.R. 378, CA, it was held that where S (who was charged with murder) had been seen prior to the trial by two psychiatrists with a view to them reporting to the authorities upon his state of mind at the time of the alleged offence, S could be cross-examined upon what he had said to them on those occasions (as revealed in their reports) in the following circumstances. Although each psychiatrist had concluded that S could properly avail himself of the defence of diminished responsibility, S at his trial refused to pursue it. His defences at the trial were self-defence, provocation and automatism, the latter only emerging effectively when S himself gave evidence. The prosecution in view of this development applied successfully to cross-examine S as to certain remarks he had made to the two doctors about the incident in question. The prosecution's purpose was to demonstrate that "automatism" was a recently conceived idea and was not in his mind when interviewed by the doctors. Thereafter, the prosecution were given leave to call both doctors who gave their views upon the defence being run, and in effect they rejected it on the grounds (a) that what S had told the police and later told them was inconsistent with it; and (b) that S's own account to the jury was not physically possible. Both rulings (*i.e.* as to cross-examination and the rebuttal evidence) were upheld.

[The next paragraph is § 8–247.]

D. RE-EXAMINATION

There is a right, in re-examination, to ask all questions which may be proper to draw forth an explanation of the sense and meaning of the expressions used by the witness in cross-examination, if they be in themselves doubtful, and, also, of the motive, by which the witness was induced to use those expressions; but there is no right to go further and to introduce matter new in itself, and not suited to the purpose of explaining either the expressions or the motives of the witness: *Queen Caroline's Case* (1820) 2 B. & B. 284 at 297. Questions falling outside these limitations require the leave of the judge. **8–247**

If a witness is called merely to allow the defendant to cross-examine him, any question put by prosecuting counsel afterwards must be considered as a re-examination, and nothing can be asked which does not arise out of the cross-examination: *R. v. Beezley* (1830) 4 C. & P. 220.

Leading questions should not be asked in re-examination: see *Ireland v. Taylor* [1949] 1 K.B. 300 at 313. Provided a proper foundation is laid (*ante*, §§ 8–74 *et seq.*) documents, etc., may be used for the purposes of refreshing memory in re-examination in the same way as in examination-in-chief: *R. v. Sutton*, 94 Cr.App.R. 70, CA. As to the admissibility of previous consistent statements in re-examination, see *ante*, §§ 8–108 *et seq.*, for the grounds of admissibility. As to treating a witness as hostile in re-examination, see *R. v. Little* (1883) 15 Cox 319, and *R. v. Powell* [1985] Crim.L.R. 592, CA, *ante*, § 8–95.

Where, at the end of the defendant's cross-examination, in the course of which damaging admissions were made, his solicitor, without giving any indication that he had any re-examination, asked for an opportunity to speak to his client and a short adjournment was granted for this purpose, the stipendiary magistrate had been entitled to refuse to allow the solicitor to re-examine the defendant on the resumption of the hearing; consultation with the defendant during the course of his evidence is generally inappropriate; and (*per* Smith J.) if an advocate wishes to speak to his client during the course of his evidence, the onus is on him to make his intention plain to the court (*i.e.* that he wishes to reserve his position as to re-examination), and to give appropriate assurances as to the extent of the proposed discussion: *R. v. Reading and West Berkshire Stipendiary Magistrate, ex p. Dyson*, 164 J.P. 117, DC.

E. POWER OF JUDGE AND JURY TO QUESTION WITNESSES

(1) Judge

The judge may question any witness at any stage in the course of the trial; and, even though counsel for the prosecution has closed his case, and counsel for the defence has taken an objection to the evidence, the judge may make any further inquiries of the witness that he thinks fit, in order to answer the objection: *R. v. Remnant* (1807) R. & R. 136; see also *R. v. Wilson*, 18 Cr.App.R. 108, CCA. **8–248**

It has, however, frequently been said by the appellate courts that the judge must exercise considerable restraint in his interventions. In *R. v. Marsh*, *The Times*, July 6, 1993, the Court of Appeal stated that it was most undesirable that a judge should interrupt a witness, particularly a defendant, when giving evidence-in-chief or being cross-examined. The court cited with approval the following passage from the judgment of the court in *R. v. Hulusi and Purvis*, 58 Cr.App.R. 378 at 385:

> "It is a fundamental principle of an English trial that, if an accused gives evidence he must be allowed to do so without being badgered and interrupted. Judges should remember that most people go into the witness-box, whether they be witnesses for the Crown or defence, in a state of nervousness. They are anxious to do their best. They expect to receive a courteous hearing, and when they find, almost as soon as they get into the witness-box and are starting to tell their story, that the judge of all people is intervening in a hostile way, then, human nature being what it is, they are liable to become confused and not to do so well as they would have done had they not been badgered and interrupted."

The court went on to say that the whole purpose of the adversarial process was that the judge sat and held the ring. It was for counsel on each side to conduct examination and cross-examination and for the judge to see that they did it fairly. It was most undesirable for the judge to anticipate cross-examination or to interrupt the flow of evidence-in-chief of a witness.

Similar observations were made in *Jahree v. State of Mauritius* [2005] 1 W.L.R. 1952, PC, where it was said that observation of this principle was of particular importance in jury trials, where strongly adverse questioning by the judge might unfairly influence the jury's thinking.

Where the judge does find it necessary to intervene in the course of the examination of a witness with questions which may suggest that the evidence of the witness is not to be believed, he should remind the jury that the question of believing or not believing any particular witness is, like all other matters of fact, a question for them: *R. v. Gilson and Cohen*, 29 Cr.App.R. 174, CCA; *R. v. Bateman*, 31 Cr.App.R. 106, CCA.

8–249 Excessive intervention by the judge is commonly advanced as a ground of appeal: see the cases cited *ante*, § 7–81, as to the circumstances in which the Court of Appeal may quash a conviction on account of the conduct of the trial judge, and *R. v. Clewer*, 37 Cr.App.R. 37, CCA; *Jones v. National Coal Board* [1957] 2 Q.B. 55; *R. v. Ptohopoulos*, 52 Cr.App.R. 47, CA; *R. v. Hircock*, 53 Cr.App.R. 51, CA; *R. v. Whybrow and Saunders*, *The Times*, February 14, 1994, CA; *R. v. Roncoli* [1998] Crim.L.R. 584, CA; and *R. v. Wiggan*, *The Times*, March 22, 1999, CA.

Where a prosecution witness refuses, without good reason, to answer questions in cross-examination, it would normally be inappropriate for the judge to seek to take over (having ascertained from defence counsel the matters which it was intended to put), but such a procedure might be justified in the case of a 14-year-old complainant of a sexual offence (as here), or, possibly, in the case of an adult witness who was mentally handicapped or was a frightened or traumatised witness in the case of a sexual offence; but it would be incumbent on the judge to direct the jury as to the unusual and unsatisfactory nature of the procedure: *R. v. Cameron* [2001] Crim.L.R. 587, CA.

Judges who wish to commend witnesses for their actions in connection with the offence being tried should make their commendation in the absence of the jury: *R. v. Newman* [1990] Crim.L.R. 203, CA

(2) Jury

8–250 The jury may ask questions to a limited extent: *R. v. Lillyman* [1896] 2 Q.B. 167 at 177. The practice of inviting the jury to ask questions is generally speaking to be deprecated. Jurors are not familiar with the rules of evidence and might ask questions which would be difficult to deal with: *R. v. Barnes* [1991] Crim.L.R. 132, CA. As to questions asked after retirement, see *ante*, § 4–427.

V. RECALLING WITNESSES (INCLUDING DEFENDANT)

8–251 The judge has a discretionary power to recall, or allow the recall of, witnesses at any stage of the trial prior to the conclusion of the summing up and of putting such questions to them as the exigencies of justice require, and the Court of Appeal will not interfere with the exercise of that discretion unless it appears that an injustice has thereby resulted: *R. v. Sullivan*, 16 Cr.App.R. 121, CCA; *R. v. McKenna*, 40 Cr.App.R. 65, CCA. If a witness for the Crown is recalled by the judge or by leave of the judge, the defendant's counsel is allowed to cross-examine him on the new evidence given: *R. v. Watson* (1834) 6 C. & P. 653. It is highly irregular in a trial before a jury to recall a witness who has already given evidence merely for the purpose of giving the evidence again, see *R. v. Sullivan*, *ante*; *cf. Phelan v. Back*, 56 Cr.App.R. 257, DC, *post*. Where a witness is recalled to give evidence in rebuttal, it would appear that the judge's discretion should be exercised within the framework of the relevant principles, see *ante*, § 4–338, and *R. v. Sullivan*, *ante*. Another reason for recalling a witness is to deal with an assertion by counsel which is unsupported by the evidence, see *R. v. Sullivan*, *ante* (assertion in defence counsel's closing speech) and *R. v. Joseph*, 56 Cr.App.R. 60 (assertion in defence counsel's opening speech), where the Court of Appeal upheld the judge's decision to allow the recall of a prosecution witness on the basis that the matter relating to the recall of the witness had arisen *ex improviso*.

8–252 A defendant, once he has made himself a witness, is liable, like any other witness, to be recalled for the purpose of answering such questions as the judge permits to be put to him: *R. v. Seigley*, 6 Cr.App.R. 106, CCA; and *R. v. Wilson* [1977] Crim.L.R. 553, CA. In both *Seigley* and *Wilson*, the defendant was recalled for cross-examination on his previous convictions. In *Wilson*, the Court of Appeal doubted that they would have exercised their discretion in the same way as the judge where counsel for the prosecution had inadvertently omitted to ask about the defendant's record at the proper time.

A defendant has no right to be re-called in order to rebut evidence given by a defence witness: *R. v. Tuegel* [2000] 2 All E.R. 872, CA (upholding judge's refusal to allow a defendant to be recalled to "put in context" evidence given by one of his witnesses); and see *R. v. Ikram*, unreported, March 19, 2008, CA ([2008] EWCA Crim. 586) (defendant's opportunity to give a full account is available once only; difficult to imagine circumstances, unless bizarre in the extreme, in which the defendant should be granted the privilege of giving evidence twice in order to advance contradictory defences).

In *R. v. Grant* [1958] Crim.L.R. 42, CCA, both counsel went to see the judge during **8–253** an adjournment in the course of the summing up. They told him of certain information they had which indicated that two prosecution witnesses might have committed perjury. The judge felt there was nothing he could do but conclude his summing up. *Held*, allowing the appeal, the witnesses should have been recalled.

In *Phelan v. Back*, *ante*, a recorder, hearing an appeal against conviction, recalled and questioned a prosecution witness at the conclusion of all the evidence and after the speech of counsel for the appellant. The purpose was to enable him to refresh his memory of a witness's evidence. No shorthand note was available and, if the witness had not been recalled, the recorder would not have found the case proved. Counsel for the appellant declined the recorder's invitation to cross-examine and address him further. *Held*, a judge when sitting alone or with magistrates and without a jury has a discretion to allow evidence to be called after the normal point at which such evidence would be excluded, if the interests of justice require it and if, in the exercise of his discretion, he thinks it is proper to do so.

A witness who has given evidence for the Crown cannot subsequently be called by the defence. It is a matter for the judge's discretion whether a witness who has given evidence could be interviewed by either side. The maxim that there is "no property in a witness" has no application to such a situation. The judge controls the trial and the witnesses who give evidence; it is only by his leave that a witness may be approached afterwards: *R. v. Kelly*, *The Times*, July 27, 1985, CA.

VI. WITNESS BECOMING ILL

In *R. v. Stretton and McCallion*, 86 Cr.App.R. 7, CA, it was held that where a wit- **8–254** ness became incapable through illness of giving further evidence after having given evidence-in-chief and having been cross-examined for some hours, the judge had a discretion to allow the trial to continue on the basis of the evidence already given. The Court of Appeal clearly regarded it as relevant that there had been evidence that it would be medically and forensically impossible for the witness to go back into the witness box or to be called as a witness in a new trial. The judge had given the jury the clearest possible warning as to how they were to approach their task in that very unusual situation—conviction upheld.

See also *R. v. Wyatt* [1990] Crim.L.R. 343, CA: seven-year-old girl becoming distressed and unable to continue cross-examination. The judge, having initially adjourned the case for about 20 minutes, decided when the girl continued to cry that her evidence should proceed no further. The case was allowed to continue. *Held*, the judge had a discretion as to how long he adjourned the case and whether to permit the case to continue. The submission, based on *Stretton and McCallion*, that a lengthy warning about the effect of truncated evidence should be given to the jury was rejected. The judge had directed the jury fairly on the evidence of the girl and left it to them to determine her credibility.

For a case on the other side of the line, see *R. v. Lawless and Basford*, 98 Cr.App.R. 342, CA (accomplice who gave only direct evidence of corruption becoming ill at conclusion of examination-in-chief).

CHAPTER 9

DOCUMENTARY AND REAL EVIDENCE

I. DOCUMENTS: GENERAL

A. CONSTRUCTION

In general, the construction of documents is a matter for the jury (see, for example, *R. v. Adams*, *The Times*, January 28, 1993, *post*, § 21–182); but from that generality are excluded binding agreements between parties and all forms of legislation, in respect of which the process of construction by a judge is indispensable: *R. v. Spens*, 93 Cr.App.R. 194, CA (City Code on Take-overs and Mergers both sufficiently resembled legislation to be likewise regarded as demanding construction by a judge and constituted form of consensual agreement between parties with penal consequences.) **9–1**

B. ORIGINAL EVIDENCE OR HEARSAY

(1) Identifying purpose for which document tendered

The hearsay rule is examined in detail in Chapter 11, *post*. Having regard to the effective definition of hearsay in section 114(1) of the *CJA* 2003 (*viz*. "a statement not made in oral evidence in the proceedings") (*post*, § 11–3), any statement in a document will be hearsay and inadmissible if the purpose for which it is sought to tender it in evidence is to rely on the truth of the statement, unless the document can be brought within one of paragraphs (a) to (d) of that subsection. **9–2**

Whether public documents or private documents are being considered, two issues arise. (a) How may the document be proved? This includes questions such as whether a copy will suffice, whether parol evidence of the contents may be given and how to prove the execution of a private document. (b) Once the document has been proved or secondary evidence of its contents given, what use may be made of the contents? It is only in relation to the second question that the issue of hearsay arises. If objection is successfully taken to the admissibility of a document on the ground of hearsay, then, of course, it will not be put in evidence at all. **9–3**

Questions of hearsay usually arise in the context of private documents. Public documents can be regarded as constituting in themselves an exception to the hearsay rule: see *Sturla v. Freccia* (1880) 5 App.Cas. 623, HL; *Irish Society v. Bishop of Derry* (1846) 12 Cl. & F. 641; and *Wilton & Co. v. Phillips* (1903) 19 T.L.R. 390; which exception is expressly preserved by the *CJA* 2003, s.118(1) (*post*, § 11–70). The common law is supplemented, however, by a mass of legislation making specific provision for the admissibility in evidence of particular categories of document, or of copies thereof. Many of the statutes also make specific provision as to the use which may be made of the documents in question. The common law rules relating to public documents, the use that can be made of copies thereof and the miscellany of statutory provisions are dealt with in the second section of this chapter.

9–4 It is in the case of private documents that the purpose for which the documents are being tendered has to be identified. Often, the documents are being put in evidence for a reason which has nothing to do with the hearsay rule. Correspondence with the defendant is an obvious example: see *R. v. Rouse* [1957] Crim.L.R. 112, CCA. A letter written by the witness to the defendant may be exhibited by the witness. Its significance is that it is what was said to the defendant. The letter may contain assertions of fact. Putting it in evidence does not make it evidence of the truth of those assertions. That is hearsay. If the matter is within the knowledge of the witness he may, of course, give direct evidence thereof. This assumes that the document in question can be properly proved and that there is no other reason for its exclusion. Examples would be that the letter contained assertions of fact prejudicial to the accused which could not be supported by other admissible evidence or that it contained prejudicial and irrelevant material, such as the author's knowledge of the accused's previous convictions. In either case, editing might solve the problem. These are matters for the discretion of the judge: they have nothing to do with the principle.

(2) Documents as "real evidence"

9–5 Apart from cases, such as correspondence, where it is the fact of the document's existence and what was done with it, or what happened to it, that is relevant and which do not constitute an exception to the hearsay rule because they are not being put in to prove the truth of their contents, there is another class of document where no question of hearsay arises. This comprises documents which constitute "real" evidence. Indeed, it may be convenient to regard the former class as being admissible because it constitutes "real" evidence. The remainder of this section of this chapter is devoted to this topic. The third section of this chapter is concerned with private documents generally. It covers proof of the contents of such documents and proof of their execution. The principal statutory exceptions to the hearsay rule in relation to private documents, namely the *Bankers' Books Evidence Act* 1879 and the *CJA* 2003 are dealt with in Chapter 11, *post*.

9–6 The presence of a document at a particular location together with the word or words upon it may often be of evidential significance.

> "Sometimes it is possible to avoid [*the application of*] the hearsay rule by showing that a statement made in a document is being used as an original and independent fact for instance, that a person who made use of the document had certain information in his possession at a relevant time—and not as evidence of the facts stated. It is always important therefore, whenever an objection is taken on hearsay grounds, to ascertain for precisely what purpose the evidence is being tendered. It may be hearsay for one purpose and not, and therefore admissible, for another," *per* Cox J. in *R. v. Romeo* (1982) 30 S.A.S.R. 243.

This approach was adopted in *R. v. Lydon*, 85 Cr.App.R. 221, CA. The court also relied on the following passage in *Cross on Evidence* (6th ed., p. 464):

> "In these cases it seems that the writing when properly admissible at all, is relevant not as an assertion of the state of facts but as itself a fact which affords circumstantial evidence upon the basis of which the jury may draw an inference as it may from any other relevant circumstance of the case."

9–7 In order to put a document in evidence as "real evidence" under this principle a sufficient foundation must be laid to link the defendant to the document. Thus, it is submitted, there must be prima facie evidence that he was the author of the document, or that he was in, or had been in possession or control of the document, or that he knew of the document or was in some other way connected with it: *Howey v. Bradley* [1970] Crim.L.R. 223, DC; *R. v. Horne* [1992] Crim.L.R. 304, CA. *Cf. R. v. Podmore*, 22 Cr.App.R. 36, CCA.

9–8 Where the prosecution are in possession of a potentially incriminating document, the provenance of which they can prove but the contents of which they cannot prove against the defendant as part of their case, it does not follow that no use at all can be made of the document. The appropriate procedure is for the finding of the document to be proved as part of the prosecution case with no reference to the contents (so as to give notice to the defence of the use which might eventually be made of the document). If the defendant gives evidence, he may be asked if he was aware of the document and of its contents; if he answers in the affirmative, he may be asked about the meaning thereof: *R. v. Gillespie and Simpson*, 51 Cr.App.R. 172, CA; *R. v. Cooper (W.J.)*, 82 Cr.App.R. 74, CA (letter signed in the name of the defendant and his wife, but in the handwriting of his wife only); *R. v. Cross*, 91 Cr.App.R. 115, CA (note of a telephone call between the defendant and another, made by the other).

(3) Absence of an entry in a particular record

Where it is the absence of an entry in a particular record that is relied on, the record itself may be regarded as "real evidence". To have any evidential value, however, it will have to be properly produced by a person responsible for maintaining it who can explain the significance of the entries and omissions: see *R. v. Patel*, 73 Cr.App.R. 117, CA (for the purpose of proving that a named man is an illegal immigrant it is insufficient for an immigration officer to state that he has examined the Home Office records; it is necessary for an officer responsible for the compilation and custody of the records to testify as to the method of compilation and as to it being such that if the man's name is not there, he is an illegal immigrant). **9–9**

Similarly, where the appropriate witness produced stock cards under the *Criminal Evidence Act* 1965 (*rep.*) as evidencing the receipt of certain items into stock, it was held that there was no infringement of the hearsay rule for the witness to go further and state that the disappearance of those items from stock could not be accounted for by sale or internal use because if that had been so the cards would have been appropriately marked, which they were not. Such evidence was direct evidence from which the jury were entitled to infer that the items were stolen: *R. v. Shone*, 76 Cr.App.R. 72, CA. **9–10**

(4) Computers

Information obtained from a computer, whether printed out or read from a display, may be divided into three categories. The first is where the computer has been used simply as a calculator to process information: see *R. v. Wood (S.W.)*, 76 Cr.App.R. 23, CA, and *Sophocleous v. Ringer* [1988] R.T.R. 52, DC. **9–11**

The second category is information which the computer has been programmed to record: see *R. v. Pettigrew*, 71 Cr.App.R. 39, CA (recording of serial numbers of bank notes); *R. v. Spiby*, 91 Cr.App.R. 186, CA (recording of details of outgoing telephone calls from hotel rooms); and *R. (O.) v. Coventry Magistrates' Court* [2004] Crim.L.R. 948, DC (computer printout with breakdown of defendant's attempts to enter a website and of charges to be made to his credit card). Apart from the programming, installation and maintenance of the computer, there is no human input in the information produced. **9–12**

The third category is information recorded and processed by the computer which has been entered by a person, whether directly or indirectly. It is only information from a computer in this third category which is hearsay: to be admissible, it must be brought within one of the exceptions to the rule against hearsay (as to which, see also the *CJA* 2003, s.129, *post*, § 11–50). The computer output in the first two categories is sometimes referred to as "real evidence": as to whether this is helpful or not, see the commentary by Professor J.C. Smith on *Spiby* ([1991] Crim.L.R. 199 at 200). **9–13**

Prior to the repeal of section 69 of the *PACE Act* 1984 by the *YJCEA* 1999, s.60, it was necessary to prove the reliability of the computer before any statement in a document produced by a computer could be admitted in evidence. This applied whichever category the information fell within: see *R. v. Shephard* [1993] A.C. 380, HL. The repeal of section 69 means that any evidence pertaining to the reliability of a computer will go to weight. In the absence of any evidence to raise the issue of reliability it would seem that the maxim *omnia praesumuntur rite esse acta* will apply. **9–14**

9–15 In his commentary on *Shephard* ([1993] Crim.L.R. 295 at 296), Professor Smith identified another situation where it is sought to put in evidence a computer print-out, and in which there is no hearsay element. This is where the print-out is the fact to be proved. Such a situation is exemplified by *R. v. Governor of Brixton Prison, ex p. Levin* [1997] A.C. 741, HL, in which it was held that where a bank's computer transfers funds from one account to another (as a result of a payment request by a customer made via a computer linked to the bank's computer) and the computer records the transaction automatically, a print-out of the record is not a hearsay assertion that the transfer occurred; it is a record of the transfer itself; production of the record is evidence in proof of the transfer with no hearsay element involved.

In *ex p. Levin*, it was assumed that section 69 of the 1984 Act would have to be (and had been) complied with. In such a case, the reliability and accuracy of the computer are obviously relevant. In other cases, however, they have no relevance at all. The significance of the computer generated document lies not in its accuracy, but in the defendant's behaviour in relation to it. He may have produced it and used it; he may have used it although not responsible for its production; he may have acted on it, or in response to it; he may have annotated it; he may have been asked to explain it, etc. In such cases, it is the defendant's behaviour in relation to the print-out that is important; as such, there is no hearsay element involved and no reliability issue.

II. PUBLIC DOCUMENTS

A. DEFINITION

9–16 For the purposes of the law of evidence, a public document is a document that is made by a public officer for the purpose of the public making use of it and being able to refer to it: *Sturla v. Freccia* (1880) 5 App.Cas. 623 at 643 (*per* Lord Blackburn).

As to public documents being admissible evidence of the facts stated therein, see *ante*, § 9–3.

B. COPIES

(1) General

9–17 As a general rule it is unnecessary to produce in evidence the original of any public document. The common law and various statutes and rules of court make comprehensive provision for the use of copies. In addition, section 14 of the *Evidence Act* 1851 (*post*, § 9–24) contains a general permission as to the use of copies where there is no specific permission. It is unlikely that in the case of public documents resort would ever need to be had to section 133 of the *CJA* 2003 (*post*, § 11–5). On a literal reading, however, it applies to all documents. As to the use of microfilm copies, see *post*, § 9–102a.

(2) Classes of copy

9–18 Copies of public documents admissible in evidence fall into four classes.

Exemplification (i.e. copies under seals of State)

9–19 An exemplification under the Great Seal is itself a record, and needs no further proof: *Leyfield's case* (1610) 10 Co.Rep. 88a; Taylor, *Evid.*, 12th ed., s.1537. Exemplifications under the seal of the court to which the record belongs are in the same position: *Olive v. Guin* (1658) 2 Sid. 145.

Office copies (i.e. copies made by an officer of the court to which the document belongs)

9–20 See Taylor, *Evid.*, 12th ed., s.1538. These are admissible without proof of comparison of the copy with the original.

9–21 By the *Supreme Court [Senior Courts] Act* 1981, s.132 (renamed as from a day to be appointed: *Constitutional Reform Act* 2005, s.59(5), and Sched. 11, para. 1), every document purporting to be sealed or stamped with the seal or stamp of the Supreme Court (or of any office of the Supreme Court) shall be received in evidence in all parts of the United Kingdom without further proof. Section 136 sanctions the making of rules for providing that, in any case where a document filed in, or in the custody of, any office of the Supreme Court is required to be produced to any court or tribunal (including an umpire or arbitrator) sitting elsewhere than at the Royal Courts of Justice, (a) it shall not be necessary for any officer, whether served with a *subpoena* in that behalf or not, to attend for the purpose of producing the document; but (b) the document may be produced to the court or tribunal by sending it to the court or tribunal, in the manner prescribed in the rules, together with a certificate, in the form so prescribed, to the effect that the document has been filed in, or is in the custody of, the office. See the *Supreme Court Documents (Production) Rules* 1926 (S.R. & O. 1926 No. 461) which, by virtue of the *Interpretation Act* 1978, s.17(2)(b), have effect as if made under this section.

An office copy has been rejected for contractions and abbreviations: *R. v. Christian* (1842) C. & Mar. 388.

Record Office copies

See the *Public Records Act* 1958, s.9(2) (as amended by the *Public Records Act 1958 (Admissibility of Electronic Copies of Public Records) Order* 2001 (S.I. 2001 No. 4058)). **9–22**

Examined copies (i.e. copies made by any person from the record itself)

The person to prove such a copy at the trial must examine the copy while the officer reads the record; but the officer need not also read the copy while the witness examines the record: *Reid v. Margison* (1808) 1 Camp. 469; *Gyles v. Hill* (1809) 1 Camp. 471n.; *Rolf v. Dart* (1809) 2 Taunt. 52; Taylor, *Evid.*, 12th ed., s.1545. **9–23**

(3) General permission for use of copies

Evidence Act 1851, s.14

14. Whenever any book or other document is of such a public nature as to be admissible in evidence on its mere production from the proper custody, and no statute exists which renders its contents provable by means of a copy, any copy thereof or extract therefrom shall be admissible in evidence in any court of justice, or before any person now or hereafter having by law or by consent of parties authority to hear, receive, and examine evidence, provided it be proved to be an examined copy or extract, or provided it purport to be signed and certified as a true copy or extract by the officer to whose custody the original is entrusted, and which officer is hereby required to furnish such certified copy or extract to any person applying at a reasonable time for the same, upon payment of a reasonable sum for the same … . **9–24**

See *Re Hall's Estate* (1852) 22 L.J.Ch. 177; *Reeve v. Hodson* (1853) 10 Hare, App. XIX; *Re Porter's Trusts* (1856) 25 L.J.Ch. 688; *R. v. Weaver* (1873) L.R. 2 C.C.R. 85 (*post*, § 9–52); and Taylor, *Evid.*, 12th ed., ss.1599, 1600.

When a copy of a document, the original of which is not evidence at common law, is made evidence by statute, a copy must be produced; the original is not made evidence by implication: *Burdon v. Rickets* (1809) 2 Camp. 121n.

C. DISPENSATION ON PROOF OF FORMALITIES

Section 1 of the *Evidence Act* 1845 has facilitated the production in evidence of many of the documents mentioned in this section. **9–25**

Evidence Act 1845, s.1

1. Whenever by any Act now in force, or hereafter to be in force, any certificate, official or public document, or document or proceeding of any corporation or joint-stock or other company, or any certified copy of any document, by-law, entry in any register or other book, or of any other proceeding, shall be receivable in evidence of any particular in any court of justice, or before any legal tribunal, or either House of Parliament, or any committee of either House, or in any judicial proceeding, the same shall respectively be admitted in evidence, provided they **9–25a**

respectively purport to be sealed or impressed with a stamp, or sealed and signed, or signed alone, as required, or impressed with a stamp and signed, as directed by the respective Acts made or to be hereafter made, without any proof of the seal or stamp, where a seal or stamp is necessary, or of the signature or of the official character of the person appearing to have signed the same, and without further proof thereof, in every case in which the original record could have been received in evidence.

See Taylor, *Evid.*, 12th ed., ss.7, 1602–1607.

D. CATEGORIES OF PUBLIC DOCUMENTS

(1) Statutes and laws

Statutes

9–26 Public general statutes, like the rules of the common law or general customs of the realm, need not be either pleaded or proved, because the courts are bound *ex officio* to take judicial notice of them: see *post*, § 10–75. In order to assure the correctness of the text of a statute, reference may be made to printed copies purporting to be published by authority, or to the official editions of the statutes; but no statutory provision exists as to proof of the public general statutes of England, Great Britain, or the United Kingdom. In the case of early statutes, an exemplification can be obtained of the Act as appearing on the chancery roll, or a certified or examined copy can be made from the parliament roll, or in case of need the original roll can be produced or referred to: Taylor, *Evid.*, 12th ed., s.21; *The Prince's case* (1606) 8 Co.Rep. 18a, 20b; Craies, *Statute Law*, 7th ed., pp. 44 *et seq.* It seems that the preamble of a public general statute is admissible, but not conclusive evidence of the facts therein recited: *R. v. Sutton* (1816) 4 M. & Sel. 532.

Statutory instruments

Making thereof

9–27 By section 2(1) of the *Statutory Instruments Act* 1946 it is provided that immediately after the making of any statutory instrument (as defined in section 1) it shall be sent to the Queen's Printer of Acts of Parliament and numbered in accordance with regulations made under the Act and that, except in such cases as may be provided by any subsequent Act or prescribed by regulations made under that Act, copies thereof shall as soon as possible be printed and sold by or under the authority of the Queen's Printer. In cases where such rules are required by any Act to be published or notified in the *London*, *Edinburgh* or *Belfast Gazette*, a notice in the *Gazette* of the rules having been made, and of the place where copies can be purchased, is now sufficient compliance with such requirement (s.12(2)). By section 3(1), regulations under the Act are to make provision for the publication of lists by Her Majesty's Stationery Office showing the date on which every such instrument was first issued by or under the authority of the office. A copy of any such list is admissible in evidence as a true copy, and an entry therein is to be conclusive evidence of the date on which any such instrument was first issued.

9–28 It appears that a statutory instrument is legally operative from the moment when it is "made" unless a later date for its operation has been specified. The meaning of "made" has not been decided but it has been held at assizes that a statutory instrument acquired validity within the Act of 1946 as soon as it was made by the Minister and laid before Parliament; that the other requirements of the Act and of the regulations with regard to printing, publishing and issue were matters of procedure only, and did not affect the validity of the instrument: *R. v. Sheer Metalcraft* [1954] 1 Q.B. 586, Assizes (Streatfeild J.).

By section 3(2) of the Act of 1946, it is a defence to prove that at the time of an alleged contravention of a statutory instrument, the instrument had not been issued by or under the authority of H.M. Stationery Office, unless the prosecution prove that at that date reasonable steps had been taken for the purpose of bringing the purport of the instrument to the notice of the public, or of persons likely to be affected by it, or of the person charged (see *R. v. Sheer Metalcraft*, *ante*).

Proof thereof

9–29 On a prosecution for an offence under a statutory instrument, the instrument itself must be proved: see *R. v. Ashley*, 52 Cr.App.R. 42, CA; *Royal v. Prescott-Clarke* [1966] 1 W.L.R. 788, DC; *cf. Palastanga v. Solman* [1962] Crim.L.R. 334, DC. But non-compliance is unlikely to render a conviction "unsafe": see *R. v. Koon Cheung Tang* [1995] Crim.L.R. 813, CA (where the court had relied on a photocopy from a commercial publication).

Documentary Evidence Act 1868, s.2

9–30 **2.** Prima facie evidence of any proclamation, order, or regulation issued before or after the passing of this Act by Her Majesty, or by the Privy Council, also of any proclamation, order, or regulation issued before or after the passing of this Act by or under the authority of any such department of the government or officer as is mentioned in the first column of the Schedule hereto, may be given in all courts of justice and in all legal proceedings whatsoever, in all or any of the modes hereinafter mentioned; that is to say—

(1) By the production of a copy of the *Gazette* purporting to contain such proclamation, order, or regulation.

(2) By the production of a copy of such proclamation, order, or regulation purporting to be printed by the Government printer, or, where the question arises in a court in any British colony or possession, of a copy purporting to be printed under the authority of the legislature of such British colony or possession.

(3) By the production, in the case of any proclamation, order, or regulation issued by Her Majesty or by the Privy Council, of a copy or extract purporting to be certified to be true by the clerk of the Privy Council, or by any one of the Lords or others of the Privy Council, and, in the case of any proclamation, order, or regulation issued by or under the authority of any of the said departments or officers, by the production of a copy or extract purporting to be certified to be true by the person or persons specified in the second column of the said Schedule, in connection with such department or office.

Any copy or extract made in pursuance of this Act may be in print or in writing, or partly in print and partly in writing.

No proof shall be required of the handwriting or official position of any person certifying, in pursuance of this Act, to the truth of any copy of or extract from any proclamation, order, or regulation.

9–31 An "order" within the meaning of the 1868 Act is not necessarily a statutory instrument: *R. v. Clarke (J.F.)* [1969] 2 Q.B. 91, 53 Cr.App.R. 251, CA. The word should be given a wide meaning covering, at any rate, any executive act of government performed by the bringing into existence of a public document (see Lord Blackburn in *Sturla v. Freccia, ante*, § 9–16), for the purpose of giving effect to an Act of Parliament: *ibid.*

For the Schedule to the Act and the various extensions thereof, see *Halsbury's Statutes*, 4th ed., Vol. 18 (2005 Reissue), p. 135. Note, in particular, section 24(5) to (7) of the *Commissioners for Revenue and Customs Act* 2005 (*post*, § 25–436).

Section 5 provides for the interpretation of the following words and expressions: "British colony and possession", "legislature", "Privy Council", "Government printer" (shall mean and include "the printer to Her Majesty, and any printer purporting to be the printer authorised to print the statutes, ordinances, Acts of State, or other public Acts of the legislature of any British colony or possession, or otherwise to be the Government printer of such colony or possession" and "*Gazette*" (the *London Gazette*, the *Edinburgh Gazette*, and the *Belfast Gazette*).

By section 6 of the Act the provisions thereof are deemed to be in addition to, and not in derogation of, any powers of proving documents given by any existing statute, or existing at common law.

Documentary Evidence Act 1882, s.2

Documents printed under superintendence of stationery office

9–32 **2.** Where any enactment, whether passed before or after [June 19, 1882], provides that a copy of any Act of Parliament, proclamation, order, regulation, rule, warrant, circular, list, gazette, or document shall be conclusive evidence, or be evidence, or have any other effect, when purporting to be printed by the Government printer, or the Queen's printer, or a printer authorised by Her Majesty, or otherwise under Her Majesty's authority, whatever may be the precise expression used, such copy shall also be conclusive evidence, or evidence, or have the said effect (as the case may be) if it purports to be printed under the superintendence or authority of Her Majesty's Stationery Office.

Byelaws

Local Government Act 1972, s.238

9–33 **238.** The production of a printed copy of a byelaw purporting to be made by a local authority, or a metropolitan county passenger transport authority, upon which is endorsed a certificate purporting to be signed by the proper officer of the authority stating—

(a) that the byelaw was made by the authority;
(b) that the copy is a true copy of the byelaw;
(c) that on a specified date the byelaw was confirmed by the authority named in the certificate or, as the case may require, was sent to the Secretary of State and has not been disallowed;
(d) the date, if any, fixed by the confirming authority for the coming into operation of the byelaw;

shall be prima facie evidence of the facts stated in the certificate, and without proof of the handwriting or official position of any person purporting to sign the certificate.

[This section is printed as amended by the *Local Government Act* 1985, s.84, and Sched. 14; and the *Education Reform Act* 1988, s.237(1), and Sched.12.]

The proof of other byelaws depends on the statutes under which they are made, and on section 1 of the *Evidence Act* 1845, *ante*, § 9–25.

Colonial and foreign laws

9–34 See *post*, § 10–69.

(2) Proceedings in Parliament

9–35 Entries in the journals of the House of Lords and House of Commons may be proved by examined copies from their minute books: *R. v. Lord G. Gordon* (1781) 21 St.Tr. 485; *R. v. Lord Melville* (1806) 29 St.Tr. 549, 683; or by copies purporting to be printed by the printers to the Crown or to either House of Parliament, or under the superintendence or authority of the Stationery Office, without any proof being given that such copies were so printed: *Evidence Act* 1845, s.3; *Documentary Evidence Act* 1882, s.2. But the resolutions of either House, with a view to ulterior proceedings, are no evidence of the facts therein stated; as, for instance, when the House of Commons resolved that a plot against the Government existed, the resolution was held to be no evidence of the existence of such a plot: *Titus Oates' case* (1685) 10 St.Tr. 1073, 1165.

9–36 In *Pepper v. Hart* [1993] A.C. 593, HL, it was held that the rule excluding reference to Parliamentary material as an aid to statutory construction should be relaxed so as to permit such reference where (a) legislation was ambiguous or obscure or led to absurdity; (b) the material relied upon consisted of one or more statements by a minister or other promoter of the Bill together if necessary with such other Parliamentary material as was necessary to understand such statements and their effect; and (c) the statements relied upon were clear.

In *R. v. Secretary of State for the Environment, Transport and the Regions, ex p. Spath Holme Ltd* [2001] 2 A.C. 349, the House of Lords reiterated that the conditions in *Pepper v. Hart* should be strictly insisted upon, and held that where the issue turned not on the meaning of statutory words but on the scope of a power conferred by a statute, a ministerial statement as to the scope of the power would only be admissible if it amounted to a categorical assurance that the power would not be used in a given situation, because Parliament could then be taken to have legislated on that basis.

In *Thet v. DPP* [2007] 1 W.L.R. 2022, DC, there was an *obiter* observation that it is "at least arguable" that the defendant in a criminal prosecution should have the benefit of any ambiguity in a criminal statute, and that it is open to question whether it would ever be appropriate to refer to parliamentary material by reference to *Pepper v. Hart*, so as to impose criminal liability upon a defendant where, in the absence of such material, the court would not impose such liability.

9–37 Where the court is considering the purpose or object of a statute for some reason other than the construction of a particular domestic statutory provision, the strict criteria for admissibility in *Pepper v. Hart* do not apply: *Three Rivers District Council v. Bank of England (No. 2)* [1996] 2 All E.R. 363, QBD (Clarke J.). Nor do the strict criteria for admissibility necessarily apply where the purpose of the legislation is to introduce into English law the provisions of an international convention or of an European directive, even where the question is one of construction: *ibid.*

Practice Direction (Criminal Proceedings: Consolidation), paras II.20, IV.37 [2002] 1 W.L.R. 2870

Citation of Hansard [Court of Appeal]

II.20.1 Where any party intends to refer to the reports of parliamentary proceedings as reported in the Official Reports of either House of Parliament ("Hansard") in support of any such argument as is permitted by the decisions in *Pepper v. Hart* [1993] A.C. 593 and *Pickstone v. Freemans Plc* [1989] A.C. 66 or otherwise he must, unless the judge otherwise directs, serve upon all other parties and the court copies of any such extract together with a brief summary of the argument intended to be based upon such extract. No other report of parliamentary proceedings may be cited. **9–38**

II.20.2 Unless the court otherwise directs, service of the extract and summary of the argument shall be effected not less than five clear working days before the first day of the hearing, whether or not it has a fixed date. Advocates must keep themselves informed as to the state of the lists where no fixed date has been given. Service on the court shall be effected by sending three copies to the Registrar of Criminal Appeals, Room C212, Royal Courts of Justice, Strand, London WC2A 2LL. If any party fails to do so the court may make such order (relating to costs or otherwise) as is in all the circumstances appropriate.

Citation of Hansard [Crown Court]

IV.37.1 [*Identical to para. II.20.1,* ante.]

IV.37.2 [*Identical to para. II.20.2,* ante, *save that service on the court is to be effected by sending three copies to the chief clerk of the relevant Crown Court centre.*]

(3) Executive acts

Of British Government

The *London Gazette* printed and published by the Queen's Printer, is evidence of all Acts of State, or public matters therein notified: *Att.-Gen. v. Theakston* (1820) 8 Price 89; and *R. v. Holt* (1793) 5 T.R. 436. But in *R. v. Gardner* (1810) 2 Camp. 513, it was held not to be evidence of military appointments notified therein. And it is not evidence of a private matter contained therein, unless it be shown that the party to be affected has read the article: *Harratt v. Wise* (1829) 9 B. & C. 712. The mere production of the *Gazette* would seem to be sufficient. Where the production of the *Gazette* is made evidence of any matter, it is not sufficient to produce a whole leaf cut from the *Gazette* containing the matter sought to be proved, but not bearing the imprint of any printer or purporting to be published by authority: *R. v. Lowe* (1883) 52 L.J.M.C. 122. **9–39**

Letters patent

Letters patent may be given in evidence without further proof; or they may be proved by exemplifications under the great seal (see 1 Saund. 119n.), or the wafer great seal: *Great Seal Act* 1884. And see Taylor, *Evid.*, 12th ed., s.1526. **9–40**

Proclamations

It seems doubtful whether the courts will take judicial notice of royal proclamations without proof: *Dupays v. Shepherd* (1698) 12 Mod. 216; and *Van Omeron v. Dowick* (1809) 2 Camp. 42. Such proclamations may be proved by the *London Gazette*, or by copies purporting to be printed by the printers to the Crown, or by the printers to either House of Parliament, or by any or either of them or purporting to be printed under the superintendence or authority of H.M.'s Stationery Office (*Documentary Evidence Act* 1882, s.2, *ante*, § 9–32), without proof being given that such copies were so printed: *Documentary Evidence Act* 1868, s.2, *ante*, § 9–30; and see Taylor, *Evid.*, 12th ed., s.1527. **9–41**

Treaties

9–42 As a treaty has no binding effect until confirmed by statute (*Walker v. Baird* [1892] A.C. 491), it is rarely needed in evidence. Extradition treaties, however, are brought into operation by Order in Council, and can be proved by a Queen's Printer's copy of the order, under the *Documentary Evidence Act* 1868, s.2 (*ante*, § 9–30).

Of colonial or foreign governments

9–43 See the *Evidence Act* 1851, s.7 (proof by examined or authenticated copies).

[The next paragraph is § 9–47.]

(4) Public registers

Births, marriages, deaths, etc.

9–47 Baptisms, marriages, and burials may be proved by the parish register in which they are entered, by giving in evidence either the register itself or an examined copy of it (2 Bac.Abr.Evid.(F.); *Doe v. Barnes* (1834) 1 M. & Rob. 386); if the original is in the proper custody, that is, in the church itself, or in the custody of the rector, vicar, curate, or other officiating minister (see *Parochial Registers and Records Measure* 1978 (1978 No. 2); see also *Doe v. Fowler* (1850) 14 Q.B. 700; *Walker v. Countess Beauchamp* (1834) 6 C. & P. 552); or a copy certified by the incumbent or other person to whose custody the original register is entrusted, under the *Evidence Act* 1851, s.14 (*ante*, § 9–24). Before such books or examined copies are received the court must be satisfied that there was a public duty on the person keeping the register to satisfy himself of the truth of the entries made therein: *Doe v. Andrews* (1850) 17 Q.B. 756 at 759. Besides the register, some proof must be given of the identity of the parties married, etc.: *Birt v. Barlow* (1779) 1 Doug. 171. See also *R. v. Bellis*, 6 Cr.App.R. 283, CCA; *R. v. Rogers*, 10 Cr.App.R. 276, CCA. It would seem that a certificate of baptism does not prove the age of the party or the date of birth: *Wihen v. Law* (1821) 3 Stark.N.P. 63; but see *R. v. North Petherton* (1826) 5 B. & C. 508.

Births and Deaths Registration Act 1953, s.34

9–48 **34.**—(1) The following provisions of this section shall have effect in relation to entries in registers under this Act or any enactment repealed by this Act.

(2) An entry or a certified copy of an entry of a birth or death in a register, or in a certified copy of a register, shall not be evidence of the birth or death unless the entry purports to be signed by some person professing to be the informant and to be such a person as might be required or permitted by law at the date of the entry to give to the registrar information concerning that birth or death:

Provided that this subsection shall not apply—

(a) in relation to an entry of a birth which, not being an entry signed by a person professing to be a superintendent registrar, purports to have been made with the authority of the Registrar General; or

(b) in relation to an entry of a death which purports to have been made upon a certificate from a coroner; or

(c) in relation to an entry of a birth or death which purports to have been made in pursuance of the enactments with respect to the registration of births and deaths at sea,

(d) in relation to the re-registration of a birth under section 9 (5) of this Act.

(3) Where more than three months have intervened between the date of the birth of any child or the date when any living new-born child or still-born child was found exposed and the date of the registration of the birth of that child, the entry or a certified copy of the entry of the birth of the child in the register, or in a certified copy of the register, shall not be evidence of the birth unless—

(a) if it appears that not more than twelve months have so intervened, the entry purports either to be signed by the superintendent registrar as well as by the registrar or to have been made with the authority of the Registrar General;

(b) if more than twelve months have so intervened, the entry purports to have been made with the authority of the Registrar General:

Provided that this subsection shall not apply in any case where the original entry in the register was made before the first day of January, eighteen hundred and seventy-five.

(4) Where more than twelve months have intervened between the date of the death or of the finding of the dead body of any person and the date of the registration of that person's death, the entry or a certified copy of the entry of the death in the register, or in a certified copy of the register, shall not be evidence of the death unless the entry purports to have been made with the authority of the Registrar General: **9–49**

[*Proviso as in subs. (3)*, ante].

(5) A certified copy of an entry in a register or in a certified copy of a register shall be deemed to be a true copy notwithstanding that it is made on a form different from that on which the original entry was made if any differences in the column headings under which the particulars appear in the original entry and the copy respectively are differences of form only and not of substance.

(6) The Registrar General shall cause any certified copy of an entry given in the General Register Office to be sealed or stamped with the seal of that Office; and, subject to the foregoing provisions of this section, any certified copy of an entry purporting to be sealed or stamped with the said seal shall be received as evidence of the birth or death to which it relates without any further or other proof of the entry, and no certified copy purporting to have been given in the said Office shall be of any force or effect unless it is sealed or stamped as aforesaid.

[This section is printed as amended by the *Children Act* 1975, s.108(1)(a), and Sched. 3, para. 13(5); and the *Family Law Reform Act* 1987, s.33(1), and Sched. 2, para. 17.]

As to the proof of the date of birth of an adopted child by a certified copy of an entry in the Adopted Children Register, see the *Adoption and Children Act* 2002, s.77(5). **9–50**

By the *Non-Parochial Registers Act* 1840, s.6, all registers and records deposited in the General Register Office by virtue of that Act shall be deemed to be in legal custody, and be receivable in evidence in all courts of justice: and provision is made for the production of them by the Registrar-General. Section 17 provides that in all criminal cases the original register or record shall be produced: but see the *Evidence Act* 1851, s.14 (*ante*, § 9–24). **9–51**

As to proof of births and deaths at sea, see the *Merchant Shipping Act* 1995, s.108, and the *Merchant Shipping (Returns of Births and Deaths) Regulations* 1979 (S.I. 1979 No. 1577). **9–52**

As to marriages, see the *Marriage Act* 1949, s.65. As to marriages abroad under British law, see the *Foreign Marriage Act* 1892, s.16. As to proof of a marriage on a prosecution for bigamy, see also *post*, §§ 31–11 *et seq.*

As to proof of births, deaths and marriages out of England, see *Lyell v. Kennedy* (1889) 14 App.Cas. 437 at 448; *Brinkley v. Att.-Gen.* (1890) 15 P.D. 76. As to Scotland, see the *Registration of Births, Deaths and Marriages (Scotland) Act* 1965, s.41(3) and the *Marriage (Scotland) Act* 1977. Both Acts extend to Scotland only, but see *Drew v. Drew* [1912] P. 175 and *Whitton v. Whitton* [1900] P. 178.

Certified copies under section 34(6) of the 1953 Act, *ante*, are, in the case of death, evidence of the death only, not of the cause of death: *Bird v. Keep* [1918] 2 K.B. 692. Nor is the record of a coroner's inquisition, nor the certificate concerning the death sent to the registrar under section 23 of the 1953 Act, evidence of the cause of death: *ibid.* followed in *Re Pollock* [1941] Ch. 219 at 222. A copy of an entry in the register book of births in a registrar's district within a Superintendent Registrar's larger district, certified to be a true copy under the hand of the Deputy Superintendent Registrar, who also certified under his hand that the register book was in his lawful custody, was held to be admissible evidence, under section 14 of the *Evidence Act* 1851 (*ante*, § 9–24), of the entry in the register book upon the mere production of such copy: *R. v. Weaver* (1873) L.R. 2 C.C.R. 85. Where the age of the victim is an essential ingredient of an offence, the age must be strictly proved, and if a certificate of birth is produced, evidence must be given positively identifying the alleged victim with the child whose birth is registered in such certificate: *R. v. Rogers*, 10 Cr.App.R. 276, CCA.

Shipping

See section 10(8) of the *Merchant Shipping Act* 1995 (admissibility of entries in register of British ships). **9–53**

Newspaper proprietors

9–54 See section 15 of the *Newspaper Libel and Registration Act* 1881 (admissibility of certified copies of entries in, or extracts from, the register of newspaper proprietors).

Shareholders

9–55 As to the admissibility of a company's register of shareholders as evidence of the facts stated therein, see the *Companies Act* 1985, s.361 (replaced, as from a day to be appointed, by the *Companies Act* 2006, s.127).

(5) Registers of professional qualifications

Barristers

9–56 The proof that a person is a barrister is by certificate of his or her call issued by the Inn to which the person belongs.

Solicitors

9–57 The Records Department of the Law Society should be consulted. This would seem to be the only authoritative source of evidence as to the inclusion of an individual on the roll or his or her possession of a practising certificate on any given date.

Medical practitioners

9–58 Section 2 of the *Medical Act* 1983 makes provision for the keeping of a register of medical practititoners by the registrar of the General Medical Council. Section 34A (as inserted by the *Medical Act 1983 (Amendment) Order* 2002 (S.I. 2002 No. 3135)) provides that a certificate issued by the registrar that a person is registered, is not registered, was registered at a particular date, etc., shall be evidence of the matters certified: s.34A(2).

Dentists

9–59 A certificate purporting to be a certificate under the hand of the registrar under the *Dentists Act* 1984, s.14(6), is prima facie evidence of the facts stated in the certificate.

Pharmacists

9–60 A certificate under the hand of the registrar, and countersigned by the president or two members of the council of the Pharmaceutical Society, is evidence that the person therein specified is a registered pharmaceutical chemist under the *Pharmacy Act* 1954, s.6(2).

Veterinary surgeons

9–61 See the *Veterinary Surgeons Act* 1966, ss.2 and 9.

Nurses, midwives and other health care workers

9–62 As to nurses and midwives, see article 8 of the *Nursing and Midwifery Order* 2001 (S.I. 2002 No. 253); as to other health care workers, see article 8 of the *Health Professions Order* 2001 (S.I. 2002 No. 254).

Opticians

9–63 See the *Opticians Act* 1989, s.11(3).

Osteopaths

9–64 See the *Osteopaths Act* 1993, s.9(3).

(6) Certificates given under public authority

General

9–65 The certificates of bishops with respect to marriage and other like matters, have been received in evidence: Co.Litt. 74; *R. v. Mawbey* (1796) 6 T.R. 619 at 637.

The certificate of a British consul abroad is not admissible as evidence in the courts of this country: *Waldron v. Coombe* (1810) 3 Taunt. 162; *ex p. Church* (1822) 1 D. & R. 324; except under specific statutory provisions, *e.g. Commissioners for Oaths Act* 1889, s.6; *Foreign Marriage Act* 1892, s.16.

Elections

See the *Representation of the People Act* 1983, s.180 (certificate that election duly held; that person named in certificate was candidate). **9–66**

[The next paragraph is § 9–68.]

Companies

The certificate of incorporation issued to a company by the Registrar of Companies is conclusive evidence that the requirements for initial registration have been complied with and if it contains a statement that the company is a public company, that it is such a company: *Companies Act* 1985, s.13(7) (replaced, as from a day to be appointed, by the *Companies Act* 2006, s.15(4)). **9–68**

(7) Acts of public bodies

Corporation books, etc.

Entries in corporation books, and in the books of public companies, relating to things public and general, and entries in other public books may be proved by examined copies: *R. v. Morsell* (1718) 1 Str. 93; *Brocas v. London Corpn*, *ibid.* 307; *Mercers of Shrewsbury v. Hart* (1823) 1 C. & P. 113 (and see *ante*, § 9–23). Entries in the books of the Custom House, of the Bank of England, or the like, may be proved in the same manner. See *Hodgson v. Fullarton* (1813) 4 Taunt. 787; *Mortimer v. M'Callan* (1840) 6 M. & W. 58. But instruments of a private nature, such as a letter found in the corporation chest (*R. v. Gwyn* (1720) 1 Str. 401), or the like, must be proved in the ordinary way as any other instrument. Where under any Act, a document or proceeding of any corporation or joint stock or other company is receivable in evidence, it shall be admitted if it purports to bear the seal, or stamp, or signature directed by the Act, without proof of the seal, stamp, or signature, or official character of the person purporting to have signed: *Evidence Act* 1845, s.1 (*ante*, § 9–25a). **9–69**

Inspection of corporation books and other public writings is granted in civil actions, but not in criminal cases where the corporation is defendant, as it might have the effect of making the corporation furnish evidence to criminate itself: *R. v. Heydon* (1762) 1 W.Bl. 351; *R. v. Purnell*, *ibid.* at 37; and see *Spokes v. Grosvenor Hotel Co.* [1897] 2 Q.B. 124.

In *R. v. Halpin* [1975] Q.B. 907, 61 Cr.App.R. 97, CA, the court held that a statutory return made by a limited company and filed at the companies registry was admissible as a public document, although the registrar was under no duty to check its accuracy. When a duty is cast upon a limited company by statute to make accurate returns of company matters to the registrar so that those returns can be filed and inspected by the public, the necessary conditions have been fulfilled for that document to be admissible. All statements made on the return are prima facie proof of the truth of their contents. The fact that the return is made out of time may affect their weight but not their admissibility. **9–70**

Proceedings of local authority

See the *Local Government Act* 1972, Sched. 12, Pt VI, para. 41. **9–71**

By section 270 of the Act, "local authority" means a county council, a district council, a London Borough Council or a parish or community council.

As to proof of local authority byelaws, see *ante*, § 9–33.

(8) Judicial documents

(a) *House of Lords*

A judgment by the House of Lords is proved by an examined copy from the journal **9–72** of the House: *Jones v. Randall* (1774) 1 Cowp. 17; or by a copy purporting to be printed by authority.

(b) *Supreme Court [Senior Courts] of England and Wales*

9–73 The Supreme Court consists of the Court of Appeal, the High Court and the Crown Court which was established by the *Courts Act* 1971: *Supreme Court Act* 1981, s.1. As to the proof of documents bearing the seal or stamp of the Supreme Court (or any office thereof) and the production of documents filed in or in the custody of the Supreme Court, see the *Supreme Court Act* 1981, ss.132 and 136, *ante*, § 9–21. As from a day to be appointed, the Supreme Court of England and Wales is renamed the Senior Courts of England and Wales, and the Act of 1981 is renamed the *Senior Courts Act* 1981: see the *Constitutional Reform Act* 2005, s.59(1) and (5), and Sched. 11, para. 1.

As to the obtaining of office copies or sealed and certified copies of any will or part of a will open to inspection under section 124 of the 1981 Act, see section 125 thereof.

In Admiralty proceedings, the judgment is conclusive evidence of the facts it establishes, not only against those concerned in interest and persons claiming under them but also against strangers. Thus, a sentence condemning goods as captured from the enemy is conclusive evidence that they were so captured: *Castrique v. Imrie* (1870) L.R. 4 H.L. 414; *Minna Craig S.S. Co. v. Chartered Mercantile Bank* [1897] 1 Q.B. 55, 460; and see Dicey and Morris, *Conflict of Laws*, 11th ed., pp. 377 *et seq.*

(c) *County courts*

9–74 See the *County Courts Act* 1984, s.12.

(d) *Magistrates' courts*

Criminal Procedure Rules 2005 (S.I. 2005 No. 384), r.6.4

9–75 **6.4.** The register of a magistrates' court, or an extract from the register certified by the magistrates' court as a true extract, shall be admissible in any legal proceedings as evidence of the proceedings of the court entered in the register.

Where, on an appeal to the Crown Court, there is an issue as to the precise nature of the charge of which the appellant was convicted, a document admissible under this rule is not to be treated as conclusive; the Crown Court is entitled also to look at other material bearing on the issue: *Gill v. DPP (Note—1995)* [1998] R.T.R. 166, DC.

(e) *Records*

9–76 It used to be the rule that in all cases not provided for by statute, where a copy of a record was given in evidence, it must be a copy of the whole record, because the omission of part might have the effect of altering the sense and import of the residue: 3 Co.Inst. 173. The scope of this rule now seems to be limited to a requirement that where a verdict is sought to be proved, so as to set up an estoppel or to establish the facts found, the judgment also must be proved: *Banner v. Banner* (1865) 34 L.J.P. & M. 14; *Robinson v. Duleep Singh* (1879) 11 Ch.D. 798.

Upon an indictment for perjury, charged as having been committed on the trial of an action in the High Court, the existence and trial of the action are sufficiently proved by the production, by the officer of the court, of the copy writ and the copy pleadings filed, and by the production, by the solicitor of the defendants in the action, of the original order to dismiss the action: *R. v. Scott* (1877) 2 Q.B.D. 415. As to proof of the former trial, where perjury is assigned in respect of a trial on indictment, see the *Perjury Act* 1911, s.14 (*post*, § 28–169). If it is necessary to prove what a witness said upon a former trial it may be proved upon oath from the notes or recollections of any person who was present at the time: *Mayor of Doncaster v. Day* (1810) 3 Taunt. 262; but in order to let in such evidence it must be first proved that the former trial took place. The normal method today will be to call evidence from whoever made the official record, whether that was a shorthand note, a tape-recording or any other form of record.

(f) *Proceedings not being records*

9–77 Rules or orders of court not amounting to judgments are proved by examined or office copies: *Streeter v. Bartlett* (1848) 5 C.B. 562. A rule of court is evidence that the court has ordered as is therein stated: *Woodroffe v. Williams* (1815) 6 Taunt. 19.

Affidavits, being admissions upon oath, are evidence as such against the parties who made them: *Harmar v. Davis* (1817) 7 Taunt. 577. When filed in the central office of the High Court, they may be proved by office copies, or by examined copies, or by production of the original from the proper custody. Affidavits not filed can be proved only by production of the affidavits themselves, and by parol evidence of their having been sworn. Even if not proved to be sworn, yet perhaps they may be received as admissions of the deponents, upon proof of their handwriting. Upon an indictment for perjury in an affidavit, the affidavit, if in existence, must in all cases be produced, whether filed or not, and must be proved: *Rees v. Bowen* (1825) M'Clel. & Y. 383. But upon proof that it has been lost or destroyed, secondary evidence may be given of its contents and of the defendant's signature to it: *R. v. Milnes* (1860) 2 F. & F. 10. Where an affidavit purported to have been sworn before a commissioner for oaths, but his commission was not proved, Patteson J. held the affidavit to be admissible, and that proof of the commissioner's acting was sufficient: *R. v. Howard* (1832) 1 M. & Rob. 187. On the trial of an indictment for perjury in relation to an affidavit sworn in the Court of Queen's Bench, proof of the defendant's signature was held sufficient evidence of the swearing of the affidavit in that court, without any further proof that the master was in court when the affidavit was sworn: *R. v. Turner* (1848) 2 C. & K. 732; see also *R. v. Spencer* (1824) 1 C. & P. 260. **9–78**

Where an affidavit is sworn abroad by a person having authority to administer an oath not derived from the law of a foreign State, judicial or official notice is to be taken of his seal or signature affixed, impressed or subscribed to the affidavit: *Commissioners for Oaths Act* 1889, s.3(2).

(g) *Convictions and acquittals*

Police and Criminal Evidence Act 1984

The principal provision relating to the manner of proof of convictions and acquittals is now section 73 of the 1984 Act. **9–79**

Police and Criminal Evidence Act 1984, s.73

Proof of convictions and acquittals

73.—(1) Where in any proceedings the fact that a person has in the United Kingdom been convicted or acquitted of an offence otherwise than by a Service court is admissible in evidence, it may be proved by producing a certificate of conviction or, as the case may be, of acquittal relating to that offence, and proving that the person named in the certificate as having been convicted or acquitted of the offence is the person whose conviction or acquittal of the offence is to be proved. **9–80**

(2) For the purposes of this section a certificate of conviction or of acquittal—

(a) shall, as regards a conviction or acquittal on indictment, consist of a certificate, signed by the proper officer of the court where the conviction or acquittal took place, giving the substance and effect (omitting the formal parts) of the indictment and of the conviction or acquittal; and

(b) shall, as regards a conviction or acquittal on a summary trial, consist of a copy of the conviction or of the dismissal of the information, signed by the proper officer of the court where the conviction or acquittal took place or by the proper officer of the court, if any, to which a memorandum of the conviction or acquittal was sent;

and a document purporting to be a duly signed certificate of conviction or acquittal under this section shall be taken to be such a certificate unless the contrary is proved.

(3) In subsection (2) above "proper officer" means—

(a) in relation to a magistrates' court in England and Wales, the designated officer for the court; and

(b) in relation to any other court, the clerk of the court, his deputy or any other person having custody of the court record.

(4) The method of proving a conviction or acquittal authorised by this section shall be in addition to and not to the exclusion of any other authorised manner of proving a conviction or acquittal.

[This section is printed as amended by the *Access to Justice Act* 1999, s.90(1), and Sched. 13, para. 12; and the *Courts Act* 2003, s.109(1), and Sched. 8, para. 285.]

9–81 As to the interpretation of this section, see section 82, *post*, § 9–84.

Section 73 is concerned solely with how convictions and acquittals may be proved. It says nothing about when they may be proved or what a conviction—if put in evidence—may be taken as proving. An acquittal is not conclusive evidence of innocence: see *R. v. Terry* [2005] 2 Cr.App.R. 7, CA (*ante*, § 4–331).

As to how to prove that the person named in the certificate is the person whose conviction or acquittal is to be proved, see the cases collected at § 32–118, *post*.

As to what should be included in a certificate of conviction, see *R. v. Hacker* [1995] 1 Cr.App.R. 332, HL (*post*, § 21–317).

Section 74, which is supplemented by section 75, is relevant to the second point. Subsections (2) and (3) effectively state that where a person's conviction is proved, he is to be taken to have committed the offence of which he was convicted unless he proves that he did not commit the offence. The burden of proof is cast upon the person seeking to show that the original court's finding was wrong.

Police and Criminal Evidence Act 1984, ss.74, 75

Conviction as evidence of commission of offence

9–82 **74.**—(1) In any proceedings the fact that a person other than the accused has been convicted of an offence by or before any court in the United Kingdom or by a Service court outside the United Kingdom shall be admissible in evidence for the purpose of proving, that that person committed that offence, where evidence of his having done so is admissible, whether or not any other evidence of his having committed that offence is given.

(2) In any proceedings in which by virtue of this section a person other than the accused is proved to have been convicted of an offence by or before any court in the United Kingdom or by a Service court outside the United Kingdom, he shall be taken to have committed that offence unless the contrary is proved.

(3) In any proceedings where evidence is admissible of the fact that the accused has committed an offence, ..., if the accused is proved to have been convicted of the offence—

(a) by or before any court in the United Kingdom; or

(b) by a Service court outside the United Kingdom,

he shall be taken to have committed that offence unless the contrary is proved.

(4) Nothing in this section shall prejudice—

(a) the admissibility in evidence of any conviction which would be admissible apart from this section; or

(b) the operation of any enactment whereby a conviction or a finding of fact in any proceedings is for the purposes of any other proceedings made conclusive evidence of any fact.

[This section is printed as amended by the *CJA* 2003, s.331, and Sched. 36, para. 85.]

Provisions supplementary to section 74

9–83 **75.**—(1) Where evidence that a person has been convicted of an offence is admissible by virtue of section 74 above, then without prejudice to the reception of any other admissible evidence for the purpose of identifying the facts on which the conviction was based—

(a) the contents of any document which is admissible as evidence of the conviction; and

(b) the contents of the information, complaint, indictment or charge-sheet on which the person in question was convicted,

shall be admissible in evidence for that purpose.

(2) Where in any proceedings the contents of any document are admissible in evidence by virtue of subsection (1) above, a copy of that document, or of the material part of it, purporting to be certified or otherwise authenticated by or on behalf of the court or authority having custody of that document shall be admissible in evidence and shall be taken to be a true copy of that document or part unless the contrary is shown.

(3) Nothing in any of the following—

(a) section 14 of the *Powers of Criminal Courts (Sentencing) Act* 2000 (under which a conviction leading to probation or discharge is to be disregarded except as mentioned in that section);

[(aa) section 187 of the *Armed Forces Act* 2006 (which makes similar provision in relation to service convictions);]

(b) [*Scotland*]; and

(c) [*Northern Ireland*],

shall affect the operation of section 74 above; and for the purposes of that section any order made by a court of summary jurisdiction in Scotland under section 182, or section 183 of the said Act of 1975 shall be treated as a conviction.

(4) Nothing in section 74 above shall be construed as rendering admissible in any proceedings evidence of any conviction other than a subsisting one.

[This section is printed as amended by the *PCC(S)A* 2000, s.165(1), and Sched. 9, para. 98; and as amended, as from a day to be appointed, by the *AFA* 2006, s.378(1), and Sched. 16, para. 103 (insertion of subs. (3)(aa)).]

Police and Criminal Evidence Act 1984, s.82

Part VIII—interpretation

82.—(1) In this Part of this Act— **9–84**

"confession", [*see* post , *§ 15–354*];

"court-martial" means a court-martial constituted under the Army Act *1955, the* Air Force Act *1955 or the* Naval Discipline Act *1957 or a disciplinary court constituted under section 50 of the said Act of 1957*;

"proceedings" means criminal proceedings, including [service proceedings; and]—

(a) *proceedings in the United Kingdom or elsewhere before a court-martial constituted under the* Army Act *1955 or the* Air Force Act *1955*;

(b) *proceedings in the United Kingdom or elsewhere before the Courts-Martial Appeal Court—*

(i) *on an appeal from a court-martial so constituted or from a court-martial constituted under the* Naval Discipline Act *1957; or*

(ii) *on a reference under section 34 of the* Courts-Martial (Appeals) Act *1968; and*

(c) *proceedings before a Standing Civilian Court; and*

"Service court" *means a court-martial or a Standing Civilian Court* [the Court Martial or the Service Civilian Court].

[(1A) In subsection (1) "service proceedings" means proceedings before a court (other than a civilian court) in respect of a service offence; and "service offence" and "civilian court" here have the same meanings as in the *Armed Forces Act* 2006.]

(2) *In this Part of this Act references to conviction before a Service court are references—*

(a) *as regards a court-martial constituted under the* Army Act *1955 or the* Air Force Act *1955, to a finding of guilty which is, or falls to be treated as, a finding of the court duly confirmed;*

(b) *as regards—*

(i) *a court-martial; or*

(ii) *a disciplinary court,*

constituted under the Naval Discipline Act *1957, to a finding of guilty which is, or falls to be treated as, the finding of the court;*

and "convicted" shall be construed accordingly.

(3) [*See* post, *§ 15–535*.]

[In the definition of "proceedings", the words following "a court-martial" in para. (a), and the words "so constituted" in para. (b) are repealed, as from a day to be appointed, by the *YJCEA* 1999, s.67(3), and Sched. 6. The definition of "court-martial", paras (a) to (c) of the definition of "proceedings" and subs. (2) are repealed, as from a day to be appointed, by the *AFA* 2006, s.378(1) and (2), Sched. 16, para. 104(1) and (2), and Sched. 17. The words in square brackets are inserted, as from a day to be appointed, by *ibid.*, s.378(1), and Sched. 16, para. 104(1) and (3).]

Section 74(1), (2)

"convicted"

For the purposes of section 74, "convicted" does not mean "convicted and sentenced": *R. v. Robertson*; *R. v. Golder* [1987] Q.B. 920, 85 Cr.App.R. 304, CA. **9–85**

In *R. v. Hayter* [2005] 2 Cr.App.R. 3, HL, it was held that where the prosecution case against the appellant was that he had procured his co-defendant to commit murder, and it was accepted by the prosecution that their case against him must fail if they failed to prove, as against him, that the co-defendant had committed the murder, and the only evidence that the co-defendant had committed the murder consisted of an out-of-court confession, the judge had been correct to direct the jury that if they found the co-defendant guilty, then they could use that finding of fact against the appellant, notwithstanding the general inadmissibility of the confession of one co-accused as against another. There was no infringement of that rule where the judge clearly directed the jury that they could not use the content or words of the confession as evidence against the appellant; section 74 of the 1984 Act gave the prosecution the right to adduce in evidence against an accused another person's prior conviction, and while that section had no direct effect where both accused stand trial together, it was hardly to be thought that Parliament, had it turned its mind to the comparatively rare cases where the question arises of using evidentially against one defendant the jury's already formed conclusion that his co-defendant is guilty, would have proposed a different approach; there was no logical reason why it should have done so, but rather every reason why it would have legislated for a similar approach; and the policy underlying section 74 suggests that it would be wrong and anomalous to give an unnecessarily expansive reach to the rule about out of court confessions. It was further held that not only could such a confession contribute to the case against the co-accused when the jury retire, but it could assist the prosecution when a judge considered whether there was a case to answer at the close of the prosecution evidence; it is sometimes necessary for a judge to make a conditional ruling on issues or the relevance or admissibility of evidence.

Hayter, *ante*, does not permit a jury to make a finding of fact in favour of one defendant, such finding being based on the exculpatory parts of a mixed statement made by that defendant, and then to use that finding against a co-defendant by a process of elimination: *Persad v. State of Trinidad and Tobago* [2008] 1 Cr.App.R. 9, PC.

"where evidence of his having done so is admissible"

9–86 Prior to its amendment by the *CJA* 2003, section 74(1) and (2) not only provided for proof that a person other than the accused committed an offence by proof that he was convicted of it, but also stipulated when such proof could be given, *viz.* where it was "relevant to any issue" in the proceedings in question. As amended, subsection (1) no longer helps as to when evidence of a person other than the accused committed an offence is admissible, merely providing that evidence that such person was convicted of the offence is admissible where evidence that he committed the offence is admissible, for the purpose of proving that he did indeed commit it.

9–87 Admissibility will now depend on a combination of the general law and of the terms of the 2003 Act. Where the evidence that a person other than the accused committed an offence amounts to evidence of "bad character" within section 98 of the 2003 Act (*post*, § 13–5), its admissibility will be governed by section 100 of that Act (*post*, § 13–11). Such evidence will not, however, constitute "bad character" evidence within those provisions if it "has to do with the alleged facts of the offence with which the defendant is charged" (s.98(a)). This exclusion is considered in more detail at § 13–6, *post*. In essence, however, it is submitted that wherever it is essential to prove the guilt of a person other than the defendant of a particular offence, evidence tendered for that purpose is directly relevant to the guilt of the defendant on the charge that he faces and is thus not evidence of bad character that is subject to section 100. Furthermore, where there is evidence of a joint enterprise, it has always been legitimate at common law to prove against one defendant the acts and declarations of his joint venturers done in furtherance of the common enterprise (see *post*, §§ 33–65 *et seq.*). This rule was specifically saved by the 2003 Act: see s.118(1) (*post*, § 11–70); and evidence of such acts and declarations is clearly not to be subject to the requirements of section 100.

9–88 Where, therefore, there is an allegation of a joint enterprise (two people are seen to set upon, assault and rob the victim in an unprovoked attack), and there is evidence of A and B being together in the vicinity before the attack and of them running away from the area shortly after the attack, evidence that B participated in the attack would be admissible on the trial of A. In the language of section 74, "evidence of [B's] having [committed the offence] is admissible" on the trial of A, and, if B has been convicted, whether in a separate trial or by virtue of a plea of guilty, the fact that he committed the offence may be proved by proof of his conviction. In all such cases, it is submitted, that the evidence that the person other than the defendant committed an offence is evidence that "has to do with the alleged facts of the offence with which the defendant is charged" and is admissible under the general law, and is not subject to section 100 (and this has now been confirmed in *R. v. S.* (2007) 151 S.J. 1260, CA), though it will be subject the judge's discretion to exclude evidence the admission of which may adversely affect the fairness of the proceedings (*post*). Pre-2003 Act cases such as *R. v. Gummerson and Steadman* [1999] Crim.L.R. 680, CA; *R. v. Grey*, 88 Cr.App.R. 385, CA; and *R. v. Kempster*, 90 Cr.App.R. 14, CA (*post*, § 13–18), would all appear to fall within this principle.

In any case where there is an issue as to the admissibility of evidence of the conviction of a person other than the defendant under section 74, it is important to note that section 74 is concerned with the admissibility of the fact that that person committed the offence, not with the fact that he was convicted of it. If the fact that he committed it is admissible, then this may be proved by evidence that he was convicted of it.

Discretionary exclusion

In a series of cases decided prior to the amendment of section 74 by the 2003 Act, it was held that it was open to the judge to exclude evidence which was admissible under section 74 pursuant to the discretion conferred by section 78 of the 1984 Act (*post*, § 15–452): *R. v. O'Connor*, 85 Cr.App.R. 298, CA; *R. v. Curry* [1988] Crim.L.R. 527, CA; *R. v. Mattison* [1990] Crim.L.R. 117, CA; *R. v. Kempster*, *ante*; *R. v. Hillier and Farrer*, 97 Cr.App.R. 349, CA; *R. v. Skinner* [1995] Crim.L.R. 805, CA. It was said to be important to ascertain at the outset the purpose for which it was sought to adduce the evidence; as only then could an informed decision be made as to whether the evidence should be excluded under section 78: *Kempster*, *ante*; *R. v. Wardell* [1997] Crim.L.R. 450, CA. In *Kempster* it was said that, if admitted, the judge should ensure that counsel did not seek to use the evidence for any other purpose, although it might happen that the judge would either limit or extend that purpose at a later stage of the trial. **9–89**

In *Curry*, *ante*, the court endorsed observations in *R. v. Robertson*; *R. v. Golder* [1987] Q.B. 920, 85 Cr.App.R. 304, CA, that section 74 should be sparingly used, and particularly so in relation to joint offences such as conspiracy and affray (riot and violent disorder would have been better examples). Where the evidence sought to be put before the jury by virtue of section 74 expressly or by necessary inference imported the complicity of the person on trial, the exclusionary discretion under section 78 should be exercised. As to this, see also *O'Connor*, *ante*. **9–90**

In *Curry* (a conspiracy case), the conviction was quashed despite the fact that there were two defendants who had pleaded not guilty and one who had pleaded guilty; it was, therefore, possible that one of the two defendants contesting the charge was not guilty, but it inevitably followed from the admission of the plea of guilty (there being no other alleged conspirators) that one of the two must have been guilty. In *R. v. Lunnon*, 88 Cr.App.R. 71, CA, evidence of the conviction of one of four alleged conspirators was admitted on the trial of the other three. The Court of Appeal upheld the judge's decision; the court seems to have been influenced by the fact that the judge had significantly watered down the effect of his ruling by directing the jury that the evidence of the conviction went only to the issue of whether there had been a conspiracy and—somewhat illogically (as the judge himself said)—that it was open to them to acquit all three of the accused they were trying (*i.e.* find that there was no conspiracy). Where the allegation is of a conspiracy with persons not charged, whether named or not, there is unlikely to be any unfairness in admitting evidence of a conviction of a defendant who has pleaded guilty; there is no necessary inference that any of the other defendants is guilty.

In *Mattison*, *ante*, it was held that the co-defendant's plea of guilty was admissible on the appellant's trial for gross indecency with him, but, his defence having been one of complete denial, the evidence should have been excluded under section 78. It is difficult to see why the nature of the defence is relevant. For a case in which the evidence seems to have been just as damning, where its admission was upheld, see *R. v. Bennett* [1988] Crim.L.R. 686, CA.

In *R. v. Stewart* [1999] Crim.L.R. 746, CA, the defence to charges of kidnapping and robbery involved the assertion that no offences had taken place. The admission of a co-defendant's pleas of guilty was upheld notwithstanding that this effectively determined the case by destroying the defence. The discretion given to the court is to be exercised so as to take account of the interests of justice as a whole.

9–90a In *R. v. S., ante*, § 9–88, it was held that the law as summarised in *R. v. Kempster* is still the law (*i.e.* a judge should exercise his discretion so as to admit the guilty plea of a co-defendant only sparingly, taking into account the enormous weight such a conviction may have in the minds of the jury and the difficulty of properly testing it at trial, especially where its admission would close off many or all of the issues which the jury are trying on the basis that the co-defendant could not, or could scarcely, have been guilty unless the defendant was also guilty).

Directing the jury

9–91 Where evidence is admitted under section 74, it is incumbent on the trial judge to explain to the jury the purpose for which it has been admitted and its limitations: *R. v. Kempster, ante*; *R. v. Skinner, ante*.

Change of plea

9–92 In *R. v. Fedrick* [1990] Crim.L.R. 403, the appellant's co-defendant changed his plea to guilty during the trial. It was held that the jury should have been discharged; in the circumstances, the plea of guilty, had it been tendered at the outset, would not have been admissible under section 74. See also *R. v. Marlow* [1997] Crim.L.R. 457, CA, to similar effect. It is submitted, however, that no general rule can be inferred from these decisions; the discharge of the jury is peculiarly a matter within the judge's discretion to be decided in the light of the facts of the particular case (see generally *ante*, §§ 4–253 *et seq.*).

The need to discharge the jury may be avoided by the device adopted by the judge in *R. v. McCarthy* [1998] 2 *Archbold News* 1, CA (96/8158/Y5). Upon it being indicated that one of two defendants charged with conspiracy wished to change his plea to guilty, the judge discharged the jury in relation to that defendant with nothing being said to the jury as to the reasons for their being discharged in relation to one defendant. They were told not to speculate. It was held that the course taken was proper, and, there being no reason to suppose that the jury had in fact speculated that the defendant had changed his plea, knowledge of which, it was agreed, would have had damning consequences for the appellant, the conviction was safe.

Section 74(3)

9–93 In *R. v. Harris, The Independent*, May 5, 2000, CA, it was held that the purpose of section 74(3) is not to define or enlarge the circumstances in which evidence of the fact that the accused had committed an offence is admissible, but simply to assist in the mode of proof of that fact. This applies *a fortiori* to the amended version of the subsection. The admissibility of evidence of the defendant having committed an offence or offences other than the offence or offences with which he is charged is now governed by section 101 of the *CJA* 2003 (*post*, § 13–25).

Section 75

9–94 Where evidence of a co-accused's conviction is admissible under section 74(1) for the purpose of proving that he committed the offence of which he was convicted, there is no further test of relevance under section 75; where the conviction is admissible, then the materials referred to in section 75(1) (*e.g.* the indictment) are admissible for the purpose of identifying the facts on which the conviction was based: *R. v. Hinchcliffe, Leckie, Brady and Doherty* [2002] 4 *Archbold News* 1, CA.

In *R. v. Ali; R. v. Bhatti* [2006] 1 Cr.App.R. 8, CA, it was said that where the conviction of a person other than the defendant is proved under section 74, the facts upon which the conviction was based may be proved by reference to the judge's summing up; section 75 allows for proof of such facts by reference to documents such as the indictment, but declares that this is "without prejudice to the reception of any other admissible evidence". As, however, the convictions of all the appellants were quashed on other grounds, what was said on this issue was *obiter*, and should be treated with caution.

Proof of convictions in various parts of United Kingdom

A conviction in any one part of the United Kingdom may be proved against a defendant in any other part thereof: *Prevention of Crimes Act* 1871, s.18. **9–95**

Proof of convictions in magistrates' courts

See also section 104 of the *MCA* 1980 and rule 37.5 of the *Criminal Procedure Rules* 2005 (S.I. 2005 No. 384). **9–96**

Proceedings in colonial and foreign courts

Foreign convictions are provable under section 7 of the *Evidence Act* 1851 (*i.e.* by examined copy or a copy authenticated in the manner prescribed therein), together with appropriate evidence to identify the person said to have been convicted as the person who was convicted: *R. v. Mauricia* [2002] 2 Cr.App.R. 27, CA. **9–97**

Section 7 of the Act of 1851 does not apply to the proceedings of the courts of Scotland or Ireland, nor, it would seem, to those of the Isle of Man or Channel Islands, and judgments of these courts must in criminal cases ordinarily be proved as those of foreign courts were at common law, *i.e.* by exemplifications under the seal of the court, if the court has a seal, and evidence must also be given that the seal affixed to the exemplification is in fact the seal of the court: *Henry v. Adey* (1803) 3 East 221; *Alves v. Banbury* (1814) 4 Camp. 28; *Cavan v. Stewart* (1816) 1 Stark.N.P. 525; *Appleton v. Lord Braybrook* (1816) 2 Stark.N.P. 6; *Flindt v. Atkins* (1811) 3 Camp. 215n; and *Alivon v. Furnival* (1834) 1 Cr.M. & R. 277.

III. PRIVATE DOCUMENTS

A. PROOF OF CONTENTS

(1) Primary and secondary evidence

The old rule that only the "best" evidence is admissible now survives only in the rule that secondary evidence of the contents of a private document cannot be given without accounting for the non-production of the original. Otherwise all admissible evidence is in general equally accepted, though its weight may be a matter of comment: see *Kajala v. Noble*, 75 Cr.App.R. 149, DC (video recordings and copies thereof), and *R. v. Wayte*, 76 Cr.App.R. 110, CA. For a recent application of the rule, see *Smakowski and Zestfair Ltd v. Westminster City Council* [1990] Crim.L.R. 419, DC. **9–98**

When a deed or other document or writing is to be given in evidence, the document itself must be produced at the trial: *Leyfield's case* (1610) 10 Co.Rep. 88a, except in the following cases: (a) where the document is in the hands of the opposite party: *Reed v. Brookman* (1788) 3 T.R. 151; *Wymark's Case* (1593) 5 Co.Rep. 74a; provided that notice to produce has been given: *post*; (b) where the document is in the possession of a person who cannot be compelled to produce it, as, for example, a person entitled to claim diplomatic immunity (see *R. v. Nowaz*, 63 Cr.App.R. 178, CA); (c) where the writing is physically impossible to produce, as, for example, inscriptions on tombstones, a pedigree hung up in a family mansion, or a writing on a wall (see *Goodright v. Moss* (1777) 2 Cowp. 591; *Berkeley Peerage Claim* (1811) 4 Camp. 401; *Mortimer v. M'Callan* (1840) 6 M. & W. 58); and (d) where it has been lost by time or accident, or by any other casualty, as by fire, etc. (*Reed v. Brookman*, *ante*) (and as to proof of loss, **9–99** see *Freeman v. Arkell* (1824) 2 B. & C. 494). In such cases, its contents may be proved by a copy or other secondary evidence: *Leyfield's case*, *ante*; *Medlicot v. Joyner* (1669) 1 Mod. 4.

In the above cases, the purpose for which it is sought to put the document or writing in evidence is as real evidence: hence the problem is literally one of how to prove the contents of the document or writing.

9–100 Where it is sought to rely on the contents to prove the truth of any statement therein, the issue is one of hearsay. All statements in documents are hearsay (but see §§ 9–11, 9–12, *ante*, as to certain computer-produced information) and inadmissible unless an exception to the hearsay rule applies (as to which, see s.114 of the *CJA* 2003, *post*, § 11–3). Once, however, it has been decided that a statement in a document is admissible in evidence it may be proved either by production of the original or by production of a copy thereof, or of the material part thereof, authenticated in such a manner as the court may approve: *CJA* 2003, s.133 (*post*, § 11–5). For the purposes of this section it is immaterial how many removes there are between a copy and the original: *ibid*. This section is wide in its terms, but it is submitted that it is not a convenient provision whereunder the restrictions on the production of copies can be avoided where the document or writing is being tendered as real evidence.

9–101 There are no degrees of secondary evidence and therefore a party who has laid the foundation for such evidence may prove the contents of a deed by parol, though it appears that there is an attested copy in existence: *Brown v. Woodman* (1834) 6 C. & P. 206. Parol evidence of the contents of a document may be admitted as secondary evidence, although a copy of the document is in existence: *R. v. Collins*, 44 Cr.App.R. 170, CCA. Further, it would seem that, where secondary evidence is going to be given by means of a copy, it is not essential that the original copy should be produced and that a copy of a copy may suffice, provided that a witness is called who can verify, not only that the copy produced is a true copy of the original copy, but also that it is in the same terms as the original: *ibid*. p. 174. Parol evidence cannot be substituted for any instrument which the law requires to be in writing: Taylor, *Evid*., 12th ed., s.396; nor for the written evidence of any contract which the parties have put in writing: *ibid*. s.401; nor for any writing, the existence or contents of which are disputed, and which is material to the issue between the parties, and is not merely the memorandum of some other fact: *ibid*. s.409; yet where the writing does not fall within either of these three classes, no reason exists for excluding parol evidence of its existence and contents: *ibid*. s.415. Thus, although a written receipt may have been given for the payment of money, proof of the fact of payment may be made by any person who witnessed it: *Rambert v. Cohen* (1802) 4 Esp. 213. So the fact of marriage may be proved by the evidence of a person who was present at it, although the marriage may have been registered: *R. v. Manwaring* (1856) Dears. & B. 132. Also, where three witnesses stated that a vessel was a British ship of Shields and that she was sailing under the British flag, but no proof was given of the register of the vessel or of the ownership, it was held that this was sufficient proof that the vessel was British: *R. v. Seberg* (1870) L.R. 1 C.C.R. 264. Also, on an indictment for unlawful assembly, parol evidence of proclamations and inscriptions has been admitted without producing copies: *R. v. Hunt* (1820) 1 St.Tr.(n.s.) 171; *R. v. Fursey* (1833) 3 St.Tr.(n.s.) 543, 561; and *O'Connell v. R.* (1844) 5 St.Tr.(n.s.) 1, 278.

9–102 When a copy of a document, the original whereof is not evidence at common law, is made evidence by Act of Parliament, a copy must be produced; the original is not made admissible evidence by implication: *Burdon v. Rickets* (1809) 2 Camp. 121n.

Microfilm copies

Police and Criminal Evidence Act 1984, ss.71, 72

Microfilm copies

9–102a **71.** In any proceedings the contents of a document may (whether or not the document is still in existence) be proved by the production of an enlargement of a microfilm copy of that document or of the material part of it, authenticated in such manner as the court may approve.

Where the proceedings concerned are proceedings before a magistrates' court inquiring into an offence as examining justices this section shall have effect with the omission of the words "authenticated in such manner as the court may approve".

[This section is printed as amended (insertion of second paragraph) by the *CPIA* 1996, s.47 and Sched. 1, para. 24. As amended, it applies only in relation to alleged offences into which no criminal investigation had begun before April 1, 1997: S.I. 1997 Nos 682 & 683, *post*, § 9–118. The second paragraph is repealed as from a day to be appointed: *CJA* 2003, s.332, and Sched. 37, Pt 4.]

Part VII—supplementary

72.—(1) In this Part of this Act— 9–102b

"copy", in relation to a document, means anything onto which information recorded in the document has been copied, by whatever means and whether directly or indirectly, and

"statement" means any representation of fact, however made; and

"proceedings" means criminal proceedings, including [service proceedings]—

(a) *proceedings in the United Kingdom or elsewhere before a court-martial constituted under the* Army Act *1955 or the* Air Force Act *1955*;

(b) *proceedings in the United Kingdom or elsewhere before the Courts-Martial Appeal Court—*

(i) *on an appeal from a court-martial so constituted or from a court-martial constituted under the* Naval Discipline Act *1957*; *or*

(ii) *on a reference under section 34 of the* Courts-Martial (Appeals) Act *1968*; *and*

(c) *proceedings before a Standing Civilian Court.*

[(1A) [*Identical to s.82(1A)*, ante, *§ 9–84*.]]

(2) Nothing in this Part of this Act shall prejudice any power of a court to exclude evidence (whether by preventing questions from being put or otherwise) at its discretion.

[This section is printed as amended by the *Civil Evidence Act* 1995, s.15(1), and Sched. 1, para. 9(1) and (2); and as amended, as from a day to be appointed, by the *AFA* 2006, s.378(1), and Sched. 16, para. 102 (insertion of words in square brackets in subs. (1), and of subs. (1A), and omission of paras (a) to (c) in definition of "proceedings").]

(2) Notice to produce

Where a written instrument is in the hands of the opposite party, it is necessary to serve him or his solicitor with a notice to produce it: and if he does not produce it at the trial, in pursuance of the notice, then, upon proving the service of the notice, secondary evidence of its contents may be given. The rule in this respect is the same in criminal as in civil cases: *Att.-Gen. v. Le Merchant* (1772) 2 T.R. 201n.; subject to the qualification that the rules for compelling discovery of documents by the defendant do not apply to criminal cases. If the defendant refuses to produce the original and invites the prosecution to rely on secondary evidence, the court is entitled to suggest that the production of the original is desirable, but has no power to order the defendant to produce the original and so provide evidence against himself: *Trust Houses Ltd v. Postlethwaite*, 109 J.P. 12. The notice to produce must be served a reasonable time before the trial. What is such reasonable time must depend on the circumstances of each case. 9–103

Where the indictment gives sufficient notice to the defendant of the subject of inquiry, so that he may prepare himself to produce the written instrument, if necessary for his defence, a notice to produce it is not required. So, upon an indictment for stealing a bill of exchange, parol evidence of it was admitted without a notice to produce it: *R. v. Aickles* (1784) 1 Leach 294. And on an indictment for stealing a letter described as addressed in a certain way, Pollock C.B. held that a witness might be asked how the letter was addressed, although no notice to produce it had been given: *R. v. Clube* (1857) 3 Jur.(n.s.) 698. So, upon an indictment for administering an unlawful oath, where it appeared that the defendant read the oath from a paper, parol evidence of what the defendant in fact said was held sufficient, without giving him notice to produce the paper: *R. v. Moors* (1801) 6 East 419n. at 421n. Where a seditious meeting came to certain resolutions, and the defendant, who was chairman, gave a copy of these resolutions to another person, it was held that this copy might be given in evidence without a notice to produce the original: *R. v. Hunt* (1820) 1 St.Tr.(n.s.) 171. Nor is it necessary 9–104 to produce or account for banners bearing certain inscriptions, etc., exhibited at such meetings; parol evidence of such matters by eye-witnesses is perfectly admissible to show the general character and intention of the assembly: *ibid*.

9–105 On the other hand, upon an indictment for setting fire to a house, with intent to defraud an insurance office, secondary evidence of the policy of insurance cannot be given, without proof of proper notice to produce the original: *R. v. Kitson* (1853) Dears. 187. And in the case of an indictment for perjury, in falsely swearing that there was no draft of a statutory declaration which had been prepared by the defendant, and the materiality of the existence of such draft turned upon its contents and the fact of certain alterations having been made upon it, parol evidence of the contents of the draft and of the alterations made in it was held inadmissible, no notice to produce such draft having been given to the defendant: *R. v. Elworthy* (1867) L.R. 1 C.C.R. 103. The best evidence rule does not apply to chattels: see *post*, § 9–154.

[The next paragraph is § 9–107.]

(3) Defendant unrepresented

9–107 In *R. v. Wayte*, 76 Cr.App.R. 110, CA, the court gave guidance upon the procedure to be adopted when it is sought to produce in evidence photostat copies of documents in cases where their admissibility may be in question and the defendant is unrepresented.

B. PROOF OF EXECUTION

(1) By an attesting witness

9–108 If there was no subscribing witness, proof of the handwriting of the parties is sufficient, the law in such a case presuming a delivery. In the case of an instrument which is attested, but to the validity of which attestation is not requisite, it may be proved as if there had been no attesting witness: *Criminal Procedure Act* 1865, s.7. An instrument, to the validity of which attestation is required, may, instead of being proved by an attesting witness, be proved in the manner in which it might be proved if no attesting witness were alive: *Evidence Act* 1938, s.3; but this exception does not apply to wills and other testamentary documents. If an attesting witness be called, it does not appear necessary that he should swear that the deed was actually executed in his presence, if he were afterwards desired to attest it by the party who executed it (*Grellier v. Neale* (1792) Peake, 3rd ed., 198 (N.P.); *Powell v. Blackett* (1794) 1 Esp. 97), or in the presence of the party (*Park v. Mears* (1800) 3 Esp. 171), and attested it accordingly, this will be sufficient, provided that the attestation and execution be done so nearly at the same time as fairly to be deemed parts of the same transaction. On the other hand, a party who sees an instrument executed, but who is not desired by the parties to attest it, cannot, by afterwards putting his name to it, prove it as an attesting witness: *M'Craw v. Gentry* (1812) 3 Camp. 232.

(2) Exceptions to rule as to proof by attesting witness

9–109 (a) Where a deed (and the same as to a will, *Doe d. Oldham v. Woolley* (1828) 8 B. & C. 22) is 20 years old or upwards, the court will presume that it has been duly executed, and will not require it to be proved (*Evidence Act* 1938, s.4), provided possession has followed the deed, or some satisfactory account is given of it, and provided there is no erasure or interlineation in it, and that it does not import fraud; otherwise it must be proved as in ordinary cases, either by the attesting witness, or by evidence of his and the party's handwriting: 2 Bac.Abr.Ev.(F.); and see *Swinnerton v. Marquis of Stafford* (1810) 3 Taunt. 91.

(b) Where a deed enrolled (and to which enrolment was necessary) is given in evidence, it is not necessary to prove the execution of it by the subscribing witness; but it may be proved by enrolment indorsed on it, or if the deed is lost, by an examined copy of the enrolment, as already mentioned, *ante*, § 9–23.

(c) Where one deed is recited in another, proof of the second deed is deemed proof of the one recited, as against the parties to the second deed and those claiming under them: 2 Bac.Abr.Ev.(F.).

(d) Secondary evidence of the execution may be given by proving the handwriting of the witness and the party (see *post*, §§ 14–60 *et seq.*, as to how this may be done), upon proof of any of the following circumstances: that the subscribing witness is dead; *Nelson v. Whittall* (1817) 1 B. & Ald. 19, or has become insane; *Currie v. Child* (1812) 3 Camp. 283, or is abroad out of reach of the process of the court; *Holmes v. Pontin* (1791) Peake, 3rd ed., 135; *Cooper v. Marsden* (1793) 1 Esp. 1; and see *Hodnett v. Forman* (1815) 1 Stark.N.P. 90, whether domiciled abroad or not; *Prince v. Blackburn* (1802) 2 East 250, or that from circumstances it may fairly be presumed that he had left the kingdom; *Wyatt v. Bateman* (1836) 7 C. & P. 586, or that after a bona fide serious and diligent inquiry he cannot be found; *Willman v. Worrall* (1838) 8 C. & P. 380; *Earl of Falmouth v. Roberts* (1842) 9 M. & W. 469, or that he is or has become incompetent as a witness from any cause; *Jones v. Mason* (1729) 2 Str. 833. The declarations of the witness himself as to the place of his residence, or hearsay statements of others on the subject, are not admitted to prove that he is abroad: *Doe d. Beard v. Powell* (1836) 7 C. & P. 617. **9–110**

In *Page v. Mann* (1827) M. & M. 79, Lord Tenterden held that proof of the handwriting of the subscribing witness, who was dead, was sufficient, without any further proof of the identity of the parties than the identity of the name and description. Where the subscribing witness is unable, or refuses to disclose the truth at the trial, the deed may be proved by other witnesses: *Talbot v. Hodson* (1816) 7 Taunt. 251. **9–111**

(3) Wills

Wills of land over 20 years old require no proof (*Evidence Act* 1938, s.4); and the ordinary mode of proving wills, whether of lands or of personal estate, is by production of the probate. **9–112**

(4) Writings not under seal

All other writings, not under seal, are proved in the same manner as deeds (see *ante*, §§ 9–108, 9–109; *Wetherston v. Edginton* (1809) 2 Camp. 94; and see *Stone v. Metcalfe* (1815) 1 Stark.N.P. 53; *Higgs v. Dixon* (1817) 2 Stark.N.P. 180). A writing of this kind, if 20 years old and produced from proper custody and free from suspicion, may be received in evidence without proof, in the same manner as an ancient deed (*Evidence Act* 1938, s.4). **9–113**

(5) Methods of proving handwriting

See *post*, §§ 14–60 *et seq.* **9–114**

(6) Unstamped instruments

The *Stamp Act* 1891, s.14(4), enacts that: **9–115**

> "... an instrument executed in any part of the United Kingdom, or relating, wheresoever executed, to any property situate, or to any matter or thing done or to be done, in any part of the United Kingdom, shall not, *except in criminal proceedings*, be given in evidence, or be available for any purpose whatever, unless it is duly stamped in accordance with the law in force at the time when it was first executed."

See also the *Finance Act* 1984, ss.109(3), 110(4).

IV. EXHIBITS

A. PRODUCTION OF CHATTELS

The production in court of chattels or physical objects is not required in order to render parol evidence as to their nature admissible: *Hocking v. Ahlquist* [1944] K.B. 120, DC. The rule that secondary evidence of the contents of a document cannot be given in evidence unless the non-production of the original is accounted for (see *ante*, § 9–98) is a long way from any supposed rule that in every case the object about which **9–116** evidence is being given must be produced: *ibid*. See also *R. v. Hunt* (1820) 3 B. & Ald. 566 (*ante*, § 9–104); *R. v. Francis* (1874) L.R. 2 C.C.R. 128; and *R. v. Orrell* [1972] R.T.R. 14, CA. Non-production of the article goes to weight only.

B. DUTIES OF COURT AND PROSECUTION

9–117 As to the duties of the court and prosecution in relation to the preservation and retention of exhibits, see *R. v. Lambeth Metropolitan Stipendiary Magistrate, ex p. McComb* [1983] Q.B. 551, CA (Civ. Div.) (where the articles in question were exhibits in criminal proceedings both in England and the Republic of Ireland), *R. v. Lushington, ex p. Otto* [1894] 1 Q.B. 420, and *R. v. Uxbridge JJ., ex p. Sofaer*, 85 Cr.App.R. 367, CA, *post*, § 25–426.

There is no overriding duty on the prosecution to preserve evidence, although that is a desirable standard. Exhibits sometimes go astray. Sometimes it is only by their destruction that it is possible to get at the evidence. In those circumstances, it is customary to rely on secondary evidence, such asphotographs: *ex p. Sofaer*, *ante*. The police should never give permission for a car to be scrapped where serious charges are to be brought which might involve the possibility of some mechanical defect in the car: *R. v. Beckford* [1996] 1 Cr.App.R. 94, CA.

9–118 Where it is necessary for an expert to carry out examination of an exhibit which involves a permanent alteration to the condition of that exhibit, the expert's evidence is not rendered inadmissible merely because the defence have not had an opportunity to examine the exhibit in its original unaltered condition. It may be prudent, although there is no obligation to do so, to give the defence an opportunity to be present. Failure to do so would not render the evidence inadmissible, but might affect its weight: *DPP v. British Telecommunications plc*, *The Times*, November 26, 1990, DC.

9–119 Where an exhibit is capable of being copied, there is a presumption that the defence should be supplied with a copy; but there may be circumstances in which a fair trial can be achieved with only supervised inspection being permitted; whether this is appropriate in any given case is for the judge at trial to determine in the light of the issues in the case, the burden of displacing the presumption being on the prosecution: *R. v. DPP, ex p. J* [2000] 1 W.L.R. 1215, DC (holding that the legitimate desire to protect the anonymity of undercover police officers, for their safety and future usefulness, might justify supervised inspection, provided that there was no risk to a fair trial).

9–120 As to the loss or destruction of disclosable material as a basis for an application for a stay of the proceedings as constituting an abuse of process, see *ante*, § 4–65.

CHAPTER 10

MISCELLANEOUS SOURCES OF EVIDENCE

I. PRESUMPTIONS

A. PRESUMPTIONS OF FACT

When arising

A presumption arises where from the proof of some fact the existence of another fact may naturally be inferred without further proof from the mere probability of its having occurred. The fact thus inferred to have occurred is said to be presumed, *i.e.* is taken for granted until the contrary is proved by the opposite party: 4 Co.Rep. 71 b. And it is presumed the more readily, in proportion to the difficulty of proving the fact by positive evidence, and to the facility of disproving it or of proving facts inconsistent with it, if it really never occurred. **10–1**

Presumption of life

The *fact* that a person is alive on a given day may be presumed from proof of his being alive on an antecedent day. The question, however, is one entirely for the jury, the *law* making no presumption either way: *R. v. Lumley* (1869) L.R. 1 C.C.R. 196. Nor is there any presumption of *law* in favour of or against the continuance of life for any given period: *ibid.*; *R. v. Tolson* (1889) 23 Q.B.D. 168, CCR, unless contained in a particular enactment. Such questions have most frequently arisen on prosecutions for bigamy: in relation thereto, see also *post*, § 31–29. **10–2**

Circumstantial evidence in general

10–3 Circumstantial evidence is receivable in criminal as well as in civil cases; and, indeed, the necessity of admitting such evidence is more obvious in the former than the latter; for, in criminal cases, the possibility of proving the matter charged by the direct and positive testimony of eye-witnesses or by conclusive documents is much more rare than in civil cases; and where such testimony is not available, the jury are permitted to infer from the facts proved other facts necessary to complete the elements of guilt or establish innocence. "It must always be narrowly examined, if only because evidence of this kind may be fabricated to cast suspicion on another. … It is also necessary before drawing the inference of the accused's guilt from circumstantial evidence to be sure that there are no other co-existing circumstances which would weaken or destroy the inference": *per* Lord Normand in *Teper v. R.* [1952] A.C. 480 at 489, PC. On the other hand, it has been said that circumstantial evidence is often the best evidence. It is evidence of surrounding circumstances which, by undesigned coincidence, is capable of proving a proposition with the accuracy of mathematics. It is no derogation of evidence to say that it is circumstantial: *R. v. Taylor, Weaver and Donovan*, 21 Cr.App.R. 20, CCA.

Where circumstantial evidence is the basis for the prosecution case, the direction to the jury need be in no special form, provided always that in suitable terms it is made plain to them that they must not convict unless they are satisfied beyond all reasonable doubt; a jury can readily understand that from one piece of evidence which they accept various inferences might be drawn, and it requires no more than ordinary common sense for a jury to understand that, if one suggested inference leads to a conclusion of guilt and another suggested inference leads to a conclusion of innocence, they could not on that piece of evidence alone be satisfied of guilt beyond all reasonable doubt unless they wholly rejected and excluded the latter suggestion; furthermore, a jury can fully understand that if the facts which they accept are consistent with guilt but also consistent with innocence they could not say that they were satisfied beyond all reasonable doubt; equally, a jury can fully understand that if a fact that they accept is inconsistent with guilt or may be so they could not say that they were satisfied of guilt beyond all reasonable doubt: *McGreevy v. DPP* [1973] 1 W.L.R. 276, HL. On a submission of no case, the correct approach is to look at the evidence in the round, and ask the question whether, looking at all the evidence and treating it with appropriate care and scrutiny, there is a case on which a properly directed jury could convict: *R. v. P.* [2008] 2 Cr.App.R. 6, CA.

As to the imperative need to avoid piecemeal consideration of a circumstantial case, see *R. v. Hillier* (2007) 233 A.L.R. 63, High Court of Australia.

B. PRESUMPTIONS OF LAW

10–4 For the most part, these are dealt with elsewhere, *e.g.* the presumption of innocence, *ante*, §§ 4–380 *et seq.*, and that a child under 10 cannot commit a crime, *ante*, § 1–90.

Omnia praesumuntur rite esse acta

10–5 It is a maxim of law that "*omnia praesumuntur rite et solemniter esse acta donec probetur in contrarium*"; upon which ground, until the contrary is proved, it will be presumed, even in a case of murder, that a man who has acted in a public capacity or situation was duly appointed, and has properly discharged his official duties: *R. v. Gordon* (1789) 1 Leach 515; *R. v. Rees* (1834) 6 C. & P. 606; *R. v. Jones* (1806) 2 Camp. 131; *R. v. Verelst* (1813) 3 Camp. 432; *R. v. Murphy* (1837) 8 C. & P. 297; *R. v. Catesby* (1824) 2 B. & C. 814; *R. v. Newton* (1843) 1 C. & K. 469; *R. v. Townsend* (1841) C. & Mar. 178; *R. v. Cresswell* (1876) 1 Q.B.D. 446; *R. v. Manwaring* (1856) Dears. & B. 132; *R. v. Stewart* (1876) 13 Cox 296; and *R. v. Roberts* (1878) 14 Cox 101, CCR.

For a more recent application of the rule in a criminal case, see *Campbell v. Wallsend Shipway and Engineering Co. Ltd* [1977] Crim.L.R. 351, DC, where the court held that the presumption applied to the validity of appointment of a Health and Safety Inspector and could not be weakened by mere challenge.

See also *Gage v. Jones* [1983] R.T.R. 508, DC (proof that a constable was in uniform), and, more controversially (see *post*, § 15–165), *Kynaston v. DPP*, 87 Cr.App.R. 200, DC (proof of "reasonable grounds for suspicion" under the *PACE Act* 1984).

This principle will not operate so as to prove a fact, proof of which is central to an offence: *Dillon v. R.* [1982] A.C. 484, PC (on a charge of negligently permitting escape, the fact that the prisoner was in lawful custody, an essential ingredient of the offence). **10–6**

II. ADMISSIONS

Criminal Justice Act 1967, s.10

10.—(1) Subject to the provisions of this section, any fact of which oral evidence may be given in any criminal proceedings may be admitted for the purpose of those proceedings by or on behalf of the prosecutor or defendant, and the admission by any party of any such fact under this section shall as against that party be conclusive evidence in those proceedings of the fact admitted. **10–7**

(2) An admission under this section—

(a) may be made before or at the proceedings;

(b) if made otherwise than in court, shall be in writing;

(c) if made in writing by an individual, shall purport to be signed by the person making it and, if so made by a body corporate, shall purport to be signed by a director or manager, or the secretary or clerk, or some other similar officer of the body corporate;

(d) if made on behalf of a defendant who is an individual, shall be made by his counsel or solicitor;

(e) if made at any stage before the trial by a defendant who is an individual, must be approved by his counsel or solicitor (whether at the time it was made or subsequently) before or at the proceedings in question.

(3) An admission under this section for the purpose of proceedings relating to any matter shall be treated as an admission for the purpose of any subsequent criminal proceedings relating to that matter (including any appeal or retrial).

(4) An admission under this section may with the leave of the court be withdrawn in the proceedings for the purpose of which it is made or any subsequent criminal proceedings relating to the same matter.

Where, under section 10, a fact is admitted orally in court by or on behalf of the prosecutor or defendant for the purposes of summary trial of an offence, the court shall cause the admission to be written down and signed by or on behalf of the party making the admission: *Criminal Procedure Rules* 2005 (S.I. 2005 No. 384), r.37.4.

Where an admission is made otherwise than in writing, what has been admitted should appear clearly in the record of the proceedings: *R. v. Lennard*, 57 Cr.App.R. 542, CA. Where it is reduced to writing, it should be supplied to the jury, provided that it is relevant to an issue before the jury and does not contain material the jury ought not to have: *R. v. Pittard* [2006] 9 *Archbold News* 3, CA. **10–8**

An admission made with the benefit of legal advice is an important part of the evidence in a trial; where leave is sought to withdraw such an admission, it is unlikely to be given absent cogent evidence from the accused and his legal advisers that the admission was made as a result of an error or misunderstanding: *R. v. Kolton* [2000] Crim.L.R. 761, CA.

Conduct of a trial with the entirety of the prosecution case consisting of admissions under section 10 should be rare; if done, it should be done with caution, since jurors might have difficulty in distinguishing what in a speech was fact and what was law, or mixed law and fact, or comment: *R. v. Lewis* [1971] Crim.L.R. 414, CA.

The practice of the prosecution being prepared to make admissions in relation to facts which "might" point to a third party having committed the crime, which the defendant denies having committed, is long-standing; such evidence is relevant and admissible; by making such admissions the prosecution prevent the potential unfairness which could arise where the defendant might have had difficulty in establishing the facts, having regard to the hearsay rule; the prosecution cannot be forced to make admissions if they do not accept that the admission points to the possibility of a third party being the perpetrator; and if they are prepared to make an admission they can seek other admissions from the defence or put in evidence of their own in order to put the admission fairly in its context; the question of what admissions the prosecution are prepared to make, or what evidence the prosecution should call, should be left to them, albeit that the judge is entitled to express a view on whether evidence is admissible or relevant: *R. v. Greenwood* [2005] 1 Cr.App.R. 7, CA.

III. WRITTEN STATEMENTS AND DEPOSITIONS

A. COMMITTAL PROCEEDINGS

(1) General

Magistrates' Courts Act 1980 s.6(1), (2)

Discharge or committal for trial

10–9 **6.**—(1) *A magistrates' court inquiring into an offence as examining justices shall on consideration of the evidence—*

(a) *commit the accused for trial if it is of opinion that there is sufficient evidence to put him on trial by jury for any indictable offence;*

(b) *discharge him if it is not of that opinion and he is in custody for no other cause than the offence under inquiry;*

but the preceding provisions of this subsection have effect subject to the provisions of this and any other Act relating to the summary trial of indictable offences.

(2) *If a magistrates' court inquiring into an offence as examining justices is satisfied that all the evidence tendered by or on behalf of the prosecutor falls within section 5A(3) above, it may commit the accused for trial for the offence without consideration of the contents of any statements, depositions or other documents, unless—*

(a) *the accused or one of the accused has no legal representative acting for him in the case, or*

(b) *a legal representative for the accused or one of the accused, as the case may be, has requested the court to consider a submission that there is insufficient evidence to put that accused on trial by jury for the offence;*

and subsection (1) above shall not apply to a committal for trial under this subsection.

[Subss. (1) and (2) are printed as substituted by the *CPIA* 1996, s.47, and Sched. 1, para. 4. As substituted, they apply only in relation to alleged offences into which no criminal investigation had begun before April 1, 1997: *Criminal Procedure and Investigations Act 1996 (Commencement) (Section 65 and Schedules 1 and 2) Order* 1997 (S.I. 1997 No. 683) and *Criminal Procedure and Investigations Act 1996 (Appointed Day No. 3) Order* 1997 (S.I. 1997 No. 682). The whole section is repealed, as from a day to be appointed, by the *CJA* 2003, s.332, and Sched. 37, Pt 4.]

As to the transitional provision, see *R. v. Uxbridge Magistrates' Court, ex p. Patel*; *R. v. City of London Magistrates' Court, ex p. Cropper*, 164 J.P. 209, DC, *post*, § 12–52. For section 5A of the 1980 Act, see *post*, § 10–15.

As to the bypassing of committal proceedings under the provisions of the *CJA* 1987 (cases of serious fraud), see *ante*, §§ 1–41 *et seq.*; or of the *CJA* 1991 (certain cases involving children), see *ante*, §§ 1–53 *et seq.* As to the sending of indictable offences to the Crown Court for trial without committal proceedings under the provisions of the *CDA* 1998, see *ante*, §§ 1–15 *et seq.*

The function of examining justices may be discharged by a single justice: *MCA* 1980, s.4(1).

10–10 A magistrate who is to sit as an examining magistrate may properly be given to read (in order to familiarise himself with the case) in advance of the hearing the copies of the statements made by, and documents produced by, prosecution witnesses which have been given to the clerk of the magistrates' court in accordance with rule 27.2(2) of the *Criminal Procedure Rules* 2005 (S.I. 2005 No. 384) (*post*, § 10–39). The fact that this occurs either unknown to or without the consent of the defence is immaterial: *R. v. Colchester Stipendiary Magistrate, ex p. Beck* [1979] Q.B. 674, 69 Cr.App.R. 128, DC.

Examining magistrates must receive and consider any admissible evidence which is put before them. The duty of determining any issue of admissibility may not be delegated to another bench: *R. v. Ormskirk JJ., ex p. Davies*, *The Times*, June 23, 1994, DC.

At common law, justices had no discretion in committal proceedings to refuse to admit admissible evidence: see *R. v. Horsham JJ., ex p. Bukhari*, 74 Cr.App.R. 291, DC; and section 78 of the *PACE Act* 1984 (*post*, § 15–452) (as amended by the *CPIA* 1996, s.47 and Sched. 1, para. 26) does not apply to committal proceedings: see subsection (3).

The prosecution may choose which witnesses to rely upon for the purposes of committal proceedings: *R. v. Epping and Harlow JJ., ex p. Massaro* [1973] Q.B. 433, 57 Cr.App.R. 499, DC; *R. v. Grays JJ., ex p. Tetley*, 70 Cr.App.R. 11, DC; *Wilkinson v. DPP*, 162 J.P. 591, DC. **10–11**

Two or more defendants can properly be before the court for the purposes of committal proceedings, provided they could properly be tried jointly on indictment: *R. v. Camberwell Green JJ., ex p. Christie* [1978] Q.B. 602, DC.

In deciding whether committal proceedings at which there has been an irregularity were so defective as to be no committal at all, the question which has to be asked is whether the defect that occurred was one that worked injustice to the defendant: *R. v. Raynor*, 165 J.P. 149, CA.

General requirement to sit in open court

As to the duty to sit in open court, see the *MCA* 1980, s.4(2) (repealed, as from a day to be appointed, by the *CJA* 2003, s.332, and Sched. 37, Pt 4). **10–12**

Proceedings in absence of accused

Magistrates' Courts Act 1980 s.4(3), (4)

4.—(3) *Subject to subsection (4) below, evidence tendered before examining justices shall be tendered in the presence of the accused.* **10–13**

(4) *Examining justices may allow evidence to be tendered before them in the absence of the accused if—*

(a) *they consider that by reason of his disorderly conduct before them it is not practicable for the evidence to be tendered in his presence; or*

(b) *he cannot be present for reasons of health but is represented by a legal representative and has consented to the evidence being tendered in his absence.*

[These subsections are printed as amended by the *Courts and Legal Services Act* 1990, Sched. 18, para. 25(3); and the *CPIA* 1996, Sched. 1, para. 2. The whole section is repealed, as from a day to be appointed, by the *CJA* 2003, s.332, and Sched. 37, Pt 4.]

Where a person remanded in custody by a magistrates' court has been made the subject of a transfer direction under section 48 of the *MHA* 1983 (*ante*, § 3–81), the magistrates' court may, in his absence, [inquire as examining justices into an offence alleged to have been committed by him and commit him for trial in accordance with section 6 of the 1980 Act] (*ante*, § 10–9) [[send him to the Crown Court for trial under section 51 or 51A of the *CDA* 1998]] if:

(a) the court is satisfied, on the written or oral evidence of the responsible clinician, that the accused is unfit to take part in the proceedings; and

(b) [where the court proceeds under section 6(1)], the accused is legally represented: *MHA* 1983, s.52(7) (as amended by the *MHA* 2007, s.11(1) and (4), and as amended, as from a day to be appointed, by the *CJA* 2003, s.41, and Sched. 3, para. 55(1) and (3)(d), so as to omit the words in single square brackets and to insert the words in double square brackets).

As to "the responsible clinician", see section 55(1) of the 1983 Act.

In *R. v. Liverpool City Magistrates' Court, ex p. Quantrell* [1999] 2 Cr.App.R. 24, DC, it was held that a valid committal for trial may take place in the absence of a legally represented accused, even without express statutory provision to such effect. See also *R. v. Bow Street Magistrates' Court, ex p. Government of Germany* [1998] Q.B. 556, DC, where reliance was placed on section 122(2) of the 1980 Act (legally represented absent party deemed not to be absent).

(2) Judicial review of committal proceedings

It is not the practice of the High Court to interfere with committal proceedings which **10–14** have not been concluded, see *R. v. Carden* (1879) 5 Q.B.D. 1; *R. v. Wells Street Stipendiary Magistrate, ex p. Seillon*, 69 Cr.App.R. 77, DC; *R. v. Horsham JJ., ex p. Bukhari, ante*, § 10–10.

Judicial review lies in respect of committal proceedings where there has been a procedural flaw: see *R. v. Oxford City JJ., ex p. Berry, ante*, § 10–10; *R. v. Barnet Magistrates' Court, ex p. Wood* [1993] Crim.L.R. 78, DC (accused not informed of his rights); *R. v. Horseferry Road Magistrates' Court, ex p. Doung, The Times*, March 22, 1996 (magistrate overrode objection to admissibility of statements under the *MCA* 1980, s.102 (*rep.*)); and *R. v. Wigan JJ., ex p. Sullivan* [1999] C.O.D. 21, DC (adjournment refused where legal representatives had had inadquate time to prepare, thereby denying defendants proper opportunity to present their case). The remedy is discretionary and is unlikely to issue if the accused's own conduct has contributed to the failure of procedure, or if an application to quash the indictment is an adequate alternative remedy (see *ex p. Wood, ante*).

As to the availability of judicial review to quash a committal on the ground of the inadmissibility of evidence or the insufficiency of the evidence, see *Neill v. North Antrim Magistrates' Court*, 97 Cr.App.R. 121, HL; and *R. v. Bedwellty JJ., ex p. Williams* [1997] A.C. 225, HL, *ante*, §§ 1–211, 1–212. The authorities plainly establish, however, that it is an inappropriate use of judicial review to challenge a committal for trial on the basis of insufficiency of evidence save in the clearest of cases: *R. v. Whitehaven JJ., ex p. Thompson* [1999] C.O.D. 15, DC.

Where commital proceedings are regular to begin with, but the committal for trial is quashed on judicial review in consequence of a subsequent irregularity, this does not render the proceedings void *ab initio*: *Re Najam* [1998] 10 *Archbold News* 2, DC (CO/3773/98) (important for the purposes of the custody time limit provisions, *ante*, § 3–58).

(3) Admissibility of evidence

Magistrates' Courts Act 1980, ss.5A–5F

Evidence which is admissible

10–15 **5A.**—(1) *Evidence falling within subsection (2) below, and only that evidence, shall be admissible by a magistrates' court inquiring into an offence as examining justices.*

(2) *Evidence falls within this subsection if it—*

(a) *is tendered by or on behalf of the prosecutor, and*

(b) *falls within subsection (3) below.*

(3) *The following evidence falls within this subsection—*

(a) *written statements complying with section 5B below;*

(b) *the documents or other exhibits (if any) referred to in such statements;*

(c) *depositions complying with section 5C below;*

(d) *the documents or other exhibits (if any) referred to in such depositions;*

(e) *statements complying with section 5D below;*

(f) *documents falling within section 5E below.*

(4) *In this section "document" means anything in which information of any description is recorded.*

Written statements

10–16 **5B.**—(1) *For the purposes of section 5A above a written statement complies with this section if—*

(a) *the conditions falling within subsection (2) below are met, and*

(b) *such of the conditions falling within subsection (3) below as apply are met.*

(2) *The conditions falling within this subsection are that—*

(a) *the statement purports to be signed by the person who made it;*

(b) *the statement contains a declaration by that person to the effect that it is true to the best of his knowledge and belief and that he made the statement knowing that, if it were tendered in evidence, he would be liable to prosecution if he wilfully stated in it anything which he knew to be false or did not believe to be true;*

(c) *before the statement is tendered in evidence a copy of the statement is given, by or on behalf of the prosecutor, to each of the other parties to the proceedings.*

(3) *The conditions falling within this subsection are that—*

(a) *if the statement is made by a person under 18 years old, it gives his age;*
(b) *if it is made by a person who cannot read it, it is read to him before he signs it and is accompanied by a declaration by the person who so read the statement to the effect that it was so read;*
(c) *if it refers to any other document as an exhibit, the copy given to any other party to the proceedings under subsection (2)(c) above is accompanied by a copy of that document or by such information as may be necessary to enable the party to whom it is given to inspect that document or a copy of it.*

[(3A) [*Identical to* Criminal Justice Act *1967, s.9(3A),* post, *§ 10–50 (inserted herein as from a day to be appointed by the* Children and Young Persons Act *1969, Sched. 5, para. 55, as amended by the* CPIA *1996, Sched. 1, para. 21).*]]

(4) *So much of any statement as is admitted in evidence by virtue of this section shall, unless the court commits the accused for trial by virtue of section 6(2) below or the court otherwise directs, be read aloud at the hearing; and where the court so directs an account shall be given orally of so much of any statement as is not read aloud.*

(5) *Any document or other object referred to as an exhibit and identified in a statement admitted in evidence by virtue of this section shall be treated as if it had been produced as an exhibit and identified in court by the maker of the statement.*

(6) [*Identical to s.5A(4),* ante.]

In connection with this section, see rule 27.1 of the *Criminal Procedure Rules* 2005 (S.I. 2005 No. 384) (*post*, § 10–39).

In this section and sections 5C and 5D (*post*), any reference to a copy of a document (within the meaning of the 1980 Act) being given by or on behalf of the prosecutor to each of the other parties, or any other party, to the proceedings in question, shall be construed, in the case of any disclosure in relation to which section 3(1) of the *Sexual Offences (Protected Material) Act* 1997 applies, as a reference to the document being disclosed under the 1997 Act in accordance with section 3(2) or (3): *Sexual Offences (Protected Material) Act* 1997, s.9(1) (not in force as at September 1, 2006). For section 3 of the 1997 Act, see *post*, § 12–114.

Where a witness does not speak English sufficiently well to make a statement in the English language, his statement should be recorded in his own language; a statement consisting of a translation into English of what the witness said orally in his own language and which is then signed by the witness having been translated back to him by the interpreter does not fall within section 5A(3): *R. v. Raynor*, 165 J.P. 149, CA.

A statement under section 5B does not require a separate signature on the declaration. Provided the declaration is truly contained in the statement, its actual position cannot affect the validity of the statement, although in practice it might be more conveniently situated at the end: see *Chapman v. Ingleton*, 57 Cr.App.R. 476, DC (considering the absence of a signature after a declaration at the head of a statement under the *CJA* 1967, s.9, *post*, § 10–50).

The statement of a person who had since died was admissible under section 102 of the *MCA* 1980 (effectively replaced now by section 5B): *R. v. Sinclair* [1995] Crim.L.R. 825, CA.

Where a witness statement is admitted (otherwise than by agreement), the jury should be directed to treat it with particular care as the maker was not available for cross-examination; failure to give such direction was fatal to a conviction where the statement was vital to the prosecution case: *R. v. Curry*, *The Times*, March 23, 1998, CA.

Depositions

5C.—(1) *For the purposes of section 5A above a deposition complies with this section if*— **10–17**
(a) *a copy of it is sent to the prosecutor under section 97A(9) below,*
(b) *the condition falling within subsection (2) below is met, and*
(c) *the condition falling within subsection (3) below is met, in a case where it applies.*

(2) *The condition falling within this subsection is that before the magistrates' court begins to inquire into the offence concerned as examining justices a copy of the deposition is given, by or on behalf of the prosecutor, to each of the other parties to the proceedings.*

(3) *The condition falling within this subsection is that, if the deposition refers to any other document as an exhibit, the copy given to any other party to the proceedings under subsection*

(2) above is accompanied by a copy of that document or by such information as may be necessary to enable the party to whom it is given to inspect that document or a copy of it.

(4) [*Identical to s.5B(4),* ante, *save for substitution of "deposition" for "statement".*]

(5) [*Identical to s.5B(5),* ante, *save for substitution of "deposition" for "statement" and "person whose evidence is taken as a deposition" for "maker of the statement".*]

(6) [*Identical to s.5A(4),* ante.]

As to the construction of this section, see the effect of section 9(1) of the *Sexual Offences (Protected Material) Act* 1997 (*ante*, § 10–16).

Statements

10–18 **5D.**—(1) *For the purposes of sections 5A above a statement complies with this section if the conditions falling within subsections (2) to (4) below are met.*

(2) *The condition falling within this subsection is that, before the committal proceedings begin, the prosecutor notifies the magistrates' court and each of the other parties to the proceedings that he believes—*

(a) *that the statement might by virtue of section 23 or 24 of the* Criminal Justice Act *1988 (statements in certain documents) be admissible as evidence if the case came to trial, and*

(b) *that the statement would not be admissible as evidence otherwise than by virtue of section 23 or 24 of that Act if the case came to trial.*

(3) *The condition falling within this subsection is that—*

(a) *the prosecutor's belief is based on information available to him at the time he makes the notification,*

(b) *he has reasonable grounds for his belief, and*

(c) *he gives the reasons for his belief when he makes the notification.*

(4) *The condition falling within this subsection is that when the court or a party is notified as mentioned in subsection (2) above a copy of the statement is given, by or on behalf of the prosecutor, to the court or the party concerned.*

(5) [*Identical to s.5B(4),* ante, *save for addition of words "in writing and is" before "admitted".*]

As to the construction of this section, see the effect of section 9(1) of the *Sexual Offences (Protected Material) Act* 1997 (*ante*, § 10–16). As to subsection (2), see *R. (CPS) v. City of London Magistrates' Court, post*, § 10–20a.

Other documents

10–19 **5E.**—(1) *The following documents fall within this section—*

(a) *any document which by virtue of any enactment is evidence in proceedings before a magistrates' court inquiring into an offence as examining justices;*

(b) *any document which by virtue of any enactment is admissible, or may be used, or is to be admitted or received, in or as evidence in such proceedings;*

(c) *any document which by virtue of any enactment may be considered in such proceedings;*

(d) *any document whose production constitutes proof in such proceedings by virtue of any enactment;*

(e) *any document by the production of which evidence may be given in such proceedings by virtue of any enactment.*

(2) *In subsection (1) above—*

(a) *references to evidence include references to prima facie evidence;*

(b) *references to any enactment include references to any provision of this Act.*

(3) [*Identical to s.5B(4),* ante, *save for substitution of "document" for "statement".*]

(4) [*Identical to s.5(A)(4),* ante.]

Proof by production of copy

10–20 **5F.**—(1) *Where a statement, deposition or document is admissible in evidence by virtue of section 5B , 5C , 5D or 5E above it may be proved by the production of—*

(a) *the statement, deposition or document, or*

(b) *a copy of it or the material part of it.*

(2) *Subsection (1)(b) above applies whether or not the statement, deposition or document is still in existence.*

(3) *It is immaterial for the purposes of this section how many removes there are between a copy and the original.*

(4) *In this section "copy", in relation to a statement, deposition or document, means anything onto which information recorded in the statement, deposition or document has been copied, by whatever means and whether directly or indirectly.*

[Ss.5A to 5F were inserted by the *CPIA* 1996, s.47, and Sched. 1, para. 3. They are repealed, as from a day to be appointed, by the *CJA* 2003, s.332, and Sched. 37, Pt 4.]

In *R. (CPS) v. City of London Magistrates' Court, The Times*, April 17, 2006, DC, it was said that where charges against the accused had been discharged in committal proceedings brought before the hearsay provisions of the *CJA* 2003 had been brought into force (on April 4, 2005), on the basis that the prosecutor had failed to comply with the requirement in section 5D(2) to notify the court and each of the parties to the proceedings of his belief that hearsay evidence might be admissible in any trial by virtue of section 23 or 24 of the 1988 Act, section 5D of the 1980 Act did not continue to apply in fresh committal proceedings brought after the provisions of the 2003 Act had been brought into force and sections 23 and 24 of the 1988 Act had been repealed; the hearsay provisions applicable to the case after April 4, 2005, were those of the 2003 Act (*R. v. Bradley* [2005] 1 Cr.App.R. 24, CA, and *R. v. H. (P.G.)* [2006] 1 Cr.App.R. 50(4), CA (see *post*, § 11–2)); and whilst section 5D had not itself been repealed, it had ceased to have potency after that date and it was therefore otiose to contemplate service of a notice under that section. The court observed, *obiter*, that Part 34 of the *Criminal Procedure Rules* 2005 (S.I. 2005 No. 384) (*post*, §§ 11–52 *et seq.*) (with its own notice requirements), which had come into force on the same day as the relevant provisions of the 2003 Act, would apply to committal proceedings and would therefore have applied to the prosecutor here; but, the court added, the overriding objective under rule 1.1 was indicative that a reasonable magistrate should have dispensed with or abbreviated the notice requirement under rule 34.7. For the submission that section 5D of the 1980 Act continues to have full effect (pending its repeal) and that the references to sections 23 and 24 of the 1988 Act merely require to be read as references to sections 116 and 117 of the 2003 Act, in accordance with section 17(2)(a) of the *Interpretation Act* 1978 (Appendix B–17), see *Criminal Law Week* 2006/15/6. **10–20a**

Magistrates' Courts Act 1980, s.97A

Summons or warrant to committal proceedings

97A.—(1) *Subsection (2) below applies where a justice of the peace for any commission area is satisfied that—* **10–21**

(a) *any person in England or Wales is likely to be able to make on behalf of the prosecutor a written statement containing material evidence, or produce on behalf of the prosecutor a document or other exhibit likely to be material evidence, for the purposes of proceedings before a magistrates' court inquiring into an offence as examining justices, and*

(b) *it is in the interests of justice to issue a summons under this section to secure the attendance of the witness to have his evidence taken as a deposition or to produce the document or other exhibit.*

(2) *In such a case the justice shall issue a summons directed to that person requiring him to attend before a justice at the time and place appointed in the summons to have his evidence taken as a deposition or to produce the document or other exhibit.*

(3)–(5) [Further process to secure attendance (arrest warrant, etc.).]

(6) *Where—*

(a) *a summons is issued under subsection (2) above or a warrant is issued under subsection (3) or (5) above, and*

(b) *the summons or warrant is issued with a view to securing that a person has his evidence taken as a deposition,*

the time appointed in the summons or specified in the warrant shall be such as to enable the evidence to be taken as a deposition before a magistrates' court begins to inquire into the offence concerned as examining justices.

(7), (8) [Punishment for refusal to give evidence.]

(9) *If in pursuance of this section a person has his evidence taken as a deposition, the designated officer for the justice concerned shall as soon as is reasonably practicable send a copy of the deposition to the prosecutor.*

(10) *If in pursuance of this section a person produces an exhibit which is a document, the*

designated officer for the justice concerned shall as soon as is reasonably practicable send a copy of the document to the prosecutor.

(11) *If in pursuance of this section a person produces an exhibit which is not a document, the designated officer for the justice concerned shall as soon as is reasonably practicable inform the prosecutor of the fact and of the nature of the exhibit.*

[This section was inserted by the *CPIA* 1996, s.47, and Sched. 1, para. 8. It is printed as amended by the *Access to Justice Act* 1999, s.90(1), and Sched. 13, para. 111; the *Courts Act* 2003, s.109(1), and Sched. 8, para. 231; and the *SOCPA* 2005, s.169(3). It is repealed as from a day to be appointed by the *CJA* 2003, s.332, and Sched. 37, Pt 4.]

10–22 In connection with this section, see rule 28.2 of the *Criminal Procedure Rules* 2005, *post*, § 10–38.

Criminal Justice Act 1972, s.46

Admissibility of written statements made outside England and Wales

10–23 **46.**—(1) ... section 9 of the *Criminal Justice Act* 1967 (... written statements to be used as evidence in ... criminal proceedings) ... and section 89 of the said Act of 1967 (... false statements which are tendered in evidence under the said section ... 9, ...) shall apply to written statements made in Scotland or Northern Ireland as well as to written statements made in England and Wales.

(1A) *The following provisions, namely—*

(a) *so much of section 5A of the* Magistrates' Courts Act *1980 as relates to written statements and to documents or other exhibits referred to in them,*

(b) *section 5B of that Act, and*

(c) *section 106 of that Act,*

shall apply where written statements are made in Scotland or Northern Ireland as well as where written statements are made in England and Wales.

(1B) *The following provisions, namely—*

(a) *so much of section 5A of the* Magistrates' Courts Act *1980 as relates to written statements and to documents or other exhibits referred to in them, and*

(b) *section 5B of that Act,*

shall (subject to subsection (1C) below) apply where written statements are made outside the United Kingdom.

(1C) *Where written statements are made outside the United Kingdom—*

(a) *section 5B of the* Magistrates' Courts Act *1980 shall apply with the omission of subsections (2)(b) and (3A);*

(b) *paragraph 1 of Schedule 2 to the* Criminal Procedure and Investigations Act *1996 (use of written statements at trial) shall not apply.*

(2) [*Repealed by* CPIA *1996, Sched. 1, para. 22.*]

[This section is printed as amended by the *MCA* 1980, s.154 and Sched. 7, para. 114; and the *CPIA* 1996, s.47 and Sched. 1, para. 22. Subss. (1A) to (1C) are repealed as from a day to be appointed by the *CJA* 2003, s.332, and Sched. 37, Pt 4.]

For section 9 of the 1967 Act, see *post*, § 10–50.

Magistrates' Courts Act 1980, s.103

Evidence of persons under 14 in committal proceedings for assault, sexual offences, etc.

10–24 **103.**—(1) *In any proceedings before a magistrates' court inquiring as examining justices into an offence to which this section applies, a statement made in writing by or taken in writing from a child shall be admissible in evidence of any matter.*

(2) *This section applies—*

(a) *to an offence which involves an assault, or injury or a threat of injury to, a person;*

(b) *to an offence under section 1 of the* Children and Young Persons Act *1933 (cruelty to persons under 16);*

(c) *to an offence under the* Sexual Offences Act *1956, the* Protection of Children Act *1978 or Part I of the* Sexual Offences Act *2003; and*

(d) *to an offence which consists of attempting or conspiring to commit, or of aiding, abetting, counselling, procuring or inciting the commission of, an offence falling within paragraph (a), (b) or (c) above.*

(3), (4) [*Repealed by* CPIA *1996, Sched. 1, para. 10.*]

(5) *In this section "child" has the same meaning as in section 53 of the* Criminal Justice Act *1991.*

[This section is printed as substituted by the *CJA* 1988, s.33; and as subsequently amended and repealed in part by the *CJA* 1991, s.55(1); the *CPIA* 1996, s.47, and Sched. 1, para. 10; and the *SOA* 2003, ss.139 and 140, and Scheds 6, para. 26(1) and (2), and 7. It is repealed, as from a day to be appointed, by the *CJA* 2003, s.332, and Sched. 37, Pt 4.]

For section 53 of the 1991 Act, see *ante*, § 1–53.

The reference to the common law offence of incitement in section 103(2)(d) has effect as a reference to the offences under Part 2 of the *SCA* 2007: 2007 Act, s.63(1), and Sched. 6, para. 5(b).

(4) Miscellaneous provisions relating to taking of depositions

Special provisions relating to children and young persons

Evidence of children

Any person of whatever age is competent to give evidence in criminal proceedings, unless it appears to the court that he is not a person who is able to understand questions put to him as a witness, and give answers to them which can be understood: *YJCEA* 1999, s.53(1) (*ante*, § 8–36a). The evidence of a child under 14 who is competent to give evidence in criminal proceedings shall be given unsworn; and a deposition of unsworn evidence given by a child under 14 may be taken for the purposes of criminal proceedings as if that evidence had been given on oath: *ibid.*, s.56(1)–(3) (*ante*, § 8–32). Unsworn evidence admitted by virtue of section 56 of the 1999 Act may corroborate evidence (sworn or unsworn) given by any other person: *CJA* 1988, s.34(3) (*ante*, § 8–32). **10–25**

Children and Young Persons Act 1933, s.42

Extension of power to take deposition of child or young person

42.—(1) Where a justice of the peace is satisfied by the evidence of a duly qualified medical practitioner that the attendance before a court of any child or young person in respect of whom any of the offences mentioned in the First Schedule to this Act is alleged to have been committed would involve serious danger to his life or health, the justice may take in writing the deposition of the child or young person on oath, and shall thereupon subscribe the deposition and add thereto a statement of his reason for taking it and of the day when and place where it was taken, and of the names of the persons (if any) present at the taking thereof. **10–26**

(2) The justice taking any such deposition shall transmit it with his statement—

(a) if the deposition relates to an offence for which any accused person is already *committed* [sent] for trial, to the proper officer of the court for trial at which the accused person has been *committed* [sent]; and

(b) in any other case, to the proper officer of the court before which proceedings are pending in respect of the offence.

[This section is printed as amended by the *Access to Justice Act* 1999, s.90(1), and Sched. 13, para. 9. The word "sent" is substituted for the word "committed" in both places in subs. (2)(a) by the *CJA* 2003, s.41, and Sched. 3, para. 33. These amendments came into force on May 9, 2005, in relation to cases sent for trial under section 51 or 51A(3)(d) of the *CDA* 1998: *Criminal Justice Act 2003 (Commencement No. 9) Order* 2005 (S.I. 2005 No. 1267). Otherwise they come into force on a day to be appointed.]

For the admissibility of a deposition taken under this section at the trial, see section 43 of the 1933 Act, *post*, § 10–47.

For Schedule 1 to the 1933 Act, see *post*, § 19–322.

In view of the width of the provisions of section 103 of the *Magistrates' Courts Act* 1980 (*ante*, § 10–24) it will rarely be necessary to rely on section 42 in the case of children, but section 43, which applies to section 42, but not to section 103, should be kept in mind. If section 42 is resorted to, the deposition of a child will not be taken on oath: see section 56(1)–(3) of the *YJCEA* 1999, *ante*.

The expression "young person" means a person who has attained the age of 14 and is under the age of 18 years: s.107(1), *post*, § 19–328.

Admissibility of statements of children in proceedings for certain offences

10–27 See section 103 of the *MCA* 1980, *ante*, § 10–24.

Depositions taken abroad

10–28 Section 283 of the *Merchant Shipping Act* 1995 provides for the taking of evidence abroad in cases of offences at sea, or by British seamen. As to the admissibility of depositions so taken, see section 286 of that Act, *post*, § 10–48.

See also the *Civil Aviation Act* 1982, s.95, *post*, § 10–49.

(5) Relevant provisions of the Criminal Procedure Rules 2005 (S.I. 2005 No. 384)

Criminal Procedure Rules 2005 (S.I. 2005 No. 384), rr.10.2, 10.3

Committal for trial without consideration of the evidence

10–29 **10.2.**—(1) This rule applies to committal proceedings where the accused has a solicitor acting for him in the case and where the court has been informed that all the evidence falls within section 5A(2) of the *Magistrates'* Courts Act 1980.

(2) A magistrates' court inquiring into an offence in committal proceedings to which this rule applies shall cause the charge to be written down, if this has not already been done, and read to the accused and shall then ascertain whether he wishes to submit that there is insufficient evidence to put him on trial by jury for the offence with which he is charged.

(3) If the court is satisfied that the accused or, as the case may be, each of the accused does not wish to make such a submission as is referred to in paragraph (2) it shall, after receiving any written evidence falling within section 5A(3) of the 1980 Act, determine whether or not to commit the accused for trial without consideration of the evidence, and where it determines not to so commit the accused it shall proceed in accordance with rule 10.3.

Consideration of evidence at committal proceedings

10–30 **10.3.**—(1) This rule does not apply to committal proceedings where under section 6(2) of the *Magistrates'* Courts Act of 1980 a magistrates' court commits a person for trial without consideration of the evidence.

(2) A magistrates' court inquiring into an offence as examining justices, having ascertained—

(a) that the accused has no legal representative acting for him in the case; or

(b) that the accused's legal representative has requested the court to consider a submission that there is insufficient evidence to put the accused on trial by jury for the offence with which he is charged, as the case may be,

shall permit the prosecutor to make an opening address to the court, if he so wishes, before any evidence is tendered.

(3) After such opening address, if any, the court shall cause evidence to be tendered in accordance with sections 5B(4), 5C(4), 5D(5) and 5E(3) of the 1980 Act, that is to say by being read out aloud, except where the court otherwise directs or to the extent that it directs that an oral account be given of any of the evidence.

(4) The court may view any exhibits produced before the court and may take possession of them.

(5) After the evidence has been tendered the court shall hear any submission which the accused may wish to make as to whether there is sufficient evidence to put him on trial by jury for any indictable offence.

(6) The court shall permit the prosecutor to make a submission—

(a) in reply to any submission made by the accused in pursuance of paragraph (5); or

(b) where the accused has not made any such submission but the court is nevertheless minded not to commit him for trial.

(7) After hearing any submission made in pursuance of paragraph (5) or (6) the court shall, unless it decides not to commit the accused for trial, cause the charge to be written down, if this has not already been done, and, if the accused is not represented by counsel or a solicitor, shall read the charge to him and explain it in ordinary language.

A committal will not be rendered invalid in consequence of the justices having admitted evidence which was inadmissible in law or having heard a witness who was not competent to give evidence: *R. v. Norfolk Q.S., ex p. Brunson* [1953] 1 Q.B. 503, 37 Cr.App.R. 6, DC (and see *ante*, §§ 1–211, 1–212). **10–31**

Where a submission of no case is made on the charge or charges preferred against the defendant, but there is the possibility of committal for trial upon lesser or different charges instead of, or, possibly, as well as the original charge or charges, the defence should be given the opportunity of addressing the court on those possibilities before the court considers its decision on the original submissions: *R. v. Gloucester Magistrates' Court, ex p. Chung*, 153 J.P. 75, DC. **10–32**

Criminal Procedure Rules 2005 (S.I. 2005 No. 384), rr.10.4, 10.5

Court's reminder to a defendant of right to object to evidence being read at trial without further proof

10.4. A magistrates' court which commits a person for trial shall forthwith remind him of his right to object, by written notification to the prosecutor and the Crown Court within 14 days of being committed unless that court in its discretion permits such an objection to be made outside that period, to a statement or deposition being read as evidence at the trial without oral evidence being given by the person who made the statement or deposition, and without the opportunity to cross-examine that person. **10–33**

Material to be sent to court of trial

10.5.—(1) As soon as practicable after the committal of any person for trial, and in any case within 4 days from the date of his committal (not counting Saturdays, Sundays, Good Friday, Christmas Day or Bank Holidays), the magistrates' court officer shall, subject to the provisions of section 7 of the *Prosecution of Offences Act* 1985 (which relates to the sending of documents and things to the Director of Public Prosecutions), send to the Crown Court officer— **10–34**

(a) the information, if it is in writing;

(b) (i) the evidence tendered in accordance with section 5A of the *Magistrates' Courts Act* 1980 and, where any of that evidence consists of a copy of a deposition or documentary exhibit which is in the possession of the court, any such deposition or documentary exhibit, and

(ii) a certificate to the effect that that evidence was so tendered;

(c) any notification by the prosecutor under section 5D(2) of the 1980 Act regarding the admissibility of a statement under section 23 or 24 of the *Criminal Justice Act* 1988 (first hand hearsay; business documents);

(d) a copy of the record made in pursuance of section 5 of the *Bail Act* 1976 relating to the grant or withholding of bail in respect of the accused on the occasion of the committal;

(e) any recognizance entered into by any person as surety for the accused together with a statement of any enlargement thereof under section 129(4) of the 1980 Act;

(f) a list of the exhibits produced in evidence before the justices or treated as so produced;

(g) such of the exhibits referred to in paragraph (1)(f) as have been retained by the justices;

(h) the names and addresses of any interpreters engaged for the defendant for the purposes of the committal proceedings, together with any telephone numbers at which they can be readily contacted, and details of the languages or dialects in connection with which they have been so engaged;

(i) if the committal was under section 6(2) of the 1980 Act (committal for trial without consideration of the evidence), a statement to that effect;

(j) if the magistrates' court has made an order under section 8(2) of the 1980 Act (removal of restrictions on reports of committal proceedings), a statement to that effect;

(k) the certificate of the examining justices as to the costs of the prosecution under the *Costs in Criminal Cases (General) Regulations* 1986;

(l) if any person under the age of 18 is concerned in the committal proceedings, a statement whether the magistrates' court has given a direction under section 39 of the *Children and Young Persons Act* 1933 (prohibition of publication of certain matter in newspapers);

(m) a copy of any representation order previously made in the case;

(n) a copy of any application for a representation order previously made in the case which has been refused; and

(o) any documents relating to an appeal by the prosecution against the granting of bail.

(2) The period of 4 days specified in paragraph (1) may be extended in relation to any committal for so long as the Crown Court officer directs, having regard to the length of any document mentioned in that paragraph or any other relevant circumstances.

Criminal Procedure Rules 2005 (S.I. 2005 No. 384), r.12.1

Documents to be sent to the Crown Court

10–35 **12.1.**—(1) As soon as practicable after any person is sent for trial (pursuant to section 51 of the *Crime and Disorder Act* 1998), and in any event within 4 days from the date on which he is sent (not counting Saturdays, Sundays, Good Friday, Christmas Day or Bank Holidays), the magistrates' court officer shall, subject to section 7 of the *Prosecution of Offences Act* 1985 (which relates to the sending of documents and things to the Director of Public Prosecutions), send to the Crown Court officer—

(a) the information, if it is in writing;

(b) the notice required by section 51(7) of the 1998 Act;

(c) a copy of the record made in pursuance of section 5 of the *Bail Act* 1976 relating to the granting or withholding of bail in respect of the accused on the occasion of the sending;

(d) any recognizance entered into by any person as surety for the accused together with any enlargement thereof under section 129(4) of the *Magistrates'* Courts Act 1980;

(e) the names and addresses of any interpreters engaged for the defendant for the purposes of the appearance in the magistrates' court, together with any telephone numbers at which they can be readily contacted, and details of the languages or dialects in connection with which they have been so engaged;

(f) if any person under the age of 18 is concerned in the proceedings, a statement whether the magistrates' court has given a direction under section 39 of the *Children and Young Persons Act* 1933 (prohibition of publication of certain matter in newspapers);

(g) a copy of any representation order previously made in the case;

(h) a copy of any application for a representation order previously made in the case which has been refused; and

(i) any documents relating to an appeal by the prosecution against the granting of bail.

(2) The period of 4 days specified in paragraph (1) may be extended in relation to any sending for trial for so long as the Crown Court officer directs, having regard to any relevant circumstances.

Criminal Procedure Rules 2005 (S.I. 2005 No. 384), Pt 27

Witness statements in magistrates' courts

10–36 **27.1.**—(1) Written statements to be tendered in evidence in accordance with section 5B of the *Magistrates'* Courts Act 1980 or section 9 of the *Criminal Justice Act* 1967 shall be in the form set out in the Practice Direction.

(2) When a copy of any of the following evidence, namely—

(a) evidence tendered in accordance with section 5A of the 1980 Act (committal for trial); or

(b) a written statement tendered in evidence under section 9 of the 1967 Act (proceedings other than committal for trial),

is given to or served on any party to the proceedings a copy of the evidence in question shall be given to the court officer as soon as practicable thereafter, and where a copy of any such statement as is referred to in sub-paragraph (b) is given or served by or on behalf of the prosecutor, the accused shall be given notice by or on behalf of the prosecutor of his right to object to the statement being tendered in evidence.

(3) Where—

(a) a statement or deposition to be tendered in evidence in accordance with section 5A of the 1980 Act; or

(b) a written statement to be tendered in evidence under section 9 of the 1967 Act, refers to any document or object as an exhibit, that document or object shall wherever possible be identified by means of a label or other mark of identification signed by the maker of the statement or deposition, and before a magistrates' court treats any document or object referred to as an exhibit in such a statement or deposition as an exhibit produced and identified in court by the maker of the statement or deposition, the court shall be satisfied that the document or object is sufficiently described in the statement or deposition for it to be identified.

(4) If it appears to a magistrates' court that any part of any evidence tendered in accordance with section 5A of the 1980 Act or a written statement tendered in evidence under section 9 of the 1967 Act is inadmissible there shall be written against that part—

(a) in the case of any evidence tendered in accordance with section 5A of the 1980 Act, but subject to paragraph (5) of this rule, the words "Treated as inadmissible" together with the signature and name of the examining justice or, where there is more than one examining justice, the signature and name of one of the examining justices by whom the evidence is so treated;

(b) in the case of a written statement tendered in evidence under section 9 of the 1967 Act the words "Ruled inadmissible" together with the signature and name of one of the justices who ruled the statement to be inadmissible.

(5) Where the nature of the evidence referred to in paragraph (4)(a) is such that it is not possible to write on it, the words set out in that sub-paragraph shall instead be written on a label or other mark of identification which clearly identifies the part of the evidence to which the words relate and contains the signature and name of an examining justice in accordance with that sub-paragraph.

(6) Where, before a magistrates' court—

(a) a statement or deposition is tendered in evidence in accordance with section 5A of the 1980 Act; or

(b) a written statement is tendered in accordance with section 9 of the 1967 Act,

the name of the maker of the statement or deposition shall be read aloud unless the court otherwise directs.

(7) Where—

(a) under section 5B(4), 5C(4), 5D(5) or 5E(3) of the 1980 Act; or

(b) under section 9(6) of the 1967 Act,

in any proceedings before a magistrates' court any part of the evidence has to be read out aloud, or an account has to be given orally of so much of any evidence as is not read out aloud, the evidence shall be read or the account given by or on behalf of the party which has tendered the evidence.

(8) Statements and depositions tendered in evidence in accordance with section 5A of the 1980 Act before a magistrates' court acting as examining justices shall be authenticated by a certificate signed by one of the examining justices.

(9) Where, before a magistrates' court—

(a) evidence is tendered as indicated in paragraph (2)(a) of this rule, retained by the court, and not sent to the Crown Court under rule 10.5; or

(b) a written statement is tendered in evidence as indicated in paragraph (2)(b) of this rule and not sent to the Crown Court under rule 43.1 or 43.2,

all such evidence shall, subject to any direction of the court in respect of non-documentary exhibits falling within paragraph (9)(a), be preserved for a period of three years by the magistrates' court officer for the magistrates' court.

Right to object to evidence being read in Crown Court trial

27.2.—(1) The prosecutor shall, when he serves on any other party a copy of the evidence to be tendered in committal proceedings, notify that party that if he is committed for trial he has the right to object, by written notification to the prosecutor and the Crown Court within 14 days of being so committed unless the court in its discretion permits such an objection to be made outside that period, to a statement or deposition being read as evidence at the trial without oral evidence being given by the person who made the statement or deposition and without the opportunity to cross-examine that person. **10–37**

(2) The prosecutor shall, on notifying a party as indicated in paragraph (1), send a copy of such notification to the magistrates' court officer.

(3) Any objection under paragraph 1(3)(c) or paragraph 2(3)(c) of Schedule 2 to the *Criminal Procedure and Investigations Act* 1996 to the reading out at the trial of a statement or deposition without further evidence shall be made in writing to the prosecutor and the Crown Court within 14 days of the accused being committed for trial unless the court at its discretion permits such an objection to be made outside that period.

In connection with the editing of statements, see also paragraph III.24 of the consolidated criminal practice direction, *ante*, §§ 4–283 *et seq.*

Taking deposition in a magistrates' court

10–38 Rule 28.2 of the *Criminal Procedure Rules* 2005 (S.I. 2005 No. 384) made provision for the procedure to be followed where a person attended before a justice of the peace in pursuance of section 97A of the *MCA* 1980 (*ante*, § 10–21) or paragraph 4 of Schedule 3 to the *CDA* 1998 (*ante*, § 1–30). The *Criminal Procedure (Amendment) Rules* 2007 (S.I. 2007 No. 699) substituted a new Part 28 in the 2005 rules, but without any provision corresponding to the former rule 28.2.

[The next paragraph is § 10–41.]

B. READING DEPOSITIONS AND STATEMENTS AT TRIAL

(1) General permission in relation to committal evidence

Introduction

10–41 Section 68 of the *CPIA* 1996 (repealed, as from a day to be appointed, by the *CJA* 2003, s.332, and Sched. 37, Pt 4) gives effect to Schedule 2 to the Act (*post*). The effect of paragraphs 1 and 2 is wide-reaching in that they make any statement falling within section 5B of the *MCA* 1980 (*ante*, § 10–16) and any deposition taken under section 97A of that Act (*ante*, § 10–21) admissible at trial. This is subject to objection by the defence, but any such objection may be overridden by the judge "in the interests of justice".

This provision goes further than any previous legislation on the admissibility of witness statements and depositions. First, there is no restriction of admissibility to cases where the witness is dead, too sick to attend court or too frightened to give evidence (as under the *CJA* 1925, s.13(3) (the provision repealed by the 1996 Act which formerly governed the admissibility of committal depositions and statements), and the *CJA* 2003, s.116, *post*, § 11–15). Secondly, there is no restriction on the discretion of the judge and no indication as to what factors he should consider. Thirdly, the presumption seems to be in favour of admission of such evidence, with the onus being on the defence to object. This is confirmed by rule 27.2 of the *Criminal Procedure Rules* 2005 (S.I. 2005 No. 384) (*ante*, § 10–37) which prescribes a period of 14 days from committal in which the defendant is to notify any objection to the prosecutor and the Crown Court.

It should be borne in mind that under the new regime introduced by the 1996 Act, the old system whereunder a magistrates' court committing an accused for trial would make a series of witness orders (full or conditional) in respect of the witnesses has been abolished, and that, therefore, the provisions of Schedule 2 are not confined to the statements or depositions of non-contentious witnesses the subject of conditional witness orders.

It appears, however, that the introduction of such a draconian system was not what was intended. These provisions were introduced at a late stage in the life of the bill in the House of Commons. Upon the House of Lords' subsequent consideration of the Commons' amendments, the apparent defects were pointed out. Although the Government were unwilling to accept any amendment to the bill, Baroness Blatch (Minister of State, Home Office) said (*Hansard*, HL, Vol. 573, col. 949):

> "If the evidence … has been admitted in earlier committal hearings and is not disputed by any parties at the trial, it would be both unnecessary and wasteful to require the presence of witnesses to give that evidence again orally. That is a practice which already exists and we are not seeking to introduce anything new or revolutionary… ."

Criminal Procedure and Investigations Act 1996, Sched. 2, paras 1–4

Section 68 SCHEDULE 2

STATEMENTS AND DEPOSITIONS

Statements

10–42 1.—(1) *Sub-paragraph (2) applies if—*

(a) *a written statement has been admitted in evidence in proceedings before a magistrates' court inquiring into an offence as examining justices,*

(b) *in those proceedings a person has been committed for trial,*

(c) *for the purposes of section 5A of the* Magistrates' Courts Act *1980 the statement complied with section 5B of that Act prior to the committal for trial,*

(d) *the statement purports to be signed by a justice of the peace, and*

(e) *sub-paragraph (3) does not prevent sub-paragraph (2) applying.*

(2) *Where this sub-paragraph applies the statement may without further proof be read as evidence on the trial of the accused, whether for the offence for which he was committed for trial or for any other offence arising out of the same transaction or set of circumstances.*

(3) *Sub-paragraph (2) does not apply if—*

(a) *it is proved that the statement was not signed by the justice by whom it purports to have been signed,*

(b) *the court of trial at its discretion orders that sub-paragraph (2) shall not apply, or*

(c) *a party to the proceedings objects to sub-paragraph (2) applying.*

(4) *If a party to the proceedings objects to sub-paragraph (2) applying the court of trial may order that the objection shall have no effect if the court considers it to be in the interests of justice so to order.*

Depositions

2.—(1) *Sub-paragraph (2) applies if—* **10–43**

(a) *in pursuance of section 97A of the* Magistrates' Courts Act *1980 (summons or warrant to have evidence taken as a deposition etc.) a person has had his evidence taken as a deposition for the purposes of proceedings before a magistrates' court inquiring into an offence as examining justices,*

(b) *the deposition has been admitted in evidence in those proceedings,*

(c) *in those proceedings a person has been committed for trial,*

(d) *for the purposes of section 5A of the* Magistrates' Courts Act *1980 the deposition complied with section 5C of that Act prior to the committal for trial,*

(e) *the deposition purports to be signed by the justice before whom it purports to have been taken, and*

(f) *sub-paragraph (3) does not prevent sub-paragraph (2) applying.*

(2) [Identical to para. 1(2), *ante*, save for substitution of "deposition" for "statement".]

(3) [Identical to para. 1(3), *ante*, save for substitution of "deposition" for "statement".]

(4) [Identical to para. 1(4), *ante*.]

Signatures

3.—(1) *A justice who signs a certificate authenticating one or more relevant statements or depositions shall be treated for the purposes of paragraphs 1 and 2 as signing the statement or deposition or (as the case may be) each of them.* **10–44**

(2) *For this purpose—*

(a) *a relevant statement is a written statement made by a person for the purposes of proceedings before a magistrates' court inquiring into an offence as examining justices;*

(b) *a relevant deposition is a deposition made in pursuance of section 97A of the* Magistrates' Courts Act *1980 for the purposes of such proceedings.*

Time limit for objection

4. *Criminal Procedure Rules may make provision—* **10–45**

(a) *requiring an objection under paragraph 1(3)(c) or 2(3)(c) to be made within a period prescribed in the rules;*

(b) *allowing the court of trial at its discretion to permit such an objection to be made outside any such period.*

[This Schedule is printed as amended by the *Courts Act* 2003, s.109(1), and Sched. 8, para. 380. As from a day to be appointed, it is repealed by the *CJA* 2003, s.332, and Sched. 37, Pt 4.]

As to the manner of objection under paragraph 1(3)(c) or 2(3)(c), see rule 27.2 of the *Criminal Procedure Rules* 2005 (S.I. 2005 No. 384) (*ante*, § 10–37). **10–46**

(2) Where deposition of child or young person taken under the Children and Young Persons Act 1933, s.42

10–47 For section 42, see *ante*, § 10–26.

Children and Young Persons Act 1933, s.43

Admission of deposition of a child or young person in evidence

43. Where, in any proceedings in respect of any of the offences mentioned in the First Schedule to this Act the court is satisfied by the evidence of a duly qualified medical practitioner that the attendance before the court of any child or young person in respect of whom the offence is alleged to have been committed would involve serious danger to his life or health, any deposition of the child or young person taken under the *Indictable Offences Act* 1848, or this Part of this Act, shall be admissible in evidence either for or against the accused person without further proof thereof if it purports to be signed by the justice by or before whom it purports to be taken.

Provided that the deposition shall not be admissible in evidence against the accused person unless it is proved that reasonable notice of the intention to take the deposition has been served upon him and that he or his *counsel or solicitor* [legal representative] had, or might have had if he had chosen to be present, an opportunity of cross-examining the child or young person making the deposition.

[This section is printed as amended, as from a day to be appointed, by the *Legal Services Act* 2007, s.208(1), and Sched. 21, paras 15 and 17 (omission of italicised words, insertion of words in square brackets).]

The relevant provisions of the *Indictable Offences Act* 1848 were repealed by the *MCA* 1952, s.132, and Sched. 6; as to a deposition under "this Part of this Act", see section 42, *ante*, § 10–26.

For Schedule 1 to the 1933 Act, see *post*, § 19–322.

(3) Where deposition taken abroad

10–48 Section 283 of the *Merchant Shipping Act* 1995 provides for the taking of evidence abroad in cases of offences at sea, or by British seamen.

Merchant Shipping Act 1995, s.286

Depositions of persons abroad admissible

286.—(1) If the evidence of any person is required in the course of any legal proceeding before a judge or magistrate in relation to the subject matter of the proceeding and it is proved that that person cannot be found in the United Kingdom, any deposition that he may have previously made at a place outside the United Kingdom in relation to the same subject matter shall, subject to subsection (2) below, be admissible in evidence in those proceedings.

(2) For a deposition to be admissible under subsection (1) above in any proceedings, the deposition—

(a) must have been taken on oath;

(b) must have been taken before a justice or magistrate in any colony or a British consular officer in any other place;

(c) must be authenticated by the signature of the justice, magistrate or officer taking it; and

(d) must, if the proceedings are criminal proceedings, have been taken in the presence of the accused;

and, in a case falling within paragraph (d) above, the deposition shall be certified by the justice, magistrate or other officer taking it to have been taken in the presence of the accused.

(3) No proof need be given of the signature or official character of the person appearing to have signed any such deposition and, in any criminal proceedings, a certificate stating that the deposition was taken in the presence of the accused shall, unless the contrary is proved, be evidence (and in Scotland sufficient evidence) of that fact.

(4) [*Not applicable to criminal proceedings.*]

(5) Nothing in this section affects the admissibility in evidence of depositions under any other enactment or the practice of any court.

10–49 Where witnesses whose evidence had been taken abroad by a British vice-consul under the *Merchant Shipping Act* 1854 (rep.), s.270 (of which this section is a re-enactment), were the officers of a British sailing vessel, which was stated by a clerk in the office of the Registrar-General for seamen, from his examination of official records, never to have been in this country, this was held to be sufficient evidence that the witnesses could not be found in the United Kingdom: *R. v. Conning* (1868) 11 Cox 134; see also *R. v. Anderson* (1868) 11 Cox 154; *R. v. Stewart* (1876) 13 Cox 296.

Civil Aviation Act 1982, s.95

Provisions as to evidence in connection with aircraft

95.—(1) Where in any proceedings before a court in the United Kingdom for an offence committed on board an aircraft the testimony of any person is required and the court is satisfied that the person in question cannot be found in the United Kingdom, there shall be admissible in evidence before that court any deposition relating to the subject matter of those proceedings previously made on oath by that person outside the United Kingdom which was so made—

(a) in the presence of the person charged with the offence; and

(b) before a judge or magistrate of a country such as is mentioned in Schedule 3 to the *British Nationality Act* 1981 as for the time being in force or which was part of Her Majesty's dominions at the time the deposition was made or in which Her Majesty had jurisdiction at that time, or before a consular officer of Her Majesty's Government in the United Kingdom.

(2) Any such deposition shall be authenticated by the signature of the judge, magistrate or consular officer before whom it was made who shall certify that the person charged with the offence was present at the taking of the deposition.

(3) [*Corresponds to* Merchant Shipping Act *1995, s.286(3),* ante.]

(4) If a complaint is made to such a consular officer as aforesaid that any offence has been committed on a British-controlled aircraft while in flight elsewhere than in or over the United Kingdom, that officer may inquire into the case upon oath.

(5) In this section—

"deposition" includes any affidavit, affirmation or statement made upon oath; and

"oath" includes an affirmation or declaration in the case of persons allowed by law to affirm or declare instead of swearing;

and subsections (4) and (5) of section 92 above shall apply for the purposes of this section as they apply for the purposes of that section.

(6) [*Corresponds to* Merchant Shipping Act *1995, s.286(5),* ante.]

(4) Statements served under the Criminal Justice Act 1967, s.9

Criminal Justice Act 1967, s.9

Proof by written statement

9.—(1) In any criminal proceedings, *other than committal proceedings,* a written statement by any person shall, if such of the conditions mentioned in the next following subsection as are applicable are satisfied, be admissible as evidence to the like extent as oral evidence to the like effect by that person. **10–50**

(2) The said conditions are—

(a) the statement purports to be signed by the person who made it;

(b) the statement contains a declaration by that person to the effect that it is true to the best of his knowledge and belief and that he made the statement knowing that if it were tendered in evidence, he would be liable to prosecution if he wilfully stated in it anything which he knew to be false or did not believe to be true;

(c) before the hearing at which the statement is tendered in evidence, a copy of the statement is served, by or on behalf of the party proposing to tender it, on each of the other parties to the proceedings; and

(d) none of the other parties or their solicitors, within seven days from the service of the copy of the statement, serves a notice on the party so proposing objecting to the statement being tendered in evidence under this section.

Provided that the conditions mentioned in paragraphs (c) and (d) of this subsection shall not apply if the parties agree before or during the hearing that the statement shall be so tendered.

(3) The following provisions shall also have effect in relation to any written statement tendered in evidence under this section, that is to say—

(a) if the statement is made by a person under the age of eighteen, it shall give his age;

(b) if it is made by a person who cannot read it, it shall be read to him before he signs it and shall be accompanied by a declaration by the person who so read the statement to the effect that it was so read; and

(c) if it refers to any other document as an exhibit, the copy served on any other party to the proceedings under paragraph (c) of the last foregoing subsection shall be accompanied by a copy of that document or by such information as may be necessary in order to enable the party on whom it is served to inspect that document or a copy thereof.

[(3A) In the case of a statement which indicates in pursuance of subsection (3)(a) of this section that the person making it has not attained the age of 14, subsection (2)(b) of this section shall have effect as if for the words from "made" onwards there were substituted the words "understands the importance of telling the truth in it".]

(4) Notwithstanding that a written statement made by any person may be admissible as evidence by virtue of this section—

(a) the party by whom or on whose behalf a copy of the statement was served may call that person to give evidence; and

(b) the court may, of its own motion or on the application of any party to the proceedings, require that person to attend before the court and give evidence.

(5) An application under paragraph (b) of the last foregoing subsection to a court other than a magistrates' court may be made before the hearing and on any such application the powers of the court shall be exercisable by *a puisne judge of the High Court, a Circuit judge or Recorder sitting alone* [any one of the following sitting alone—

(a) a puisne judge of the High Court;

(b) a Circuit judge;

(c) a District Judge (Magistrates' Courts);

(d) a Recorder].

(6) So much of any statement as is admitted in evidence by virtue of this section shall, unless the court otherwise directs, be read aloud at the hearing and where the court so directs an account shall be given orally of so much of any statement as is not read aloud.

(7) Any document or object referred to as an exhibit and identified in a written statement tendered in evidence under this section shall be treated as if it had been produced as an exhibit and identified in court by the maker of the statement.

(8) A document required by this section to be served on any person may be served—

(a) by delivering it to him or to his solicitor; or

(b) by addressing it to him and leaving it at his usual or last known place of abode or place of business or by addressing it to his solicitor and leaving it at his office; or

(c) by sending it in a registered letter or by the recorded delivery service addressed to him at his usual or last known place of abode or place of business or addressed to his solicitor at his office; or

(d) in the case of a body corporate, by delivering it to the secretary or clerk of the body at its registered or principal office or sending it in a registered letter or by the recorded delivery service addressed to the secretary or clerk of that body at that office.

[Subs. (3) is printed as amended by the *CPIA* 1996, s.69. Subs. (3A) is inserted as from a day to be appointed by the *CYPA* 1969, s.72(3), and Sched. 5, para. 55. The italicised words in subs. (1) are repealed as from a day to be appointed by the *CJA* 2003, s.332, and Sched. 7, Pt 4. The italicised words in subs. (5) are repealed, and the words in square brackets are inserted, as from a day to be appointed, by the *Courts Act* 2003, s.65, and Sched. 4, para. 1.]

10–51 As to the signature requirement in subsection (2)(b), see *Chapman v. Ingleton*, 57 Cr.App.R. 476, DC, *ante*, § 10–16.

Section 9(7) was considered in *Smakowski and Zestfair Ltd v. Westminster City Council* [1990] Crim.L.R. 419, DC (inadmissible document does not become admissible because the statement of the witness producing it is read under s.9).

The circumstances in which these statements should be used and their evidential value were considered in *Lister v. Quaife*, 75 Cr.App.R. 313, DC.

Where a statement under this section refers to a person by name and the name is that of the accused, it is wholly inappropriate in the absence of any suggestion that the person referred to and the accused are two different people, to make a submission of "no case" on the basis that there has been no positive evidence to identify the person in the statement with the accused: *Ellis v. Jones* [1973] 2 All E.R. 893, DC; *cf. Samuda v. Raven* [1973] Crim.L.R. 112, DC; and *R. v. Derwentside JJ., ex p. Swift*; *R. v. Sunderland JJ., ex p. Bate* [1997] R.T.R. 89, DC.

Justices calling evidence under this provision should observe the general rules as to the time at which that evidence is ordinarily called: *French's Dairies Ltd v. Davis* [1973] Crim.L.R. 630, DC.

As to "Notices of Further Evidence", see *ante*, § 4–279. See also in relation to such statements, *Practice Direction (Criminal Proceedings: Consolidation)*, para. III.24, *ante*, § 4–283.

Statements made outside England and Wales

See section 46 of the *CJA* 1972, *ante*, § 10–23. **10–52**

IV. CERTIFICATES AND STATUTORY DECLARATIONS

A. EVIDENCE BY CERTIFICATE

Various matters are by statute provable by certificate. Provisions relevant to the subject matter of this work are dealt with at the appropriate place in the text: for example, certificates as to certain professional qualifications (*ante*, §§ 9–56 *et seq.*), a certificate as to the driver, user or owner of a motor vehicle under section 11 of the *RTOA* 1988 (*post*, § 32–160). **10–53**

Where one subsection of a section of a statute provides that a certificate as to certain matter "shall be admissible in evidence" in proof of its contents, and the following subsection provides that such certificate "shall not be received in evidence" unless certain steps have been taken (*e.g.* service of a copy on the defence), admissibility does not depend upon proof by the prosecution that such steps have been taken; it is for the defence to object to admissibility prior to the end of the prosecution case; and, if no objection is taken at trial, it is no ground of appeal against conviction that the requisite steps had not been taken; if, however, the defendant was unrepresented at trial, a failure to object should not be held against him on appeal; and as to admissibility, it would be otherwise where the statutory provision governing admissibility was to the effect that a certificate "is admissible only if" certain steps have been taken: *Att.-Gen. for the Cayman Islands v. Roberts* [2002] 1 W.L.R. 1842, PC. See also *McCormack v. DPP* [2002] R.T.R. 20, QBD (Maurice Kay J.).

Criminal Justice Act 1948, s.41

41.—(1) In any criminal proceedings, a certificate purporting to be signed by a constable, or by a person having the prescribed qualifications, and certifying that a plan or drawing exhibited thereto is a plan or drawing by him of the place or object specified in the certificate, and that the plan or drawing is correctly drawn to a scale so specified, shall be evidence of the relative position of the things shown on the plan or drawing.

(4) Nothing in this section shall be deemed to make a certificate … admissible as evidence in proceedings for an offence except in a case where and to the extent to which oral evidence to the like effect would have been admissible in those proceedings.

(5) Nothing in this section shall be deemed to make a certificate … admissible as evidence in proceedings for any offence—

(a) unless a copy thereof has, not less than seven days before the hearing or trial, been served in the prescribed manner on the person charged with the offence; or

(b) if that person, not later than three days before the hearing or trial or within such further time as the court may in special circumstances allow, serves notice in the prescribed form and manner on the prosecutor requiring the attendance at the trial of the person who signed the certificate …

(5A) *Where the proceedings mentioned in subsection (1) above are proceedings before a magistrates' court inquiring into an offence as examining justices this section shall have effect with the omission of—*

(a) *subsection (4), and*

(b) *in subsection (5), paragraph (b) and the word "or" immediately preceding it.*

(6) In this section the expression "prescribed" means prescribed by rules made by the Secretary of State.

[This section is printed as amended, and repealed in part, by the *RTA* 1960, s.267, and Sched. 18; the *Theft Act* 1968, s.33(3), and Sched. 3; and the *CPIA* 1996, s.47, and Sched. 1, para. 18. Subs. (5A) is repealed, as from a day to be appointed, by the *CJA* 2003, s.332, and Sched. 37, Pt 4.]

Evidence by Certificate Rules 1961 (S.I. 1961 No. 248), rr.1–3

10–54 **1.** The prescribed qualifications for the purpose of subsection (1) of section forty-one of the *Criminal Justice Act* 1948 (which relates to the admissibility of certified plans and drawings in criminal proceedings), shall be—

(a) registration as an architect under the *Architects (Registration) Acts* 1931 to 1938, or

(b) membership of any of the following bodies, that is to say, the Royal Institution of Chartered Surveyors, the Institution of Civil Engineers, the Institution of Municipal Engineers and the Land Agents Society.

2. A certificate under subsection (1) of section eleven of the *Road Traffic Offenders Act* 1988, shall be in the form numbered 1 in the Schedule hereto or in a form to the like effect and a notice under paragraph (b) of subsection (3) of that section or under paragraph (b) of subsection (5) of section forty-one of the *Criminal Justice Act* 1948, shall be in the form numbered 2 in the Schedule hereto or in a form to the like effect.

3. Any certificate or other document required to be served by subsection (3) of the said section eleven or by subsection (5) of the said section forty-one shall be served in the following manner, that is to say:—

(a) where the person to be served is a corporation, by addressing it to the corporation and leaving it at, or sending it by registered post or by the recorded delivery service to, the registered office of the corporation or, if there be no such office, its principal office or place at which it conducts its business;

(b) in any other case, by delivering it personally to the person to be served or by addressing it to him and leaving it at, or sending it by registered post or by the recorded delivery service to, his last or usual place of abode or place of business.

[These rules are printed as amended by the *Evidence by Certificate Rules* 1962 (S.I. 1962 No. 2319). The reference to the *Road Traffic Offenders Act* 1988 is substituted by virtue of the *Road Traffic (Consequential Provisions) Act* 1988, s.2(4).]

As to section 11 of the 1988 Act, see *post*, § 32–160.

B. STATUTORY DECLARATIONS

10–55 For general provisions relating to statutory declarations, see the *Interpretation Act* 1978, Sched. 1 (Appendix B–28) and the *Statutory Declarations Act* 1835.

The most important provision for proof by statutory declaration in the criminal law is the *Theft Act* 1968, s.27(4) (*post*, § 21–332), which is applied in relation to proceedings for an offence under section 83 or 84 of the *Postal Services Act* 2000 (*post*, §§ 25–350, 25–351) by section 109(2) of that Act.

V. TRANSCRIPT OF EVIDENCE

A. RETRIAL ORDERED BY COURT OF APPEAL

10–56 The *CAA* 1968 empowers the Court of Appeal to order a retrial in certain circumstances (see ss.7 and 8, *ante*, §§ 7–112 *et seq.*). Schedule 2 has effect with respect to, *inter alia*, the procedure to be followed upon the retrial: s.8(4).

Criminal Appeal Act 1968, Sched. 2, para. 1

1.—(1) Evidence given at a retrial must be given orally if it was given orally at the original trial, unless—

(a) all the parties to the retrial agree otherwise;

(b) section 116 of the *Criminal Justice Act* 2003 applies (admissibility of hearsay evidence where a witness is unavailable); or

(c) the witness is unavailable to give evidence, otherwise than as mentioned in subsection (2) of that section, and section 114(1)(d) of that Act applies (admission of hearsay evidence under residual discretion).

(2) Paragraph 5 of Schedule 3 to the *Crime and Disorder Act* 1998 (use of depositions) does not apply at a retrial to a deposition read as evidence at the original trial.

[This paragraph is printed as substituted by the *CJA* 2003, s.131.]

For paragraph 5 of Schedule 3 to the 1998 Act, see *ante*, § 1–31.

B. RETRIAL FOLLOWING DISCHARGE OF JURY

As from the commencement of Part 2 of Chapter 11 of the *CJA* 2003 (*post*, §§ 11–2 *et seq.*), the admissibility at a retrial not ordered under the *CAA* 1968 of a transcript of evidence given at the first trial will be governed by sections 114 and 116 (witness unavailable). **10–57**

VI. LETTERS OF REQUEST

Crime (International Co-operation) Act 2003, s.7

Requests for assistance in obtaining evidence abroad

7.—(1) If it appears to a judicial authority in the United Kingdom on an application made by a person mentioned in subsection (3)— **10–58**

(a) that an offence has been committed or that there are reasonable grounds for suspecting that an offence has been committed, and

(b) that proceedings in respect of the offence have been instituted or that the offence is being investigated,

the judicial authority may request assistance under this section.

(2) The assistance that may be requested under this section is assistance in obtaining outside the United Kingdom any evidence specified in the request for use in the proceedings or investigation.

(3) The application may be made—

(a) in relation to England and Wales and Northern Ireland, by a prosecuting authority,

(b) in relation to Scotland, by the Lord Advocate or a procurator fiscal,

(c) where proceedings have been instituted, by the person charged in those proceedings.

(4) The judicial authorities are—

(a) in relation to England and Wales, any judge or justice of the peace,

(b), (c) [*Scotland, Northern Ireland*].

(5) In relation to England and Wales or Northern Ireland, a designated prosecuting authority may itself request assistance under this section if—

(a) it appears to the authority that an offence has been committed or that there are reasonable grounds for suspecting that an offence has been committed, and

(b) the authority has instituted proceedings in respect of the offence in question or it is being investigated.

"Designated" means designated by an order made by the Secretary of State.

(6) [*Scotland*].

(7) If a request for assistance under this section is made in reliance on Article 2 of the 2001 Protocol (requests for information on banking transactions) in connection with the investigation of an offence, the request must state the grounds on which the person making the request considers the evidence specified in it to be relevant for the purposes of the investigation.

The "2001 Protocol" is the Protocol to the Mutual Legal Assistance Convention, established by Council Act of October 16, 2001 (2001/C326/01); and "the Mutual Legal Assistance Convention" is the Convention on Mutual Assistance in Criminal Matters, established by Council Act of May 29, 2000 (2000/C197/01): s.51(1).

Designation of prosecuting authorities

The *Crime (International Co-operation) Act 2003 (Designation of Prosecuting Authorities) Order* 2004 (S.I. 2004 No. 1034) (as amended by the *Crime (International Co-operation) Act 2003 (Designation of Prosecuting Authorities) (Amendment) Order* 2005 (S.I. 2005 No. 1130), and the *Secretaries of State for Children, Schools and* **10–59**

Families, for Innovation, Universities and Skills and for Business, Enterprise and Regulatory Reform Order 2007 (S.I. 2007 No. 3224)) designates as prosecuting authorities for the purposes of section 7(5), the Attorneys General of England and Wales and Northern Ireland, the Director of Revenue and Customs Prosecutions and any person designated under the *Commissioners for Revenue and Customs Act* 2005, s.37(1), the Directors of the Financial Services Authority, the Serious Fraud Office and of Public Prosecutions (of England and Wales and of Northern Ireland), any crown prosecutor, any person designated under the *CJA* 1987, s.1(7), and the Secretary of State for Business, Enterprise and Regulatory Reform.

Sending requests for assistance

10–60 Section 8 makes provision for the transmission of United Kingdom requests to overseas authorities.

Crime (International Co-operation) Act 2003, ss.9, 10

Use of evidence obtained

10–60a **9.**—(1) This section applies to evidence obtained pursuant to a request for assistance under section 7.

(2) The evidence may not without the consent of the appropriate overseas authority be used for any purpose other than that specified in the request.

(3) When the evidence is no longer required for that purpose (or for any other purpose for which such consent has been obtained), it must be returned to the appropriate overseas authority, unless that authority indicates that it need not be returned.

(4) In exercising the discretion conferred by … Article 5 of the *Criminal Justice (Evidence, Etc.) (Northern Ireland) Order* 1988 (S.I. 1988/ 1847 (N.I. 17)) (exclusion of evidence otherwise admissible) in relation to a statement contained in the evidence, the court must have regard—

(a) to whether it was possible to challenge the statement by questioning the person who made it, and

(b) if proceedings have been instituted, to whether the local law allowed the parties to the proceedings to be legally represented when the evidence was being obtained.

(5) [*Scotland.*]

(6) In this section, the appropriate overseas authority means the authority recognised by the government of the country in question as the appropriate authority for receiving requests of the kind in question.

[The words omitted from subs. (4) were repealed by the *CJA* 2003, s.332, and Sched. 37, Pt 6.]

[Domestic freezing orders

10–60b **10.**—(1) If it appears to a judicial authority in the United Kingdom, on an application made by a person mentioned in subsection (4)—

(a) that proceedings in respect of a listed offence have been instituted or such an offence is being investigated,

(b) that there are reasonable grounds to believe that there is evidence in a participating country which satisfies the requirements of subsection (3), and

(c) that a request has been made, or will be made, under section 7 for the evidence to be sent to the authority making the request,

the judicial authority may make a domestic freezing order in respect of the evidence.

(2) A domestic freezing order is an order for protecting evidence which is in the participating country pending its transfer to the United Kingdom.

(3) The requirements are that the evidence—

(a) is on premises specified in the application in the participating country,

(b) is likely to be of substantial value (whether by itself or together with other evidence) to the proceedings or investigation,

(c) is likely to be admissible in evidence at a trial for the offence, and

(d) does not consist of or include items subject to legal privilege.

(4) The application may be made—

(a) in relation to England and Wales and Northern Ireland, by a constable,

(b) in relation to Scotland, by the Lord Advocate or a procurator fiscal.

(5) [*Identical to s.7(4)*, ante, *§ 10–58*.]

(6) This section does not prejudice the generality of the power to make a request for assistance under section 7.]

This section comes into force on a day to be appointed.

Sending freezing orders

Section 11 (into force on a day to be appointed) makes provision for the sending of freezing orders. This must be done via the Secretary of State. **10–60c**

Variation or revocation of freezing orders

Under section 12 (into force on a day to be appointed), a judicial authority which makes a freezing order under section 10 may vary or revoke it on application by the persons mentioned in this section. **10–60d**

Rules of court

In connection with section 7 of the 2003 Act, see rule 32.3 of the *Criminal Procedure Rules* 2005 (S.I. 2005 No. 384). This requires a copy of a request under section 7, which is sent directly abroad, to be sent to the Secretary of State. **10–60e**

VII. EXPERT EVIDENCE

A. LEGISLATION

Criminal Justice Act 1988, s.30

Expert reports

30.—(1) An expert report shall be admissible as evidence in criminal proceedings, whether or not the person making it attends to give oral evidence in those proceedings. **10–61**

(2) If it is proposed that the person making the report shall not give oral evidence, the report shall only be admissible with the leave of the court.

(3) For the purpose of determining whether to give leave the court shall have regard—

(a) to the contents of the report;

(b) to the reasons why it is proposed that the person making the report shall not give oral evidence;

(c) to any risk, having regard in particular to whether it is likely to be possible to controvert statements in the report if the person making it does not attend to give oral evidence in the proceedings, that its admission or exclusion will result in unfairness to the accused or, if there is more than one, to any of them; and

(d) to any other circumstances that appear to the court to be relevant.

(4) An expert report, when admitted, shall be evidence of any fact or opinion of which the person making it could have given oral evidence.

(4A) *Where the proceedings mentioned in subsection (1) above are proceedings before a magistrates' court inquiring into an offence as examining justices this section shall have effect with the omission of—*

(a) *in subsection (1) the words "whether or not the person making it attends to give oral evidence in those proceedings", and*

(b) *subsections (2) to (4).*

(5) In this section "expert report" means a written report by a person dealing wholly or mainly with matters on which he is (or would if living be) qualified to give expert evidence.

[Subs. (4A) was inserted by the *CPIA* 1996, s.47, and Sched. 1, para. 32. It applies only in relation to alleged offences into which no criminal investigation had begun before April 1, 1997: S.I. 1997 Nos 682 & 683 (*ante*, § 10–9). It is repealed as from a day to be appointed: *CJA* 2003, s.332, and Sched. 7, Pt 4.]

Advance notice of expert evidence

The *PACE Act* 1984, s.81, provided for the making of rules: (a) requiring a party to proceedings before the Crown Court to give advance notice of any expert evidence he **10–62** proposes to adduce; and (b) prohibiting a party from adducing such evidence if he does not make the necessary advance disclosure, except with the leave of the court. The *Crown Court (Advance Notice of Expert Evidence) Rules* 1987 (S.I. 1987 No. 716) were made in pursuance of section 81. They have been replaced by Part 24 of the *Criminal Procedure Rules* 2005 (S.I. 2005 No. 384).

Criminal Procedure Rules 2005 (S.I. 2005 No. 384), Pt 24

Requirement to disclose expert evidence

10–63 **24.1.**—(1) Following—

(a) a plea of not guilty by any person to an alleged offence in respect of which a magistrates' court proceeds to summary trial;
(b) the committal for trial of any person;
(c) the transfer to the Crown Court of any proceedings for the trial of a person by virtue of a notice of transfer given under section 4 of the *Criminal Justice Act* 1987;
(d) the transfer to the Crown Court of any proceedings for the trial of a person by virtue of a notice of transfer served on a magistrates' court under section 53 of the *Criminal Justice Act* 1991;
(e) the sending of any person for trial under section 51 of the *Crime and Disorder Act* 1998;
(f) the preferring of a bill of indictment charging a person with an offence under the authority of section 2(2)(b) of the *Administration of Justice (Miscellaneous Provisions) Act* 1933; or
(g) the making of an order for the retrial of any person,

if any party to the proceedings proposes to adduce expert evidence (whether of fact or opinion) in the proceedings (otherwise than in relation to sentence) he shall as soon as practicable, unless in relation to the evidence in question he has already done so or the evidence is the subject of an application for leave to adduce such evidence in accordance with section 41 of the *Youth Justice and Criminal Evidence Act* 1999—

(i) furnish the other party or parties and the court with a statement in writing of any finding or opinion which he proposes to adduce by way of such evidence and notify the expert of this disclosure, and
(ii) where a request in writing is made to him in that behalf by any other party, provide that party also with a copy of (or if it appears to the party proposing to adduce the evidence to be more practicable, a reasonable opportunity to examine) the record of any observation, test, calculation or other procedure on which such finding or opinion is based and any document or other thing or substance in respect of which any such procedure has been carried out.

(2) A party may by notice in writing waive his right to be furnished with any of the matters mentioned in paragraph (1) and, in particular, may agree that the statement mentioned in paragraph (1)(a) may be furnished to him orally and not in writing.

(3) In paragraph (1), "document" means anything in which information of any description is recorded.

[This rule is printed as amended by the *Criminal Procedure (Amendment No. 2) Rules* 2006 (S.I. 2006 No. 2636).]

Withholding evidence

24.2.—(1) If a party has reasonable grounds for believing that the disclosure of any evidence in compliance with the requirements imposed by rule 24.1 might lead to the intimidation, or attempted intimidation, of any person on whose evidence he intends to rely in the proceedings, or otherwise to the course of justice being interfered with, he shall not be obliged to comply with those requirements in relation to that evidence.

(2) Where, in accordance with paragraph (1), a party considers that he is not obliged to comply with the requirements imposed by rule 24.1 with regard to any evidence in relation to any other party, he shall give notice in writing to that party to the effect that the evidence is being withheld and the grounds for doing so.

Effect of failure to disclose

24.3. A party who seeks to adduce expert evidence in any proceedings and who fails to comply with rule 24.1 shall not adduce that evidence in those proceedings without the leave of the court.

These rules are applied by section 127 of the *CJA* 2003, *post*, § 11–47.

As to these rules, see *R. v. Ward*, 96 Cr.App.R. 1, CA, *post*, § 10–68.

Funding

See *ante*, §§ 6–173, 6–176 and 6–202; and, as to appellate proceedings, *post*, §§ 7–173, 7–215b. **10–63a**

Expert's duty and content of report

As from November 6, 2006, the *Criminal Procedure (Amendment No. 2) Rules* 2006 (S.I. 2006 No. 2636) inserted a new Part 33 in the *Criminal Procedure Rules* 2005 (S.I. 2005 No. 384). **10–63b**

Criminal Procedure Rules 2005 (S.I. 2005 No. 384), Pt 33 (as inserted by the Criminal Procedure (Amendment No. 2) Rules 2006 (S.I. 2006 No. 2636))

Reference to expert

33.1. A reference to an "expert" in this Part is a reference to a person who is required to give or prepare expert evidence for the purpose of criminal proceedings, including evidence required to determine fitness to plead or for the purpose of sentencing. **10–63c**

Expert's duty to the court

33.2—(1) An expert must help the court to achieve the overriding objective by giving objective, unbiased opinion on matters within his expertise. **10–63d**

(2) This duty overrides any obligation to the person from whom he receives instructions or by whom he is paid.

(3) This duty includes an obligation to inform all parties and the court if the expert's opinion changes from that contained in a report served as evidence or given in a statement under Part 24 or Part 29.

Content of expert's report

33.3—(1) An expert's report must— **10–63e**

(a) give details of the expert's qualifications, relevant experience and accreditation;

(b) give details of any literature or other information which the expert has relied on in making the report;

(c) contain a statement setting out the substance of all facts given to the expert which are material to the opinions expressed in the report or upon which those opinions are based;

(d) make clear which of the facts stated in the report are within the expert's own knowledge;

(e) say who carried out any examination, measurement, test or experiment which the expert has used for the report and—

  (i) give the qualifications, relevant experience and accreditation of that person,

  (ii) say whether or not the examination, measurement, test or experiment was carried out under the expert's supervision, and

  (iii) summarise the findings on which the expert relies;

(f) where there is a range of opinion on the matters dealt with in the report—

  (i) summarise the range of opinion, and

  (ii) give reasons for his own opinion;

(g) if the expert is not able to give his opinion without qualification, state the qualification;

(h) contain a summary of the conclusions reached;

(i) contain a statement that the expert understands his duty to the court, and has complied and will continue to comply with that duty; and

(j) contain the same declaration of truth as a witness statement.

(2) Only sub-paragraphs (i) and (j) of rule 33.3(1) apply to a summary by an expert of his conclusions served in advance of that expert's report.

Expert to be informed of service of report

33.4. A party who serves on another party or on the court a report by an expert must, at once, inform that expert of that fact. **10–63f**

Pre-hearing discussion of expert evidence

10–63g **33.5**—(1) This rule applies where more than one party wants to introduce expert evidence.

(2) The court may direct the experts to—

(a) discuss the expert issues in the proceedings; and

(b) prepare a statement for the court of the matters on which they agree and disagree, giving their reasons.

(3) Except for that statement, the content of that discussion must not be referred to without the court's permission.

Failure to comply with directions

10–63h **33.6.** A party may not introduce expert evidence without the court's permission if the expert has not complied with a direction under rule 33.5.

Court's power to direct that evidence is to be given by a single joint expert

10–63i **33.7.**—(1) Where more than one defendant wants to introduce expert evidence on an issue at trial, the court may direct that the evidence on that issue is to be given by one expert only.

(2) Where the co-defendants cannot agree who should be the expert, the court may—

(a) select the expert from a list prepared or identified by them; or

(b) direct that the expert be selected in such other manner as the court may direct.

Instructions to a single joint expert

10–63j **33.8.**—(1) Where the court gives a direction under rule 33.7 for a single joint expert to be used, each of the co-defendants may give instructions to the expert.

(2) When a co-defendant gives instructions to the expert he must, at the same time, send a copy of the instructions to the other co-defendant(s).

(3) The court may give directions about—

(a) the payment of the expert's fees and expenses; and

(b) any examination, measurement, test or experiment which the expert wishes to carry out.

(4) The court may, before an expert is instructed, limit the amount that can be paid by way of fees and expenses to the expert.

(5) Unless the court otherwise directs, the instructing co-defendants are jointly and severally liable for the payment of the expert's fees and expenses.

B. OPINION EVIDENCE

Test of admissibility

10–64 As a general rule, parol evidence is not admissible with regard to anything not immediately within the knowledge of the witness; he must speak of facts which happened in his presence, or within his hearing. This rule excludes both hearsay and the expression of opinion or belief. But to this rule there is a necessary exception on questions of the identity of things or persons, or the genuineness of handwriting, where the witness is qualified to express a credible opinion or belief on the subject: *R. v. Silverlock* [1894] 2 Q.B. 766, CCR; Taylor, Evid., 12th ed., ss.1414 *et seq.*, *post*, § 14–64.

In matters of science or trade, the opinion of an expert, or person intimately acquainted with it, is admissible to furnish the court with information which is likely to be outside the experience and knowledge of a judge or jury. If, on the proven facts, a judge or jury can form their own conclusions without help, then the opinion of an expert is unnecessary: *R. v. Turner (T.)* [1975] Q.B. 834, 60 Cr.App.R. 80, CA. For a recent example of the application of this principle, see *R. v. Loughran* [1999] Crim.L.R. 404, CA.

The topics upon which expert evidence has been received are manifold. Apart from the matters dealt with specifically in § 10–69, *post*, no attempt is made in this section to provide a definitive list of such topics. However, reference may be made to the following paragraphs: §§ 4–326 *et seq.*, *ante* (defendant's mental state, I.Q., etc.); § 8–26, *ante* (whether witness may be sworn); § 8–36a, *ante* (competency); §§ 8–154 *et seq.*, *ante* (witness's reliability); §§ 14–47a, 14–48, 14–52, 14–53, 14–63 *et seq.*, *post* (identification issues); § 17–99, *post* (insanity); § 17–125, *post* (duress); § 19–76, *post* (diminished responsibility); § 19–197, *post* (psychiatric injury as bodily harm); § 24–86, *post* (firearms); §§ 27–77, 27–107b, *post* (drugs); § 30–254, *post* (insider trading); §§ 31–17,

31–21, 31–23, *post* (foreign marriages, *etc.*); §§ 31–64 *et seq.*, *post* (obscenity); § 31–109, *post* (indecent photographs); and §§ 32–21, 32–83, 32–104, 32–162, 32–187, *post* (road traffic issues).

As to proof of the facts on which an expert bases his opinion, see *post*, §§ 11–47, 11–48.

Qualification

Whether a witness is competent to give evidence as an expert is for the judge to determine: *R. v. Silverlock, ante.* **10–65**

In *R. v. Bonython* (1984) 38 S.A.S.R. 45, King C.J., giving the principal judgment of the South Australia Supreme Court, said that there were two questions for the judge to decide.

"The first is whether the subject matter of the opinion falls within the class of subjects upon which expert testimony is permissible. This … may be divided into two parts: (a) whether the subject matter of the opinion is such that a person without instruction or experience in the area of knowledge or human experience would be able to form a sound judgment on the matter without the assistance of witnesses possessing special knowledge or experience in the area, and (b) whether the subject matter of the opinion forms part of a body of knowledge or experience which is sufficiently organized or recognized to be accepted as a reliable body of knowledge or experience, a special acquaintance with which by the witness would render his opinion of assistance to the court. The second question is whether the witness has acquired by study or experience sufficient knowledge of the subject to render his opinion of value in resolving the issues before the court.

An investigation of the methods used by the witness in arriving at his opinion may be pertinent, in certain circumstances, to the answers to both the above questions. If the witness has made use of new or unfamiliar techniques or technology, the court may require to be satisfied that such techniques or technology have a sufficient scientific basis to render results arrived at by that means part of a field of knowledge which is a proper subject of expert evidence … . Where the witness possesses the relevant formal qualifications to express an opinion on the subject, an investigation on the *voir dire* of his methods will rarely be permissible on the issue of his qualifications. There may be greater scope for such examination where the alleged qualifications depend upon experience or informal studies … . Generally speaking, once the qualifications are established, the methodology will be relevant to the weight of the evidence and not to the competence of the witness to express an opinion ….

If the qualifications of a witness to give expert evidence are in issue, it may be necessary to hear evidence on the *voir dire* in order to make a finding as to those qualifications. If there is an issue as to whether the subject matter upon which the opinion is sought is a proper subject of expert evidence, any disputed facts relevant to the determination of that issue should be resolved by the reception of evidence on the *voir dire*" (at pp. 46–48).

In *R. v. Hodges* [2003] 2 Cr.App.R. 15, CA, it was held that a drugs squad police officer giving evidence in relation to the street value of drugs, etc., met the *Bonython* test of admissibility. As to drugs, see also *post*, §§ 27–77, 27–77a.

If the prosecution are permitted to call a witness of tenuous qualifications, the burden of proof might shift imperceptibly, and a burden be cast on the defendant to rebut a case which should never have been before the jury at all; a defendant could not fairly be asked to meet evidence of opinion given by a quack, a charlatan or an enthusiastic amateur: *R. v. Robb*, 93 Cr.App.R. 161, CA (evidence of voice identification by expert, well-qualified by academic training and practical experience, admissible, despite reliance upon technique accepted as unreliable by majority of professional opinion).

"It would be entirely wrong to deny to the law of evidence the advantages to be gained from new techniques and … advances in science", *per* Steyn L.J., in *R. v. Clarke (R.L.)* [1995] 2 Cr.App.R. 425 at 430, CA (facial mapping by video superimposition); following *R. v. Stockwell*, 97 Cr.App.R. 260, CA (evidence of facial mapping expert properly admitted where offender caught on video was disguised; *aliter*, in the case of a clear photograph with no suggestion of a change of appearance). See also *R. v. Luttrell; R. v. Dawson and Hamberger* [2004] 2 Cr.App.R. 31, CA (lip-reading was a well recognised skill and lip-reading from video footage was no more than an application of that skill).

As to the need to establish the reliability of the underlying scientific technique, and as to the criteria for assessing reliability, see also *Trochym v. The Queen*, *post*, § 10–70.

The fact that the witness was a member of the team that investigated the offence does not disqualify him as an expert witness, although it might go to the weight to be attached to his evidence: *R. v. Gokal* [1999] 6 *Archbold News* 2, CA (97 04132 S2). As to the distinction between matters that go to the entitlement of a witness to give evidence as an expert and matters that go to the weight of any evidence given, see, in particular, *R. (Doughty) v. Ely Magistrates' Court, CPS (interested party)*, 172 J.P. 259, DC, where the justices had wrongly excluded the evidence of a former police officer whom the defence had wished to call as to the workings of a speed detection device. His alleged lack of equivalent experience as compared with the prosecution expert, his non-attendance on courses run by the manufacturer and an alleged error in his written report were all matters that would go to the weight to be attached to his evidence, not to its admissibility in the first place.

A judge has a discretion to direct a *voire dire* for the purpose of deciding whether a purported expert should be allowed to give evidence as an expert witness; but the discretion should be exercised sparingly, as the judge should be astute to avoid unnecessary satellite litigation; in the vast majority of cases, the judge would be able to decide the issue on the basis of the written material before him: *R. v. G.* [2004] 2 Cr.App.R. 38, CA.

Scope

10–66 An expert is now permitted to give his opinion on what has been called "the ultimate issue", but the judge should make it clear to the jury that they are not bound by the expert's opinion, and that the issue is for them to decide: *R. v. Stockwell, ante* (declining to follow the former common law rule (see *R. v. Wright* (1821) Russ. & Ry. 456 at 458), long since honoured more in the breach than in the observance); but a failure slavishly to follow this formula does not automatically render a conviction unsafe: *R. v. Fitzpatrick* [1999] Crim.L.R. 832, CA.

In *R. v. Gokal, ante*, it was held to have been permissible for an accountancy expert who gave evidence in relation to transactions of great complexity to have expressed the opinion that the arrangements were such as to demonstrate dishonest collusion between various parties to the transactions. It had been conceded that it was proper for him to say that the mechanics of the arrangements were such that there could have been no legitimate purpose, and that their only purpose could have been to hide the truth. The court said that the distinction between this and saying that there was dishonest collusion was one without a difference. It should be noted, however, that the dishonesty of the transactions did not go directly to the issue of the guilt of the defendant, whose defence was not so much that the transactions were honest, but that if there was a fraud, he was not part of it. It must be at least doubtful if such evidence would be allowed to be given where it goes directly to the honesty of the defendant. The line may be a fine one, but the evidence of the expert should be confined to his area of expertise; in this case, that was accountancy, not honesty.

Before a court can assess the value of an opinion it must know the facts upon which it is based. If the expert has been misinformed, or has taken irrelevant facts into consideration, or has failed to consider relevant ones, the opinion is likely to be valueless. An expert witness should, therefore, be asked to state the facts upon which his opinion is based. As to the need for a proper factual basis to be established by other evidence, see *R. v. J.P.* [1999] Crim.L.R. 401, CA; as to the need for such evidence to be admissible, see *post*, § 11–48.

The witness need not have conducted any test or examination himself; he may give his opinion on the basis of the facts proved in court: see *R. v. Mason*, 7 Cr.App.R. 67, CCA (opinion as to cause of death though witness had never seen the body); and *R. v. Pinfold and Mackenney* [2004] 2 Cr.App.R. 5, CA (expert may give evidence as to the reliability of witness notwithstanding that he had not examined the witness). The fact that the witness has not himself conducted any test or examination may naturally go to the weight to be attached to his opinion.

Proper approach

10–67 An expert witness should give reasons for his conclusion: *R. v. Hipson* [1969] Crim.L.R. 85, CA. If the statement of an expert witness, who has not been required to give oral evidence, does not give full details of his reasoning, it is for the prosecution, or sometimes the court, to look at the evidence and decide whether it is right to call the witness lest the jury reach a decision of their own without proper expert assistance: *ibid.*

Although an expert may be regarded as giving independent evidence to assist the court, it is wrong for the jury to be directed that his evidence should be accepted in the absence of reasons for rejecting it: *R. v. Lanfear* [1968] 2 Q.B. 77, 52 Cr.App.R. 176, CA; and see *Stockwell*, *ante*.

In *R. v. Cannings* [2004] 2 Cr.App.R. 7, CA, a case of the alleged murder of a baby, it was said that if the outcome of the trial depends exclusively or almost exclusively on a serious disagreement between distinguished and reputable experts, it will often be unwise, and therefore unsafe, to proceed; and this was particularly so, in a field of learning, where the experts were still at the "frontiers of knowledge". *Cannings* is not, however, authority for a proposition, in cases where the issue is whether a child was the victim of a deliberate killing by its mother or had died from natural, even if unexplained, causes, that whenever there is a genuine conflict of opinion between reputable experts, the prosecution should not proceed, or should be stopped, or that the evidence of the prosecution experts should be disregarded; in *Cannings*, there was nothing to establish unnatural as opposed to natural death and the basis of the case depended on inferences by one group of experts which were disputed by another reasonable body of medical opinion: *R. v. Kai-Whitewind* [2005] 2 Cr.App.R. 31, CA.

As to the particular caution that is needed where the scientific knowledge of the process or processes involved is or may be incomplete, and where expert opinion evidence is not just relied upon as additional material to support a prosecution but is fundamental to it, see *R. v. Holdsworth* [2008] 5 *Archbold News* 1, CA (quashing a conviction for murder where the foundation of the prosecution case had been the uncontradicted medical evidence, and where fresh evidence provided a credible alternative medical explanation consistent with the appellant's account of events).

In *R. v. Harris*; *R. v. Rock*; *R. v. Cherry*; *R. v. Faulder* [2006] 1 Cr.App.R. 5, the Court of Appeal said that in cases of alleged non-accidental head injury to infants, the accepted hypothesis that non-accidental head injury depended on the finding of a triad of intracranial injuries consisting of encephalopathy, subdural haemorrhages and retinal haemorrhages had not been undermined by the so-called unified hypothesis (that there was a unified cause of such injuries which was not necessarily trauma); but, whilst it had not been undermined, the triad remained no more than a strong pointer; on its own, it was not possible to find that the triad automatically and necessarily led to a diagnosis of non-accidental head injury; in such cases, it was for the jury to resolve differences of medical opinion, taking account of all the circumstances, including the clinical picture.

Duty of disclosure

It is the duty of an expert instructed by the prosecution to act in the cause of justice: **10–68**
R. v. Ward, 96 Cr.App.R. 1, CA. It follows that if an expert has carried out a test which casts doubt on his opinion, or if such a test has been carried out in his laboratory and is known to him, he is under a duty to disclose this to the solicitor instructing him who has a duty to disclose it to the defence. This duty exists irrespective of any request by the defence. It is not confined to documentation on which the opinion or findings of the expert are based; it extends to anything which might arguably assist the defence. It is, therefore, wider in scope than the obligations imposed by Part 24 of the *Criminal Procedure Rules* 2005 (S.I. 2005 No. 384) (*ante*, § 10–63). Moreover, it is a positive duty, which in the context of scientific evidence, obliges the prosecution to make full and proper inquiries from forensic scientists to ascertain whether there is discoverable material: *ibid.*

In *R. v. Harris*; *R. v. Rock*; *R. v. Cherry*; *R. v. Faulder*, *ante*, the Court of Appeal said that expert evidence should be seen to be the independent product of the expert uninfluenced as to form or content by the exigencies of litigation; an expert should provide independent assistance to the court by way of objective unbiased opinion in relation to matters within his expertise and should never assume the role of advocate; the facts or assumptions on which his opinion is based should be stated and he should not omit to consider material facts which detract from his concluded opinion; an expert should make it clear when a particular question or issue falls outside his expertise, and if his opinion has not been properly researched because he considers that insufficient data are available then he should say so with an indication that his opinion is no more than a provisional one; and if, after exchange of reports, an expert changes his view on material matters, such change of view should be communicated to the other side without delay and, when appropriate, to the court; in cases where there is a genuine disagreement on a scientific or medical issue, or where it is necessary for a party to advance a particular hypothesis to explain a given set of facts, the tribunal of fact will have to resolve the issue which is raised, but the expert who advances such a hypothesis owes a heavy duty to explain to the court that what he is advancing is a hypothesis, that it is controversial (if it is) and to place before the court any material which contradicts the hypothesis; and he must make his material available to the other experts in the case.

The court added that rule 24.1 of the 2005 rules (*ante*) and the plea and case management hearing form (Appendix D–2) make provision for experts to consult together and, if possible, to agree points of agreement and disagreement with a summary of reasons; in cases of alleged child abuse, it was said that the judge should be prepared to give directions in respect of expert evidence taking account of the foregoing general guidance, with a view to narrowing the areas of dispute and limiting the volume of expert evidence.

In *R. v. B. (T.)* [2006] 2 Cr.App.R. 3, the Court of Appeal approved the statement of an expert witness's duties at trial contained in *R. v. Harris*, *ante*, and added that the report of an expert should include, (i) details of the witness's qualifications, experience and accreditation relevant to the opinions expressed in the report and the range and extent of expertise and any limitations thereon; (ii) a statement setting out the substance of the instructions received, however received, the questions upon which an opinion was sought, the materials provided, and the materials which were relevant to the opinions expressed or upon which they were based; (iii) information as to who had carried out any tests, etc., and their methodology, and whether such work was carried out under the supervision of the witness; (iv) where there was a range of opinion in the matters dealt with in the report, a summary of the range of opinion and the reasons for the opinion given; any material facts or matters which detracted from the witness's opinion and any points which should be made against it; (v) relevant extracts from the literature or other material which might assist the court; (vi) a statement that the witness had complied with the duty to the court to provide independent assistance by way of objective unbiased opinion in relation to matters within his or her expertise and an acknowledgment that the witness would inform all parties and, where appropriate, the court in the event of any change of opinion on the material issues. The court said that these guidelines applied equally to supplementary reports.

In *R. v. Puaca* [2006] Crim.L.R. 341, CA, it was said that all pathologists are under a duty to comply with the obligations imposed on expert witnesses from the start; it would be wholly wrong for a pathologist carrying out the first post-mortem at the request of the police or the coroner merely to leave it to the defence to instruct a pathologist to prepare a report setting out contrary arguments.

Conflicts of interest

10–68a A conflict of interest on the part of an expert witness does not operate so as automatically to disqualify him from giving evidence in the proceedings; the key question is whether his expression of opinion is independent of the parties and the pressures of litigation; and this does not infringe the requirement in Article 6 of the ECHR (*post*, § 16–57) for an "independent and impartial tribunal", which is concerned with the integrity of the tribunal and does not require that the same tests of independence applicable to a judge be satisfied by an expert witness; but (ii) a potential conflict of interest must be disclosed by the relevant party, even if the view is taken that any such conflict is not material: *Toth v. Jarman (Note)* [2006] 4 All E.R. 1276, CA (Civ. Div.).

C. Colonial and Foreign Laws

The law of a foreign country must be proved by the testimony of witnesses of competent skill; and foreign *written* law cannot be proved by the production of the written law itself, or of an authenticated copy, but must be proved by some skilled witness who describes the law: *Dalrymple v. Dalrymple* (1811) 2 Hagg. (Consist.Rep.) 54; *Sussex Peerage Claim* (1844) 6 St.Tr.(n.s.) 79; *Baron de Bode v. R.* (1851) 6 St.Tr.(n.s.) 237; *Castrique v. Imrie* (1870) L.R. 4 H.L. 414; Taylor, *Evid.*, 12th ed., ss.1423, 1424; unless the evidence is agreed: *R. v. Okolie, The Times*, June 16, 2000, CA. The witness to prove a foreign law must be a person *peritus virtute officii*, or *virtute professionis*: *Sussex Peerage Claim, ante*. But a witness, whose knowledge of the law of a foreign country is derived solely from his having studied it at a university in another country, is not a good witness to prove it: *Bristow v. Sequeville* (1850) 5 Ex. 275; *In the Goods of Bonelli* (1875) 1 P.D. 69; and see Taylor, *Evid.*, 12th ed., s.1425. A witness competent to give evidence on a point of foreign law may refer to foreign law books to refresh his memory, or to correct or confirm his opinion, but the law itself must be taken from his evidence: *Sussex Peerage Claim, ante*. The law of one part of the Queen's dominions for the purposes of judicial proceedings in another part may be ascertained under the *British Law Ascertainment Act* 1859. 10–69

Any question as to the effect of any such evidence is to be decided by the judge, without being submitted to the jury: *Administration of Justice Act* 1920, s.15.

A conflict of interest on the part of an expert witness does not operate so as automatically to disqualify him from giving evidence in the proceedings; the key question is whether his expression of opinion is independent of the parties and the pressures of litigation; and this does not infringe the requirement in Article 6 of the ECHR (*post*, § 16–57) for an "independent and impartial tribunal", which is concerned with the integrity of the tribunal and does not require that the same tests of independence applicable to a judge be satisfied by an expert witness; but (ii) a potential conflict of interest must be disclosed by the relevant party, even if the view is taken that any such conflict is not material: *Toth v. Jarman (Note), ante*, § 10–68a.

D. Application of Scientific Techniques to Testimony of Lay Witnesses

In *Fennell v. Jerome Property Maintenance Ltd, The Times*, November 26, 1986, QBD, it was held that evidence produced by the administration of a mechanically, chemically or hypnotically induced test on a witness so as to show the veracity or otherwise of that witness is inadmissible. And as to the inadmissibility of evidence obtained during a polygraph session conducted as a condition of release on licence, see the *Offender Management Act* 2007, s.30. 10–70

In *Trochym v. The Queen*, 216 C.C.C. (3d) 225, the Supreme Court of Canada held that whilst a party wishing to rely on novel, scientific evidence must first establish that the underlying science is sufficiently reliable to be admitted in a court of law, the same applied to the application of a scientific technique to the testimony of a lay witness; and reliability is to be evaluated according to (a) whether the technique can be and has been tested, (b) whether it has been subjected to peer review and publication, (c) the known or potential rate of error, and (d) whether the theory or technique has been generally accepted. Applying these principles to post-hypnosis evidence, the court held that such evidence was inadmissible, the general consensus being that most individuals were more susceptible under hypnosis, that any increase in accurate memories was accompanied by an increase in inaccurate memories, that hypnosis could compromise the subject's ability to distinguish memory from imagination and that subjects frequently reported being more confident of post-hypnotic memories, regardless of their accuracy; in relation to the admission of post-hypnosis evidence on a topic not broached during the hypnosis, a judge must be satisfied that any detrimental effect arising from the risk of such evidence being tainted by post-hypnosis memories was outweighed by the probative value of the evidence.

E. Immunity

In *Meadow v. General Medical Council* [2007] Q.B. 462, CA (Civ. Div.), it was held that it would be wrong in principle to extend the common law immunity of a witness 10–70a from suit in civil proceedings in respect of both honest and dishonest evidence given in court, so as to confer blanket immunity on expert witnesses from disciplinary fitness to practise proceedings arising out of their evidence in court.

F. Appellate Proceedings

10–70b As to the admissibility of expert evidence on appeal, see, in particular, *ante*, § 7–214; and as to the funding of such evidence, see *ante*, §§ 7–173, 7–215b.

VIII. JUDICIAL NOTICE

A. Principle

10–71 Courts may take judicial notice of matters which are so notorious, or clearly established, or susceptible of demonstration by reference to a readily obtainable and authoritative source that evidence of their existence is unnecessary; and local courts are not merely permitted to use their local knowledge, but are to be regarded as fulfilling a constitutional function if they do so: *Mullen v. Hackney L.B.C.* [1997] 1 W.L.R. 1103, CA (Civ. Div.).

When a court takes judicial notice of a fact, it finds (or directs the jury to find) that the fact exists although its existence has not been established by evidence. The doctrine applies not only to judges but also to juries with respect to matters coming within the sphere of their everyday knowledge and experience: *R. v. Rosser* (1836) 7 C. & P. 648; *R. v. Jones (R.W.)*, 54 Cr.App.R. 63, CA; but courts should be cautious in treating a factual conclusion as obvious, even though the man in the street would unhesitatingly hold it to be so: *Carter v. Eastbourne B.C.*, 164 J.P. 273, DC.

10–72 Although judges and juries may, in arriving at their decisions, use their general information and that knowledge of the common affairs of life which men of ordinary intelligence possess (see *Jones, ante*), they may not act on their own private knowledge or belief regarding the facts of the particular case: *R. v. Sutton* (1816) 4 M. & S. 532; *Ingram v. Percival* [1969] 1 Q.B. 548, DC; *Wetherall v. Harrison* [1976] Q.B. 773, DC (proper for a justice with specialised knowledge of the circumstances forming the background to a particular case to draw upon that knowledge in interpreting the evidence, but improper in effect to give evidence to himself and the other justices which is at variance with the evidence given, for to do so would offend the fundamental principle that evidence should be given in the presence of the parties and be subject to cross-examination); *Paul v. DPP*, 90 Cr.App.R. 173, DC (justices entitled to rely on knowledge of area in concluding that residents likely to be caused nuisance by practice of kerb-crawling); and *R. v. Fricker*, *The Times*, July 13, 1999, CA (principle in *Wetherall v. Harrison* applies equally to juries). Where, however, a juror passed a note to the judge indicating that his knowledge of a particular locality was at variance with the evidence of the defendant, the judge's decision to allow the prosecution to call rebuttal evidence to this effect was upheld on appeal: *R. v. Blick*, 50 Cr.App.R. 280, CCA.

10–73 As to the need for justices to be circumspect in their use of local knowledge and to inform the parties when reliance is being placed upon local knowledge, see *Bowman v. DPP* [1990] Crim.L.R. 600, DC; *Norbrook Laboratories (G.B.) Ltd v. Health and Safety Executive*, *The Times*, February 23, 1998, DC.

B. Scope

10–74 For a full examination of the areas of law and fact to which the doctrine of judicial notice applies, see *Phipson on Evidence*, 16th ed., paras 3–02 *et seq.*

C. Statutes

10–75 Every Act passed since 1850 is a public Act to be judicially noted as such, unless the contrary is expressly provided: *Interpretation Act* 1978, s.3 and Sched. 2, para. 2, and see *Pillai v. Mudanayaka* [1953] A.C. 514 at 528, PC.

As to the proof of statutory instruments, see *ante*, § 9–29.

D. SIGNATURES OF JUDGES

Evidence Act 1845, s.2

2. All courts, judges, justices, masters in Chancery, masters of courts, commissioners judicially acting and other judicial officers, are henceforth to take judicial notice of the signature of any of the equity or common law judges of the superior courts at Westminster, provided such signature be attached or appended to any decree, order, certificate, or other judicial or official document. **10–76**

The reference to "any of the equity or common law judges of the superior courts at Westminster" should be construed as referring to judges of the High Court and Court of Appeal: see the *Supreme Court of Judicature (Consolidation) Act* 1925, ss.18(2), 26(2), and the *Supreme Court [Senior Courts] Act* 1981, s.151(5), and Sched. 4, para. 1(1) (renamed as from a day to be appointed: *Constitutional Reform Act* 2005, s.59(5), and Sched. 11, para. 1).

CHAPTER 11

HEARSAY EVIDENCE

I. INTRODUCTION

The basic rule at common law was that hearsay evidence was inadmissible in criminal proceedings. The rule rendered inadmissible "any statement other than one made by a person while giving oral evidence in the proceedings ... as evidence of any fact or opinion stated": see *Cross & Tapper on Evidence*, 10th ed., p.578; and *R. v. Sharp (Colin)*, 86 Cr.App.R. 274 at 278, HL (approving a similar statement of the rule in earlier editions). To the basic rule, there were many exceptions, both common law (*e.g.* the *res gestae* principle) and statutory (*e.g.* Pt II of the *CJA* 1988). The House of Lords had made clear, however, that any new exceptions must be the result of legislation: see *Myers v. DPP* [1965] A.C. 1001; and *R. v. Kearley* [1992] 2 A.C. 228, HL. And as to the impropriety of admitting hearsay simply because it assisted the defence, see *R. v. Van Vreden*, 57 Cr.App.R. 818, CA; and *R. v. Turner (B.J.)*, 61 Cr.App.R. 67 at 88, CA. **11–1**

The admissibility of hearsay in criminal proceedings is now governed by the *CJA* 2003. Chapter 2 (ss.114–136) of Part 11 of the Act is headed "Hearsay". Whilst the legislation does not contain an express definition of "hearsay", the opening words of section 114(1) (*post*, § 11–3), taken together with section 115 (*post*, § 11–4), effectively define it as any representation of fact or opinion made by a person otherwise than in oral evidence in the proceedings in question when tendered as evidence of any matter stated therein (*cf.* s.121(2), *post*, § 11–41). As with the common law, section 114(1) enacts a basic rule that hearsay, as so defined, is inadmissible in criminal proceedings unless (a) it can be brought within a statutory exception, including the following provisions of this chapter of the Act, (b) it is admissible under one of the common law exceptions preserved by section 118, (c) all parties to the proceedings agree to it being admissible, or (d) "the court is satisfied that it is in the interests of justice for it to be admissible". In making a decision under paragraph (d), a court is obliged to have regard to the matters listed in subsection (2). Section 118(2) provides that, with the exception of the rules preserved by subsection (1), the common law rules governing the admissibility of hearsay evidence in criminal proceedings are abolished.

II. STATUTE

A. CRIMINAL JUSTICE ACT 2003

(1) Commencement

Apart from section 132 (which came into force on January 29, 2004), Chapter 2 of Part 11 of the 2003 Act was brought into force on April 4, 2005: *Criminal Justice Act 2003 (Commencement No. 8 and Transitional and Saving Provisions) Order* 2005 (S.I. 2005 No. 950). Section 141 of the Act stipulates that no provision of Part 11 has effect in relation to criminal proceedings begun before the commencement of that provision. In *R. v. Bradley* [2005] 1 Cr.App.R. 24, CA, the court was concerned with the commencement of Chapter 1 (*post*, §§ 13–1 *et seq.*). It held that the definition of **11–2** "criminal proceedings" in sections 112 and 140 as "criminal proceedings in relation to which the strict rules of evidence apply" meant that the new legislation would apply to any trial or dispute as to the facts following a guilty plea that began on or after the commencement date. *Bradley* was followed in relation to Chapter 2 in *R. v. H. (P.G.)* [2006] 1 Cr.App.R. 4, CA, where it was held the hearsay provisions of the 2003 Act apply to all trials beginning on or after the date of commencement, even if a preparatory hearing in relation to the trial had taken place before that date, in relation to which section 8(1) of the *CJA* 1987 (*ante*, § 4–84n), and section 30 of the *CPIA* 1996 (*ante*, § 4–84u) provide that where a preparatory hearing is ordered, "the trial shall begin with that hearing".

(2) The basic rules

Criminal Justice Act 2003, ss.114, 115, 133, 134

Admissibility of hearsay evidence

11–3 **114.**—(1) In criminal proceedings a statement not made in oral evidence in the proceedings is admissible as evidence of any matter stated if, but only if—

(a) any provision of this Chapter or any other statutory provision makes it admissible,
(b) any rule of law preserved by section 118 makes it admissible,
(c) all parties to the proceedings agree to it being admissible, or
(d) the court is satisfied that it is in the interests of justice for it to be admissible.

(2) In deciding whether a statement not made in oral evidence should be admitted under subsection (1)(d), the court must have regard to the following factors (and to any others it considers relevant)—

(a) how much probative value the statement has (assuming it to be true) in relation to a matter in issue in the proceedings, or how valuable it is for the understanding of other evidence in the case;
(b) what other evidence has been, or can be, given on the matter or evidence mentioned in paragraph (a);
(c) how important the matter or evidence mentioned in paragraph (a) is in the context of the case as a whole;
(d) the circumstances in which the statement was made;
(e) how reliable the maker of the statement appears to be;
(f) how reliable the evidence of the making of the statement appears to be;
(g) whether oral evidence of the matter stated can be given and, if not, why it cannot;
(h) the amount of difficulty involved in challenging the statement;
(i) the extent to which that difficulty would be likely to prejudice the party facing it.

(3) Nothing in this Chapter affects the exclusion of evidence of a statement on grounds other than the fact that it is a statement not made in oral evidence in the proceedings.

In *R. v. Xhabri* [2006] 1 Cr.App.R. 26, CA, it was held that this section is not incompatible with Article 6(3)(d) of the ECHR (*post*, § 16–57), on account of the fact that it allows for the admission of a statement by a witness who is not available for cross-examination; Article 6(3)(d) is not an absolute right, the touchstone being whether the fairness of the trial requires the availability for cross-examination of the witness; a court has a power under section 126 (*post*, § 11–46), and a duty under the *Human Rights Act* 1998, to exclude evidence in a particular case where its admission would lead to an unfair trial; furthermore, there is no inherent inequality about the provisions since they apply equally to all parties. As to this, see also *post*, §§ 11–15 *et seq.*

For the purposes of subsection (1)(c), "agreement" does not require a contract law analysis of offer and acceptance, nor does it require some formal recording of the position by the court, nor does it necessarily require express agreement; rather, where hearsay is relied on by a party, the court is entitled to infer, in the absence of objection by another party, that there is no objection to its admissibility, and thus that there is agreement to its admissibility; such an inference, however, should not be drawn automatically or in all circumstances; in particular, it would be difficult, and in most cases impossible, to draw such an inference if the defendant were unrepresented: *Emlyn Williams t/a Williams of Porthmadog v. Vehicle and Operator Services Agency*, 172 J.P. 328, DC.

In *R. v. Taylor* [2006] 2 Cr.App.R. 14, CA, it was held that whilst section 114(2) provides that "the court must have regard" to nine factors when determining whether it was in the "interests of justice" for hearsay to be admitted under section 114(1)(d), there was no obligation on the court to reach a conclusion on all nine factors or to embark on an investigation in order to do so; to reach a proper conclusion on whether the evidence should be admitted, the court was required to exercise its judgment in the light of those particular factors, to give consideration to them and to others which the court considered relevant, and to assess their significance and the weight which in the court's judgment they bore individually and in relation to each other.

An out-of-court accusation by one defendant against another is capable of being admitted under section 114(1)(d), and if it is so admitted, it is evidence in the case generally: *R. v. Mclean* [2008] 1 Cr.App.R. 11, CA, as explained in *R. v. Y.* [2008] 1 Cr.App.R. 34, CA, in which it was held that paragraphs (a) to (d) of section 114(1) are alternatives, and hearsay is admissible if it falls within any one of them; that there is no basis on which paragraph (d) can be read so as to be subject to the provisions of another paragraph, and it is available in law for all types of hearsay, and on application by any party to a criminal trial. The court said that the nature of the hearsay is certainly relevant to whether it is in the interests of justice to admit it, but is irrelevant to whether section 114(1)(d) is capable of applying to it; consequently, section 118(1) (which preserves, *inter alia*, "any rule of law relating to the admissibility of confessions or mixed statements in criminal proceedings" (*post*, § 11–70)) cannot exclude the application of section 114(1)(d) to a confession (*e.g.* of an absent co-accused) not admissible under the preserved common law rules; and indeed, a hearsay accusation against the accused will be capable of falling within section 114(1)(d), whether associated with a confession by the accuser or not. The court added, however, that care should still be taken to ensure that the factors set out in section 114(2) are fully considered, and it is not the effect of section 114(1)(d) that hearsay statements are routinely to be admitted; in considering those factors, a judge must remember why the Act does not render hearsay automatically admissible (*viz.*, broadly, because it is necessarily second-best evidence, being as such much more difficult to test and to assess, and because the jury never see the person whose word is being relied upon, and who cannot be asked a single exploratory or challenging question about what he has said), and the real disadvantages of hearsay remain critical to the assessment of whether the interests of justice call for its admission; in particular, if it is the prosecution who wish to adduce the hearsay in question, if it is an accusation against the defendant rather than an admission against interest by the maker, or if it is contained in a police interview of a person other than the defendant, those circumstances are important factors to be taken into account; indeed, (a) in the great majority of cases, it will not be in the interests of justice for such police interviews to be admitted, (b) it will be an unusual case where it will be in the interests of justice for a hearsay accusation to be admitted, and (c) since the burden of proving the case is upon the prosecution and to a high standard, considerable care should be taken where the prosecution seek to rely upon hearsay to supply a case where otherwise they would have none.

The observations of the court in *McEwan v. DPP*, 171 J.P. 308, DC (section 114(1)(d) is a "safety valve" and that "it would have to be an exceptional case for it to be relied upon … to rescue the prosecution from the consequences of its own failures") must be seen as observations made in the context of that case and applicable solely to the facts of that case, and not as observations of general application, there being nothing in the section to indicate that it is to be generally interpreted in such a way: *Sak v. CPS*, 172 J.P. 89, DC.

The statement of a non-compellable wife is potentially admissible against her husband under section 114(1)(d) where she refuses to give oral evidence; but it could well be objectionable to admit a woman's statement if the police take it, intending to call her to give evidence, and then seek to place it in evidence when she states that she does not wish to give evidence against her husband; there is an obvious paradox in excusing the wife from giving evidence, but then placing before the jury in the form of a statement the very evidence that she does not wish to give and cannot be compelled to give; whether or not it is just to admit the statement in any such case must depend upon the individual facts: *R. v. L. (R.)* [2008] 2 Cr.App.R. 18, CA. As to this case, see also *ante*, § 8–48.

The Court of Appeal will only interfere with a judge's decision as to the "interests of justice" test, if it was outwith the range of reasonable decisions: *R. v. Musone* [2007] 2 Cr.App.R. 29, CA. It is important that a judge should give himself an opportunity clearly to identify the reasons by which he reached his conclusion as to the admissibility of hearsay; to that end, postponing the giving of reasons in order to maintain the impetus of a trial is to be commended: *ibid*.

As to the potential admissibility of the statement of an absent witness via section 114(1)(d), where it is inadmissible under section 116 (*post*, § 11–15), see *R. v. Adams*, *post*, § 11–21; and as to the potential admissibility via the same paragraph of a statement prepared by the prosecution as to the circumstances of a previous offence for the purposes of proving the defendant's bad character under Chapter 1 of Part 11 of the 2003 Act, see *R. v. Steen*, *post*, § 13–66.

Valuable assistance as to the assessment of the twin criteria of necessity and reliability (which feature prominently among the factors listed in section 114(2)) may be gained from the judgment of the Supreme Court of Canada in *R. v. Khelawon* [2006] 2 S.C.R. 787.

Statements and matters stated

11–4 **115.**—(1) In this Chapter references to a statement or to a matter stated are to be read as follows.

(2) A statement is any representation of fact or opinion made by a person by whatever means; and it includes a representation made in a sketch, photofit or other pictorial form.

(3) A matter stated is one to which this Chapter applies if (and only if) the purpose, or one of the purposes, of the person making the statement appears to the court to have been—

(a) to cause another person to believe the matter, or

(b) to cause another person to act or a machine to operate on the basis that the matter is as stated.

Proof of statements in documents

11–5 **133.** Where a statement in a document is admissible as evidence in criminal proceedings, the statement may be proved by producing either—

(a) the document, or

(b) (whether or not the document exists) a copy of the document or of the material part of it,

authenticated in whatever way the court may approve.

Interpretation of Chapter 2

11–6 **134.**—(1) In this Chapter—

"copy", in relation to a document, means anything on to which information recorded in the document has been copied, by whatever means and whether directly or indirectly;

"criminal proceedings" means criminal proceedings in relation to which the strict rules of evidence apply;

"defendant", in relation to criminal proceedings, means a person charged with an offence in those proceedings;

"document" means anything in which information of any description is recorded;

"oral evidence" includes evidence which, by reason of any disability, disorder or other impairment, a person called as a witness gives in writing or by signs or by way of any device;

"statutory provision" means any provision contained in, or in an instrument made under, this or any other Act, including any Act passed after this Act.

(2) Section 115 (statements and matters stated) contains other general interpretative provisions.

(3) Where a defendant is charged with two or more offences in the same criminal proceedings, this Chapter has effect as if each offence were charged in separate proceedings.

Proceedings under the *Criminal Procedure (Insanity) Act* 1964, s.4A (*ante*, § 4–168), for determining whether the defendant did the act or made the omission charged, fall within the definition of "criminal proceedings": *R. v. Chal* [2008] 1 Cr.App.R. 18, CA.

The definition of "document" is identical to that contained in Schedule 2 to the *CJA* 1988. In *R. v. Nazeer* [1998] Crim.L.R. 750, CA, it was held that where a computer contained records which, if printed out, would be admissible as complying with (what is now) section 117 of the 2003 Act, but the computer was unable to produce a print out and it was physically impossible to produce the computer itself in court, the statements could be proved by a witness giving oral evidence of what he read on the computer screen; having regard to the definition of "document", the computer was itself a document, and it being impossible to produce the original, secondary evidence was admissible; (what is now) section 133 (*ante*) was permissive and did not preclude proof by oral evidence.

Limitations on the exclusionary rule

As has been seen (*ante*, § 11–1), section 114(1), when taken together with section 115, effectively enacts a hearsay rule that coincides with the common law rule. The exclusionary rule will have no application where (a) the statement is the fact to be proved (as in the case of certain computer generated documents, sometimes referred to as "real evidence" (*ante*, §§ 9–11 *et seq.*)), (b) the purpose for which the statement is tendered is not to prove the truth of any matter stated in it (*post*), (c) the statement does not constitute an assertion of fact, (d) the statement does constitute an assertion of fact, but it was not the purpose, or one of the purposes of the maker of the statement to cause another person to believe the matter stated in it or (e) the statement, whilst not asserting a fact, is of such a nature that a fact may be implied from it. Statements in the first three of these categories were admissible at common law (as not being hearsay), and the provisions of the 2003 Act do not affect this. As to statements not intended to be believed by another, see *post*, § 11–12a. As to implied assertions, see *post*, §§ 11–13, 11–14. **11–7**

Purpose for which statement tendered

"Evidence of a statement made to a witness ... may or may not be hearsay. It is hearsay and inadmissible when the object of the evidence is to establish the truth of what is contained in the statement. It is not hearsay and is admissible when it is proposed to establish by the evidence, not the truth of the statement, but the fact that it was made": *Subramaniam v. Public Prosecutor* [1956] 1 W.L.R. 956 at 969, PC; and *Ratten v. R.*, *ante*. Where, for example, the purpose is to tender the statement as evidence of the hearer's state of mind (see *Subramaniam*, *ante*), then it may be admissible as original evidence, *i.e.* the statement will be in issue or relevant for a reason quite independent of whether any assertions contained in the statement are true or false. **11–8**

As to when the evidence is tendered as evidence of the speaker's state of mind, see also *post*, §§ 11–82, 11–83.

Mawaz Khan v. R. [1967] 1 A.C. 454, PC, further illustrates the importance of establishing the purpose for which the evidence is tendered. Two men were charged with murder. Each made a statement to the police in the absence of the other. Both statements set up identical alibis and offered identical explanations for the injuries which each had sustained. Many of the details of their statements were contradicted by the evidence of witnesses. Neither gave evidence and the jury were initially directed that a statement made by a defendant in the absence of his co-defendant is only evidence against the maker. The judge then went on to direct the jury that in one respect the statement of each defendant could be used against the other. "What the Crown says is that these statements have been shown to be a tissue of lies and that they disclose an attempt to fabricate a joint story ... the fabrication of a joint story would be evidence against both. It would be evidence that they had co-operated after the alleged crime." The Privy Council upheld the direction. **11–9**

Statement not constituting assertion of fact

In *R. v. Chapman* [1969] 2 Q.B. 436, 53 Cr.App.R. 336, CA, police evidence relating to the *RSA* 1967, s.2(2)(b) (*rep.*) was, "we notified Dr Din, he made an examination **11–10** and raised no objection to the taking of a specimen." This was held to be admissible to establish that the doctor made no objection. The evidence did not contravene the rule against hearsay because the purpose in tendering it was to establish the fact that a statement (*e.g.* "I have no objection") was made. See also *R. v. Holt* [1968] 1 W.L.R. 1942, CA; *R. v. Skinner* [1968] 2 Q.B. 700 at 709, 52 Cr.App.R. 599 at 606, CA; and *R. v. Orrell* [1972] R.T.R. 14, CA.

11–11 In *Ratten v. R.* [1972] A.C. 378, PC, R's wife died from a gunshot wound. R asserted that the discharge was accidental and had occurred while he was cleaning the gun. R was charged with murder. Evidence relating to three telephone calls was adduced at the trial. (a) At 1.09 p.m., R's father telephoned, spoke to R and heard the deceased's voice in the background. All appeared to be normal. (b) At 1.15 p.m., a telephone call from R's house was received at the local exchange. The caller was hysterical, said "Get me the police," gave R's address as the telephonist was connecting the call to the police, and then hung up. The telephonist gave the police the address. The telephonist, in her evidence, referred to the caller as "she" and the jury were properly directed upon the question as to whether they should accept that evidence as establishing that the caller was the deceased. (c) At 1.20 p.m., the police telephoned R's house and spoke to R who asked them to come immediately. R's wife, by then, was dead. The appellant, who denied that the second call was ever made, contended that the evidence relating thereto was hearsay and did not fall within any recognised exception thereto. *Held*, (a) the evidence was not hearsay. It was admissible as evidence of fact relevant to an issue. The mere fact that the evidence of a witness includes evidence as to words spoken by another person who is not called is no objection to its admissibility. Words spoken are facts just as much as any other action by a human being. If the speaking of the words is a relevant fact, a witness may give evidence that they were spoken. The question of hearsay only arises when the words spoken are relied on "testimonially", *i.e.* as establishing some fact narrated by the words. (b) Even assuming that there was a hearsay element (*i.e.* that the words said to have been used involve an assertion of the truth of some facts stated in them, *viz.* that the deceased was being attacked by R) in the evidence, it was properly admitted as part of the *res gestae* (for the relevant principles, see *post*, §§ 11–74 *et seq.*).

11–12 As to the admissibility of offers of immoral services to undercover police officers by women ostensibly employed as masseuses at a massage parlour in order to show the true purpose for which the premises were used, see *Woodhouse v. Hall*, 72 Cr.App.R. 39, DC (*post*, § 20–235), in which *Ratten* was applied.

Statements made without the purpose of causing another to believe them

11–12a In *R. v. N. (K.)*, 171 J.P. 158, CA, it was held that an out of court statement made by a witness in the form of a diary entry would not amount to a "matter stated" within section 115 (*ante*, § 11–4) if it was not intended to be read by anyone but the author; such a statement would thus be admissible (if relevant) as real or direct evidence outside the scope of the hearsay rules in Chapter 2 of Part 11 of the Act. For criticism of this decision, see *Criminal Law Week* 2007/12/3.

In *R. v. Isichei*, 170 J.P. 753, CA, it was said (without deciding the point) that whereas section 115(2) provides that a "statement" for the purposes of Chapter 2 is any representation of fact or opinion made by a person by whatever means, and whereas section 115(3) provides that a "matter stated" is one to which the chapter applies if (and only if) the purpose, or one of the purposes, of the person making the statement appears to the court to have been, *inter alia*, to cause another person to believe the matter, where a person said to another that he was going to make a telephone call to a third person, whom he named, before then making a telephone call, it would arguably require a semantically correct and highly artificial application of the provision to conclude that the remark was not a statement governed by the Act and thus admissible without reference to its other provisions; on the assumption that it was covered by the Act, what had been said, on the facts of the case, was, the court said, part of the story of a common sense series of events and had been admissible in the "interests of justice" under section 114(1)(d) (*ante*, § 11–3); but, the court added, if the maker of the telephone call had not had the purpose before he made the call of causing the other person to know that he was calling the person whom he had named, the evidence would, if anything, have been even more probative and would have been admissible as being outside the Act. For further analysis of this aspect of this case, see *Criminal Law Week* 2007/01/6.

Implied assertions

Ratten and *Woodhouse v. Hall* were distinguished by the House of Lords in *R. v. Kearley* [1992] 2 A.C. 228. The certified question was: **11–13**

> "Whether evidence may be adduced at a trial of words spoken (namely a request for drugs to be supplied by the defendant), not spoken in the presence or hearing of the defendant, by a person not called as a witness, for the purpose not of establishing the truth of any fact narrated by the words, but of inviting the jury to draw an inference from the fact that the words were spoken (namely that the defendant was a supplier of drugs)."

Evidence had been given of telephone calls and personal calls to the defendant's house when the police, but not the defendant, were present, in which the callers requested to speak to him and asked to be supplied with drugs. None of these persons were witnesses. *Held* (Lords Griffiths and Browne-Wilkinson dissenting), that, in so far as the requests merely manifested the callers' state of mind, *viz.* their belief or opinion that the defendant would supply them with drugs, such state of mind was irrelevant and evidence as to it was, accordingly, inadmissible; that, in so far as the requests could be treated as having impliedly asserted the fact that the defendant was a supplier of drugs, evidence thereof was hearsay, the rule against which applied equally to implied as well as express assertions; and the fact that a multiplicity of requests for drugs might have greater probative force than a single request was not a ground for disregarding it.

Lord Ackner (at p. 257), distinguished *Woodhouse v. Hall*, *ante*, on the basis that in order to prove premises to be a brothel, it is enough to prove that at the premises more than one woman *offers* herself as a participant in physical acts of indecency. The evidence of such offers was "original" not hearsay. As to *Ratten*, his Lordship said that it was important to understand the issues in the case in order to appreciate the relevance of the evidence. The defendant was asserting that the death was an accident and was denying that the telephone call at 1.15 p.m. had taken place. The fact of the phone call and the caller's apparent state of fear were relevant to the issue of accident. Lord Oliver said, in relation to *Ratten*:

> "That is a long way from the instant case where the conversation is relied upon not as a circumstance surrounding an act of the accused but as indicative of the speaker's view of the accused's intentions. In so far as it was considered permissible in *Ratten* to draw from the contents of the call the inference that the deceased was saying that she was under attack from her husband and that that was true, that could be justified only by treating the contents as part of the *res gestae*" (at p. 267).

Kearley was applied in *R. v. O'Connell* [2003] 6 *Archbold News* 2, CA, where it was held that it made no difference that the defendant was present at the time of the telephone calls if he had been unable to hear what was being said; but his reaction (shouting warnings to the effect that he was in police custody) was admissible.

The exclusion from section 115 of the 2003 Act of implied assertions has been taken to be indicative of an intention on the part of Parliament to reverse the decision in *Kearley*. Whilst there was some initial uncertainty as to whether the drafting had in fact achieved this result (see the 2007 edition of this work), the matter has now been resolved by *R. v. Sukadeve Singh* [2006] 2 Cr.App.R. 12, CA. It was held that when sections 114 (*ante*, § 11–3) and 118 (*post*, § 11–70) were read together, they abolished the common law hearsay rules (save for those which had been preserved expressly) and created instead a new rule against hearsay, which did not extend to implied assertions; an unintentional implied assertion was not a "matter stated" to which the hearsay provisions in the Act applied, and it followed that the view of the majority in *Kearley* (*viz.* that an unintentional implied assertion was inadmissible hearsay), had been set aside by the Act and that unintentional implied assertions were now admissible because they were no longer to be regarded as hearsay. **11–14**

(3) Principal categories of admissibility

(a) *Absent witnesses*

Criminal Justice Act 2003, s.116

Cases where a witness is unavailable

11–15 **116.**—(1) In criminal proceedings a statement not made in oral evidence in the proceedings is admissible as evidence of any matter stated if—

(a) oral evidence given in the proceedings by the person who made the statement would be admissible as evidence of that matter,

(b) the person who made the statement (the relevant person) is identified to the court's satisfaction, and

(c) any of the five conditions mentioned in subsection (2) is satisfied.

(2) The conditions are—

(a) that the relevant person is dead;

(b) that the relevant person is unfit to be a witness because of his bodily or mental condition;

(c) that the relevant person is outside the United Kingdom and it is not reasonably practicable to secure his attendance;

(d) that the relevant person cannot be found although such steps as it is reasonably practicable to take to find him have been taken;

(e) that through fear the relevant person does not give (or does not continue to give) oral evidence in the proceedings, either at all or in connection with the subject matter of the statement, and the court gives leave for the statement to be given in evidence.

(3) For the purposes of subsection (2)(e) "fear" is to be widely construed and (for example) includes fear of the death or injury of another person or of financial loss.

(4) Leave may be given under subsection (2)(e) only if the court considers that the statement ought to be admitted in the interests of justice, having regard—

(a) to the statement's contents,

(b) to any risk that its admission or exclusion will result in unfairness to any party to the proceedings (and in particular to how difficult it will be to challenge the statement if the relevant person does not give oral evidence),

(c) in appropriate cases, to the fact that a direction under section 19 of the *Youth Justice and Criminal Evidence Act* 1999 (special measures for the giving of evidence by fearful witnesses etc) could be made in relation to the relevant person, and

(d) to any other relevant circumstances.

(5) A condition set out in any paragraph of subsection (2) which is in fact satisfied is to be treated as not satisfied if it is shown that the circumstances described in that paragraph are caused—

(a) by the person in support of whose case it is sought to give the statement in evidence, or

(b) by a person acting on his behalf,

in order to prevent the relevant person giving oral evidence in the proceedings (whether at all or in connection with the subject matter of the statement).

Interpretation

11–16 As to the meaning of "statement" and "matter stated", see section 115, *ante*, § 11–4; as to "oral evidence", see section 134(1), *ante*, § 11–6.

Standard of proof

11–17 It was held in relation to corresponding provisions of earlier legislation (*PACE Act* 1984, s.68, and *CJA* 1988, ss.23 and 24), that the standard of proof in relation to the statutory requirements was the criminal standard: *R. v. Minors*; *R. v. Harper*, 89 Cr.App.R. 102, CA; *R. v. Acton Magistrates' Court, ex p. McMullen*; *R. v. Tower Bridge Magistrates' Court, ex p. Lawlor*, 92 Cr.App.R. 98, DC; but that, where the evidence is sought to be introduced by the defence, it is the civil standard: *R. v. Mattey and Queeley* [1995] 2 Cr.App.R. 409, CA.

If there is a dispute about admissibility, the judge should conduct a trial-within-a-trial: *R. v. Minors*; *R. v. Harper*, *ante*. There is a right of cross-examination in respect of any evidence relied on to establish the conditions of admissibility: *R. v. Wood and Fitzsimmons* [1998] Crim.L.R. 213, CA; and *R. v. Elliott, Pearce and McGee*, *The Times*, May 15, 2003, CA.

As to the need to lay the requisite factual foundation and the insufficiency of paying lip service to the conditions of admissibility, see *R. v. Governnor of Pentonville Prison, ex p. Osman*, 90 Cr.App.R. 281, DC; and as to the manner of proof, see also *Bermudez v. Chief Constable of Avon and Somerset* [1988] Crim.L.R. 452, DC.

In *R. v. J.P.* [1999] Crim.L.R. 401, CA, it was held that where a sentence within a statement, otherwise admissible under section 23 of the 1988 Act, was ambiguous as to whether it was itself hearsay, and there was no firm ground upon which to resolve the ambiguity, the sentence should be excluded.

Directing the jury

The following propositions are based on authorities decided in relation to the provisions of the *CJA* 1988. Whilst it is not appropriate to lay down precise directions to be given to the jury in all cases (see *R. v. Hardwick*, *The Times*, February 28, 2001, CA), and whilst the strength of any warning is to be decided upon the basis of the facts of the individual case, the issues and the significance of the statement in the context of the case as a whole, the jury should be warned, especially in a case where the evidence in the statement is disputed, that in assessing the weight of the evidence they should take account of (a) the fact that, unlike evidence given orally in court, it will not normally have been given on oath or affirmation, (b) the fact that it has not been subject to cross-examination, and (c) the circumstances in which the statement was made, particularly if it is apparent that it was made for the purposes of pending or contemplated judicial proceedings, or of a criminal investigation. It will often be appropriate to develop the warning by pointing out particular features of the evidence which conflict with other evidence and which could have been explored in cross-examination. In an identification case it will in addition be necessary to give the appropriate warning as to the dangers of identification evidence: see *Scott v. R.* [1989] A.C. 1242, PC; *R. v. Cole*, 90 Cr.App.R. 478, CA; *R. v. McCoy* [2000] 6 *Archbold News* 2, CA. **11–18**

There is no rule of law that a judge is bound to direct the jury that they could not possibly pay as much attention to a witness statement as to other evidence: *R. v. Greer (James)* [1998] Crim.L.R. 572, CA.

Witness dead (s.116(2)(a))

It should be noted that in the case of a statement falling within sub-paragraphs (a) to (d) of subsection (2), the Act itself gives the court no discretion, merely providing that a statement "is admissible" if the relevant conditions are satisfied. This is a significant difference as compared with the 1988 Act which rendered all such statements subject to an "interests of justice" discretion, with the presumption being against admission where it was apparent that the statement in question had been prepared for the purposes of criminal proceedings or a criminal investigation. **11–18a**

The court's discretion to exclude statements within sub-paragraphs (a) to (d) will derive from section 78 of the *PACE Act* 1984 (exclusion of unfair evidence (*post*, § 15–452)), specifically preserved by section 126(2)(a) (*post*, § 11–46), and from the specific discretion to exclude a statement on the ground that its admission would be likely to lead to disproportionate waste of time for little benefit (see s.126(1), *post*). In *R. v. Cole*; *R. v. Keet* [2008] 1 Cr.App.R. 5, CA, it was said that, in practice, application of the test in section 78 would be unlikely to produce a different result from application of the "interests of justice" test in section 114, and that a court would be likely to take account of the matters in section 114(2) in considering fairness under section 78 or in relation to the jurisprudence of the European Court of Human Rights as to the requirements of a fair trial.

As to the European jurisprudence, the court in *R. v. Cole*; *R. v. Keet*, *ante*, said that it did not follow from the decision in *Luca v. Italy* (2003) 36 E.H.R.R.46, ECtHR, that the requirements of a fair trial, as laid down by Article 6 of the ECHR (*post*, § 16–57), preclude the admission of hearsay under section 116 in any circumstance where the source of the evidence is unavailable to be cross-examined and where the evidence of the missing witness is the only, and potentially decisive, evidence; Article 6(3)(d) does not lay down an absolute rule that evidence of a statement cannot be admitted unless the defendant has had an opportunity to examine the maker, the only governing criterion being whether the admission of the evidence was compatible with a fair trial; and whether the fairness of a trial will be impaired by admitting evidence of an absent witness will depend on the facts of the case. As to the European jurisprudence, see also *R. v. Xhabri*, *ante*, § 11–3, *R. v. Arnold*, *post*, § 11–24, *Grant v. The State*, *post*, § 11–25, and *R. v. Al-Khawaja* [2006] 1 Cr.App.R. 9, CA, in which it was held that where the sole witness to an alleged crime died before trial, the case law of the European Court of Human Rights on Article 6 did not require the conclusion that the admission, under the 1988 Act, ss.23, 25 and 26, of a statement made by the witness for the purposes of any prosecution that might ensue, would render the trial unfair; the provision in Article 6(3)(d) that an accused should be able to have any witness against him examined is one specific aspect of a fair trial, but where that opportunity was not provided, the question was "whether the proceedings as a whole, including the way the evidence was taken, were fair" (*Doorson v. Netherlands*, 22 E.H.R.R. 330, ECtHR).

Evidence of a dying declaration is admissible under this paragraph: *R. v. Musone* [2007] 2 Cr.App.R. 29, CA.

Witness unfit (s.116(2)(b))

11–19 As to the inadmissibility of a statement under this section, if the maker of the statement did not have the "required capability" at the time he made it, see section 123 of the 2003 Act, *post*, § 11–43.

A statement from a doctor that it would be in the best interests of the witness if she were able to submit written evidence was hardly equivalent to proof that she was unfit to attend because of her mental condition; whilst pointing in that direction, it was not sufficient; the provision in question is important as it is necessary that statements of witnesses who are indeed unfit should be able to be given, but it is equally important that there is proper protection against the admission of such statements unless the relevant conditions are indeed satisfied: *R. (Meredith) v. Harwich JJ.*, 171 J.P. 249, QBD (Collins J.).

Where a witness attended court but was unfit, through mental illness, to give evidence, his statement was admissible: *R. v. Setz-Dempsey*, 98 Cr.App.R. 23, CA (decided on section 23(2)(a) of the 1988 Act, the conviction being quashed, *inter alia*, on the ground that the jury should have heard the medical evidence, which went incidentally to the reliability of the statement).

As to the extent to which the court has a discretion in relation to this paragraph, see *ante*, § 11–18a, and *Grant v. The State*, *post*, § 11–25.

Witness outside United Kingdom (s.116(2)(c))

11–20 Section 116(2)(c) corresponds to section 23(2)(b) of the 1988 Act. In *R. v. Hurst* [1995] 1 Cr.App.R. 82, the Court of Appeal said that an application based on section 23(2)(b) could be made before trial or at trial. In the former case, the court would have to look to the future to see whether it would be practicable for the witness's attendance to be secured at the date of the trial. The words "reasonably practicable" involve a consideration of the normal steps which would be taken to secure the attendance of a witness, and the qualification of reasonableness includes other circumstances such as the cost and the steps which may be available to secure attendance. Circumstances may occur at short notice which render it impracticable to secure the attendance of the witness on the day when he is required to testify although practicable arrangements had already been made; faced with an application at trial, all the circumstances will have to be considered, including, in particular, what steps had previously been taken.

The mere fact that it is possible for the witness to attend is not conclusive: *R. v. Castillo* [1996] 1 Cr.App.R. 438, CA. The importance of the evidence and how prejudicial it is to the defendant are factors to be considered: *ibid*; and *R. v. Yu* [2006] Crim.L.R. 643, CA.

In *R. v. C. and K.* [2006] Crim.L.R. 637, CA, it was said that whether it is "reasonably practicable" to secure the attendance of a witness who is outside the United Kingdom must be judged on the basis of the steps taken by the party seeking to secure his attendance; but that, even if a statement is admissible under section 116(2)(c)), the court has an exclusionary discretion under section 126(1) (*post*, § 11–46), as well as a general exclusionary discretion under section 78 of the *PACE Act* 1984; whether it would be fair to admit a statement under section 116(2)(c) would depend in part on what efforts should reasonably be made to secure the attendance of the witness or, at least, to arrange a procedure whereby the contents of the statement can be clarified and challenged. As to the limits of this case, and as to whether the discretion under section 126 is completely general, see the commentary in *Criminal Law Week* 2006/25/8.

For examples of steps which the Court of Appeal thought might have been taken with a view to securing the attendance of witnesses from South America in a drug smuggling case, see *R. v. Gonzales de Arango*, 96 Cr.App.R. 399, CA.

The fact that it is not reasonably practicable to secure the attendance of one witness may be established by the statement of another witness admitted pursuant to section 116: *R. v. Castillo, ante*.

As to the extent to which the court has a discretion in relation to this paragraph, see *ante*, § 11–18a, and *Grant v. The State*, *post*, § 11–25.

Witness cannot be found (s.116(2)(d))

In *R. v. Adams* [2008] 1 Cr.App.R. 35, CA, it was held that it was not sufficient to leave contacting a witness (who had been informed of the fixed date of trial four months earlier) to ensure his attendance at court on the fixed day until the last working day before that day, nor was it sufficient simply to leave a voicemail message when he did not answer his mobile telephone. Those responsible for getting witnesses to court should take account of the fact that it is notorious that witnesses are not invariably organised people with settled addresses who respond promptly to correspondence and messages; that often they do not want to come to court; that, even if they are willing, they may not accord the commitment the priority it warrants; but that even if they do, "it is only too foreseeable" that something (holidays, work, illness being routine examples) may intervene to push the matter out of their minds or to cause a clash of commitments. The court further held, however, that a statement that is inadmissible under section 116(2)(d) may nevertheless be admissible "in the interests of justice" under section 114(1)(d) (*ante*, § 11–3). Where, therefore, admitting the statement of an absent witness had done no more than prove the uncontentious, and shut off an entirely technical escape route, this had been in the "interests of justice" (observing, however, that it is quite likely that it would not be in the interests of justice for disputed parts of the prosecution case to be proved by a hearsay statement when the witness is not available for cross-examination). **11–21**

In deciding whether such steps as were "reasonably practicable" to find a witness have been taken, a judge may legitimately take account of the relative importance of the witness, and of police resources; but not of the seriousness of the charge: *R. v. Coughlan* [1999] 5 *Archbold News* 2, CA (98 05345 Y3).

As to the extent to which the court has a discretion in relation to this paragraph, see *ante*, § 11–18a. For an authority (decided under the 1988 Act) as to how the discretion should be exercised, see *R. v. Sellick and Sellick*, *post*, § 11–25.

Witness in fear (s.116(2)(e))

When it is sought to admit the statement of a witness under section 116(2)(e), the inquiry to be conducted by the judge should focus on the time when the witness would give evidence, subject to a degree of give and take to allow for the practical realities; before a court could be properly satisfied as to the conditions of admissibility, it should be informed what steps had been taken to persuade the witness to attend or to alleviate his fears; and ideally, there should be some direct evidence from the witness; if oral evidence from the witness was not to be forthcoming, then some form of recorded interview would be of assistance: *R. v. H., W. and M.* [2001] Crim.L.R. 815, CA. Whilst a court **11–22** should not skew justice by accepting any proclamation of fear, seeking to test the basis of the fear would be ill-advised as it would undermine the very purpose of section 116: *R. v. Davies* [2007] 2 All E.R. 1070, CA.

In *R. v. Acton Magistrates' Court, ex p. McMullen*; *R. v. Tower Bridge Magistrates' Court, ex p. Lawlor*, 92 Cr.App.R. 98, DC, it was held that where a witness through fear was unable to give oral evidence, a written statement was admissible where the witness was in fear as a consequence of the material offence, or had been put in fear subsequently in relation to that offence and the possibility of having to testify to it. In *R. v. Fairfax* [1995] Crim.L.R. 949, CA, it appears to have been held that the fear need not relate to the offence. Nor need it relate to action by or on behalf of the accused: *R. v. Rutherford* [1998] Crim.L.R. 490, CA.

In *Fairfax, ante*, it was held that a written or oral statement by the witness that he was in fear was admissible for the purpose of proving that he was in fear; such statements are not hearsay, being tendered as direct evidence of the maker's state of mind (see *R. v. Blastland* [1986] A.C. 41, HL; and *post*, § 11–82). In *R. v. Belmarsh Magistrates' Court, ex p. Gilligan* [1998] 1 Cr.App.R. 14, however, the Divisional Court held that a written statement by the witness was not admissible for this purpose; but it is submitted that if the *Blastland* principle applies, it can make no difference whether the witness makes an oral or a written statement that he is in fear.

A magistrate may satisfy himself that a witness is not giving evidence through fear by his own observation of the demeanour of the witness: *R. v. Ashford Magistrates' Court, ex p. Hilden*, 96 Cr.App.R. 92, DC.

A witness may fall within section 116(2)(e) although he attends court to tell the judge (unsworn) of his fear: *R. v. Greer (James)* [1998] Crim.L.R. 572, CA. Where a witness gives some evidence but does not "come up to proof" on relevant matters (the identity of his attacker), and it can be shown that this is on account of fear, the case will fall within section 116(2)(e), and a previous statement made by him will be admissible in evidence (subject to the discretion of the judge): *R. v. Waters*, 161 J.P. 249, CA.

Where it is known in advance that a witness is unwilling to give evidence, it is highly desirable that any investigation of his reasons should be conducted in the absence of the jury, and some innocuous form of words used to explain his absence: *R. v. Jennings and Miles* [1995] Crim.L.R. 810, CA. If the witness unexpectedly says that he is unwilling to give evidence through fear for his safety, or that of his family, it seems the judge should continue with an inquiry in the absence of the jury; if the statement is admitted, the jury will have to be directed to ignore the witness's remarks and, assuming it to be the case, they should be directed that there is no evidence to link the defendant with the witness's fear: see *Jennings and Miles, ante*.

The "interests of justice" (s.116(4))

11–23 The onus is on the party seeking to have the statement admitted to satisfy the court that it "ought to be admitted in the interests of justice": *R. v. Patel*, 97 Cr.App.R.294, CA. The exercise to be performed by the court is one of balancing the risk of unfairness to the defendant because the evidence cannot be challenged, as against the risk of unfairness to the prosecution because they cannot put before the jury all the available evidence; whilst this is not strictly an exercise of discretion, it is something similar to it, in that it is evaluative and fact sensitive and the sort of exercise which the trial judge is in the best position to perform; to that end, such a decision would only be interfered with on appeal if it was obviously wrong, or perverse or unreasonable; and, so far as concerns cases in which the statement is the sole or decisive evidence against the defendant, there being no absolute rule that such evidence should not be read to the jury (*R. v. Sellick and Sellick*, *post*, § 11–25), such cases must be considered with care on their own facts, bearing in mind that the legislation does not give the prosecution "*carte blanche*": *R. v. Doherty*, 171 J.P. 79, CA.

Where a witness gives evidence on a *voire dire* that he is unwilling to give evidence as a result of a threat which had been made to him, it is an inference which the judge may draw, in the absence of any other evidence, that the threat was made, if not at the instigation of the defendant, with his approval; and if the judge so concludes, this should normally be conclusive as to how the discretion under section 116(4) should be exercised; if, however, the defendant gives evidence on the *voire dire*, in consequence of which the judge is left in doubt as to whether he had anything to do with the making of the threat, this would be a relevant factor to the exercise of that discretion: *R. v. Harvey* [1998] 10 *Archbold News* 2, CA.

The obligation to have regard to the contents of the statement does not require the court to look at it. It is enough that the court has been informed of its contents: *R. v. Ashford Magistrates' Court, ex p. Hilden*, 96 Cr.App.R. 92, DC.

In considering the admissibility of a statement by a prosecution witness under this section, it is proper to have regard to the likelihood of it being possible for the defendant to controvert the statement of the witness by himself giving evidence and by calling the evidence of other witnesses: *R. v. Cole*, 90 Cr.App.R. 478, CA.

The weight to be attached to the inability to cross-examine and the magnitude of any consequential risk that admission of the statement will result in unfairness to the accused must depend in part on the court's assessment of the quality of the evidence shown by the contents of the statement: *Cole, ante*; *R. v. Fairfax* [1995] Crim.L.R. 949, CA; *R. v. Batt and Batt* [1995] Crim.L.R. 240, CA (where the evidence is of considerable significance as implicating the defendants, the judge is entitled to take this into account in support of admission of the statement).

The fact that the absent witness provides the only significant evidence against the accused and that his evidence is identification evidence is not sufficient to render the admission of written evidence from that witness contrary to the interests of justice *per se*: *R. v. Dragic* [1996] 2 Cr.App.R. 232, CA.

In *R. v. Arnold* [2004] 6 *Archbold News* 2, CA, the court observed, *obiter*, that it is **11–24**
not the case that what was said in *Luca v. Italy, ante*, § 11–18a, to the effect that where a conviction is solely or to a decisive degree based on depositions that have been made by a person whom the accused has had no opportunity to examine or to have examined, the rights of the defence are restricted to an extent that is incompatible with the guarantees provided by Article 6, admits of no exceptions; if that were so, then section 116(2)(e) could never be relied on where the essential or only witness is kept out of the way by fear; such would be an intolerable result as a general proposition and would only encourage the intimidation which this provision was designed to defeat; no invariable rule to that effect should be propounded or followed; but this is not to be taken as a licence to prosecutors; great care must be taken in each case to ensure that attention is paid to the letter and spirit of the Convention, and judges should not easily be persuaded that it is in the interests of justice to permit evidence to be read; where the witness provides the sole or determinative evidence against the accused, permitting it to be read may well, depending on the circumstances, jeopardise infringing the defendant's rights under Article 6(3)(d), and even if it is not the only evidence, care must be taken to ensure that the ultimate aim of each and every trial, namely, a fair hearing, is achieved.

In *R. v. Sellick and Sellick* [2005] 2 Cr.App.R. 15, CA (a case on the 1988 Act), it **11–25**
was held that where a court is sure that a witness for the prosecution does not give evidence through fear occasioned by the defendant, or persons acting on his behalf, then a statement made by such a witness may be admitted, even though the evidence may be the sole and decisive evidence against the defendant; but the court must be astute to examine the quality and reliability of the evidence, must have regard to the taking of appropriate counter-balancing measures pursuant to what is now section 124 of the 2003 Act (*post*, § 11–44), and must warn the jury as to the disadvantage to the accused of not being able to cross-examine the witness; but the defendant can have no cause for complaint that his rights under Article 6(3)(d) have been infringed where it is his own action, or action taken on his behalf, that has given rise to the situation in which the witness is absent; and where the court is sure that all reasonable steps have been taken to find a witness (s.23(2)(c) of the 1988 Act (now "such steps as it is reasonably practicable to take")), and believes to a high degree of probability (but is not sure) that the witness is being intimidated by or on behalf of the defence, it still cannot be right, having regard to the rights of victims and their families, and the safety of the public generally, for there to be an absolute rule that, where compelling evidence is the sole or decisive evidence, admission of such evidence must automatically lead to infringement of the defendant's

Article 6 rights; that would lead to a situation where the more successful the intimidation, the stronger the argument becomes that the statement cannot be read; the more subtle and less easily established intimidation would provide a defendant with the opportunity of excluding the most material evidence against him; however, care must be taken to see that the legislation is not abused; where intimidation is alleged, the court must examine the circumstances with care; and the more "decisive" the evidence, the greater the care that will be needed to be sure why it is that a witness cannot attend to give evidence.

In *Grant v. The State* [2007] 1 A.C. 1, PC, it was held that whilst the European Court of Human Rights had strongly favoured the calling of live witnesses, available for cross-examination by the defence, it had been astute to avoid treating the rights set out in Article 6(3)(d) as laying down strict rules from which no derogation or deviation was possible in any circumstances; although the rights of the individual had to be safeguarded, the interests of the community and the victims of crime had also to be respected; thus, the focus of inquiry in any given case was not on whether there had been a deviation from the strict letter of Article 6(3)(d), but on whether any deviation had operated unfairly to the defendant in the context of the proceedings as a whole; it would be intolerable if a defendant, shown to have induced fear in a witness thereby causing his non-attendance at trial, could rely on Article 6 to prevent the admission of hearsay evidence; where, however, a witness was unavailable to give evidence in person because he was dead, or too ill to attend, or abroad, or could not be traced, the argument for admitting hearsay was less irresistible (although there may still be a compelling argument for admitting it, provided always that its admission does not place the defendant at an unfair disadvantage). Their Lordships approved the approach to Article 6(3)(d) in *R. v. D.* [2003] Q.B. 90, CA, *R. v. M. (K.J.)* [2003] 2 Cr.App.R. 21, CA, *R. v. Al-Khawaja*, *ante*, § 11–18a, and *R. v. Sellick and Sellick*, *ante*.

(b) *Documents created or received in the course of a trade, business or profession*

Criminal Justice Act 2003, s.117

Business and other documents

11–26 **117.**—(1) In criminal proceedings a statement contained in a document is admissible as evidence of any matter stated if—

(a) oral evidence given in the proceedings would be admissible as evidence of that matter,

(b) the requirements of subsection (2) are satisfied, and

(c) the requirements of subsection (5) are satisfied, in a case where subsection (4) requires them to be.

(2) The requirements of this subsection are satisfied if—

(a) the document or the part containing the statement was created or received by a person in the course of a trade, business, profession or other occupation, or as the holder of a paid or unpaid office,

(b) the person who supplied the information contained in the statement (the relevant person) had or may reasonably be supposed to have had personal knowledge of the matters dealt with, and

(c) each person (if any) through whom the information was supplied from the relevant person to the person mentioned in paragraph (a) received the information in the course of a trade, business, profession or other occupation, or as the holder of a paid or unpaid office.

(3) The persons mentioned in paragraphs (a) and (b) of subsection (2) may be the same person.

(4) The additional requirements of subsection (5) must be satisfied if the statement—

(a) was prepared for the purposes of pending or contemplated criminal proceedings, or for a criminal investigation, but

(b) was not obtained pursuant to a request under section 7 of the *Crime (International Co-operation) Act* 2003 or an order under paragraph 6 of Schedule 13 to the *Criminal Justice Act* 1988 (which relate to overseas evidence).

(5) The requirements of this subsection are satisfied if—

(a) any of the five conditions mentioned in section 116(2) is satisfied (absence of relevant person etc), or

(b) the relevant person cannot reasonably be expected to have any recollection of the matters dealt with in the statement (having regard to the length of time since he supplied the information and all other circumstances).

(6) A statement is not admissible under this section if the court makes a direction to that effect under subsection (7).

(7) The court may make a direction under this subsection if satisfied that the statement's reliability as evidence for the purpose for which it is tendered is doubtful in view of—

(a) its contents,

(b) the source of the information contained in it,

(c) the way in which or the circumstances in which the information was supplied or received, or

(d) the way in which or the circumstances in which the document concerned was created or received.

Whether a statement in a document is admissible under this section is a matter of law for determination by the judge alone: *R. v. Lewendon* [2006] 2 Cr.App.R. 19, CA.

Interpretation

As to the meaning of "statement" and "matter stated", see section 115, *ante*, § 11–4; as to "document" and "oral evidence", see section 134(1), *ante*, § 11–6. **11–27**

Standard of proof

See *ante*, § 11–17. **11–28**

In determining the conditions of admissibility of a document under this section, direct evidence is not essential, though it may often be desirable; the court may, as Parliament clearly intended, draw inferences from the documents themselves and from the method or route by which the documents have been produced before the court: *R. v. Foxley* [1995] 2 Cr.App.R. 523, CA (the documents in question did not fall within section 117(4)).

Directing the jury

See *ante*, § 11–18. **11–29**

Section 117(2)

Section 117(1) and (2) coincide closely with section 24(1) and (2) of the *CJA* 1988. In *R. v. McCarthy* [1998] R.T.R. 374, CA, it was held that where, on a vehicle production line, a computer controlled a machine which automatically stamped a unique number on each vehicle and generated a corresponding bar code label which was attached to the vehicle, and thereafter as parts were added to the vehicle, an operator either scanned the bar code on the part, if already in existence, together with the bar code on the vehicle, or, if there was no bar code, the operator scanned the vehicle number and keyed in the part number, so as to construct a database which would, *inter alia*, contain information as to the part numbers of all the major parts of each vehicle correlated to the unique vehicle number, a print-out of the database was admissible under section 24; to the extent that the information consisted of the automatically generated unique vehicle numbers, there was no human input and no question of hearsay; to the extent that it consisted of the corresponding part numbers, it depended on human input, *i.e.* the scanning of bar codes or the keying in of part numbers; but such was supplied by a person (the operator) who "had, or may reasonably be supposed to have had, personal knowledge of the matters dealt with", and accordingly fell within what is now section 117(2)(b). **11–30**

Where X left a note on the windscreen of a stationary vehicle in a car park in which she recorded the registration number of a second vehicle that she had seen collide with the stationary vehicle, where Y, on finding the note, telephoned the police and recited the recorded registration number, where the registration number was further recorded in the police incident log by Z, where the owner of the second vehicle admitted being in the car park at the material time but denied colliding with the stationary vehicle, and where, by the time of the trial, the original note had been lost, the justices had been right to admit the police record as hearsay evidence, but they had been wrong to do so under section 117; the requirements of section 117(2) were not satisfied, since, although Z had compiled the police record in the course of his occupation, neither X nor Y had themselves received the information in the course of any business, etc.; but the police record would have been admissible under section 114(1)(d) (*ante*, § 11–3) and, as it was multiple hearsay, under section 121(1)(c) (*post*, § 11–41); it could be inferred by their purported admission of the evidence under section 117 that the justices had had no concerns about the reliability of the evidence (as they had made no direction under section 117(7)), and considering the interests of justice cumulatively with the criteria in section 114(2), it was inevitable that they would have admitted the evidence under sections 114 and 121: *Maher v. DPP*, 170 J.P. 441, DC.

In *R. v. Humphris*, 169 J.P. 441, CA, it was held that whereas section 117 might be relied on for the purpose of proving a defendant's previous convictions, where they were admissible under section 101 (*post*, § 13–25), as an alternative to the more conventional method of proving them under the *PACE Act* 1984, ss.73 and 74 (*ante*, §§ 9–80, 9–81), it could not be relied upon to justify the admission of a computerised police record providing details of the methods used by the defendant to commit those previous offences. The decision may, however, have turned on a lack of evidence as to the source of the information. For a suggestion that, given proper proof of the chain of information, such a record could in fact be relied upon for such a purpose, see the commentary in *Criminal Law Week* 2005/32/1; and *R. v. Humphris* was distinguished in *Wellington v. DPP*, 171 J.P. 497, QBD (Jackson J.), in which it was held that a record in the police national computer stating that a person had used a particular alias could be proved under section 117; for the purposes of subsection (2)(b) and (c), the inescapable inference would be that the police officer who supplied the information "had or may reasonably be supposed to have had personal knowledge of" the fact that an alias was being used. In *Wellington* it was assumed that the case would also fall within subsection (4), but this, it is submitted, is incorrect. A standard police national computer record is plainly not "prepared for the purposes of pending or contemplated criminal proceedings."

Section 117(4)

11–31 A custody record falls within this subsection: *R. v. Hogan* [1997] Crim.L.R. 349, CA; as does a transcript of a person's evidence in an earlier trial: *R. v. Lockley and Corah* [1995] 2 Cr.App.R. 554, CA (*sed quaere*).

(c) *Preservation of certain common law categories of admissibility*

11–32 Section 118(1) preserves certain categories of admissibility that were established under the common law. The text of the section is set out in full, *post*, § 11–70, and the rules preserved thereby are examined at §§ 11–71 *et seq*. Section 118(2) provides that, with the exception of the rules preserved by subsection (1), the common law rules governing the admissibility of hearsay evidence in criminal proceedings are abolished. As to subsection (2), see *ante*, § 11–14.

(d) *Previous statements of witnesses*

Criminal Justice Act 2003, ss.119, 120

Inconsistent statements

11–33 **119.**—(1) If in criminal proceedings a person gives oral evidence and—

(a) he admits making a previous inconsistent statement, or
(b) a previous inconsistent statement made by him is proved by virtue of section 3, 4 or 5 of the *Criminal Procedure Act* 1865,

the statement is admissible as evidence of any matter stated of which oral evidence by him would be admissible.

(2) If in criminal proceedings evidence of an inconsistent statement by any person is given under section 124(2)(c), the statement is admissible as evidence of any matter stated in it of which oral evidence by that person would be admissible.

In connection with this section, see, in particular, section 122 of the 2003 Act (*post*, § 11–42).

Other previous statements of witnesses

120.—(1) This section applies where a person (the witness) is called to give evidence in criminal proceedings. **11–34**

(2) If a previous statement by the witness is admitted as evidence to rebut a suggestion that his oral evidence has been fabricated, that statement is admissible as evidence of any matter stated of which oral evidence by the witness would be admissible.

(3) A statement made by the witness in a document—

(a) which is used by him to refresh his memory while giving evidence,

(b) on which he is cross-examined, and

(c) which as a consequence is received in evidence in the proceedings,

is admissible as evidence of any matter stated of which oral evidence by him would be admissible.

(4) A previous statement by the witness is admissible as evidence of any matter stated of which oral evidence by him would be admissible, if—

(a) any of the following three conditions is satisfied, and

(b) while giving evidence the witness indicates that to the best of his belief he made the statement, and that to the best of his belief it states the truth.

(5) The first condition is that the statement identifies or describes a person, object or place.

(6) The second condition is that the statement was made by the witness when the matters stated were fresh in his memory but he does not remember them, and cannot reasonably be expected to remember them, well enough to give oral evidence of them in the proceedings.

(7) The third condition is that—

(a) the witness claims to be a person against whom an offence has been committed,

(b) the offence is one to which the proceedings relate,

(c) the statement consists of a complaint made by the witness (whether to a person in authority or not) about conduct which would, if proved, constitute the offence or part of the offence,

(d) the complaint was made as soon as could reasonably be expected after the alleged conduct,

(e) the complaint was not made as a result of a threat or a promise, and

(f) before the statement is adduced the witness gives oral evidence in connection with its subject matter.

(8) For the purposes of subsection (7) the fact that the complaint was elicited (for example, by a leading question) is irrelevant unless a threat or a promise was involved.

In connection with this section, see, in particular, section 122 of the 2003 Act (*post*, § 11–42).

Previous inconsistent statements (s.119)

As to cross-examination of a witness on a previous inconsistent statement, see *ante*, §§ 8–94a (by the party calling the witness in the event that he proves hostile), and 8–124 *et seq.* (by the opposing party). As to proof of such statements where they are not admitted, see sections 3 (hostile witness), 4 (oral statements) and 5 (written statements) of the *Criminal Procedure Act* 1865 (*ante*, §§ 8–94a, 8–124a and 8–127). **11–35**

Section 119(2) reverses the common law rule whereby a previous inconsistent statement was not evidence of its contents, but went merely to the weight to be given to the witness's oral evidence. As to this, see *ante*, §§ 8–100, 8–130. But a judge may exercise his exclusionary discretion under the *PACE Act* 1984, s.78 (*post*, § 15–452), so as to rule that its contents are not admissible as evidence of the matters stated, notwithstanding the terms of section 119(1); and this course should have been taken where the complainant in a case of rape gave evidence in accordance with her fourth statement (made following therapy with a psychologist), in which she alleged for the first time having been raped despite her physical resistance, and where she was cross-examined on her first statement (alleging rape following submission), the contents of which she then disavowed: *R. v. Coates* [2008] 1 Cr.App.R. 3, Ct-MAC.

As to the directions to be given to the jury where a previous inconsistent statement is admitted under this section, see *R. v. Hulme*, *post*, § 11–42.

Other prior statements (s.120)

Rebuttal of suggestion of recent fabrication (s.120(2))

11–36 As to the admission of a prior statement of a witness giving oral evidence for the purpose of rebutting a suggestion of recent fabrication, see *ante*, §§ 8–108 *et seq.* Section 120(2) reverses the common law rule that a statement admitted for this purpose was not evidence as to the truth of its contents.

Cross-examination on memory refreshing documents (s.120(3))

11–37 As to when a document may be used by a witness giving oral evidence for the purpose of refreshing his memory, see section 139 of the 2003 Act (*ante*, § 8–74). As to when such document may be exhibited, see *ante*, §§ 8–86, 8–87. The provision of section 120(3) to the effect that once such document is exhibited, it becomes evidence of any matter stated of which oral evidence by the witness would be admissible goes further than the common law (as to which, see *ante*, §§ 8–86, 8–87).

Statements identifying/ describing person, object or place (s.120(4), (5))

11–38 This category is entirely new, and it is not clear what its rationale is. It would appear, however, to be catering for the situation where a witness cannot remember relevant details unaided (if he could, there would be no need to resort to the statement), but it is impossible to bring the case within the memory refreshing rule, so as to allow him to use the statement as an aid to his oral evidence. Such situations are likely to be rare, as it will be unusual for it not to be possible to use a statement as a memory refreshing aid, since it is only necessary, for that rule to be invoked, that the witness should be able to say that the statement records his recollection of the matter at the time he made it, and that the court should conclude that his recollection of the matter was likely to have been significantly better at that time than it is at the time of giving his evidence.

Witness who cannot reasonably be expected to remember events (s.120(4), (6))

11–39 In a case falling within subsection (6), the witness would be able to give oral evidence using the statement as a memory refresher, but the purpose of the provision seems to be that the process should be short-circuited and the statement should simply become the witness's evidence. There is an obvious danger, however, that this subsection could trigger the routine substitution of a witness's statement for oral evidence-in-chief. Where the matters dealt with by the witness are routine, then the case may well be brought within this provision, but where the witness was at the heart of the drama that gave rise to the prosecution, the requirement that the witness "does not remember … and cannot reasonably be expected to remember" the matters dealt with in the statement well enough to give oral evidence of them is most unlikely ever to be satisfied.

Recent complaint (s.120(4), (7) and (8))

11–40 These provisions effect a radical revision of the common law (see *R. v. O.* [2006] 2 Cr.App.R. 27, CA). At common law, recent complaint evidence was admissible only in cases of alleged sexual offences, and the complaint was admitted only to show consistency and to rebut consent. Furthermore, since the purpose of the rule was to show consistency, it was a requirement that the complainant should have given evidence of the alleged offence; otherwise, there was nothing with which the complaint could be said to be consistent.

Under section 120, there is a requirement that before the statement is adduced, that the witness should have given oral evidence in connection with its subject matter. But is this to be taken to be a full account of the alleged offence? Apart from that, the legislation goes further than the common law in that, first, it is not restricted to sexual offences, and, secondly, the statement is admitted as evidence of the truth of its contents (see *R. v. O.*, *ante* (confirming these points)).

Whilst subsection (8) provides that the fact that the complaint was "elicited" (unless by threat or promise) is irrelevant for the purposes of subsection (7) (*i.e.* admissibility), the circumstances in which it came to be made will be highly material to the court's consideration of the significance to be attached to it. A complaint that results from a leading question may be admissible, but as with any answer to leading questions, the tribunal of fact would be wise to treat it with the utmost caution.

In *R. v. O.*, *ante*, it was said that whilst there is obviously a need, in fairness, to restrict evidence of repeated complaints, the circumstances of a complaint subsequent to the first complaint may be such that it too could be said to have been made "as soon as could reasonably be expected after the alleged conduct" (*e.g.* because made to a different person), so as to make it admissible, subject to careful directions as to how the jury should approach it.

(4) Supplementary

(a) *Multiple hearsay*

Criminal Justice Act 2003, s.121

Additional requirement for admissibility of multiple hearsay

121.—(1) A hearsay statement is not admissible to prove the fact that an earlier hearsay statement was made unless— **11–41**

(a) either of the statements is admissible under section 117, 119, or 120,

(b) all parties to the proceedings so agree, or

(c) the court is satisfied that the value of the evidence in question, taking into account how reliable the statements appear to be, is so high that the interests of justice require the later statement to be admissible for that purpose.

(2) In this section "hearsay statement" means a statement, not made in oral evidence, that is relied on as evidence of a matter stated in it.

When making a decision under subsection (1)(c), a court should refer to the factors set out in section 114(2) (*ante*, § 11–3) to be considered when deciding whether it would be in the interests of justice to admit primary hearsay under section 114(1)(d): *R. v. Musone* [2007] 2 Cr.App.R. 29, CA.

In connection with this section, see also *Maher v. DPP*, *ante*, § 11–30.

(b) *Exhibiting statements made in documents*

Criminal Justice Act 2003, s.122

Documents produced as exhibits

122.—(1) This section applies if on a trial before a judge and jury for an offence— **11–42**

(a) a statement made in a document is admitted in evidence under section 119, or 120, and

(b) the document or a copy of it is produced as an exhibit.

(2) The exhibit must not accompany the jury when they retire to consider their verdict unless—

(a) the court considers it appropriate, or

(b) all the parties to the proceedings agree that it should accompany the jury.

In *R. v. Hulme* [2007] 1 Cr.App.R. 26, CA, it was held: (i) that where a previous inconsistent statement was admitted as proof of matters stated in accordance with section 119 (*ante*, § 11–33) and the judge was considering whether, in accordance with section 122(2)(a), it was appropriate to allow the jury to retire with the statement as an exception to the general rule (in s.122(2)) against doing so, the fact that the jury may attach disproportionate weight to the contents of the statement, as compared with the oral evidence in the case, had to be taken into account by the judge with due weight being given to it; for the same reason (albeit to a lesser degree and though the general rule in s.122(2) does not encompass it), the jury should not be entitled to read the statement in the jury box before retiring to consider their verdict; and (ii) that whereas a general direction to the jury would be necessary where a previous inconsistent statement was admitted under section 119 (*i.e.* to the effect that careful consideration was needed as to whether reliance could be placed on the witness's oral evidence or on what was said in the witness statement, or whether the conflict was so great that the evidence of the witness could not be relied on at all), further directions would be necessary where the jury were permitted to retire with the statement; such directions must impress on the jury the reason why they were being given the document and the importance of not attaching disproportionate weight to it simply because they had it before them, given that they had to rely on their recollection of the oral evidence and of the judge's summing up of that evidence.

(c) *Capability to make statement*

Criminal Justice Act 2003, s.123

Capability to make statement

11–43 **123.**—(1) Nothing in section 116, 119, or 120 makes a statement admissible as evidence if it was made by a person who did not have the required capability at the time when he made the statement.

(2) Nothing in section 117 makes a statement admissible as evidence if any person who, in order for the requirements of section 117(2) to be satisfied, must at any time have supplied or received the information concerned or created or received the document or part concerned—

(a) did not have the required capability at that time, or

(b) cannot be identified but cannot reasonably be assumed to have had the required capability at that time.

(3) For the purposes of this section a person has the required capability if he is capable of—

(a) understanding questions put to him about the matters stated, and

(b) giving answers to such questions which can be understood.

(4) Where by reason of this section there is an issue as to whether a person had the required capability when he made a statement—

(a) proceedings held for the determination of the issue must take place in the absence of the jury (if there is one);

(b) in determining the issue the court may receive expert evidence and evidence from any person to whom the statement in question was made;

(c) the burden of proof on the issue lies on the party seeking to adduce the statement, and the standard of proof is the balance of probabilities.

(d) *Credibility of maker of statement*

Criminal Justice Act 2003, s.124

Credibility

11–44 **124.**—(1) This section applies if in criminal proceedings—

(a) a statement not made in oral evidence in the proceedings is admitted as evidence of a matter stated, and

(b) the maker of the statement does not give oral evidence in connection with the subject matter of the statement.

(2) In such a case—

(a) any evidence which (if he had given such evidence) would have been admissible as relevant to his credibility as a witness is so admissible in the proceedings;

(b) evidence may with the court's leave be given of any matter which (if he had given such evidence) could have been put to him in cross-examination as relevant to his credibility as a witness but of which evidence could not have been adduced by the cross-examining party;

(c) evidence tending to prove that he made (at whatever time) any other statement inconsistent with the statement admitted as evidence is admissible for the purpose of showing that he contradicted himself.

(3) If as a result of evidence admitted under this section an allegation is made against the maker of a statement, the court may permit a party to lead additional evidence of such description as the court may specify for the purposes of denying or answering the allegation.

(4) In the case of a statement in a document which is admitted as evidence under section 117 each person who, in order for the statement to be admissible, must have supplied

or received the information concerned or created or received the document or part concerned is to be treated as the maker of the statement for the purposes of subsections (1) to (3) above.

(e) *Stopping the case where evidence unconvincing*

Criminal Justice Act 2003, s.125

Stopping the case where evidence is unconvincing

125.—(1) If on a defendant's trial before a judge and jury for an offence the court is satisfied at any time after the close of the case for the prosecution that— **11–45**

(a) the case against the defendant is based wholly or partly on a statement not made in oral evidence in the proceedings, and

(b) the evidence provided by the statement is so unconvincing that, considering its importance to the case against the defendant, his conviction of the offence would be unsafe,

the court must either direct the jury to acquit the defendant of the offence or, if it considers that there ought to be a retrial, discharge the jury.

(2) Where—

(a) a jury is directed under subsection (1) to acquit a defendant of an offence, and

(b) the circumstances are such that, apart from this subsection, the defendant could if acquitted of that offence be found guilty of another offence,

the defendant may not be found guilty of that other offence if the court is satisfied as mentioned in subsection (1) in respect of it.

(3) If—

(a) a jury is required to determine under section 4A(2) of the *Criminal Procedure (Insanity) Act* 1964 whether a person charged on an indictment with an offence did the act or made the omission charged, and

(b) the court is satisfied as mentioned in subsection (1) above at any time after the close of the case for the prosecution that—

(i) the case against the defendant is based wholly or partly on a statement not made in oral evidence in the proceedings, and

(ii) the evidence provided by the statement is so unconvincing that, considering its importance to the case against the person, a finding that he did the act or made the omission would be unsafe,

the court must either direct the jury to acquit the defendant of the offence or, if it considers that there ought to be a rehearing, discharge the jury.

(4) This section does not prejudice any other power a court may have to direct a jury to acquit a person of an offence or to discharge a jury.

Where, following the retraction in oral evidence by a witness of a previous out of court witness statement in which he had made a positive identification of the defendant (as someone he recognised) as the person who had committed the offence being tried, a judge ruled, (a) in accordance with sections 3 and 4 of the *Criminal Procedure Act* 1865 (*ante*, §§ 8–94a, 8–125), that the witness was to be treated as hostile, so as to permit proof of the previous inconsistent statement, and (b) in accordance with sections 114 and 119 of the 2003 Act (*ante*, §§ 11–3, 11–33), that the previous inconsistent statement was admissible as proof of the matters stated, for the purposes of determining whether a not guilty verdict should be directed at the close of the prosecution case, either under section 125(1) of the 2003 Act or in the light of *R. v. Turnbull* [1977] Q.B. 224, 63 Cr.App.R. 132, CA (*post*, §§ 14–2 *et seq.*), the judge was entitled to take into consideration the terrifying circumstances of the offence; and, on the facts, in the light of the new statutory provisions in relation to hearsay, it would have been an affront to the administration of justice if the jury had not been permitted to evaluate, separately and together, the quality of the witness's oral evidence and to be able to rely, if they thought fit, on the terms of the original statement: *R. v. Joyce and Joyce*, unreported, June 27, 2005, CA ([2005] EWCA Crim. 1785).

(f) *General discretion to exclude evidence*

Criminal Justice Act 2003, s.126

Court's general discretion to exclude evidence

126.—(1) In criminal proceedings the court may refuse to admit a statement as evidence of a matter stated if— **11–46**

(a) the statement was made otherwise than in oral evidence in the proceedings, and
(b) the court is satisfied that the case for excluding the statement, taking account of the danger that to admit it would result in undue waste of time, substantially outweighs the case for admitting it, taking account of the value of the evidence.

(2) Nothing in this Chapter prejudices—
(a) any power of a court to exclude evidence under section 78 of the *Police and Criminal Evidence Act* 1984 (exclusion of unfair evidence), or
(b) any other power of a court to exclude evidence at its discretion (whether by preventing questions from being put or otherwise).

As to the nature of the discretion under subsection (1), see *R. v. C. and K., ante*, § 11–20, and the commentary thereto in *Criminal Law Week* 2006/25/8.

(g) *Expert evidence*

Criminal Justice Act 2003, s.127

Expert evidence: preparatory work

11–47 **127.**—(1) This section applies if—
(a) a statement has been prepared for the purposes of criminal proceedings,
(b) the person who prepared the statement had or may reasonably be supposed to have had personal knowledge of the matters stated,
(c) notice is given under the appropriate rules that another person (the expert) will in evidence given in the proceedings orally or under section 9 of the *Criminal Justice Act* 1967 base an opinion or inference on the statement, and
(d) the notice gives the name of the person who prepared the statement and the nature of the matters stated.

(2) In evidence given in the proceedings the expert may base an opinion or inference on the statement.

(3) If evidence based on the statement is given under subsection (2) the statement is to be treated as evidence of what it states.

(4) This section does not apply if the court, on an application by a party to the proceedings, orders that it is not in the interests of justice that it should apply.

(5) The matters to be considered by the court in deciding whether to make an order under subsection (4) include—
(a) the expense of calling as a witness the person who prepared the statement;
(b) whether relevant evidence could be given by that person which could not be given by the expert;
(c) whether that person can reasonably be expected to remember the matters stated well enough to give oral evidence of them.

(6) Subsections (1) to (5) apply to a statement prepared for the purposes of a criminal investigation as they apply to a statement prepared for the purposes of criminal proceedings, and in such a case references to the proceedings are to criminal proceedings arising from the investigation.

(7) The appropriate rules are Criminal Procedure Rules made by virtue of—
(a) section 81 of the *Police and Criminal Evidence Act* 1984 (advance notice of expert evidence in Crown Court), or
(b) section 20(3) of the *Criminal Procedure and Investigations Act* 1996 (advance notice of expert evidence in magistrates' courts).

[This section is printed as amended by the *Courts Act 2003 (Consequential Amendments) Order* 2004 (S.I. 2004 No. 2035).]

11–48 For section 81 of the 1984 Act, see *ante*, § 10–62.

An expert witness should state the facts on which his opinion is based; and such facts should be proved by admissible evidence: *English Exporters Ltd v. Eldonwall Ltd* [1973] Ch. 415 at 421, Ch D; *R. v. Turner (T.)* [1975] Q.B. 834, 60 Cr.App.R. 80, CA. The purpose of this section is to assist in the proving of the facts on which the expert's opinion is based. The basic facts can be dealt with in the statements of one or more persons with first-hand knowledge of the matters in question. Notice under the relevant rules can then allude to these statements, and then, subject to the discretion of the judge, the statement(s) may be taken as proving the primary facts, and the expert may then give his opinion thereon.

In a case that preceded the 2003 Act, it was said that where proof of the facts is likely to be time-consuming and expensive, *e.g.* because it would involve taking statements from a large number of laboratory assistants upon whose work the expert has relied, the prosecution should invite the defence to make suitable admissions: see *R. v. Jackson* [1996] 2 Cr.App.R. 420, CA.

Once the primary facts on which his opinion is based are proved, the expert is entitled to draw on the work of others in his field of experience as part of the process of arriving at a conclusion: *R. v. Abadom*, 76 Cr.App.R. 48, CA; and see *R. v. Somers*, 48 Cr.App.R. 11, CCA (doctor entitled to refresh memory from publication of British Medical Association giving current knowledge on particular subject—destruction of alcohol in body); and *R. v. Hodges* [2003] 2 Cr.App.R. 15, CA (police officer giving evidence as to street value of drugs, etc.) (*post*, § 27–77). Where an expert does draw on the work of others, he should refer to such material so that the cogency and probative value of his conclusion can be tested and evaluated by reference to it: *Abadom*, *ante*.

As to the preservation of the common law rules in this regard, see section 118(1), *post*, § 11–70.

(h) *Confessions*

Section 128(1) of the 2003 Act inserts a new section 76A (confessions may be given in evidence for co-accused) into the *PACE Act* 1984 (*post*, § 15–353a). Subsection (2) provides that subject to the insertion of the new section 76A into the 1984 Act by subsection (1), nothing in Chapter 2 of Part 11 of the 2003 Act makes a confession by a defendant admissible if it would not be admissible under section 76 of the 1984 Act (*post*, § 15–352), and subsection (3) provides that in subsection (2), "confession" has the meaning given to it by section 82 of the 1984 Act (*post*, § 15–354). **11–49**

At common law, evidence of a confession by a third party was inadmissible as hearsay: *R. v. Turner (B.J.)*, 61 Cr.App.R. 67, CA; *R. v. Blastland* [1986] A.C. 41, HL. Whether such a confession will be admissible under the 2003 Act will depend on whether it can be brought within any of paragraphs (a) to (d) of section 114(1), *ante*, § 11–3.

(i) *Representions other than by a person*

Criminal Justice Act 2003, s.129

Representations other than by a person

129.—(1) Where a representation of any fact— **11–50**

(a) is made otherwise than by a person, but

(b) depends for its accuracy on information supplied (directly or indirectly) by a person,

the representation is not admissible in criminal proceedings as evidence of the fact unless it is proved that the information was accurate.

(2) Subsection (1) does not affect the operation of the presumption that a mechanical device has been properly set or calibrated.

(5) Rules of court

Criminal Justice Act 2003, s.132

Rules of court

132.—(1) Rules of court may make such provision as appears to the appropriate authority to be necessary or expedient for the purposes of this Chapter; and the appropriate authority is the authority entitled to make the rules. **11–51**

(2) The rules may make provision about the procedure to be followed and other conditions to be fulfilled by a party proposing to tender a statement in evidence under any provision of this Chapter.

(3) The rules may require a party proposing to tender the evidence to serve on each party to the proceedings such notice, and such particulars of or relating to the evidence, as may be prescribed.

(4) The rules may provide that the evidence is to be treated as admissible by agreement of the parties if—

(a) a notice has been served in accordance with provision made under subsection (3), and

(b) no counter-notice in the prescribed form objecting to the admission of the evidence has been served by a party.

(5) If a party proposing to tender evidence fails to comply with a prescribed requirement applicable to it—

(a) the evidence is not admissible except with the court's leave;

(b) where leave is given the court or jury may draw such inferences from the failure as appear proper;

(c) the failure may be taken into account by the court in considering the exercise of its powers with respect to costs.

(6) In considering whether or how to exercise any of its powers under subsection (5) the court shall have regard to whether there is any justification for the failure to comply with the requirement.

(7) A person shall not be convicted of an offence solely on an inference drawn under-subsection (5)(b).

(8) Rules under this section may—

(a) limit the application of any provision of the rules to prescribed circumstances;

(b) subject any provision of the rules to prescribed exceptions;

(c) make different provision for different cases or circumstances.

(9) Nothing in this section prejudices the generality of any enactment conferring power to make rules of court; and no particular provision of this section prejudices any general provision of it.

(10) In this section "prescribed" means prescribed by rules of court.

[This section is printed as amended by the *Courts Act 2003 (Consequential Amendments) Order* 2004 (S.I. 2004 No. 2035).]

Whereas section 132(5) envisages circumstances in which a court may refuse to admit evidence where the requirements of Part 34 of the 2005 rules (*post*), as to the giving of notice, have not been complied with, that sanction should not be used to discipline a party for a failure to comply where any unfairness to other parties can be cured (including by the grant of an adjournment) and where the interests of justice would otherwise require the evidence to be admitted: *R. v. Musone* [2007] 2 Cr.App.R. 29, CA.

Criminal Procedure Rules 2005 (S.I. 2005 No. 384), Pt 34

When this Part applies

11–52 **34.1.** This Part applies in a magistrates' court and in the Crown Court where a party wants to introduce evidence on one or more of the grounds set out in section 114(1)(d), section 116, section 117 and section 121 of the *Criminal Justice Act* 2003, and in this Part that evidence is called "hearsay evidence".

Notice of hearsay evidence

11–53 **34.2.** The party who wants to introduce hearsay evidence must give notice in the form set out in the Practice Direction to the court officer and all other parties.

When the prosecutor must give notice of hearsay evidence

11–54 **34.3.** The prosecutor must give notice of hearsay evidence—

(a) in a magistrates' court, at the same time as he complies or purports to comply with section 3 of the *Criminal Procedure and Investigations Act* 1996 (disclosure by prosecutor); or

(b) in the Crown Court, not more than 14 days after—

(i) the committal of the defendant, or

(ii) the consent to the preferment of a bill of indictment in relation to the case, or

(iii) the service of a notice of transfer under section 4 of the *Criminal Justice Act* 1987 (serious fraud cases) or under section 53 of the *Criminal Justice Act* 1991 (certain cases involving children), or

(iv) where a person is sent for trial under section 51 of the *Crime and Disorder Act* 1998 (indictable-only offences sent for trial), the service of copies of the documents containing the evidence on which the charge or charges are based under paragraph 1 of Schedule 3 to the 1998 Act.

When a defendant must give notice of hearsay evidence

11–55 **34.4.** A defendant must give notice of hearsay evidence not more than 14 days after the prosecutor has complied with or purported to comply with section 3 of the *Criminal Procedure and Investigations Act* 1996 (disclosure by prosecutor).

Opposing the introduction of hearsay evidence

34.5. A party who receives a notice of hearsay evidence may oppose it by giving notice within 14 days in the form set out in the Practice Direction to the court officer and all other parties. **11–56**

34.6. [*Revoked by* Criminal Procedure (Amendment) Rules *2007 (S.I. 2007 No. 699), r. 38 and Sched. 4.*] **11–57**

Court's power to vary requirements under this Part

34.7. The court may— **11–58**

(a) dispense with the requirement to give notice of hearsay evidence;
(b) allow notice to be given in a different form, or orally; or
(c) shorten a time limit or extend it (even after it has expired).

Waiving the requirement to give a notice of hearsay evidence

34.8. A party entitled to receive a notice of hearsay evidence may waive his entitlement by so informing the court and the party who would have given the notice. **11–59**

[This part is printed as amended by the *Criminal Procedure (Amendment) Rules* 2006 (S.I. 2006 No. 353).]

B. Bankers' Books Evidence Act 1879

(1) Introduction

This Act was passed in order to obviate the inconvenience caused by the removal of ledgers and other account books from banks for the purpose of production in legal proceedings, and in order to facilitate proof of transactions recorded in such ledgers and books. **11–60**

(2) Mode of proof of entries in bankers' books

Bankers' Books Evidence Act, 1879, s.3

3. Subject to the provisions of this Act, a copy of any entry in a banker's book shall in all legal proceedings be received as prima facie evidence of such entry, and of the matters, transactions, and accounts therein recorded. **11–61**

This section must be read in conjunction with sections 4, 5 and 9, below. The original records will not be admissible as such—see *ante*, § 9–102.

Section 10 defines "legal proceeding" as including "any civil or criminal proceeding or inquiry in which evidence is or may be given".

(3) Proof that book is a banker's book; verification of copy

Bankers' Books Evidence Act 1879, ss.4, 5

4. A copy of an entry in a banker's book shall not be received in evidence under this Act unless it be first proved that the book was at the time of the making of the entry one of the ordinary books of the bank, and that the entry was made in the usual and ordinary course of business, and that the book is in the custody or control of the bank. Such proof may be given by a partner or officer of the bank, and may be given orally or by an affidavit sworn before any commissioner or person authorised to take affidavits. **11–62**

Where the proceedings concerned are proceedings before a magistrates' court inquiring into an offence as examining justices, this section shall have effect with the omission of the words "orally or".

5. A copy of an entry in a banker's book shall not be received in evidence under this Act unless it be further proved that the copy has been examined with the original entry and is correct. Such proof shall be given by some person who has examined the copy with the original entry, and may be given either orally or by an affidavit sworn before any commissioner or person authorised to take affidavits.

[*Identical to second para. of s.4,* ante.]

[These sections are printed as amended (insertion of second paragraph in each section) by the *CPIA* 1996, s.47 and Sched. 1, paras 15 and 16. As amended, they apply only in relation to alleged offences into which no criminal investigation had begun before April 1, 1997: *Criminal Procedure and Investigations Act 1996 (Commencement) (Sections 65 and Schedules 1 and 2) Order* 1997 (S.I. 1997 No. 683) and *Criminal Procedure and Investigations Act 1996 (Appointed Day No. 3) Order* 1997

(S.I. 1997 No. 682). The inserted paragraphs are repealed as from a day to be appointed: *CJA* 2003, s.332, and Sched. 37, Pt 4.]

The expression "some person" in section 5 is not limited to an officer of the bank: *R. v. Albutt and Screen*, 6 Cr.App.R. 55, CCA.

(4) Case in which banker, etc. not compellable to produce book, etc.; court order for inspection

Bankers' Books Evidence Act 1879, ss.6, 7

11–63 **6.** A banker or officer of a bank shall not, in any legal proceeding to which the bank is not a party, be compellable to produce any banker's book the contents of which can be proved under this Act or under the *Civil Evidence (Scotland) Act* 1988, or Schedule 3 to the *Prisoners and Criminal Proceedings (Scotland) Act* 1993 or Schedule 8 to the *Criminal Procedure (Scotland) Act* 1995, or to appear as a witness to prove the matters, transactions, and accounts therein recorded, unless by order of a judge made for special cause.

[This section is printed as amended by the *Civil Evidence (Scotland) Act* 1988, s.7(3); the *Prisoners and Criminal Proceedings (Scotland) Act* 1993, s.29 and Sched. 3, para. 7(3); and the *Criminal Procedure (Consequential Provisions) (Scotland) Act* 1995, ss.4 and 5, and Scheds 3 and 4, para. 2.]

7. On the application of any party to a legal proceeding a court or judge may order that such party be at liberty to inspect and take copies of any entries in a banker's book for any of the purposes of such proceedings. An order under this section may be made either with or without summoning the bank or any other party, and shall be served on the bank three clear days before the same is to be obeyed, unless the court or judge otherwise directs.

As to the making of an application under this section, see Part 28 of the *Criminal Procedure Rules* 2005 (S.I. 2005 No. 384) (*ante*, §§ 8–7 *et seq.*).

Section 10 provides that in the Act the expression "the court" means the court, judge, arbitrator, persons, or person before whom a legal proceeding is held or taken, and the expression "a judge" means with respect to England a judge of the High Court. Examining justices are a court within this section: *R. v. Kinghorn* [1908] 2 K.B. 949.

Whilst the purpose of an order under this section is to enable bankers' books to be inspected and copied despite the duty of confidentiality owed by the bank to the customer, an order under the section is unnecessary where the customer waives his right to confidentiality and the bank agrees to the inspection and copying of its books; an order under this section is not, therefore, a precondition to adducing the evidence under section 3: *Wheatley v. Commr of Police of the British Virgin Islands* [2006] 1 W.L.R. 1683, PC.

11–64 See *R. v. Bono* (1913) 29 T.L.R. 635; and *Williams v. Summerfield* [1972] 2 Q.B. 513, 56 Cr.App.R. 597, DC (justices must satisfy themselves that the application is not solely a fishing expedition to find material on which to hang a charge; they should take into account whether the prosecution have in their possession other evidence against the defendant; they should limit the period of disclosure of the bank account to a period which is strictly relevant to the charge before them). In a difficult case, justices may refuse to make an order and state that the application should be made to the High Court: *ibid. Williams v. Summerfield* was applied in *R. v. Nottingham City JJ., ex p. Lynn*, 79 Cr.App.R. 238, DC (the "fishing" principle will apply equally to the *period* which is the subject of the application as to the propriety of seeking an order at all).

Although section 7 expressly permits an *ex parte* application, "there is much to be said for notice being given. There is much to be said for a frank attitude in all criminal proceedings": *R. v. Marlborough Street Magistrates' Court Metropolitan Stipendiary Magistrate, ex p. Simpson*, 70 Cr.App.R. 291, DC.

In *R. v. Andover JJ., ex p. Rhodes* [1980] Crim.L.R. 644, DC, the court upheld an order made in respect of a husband's account because his wife, who had been charged with theft, had told the police that the stolen money had been credited to his account. He had refused to co-operate in the inquiry.

11–65 The fact that a defendant gives notice of an intention to plead guilty is not a proper reason for the court refusing to make an order—he may change his mind. It is the duty of the prosecution to go on inquiring into the case until a plea is in fact made: *Owen v. Sambrook* [1981] Crim.L.R. 329, DC.

In *R. v. Grossman*, 73 Cr.App.R. 302, CA (Civ.Div.), the Inland Revenue had obtained an order under section 7 addressed to the London headquarters of an English bank but relating to an account held at its branch in the Isle of Man. The account was that of an Isle of Man bank, who collected and paid cheques through the medium of the English bank as a clearing house. The object was to obtain evidence against G. *Held*, discharging the order, an order could be made under section 7 in respect of a bank's customer who was not a party to the proceedings, but only exceptionally. It was important that the court should respect the confidence of a bank account and only if the public interest in helping the prosecution outweighed the private interest of confidentiality should inspection be ordered. As the branch was subject to Manx law it was to be considered as a different entity from its headquarters; thus it should be considered as a foreign bank and, therefore, not subject to the court's jurisdiction. Accordingly, in its discretion, the court should not have made the order under section 7. Where the accounts of third parties are affected by the application, it should ordinarily be made upon notice to the customer: *ibid.*, *per* Shaw and Oliver L.JJ. (As to the lack of jurisdiction of the civil division of the Court of Appeal, see *ante*, § 7–22.) *Grossman* was considered and applied by Hoffmann J. in *Mackinnon v. Donaldson, Lufkin and Jenrette Securities Corpn* [1986] Ch. 482. His Lordship considered the remedies available to a bank or third party customer affected by an order under section 7 made on an *ex parte* application. Having referred to the lack of jurisdiction in the civil division of the Court of Appeal in *Grossman*, *ante*, he said that, if any person affected may apply to discharge an injunction (see *Halsbury's Laws*, 4th ed., Vol. 24, para. 1111 (para. 1020 in the 1991 reissue volume)), he saw no reason why the same should not apply to an order under section 7 (at p. 492). His Lordship was concerned with civil proceedings, but it is submitted that the reasoning applies equally to criminal proceedings. The first step should be to apply to the court that made the order under section 7 to discharge it.

(5) Costs, interpretation

Bankers' Books Evidence Act 1879, ss.8, 9

8. The costs of any application to a court or judge under or for the purposes of this Act, and the costs of anything done or to be done under an order of a court or judge made under or for the purposes of this Act shall be in the discretion of the court or judge, who may order the same or any part thereof to be paid to any party by the bank, where the same have been occasioned by any default or delay on the part of the bank. Any such order against a bank may be enforced as if the bank was a party to the proceeding. **11–66**

9.—(1) In this Act the expressions "bank" and "banker" mean—

(a) a deposit-taker;

(b) [*repealed by* Trustee Savings Bank Act *1985, Sched. 4*];

(c) the National Savings Bank; ...

(1A) "Deposit taker" means—

(a) a person who has permission under Part 4 of the *Financial Services and Markets Act* 2000 to accept deposits; or

(b) an EEA firm of the kind mentioned in paragraph 5(b) of Schedule 3 to that Act which has permission under paragraph 15 of that Schedule (as a result of qualifying for authorisation under paragraph 12(1) of that Schedule) to accept deposits or other repayable funds from the public.

(1B) But a person is not a deposit-taker if he has permission to accept deposits only for the purpose of carrying on another regulated activity in accordance with that permission.

(1C) Subsections (1A) and (1B) must be read with—

(a) section 22 of the *Financial Services and Markets Act* 2000;

(b) any relevant order under that section; and

(c) Schedule 2 to that Act.

(2) Expressions in this Act relating to "bankers' books" include ledgers, day books, cash books, account books and other records used in the ordinary business of the bank, whether those records are in written form or are kept on microfilm, magnetic tape or any other form of mechanical or electronic data retrieval mechanism.

[Section 9 is printed as substituted by the *Banking Act* 1979, Sched. 6; and as subsequently amended by the *Trustee Savings Banks Act* 1981, Sched. 6; the *Building Societies Act* 1986, Sched. 18; the *Banking Act* 1987, Sched. 6; the *Postal Services Act 2000 (Consequential Modifications No. 1) Order* 2001 (S.I. 2001 No. 1149), Sched. 1, para. 3; and the *Financial Services and Markets Act 2000 (Consequential Amendments and Repeals) Order* 2001 (S.I. 2001 No. 3649).]

11–67 The reference to "an institution authorised under the *Banking Act* 1987" is to take effect as if it included a reference to "a European deposit taker": *Banking Coordination (Second Council Directive) Regulations* 1992 (S.I. 1992 No. 3218).

11–68 Prior to amendment by the 1979 Act, section 9 defined "bankers' books" as including "ledgers, day books, cash books, account books, and all other books used in the ordinary business of the bank." In *R. v. Dadson*, 77 Cr.App.R. 91, CA, it was held that letters contained in a bank correspondence file were not "bankers' books" within the old provision. Whether the new provision will be held to embrace such documents remains to be seen—the reasoning in *Dadson* suggests that it is doubtful. And in *Re Howglen Ltd* [2001] 1 All E.R. 376, Ch D, it was held that the words "other records" in section 9(2) are not apt to cover records kept by a bank of conversations between its employees, however senior, and its customers; they were to be interpreted *eiusdem generis* with the preceding words, which referred to the means by which a bank recorded day-to-day financial transactions; records which were essentially records of meetings could not properly be regarded as entries in the books kept by a bank for the purpose of its ordinary business within the definition in section 9(2).

11–69 Cheques and paying-in slips are not within the provision: *Williams v. Williams* [1988] Q.B. 161, CA (Civ. Div.).

III. COMMON LAW

(1) Preservation of rules

Criminal Justice Act 2003, s.118

Preservation of certain common law categories of admissibility

11–70 **118.**—(1) The following rules of law are preserved.

1 *Public information etc*

Any rule of law under which in criminal proceedings—

(a) published works dealing with matters of a public nature (such as histories, scientific works, dictionaries and maps) are admissible as evidence of facts of a public nature stated in them,

(b) public documents (such as public registers, and returns made under public authority with respect to matters of public interest) are admissible as evidence of facts stated in them,

(c) records (such as the records of certain courts, treaties, Crown grants, pardons and commissions) are admissible as evidence of facts stated in them, or

(d) evidence relating to a person's age or date or place of birth may be given by a person without personal knowledge of the matter.

2 *Reputation as to character*

Any rule of law under which in criminal proceedings evidence of a person's reputation is admissible for the purpose of proving his good or bad character.

Note

The rule is preserved only so far as it allows the court to treat such evidence as proving the matter concerned.

3 *Reputation or family tradition*

Any rule of law under which in criminal proceedings evidence of reputation or family tradition is admissible for the purpose of proving or disproving—

(a) pedigree or the existence of a marriage,

(b) the existence of any public or general right, or

(c) the identity of any person or thing.

Note

The rule is preserved only so far as it allows the court to treat such evidence as proving or disproving the matter concerned.

4 *Res gestae*

Any rule of law under which in criminal proceedings a statement is admissible as evidence of any matter stated if—

(a) the statement was made by a person so emotionally overpowered by an event that the possibility of concoction or distortion can be disregarded,

(b) the statement accompanied an act which can be properly evaluated as evidence only if considered in conjunction with the statement, or

(c) the statement relates to a physical sensation or a mental state (such as intention or emotion).

5 *Confessions etc*

Any rule of law relating to the admissibility of confessions or mixed statements in criminal proceedings.

6 *Admissions by agents etc*

Any rule of law under which in criminal proceedings—

(a) an admission made by an agent of a defendant is admissible against the defendant as evidence of any matter stated, or

(b) a statement made by a person to whom a defendant refers a person for information is admissible against the defendant as evidence of any matter stated.

7 *Common enterprise*

Any rule of law under which in criminal proceedings a statement made by a party to a common enterprise is admissible against another party to the enterprise as evidence of any matter stated.

8 *Expert evidence*

Any rule of law under which in criminal proceedings an expert witness may draw on the body of expertise relevant to his field.

(2) Public information

See generally, *ante*, §§ 9–16 *et seq*. **11–71**

(3) Reputation as to character

For the purpose of proving the good or bad character of a person, where it is relevant and permissible to do so, a witness may give evidence as to his general reputation: see *R. v. Rowton* (1865) L. & C. 520. It is self-evident that, in order to be able to give evidence of a person's general reputation, reliance will have to be placed on the opinions of others. **11–72**

(4) Reputation or family tradition

At common law, evidence was admissible of reputation or of family tradition for the purpose of proving or disproving pedigree or the existence of a marriage, the existence of any public or general right, or the identity of any person or thing. According to *Phipson on Evidence*, 16th ed., 2005, para. 33–04, evidence of general reputation is admissible to prove such matters, partly by reason of the difficulty of obtaining better evidence in such cases, and partly because "the concurrence of many voices" among those most favourably situated for knowing, raises a reasonable presumption that the facts concurred in are true. As to what constitute matters of public and general rights, see *ibid.*, para. 32–28; as to what constitute matters of pedigree, see *ibid.*, para. 32–11; as to marriage, see *ibid.*, para. 33–07; and as to the identification of persons and things, see *ibid.*, para. 33–08. **11–73**

The *Civil Partnership Act* 2004, s.84(5) provides that any rule of law which is preserved by section 118(1), and under which in any proceedings evidence of reputation or family tradition is admissible for the purpose of proving or disproving the existence of a marriage, is to be treated as applying in an equivalent way for the purpose of proving or disproving the existence of a civil partnership.

(5) Res gestae

(a) *Possibility of concoction or distortion can be disregarded by reason of emotional involvement in events*

The principle

In *Ratten v. R.* [1972] A.C. 378, Lord Wilberforce, delivering the opinion of the **11–74**

Privy Council said (at p. 389) that where a hearsay statement is made either by the victim of an attack or by a bystander, indicating directly or indirectly the identity of the attacker, the admissibility of the statement is said to be dependent on whether it was made as part of the *res gestae* (all facts so connected with a fact in issue as to introduce it, explain its nature, or form in connection with it one continuous transaction).

His Lordship said that there were two objections to such evidence. The first was that there may be uncertainty as to the exact words used because of their transmission through the evidence of another person than the speaker. The second was the risk of concoction of false evidence by persons who have been the victims of assault or accident. The first matter goes to weight. The person testifying to the words used is liable to cross-examination; the accused, if he was present, can give his own account, if different. There is no such difference in kind or substance between evidence of what was said and evidence of what was done (for example between evidence of what the victim said as to an attack and evidence that he was seen in a terrified state or was heard to shriek) as to require a total rejection of one and admission of the other.

11–75 His Lordship continued by saying that the possibility of concoction, where it exists, is an entirely valid reason for exclusion. It was their Lordships' opinion that this should be recognised as the relevant test; the test should not be the uncertain one of whether the making of the statement was in some sense part of the event or transaction. This may often be difficult to establish: such external matters as the time which elapses between the events and the speaking of the words (or vice versa), and differences in location being relevant factors but not, taken by themselves, decisive criteria. As regards statements made after the event, it must be for the judge, by preliminary ruling, to satisfy himself that the statement was so clearly made in circumstances of spontaneity or involvement in the event that the possibility of concoction can be disregarded. Conversely, if the judge considers that the statement was made by way of narrative of a detached prior event so that the speaker was so disengaged from it as to be able to construct or adapt his account, he should exclude it. The same must in principle be true of statements made before the event. If the drama, leading up to the climax, has commenced and assumed such intensity and pressure that the utterance can safely be regarded as a true reflection of what was unrolling or actually happening, it ought to be received.

As to the nature of proof required to establish the involvement of the speaker in the pressure of the drama, or the concatenation of events leading up to the crisis, facts differ so greatly that it is impossible to lay down any precise general rule: "It is difficult to imagine a case where there is no evidence at all of connection between statement and principal event other than the statement itself, but whether this is sufficiently shown must be a matter for the trial judge. Their Lordships would be disposed to agree that, amongst other things, he may take the statement itself into account" ([1972] A.C. 378 at 391).

11–76 For the facts in *Ratten*, see *ante*, § 11–11. It is implicit in the reasoning of the Privy Council that statements admitted pursuant to this principle are evidence of the truth of the facts asserted in them. This was made explicit by the House of Lords in *R. v. Andrews*, *post*, § 11–78.

The principle is a single principle: *R. v. Callender* [1998] Crim.L.R. 337, CA (rejecting a submission that the conditions of admissibility specified in *Ratten* and *Andrews* have no application where the statement is tendered as one which accompanied and explained a relevant act).

Application of rule

11–77 For instances of the application of *Ratten* so as to admit statements identifying the speaker's assailant, see *R. v. Nye and Loan*, 66 Cr.App.R. 252, CA, and *R. v. Turnbull (R.)*, 80 Cr.App.R. 104, CA. In the former, the statement of the victim of an assault which had taken place during an altercation after a road accident, identifying one of the appellants as the assailant, was admitted. The statement had been made to a police officer shortly after the event. The Court of Appeal said that it was difficult to imagine a more spontaneous identification, there having been no opportunity for concoction. In *Turnbull*, *ante*, the statement of the victim of a lethal assault was admitted despite extreme difficulty in determining what he was saying on account of his inebriation and heavy accent, and despite the fact that he never actually said the defendant's name. These were matters which went to the weight of the evidence only.

In *R. v. Newport* [1998] Crim.L.R. 581, CA, it was held that evidence from a friend of the victim of an alleged murder (the defence being accident) of a telephone call from the deceased 20 minutes before the killing in which she sounded agitated and frightened and asked if she could come to the friend's house if she had to leave in a hurry (the defendant being the husband of the deceased) was inadmissible as part of the *res gestae* as it was not part of the immediate incident and was not a spontaneous and unconsidered reaction to an immediately impending emergency. No consideration appears to have been given to the question whether the evidence was admissible as a statement as to health or feelings (*post*, § 11–82). The case should be treated with some caution as the appeal against conviction was in any event dismissed in view of the other evidence.

Practical considerations

The House of Lords in *R. v. Andrews (D.)* [1987] A.C. 281, applied the decision in *Ratten*. Lord Ackner, with whose speech the remainder of their Lordships concurred, having reviewed the authorities, summarised "the position which confronts the trial judge when faced in a criminal case with an application under the *res gestae* doctrine to admit evidence of statements, with a view to establishing the truth of some fact thus narrated, such evidence being truly categorised as 'hearsay evidence'". **11–78**

> "1. The primary question which the judge must ask himself is—can the possibility of concoction or distortion be disregarded?
>
> 2. To answer that question the judge must first consider the circumstances in which the particular statement was made, in order to satisfy himself that the event was so unusual or startling or dramatic as to dominate the thoughts of the victim, so that his utterance was an instinctive reaction to that event thus giving no real opportunity for reasoned reflection. In such a situation the judge would be entitled to conclude that the involvement or the pressure of the event would exclude the possibility of concoction or distortion, providing that the statement was made in conditions of approximate but not exact contemporaneity.
>
> 3. In order for the statement to be sufficiently 'spontaneous' it must be so closely associated with the event which has excited the statement, that it can be fairly stated that the mind of the declarant was still dominated by the event. Thus the judge must be satisfied that the event, which provided the trigger mechanism for the statement, was still operative. The fact that the statement was made in answer to a question is but one factor to consider under this heading.
>
> 4. Quite apart from the time factor, there may be special features in the case, which relate to the possibility of concoction or distortion .... The judge must be satisfied that the circumstances were such that having regard to the special feature of malice there was no possibility of any concoction or distortion to the advantage of the maker or the disadvantage of the accused.
>
> 5. As to the possibility of error in the facts narrated in the statement, if only the ordinary fallibility of human recollection is relied upon, this goes to the weight to be attached to and not to the admissibility of the statement and is therefore a matter for the jury. However, here again there may be special features that may give rise to the possibility of error. In the instant case there was evidence that the deceased had drunk in excess .... Another example would be where the identification was made in circumstances of particular difficulty or where the declarant suffered from defective eyesight. In such circumstances the trial judge must consider whether he can exclude the possibility of error" (pp. 300–301).

His Lordship added that once the trial judge had ruled that the statement was admissible it was his duty to make it clear to the jury that it was for them to decide what was said and to be sure that the witnesses were not mistaken in what they believed had been said to them. Further, they must be satisfied that the declarant did not concoct or distort to his advantage or the disadvantage of the accused the statement relied upon and where there was material to raise the issue, that he was not actuated by any malice or ill will. Where there were special features that bear on the possibility of mistake then the jury's attention must be invited to those matters.

His Lordship concluded (at p. 302) by saying that any attempt to use the doctrine as a device to avoid calling the maker of the statement, when he is available, is to be deprecated. Thus to deprive the defence of the opportunity to cross-examine him, would not be consistent with the fundamental duty of the prosecution to place all the relevant material facts before the court.

Where the prosecution seek to rely on a *res gestae* statement, but are unwilling to call the maker of the statement because they have reasonable grounds for believing that he will not give truthful evidence, it is a matter for the discretion of the judge to be exercised in accordance with section 78 of the *PACE Act* 1984; if the prosecution are not even prepared to tender the witness for cross-examination, then a court might well conclude that the discretion would be exercised against admission; fairness, however, is likely to be achieved if the prosecution tender the maker of the statement for cross-examination: *Att.-Gen.'s Reference (No. 1 of 2003)* [2003] 2 Cr.App.R. 29, CA.

11–79 Whilst it is obviously desirable to call the maker of the statement, as indicated by Lord Ackner (*ante*), it is submitted that the fact that the maker of the statement is called does not preclude another witness from giving evidence of the statement. It frequently happens that witnesses forget the detail of what happened or of what they said: this is particularly likely to be the case if the witness has been involved in the actual incident. He or she may well say something quite spontaneously (the rationale of the rule) yet have no recollection of saying it when making a statement to the police, let alone months later at trial. If the maker of the statement has no recollection of making the statement, or recalls saying something different to what the witness recalls having been said or the maker of the statement's evidence at trial is inconsistent with the statement, these are matters which go to weight, not admissibility. The rationale of the rule is that the excitement of involvement gives the statement authenticity: if the court were to exclude the evidence of a credible witness to what was said because the maker of the statement is himself a witness, or being a witness cannot remember making the statement or remembers saying something different, this would be to take a course more likely to defeat, rather than to further, the ends of justice.

11–80 It was said in *R. v. Elliott (Denrick)* [2000] Crim.L.R. 51, CA, that where there is no suggestion on the part of the defence that the maker of the statement was motivated by malice or ill-will, but was simply mistaken, there is no need to direct the jury in accordance with *Andrews*. *Sed quaere*: the conditions of admissibility are as stated by the House of Lords, and the fact that the defence take no point on the issue of admissibility does not absolve the judge from his responsibility not to admit inadmissible evidence. If admitted, it is his duty to direct the jury in relation to such evidence, although the precise nature of the direction should obviously be tailored to the particular facts and issues.

(b) *Statements accompanying acts*

11–81 "Though you cannot give in evidence a declaration *per se*, yet when there is an act accompanied by a statement which is so mixed up with it as to become part of the *res gestae*, evidence of such a statement may be given", *per* Grove J. in *Howe v. Malkin* (1878) 40 L.T. 196. As to the *res gestae* comprising all facts so connected with a fact in issue as to introduce it, explain its nature, or form in connection with it one continuous transaction, see *ante*, § 11–74. See also *R. v. Callender*, *ante*, § 11–76, as to there being a single principle in play.

(c) *Statements as to health or feelings*

11–82 Whenever it is relevant to prove the physical condition, emotions, opinions or state of mind of a person (for example a deceased person whose death resulted in financial benefit being accorded to the accused person or his business), statements of that person which are indicative thereof which were made at or about the material time (or during the material period) may be given in evidence. Such statements are admissible as being evidence of conduct from which the physical condition or emotion of the speaker can be inferred. They are admissible, in other words, as original evidence and not as an exception to the hearsay rule, see *Gilbey v. Great Western Ry Co.* (1910) 102 L.T. 202; *Ratten v. R.*, *ante*, § 11–11; and *Process Church of the Final Judgment v. Rupert Hart Davis Ltd*, *The Times*, January 29, 1975, CA. Narrative statements of past symptoms are not admissible under this principle: see *R. v. Black*, 16 Cr.App.R. 118, CCA (where the admission of such statements was upheld on the alternative ground that they were made in the accused's presence in circumstances which called for a reply).

On a trial for murder by poisoning, statements by the deceased, shortly before he took poison, are admissible to prove the state of his health at that time: *R. v. Johnson* (1847) 2 C. & K. 354. On an indictment for murder alleged to have been committed by withholding proper food from a child, a complaint by the child of being hungry is admissible: *R. v. Condé* (1867) 10 Cox 547. On an indictment for murder, where the defence was suicide, a statement by the deceased to a friend relating that her husband, the accused (who had produced an apparent suicide note), had asked her for help in writing examples of suicide notes in conjunction with a psychology project was admissible as showing that she was not in a suicidal state of mind and that she wrote them in the belief that she was assisting him in the course of his work: *R. v. Gilfoyle* [1996] 1 Cr.App.R. 302, CA. **11–83**

Such expressions, statements and complaints, although admissible in evidence so far as they show the bodily condition of the person making them, at the time when they are made, cannot be given in evidence to show who caused such condition, or how it was caused: *R. v. Gloster* (1888) 16 Cox 471; *R. v. Abbott*, 67 J.P. 151; *R. v. Thomson* [1912] 3 K.B. 19, 7 Cr.App.R. 276, CCA.

See also *R. v. Blastland* [1986] A.C. 41, HL, in which the authorities were reviewed.

(6) Confessions

See generally, *post*, §§ 15–350 *et seq.* As to this provision not operating so as to exclude the application of section 114(1)(d) to a confession, see *R. v. Y.*, *ante*, § 11–3. **11–84**

(7) Admissions by agents

See *R. v. Downer* (1880) 14 Cox 886, CCR (letter written by solicitor for his client is admissible against the latter if it can be shown that it was written in pursuance of the client's instructions; insufficient merely to show that it was written following a meeting with a client interview); and *R. v. Turner (B.J.)*, 61 Cr.App.R. 67, CA, *post*, § 15–447. Where the defendant refers a request for information to a third party, it is submitted that the same principle will apply. An answer given by the third party will be admissible if it is proved that the answer given was given on the authority of the defendant, or if the defendant adopts the answer. **11–85**

(8) Common enterprise

See *post*, §§ 33–65 *et seq.* **11–86**

(9) Expert evidence

See *ante*, § 11–48. **11–87**

the admission of such statements was upheld on the alternative ground that they were made in the accused's presence in circumstances which called for a reply).

11-83 On a trial for murder by poisoning, statements by the deceased shortly before he took poison, are admissible to prove the state of his health at that time. *R. v. Johnson* (1847) 2 C. & K. 354. On an indictment for murder alleged to have been committed by a [illegible] people, [illegible] from a child, a complaint by the child of being hungry is admissible. *R. v. Gould* (1867) 10 Cox 525. On an indictment for murder, where the deceased was [illegible], a statement by the deceased to a friend relating that her husband, the accused (who had produced an apparent suicide note), had asked her for help in writing examples of suicide notes in connection with a psychology project was admissible as showing that she was not in a suicidal state of mind and that she wrote them in the belief that she was assisting him in the course of his work. *R. v. Gilfoyle* [1996] 1 Cr.App.R. 302, CA.

Such expressions, statements and complaints, although admissible in evidence so far as they show the bodily condition of the person making them at the time when they are made, cannot be given in evidence to show who caused such condition, or how it was caused. *R. v. Gloster* (1888) 16 Cox 471; *R. v. Thomson* 67 J.P. 15 [illegible]; *R. v. Thomson* [1912] 3 K.B. 19, 7 Cr.App.R. 276, CCA.

See also *R. v. Blastland* [1986] A.C. 41, HL, in which the authorities were reviewed.

(6) Confessions

11-84 See generally *ante*, §§ 15-350 *et seq.* As to the provision not operating so as to exclude the application of section 11(4)(d) to a confession, see *R. v. [illegible]*, *ante*, § 11-3.

(7) Admissions by agents

11-85 See *R. v. Downer* (1880) 14 Cox 486, CCR (letter written by solicitor for his client is admissible against the latter if it can be shown that it was written in pursuance of the client's instructions; insufficient merely to show that it was written following a meeting with a client (interview)), and *R. v. Turner* (1975) 61 Cr.App.R. 67, CA, *post*, § 15-417. Where the defendant refers a request for information to a third party, it is submitted that the same principle will apply: an answer given by the third party will be admissible if it is proved that the answer given was given on the authority of the defendant or if the defendant adopts the answer.

(8) Common enterprise

11-86 See *post*, §§ 33-65 *et seq.*

(9) Expert evidence

11-87 See *ante*, § 11-18.

Chapter 12

PRIVILEGE, PUBLIC INTEREST IMMUNITY AND DISCLOSURE

I. PRIVILEGE

A. The Nature of Privilege

A witness may refuse to produce documents or give evidence on the ground that the information sought is privileged. In respect of documents, he is protected from giving evidence as to their content, or his knowledge or belief founded thereon. Privilege prevents the production of evidence; it is not concerned with its admissibility, which depends upon its relevance: *Calcraft v. Guest* [1898] 1 Q.B. 759; *R. v. Tompkins*, 67 Cr.App.R. 181, CA; *R. v. Governor of Pentonville Prison, ex p. Osman*, 90 Cr.App.R. 281 at 310, DC. As to the nature of privilege generally, see *Cross & Tapper on Evidence*, 11th ed., pp. 447–449, and as to the nature of legal professional privilege, see *Phipson on Evidence*, 16th ed., paras 23–01 *et seq*. **12–1**

B. Answers Which May Incriminate a Witness

Privilege against self-incrimination

A witness is entitled to claim the privilege against self-incrimination in respect of any piece of information or evidence on the basis of which the prosecution might wish to establish guilt or decide to prosecute under English law: *Den Norske Bank A.S.A. v. Antonatos* [1999] Q.B. 271 at 287, CA (Civ. Div.), and see Article 6 of the ECHR, *post* §§ 16–57, 16–69 *et seq.* It is equally available to the guilty person who wishes to avoid conviction and to the innocent who wishes to avoid the inconvenience of a prosecution: *R. v. Khan* [2008] Crim.L.R. 391, CA. **12–2**

The rule does not prevent the production of public documents: *Bradshaw v. Murphy* (1836) 7 C. & P. 612; the incrimination of others: *R. v. Minihane*, 16 Cr.App.R. 38, CCA; eliciting previous criminal convictions which go to the witness's credit: see *ante*, § 8–138; or the obtaining of physical evidence from the accused, such as samples of hair: *R. v. Apicella*, 82 Cr.App.R. 295, CA. Nor does it permit a witness to refuse to take the oath: *Serves v. France*, 3 B.H.R.C. 446, ECtHR; nor the keeper of a vehicle to refuse to give information as to the identity of the driver of a vehicle alleged to be guilty of an offence under the *RTA* 1988: *O'Halloran and Francis v. U.K.* (2008) 46 E.H.R.R. 21, ECtHR (as to which, see also *post*, § 16–69). The compulsory production of pre-existing documents or other material which existed independently of the will of the suspect or the accused does not infringe against the right to silence and the right not to incriminate oneself: *Att.-Gen.'s Reference (No. 7 of 2000)* [2001] 2 Cr.App.R. 19, CA; *R. v. Kearns* [2003] 1 Cr.App.R. 7, CA; and *C. plc v. P. (Att.-Gen. intervening)* [2008] Ch. 1, CA (Civ. Div.) (there was no warrant for suggesting that the privilege was any different in civil proceedings than it was in criminal proceedings, and, to that end, the privilege was confined to testimonial oral and written evidence obtained by the use of powers of compulsion (leave to appeal to the House of Lords: see [2008] 1 W.L.R. 153)); *per contra J.B. v. Switzerland* [2001] Crim.L.R. 748, ECtHR; and *Jalloh v. Germany* (2007) 44 E.H.R.R. 32, ECtHR (*post*, § 16–69). As to the evolution and rationale of this immunity and the "right of silence" generally, see *R. v. Director of Serious Fraud Office, ex p. Smith* [1993] A.C. 1 at 30, HL.

The privilege may be expressly removed by statute, although attempts to do so have frequently been held to be incompatible with Article 6: see *ante*, § 1–286, and *post*, §§ 15–448 *et seq.* and §§ 16–69 *et seq.*

Penalty, punishment or forfeiture under English law

12–3 The privilege relates to any risk of prosecution arising under English law: *Den Norske Bank A.S.A. v. Antonatos, ante*; but there must be a real risk of incrimination or a material increase of an existing risk (*Khan v. Khan* [1982] 1 W.L.R. 513, CA (Civ. Div.), applied in *R. v. Khan, ante*). Thus, no privilege arises where matters are covered by a general pardon: *R. v. Boyes* (1861) 1 B. & S. 311; or by undertakings and immunities from prosecution given by the Director of Public Prosecutions; or where the questions asked relate to an offence to which the witness has pleaded guilty and to the basis of plea which he has provided (*R. v. Khan, ante*). If the danger of incrimination has already arisen and is independent of any question which a witness is required to answer, or if his position is made no worse by answering a question, then there can be no basis for him to invoke the privilege: *ibid*.

The privilege is not available in respect of a risk of liability for debt in civil proceedings: *Witnesses Act* 1806, s.1; but was preserved in criminal proceedings in respect of liability to forfeiture by the *Civil Evidence Act* 1968, s.16(1)(a).

The privilege does not extend to incrimination under foreign law. However, a court has a discretion to excuse a witness from giving evidence or producing documents which may thus incriminate him: *Brannigan v. Davison* [1997] A.C. 238 PC; *Att.-Gen. for Gibraltar v. May* [1999] 1 W.L.R. 998, CA (Civ. Div.).

12–4 A defendant called on his own behalf under the *Criminal Evidence Act* 1898 cannot claim privilege so far as the answer relates to the offence then charged against him: s.1(2), *ante*, § 8–161.

Taking and assessing the objection

12–5 The objection must be taken by the claimant personally on oath: *Downie v. Coe, The Times*, November 28, 1997, CA (Civ. Div.). Although a witness is presumed to know the law sufficiently to enable him to object: *R. v. Coote* (1873) L.R. 4 P.C. 599, the usual and better course is for the court to warn him that he need not respond if the answer may clearly tend to incriminate him.

A mere assertion of the privilege is insufficient; the court must be satisfied that there is a reasonable ground to apprehend a real and appreciable danger to the witness, and not one of an imaginary or insubstantial character. A mere claim of privilege, even when based on legal advice, is insufficient. The court must be satisfied that such a danger exists from all the circumstances of the case and the nature of the evidence which the witness is called to give: *R. (CPS) v. Bolton Magistrates' Court* [2004] 1 Cr.App.R. 33, DC. Once satisfied, the court must uphold the privilege even if the witness is acting from mixed motives, or refusing to answer in bad faith and failing to appreciate the risk of incrimination. Great latitude should be allowed to the witness in judging whether the effect of any particular question may lead to further investigation or risk. The proper procedure is to object to each question as it is asked, although there will come a point when continued questioning is clearly futile: *Den Norske Bank A.S.A. v. Antonatos ante*, at pp. 285–289. The privilege may be asserted at any stage, even after some answers have been given which tend to incriminate; a valid claim protects past and future answers alike: *R. v. Garbett* (1847) 2 C. & K. 474. Counsel for the other party is not entitled to argue the question: *R. v. Adey* (1831) 1 M. & Rob. 94; *Thomas v. Newton* (1827) M. & M. 48n.

Answers given without objection are admissible against the witness on a subsequent charge as to the offence admitted: *R. v. Sloggett* (1856) Dears 656. Anything a witness is wrongly compelled to say after claiming privilege will be treated as having been said involuntarily and will not be admissible against him subsequently: *R. v. Garbett, ante*; but it remains admissible in the trial in which it was given: *R. v. Kinglake* (1870) 11 Cox 499. **12–6**

C. Legal Professional Privilege

(1) The nature of legal professional privilege

Legal professional privilege is commonly classified in modern usage under the two sub-headings of litigation privilege, which attaches to communications in connection with, in contemplation of, and for the purpose of adversarial legal proceedings, and legal advice privilege, which attaches to communications between a professional legal adviser, acting as such, and his client. There is considerable overlap between the two, but their scope is different, principally in that legal advice privilege (*post*, § 12–12) is not restricted to communications in connection with litigation, whereas litigation privilege (*post*, § 12–9) is not restricted to communications between legal adviser and client. This classification is reflected in section 10(1)(a) and (b) of the *PACE Act* 1984 (*post*, § 15–90), which was intended to express the common law rule: *R. v. Central Criminal Court, ex p. Francis & Francis (a firm)* [1989] A.C. 346, HL (*per* Lord Goff at p. 396). The history, case law, and present day scope of each form of the privilege were extensively reviewed in *Three Rivers D.C. v. Governor and Company of the Bank of England (No. 5)* [2003] Q.B. 1556, CA (Civ. Div.), and *Three Rivers D.C. v. Governor and Company of the Bank of England (No. 6)* [2005] 1 A.C. 610, HL. **12–7**

It is not necessary for a communication to have been received before privilege can be claimed; a document intended to be a communication between solicitor and client is privileged even it if is never communicated: *Three Rivers D.C. (No.5), ante*.

This common law right to consult legal advisers without fear of the communication being revealed is a fundamental condition on which the administration of justice rests; once established, no exception should be allowed to its absolute nature: *R. v. Derby Magistrates' Court, ex p. B* [1996] A.C. 487, HL; and *B. v. Auckland District Law Society* [2003] 2 A.C. 736, PC. Consultations with lawyers should take place in a manner which favours full and uninhibited disclosure: *Campbell v. UK*, 15 E.H.R.R. 137, ECtHR; and see *post*, § 16–111. The right to legal confidentiality cannot be overidden by general or ambiguous statutory words; an intention to override must be expressly stated or appear by necessary implication: *R. (Morgan Grenfell & Co. Ltd) v. Special Commr of Income Tax* [2003] 1 A.C. 563, HL; and *B. v. Auckland District Law Society, ante*.

A document does not become privileged merely by being handed to a lawyer (see *Bursill v. Tanner* (1885) 16 Q.B.D. 1). A solicitor who holds a document for or relating to his client can assert in respect of its seizure no greater authority than the client possesses: *R. v. Peterborough Justice, ex p. Hicks* [1977] 1 W.L.R. 1371, DC; *R. v. King (D.A.)*, 77 Cr.App.R. 1 (*post*, § 12–11). If an unprivileged document in counsel's hands is called for in court, it must be produced: *Bursill v. Tanner, ante*. **12–8**

Neither does legal professional privilege attach to the identity of the client: *Bursill v. Tanner, ante*; *R. (Howe) v. South Durham Magistrates' Court*, 168 J.P. 424, DC (solicitor acting for client when he was disqualified from driving); or the date, time and length of attendances with his solicitor: *R. v. Manchester Crown Court, ex p. R.* [1999] 2 Cr.App.R. 267, DC. A mere record of a client's name, address and contact details is not privileged; and it follows that the identity of the person who makes a particular telephone call to a solicitor's office is not privileged, nor are the telephone numbers of the clients of the firm or the dates on which they made contact with the office: *R. (Miller Gardner Solicitors) v. Minshull Street Crown Court*, 67 J.C.L. 370, DC ([2002] EWHC 3077 (Admin.)). A solicitor who witnesses his client's deed may also be examined as to its execution: *Doe v. Roe* (1808) 2 Dowl. 449.

As to the seizure of privileged material under the 1984 Act, see *post*, §§ 15–90 *et seq.*, §§ 15–124 *et seq.*

Litigation privilege

12–9 Litigation privilege is essentially a creature of adversarial proceedings and thus cannot exist in the context of non-adversarial proceedings: *Re L. (A Minor) (Police Investigation: Privilege)* [1997] 1 A.C. 16, HL. Accordingly, litigation privilege does not apply to communications in investigative proceedings such as those under Part IV of the *Children Act* 1989: *ibid.*; or private non-statutory enquiries: *Three Rivers D.C. (No. 5), ante*. Thus, an expert's report prepared by a party in proceedings under Part IV of the 1989 Act is not protected by privilege from disclosure to the police, even if a similar report prepared for the purpose of criminal, and therefore adversarial proceedings, would be protected from disclosure in the *Children Act* 1989 or any other proceedings: *S. County Council v. B.* [2000] Fam. 76, Fam D (Charles J.).

Where litigation privilege does apply, it includes communications made between the professional adviser, his client or his client's representative, and any other person (see *Wheeler v. Le Marchant* (1881) 17 Ch.D. 675), provided the communication was made in connection with and for the purpose of existing or contemplated legal proceedings. That purpose does not have to be the sole purpose of the communication, provided it was the dominant purpose: *Waugh v British Railways Board* [1980] A.C. 521, HL.The dominant purpose of a communication must be determined objectively on the evidence, and is not necessarily that of its author: *Guinness Peat Ltd v. Fitzroy Robinson* [1987] 1 W.L.R. 1027, CA (Civ. Div.) (dominant purpose of a letter complying with the terms of an insurance policy by notifying insurers of a claim was that of the insurers who required notification so that they might obtain legal advice on the claim).

The identity and other details of witnesses intended to be called in adversarial litigation (whether or not their identity was the fruit of legal advice) are covered by litigation privilege: *R. (Kelly) v. Warley Magistrates' Court* [2008] 1 Cr.App.R. 14, DC (*ante*, § 4–84a).

12–10 Litigation privilege does not attach to a document which was not created for the purposes of litigation by virtue of its being obtained by a client or his legal adviser for such a purpose, nor to a copy of such a document by virtue of its being copied for such a purpose: *Ventouris v. Mountain* [1991] 1 W.L.R. 607, CA (Civ. Div.) (save, possibly, for such copies of originals which were never in the control of the party claiming privilege: *Watson v. Cammell Laird & Co. Ltd* [1959] 1 W.L.R. 702, CA, doubted in *Ventouris v. Mountain*, and distinguished by Aldous J. in *Lubrizol Corporation v. Esso Petroleum Co. Ltd.* [1992] 1 W.L.R. 957, Ch D). However, where the selection of documents copied or assembled by a solicitor betrays the trend of his advice to his client, the documents so selected are privileged: *Lyell v. Kennedy (No. 3)* (1884) 27 Ch.D. 1; *Ventouris v. Mountain, ante*, at p.615; provided that the documents are third party and not own client documents: *Sumitomo Corporation v. Credit Lyonnais Rouse Ltd* [2002] 1 W.L.R. 479, CA (Civ. Div.).

Translations of documents should be treated in the same manner as copies: *Sumitomo Corporation v. Credit Lyonnais Rouse Ltd, ante*.

12–11 Litigation privilege attaches to confidential communications between solicitors and expert witnesses but not to an expert's opinion based upon non-privileged material, nor to the non-privileged chattels or documents upon which the opinion was based. Thus, no privilege attaches to a document in the possession of a handwriting expert which emanated from a defendant and was sent by him to his solicitors for examination by the expert: *R. v. King (D.A.)*, 77 Cr.App.R. 1, CA: see also *Harmony Shipping Co. S.A. v. Saudi Europe Line Ltd* [1979] 1 W.L.R. 1380 at 1385, CA (Civ. Div.).

Where the expert's opinion is, at least to a significant extent, based upon privileged material, the opinion itself is also privileged. Consequently the defence can object if the prosecution seek to elicit evidence from an expert who has been abandoned and not relied upon by the defence: *R. v. Davies*, 166 J.P. 243, CA. A person interviewed by a doctor at the instigation of his own lawyers for the purpose of his defence is entitled to assume that what he says has the same status as his communications with his lawyers.

Both the interview and the opinion based thereon are privileged: *ibid.* Similarly, an expert's opinion on DNA is privileged where it is based upon a blood sample taken from the accused and sent to the expert by his solicitors in contemplation of criminal proceedings, because the blood sample itself is an item subject to legal professional privilege within the meaning of the *PACE Act* 1984, s.10 (*post*, § 15–90): *R. v. R.* [1995] 1 Cr.App.R. 183, CA. As to waiver of privilege by service of an expert report, see *post*, § 12–17.

Legal advice privilege

All confidential communications between a lawyer and his client relating to a transaction in which the lawyer has been instructed for the purpose of obtaining legal advice will be privileged, provided that they are directly related to the performance by the lawyer of his professional duty as legal adviser of his client: *Three Rivers D.C. (No. 6)*, *ante*; however, this requires there to be a "relevant legal context", and in cases of doubt the judge should ask himself whether the advice related to the rights, liabilities, obligations or remedies of the client under either private or public law, and, if so, whether the communication fell within the policy underlying the justification for the privilege: *ibid.* **12–12**

Legal advice privilege does not apply to documents communicated by a third party to a client or his solicitor for advice to be taken upon them (such as a surveyor's report to a solicitor administering an estate: *Wheeler v. Le Marchant* (1881) 17 Ch. D. 675), but only to communications passing between the client and his solicitor (whether or not through any intermediary) and documents evidencing such communications: *Three Rivers (No. 5), ante* (in which the Court of Appeal held that for these purposes employees of the client were third parties). **12–13**

The privilege is that of the client, and the lawyer is not entitled to withhold information or documents which the client himself would not be entitled to withhold: *Bursill v. Tanner* (1885) 16 Q.B.D. 1, CA; *R. v. Peterborough Justice, ex p. Hicks* [1977] 1 W.L.R. 1371, DC.

(2) Communications in furtherance of crime

The privilege does not extend to communications which are made for the purpose of obtaining advice on the commission of a future crime, or which are themselves part of a crime: *R. v. Cox and Railton* (1884) 14 Q.B.D. 153; *Bullivant v. Att.-Gen. for Victoria* [1901] A.C. 196 at 200, *per* Lord Halsbury L.C.; and *C. v. C. (Privilege: Criminal Communications)* [2002] Fam. 42, C.A. (Civ. Div.) (indecent, obscene, abusive and menacing telephone call by client to solicitor constituting an offence contrary to the *Telecommunications Act* 1984, s.3). Whether the solicitor was aware of the illicit purpose is immaterial, as such matters are otherwise than in the ordinary course of professional communications: *Banque Keyser Ullmann S.A. v. Skandia (U.K.) Insurance Co. Ltd* [1986] 1 Lloyd's Rep. 336, CA (Civ. Div.). Similarly, documents or information obtained in contravention of domestic or foreign law cannot be privileged: *Dubai Aluminium Co. Ltd v. Al-Alwai* [1999] 1 W.L.R. 1964, QBD (Rix J.). Whilst litigation privilege is not displaced solely by virtue of a client's antecedent fraud or crime, if the client seeks to further it in civil proceedings by advancing bogus defences to his solicitors, his communications for this purpose are not privileged: *Dubai Bank Ltd v. Galadari (No. 6)*, *The Times*, April 22, 1991, Ch D (reversed on appeal on another issue, *The Times*, October 14, 1992). *Quaere*, whether advice on how to avoid committing a crime, or that certain conduct could lead to prosecution is privileged: see *R. v. Haydn* (1825) 2 Fox and Sm. 379 (Ir.); *Butler v. Board of Trade* [1971] Ch. 680, Ch D. **12–14**

Before the principle can be relied upon, there must be prima facie evidence that it was the client's intention to obtain advice in furtherance of his criminal purpose, see *O'Rourke v. Darbishire* [1920] A.C. 581, HL; and not simply an allegation of fraudulent conduct: *Istil Group Inc. v. Zahoor* [2003] 2 All E.R. 252, Ch D. In deciding whether a document came into existence in furtherance of a criminal purpose, the court should ask itself whether there is prima facie evidence of fraud and prima facie evidence that the document came into existence as part of that fraudulent or criminal purpose: *R. v. Gibbins* [2004] 2 *Archbold News* 1, CA. In determining the second question, the **12–15** court may be entitled to look at the document itself: see *R. v. Governor of Pentonville Prison, ex p. Osman*, 90 Cr.App.R. 281, DC, where, however, the matter was not fully argued.

In *R. (Hallinan Blackburn Gittings & Nott (a firm)) v. Middlesex Guildhall Crown Court* [2005] 1 W.L.R. 766, CA, it was held that on an application for a production order under Schedule 1 to the *PACE Act* 1984 (*post*, § 15–75) in relation to documents in the hands of the solicitor acting for a defendant in a pending criminal trial, a claim to legal professional privilege may be defeated where there is evidence of a specific agreement to pervert the course of justice, which is freestanding and independent, in the sense that it does not require any judgment to be reached in relation to the issues to be tried in the pending proceedings. As to this, see also *Kuwait Airways Corp. v. Iraqi Airways Co. (No. 6)*, *The Times*, April 25, 2005, CA (Civ. Div.).

(3) Duration and waiver of privilege

Duration

12–16 A document or communication is "once privileged, always privileged": *Calcraft v. Guest* [1898] 1 Q.B. 759 at 761. The principle that a client should be free to consult his legal advisers without fear of his communications being revealed is a fundamental condition on which the administration of justice as a whole rests. Legal professional privilege is the predominant public interest to be upheld, even where the witness no longer has any recognisable interest in preserving the confidentiality: *R. v. Derby Magistrates' Court, ex p. B.* [1996] A.C. 487, HL. Documents privileged in respect of civil proceedings remain privileged in respect of later criminal proceedings: *cf. Companies Act* 2006, s.1129 (*post*, § 30–107).

Waiver

12–17 The privilege may be expressly or impliedly waived by the witness or, after death, by his personal representatives or heirs: *R. v. Molloy* [1997] 2 Cr.App.R. 283, CA. Where a witness ventures into an area of privilege, judges frequently inform the witness of his rights. It is submitted that this is the better course. Evidence of earlier instructions given by a solicitor to rebut an allegation of recent fabrication does not amount to a waiver of privilege: *R. v. Wilmot*, 89 Cr.App.R. 341, CA; and does not therefore entitle the Crown to trespass upon privileged communications between solicitor and client. A defendant's bare assertion that he did not answer questions during an interview because he was following his solicitor's advice does not amount to a waiver of privilege: *R. v. Condron and Condron* [1997] 1 Cr.App.R. 185, CA. But if he, or his solicitor in his presence, elaborates on the basis of such advice, privilege is waived: *R. v. Bowden* [1999] 2 Cr.App.R. 176, CA (*post*, § 15–424); and *R. v. Hall-Chung* (2007) 151 S.J. 1020, CA.

It does not follow that privilege has been waived generally because a privileged document has been disclosed for a limited purpose; it must often be in the interests of justice that a partial or limited waiver of privilege should be made by a party who would not contemplate anything which might cause privilege to be lost: *B. v. Auckland District Law Society* [2003] 2 A.C. 736, PC, following *British Coal Corp. v. Dennis Rye Ltd (No. 2)* [1988] 1 W.L.R. 1113, CA (Civ. Div.). A court should not be astute to hold that privilege has been lost, save to the extent that justice and the right to a fair trial make that necessary; the judge must identify the confidential communications which the person claiming privilege chose to disclose and see to what extent fairness demands that other documents or communications should also be disclosed: *R. v. Ahmed*, unreported, November 11, 2007, CA ([2007] EWCA Crim 2870). Where that person is a third party, such as a prosecution witness, he should be given an opportunity to be heard: *ibid.*

Disclosure of an expert's report waives any privilege existing in any background document or material referred to in the report: *Clough v. Tameside and Glossop Health Authority* [1998] 1 W.L.R. 1478 (Bracewell J.); but a passing reference in a report that is disclosed to another document which is privileged would not necessarily amount to a waiver of privilege: *R. v. Davies*, 166 J.P. 243, CA (*obiter* expression of opinion, considering *Clough*).

Where there has been a waiver in law, the judge will have to decide whether it would be fair to permit the prosecution to exploit the waiver; and, in deciding on what is fair, the judge should consider the circumstances in which the waiver occurred, and whether the fact-finding tribunal would be misled by the partial nature of the information voluntarily provided by the defence: *R. v. Loizou* [2006] 9 *Archbold News* 2, CA, and *Hall-Chung, ante* (in each of which it would have been misleading for the jury to have been given a reason for the solicitor's advice that the defendant should not answer questions in interview without the prosecution being able to cross-examine as to what the defendant had told his solicitor at the time). **12–18**

Where solicitors are retained by joint clients, the waiver of privilege implied at the outset of the joint retainer is limited so as to exclude communications made after the emergence of an actual conflict of interest: *TSB Bank plc v. Robert Irving & Burns (a firm) (Colonia Baltica Insurance Ltd, third party)* [2000] 2 All E.R. 826, CA (Civ. Div.).

(4) Secondary evidence of privileged material

A privileged document is admissible in evidence, if relevant, once it is in the possession of the other side: *Butler v. Board of Trade* [1971] Ch. 680, Ch D; *R. v. Tompkins*, 67 Cr.App.R. 181, CA; *R. v. Cottrill* [1997] Crim.L.R. 56, CA. Admissibility depends upon the relevance of the document; the method by which it has been obtained is immaterial: *Kuruma v. R.* [1955] A.C. 197 at 203, PC. In civil proceedings, an injunction may be available to restrain the use of a privileged document or secondary evidence thereof: *Lord Ashburton v. Pape* [1913] 2 Ch. 469; *Goddard v. Nationwide Building Society* [1987] Q.B. 670, CA (Civ. Div.). No such remedy is available in criminal proceedings, although the position in the case of a private prosecution has been left open: *Butler v. Board of Trade, ante*. A party may be restrained from using a privileged document in civil proceedings if it has been obtained by a trick or by stealth: *I.T.C. Film Distributors v. Video Exchange Ltd* [1982] Ch. 431, Ch D; or where it has clearly been disclosed in error: *Al-Fayed v Commr of Police of the Metropolis, The Times*, June 17, 2002, CA (Civ. Div.), and the cases cited therein. In criminal proceedings the same restraint can be effected by an application under the *PACE Act* 1984, s.78 (*post*, § 15–452): see *R. v. Governor of Pentonville Prison, ex p. Osman*, 90 Cr.App.R. 281 at 310, DC; *Kuruma v. R., ante*, at p. 204; and *R. v. Cottrill, ante*. **12–19**

(5) Statutory extensions

Legal professional privilege has been extended by statute to include communications to or by: (i) licensed conveyancers or a recognised body in the course of acting as such for a client: *Administration of Justice Act* 1985, s.33 (as amended, from a day to be appointed, by the *Legal Services Act* 2007, s.182, and Sched. 17, para. 22); (ii) authorised advocates and authorised litigators providing advocacy or litigation services: *Courts and Legal Services Act* 1990, s.63 (repealed as from a day to be appointed by the *Legal Services Act* 2007, ss.208(1) and 210, Sched. 21, paras 83 and 91, and Sched. 23); and (iii) as from a day to be appointed, authorised persons providing advocacy, litigation, conveyancing or probate services, and bodies holding a licence under Part 4 of the *Legal Services Act* 2007: 2007 Act, s.190. As to the privilege from disclosure in legal proceedings of communications with patent agents and registered trade mark agents, see the *Copyright, Designs and Patents Act* 1988, ss.280 (as amended, as from a day to be appointed, by the 2007 Act, ss.185(6), 208(1) and 210, Sched. 21, para. 77, and Sched. 23) and 284. **12–20**

(6) Prison legal aid officers

No privilege analogous to that between lawyer and client arises between a prisoner and a prison legal aid officer. However, it is in the public interest that formal interviews with a legal aid officer for the purpose of making an application should, save in exceptional circumstances, be treated as confidential discussions to which public interest immunity attaches: *R. v. Umoh*, 84 Cr.App.R. 138, CA. **12–21**

D. CONFIDENTIAL RELATIONSHIPS

General

12–22 No legal privilege arises out of the relationship between a patient and doctor: *Wilson v. Rastall* (1792) 4 T.R. 753; *Duchess of Kingston's case* (1776) 20 St.Tr. 355 at 472. (As to statements made to a doctor examining a suspect or defendant, see *R. v. McDonald* [1991] Crim.L.R. 122, CA and *R. v. Gayle* [1994] Crim.L.R. 679, CA, *post*, § 15–496.) Nor does it arise between journalist and informant: *Att.-Gen. v. Mulholland and Foster* [1963] 2 Q.B. 477; *British Steel Corp v. Granada Television Ltd* [1981] A.C. 1096, HL, although the common law position has been modified by the *Contempt of Court Act* 1981, s.10, *post*, § 28–94. The position of priest and penitent has not been authoritatively decided, but the tendency of judicial dicta is that, while in strict law the privilege does not exist, a minister of religion should not be required to give evidence as to a confession made to him: *R. v. Griffin* (1853) 6 Cox 219; *R. v. Hay* (1896) 2 F. & F. 4.

12–23 As to the competence and compellability of the defendant's spouse (or civil partner), see the *PACE Act* 1984, s.80 (*ante*, § 8–46); and the *YJCEA* 1999, s.53 (*ante*, § 8–36).

A father or mother may be a witness for or against a child: *R. v. Mayor of Okehampton* (1752) 1 Wils. K.B. 332; and see *R. v. Bramley* (1795) 6 T.R. 330; *Goodright v. Moss* (1777) 2 Cowp. 591. A child may also be a witness for or against his father or mother.

Discretion of court

12–24 The court has a discretion to excuse a witness from answering a question when to do so would involve a breach of confidence: see the *obiter* observations of Lord Widgery C.J. in relation to doctors in *Hunter v. Mann* [1974] Q.B. 767, 59 Cr.App.R. 37, DC (at pp. 775, 41).

Before compelling disclosure, a court should be satisfied that the potential answer is relevant and will serve a useful purpose in relation to the proceedings, and then weigh the conflicting interests to determine whether confidentiality be overridden or respected: see *Att.-Gen. v. Mulholland and Foster*, *ante*, *per* Lord Denning M.R. at pp. 489, 490, and *per* Donovan L.J. at p. 492; *Att.-Gen. v. Clough* [1963] 1 Q.B. 773, *per* Lord Parker C.J. at p. 792; *Att.-Gen. v. Lundin*, 75 Cr.App.R. 90, DC, *per* Watkins L.J. at p. 100; and *British Steel Corp. v. Granada Television Ltd*, *ante*, *per* Lord Wilberforce (at pp. 1168–1169).

Search and seizure

12–25 The *PACE Act* 1984 imposed strict restrictions on the extent to which access may be obtained to confidential information for the purposes of a criminal investigation: see, in particular, sections 8 to 13, and Schedule 1, *post*, §§ 15–72 *et seq.* These restrictions must now be read subject to the provisions of Part 2 of the *CJPA* 2001, *post*, §§ 15–124 *et seq.*

II. PUBLIC INTEREST IMMUNITY

A. GENERAL PRINCIPLES

(1) Introduction

12–26 Public interest immunity was previously called "Crown privilege". This expression is no longer used, as "it is not a matter of privilege and it is not confined to the Crown": *per* Brightman L.J. in *Buttes Gas & Oil Co. v. Hammer (No. 3)* [1981] Q.B. 223 at 262, CA (Civ. Div.), reversed on a different point at [1982] A.C. 888, HL; see also *R. v. Ward*, 96 Cr.App.R. 1 at 26–27, CA; *R. v. Chief Constable of the West Midlands Police, ex p. Wiley* [1995] 1 A.C. 274 at 290–291, HL.

12–27 The doctrine of public interest immunity, as it operates in criminal proceedings, was summarised in *R. v. H.* [2004] 2 A.C. 134, HL, as follows:

"Circumstances may arise in which material held by the prosecution and tending to undermine the prosecution or assist the defence cannot be disclosed to the defence, fully or even at all, without the risk of serious prejudice to an important public interest. The public interest most regularly engaged is that in the effective investigation and prosecution of serious crime, which may involve resort to informers and under-cover agents, or the use of scientific or operational techniques (such as surveillance) which cannot be disclosed without exposing individuals to the risk of personal injury or jeopardising the success of future operations. In such circumstances some derogation from the golden rule of full disclosure may be justified but such derogation must always be the minimum derogation necessary to protect the public interest in question and must never imperil the overall fairness of the trial" (at [18]).

In accordance with the code of practice under Part II of the *CPIA* 1996, material the disclosure of which would give rise to a real risk of serious prejudice to an important public interest, known as sensitive material, must be listed on a schedule of such material, or, in exceptional circumstances, be revealed to the prosecutor separately (Appendix A–237). The code sets out numerous examples of such material (*post*, § 12–33). No such list can be exhaustive: see *D. v. NSPCC* [1978] A.C. 171 at 230, HL, where Lord Hailsham observed that the "categories of public interest are not closed, and must alter from time to time whether by restriction or extension as social conditions and social legislation develop" (cited in *ex p. Wiley*, *ante*, at p. 305). **12–28**

(2) Foreign interests

The particular public interest requiring protection must be an interest relevant to the United Kingdom. Public interest immunity cannot be claimed by a foreign state or on the ground that it would infringe the public interest of a foreign state: *Buttes Gas & Oil Co. v. Hammer (No. 3)*, *ante*, at pp. 247, 251, 262. However, as the public interest of the United Kingdom requires continued co-operation, and recognises a convergence of interests, with foreign sovereign states (*ibid.* at p. 256), public interest immunity can apply to various communications between British and foreign government departments (*R. v. Governor of Brixton Prison, ex p. Osman*, 93 Cr.App.R. 202, DC (at pp. 206–207)) or between British and foreign prosecuting authorities (*R. v. Horseferry Road Magistrates' Court, ex p. Bennett (No. 2)*, 99 Cr.App.R. 123 at 126, DC). **12–29**

(3) "Class" and "contents" claims

At one time "class immunity" might be claimed by the government or others (*e.g. D. v. NSPCC*, *ante*) for a document by virtue of the class to which it belonged, regardless of its contents, and without reference to any harm which disclosure of the particular document might cause: *Conway v. Rimmer* [1968] A.C. 910, HL. However, this approach has no place within modern criminal proceedings in which disclosure is governed by the regime imposed by the 1996 Act and implemented in accordance with *R. v. H.*, *post*, § 12–44d. Sensitive material is now defined by reference to the risk of serious prejudice to an important public interest that would arise if the material in question were disclosed, and the determination of any issue as to the disclosure of a document must involve a consideration of its contents (see too the Attorney-General's guidelines on disclosure, paras 20 to 22, Appendix A–247). It is submitted, however, that "class reasoning" can still be relevant, such as where disclosure of a document would harm the public interest in promoting frankness in documents of that type (*e.g. Taylor v. Anderton (Police Complaints Authority intervening)* [1995] 1 W.L.R. 447 (Civ. Div.) (investigating officers' reports in respect of complaints against the police)), but the relevant consideration is the harm which might be caused by disclosure, rather than the class of document *per se*, and where there is no additional sensitivity in the contents of the document, often the fact that such a document would not be disclosed without an order from the court, in accordance with *R. v. H.*, is a sufficient protection; thus, where the contents of such a document satisfy the test for disclosure, to that extent, disclosure is likely to be ordered. **12–30**

(4) Matter within the public domain

If there has been publication to the whole world, then that side of any balancing exercise concerned with the public interest must collapse: see *Sankey v. Whitlam* (1978) **12–31**

42 A.L.R. 1; and any prior dissemination of a document is a matter to be taken into account in the balance: see *R. v. Governor of Brixton Prison, ex p. Osman*, 93 Cr.App.R. 202 at 210, DC. Immunity is not, however, lost simply because the material in question is used in proceedings contemplated when it was created: see *Makanjuola v. Commr of Police of the Metropolis* [1992] 3 All E.R. 617, CA (Civ. Div.), *per* Bingham L.J., at p.623.

12–32 The fact that the information is already known to both parties, as opposed to being in the public domain is irrelevant: *Halford v. Sharples* [1992] 1 W.L.R. 736, CA (Civ. Div.) (overruled on unrelated grounds in *R. v. Chief Constable of West Midlands Police, ex p. Wiley* [1995] 1 A.C. 274, HL).

B. CATEGORIES OF PUBLIC INTEREST IMMUNITY

Categories listed in the code of practice

12–33 The list of examples of sensitive material provided in the code of practice under Part II of the *CPIA* 1996, para. 6.12, reads as follows (numbering added):

(i) material relating to national security;
(ii) material received from the intelligence and security agencies;
(iii) material relating to intelligence from foreign sources which reveals sensitive intelligence gathering methods;
(iv) material given in confidence;
(v) material relating to the identity or activities of informants, or undercover police officers, or witnesses, or other persons supplying information to the police who may be in danger if their identities are revealed;
(vi) material revealing the location of any premises or other place used for police surveillance, or the identity of any person allowing a police officer to use them for surveillance;
(vii) material revealing, either directly or indirectly, techniques and methods relied upon by a police officer in the course of a criminal investigation, for example covert surveillance techniques, or other methods of detecting crime;
(viii) material whose disclosure might facilitate the commission of other offences or hinder the prevention and detection of crime;
(ix) material upon the strength of which search warrants were obtained;
(x) material containing details of persons taking part in identification parades;
(xi) material supplied to an investigator during a criminal investigation which has been generated by an official of a body concerned with the regulation or supervision of bodies corporate or of persons engaged in financial activities, or which has been generated by a person retained by such a body;
(xii) material supplied to an investigator during a criminal investigation which relates to a child or young person and which has been generated by a local authority social services department, an area child protection committee or other party contacted by an investigator during the investigation;
(xiii) material relating to the private life of a witness.

12–34 As to (v), the public interest in preserving the anonymity of informants has long been recognised: *Marks v. Beyfus* [1890] 25 Q.B.D. 494, CA; *D. v. NSPCC* [1978] A.C. 171, HL (applying the principle in respect of police informants to those providing information to the NSPCC). The general policy of neither confirming nor denying the existence of an informant was approved in *R. v. Roussow*, unreported, November 14, 2006, CA ([2006] EWCA Crim. 2980): simply revealing the fact of there being an informant, if it be the case, could of itself be dangerous, and if the answer were to be that there was no informant, that might have grave implications when a like statement could not be made in other cases.

The need for judges to scrutinise with great care applications by the defence for disclosure of details about informants and to adopt a robust approach in declining to order disclosure when they were not justified was emphasised in *R. v. Turner* [1995] 2 Cr.App.R. 94, CA (in which the informant's participation in the events with which the trial was concerned and the defendant's claim that he had been set up made disclosure necessary). Where a participating informant is a prosecution witness called at trial it is extremely likely that his status will have to be disclosed; failure to do so would give rise to a serious risk that the jury would be misled and that the witness would give misleading answers: *R. v. Patel* [2002] Crim.L.R. 304, CA. See also *R. v. Early* [2003] 1 Cr.App.R. 19, CA.

Public interest immunity does not prevent an informant from revealing his status himself: *Savage v. Chief Constable of Hampshire* [1997] 1 W.L.R. 1061, CA (Civ. Div.).

As to (vi), public interest immunity protects the identity of a person who has allowed his premises to be used for surveillance, and therefore the location of those premises or any other information which might reveal his identity: *R. v. Rankine* [1986] Q.B. 861, 83 Cr.App.R. 18, CA. The rationale is the same as that in relation to informers, and public interest immunity applies where occupiers fear only harassment as opposed to actual violence: *Blake and Austin v. DPP*, 97 Cr.App.R. 169 at 175, DC. Information which can be revealed without identifying the occupier should be revealed (*R. v. Johnson (Kenneth)*, 88 Cr.App.R. 131 at 134, CA; *R. v. Grimes* [1994] Crim.L.R. 213, CA), unless public interest immunity can be justified on another ground, such as protection of police methods. **12–35**

In *R. v. Johnson, ante*, at p. 139, the Court of Appeal gave guidance on the evidential requirements for excluding evidence which identifies places of observation and occupiers of premises.

> "The minimum evidential requirements seem to us to be the following:
>
> (a) The police officer in charge of the observations to be conducted, one of no lower rank than a sergeant should usually be acceptable for this purpose, must be able to testify that beforehand he visited all observation places to be used and ascertained the attitude of occupiers of the premises, not only to the use to be made of them, but to the possible disclosure thereafter of the use made and facts which could lead to the identification of the premises thereafter and of the occupiers. He may of course in addition inform the court of difficulties, if any, usually encountered in the particular locality of obtaining assistance from the public.
>
> (b) A police officer of no lower rank than a chief inspector must be able to testify that immediately prior to the trial he visited the places used for observations, the results of which it is proposed to give in evidence, and ascertained whether the occupiers are the same as when the observations took place and whether they are or are not, what the attitude of the occupiers is to the possible disclosure of the use previously made of the premises and of facts which could lead at the trial to identification of premises and occupiers.
>
> Such evidence will of course be given in the absence of the jury when the application to exclude the material evidence is made. The judge should explain to the jury, as this judge did, when summing up or at some appropriate time before that, the effect of his ruling to exclude, if he so rules."

As to warning a jury of the possible handicap imposed on the defence by the restraints on cross-examination resulting from a ruling upholding a claim to public interest immunity, and the consequent need to pay special attention to any disadvantage that may have caused, see *R. v. Johnson, ante*, at p. 138, and *R. v. Hewitt; R. v. Davis*, 95 Cr.App.R. 81 at 86, CA.

As to (vii), for an example (pre-dating the 1996 Act) of over-zealous protection of surveillance techniques, see *R. v. Brown and Daley*, 87 Cr.App.R. 52, CA (judge wrongly prevented questions as to the colour and make of an unmarked surveillance vehicle). **12–36**

As to (viii), public interest immunity has been found to attach to the police force *Public Order Manual*, containing details of police techniques for dealing with disorder, demonstrations and riots, on the basis that publication would enable such offenders to frustrate police efforts to control them: see *Goodwin v. Chief Constable of Lancashire*, *The Times*, November 3, 1992, CA (Civ. Div.). **12–37**

The mere fact that material falls within one of the categories listed does not mean that public interest immunity attaches (see *ante*, § 12–30); for example, whether material upon the strength of which search warrants were obtained ((ix) above) is sensitive will depend upon the nature of the material, rather than the fact that it led to a search warrant being obtained. **12–38**

12–39 As to (xi), the mere fact that information or documents have come into the possession of a government department as a result of the exercise by it of statutory powers to obtain information or documents does not prohibit their disclosure in the absence of a statutory prohibition thereon: *Norwich Pharmacal Co. v. Customs and Excise Commrs* [1974] A.C. 133, HL.

Material obtained by Department of Trade inspectors during investigations under section 165 of the *Companies Act* 1948 (now the *Companies Act* 1985, s.432, *post*, § 30–3) has been held to be subject to public interest immunity: *R. v. Cheltenham JJ., ex p. Secretary of State for Trade* [1977] 1 W.L.R. 95, DC. Material obtained by liquidators at voluntarily attended interviews during insolvency proceedings has similarly been held to be subject to public interest immunity: *Re Barlow Clowes Gilt Managers Ltd* [1992] Ch. 208, Ch D, and *R. v. Clowes*, 95 Cr.App.R. 440, CCC (Phillips J.). However, transcripts of examinations under section 236 of the *Insolvency Act* 1986 are not covered by public interest immunity: *Re Arrows Ltd (No. 4)* [1995] 2 A.C. 75, HL.

12–40 As to (xii), it is well established that various categories of documents and records maintained by the social services and organisations such as the NSPCC in relation to children are subject to public interest immunity. This is justified by the particular circumstances of the welfare of children and the risk that frankness would be imperilled if such records were liable to be disclosed without the "protection" of public interest immunity: *Re D. (Infants)* [1970] 1 W.L.R. 599, CA (Civ. Div.); *D. v. NSPCC* [1978] A.C. 171, HL; *Re M (A Minor) (Disclosure of Material)* [1990] 2 F.L.R. 36, CA (Civ. Div.). As to information relating to family proceedings, see *post*, § 12–51a.

Police complaints investigations

12–41 Documents obtained for the purposes of an investigation into a complaint against the police under Part IV of the *Police Act* 1996 no longer attract public interest immunity as a class: *R. v. Chief Constable of the West Midlands Police, ex p. Wiley* [1995] 1 A.C. 274, HL. However, the reports of investigating officers, made for the same purpose, do form a class which is entitled to public interest immunity. The rationale behind such public interest immunity is that "the prospect of disclosure in other than unusual circumstances would have an undesirably inhibiting effect on investigating officers' reports": *per* Sir Thomas Bingham M.R. in *Taylor v. Anderton (Police Complaints Authority intervening)* [1995] 1 W.L.R. 447, CA (Civ. Div.), at p. 465.

Material relating to intercepted communications

12–42 For the statutory restrictions on the disclosure of material tending to suggest that interception of communications has taken place, whether lawfully or otherwise, see the *RIPA* 2000, ss.17 and 18, *post*, §§ 25–377 *et seq.*

Information relating to the judicial process

12–43 The function of a judge would now be regarded as wholly incompatible with his being called as a witness with regard to any proceedings in which he has adjudicated: see Taylor, *Evid.*, 12th ed., s.938. If, however, a judge's evidence in regard to such matters is vital, he should not allow the fact that he cannot be compelled to give it to stand in the way of his doing so: *Warren v. Warren* [1996] 4 All E.R. 664, CA (Civ. Div.). As to jurors, see *ante*, §§ 4–263, 7–215, and the *Contempt of Court Act* 1981, s.8, *post*, § 28–90.

C. THE DECISION AS TO NON-DISCLOSURE

Introduction

12–44 The *Criminal Procedure Rules* 2005 (S.I. 2005 No. 384), *post*, §§ 12–77 *et seq.*, make provision in relation to the procedure to be followed where the prosecution make an application for an order for non-disclosure. The rules of common law governing the approach which should be adopted when a court decides whether to accede to such an application are unaffected by the Act: s.21(2), *post*, § 12–71.

Voluntary disclosure

12–44a Whilst it is clear that under the *CPIA* 1996 it is for the court, not the prosecution, to determine that material should not be disclosed on grounds of public interest immunity (ss.3(6) and 7A(8), *post*, §§ 12–54, 12–58a), thus maintaining the common law position (see, *e.g.*, *R. v. Ward*, 96 Cr.App.R. 1, CA), the 1996 Act does not indicate whether or to what extent the prosecution are bound to apply for a ruling even when of the view that disclosure should be made notwithstanding the pubic interest in non-disclosure. The view expressed in *R. v. H.* (*post*, § 12–80a) that "only in truly borderline cases should the prosecution seek a judicial ruling on the disclosability of material in its hands" would appear to endorse voluntary disclosure where it is clear to the prosecution that non-disclosure could not be justified.

Historically, the rule was that the assertion of public interest immunity was a duty and not a right: in *Marks v. Beyfus* [1890] 25 Q.B.D. 494, CA, Lord Esher stated (at p.500) that even if the DPP had been willing to answer questions about informants the judge ought not to have allowed him to do so; and in *Makanjuola v. Commr of Police of the Metropolis* [1992] 3 All E.R. 617, CA (Civ. Div.), it was said (at p.623) that "public interest immunity is not a trump card vouchsafed to certain privileged players to play when and as they wish. It is an exclusionary rule, imposed on parties in certain circumstances, even where it is to their disadvantage in litigation"; and that where a litigant held documents in a class prima facie immune he should (save perhaps in a very exceptional case) assert that the documents are immune and decline to disclose them, since the ultimate judge of where the public interest lay was not him but the court. However, this position was distinguished by Lord Woolf in *R. v. Chief Constable of West Midlands Police, ex p. Wiley* [1995] 1 A.C. 274, HL, at p.296, as applying to litigants, such as the chief constable in *Makanjuola*; if the decision of the chief constable were endorsed by the Attorney-General and possibly the Home Secretary as well it would be unobjectionable for the chief constable to make disclosure as the court would take their views as the evidence of those best able to assess the public interest involved. Lord Templeman took the wider view (at p.281) that when a document was known to be relevant and material, the holder of the document should voluntarily disclose it unless he is satisfied that disclosure would cause substantial harm, and that a rubber stamp approach to public interest immunity by the holder of a document was neither necessary nor appropriate. The Divisional Court had also given its blessing to some measure of voluntary disclosure by the prosecution of material which was prima facie immune in *R. v. Horseferry Road Magistrates' Court, ex p. Bennett (No. 2)*, 99 Cr.App.R. 123, DC (which was not cited to the House of Lords in *ex p. Wiley*, *ante*), but only with the express written approval of the Treasury Solicitor. The court issued guidance as to the procedure to be followed by the prosecution and the Treasury Solicitor in such circumstances.

In *R. v. Adams* [1997] Crim.L.R. 292, CA (also a pre-1996 Act case), the court considered that where a defendant who was an informant sought disclosure of his own contact sheets, the decision to disclose could properly be taken at the level of Detective Chief Inspector, provided that disclosure was not made of the identity of any other informant or any material that might attract public interest immunity on other grounds; however, different considerations applied to disclosure of one defendant's contact sheets to a co-defendant, which, even though the prosecution considered that such disclosure ought to be made, was an issue which ought to have been determined by the judge (reiterating the warning in *R. v. Turner*, *ante*, § 12–34, as to the need to be robust when requests for such disclosure are made), with all three parties being heard. Such a situation is now provided for by the *Criminal Procedure Rules* 2005 (S.I. 2005 No. 384), r.25.4 (*post*, § 12–82).

12–44b Voluntary disclosure of material to which public interest immunity attaches is to be distinguished from disclosure of that part of the material which meets the test for disclosure (under the 1996 Act, ss.3 and 7A, *post*, §§ 12–54, 12–58a) in a form which does not harm the public interest requiring protection; prosecutors are urged by the Attorney-General's guidelines to aim to disclose as much of the material as they properly can (for example, by giving the defence redacted or edited copies or summaries)

(Appendix A–247). Where the undisclosed part of the material does not itself meet the test for disclosure no application for non-disclosure will then be necessary.

Inspection

12–44c In order to make a decision as to non-disclosure, the court must necessarily study the material in respect of which public interest immunity is asserted: *R. v. K. (T. D.)*, 97 Cr.App.R. 342, CA; *R. v. Brown (W.)* [1995] 1 Cr.App.R. 191 at 200, CA (on appeal to the House of Lords ([1998] A.C. 367, *sub nom. R. v. Brown (Winston)*), this issue was not the subject of argument); and *R. v. H.* [2004] 2 A.C. 134, HL.

The issue for the court

12–44d It was formerly said that the decision as to whether to order disclosure of material that attracted public interest immunity involved a balancing exercise, weighing the public interest in maintaining the secrecy of the material against the public interest in the administration of justice, which requires that relevant material is available to the parties to the litigation. However, such language no longer seems appropriate in the light of the consideration given to the topic by the House of Lords in *R. v. H., ante.* Their Lordships held that where any issue of derogation from the golden rule of full disclosure comes before a court, it must address a series of questions.

"(1) What is the material which the prosecution seek to withhold? This must be considered by the court in detail.

(2) Is the material such as may weaken the prosecution case or strengthen that of the defence? If No, disclosure should not be ordered. If Yes, full disclosure should (subject to (3), (4) and (5) below) be ordered.

(3) Is there a real risk of serious prejudice to an important public interest (and, if so, what) if full disclosure of the material is ordered? If No, full disclosure should be ordered.

(4) If the answer to (2) and (3) is Yes, can the defendant's interest be protected without disclosure or disclosure be ordered to an extent or in a way which will give adequate protection to the public interest in question and also afford adequate protection to the interests of the defence? This question requires the court to consider, with specific reference to the material which the prosecution seek to withhold and the facts of the case and the defence as disclosed, whether the prosecution should formally admit what the defence seek to establish or whether disclosure short of full disclosure may be ordered. This may be done in appropriate cases by the preparation of summaries or extracts of evidence, or the provision of documents in an edited or anonymised form, provided the documents supplied are in each instance approved by the judge. In appropriate cases the appointment of special counsel may be a necessary step to ensure that the contentions of the prosecution are tested and the interests of the defendant protected (*as to the appointment of special counsel, see* post, *§ 12–80d*). In cases of exceptional difficulty the court may require the appointment of special counsel to ensure a correct answer to questions (2) and (3) as well as (4).

(5) Do the measures proposed in answer to (4) represent the minimum derogation necessary to protect the public interest in question? If No, the court should order such greater disclosure as will represent the minimum derogation from the golden rule of full disclosure.

(6) If limited disclosure is ordered pursuant to (4) or (5), may the effect be to render the trial process, viewed as a whole, unfair to the defendant? If Yes, then fuller disclosure should be ordered even if this leads or may lead the prosecution to discontinue the proceedings so as to avoid having to make disclosure.

(7) If the answer to (6) when first given is No, does that remain the correct answer as the trial unfolds, evidence is adduced and the defence advanced?

It is important that the answer to (6) should not be treated as a final, once-and-for-all, answer but as a provisional answer which the court must keep under review" (at [36]).

The importance of the rigorous application of these principles, first by the prosecution, and then by the court considering the material, is stressed in the Attorney-General's guidelines on disclosure (see *post*, § 12–76a, and the full text in Appendix A–243 *et seq.*). See also *R. v. West (Ricky)*, 69 J.C.L. 309, CA ([2005] EWCA Crim. 517), where the Court of Appeal said that great caution is necessary in the handling of public interest immunity applications made in the absence of the defence; and that there should be the most searching investigation by the police, by prosecuting authorities and by courts of the facts relating to matters in respect of which public interest immunity is claimed, coupled with the most searching consideration of their possible relevance in the light of whatever defence is being advanced.

For further consideration of *R. v. H.*, *ante*, and the exceptional use of special counsel, see *post*, § 12–80d.

Whether a trial can be fair despite the non-disclosure of material that would otherwise have been disclosed will depend on all the circumstances of the particular case. Where, however, the material may prove the defendant's innocence or avoid a miscarriage of justice, non-disclosure is unlikely ever to be justifiable, whatever the circumstances: see *R. v. Keane*, 99 Cr.App.R. 1, CA; and *R. v. Brown (W.)* [1995] 1 Cr.App.R. 191, CA. As to material allowing a defendant to put forward "a tenable case in the best possible light", see *R. v. Agar*, 90 Cr.App.R. 318 at 323, CA. **12–44e**

III. DISCLOSURE

A. PRELIMINARY

Introduction

In relation to offences into which a criminal investigation was commenced on or after April 4, 2005, the duties and responsibilities of parties with regard to disclosure are now governed by Parts I and II of the *CPIA* 1996, as amended by the *CJA* 2003. Part I (ss.1–21) has created a staged approach (initial prosecution disclosure, defence disclosure, continual review by the prosecution). Part II (ss.22–27) provides for a code of practice for regulating action the police must take in recording and retaining material obtained in the course of a criminal investigation and revealing it to the prosecution for a decision on disclosure. A revised code of practice, taking account of the amendments made by the 2003 Act, was brought into operation on April 4, 2005 (see Appendix A–231 *et seq.*). The Attorney-General issued new guidelines on disclosure of information in criminal proceedings, also taking the 2003 Act amendments into account, in April 2005 (see *post*, § 12–76a, and Appendix A–243 *et seq.*). A protocol for the control and management of unused material in the Crown Court was published under the auspices of the Court of Appeal on February 20, 2006 (see Appendix N–52 *et seq*). In *R. v. K. (Note)* [2006] 2 All E.R. 552, CA, it was said that the protocol clearly sets out the principles relating to disclosure, that those who act for the prosecution and the defence should familiarise themselves with it, and that it should be applied by trial judges. **12–45**

For the Act as it applies to criminal investigations commenced before April 4, 2005, reference should be made to the 2005 edition of this work, at §§ 12–45 *et seq.*

Surviving common law

The disclosure required by the 1996 Act is, and is intended to be, less extensive than would have been required prior to the Act at common law: *R. v. DPP, ex p. Lee* [1999] 2 Cr.App.R. 304, DC. **12–46**

However, the Act does not render the common law rules inapplicable to cases where the investigation began before the appointed day for the commencement of Parts I and II of the 1996 Act, *i.e.* April 1, 1997 (for guidance on this topic, reference should be made to the 1997 edition of this work, at §§ 12–46 *et seq.*), or, in other cases, to things falling to be done before "the relevant time" in relation to the alleged offence (see s.21(1) (*post*, § 12–71)). For most either way offences, "the relevant time" is presently the time of committal (s.21(3)(b)). **12–47**

In *ex p. Lee*, *ante*, it was held that the Act did not abolish common law obligations relating to the disclosure of material by the prosecutor prior to committal. However, the considerably reduced ability of the defence to take an active part in committal proceedings after the insertion of sections 5A to 5F of the *MCA* 1980 (*ante*, §§ 10–15 *et seq.*) meant that the disclosure required prior to committal was correspondingly reduced. Section 41 of, and Schedule 3 to, the *CJA* 2003 provide (as from a day to be appointed) for the sending of either way offences to the Crown Court under section 51 of the *CDA* 1998 (*ante*, § 1–17). The practical result will be that the vast majority of cases heard by **12–48** the Crown Court will arrive there shortly after an offence is alleged to have occurred. The "relevant time" will be reached quickly and there will be little scope for disclosure before it is reached.

12–49 What is required before the "relevant time" is that the prosecutor must always be alive to the need to make disclosure of material of which he is aware (either from his own consideration of the papers or because his attention has been drawn to it by the defence) and which he, as a responsible prosecutor, recognises should be disclosed at an early stage. He should ask himself what, if any, immediate disclosure justice and fairness require him to make in the particular circumstances of the case. Examples given in *ex p. Lee* which will survive the effective demise of committal proceedings would be the previous convictions of a complainant or deceased if that information could reasonably be expected to assist the defence when applying for bail, and material which would enable the defendant and his representatives to make preparations for trial which may be significantly less effective if disclosure is delayed (*e.g.* names of eye-witnesses whom the prosecution do not intend to use). In relation to this last category, disclosure would largely depend on what the defendant chose to reveal about his case.

As to post-trial disclosure, see *R. v. Makin* (2004) 148 S.J. 821, CA, *post*, § 12–60.

Sensitive material

12–50 The 1996 Act does not alter the rules of common law as to whether disclosure is in the public interest (s.21(2), *ante*, §§ 12–44 *et seq.*), although it does regulate the procedure for making an application to the courts for permission to withhold material for which public interest immunity is claimed.

Third party disclosure

12–51 Where it is sought to obtain material from third parties (upon whom there is no duty of disclosure), the appropriate procedure is to obtain a summons under the *Criminal Procedure (Attendance of Witnesses) Act* 1965: see *ante*, §§ 8–2 *et seq.* The drawbacks to such procedure were highlighted by the Court of Appeal in *R. v. Alibhai* [2004] 5 *Archbold News* 1, where the court stressed that if frauds were to be prosecuted effectively it is important that the alleged victims should not only be willing to disclose relevant material comprehensively and promptly, but that they should also be prepared to take all proper and efficient steps to bring about such disclosure. The court added that mere commercial confidentiality does not give rise to a right to withhold information and documents.

As to the desirability of prosecutors taking appropriate steps to obtain material in the hands of third parties which might reasonably be considered capable of undermining the prosecution case or of assisting the case for the accused, see, generally, the Attorney-General's guidelines (Appendix A–242) and, in a case of childhood sexual abuse with numerous complainants, *R. v. Brushett* [2001] Crim.L.R. 471, CA. Where pivotal evidence comes from a man with a known prison record, the prosecution should at an early stage equip themselves with his prison records; not only might they include matters prejudicial to their case and disclosable to the defence, but they might find their own case strengthened: *R. v. McCartney and Hamlett* [2003] 6 *Archbold News* 2, CA.

For an overview of the difficulties that can arise in respect of third party material, see also the protocol for the control and management of unused material in the Crown Court, paragraphs 52 to 62 (Appendix N–59 *et seq.*).

Information relating to family proceedings

12–51a Properly construed, rule 10.20A of the *Family Proceedings Rules* 1991 (S.I. 1991 No. 1247) does not permit the onward disclosure of information relating to family proceedings, which has been disclosed to the police, to a lawyer representing a party in criminal proceedings; a defence lawyer wishing to obtain permission to use such information may apply through a party to the family proceedings provided that notice is given to the other parties and that the application identifies the documents concerned: *Borough Council v A. (Chief Constable intervening)* [2007] 1 All E.R. 293, Fam D (Sumner J.); and see generally, *ante*, §§ 8–21 *et seq.*

European Convention on Human Rights

As to the disclosure requirements of the ECHR (an aspect of the right to a fair trial), see *post*, §§ 16–83 *et seq*. **12–51b**

The principle of tying prosecution disclosure to material that is relevant to the issues of guilt or innocence does not violate the ECHR or the jurisprudence of the European Court; there is nothing therein to equate the notion of a fair trial, including the requirement of the prosecution to prove their case, with the notion that the defence, while keeping their cards close to their chest, can demand sight of all the prosecution material, however irrelevant to any issue that could be guessed at: *R. v. M. (Michael)*, unreported, November 4, 2003, CA ([2003] EWCA Crim. 3764) (considering the statutory provisions in force prior to April 4, 2005).

As to the compatibility of the *ex parte* procedure for obtaining rulings as to the non-disclosure of material on the grounds of public interest immunity, with the requirements of the Convention, see *post*, § 12–80c.

B. LEGISLATION

(1) Criminal Procedure and Investigations Act 1996

Criminal Procedure and Investigations Act 1996, ss.1, 2

PART I

DISCLOSURE

Introduction

Application of this Part

1.—(1) This Part applies where— **12–52**

(a) a person is charged with a summary offence in respect of which a court proceeds to summary trial and in respect of which he pleads not guilty,

(b) a person who has attained the age of 18 is charged with an offence which is triable either way, in respect of which a court proceeds to summary trial and in respect of which he pleads not guilty, or

(c) a person under the age of 18 is charged with an indictable offence in respect of which a court proceeds to summary trial and in respect of which he pleads not guilty.

(2) This Part also applies where—

(a) *a person is charged with an indictable offence and he is committed for trial for the offence concerned,*

(b) *a person is charged with an indictable offence and proceedings for the trial of the person on the charge concerned are transferred to the Crown Court by virtue of a notice of transfer given under section 4 of the* Criminal Justice Act *1987 (serious or complex fraud),*

(c) *a person is charged with an indictable offence and proceedings for the trial of the person on the charge concerned are transferred to the Crown Court by virtue of a notice of transfer served on a magistrates' court under section 53 of the* Criminal Justice Act *1991 (certain cases involving children),*

(cc) a person is charged with an offence for which he is sent for trial *under section 51 (no committal proceedings for indictable-only offences) of the* Crime and Disorder Act *1998*,

(d) a count charging a person with a summary offence is included in an indictment under the authority of section 40 of the *Criminal Justice Act* 1988 (common assault etc.), or

(e) a bill of indictment charging a person with an indictable offence is preferred under the authority of section 2(2)(b) of the *Administration of Justice (Miscellaneous Provisions) Act* 1933 (bill preferred by direction of Court of Appeal, or by direction or with consent of a judge), or

(f) a bill of indictment charging a person with an indictable offence is preferred under section 22B(3)(a) of the *Prosecution of Offences Act* 1985.

(3) This Part applies in relation to alleged offences into which no criminal investigation has begun before the appointed day.

(4) For the purposes of this section a criminal investigation is an investigation which police officers or other persons have a duty to conduct with a view to it being ascertained—

(a) whether a person should be charged with an offence, or

(b) whether a person charged with an offence is guilty of it.

(5) The reference in subsection (3) to the appointed day is to such day as is appointed for the purposes of this Part by the Secretary of State by order.

[(6) In this Part—

(a) subsections (3) to (5) of section 3 (in their application for the purposes of section 3, 7 or 9), and

(b) sections 17, and 18,

have effect subject to subsections (2) and (3) of section 9 of the *Sexual Offences (Protected Material) Act* 1997 (by virtue of which those provisions of this Act do not apply in relation to disclosures regulated by that Act).]

[This section is printed as amended by the *CDA* 1998, s.119, and Sched. 8, para. 125(a), (b); and, as from a day to be appointed, by the *Sexual Offences (Protected Material) Act* 1997, s.9 (insertion of subs. (6)); and the *CJA* 2003, s.41, and Sched. 3, para. 66(1) and (2) (omission of subs. (2)(a) to (c) and the words from "under" to the end of subs. (2)(cc)). The amendment of subs. (2)(cc) came into force on May 9, 2005, in relation to cases sent for trial under s.51 or s.51A of the *CDA* 1998: *Criminal Justice Act 2003 (Commencement No. 9) Order* 2005 (S.I. 2005 No. 1267).]

When a criminal investigation into an offence begins is a question of fact. It may begin before the offence is committed, particularly in a surveillance case or one involving a series of offences: *R. v. Uxbridge Magistrates' Court, ex p. Patel*; *R. v. City of London Magistrates' Court, ex p. Cropper*, 164 J.P. 209, DC. In so far as it decided to the contrary, *R. v. Norfolk Stipendiary Magistrate, ex p. Keable* [1998] Crim.L.R. 510, DC, should not be followed: *ibid*.

General interpretation

12–53 **2.**—(1) References to the accused are to the person mentioned in section 1(1) or (2).

(2) Where there is more than one accused in any proceedings this Part applies separately in relation to each of the accused.

(3) References to the prosecutor are to any person acting as prosecutor, whether an individual or a body.

(4) References to material are to material of all kinds, and in particular include references to—

(a) information, and

(b) objects of all descriptions.

(5) References to recording information are to putting it in a durable or retrievable form (such as writing or tape).

(6) This section applies for the purposes of this Part.

Subsection (3) is apt to include a private prosecutor; this is in accordance with the general principle that a private prosecutor is subject to the same obligations as a minister of justice as are the public prosecuting authorities: *R. v. Belmarsh Magistrates' Court, ex p. Watts* [1999] 2 CrApp.R. 188, DC; *R. (Dacre and Associated Newspapers) v. City of Westminster Magistrates' Court* [2008] 8 *Archbold News* 2, DC.

Criminal Procedure and Investigations Act 1996, ss.3, 4

The main provisions

Initial duty of prosecutor to disclose

12–54 **3.**—(1) The prosecutor must—

(a) disclose to the accused any prosecution material which has not previously been disclosed to the accused and which might reasonably be considered capable of undermining the case for the prosecution against the accused or of assisting the case for the accused, or

(b) give to the accused a written statement that there is no material of a description mentioned in paragraph (a).

(2) For the purposes of this section prosecution material is material—

(a) which is in the prosecutor's possession, and came into his possession in connection with the case for the prosecution against the accused, or

(b) which, in pursuance of a code operative under Part II, he has inspected in connection with the case for the prosecution against the accused.

(3) Where material consists of information which has been recorded in any form the prosecutor discloses it for the purposes of this section—

(a) by securing that a copy is made of it and that the copy is given to the accused, or

(b) if in the prosecutor's opinion that is not practicable or not desirable, by allowing the accused to inspect it at a reasonable time and a reasonable place or by taking steps to secure that he is allowed to do so;

and a copy may be in such form as the prosecutor thinks fit and need not be in the same form as that in which the information has already been recorded.

(4) Where material consists of information which has not been recorded the prosecutor discloses it for the purposes of this section by securing that it is recorded in such form as he thinks fit and—

(a) by securing that a copy is made of it and that the copy is given to the accused, or

(b) if in the prosecutor's opinion that is not practicable or not desirable, by allowing the accused to inspect it at a reasonable time and a reasonable place or by taking steps to secure that he is allowed to do so.

(5) Where material does not consist of information the prosecutor discloses it for the purposes of this section by allowing the accused to inspect it at a reasonable time and a reasonable place or by taking steps to secure that he is allowed to do so.

(6) Material must not be disclosed under this section to the extent that the court, on an application by the prosecutor, concludes it is not in the public interest to disclose it and orders accordingly.

(7) Material must not be disclosed under this section to the extent that it is material the disclosure of which is prohibited by section 17 of the *Regulation of Investigatory Powers Act* 2000.

(8) The prosecutor must act under this section during the period which, by virtue of section 12, is the relevant period for this section.

[This section is printed as amended by the *RIPA* 2000, s.82, and Sched. 4, para. 7; and the *CJA* 2003, ss.32 and 331, and Sched. 36, paras 20 and 21. The "coming into force of the [amendments made by sections 32, 33(1) and (2), 36 to 38 and 39, and Sched. 36, paras 17 to 39, and the repeals effected by Sched. 37, Pt 3] is of no effect in relation to alleged offences into which a criminal investigation within the meaning of section 1(4) of the" 1996 Act began before April 4, 2005: *Criminal Justice Act 2003 (Commencement No. 8 and Transitional and Saving Provisions) Order* 2005 (S.I. 2005 No. 950), Sched. 2, para. 2; and the *Criminal Justice Act 2003 (Commencement No. 13 and Transitional Provisions) Order* 2006 (S.I. 2006 No. 1835). As to this saving, see *ante*, § 12–45.]

Subsections (3) to (5) do not apply in relation to any disclosure required by sections 3, 7 or 9 of this Act if section 3(1) of the *Sexual Offences (Protected Material) Act* 1997 (*post*, § 12–104) applies in relation to that disclosure: *Sexual Offences (Protected Material) Act* 1997, s.9(2) (*post*, § 12–110).

A court has no power to order to make an order as to the extent of primary disclosure **12–54a**
under this section: *R. v. M. (Michael)*, unreported, November 4, 2003, CA ([2003] EWCA Crim. 3764) (as to which, see also *ante*, § 12–51b).

The protocol for the control and management of unused material in the Crown Court states (see paras 4, 18, 30 and 37) that the overarching principle of disclosure is that unused prosecution material will fall to be disclosed if, and only if, it satisfies the test for disclosure; thus not only is there no requirement to disclose material which might not reasonably be considered capable of undermining the case for the prosecution or of assisting the case for the accused (see s.3(1)(a), *ante*), but wider disclosure is an abdication by the prosecution of their statutory responsibility which judges should not allow (Appendix N–52 *et seq.*; see too the Attorney-General's guidelines, para. 44, Appendix A–250, and the protocol for the control and management of heavy fraud and other complex criminal cases, Appendix N–19).

In determining whether material falls within section 3(1)(a), the parties' respective cases must be carefully, but not restrictively, analysed, to ascertain the specific facts the prosecution seek to establish and the specific grounds on which the charges are resisted: *R. v. H.* [2004] 2 A.C. 134, HL. Material may assist the case for the accused not only where it could be used to explain the accused's actions, support his case, or provide material for cross-examination of prosecution witnesses, but also where it might support submissions that could lead to the exclusion of evidence, a stay of proceedings, or a finding that any public authority had acted incompatibly with the accused's rights under the ECHR (see the Attorney-General's guidelines, *ante*, at paras 10 to 14).

Material which has been held to be disclosable under section 3 has included previous convictions of prosecution witnesses (*R. v. Vasilou* [2000] Crim.L.R. 845, CA, and *R. v. Underwood* [2003] 6 *Archbold News* 1, CA, in each of which it was assumed that these were covered by the Act); the identity of persons who might have witnessed an incident giving rise to criminal charges, including those who dial 999 to report such an incident (*R. v. Heggart* [2001] 4 *Archbold News* 2, CA); and information as to the reward to be paid, after the trial, to a registered police informant who was a prosecution witness (*R. v. Allan* [2005] Crim.L.R. 716, CA), or to a co-defendant giving evidence for the prosecution (*R. v. Smith* [2004] 8 *Archbold News* 1, CA, where the information could have had a causative effect on a tenable abuse argument).

As to whether section 3 requires disclosure of the results of a preliminary roadside breath test under the *RTA* 1988, s.6A, see *Smith v. DPP* [2007] R.T.R. 36, DC (*post*, § 32–89a).

Initial duty to disclose: further provisions

12–55 **4.**—(1) This section applies where—

(a) the prosecutor acts under section 3, and

(b) before so doing he was given a document in pursuance of provision included, by virtue of section 24(3), in a code operative under Part II.

(2) In such a case the prosecutor must give the document to the accused at the same time as the prosecutor acts under section 3.

[This section is printed as amended by the *CJA* 2003, s.331, and Sched. 36, paras 20, and 22.]

Criminal Procedure and Investigations Act 1996, ss.5, 6

Compulsory disclosure by accused

12–56 **5.**—(1) Subject to subsections *(2) to* [(3A) and] (4), this section applies where—

(a) this Part applies by virtue of section 1(2), and

(b) the prosecutor complies with section 3 or purports to comply with it.

(2) *Where this Part applies by virtue of section 1(2)(b), this section does not apply unless—*

(a) *a copy of the notice of transfer, and*

(b) *copies of the documents containing the evidence,*

have been given to the accused under regulations made under section 5(9) of the Criminal Justice Act *1987.*

(3) *Where this Part applies by virtue of section 1(2)(c), this section does not apply unless—*

(a) *a copy of the notice of transfer, and*

(b) *copies of the documents containing the evidence,*

have been given to the accused under regulations made under paragraph 4 of Schedule 6 to the Criminal Justice Act *1991.*

(3A) Where this Part applies by virtue of section 1(2)(cc), this section does not apply unless—

(a) copies of the documents containing the evidence have been served on the accused under regulations made under paragraph 1 of Schedule 3 to the *Crime and Disorder Act* 1998; and

(b) a copy of the notice under *subsection (7) of section 51* [subsection (1) of section 51D] of that Act has been served on him under that subsection.

(4) Where this Part applies by virtue of section 1(2)(e), this section does not apply unless the prosecutor has served on the accused a copy of the indictment and a copy of the set of documents containing the evidence which is the basis of the charge.

(5) Where this section applies, the accused must give a defence statement to the court and the prosecutor.

[(5A) Where there are other accused in the proceedings and the court so orders, the accused must also give a defence statement to each other accused specified by the court.

(5B) The court may make an order under subsection (5A) either of its own motion or on the application of any party.]

(5C) A defence statement that has to be given to the court and the prosecutor (under subsection (5)) must be given during the period which, by virtue of section 12, is the relevant period for this section.

[(5D) A defence statement that has to be given to a co-accused (under subsection (5A)) must be given within such period as the court may specify.]

[This section is printed as amended by the *CDA* 1998, s.119, and Sched. 8, para. 126; and the *CJA* 2003, ss.33(1) and 331, and Sched. 36, paras 20 and 23; and as amended, as from a day to be appointed, by *ibid.*, ss.33(1) (insertion of subss. (5A), (5B) and (5D)) and 41, and Sched. 3, para. 66(1) and (3) (substitution of words in square brackets for italicised words in subss. (1) and (3A), omission of subss. (2) and (3)). The amendment of subs. (3A) came into force on May 9, 2005, in relation to cases sent for trial under the *CDA* 1998, s.51A(3)(d): *Criminal Justice Act 2003 (Commencement No. 9) Order* 2005 (S.I. 2005 No. 1267). As to the saving of the legislation prior to its amendment by the 2003 Act in relation to criminal investigations begun before April 4, 2005, see the note to s.3, *ante*, § 12–54.]

Voluntary disclosure by accused

6.—(1) This section applies where— **12–57**

(a) this Part applies by virtue of section 1(1), and

(b) the prosecutor complies with section 3 or purports to comply with it.

(2) The accused—

(a) may give a defence statement to the prosecutor, and

(b) if he does so, must also give such a statement to the court.

(4) If the accused gives a defence statement under this section he must give it during the period which, by virtue of section 12, is the relevant period for this section.

[Subs. (3) was repealed by the *CJA* 2003, s.331, and Sched. 36, paras 20 and 24. As to the saving provision in respect of this repeal, see the note to s.3, *ante*, § 12–54.]

Criminal Procedure and Investigations Act 1996, ss.6A–6E

Contents of defence statement

6A.—(1) For the purposes of this Part a defence statement is a written statement— **12–57a**

(a) setting out the nature of the accused's defence, including any particular defences on which he intends to rely,

(b) indicating the matters of fact on which he takes issue with the prosecution,

(c) setting out, in the case of each such matter, why he takes issue with the prosecution,

[(ca) setting out particulars of the matters of fact on which he intends to rely for the purposes of his defence,] and

(d) indicating any point of law (including any point as to the admissibility of evidence or an abuse of process) which he wishes to take, and any authority on which he intends to rely for that purpose.

(2) A defence statement that discloses an alibi must give particulars of it, including—

(a) the name, address and date of birth of any witness the accused believes is able to give evidence in support of the alibi, or as many of those details as are known to the accused when the statement is given;

(b) any information in the accused's possession which might be of material assistance in identifying or finding any such witness in whose case any of the details mentioned in paragraph (a) are not known to the accused when the statement is given.

(3) For the purposes of this section evidence in support of an alibi is evidence tending to show that by reason of the presence of the accused at a particular place or in a particular area at a particular time he was not, or was unlikely to have been, at the place where the offence is alleged to have been committed at the time of its alleged commission.

(4) The Secretary of State may by regulations make provision as to the details of the matters that, by virtue of subsection (1), are to be included in defence statements.

[This section was inserted by the *CJA* 2003, s.33(2). As to the saving provision in relation to this amendment, see the note to s.3, *ante*, § 12–54. Subs. (1)(ca) is inserted, as from a day to be appointed, by the *CJIA* 2008, s.60(1).]

Whilst it is good practice for a defence statement to be signed by the defendant (*R. v. Wheeler* [2001] 1 Cr.App.R. 10, CA), a judge has no power to issue a practice direction to the effect that defence statements must be signed by the defendant. However, where a defence statement is unsigned a judge may require the defendant to satisfy him that he has complied with his obligations under the Act by confirming that the document really is his statement: *R. (Sullivan) v. Maidstone Crown Court* [2002] 2 Cr.App.R. 31, DC.

Guidance issued by the Bar Council as to the duties of counsel in relation to the preparation of defence statements is set out at § 12–99a, *post*.

A defence statement that consisted in merely a general denial of the counts in the indictment accompanied by the assertion that the defendant took issue with any witness purporting to give evidence contrary to his denials did not meet the purpose of a defence statement and was described as woefully inadequate in *R. v. Bryant*, unreported, July 28, 2005, CA ([2005] EWCA Crim. 2079). Judges are urged by the protocol for the control and management of unused material in the Crown Court to ensure that defence statements comply with the requirements of section 6A, and, if they do not, to consider giving a warning under section 6E (*post*, § 12–57e) that an adverse inference might be drawn (Appendix N–56).

[Updated disclosure by accused

12–57b **6B.**—(1) Where the accused has, before the beginning of the relevant period for this section, given a defence statement under section 5, or 6, he must during that period give to the court and the prosecutor either—

(a) a defence statement under this section (an "updated defence statement"), or

(b) a statement of the kind mentioned in subsection (4).

(2) The relevant period for this section is determined under section 12.

(3) An updated defence statement must comply with the requirements imposed by or under section 6A by reference to the state of affairs at the time when the statement is given.

(4) Instead of an updated defence statement, the accused may give a written statement stating that he has no changes to make to the defence statement which was given under section 5, or 6.

(5) Where there are other accused in the proceedings and the court so orders, the accused must also give either an updated defence statement or a statement of the kind mentioned in subsection (4), within such period as may be specified by the court, to each other accused so specified.

(6) The court may make an order under subsection (5) either of its own motion or on the application of any party.]

[This section is inserted, as from a day to be appointed, by the *CJA* 2003, s.33(3).]

[Notification of intention to call defence witnesses

12–57c **6C.**—(1) The accused must give to the court and the prosecutor a notice indicating whether he intends to call any persons (other than himself) as witnesses at his trial and, if so—

(a) giving the name, address and date of birth of each such proposed witness, or as many of those details as are known to the accused when the notice is given;

(b) providing any information in the accused's possession which might be of material assistance in identifying or finding any such proposed witness in whose case any of the details mentioned in paragraph (a) are not known to the accused when the notice is given.

(2) Details do not have to be given under this section to the extent that they have already been given under section 6A(2).

(3) The accused must give a notice under this section during the period which, by virtue of section 12, is the relevant period for this section.

(4) If, following the giving of a notice under this section, the accused—

(a) decides to call a person (other than himself) who is not included in the notice as a proposed witness, or decides not to call a person who is so included, or

(b) discovers any information which, under subsection (1), he would have had to include in the notice if he had been aware of it when giving the notice,

he must give an appropriately amended notice to the court and the prosecutor.]

[This section is inserted, as from a day to be appointed, by the *CJA* 2003, s.34.]

As to whether—in advance of the commencement of this section—rule 3.5(1) of the *Criminal Procedure Rules* 2005 (S.I. 2005 No. 384), when read with rule 3.10 and the overriding objective in rule 1.1 (*ante*, §§ 4–84d, 4–84e, 4–84b respectively), confers on a court a power to make an unconditional direction that "the defence" are to disclose to the prosecution full details of all defence witnesses, see *R. (Kelly) v. Warley Magistrates' Court* [2008] 1 Cr.App.R. 14, DC (*ante*, § 4–84a).

[Notification of names of experts instructed by accused

6D.—(1) If the accused instructs a person with a view to his providing any expert opinion for possible use as evidence at the trial of the accused, he must give to the court and the prosecutor a notice specifying the person's name and address. **12–57d**

(2) A notice does not have to be given under this section specifying the name and address of a person whose name and address have already been given under section 6C.

(3) A notice under this section must be given during the period which, by virtue of section 12, is the relevant period for this section.]

[This section is inserted, as from a day to be appointed, by the *CJA* 2003, s.35.]

Disclosure by accused: further provisions

6E.—(1) Where an accused's solicitor purports to give on behalf of the accused— **12–57e**

(a) a defence statement under section 5, 6, or 6B, or

(b) a statement of the kind mentioned in section 6B(4),

the statement shall, unless the contrary is proved, be deemed to be given with the authority of the accused.

(2) If it appears to the judge at a pre-trial hearing that an accused has failed to comply fully with section 5, 6B, or 6C, so that there is a possibility of comment being made or inferences drawn under section 11(5), he shall warn the accused accordingly.

(3) In subsection (2) "pre-trial hearing" has the same meaning as in Part 4 (see section 39).

(4) The judge in a trial before a judge and jury—

(a) may direct that the jury be given a copy of any defence statement, and

(b) if he does so, may direct that it be edited so as not to include references to matters evidence of which would be inadmissible.

(5) A direction under subsection (4)—

(a) may be made either of the judge's own motion or on the application of any party;

(b) may be made only if the judge is of the opinion that seeing a copy of the defence statement would help the jury to understand the case or to resolve any issue in the case.

(6) The reference in subsection (4) to a defence statement is a reference—

(a) where the accused has given only an initial defence statement (that is, a defence statement given under section 5 or 6), to that statement;

(b) where he has given both an initial defence statement and an updated defence statement (that is, a defence statement given under section 6B), to the updated defence statement;

(c) where he has given both an initial defence statement and a statement of the kind mentioned in section 6B(4), to the initial defence statement.

[This section was inserted by the *CJA* 2003, s.36. As to the saving provision in relation to this amendment, see the note to s.3, *ante*, § 12–54.]

Criminal Procedure and Investigations Act 1996, ss.7–9

Secondary disclosure by prosecutor

7. [*Repealed by* CJA *2003, s.331, and Sched. 36, paras 20 and 25. As to the saving provision in relation to this repeal, see the note to s.3*, ante, *§ 12–54*.] **12–58**

Continuing duty of prosecutor to disclose

7A.—(1) This section applies at all times— **12–58a**

(a) after the prosecutor has complied with section 3 or purported to comply with it, and

(b) before the accused is acquitted or convicted or the prosecutor decides not to proceed with the case concerned.

(2) The prosecutor must keep under review the question whether at any given time (and, in particular, following the giving of a defence statement) there is prosecution material which—

(a) might reasonably be considered capable of undermining the case for the prosecution against the accused or of assisting the case for the accused, and

(b) has not been disclosed to the accused.

(3) If at any time there is any such material as is mentioned in subsection (2) the prosecutor must disclose it to the accused as soon as is reasonably practicable (or within the period mentioned in subsection (5)(a), where that applies).

(4) In applying subsection (2) by reference to any given time the state of affairs at that time (including the case for the prosecution as it stands at that time) must be taken into account.

(5) Where the accused gives a defence statement under section 5, 6, or 6B—

(a) if as a result of that statement the prosecutor is required by this section to make any disclosure, or further disclosure, he must do so during the period which, by virtue of section 12, is the relevant period for this section;

(b) if the prosecutor considers that he is not so required, he must during that period give to the accused a written statement to that effect.

(6) For the purposes of this section prosecution material is material—

(a) which is in the prosecutor's possession and came into his possession in connection with the case for the prosecution against the accused, or

(b) which, in pursuance of a code operative under Part 2, he has inspected in connection with the case for the prosecution against the accused.

(7) Subsections (3) to (5) of section 3 (method by which prosecutor discloses) apply for the purposes of this section as they apply for the purposes of that.

(8) Material must not be disclosed under this section to the extent that the court, on an application by the prosecutor, concludes it is not in the public interest to disclose it and orders accordingly.

(9) Material must not be disclosed under this section to the extent that it is material the disclosure of which is prohibited by section 17 of the *Regulation of Investigatory Powers Act* 2000.

[This section was inserted by the *CJA* 2003, s.37. As to the saving provision in relation to this amendment, see the note to s.3, *ante*, § 12–54.]

12–58b Subject to any issue of public interest immunity, the prosecution have an obligation to disclose a defendant's defence statement to a co-defendant if it might reasonably be expected to assist the co-defendant's defence: *R. v. Cairns* [2003] 1 Cr.App.R. 38, CA. And as to the requirement that a prosecutor's response to a defence application for a witness anonymity order should include confirmation that the prosecution have considered whether the continuing duty to disclose material under this section has been triggered by the application, see paragraph I.15.9 of the consolidated criminal practice direction, *ante*, § 8–71r.

In *R. v. Makin* (2004) 148 S.J. 821, CA, it was said that the duty of disclosure continues so long as proceedings remain whether at first instance or on appeal. In relation to the post-trial period, such duty must derive from the general common law duty of the prosecution to act fairly and to assist in the administration of justice (as to which, see *R. v. Banks* [1916] 2 K.B. 621 at 623, 12 Cr.App.R. 74 at 76, CCA; *Dallison v. Caffery* [1965] 1 Q.B. 348 at 369, DC; *R. v. Brown (Winston)* [1998] A.C. 367 at 374, HL; *R. v. Mills and Poole* [1998] A.C. 382, HL; *R. v. Ward*, 96 Cr.App.R. 1, CA), as it plainly does not derive from the 1996 Act.

Application by accused for disclosure

12–59 **8.**—(1) This section applies where the accused has given a defence statement under section 5, 6, or 6B and the prosecutor has complied with section 7A(5) or has purported to comply with it or has failed to comply with it.

(2) If the accused has at any time reasonable cause to believe that there is prosecution

material which is required by section 7A to be disclosed to him and has not been, he may apply to the court for an order requiring the prosecutor to disclose it to him.

(3) For the purposes of this section prosecution material is material—

(a) which is in the prosecutor's possession and came into his possession in connection with the case for the prosecution against the accused,

(b) which, in pursuance of a code operative under Part II, he has inspected in connection with the case for the prosecution against the accused, or

(c) which falls within subsection (4).

(4) Material falls within this subsection if in pursuance of a code operative under Part II the prosecutor must, if he asks for the material, be given a copy of it or be allowed to inspect it in connection with the case for the prosecution against the accused.

(5) [*Identical to s.3(6),* ante, *§ 12–54.*]

(6) [*Identical to s.3(7),* ante, *§ 12–54 (including the amendment).*]

[This section is printed as amended by the *CJA* 2003, s.38. As to the saving provision in relation to this amendment, see the note to s.3, *ante*, § 12–54.]

Applications for disclosure under this section do not of themselves raise a "question of law relating to the case" within the terms of section 9(3)(c) of the *CJA* 1987 (*ante*, § 4–84m), or section 31(3)(c) of the *CPIA* 1996 (*ante*, § 4–84v), and thus do not fall within the ambit of a preparatory hearing under either Act: *R. v. H.* [2007] 2 A.C. 270, HL (*ante*, § 4–85f).

The procedure for an application under this section is to be found in the *Criminal Procedure Rules* 2005 (S.I. 2005 No. 384), r.25.6 (*post*, § 12–84). No application can be made unless a defence statement has been served; but late service is sufficient (*DPP v. Wood; DPP v. McGillicuddy*, 170 J.P. 177, DC). Judges are urged by the protocol for the control and management of unused material in the Crown Court to reject any application which is not referable to any issue in the case identified by the defence statement or is otherwise not in accordance with rule 25.6 (see Appendix N–56); similarly, disclosure of material concerning the accuracy of a breath-testing device should have been refused where the defence statement did not raise an issue to which reliability was relevant (*DPP v. Wood; DPP v. McGillicuddy, ante*).

"The prosecutor", for the purposes of subsection (3), is defined in section 2(3) (*ante*, § 12–53); in a prosecution by the CPS for an offence of driving with excess alcohol it was not the police, nor the third party with a contract to provide the police with breath-testing devices; there was thus no power to order disclosure of material in the possession of the third party (*DPP v. Wood; DPP v. McGillicuddy, ante*).

Continuing duty of prosecutor to disclose

9. [*Repealed by* CJA *2003, s.331, and Sched. 36, paras 20 and 26. As to the saving provision in relation to this repeal, see the note to s.3,* ante, *§ 12–54.*] **12–60**

Criminal Procedure and Investigations Act 1996, ss.10, 11

Prosecutor's failure to observe time limits

10.—(1) This section applies if the prosecutor— **12–61**

(a) purports to act under section 3 after the end of the period which, by virtue of section 12, is the relevant period for section 3, or

(b) purports to act under section 7A(5) after the end of the period which, by virtue of section 12, is the relevant period for section 7A.

(2) Subject to subsection (3), the failure to act during the period concerned does not on its own constitute grounds for staying the proceedings for abuse of process.

(3) Subsection (2) does not prevent the failure constituting such grounds if it involves such delay by the prosecutor that the accused is denied a fair trial.

[This section is printed as amended by the *CJA* 2003, s.331, and Sched. 36, paras 20 and 27. As to the saving provision in relation to this amendment, see the note to s.3, *ante*, § 12–54.]

Faults in disclosure by accused

11.—(1) This section applies in the three cases set out in subsections (2), (3) and (4). **12–62**

(2) The first case is where section 5 applies and the accused—

(a) fails to give an initial defence statement,

(b) gives an initial defence statement but does so after the end of the period which, by virtue of section 12, is the relevant period for section 5,

(c) is required by section 6B to give either an updated defence statement or a statement of the kind mentioned in subsection (4) of that section but fails to do so,

(d) gives an updated defence statement or a statement of the kind mentioned in section 6B(4) but does so after the end of the period which, by virtue of section 12, is the relevant period for section 6B,

(e) sets out inconsistent defences in his defence statement, or

(f) at his trial—

(i) puts forward a defence which was not mentioned in his defence statement or is different from any defence set out in that statement,

(ii) relies on a matter [(or any particular of any matter of fact)] which, in breach of the requirements imposed by or under section 6A, was not mentioned in his defence statement,

(iii) adduces evidence in support of an alibi without having given particulars of the alibi in his defence statement, or

(iv) calls a witness to give evidence in support of an alibi without having complied with section 6A(2)(a) or (b) as regards the witness in his defence statement.

(3) The second case is wheresection 6 applies, the accused gives an initial defence statement, and the accused—

(a) gives the initial defence statement after the end of the period which, by virtue of section 12, is the relevant period for section 6, or

(b) does any of the things mentioned in paragraphs (c) to (f) of subsection (2).

[(4) The third case is where the accused—

(a) gives a witness notice but does so after the end of the period which, by virtue of section 12, is the relevant period for section 6C, or

(b) at his trial calls a witness (other than himself) not included, or not adequately identified, in a witness notice.]

(5) Where this section applies—

(a) the court or any other party may make such comment as appears appropriate;

(b) the court or jury may draw such inferences as appear proper in deciding whether the accused is guilty of the offence concerned.

(6) Where—

(a) this section applies by virtue of subsection (2)(f)(ii) (including that provision as it applies by virtue of subsection (3)(b)), and

(b) the matter which was not mentioned is a point of law (including any point as to the admissibility of evidence or an abuse of process) or an authority,

comment by another party under subsection (5)(a) may be made only with the leave of the court.

[(7) Where this section applies by virtue of subsection (4), comment by another party under subsection (5)(a) may be made only with the leave of the court.]

(8) Where the accused puts forward a defence which is different from any defence set out in his defence statement, in doing anything under subsection (5) or in deciding whether to do anything under it the court shall have regard—

(a) to the extent of the differences in the defences, and

(b) to whether there is any justification for it.

(9) Where the accused calls a witness whom he has failed to include, or to identify adequately, in a witness notice, in doing anything under subsection (5) or in deciding whether to do anything under it the court shall have regard to whether there is any justification for the failure.

(10) A person shall not be convicted of an offence solely on an inference drawn under subsection (5).

[(11) Where the accused has given a statement of the kind mentioned in section 6B(4), then, for the purposes of subsections (2)(f)(ii) and (iv), the question as to whether there has been a breach of the requirements imposed by or under section 6A or a failure to comply with section 6A(2)(a) or (b) shall be determined—

(a) by reference to the state of affairs at the time when that statement was given, and

(b) as if the defence statement was given at the same time as that statement.]

(12) In this section—

(a) "initial defence statement" means a defence statement given under section 5, or 6;

(b) "updated defence statement" means a defence statement given under section 6B;

(c) a reference simply to an accused's "defence statement" is a reference—

(i) where he has given only an initial defence statement, to that statement;

(ii) where he has given both an initial and an updated defence statement, to the updated defence statement;

(iii) where he has given both an initial defence statement and a statement of the kind mentioned in section 6B(4), to the initial defence statement;

(d) a reference to evidence in support of an alibi shall be construed in accordance with section 6A(3);

(e) "witness notice" means a notice given under section 6C.

[This section is printed as substituted by the *CJA* 2003, s.39, save that subss. (4), (7) and (11) had not been brought into force as at October 1, 2008. As to the saving provision in relation to this amendment, see the note to s.3, *ante*, § 12–54. The words in square brackets in subs. (2)(f)(ii) are inserted, as from a day to be appointed, by the *CJIA* 2008, s.60(2).]

Section 11 does not disallow, or require leave for, cross-examination of an accused on differences between his defence at trial and his defence statement: *R. v. Tibbs* [2000] 2 Cr.App.R. 309, CA (decided under the previous version of s.11, which required the leave of the court to be obtained before making such comment as appeared appropriate whenever the section applied). Such cross-examination may now be assisted by an application under section 6E(5) (*ante*, § 12–57e) for the jury to be given a copy of the defence statement. Prosecutors are encouraged by the protocol for the control and management of unused material in the Crown Court to consider commenting upon failures in defence disclosure in suitable cases more readily than was the practice in respect of investigations which commenced before April 4, 2005 (Appendix N–56).

No use should be made of a defence statement if the defendant denies knowledge of it and it cannot be shown that he knew of its contents: *R. v. V.* (2005) 149 S.J. 301, CA. In *R. v. Wheeler* [2001] 1 Cr.App.R. 10, CA, it was held that where the defendant, upon being confronted with a contradiction between his evidence and the statement, asserts that the latter contains a mistake, a judge would be wise to raise the issue with counsel and, if appropriate, to direct the jury to accept the defendant's evidence as to the statement. Following the insertion of section 6E, *ante*, it would appear that in such cases the burden would now be on the defendant to prove his lack of knowledge and the mistake respectively.

Criminal Procedure and Investigations Act 1996, ss.12, 13

Time limits

Time limits

12.—(1) This section has effect for the purpose of determining the relevant period for sections 3, 5, 6, 6B, 6C, and 7A(5). **12–63**

(2) Subject to subsection (3), the relevant period is a period beginning and ending with such days as the Secretary of State prescribes by regulations for the purposes of the section concerned.

(3) The regulations may do one or more of the following—

(a) provide that the relevant period for any section shall if the court so orders be extended (or further extended) by so many days as the court specifies;

(b) provide that the court may only make such an order if an application is made by a prescribed person and if any other prescribed conditions are fulfilled;

(c) provide that an application may only be made if prescribed conditions are fulfilled;

(d) provide that the number of days by which a period may be extended shall be entirely at the court's discretion;

(e) provide that the number of days by which a period may be extended shall not exceed a prescribed number;

(f) provide that there shall be no limit on the number of applications that may be made to extend a period;

(g) provide that no more than a prescribed number of applications may be made to extend a period;

and references to the relevant period for a section shall be construed accordingly.

(4) Conditions mentioned in subsection (3) may be framed by reference to such factors as the Secretary of State thinks fit.

(5) Without prejudice to the generality of subsection (4), so far as the relevant period for section 3 or 7A(5) is concerned—

(a) conditions may be framed by reference to the nature or volume of the material concerned;

(b) the nature of material may be defined by reference to the prosecutor's belief that the question of non-disclosure on grounds of public interest may arise.

(6) In subsection (3) "prescribed" means prescribed by regulations under this section.

[This section is printed as amended by the *CJA* 2003, s.331, and Sched. 36, paras 20 and 28. As to the saving provision in relation to this amendment, see the note to s.3, *ante*, § 12–54.]

For regulations made under this subsection, see *post*, §§ 12–94 *et seq.*

Time limits: transitional

12–64 **13.**—(1) As regards a case in relation to which no regulations under section 12 have come into force for the purposes of section 3, section 3(8) shall have effect as if it read—

"(8) The prosecutor must act under this section as soon as is reasonably practicable after—

(a) *the accused pleads not guilty (where this Part applies by virtue of section 1(1)),*

(b) *the accused is committed for trial (where this Part applies by virtue of section 1(2)(a)),*

(c) *the proceedings are transferred (where this Part applies by virtue of section 1(2)(b) or (c)),*

(ca) copies of the documents containing the evidence on which the charge or charges are based are served on the accused (where this Part applies by virtue of section 1(2)(cc)),

(d) the count is included in the indictment (where this Part applies by virtue of section 1(2)(d)), or

(e) the bill of indictment is preferred (where this Part applies by virtue of section 1(2)(e) or (f))."

(2) As regards a case in relation to which no regulations under section 12 have come into force for the purposes of section 7A, section 7A(5) shall have effect as if—

(a) in paragraph (a) for the words from "during the period" to the end, and

(b) in paragraph (b) for "during that period",

there were substituted "as soon as is reasonably practicable after the accused gives the statement in question".

[This section is printed as amended by the *CDA* 1998, s.119, and Sched. 8, para. 127(b); the *Access to Justice Act* 1999, s.67(2); and the *CJA* 2003, s.331, and Sched. 36, paras 20 and 29. As to the saving provision in relation to the latter amendment, see the note to s.3, *ante*, § 12–54. The section is further amended, as from a day to be appointed, by the *CJA* 2003, s.41, and Sched. 3, para. 66 (repeal of subss. (a) to (c) of the modified s.3(8)).]

Criminal Procedure and Investigations Act 1996, ss.14–16

Public interest

Public interest: review for summary trials

12–65 **14.**—(1) This section applies where this Part applies by virtue of section 1(1).

(2) At any time—

(a) after a court makes an order under section 3(6), 7A(8) or 8(5), and

(b) before the accused is acquitted or convicted or the prosecutor decides not to proceed with the case concerned, the accused may apply to the court for a review of the question whether it is still not in the public interest to disclose material affected by its order.

(3) In such a case the court must review that question, and if it concludes that it is in the public interest to disclose material to any extent—

(a) it shall so order, and

(b) it shall take such steps as are reasonable to inform the prosecutor of its order.

(4) Where the prosecutor is informed of an order made under subsection (3) he must act accordingly having regard to the provisions of this Part (unless he decides not to proceed with the case concerned).

[This section is printed as amended by the *CJA* 2003, s.331, and Sched. 36, paras 20, and 30. As to the saving provision in relation to this amendment, see the note to s.3, *ante*, § 12–54.]

Public interest: review in other cases

15.—(1) This section applies where this Part applies by virtue of section 1(2). **12–66**

(2) This section applies at all times—

(a) after a court makes an order under section 3(6), 7A(8) or 8(5), and

(b) before the accused is acquitted or convicted or the prosecutor decides not to proceed with the case concerned.

(3) The court must keep under review the question whether at any given time it is still not in the public interest to disclose material affected by its order.

(4) The court must keep the question mentioned in subsection (3) under review without the need for an application; but the accused may apply to the court for a review of that question.

(5) If the court at any time concludes that it is in the public interest to disclose material to any extent—

(a) it shall so order, and

(b) it shall take such steps as are reasonable to inform the prosecutor of its order.

(6) [*Identical to s.14(4),* ante, *§ 12–65, save for* "(5)" *in lieu of* "(3)".]

[This section is printed as amended by the *CJA* 2003, s.331, and Sched. 36, paras 20 and 31. As to the saving provision in relation to this amendment, see the note to s.3, *ante*, § 12–54.]

Applications: opportunity to be heard

16. Where— **12–67**

(a) an application is made under section 3(6), 7A(8), 8(5), 14(2) or 15(4),

(b) a person claiming to have an interest in the material applies to be heard by the court, and

(c) he shows that he was involved (whether alone or with others and whether directly or indirectly) in the prosecutor's attention being brought to the material,

the court must not make an order under section 3(6), 7A(8), 8(5), 14(3) or 15(5) (as the case may be) unless the person applying under paragraph (b) has been given an opportunity to be heard.

[This section is printed as amended by the *CJA* 2003, s.331, and Sched. 36, paras 20 and 32. As to the saving provision in relation to this amendment, see the note to s.3, *ante*, § 12–54.]

For the requirement to give notice to a person who may fall within this section, see the *Criminal Procedure Rules* 2005 (S.I. 2005 No. 384), r.25.5 (*post*, § 12–83).

Criminal Procedure and Investigations Act 1996, ss.17, 18

Confidentiality

Confidentiality of disclosed information

17.—(1) If the accused is given or allowed to inspect a document or other object under— **12–68**

(a) section 3, 4, 7A, 14 or 15, or

(b) an order under section 8,

then, subject to subsections (2) to (4), he must not use or disclose it or any information recorded in it.

(2) The accused may use or disclose the object or information—

(a) in connection with the proceedings for whose purposes he was given the object or allowed to inspect it,

(b) with a view to the taking of further criminal proceedings (for instance, by way of appeal) with regard to the matter giving rise to the proceedings mentioned in paragraph (a), or

(c) in connection with the proceedings first mentioned in paragraph (b).

(3) The accused may use or disclose—

(a) the object to the extent that it has been displayed to the public in open court, or

(b) the information to the extent that it has been communicated to the public in open court;

but the preceding provisions of this subsection do not apply if the object is displayed or the information is communicated in proceedings to deal with a contempt of court under section 18.

(4) If—

(a) the accused applies to the court for an order granting permission to use or disclose the object or information, and

(b) the court makes such an order,

the accused may use or disclose the object or information for the purpose and to the extent specified by the court.

(5) An application under subsection (4) may be made and dealt with at any time, and in particular after the accused has been acquitted or convicted or the prosecutor has decided not to proceed with the case concerned; but this is subject to rules made by virtue of section 19(2).

(6) Where—

(a) an application is made under subsection (4), and

(b) the prosecutor or a person claiming to have an interest in the object or information applies to be heard by the court,

the court must not make an order granting permission unless the person applying under paragraph (b) has been given an opportunity to be heard.

(7) References in this section to the court are to—

(a) a magistrates' court, where this Part applies by virtue of section 1(1);

(b) the Crown Court, where this Part applies by virtue of section 1(2).

(8) Nothing in this section affects any other restriction or prohibition on the use or disclosure of an object or information, whether the restriction or prohibition arises under an enactment (whenever passed) or otherwise.

[This section is printed as amended by the *CJA* 2003, s.331, and Sched. 36, paras 20 and 33. As to the saving provision in relation to this amendment, see the note to s.3, *ante*, § 12–54.]

This section does not apply to any material disclosed under the *Sexual Offences (Protected Material) Act* 1997 in accordance with section 3(2) or (3) of that Act (which is subject instead to the greater restrictions imposed by section 8 of that Act): *Sexual Offences (Protected Material) Act* 1997, s.9(3). Other disclosure not falling within section 17(1) (such as that made before "the relevant time", *ante*, § 12–47) is subject to an implied undertaking not to use the material for any purposes other than the proper conduct of the particular case (*Taylor v. Director of the Serous Fraud Office* [1999] 2 A.C. 177, HL).

12–68a Where material has been inadvertently disclosed, there is no reason in principle why the Crown Court should not restrain the use of the material, although the particular circumstances of the case which dictate whether justice requires an order, will be different; and, in particular, in a criminal case where there is more than one defendant, regard must be had to the position both as between prosecution and defendants, and as between defendants: *R. v. G. and B.* [2004] 2 Cr.App.R. 37, CA. Before making an order restraining use of material inadvertently disclosed, regard must be had to the potential consequences, which were (in a case where there had been disclosure to counsel for two of five defendants), first, that counsel in the know would be unable to discuss the sensitive information with their client, obtain their instructions as to its accuracy, advise their client about his rights in relation to it, or use it in cross-examination or otherwise; secondly, that it would be necessary for lawyers in the know to take care not to let slip the sensitive material to their clients or anyone else not in the know, including counsel for the other defendants, otherwise they would be in contempt; thirdly, that policing the behaviour of those restrained would be virtually impossible, particularly bearing in mind that any communication to the client would be protected by legal privilege; fourthly, that the relationship between the lawyer in the know and his client would be bound to be damaged because, in addition to preventing frankness and fettering the free flow of information between lawyer and client, the order would be likely to nurture in the client a belief that his lawyers are putting other interests, possibly including those of the prosecution, above his own; and a client's perception of the relationship is a matter of importance; fifthly, that, the judge having a continuing duty to keep the public interest immunity order under review, submissions from those in the know would be entirely artificial if they were prevented from referring to the material in question; finally, that the creation of an "asymmetrical Chinese wall" between some but not all of the lawyers and their clients would make it impossible for the other defendants, whose lawyers were not in the know, to avoid a sense of unfairness if those representing their co-accused were in possession of information which was denied to their lawyers and which might be of benefit to the conduct of their defence: *ibid*.

Confidentiality: contravention

18.—(1) It is a contempt of court for a person knowingly to use or disclose an object or information recorded in it if the use or disclosure is in contravention of section 17. **12–69**

(2) The following courts have jurisdiction to deal with a person who is guilty of a contempt under this section—

(a) a magistrates' court, where this Part applies by virtue of section 1(1);

(b) the Crown Court, where this Part applies by virtue of section 1(2).

(3) A person who is guilty of a contempt under this section may be dealt with as follows—

(a) a magistrates' court may commit him to custody for a specified period not exceeding six months or impose on him a fine not exceeding £5,000 or both;

(b) the Crown Court may commit him to custody for a specified period not exceeding two years or impose a fine on him or both.

(4) If—

(a) a person is guilty of a contempt under this section, and

(b) the object concerned is in his possession,

the court finding him guilty may order that the object shall be forfeited and dealt with in such manner as the court may order.

(5) The power of the court under subsection (4) includes power to order the object to be destroyed or to be given to the prosecutor or to be placed in his custody for such period as the court may specify.

(6) If—

(a) the court proposes to make an order under subsection (4), and

(b) the person found guilty, or any other person claiming to have an interest in the object, applies to be heard by the court,

the court must not make the order unless the applicant has been given an opportunity to be heard.

(7) If—

(a) a person is guilty of a contempt under this section, and

(b) a copy of the object concerned is in his possession,

the court finding him guilty may order that the copy shall be forfeited and dealt with in such manner as the court may order.

(8) Subsections (5) and (6) apply for the purposes of subsection (7) as they apply for the purposes of subsection (4), but as if references to the object were references to the copy.

(9) [*Civil proceedings*.]

(10) The powers of a magistrates' court under this section may be exercised either of the court's own motion or by order on complaint.

This section does not apply to any material disclosed under the *Sexual Offences (Protected Material) Act* 1997 in accordance with section 3(2) or (3) of that Act: *Sexual Offences (Protected Material) Act* 1997, s.9(3).

Criminal Procedure and Investigations Act 1996, ss.19–21

12–69a **19.** [*Provision for rules of court.*]

For criminal procedure rules made pursuant to this subsection, see *post*, §§ 12–77 *et seq.*

Other statutory rules as to disclosure

12–70 **20.**—(1) A duty under any of the disclosure provisions shall not affect or be affected by any duty arising under any other enactment with regard to material to be provided to or by the accused or a person representing him; but this is subject to subsection (2).

(3), (4) [*Make corresponding provision in relation to expert evidence in magistrates' courts as* Police and Criminal Evidence Act *1984, s.81* (ante, *§ 10–62) made for Crown Court.*]

(5) For the purposes of this section—

(a) the disclosure provisions are sections 3 to 8;

(b) "enactment" includes an enactment comprised in subordinate legislation (which here has the same meaning as in the *Interpretation Act* 1978).

[This section is printed as amended, and repealed in part, by the *CJA* 2003, s.331, and Sched. 36, paras 20 and 35. As to the saving provision in relation to this amendment, see the note to s.3, *ante*, § 12–54.]

As to the limitation of subsection (1), see the *Sexual Offences (Protected Material) Act* 1997, s.9(2), *post*, § 12–110.

Common law rules as to disclosure

12–71 **21.**—(1) Where this Part applies as regards things falling to be done after the relevant time in relation to an alleged offence, the rules of common law which—

(a) were effective immediately before the appointed day, and

(b) relate to the disclosure of material by the prosecutor,

do not apply as regards things falling to be done after that time in relation to the alleged offence.

(2) Subsection (1) does not affect the rules of common law as to whether disclosure is in the public interest.

(3) References in subsection (1) to the relevant time are to the time when—

(a) the accused pleads not guilty (where this Part applies by virtue of section 1(1)),

(b) the accused is *committed* [sent] for trial (where this Part applies by virtue of section *1(2)(a)* [1(2)(cc)])

(c) *the proceedings are transferred (where this Part applies by virtue of section 1(2)(b) or (c)),*

(d) the count is included in the indictment (where this Part applies by virtue of section 1(2)(d)), or

(e) the bill of indictment is preferred (where this Part applies by virtue of section 1(2)(e)).

(4) The reference in subsection (1) to the appointed day is to the day appointed under section 1(5).

[This section is printed as amended, as from a day to be appointed, by the *CJA* 2003, s.41, and Sched. 3, para. 66 (omission of italicised text, insertion of text in square brackets).]

Criminal Procedure and Investigations Act 1996, s.21A

Code of practice for police interviews of witnesses notified by accused

12–71a **21A.**—(1) The Secretary of State shall prepare a code of practice which gives guidance to police officers, and other persons charged with the duty of investigating offences, in relation to the arranging and conducting of interviews of persons–

(a) particulars of whom are given in a defence statement in accordance with section 6A(2), or

(b) who are included as proposed witnesses in a notice given under section 6C.

(2) The code must include (in particular) guidance in relation to–

(a) information that should be provided to the interviewee and the accused in relation to such an interview;

(b) the notification of the accused's solicitor of such an interview;

(c) the attendance of the interviewee's solicitor at such an interview;

(d) the attendance of the accused's solicitor at such an interview;

(e) the attendance of any other appropriate person at such an interview taking into account the interviewee's age or any disability of the interviewee.

(3) Any police officer or other person charged with the duty of investigating offences who arranges or conducts such an interview shall have regard to the code.

(4) [*Duty to consult in preparation of code.*]

(5) The code shall not come into operation until the Secretary of State by order so provides.

(6) [*Revision of Code.*]

(7) [*Requirement of approval of each House of Parliament.*]

(8) [*Requirement of approval of each House of Parliament for revised code.*]

(9) [*Code to be laid before each House of Parliament.*]

(10) No order or draft of an order may be laid until the consultation required by subsection (4) has taken place.

(11) A failure by a person mentioned in subsection (3) to have regard to any provision of a code for the time being in operation by virtue of an order under this section shall not in itself render him liable to any criminal or civil proceedings.

(12) In all criminal and civil proceedings a code in operation at any time by virtue of an order under this section shall be admissible in evidence.

(13) If it appears to a court or tribunal conducting criminal or civil proceedings that—

(a) any provision of a code in operation at any time by virtue of an order under this section, or

(b) any failure mentioned in subsection (11),

is relevant to any question arising in the proceedings, the provision or failure shall be taken into account in deciding the question.

[This section was inserted by the *CJA* 2003, s.40.]

No defence witness interview code had been laid before Parliament as at October 1, 2008.

Criminal Procedure and Investigations Act 1996, s.22

PART II

CRIMINAL INVESTIGATIONS

Introduction

22.—(1) For the purposes of this Part a criminal investigation is an investigation conducted by police officers with a view to it being ascertained— **12–72**

(a) whether a person should be charged with an offence, or

(b) whether a person charged with an offence is guilty of it.

(2) In this Part references to material are to material of all kinds, and in particular include references to—

(a) information, and

(b) objects of all descriptions.

(3) In this Part references to recording information are to putting it in a durable or retrievable form (such as writing or tape).

Where police officers had themselves witnessed behaviour on the part of a defendant which led to his arrest by them and his subsequent charging with an offence, there was no deliberation involved by the officers which could be described as an "investigation" for the purposes of section 22 of the Act, or paragraph 2.1 of the code of practice (Appendix A–233 *et seq.*), as to whether he should be charged with the offence: *DPP v. Metten*, unreported, January 22, 1999, DC. There was therefore no duty imposed on the officers by what is now paragraph 3.5 of the code (Appendix A–234) to take the names of other people who had witnessed the incident.

Code of practice

Section 23 of the Act imposed an obligation on the Secretary of State to prepare a code of practice. Section 24 gave examples of the kinds of provision to be included in the code. See *post*, § 12–100 and Appendix A–232 *et seq.* **12–73**

Criminal Procedure and Investigations Act 1996, ss.25–27

Operation and revision of code

12–74 **25.**—(1) When the Secretary of State has prepared a code under section 23—

(a) he shall publish it in the form of a draft,

(b) he shall consider any representations made to him about the draft, and

(c) he may modify the draft accordingly.

(2) When the Secretary of State has acted under subsection (1) he shall lay the code before each House of Parliament, and when he has done so he may bring it into operation on such day as he may appoint by order.

(3) A code brought into operation under this section shall apply in relation to suspected or alleged offences into which no criminal investigation has begun before the day so appointed.

(4) [*Revision of code.*]

For the revised code of practice published and brought into operation pursuant to section 25 of the Act, see *post*, § 12–100, and Appendix A–232.

Effect of code

12–75 **26.**—(1) A person other than a police officer who is charged with the duty of conducting an investigation with a view to it being ascertained—

(a) whether a person should be charged with an offence, or

(b) whether a person charged with an offence is guilty of it,

shall in discharging that duty have regard to any relevant provision of a code which would apply if the investigation were conducted by police officers.

(2) A failure—

(a) by a police officer to comply with any provision of a code for the time being in operation by virtue of an order under section 25, or

(b) by a person to comply with subsection (1),

shall not in itself render him liable to any criminal or civil proceedings.

(3) In all criminal and civil proceedings a code in operation at any time by virtue of an order under section 25 shall be admissible in evidence.

(4) [*Identical to s.21A(13),* ante, *§ 12–71a, save for references to* "section 25" *and* "subsection (2)(a) or (b)" *in lieu of the references to* "this section" *and* "subsection (11)".]

Common law rules as to criminal investigations

12–76 **27.**—(1) Where a code prepared under section 23 and brought into operation under section 25 applies in relation to a suspected or alleged offence, the rules of common law which—

(a) were effective immediately before the appointed day, and

(b) relate to the matter mentioned in subsection (2),

shall not apply in relation to the suspected or alleged offence.

(2) The matter is the revealing of material—

(a) by a police officer or other person charged with the duty of conducting an investigation with a view to it being ascertained whether a person should be charged with an offence or whether a person charged with an offence is guilty of it;

(b) to a person involved in the prosecution of criminal proceedings.

(3) In subsection (1) "the appointed day" means the day appointed under section 25 with regard to the code as first prepared.

Attorney-General's guidelines on disclosure of information in criminal proceedings

12–76a Revised guidelines were issued by the Attorney-General in April, 2005, applicable with immediate effect to all cases, save where they specifically refer to statutory or code provisions brought in by the *CJA* 2003 that do not yet apply to the particular case. The guidelines themselves are printed in full in Appendix A–243 *et seq.*

For guidelines on disclosure to the defence and to the court in respect of applications for witness anonymity orders, see Appendix A–273.

(2) Rules and regulations

Disclosure rules

12–77 The *Criminal Procedure Rules* 2005 (S.I. 2005 No. 384) which came into force on

April 4, 2005, effectively reproduce the *Crown Court (Criminal Procedure and Investigations Act 1996) (Disclosure) Rules* 1997 (S.I. 1997 No. 698) which had come into force on April 1, 1997.

Criminal Procedure Rules 2005 (S.I. 2005 No. 384), rr.25.1, 25.2

Public interest: application by prosecutor

25.1.—(1) This rule applies to the making of an application by the prosecutor under section 3(6), 7A(8) or 8(5) of the *Criminal Procedure and Investigations Act* 1996. **12–78**

(2) Notice of such an application shall be served on the court officer and shall specify the nature of the material to which the application relates.

(3) Subject to paragraphs (4) and (5) below, a copy of the notice of application shall be served on the accused by the prosecutor.

(4) Where the prosecutor has reason to believe that to reveal to the accused the nature of the material to which the application relates would have the effect of disclosing that which the prosecutor contends should not in the public interest be disclosed, paragraph (3) above shall not apply but the prosecutor shall notify the accused that an application to which this rule applies has been made.

(5) Where the prosecutor has reason to believe that to reveal to the accused the fact that an application is being made would have the effect of disclosing that which the prosecutor contends should not in the public interest be disclosed, paragraph (3) above shall not apply.

(6) Where an application is made in the Crown Court to which paragraph (5) above applies, notice of the application may be served on the trial judge or, if the application is made before the start of the trial, on the judge, if any, who has been designated to conduct the trial instead of on the court officer.

Applications under paragraphs (2), (4) and (5) are commonly referred to as type 1, type 2 and type 3 applications, respectively. Judges are urged by the protocol for the control and management of unused material in the Crown Court always to ask the prosecution to justify the form of notice given (Appendix N–58).

Public interest: hearing of application by prosecutor

25.2.—(1) This rule applies to the hearing of an application by the prosecutor under section 3(6), 7A(8) or 8(5) of the *Criminal Procedure and Investigations Act* 1996. **12–79**

(2) Where notice of such an application is served on the Crown Court officer, the officer shall on receiving it refer it—

(a) if the trial has started, to the trial judge; or

(b) if the application is received before the start of the trial either—

(i) to the judge who has been designated to conduct the trial, or

(ii) if no judge has been designated for that purpose, to such judge as may be designated for the purposes of hearing the application.

(3) Where such an application is made and a copy of the notice of application has been served on the accused in accordance with rule 25.1(3), then subject to paragraphs (4) and (5) below—

(a) the court officer shall on receiving notice of the application give notice to—

(i) the prosecutor,

(ii) the accused, and

(iii) any person claiming to have an interest in the material to which the application relates who has applied under section 16(b) of the 1996 Act to be heard by the court,

of the date and time when and the place where the hearing will take place and, unless the court orders otherwise, such notice shall be given in writing;

(b) the hearing shall be *inter partes*; and

(c) the prosecutor and the accused shall be entitled to make representations to the court.

(4) Where the prosecutor applies to the court for leave to make representations in the absence of the accused, the court may for that purpose sit in the absence of the accused and any legal representative of his.

(5) Subject to rule 25.5(4) (interested party entitled to make representations), where a copy of the notice of application has not been served on the accused in accordance with rule 25.1(3)—

(a) the hearing shall be *ex parte*;
(b) only the prosecutor shall be entitled to make representations to the court;
(c) the accused shall not be given notice as specified in paragraph (3)(a)(ii) of this rule; and
(d) where notice of the application has been served in the Crown Court in pursuance of rule 25.1(6), the judge on whom it is served shall take such steps as he considers appropriate to ensure that notice is given as required by paragraph (3)(a)(i) and (iii) of this rule.

12–80 Where the prosecutor makes an *ex parte* application for an order for non-disclosure under the Act and these rules, the dicta of the Court of Appeal in *R. v. Davis, Johnson and Rowe*, 97 Cr.App.R. 110 at 114, continue to apply. The court there laid down the procedure, which is adopted by these rules, to be followed where the prosecution seek to withhold material from the defence on the grounds of public interest immunity. The court emphasised that open justice requires maximum disclosure and, whenever possible, the opportunity for the defence to make representations on the basis of the fullest information. It follows that if the judge takes the view that the defence should have had notice of the application, or of the nature of the material, or that the application should be made *inter partes*, he should so direct.

12–80a As there is no requirement to disclose material which might not reasonably be considered capable of undermining the case for the prosecution or of assisting the case for the accused, neutral material or material damaging to the defendant need not be disclosed and should not be brought to the attention of the court; only in truly borderline cases should the prosecution seek a judicial ruling on the disclosability of material in its hands: *R. v. H.* [2004] 2 A.C. 134, HL (at [35]).

For the additional statutory hurdles to be crossed before material tending to suggest that interception of communications has taken place, whether lawfully or otherwise, can be disclosed to the judge, see the *RIPA* 2000, s.18, *post*, § 25–378.

12–80b Prosecution counsel should not go alone to a judge in chambers if there is no basis for an *ex parte* application; and a shorthand writer should always be present: *R. v. Smith (David James)* [1998] 2 Cr.App.R. 1, CA. Unless there is an issue of public interest immunity, it is wrong for a prosecutor to ask the judge for advice on disclosure. The responsibility for deciding such questions rests with the prosecution: *R. v. B.* [2000] Crim.L.R. 50, CA. Given the nature of the procedure, the requirement that the information provided to the judge is accurate cannot be over-stressed: *R. v. Jackson* [2000] Crim.L.R. 377, CA; and *R. v. Early* [2003] 1 Cr.App.R. 19, CA.

12–80c The *ex parte* procedure has been considered by the European Court of Human Rights in *Jasper v. U.K.*, 30 E.H.R.R. 441, and *Fitt v. U.K.*, 30 E.H.R.R. 480. Both cases post-dated *Davis, Johnson and Rowe*, *ante*, but pre-dated the Act. In both cases the court by a majority of nine votes to eight found no violation of Article 6 of the ECHR (*post*, §§ 16–57 *et seq.*). The court recognised the need for any difficulties caused by limitations on defence rights to be counter-balanced by the procedures followed by the judicial authorities. In *P.G. v. U.K.* (2008) 46 E.H.R.R. 51, the European Court of Human Rights confirmed the decisions in *Jasper* and *Fitt*, finding that the procedure followed by the trial judge had been sufficient to protect the interests of the accused.

Jasper was distinguished in *Edwards and Lewis v. U.K.* [2003] Crim.L.R. 891, ECtHR, where the non-disclosure of otherwise disclosable material on public interest immunity grounds following an *ex parte* application to the trial judge was held to have rendered a trial unfair as violating the requirement that the proceedings should be adversarial in nature with equality of arms as between prosecution and defence, where the defendant wished to make an abuse of process application and/or apply for the exclusion of certain prosecution evidence (under the *PACE Act* 1984, s.78) on the ground that he had been entrapped into committing the offence with which he was charged, and where the material not disclosed might have assisted on that issue; and this was so even though the judge had been apprised by the defence of the fact that entrapment was an issue, and even though both the judge and (in one case) the Court of Appeal (who had seen the material) were categorical as to there being nothing in the material which could have assisted the defence on this issue; *Jasper* could be distinguished in that there the undisclosed evidence was never seen by the tribunal of fact (*i.e.* the jury), whereas here it was the trial judge (who had seen the material) who was to rule on any abuse/section 78 submissions; and he may have been unconsciously influenced by knowledge of what was in the undisclosed material, which the defence had had no opportunity to challenge.

The House of Lords in *R. v. H.* [2004] 2 A.C. 134, said that to contend, on the basis of *Edwards and Lewis,* that it is automatically incompatible with Article 6 of the ECHR (*post*, § 16–57) for a judge to rule on a claim to public interest immunity in the absence of adversarial argument on behalf of the accused where the material which the prosecution is seeking to withhold is, or may be, relevant to a disputed issue of fact which the judge has to decide in order to rule on an application which will effectively determine the outcome of the proceedings, was to seek to place the trial judge in a straitjacket; the consistent practice of the European Court, in this and other fields, has been to declare principles, and apply those principles on a case-by-case basis according to the particular facts of the case before it, and to avoid laying down rigid or inflexible rules. **12–80d**

The overriding requirement was that the guiding principles should be respected and observed, in the infinitely diverse situations with which trial judges have to deal, in all of which the touchstone was to ascertain what justice requires in the circumstances of the particular case. Cases would arise in which the appointment of an approved advocate as special counsel was necessary, but such an appointment should be exceptional, never automatic, and not ordered unless the judge is satisfied that no other course will adequately meet the overriding requirement of fairness to the defendant. Where the disclosure test (set out at § 12–44d, *ante*) is faithfully applied, the occasions on which a judge will be obliged to recuse himself because he has been privately shown material damning to the defendant will be rare.

Edwards and Lewis, ante, was distinguished in *R. v. May* [2005] 3 All E.R. 523, CA, as relating to a situation where a determinative ruling on an issue of fact had to be decided by the trial judge by reference to the undisclosed material, in which case consideration should be given to the appointment of special counsel. In *May*, on the other hand, the judge had expressly stated that he was ignoring anything revealed to him which attracted public interest immunity. The court said that there was no reason not to accept this statement; judges were able to put such material out of their minds when dealing with substantive issues arising in the proceedings; if, however, a judge were to form the view that, despite his best efforts, he would be unlikely to be able to ignore the undisclosed material, then consideration may have to be given to the appointment of special counsel. The test is one of fairness. In *R. v. Dawson* [2007] 4 *Archbold News* 3, where the judge, ruling on an application for a stay on the basis of entrapment, had similarly made it clear that he had not relied upon any of the material which he had been shown *ex parte* and which had not been disclosed to the defence, the Court of Appeal stated that whilst a judge was of course entitled to recuse himself if he felt that the interests of justice so required (such as if he believed that his study of undisclosed material would lead him to conclude that he could not dissociate his own fair judgment of the admissible evidence from the undisclosed facts that had been revealed to him), it was difficult to think of any circumstances in which a judge might reach that conclusion, and the virtually invariable rule was that the judge who had examined undisclosed material should continue to act as the trial judge.

In *Atlan v. U.K.* (2002) 34 E.H.R.R. 33, ECtHR, it was held that the prosecution's false denials of the existence of undisclosed relevant information and their failure to inform the trial judge of the true position had violated Article 6. An *ex parte* procedure conducted before the Court of Appeal after matters came to light had been insufficient to remedy the unfairness at first instance. The trial judge was best placed to decide whether the non-disclosure of relevant material would be unfairly prejudicial to the defence. In *R. v. Botmeh and Alami* (2008) 46 E.H.R.R. 31, ECtHR, however, it was held that there had been no violation of Article 6 where material which had not been in the possession of the prosecution at the time of trial was first considered by the Court of Appeal in an *ex parte* hearing; the fact that that court had been able to consider the impact of the new material on the safety of the applicants' convictions in the light of detailed argument from their counsel and the fact that the undisclosed material had been found to add nothing of significance to what had been disclosed at trial, meant **12–80e** that the failure to place the material before the trial judge was in the particular circumstances of the case remedied by the subsequent procedure before the Court of Appeal. To similar effect, see *Dowsett v. U.K.* (2004) 38 E.H.R.R. 41, ECtHR.

As to the procedure to be adopted where an issue arises as to the manner in which the judge in the Crown Court dealt with an issue of public interest immunity, see *R. v. McDonald, Rafferty and O'Farrell*, *The Times*, November 8, 2004, CA, *ante*, § 7–200b.

Criminal Procedure Rules 2005 (S.I. 2005 No. 384), rr.25.3–25.8

Public interest: non-disclosure order

12–81 **25.3.**—(1) This rule applies to an order under section 3(6), 7A(8) or 8(5) of the *Criminal Procedure and Investigations Act* 1996.

(2) On making an order to which this rule applies, the court shall state its reasons for doing so. Where such an order is made in the Crown Court, a record shall be made of the statement of the court's reasons.

(3) In a case where such an order is made following—

(a) an application to which rule 25.1(4) (nature of material not to be revealed) applies; or

(b) an application notice of which has been served on the accused in accordance with rule 25.1(3) but the accused has not appeared or been represented at the hearing of that application,

the court officer shall notify the accused that an order has been made. No notification shall be given in a case where an order is made following an application to which rule 25.1(5) (fact of application not to be revealed) applies.

Review of non-disclosure order: application by accused

12–82 **25.4.**—(1) This rule applies to an application by the accused under section 14(2) or section 15(4) of the *Criminal Procedure and Investigations Act* 1996.

(2) Such an application shall be made by notice in writing to the court officer for the court that made the order under section 3(6), 7A(8) or 8(5) of the 1996 Act and shall specify the reason why the accused believes the court should review the question whether it is still not in the public interest to disclose the material affected by the order.

(3) A copy of the notice referred to in paragraph (2) shall be served on the prosecutor at the same time as it is sent to the court officer.

(4) Where such an application is made in a magistrates' court, the court officer shall take such steps as he thinks fit to ensure that the court has before it any document or other material which was available to the court which made the order mentioned in section 14(2) of the 1996 Act.

(5) Where such an application is made in the Crown Court, the court officer shall refer it—

(a) if the trial has started, to the trial judge; or

(b) if the application is received before the start of the trial either—

(i) to the judge who has been designated to conduct the trial, or

(ii) if no judge has been designated for that purpose, to the judge who made the order to which the application relates.

(6) The judge to whom such an application has been referred under paragraph (5) shall consider whether the application may be determined without a hearing and, subject to paragraph (7), may so determine it if he thinks fit.

(7) No application to which this rule applies shall be determined by the Crown Court without a hearing if it appears to the judge that there are grounds on which the court might conclude that it is in the public interest to disclose material to any extent.

(8) Where a magistrates' court considers that there are no grounds on which it might conclude that it is in the public interest to disclose material to any extent it may determine an application to which this rule applies without hearing representations from the accused, the prosecutor or any person claiming to have an interest in the material to which the application relates.

(9) Subject to paragraphs (10) and (11) of this rule and to rule 25.5(4) (interested party entitled to make representations), the hearing of an application to which this rule applies shall be inter partes and the accused and the prosecutor shall be entitled to make representations to the court.

(10) Where after hearing the accused's representations the prosecutor applies to the

court for leave to make representations in the absence of the accused, the court may for that purpose sit in the absence of the accused and any legal representative of his.

(11) Subject to rule 25.5(4), where the order to which the application relates was made following an application of which the accused was not notified under rule 25.1(3) or (4), the hearing shall be ex parte and only the prosecutor shall be entitled to make representations to the court.

(12) The court officer shall give notice in writing to—

(a) the prosecutor;

(b) except where a hearing takes place in accordance with paragraph (11), the accused; and

(c) any person claiming to have an interest in the material to which the application relates who has applied under section 16(b) of the 1996 Act to be heard by the court,

of the date and time when and the place where the hearing of an application to which this rule applies will take place and of any order which is made by the court following its determination of the application.

(13) Where such an application is determined without a hearing in pursuance of paragraph (6), the court officer shall give notice in writing in accordance with paragraph (12) of any order which is made by the judge following his determination of the application.

Public interest applications: interested persons

25.5.—(1) Where the prosecutor has reason to believe that a person who was involved (whether alone or with others and whether directly or indirectly) in the prosecutor's attention being brought to any material to which an application under section 3(6), 7A(8), 8(5), 14(2) or 15(4) of the *Criminal Procedure and Investigations Act* 1996 relates may claim to have an interest in that material, the prosecutor shall— **12–83**

(a) in the case of an application under section 3(6), 7A(8) or 8(5) of the 1996 Act, at the same time as notice of the application is served under rule 25.1(2) or (6); or

(b) in the case of an application under section 14(2) or 15(4) of the 1996 Act, when he receives a copy of the notice referred to in rule 25.4(2),

give notice in writing to—

(i) the person concerned of the application, and

(ii) the court officer or, as the case may require, the judge of his belief and the grounds for it.

(2) An application under section 16(b) of the 1996 Act shall be made by notice in writing to the court officer or, as the case may require, the judge as soon as is reasonably practicable after receipt of notice under paragraph (1)(i) above or, if no such notice is received, after the person concerned becomes aware of the application referred to in that sub-paragraph and shall specify the nature of the applicant's interest in the material and his involvement in bringing the material to the prosecutor's attention.

(3) A copy of the notice referred to in paragraph (2) shall be served on the prosecutor at the same time as it is sent to the court officer or the judge as the case may require.

(4) At the hearing of an application under section 3(6), 7A(8), 8(5), 14(2) or 15(4) of the 1996 Act a person who has made an application under section 16(b) in accordance with paragraph (2) of this rule shall be entitled to make representations to the court.

Disclosure: application by accused and order of court

25.6.—(1) This rule applies to an application by the accused under section 8(2) of the *Criminal Procedure and Investigations Act* 1996. **12–84**

(2) Such an application shall be made by notice in writing to the court officer and shall specify—

(a) the material to which the application relates;

(b) that the material has not been disclosed to the accused;

(c) the reason why the material might be expected to assist the applicant's defence as disclosed by the defence statement given under section 5 or 6 of the 1996 Act; and

(d) the date of service of a copy of the notice on the prosecutor in accordance with paragraph (3).

(3) A copy of the notice referred to in paragraph (2) shall be served on the prosecutor at the same time as it is sent to the court officer.

(4) Where such an application is made in the Crown Court, the court officer shall refer it—

(a) if the trial has started, to the trial judge, or
(b) if the application is received before the start of the trial—
(i) to the judge who has been designated to conduct the trial, or
(ii) if no judge has been designated for that purpose, to such judge as may be designated for the purposes of determining the application.

(5) A prosecutor receiving notice under paragraph (3) of an application to which this rule applies shall give notice in writing to the court officer within 14 days of service of the notice that—
(a) he wishes to make representations to the court concerning the material to which the application relates; or
(b) if he does not so wish, that he is willing to disclose that material,

and a notice under paragraph 5(a) shall specify the substance of the representations he wishes to make.

(6) A court may determine an application to which this rule applies without hearing representations from the applicant or the prosecutor unless—
(a) the prosecutor has given notice under paragraph (5)(a) and the court considers that the representations should be made at a hearing; or
(b) the court considers it necessary to hear representations from the applicant or the prosecutor in the interests of justice for the purposes of determining the application.

(7) Subject to paragraph (8), where a hearing is held in pursuance of this rule—
(a) the court officer shall give notice in writing to the prosecutor and the applicant of the date and time when and the place where the hearing will take place;
(b) the hearing shall be inter partes; and
(c) the prosecutor and the applicant shall be entitled to make representations to the court.

(8) Where the prosecutor applies to the court for leave to make representations in the absence of the accused, the court may for that purpose sit in the absence of the accused and any legal representative of his.

(9) A copy of any order under section 8(2) of the 1996 Act shall be served on the prosecutor and the applicant.

Disclosure: application for extension of time limit and order of the court

12–85 **25.7.**—(1) This rule applies to an application under regulation 3(2) of the *Criminal Procedure and Investigations Act 1996 (Defence Disclosure Time Limits) Regulations* 1997 (S.I. 1997 No. 684), including that regulation as applied by regulation 4(2).

(2) An application to which this rule applies shall be made by notice in writing to the court officer and shall, in addition to the matters referred to in regulation 3(3)(a) to (c) of the 1997 Regulations, specify the date of service of a copy of the notice on the prosecutor in accordance with paragraph (3) of this rule.

(3) A copy of the notice referred to in paragraph (2) of this rule shall be served on the prosecutor at the same time as it is sent to the court officer.

(4) The prosecutor may make representations to the court concerning the application and if he wishes to do so he shall do so in writing within 14 days of service of a notice under paragraph (3) of this rule.

(5) On receipt of representations under paragraph (4) above, or on the expiration of the period specified in that paragraph if no such representations are received within that period, the court shall consider the application and may, if it wishes, do so at a hearing.

(6) Where a hearing is held in pursuance of this rule—
(a) the court officer shall give notice in writing to the prosecutor and the applicant of the date and time when and the place where the hearing will take place;
(b) the hearing shall be inter partes; and
(c) the prosecutor and the applicant shall be entitled to make representations to the court.

(7) A copy of any order under regulation 3(1) or 4(1) of the 1997 Regulations shall be served on the prosecutor and the applicant.

Public interest and disclosure applications: general

12–86 **25.8.**—(1) Any hearing held under this Part may be adjourned from time to time.

(2) Any hearing referred to in paragraph (1) other than one held under rule 25.7 may be held in private.

(3) Where a Crown Court hearing, or any part thereof, is held in private under paragraph (2), the court may specify conditions subject to which the record of its statement of reasons made in pursuance of rule 25.3(2) is to be kept.

(4) Where an application or order to which any provision of this rule applies is made after the start of a trial in the Crown Court, the trial judge may direct that any provision of this rule requiring notice of the application or order to be given to any person shall not have effect and may give such direction as to the giving of notice in relation to that application or order as he thinks fit.

Confidentiality rules

Part 26 of the *Criminal Procedure Rules* 2005 (S.I. 2005 No. 384) which came into force on April 4, 2005, effectively reproduces the *Crown Court (Criminal Procedure and Investigations Act 1996) (Confidentiality) Rules* 1997 (S.I. 1997 No. 699) which came into force on April 1, 1997. **12–87**

Criminal Procedure Rules 2005 (S.I. 2005 No. 384), Pt 26

Application for permission to use or disclose object or information

26.1.—(1) This rule applies to an application under section 17(4) of the *Criminal Procedure and Investigations Act* 1996. **12–88**

(2) Such an application shall be made by notice in writing to the court officer for the court which conducted or is conducting the proceedings for whose purposes the applicant was given, or allowed to inspect, the object to which the application relates.

(3) The notice of application shall—

(a) specify the object which the applicant seeks to use or disclose and the proceedings for whose purposes he was given, or allowed to inspect, it;

(b) where the applicant seeks to use or disclose any information recorded in the object specified in pursuance of paragraph (3)(a), specify that information;

(c) specify the reason why the applicant seeks permission to use or disclose the object specified in pursuance of paragraph (3)(a) or any information specified in pursuance of paragraph (3)(b);

(d) describe any proceedings in connection with which the applicant seeks to use or disclose the object or information referred to in paragraph (3)(c); and

(e) specify the name and address of any person to whom the applicant seeks to disclose the object or information referred to in paragraph (3)(c).

(4) Where the court officer receives an application to which this rule applies, the court officer or the clerk of the magistrates' court shall fix a date and time for the hearing of the application.

(5) The court officer shall give the applicant and the prosecutor at least 28 days' notice of the date fixed in pursuance of paragraph (4) and shall at the same time send to the prosecutor a copy of the notice given to him in pursuance of paragraph (2).

(6) Where the prosecutor has reason to believe that a person may claim to have an interest in the object specified in a notice of application in pursuance of paragraph (3)(a), or in any information so specified in pursuance of paragraph (3)(b), he shall, as soon as reasonably practicable after receipt of a copy of that notice under paragraph (5), send a copy of the notice to that person and inform him of the date fixed in pursuance of paragraph (4).

Prosecutor or interested party wishing to be heard

26.2.—(1) This rule applies to an application under section 17(6)(b) of the *Criminal Procedure and Investigations Act* 1996. **12–89**

(2) An application to which this rule applies shall be made by notice in writing to the court officer of the court referred to in rule 26.1(2) not less than 7 days before the date fixed in pursuance of rule 26.1(4).

(3) The applicant shall at the same time send to the person whose application under section 17(4) of the 1996 Act is concerned a copy of the notice given in pursuance of paragraph (2).

Decision on application for use or disclosure

26.3.—(1) Where no application to which rule 26.2 applies is made in accordance with paragraph (2) of that rule, the court shall consider whether the application under section 17(4) of the *Criminal Procedure and Investigations Act* 1996 may be determined without hearing **12–90**

representations from the accused, the prosecutor or any person claiming to have an interest in the object or information to which the application relates, and may so determine it if the court thinks fit.

(2) Where an application to which rule 26.1 applies is determined without hearing any such representations the court officer shall give notice in writing to the person who made the application and to the prosecutor of any order made under section 17(4) of the 1996 Act or, as the case may be, that no such order has been made.

Unauthorised use or disclosure

12–91 **26.4.**—(1) This rule applies to proceedings to deal with a contempt of court under section 18 of the *Criminal Procedure and Investigations Act* 1996.

(2)–(7) [*Proceedings before a magistrates' court.*]

(8) An application to the Crown Court for an order of committal or for the imposition of a fine in proceedings to which this rule applies may be made by the prosecutor or by any other person claiming to have an interest in the object, or in any information recorded in an object, the use or disclosure of which is alleged to contravene section 17 of the 1996 Act. Such an application shall be made in accordance with paragraphs (9) to (20).

(9) An application such as is referred to in paragraph (8) shall be made by notice in writing to the court officer at the same place as that in which the Crown Court sat or is sitting to conduct the proceedings for whose purposes the object mentioned in paragraph (2) was given or inspected.

(10) The notice referred to in paragraph (9) shall set out the name and a description of the applicant, the name, description and address of the person sought to be committed or fined and the grounds on which his committal or the imposition of a fine is sought and shall be supported by an affidavit verifying the facts.

(11) Subject to paragraph (12), the notice referred to in paragraph (9), accompanied by a copy of the affidavit in support of the application, shall be served personally on the person sought to be committed or fined.

(12) The court may dispense with service of the notice under this rule if it is of the opinion that it is necessary to do so in order to protect the applicant or for another purpose identified by the court.

(13) Nothing in the foregoing provisions of this rule shall be taken as affecting the power of the Crown Court to make an order of committal or impose a fine of its own motion against a person guilty of a contempt under section 18 of the 1996 Act.

(14) Subject to paragraph (15), proceedings to which this rule applies shall be heard in open court.

(15) Proceedings to which this rule applies may be heard in private where—

(a) the object, the use or disclosure of which is alleged to contravene section 17 of the 1996 Act, is; or

(b) the information, the use or disclosure of which is alleged to contravene that section, is recorded in,

an object which is, or forms part of, material in respect of which an application was made under section 3(6), 7A(8) or 8(5) of the 1996 Act, whether or not the court made an order that the material be not disclosed:

Provided that where the court hears the proceedings in private it shall nevertheless, if it commits any person to custody or imposes a fine on him in pursuance of section 18(3) of the 1996 Act, state in open court the name of that person, the period specified in the order of committal or, as the case may be, the amount of the fine imposed, or both such period and such amount where both are ordered.

(16) Except with the leave of the court hearing an application for an order of committal or for the imposition of a fine no grounds shall be relied upon at the hearing except the grounds set out in the notice referred to in paragraph (9).

(17) If on the hearing of the application the person sought to be committed or fined expresses a wish to give oral evidence on his own behalf, he shall be entitled to do so.

(18) The court by whom an order of committal is made may by order direct that the execution of the order of committal shall be suspended for such period or on such terms or conditions as it may specify.

(19) Where execution of an order of committal is suspended by an order under paragraph (18), the applicant for the order of committal must, unless the court otherwise directs, serve on the person against whom it was made a notice informing him of the making and terms of the order under that paragraph.

(20) The court may, on the application of any person committed to custody for a contempt under section 18 of the 1996 Act, discharge him.

Forfeiture of object used or disclosed without authority

26.5.—(1) Where the Crown Court finds a person guilty of contempt under section 18 of the *Criminal Procedure and Investigations Act* 1996 and proposes to make an order under section 18(4) or (7), the court may adjourn the proceedings. **12–92**

(2) Where the court adjourns the proceedings under paragraph (1), the court officer shall give notice to the person found guilty and to the prosecutor—

(a) that the court proposes to make such an order and that, if an application is made in accordance with paragraph (5), it will before doing so hear any representations made by the person found guilty, or by any person in respect of whom the prosecutor gives notice to the court under paragraph (3); and

(b) of the time and date of the adjourned hearing.

(3) Where the prosecutor has reason to believe that a person may claim to have an interest in the object which has been used or disclosed in contravention of section 17 of the 1996 Act he shall, on receipt of notice under paragraph (2), give notice of that person's name and address to the court office for the court which made the finding of guilt.

(4) Where the court officer receives a notice under paragraph (3), he shall, within 7 days of the finding of guilt, notify the person specified in that notice—

(a) that the court has made a finding of guilt under section 18 of the 1996 Act, that it proposes to make an order under section 18(4) or, as the case may be, 18(7) and that, if an application is made in accordance with paragraph (5), it will before doing so hear any representations made by him; and

(b) of the time and date of the adjourned hearing.

(5) An application under section 18(6) of the 1996 Act shall be made by notice in writing to the court officer not less than 24 hours before the time set for the adjourned hearing.

[The next paragraph is § 12–94.]

Time limits

The *Criminal Procedure and Investigations Act 1996 (Defence Disclosure Time Limits) Regulations* 1997 (S.I. 1997 No. 684) were made in pursuance of sections 12 and 77(2) of the Act. They came into force on April 1, 1997. **12–94**

S.I. 1997 No. 684

1.—(1) [*Citation and commencement.*] **12–95**

(2) These Regulations extend to England and Wales only.

(3) In these Regulations, the expression "the Act" means the *Criminal Procedure and Investigations Act* 1996.

2. Subject to regulations 3, 4, and 5, the relevant period for sections 5, and 6 of the Act (disclosure by the accused) is a period beginning with the day on which the prosecutor complies, or purports to comply, with section 3 of that Act and ending with the expiration of 14 days from that day. **12–96**

3.—(1) The period referred to in regulation 2 shall, if the court so orders, be extended by so many days as the court specifies. **12–97**

(2) The court may only make such an order if an application which complies with paragraph (3) below is made by the accused before the expiration of the period referred to in regulation 2.

(3) An application under paragraph (2) above shall—

(a) state that the accused believes, on reasonable grounds, that it is not possible for him to give a defence statement under section 5 or, as the case may be, 6 of the Act during the period referred to in regulation 2;

(b) specify the grounds for so believing; and

(c) specify the number of days by which the accused wishes that period to be extended.

(4) The court shall not make an order under paragraph (1) above unless it is satisfied that the accused cannot reasonably give or, as the case may be, could not reasonably have given a defence statement under section 5 or, as the case may be, 6 of the Act during the period referred to in regulation 2.

(5) The number of days by which the period referred to in regulation 2 may be extended shall be entirely at the court's discretion.

4.—(1) Where the court has made an order under regulation 3(1), the period referred to in **12–98**

regulation 2 as extended in accordance with that order shall, if the court so orders, be further extended by so many days as the court specifies.

(2) Paragraphs (2) to (5) of regulation 3 shall, subject to paragraph (4) below, apply for the purposes of an order under paragraph (1) above as they apply for the purposes of an order under regulation 3(1).

(3) There shall be no limit on the number of applications that may be made under regulation 3(2) as applied by paragraph (2) above; and on a second or subsequent such application the court shall have the like powers under paragraph (1) above as on the first such application.

(4) In the application of regulation 3(2) to (5) in accordance with paragraph (2) above, any reference to the period referred to in regulation 2 shall be construed as a reference to that period as extended or, as the case may be, further extended by an order of the court under regulation 3(1) or paragraph (1) or (3) above.

12–99 **5.**—(1) Where the period referred to in regulation 2 or that period as extended or, as the case may be, further extended by an order of the court under regulation 3(1) or 4(1) or (3) would, apart from this regulation, expire on any of the days specified in paragraph (2) below, that period shall be treated as expiring on the next following day which is not one of those days.

(2) The days referred to in paragraph (1) above are Saturday, Sunday, Christmas Day, Good Friday and any day which under the *Banking and Financial Dealings Act* 1971 is a bank holiday in England and Wales.

Where the prosecutor gave a written statement that there was no material falling to be disclosed by way of initial disclosure, and subsequently served a schedule of unused material, the relevant period under regulation 2 began with the service of the written statement: *DPP v. Wood; DPP v. McGillicuddy*, 170 J.P. 177, DC.

Preparation of defence statements

12–99a On September 24, 1997, the Professional Conduct and Complaints Committee of the Bar Council approved the following guidance as to the duties of counsel in relation to the preparation of defence statements (incorrectly referred to throughout as "defence case statements") pursuant to the *CPIA* 1996.

1. It is becoming increasingly common for solicitors to instruct counsel to draft or settle defence case statements, required under section 5 of the *Criminal Procedure and Investigations Act* 1996. Often these instructions are given to counsel with no or little previous involvement in the case shortly before the expiry of the time limit.

2. The relevant legislation is set out at §§ 12–82 *et seq.* of the 1997 edition of *Archbold* [see §§ 12–52 *et seq.*, *ante*]. In summary, however:

(i) the time limit for compliance is short—14 days from service of prosecution material or a statement that there is none; the permitted grounds for an extension of time are limited;

(ii) the contents of the defence case statement are obviously of great importance to the defendant; an inaccurate or inadequate statement of the defence could have serious repercussions for the defendant, if the trial judge permits "appropriate" comment;

(iii) whilst it will the [*sic*] natural instinct of most defence counsel to keep the defence case statement short, a short and anodyne statement may be insufficient to trigger any obligation on the prosecution to give secondary disclosure of prosecution material.

3. Normally it will be more appropriate for instructing solicitors to draft the defence case statement, since typically counsel will have had little involvement at this stage.

4. However, there is nothing unprofessional about counsel drafting or settling a defence case statement, although it must be appreciated that there is no provision in the current regulations for graduated fees allowing for counsel to be paid a separate fee for this work. This most unsatisfactory situation (which has arisen, as a result of the 1996 Act, since the graduated fees regulations were negotiated) is being addressed urgently by the Legal Aid and Fees Committee. A barrister has no obligation to accept work for which he will not be paid. The absence of a fee will justify refusal of the instructions by counsel who are not to be retained for the trial and are simply asked to do no more than draft or settle the defence case statement. Where counsel is retained for the trial, rule 502(b) of the Code of Conduct deems instructions in a legally aided matter to be at a proper fee and counsel would not be justified in refusing to draft or settle a defence case statement on the sole ground that there is no separate fee payable for this work.

12–99b 5. Many members of the Bar will nevertheless feel that, in the interests of their lay client and or of good relations with instructing solicitors, they cannot refuse the work, even where they would otherwise be entitled to do so. Those who do so need to recognise the crucial importance of:

(i) obtaining all prosecution statements and documentary exhibits;

(ii) getting instructions from the lay client, from a properly signed proof and preferably a conference. Those instructions need to explain the general nature of the defence, to indicate the matters on which issue is taken with the prosecution and to give an explanation of the reason for taking issue. They must also give details of any alibi defence, sufficient to give the information required by section 5(7) [now6A(2)] of the 1996 Act;

(iii) getting statements from other material witnesses;

(iv) ensuring that the client realises the importance of the defence case statement and the potential adverse consequences of an inaccurate or inadequate statement;

(v) getting proper informed approval for the draft from the client. This is particularly important, given the risks of professional embarrassment if the client seeks to disown the statement during the course of the trial, perhaps when the trial is not going well or when under severe pressure in cross-examination. Counsel ought to insist on getting written acknowledgement from the lay client that:

(a) he understands the importance of the accuracy and adequacy of the defence case statement for this case;

(b) he has had the opportunity of considering the contents of the statement carefully and approves it.

This may often mean having a conference with the lay client to explain the defence case statement and to get informed approval, although in straightforward cases where counsel has confidence in the instructing solicitor, this could be left to the solicitor. Where this latter course is taken, a short written advice (which can be in a standard form) as to the importance of obtaining the written acknowledgement before service of the statement should accompany the draft defence case statement. A careful record should be kept of work done and advice given;

(vi) if there is inadequate time, counsel should ask the instructing solicitor to apply for an extension of time. This needs to be considered at a very early stage, since the application must be made before the expiry of the time limit.

6. It follows that counsel ought not to accept any instructions to draft or settle a defence case statement unless given the opportunity and adequate time to gain proper familiarity with the case and to comply with the fundamental requirements set out above. In short, there is no halfway house. If instructions are accepted, then the professional obligations on counsel are considerable.

REPRODUCED FROM *BAR NEWS* WITH KIND PERMISSION OF THE GENERAL COUNCIL OF THE BAR.

(3) Codes of practice

Pursuant to sections 23 and 25 of the 1996 Act, the Secretary of State has prepared and published a revised code of practice setting out "the manner in which police officers are to record, retain and reveal to the prosecutor material obtained in a criminal investigation and which may be related to the investigation, and related matters" (see the preamble). It was brought into force by the *Criminal Procedure and Investigations Act 1996 (Code of Practice) Order* 2005 (S.I. 2005 No. 985), in respect of criminal investigations conducted by police officers which began on or after April 4, 2005. **12–100**

[For the full text of this Code, see Appendix A–232 *et seq.*]

Further, more detailed guidance for the carrying out of the duties of disclosure by the police and the CPS, albeit predating the changes brought in by the *CJA* 2003, can be found in the joint operational instructions agreed between the Association of Chief Police Officers and the CPS for the disclosure of unused material, available from the CPS website (www.cps.gov.uk). **12–100a**

The *Criminal Procedure and Investigations Act 1996 (Code of Practice) (Armed Forces) Order* 2008 (S.I. 2008 No. 648) brought into force on April 1, 2008, a code of **12–100b** practice for the conduct of service investigations by service policemen. The code is equivalent to that in respect of criminal investigations issued under section 23(1) of the 1996 Act, subject to modifications to take account of the structure and operation of service courts and of the service police.

(4) Sexual offences

Introduction

12–101 The *Sexual Offences (Protected Material) Act* 1997 received Royal Assent on March 21, 1997. It makes provision for regulating access by defendants and others to certain categories of material disclosed by the prosecution or by the Criminal Cases Review Commission in connection with proceedings relating to certain sexual and other offences, a list of which is contained in the Schedule to the Act.

The Act comes into force on such day as the Secretary of State may appoint. Nothing in the Act applies to any proceedings for a sexual offence where the defendant was charged with the offence before the commencement of the Act.

Sexual Offences (Protected Material) Act 1997

Introductory

Meaning of "protected material"

12–102 **1.**—(1) In this Act "protected material", in relation to proceedings for a sexual offence, means a copy (in whatever form) of any of the following material, namely—

(a) a statement relating to that or any other sexual offence made by any victim of the offence (whether the statement is recorded in writing or in any other form),

(b) a photograph or pseudo-photograph of any such victim, or

(c) a report of a medical examination of the physical condition of any such victim,

which is a copy given by the prosecutor to any person under this Act.

(2) For the purposes of subsection (1) a person is, in relation to any proceedings for a sexual offence, a victim of that offence if—

(a) the charge, summons or indictment by which the proceedings are instituted names that person as a person in relation to whom that offence was committed; or

(b) that offence can, in the prosecutor's opinion, be reasonably regarded as having been committed in relation to that person;

and a person is, in relation to any such proceedings, a victim of any other sexual offence if that offence can, in the prosecutor's opinion, be reasonably regarded as having been committed in relation to that person.

(3) In this Act, where the context so permits (and subject to subsection (4))—

(a) references to any protected material include references to any part of any such material; and

(b) references to a copy of any such material include references to any part of any such copy.

(4) Nothing in this Act—

(a) so far as it refers to a defendant making any copy of—

(i) any protected material, or

(ii) a copy of any such material,

applies to a manuscript copy which is not a verbatim copy of the whole of that material or copy; or

(b) so far as it refers to a defendant having in his possession any copy of any protected material, applies to a manuscript copy made by him which is not a verbatim copy of the whole of that material.

Meaning of other expressions

12–103 **2.**—(1) In this Act—

"contracted out prison" means a contracted out prison within the meaning of Part IV of the *Criminal Justice Act* 1991;

"defendant", in relation to any proceedings for a sexual offence, means any person charged with that offence (whether or not he has been convicted);

"governor", in relation to a contracted out prison, means the director of the prison;

"inform" means inform in writing;

"legal representative", in relation to a defendant, means *any authorised advocate or authorised litigator (as defined by section 119(1) of the* Courts and Legal Services Act *1990*) [a person who, for the purposes of the *Legal Services Act* 2007, is an authorised person in relation to an activity which constitutes the exercise of a right of audience or the conduct of litigation (within the meaning of that Act) and who is] acting for the defendant in connection with any proceedings for the sexual offence in question;

"photograph" and "pseudo-photograph" shall be construed in accordance with section 7(4) and (7) of the *Protection of Children Act* 1978;

"prison" means any prison, young offender institution or remand centre which is under the general superintendence of, or is provided by, the Secretary of State under the *Prison Act* 1952, including a contracted out prison;

"proceedings" means (subject to subsection (2)) criminal proceedings;

"the prosecutor", in relation to any proceedings for a sexual offence, means any person acting as prosecutor (whether an individual or a body);

"relevant proceedings", in relation to any material which has been disclosed by the prosecutor under this Act, means any proceedings for the purposes of which it has been so disclosed or any further proceedings for the sexual offence in question;

"sexual offence" means one of the offences listed in the Schedule to this Act.

(2) For the purposes of this Act references to proceedings for a sexual offence include references to—

(a) any appeal or application for leave to appeal brought or made by or in relation to a defendant in such proceedings;

(b) any application made to the Criminal Cases Review Commission for the reference under section 9 or 11 of the *Criminal Appeal Act* 1995 of any conviction, verdict, finding or sentence recorded or imposed in relation to any such defendant; and

(c) any petition to the Secretary of State requesting him to recommend the exercise of Her Majesty's prerogative of mercy in relation to any such defendant.

(3) In this Act, in the context of the prosecutor giving a copy of any material to any person—

(a) references to the prosecutor include references to a person acting on behalf of the prosecutor; and

(b) where any such copy falls to be given to the defendant's legal representative, references to the defendant's legal representative include references to a person acting on behalf of the defendant's legal representative.

[The definition of "legal representative" is printed as amended, as from a day to be appointed, by the *Legal Services Act* 2007, s.208(1), and Sched 21, para. 123 (omission of italicised words, insertion of words in square brackets).]

Regulation of disclosures to defendant

Regulation of disclosures by prosecutor

3.—(1) Where, in connection with any proceedings for a sexual offence, any statement or other material falling within any of paragraphs (a) to (c) of section 1(1) would (apart from this section) fall to be disclosed by the prosecutor to the defendant— **12–104**

(a) the prosecutor shall not disclose that material to the defendant; and

(b) it shall instead be disclosed under this Act in accordance with whichever of subsections (2) and (3) below is applicable.

(2) If—

(a) the defendant has a legal representative, and

(b) the defendant's legal representative gives the prosecutor the undertaking required by section 4 (disclosure to defendant's legal representative),

the prosecutor shall disclose the material in question by giving a copy of it to the defendant's legal representative.

(3) If subsection (2) is not applicable, the prosecutor shall disclose the material in question by giving a copy of it to the appropriate person for the purposes of section 5 (disclosure to unrepresented defendant) in order for that person to show that copy to the defendant under that section.

(4) Where under this Act a copy of any material falls to be given to any person by the prosecutor, any such copy—

(a) may be in such form as the prosecutor thinks fit, and
(b) where the material consists of information which has been recorded in any form, need not be in the same form as that in which the information has already been recorded.

(5) Once a copy of any material is given to any person under this Act by the prosecutor, the copy shall (in accordance with section 1(1)) be protected material for the purposes of this Act.

Disclosure to defendant's legal representative

12–105 **4.**—(1) For the purposes of this Act the undertaking which a defendant's legal representative is required to give in relation to any protected material given to him under this Act is an undertaking by him to discharge the obligations set out in subsections (2) to (7).

(2) He must take reasonable steps to ensure—
(a) that the protected material, or any copy of it, is only shown to the defendant in circumstances where it is possible to exercise adequate supervision to prevent the defendant retaining possession of the material or copy or making a copy of it, and
(b) that the protected material is not shown and no copy of it is given, and its contents are not otherwise revealed, to any person other than the defendant, except so far as it appears to him necessary to show the material or give a copy of it to any such person—
(i) in connection with any relevant proceedings, or
(ii) for the purposes of any assessment or treatment of the defendant (whether before or after conviction).

(3) He must inform the defendant—
(a) that the protected material is such material for the purposes of this Act,
(b) that the defendant can only inspect that material, or any copy of it, in circumstances such as are described in subsection (2)(a), and
(c) that it would be an offence for the defendant—
(i) to have that material, or any copy of it, in his possession otherwise than while inspecting it or the copy in such circumstances, or
(ii) to give that material or any copy of it, or otherwise reveal its contents, to any other person.

(4) He must, where the protected material or a copy of it has been shown or given in accordance with subsection (2)(b)(i) or (ii) to a person other than the defendant, inform that person—
(a) that that person must not give any copy of that material, or otherwise reveal its contents—
(i) to any other person other than the defendant, or
(ii) to the defendant otherwise than in circumstances such as are described in subsection (2)(a); and
(b) that it would be an offence for that person to do so.

(5) He must, where he ceases to act as the defendant's legal representative at a time when any relevant proceedings are current or in contemplation—
(a) inform the prosecutor of that fact, and
(b) if he is informed by the prosecutor that the defendant has a new legal representative who has given the prosecutor the undertaking required by this section, give the protected material, and any copies of it in his possession, to the defendant's new legal representative.

(6) He must, at the time of giving the protected material to the new legal representative under subsection (5), inform that person—
(a) that that material is protected material for the purposes of this Act, and
(b) of the extent to which—
(i) that material has been shown by him, and
(ii) any copies of it have been given by him,
to any other person (including the defendant).

(7) He must keep a record of every occasion on which the protected material was shown, or a copy of it was given, as mentioned in subsection (6)(b).

Disclosure to unrepresented defendant

12–106 **5.**—(1) This section applies where, in accordance with section 3(3), a copy of any material falls to be given by the prosecutor to the appropriate person for the purposes of this section in order for that person to show that copy to the defendant under this section.

(2) Subject to subsection (3), the appropriate person in such a case is—

(a) if the defendant is detained in a prison, the governor of the prison or any person nominated by the governor for the purposes of this section; and

(b) otherwise the officer in charge of such police station as appears to the prosecutor to be suitable for enabling the defendant to have access to the material in accordance with this section or any person nominated by that officer for the purposes of this section.

(3) The Secretary of State may by regulations provide that, in such circumstances as are specified in the regulations, the appropriate person for the purposes of this section shall be a person of any description so specified.

(4) The appropriate person shall take reasonable steps to ensure—

(a) that the protected material, or any copy of it, is only shown to the defendant in circumstances where it is possible to exercise adequate supervision to prevent the defendant retaining possession of the material or copy or making a copy of it,

(b) that, subject to paragraph (a), the defendant is given such access to that material, or a copy of it, as he reasonably requires in connection with any relevant proceedings, and

(c) that that material is not shown and no copy of it is given, and its contents are not otherwise revealed, to any person other than the defendant.

(5) The prosecutor shall, at the time of giving the protected material to the appropriate person, inform him—

(a) that that material is protected material for the purposes of this Act, and

(b) that he is required to discharge the obligations set out in subsection (4) in relation to that material.

(6) The prosecutor shall at that time also inform the defendant—

(a) that that material is protected material for the purposes of this Act,

(b) that the defendant can only inspect that material, or any copy of it, in circumstances such as are described in subsection (4)(a), and

(c) that it would be an offence for the defendant—

(i) to have that material, or any copy of it, in his possession otherwise than while inspecting it or the copy in such circumstances, or

(ii) to give that material or any copy of it, or otherwise reveal its contents, to any other person,

as well as informing him of the effect of subsection (7).

(7) If—

(a) the defendant requests the prosecutor in writing to give a further copy of the material mentioned in subsection (1) to some other person, and

(b) it appears to the prosecutor to be necessary to do so—

(i) in connection with any relevant proceedings, or

(ii) for the purposes of any assessment or treatment of the defendant (whether before or after conviction),

the prosecutor shall give such a copy to that other person.

(8) The prosecutor may give such a copy to some other person where no request has been made under subsection (7) but it appears to him that in the interests of the defendant it is necessary to do so as mentioned in paragraph (b) of that subsection.

(9) The prosecutor shall, at the time of giving such a copy to a person under subsection (7) or (8), inform that person—

(a) that the copy is protected material for the purposes of this Act,

(b) that he must not give any copy of the protected material or otherwise reveal its contents—

(i) to any person other than the defendant, or

(ii) to the defendant otherwise than in circumstances such as are described in subsection (4)(a); and

(c) that it would be an offence for him to do so.

(10) If the prosecutor—

(a) receives a request from the defendant under subsection (7) to give a further copy of the material in question to another person, but

(b) does not consider it to be necessary to do so as mentioned in paragraph (b) of that subsection and accordingly refuses the request,

he shall inform the defendant of his refusal.

(11) [*Making of regulations under subs. (3).*]

Further disclosures by prosecutor

12–107 **6.**—(1) Where—

(a) any material has been disclosed in accordance with section 3(2) to the defendant's legal representative, and

(b) at a time when any relevant proceedings are current or in contemplation the legal representative either—

(i) ceases to act as the defendant's legal representative in circumstances where section 4(5)(b) does not apply, or

(ii) dies or becomes incapacitated,

that material shall be further disclosed under this Act in accordance with whichever of section 3(2) or (3) is for the time being applicable.

(2) Where—

(a) any material has been disclosed in accordance with section 3(3), and

(b) at a time when any relevant proceedings are current or in contemplation the defendant acquires a legal representative who gives the prosecutor the undertaking required by section 4,

that material shall be further disclosed under this Act, in accordance with section 3(2), to the defendant's legal representative.

12–108 **7.** [*Regulation of disclosures by Criminal Cases Review Commission.*]

Supplementary

Offences

12–109 **8.**—(1) Where any material has been disclosed under this Act in connection with any proceedings for a sexual offence, it is an offence for the defendant—

(a) to have the protected material, or any copy of it, in his possession otherwise than while inspecting it or the copy in circumstances such as are described in section 4(2)(a) or 5(4)(a), or

(b) to give that material or any copy of it, or otherwise reveal its contents, to any other person.

(2) Where any protected material, or any copy of any such material, has been shown or given to any person in accordance with section 4(2)(b)(i) or (ii) or section 5(7) or (8), it is an offence for that person to give any copy of that material or otherwise reveal its contents—

(a) to any person other than the defendant, or

(b) to the defendant otherwise than in circumstances such as are described in section 4(2)(a) or 5(4)(a).

(3) Subsections (1) and (2) apply whether or not any relevant proceedings are current or in contemplation (and references to the defendant shall be construed accordingly).

(4) A person guilty of an offence under this section is liable—

(a) on summary conviction, to imprisonment for a term not exceeding *six* [12] months or a fine not exceeding the statutory maximum or both;

(b) on conviction on indictment, to imprisonment for a term not exceeding two years or a fine or both.

(5) Where a person is charged with an offence under this section relating to any protected material or copy of any such material, it is a defence to prove that, at the time of the alleged offence, he was not aware, and neither suspected nor had reason to suspect, that the material or copy in question was protected material or (as the case may be) a copy of any such material.

(6) The court before which a person is tried for an offence under this section may (whether or not he is convicted of that offence) make an order requiring him to return any protected material, or any copy of any such material, in his possession to the prosecutor.

(7) Nothing in subsection (1) or (2) shall be taken to apply to—

(a) any disclosure made in the course of any proceedings before a court or in any report of any such proceedings, or

(b) any disclosure made or copy given by a person when returning any protected material, or a copy of any such material, to the prosecutor or the defendant's legal representative;

and accordingly nothing in section 4, or 5 shall be read as precluding the making of any disclosure or the giving of any copy in circumstances falling within paragraph (a) or (as the case may be) paragraph (b) above.

[In subs. (4)(a), "12" is substituted for "six", as from a day to be appointed, by the *CJA* 2003, s.282(2) and (3). The increase has no application to offences committed before the substitution takes effect: s.282(4).]

Modification and amendment of other enactments

9.—(1) [*Modifies ss.5B to 5D of the* Magistrates' Courts Act *1980,* ante, *§§ 10–16* et seq.; *and repealed, as from a day to be appointed, by the* CJA *2003, s.332, and Sched. 37, Pt 4.*] **12–110**

(2) Despite section 20(1) of the *Criminal Procedure and Investigations Act* 1996 (disclosure provisions of the Act not affected by other statutory duties), section 3(3) to (5) of that Act (manner of disclosure) shall not apply in relation to any disclosure required by section 3, 7 or 9 of that Act if section 3(1) above applies in relation to that disclosure.

(3) [*See ss.17 and 18 of the* Criminal Procedure and Investigations Act *1996,* ante, *§§ 12–68* et seq.]

(4) [*Inserts subs. 1(6) into the* Criminal Procedure and Investigations Act *1996,* ante, *§ 12–52.*]

10. [*Financial provision.*] **12–111**

Short title, commencement and extent

11.—(1) [*Short title.*] **12–112**

(2) This Act shall come into force on such day as the Secretary of State may appoint by order made by statutory instrument.

(3) Nothing in this Act applies to any proceedings for a sexual offence where the defendant was charged with the offence before the commencement of this Act.

(4) This Act extends to England and Wales only.

Section 2 SCHEDULE

SEXUAL OFFENCES FOR PURPOSES OF THIS ACT

5. Any offence under section 1 of the *Protection of Children Act* 1978 or section 160 of the *Criminal Justice Act* 1988 (indecent photographs of children). **12–113**

5A. Any offence under any provision of Part 1 of the *Sexual Offences Act* 2003 except section 64, 65, 69 or 71.

6. Any offence under section 1 of the *Criminal Law Act* 1977 of conspiracy to commit any of the offences mentioned in paragraphs 5 and 5A.

7. Any offence under section 1 of the *Criminal Attempts Act* 1981 of attempting to commit any of those offences.

8. Any offence of inciting another to commit any of those offences.

[This schedule is printed as amended, and repealed in part, by the *SOA* 2003, ss.139 and 140, and Scheds 6, para. 36, and 7. The reference in para. 8 to inciting another to commit an offence has effect as a reference to the offences under Part 2 of the *SCA* 2007: 2007 Act, s.63(1), and Sched. 6, para. 34.]

(5) Miscellaneous

Advance information

The *CLA* 1977, s.48(1), (2), provides that *Criminal Procedure Rules* may make provision requiring the prosecution to give advance information as to the nature of their case, and requiring a magistrates' court to grant an adjournment in the event of non-compliance by the prosecution with their obligations under any rules so made, unless satisfied that the accused would not be substantially prejudiced by the non-compliance. The rule-making power was cast in the customary broad terms, allowing, *inter alia*, for different provision for different offences. Section 48(3) provides that it shall not be open to a person convicted of an offence to appeal against the conviction on the ground that **12–114** a requirement imposed by virtue of subsection (1) was not complied with by the prosecutor. Part 21 of the *Criminal Procedure Rules* 2005 (S.I. 2005 No. 384) which came into force on April 4, 2005, effectively reproduces the *Magistrates' Courts (Advance Information) Rules* 1985 (S.I. 1985 No. 601).

Criminal Procedure Rules 2005 (S.I. 2005 No. 384), Pt 21

Scope of procedure for furnishing advance information

12–115 **21.1.** This Part applies in respect of proceedings against any person ("the accused") for an offence triable either way.

Notice to accused regarding advance information

21.2. As soon as practicable after a person has been charged with an offence in proceedings in respect of which this Part applies or a summons has been served on a person in connection with such an offence, the prosecutor shall provide him with a notice in writing explaining the effect of rule 21.3 and setting out the address at which a request under that section may be made.

Request for advance information

21.3.—(1) If, in any proceedings in respect of which this Part applies, either before the magistrates' court considers whether the offence appears to be more suitable for summary trial or trial on indictment or, where the accused has not attained the age of 18 years when he appears or is brought before a magistrates' court, before he is asked whether he pleads guilty or not guilty, the accused or a person representing the accused requests the prosecutor to furnish him with advance information, the prosecutor shall, subject to rule 21.4, furnish him as soon as practicable with either—

(a) a copy of those parts of every written statement which contain information as to the facts and matters of which the prosecutor proposes to adduce evidence in the proceedings; or

(b) a summary of the facts and matters of which the prosecutor proposes to adduce evidence in the proceedings.

(2) In paragraph (1) above, "written statement" means a statement made by a person on whose evidence the prosecutor proposes to rely in the proceedings and, where such a person has made more than one written statement one of which contains information as to all the facts and matters in relation to which the prosecutor proposes to rely on the evidence of that person, only that statement is a written statement for purposes of paragraph (1) above.

(3) Where in any part of a written statement or in a summary furnished under paragraph (1) above reference is made to a document on which the prosecutor proposes to rely, the prosecutor shall, subject to rule 21.4, when furnishing the part of the written statement or the summary, also furnish either a copy of the document or such information as may be necessary to enable the person making the request under paragraph (1) above to inspect the document or a copy thereof.

Refusal of request for advance information

12–116 **21.4.**—(1) If the prosecutor is of the opinion that the disclosure of any particular fact or matter in compliance with the requirements imposed by rule 21.3 might lead to any person on whose evidence he proposes to rely in the proceedings being intimidated, to an attempt to intimidate him being made or otherwise to the course of justice being interfered with, he shall not be obliged to comply with those requirements in relation to that fact or matter.

(2) Where, in accordance with paragraph (1) above, the prosecutor considers that he is not obliged to comply with the requirements imposed by rule 21.3 in relation to any particular fact or matter, he shall give notice in writing to the person who made the request under that section to the effect that certain advance information is being withheld by virtue of that paragraph.

Duty of court regarding advance information

21.5.—(1) Subject to paragraph (2), where an accused appears or is brought before a magistrates' court in proceedings in respect of which this Part applies, the court shall, before it considers whether the offence appears to be more suitable for summary trial or trial on indictment, satisfy itself that the accused is aware of the requirements which may be imposed on the prosecutor under rule 21.3.

(2) Where the accused has not attained the age of 18 years when he appears or is brought before a magistrates' court in proceedings in respect of which this rule applies, the

court shall, before the accused is asked whether he pleads guilty or not guilty, satisfy itself that the accused is aware of the requirements which may be imposed on the prosecutor under rule 21.3.

Adjournment pending furnishing of advance information

21.6.—(1) If, in any proceedings in respect of which this Part applies, the court is satisfied that, a request under rule 21.3 having been made to the prosecutor by or on behalf of the accused, a requirement imposed on the prosecutor by that section has not been complied with, the court shall adjourn the proceedings pending compliance with the requirement unless the court is satisfied that the conduct of the case for the accused will not be substantially prejudiced by non-compliance with the requirement. **12–117**

(2) Where, in the circumstances set out in paragraph (1) above, the court decides not to adjourn the proceedings, a record of that decision and of the reasons why the court was satisfied that the conduct of the case for the accused would not be substantially prejudiced by non-compliance with the requirement shall be entered in the register kept under rule 6.1.

For the purposes of rule 21.3, "document" may include a video: *R. v. Calderdale Magistrates' Court ex p. Donahue and Cutler* [2001] Crim.L.R. 141, DC. Where a summary supplied in accordance with rule 21.3(1)(b) contains a reference to DNA profiles, that is not a reference to a document on which the prosecutor proposes to rely within the meaning of rule 21.3(3): *R. (DPP) v. Croydon Magistrates' Court* [2001] Crim.L.R. 980, DC. **12–118**

Where a prosecutor fails to provide adequate advance information pursuant to rule 21.3, the plea before venue procedure under the *MCA* 1980, s.17A (*ante*, § 1–67) should be adjourned "unless the court is satisfied that the conduct of the case will not be substantially prejudiced by non-compliance with the requirement" (r.21.6(1)) for advance disclosure: *R. v. Calderdale Magistrates' Court, ex p. Donahue and Cutler*, *ante*. And it is not open to justices, on the basis of the rules alone, to hold that the prosecution amounted to an abuse of process. The proper course is for the justices either to adjourn the case or to proceed, on satisfying themselves that no prejudice would be caused to the defendant by proceeding: *King v. Kucharz* [1989] C.O.D. 469, DC; and *R. (P.(A.), D.(M.) and S.(J.)) v. Leeds Youth Court*, 165 J.P. 684, DC. Nor is it a consequence of Article 6 of the ECHR (*post*, § 16–57) that prosecution witness statements in summary proceedings have to be disclosed to the defence before trial: *R. v. Stratford JJ., ex p. Imbert* [1999] 2 Cr.App.R. 276, DC.

A prosecuting authority, including local government authorities, should reveal the identity of a complainant to a defendant at an early stage and well before advance disclosure: *Daventry District Council v. Olins* [1990] C.O.D. 244, DC.

In *R. v. Serious Fraud Office, ex p. Maxwell (K.), The Times*, October 9, 1992, DC, it was held that there was no duty on the Serious Fraud Office to provide advance information under the equivalent to rule 21.3 where a case was to be transferred to the Crown Court pursuant to section 4 of the *CJA* 1987 (*ante*, § 1–41). The purpose of the rule was to enable an accused to make an informed choice as to the mode of his trial, but a defendant had no such choice in a case where a notice of transfer was served. In any event, it was to be doubted whether rule 21.3 was enforceable by a mandatory order, since the justices had no power to direct that advance information be given: in default of compliance, their power was to adjourn the proceedings (see also *R. v. Dunmow JJ., ex p. Nash, The Times*, May 17, 1993, DC). The Divisional Court also considered whether the Crown was in breach of its common law duty of disclosure in this case: see *ante*, § 1–285.

Serious fraud cases

See the *CJA* 1987, s.9, *ante*, § 4–84o. **12–119**

Expert evidence

See the *PACE Act* 1984, s.81, and Part 24 of the *Criminal Procedure Rules* 2005 (S.I. 2005 No. 384), *ante*, §§ 10–62 *et seq*. **12–120**

Long, complex or serious cases

Part III (ss.28–38) of the *CPIA* 1996 makes provision for preparatory hearings in **12–121** cases which are likely to be long, complex or serious (other than fraud cases). The details follow closely those in the *CJA* 1987 (fraud cases), including in relation to the judge's power to order a defence statement. As to the relationship of this power to order disclosure to the general power under Part I of the 1996 Act, see section 20(1), (2) (*ante*, § 12–70). For Part III of the Act, see *ante*, §§ 4–84s *et seq.*

Summary offences

12–122 The extent of the disclosure of the prosecution case that is necessary to ensure a fair trial depends on the evidence and the issues in the case; for the purposes of summary trials, the prosecution case must be revealed in sufficient detail to enable the defendant properly to prepare his defence; but the precise wording or content of disclosed statements, exhibits or other documentation does not limit what questions the prosecution may ask of their witnesses or the evidence they may introduce; provided that the requirements of natural justice are not breached, supplementary questions may be asked and areas may be explored in greater detail than revealed in the disclosed material: *Filmer v. DPP* [2007] R.T.R. 28, DC.

Chapter 13

EVIDENCE OF BAD CHARACTER

I. INTRODUCTION

A. Abolition of Common Law Rules

Criminal Justice Act 2003, s.99

Abolition of common law rules

99.—(1) The common law rules governing the admissibility of evidence of bad character in criminal proceedings are abolished. **13–1**

(2) Subsection (1) is subject to section 118(1) in so far as it preserves the rule under which in criminal proceedings a person's reputation is admissible for the purposes of proving his bad character.

As to what constitutes "evidence of bad character", see section 98, *post*, § 13–5. As to the survival of the common law in relation to evidence falling outwith the definition of "evidence of bad character" for the purposes of the 2003 Act, see, *post*, § 13–8.

Section 99(1) extends to abolition of the rule in *Hollington v. Hewthorn & Co. Ltd* [1943] 1 K.B. 587, CA (the prior conviction of a party was not even evidence of his having committed the offence that gave rise to the charge), if that rule ever applied to criminal proceedings; accordingly, it had no application to foreign convictions; such convictions, where they were otherwise admissible against the defendant via one of the gateways in section 101 of the 2003 Act (*post*, § 13–25), would be admissible provided that they were properly proved; and the method of proof was provided for by the *Evidence Act* 1851, s.7 (*ante*, § 9–97): *R. v. Kordasinski* [2007] 1 Cr.App.R. 17, CA. For criticism of this decision, see *Criminal Law Week* 2006/42/2. As to convictions abroad, see also *post*, § 13–99.

Commencement

Part 11 of the 2003 Act comprises sections 98 to 141. It is divided into three chapters, the first of which (evidence of bad character) consists of sections 98 to 113, the second of which (hearsay) consists of sections 114 to 136 (*ante*, §§ 11–2 *et seq.*)), and the third of which (ss.137–141) contains supplementary provisions. Section 141 provides that no provision of Part 11 has effect in relation to criminal proceedings begun before the commencement of that provision, and section 140 defines "criminal proceedings" for the purposes of Chapter 3 in identical terms to the definition in section 112 (*post*, § 13–8) for the purposes of Chapter 1 (*i.e.* "criminal proceedings in relation to which the strict rules of evidence apply"). **13–2**

In *R. v. Bradley* [2005] 1 Cr.App.R. 24, CA, it was held that the effect of section 141, when taken together with the definition of "criminal proceedings", was that the provisions of the Act would apply, and the common law rules would cease to apply, in relation to any trial or *Newton* hearing (as to which, see *ante*, § 5–74) that begins after the commencement date for the provision. *Bradley* (decided in relation to Chapter 1) was followed and applied in relation to Chapter 2 in *R. v. H. (P.G.)* [2006] 1 Cr.App.R. 4, CA, where it was held the provisions of the 2003 Act apply to all trials beginning on or after the date of commencement, even if a preparatory hearing in relation to the trial had taken place before that date, in relation to which section 8(1) of the *CJA* 1987 (*ante*, § 4–84n), and section 30 of the *CPIA* 1996 (*ante*, § 4–84u) provide that where a preparatory hearing is ordered, "the trial shall begin with that hearing".

The *Criminal Justice Act 2003 (Commencement No. 6 and Transitional Provisions) Order* 2004 (S.I. 2004 No. 3033) brought sections 98 to 110, and 112 into force on December 15, 2004, and section 113 into force on January 1, 2005. The provision for the making of rules of court in section 111 had already been brought into force.

For a case in which the judge applied the former statutory provisions, then had to reconsider the position upon the case of *R. v. Bradley* being reported, see *R. v. Lambrou, Constantinou and Gun* [2006] 2 *Archbold News* 2, CA.

Where a defendant was convicted before the bad character provisions in the 2003 Act had been brought into force, in a trial at which no evidence of bad character had been adduced against him, there was no unfairness where, following a successful appeal, he was retried after the commencement of those provisions, and evidence of bad character was admitted against him, pursuant to those provisions; it was a matter of chance whether a defendant faced trial before or after the change in the law; had there been any delay in hearing the appeal, however, this may have rendered an order for a retrial an abuse of process: *R. v. Campbell (Marvin)*, *The Times*, May 30, 2006, CA.

Reputation

13–3 The only qualification to the abolition of the common law rules is in section 99(2), which subjects the general abolition to section 118(1) of the 2003 Act (*ante*, § 11–70). That subsection saves, *inter alia*, the common law rule that allowed for proof of a person's bad character by the calling of evidence as to his reputation. Section 99(2) says nothing about when evidence of bad character may be given. That is dictated by the other provisions of Chapter 1 of Part 11, and, in particular, by sections 100 and 101. It merely provides that, where it is permissible to prove a person's bad character, it is legitimate to do so by calling evidence as to his reputation.

B. RELATIONSHIP TO OTHER STATUTORY PROVISIONS

13–4 There are various other statutory provisions that make provision for, or in relation to, evidence that may constitute evidence of bad character within section 98 of the 2003 Act (*post*, § 13–5). Three of them are mentioned in the provisions of Chapter 1 of Part 11. First, there is the reference to section 118(1) of the 2003 Act (*ante*, § 13–3). Secondly, section 112(3) (*post*, § 13–8) provides that nothing in Chapter 1 affects the exclusion of evidence under the rule in section 3 of the *Criminal Procedure Act* 1865 against a party impeaching the credit of his own witness by general evidence of bad character, or under section 41 of the *YJCEA* 1999. As to section 3 of the 1865 Act, see *ante*, § 8–94a. As to section 41 of the 1999 Act, see *ante*, §§ 8–123m *et seq.* Where, upon the trial of a sexual offence, it is sought to cross-examine the complainant as to sexual behaviour or to adduce evidence on that matter, if the matter also falls within the definition of bad character evidence, the judge will have to be satisfied as to both the requirements of the 1999 Act, and of section 100 of this Act (*post*, § 13–11): see *R. v. V.*, unreported, July 27, 2006, CA ([2006] EWCA Crim. 1901).

Section 6 of the *Criminal Procedure Act* 1865 (*ante*, § 8–151) provides that where a witness, upon being lawfully cross-examined as whether he has been convicted of an offence, denies the suggestion or does not admit it or does not answer, the cross-examining party may then call evidence to prove the conviction.

Sections 73 to 75 of the *PACE Act* 1984 (*ante*, §§ 9–80 *et seq.*) make provision for the manner of proof of convictions and acquittals, and as to what may be taken to be established by proof of a conviction.

Section 27(3) of the *Theft Act* 1968 (*post*, § 21–313) makes provision for proof of guilty knowledge on a charge of handling stolen goods by proof of previous convictions for handling or theft. See *post*, § 21–314, as to the relationship of that provision to the provisions of the 2003 Act.

The *Rehabilitation of Offenders Act* 1974 (*post*, §§ 13–120 *et seq.*) makes provision for the rehabilitation of offenders who have not been convicted of an offence for specified periods, which vary according to the severity of the punishment imposed. The fact that a defendant's previous convictions have become spent may be relevant in a number of ways in criminal proceedings. Typically, however, such a defendant may wish to be allowed to present himself to the court as a person of good character (as to this, see *post*, § 13–77), or the fact that the convictions are spent, or nearly spent, may be advanced as one reason for refusing a prosecution application to admit evidence of the defendant's bad character.

C. INTERPRETATION

Criminal Justice Act 2003, s.98

"Bad character"

98. References in this Chapter to evidence of a person's "bad character" are to evidence of, or of a disposition towards, misconduct on his part, other than evidence which— **13–5**

(a) has to do with the alleged facts of the offence with which the defendant is charged, or

(b) is evidence of misconduct in connection with the investigation or prosecution of that offence.

As to "misconduct", see *post*, § 13–8.

Evidence having to do with alleged facts of offence charged

Whether evidence "has to do with the alleged facts of the offence with which the defendant is charged" may itself be subject to argument. It is an important issue, because if the evidence does relate to the alleged facts, it does not have to pass through any of the various gateways in section 100 (non-defendants) or 101 (defendants) (the importance of this point being emphasised in *R. v. Edwards and Rowlands*; *R. v. McLean*; *R. v. Smith (David)*; *R. v. Enright and Gray* [2006] 2 Cr.App.R. 4, CA). Where the charge laid against the defendant cannot be proved without establishing the bad character of the defendant or another, then it is submitted that evidence to that effect must be taken to fall within paragraph (a). In the case of the defendant, an example would be driving whilst disqualified. Proof of the defendant's prior conviction and disqualification is not evidence as to bad character within this section. Examples of charges where proof of a person other than the defendant's misconduct is essential to proof of the charge would be allegations of offences contrary to section 4(1) (assisting offenders) or 5(1) (concealment of evidence) of the *CLA* 1967 (*post*, §§ 18–34, 28–29 respectively). Equally, where the allegation is that the defendant acted as a secondary party, aiding or abetting, counselling or procuring the offence, it will normally be essential to prove the commission of the offence by the principal (see *R. v. Turner* [1991] Crim.L.R. 57, CA). **13–6**

Another example, it is submitted, would be a charge of conspiracy. Conspiracy requires agreement by at least two people. It is essential, therefore, where a sole defendant is charged with conspiracy that the prosecution prove the guilt of at least one other person (identified or unidentified). Where an alleged co-conspirator has been convicted of participation in the conspiracy, his guilt of the offence may be proved under section 74 of the *PACE Act* 1984 (*ante*, § 9–82). The fact that such evidence might be damning, as where there are only two alleged conspirators, does not affect the admissibility of the evidence, but it may go to the discretion given to a judge under section 78 of the 1984 Act (*post*, § 15–452) to exclude evidence otherwise admissible under section 74. As to this discretion, see *ante*, §§ 9–89 *et seq.*

Further examples are provided by the offences of riot and violent disorder, contrary to sections 1 and 2 of the *Public Order Act* 1986 (*post*, §§ 29–4, 29–10), both of which require proof of participation by a minimum number of persons. Upon a charge against a single defendant for participation in either such offence, the prosecution must prove that others (to the required number) participated. As with conspiracy, the process of proof may be short-circuited where others have been convicted by proving their convictions under section 74 of the 1984 Act.

In all such cases, it is essential that the prosecution prove the guilt of the defendant (driving whilst disqualified), or of the principal offender or of the joint offender. Proof of such matters must be taken to fall outside the scope of Chapter 1 of Part 11 of the 2003 Act. It is not subject to the conditions of admissibility laid out in sections 100 and 101, nor is it subject to the discretion given to the judge in either of those sections or in section 103; but it may be subject to the overriding discretion given to judges in section 78 of the 1984 Act.

In other cases, evidence of misconduct on the part of a person other than the defendant may not be essential to proof of the defendant's guilt, but it may be directly relevant to it. Where the defendant is alleged to have been one of several joint venturers, it has always been open to the prosecution to prove the joint venturers' acts and declarations in furtherance of the joint enterprise. This rule was expressly preserved by section 118(1) of the *CJA* 2003 (*ante*, § 11–70), and it is submitted that evidence that is admissible under it, is evidence that "has to do with the alleged facts of the offence with which the defendant is charged" within section 98(a), and is thus outside the scope of Chapter 1 of Part 11. This was effectively confirmed in *R. v. S.* (2007) 151 S.J. 1260, CA (evidence of a co-defendant's guilty plea falls within s.98(a)).

Apart from the above, evidence which would have been admissible at common law, outside the rules relating to background or similar fact evidence, and evidence directly relating to the offence charged, provided it is of matters that are reasonably contemporaneous, and closely associated, with the alleged facts, will come within section 98(a): *R. v. McNeill*, 172 J.P. 50, CA. See also *R. v. Tirnaveanu* [2007] 2 Cr.App.R. 23, CA (to come within s.98(a), the evidence must have some nexus in time with the offence charged); and *R. v. Machado*, 170 J.P. 400, CA (evidence of reprehensible conduct on the part of the alleged victim that was contemporaneous with, and closely associated with, the alleged facts of the offence, fell within s.98(a)).

As to whether evidence falls within section 98(a), see also *ante*, § 9–86, and *post*, § 13–18.

Convictions overseas

13–7 See *ante*, § 13–1, and *post*, § 13–99.

Criminal Justice Act 2003, s.112

Interpretation of Chapter 1

13–8 **112.**—(1) In this Chapter—

"bad character" is to be read in accordance with section 98;

"criminal proceedings" means criminal proceedings in relation to which the strict rules of evidence apply;

"defendant", in relation to criminal proceedings, means a person charged with an offence in those proceedings; and "co-defendant", in relation to a defendant, means a person charged with an offence in the same proceedings;

"important matter" means a matter of substantial importance in the context of the case as a whole;

"misconduct" means the commission of an offence or other reprehensible behaviour;

"offence" includes a service offence;

"probative value", and "relevant" (in relation to an item of evidence), are to be read in accordance with section 109;

"prosecution evidence" means evidence which is to be (or has been) adduced by the prosecution, or which a witness is to be invited to give (or has given) in cross-examination by the prosecution;

"service offence" *means an offence under the* Army Act *1955, the* Air Force Act *1955 or the* Naval Discipline Act *1957* [has the same meaning as in the *Armed Forces Act* 2006];

"written charge" has the same meaning as in section 29 and also includes an information.

(2) Where a defendant is charged with two or more offences in the same criminal proceedings, this Chapter (except section 101(3)) has effect as if each offence were charged in separate proceedings; and references to the offence with which the defendant is charged are to be read accordingly.

(3) Nothing in this Chapter affects the exclusion of evidence—

(a) under the rule in section 3 of the *Criminal Procedure Act* 1865 against a party impeaching the credit of his own witness by general evidence of bad character,

(b) under section 41 of the *Youth Justice and Criminal Evidence Act* 1999 (restriction on evidence or questions about complainant's sexual history), or

(c) on grounds other than the fact that it is evidence of a person's bad character.

[In the definition of "service offence", the words in square brackets are substituted for the words from "means" to "Act 1957", as from a day to be appointed, by the *AFA* 2006, s.378(1), and Sched. 16, para. 215.]

As to section 3 of the 1865 Act, see *ante*, § 8–94a. **13–9**

As to section 41 of the 1999 Act, see *ante*, § 8–123m.

As to the definition of "criminal proceedings", see *R. v. Bradley*, *ante*, § 13–2.

In *R. v. Renda* [2006] 2 All E.R. 553, CA, it was held that "reprehensible behaviour" could include conduct of the defendant which had given rise to a charge, in relation to which juries had made findings that he was unfit to plead but that he had done the act charged against him.

As to the admissibility of facts giving rise to allegations that have never been tried, see *R. v. Edwards and Rowlands*; *R. v. McLean*; *R. v. Smith (David)*; *R. v. Enright and Gray* [2006] 2 Cr.App.R. 4, CA (stay on grounds of abuse of process); and *R. v. Ngyuen* [2008] 2 Cr.App.R. 9, CA (deliberate decision by prosecution not to make other matter the subject of a separate charge).

As to non-criminal conduct, see also *post*, § 13–61. As to conduct the subject of a separate charge on which a defendant is awaiting a separate trial, see *R. v. Rafiq*, *post*, § 13–72a.

In *R. v. Weir* [2006] 2 All E.R. 570, CA, it was held that, (i) evidence in one case that the 39-year-old defendant (charged with sexual offences against a 13-year-old girl) had had a three-year consensual sexual relationship with a girl who had been 16 at the outset of the relationship and of a suggestive remark made to the 15-year-old sister of the complainant, did not constitute evidence of "misconduct" where there was no particular feature (such as grooming, parental disapproval or particular immaturity of the girl) of an otherwise lawful relationship with the first girl to make it "reprehensible" and where the conversation with the sister was no more than "unattractive", but the evidence, not therefore being evidence of "bad character" within the 2003 Act, was potentially admissible at common law, and was so admissible as being relevant to the issue of whether or not the defendant would have had an interest in young girls; but (ii) evidence in a case of violent disorder, in which the four defendants were blaming each other, that the two appellants had on previous occasions come to the attention of the police as the victims of a knife attack, when they had refused to make statements, and as persons arrested on suspicion of a serious assault in relation to which the alleged victim refused to make a statement, could not amount to evidence of "misconduct"; it did not show a propensity to violence, and it would only have been relevant to the co-defendant's case (who had been responsible for adducing it) if it had so shown; accordingly, it had been wrongly admitted under the 2003 Act, and it was equally inadmissible at common law.

Evidence that the appellant snapped at his partner and was aggressive (but never violent) when he failed to take his medication for schizophrenia was irrelevant where the appellant was charged with the brutal murder of his close friend in circumstances which suggested that the killer had been known to the deceased and had attacked him unexpectedly (considering *R. v. Dolan* (*post*, § 13–35), and distinguishing *R. v. Fulcher* (*post*, § 13–30)); the evidence was not of "reprehensible behaviour" within the meaning of the Act; and, even if it was, it did not amount to "important explanatory evidence" within sections 101(1)(c) and 102 (*post*, §§ 13–25, 13–29): *R. v. Osbourne* [2007] Crim.L.R. 710, CA.

Evidence that a witness had taken an overdose was not evidence of "reprehensible behaviour": *R. v. Hall-Chung* (2007) 151 S.J. 1020, CA (considering *R. v. Osbourne*, *ante*).

The effect of section 112(2) is that, in a case where the defendant is charged upon several counts, the evidence going to one count is bad character evidence within the meaning of the Act, so far as the other counts are concerned: *R. v. Chopra* [2007] 1 Cr.App.R. 16, CA. And in *R. v. Wallace* [2007] 2 Cr.App.R. 30, CA, it was held that this would extend to a case where a defendant was charged on a multi-count indictment and the reality was that no count was self-contained and capable of being proved individually, but that the counts stood or fell together on the basis of the totality of the circumstantial evidence; and that technically a "bad character" application should be made although it would inevitably be granted. However, the court said that, since the purpose of the admission of the evidence in such circumstances was not to prove that the appellant was of bad character in the sense that the expression was commonly used, it would not be one in which the judge would be required to give any bad character direction to the jury.

D. ARMED FORCES

13–10 Section 113 of the 2003 Act gives effect to Schedule 6 (amended, as from a day to be appointed, by the *AFA* 2006, s.378(1), and Sched. 16, para. 234). This makes provision for the application of Chapter 1 of Part 11 to proceedings before service courts, subject to the various modifications set out therein. As to the commencement of section 113, see *ante*, § 13–2.

II. PERSONS OTHER THAN DEFENDANTS

(1) Statute

Criminal Justice Act 2003, s.100

Non-defendant's bad character

13–11 **100.**—(1) In criminal proceedings evidence of the bad character of a person other than the defendant is admissible if and only if—

(a) it is important explanatory evidence,

(b) it has substantial probative value in relation to a matter which—

(i) is a matter in issue in the proceedings, and

(ii) is of substantial importance in the context of the case as a whole, or

(c) all parties to the proceedings agree to the evidence being admissible.

(2) For the purposes of subsection (1)(a) evidence is important explanatory evidence if—

(a) without it, the court or jury would find it impossible or difficult properly to understand other evidence in the case, and

(b) its value for understanding the case as a whole is substantial.

(3) In assessing the probative value of evidence for the purposes of subsection (1)(b) the court must have regard to the following factors (and to any others it considers relevant)—

(a) the nature and number of the events, or other things, to which the evidence relates;

(b) when those events or things are alleged to have happened or existed;

(c) where—

(i) the evidence is evidence of a person's misconduct, and

(ii) it is suggested that the evidence has probative value by reason of similarity between that misconduct and other alleged misconduct,

the nature and extent of the similarities and the dissimilarities between each of the alleged instances of misconduct;

(d) where—

(i) the evidence is evidence of a person's misconduct,

(ii) it is suggested that that person is also responsible for the misconduct charged, and

(iii) the identity of the person responsible for the misconduct charged is disputed, the extent to which the evidence shows or tends to show that the same person was responsible each time.

(4) Except where subsection (1)(c) applies, evidence of the bad character of a person other than the defendant must not be given without leave of the court.

(2) Witnesses and non-witnesses

Section 100 regulates the admissibility of evidence as to the bad character of both witnesses (including those who do not give oral evidence) and non-witnesses. The principal distinction between the two will be in relation to evidence of bad character which goes only to credibility. Since the credibility of a non-witness will never be in issue, such evidence will be inadmissible. **13–12**

(3) Important explanatory evidence (subss. 1(a) and (2))

This head of admissibility coincides with one of the heads of admissibility in relation to a defendant: see sections 101(1)(c) and 102 (*post*, §§ 13–25, 13–29). This in turn was founded on the common law principle, for which *R. v. Pettman*, unreported, May 2, 1985, CA (5048/C/82) (*post*, § 13–30) is commonly cited as the leading authority. The principle is considered in more detail in relation to defendants, *post*, as it is in relation to defendants that the principles were elaborated in the authorities. The effect of section 100(1)(a) and (2) is that no different principle should operate in relation to persons other than the defendant. **13–13**

(4) Matter in issue (subss. (1)(b) and (3))

The principal matters in issue in criminal proceedings are whether the defendant did the act or made the omission charged against him, and, if he did, whether he did so with the relevant state of mind (intentionally, recklessly, knowingly, wilfully, dishonestly, with fraudulent intent, etc.), or whether he did so by mistake, by accident, through inadvertence or even in a state of automatism. If he did do the act or make the omission charged against him, and did so with the relevant state of mind, this will not necessarily be the end of the case, for the law may provide for excuses in the form of defences such as self-defence, duress or necessity, or, in a case of murder, provocation or diminished responsibility, and a host of other statutory provisions allowing for particular defences to particular offences. Not all of these issues will be live issues in any given case. Commonly, there will only be one live issue. Was it the defendant who did it? Was he acting dishonestly? Was he acting in self-defence? Where the issue is as to whether the defendant was responsible, a related issue will be as to who did do it (assuming there is no doubt that the crime was committed) if it was not the defendant. **13–14**

Where any of the foregoing issues are live issues in the particular case, it may safely be said that they are important issues. Resolution of any of them in favour of the defendant will be likely to be determinative of the outcome of the case. They are primary issues. There will be other issues in the case of a lesser order of importance in that their resolution one way or the other will not be determinative of the outcome of the case. Such issues may include matters such as whether or not the defendant has concocted his alibi, whether he lied during his interviews with the police, whether he mentioned a fact which he has relied on at trial, whether he lied during the course of his evidence, whether he opted to say nothing in police interview because he had been advised to do so by his solicitor or because he had not thought up a defence at the time or realised that any defence he might advance would be shown to be a pack of lies. Such issues may be called secondary issues.

The common law distinguished between matters going to the issue and matters going only to credit; and such distinction was also recognised in previous statute law. Thus both sections 4 and 5 of the *Criminal Procedure Act* 1865 (*ante*, §§ 8–125, 8–127) make provision for cross-examination on prior inconsistent statements "relative to the subject matter of the indictment" and for their proof if the making of such statement is denied. All of the matters mentioned above would be matters "relative to the subject matter of the indictment".

The language of section 100 does not recognise any distinction between matters going to the issue and matters going to credit only. The language, taken on its own, strongly suggests that it is only concerned with the admissibility of bad character evidence where such evidence is relevant to a matter in issue that is a matter relative to the subject matter of the indictment, *i.e.* that it is not concerned at all with evidence that is relevant only to credit. At common law, evidence that went only to credibility was never spoken of as having "probative value". Evidence only had "probative value" if it went to proving or disproving one of the primary or secondary issues in the case. Such a view of the legislation is borne out by subsection (3), the language of which is redolent of the common law rules relating to the admissibility of similar fact evidence. None of it is suggestive of evidence that goes only to the credibility of the witness.

13–15 In *R. v. S. (Andrew)* [2006] 2 Cr.App.R. 31, CA (and see *R. v. Weir* [2006] 2 All E.R. 570, CA, to similar effect) it was confirmed that this is not a correct reading of the legislation, and that section 100(1)(b) must be read on the basis that the creditworthiness of a witness is "a matter in issue in the proceedings" within paragraph (b)(i). The issue for the judge will then be to decide, upon an application to cross-examine the witness on his previous convictions, whether the matter is one of "substantial importance in the case as a whole", and, if it is, whether the matters which it is proposed should be put to the witness have "substantial probative value" in relation to that issue. Thus, on the first point, the judge may disallow the questions if of the opinion that whilst there is an issue as to the witness's credibility, it is a side-issue which could not possibly influence the outcome of the case; and, on the second point, the judge may disallow the question if of the opinion that, whilst the witness's credibility is right at the heart of the case, the matter that it is proposed should be put to him could not possibly influence the jury's assessment of the witness's evidence.

Credit as a matter in issue

13–16 As has been seen (*ante*), the credit-worthiness of a witness is to be regarded as a matter in issue in the proceedings for the purposes of section 100(1)(b). If the judge concludes that it is "of substantial importance in the context of the case as whole" and that the bad character evidence has "substantial probative value" in relation to this issue, then such evidence is admissible. In *R. v. Sweet-Escott*, 55 Cr.App.R. 316, Assizes, Lawton J. stated that the test to be applied was whether or not the matter which it was sought to put to the witness would affect his likely standing with the tribunal of fact. This test was approved by the Court of Appeal in *R. v. Funderburk*, 90 Cr.App.R. 466, and it seems probable that the Court of Appeal will equate it to the requirement that the bad character evidence should have "substantial probative value".

Complaints, disciplinary proceedings, acquittals, etc.

13–17 The following cases were decided at common law. Any application to cross-examine a police officer as to allegedly improper conduct will now be governed by section 100, but the approach of the courts to such issues prior to the enactment of the 2003 Act is likely to prove instructive. In *R. v. Edwards* [1991] 1 W.L.R. 207, CA, it was held that a police officer could be questioned as to any relevant criminal offences or disciplinary charges found proved against him, but charges which have not yet been adjudicated upon should not be put in cross-examination (under the 2003 Act a mere allegation would be held to have no "probative value" in relation to the issue of the witness's credit). A police officer who has allegedly fabricated an admission may be cross-examined to make the tribunal of fact aware that his evidence of an admission in a previous case was demonstrably disbelieved; where, however, the previous acquittal did not necessarily indicate that the officer had been disbelieved, such cross-examination was not to be allowed: *ibid.* (considering *R. v. Thorne*, *post*, and *R. v. Cooke*, 84 Cr.App.R. 286, CA, *ante*, § 4–331). Any answers given by police officers to questions directed to such collateral issues would be relevant to their credit only, and it would not be open to the defence to call evidence to contradict them: *ibid.*, rejecting a suggestion (based on *R. v. Busby*, 75 Cr.App.R. 79, CA, *ante*, § 8–150) that, apart from the exception in the case of bias (*ante*, § 8–148), there was a further exception to the rule as to the finality of answers going only to credit, namely "to show that the police are prepared to go to improper lengths to secure a conviction." The court said that a close study of

Busby seemed to show that its true basis may well have been the suggestion of bias against the particular defendants in that particular case.

Where a previous acquittal necessarily indicated that a police officer's evidence had been disbelieved, cross-examination of that officer in relation to that matter should be permitted notwithstanding that in the instant case the misconduct alleged against the police officer was of a different nature to that alleged in the earlier case: *R. v. Malik* [2000] 2 Cr.App.R. 8, CA.

In *R. v. Thorne*, 66 Cr.App.R. 6, CA, counsel sought leave to cross-examine a police officer about the verdicts of acquittal which had been returned by other juries in other cases in which the informer witness in the instant case had given evidence for the prosecution. The court, in upholding the judge's refusal to permit such cross-examination, held that the acquittals did not begin to prove that the informer was biased—as alleged—against any of the defendants in the instant case. Further, the fact that a jury return a verdict of not guilty does not go to prove that an important witness for the prosecution (albeit the sole witness) is a liar; nor could the pattern of acquittals properly assist in destroying the informer's credibility.

Matters in issue other than credit

Prosecution applications

If the evidence of misconduct on the part of the person other than the defendant "has to do with the alleged facts of the offence with which the defendant is charged", then it will not be subject to the requirements of section 100 (see s.98(a) (*ante*, § 13–6)). As to whether evidence does or does not have "to do with the alleged facts of the offence with which the defendant is charged", see *ante*, §§ 9–86, 13–6, where it is suggested that if it is essential, in order to prove the defendant's guilt, to prove that a person other than the defendant was guilty of an offence, then evidence adduced for that purpose would fall within section 98(a), as would evidence admissible pursuant to the rule that the acts and declarations of joint venturers in furtherance of the joint venture are admissible against each other. **13–18**

Apart from evidence falling within section 98(a) (and thus outside the provisions of Chapter 1 of Part 11 altogether), evidence of a person's bad character (within the sense of section 98) may be relevant to the prosecution's case in a variety of ways. Upon a charge of handling, it is an essential requirement that the goods should be proved to have been stolen. It will always be admissible on such a charge, therefore, to prove the commission of the theft by another; and in *R. v. Pigram* [1995] Crim.L.R. 808, CA, it was held to be legitimate to prove that another person committed the offence of handling the same goods for the purpose of proving that they were stolen goods. Similarly, on a charge of driving (or allowing oneself to be carried) in a conveyance taken without consent, contrary to the *Theft Act* 1968, s.12 (*post*, § 21–141), the prosecution may prove the non-consensual taking of the conveyance by another: see *DPP v. Parker* [2006] R.T.R. 26, DC. Where it is relevant to prove the commission of an offence by another, then this may be done by proving his conviction of that offence (see the *PACE Act* 1984, s.74, *ante*, § 9–82).

Prior to the enactment of the 2003 Act, section 74(1) of the 1984 Act did not merely provide that where evidence of the commission of an offence by a person other than the defendant was admissible, then this could be proved by proving his conviction of the offence. It stipulated a condition for the admissibility of evidence of another person's conviction for such purpose, *viz.* that proof of that other person's commission of the offence be "relevant to any issue" in the proceedings against the defendant. That condition has been removed from section 74 because it is now section 100 that provides for the conditions of admissibility of evidence not falling within section 98(a). Three cases decided in relation to section 74 illustrate, however, the potential operation of section 100(1)(b).

In *R. v. Robertson*; *R. v. Golder* [1987] Q.B. 920, 85 Cr.App.R. 304, CA, evidence was admitted (in the case of *Golder*) of the conviction of two co-accused of two offences (one of which was the offence with which the appellant was jointly charged) on the ground that the details fitted with the admissions alleged to have been made by the appellant, which were disputed; the effect of the evidence was to tend to rebut, therefore, the allegation that the admissions had been fabricated by the police.

In *R. v. Warner and Jones*, 96 Cr.App.R. 324, CA, the appellants had been convicted of conspiracy to supply controlled drugs. Observation evidence had been given of a large number of people visiting the address of one of the appellants. Many of the visitors were inside for only a minute or two. There was other evidence to suggest that the visits were not purely social. Evidence was admitted under section 74 to the effect that eight of the visitors had convictions for possession of, or supplying, heroin. It was held, distinguishing *R. v. Kearley* [1992] 2 A.C. 228, HL (*ante*, § 11–13), that no element of hearsay was involved. What the police were observing was the actual carrying on of a business by the appellants; evidence was being accumulated from which it could be inferred that actual sales were taking place involving both the visitors and the appellants. The character of the visitors was relevant to provide supporting evidence of the character of the transactions and of the purpose for which the appellants were letting the visitors into the house and, apparently, doing business with them. To similar effect, see *R. v. Rothwell*, 99 Cr.App.R. 388, CA.

In *R. v. Gummerson and Steadman* [1999] Crim.L.R. 680, CA, it was held that where the victim of a robbery had purported to recognise the voices of three offenders (A, B and C), the guilty plea of C was admissible under section 74 on two bases; first, it tended to make it more likely that the recognition of the other two offenders was accurate, especially where those identifications were made with more confidence (*R. v. Castle* [1989] Crim.L.R. 567, CA); secondly, there was evidence to link A and B with C both before and after the offence; where the identity of one of several offenders is known, it is relevant to prove the identity of the persons whom he was with before and after the offence, especially if they are the same persons.

For the suggestion that the evidence of C's guilt in *Gummerson and Steadman* is best regarded as evidence that had "to do with the alleged facts of the offence" with which A and B were charged, and thus would not be subject to section 100, see *ante*, § 9–86. The same applies to the disputed evidence in *R. v. Grey*, 88 Cr.App.R. 375, CA, and *R. v. Kempster*, 90 Cr.App.R. 14, CA. What emerges from these cases is that where there is evidence of the commission of an offence by two or more persons, evidence that a person other than the defendant committed the offence will be admissible as against the defendant, where there is evidence to connect the defendant with that other person in a material manner (as where they were seen together both shortly before and shortly after the commission of the offence).

Defence applications

13–19 Apart from cross-examination directed to credit only (*ante*), the defence may wish to elicit evidence of the bad character of a witness or non-witness for one of a number of reasons. Typically, the purpose sought to be achieved will be either to suggest that someone else committed the crime with which the defendant is charged, or to bolster a particular defence such as self-defence or duress, or to lend weight to the defendant's allegation of police malpractice in their investigation of the case against him.

13–20 **Suggestion that third party responsible.** At common law, it was always open to a defendant to suggest that someone other than himself was responsible for the crime with which he was charged (see *R. v. Greenwood*, *ante*, § 10–8; and *R. v. Lee*, 62 Cr.App.R. 33, CA, where evidence was admitted, on a charge of burglary, of the bad character of persons who were not called as witnesses, who had had access to premises). If the evidence is direct evidence to the effect that the third party was responsible, then such evidence will not fall within section 100 at all. Such direct evidence will have "to do with the facts of the offence with which the defendant is charged" within section 98(a) (*ante*, § 13–5) and will thus fall outwith the provisions of Chapter 1 of Part 11 of the Act. Section 100 is concerned with evidence of misconduct not connected to the particular offence that has probative value in relation to the identity of the perpetrator of the offence charged against the defendant. It opens the door to what may perhaps be called reverse propensity evidence. Subsection (3)(d) is directly concerned with such issues.

Bolstering particular defence. Prior to the enactment of the 2003 Act, cross-examination of—typically—the investigating police officer to establish the bad character of a person who was neither a party nor a witness commonly occurred in practice. The most obvious example was in cases of homicide. Where the defence to a charge of murder is self-defence and it is elicited that the deceased had a series of convictions for serious offences of violence, the relevance of this evidence is that it goes to disposition (see *R. v. Randall* [2004] 1 Cr.App.R. 26 (at [24]), HL). **13–21**

In *R. v. Murray* [1995] R.T.R. 239, the Court of Appeal had to consider the admissibility of the convictions of an absent witness. The accused was charged with reckless driving; his defence was "duress of circumstance" or necessity (see *post*, § 17–128), on account of the driving of the absent witness. The court ruled that evidence of the convictions of the other driver (all for dishonesty, except one of possession of a firearm within five years of release from Borstal) should have been admitted. The test was relevance, and knowledge of his character might well have coloured the jury's deliberations and bolstered the credibility of the appellant's account.

In *R. v. S. (Andrew)* (*ante*, § 13–15), it was held that a propensity on the part of a complainant to behave in the manner suggested by the defence as part of the defence must be a "matter in issue" within section 100(1)(b)(i).

Lending weight to suggestion of police malpractice. Prior to the 2003 Act, there had been a number of cases in which the defence had wished to elicit evidence of police malpractice in other investigations where it was being said that that malpractice bore striking similarities to the malpractice alleged by the defendant in the instant case. The allegation may have been in relation to the same officers or in relation to officers belonging to a particular squad—the suggestion in such cases being that such practices were endemic in the squad or even force concerned. In *R. v. Clancy* [1997] Crim.L.R. 290, the Court of Appeal regarded *R. v. Edwards* (*ante*, § 13–17) as decisive in relation to the question of whether evidence was admissible of discreditable conduct of police officers who were not witnesses but who belonged to the same squad as the officers who were witnesses to show a pattern of conduct common to the squad and designed to circumvent the protections afforded by the *PACE Act* 1984. In *R. v. Edwards (M.)* [1996] 2 Cr.App.R. 345 (referred to approvingly in *R. v. Whelan* [1997] Crim.L.R. 353, CA), however, the judgment of the Court of Appeal concluded (at p. 350G) that "it is impossible to be confident that had the jury which convicted this appellant known of the facts and circumstances in the other cases in which Constable C. had been involved, that they would have been bound to convict ...". The officer in question had been subject to an investigation, but no proceedings had been brought against him. This seemed to give the green light to what has been called (*Cross & Tapper on Evidence* (11th ed.), p. 391) "reverse similar fact" evidence applying to the previous conduct of a witness; but the prohibition on evidence relating to the previous conduct of other officers remained in place. **13–22**

Section 100(3)(c) would appear to open the way to such "reverse similar fact" evidence and without restriction as to whose conduct it relates to, provided only that it carries sufficient cogency. Where, therefore, it could be established that the defendant was alleging he had confessed only as a result of some peculiar misconduct on behalf of a police officer, and that he would have had no way of knowing that on 20 previous occasions similar misconduct by various officers in the same squad as the officer in question had preceded confessions by other persons in custody, all of whom had subsequently retracted their confessions, proof of those facts would provide cogent support for the defendant's case, and it is submitted that section 100 would allow for proof of them. That any evidence that the defence seek to introduce under this head must have "enhanced" probative value (as with common law similar fact evidence) is manifest from the terms of the legislation, and was confirmed (albeit *obiter*) by the House of Lords in *O'Brien v. Chief Constable of South Wales Police* [2005] 2 A.C. 534.

(5) Agreement of parties (subs. (1)(c))

This head of admissibility needs no elaboration. The purpose for which the evidence may be used will be delimited by the purpose of the parties in agreeing to its admissibility. **13–23**

(6) Requirement of leave

13–24 Apart from cases of agreed admissibility, there is a requirement that leave is obtained from the court (s.100(4)). The purpose of this provision, it is submitted, is to ensure that a ruling is obtained from the court as to the admissibility criteria being met. It is not the purpose of the provision to give the court a discretion to refuse leave despite the admissibility criteria being met. Evidence will not be admissible under section 100 unless, for example, it is *important* explanatory evidence, *i.e.* without it, the court or jury would find it impossible or difficult properly to understand other evidence in the case, and its value for understanding the case is substantial. Once the court has made the judgment that those criteria are met, there should be no question of a general discretion to refuse to allow the evidence in. And the same applies to section 100(1)(b)—the evidence must have *substantial* probative value to a matter in issue which is one of *substantial* importance to the case as a whole.

III. DEFENDANTS

A. ADMISSIBILITY

Criminal Justice Act 2003, ss.101, 108

Defendant's bad character

13–25 **101.**—(1) In criminal proceedings evidence of the defendant's bad character is admissible if, but only if—

(a) all parties to the proceedings agree to the evidence being admissible,
(b) the evidence is adduced by the defendant himself or is given in answer to a question asked by him in cross-examination and intended to elicit it,
(c) it is important explanatory evidence,
(d) it is relevant to an important matter in issue between the defendant and the prosecution,
(e) it has substantial probative value in relation to an important matter in issue between the defendant and a co-defendant,
(f) it is evidence to correct a false impression given by the defendant, or
(g) the defendant has made an attack on another person's character.

(2) Sections 102 to 106 contain provision supplementing subsection (1).

(3) The court must not admit evidence under subsection (1)(d) or (g) if, on an application by the defendant to exclude it, it appears to the court that the admission of the evidence would have such an adverse effect on the fairness of the proceedings that the court ought not to admit it.

(4) On an application to exclude evidence under subsection (3) the court must have regard, in particular, to the length of time between the matters to which that evidence relates and the matters which form the subject of the offence charged.

13–25a In *R. v. Renda* [2006] 2 All E.R. 553, CA, it was said that the circumstances were limited in which the Court of Appeal would interfere with decisions or rulings arising from the bad character provisions of the 2003 Act, which represented either judgments by a trial judge in the specific factual context of an individual case, or the exercise of a judicial discretion; a judge's "feel" for the case was usually the critical ingredient of the decision at first instance which the appellate court lacked, and context therefore was vital; further, the creation of, and subsequent citation from, a vast body of so-called "authority", in reality representing no more than observations on a fact-specific decision of a judge in the Crown Court, was unnecessary and may well be counter-productive; and even if it was positively established that there had been an incorrect ruling or misdirection by the judge, the Court of Appeal was required to analyse its impact (if any) on the safety of any subsequent conviction; it did not follow from any proved error that a conviction would be quashed.

To similar effect, see *R. v. Hanson*; *R. v. Gilmore*; *R. v. P.* [2005] 2 Cr.App.R. 21, CA (*post*, § 13–68); and *R. v. Campbell* [2007] 2 Cr.App.R. 28, CA (failure to give a direction that is no more than assistance in applying common sense to the evidence should not automatically be treated as a ground of appeal, let alone as a reason to allow the appeal); and the approach of the High Court, on an appeal by way of case stated, will be the same as that of the Court of Appeal: see *DPP v. Chand*, 171 J.P. 285, DC (unless court concluded that no reasonable tribunal could have decided as the magistrates' court had done, an appeal would be unsuccessful).

In *R. v. M.* [2007] Crim.L.R. 637, however, the Court of Appeal held that whilst a trial judge had a certain latitude when making a decision as to the admissibility of evidence of bad character through section 101(1)(d), on a propensity basis, the decision was not solely an exercise of discretion, and it would be interfered with on an appeal if his view as to the capacity of the prior events to establish the propensity was plainly wrong. Furthermore, the court said that where bad character evidence had wrongly been admitted via one gateway, a conviction could not be upheld on the basis that the evidence might properly have been admitted via another gateway, as the jury would have had to have been directed accordingly. As to this case, see also *post*, § 13–67; and, as to the relationship between the different gateways, see also *post*, § 13–102.

Where bad character evidence is admitted as being relevant to both propensity and credibility it would make no sense to give a standard good character direction, the effect of which would be the exact opposite of the direction on bad character. An appropriately modified direction would remind the jury that the defendant had no prior convictions and that, ordinarily, that would entitle him to a direction that that should be counted in his favour on both propensity and credibility. The jury should then be told that it was for them to consider which counted with them more, the absence of previous convictions or the evidence of bad character. If the former, then they should take that into account in the defendant's favour. If the latter, then they would be entitled to take that into account against him: *R. v. Doncaster*, 172 J.P. 202, CA.

Offences committed by defendant when a child

108.—(1) [*Repeal of* Children and Young Persons Act *1963*, *s.16(2)*, *(3)*, ante, *§ 8–163*.] **13–26**

(2) In proceedings for an offence committed or alleged to have been committed by the defendant when aged 21 or over, evidence of his conviction for an offence when under the age of 14 is not admissible unless—

(a) both of the offences are triable only on indictment, and

(b) the court is satisfied that the interests of justice require the evidence to be admissible.

(3) Subsection (2) applies in addition to section 101.

B. THE SEVEN GATEWAYS

(1) Agreement of parties (s.101(1)(a))

As in the case of section 100 (*ante*, § 13–23), this gateway needs no elaboration. **13–27** Subject to the decisions of the Court of Appeal in *R. v. Highton*; *R. v. Van Nguyen*; *R. v. Carp* and *R. v. Campbell* (*post*, § 13–102), the purpose for which the evidence may be used will be delimited by the purpose of the parties in agreeing to its admissibility.

(2) Evidence adduced or elicited by defendant (s.101(1)(b))

A defendant charged with a sex offence may wish to establish that he has no convic- **13–28** tions for any such offence, but he recognises that he must also own up to the fact that he has a conviction for excess alcohol and for a minor public order offence. This gateway allows him to "come clean" about those matters. The judge will be bound to give a character direction, which may by slightly modified as compared with the standard two-limb good character direction to which the defendant with no convictions and who gives evidence in his own defence is entitled.

A defendant may have other reasons for wishing to put in evidence some or all of his previous convictions (*e.g.* to suggest that the police simply picked on him because they knew he had convictions for like offences) in evidence. Whatever his reason, this paragraph allows him to do so. If evidence of his bad character is not and does not become admissible via any of the other gateways, then, subject to *R. v. Highton*; *R. v. Van Nguyen*; *R. v. Carp* and *R. v. Campbell* (*post*, 13–102), the use that may be made of the evidence will be determined by the purpose for which the defendant has introduced the evidence.

(3) Important explanatory evidence (ss.101(1)(c), 102)

Criminal Justice Act 2003, s.102

"Important explanatory evidence"

13–29 **102.** For the purposes of section 101(1)(c) evidence is important explanatory evidence if—

(a) without it, the court or jury would find it impossible or difficult properly to understand other evidence in the case, and

(b) its value for understanding the case as a whole is substantial.

13–30 This gateway coincides with the common law rule that permitted evidence to be adduced as to the background to an offence, where this was relevant to the offence charged and where the account to be placed before the court would be incomplete and incomprehensible without the background evidence, and this was so notwithstanding that such background evidence might include evidence establishing that the accused was guilty of an offence with which he was not charged: see *R. v. Pettman*, unreported, May 2, 1985, CA (5048/C/82); and *R. v. Fulcher* [1995] 2 Cr.App.R. 251, CA.

"Background" or "explanatory" evidence, for this purpose, includes evidence as to motive (although in *R. v. Edwards and Rowlands*; *R. v. McLean*; *R. v. Smith (David)*; *R. v. Enright and Gray*, *ante*, § 13–6, the possibility was canvassed of evidence as to motive being evidence that "has to do with the alleged facts of the offence" within s.98(a)). Although the prosecution do not have to prove motive, evidence of motive was always admissible at common law in order to show that it was more probable that the accused committed the offence charged. The position was well stated in a dictum of Lord Atkinson during argument in *R. v. Ball* [1911] A.C. 47, HL:

> "Surely in an ordinary prosecution for murder you can prove previous acts or words of the accused to show that he entertained feelings of enmity towards the deceased, and this is evidence not merely of the malicious mind with which he killed the deceased, but of the fact that he killed him. You can give in evidence the enmity of the accused towards the deceased to prove that the accused took the deceased's life. Evidence of motive necessarily goes to prove the fact of the homicide by the accused, as well as his 'malice aforethought,' in as much as it is more probable that men are killed by those that have some motive for killing them than by those who have not" (at p. 68).

As *Ball* was a case of incest, it is clear that Lord Atkinson's remarks were of general application, and not confined to murder. In *R. v. Buckley* (1873) 13 Cox 293, on a trial for murder, the deposition of the deceased against the defendant, taken on another charge against him, for which he was afterwards convicted, was held to be admissible evidence for the prosecution in order to prove malice or motive against the defendant.

13–31 The passage in *Ball* cited above was for long regarded as authority (together with *Buckley*, and the cases cited in the note to *R. v. Dosett* (1846) 3 C. & K. 306) for the proposition that evidence of motive is admissible and that motive can be established by previous words and acts notwithstanding that some or all of what is proved may reveal that the accused has committed other offences. Obviously, the evidence must have clear probative value and the more remote from the date of the offence the incident sought to be proved is, the clearer the probative value must be.

13–32 Some doubt about *Ball* having been expressed in *R. v. Berry (D.R.)*, 83 Cr.App.R. 7, CA, the issue was re-examined in *R. v. Williams (C.I.)*, 84 Cr.App.R. 299, CA. The court said that there was a good deal of authority to support the dicta of Lord Atkinson in *Ball* (that evidence of motive was admissible to show that it was more probable that the accused committed the offence charged) and of Kennedy J. in *R. v. Bond* [1906] 2 K.B. 389 at 401 (that relations of a murdered man to his assailant were properly admitted to proof as integral parts of the history of the alleged crime, so far as they might reasonably be treated as explanatory of the conduct of the accused). The court concluded that those dicta correctly represented the law, and that no further doubt about the matter need be felt. It was held, therefore, that on a charge of making threats to kill, contrary to the *Offences against the Person Act* 1861, s.16 (*post*, § 19–124), evidence of previous history was admissible as tending to prove that the defendant intended his words to be taken seriously.

13–33 *Pettman* (*ante*, § 13–30) was applied in *R. v. Sidhu*, 98 Cr.App.R. 59, CA: the appellant had been charged with two others with conspiracy to possess explosives in such circumstances as to give rise to a reasonable suspicion that they were not in their possession or under their control for a lawful purpose (*Explosive Substances Act* 1883, s.4(1), *post*, § 23–72). He had been seen with his co-accused at the house where they had taken explosives supplied to them by an undercover police officer, and his fingerprints were found on some of the notes with which they had paid for the explosives. In interview, he denied all knowledge of the explosives. He claimed to be a law-abiding citizen and denied being involved in any terrorist organisation, saying that he did not believe in violence as it was against his religious principles. He did not give evidence. The judge admitted a video, apparently made in Pakistan, which showed the appellant as one of a group of heavily armed people practising using various weapons, and singing in support of the Khalistan Liberation Force. The Court of Appeal upheld this decision on the ground that the video was clearly relevant to the reasonableness of the suspicion that the explosives were possessed for an unlawful purpose. It was evidence of a continual background relevant to the appellant's part in the conspiracy, without the totality of which the account placed before the jury would have been incomplete since, on the facts, the events shown on the video could not be said to be too remote in time.

For further illustrations of the application of the principle in *Pettman*, see *R. v. B.* [1997] Crim.L.R. 220, CA; *R. v. M. (T.)*; *R. v. M. (P.A.)* [2000] 1 W.L.R. 421, CA; *R. v. Shaw* [2003] Crim.L.R. 278, CA; and *R. v. W.* [2003] 10 *Archbold News* 2, CA (it made no difference to admissibility of such evidence that at material time the defendant would have been presumed to have been *doli incapax*, and to have been incapable of sexual intercourse); and, for what appears to have been an extreme example, see *R. v. Underwood* [1999] Crim.L.R. 227, CA. The principle was re-affirmed by the Court of Appeal in *R. v. Sawoniuk* [2000] 2 Cr.App.R. 220, where it was said that in order to make a rational assessment of evidence directly relating to a charge, it may often be necessary for a jury to receive evidence describing, perhaps in some detail, the context and circumstances in which the offence charged is said to have been committed; and in *R. v. Phillips (Alun)* [2003] 2 Cr.App.R. 35, CA, where the defendant had been charged with the murder of his wife, and it was held that evidence that the marriage had broken down was admissible both to rebut his claim that it was a happy marriage, and to show that he had a motive for killing her; a motive was not disqualified from being such simply because it would not move a rational person to act in a particular way (not following *R. v. Berry*, *ante*, to the extent that it suggested the contrary); in such a case, it will often be relevant for the jury to know about the matrimonial relationship in order to make a properly informed assessment of the entire evidence. **13–34**

In *R. v. Dolan* [2003] Crim.L.R. 41, CA, where the appellant had been charged with the murder of his baby by forceful shaking, and it was clear that the killing was the responsibility of one or both parents, it was held that evidence of various episodes, spoken to by the baby's mother and a former girlfriend of the appellant, in which he had lost his temper and displayed significant violence towards inanimate objects when they did not work had not been admissible under the *Pettman* principle; the fact that a man who was not shown to have any tendency to lose his temper and react violently towards human beings became frustrated and violent towards inanimate objects was irrelevant and inadmissible. See also *R. v. Osbourne*, *ante*, § 13–9. **13–35**

Where, at the appellant's trial for conspiracy to contravene the prohibition on the importation of cocaine, it had been the prosecution case that he had been stopped by police in a car in which he was knowingly transporting a drugs courier (carrying a kilogram of cocaine) and her principal from an airport, and where the appellant's case had been that he had innocently been giving a lift to a friend as a favour, the fact that he had, three-and-a-half years before, pleaded guilty to an offence of possession of cannabis with intent to supply (the facts being that he and two others had been stopped in a car in which a quantity of cannabis and cash had been found) and, two years before, had pleaded guilty to simple possession of cannabis, was not admissible as important explanatory evidence; whilst the evidence of the two convictions might have made it more likely that the jury would disbelieve the appellant's account, there was no basis for saying that the requirements of section 102 were satisfied in that the jury would have been disabled from, or at a disadvantage in, understanding any of the evidence allegedly connecting the appellant with the offence if they did not have the convictions before them:

R. v. Beverley [2006] Crim.L.R. 1064, CA. No consideration was given to the long line of authorities arising from customs prosecutions in which similar evidence has been admitted for the precise purpose of rebutting a defence of innocent coincidence (see *post*, §§ 25–471 *et seq.*). Whilst the court rejected an alternative prosecution argument that the convictions were admissible under section 101(1)(d) as establishing a propensity (see s.103(1), *post*, § 13–37), the customs authorities would have supported an argument that the convictions were admissible under section 101(1)(d), as being relevant to *the* matter in issue between prosecution and defendant, namely knowledge (*cf. R. v. Atkinson*, *post*, § 13–67, where a similar issue arose and where, as here, no reference was made to the customs cases).

In *R. v. Butler (Diana)* [2000] Crim.L.R. 835, CA, the court said that in the event of an issue arising as to the admissibility of evidence under this principle, counsel should endeavour to agree an account of the background so as not to distract the jury's attention from the central events. Failing agreement of which the judge approves, there should be a fuller analysis of the situation in the absence of the jury.

13–36 As to the particular need for caution where there is an application to adduce evidence via this gateway, but there is a risk that, once admitted, it will be used as evidence of propensity, see *R. v. Davis*, *post*, § 13–102.

(4) Important matter in issue between defendant and prosecution (ss.101(1)(d), 103)

Criminal Justice Act 2003, s.103

"Matter in issue between the defendant and the prosecution"

13–37 **103.**—(1) For the purposes of section 101(1)(d) the matters in issue between the defendant and the prosecution include—

(a) the question whether the defendant has a propensity to commit offences of the kind with which he is charged, except where his having such a propensity makes it no more likely that he is guilty of the offence;

(b) the question whether the defendant has a propensity to be untruthful, except where it is not suggested that the defendant's case is untruthful in any respect.

(2) Where subsection (1)(a) applies, a defendant's propensity to commit offences of the kind with which he is charged may (without prejudice to any other way of doing so) be established by evidence that he has been convicted of—

(a) an offence of the same description as the one with which he is charged, or

(b) an offence of the same category as the one with which he is charged.

(3) Subsection (2) does not apply in the case of a particular defendant if the court is satisfied, by reason of the length of time since the conviction or for any other reason, that it would be unjust for it to apply in his case.

(4) For the purposes of subsection (2)—

(a) two offences are of the same description as each other if the statement of the offence in a written charge or indictment would, in each case, be in the same terms;

(b) two offences are of the same category as each other if they belong to the same category of offences prescribed for the purposes of this section by an order made by the Secretary of State.

(5) A category prescribed by an order under subsection (4)(b) must consist of offences of the same type.

(6) Only prosecution evidence is admissible under section 101(1)(d).

(a) *Matters in issue*

13–38 Prior to the 2003 Act, it was safe to say that the matters in issue between prosecution and defendant were (a) whether he did the act or made the omission charged against him, and (b) whether he did so with the state of mind alleged (knowingly, intentionally, recklessly, dishonestly, wilfully, etc.) or whether he may have done it by accident, by mistake or even, possibly, whilst in a state of automatism. In particular cases, such as murder, there might be other issues. Thus, there might be no dispute that the defendant killed the deceased intentionally, the only issue being whether he was provoked or in a state of diminished responsibility. For further consideration of the matters that may be said to be in issue between prosecution and defendant in a criminal trial, see *ante*, § 13–14.

In considering matters in issue between prosecution and defendant, the one thing that the 2003 Act changes is that it deems (s.103(1)) propensity to commit offences of the type charged or to be untruthful to be a matter in issue for the purposes of gateway (d). Significantly, however, section 103(1) does not say that for the purposes of gateway (d) "the *important* matters in issue" include propensity. Propensity is thus deemed always to be "a matter in issue", save where the defendant having a propensity to commit offences of the type charged makes it no more likely that he is guilty of the offence charged, but not necessarily an "important matter in issue". That the omission of the word "important" in section 103(1) was deliberate tends to be confirmed by its inclusion in section 102, which begins "For the purposes of section 101(1)(c) evidence is important explanatory evidence if . . .". Furthermore, the heading to section 102 is "*Important explanatory evidence*" whereas the heading to section 103 is "*Matter in issue between the defendant and the prosecution*".

Thus, under the Act of 2003, the matters in issue between prosecution and defence are, as before, (i) did the defendant do the act, make the omission charged (though this frequently is not a live issue), and (ii) did he have the relevant state of mind? As before, there will be subsidiary issues (*e.g.* has the defendant fabricated an alibi?). Such subsidiary issues may or may not be rated "important", whereas the first two issues (provided they are live) are invariably going to be important. To these issues, the Act has added an issue, *viz.* whether or not the defendant has one of the stated propensities. On the assumption that this is rated an important issue, the important issues in the case will then be: Did he do it? Did he mean to do it? Does he have a propensity to do it?

Bad character evidence will be admissible via gateway (d) if it is relevant to any of these issues (as to which, see *R. v. Freeman*; *R. v. Crawford* [2008] 8 *Archbold News* 1, CA ([2008] EWCA Crim. 1863), where it was said that it was not always helpful to concentrate on propensity when considering section 101(1)(d)), and if it is relevant to either of the first two issues, reference to section 103 is entirely beside the point. If the evidence of previous offending reveals the commission of offences in a unique fashion (so-called leaving a signature at the scene) and the current offence was committed in an identical manner, the evidence of the previous offences by the defendant is relevant to the issue of who committed the offence. If the swimming instructor's defence to a charge of sexual assault is that he accidentally touched the complainant between her legs, evidence that he had 27 previous similar "accidents" would be admissible to prove that this was no accident.

Failing such direct relevance, evidence of bad character may be admissible to prove that the defendant had a propensity to commit offences of the type charged (provided, of course, that such issue has been rated "important" by the judge). Where the offender is charged with sex offences, evidence that he has a string of convictions for dishonesty will be irrelevant for this purpose, but evidence that he has convictions for sex offences will, pursuant to section 101(1)(d), be "relevant" to this issue.

At common law, evidence of previous misconduct ("similar fact evidence") was admissible to prove identity, or to rebut a defence of mistake, accident or innocent association, or to rebut a suggestion of mistake or fabrication on the part of the complainant or complainants. Evidence that was admissible at common law under this principle undoubtedly remains admissible under the 2003 Act. It is convenient, therefore, to set out the scope of the common law principles, and then, against that background, to consider when "mere propensity" evidence is to be rated an "important matter in issue", so as to permit evidence to establish such propensity. In *O'Brien v. Chief Constable of South Wales Police* [2005] 2 A.C. 534, HL, it was suggested, *obiter*, that the Act of 2003 had preserved the common law requirement of enhanced probative value in relation to similar fact evidence, but this view was rejected in *R. v. Weir* [2006] 2 All E.R. 570, CA, in which it was held that the common law test had been made obsolete by the Act, and that where evidence of the defendant's bad character was relevant to an important matter in issue between the defendant and the prosecution, then it was admissible subject only to the discretion given to the court by section 101(3).

(b) *Evidence that would have been admissible at common law*

Sufficient probative force

13–39 The leading case was the decision of the House of Lords in *DPP v. P.* [1991] 2 A.C. 447. The sole speech was delivered by Lord Mackay L.C. His Lordship concluded (at p. 460) that the essential feature of evidence to be admitted under the "similar fact" rule was that its probative force in support of the allegation being tried was sufficiently great to make it just to admit the evidence, notwithstanding that it was prejudicial to the accused in tending to show that he was guilty of another crime. Such probative force could be derived from striking similarities in the evidence about the manner in which the crime was committed, but restricting the circumstances in which there was sufficient probative force to overcome the prejudice of evidence relating to another crime to cases where there was some striking similarity between them was to restrict the operation of the principle in a way that gave too much effect to a particular manner of stating it, and was not justified in principle.

The great advantage of *P.* was that it rid the law of the notion that had developed in the years since the decision of the House of Lords in *DPP v. Boardman* [1975] A.C. 421, that the test of admissibility was that there should be a "striking similarity" between the similar fact evidence and the evidence relating to the charge being tried. What was now clear was that the degree of similarity required would vary according to the issues in the case and the nature of the other evidence.

The disadvantage of *P.* was that it gave little assistance as to what should be taken to invest the similar fact evidence with a sufficient degree of probative value. This disadvantage was more apparent than real because the Lord Chancellor's conclusion was expressed to derive from the five speeches in *Boardman*, from which his Lordship quoted at length. Perusal of those speeches gives a clear indication of what was to be regarded as investing the evidence with the requisite degree of probative force.

The unlikelihood of coincidence

13–40 There was abundant authority for the view that evidence would be admissible under the similar fact rule if explanation of it on the basis of coincidence would be an "affront to common sense", or would be "against all probabilities" or would be an explanation subscribed to only by an "ultra-cautious jury". If this were the case, then the evidence had the necessary probative force.

The leading authority for this proposition is *Boardman, ante*. The starting point, however, in any consideration of similar fact evidence had long been the opinion of Lord Herschell in *Makin v. Att.-Gen. for New South Wales* [1894] A.C. 57, PC.

> "The mere fact that evidence adduced tends to show the commission of other crimes does not render it inadmissible if it be relevant to an issue before the jury, and it may be so relevant if it bears on the question whether the acts alleged to constitute the crime charged in the indictment were designed or accidental, or to rebut a defence which would be otherwise open to the accused" (at p. 65).

The similar fact evidence would be relevant to the issue of whether the accused's conduct was accidental on the basis that a person may have one accident, but is unlikely to have two or more accidents of a similar nature. Although, therefore, his Lordship did not expressly mention "coincidence", it is plain that the unlikelihood of coincidence was the rationale justifying reception of the evidence.

13–41 In *Boardman*, the significance of coincidence to the decision about admissibility was expressly referred to by all five Law Lords. Lord Morris referred to the fact that Lord Herschell in *Makin* had given certain examples of when similar fact evidence might be admissible. His Lordship continued:

> "In his speech in *Harris v. DPP* [1952] A.C. 694, Viscount Simon pointed out, at p. 705, that it would be an error to attempt to draw up a closed list of the sorts of cases in which the principle operates. Just as a closed list need not be contemplated so also, where what is important is the application of principle, the use of labels or definitive descriptions cannot be either comprehensive or restrictive. While there may be many reasons why what is called 'similar fact' evidence is admissible there are some cases where words used by Hallett J. are

apt. In *R. v. Robinson* (1953) 37 Cr.App.R. 95 he said, at 106–107:

'If a jury are precluded by some rule of law from taking the view that something is coincidence which is against all probabilities if the accused person is innocent, then it would seem to be a doctrine of law which prevents a jury from using what looks like ordinary common sense.'

But as Viscount Simon pointed out in *Harris v. DPP* [1952] A.C. 694, 708 evidence of other occurrences which merely tend to deepen suspicion does not go to prove guilt: so evidence of 'similar facts' should be excluded unless such evidence has a really material bearing on the issues to be decided" (at p. 439).

His Lordship later referred to the summing up:

"The ... judge left the matter fairly to the jury. He mentioned the possibility of two or more people conspiring together and he examined the question whether there were or were not any indications that S and H had conspired together. That was important because one question which the jury may have wished to consider was whether it was against all the probabilities, if the defendant was innocent, that two boys, unless they had collaborated, would tell stories having considerable features of similarity" (at pp. 441–442).

Lord Wilberforce said that the basic principle must be that the admission of similar fact evidence is exceptional and requires a strong degree of probative force.

"This probative force is derived, if at all, from the circumstance that the facts testified to by the several witnesses bear to each other such a striking similarity that they must when judged by experience and common sense, either all be true, or have arisen from a cause common to the witnesses or from pure coincidence" (at p. 444).

Lord Hailsham said:

"In all these cases it is for the judge to ensure as a matter of law in the first place, and as a matter of discretion where the matter is free, that a properly instructed jury, applying their minds to the facts, can come to the conclusion that they are satisfied so that they are sure that to treat the matter as pure coincidence by reason of the 'nexus', 'pattern', 'system', 'striking resemblances' or whatever phrase is used is 'an affront to common sense' [*(DPP) v. Kilbourne* [1973] A.C. 729, *per* Lord Simon, at p. 759]. In this the ordinary rules of logic and common sense prevail ... Attempts to codify the rules of common sense are to be resisted" (at pp. 453–454).

Lord Cross said (at p. 457) that the question must always be whether the similar fact evidence taken together with the other evidence would do no more than raise or strengthen a suspicion that the accused committed the crime with which he is charged or would point so strongly to guilt that only an ultra-cautious jury if they accepted it as true, would acquit in face of it. Although the admissibility of such evidence is a question of law, not of discretion, the question must be one of degree. **13–42**

His Lordship then contrasted the issues arising in cases such as the instant case and *R. v. Sims* [1946] K.B. 531, 31 Cr.App.R. 158, CCA, with those arising in cases such as *R. v. Straffen* [1952] 2 Q.B. 911, 36 Cr.App.R. 132, CCA, and *R. v. Smith (G.J.)*, 11 Cr.App.R. 229, CCA (the "brides in the bath" case).

"In those cases there was no direct evidence that the accused had committed the offence with which he was charged but equally there was no question of any witness for the prosecution telling lies. In the first case one started with the undoubted fact that the child had been murdered by someone and in the second case with the undoubted fact that Mrs Smith had been drowned in her bath on her honeymoon. The 'similar fact' evidence was equally indisputable—namely, in the first case that Straffen had committed two identical murders and in the second that two other brides of Mr Smith had been drowned in their baths on their honeymoons. If it was admitted, this evidence, the truth of which was not open to challenge, provided very strong circumstantial evidence that in each case the accused had committed murder. In such cases as *R. v. Sims* ... or this case on the other hand there is, it is true, some direct evidence that the offence was committed by the accused but he says that that evidence is false and the similar fact evidence—which he says is also false—is sought to be let in in order to strengthen the case for saying that his denials are untrue. In such circumstances the first question which arises is obviously whether his accusers may not have put their heads together to concoct false evidence and if there is any real chance of this having occurred the similar fact evidence must be excluded ... . But even if collaboration is out of the way it remains possible that the charge made by the complainant is false and that it is simply a coincidence that others should be making or should have made independently allegations of a similar character against the accused. The likelihood of such a coincidence obviously

> becomes less and less the more people there are who make the similar allegations and the more striking are the similarities in the various stories. In the end … it is a question of degree" (at pp. 458–459).

Finally, Lord Salmon said:

> "The test must be—is the evidence capable of tending to persuade a reasonable jury of the accused's guilt on some ground other than his bad character and disposition to commit the sort of crime with which he is charged? … [E]vidence which proves merely that the accused has committed crimes in the past and is therefore disposed to commit the crime charged is clearly inadmissible. It has however never been doubted that if the crime charged is committed in a uniquely or strikingly similar manner to other crimes committed by the accused, the manner in which the other crimes were committed may be evidence on which a jury could reasonably conclude that the accused was guilty of the crime charged. The similarity would have to be so unique or striking that common sense makes it inexplicable on the basis of coincidence … the question of whether the evidence is capable of being so regarded by a reasonable jury is a question of law" (at p. 462).

The unlikelihood of coincidence as the basis for the admission of similar fact evidence was recognised by the Court of Appeal in *R. v. Groves* [1998] Crim.L.R. 200; and *R. v. Arnold* [2004] 6 *Archbold News* 2; and in *R. v. Chopra* [2007] 1 Cr.App.R. 16, the Court of Appeal acknowledged that it continued to be relevant, and would sometimes be critical, under the 2003 Act. "Mere coincidence" would not, however, suffice: see *R. v. Musquera* [1999] Crim.L.R. 857, in which the Court of Appeal observed that whilst *P.* had got rid of the necessity to identify a "striking similarity", it was still necessary to invoke some identifiable common feature or features constituting a significant connection and going beyond mere propensity or coincidence.

An Australian perspective

13–43 In *Pfennig v. R.* (1995) 127 A.L.R. 99, the High Court of Australia concluded that the basis for admitting similar fact evidence lay in its possessing a particular probative value or cogency such that, if accepted, it bore no reasonable explanation other than the inculpation of the accused in the offence charged; in other words, for propensity or similar fact evidence to be admissible, the objective improbability of its having some innocent explanation was such that there was no reasonable view of it other than as supporting an inference that the accused was guilty of the offence charged. Only if there was no such view could one safely say that the probative force of the evidence outweighed its prejudicial effect and admit the evidence. The High Court took the view that their formulation was entirely consistent with the English law as laid down in *Boardman* (properly understood) and *P.*

Practical application

Issues and evidence

13–44 When the topic is considered in the context of the issues which typically arise in a criminal case, the practical application of the principles involved becomes clearer. Before any judgment could be made about the admissibility of similar fact evidence in a given case, it was vital that there should have been a proper appreciation of what the issue was or was likely to be, and what the other evidence against the defendant was (see *per* Steyn L.J. in *R. v. Clarke (R.L.)* [1995] 2 Cr.App.R. 425 at 435, CA).

The issue in a case where there was some question of admitting similar fact evidence would probably be one of the following. First, as in *Straffen* (*ante*), it may have been clear that a crime had been committed and the only issue for the jury to determine would have been whether the defendant committed it. Secondly, the acts alleged against the accused may have been clear, or disputed as to matters of detail only, with the "live" issue being whether the acts were designed or accidental, or whether the defendant was acting under some mistake of fact. Where the case fell in this category, it was, of course, denied that a crime occurred, but this was because the physical act (of touching a girl's breasts or of receiving stolen goods) was said to have an innocent explanation. In a third category were cases where again the occurrence of any crime was denied, but this time it was because the evidence of the witness speaking to the facts alleged to constitute the crime was denied. It may have been said that the witness had deliberately invented the evidence, had imagined it, or was simply mistaken.

This summary of the issues which typically arose at common law (and will continue to arise under the 2003 legislation) does not purport to be exhaustive. In the following paragraphs, these categories are looked at more closely. This is done for the purposes of illustration; as has been repeatedly stressed in the authorities, it was an error to attempt to compose a definitive list of the sorts of cases in which the similar fact principle operated: see, especially, the speech of Lord Morris in *Boardman*, *ante*, § 13–41.

Identity

R. v. Straffen (*ante*, § 13–8) is perhaps the best known example of evidence of other crimes committed by the accused being given in evidence for the express purpose of proving that he committed the crime for which he was being tried, the only other evidence being of opportunity. **13–45**

Where identity is in issue, the degree of similarity required would vary according to the other evidence in the case: see *R. v. W. (John)* [1998] 2 Cr.App.R. 289, CA. If there was no other evidence in the case, something akin to a signature or fingerprint may have been necessary: *ibid.*

In *Thompson v. R.* [1918] A.C. 221, HL, offences of gross indecency were committed by a man against two boys in a public lavatory on a Friday. The man said he would meet them at the same place on the Monday. Their evidence on this was not in issue. The police were informed and were present watching on the Monday. The appellant arrived at the scene with two other men and engaged in some equivocal conduct and conversation with the boys. The boys indicated this was the man from the Friday and the police intervened. In his possession were found powder puffs and, at his home, were found photographs of naked boys. His defence was that he was not the man on the Friday and his conduct on the Monday was entirely innocent. The reasoning of their Lordships varied. There is little doubt that the case was regarded as close to the line. One view of the decision is that the finding of the articles, without more, effectively negatived the possibility that the boys had made a mistake in their identification: the chances of them picking out the wrong man and that man having articles of the sort that the right man might be expected to have had was so remote, that common sense dictated the view that there was no mistake. However, the better (and safer) view is that their Lordships were not, in fact, prepared to go that far. Without the appellant's equivocal conduct on the Monday, it is doubtful that the evidence would have been held to be admissible. One of the principal speeches was delivered by Lord Atkinson, whose line of reasoning involved an extra step. The man on the Friday made an appointment for the Monday. The appellant's conduct and conversation on the Monday were equivocal: the articles found rebutted the suggestion that the conduct on the Monday was innocent. What were the chances of one man making an appointment for an obviously immoral purpose and of another man being wrongly identified as that man, yet happening to harbour exactly the same intent as the first man? **13–46**

Consideration of *Thompson* merely serves to underline the vital importance of considering all the evidence, the issue to which the disputed evidence was said to relate and how it was said to relate thereto. In every case where identity was in issue, the judge should ask himself a question along the lines: if this evidence were added to the equation, would it be an affront to common sense to reject it as coincidence? Or, would only an ultra-cautious jury fail to act on it? It followed that a high degree of cogency was required, always having regard to the context. Judges would obviously take great care in considering the admissibility of such evidence. In particular, any suggestion that particular facts could not be sensibly explained as coincidence needed to be examined with particular care, lest there be an element of self-fulfilment. If, in circumstances similar to those in *Thompson*, a boy complained of being accosted in a public lavatory, which happened to be notorious as a location where homosexuals congregated, and the boy, having returned to the scene with the police, picked out a man as the offender, there would be little value in discovering that that man had convictions for homosexual offences or was in possession of articles suggestive of indulgence in homosexual practices. There would be a reasonable prospect that the same would be true of any man picked at random in that particular lavatory.

13–46a Where the issue at the appellant's trial for an offence of robbery was one of identification, and where the evidence of a victim of the alleged offence was that one of her assailants had said that he wanted his "coke" back, evidence of the appellant's previous conviction for being concerned in the importation of cocaine some seven years before the trial had been admissible, on the basis that it was relevant to an important matter in issue between the defence and prosecution by supporting the accuracy of the victim's identification as a connecting factor placing the appellant in a discrete category of persons interested in cocaine: *R. v. Isichei*, 170 J.P. 753, CA.

Accident, mistake, etc.

13–47 Where mistake, accident or innocent association was in issue it was obvious that a lesser degree of similarity may have been required, though the effect of the evidence must have been equally compelling. In a note on the case of *R. v. Lewis (P.A.)*, 76 Cr.App.R. 33, in 99 L.Q.R. 349, T.R.S. Allan takes as an example the case of *R. v. Francis* (1874) L.R. 2 C.C.R. 128, in relation to which he says:

> "Where, for example, the defendant is accused of defrauding a pawnbroker by representing a worthless ring to be a real diamond ring, evidence that he has previously made untrue assertions to other pawnbrokers concerning the value of other articles is likely to be highly probative in relation to his defence of mistake" (at p. 352).

13–48 In the following paragraphs some examples are given of cases where evidence was held to be admissible under the similar fact principle for the purpose of proving system or design, or of rebutting some such defence as accident or mistake. The examples relate to all types of allegations. They are included for the purposes of illustration. The key points to remember are that there were no special rules for particular offences and that, whatever the allegation, the issue for the judge would be whether the "similar fact" evidence so effectively proved intent or system, or negatived accident or mistake that only an ultra-cautious jury would fail to act on it; alternatively, would explanation of the evidence on the basis of coincidence be an affront to common sense? In these cases, as in cases where the issue was identity, it was vital that the judge had in mind the evidence in the case as a whole and the precise issue to which the disputed evidence was said to be relevant.

13–49 Where four indictments were found against a woman, which respectively charged her with poisoning her husband and two of her sons, and with attempting to poison a third son, evidence was tendered on the trial of the first indictment that arsenic had been taken by the three sons a few months after their father's death, that all four persons when taken ill exhibited the same symptoms, and that the defendant had been in the habit of preparing their meals. The court held the evidence admissible for the purpose of proving that the husband died of arsenic, and that his death had not been accidental: *R. v. Geering* (1849) 18 L.J.M.C. 215. In *Makin v. Att.-Gen. for New South Wales*, *ante*, § 13–40, *Geering* was approved, and the Privy Council held that on an indictment for the murder of an infant, in order to prove malice or meet the defence of accident, the prosecution could properly adduce evidence that other infants had been received by the defendants for a small sum, on a representation that they desired to adopt them, that the payments were insufficient to support the infants long, and that several bodies of infants had been found buried in the defendants' garden. See also the facts of the "brides in the bath" case (*R. v. Smith (G. J.)*) referred to in the extract from the speech of Lord Cross in *Boardman*, *ante*, § 13–42.

13–50 Where a brother and sister were indicted for incest committed in July and September, 1910, and it was proved that at these times they were living together and occupying the same bed, evidence was held to have been rightly admitted which showed that they had had a child in 1908, since it went to establish the existence of sexual passion between the parties as an element in proving that they had illicit connection in fact on or between the dates charged, and as negativing the defence of living together innocently: *R. v. Ball* [1911] A.C. 47, HL.

Upon the trial of an indictment under the *Offences against the Person Act* 1861, s.58, for "feloniously and unlawfully using a certain instrument, with intent to procure a miscarriage", in order to prove the intent, evidence may be given that at other times the defendant had caused miscarriages by similar means, and had then used expressions tending to show that he was in the habit of performing similar operations for the same illegal purpose: *R. v. Bond* [1906] 2 K.B. 389. Evidence that the defendant administered drugs to one woman with intent to procure her abortion may be admissible in support of a charge of having used an instrument with the like intent on another woman, and vice versa in order to refute the contention of the defence that the acts were done innocently: *R. v. Starkie* [1922] 2 K.B. 275, 16 Cr.App.R. 61, CCA. **13–51**

Where the defendant was indicted for arson with intent to defraud an insurance company, for the purpose of throwing light upon his intention, and proving that the fire was the result of design and not of accident, evidence was admitted that the defendant had previously occupied two houses in succession, both of which had been insured, that fires had broken out in both, and that the defendant had made claims upon and been paid by the insurance companies in respect of the loss caused by each fire: *R. v. Gray* (1866) 4 F. & F. 1102; approved in *Makin v. Att.-Gen. for New South Wales*, *ante*, § 13–40. The same rule applied where it was necessary to prove malice or intent on the part of the defendant. In *R. v. Harrison-Owen*, 35 Cr.App.R. 108, CCA, the defence to a charge of burglary was automatism; it was held that it was not permissible to cross-examine the defendant as to convictions for similar offences in order to rebut this defence. This decision was, however, doubted by Lord Denning in *Bratty v. Att.-Gen. for Northern Ireland* [1963] A.C. 386 at 410, HL. **13–52**

As to the application of these principles in the context of prosecutions relating to controlled drugs, see *post*, §§ 25–471 *et seq.* **13–53**

Allegation that prosecution witnesses mistaken or lying

This is the third broad type of defence that there may be to a criminal charge. The first (*ante*, § 13–45) involves admission that the offence was committed but denial that the perpetrator was the defendant. The second (*ante*, § 13–47) involves admission of many of the facts alleged, but putting an innocent gloss thereon. The third involves denial of the truth of the accounts given by the prosecution witnesses, whether it is said that they are mistaken (as a result of a vivid imagination or otherwise) or lying. **13–54**

Boardman (§§ 13–40 *et seq.*, *ante*) was itself such a case; *R. v. Sims* (*ante*, § 13–42) was another. The rationale of similar fact evidence in such cases was simply stated. Two or more people do not make up, or mistakenly make, similar allegations against the same person independently of each other. In *Sims*, Lord Goddard C.J., giving the judgment of a full Court of Criminal Appeal, said: **13–55**

> "The evidence of each man was that the accused invited him into the house and there committed the acts charged. The acts they describe bear a striking similarity … . The probative force of all the acts together is much greater than one alone; for, whereas the jury might think one man might be telling an untruth, three or four are hardly likely to tell the same untruth unless they are conspiring. If there is nothing to suggest a conspiracy their evidence would seem to be overwhelming" (at pp. 539–540, 168).

This reasoning was approved by Lord Cross in *Boardman*: see *ante*, § 13–42 for his Lordship's analysis of the problem. See also the reasoning in the Scottish cases of *Moorov v. H.M. Advocate* [1930] J.C. 68, and *H.M. Advocate v. A.E.* [1937] J.C. 96, which were specifically approved by Lord Hailsham L.C. in *DPP v. Kilbourne* [1973] A.C. 729.

In many of these cases, the suggestion would have been that the witnesses were lying. Sometimes, however, it would simply be alleged that they were mistaken. This was more likely to occur in cases of fraud, when a number of witnesses said that similar representations were made by the defendant. The defence may have been that no such thing was said; provided the witnesses were independent, the jury should have been allowed to take account of the evidence of A when considering whether B had made a mistake; and of the evidence of B when deciding whether A had made the same mistake. **13–56**

In such cases, the task of the judge would have been to assume that the evidence of the witnesses was true (*R. v. H.* [1995] 2 A.C. 596, HL, and see now section 109 of the **13–57**

2003 Act, *post*, § 13–104), and then ask himself whether explanation of the common allegations on the basis of chance or coincidence would have been an affront to common sense. No particular degree of similarity was required. The reality was that independent people do not make false allegations of a like nature against the same person.

Particular topics

Independent source

13–58 In *R. v. H.*, *ante*, Lord Mackay L.C. said (at p. 604) that unlike corroboration under the old corroboration rules, similar fact evidence did not have to come from a source independent of the witness giving evidence in relation to the offence charged. This, it is submitted, had to be seen in its proper perspective. As in all cases, much would depend on the nature of the issue. Where there was a complete denial of the evidence of the witnesses, it was inconceivable that if A gave evidence of ten identical offences committed against her by the defendant, the evidence of each offence should have been admissible as similar fact evidence in relation to all the other offences. There was no coincidence factor at all. It was only if another person (or other people) independently made like allegations that coincidence and similar fact came into play. If, however, the defence was one of admitting the essence of the evidence of the complainant, but putting an innocent explanation on it, the matter would be different. A swimming instructor may accidentally touch a girl between her legs on one or two occasions; but if his explanation of so touching a girl on a regular basis over a period of weeks is pure accident or inadvertence, the tribunal of fact would be entitled to take into account the whole of the girl's evidence in evaluating whether this was indeed accidental or whether to explain it on the basis of a series of similar accidents would be an affront to common sense, the true explanation being that the defendant was engaged in a systematic course of conduct.

At what stage to admit the evidence?

13–59 In *R. v. Bond* [1906] 2 K.B. 389, Darling J. said, with reference to *Makin's* case (*ante*, § 13–40): "I do not suppose that Lord Herschell meant that such evidence might be called to rebut any defence possibly open, but of an intention to rely on which there was no probability whatever" (at p. 409).

In *Thompson v. R.* [1918] A.C. 221 at 232, Lord Sumner said:

> "Sometimes, for one reason or another, evidence is admissible, notwithstanding that its general character is to show that the accused had in him the makings of a criminal, for example, in proving guilty knowledge or intent or system or in rebutting an appearance of innocence which, unexplained, the facts might wear. In cases of coining, uttering, procuring abortion, demanding by menaces, false pretences and sundry species of frauds, such evidence is constantly properly admitted. Before an issue can be said to be raised which would permit the introduction of such evidence, so obviously prejudicial to the accused, it must have been raised in substance if not in so many words, and the issue so raised must be one to which the prejudicial evidence is relevant. The mere theory that a plea of not guilty puts everything material in issue is not enough for this purpose. The prosecution cannot credit the accused with fancy defences in order to rebut them at the outset with some damning piece of evidence."

13–60 In *Harris v. DPP* [1952] A.C. 694, HL, it was laid down that the prosecution may adduce all proper evidence tending to prove the charge against the defendant, including evidence tending to show that the defendant has been guilty of criminal acts other than those covered by the indictment, without waiting for the defendant to set up a specific defence calling for rebuttal. It is submitted, however, that this was subject to the judge being satisfied that such evidence did in fact go to an issue before the jury. If not, he could hardly have been satisfied that the evidence had any probative value, let alone such compelling value as was necessary to justify its reception. As to the timing of the evidence, see also *R. v. Anderson (M.)* [1988] Q.B. 678, 87 Cr.App.R. 349, CA (a decision with less significance in an age of defence disclosure).

Non-criminal conduct

13–61 Evidence admitted under the similar fact principle was not confined to evidence which disclosed other criminal offences: see *Thompson v. R.*, *ante*, § 13–46; *R. v. Butler*, 84 Cr.App.R. 12, CA (on a charge of rape, evidence of similar conduct, but done with consent); *R. v. Ollis* [1900] 2 Q.B. 758; and *R. v. Downey* [1995] 1 Cr.App.R. 547, CA. Nor would evidence which revealed, or tended to reveal, the commission of another offence be excluded merely because a prosecution in respect thereof would be time-barred: see *R. v. Shellaker* [1914] 1 K.B. 414, 9 Cr.App.R. 240, CCA, and *R. v. Adams*, *The Times*, April 8, 1993, CA; or because the defendant had previously been tried and acquitted in respect thereof: *R. v. Z.* [2000] 2 A.C. 483, HL. *Cf.* the authorities under the 2003 Act, *ante*, § 13–9. For proof of propensity under the 2003 Act by reference to conduct that has not given rise to a conviction, see *R. v. McKenzie*, *post*, § 13–67.

As to how to direct the jury when non-conviction evidence is admitted in the case of a defendant with no previous convictions, see *R. v. Doncaster*, *post*, § 13–68.

Possession of incriminating articles

These cases typically consisted of the arrest of the defendant in respect of one matter and the finding of articles on him or at his home, his office or in his car which suggested involvement in, or close association with, some form of disreputable conduct. *Thompson v. R.* (*ante*, § 13–46) was such a case. **13–62**

If there was evidence to justify linking the articles to the crime charged, evidence of the finding of the articles was plainly admissible. If not, it was submitted that the general rules (*i.e.* those in *Makin*, *Boardman* and *P.*, *ante*, §§ 13–39 *et seq.*) applied. In *R. v. B. (R.A.)* [1997] 2 Cr.App.R. 88, however, the Court of Appeal held that where it was denied that the alleged criminal act took place, evidence of possession by the defendant of incriminating articles was inadmissible for the purpose of proving that the defendant had a leaning towards such acts as the act alleged.

The Court of Appeal referred to *R. v. Wright*, 90 Cr.App.R. 325, in which the headmaster of a school was charged with a large number of offences of buggery and gross indecency with male pupils. His defence was a complete denial of the alleged acts. One of the issues in the case related to the admissibility of a booklet found in his study; the booklet was clearly intended to appeal to a person with homosexual inclinations. In the course of giving the judgment of the Court of Appeal, Mustill L.J. said (at p. 329) that there was no need to burden the judgment "with the numerous and difficult authorities on the similar facts rule: a rule which has nothing to do with the present case". At page 331, however, his Lordship referred, in the context of the admissibility of incriminating articles, to *Makin* (*ante*, § 13–40, the starting point for any serious consideration of similar fact evidence). His Lordship then said that whilst such evidence might well be admissible where the essence of the defence was either identity or that the act had an innocent explanation, it was inadmissible where the defence was a simple denial that the acts in question ever happened at all. In *B.*, the court referred to this part of the judgment and said that it should be more widely known.

It is submitted, however, that there was no different principle for cases where the nature of the defence was a complete denial. It is further submitted that, contrary to what was said by Mustill L.J., the issue was one of (what was commonly understood to be) similar fact evidence. The view that some different principle applied according to the nature of the defence was rejected by Lord Cross in *Boardman* ("why should it make any difference to the admissibility ... of similar fact evidence whether my case is that the meeting at which the offence is said to have been committed never took place or that I committed no offence in the course of it?" (p. 458)): see also Lord Hailsham ("I do not see the logical distinction between innocent association cases and cases of complete denial" (p. 452)). The approach of the Court of Appeal in *R. v. Clarke (R.L.)* [1995] 2 Cr.App.R. 425 to evidence of possession of incriminating articles was that there was only one principle to be applied, namely that to be derived from *Boardman* and *P. Clarke* was a case where the identity of the offender was in issue, but the decision did not depend on a special rule applying to such cases. In *Wright*, the Court of Appeal accepted that where identity was in issue, evidence of similar fact or disposition (if sufficiently cogent) would be admissible (referring to *Thompson v. R.*, *ante*), but Lord Cross might as well have asked why it should make any difference that the defence is one of disputed identity as opposed to a complete denial of the allegation.

The assertion that the same principle applied to all cases regardless of the nature of the defence was not to assert that the application of that principle would lead to the same conclusion in all such cases. The probative value of the disputed evidence had to be assessed in the light of all the evidence and the issues in the case; to be admissible it had to be so cogent that if added to all the other evidence, only an ultra-cautious jury would acquit in the face of it. If a complainant made an allegation of a sexual offence against a person previously unknown to him, and the defence was one of complete denial, it is submitted that evidence of the finding in the accused's possession of a magazine depicting the commission of acts of exactly the same type as those alleged would be admissible. What are the chances of the complainant making an allegation of a serious sexual offence against a complete stranger, and that person turning out to have an interest in exactly the type of conduct of which he is accused? The practical application of the principle is unlikely ever to be so straightforward. In the majority of cases, the allegation is against someone (headmaster, scout leader, swimming instructor, etc.) who is known to the accuser, and a judge will no doubt bear in mind that if a false accusation is to be made, it is perhaps more likely to be made against a person known (or believed) to have a homosexual or paedophilic propensity; if the accused has been picked on for this reason, there would, of course, be no coincidence factor at all in the discovery of incriminating magazines or articles in his possession (*aliter*, of course, if the items were referable to the particular allegation).

13–63 In so far as the decision in *B. (R.A.)* suggests that different principles applied according to the nature of the defence, it is submitted that it is wrong. It was the practice of categorising allegations and defences which bedevilled this area of the law for so many years and which was condemned in *Boardman*.

Directing the jury

13–63a Where a number of independent allegations are before the jury, and they are being invited to conclude that they must all be true on the basis that independent people do not make up like, false allegations against the same person, it is not incumbent on the judge to anticipate in advance that the jury might acquit on some counts, and to warn them that if they do so the evidence of the relevant witnesses should be disregarded so that there are fewer allegations to support each other; the proposition which the jury have to consider is not that there could not be independent similar false complaints, but that each similar complaint makes each other similar complaint the more likely: *R. v. Chopra* [2007] 1 Cr.App.R. 16, CA.

To the extent that *R. v. S.*, unreported, February 29, 2008, CA ([2008] EWCA Crim. 544), suggested that the jury, in their decision-making process in such cases, should always first determine whether they were satisfied on the evidence in relation to one of the counts of the defendant's guilt before proceeding to use that evidence in dealing with any other count in the indictment, that approach was too restrictive; the jury should be reminded that they have to reach a verdict on each count separately, but they are nevertheless entitled, when determining guilt in respect of a count, to have regard to evidence relating to any other count or any other bad character evidence, provided that such evidence is relevant and admissible: *R. v. Freeman*; *R. v. Crawford* [2008] 8 *Archbold News* 1, CA ([2008] EWCA Crim. 1863).

(c) *Propensity evidence*

Whether propensity is a matter in issue and whether it is an "important" such matter

13–64 As to propensity being just one issue that may arise in a criminal case, see *ante*, § 13–38.

Whether the defendant has a propensity to commit offences of the kind with which he is charged is deemed by section 103(1)(a) to be a matter in issue between the defendant and the prosecution, "except where his having such propensity makes it no more likely that he is guilty of the offence charged". Similarly, whether the defendant has a propensity to be untruthful is deemed by section 103(1)(b) to be a matter in issue between defendant and prosecution, "except where it is not suggested that the defendant's case is untruthful in any respect."

The first question for the court to decide, therefore, when confronted by an application to admit evidence for the purpose of proving one or other propensity will be as to whether or not the relevant exception applies. If it does, then that is an end of the matter. If the judgment is that it does not, this does not determine the application in favour of the prosecution. It remains a matter for the judge to decide whether the defendant having the propensity in question is an "important" matter in issue (this point being underlined in *R. v. Bullen*, *post*, § 13–65a (at [33])). If not, then again, the application must fail. If, however, the prosecution surmount this hurdle, there is still the possibility of exclusion by virtue of the exercise of the discretion given to the court under section 101(4) and 103(3).

When should the propensity of the defendant to commit offences of the type charged be adjudged an "important" matter in issue? The answer, it is submitted, is when the fact of such propensity may, when combined with the other evidence in the case, serve to eliminate doubt or, occasionally, to found a convincing case. In the former category might be the case of the alleged burglar who seeks to undermine the reliability of the fingerprint evidence against him. A jury without knowledge of his several previous convictions for burglary might just have a nagging doubt. With such knowledge, they might be confident that all doubt is eliminated. In the latter category might be a case of theft in which it was possible to prove that only three people had the opportunity to commit the offence. It might be further possible to prove that those three people knew nothing of each other and that two of them had impeccable characters, but the third had a history of dishonesty. A jury would be entitled to conclude that it was against all common sense and reason to suppose that suddenly one of the other two candidates had done an act which was totally "out of character" and had happened to do so when, unknown to him, there was available an alternative candidate for whom such conduct would have been very much "in character".

As was the case at common law (*ante*), it is submitted that decisions as to the "importance" of propensity should be decided in the context of the facts of the particular case, the other evidence available to the prosecution and the issues in the case.

Authorities

The proper approach

To date, the Court of Appeal has steered clear of examination of the minutiae of the legislation. The leading case on the propensity provisions is *R. v. Hanson*; *R. v. Gilmore*; *R. v. P.* [2005] 2 Cr.App.R. 21, CA. The court issued the following guidance. First, when considering an application to adduce evidence of a defendant's previous convictions to establish propensity to commit offences of the kind with which the defendant is charged, a judge should consider whether the history of his convictions establish a propensity to commit offences of the kind charged, whether that propensity made it more likely that the defendant had committed the offence charged (see the exception in s.103(1)(a)), whether it was unjust to rely on convictions of the same description or category (see s.103(3)), and, in any event, whether the proceedings would be unfair if they were admitted (see s.101(3)); as to propensity to be untruthful, previous convictions were likely to be capable of showing such propensity only where, in the earlier cases, either there was a plea of not guilty and the defendant gave an account which the jury must have disbelieved, or the way in which the offence was committed showed such propensity, *e.g.* by making false representations. Secondly, applications to adduce such evidence should not be made routinely, simply because a defendant had previous convictions, but should be based on the particular circumstances of each case. Thirdly, in ruling on any such application, judges should bear in mind, (a) that, in referring to offences of the same description or category, section 103(2) was not exhaustive of the **13–65** types of conviction which might be relied upon; (b) that it was not necessarily sufficient, however, in order to show such propensity that a conviction should be of the same description or category as that charged; (c) that there was no minimum number of events necessary to demonstrate such a propensity; though the fewer the number of convictions, the weaker was likely to be the evidence of propensity; a single previous conviction for an offence of the same description or category would often not show propensity, but it might do so where, for example, it showed a tendency to unusual behaviour; (d) that the strength of the prosecution case must be considered; if there was no, or little, other evidence against a defendant it was unlikely to be just to admit his previous convictions, whatever they were; (e) that if there was a substantial gap between the date of the commission and the date of conviction for the earlier offence(s), the date of commission would generally be of more significance than the date of conviction when assessing admissibility; (f) that it would often be necessary to examine each individual conviction rather than merely looking at the name of the offence, and that the sentence passed would not normally be probative or admissible; (g) that where past events were disputed (as to which, see also *post*, § 13–66), the judge had to take care not to permit the trial to be unreasonably diverted into an investigation of matters not charged in the indictment; and (h) that, as to a propensity to untruthfulness, that was not the same as a propensity to dishonesty. As to directing the jury, see *post*, § 13–68.

In *R. v. Campbell* [2007] 2 Cr.App.R. 28, CA, it was said that the question of whether the defendant has a propensity to be untruthful will not normally be capable of being described as an *important* matter in issue between the defendant and the prosecution; the only circumstance in which there is likely to be an *important* issue as to whether a defendant has a propensity to be untruthful is where telling lies is an important element of the offence charged (but even then, the propensity to tell lies is only likely to be significant if the lying is in the context of committing criminal offences, in which case the evidence is likely to be admissible under s.103(1)(a)). It is submitted, however, that this approach is too restrictive for the reasons given in the commentary in *Criminal Law Week* 2007/26/1, and in *R. v. Jarvis* [2008] Crim.L.R. 632, CA, where it was held, without making reference to *Campbell*, that there is no warrant in the Act for restricting bad character evidence going to a propensity to untruthfulness to evidence of past untruthfulness as a witness; and that such an interpretation would largely and unwarrantably restrict the admission of relevant evidence. If, the court added, a witness or defendant has a proven history of untruthful dealing with other people, that would plainly be relevant and ought to be admitted, so long as it has substantial probative value on an issue arising between the relevant parties.

Function of the judge

13–65a The task of the trial judge was not to determine whether the evidence did in fact establish such a propensity, but was merely to determine whether it was capable of doing so; and whilst it was likely to be unjust to admit such evidence where the other evidence in the case against the defendant was weak (*R. v. Hanson*; *R. v. Gilmore*; *R. v. P.*, *ante*), where the judge had postponed dealing with the application until he had heard the bulk of the evidence called by the prosecution, he would be in the best position to determine whether the prosecution case was properly to be described as "weak" for this purpose: *R. v. Brima* [2007] 1 Cr.App.R. 24, CA.

As to the importance of ensuring that the evidence of reprehensible conduct is relevant to the particular matter in issue, see *R. v. Leaver*, 71 J.C.L. 124, CA ([2006] EWCA Crim. 2988) (evidence showed that defendant behaved in a contemptuous and degrading manner towards women; however, issue in case was "intent" on a charge of causing grievous bodily harm with intent to do so, an assault being admitted), and *R. v. Bullen* [2008] 2 Cr.App.R. 25, CA (on a charge of murder, whether defendant had propensity to violence was not an important matter in issue where only issue was whether he had specific intent required for murder).

Giving of appropriate notice and information

13–65b In *R. v. Bovell*; *R. v. Dowds* [2005] 2 Cr.App.R. 27, CA, it was said to be necessary for all parties to provide information in relation to convictions and other evidence of bad character whether in relation to a defendant or to some other person in good time; this could be achieved if the rules in relation to the giving of notice were complied with (as to which, see *post*, §§ 13–111 *et seq.*); in this connection, the court said that it should be noted that the basis of plea in relation to earlier convictions might be relevant where it demonstrated differences from the way in which the prosecution initially put the case.

There is no rule, however, that full details of previous convictions are necessary in every case where the prosecution seek to rely on them to demonstrate propensity; it is certainly good practice for such details to be available in case they are required, but whether they are necessary in order for the jury fairly to assess the convictions' relevance to propensity will depend on the facts of the case: *R. v. Lamaletie and Royce*, 172 J.P. 249, CA.

Resolution of factual disputes

In *R. v. Ainscough*, 170 J.P. 517, CA, it was said that disputes as to the facts of a previous conviction should, in almost all cases, be dealt with in accordance with *R. v. Humphris*, 169 J.P. 441, CA (*ante*, § 11–30) (*viz.* by having available a statement from the complainant in the previous case or the complainant in person); but this may not always be dispositive of the issue, since a complainant's evidence may be inconsistent with the basis upon which the defendant was sentenced (a fact also recognised in *R. v. Bovell*; *R. v. Dowds*, *ante*); in such cases, the court said, there would be a need for caution, a need to have regard to *Humphris*, and a need to ensure that the trial did not give rise to satellite issues as to what happened in a previous trial. **13–66**

In *R. v. Steen* [2008] 2 Cr.App.R. 26, CA, where the prosecution sought to prove the circumstances of a fraud of which the defendant had been convicted and which was similar to that alleged in the indictment, and where the defence would make no agreement as to those circumstances, it was held that a document which summarised the prosecution case, the facts which had clearly been admitted by the defendant and the manner in which the issues had been left to the jury by the judge, had been admissible for the purpose of proving the conduct underlying the conviction. The document was hearsay within the *CJA* 2003, but was admissible "in the interests of justice" under section 114(1)(d) (*ante*, § 11–3), where the underlying material (the defendant's interviews and evidence) could easily have been put before the jury in unredacted form, but where there was no reason why the jury should have been encumbered with unnecessary detail.

Establishing a propensity (s.103(2)–(6))

The *Criminal Justice Act 2003 (Categories of Offences) Order* 2004 (S.I. 2004 No. 3346) was made under section 103(4)(b), and came into force on December 29, 2004. It provides that the categories of offences set out in Parts 1 and 2 of the schedule are prescribed for the purposes of section 103(4)(b): art. 2(1); and that two offences are of the same category as each other if they are included in the same part of the schedule. Part 1 is headed "Theft Category", and lists offences contrary to sections 1, 8, 9(1)(a), if committed with intent to commit an offence of stealing anything in the building or part of a building in question, 9(1)(b), if committed by stealing or attempting to steal anything in the building or that part of it, 10, if the offender stole, attempted to steal or intended to steal, 12, 12A, 22 and 25 of the *Theft Act* 1968, and contrary to section 3 of the *Theft Act* 1978, and offences of aiding, abetting, counselling, procuring or inciting the commission of any of these offences, and attempts to commit any such offence. Part 2 is headed "Sexual Offences (persons under the age of 16) Category". It lists offences under the *SOA* 1956, ss.1, 5, 6, 7 and 10 to 15 (if, in the case of sections 1, 7 and 10 to 15, the offence was committed in relation to a person under the age of 16), under the *MHA* 1959, s.128 (if committed in relation to a person under the age of 16), under the *Indecency with Children Act* 1960, s.1, under the *CLA* 1977, s.54, under the *Sexual Offences (Amendment) Act* 2000, s.3, and under the *SOA* 2003, ss.1 to 4, 5 to 10, 14, 16, 17, 25, 26, 30, 31, 34, 35, 38 and 39 (if, in the case of ss.1 to 4, 16, 17, 25, 26, 30, 31, 34, 35, 38 and 39 the offence was committed in relation to a person under the age of 16, and if, in the case of section 14, doing it will involve the commission of an offence **13–67** under section 9 or 10), and offences of aiding, abetting, counselling, procuring or inciting the commission of any of these offences, and attempts to commit any such offence.

Where the defendant was charged with sexual assault on a child under 13, contrary to the *SOA* 2003, s.7, evidence that he had previously been cautioned for an offence of taking an indecent photograph of a child was admissible for the purpose of establishing a propensity on the part of the defendant to commit offences of the kind with which he was charged notwithstanding that such an offence was not included in the above order as being an offence of the same category as the other offences in the "sexual offences (persons under the age of 16)" category; if a propensity to commit an offence in a category prescribed by an order under section 103(4) could only be established by proof of a conviction of an offence in the same category, the use of the words "may (without prejudice to any other way of doing so)" in section 103(2) would be devoid of all significance: *R. v. Weir* [2006] 2 All E.R. 570, CA.

The fact that past convictions are of the same "description" or "category" does not automatically mean that they should be admitted; there must be a degree of similarity between the past offence and the current allegation, although the similarity does not have to be striking in the way that similar fact evidence had to be: *R. v. Tully and Wood*, 171 J.P. 25, CA (where appellants charged with robbery, judge had been wrong to rule that all their convictions for dishonesty could be admitted on the basis that a propensity to obtain other people's property by one means or another made it more likely that they would have committed the offence).

Where the appellants were charged with offences of violence arising out of an attack on the two complainants in a street late at night, and where the issue in both cases was identification, the judge had been entitled to admit evidence of the appellants' previous convictions for offences involving "street violence" as tending to show that they had a propensity to commit offences of the type with which they were charged: *R. v. Eastlake (Nicky) and Eastlake (Kevin Scott)* (2007) 151 S.J. 258, CA.

In *R. v. Atkinson*, 170 J.P. 605, CA, it was held that evidence that the defendant had previously been convicted of two offences of possession of class A drugs with intent to supply (which arose out of a single incident in which he had been stopped in a car in which crack cocaine and heroin were found to be concealed, and in relation to which he had pleaded guilty on the basis that he had been a custodian for another) did not demonstrate a propensity to commit an offence of being in possession of heroin with intent to supply where the material facts were that police officers had stopped the defendant in a car in which the drugs were concealed. For the suggestion that the evidence as to the previous conviction may have been relevant to the issue of knowledge, rather than propensity, see *Criminal Law Week* 2006/37/2; and see *ante*, § 13–38, for a discussion of "matters in issue". The court considered *R. v. Hanson*; *R. v. Gilmore*; *R. v. P.* (*ante*, § 13–65), but not the authorities referred to at §§ 25–471 *et seq.*, *post*. As to the issues in this case, see also *R. v. Beverley*, *ante*, § 13–35.

In *R. v. M.* [2007] Crim.L.R. 637, CA, it was held that whilst there may be cases where the factual circumstances of just one conviction (even as long ago as 20 years earlier) might establish a propensity, such cases would be rare and they would be those where the earlier conviction showed some special distinctive feature, such as a predilection on the part of the defendant for a highly unusual form of sexual activity, or some arcane highly specialised knowledge relevant to the present offence; where there were less distinctive features in common, evidence of the propensity manifesting itself during the intervening period would be necessary, in order to render the earlier evidence admissible as evidence of a "continuing propensity". As to this case, see also *ante*, § 13–25a. For an example of convictions in 1968 and 1974 being relied on to establish propensity, see *R. v. Sully* (2007) 151 S.J. 1564, CA (for the suggestion, however, that there had been no need to rely on the propensity head of admissibility, see *Criminal Law Week* 2007/46/2).

A propensity to commit offences of the kind with which the defendant is charged may be established by reference to offences committed after the date of the offence charged: *R. v. Adenusi*, 171 J.P. 169, CA; and see *R. v. Coltress*, 68 Cr.App.R. 193, CA.

As to the possibility of establishing a propensity to deal in drugs by proof that the defendant was in possession of a large quantity of cash, see *post*, § 27–75.

Where conduct that has not resulted in a conviction is relied on by the prosecution, particular care is required. First, there is a risk that such reliance will give rise to the trial of satellite issues, with the added dilemma that the more evidence there is of earlier reprehensible conduct, the more likely it is that the prosecution will be able to establish the alleged propensity, but the greater the risk of the focus of the trial being diverted onto such satellite issues. Secondly, where the previous matters were not even the subject of an investigation at the time, the evidence is liable to be stale and incomplete and the defendant is likely to be prejudiced in his efforts to deal with it by virtue of the passage of time and consequent inability to pinpoint details: *R. v. McKenzie* [2008] R.T.R. 22, CA.

Directing the jury

In *R. v. Hanson*; *R. v. Gilmore*; *R. v. P.*, *ante*, § 13–65, it was said that in any case **13–68** in which evidence of bad character was admitted to show propensity to commit offences or to be untruthful, the summing up should warn the jury clearly against placing undue reliance on previous convictions, and should, in particular, direct them that, (a) they should not conclude that the defendant was guilty or untruthful merely because he had those convictions, (b) although the convictions might show propensity, that did not mean that he had committed the offences or been untruthful in this case, (c) whether they in fact showed a propensity was for them to decide, (d) they must take into account what the defendant said about his previous convictions, and (e) although they were entitled, if they found propensity shown, to take that into account when determining guilt, propensity was only one relevant factor and they should assess its significance in light of all other evidence in the case. The court added that if a judge directed himself correctly, it would be slow to interfere with a ruling either as to admissibility or as to the consequences of non-compliance with the regulations for giving of notice of intention to rely on bad character evidence (as to which, see *post*, §§ 13–111 *et seq.*).

In *R. v. Edwards*; *R. v. Fysh*; *R. v. Duggan*; *R. v. Chohan* [2006] 1 Cr.App.R. 3, CA, it was said that the guidelines in *R. v. Hanson*; *R. v. Gilmore*; *R. v. P.*, as to what a summing up should contain, were not a rigid blueprint, departure from which would result in a conviction being quashed; what was required was (i) a clear warning to the jury not to place undue reliance on previous convictions, (ii) an explanation as to why they had heard evidence of the convictions and their relevance to the case (which would depend primarily, but not exclusively (as to which, see also *post*, § 13–102), on the gateway through which they had been admitted); provided the judge gives a clear warning to the jury, the terms in which he does so may differ from case to case.

In *R. v. Campbell* [2007] 2 Cr.App.R. 28, CA, it was said that the jury should be given assistance as to the relevance of bad character evidence which is tailored to the facts of the individual case; relevance can normally be deduced from the application of common sense; and, as to identifying the gateway through which the evidence was admitted, if the jury are told in simple language and with reference, where appropriate, to the particular facts of the case, why the bad character evidence may be relevant, this will necessarily encompass the gateway by which the evidence was admitted. As to this case, see also *ante*, § 13–65, and *post*, §§ 13–101, 13–102.

Where bad character evidence is admitted as being relevant to both propensity and credibility it would make no sense to give a standard good character direction, the effect of which would be the exact opposite of the direction on bad character. An appropriately modified direction would remind the jury that the defendant had no prior convictions and that, ordinarily, that would entitle him to a direction that that should be counted in his favour on both propensity and credibility. The jury should then be told that it was for them to consider which counted with them more, the absence of previous convictions or the evidence of bad character. If the former, then they should take that into account in the defendant's favour. If the latter, then they would be entitled to take that into account against him: *R. v. Doncaster*, 172 J.P. 202, CA.

(5) Important matter in issue between defendant and co-defendant (ss.101(1)(e), 104))

Criminal Justice Act 2003, s.104

"Matter in issue between the defendant and a co-defendant"

104.—(1) Evidence which is relevant to the question whether the defendant has a propensity **13–69**

to be untruthful is admissible on that basis under section 101(1)(e) only if the nature or conduct of his defence is such as to undermine the co-defendant's defence.

(2) Only evidence—

(a) which is to be (or has been) adduced by the co-defendant, or

(b) which a witness is to be invited to give (or has given) in cross-examination by the co-defendant,

is admissible under section 101(1)(e).

13–70 This gateway is intended to deal with "cut-thoat" defences. It does not, however, permit evidence that goes to mere propensity to commit offences of the type charged or of any other type (*i.e.* it must go to an "important matter in issue" between the defendants; mere propensity is not such an issue, and, unlike as between prosecution and defence, it is not deemed to be such an issue). Evidence of a propensity to be untruthful is, however, admissible under this head, but only if the nature or conduct of the defendant's case has been such as to undermine the co-defendant's case. Even if this is deemed to be the case, the co-defendant will not have licence to cross-examine the defendant as to all his previous convictions: see *R. v. Hanson*; *R. v. Gilmore*; *R. v. P.*, *ante*, § 13–65, as to the limited range of convictions that may be said to establish a propensity to untruthfulness.

13–71 Under the *Criminal Evidence Act* 1898, one ground for the admission of evidence of the defendant's bad character was that he had "given evidence against any other person charged in the same proceeding". The new formulation differs in one obvious respect, *viz.* there is no need for the defendant to have given evidence, although if he does not do so, there will be little scope for the operation of section 104(1) in any event. The leading case on the former provision was *R. v. Varley*, 75 Cr.App.R. 241, CA, where it was held that "evidence against" meant evidence which supported the prosecution case in a material particular or which undermined the defence of the co-defendant. The following points would seem to carry across to the new provision. First, the question whether one defendant's case has undermined the defence of another has to be judged objectively; hostile intent is irrelevant. Secondly, where it is suggested that a defence has been undermined, care must be taken to see if that really is the effect. Inconvenience to, or inconsistency with, the co-defendant's defence are not in themselves enough (see *R. v. Kirkpatrick* [1998] Crim.L.R. 63, CA). Thirdly, a mere denial in a joint venture did not rank as evidence against a co-defendant.

In *R. v. Crawford (Charisse)* [1998] 1 Cr.App.R. 338, CA, it was said that the essential question was whether the evidence damaged in a significant way the co-defendant's defence; if, on any factual matter, there was no issue between the Crown and a co-defendant, the defendant's evidence did not damage the defence of the co-defendant if it was to the same effect; if the evidence supports the Crown's case in a respect which is not contentious, that is not a material respect; if, however, the defendant's case supports the prosecution on a significant matter in issue between the Crown and the co-defendant and relative to proof of the commission of the offence by the co-defendant, that was evidence potentially damaging to the co-defendant and to be regarded as falling within the former statutory provision (considering *Murdoch v. Taylor* [1965] A.C. 574, HL, *R. v. Bruce*, 61 Cr.App.R. 123, CA, and *R. v. Varley*, *ante*).

In *R. v. Hatton*, 64 Cr.App.R. 88, CA, it was held that cross-examination under the former provision was attracted when the evidence was such that it did more to undermine the co-accused's defence than the Crown's case and thereby rendered his acquittal less likely.

In *R. v. Edwards and Rowlands*; *R. v. McLean*; *R. v. Smith (David)*; *R. v. Enright and Gray* [2006] 2 Cr.App.R. 4, CA, it was held that simply because an application is made by a co-defendant, a judge is not bound to admit it; the gateway in section 101(1)(e) must be gone through; but, in determining an application under section 101(1)(e), analysis with a fine tooth comb is unlikely to be helpful; it is the context of the case as a whole that matters; and section 104(1) is not exhaustive of the scope of section 101(1)(e); it limits evidence relevant to a defendant's propensity to be untruthful;

whether a defendant's stance amounts to no more than a denial of participation (see *R. v. Varley*, *ante*), or gives rise to an important matter in issue between a defendant and a co-defendant will inevitably turn on the facts of the individual case.

Apart from cases where the defence of one defendant undermines the defence of another defendant, there was a line of authority at common law that permitted one defendant to adduce evidence that was relevant to his defence, notwithstanding that it might reveal the bad character of a co-defendant. This line of cases, which began with *R. v. Miller*, 36 Cr.App.R. 169, Assizes (Devlin J.), and included the Privy Council decision in *Lowery v. R.* [1974] A.C. 85, culminated in the decision of the House of Lords in *R. v. Randall* [2004] 1 Cr.App.R. 26, in which it was held that whilst the prosecution were precluded from leading evidence that does no more than show an accused's propensity to commit the crime charged, no reason of policy or fairness required the exclusion of such evidence when tendered by a co-accused in disproof of his own guilt. A defendant was entitled to disprove his own guilt and might do so by tendering evidence of propensity on the part of a co-accused where to do so would show that his version of the facts was more probable than that put forward by a co-accused. **13–72**

It seems likely that the courts will adapt the *Randall* test to gateway (e). Where there is an important matter in issue between co-defendants (as where they directly blame each other and exculpate themselves), evidence of the bad character of one of the defendants will be said to have "substantial probative value" in relation to that issue if it tends to show that the version of the facts put forward by the other defendant is more likely to be true than the version put forward by that defendant.

In *R. v. Robinson* [2006] 1 Cr.App.R. 14, CA, it was held that where evidence of one defendant's bad character was adduced by another defendant, pursuant to the decision in *R. v. Randall, ante*, it was not a misdirection for the judge to instruct the jury that when considering the case against the first defendant, all the evidence in the case could be taken into account (*Randall* and *R. v. Price* [2005] Crim.L.R. 304, CA); whilst accepting that *R. v. Mertens* [2005] Crim.L.R. 301, CA, established that it would not be a misdirection to direct the jury to ignore such evidence when considering the case against the defendant to whom the evidence of bad character relates, that did not mean that *Price* was wrong; the effect of *Mertens*, supported by *R. v. Murrell* [2005] Crim.L.R. 869, CA, was that trial judges should consider carefully how the interests of justice for all defendants may properly be met in a "cut-throat" trial; but, in accordance, with *Randall*, the judge must also consider the necessity to give directions which will not "needlessly perplex juries". **13–72a**

In *R. v. Rafiq* [2005] Crim.L.R. 963, CA, evidence was admitted, pursuant to the principle in *Randall*, as to a matter for which one defendant was awaiting trial. Distinguishing *R. v. Smith* [1989] Crim.L.R. 900, CA (questions about a pending charge are improper) on the basis that it applied to a single defendant case and not to a *Randall*-type case, it was said that what mattered was not the fact or otherwise of conviction, but the particular circumstances in which the offence (if it had been committed by the defendant) had in fact been committed; and there could be circumstances in which the facts of a previous case could be relevant even though there had been an acquittal.

As to the discretionary exclusion of evidence admissible under this head, see *R. v. Musone*, *post*, § 13–110a.

(6) Correcting a false impression (ss.101(1)(f), 105)

Criminal Justice Act 2003, s.105

Evidence to correct a false impression

105.—(1) For the purposes of section 101(1)(f)— **13–73**

(a) the defendant gives a false impression if he is responsible for the making of an express or implied assertion which is apt to give the court or jury a false or misleading impression about the defendant;

(b) evidence to correct such an impression is evidence which has probative value in correcting it.

(2) A defendant is treated as being responsible for the making of an assertion if—

(a) the assertion is made by the defendant in the proceedings (whether or not in evidence given by him),

(b) the assertion was made by the defendant—

(i) on being questioned under caution, before charge, about the offence with which he is charged, or

(ii) on being charged with the offence or officially informed that he might be prosecuted for it,

and evidence of the assertion is given in the proceedings,

(c) the assertion is made by a witness called by the defendant,

(d) the assertion is made by any witness in cross-examination in response to a question asked by the defendant that is intended to elicit it, or is likely to do so, or

(e) the assertion was made by any person out of court, and the defendant adduces evidence of it in the proceedings.

(3) A defendant who would otherwise be treated as responsible for the making of an assertion shall not be so treated if, or to the extent that, he withdraws it or disassociates himself from it.

(4) Where it appears to the court that a defendant, by means of his conduct (other than the giving of evidence) in the proceedings, is seeking to give the court or jury an impression about himself that is false or misleading, the court may if it appears just to do so treat the defendant as being responsible for the making of an assertion which is apt to give that impression.

(5) In subsection (4) "conduct" includes appearance or dress.

(6) Evidence is admissible under section 101(1)(f) only if it goes no further than is necessary to correct the false impression.

(7) Only prosecution evidence is admissible under section 101(1)(f).

Misleading impression about the defendant

13–74 Under the *Criminal Evidence Act* 1898, the defendant could be cross-examined as to his bad character if, *inter alia*, he or his advocate had "asked questions of the witnesses for the prosecution with a view to establish his good character, or has given evidence of his good character". Under the 2003 legislation, correcting evidence may be given notwithstanding that the defendant himself does not give evidence.

In *R. v. Renda* [2006] 2 All E.R. 553, CA, it was said that, for the purposes of section 101(1)(f), the question whether the defendant had given a "false impression" about himself, and whether there was evidence which may properly serve to correct such a false impression within section 105(1)(a) and (b) was fact-specific; and it was most unlikely to be useful to refer to authorities (including those considering the 1898 Act) which were no more than factual examples of occasions when it was decided that an individual defendant had put his character in issue; and, for the purposes of section 105(3), there was a significant difference between the defendant who made a specific and positive decision to correct a false impression for which he was responsible, or to disassociate himself from false impressions conveyed by the assertions of others, and the defendant who in cross-examination was obliged to concede that he had been misleading the jury; a concession extracted in cross-examination that the defendant had not been telling the truth in part of his examination-in-chief would not normally amount to a withdrawal or disassociation from the original assertion for the purposes of that subsection.

13–75 In deference to what was said *Renda*, *ante*, decisions under the 1898 Act as to what did or did not put the defendant's character in issue have been omitted from this edition, although it is submitted that they may still prove useful as a guide. The following cases under the former legislation would appear, however, to have continuing relevance as to the consequences of putting character in issue. A defendant could not claim to be entitled to put in issue part of his character only. Thus, if he called a witness to establish his good character with regard to sexual morality, the witness could be cross-examined by the prosecution on the defendant's convictions for offences involving dishonesty: *R. v. Winfield*, 27 Cr.App.R. 139, CCA, and *R. v. Morris*, 43 Cr.App.R. 206, CCA. A defendant could not assert his good character in certain respects without exposing himself to inquiry as to the rest of his record so far as this tended to disprove his claim to good character: *Stirland v. DPP* [1944] A.C. 315, HL.

13–76 It is no disproof of good character that a person has been suspected or accused of a previous crime. Accordingly, such questions as "Were you suspected?" or "Were you accused?" are permissible only if the defendant has expressly or impliedly asserted the contrary: see section 105(1)(a), and *Stirland v. DPP* [1944] A.C. 315, HL; and *R. v. Meehan and Meehan* [1978] Crim.L.R. 690, CA.

Where a defendant had made an assertion in interview which would be apt to give the court or jury a false or misleading impression about him, a judge would be entitled to admit evidence of his bad character before evidence of the assertion was adduced, notwithstanding the language of section 105(2)(b); the sensible procedure to adopt in such cases would be for the prosecution to make their application before evidence of the interviews was adduced: *R. v. Ullah*, unreported, July 18, 2006, CA ([2006] EWCA Crim. 2003). **13–76a**

In *R. v. Spartley* (2007) 151 S.J. 670, the Court of Appeal upheld a judge's decision to admit evidence of an admission against interest made by the defendant in an interview by an overseas police force several years previously for the purpose of contradicting his assertion of never having been involved in the type of activity alleged against him.

Effect of previous convictions being "spent"

As to when convictions become "spent", see the *Rehabilitation of Offenders Act* 1974, *post*, §§ 13–120 *et seq*. See also paragraph I.6 of the consolidated criminal practice direction, *post*, § 13–121. As to the appropriate directions to the jury, see *ante*, §§ 4–406 *et seq*. **13–77**

Defence counsel frequently invite judges to approve a formula which could be put to the relevant police officer or admitted by the Crown which in effect puts the defendant before the jury as a man of good character despite his previous, though spent, convictions. This issue was considered by the Court of Appeal in *R. v. Nye*, 75 Cr.App.R. 247. The court rejected the submission that when a man, who has previously been convicted, has reached the stage when his conviction or convictions are spent, he should as of right be entitled to present himself as a man of good character and to claim as much if he comes again to be tried for some offence.

> "(I)t is entirely a question for the discretion of the judge. It may well be that the past spent conviction happened when the defendant being tried was a juvenile, for instance for stealing apples, a conviction of many years before. In those circumstances quite plainly a trial judge would rule that such a person ought to be permitted to present himself as a man of good character. At the other end of the scale, if a defendant is a man who has been convicted of some offence of violence and his conviction has only just been spent and the offence for which he is then standing trial involves some violence, then it would be plain that a trial judge would rule that it would not be right for such a person to present himself as a man of good character. The essence of this matter is that the jury must not be misled and no lie must be told to them about this matter. The exercise of discretion of the trial judge in the cases which fall between the two extremes referred to must be carried out having regard to the 1974 Act and to the practice direction. It should be exercised, so far as it can be, favourably towards the accused person" (*per* Talbot J. at pp. 250, 251).

In *R. v. O'Shea*, *The Times*, June 8, 1993, CA, it was said that whatever formula the judge chooses to adopt, there must be no question of the jury being misled and they must certainly not be told that the defendant has no previous convictions. See also *R. v. M. (Ian)* [1999] 6 *Archbold News* 3, CA, to similar effect. In *R. v. M. (Ian)*, the court added that in the normal case the jury should be told of the convictions, that they are spent, and, if it be the case, that they are of an entirely different nature and that the accused pleaded guilty; and the judge should direct the jury that they may think it right to treat the accused as a person of good character, and, if they so think, then that is a matter that they should take into account in evaluating his evidence, and in considering whether he is the sort of person who is likely to have committed the offence with which he is charged.

As a general rule, where the question of how to deal with spent convictions arises, the best course is to get the judge's ruling at the outset.

(7) Attack on another person's character (ss.101(1)(g), 106)

Criminal Justice Act 2003, s.106

Attack on another person's character

13–78 **106.**—(1) For the purposes of section 101(1)(g) a defendant makes an attack on another person's character if—

(a) he adduces evidence attacking the other person's character,

(b) he (or any legal representative appointed under section 38(4) of the *Youth Justice and Criminal Evidence Act* 1999 to cross-examine a witness in his interests) asks questions in cross-examination that are intended to elicit such evidence, or are likely to do so, or

(c) evidence is given of an imputation about the other person made by the defendant—

(i) on being questioned under caution, before charge, about the offence with which he is charged, or

(ii) on being charged with the offence or officially informed that he might be prosecuted for it.

(2) In subsection (1) "evidence attacking the other person's character" means evidence to the effect that the other person—

(a) has committed an offence (whether a different offence from the one with which the defendant is charged or the same one), or

(b) has behaved, or is disposed to behave, in a reprehensible way;

and "imputation about the other person" means an assertion to that effect.

(3) Only prosecution evidence is admissible under section 101(1)(g).

Fairness

13–79 Apart from the requirement that the defendant should have made an attack on another person's character within section 106 before evidence of his own bad character can be admitted through gateway (g), any prosecution application under section 101(1)(g) may be opposed under section 101(3) on the ground that the admission of such evidence would have such an adverse effect on the fairness of the proceedings that the court ought not to admit it. This confers a discretion on the court to exclude character evidence though the conditions of admissibility are met, and this coincides with the discretion that had been held to exist in relation to the corresponding head of admissibility under the *Criminal Evidence Act* 1898 (*viz.* "the nature or conduct of the defence is such as to involve imputations on the character of the prosecutor or the witnesses for the prosecution; or the deceased victim of the alleged crime").

13–80 The existence of a discretion to exclude evidence under the 1898 Act, even though admissible in law was clearly established: see *Selvey v. DPP* [1970] A.C. 304, HL; *Noor Mohamed v. R.* [1949] A.C. 182, PC; *Maxwell v. DPP* [1935] A.C. 309, HL; *Harris v. DPP* [1952] A.C. 694, HL; *Jones v. DPP* [1962] A.C. 635, HL; *R. v. Jenkins*, 31 Cr.App.R. 1, CCA; *R. v. Cook* [1952] 2 Q.B. 340, 43 Cr.App.R. 138, CCA. There was no general rule for the exercise of such discretion; it depended on the circumstances of the case and the overriding duty of the judge to secure that the trial was fair. Where, however, a defendant had a particularly bad or damaging record, a judge was likely to admit it only if the imputations made against the prosecution witnesses were correspondingly grave: see *R. v. Taylor and Goodman* [1999] 2 Cr.App.R. 163, CA. A supposed general rule suggested in *R. v. Flynn*, 45 Cr.App.R. 268, CCA, that where the very nature of the defence necessarily involved the imputation, the discretion should be exercised in favour of the defendant, had come to be regarded as non-existent: *Selvey v. DPP*, *ante*, in which the following principles laid down in *Jenkins*, *ante*, were approved:

> "[The judge] may feel that even though the position is established in law, still the putting of such questions as to the character of the accused person may be fraught with results which immeasurably outweigh the result of questions put by the defence and which make a fair trial of the accused person almost impossible. On the other hand, in the ordinary and normal case he may feel that if the credit of the prosecutor or his witnesses has been attacked, it is only fair that the jury should have before them material on which they can form their judgment whether the accused person is any more worthy to be believed than those he has attacked" (31 Cr.App.R. 1, 15).

The Court of Appeal would not interfere with the exercise of the discretion of the trial judge unless he had erred in principle or there was no material on which he could properly have exercised his discretion: *R. v. Jenkins*, *ante*; *R. v. Cook*, *ante*; and see observations in *Selvey*, *ante*.

A factor to bear in mind is section 4(1) of the *Rehabilitation of Offenders Act* 1974 notwithstanding that section 7(2) of the Act excludes the application of section 4 to criminal proceedings: see *post*, §§ 13–121 (practice direction), 13–125 (s.4), 13–133 (s.7(2)), and *R. v. Nye*, 75 Cr.App.R. 247, CA (*ante*, § 13–77). **13–81**

Evidence/ imputation that another has committed offence/ behaved reprehensibly

Because of the parallels with the former legislation (see *ante*, § 13–79), authorities on the 1898 Act are likely to prove instructive in relation to the application of the 2003 legislation; but it should be noted that, unlike the position under the 1898 Act, if an attack is made on the character of another by the defendant, the prosecution will not be dependent on the defendant giving evidence for the opportunity to put in evidence the defendant's character by way of cross-examination. However, in *R. v. Nelson*, unreported, December 19, 2006, CA ([2006] EWCA Crim. 3412), it was said that whilst the effect of section 106(1)(c) is that imputations made by a defendant in interview will only amount to an attack on another person's character for the purposes of section 101(1)(g) if "evidence is given" of the imputation, the imputation must first be relevant to a matter in issue before it can be given; it will be improper for the prosecution to seek to adduce evidence of the imputation simply in order to adduce evidence of the defendant's bad character under section 101(1)(g). **13–82**

The leading case on the interpretation of the relevant provision of the 1898 Act (s.1(3)(ii)) was *Selvey v. DPP*, *ante*, which established the following principles. **13–83**

(a) The words of the statute were to be given their ordinary and natural meaning (as to which, see also *R. v. Hudson* [1912] 2 K.B. 464, 7 Cr.App.R. 256, CCA; *R. v. Jenkins*, *ante*, § 13–80; and *R. v. Cook*, *ante*, § 13–80).

(b) The statute permitted cross-examination of a defendant as to character both when the imputation on the character of the prosecutor or a witness was cast to show his unreliability as a witness independently of the evidence given by him and also when the casting of the imputation was necessary to enable the defendant to establish his defence.

(c) In cases of rape, the defendant could allege consent without placing himself in peril of such cross-examination (as to which, see also *R. v. Sheean* (1908) 21 Cox 561; *R. v. Turner (J.)*, 30 Cr.App.R. 9, CCA; and *post*, § 13–86).

(d) If what was said amounted in reality to no more than an emphatic denial of the charge, it was not to be regarded as an imputation. As to this, see also *R. v. Rouse* [1904] 1 K.B. 184; *R. v. Grant*, 30 Cr.App.R. 99, CCA; *R. v. Jones (W.)*, 17 Cr.App.R. 117, CCA; and *R. v. Desmond* [1999] Crim.L.R. 313, CA (it makes no difference that counsel spells out the suggestion since he has a certain latitude as to how to frame his questions, nor that he draws on inconsistencies in the accounts given by the witness to lend substance to the suggestion that he is lying). Where attacks were mounted upon the conduct of police witnesses, see particularly, *R. v. Clark* [1955] 2 Q.B. 469, 39 Cr.App.R. 120, CCA; *R. v. Cook*, *ante*; *R. v. Levy*, 50 Cr.App.R. 238, CCA; *R. v. Tanner*, 66 Cr.App.R. 56, CA; *R. v. Nelson*, 68 Cr.App.R. 12, CA; *R. v. McGee and Cassidy*, 70 Cr.App.R. 247, CA; *R. v. Britzman*, 76 Cr.App.R. 134, CA; and *R. v. Owen*, 83 Cr.App.R. 100, CA, and *post*, § 13–91.

A defendant who gave evidence of a homosexual relationship between himself and a prosecution witness (it having been put to the witness who emphatically denied it), to explain his presence in the room of the witness where his fingerprints had been found, still brought himself within section 1(3)(ii) of the 1898 Act. The fact that it was said that the allegation was made to explain the defendant's presence in the room and not to discredit the witness's testimony, was immaterial: *R. v. Bishop* [1975] Q.B. 274, 59 Cr.App.R. 246, CA. An imputation on character included charges of faults or vices, whether reputed or real, which are not criminal offences: *ibid*. However, merely to put to a man in cross-examination that he was intoxicated or swearing on a particular **13–84** occasion did not amount to the sort of imputations on character upon which the 1898 Act was based: *R. v. McLean* [1978] Crim.L.R. 430, CA. The question in such cases under the 2003 Act would be as to whether such charges amounted to an allegation of "reprehensible behaviour" (see s.106(2)(b)).

13–85 Prima facie, answers given by a defendant to questions put in cross-examination are not a part of the "nature or conduct of the defence", but are part of the case for the prosecution: *R. v. Jones (Richard)*, 3 Cr.App.R. 67, CCA. If such questions were in the nature of a trap, an involuntary imputation on the character of a prosecution witness made in the answer would not justify putting in evidence of the bad character of the defendant: *ibid.*; *R. v. Grout*, 3 Cr.App.R. 64, CCA; *R. v. Seigley*, 6 Cr.App.R. 106, CCA; *R. v. Baldwin*, 18 Cr.App.R. 175, CCA; and *R. v. Eidinow*, 23 Cr.App.R. 145, CCA.

Defence of consent in rape

13–86 For the rule under the 1898 Act, see *ante*, § 13–83 (para. (c)). The reason given for the rule in *Turner* was that by alleging consent the accused was doing no more than denying one of the elements of the offence (non-consent) which the prosecution have to prove. If the accused made imputations on the character of the complainant that went beyond his allegation of consent, he would lose the protection of the statute. *Turner* was approved by the House of Lords in *Selvey v. DPP*, *ante*.

13–87 With the re-definition of rape to include buggery of a man, it remained to be seen whether the courts would hold that an allegation of consent to an act of buggery exposed the defendant to the risk of cross-examination under section 1(3)(ii). On the one hand, Parliament having chosen to re-define rape, the principle in *Turner* and *Selvey* would seem to have applied. On the other hand, the reality was that for a heterosexual man an allegation of consent to a homosexual act undoubtedly carried an imputation on character beyond that which is implicit in an allegation of consent to a heterosexual act. If the victim was homosexual, there would seem to have been no reason why the principle in *Turner* should not have applied.

13–88 Under the 2003 Act, the question will be whether the suggestion that the complainant consented amounts to a suggestion of "reprehensible" behaviour. This, it is submitted, will involve a judgment being made in the context of the particular factual allegations. It is certainly open to the courts to depart from the hard and fast rule that operated under the 1898 Act, as there will undoubtedly be cases where an allegation of consent involves an allegation of what any right-thinking person would regard as "reprehensible" conduct.

13–89 In *R. v. Renda*, *ante*, § 13–74, however, the Court of Appeal stuck close to the approach under the 1898 Act. It was held that where in interview, a defendant, charged with rape, had not merely asserted that the complainant had consented (and was motivated by a desire for revenge) but had referred to her in most disparaging terms, the judge had been correct to refuse a prosecution application based on the defence of consent; but he had been correct to allow it on account of the sweeping attack on the complainant's character in interview; such evidence had properly been part of the prosecution case (although formally exculpatory, it had obvious incriminatory potential) and putting it in as part of their case could not be said to have been a mere device for setting up an application to put in the defendant's bad character.

Self-defence

13–90 An allegation by the defendant that he was defending himself against an unprovoked attack by the complainant is "an attack on another person's character" within section 101(1)(g): *R. v. Lamaletie and Royce*, 172 J.P. 249, CA. The fact that such an allegation is necessary in order to raise the defence of self-defence would be relevant only to the exercise by the judge of his exclusionary discretion under section 101(3): *ibid.* See also *R. v. Stone* [2002] 1 *Archbold News* 1, CA (allegation that victim attacked defendant with a knife involved more than an "emphatic denial").

Challenging police evidence

13–91 In *R. v. Tanner*, *ante*, § 13–83 (para. (d)), the case against T depended entirely upon admissions he was alleged to have made to police officers. The officers were cross-examined upon the basis that they were wrong in saying that the admissions were made—it was not put to them that they were lying. In evidence-in-chief, T confined himself to saying that what the police alleged he had said by way of admission, he had not said. The judge interposed with the following question: "It follows from that, does it not ... that the whole of this evidence of these ... officers where they say you admitted this offence, is made up?" A. "Yes." In cross-examination, it was put to him: Q. "So again this is all complete invention by the police officer?" A. "Yes." Counsel for the Crown was then given leave to cross-examine as to character. In upholding this ruling, the Court of Appeal drew attention to the distinction, drawn in the authorities, between "an emphatic denial of guilt" (see *Rouse*, *ante*, § 13–83 (para. (d)), and *Grout*, *ante*, § 13–85), and alleging that a prosecution witness is a liar can amount to no more than that (*ibid.*), which did not bring the defendant within the section (*Selvey*, *ante*), and an allegation of serious impropriety on the part of the police, where the position differed: see *R. v. Wright*, 5 Cr.App.R. 131, CCA; *Jones (W.)*, *ante*; *Cook*, *ante*; and *Levy*, *ante*. See also Lord Goddard C.J. in *R. v. Clark*, *ante*, at pp. 477–478, 129.

The distinction may be a narrow one; which side of the line any particular case fell would depend upon its particular facts. In *Tanner*, the nature and conduct of the defence did involve imputations upon the character of the police officers. It was not a case of the denial of a single answer, nor was there any suggestion or possibility of mistake or misunderstanding. T denied not only his admission but in the case of each interview a series of subsequent important answers attributed to him by the police. It necessarily followed from the cross-examination of the police and T's evidence-in-chief that he was saying impliedly that the police had made up a substantial and vital part of their evidence and that they had conspired to do so. The judge's interventions merely brought into the open what was already implicit. **13–92**

Doubt was cast on this approach in *R. v. Nelson*, *ante*, § 13–83 (para. (d)), but the court adopted the stricter approach exemplified in *Tanner* in the subsequent cases of *R. v. McGee and Cassidy* and *R. v. Britzman*, *ante*, § 13–83 (para. (d)). All of these cases were considered in *R. v. Owen*, *ante*, § 13–83 (para. (d)). This was among the many authorities reviewed by the Court of Appeal in *R. v. McLeod* [1995] 1 Cr.App.R. 591 (*post*, § 13–95). Whilst the court was principally concerned with a different question, it approved the general approach in *Owen*, which, it is submitted, was thereafter to be regarded as the leading authority on this particular point. **13–93**

The court adopted the approach of *Tanner* and *Britzman* to the effect that if the reality of the position was that the jury would have to decide whether the evidence of the witness whose testimony had been challenged had been made up, then there was no room for drawing a distinction between a defence which was so conducted as to make specific allegations of fabrication and one in which the allegation arose by way of necessary and reasonable implication. In deciding whether imputations had been made on the character of another person, the manner in which counsel put questions in cross-examination was irrelevant: the effect and purport of the cross-examination had to be judged objectively. **13–94**

The nature of the previous convictions as a factor in the exercise of discretion, scope of cross-examination and evidential significance of matters cross-examined to

In *R. v. McLeod*, *ante*, § 13–93, it was submitted that where cross-examination was permitted under section 1(3)(ii) of the 1898 Act, it was nevertheless impermissible to elicit: (a) facts similar to some of those in the instant case (not otherwise admissible as similar fact evidence); (b) that a defence similar to the instant one had been advanced but rejected on a previous occasion; or (c) that the circumstances of the prior offence, although in no way similar to the instant offence, disclosed exceptionally vicious, depraved or scandalous behaviour. In the years since *Selvey v. DPP*, *ante*, § 13–83, there had been a series of conflicting decisions. These were reviewed by the court; included in the review were *Maxwell v. DPP* [1935] A.C. 309, HL; *R. v. Jenkins*, 31 Cr.App.R. 1, CCA; *R. v. Vickers* [1972] Crim.L.R. 101, CA; *R. v. France and France* [1979] Crim.L.R. 48, CA; *R. v. Duncalf*, 69 Cr.App.R. 206, CA; *R. v. Watts (W.)*, 77 Cr.App.R. 12, CA; *R. v. John and Braithwaite*, unreported, November 24, 1983, CA; **13–95**

R. v. Burke, 82 Cr.App.R. 156, CA; *R. v. Powell*, 82 Cr.App.R. 165, CA; *R. v. Owen*, *ante*, § 13–93; and *R. v. Khan* [1991] Crim.L.R. 51, CA.

13–96 For the general principles upon which the discretion should be exercised, Stuart-Smith L.J., giving the judgment of the court, said that the court could not improve on the analysis in the judgment of Ackner L.J. in *Burke*, *ante*, at p. 161. Ackner L.J. reaffirmed that the leading case was *Selvey v. DPP*, from which he deduced the following principles.

(a) The judge has to weigh the prejudicial effect of the questions against the damage done by the attack on the prosecution's witnesses and has to exercise his discretion so as to secure a trial fair to both prosecution and defence (see *R. v. Cook* [1959] 2 Q.B. 340 at 344–348, 43 Cr.App.R. 138 at 143, CCA).

(b) Cases occurred in which it would be unjust to admit evidence of a character gravely prejudicial to the accused even though there might be some tenuous grounds for holding it technically admissible (*Noor Mohamed v. R.* [1949] A.C. 182 at 192, PC). [The second half of principle (b) was a restatement of the first sentence of the quotation from *Jenkins* at § 13–80, *ante*.]

(c) [The third principle was a restatement of the second sentence of the same quotation.]

(d) In the Court of Appeal, it is not enough that the court thinks it would have exercised its discretion differently. It will only interfere if the judge erred in principle or if there was no material on which he could properly have arrived at his decision (*R. v. Watson*, 8 Cr.App.R. 249 at 254, CCA, and *Cook*, *ante*).

13–97 The court in *McLeod* then dealt with the particular issues raised by the appeal. It set out its conclusions in a series of further propositions.

(a) The primary purpose of cross-examination on the bad character of the accused was to show that he was not worthy of belief. It was not to show that he had a disposition to commit the type of offence with which he was charged: see *Vickers* and *Khan*, *ante*. But the mere fact that the offences were of a similar type to that charged or, because of their number and type, had the incidental effect of suggesting a tendency or disposition to commit the offence charged did not make questions about them improper: see *Powell*, *Owen* and *Selvey v. DPP*, *ante*.

(b) It was undesirable that there should be prolonged or extensive cross-examination in relation to previous offences. (As to this, see also *R. v. Lamaletie and Royce*, 172 J.P. 249, CA (the concept underlying the gateway in s.101(1)(g) being that where the defendant has impugned the character of a prosecution witness, the jury will be assisted in deciding who to believe by knowing of the defendant's bad character, what is relevant is "character" in a broad, general sense, and so the details are unnecessary and potentially distracting).)

(c) Similarities of defences which had been rejected by juries on previous occasions, and whether or not the accused pleaded guilty or was disbelieved having given evidence on oath, could be a legitimate matter for questions. Such matters were clearly relevant to credibility.

(d) Underlying facts that showed particularly bad character over and above the bare facts of the case were not necessarily to be excluded. The judge should be careful to balance the gravity of the attack on the prosecution with the degree of prejudice to the defendant which would result from the disclosure of the facts in question. Details of sexual offences against children were likely to be regarded by a jury as particularly prejudicial and might well be the reason why in *Watts (W.)*, *ante*, the court thought the questions impermissible.

(e) If objection was to be taken to a particular line of cross-examination about the underlying facts of a previous offence, it should be taken as soon as it was apparent that there was a danger of going too far. There was little point in taking it subsequently for it would not normally be a ground for discharging the jury.

(f) While it was the duty of the judge to keep cross-examination within bounds, if no objection was taken at the time, it would be difficult to contend later that the judge had wrongly exercised his discretion. In any event, the Court of Appeal would not interfere with the exercise of the judge's discretion save on well established principles.

(g) Where the accused had been cross-examined as to his character and previous offences, the judge must in the summing up tell the jury that the purpose of the questioning went only to credit and that they should not consider that it showed a propensity to commit the offence they were considering. As to this see also *post*, § 13–101.

Attack on non-witness, non-victim

In *R. v. Nelson*, unreported, December 19, 2006, CA ([2006] EWCA Crim. 3412), it was held that whereas there is no doubt that section 101(1)(g) was deliberately worded so that the gateway should not be confined to cases where an attack is made on the character of a prosecution witness, it would be most unusual for a judge not to exercise his discretion to exclude evidence of bad character under section 101(3) of the 2003 Act and section 78 of the *PACE Act* 1984 where the only basis on which the evidence could be admitted was an attack on a non-witness who was also a non-victim; otherwise, the fairness of the proceedings would be materially damaged; but a rare situation where it might be appropriate not to exclude such evidence would be where the imputations made by the defendant about a non-witness might influence the view of the jury as to the evidence of a witness. **13–98**

Convictions, etc., abroad

A plea of *nolo contendere* in the United States of America is not the equivalent of a conviction, even though it leads to the imposition of a penalty: *R. v. McGregor*, 95 Cr.App.R. 240, CA. **13–99**

Where a defendant has been convicted of an offence in a foreign jurisdiction whose law provides that a finding of guilt does not rank as a conviction until such time as there is no possibility of the finding of guilt being set aside on appeal, he may, if he gives evidence of his good character, be asked about such finding of guilt and as to the underlying facts; whether or not it was properly to be regarded as a conviction for the purposes of section 1 of the 1898 Act, it was held that it certainly came within the broader category of matters about which questions may be asked under that section once a defendant had put his character in issue: *R. v. El-Delbi* [2003] 7 *Archbold News* 1, CA.

As to convictions abroad, see also *R. v. Kordasinski*, *ante*, § 13–1.

Warning by judge

It is desirable that a warning should be given by the judge when it becomes apparent that the defence is taking a course which may expose the defendant to the risk of cross-examination as to character: *Selvey v. DPP*, *ante*, and see *R. v. Cook* [1959] 2 Q.B. 340 at 349, 43 Cr.App.R. 138 at 147, CCA. For the procedure at a summary trial where the defendant is unrepresented, see *R. v. Weston-super-Mare JJ., ex p. Townsend* [1968] 3 All E.R. 225n, DC. **13–100**

Failure to give a warning is not fatal to a conviction: see *R. v. Benson*, 3 Cr.App.R. 70, CCA (unrepresented defendant).

Directing the jury

The classic direction in relation to character evidence that had been admitted under section 1(3)(ii) of the 1898 Act, on the ground of an attack by the defendant on the character of a prosecution witness, was that of the trial judge in *R. v. Cook*, *ante* (not set out in any of the reports): **13–101**

> "When allegations are made against … witnesses for the prosecution, you should consider the person who is making them, and for that purpose you are entitled to take into consideration that he admits that he is a convicted criminal … it does not make it any more likely that he committed this crime but it may mean that it is more unlikely that the allegations made against [the witness] are true than if they were made by a person of good character."

See also *R. v. McLeod*, *ante*, § 13–97 (point ((g)), and *R. v. Jenkins*, *ante*, § 13–80, as to the rationale for admitting the evidence being that fairness would require that the jury should have before them material on which they could form a judgment as to whether the accused was any more worthy of belief than those he attacked.

Under the 2003 Act, the position has been confused by the judgment of the Court of Appeal in *R. v. Campbell* [2007] 2 Cr.App.R. 28, where it was said that once evidence has been admitted through one of the gateways in section 101(1), it may be used by the jury for any relevant purpose without limit as to the gateway through which the evidence was admitted (referring to *R. v. Highton*; *R. v. Van Nguyen*; *R. v. Carp*, *post*, § 13–102); to direct the jury only to have regard to the evidence for some purposes, and to disregard its relevance in other respects would be to revert to the "unsatisfactory practices" that prevailed under the old law; and, as to the extent to which evidence of bad character will be relevant once admitted, the court said that the distinction drawn in the past between a propensity to commit criminal acts and credibility is usually unrealistic; if the jury learn that a defendant has a propensity to commit criminal acts, they may well at one and the same time conclude that it is more likely that he is guilty and that he is less likely to be telling the truth when he says that he is not. For criticism of this decision as being self-defeating (if the evidence is relevant for more than one purpose, then it should have qualified for admission via more than one gateway), and as confusing the issues as to whether the defendant is *in fact* telling the truth with the issue whether he has the *ability* to tell the truth or is worthy of belief, see *Criminal Law Week* 2007/26/1.

Where the only basis for admitting evidence of the defendant's bad character is that he has attacked another person's character, it is submitted that it is imperative that the jury should be directed in accordance with the former law, as it is imperative that the direction to the jury should reflect the rationale for admitting the evidence in the first place.

(8) Relationship between the seven gateways

13–102 Whilst it is undoubtedly the case that bad character evidence may be admissible via more than one gateway, there are two lines of authority as to the use to which such evidence may be put once admitted via one or more particular gateways. In *R. v. Highton*; *R. v Van Nguyen*; *R. v. Carp* [2006] 1 Cr.App.R. 7, CA, it was held that once evidence of a defendant's bad character has been admitted through one of the seven gateways, it can be used for any purpose for which bad character evidence is relevant in the particular case; that was so because, (i) the use of the word "include" in section 103(1) (*ante*, § 13–37) indicated that the matters in issue for the purposes of gateway (d) might extend beyond the two areas mentioned, and the same argument might also be advanced in respect of other gateways, particularly gateways (a) and (b); (ii) section 101(1) stated that it dealt with admissibility of bad character through the seven gateways, without referring to the effect that such evidence, if admissible, was to have; (iii) the width of the definition in section 98 of evidence of bad character suggested that, wherever such evidence was admitted, it could be admitted for any purpose for which it was relevant in the case in which it was admitted; (iv) accordingly, a distinction was to be drawn between the *admissibility* of evidence of bad character (which depended upon it getting through one of the gateways) and the *use* to which it might be put once it had been admitted (which depended upon the matters to which it was relevant, rather than upon the gateway through which it was admitted); (v) although, therefore, it was true that the reasoning leading to the admission of evidence under gateway (d) might also determine the matters to which the evidence was relevant or primarily relevant once admitted, the same was not true of all the gateways; under gateway (g), for example, admissibility depended on the defendant having made an attack on another person's character, but once the evidence was admitted, it might, depending on the facts, be relevant not only to credibility, but also to propensity to commit the offences with which he was charged. The court said that the defendant was protected by the requirement that a judge in summing up must explain why the jury had heard the evidence and the ways in which it might be relevant to their decision (as to which see *R. v. Hanson*; *R. v. Gilmore*; *R. v. P.*, and *R. v. Edwards*; *R. v. Fysh*; *R. v. Duggan*; *R. v. Chohan*, *ante*, § 13–68), by section 101(3), which prohibits such evidence if it would cause unfairness, and by the disapplication of section 103(1)(a) and (2) by section 103(3) where it would be "unjust". For a criticism of this decision as going too far, see *Criminal Law Week* 2005/31/3; but it was adopted in *R. v. Campbell* (as to which, see *ante*, §§ 13–25a, 13–65, 13–68 and 13–101).

For a different approach, see *R. v. M., ante*, § 13–25a, where the court underscored the need for the direction to the jury to be related to the gateway through which the evidence was admitted; and *R. v. Davis*, 172 J.P. 358, CA, where it was said that bad character evidence admitted under one gateway should not readily be used, once admitted, for a purpose, such as propensity, for which additional safeguards or different tests have first to be met. In *Davis*, the court was concerned, in particular, with gateway (c) (*ante*, §§ 13–29 *et seq.*), in relation to which it said that there must be a danger in admitting bad character evidence merely as "explanatory" evidence, no matter how important it is, if the use to which it is really intended to put it is as evidence of propensity, where the statutory tests and safeguards (in particular under ss.101(3) and (4) and 103(3)) are different. Accordingly, the court said that the test for gateway (c) should be applied cautiously where there is potential to use the evidence as evidence of propensity; alternatively, section 78 of the *PACE Act* 1984 might well require the exclusion of such evidence where it really amounts to evidence of propensity which would not be admitted as such. The court pointed out that similar considerations applied to gateways (f) (correcting a false impression) and (g) (attack on another person's character).

(9) Defendant's bad character referred to inadvertently

Where it is accidentally elicited during the course of the case for the Crown that the defendant has been previously convicted, the decision whether or not to discharge the jury is one for the discretion of the judge on the particular facts, and the Court of Appeal will not lightly interfere with the exercise of that discretion. Every case depends on its own facts and it is far from being the rule that in every case where something prejudicial to the defendant has been admitted in evidence through inadvertence, the jury must be discharged: *R. v. Weaver and Weaver* [1968] 1 Q.B. 353, 51 Cr.App.R. 77, CA, followed in *R. v. Palin*, 53 Cr.App.R. 535, CA. Where such irregularity occurs during the trial of a defendant who is not represented by counsel, it is the duty of the judge to warn him that he has the right to apply that the jury should be discharged and the trial started afresh: *R. v. Featherstone*, 28 Cr.App.R. 176, CCA; *R. v. Fripp and Jones*, 29 Cr.App.R. 6, CCA. There is no general rule that where one defendant refers to the fact that a co-defendant has a criminal record, the jury must be discharged; the matter is one for the discretion of the trial judge: *R. v. Sutton*, 53 Cr.App.R. 504, CA. The court would be slow to lay down such a general rule because it would make it too easy, if a trial were not going well, for one defendant to say something which would secure his co-defendant the advantages of a new trial. The court is always slow to interfere with such an exercise of discretion by the judge: *ibid*. Knowledge of the defendant's bad character does not automatically disqualify a juror, see *R. v. Box and Box* [1964] 1 Q.B. 430, 47 Cr.App.R. 284, CCA, and other cases dealing with a juror's knowledge of the defendant's bad character gained otherwise than in court during the proceedings, *ante*, § 4–258. 13–103

In *R. v. Coughlan and Young*, 63 Cr.App.R. 33, CA, a defendant during cross-examination by the Crown referred to the fact that a co-defendant [C] had a previous conviction of some gravity. "[Prosecuting counsel] sensibly went on with his cross-examination as if nothing untoward had happened; and [defending counsel] just as sensibly did not intervene at once. He waited until G had completed his evidence. He then asked the judge to allow the jury to retire" (at p. 38). The judge's refusal to order a fresh trial was upheld. "The judge made his own assessment of the impact which [G's] outburst may have made on the jury. It is our experience that if this kind of casual remark is made and no notice is taken of it at the time, it tends to be forgotten particularly when the trial is a long one and there are a number of defendants. The judge was in a far better position to assess the likelihood of prejudice to [C] than this court is."

IV. PROCEDURE

(1) Timing of applications

13–103a In *R. v. Gyima* [2007] Crim.L.R. 890, CA, it was said that whilst there will normally be good practical reasons for a judge to rule on the admissibility of evidence of bad character at the outset of a trial, judges and practitioners should be astute to recognise that in weak or potentially weak cases it may be important to defer such a ruling until the whole of the prosecution evidence has been adduced in order that the court is better placed to assess that evidence and to determine the application in the light thereof.

As to the timing of applications, see also *R. v. Brima, ante*, § 13–65a, *R. v. Ullah, ante*, § 13–76a, and *R. v. Card, post*, § 13–106.

(2) Assumption of truth in assessment of relevance or probative value

Criminal Justice Act 2003, s.109

Assumption of truth in assessment of relevance or probative value

13–104 **109.**—(1) Subject to subsection (2), a reference in this Chapter to the relevance or probative value of evidence is a reference to its relevance or probative value on the assumption that it is true.

(2) In assessing the relevance or probative value of an item of evidence for any purpose of this Chapter, a court need not assume that the evidence is true if it appears, on the basis of any material before the court (including any evidence it decides to hear on the matter), that no court or jury could reasonably find it to be true.

As to this section, see *R. v. Edwards and Rowlands*; *R. v. McLean*; *R. v. Smith (David)*; *R. v. Enright and Gray, ante*, § 13–8.

As to the position at common law, see *ante*, § 13–57.

In *R. v. Naylor* [1998] Crim.L.R. 662, CA, it was said that where a judge ruled at the outset of a trial on the basis of the written evidence that evidence in relation to a previous offence was admissible as similar fact, but the evidence given, varying from the written evidence, removed the basis for the ruling, the correct course (assuming that the evidence of the earlier offence had been put before the jury, or they had been told about it, *e.g.* in opening) was to discharge the jury.

(3) Stopping the case where evidence contaminated

Criminal Justice Act 2003, s.107

Stopping the case where evidence contaminated

13–105 **107.**—(1) If on a defendant's trial before a judge and jury for an offence—

(a) evidence of his bad character has been admitted under any of paragraphs (c) to (g) of section 101(1), and

(b) the court is satisfied at any time after the close of the case for the prosecution that—

(i) the evidence is contaminated, and

(ii) the contamination is such that, considering the importance of the evidence to the case against the defendant, his conviction of the offence would be unsafe,

the court must either direct the jury to acquit the defendant of the offence or, if it considers that there ought to be a retrial, discharge the jury.

(2) Where—

(a) a jury is directed under subsection (1) to acquit a defendant of an offence, and

(b) the circumstances are such that, apart from this subsection, the defendant could if acquitted of that offence be found guilty of another offence,

the defendant may not be found guilty of that other offence if the court is satisfied as mentioned in subsection (1)(b) in respect of it.

(3) If—

(a) a jury is required to determine under section 4A(2) of the *Criminal Procedure (Insanity) Act* 1964 whether a person charged on an indictment with an offence did the act or made the omission charged,

(b) evidence of the person's bad character has been admitted under any of paragraphs (c) to (g) of section 101(1), and

(c) the court is satisfied at any time after the close of the case for the prosecution that—

(i) the evidence is contaminated, and

(ii) the contamination is such that, considering the importance of the evidence to the case against the person, a finding that he did the act or made the omission would be unsafe,

the court must either direct the jury to acquit the defendant of the offence or, if it considers that there ought to be a rehearing, discharge the jury.

(4) This section does not prejudice any other power a court may have to direct a jury to acquit a person of an offence or to discharge a jury.

(5) For the purposes of this section a person's evidence is contaminated where—

(a) as a result of an agreement or understanding between the person and one or more others, or

(b) as a result of the person being aware of anything alleged by one or more others whose evidence may be, or has been, given in the proceedings,

the evidence is false or misleading in any respect, or is different from what it would otherwise have been.

As to the court's duty to give reasons for a ruling under this section, see section 110, *post*, § 13–109.

Section 107 did not justify the making of a submission which, in substance, was no more than the reiteration of the argument for not admitting evidence of bad character in the first place; section 107 deals with a particular situation where evidence of "bad character" has been admitted and proves to be false or misleading (see subs. (5)); unless the case fell squarely within that provision, the Court of Appeal was the appropriate forum in which to challenge the correctness of the admissibility ruling: *R. v. Renda*, *ante*, § 13–74. **13–106**

In *R. v. Card* [2006] 2 Cr.App.R. 28, the Court of Appeal made the following observations in relation to section 107: (i) contamination may arise from deliberate collusion, the exercise of improper pressure, through inadvertence or innocently; (ii) the section required the judge to make what was in effect a finding of fact after the admission of the evidence (based on an assessment as to whether the evidence of a witness was false or misleading, or different from what it would have been had it not been contaminated); (iii) the purpose of the section is to reduce the risk of conviction based on over-reliance on evidence of bad character and the provision acknowledges the potential danger that, where the evidence is contaminated, the evidence of bad character may have a disproportionate impact on the evaluation of the case by the jury; (iv) although the duty to stop the case does not arise unless the judge is satisfied that there has been an important contamination of the evidence, if he is so satisfied, he has no discretion and he must stop the case (whether or not there would, on a conventional approach, be a case to answer); (v) an order for a retrial, rather than a direction to acquit, would not normally be susceptible to a subsequent application based on an asserted abuse of process, since, without something fresh emerging, that would amount to an appeal of the order for a retrial; and (vi) where the prosecution make an application to adduce evidence of the defendant's bad character at the start of the trial and the defence make a responsible submission that there is material in the prosecution case to suggest that there was or may have been witness contamination, it would normally be sensible for the judge to postpone a decision on the application until the allegedly contaminated evidence has been examined in the trial; by doing so, the judge will have well in mind the precise details of the evidence actually given, rather than anticipated, with such weaknesses and problems as may have emerged. As to (vi), it is apparent that what the court had in mind was an application by the prosecution to adduce evidence of a defendant's previous convictions. There can be no question of postponing all evidence of bad character, as the issue of contamination under section 107 only arises in relation to evidence of bad character admitted under the provisions of the 2003 Act. If no such evidence has been admitted, section 107 has no application.

In order to assist the judge and jury to make decisions about collusion or contamination, it is submitted that those responsible for the collection of evidence should, as a mater of routine, keep detailed records of the circumstances in which the various allegations came to the attention of the authorities. It should be standard procedure in taking **13–107** a proof of evidence from an alleged victim, whether in a written statement or in a video recording, to include therein the victim's account of what prompted him or her to report the matter and how he or she did so. There should then be continuity of evidence through to the report to the police. Each person involved should also deal with the question of whether he or she spoke to anybody else about the allegations. By doing this, judge and jury will be in a much better position to make an informed decision on these issues.

Where there is an issue as to contamination (innocent or otherwise) in a case which is left to the jury, the issue should be left to them, with a direction not to accept the allegedly contaminated evidence unless satisfied that it is reliable and true and not tainted by collusion or innocent contamination: see *R. v. H.* [1995] 2 A.C. 596, HL.

13–108 In *R. v. R. (David)* [1999] Crim.L.R. 909, CA, it was said that where the defence to an allegation of a sexual offence against a child involves the suggestion that the complainant may "have got the idea" as a result of contamination (innocent or otherwise) resulting from contact with a particular person, a judge should hesitate long before shutting out evidence which arguably went to that issue, notwithstanding that the complainant denies in cross-examination that there has been any collusion; and where there is a possibility of such evidence being adduced, it is preferable that it is the subject of agreement between the parties, rather than the subject of a prescriptive ruling from the judge as to what form of words should be adopted by a particular witness.

(4) Duty to give reasons for rulings

Criminal Justice Act 2003, s.110

Court's duty to give reasons for rulings

13–109 **110.**—(1) Where the court makes a relevant ruling—

(a) it must state in open court (but in the absence of the jury, if there is one) its reasons for the ruling;

(b) if it is a magistrates' court, it must cause the ruling and the reasons for it to be entered in the register of the court's proceedings.

(2) In this section "relevant ruling" means—

(a) a ruling on whether an item of evidence is evidence of a person's bad character;

(b) a ruling on whether an item of such evidence is admissible under section 100, or 101 (including a ruling on an application under section 101(3));

(c) a ruling under section 107.

Where a judge's decision to permit a defence witness to be cross-examined on his bad character had been correct, the absence of detailed reasons did not impinge on the safety of the conviction: *R. v. Renda, ante*, § 13–74.

(5) Rules of court

Criminal Justice Act 2003, s.111

Rules of court

13–110 **111.**—(1) Rules of court may make such provision as appears to the appropriate authority to be necessary or expedient for the purposes of this Act; and the appropriate authority is the authority entitled to make the rules.

(2) The rules may, and, where the party in question is the prosecution, must, contain provision requiring a party who—

(a) proposes to adduce evidence of a defendant's bad character, or

(b) proposes to cross-examine a witness with a view to eliciting such evidence,

to serve on the defendant such notice, and such particulars of or relating to the evidence, as may be prescribed.

(3) The rules may provide that the court or the defendant may, in such circumstances as may be prescribed, dispense with a requirement imposed by virtue of subsection (2).

(4) In considering the exercise of its powers with respect to costs, the court may take into account any failure by a party to comply with a requirement imposed by virtue of subsection (2) and not dispensed with by virtue of subsection (3).

(5) The rules may—

(a) limit the application of any provision of the rules to prescribed circumstances;

(b) subject any provision of the rules to prescribed exceptions;

(c) make different provision for different cases or circumstances.

(6) Nothing in this section prejudices the generality of any enactment conferring power to make rules of court; and no particular provision of this section prejudices any general provision of it.

(7) In this section "prescribed" means prescribed by rules of court.

In *R. v. Spartley* (2007) 151 S.J. 670, CA, it was held that evidence of bad character had been properly admitted (as to which, see *ante*, § 13–76a), despite a failure to comply with the notice requirements of Part 35 of the *Criminal Procedure Rules* 2005 (S.I. 2005 No. 384) (*post*), where the prosecution had fulfilled their disclosure obligations under the *CPIA* 1996, s.3 (*ante*, § 12–54) in relation to that evidence in sufficient time for the defendant to have responded to it. **13–110a**

In *R. v. Musone* [2007] 2 Cr.App.R. 29, CA, it was held that whereas neither section 101(3) of the 2003 Act (*ante*, § 13–25) nor section 78 of the *PACE Act* 1984 (*post*, § 15–452) provide an exclusionary power in respect of evidence of bad character admissible at the behest of a defendant as against a co-defendant under section 101(1)(e), and whereas section 111 of the 2003 Act makes no provision for any sanction (other than in relation to costs (see subs. (4)) where a defendant fails to comply with the notice requirements, *etc.*, of the Part 35 rules, and ambushes a co-defendant by making a late application under section 101(1)(e), there is an implicit power in the rules to refuse to admit evidence which a defendant seeks to adduce in deliberate manipulation of those rules; the cases in which a breach of the procedural rules would entitle a court to exclude evidence of substantial probative value would be rare, but there will be cases where the only way in which the court can ensure fairness and further the overriding objective in rule 1.1 of the 2005 rules (*ante*, § 4–84b) will be by excluding the evidence. To similar effect, see *R. v. Jarvis* [2008] Crim.L.R. 632, CA (whilst it will often be the case that an application has to be made later than the rules provide for, if it is made so late that the judge takes the view that the target of the application would unfairly be unable to deal with the evidence, r.35.8 (*post*, § 13–118) gives the judge a wide discretion whether to allow the application). For criticism of this aspect of the decision in *Musone* (comparing the lack of an exclusionary power in section 111 with the express provision of such a power in section 132 (hearsay)), see *Criminal Law Week* 2007/21/3.

Criminal Procedure Rules (S.I. 2005 No. 384), Pt 35

When this Part applies

35.1. This Part applies in a magistrates' court and in the Crown Court when a party wants to introduce evidence of bad character as defined in section 98 of the *Criminal Justice Act* 2003. **13–111**

Introducing evidence of non-defendant's bad character

35.2. A party who wants to introduce evidence of a non-defendant's bad character or who wants to cross-examine a witness with a view to eliciting that evidence, under section 100 of the *Criminal Justice Act* 2003 must apply in the form set out in the Practice Direction and the application must be received by the court officer and all other parties to the proceedings— **13–112**

(a) not more than 14 days after the prosecutor has—

(i) complied or purported to comply with section 3 of the *Criminal Procedure and Investigations Act* 1996 (initial disclosure by the prosecutor), or

(ii) disclosed the previous convictions of that non-defendant; or

(b) as soon as reasonably practicable, where the application concerns a non-defendant who is to be invited to give (or has given) evidence for a defendant.

[This rule is printed as amended by the *Criminal Procedure (Amendment) Rules* 2006 (S.I. 2006 No. 353).]

Opposing introduction of evidence of non-defendant's bad character

35.3. A party who receives a copy of an application under rule 35.2 may oppose that application by giving notice in writing to the court officer and all other parties to the proceedings not more than 14 days after receiving that application. **13–113**

Prosecutor introducing evidence of defendant's bad character

13–114 **35.4.**—(1) A prosecutor who wants to introduce evidence of a defendant's bad character or who wants to cross-examine a witness with a view to eliciting that evidence, under section 101 of the *Criminal Justice Act* 2003 must give notice in the form set out in the Practice Direction to the court officer and all other parties to the proceedings.

(2) Notice under paragraph (1) must be given—

(a) in a case to be tried in a magistrates' court, at the same time as the prosecutor complies or purports to comply with section 3 of the *Criminal Procedure and Investigations Act* 1996; and

(b) in a case to be tried in the Crown Court, not more than 14 days after—

(i) the committal of the defendant, or

(ii) the consent to the preferment of a bill of indictment in relation to the case, or

(iii) the service of notice of transfer under section 4(1) of the *Criminal Justice Act* 1987 (notices of transfer) or under section 53(1) of the *Criminal Justice Act* 1991 (notices of transfer in certain cases involving children), or

(iv) where a person is sent for trial under section 51 of the *Crime and Disorder Act* 1998 (sending cases to the Crown Court) the service of copies of the documents containing the evidence on which the charge or charges are based under paragraph 1 of Schedule 3 to that Act.

Co-defendant introducing evidence of defendant's bad character

13–115 **35.5.** A co-defendant who wants to introduce evidence of a defendant's bad character or who wants to cross-examine a witness with a view to eliciting that evidence under section 101 of the *Criminal Justice Act* 2003 must give notice in the form set out in the Practice Direction to the court officer and all other parties to the proceedings not more than 14 days after the prosecutor has complied or purported to comply with section 3 of the *Criminal Procedure and Investigations Act* 1996.

Defendant applying to exclude evidence of his own bad character

13–116 **35.6.** A defendant's application to exclude bad character evidence must be in the form set out in the Practice Direction and received by the court officer and all other parties to the proceedings not more than 14 days after receiving a notice given under rules 35.4 or 35.5.

[This rule is printed as amended by S.I. 2006 No. 353 (*ante*, § 13–112).]

13–117 **35.7.** [*Revoked by* Criminal Procedure (Amendment) Rules *2007 (S.I. 2007 No. 699), r.38 and Sched. 4.*]

Court's power to vary requirements under this part

13–118 **35.8.** The court may—

(a) allow a notice or application required under this rule to be given in a different form, or orally; or

(b) shorten a time-limit under this rule or extend it even after it has expired.

See *R. (Robinson) v. Sutton Coldfield Magistrates' Court*, 170 J.P. 336, DC, *ante*, § 4–84a, and *R. v. Jarvis*, *ante*, § 13–110a.

Defendant waiving right to receive notice

13–119 **35.9.** A defendant entitled to receive a notice under this Part may waive his entitlement by so informing the court and the party who would have given the notice.

V. REHABILITATION OF OFFENDERS

(1) Introduction

13–120 The *Rehabilitation of Offenders Act* 1974 should be read in conjunction with the *Rehabilitation of Offenders Act 1974 (Exceptions) Order* 1975 (S.I. 1975 No. 1023), as amended bythe *Postal Services Act 2000 (Consequential Modifications No. 1) Order* 2001 (S.I. 2001 No. 1149), the *Rehabilitation of Offenders Act 1974 (Exceptions) (Amendment) Order* 2001 (S.I. 2001 No. 1192), the *Rehabilitation of Offenders Act 1974 (Exceptions) (Amendment) (No. 2) Order* 2001 (S.I. 2001 No. 3816), the *Rehabilitation of Offenders Act 1974 (Exceptions) (Amendment) Order* 2002 (S.I. 2002 No. 441), the *Rehabilitation of Offenders Act 1974 (Exceptions) (Amendment)*

(England and Wales) Order 2003 (S.I. 2003 No. 965), the *Rehabilitation of Offenders Act 1974 (Exceptions) (Amendment) (England and Wales) Order* 2006 (S.I. 2006 No. 2143); and the *Rehabilitation of Offenders Act 1974 (Exceptions) (Amendment) (England and Wales) Order* 2007 (S.I. 2007 No. 2149). Section 4 provides for the effect of rehabilitation. The 1975 order excepts from the operation of section 4(1), (2) and (3)(b) certain types of work, certain licences, certificates and permits and certain types of proceedings.

(2) Practice direction

On the day before the Act came into force, Lord Widgery C.J. issued a practice direction on its operation. This has been reproduced as paragraph I.6 of the consolidated criminal practice direction. Sub-paragraph 6 is of particular practical significance. **13–121**

Practice Direction (Criminal Proceedings: Consolidation), para. I.6 [2002] 1 W.L.R. 2870

I.6.1 The effect of section 4(1) of the *Rehabilitation of Offenders Act* 1974 is that a person who has become a rehabilitated person for the purpose of the Act in respect of a conviction (known as a "spent" conviction) shall be treated for all purposes in law as a person who has not committed or been charged with or prosecuted for or convicted of or sentenced for the offence or offences which were the subject of that conviction.

I.6.2 Section 4(1) of the 1974 Act does not apply however to evidence given in criminal proceedings (s.7(2)(a)). Convictions are often disclosed in such criminal proceedings. When the Bill was before the House of Commons on 28 June, 1974 the hope was expressed that the Lord Chief Justice would issue a practice direction for the guidance of the Crown Court with a view to reducing disclosure of spent convictions to a minimum and securing uniformity of approach. The direction is set out in the following paragraphs. The same approach should be adopted in all courts of criminal jurisdiction.

I.6.3 During the trial of a criminal charge reference to previous convictions (and therefore to spent convictions) can arise in a number of ways. The most common is when the character of the accused or a witness is sought to be attacked by reference to his criminal record, but there are, of course, cases where previous convictions are relevant and admissible as, for instance, to prove system.

I.6.4 It is not possible to give general directions which will govern all these different situations, but it is recommended that both court and advocates should give effect to the general intention of Parliament by never referring to a spent conviction when such reference can reasonably be avoided.

I.6.5 After a verdict of guilty the court must be provided with a statement of the defendant's record for the purposes of sentence. The record supplied should contain all previous convictions, but those which are spent should, so far as practicable, be marked as such.

I.6.6 No one should refer in open court to a spent conviction without the authority of the judge, which authority should not be given unless the interests of justice so require.

I.6.7 When passing sentence the judge should make no reference to a spent conviction unless it is necessary to do so for the purpose of explaining the sentence to be passed.

The question of when a defendant whose previous convictions are "spent" can be put forward as a person of good character was considered in *R. v. Nye*, *ante*, § 13–77. **13–122**

In *R. v. Evans* [1992] Crim.L.R. 125, CA, a conviction was quashed because of the trial judge's refusal to permit cross-examination of the alleged victim of an offence of violence about his previous convictions, which were spent. The court said that whatever may be the effect of the practice direction read against the words of the statute, the case was clearly one where the judge, if he had a discretion at all, should have allowed the convictions to be put. There was a head-on conflict of evidence between the appellant and the principal prosecution witness. The jury were entitled to know the latter's criminal record.

In *R. v. Corelli* [2001] Crim.L.R. 913, CA, it was held that the provisions of a statute cannot be cut down by those of a practice direction, and since section 7 (*post*, § 13–133), provides that nothing in section 4(1) (*post*, § 13–125) "shall affect the determination of any issue, or prevent the admission … of any evidence, relating to a person's previous convictions ... in any criminal proceedings", the law governing cross-examination by one defendant of another defendant on spent convictions was as stated in *Murdoch v. Taylor* [1965] A.C. 574, HL (*ante*, § 13–71), *i.e.* if a defendant has "given evidence against" a co-defendant within the meaning of section 1(3)(iii) of the *Criminal Evidence Act* 1898 (see now s.101(1)(g) of the *CJA* 2003, *ante*, §§ 13–69 *et seq.*), and if the question which it is proposed to put is relevant, the judge has no discretion to disallow it.

(3) Statute

Rehabilitation of Offenders Act 1974, s.1

Rehabilitated persons and spent convictions

13–123 **1.**—(1) Subject to subsection (2) below, where an individual has been convicted, whether before or after the commencement of this Act, of any offence or offences, and the following conditions are satisfied, that is to say—

(a) he did not have imposed on him in respect of that conviction a sentence which is excluded from rehabilitation under this Act; and

(b) he has not had imposed on him in respect of a subsequent conviction during the rehabilitation period applicable to the first-mentioned conviction in accordance with section 6 below a sentence which is excluded from rehabilitation under this Act;

then, after the end of the rehabilitation period so applicable (including, where appropriate, any extension under section 6(4) below of the period originally applicable to the first-mentioned conviction) or, where that rehabilitation period ended before the commencement of this Act, after the commencement of this Act, that individual shall for the purposes of this Act be treated as a rehabilitated person in respect of the first-mentioned conviction and that conviction shall for those purposes be treated as spent.

(2) A person shall not become a rehabilitated person for the purposes of this Act in respect of a conviction unless he has served or otherwise undergone or complied with any sentence imposed on him in respect of that conviction; but the following shall not, by virtue of this subsection, prevent a person from becoming a rehabilitated person for those purposes—

(a) failure to pay a fine or other sum adjudged to be paid by or imposed on a conviction, or breach of a condition of a recognizance or of a bond of caution to keep the peace or be of good behaviour;

(b) breach of any condition or requirement applicable in relation to a sentence which renders the person to whom it applies liable to be dealt with for the offence for which the sentence was imposed, or, where the sentence was a suspended sentence of imprisonment, liable to be dealt with in respect of that sentence (whether or not, in any case, he is in fact so dealt with);

(c) failure to comply with any requirement of a suspended sentence supervision order.

(2A) Where in respect of a conviction a person has been sentenced to imprisonment with an order under section 47(1) of the *Criminal Law Act* 1977, he is to be treated for the purposes of subsection (2) above as having served the sentence as soon as he completes service of so much of the sentence as was by that order required to be served in prison.

(2B) In subsection (2)(a) above the reference to a fine or other sum adjudged to be paid by or imposed on a conviction does not include a reference to an amount payable under a confiscation order made under Part 2 of the *Proceeds of Crime Act* 2002.

(3) In this Act "sentence" includes any order made by a court in dealing with a person in respect of his conviction of any offence or offences, other than—

(za) a surcharge imposed under section 161A(3) of the *Criminal Justice Act* 2003;

(a) an order for committal or any other order made in default of payment of any fine or other sum adjudged to be paid by or imposed on a conviction, or for want of sufficient distress to satisfy any such fine or other sum;

(b) an order dealing with a person in respect of a suspended sentence of imprisonment.

[(3A) In subsection (3)(a), the reference to want of sufficient distress to satisfy a fine or other sum includes a reference to circumstances where—

(a) there is power to use the procedure in Schedule 12 to the *Tribunals, Courts and Enforcement Act* 2007 to recover the fine or other sum from a person, but

(b) it appears, after an attempt has been made to exercise the power, that the person's goods are insufficient to pay the amount outstanding (as defined by paragraph 50(3) of that Schedule).]

(4) In this Act, references to a conviction, however expressed, include references—

(a) to a conviction by or before a court outside Great Britain; and

(b) to any finding (other than a finding linked with a finding of insanity) in any criminal proceedings ... that a person has committed an offence or done the act or made the omission charged;

and notwithstanding anything in section 9 of the *Criminal Justice (Scotland) Act* 1949 or section 14 of the *Powers of Criminal Courts (Sentencing) Act* 2000 [or section 187 of the *Armed Forces Act* 2006] (conviction of a person ... discharged to be deemed not to be a conviction) a conviction in respect of which an order is made discharging the person concerned absolutely or conditionally shall be treated as a conviction for the purposes of this Act and the person in question may become a rehabilitated person in respect of that conviction and the conviction a spent conviction for those purposes accordingly.

[This section is printed as amended or repealed in part by the *CLA* 1977, Sched. 9; the *Children Act* 1989, s.108(7), and Sched. 15; the *CJA* 1991, s.100, and Sched. 11, para. 20; the *PCC(S)A* 2000, s.165(1), and Sched. 9, para. 47; the *PCA* 2002, s.456, and Sched. 11, para. 7; and the *Domestic Violence, Crime and Victims Act* 2004, s.58(1), and Sched. 10, para. 9; and as amended, as from a day to be appointed, by the *AFA* 2006, s.378(1), and Sched. 16, para. 63 (insertion of words in square brackets in subs. (4)); and the *Tribunals, Courts and Enforcement Act* 2007, s.62(3), and Sched. 13, para. 38 (insertion of subs. (3A)).]

In subsection (2)(a), the reference to a fine or other sum adjudged to be paid by or imposed on a conviction does not include a reference to an amount payable under a confiscation order: *DTA* 1994, s.65(2).

Rehabilitation of Offenders Act 1974, s.2

Rehabilitation of persons dealt with in service disciplinary proceedings

2.—(1) ... for the purposes of this Act any finding that a person is guilty of an offence in respect of any act or omission which was the subject of service disciplinary proceedings shall be treated as a conviction and any punishment awarded or order made by virtue of Schedule 5A to the *Army Act* 1955 or the *Air Force Act* 1955 or Schedule 4A to the *Naval Discipline Act* 1957, in respect of any such finding shall be treated as a sentence. **13–124**

(2)–(4) [*Repealed by* Armed Forces Act *1996, s.13(2).*]

(5) In this Act, "service disciplinary proceedings" means any of the following—

[(za) any proceedings (whether or not before a court) in respect of a service offence within the meaning of the *Armed Forces Act* 2006 (except proceedings before a civilian court within the meaning of that Act);]

(a) any proceedings under the *Army Act* 1955, the *Air Force Act* 1955, or the *Naval Discipline Act* 1957, whether before a court-martial or before any other court or person authorised thereunder to award a punishment in respect of any offence;

(b) any proceedings under any Act previously in force corresponding to any of the Acts mentioned in paragraph (a) above;

(bb) any proceedings before a Standing Civilian Court established under the *Armed Forces Act* 1976;

(c) any proceedings under any corresponding enactment or law applying to a force, other than a home force, to which section 4 of the *Visiting Forces (British Commonwealth) Act* 1933 applies or applied at the time of the proceedings, being proceedings in respect of a member of a home force who is or was at that time attached to the first-mentioned force under that section;

whether in any event those proceedings take place in Great Britain or elsewhere.

[(6) Section 376(1) to (3) of the *Armed Forces Act* 2006 ("conviction" and "sentence" in relation to summary hearings and the SAC) apply for the purposes of this Act as they apply for the purposes of that Act.]

[This section is printed as amended by the *AFA* 1976, s.22(5), and Sched. 9; and the *AFA* 1981, Sched. 4; as repealed in part by the *AFA* 1996, s.13, and Sched. 7, Pt III; and as amended, as from a day to be appointed, by the *AFA* 2006, s.378(1), and Sched. 16, para. 64 (insertion of subss. (2)(za) and (6)).]

Section 3 makes special provision with respect to certain disposals by children's hearings under the *Social Work (Scotland) Act* 1968.

Rehabilitation of Offenders Act 1974, s.4

Effect of rehabilitation

13–125 **4.**—(1) Subject to sections 7 and 8 below, a person who has become a rehabilitated person for the purposes of this Act in respect of a conviction shall be treated for all purposes in law as a person who has not committed or been charged with or prosecuted for or convicted of or sentenced for the offence or offences which were the subject of that conviction; and, notwithstanding the provisions of any other enactment or rule of law to the contrary, but subject as aforesaid—

(a) no evidence shall be admissible in any proceedings before a judicial authority exercising its jurisdiction or functions in Great Britain to prove that any such person has committed or been charged with or prosecuted for or convicted of or sentenced for any offence which was the subject of a spent conviction; and

(b) a person shall not, in any such proceedings, be asked, and, if asked, shall not be required to answer, any question relating to his past which cannot be answered without acknowledging or referring to a spent conviction or spent convictions or any circumstances ancillary thereto.

(2) Subject to the provisions of any order made under subsection (4) below, where a question seeking information with respect to a person's previous convictions, offences, conduct or circumstances is put to him or to any other person otherwise than in proceedings before a judicial authority—

(a) the question shall be treated as not relating to spent convictions or to any circumstances ancillary to spent convictions, and the answer thereto may be framed accordingly; and

(b) the person questioned shall not be subjected to any liability or otherwise prejudiced in law by reason of any failure to acknowledge or disclose a spent conviction or any circumstances ancillary to a spent conviction in his answer to the question.

(3) Subject to the provisions of any order made under subsection (4) below,—

(a) any obligation imposed on any person by any rule of law or by the provisions of any agreement or arrangement to disclose any matters to any other person shall not extend to requiring him to disclose a spent conviction or any circumstances ancillary to a spent conviction (whether the conviction is his own or another's); and

(b) a conviction which has become spent or any circumstances ancillary thereto, or any failure to disclose a spent conviction or any such circumstances, shall not be a proper ground for dismissing or excluding a person from any office, profession, occupation or employment, or for prejudicing him in any way in any occupation or employment.

13–126 (4) The Secretary of State may by order—

(a) make such provision as seems to him appropriate for excluding or modifying the application of either or both of paragraphs (a) and (b) of subsection (2) above in relation to questions put in such circumstances as may be specified in the order;

(b) provide for such exceptions from the provisions of subsection (3) above as seem to him appropriate, in such cases or classes of case, and in relation to convictions of such a description, as may be specified in the order.

(5) For the purposes of this section and section 7 below any of the following are circumstances ancillary to a conviction, that is to say—

(a) the offence or offences which were the subject of that conviction;

(b) the conduct constituting that offence or those offences; and

(c) any process or proceedings preliminary to that conviction, any sentence imposed in respect of that conviction, any proceedings (whether by way of appeal or otherwise) for reviewing that conviction or any such sentence, and anything done in pursuance of or undergone in compliance with any such sentence.

(6) For the purposes of this section and section 7 below "proceedings before a judicial authority" includes, in addition to proceedings before any of the ordinary courts of law, proceedings before any tribunal, body or person having power—

(a) by virtue of any enactment, law, custom or practice;

(b) under the rules governing any association, institution, profession, occupation or employment; or

(c) under any provision of an agreement providing for arbitration with respect to questions arising thereunder;

to determine any question affecting the rights, privileges, obligations or liabilities of any person, or to receive evidence affecting the determination of any such question.

For limitations on the operation of this section, see *post*, § 13–133.

As to the disapplication of this section in relation to the disclosure to the public of information about child sex offenders, see section 327B(8) of the *CJA* 2003.

Rehabilitation of Offenders Act 1974, s.5

Rehabilitation periods for particular sentences

5.—(1) The sentences excluded from rehabilitation under this Act are— **13–127**

(a) a sentence of imprisonment for life;

(b) a sentence of imprisonment, youth custody detention in a young offender institution or corrective training for a term exceeding thirty months;

(c) a sentence of preventive detention;

(d) a sentence of detention during Her Majesty's pleasure or for life under section 90 or 91 of the *Powers of Criminal Courts (Sentencing) Act* 2000 [, or under section 209 or 218 of the *Armed Forces Act* 2006], or under section 205(2) or (3) of the *Criminal Procedure (Scotland) Act* 1975, or a sentence of detention for a term exceeding thirty months passed under section 91 of the said Act of 2000 [or section 209 of the said Act of 2006] (young offenders convicted of grave crimes) or under section 206 of the said Act of 1975 (detention of children convicted on indictment), *or a corresponding court-martial punishment*, and

(e) a sentence of custody for life, and

(f) a sentence of imprisonment for public protection under section 225 of the *Criminal Justice Act* 2003, a sentence of detention for public protection under section 226 of that Act or an extended sentence under section 227 or 228 of that Act [(including any sentence within this paragraph passed as a result of any of sections 219 to 222 of the *Armed Forces Act* 2006)],

and any other sentence is a sentence subject to rehabilitation under this Act.

(1A) *In subsection (1)(d) above "corresponding court-martial punishment" means a punishment awarded under section 71A(3) or (4) of the* Army Act *1955, section 71A(3) or (4) of the* Air Force Act *1955 or section 43A(3) or (4) of the* Naval Discipline Act *1957.*

[(1A) In subsection (1)(d)—

(a) references to section 209 of the *Armed Forces Act* 2006 include references to section 71A(4) of the *Army Act* 1955 or *Air Force Act* 1955 or section 43A(4) of the *Naval Discipline Act* 1957;

(b) the reference to section 218 of the *Armed Forces Act* 2006 includes a reference to section 71A(3) of the *Army Act* 1955 or *Air Force Act* 1955 or section 43A(3) of the *Naval Discipline Act* 1957.]

(2) For the purposes of this Act—

(a) the rehabilitation period applicable to a sentence specified in the first column of Table A below is the period specified in the second column of that Table in relation to that sentence, or, where the sentence was imposed on a person who was under eighteen years of age at the date of his conviction, half that period; and

(b) the rehabilitation period applicable to a sentence specified in the first column of Table B below is the period specified in the second column of that Table in relation to that sentence;

reckoned in either case from the date of the conviction in respect of which the sentence was imposed.

TABLE A

REHABILITATION PERIODS SUBJECT TO REDUCTION BY HALF FOR PERSONS UNDER 18

13–128

Sentence	*Rehabilitation period*
A sentence of imprisonment detention in a young offender institution or youth custody or corrective training for a term exceeding six months but not exceeding thirty months.	Ten years
A sentence of cashiering, discharge with ignominy or dismissal with disgrace from Her Majesty's service.	Ten years
A sentence of imprisonment detention in a young offender institution or youth custody for a term not exceeding six months.	Seven years
A sentence of dismissal from Her Majesty's service.	Seven years
Any sentence of [service] detention [within the meaning of the *Armed Forces Act* 2006, or any sentence of detention corresponding to such a sentence,] in respect of a conviction in service disciplinary proceedings.	Five years
A fine or any other sentence subject to rehabilitation under this Act, not being a sentence to which Table B below or any of subsections (3) to (8) below applies.	Five years

TABLE B

REHABILITATION PERIODS FOR CERTAIN SENTENCES CONFINED TO YOUNG OFFENDERS

13–129

Sentence	*Rehabilitation period*
A sentence of Borstal training.	Seven years
A custodial order under Schedule 5A to the *Army Act* 1955 or the *Air Force Act* 1955, or under Schedule 4A to the *Naval Discipline Act* 1957, where the maximum period of detention specified in the order is more than six months.	Seven years
A custodial order under section 71AA of the *Army Act* 1955 or the *Air Force Act* 1955, or under section 43AA of the *Naval Discipline Act* 1957, where the maximum period of detention specified in the order is more than six months.	Seven years
A sentence of detention for a term exceeding six months but not exceeding thirty months passed under section 91 of the *Powers of Criminal Courts (Sentencing) Act* 2000 [or under section 209 of the *Armed Forces Act* 2006] or under section 206 of the *Criminal Procedure (Scotland) Act* 1975.	Five years
Any sentence of detention for a term not exceeding six months passed under *either of those provisions* [any provision mentioned in the fourth entry in this Table].	Three years
An order for detention in a detention centre made under section 4 of the *Criminal Justice Act* 1982 or section 4 of the *Criminal Justice Act* 1961.	Three years
A custodial order under any of the Schedules to the said Acts of 1955 and 1957 mentioned above, where the maximum period of detention specified in the order is six months or less.	Three years
A custodial order under section 71AA of the said Acts of 1955, or section 43AA of the said Act of 1957, where the maximum period of detention specified in the order is six months or less.	Three years

[(2A) Table B applies in relation to a sentence under section 71A(4) of the *Army Act* 1955 or *Air Force Act* 1955 or section 43A(4) of the *Naval Discipline Act* 1957 as it applies in relation to one under section 209 of the *Armed Forces Act* 2006.]

(3) The rehabilitation period applicable—

(a) to an order discharging a person absolutely for an offence; and

(b) to the discharge by a children's hearing under section 43(2) of the *Social Work (Scotland) Act* 1968 of the referral of a child's case;

shall be six months from the date of conviction.

(4) Where in respect of a conviction a person was conditionally discharged, bound over to keep the peace or be of good behaviour, ... the rehabilitation period applicable to the sentence shall be one year from the date of conviction or a period beginning with that date and ending when the order for conditional discharge ... or (as the case may be) the recognizance or bond of caution to keep the peace or be of good behaviour ceases or ceased to have effect, whichever is the longer.

(4A) Where in respect of a conviction a probation order or a community order under section 177 of the *Criminal Justice Act* 2003 [or a service community order or overseas community order under the *Armed Forces Act* 2006] was made, the rehabilitation period applicable to the sentence shall be—

(a) in the case of a person aged eighteen years or over at the date of his conviction, five years from the date of his conviction;

(b) in the case of a person aged under the age of eighteen years at the date of his conviction, two and a half years from the date of conviction or a period beginning with the date of conviction and ending when the order in question ceases or ceased to have effect whichever is the longer.

(4B) Where in respect of a conviction a referral order (within the meaning of the *Powers of Criminal Courts (Sentencing) Act* 2000) is made in respect of the person convicted, the rehabilitation period applicable to the sentence shall be—

(a) if a youth offender contract takes effect under section 23 of that Act between him and a youth offender panel, the period beginning with the date of conviction and ending on the date when (in accordance with section 24 of that Act) the contract ceases to have effect;

(b) if no such contract so takes effect, the period beginning with the date of conviction and having the same length as the period for which such a contract would (ignoring any order under paragraph 11 or 12 of Schedule 1 to that Act) have had effect had one so taken effect.

(4C) Where in respect of a conviction an order is made in respect of the person convicted under paragraph 11 or 12 of Schedule 1 to the *Powers of Criminal Courts (Sentencing) Act* 2000 (extension of period for which youth offender contract has effect), the rehabilitation period applicable to the sentence shall be—

(a) if a youth offender contract takes effect under section 23 of that Act between the offender and a youth offender panel, the period beginning with the date of conviction and ending on the date when (in accordance with section 24 of that Act) the contract ceases to have effect

(b) if no such contract so takes effect, the period beginning with the date of conviction and having the same length as the period for which, in accordance with the order, such a contract would have had effect had one so taken effect.

(5) Where in respect of a conviction any of the following sentences was imposed, that is to say— **13–130**

(a) an order under section 57 of the *Children and Young Persons Act* 1933 or section 61 of the *Children and Young Persons (Scotland) Act* 1937 committing the person convicted to the care of a fit person;

(b) a supervision order under any provision of either of those Acts or of the *Children and Young Persons Act* 1963;

(c) an order under section 413 of the *Criminal Procedure (Scotland) Act* 1975 committing a child for the purpose of his undergoing residential training;

(d) an approved school order under section 61 of the said Act of 1937;

[(da) a youth rehabilitation order under Part 1 of the *Criminal Justice and Immigration Act* 2008;]

(e) ... a supervision order under section 63(1) of the *Powers of Criminal Courts (Sentencing) Act* 2000; or

(f) a supervision requirement under any provision of the *Social Work (Scotland) Act* 1968;

(g) a community supervision order under Schedule 5A to the *Army Act* 1955 or the *Air Force Act* 1955, or under Schedule 4A to the *Naval Discipline Act* 1957;

(h) [*repealed by* Armed Forces Act *1991, s.26(2) and Sched. 3*];

the rehabilitation period applicable to the sentence shall be one year from the date of conviction or a period beginning with that date and ending when the order or requirement ceases or ceased to have effect, whichever is the longer.

(6) Where in respect of a conviction any of the following orders was made, that is to say—

(a) an order under section 54 of the said Act of 1933 committing the person convicted to custody in a remand home;

(b) an approved school order under section 57 of the said Act of 1933; or

(c) an attendance centre order under section 60 of the *Powers of Criminal Courts (Sentencing) Act* 2000;

(d) a secure training order under section 1 of the *Criminal Justice and Public Order Act* 1994;

the rehabilitation period applicable to the sentence shall be a period beginning with the date of conviction and ending one year after the date on which the order ceases or ceased to have effect.

(6A) Where in respect of a conviction a detention and training order was made under section 100 of the *Powers of Criminal Courts (Sentencing) Act* 2000 [, or an order under section 211 of the *Armed Forces Act* 2006 was made], the rehabilitation period applicable to the sentence shall be—

(a) in the case of a person aged fifteen years or over at the date of his conviction, five years if the order was, and three and a half years if the order was not, for a term exceeding six months;

(b) in the case of a person aged under fifteen years at the date of his conviction, a period beginning with that date and ending one year after the date on which the order ceases to have effect.

(7) Where in respect of a conviction a hospital order under Part III of the *Mental Health Act* 1983 or under Part VI of the *Mental Health (Scotland) Act* 1984 (with or without a restriction order) was made, the rehabilitation period applicable to the sentence shall be the period of five years from the date of conviction or a period beginning with that date and ending two years after the date on which the hospital order ceases or ceased to have effect, whichever is the longer.

(8) Where in respect of a conviction an order was made imposing on the person convicted any disqualification, disability, prohibition or other penalty, the rehabilitation period applicable to the sentence shall be a period beginning with the date of conviction and ending on the date on which the disqualification, disability, prohibition or penalty (as the case may be) ceases or ceased to have effect.

13–131 (9) For the purposes of this section—

(a) "sentence of imprisonment" includes a sentence of detention under section 207 or 415 of the *Criminal Procedure (Scotland) Act* 1975 and a sentence of penal servitude, and "term of imprisonment" shall be construed accordingly;

(b) consecutive terms of imprisonment or of detention under section 91 of the *Powers of Criminal Courts (Sentencing) Act* 2000 [or section 209 of the *Armed Forces Act* 2006] or section 206 of the said Act of 1975, and terms which are wholly or partly concurrent (being terms of imprisonment or detention imposed in respect of offences of which a person was convicted in the same proceedings) shall be treated as a single term;

(c) no account shall be taken of any subsequent variation, made by a court in dealing with a person in respect of a suspended sentence of imprisonment, of the term originally imposed; and

(d) a sentence imposed by a court outside Great Britain shall be treated as a sentence of that one of the descriptions mentioned in this section which most nearly corresponds to the sentence imposed.

(10) References in this section to the period during which a probation order, or a ... supervision order under the *Powers of Criminal Courts (Sentencing) Act* 2000, or a supervision requirement under the *Social Work (Scotland) Act* 1968, is or was in force include references to any period during which any order or requirement to which this subsection applies, being an order or requirement made or imposed directly or indirectly in substitution for the first-mentioned order or requirement, is or was in force.

This subsection applies—

(a) to any such order or requirement as is mentioned above in this subsection;

(b) to any order having effect under section 25(2) of the *Children and Young Persons Act* 1969 as if it were a training school order in Northern Ireland; and

(c) to any supervision order made under section 72(2) of the said Act of 1968 and having effect as a supervision order under the *Children and Young Persons Act (Northern Ireland)* 1950.

(10A) The reference in subsection (5) above to the period during which a reception order has effect includes a reference to any subsequent period during which by virtue of the order having been made the *Social Work (Scotland) Act* 1968 or the *Children and Young Persons Act (Northern Ireland)* 1968 has effect in relation to the person in respect of whom the order was made and subsection (10) above shall accordingly have effect in relation to any such subsequent period.

(11) The Secretary of State may by order—

(a) substitute different periods or terms for any of the periods or terms mentioned in subsections (1) to (8) above; and

(b) substitute a different age for the age mentioned in subsection (2)(a) above.

[This section is printed as amended and repealed in part by the *AFA* 1976, Sched. 9; the *Criminal Justice (Scotland) Act* 1980, Scheds 7 and 8; the *AFA* 1981, Sched. 4; the *CJA* 1982, Scheds 14 and 16; the *Mental Health (Amendment) Act* 1982, Sched. 3; the *MHA* 1983, Sched. 4; the *Mental Health (Scotland) Act* 1984, Sched. 3; the *CJA* 1988, Sched. 8, para. 9; the *Children Act* 1989, s.108(7), and Sched. 15; the *CJA* 1991, s.68, and Sched. 8; the *AFA* 1991, s.26(2), and Sched. 3; the *CJPOA* 1994, s.168(1) and (2), and Scheds 9, para. 11(1), and 10, para. 30; the *CDA* 1998, s.119, and Sched. 8, para. 35; the *YJCEA* 1999, s.67(1), and Sched. 4, para. 6; the *PCC(S)A* 2000, s.165(1), and Sched. 9, para. 48; the *CJCSA* 2000, s.74, and Sched. 7, paras 48 and 49; and the *CJA* 2003, s.304, and Sched. 32, para. 18; and as amended, as from a day to be appointed, by the *AFA* 2006, s.378(1) and (2), Sched. 16, para. 65, and Sched. 17 (omission of italicised words (other than short titles of Acts) and insertion of words in square brackets (other than subs. (5)(da)); and the *CJIA* 2008, s.6(2), and Sched. 4, paras 20 and 21 (insertion of subs. (5)(da)). The amendment made by the 2008 Act is of no effect in relation to any offence committed before it comes into force or any failure to comply with an order made in respect of an offence committed before it comes into force: s.148(2), and Sched. 27, para. 1(1)).]

Suspended sentences are treated as if they had been sentences of immediate imprisonment.

An order for endorsement of a licence is not an order imposing on the convicted person a "disability, prohibition or other penalty" within the meaning of section 5(8): *Power v. Provincial Insurance plc* [1998] R.T.R. 60, CA (Civ. Div.).

Rehabilitation of Offenders Act 1974, s.6

The rehabilitation period applicable to a conviction

6.—(1) Where only one sentence is imposed in respect of a conviction (not being a sentence excluded from rehabilitation under this Act) the rehabilitation period applicable to the conviction is, subject to the following provisions of this section, the period applicable to the sentence in accordance with section 5 above. **13–132**

(2) Where more than one sentence is imposed in respect of a conviction (whether or not in the same proceedings) and none of the sentences imposed is excluded from rehabilitation under this Act, then, subject to the following provisions of this section, if the periods applicable to those sentences in accordance with section 5 above differ, the rehabilitation period applicable to the conviction shall be the longer or the longest (as the case may be) of those periods.

(3) Without prejudice to subsection (2) above, where in respect of a conviction a person was conditionally discharged or a probation order was made and after the end of the rehabilitation period applicable to the conviction in accordance with subsection (1) or (2) above he is dealt with, in consequence of a breach of conditional discharge or a breach of the order, for the offence for which the order for conditional discharge or probation order was made, then, if the rehabilitation period applicable to the conviction in accordance with subsection (2) above (taking into account any sentence imposed when he is so dealt with) ends later than the rehabilitation period previously applicable to the conviction, he shall be treated for the purposes of this Act as not having become a rehabilitated person in respect of that conviction, and the conviction shall for those purposes be treated as not having become spent, in relation to any period falling before the end of the new rehabilitation period.

(4) Subject to subsection (5) below, where during the rehabilitation period applicable to a conviction—

(a) the person convicted is convicted of a further offence; and

(b) no sentence excluded from rehabilitation under this Act is imposed on him in respect of the later conviction;

if the rehabilitation period applicable in accordance with this section to either of the convictions would end earlier than the period so applicable in relation to the other, the rehabilitation period which would (apart from this subsection) end the earlier shall be extended so as to end at the same time as the other rehabilitation period.

(5) Where the rehabilitation period applicable to a conviction is the rehabilitation period applicable in accordance with section 5(8) above to an order imposing on a person any disqualification, disability, prohibition or other penalty, the rehabilitation period applicable to another conviction shall not by virtue of subsection (4) above be extended by reference to that period; but if any other sentence is imposed in respect of the first-mentioned conviction for which a rehabilitation period is prescribed by any other provision of section 5 above, the rehabilitation period applicable to another conviction shall, where appropriate, be extended under subsection (4) above by reference to the rehabilitation period applicable in accordance with that section to that sentence or, where more than one such sentence is imposed, by reference to the longer or longest of the periods so applicable to those sentences, as if the period in question were the rehabilitation period applicable to the first-mentioned conviction.

(6) … for the purposes of subsection (4)(a) above there shall be disregarded—

(a) any conviction in England and Wales of a summary offence or of a scheduled offence (within the meaning of section 22 of the *Magistrates' Courts Act* 1980) tried summarily in pursuance of subsection (2) of that section (summary trial where value involved is small);

(b) any conviction in Scotland of an offence which is not excluded from the jurisdiction of inferior courts of summary jurisdiction by virtue of section 4 of the *Summary Jurisdiction (Scotland) Act* 1954 (certain crimes not to be tried in inferior courts of summary jurisdiction); and

(bb) any conviction in service disciplinary proceedings for an offence listed in *the* Schedule [1] to this Act;

(c) any conviction by or before a court outside Great Britain of an offence in respect of conduct which, if it had taken place in any part of Great Britain, would not have constituted an offence under the law in force in that part of Great Britain.

(7) [*Repealed by* Armed Forces Act *1996, Sched. 7 Pt III.*]

[This section is printed as amended by the *CLA* 1977, Sched. 12; and the *MCA* 1980, Sched. 7; and as amended and repealed in part by the *AFA* 1996, s.13, and Sched. 7, Pt III; and the *CJCSA* 2000, s.74, and Sched. 7, paras 48 and 50; and as amended, as from a day to be appointed, by the *CJIA* 2008, s.49, and Sched. 10, paras 1 and 2 (substitution of reference to "Schedule 1" for the reference to "the Schedule" in subs. (6)).]

The Schedule [Schedule 1] to the Act (inserted by the *AFA* 1996, s.13(4)) is not printed in this work.

Rehabilitation of Offenders Act 1974, s.7(1), (2), (4), (5)

Limitations on rehabilitation under this Act, etc.

13–133 **7.**—(1) Nothing in section 4(1) above shall affect—

(a) any right of Her Majesty, by virtue of Her Royal prerogative or otherwise, to grant a free pardon, to quash any conviction or sentence, or to commute any sentence;

(b) the enforcement by any process or proceedings of any fine or other sum adjudged to be paid by or imposed on a spent conviction;

(c) the issue of any process for the purpose of proceedings in respect of any breach of a condition or requirement applicable to a sentence imposed in respect of a spent conviction; or

(d) the operation of any enactment by virtue of which, in consequence of any conviction, a person is subject, otherwise than by way of sentence, to any disqualification, disability, prohibition or other penalty the period of which extends beyond the rehabilitation period applicable in accordance with section 6 above to the conviction.

(2) Nothing in section 4(1) above shall affect the determination of any issue, or prevent the admission or requirement of any evidence, relating to a person's previous convictions or to circumstances ancillary thereto—

(a) in any criminal proceedings before a court in Great Britain (including any appeal or reference in a criminal matter);

(b) in any service disciplinary proceedings or in any proceedings on appeal from any service disciplinary proceedings;

(bb) in any proceedings under Part 2 of the *Sexual Offences Act* 2003, or on appeal from any such proceedings;

(c) [*certain family proceedings and proceedings relating to minors*];

(cc) in any proceedings brought under the *Children Act* 1989;

(d) in any proceedings *relating to* [for] the variation or discharge of a *supervision order under the* Powers of Criminal Courts (Sentencing) Act *2000* [youth rehabilitation order under Part 1 of the *Criminal Justice and Immigration Act* 2008], or on appeal from any such proceedings;

(e) [*certain Scottish children's proceedings*];

(f) in any proceedings in which he is a party or a witness, provided that, on the occasion when the issue or the admission or requirement of the evidence falls to be determined, he consents to the determination of the issue or, as the case may be, the admission or requirement of the evidence notwithstanding the provisions of section 4(1); or

(g) [*repealed by* Banking Act *1987*, *Sched. 7*].

In the application of this subsection to Scotland, "minor" means a child under the age of eighteen, including a pupil child.

(4) The Secretary of State may by order exclude the application of section 4(1) above in relation to any proceedings specified in the order (other than proceedings to which section 8 below applies) to such extent and for such purposes as may be so specified.

(5) No order made by a court with respect to any person otherwise than on a conviction shall be included in any list or statement of that person's previous convictions given or made to any court which is considering how to deal with him in respect of any offence.

[These subsections are printed as amended by the *Children Act* 1989, s.108(5), and Sched. 13, para. 35; the *CDA* 1998, s.119, and Sched. 8, para. 36; the *PCC(S)A* 2000, s.165(1), and Sched. 9, para. 49; the *Police Reform Act* 2002, s.107(1), and Sched. 7, para. 4; and the *SOA* 2003, s.139, and Sched. 6, para. 19; and as repealed in part by the *Banking Act* 1987, Sched. 7; and as amended, as from a day to be appointed (as to which, see *ante*, § 5–1), by the *CJIA* 2008, s.6(2), and Sched. 4, paras 20 and 22 (substitution of words in square brackets for italicised words in subs. (2)(d)).]

Subsection (3) confers a general judicial discretion to admit evidence of spent convictions if justice cannot otherwise be done; this does not apply to proceedings listed in subsection (2), referred to in an order under subsection (4) or defamation actions.

Summary offences relating to spent convictions

Section 9 creates two summary offences. One (s.9(2)) relates to unauthorised **13–134**
disclosure of spent convictions; the other (s.9(4)) relates to the obtaining of information about such convictions by means of "any fraud, dishonesty or bribe."

Cautions, etc.

Section 49 of, and Schedule 10 to, the *CJIA* 2008 amend the 1974 Act, by inserting **13–135**
new sections 8A (protection afforded to spent cautions) and 9A (unauthorised disclosure of spent cautions) and a new Schedule 2 (protection for spent cautions), so as to bring warnings, reprimands, simple cautions and conditional cautions within its ambit. Section 8A gives effect to Schedule 2. Section 9A broadly corresponds to section 9 (*ante*) and creates summary offences relating to the unauthorised disclosure of caution information and the obtaining of such information by any fraud, dishonesty or bribe. As to the penalties, there is a transitional provision in Schedule 27, para. 20, in relation to an offence committed before the commencement of the *CJA* 2003, s.281(5). The new Schedule 2 makes broadly corresponding provision to section 4 (*ante*, § 13–125), in particular providing that a conditional caution becomes spent three months after it is given (unless

the person concerned is subsequently convicted of the offence in respect of which it was given) and that all other cautions become spent when they are given, and additionally applies various provisions of section 7, including in particular subsection (2) (other than paras. (b) and (d)) to spent cautions. These amendments come into force on a day to be appointed. As to the application of these provisions to cautions given before the date on which section 49 comes into force, see Schedule 27, para. 19, to the 2008 Act.

Chapter 14

EVIDENCE OF IDENTIFICATION

I. VISUAL IDENTIFICATION

A. Background

The mistaken identification of Adolf Beck by 15 witnesses led to a Committee of Inquiry in 1905 (Cmnd. 2315) and was directly responsible for the establishment of the Court of Criminal Appeal by the *CAA* 1907. Similar concerns led to the establishment of Lord Devlin's Committee on Evidence of Identification in 1976, to which the Attorney-General responded by instituting special procedures in identification cases (*Hansard*, Vol. 912, col. 115, set out in previous editions of this work). Shortly thereafter came the response of the Court of Appeal in *R. v. Turnbull* [1977] Q.B. 224, 63 Cr.App.R. 132, CA, *post*, § 14–2, and, in 1984, Code D of the codes of practice, issued under the *PACE Act* 1984 (Appendix A–112 *et seq.*). The later history on the topic is reviewed in *R. v. Forbes* [2001] 1 A.C. 473, HL. **14–1**

B. The Turnbull Guidelines

(1) R. v. Turnbull

The following guidelines, to be observed by trial judges when "identity" is an issue, were laid down by the Court of Appeal (a full court) in *R. v. Turnbull* [1977] Q.B. 224 at 228–231, 63 Cr.App.R. 132 at 137–140. In the view of the court, they involved changes of practice, but not of law (see pp. 228, 137). **14–2**

> "First, whenever the case against an accused depends wholly or substantially on the correctness of one or more identifications of the accused which the defence alleges to be mistaken, the judge should warn the jury of the special need for caution before convicting the accused in reliance on the correctness of the identification or identifications. In addition he should instruct them as to the reason for the need for such a warning and should make some reference to the possibility that a mistaken witness can be a convincing one and that a number of such witnesses can all be mistaken. Provided this is done in clear terms the judge need not use any particular form of words.
>
> Secondly, the judge should direct the jury to examine closely the circumstances in which the identification by each witness came to be made. How long did the witness have the accused under observation? At what distance? In what light? Was the observation impeded in any way, as for example, by passing traffic or a press of people? Had the witness ever seen the accused before? How often? If only occasionally, had he any special reason for remembering the accused? How long elapsed between the original observation and the subsequent identification to the police? Was there any material discrepancy between the description of **14–3**

the accused given to the police by the witness when first seen by them and his actual appearance? If in any case, whether it is being dealt with summarily or on indictment, the prosecution have reason to believe that there is such a material discrepancy they should supply the accused or his legal advisers with particulars of the description the police were first given … . Finally, he should remind the jury of any specific weaknesses which had appeared in the identification evidence.

14–4 Recognition may be more reliable than identification of a stranger; but even when the witness is purporting to recognise someone whom he knows, the jury should be reminded that mistakes in recognition of close relatives and friends are sometimes made.

14–5 All these matters go to the quality of identification evidence. If the quality is good and remains good at the close of the accused's case, the danger of a mistaken identification is lessened; but the poorer the quality, the greater the danger.

14–6 In our judgment when the quality is good, as for example when the identification is made after a long period of observation, or in satisfactory conditions by a relative, a neighbour, a close friend, a workmate and the like, the jury can safely be left to assess the value of the identifying evidence even though there is no other evidence to support it: provided always, however, that an adequate warning has been given about the special need for caution … .

14–7 When, in the judgment of the trial judge, the quality of the identifying evidence is poor, as for example when it depends solely on a fleeting glance or on a longer observation made in difficult conditions, the situation is very different. The judge should then withdraw the case from the jury and direct an acquittal unless there is other evidence which goes to support the correctness of the identification. This may be corroboration in the sense lawyers use that word; but it did not need to be so if its effect is to make the jury sure that there had been no mistaken identification: for example, X sees the accused snatch a woman's handbag; he gets only a fleeting glance of the thief's face as he runs off but he does see him entering a nearby house. Later he picks out the accused on an identity parade. If there was no more evidence than this, the poor quality of the identification would require the judge to withdraw the case from the jury; but this would not be so if there was evidence that the house into which the accused was alleged by X to have run was his father's. Another example of supporting evidence not amounting to corroboration in a technical sense is to be found in *R. v. Long*, 57 Cr.App.R. 871 … .

14–8 The trial judge should identify to the jury the evidence which he adjudges is capable of supporting the evidence of identification. If there is any evidence or circumstances which the jury might think was supporting when it did not have that quality, the judge should say so … .

14–9 Care should be taken by the judge when directing the jury about the support for an identification which may be derived from the fact they have rejected an alibi. False alibis may be put forward for many reasons: an accused, for example, who has only his own truthful evidence to rely on may stupidly fabricate an alibi and get lying witnesses to support it out of fear that his own evidence will not be enough. Further, alibi witnesses can make genuine mistakes about dates and occasions like any other witnesses can. It is only when the jury is satisfied that the sole reason for the fabrication was to deceive them and there is no other explanation for its being put forward can fabrication provide any support for identification evidence. The jury should be reminded that proving the accused has told lies about where he was at the material time does not by itself prove that he was where the identifying witness says he was …

14–10 A failure to follow these guidelines is likely to result in a conviction being quashed and will do so if in the court's judgment on all the evidence the verdict is unsafe. …"

As to the court's opinion as to its jurisdiction to interfere in such cases, see *ante*, §§ 7–55, 7–63.

(2) Disclosure and evidential issues

Disclosure of material relevant to identification

14–11 Where identification was or may have been in issue, the prosecution's common law duty of disclosure extended to photographs taken on arrest and initial crime reports containing details of eye-witness descriptions: *R. v. Fergus (Ivan)*, 98 Cr.App.R. 313, CA; and to photofits and identikits: *R. v. Wright* [1994] Crim.L.R. 131, CA. Public interest immunity does not attach to such materials: *Fergus (Ivan)*, *ante*. As to disclosure under the *CPIA* 1996, see *ante* §§ 12–52 *et seq*.

"Trial-within-a-trial"

As to the holding of a *voire dire* on identification issues, see *post*, § 14–35. 14–11a

Inadvertent failure by the Crown to identify the defendant

See *ante*, § 4–353. 14–11b

(3) Withdrawing the case from the jury

When the quality of the identifying evidence is poor and unsupported, the trial judge should withdraw the case from the jury: *R. v. Turnbull*, *ante*, § 14–7. *Turnbull* protects a jury from acting upon the type of evidence which, even if believed, experience has shown to be a possible source of injustice: *Daley v. R.* [1994] 1 A.C. 117, PC. Where the judge forms the view that the identification evidence is poor and unsupported, he is under a duty to invite submissions and, if appropriate, to withdraw the case from the jury: *R. v. Fergus (Ivan)*, *ante*. Identification evidence needs to be assessed not only at the close of the prosecution's case, but also at the close of the accused's case: *R. v. Turnbull*, *ante*, § 14–5; *R. v. Fergus*, *ante*. A distinction is, however, to be drawn between cases where the integrity of the identifying witness(es) is not in issue and those where it is; credibility is a matter for the jury: *R. v. Macmath* [1997] Crim.L.R. 586, CA. 14–12

Identification evidence can be poor even if given by a number of witnesses. Where the evidence is of sufficient quality to justify the case being left to the jury, though there is no other evidence to support it, the judge is entitled to direct the jury that an identification by one witness can constitute support for an identification by another, provided that he warns them in clear terms that even a number of honest witnesses can all be mistaken: *R. v. Weeder*, 71 Cr.App.R. 228 at 231, CA; *R. v. Breslin*, 80 Cr.App.R. 226, CA. 14–13

In *R. v. Tyler*, 96 Cr.App.R. 332, CA, it was said that identification by two witnesses carries more weight than by one alone. This, it is submitted, is common sense: honest witnesses do not tend to make the same mistake, especially if the identification procedures (designed to provide a fair test) are properly carried out and there has been no opportunity for innocent contamination. It is submitted, however, that *R. v. Tyler* is not authority for the bald proposition that a judge is under no duty to withdraw a case from the jury whenever there are two or more identification witnesses. Identification by more than one witness is clearly a factor in determining whether the quality of the identification evidence as a whole justifies leaving the issue to the jury, but inherently poor identification evidence is not improved by mere repetition from different witnesses. The trial judge must consider the cumulative effect of any specific weaknesses in the quality of the identification evidence: *R. v. Fergus (Ivan)*, *ante*.

Where a prosecution case is entirely dependent on the victim's identification of the defendant, the judge should analyse the identification issues and should set out his reasons for allowing the case to proceed; but a failure to do so is not in itself a ground for quashing a conviction, as it then falls to be asked whether the judge erred in his approach or reached an unreasonable decision: *R. v. Shervington* [2008] Crim.L.R. 581, CA.

(4) When a Turnbull warning is appropriate

Issue as to honest mistake

A *Turnbull* direction is generally required in all cases where identification is a substantial issue. Only in the most exceptional circumstances would a conviction based on uncorroborated identification evidence be sustained in the absence of a *Turnbull* warning: *Scott v. R.* [1989] A.C. 1242 at 1261, PC; *Beckford v. R.*, 97 Cr.App.R. 409 at 415, PC; *Turnbull*, *ante*, § 14–10; and *R. v. Hunjan*, 68 Cr.App.R. 99, CA. For an example of an appeal being dismissed despite a failure to give the requisite *Turnbull* direction, see *Freemantle v. R.* [1995] 1 Cr.App.R. 1, PC. Adapting what was said by the Privy Council to the test in the *CAA* 1968, s.2 (*ante*, § 7–43) and to the English case law relating to non-direction, the question for the Court of Appeal will be: was the 14–14 identification evidence of such exceptional quality that the jury would inevitably have convicted had a *Turnbull* direction been given? If not, the conviction will be unsafe and should be quashed.

Issue as to veracity

14–15 A *Turnbull* warning is not required and would only confuse a jury where, (a) the defence attack the veracity and not the accuracy of the identifying witness; (b) there is no evidence to support the possibility of mistaken identification: *R. v. Cape* [1996] 1 Cr.App.R. 191, CA; or (c) the identifying witness states that he was mistaken and the prosecution do not rely upon his earlier statement: *R. v. Davis* [2006] 8 *Archbold News* 4, CA. There is, however, an obvious need to give a general warning even in recognition cases where the main challenge is to the truthfulness of the witness. The first question for the jury is whether the witness is honest; if he is, the next question is the same as that which must be asked of every honest witness who purports to make an identification, namely, whether he is right or might be mistaken: *Beckford v. R.*, 97 Cr.App.R. 409, PC; but the judge need not go on to give an adapted *Turnbull* direction (reminding the jury that people can make mistakes in recognising relatives, *etc.*) where such a direction would add nothing of substance to the judge's other directions: *Capron v. The Queen*, unreported, June 29, 2006, PC ([2006] UKPC 34) (considering *Beckford*, *ante*, and *Shand v. The Queen* [1996] 2 Cr.App.R. 204, PC); and see *R. v. Giga* [2007] Crim.L.R. 571, CA.

Minor identification problems

14–16 *Turnbull* "is intended primarily to deal with the ghastly risk run in cases of fleeting encounters": *R. v. Oakwell*, 66 Cr.App.R. 174, CA. It does not apply to every case involving a minor identification problem: *R. v. Curry and Keeble* [1983] Crim.L.R. 737, CA. Both *Oakwell* and *Curry* involved assaults on police officers who had arrested their alleged assailants at the scene of the crime. The presence of the appellants was not disputed; the issues concerned the degree and nature of their involvement, and in each case, the judge had given some warning to the jury relevant to the issue of identification. Although the Court of Appeal has held that no *Turnbull* direction is required where defendants admit presence at a melee but deny criminal liability (*R. v. Linegar* [2002] 1 *Archbold News* 1), it is submitted that the better and safer course is to give a warning appropritately modified to meet the facts of the case: see, for example, *R. v. O'Leary and Lloyd-Evans*, 67 J.C.L. 115, CA ([2002] EWCA Crim. 2055). These cases should not be regarded as driving a wedge into the clear and specific directions enjoined upon courts by *Turnbull* and the many cases that followed it: *R. v. Bowden* [1993] Crim.L.R. 379, CA. The full warning should be given where a defendant denies that he was present at the commission of the offence (*R. v. Curry*, *ante*), or where there exists a possibility of mistaken identification: *R. v. Slater* [1995] 1 Cr.App.R. 584, CA; *cf. R. v. Thornton* [1995] 1 Cr.App.R. 578, CA.

(5) Directions to the jury

14–17 Where the case depends wholly or substantially upon the correctness of identification evidence, *Turnbull* requires that a judge should:

(a) warn the jury of the special need for caution before convicting on that evidence (*ante*, § 14–2);

(b) instruct the jury as to the reason for such need (*ante*, § 14–2);

(c) refer the jury to the fact that a mistaken witness can be a convincing witness, and that a number of witnesses can be mistaken (*ante*, § 14–2);

(d) direct the jury to examine closely the circumstances in which each identification was made (*ante*, § 14–3);

(e) remind the jury of any specific weaknesses in the identification evidence (*ante*, § 14–3);

(f) where appropriate, remind the jury that mistaken recognition can occur even of close relatives and friends (*ante*, § 14–4);

(g) identify to the jury the evidence capable of supporting the identification (*ante*, § 14–8); and

(h) identify evidence which might appear to support the identification but which does not in fact have that quality (*ante*, §§ 14–8 *et seq.*).

A *Turnbull* direction should be given if the evidence justifies it, even in the shortest of cases: *R. v. Stanton*, *The Times*, April 28, 2004, CA; and even though the defence have not raised the issue: *Beckford v. R.*, *ante*, at p. 416.

To direct a jury that it is just as possible mistakenly to fail to identify a suspect as it is to make a mistaken identification effectively amounts to a reversal of the burden of proof and is a misdirection: *R. v. Speede*, *The Times*, April 3, 1991, CA. Where, however, the defence rely upon the mistaken identification of others at an identification parade, a judge is not precluded from pointing out relevant factors, which reduced the likelihood of accurate observation: *R. v. Trew* [1996] 2 Cr.App.R. 138, CA. **14–18**

The need for special caution and the reason for such need

See *Turnbull*, *ante*, § 14–2. The summing up must warn the jury as to the need for special caution, and expose to them the weaknesses and dangers of identification evidence both in general and as related to the circumstances of the particular case: *R. v. Keane*, 65 Cr.App.R. 247, CA; *R. v. Bentley* [1991] Crim.L.R. 620, CA; *R. v. Fergus (Ivan)*, 98 Cr.App.R. 313, CA. A judge must ensure that the full force of the *Turnbull* direction is conveyed, whatever words are used. The jury must be told not only that a convincing witness may be wrong, but also that the need for special caution is rooted in the court's actual experience of miscarriages of justice. The specimen direction advised by the Judicial Studies Board is the briefest permissible summary of the dangers inherent in identification evidence: *R. v. Nash* [2005] Crim.L.R. 232, CA; and it would be wrong for a judge to put his own gloss on it: *R. v. Shervington* [2008] Crim.L.R. 581, CA (where the judge prefaced his direction by saying that the jury should not allow an "over-sophisticated approach" to become "a mugger's charter"). **14–18a**

Identification of strangers and recognition

See *Turnbull*, *ante*, § 14–4. The fact that recognition may be more reliable than identification of a stranger does not absolve a judge from reminding the jury that mistakes in recognition of close relatives and friends are sometimes made: *R. v. Bowden* [1993] Crim.L.R. 379, CA; *Beckford v. R.*, *ante*, § 14–15. In *R. v. Bentley* [1991] Crim.L.R. 620, CA, Lord Lane C.J. observed that recognition evidence could not be regarded as trouble free. Many people had experienced seeing someone in the street whom they knew, only to discover they were wrong. The expression "I could have sworn it was you" indicated the sort of warning a judge should give, because that was exactly what a witness did—he swore that it was the person he thought it was. But he may have been mistaken even in recognition. In the narrow field of recognition there were degrees of danger; perhaps less so where the parties had known each other for many years, or where the person identified was at the scene. Even here, it is advisable to alert the jury to the possibility of honest mistake and to the dangers, and the reasons why such dangers exist in identification evidence. In a recognition case, the risk is not that the witness will pick out the wrong person on a parade, but that at the time of the offence he mistakenly thinks he recognises the offender; this danger should be brought home to the jury: see *R. v. Thomas* [1994] Crim.L.R. 128, CA. See also *R. v. Aurelio Pop* (2003) 147 S.J. 692, PC (fact that an identification of the accused depends on a purported recognition of him by an acquaintance of several years' standing does not diminish the need for an appropriate *Turnbull* direction); and *R. v. Mason and Cummins* [2005] 1 Cr.App.R. 11, CA (not sufficient, even where witness and accused were well-known to each other, to warn the jury to approach the evidence of recognition with considerable care; necessary to tell them why care was needed, and in particular that a mistaken witness can be a convincing one and that mistakes in recognition are made even in a case of purported recognition of close relatives). **14–19**

Recognition by name

Recognition cases include those where a witness knows the defendant sufficiently well **14–20** to identify him by name. However, not all cases of identification by name are recognition cases. Care should be taken to ensure that the witness knows the defendant's name of his own knowledge. Identification through a name which is known to the witness only by hearsay is almost equivalent to a dock identification: *R. v. Fergus* [1992] Crim.L.R. 363, CA.

Identifying specific weaknesses in the evidence

14–21 See *Turnbull*, *ante*, § 14–3. Whilst it is neither necessary to catalogue every minor discrepancy, nor to adopt any particular format (*R. v. Barnes* [1995] 2 Cr.App.R. 491, CA), a judge must place before the jury any specific weaknesses which could be said to have been exposed in the evidence, and he must do so in a coherent manner so that the cumulative impact of the weaknesses is fairly laid out: *R. v. Fergus (Ivan)*, *ante*, § 14–18; *R. v. Pattinson and Exley* [1996] 1 Cr.App.R. 51, CA; *Stanton*, *ante*, § 14–18; and *R. v. I.* [2007] 2 Cr.App.R. 24, CA (judge should explain clearly why they are weaknesses). It is usually desirable to put before the jury a coherent list of the points against a correct identification. Dealing with them in the course of recounting the evidence may lead to points being overlooked and may dissipate their combined force. It should also be made clear that such a list constitutes material which the judge considers the jury should weigh carefully in reaching a verdict, and not merely submissions or points raised by defence counsel: *R. v. Elliott* [1998] 1 *Archbold News* 2, CA (97/2718/W3). The Court of Appeal have suggested that before summing up the judge should always discuss these issues with the advocates, so that he might ascertain the points they intend to make in their speeches to support or undermine the identification, and so that they will know the judge's view as to whether any particular piece of evidence is capable of having either effect: *Stanton*, *ante*.

Evidence capable of supporting the identification

14–22 See *R. v. Turnbull*, *ante*, § 14–8. Where the identification evidence is poor but there is other evidence supporting its correctness, it is essential that it is made clear to the jury that it is for them to decide, if they accept that evidence, whether in fact it does support the identification: *R. v. Akaidere* [1990] Crim.L.R. 808, CA. Where a judge would have directed an acquittal, but for the existence of evidence capable of supporting the identification, there is no principle that he should direct the jury that they should acquit if they reject the supporting evidence: *R. v. Ley* [2007] 1 Cr.App.R. 25, CA.

(i) *Identification by two or more witnesses*

14–22a See *ante*, § 14–13.

(ii) *Similar fact and multiple offences committed by the same person*

14–22b See *ante*, §§ 13–45 *et seq.*, § 13–62.

(iii) *Alibi evidence*

14–22c See *R. v. Turnbull*, *ante*, § 14–9. Where the collapse of an alibi forms no part of the Crown's case, it may not be necessary to give a warning about a false alibi: see *R. v. Penman*, 82 Cr.App.R. 44, CA; and *R. v. Francis*, 91 Cr.App.R. 271, CA. The safer course, however, will be to give such a warning if there is any risk that the jury may regard the collapsed alibi as confirming a disputed identification or, in the view of the judge, the collapsed alibi is likely to have a significant impact on the jury: see *R. v. Duncan*, *The Times*, July 24, 1992, CA; *R. v. Pemberton*, 99 Cr.App.R. 228, CA; *R. v. Drake* [1996] Crim.L.R. 109, CA; *R. v. Brown* [1997] Crim.L.R. 502, CA. See generally, *ante*, § 4–402.

(iv) *Lies*

14–23 Lies told by a defendant may provide support for identification evidence if the jury are satisfied that the lies are deliberate and relate to that issue. The jury must be given a direction along the general lines indicated in *R. v. Lucas*, 73 Cr.App.R. 159 at 162, CA: *R. v. Goodway*, 98 Cr.App.R. 11, CA, *ante*, § 4–402.

(v) *Correct identification of other participants in the offence*

It is permissible under section 74(1) of the *PACE Act* 1984 (*ante*, § 9–82) to corroborate the evidence of an identifying witness by proof that a co-accused, identified by the same witness as being a participant in the same offence, has pleaded guilty to that offence: *R. v. Castle* [1989] Crim.L.R. 567, CA; *R. v. Jones (Terrence)* [1992] Crim.L.R. 365, CA; and *R. v. Gummerson and Steadman* [1999] Crim.L.R. 680, CA. It is submitted that a successful identification of a co-accused in difficult circumstances may be admissible to show that the circumstances were not so difficult as to make unreliable an identification of the accused at the same time and place. Alternatively, on the assumption that some link between the two accused can be independently established, proof of the co-accused's guilt may tend to rebut mistake (see the example in *Turnbull*, *ante*, § 14–2 and the judgment of Lawton L.J. in *R. v. Long*, 57 Cr.App.R. 871 at 879; and see also *R. v. Grey (Kenneth)*, 88 Cr.App.R. 385, CA, *ante*, §§ 9–86, 13–18; and *R. v. Gummerson and Steadman*, *ante*): this will be so regardless of whether the identifying witness also identified the co-accused. However, simply to suggest that because one identification was correct, the other is more likely to be correct involves the very dangers identified in *Turnbull*: see *R. v. Turnbull*, *ante*, § 14–2. **14–23a**

(vi) *Previous convictions*

A defendant's previous convictions may be relevant to show that he falls into a discrete category of persons having an interest in an issue relevant to the purported identification, or having a propensity to commit the offence charged: see *R. v. Isichei*, 170 J.P. 753, CA (*ante*, § 13–46a); and *R. v. Eastlake (Nicky) and Eastlake (Kevin Scott)* (2007) 151 S.J. 258, CA (*ante*, § 13–67). **14–23b**

Evidence incapable of supporting the identification

See *R. v. Turnbull*, *ante*, § 14–8. Evidence which is not independent of the identification is not capable of supporting it. Thus, where a witness described a burglar in her premises as resembling her cleaner, causing suspicion to fall on her cleaner's son, and two months later identified the son at an identification parade, it was undesirable to import, as a separate point confirming a weak identification, the fact that the defendant could have had the inside knowledge displayed by the burglars: *R. v. Jamel* [1993] Crim.L.R. 52, CA. **14–24**

(6) Application of the guidelines to specific circumstances

Identification by police officers

The *Turnbull* guidelines apply equally to police officers who are identifying witnesses: *Reid v. R.* [1990] A.C. 363, PC. Whilst all witnesses are subject to the same rules, the tribunal of fact, in assessing reliability, is entitled to take account of the reasons given for a positive identification, and a judge is entitled to draw the attention of the jury to any such reasons. An identifying witness who is involved in the criminal justice system is likely to have a greater appreciation of the importance of identification, and so to look for some particular identifying feature. Honest police officers are likely to be more reliable than the general public, being trained and less likely to have their observations and recollections affected by the excitement of the situation. Provided that the usual warnings are given, the reasons scrutinised, and the integrity of the witness is not in doubt, the tribunal can give effect to what is only common sense: *R. v. Ramsden* [1991] Crim.L.R. 295, CA; *R. v. Tyler*, 96 Cr.App.R. 332, CA; and *Powell v. DPP* [1992] R.T.R. 270, DC. **14–25**

As to police officers making identifications from CCTV recordings of offences being committed, see *R. v. Smith*, *post*, § 14–47.

Identification of companions

Where the identification of an offender is in issue, a purported identification of the offender's companion should generally be subject to a *Turnbull* direction. Where the identification of the companion is unchallenged, there is no duty to give any such direction: *R. v. Bath* [1990] Crim.L.R. 716, CA. **14–26**

Identification of motor cars

14–27 A direction analogous to a *Turnbull* direction is not required in relation to the identification of motor cars. However, a trial judge should draw the jury's attention to: (a) the opportunity that each witness had to identify the car; (b) each witness's apparent ability to distinguish between makes of car; (c) how far each witness can be relied on as to what he remembered: *R. v. Browning*, 94 Cr.App.R. 109, CA. Nor is a *Turnbull* direction required for number plates; it is sufficient to remind the jury of the circumstances in which the observation was made, and of any factors which might render the testimony less reliable than would otherwise be the case, together with any other special warning which the trial judge may consider is merited by the particular facts of the case: *R. v. Hampton and Brown* [2006] Crim.L.R. 60, CA.

Identification by clothing

14–28 The recognition of clothing can be a valuable aid to identification: *R. v. Hickin* [1996] Crim.L.R. 584, CA. However, where a witness does no more than describe the offender's clothing, an identification procedure would serve no useful purpose: *Marsh v. DPP* [2007] Crim.L.R. 162, CA.

Identification by continuity of presence

14–28a Where an eye-witness observes a crime being committed, calls the police and keeps the offenders under surveillance until the police arrest them, but does not purport to recognise them or identify their facial features, a judge is not obliged to comply fully with the classic *Turnbull* requirements and give a full and separate analysis of the weaknesses and strengths of the identification evidence. A general *Turnbull* direction, followed by appropriate warnings and an analytical review of the evidence of the eye-witness is sufficient: *R. v. Nyanteh* [2005] Crim.L.R. 651, CA. For similar examples of such circumstantial evidence leading to identification, see *R. v. Oscar* [1991] Crim.L.R. 778, CA; and *R. v. Gayle* [1999] 2 Cr.App.R. 130, CA.

C. Police and Criminal Evidence Act 1984: Code D

[For the full text of Code D, see Appendix A–112 *et seq.*]

(1) Application of Code D

General

14–29 The specific provisions of Code D are designed to test the ability of the witness to identify the person seen on a previous occasion and to provide safeguards against mistaken identification: Code D:1.2. They are not all-embracing, and there are situations which fall outside them. Where Code D does apply, it is intended to be an intensely practical document, giving police officers clear instructions on the approach they should follow in specified circumstances. It is not old-fashioned literalism but sound interpretation to read the code as meaning what it says: *R. v. Forbes* [2001] 1 A.C. 473, HL.

Revisions and modifications of the code

14–29a Code D formed part of the original codes of practice introduced in 1985: *Police and Criminal Evidence Act 1984 (Codes of Practice) (No. 1) Order* 1985 (S.I. 1985 No. 1937). Revisions of Code D came into force on April 1, 1991 (*Police and Criminal Evidence Act 1984 (Codes of Practice) (No. 2) Order* 1990 (S.I. 1990 No. 2580)); on April 10, 1995 (*Police and Criminal Evidence Act 1984 (Codes of Practice) (No. 3) Order* 1995 (S.I. 1995 No. 450)); on April 1, 2003 (*Police and Criminal Evidence Act 1984 (Codes of Practice) (Codes B to E) (No. 2) Order* 2003 (S.I. 2003 No. 703)); on August 1, 2004 (*Police and Criminal Evidence Act 1984 (Codes of Practice) Order* 2004 (S.I. 2004 No. 1887)); on January 1, 2006 (*Police and Criminal Evidence Act 1984 (Codes of Practice) Order* 2005 (S.I. 2005 No. 3503)); and, most recently, on February 1, 2008 (*Police and Criminal Evidence Act 1984 (Codes of Practice) Order* 2008 (S.I. 2008 No. 167)). The current version applies to any procedure to which the code relates carried out after January 31, 2008. As to the codes' history, see *post*, § 15–7.

All references in this chapter to Code D or its annexes are references to the current code which came into effect on February 1, 2008. A degree of caution needs to be exercised in citing authorities relating to earlier versions, but it may be noted that the changes of substance introduced by the 2006 code were limited to paragraphs 4.16 *et seq.* (taking footwear impressions) and 5.12 (photographing suspects other than at a police station); and the 2008 changes reflect the power to take a photograph elsewhere than at a police station of a person given a direction to leave, and not to return to, a specified location under the *VCRA* 2006, s.27. The full text of Code D is set out at Appendix A–112 *et seq.*

Categories of suspect

(i) *Suspects known and available to the police*

The code imposes specific identification procedures in respect of suspects known and available to the police: Code D:3.4 *et seq.* A suspect is "known" if there is sufficient information known to the police to justify the arrest of a particular person for suspected involvement in the offence and is "available" if he is immediately available or will become available within a reasonably short time and is willing to take an effective part in at least one of the following identification procedures which it is practicable to arrange, *viz.* a video identification, an identification parade or a group identification: Code D:3.4. **14–30**

In *R. v. Nunes* [2001] 10 *Archbold News* 1, CA, a similar provision in the 1995 code (D:2.1) was held to have been breached where a police officer, who had witnessed a person committing an offence, but had been unable to effect an arrest, was allowed to identify the defendant at the scene of his arrest by other officers who, having sealed off the area, had arrested him on suspicion of having committed the offence, in response to which he had said that he had done nothing.

A person is not a "known suspect" merely because he matches the description of an offender circulated to police officers: *Coulman v. DPP* [1997] C.O.D. 91, DC.

(ii) *Suspects not available to the police*

As to the procedures to be adopted in the case of known suspects not available to the police, see Code D:3.21 (Appendix A–124). **14–30a**

(iii) *Suspects whose identity is not known to the police*

As to the procedures to be adopted in the case of suspects not known to the police, see Code D:3.2 (Appendix A–120). The requirement that, where practicable, a record shall be made of any description of the suspect given by the witness is not mere bureaucracy; it affords the best safeguard against the possibility of autosuggestion: *R. v. Vaughan, The Independent*, May 12, 1997, CA (96 06431 Y3). The code is not breached if it is impracticable to make such a record: *R. v. El-Hannachi* [1998] 2 Cr.App.R. 226, CA. Identification evidence is likely to be excluded where an officer draws a witness's attention to an individual in breach of Code D:3.2(b) and there was a subsequent failure to hold an identification parade: see *R. v. K.* [2003] 4 *Archbold News* 1, DC (decided in relation to the unmodified version of the 1995 code); *per contra, R. v. Williams* (2003) 147 S.J. 1305, CA (criticised at *Criminal Law Week* 2003/42/3). **14–31**

Identification procedures in foreign jurisdictions

Code D does not apply to identifications outside the jurisdiction. The fact that an identification abroad was carried out otherwise than in accordance with the code was something that could be taken into account if, and in so far as, it affected the intrinsic fairness of the procedures actually adopted. Further, the judge, in deciding whether to admit the evidence could take into account that both he and the defence could warn the jury of the disadvantages of the procedure adopted and the consequent danger of relying on the evidence: *R. v. Quinn* [1990] Crim.L.R. 581, CA. **14–32**

(2) Identification procedures

Holding an identification procedure

14–33 When a suspect is known and available, an identification procedure must be held when either (i) a witness has identified the suspect or purports to have done so prior to a video identification, an identification parade or a group identification having taken place, or (ii) there is a witness available who expresses an ability to identify the suspect (this should read "offender") or where there is a reasonable chance of the witness being able to do so, and the witness has not been given the opportunity to identify the suspect in any of the aforementioned procedures, and in either case, the suspect disputes being the person the witness claims to have seen; but an identification procedure need not be held where it is not practicable to hold one or it would serve no useful purpose in proving or disproving whether the suspect was involved in committing the offence, *e.g.* where it is not disputed that the suspect is already well known to the witness: Code D:3.12; or where the witness merely describes a specific piece of clothing: see *Marsh v. DPP*, *ante*, § 14–28. As to the mandatory nature of the corresponding provision in the 1995 version of Code D, see *R. v. Forbes* [2001] 1 A.C. 473, HL.

In *R. v. Rutherford and Palmer*, 98 Cr.App.R. 191, CA (approved in *R. v. Harris* (2003) 147 S.J. 237, CA), it was held that the duty to hold an identification procedure applies equally where a dispute as to identity may reasonably be anticipated. Such a dispute was not reasonably to be anticipated, however, where the suspect had declined to participate in a parade, and did not thereafter deny presence at the scene of the offence: *R. v. McCartney* [2003] 6 *Archbold News* 2, CA. For the provisions of the code to be triggered, the suspect had to make some positive assertion that put identification in issue: *ibid.* In *R. v. Lambert*, unreported, January 13, 2004, CA ([2004] EWCA Crim. 154) it was said that the question of whether a suspect disputes an identification made or purported to have been made by a witness, falls for consideration at the time that the police were investigating the offence, rather than in the light of the evidence actually given at trial; there does not necessarily have to be a positive dispute as to identification raised by the particular suspect; it is sufficient if the circumstances are such that it is clear to the police that there is an identification issue; but where there is no such issue, it would be time-consuming, expensive and unnecessary to conduct an identification procedure; where, therefore, all the defendants in interview either made no comment, admitted to having been present at the time of the offence, or admitted limited participation, it was held that there had not been a breach of Code D:3.12 by virtue of the failure to conduct an identification procedure; it had been reasonable on the facts of the case for the police to conclude that participation, not identification, was the issue, albeit it is perfectly possible for there still to be a serious identification issue notwithstanding that presence at the scene is admitted.

Where it is not disputed that the suspect is already well known to the witness who claims to have seen him commit the offence, a positive idenfication establishes no more than the uncontroversial fact that the witness is able to identify the person he knows and does not resolve the question of whether that person committed the offence: *Goldson v. R.*, unreported, March 23, 2000, PC ([2000] UKPC 9); and *Brown and Isaac v. The State*, 67 J.C.L. 469, PC ([2003] UKPC 10).

In *Harris*, *ante*, it was held that an identification procedure should have been conducted where a 16-year-old suspect disputed recognition by a witness who had not seen him for slightly over two years. Although a positive identification at a parade would not have advanced the prosecution's case, in the circumstances, the possibility of a failure to identify at an identification parade should not have been discounted. Similarly, identification of a suspect by a witness who had known him 14 years earlier, but who had seen him only once since, could not be a case of recognition of someone "well known": *McKenna v. DPP* [2005] 5 *Archbold News* 2, QBD (Newman J.).

An identification procedure may also be held if the officer in charge of the investigation considers that it would be useful: Code D:3.13. The decision to hold such a discretionary identification procedure is that of the investigating officer, who may be called upon to justify a decision not to hold one: *R. v. Gayle (Nicholas Nehemiah)* [1999] 2 Cr.App.R. 130, CA.

If it is not practicable to hold the procedure on one day, it does not follow that it is impracticable to hold it on another day. Nor does a suspect's agreement to take part in a group identification necessarily mean that he accepts that it is impracticable to hold a parade (or a video identification): *R. v. Penny*, 94 Cr.App.R. 345, CA. Time constraints may affect the determination of what is practicable (*R. v. Jamel* [1993] Crim.L.R. 52, CA), to which the trial judge may have regard in exercising his discretion: *R. v. Penny*, *ante*.

Where known suspects admitted presence at the scene of criminal activity but denied criminal participation therein, they were not disputing identification for the purposes of Code D:3.12; accordingly, it had been proper to show to witnesses a video-recording of the suspects coming and going at the scene of the crime (a house) in order that they could make further statements ascribing particular roles to the various persons shown: *R. v. Chen* [2001] 5 *Archbold News* 3, CA.

Selection of identification procedures

Where an identification procedure is to be held, the current code requires the identification officer and the officer in charge of the investigation to consult and decide whether it would be more suitable or practicable to offer a video identification or an identification parade (Code D:3.14). As to the position when a suspect refuses the first identification procedure offered, see Code D:3.15. A group identification may be offered if the officer in charge considers that it would be more satisfactory and the identification officer considers that it would be practicable to arrange (Code D:3.16). If none of these procedures are available, then the identification officer may arrange a covert video identification or covert group identification (Code D:3.17(v) and Code D:3.21). A confrontation remains the last resort (Code D:3.33). **14–33a**

The effect of a failure to hold an identification procedure

In the case of a breach of Code D the trial judge should explain that there has been a breach of the code and how it has arisen. Where there has been a failure to hold a required identification procedure, the jury should ordinarily be told that, in assessing the whole of the case, they should take account of the fact that the defendant had lost the safeguard of putting the eye-witnesses's identification to the test, giving it such weight as they think fit: *R. v. Forbes* [2001] 1 A.C. 473, HL. A failure to give a *Forbes* direction may render a conviction unsafe: *R. v. O'Leary and Lloyd-Evans*, 67 J.C.L. 115, CA ([2002] EWCA Crim. 2055); *R. v. Muhidinz*, 70 J.C.L 197, CA ([2005] EWCA Crim. 2758). **14–33b**

Where a defendant is unreasonably denied an identification procedure, a court should be slow to permit the prosecution to call evidence, such as facial mapping, to fill a gap in the identification evidence. There may be circumstances in which it would be appropriate. But where such evidence is called to circumvent a clear breach of Code D, the prosecution should not be entitled to do so: *R. v. Walker*, unreported, November 14, 1994, CA (94 01733 Y2), considered in *R. v. Donald* [2004] Crim.L.R. 841, CA.

Directions following a positive identification

Where an eye-witness has identified the defendant at an identification procedure in circumstances involving no breach of the code, the trial judge will ordinarily tell the jury that they can view that identification as strengthening the prosecution case. But where the defendant was arrested following an eye-witness identification, the judge may also wish to alert the jury to the risk that the witness was re-identifying the person who was arrested, and not the culprit who committed the crime: *R. v. Forbes*, *ante*. See also *R. v. I.* [2007] 2 Cr.App.R. 24, CA (where a formal identification follows an informal identification, as where the witness has identified the defendant as the offender from a photograph in a procedure not organised by the police, it will not necessarily be unfair to admit evidence of the formal identification, but it is incumbent on the judge to highlight the risk that it may be tainted by the earlier identification of the photograph). **14–33c**

Qualified identification

A failure to make a positive identification is no bar to the witness describing the **14–33d** offence, the offender or an identification procedure. A qualified identification may be both relevant and probative where: (a) it supports or is at least consistent with other evidence that indicates that the defendant committed the crime; or (b) the explanation for the non- or qualified identification may help to place it in its proper context, and so, for example, show that the other evidence given by the witness may still be correct. The judge must decide whether the evidence is more prejudicial than relevant and probative bearing in mind the importance of protecting the position of a defendant against unfairness: *R. v. George* [2003] Crim.L.R. 282, CA. Where a witness makes a qualified identification, the prosecution must not seek to transform it into an unqualified identification by careful questioning. They should avoid examining the witness in a manner which suggests a positive identification would have been made but for some fact (*e.g.* the subsequent growth of facial hair): *ibid*.

(3) Video identification

14–33e As to video identification: see Code D:3.5, D:3.6 and D:3.14 *et seq.*; and Annex A (Appendix A–121, A–139 *et seq.*). Evidence of a video identification procedure should be excluded where it is blatantly unfair: *R. v. Marcus* [2005] Crim.L.R. 384, CA (defendant agreed to video identification procedure with certain parts of the faces of all images obscured, but police deliberately conducted a parallel procedure with no facial obscuring, thus making defendant stand out).

As to the use of film for identification other than film created by the police for such purposes, see Code D:3.28, and *post*, §§ 14–45 *et seq.*

(4) Identification parades

Identification of suspects at identification parades

14–34 The identification of a suspect by a witness after the parade has ended is admissible providing the witness can satisfy the court that he genuinely recognised the accused and had refrained from showing it for no improper motive: see Annex B, para. D:20 (Appendix A–145 *et seq.*). A suspect or his solicitor should be informed as soon as practicable where a witness modifies in any significant way an identification made on or after the parade: *R. v. Willoughby* [1999] 2 Cr.App.R. 82, CA. Where a witness cannot recall the number of the person he picked out at a parade, or even cannot remember picking out any suspect at all, it is permissible for another witness to give that evidence: *R. v. McCay*, 91 Cr.App.R. 84, CA; *R. v. Osbourne and Virtue* [1973] 1 Q.B. 678, 57 Cr.App.R. 297, CA. The safe way to avoid any such difficulty is to ensure that an identifying witness makes a statement immediately after the parade. A witness should not be told whether an identification is "correct" until he has made any further statement that he may wish: *Willoughby*, *ante*.

Determining the admissibility of identification parade evidence

14–35 In *R. v. Beveridge*, 85 Cr.App.R. 255, and *R. v. Flemming*, 86 Cr.App.R. 32, the Court of Appeal said that a *voire dire* was inappropriate where the admissibility of identification parade evidence was in issue. These authorities were frequently overlooked: see *R. v. Ryan* [1992] Crim.L.R. 187, CA, and *R. v. Penny*, *ante*, § 14–33. However, in *R. v. Martin and Nicholls* [1994] Crim.L.R. 218, the court restated its former position, saying that occasions for conducting a trial-within-a-trial would be rare; in general, the judge should make his decision upon the depositions, statements and submissions of counsel. As to the hearing of evidence in the absence of the jury generally, see *ante*, §§ 4–287 *et seq.*

Conduct of identification parades

14–36 See generally Annex B (Appendix A–143 *et seq.*). Code D is a statutory code which lays down a detailed regime and it is not for the police to substitute their own procedures or rules: *R. v. Quinn* [1995] 1 Cr.App.R. 480, CA.

In *R. v. Marrin*, *The Times*, March 5, 2002, CA, it was held that the use of make-up on identification parade volunteers in order to enhance their resemblance to the suspect, done in good faith and without objection, was compliant with paragraph 9 of Annex B (volunteers should "so far as possible resemble the suspect in age, height and general appearance" (Appendix A–143)), and led to no unfairness.

It is a breach of the code for an investigating officer, having brought a potential identifying witness to a parade, to speak to the inspector in charge and have the opportunity of speaking to the witness before the witness entered the parade room: *R. v. Gall*, 90 Cr.App.R. 64, CA. Where investigating officers breach D:3.11 (formerly D:2.2) by participating in a parade, it would be wise if the witnesses to whom the officers had the opportunity of speaking were called to give evidence about what had happened: *R. v. Ryan* [1992] Crim.L.R. 187, CA. An investigating officer who merely escorted a suspect from his cell to an identification parade did not thereby breach the former Code D:2.2: *R. v. Jones (Terrence)* [1992] Crim.L.R. 365, CA; but this is not necessarily conclusive in relation to the differently worded Code D:3.11. The cumulative effect of breaches, such as a failure to warn witnesses not to discuss the case or to keep them apart, can render the evidence of identification inadequate: *R. v. Finley* [1993] Crim.L.R. 50, CA.

[The next paragraph is § 14–38.]

(5) Group identification and confrontations

A suspect has no statutory right to demand a confrontation (*R. v. Joseph* [1994] Crim.L.R. 48, CA), or group identification. As to group identifications, see Code D, paras D:3.9, D:3.10, D:3.16 (Appendix A–121, A–122). Group identifications should follow the principles and procedures for an identification parade as set out in Annex C (Appendix A–146 *et seq.*). A group identification could be faulted if it was mounted in a street where there was no reasonable prospect of finding anyone who resembled the suspect: *R. v. Jamel* [1993] Crim.L.R. 52, CA. **14–38**

As to confrontations, see Code D, para. 3.23 and Annex D (Appendix A–124, A–154). Neither reasonable force nor the threat of force may be used to bring about a confrontation: *R. v. Jones and Nelson*, *The Times*, April 21, 1999, CA. The fact that a confrontation occurred at the insistence of the defence does not *per se* render the evidence of confrontation admissible; it is only one factor to consider: *R. v. Joseph*, *ante*. A note of the witness's description of the offender should be made and retained before any confrontation as the best means of assessing the possibility of auto-suggestion: *R. v. Vaughan*, *The Independent*, May 12, 1997, CA (96 06431 Y3).

Showing the victim a security video recording of the suspect near the time and the scene of the offence effectively amounts to a confrontation by video: *R. v. Johnson* [1996] Crim.L.R. 504, CA.

(6) Covert identification procedures

Where a known suspect is not available or has ceased to be available (see *ante*, § 14–30), the identification officer may arrange a covert video identification or covert group identification: Code D:3.21 and Annex C, para. D:34 *et seq.* (Appendix A–124 and A–152 *et seq.*). Section 64A of the *PACE Act* 1984 (*post*, § 15–248a) permits use of photographs or videotapes of suspects detained at police stations for the purposes of identification procedures: Code D:3.30 (Appendix A–126). **14–39**

In *R. v. Kennedy*, unreported, March 20, 1992, CA (90 02296 Y4), the appellant, having refused an identification parade and thwarted police attempts to effect a confrontation, was videoed walking down a passageway in a police station, handcuffed to a police officer. The police then made similar video recordings of eight men of similar appearance, similarly handcuffed. The recordings were then shown to the witnesses. The court commented that this was the "fairest possible method which in the circumstances could have been devised. It was certainly a great deal fairer than any sort of group identification… (or) confrontation."

The covert filming of a defendant in the cell area of a magistrates' court for the purpose of having the film compared with pictures taken by a closed circuit television camera of a person committing a robbery was unlawful because it breached both section 41 of the *CJA* 1925 (prohibition on the taking of photographs, etc., in court or any part of the court building) and the right to privacy guaranteed by Article 8 of the ECHR (*post*, § 16–101). Covert filming in a public place could amount to an infringement of the right of privacy even when there was no private element to the events filmed. However, the unlawfulness of such filming was only relevant to the trial process if it interfered with the right of the defendant to a fair hearing; and the trial judge's decision to admit expert comparison evidence on the basis that there was no prejudice to the fairness of the proceedings could not be impugned: *R. v. Loveridge (William), Lee (Charles) and Loveridge (Christine)* [2001] 2 Cr.App.R. 29, CA. See also *Perry v. U.K.* [2003] Crim.L.R. 281, ECtHR.

(7) Effect of breaches of Code D

14–40 While it is important that the codes of practice should be observed, it is equally important to see whether any unfairness resulted from a breach. Where there is a breach, the trial judge, having heard submissions, should exercise his discretion whether or not to allow the evidence to be given, by applying the test prescribed by section 78 of the *PACE Act* 1984 (*post*, § 15–452): *R. v. Grannell*, 90 Cr.App.R. 149, CA. The fundamental issue, whether the code applies or not, is whether the identification would have such an adverse effect on the fairness of the proceedings that it should be excluded: *R. v. Hickin* [1996] Crim.L.R. 584, CA; *R. v. Malashev* [1997] Crim.L.R. 587, CA. Where insufficient regard is had to fair identification practices, and adducing reliable identification evidence, the discretion to exclude evidence under section 78 is likely to be exercised and convictions will be liable to be treated as unsafe: *R. v. Popat* [1998] 2 Cr.App.R. 208, CA.

Although every case has to be determined on its own facts, it is submitted that whenever Code D is breached, the resolution of two preliminary issues should be of considerable assistance in determining the fundamental issue as to the fairness of the proceedings. First, did the breach occasion the mischief which the code was designed to prevent? If so, the identification may be flawed. Secondly, was the breach caused by a flagrant disregard of the code, or was the breach, or the cumulative effect of more than one breach, capable of engendering considerable suspicion that the identification procedure was unfair? If so, even if the breach of a particular provision did not lead to the mischief intended to be prevented, the evidence of identification might be so tainted with unfairness that it should not be admitted, as in *R. v. Gall* and *R. v. Finley* (*ante*, § 14–36).

The admissibility of informal identification procedures which deprive suspects of the safeguards provided by the code is always liable to be challenged. Each case depends upon its own facts, but a valuable precaution is, where practicable, to have some record of a witness's description of a culprit before embarking upon such an informal identification, thus providing at least some yardstick for testing the accuracy of any subsequent identification: *R. v. Hickin*, *ante*.

14–41 Where identification evidence obtained in breach of Code D is admitted, the judge ought to draw the jury's attention to the breaches, invite them to consider the reasons why the code had been drawn in the way it had been, and whether in their estimation the breaches were such as to cause them to have doubts about the safety of the identification: *R. v. Quinn* [1995] 1 Cr.App.R. 480, CA, specifically approved in *R. v. Forbes* [2001] 1 A.C. 473, HL. The trial judge should not only explain that there has been a breach of the code, but how it has arisen: *ibid*. See also *ante*, § 14–33b.

D. DOCK IDENTIFICATION

14–42 The identification of a defendant for the first time in the dock is both an undesirable practice: see *R. v. Cartwright*, 10 Cr.App.R. 219, CCA; and a serious irregularity: see *R. v. Edwards* (2006) 150 S.J. 570, PC. Although a trial judge retains a discretion to permit a dock identification, it is submitted that in practice the exercise of such discretion should not even be considered unless: (a) a defendant has refused to comply with a formal request to attend an identification parade, and (b) none of the other identification procedures has been carried out as a result of the defendant's default. As the police may adopt a satisfactory identification procedure in respect of a refractory defendant (see, for example, the method adopted in *R. v. Kennedy*, *ante*, § 14–39), it is now difficult to conceive of circumstances in which a trial judge would permit a dock identification. Where a witness volunteers a dock identification, the summing up should make it plain that such evidence is undesirable; that the proper practice is to hold a parade; and that the evidence should be approached with great care: *Williams (Noel) v. R.* [1997] 1 W.L.R. 548, PC. If a jury are not discharged after such an identification, it is incumbent upon the judge to direct them to give it little or no weight: *R. v. Edwards*, *ante*.

Different considerations apply in summary trials: see *Barnes v. Chief Constable of Durham* [1997] 2 Cr.App.R. 505, DC; and *Karia v. DPP*, 166 J.P. 753, QBD (Stanley Burnton J.) (where there has been no prior indication that identity is in issue, it is permissible for the prosecution to seek, and rely on, a dock identification).

For an analysis of the dangers of dock identifications, see *Holland v. H.M. Advocate*, *The Times*, June 1, 2005, PC, where it was, nevertheless, held that permitting such an identification was not *per se* incompatible with the right to a fair trial. Factors to weigh in the equation of whether an accused had had a fair trial would include whether he was legally represented, what directions the judge had given about identification evidence and the significance of the contested evidence in the context of the prosecution evidence as a whole.

As to the circumstances where a jury may compare a photograph or video recording with the defendant in the dock, see *post*, §§ 14–45, 14–49.

E. IDENTIFICATION AND THE USE OF VISUAL AIDS

(1) Identification of a suspect

Using photographs to identify a suspect

Photographs may be shown to a witness in accordance with the provisions of Code D, para. D:3.28, and Annex E (Appendix A–126 and A–155 *et seq.*). Where a suspect is so identified, an identification parade or group or video identification should be held: Annex E, para. D:6 (Appendix A–155). **14–43**

Subsequent use of photographs used to identify a suspect

As a general rule, the Crown should neither adduce evidence of, nor refer to, police photographs: *R. v. Lamb*, 71 Cr.App.R. 198, CA. The prejudicial effect of adducing such evidence of bad character usually outweighs any probative value. However, the Crown might, unusually, lead such evidence where the accused's criminal record has been adduced by the defence: *R. v. Allen* [1996] Crim.L.R. 426, CA; or where the defence take an unfair advantage from the Crown's proper omission to adduce the photographs: *R. v. Bleakley* [1993] Crim.L.R. 203, CA. The defence must always be informed if photographs have been shown at any stage to a witness (Annex E, para. D:9 (Appendix A–156)) and it is for the defence to decide whether any reference should be made to the fact that photographs had been seen by the witnesses who identified the defendant: *R. v. Lamb*, *ante*. **14–44**

Using video recordings to identify a suspect

See Code D, paras D:3.28, D:3.29 (Appendix A–126). As to the use of video recordings as an alternative to identification parades, see *ante*, § 14–33e. **14–44a**

A video film of a group identification made by a witness should not be shown to that witness subsequently to try to improve the quality of the witness's identification evidence at trial: *R. v. Smith and Doe*, 85 Cr.App.R. 197, CA.

(2) Identification of the defendant

Permissible use of photographs, etc.

The authorities concerning the use of images of offenders were reviewed in *Att.-Gen.'s Reference (No. 2 of 2002)* [2003] 1 Cr.App.R. 21, CA. The court identified at **14–45** least three circumstances where a jury may be invited to conclude that a defendant committed the offence on the basis of an image taken from the scene of the crime: (a) where the image is sufficiently clear to allow comparison with the defendant in the dock; (b) where the image is identified by a witness who knows the defendant sufficiently well to recognise him; and this may be so even if the image is no longer available for the jury; or (c) where the identification is based on opinion evidence. Opinion evidence may be given on the basis of comparisons of the images with a reasonably contemporary photograph of the defendant either (i) by a witness who did not know the defendant, but had acquired specialist knowledge by spending substantial time viewing and analysing the images from the scene, or (ii) by a facial mapping expert. Opinion evidence is inadmissible unless the images and the photograph are available for the jury: see *post*, § 14–48.

Identification by the jury

14–46 Where a jury are invited to make the identification by comparing the image with the defendant in the dock, it is imperative that they should be warned by the judge of the perils of deciding, whether by this means alone, or with some form of supporting evidence, that a defendant has committed the crime alleged. No particular form of words or formula is required provided that the jury are warned of the dangers and difficulties of making an identification from photographs, and the fact that photographs may give different impressions of the same person: *ibid.*, and *R. v. Downey* [1995] 1 Cr.App.R. 547, CA. Although in *Downey* it was stated that there was no requirement that something had to be said in every case, in *R. v. Blenkinsop* [1995] 1 Cr.App.R. 7, CA, the court observed that there was a general and invariable requirement that the jury should be warned of the risk of mistaken identification, and of the need to exercise particular care in any identification which they make for themselves.

Where a defendant refused to comply with a jury's request made during a summing-up that he stand up and turn around so that they could make comparisons with video evidence, the jury should not be invited to draw an adverse inference from such refusal. Such a direction reversed the burden of proof: *R. v. McNamara* [1996] Crim.L.R. 750, CA.

Recognition by a witness

14–47 There is no effective distinction in principle between the evidence of a man who looks at a video tape, or a security officer who sees the incident on a security monitor, and that of a bystander who observes the primary facts. Thus a witness may give evidence that he recognises or identifies a person from his viewing of a video recording of the alleged offence. In such circumstances, the tribunal of fact has to apply the *Turnbull* directions having regard not only to the witness, but also to the position of the camera, the opportunity for viewing which it depicts, and to the nature and clarity of the film or recording: *Taylor v. Chief Constable of Cheshire*, 84 Cr.App.R. 191, DC.

In *R. v. Smith* [2008] 7 *Archbold News* 2, CA, the court observed *obiter* that, although a police officer asked to view a CCTV recording in order to see whether he recognises anyone in it is not in the same shoes as a witness asked to identify someone he has seen committing a crime, the safeguards of Code D are equally important; in particular, where an officer does recognise someone, there must be some record to assist in gauging the reliability of the recognition, and so it is important that the officer's initial reactions to the recording are set out and available for scrutiny, including whether he fails to recognise anyone on first viewing but succeeds in doing so subsequently, what words he uses by way of recognition, whether he recognises anyone else, whether he expresses any doubt, and what it is about the image that he says has triggered the recognition; without a protocol for measuring the recognition against an objective standard, there can be no assurance that an officer is not merely asserting that which he wishes and hopes, however subconsciously, to achieve, *viz.* the recognition of a guilty participant.

Facial mapping

14–47a Evidence of facial mapping may of itself be sufficient to justify leaving a case to the jury: *R. v. Hookway* [1999] Crim.L.R. 750, CA. In *R. v. Grey*, unreported, March 27, 2003, CA ([2003] EWCA Crim. 1001), it was said that facial imaging or mapping, including opinion evidence, is admissible to demonstrate, if necessary using enhancement techniques afforded by specialist equipment, particular facial characteristics or combinations of such characteristics, so as to permit a jury to reach their own conclusions. However, there is no national database or agreed formula from which conclusions as to the probability of occurrence of particular facial characteristics or combinations of facial characteristics can safely be drawn. Accordingly, any estimate of such probabilities or any expression of the degree of support provided by particular facial characteristics or combinations thereof must be only the subjective opinion of the witness; and, as there is no means of determining objectively whether or not such opinion is justified the court doubted whether or not such opinions should ever be expressed by such witnesses. In *R. v. Gardner*, 68 J.C.L. 372, CA ([2004] EWCA Crim. 1639), however, the court said that there is no rule that in such cases an expert witness cannot go further than saying "there are the following similarities", as opposed to giving a view as to the degree of probability of the images being the same. Nevertheless, the court then referred at length to the strong warning given, and note of caution sounded, in *Grey*. In a comprehensively reasoned judgment, the New South Wales Court of Criminal Appeal in *R. v. Tang*, 65 N.S.W.L.R. 681, adopted (at [155]) the reasoning of the Court of Appeal in *Grey*. On the basis that the New South Wales legislation effectively restated the common law rules, the decision provides compelling support for an argument that *Gardner* contained an inaccurate statement of the law.

As to the use of facial mapping to circumvent the codes, see *Walker* and *Donald*, *ante*, § 14–33b.

Loss of the image

An expert can only give opinion evidence if the images used for the purposes of comparison are available for the jury, but a witness who knows the defendant sufficiently well to have recognised him in the image may still give that evidence, even though the image is no longer available: *Att.-Gen.'s Reference (No. 2 of 2002)*, *ante*, § 14–45. In *Taylor v. Chief Constable of Cheshire*, 84 Cr.App.R. 191, DC, the court observed: **14–48**

> "Where there is a recording, a witness has the opportunity to study again and again what may be a fleeting glimpse of a short incident, and that study may affect greatly both his ability to describe what he saw and his confidence in an identification. When the film or recording is shown to the court, his evidence and the validity of his increased confidence, if he has any, can be assessed in the light of what the court itself can see. When the film or recording is not available, or is not produced, the court will, and in my view must, hesitate and consider very carefully indeed before finding themselves made sure of guilt upon such evidence. But if they are made sure of guilt by such evidence, having correctly directed themselves with reference to it, there is no reason in law why they should not convict" (*per* Ralph Gibson L.J. at p. 199).

Video recordings made later at the scene of the crime

Identification may also be made from video recordings made on a later occasion than when the crime was committed. Such recordings fall outside the code. Their admissibility is subject to the discretion of the trial judge. To ask a witness to view such a recording is a natural part of the investigation process and involves no unfairness to a defendant if carried out in an acceptable manner: *R. v. Jones (M.A.)*, 158 J.P. 293, CA. It was said that the process of identification by a witness in such circumstances involves at least three stages: did the witness recognise a person filmed on the later occasion? If so, did he identify or recognise that person as having been present on the earlier occasion when the crime was committed? Finally, could he identify that person as participating in the crime as opposed to merely being present? See also *ante*, § 14–45. **14–49**

A video recording of an accused's confession, made with his consent in the form of a re-enactment of the crime is admissible: *Li Shu Ling v. R.* [1989] A.C. 270, PC.

The use of video recordings in court

Where a video recording or film is relevant to an issue in dispute, it should be shown **14–50** to the jury: see *Taylor v. Chief Constable of Cheshire*, *ante*, § 14–48. The best evidence rule in its old form has no relevance to video tapes and films. A video recording of an original film is admissible: *Kajala v. Noble*, 75 Cr.App.R. 149, DC.

As to jury retirement with a video recording of the scene, see *ante*, § 4–423a.

(3) Photofits, identikits and sketches

14–51 Photofits, identikits and sketches produced by a police officer are generally admissible and may go before a jury: see *R. v. Cook* [1987] Q.B. 417 at 425, 84 Cr.App.R. 369 at 375, CA. No *Turnbull* warning is required in respect of a photofit: it is sufficient to direct the jury that it is not a photograph, but an attempt to reconstruct the features of a person to the best of the witness's ability: *R. v. Constantinou*, 91 Cr.App.R. 74, CA.

II. IDENTIFICATION BY OTHER PERSONAL CHARACTERISTICS

A. VOICE IDENTIFICATION

Introduction

14–52 Where voice identification (now commonly referred to by speech scientists as "speaker comparisons") is in issue, the jury should be given the full *Turnbull* warning, appropriately modified: *R. v. Hersey* [1998] Crim.L.R. 281, CA. Accurate voice identification is more difficult than visual identification (although it is more likely to be reliable when carried out by experts (as to which, see *post*) using acoustic, spectrographic and sophisticated auditory techniques: *R. v. Flynn and St John* [2008] 2 Cr.App.R. 20, CA); accordingly, a warning to a jury should be even more stringent than that given in relation to visual identification: *R. v. Roberts* [2000] Crim.L.R. 183, CA.

Expert evidence

14–52a Expert evidence is admissible in respect of matters outside the experience of the jury, or where an expert has himself made the identification: *R. v. Robb*, 93 Cr.App.R. 161, CA; and see *ante*, § 10–65. A jury should be permitted to hear prepared tapes on which expert opinion is based: *R. v. Bentum*, *The Times*, May 25, 1989, CA.

In *R. v. O'Doherty* [2003] 1 Cr.App.R. 5, the Northern Ireland Court of Appeal held that: (i) the state of scientific knowledge having advanced since *R. v. Robb*, no prosecution should be brought in which one of the planks was voice identification evidence given by an expert which was solely confined to auditory analysis (dialect/ accent of the speaker); there should also be expert evidence of acoustic analysis (examination of differences in acoustic properties of the speech which depended on the individual's vocal tract, mouth and throat); but this would not apply where a known group was listened to and the question was who among that group had spoken particular words, or where there were rare characteristics to identify the speaker or where the issue related to accent or dialect; (ii) if evidence of voice recognition was relied on, the jury should be allowed to listen to a tape-recording on which the recognition was based, assuming that the jury had heard the defendant give evidence; (iii) the jury might also listen to a tape-recording of the voice of the suspect in order to assist them in evaluating expert evidence and in making up their own minds as to whether the voice on the tape was the voice of the defendant; but (iv) there should be a specific warning of the dangers of relying on their own untrained ears.

The advantage of expert evidence is that the expert can draw up an overall profile of an individual's speech patterns, in which the significance of each parameter is assessed individually, and which will be backed up with instrumental analysis and reference research, whereas a lay listener's identification is fundamentally opaque, making it more difficult to challenge: see *R. v. Flynn and St John*, *ante* (at [16]).

Lay listeners (including police officers)

14–52b The factors relevant to the ability of a lay listener correctly to identify voices include: (a) the quality of the recording of the disputed voice, (b) the gap in time between the listener hearing the known voice and his attempt to recognise the disputed voice, (c) the ability of the individual to identify voices in general (research showing that this varies from person to person), (d) the nature and duration of the speech which is sought to be identified and (e) the familiarity of the listener with the known voice; and even a confident recognition of a familiar voice by a lay listener may nevertheless be wrong: see *R. v. Flynn and St John, ante*.

Evidence of police officers that during the course of conversations with the accused they recognised his voice as that of a person recorded on tapes is admissible: *Robb, ante*, and see *ante*, § 10–65. However, there would be strong grounds for excluding that evidence:

> "... in any case where police officers' evidence of recognition appears suspect or procured for ulterior motives, or in any case where unfair advantage has been taken of the defendant to strengthen the case against him" (at p. 168).

Where the prosecution assert that police officers recognised or identified a particular speaker, witness statements should be made and served setting out the basis for their opinion: *R. v. Chenia* [2003] 2 Cr.App.R. 6, CA; and (*per R. v. Flynn and St John, ante*) the following minimum safeguards should be observed: (a) the voice recognition exercise should be carried out by someone other than the officer investigating the offence; (b) proper records should be kept of the amount of time spent in contact with the suspect by any officer giving voice recognition evidence, of the date and time spent by any such officer in compiling any transcript of a covert recording, and of any annotations on a transcript made by a listening officer as to his views as to the identity of a speaker; and (c) any officer attempting a voice recognition exercise should not be provided with a transcript bearing the annotations of any other officer.

Directing the jury

Where voice recognition evidence is admitted, juries are entitled to listen to recordings to try to identify who said what, provided that they are directed that when they listen to the tapes, they should bear in mind the evidence of the voice recognition witnesses (expert and lay): *R. v. Flynn and St John, ante*. The dicta in *Chenia, ante*, to the effect that a jury unassisted by expert (*i.e.* scientific) evidence should be directed that they should not compare one voice with another by comparing the characteristics of each because of the dangers in doing so, were disapproved in *Flynn and St John, ante*, but the point was not argued. It is submitted that the approach adopted in *R. v. Korgbara*, unreported, March 30, 2007 ([2007] NSWCCA 84), is to be preferred, namely, that the test to be applied by a trial judge when deciding whether to permit voice comparison by the jury was whether the quality and quantity of material was sufficient to enable a useful comparison to be made. In the vast majority of cases, the approach in *Flynn and St John* will undoubtedly be appropriate. Where, however, the quantity and quality of the evidence is such that no useful comparison can be made, it would seem perverse to permit the jury to undertake a recognition exercise where experts or those familiar with the defendant's voice have been unable to reach any conclusions. **14–52c**

For expert and opinion evidence generally, see *ante*, §§ 10–64 *et seq*.

B. Fingerprints, Palm-prints and Footwear Impressions

(1) Fingerprints

A person may be identified by fingerprints alone: *R. v. Castleton*, 3 Cr.App.R. 74, CCA. As from June 11, 2001, the National Fingerprint Standards (1953) which required a match of 16 ridge characteristics on any one digit or, where prints are uplifted from two digits, not less than 10 matches for each digit, ceased to apply. Identification is now a matter for the opinion and expertise of fingerprint experts, in relation to which the Court of Appeal in *R. v. Buckley*, 163 J.P. 561, CA, issued the following guidance: **14–53**

> "If there are fewer than eight similar ridge characteristics, it is highly unlikely that a judge will exercise his discretion to admit such evidence and, save in wholly exceptional circumstances, the prosecution should not seek to adduce such evidence. If there are eight or more similar ridge characteristics, a judge may or may not exercise his or her discretion in favour of admitting the evidence. How the discretion is exercised will depend on all the

> circumstances of the case, including in particular: (i) the experience and expertise of the witness; (ii) the number of similar ridge characteristics; (iii) whether there are dissimilar characteristics; (iv) the size of the print relied on, in that the same number of similar ridge characteristics may be more compelling in a fragment of print than in an entire print; and (v) the quality and clarity of the print on the item relied on, which may involve, for example, consideration of possible injury to the person who left the print, as well as factors such as smearing or contamination.
>
> In every case where fingerprint evidence is admitted, it will generally be necessary, as in relation to all expert evidence, for the judge to warn the jury that it is evidence opinion [*sic*] only, that the expert's opinion is not conclusive and that it is for the jury to determine whether guilt is proved in the light of all the evidence" (at p. 568).

The Crown must show that the fingerprints taken from the scene of the crime match those on the fingerprint form, and also identify the fingerprints on the form. An inability to explain the presence of fingerprints, or a failure specifically to deny the fingerprints in question, does not amount to an admission by the defence. Strict proof is required: *Chappell v. DPP*, 89 Cr.App.R. 82, DC.

Statutory provisions

14–54 As to the taking of fingerprints (including palm-prints) under the *PACE Act* 1984, see sections 27 (*post*, § 15–174), 61 (*post*, §§ 15–232 *et seq.*) and 65 (*post*, § 15–249).

For the provisions in Code D relating to fingerprints, see Code D, paras D:4.1–D:4.7 and Annex F (Appendix A–128 *et seq.*, and A–158).

As to the destruction of fingerprints, see Code D:4.7 and Annex F, and the *PACE Act* 1984, s.64, *post*, §§ 15–246 *et seq.*

(2) Palm and other prints

14–55 There is no reason why the standards for the presentation of fingerprint evidence, *ante*, § 14–53, should not be adopted in respect of all other forms of prints, including palm and foot prints. Whether part of the side or front of the hand forms part of the palm is a question of fact and degree: *R. v. Tottenham JJ., ex p. M.L.*, 82 Cr.App.R. 277, DC. As to the taking of palm-prints, see *ante*, § 14–54. As to identification by ear prints, see *R. v. Dallagher* [2003] 1 Cr.App.R. 12, CA, and *R. v. Kempster (No. 2)* [2008] 2 Cr.App.R. 19, CA (such evidence was capable of identifying the person who had left such a print on a surface, where minutiae (*i.e.* small anatomical features such as notches, nodules or creases in the ear structure) could be identified and matched; where, however, the only information came from gross features (*i.e.* the main cartilaginous folds), there was likely to be less confidence, because of the flexibility of the ear and the uncertainty of the pressure that would have been applied at the time the mark was made).

(3) Footwear impressions

14–55a As to the taking and destruction of footwear impressions, see sections 61A and 64 of the *PACE Act* 1984, *post*, §§ 15–234a, 15–246. For the provisions of Code D relating to footwear impressions, see paras D4.16–D4.21 and Annex F.

C. BLOOD, BODY SAMPLES, SECRETIONS, SCENT AND ODONTOLOGY

14–56 The requirements for taking body samples and impressions, including dental impressions, are set out in Code D, para. D:6 (Appendix A–135), and the *PACE Act* 1984, ss.62 and 63, *post*, §§ 15–235 *et seq.* As to the destruction of such samples, see the 1984 Act, s.64, *post*, §§ 15–246 *et seq.*, and Code D, para. D:6.8, and Annex F (Appendix A–137 and A–158).

Blood

14–57 Blood grouping and the detection and identification of the constituents or characteristics of a blood sample can indicate the degree of probability that the sample emanated from a proportion of the population which includes or excludes a suspect. The value of any such evidence will vary according to the circumstances, but it is submitted that evidence of mere probability alone is insufficient to justify a conviction: see the observations of Lord Reid in *S. v. McC.*; *W. v. W.* [1972] A.C. 24 at 41E–42B, HL (blood tests in a paternity suit).

DNA

A DNA profile is not unique; it expresses probabilities. It is a fallacy to confuse the match probability with what is known as the likelihood ratio. There are two distinct questions: (a) what is the probability that an individual would match the DNA profile from the crime sample given that he is innocent? (b) What is the probability that an individual is innocent, if he matches the DNA profile from the crime sample? The "prosecutor's fallacy" consisted of giving the answer to the first question as the answer to the second: *R. v. Deen, The Times*, January 10, 1994, CA; and see *R. v. Gordon* [1995] 1 Cr.App.R. 290, CA. In the absence of special features, expert evidence should not be admitted to induce juries to attach mathematical values to probabilities arising from non-scientific evidence (*i.e.* Bayes's theorem) to support or counter DNA evidence or other evidence: *R. v. Adams (No. 2)* [1998] 1 Cr.App.R. 377, CA. **14–58**

The cogency of DNA evidence makes it particularly important that: (a) DNA testing is rigorously conducted to obviate the risk of laboratory error; (b) the method of DNA analysis and the basis of subsequent statistical calculation should, as far as possible, be transparent to the defence; and (c) the true import of the resultant conclusion is accurately and fairly explained to the jury. To achieve these ends, the following procedural guidelines were laid down in *R. v. Doheny*; *R. v. Adams* [1997] 1 Cr.App.R. 369, CA.

First, the scientist should adduce the evidence of DNA comparisons together with calculations of the random occurrence ratio. Secondly, the Crown should serve on the defence sufficient details of how the calculations were carried out so as to allow the basis of those calculations to be scrutinised. Thirdly, on request the forensic science service should make available to a defence expert the databases upon which the calculations were based.

When the scientist testifies, it is important that he should not overstep the line which separates his province from that of the jury. He should explain the nature of the match between the DNA in the crime stain and the defendant's DNA. He should, on the basis of empirical statistical data, give the jury the random occurrence ratio, the frequency with which the matching DNA characteristics were likely to be found in the population at large. If the necessary data are available, it might be appropriate to state how many people with those matching characteristics were likely to be found within the United Kingdom, or perhaps within a more limited sub-group. That would often be the limit of the evidence which could properly be adduced. A scientist should not be asked his opinion on the likelihood that it was the defendant who left the crime stain, nor when giving evidence should he use terminology which might lead a jury to believe that he was expressing an opinion.

In summing up, the judge should explain the relevance of the random occurrence ratio; and he should draw attention to the extraneous circumstances which gave that ratio its significance; and to any extraneous evidence which conflicted with the suggestion that the defendant was responsible for the crime stain. For recent confirmation of these principles, see *Pringle v. R.*, unreported, January 27, 2003, PC ([2003] UKPC 17).

In *R. v. Bates* [2006] 9 *Archbold News* 2, CA, it was held that partial profile DNA evidence may plainly be relevant in the sense of being probative of a matter in issue between the prosecution and the defence; that there is no reason in principle why such evidence should automatically be excluded on the basis that analysis of a fuller profile might have exculpated the accused altogether; but that there may be cases where the probability of a match between the crime scene sample and any given person was so great that the judge would consider the probative value of the DNA evidence to be minimal and that it should, therefore, be excluded in the exercise of his discretion. Where such evidence is admitted, however, the court said that the jury should be given sufficient information to enable them to evaluate it properly; as was observed in *R. v. Doheny*; *R. v. Adams*, *ante*, the significance of DNA evidence depends to a large extent upon the other evidence in the case; by itself, particularly if based on a partial profile, it may not take the matter far, but, in conjunction with other evidence, it may be of considerable significance.

DNA evidence taken from a crime scene that does not match the accused is powerful evidence which the jury should be invited to consider carefully and weigh in the scales against the prosecution evidence of identification. To raise against a defendant theoretical or speculative possibilities that the sample had been contaminated and to use such speculation to neutralise the significance of the non-matching profile was wrong. Judges should consider with great care the way in which they present scientific evidence to the jury: *R. v. Mitchell*, *The Times*, July 8, 2004, CA.

Tracker dogs and scent

14–59 See *R. v. Pieterson and Holloway* [1995] 2 Cr.App.R. 11, CA, and *R. v. Sykes* [1997] Crim.L.R. 752, CA.

D. BODILY MARKS, FEATURES, INJURIES

14–59a Section 54A of the *PACE Act* 1984 (*post*, § 15–193a) empowers the police to search, but not intimately search, and examine persons detained at a police station to establish whether they have any marks, features or injuries which would tend to identify them as the person involved in the commission of an offence. These powers are regulated by Code D:5 (Appendix A–130 *et seq.*). In certain circumstances, such examination may be carried out without the suspect's consent; and reasonable force may be used to expose the identifying feature or take photographs: see s.117 of the 1984 Act (*post*, § 15–26), and paras D:5.2, D:5.9 and D:5.14 (Appendix A–130, A–131). A different regime applies to persons voluntarily present at a police station (Code D:5.19).

E. HANDWRITING

Proof by a person having knowledge of it

14–60 Handwriting may be proved either by the admission of the author or by any person who saw the author write or sign the document in question. In addition it may be proved by any witness who will at least swear that he believes the writing to be that of the party (*Eagleton v. Kingston* (1803) 8 Ves. 438 at 475, *per* Eldon L.C.), and has either seen the person write, or corresponded regularly with him, or acted upon such correspondence: *R. v. O'Brien*, 7 Cr.App.R. 29, CCA. A mere statement that the writing is like that of the party is not enough: *Drew v. Prior* (1843) 5 M. & Gr. 264.

(i) *Observation of the act of writing*

A single observation of the act of writing is sufficient: *Burr v. Harper* (1816) Holt N.P. 240; *William v. Worall* (1838) 8 C. & P. 380; *Warren v. Anderson* (1839) 8 Scott 384. The same applies to the writing of a surname only: *Lewis v. Sapio* (1827) M. & M. 39.

(ii) *Regular correspondence*

Acquaintance with handwriting from the habit of regular correspondence is sufficient: *Gould v. Jones* (1762) 1 W.Bl. 384; *Harrington v. Fry* (1824) Ry. & M. 90, or where acquaintance has been acquired in the course of business from a number of documents purporting to have been written by the party: *Doe v. Suckermore* (1837) 5 A. & E. 703; *Fitzwalter Peerage Claim* (1843) 10 Cl. & F. 193. Handwritten replies to correspondence addressed to the party may lead to the inference that the reply was written by the person whose handwriting it purports to be: *Carey v. Pitt* (1797) Peake Add.Cas. 130.

(iii) *Acting upon correspondence*

14–61 A witness who acts upon correspondence may identify the handwriting of the correspondent, even though the witness was not a party to that correspondence: *R. v. Slaney* (1832) 5 C. & P. 213. Similarly, where letters are sent direct to a party in the course of business, it is permissible to presume that answers received from the addressee are written by him: *Carey v. Pitt*, *ante*.

Many of the above cases derive from a period when communications and business documents were written by hand and literacy was infrequent. These authorities should be viewed with caution. It is submitted that identification of handwriting by a lay witness based upon a single or even a few previous observations of the act of writing is of such poor evidential quality that, save in exceptional circumstances, it should not be adduced. What is required is a familiarity with the party's handwriting.

A non-expert, including a police officer, who acquires knowledge of the handwriting for the purpose of identifying it at trial, or in the course of a particular case, is not entitled to give such evidence at trial: *R. v. Crouch* (1850) 4 Cox 163; *R. v. Rickard*, 13 Cr.App.R. 140, CCA. These cases should be viewed in the context of their particular facts. It is submitted that there is no reason why a police officer who has, for example, investigated a large fraud over many months should not be allowed to say that during the course of the investigation, he has got to know the defendant's handwriting. If he recognises handwriting as the defendant's, he should be allowed to say so, in the same manner as any other witness. All that is required is a proper foundation; if the evidence is disputed, the weight of the opinion is for the jury to determine. **14–62**

Proof by comparison and expert evidence

Criminal Procedure Act 1865, s.8

8. Comparison of a disputed writing with any writing proved to the satisfaction of the judge to be genuine shall be permitted to be made by witnesses: and such writings, and the evidence of witnesses respecting the same, may be submitted to the court and jury as evidence of the genuineness or otherwise of the writing in dispute. **14–63**

Section 8 requires the judge, not the jury, to determine whether a piece of writing required for comparison is genuine. In so deciding, the judge must be satisfied according to the criminal standard of proof: *R. v. Ewing* [1983] Q.B. 1039, 77 Cr.App.R. 47, CA. Similarly, it is for the judge to determine whether a witness is competent to give evidence as a handwriting expert: *R. v. Silverlock* [1894] 2 Q.B. 766, CCR, *ante*, § 10–65. However, it is for the jury, not the judge, to determine the authorship of the disputed handwriting, forgeries, the decipherment of obliterated words, erasures or alterations. A handwriting expert should give reasons for his conclusions: *R. v. Hipson* [1969] Crim.L.R. 85, CA; but a jury should not be directed that expert evidence should be accepted in the absence of reasons for rejecting it: *R. v. Lanfear* [1968] 2 Q.B. 77, 52 Cr.App.R. 176, CA. **14–64**

A jury should be warned in clear and stringent terms not to draw their own unaided conclusion from a comparison between disputed and genuine writings: *R. v. Tilley and Tilley*, 45 Cr.App.R. 360, CCA; *R. v. O'Sullivan*, 53 Cr.App.R. 274, CA. Nor should the judge purport or appear to be a handwriting expert by comparing examples of signatures: *R. v. Tilley and Tilley*, *ante*; *R. v. Simbodyal*, *The Times*, October 10, 1991, CA. It is submitted that the same principle applies in the Court of Appeal, notwithstanding *R. v. Smith*, 3 Cr.App.R. 87, and *R. v. Rickard*, 13 Cr.App.R. 140. **14–65**

Where it is or should be anticipated that there will be a dispute as to handwriting, the prosecution should call expert evidence: *R. v. O'Sullivan*, *ante*. It is permissible for an expert to compare genuine and admitted writings with a photocopy of the disputed writing where the latter has been lost and give an opinion as to the authorship of the lost original: *Lockheed Arabia v. Owen* [1993] Q.B. 806, CA. However, a photocopy will rarely if ever reveal pressure marks, tracings, overwritten words, pen lifts or other signs used to identify or eliminate the possibility of forgery.

Both the genuine and the disputed documents should normally be made available to both parties; privilege does not attach to documents supplied by one party to the expert for the purposes of comparison.

III. IDENTIFICATION BY OTHER EVIDENCE

Possession of incriminating articles

The use of incriminating articles found in the possession of an accused as evidence of **14–66** identification depends upon a number of factors. It is submitted that the following principles apply:

(a) where the article was used in connection with the offence, it may be adduced as evidence tending to show the identity of the offender;

(b) where the article is not connected with the offence charged, it is admissible only by way of "similar fact" evidence (see *ante*, § 13–62).

14–67 If there is evidence to support the assertion, it is a matter for the jury to determine if the article was both used in connection with the offence and was found in the possession of the accused. This, it is submitted, is a matter of common sense. It often appears as evidence arising by way of transference, *i.e.* the forensic axiom that each offender leaves some residual trace of his presence at the scene of the crime (*e.g.* hairs, prints, etc.), and on departing, takes with him some detritus (*e.g.* paint, glass fragments, soil, etc.). Such evidence is commonplace. It is admissible because it is relevant evidence going to prove the identity of the accused as the offender, or at least as being present at the scene of the crime.

"Similar fact" evidence

14–68 See *ante*, §§ 13–39 *et seq.*, 13–45 *et seq.*, 13–62.

Identification and judicial notice of the legal process

14–69 A magistrate can take judicial notice of the ordinary processes of arrest, charge and bail within his jurisdiction so as to raise a prima facie case that a person surrendering to bail and answering to the name laid in the charge is the same person as the person who has been arrested, charged and bailed: *Allan v. Ireland*, 79 Cr.App.R. 206, DC. See also *Creed v. Scott* [1976] R.T.R. 485, DC.

CHAPTER 15

INVESTIGATORY POWERS; CONFESSIONS; DISCRETION TO EXCLUDE EVIDENCE, ETC.

I. INVESTIGATORY POWERS

A. POLICE AND CRIMINAL EVIDENCE ACT 1984

(1) Introduction

The law relating to the police's powers to stop and search persons, to enter and search premises and to seize property therein, to make arrests, to detain persons without charge and after charge and to question persons who have been detained is largely contained in the *PACE Act* 1984. The Act defines the limits of the powers of police officers in these areas and provides a series of checks and controls on the exercise of those powers. The Act has been supplemented by a series of codes of practice: see *post*, § 15–4. **15–1**

The following parts of the Act are dealt with in this Chapter: Part I (ss.1–7: Power to Stop and Search), Part II (ss.8–23: Powers of Entry, Search and Seizure), Part III (ss.24–33: Arrest), and Part V (ss.53–65: Questioning and Treatment of Persons by Police). The only other part specifically concerned with the police's powers and duties is Part IV (ss.34–52: Detention): as to this, see *ante*, §§ 3–93 *et seq.*

The 1984 Act is not, however, a complete code of a police officer's powers or duties. Many provisions at common law (see, *e.g.*, breach of the peace arrest power, *post*) and under statute were retained; further powers have subsequently been enacted (*e.g.* the *Police Act* 1997, Pt III, the *RIPA* 2000, the *CJPA* 2001, Pt 2, the *PCA* 2002, and the *SOCPA* 2005, ss.60–70). **15–2**

(2) Codes of practice

(a) *Statute*

Police and Criminal Evidence Act 1984, ss.66, 67

Codes of practice

66.—(1) The Secretary of State shall issue codes of practice in connection with— **15–3**

(a) the exercise by police officers of statutory powers—
  (i) to search a person without first arresting him;
  (ii) to search a vehicle without making an arrest; or
  (iii) to arrest a person;
(b) the detention, treatment, questioning and identification of persons by police officers;
(c) searches of premises by police officers; and
(d) the seizure of property found by police officers on persons or premises.

(2) Codes shall (in particular) include provision in connection with the exercise by police officers of powers under section 63B above.

[This section is printed as amended and repealed in part by the *CJCSA* 2000, s.57(4); and the *SOCPA* 2005, ss.110(3) and 174(2), and Sched. 17.]

Codes of practice—supplementary

15–4 **67.**—(1) In this section, "code" means a code of practice under section 60, 60A or 66.

(2) The Secretary of State may at any time revise the whole or any part of a code.

(3) A code may be made or revised, so as to—
(a) apply only in relation to one or more specified areas,
(b) have effect only for a specified period,
(c) apply only in relation to specified offences or descriptions of offences.

(4) [*Duty to consult before issuing, revising code; persons, organizations to be consulted.*]

(5)–(7D) [*Procedural provision in relation to the making, revision of code, and its commencement.*]

15–5 (8) [*Repealed by* Police Act *1996, Sched. 9.*]

(9) Persons other than police officers who are charged with the duty of investigating offences or charging offenders shall in the discharge of that duty have regard to any relevant provision of … a code.

(9A) Persons on whom powers are conferred by—
(a) any designation under section 38 or 39 of the *Police Reform Act* 2002 (police powers for police authority employees), or
(b) any accreditation under section 41 of that Act (accreditation under community safety accreditation schemes),

shall have regard to any relevant provision of a code … in the exercise or performance of the powers and duties conferred or imposed on them by that designation or accreditation.

(10) A failure on the part—
(a) of a police officer to comply with any provision of … a code;
(b) of any person other than a police officer who is charged with the duty of investigating offences or charging offenders to have regard to any relevant provision of … a code in the discharge of that duty, or
(c) of a person designated under section 38 or 39 or accredited under section 41 of the *Police Reform Act* 2002 to have regard to any relevant provision of … a code in the exercise or performance of the powers and duties conferred or imposed on him by that designation or accreditation,

shall not of itself render him liable to any criminal or civil proceedings.

(11) In all criminal and civil proceedings any … code shall be admissible in evidence; and if any provision of … a code appears to the court or tribunal conducting the proceedings to be relevant to any question arising in the proceedings it shall be taken into account in determining that question.

(12) *In this section "criminal proceedings" includes—*
(a) *proceedings in the United Kingdom or elsewhere before a court-martial constituted under the* Army Act *1955, the* Air Force Act *1955 or the* Naval Discipline Act *1957 or a disciplinary court constituted under section 52G of the said Act of 1957;*
(b) *proceedings before the Courts-Martial Appeal Court; and*
(c) *proceedings before a Standing Civilian Court.*

[(12) In subsection (11) "criminal proceedings" includes service proceedings.

(13) In this section "service proceedings" means proceedings before a court (other than a civilian court) in respect of a service offence; and "service offence" and "civilian court" here have the same meanings as in the *Armed Forces Act* 2006.]

[This section is printed as amended, and repealed in part, by the *AFA* 1996, s.5 and

Sched. 1, Pt IV, para. 105; the *CJPA* 2001, ss.76(2) and 77; the *Police Reform Act* 2002, s.107(1) and (2), Sched. 7, para. 9(6)–(8), and Sched. 8; and the *CJA* 2003, ss.11(1) and 332, and Sched. 37, Pt 1; and as amended, as from a day to be appointed, by the *AFA* 2006, s.378(1) and Sched. 16, para. 101 (substitution of subs. (12) by new subss. (12) and (13).]

For section 60 (tape-recording of interviews), see *post*, § 15–223.

Eight codes of practice have been issued by the Secretary of State under sections 60(1)(a), 60A(1) and 66. Each code has been given a key letter, as follows: **15–6**

A. Code of Practice for the Exercise by: Police Officers of Statutory Powers of Stop and Search; Police Officers and Police Staff of Requirements to Record Public Encounters.
B. Code of Practice for the Searching of Premises by Police Officers and the Seizure of Property found by Police Officers on Persons or Premises.
C. Code of Practice for the Detention, Treatment and Questioning of Persons by Police Officers.
D. Code of Practice for the Identification of Persons by Police Officers.
E. Code of Practice on Tape Recording of Interviews with Suspects.
F. Code of Practice on Visual Recording of Interviews with Suspects.
G. Code of Practice for the Statutory Power of Arrest by Police Officers.
H. Code of Practice for the Detention, Treatment and Questioning by Police Officers of Persons under Section 41 of, and Schedule 8 to, the *Terrorism Act* 2000.

The full text of the codes is set out in Appendix A and also on the Home Office website at www.homeoffice.gov.uk.

(b) *Commencement*

The original (red) Codes A to D came into force on January 1, 1986. They were replaced by (blue) Codes A to D which came into force on April 1, 1991. The original Code E came into force on July 29, 1988. Revised Codes A to D and the original Code E were replaced by (green) Codes A to E as from April 10, 1995: *Police and Criminal Evidence Act 1984 (Codes of Practice) (No. 3) Order* 1995 (S.I. 1995 No. 450). As from May 15, 1997, a revised Code A came into force: *Police and Criminal Evidence Act 1984 (Codes of Practice No. 4) Order* 1997 (S.I. 1997 No. 1159), with a further revision coming into force on March 1, 1999: *Police and Criminal Evidence Act 1984 (Codes of Practice No. 5) Order* 1999 (S.I. 1999 No. 291). **15–7**

The *Police and Criminal Evidence Act 1984 (Codes of Practice) (Modification) Order* 2001 (S.I. 2001 No. 2254) modified Codes C and D for a period of two years from the date of commencement of the order (July 16, 2001) but so as to have effect only in the police areas of Staffordshire, Nottinghamshire and the metropolitan police district. The modifications related to the testing of persons in police detention for the presence of specified Class A drugs in accordance with the provisions of sections 63B and 63C of the *PACE Act* 1984 (inserted by the *CJCSA* 2000, s.57). The *Police and Criminal Evidence Act 1984 (Codes of Practice) (Modifications to Code C and Code D) (Certain Police Areas) Order* 2002 (S.I. 2002 No. 1150) revoked and replaced S.I. 2001 No. 2254, as from May 20, 2002. The effect was to extend the modifications made by that order to include also the police areas of Bedfordshire, Devon and Cornwall, Lancashire, Merseyside, South Yorkshire and North Wales. The *Police and Criminal Evidence Act 1984 (Codes of Practice) (Modifications to Code C and Code D) (Certain Police Areas) (Amendment) Order* 2002 (S.I. 2002 No. 1863) extended the application of the modifications to the police areas of Avon and Somerset, Greater Manchester, Thames Valley and West Yorkshire as from September 2, 2002.

Revised (blue) Codes A to E came into force on April 1, 2003: see the *Police and Criminal Evidence Act 1984 (Codes of Practice) (Statutory Powers of Stop and Search) Order* 2002 (S.I. 2002 No. 3075), and the *Police and Criminal Evidence Act 1984 (Codes of Practice) (Codes B to E) (No. 2) Order* 2003 (S.I. 2003 No. 703).

As from April 1, 2003, the *Police and Criminal Evidence Act 1984 (Codes of Practice) (Modifications to Codes C and D) (Certain Police Areas) Order* 2003 (S.I. 2003 No. 704) revoked S.I. 2002 No. 1150 and S.I. 2002 No. 1863 (*ante*), so as to effect corresponding modifications to the new Codes C and D as were originally made to the former codes by S.I. 2001 No. 2254 (*ante*). The modifications had effect in all of the afore-mentioned police areas, plus Cleveland and Humber. They were extended to the police areas of Cambridgeshire, Leicestershire, Northumbria, and West Midlands as from April 1, 2004 by the *Police and Criminal Evidence Act 1984 (Codes of Practice) (Modifications to Codes C and D) (Certain Police Areas) (Amendment) Order* 2004 (S.I. 2004 No. 78).

The *Police and Criminal Evidence Act 1984 (Codes of Practice) (Visual Recording of Interviews) Order* 2002 (S.I. 2002 No. 1266) appointed May 7, 2002, as the date on which the code of practice for the visual recording of interviews under section 60A(1) of the 1984 Act (*post*, § 15–231) would come into operation. As at September 20, 2006, there was nowhere that such recording was required, although it had been mandatory (as an experimental project) at certain police stations between May 7, 2002, and October 31, 2003. For further details in relation thereto, see Appendix A–180.

The *Police and Criminal Evidence Act 1984 (Codes of Practice) Order* 2004 (S.I. 2004 No. 1887) revoked S.I. 2002 No. 1266, S.I. 2002 No. 3075, S.I. 2003 No. 703, S.I. 2003 No. 704 and S.I. 2004 No. 78 (*ante*), and brought into force (crimson) Codes A to F on August 1, 2004. The former modifications of Codes C and D became a permanent part of the codes, but only in those areas in which the relevant legislation was in force. From April 1, 2005, these were the police areas mentioned above, plus Gwent, Northamptonshire and South Wales. From December 1, 2005, the legislation was in force in all police areas.

On January 1, 2006, revised Codes A to F came into force; new Code G (exercise by police officers of statutory power of arrest) came into force; and S.I. 2004 No. 1887 (*ante*) and the *Police and Criminal Evidence Act 1984 (Codes of Practice) (Revisions to Code C) Order* 2005 (S.I 2005 No. 602) were revoked: *Police and Criminal Evidence Act 1984 (Codes of Practice) Order* 2005 (S.I 2005 No. 3503).

The *Police and Criminal Evidence Act 1984 (Code of Practice C and Code of Practice H) Order* 2006 (S.I. 2006 No. 1938) brought a revised Code C and a new Code H (on the detention, treatment and questioning by police officers of persons under section 41 of, and Schedule 8 to, the *Terrorism Act* 2000) into force on July 25, 2006. This was consequential upon the commencement of the final provisions of the *Terrorism Act* 2006, which are concerned with the 28-day detention of those arrested under section 41 of the 2000 Act. Whereas Code C had previously regulated detention following arrest under section 41, this is now regulated by Code H. Code C was revised so as to remove references to detention under section 41 of, and Schedule 8 to, the 2000 Act; and Code H largely mirrors the provisions of old Code C, but with various differences.

The *Police and Criminal Evidence Act 1984 (Codes of Practice) (Revisions to Code A) Order* 2006 (S.I. 2006 No. 2165) provided for revisions to Code A with effect from August 31, 2006.

As from February 1, 2008, revised Codes A to E came into force: *Police and Criminal Evidence Act 1984 (Codes of Practice) Order* 2008 (S.I. 2008 No. 167). However, the legal advice changes in Code C took effect on that day only in Greater Manchester, the West Midlands and West Yorkshire; they took effect elsewhere on April 21, 2008. Also, the variation of Code E allowing the recording of interviews by a secure digital network rather than on removable media applies only in part of Lancashire as part of a pilot scheme.

For the full text of the current codes, see Appendix A.

A court can have regard to a current code of practice in considering events before that code came into force, because the provisions of the new code reflect current thinking as to what is fair: *R. v. Ward*, 98 Cr.App.R. 337, CA.

(c) *Status of the codes*

15–8 The foreword to the original Codes A to D stated:

> "The Codes supersede some existing provisions (including the Judges' Rules) as well as including wholly new material. They reflect the views of the Royal Commission on Criminal Procedure, which reported in 1981, and the philosophy of the *Police and Criminal Evidence Act* 1984, in providing for clear and workable guidelines for the police, balanced by strengthened safeguards for the public."

The codes are not subordinate legislation. They are issued in accordance with section 67 of the 1984 Act, *ante*. The true status of the codes is, it is submitted, clear from sections 60, 66, and 67: they are codes of practice designed to regulate the conduct of persons charged with the duty of investigating offences. Non-observance of the codes does not of itself give rise to any criminal or civil liability; but compliance therewith or breach thereof may be relevant to decisions about the admissibility of evidence.

The codes include notes for guidance which are not provisions of the codes. Nevertheless, the notes are important and should be complied with wherever possible. The annexes to the codes are part of the codes (see the opening paragraphs of each code). **15–9**

(d) *Who is bound by the codes?*

The codes of practice apply to: **15–10**

(a) police officers (ss.60(1), 60A(1), 66(1) and 67(10))—this includes police forces such as the British Transport Police; and
(b) persons "other than police officers who are charged with the duty of investigating offences or charging offenders" (s.67(9)).

Category (b) includes Revenue and Customs officers: *R. v. Okafor*, 99 Cr.App.R. 97, CA; *R. v. Weerdesteyn* [1995] 1 Cr.App.R. 405, CA; officers of the Serious Fraud Office: *R. v. Director of Serious Fraud Office, ex p. Saunders* [1988] Crim.L.R. 837, DC; and Inland Revenue special compliance officers investigating tax fraud: *R. v. Gill* [2004] 1 Cr.App.R. 20, CA; but not local tax inspectors: *R. v. Doncaster*, 172 J.P. 202, CA. The codes can also apply to store detectives or similar security officers, and are not just restricted to officers of central government or other persons acting under statutory powers: *R. v. Bayliss*, 98 Cr.App.R. 235, CA. It is a question of fact whether or not a particular individual is a person "charged with the duty of investigating offences": *ibid.*

In *Joy v. Federation against Copyright Theft Ltd* [1993] Crim.L.R. 588, DC, it was held that the duty referred to in section 67(9) was any type of legal duty, whether imposed by statute, common law or by contract. Accordingly, an investigator employed by the respondents was held to be subject to such a duty. As to commercial investigators, see *R. v. Twaites and Brown*, 92 Cr.App.R. 106, CA (bookmakers' investigators). In *R. v. Welcher* [2007] Crim.L.R. 804, CA, it was held that a line manager conducting interviews in accordance with his employers' disciplinary policy, with a view to reporting to the employers' disciplinary panel as to whether the defendant should be dismissed, was not "charged with the duty of investigating offences". **15–11**

In *R. v. Devani* [2008] 1 Cr.App.R. 4, CA, it was held that the codes applied to a prison officer with powers of arrest equivalent to a constable (apparently a reference to the *Prison Act* 1952, s.8 (*post*, § 28–199)), but not to operational support grade officers within the same prison who had no such powers. However, even though the codes do not apply to the latter, a judge should consider whether there has been a breach of the spirit or substance of the codes: *ibid.*, and *R. v. Ristic* [2004] 2 *Archbold News* 3, CA.

An inspector of the RSPCA may be bound by the codes: *RSPCA v. Eager* [1995] Crim.L.R. 59, DC. A head teacher, however, has no duty to investigate incidents at school and, thus, in the absence of any contractual duty to investigate, is not a person "charged with the duty of investigating offences": *DPP v. G. (Duty to investigate)*, *The Times*, November 24, 1997, DC.

Neither DTI inspectors asking questions under the *Companies Act* 1985, s.434 (*post*, § 30–4) (*R. v. Seelig and Lord Spens*, 94 Cr.App.R. 17, CA), nor a Bank of England manager exercising supervisory powers over a bank under the *Banking Act* 1987 (*R. v. Smith (W.D.)*, 99 Cr.App.R. 223, CA) were "investigating offences" within section 67(9).

A police officer effecting an arrest for contempt of court on a judge's direction acts as if he is a jailer rather than an investigating officer and thus is not obliged to go through the formalities required by the 1984 Act and the codes: *R. v. Jones* [1996] Crim.L.R. 806, CA.

The duty on investigators other than police officers is "to have regard to any relevant provision" of the codes. Compliance with the letter of the codes will sometimes be impossible by virtue of the codes being expressed to apply to police officers and to police stations. For example, in *R. (Social Security Secretary) v. South Central Division Magistrates*, *The Daily Telegraph*, November 28, 2000, DC, it was held that there was no breach of Code C:3.21 (Appendix A–47) where a social security investigator failed to tell an interviewee who attended a social security office voluntarily that he was entitled to free legal advice, because there was no such entitlement. See also *R. (Beale) v. South East Wiltshire Magistrates' Court*, 167 J.P. 41, DC (trading standards inspector not obliged to tell interviewee at latter's farm that the legal advice to which he was entitled was free).

(e) *Admissibility*

15–12 The codes are admissible in evidence in all criminal and civil proceedings, and any provision of a code if "relevant to any question arising in the proceedings" shall be "taken into account in determining that question" (s.67(11)). This does not just apply to questions for the judge to determine: *R. v. Kenny* [1992] Crim.L.R. 800, CA (where relevant, the jury must be directed as to the fact of a breach and its significance). However, section 67(11) does not render admissible something which would otherwise be hearsay, merely because the statement is made during processes properly conducted in accordance with the relevant code: *R. v. Lynch* [2008] 1 Cr.App.R. 24, CA (not following *R. v. McCay*, 91 Cr.App.R. 84, CA).

Even if a particular questioner is not required to have regard to Code C (because he is not a person "charged with the duty of investigating offences", *ante*), the principles of fairness enshrined in Code C are nonetheless of assistance when the court is considering its discretion to exclude unfair evidence under section 78 (*post*, § 15–452): *R. v. Smith (W.D.), ante*.

(f) *Breaches of the codes*

Police discipline

15–13 Non-compliance with a code provision does not *per se* give rise to any criminal or civil liability: s.67(10).

Exclusion of evidence obtained in breach

15–14 Evidence obtained in breach of a code may be excluded by the trial judge under section 76 (confessions, *post*, § 15–350), under section 78 (exclusion of unfair evidence, *post*, § 15–452), or at common law (*post*, § 15–535). The effect of a breach of the provisions has been considered in numerous authorities: see, in particular, in relation to Code C, *post*, §§ 15–251 *et seq.*, and, in relation to Code D, *ante*, §§ 14–40 *et seq.*

15–15 General principles which still apply can be derived from two early Court of Appeal cases which dealt with breaches of the codes—*R. v. Absolam*, 88 Cr.App.R. 332, and *R. v. Delaney*, 88 Cr.App.R. 338. They are as follows: (a) a breach of a code does not lead automatically to exclusion (*Delaney*); (b) where there is a breach, the judge has a discretion to exclude the evidence (*Absolam/Delaney*); (c) the breach must be significant and substantial, and the more so, the more likely the judge is to exclude the evidence (*Absolam*); (d) bad faith/flagrant disregard of the codes' provisions will make exclusion more likely (*Delaney*); (e) the test to be applied is the section 78 test (*R. v. Grannell*, 90 Cr.App.R. 149, CA); (f) in applying the test, the judge should have regard to the rationale of the provisions of the code (*e.g.* Code D is generally designed to ensure that identification procedures provide a fair test of ability to identify) and the extent to which the breach is likely to defeat that rationale (*Delaney*); (g) if there is a breach but the judge admits the evidence, he should give reasons for so doing: *R. v. Allen* [1995] Crim.L.R. 643, CA; (h) if the evidence is allowed in despite the breach, the judge should explain the significance of the breach to the jury, as it may go to the weight they attach to the evidence (see *R. v. Graham* [1994] Crim.L.R. 212, CA, and *R. v. Quinn ante*, § 14–41).

15–16 For further details of *Absolam*, see section 58 of the *PACE Act* 1984, *post*, § 15–206. For further details of *Delaney*, see *post*, § 15–501 (the "verballing" provisions), and for many further examples of the exclusion of evidence obtained in breach of a code of conduct, see *post*, §§ 15–366, 15–478 *et seq.*

[The next paragraph is § 15–23.]

(3) "Reasonable grounds for suspicion"

"Reasonable grounds for suspicion" is an important phrase within the framework of the Act and the codes of practice. A constable cannot exercise the powers of stop and search under Part I, for example, unless he has "reasonable grounds for suspicion" that he will find stolen or prohibited articles (s.1(3), *post*, § 15–49). Certain arrest powers require "reasonable grounds for suspicion" before they can be exercised (*post*, §§ 15–161 *et seq.*). **15–23**

"Reasonable grounds for suspicion" is not defined in the Act. For the purposes of stop and search powers, Code A provides some guidance at paragraphs A:2.2 to A:2.9 (Appendix A–5). The test is described in A:2.2 as an objective one. The officer must consider all the circumstances, including the nature of the article suspected of being carried, the context of its being carried including time and place, and the behaviour of the person concerned. A:2.2 emphasises that reasonable suspicion can "never be supported on the basis of personal factors alone", such as race, age, appearance, or a known previous conviction for possession of an unlawful article. Nor may it be founded upon stereotyped images of those considered more likely to commit offences.

The test as to whether reasonable grounds for the suspicion to justify an arrest existed is partly subjective, in that the arresting officer must have formed a genuine suspicion that the person being arrested was guilty of an offence, and partly objective, in that there had to be reasonable grounds for forming such a suspicion; such grounds could arise from information received from another (even if it subsequently proves to be false), provided that a reasonable man, having regard to all the circumstances, would regard them as reasonable grounds for suspicion; but a mere order from a superior officer to arrest a particular individual could not constitute reasonable grounds for such suspicion: *O'Hara v. Chief Constable of the Royal Ulster Constabulary* [1997] A.C. 286, HL. **15–24**

See also *Siddiqui v. Swain* [1979] R.T.R. 454, 457, DC, in which "reasonable grounds to suspect" in the *RTA* 1972, s.8(5) (now the *RTA* 1988, s.7) were said to "import the further requirement that the constable in fact suspects"; *Parker v. Chief Constable of the Hampshire Constabulary*, unreported, June 25, 1999, CA (Civ. Div.), where it was held that an officer who had reasonable grounds to think it "possible" that one of two people in a car was someone he was entitled to arrest had been justified in arresting that person; and *Cumming v. Chief Constable of Northumbria Police, The Times*, January 2, 2004, CA (Civ. Div.) (there is nothing in principle to prevent (a) opportunity from amounting to reasonable grounds for suspicion, or (b) the police arresting more than one person even if the crime can only have been committed by one person).

As to having reasonable grounds for suspecting that an offence has been committed (see s.24(2), *post*, § 15–161), it is not necessary that an officer should have in mind specific statutory provisions, or that he should mentally identify specific offences with technicality or precision. He must, however, reasonably suspect the existence of facts amounting to an offence of a kind that he has in mind; unless he can do that, he cannot comply with his obligation under section 28(3) (*post*, § 15–176) to inform the suspect of the grounds of arrest: *Chapman v. DPP*, 89 Cr.App.R. 190, DC; *Mossop v. DPP* [2003] 6 *Archbold News* 1, DC.

If the arresting officer knows at the time of arrest that there is no possibility of a charge being made, the arrest would be unlawful as he must have acted on an irrelevant consideration or for some improper motive: *Plange v. Chief Constable of South Humberside Police, The Times*, March 23, 1992, CA (Civ. Div.). *Plange* was referred to, without disapproval, in *R. v. Chalkley and Jeffries* [1998] 2 Cr.App.R. 79, CA, but the court seems to have thought that an arrest would be lawful if there were reasonable grounds to suspect the person arrested to be guilty of the offence for which he was told he was being arrested, even though the arresting officer knew that there was no intention to prosecute him for that offence, provided that the true reason for the arrest was to facilitate the investigation and prevention of more serious crime. This was, however, *obiter*, as the officers who made the arrest knew nothing of their superiors' motives, and because, in any event, the validity of the arrest was irrelevant to the determination of the appeal.

In *Kynaston v. DPP*, 87 Cr.App.R. 200, DC, it was held that where the validity of an arrest is in issue, if the defence do not raise the question whether there were reasonable grounds for suspicion, it is open to the court, in appropriate circumstances, to infer that such grounds existed.

(4) Police officers performing duties of higher rank

15–25 Section 107 of the Act provides that for the purpose of any provision of the Act or any other Act under which a power in respect of the investigation of offences or the treatment of persons in police custody is exercisable only by or with the authority of a police officer of at least the rank of superintendent, an officer of the rank of chief inspector shall be treated as holding the rank of superintendent if he has been authorised by an officer holding a rank above the rank of superintendent to exercise the power or, as the case may be, to give his authority for its exercise, or he is acting during the absence of an officer holding the rank of superintendent who has authorised him, for the duration of that absence, to exercise the power or, as the case may be, to give his authority for its exercise. By subsection (2), a sergeant may exercise the powers of an inspector if he has been authorised to do so by a superintendent or above.

The holder of an acting rank, so far as authority and powers are concerned, is to be treated as if he were the holder of the substantive rank, unless his appointment to the acting rank was a colourable pretence: *R. v. Alladice*, 87 Cr.App.R. 380, CA.

(5) Use of force

Police and Criminal Evidence Act 1984, s.117

Power of constable to use reasonable force

15–26 **117.** Where any provision of this Act—

(a) confers a power on a constable; and

(b) does not provide that the power may only be exercised with the consent of some person, other than a police officer,

the officer may use reasonable force, if necessary, in the exercise of the power.

(6) Interpretation

Police and Criminal Evidence Act 1984, s.118

General interpretation

15–27 **118.**—(1) In this Act—

"British Transport Police Force" means the constables appointed under section 53 of the *British Transport Commission Act* 1949;

"designated police station" has the meaning assigned to it by section 35 above;

"document" means anything in which information of any description is recorded;

…

"item subject to legal privilege" has the meaning assigned to it by section 10 above;

"parent or guardian" means—

(a) in the case of a child or young person in the care of a local authority, that authority;

(b) [*repealed by* Children Act *1989, s.108(7) and Sched. 15*];

"premises" has the meaning assigned to it by section 23 above;

"recordable offence" means any offence to which regulations under section 27 above apply;

"vessel" includes any ship, boat, raft or other apparatus constructed or adapted for floating on water.

(2) Subject to subsection (2A) a person is in police detention for the purposes of this Act if—

(a) he has been taken to a police station after being arrested for an offence or after being arrested under section 41 of the *Terrorism Act* 2000, or,

(b) he is arrested at a police station after attending voluntarily at the station or accompanying a constable to it,

and is detained there or is detained elsewhere in the charge of a constable, except that a person who is at a court after being charged is not in police detention for those purposes.

(2A) Where a person is in another's lawful custody by virtue of paragraph 22, 34(1) or 35(3) of Schedule 4 to the *Police Reform Act* 2002, he shall be treated as in police detention.

[This section is printed as amended by the *Civil Evidence Act* 1995; the *Anti-Terrorism, Crime and Security Act* 2001, s.101, and Sched. 7, para. 14; and the *Police Reform Act* 2002, s.107(1),and Sched. 7, para. 9(9); and as repealed in part by the *CJPOA* 1994, s.168(3), and Sched. 11; the *Terrorism Act* 2000, s.125, and Sched. 15, para. 5(12); and the *SOCPA* 2005, ss.111 and 174(2), Sched. 7, para. 24(1) and (2), and Sched. 17.]

For section 24, see *post*, § 15–161; for section 35, see *ante*, § 3–94; for section 10, see *post*, § 15–90; for section 23, see *post*, § 15–123; and for section 27, see *post*, § 15–174.

A serving prisoner brought to a police station pursuant to a production order (issued under the *C(S)A* 1997, s.41 and Sched. 1, para. 3(1) (*ante*, § 8–15)), in order that the police may ask questions relating to evidence that the prisoner might give for the prosecution in another's trial, is not in police detention within the meaning of section 118(2): *R. v. Drury* [2001] Crim.L.R. 847, CA.

(7) Application of Act to Armed Forces

Police and Criminal Evidence Act 1984, s.113

Application of Act to Armed Forces

113.—(1) *The Secretary of State may by order direct that any provision of Part 5 of this Act or Part 11 of this Act so far as relating to that Part which relates to investigations of offences conducted by police officers or to persons detained by the police shall apply, subject to such modifications as he may specify, to investigations of offences conducted under the* Army Act *1955, the* Air Force Act *1955 or the* Naval Discipline Act *1957 or to persons under arrest under any of those Acts.* **15–28**

[(1) The Secretary of State may by order make provision in relation to—

(a) investigations of service offences,

(b) persons arrested under a power conferred by or under the *Armed Forces Act* 2006,

(c) persons charged under that Act with service offences,

(d) persons in service custody, or

(e) persons convicted of service offences,

which is equivalent to that made by any provision of Part 5 of this Act (or this Part of this Act so far as relating to that Part), subject to such modifications as the Secretary of State considers appropriate.]

(2) Section 67(9) above shall not have effect in relation to investigations of *offences conducted under the* Army Act *1955, the* Air Force Act *1955 or the* Naval Discipline Act *1957* [service offences].

(3) The Secretary of State shall issue a code of practice, or a number of such codes, for persons other than police officers who are concerned with—

(a) the exercise of powers conferred by *Part 2 of the* Armed Forces Act *2001* [or under Part 3 of the *Armed Forces Act* 2006]; or

(b) *enquiries into offences under the* Army Act *1955, the* Air Force Act *1955 or the* Naval Discipline Act *1957* [investigations of service offences].

(3A) In subsections (4) to (10), "code" means a code of practice under subsection (3).

(4) Without prejudice to the generality of subsection (3) above, a code may contain provisions, in connection with the powers mentioned in subsection (3)(a) above or the *enquiries* [investigations] mentioned in subsection (3)(b) above, as to the following matters—

(a) the tape-recording of interviews;

(b) searches of persons and premises; and

(c) the seizure of things found on searches.

(5) [*Identical to s.67(2),* ante, *§ 15–4.*] **15–29**

(6) [*Identical to s.67(3),* ante, *§ 15–4.*]

(7) [*Any code, or revision thereof, to be laid before Parliament.*]

(8) A failure on the part of any person to comply with any provision of a code shall not of itself render him liable to any criminal or civil proceedings except those to which this subsection applies.

(9) *Subsection (8) above applies—*

(a) *to proceedings under any provision of the* Army Act *1955 or the* Air Force Act *1955 other than section 70; and*

(b) *to proceedings under any provision of the* Naval Discipline Act *1957 other than section 42.*

[(9) Subsection (8) above applies to proceedings in respect of an offence under a provision of Part 1 of the *Armed Forces Act* 2006 other than section 42 (criminal conduct).]

15–30 (10) [*Identical to s.67(11)*, ante, *§ 15–5.*]

(11) *In subsection (10) above "criminal proceedings" includes*—[*as s.67(12)*, ante, *§ 15–5*].

(12) Parts VII and VIII of this Act have effect for the purposes of [service] proceedings—

(a) *before a court-martial constituted under the* Army Act *1955 or the* Air Force Act *1955;*

(b) *before the Courts-Martial Appeal Court; and*

(c) *before a Standing Civilian Court,*

subject to any modifications which the Secretary of State may by order specify.

[(12A) In this section—

"service offence" has the meaning given by section 50 of the *Armed Forces Act* 2006;

"criminal proceedings" includes service proceedings;

"service proceedings" means proceedings before a court (other than a civilian court) in respect of a service offence; and

"civilian court" has the meaning given by section 374 of the *Armed Forces Act* 2006;

and section 376(1) and (2) of that Act (meaning of "convicted" in relation to summary hearings and the SAC) apply for the purposes of subsection (1)(e) above as they apply for the purposes of that Act.]

(13), (14) [*Procedure for making an order under this section.*]

[This section is printed as amended, and repealed in part, by the *AFA* 2001, s.13; and the *CJA* 2003, ss.11(2)–(4) and 332, and Sched. 37, Pt 1; and as amended, as from a day to be appointed, by the *AFA* 2006, s.378(1) and (2), Sched. 16, para. 105, and Sched. 17 (omission of subs. (11), substitution of new subss. (1) and (9), insertion of new subss. (12A) and (14), omission of italicised words, insertion of words in square brackets in subss. (2), (3), (4) and (12)).]

15–31 The Secretary of State in exercise of the power conferred by section 113 has made the *Police and Criminal Evidence Act 1984 (Application to the Armed Forces) Order* 2006 (S.I. 2006 No. 2015). This applies specified provisions of the 1984 Act (with extensive modifications) to the investigation of offences conducted by a service policeman under either of the 1955 Acts or the Act of 1957 and to persons arrested in connection with such an investigation. The provisions applied are: sections 54 (searches of detained persons (*post*, § 15–192)), 54A (searches and examination to ascertain identity (*post*, § 15–193a)), 55 (intimate searches (*post*, § 15–194)), 55A (x-rays and ultrasound scans (*post*, § 15–198a)), 56 (right to have someone informed of arrest (*post*, § 15–199)), 58 (legal advice (*post*, § 15–206)), 61 (fingerprinting (*post*, § 15–232)), 61A (footwear impressions (*post*, § 15–234a)), 62 (intimate samples (*post*, § 15–235)), 63 (other samples (*post*, § 15–238)), 63A (fingerprints and samples: supplementary provisions (*post*, § 15–241)), 64 (destruction of fingerprints and samples (*post*, § 15–246)), 64A (photographing suspects (*post*, § 15–248a)), 65 (Pt V: supplementary (*post*, § 15–249)) and 117 (power of constable to use reasonable force (*ante*, § 15–26)). Of those provisions, sections 54A, 55A, 61A and 64A are applied for the first time. What are referred to as "recordable offences" in the 1984 Act are referred to in the modified provisions as "recordable service offences", and these are listed in Schedule 2 to the order. Schedule 3 sets out the full text of the provisions of the Act applied by the order, as modified. The order took effect on December 31, 2006, and replaced the 1997 order of the same name (S.I. 1997 No. 15). It has been amended by the *Armed Forces (Service Police Amendments) Order*

2007 (S.I. 2007 No. 1861) to reflect the change of title of the Royal Naval Regulating Branch to that of the Royal Navy Police.

[The next paragraph is § 15–39.]

Codes of practice

Section 113(3) of the 1984 Act, *ante*, provides that the Secretary of State is under a duty to issue a code of practice, or a number of such codes, for persons other than police officers who are concerned with inquiries into offences under either of the 1955 Acts or the Act of 1957, or with the excercise of the powers conferred by the *AFA* 2001, Pt 2. Revised codes of practice (not set out in this work) were brought into force by the *Police and Criminal Evidence Act 1984 (Codes of Practice) (Armed Forces) Order* 1997 (S.I. 1997 No. 17); and as to Part 2 of the 2001 Act, see the *Police and Criminal Evidence Act 1984 (Codes of Practice) (Armed Forces) Order* 2003 (S.I. 2003 No. 2315). **15–39**

(8) Application of Act to Revenue and Customs

Police and Criminal Evidence Act 1984, s.114

Application of Act to Revenue and Customs

114.—(1) [*Amends customs and excise Acts.*] **15–40**

(2) The Treasury may by order direct—

(a) that any provision of this Act which relates to investigations of offences conducted by police officers or to persons detained by the police shall apply, subject to such modifications as the order may specify, to investigations conducted by officers of Revenue and Customs, or to persons detained by officers of Revenue and Customs; and

(b) that, in relation to investigations of offences conducted by officers of Revenue and Customs—

(i) this Act shall have effect as if the following sections were inserted after section 14—

"*Exception for the Commissioners for Her Majesty's Revenue and Customs*

14A. Material in the possession of a person who acquired or created it in the course of any trade, business, profession or other occupation or for the purpose of any paid or unpaid office and which relates to a matter in relation to which Her Majesty's Revenue and Customs have functions, is neither excluded material nor special procedure material for the purposes of any enactment such as is mentioned in section 9(2) above.

Revenue and Customs: restriction on other powers to apply for production of documents

14B.—(1) An officer of Revenue and Customs may make an application for the delivery of, or access to, documents under a provision specified in subsection (3) only if the condition in subsection (2) is satisfied.

(2) The condition is that the officer thinks that an application under Schedule 1 would not succeed because the material required does not consist of or include special procedure material.

(3) The provisions are—

(a) section 20BA of, and Schedule 1AA to, the *Taxes Management Act* 1970 (serious tax fraud);

(b) paragraph 11 of Schedule 11 to the *Value Added Tax Act* 1994 (VAT);

(c) paragraph 4A of Schedule 7 to the *Finance Act* 1994 (insurance premium tax);

(d) paragraph 7 of Schedule 5 to the *Finance Act* 1996 (landfill tax);

(e) paragraph 131 of Schedule 6 to the *Finance Act* 2000 (climate change levy);

(f) paragraph 8 of Schedule 7 to the *Finance Act* 2001 (aggregates levy);

(g) Part 6 of Schedule 13 to the *Finance Act* 2003 (stamp duty land tax)."; and

(ii) section 55 above shall have effect as if it related only to things such as are mentioned in subsection (1)(a) of that section [, and

(c) that in relation to Revenue and Customs detention (as defined in any order made under this subsection) the *Bail Act* 1976 shall have effect as if references in it to a constable were references to an officer of Revenue and Customs of such grade as may be specified in the order],

(d) that where an officer of Revenue and Customs searches premises in reliance on a warrant under section 8 of, or paragraph 12 of Schedule 1 to, this Act (as applied by an order under this subsection) the officer shall have the power to search persons found on the premises—

(i) in such cases and circumstances as are specified in the order, and

(ii) subject to any conditions specified in the order; and

(e) that powers and functions conferred by a provision of this Act (as applied by an order under this subsection) may be exercised only by officers of Revenue and Customs acting with the authority (which may be general or specific) of the Commissioners for Her Majesty's Revenue and Customs.

(2A) A certificate of the Commissioners that an officer of Revenue and Customs had authority under subsection (2)(e) to exercise a power or function conferred by a provision of this Act shall be conclusive evidence of that fact.

(3) An order under subsection (2)—

(a) may make provision that applies generally or only in specified cases or circumstances,

(b) may make different provision for different cases or circumstances,

(c) may, in modifying a provision, in particular impose conditions on the exercise of a function, and

(d) shall not be taken to limit a power under section 164 of the *Customs and Excise Management Act* 1979.

(5) [*Procedure for making an order under this section.*]

[This section is printed as amended by the *Finance Act* 2007, s.82; and as amended, as from a day to be appointed, by the *CJA* 1988, s.150 (insertion of subs. (2)(c))). The references to "officers of Revenue and Customs" and to "the Commissioners for Her Majesty's Revenue and Customs" have been substituted by virtue of the *Commissioners for Revenue and Customs Act* 2005, s.50(1) and (2).]

Section 84(2) and (3) of the *Finance Act* 2007 (in force on December 1, 2007) provide that nothing in section 6 or 7 of the *Commissioners for Revenue and Customs Act* 2005 (which had been intended to prevent powers previously used by Customs and Excise from being used in respect of matters inherited from the Inland Revenue, and *vice versa*) restricts the functions in connection with which officers of Revenue and Customs may exercise a power under the 1984 Act by virtue of section 114 (as amended by s.82), but that an order under section 114 does not have effect in relation to a matter specified in the 2005 Act, s.54(4)(b) or (f), or Sched. 1, paras 3, 7, 10, 13 to 15, 19 or 24 to 29 (former Inland Revenue matters).

15–41 The powers conferred by section 114(2) have effect in relation to the provisions of Part 2 of the *CJPA* 2001 (*post*, §§ 15–124 *et seq.*) as they have effect in relation to the provisions of the 1984 Act: s.67 of the 2001 Act.

In exercise of the powers conferred by section 114(2), the Treasury have made the *PACE Act 1984 (Application to Revenue and Customs) Order* 2007 (S.I. 2007 No. 3175), which revokes and replaces earlier statutory instruments made under the same provision: for details, see the 2008 edition of this work.

S.I. 2007 No. 3175

Interpretation

15–42 2.—(1) In this Order—

"the Act" means the *Police and Criminal Evidence Act* 1984;

"the Commissioners" means the Commissioners for Her Majesty's Revenue and Customs;

"the customs and excise Acts" has the meaning given to it by section 1 of the *Customs and Excise Management Act* 1979;

"former Inland Revenue matter" means a matter specified in section 54(4)(b) or (f) of, or in paragraphs 3, 7, 10, 13 to 15, 19 or 24 to 29 of Schedule 1 to, the *Commissioners for Revenue and Customs Act* 2005;

"office of Revenue and Customs" means premises wholly or partly occupied by Her Majesty's Revenue and Customs;

"relevant indictable offence" means an indictable offence which relates to a matter in relation to which Her Majesty's Revenue and Customs have functions apart from a former Inland Revenue matter;

"relevant investigation" means a criminal investigation conducted by officers of Revenue and Customs which relates to a matter in relation to which Her Majesty's Revenue and Customs have functions apart from a former Inland Revenue matter.

(2) A person is in Revenue and Customs detention for the purpose of this Order if—

(a) he has been taken to an office of Revenue and Customs after being arrested for an offence; or

(b) he is arrested at an office of Revenue and Customs after attending voluntarily at the office or accompanying an officer of Revenue and Customs to it,

and is detained there or detained elsewhere in the charge of an officer of Revenue and Customs, and nothing shall prevent a detained person from being transferred between Revenue and Customs detention and police detention.

Application

3.—(1) The provisions of the Act contained in Schedule 1 to this Order which relate to investigations of offences conducted by police officers or to persons detained by the police shall apply to relevant investigations conducted by officers of Revenue and Customs and to persons detained by such officers.

This is subject to the modifications in paragraphs (2) and (3) and articles 4 to 19 and Schedule 2.

(2) The Act shall have effect as if the words and phrases in Column 1 of Part 1 of Schedule 2 to this Order were replaced by the substitute words and phrases in Column 2 of that Part.

(3) Where in the Act any act or thing is to be done by a constable of a specified rank, that act or thing shall be done by an officer of Revenue and Customs of at least the grade specified in Column 2 of Part 2 of Schedule 2 to this Order, and the Act shall be construed accordingly.

Exceptions

4. Nothing in the application of the Act to Revenue and Customs confers on an officer of Revenue and Customs any power—

(a) to charge a person with any offence;

(b) to release a person on bail; or

(c) to detain a person for an offence after he has been charged with that offence.

Seizure and retention of things found

5.—(1) Where in the Act a constable is given power to seize and retain any thing found upon a lawful search of person or premises, an officer of Revenue and Customs shall have the same power notwithstanding that the thing found is not evidence of an offence which relates to a matter in relation to which Her Majesty's Revenue and Customs have functions. **15–43**

(2) Nothing in the application of the Act to Revenue and Customs prevents any thing lawfully seized by a person under any enactment from being accepted and retained by an officer of Revenue and Customs.

(3) Section 21 of the Act (access and copying) shall not apply to any thing seized as liable to forfeiture under the customs and excise Acts.

Excluded and special procedure material

6. In its application by virtue of article 3 above the Act shall have effect as if the following section were inserted after section 14—

[*See s.114(2)(b)(i) of the 1984 Act,* ante, *§ 15–40, for text of section 14A.*]

Restriction on other powers to apply for document

7. In its application by virtue of article 3 above the Act shall have effect as if the following section were inserted after section 14A—

[*See s.114(2)(b)(i) of the 1984 Act, ante, § 15–40, for text of section 14B.*]

Modification of section 18 of the Act (entry and search after arrest)

8.—(1) Section 18 of the Act (entry and search after arrest) is modified as follows.

(2) For subsection 18 (1) substitute—

"(1) Subject to the following provisions of this section, an officer of Revenue and Customs may enter and search any premises occupied or controlled by a person who is under arrest for any relevant indictable offence if he has reasonable grounds for suspecting that there is on the premises evidence, other than items subject to legal privilege, that relates—

(a) to that offence; or

(b) to some other indictable offence which is connected with or similar to that offence.".

Modification of section 35 of the Act (designated police stations)

9.—(1) Section 35 of the Act (designated police stations) is modified as follows.

(2) For subsection 35(1) substitute—

"(1) The Director of Detection shall designate offices of Revenue and Customs which, subject to sections 30(3) and (5), are to be the offices to be used for the purposes of detaining arrested persons.".

(3) For subsection 35(2) substitute—

"(2) The Director of Detection's duty under subsection (1) above is to designate offices of Revenue and Customs appearing to him to provide enough accommodation for that purpose.".

(4) For subsection 35(3) substitute—

"(3) Without prejudice to section 12 of the *Interpretation Act* 1978 (continuity of duties) the Director of Detection—

(a) may designate an office which was not previously designated; and

(b) may direct that a designation of an office previously made shall cease to operate.".

Modification of section 36 of the Act (custody officers at police stations)

10.—(1) Section 36 of the Act (custody officers at police stations) is modified as follows.

(2) For subsection (2) substitute—

"(2) A custody officer for an office of Revenue and Customs designated under section 35(1) above shall be appointed—

(a) by the Director of Detection; or

(b) by such other officer of Revenue and Customs as the Director of Detection may direct.".

Modification of section 41 of the Act (limits on period of detention without charge)

11.—(1) Section 41 of the Act (limits on period of detention without charge) is modified as follows.

(2) For subsection (2)(b) substitute—

"(b) in the case of a person arrested outside England and Wales, shall be—

(i) the time at which that person arrives at the office of Revenue and Customs in England and Wales in which the offence for which he was arrested is being investigated; or

(ii) the time 24 hours after the time of that person's entry into England and Wales".

12. [*Modification of section 50 of the Act (keeping of records of detention).*]

Modification of section 55 of the Act (intimate searches)

15–43a **13.**—(1) Section 55 of the Act (intimate searches) shall have effect as if it related only to things such as are mentioned in subsection (1)(a) of that section.

(2) [*Information to be included in Commissioners' annual report (s.55(15)).*]

Modification of section 64 of the Act (destruction of fingerprints and samples)

14.—(1) Section 64 of the Act (destruction of fingerprints and samples) is modified as follows.

(2) For subsection (5)(b) substitute—

"(b) the Director of Risk and Intelligence shall make access to the data impossible, as soon as it is practicable to do so".

(3) For subsection (6A) substitute—

"(6A) If—

(a) subsection (5)(b) above falls to be complied with; and

(b) the person to whose fingerprints or impressions of footwear the data relates asks for a certificate that it has been complied with,

such a certificate shall be issued to him, not later than the end of the period of three months beginning with the day on which he asks for it, by the Director of Risk and Intelligence or a person authorised by him or on his behalf for the purposes of this section.".

Modification of section 77 of the Act (definition of independent person)

15. Section 77(3) of the Act (definition of independent person) shall be modified to the extent that the definition of "independent person" shall, in addition to the persons mentioned therein, also include an officer of Revenue and Customs or any other person acting under the authority of the Commissioners. **15–43b**

Use of reasonable force

16. Where any provision of the Act as applied to Revenue and Customs—

(a) confers a power on an officer of Revenue and Customs, and

(b) does not provide that the power may only be exercised with the consent of some person other than that officer,

the officer may use reasonable force, if necessary, in the exercise of the power.

Arrest without warrant

17. Section 24(2) of the Act (arrest without warrant) does not limit— **15–43c**

(a) section 138(1) of the *Customs and Excise Management Act* 1979;

(b) section 20 and paragraph 4 of Schedule 3 to the *Criminal Justice (International Co-operation) Act* 1990;

(c) any other enactment, including any enactment contained in subordinate legislation, for the time being in force which confers upon officers of Revenue and Customs the power to arrest or detain persons.

Search of persons

18. Where an officer of Revenue and Customs searches premises in reliance on a warrant under section 8 of, or paragraph 12 of Schedule 1 to, the Act (power of justice of the peace to authorise entry and search of premises), he may search any person found on the premises—

(a) where he has reasonable cause to believe that person to be in possession of material which is likely to be of substantial value (whether by itself or together with other material) to the investigation of the offence;

(b) but no person should be searched except by a person of the same sex.

Authorisation

19. Powers and functions in the provisions of the Act contained in Schedule 1 to this Order may be exercised only by officers of Revenue and Customs acting with the authority (which may be general or specific) of the Commissioners.

20. [*Revocation of statutory instruments referred to at § 15–41,* ante.]

Provisions of the Act applied to Revenue and Customs

Article 3(1) of S.I. 2007 No. 3175 (*ante*, § 15–42) stipulates that the following provisions of the 1984 Act (listed in Schedule 1 to the order) shall apply (subject to the modifications in paras (2) and (3) and arts 4 to 19 and Sched. 2) to relevant investigations (as to which, see art. 2(1), *ante*, § 15–42) conducted by officers of Revenue and Customs and to persons detained by such officers: section 8, section 9 and Schedule 1, sections 15 and 16, section 17(1)(b), (2) and (4), section 18 (subject to the modification in art. 8), sections 19 to 21, section 22(1) to (4), section 24(2) (subject to the modification in art. 17), sections 28 and 29, section 30(1) to (4)(a) and (5) to (11), section 31, section 32(1) to (9) (subject to the modifications in art. 5), section 34(1) to (5), section 35(1), (2), **15–44**

(3) and (4) (subject to the modifications in art. 9), section 36(1), (2), (3), (4), (5), (6), (7), (8), (9) and (10) (subject to the modification in art. 10), sections 37, 39 and 40, section 41(1), (2), (4) and (6) to (9) (subject to the modification in art. 11), section 42(1), (2) and (4) to (11), section 43(1) to (12) and (14) to (19), section 44, section 50 (subject to the modification in art. 12), section 51(d), section 54, section 55 (subject to the modifications in arts 5 and 13), section 56(1) to (9), section 57, section 58(1) to (11), sections 62 and 63, section 64, except subsection (6B), (subject to the modifications in art. 14), sections 66 and 67, section 77 (subject to the modification in art. 15), and section 107.

Equivalent words and phrases

15–45 Part 1 of Schedule 2 to S.I. 2007 No. 3175 (given effect by art. 3(2), *ante*, § 15–42) provides that where in the Act one of the following words or phrases is used, in the application of the Act to Revenue and Customs, there shall be substituted the word or phrase in square brackets: chief officer of police [director]; constable [officer of Revenue and Customs]; designated police station [designated office of Revenue and Customs]; officer of a force maintained by a police authority [officer of Revenue and Customs]; police detention (except in s.118 and in s.39(1)(a) the second time the word occurs) [Revenue and Customs detention]; police officer [officer of Revenue and Customs]; police station [office of Revenue and Customs]; rank [grade]; station [office of Revenue and Customs]; the police [Her Majesty's Revenue and Customs].

Equivalent grades

15–45a Part 2 of Schedule 2 to S.I. 2007 No. 3175 (given effect by art. 3(3), *ante*, § 15–42) provides that where in the Act an act or thing is to be done by a constable of one of the following ranks, that same act or thing shall, in the application of the Act to Revenue and Customs, be done by an officer of at least an equivalent grade specified in square brackets: sergeant [officer], inspector [higher officer], chief inspector [higher officer], and superintendent [senior officer].

(9) Application of Act to Department of Business, Enterprise and Regulatory Reform investigations

Police and Criminal Evidence Act 1984, s.114A

Power to apply Act to officers of the Secretary of State, etc.

15–46 **114A.**—(1) The Secretary of State may by order direct that—

(a) the provisions of Schedule 1 to this Act so far as they relate to special procedure material, and

(b) the other provisions of this Act so far as they relate to the provisions falling within paragraph (a) above,

shall apply, with such modifications as may be specified in the order, for the purposes of investigations falling within subsection (2) as they apply for the purposes of investigations of offences conducted by police officers.

(2) An investigation falls within this subsection if—

(a) it is conducted by an officer of the department of the Secretary of State for Business, Enterprise and Regulatory Reform or by another person acting on that Secretary of State's behalf;

(b) it is conducted by that officer or other person in the discharge of a duty to investigate offences; and

(c) the investigation relates to an indictable offence or to anything which there are reasonable grounds for suspecting has involved the commission of an indictable offence.

(3) The investigations for the purposes of which provisions of this Act may be applied with modifications by an order under this section include investigations of offences committed, or suspected of having been committed, before the coming into force of the order or of this section.

(4) [*Order to be made by statutory instrument.*]

[This section was inserted by the *CJPA* 2001, s.85. It is printed as amended by the *SOCPA* 2005, s.111, and Sched. 7, para. 43(1) and (11); and the *Secretaries of State for Children, Schools and Families, for Innovation, Universities and Skills and for Business, Enterprise and Regulatory Reform Order* 2007 (S.I. 2007 No. 3224).]

The *Police and Criminal Evidence Act 1984 (Department of Trade and Industry Investigations) Order* 2002 (S.I. 2002 No. 2326), as amended by S.I. 2007 No. 3224, *ante*, provides that, subject to the modifications set out in article 4, the provisions of Schedule 1 to the Act, so far as they relate to special procedure material, and the other provisions of the Act so far as they relate to those provisions, shall apply for the purposes of Department of Business, Enterprise and Regulatory Reform investigations as they apply for the purposes of investigations conducted by police officers: art.3(1). Article 3(2) provides that the investigations for the purpose of which those provisions are applied by this order include investigations of offences committed, or suspected of having been committed, before the coming into force of the order or of section 114A of the Act. The order came into force on October 14, 2002.

(10) Special police forces

Section 30 of the *Police Act* 1996 provides that a member of a police force shall have all the powers and privileges of a constable throughout England and Wales and the adjacent United Kingdom waters. A special constable has all the powers and privileges of a constable in the police area for which he is appointed: s.30(2). Section 101(1) provides that in the 1996 Act, except where the context otherwise requires, "police force" means a force maintained by a police authority; "police authority" is itself defined as the authority established under section 3, in relation to a police area listed in Schedule 1, the Secretary of State, in relation to the metropolitan police district, and the Common Council, in relation to the City of London police area. **15–47**

Apart from the ordinary police forces, *i.e.* those maintained by a police authority, the appointment of special police forces for specific limited purposes is authorised by a number of statutory provisions. Constables belonging to such a special police force have the powers of a constable, but only when acting within the limits of their jurisdiction. Thus there are docks and harbour police, transport police, airport police and university police. In addition, the powers of a constable are in certain circumstances conferred on persons who are not constables at all, but only for specific purposes: see the *Salmon and Freshwater Fisheries Act* 1975, s.36(1), (2). For a full list of such special police forces and powers, see *Halsbury's Statutes*, 4th ed., Vol. 33(2) (2007 Reissue), pp. 27–29.

One of the most important of the special police forces is the defence police: see the *Ministry of Defence Police Act* 1987.

B. STOP AND SEARCH

(1) Police and Criminal Evidence Act 1984, Pt I (ss.1–7)

Section 1 of the *PACE Act* 1984 creates a uniform power to stop and search in England and Wales. It does not, however, replace all other statutory powers of stop and search, for example, under the *Firearms Act* 1968, s.47(3) (*post*, § 24–79); the *Misuse of Drugs Act* 1971, s.23(2) (*post*, § 27–102); the *Terrorism Act* 2000, s.43 (*post*, § 25–87); and the *Aviation Security Act* 1982, ss.13(3) and 24B. As a general power, it has now been supplemented by the *CJPOA* 1994, s.60 (*post*, § 15–65). **15–48**

Sections 2 and 3, coupled with the Code of Practice for the Exercise by Police Officers of Statutory Powers of Stop and Search (Code A, see Appendix A–2 *et seq.*), set out the safeguards required under the 1984 Act, and for almost all other stop and search provisions.

Police and Criminal Evidence Act 1984, s.1

Power of constable to stop, search persons, vehicles etc.

1.—(1) A constable may exercise any power conferred by this section— **15–49**

(a) in any place to which at the time when he proposes to exercise the power the public or any section of the public has access, on payment or otherwise, as of right or by virtue of express or implied permission; or

(b) in any other place to which people have ready access at the time when he proposes to exercise the power but which is not a dwelling.

(2) Subject to subsections (3) to (5) below, a constable—

(a) may search

(i) any person or vehicle;

(ii) anything which is in or on a vehicle,

for stolen or prohibited articles, any article to which subsection (8A) below applies or any firework to which subsection (8B) below applies; and

(b) may detain a person or vehicle for the purpose of such a search.

(3) This section does not give a constable power to search a person or vehicle or anything in or on a vehicle unless he has reasonable grounds for suspecting that he will find stolen or prohibited articles, any article to which subsection (8A) below applies or any firework to which subsection (8B) below applies.

(4) If a person is in a garden or yard occupied with and used for the purposes of a dwelling or on other land so occupied and used, a constable may not search him in the exercise of the power conferred by this section unless the constable has reasonable grounds for believing—

(a) that he does not reside in the dwelling; and

(b) that he is not in the place in question with the express or implied permission of a person who resides in the dwelling.

15–50 (5) If a vehicle is in a garden or yard occupied with and used for the purposes of a dwelling or on other land so occupied and used, a constable may not search the vehicle or anything in or on it in the exercise of the power conferred by this section unless he has reasonable grounds for believing—

(a) that the person in charge of the vehicle does not reside in the dwelling; and

(b) that the vehicle is not in the place in question with the express or implied permission of a person who resides in the dwelling.

(6) If in the course of such a search a constable discovers an article which he has reasonable grounds for suspecting to be a stolen or prohibited article, an article to which subsection (8A) below applies or a firework to which subsection (8B) below applies, he may seize it.

(7) An article is prohibited for the purposes of this Part of this Act if it is—

(a) an offensive weapon; or

(b) an article—

(i) made or adapted for use in the course of or in connection with an offence to which this sub-paragraph applies; or

(ii) intended by the person having it with him for such use by him or by some other person.

15–51 (8) The offences to which subsection (7)(b)(i) above applies are—

(a) burglary;

(b) theft;

(c) offences under section 12 of the *Theft Act* (taking motor vehicle or other conveyance without authority);

(d) fraud (contrary to section 1 of the *Fraud Act* 2006); and

(e) offences under section 1 of the *Criminal Damage Act* 1971 (destroying or damaging property).

(8A) This subsection applies to any article in relation to which a person has committed, or is committing or is going to commit an offence under section 139 of the *Criminal Justice Act* 1988.

(8B) This subsection applies to any firework which a person possesses in contravention of a prohibition imposed by fireworks regulations.

(8C) In this section—

(a) "firework" shall be construed in accordance with the definition of "fireworks" in section 1(1) of the *Fireworks Act* 2003; and

(b) "fireworks regulations" has the same meaning as in that Act.

(9) In this Part of this Act "offensive weapon" means any article—

(a) made or adapted for use for causing injury to persons; or

(b) intended by the person having it with him for such use by him or by some other person.

[This section is printed as amended, and repealed in part, by the *CJA* 1988, s.140; the *CJA* 2003, ss.1 and 332, and Sched. 37, Pt 1; the *SOCPA* 2005, s.115; and the *Fraud Act* 2006, s.14(1), and Sched. 1, para. 21.]

Every police officer in England and Wales of whatever rank holds the office of constable: *Lewis v. Cattle* [1938] 2 K.B. 454 at 457, DC.

As to "reasonable grounds for suspecting", see *ante*, § 15–23.

As to section 139 of the *CJA* 1988, see *post*, § 24–125.

Police and Criminal Evidence Act 1984, s.2

Provisions relating to search under section 1 and other powers

2.—(1) A constable who detains a person or vehicle in the exercise— 15–52

(a) of the power conferred by section 1 above, or

(b) of any other power—

(i) to search a person without first arresting him; or

(ii) to search a vehicle without making an arrest,

need not conduct a search if it appears to him subsequently—

(i) that no search is required; or

(ii) that a search is impracticable.

(2) If a constable contemplates a search, other than a search of an unattended vehicle, in the exercise—

(a) of the power conferred by section 1 above; or

(b) of any other power, except the power conferred by section 6 below and the power conferred by section 27(2) of the *Aviation Security Act* 1982—

(i) to search a person without first arresting him; or

(ii) to search a vehicle without making an arrest,

it shall be his duty, subject to subsection (4) below, to take reasonable steps before he commences the search to bring to the attention of the appropriate person—

(i) if the constable is not in uniform, documentary evidence that he is a constable; and

(ii) whether he is in uniform or not, the matters specified in subsection (3) below;

and the constable shall not commence the search until he has performed that duty.

(3) The matters referred to in subsection (2)(ii) above are— 15–53

(a) the constable's name and the name of the police station to which he is attached;

(b) the object of the proposed search;

(c) the constable's grounds for proposing to make it; and

(d) the effect of section 3(7) or (8) below, as may be appropriate.

(4) A constable need not bring the effect of section 3(7) or (8) below to the attention of the appropriate person if it appears to the constable that it will not be practicable to make the record in section 3(1) below.

(5) In this section "the appropriate person" means—

(a) if the constable proposes to search a person, that person; and

(b) if he proposes to search a vehicle, or anything in or on a vehicle, the person in charge of the vehicle.

(6) On completing a search of an unattended vehicle or anything in or on such a vehicle in the exercise of any such power as is mentioned in subsection (2) above a constable shall leave a notice—

(a) stating that he has searched it;

(b) giving the name of the police station to which he is attached;

(c) stating that an application for compensation for any damage caused by the search may be made to that police station; and

(d) stating the effect of section 3(8) below.

(7) The constable shall leave the notice inside the vehicle unless it is not reasonably practicable to do so without damaging the vehicle.

(8) The time for which a person or vehicle may be detained for the purposes of such a search is such time as is reasonably required to permit a search to be carried out either at the place where the person or vehicle was first detained or nearby. 15–54

(9) Neither the power conferred by section 1 above nor any other power to detain and search a person without first arresting him or to detain and search a vehicle without making an arrest is to be construed—

(a) as authorising a constable to require a person to remove any of his clothing in public other than an outer coat, jacket or gloves; or

(b) as authorising a constable not in uniform to stop a vehicle.

(10) This section and section 1 above apply to vessels, aircraft and hovercraft as they apply to vehicles.

Where a constable purports to search a person in the exercise of a power to search him without first arresting him, a failure to give the person the information required by section 2(3) will render the search unlawful and take him outside the execution of his duty: *Osman v. DPP*, 163 J.P. 725, DC, followed in *R. (Bonner) v. DPP* [2005] A.C.D. 56, QBD (McCombe J.), *R. v. Bristol*, 172 J.P. 161, CA, and *B. v. DPP*, 172 J.P. 449, DC (duty of plain-clothes officer to produce documentary evidence applies even where he is well-known to the person to be searched).

As to the admissibility of evidence obtained in consequence of an unlawful search, see *post*, § 15–525.

Police and Criminal Evidence Act 1984, s.3

Duty to make records concerning searches

15–55 **3.**—(1) Where a constable has carried out a search in the exercise of any such power as is mentioned in section 2(1) above, other than a search—

(a) under section 6 below; or

(b) under section 27(2) of the *Aviation Security Act* 1982,

he shall make a record of it in writing unless it is not practicable to do so.

(2) If—

(a) a constable is required by subsection (1) above to make a record of a search; but

(b) it is not practicable to make the record on the spot,

he shall make it as soon as practicable after the completion of the search.

(3) The record of a search of a person shall include a note of his name, if the constable knows it, but a constable may not detain a person to find out his name.

(4) If a constable does not know the name of a person whom he has searched, the record of the search shall include a note otherwise describing that person.

(5) The record of a search of a vehicle shall include a note describing the vehicle.

15–56 (6) The record of a search of a person or a vehicle—

(a) shall state—

(i) the object of the search;

(ii) the grounds for making it;

(iii) the date and time when it was made;

(iv) the place where it was made;

(v) whether anything, and if so what, was found;

(vi) whether any, and if so what, injury to a person or damage to property appears to the constable to have resulted from the search; and

(b) shall identify the constable making it.

(7) If a constable who conducted a search of a person made a record of it, the person who was searched shall be entitled to a copy of the record if he asks for one before the end of the period specified in subsection (9) below.

(8) If—

(a) the owner of a vehicle which has been searched or the person who was in charge of the vehicle at the time when it was searched asks for a copy of the record of the search before the end of the period specified in subsection (9) below; and

(b) the constable who conducted the search made a record of it,

the person who made the request shall be entitled to a copy.

(9) The period mentioned in subsections (7) and (8) above is the period of 12 months beginning with the date on which the search was made.

(10) The requirements imposed by this section with regard to records of searches of vehicles shall apply also to records of searches of vessels, aircraft and hovercraft.

Police and Criminal Evidence Act 1984, s.4

Road checks

15–57 **4.**—(1) This section shall have effect in relation to the conduct of road checks by police officers for the purpose of ascertaining whether a vehicle is carrying—

(a) a person who has committed an offence other than a road traffic or a vehicle excise offence;

(b) a person who is a witness to such an offence;

(c) a person intending to commit such an offence; or

(d) a person who is unlawfully at large.

(2) For the purposes of this section a road check consists of the exercise in a locality of the power conferred by section 163 of the *Road Traffic Act* 1988 in such away as to stop during the period for which its exercise in that way in that locality continues all vehicles or vehicles selected by any criterion.

(3) Subject to subsection (5) below, there may only be such a road check if a police officer of the rank of superintendent or above authorises it in writing.

(4) An officer may only authorise a road check under subsection (3) above— **15–58**

(a) for the purpose specified in subsection (1)(a) above, if he has reasonable grounds—

(i) for believing that the offence is an indictable offence; and

(ii) for suspecting that the person is, or is about to be, in the locality in which vehicles would be stopped if the road check were authorised;

(b) for the purpose specified in subsection (1)(b) above, if he has reasonable grounds for believing that the offence is an indictable offence;

(c) for the purpose specified in subsection (1)(c) above, if he has reasonable grounds—

(i) for believing that the offence would be an indictable offence; and

(ii) for suspecting that the person is, or is about to be, in the locality in which vehicles would be stopped if the road check were authorised;

(d) for the purpose specified in subsection (1)(d) above, if he has reasonable grounds for suspecting that the person is, or is about to be, in that locality.

(5) An officer below the rank of superintendent may authorise such a road check if it appears to him that it is required as a matter of urgency for one of the purposes specified in subsection (1) above. **15–59**

(6) If an authorisation is given under subsection (5) above, it shall be the duty of the officer who gives it—

(a) to make a written record of the time at which he gives it; and

(b) to cause an officer of the rank of superintendent or above to be informed that it has been given.

(7) The duties imposed by subsection (6) above shall be performed as soon as it is practicable to do so.

(8) An officer to whom a report is made under subsection (6) above may, in writing, authorise the road check to continue.

(9) If such an officer considers that the road check should not continue, he shall record in writing—

(a) the fact that it took place; and

(b) the purpose for which it took place.

(10) An officer giving an authorisation under this section shall specify the locality in which vehicles are to be stopped.

(11) An officer giving an authorisation under this section, other than an authorisation under subsection (5) above—

(a) shall specify a period, not exceeding seven days, during which the road check may continue; and

(b) may direct that the road check—

(i) shall be continuous; or

(ii) shall be conducted at specified times,

during that period.

(12) If it appears to an officer of the rank of superintendent or above that a road check ought to continue beyond the period for which it has been authorised he may, from time to time, in writing specify a further period, not exceeding seven days, during which it may continue. **15–60**

(13) Every written authorisation shall specify—

(a) the name of the officer giving it;

(b) the purpose of the road check; and

(c) the locality in which vehicles are to be stopped.

(14) The duties to specify the purposes of a road check imposed by subsections (9) and (13) above include duties to specify any relevant indictable offence.

(15) Where a vehicle is stopped in a road check, the person in charge of the vehicle at

the time when it is stopped shall be entitled to obtain a written statement of the purpose of the road check if he applies for such a statement not later than the end of the period of twelve months from the day on which the vehicle was stopped.

(16) Nothing in this section affects the exercise by police officers of any power to stop vehicles for purposes other than those specified in subsection (1) above.

[This section is printed as amended by the *Road Traffic (Consequential Provisions) Act* 1988, s.4, and Sched. 3, para. 27(1); and the *SOCPA* 2005, s.111, and Sched. 7, para. 43(1) and (2).]

15–61 There is no general police power to set up road blocks. Apart from section 4, specific powers to stop vehicles include:

(a) the *RTA* 1988, s.163 (*post*, § 32–136);
(b) the *CJPOA* 1994, s.60 (*post*, § 15–65);
(c) the *Terrorism Act* 2000, s.44 (*post*, § 25–88);
(d) common law powers of constables to control traffic on public roads (see *Johnson v. Phillips* [1976] 1 W.L.R. 65, DC), and to stop and turn back motor vehicles on reasonable grounds for apprehending an imminent breach of the peace (*R. (Laporte) v. Chief Constable of Gloucestershire Constabulary* [2007] 2 A.C. 105, HL ("imminent" meaning "about to happen")).

15–62 Section 4(2) specifically states that the road check is no more than the exercise in a locality of the power under section 163 of the *RTA* 1988. Section 163 (*post*, § 32–136) is the power most often used to stop vehicles. It provides that a constable in uniform may stop a person driving (or cycling) on a road. No specific purpose for stopping the vehicle need be stated by the constable. Failure to comply is a criminal offence (s.163(3)). The constable is entitled to detain the vehicle for a reasonable time so as to enable him, if he suspects the vehicle to be stolen, to effect an arrest and explain to the driver the reason for the arrest: *Lodwick v. Saunders*, 80 Cr.App.R. 304, DC.

Neither section 163 nor section 4 confers a power to search the vehicle. Any search must therefore come within the provisions of section 1 of the *PACE Act* 1984 (stop and search, *ante*, § 15–49) or of some other specific statutory power (*e.g.* the *Misuse of Drugs Act* 1971, s.23, *post*, § 27–102).

Police and Criminal Evidence Act 1984, ss.6, 7

Statutory undertakers, etc.

15–63 **6.**—(1) A constable employed by statutory undertakers may stop, detain and search any vehicle before it leaves a goods area included in the premises of the statutory undertakers.

(1A) Without prejudice to any powers under subsection (1) above, a constable employed by the British Transport Police Authority may stop, detain and search any vehicle before it leaves a goods area which is included in the premises of any successor of the British Railways Board and is used wholly or mainly for the purposes of a relevant undertaking.

(2) In this section "goods area" means any area used wholly or mainly for the storage or handling of goods; and "successor of the British Railways Board" and "relevant undertaking" have the same meanings as in the *Railways Act 1993 (Consequential Modifications) Order* 1999.

(3) For the purposes of section 6 of the *Public Stores Act* 1875, any person appointed under the *Special Constables Act* 1923 to be a special constable within any premises which are in the possession or under the control of British Nuclear Fuels Limited shall be deemed to be a constable deputed by a public department and any goods and chattels belonging to or in the possession of British Nuclear Fuels Limited shall be deemed to be Her Majesty's Stores.

(4) [*Application of subsection (3) to Northern Ireland.*]

[This section is printed as amended by the *Railways Act 1993 (Consequential Modifications) Order* 1999 (S.I. 1999 No. 1998); the *Transport Act* 2000, s.217, and Sched. 18, para. 5; and the *British Transport Police (Transitional and Consequential Provisions) Order* 2004 (S.I. 2004 No. 1573), art. 12(1)(e) (purporting to amend subs. (1), but in fact amending subs. (1A)).]

Part I—supplementary

15–64 **7.**—(1) [*Repeals of particular enactments.*]

(2) There shall also cease to have effect—

(a) so much of any enactment contained in an Act passed before 1974, other than—
   (i) an enactment contained in a public general Act; or
   (ii) an enactment relating to statutory undertakers,
 as confers power on a constable to search for stolen or unlawfully obtained goods; and

(b) so much of any enactment relating to statutory undertakers as provides that such a power shall not be exercisable after the end of a specified period.

(3) In this Part of this Act "statutory undertakers" means persons authorised by any enactment to carry on any railway, light railway, road transport, water transport, canal, inland navigation, dock or harbour undertaking.

(2) Criminal Justice and Public Order Act 1994

Criminal Justice and Public Order Act 1994, s.60

Powers to stop and search in anticipation of, or after, violence

60.—(1) If a police officer of or above the rank of inspector reasonably believes— **15–65**

(a) that incidents involving serious violence may take place in any locality in his police area, and that it is expedient to give an authorisation under this section to prevent their occurrence,

(aa) that—
   (i) an incident involving serious violence has taken place in England and Wales in his police area;
   (ii) a dangerous instrument or offensive weapon used in the incident is being carried in any locality in his police area by a person; and
   (iii) it is expedient to give an authorisation under this section to find the instrument or weapon; or

(b) that persons are carrying dangerous instruments or offensive weapons in any locality in his police area without good reason,

he may give an authorisation that the powers conferred by this section are to be exercisable at any place within that locality for a specified period not exceeding 24 hours.

(2) [*Repealed by* Knives Act *1997, s.8*.]

(3) If it appears to an officer of or above the rank of superintendent that it is expedient to do so, having regard to offences which have, or are reasonably suspected to have, been committed in connection with any activity falling within the authorisation, he may direct that the authorisation shall continue in being for a further 24 hours.

(3A) If an inspector gives an authorisation under subsection (1) he must, as soon as it is practicable to do so, cause an officer of or above the rank of superintendent to be informed.

(4) This section confers on any constable in uniform power—

(a) to stop any pedestrian and search him or anything carried by him for offensive weapons or dangerous instruments;

(b) to stop any vehicle and search the vehicle, its driver and any passenger for offensive weapons or dangerous instruments.

(4A) [*Repealed by* Anti-terrorism, Crime and Security Act *2001, s.125 and Sched. 8*.] **15–66**

(5) A constable may, in the exercise of the powers conferred by subsection (4) above, stop any person or vehicle and make any search he thinks fit whether or not he has any grounds for suspecting that the person or vehicle is carrying weapons or articles of that kind.

(6) If in the course of a search under this section a constable discovers a dangerous instrument or an article which he has reasonable grounds for suspecting to be an offensive weapon, he may seize it.

(7) This section applies (with the necessary modifications) to ships, aircraft and hovercraft as it applies to vehicles.

(8) A person who fails

(a) to stop, or to stop a vehicle;

(b) [*repealed by* Anti-terrorism, Crime and Security Act *2001, s.125 and Sched. 8*]

when required to do so by a constable in the exercise of his powers under this section shall be liable on summary conviction to imprisonment for a term not exceeding *one month* [51 weeks] or to a fine not exceeding level 3 on the standard scale or both.

(9) Subject to subsection (9ZA), any authorisation under this section shall be in writing signed by the officer giving it and shall specify [the grounds on which it is given and] the locality in which and the period during which the powers conferred by this section are

exercisable and a direction under subsection (3) shall also be given in writing or, where that is not practicable, recorded in writing as soon as it is practicable to do so.

(9ZA) An authorisation under subsection (1)(aa) need not be given in writing where it is not practicable to do so but any oral authorisation must state the matters which would otherwise have to be specified under subsection (9) and must be recorded in writing as soon as it is practicable to do so.

(9A) The preceding provisions of this section, so far as they relate to an authorisation by a member of the British Transport Police Force (including one who for the time being has the same powers and privileges as a member of a police force for a police area), shall have effect as if the references to a locality in his police area were references to a place in England and Wales specified in section 31(1)(a) to (f) of the *Railways and Transport Safety Act* 2003 and as if the reference in subsection (1)(aa)(i) above to his police area were a reference to any place falling within section 31(1)(a) to (f) of the Act of 2003.

(10) Where a vehicle is stopped by a constable under this section, the driver shall be entitled to obtain a written statement that the vehicle was stopped under the powers conferred by this section if he applies for such a statement not later than the end of the period of twelve months from the day on which the vehicle was stopped ….

(10A) A person who is searched by a constable under this section shall be entitled to obtain a written statement that he was searched under the powers conferred by this section if he applies for such a statement not later than the end of the period of twelve months from the day on which he was searched.

15–67 (11) In this section—

"dangerous instruments" means instruments which have a blade or are sharply pointed;

"offensive weapon" has the meaning given by section 19 of the *Police and Criminal Evidence Act* 1984 or, in relation to Scotland, section 47(4) of the *Criminal Law (Consolidation) (Scotland) Act* 1995; but in subsections (1)(aa), (4), (5) and (6) above and subsection (11A) below includes, in the case of an incident of the kind mentioned in subsection (1)(aa)(i) above, any article used in the incident to cause or threaten injury to any person or otherwise to intimidate; and

"vehicle" includes a caravan as defined in section 29(1) of the *Caravan Sites and Control of Development Act* 1960.

(11A) For the purposes of this section, a person carries a dangerous instrument or an offensive weapon if he has it in his possession.

(12) The powers conferred by this section are in addition to and not in derogation of, any power otherwise conferred.

[This section is printed as amended and repealed in part by the *Knives Act* 1997, s.8; the *CDA* 1998, s.25; the *Anti-Terrorism, Crime and Security Act* 2001, ss.101 and 125, Sched. 7, paras 15 and 16, and Sched. 8; the *Railways and Transport Safety Act* 2003, s.73(1), and Sched. 5, para. 4(1) and (2)(f); the *British Transport Police (Transitional and Consequential Provisions) Order* 2004 (S.I. 2004 No. 1573), art. 12(3)(a); and the *SCA* 2007, s.87; and, as from a day to be appointed, by the *CJA* 2003, s.280(2), and Sched. 26, para. 45(1) and (2) (substitution of words in square brackets for italicised words in subs. (8)); but this amendment does not affect the penalty for an offence committed before it takes effect: *ibid.*, s.280(3).]

Criminal Justice and Public Order Act 1994, s.60AA

Powers to require removal of disguises

15–67a **60AA.**—(1) Where—

(a) an authorisation under section 60 is for the time being in force in relation to any locality for any period, or

(b) an authorisation under subsection (3) that the powers conferred by subsection (2) shall be exercisable at any place in a locality is in force for any period,

those powers shall be exercisable at any place in that locality at any time in that period.

(2) This subsection confers power on any constable in uniform—

(a) to require any person to remove any item which the constable reasonably believes that person is wearing wholly or mainly for the purpose of concealing his identity;

(b) to seize any item which the constable reasonably believes any person intends to wear wholly or mainly for that purpose.

(3) If a police officer of or above the rank of inspector reasonably believes—

(a) that activities may take place in any locality in his police area that are likely (if they take place) to involve the commission of offences, and

(b) that it is expedient, in order to prevent or control the activities, to give an authorisation under this subsection,

he may give an authorisation that the powers conferred by this section shall be exercisable at any place within that locality for a specified period not exceeding twenty-four hours.

(4) If it appears to an officer of or above the rank of superintendent that it is expedient to do so, having regard to offences which—

(a) have been committed in connection with the activities in respect of which the authorisation was given, or

(b) are reasonably suspected to have been so committed,

he may direct that the authorisation shall continue in force for a further twenty-four hours.

(5) If an inspector gives an authorisation under subsection (3), he must, as soon as it is practicable to do so, cause an officer of or above the rank of superintendent to be informed.

(6) Any authorisation under this section—

(a) shall be in writing and signed by the officer giving it; and

(b) shall specify—

(i) the grounds on which it is given;

(ii) the locality in which the powers conferred by this section are exercisable;

(iii) the period during which those powers are exercisable;

and a direction under subsection (4) shall also be given in writing or, where that is not practicable, recorded in writing as soon as it is practicable to do so.

(7) A person who fails to remove an item worn by him when required to do so by a constable in the exercise of his power under this section shall be liable, on summary conviction, to imprisonment for a term not exceeding *one month* [51 weeks] or to a fine not exceeding level 3 on the standard scale or both.

(8) The preceding provisions of this section, so far as they relate to an authorisation by a member of the British Transport Police Force (including one who for the time being has the same powers and privileges as a member of a police force for a police area), shall have effect as if references to a locality or to a locality in his police area were references to any locality in or in the vicinity of any policed premises, or to the whole or any part of any such premises.

(9) [*Repealed by* Railways and Transport Safety Act *2003, s.73 , and Sched. 5, para. 4(1) and (2)(f).*]

(10) The powers conferred by this section are in addition to, and not in derogation of, any power otherwise conferred.

(11) This section does not extend to Scotland.

[This section was inserted by the *Anti-terrorism, Crime and Security Act* 2001, s.94(1). It is printed as amended, as from a day to be appointed, by the *CJA* 2003, s.280(2), and Sched. 26, para. 45(1) and (3) (substitution of words in square brackets for italicised words); but this amendment does not affect the penalty for an offence committed before it takes effect: *ibid.*, s.280(3).]

A police officer asking a person to remove a mask pursuant to section 60(4A) (now repealed, but the reasoning presumably applies to section 60AA(2)) is not performing a search pursuant to the *PACE Act* 1984, s.2: *DPP v. Avery* [2002] 1 Cr.App.R. 31, DC.

Retention and disposal of things seized under section 60

Section 60A of the *CJPOA* 1994 (as amended by the *Anti-terrorism, Crime and Security Act* 2001, s.94(2)) provides that things seized under section 60 or section 60AA may be retained in accordance with regulations made by the Secretary of State. **15–67b**

(3) Code of practice

For the codes of practice generally, see *ante*, §§ 15–3 *et seq.* The current Code A came into force on February 1, 2008, replacing the version which came into force on January 1, 2006 (and which was revised with effect from August 31, 2006). It applies to any search commencing after midnight on January 31, 2008. **15–68**

[For the full text of Code A, see Appendix A–3 *et seq.*]

C. ENTRY, SEARCH AND SEIZURE

(1) Introduction

15–69 Part II of the *PACE Act* 1984 (ss.8–23) consolidates many, but not all, police powers of entry, search and seizure. It enacts provisions relating to search warrants, privileged material (ss.8–16), and seizure (ss.19–22). Section 8 creates a general power to obtain a search warrant in the case of an indictable offence. Sections 15 (search warrants—safeguards), 16 (execution of warrants) and 19 (general power of seizure), relate to all powers of entry including those not repealed by the 1984 Act. These include a variety of statutes authorising a justice of the peace to issue a warrant authorising a constable to search for and seize certain items and to enter premises for the purpose of doing so. Examples in this work are the *Obscene Publications Act* 1959, s.3 (*post*, § 31–84), the *Theft Act* 1968, s.26 (*post*, § 21–331) and the *Misuse of Drugs Act* 1971, s.23 (*post*, § 27–102).

15–70 The 1984 Act left unaffected a great range of other powers of entry and search conferred by primary and subordinate legislation on an equally wide range of people, but including in particular officers of Revenue and Customs and of central and local government. Almost all legislation relating to any aspect of public health or safety contains enforcement provisions, including powers of inspection, entry and search. For a list of such provisions, see Stone, *Entry, Search and Seizure* (4th ed., 2005).

15–71 The powers of seizure under the *PACE Act* 1984 and many other statutes were considerably extended by the provisions of *CJPA* 2001, Pt 2. The intention was first to remedy the problem highlighted by the decision in *R. v. Chesterfield JJ., ex p. Bramley* [2000] Q.B. 576, DC (no entitlement to seize items for purpose of sifting through them later to see whether they fall within scope of warrant), and secondly, to give the police and others power to seize and retain material which could not itself be seized but which is inextricably linked with material which is liable to be seized. The second of these purposes is peculiarly related to the difficulties encountered with modern technology and the increasing use of computers. For the text of Part 2, see *post*, §§ 15–124 *et seq*.

Guidance in relation to the new powers is included in the Code of Practice for the Searching of Premises by Police Officers and the Seizure of Property found by Police Officers on Persons or Premises (Code B): see paras B:7.7 *et seq*. (Appendix A–33).

As to entry on or interference with property for the purpose of preventing or detecting serious crime under the *Police Act* 1997, see *post*, § 15–252. As to entry under a warrant to search for and seize documents required under a disclosure notice issued pursuant to the *SOCPA* 2005, see *post*, § 15–338.

(2) Statute

Police and Criminal Evidence Act 1984, s.8

Power of justice of the peace to authorise entry and search of premises

15–72 **8.**—(1) If on an application made by a constable a justice of the peace is satisfied that there are reasonable grounds for believing—

(a) that an indictable offence has been committed; and

(b) that there is material on premises mentioned in subsection (1A) below which is likely to be of substantial value (whether by itself or together with other material) to the investigation of the offence; and

(c) that the material is likely to be relevant evidence; and

(d) that it does not consist of or include items subject to legal privilege, excluded material or special procedure material; and

(e) that any of the conditions specified in subsection (3) below applies in relation to each set of premises specified in the application,

he may issue a warrant authorising a constable to enter and search the premises.

(1A) The premises referred to in subsection (1)(b) above are—

(a) one or more sets of premises specified in the application (in which case the application is for a "specific premises warrant"); or

(b) any premises occupied or controlled by a person specified in the application, including such sets of premises as are so specified (in which case the application is for an "all premises warrant").

(1B) If the application is for an all premises warrant, the justice of the peace must also be satisfied—

(a) that because of the particulars of the offence referred to in paragraph (a) of subsection (1) above, there are reasonable grounds for believing that it is necessary to search premises occupied or controlled by the person in question which are not specified in the application in order to find the material referred to in paragraph (b) of that subsection; and

(b) that it is not reasonably practicable to specify in the application all the premises which he occupies or controls and which might need to be searched.

(1C) The warrant may authorise entry to and search of premises on more than one occasion if, on the application, the justice of the peace is satisfied that it is necessary to authorise multiple entries in order to achieve the purpose for which he issues the warrant.

(1D) If it authorises multiple entries, the number of entries authorised may be unlimited, or limited to a maximum.

(2) A constable may seize and retain anything for which a search has been authorised under subsection (1) above.

(3) The conditions mentioned in subsection (1)(e) above are—

(a) that it is not practicable to communicate with any person entitled to grant entry to the premises;

(b) that it is practicable to communicate with a person entitled to grant entry to the premises but it is not practicable to communicate with any person entitled to grant access to the evidence;

(c) that entry to the premises will not be granted unless a warrant is produced;

(d) that the purpose of a search may be frustrated or seriously prejudiced unless a constable arriving at the premises can secure immediate entry to them.

(4) In this Act "relevant evidence", in relation to an offence, means anything that would be admissible in evidence at a trial for the offence.

(5) The power to issue a warrant conferred by this section is in addition to any such power otherwise conferred.

(6) This section applies in relation to a relevant offence (as defined in section 28D(4) of the *Immigration Act* 1971) as it applies to an indictable offence.

(7) Section 4 of the *Summary Jurisdiction (Process) Act* 1881 (execution of process of English courts in Scotland) shall apply to a warrant issued on the application of an officer of Revenue and Customs under this section by virtue of section 114 below.

[This section is printed as amended by the *Immigration and Asylum Act* 1999, s.169(1), and Sched. 14, para. 80(1) and (2); the *SOCPA* 2005, ss.111, 113(1)–(4) and 114(1) and (2), and Sched. 7, para. 43(1) and (3); and the *Finance Act* 2007, s.86.]

For the meaning of "items subject to legal privilege", see section 10, *post*, § 15–90; for "excluded material", see sections 11 to 13, *post*, §§ 15–96 *et seq.*; and for "special procedure material", see section 14, *post*, § 15–99. As to the extension of Part II so as to have effect as if the references to indictable offences in section 8 and in Schedule 1 (*post*, § 15–75) included any conduct which is an offence under the law of a country or territory outside the United Kingdom and would constitute an indictable offence if it had occurred in any part of the United Kingdom, see section 16 of the *Crime (International Co-operation) Act* 2003 (as amended by *SOCPA* 2005, s.111, and Sched. 7, para. 51(1) and (2)).

In *Redknapp v. Commr of the City of London Police and City of London Magistrates' Court (McKay, Storrie, Mandaric and Faye (interested parties))*, 172 J.P. 388, DC (see also *post*, § 15–104), it was said that obtaining a search warrant is never a formality; all the material necessary to justify the warrant's grant should be contained in the information provided on the application form; if the magistrate (or judge in the case of an application under section 9 of the 1984 Act) requires any further information to satisfy himself that the warrant is justified, a note should be made of the additional information so that there is a proper record of the full basis upon which the warrant has been granted; where the required information is not contained in the application form or in such a note, the warrant is unlawfully issued.

Before issuing a warrant under section 8, a justice has to be satisfied that the material **15–73**

9. Such a notice may be served—

(a) on a body corporate, by serving it on the body's secretary or clerk or other similar officer; and

(b) on a partnership, by serving it on one of the partners.

10. For the purposes of this Schedule, and of section 7 of the *Interpretation Act* 1978 in its application to this Schedule, the proper address of a person, in the case of secretary or clerk or other similar officer of a body corporate, shall be that of the registered or principal office of that body, in the case of a partner of a firm shall be that of the principal office of the firm, and in any other case shall be the last known address of the person to be served.

11. Where notice of an application for an order under paragraph 4 above has been served on a person, he shall not conceal, destroy, alter or dispose of the material to which the application relates except—

(a) with the leave of a judge; or

(b) with the written permission of a constable,

until—

(i) the application is dismissed or abandoned; or

(ii) he has complied with an order under paragraph 4 above made on the application.

Issue of warrants by circuit judge

15–78 12. If on an application made by a constable a *circuit* judge—

(a) is satisfied—

(i) that either set of access conditions is fulfilled; and

(ii) that any of the further conditions set out in paragraph 14 below is also fulfilled [in relation to each set of premises specified in the application]; or

(b) is satisfied—

(i) that the second set of access conditions is fulfilled; and

(ii) that an order under paragraph 4 above relating to the material has not been complied with,

he may issue a warrant authorising a constable to enter and search the premises or (as the case may be) all premises occupied or controlled by the person referred to in paragraph 2(a)(ii) or 3(a), including such sets of premises as are specified in the application (an "all premises warrant").

12A. The judge may not issue an all premises warrant unless he is satisfied—

(a) that there are reasonable grounds for believing that it is necessary to search premises occupied or controlled by the person in question which are not specified in the application, as well as those which are, in order to find the material in question; and

(b) that it is not reasonably practicable to specify all the premises which he occupies or controls which might need to be searched.

13. A constable may seize and retain anything for which a search has been authorised under paragraph 12 above.

14. The further conditions mentioned in paragraph 12(a)(ii) above are—

(a) that it is not practicable to communicate with any person entitled to grant entry to the premises;

(b) that it is practicable to communicate with a person entitled to grant entry to the premises but it is not practicable to communicate with any person entitled to grant access to the material;

(c) that the material contains information which—

(i) is subject to a restriction or obligation such as is mentioned in section 11(2)(b) above; and

(ii) is likely to be disclosed in breach of it if a warrant is not issued;

(d) that service of notice of an application for an order under paragraph 4 above may seriously prejudice the investigation.

15.—(1) If a person fails to comply with an order under paragraph 4 above, a *circuit* judge may deal with him as if he had committed a contempt of the Crown Court.

(2) Any enactment relating to contempt of the Crown Court shall have effect in relation to such a failure as if it were such a contempt.

Costs

16. The costs of any application under this Schedule and of anything done or to be done in pursuance of an order made under it shall be in the discretion of the judge.

[Interpretation

17. In this Schedule, "judge" means *a Circuit Judge* [a judge of the High Court, a Circuit judge, a Recorder] or a District Judge (Magistrates' Courts)].

[This Schedule is printed as amended and repealed in part by the *CJPA* 2001, s.70, and Sched. 2, para. 14; and the *SOCPA* 2005, ss.111, 113(1) and (10)–(15), and 174(2), Sched. 7, para. 43(1) and (13), and Sched. 17; and, as from a day to be appointed, by the *Courts Act* 2003, s.65, and Sched. 4, para. 6 (omission of references to a "circuit" judge in paras 1 to 16 and insertion of para. 17); and the *SOCPA* 2005, s.114(1) and (9) (deletion of words in italics, and insertion of words in square brackets, in para. 17).]

Procedure

A judge has a discretion to hear an application for access to excluded material or special procedure material in chambers: *R. v. Central Criminal Court, ex p. DPP, The Times*, April 1, 1988, DC. **15–79**

There is no requirement to give notice of the proceedings to the accused or suspected person. Paragraph 7 of Schedule 1 applies as between the applicant and the person or institution in whose custody special procedure material is believed to be held: *R. v. Crown Court at Leicester, ex p. DPP*, 86 Cr.App.R. 254, DC. In *R. v. Manchester Crown Court, ex p. Taylor*, 87 Cr.App.R. 358, the Divisional Court left open the question whether the suspect has any *locus standi* to complain about breaches of procedure by the applicant in relation to the respondent party who had control of the information.

As to the duty to record relevant information on the application form or in an additional note, see *Redknapp v. Commr of the City of London Police and City of London Magistrates' Court (McKay, Storrie, Mandaric and Faye (interested parties)), ante*, § 15–73.

Where it is sought to gain access to special procedure material located in the offices of a firm of solicitors, there is no rule that where it is not the firm itself that is under investigation, an application under Schedule 1 should be made on notice, albeit that should be regarded as the preferred method of procedure: *R. (Miller Gardner Solicitors) v. Minshull Street Crown Court*, unreported, December 20, 2002, DC ([2002] EWHC 3077 (Admin.)). On the assumption that Article 8 of the ECHR (*post*, § 16–101) was engaged by a search of a solicitor's office on the basis that a person's home and private life may extend, in some circumstances, to professional or business life, the matters that a judge must find established under Schedule 1 before issuing a warrant will usually ensure that the individual's Article 8 rights are fully protected: *ibid*.

It is the duty of the applicant to set out, either in the notice itself or in further documentation, such as the "information in support", a description of all that is sought to be produced: *R. v. Central Criminal Court, ex p. Adegbesan*, 84 Cr.App.R. 219, DC. But in *ex p. Taylor, ante*, it was said that whilst it was preferable that the information was given in writing, it could be given orally; it was held to be sufficient that the information was given to an employee of the recipient of the notice on an earlier occasion, the recipient being referred to that employee at the time of service of the notice. The court emphasised, however, that it was vital that the respondent should know before the order was made what he had to produce or allow access to as well as the nature of the offence being investigated. **15–80**

In *R. v. Inner London Crown Court, ex p. Baines and Baines (a Firm)* [1988] Q.B. 579, 87 Cr.App.R. 111, DC, it was held that it was not sufficient information merely to serve upon the respondent notice of intention to make the application and a copy of the proposed order. The applicant had in fact sent to the Crown Court, but not to the respondent, "an information" containing a proof of evidence by a constable to show that the conditions for making an order were satisfied. The police are not required by the Act to provide the evidence in support of the application in advance of the hearing. It is, however, wrong to send information to the Crown Court which is not sent to the respondent. A document dealing with each condition which has to be satisfied is appropriate, providing it contains no inadmissible or prejudicial material. In making the application, "compliance with strict rules of evidence is not to be expected but statements which have no substance to the prejudice of the party who is the subject of the **15–81** order sought are impermissible. They ought not to be made and if made should be ruled out by the judge" (*per* Watkins L.J. at pp. 584–5, 116). It would be open to the respondent to seek an adjournment of the hearing if evidence was given which could not be adequately responded to there and then.

As to the importance of the police making full disclosure in applying for a production order, see also *R. v. Acton Crown Court, ex p. Layton* [1993] Crim.L.R. 458, DC.

Further guidance to police officers on the question of warrants was given in *R. v. Central Criminal Court, ex p. A.J.D. Holdings* [1992] Crim.L.R. 669, DC. The court said that it is important before any search warrant is applied for that careful consideration is given to what material it is hoped a search might reveal, so as to be clear to anyone subsequently considering the lawfulness of the warrant. The application should make clear that the material sought related to the crime under investigation. A written note should be made of anything said in support of the application beyond what was set out in the written application. There should be careful briefing of the officers who were to execute the search, including how material to be searched for might be thought to relate to the crime under investigation. A power of search was a necessary but draconian power.

15–82 It is not enough for a constable simply to assert that the access conditions have been met. The judge should not make an order unless satisfied that one or other of the sets of access conditions is fulfilled: *R. v. Crown Court at Lewes, ex p. Hill*, 93 Cr.App.R. 60, DC. Once a judge has concluded under paragraph (2)(a)(i) of Schedule 1 that a serious arrestable offence has been committed, it is inconsistent to refuse an application for access to material by finding under paragraph 2(c) that it is not in the public interest that access should be given: *R. v. Crown Court at Northampton, ex p. DPP*, *ibid.* at 376, DC.

A judge does not have power under section 9 and Schedule 1 to order production of a medical report by the administrator of a hospital: *R. v. Central Criminal Court, ex p. Brown*, *The Times*, September 7, 1992, DC. Paragraph 3(b) was not satisfied, because prior to the enactment of section 9(2), no enactment would have authorised the issue of a warrant to seize the material in question.

15–83 In *R. v. Preston Crown Court, ex p. McGrath*, *The Times*, October 27, 1992, DC, it was held that, where the material the subject of the application is mixed in that it consists of special procedure material and other material, all of the material can be the subject of a special procedure order under Schedule 1. Parliament could not have intended sequential applications under Schedule 1 and section 8 (applications to a justice of the peace). However, notwithstanding the decision in *ex p. McGrath*, a judge should still have regard to the desirability of confining access to material of substantial value to, and relevant evidence in, the investigation: *R. v. Southampton Crown Court, ex p. J. and P.* [1993] Crim.L.R. 962, DC, where warrants were quashed because, *inter alia*, they were too widely drawn. The court also quashed the warrants on two other grounds, namely that they wrongly included material subject to legal privilege (*post*, § 15–90), and that in any event they should have been applied for *inter partes*. As for making the order *ex parte*, the court observed that the scheme of Schedule 1 is that applications should normally be made *inter partes* save for certain exceptions. Circuit judges have a responsibility, heaviest on an *ex parte* application, to see that the procedure is not abused. The fact that a solicitor is under investigation does not of itself justify intruding *ex parte* into his affairs and those of his clients. All the circumstances must be considered, including the seriousness of the matter being investigated, evidence already available to the police, and the extent to which the solicitor already knows of the interest in his affairs such as might cause him to destroy or interfere with documents. The judge had failed to explain his reasons for exercising, *ex parte*, such highly intrusive powers. The court recommended that judges give reasons when making such orders, notwithstanding the absence of any such requirement in the Act.

15–84 As to the heavy responsibility on the judge, see also *R. v. Maidstone Crown Court, ex p. Waitt* [1988] Crim.L.R. 384, DC (*ex parte* applications should never become a matter of common form). *Ex p. Waitt* was distinguished on the facts in *R. v. Leeds Crown Court, ex p. Switalski* [1991] C.O.D. 199, DC, in which it was said that where a search was to be made of solicitors' premises one would expect the application to be *inter partes*, but not where the firm itself was under investigation. In this context "practicable" in paragraph 14(a) bore a wider meaning than feasible or physically possible.

In *Barclays Bank plc (Trading as Barclaycard) v. Taylor* [1989] 1 W.L.R. 1066, CA (Civ. Div.), it was held that, irrespective of whether a notice under Schedule 1 to the 1984 Act is defective, an access order once made, being valid on its face, is fully effective until set aside by due process; and that since a banker's duty of confidentiality to his client is qualified by the exception of disclosure under compulsion of law, a bank which complies with an access order is not thereby in breach of its duty to its client. It was further held that since such an order could not be made by consent and the responsibility for deciding whether the access conditions were satisfied rested with the judge making the order, and since the public interest in assisting the police investigation of crime might be frustrated if the account holder knew of the application, it is not necessary for the purpose of giving business efficacy to the banker-client relationship to imply an obligation that the bank, in the absence of special circumstances known only to itself, should either oppose or probe the application or supporting evidence, or that it should inform its client of the application.

Barclays Bank v. Taylor was not referred to in *R. v. Singleton* [1995] 1 Cr.App.R. **15–85**
431, CA, in which it was held that excluded material could be disclosed voluntarily even though an application under section 9 would have been unsuccessful. This conclusion was reached on the basis of the questionable view that the person whom the duty of confidence is designed to protect is the person who has acquired or created the record, not the person to whom it relates (*i.e.* doctor as opposed to patient) (at p. 439A).

Once a circuit judge has made an *ex parte* order issuing a warrant, pursuant to paragraph 12, he has no power to review or rescind the order, even if it can be shown that he made it on an erroneous basis, having been given inaccurate or incomplete information. Instead, the aggrieved party should apply directly for judicial review: *R. v. Liverpool Crown Court, ex p. Wimpey plc* [1991] C.O.D. 370, DC. *Cf. DPP v. Channel 4, post.*

See also *R. v. Middlesex Guildhall Crown Court, ex p. Salinger* [1993] Q.B. 564, 97 Cr.App.R. 34, DC, and *DPP v. Channel 4 Television Co. Ltd* [1993] 2 All E.R. 517, DC (decisions under the *Prevention of Terrorism (Temporary Provisions) Act* 1989, Sched. 7). In the *Channel 4* case, it was held that, on an application to commit a person for contempt of court in refusing to comply with an order to produce material relating to a programme, the court could not set aside the order. Until the order was set aside by the same judge or quashed by judicial review, it had to be obeyed.

Police and the media

In *R. v. Bristol Crown Court, ex p. Bristol Press and Picture Agency Ltd*, 85 **15–86**
Cr.App.R. 190, DC, it was held that a judge, exercising his powers under Schedule 1 to order production of material for the purposes of a criminal investigation, was entitled to draw the inference that press photographs of riots were likely to be of newsworthy incidents which might be of value in a criminal investigation and to conclude that the access conditions in paragraph 2(a)(iii) and (iv) were satisfied. So far as concerns the public interest condition, set out in sub-paragraph (c), the judge had said:

> "There is a very great public interest that those guilty of crime, and particularly of serious crime involving widespread public disorder, should be brought to justice. Equally, there is a great public interest that those who are innocent but who may be suspected of crime should be cleared and, if possible, eliminated from the criminal process. Photographs that are likely to advance either of these objects are of benefit to the investigation."

The judge had concluded in favour of granting the application and it was a matter for his discretion. He had applied the right test, made no error of law, and had taken account of relevant matters only.

Relevant matters included differing aspects of the public interest: **15–87**

> "As to the public interest in sub-paragraph (c), the balancing exercise which has to be carried out is between the public interest in the investigation and prevention of crime and the public interest in the press being free to report and to photograph as much as they can of what is going on in our great cities, and particularly in the deprived areas of cities. There is also

public interest in the press being able to go about that activity in safety" (*per* Glidewell L.J. at p. 195).

15–88 A notice of application by the police for the production of special procedure material by a newspaper or television company or news agency will contain a request in the following or similar terms: "All transmitted, published, non-transmitted and/or unpublished cine film, video tape, still photographs and negatives of the [march/procession/assembly/demonstration and subsequent disturbances] which took place on [date] at/between [place(s)], which was obtained with a view to being of newsworthy interest."

An order to produce or to allow access to special procedure material is likely to include the following or similar terms:

(a) that the respondent deliver up all special procedure material in their possession to the applicant within seven days;

(b) that the applicant return to the respondent any material delivered to him pursuant to this order as soon as reasonably practicable after the conclusion of the investigation or criminal proceedings as the case may be, or as soon as practicable after it is apparent to the applicant that this material or any significant part of it will be of no value to the investigation;

(c) that the material is used only for the purposes of the applicant's criminal investigation and any resulting criminal proceedings.

Privilege against self-incrimination

15–89 Where the first set of access conditions is found to be fulfilled, the fact that compliance with the order by the person ordered to make production may involve him in incriminating himself is not *per se* a reason for not making an order: *R. (Bright) v. Central Criminal Court*; *R. (Alton) v. Same*; *R. (Rusbridger) v. Same* [2001] 1 W.L.R. 662, DC.

Interception of email

15–89a See *R. (NTL Group Ltd) v. Ipswich Crown Court* [2003] 1 Cr.App.R. 14, DC, *post*, § 25–368.

Police and Criminal Evidence Act 1984, s.10

Meaning of "items subject to legal privilege"

15–90 **10.**—(1) Subject to subsection (2) below, in this Act "items subject to legal privilege" means—

(a) communications between a professional legal adviser and his client or any person representing his client made in connection with the giving of legal advice to the client;

(b) communications between a professional legal adviser and his client or any person representing his client or between such an adviser or his client or any such representative and any other person made in connection with or in contemplation of legal proceedings and for the purposes of such proceedings; and

(c) items enclosed with or referred to in such communications and made—

(i) in connection with the giving of legal advice; or

(ii) in connection with or in contemplation of legal proceedings and for the purposes of such proceedings,

when they are in the possession of a person who is entitled to possession of them.

(2) Items held with the intention of furthering a criminal purpose are not items subject to legal privilege.

15–91 The leading case at common law, *R. v. Cox and Railton* (1884) 14 Q.B.D. 153, decided that legal professional privilege did not extend to advice given by the innocent lawyers to a client who wanted guidance in the commission of a crime or fraud. See generally *ante*, §§ 12–10 *et seq*.

In *R. v. Central Criminal Court, ex p. Francis and Francis (a Firm)* [1989] A.C. 346, the majority of the House of Lords held that section 10(2) had left the rule in *Cox and Railton* unaffected. Communications made by a client to his solicitor with the intention of furthering a criminal purpose were excluded from the protection of legal professional privilege.

The majority held that on a purposive rather than a literal construction of section 10(2), items which would otherwise come within the definition of "items subject to legal privilege" contained in section 10(1) were excluded from that definition if they were held with the intention of either the holder or any other person of furthering a criminal purpose, whether the purpose be that of the client, the solicitor or any other person.

The decision of the majority disapproved the reasoning of the Divisional Court in *R. v. Snaresbrook Crown Court, ex p. DPP*, 86 Cr.App.R. 227 (that the intention referred to in section 10(2) must be that of the holder of the item), but not necessarily the conclusion therein. Lord Goff, with whom Lord Griffiths agreed, said (at p. 392) that he was inclined to agree with the view of Glidewell L.J. in that case that the common law principle of legal professional privilege cannot be excluded, by the exception established in *Cox and Railton*, in cases where a communication is made by a client to his legal adviser regarding the conduct of his case in criminal or civil proceedings, merely because such communication is untrue and would, if acted upon, lead to the commission of the crime of perjury in such proceedings. **15–92**

On the issue of how to determine whether an item is held with the intention of furthering a criminal purpose, see *R. v. Governor of Pentonville Prison, ex p. Osman*, 90 Cr.App.R. 281, DC, *ante*, § 12–11. In relation to documents held by a solicitor acting for a defendant in pending criminal proceedings, a claim to legal professional privilege can be defeated where there is evidence of a specific agreement to pervert the course of justice, which is freestanding and independent, in the sense that it does not require any judgment to be reached in relation to the issues to be tried in the pending proceedings: *R. (Hallinan Blackburn Gittings & Nott (a firm)) v. Crown Court at Middlesex Guildhall* [2005] 1 W.L.R. 766, DC (applied in *Kuwait Airways Corp. v. Iraqi Airways Co. (No. 6)* [2005] 1 W.L.R. 2734, CA (Civ. Div.)).

In *R. v. Inner London Crown Court, ex p. Baines and Baines (a Firm)*, *ante*, § 15–81, it was held that the actual document known as the conveyance of a house and the records showing how the transaction was financed were not subject to legal privilege within section 10. They themselves did not amount to the giving of advice: however, correspondence between solicitor and client as to how a conveyancing transaction could or should be financed and successfully completed might well be privileged. A document which indicates the fact of attendance by a client upon his solicitor, the date and time thereof or the length thereof, whether in the form of an appointments diary, an attendance note or a time-sheet, is not privileged: *R. v. Manchester Crown Court, ex p. Rogers* [1999] 2 Cr.App.R. 267, DC.

In *R. v. Guildhall Magistrates' Court, ex p. Primlaks Holdings Co. (Panama) Inc.* [1990] 1 Q.B. 261, 89 Cr.App.R. 215, DC (*ante*, § 15–72), the court said that if legal privilege was lost under section 10(2), it would not necessarily follow that the material is not special procedure material on the basis that it is held subject to an express or implied undertaking as to confidence. It also said that documents which were not "made" as stated in section 10(1)(c) but which were pre-existing would not be subject to legal privilege despite being enclosed with communications referred to in paragraphs (a) and (b), but they would, prima facie, be special procedure material within section 14(2). **15–93**

A forgery made for the purpose of supporting a civil claim cannot be subject to legal privilege; "made in connection with legal proceedings" means lawfully made: *R. v. Leeds Magistrates' Court, ex p. Dumbleton* [1993] Crim.L.R. 866, DC. Nor will it become privileged by being enclosed with a communication made in connection with legal proceedings: *ibid*. A copy of such forgery could stand in no better position than the forgery itself (*Dubai Bank Ltd v. Galadari* [1990] 1 Ch. 98, CA (Civ. Div.)): *ibid*. **15–94**

In *R. v. Southampton Crown Court, ex p. J. and P.* [1993] Crim.L.R. 962, DC, the court gave the following guidance. It is necessary to balance the competing interests of the investigation of crime and the confidentiality of communications between solicitor and client. The police should draw the judge's attention to material arguably subject to legal privilege and provide him with sufficient information to reach a decision as to whether or not that material is privileged. Where there is doubt, legal advice should be obtained for the judge's assistance. It may not be possible to satisfy a judge that there are reasonable grounds for believing that every document in a file, or every file in a **15–95** category, is not legally privileged. If an investigation is relatively narrow, it should be possible to exclude privileged material with some precision.

An expert's opinion obtained at the request of solicitors to a party to litigation in circumstances to which section 10(1)(b) applied, and which is based on privileged information is itself privileged; accordingly, the opinion of a doctor instructed on behalf of a defendant charged with murder in connection with a possible defence of diminished responsibility was privileged, and whilst there was no property in a witness, the prosecution was not entitled to call the doctor to give evidence of her opinion when the defence failed to do so: *R. v. Davies*, 166 J.P. 243, CA.

Where a scientist carried out DNA tests at the request of defence solicitors on a blood sample provided by the defendant to his general practitioner for that purpose, that blood sample was "an item ... made" for the purposes of legal proceedings within section 10(1)(c): *R. v. R.* [1995] 1 Cr.App.R. 183, CA.

For the general restriction on seizure of items believed to be subject to legal privilege, see section 19(6), *post*, § 15–112.

Police and Criminal Evidence Act 1984, ss.11, 12

Meaning of "excluded material"

15–96 **11.**—(1) Subject to the following provisions of this section, in this Act "excluded material" means—

(a) personal records which a person has acquired or created in the course of any trade, business, profession or other occupation or for the purposes of any paid or unpaid office and which he holds in confidence;
(b) human tissue or tissue fluid which has been taken for the purposes of diagnosis or medical treatment and which a person holds in confidence;
(c) journalistic material which a person holds in confidence and which consists—
  (i) of documents; or
  (ii) of records other than documents.

(2) A person holds material other than journalistic material in confidence for the purposes of this section if he holds it subject—

(a) to an express or implied undertaking to hold it in confidence; or
(b) to a restriction on disclosure or an obligation of secrecy contained in any enactment, including an enactment contained in an Act passed after this Act.

(3) A person holds journalistic material in confidence for the purposes of this section if—

(a) he holds it subject to such an undertaking, restriction or obligation; and
(b) it has been continuously held (by one or more persons) subject to such an undertaking, restriction or obligation since it was first acquired or created for the purposes of journalism.

Meaning of "personal records"

15–97 **12.** In this Part of this Act "personal records" means documentary and other records concerning an individual (whether living or dead) who can be identified from them and relating—

(a) to his physical or mental health;
(b) to spiritual counselling or assistance given or to be given to him; or
(c) to counselling or assistance given or to be given to him, for the purposes of his personal welfare, by any voluntary organisation or by any individual who—
  (i) by reason of his office or occupation has responsibilities for his personal welfare; or
  (ii) by reason of an order of a court has responsibilities for his supervision.

Hospital records of patients' admission and discharge from a mental hospital are "personal records" because they are records "relating to" their "mental health": *R. v. Cardiff Crown Court, ex p. Kellam*, *The Times*, May 3, 1993, DC.

Police and Criminal Evidence Act 1984, ss.13, 14

Meaning of "journalistic material"

15–98 **13.**—(1) Subject to subsection (2) below, in this Act "journalistic material" means material acquired or created for the purposes of journalism.

(2) Material is only journalistic material for the purposes of this Act if it is in the possession of a person who acquired or created it for the purposes of journalism.

(3) A person who receives material from someone who intends that the recipient shall use it for the purposes of journalism is to be taken to have acquired it for those purposes.

Meaning of "special procedure material"

14.—(1) In this Act "special procedure material" means— 15–99

(a) material to which subsection (2) below applies; and

(b) journalistic material, other than excluded material.

(2) Subject to the following provisions of this section, this subsection applies to material, other than items subject to legal privilege and excluded material, in the possession of a person who—

(a) acquired or created it in the course of any trade, business, profession or other occupation or for the purpose of any paid or unpaid office; and

(b) holds it subject—

(i) to an express or implied undertaking to hold it in confidence; or

(ii) to a restriction or obligation such as is mentioned in section 11(2)(b) above.

(3) Where material is acquired—

(a) by an employee from his employer and in the course of his employment; or

(b) by a company from an associated company,

it is only special procedure material if it was special procedure material immediately before the acquisition.

(4) Where material is created by an employee in the course of his employment, it is only special procedure material if it would have been special procedure material had his employer created it.

(5) Where material is created by a company on behalf of an associated company, it is only special procedure material if it would have been special procedure material had the associated company created it.

(6) A company is to be treated as another's associated company for the purposes of this section if it would be so treated under section 302 of the *Income and Corporation Taxes Act* 1970.

Applications to seize special procedure material have been made frequently in relation to records held by banks and building societies, conveyancing documents held by solicitors, photographs held by newspapers and news footage held by television companies. 15–100

In *R. v. Leeds Magistrates' Court, ex p. Dumbleton*, § 15–94, *ante*, it was held that letters forged to support a civil claim which were in the possession of the claimant's solicitor could not be special procedure material because from their nature they could not have been acquired or created in the course of the profession of a solicitor. Parliament cannot have intended to protect forged documents on the grounds that they were forged by a solicitor or supplied to him by a fraudulent client. Furthermore, a dishonest solicitor could not be said to hold a forged document subject to an express or implied undertaking to hold it in confidence, there being no confidence in iniquity.

For section 14A, which relates only to investigations by officers of Revenue and Customs of offences relating to assigned matters, see *ante*, § 15–40.

Police and Criminal Evidence Act 1984, ss.15, 16

Search warrants—safeguards

15.—(1) This section and section 16 below have effect in relation to the issue to constables under any enactment, including an enactment contained in an Act passed after this Act, of warrants to enter and search premises; and an entry on or search of premises under a warrant is unlawful unless it complies with this section and section 16 below. 15–101

(2) Where a constable applies for any such warrant, it shall be his duty—

(a) to state—

(i) the ground on which he makes the application;

(ii) the enactment under which the warrant would be issued;

(iii) if the application is for a warrant authorising entry and search on more than one occasion, the ground on which he applies for such a warrant, and whether he seeks a warrant authorising an unlimited number of entries, or (if not) the maximum number of entries desired;

(b) to specify the matters set out in subsection (2A) below; and

(c) to identify, so far as is practicable, the articles or persons to be sought.

(2A) The matters which must be specified pursuant to subsection (2)(b) above are—

(a) if the application relates to one or more sets of premises specified in the application, each set of premises which it is desired to enter and search;

(b) if the application relates to any premises occupied or controlled by a person specified in the application—

(i) as many sets of premises which it is desired to enter and search as it is reasonably practicable to specify;

(ii) the person who is in occupation or control of those premises and any others which it is desired to enter and search;

(iii) why it is necessary to search more premises than those specified under sub-paragraph (i); and

(iv) why it is not reasonably practicable to specify all the premises which it is desired to enter and search.

(3) An application for such a warrant shall be made *ex parte* and supported by an information in writing.

(4) The constable shall answer on oath any question that the justice of the peace or judge hearing the application asks him.

(5) A warrant shall authorise an entry on one occasion only unless it specifies that it authorises multiple entries.

(5A) If it specifies that it authorises multiple entries, it must also specify whether the number of entries authorised is unlimited, or limited to a specified maximum.

(6) A warrant—

(a) shall specify—

(i) the name of the person who applies for it;

(ii) the date on which it is issued;

(iii) the enactment under which it is issued; and

(iv) each set of premises to be searched, or (in the case of an all premises warrant) the person who is in occupation or control of premises to be searched, together with any premises under his occupation or control which can be specified and which are to be searched; and

(b) shall identify, so far as is practicable, the articles or persons to be sought.

(7) Two copies shall be made of a warrant which specifies only one set of premises and does not authorise multiple entries; and as many copies as are reasonably required may be made of any other kind of warrant.

(8) The copies shall be clearly certified as copies.

[This section is printed as amended and repealed in part by the *SOCPA* 2005, ss.113(1) and (5)–(8), 114(1) and (3)–(7), and 174(2), and Sched. 17; and the *Serious Organised Crime and Police Act 2005 (Amendment) Order* 2005 (S.I. 2005 No. 3496).]

Subject to modifications, sections 15 and 16 (*post*, § 15–102) of the 1984 Act have effect in relation to the issue of a warrant under section 19(4) or 23(1) of the *Animal Welfare Act* 2006: see the 2006 Act, s.53, and Sched. 2, para. 1.

As to the documents or information upon the strength of which search warrants are obtained being protected by public interest immunity, see *Taylor v. Anderton*, *The Times*, October 16, 1986, Ch D.

In *R. v. Longman*, 88 Cr.App.R. 148, CA, the court expressed the view that the word "it" in section 15(1) referred to the warrant rather than the entry or search. Their Lordships thought (see p. 152) that the real intention had probably been to provide that the warrant should comply with section 15 and the entry and search should comply with section 16. Although they said they were leaving the point unresolved (see p. 153), the Divisional Court in *R. v. Central Criminal Court, ex p. A.J.D. Holdings Ltd*, *ante* § 15–81, refused to accept that *Longman* left it open to the court to hold that the invalidity of a warrant did not necessarily make a search unlawful.

A search warrant referring to items in general terms (*e.g.* "bank accounts") did not contravene section 15(6)(b) where it was clear, reading the warrant as a whole, that the references related to the suspected offences identified in the supporting information: *R. (Paul da Costa & Co. (a firm)) v. Thames Magistrates' Court* [2002] S.T.C. 267, DC.

In *R. v. Chief Constable of Lancashire, ex p. Parker*, 97 Cr.App.R. 90, DC, the court observed that it is highly desirable for the copying and certification of copies under section 15(7) and (8) to be carried out by the issuing court, compliance with those provisions being the responsibility of the judge or magistrate who issues the warrant (although he can delegate the issuing process to court staff). The court went on to hold that copies of the warrant have to be clearly certified as such, and that it would be contrary to the purpose of the legislation if a judge could authorise the police to replace the whole or part of the original warrant, for the purpose of its execution, by an uncertified photocopy which he has not seen. Their Lordships suggested *obiter* that, where a warrant consists of more than one page, something more than the judge's signature and the court stamp on one page would be desirable as a means of authenticating the whole: the judge might, for example, initial the other pages, and in the case of a three-page warrant the pages might be numbered 1/3, etc.

Execution of warrants

16.—(1) A warrant to enter and search premises may be executed by any constable. **15–102**

(2) Such a warrant may authorise persons to accompany any constable who is executing it.

(2A) A person so authorised has the same powers as the constable whom he accompanies in respect of—

(a) the execution of the warrant, and

(b) the seizure of anything to which the warrant relates.

(2B) But he may exercise those powers only in the company, and under the supervision, of a constable.

(3) Entry and search under a warrant must be within three months from the date of its issue.

(3A) If the warrant is an all premises warrant, no premises which are not specified in it may be entered or searched unless a police officer of at least the rank of inspector has in writing authorised them to be entered.

(3B) No premises may be entered or searched for the second or any subsequent time under a warrant which authorises multiple entries unless a police officer of at least the rank of inspector has in writing authorised that entry to those premises.

(4) Entry and search under a warrant must be at a reasonable hour unless it appears to the constable executing it that the purpose of a search may be frustrated on an entry at a reasonable hour.

(5) Where the occupier of premises which are to be entered and searched is present at the time when a constable seeks to execute a warrant to enter and search them, the constable—

(a) shall identify himself to the occupier and, if not in uniform, shall produce to him documentary evidence that he is a constable;

(b) shall produce the warrant to him; and

(c) shall supply him with a copy of it.

(6) Where—

(a) the occupier of such premises is not present at the time when a constable seeks to execute such a warrant; but

(b) some other person who appears to the constable to be in charge of the premises is present,

subsection (5) above shall have effect as if any reference to the occupier were a reference to that other person.

(7) If there is no person present who appears to the constable to be in charge of the premises, he shall leave a copy of the warrant in a prominent place on the premises.

(8) A search under a warrant may only be a search to the extent required for the purpose for which the warrant was issued. **15–103**

(9) A constable executing a warrant shall make an endorsement on it stating—

(a) whether the articles or persons sought were found; and

(b) whether any articles were seized, other than articles which were sought and, unless the warrant is a warrant specifying one set of premises only, he shall do so separately in respect of each set of premises entered and searched, which he shall in each case state in the endorsement.

(10) A warrant shall be returned to the appropriate person mentioned in subsection (10A) below—

(a) when it has been executed; or

(b) in the case of a specific premises warrant which has not been executed,

or an all premises warrant, or any warrant authorising multiple entries, upon the expiry of the period of three months referred to in subsection (3) above or sooner.

(10A) The appropriate person is—

(a) if the warrant was issued by a justice of the peace, the designated officer for the local justice area in which the justice was acting when he issued the warrant;

(b) if it was issued by a judge, the appropriate officer of the court from which he issued it.

(11) A warrant which is returned under subsection (10) above shall be retained for 12 months from its return—

(a) by the designated officer for the local justice area, if it was returned under paragraph (i) of that subsection; and

(b) by the appropriate officer, if it was returned under paragraph (ii).

(12) If during the period for which a warrant is to be retained the occupier of premises to which it relates asks to inspect it, he shall be allowed to do so.

[This section is printed as amended by the *Access to Justice Act* 1999, s.90(1), and Sched. 13, para. 126; the *CJA* 2003, s.2; the *Courts Act* 2003, s.109(1), and Sched. 8, para. 281; the *SOCPA* 2005, ss.113(1) and (9), and 114(1) and (8); and the *Serious Organised Crime and Police Act 2005 (Amendment) Order* 2005 (S.I. 2005 No. 3496).]

As to the application of this section to warrants under the *Animal Welfare Act* 2006, see *ante*, § 15–101.

15–104 Where police officers failed to show the occupier of premises which were being searched the whole of the warrant, and failed to supply her with a copy of it, there was a breach of section 16(5), making the execution of the search unlawful; and this was so even where the police did not wish the occupier to see the addresses of other premises listed in the warrant, because the police could avoid that problem by obtaining separate warrants or by redacting those addresses: *Redknapp v. Commr of the City of London Police and City of London Magistrates' Court (McKay, Storrie, Mandaric and Faye (interested parties))*, 172 J.P. 388, DC (see also *ante*, § 15–73).

The practice of taking pre-prepared questionnaires for service on staff when executing search warrants might breach section 16(8) if in reality the warrant is only an excuse to enable the investigator to contact witnesses who might not otherwise be traced; if it is intended to serve such questionnaires, the court should be informed at the time of making the application or in any event before it is executed: *R. (Paul da Costa & Co. (a firm)) v. Thames Magistrates' Court* [2002] S.T.C. 267, DC.

[The next paragraph is § 15–107.]

Police and Criminal Evidence Act 1984, s.17

Entry for purpose of arrest, etc.

15–107 **17.**—(1) Subject to the following provisions of this section, and without prejudice to any other enactment, a constable may enter and search any premises for the purpose—

(a) of executing—

(i) a warrant of arrest issued in connection with or arising out of criminal proceedings; or

(ii) a warrant of commitment issued under section 76 of the *Magistrates' Courts Act* 1980;

(b) of arresting a person for an indictable offence;

(c) of arresting a person for an offence under—

(i) section 1 (prohibition of uniforms in connection with political objects), … of the *Public Order Act* 1936;

(ii) any enactment contained in sections 6 to 8 or 10 of the *Criminal Law Act* 1977 (offences relating to entering and remaining on property);

(iii) section 4 of the *Public Order Act* 1986 (fear or provocation of violence);

(iiia) section 4 (driving etc. when under influence of drink or drugs) or 163 (failure to stop when required to do so by constable in uniform) of the *Road Traffic Act* 1988;

(iiib) section 27 of the *Transport and Works Act* 1992 (which relates to offences involving drink or drugs);

(iv) section 76 of the *Criminal Justice and Public Order Act* 1994 (failure to comply with interim possession order);

(v) any of sections 4, 5, 6(1) and (2), 7 and 8(1) and (2) of the *Animal Welfare Act* 2006 (offences relating to the prevention of harm to animals);

(ca) of arresting, in pursuance of section 32(1A) of the *Children and Young Persons Act* 1969, any child or young person who has been remanded or committed to local authority accommodation under section 23(1) of that Act;

(caa) of arresting a person for an offence to which section 61 of the *Animal Health Act* 1981 applies;

(cb) of recapturing any person who is, or is deemed for any purpose to be, unlawfully at large while liable to be detained—

(i) in a prison, remand centre, young offender institution or secure training centre, or

(ii) in pursuance of section 92 of the *Powers of Criminal Courts (Sentencing) Act* 2000 (dealing with children and young persons guilty of grave crimes), in any other place;

(d) of recapturing any person whatsoever who is unlawfully at large and whom he is pursuing; or

(e) of saving life or limb or preventing serious damage to property.

15–108 (2) Except for the purpose specified in paragraph (e) of subsection (1) above, the powers of entry and search conferred by this section—

(a) are only exercisable if the constable has reasonable grounds for believing that the person whom he is seeking is on the premises; and

(b) are limited, in relation to premises consisting of two or more separate dwellings, to powers to enter and search—

(i) any parts of the premises which the occupiers of any dwelling comprised in the premises use in common with the occupiers of any other such dwelling; and

(ii) any such dwelling in which the constable has reasonable grounds for believing that the person whom he is seeking may be.

(3) The powers of entry and search conferred by this section are only exercisable for the purposes specified in subsection (1)(c)(ii) or (iv) above by a constable in uniform.

(4) The power of search conferred by this section is only a power to search to the extent that is reasonably required for the purpose for which the power of entry is exercised.

(5) Subject to subsection (6) below, all the rules of common law under which a constable has power to enter premises without a warrant are hereby abolished.

(6) Nothing in subsection (5) above affects any power of entry to deal with or prevent a breach of the peace.

[This section is printed as amended and repealed in part by the *Public Order Act* 1986, s.40(2) and Sched. 2, para. 7; the *CJPOA* 1994, s.168(2) and Sched. 1, para. 53; the *Prisoners (Return to Custody) Act* 1995, s.2(1); the *PCC(S)A* 2000, s.165(1) and Sched. 9, para. 95; the *Police Reform Act* 2002, s.49(2); the *SOCPA* 2005, s.111, and Sched. 7, paras 43(1) and (4), and 58; and the *Animal Welfare Act* 2006, s.24.]

15–109 The power of entry pursuant to section 17(1)(b) is only available to an officer who has reasonable grounds for suspicion, but such grounds can be inferred: *Kynaston v. DPP*, 87 Cr.App.R. 200, DC, *post*, § 15–165.

A police officer exercising his power to enter premises by the use of reasonable force, pursuant to sections 17 and 117 (*ante*, § 15–26), should, unless the circumstances make it impossible, impracticable or undesirable, give any occupant present the reason for his exercising that power of entry: *O'Loughlin v. Chief Constable of Essex* [1998] 1 W.L.R. 374, CA (Civ. Div.). If the real reason is to arrest a person inside for an indictable offence (s.17(1)(b)), it is insufficient for the officer to tell the occupants that he wishes to "speak to" that person about the offence: *ibid*.

Where police officers are invited onto premises by an occupier or other person authorised to do so, who had been told by them the reason for their entry, they are lawfully on the premises, and they do not have to comply with section 17, which applies to entry and search in the absence of consent: *Riley v. DPP*, 91 Cr.App.R. 14, DC; *Hobson v. Chief Constable of the Cheshire Constabulary*, 168 J.P. 111, DC.

Section 17(1)(d) contemplates an act of pursuit, a chase, however short in time and distance, and does not cover a situation where the police form an intention to arrest and decide to put it into practice by resorting to the premises where they believe that the person sought might be found: *D'Souza v. DPP*, 96 Cr.App.R. 278, HL.

For an example of justifiable entry under section 17(1)(e) (saving life or limb), see *Blench v. DPP*, 69 J.C.L. 98, DC.

Police and Criminal Evidence Act 1984, s.18

Entry and search after arrest

15–110 **18.**—(1) Subject to the following provisions of this section, a constable may enter and search any premises occupied or controlled by a person who is under arrest for an indictable offence, if he has reasonable grounds for suspecting that there is on the premises evidence, other than items subject to legal privilege, that relates—

(a) to that offence; or

(b) to some other indictable offence which is connected with or similar to that offence.

(2) A constable may seize and retain anything for which he may search under subsection (1) above.

(3) The power to search conferred by subsection (1) above is only a power to search to the extent that is reasonably required for the purpose of discovering such evidence.

(4) Subject to subsection (5) below, the powers conferred by this section may not be exercised unless an officer of the rank of inspector or above has authorised them in writing.

(5) A constable may conduct a search under subsection (1)—

(a) before the person is taken to a police station or released on bail under section 30A, and

(b) without obtaining an authorisation under subsection (4),

if the condition in subsection (5A) is satisfied.

(5A) The condition is that the presence of the person at a place (other than a police station) is necessary for the effective investigation of the offence.

(6) If a constable conducts a search by virtue of subsection (5) above, he shall inform an officer of the rank of inspector or above that he has made the search as soon as practicable after he has made it.

(7) An officer who—

(a) authorises a search; or

(b) is informed of a search under subsection (6) above,

shall make a record in writing—

(i) of the grounds for the search; and

(ii) of the nature of the evidence that was sought.

(8) If the person who was in occupation or control of the premises at the time of the search is in police detention at the time the record is to be made, the officer shall make the record as part of his custody record.

[This section is printed as amended by the *Police Reform Act* 2002, s.107(1), and Sched. 7, para. 9(1); the *CJA* 2003, s.12, and Sched. 1, paras 1 and 2; and the *SOCPA* 2005, s.111, and Sched. 7, para. 43(1) and (5).]

15–111 For the power to search premises where an arrest takes place, see section 32 of the Act, *post*, § 15–186. For the modification of section 18 in relation to investigations by Revenue and Customs officers of offences relating to assigned matters, see *ante*, § 15–43.

The power of entry and search under section 18 applies only where the premises searched are in fact occupied or controlled by the person under arrest; if they are not, the search is unlawful, even if the officer conducting the search has a reasonable belief that they are: *Khan v. Commr of Police of the Metropolis*, *The Times*, June 16, 2008, CA (Civ. Div.).

The reasoning in *O'Loughlin v. Chief Constable of Essex*, *ante*, § 15–109, applies equally to section 18: *Linehan v. DPP* [2000] Crim.L.R. 861, DC (officers proposing to enter premises by force should have told the occupier their purpose, *i.e.* to search for the proceeds of a burglary for which the occupier's son had been arrested).

The word "anything" in section 18(2) entitles a constable to seize a vehicle and not just its parts or contents, even though the vehicle itself is "premises" for the purposes of the Act (s.23, *post*, § 15–123): *Cowan v. Condon* [2000] 1 W.L.R. 254, CA (Civ. Div.).

Section 18(7) is directory only; non-compliance does not automatically invalidate the search: *Krohn v. DPP* [1997] C.O.D. 345, DC.

For a case where evidence obtained through a search was held to be properly admitted notwithstanding a breach of section 18(8), see *R. v. Wright* [1994] Crim.L.R. 55, CA.

Section 18 does not have the effect of abolishing common law rules as to entry and search after arrest, it being a well established principle that a rule of law was not extinguished by a statute unless the statute made that clear by express provision or clear implication: *R. (Rottman) v. Commr of Police of the Metropolis* [2002] 2 A.C. 692, HL. At common law, a police officer who entered a house and arrested a suspect pursuant to a warrant of arrest had power to search the entire house and seize any articles which provided evidence against the suspect; that power applied to extradition crimes as well as domestic crimes; and it survived the 1984 Act: *ibid.*

In *R. (Hewitson) v. Chief Constable of the Dorset Police*, *The Times*, January 6, 2004, DC, the court refused to extend the police's common law power of search, as explained in *Rottman*, *ante*, to searching a flat in circumstances where (a) the suspect was arrested away from the flat and its curtilage, (b) the search was more than two hours after the arrest, and (c) the link between the suspect and the flat was tenuous, the flat belonging to a friend and the suspect being only an occasional visitor.

Police and Criminal Evidence Act 1984, s.19

General power of seizure, etc.

19.—(1) The powers conferred by subsections (2), (3) and (4) below are exercisable by a constable who is lawfully on any premises. **15–112**

(2) The constable may seize anything which is on the premises if he has reasonable grounds for believing—

(a) that it has been obtained in consequence of the commission of an offence; and

(b) that it is necessary to seize it in order to prevent it being concealed, lost, damaged, altered or destroyed.

(3) The constable may seize anything which is on the premises if he has reasonable grounds for believing—

(a) that it is evidence in relation to an offence which he is investigating or any other offence; and

(b) that it is necessary to seize it in order to prevent the evidence being concealed, lost, altered or destroyed.

(4) The constable may require any information which is stored in any electronic form and is accessible from the premises to be produced in a form in which it can be taken away and in which it is visible and legible or from which it can readily be produced in a visible and legible form if he has reasonable grounds for believing—

(a) that—

(i) it is evidence in relation to an offence which he is investigating or any other offence; or

(ii) it has been obtained in consequence of the commission of an offence; and

(b) that it is necessary to do so in order to prevent it being concealed, lost, tampered with or destroyed.

(5) The powers conferred by this section are in addition to any power otherwise conferred.

(6) No power of seizure conferred on a constable under any enactment (including an enactment contained in an Act passed after this Act) is to be taken to authorise the seizure of an item which the constable exercising the power has reasonable grounds for believing to be subject to legal privilege.

[This section is printed as amended by the *CJPA* 2001, s.70 and Sched. 2, para. 13.]

For the disapplication of subsection (6) in relation to the powers of seizure under sections 50 and 51 of the *CJPA* 2001, see subsection (4) of those sections, *post*, §§ 15–127, 15–128. **15–113**

Unlike section 17, *ante*, § 15–107, which by subsection (5) expressly abolished with one exception all the rules of common law under which a constable had power to enter premises, section 19 contains no corresponding provision in relation to common law powers of seizure. On the contrary, subsection (5) provides that the powers conferred by the section are in addition to any power otherwise conferred. It appears to have been the intention of Parliament that in relation to the general power of seizure—as opposed to specific powers given by particular provisions such as section 26(3) of the *Theft Act* 1968 (*post*, § 21–331)—there would be no need to look further than the 1984 Act.

For the meaning of "anything" (s.19(2)), see *Cowan v. Condon*, *ante*, § 15–111.

Section 19 refers to "evidence" (s.19(3), (4)), as opposed to "relevant evidence", which is defined in section 8(4) (*ante*, § 15–72), in relation to an offence, as "anything that would be admissible in evidence at a trial for the offence".

The references to an "offence" in section 19(3) do not include foreign offences; in the absence of an express provision to the contrary, "offence" in a statute means a domestic offence: *R. (Rottman) v. Commr of Police of the Metropolis* [2002] 2 A.C. 692, HL.

Police and Criminal Evidence Act 1984, ss.20, 21

Extension of powers of seizure to computerised information

15–114 **20.**—(1) Every power of seizure which is conferred by an enactment to which this section applies on a constable who has entered premises in the exercise of a power conferred by an enactment shall be construed as including a power to require any information stored in any electronic form and accessible from the premises to be produced in a form in which it can be taken away and in which it is visible and legible or from which it can readily be produced in a visible and legible form.

(2) This section applies—

(a) to any enactment contained in an Act passed before this Act;

(b) to sections 8 and 18 above;

(c) to paragraph 13 of Schedule 1 to this Act; and

(d) to any enactment contained in an Act passed after this Act.

[This section is printed as amended by the *CJPA* 2001, s.70, and Sched. 2, para. 13.]

Access and copying

15–115 **21.**—(1) A constable who seizes anything in the exercise of a power conferred by any enactment, including an enactment contained in an Act passed after this Act, shall, if so required by a person showing himself—

(a) to be the occupier of premises on which it was seized; or

(b) to have had custody or control of it immediately before the seizure,

provide that person with a record of what he seized.

(2) The officer shall provide the record within a reasonable time from the making of the request for it.

(3) Subject to subsection (8) below, if a request for permission to be granted access to anything which—

(a) has been seized by a constable; and

(b) is retained by the police for the purpose of investigating an offence,

is made to the officer in charge of the investigation by a person who had custody or control of the thing immediately before it was so seized or by someone acting on behalf of such a person, the officer shall allow the person who made the request access to it under the supervision of a constable.

15–116 (4) Subject to subsection (8) below, if a request for a photograph or copy of any such thing is made to the officer in charge of the investigation by a person who had custody or control of the thing immediately before it was so seized, or by someone acting on behalf of such a person, the officer shall—

(a) allow the person who made the request access to it under the supervision of a constable for the purpose of photographing or copying it; or

(b) photograph or copy it, or cause it to be photographed or copied.

(5) A constable may also photograph or copy, or have photographed or copied, anything which he has power to seize, without a request being made under subsection (4) above.

(6) Where anything is photographed or copied under subsection (4)(b) above, the photograph or copy shall be supplied to the person who made the request.

(7) The photograph or copy shall be so supplied within a reasonable time from the making of the request.

(8) There is no duty under this section to grant access to, or to supply a photograph or copy of, anything if the officer in charge of the investigation for the purposes of which it was seized has reasonable grounds for believing that to do so would prejudice—

(a) that investigation;

(b) the investigation of an offence other than the offence for the purposes of investigating which the thing was seized; or

(c) any criminal proceedings which may be brought as a result of—

(i) the investigation of which he is in charge; or

(ii) any such investigation as is mentioned in paragraph (b) above.

(9) The references to a constable in subsections (1), (2), (3)(a) and (5) include a person authorised under section 16(2) to accompany a constable executing a warrant.

[This section is printed as amended by the *CJA* 2003, s.12, and Sched. 1, paras 1 and 3.]

Where complainants seek to challenge a chief constable's refusal under section 21(8) to permit copies to be made of documents seized from them by the police, they should do so by way of judicial review, and not as an application in a private law action begun by writ: *Allen v. Chief Constable of Cheshire Constabulary*, *The Times*, July 16, 1988, CA (Civ. Div.). **15–117**

Where company documents are seized the person who may ask the police for access to them or for copies of them under section 21(3) and (4) as having had "custody or control" of the documents immediately before their seizure is the company itself. The directors or former directors of the company do not possess this right in their capacity as such: see *Re D.P.R. Futures Ltd* [1989] 1 W.L.R. 778, Ch D.

Police and Criminal Evidence Act 1984, s.22

Retention

22.—(1) Subject to subsection (4) below, anything which has been seized by a constable or taken away by a constable following a requirement made by virtue of section 19 or 20 above may be retained so long as is necessary in all the circumstances. **15–118**

(2) Without prejudice to the generality of subsection (1) above—

(a) anything seized for the purposes of a criminal investigation may be retained, except as provided by subsection (4) below—

(i) for use as evidence at a trial for an offence; or

(ii) for forensic examination or for investigation in connection with an offence; and

(b) anything may be retained in order to establish its lawful owner, where there are reasonable grounds for believing that it has been obtained in consequence of the commission of an offence.

(3) Nothing seized on the ground that it may be used—

(a) to cause physical injury to any person;

(b) to damage property;

(c) to interfere with evidence; or

(d) to assist in escape from police detention or lawful custody,

may be retained when the person from whom it was seized is no longer in police detention or the custody of a court or is in the custody of a court but has been released on bail.

(4) Nothing may be retained for either of the purposes mentioned in subsection (2)(a) above if a photograph or copy would be sufficient for that purpose.

(5) Nothing in this section affects any power of a court to make an order under section 1 of the *Police (Property) Act* 1897.

(6) This section also applies to anything retained by the police under section 28H(5) of the *Immigration Act* 1971.

(7) The reference in subsection (1) to anything seized by a constable includes anything seized by a person authorised under section 16(2) to accompany a constable executing a warrant.

[This section is printed as amended by the *Immigration and Asylum Act* 1999, s.169(1), and Sched. 14, para. 80(1) and (3); and the *CJA* 2003, s.12, and Sched. 1, paras 1 and 4.]

For the purposes of sections 21 and 22 material produced in pursuance of an order under paragraph 4(a) of Schedule 1 shall be treated as if it were material seized by a constable: Sched. 1, para. 6, *ante*, § 15–76.

15–119 Judicial guidance on the return of seized property required for the defence was given in *R. v. Southampton JJ., ex p. Newman*, 88 Cr.App.R. 202, DC. If the property was taken from the defendant's person, an application may be made under section 48 of the *Magistrates' Courts Act* 1980. If the property was seized by the police and is in their possession, an application may be made under section 1 of the *Police (Property) Act* 1897 (see s.22(5), *ante*, and Note for Guidance 7A in Code B (Appendix A–35)). If neither of these options is open to an accused, he is not without remedy. A magistrates' court has inherent jurisdiction and can to some extent control its own procedures. If an accused indicates that without his documents, or without certain identified documents, he will not be able to prepare his defence, the court can always refuse to proceed until the prosecution hands over such documents as the court finds necessary for justice to be done. Alternatively, a civil action can be brought.

15–120 For the meaning of "retained" in section 22(1), as applied to material produced under an order to make material available under section 55 of the *DTA* 1994, see *R. v. Southwark Crown Court, ex p. Customs and Excise* [1990] 1 Q.B. 650, DC, *post*, § 15–260. "Trial for an offence" (s.22(a)(i)) means a trial in this jurisdiction: *ibid.*

The police do not have a general right to retain unlawfully seized material as against its owner for use as evidence under section 22(2), as the subsection has to be read in conjunction with the rest of section 22 and is thus only concerned with material that has been lawfully seized, under whatever power, or that has been taken away following a requirement made under section 19(4) or 20(1): *R. v. Chief Constable of Lancashire, ex p. Parker*, 97 Cr.App.R. 90, DC.

As to the use to which material acquired during the course of a criminal investigation may be put, other than for the purpose of such investigation or any resulting criminal proceedings, see *Marcel v. Commr of Police of the Metropolis* [1992] Ch. 225, CA (Civ. Div.), and *Preston B.C. v. McGrath, The Times*, May 19, 2000, CA (Civ. Div.).

Prosecution's duties in relation to exhibits

15–121 The extent of the prosecution's duty to retain control over exhibits and preserve evidence generally pending trial was considered in *R. v. Lushington, ex p. Otto* [1894] 1 Q.B. 420, *per* Wright J. at 423, 424; *R. v. Lambeth Metropolitan Stipendiary Magistrate, ex p. McComb* [1983] Q.B. 551, 76 Cr.App.R. 246, CA (Civ. Div.); and *R. v. Uxbridge JJ., ex p. Sofaer*, 85 Cr.App.R. 367, DC. See also *post*, § 25–426.

Injunctions

15–122 The High Court may by order (whether interlocutory or final) grant an injunction or appoint a receiver in all cases in which it appears to the court to be just and convenient to do so: *Supreme Court Act* 1981, s.37(1). In *Chief Constable of Kent v. V.* [1983] Q.B. 34, CA (Civ. Div.), an injunction was granted pursuant to this section so as to freeze a bank account into which stolen cheques had been paid. However, the limited utility of this provision for the purposes of recovering the proceeds of crime is illustrated by *Chief Constable of Hampshire v. A. Ltd* [1985] Q.B. 132, 79 Cr.App.R. 30, CA (Civ. Div.), *Chief Constable of Leicestershire v. M.* [1989] 1 W.L.R. 20, Ch D, and *Chief Constable of Surrey v. A., The Times*, October 27, 1988, QBD.

In practice, it will rarely now be necessary to resort to section 37, having regard to the provision for the making of restraint orders under the *PCA* 2002. See, in particular, sections 40 to 47, *ante*, §§ 5–601 *et seq.*

Police and Criminal Evidence Act 1984, s.23

Meaning of "premises" etc.

15–123 **23.** In this Act—

"premises" includes any place and, in particular, includes—

(a) any vehicle, vessel, aircraft or hovercraft;

(b) any offshore installation;

(ba) any renewable energy installation;

(c) any tent or movable structure; and

"offshore installation" has the meaning given to it by section 1 of the *Mineral Workings (Offshore Installations) Act* 1971;

"renewable energy installation" has the same meaning as in Chapter 2 of Part 2 of the *Energy Act* 2004.

[This section is printed as amended by the *Energy Act* 2004, s.103(2).]

Criminal Justice and Police Act 2001, ss.50–52

PART 2

POWERS OF SEIZURE

Additional powers of seizure

Additional powers of seizure from premises

50.—(1) Where— 15–124

(a) a person who is lawfully on any premises finds anything on those premises that he has reasonable grounds for believing may be or may contain something for which he is authorised to search on those premises,

(b) a power of seizure to which this section applies or the power conferred by subsection (2) would entitle him, if he found it, to seize whatever it is that he has grounds for believing that thing to be or to contain, and

(c) in all the circumstances, it is not reasonably practicable for it to be determined, on those premises—

(i) whether what he has found is something that he is entitled to seize, or

(ii) the extent to which what he has found contains something that he is entitled to seize,

that person's powers of seizure shall include power under this section to seize so much of what he has found as it is necessary to remove from the premises to enable that to be determined.

(2) Where— 15–125

(a) a person who is lawfully on any premises finds anything on those premises ("the seizable property") which he would be entitled to seize but for its being comprised in something else that he has (apart from this subsection) no power to seize,

(b) the power under which that person would have power to seize the seizable property is a power to which this section applies, and

(c) in all the circumstances it is not reasonably practicable for the seizable property to be separated, on those premises, from that in which it is comprised,

that person's powers of seizure shall include power under this section to seize both the seizable property and that from which it is not reasonably practicable to separate it.

(3) The factors to be taken into account in considering, for the purposes of this section, whether or not it is reasonably practicable on particular premises for something to be determined, or for something to be separated from something else, shall be confined to the following— 15–126

(a) how long it would take to carry out the determination or separation on those premises;

(b) the number of persons that would be required to carry out that determination or separation on those premises within a reasonable period;

(c) whether the determination or separation would (or would if carried out on those premises) involve damage to property;

(d) the apparatus or equipment that it would be necessary or appropriate to use for the carrying out of the determination or separation; and

(e) in the case of separation, whether the separation—

(i) would be likely, or

(ii) if carried out by the only means that are reasonably practicable on those premises, would be likely,

to prejudice the use of some or all of the separated seizable property for a purpose for which something seized under the power in question is capable of being used.

(4) Section 19(6) of the 1984 Act and Article 21(6) of the *Police and Criminal Evidence (Northern Ireland) Order* 1989 (powers of seizure not to include power to seize anything that a person has reasonable grounds for believing is legally privileged) shall not apply to the power of seizure conferred by subsection (2). 15–127

(5) This section applies to each of the powers of seizure specified in Part 1 of Schedule 1.

(6) Without prejudice to any power conferred by this section to take a copy of any document, nothing in this section, so far as it has effect by reference to the power to take copies of documents under section 28(2)(b) of the *Competition Act* 1998, shall be taken to confer any power to seize any document.

As to the commencement of, and background to, this legislation, see *ante*, § 15–71.

Additional powers of seizure from the person

15–128 **51.**—(1) Where—

(a) a person carrying out a lawful search of any person finds something that he has reasonable grounds for believing may be or may contain something for which he is authorised to search,

(b) a power of seizure to which this section applies or the power conferred by subsection (2) would entitle him, if he found it, to seize whatever it is that he has grounds for believing that thing to be or to contain, and

(c) in all circumstances it is not reasonably practicable for it to be determined, at the time and place of the search—

(i) whether what he has found is something that he is entitled to seize, or

(ii) the extent to which what he has found contains something that he is entitled to seize,

that person's powers of seizure shall include power under this section to seize so much of what he has found as it is necessary to remove from that place to enable that to be determined.

(2) Where—

(a) a person carrying out a lawful search of any person finds something ("the seizable property") which he would be entitled to seize but for its being comprised in something else that he has (apart from this subsection) no power to seize,

(b) the power under which that person would have power to seize the seizable property is a power to which this section applies, and

(c) in all the circumstances it is not reasonably practicable for the seizable property to be separated, at the time and place of the search, from that in which it is comprised,

that person's powers of seizure shall include power under this section to seize both the seizable property and that from which it is not reasonably practicable to separate it.

(3) The factors to be taken into account in considering, for the purposes of this section, whether or not it is reasonably practicable, at the time and place of a search, for something to be determined, or for something to be separated from something else, shall be confined to the following—

(a) how long it would take to carry out the determination or separation at that time and place;

(b) the number of persons that would be required to carry out that determination or separation at that time and place within a reasonable period;

(c) whether the determination or separation would (or would if carried out at that time and place) involve damage to property;

(d) the apparatus or equipment that it would be necessary or appropriate to use for the carrying out of the determination or separation; and

(e) in the case of separation, whether the separation—

(i) would be likely, or

(ii) if carried out by the only means that are reasonably practicable at that time and place, would be likely,

to prejudice the use of some or all of the separated seizable property for a purpose for which something seized under the power in question is capable of being used.

(4) [*Identical to s.50(4)*, ante.]

(5) This section applies to each of the powers of seizure specified in Part 2 of Schedule 1.

Notice of exercise of power under s.50 or 51

15–129 **52.**—(1) Where a person exercises a power of seizure conferred by section 50, it shall (subject to subsections (2) and (3)) be his duty, on doing so, to give to the occupier of the premises a written notice—

(a) specifying what has been seized in reliance on the powers conferred by that section;

(b) specifying the grounds on which those powers have been exercised;
(c) setting out the effect of sections 59 to 61;
(d) specifying the name and address of the person to whom notice of an application under section 59(2) to the appropriate judicial authority in respect of any of the seized property must be given; and
(e) specifying the name and address of the person to whom an application may be made to be allowed to attend the initial examination required by any arrangements made for the purposes of section 53(2).

(2) Where it appears to the person exercising on any premises a power of seizure conferred by section 50—

(a) that the occupier of the premises is not present on the premises at the time of the exercise of the power, but
(b) that there is some other person present on the premises who is in charge of the premises,

subsection (1) of this section shall have effect as if it required the notice under that subsection to be given to that other person.

(3) Where it appears to the person exercising a power of seizure conferred by section 50 that there is no one present on the premises to whom he may give a notice for the purposes of complying with subsection (1) of this section, he shall, before leaving the premises, instead of complying with that subsection, attach a notice such as is mentioned in that subsection in a prominent place to the premises.

(4) Where a person exercises a power of seizure conferred by section 51 it shall be his duty, on doing so, to give a written notice to the person from whom the seizure is made—

(a) specifying what has been seized in reliance on the powers conferred by that section;
(b) specifying the grounds on which those powers have been exercised;
(c) setting out the effect of sections 59 to 61;
(d) specifying the name and address of the person to whom notice of any application under section 59(2) to the appropriate judicial authority in respect of any of the seized property must be given; and
(e) specifying the name and address of the person to whom an application may be made to be allowed to attend the initial examination required by any arrangements made for the purposes of section 53(2).

(5) The Secretary of State may by regulations made by statutory instrument, after consultation with the Scottish Ministers, provide that a person who exercises a power of seizure conferred bysection 50 shall be required to give a notice such as is mentioned in subsection (1) of this section to any person, or send it to any place, described in the regulations.

(6) Regulations under subsection (5) may make different provision for different cases.

(7) [*Statutory instrument procedure.*]

Criminal Justice and Police Act 2001, ss.53–58

Return or retention of seized property

Examination and return of property seized under s.50 or 51

53.—(1) This section applies where anything has been seized under a power conferred by section 50 or 51. **15–130**

(2) It shall be the duty of the person for the time being in possession of the seized property in consequence of the exercise of that power to secure that there are arrangements in force which (subject to section 61) ensure—

(a) that an initial examination of the property is carried out as soon as reasonably practicable after the seizure;
(b) that that examination is confined to whatever is necessary for determining how much of the property falls within subsection (3);
(c) that anything which is found, on that examination, not to fall within subsection (3) is separated from the rest of the seized property and is returned as soon as reasonably practicable after the examination of all the seized property has been completed; and
(d) that, until the initial examination of all the seized property has been completed and anything which does not fall within subsection (3) has been returned, the seized property is kept separate from anything seized under any other power.

(3) The seized property falls within this subsection to the extent only—

(a) that it is property for which the person seizing it had power to search when he made the seizure but is not property the return of which is required by section 54;

(b) that it is property the retention of which is authorised by section 56; or

(c) that it is something which, in all the circumstances, it will not be reasonably practicable, following the examination, to separate from property falling within paragraph (a) or (b).

(4) In determining for the purposes of this section the earliest practicable time for the carrying out of an initial examination of the seized property, due regard shall be had to the desirability of allowing the person from whom it was seized, or a person with an interest in that property, an opportunity of being present or (if he chooses) of being represented at the examination.

(5) In this section, references to whether or not it is reasonably practicable to separate part of the seized property from the rest of it are references to whether or not it is reasonably practicable to do so without prejudicing the use of the rest of that property, or a part of it, for purposes for which (disregarding the part to be separated) the use of the whole or of a part of the rest of the property, if retained, would be lawful.

Obligation to return items subject to legal privilege

15–131 **54.**—(1) If, at any time after a seizure of anything has been made in exercise of a power of seizure to which this section applies—

(a) it appears to the person for the time being having possession of the seized property in consequence of the seizure that the property—

(i) is an item subject to legal privilege, or

(ii) has such an item comprised in it, and

(b) in a case where the item is comprised in something else which has been lawfully seized, it is not comprised in property falling within subsection (2),

it shall be the duty of that person to secure that the item is returned as soon as reasonably practicable after the seizure.

(2) Property in which an item subject to legal privilege is comprised falls within this subsection if—

(a) the whole or a part of the rest of the property is property falling within subsection (3) or property the retention of which is authorised by section 56; and

(b) in all the circumstances, it is not reasonably practicable for that item to be separated from the rest of that property (or, as the case may be, from that part of it) without prejudicing the use of the rest of that property, or that part of it, for purposes for which (disregarding that item) its, use, if retained, would be lawful.

(3) Property falls within this subsection to the extent that it is property for which the person seizing it had power to search when he made the seizure, but is not property which is required to be returned under this section or section 55.

(4) This section applies—

(a) to the powers of seizure conferred by sections 50 and 51;

(b) to each of the powers of seizure specified in Parts 1 and 2 of Schedule 1; and

(c) to any power of seizure (not falling within paragraph (a) or (b)) conferred on a constable by or under any enactment, including an enactment passed after this Act.

Obligation to return excluded and special procedure material

15–132 **55.**—(1) If, at any time after a seizure of anything has been made in exercise of a power to which this section applies—

(a) it appears to the person for the time being having possession of the seized property in consequence of the seizure that the property—

(i) is excluded material or special procedure material, or

(ii) has any excluded material or any special procedure material comprised in it,

(b) its retention is not authorised by section 56, and

(c) in a case where the material is comprised in something else which has been lawfully seized, it is not comprised in property falling within subsection (2) or (3),

it shall be the duty of that person to secure that the item is returned as soon as reasonably practicable after the seizure.

(2) Property in which any excluded material or special procedure material is comprised falls within this subsection if—

(a) the whole or a part of the rest of the property is property for which the person seizing it had power to search when he made the seizure but is not property the return of which is required by this section or section 54; and

(b) in all the circumstances, it is not reasonably practicable for that material to be separated from the rest of that property (or, as the case may be, from that part of it) without prejudicing the use of the rest of that property, or that part of it, for purposes for which (disregarding that material) its use, if retained, would be lawful.

(3) Property in which any excluded material or special procedure material is comprised falls within this subsection if—

(a) the whole or a part of the rest of the property is property the retention of which is authorised by section 56; and

(b) in all the circumstances, it is not reasonably practicable for that material to be separated from the rest of that property (or, as the case may be, from that part of it) without prejudicing the use of the rest of that property, or that part of it, for purposes for which (disregarding that material) its use, if retained, would be lawful.

(4) This section applies (subject to subsection (5)) to each of the powers of seizure specified in Part 3 of Schedule 1.

(5) In its application to the powers of seizure conferred by—

(a) [*repealed by* Proceeds of Crime Act *2002, s.457, Sched. 12*],

(b) section 56(5) of the *Drug Trafficking Act* 1994,

(c) [*Northern Ireland*], and

(d) section 352 (4) of the *Proceeds of Crime Act* 2002,

this section shall have effect with the omission of every reference to special procedure material.

(6) In this section, except in its application to—

(a) the power of seizure conferred by section 8(2) of the 1984 Act,

(b) [*Northern Ireland*],

(c) each of the powers of seizure conferred by the provisions of paragraphs 1 and 3 of Schedule 5 to the *Terrorism Act* 2000, and

(d) the power of seizure conferred by paragraphs 15 and 19 of Schedule 5 to that Act of 2000, so far only as the power in question is conferred by reference to paragraph 1 of that Schedule,

"special procedure material" means special procedure material consisting of documents or records other than documents.

[This section is printed as amended by the *PCA* 2002, ss.456 and 457, and Scheds 11, para. 40(2), and 12.]

Property seized by constables etc.

56.—(1) The retention of— **15–133**

(a) property seized on any premises by a constable who was lawfully on the premises,

(b) property seized on any premises by a relevant person who was on the premises accompanied by a constable, and

(c) property seized by a constable carrying out a lawful search of any person,

is authorised by this section if the property falls within subsection (2) or (3).

(2) Property falls within this subsection to the extent that there are reasonable grounds for believing—

(a) that it is property obtained in consequence of the commission of an offence; and

(b) that it is necessary for it to be retained in order to prevent its being concealed, lost, damaged, altered or destroyed.

(3) Property falls within this subsection to the extent that there are reasonable grounds for believing—

(a) that it is evidence in relation to any offence; and

(b) that it is necessary for it to be retained in order to prevent its being concealed, lost, altered or destroyed.

(4) Nothing in this section authorises the retention (except in pursuance of section 54(2)) of anything at any time when its return is required by section 54.

(4A) Subsection (1)(a) includes property seized on any premises—

(a) by a person authorised under section 16(2) of the 1984 Act to accompany a constable executing a warrant, or

(b) by a person accompanying a constable under section 2(6) of the *Criminal Justice Act* 1987 in the execution of a warrant under section 2(4) of that Act.

(5) In subsection (1)(b) the reference to a relevant person's being on any premises accompanied by a constable is a reference only to a person who was so on the premises under the authority of—

(a) a warrant under section 448 of the *Companies Act* 1985 authorising him to exercise together with a constable the powers conferred by subsection (3) of that section;

(b) [*Northern Ireland*];

(c)–(e) [*repealed by* Financial Services and Markets Act 2000 (Consequential Amendments and Repeals) Order *2001 (S.I. 2001 No. 3649), art. 364*].

[This section is printed as amended by the *CJA* 2003, s.12, and Sched. 1, para. 14.]

Retention of seized items

15–134 **57.**—(1) This section has effect in relation to the following provisions (which are about the retention of items which have been seized and are referred to in this section as "the relevant provisions")—

(a)–(q) [*see* post].

(2) The relevant provisions shall apply in relation to any property seized in exercise of a power conferred by section 50 or 51 as if the property had been seized under the power of seizure by reference to which the power under that section was exercised in relation to that property.

(3) Nothing in any of sections 53 to 56 authorises the retention of any property at any time when its retention would not (apart from the provisions of this Part) be authorised by the relevant provisions.

(4) Nothing in any of the relevant provisions authorises the retention of anything after an obligation to return it has arisen under this Part.

15–135 The provisions listed in subsection (1) (as amended) are: (a) the *PACE Act* 1984, s.22; (f) the *Companies Act* 1985, s.448(6); (g) the *Weights and Measures (Packaged Goods) Regulations* 2006 (S.I. 2006 No. 659), Sched. 7; (k) the *Human Fertilisation and Embryology Act* 1990, s.40(4); (l) the *Knives Act* 1997, s.5(4); (m) the *Data Protection Act* 1998, Sched. 9, para. 7(2); (n) the *Competition Act* 1998, s.28(7); (o) the *FSMA* 2000, s.176(8); (p) the *Freedom of Information Act* 2000, Sched. 3, para. 7(2); (pa) the *Enterprise Act* 2002, s.227F; (q) the *Human Tissue Act* 2004, Sched. 5, para. 5(4); and (r) the *Animal Welfare Act* 2006, Sched. 2, para. 12(3). Paragraphs (b), (d) and (i) relate to Northern Ireland. Paragraphs (e), (h) and (j) were repealed by S.I. 2001 No. 3649 (*ante*, § 15–133), art. 364. Paragraph (c) was repealed by the *Finance Act* 2007, ss.84(4) and 114, Sched. 22, paras. 3 and 13(1)(a), and Sched. 27, Pt 5.

Person to whom seized property is to be returned

15–136 **58.**—(1) Where—

(a) anything has been seized in exercise of any power of seizure, and

(b) there is an obligation under this Part for the whole or any part of the seized property to be returned,

the obligation to return it shall (subject to the following provisions of this section) be an obligation to return it to the person from whom it was seized.

(2) Where—

(a) any person is obliged under this Part to return anything that has been seized to the person from whom it was seized, and

(b) the person under that obligation is satisfied that some other person has a better right to that thing than the person from whom it was seized,

his duty to return it shall, instead, be a duty to return it to that other person or, as the case may be, to the person appearing to him to have the best right to the thing in question.

(3) Where different persons claim to be entitled to the return of anything that is required to be returned under this Part, that thing may be retained for as long as is reasonably necessary for the determination in accordance with subsection (2) of the person to whom it must be returned.

(4) References in this Part to the person from whom something has been seized, in rela-

tion to a case in which the power of seizure was exercisable by reason of that thing's having been found on any premises, are references to the occupier of the premises at the time of the seizure.

(5) References in this section to the occupier of any premises at the time of a seizure, in relation to a case in which—

(a) a notice in connection with the entry or search of the premises in question, or with the seizure, was given to a person appearing in the occupier's absence to be in charge of the premises, and

(b) it is practicable, for the purpose of returning something that has been seized, to identify that person but not to identify the occupier of the premises,

are references to that person.

Criminal Justice and Police Act 2001, ss.59–62

Remedies and safeguards

Application to the appropriate judicial authority

59.—(1) This section applies where anything has been seized in exercise, or purported exercise, of a relevant power of seizure. **15–137**

(2) Any person with a relevant interest in the seized property may apply to the appropriate judicial authority, on one or more of the grounds mentioned in subsection (3), for the return of the whole or a part of the seized property.

(3) Those grounds are—

(a) that there was no power to make the seizure;

(b) that the seized property is or contains an item subject to legal privilege that is not comprised in property falling within section 54(2);

(c) that the seized property is or contains any excluded material or special procedure material which—

(i) has been seized under a power to which section 55 applies;

(ii) is not comprised in property falling within section 55(2) or (3); and

(iii) is not property the retention of which is authorised by section 56;

(d) that the seized property is or contains something seized under section 50 or 51 which does not fall within section 53(3);

and subsections (5) and (6) of section 55 shall apply for the purposes of paragraph (c) as they apply for the purposes of that section.

(4) Subject to subsection (6), the appropriate judicial authority, on an application under subsection (2), shall—

(a) if satisfied as to any of the matters mentioned in subsection (3), order the return of so much of the seized property as is property in relation to which the authority is so satisfied; and

(b) to the extent that that authority is not so satisfied, dismiss the application.

(5) The approriate judicial authority—

(a) on an application under subsection (2),

(b) on an application made by the person for the time being having possession of anything in consequence of its seizure under a relevant power of seizure, or

(c) on an application made—

(i) by a person with a relevant interest in anything seized under section 50 or 51, and

(ii) on the grounds that the requirements of section 53(2) have not been or are not being complied with,

may give such directions as the authority thinks fit as to the examination, retention, separation or return of the whole or any part of the seized property.

(6) On any application under this section, the appropriate judicial authority may authorise the retention of any property which—

(a) has been seized in exercise, or purported exercise, of a relevant power of seizure, and

(b) would otherwise fall to be returned,

if that authority is satisfied that the retention of the property is justified on grounds falling within subsection (7).

(7) Those grounds are that (if the property were returned) it would immediately become appropriate— **15–138**

(a) to issue, on the application of the person who is in possession of the property at the time of the application under this section, a warrant in pursuance of which, or of the exercise of which, it would be lawful to seize the property; or
(b) to make an order under—
(i) paragraph 4 of Schedule 1 to the 1984 Act,
(ii) [*Northern Ireland*],
(iii) section 20BA of the *Taxes Management Act* 1970, or
(iv) paragraph 5 of Schedule 5 to the *Terrorism Act* 2000,
under which the property would fall to be delivered up or produced to the person mentioned in paragraph (a).

(8) Where any property which has been seized in exercise, or purported exercise, of a relevant power of seizure has parts ("part A" and "part B") comprised in it such that—
(a) it would be inappropriate, if the property were returned, to take any action such as is mentioned in subsection (7) in relation to part A,
(b) it would (or would but for the facts mentioned in paragraph (a)) be appropriate, if the property were returned, to take such action in relation to part B, and
(c) in all the circumstances, it is not reasonably practicable to separate part A from part B without prejudicing the use of part B for purposes for which it is lawful to use property seized under the power in question,
the facts mentioned in paragraph (a) shall not be taken into account by the appropriate judicial authority in deciding whether the retention of the property is justified on grounds falling within subsection (7).

(9) If a person fails to comply with any order or direction made or given by a judge of the Crown Court in exercise of any jurisdiction under this section—
(a) the authority may deal with him as if he had committed a contempt of the Crown Court; and
(b) any enactment relating to contempt of the Crown Court shall have effect in relation to the failure as if it were such a contempt.

(10) The relevant powers of seizure for the purposes of this section are—
(a) the powers of seizure conferred by sections 50 and 51;
(b) each of the powers of seizure specified in Parts 1 and 2 of Schedule 1; and
(c) any power of seizure (not falling within paragraph (a) or (b)) conferred on a constable by or under any enactment, including an enactment passed after this Act.

(11) References in this section to a person with a relevant interest in seized property are references to—
(a) the person from whom it was seized;
(b) any person with an interest in the property; or
(c) any person, not falling within paragraph (a) or (b), who had custody or control of the property immediately before the seizure.

(12) For the purposes of subsection (11)(b), the persons who have an interest in seized property shall, in the case of property which is or contains an item subject to legal privilege, be taken to include the person in whose favour that privilege is conferred.

In connection with this section, see rule 39 of the *Crown Court Rules* 1982 (S.I. 1982 No. 1109), *post*, § 15–150a.

Cases where duty to secure arises

15–139 **60.**—(1) Where property has been seized in exercise, or purported exercise, of any power of seizure conferred by section 50 or 51, a duty to secure arises under section 61 in relation to the seized property if—
(a) a person entitled to do so makes an application under section 59 for the return of the property;
(b) in relation to England, Wales and Northern Ireland, at least one of the conditions set out in subsections (2) and (3) is satisfied;
(c) in relation to Scotland, the condition set out in subsection (2) is satisfied; and
(d) notice of the application is given to a relevant person.

(2) The first condition is that the application is made on the grounds that the seized property is or contains an item subject to legal privilege that is not comprised in property falling within section 54(2).

(3) The second condition is that—
(a) the seized property was seized by a person who had, or purported to have,

power under this Part to seize it by virtue only of one or more of the powers specified in subsection (6); and

(b) the application—

(i) is made on the ground that the seized property is or contains something which does not fall within section 53(3); and

(ii) states that the seized property is or contains special procedure material or excluded material.

(4) In relation to property seized by a person who had, or purported to have, power under this Part to seize it by virtue only of one or more of the powers of seizure conferred by—

(a) [*repealed by* Proceeds of Crime Act *2002, s.457 and Sched. 12*],

(b) section 56(5) of the *Drug Trafficking Act* 1994,

(c) [*Northern Ireland*], or

(d) section 352(4) of the *Proceeds of Crime Act* 2002,

the second condition is satisfied only if the application states that the seized property is or contains excluded material.

(5) In relation to property seized by a person who had, or purported to have, power under this Part to seize it by virtue only of one or more of the powers of seizure specified in Part 3 of Schedule 1 but not by virtue of—

(a) the power of seizure conferred by section 8(2) of the 1984 Act,

(b) [*Northern Ireland*],

(c) either of the powers of seizure conferred by paragraphs 1 and 3 of Schedule 5 to the *Terrorism Act* 2000, or

(d) either of the powers of seizure conferred by paragraphs 15 and 19 of Schedule 5 to that Act of 2000 so far as they are conferred by reference to paragraph 1 of that Schedule,

the second condition is satisfied only if the application states that the seized property is or contains excluded material or special procedure material consisting of documents or records other than documents.

(6) The powers mentioned in subsection (3) are—

(a) the powers of seizure specified in Part 3 of Schedule 1;

(b) the powers of seizure conferred by the provisions of Parts 2 and 3 of the 1984 Act (except section 8(2) of that Act);

(c) [*Northern Ireland*];

(d) the powers of seizure conferred by the provisions of paragraph 11 of Schedule 5 to the *Terrorism Act* 2000; and

(e) the powers of seizure conferred by the provisions of paragraphs 15 and 19 of that Schedule so far as they are conferred by reference to paragraph 11 of that Schedule.

(7) In this section "a relevant person" means any one of the following—

(a) the person who made the seizure;

(b) the person for the time being having possession, in consequence of the seizure, of the seized property;

(c) the person named for the purposes of subsection (1)(d) or (4)(d) of section 52 in any notice given under that section with respect to the seizure.

[This section is printed as amended by the *PCA* 2002, ss.456 and 457, and Scheds 11, para. 40(3), and 12.]

The duty to secure

61.—(1) The duty to secure that arises under this section is a duty of the person for the time being having possession, in consequence of the seizure, of the seized property to secure that arrangements are in force that ensure that the seized property (without being returned) is not, at any time after the giving of the notice of the application under section 60(1), either— **15–140**

(a) examined or copied, or

(b) put to any use to which its seizure would, apart from this subsection, entitle it to be put,

except with the consent of the applicant or in accordance with the directions of the appropriate judicial authority.

(2) Subsection (1) shall not have effect in relation to any time after the withdrawal of the application to which the notice relates.

(3) Nothing in any arrangements for the purposes of this section shall be taken to prevent the giving of a notice under section 49 of the *Regulation of Investigatory Powers Act* 2000 (notices for the disclosure of material protected by encryption etc.) in respect of any information contained in the seized material; but subsection (1) of this section shall apply to anything disclosed for the purpose of complying with such a notice as it applies to the seized material in which the information in question is contained.

(4) Subsection (9) of section 59 shall apply in relation to any jurisdiction conferred on the appropriate judicial authority by this section as it applies in relation to the jurisdiction conferred by that section.

Use of inextricably linked property

15–141 **62.**—(1) This section applies to property, other than property which is for the time being required to be secured in pursuance of section 61, if—

(a) it has been seized under any power conferred by section 50 or 51 or specified in Part 1 or 2 of Schedule 1, and
(b) it is inextricably linked property.

(2) Subject to subsection (3), it shall be the duty of the person for the time being having possession, in consequence of the seizure, of the inextricably linked property to ensure that arrangements are in force which secure that that property (without being returned) is not at any time, except with the consent of the person from whom it was seized, either—

(a) examined or copied, or
(b) put to any other use.

(3) Subsection (2) does not require that arrangements under that subsection should prevent inextricably linked property from being put to any use falling within subsection (4).

(4) A use falls within this subsection to the extent that it is use which is necessary for facilitating the use, in any investigation or proceedings, of property in which the inextricably linked property is comprised.

(5) Property is inextricably linked property for the purposes of this section if it falls within any of subsections (6) to (8).

(6) Property falls within this subsection if—

(a) it has been seized under a power conferred by section 50 or 51; and
(b) but for subsection (3)(c) of section 53, arrangements under subsection (2) of that section in relation to the property would be required to ensure the return of the property as mentioned in subsection (2)(c) of that section.

(7) Property falls within this subsection if—

(a) it has been seized under a power to which section 54 applies; and
(b) but for paragraph (b) of subsection (1) of that section, the person for the time being having possession of the property would be under a duty to secure its return as mentioned in that subsection.

(8) Property falls within this subsection if—

(a) it has been seized under a power of seizure to which section 55 applies; and
(b) but for paragraph (c) of subsection (1) of that section, the person for the time being having possession of the property would be under a duty to secure its return as mentioned in that subsection.

Criminal Justice and Police Act 2001, ss.63–66

Construction of Part 2

Copies

15–142 **63.**—(1) Subject to subsection (3)—

(a) in this Part, "seize" includes "take a copy of", and cognate expressions shall be construed accordingly;
(b) this Part shall apply as if any copy taken under any power to which any provision of this Part applies were the original of that of which it is a copy; and
(c) for the purposes of this Part, except sections 50 and 51, the powers mentioned in subsection (2) (which are powers to obtain hard copies etc. of information which is stored in electronic form) shall be treated as powers of seizure, and references to seizure and to seized property shall be construed accordingly.

(2) The powers mentioned in subsection (1)(c) are any powers which are conferred by—

(a)–(i) [*see* post].

(3) Subsection (1) does not apply to section 50(6) or 57.

The provisions listed in subsection (1) are: (a) the *PACE Act* 1984, ss.19(4) and 20; (c) the *Firearms Act* 1968, s.46(3); (d) the *Gaming Act* 1968, s.43(5)(aa); (f) the *Food Safety Act* 1990, s.32(6)(b); (h) the *Competition Act* 1998, s.28(2)(f); and (i) the *Nuclear Safeguards Act* 2000, s.8(2)(c). Paragraphs (b) and (g) relate to Northern Ireland. Paragraph (e) was repealed by the *Finance Act* 2007, ss.84(4) and 114, Sched. 22, paras. 3 and 13(1)(b), and Sched. 27, Pt 5.

Meaning of "appropriate judicial authority"

64.—(1) Subject to subsection (2), in this Part "appropriate judicial authority" means— **15–143**

(a) in relation to England and Wales and Northern Ireland, a judge of the Crown Court;

(b) [*Scotland*].

(2) In this Part "appropriate judicial authority", in relation to the seizure of items under any power mentioned in subsection (3) and in relation to items seized under any such power, means—

(a) in relation to England and Wales and Northern Ireland, the High Court;

(b) [*Scotland*].

(3) Those powers are—

(a) the powers of seizure conferred by—

(i) section 448(3) of the *Companies Act* 1985;

(ii) [*Northern Ireland*];

(iii) section 28(2) of the *Competition Act* 1998;

(aa) the power of seizure conferred by section 352(4) of the *Proceeds of Crime Act* 2002, if the power is exercisable for the purposes of a civil recovery investigation or a detained cash investigation (within the meaning of Part 8 of that Act);

(b) any power of seizure conferred by section 50, so far as that power is exercisable by reference to any power mentioned in paragraph (a).

[This section is printed as amended by the *PCA* 2002, ss.456 and 457, and Scheds 11, para. 40(4), and 12; and the *SCA* 2007, s.77, and Sched. 10, para. 27.]

Meaning of "legal privilege"

65.—(1) Subject to the following provisions of this section, references in this Part to an item subject to legal privilege shall be construed— **15–144**

(a) for the purposes of the application of this Part to England and Wales, in accordance with section 10 of the 1984 Act (meaning of "legal privilege");

(b), (c) [*Scotland and Northern Ireland*].

(2) In relation to property which has been seized in exercise, or purported exercise, of—

(a) the power of seizure conferred by section 28(2) of the *Competition Act* 1998, or

(b) so much of any power of seizure conferred by section 50 as is exercisable by reference to that power,

references in this Part to an item subject to legal privilege shall be read as references to a privileged communication within the meaning of section 30 of that Act.

(3) [*Repealed by* Finance Act *2007, ss.84(4) and 114, Sched. 22, paras. 3 and 13(1)(c), and Sched. 27, Pt 5.*]

(3A) In relation to property which has been seized in exercise, or purported exercise, of—

(a) the power of seizure conferred by section 352(4) of the *Proceeds of Crime Act* 2002, or

(b) so much of any power of seizure conferred by section 50 as is exercisable by reference to that power,

references in this Part to an item subject to legal privilege shall be read as references to privileged material within the meaning of section 354(2) of that Act.

(4) An item which is, or is comprised in, property which has been seized in exercise, or purported exercise, of the power of seizure conferred by section 448(3) of the *Companies Act* 1985 shall be taken for the purposes of this Part to be an item subject to legal privilege if, and only if, the seizure of that item was in contravention of section 452(2) of that Act (privileged information). **15–145**

(5) [*Northern Ireland*.]

(6) [*Corresponds to subs. (4) with substitution of references to* Timeshare Act *1992, Sched. 2, para. 3(2) and para. 3(4).*]

(7) [*Corresponds to subs. (4) with substitution of references to* Data Protection Act *1998, Sched. 9, para. 1 and para. 9.*]

(8) [*Corresponds to subs. (4) with substitution of references to* Freedom of Information Act *2000, Sched. 3, para. 1 and para. 9.*]

(8A) [*Corresponds to subs. (4) with substitution of references to* Enterprise Act *2002, ss.227C and 227B(4).]*

(9) An item which is, or is comprised in, property which has been seized in exercise, or purported exercise, of so much of any power of seizure conferred by section 50 as is exercisable by reference to a power of seizure conferred by—

(a)–(f) [*the powers of seizure mentioned in subss. (4) to (8A) respectively*],

shall be taken for the purposes of this Part to be an item subject to legal privilege if, and only if, the item would have been taken for the purposes of this Part to be an item subject to legal privilege had it been seized under the power of seizure by reference to which the power conferred by section 50 was exercised.

[This section is printed as amended by the *PCA* 2002, s.456, and Sched. 11, para. 40(5); and the *Enterprise Act 2002 (Amendment) Regulations* 2006 (S.I. 2006 No. 3363), regs. 24 and 26.]

General interpretation of Part 2

15–146 **66.**—(1) In this Part—

"appropriate judicial authority" has the meaning given by section 64;

"documents" includes information recorded in any form;

"item subject to legal privilege" shall be construed in accordance with section 65;

"premises" includes any vehicle, stall or moveable structure (including an offshore installation) and any other place whatever, whether or not occupied as land;

"offshore installation" has the same meaning as in the *Mineral Workings (Offshore Installations) Act* 1971;

"return", in relation to seized property, shall be construed in accordance with section 58, and cognate expressions shall be construed accordingly;

"seize", and cognate expressions, shall be construed in accordance with section 63(1) and subsection (5) below;

"seized property", in relation to any exercise of a power of seizure, means (subject to subsection (5)) anything seized in exercise of that power; and

"vehicle" includes any vessel, aircraft or hovercraft.

(2) In this Part references, in relation to a time when seized property is in any person's possession in consequence of a seizure ("the relevant time"), to something for which the person making the seizure had power to search shall be construed—

(a) where the seizure was made on the occasion of a search carried out on the authority of a warrant, as including anything of the description of things the presence or suspected presence of which provided grounds for the issue of the warrant;

(b) where the property was seized in the course of a search on the occasion of which it would have been lawful for the person carrying out the search to seize anything which on that occasion was believed by him to be, or appeared to him to be, of a particular description, as including—

(i) anything which at the relevant time is believed by the person in possession of the seized property, or (as the case may be) appears to him, to be of that description; and

(ii) anything which is in fact of that description;

(c) where the property was seized in the course of a search on the occasion of which it would have been lawful for the person carrying out the search to seize anything which there were on that occasion reasonable grounds for believing was of a particular description, as including—

(i) anything which there are at the relevant time reasonable grounds for believing is of that description; and

(ii) anything which is in fact of that description;

(d) where the property was seized in the course of a search to which neither paragraph (b) nor paragraph (c) applies, as including anything which is of a description of things which, on the occasion of the search, it would have been lawful for the person carrying it out to seize otherwise than under section 50 and 51; and

(e) where the property was seized on the occasion of a search authorised under section 82 of the *Terrorism Act* 2000 (seizure of items suspected to have been, or to be intended to be, used in commission of certain offences), as including anything—

(i) which is or has been, or is or was intended to be, used in the commission of an offence such as is mentioned in subsection (3)(a) or (b) of that section; or

(ii) which at the relevant time the person who is in possession of the seized property reasonably suspects is something falling within sub-paragraph (i).

(3) For the purpose of determining in accordance with subsection (2), in relation to any time, whether or to what extent property seized on the occasion of a search authorised under section 9 of the *Official Secrets Act* 1911 (seizure of evidence of offences under that Act having been or being about to be committed) is something for which the person making the seizure had power to search, subsection (1) of that section shall be construed— **15–147**

(a) as if the reference in that subsection to evidence of an offence under that Act being about to be committed were a reference to evidence of such an offence having been, at the time of the seizure, about to be committed; and

(b) as if the reference in that subsection to reasonable ground for suspecting that such an offence is about to be committed were a reference to reasonable ground for suspecting that at the time of the seizure such an offence was about to be committed.

(4) References in subsection (2) to a search include references to any activities authorised by virtue of any of the following—

(a)–(r) [*see* post].

(5) References in this Part to a power of seizure include references to each of the powers to take possession of items under—

(b)–(i) [*see* post],

and references in this Part to seizure and to seized property shall be construed accordingly.

(6) In this Part, so far as it applies to England and Wales—

(a) references to excluded material shall be construed in accordance with section 11 of the 1984 Act (meaning of "excluded material"); and

(b) references to special procedure material shall be construed in accordance with section 14 of that Act (meaning of "special procedure material").

(7) [*Northern Ireland.*]

(8) References in this Part to any item or material being comprised in other property include references to its being mixed with that other property.

(9) [*Northern Ireland.*]

The provisions listed in subsection (4) (as amended) are: (a) the *Trade Descriptions Act* 1968, s.28(1); (b) the *Fair Trading Act* 1973, s.29(1); (c) the *Prices Act* 1974, Sched., para. 9; (d) the *Consumer Credit Act* 1974, s.162(1); (e) the *Estate Agents Act* 1979, s.11(1) (amended, as from a day to be appointed, so as to substitute a reference to subss. (1) to (1C): *Consumers, Estate Agents and Redress Act* 2007, s.63(1), and Sched. 7, para. 22(a)); (g) the *Weights and Measures Act* 1985, s.79, and the *Weights and Measures (Packaged Goods) Regulations* 2006 (S.I. 2006 No. 659), Sched. 7; (h) the *Consumer Protection Act* 1987, s.29; (j) the *Food Safety Act* 1990, s.35(2); (k) the *Property Misdescriptions Act* 1991, Sched., para. 3; (m) the *Timeshare Act* 1992, Sched. 2, para. 3; (ma) the *Enterprise Act* 2002, s.227C; (n) the *Human Tissue Act* 2004, Sched. 5, para. 2; (o) the *General Product Safety Regulations* 2005 (S.I. 2005 No. 1803), reg. 22; (p) the *Animal Welfare Act* 2006, ss.26(1), 27(1), 28(1) and 29(1); (q) the *Business Protection from Misleading Marketing Regulations* 2008 (S.I. 2008 No. 1276), reg. 23; and (r) the *Consumer Protection from Unfair Trading Regulations* 2008 (S.I. 2008 No. 1277), reg. 21. Paragraphs (f), (i) (repealed) and (l) relate to Northern Ireland.

The provisions listed in subsection (5) are: (b) the *Companies Act* 1985, s.448(3); (f) the *CJA* 1987, s.2(5); (g) the *Human Fertilisation and Embryology Act* 1990, s.40(2); (h) the *Competition Act* 1998, s.28(2)(c); and (i) the *FSMA* 2000, s.176(5). Paragraphs (a), (c) and (e) were repealed by S.I. 2001 No. 3649 (*ante*, § 15–133), art. 364. Paragraph (d) relates to Northern Ireland.

Powers of seizure (Schedule 1, Parts 1, 2 and 3)

Powers to which section 50 applies (list 1)

Schedule 1, Part 1, lists the powers of seizure conferred by the following enactments: (1) the *PACE Act* 1984, Pts II and III; (3) the *Official Secrets Act* 1911, s.9(1); **15–148**

(4) the *Children and Young Persons (Harmful Publications) Act* 1955, s.3(1); (5) the *Obscene Publications Act* 1959, s.3(1) and (2); (8) the *Firearms Act* 1968, s.46; (9) the *Trade Descriptions Act* 1968, s.28(1)(c) and (d); (10) the *Theft Act* 1968, s.26(3); (14) the *Misuse of Drugs Act* 1971, s.23(2) and (3); (15) the *Immigration Act* 1971, ss.28D(3), 28E(5) and 28F(6); (16) the *Fair Trading Act* 1973, s.29(1)(c) and (d); (17) the *Biological Weapons Act* 1974, s.4(1)(b), (c) and (d); (18) the *Prices Act* 1974, Sched., para. 9(2); (19) the *Consumer Credit Act* 1974, s.162(1)(c) and (d); (21) the *Protection of Children Act* 1978, s.4(2); (23) the *CEMA* 1979, s.118C(4); (24) the *Estate Agents Act* 1979, s.11(1)(c) (replaced, as from a day to be appointed, by a reference to subs. (1B): *Consumers, Estate Agents and Redress Act* 2007, s.63(1), and Sched. 7, para. 22(b)); (25) the *Indecent Displays (Control) Act* 1981, s.2(3); (26) the *Forgery and Counterfeiting Act* 1981, ss.7(1) and 24(1); (27) the *Betting and Gaming Duties Act* 1981, Sched. 1, para. 16(2); (34) the *Video Recordings Act* 1984, s.17(2); (35) the *Companies Act* 1985, s.448(3); (36) the *Weights and Measures Act* 1985, s.79(2)(b); (39) the *Protection of Military Remains Act* 1986, s.6(3); (41) the *Greater London Council (General Powers) Act* 1986, s.12; (44) the *CJA* 1987, s.2(5); (45) the *Consumer Protection Act* 1987, s.29(4), (5) and (6); (48) the *Copyright, Designs and Patents Act* 1988, ss.109(4), 200(3A) and 297B(4); (50) the *Food Safety Act* 1990, s.32(6); (51) the *Computer Misuse Act* 1990, s.14(4); (52) the *Human Fertilisation and Embryology Act* 1990, s.40(2); (53) the *Property Misdescriptions Act* 1991, Sched., para. 3(3); (54) the *Dangerous Dogs Act* 1991, s.5(2); (56) the *Timeshare Act* 1992, Sched. 2, para. 3(2); (56A) the *Charities Act* 1993, s.31A(3); (58A) the *Trade Marks Act* 1994, s.92A(4); (59) the *DTA* 1994, s.56(5); (60) the *Chemical Weapons Act* 1996, s.29(2)(c), (d) and (e); (63) the *Knives Act* 1997, s.5(2); (64) the *Nuclear Explosions (Prohibitions and Inspections) Act* 1998, s.10(2)(c), (d) and (e); (65) the *Data Protection Act* 1998, Sched. 9, para. 1; (66) the *Landmines Act* 1998, s.18(3)(c), (d) and (e); (67) the *Competition Act* 1998, s.28(2); (68) the *Nuclear Safeguards Act* 2000, s.8(2); (69) the *FSMA* 2000, s.176(5); (70) the *Terrorism Act* 2000, s.82(3); (71) *ibid.*, Sched. 5, paras 1, 3, 11, 15 and 19; (73) the *Freedom of Information Act* 2000, Sched. 3, para. 1; (73A) the *PCA* 2002, s.352; (73A [*sic*]) the *International Criminal Court Act* 2001, Sched. 5, para. 9; (73B) the *Enterprise Act* 2002, s.194(2); (73BA) *ibid.*, s.227C; (73C) the *Crime (International Co-operation) Act* 2003, ss.17 and 22; (73D) the *Extradition Act* 2003, ss.156(5), 160(5), 161(4), 162(6) and (7), and 164(6) and (7); (73E) the *Human Tissue Act* 2004, s.56, and Sched. 6, para. 5(1) and (2); (73E [*sic*]) the *Licensing Act* 2003, s.90; (73F) the *SOCPA* 2005, s.66; (73F [*sic*]) the *Gambling Act* 2005, s.317; (73G) the *General Product Safety Regulations* 2005 (S.I. 2005 No. 1803), reg. 22(4)–(6); (73G [*sic*]) the *Weights and Measures (Packaged Goods) Regulations* 2006 (S.I. 2006 No. 659), Sched. 5, para. 4; (73H) the *Terrorism Act* 2006, s.28; (73I) the *Animal Welfare Act* 2006, Sched. 2, para. 10(2)(j); (73J) the *Money Laundering Regulations* 2007 (S.I. 2007 No. 2157), reg. 39(6); (73J [*sic*]) the *Business Protection from Misleading Marketing Regulations* 2008 (S.I. 2008 No. 1276), reg. 23(1)(c) and (d); (73K) the *Transfer of Funds (Information on the Payer) Regulations* 2007 (S.I. 2007 No. 3298), reg. 9(6); and (73K [*sic*]) the *Consumer Protection from Unfair Trading Regulations* 2008 (S.I. 2008 No. 1277), reg. 21(1)(c) and (d).

Paragraph 7 was repealed by the *Licensing Act* 2003, s.199, and Sched. 7. Paragraphs 6, 11 and 20 were repealed by the *Gambling Act* 2005, s.356, and Sched. 16, para. 18. Paragraphs 13, 28, 29, 57, 58, 61 and 72 were repealed by the *Finance Act* 2007, ss.84(4) and 114, Sched. 22, paras 3 and 13(2), and Sched. 27, Pt 5. Paragraphs 32, 40 and 43 were repealed by S.I. 2001 No. 3649 (*ante*, § 15–133), art. 364. Paragraph 37 was repealed by the *Weights and Measures (Packaged Goods) Regulations* 2006 (S.I. 2006 No. 659), reg. 1(2), and Sched. 1, Pt 2, paras (24) and (27)(b). Paragraph 47 was repealed by the *PCA* 2002, s.457 and Sched. 12. Paragraph 49 was repealed by the *Crime (International Co-operation) Act* 2003, s.91, and Sched. 6. Paragraph 56A was inserted by the *Charities Act* 2006, s.26(2). The first paragraph 73A was inserted by the *PCA* 2002, s.456, and Sched. 11, para. 40(6). Paragraph 48 was amended, and paragraph 58A and the second paragraph 73A were inserted, by the *Criminal Justice and Police Act 2001 (Powers of Seizure) Order* 2003 (S.I. 2003 No. 934). Paragraph

73B (renumbered by a correction slip) was inserted by the *Enterprise Act* 2002, s.194(5). Paragraph 73BA was inserted by the *Enterprise Act 2002 (Amendment) Regulations* 2006 (S.I. 2006 No. 3363), regs 24 and 28. Paragraphs 73C and 73D were inserted by the *Crime (International Co-operation) Act* 2003, s.26(3), and the *Extradition Act* 2003, s.165(2), respectively. Paragraph 73E was inserted by the *Human Tissue Act* 2004, s.56, and Sched. 6, para. 5(1) and (4). A second paragraph 73E (renumbered erroneously by the *Gambling Act* 2005, s.356, and Sched. 16, para. 18) was inserted by the *Licensing Act* 2003, s.198, and Sched. 6, paras 119 and 128(a). Paragraph 73F was inserted by the *SOCPA* 2005, s.68. A second paragraph 73F was inserted by the *Gambling Act* 2005, s.356, and Sched. 16, para. 18. The first paragraph 73G was inserted by the *General Product Safety Regulations* 2005 (S.I. 2005 No. 1803), reg. 47(3). A second paragraph 73G was inserted by S.I. 2006 No. 659 (*ante*), reg. 1(2), and Sched. 1, Pt 2, paras (24) and (27)(c). Paragraph 73H was inserted by the *Terrorism Act* 2006, s.28(6)(a). Paragraph 73I was inserted by the *Animal Welfare Act* 2006, s.64, and Sched. 3, para. 14. The first paragraph 73J was inserted by the *Money Laundering Regulations* 2007 (S.I. 2007 No. 2157), reg. 51,. and Sched. 6, para. 3. The first paragraph 73K was inserted by the *Transfer of Funds (Information on the Payer) Regulations* 2007 (S.I. 2007 No. 3298), reg. 19, and Sched. 3, para. 3. The second paragraphs 73J and 73K were inserted by the *Consumer Protection from Unfair Trading Regulations* 2008 (S.I. 2008 No. 1277), reg. 30, and Sched. 2, para. 64.

Paragraphs 2, 12, 22, 30, 31, 33, 38, 42, 46 (repealed), 55 and 62 relate to Northern Ireland.

Powers to which section 51 applies (list 2)

Schedule 1, Part 2, lists the powers of seizure conferred by the following enactments: (74) the *PACE Act* 1984, Pt III; (76) as (8) in list 1; (77) as (14) in list 1; (78) the *Immigration Act* 1971, s.28G(7); (79) as (17) in list 1; (81) the *CJPOA* 1994, s.139(10); (82) the *Terrorism Act* 2000, s.43(4); (83) as (71) in list 1; and (83A) the *Extradition Act* 2003, s.163(6) and (7) (inserted by s.165(3) of that Act). Paragraphs 75 and 80 relate to Northern Ireland. **15–149**

Powers to which section 55 applies (list 3)

Schedule 1, Part 3, lists the powers of seizure conferred by the following enactments: (*84*) the *PACE Act* 1984, s.8(2); (*86*) as (3) in list 1; (87) as (4) in list 1; (*88*) as (5) in list (1); (*91*) as (8) in list 1; (*92*) as (10) in list 1; (*95*) the *Immigration Act* 1971, s.28D(3); (*96*) as (17) in list 1; (*98*) as (21) in list 1; (*100*) as (25) in list 1; (*101*) as (26) in list 1; (*103*) as (34) in list 1; (*106*) as (48) in list 1; (*107*) as (51) in list 1; (*107A*) as (58A) in list 1; (*108*) as (59) in list 1; (*109*) (i) the *Terrorism Act* 2000, Sched. 5, paras 1 and 3, and (ii) *ibid.*, paras 15 and 19, but so far only as the power in question is conferred by reference to para. 1 of that Schedule; (*110*) the *PCA* 2002, s.352(4); (*111*) the *Licensing Act* 2003, s.90; (*112*) the *Gambling Act* 2005, s.317; (*113*) the *Terrorism Act* 2006, s.28. Paragraphs 85, 94, 99, 102 and 104 relate to Northern Ireland. **15–150**

Paragraphs 89, 93 and 97 were repealed by the *Gambling Act* 2005, s.356, and Sched. 16, para. 18. Paragraph 90 was repealed, and paragraph 111 (as renumbered by the *Gambling Act*, s.356, and Sched. 16, para. 18) was inserted, by the *Licensing Act* 2003, ss.198 and 199, Sched. 6, paras 119 and 128(b), and Sched. 7. Paragraph 105 was repealed, and paragraph 110 was added, by the *PCA* 2002, ss.456 and 457, and Scheds 11, para. 40(7), and 12. Paragraph 106 was amended, and paragraph 107A was inserted, by S.I. 2003 No. 934 (*ante*, § 15–148). Paragraph *112* was inserted by the *Gambling Act* 2005, s.356, and Sched. 16, para. 18.

Applications under section 59

Rule 39 of the *Crown Court Rules* 1982 (S.I. 1982 No. 1109) makes procedural provision in relation to the making of applications under section 59 of the 2001 Act (*ante*, § 15–137). Such applications may be heard in chambers: see rule 27(2)(d) of the 1982 rules. Rule 39 has not been incorporated into the *Criminal Procedure Rules* 2005 (S.I. 2005 No. 384). It survives as a Crown Court rule. The Criminal Procedure Rule **15–150a**

Committee appear to consider applications under section 59 to be civil proceedings (*sed quaere*).

Crown Court Rules 1982 (S.I. 1982 No. 1109), r.39

Applications relating to property seized in accordance with the provisions of Part 2 of the Criminal Justice and Police Act 2001

39.—(1) This rule applies to any application made under section 59 of the *Criminal Justice and Police Act* 2001 ("the 2001 Act") and expressions used in this rule shall have the same meaning as in the 2001 Act.

(2) Notice of an application shall be given to the appropriate officer of the Crown Court and shall—

(a) be made in writing;

(b) where the application is made under section 59(2) of the 2001 Act specify under which of the grounds in section 59(3) of the 2001 Act it is made and—

(i) where it is made under section 59(3)(a) of the 2001 Act specify why the applicant considers there was no power to make the seizure;

(ii) where it is made under section 59(3)(b), (c) or (d) of the 2001 Act describe the property and specify why the return of the property is required;

(c) where the application is made to authorise the retention of property by a person for the time being in possession of it, specify which of the grounds in section 59(7) is relied upon.

(3) Copies of an application made under section 59(2) of the 2001 Act by a person with a relevant interest in the property shall be served upon—

(a) the person for the time being in possession of the property;

(b) the person (if any) identified as being the person to whom notice of such an application should be given by a notice served under section 52 of the 2001 Act when the property was seized; and

(c) any other person appearing to be the owner of the property.

(4) Copies of an application made under section 59(2) of the 2001 Act by a person for the time being in possession of property which has been seized shall be served upon—

(a) the person from whom the property was seized;

(b) any person appearing to have a relevant interest in the property; and

(c) any other person appearing to be the owner of the property.

(5) Any person served with a copy of an application under this rule shall within 7 days of being served—

(a) notify the applicant and the appropriate officer of the Crown Court whether or not he wishes to make representations concerning the application and appear at the hearing of the application; and

(b) if he wishes to make representations, give the applicant and the appropriate officer of the Crown Court a written statement setting out such representations.

(6) The appropriate officer of the Crown Court shall—

(a) fix a date, time and place for the hearing of the application; and

(b) notify the applicant and any other party wishing to make representations at the hearing of the application of the date, time and place fixed for the hearing of the application.

(7) When hearing the application the court may, if it thinks necessary in the interests of justice, direct that the public be excluded from the court.

[This rule was inserted as rule 38 by the *Crown Court (Amendment) (No. 2) Rules* 2003 (S.I. 2003 No. 639). It was renumbered as rule 39 by the *Crown Court (Amendment) (No. 3) Rules* 2003 (S.I. 2003 No. 1664).]

(3) Code of practice

15–151 For the codes of practice generally, see *ante*, §§ 15–3 *et seq.* The current Code B (Code of Practice for the Searching of Premises by Police Officers and the Seizure of Property found by Police Officers on Persons or Premises) came into force on February 1, 2008.

It should be noted that paragraph B:2.5 was introduced (in the 1995 edition, as para. B:1.3B) to reverse the decision in *Dudley M.B.C. v. Debenhams plc*, *The Times*, August 16, 1994, DC, in which it was held that trading standards officers entering a shop pursuant to their right to do so under section 29 of the *Consumer Protection Act* 1987 were subject to Code B. It is submitted that this was unnecessary as that decision was in any event wrong: Code B only bites in relation to searches falling within paragraph B:2.3. A search pursuant to a particular statutory power clearly does not fall within these provisions: as is pointed out in *Walkers Snack Foods Ltd v. Coventry City Council* [1998] 3 All E.R. 163, DC (considering a similar provision in the *Food Safety Act* 1990), the exercise of the statutory power is not by virtue of the occupier's consent, but by virtue of the specific statutory entitlement. There are countless such provisions in primary and subordinate legislation; they invariably contain their own safeguards; for example, section 29(1) of the 1987 Act requires the officer to produce his credentials if required, and limits the exercise of the power to "any reasonable hour".

If during a routine scene of crime search (as to which see paragraph B:2.3(a)), the police discover evidence appearing to implicate the occupier, any further search should be conducted in accordance with Code B, which will involve obtaining the occupier's written consent for the continuance of the search: *R. v. Sanghera* [2001] 1 Cr.App.R. 20, CA.

[For the full text of Code B, see Appendix A–19 *et seq.*]

D. ARREST

(1) Summary

Police powers of arrest are now mainly as follows: **15–152**

(a) arrest without warrant under Part III (ss.24–33) of the *PACE Act* 1984 (*post*, §§ 15–161 *et seq.*);

(b) arrest without warrant under a limited number of statutory enactments specifically preserved by the *PACE Act* 1984, s.26(2) and Sched. 2 (*post*, § 15–172);

(c) arrest with a warrant issued by a justice of the peace or a judge (see generally *post*, §§ 19–342 *et seq.*);

(d) arrest with or without a warrant under Part X of the *CJPOA* 1994 (cross-border enforcement) (*post*, § 15–189); and

(e) the common law power of arrest for a breach of the peace (*post*, §§ 19–343, 19–344).

(2) The Police and Criminal Evidence Act 1984

Powers of arrest

The powers of arrest without warrant provided for by Part III of the 1984 Act may be divided into four categories: arrest without warrant by constables (s.24, *post* § 15–161); arrest without warrant by other persons (s.24A, *post* § 15–162); other statutory powers of arrest (s.26, Sched. 2, *post*, §§ 15–171 *et seq.*); and arrest for fingerprinting (s.27, *post*, § 15–174). **15–153**

[The next paragraph is § 15–159.]

What constitutes lawful arrest

In general, an arrest is constituted by a physical seizure or touching of the arrested person's body, with a view to his detention; see, for example, *R. v. Brosch* [1988] Crim.L.R. 743, CA. But there may also be an arrest by mere words: see *Alderson v. Booth* [1969] 2 Q.B. 216, 53 Cr.App.R. 301, DC (arrest is constituted when any form of words is used which is calculated to bring to the suspect's notice, and does so, that he is under compulsion, and he thereafter submits to that compulsion); and *R. v. Inwood*, 57 Cr.App.R. 529, CA (no magic formula, only the obligation to make it plain to the suspect by what is said and done that he is no longer a free man; different procedures might be needed according to the person's age, ethnic origin, knowledge of English, intellectual qualities, physical or mental disabilities). Where a police officer restrains a person, but does not at that time intend or purport to arrest him, then he commits an **15–159** assault, even if an arrest would have been justified: *Wood v. DPP* [2008] 6 *Archbold News* 2, DC (following *Kenlin v. Gardner* [1967] 2 Q.B. 510, DC).

A constable may use reasonable force, if necessary, to effect an arrest (s.117, *ante*, § 15–26).

An arrest is unlawful unless at the time of the arrest or as soon as practicable after the arrest the arrested person is informed that he is under arrest and of the ground of the arrest, regardless of whether the fact of arrest is obvious (*PACE Act* 1984, s.28 (*post*, § 15–176)). This is subject to an exception in the case of a person who escapes (s.28(5)).

Consequences of arrest

15–160 Where a private citizen makes a lawful arrest either at common law or under statute, he should take the arrested person before a justice of the peace or a police officer, not necessarily forthwith, but as soon as reasonably possible: *John Lewis & Co. Ltd v. Tims* [1952] A.C. 676, HL.

As to the obligations of a constable when he arrests someone for an offence, or takes someone into custody after he has been arrested for an offence by a person other than a constable, at any place other than at a police station, see section 30 of the *PACE Act* 1984 (*post*, § 15–182).

A person who is at a police station under arrest must be further arrested where it appears that if he were released he would be liable to arrest for some other offence (*PACE Act* 1984, s.31, *post*, § 15–185).

Section 32 provides for the search of a person upon arrest and for entry and search of any premises in which he was when arrested or immediately before he was arrested (*post*, § 15–186).

For the conditions and duration of the detention of an arrested person, see the *PACE Act* 1984, Pt IV, ss.34–52, *ante*, §§ 3–93 *et seq.* For bail after arrest, see section 47, *ante*, § 3–130. For the questioning and treatment of persons in custody, see the *PACE Act* 1984, Pt V, ss.53–65, *post*, §§ 15–190 *et seq.*

Police and Criminal Evidence Act 1984, s.24

Arrest without warrant: constables

15–161 **24.**—(1) A constable may arrest without a warrant—

(a) anyone who is about to commit an offence;

(b) anyone who is in the act of committing an offence;

(c) anyone whom he has reasonable grounds for suspecting to be about to commit an offence;

(d) anyone whom he has reasonable grounds for suspecting to be committing an offence.

(2) If a constable has reasonable grounds for suspecting that an offence has been committed, he may arrest without a warrant anyone whom he has reasonable grounds to suspect of being guilty of it.

(3) If an offence has been committed, a constable may arrest without a warrant—

(a) anyone who is guilty of the offence;

(b) anyone whom he has reasonable grounds for suspecting to be guilty of it.

(4) But the power of summary arrest conferred by subsection (1), (2) or (3) is exercisable only if the constable has reasonable grounds for believing that for any of the reasons mentioned in subsection (5) it is necessary to arrest the person in question.

(5) The reasons are—

(a) to enable the name of the person in question to be ascertained (in the case where the constable does not know, and cannot readily ascertain, the person's name, or has reasonable grounds for doubting whether a name given by the person as his name is his real name);

(b) correspondingly as regards the person's address;

(c) to prevent the person in question—

(i) causing physical injury to himself or any other person;

(ii) suffering physical injury;

(iii) causing loss of or damage to property;

(iv) committing an offence against public decency (subject to subsection (6)); or

(v) causing an unlawful obstruction of the highway;

(d) to protect a child or other vulnerable person from the person in question;
(e) to allow the prompt and effective investigation of the offence or of the conduct of the person in question;
(f) to prevent any prosecution for the offence from being hindered by the disappearance of the person in question.

(6) Subsection (5)(c)(iv) applies only where members of the public going about their normal business cannot reasonably be expected to avoid the person in question.

[This section was substituted by the *SOCPA* 2005, s.110(1) and (4).]

Police and Criminal Evidence Act 1984, s.24A

Arrest without warrant: other persons

24A.—(1) A person other than a constable may arrest without a warrant— **15–162**
(a) anyone who is in the act of committing an indictable offence;
(b) anyone whom he has reasonable grounds for suspecting to be committing an indictable offence.

(2) Where an indictable offence has been committed, a person other than a constable may arrest without a warrant—
(a) anyone who is guilty of the offence;
(b) anyone whom he has reasonable grounds for suspecting to be guilty of it.

(3) But the power of summary arrest conferred by subsection (1) or (2) is exercisable only if—
(a) the person making the arrest has reasonable grounds for believing that for any of the reasons mentioned in subsection (4) it is necessary to arrest the person in question; and
(b) it appears to the person making the arrest that it is not reasonably practicable for a constable to make it instead.

(4) The reasons are to prevent the person in question—
(a) causing physical injury to himself or any other person;
(b) suffering physical injury;
(c) causing loss of or damage to property; or
(d) making off before a constable can assume responsibility for him.

(5) This section does not apply in relation to an offence under Part 3 or 3A of the *Public Order Act* 1986.

[This section was inserted by the *SOCPA* 2005, s.110(1) and (4). Subs. (5) was inserted by the *Racial and Religious Hatred Act* 2006, s.2.]

As to "reasonable grounds for suspecting", see *ante*, §§ 15–23 *et seq.*

Section 71 of the *Electoral Administration Act* 2006 disapplies section 24A in relation to the arrest of a person inside a polling station who has committed or is suspected of committing an offence contrary to section 60 (personation) of the *Representation of the People Act* 1983.

For an arrest to be justified under subsection (2), it is essential that an indictable offence has been committed: see *R. v. Self*, 95 Cr.App.R. 42, CA.

[The next paragraph is § 15–171.]

Police and Criminal Evidence Act 1984, s.26, Sched. 2

Repeal of statutory powers of arrest without warrant or order

26.—(1) Subject to subsection (2) below, so much of any Act (including a local Act) passed before this Act as enables a constable— **15–171**
(a) to arrest a person for an offence without a warrant; or
(b) to arrest a person otherwise than for an offence without a warrant or an order of a court,

shall cease to have effect.

(2) Nothing in subsection (1) above affects the enactments specified in Schedule 2 to this Act.

SCHEDULE 2

PRESERVED POWERS OF ARREST

Section 2 of the *Emergency Powers Act* 1920. **15–172**
Section 49 of the *Prison Act* 1952.

Section 13 of the *Visiting Forces Act* 1952.

Sections 186 and 190B of the Army Act *1955.*

Sections 186 and 190B of the Air Force Act *1955.*

Sections 104 and 105 of the Naval Discipline Act *1957.*

Section 32 of the *Children and Young Persons Act* 1969.

Section 24(2) of the *Immigration Act* 1971 and paragraphs 17, 24 and 33 of Schedule 2 and paragraph 7 of Schedule 3 to that Act.

Section 7 of the *Bail Act* 1976.

Schedule 5 to the *Reserve Forces Act* 1980.

Sections 18, 35(10), 36(8), 38(7), 136(1) and 138 of the *Mental Health Act* 1983.

Section 5(5) of the *Repatriation of Prisoners Act* 1984.

[This Schedule is printed as amended, and repealed in part, by the *Representation of the People Act* 1985, s.25(1); the *Prevention of Terrorism (Temporary Provisions) Act* 1989, s.25(2) and Sched. 9, Pt I; the *Road Traffic (Consequential Provisions) Act* 1988, s.4 and Sched. 1; the *Children Act* 1989, s.108(5) and (7), Sched. 13 and Sched. 15; the *SOCPA* 2005, ss.111 and 174(2), Sched. 7, para. 24(1) and (4), and Sched. 17; and the *Electoral Administration Act* 2006, s.74(2), and Sched. 2. The entries relating to the 1955 and 1957 Acts are repealed as from a day to be appointed: *AFA* 2006, s.378(2), and Sched. 17.]

[The next paragraph is § 15–174.]

Police and Criminal Evidence Act 1984, s.27

Fingerprinting of certain offenders

15–174 **27.**—(1) If a person—

(a) has been convicted of a recordable offence;

(b) has not at any time been in police detention for the offence; and

(c) has not had his fingerprints taken—

(i) in the course of the investigation of the offence by the police; or

(ii) since the conviction,

any constable may at any time not later than one month after the date of the conviction require him to attend a police station in order that his fingerprints may be taken.

(1A) Where a person convicted of a recordable offence has already had his fingerprints taken as mentioned in paragraph (c) of subsection (1) above, that fact (together with any time when he has been in police detention for the offence) shall be disregarded for the purposes of that subsection if—

(a) the fingerprints taken on the previous occasion do not constitute a complete set of his fingerprints; or

(b) some or all of the fingerprints taken on the previous occasion are not of sufficient quality to allow satisfactory analysis, comparison or matching.

(1B) Subsections (1) and (1A) above apply—

(a) where a person has been given a caution in respect of a recordable offence which, at the time of the caution, he has admitted, or

(b) where a person has been warned or reprimanded under section 65 of the *Crime and Disorder Act* 1998 for a recordable offence,

as they apply where a person has been convicted of an offence, and references in this section to a conviction shall be construed accordingly.

(2) A requirement under subsection (1) above—

(a) shall give the person a period of at least 7 days within which he must so attend; and

(b) may direct him to so attend at a specified time of day or between specified times of day.

(3) Any constable may arrest without warrant a person who has failed to comply with a requirement under subsection (1) above.

(4) The Secretary of State may by regulations make provision for recording in national police records convictions for such offences as are specified in the regulations.

(4A) [*Repealed by* Criminal Justice and Police Act *2001, s.137 and Sched. 7, Pt II.*]
(5) [*Making of regulations.*]

[Subss. (1A) and (1B) were inserted by the *CJPA* 2001, s.78(1).]

For the meaning of "police detention", see section 118(2), *ante*, § 15–27. **15–175**
The actual taking of fingerprints is provided for by section 61, *post*, § 15–232.

By section 118(1) (*ante*, § 15–27), "recordable offence" means any offence to which regulations under section 27 apply. The *National Police Records (Recordable Offences) Regulations* 2000 (S.I. 2000 No. 1139) (as amended by the *National Police Records (Recordable Offences) (Amendment) Regulations* 2003 (S.I. 2003 No. 2823)) were made under subsection (4). They provide that there may be recorded in national police records convictions for, or cautions, reprimands and warnings given in respect of, offences punishable with imprisonment or for an offence included in a list of over 40 non-imprisonable offences. The reference to offences punishable with imprisonment is to be construed without regard to any prohibition or restriction imposed by or under any enactment on the punishment of young offenders. The regulations also provide that where a person's convictions are recordable, there may also be recorded his convictions for any other offences in the same proceedings.

Police and Criminal Evidence Act 1984, s.28

Information to be given on arrest

28.—(1) Subject to subsection (5) below, where a person is arrested, otherwise than by being informed that he is under arrest, the arrest is not lawful unless the person arrested is informed that he is under arrest as soon as is practicable after his arrest. **15–176**

(2) Where a person is arrested by a constable, subsection (1) above applies regardless of whether the fact of the arrest is obvious.

(3) Subject to subsection (5) below, no arrest is lawful unless the person arrested is informed of the ground for the arrest at the time of, or as soon as is practicable after, the arrest.

(4) Where a person is arrested by a constable, subsection (3) above applies regardless of whether the ground for the arrest is obvious.

(5) Nothing in this section is to be taken to require a person to be informed—

(a) that he is under arrest; or
(b) of the ground for the arrest,

if it was not reasonably practicable for him to be so informed by reason of his having escaped from arrest before the information could be given.

In *Taylor v. Chief Constable of Thames Valley Police* [2004] 1 W.L.R. 3155, CA (Civ. Div.), the court said that section 28(3) reflects the common law as laid down in *Christie v. Leachinsky* [1947] A.C. 573, HL, and explained that the underlying rationale is that a person is entitled to know why he is being arrested; one reason for that is that he should have the opportunity of explaining any misunderstanding, or of calling attention to others for whom he might have been mistaken. The court said that the modern approach to section 28(3) is to ask whether, having regard to all the circumstances, the person arrested was told in simple, non-technical language that he could understand, the essential legal and factual grounds for his arrest (*Fox, Campbell and Hartley v. U.K.*, 13 E.H.R.R. 157, ECtHR, para. 40, considering Article 5(2) of the European Convention); in future wrongful arrest cases, it will be unnecessary and undesirable to consider authority besides *Fox*, *ante*; thus, upon making an arrest for violent disorder, it had been sufficient to refer to "violent disorder" with a reference to the time and place; there had been no need to specify the precise way in which the arrestee was said to be taking part in the disorder. **15–177**

As to there being no intent to prosecute the suspect for the offence for which he is arrested, see *ante*, § 15–166. As to the unfairness of arresting and questioning for a lesser offence, when in fact the investigation relates to a more serious offence arising out of the same incident, see *R. v. Kirk* [2000] 1 Cr.App.R. 400, CA, *post*, § 15–484. **15–178**

In *Wheatley v. Lodge* [1971] 1 W.L.R. 29, DC, it was held that a police officer arresting a deaf person or somebody who could not speak English had to do what a reasonable person would do in the circumstances.

15–179 Where an arrest is unlawful, on the ground that the accused has not been told what acts are alleged to have constituted the offence for which he was arrested, this unlawfulness ceases when he is informed of the details at the police station: *R. v. Kulynycz* [1971] 1 Q.B. 367, 55 Cr.App.R. 34, CA. Where the initial arrest is valid and at the time of the arrest it is impracticable, because of the accused's physical resistance to the arrest, to inform him of the reason for the arrest, the initial arrest does not become invalid retrospectively when the officer fails to state the ground of arrest at the police station: *DPP v. Hawkins*, 88 Cr.App.R. 166, DC (applied in *Blench v. DPP*, 69 J.C.L. 98, DC).

15–180 In *Dawes v. DPP* [1995] 1 Cr.App.R. 65, DC, the defendant was detained by the automatic activation of the door locks inside a car specially adapted by the police as a trap. It was held on appeal that he was arrested the moment that he was trapped inside the car, and that at that point the police were obliged to inform him of his arrest and his grounds of arrest as soon as practicable. Once the police discharged this duty, the arrest was made lawful. On the facts, the police had fulfilled the duty, but the court recommended that in future the police fix such cars with a device which automatically tells the offender that he has been arrested and why.

Police and Criminal Evidence Act 1984, ss.29, 30

Voluntary attendance at police station etc.

15–181 **29.** Where for the purpose of assisting with an investigation a person attends voluntarily at a police station or at any other place where a constable is present or accompanies a constable to a police station or any such other place without having been arrested—

(a) he shall be entitled to leave at will unless he is placed under arrest;

(b) he shall be informed at once that he is under arrest if a decision is taken by a constable to prevent him from leaving at will.

Arrest elsewhere than at police station

15–182 **30.**—(1) Subsection (1A) applies where a person is, at any place other than a police station—

(a) arrested by a constable for an offence, or

(b) taken into custody by a constable after being arrested for an offence by a person other than a constable.

(1A) The person must be taken by a constable to a police station as soon as practicable after the arrest.

(1B) Subsection (1A) has effect subject to section 30A (release on bail) and subsection (7) (release without bail).

(2) Subject to subsections (3) to (5) below, the police station to which an arrested person is taken under subsection (1A) above shall be a designated police station.

(3) A constable to whom this subsection applies may take an arrested person to any police station unless it appears to the constable that it may be necessary to keep the arrested person in police detention for more than six hours.

(4) Subsection (3) above applies—

(a) to a constable who is working in a locality covered by a police station which is not a designated police station; and

(b) to a constable belonging to a body of constables maintained by an authority other than a police authority.

(5) Any constable may take an arrested person to any police station if—

(a) either of the following conditions is satisfied—

(i) the constable has arrested him without the assistance of any other constable and no other constable is available to assist him;

(ii) the constable has taken him into custody from a person other than a constable without the assistance of any other constable and no other constable is available to assist him; and

(b) it appears to the constable that he will be unable to take the arrested person to a designated police station without the arrested person injuring himself, the constable or some other person.

15–183 (6) If the first police station to which an arrested person is taken after his arrest is not a designated police station, he shall be taken to a designated police station not more than six hours after his arrival at the first police station unless he is released previously.

(7) A person arrested by a constable at any place other than a police station must be released without bail if the condition in subsection (7A) is satisfied.

Section 30C is another provision applied to arrest for failure to comply with conditions attached to a conditional caution: see *ante*, § 15–183.

Bail under section 30A: variation of conditions by police

30CA.—(1) Where a person released on bail under section 30A(1) is on bail subject to conditions— **15–184ca**

(a) a relevant officer at the police station at which the person is required to attend, or

(b) where no notice under section 30B specifying that police station has been given to the person, a relevant officer at the police station specified under section 30B(4A)(c), may, at the request of the person but subject to subsection (2), vary the conditions.

(2) On any subsequent request made in respect of the same grant of bail, subsection (1) confers power to vary the conditions of the bail only if the request is based on information that, in the case of the previous request or each previous request, was not available to the relevant officer considering that previous request when he was considering it.

(3) Where conditions of bail granted to a person under section 30A(1) are varied under subsection (1)—

(a) paragraphs (a) to (d) of section 30A(3A) apply,

(b) requirements imposed by the conditions as so varied must be requirements that appear to the relevant officer varying the conditions to be necessary for any of the purposes mentioned in paragraphs (a) to (d) of section 30A(3B), and

(c) the relevant officer who varies the conditions must give the person notice in writing of the variation.

(4) Power under subsection (1) to vary conditions is, subject to subsection (3)(a) and (b), power—

(a) to vary or rescind any of the conditions, and

(b) to impose further conditions.

(5) In this section "relevant officer", in relation to a designated police station, means a custody officer but, in relation to any other police station—

(a) means a constable, or a person designated as a staff custody officer under section 38 of the *Police Reform Act* 2002, who is not involved in the investigation of the offence for which the person making the request under subsection (1) was under arrest when granted bail under section 30A(1), if such a constable or officer is readily available, and

(b) if no such constable or officer is readily available—

(i) means a constable other than the one who granted bail to the person, if such a constable is readily available, and

(ii) if no such constable is readily available, means the constable who granted bail.

[This section is inserted by the *PJA* 2006, s.10, and Sched. 6, paras 1 and 4.]

Section 30CA is another provision applied to arrest for failure to comply with conditions attached to a conditional caution: see *ante*, § 15–183. This is subject to section 24B(3)(a) of the 2003 Act, which modifies section 30CA(5)(a) to substitute, for the reference to being involved in the investigation of the offence, a reference to being involved:

"(i) in the investigation of the offence in respect of which the person was given the conditional caution, or

(ii) in investigating whether the person has failed, without reasonable excuse, to comply with any of the conditions attached to the conditional caution".

Bail under section 30A: variation of conditions by court

30CB.—(1) Where a person released on bail under section 30A(1) is on bail subject to conditions, a magistrates' court may, on an application by or on behalf of the person, vary the conditions if— **15–184cb**

(a) the conditions have been varied under section 30CA(1) since being imposed under section 30A(3B),

(b) a request for variation under section 30CA(1) of the conditions has been made and refused, or

(c) a request for variation under section 30CA(1) of the conditions has been made and the period of 48 hours beginning with the day when the request was made has expired without the request having been withdrawn or the conditions having been varied in response to the request.

(2) In proceedings on an application for a variation under subsection (1), a ground may not be relied upon unless—

(a) in a case falling within subsection (1)(a), the ground was relied upon in the request in response to which the conditions were varied under section 30CA(1), or

(b) in a case falling within paragraph (b) or (c) of subsection (1), the ground was relied upon in the request mentioned in that paragraph,

but this does not prevent the court, when deciding the application, from considering different grounds arising out of a change in circumstances that has occurred since the making of the application.

(3) Where conditions of bail granted to a person under section 30A(1) are varied under subsection (1)—

(a) paragraphs (a) to (d) of section 30A(3A) apply,

(b) requirements imposed by the conditions as so varied must be requirements that appear to the court varying the conditions to be necessary for any of the purposes mentioned in paragraphs (a) to (d) of section 30A(3B), and

(c) that bail shall not lapse but shall continue subject to the conditions as so varied.

(4) [*Identical to s.30CA(4),* ante, *§ 15–184ca.*]

[This section is inserted by the *PJA* 2006, s.10, and Sched. 6, paras 1 and 4.]

Section 30CB is another provision applied to arrest for failure to comply with conditions attached to a conditional caution: see *ante*, § 15–183.

Failure to answer to bail under section 30A

15–184d **30D.**—(1) A constable may arrest without a warrant a person who—

(a) has been released on bail under section 30A subject to a requirement to attend a specified police station, but

(b) fails to attend the police station at the specified time.

(2) A person arrested under subsection (1) must be taken to a police station (which may be the specified police station or any other police station) as soon as practicable after the arrest.

(2A) A person who has been released on bail under section 30A may be arrested without a warrant by a constable if the constable has reasonable grounds for suspecting that the person has broken any of the conditions of bail.

(2B) A person arrested under subsection (2A) must be taken to a police station (which may be the specified police station mentioned in subsection (1) or any other police station) as soon as practicable after the arrest.

(3) In subsection (1), "specified" means specified in a notice under subsection (1) or (5) of section 30B or, if notice of change has been given under subsection (7) of that section, in that notice.

(4) For the purposes of—

(a) section 30 (subject to the obligations in subsections (2) and (2B)), and

(b) section 31,

an arrest under this section is to be treated as an arrest for an offence.

[This section was inserted by the *CJA* 2003, s.4(1) and (7). It is printed as amended by the *PJA* 2006, s.10, and Sched. 6, paras 1 and 5.]

Section 30D is another provision applied to arrest for failure to comply with conditions attached to a conditional caution: see *ante*, § 15–183.

Police and Criminal Evidence Act 1984, s.31

Arrest for further offence

15–185 **31.** Where—

(a) a person—

(i) has been arrested for an offence; and

(ii) is at a police station in consequence of that arrest; and

(b) it appears to a constable that, if he were released from that arrest, he would be liable to arrest for some other offence,

he shall be arrested for that other offence.

Section 31 is another provision applied to arrest for failure to comply with conditions attached to a conditional caution: see *ante*, § 15–183.

In connection with section 31, see also section 41(4) of the Act, *ante*, § 3–111.

In *R. v. Samuel* [1988] Q.B. 615, 87 Cr.App.R. 232, the Court of Appeal said *obiter* (at pp. 622, 238) that there was nothing in section 31 to prevent the further arrest being delayed until such time as release from the initial arrest was imminent; the "obvious purpose" of the section being to prevent the release and immediate re-arrest of an alleged offender.

Police and Criminal Evidence Act 1984, s.32

Search upon arrest

32.—(1) A constable may search an arrested person, in any case where the person to be searched has been arrested at a place other than a police station, if the constable has reasonable grounds for believing that the arrested person may present a danger to himself or others. **15–186**

(2) Subject to subsections (3) to (5) below, a constable shall also have power in any such case—

(a) to search the arrested person for anything—
  (i) which he might use to assist him to escape from lawful custody; or
  (ii) which might be evidence relating to an offence; and
(b) if the offence for which he has been arrested is an indictable offence, to enter and search any premises in which he was when arrested or immediately before he was arrested for evidence relating to the offence.

(3) The power to search conferred by subsection (2) above is only a power to search to the extent that is reasonably required for the purpose of discovering any such thing or any such evidence.

(4) The powers conferred by this section to search a person are not to be construed as authorising a constable to require a person to remove any of his clothing in public other than an outer coat, jacket or gloves but they do authorise a search of a person's mouth.

(5) A constable may not search a person in the exercise of the power conferred by subsection (2)(a) above unless he has reasonable grounds for believing that the person to be searched may have concealed on him anything for which a search is permitted under that paragraph.

(6) A constable may not search premises in the exercise of the power conferred by subsection (2)(b) above unless he has reasonable grounds for believing that there is evidence for which a search is permitted under that paragraph on the premises.

(7) In so far as the power of search conferred by subsection (2)(b) above relates to premises consisting of two or more separate dwellings, it is limited to a power to search— **15–187**

(a) any dwelling in which the arrest took place or in which the person arrested was immediately before his arrest; and
(b) any parts of the premises which the occupier of any such dwelling uses in common with the occupiers of any other dwellings comprised in the premises.

(8) A constable searching a person in the exercise of the power conferred by subsection (1) above may seize and retain anything he finds, if he has reasonable grounds for believing that the person searched might use it to cause physical injury to himself or to any other person.

(9) A constable searching a person in the exercise of the power conferred by subsection (2)(a) above may seize and retain anything he finds, other than an item subject to legal privilege, if he has reasonable grounds for believing—

(a) that he might use it to assist him to escape from lawful custody; or
(b) that it is evidence of an offence or has been obtained in consequence of the commission of an offence.

(10) Nothing in this section shall be taken to affect the power conferred by section 43 of the *Terrorism Act* 2000.

[This section is printed as amended by the *CJPOA* 1994, s.59(2); the *Terrorism Act* 2000, s.125, and Sched. 15, para. 5(3); and the *SOCPA* 2005, s.111, and Sched. 7, para. 43(1) and (6).]

For the extended powers of seizure under this section, see section 51 of the *CJPA* 2001 (*ante*, § 15–128).

In its application to an offence under section 31(1) of the *London Olympic Games* **15–188** *and Paralympic Games Act* 2006 (selling an Olympic ticket in a public place or in the course of a business otherwise than in accordance with a written authorisation issued by the London Organising Committee), this section permits the searching of a vehicle which a constable reasonably thinks was used in connection with the offence: 2006 Act, s.31(7).

A search under section 32 must be made at the time of the arrest and not several hours later: *R. v. Badham* [1987] Crim.L.R. 202, Crown Court (H.H. Judge Compston). *Cf.* section 18, *ante*, § 15–110.

A suspected burglar's car keys were not "evidence relating to an offence" under section 32(2)(a)(ii): *R. v. Churchill* [1989] Crim.L.R. 226, CA.

It is a question of fact where officers rely on section 32 to justify a search whether that was the genuine reason for the officers in making the entry: *R. v. Beckford (Junior)*, 94 Cr.App.R. 43, CA. If a judge admits evidence in the face of a challenge based on a breach of section 32, he should nevertheless leave the issue as to the officers' motive to the jury as being a matter which may go to the weight to be attached to their evidence: *ibid.*

"Premises" includes "any vehicle": s.23, *ante*, § 15–123. As to the use of force, see section 117, *ante*, § 15–26.

As to the extent of the power of seizure where a constable is making a search of premises in exercise of the power conferred by subsection (2)(b), see section 19 of the Act, *ante*, § 15–112.

(3) The Criminal Justice and Public Order Act 1994

15–189 Part X of the 1994 Act (ss.136–141) is headed "Cross-border enforcement". Section 136 (amended by the *YJCEA* 1999, s.67(1) and Sched. 4, para. 23) is concerned with the execution of warrants issued in one of the three United Kingdom jurisdictions (England and Wales, Scotland and Northern Ireland) in one of the other jurisdictions. It may be executed either by a constable of a police force in the country of issue, or by a constable of a police force of the country in which it is to be executed, or by a person authorised in the warrant to do so. Where a Scottish warrant is executed in England or Wales, the person arrested has the same rights as he would have if execution had been in Scotland by a constable of a police force in Scotland.

Section 137(1) (amended by the *SOCPA* 2005, s.111, and Sched. 7, para. 47(1) and (2)) provides that if certain conditions are satisfied a constable of a police force in England and Wales may arrest a person without a warrant in Scotland or Northern Ireland for an offence committed in England and Wales. There are reciprocal provisions for officers of a police force in Scotland or Northern Ireland. Where an officer of a Scottish police force effects an arrest outside Scotland pursuant to these provisions, the person arrested has the same rights as he would have had if the arrest had been in Scotland. Section 138 supplements section 137 (elaboration of justifications for arrest without warrant).

Section 139 governs the powers of search, entry and seizure available to a constable of a police force in England and Wales or Northern Ireland when executing a warrant or effecting an arrest without warrant under sections 136 or 137. These broadly correspond to the powers available under the *PACE Act* 1984. Thus a constable to whom the section applies may search the person arrested if he has reasonable grounds for believing that he may present a danger to himself; he may also search him for anything which he might use to assist him to escape or which might be evidence relating to an offence; and he may enter and search any premises in which the arrested person was when, or was immediately before, he was arrested for evidence relating to the offence for which he was arrested.

As to the application of sections 136 to 139 to officers of Revenue and Customs, see the *Finance Act* 2007, s.87.

Section 140 confers reciprocal powers of arrest on constables of the police forces in the three jurisdictions of the United Kingdom. A constable from one jurisdiction who is present in another jurisdiction may arrest a person in that jurisdiction using the police powers of arrest of the local jurisdiction.

E. Questioning and Treatment of Persons

(1) Introduction

Part V of the *PACE Act* 1984 (ss.53–65) creates a number of police powers, includ- 15–190
ing the search of detained persons (s.54), "intimate" searches (s.55), and the taking of fingerprints (s.61), "intimate" (s.62) and other samples (s.63). It also creates safeguards for the suspect in relation to these searches and provides certain rights for detained persons: the right to have someone informed when arrested (s.56), the right to legal advice (s.58), and the right to have fingerprints and samples destroyed in certain circumstances (s.64). Additional rights are given to children and young persons, and steps must be taken to ascertain the identity of a person responsible for the welfare of a child or young person in police detention (s.57). The original provisions have been substantially amended and added to since first enactment.

These powers and rights are collected together under the heading "Questioning and Treatment of Persons by Police". They must be read in conjunction with the further powers and safeguards in Code C, the Code of Practice for the Detention, Treatment and Questioning of Persons by Police Officers (*post*, § 15–251 and Appendix A–39 *et seq.*) and in Code H (the corresponding code relating to the detention, treatment and questioning of persons under section 41 of, and Schedule 8 to, the *Terrorism Act* 2000) (Appendix A–213 *et seq.*).

(2) Searches of detained persons

Police and Criminal Evidence Act 1984, ss.53, 54

Abolition of certain powers of constables to search persons

53.—(1) Subject to subsection (2) below, there shall cease to have effect any Act (including a 15–191
local Act) passed before this Act in so far as it authorises—

(a) any search by a constable of a person in police detention at a police station; or

(b) an intimate search of a person by a constable;

and any rule of common law which authorises a search such as is mentioned in paragraph (a) or (b) above is abolished.

(2) [*Repealed by* Prevention of Terrorism (Temporary Provisions) Act *1989, s.25(2) and Sched. 9, Pt I.*]

[This section is printed as amended by the *CJA* 1988, s.147, s.170(1), and Sched. 15, para. 99.]

Searches of detained persons

54.—(1) The custody officer at a police station shall ascertain ... everything which a person 15–192
has with him when he is—

(a) brought to the station after being arrested elsewhere or after being committed to custody by an order or sentence of a court; or

(b) arrested at the station or detained there, as a person falling within section 34(7), under section 37 above [or as a person to whom section 46ZA(4) or (5) applies].

(2) The custody officer may record or cause to be recorded all or any of the things which he ascertains under subsection (1).

(2A) In the case of an arrested person, any such record may be made as part of his custody record.

(3) Subject to subsection (4) below, a custody officer may seize and retain any such thing or cause any such thing to be seized and retained.

(4) Clothes and personal effects may only be seized if the custody officer—

(a) believes that the person from whom they are seized may use them—

(i) to cause physical injury to himself or any other person;

(ii) to damage property;

(iii) to interfere with evidence; or

(iv) to assist him to escape; or

(b) has reasonable grounds for believing that they may be evidence relating to an offence.

(5) Where anything is seized, the person from whom it is seized shall be told the reason for the seizure unless he is—

(a) violent or likely to become violent; or

(b) incapable of understanding what is said to him.

15–193 (6) Subject to subsection (7) below, a person may be searched if the custody officer considers it necessary to enable him to carry out his duty under subsection (1) above and to the extent that the custody officer considers necessary for that purpose.

(6A) A person who is in custody at a police station or is in police detention otherwise than at a police station may at any time be searched in order to ascertain whether he has with him anything which he could use for any of the purposes specified in subsection (4)(a) above.

(6B) Subject to subsection (6C) below, a constable may seize and retain, or cause to be seized and retained, anything found on such a search.

(6C) A constable may only seize clothes and personal effects in the circumstances specified in subsection (4) above.

(7) An intimate search may not be conducted under this section.

(8) A search under this section shall be carried out by a constable.

(9) The constable carrying out a search shall be of the same sex as the person searched.

[This section is printed as amended, and repealed in part, by the *CJA* 1988, s.147; the *CJPOA* 1994, s.168(2), and Sched. 10, para. 55; the *CJA* 2003, s.8; and the *PJA* 2006, s.47(1) and (6) (insertion of words in square brackets in subs. (1)(b)). The 2006 Act amendment came into force on April 1, 2007, but only in the local justice area of Lambeth and Southwark: *Police and Justice Act 2006 (Commencement No. 2, Transitional and Saving Provisions) Order* 2007 (S.I. 2007 No. 709).]

As from June 29, 2007 (*Police and Justice Act 2006 (Commencement No. 3) Order* 2007 (S.I. 2007 No. 1614)), section 54 of the 1984 Act applies to a person falling within the *CJA* 2003, s.24A(3) ((i) a person arrested for breach of conditional caution, then bailed, at police station in answer to his bail or otherwise in detention at a police station, (ii) a person bailed elsewhere than at police station attending to answer bail or otherwise in detention at police station, and (iii) a person arrested for failure to answer to police bail), and who is detained under that section, as it applies to a person falling within the 1984 Act, s.34(7) (*ante*, § 3–93), and who is detained under section 37 of that Act (*ante*, § 3–97): 2003 Act, s.24B(6), as inserted by the *PJA* 2006, s.18(1).

For the meaning of "intimate search", see section 65, *post*, § 15–249.

Police and Criminal Evidence Act 1984, s.54A

Searches and examination to ascertain identity

15–193a **54A.**—(1) If an officer of at least the rank of inspector authorises it, a person who is detained in a police station may be searched or examined, or both—

(a) for the purpose of ascertaining whether he has any mark that would tend to identify him as a person involved in the commission of an offence; or

(b) for the purpose of facilitating the ascertainment of his identity.

(2) An officer may only give an authorisation under subsection (1) for the purpose mentioned in paragraph (a) of that subsection if—

(a) the appropriate consent to a search or examination that would reveal whether the mark in question exists has been withheld; or

(b) it is not practicable to obtain such consent.

(3) An officer may only give an authorisation under subsection (1) in a case in which subsection (2) does not apply if—

(a) the person in question has refused to identify himself; or

(b) the officer has reasonable grounds for suspecting that that person is not who he claims to be.

(4) An officer may give an authorisation under subsection (1) orally or in writing but, if he gives it orally, he shall confirm it in writing as soon as is practicable.

(5) Any identifying mark found on a search or examination under this section may be photographed—

(a) with the appropriate consent; or

(b) if the appropriate consent is withheld or it is not practicable to obtain it, without it.

(6) Where a search or examination may be carried out under this section, or a

photograph may be taken under this section, the only persons entitled to carry out the search or examination, or to take the photograph, are constables.

(7) A person may not under this section carry out a search or examination of a person of the opposite sex or take a photograph of any part of the body of a person of the opposite sex.

(8) An intimate search may not be carried out under this section.

(9) A photograph taken under this section—

- (a) may be used by, or disclosed to, any person for any purpose related to the prevention or detection of crime, the investigation of an offence or the conduct of a prosecution; and
- (b) after being so used or disclosed, may be retained but may not be used or disclosed except for a purpose so related.

(10) In subsection (9)—

- (a) the reference to crime includes a reference to any conduct which—
  - (i) constitutes one or more criminal offences (whether under the law of a part of the United Kingdom or of a country or territory outside the United Kingdom); or
  - (ii) is, or corresponds to, any conduct which, if it all took place in any one part of the United Kingdom, would constitute one or more criminal offences; and
- (b) the references to an investigation and to a prosecution include references, respectively, to any investigation outside the United Kingdom of any crime or suspected crime and to a prosecution brought in respect of any crime in a country or territory outside the United Kingdom.

(11) In this section—

- (a) references to ascertaining a person's identity include references to showing that he is not a particular person; and
- (b) references to taking a photograph include references to using any process by means of which a visual image may be produced, and references to photographing a person shall be construed accordingly.

(12) In this section "mark" includes features and injuries; and a mark is an identifying mark for the purposes of this section if its existence in any person's case facilitates the ascertainment of his identity or his identification as a person involved in the commission of an offence.

(13) Nothing in this section applies to a person arrested under an extradition arrest power.

[This section was inserted by the *Anti-Terrorism, Crime and Security Act* 2001, s.90(1). It is printed as amended by the *Police Reform Act* 2002, s.107(1) and Sched. 7, para. 9(2); and the *Extradition Act* 2003, s.169(2).]

As to the "appropriate consent", see section 65 of the 1984 Act, *post*, § 15–249.

As from June 29, 2007 (*Police and Justice Act 2006 (Commencement No. 3) Order* 2007 (S.I. 2007 No. 1614)), the *CJA* 2003, s.24B(7) (inserted by the *PJA* 2006, s.18(1)) applies section 54A of the 1984 Act to a person detained at a police station under section 24A of the 2003 Act (arrest for breach of a conditional caution), with the following modifications:

- (a) in subsections (1)(a) and (12), after "as a person involved in the commission of an offence", insert "or as having failed to comply with any of the conditions attached to his conditional caution";
- (b) in subsection (9)(a), after "the investigation of an offence", insert ", the investigation of whether the person in question has failed to comply with any of the conditions attached to his conditional caution".

Police and Criminal Evidence Act 1984, s.55

Intimate searches

55.—(1) Subject to the following provisions of this section, if an officer of at least the rank of inspector has reasonable grounds for believing— **15–194**

- (a) that a person who has been arrested and is in police detention may have concealed on him anything which—
  - (i) he could use to cause physical injury to himself or others; and

(ii) he might so use while he is in police detention or in the custody of a court; or

(b) that such a person—

(i) may have a Class A drug concealed on him; and

(ii) was in possession of it with the appropriate criminal intent before his arrest,

he may authorise an intimate search of that person.

15–195 (2) An officer may not authorise an intimate search of a person for anything unless he has reasonable grounds for believing that it cannot be found without his being intimately searched.

(3) An officer may give an authorisation under subsection (1) above orally or in writing but, if he gives it orally, he shall confirm it in writing as soon as is practicable.

(3A) A drug offence search shall not be carried out unless the appropriate consent has been given in writing.

(3B) Where it is proposed that a drug offence search be carried out, an appropriate officer shall inform the person who is to be subject to it—

(a) of the giving of the authorisation for it; and

(b) of the grounds for giving the authorisation.

(4) An intimate search which is only a drug offence search shall be by way of examination by a suitably qualified person.

(5) Except as provided by subsection (4) above, an intimate search shall be by way of examination by a suitably qualified person unless an officer of at least the rank of inspector considers that this is not practicable.

(6) An intimate search which is not carried out as mentioned in subsection (5) above shall be carried out by a constable.

(7) A constable may not carry out an intimate search of a person of the opposite sex.

(8) No intimate search may be carried out except—

(a) at a police station;

(b) at a hospital;

(c) at a registered medical practitioner's surgery; or

(d) at some other place used for medical purposes.

(9) An intimate search which is only a drug offence search may not be carried out at a police station.

15–196 (10) If an intimate search of a person is carried out, the custody record relating to him shall state—

(a) which parts of his body were searched; and

(b) why they were searched.

(10A) If the intimate search is a drug offence search, the custody record relating to that person shall also state—

(a) the authorisation by virtue of which the search was carried out;

(b) the grounds for giving the authorisation; and

(c) the fact that the appropriate consent was given.

(11) The information required to be recorded by subsections (10) and (10A) above shall be recorded as soon as practicable after the completion of the search.

(12) The custody officer at a police station may seize and retain anything which is found on an intimate search of a person, or cause any such thing to be seized and retained—

(a) if he believes that the person from whom it is seized may use it—

(i) to cause physical injury to himself or any other person;

(ii) to damage property;

(iii) to interfere with evidence; or

(iv) to assist him to escape; or

(b) if he has reasonable grounds for believing that it may be evidence relating to an offence.

15–197 (13) Where anything is seized under this section, the person from whom it is seized shall be told the reason for the seizure unless he is—

(a) violent or likely to become violent; or

(b) incapable of understanding what is said to him.

(13A) Where the appropriate consent to a drug offence search of any person was refused without good cause, in any proceedings against that person for an offence—

(a) the court, in determining whether there is a case to answer;

(b) a judge, in deciding whether to grant an application made by the accused under paragraph 2 of Schedule 3 to the *Crime and Disorder Act* 1998 (applications for dismissal); and

(c) the court or jury, in determining whether that person is guilty of the offence charged,

may draw such inferences from the refusal as appear proper.

(14), (14A), (15), (16) [*Information to be contained in annual reports.*]

(17) In this section—

"the appropriate criminal intent" means an intent to commit an offence under—

(a) section 5(3) of the *Misuse of Drugs Act* 1971 (possession of controlled drug with intent to supply to another); or

(b) section 68(2) of the *Customs and Excise Management Act* 1979 (exportation etc. with intent to evade a prohibition or restriction);

"appropriate officer" means—

(a) a constable,

(b) a person who is designated as a detention officer in pursuance of section 38 of the *Police Reform Act* 2002 if his designation applies paragraph 33D of Schedule 4 to that Act, or

(c) a person who is designated as a staff custody officer in pursuance of section 38 of that Act if his designation applies paragraph 35C of Schedule 4 to that Act;

"Class A drug" has the meaning assigned to it by section 2(1)(b) of the *Misuse of Drugs Act* 1971;

"drug offence search" means an intimate search for a Class A drug which an officer has authorised by virtue of subsection (1)(b) above; and

"suitably qualified person" means—

(a) a registered medical practitioner; or

(b) a registered nurse.

[This section is printed as amended by the *CJA* 1988, Sched. 15, para. 99; the *CJPA* 2001, s.79; and the *Drugs Act* 2005, s.3.]

For the meaning of "intimate search", see section 65, *post*, § 15–249.

For the modification of section 55 in relation to investigations by officers of Revenue and Customs of offences relating to assigned matters, see *ante*, § 15–43.

Code C, Annex A, contains specific guidance on the conduct of intimate searches and strip searches (Appendix A–92). **15–198**

Police and Criminal Evidence Act 1984, s.55A

X-rays and ultrasound scans

55A.—(1) If an officer of at least the rank of inspector has reasonable grounds for believing that a person who has been arrested for an offence and is in police detention— **15–198a**

(a) may have swallowed a Class A drug, and

(b) was in possession of it with the appropriate criminal intent before his arrest,

the officer may authorise that an x-ray is taken of the person or an ultrasound scan is carried out on the person (or both).

(2) An x-ray must not be taken of a person and an ultrasound scan must not be carried out on him unless the appropriate consent has been given in writing.

(3) If it is proposed that an x-ray is taken or an ultrasound scan is carried out, an appropriate officer must inform the person who is to be subject to it—

(a) of the giving of the authorisation for it, and

(b) of the grounds for giving the authorisation.

(4) An x-ray may be taken or an ultrasound scan carried out only by a suitably qualified person and only at—

(a) a hospital,

(b) a registered medical practitioner's surgery, or

(c) some other place used for medical purposes.

(5) The custody record of the person must also state—

(a) the authorisation by virtue of which the x-ray was taken or the ultrasound scan was carried out,

(b) the grounds for giving the authorisation, and

(c) the fact that the appropriate consent was given.

(6) The information required to be recorded by subsection (5) must be recorded as soon as practicable after the x-ray has been taken or ultrasound scan carried out (as the case may be).

(7), (8) [*Information to be contained in annual reports.*]

(9) If the appropriate consent to an x-ray or ultrasound scan of any person is refused without good cause, in any proceedings against that person for an offence—

(a)–(c) [*identical to section 55(13A)(a)–(c)*, ante, *§ 15–197*].

(10) In this section "the appropriate criminal intent", "appropriate officer", "Class A drug" and "suitably qualified person" have the same meanings as in section 55 above.

[This section was inserted by the *Drugs Act* 2005, s.5.]

(3) Right to have someone informed when arrested

Police and Criminal Evidence Act 1984, s.56

15–199 **56.**—(1) Where a person has been arrested and is being held in custody in a police station or other premises, he shall be entitled, if he so requests, to have one friend or relative or other person who is known to him or who is likely to take an interest in his welfare told, as soon as is practicable except to the extent that delay is permitted by this section, that he has been arrested and is being detained there.

(2) Delay is only permitted—

(a) in the case of a person who is in police detention for an indictable offence; and
(b) if an officer of at least the rank of inspector authorises it.

(3) In any case the person in custody must be permitted to exercise the right conferred by subsection (1) above within 36 hours from the relevant time, as defined in section 41(2) above.

(4) An officer may give an authorisation under subsection (2) above orally or in writing but, if he gives it orally, he shall confirm it in writing as soon as is practicable.

(5) Subject to subsection (5A) below an officer may only authorise delay where he has reasonable grounds for believing that telling the named person of the arrest—

(a) will lead to interference with or harm to evidence connected with an indictable offence or interference with or physical injury to other persons; or
(b) will lead to the alerting of other persons suspected of having committed such an offence but not yet arrested for it; or
(c) will hinder the recovery of any property obtained as a result of such an offence.

15–200 (5A) An officer may also authorise delay where he has reasonable grounds for believing that—

(a) the person detained for the indictable offence has benefited from his criminal conduct, and
(b) the recovery of the value of the property constituting the benefit will be hindered by telling the named person of the arrest.

(5B) For the purposes of subsection (5A) above the question whether a person has benefited from his criminal conduct is to be decided in accordance with Part 2 of the *Proceeds of Crime Act* 2002.

15–201 (6) If a delay is authorised—

(a) the detained person shall be told the reason for it; and
(b) the reason shall be noted on his custody record.

(7) The duties imposed by subsection (6) above shall be performed as soon as is practicable.

(8) The rights conferred by this section on a person detained at a police station or other premises are exercisable whenever he is transferred from one place to another; and this section applies to each subsequent occasion on which they are exercisable as it applies to the first such occasion.

(9) There may be no further delay in permitting the exercise of the right conferred by subsection (1) above once the reason for authorising delay ceases to subsist.

15–202 (10) Nothing in this section applies to a person arrested or detained under the terrorism provisions.

[This section is printed as amended and repealed in part by the *DTOA* 1986, s.32; the *CJA* 1988, s.99(2); the *Terrorism Act* 2000, s.125, and Sched. 15, para. 5(5); the *CJPA* 2001, s.74; the *PCA* 2002, s.456, and Sched. 11, para. 14(2); and the *SOCPA* 2005, s.111, and Sched. 7, para. 43(1) and (9).]

For section 41(2) of the Act, see *ante*, § 3–111.

(4) Additional rights of children and young persons

Children and Young Persons Act 1933, s.34

34.—(1) [*Repealed by* CJA *1991, s.56.*] 15–203

(2) Where a child or young person is in police detention, such steps as are practicable shall be taken to ascertain the identity of a person responsible for his welfare.

(3) If it is practicable to ascertain the identity of a person responsible for the welfare of the child or young person, that person shall be informed, unless it is not practicable to do so—

- (a) that the child or young person has been arrested;
- (b) why he has been arrested; and
- (c) where he is being detained.

(4) Where information falls to be given under subsection (3) above, it shall be given as soon as it is practicable to do so.

(5) For the purposes of this section the persons who may be responsible for the welfare of a child or young person are—

- (a) his parent or guardian; or
- (b) any other person who has for the time being assumed responsibility for his welfare.

(6) If it is practicable to give a person responsible for the welfare of the child or young person the information required by subsection (3) above, that person shall be given it as soon as it is practicable to do so. 15–204

(7) If it appears that at the time of his arrest a supervision order, as defined in section 163 of the *Powers of Criminal Courts (Sentencing) Act* 2000 or Part IV of the *Children Act* 1989, is in force in respect of him, the person responsible for his supervision shall also be informed as described in subsection (3) above as soon as it is reasonably practicable to do so.

(7A) If it appears that at the time of his arrest the child or young person is being provided with accommodation by or on behalf of a local authority under section 20 of the *Children Act* 1989, the local authority shall also be informed as described in subsection (3) above as soon as it is reasonably practicable to do so.

(8) The reference to a parent or guardian in subsection (5) above is ... in the case of a child or young person in the care of a local authority, a reference to that authority ....

(9) The rights conferred on a child or young person by subsections (2) to (8) above are in addition to his rights under section 56 of the *Police and Criminal Evidence Act* 1984.

(10) The reference in subsection (2) above to a child or young person who is in police detention includes a reference to a child or young person who has been detained under the terrorism provisions; and in subsection (3) above "arrest" includes such detention.

(11) In subsection (10) above "the terrorism provisions" has the meaning assigned to it by section 65 of the *Police and Criminal Evidence Act* 1984.

[Subss. (2) to (11) were substituted by the *PACE Act* 1984, s.57. They are printed as subsequently amended and repealed in part by the *Children Act* 1989, s.108(5) and (7), and Scheds 13, para. 6(2) and (3), and 15; and the *PCC(S)A* 2000, s.165(1), and Sched. 9, para. 1.]

Section 107(1) of the 1933 Act (*post*, § 19–328) was amended by the *CJA* 1991, s.68, and Sched. 8, para. 1(3), so as to define "young person" as "a person who has attained the age of fourteen and is under the age of eighteen years". Section 31(2) of the Act (inserted by the 1991 Act, s.68, and Sched. 8, para. 1(1)) provides, however, that in that section and in section 34, "young person" is to mean "a person who has attained the age of fourteen and is under the age of seventeen years". The amended section 107(1) came into force on October 1, 1992 (*Criminal Justice Act 1991 (Commencement No. 2 and Transitional Provisions) Order* 1992 (S.I. 1992 No. 333)), but the new section 31(2) of the 1933 Act was not brought into force on that day. Accordingly, in order to ensure that "young person" in section 34 refers only to persons under the age of 17 years, the amended definition of "young person" in section 107(1) was excluded from coming into force to the extent that it would otherwise apply to section 34: S.I. 1992 No. 333, art. 2(4). 15–205

(5) Access to legal advice

Police and Criminal Evidence Act 1984, s.58

15–206 **58.**—(1) A person arrested and held in custody in a police station or other premises shall be entitled, if he so requests, to consult a solicitor privately at any time.

(2) Subject to subsection (3) below, a request under subsection (1) above and the time at which it was made shall be recorded in the custody record.

(3) Such a request need not be recorded in the custody record of a person who makes it at a time while he is at a court after being charged with an offence.

(4) If a person makes such a request, he must be permitted to consult a solicitor as soon as is practicable except to the extent that delay is permitted by this section.

(5) In any case he must be permitted to consult a solicitor within 36 hours from the relevant time, as defined in section 41(2) above.

(6) Delay in compliance with a request is only permitted—

(a) in the case of a person who is in police detention for an indictable offence; and

(b) if an officer of at least the rank of superintendent authorises it.

15–207 (7) An officer may give an authorisation under subsection (6) above orally or in writing but, if he gives it orally, he shall confirm it in writing as soon as is practicable.

(8) Subject to subsection (8A) below an officer may only authorise delay where he has reasonable grounds for believing that the exercise of the right conferred by subsection (1) above at the time when the person detained desires to exercise it—

(a)–(c) [*identical to s.56(5)(a)–(c),* ante, *§ 15–199*].

(8A) An officer may also authorise delay where he has reasonable grounds for believing that—

(a) the person detained for the indictable offence has benefited from his criminal conduct, and

(b) the recovery of the value of the property constituting the benefit will be hindered by the exercise of the right conferred by subsection (1) above.

(8B) For the purposes of subsection (8A) above the question whether a person has benefited from his criminal conduct is to be decided in accordance with Part 2 of the *Proceeds of Crime Act* 2002.

15–208 (9) [*Identical to s.56(6),* ante, *§ 15–201.*]

(10) The duties imposed by subsection (9) above shall be performed as soon as is practicable.

(11) There may be no further delay in permitting the exercise of the right conferred by subsection (1) above once the reason for authorising delay ceases to subsist.

15–209 (12) Nothing in this section applies to a person arrested or detained under the terrorism provisions.

[This section is printed as amended by the *DTOA* 1986, s.32; the *CJA* 1988, s.99(3); the *Terrorism Act* 2000, s.125, and Sched. 15, para. 5(6); the *PCA* 2002, s.456, and Sched. 11, para. 14(3); and the *SOCPA* 2005, s.111, and Sched. 7, para. 43(1) and (9).]

For "the relevant time" and section 41(2) of the Act, see *ante*, § 3–111.

Right of access to solicitor

15–210 Section 58 grants a person arrested and "held in custody in a police station or other premises" the right to consult a solicitor "if he so requests". Section 23 (*ante*, § 15–123) defines "premises" as including "any place" and specifies a number of examples such as vehicles. In *R. v. Kerawalla* [1991] Crim.L.R. 451, CA, it was held that the expression "held in custody" is narrower than "in custody", so that a person arrested and detained may be in custody but not yet "held in custody" for the purposes of section 58 until his custody has been authorised, as by a custody officer who satisfies himself that continued detention is authorised. *Cf. R. v. Sanusi* [1992] Crim.L.R. 43, CA (customs officers' area at airport tantamount to a police station).

As to the duty to inform a person under arrest at a police station of his right to consult privately with a solicitor and that free independent legal advice is available, see Code C:3.1 and 6.1 (Appendix A–46, A–54); and as to the duty to remind a person being interviewed at a police station or other authorised place of detention of these rights, see Code C:11.2 (Appendix A–73). As to the duty to take an arrestee to a police station as soon as practicable after arrest, see section 30 of the 1984 Act (*ante*, § 15–182).

The right of access to a solicitor under section 58(1) does not extend to a person on remand in custody at a magistrates' court (see section 118(2), *ante*, § 15–27), but there is a right of access at common law which was not abrogated by the passing of the 1984 Act. The right is, on request, to be permitted to consult a solicitor as soon as reasonably practicable: *R. v. Chief Constable of South Wales, ex p. Merrick* [1994] 1 W.L.R. 663, DC.

A person, not under arrest, who is interviewed under caution by a trading standards officer other than at a police station, has no entitlement to non-means tested free legal advice: *R. (Beale) v. South East Wiltshire Magistrates' Court*, 167 J.P. 41, DC.

Denial of access

Access to legal advice may only be delayed for up to 36 hours (s.58(5)) and only if a person is detained for an indictable offence, and such delay is authorised by an officer of at least the rank of superintendent: s.58(6), Code C:6 (Appendix A–54 *et seq.*). The grounds upon which such delay is permitted are contained in section 58(8) and (8A), and paragraph 6 of, and Annex B to, Code C (Appendix A–54, A–99 *et seq.*). A different regime applies to those held under the *Terrorism Act* 2000: see s.58(12) and Annex B, paras 8 to 12. **15–211**

In *R. v. Samuel* [1988] Q.B. 615, 87 Cr.App.R. 232, CA, the right of access to legal advice was described as "one of the most important and fundamental rights of a citizen" (at pp. 630, 245). Where it was sought to justify denial of the right of access to a solicitor on "reasonable grounds", that could not be done except by reference to specific circumstances including evidence about the person detained or the actual solicitor involved.

The choice by the draftsman of the word "will" in section 58(8)(a), (b) and (c), as opposed to "might", "could", "there was a risk", "there was a substantial risk", etc., must have been deliberately restrictive. The word "will" in conjunction with "belief" implied in the believer a belief that it would very probably happen.

> "Therefore, inadvertent or unwitting conduct apart, the officer must believe that a solicitor will, if allowed to consult with a detained person, thereafter commit a criminal offence. Solicitors are officers of the court. We think that the number of times that a police officer could genuinely be in that state of belief will be rare. Moreover it is our view that, to sustain such a basis for refusal, the grounds put forward would have to have reference to a specific solicitor. We do not think they could ever be successfully advanced in relation to solicitors generally" (*ibid.* at pp. 626, 242).

As to a solicitor who might be caused to pass on unwittingly some form of coded message, Hodgson J. continued: **15–212**

> "Whether there is any evidence that this has or may have happened in the past we have no way of knowing. Solicitors are intelligent professional people; persons detained by the police are frequently not very clever and the expectation that one of (a) to (c) will be brought about in this way seems to contemplate a degree of intelligence and sophistication in persons detained, and perhaps a naïveté and lack of common sense in solicitors, which we doubt often occurs. When and if it does, we think it would have to have reference to the specific person detained. The archetype would, we imagine, be the sophisticated criminal who is known or suspected of being a member of a gang of criminals" (*ibid.*).

By contrast, in *R. v. Alladice*, 87 Cr.App.R. 380, CA, the court said that it did not share the apparent scepticism of the court in *Samuel* about solicitors being used as unwilling channels of communication; that such things happened was within the experience of the members of the court (at p. 384).

As to the use of duty solicitors, Hodgson J. said: **15–213**

> "Duty solicitors will be well known to the police, and we think it will therefore be very difficult to justify consultation with the duty solicitor being delayed. If the duty solicitor has the reputation, deserved or not, for advising persons detained to refuse to answer questions that would, of course, be no reason for delaying consultation" (at pp. 627, 243).

In *R. v. Silcott, Braithwaite and Raghip*, *The Times*, December 9, 1991 (91/4944/S1; 91/4945/S1; 90/5920/S1), the Court of Appeal said that, inadvertent or unwitting conduct apart, the police officer must believe that a solicitor would, if allowed to consult the person in police detention, thereafter commit a criminal offence and that, to sustain such a basis for refusal, the grounds put forward would have to be by reference to a specific solicitor. The reference to inadvertent or unwitting conduct is absent from *The Times* report.

Code C, Annex B, para. 3 (Appendix A–99) states that an authorising officer may delay access to legal advice if he has reasonable grounds to believe that the solicitor the detainee wants to consult will, inadvertently or otherwise, pass on a message from the detainee, or act in some other way which will have any of the consequences specified in paragraphs 1 or 2 of Annex B. In these circumstances the detainee must be allowed to choose another solicitor. See also, Note B3 (Appendix A–101).

A chief constable is not entitled to make a blanket order banning a probationary solicitor's representative from attending the police station to advise persons in custody. He could, however, under Code C:6.12A and 6.13 (Appendix A–55), advise his officers that a particular representative was likely to hinder an investigation and the appropriate officer in a particular case could then decide whether he should be excluded: *R. (Thompson) v. Chief Constable of Northumbria Police* [2001] 1 W.L.R. 1342, CA. As to the effect of excluding a solicitor's representative in the context of adverse inferences from silence, see *post*, § 15–222.

That there might be a conflict of interest between a particular solicitor and the detainee is not a ground for excluding the solicitor; such considerations are for the solicitor and the Law Society: *R. (Malik) v. Chief Constable of Greater Manchester* [2007] A.C.D. 15, QBD (Beatson J.). Where, however, the police were investigating a conspiracy, and where they considered that what transpired at a particular meeting might be of central relevance to the alleged conspiracy, the fact that a particular solicitor was present at that meeting and that his role at the meeting was not clear, would justify a decision to exclude him as a legal adviser to one of the suspected conspirators: *ibid.*

Consequences of breach of section 58

15–214 Where there is a breach of section 58, a decision about admissibility will be governed by sections 76 and 78 of the 1984 Act (*post*, §§ 15–352, 15–452 respectively): *R. v. Alladice*, 87 Cr.App.R. 380, CA. For cases where it was held on appeal that interviews in breach of section 58 should have been excluded under section 76, see *R. v. McGovern*, 92 Cr.App.R. 228, CA (defendant aged 19, six months' pregnant, of limited intelligence), and *R. v. Chung*, 92 Cr.App.R. 314, CA; and, under section 78, see *R. v. Samuel*, *ante*, §§ 15–211 *et seq.*, *R. v. Absolam*, 88 Cr.App.R. 332, CA (see *post*, § 15–463), *R. v. Parris*, 89 Cr.App.R. 68, CA, *R. v. Walsh*, 91 Cr.App.R. 161, CA (see *post*, § 15–463), and *R. v. Beycan* [1990] Crim.L.R. 185, CA. For cases where breaches of section 58 did not prevent the interviews' admissibility, see *R. v. Alladice*, *ante*, and *R. v. Dunford*, 91 Cr.App.R. 150, CA. For more detailed discussion of these authorities, see the 2004 edition of this work.

[The next paragraph is § 15–221.]

Section 58 and drink driving cases

15–221 In *DPP v. Billington*, 87 Cr.App.R. 68, DC, it was held:

(a) that there was nothing in section 58 or Code C which required the police to delay the taking of a specimen of breath, blood or urine for analysis under the *RTA* 1988, s.7; and

(b) that failure to accord the defendant the right of consulting a solicitor as soon as practicable under section 58 did not thereby furnish the defendant with a reasonable excuse for failing to provide a specimen for analysis.

Billington was applied in *DPP v. Skinner*; *DPP v. Cornell* [1990] R.T.R. 254, DC, which was itself followed in *DPP v. Whalley* [1991] R.T.R. 161, DC: the effect of these decisions is that an arrested person cannot justify failure to supply a specimen on the ground that he is reading the codes of practice. This also applies to specimens taken under section 8 of the 1988 Act: *DPP v. Ward* [1999] R.T.R. 11, DC. See also *DPP v. Varley*, 163 J.P. 443, DC.

Whilst the public interest requires that the breath test procedure cannot be delayed to any significant extent, if there happens to be a solicitor in the charge room whom the detainee wishes to consult "for a couple of minutes" before deciding whether or not to provide specimens of breath he must be allowed to do so; similarly, if the detainee asks at that stage to speak to his solicitor or to the duty solicitor on the telephone for a couple of minutes and the solicitor is immediately available, he should be allowed to do so. If the detainee does no more than indicate a general desire to have legal advice, this is not a reason to delay the procedure: *Kennedy v. DPP* [2004] R.T.R. 6, DC; followed in *Kirkup v. DPP* [2004] Crim.L.R. 230, DC (where it was observed that a duty solicitor will not necessarily be immediately available or respond promptly), *Whitley v. DPP* [2004] Crim.L.R. 585, DC (what is practicable should be considered from the point of view of those at the police station at the time, rather than in hindsight), *Myles v. DPP* [2005] R.T.R. 1, DC (Commonwealth cases of limited assistance) and *Causey v. DPP*, 169 J.P. 331, DC (where the authorities are summarised).

Compatibility with the European Convention on Human Rights

Article 6(3) of the ECHR normally requires that an accused be allowed the benefit of legal advice in the initial stages of interrogation. The right of private consultation may be limited for good cause: *Murray v. U.K.*, 22 E.H.R.R. 29, ECtHR. If an accused's right to an effective exercise of his defence rights has been infringed, it is not necessary to prove that the restriction had a prejudicial effect on the course of the trial: *Brennan v. U.K.* (2002) 34 E.H.R.R. 18, ECtHR. **15–222**

In the context of legislation which permits adverse inferences to be drawn from silence, the right of access to legal advice is of "paramount importance": *Murray v. U.K.*, *ante*, at 67. Delaying access to legal advice in such cases, whatever the justification, is incompatible with the right to a fair trial guaranteed by Article 6(1) of the Convention and the right of access to legal advice under Article 6(3)(c) (*post*, § 16–57): *ibid.*; and reiterated in a number of subsequent European Court of Human Rights cases: see *Condron v. U.K.* (2001) 31 E.H.R.R. 1; *Magee v. U.K.* (2001) 31 E.H.R.R. 35; *Averill v. U.K.* (2001) 31 E.H.R.R. 36. See also *R. v. Aspinall* [1999] 2 Cr.App.R. 115 at 121–122, CA; and Code C:10, and Annex C.

(6) Tape-recording of interviews

(a) *Statute*

Police and Criminal Evidence Act 1984, s.60

60.—(1) It shall be the duty of the Secretary of State— **15–223**

(a) to issue a code of practice in connection with the tape-recording of interviews of persons suspected of the commission of criminal offences which are held by police officers at police stations; and

(b) to make an order requiring the tape-recording of interviews of persons suspected of the commission of criminal offences, or of such descriptions of criminal offences as may be specified in the order, which are so held, in accordance with the code as it has effect for the time being.

(2) An order under subsection (1) above shall be made by statutory instrument and shall be subject to annulment in pursuance of a resolution of either House of Parliament.

(b) *Code of practice*

For the codes of practice generally, see *ante*, §§ 15–3 *et seq.* The current Code of Practice on Tape Recording of Interviews with Suspects, Code E (Appendix A–162), came into force on February 1, 2008. It applies to interviews carried out after midnight on January 31, 2008, notwithstanding that the interview may have commenced before that time: see the preamble to the code itself (Appendix A–162a). **15–224**

The *Police and Criminal Evidence Act 1984 (Codes of Practice) (Code E) Order* 2003 (S.I. 2003 No. 705) applies to interviews of persons suspected of the commission of indictable offences which are held by police officers at police stations and which commence after March 31, 2003. It provides that interviews to which it applies shall be tape-recorded in accordance with Code E, except where the interviewee has been arrested under section 41 of the *Terrorism Act* 2000, or is detained under Schedule 7 to that Act. **15–225**

[For the full text of Code E, see Appendix A–162 *et seq.*]

(c) *Practice direction*

Practice Direction (Criminal Proceedings: Consolidation), para. IV.43
[2002] 1 W.L.R. 2870

15–226 **IV.43.1** Where a suspect is to be interviewed by the police, the Code of Practice on Tape Recording of Interviews with Suspects (Code E) effective from 10 April 1995 and issued under section 60 of the *Police and Criminal Evidence Act* 1984 applies. Where a record of the interview is to be prepared this should be in accordance with the national guidelines approved by the Secretary of State, as envisaged by Note E:5A of the Code.

IV.43.2 Where the prosecution intends to adduce evidence of the interview in evidence, and agreement between the parties has not been reached about the record, sufficient notice must be given to allow consideration of any amendment to the record or the preparation of any transcript of the interview or the preparation of any transcript of a tape recorded interview or any editing of a tape for the purpose of playing it back in court. To that end, the following practice should be followed. (a) Where the defence is unable to agree a record of interview or transcript (where one is already available) the prosecution should be notified no more than 21 days from the date of committal or date of transfer, or at the PDH if earlier, with a view to securing agreement to amend. The notice should specify the part to which objection is taken or the part omitted which the defence consider should be included. A copy of the notice should be supplied to the court within the period specified above. (b) If agreement is not reached and it is proposed that the tape or part of it be played in court, notice should be given to the prosecution by the defence no more than 14 days after the expiry of the period in (a), or as ordered at the PDH, in order that counsel for the parties may agree those parts of the tape that should not be adduced and that arrangements may be made, by editing or in some other way, to exclude that material. A copy of the notice should be supplied to the court within the period specified above. (c) Notice of any agreement reached under (a) or (b) should be supplied to the court by the prosecution as soon as is practicable. (d) Alternatively, if, in any event, prosecuting counsel proposes to play the tape or part of it, the prosecution should, within 28 days of the date of committal or date of transfer or, if earlier, at the PDH, notify the defence and the court. The defence should notify the prosecution and the court within 14 days of receiving the notice if they object to the production of the tape on the basis that a part of it should be excluded. If the objections raised by the defence are accepted, the prosecution should prepare an edited tape or make other arrangements to exclude the material part and should notify the court of the arrangements made. (e) Whenever editing or amendment of a record of interview or of a tape or of a transcript takes place, the following general principles should be followed: (i) where a defendant has made a statement which includes an admission of one or more other offences, the portion relating to other offences should be omitted unless it is or becomes admissible in evidence; (ii) where the statement of one defendant contains a portion which is partly in his favour and partly implicatory of a co-defendant in the trial, the defendant making the statement has the right to insist that everything relevant which is in his favour goes before the jury. In such a case the judge must be consulted about how best to protect the position of the co-defendant.

15–227 **IV.43.3** If there is a failure to agree between counsel under paragraph 43.2(a) to (e), or there is a challenge to the integrity of the master tape, notice and particulars should be given to the court and to the prosecution by the defence as soon as is practicable. The court may then, at its discretion, order a pre-trial review or give such other directions as may be appropriate.

IV.43.4 If a tape is to be adduced during proceedings before the Crown Court it should be produced and proved by the interviewing officer or any other officer who was present at the interview at which the recording was made. The prosecution should ensure that such an officer will be available for this purpose.

IV.43.5 Where such an officer is unable to act as the tape machine operator it is for the prosecution to make some other arrangement.

IV.43.6 In order to avoid the necessity for the court to listen to lengthy or irrelevant material before the relevant part of a tape recording is reached, counsel shall indicate to the tape machine operator those parts of a recording which it may be necessary to play. Such an indication should, so far as possible, be expressed in terms of the time track or other identifying process used by the interviewing police force and should be given in time for the operator to have located those parts by the appropriate point in the trial.

IV.43.7 Once a trial has begun, if, by reason of faulty preparation or for some other cause, the procedures above have not been properly complied with, and an application is made to amend the record of interview or transcript or to edit the tape, as the case may be, thereby making necessary an adjournment for the work to be carried out, the court may make at its discretion an appropriate award of costs.

IV.43.8 Where a case is listed for hearing on a date which falls within the time limits set out above, it is the responsibility of the parties to ensure that all the necessary steps are taken to comply with this practice direction within such shorter period as is available.

IV.43.9 In paragraph 43.2(a)(d), "date of transfer" is the date on which notice of transfer is given in accordance with the provisions of section 4(1)(c) of the *Criminal Justice Act* 1987.

IV.43.10 This direction should be read in conjunction with the Code of Practice on Tape Recording referred to in paragraph 43.1 and with the Home Office Circular 26/1995.

For section 4(1)(c) of the *CJA* 1987 (notice of transfer in serious fraud cases), see *ante*, § 1–41. As to Home Office Circular 26/1995 see *post*, § 15–230.

As to the use in trials of tape recordings and transcripts, see *ante*, §§ 4–421 *et seq.* **15–228**

[The next paragraph is § 15–230.]

(d) *Home Office circulars*

Home Office Circular 26/1995 (referred to in para. IV.43.10 of the practice direction, *ante*, and set out in full at (1995) 159 J.P.N. 303) provides police forces with national guidelines on the preparation of records of interviews in accordance with Note for Guidance 5A of Code E (Appendix A–176). They are an amended version of the annex attached to Home Office Circular 21/1992, which is withdrawn. The significant changes from the previous guidance are to allow for the involvement of people other than the investigating officer, including civilians, in the preparation of records, and to give advice on how to record matters which may give rise to an inference being drawn under sections 34, 36 or 37 of the *CJPOA* 1994 (*post*, §§ 15–414 *et seq.*). The guidelines make clear that where a person other than the interviewing officer prepares the record, it remains the responsibility of the interviewing officer to ensure its accuracy. **15–230**

The guidelines contain advice as to the need for police officers to remind themselves before interview of the main elements of the offence they are investigating. Police officers are advised that during the interview they should make a note of the counter time at which anything is said which might later need to be retrieved for verbatim transcription or in order to check the accuracy of a third person summary. The circular contains detailed advice as to the content of a summary of an interview, setting out what matters should be transcribed verbatim: these include all admissions (including ambiguous admissions) and "the main salient points", *i.e.* statements or questions about intent, dishonesty or possible defence, knowledge of key facts, presence at scene of crime on other occasions, assertion that others were involved, questions aimed at demonstrating that an offender under 14 knew that what he was doing was seriously wrong. A verbatim record should also be made of any questions or answers relating to a failure by the interviewee to answer questions, whether adequately or at all, or to account for any object, substance of mark or his presence at a particular place (see the *CJPOA* 1994, ss.34, 36, 37 (*post*, §§ 15–414 *et seq.*)).

The circular advises that questions of bail and alternative pleas or charges should not normally be discussed in interview, but if they are, they should be recorded verbatim. Other matters (aggravating factors/mitigating circumstances) may be summarised in the third person, with relevant tape counter times noted in the margin of the record.

Home Office Circular 47/1995 provides that in cases where the police supply the Crown Prosecution Service with an "abbreviated file", it is only necessary to include a short descriptive note of an interview. A "full file" will be required for all cases except those which are likely to be disposed of by way of a guilty plea in a magistrates' court; even then, a full file will be required if the offence charged is an offence of assault triable either way, other than one contrary to section 38 or 47 of the *Offences against the Person Act* 1861.

(7) Visual recording of interviews

Police and Criminal Evidence Act 1984, s.60A

Visual recording of interviews

15–231 **60A.**—(1) The Secretary of State shall have power—

(a) to issue a code of practice for the visual recording of interviews held by police officers at police stations; and

(b) to make an order requiring the visual recording of interviews so held, and requiring the visual recording to be in accordance with the code for the time being in force under this section.

(2) A requirement imposed by an order under this section may be imposed in relation to such cases or police stations in such areas, or both, as may be specified or described in the order.

(3) [*Order to be made by statutory instrument.*]

(4) In this section—

(a) references to any interview are references to an interview of a person suspected of a criminal offence; and

(b) references to a visual recording include references to a visual recording in which an audio recording is comprised.

[This section is inserted by the *CJPA* 2001, s.76(1).]

For Code F, the Code of Practice on Visual Recording of Interviews with Suspects, see Appendix A–180 *et seq.*

(8) Fingerprints, photographs, intimate and other samples

Police and Criminal Evidence Act 1984, s.61

Fingerprinting

15–232 **61.**—(1) Except as provided by this section no person's fingerprints may be taken without the appropriate consent.

(2) Consent to the taking of a person's fingerprints must be in writing if it is given at a time when he is at a police station.

(3) The fingerprints of a person detained at a police station may be taken without the appropriate consent if—

(a) he is detained in consequence of his arrest for a recordable offence; and

(b) he has not had his fingerprints taken in the course of the investigation of the offence by the police.

(3A) Where a person mentioned in paragraph (a) of subsection (3) or (4) has already had his fingerprints taken in the course of the investigation of the offence by the police, that fact shall be disregarded for the purposes of that subsection if—

(a) the fingerprints taken on the previous occasion do not constitute a complete set of his fingerprints; or

(b) some or all of the fingerprints taken on the previous occasion are not of sufficient quality to allow satisfactory analysis, comparison or matching (whether in the case in question or generally).

(4) The fingerprints of a person detained at a police station may be taken without the appropriate consent if—

(a) he has been charged with a recordable offence or informed that he will be reported for such an offence; and

(b) [*identical to subs. (3)(b)*, ante].

(4A) The fingerprints of a person who has answered to bail at a court or police station may be taken without the appropriate consent at the court or station if—

(a) the court, or

(b) an officer of at least the rank of inspector,

authorises them to be taken.

(4B) A court or officer may only give an authorisation under subsection (4A) if—

(a) the person who has answered to bail has answered to it for a person whose fingerprints were taken on a previous occasion and there are reasonable grounds for believing that he is not the same person; or

(b) the person who has answered to bail claims to be a different person from a person whose fingerprints were taken on a previous occasion.

(5) An officer may give an authorisation under subsection ... (4A) above orally or in writing but, if he gives it orally, he shall confirm it in writing as soon as is practicable.

(6) Any person's fingerprints may be taken without the appropriate consent if—

(a) he has been convicted of a recordable offence;

(b) he has been given a caution in respect of a recordable offence which, at the time of the caution, he has admitted; or

(c) he has been warned or reprimanded under section 65 of the *Crime and Disorder Act* 1998 for a recordable offence.

[(6A) A constable may take a person's fingerprints without the appropriate consent if—

(a) the constable reasonably suspects that the person is committing or attempting to commit an offence, or has committed or attempted to commit an offence; and

(b) either of the two conditions mentioned in subsection (6B) is met.

(6B) The conditions are that—

(a) the name of the person is unknown to, and cannot be readily ascertained by, the constable;

(b) the constable has reasonable grounds for doubting whether a name furnished by the person as his name is his real name.

(6C) The taking of fingerprints by virtue of subsection (6A) does not count for any of the purposes of this Act as taking them in the course of the investigation of an offence by the police.]

(7) In a case where by virtue of subsection (3), (4) *or (6)* [, (6) or (6A)] above a person's fingerprints are taken without the appropriate consent—

(a) he shall be told the reason before his fingerprints are taken; and

(b) the reason shall be recorded as soon as is practicable after the fingerprints are taken.

(7A) If a person's fingerprints are taken at a police station, [or by virtue of subsection (6A) at a place other than a police station,] whether with or without the appropriate consent—

(a) before the fingerprints are taken, an officer [(or, in a subsection (6A) case, the constable)] shall inform him that they may be the subject of a speculative search; and

(b) the fact that the person has been informed of this possibility shall be recorded as soon as possible after the fingerprints have been taken.

(8) If he is detained at a police station when the fingerprints are taken, the reason for taking them and, in the case falling within subsection (7A) above, the fact referred to in paragraph (b) of that subsection shall be recorded on his custody record.

(8A) Where a person's fingerprints are taken electronically, they must be taken in such a manner, and using such devices, as the Secretary of State has approved for the purposes of electronic fingerprinting.

(8B) The power to take the fingerprints of a person detained at a police station without the appropriate consent shall be exercisable by any constable.

(9) Nothing in this section—

(a) affects any power conferred by paragraph 18(2) of Schedule 2 to the *Immigration Act* 1971[, section 141 of the *Immigration and Asylum Act* 1999 or regulations made under section 144 of that Act]; or

(b) applies to a person arrested or detained under the terrorism provisions.

(10) Nothing in this section applies to a person arrested under an extradition arrest power.

[This section is printed as amended by the *CJPOA* 1994, s.168(2) and Sched. 10, para. 56; the *Terrorism Act* 2000, s.125 and Sched. 15, para. 5(7); the *Anti-Terrorism, Crime and Security Act* 2001, s.90(2); the *CJPA* 2001, s.78(2)–(7); the *Police Reform Act* 2002, s.107(1), and Sched. 7, para. 9(3); the *Extradition Act* 2003, s.169(3); and the *CJA* 2003, s.9; and, as from a day to be appointed, by the *Immigration and Asylum Act* 1999, s.169(1), and Sched. 14, para. 80(1) and (4) (insertion of words in square brackets in subs. (9)); and the *SOCPA* 2005, s.117(1)–(4) (insertion of words in square brackets, omission of italicised words in remainder of section).]

As to the meaning of "appropriate consent", "fingerprints" and "the terrorism provisions", see section 65, *post*, §§ 15–249 *et seq*. **15–233**

As to the taking of fingerprints after conviction, see also section 27, *ante*, § 15–174.

As to identification by fingerprints, see Code D, para. 4 (Appendix A–128) and generally, *ante*, §§ 14–53 *et seq*.

As to the destruction of fingerprints, see section 64, *post*, §§ 15–246 *et seq.*

As to the exclusion of fingerprint evidence, see *R. v. Buckley*, 163 J.P. 561, CA, *ante*, § 14–53.

15–234 The words "detained at" a police station in section 61(3) include a person detained temporarily at a police station after having been remanded in custody by a magistrates' court: *R. v. Seymour* [1995] 9 *Archbold News* 1, CA (94/6544/W3).

Police and Criminal Evidence Act 1984, s.61A

Impressions of footwear

15–234a **61A.**—(1) Except as provided by this section, no impression of a person's footwear may be taken without the appropriate consent.

(2) Consent to the taking of an impression of a person's footwear must be in writing if it is given at a time when he is at a police station.

(3) Where a person is detained at a police station, an impression of his footwear may be taken without the appropriate consent if—

(a) he is detained in consequence of his arrest for a recordable offence; and

(b) he has not had an impression taken of his footwear in the course of the investigation of the offence by the police.

(4) Where a person mentioned in paragraph (a) of subsection (3) above has already had an impression taken of his footwear in the course of the investigation of the offence by the police, that fact shall be disregarded for the purposes of that subsection if the impression of his footwear taken previously is—

(a) incomplete; or

(b) is not of sufficient quality to allow satisfactory analysis, comparison or matching (whether in the case in question or generally).

(5) If an impression of a person's footwear is taken at a police station, whether with or without the appropriate consent—

(a) before it is taken, an officer shall inform him that it may be the subject of a speculative search; and

(b) the fact that the person has been informed of this possibility shall be recorded as soon as is practicable after the impression has been taken, and if he is detained at a police station, the record shall be made on his custody record.

(6) In a case where, by virtue of subsection (3) above, an impression of a person's footwear is taken without the appropriate consent—

(a) he shall be told the reason before it is taken; and

(b) the reason shall be recorded on his custody record as soon as is practicable after the impression is taken.

(7) The power to take an impression of the footwear of a person detained at a police station without the appropriate consent shall be exercisable by any constable.

(8) Nothing in this section applies to any person—

(a) arrested or detained under the terrorism provisions;

(b) arrested under an extradition arrest power.

[This section was inserted by the *SOCPA* 2005, s.118(1) and (2).]

Police and Criminal Evidence Act 1984, s.62

Intimate samples

15–235 **62.**—(1) Subject to section 63B below an intimate sample may be taken from a person in police detention only—

(a) if a police officer of at least the rank of inspector authorises it to be taken; and

(b) if the appropriate consent is given.

(1A) An intimate sample may be taken from a person who is not in police detention but from whom, in the course of the investigation of an offence, two or more non-intimate samples suitable for the same means of analysis have been taken which have proved insufficient—

(a) if a police officer of at least the rank of inspector authorises it to be taken; and

(b) if the appropriate consent is given.

(2) An officer may only give an authorisation under subsection (1) or (1A) above if he has reasonable grounds—

(a) for suspecting the involvement of the person from whom the sample is to be taken in a recordable offence; and

(b) for believing that the sample will tend to confirm or disprove his involvement.

(3) An officer may give an authorisation under subsection (1) or (1A) above orally or in writing but, if he gives it orally, he shall confirm it in writing as soon as is practicable.

(4) The appropriate consent must be given in writing.

(5) Where—

(a) an authorisation has been given; and

(b) it is proposed that an intimate sample shall be taken in pursuance of the authorisation,

an officer shall inform the person from whom the sample is to be taken—

(i) of the giving of the authorisation; and

(ii) of the grounds for giving it.

(6) The duty imposed by subsection (5)(ii) above includes a duty to state the nature of the offence in which it is suspected that the person from whom the sample is to be taken has been involved. **15–236**

(7) If an intimate sample is taken from a person—

(a) the authorisation by virtue of which it was taken;

(b) the grounds for giving the authorisation; and

(c) the fact that the appropriate consent was given,

shall be recorded as soon as is practicable after the sample is taken.

(7A) If an intimate sample is taken from a person at a police station—

(a) before the sample is taken, an officer shall inform him that it may be the subject of a speculative search; and

(b) the fact that the person has been informed of this possibility shall be recorded as soon as practicable after the sample has been taken.

(8) If an intimate sample is taken from a person detained at a police station, the matters required to be recorded by subsection (7) or (7A) above shall be recorded in his custody record.

(9) In the case of an intimate sample which is a dental impression, the sample may be taken from a person only by a registered dentist.

(9A) In the case of any other form of intimate sample, except in the case of a sample of urine, the sample may be taken from a person only by—

(a) a registered medical practitioner; or

(b) a registered health care professional.

(10) Where the appropriate consent to the taking of an intimate sample from a person was refused without good cause, in any proceedings against that person for an offence—

(a) the court, in determining—

(i) *whether to commit that person for trial; or*

(ii) whether there is a case to answer; and

(aa) a judge, in deciding whether to grant an application made by the accused under—

(i) *section 6 of the* Criminal Justice Act *1987 (application for dismissal of charges of serious fraud in respect of which notice of transfer has been given under section 4 of that Act); or*

(ii) *paragraph 5 of Schedule 6 to the* Criminal Justice Act *1991 (application for dismissal of charge of violent or sexual offence involving child in respect of which notice of transfer has been given under section 53 of that Act); and*

[paragraph 2 of Schedule 3 to the *Crime and Disorder Act* 1998 (applications for dismissal); and]

(b) the court or jury, in determining whether that person is guilty of the offence charged,

may draw such inferences from the refusal as appear proper… .

(11) Nothing in this section applies to the taking of a specimen for the purposes of any of the provisions of sections 4 to 11 of the *Road Traffic Act* 1988 or of sections 26 to 38 of the *Transport and Works Act* 1992.

(12) Nothing in this section applies to a person arrested or detained under the terrorism procedures; and subsection (1A) shall not apply where the non-intimate samples mentioned in that subsection were taken under paragraph 10 of Schedule 8 to the *Terrorism Act* 2000.

[This section is printed as amended and repealed in part by the *Road Traffic (Consequential Provisions) Act* 1988, s.4 and Sched. 3, para. 27(4); the *CJPOA* 1994, ss.54(1)–(5) and 168(1)–(3), and Scheds 9, para. 24, 10, paras 57 and 62(4)(a), and 11;

the *Terrorism Act* 2000, s.125 and Sched. 15, para. 5(8); the *CJCSA* 2000, s.74 and Sched. 7, para. 78; the *CJPA* 2001, s.80(1); and the *Police Reform Act* 2002, ss.53(2) and 54(1). Sub-paras (i) and (ii) of subs. (10)(aa) are replaced by the words in square brackets that follow them by the *CJA* 2003, s.41, and Sched. 3, para. 56(1) and (2)(b). This amendment came into force on May 9, 2005 (*Criminal Justice Act 2003 (Commencement No. 9) Order* 2005 (S.I. 2005 No. 1267)) in relation to cases sent for trial under s.51 or 51A(3)(d) of the *CDA* 1998. Otherwise, it comes into force on a day to be appointed. Subs. (10)(a)(i) is repealed as from a day to be appointed by the *CJA* 2003, ss.41 and 332, Sched. 3, para. 56(2)(a), and Sched. 37, Pt 4.]

15–237 As to the meaning of "appropriate consent" and "intimate sample", see section 65, *post*, §§ 15–249 *et seq*. As to "police detention", see section 118(2), *ante*, § 15–27. A "recordable offence" is any offence to which regulations under section 27 (*ante*, § 15–174) apply: s.118(1) (*ante*, § 15–27).

As to the destruction of samples, see section 64, *post*, §§ 15–246 *et seq*.

For identification by body samples and impressions, see Code D:6 (Appendix A–135), and generally, *ante*, §§ 14–56 *et seq*. For intimate and strip searches, see Code C: Annex A (Appendix A–92 *et seq*.).

Section 62 does not expressly require authorisation to precede consent, though it is possible to foresee circumstances in which authorisation could affect the basis upon which consent was given: *R. v. Butt*, unreported, February 20, 1998, CA (96/07877/Z2).

An analysis of the result of an intimate sample taken under section 62 in the course of one investigation may be used for the purposes of a separate investigation into a different offence: *R. v. Kelt*, 99 Cr.App.R. 372, CA.

Police and Criminal Evidence Act 1984, s.63

Other samples

15–238 **63.**—(1) Except as provided by this section, a non-intimate sample may not be taken from a person without the appropriate consent.

(2) Consent to the taking of a non-intimate sample must be given in writing.

(2A) A non-intimate sample may be taken from a person without the appropriate consent if two conditions are satisfied.

(2B) The first is that the person is in police detention in consequence of his arrest for a recordable offence.

(2C) The second is that—

(a) he has not had a non-intimate sample of the same type and from the same part of the body taken in the course of the investigation of the offence by the police, or

(b) he has had such a sample taken but it proved insufficient.

(3) A non-intimate sample may be taken from a person without the appropriate consent if—

(a) he … is being held in custody by the police on the authority of a court; and

(b) an officer of at least the rank of inspector authorises it to be taken without the appropriate consent.

(3A) A non-intimate sample may be taken from a person (whether or not he is in police detention or held in custody by the police on the authority of a court) without the appropriate consent if—

(a) he has been charged with a recordable offence or informed that he will be reported for such an offence; and

(b) either he has not had a non-intimate sample taken from him in the course of the investigation of the offence by the police or he has had a non-intimate sample taken from him but either it was not suitable for the same means of analysis or, though so suitable, the sample proved insufficient.

(3B) A non-intimate sample may be taken from a person without the appropriate consent if he has been convicted of a recordable offence.

(3C) A non-intimate sample may also be taken from a person without the appropriate consent if he is a person to whom section 2 of the *Criminal Evidence (Amendment) Act* 1997 applies (persons detained following acquittal on grounds of insanity or finding of unfitness to plead).

(4) An officer may only give an authorisation under subsection (3) above if he has reasonable grounds—

(1C) Where—

(a) fingerprints, impressions of footwear or samples have been taken from any person in connection with the investigation of an offence but otherwise than in circumstances to which subsection (1) above applies, and

(b) that person has given his consent in writing to the use in a speculative search of the fingerprints, of the impressions of footwear or of the samples and of information derived from them,

the fingerprints or impressions of footwear or, as the case may be, those samples and that information may be checked against any of the fingerprints, impressions of footwear, samples or information mentioned in paragraph (a) or (b) of that subsection.

(1D) A consent given for the purposes of subsection (1C) above shall not be capable of being withdrawn.

(2) Where a sample of hair other than pubic hair is to be taken the sample may be taken either by cutting hairs or by plucking hairs with their roots so long as no more are plucked than the person taking the sample reasonably considers to be necessary for a sufficient sample.

(3) Where any power to take a sample is exercisable in relation to a person the sample may be taken in a prison or other institution to which the *Prison Act* 1952 applies.

(3A) Where— **15–242**

(a) the power to take a non-intimate sample under section 63(3B) above is exercisable in relation to any person who is detained under Part III of the *Mental Health Act* 1983 in pursuance of—

(i) a hospital order or interim hospital order made following his conviction for the recordable offence in question, or

(ii) a transfer direction given at a time when he was detained in pursuance of any sentence or order imposed following that conviction, or

(b) the power to take a non-intimate sample under section 63(3C) above is exercisable in relation to any person,

the sample may be taken in the hospital in which he is detained under that Part of that Act.

Expressions used in this subsection and in the *Mental Health Act* 1983 have the same meaning as in that Act.

(3B) Where the power to take a non-intimate sample under section 63(3B) above is exercisable in relation to a person detained in pursuance of directions of the Secretary of State under section 92 of the *Powers of Criminal Courts (Sentencing) Act* 2000 the sample may be taken at the place where he is so detained.

(4) Any constable may, within the allowed period, require a person who is neither in police detention nor held in custody by the police on the authority of a court to attend a police station in order to have a sample taken where—

(a) the person has been charged with a recordable offence or informed that he will be reported for such an offence and either he has not had a sample taken from him in the course of the investigation of the offence by the police or he has had a sample so taken from him but either it was not suitable for the same means of analysis or, though so suitable, the sample proved insufficient; or

(b) the person has been convicted of a recordable offence and either he has not had a sample taken from him since the conviction or he has had a sample taken from him (before or after his conviction) but either it was not suitable for the same means of analysis or, though so suitable, the sample proved insufficient.

(5) The period allowed for requiring a person to attend a police station for the purpose specified in subsection (4) above is—

(a) in the case of a person falling within paragraph (a), one month beginning with the date of the charge or of his being informed as mentioned in that paragraph or one month beginning with the date on which the appropriate officer is informed of the fact that the sample is not suitable for the same means of analysis or has proved insufficient, as the case may be;

(b) in the case of a person falling within paragraph (b), one month beginning with the date of the conviction or one month beginning with the date on which the appropriate officer is informed of the fact that the sample is not suitable for the same means of analysis or has proved insufficient, as the case may be.

(6) A requirement under subsection (4) above—

(a) shall give the person at least 7 days within which he must so attend; and

(b) may direct him to attend at a specified time of day or between specified times of day.

(7) Any constable may arrest without a warrant a person who has failed to comply with a requirement under subsection (4) above.

(8) In this section "the appropriate officer" is—

(a) in the case of a person falling within subsection (4)(a), the officer investigating the offence with which that person has been charged or as to which he was informed that he would be reported;

(b) in the case of a person falling within subsection (4)(b), the officer in charge of the police station from which the investigation of the offence of which he was convicted was conducted.

[This section was inserted by the *CJPOA* 1994, s.56; and is printed as amended by the *CPIA* 1996, s.64(1); the *Criminal Evidence (Amendment) Act* 1997, ss.3 and 4; the *PCC(S)A* 2000, s.165(1) and Sched. 9, para. 97; the *CJPA* 2001, s.81; the *SOCPA* 2005, ss.59 and 118(1) and (3), and Sched. 4, paras 43 and 46; and the *AFA* 2006, s.378(1), and Sched. 16, para. 100; and as amended, as from a day to be appointed, by the *SOCPA* 2005, s.117(5) (insertion of words in square brackets).]

Police and Criminal Evidence Act 1984, ss.63B, 63C

Testing for presence of Class A drugs

15–243 **63B.**—(1) A sample of urine or a non-intimate sample may be taken from a person in police detention for the purpose of ascertaining whether he has any specified Class A drug in his body—

(a) either the arrest condition or the charge condition is met;

(b) both the age condition and the request condition are met; and

(c) the notification condition is met in relation to the arrest condition, the charge condition or the age condition (as the case may be).

(1A) The arrest condition is that the person concerned has been arrested for an offence but has not been charged with that offence and either—

(a) the offence is a trigger offence; or

(b) a police officer of at least the rank of inspector has reasonable grounds for suspecting that the misuse by that person of a specified Class A drug caused or contributed to the offence and has authorised the sample to be taken.

(2) The charge condition is either—

(a) that the person concerned has been charged with a trigger offence; or

(b) that the person concerned has been charged with an offence and a police officer of at least the rank of inspector, who has reasonable grounds for suspecting that the misuse by that person of any specified Class A drug caused or contributed to the offence, has authorised the sample to be taken.

(3) The age condition is—

(a) if the arrest condition is met, that the person concerned has attained the age of 18;

(b) if the charge condition is met, that he has attained the age of 14.

(4) The request condition is that a police officer has requested the person concerned to give the sample.

(4A) The notification condition is that—

(a) the relevant chief officer has been notified by the Secretary of State that appropriate arrangements have been made for the police area as a whole, or for the particular police station, in which the person is in police detention, and

(b) the notice has not been withdrawn.

(4B) For the purposes of subsection (4A) above, appropriate arrangements are arrangements for the taking of samples under this section from whichever of the following is specified in the notification—

(a) persons in respect of whom the arrest condition is met;

(b) persons in respect of whom the charge condition is met;

(c) persons who have not attained the age of 18.

(5) Before requesting the person concerned to give a sample, an officer must—

(a) warn him that if, when so requested, he fails without good cause to do so he may be liable to prosecution, and

(b) in a case within subsection (1A)(b) or (2)(b) above, inform him of the giving of the authorisation and of the grounds in question.

(5A) In the case of a person who has not attained the age of 17—

(a) the making of the request under subsection (4) above;

(b) the giving of the warning and (where applicable) the information under subsection (5) above; and

(c) the taking of the sample,

may not take place except in the presence of an appropriate adult.

(5B) If a sample is taken under this section from a person in respect of whom the arrest condition is met no other sample may be taken from him under this section during the same continuous period of detention but—

(a) if the charge condition is also met in respect of him at any time during that period, the sample must be treated as a sample taken by virtue of the fact that the charge condition is met;

(b) the fact that the sample is to be so treated must be recorded in the person's custody record.

(5C) Despite subsection (1)(a) above, a sample may be taken from a person under this section if—

(a) he was arrested for an offence (the first offence),

(b) the arrest condition is met but the charge condition is not met,

(c) before a sample is taken by virtue of subsection (1) above he would (but for his arrest as mentioned in paragraph (d) below) be required to be released from police detention,

(d) he continues to be in police detention by virtue of his having been arrested for an offence not falling within subsection (1A) above, and

(e) the sample is taken before the end of the period of 24 hours starting with the time when his detention by virtue of his arrest for the first offence began.

(5D) A sample must not be taken from a person under this section if he is detained in a police station unless he has been brought before the custody officer.

(6) A sample may be taken under this section only by a person prescribed by regulations made by the Secretary of State by statutory instrument.

No regulations shall be made under this subsection unless a draft has been laid before, and approved by resolution of, each House of Parliament.

(6A) [*Power to amend age specified in subs. (3) by statutory instrument.*]

(6B) [*Statutory instrument procedure.*]

(7) Information obtained from a sample taken under this section may be disclosed—

(a) for the purpose of informing any decision about granting bail in criminal proceedings (within the meaning of the *Bail Act* 1976) to the person concerned;

(aa) for the purpose of informing any decision about the giving of a conditional caution under Part 3 of the *Criminal Justice Act* 2003 [or a youth conditional caution under Chapter 1 of Part 4 of the *Crime and Disorder Act* 1998] to the person concerned;

(b) where the person concerned is in police detention or is remanded in or committed to custody by an order of a court or has been granted such bail, for the purpose of informing any decision about his supervision;

(c) where the person concerned is convicted of an offence, for the purpose of informing any decision about the appropriate sentence to be passed by a court and any decision about his supervision or release;

(ca) for the purpose of an assessment which the person concerned is required to attend by virtue of section 9(2) or 10(2) of the *Drugs Act* 2005;

(cb) for the purpose of proceedings against the person concerned for an offence under section 12(3) or 14(3) of that Act;

(d) for the purpose of ensuring that appropriate advice and treatment is made available to the person concerned.

(8) A person who fails without good cause to give any sample which may be taken from him under this section shall be guilty of an offence.

(9) [*Repealed by* Drugs Act *2005, ss.7(12) and 23, and Sched. 2.*]

(10) In this section—

"appropriate adult", in relation to a person who has not attained the age of 17, means—

(a) his parent or guardian or, if he is in the care of a local authority or voluntary organisation, a person representing that authority or organisation; or

(b) a social worker of a local authority ...; or

(c) if no person falling within paragraph (a) or (b) is available, any responsible person aged 18 or over who is not a police officer or a person employed by the police;

"relevant chief officer" means—

(a) in relation to a police area, the chief officer of police of the police force for that police area; or

(b) in relation to a police station, the chief officer of police of the police force for the police area in which the police station is situated.

[This section was inserted by the *CJCSA* 2000, s.57(1) and (2). It is printed as amended by the *CJA* 2003, s.5(1) and (3); the *Children Act* 2004, s.64, and Sched. 5, Pt 4; and the *Drugs Act* 2005, ss.7(1)–(12) and 23(1) and (2), Sched. 1, paras 1, 4 and 5, and Sched. 2; and as amended, as from a day to be appointed, by the *CJIA* 2008, s.148(1), and Sched. 26, para. 20(2) (insertion of words in square brackets).]

15–243a Part 3 (ss.9 to 19) of the *Drugs Act* 2005 (in force in part from December 1, 2005; fully in force from April 1, 2007: *Drugs Act 2005 (Commencement No. 5) Order* 2007 (S.I. 2007 No. 562)) is headed "Assessment of Misuse of Drugs". Section 9 applies if a sample is taken under section 63B of the 1984 Act, analysis of the sample reveals the presence of a Class A drug, and certain other conditions are met. Before such person is released from a police station, a police officer may require him to attend an "initial assessment" with a suitably qualified assessor for specified purposes. Section 10 allows the police officer, at the same time as imposing an initial assessment requirement, to impose a follow up requirement. Section 11 contains supplemental provisions as to the manner of imposing requirements. Section 12 creates a summary offence of not attending or failing to stay for the duration of the appointment with the assessor. Section 13 concerns the making of arrangements for the follow-up assessment, with section 14 corresponding to section 12. Section 15 restricts the disclosure of information obtained during an assessment. Section 16 makes provision for a requirement imposed under section 9 or 10 to cease to have effect if further analysis of the sample does not reveal that a Class A drug was present. Section 17 provides for a requirement under either section to cease to have effect if at any time before the person has complied fully with the requirement, he is charged with the related offence, or a court imposes on him a condition of bail pursuant to the *Bail Act* 1976, s.3(6D) (duty to impose condition to undergo relevant assessment) (*ante*, § 3–10). Section 18 makes provision for the issuing of guidance to the police and suitably qualified persons. Section 19 is an interpretation section.

15–244 The *Police and Criminal Evidence Act 1984 (Drug Testing of Persons in Police Detention) (Prescribed Persons) Regulations* 2001 (S.I. 2001 No. 2645) prescribe the persons who may take samples pursuant to the power to request samples under this section.

Testing for presence of Class A drugs: supplementary

15–245 **63C.**—(1) A person guilty of an offence under section 63B above shall be liable on summary conviction to imprisonment for a term not exceeding *three months* [51 weeks], or to a fine not exceeding level 4 on the standard scale, or to both.

(2) A police officer may give an authorisation under section 63B above orally or in writing but, if he gives it orally, he shall confirm it in writing as soon as practicable.

(3) If a sample is taken under section 63B above by virtue of an authorisation, the authorisation and the grounds for the suspicion shall be recorded as soon as is practicable after the sample is taken.

(4) If the sample is taken from a person detained at a police station, the matters required to be recorded by subsection (3) above shall be recorded in his custody record.

(5) Subsections (11) and (12) of section 62 above apply for the purposes of section 63B above as they do for the purposes of that section; and section 63B above does not prejudice the generality of sections 62 and 63 above.

(6) In section 63B above—

"Class A drug" and "misuse" have the same meanings as the *Misuse of Drugs Act* 1971;

"specified" (in relation to a Class A drug) and "trigger offence" have the same meanings as in Part III of the *Criminal Justice and Court Services Act* 2000.

[This section was inserted by the *CJCSA* 2000, s.57(1) and (2). It is printed as amended, as from a day to be appointed, by the *CJA* 2003, s.280(2), and Sched. 26, para. 35 (substitution of "51 weeks" for "six months" in subs. (1), but not in relation to any offence committed before the date of commencement: s.280(3)).]

As to the definitions in subsection (6), see section 70 of, and Schedule 6 to, the 2000 Act, *post*; and sections 2(1) and 37(2) of the *Misuse of Drugs Act* 1971, *post*, §§ 27–5, 27-127.

Criminal Justice and Court Services Act 2000, s.70

Interpretation, etc.

70.—(1) In this Part— **15–245a**

"Class A drug" has the same meaning as in the *Misuse of Drugs Act* 1971,

"specified", in relation to a Class A drug, means specified by an order made by the Secretary of State,

"trigger offence" has the meaning given by Schedule 6.

(2) The Secretary of State may by order amend Schedule 6 so as to add, modify or omit any description of offence.

(3) In this Part (except in section 69), references to release include temporary release.

(4) [*Amends* PCC(S)A *2000, s.163*, ante, *§ 5–4*.]

(5) *Section 53 does not apply in relation to any community order made before that section comes into force.*

[As from a day to be appointed (as to which, see *ante*, § 5–1), subs. (5) is repealed by the *CJIA* 2008, ss.6(2) and 149, Sched. 4, paras 68 and 70, and Sched. 28, Pt 1.]

Criminal Justice and Court Services Act 2000, Sched. 6

SCHEDULE 6

TRIGGER OFFENCES

1. Offences under the following provisions of the *Theft Act* 1968 are trigger offences: **15–245b**

section 1 (theft)
section 8 (robbery)
section 9 (burglary)
section 10 (aggravated burglary)
section 12 (taking motor vehicle or other conveyance without authority)
section 12A (aggravated vehicle-taking)
section 22 (handling stolen goods)
section 25 (going equipped for stealing, etc.)

2. Offences under the following provisions of the *Misuse of Drugs Act* 1971 are trigger offences, if committed in respect of a specified Class A drug:

section 4 (restriction on production and supply of controlled drugs)
section 5(2) (possession of controlled drug)
section 5(3) (possession of controlled drug with intent to supply).

3. Offences under the following provisions of the *Fraud Act* 2006 are trigger offences—

section 1 (fraud)
section 6 (possession etc. of articles for use in frauds)
section 7 (making or supplying articles for use in frauds).

3A. An offence under section 1(1) of the *Criminal Attempts Act* 1981 is a trigger offence, if committed in respect of an offence under—

(a) any of the following provisions of the *Theft Act* 1968:
section 1 (theft)
section 8 (robbery)
section 9 (burglary)
section 22 (handling stolen goods), or
(b) section 1 of the *Fraud Act* 2006 (fraud).

4. Offences under the following provisions of the *Vagrancy Act* 1824 are trigger offences:

section 3 (begging)
section 4 (persistent begging).

[This schedule is printed as amended by the *Criminal Justice and Court Services*

Act 2000 (Amendment) Order 2004 (S.I. 2004 No. 1892); the *Fraud Act* 2006, s.14(1) and (3), Sched. 1, para. 32, and Sched. 3; and the *Criminal Justice and Court Services Act 2000 (Amendment) Order* 2007 (S.I. 2007 No. 2171).]

Criminal Justice (Specified Class A Drugs) Order 2001 (S.I. 2001 No. 1816), art. 2

15–245C **2.** For the purposes of section 70(1) of the *Criminal Justice and Court Services Act* 2000 (and accordingly for the purposes of section 63C(6) of the *Police and Criminal Evidence Act* 1984, section 65(10) of the *Criminal Justice Act* 1991 and section 163 of the *Powers of Criminal Courts (Sentencing) Act* 2000), the term "specified class A drugs" shall refer to the following drugs:

(a) cocaine, its salts and any preparation or other product containing cocaine or its salts; and

(b) diamorphine, its salts and any preparation or other product containing diamorphine or its salts.

Police and Criminal Evidence Act 1984, s.64

Destruction of fingerprints and samples

15–246 **64.**—(1A) Where—

(a) fingerprints, impressions of footwear or samples are taken from a person in connection with the investigation of an offence, and

(b) subsection (3) below does not require them to be destroyed,

the fingerprints, impressions of footwear or samples may be retained after they have fulfilled the purposes for which they were taken but shall not be used by any person except for purposes related to the prevention or detection of crime, the investigation of an offence *or the conduct of a prosecution* [, the conduct of a prosecution or the identification of a deceased person or of the person from whom a body part came].

(1B) In subsection (1A) above—

(a) the reference to using a fingerprint or an impression of footwear includes a reference to allowing any check to be made against it under section 63A(1) or (1C) above and to disclosing it to any person;

(b) the reference to using a sample includes a reference to allowing any check to be made under section 63A(1) or (1C) above against it or against information derived from it and to disclosing it or any such information to any person;

(c) the reference to crime includes a reference to any conduct which—

(i) constitutes one or more criminal offences (whether under the law of a part of the United Kingdom or of a country or territory outside the United Kingdom); or

(ii) is, or corresponds to, any conduct which, if it all took place in any one part of the United Kingdom, would constitute one or more criminal offences; and

(d) the references to an investigation and to a prosecution include references, respectively, to any investigation outside the United Kingdom of any crime or suspected crime and to a prosecution brought in respect of any crime in a country or territory outside the United Kingdom.

[(1BA) Fingerprints taken from a person by virtue of section 61(6A) above must be destroyed as soon as they have fulfilled the purpose for which they were taken.]

(3) If—

(a) fingerprints, impressions of footwear or samples are taken from a person in connection with the investigation of an offence; and

(b) that person is not suspected of having committed the offence,

they must, except as provided in the following provisions of this section, be destroyed as soon as they have fulfilled the purpose for which they were taken.

(3AA) Samples, fingerprints and impressions of footwear are not required to be destroyed under subsection (3) above if—

(a) they were taken for the purposes of the investigation of an offence of which a person has been convicted; and

(b) a sample, fingerprint, (or as the case may be) an impression of footwear was also taken from the convicted person for the purposes of that investigation.

(3AB) Subject to subsection (3AC) below, where a person is entitled under *subsection (3)* [subsection (1BA) or (3)] above to the destruction of any fingerprint, impression of footwear or sample taken from him (or would be but for subsection (3AA) above), neither the fingerprint, nor the impression of footwear, nor the sample, nor any information derived from the sample, shall be used—

(a) in evidence against the person who is or would be entitled to the destruction of that fingerprint, impression of footwear or sample; or

(b) for the purposes of the investigation of any offence;

and subsection (1B) above applies for the purposes of this subsection as it applies for the purposes of subsection (1A) above.

(3AC) Where a person from whom a fingerprint, impression of footwear or sample has been taken consents in writing to its retention—

(a) that [fingerprint,] impression of footwear or sample need not be destroyed under subsection (3) above;

(b) subsection (3AB) above shall not restrict the use that may be made of the fingerprint, impression of footwear or sample or, in the case of a sample, of any information derived from it; and

(c) that consent shall be treated as comprising a consent for the purposes of section 63A(1C) above;

and a consent given for the purpose of this subsection shall not be capable of being withdrawn.

[This subsection does not apply to fingerprints taken from a person by virtue of section 61(6A) above.]

(3AD) For the purposes of subsection (3AC) above it shall be immaterial whether the consent is given at, before or after the time when the entitlement to the destruction of the fingerprint, impression of footwear or sample arises.

(4) [*Repealed by* Criminal Justice and Police Act *2001, s.137, and Sched. 7, Pt 2.*]

(5) If fingerprints or impressions of footwear are destroyed— **15–247**

(a) any copies of the fingerprints or impressions of footwear shall also be destroyed; and

(b) any chief officer of police controlling access to computer data relating to the fingerprints or impressions of footwear shall make access to the data impossible, as soon as it is practicable to do so.

(6) A person who asks to be allowed to witness the destruction of his fingerprints or impressions of footwear or copies of them shall have a right to witness it.

(6A) If—

(a) subsection (5)(b) above falls to be complied with; and

(b) the person to whose fingerprints or impressions of footwear the data relate asks for a certificate that it has been complied with,

such a certificate shall be issued to him, not later than the end of the period of three months beginning with the day on which he asks for it, by the responsible chief officer of police or a person authorised by him or on his behalf for the purposes of this section.

(6B) In this section—

...

"the responsible chief officer of police" means the chief officer of police in whose police area the computer data were put onto the computer.

(7) Nothing in this section—

(a) affects any power conferred by paragraph 18(2) of Schedule 2 to the *Immigration Act* 1971 or section 20 of the *Immigration and Asylum Act* 1999 (disclosure of police information to the Secretary of State for use for immigration purposes); or

(b) applies to a person arrested or detained under the terrorism provisions.

[This section is printed as amended by the *CJA* 1988, s.148; the *CJPOA* 1994, s.57; the *Police Act* 1996, s.103, and Sched. 7, para. 37; the *CJPA* 2001, s.82; and the *SOCPA* 2005, s.118(1) and (4); and as amended, as from a day to be appointed, by the *SOCPA* 2005, s.117(6)–(10).]

The fingerprints, samples and information the retention and use of which, in accordance with section 64 is authorised by section 82 of the 2001 Act, include (a) fingerprints and samples the destruction of which should have taken place before the commencement of section 82 (May 11, 2001), but did not, and (b) information deriving from any such samples or from samples the destruction of which did take place, in accordance with section 64, before the commencement of section 82: s.82(6).

For definitions of "fingerprints", "intimate sample", "non-intimate sample" and "the terrorism provisions", see section 65, *post*, § 15–249. **15–248**

The restriction in subsection (1A) on the use that may be made of retained fingerprints or samples, and information derived from them, applies to both fingerprints and samples taken from a suspect and also to fingerprints and samples taken from volunteers and victims: *Lambeth London Borough v. S., C., V. and J. (by his guardian)* [2007] 1 F.L.R. 152, Fam D (Ryder J.). Where a print or sample, or information relating to such print or sample, is improperly retained in breach of the requirements of this section, evidence derived therefrom will not be automatically excluded, but the breach will be a factor to be taken into account by the judge in exercising his discretion to exclude it: see *Att.-Gen.'s Reference (No. 3 of 1999)* [2001] 2 A.C. 91, HL (decided in relation to this section, as it read prior to its amendment by the 2001 Act).

Section 64 applies to DNA profiles: *R. v. Nathaniel* [1995] 2 Cr.App.R. 565, CA. The use of DNA profiles from destroyed samples to form a database for use for statistical purposes does not breach section 64: *R. v. Willoughby* [1997] 1 *Archbold News* 2, CA.

Section 64(1A) is not incompatible with Article 8(1) of the ECHR (*post*, § 16–101). Even if Article 8 was engaged, the interference was justified under Article 8(2): *R. (S.) v. Chief Constable of South Yorkshire Police*; *R. (Marper) v. Same* [2004] 1 W.L.R. 2196, HL.

Police and Criminal Evidence Act 1984, s.64A

Photographing of suspects etc.

15–248a **64A.**—(1) A person who is detained at a police station may be photographed—

(a) with the appropriate consent; or
(b) if the appropriate consent is withheld or it is not practicable to obtain it, without it.

(1A) A person falling within subsection (1B) below may, on the occasion of the relevant event referred to in subsection (1B), be photographed elsewhere than at a police station—

(a) with the appropriate consent; or
(b) if the appropriate consent is withheld or it is not practicable to obtain it, without it.

(1B) A person falls within this subsection if he has been—

(a) arrested by a constable for an offence;
(b) taken into custody by a constable after being arrested for an offence by a person other than a constable;
(c) made subject to a requirement to wait with a community support officer under paragraph 2(3) or (3B) of Schedule 4 to the *Police Reform Act* 2002 ("the 2002 Act");
(ca) given a direction by a constable under section 27 of the *Violent Crime Reduction Act* 2006;
(d) given a penalty notice by a constable in uniform under Chapter 1 of Part 1 of the *Criminal Justice and Police Act* 2001, a penalty notice by a constable under section 444A of the *Education Act* 1996, or a fixed penalty notice by a constable in uniform under section 54 of the *Road Traffic Offenders Act* 1988;
(e) given a notice in relation to a relevant fixed penalty offence (within the meaning of paragraph 1 of Schedule 4 to the 2002 Act) by a community support officer by virtue of a designation applying that paragraph to him;
(f) given a notice in relation to a relevant fixed penalty offence (within the meaning of paragraph 1 of Schedule 5 to the 2002 Act) by an accredited person by virtue of accreditation specifying that that paragraph applies to him; or
(g) given a notice in relation to a relevant fixed penalty offence (within the meaning of Schedule 5A to the 2002 Act) by an accredited inspector by virtue of accreditation specifying that paragraph 1 of Schedule 5A to the 2002 Act applies to him.

(2) A person proposing to take a photograph of any person under this section—

(a) may, for the purpose of doing so, require the removal of any item or substance worn on or over the whole or any part of the head or face of the person to be photographed; and
(b) if the requirement is not complied with, may remove the item or substance himself.

(3) Where a photograph may be taken under this section, the only persons entitled to take the photograph are constables.

(4) A photograph taken under this section—

(a) may be used by, or disclosed to, any person for any purpose related to the prevention or detection of crime, the investigation of an offence or the conduct of a prosecution or to the enforcement of a sentence; and

(b) after being so used or disclosed, may be retained but may not be used or disclosed except for a purpose so related.

(5) In subsection (4)—

(a) the reference to crime includes a reference to any conduct which—

(i) constitutes one or more criminal offences (whether under the law of a part of the United Kingdom or of a country or territory outside the United Kingdom); or

(ii) is, or corresponds to, any conduct which, if it all took place in any one part of the United Kingdom, would constitute one or more criminal offences; and

(b) the references to an investigation and to a prosecution include references, respectively, to any investigation outside the United Kingdom of any crime or suspected crime and to a prosecution brought in respect of any crime in a country or territory outside the United Kingdom; and

(c) "sentence" includes any order made by a court in England and Wales when dealing with an offender in respect of his offence.

(6) References in this section to taking a photograph include references to using any process by means of which a visual image may be produced; and references to photographing a person shall be construed accordingly.

(6A) In this section, a "photograph" includes a moving image, and corresponding expressions shall be construed accordingly.

(7) Nothing in this section applies to a person arrested under an extradition arrest power.

[This section was inserted by the *Anti-Terrorism, Crime and Security Act* 2001, s.92. It is printed as amended by the *Police Reform Act* 2002, s.107(1), and Sched. 7, para. 9(5); the *Extradition Act* 2003, s.169(5); the *SOCPA* 2005, s.116; the *PJA* 2006, s.52, Sched. 14, para. 11, and Sched. 15, Pt 2; and the *VCRA* 2006, s.27(7).]

As to the "appropriate consent", see section 65(1), *post*, § 15–249.

In connection with this section, see Code D:5.12 *et seq.* (Appendix A–131). As to the use that may be made of photographs taken before section 64A's commencement, see *Hellewell v. Chief Constable of Derbyshire* [1995] 1 W.L.R. 804, QBD (Laws J.). **15–248b**

As to the taking of a photograph of an indentifying mark found on a search or examination under section 54A, see *ante*, § 15–193a.

(9) Definitions

Police and Criminal Evidence Act 1984, s.65

Part V: supplementary

65.—(1) In this Part of this Act— **15–249**

"analysis", in relation to a skin impression, includes comparison and matching;

"appropriate consent" means—

(a) in relation to a person who has attained the age of 17 years, the consent of that person;

(b) in relation to a person who has not attained that age but has attained the age of 14 years, the consent of that person and his parent or guardian; and

(c) in relation to a person who has not attained the age of 14 years, the consent of his parent or guardian;

"extradition arrest power" means any of the following—

(a) a Part 1 warrant (within the meaning given by the *Extradition Act* 2003) in respect of which a certificate under section 2 of that Act has been issued;

(b) section 5 of that Act;

(c) a warrant issued under section 71 of that Act;

(d) a provisional warrant (within the meaning given by that Act);

...

"fingerprints", in relation to any person, means a record (in any form and produced by any method) of the skin pattern and other physical characteristics or features of—

(a) any of that person's fingers; or
(b) either of his palms;

"intimate sample" means—

(a) a sample of blood, semen or any other tissue fluid, urine or pubic hair;
(b) a dental impression;
(c) a swab taken from any part of a person's genitals (including pubic hair) or from a person's body orifice other than the mouth;

"intimate search" means a search which consists of the physical examination of a person's body orifices other than the mouth;

"non-intimate sample" means—

(a) a sample of hair other than pubic hair;
(b) a sample taken from a nail or from under a nail;
(c) a swab taken from any part of a person's body other than a part from which a swab taken would be an intimate sample;
(d) saliva;
(e) a skin impression;

"registered dentist" has the same meaning as in the *Dentists Act* 1984;

"registered health care professional" means a person (other than a medical practitioner) who is—

(a) a registered nurse; or
(b) a registered member of a health care profession which is designated for the purposes of this paragraph by an order made by the Secretary of State;

"skin impression", in relation to any person, means any record (other than a fingerprint) which is a record (in any form and produced by any method) of the skin pattern and other physical characteristics or features of the whole or any part of his foot or of any other part of his body;

"speculative search", in relation to a person's fingerprints or samples, means such a check against other fingerprints or samples or against information derived from other samples as is referred to in section 63A(1) above;

"sufficient" and "insufficient", in relation to a sample, means subject to subsection (2) below sufficient or insufficient (in point of quantity or quality) for the purpose of enabling information to be produced by the means of analysis used or to be used in relation to the sample;

"the terrorism provisions" means section 41 of the *Terrorism Act* 2000, and any provision of Schedule 7 to that Act conferring a power of arrest or detention; and

"terrorism" has the meaning given in section 1 of that Act,

and … .

(1A) A health care profession is any profession mentioned in section 60(2) of the *Health Act* 1999 other than the profession of practising medicine and the profession of nursing.

(1B) [*Making of orders under subs. (1).*]

(2) References in this Part of this Act to a sample's proving insufficient include references to where, as a consequence of—

(a) the loss, destruction or contamination of the whole or any part of the sample,
(b) any damage to the whole or a part of the sample, or
(c) the use of the whole or a part of the sample for an analysis which produced no results or which produced results some or all of which must be regarded, in the circumstances, as unreliable,

the sample has become unavailable or insufficient for the purpose of enabling information, or information of a particular description, to be obtained by means of analysis of the sample.

[This section is printed as amended and repealed in part by the *DTOA* 1986, s.32; the *CJA* 1988, s.170(1), (2), and Scheds 15 and 16; the *DTA* 1994, s.65(1) and Sched. 9, para. 8; the *CJPOA* 1994, ss.58(2)–(4) and 59(1); the *Terrorism Act* 2000, s.125 and Sched. 15, para. 5(10); the *CJPA* 2001, ss.78(5) and 80(5), (6); the *Police Reform Act* 2002, s.54(2), (3); the *PCA* 2002, s.457, and Sched. 12; the *Extradition Act* 2003, s.169(6); and the *SOCPA* 2005, s.119.]

15–250 For section 41 of, and Schedule 7 to, the 2000 Act, see *post*, §§ 25–85, 25–127.

As to fingerprints and palm-prints, see *ante*, § 14–55.

Mere visual examination or an attempt to get a person to extrude what is contained in the body through one of its orifices is not an intimate search: *R. v. Hughes*, 99 Cr.App.R. 160, CA. (The case concerned drugs concealed in a person's mouth and was decided prior to the addition of the words "other than the mouth" in the definition of "intimate search" by the *CJPOA* 1994, s.59. It is doubtful whether this decision would be applied to other body orifices.)

(10) Code of practice

Introduction

For the codes of practice generally, see *ante*, §§ 15–3 *et seq.* The current Code C came into force on February 1, 2008. As to its commencement, see *ante*, § 15–7. In *R. v. Ward*, 98 Cr.App.R. 337, CA, it was said that a court could have regard to the text of a new code even though it was not in force at the relevant time, because it will reflect current thinking as to what is fair. For the statutory provisions governing the detention of suspects, see *ante*, §§ 3–93 *et seq.* **15–251**

Code C is particularly important in considering the admissibility of admissions and confessions under sections 76 and 78 of the *PACE Act* 1984. Its provisions on the right to legal advice, cautions, and the recording of interviews have been invoked in many cases where alleged confessions have been challenged. For cases on confessions under section 76 and Code C, see *post*, §§ 15–352 *et seq.*; for cases on the exclusion of unfair evidence under section 78 and Code C, see *post*, §§ 15–452 *et seq.* The overlap between the provisions of the code and of sections 58, 76 and 78 of the Act necessitates a number of cross-references in the text.

The provisions of Code C extend beyond the treatment of those in detention: *R. v. Christou and Wright* [1992] Q.B. 979, 95 Cr.App.R. 264, CA, *post*, § 15–527.

Code H (as to which, see *ante*, § 15–7) contains corresponding provisions in relation to the detention, treatment and questioning by police officers of persons under section 41 of, and Schedule 8 to, the *Terrorism Act* 2000. The principal differences in Code H are: (i) that less detail as to the grounds of arrest is required; (ii) that the detainee is to be transferred to prison and dealt with under the *Prison Rules* 1999 (S.I. 1999 No. 728) where a warrant has been issued providing for detention beyond 14 days; (iii) that there is more detailed provision as to visiting rights and exercise, and a clear demarcation is made between visits from friends and family, and official visits; (iv) that moving a detainee from a police station for medical treatment or any other reason does not "stop the clock" as it would in the case of a non-terrorism detainee; (v) there is specific provision as to the allocation of reading material; (vi) there is a requirement that the detainee is to receive daily healthcare visits; and (vii) there are notes for guidance concerning applications to extend the period of detention.

[For the full text of Code C, see Appendix A–38 *et seq.* For Code H, see Appendix A–213 *et seq.*]

F. POLICE ACT 1997 AND REGULATION OF INVESTIGATORY POWERS ACT 2000

Part III of the *Police Act* 1997 (ss.91–108) allows for authorisation of covert entry upon and interference with property or with wireless telegraphy by the police, Revenue and Customs and others. The Act in part attempts to meet the astonishment expressed by Lord Nolan in *R. v. Khan (Sultan)* [1997] A.C. 558 at 582, HL, at the lack of a statutory system regulating the use of surveillance devices by the police. Such a system has existed in this field in relation to the intelligence services since the *Security Services Act* 1989 and the *Intelligence Services Act* 1994. **15–252**

The powers contained in the Act are supplementary to existing police powers: s.93(7).

All forms of covert surveillance which do not involve covert entry upon or interference with property or wireless telegraphy come under the *RIPA* 2000 (*Regulation of Investigatory Powers Act 2000 (Commencement No. 1 and Transitional Provisions) Order* 2000 (S.I. 2000 No. 2543)). The Act is an attempt to put covert policing on a statutory footing and an implicit acceptance that a non-statutory basis for such activity would breach the *Human Rights Act* 1998: see *Hansard*, H.C., Vol. 345, col. 677, and **15–253** the remarks of the Home Office Minister in the press notice accompanying the draft codes (Notice 291/2000). See further *post*, § 15–529.

15–254 The Act distinguishes between directed (s.26(2)) and intrusive surveillance (s.26(3)–(5)). "Directed surveillance" is defined as covert surveillance that is undertaken in relation to a specific investigation or a specific operation which is likely to result in the obtaining of private information about a person. "Intrusive surveillance" is defined as covert surveillance carried out in relation to anything taking place on residential premises. The Act also provides for the use of "covert human intelligence sources". This is defined as a person who establishes or maintains a personal relationship with a person for the covert purpose of using the relationship to obtain information or provide access to information to another person or covertly disclosing information obtained by the use of such a relationship or as a consequence of the existence of such a relationship (s.26(8)); and it has been held to include an undercover police officer: *R. v. Hardy* [2003] 1 Cr.App.R. 30, CA. The protections for any suspect are greater in respect of intrusive surveillance than in respect of directed surveillance or the use of covert human intelligence sources.

15–255 All conduct defined in section 26 will be lawful provided it is carried out in relation to the authorisation to which it relates (s.27). The Act does not make a failure to obtain an authorisation a criminal offence, but the explanatory notes accompanying the Act (para. 180) recognise that such a failure may mean that the law enforcement agency had acted unlawfully under the *Human Rights Act* 1998, s.6. Such covert activity must be both necessary and proportionate (ss.28, 29 and 32) and the Act sets out specific criteria. The Act sets up a system of authorisations and supervision by a number of commissioners and tribunals. Codes of practice in relation to the exercise of covert surveillance powers and the use of human intelligence sources under Part II of the Act were brought into force on August 1, 2002: see the *Regulation of Investigatory Powers (Covert Surveillance: Code of Practice) Order* 2002 (S.I. 2002 No. 1933), and the *Regulation of Investigatory Powers (Covert Human Intelligence Sources: Code of Practice) Order* 2002 (S.I. 2002 No. 1932). Both codes are on the Home Office website (www.homeoffice.gov.uk). The first of these codes covers not only activity under Part II of the 2000 Act, but also activity under Part III of the 1997 Act, replacing the code of practice issued under section 101. As to the importance of compliance with the Act and the codes, see *R. v. Harmes and Crane* [2006] 7 *Archbold News* 1, CA (*ante*, § 4–63).

15–256 Neither the *Police Act* 1997 nor the 2000 Act purports to deal with the question of the admissibility of evidence obtained under their provisions. Their relevance is confined to the fact that they provide a framework of law by which the legality of the actions of the police may be judged; where evidence has been unlawfully obtained, this is a matter to be taken into account by a court in deciding whether it is fair to admit it (*PACE Act* 1984, s.78, *post*, § 15–452). It is the effect of the behaviour of the police on the fairness of the proceedings that is important, rather than the illegality of their conduct: *per* Lord Nolan in *Khan*, *ante*, at p. 582. Fairness, however, is not to be confined to procedural fairness and evidence may be excluded because it has been obtained by unfair means: *per* Lord Nicholls (paras 11 and 12) and Lord Scott (para. 122) in *R. v. Looseley* (*post*, § 15–430). As to the effect of the *Human Rights Act* 1998, see *post*, §§ 15–531 *et seq.*

G. DRUG TRAFFICKING ACT 1994

(1) Introduction

15–257 Sections 1 to 54 of the 1994 Act were repealed as from February 24, 2003, by the *PCA* 2002, s.457, and Sched. 12, and the *Proceeds of Crime Act 2002 (Commencement No. 4, Transitional Provisions and Savings) Order* 2003 (S.I. 2003 No. 120).

Sections 55 and 56 of the 1994 Act remain in force, together with certain ancillary provisions. They permit the police and H.M. Customs and Excise to obtain production orders and search warrants for the purpose of investigations into drug trafficking offences, with a view to a prosecution, as well as into the proceeds of drug trafficking. The 2002 Act (*post*, § 15–279 *et seq.*) provides for a new power for the enforcement authorities to obtain a production order and a search warrant for the purposes of an investigation into the proceeds of any criminal conduct, which would include drug trafficking proceeds, but the new power does not cover investigations into drug trafficking offences (as defined in the new section 59A of the 1994 Act, *post*, § 15–268). This provides the rationale for the retention of the existing powers.

See also section 63(3)(b) of the 1994 Act (also unrepealed), which provides that in the 1994 Act any reference to "drug trafficking" includes a reference to drug trafficking carried out before the commencement of the Act.

(2) Investigation of offences

Drug Trafficking Act 1994, s.55

Order to make material available

55.—(1) A constable may, for the purpose of an investigation into drug trafficking, apply to a Circuit judge for an order under subsection (2) below in relation to particular material or material of a particular description. **15–258**

(2) If on such an application the judge is satisfied that the conditions in subsection (4) below are fulfilled, he may make an order that the person who appears to him to be in possession of the material to which the application relates shall—

(a) produce it to a constable for him to take away, or

(b) give a constable access to it,

within such period as the order may specify.

This subsection has effect subject to section 59(11) of this Act.

(3) The period to be specified in an order under subsection (2) above shall be seven days unless it appears to the judge that a longer or shorter period would be appropriate in the particular circumstances of the application.

(4) The conditions referred to in subsection (2) above are—

(a) that there are reasonable grounds for suspecting that a specified person has carried on … drug trafficking;

(b) that there are reasonable grounds for suspecting that the material to which the application relates—

(i) is likely to be of substantial value (whether by itself or together with other material) to the investigation for the purpose of which the application is made; and

(ii) does not consist of or include items subject to legal privilege or excluded material; and

(c) that there are reasonable grounds for believing that it is in the public interest, having regard—

(i) to the benefit likely to accrue to the investigation if the material is obtained, and

(ii) to the circumstances under which the person in possession of the material holds it,

that the material should be produced or that access to it should be given.

(5) Where the judge makes an order under subsection (2)(b) above in relation to material on any premises he may, on the application of a constable, order any person who appears to him to be entitled to grant entry to the premises to allow a constable to enter the premises to obtain access to the material. **15–259**

(6) An application under subsection (1) or (5) above may be made *ex parte* to a judge in chambers.

(7) [*Provision for rules of court.*]

(8) An order of a Circuit judge under this section shall have effect as if it were an order of the Crown Court.

(9) Where the material to which an application under subsection (1) above relates consists of information contained in a computer—

(a) an order under subsection (2)(a) above shall have effect as an order to produce the material in a form in which it can be taken away and in which it is visible and legible; and

(b) an order under subsection (2)(b) above shall have effect as an order to give access to the material in a form in which it is visible and legible.

(10) An order under subsection (2) above—

(a) shall not confer any right to production of, or access to, items subject to legal privilege or excluded material;

(b) shall have effect notwithstanding any obligation as to secrecy or other restriction upon the disclosure of information imposed by statute or otherwise; and

(c) may be made in relation to material in the possession of an authorised government department;

and in this subsection "authorised government department" means a government department which is an authorised department for the purposes of the *Crown Proceedings Act* 1947.

[The words omitted from subs. (4)(a) were repealed by the *PCA* 2002, s.457 and Sched. 12.]

15–260 In *R. v. Southwark Crown Court, ex p. Customs and Excise*; *R. v. Southwark Crown Court, ex p. Bank of Credit and Commerce International S.A.* [1990] 1 Q.B. 650, DC, it was held that there was nothing in section 27(1) of the 1986 Act (now s.55(1) of the 1994 Act) which required that the relevant investigation should necessarily be one being conducted by United Kingdom customs officers. It was not surprising that Parliament should have legislated to permit a customs officer to apply to a circuit judge for a production order in respect of the suspected passage of money, laundered from drug trafficking abroad, into a London bank account. Secondly, the court held that there was nothing in the words of section 27(2) (now s.55(2) of the 1994 Act) to suggest that Parliament did not intend the judge to have a discretion either to grant, or to refuse an order although he was persuaded that the conditions in subsection (4) were satisfied; but it was not easy to identify circumstances in which a judge might properly refuse to make an order when those conditions had been satisfied; once a judge had decided to make an order, he had to make it in the simple terms set out in subsection (2). Exceptionally, a judge would be entitled to refuse to make an order at all unless the applicant was willing to give satisfactory undertakings.

15–261 The word "retained" in section 22(1) of the *PACE Act* 1984 (*ante*, § 15–131), as applied by section 29(1)(a) (now s.57(1)(a) of the 1994 Act, *post*, § 15–265) to material produced in pursuance of an order under section 27(2)(a), meant that the customs officer was entitled to keep the produced material back as against the owner or possessor of it for so long as the Act permitted. Thus the information in the produced material could, without parting with the material itself, be made available, either by sending copies or by other means, to the foreign agency for whose investigation the production of the material was sought or whose co-operation was required for the purposes of an investigation being conducted here: *ibid*.

It was further held that the words "trial for an offence" in section 22(2)(a)(i) of the 1984 Act meant trial for an offence against the law of this country. Accordingly, in the absence of any further order, customs officers were not at liberty to send the originals of any produced material overseas for the purpose of criminal trials in other jurisdictions.

In connection with section 55, reference should also be made to rule 56.4 of the *Criminal Procedure Rules* 2005, *post*.

Criminal Procedure Rules 2005 (S.I. 2005 No. 384), r.56.4

Investigation into drug trafficking or into the proceeds of criminal conduct

15–262 **56.4.**—(1) Where an order under section 93H of the *Criminal Justice Act* 1988 (order to make material available), section 55 of the *Drug Trafficking Act* 1994 (order to make material available), or section 345 of the *Proceeds of Crime Act* 2002 (production orders) has been made by the Crown Court, any person affected by it may apply in writing to the court officer for the order to be discharged or varied, and on hearing such an application a circuit judge or, in the case of an order under the 2002 Act, a judge entitled to exercise the jurisdiction of the Crown Court may discharge the order or make such variations to it as he thinks fit.

(2) Subject to paragraph (3), where a person proposes to make an application under paragraph (1) for the discharge or variation of an order, he shall give a copy of the application, not later than 48 hours before the making of the application—

(a) to a constable at the police station specified in the order; or

(b) where the application for the order was made under the 2002 Act and was not made by a constable, to the office of the appropriate officer who made the application, as specified in the order,

in either case together with a notice indicating the time and place at which the application for discharge or variation is to be made.

(3) A circuit judge or, in the case of an order under the 2002 Act, a judge entitled to exercise the jurisdiction of the Crown Court may direct that paragraph (2) need not be complied with if he is satisfied that the person making the application has good reason to seek a discharge or variation of the order as soon as possible and it is not practicable to comply with that paragraph.

(4) In this rule—

"appropriate officer" has the meaning given to it by section 378 of the 2002 Act;

"constable" includes a person commissioned by the Commissioners for Her Majesty's Revenue and Customs;

"police station" includes a place for the time being occupied by Her Majesty's Revenue and Customs.

[This rule is printed as amended by the *Criminal Procedure Rules (Amendment No. 3) Rules* 2007 (S.I. 2007 No. 3662), r.13.]

For section 93H of the 1988 Act, see § 5–520 in the 2003 edition of this work. For section 345 of the 2002 Act, see *post*, § 15–283.

Drug Trafficking Act 1994, s.56

Authority for search

56.—(1) A constable may, for the purpose of an investigation into drug trafficking, apply to a Circuit judge for a warrant under this section in relation to specified premises. **15–263**

(2) On such application the judge may issue a warrant authorising a constable to enter and search the premises if the judge is satisfied—

(a) that an order made under section 55 of this Act in relation to material on the premises has not been complied with;

(b) that the conditions in subsection (3) below are fulfilled; or

(c) that the conditions in subsection (4) below are fulfilled.

(3) The conditions referred to in subsection (2)(b) above are—

(a) that there are reasonable grounds for suspecting that a specified person has carried on ... drug trafficking;

(b) that the conditions in subsection (4)(b) and (c) of section 55 of this Act are fulfilled in relation to any material on the premises; and

(c) that it would not be appropriate to make an order under that section in relation to the material because—

(i) it is not practicable to communicate with any person entitled to produce the material;

(ii) it is not practicable to communicate with any person entitled to grant access to the material or entitled to grant entry to the premises on which the material is situated; or

(iii) the investigation for the purpose of which the application is made might be seriously prejudiced unless a constable could secure immediate access to the material.

(4) The conditions referred to in subsection (2)(c) above are— **15–264**

(a) that there are reasonable grounds for suspecting that a specified person has carried on ... drug trafficking;

(b) that there are reasonable grounds for suspecting that there is on the premises material relating to the specified person or to drug trafficking which is likely to be of substantial value (whether by itself or together with other material) to the investigation for the purpose of which the application is made, but that the material cannot at the time of the application be particularised; and

(c) that—

(i) it is not practicable to communicate with any person entitled to grant entry to the premises;

(ii) entry to the premises will not be granted unless a warrant is produced; or

(iii) the investigation for the purpose of which the application is made might be seriously prejudiced unless a constable arriving at the premises could secure immediate entry to them.

(5) Where a constable has entered premises in the execution of a warrant issued under this section, he may seize and retain any material, other than items subject to legal privilege and excluded material, which is likely to be of substantial value (whether by itself or

together with other material) to the investigation for the purpose of which the warrant was issued.

[The words omitted from subss. (3)(a) and (4)(a) were repealed by the *PCA* 2002, s.457, and Sched. 12.]

Drug Trafficking Act 1994, s.57

Provisions supplementary to sections 55 and 56

15–265 **57.**—(1) For the purposes of sections 21 and 22 of the *Police and Criminal Evidence Act* 1984 (access to, and copying and retention of, seized material)—

(a) an investigation into drug trafficking shall be treated as if it were an investigation of or in connection with an offence; and

(b) material produced in pursuance of an order under section 55(2)(a) of this Act shall be treated as if it were material seized by a constable.

(2) In sections 55 and 56 of this Act "excluded material", "items subject to legal privilege" and "premises" have the same meaning as in the 1984 Act.

Drug Trafficking Act 1994, s.58

Offence of prejudicing investigation

15–266 **58.**—(1) Where, in relation to an investigation into drug trafficking—

(a) an order under section 55 of this Act has been made or has been applied for and has not been refused, or

(b) a warrant under section 56 of this Act has been issued,

a person is guilty of an offence if, knowing or suspecting that the investigation is taking place, he makes any disclosure which is likely to prejudice the investigation.

(2) In proceedings against a person for an offence under this section, it is a defence to prove—

(a) that he did not know or suspect that the disclosure was likely to prejudice the investigation; or

(b) that he has lawful authority or reasonable excuse for making the disclosure.

(3) Nothing in subsection (1) above makes it an offence for a professional legal adviser to disclose any information or other matter—

(a) to, or to a representative of, a client of his in connection with the giving by the legal adviser of legal advice to the client; or

(b) to any person—

(i) in contemplation of, or in connection with, legal proceedings; and

(ii) for the purposes of those proceedings.

(4) Subsection (3) above does not apply in relation to any information or other matter which is disclosed with a view to furthering a criminal purpose.

(5) A person guilty of an offence under this section shall be liable—

(a) on summary conviction, to imprisonment for a term not exceeding *six* [12] months or to a fine not exceeding the statutory maximum or to both; or

(b) on conviction on indictment, to imprisonment for a term not exceeding five years or to a fine or to both.

[In subs. (5)(a), "12" is substituted for "six", as from a day to be appointed, by the *CJA* 2003, s.282(2) and (3). The increase has no application to offences committed before the substitution takes effect: s.282(4).]

Drug Trafficking Act 1994, s.59

Disclosure of information held by government departments

15–267 **59.**—(11) ... in the case of material in the possession of an authorised government department, an order under section 55(2) of this Act may require any officer of the department (whether named in the order or not) who may for the time being be in possession of the material concerned to comply with it, and such an order shall be served as if the proceedings were civil proceedings against the department.

(12) The person on whom such an order is served—

(a) shall take all reasonable steps to bring it to the attention of the officer concerned; and

(b) if the order is not brought to that officer's attention within the period specified in an order under section 55(2), shall report the reasons for the failure to the court;

and it shall also be the duty of any other officer of the department in receipt of the order to take such steps as are mentioned in paragraph (a) above.

(13) In this section "authorised government department" means a government department which is an authorised department for the purposes of the *Crown Proceedings Act* 1947.

[Subss. (1) to (10) and the opening words of subs. (11) were repealed by the *PCA* 2002, s.457 and Sched. 12. Subs. (12) is printed as amended by *ibid.*, s.456 and Sched. 11, para. 25(1), (3).]

Drug Trafficking Act 1994, s.59A

Construction of sections 55 to 59

59A.—(1) This section has effect for the purposes of sections 55 to 59. **15–268**

(2) A reference to a constable includes a reference to an office of Revenue and Customs.

(3) A customs officer is a person commissioned by the Commissioners for Her Majesty's Revenue and Customs under section 6(3) of the *Customs and Excise Management Act* 1979.

(4) Drug trafficking means doing or being concerned in any of the following (whether in England and Wales or elsewhere)—

(a) producing or supplying a controlled drug where the production or supply contravenes section 4(1) of the *Misuse of Drugs Act* 1971 or a corresponding law;

(b) transporting or storing a controlled drug where possession of the drug contravenes section 5(1) of that Act or a corresponding law;

(c) importing or exporting a controlled drug where the importation or exportation is prohibited by section 3(1) of that Act or a corresponding law;

(d) manufacturing or supplying a scheduled substance within the meaning of section 12 of the *Criminal Justice (International Co-operation) Act* 1990 where the manufacture or supply is an offence under that section or would be such an offence if it took place in England and Wales;

(e) using any ship for illicit traffic in controlled drugs in circumstances which amount to the commission of an offence under section 19 of that Act.

(5) In this section "corresponding law" has the same meaning as in the *Misuse of Drugs Act* 1971.

[This section was inserted by the *PCA* 2002, s.456, and Sched. 11, para. 25(1) and (4). It is printed as amended by the *Commissioners for Revenue and Customs Act* 2005, s.50(1) and (2).]

In connection with the meaning of "drug trafficking", see *ante*, § 15–257.

(3) Prosecution of offences, etc.

Drug Trafficking Act 1994, s.60

Revenue and Customs prosecutions

60.—(1) Proceedings for a specified offence may be instituted by the Director of Revenue and Customs Prosecutions or by order of the Commissioners for Her Majesty's Revenue and Customs ("the Commissioners"). **15–269**

(2) Any proceedings for a specified offence which are instituted by order of the Commissioners shall be commenced in the name of an officer of Revenue and Customs.

(4) Where the Commissioners investigate, or propose to investigate, any matter with a view to determining—

(a) whether there are grounds for believing that a specified offence has been committed, or

(b) whether a person should be prosecuted for a specified offence,

that matter shall be treated as an assigned matter within the meaning of the *Customs and Excise Management Act* 1979.

(5) Nothing in this section shall be taken—

(a) to prevent any person (including any officer) who has power to arrest, detain or prosecute any person for a specified offence from doing so; or

(b) to prevent a court from proceeding to deal with a person brought before it following his arrest by an officer for a specified offence, even though the proceedings have not been instituted in accordance with this section.

(6) In this section—

["public prosecutor", "requisition" and "written charge" have the same meaning as in section 29 of the *Criminal Justice Act* 2003;]

"specified offence" means—

(a) an offence under … section 58 of this Act;

(b) attempting to commit, conspiracy to commit or incitement to commit any such offence; …

(6A) Proceedings for an offence are instituted—

(a) when a justice of the peace issues a summons or warrant under section 1 of the *Magistrates' Courts Act* 1980 (issue of summons to, or warrant for arrest of, accused) in respect of the offence;

[(aa) when a public prosecutor issues a written charge and requisition in respect of the offence;]

(b) when a person is charged with the offence after being taken into custody without a warrant;

(c) when a bill of indictment is preferred under section 2 of the *Administration of Justice (Miscellaneous Provisions) Act* 1933 in a case falling within paragraph (b) of subsection (2) of that section (preferment by direction of the criminal division of the Court of Appeal or by direction, or with the consent, of a High Court judge).

(6B) Where the application of subsection (6A) would result in there being more than one time for the institution of proceedings they must be taken to have been instituted at the earliest of those times.

[This section is printed as amended, and repealed in part, by the *PCA* 2002, ss.456 and 457, Sched. 11, para. 25(1) and (5), and Sched. 12; and the *Commissioners for Revenue and Customs Act* 2005, ss.50(6) and 52(2), Sched. 4, para. 59, and Sched. 5; and as amended, as from a day to be appointed, by the *CJA* 2003, s.331, and Sched. 36, para. 12 (insertion of words in square brackets in subss. (6) and (6A)).]

The reference to the common law offence of incitement in section 60(6) has effect as a reference to the offences under Part 2 of the *SCA* 2007: 2007 Act, s.63(1), and Sched. 6, para. 25.

Drug Trafficking Act 1994, s.61

Extension of certain offences to Crown servants and exemptions for regulators etc.

15–270 **61.**—(1) The Secretary of State may by regulations provide that, in such circumstances as may be prescribed, section … 58 of this Act shall apply to such persons in the public service of the Crown, or such categories of person in that service, as may be prescribed.

(5) In this section—

"the Crown" includes the Crown in right of Her Majesty's Government in Northern Ireland; and

"prescribed" means prescribed by regulations made by the Secretary of State.

(6), (7) [*Procedure for making regulations under this section*.]

[Subs. (1) is printed as amended by the *PCA* 2002, s.456, and Sched. 11, para. 25(1), (6). Subss. (2) to (4) were repealed by *ibid*., s.457 and Sched. 12.]

Various financial institutions are operated by the public sector and section 61 is designed, in part, to permit the extension of the provisions of section 58 to such institutions.

H. PROCEEDS OF CRIME ACT 2002

(1) Summary

Introduction

15–271 Part 8 of the 2002 Act is headed "Investigations" and is divided into four Chapters. It came into force on February 24, 2003: *Proceeds of Crime Act 2002 (Commencement No. 4, Transitional Provisions and Savings) Order* 2003 (S.I. 2003 No. 120). Chapter 1 (ss.341–342) is entitled "Introduction". Section 341 defines the types of investigations that are relevant to this part, *viz.* confiscation investigations, civil recovery investigations, detained cash investigations and money laundering investigations. A person commits an offence if, knowing or suspecting that one of these investigations is being, or is about to be, conducted, he makes a disclosure which is likely to prejudice the investigation, or falsifies, conceals, destroys or otherwise disposes of, or causes or permits the falsification, concealment, destruction or disposal of, documents which are relevant to the investigation, unless he does not know or suspect that the disclosure is likely to prejudice the investigation, or where documents are concerned, he does not know or suspect that the documents are relevant to the investigation, or he does not intend to conceal them (s.342 (*post*, § 26–22)).

Judges and courts

Chapter 2 (ss.343–379) is entitled "England and Wales and Northern Ireland". Sections 343 and 344 concern judges and courts. Section 343 states that applications for the purpose of a confiscation investigation or a money laundering investigation should be made to a Crown Court judge, and for a civil recovery investigation or a detained cash investigation to a High Court judge. Section 344 provides that in this Chapter references to the court are to the Crown Court, in relation to an order for the purposes of a confiscation or money laundering investigation, and to the High Court, in relation to an order for the purposes of a civil recovery investigation or a detained cash investigation. **15–272**

Production orders

Sections 345 to 351 concern production orders. Section 345(4) states that a production order either requires the person to produce the property to an appropriate officer for him to take away, or requires that person to give an appropriate officer access to that material. Section 346 states that a production order can only be made where, *inter alia*, there are reasonable grounds for suspecting that the person who is subject to the investigation has benefited from his criminal conduct, or has committed a money laundering offence, or in the case of civil recovery, the property is recoverable or associated property, or, in the case of detained cash, the property is either recoverable or is intended to be used in unlawful conduct. Section 347 allows a judge making the production order requiring the delivery up of certain material that is on premises, to make an order to grant entry to premises to an appropriate officer. Section 348 excludes privileged and excluded material from production orders and makes further provisions in relation to such orders. Section 349 deals with material applied for on a production order that is contained in a computer. Section 350 allows for production orders to be made in relation to material in the possession or control of a government department, where such an order must be served as if the proceedings are civil proceedings. **15–273**

Search and seizure warrants

Sections 352 to 356 are entitled "Search and seizure warrants". Section 352 allows for the issue by a judge of a search and seizure warrant to enter and search premises and seize and retain material where a production order has not been complied with and there are reasonable grounds for believing that the material is on the premises, or where section 353 applies. Section 353 applies either where a production order is not appropriate, such as where it is not practicable to communicate with any person against whom a production order would be made, or where the investigation might be seriously prejudiced unless an appropriate person is able to secure immediate access to the material. Section 354 excludes privileged and excluded material from search and seizure warrants. Section 355 empowers the Secretary of State to modify the *PACE Act* 1984 in respect of search and seizure warrants sought for the purposes of confiscation or money laundering investigations. Section 356 makes further provision in respect of warrants sought for the purposes of civil recovery investigations. **15–274**

Disclosure orders

Sections 357 to 362 are headed "Disclosure orders". Section 357 enables a judge to make a disclosure order, except in relation to a money laundering investigation. Subsection (4) defines a disclosure order as an order requiring a specified person to answer **15–275** questions, provide information and/or produce documents. Section 359 creates two offences in relation to non-compliance with a disclosure order. Subsections (1) and (2) make it a summary offence to fail to comply with a requirement made under a disclosure order without reasonable excuse (six months' imprisonment or a level 5 fine, or both). Subsections (3) and (4) create an offence triable either way of knowingly or recklessly making a misleading statement in respect of a requirement under a disclosure order (maximum penalty on conviction on indictment, two years' imprisonment or a fine, or both). Section 360 states that, subject to a number of exceptions (including the offences created by s.359 above), statements made by a person in response to a requirement imposed under a disclosure order may not be used as evidence against him in criminal proceedings.

Customer information orders

15–276 Sections 363 to 369 deal with customer information orders. Section 363 entitles an appropriate officer in the circumstances outlined in subsections (2) and (3) and section 365, to apply to the court for a customer information order, requiring a financial institution covered by the application, to provide any customer information it has relating to the person specified in the application. Section 364 defines the term "customer information" as including an individual's or company's name, address, account numbers, and details of any person holding an account jointly with the specified person. Section 366 creates two offences, one summary offence of failing to comply with a customer information order without reasonable excuse (level 5 fine), and an either way offence of knowingly or recklessly providing false or misleading information (maximum penalty on conviction on indictment, a fine). Section 367 deals with the general inadmissibility of customer information order statements as evidence against the financial institution in criminal proceedings. Section 368 states that a customer information order has effect in spite of any restriction on the disclosure of information.

Account monitoring orders

15–277 Sections 370 to 375 concern account monitoring orders. Section 370 allows an appropriate officer in certain circumstances to apply to the court for such an order requiring the provision of information relating to the account or accounts held at a specified financial institution by a specified person for a period not exceeding 90 days. Section 371 sets out the requirements that must be met before such an order can be made, which include that there must be reasonable grounds for believing that the account information is likely to be of substantial value to the investigation.

Miscellaneous

15–278 Section 377 requires the Secretary of State to prepare a code of practice as to the exercise by the Director, members of staff of the Agency, accredited financial investigators, constables and customs officers of their functions under this Chapter. Failure to comply with the code will not, *per se*, give rise to any liability in civil or criminal proceedings, but the code is admissible as evidence in any such proceedings. Section 378 deals with the interpretation of the term "officer" in respect of different types of investigation within this Chapter.

Chapter 4 (ss.413–416) is entitled "Interpretation". It provides definitions of, *inter alia*, "criminal conduct", "property", and "money laundering offences".

(2) Statute

Proceeds of Crime Act 2002, ss.341–345

PART 8

INVESTIGATIONS

CHAPTER 1

INVESTIGATIONS

Investigations

15–279 **341.**—(1) For the purposes of this Part a confiscation investigation is an investigation into—

(a) whether a person has benefited from his criminal conduct, or
(b) the extent or whereabouts of his benefit from his criminal conduct.

(2) For the purposes of this Part a civil recovery investigation is an investigation into—
(a) whether property is recoverable property or associated property,
(b) who holds the property, or
(c) its extent or whereabouts.

(3) But an investigation is not a civil recovery investigation if—
(a) proceedings for a recovery order have been started in respect of the property in question,
(b) an interim receiving order applies to the property in question,
(c) an interim administration order applies to the property in question, or
(d) the property in question is detained under section 295.

(3A) For the purposes of this Part a detained cash investigation is—
(a) an investigation for the purposes of Chapter 3 of Part 5 into the derivation of cash detained under section 295 or a part of such cash, or
(b) an investigation for the purposes of Chapter 3 of Part 5 into whether cash detained under section 295, or a part of such cash, is intended by any person to be used in unlawful conduct.

(4) For the purposes of this Part a money laundering investigation is an investigation into whether a person has committed a money laundering offence.

[This section is printed as amended by the *SCA* 2007, s.75(1).]

Offences of prejudicing investigation

342. [*See* post, *§ 26–22*.] **15–280**

CHAPTER 2

ENGLAND AND WALES AND NORTHERN IRELAND

Judges and courts

Judges

343.—(1) In this Chapter references to a judge in relation to an application must be construed in accordance with this section. **15–281**

(2) In relation to an application for the purposes of a confiscation investigation or a money laundering investigation a judge is—
(a) in England and Wales, a judge entitled to exercise the jurisdiction of the Crown Court;
(b) in Northern Ireland, a Crown Court judge.

(3) In relation to an application for the purposes of a civil recovery investigation or a detained cash investigation a judge is a judge of the High Court.

[This section is printed as amended by the *SCA* 2007, s.77, and Sched. 10, paras 1 and 3.]

Courts

344. In this Chapter references to the court are to— **15–282**
(a) the Crown Court, in relation to an order for the purposes of a confiscation investigation or a money laundering investigation;
(b) the High Court, in relation to an order for the purposes of a civil recovery investigation or a detained cash investigation.

[This section is printed as amended by the *SCA* 2007, s.77, and Sched. 10, paras 1 and 4.]

Production orders

Production orders

345.—(1) A judge may, on an application made to him by an appropriate officer, make a production order if he is satisfied that each of the requirements for the making of the order is fulfilled. **15–283**

(2) The application for a production order must state that—

(a) a person specified in the application is subject to a confiscation investigation or a money laundering investigation, or

(b) property specified in the application is subject to a civil recovery investigation or a detained cash investigation.

(3) The application must also state that—

(a) the order is sought for the purposes of the investigation;

(b) the order is sought in relation to material, or material of a description, specified in the application;

(c) a person specified in the application appears to be in possession or control of the material.

(4) A production order is an order either—

(a) requiring the person the application for the order specifies as appearing to be in possession or control of material to produce it to an appropriate officer for him to take away, or

(b) requiring that person to give an appropriate officer access to the material,

within the period stated in the order.

(5) The period stated in a production order must be a period of seven days beginning with the day on which the order is made, unless it appears to the judge by whom the order is made that a longer or shorter period would be appropriate in the particular circumstances.

[This section is printed as amended by the *SCA* 2007, s.75(2).]

As to applications for the discharge or variation of an order under section 345, see *ante*, § 15–262.

15–283a In connection with the making of applications under this section, reference should be made to rule 62.3 of the *Criminal Procedure Rules* 2005.

Criminal Procedure Rules 2005 (S.I. 2005 No. 384), r.62.3

Proof of identity and accreditation

62.3.—(1) This rule applies where—

(a) an appropriate officer makes an application under section 345 (production orders), section 363 (customer information orders) or section 370 (account monitoring orders) of the *Proceeds of Crime Act* 2002 for the purposes of a confiscation investigation or a money laundering investigation; or

(b) a prosecutor makes an application under section 357 of the 2002 Act (disclosure orders) for the purposes of a confiscation investigation.

(2) Subject to sections 449 and 449A of the 2002 Act (which make provision for a member of—

(a) the Serious Organised Crime Agency's staff; and

(b) the staff of the relevant Director,

to use pseudonyms), the appropriate officer or an authorised person, as the case may be, must provide the judge with proof of his identity and, if he is an accredited financial investigator, his accreditation under section 3 of the 2002 Act.

(3) In this rule—

"appropriate officer" has the meaning given to it by 378 of the 2002 Act;

"confiscation investigation" and "money laundering investigation" have the meanings given to them by section 341 of the 2002 Act.

[This rule is printed as substituted by the *Criminal Procedure (Amendment No. 3) Rules* 2007 (S.I. 2007 No. 3662), r.23.]

Proceeds of Crime Act 2002, ss.346–369

Requirements for making of production order

15–284 **346.**—(1) These are the requirements for the making of a production order.

(2) There must be reasonable grounds for suspecting that—

(a) in the case of a confiscation investigation, the person the application for the order specifies as being subject to the investigation has benefited from his criminal conduct;

(b) in the case of a civil recovery investigation, the property the application for the order specifies as being subject to the investigation is recoverable property or associated property;

(ba) in the case of a detained cash investigation into the derivation of cash, the property the application for the order specifies as being subject to the investigation, or a part of it, is recoverable property;

(bb) in the case of a detained cash investigation into the intended use of cash, the property the application for the order specifies as being subject to the investigation, or a part of it, is intended by any person to be used in unlawful conduct;

(c) in the case of a money laundering investigation, the person the application for the order specifies as being subject to the investigation has committed a money laundering offence.

(3) There must be reasonable grounds for believing that the person the application specifies as appearing to be in possession or control of the material so specified is in possession or control of it.

(4) There must be reasonable grounds for believing that the material is likely to be of substantial value (whether or not by itself) to the investigation for the purposes of which the order is sought.

(5) There must be reasonable grounds for believing that it is in the public interest for the material to be produced or for access to it to be given, having regard to—

(a) the benefit likely to accrue to the investigation if the material is obtained;

(b) the circumstances under which the person the application specifies as appearing to be in possession or control of the material holds it.

[This section is printed as amended by the *SCA* 2007, s.75(3).]

Order to grant entry

347.—(1) This section applies if a judge makes a production order requiring a person to give an appropriate officer access to material on any premises. **15–285**

(2) The judge may, on an application made to him by an appropriate officer and specifying the premises, make an order to grant entry in relation to the premises.

(3) An order to grant entry is an order requiring any person who appears to an appropriate officer to be entitled to grant entry to the premises to allow him to enter the premises to obtain access to the material.

Further provisions

348.—(1) A production order does not require a person to produce, or give access to, privileged material. **15–286**

(2) Privileged material is any material which the person would be entitled to refuse to produce on grounds of legal professional privilege in proceedings in the High Court.

(3) A production order does not require a person to produce, or give access to, excluded material.

(4) A production order has effect in spite of any restriction on the disclosure of information (however imposed).

(5) An appropriate officer may take copies of any material which is produced, or to which access is given, in compliance with a production order.

(6) Material produced in compliance with a production order may be retained for so long as it is necessary to retain it (as opposed to copies of it) in connection with the investigation for the purposes of which the order was made.

(7) But if an appropriate officer has reasonable grounds for believing that—

(a) the material may need to be produced for the purposes of any legal proceedings, and

(b) it might otherwise be unavailable for those purposes,

it may be retained until the proceedings are concluded.

Computer information

349.—(1) This section applies if any of the material specified in an application for a production order consists of information contained in a computer. **15–287**

(2) If the order is an order requiring a person to produce the material to an appropriate officer for him to take away, it has effect as an order to produce the material in a form in which it can be taken away by him and in which it is visible and legible.

(3) If the order is an order requiring a person to give an appropriate officer access to the material, it has effect as an order to give him access to the material in a form in which it is visible and legible.

Government departments

15–288 **350.**—(1) A production order may be made in relation to material in the possession or control of an authorised government department.

(2) An order so made may require any officer of the department (whether named in the order or not) who may for the time being be in possession or control of the material to comply with it.

(3) An order containing such a requirement must be served as if the proceedings were civil proceedings against the department.

(4) If an order contains such a requirement—

(a) the person on whom it is served must take all reasonable steps to bring it to the attention of the officer concerned;

(b) any other officer of the department who is in receipt of the order must also take all reasonable steps to bring it to the attention of the officer concerned.

(5) If the order is not brought to the attention of the officer concerned within the period stated in the order (in pursuance of section 345(4)) the person on whom it is served must report the reasons for the failure to—

(a) a judge entitled to exercise the jurisdiction of the Crown Court or (in Northern Ireland) a Crown Court judge, in the case of an order made for the purposes of a confiscation investigation or a money laundering investigation;

(b) a High Court judge, in the case of an order made for the purposes of a civil recovery investigation or a detained cash investigation.

(6) An authorised government department is a government department, or a Northern Ireland department, which is an authorised department for the purposes of the *Crown Proceedings Act* 1947.

[This section is printed as amended by the *SCA* 2007, s.77, and Sched. 10, paras 1 and 5.]

Supplementary

15–289 **351.**—(1) An application for a production order or an order to grant entry may be made *ex parte* to a judge in chambers.

(2) Rules of court may make provision as to the practice and procedure to be followed in connection with proceedings relating to production orders and orders to grant entry.

(3) An application to discharge or vary a production order or an order to grant entry may be made to the court by—

(a) the person who applied for the order;

(b) any person affected by the order.

(4) The court—

(a) may discharge the order;

(b) may vary the order.

(5) If an accredited financial investigator, a member of SOCA's staff, a constable or a customs officer applies for a production order or an order to grant entry, an application to discharge or vary the order need not be by the same accredited financial investigator, member of SOCA's staff, constable or customs officer.

(6) References to a person who applied for a production order or an order to grant entry must be construed accordingly.

(7) Production orders and orders to grant entry have effect as if they were orders of the court.

(8) Subsections (2) to (7) do not apply to orders made in England and Wales for the purposes of a civil recovery investigation or a detained cash investigation.

[This section is printed as amended by the *SCA* 2007, ss.74(2) and 77, Sched. 8, paras 103 and 104, and Sched. 10, paras 1 and 6.]

Search and seizure warrants

Search and seizure warrants

15–290 **352.**—(1) A judge may, on an application made to him by an appropriate officer, issue a search and seizure warrant if he is satisfied that either of the requirements for the issuing of the warrant is fulfilled.

(2) The application for a search and seizure warrant must state that—

(a) a person specified in the application is subject to a confiscation investigation or a money laundering investigation, or

(b) property specified in the application is subject to a civil recovery investigation or a detained cash investigation.

(3) The application must also state—

(a) that the warrant is sought for the purposes of the investigation;

(b) that the warrant is sought in relation to the premises specified in the application;

(c) that the warrant is sought in relation to material specified in the application, or that there are reasonable grounds for believing that there is material falling within section 353(6), (7), (7A), (7B) or (8) on the premises.

(4) A search and seizure warrant is a warrant authorising an appropriate person—

(a) to enter and search the premises specified in the application for the warrant, and

(b) to seize and retain any material found there which is likely to be of substantial value (whether or not by itself) to the investigation for the purposes of which the application is made.

(5) An appropriate person is—

(a) a constable, an accredited financial investigator or an officer of Revenue and Customs, if the warrant is sought for the purposes of a confiscation investigation or a money laundering investigation;

(b) a member of SOCA's staff or of the staff of the relevant director, if the warrant is sought for the purposes of a civil recovery investigation;

(c) a constable, an accredited financial investigator or an officer of Revenue and Customs, if the warrant is sought for the purposes of a detained cash investigation.

(5A) In this Part "relevant Director"—

(a) in relation to England and Wales, means the Director of Public Prosecutions, the Director of Revenue and Customs Prosecutions or the Director of the Serious Fraud Office; and

(b) [*Northern Ireland*].

(6) The requirements for the issue of a search and seizure warrant are—

(a) that a production order made in relation to material has not been complied with and there are reasonable grounds for believing that the material is on the premises specified in the application for the warrant, or

(b) that section 353 is satisfied in relation to the warrant.

(7) The reference in paragraph (a) or (c) of subsection (5) to an accredited financial investigator is a reference to an accredited financial investigator who falls within a description specified in an order made for the purposes of that paragraph by the Secretary of State under section 453.

[This section is printed as amended by the *Commissioners for Revenue and Customs Act* 2005, s.50(2); and the *SCA* 2007, ss.74(2), 76(1), 77 and 80(1) and (2), Sched. 8, paras 103 and 105, and Sched. 10, paras 1 and 7.]

Requirements where production order not available

353.—(1) This section is satisfied in relation to a search and seizure warrant if— **15–291**

(a) subsection (2) applies, and

(b) either the first or the second set of conditions is complied with.

(2) This subsection applies if there are reasonable grounds for suspecting that—

(a) in the case of a confiscation investigation, the person specified in the application for the warrant has benefited from his criminal conduct;

(b) in the case of a civil recovery investigation, the property specified in the application for the warrant is recoverable property or associated property;

(ba) in the case of a detained cash investigation into the derivation of cash, the property specified in the application for the warrant, or a part of it, is recoverable property;

(bb) in the case of a detained cash investigation into the intended use of cash, the property specified in the application for the warrant, or a part of it, is intended by any person to be used in unlawful conduct;

(c) in the case of a money laundering investigation, the person specified in the application for the warrant has committed a money laundering offence.

(3) The first set of conditions is that there are reasonable grounds for believing that—

(a) any material on the premises specified in the application for the warrant is likely to be of substantial value (whether or not by itself) to the investigation for the purposes of which the warrant is sought,

(b) it is in the public interest for the material to be obtained, having regard to the benefit likely to accrue to the investigation if the material is obtained, and

(c) it would not be appropriate to make a production order for any one or more of the reasons in subsection (4).

(4) The reasons are—

(a) that it is not practicable to communicate with any person against whom the production order could be made;

(b) that it is not practicable to communicate with any person who would be required to comply with an order to grant entry to the premises;

(c) that the investigation might be seriously prejudiced unless an appropriate person is able to secure immediate access to the material.

(5) The second set of conditions is that—

(a) there are reasonable grounds for believing that there is material on the premises specified in the application for the warrant and that the material falls within subsection (6), (7), (7A), (7B) or (8),

(b) there are reasonable grounds for believing that it is in the public interest for the material to be obtained, having regard to the benefit likely to accrue to the investigation if the material is obtained, and

(c) any one or more of the requirements in subsection (9) is met.

(6) In the case of a confiscation investigation, material falls within this subsection if it cannot be identified at the time of the application but it—

(a) relates to the person specified in the application, the question whether he has benefited from his criminal conduct or any question as to the extent or whereabouts of his benefit from his criminal conduct, and

(b) is likely to be of substantial value (whether or not by itself) to the investigation for the purposes of which the warrant is sought.

(7) In the case of a civil recovery investigation, material falls within this subsection if it cannot be identified at the time of the application but it—

(a) relates to the property specified in the application, the question whether it is recoverable property or associated property, the question as to who holds any such property, any question as to whether the person who appears to hold any such property holds other property which is recoverable property, or any question as to the extent or whereabouts of any property mentioned in this paragraph, and

(b) is likely to be of substantial value (whether or not by itself) to the investigation for the purposes of which the warrant is sought.

(7A) In the case of a detained cash investigation into the derivation of cash, material falls within this subsection if it cannot be identified at the time of the application but it—

(a) relates to the property specified in the application, the question whether the property, or a part of it, is recoverable property or any other question as to its derivation, and

(b) is likely to be of substantial value (whether or not by itself) to the investigation for the purposes of which the warrant is sought.

(7B) In the case of a detained cash investigation into the intended use of cash, material falls within this subsection if it cannot be identified at the time of the application but it—

(a) relates to the property specified in the application or the question whether the property, or a part of it, is intended by any person to be used in unlawful conduct, and

(b) is likely to be of substantial value (whether or not by itself) to the investigation for the purposes of which the warrant is sought.

(8) In the case of a money laundering investigation, material falls within this subsection if it cannot be identified at the time of the application but it—

(a) relates to the person specified in the application or the question whether he has committed a money laundering offence, and

(b) is likely to be of substantial value (whether or not by itself) to the investigation for the purposes of which the warrant is sought.

(9) The requirements are—

(a) that it is not practicable to communicate with any person entitled to grant entry to the premises;

(b) that entry to the premises will not be granted unless a warrant is produced;
(c) that the investigation might be seriously prejudiced unless an appropriate person arriving at the premises is able to secure immediate entry to them.

(10) [*Identical to s.352(5)*, ante, *§ 15–290*.]

(11) [*Identical to s.352(7)*, ante, *§ 15–290 save for reference to* "subsection (10)" *in lieu of reference to* "subsection (5)".]

[This section is printed as amended by the *Commissioners for Revenue and Customs Act* 2005, s.50(2); and the *SCA* 2007, ss.74(2), 76(2) and (3), 77 and 80(3) and (4), Sched. 8, paras 103 and 106, and Sched. 10, paras 1 and 8.]

Further provisions: general

354.—(1) A search and seizure warrant does not confer the right to seize privileged material. **15–292**

(2) Privileged material is any material which a person would be entitled to refuse to produce on grounds of legal professional privilege in proceedings in the High Court.

(3) A search and seizure warrant does not confer the right to seize excluded material.

Further provisions: confiscation and money laundering

355.—(1) This section applies to— **15–293**

(a) search and seizure warrants sought for the purposes of a confiscation investigation or a money laundering investigation, and
(b) powers of seizure under them.

(2) In relation to such warrants and powers, the Secretary of State may make an order which applies the provisions to which subsections (3) and (4) apply subject to any specified modifications.

(3) This subsection applies to the following provisions of the *Police and Criminal Evidence Act* 1984—

(a) section 15 (search warrants—safeguards);
(b) section 16 (execution of warrants);
(c) section 21 (access and copying);
(d) section 22 (retention).

(4) [*Northern Ireland*.]

Further provisions: civil recovery and detained cash

356.—(1) This section applies to search and seizure warrants sought for the purposes of civil recovery investigations or detained cash investigations. **15–294**

(2) An application for a warrant may be made ex parte to a judge in chambers.

(3) A warrant may be issued subject to conditions.

(4) A warrant continues in force until the end of the period of one month starting with the day on which it is issued.

(5) A warrant authorises the person it names to require any information which is held in a computer and is accessible from the premises specified in the application for the warrant, and which the named person believes relates to any matter relevant to the investigation, to be produced in a form—

(a) in which it can be taken away, and
(b) in which it is visible and legible.

(7) A warrant may include provision authorising a person who is exercising powers under it to do other things which—

(a) are specified in the warrant, and
(b) need to be done in order to give effect to it.

(8) Copies may be taken of any material seized under a warrant.

(9) Material seized under a warrant may be retained for so long as it is necessary to retain it (as opposed to copies of it) in connection with the investigation for the purposes of which the warrant was issued.

(10) But if the appropriate person has reasonable grounds for believing that—

(a) the material may need to be produced for the purposes of any legal proceedings, and
(b) it might otherwise be unavailable for those purposes,

it may be retained until the proceedings are concluded.

(11) The appropriate person is—

(a) an appropriate officer, if the warrant was issued for the purposes of a civil recovery investigation;

(b) a constable, an accredited financial investigator or an officer of Revenue and Customs, if the warrant was issued for the purposes of a detained cash investigation.

(12) The reference in paragraph (b) of subsection (11) to an accredited financial investigator is a reference to an accredited financial investigator who falls within a description specified in an order made for the purposes of that paragraph by the Secretary of State under section 453.

[This section is printed as amended by the *SCA* 2007, ss.74(2), 77, 80(5) and (6), and 92, Sched. 8, paras 103 and 107, Sched. 10, paras 1 and 9, and Sched. 14.]

Disclosure orders

Disclosure orders

15–295 **357.**—(1) A judge may, on an application made to him by the relevant authority, make a disclosure order if he is satisfied that each of the requirements for the making of the order is fulfilled.

(2) No application for a disclosure order may be made in relation to a detained cash investigation or a money laundering investigation.

(2A) The relevant authority may only make an application for a disclosure order in relation to a confiscation investigation if the relevant authority is in receipt of a request to do so from an appropriate officer.

(3) The application for a disclosure order must state that—

(a) a person specified in the application is subject to a confiscation investigation which is being carried out by the appropriate officer and the order is sought for the purposes of the investigation, or

(b) property specified in the application is subject to a civil recovery investigation and the order is sought for the purposes of the investigation.

(4) A disclosure order is an order authorising an appropriate officer to give to any person the appropriate officer considers has relevant information notice in writing requiring him to do, with respect to any matter relevant to the investigation for the purposes of which the order is sought, any or all of the following—

(a) answer questions, either at a time specified in the notice or at once, at a place so specified;

(b) provide information specified in the notice, by a time and in a manner so specified;

(c) produce documents, or documents of a description, specified in the notice, either at or by a time so specified or at once, and in a manner so specified.

(5) Relevant information is information (whether or not contained in a document) which the appropriate officer concerned considers to be relevant to the investigation.

(6) A person is not bound to comply with a requirement imposed by a notice given under a disclosure order unless evidence of authority to give the notice is produced to him.

(7) In this Part "relevant authority" means—

(a) in relation to a confiscation investigation, a prosecutor; and

(b) in relation to a civil recovery investigation, a member of SOCA's staff or the relevant Director.

(8) For the purposes of subsection (7)(a) a prosecutor is—

(a) in relation to a confiscation investigation carried out by a member of SOCA's staff, the relevant Director or any specified person;

(b) in relation to a confiscation investigation carried out by an accredited financial investigator, the Director of Public Prosecutions, the Director of Public Prosecutions for Northern Ireland or any specified person;

(c) in relation to a confiscation investigation carried out by a constable, the Director of Public Prosecutions, the Director of Public Prosecutions for Northern Ireland, the Director of the Serious Fraud Office or any specified person; and

(d) in relation to a confiscation investigation carried out by an officer of Revenue and Customs, the Director of Revenue and Customs Prosecutions, the Director of Public Prosecutions for Northern Ireland or any specified person.

(9) In subsection (8) "specified person" means any person specified, or falling within a description specified, by an order of the Secretary of State.

[This section is printed as amended by the *SCA* 2007, ss.74(2) and 77, Sched. 8, paras 103 and 108, and Sched. 10, paras 1 and 10.]

For disclosure order applications, see rule 62.3 of the *Criminal Procedure Rules* 2005 (S.I. 2005 No. 384), *ante*, § 15–283a.

Requirements for making of disclosure order

358.—(1) These are the requirements for the making of a disclosure order. 15–296

(2) There must be reasonable grounds for suspecting that—

(a) in the case of a confiscation investigation, the person specified in the application for the order has benefited from his criminal conduct;

(b) in the case of a civil recovery investigation, the property specified in the application for the order is recoverable property or associated property.

(3) There must be reasonable grounds for believing that information which may be provided in compliance with a requirement imposed under the order is likely to be of substantial value (whether or not by itself) to the investigation for the purposes of which the order is sought.

(4) There must be reasonable grounds for believing that it is in the public interest for the information to be provided, having regard to the benefit likely to accrue to the investigation if the information is obtained.

Offences

359.—(1) A person commits an offence if without reasonable excuse he fails to comply with a requirement imposed on him under a disclosure order. 15–297

(2) A person guilty of an offence under subsection (1) is liable on summary conviction to—

(a) imprisonment for a term not exceeding *six months* [51 weeks],

(b) a fine not exceeding level 5 on the standard scale, or

(c) both.

(3) A person commits an offence if, in purported compliance with a requirement imposed on him under a disclosure order, he—

(a) makes a statement which he knows to be false or misleading in a material particular, or

(b) recklessly makes a statement which is false or misleading in a material particular.

(4) A person guilty of an offence under subsection (3) is liable—

(a) on summary conviction, to imprisonment for a term not exceeding *six* [12] months or to a fine not exceeding the statutory maximum or to both, or

(b) on conviction on indictment, to imprisonment for a term not exceeding two years or to a fine or to both.

[This section is printed as amended, as from a day to be appointed, by the *CJA* 2003, s.281(4), (5) (substitution of "51 weeks" for "six months" in subs. (2)), and s.282(2), (3) (substitution of "12" for "six" in subs. (4)), but not in relation to any offence committed before the date of commencement: *ibid.*, ss.281(6), 282(4).]

Statements

360.—(1) A statement made by a person in response to a requirement imposed on him under a disclosure order may not be used in evidence against him in criminal proceedings. 15–298

(2) But subsection (1) does not apply—

(a) in the case of proceedings under Part 2 or 4,

(b) on a prosecution for an offence under section 359(1) or (3),

(c) on a prosecution for an offence under section 5 of the *Perjury Act* 1911 or [*Northern Ireland*] (false statements), or

(d) on a prosecution for some other offence where, in giving evidence, the person makes a statement inconsistent with the statement mentioned in subsection (1).

(3) A statement may not be used by virtue of subsection (2)(d) against a person unless—

(a) evidence relating to it is adduced, or

(b) a question relating to it is asked,

by him or on his behalf in the proceedings arising out of the prosecution.

Further provisions

361.—(1) A disclosure order does not confer the right to require a person to answer any privileged question, provide any privileged information or produce any privileged document, except that a lawyer may be required to provide the name and address of a client of his. 15–299

(2) A privileged question is a question which the person would be entitled to refuse to answer on grounds of legal professional privilege in proceedings in the High Court.

(3) Privileged information is any information which the person would be entitled to refuse to provide on grounds of legal professional privilege in proceedings in the High Court.

(4) Privileged material is any material which the person would be entitled to refuse to produce on grounds of legal professional privilege in proceedings in the High Court.

(5) A disclosure order does not confer the right to require a person to produce excluded material.

(6) A disclosure order has effect in spite of any restriction on the disclosure of information (however imposed).

(7) The appropriate officer may take copies of any documents produced in compliance with a requirement to produce them which is imposed under a disclosure order.

(8) Documents so produced may be retained for so long as it is necessary to retain them (as opposed to a copy of them) in connection with the investigation for the purposes of which the order was made.

(9) But if the appropriate officer has reasonable grounds for believing that—

(a) the documents may need to be produced for the purposes of any legal proceedings, and

(b) they might otherwise be unavailable for those purposes,

they may be retained until the proceedings are concluded.

[This section is printed as amended by the *SCA* 2007, s.74(2), and Sched. 8, paras 103 and 109.]

Supplementary

15–300 **362.**—(1) An application for a disclosure order may be made ex parte to a judge in chambers.

(2) Rules of court may make provision as to the practice and procedure to be followed in connection with proceedings relating to disclosure orders.

(3) An application to discharge or vary a disclosure order may be made to the court by—

(a) the person who applied for the order;

(b) any person affected by the order.

(4) The court—

(a) may discharge the order;

(b) may vary the order.

(4A) If a member of SOCA's staff or a person falling within a description of persons specified by virtue of section 357(9) applies for a disclosure order, an application to discharge or vary the order need not be by the same member of SOCA's staff or (as the case may be) the same person falling within that description.

(4B) References to a person who applied for a disclosure order must be construed accordingly.

(5) Subsections (2) to (4) do not apply to orders made in England and Wales for the purposes of a civil recovery investigation.

[This section is printed as amended by the *SCA* 2007, s.74(2), and Sched. 8, paras 103 and 110.]

Customer information orders

Customer information orders

15–301 **363.**—(1) A judge may, on an application made to him by an appropriate officer, make a customer information order if he is satisfied that each of the requirements for the making of the order is fulfilled.

(1A) No application for a customer information order may be made in relation to a detained cash investigation.

(2) The application for a customer information order must state that—

(a) a person specified in the application is subject to a confiscation investigation or a money laundering investigation, or

(b) property specified in the application is subject to a civil recovery investigation and a person specified in the application appears to hold the property.

(3) The application must also state that—

(a) the order is sought for the purposes of the investigation;

(b) the order is sought against the financial institution or financial institutions specified in the application.

(4) An application for a customer information order may specify—
(a) all financial institutions,
(b) a particular description, or particular descriptions, of financial institutions, or
(c) a particular financial institution or particular financial institutions.

(5) A customer information order is an order that a financial institution covered by the application for the order must, on being required to do so by notice in writing given by an appropriate officer, provide any such customer information as it has relating to the person specified in the application.

(6) A financial institution which is required to provide information under a customer information order must provide the information to an appropriate officer in such manner, and at or by such time, as an appropriate officer requires.

(7) If a financial institution on which a requirement is imposed by a notice given under a customer information order requires the production of evidence of authority to give the notice, it is not bound to comply with the requirement unless evidence of the authority has been produced to it.

[This section is printed as amended by the *SCA* 2007, s.77, and Sched. 10, paras 1 and 11.]

For customer information order applications, see rule 62.3 of the *Criminal Procedure Rules* 2005 (S.I. 2005 No. 384), *ante*, § 15–283a.

Meaning of customer information

364.—(1) "Customer information", in relation to a person and a financial institution, is information whether the person holds, or has held, an account or accounts at the financial institution (whether solely or jointly with another) and (if so) information as to— **15–302**
(a) the matters specified in subsection (2) if the person is an individual;
(b) the matters specified in subsection (3) if the person is a company or limited liability partnership or a similar body incorporated or otherwise established outside the United Kingdom.

(2) The matters referred to in subsection (1)(a) are—
(a) the account number or numbers;
(b) the person's full name;
(c) his date of birth;
(d) his most recent address and any previous addresses;
(e) the date or dates on which he began to hold the account or accounts and, if he has ceased to hold the account or any of the accounts, the date or dates on which he did so;
(f) such evidence of his identity as was obtained by the financial institution under or for the purposes of any legislation relating to money laundering;
(g) the full name, date of birth and most recent address, and any previous addresses, of any person who holds, or has held, an account at the financial institution jointly with him;
(h) the account number or numbers of any other account or accounts held at the financial institution to which he is a signatory and details of the person holding the other account or accounts.

(3) The matters referred to in subsection (1)(b) are—
(a) the account number or numbers;
(b) the person's full name;
(c) a description of any business which the person carries on;
(d) the country or territory in which it is incorporated or otherwise established and any number allocated to it under the *Companies Act* 1985 or the *Companies (Northern Ireland) Order* 1986 (S.I. 1986/1032 (N.I. 6)) or corresponding legislation of any country or territory outside the United Kingdom;
(e) any number assigned to it for the purposes of value added tax in the United Kingdom;
(f) its registered office, and any previous registered offices, under the *Companies Act* 1985 or the *Companies (Northern Ireland) Order* 1986 (S.I. 1986/1032 (N.I. 6)) or anything similar under corresponding legislation of any country or territory outside the United Kingdom;
(g) its registered office, and any previous registered offices, under the *Limited Liability Partnerships Act* 2000 or anything similar under corresponding legislation of any country or territory outside Great Britain;

(h) the date or dates on which it began to hold the account or accounts and, if it has ceased to hold the account or any of the accounts, the date or dates on which it did so;

(i) such evidence of its identity as was obtained by the financial institution under or for the purposes of any legislation relating to money laundering;

(j) the full name, date of birth and most recent address and any previous addresses of any person who is a signatory to the account or any of the accounts.

(4) The Secretary of State may by order provide for information of a description specified in the order—

(a) to be customer information, or

(b) no longer to be customer information.

(5) Money laundering is an act which—

(a) constitutes an offence under section 327, 328 or 329 of this Act or section 18 of the *Terrorism Act* 2000, or

(aa) constitutes an offence specified in section 415(1A) of this Act;

(b) would constitute an offence specified in paragraph (a) or (aa) if done in the United Kingdom.

[This section is printed as amended by the *SOCPA* 2005, s.107(1) and (2).]

Requirements for making of customer information order

15–303 **365.**—(1) These are the requirements for the making of a customer information order.

(2) In the case of a confiscation investigation, there must be reasonable grounds for suspecting that the person specified in the application for the order has benefited from his criminal conduct.

(3) In the case of a civil recovery investigation, there must be reasonable grounds for suspecting that—

(a) the property specified in the application for the order is recoverable property or associated property;

(b) the person specified in the application holds all or some of the property.

(4) In the case of a money laundering investigation, there must be reasonable grounds for suspecting that the person specified in the application for the order has committed a money laundering offence.

(5) In the case of any investigation, there must be reasonable grounds for believing that customer information which may be provided in compliance with the order is likely to be of substantial value (whether or not by itself) to the investigation for the purposes of which the order is sought.

(6) In the case of any investigation, there must be reasonable grounds for believing that it is in the public interest for the customer information to be provided, having regard to the benefit likely to accrue to the investigation if the information is obtained.

Offences

15–304 **366.**—(1) A financial institution commits an offence if without reasonable excuse it fails to comply with a requirement imposed on it under a customer information order.

(2) A financial institution guilty of an offence under subsection (1) is liable on summary conviction to a fine not exceeding level 5 on the standard scale.

(3) A financial institution commits an offence if, in purported compliance with a customer information order, it—

(a) makes a statement which it knows to be false or misleading in a material particular, or

(b) recklessly makes a statement which is false or misleading in a material particular.

(4) A financial institution guilty of an offence under subsection (3) is liable—

(a) on summary conviction, to a fine not exceeding the statutory maximum, or

(b) on conviction on indictment, to a fine.

Statements

15–305 **367.**—(1) A statement made by a financial institution in response to a customer information order may not be used in evidence against it in criminal proceedings.

(2) But subsection (1) does not apply—

(a) in the case of proceedings under Part 2 or 4,

(b) on a prosecution for an offence under section 366(1) or (3), or

(c) on a prosecution for some other offence where, in giving evidence, the financial institution makes a statement inconsistent with the statement mentioned in subsection (1).

(3) A statement may not be used by virtue of subsection (2)(c) against a financial institution unless—

(a) evidence relating to it is adduced, or

(b) a question relating to it is asked,

by or on behalf of the financial institution in the proceedings arising out of the prosecution.

Disclosure of information

368. A customer information order has effect in spite of any restriction on the disclosure of information (however imposed). **15–306**

Supplementary

369.—(1) An application for a customer information order may be made ex parte to a judge in chambers. **15–307**

(2) Rules of court may make provision as to the practice and procedure to be followed in connection with proceedings relating to customer information orders.

(3) An application to discharge or vary a customer information order may be made to the court by—

(a) the person who applied for the order;

(b) any person affected by the order.

(4) The court—

(a) may discharge the order;

(b) may vary the order.

(5) If an accredited financial investigator, a member of SOCA's staff, a constable or an officer of Revenue and Customs applies for a customer information order, an application to discharge or vary the order need not be by the same accredited financial investigator, member of SOCA's staff, constable or officer of Revenue and Customs.

(6) References to a person who applied for a customer information order must be construed accordingly.

(7) An accredited financial investigator, a member of SOCA's staff, a constable or an officer of Revenue and Customs may not make an application for a customer information order or an application to vary such an order unless he is a senior appropriate officer or he is authorised to do so by a senior appropriate officer.

(8) Subsections (2) to (6) do not apply to orders made in England and Wales for the purposes of a civil recovery investigation.

[This section is printed as amended by the *Commissioners for Revenue and Customs Act* 2005, s.50(2); and the *SCA* 2007, s.74(2), and Sched. 8, paras 103 and 111.]

In connection with applications under this section, reference should be made to rule 62.2 of the *Criminal Procedure Rules* 2005. **15–307a**

Criminal Procedure Rules 2005 (S.I. 2005 No. 384), r.62.2

Customer information orders under the Proceeds of Crime Act 2002

62.2.—(1) Where any person other than the person who applied for the customer information order proposes to make an application under section 369(3) of the *Proceeds of Crime Act* 2002 for the discharge or variation of a customer information order, he shall, not later than 48 hours before the application is to be made, give a copy of the proposed application—

(a) to a police officer at the police station specified in the customer information order; or

(b) where the application for the customer information order was not made by a constable, to the office of the appropriate officer who made the application, as specified in the customer information order,

in either case together with a notice indicating the time and place at which the application for a discharge or variation is to be made.

(2) In this rule—

"appropriate officer" has the meaning given to it by section 378 of the 2002 Act;

references to the person who applied for the customer information order must be construed in accordance with section 369(5) and (6) of the 2002 Act.

[This rule is printed as substituted (in identical terms) by the *Criminal Procedure (Amendment No. 3) Rules* 2007 (S.I. 2007 No. 3662), r.23.]

Proceeds of Crime Act 2002, ss.370–379

Account monitoring orders

Account monitoring orders

15–308 **370.**—(1) A judge may, on an application made to him by an appropriate officer, make an account monitoring order if he is satisfied that each of the requirements for the making of the order is fulfilled.

(1A) No application for an account monitoring order may be made in relation to a detained cash investigation.

(2) The application for an account monitoring order must state that—

(a) a person specified in the application is subject to a confiscation investigation or a money laundering investigation, or

(b) property specified in the application is subject to a civil recovery investigation and a person specified in the application appears to hold the property.

(3) The application must also state that—

(a) the order is sought for the purposes of the investigation;

(b) the order is sought against the financial institution specified in the application in relation to account information of the description so specified.

(4) Account information is information relating to an account or accounts held at the financial institution specified in the application by the person so specified (whether solely or jointly with another).

(5) The application for an account monitoring order may specify information relating to—

(a) all accounts held by the person specified in the application for the order at the financial institution so specified,

(b) a particular description, or particular descriptions, of accounts so held, or

(c) a particular account, or particular accounts, so held.

(6) An account monitoring order is an order that the financial institution specified in the application for the order must, for the period stated in the order, provide account information of the description specified in the order to an appropriate officer in the manner, and at or by the time or times, stated in the order.

(7) The period stated in an account monitoring order must not exceed the period of 90 days beginning with the day on which the order is made.

[This section is printed as amended by the *SCA* 2007, s.77, and Sched. 10, paras 1 and 12.]

For account monitoring order applications, see rule 62.3 of the *Criminal Procedure Rules* 2005 (S.I. 2005 No. 384), *ante*, § 15–283a.

Requirements for making of account monitoring order

15–309 **371.**—(1) These are the requirements for the making of an account monitoring order.

(2) In the case of a confiscation investigation, there must be reasonable grounds for suspecting that the person specified in the application for the order has benefited from his criminal conduct.

(3) In the case of a civil recovery investigation, there must be reasonable grounds for suspecting that—

(a) the property specified in the application for the order is recoverable property or associated property;

(b) the person specified in the application holds all or some of the property.

(4) In the case of a money laundering investigation, there must be reasonable grounds for suspecting that the person specified in the application for the order has committed a money laundering offence.

(5) In the case of any investigation, there must be reasonable grounds for believing that account information which may be provided in compliance with the order is likely to be of substantial value (whether or not by itself) to the investigation for the purposes of which the order is sought.

(6) In the case of any investigation, there must be reasonable grounds for believing that it is in the public interest for the account information to be provided, having regard to the benefit likely to accrue to the investigation if the information is obtained.

Statements

15–310 **372.**—(1) A statement made by a financial institution in response to an account monitoring order may not be used in evidence against it in criminal proceedings.

money laundering investigation: section 341(4)

(2) In the application of this Part to England and Wales and Northern Ireland, these expressions are to be construed in accordance with these provisions of this Part—

account information: section 370(4)
account monitoring order: section 370(6)
appropriate officer: section 378
customer information: section 364
customer information order: section 363(5)
disclosure order: section 357(4)
document: section 379
order to grant entry: section 347(3)
production order: section 345(4)
relevant authority: section 357(7) to (9)
relevant Director: section 352(5A)
search and seizure warrant: section 352(4)
senior appropriate officer: section 378
senior member of SOCA's staff: section 378(8).

(3) [*Scotland.*]

(4) "Financial institution" means a person carrying on a business in the regulated sector.

(5) But a person who ceases to carry on a business in the regulated sector (whether by virtue of paragraph 5 of Schedule 9 or otherwise) is to continue to be treated as a financial institution for the purposes of any requirement under—

(a) a customer information order, or

(b) an account monitoring order,

to provide information which relates to a time when the person was a financial institution.

(6) References to a business in the regulated sector must be construed in accordance with Schedule 9.

(7) "Recovery order", "interim receiving order" and "interim administration order" have the same meanings as in Part 5.

(7A) "Unlawful conduct" has the meaning given by section 241.

(8) References to notice in writing include references to notice given by electronic means.

(9) This section and sections 413 to 415 apply for the purposes of this Part.

[This section is printed as amended by the *SCA* 2007, ss.74(2) and 77, Sched. 8, paras 103 and 117, and Sched. 10, paras 1 and 24.]

[The next paragraph is § 15–330.]

I. SERIOUS ORGANISED CRIME AND POLICE ACT 2005

(1) Disclosure notices

(a) *Summary*

Section 60 of the 2005 Act provides for the DPP, the Director of Revenue and Customs Prosecutions, and the Lord Advocate to give "disclosure notices" in connection with the investigation of offences to which Chapter 1 of Part 2 applies. Each may delegate such powers. Section 61 lists the offences to which the powers apply. They are "lifestyle offences" under the *PCA* 2002 (*ante*, §§ 5–653 *et seq.*), offences under the *Terrorism Act* 2000, ss.15 to 18, any offence which is a qualifying offence (as to which see subs. (2)) under the *CEMA* 1979, s.170, the *Value Added Tax Act* 1994, s.72, the *Theft Act* 1968, s.17, or any qualifying common law offence of cheating in relation to the public revenue, or an attempt or conspiracy to commit any such offence. **15–330**

Section 62 provides for a disclosure notice (as to which, see s.62(3)) to be given to a person where it appears to the investigating authority that there are reasonable grounds for suspecting that an offence to which Chapter 1 applies has been committed, that any person has information which relates to a matter relevant to the investigation of that offence, and that there are reasonable grounds for believing that information which may be provided by that person in compliance with a disclosure notice is likely to be of substantial value (whether or not by itself) to that investigation. Section 63 contains provision as to the production of documents where a disclosure notice has been given. Section 64 contains restrictions on the requirement to produce information (privileged information, "excluded material" within the *PACE Act* 1984, information subject to obligation of confidence, etc.). Section 65 restricts the use of statements made in response to a requirement imposed under section 62 or 63. The statement may not be used against the maker in criminal proceedings, except in the specified circumstances. Sections 66 and 67 provide for enforcement. Section 66 sets out the procedure for the issue and execution of a warrant in order to seize documents subject to a disclosure notice. Section 67(1) makes it a summary offence for a person, without reasonable excuse, to fail to comply with a requirement imposed on him under section 62 or 63. Section 67(2) provides for an either way offence where a person, in purported compliance with any such requirement, knowingly or recklessly makes a statement that is false or misleading in a material particular. Section 67(3) creates a summary offence of wilfully obstructing any person in the exercise of any rights conferred by a warrant under section 66. Section 68 inserts a reference to the power of seizure under section 66 into Part 1 of Schedule 1 to the *CJPA* 2001 (*ante*, § 15–148). Section 69 prescribes the manner in which a disclosure notice may be given. Section 70 provides for the interpretation of Chapter 1.

(b) *Commencement*

15–331 Sections 60 to 70 came into force on April 1, 2006: *Serious Organised Crime and Police Act 2005 (Commencement No. 1, Transitional and Transitory Provisions) Order* 2005 (S.I. 2005 No. 1521).

(c) *Legislation*

Serious Organised Crime and Police Act 2005, ss.60–70

PART 2

INVESTIGATIONS, PROSECUTIONS, PROCEEDINGS AND PROCEEDS OF CRIME

CHAPTER 1

INVESTIGATORY POWERS OF DPP, ETC.

Investigatory powers of DPP etc.

15–332 **60.**—(1) This Chapter confers powers on—

(a) the Director of Public Prosecutions,
(b) the Director of Revenue and Customs Prosecutions, *and*
(c) the Lord Advocate, and
(d) the Director of Public Prosecutions for Northern Ireland,

in relation to the giving of disclosure notices in connection with the investigation of offences to which this Chapter applies or in connection with a terrorist investigation.

(2) The Director of Public Prosecutions may, to such extent as he may determine, delegate the exercise of his powers under this Chapter to a Crown prosecutor.

(3) The Director of Revenue and Customs Prosecutions may, to such extent as he may determine, delegate the exercise of his powers under this Chapter to a Revenue and Customs Prosecutor.

(4) [*Scotland.*]

(4A) [*Northern Ireland.*]

(5) In this Chapter "the Investigating Authority" means—

(a) the Director of Public Prosecutions,
(b) the Director of Revenue and Customs Prosecutions, *or*
(c) the Lord Advocate, or
(d) the Director of Public Prosecutions for Northern Ireland.

(6) But, in circumstances where the powers of any of those persons are exercisable by any other person by virtue of subsection (2), (3), (4) or (4A), references to "the Investigating Authority" accordingly include any such other person.

(7) In this Chapter "terrorist investigation" means an investigation of—

(a) the commission, preparation or instigation of acts of terrorism,

(b) any act or omission which appears to have been for the purposes of terrorism and which consists in or involves the commission, preparation or instigation of an offence, or

(c) the commission, preparation or instigation of an offence under the *Terrorism Act* 2000 or under Part 1 of the *Terrorism Act* 2006 other than an offence under section 1 or 2 of that Act.

[This section is printed as amended by the *Terrorism Act* 2006, s.33(1) and (2); and by the *Northern Ireland (Miscellaneous Provisions) Act* 2006, s.26(2), and Sched. 3, paras 1 and 2. The italicised words are repealed as from a day to be appointed: *ibid.*, s.30(2), and Sched. 5.]

Offences to which this Chapter applies

61.—(1) This Chapter applies to the following offences— **15–333**

(a) any offence listed in Schedule 2 to the *Proceeds of Crime Act* 2002 (lifestyle offences: England and Wales);

(b) any offence listed in Schedule 4 to that Act (lifestyle offences: Scotland);

(ba) any offence listed in Schedule 5 to that Act (lifestyle offences: Northern Ireland;

(c) any offence under sections 15 to 18 of the *Terrorism Act* 2000 (offences relating to fund-raising, money laundering etc.);

(d) any offence under section 170 of the *Customs and Excise Management Act* 1979 (fraudulent evasion of duty) or section 72 of the *Value Added Tax Act* 1994 (offences relating to VAT) which is a qualifying offence;

(e) any offence under section 17 of the *Theft Act* 1968 or section 17 of the *Theft Act (Northern Ireland)* 1969 (false accounting), or any offence at common law of cheating in relation to the public revenue, which is a qualifying offence;

(f) any offence under section 1 of the *Criminal Attempts Act* 1981 or Article 3 of the *Criminal Attempts and Conspiracy (Northern Ireland) Order* 1983, or in Scotland at common law, of attempting to commit any offence in paragraph (c) or any offence in paragraph (d) or (e) which is a qualifying offence;

(g) any offence under section 1 of the *Criminal Law Act* 1977 or Article 9 of the *Criminal Attempts and Conspiracy (Northern Ireland) Order* 1983, or in Scotland at common law, of conspiracy to commit any offence in paragraph (c) or any offence in paragraph (d) or (e) which is a qualifying offence;

(h) in England and Wales—

(i) any common law offence of bribery;

(ii) any offence under section 1 of the *Public Bodies Corrupt Practices Act* 1889 (corruption in office);

(iii) the first two offences under section 1 of the *Prevention of Corruption Act* 1906 (bribes obtained by or given to agents).

(2) For the purposes of subsection (1) an offence in paragraph (d) or (e) of that subsection is a qualifying offence if the Investigating Authority certifies that in his opinion—

(a) in the case of an offence in paragraph (d) or an offence of cheating the public revenue, the offence involved or would have involved a loss, or potential loss, to the public revenue of an amount not less than £5,000;

(b) in the case of an offence under section 17 of the *Theft Act* 1968 or section 17 of the *Theft Act (Northern Ireland)* 1969, the offence involved or would have involved a loss or gain, or potential loss or gain, of an amount not less than £5,000.

(3) A document purporting to be a certificate under subsection (2) is to be received in evidence and treated as such a certificate unless the contrary is proved.

(4), (5) [*Provision for amendment of subss. (1) and (2) by order.*]

[This section is printed as amended by the *Serious Organised Crime and Police Act 2005 (Amendment of Section 61(1)) Order* 2006 (S.I. 2006 No. 1629); and the *Northern Ireland (Miscellaneous Provisions) Act* 2006, s.26(2), and Sched. 3, paras 1 and 3.]

Disclosure notices

62.—(1) If it appears to the Investigating Authority— **15–334**

(a) that there are reasonable grounds for suspecting that an offence to which this Chapter applies has been committed,

(b) that any person has information (whether or not contained in a document) which relates to a matter relevant to the investigation of that offence, and

(c) that there are reasonable grounds for believing that information which may be provided by that person in compliance with a disclosure notice is likely to be of substantial value (whether or not by itself) to that investigation,

he may give, or authorise an appropriate person to give, a disclosure notice to that person.

(1A) If it appears to the Investigating Authority—

(a) that any person has information (whether or not contained in a document) which relates to a matter relevant to a terrorist investigation, and

(b) that there are reasonable grounds for believing that information which may be provided by that person in compliance with a disclosure notice is likely to be of substantial value (whether or not by itself) to that investigation,

he may give, or authorise an appropriate person to give, a disclosure notice to that person.

(2) In this Chapter "appropriate person" means—

(a) a constable,

(b) a member of the staff of SOCA who is for the time being designated under section 43, or

(c) an officer of Revenue and Customs.

But in the application of this Chapter to Northern Ireland, this subsection has effect as if paragraph (b) were omitted.

(3) In this Chapter "disclosure notice" means a notice in writing requiring the person to whom it is given to do all or any of the following things in accordance with the specified requirements, namely—

(a) answer questions with respect to any matter relevant to the investigation;

(b) provide information with respect to any such matter as is specified in the notice;

(c) produce such documents, or documents of such descriptions, relevant to the investigation as are specified in the notice.

(4) In subsection (3) "the specified requirements" means such requirements specified in the disclosure notice as relate to—

(a) the time at or by which,

(b) the place at which, or

(c) the manner in which,

the person to whom the notice is given is to do any of the things mentioned in paragraphs (a) to (c) of that subsection; and those requirements may include a requirement to do any of those things at once.

(5) A disclosure notice must be signed or counter-signed by the Investigating Authority.

(6) This section has effect subject to section 64 (restrictions on requiring information etc.).

[This section is printed as amended by the *Terrorism Act* 2006, s.33(3); and the *Northern Ireland (Miscellaneous Provisions) Act* 2006, s.26(2), and Sched. 3, paras 1 and 4.]

Production of documents

15–335 **63.**—(1) This section applies where a disclosure notice has been given under section 62.

(2) An authorised person may—

(a) take copies of or extracts from any documents produced in compliance with the notice, and

(b) require the person producing them to provide an explanation of any of them.

(3) Documents so produced may be retained for so long as the Investigating Authority considers that it is necessary to retain them (rather than copies of them) in connection with the investigation for the purposes of which the disclosure notice was given.

(4) If the Investigating Authority has reasonable grounds for believing—

(a) that any such documents may have to be produced for the purposes of any legal proceedings, and

(b) that they might otherwise be unavailable for those purposes,

they may be retained until the proceedings are concluded.

(5) If a person who is required by a disclosure notice to produce any documents does not produce the documents in compliance with the notice, an authorised person may require that person to state, to the best of his knowledge and belief, where they are.

(6) In this section "authorised person" means any appropriate person who either—

(a) is the person by whom the notice was given, or

(b) is authorised by the Investigating Authority for the purposes of this section.

(7) This section has effect subject to section 64 (restrictions on requiring information etc.).

Restrictions on requiring information etc.

64.—(1) A person may not be required under section 62 or 63— **15–336**

(a) to answer any privileged question,

(b) to provide any privileged information, or

(c) to produce any privileged document,

except that a lawyer may be required to provide the name and address of a client of his.

(2) A "privileged question" is a question which the person would be entitled to refuse to answer on grounds of legal professional privilege in proceedings in the High Court.

(3) "Privileged information" is information which the person would be entitled to refuse to provide on grounds of legal professional privilege in such proceedings.

(4) A "privileged document" is a document which the person would be entitled to refuse to produce on grounds of legal professional privilege in such proceedings.

(5) A person may not be required under section 62 to produce any excluded material (as defined by section 11 of the *Police and Criminal Evidence Act* 1984 or, in relation to Northern Ireland, Article 13 of the *Police and Criminal Evidence (Northern Ireland) Order* 1989).

(6), (7) [*Scotland.*]

(8) A person may not be required under section 62 or 63 to disclose any information or produce any document in respect of which he owes an obligation of confidence by virtue of carrying on any banking business, unless—

(a) the person to whom the obligation of confidence is owed consents to the disclosure or production, or

(b) the requirement is made by, or in accordance with a specific authorisation given by, the Investigating Authority.

(9) Subject to the preceding provisions, any requirement under section 62 or 63 has effect despite any restriction on disclosure (however imposed).

[This section is printed as amended by the *Northern Ireland (Miscellaneous Provisions) Act* 2006, s.26(2), and Sched. 3, paras 1 and 5.]

Restrictions on use of statements

65.—(1) A statement made by a person in response to a requirement imposed under section 62 or 63 ("the relevant statement") may not be used in evidence against him in any criminal proceedings unless subsection (2) or (3) applies. **15–337**

(2) This subsection applies where the person is being prosecuted—

(a) for an offence under section 67 of this Act, or

(b) for an offence under section 5 of the *Perjury Act* 1911 (false statements made on oath otherwise than in judicial proceedings or made otherwise than on oath), or

(c) for an offence under section 2 of the *False Oaths (Scotland) Act* 1933 (false statutory declarations and other false statements without oath) or at common law for an offence of attempting to pervert the course, or defeat the ends, of justice.

(3) This subsection applies where the person is being prosecuted for some other offence and—

(a) the person, when giving evidence in the proceedings, makes a statement inconsistent with the relevant statement, and

(b) in the proceedings evidence relating to the relevant statement is adduced, or a question about it is asked, by or on behalf of the person.

Power to enter and seize documents

66.—(1) A justice of the peace may issue a warrant under this section if, on an information on oath laid by the Investigating Authority, he is satisfied— **15–338**

(a) that any of the conditions mentioned in subsection (2) is met in relation to any documents of a description specified in the information, and

(b) that the documents are on premises so specified.

(2) The conditions are—

(a) that a person has been required by a disclosure notice to produce the documents but has not done so;

(b) that it is not practicable to give a disclosure notice requiring their production;

(c) that giving such a notice might seriously prejudice the investigation of an offence to which this Chapter applies.

(3) A warrant under this section is a warrant authorising an appropriate person named in it—

(a) to enter and search the premises, using such force as is reasonably necessary;

(b) to take possession of any documents appearing to be documents of a description specified in the information, or to take any other steps which appear to be necessary for preserving, or preventing interference with, any such documents;

(c) in the case of any such documents consisting of information recorded otherwise than in legible form, to take possession of any computer disk or other electronic storage device which appears to contain the information in question, or to take any other steps which appear to be necessary for preserving, or preventing interference with, that information;

(d) to take copies of or extracts from any documents or information falling within paragraph (b) or (c);

(e) to require any person on the premises to provide an explanation of any such documents or information or to state where any such documents or information may be found;

(f) to require any such person to give the appropriate person such assistance as he may reasonably require for the taking of copies or extracts as mentioned in paragraph (d).

(4) A person executing a warrant under this section may take other persons with him, if it appears to him to be necessary to do so.

(5) A warrant under this section must, if so required, be produced for inspection by the owner or occupier of the premises or anyone acting on his behalf.

(6) If the premises are unoccupied or the occupier is temporarily absent, a person entering the premises under the authority of a warrant under this section must leave the premises as effectively secured against trespassers as he found them.

(7) Where possession of any document or device is taken under this section—

(a) the document may be retained for so long as the Investigating Authority considers that it is necessary to retain it (rather than a copy of it) in connection with the investigation for the purposes of which the warrant was sought, or

(b) the device may be retained for so long as he considers that it is necessary to retain it in connection with that investigation,

as the case may be.

(8) If the Investigating Authority has reasonable grounds for believing—

(a) that any such document or device may have to be produced for the purposes of any legal proceedings, and

(b) that it might otherwise be unavailable for those purposes,

it may be retained until the proceedings are concluded.

(9) Nothing in this section authorises a person to take possession of, or make copies of or take extracts from, any document or information which, by virtue of section 64, could not be required to be produced or disclosed under section 62 or 63.

(10), [11] [*Scotland and [Northern Ireland]*.]

Offences in connection with disclosure notices or search warrants

15–339 **67.**—(1) A person commits an offence if, without reasonable excuse, he fails to comply with any requirement imposed on him under section 62 or 63.

(2) A person commits an offence if, in purported compliance with any requirement imposed on him under section 62 or 63—

(a) he makes a statement which is false or misleading, and

(b) he either knows that it is false or misleading or is reckless as to whether it is false or misleading.

"False or misleading" means false or misleading in a material particular.

(3) A person commits an offence if he wilfully obstructs any person in the exercise of any rights conferred by a warrant under section 66.

(4) A person guilty of an offence under subsection (1) or (3) is liable on summary conviction—

(a) to imprisonment for a term not exceeding 51 weeks, or

(b) to a fine not exceeding level 5 on the standard scale,

or to both.

(5) A person guilty of an offence under subsection (2) is liable—

(a) on conviction on indictment, to imprisonment for a term not exceeding two years or to a fine, or to both;

(b) on summary conviction, to imprisonment for a term not exceeding 12 months or to a fine not exceeding the statutory maximum, or to both.

(6), [7] [*Scotland and [Northern Ireland]*.]

Procedure applicable to search warrants

68. [*Amends* CJPA *2001, Sched. 1*, ante, *§ 15–148*.] **15–340**

Manner in which disclosure notice may be given

69.—(1) This section provides for the manner in which a disclosure notice may be given under section 62. **15–341**

(2) The notice may be given to a person by—

(a) delivering it to him,

(b) leaving it at his proper address,

(c) sending it by post to him at that address.

(3) The notice may be given—

(a) in the case of a body corporate, to the secretary or clerk of that body;

(b) in the case of a partnership, to a partner or a person having the control or management of the partnership business;

(c) in the case of an unincorporated association (other than a partnership), to an officer of the association.

(4) For the purposes of this section and section 7 of the *Interpretation Act* 1978 (service of documents by post) in its application to this section, the proper address of a person is his usual or last-known address (whether residential or otherwise), except that—

(a) in the case of a body corporate or its secretary or clerk, it is the address of the registered office of that body or its principal office in the United Kingdom,

(b) in the case of a partnership, a partner or a person having the control or management of the partnership business, it is that of the principal office of the partnership in the United Kingdom, and

(c) in the case of an unincorporated association (other than a partnership) or an officer of the association, it is that of the principal office of the association in the United Kingdom.

(5) This section does not apply to Scotland.

Interpretation of Chapter 1

70.—(1) In this Chapter— **15–342**

"act of terrorism" includes anything constituting an action taken for the purposes of terrorism, within the meaning of the *Terrorism Act* 2000 (see section 1(5) of that Act);

"appropriate person" has the meaning given by section 62(2);

"the Investigating Authority" is to be construed in accordance with section 60(5) and (6);

"disclosure notice" has the meaning given by section 62(3);

"document" includes information recorded otherwise than in legible form;

"terrorism" has the same meaning as in the *Terrorism Act* 2000 (see section 1(1) to (4) of that Act);

"terrorist investigation" has the meaning given by section 60(7).

(2) In relation to information recorded otherwise than in legible form, any reference in this Chapter to the production of documents is a reference to the production of a copy of the information in legible form.

[This section is printed as amended by the *Terrorism Act* 2006, s.33(4).]

(2) Offenders assisting investigations and prosecutions; undertakings as to use of evidence

(a) *Summary*

Section 71 of the 2005 Act (*ante*, § 1–94) provides that a specified prosecutor may offer any person immunity from prosecution by means of a written notice where it is appropriate to do so for the purposes of the investigation or prosecution of any offence. Section 72(1) provides that if a specified prosecutor thinks that for the purposes of an **15–343** investigation or prosecution of any offence it is appropriate to offer any person an undertaking that information of any description will not be used against the person in any proceedings a written "restricted use undertaking" notice may be given. A notice may be given in criminal proceedings or in proceedings under Part 5 of the *PCA* 2002 (civil recovery). If an undertaking is given, the information described must not be used in any proceedings to which section 72 applies except in circumstances specified in the undertaking (s.72(3)), but the undertaking ceases to have effect if the person fails to comply with any conditions specified therein (s.72(4)).

(b) *Legislation*

Serious Organised Crime and Police Act 2005, s.72

Assistance by offender: undertakings as to use of evidence

15–344 **72.**—(1) If a specified prosecutor thinks that for the purposes of the investigation or prosecution of any offence it is appropriate to offer any person an undertaking that information of any description will not be used against the person in any proceedings to which this section applies he may give the person a written notice under this subsection (a "restricted use undertaking").

(2) This section applies to—

(a) criminal proceedings;

(b) proceedings under Part 5 of the *Proceeds of Crime Act* 2002.

(3) If a person is given a restricted use undertaking the information described in the undertaking must not be used against that person in any proceedings to which this section applies brought in England and Wales or Northern Ireland except in the circumstances specified in the undertaking.

(4) A restricted use undertaking ceases to have effect in relation to the person to whom it is given if the person fails to comply with any conditions specified in the undertaking.

(5) [*Northern Ireland*.]

(6) The Director of Public Prosecutions or a person designated by him under section 71(4)(e) may not give a restricted use undertaking in relation to proceedings in Northern Ireland.

(7) Specified prosecutor must be construed in accordance with section 71(4).

[The next paragraph is § 15–350.]

II. *CONFESSIONS AND RELATED TOPICS*

A. CONFESSIONS

(1) Police and Criminal Evidence Act 1984

(a) *Admissibility*

15–350 Part VIII of the *PACE Act* 1984 (ss.73–82) is headed "Evidence in Criminal Proceedings—General". Section 76 governs the admissibility of confessions. For the meaning of "confession" and other words and phrases used in section 76, see *post*, §§ 15–354 *et seq.*

The admissibility of a confession may be challenged in one or more of four ways: (a) under section 76(2)(a), the prosecution has not proved that the confession was not or may not have been obtained by oppression of the person who made it; (b) under section 76(2)(b), the prosecution has not proved that the confession was not or may not have been obtained in consequence of anything said or done which was likely, in the circumstances existing at the time, to render unreliable any confession which might be made in consequence thereof; (c) under section 78, if it appears to the court that, having regard to all the circumstances, including the circumstances in which the evidence was obtained, the admission of the evidence would have such an adverse effect on the fairness of the proceedings that the court ought not to admit it (*post*, § 15–452); or (d) at common law, in the discretion of the trial judge, the evidence ought to be excluded so as to protect the defendant from an unfair trial (*post*, § 15–535).

15–351 As to the law and procedure in relation to a challenge to a confession's admissibility, see *post*, §§ 15–374 *et seq.*

As to a confession by a mentally handicapped person, see *post*, §§ 15–368 *et seq.*; as to a confession based on hearsay, see *post*, § 15–399; as to the embargo on cross-examination on an inadmissible confession, see *post*, § 15–386; as to the use of a confession against a co-defendant, see *post*, §§ 15–388 *et seq.*; as to its use by a co-defendant, see section 76A, *post*, § 15–353a; as to editing a defendant's statement to exclude matters improperly prejudicial to him, see *post*, § 15–392; as to partial admissions and self-serving statements, see *post*, § 15–400; as to exhibiting contemporaneous notes of interview, see *post*, §§ 15–393 *et seq.*

Police and Criminal Evidence Act 1984, ss.76, 76A

Confessions

76.—(1) In any proceedings a confession made by an accused person may be given in evidence against him in so far as it is relevant to any matter in issue in the proceedings and is not excluded by the court in pursuance of this section. **15–352**

(2) If, in any proceedings where the prosecution proposes to give in evidence a confession made by an accused person, it is represented to the court that the confession was or may have been obtained—

(a) by oppression of the person who made it; or

(b) in consequence of anything said or done which was likely, in the circumstances existing at the time, to render unreliable any confession which might be made by him in consequence thereof,

the court shall not allow the confession to be given in evidence against him except in so far as the prosecution proves to the court beyond reasonable doubt that the confession (notwithstanding that it may be true) was not obtained as aforesaid.

(3) In any proceedings where the prosecution proposes to give in evidence a confession made by an accused person, the court may of its own motion require the prosecution, as a condition of allowing it to do so, to prove that the confession was not obtained as mentioned in subsection (2) above.

(4) The fact that a confession is wholly or partly excluded in pursuance of this section shall not affect the admissibility in evidence— **15–353**

(a) of any facts discovered as a result of the confession; or

(b) where the confession is relevant as showing that the accused speaks, writes or expresses himself in a particular way, of so much of the confession as is necessary to show that he does so.

(5) Evidence that a fact to which this subsection applies was discovered as a result of a statement made by an accused person shall not be admissible unless evidence of how it was discovered is given by him or on his behalf.

(6) Subsection (5) above applies—

(a) to any fact discovered as a result of a confession which is wholly excluded in pursuance of this section; and

(b) to any fact discovered as a result of a confession which is partly so excluded, if the fact is discovered as a result of the excluded part of the confession.

(7) Nothing in Part VII of this Act shall prejudice the admissibility of a confession made by an accused person.

(8) In this section "oppression" includes torture, inhuman or degrading treatment, and the use or threat of violence (whether or not amounting to torture).

(9) *Where the proceedings mentioned in subsection (1) above are proceedings before a magistrates' court inquiring into an offence as examining justices this section shall have effect with the omission of—*

(a) *in subsection (1) the words "and is not excluded by the court in pursuance of this section", and*

(b) *subsections (2) to (6) and (8).*

[This section is printed as amended by the *CPIA* 1996, s.47 and Sched. 1, para. 25 (insertion of subs. (9)). As from a day to be appointed, subs. (9) is repealed by the *CJA* 2003, ss.41 and 332, Sched. 3, para. 56(1), (4), and Sched. 37, Pt 4.]

Confessions may be given in evidence for co-accused

76A.—(1) In any proceedings a confession made by an accused person may be given in evidence for another person charged in the same proceedings (a co-accused) in so far as it is relevant to any matter in issue in the proceedings and is not excluded by the court in pursuance of this section. **15–353a**

(2) If, in any proceedings where a co-accused proposes to give in evidence a confession made by an accused person, it is represented to the court that the confession was or may have been obtained—

(a) by oppression of the person who made it; or

(b) in consequence of anything said or done which was likely, in the circumstances existing at the time, to render unreliable any confession which might be made by him in consequence thereof,

the court shall not allow the confession to be given in evidence for the co-accused except in so far as it is proved to the court on the balance of probabilities that the confession (notwithstanding that it may be true) was not so obtained.

(3) Before allowing a confession made by an accused person to be given in evidence for a co-accused in any proceedings, the court may of its own motion require the fact that the confession was not obtained as mentioned in subsection (2) above to be proved in the proceedings on the balance of probabilities.

(4)–(6) [*Identical to s.76(4)–(6),* ante, *§ 15–353.*]

(7) [*Identical to s.76(8),* ante, *§ 15–353.*]

[This section is inserted by the *CJA* 2003, s.128(1).]

See further, *post*, §§ 15–386 *et seq.*, as to the consequences of admitting a co-accused's confession under section 76A.

Section 76A does not entitle a defendant to adduce in evidence a confession of a co-accused who has pleaded guilty because, once a co-accused has pleaded guilty, he can be compelled to give evidence for the defendant at the latter's trial; the section is designed to cater for the joint trial of the defendant and the co-accused, because in that situation the co-accused cannot be compelled to give evidence: *R. v. Finch* [2007] 1 Cr.App.R. 33, CA. However, where a defendant pleaded guilty on a written basis, and then withdrew his plea, his co-accused was entitled to adduce both the plea and the written basis pursuant to section 76A: *R. v. Johnson*, 171 J.P. 574, CA (see also *post*, § 15–354).

(b) *Words and phrases*

"confession"

15–354 Section 82(1) (interpretation—Pt VIII) (*ante*, § 9–84), provides:

"'confession' includes any statement wholly or partly adverse to the person who made it, whether made to a person in authority or not and whether made in words or otherwise."

A guilty plea (subsequently withdrawn) and an accompanying written basis of plea were both held to be confessions in the context of section 76A of the 1984 Act (*ante*, § 15–353a): *R. v. Johnson*, 171 J.P. 574, CA.

A wholly exculpatory statement is not a confession: *R. v. Z.* [2005] 2 A.C. 467, HL. Where the prosecution seek to rely on such a statement, for example to show inconsistency by the defendant, the evidence cannot be excluded under section 76 but, in appropriate circumstances, it can be excluded under section 78: *ibid.*

15–355 A form completed pursuant to a requirement under the *RTA* 1988, s.172(2) (*post*, § 32–133), but not signed by the accused, is nonetheless admissible as a confession within the meaning of section 82(1) if there is sufficient evidence that he completed it (such as the form being sent to his address and being returned with detailed information relating to him, *e.g.* his name, address and date of birth): *Mawdesley v. Chief Constable of Cheshire Constabulary*; *Yorke v. Same* [2004] 1 W.L.R. 1035, QBD (Owen J.).

"proposes to give in evidence"

15–356 See *R. v. Sat-Bhambra*, *post*, § 15–377 (section 76 ceases to be applicable once the confession has been given in evidence).

"it is represented to the court"

15–357 See *R. v. Liverpool Juvenile Court, ex p. R.* [1988] Q.B. 1, 86 Cr.App.R. 1, CA, *post*, § 15–374.

"oppression"—section 76(2)(a) and (8)

In *R. v. Fulling* [1987] Q.B. 426, 85 Cr.App.R. 136, the Court of Appeal held that "oppression" in section 76(2)(a) was to be given its ordinary dictionary meaning: **15–358**

> "The *Oxford English Dictionary* as its third definition of the word runs as follows: 'exercise of authority or power in a burdensome, harsh, or wrongful manner; unjust or cruel treatment of subjects, inferiors, etc., or the imposition of unreasonable or unjust burdens'" (*per* Lord Lane C.J. at pp. 432, 142).

The court found it hard to envisage any circumstances in which such oppression would not entail some impropriety on the part of the interrogator.

There is no reference in the judgment to section 76(8), which reflects the wording of Article 3 of the ECHR (*post*, § 16–39). The words "the use or threat of violence" in section 76(8) are not further defined in the 1984 Act. But "violence" is broadly defined in the *Public Order Act* 1986, s.8 (*post*, § 29–38).

In *R. v. Mushtaq* [2005] 2 Cr.App.R. 32, HL (see *post*, § 15–385), Lord Carswell used the following definition (taken from a 1968 speech by Lord MacDermott and quoted in *R. v. Prager* [1972] 1 W.L.R. 260, CA, at 266): **15–359**

> "... questioning which by its nature, duration or other circumstances (including the fact of custody) excites hopes (such as the hope of release) or fears, or so affects the mind of the subject that his will crumbles and he speaks when otherwise he would have stayed silent."

For an example of police shouting during interview being held to be oppression, see *R. v. Paris*, 97 Cr.App.R. 99, CA. However, raised police voices are not necessarily oppressive: *R. v. Emmerson*, 92 Cr.App.R. 284, CA; *R. v. Heaton* [1993] Crim.L.R. 593, CA. **15–360**

In *R. v. Parker* [1995] Crim.L.R. 233, CA, it was held that the phrase "exercise of authority in a burdensome, harsh or wrongful manner" (see *Fulling*, *ante*) does not mean that any wrongful breach of the codes amounts to oppression. The court said that it is important to look at the context in which this expression was used in *Fulling*.

Oppression at one interview may taint subsequent interviews: see *Burut v. Public Prosecutor* [1995] 2 A.C. 579, PC.

"in consequence of anything said or done"

As to the correct judicial approach to section 76(2)(b), see *post*, § 15–384. **15–361**

The words "said or done" in section 76(2) do not include anything said or done by the person making the confession; it is clear from the section's wording, and the words "in consequence", that a causal link has to be shown between what is said and done and the confession; so "anything said or done" is limited to something external to the person making the confession and to something which is likely to have some influence on him: *R. v. Goldenberg*, 88 Cr.App.R. 285, CA; *R. v. Crampton*, 92 Cr.App.R. 369, CA (doubtful whether mere holding of interview with addict in withdrawal can be something "said or done" within s.76(2)(b)); and *R. v. Wahab* [2003] 1 Cr.App.R. 15, CA (appellant instructed his solicitor to approach police as to whether convenient arrangement possible in relation to his relatives in custody; police made no promises; *held*, subsequent confession admissible because, when instructions given, appellant was uninfluenced by anything said or done by anybody else, and everything thereafter originated from himself).

Although section 76(2) will usually involve considering what the police had said or done, this is not necessarily so: *R. v. M.* [2000] 8 *Archbold News* 2, CA, where the defendant's legal representative's interjections during interview rendered the subsequent confession unreliable. But proper advice from a solicitor will rarely provide a basis for excluding a confession under section 76(2): *Wahab*, *ante*. **15–362**

Nor does section 76(2) necessarily require wrongdoing by the police: *R. v. Walker* [1998] Crim.L.R. 211, CA (police conducting interview shortly after, unknown to them, mentally unstable defendant had smoked crack (see also *post*, § 15–368)).

"circumstances existing at the time"

"Circumstances existing at the time" within the meaning of section 76(2)(b) include **15–363** the defendant's mental state, which should be assessed with the help of medical evidence rather than the judge's own view of the defendant's performance in interview; such medical evidence is also relevant as to whether the prosecution have proved that the confession was not made as a result of what was said or done: *R. v. Everett* [1988] Crim.L.R. 826, CA; *R. v. Silcott, Braithwaite and Raghip*, *The Times*, December 9, 1991, CA.

"likely ... to render unreliable any confession which might be made by him in consequence thereof"

15–364 These words from section 76(2)(b) create an objective test, in a sense hypothetical, since they relate not to the confession but to any confession: *R. v. Barry*, 95 Cr.App.R. 384, CA (see also *post*, § 15–384). However, the reference to "any" confession does not mean that the subject matter or nature of the confession can be disregarded; "any" means "any such" or "such a" confession as the defendant made: *Re Proulx*; *R. v. Bow Street Magistrates' Court, ex p. Proulx* [2001] 1 All E.R. 57, DC.

"Unreliable" means "cannot be relied upon as being the truth": *R. v. Crampton*, *ante*, § 15–361 (at p. 372). The question of reliability is always fact specific, and, in particular, defendant specific: *R. v. Wahab*, *ante*, § 15–361.

15–365 The truth of the confession is immaterial. If the judge concludes that what was said and done was likely to render any resulting confession unreliable and the prosecution fail to prove that the confession was not obtained in consequence thereof, he has no discretion: *R. v. Kenny* [1994] Crim.L.R. 284, CA; *R. v. Cox* [1991] Crim.L.R. 276, CA (judge should have excluded confession under section 76 even though mentally handicapped defendant repeated it in the *voire dire*); and *R. v. Blackburn* [2005] 2 Cr.App.R. 30, CA. For an example of a case where a judge properly admitted an interview notwithstanding his conclusion that a police officer's remark was likely to induce an unreliable confession, see *R. v. Weeks* [1995] Crim.L.R. 52, CA (where, despite the police officer's remark, an astute and experienced defendant had continued to deny many allegations made against him).

(c) *Codes of practice*

15–366 A failure to comply with Code C may lead directly or indirectly to the exclusion of evidence under section 76. The breach may itself be that which renders the confession unreliable, as in the case of a failure to caution (as in *R. v. Doolan* [1988] Crim.L.R. 747, CA); or of an improper denial of access to a solicitor (*R. v. McGovern*, 92 Cr.App.R. 228, CA; *R. v. Chung*, 92 Cr.App.R. 314, CA). Alternatively, a breach of the "anti-verballing" provisions (*post*, §§ 15–501 *et seq.*), such as a failure to record an interview, may prevent the judge from being sure that the confession was not induced as alleged by the accused: see the extract from the judgment of Lord Lane C.J. in *R. v. Delaney*, 88 Cr.App.R. 338, CA, quoted at § 15–506, *post*.

(d) *The "fruit of the poisoned tree"*

15–367 Under the law prior to the *PACE Act* 1984, evidence of facts discovered as a result of an inadmissible confession could be given but without calling in aid any part of the confession from which they may have been derived: *R. v. Warwickshall* (1783) 1 Leach 298; *R. v. Berriman* (1854) 6 Cox 388. The admissibility of facts discovered as a result of an inadmissible confession is now covered by section 76(4)–(6) of the 1984 Act (*ante*, § 15–353). Section 76(4) retains the law as established in *Warwickshall* and *Berriman*, *ante*. In *Lam Chi-Ming v. R.* [1991] 2 A.C. 212, PC, the trial judge having ruled the three defendants' confessions inadmissible, it was held to be wrong to have allowed in evidence a subsequent video recording of the defendants directing the police to the water front and making gestures indicating throwing the knife into the water, and also to have allowed police evidence describing those actions which resulted in the recovery of the murder weapon in the sea at that place. The Privy Council observed that the evidence would have been inadmissible in English law by reason of section 76(4) to (6) of the 1984 Act. See also, *Timothy v. R.* [2000] 1 W.L.R. 485, PC.

(e) *Mentally handicapped persons*

15–368 A defendant's mental condition is one of the factors to be taken into account in deciding if the confession is unreliable; nothing in the authorities limits or defines the particular form of mental or psychological condition or disorder: *R. v. Walker* [1998] Crim.L.R. 211, CA (*ante*, § 15–362). The disorder must not only be of a type which might render a confession unreliable, but there must also be a significant deviation from the norm shown; and there must be a history pre-dating making of admissions which is not based solely on a history given by the subject and which points to or explains the abnormality or abnormalities: *R. v. O'Brien* [2000] Crim.L.R. 676, CA. As to the admissibility of psychiatric evidence, see *ante*, §§ 4–326 *et seq.*

Submission of no case

In *R. v. Mackenzie*, 96 Cr.App.R. 98, CA, it was held that a judge should withdraw **15–369** the case from the jury where the following three conditions apply at any stage of the case: (a) the prosecution case depends wholly upon confessions; (b) the defendant suffers from a significant degree of mental handicap; and (c) the confessions are unconvincing to a point where a jury properly directed could not properly convict upon them. Lord Taylor C.J. gave as examples of unconvincing confessions those which lack incriminating details to be expected of a guilty and willing confessor, or which are inconsistent with other evidence, or which are otherwise inherently improbable. The principles in *Mackenzie* were applied in *R. v. Campbell* and *R. v. Bailey* (*post*, §§ 15–372 *et seq.*); and *R. v. Wood* [1994] Crim.L.R. 222, CA.

Police and Criminal Evidence Act 1984, s.77

Confessions by mentally handicapped persons

77.—(1) Without prejudice to the general duty of the court at a trial on indictment with a **15–370** jury to direct the jury on any matter on which it appears to the court appropriate to do so, where at such a trial—

(a) the case against the accused depends wholly or substantially on a confession by him; and

(b) the court is satisfied—

(i) that he is mentally handicapped; and

(ii) that the confession was not made in the presence of an independent person,

the court shall warn the jury that there is special need for caution before convicting the accused in reliance on the confession, and shall explain that the need arises because of the circumstances mentioned in paragraphs (a) and (b) above.

(2) In any case where at the summary trial of a person for an offence it appears to the court that a warning under subsection (1) above would be required if the trial were on indictment with a jury, the court shall treat the case as one in which there is a special need for caution before convicting the accused on his confession.

(2A) In any case where at the trial on indictment without a jury of a person for an offence it appears to the court that a warning under subsection (1) above would be required if the trial were with a jury, the court shall treat the case as one in which there is a special need for caution before convicting the accused on his confession.

(3) In this section—

"independent person" does not include a police officer or a person employed for, or engaged on, police purposes;

"mentally handicapped," in relation to a person, means that he is in a state of arrested or incomplete development of mind which includes significant impairment of intelligence and social functioning; and

"police purposes" has the meaning assigned to it by section 101(2) of the *Police Act* 1996.

[This section is printed as amended by the *Police Act* 1996, s.103 and Sched. 7, para. 38; and the *CJA* 2003, s.331, and Sched. 36, para. 48.]

For the meaning of "confession", see *ante*, § 15–354. For modification of subs. (3) in **15–371** relation to investigations by officers of Revenue and Customs of offences relating to assigned matters, see *ante*, § 15–43.

The provisions for mentally disordered and otherwise mentally vulnerable people in Code C are summarised at Annex E (Appendix A–105 *et seq.*). For authorities on mental handicap and Code C, see *post*, § 15–490. For cases on section 77, see *R. v.*

Lamont [1989] Crim.L.R. 813, CA (conviction quashed because judge had failed to give a warning under section 77); *R. v. Moss*, 91 Cr.App.R. 371, CA; and *R. v. Ham* (1995) 36 B.M.L.R. 169, CA (*post*, § 15–490).

15–372 In *R. v. Campbell* [1995] 1 Cr.App.R. 522, CA, it was held that the test for warning the jury under section 77(1), of the special need for caution in relation to a confession made by a mentally handicapped person in the absence of an appropriate adult, is whether the case for the Crown is substantially less strong without the confession. The court gave the following guidance for cases where the warning should be given. Although no specific wording need be used, the judge would be wise to use the phrase "special need for caution". He should also explain why a confession from a mentally handicapped person might be unreliable, and that is best done by indicating that persons who are mentally handicapped or disordered might, without wishing to do so, provide information which is unreliable, misleading or self-incriminating. The explanation should be tailored to the particular evidence in the case, *e.g.* if there is evidence that the accused is suggestible, or prone to acquiesce, comply, or give in to pressure. The judge should go on to explain that the appropriate adult's function is designed to minimise the risk of the accused giving unreliable information by seeing that the interview is conducted properly and fairly and facilitating, if need be, communication between the police and the suspect.

Campbell was applied in *R. v. Bailey* [1995] 2 Cr.App.R. 262, CA, where further guidance was given as to the direction to be given to the jury in cases of confessions by persons who are significantly mentally handicapped and in which the Crown would not have a case in the absence of those confessions:

> "What is required of a judge in a summing up in such cases … is a full and proper statement of the mentally handicapped defendant's case against the confessions being accepted by the jury as true and accurate. Because the defendant is significantly mentally handicapped, this duty will include a duty to see that points made on the defendant's behalf and other points which appear to the judge to be appropriate to his defence that the confessions are unreliable or untrue, are placed before the jury. That, in our view, is consistent with the general duty referred to at the start of section 77 of the court at trial on indictment to direct the jury on any matter on which it appears to the court appropriate to do so and with the observations of Lord Ackner in *R. v. Spencer and Smails* [1987] A.C. 128, 141(A) to 142(H). We would draw attention particularly to this observation by his Lordship at p.142(H): 'The overriding rule is that he [the trial judge] must put the defence case fairly and adequately'" (*per* Roch L.J. at p. 275).

In *R. v. Qayyum* [2007] Crim.L.R. 160, CA, it was held that the absence of a formal warning did not make a conviction unsafe where the judge had directed the jury several times about the importance of taking into account the defendant's linguistic and intellectual difficulties (English not his first language, I.Q. of 67).

15–373 In *Bailey*, *ante*, it was held that confessions made to friends are not made "in the presence of an independent person" within section 77, because, for the purposes of the section, such a person has to be independent of the person to whom the confession is made. The independent person is required because the mentally handicapped person might have difficulty in recalling what he or she said and independent evidence as to the emotional and mental state of the mentally handicapped person might be desirable. Further, an independent person might, if the mentally handicapped person is or becomes obviously unfit to speak, give sensible advice to that person.

A solicitor present at a police station in a professional capacity can be an "independent person" for the purposes of section 77, even though he is excluded from the definition of "appropriate adult" in Code C (Note C:1F, Appendix A–43): *R. v. Lewis (M.)* [1996] Crim.L.R. 260, CA.

In establishing whether a defendant was mentally handicapped within the meaning of section 77(3), it is not appropriate to take intelligence quotients from one case (such as *R. v. Silcott, Braithwaite and Raghip*, *ante*, § 15–213) and apply them slavishly to another, because each case must be looked at on its own facts: *R. v. Kenny* [1994] Crim.L.R. 284, CA. See also *ante*, § 15–365.

(2) Challenging a confession

(a) *Making the objection*

15–374 A challenge to the admissibility of a confession under section 76 of the *PACE Act*

1984 is made by representation to the court (s.76(2)) that the confession was or may have been obtained either:

(a) by oppression (s.76(2)(a)), or

(b) in consequence of anything said or done which was likely, in the circumstances existing at the time, to render unreliable any confession which might be made by him in consequence thereof (s.76(2)(b)).

In *R. v. Liverpool Juvenile Court, ex p. R.* [1988] Q.B. 1, 86 Cr.App.R. 1, CA, Russell L.J. said at pp. 10–11, 6–7:

> "For the avoidance of doubt, I consider that 'representation' is not the same as, nor does it include, cross-examination. Thus the court is not required to embark upon, nor is the defence bound to proceed upon, a *voire dire* merely because of a suggestion in cross-examination that the alleged confession was obtained improperly."

The trial judge may of his own motion require the prosecution to prove that the confession was not obtained in breach of section 76(2)(a) or (b): s.76(3).

(b) *Making the objection: pre-PACE Act 1984*

In *Adjodha v. The State* [1982] A.C. 204, PC, Lord Bridge (at p. 223) indicated the normal procedure to be followed where the admissibility of a confession is to be challenged. The confession would not be opened to the jury and the trial judge would determine its admissibility on a *voire dire*. The defence could, however, opt for the tactic of allowing the jury to hear the evidence relating to the confession. At the end of the prosecution case the defence could apply to the judge to tell the jury to disregard the confession or the judge could do this of his own initiative if he doubted the "voluntariness" of the confession (the pre-*PACE Act* 1984 test). **15–375**

(c) *Making the objection: under the PACE Act*

The initial reaction to section 76 of the 1984 Act was to continue to adopt the procedure outlined in *Ajodha, ante*, namely for the defence to choose whether to make the objection to the admissibility of a confession either in a trial-within-a-trial in the absence of the jury (*post*, § 15–380) or with the evidence heard only in front of the jury. Support for this approach appears to have come from the decision in *R. v. Liverpool Juvenile Court, ex p. R.* [1988] Q.B. 1, 86 Cr.App.R. 1 (*post*, § 15–396). **15–376**

In *R. v. Sat-Bhambra*, 88 Cr.App.R. 55, CA, however, a decision in which no reference is made to *Ajodha* or *R. v. Liverpool Juvenile Court, ex p. R., ante*, Lord Lane C.J. did not see the defendant's position as one of choice. If objection to the admissibility of a confession was to be taken under section 76, the time to take the objection was before the confession was given in evidence. If the confession was admitted, whether after objection or not, and evidence subsequently emerged during the trial which called into question the "admissibility" of the confession, the judge was precluded from re-opening the section 76 issue, but he was not powerless. He could direct the jury to disregard the statement; he could direct their attention to the matters which might affect the weight to be attached to the confession; or, if he thought the matter could not be resolved by a suitable direction to the jury, he could discharge the jury. See, to similar effect, *R. v. Davis* [1990] Crim.L.R. 860, CA (*post*, § 15–380). **15–377**

Objection to the admissibility of the evidence should normally be taken immediately prior to the moment when the prosecution would begin to lead the evidence. Sometimes, and it is a matter entirely for the discretion of the judge, it will be more convenient to hear argument as to admissibility at an earlier stage of the trial, for example prior to the opening to the jury: see *R. v. Hammond*, 28 Cr.App.R. 84, 85–86, CCA; *R. v. Murray*, 34 Cr.App.R. 203 at 206, CCA. This is done when prosecuting counsel would be unable otherwise to explain the case for the Crown in opening. The effect of sections 39 and 40 of the *CPIA* 1996 (*ante*, §§ 4–84o *et seq.*) is that a judge may determine the admissibility of evidence at a pre-trial hearing. **15–378**

No discussion of an intended objection must take place in front of the jury: *Mitchell v. R.* [1998] A.C. 695, PC. **15–379**

There is nothing to stop the defence avoiding a trial-within-a-trial and by-passing the judge altogether by simply arguing the various points in front of the jury.

(d) *The voire dire*

15–380 At the appropriate time, usually just before the challenged evidence is due to be given, the judge conducts a trial on the *voire dire* to decide the question of admissibility in the absence of the jury. Although pre-*PACE Act* 1984 cases suggested that a hearing in the absence of the jury should only take place at the request or with the consent of the defence (see *Ajodha v. The State*, *ante*, and *R. v. Anderson*, 21 Cr.App.R. 178, CCA), the modern position is otherwise. The defence are not entitled to hold the *voire dire* in the jury's presence: *R. v. Davis* [1990] Crim.L.R. 860, CA.

When the *voire dire* has been completed, the judge should give no explanation of the outcome thereof to the jury: *Mitchell v. R.*, *ante*.

(e) *Evidence*

15–381 The prosecution call their evidence first in the usual way, unless the application is to be argued on the papers alone. The defendant must put his case to the prosecution witnesses called on the *voire dire*: *R. v. Davis*, *ante*. There is no requirement for the defence to tell the judge on the *voire dire* what the defendant's response would be if the evidence were admitted: *R. v. Keenan* [1990] 2 Q.B. 54 at 69; 90 Cr.App.R. 1 at 12, CA (see also *post*, § 15–506). The defendant does not have to give evidence: *Davis*, *ante*; but in practice the defendant often does: see *Wong Kam-Ming v. R.* [1980] A.C. 247, PC; *R. v. Brophy* [1982] A.C. 476, HL, *post*. The failure of the defendant to give evidence may leave the trial judge with a one-sided picture, although calling the defendant may, too, have disastrous consequences for the defence submission (as in *R. v. Alladice*, 87 Cr.App.R. 380, CA). Where, however, there are clear breaches of the codes of practice, the evidence of the defendant may add little weight to an attack upon the confession evidence: see, for example, *R. v. Walsh*, 91 Cr.App.R. 161, CA. For a full discussion of these points, see the reference to *Keenan* at § 15–506, *post*. This approach, it is submitted, envisages that it will be more common for challenges to confession evidence to be based upon a scrutiny of the police case rather than defence evidence. The scrutiny will be made either on the papers (the custody record and the witness statements) or from live evidence, particularly evidence which the prosecution may wish to call in order to justify what appears to be a prima facie breach (see *Keenan*, at pp. 64, 8).

(f) *Cross-examination of the defendant*

15–382 If the defendant gives evidence on the *voire dire* he may be cross-examined. He may not be cross-examined as to the truth of the confession: *Wong Kam-Ming v. R.* [1980] A.C. 247, PC; *R. v. Liverpool Juvenile Court, ex p. R.*, *ante*; *R. v. Davis*, *ante*.

The majority opinion in *Wong Kam-Ming*, delivered by Lord Edmund-Davies, appears to support the following propositions.

(a) During the cross-examination of an accused on the *voire dire* as to the admissibility of his challenged statement, questions may not be put as to the truth of the challenged statement.

(b) The prosecution is not permitted to lead, as part of its case, evidence of what the accused said on the *voire dire*, whether the judge has excluded or admitted the challenged statement.

(c) If the judge has admitted the challenged statement (but not if he has excluded it), *and* if the accused subsequently gives evidence in the main trial before the jury, the accused may be cross-examined by prosecuting counsel as to discrepancies between his present evidence and what he said on the *voire dire*, and *semble*, if he does not admit saying what he said on the *voire dire*, proof of what he said may be given in rebuttal, provided always that any relevant statutory provisions, *e.g.* Lord Denman's Act, are strictly complied with, and subject to the right of the judge to exclude such cross-examination and evidence as unfair or oppressive to the accused.

15–383 In *R. v. Brophy* [1982] A.C. 476, HL, it was held that where an accused makes an admission in the course of a *voire dire* and the confession is subsequently ruled inadmissible, then that admission cannot be introduced by the prosecution providing it was relevant to an issue on the *voire dire*.

It is open to question whether *Wong Kam-Ming* and *Brophy* have survived the introduction of section 76, which seems to allow the admission of judicial confessions at whatever stage they have been made. Section 78 or 82(3) could, of course, be employed to achieve the same position as existed at common law prior to the 1984 Act.

(g) *The judge decides*

In *R. v. Barry*, 95 Cr.App.R. 384, CA, it was said that section 76(2)(b) requires the judge to adopt a three-step process: (1) identifying what was said or done, *i.e.* taking into account everything said and done by the police; (2) asking whether what was said and done was likely in the circumstances to render unreliable a confession made in consequence, the test being objective; and (3) asking whether the prosecution have proved beyond reasonable doubt that the particular confession was not obtained in consequence of the thing said or done. The matter should be approached in a common sense way rather than on any refined analysis of causation concepts: *ibid.*, and see *R. v. Rennie*, 74 Cr.App.R. 207, CA. **15–384**

(h) *After the voire dire*

If the challenge to the admissibility of the confession succeeds, the trial continues without the evidence of the confession. If the challenge fails, the prosecution evidence of the confession and the circumstances in which it was obtained will be given in the presence of the jury. The defence are entitled to cross-examine the witnesses who gave evidence on the *voire dire*: *R. v. Murray* [1951] 1 K.B. 391, 34 Cr.App.R. 203, CCA. **15–385**

The jury must consider the probative value and effect of the evidence of the confession. Where the issues explored in the trial-within-a-trial are explored again in front of the jury, the trial judge should give appropriate directions to the jury. The logic of section 76(2) requires that they should be directed that, if they consider that a confession was, or may have been, obtained by oppression or in consequence of anything said or done which was likely to render it unreliable, they should disregard it: *R. v. Mushtaq* [2005] 2 Cr.App.R. 32, HL. If a judge is not satisfied beyond reasonable doubt that a confession was not obtained by oppression or any other improper means it is excluded as Parliament considers that in those circumstances it should not play any part in the jury's verdict; but it would fly in the face of such a policy to say that a jury are entitled to rely on a confession even though, as the ultimate arbiters of all matters of fact, they properly consider that it was, or may have been, obtained by oppression or any other improper means: *ibid.* Where the only real dispute is whether the defendant's account of the interview is true, it may well be enough for the judge to indicate that, if the jury consider that the confession was, or may have been, obtained in the way described by the defendant, they must disregard it (*ibid.*, at [55]).

(i) *Limited use of inadmissible confession*

A distinction has to be drawn between use by the prosecution and use by a co-defendant. **15–386**

In the case of the prosecution, there should be no cross-examination on an inadmissible confession, of which no more should be heard: *R. v. Treacy*, 30 Cr.App.R. 93, CCA. Information derived from such a confession may be used, provided that it is not revealed that it is derived from a statement of the defendant: *R. v. Rice* [1963] 1 Q.B. 857 at 869, 47 Cr.App.R. 79 at 86, CCA (and see section 76(4) and (5), *ante*, § 15–353).

A confession which is inadmissible on behalf of the prosecution may nonetheless be admissible on behalf of a co-defendant under section 76A of the 1984 Act (see *ante*, § 15–353a), which appears to have overtaken cases such as *R. v. Myers* [1998] A.C. 124, HL. Where a confession is admitted pursuant to section 76A, it seems that everything said in it is evidence: see the *CJA* 2003, s.114(1)(a), *ante*, § 11–3 (section 76A having been inserted into the 1984 Act by the *CJA* 2003, s.128(1)). **15–387**

The power to order separate trials may have to be used more frequently in order to give effect to the competing rights of co-defendants to a fair trial under Article 6 of the

ECHR (*post*, § 16–57). See also *R. v. O'Boyle*, 92 Cr.App.R. 202, CA, a "wholly exceptional, if not unique" case, in which the trial judge wrongly refused an application for separate trials when a co-defendant sought to cross-examine the appellant on a confession allegedly made by the appellant in the United States and which the trial judge had ruled inadmissible.

(j) *Use of defendant's confession against a co-defendant*

General rule

15–388 It is a fundamental rule that statements made by one defendant, either to the police or to others (other than statements, whether in the presence or absence of a co-defendant, made in the course and pursuance of a joint criminal enterprise to which the co-defendant was a party: see *post*, §§ 33–65 *et seq.*), are not evidence against a co-defendant unless the co-defendant either expressly or by implication adopts the statements and thereby makes them his own: see generally *R. v. Rudd*, 32 Cr.App.R. 138, CCA; *R. v. Gunewardene* [1951] 2 K.B. 600, 35 Cr.App.R. 80, CCA; *R. v. Rhodes*, 44 Cr.App.R. 23, CCA. But the rule may have to be qualified in the light of *R. v. Hayter*, *ante*, § 9–85.

15–389 Once a defendant goes into the witness-box and gives evidence in the course of a joint trial, then what he says becomes evidence for all the purposes of the case including the purpose of being evidence against his co-defendant: *R. v. Rudd*, *ante*. As to directing the jury in relation to the evidence of one defendant incriminating another, see *ante*, § 4–404n.

The practice of cross-examining one defendant on another defendant's interview is impermissible, although this is not to say that it would never be appropriate to ask questions about what appeared in a co-defendant's interview: *R. v. Gray and Evans* [1998] Crim.L.R. 570, CA.

Mitigation of general rule

15–390 Notwithstanding the general rule referred to *ante*, § 15–388, and the judge's duty to direct the jury upon it, in some cases further steps are taken to minimise the highly prejudicial effect which a defendant's statement may have upon the case of a co-defendant. One possibility is to edit the statement so as to remove passages which incriminate the co-defendant: see *R. v. Gunewardene* [1951] 2 K.B. 600, 35 Cr.App.R. 80, CCA (*per* Lord Goddard C.J. at pp. 610–611, 91–92); *R. v. Jefferson*, 99 Cr.App.R. 13, CA; or to substitute letters of the alphabet for the names of other persons named in the statement, as was done in *R. v. Silcott* [1987] Crim.L.R. 765, CCC (Hodgson J.). However, the judge has no discretion to edit a statement in either of these ways if the maker of the statement objects; if the prosecution seek to put the statement in against him, he has a right to have the whole of the statement put in evidence: *Lobban v. R.* [1995] 2 Cr.App.R. 573, PC. See also *ante*, §§ 4–280 *et seq.*

15–391 As to the prejudicial nature of a co-defendant's statement founding the basis of an application for separate trials, see *ante*, §§ 1–178 *et seq.*

(k) *Editing of defendant's statement to exclude prejudicial material*

15–392 It has been recognised that it is permissible to edit a defendant's statement to exclude prejudicial or irrelevant material. Any dispute can be adjudicated upon by the trial judge: *R. v. Weaver and Weaver* [1968] 1 Q.B. 353, 51 Cr.App.R. 52, CA; *R. v. Knight and Thompson*, 31 Cr.App.R. 52, CCA.

(l) *Exhibiting contemporaneous notes of interviews*

Notes signed by the accused

15–393 Contemporaneous notes of an interview which have been signed by the accused may go before the jury as an exhibit: *R. v. Todd*, 72 Cr.App.R. 299, CA. Although police officers' notebooks (*ante*, § 8–87) are now more commonly signed by suspects, as required by Code C in certain circumstances (see, in particular, C:11.13, Appendix A–74), it is still not common practice to have the notebook copied or even shown to the jury unless there is some good reason for them to see the entry.

Notes not signed by the accused

In the era of tape recorded interviews the importance of exhibiting notes of interview has diminished. Such notes, however, will still arise in relation to interviews conducted outside the police station. Ordinarily, such documents are no more than memory-refreshing documents which cannot be exhibited: *R. v. Fenlon*, 71 Cr.App.R. 307, CA; *R. v. Dillon*, 85 Cr.App.R. 27, CA. In *Fenlon*, the court left open the question whether notes could be exhibited where there had been conduct by the defendant which may be said to be the equivalent of signing them (*e.g.* reading them, or having them read over, and then saying they are correct). In *R. v. Sekhon*, 85 Cr.App.R. 19, the Court of Appeal, considered both *Fenlon* and *Dillon*. Its conclusion was that notes could be exhibited in a wider range of circumstances than is suggested by those authorities. For the details of this decision, see *ante*, § 8–87. It should be noted that the court in *Sekhon* was actually concerned with observation logs, and, thus, what was said in relation to notes of interview of a defendant may be *obiter*. **15–394**

(m) *Reconsideration of the judge's ruling*

See *R. v. Sat-Bhambra*, 88 Cr.App.R. 55, CA, *ante*, § 15–377. **15–395**

(n) *Proceedings before justices*

Summary trial

In *R. v. Liverpool Juvenile Court, ex p. R.* [1988] Q.B. 1, 86 Cr.App.R. 1, DC, it was held that where a confession's admissibility was challenged under section 76 during summary proceedings, the magistrates were bound by section 76(2) to hold a trial-within-a-trial. The question of the admissibility of a confession should normally be raised on a *voire dire* before the end of the prosecution case, but the defendant is at liberty to raise the admissibility or weight of the confession at any subsequent stage of the trial (but see *ante*, §§ 15–376 *et seq.*). If there is a trial-within-a-trial, the defendant may give evidence confined to the question of admissibility and the justices will not be concerned with the truth of the confession. Whatever procedure is adopted, it should never be necessary to call the prosecution evidence relating to the obtaining of a confession twice: *ibid.* **15–396**

If there is an alternative submission under section 78 of the 1984 Act, this should be examined on the same *voire dire*: *Halawa v. Federation Against Copyright Theft* [1995] 1 Cr.App.R. 21, DC (*post*, § 15–460). **15–397**

Committal proceedings

As amended by the *CPIA* 1996, section 76 has no application to committal proceedings (*ante*, §§ 15–352, 15–353). **15–398**

(3) Confession based on hearsay

"A voluntary statement made by an accused is admissible as a 'confession'. He can confess to his own acts, knowledge or intentions, but he cannot 'confess' as to the acts of other persons which he has not seen and of which he can only have knowledge by hearsay": *Surujpaul v. R.*, 42 Cr.App.R. 266 at 273, PC. **15–399**

It has been held in a number of drugs cases that an admission by the accused that the substance in his possession is a controlled drug may be prima facie evidence of that fact provided there is sufficient evidence of his knowledge of the nature of the substance in his possession. Such an informal opinion by an accused must come from prior knowledge or experience: *post*, §§ 27–23, 27–24.

As to the distinction between proof that goods are stolen and proof of knowledge for the purposes of the *Theft Act* 1968, s.22, when the evidence as to each consists entirely of the accused's admissions, see *post*, § 21–295.

(4) Partial admissions and self-serving statements

15–400 It is important to distinguish between statements which are entirely self-serving and those which are only partly adverse to the accused. It is also important to distinguish between the issues of admissibility and evidential status if admitted. In recent years there has developed a substantial body of case law on this topic.

(a) *Partial admissions (mixed statements)*

15–401 It is submitted that the combination of the provisions of the *PACE Act* 1984 and the decisions of the House of Lords in *R. v. Sharp (C.)*, 86 Cr.App.R. 274, and *R. v. Aziz* [1996] 1 A.C. 41, has put the law on this subject beyond doubt. Section 76 (*ante*, § 15–352) provides for the admissibility of confessions. Section 82(1) defines "confession" as including "any statement wholly or partly adverse to the person who made it". Accordingly, a partial admission is admissible in evidence subject to the conditions stipulated in section 76.

The plain intention of the Act is that where a partly adverse statement is admitted in evidence pursuant to the Act, the tribunal of fact is entitled to consider the whole statement: both the incriminating parts and the excuses must be considered in determining where the truth lies: *R. v. Aziz*, *ante* (at p. 50).

In *Sharp*, *ante*, the House of Lords were concerned with the common law. Their Lordships held that it was important that a jury should be directed in a way that they could understand and follow; that they could not fairly evaluate the facts in an admission unless they could evaluate the facts in the excuse or explanation accompanying it; and that they should be directed that the whole of a "mixed" statement was to be taken into consideration as evidence in deciding where the truth lay.

15–402 Their Lordships, in both *Sharp* and *Aziz*, specifically approved the following passage in the judgment of Lord Lane C.J. in *R. v. Duncan*, 73 Cr.App.R. 359 at 365:

> "Where a 'mixed' statement is under consideration by the jury in a case where the defendant has not given evidence, it seems to us that the simplest, and therefore, the method most likely to produce a just result, is for the jury to be told that the whole statement, both the incriminating parts and the excuses or explanations, must be considered by them in deciding where the truth lies. It is ... not helpful to try to explain to the jury that the exculpatory parts of the statement are something less than evidence of the facts they state. Equally, where appropriate, as it usually will be, the judge may, and should, point out that the incriminating parts are likely to be true (otherwise why say them?), whereas the excuses do not have the same weight. Nor is there any reason why, again where appropriate, the judge should not comment in relation to the exculpatory remarks upon the election of the accused not to give evidence."

15–403 In *R. v. Garrod* [1997] Crim.L.R. 445, the Court of Appeal stated that where a statement contained an admission of fact which was significant to any issue in the case, meaning capable of adding some degree of weight to the prosecution case on an issue which was relevant to guilt, the statement must be regarded as "mixed". This must be applied by reference to what happens at trial and can therefore only be finally resolved at the close of the evidence; the rule that the exculpatory parts of a mixed statement are evidence of the facts contained therein is based on considerations of fairness to the defendant and simplicity for the jury, and if the prosecution place significant reliance on the incriminating parts of an interview it will be more likely that the jury should be told that the parts which explain or excuse those incriminating parts are also evidence; the admission of an ingredient of the offence will often constitute a significant admission, but not always (*e.g.* admitting in a murder trial that the victim is dead is unlikely to be significant), and likewise, in the absence of an admission of such an ingredient, the statement is less likely to be mixed: *R. v. Papworth and Doyle* [2008] 1 Cr.App.R. 36, CA.

In *Western v. DPP* [1997] 1 Cr.App.R. 474, DC, it was held that whether a statement was mixed or not was not determined by the purpose for which the prosecution sought to use it but upon examination of the statement itself.

(b) *Wholly self-serving statements*

15–404 As to a wholly exculpatory statement not being a confession, see *R. v. Z.* [2005] 2 A.C. 467, HL, *ante*, § 15–354.

In *R. v. Pearce*, 69 Cr.App.R. 365, CA (following *R. v. Storey*, 52 Cr.App.R. 334, CA, and *R. v. Donaldson*, 64 Cr.App.R. 59, CA), the principles were summarised as follows:

"(1) A statement which contains an admission is always admissible as a declaration against interest and is evidence of the facts admitted. With this exception a statement made by an accused is never evidence of the facts in the statement.

(2)(a) A statement that is not an admission is admissible to show the attitude of the accused at the time when he made it. This, however, is not to be limited to a statement made on the first encounter with the police. The reference in *R. v. Storey* to the reaction of the accused 'when first taxed' should not be read as circumscribing the limits of admissibility. The longer the time that has elapsed after the first encounter the less the weight which will be attached to the denial. The judge is able to direct the jury about the value of such statements. (b) [*Mixed statements*.] (c) The prosecution may wish to draw attention to inconsistent denials. A denial does not become an admission because it is inconsistent with another denial. There must be many cases, however, where convictions have resulted from such inconsistencies between two denials.

(3) Although in practice, most statements are given in evidence even when they are largely self serving, there may be a rare occasion when an accused produces a carefully prepared written statement to the police, with a view to its being made part of the prosecution evidence. The trial judge would plainly exclude such a statement as inadmissible" (pp. 369–370).

In *R. v. Tooke*, 90 Cr.App.R. 417, CA, further consideration was given to *principle (2)(a), ante*: **15–405**

"... the test which should be applied is partly that of spontaneity, partly that of relevance and partly that of asking whether the statement which is sought to be admitted adds any weight to the other testimony which has been given in the case. Of course it is not an easy task for the judge to decide in his discretion where the dividing line lies."

For an example of a statement falling within *principle (3), ante*, see *R. v. Newsome*, 71 Cr.App.R. 325, CA (accused's dictated statement to solicitor made 13 hours after the alleged offence and after several interviews held to be self-serving). **15–406**

If the prosecution seek to rely on an adverse inference from silence under sections 34, 36 or 37 of the *CJPOA* 1994 (*post*, §§ 15–414 *et seq.*), it would seem that the defendant is entitled to put in a statement falling within *principle 3*, as tending to rebut the suggestion of recent invention. It would then be for the jury to decide how much weight to attach to the initial silence, on the one hand, and to the statement, on the other. For the principles governing the admission of previous consistent statements for the purpose of rebutting an allegation of recent invention, see *ante*, §§ 8–108 *et seq.*; and see also section 120(2) of the *CJA* 2003 (*ante*, § 11–34). **15–407**

(c) *Submission of no case*

It follows that the judge cannot take into account self-serving statements in considering a submission of no case (unless, it is submitted, the question of an adverse inference from silence arises (*ante*)). Some of the authorities cited above arise out of this point: see particularly *R. v. Storey, ante*. See, however, *R. v. Hamand*, 82 Cr.App.R. 65, CA, in which a conviction was quashed where the trial judge had ruled at the end of the prosecution's evidence that a "mixed statement" made to the police was not "evidence" that the injuries which the defendant admitted inflicting upon another were inflicted in the course of self-defence. **15–408**

B. ACCUSATIONS MADE IN THE PRESENCE OF THE DEFENDANT

(1) Common law

A statement made in the presence of a defendant, accusing him of a crime, upon an occasion which may be expected reasonably to call for some explanation or denial from him, is not evidence against him of the facts stated, save in so far as he accepts the statement so as to make it in effect his own. If he accepts the statement in part only, then to that extent alone does it become his statement. He may accept the statement by word or conduct, action or demeanour, and it is for the jury to determine whether he accepted it in whole or in part. A mere denial does not necessarily render the statement inadmissible. There is no rule of law that evidence cannot be given of an accusation of **15–409** crime and of the behaviour of the defendant on hearing such accusation where that behaviour amounts to a denial of guilt. Although there is no such rule of law, the evidential value of the behaviour of the accused person where he denies the charge is very small either for or against him, and the effect on the minds of the jury of his being publicly or repeatedly charged to his face with the crime may seriously prejudice the fairness of his trial. The judge may, therefore, in most cases rightly exercise his influence in order to prevent such evidence being given where it would have little or no evidential value: *R. v. Christie* [1914] A.C. 545, HL. As to admissibility, the questions for the judge to consider are whether a jury properly directed could conclude that the defendant had in fact adopted the statement in question; if so, whether the matter is of sufficient relevance to justify its introduction in evidence; and whether its admission in evidence would have such an adverse affect on the fairness of the proceedings that it ought to be excluded: *R. v. Osborne*, *The Times*, November 17, 2005, CA.

When the statement is admitted in evidence, the following direction from *R. v. Norton* [1910] 2 K.B. 496, 5 Cr.App.R. 65, CCA, was approved in *Christie*, *ante*:

> "Where [the statement is admitted] we think the following is the proper direction to be given to the jury—that if they come to the conclusion that the defendant had acknowledged the truth of the whole or any part of the facts stated they might take the statement, or so much of it as was acknowledged to be true (but no more) into consideration as evidence in the case generally, not because the statement, standing alone, afforded any evidence of the matter contained in it, but solely because of the defendant's acknowledgment of its truth; but unless they found as a fact that there was such an acknowledgment they ought to disregard the statement altogether" (at pp. 500–501, 75–76).

15–410 Where a defendant is informed by a police officer, who does not caution him, of an allegation made by a third person (*e.g.* a co-defendant), his silence when told of the allegation cannot *per se* amount to an acknowledgment by him of the truth of the allegation within the principle enunciated in *R. v. Christie*, *ante*. The caution merely serves to remind the defendant of a right which he already possesses at common law. The fact that in a particular case he had not been reminded of it was no ground for inferring that his silence was not in exercise of that right: *Hall v. R.*, 55 Cr.App.R. 108, PC, approving *R. v. Whitehead* [1929] 1 K.B. 99, 21 Cr.App.R. 23, CCA, and *R. v. Keeling*, 28 Cr.App.R. 121, CCA; *cf. R. v. Feigenbaum* [1919] 1 K.B. 431, 14 Cr.App.R. 1, CCA (not followed).

Where the defendant's reaction to over half the questions put to him by the police was either to remain silent, shake his head or reply "no comment", the court held that it was proper for the whole "dialogue" to go before the jury. If the defendant has failed to respond to any of the questions it may well be, on the principle in *Hall v. R.*, *ante*, that the evidence of the abortive dialogue should not be admitted: *R. v. Mann*, 56 Cr.App.R. 750, CA. See also *R. v. Raviraj*, 85 Cr.App.R. 93, CA, *post*, § 15–412.

15–411 In *R. v. Chandler*, 63 Cr.App.R. 1, CA, the court declined to apply the principle of *Hall v. R.* when the defendant would not answer some questions when interrogated by a police sergeant in a police station in the presence of his solicitor and prior to caution. It was held that as the solicitor was present the defendant and the police officer were on equal terms. It could be left to the jury to decide whether the defendant's silence amounted to an acceptance of what the police officer had said and, if so, whether guilt could reasonably be inferred from what he had accepted. In *R. v. Murphy and McKinley* [1993] 4 N.I.J.B. 42, NICA, Kelly L.J. described the "contentious part of the judgment in *Chandler*" (*i.e.* that the solicitor's presence put the suspect on even terms with the police officer) as *obiter* (at p. 59) and expressed reluctance to extend the common law any further.

In *Parkes v. R.*, 64 Cr.App.R. 25, PC, the mother of a girl who was found with stab wounds asked the appellant why he had stabbed her. The appellant made no reply, but when the mother threatened to hold him until the police arrived, he drew a knife and tried to stab her. The Board approved the judge's direction that the appellant's silence, coupled with his subsequent conduct, was a matter from which it could be inferred that the appellant accepted the truth of the accusation. They distinguished *Hall v. R.*, applying *Christie v. DPP*, *ante*, and the dictum of Cave J. in *R. v. Mitchell* (1892) 17 Cox C.C. 503 at 508: "Undoubtedly when persons are speaking on even terms, and a charge is made, the accused person ought to reply, and if he does not, it is some evidence to show that he admits the charge to be true."

R. v. Horne [1990] Crim.L.R. 188, CA, appears to have been another "even terms" case. After a fight in a restaurant, T complained of being "glassed" by the defendant. The police found the defendant hiding in the car park. When they brought him back inside the restaurant, T said: "Take that bastard away, he's the one who glassed me," to which the defendant made no reply. The Court of Appeal, relying on *Christie* and *Chandler, ante*, held that in circumstances where some protest or denial might have been expected, a jury were entitled to take account of the fact that an accused had said nothing. **15–412**

Hall v. R., Chandler and *Parkes* were all considered by the Court of Appeal in *R. v. Raviraj, ante*. Stocker L.J. said, in relation to the doctrine of recent possession in allegations of theft and handling (*post*, § 21–319):

> "The doctrine is only a particular aspect of the general proposition that where suspicious circumstances appear to demand an explanation, and no explanation or an entirely incredible explanation is given, the lack of explanation may warrant an inference of guilty knowledge in the defendant. This again is only part of a wider proposition that guilt may be inferred from unreasonable behaviour of a defendant when confronted with facts which seem to accuse" (at p. 103).

However, Stocker L.J.'s above-quoted words did *not* justify drawing an adverse inference at common law from a defendant's refusal to leave his cell to be interviewed: *R. v. Johnson* [2006] Crim.L.R. 253, CA (see also *post*, § 15–416).

In *R. v. Collins and Keep* [2004] 2 Cr.App.R. 11, CA, where the authorities were reviewed, it was held that a co-defendant's lie (given in answer to a single question by a police officer who had stopped the defendants' car) could not be evidence against the appellant where the latter merely had remained silent; this was especially so as the appellant and the police officer were not on equal terms.

The common law position is preserved by section 34(5) of the *CJPOA* 1994 (*post*, § 15–414).

(2) Police and Criminal Evidence Act 1984

Where an accusation of crime is accepted in whole or in part whether by words or conduct, that part which is accepted effectively becomes the statement of the accused person. As such it will fall within the definition of "confession" in section 82(1) of the Act (see *ante*, § 15–354). The issue in such cases is almost invariably one of deciding whether the defendant did indeed adopt the accusation as opposed to why he did. **15–413**

(3) Criminal Justice and Public Order Act 1994

Adverse inferences from a failure to mention facts

Criminal Justice and Public Order Act 1994, s.34

Effect of accused's failure to mention facts when questioned or charged

34.—(1) Where, in any proceedings against a person for an offence, evidence is given that the accused— **15–414**

(a) at any time before he was charged with the offence, on being questioned under caution by a constable trying to discover whether or by whom the offence had been committed, failed to mention any fact relied on in his defence in those proceedings; or

(b) on being charged with the offence or officially informed that he might be prosecuted for it, failed to mention any such fact,

being a fact which in the circumstances existing at the time the accused could reasonably have been expected to mention when so questioned, charged or informed, as the case may be, subsection (2) below applies.

(2) Where this subsection applies—

(a) *a magistrates' court inquiring into the offence as examining justices;*

(b) a judge, in deciding whether to grant an application made by the accused under—

(i) *section 6 of the* Criminal Justice Act *1987 (application for dismissal of change of serious fraud in respect of which notice of transfer has been given under section 4 of that Act); or*

(ii) *paragraph 5 of Schedule 6 to the* Criminal Justice Act *1991 (application for dismissal of charge of violent or sexual offence involving child in respect of which notice of transfer has been given under section 53 of that Act)*;

[paragraph 2 of Schedule 3 to the *Crime and Disorder Act* 1998];

(c) the court, in determining whether there is a case to answer; and

(d) the court or jury, in determining whether the accused is guilty of the offence charged,

may draw such inferences from the failure as appear proper.

(2A) Where the accused was at an authorised place of detention at the time of the failure, subsections (1) and (2) above do not apply if he had not been allowed an opportunity to consult a solicitor prior to being questioned, charged or informed as mentioned in subsection (1) above.

(3) Subject to any directions by the court, evidence tending to establish the failure may be given before or after evidence tending to establish the fact which the accused is alleged to have failed to mention.

(4) This section applies in relation to questioning by persons (other than constables) charged with the duty of investigating offences or charging offenders as it applies in relation to questioning by constables; and in subsection (1) above "officially informed" means informed by a constable or any such person.

(5) This section does not—

(a) prejudice the admissibility in evidence of the silence or other reaction of the accused in the face of anything said in his presence relating to the conduct in respect of which he is charged, in so far as evidence thereof would be admissible apart from this section; or

(b) preclude the drawing of any inference from any such silence or other reaction of the accused which could properly be drawn apart from this section.

(6) This section does not apply in relation to a failure to mention a fact if the failure occurred before the commencement of this section.

(7) [*Repealed by* Criminal Procedure and Investigations Act *1996, s.44(4)*.]

[This section is printed as amended by the *CPIA* 1996, s.44(3), (4); and the *YJCEA* 1999, s.58(1), (2). Sub-paras (i) and (ii) of subs. (2)(b) are replaced by the words in square brackets that follow them by the *CJA* 2003, s.41, and Sched. 3, para. 64(1) and (2)(b). This amendment came into force on May 9, 2005 (*Criminal Justice Act 2003 (Commencement No. 9) Order* 2005 (S.I. 2005 No. 1267)) in relation to cases sent for trial under s.51 or 51A(3)(d) of the *CDA* 1998. Otherwise, it comes into force on a day to be appointed. Subs. (2)(a) is repealed as from a day to be appointed by the *CJA* 2003, ss.41 and 332, Sched. 3, para. 64(2)(a), and Sched. 37, Pt 4.]

Silence when questioned or charged

15–415 Sections 34 to 37 are based on the draft bill attached to the Eleventh Report of the Criminal Law Revision Committee ("CLRC") (Cmnd. 4991 (1972)) and the *Criminal Evidence (Northern Ireland) Order* 1988 (S.I. 1988 No. 1987 (N.I. 20)). A suspect still retains the right to remain silent during questioning. The right to silence is a discrete but closely related right to the privilege against self-incrimination (*ante*, § 12–2). In *R. v. Bowden* [1999] 2 Cr.App.R. 176, Lord Bingham C.J. said (at p. 181) that since these provisions "restrict rights recognised at common law as appropriate to protect defendants against the risk of injustice they should not be construed more widely than the statutory language requires." In *Averill v. U.K.* (2001) 31 E.H.R.R. 839, ECtHR, it was said that the extent to which adverse inferences may be drawn from an accused's failure to respond to police questioning must be "necessarily limited" (para. 47). For section 35 (inferences from a failure to testify), and the Court of Appeal's consideration thereof in *R. v. Cowan*; *R. v. Gayle*; *R. v. Ricciardi* [1996] 1 Cr.App.R. 1, see *ante*, §§ 4–399 *et seq.*

15–416 In *R. v. Argent* [1997] 2 Cr.App.R. 27 at 32–33, CA, Lord Bingham C.J. indicated that there were six formal conditions that had to be met before section 34 could operate (the words in square brackets are editorial insertion):

1. there had to be proceedings against a person for an offence;

2. the failure to answer had to occur before a defendant was charged [this is subject to s.34(1)(b)];
3. the failure had to occur during questioning under caution by a constable or other person within section 34(4);
4. the questioning had to be directed to trying to discover whether or by whom the offence had been committed;
5. the failure had to be to mention any fact relied on in the person's defence in those proceedings; and
6. the fact the defendant failed to mention had to be one which, in the circumstances existing at the time of the interview, he could reasonably have been expected to mention when so questioned.

Section 34 does not require an arrest to have been made, but a suspect must have been cautioned before the section applies: s.34(1)(a). As to when a caution is required, and the terms of any caution given, see Code C:10 (Appendix A–69).

In *R. v. Johnson* [2006] Crim.L.R. 253, CA (see also *ante*, § 15–412), it was held, applying *Argent*, *ante*, that section 34(1)(a) did not apply to a suspect who refused to leave his cell to be interviewed and was not asked any questions; but the position would have been otherwise had the police asked questions in the cell.

It is submitted that section 34 was intended to apply to a situation that "calls out" for **15–417** an explanation: see *Murray v. DPP*, 97 Cr.App.R. 151 at 160, HL. Where a defendant gives one account in interview and a different account at trial, this would be something upon which the prosecution would be likely to rely as indicating that his evidence was not credible, and it would be something to which the judge would be likely to draw attention in summing up, and this would be the case quite apart from section 34; in such cases, therefore, it should not normally be necessary to seek a formalised direction under that section; anything which over-formalises common sense is to be discouraged: *R. v. Maguire*, 172 J.P. 417, CA (endorsing observations to like effect in *R. v. Brizzalari*, *The Times*, March 3, 2004, CA).

Section 34 does not preclude the drawing of adverse inferences under both subsection (1)(a) and (b); where a jury have been invited to consider drawing an adverse inference at interview stage, it will in most circumstances add nothing to consider such an inference at the charging stage, but not always (*e.g.* where there is a delay between interview and charge); where no inference can be drawn under paragraph (a), subject to any issue of unfairness, there is no good reason for a judge not to leave to the jury the possibility of drawing an inference under paragraph (b); if, however, allowing such an inference would nullify the safeguards contained in the 1984 Act and the codes, or if the police had behaved in bad faith, then the judge should not permit the jury to consider drawing an inference: *R. v. Dervish* [2002] 2 Cr.App.R. 6, CA.

The objective sought to be achieved by section 34(1)(a) is early disclosure of a suspect's account and not, separately and distinctly, its subjection to police cross-examination; there was no place for any adverse inference where the defendant gave the police his full account in a pre-prepared statement from which he did not depart in evidence; and this was so notwithstanding that it was not given in response to questioning and that he said "no comment" to all subsequent police questions; but it does not follow that no adverse inference may ever be drawn where there is a prepared statement; what is said at trial may be fuller, or it may be inconsistent; and nor does it follow, in a case where there is no possibility of an adverse inference, that the prosecution are obliged to adduce a wholly self-serving prepared statement as part of their case: *R. v. Knight* [2004] 1 Cr.App.R. 9, CA; followed in *R. v. Turner (Dwaine)* [2004] 1 Cr.App.R. 24, CA (where it was said that the growing practice of submitting a pre-prepared statement and declining to answer police questions may prove dangerous for an innocent person who subsequently discovers at trial that something significant has been omitted; and that no such problems would arise where the suspect gives appropriate answers in interview).

Fact relied on and unreasonable silence

The authorities on this topic were reviewed in detail in *R. v. Webber* [2004] 1 **15–418** Cr.App.R. 40, HL. The following propositions are derived from the judgment:

(a) a defendant who does not give or call evidence, or does not advance a positive case, but merely puts the prosecution to proof, does not rely on a fact for the purpose of section 34: *R. v. Moshaid* [1998] Crim.L.R. 420, CA;
(b) but a specific and positive case put, on instructions, by a defendant's advocate to a prosecution witness, whether or not the witness accepts it, can be a fact relied on, even if the defendant does not give or call evidence; if a judge is in doubt as to whether a positive case is being put, he should clarify the matter in the jury's absence: *Webber, ante*;
(c) similarly, adopting in closing submissions a co-defendant's evidence can make section 34 applicable: *Webber, ante*;
(d) section 34 cannot apply where the fact later relied on by the defendant was not known to him when questioned: *R. v. Nickolson* [1999] Crim.L.R. 61, CA;
(e) facts not in issue cannot justify an adverse inference (because the inference is that the fact not mentioned in interview is likely to be untrue): *R. v. B.* [2003] 10 *Archbold News* 2, CA; *R. v. Wisdom*, unreported, December 10, 1999, CA;
(f) "'fact' should be given a broad and not a narrow or pedantic meaning. The word covers any alleged fact which is in issue and is put forward as part of the defence case: if the defendant advances at trial any pure fact of exculpatory explanation or account which, if it were true, he could reasonably have been expected to advance earlier, section 34 is potentially applicable": *Webber, ante* (at [33]).

As to points (a) and (b), see also *R. v. Broadhead*, unreported, June 23, 2006, CA ([2006] EWCA Crim. 1705) (*post*, § 15–426). As to (e), see also *R. v. Wheeler*, unreported, March 13, 2008, CA ([2008] EWCA Crim. 688). As to (f), *Webber* was applied, and *Nickolson* ((d), *ante*) was distinguished, in *R. v. Esimu*, 171 J.P. 452, CA (facts underlying alternative, theoretical, innocent explanations of incriminating circumstances where those circumstances had been made known to the defendant at time of interview).

"in the circumstances existing at the time"

15–419 In *R. v. Argent, ante*, § 15–416, Lord Bingham C.J. stated, at p. 33, that a court should not construe the expression "in the circumstances" (s.34(1)) restrictively. Matters such as time of day, the defendant's age, experience, mental capacity, state of health, sobriety, tiredness, personality and legal advice were all relevant circumstances; a court may conclude that it was reasonable for the defendant to have held his peace for a host of reasons, such as that he was tired, ill, frightened, drunk, drugged, unable to understand what was going on, suspicious of the police, afraid that his answer would not be fairly recorded or worried at committing himself without legal advice. In deciding about what was reasonable, a court is to consider the particular accused with such qualities, knowledge, apprehensions and advice as he was shown to have had at the time.

Particular categories of defendant

15–420 The codes of practice recognise "special groups" who have additional protections:
(a) people with hearing and speech difficulties: C:3.12 (Appendix A–47);
(b) people with limited ability to speak English: C:3.12 (*ibid.*);
(c) juveniles: C:3.13 (*ibid.*);
(d) the mentally handicapped or mentally disordered: section 77 (*ante*, § 15–370) and C:3.15 (Appendix A–47).

In the House of Lords, Lord Taylor C.J. said that the position of the very young and the vulnerable would have to be "very specially considered": *Hansard*, H.L., Vol. 555, col. 520. It is submitted that the courts should be particularly slow to draw inferences where suspects in these groups have not had full access to their legal rights. In view of the importance of section 77 of the *PACE Act* 1984 (*ante*, § 15–370), special care must be exercised in relation to the mentally handicapped or mentally disordered. If a judge felt that a defendant had not understood the caution or had some doubts about it, he should not activate section 34: *R. v. Martin* [1992] 5 N.I.J.B. 1 at 41, NICA.

Legal advice

Access to legal advice

Section 58 of the *YJCEA* 1999 amends sections 34 (*ante*, § 15–414), 36 (*post*, § 15–433) and 37 (*post*, § 15–435) of the 1994 Act to prohibit adverse inferences from failure to mention a fact or to provide an explanation, at an "authorised place of detention" (defined in s.38(2A), *post*, § 15–438), unless a suspect has had an opportunity to consult a solicitor. **15–421**

Legal advice to remain silent

In *R. v. Condron and Condron* [1997] 1 Cr.App.R. 185 at 191, the Court of Appeal said that legal advice to remain silent cannot by itself prevent an adverse inference being drawn, otherwise section 34 would be rendered wholly nugatory. Such advice is "a very relevant" circumstance to be taken into account by a court in deciding whether the defendant could reasonably have been expected to mention the fact relied on at that time: *R. v. Argent*, *ante*, § 15–416, at p. 36. Lord Bingham C.J. (in *Argent*) added that the jury are not concerned with the correctness of the solicitor's advice, nor with whether it complies with the Law Society's guidelines, but with the reasonableness of the defendant's conduct in all the circumstances. The court approved the trial judge's direction to the jury on this matter: **15–422**

> "You should consider whether or not he is able to decide for himself what he should do or having asked for a solicitor to advise him he would not challenge that advice" (at p. 34).

The direction to the jury where a solicitor has advised silence should be given in carefully considered and measured terms: *R. v. Moshaid*, *ante*, § 15–418.

If a defendant wishes the court not to draw an adverse inference, he or his solicitor may have to go further and state the basis or the reason for that advice: *R. v. Condron and Condron*, *ante*; *R. v. Roble* [1997] Crim.L.R. 449, CA (good reasons for such advice might be that the interviewing officer had disclosed little or nothing of the nature of the case against the defendant, so that the solicitor cannot usefully advise his client or, where the nature of the offence, or the material in the hands of the police is so complex, or relates to matters so long ago, that no sensible immediate response is feasible).

In *Condron v. U.K.*, *ante*, § 15–222, the European Court of Human Rights said that the fact an accused has been advised by his lawyer to remain silent must be given "appropriate weight" by the domestic court as there may be a good reason for such advice (para. 60); and a reason mentioned in *Averill v. U.K.*, *ante*, § 15–222, for not drawing an adverse inference, was "*bona fide* advice received from his lawyer" (para. 47). The current JSB specimen direction (*post*, § 15–437) has been amended to ensure that the jury are specifically directed to take legal advice to remain silent into account. **15–423**

In *R. v. Hoare and Pierce* [2005] 1 Cr.App.R. 22, CA, the court reviewed the authorities on legal advice to remain silent, including *R. v. Betts and Hall* [2001] 2 Cr.App.R. 16, CA, *R. v. Howell* [2005] 1 Cr.App.R. 1, CA, *Beckles v. U.K.* (2003) 36 E.H.R.R. 13, ECtHR, *R. v. Robinson* (2003) 153 N.L.J. 1378, CA, and *R. v. Knight* [2004] 1 Cr.App.R. 9, CA. The court held that there was no inconsistency between *Betts and Hall* on the one hand and *Howell* and *Knight* on the other:

> "It is plain from Kay L.J.'s judgment [in *Betts and Hall*] that, even where a solicitor has in good faith advised silence and a defendant has genuinely relied on it in the sense that he accepted it and believed that he was entitled to follow it, a jury may still draw an adverse inference if it is sure that the *true* reason for his silence is that he had no or no satisfactory explanation consistent with innocence to give. That is of piece with Laws L.J.'s reasoning in *Howell* and *Knight* that genuine reliance by a defendant on his solictior's advice to remain silent is not in itself enough to preclude adverse comment."

In *R. v. Beckles* [2005] 1 Cr.App.R. 23, CA (see also *post*, § 15–427), after reviewing *Hoare*, *ante*, and previous authorities, Lord Woolf C.J. said:

> "In our judgment, in a case where a solicitor's advice is relied upon by the defendant, the ultimate question for the jury remains under section 34 whether the facts relied on at the trial were facts which the defendant could reasonably have been expected to mention at interview. If they were not, that is the end of the matter. If the jury consider that the defendant

genuinely relied on the advice, that is not necessarily the end of the matter. It may still not have been reasonable for him to rely on the advice, or the advice may not have been the true explanation for his silence."

Privilege

15–424 A waiver of privilege will be involved if the defendant or his solicitor seeks to put forward, in interview or in evidence, the reason for advice given by a solicitor: *R. v. Bowden* [1999] 2 Cr.App.R. 176 at 182, 184, CA. Calling a solicitor to give evidence that a defendant communicated the fact later relied upon at the time of the interview does not involve waiving privilege: *R. v. Condron and Condron*, *ante*, at p.197; and *R. v. Bowden*, *ante*, at p.182. Nor is privilege waived where a defendant, under cross-examination, has no choice but to reveal what passed between him and his solicitor, to rebut a suggestion of recent fabrication: *R. v. Wishart and Boutcher*, unreported, May 12, 2005, CA ([2005] EWCA Crim. 1337).

Once privilege is waived, however, fairness will determine the extent to which the defendant should be required to disclose further details of the legal advice; where the issue is whether the defendant genuinely relied on legal advice to remain silent or whether an adverse inference should be drawn against him, the prosecution should normally be allowed to cross-examine as to the context in which the advice was given: *R. v. Loizou* [2006] 9 *Archbold News* 2, CA (where the authorities on privilege and section 34 are reviewed in detail). See also *R. v. Hall-Chung* (2007) 151 S.J. 1020, CA (judges should not assume that the prosecution would be entitled to take advantage of a waiver wherever there had been a waiver in law; the circumstances in which privilege had been waived had to be taken into account when deciding what fairness required).

Sufficient evidence for prosecution to succeed

15–425 Code C:11.6 (Appendix A–73) provides that interviewing must cease when the officer in charge of the investigation: (a) is satisfied all the questions he considers relevant to obtaining accurate and reliable information about the offence have been put to the suspect, and this includes allowing the suspect an opportunity to give an innocent explanation and asking questions to test whether the explanation is accurate and reliable; (b) has taken account of any other available evidence; and (c) he, or in the case of a detained person, the custody officer, reasonably believes there is sufficient evidence to provide a realistic prospect of a conviction.

These provisions reflect a marked shift in emphasis towards an overtly inquisitorial procedure, as compared with the primary legislation and the 1995 edition of the code. Thus section 37 of the *PACE Act* 1984 (*ante*, § 3–97) imposes a duty on the custody officer to consider whether there is sufficient evidence to charge the person before him; and a further duty to charge him if he does so consider. If he does not so consider, he is under a duty to release the arrestee unless he has reasonable grounds for believing that his detention without charge is necessary to secure or preserve evidence or to obtain such evidence by questioning him. As to the 1995 edition of the code, in three early decisions (*R. v. Coleman, Knight and Hochenberg*, unreported, October 20, 1995, CA (94 4814, 4816, 4817 X4); *R. v. Pointer* [1997] Crim.L.R. 676, CA; and *R. v. Gayle* [1999] Crim.L.R. 502, CA), the court took a strict line in relation to these provisions, holding that they meant what they said. In a series of subsequent decisions, however, this approach was rejected, and a practice was sanctioned which is now encapsulated in the new code provisions: see *R. v. McGuinness* [1999] Crim.L.R. 318, CA; *R. v. Ioannou* [1999] Crim.L.R. 586, CA; *R. v. Van Bokkum* [2000] 6 *Archbold News* 2, CA; *R. v. Elliott* [2002] 5 *Archbold News* 2, CA; and *R. v. Sed* [2004] 1 W.L.R. 3218, CA.

Silence and the establishment of a prima facie case

15–426 Section 34(2)(c) provides that a court in deciding whether there is a case to answer may draw such inferences from a failure to mention a fact relied upon as appear proper, but section 38(3) (*post*, § 15–438) stipulates that a finding of a case to answer shall not be based solely on such an inference.

Section 34 will seldom arise in practice in determining whether there is a case to answer. The adverse inference is restricted to a fact relied on by the defendant in his defence as opposed to his failure to explain a fact relied on by the prosecution. But see *R. v. Webber, ante*, § 15–418 (positive case put by defence advocate to prosecution witness), *R. v. Hart and McLean* [1998] 6 *Archbold News* 1, CA (cited in *Webber* at [25]), and *R. v. Broadhead*, unreported, June 23, 2006, CA ([2006] EWCA Crim. 1705) (putting a specific and positive case is to be contrasted with merely testing and probing the prosecution case).

Directing the jury

15–427 In *R. v. Condron and Condron, ante*, § 15–422, the Court of Appeal approved the Judicial Studies Board specimen direction on section 34 (the direction is unpublished but is available on the JSB website (www.jsboard.co.uk)). The current version of the direction is set out below, and is based in part on a suggestion of the Court of Appeal in *R. v. Betts and Hall, ante*, § 15–423 (para. 57). It is prefaced by a reminder as to the desirability of discussing the matter with counsel before final speeches with a view to ascertaining the precise fact or facts relied on and their materiality, and to consider the terms of the direction which will be appropriate to the circumstances of the case. The preface points out that if the fact(s) in question cannot easily be ascertained, it will be appropriate to consider whether any direction should be given at all, and that if it is decided as a matter of law that no inference direction is appropriate, the *McGarry* direction, *post*, should be given. The direction is accompanied by notes (not reproduced here) which seek to explain the authorities upon which the direction is based. The legal basis for various aspects of the direction was considered in some detail in *R. v. Petkar and Farquhar* [2004] 1 Cr.App.R. 22, CA. In *R. v. Beckles* [2005] 1 Cr.App.R. 23, CA (see also *ante*, § 15–423), it was said that the specimen direction is being redrafted. Under the revised direction the jury will be asked to consider whether the defendant *genuinely and reasonably* relied on the legal advice to remain silent.

"1. Before his interview(s) the defendant was cautioned. He was first told that he need not say anything. It was therefore his right to remain silent. However, he was also told that it might harm his defence if he did not mention when questioned something which he later relied on in court; and that anything he did say might be given in evidence.

2. As part of his defence, the defendant has relied upon (*here specify the facts to which this direction applies*). But [the prosecution/ say he admits] that he failed to mention these facts when he was interviewed about the offence(s). [If you are sure that this is so, this/ This] failure may count against him. This is because you may draw the conclusion from his failure that he had [had no answer then/had no answer that he then believed would stand up to scrutiny/has since invented his account/has since tailored his account to fit the prosecution's case/(*here refer to any other reasonable inferences contended for*)]. If you do draw that conclusion, you must not convict him wholly or mainly on the strength of it; but you may take it into account as some additional support for the prosecution's case and when deciding whether his [evidence/case] about these facts is true.

3. However, you may draw such a conclusion against him only if you think it is a fair and proper conclusion, and you are satisfied about three things: first, that when he was interviewed he could reasonably have been expected to mention the facts on which he now relies; second, that the only sensible explanation for his failure to do so is that he had no answer at the time or none that would stand up to scrutiny; third, that apart from his failure to mention those facts, the prosecution's case against him is so strong that it clearly calls for an answer by him.

4. (*Add, if appropriate*:) The defence invite you not to draw any conclusion from the defendant's silence, on the basis of the following evidence (*here set out the evidence*). If you [accept this evidence and] think this amounts to a reason why you should not draw any conclusion from his silence, do not do so. Otherwise, subject to what I have said, you may do so.

5. (*Where legal advice to remain silent is relied upon, add the following to or instead of paragraph 4*:) The defendant has given evidence that he did not answer questions on the advice of his solicitor/legal representative. If you accept the evidence that he was so advised, this is obviously an important consideration; but it does not automatically prevent you from drawing any conclusion from his silence. Bear in mind that a person given legal advice has the choice whether to accept or reject it; and that the defendant was warned that any failure to mention facts which he relied on at his trial might harm his defence. Take into account

also (*here set out the circumstances relevant to the particular case, which may include the age of the defendant, the nature of and/or the reasons for the advice given, and the complexity or otherwise of the facts on which he relied at the trial*). Having done so, decide whether the defendant could genuinely have been expected to mention the facts on which he now relies. If, for example, you considered that he had or may have had an answer to give, but genuinely relied on the legal advice to remain silent, you should not draw any conclusion against him. But if, for example, you were sure that the defendant had no answer, and merely latched onto the legal advice as a convenient shield behind which to hide, you would be entitled to draw a conclusion against him, subject to the direction I have given you."

15–428 The requirement that "the prosecution's case against him is so strong that it clearly calls for an answer" before an adverse inference is drawn is borrowed from the direction under section 35 (*ante*, § 4–398) and should be included in the summing up: *R. v. Condron and Condron* [1997] 1 Cr.App.R. 185, CA (at p. 195); *R. v. Milford* [2001] Crim.L.R. 330, CA (not following *R. v. Doldur* [2000] Crim.L.R. 178, CA); *R. v. Parchment* [2003] 9 *Archbold News* 2, CA; *R. v. Petkar and Farquhar*, *ante*.

The House of Lords has emphasised the importance of accurate directions in the face of a defendant's silence: *R. v. Webber*, *ante*, § 15–418 (at [34]). However, a misdirection in relation to section 34 does not necessarily require the quashing of a conviction: *R. v. Boyle and Ford* (2006) 150 S.J. 1151, CA. The court said (at [14]) that the essential question on appeal is whether any misdirection has rendered the conviction unsafe. For the purposes of determining this question, it may assist to analyse the direction actually given, and then to compare it with the direction that should have been given. The court should then make an assessment of whether the jury would have been bound to convict if they had been properly directed, with the conviction only being upheld if it is sure that they would have done so. *Boyle and Ford* was followed in *R. v. Lowe*, 71 J.C.L. 392, CA ([2007] EWCA Crim. 833); and in *R. v. Wheeler*, unreported, March 13, 2008, CA ([2008] EWCA Crim. 688), the court acknowledged this principle but quashed a conviction for rape where the prosecution case was otherwise entirely dependent on the evidence of the complainant and where the jury had been erroneously directed (see *ante*, § 15–418) that they could draw an adverse inference against the defendant from his failure to mention facts which were not in dispute at trial. The court said that the jury may have been influenced by the defendant's failure to mention facts that they might well have thought an innocent man would have mentioned.

Where it is open to the jury to draw an adverse inference, the judge should identify the relevant facts in respect of which such an inference arises: *R. v. Webber*, *ante*, § 15–418 (at [34] and [38]); *R. v. Chenia* [2003] 2 Cr.App.R. 6, CA (this is to be approached in a common sense way); *R. v. Petkar and Farquhar*, *ante*. Where a suspect has submitted a pre-prepared statement instead of answering questions, the summing up should identify by way of comparison any fact relied on at trial but not mentioned in the pre-prepared statement; in some cases, any discrepancy may be better considered as part of a *Lucas* direction (*ante*, §§ 4–402 *et seq.*): *R. v. Turner (Dwaine)*, *ante*, § 15–417. If no such inference is open to the jury, then the judge should specifically so direct them: *R. v. McGarry* [1999] 1 Cr.App.R. 377, CA. The specimen direction includes such a direction; but the absence of such a direction will not necessarily lead to an unsafe conviction: *R. v. Francom* [2001] 1 Cr.App.R. 17, CA.

Both the defendant and his advocate should be given the opportunity of dealing with the reason for silence in interview before a direction under section 34 is given: *R. v. Self*, unreported, May 7, 1999, CA (98 6128 W2); *R. v. Kerr and Roulstone*, unreported, January 13, 2000, CA (98 07476 X5). *Cf. R. v. Khan (Deniz)* [1999] 2 *Archbold News* 2, CA (96 0395 Y4) (judge had been entitled to direct jury on issue although prosecution had not cross-examined defendant on the point; failure to raise matter with counsel was to be deprecated, but no injustice done as judge pointed out that neither defendant nor his counsel had had opportunity to deal with matter). It is submitted that the approach in *Self* and *Kerr and Roulstone* is to be preferred particularly with regard to whether a failure to give the defence an opportunity to respond is compatible with Article 6 of the European Convention. The notes accompanying the specimen direction adopt this approach.

In *R. v. Daly* [2002] 2 Cr.App.R. 14, CA, it was held that there is nothing in the wording of section 34 that requires the issue of whether or not the defendant might reasonably have been expected to mention a fact relied on in his defence when questioned or charged to be capable of resolution independently of the issue of guilt or innocence (preferring *R. v. Hearne* [2000] 6 *Archbold News* 2, CA, to *R. v. Mountford* [1999] Crim.L.R. 575, CA, and *R. v. Gill* [2001] 1 Cr.App.R. 11, CA). See also *R. v. Gowland-Wynn* [2002] 1 Cr.App.R. 41, CA, and *R. v. Webber, ante*, § 15–418 (criticising the reasoning in *Mountford* and *Gill*), to the same effect. In *R. v. Daly*, it was further held that where the fact relied on involves an admission of part of the prosecution case (the less incriminating part) together with an innocent explanation of the more incriminating part, the statute permits the drawing of an adverse inference, although the actual inference drawn may be weaker than in a case where the fact relied on and not previously mentioned implies complete innocence; where the fact relied on is incriminating in part (as here, an admission to being a thief, but not to being a robber), the direction to the jury should alert them to the need to consider the possibility that the defendant's silence may have had as much to do with the fact that he did not wish to incriminate himself even in a relatively minor offence (theft) as with not having an innocent explanation for the allegation of robbery or not having one that would stand up to scrutiny.

Where the guilt or innocence of two or more defendants stands or falls together, it is generally desirable to direct the jury that they should not hold the silence in interview of one against the other: *R. v. McLean and McLean* [1999] 4 *Archbold News* 1, CA (98 01354 R2, 98 01609 S2).

A direction under section 34 may be combined with a *Lucas* direction (*ante*, §§ 4–402 *et seq.*): *R. v. O. (A.)* [2000] Crim.L.R. 617, CA; but see *R. v. Turner (Dwaine)*, *ante*.

Where legal advice to remain silent is relied upon, the matters set out in paragraph 5 of the specimen direction should be put before the jury, and a failure to do so may result in a successful appeal: *R. v. Bresa* [2006] Crim.L.R. 179, CA. However, where a defendant does not waive privilege, it is permissible to say, in addition to the matters set out in paragraph 5, words to the following effect (*ibid.*):

> "You have no explanation for the advice in this case. It is the defendant's right not to reveal the contents of any advice from his solicitor or what transpired between himself and his solicitor. At the same time he has a choice whether to reveal that advice and thereby reveal all that transpired between himself and his solicitor."

Summary proceedings

In *T. v. DPP*, 171 J.P. 605, DC, it was said that when justices are considering section 34, they should ask themselves three questions: "(1) Has the defendant relied in his defence on a fact which he could reasonably be expected to have mentioned in his interview, but did not? … (2) What is his explanation for not having mentioned it? (3) If that explanation is not a reasonable one, is the proper inference to be drawn that he is guilty?" **15–428a**

The nature of the adverse inference

In *R. v. Milford, ante*, § 15–428, the court reviewed conflicting authorities (for which see the 2004 edition of this work) as to whether the adverse inference was limited to recent fabrication (as suggested by Stuart-Smith L.J. in *Condron, ante*) and concluded: **15–429**

> "The significance for the jury of a failure by the defendant when first questioned to mention facts relied on at his trial is whether or not that failure is an indication that the facts which he now adopts or advances before the jury (*including* any explanation for his involvement in undisputed but equivocal events) can or cannot be relied on. We share the apparent view of the authors of the most recent JSB direction that the adverse inference which may be drawn is not limited to one of 'recent invention' strictly so described, but extends to a fact or explanation tailored to fit the prosecution case or which the defendant believed would not stand up to scrutiny at the time" (at [33]).

These observations were endorsed by the House of Lords in *R. v. Webber, ante*, § 15–418 (at [30]). However, as to where the defendant submits a pre-prepared statement instead of answering questions, see *R. v. Knight, ante*, § 15–417, and *R. v. Turner (Dwaine), ante*, § 15–428.

Rebutting the inference

15–430 In *R. v. Condron and Condron*, *ante*, the court said (at p. 197), relying on *R. v. Wilmot*, 89 Cr.App.R. 341, that an inference of subsequent fabrication could be rebutted by calling a third party to whom the relevant fact was communicated at about the time of the interview. If this third party were a solicitor then this would not involve a waiver of privilege (a point confirmed in *R. v. Bowden*, at p. 182, *ante*, § 15–415). The court added that it is always open to an accused person who has failed to mention some important fact at interview, to communicate it to the police at any time before trial; but unless it is done promptly, it is unlikely to rebut any adverse inference that might otherwise be drawn. As to defence disclosure, see *ante*, § 12–56.

Procedure

15–431 In *R. v. Condron and Condron*, *ante*, § 15–422, the Court of Appeal, at pp. 195–196, whilst stressing that there is no hard and fast procedure and that each case must be determined on its own facts, gave guidance on the procedure to be adopted in determining whether an adverse inference may be drawn in any particular case.

(a) Objection may be taken to the admissibility of a no comment interview under section 76 and/or section 78 and this may necessitate a *voire dire*.

(b) It would seldom be appropriate to rule on the question of whether a jury should be invited to draw an adverse inference before the conclusion of all the evidence. This could occur in an exceptional case, such as a defendant of very low intelligence who has been advised by his solicitor to make no comment. In *R. v. Argent*, *ante*, § 15–416, Lord Bingham C.J., at p. 31, indicated that this may also be appropriate where a judge concludes that a jury properly directed could not properly draw an inference adverse to the defendant.

(c) Normally the prosecution should simply adduce the fact that after the appropriate caution the accused did not answer questions or made no comment (see, to similar effect, *R. v. Lashley* [2006] Crim.L.R. 86, CA (at [28])). Unless the relevance of a particular point has been revealed in cross-examination, it would not seem appropriate to spend time at this stage going through the questions asked at interview. If and when the accused gives evidence and mentions a fact which, in the view of prosecuting counsel, he could reasonably have been expected to mention in interview, he may be asked why he did not mention it in interview.

The European Convention on Human Rights

15–432 In *Condron v. U.K.* (2001) 31 E.H.R.R. 1, ECtHR, it was held that the right of the applicants to a fair trial under Article 6(1) of the European Convention (*post*, § 16–57) was violated where the judge's direction to the jury in relation to section 34 failed to strike the right balance between the right to silence and the circumstances in which an adverse inference may properly be drawn from silence, including by a jury; in particular, the jury should have been directed as a matter of fairness, that if they were satisfied that the applicants' silence at interview could not sensibly be attributed to their having no answer or none that would stand up to cross-examination [questioning or investigation], they should not draw an adverse inference; and this unfairness could not be cured by the appellate proceedings, for whilst it is possible for defects at trial to be remedied by a subsequent procedure before a court of appeal (see *Edwards v. U.K.*, 15 E.H.R.R. 417, ECtHR), the Court of Appeal in this case had no means of knowing whether the applicants' silence played a significant role in the jury's decision to convict. It was the function of the jury, properly directed, to decide whether or not to draw an adverse inference from the applicants' silence, section 34 of the 1994 Act specifically entrusting this task to the jury as part of a legislative scheme designed to confine the use which can be made of an accused's silence at trial. The court added (para. 60) that "particular caution" was required before an adverse inference could be drawn from silence during questioning.

As to the European Court of Human Rights' consideration of the effect of legal advice to make no comment in interview, see, *ante*, §§ 15–422 *et seq.*

Criminal Justice and Public Order Act 1994, s.36

Effect of accused's failure or refusal to account for objects, substances or marks

36.—(1) Where— 15–433

(a) a person is arrested by a constable, and there is—
 (i) on his person; or
 (ii) in or on his clothing or footwear; or
 (iii) otherwise in his possession; or
 (iv) in any place in which he is at the time of his arrest,

any object, substance or mark, or there is any mark on any such object; and

(b) that or another constable investigating the case reasonably believes that the presence of the object, substance or mark may be attributable to the participation of the person arrested in the commission of an offence specified by the constable; and

(c) the constable informs the person arrested that he so believes, and requests him to account for the presence of the object, substance or mark; and

(d) the person fails or refuses to do so,

then if, in any proceedings against the person for the offence so specified, evidence of those matters is given, subsection (2) below applies.

(2) Where this subsection applies—

(a) *a magistrates' court inquiring into the offence as examining justices;*

(b) a judge in deciding whether to grant an application made by the accused under—
 (i) *section 6 of the* Criminal Justice Act *1987 (application for dismissal of charge of serious fraud in respect of which notice of transfer has been given under section 4 of that Act); or*
 (ii) *paragraph 5 of Schedule 6 to the* Criminal Justice Act *1991 (application for dismissal of charge of violent or sexual offence involving child in respect of which notice of transfer has been given under section 53 of that Act);*

[paragraph 2 of Schedule 3 to the *Crime and Disorder Act* 1998];

(c) the court, in determining whether there is a case to answer; and

(d) the court or jury, in determining whether the accused is guilty of the offence charged,

may draw such inferences from the failure or refusal as appear proper.

(3) Subsections (1) and (2) above apply to the condition of clothing or footwear as they apply to a substance or mark thereon.

(4) Subsections (1) and (2) above do not apply unless the accused was told in ordinary language by the constable when making the request mentioned in subsection (1)(c) above what the effect of this section would be if he failed or refused to comply with the request.

(4A) Where the accused was at an authorised place of detention at the time of the failure or refusal, subsections (1) and (2) above do not apply if he had not been allowed an opportunity to consult a solicitor prior to the request being made.

(5) This section applies in relation to officers of customs and excise as it applies in relation to constables.

(6) This section does not preclude the drawing of any inference from a failure or refusal of the accused to account for the presence of an object, substance or mark or from the condition of clothing or footwear which could properly be drawn apart from this section.

(7) This section does not apply in relation to a failure or refusal which occurred before the commencement of this section.

(8) [*Repealed by* Criminal Procedure and Investigations Act *1996, s.44(4).*]

[This section is printed as amended by the *CPIA* 1996, s.44(3), (4); and the *YJCEA* 1999, s.58(1), (3). Sub-paras (i) and (ii) of subs. (2)(b) are replaced by the words in square brackets that follow them by the *CJA* 2003, s.41, and Sched. 3, para. 64(1) and (3)(b). This amendment came into force on May 9, 2005 (*Criminal Justice Act 2003 (Commencement No. 9) Order* 2005 (S.I. 2005 No. 1267)) in relation to cases sent for trial under s.51 or 51A(3)(d) of the *CDA* 1998. Otherwise, it comes into force on a day to be appointed. Subs. (2)(a) is repealed as from a day to be appointed by the *CJA* 2003, ss.41 and 332, Sched. 3, para. 64(3)(a), and Sched. 37, Pt 4.]

Objects, substances or marks

Section 36 permits an adverse inference to be drawn when an arrested person fails or 15–434 refuses to explain an object, substance or mark on his person, clothing, footwear or in his possession or in any place where he is at the time of his arrest.

The effect of Code C:11.1A and C:11.1 is that questioning under this section should normally take place during formal interview at a police station.

Although there is substantial overlap between this provision and section 34, there are significant differences:

(a) the section only applies after arrest;

(b) the suspect must be told that the police believe the object, substance or mark is attributable to his involvement in a specified offence, and be asked to account for the object, substance or mark;

(c) the suspect must be told "in ordinary language" the effect of the section if there is no response to questioning: s.36(4) (see Code C:10.11, Appendix A–71);

(d) no qualifying provision of reasonableness is contained in the section.

In *R. v. Compton* [2003] 1 *Archbold News* 2, the Court of Appeal pointed out that section 36, unlike section 34, invites no comparison between the statement in interview and the evidence at trial, since section 36 contains no reference to the word "reasonable". The sole question is whether the suspect did account for the relevant substance. The court implicitly approved the trial judge's incorporation in his summing-up of the portion of the section 34 direction (*ante*, § 15–334) dealing with legal advice to remain silent. There is no reason as to why the dicta in *Compton* should not equally apply to section 37.

The words "an offence specified by the constable" in section 36(1)(b) do not mean that the offence specified by the officer must be identical to that charged in the indictment: *ibid*.

The Judicial Studies Board's specimen direction on section 36 is set out in the supplement.

Criminal Justice and Public Order Act 1994, s.37

Effect of accused's failure or refusal to account for presence at a particular place

15–435 **37.**—(1) Where—

(a) a person arrested by a constable was found by him at a place at or about the time the offence for which he was arrested is alleged to have been committed; and

(b) that or another constable investigating the offence reasonably believes that the presence of the person at that place and at that time may be attributable to his participation in the commission of the offence; and

(c) the constable informs the person that he so believes, and requests him to account for that presence; and

(d) the person fails or refuses to do so,

then if, in any proceedings against the person for the offence, evidence of those matters is given, subsection (2) below applies.

(2) [*Identical to s.36(2)*, ante, *§ 15–433 (including the amendments)*.]

(3) Subsections (1) and (2) do not apply unless the accused was told in ordinary language by the constable when making the request mentioned in subsection (1)(c) above what the effect of this section would be if he failed or refused to comply with the request.

(3A) Where the accused was at an authorised place of detention at the time of the failure or refusal, subsections (1) and (2) do not apply if he had not been allowed an opportunity to consult a solicitor prior to the request being made.

(4) [*Identical to s.36(5)*, ante, *§ 15–433*.]

(5) This section does not preclude the drawing of any inference from a failure or refusal of the accused to account for his presence at a place which could properly be drawn apart from this section.

(6) [*Identical to s.36(7)*, ante, *§ 15–433*.]

(7) [*Repealed by* Criminal Procedure and Investigations Act *1996, s.44(4)*.]

[This section is printed as amended by the *CPIA* 1996, s.44(3), (4); and the *YJCEA* 1999, s.58(1), (4). As to subs. (2), the amending provisions of the 2003 Act are s.41, and Sched. 3, para. 64(1) and (4).]

Presence at a particular place

15–436 This section is identical to section 36 except that it applies to a person's presence at a place at or about the time of the offence. For the meaning of "place", see section 38(1) (*post*, § 15–438).

Inferences to be drawn under sections 36 and 37

Sections 36 and 37 are not concerned with the adverse inferences that may be drawn from a defendant's possession of an object, the existence of a substance or mark, or his presence at a particular place, but with his failure to provide an explanation when asked. In *R. v. Campbell*, unreported, March 29, 1993, the Northern Ireland Court of Appeal upheld the adverse inference drawn by the trial judge (sitting without a jury), under the Northern Ireland equivalent of section 36, that the defendant's explanation at trial was a recent and false invention. It should be noted, however, that an inference may be drawn under these sections whether or not an innocent explanation is subsequently advanced. **15–437**

The Judicial Studies Board's specimen direction on section 37 is set out in the supplement.

Criminal Justice and Public Order Act 1994, s.38

Interpretation and savings for sections 34, 35, 36 and 37

38.—(1) In sections 34, 35, 36 and 37 of this Act— **15–438**

"legal representative" means *an authorised advocate or authorised litigator, as defined by section 119(1) of the* Courts and Legal Services Act *1990* [a person who, for the purposes of the *Legal Services Act* 2007, is an authorised person in relation to an activity which constitutes the exercise of a right of audience or the conduct of litigation (within the meaning of that Act)]; and

"place" includes any building or part of a building, any vehicle, vessel, aircraft or hovercraft and any other place whatsoever.

(2) In sections 34(2), 35(3), 36(2) and 37(2), references to an offence charged include references to any other offence of which the accused could lawfully be convicted on that charge.

(2A) In each of sections 34(2A), 36(4A) and 37(3A) "authorised place of detention" means—

(a) a police station; or

(b) any other place prescribed for the purposes of that provision by order made by the Secretary of State;

and the power to make an order under this subsection shall be exercisable by statutory instrument which shall be subject to annulment in pursuance of a resolution of either House of Parliament.

(3) A person shall not have the proceedings against him transferred to the Crown Court for trial, have a case to answer or be convicted of an offence solely on an inference drawn from such a failure or refusal as is mentioned in section 34(2), 35(3), 36(2) or 37(2).

(4) A judge shall not refuse to grant such an application as is mentioned in section 34(2)(b), 36(2)(b) and 37(2)(b) solely on an inference drawn from such a failure as is mentioned in section 34(2), 36(2) or 37(2).

(5) Nothing in sections 34, 35, 36 or 37 prejudices the operation of a provision of any enactment which provides (in whatever words) that any answer or evidence given by a person in specified circumstances shall not be admissible in evidence against him or some other person in any proceedings or class or proceedings (however described, and whether civil or criminal).

In this subsection, the reference to giving evidence is a reference to giving evidence in any manner, whether by furnishing information, making discovery, producing documents or otherwise.

(6) Nothing in sections 34, 35, 36 or 37 prejudices any power of a court, in any proceedings, to exclude evidence (whether by preventing questions being put or otherwise) at its discretion.

[This section is printed as amended by the *YJCEA* 1999, s.58(1) and (5); and as amended, as from a day to be appointed, by the *Legal Services Act* 2007, s.208, and Sched. 21, para. 116 (insertion of words in square brackets and omission of italicised words in definition of "legal representative").]

Section 38 came into force on April 10, 1995: *CJPOA (Commencement No. 6) Order* 1995 (S.I. 1995 No. 721).

Application to armed forces

15–439 Sections 34 to 38 of the Act apply, subject to modifications, to specified military proceedings: see s.39 of the Act and the *CJPOA 1994 (Application to the Armed Forces) Orders* 1997 (S.I. 1997 No. 16) and 2006 (S.I. 2006 No. 2326).

Other legislation

15–440 Adverse inferences also arise under the *CJA* 1987, s.10 (*ante*, § 4–84r), the *PACE Act* 1984, s.62(10), (*ante*, § 15–236), and the *CPIA* 1996, ss.11(3) (*ante*, § 12–62) and 34 (*ante*, § 4–84y).

C. JUDICIAL CONFESSIONS

(1) General

15–441 An admission made in the course of judicial proceedings, whether at an earlier stage of proceedings for the same offence or in separate proceedings, will come within the definition of "confession" in section 82(1) of the 1984 Act (*ante*, § 15–354) for the purposes of section 76 (*ante*, § 15–352).

(2) Admission in proceedings for the same offence

(a) *Plea of guilty at trial*

15–442 The defendant must in open court freely and voluntarily confess that he is guilty of the offence of which he is charged in the indictment. Confession may be made on arraignment, or at any subsequent stage of the proceedings, by withdrawal, with the consent of the court, of a plea of not guilty, and substitution of a plea of guilty: *Holdsworth's case* (1832) 1 Lew. 279.

See generally, *ante*, §§ 4–104 *et seq.*

(b) *Admission at earlier trial*

15–443 An admission made during the course of a trial is admissible at a retrial: *R. v. McGregor* [1968] 1 Q.B. 372, 51 Cr.App.R. 338, CA.

(c) *Proceedings before justices*

Summary proceedings

15–444 R, having pleaded guilty to burglary before the magistrates, was later allowed to change his plea and elected to go for trial. At the trial, evidence of his plea of guilty before the magistrates was admitted. It was held: (a) the court could not accept that a plea of guilty in court if withdrawn had no effect whatsoever; (b) whether such evidence should be admitted depended upon whether the confession had any probative value and whether that probative value exceeded its prejudicial effect. This depended upon the facts of each case and was a matter for the judge's discretion. The question must be decided by examination of the relevant facts during a trial-within-a-trial. However, occasions when the evidence would be admitted must be very rare: *R. v. Rimmer*, 56 Cr.App.R. 196, CA. In *R. v. Hetherington* [1972] Crim.L.R. 703, CA, the court stated that it was unable to accept, as applicable to all cases, the observation in *Rimmer* that the issue of admissibility should be resolved by a trial-within-a-trial.

15–445 It is submitted that the law now is that a plea of guilty in a magistrates' court comes within the meaning of a "confession" in section 82(1) (*ante*, § 15–354) in that it is a statement adverse to the maker. As such it can be given in evidence under section 76(1), subject to any representations made under section 76(2), in which case a *voire dire* should be held, and subject to such discretion as the trial judge may have to exclude it under either section 78 of the Act or the discretion to exclude evidence preserved by section 82(3). As to section 76, see *ante*, § 15–352; as to the holding of a *voire dire*, see *ante*, §§ 15–380 *et seq.*; as to sections 78 and 82(3), see *post*, §§ 15–452 *et seq.*

As to equivocal pleas and the circumstances in which a change of plea of guilty entered in a magistrates' court should be permitted, see *ante*, §§ 2–194 *et seq*.

(3) Admissions in other proceedings

(a) *Admissions other than under compulsory process of law*

General rule

15–446 At common law, admissions by the defendant on oath in another case, civil or criminal, are admissible against him: *R. v. Garbett* (1847) 1 Den. 236; *R. v. Colpus* [1917] 1 K.B. 574, 12 Cr.App.R. 193, CCA; except as to questions he objected to, but was improperly compelled to answer, when under no obligation to incriminate himself: *R. v. Chidley* (1860) 8 Cox 365; *R. v. Laurent*, 62 J.P. 250.

Mitigation in former proceedings

15–447 In *R. v. Turner (B.J.)*, 61 Cr.App.R. 67, CA, it was held the Crown was entitled to prove what counsel had said during the course of a speech in mitigation in different proceedings as it amounted to an admission of the offence charged in the instant proceedings. A duly authorised agent can make admissions on behalf of his principal, though the party seeking to rely upon the admission must prove that the agent was duly authorised. Proof of the circumstances in which the barrister said what he did amounted to prima facie evidence that he was authorised to say it: *ibid*. at p. 82.

(b) *Admissions under compulsory process of law*

15–448 Following the decision of the European Court of Human Rights in *Saunders v. U.K.*, 23 E.H.R.R. 313 (*post*, § 16–69) (see also, *I.J.L. v. U.K.* (2001) 33 E.H.R.R. 225, ECtHR, and *J.B. v. Switzerland* [2001] Crim.L.R. 748, ECtHR), the Government formed and applied a policy of not using against an accused in criminal proceedings evidence obtained by compulsory questioning whether before or after charge: see *R. v. Secretary of State for Trade and Industry, ex p. McCormick*, 2 B.C.L.C. 18, CA (Civ. Div.). This policy applied to questioning under the *Companies Act* 1985, the *Insolvency Act* 1986, the *Financial Services Act* 1986, the *Banking Act* 1987, the *CJA* 1987 and analogous powers under other provisions: *Hansard*, H.C., Vol. 305, cols 639–640. See further, *R. v. Faryab* [2000] Crim.L.R. 180, CA; *R. v. Hertfordshire C.C., ex p. Green Environmental Industries Ltd* [2000] 2 A.C. 412, HL; *Att.-Gen.'s Reference (No. 7 of 2000)* [2001] 2 Cr.App.R. 19, CA; and *R. v. Kearns* [2003] 1 Cr.App.R. 7, CA. See also *R. v. Allen* [2002] 1 A.C. 509, HL; and *Allen v. U.K.* [2003] Crim.L.R. 280, ECtHR.

15–449 Statutory effect (as from April 14, 2000) was given to this policy by the *YJCEA* 1999, s.59 and Sched. 3, which effected a series of amendments to various statutory provisions so as to restrict the use that may be made in criminal proceedings of answers and statements given under compulsion (*Youth Justice and Criminal Evidence Act 1999 (Commencement No. 2) Order* 2000 (S.I. 2000 No. 1034)). The amendment of these provisions did not provide a right of appeal where the *Human Rights Act* 1998 was not in force at the time of the trial: *R. v. Lyons* [2003] 1 A.C. 976, HL.

(c) *Admissions excluded by statute*

15–450 By certain statutes, admissions by a person on a former trial or inquiry in which he was examined as a witness cannot be given in evidence against him in subsequent proceedings. Examples are the *Explosive Substances Act* 1883, s.6(2); the *Theft Act* 1968, s.31(1) (*post*, § 21–336); the *Criminal Damage Act* 1971, s.9 (*post*, § 23–53); the *Supreme Court Act* 1981 (to be cited, as from a day to be appointed, as the *Senior Courts Act* 1981: *Constitutional Reform Act* 2005, s.59, and Sched. 11, para. 1(1)), s.72; the *Representation of the People Act* 1983, s.141(2); and the *Offender Management Act* 2007, s.30 (see *ante*, § 8–158).

D. ACTS AND STATEMENTS IN FURTHERANCE OF JOINT ENTERPRISE

15–451 The acts and declarations of any conspirator in furtherance of the common design are admissible against any other conspirator, provided there is independent evidence to prove the existence of the conspiracy and that the persons concerned are parties to it. Such evidence may not fall within the definition of "confession" in section 82(1) of the *PACE Act* 1984 but may still be excluded under section 78. This topic is dealt with more fully, *post*, §§ 33–65 *et seq.*

III. DISCRETION TO EXCLUDE EVIDENCE

A. UNDER STATUTE

(1) General

Police and Criminal Evidence Act 1984, s.78

Exclusion of unfair evidence

15–452 **78.**—(1) In any proceedings the court may refuse to allow evidence on which the prosecution proposes to rely to be given if it appears to the court that, having regard to all the circumstances, including the circumstances in which the evidence was obtained, the admission of the evidence would have such an adverse effect on the fairness of the proceedings that the court ought not to admit it.

(2) Nothing in this section shall prejudice any rule of law requiring a court to exclude evidence.

(3) *This section shall not apply in the case of proceedings before a magistrates' court inquiring into an offence as examining justices.*

[This section is printed as amended by the *CPIA* 1996, s.47 and Sched. 1, para. 26 (insertion of subs. (3)). As from a day to be appointed, subs. (3) is repealed by the *CJA* 2003, ss.41 and 332, Sched. 3, para. 56(1), (5), and Sched. 37, Pt 4.]

15–453 Section 78 is the most important provisions in the *PACE Act* 1984, and the most often referred to in practice. Together with section 76 (confessions, *ante*, § 15–352) it plays a fundamental role in the consideration of the admissibility of evidence, particularly evidence of admissions and confessions. Its precise scope is unclear, but, given that the common law discretion to exclude evidence is expressly preserved by section 82(3) (*post*, § 15–535), Parliament must have intended section 78 to be of broader application, or at the very least as broad (see *R. v. Khan* [1997] A.C. 558 at 578, HL). So, whereas at common law there was no discretion to exclude evidence obtained as a result of an *agent provocateur's* activities (*R. v. Sang* [1980] A.C. 402, HL, at 437), in *R. v. Looseley*; *Att.-Gen.'s Reference (No. 3 of 2000)* [2002] 1 Cr.App.R. 29, HL, Lord Nicholls (at [11]) said that section 78 had reversed *Sang* on the admissibility of evidence obtained unfairly; and (at [16]) that *Sang* had been overtaken by section 78 and the development of the common law doctrine of abuse of process, both of which had been reinforced by the enactment of the *Human Rights Act* 1998 (*post*, §§ 16–5 *et seq.*). See further *post*, § 15–456 (at (g) and (i)), §§ 15–518 *et seq.*

15–454 In *R. v. Quinn* [1990] Crim.L.R. 581, Lord Lane C.J. underlined the general nature of the discretion:

> "The function of the judge is therefore to protect the fairness of the proceedings, and normally proceedings are fair if a jury hears all relevant evidence which either side wishes to place before it, but proceedings may become unfair if, for example, one side is allowed to adduce relevant evidence which, for one reason or another, the other side cannot properly challenge or meet".

15–455 In the absence of definitive authority on the scope of section 78 (see the general observations of the Court of Appeal, *post*, § 15–457), the growing body of case law provides substantial guidance for the practitioner. A number of key features have emerged.

(a) The *PACE Act* 1984 is a codifying Act and therefore the principles set out in *Bank of England v. Vagliano* [1891] A.C. 107 at 144 apply: "I think the proper course is in the first instance to examine the language of the statute and to ask what is its natural meaning, uninfluenced by any considerations derived from the previous state of the law, and not to start with inquiring how the law previously stood ..." (*per* Lord Herschell): see *R. v. Fulling* [1987] Q.B. 426,

85 Cr.App.R. 136, CA (*ante*, § 15–358); and *R. v. Smurthwaite*; *R. v. Gill*, 98 Cr.App.R. 437 at 440, CA (*post*, § 15–518).

(b) Each case has to be decided on its own facts (*post*, § 15–457).

(c) "Evidence" in section 78 means all the evidence which the prosecution might seek to adduce at trial: *R. v. Mason (Carl)*, 86 Cr.App.R. 349, CA. It might have been thought that section 76 provided the complete code for the admissibility of confessions. But in *Mason* it was held that a trial judge has a discretion to deal with the admissibility of a confession under section 78 regardless of the power conferred by section 76.

(d) Section 78 has been successfully invoked, and frequently, both to exclude evidence and to quash convictions where evidence should have been excluded. By contrast, at common law few such decisions were made, at least on appeal: see *R. v. Sang* [1980] A.C. 402, HL, *per* Lord Diplock at p. 435.

(e) Section 78 has been invoked (although not always successfully) in relation to a wide range of evidential material, including confessions (*post*, § 15–478), an alibi notice (*R. v. Fields and Adams* [1991] Crim.L.R. 38, CA, *ante*, § 4–319), depositions of absent witnesses (*R. v. O'Loughlin and McLaughlin*, 85 Cr.App.R. 157, CCC (Kenneth Jones J.), *post*, § 15–535), evidence of co-defendants' pleas of guilty (*post*, § 15–512), identification evidence (*post*, § 15–513) and evidence obtained from an illegal search (*R. v. Khan, Sakkarvej and Pamarapa* [1997] Crim.L.R. 508, CA, *post*, § 15–524). **15–456**

(f) The greatest use of section 78 has been in the field of confessions. It has been applied in conjunction with breaches of the important and detailed provisions on interviewing suspects in Code of Practice C (Appendix A–38). A breach of Code C may lead to the exclusion of a confession under section 78, but not every breach will trigger exclusion. Moreover, evidence may be excluded where there has been no breach of Code C.

(g) There are two stages in the application of section 78: first, the circumstances in which the evidence came to be obtained; secondly, whether admission of the evidence would have an adverse effect upon the fairness of the proceedings. In considering fairness, a balance has to be struck between that which is fair to the prosecution and that which is fair to the defence (see *R. v. Hughes* [1988] Crim.L.R. 519, CA). The final aspect of the fairness test appears to relate only to the defendant: whether the admission of the evidence would have "such an adverse effect on the fairness of the proceedings that the court ought not to admit it". In *R. v. Looseley* (*ante*, § 15–453; *post*, §§ 15–518 *et seq.*), Lord Nicholls said (at [11]–[12]) that the concept of fairness was not limited to procedural fairness and Lord Scott added (at [122]) that evidence could be excluded because it had been obtained by unfair means.

(h) On appeal from a trial judge's refusal to exclude evidence under section 78, the Court of Appeal will only interfere with the exercise of the judge's discretion on *Wednesbury* principles: see *post*, §§ 15–471 *et seq.*

(i) The right to a fair trial under Article 6 of the ECHR involves the same criterion as applies under section 78: *R. v. P.* [2002] 1 A.C. 146, HL; *R. v. Looseley*, *ante*.

(2) Applying section 78: no general guidance

In *R. v. Samuel* [1988] Q.B. 615, 87 Cr.App.R. 232, CA (see *ante*, § 15–211), Hodgson J. said (at pp. 630, 245) that, because of the infinite variety of circumstances, it was undesirable to attempt any general guidance as to how the judge's discretion under section 78 or his inherent powers should be exercised, but unhesitatingly rejected a submission that the power under section 78 could not be exercised in the absence of impropriety, although the propriety or otherwise of the way in which the evidence was obtained is something to which the court is specifically enjoined to take into account (adopted in *R. v. O'Leary*, 87 Cr.App.R. 387 at 391, CA). **15–457**

As to every case having to be decided on its own facts, see *R. v. Parris*, 89 Cr.App.R. 68 at 72, CA; *R. v. Jelen and Katz*, 90 Cr.App.R. 456, CA ("This is not an apt field for hard case law and well founded distinctions between cases", *per* Auld J. at p. 465).

(3) Procedure

(a) *General*

15–458 Where the defence seek under section 78 to exclude evidence upon which the prosecution propose to rely, an application will be made to the judge in the absence of the jury at the appropriate time, usually just before the evidence is to be called. In some cases, the submission can be made on the face of the papers without the need for evidence. In other cases, for example those involving confessions, evidence will often have to be called on the *voire dire*. The prosecution may wish to justify an apparent breach of Code C, for example, which appears on the face of the witness statements or in the custody record. The defence may have to call evidence to assert a breach which cannot otherwise be supported without defence evidence.

The procedure for challenging confessions is set out and discussed in detail at §§ 15–374 *et seq.*, *ante* (s.76: confessions). In most cases, the defence challenge to a confession will be made in the alternative, under section 76 or section 78. Usually the procedure under the two sections will be the same. If there is a challenge under sections 76 and 78 there will be a hearing on the *voire dire* because it is required for section 76. If there is only a challenge under section 78, a judge may in his discretion refuse to hold a trial-within-a-trial. In *R. v. Manji* [1990] Crim.L.R. 512, however, the Court of Appeal held that the trial judge had been wrong to refuse to hold a trial-within-a-trial on the issue of whether the police had cautioned the defendant. It was the judge's task to make a finding as to whether the prosecution had proved that a caution had been given.

15–459 In *R. v. Keenan* [1990] 2 Q.B. 54 at 63–66, 90 Cr.App.R. 1 at 8–10, CA, Hodgson J. said that a number of different situations may face a judge when confronted by an objection based on alleged breaches of the Act or the codes. (a) One or more breaches may be apparent in the custody record or from the witness statements. In this situation, it may be that all that is necessary is for an admission by the prosecution followed by argument. (b) There may be a prima facie breach, which must be justified by evidence from the prosecution. An order refusing access to a solicitor can only be justified by evidence from the police officer who made the order. The defence may wish to call evidence from the solicitor to whom the defendant sought to have access; on occasion, the defence may feel it desirable to call the defendant himself. (c) There may be alleged breaches which can probably only be established by the evidence of the defendant himself, *e.g.* cases of alleged oppression or in relation to what is now paragraphs 11.15–11.20 of Code C (persons at risk). There is no requirement on the defence to tell the judge what the defendant's response would be if the evidence were admitted.

Where the defence had sufficient foundation to request a *voire dire*, it was wrong in principle to refuse the request on the basis of a statement made by prosecution counsel that officers of revenue and customs had a policy of not answering certain questions (as to their grounds for stopping particular passengers): *R. v. Rehman* [2007] Crim.L.R. 101, CA.

(b) *Magistrates' courts*

Summary trial

15–460 When an application is made under section 78, a magistrates' court may deal with the application when it arises or they may leave the decision until the end of the hearing; the object should always be to secure a trial which is fair to both sides: *Vel v. Owen* [1987] Crim.L.R. 496, DC; *Halawa v. Federation Against Copyright Theft* [1995] 1 Cr.App.R. 21, DC. In the latter case, the court proffered the following guidance for the assistance of magistrates' courts (the points have been re-ordered).

1. A proper understanding of what is fair will lead in some cases to the conclusion that, if the defendant wishes to proceed by way of a *voire dire*, he should be allowed to do so because, unless there are good reasons to take a different course, he should have the opportunity to secure the exclusion of unfair evidence before he decides whether to give evidence on the main issues. If he is unfairly denied that opportunity, his right to remain silent on the main issues is impaired.

2. If the application is made as alternative to a submission under section 76 of the 1984 Act (*ante*, § 15–352), it should be examined at the same time, in accordance with the procedure laid down in *R. v. Liverpool Juvenile Court, ex p. R.* [1988] Q.B. 1, 86 Cr.App.R. 1, DC (*ante*, § 15–396).
3. If the point is raised only under section 78, in most cases the better course will be for the whole of the prosecution case to be heard, including the disputed evidence, before any *voire dire* is held.
4. In order to decide what course to take, the court may ask the defence the extent of the issues to be addressed by the defendant's evidence on the *voire dire*. If the issues are limited to the circumstances in which the evidence was obtained, there would in most cases be no apparent reason why the defendant should not be heard as on a *voire dire*. If, however, the defendant intends to contradict some part of the prosecution's account of "all the circumstances" (see s.78), it would be open to the court to conclude that the proceedings on the *voire dire* might be protracted and would introduce issues which would have to be re-examined in the remaining stages of the trial if a prima facie case is held to be established, in which case the securing of a fair trial to both sides would not require a *voire dire*. For this purpose the court would be entitled to take account of the nature and extent of the cross-examination of the prosecution witnesses for an understanding of the extent of any dispute as to "all the circumstances".

By contrast, in *DPP v. Lawrence* [2008] 1 Cr.App.R. 10, DC (see also *post*, § 15–499), it was said *obiter* (and without reference to any authority) that, where a defendant challenges under section 78 the admissibility in summary proceedings of statements allegedly made by him, the justices should normally hear the evidence sought to be excluded and consider any circumstances which it is said would render its admission unfair. If they subsequently resolve to exclude the evidence, they should then consider, after seeking the views of the parties, whether the substantive hearing (if any) should be conducted by a differently constituted bench.

Committal proceedings

See section 78(3) (*ante*, § 15–452); and *R. v. King's Lynn JJ., ex p. Holland*, 96 Cr.App.R. 74, DC. **15–461**

(c) *Burden of proof*

Whereas in section 76 (*ante*, § 15–352) the wording places the burden of proof squarely upon the prosecution to prove that the confession was not obtained in breach of section 76(2)(a) or (b), the position under section 78 is less clear (as was recognised in *R. v. Anderson* [1993] Crim.L.R. 447, CA). Section 78 places no burden on the prosecution to disprove unfairness: see *Vel v. Owen* [1987] Crim.L.R. 496, DC. But does the burden fall on the defence? In *R. v. Keenan, ante*, § 15–459, the judgment of the Court of Appeal suggests, perhaps not intentionally, that the burden shifts depending on the circumstances (see pp. 63–66, 8–10). **15–462**

In *R. (Saifi) v. Governor of Brixton Prison* [2001] 1 W.L.R. 1134, DC, it was said that the concept of the burden of proof has no part to play in the exercise of the discretion under section 78.

There seems no reason why the trial court cannot exercise its discretion of its own motion, although there is no equivalent in section 78 to section 76(3). In most cases the defence will raise the issue with the trial judge. Therefore the evidential burden of satisfying the court that there is an issue to be decided, as in self-defence (*post*, § 19–43), will rest on the defence, if no more.

(d) *"Significant and substantial" breaches*

The extent to which a breach or breaches of the Act or the codes of practice will trigger the exercise of the trial judge's discretion to exclude evidence under section 78 has, in the main, been discussed on appeal on a case by case basis. Nevertheless, the expression "significant and substantial" has been used in three key cases (*Keenan, ante, Absolam* and *Walsh, post*), even though other expressions, such as "material breaches" (see **15–463**

R. v. Doolan [1988] Crim.L.R. 747, CA), have been used elsewhere. The words "significant and substantial" do not appear in the statute: see *R. v. Oliphant* [1992] Crim.L.R. 40, CA.

In *R. v. Absolam*, 88 Cr.App.R. 332, CA (see *ante*, § 15–215 on s.58: access to legal advice), "significant and substantial" breaches of Code C led to the conviction being quashed. In *R. v. Walsh*, 91 Cr.App.R. 161 (also a s.58 case, see *ante*, § 15–216), the Court of Appeal stated, at p. 163, that "significant and substantial breaches" of the Act or the codes mean that "prima facie at least the standards of fairness set by Parliament have not been met":

> "So far as a defendant is concerned, it seems to us also to follow that to admit evidence against him which has been obtained in circumstances where these standards have not been met, cannot but have an adverse effect on the fairness of the proceedings. This does not mean, of course, that in every case of a significant or substantial breach of section 58 or the Code of Practice the evidence concerned will automatically be excluded. Section 78 does not so provide. The task of the court is not merely to consider whether there would be an adverse effect on the fairness of the proceedings, but such an adverse effect that justice requires the evidence to be excluded" (at p. 163).

As to the reference to "significant and substantial" breaches in *R. v. Keenan*, *ante*, see *post*, § 15–506.

In *R. v. Stewart* [1995] Crim.L.R. 500, CA, it was pointed out that it was the nature and not the number of breaches that was the important factor.

(e) *Good faith/ bad faith*

15–464 There is no requirement for the police to have acted in bad faith before evidence is excluded. Bad faith on the part of police officers will usually lead to exclusion of the evidence: see *R. v. Alladice*, 87 Cr.App.R. 380 at 386, CA. The contrary does not follow. Good faith by the police will not excuse serious breaches of the Act and the codes: see *ibid.*; and *R. v. Samuel*, *ante*, § 15–211.

In *R. v. Walsh*, *ante*, the court said (at p. 163) that bad faith may make "substantial or significant" that which might not otherwise be so, but the contrary does not follow: breaches which are in themselves "substantial or significant" are not rendered otherwise by the good faith of the officers concerned.

15–465 In breath test cases, however, the rule seems to be different. Evidence will not be excluded unless there is bad faith on the part of the police. In *Matto v. Wolverhampton Crown Court* [1987] R.T.R. 337, DC, bad faith on the part of police officers was held to be a factor which should have led to the exclusion of evidence under section 78 in a breath test case. The police officers knew they were acting unlawfully at the time of the first breath test.

15–466 It was held that *Fox v. Chief Constable of Gwent* [1986] A.C. 281, HL (impropriety in conducting a roadside breath test cannot stop a prosecution, but the court may exercise its discretion to exclude evidence brought in support of a charge: see *R. v. Sang* [1980] A.C. 402, HL), could be distinguished because there had been no *mala fides* in that case. Section 78 required the court to have regard to the way in which the evidence was obtained. *Fox* and *Matto*, *ante*, were applied in *Sharpe v. DPP* [1993] R.T.R. 392, DC, where an excess alcohol conviction was quashed after justices had wrongly refused to issue the defence with witness summonses. The defence case was that the evidence of the breath test should have been excluded under section 78 because of the officers' behaviour in the course of stopping and arresting the motorist. The justices, by refusing the summonses, effectively had indicated that they would have admitted the evidence of the breath test however badly the officers had behaved. By so doing, the justices had not exercised their discretion under section 78. However, Buckley J. (at p. 398) rejected a defence submission that a finding of *mala fides* meant that the discretion could only be exercised one way: *mala fides* is a relevant factor under section 78, but not conclusive. The origin of the bad faith approach in breath test cases seems to have been *Fox*, *ante*, a pre-*PACE Act* 1984 case: see *R. v. Thomas* [1990] Crim.L.R. 269, DC; *DPP v. Wilson* [1991] R.T.R. 284, DC; *DPP v. McGladrigan* [1991] R.T.R. 297, DC; *Braham v. DPP* [1996] R.T.R. 30, DC; and *DPP v. Kay* [1999] R.T.R. 109, DC.

See also *post*, §§ 15–524 *et seq.*, as to evidence obtained unlawfully, unfairly or by a trick.

(f) *The judge's ruling*

There is no specific requirement for the judge to give reasons in deciding to admit confession evidence on the *voire dire* or to admit other evidence challenged under section 78. The absence of a detailed ruling will not give rise to criticism: see *R. v. Moss*, 91 Cr.App.R. 371 at 375, CA. It is submitted, however, that it would greatly assist defence counsel, in considering an appeal and in formulating grounds of appeal, and also the Court of Appeal, if an appeal proceeds, if the judge were to give a short judgment. This should include any findings of fact, a summary of the arguments, a statement as to which matters have been taken into account, and the reasons for not excluding the evidence. Support for such an approach may be found in *Flannery v. Halifax Estate Agencies Ltd, t/a Colleys Professional Services* [2000] 1 W.L.R. 377, CA (Civ. Div.); and *R. v. Snaresbrook Crown Court, ex p. Input Management Ltd*, 163 J.P. 533, DC. A duty to give a reasoned judgment now exists under Article 6 of the ECHR (*post*, § 16–75). **15–467**

(g) *Reconsideration of the judge's ruling*

The words "evidence on which the prosecution proposes to rely" in section 78 are not appropriate to something which has happened in the past. Accordingly, if the trial judge admits the evidence after an application by the defence to exclude it, he cannot reconsider his decision under section 78 even if fresh evidence given before the jury changes his mind: *R. v. Sat-Bhambra*, 88 Cr.App.R. 55 at 62, CA. However, the judge is not powerless to act: as to the options open to him, see *ante*, § 15–377. See also *R. v. Hassan* [1995] Crim.L.R. 404, CA. **15–468**

In *R. v. Allen* [1992] Crim.L.R. 297, CA, the judge excluded evidence of a conversation because of breaches of Code C, but later admitted the evidence having taken the view that counsel for the defence had opened up the position by his cross-examination of the police. The court refused to interfere with the exercise of the judge's discretion.

(h) *Subsequent interviews*

It is a feature of many cases in which admissions are sought to be excluded under section 78 that some of the interviews are improperly conducted or recorded in breach of the Act or of Code C and some are subsequently properly conducted and recorded. The first issue is whether the inadmissible interview should be regarded as tainting the subsequent interview to the extent that it should also have been ruled inadmissible. The second issue seems to be whether the Court of Appeal will refuse to interfere where there has been a wrongful decision to admit the first interview but an untainted second interview containing clear admissions of guilt. See *post*, §§ 15–471 *et seq.* **15–469**

As to the first point, the authorities (including *R. v. Canale*, 91 Cr.App.R. 1, CA; *R. v. Gillard and Barrett*, 92 Cr.App.R. 61, CA; *R. v. McGovern*, *ante*, § 15–214; *Y. v. DPP* [1991] Crim.L.R. 917, DC; and *R. v. Glaves* [1993] Crim.L.R. 685, CA) were reviewed in *R. v. Neil* [1994] Crim.L.R. 441, CA: where there is a series of interviews and the court excludes one on the grounds of unfairness, the question whether a later interview which is itself unobjectionable should also be excluded is a matter of fact and degree. It is likely to depend on whether the objections leading to the exclusion of the first interview were of a fundamental and continuing nature, and, if so, if the arrangements for the subsequent interview gave the defendant a sufficient opportunity to exercise an informed and independent choice as to whether he should repeat or retract what he said in the excluded interview or say nothing. The above passage was quoted with approval by the Court of Appeal in *R. v. Nelson and Rose* [1998] 2 Cr.App.R. 399 at 409. See also *R. v. Wood* [1994] Crim.L.R. 222, CA, *R. v. Conway* [1994] Crim.L.R. 838, CA, and *Prouse v. DPP* [1999] 10 *Archbold News* 2, DC.

(4) Appeal

(a) *The citation of authorities*

Although each case has to be determined on its own particular facts (*ante*, § 15–457), **15–470** the Court of Appeal has been prepared to consider the application of section 78 (and s.76) in other Court of Appeal cases. In particular, reference has often been made to some of the key cases which touch upon questions of principle: see *R. v. Samuel* [1988] Q.B. 615, 87 Cr.App.R. 232; *R. v. Alladice*, 87 Cr.App.R. 380; *R. v. Absolam*, 88 Cr.App.R. 332; *R. v. Parris*, 89 Cr.App.R. 68; *R. v. Walsh*, 91 Cr.App.R. 161 (all denial of access to legal advice cases under s.58: *ante*, §§ 15–210 *et seq.*); *R. v. Sat-Bhambra*, 88 Cr.App.R. 55 (ss.76 and 78 look forward not back: *ante*, §§ 15–352, 15–452); *R. v. Keenan* [1990] 2 Q.B. 54, 90 Cr.App.R. 1; *R. v. Delaney*, 88 Cr.App.R. 338; and *R. v. Canale*, 91 Cr.App.R. 1 (three cases under the "verballing" provisions of Code C: *post*, § 15–501).

The citation of first instance authorities will not normally be helpful: *R. v. Grannell*, 90 Cr.App.R. 149, CA. *Cf.* the reference to such a decision in *R. v. Davis* [1990] Crim.L.R. 860, CA (*ante*, § 15–374).

(b) *The judge's discretion: Wednesbury principles*

15–471 Where the Court of Appeal is invited to consider the exercise of the trial judge's discretion under section 78, the court will be "loth to interfere" with the judge's decision "subject to the question of *Wednesbury* reasonableness": *per* May L.J. in *R. v. O'Leary*, 87 Cr.App.R. 387 at 391.

In *Associated Provincial Picture Houses Ltd v. Wednesbury Corporation* [1948] 1 K.B. 223, Lord Greene M.R. said:

> "a person entrusted with a discretion must, so to speak, direct himself properly in law. He must call his own attention to the matters which he is bound to consider. He must exclude from his consideration matters which are irrelevant to what he has to consider. If he does not obey those rules, he may truly be said, and often is said, to be acting 'unreasonably'. Similarly, there may be something so absurd that no sensible person could ever dream that it lay within the powers of the authority. Warrington L.J. in *Short v. Poole Corporation* ([1926] Ch. 66 at pp. 90–91) gave the example of the red-haired teacher, dismissed because she had red hair. That is unreasonable in one sense. In another sense it is taking into consideration extraneous matters. It is so unreasonable that it might almost be described as being done in bad faith; and, in fact, all these things run into one another" (at p. 229).

15–472 In *R. v. O'Leary*, *ante*, the Court of Appeal held that the trial judge had applied the proper test and his decision was not perverse in the legal sense, *i.e.* a decision to which no reasonable trial judge could have come. The *Wednesbury* approach was adopted in *R. v. Christou and Wright* [1992] Q.B. 979, 95 Cr.App.R. 264 (*post*, § 15–527); *R. v. Rankin*, *The Times*, September 5, 1995, CA; *R. v. Khan, Sakkarvej and Pamarapa* [1997] Crim.L.R. 508, CA; and *Thompson v. R.* [1998] A.C. 811, PC.

References to the *Wednesbury* approach in the authorities, *ante*, and the exercise of the judge's discretion, were considered in *R. v. Middlebrook and Caygill*, unreported, February 18, 1994, CA (92/6701/Z2). The court held that section 78 did not provide a true discretion, despite the use of that word in many cases. A true discretion consists in a power which can lawfully be exercised in more than one way. Section 78 provides that "the court may refuse to allow evidence on which the prosecution proposes to rely to be given if it appears to the court that ... [its admission] would have such an adverse effect on the fairness of the proceedings that the court ought not to admit it". The word "may" must be read as meaning "shall". If the material in the case discloses a state of affairs in which a reasonable judge must have concluded that admission of the evidence would produce unfairness, the Court of Appeal will set aside a ruling which goes the other way. This is what is meant by references to *Wednesbury* in the cases.

In *R. v. Dures* [1997] 2 Cr.App.R. 247 at 261–262, the Court of Appeal quoted with approval the following passage from *R. v. Quinn* [1995] 1 Cr.App.R. 480:

> "Before this court could reach the conclusion that the judge was wrong in that respect, we would have to be satisfied that no reasonable judge, having heard the evidence that this ... judge did, could have reached the conclusion that he did" (*per* Lord Taylor C.J. at p. 489).

Rose L.J. (at p. 262) said that this passage represented the practice of the Court of Appeal and if, and in so far as, the judgment of Laws J. in *Middlebrook and Caygill*, *ante*, suggests any different approach, then the approach in *Quinn*, *ante*, should be followed. In *R. v. Chalkley and Jeffries* [1998] 2 Cr.App.R. 79 at 105, a differently constituted Court of Appeal, without considering *Dures*, *ante*, referred to the above approach of Laws J. in *Middlebrook and Caygill*, *ante*, with approval. In *Thompson v. R.*, *ante*, the Privy Council said that there was no difference between the approach in *Middlebrook* and that in *Christou and Wright* (*Chalkley and Jeffries* had not been decided at the time of argument before the Privy Council and is not referred to).

Whilst the Court of Appeal will generally defer to the view of the trial judge in relation to live evidence which it has not had the benefit of hearing, where there is an issue as to whether the trial overall matched up to the fair trial requirements of Article 6 of the ECHR (*post*, § 16–57), no deference is due to the judge of first instance, it being the function of the Court of Appeal to conduct its own independent assessment on this issue: see *R. v. Davis (Iain)*; *R. v. Ellis* [2006] 2 Cr.App.R. 32, CA (this aspect of the Court of Appeal's reasoning is unaffected by the decision's reversal: see *R. v. Davis* [2008] 3 W.L.R. 125, HL). **15–473**

(c) *The Court of Appeal's discretion*

Where the trial judge fails to exercise his discretion, the Court of Appeal will endeavour to put itself in the position of the judge and decide how the discretion should have been exercised: *R. v. Parris*, 89 Cr.App.R. 68 (*ante*, § 15–214); *R. v. Keenan* [1990] 2 Q.B. 54, 90 Cr.App.R. 1. **15–474**

For an example of the Court of Appeal applying a section 78 discretion in a confession case which had been argued at trial under section 76 alone, see *R. v. Howden-Simpson* [1991] Crim.L.R. 49, CA.

(d) *Quashing the conviction*

If confession evidence has been wrongly admitted by the trial judge and there is little or no other evidence, the Court of Appeal will have no alternative but to quash the conviction, as in *R. v. Parris*, 89 Cr.App.R. 68 (*ante*, § 15–214). Where there is other "good evidence" against the defendant, as in *R. v. Dunford*, 91 Cr.App.R. 150, this will be taken into account. **15–475**

It is clear that the mere fact that evidence has been wrongly admitted will not lead to the automatic quashing of the conviction. Under the amended section 2 of the *CAA* 1968 (*ante*, § 7–43), the only question for the Court of Appeal will be whether the conviction is unsafe: see further, *ante*, §§ 7–45 *et seq.* **15–476**

(5) Access to legal advice

As to section 58 of the *PACE Act* 1984 (right of access to legal advice), see *ante*, §§ 15–206 *et seq.* **15–477**

As to Code C and access to legal advice, see paras 3.1, 3.2 and 6 and Annex B (Appendix A–46, A–54 and A–99).

See also *R. v. Vernon* [1988] Crim.L.R. 445, Crown Court (H.H. Judge Andrew Q.C.) (failure to draw attention to duty solicitor scheme vitiated "consent" to be interviewed).

(6) Confessions

The admissibility of confessions is governed by section 76 of the *PACE Act* 1984 (*ante*, §§ 15–352 *et seq.*). It is common and approved practice to challenge a confession under section 76 and also under section 78 in the alternative. Many of the section 78 cases involve alleged breaches of the "verballing" provisions of Code C: see *post*, § 15–501. For the procedure to be adopted in confession cases, see *ante*, §§ 15–374 *et seq.* **15–478**

A "co-operation conversation", whereby a suspect is encouraged to give customs officers information about accomplices, is not an interview for the purpose of gathering evidence against the suspect, and is liable to be excluded under section 78, if not section 76: *R. v. De Silva* [2003] 2 Cr.App.R. 5, CA.

In *R. v. Elleray* [2003] 2 Cr.App.R. 11, CA, it was said that if, in the course of an interview with a probation officer who was preparing a pre-sentence report, the offender admitted having committed the offence with which he was charged or another offence, the probation officer could not ignore what was said; there was a duty to provide a full and frank report, including as to risk of commission of further offences; but if a subsequent prosecution were to be based on such admission, the admissibility of the confession would have to be judged under section 78; in deciding on the issue of fairness, it was important to bear in mind the desirability of frankness between offender and probation officer; and that if it were to become the practice for the prosecution regularly to rely on such admissions, a situation would soon arise when probation officers were unable to perform their duty; accordingly, the prosecution should carefully consider whether it was right to seek to rely on any such admission; in making its judgment under section 78, the court should bear in mind the contrast between an interview with a probation officer and one with a police officer conducted under the protection of the 1984 Act; in particular, there might have been no accurate record, no caution and no legal representation; and as to probation officers, it was not for the court to dictate what they should do in such situation, but they should take whatever action they thought appropriate to protect the position of the interviewee, including, possibly, warning the interviewee that what was said by way of admission would be included in the report to the court, and offering to pause the interview so that the offender might have legal representation.

(7) Codes C and H and section 78

(a) *Introduction*

15–479 The current Code C came into force on February 1, 2008. See *ante*, § 15–7, for the commencement dates of previous versions of Code C. Code H (Appendix A–213 *et seq.*) contains corresponding provisions in relation to the detention, treatment and questioning by police officers of persons under section 41 of, and Schedule 8 to, the *Terrorism Act* 2000, and came into force on July 25, 2006 (see *ante*, § 15–7). For a summary of the differences, see *ante*, § 15–251.

A court can have regard to the current Code C in considering events before that code came into force, because the provisions of the new code reflect current thinking as to what is fair: *R. v. Ward*, 98 Cr.App.R. 337, CA.

(b) *Summary of the provisions of Code C*

15–480 Code C contains detailed provisions on the use of custody records (C:2), the procedure and documentation for detained persons at police stations (C:3), the position of persons attending a police station voluntarily (C:3.21–C:3.22), detained persons' property (C:4), intimate and strip searches (Annex A), the right of an arrested person not to be held *incommunicado* (C:5 and Annex B), the right to legal advice (C:6 and Annex B), the rights of citizens of independent Commonwealth countries and foreign nationals (C:7 and Annex F), conditions of detention (C:8), and the treatment of detained persons (C:9). It also contains detailed provisions on cautions (C:10), interviews (C:11 and Annexes C and E) including interviews at police stations (C:12), written statements under caution (Annex D), interpreters (C:13), special restrictions on questioning (C:14), reviews and extensions of detention (C:15), charging detained persons (C:16), and testing for presence of Class A drugs (C:17).

Throughout Code C, particular provision is made for special groups of persons: juveniles, persons who appear to be blind or seriously visually handicapped, persons who are deaf, unable to read, unable to speak or who have a speech impediment, and persons who are mentally disordered or otherwise mentally vulnerable. The provisions relating to mentally disordered and mentally vulnerable persons are summarised in Annex E.

15–481 In *R. v. Keenan* [1990] 2 Q.B. 54 at 63, 90 Cr.App.R. 1 at 7, CA, Hodgson J. said:

> "Code C, in extension of the provisions of Part III (arrest), Part IV (detention) and Part V (questioning and treatment of persons by police), addresses two main concerns. First, it provides safeguards for detained persons and provides for their proper treatment with the object of ensuring that they are not subjected to undue pressure or oppression. Equally importantly, these code provisions are designed to make it difficult for a detained person to make unfounded allegations against the police which might otherwise appear credible. Secondly, it provides safeguards against the police inaccurately recording or inventing the words used in questioning a detained person."

For the "verballing" provisions, see *post*, § 15–501.

(c) *Breaching Code C*

A breach or breaches of a code of practice may lead to evidence obtained after or in consequence of the breach being excluded by the trial judge, either under section 76 (confessions: *ante*, §§ 15–352 *et seq.*), or more usually under section 78 or under the common law (*post*, § 15–535). For breaches of the codes, see generally, *ante*, §§ 15–14 *et seq.* **15–482**

(d) *Particular topics: authorities*

Information as to rights

See generally Code C:1.2, 3.1, 3.2. Where a person arrested by customs officers is detained at an airport, this is tantamount to being at a police station (Code C:3.1), and he should be informed of his rights: *R. v. Sanusi* [1992] Crim.L.R. 43, CA. **15–483**

Failure to caution

The absence of a caution in circumstances in which it should have been administered will normally amount to a significant and substantial breach of the code: *R. v. Sparks* [1991] Crim.L.R. 128, CA; *R. v. Pall* [1992] Crim.L.R. 126, CA. For a case where evidence was admitted despite no caution being administered, see *R. v. Gill* [2004] 1 Cr.App.R. 20, CA, *ante*, § 15–10 (no likelihood that the defendants would have given different answers if caution administered; prosecution wanted to adduce the answers as evidence of deliberate lies rather than as confessions). **15–484**

The thrust of C:10.1 is that before questioning a suspect the police must ensure that he is aware of the true nature of the investigation; it is only if this requirement is fulfilled that the suspect can make meaningful decisions as to whether to avail himself of legal advice and as to how to respond to questions. Where there are grounds for arresting a suspect for a number of offences of different levels of seriousness arising out of the same incident it is unfair to arrest and question only in relation to a lesser offence, and then when compromising answers have been made, to reveal that the investigation relates to a more serious offence: *R. v. Kirk* [2000] 1 Cr.App.R. 400, CA. See now the requirement in Code C:11.1A (Appendix A–73) to inform an interviewee of the nature of the offence, or further offence, about which he is being interviewed.

In *R. v. James* [1996] Crim.L.R. 650, CA, the defendant's business partner having disappeared, the police questioned him without caution and prior to arrest. The questioning included questions about inconsistencies in his account. It was held that, although C:10.1 speaks of "grounds to suspect", it is implicit that the grounds be reasonable. The concept of "reasonable grounds for suspicion" is not an absolute one, particularly where there existed at the relevant time a real possibility that no crime at all had been committed, which clearly delayed the point at which initial uncertainties about an interviewee's innocence turned into an objectively well-founded suspicion of guilt. The Court of Appeal did, however, question whether it was proper not to have administered a caution when the police sought to put inconsistencies to the interviewee. See also *R. v. Shillibier* [2006] 5 *Archbold News* 2, CA: a person spoken to pursuant to a "trace, interview and eliminate" investigative policy need only receive the full caution if there are in fact reasonable grounds to suspect him of committing the offence; the existence of a warrant to search his address is a relevant factor, but does not automatically make him a suspect in the investigation.

In *R. v. Hunt* [1992] Crim.L.R. 582, CA, police officers saw the defendant in someone else's garden putting a flick-knife into his pocket. One officer asked the defendant what the knife was for and received a reply to the effect that it belonged to the defendant and he (the defendant) would carry it if he wished. *Held*, the judge had erred in failing to exclude this exchange under section 78, because, when the officer first asked the defendant about the knife, he had ample grounds for suspecting an offence and therefore should have cautioned him then (Code C:10.1). **15–485**

As to undercover police officers not breaching Code C:10.1, see *R. v. Christou and Wright* [1992] Q.B. 979, 95 Cr.App.R. 264, CA, *post*, § 15–527.

15–486 A number of authorities in this field concern officers of revenue and customs questioning suspected drug couriers. The following propositions emerge from the authorities:

(a) Code C10.1 applies to Revenue and Customs officers as well as police officers: see *R. v. Okafor*, 99 Cr.App.R. 97, CA;
(b) the appropriate time to administer the caution is when, on an objective test, there are grounds for suspicion, falling short of evidence supporting a prima facie case of guilt, that an offence has been committed by the person questioned; a positive field test for the presence of drugs is not required before the need to caution arises: *R. v. Nelson and Rose* [1998] 2 Cr.App.R. 399, CA;
(c) where customs officers suspect two airline passengers travelling together of involvement in a drug smuggling operation, but are unsure of a suspect suitcase's ownership, the passengers can be questioned about ownership prior to any caution being administered, but any other questioning should be preceded by a caution: *R. v. Senior* [2004] 2 Cr.App.R. 12, CA;
(d) questions asked in breach of Code C will not necessarily result in the answers being excluded: *R. v. Senior, ante*, followed in *R. v. Rehman* [2007] Crim.L.R. 101, CA;
(e) the mere fact that a person comes to an airport, to meet or collect someone in whose bag drugs are identified, does not by itself constitute grounds to suspect involvement in drug smuggling so as to require a caution: *R. v. Perpont* (2004) 148 S.J. 1372, CA.

In road traffic cases, answers to questions asked by police officers prior to the administration of a roadside breath test or a caution have been held admissible: see *Whelehan v. DPP* [1995] R.T.R. 177, DC, and *Sneyd v. DPP* [2007] R.T.R. 6, DC (questions about alcohol consumed), and *Kemsley v. DPP*, 169 J.P.148, DC (questions as to whether driver of particular car).

In *R. v. Hawkins* [2005] 8 *Archbold News* 2, CA, the defendant garage manager was seriously burnt in a fire in which an employee died. Shortly after the fire, he made admissions to a fire officer in a brief conversation, and then made further admissions in a longer conversation at hospital with a police officer sent to speak to him. Neither conversation was preceded by a caution. It was held that the second conversation should have been preceded by a caution and should not have been admitted in evidence. Although the police officer did not suspect the defendant of having committed an offence, because she had no knowledge of fires or of health and safety matters, the fire officer with his specialist knowledge must have realised that the defendant's account made him a suspect. Had there been adequate liaison between the police and the fire authorities, the defendant would have been cautioned at hospital and given the other protections of a suspect. The court also took into account his physical condition at the time of the questioning.

Incorrect form of caution

15–486a Where a terrorism suspect's access to his solicitor was lawfully delayed pursuant to the *Terrorism Act* 2000, Sched. 8, para. 8 (*post*, § 25–140a), what he said in interview while such access was delayed was admissible, even though he had been wrongly cautioned to the effect that an adverse inference could be drawn against him if he failed to mention any fact subsequently relied on in his own defence: *R. v. Ibrahim* [2008] 2 Cr.App.R. 23, CA. For a criticism of this decision, see the commentary in *Criminal Law Week* 2008/18/4.

Second caution

15–487 One caution is not necessarily enough: *R. v. Miller* [1998] Crim.L.R. 209, CA (caution at scene of arrest, but not at police station). But in *R. v. Oni* [1992] Crim.L.R. 183, CA, there was no need for a second caution after a break in questioning of about two minutes.

Second caution after charge

15–488 Where a defendant has been charged and cannot therefore be interviewed further, it is nevertheless necessary, if he wishes to make a further statement, to administer a further caution and ensure in accordance with Annex D, paragraph 2 (Appendix A–105), that it is written at the head of any statement that he makes: *R. v. Pall* [1992] Crim.L.R. 126, CA.

In *R. v. Williams (M.A.)*, 156 J.P. 776, the Court of Appeal expressed disapproval of "social visits" by officers to persons in custody whose alleged offences the officers were investigating. Although there is no objection to a suspect making a statement of his own volition after being charged, the police, in order to avoid the risk of the accused retracting his statement at trial, should pay meticulous attention to the codes.

Deafness

In *R. v. Clarke* [1989] Crim.L.R. 892, CA, it was held that there could be no breach of what is now Code C:13.5 if the police officers were not aware that the suspect was deaf or if they had no doubts about his hearing ability. That was not an end to the matter, because if it subsequently appeared that the suspect did indeed have a hearing impairment which would make it unfair for the evidence to be adduced, it should be excluded under section 78. **15–489**

Mental handicap/mental disorder

In relation to an issue under section 76(2)(b) of the 1984 Act, the defendant's actual mental condition is relevant: see *ante*, § 15–363. **15–490**

Section 77 of the *PACE Act* 1984 (warnings to juries) (*ante*, § 15–370) is confined to persons who are mentally handicapped (as defined in subs. (3)) whereas Code C, Annex E (Appendix A–105) provides protection for the "mentally disordered", "mentally vulnerable" and those "mentally incapable of understanding the significance of questions put". See further *R. v. O'Brien*, *ante*, § 15–368.

Where it is necessary to make a finding as to whether a defendant was "mentally handicapped", this should be based on medical evidence; and police officers, not having expertise in the matter, should not be allowed to state their opinion: *R. v. Ham* (1995) 36 B.M.L.R. 169, CA. *Semble*, the court was confining itself to a finding of "mental handicap" within the specific definition in section 77. The approach of Code C is not to require police officers to make judgments about whether or not a suspect is mentally disordered or vulnerable, but to require them to err on the side of caution. In the current Code C the expressions "mentally vulnerable" and "mental disorder" are defined in Note 1G. If an officer has any suspicion, or is told in good faith, that a person may be mentally disordered or mentally vulnerable, then he is to be treated as if he were mentally disordered or mentally vulnerable (Code C:1.4 (Appendix A–40)). To this extent, the opinion of a police officer may obviously be relevant.

The fact that a defendant who suffered from a mental disorder exhibited no acute symptoms, had been declared probably fit for interview by a doctor, and was able to understand procedures and answer questions, did not obviate the need for an appropriate adult: *R. v. Aspinall* [1999] 2 Cr.App.R. 115, CA.

A solicitor present at a police station in a professional capacity is excluded from the definition of "appropriate adult" in Code C (Note C:1F, Appendix A–43), but in *R. v. Lewis (M.)* [1996] Crim.L.R. 260, CA, it was said that the solicitor's function is similar. Although an appropriate adult might have a greater insight into the disabilities of a mentally handicapped person with a low I.Q., both the solicitor and the appropriate adult have to ensure that the accused fully understands his rights, that the interview is conducted correctly, that the police do not abuse their position, that the accused is able to make himself clearly understood, and that he clearly understands what is put to him. The absence of an appropriate adult from an interview, at which the defendant's solicitor was present, is unlikely by itself to be a reason to exclude the interview: *R. v. Law-Thompson* [1997] Crim.L.R. 674, CA. There is no rule that a confession obtained from a mentally handicapped person in the absence of a solicitor and an appropriate adult should automatically lead to exclusion under section 78: *R. v. Ali* [1999] 2 *Archbold News* 2, CA.

For a "flagrant breach" of the original Code 11.3 (record of interview), in the case of an educationally sub-normal 17-year-old, see *R. v. Delaney*, 88 Cr.App.R. 338, CA, *post*, § 15–506. See also *R. v. McGovern*, 92 Cr.App.R. 228, CA, *ante*, § 15–214; *R. v. Harvey* [1988] Crim.L.R. 241, CCC (Farquharson J.).

Juveniles—"appropriate adult"

15–491 An arrested juvenile has the right under Code C to have the appropriate adult informed of the grounds of his detention (C:3.15) and the right not to be interviewed in the absence of the appropriate adult (C:11.15). For the meaning of "appropriate adult", see Code C:1.7.

A 17-year-old is not a "juvenile" within Code C. The absence of an appropriate adult at an interview did not *per se* involve a breach of the code. Nonetheless, the interviewing of a detainee of such an age, who is unrepresented, has no previous history of arrest and who has been in custody for 24 hours at the time of the interview, is liable to give rise to issues under sections 76 and 78 that require anxious consideration: *R. (DPP) v. Stratford Youth Court*, 165 J.P. 761, DC.

15–492 Consideration was given to the meaning of "appropriate adult" in *DPP v. Blake*, 89 Cr.App.R. 179, DC. A 16-year-old juvenile was arrested and taken to a police station for interview. The police wanted her father to be the appropriate adult. But the juvenile was estranged from her father and wanted her social worker to attend. The local social workers had a policy of not attending interviews if a parent was available. Accordingly, her father attended the interview. He took no part in the interview and the juvenile ignored him. At trial the justices ruled her confession in interview inadmissible under section 76(2)(b) (*ante*, § 15–352), on the ground, *inter alia*, that her father was not an appropriate adult. The prosecutor's appeal failed. The Divisional Court considered Code C (similar provisions are in the current Code C at C:1.7, C:3.15, C:11.15 and C:11.17), and concluded that the justices had been entitled to find that the defendant's estranged father was not an "appropriate adult" within the spirit of Code C. Further (*per* Mann L.J.), the appropriate adult could not be a person with whom the juvenile had no empathy. The court placed emphasis upon what is now paragraph C:11.17, saying that it was apparent that under the code the appropriate adult has an important role to play in any interview which he attends.

15–493 In *R. v. Jefferson*, 99 Cr.App.R. 13, CA, it was held that the appellant's father, who in interview was encouraging a juvenile to tell the truth in response to police officers' fair and proper questions, did not fail in his duty to advise the juvenile, nor did his conduct disqualify him as an appropriate adult. In *R. v. W.* [1994] Crim.L.R. 130, the Court of Appeal refused to interfere with the judge's finding that the appellant's mother, who herself required the protection of an appropriate adult, being mentally handicapped within the meaning of section 77(3) (*ante*, § 15–370), was capable of fulfilling the role of appropriate adult in an interview.

If a police officer does not inform the appropriate adult of his full role, in accordance with C:11.17, then Code C is breached: *H. and M. v. DPP* [1998] Crim.L.R. 653, DC.

Interviewing wards of court

15–494 Where a ward of court is to be interviewed or, possibly, examined as a witness or as a suspect, the relevant parts of Code C, *i.e.* in particular, paragraphs C:11.6—C:11.20, should be read in conjunction with *Practice Direction (Criminal Proceedings: Consolidation)*, para. I.5, *ante*, §§ 8–42 *et seq.*

Where a ward of court has reached the age of 17, the police do not need leave to interview him: *Re B. (a Minor)* [1990] F.C.R. 409, Fam D (Ewbank J.).

Drug addicts suffering withdrawal

15–495 For the interviewing of heroin addicts, see *R. v. Goldenberg*, 88 Cr.App.R. 285, CA, and *R. v. Crampton*, 92 Cr.App.R. 369, CA, *ante*, § 15–364; and Annex H to Code C (Appendix A–111).

Confession to doctor

15–496 For the inclusion of a confession to a psychiatrist who saw the defendant (a regular drug taker) for the purpose of determining his fitness to plead, see *R. v. McDonald* [1991] Crim.L.R. 122, CA (followed in *R. v. Gayle* [1994] Crim.L.R. 679, CA). The court expressed the view that it would be rare to seek to adduce evidence of what the defendant said to a doctor where the issue being tried was non-medical.

Prison inmates

An interview with a prisoner is governed by Code C: see *R. v. Rowe* [1994] Crim.L.R. 837, CA. H.M. Chief Inspector of Constabulary has provided guidance to chief constables and commissioners of police (July 22, 1996), that interviews with convicted prisoners must be conducted in accordance with the *PACE Act* 1984 and the codes of practice. **15–497**

(e) *Meaning of "interview"*

The term "interview" is used extensively in Code C (see, notably, paras C:11 (interviews: general) and C:12 (interviews in police stations)). If an exchange constitutes an interview then it is subject to the contemporaneity requirements in C:11.7 and any exchanges after arrest which amount to an interview must take place at a police station (C:11.1). **15–498**

"Interview" is not defined in the 1984 Act and was not defined in the first version of Code C. In the second version, there was a definition, but it appeared in one of the notes for guidance, which are not formally part of the code: this gave rise to doubts as to its status. Further confusion was generated by the apparently self-contradictory nature of the definition: see *R. v. Cox*, 96 Cr.App.R. 464, CA (*per* McCullough J. at pp. 469–470). Code C:11.1A of the previous and current codes defines "interview" as the "questioning of a person regarding his involvement or suspected involvement in a criminal offence or offences which, by virtue of paragraph 10.1 of Code C, is required to be carried out under caution". This improved definition has eliminated the need to refer to all but a few of the plethora of cases considering the meaning of "interview" under the first two versions of the code.

The codes do not apply to words said as part of an offence itself (*e.g.* under the *Public Order Act* 1986, s.5): *DPP v. Lawrence* [2008] 1 Cr.App.R. 10, DC; but any questioning (formal or informal, see *R. v. Sparks* [1991] Crim.L.R. 128, CA) of a person regarding his involvement or suspected involvement in an offence which, by virtue of C:10.1, should be under caution (*i.e.* there must be grounds for suspecting him of having committed an offence) is an interview, to which the provisions of C:11 and C:12 (if at a police station) apply. "Any questioning" means what it says and, therefore, one question may be an interview: *R. v. Miller* [1998] Crim.L.R. 209, CA; *R. v. Ward*, 98 Cr.App.R. 337, CA; *R. v. Dunn*, 91 Cr.App.R. 237, CA. A conversation will constitute an interview if a suspect is being asked to incriminate himself: *Batley v. DPP*, *The Times*, March 5, 1998, DC. A spontaneous statement made by the suspect cannot amount to an interview, but if the police put any questions as a result of such a statement, what follows plainly will be an interview. Protection in relation to allegedly spontaneous remarks is now provided by the obligation under C:11.2A to put to the suspect at the outset of any police station interview any significant statement or silence prior to arrival at the police station. (For "spontaneous exchange" cases decided before the third version of the code came into force, see *R. v. Matthews*, 91 Cr.App.R. 43, CA; *R. v. Scott* [1991] Crim.L.R. 56, CA; and *R. v. Marsh* [1991] Crim.L.R. 455, CA; as to "off the record" conversations initiated by the suspect, see *R. v. Matthews*, *ante*, and *R. v. Menard* [1995] 1 Cr.App.R. 306, CA.) **15–499**

The fact that the questioning is conducted by an officer not involved in the investigation (*e.g.* a custody officer) is irrelevant: *R. v. Absolam*, 88 Cr.App.R. 332, CA; *R. v. Oransaye* [1993] Crim.L.R. 772, CA.

The fact that questions are put out of curiosity or with a view to eliminating the suspect from inquiries does not stop the questioning from being an interview: *R. v. Hunt* [1992] Crim.L.R. 582, CA.

Code C:10.1 permits questioning without caution in furtherance of the proper and effective conduct of a search. But this plainly does not cut down the duty to caution a **15–500** person whom there are grounds to suspect of an offence. If such grounds exist, there must be a caution before any questions are put about any matter found during the course of the search; if those questions concern the person's involvement or alleged involvement in a criminal offence then they will amount to an interview (C:11.1A); and, if the person is under arrest or a decision to arrest him has been made, any questioning about what is found should take place at the police station (C:11.1), unless one of the exceptions therein applies. The strict attitude of the Court of Appeal is illustrated by the following decisions, all of which preceded the third version of the code: *R. v. Manji* [1990] Crim.L.R. 512; *R. v. Langiert* [1991] Crim.L.R. 777; *R. v. White* [1991] Crim.L.R. 779; and *R. v. Power* [1993] Crim.L.R. 206. See also *R. v. Khan* [1993] Crim.L.R. 54, CA (the fact that police officers are entitled to detain a person at premises whilst a search is conducted does not give them *carte blanche* to administer interrogation of the kind that ought properly be reserved for the police station); and *R. v. Raphaie* [1996] Crim.L.R. 812, CA (approving the dictum in *Khan*). In *R. v. Maynard*, unreported, April 2, 1998 (97 03255 W3), a decision concerning the third version of the code, the Court of Appeal said that the prohibition in C:11.1 exists for good reasons, including the tape recording of interviews and access to legal advice. It would be unacceptable for police officers to circumvent the code protections by refraining from exercising their powers of arrest even when they have decided to exercise them.

The statutory procedures under sections 7 and 8 of the *RTA* 1988 for obtaining specimens from drivers suspected of excess alcohol offences do not constitute an interview for the purposes of Code C: *DPP v. D.*; *DPP v. Rous*, 94 Cr.App.R. 185, DC, and Code C:11.1A.

(f) *The "verballing" provisions*

15–501 In *R. v. Keenan* [1990] 2 Q.B. 54, 90 Cr.App.R. 1, CA, Hodgson J. referred (at pp. 63, 7) to the slang expressions "to verbal" and "the verbals" as being used to describe the practice of police officers inaccurately recording or inventing the words used by a suspect in interview. The court's conclusion was that where there had been "significant and substantial" (see *ante*, § 15–463) breaches—

> "of the 'verballing' provisions of the Code, the evidence so obtained will frequently be excluded. We do not think that any injustice will be caused by this. It is clear that not every breach or combination of breaches of the Code will justify the exclusion of interview evidence under section 76 or section 78 ... They must be significant and substantial. If this were not the case, the courts would be undertaking a task which is no part of their duty: as Lord Lane C.J. said in *Delaney* [88 Cr.App.R. 338]: 'It is no part of the duty of the court to rule a statement inadmissible simply in order to punish the police for failure to observe the Code of Practice.'
>
> But if the breaches are 'significant and substantial', we think it makes good sense to exclude them ... . If the rest of the evidence is strong, then it may make no difference to the eventual result if he excludes the evidence. In cases when the rest of the evidence is weak or non-existent, that is just the situation where the temptation to do what the provisions are aimed to prevent is greatest, and the protection of the rules most needed" (at pp. 69–70, 13).

15–502 The provisions of Code C (referred to in *Keenan*) are C:11.7 (requirement of accurate record of each interview), C:11.10 (requirement to record reason if interview not recorded contemporaneously) (Appendix A–75) and C:11.11 (requirement that interviewee be shown at police station the record of interview with a view to his signing it). See also C:11.4 (duty to put significant statement or silence to suspect (Appendix A–73)) and C:11.13 (record of comments outside context of interview (Appendix A–74)).

15–503 The importance of the detailed provisions on interviewing suspects has been emphasised repeatedly. In *R. v. Canale*, 91 Cr.App.R. 1, CA, Lord Lane C.J. stated:

> "As this Court recently emphasised in the case of *Keenan* ... the importance of the rules relating to contemporaneous noting of interviews can scarcely be over-emphasised. The object is twofold; not merely to ensure, so far as possible, that the suspect's remarks are accurately recorded and that he has an opportunity when he goes through the contemporaneous record afterwards of checking each answer and initialling each answer, but likewise it is a protection for the police, to ensure, so far as possible, that it cannot be suggested that they induced the suspect to confess by improper approaches or improper promises. If the contemporaneous note is not made, then each of those two laudable objects is apt to be stultified" (at p. 5).

The philosophy behind Code C in this context was explained by Steyn L.J. in *R. v. Hunt* [1992] Crim.L.R. 582, CA. The following passage from the transcript of the judgment is cited in *R. v. Ward*, 98 Cr.App.R. 337 at 340: **15–504**

> "Under consideration, in the present context, are the provisions of Code C, which are commonly described as the anti-verballing provisions of Code C. The background to those provisions was of course a public perception and a legislative intention that the evil of police officers falsely attributing incriminating statements to persons in custody should be stamped out. We must also recognise that an unseen and unsigned record of what was allegedly said placed a person in custody at an unfair disadvantage. There was in real life a practicable [*sic*] burden on him to raise a reasonable doubt about what an experienced witness, the police officer, said, and as often as not there was a supporting note made by the police officer. The potential scope for miscarriages of justice are [*sic*] manifest. The balance had to be redressed, that is the principal mischief which the anti-verballing provisions of Code C were designed to cure."

On the facts in *Keenan*, *ante*, there had been breaches of these provisions, but the judge had admitted the disputed evidence, saying that any unfairness could be cured by the defendant giving evidence. It was held that the judge had been wrong in assuming unfairness could be cured by the defendant giving evidence: (a) if he had intended not to give evidence if the challenged evidence was excluded, admitting the evidence had unfairly robbed him of his right to silence (*R. v. Hamand*, 82 Cr.App.R. 65, CA); (b) if the defence case was that the evidence had been concocted, then it was unfair to admit it, because it forced the defendant to give evidence and also, by attacking the police, to put his character in evidence; and (c) if the defence case was that the interview was inaccurately recorded, then it was plainly unfair to admit it because it placed the defendant at a substantial disadvantage in that he had been given no contemporaneous opportunity to correct any inaccuracies. **15–505**

In *Keenan*, the court made particular reference to *R. v. Delaney*, 88 Cr.App.R. 338, CA, in which Lord Lane C.J. remarked that observance of the code may benefit the prosecution in a criminal case: **15–506**

> "By failing to make a contemporaneous note, or indeed any note, as soon as practicable, the officers deprived the court of what was, in all likelihood, the most cogent evidence as to what did indeed happen during these interviews and what did induce the appellant to confess. ... (T)he judge and the prosecution were *pro tanto* disabled by the omission of the officers to act in accordance with the Codes of Practice, disabled from having the full knowledge upon which the judge could base his decision. The judge of course is entitled to ask himself why the officers broke the rules. Was it mere laziness or was it something more devious? Was it perhaps a desire to conceal from the court the full truth of the suggestions they had held out to the defendant? These are matters which may well tip the scales in favour of the defendant in these circumstances and make it impossible for the judge to say that he is satisfied beyond reasonable doubt, and so require him to reject the evidence" (at p. 341).

[The next paragraph is § 15–508.]

The presence of a solicitor's clerk is a matter which a judge is entitled to take into account in deciding whether to exclude evidence on account of breaches of the anti-verballing provisions: *R. v. Dunn*, 91 Cr.App.R. 237, CA. There were three relevant considerations: first, the clerk could intervene; secondly, his or her presence would inhibit fabrication by the police; and thirdly, if the police did fabricate answers, the clerk would be available to give evidence in contradiction of the police evidence. See also *R. v. Paris*, *ante*, § 15–360. **15–508**

In *R. v. Cox*, 96 Cr.App.R. 464, CA, the court gave the police the following guidance where a conversation takes place between the police and a suspect in the absence of a solicitor and without being tape-recorded. Paragraph 11.10 provides that the person interviewed should be given the opportunity to read the interview record and sign it as correct. In general, the sooner such a note is shown to the suspect the better, because his recollection will be fresher and there will be less chance that he will deny what was said. If, however, it is expected that a solicitor will arrive soon, it may be better to wait until he comes. Fairness should be the guide. If the note has, for whatever reason, not been shown to the suspect prior to his solicitor's arrival, fairness to both the suspect and **15–509** the police requires that it be shown to him in his solicitor's presence. If it has been shown to the suspect prior to the solicitor's arrival, the solicitor should be informed of that fact when he arrives. If the police act less than fairly, the chances of the conversation being excluded materially increase. See also *R. v. Scott* [1991] Crim.L.R. 56, CA; *R. v. Weerdesteyn* [1995] 1 Cr.App.R. 405, CA; *Batley v. DPP*, *The Times*, March 5, 1998, DC.

15–510 The Court of Appeal will view with care claims by police officers that it has not been practicable to make a contemporaneous note in accordance with C:11.7: *R. v. Chung*, 92 Cr.App.R. 314, CA; *R. v. Park*, 99 Cr.App.R. 270, CA.

15–511 C:11.13 (the requirement to show remarks which are not an interview to a suspect for approval (Appendix A–74)) has also been regarded as an important protection: *R. v. Longmuir*, unreported, February 28, 1995, CA (94/3888/X3); *R. v. Thomson*, unreported, May 9, 1995, CA (94/7253/X4); *R. v. Miller* [1998] Crim.L.R. 209, CA; *DPP v. Davies*, unreported, May 13, 2002, DC (the whole purpose of C:11.13 is to avoid a dispute as to what was said). In *R. v. Edwards (M. J.)* [1997] Crim.L.R. 348, the Court of Appeal doubted whether C:11.13 applied to conversations between an undercover police officer and a suspect, but declined to decide the issue. Despite Code C:2.1 (requirement for all information to be recorded under the code to be recorded on the custody record), C:11.13 does not require entries which have been made in a police notebook and offered to the defendant for authentication to be recorded on the custody record: *R. v. Heslop* [1996] Crim.L.R. 730, CA.

Code C:11.7 and 11.13 do not apply to spontaneous remarks made by a person after being arrested at court for contempt of court, but the court may have regard to them: *R. v. Jones (P. A.)* [1996] Crim.L.R. 806, CA.

(8) Section 74: conviction of co-accused as evidence

15–512 For the operation of section 78 in the context of section 74 of the *PACE Act* 1984, see *ante*, §§ 9–89 *et seq.*

(9) Identification evidence

15–513 Identification evidence is considered in Chapter 14.

(10) Agents provocateurs

(a) *Definition*

15–514 "*Agent provocateur*" was defined by the Royal Commission on Police Powers 1928 (Cmd. 3297) as "a person who entices another to commit an express breach of the law which he would not otherwise have committed and then proceeds to inform against him in respect of such an offence"—cited without disapproval in *R. v. Mealey and Sheridan*, 60 Cr.App.R. 59, CA.

15–515 On August 1, 2002, a code of practice (issued under section 71 of the *RIPA* 2000 and replacing the draft code that had been published on September 25, 2000) governing the use of "covert human intelligence sources" (as to the definition of this expression, see *ante*, § 15–254) came into force: see *ante*, § 15–255.

(b) *Pre-PACE Act*

15–516 The fact that the defendant would not have committed the offence if it were not for the activity of an *agent provocateur* is no defence in English law, and there is no common law discretion to exclude evidence of a crime instigated by an *agent provocateur*: *R. v. Sang* [1980] A.C. 402, HL.

15–517 In *R. v. Looseley*; *Att.-Gen's Reference (No. 3 of 2000)* [2002] 2 Cr.App.R. 29, HL, Lord Nicholls (at [11]) said that although entrapment is not a substantive defence, English law has now developed remedies in respect of entrapment, *viz.* staying proceedings and excluding evidence pursuant to section 78. In these respects *Sang* has been "overtaken".

(c) *Under the PACE Act 1984*

15–518 In *R. v. Looseley*; *Att.-Gen.'s Reference (No. 3 of 2000)*, *ante*, the House of Lords extensively reviewed the issue of entrapment. Lord Nicholls and Lord Hoffmann said that the appropriate remedy would be staying the prosecution as an abuse of process rather than excluding evidence (at [16], [36]); but the use of a covert operation may affect the admissibility of particular pieces of evidence and in such circumstances section 78 would apply (*per* Lord Hoffman at [42]–[43]). The judgments are summarised in greater detail at § 4–63, *ante*.

For detailed consideration of the authorities preceding *Looseley*, see the 2005 edition of this work. The following observations are derived from the judgments in *Looseley*: **15–519**

(a) test purchases by undercover police officers are generally acceptable: *DPP v. Marshall* [1988] 3 All E.R. 683, DC (see Lord Nicholls at [3]);
(b) similarly, it is generally acceptable for police officers to pose as fare-paying passengers to catch an unlicensed taxi driver: *Nottingham City Council v. Amin* [2000] 1 Cr.App.R. 426, DC (see Lord Nicholls at [3]; but the position would be otherwise if the officers had been waving £50 notes or pretending to be in distress (see Lord Hoffman at [54]);
(c) the use of evidence obtained by entrapment ("as a result of police incitement") may deprive a defendant of the right to a fair trial embodied in Article 6: *Teixeira de Castro v. Portugal*, 28 E.H.R.R. 101 (see Lord Nicholls at [15]);
(d) "The only proper purpose of police participation is to obtain evidence of criminal acts which they suspect someone is about to commit or in which he is already engaged. It is not to tempt people to commit crimes in order to expose their bad characters and punish them" (Lord Hoffman at [56]);
(e) the police activity in *Williams v. DPP*, 98 Cr.App.R. 209, DC (investigation of thefts from vehicles in Essex; police left unattended van with back door open and cartons of cigarettes visible; defendants arrested on stealing cigarettes) was justified, "because it was an authorised investigation into actual crime, and the fact that the defendants may not have previously been suspected or even thought of offending was their hard luck"; but the trick would have been an abuse of state power if carried out in an area where such crime was not suspected to be prevalent (Lord Hoffman at [65]).

On the facts of *Looseley*, *ante*, the House of Lords held that there was no objection to the police posing as drug-users to trap an active drug dealer; but in *Att.-Gen.'s Reference (No. 3 of 2000)*, there was an abuse of process where the defendant, who had never dealt in drugs, was induced to procure heroin for an undercover officer by the prospect of a profitable trade in smuggled cigarettes—the police had caused him to commit an offence which he would not otherwise have committed. For further examples of cases falling on either side of the line, see *R. v. Moon*, 70 J.C.L. 194, CA ([2004] EWCA Crim. 2872), and *R. v. Harmes and Crane* [2006] 7 *Archbold News* 1, CA (*ante*, § 4–63). **15–520**

Where the entrapment is by journalists rather than the police, similar principles apply (see *R. v. Shannon* [2001] 1 Cr.App.R. 12, CA, upheld in *Shannon v. U.K.* [2005] Crim.L.R. 133, ECtHR), although not with the same force (*R. v. Hardwicke and Thwaites* [2001] Crim.L.R. 220, CA). In *Shannon*, the conviction was upheld, because there was no procedural unfairness in admitting the journalism evidence, and there had been no abuse of the process of the court. The following passage from Potter L.J.'s judgment was approved by Lord Hutton in *Looseley*, *ante* (at [103]): **15–521**

> "the ultimate question is not the broad one: is the bringing of proceedings fair (in the sense of appropriate) in entrapment cases. It is whether the fairness of the proceedings will be adversely affected by admitting the evidence of the agent provocateur or evidence which is available as the result of his action or activities. So, for instance, if there is good reason to question the credibility of evidence given by an agent provocateur, or which casts doubt on the reliability of other evidence procured by or resulting from his actions, and that question is not susceptible of being properly or fairly resolved in the course of the proceedings from available, admissible and 'untainted' evidence, then the judge may readily conclude that such evidence should be excluded. If, on the other hand, the unfairness complained of is no more than the visceral reaction that it is in principle unfair as a matter of policy, or wrong as a matter of law, for a person to be prosecuted for a crime which he would not have committed without the incitement or encouragement of others, then that is not itself sufficient, unless the

behaviour of the police (or someone acting on behalf of or in league with the police) and/or the prosecuting authority has been such as to justify a stay on grounds of abuse of process."

For a case where the fact-finding tribunal was held to have failed, wrongly, to distinguish between entrapment by a journalist and entrapment by the police, see *Council for the Regulation of Health Care Professionals v. General Medical Council and Saluja* [2007] 1 W.L.R. 3094, QBD (Goldring J.).

[The next paragraph is § 15–524.]

(11) Evidence obtained through unlawful act or trickery

General

15–524 At common law, the method by which evidence was obtained was strictly irrelevant. Therefore evidence was admissible which had been stolen (*R. v. Leathem* (1861) 8 Cox C.C. 498, cited in *Kuruma v. R.* [1955] A.C. 197, PC), or obtained by an illegal search (*Jones v. Owen*, 34 J.P. 759; *Kuruma v. R.*, *ante*; and *Jeffrey v. Black* [1978] Q.B. 490, 66 Cr.App.R. 81, DC).

Under the *PACE Act* 1984 evidence obtained improperly or by a trick may be excluded if its admission would have such an adverse effect on the fairness of the proceedings that the court ought not to admit it (s.78: *ante*, § 15–422). See generally *R. v. Looseley*; *Att.-Gen.'s Reference (No. 3 of 2000)*, *ante*, §§ 15–518 *et seq.* and, in relation to trickery by the police, *Williams v. DPP*, *ante*, § 15–519 at (e).

Unlawful search

15–525 Where evidence is obtained in consequence of an unlawful search, the judge has a discretion, not an obligation, to exclude the evidence under section 78. In deciding how to exercise the discretion, the judge has to make an assessment of the effect of admitting the evidence on the fairness of the proceedings; absent bad faith or a flagrant and deliberate breach of one of the codes of practice issued pursuant to the 1984 Act, or some matter affecting the quality of the evidence, the mere fact that evidence is discovered in the course of an unlawful search is unlikely to render the admission of the evidence unfair: *R. v. Khan, Sakkaravej and Pamarapa* [1997] Crim.L.R. 508, CA (considering the effect of relatively minor breaches of the Vienna Convention on Diplomatic Relations 1961 on the admissibility of evidence of the finding of drugs in the baggage of a diplomat). See also *R. v. McCarthy* [1996] Crim.L.R. 818, CA.

Trickery, etc.

15–526 The general approach of the courts to evidence obtained by trickery is to say that deceit which simply provides a defendant with an opportunity to confess to the offence, as opposed to trickery that positively induces a confession, will not result in a confession being excluded.

In *R. v. Mason*, 86 Cr.App.R. 349, CA (see *ante*, § 15–453), the defendant's conviction for arson was quashed because police officers tricked him into making a confession. They told him, and his solicitor, untruthfully, that his fingerprint had been found on fragments of a bottle used in starting the fire. The trial judge had wrongly admitted the evidence. He failed to consider, in the exercise of his discretion under section 78, the deceit. (See also the *obiter dicta* of Lord Scarman in relation to the common law in *R. v. Sang* [1980] A.C. 402 at 456–457, HL: the obtaining of evidence from a suspect by deception or a trick is likely to infringe the rule against self-incrimination.)

In *R. v. Jelen and Katz*, 90 Cr.App.R. 456, CA, one of three defendants, D, had pleaded guilty to an offence of conspiracy to commit false accounting. He had been the first to be arrested. He had admitted his part and incriminated the two persons, J and K, who subsequently became his co-defendants. At the time of D's arrest, the police took the view that there was insufficient evidence to justify arresting and charging J, but that if they interviewed him they would have to caution him. In these circumstances they sought and received the assistance of D, who agreed to meet with J while wearing a defendant's right to a fair trial, despite the fact that the evidence was obtained in violation of Article 8 (*post*, § 16–101). At each level of jurisdiction, the domestic courts had assessed the effect of admission of the evidence on the fairness of the trial by reference to section 78, and it being clear that had those courts been of the view that the admission of the evidence would have led to substantive unfairness, they would have had a discretion to exclude it, the proceedings as a whole were not unfair. As to the effect of the *Human Rights Act* 1998, see the commentary on *Khan* [2000] Crim.L.R. at 684–686.

Khan v. U.K. was considered by the House of Lords in *R. v. P.* [2002] 1 A.C. 146. **15–532**
Lord Hobhouse pointed out that a defendant is not entitled to have unlawfully obtained evidence excluded simply because it has been so obtained. The entitlement is to challenge the admission of the evidence and have a judicial assessment of the impact of the admission of such evidence on the fairness of the proceedings. His Lordship also said that the effect of *Khan v. U.K.* was that "any remedy for a breach of Article 8 lies outside the scope of the criminal trial" (p. 475). *Khan v. U.K.* was also considered by the Court of Appeal in *R. v. Bailey* [2001] 5 *Archbold News* 1, and by the European Court of Human Rights in *P.G. v. U.K.* (2008) 46 E.H.R.R. 51, ECtHR.

In *R. v. Roberts* [1997] 1 Cr.App.R. 217, CA, the appellant had remained silent when questioned about a number of armed robberies. Both he and C were later charged with a particular robbery and C asked the police to put him in a cell with the appellant in order to get him to admit the robbery and exculpate C. The appropriate authority was obtained to bug the cell and in the course of conversation the appellant admitted a number of offences. The Court of Appeal upheld the trial judge's decision to admit the evidence thereby obtained. Important factual considerations were that C was not a police agent and was still a suspect, it could not be anticipated that the appellant would admit other offences, the appropriate authority for the bugging had been obtained, neither defendant knew the cell was bugged, and no deception or ruse had been practised either by the police or by C. Consequently, the conduct of the police had not, wittingly or unwittingly, led to unfairness. The same approach was taken in *R. v. Mason* [2002] 2 Cr.App.R. 38. The Court of Appeal said that it was "highly desirable" for a statutory code to cover covert surveillance in police stations. The court also referred to the decision of Newman J. in *R. v. Sutherland*, unreported, January 29, 2002, Crown Court, to stop a trial as an abuse of process where police officers had acted in bad faith in covertly recording conversations in the exercise yard between defendants and their solicitors. As regards the use of cameras in police stations for identification purposes and potential breaches of Article 8 of the ECHR, see *Perry v. U.K.* [2003] Crim.L.R. 281, ECtHR.

In *R. v. Chalkley and Jeffries* [1998] 2 Cr.App.R. 79, CA (see also § 15–166, *ante*), the police received authorisation to install a listening device in the defendant's home. In order to do so they decided to arrest him for unrelated offences about which they had earlier received information, but taken no action, and in respect of which there was no realistic prospect of proceedings. It was held that a collateral motive for an arrest on otherwise good grounds did not necessarily make the arrest unlawful. The tapes were rightly admitted in evidence: there was no dispute as to their content or relevance, they did not result from incitement, entrapment or inducement and none of the alleged unlawful conduct by the police affected the quality of the evidence.

(12) The European Convention on Human Rights

As to the effect of the *Human Rights Act* 1998, see *post*, §§ 16–5 *et seq.* The most **15–533**
relevant articles of the Convention in this respect are Articles 3 (*post*, §§ 16–39 *et seq.*), 5 (*post*, §§ 16–43 *et seq.*), 6 (*post*, §§ 16–57 *et seq.*) and 8 (*post*, §§ 16–101 *et seq.*).

(13) Abuse of process

Improper police activity or illegally obtained evidence may alternatively fall to be **15–534**
considered in the context of an application to stay proceedings as an abuse of process, *ante*, §§ 4–48 *et seq.*; *R. v. Latif*; *R. v. Shahzad* [1996] 2 Cr.App.R. 92, HL; and *R. v. Looseley*; *Att.-Gen.'s Reference (No. 3 of 2000)*, *ante*, §§ 15–518 *et seq.*

B. At Common Law

Police and Criminal Evidence Act 1984, s.82(3)

15–535 (3) Nothing in this Part of this Act shall prejudice any power of a court to exclude evidence (whether by preventing questions from being put or otherwise) at its discretion.

The power at common law to exclude relevant evidence is specifically retained by section 82(3). Nevertheless the importance of the rule at common law is much diminished by the scope of section 78, which is at least as wide in scope as the common law rule (see *ante*, § 15–453).

At common law a judge has a discretion in a criminal trial "to exclude evidence if it is necessary in order to secure a fair trial for the accused": *per* Lord Griffiths in *Scott v. R.* [1989] A.C. 1242 at 1256, PC, referring to numerous dicta to that effect in *R. v. Selvey* [1970] A.C. 304, HL, and *R. v. Sang* [1980] A.C. 402, HL.

(2) Subsection (1) does not apply to an act if—

(a) as the result of one or more provisions of primary legislation, the authority could not have acted differently; or

(b) in the case of one or more provisions of, or made under, primary legislation which cannot be read or given effect in a way which is compatible with the Convention rights, the authority was acting so as to give effect to or enforce those provisions.

(3) In this section, "public authority" includes—

(a) a court or tribunal, and

(b) any person certain of whose functions are functions of a public nature,

but does not include either House of Parliament or a person exercising functions in connection with proceedings in Parliament.

(4) In subsection (3) "Parliament" does not include the House of Lords in its judicial capacity.

(5) In relation to a particular act, a person is not a public authority by virtue only of subsection (3)(b) if the nature of the act is private.

(6) "An act" includes a failure to act but does not include a failure to—

(a) introduce in, or lay before, Parliament a proposal for legislation; or

(b) make any primary legislation or remedial order.

Proceedings

7.—(1) A person who claims that a public authority has acted (or proposes to act) in a way which is made unlawful by section 6(1) may— **16–22**

(a) bring proceedings against the authority under this Act in the appropriate court or tribunal, or

(b) rely on the Convention right or rights concerned in any legal proceedings,

but only if he is (or would be) a victim of the unlawful act.

(2) In subsection (1)(a) "appropriate court or tribunal" means such court or tribunal as may be determined in accordance with rules; and proceedings against an authority include a counterclaim or similar proceeding.

(3) If the proceedings are brought on an application for judicial review, the applicant is to be taken to have a sufficient interest in relation to the unlawful act only if he is, or would be, a victim of that act.

(4) [*Scotland*].

(5) Proceedings under subsection (1)(a) must be brought before the end of—

(a) the period of one year beginning with the date on which the act complained of took place; or

(b) such longer period as the court or tribunal considers equitable having regard to all the circumstances,

but that is subject to any rule imposing a stricter time limit in relation to the procedure in question.

(6) In subsection (1)(b) "legal proceedings" includes—

(a) proceedings brought by or at the instigation of a public authority; and

(b) an appeal against the decision of a court or tribunal.

(7) For the purposes of this section, a person is a victim of an unlawful act only if he would be a victim for the purposes of Article 34 of the Convention if proceedings were brought in the European Court of Human Rights in respect of that act.

(8) Nothing in this Act creates a criminal offence.

(9) In this section "rules" means—

(a) in relation to proceedings before a Court or tribunal outside Scotland, rules made by the Lord Chancellor or the Secretary of State for the purposes of this section or rules of court,

(b) [*Scotland*],

(c) [*Northern Ireland*],

and includes provision made by order under section 1 of the *Courts and Legal Services Act* 1990.

By section 7(1)(a) a person who claims that a public authority has acted (or proposes to act) in a manner which is incompatible with a Convention right may bring proceedings to challenge the decision. Where the impugned decision is that of a court, the challenge must generally be brought by exercising a right of appeal or an application for **16–23** judicial review (see s.9(1), *post*, § 16–26). In addition, by section 7(1)(b) any person who claims that a court or other public authority has acted or proposes to act in a manner incompatible with a Convention right may rely on that right in any legal proceedings. Both methods of invoking Convention rights are subject to the proviso that the person concerned is (or would be) a "victim" for the purposes of Article 34 of the Convention. As to the meaning of "victim", see *post*, § 16–31. Where proceedings have been brought by or at the instigation of a public authority, the individual affected may, under section 7(1)(b), rely on a Convention right in the course of those proceedings, notwithstanding that the act complained of took place before the coming into force of section 7 (s.22(4), *ante*, § 16–9). Where the very holding of a trial would constitute a breach of a Convention right, the Court has no discretion to continue with the trial because to do so would constitute an unlawful act contrary to section 6: *Att.-Gen.'s Reference (No. 2 of 2001)* [2004] 2 A.C. 72, HL (at [33–34]). In the absence of bad faith, or other exceptional circumstances, the Divisional Court should not entertain an application for judicial review of a decision to prosecute on the ground that the offence is alleged to be incompatible with a Convention right: *R. v. DPP, ex p. Kebilene* [2000] 2 A.C. 326, HL. See also *R. (Pepushi) v. CPS, The Times*, May, 21, 2004, DC. For an example of exceptional circumstances that justified the bringing of judicial review proceedings in respect of a decision to continue a prosecution, see *R. (D.) v. Central Criminal Court* [2004] 1 Cr.App.R. 41, DC; and *post*, § 16–38.

Human Rights Act 1998, s.8

Judicial remedies

16–24 **8.**—(1) In relation to any act (or proposed act) of a public authority which the court finds is (or would be) unlawful, it may grant such relief or remedy, or make such order, within its powers as it considers just and appropriate.

(2)–(5) [*Damages to be awarded only by court having power to do so in civil proceedings and restrictions thereon.*]

(6) In this section—

"court" includes a tribunal;

"damages" means damages for an unlawful act of a public authority; and

"unlawful" means unlawful under section 6(1).

16–25 Section 8 provides that where a court finds that a public authority has acted (or proposes to act) in a manner incompatible with Convention rights, the court may grant such relief or remedy, or make such order, within its powers as it considers just and appropriate. In relation to criminal proceedings, the powers of a court to stay proceedings, to exclude evidence or to allow a submission of no case to answer may be of particular significance. As to the remedies available when there is a breach of the right to be tried within a reasonable time, see *post*, § 16–73. As to the correct approach to the admission of evidence obtained in breach of Article 8, see *post*, §§ 16–66 *et seq.* In the Court of Appeal, a conviction following a trial in which the appellant's Article 6 rights (the right to a fair trial) have been violated is likely to be deemed "unsafe" within section 2(1) of the *CAA* 1968: see *R. v. Togher* [2001] 1 Cr.App.R. 33, CA; *R. v. Forbes* [2001] 1 A.C. 473, HL; *R. v. A. (No. 2)* [2002] 1 A.C. 45, HL (*per* Lord Steyn, at [38]); and *Att.-Gen.'s Reference (No. 2 of 2001)*, *ante* (*per* Lord Bingham, at [13]).

Human Rights Act 1998, s.9

Judicial acts

16–26 **9.**—(1) Proceedings under section 7(1)(a) in respect of a judicial act may be brought only—

(a) by exercising a right of appeal;

(b) on an application (in Scotland a petition) for judicial review; or

(c) in such other forum as may be prescribed by rules.

(2) That does not affect any rule of law which prevents a court from being the subject of judicial review.

(3), (4) [*Power to award damages in respect of a judicial act confined to cases of unlawful detention pursuant to a court order.*]

(5) In this section—

"appropriate person" [*relates to subss. (3), (4)*];

"court" includes a tribunal;

"judge" includes a member of a tribunal, a justice of the peace and a clerk or other officer entitled to exercise the jurisdiction of a court;

"judicial act" means a judicial act of a court and includes an act done on the instructions, or on behalf, of a judge; and

"rules" has the same meaning as in section 7(9).

The restriction on judicial review of matters arising out of trial on indictment contained in the *Supreme [Senior Courts] Court Act* 1981 (renamed as from a day to be appointed: *Constitutional Reform Act* 2005, s.59(5), and Sched. 11, para. 1), s.29(3), *ante*, § 7–4, is not incompatible with a Convention right, and is preserved by section 9(2): *R. v. Canterbury Crown Court, ex. p. Regentford Ltd*, *The Times*, February 6, 2001, DC (concerning the refusal of a trial judge to make a defendant's costs order thereby potentially infringing Article 6(2)). See also *R. (Shields) v. Crown Court at Liverpool* [2001] U.K.H.R.R. 610, DC (concerning refusal to amend a legal aid order to provide for representation by Queen's Counsel and junior); *R. (O.) v. Central Criminal Court*, unreported, January 23, 2006, DC ([2006] EWHC 256 (Admin.)) (refusal of an application to dismiss a charge pursuant to the *CDA* 1998, Sched. 3, *ante*, §§ 1–40 and 7–12); and *R. (H.) v. Wood Green Crown Court* [2007] 2 All E.R. 259, DC, *ante*, § 8–14. **16–26a**

III. GENERAL PRINCIPLES OF INTERPRETATION

A. THE HUMAN RIGHTS ACT 1998

Constitutional human rights legislation is "*sui generis*, calling for principles of interpretation of its own, suitable to its character" (*Ministry of Home Affairs v. Fisher* [1980] A.C. 319 at 329C–E, PC). Respect must be paid to the language which has been used and to the traditions and usages which have given meaning to the language (*ibid.* at 329E–F). The guiding principle is that an enactment giving effect to fundamental rights requires "a generous interpretation avoiding what has been called 'the austerity of tabulated legalism', suitable to give to individuals the full measure of the fundamental rights and freedoms referred to" (*ibid.* at 328G–H; *Att.-Gen. of Gambia v. Momodou Jobe* [1984] A.C. 689 at 700H, PC; *Att.-Gen. of Hong Kong v. Lee Kwong-kut* [1993] A.C. 951 at 966B–E, PC; *Vasquez and O'Neil v. R.* [1994] 1 W.L.R. 1304 at 1313B *et seq.*, PC; *Flicklinger v. Crown Colony of Hong Kong* [1991] 1 N.Z.L.R. 439 at 440; *R. v. DPP, ex p. Kebilene* [2000] 2 A.C. 326, HL). Human rights legislation has a "special character" which calls for a broad and purposive approach to construction: *Ministry of Transport v. Noort* [1992] 3 N.Z.L.R. 260 at 271, 276–278; *R. v. Goodwin (No. 1)* [1993] 2 N.Z.L.R. 153. The court should look to "the substance and reality of what was involved and should not be over-concerned with what are no more than technicalities": *Huntley v. Att.-Gen. for Jamaica* [1995] 2 A.C. 1 at 12G–H, PC. At the same time the exercise remains one of judicial interpretation of the language used. "If the language used by the lawgiver is ignored in favour of a general resort to 'values' the result is not interpretation but divination": *Matadeen v. Pointu* [1999] 1 A.C. 98, 108, PC (*per* Lord Hoffmann). **16–27**

In interpreting human rights legislation, the courts should be willing to look to comparative case law since "[e]very system of law stands to benefit by an awareness of the answers given by other courts and tribunals to similar problems": *R. v. Khan (Sultan)* [1997] A.C. 558, HL, *per* Lord Nicholls at 583C. See also *R. (Daly) v. Secretary of State for the Home Department* [2001] 2 A.C 532, HL (*per* Lord Cooke at [30]); and *R. v. Lambert* [2002] 2 A.C. 545, HL (at [40]). Decisions on the interpretation of domestic constitutional human rights provisions in other jurisdictions are, however, of persuasive, rather than binding, authority: *Att.-Gen. of Hong Kong v. Lee Kwong-Kut*, *ante*, at p. 966G; *Brown v. Stott* [2003] 1 A.C. 681, PC, *per* Lord Hope at p. 724. **16–28**

B. THE EUROPEAN CONVENTION ON HUMAN RIGHTS

Approach to construction

In determining any question which has arisen in connection with a Convention right, **16–29** courts are required to take into account the decisions of the European Court and Commission of Human Rights and the Committee of Ministers of the Council of Europe on the interpretation of the Convention (*Human Rights Act* 1998, s.2(1), *ante*, § 16–13). The Court and Commission have established the following general principles.

(i) The Convention is "an instrument designed to maintain and promote the ideals and values of a democratic society" (*Kjeldsen v. Denmark*, 1 E.H.R.R. 711 at para. 53). Particularly important features of a democratic society are "pluralism, tolerance and broad-mindedness" (*Handyside v. U.K.*, 1 E.H.R.R. 737, at para. 49; *Dudgeon v. U.K.*, 4 E.H.R.R. 149, at para. 53), and the "rule of law" (*Golder v. U.K.*, 1 E.H.R.R. 524 at para. 34; *Klass v. Germany*, 2 E.H.R.R. 214, at para. 55).

(ii) The Convention has been described as "a living instrument which must be interpreted in the light of present day conditions" (*Tyrer v. U.K.*, 2 E.H.R.R. 1, at para. 31; *Airey v. Ireland*, 2 E.H.R.R. 305, at para. 26). This is of particular importance in connection with the right to a fair trial, since the requirements of fairness have undergone a "considerable evolution" in the Court's case law, particularly as regards the importance attached to the appearance of fairness, and the increased sensitivity of the public to the fair administration of justice: *Borgers v. Belgium*, 15 E.H.R.R. 92, at para. 24. See also *R. v. H.* [2004] 2 A.C. 134, HL (at [11]). Older Convention case law must be approached with this principle in mind.

(iii) The Convention "is intended to guarantee not rights that are theoretical and illusory but rights that are practical and effective" (*Marckx v. Belgium*, 2 E.H.R.R. 330, at para. 31; *Airey v. Ireland*, *ante*, at para. 24; *Artico v. Italy*, 3 E.H.R.R. 1, at para. 33; *Soering v. U.K.*, 11 E.H.R.R. 439, at para. 87). Thus, the conditions imposed for the exercise of a Convention right must not impair its very existence or deprive it of its effectiveness (*Heaney and McGuinness v.Ireland* (2001) 33 E.H.R.R. 12).

(iv) The European Court and Commission of Human Rights have adopted an "autonomous approach" to the interpretation of certain terms which does not depend on the meaning given under national law: *Engel v. Netherlands*, 1 E.H.R.R. 647, at para. 82 (on the meaning of the term "criminal" in Article 6) (*post*, § 16–60); *Deweer v. Belgium*, 2 E.H.R.R. 439, at para. 46 (on the meaning of the term "charge" in Article 6) (*post*, § 16–73); *Kostovski v. Netherlands*, 12 E.H.R.R. 434 (on the meaning of the term "witness" in Article 6(3)(d) (*post*, § 16–91)); *Welch v. U.K.*, 20 E.H.R.R. 247, at paras 27 to 35 (on the meaning of the term "penalty" in Article 7) (*post*, § 16–100). The Convention is concerned with the substance of an individual's position rather than with its formal classification, and courts may therefore need to "look behind appearances and investigate the realities of the procedure in question": *Deweer v. Belgium*, *ante*, at para. 44; *Adolf v. Austria*, 4 E.H.R.R. 315, at para. 30; *Welch v. U.K.*, *ante*, at para. 27; *Van Droogenbroeck v. Belgium*, 4 E.H.R.R. 443, at para. 38; *Duinhoff v. Netherlands*, 13 E.H.R.R. 478, at para. 34; *cf. Huntley v. Att.-Gen. for Jamaica* [1995] 2 A.C. 1 at 12G–H, PC.

(v) The existence of a "generally shared approach" in other contracting states is relevant to the application of the Convention (*Marckx v. Belgium*, *ante*; *Tyrer v. U.K.*, *ante*; *Dudgeon v. U.K.*, 4 E.H.R.R. 149; *X., Y. and Z. v. U.K.*, 24 E.H.R.R. 143; and *Ocalan v. Turkey* (2005) 41 E.H.R.R. 45), but absolute uniformity is not required (*Sunday Times v. U.K.*, 2 E.H.R.R. 245, at para. 61; *Muller v. Switzerland*, 13 E.H.R.R. 212, at para. 35; *Wingrove v. U.K.*, 24 E.H.R.R. 1, at para. 58; *F. v. Switzerland*, 10 E.H.R.R. 411, at para. 33; *Monnell and Morris v. U.K.*, 10 E.H.R.R. 205, at para. 47). See also *Brown v. Stott* [2003] 1 A.C. 681, PC, *per* Lord Hope at p.724. The Convention should so far as possible also be interpreted in harmony with other rules of public international law of which it forms part (*Al-Adsani v. U.K.* (2002) 34 E.H.R.R. 11). The court must, however, confine its primary attention to the issues of interpretation and application of the provisions of the Convention itself (*Ocalan v. Turkey*, *ante*). For examples of the Court relying on non-European jurisprudence, see *Allan v. U.K.* (2003) 36 E.H.R.R. 12; *Hurst v. U.K. (No. 2)* (2004) 38 E.H.R.R. 40; and *Jalloh v. Germany* (2007) 44 E.H.R.R. 32.

The "margin of appreciation"

The "margin of appreciation" doctrine which is applied by the European Court of Human Rights reflects the primary role which national authorities, including the courts, are intended to perform in human rights protection. It is a doctrine of restrained review at the international level which is derived from the principle that the Convention machinery is "subsidiary to the national systems safeguarding human rights" (*Handyside v. U.K.*, 1 E.H.R.R. 737, at para. 48). In *R. v. DPP, ex p. Kebilene* [2000] 2 A.C. 326, Lord Hope observed that although the margin of appreciation doctrine is not available to the national courts when applying the provisions of the 1998 Act, the Convention should nevertheless be seen as an expression of fundamental principles rather than a set of mere rules. In some circumstances it would be appropriate for the courts to recognise that there is an area of judgment within which the judiciary will defer, on democratic grounds, to the considered opinion of the elected body or person whose act or decision is said to be incompatible with the Convention. It would be easier for the courts to recognise such a "discretionary area of judgment" where the Convention itself required a balance to be struck, or where questions of social or economic policy were involved; much less so where the Convention right in issue is stated in terms which are unqualified, is of high constitutional importance, or raises questions which the court is especially well placed to determine. See also *Brown v. Stott* [2003] 1 A.C. 681, PC; *R. v. Benjafield*; *R. v. Leal*; *R. v. Rezvi*; *R. v. Milford* [2003] 1 A.C. 1099, CA; *McIntosh v. Lord Advocate* [2003] 1 A.C. 1078, PC; and *International Transport Roth GmbH v. Secretary of State for the Home Department* [2003] Q.B. 728, CA. **16–30**

In *R. v. A. (No. 2)* [2002] 1 A.C. 45, HL, Lord Steyn observed (at [36]) that whilst the courts must give weight to the legislative policy adopted by Parliament, where the question arose whether, in a criminal statute, Parliament had adopted a legislative scheme which makes an excessive inroad into the right to a fair trial, the court would be qualified to make its own judgment, and must do so. See also *R. v. Lambert* [2002] 2 A.C. 545, HL; and *Sheldrake v. DPP*; *Att.-Gen.'s Reference (No. 4 of 2002)* [2005] 1 A.C. 264, HL. In *A. v. Secretary of State for the Home Department*; *X. v. Same* [2005] 2 A.C. 68, the House of Lords underlined that the role of independent judges charged with interpreting and applying the law "is universally recognised as a cardinal feature of the modern democratic state, a cornerstone of the rule of law itself" (*per* Lord Bingham at [42]). By enacting the *Human Rights Act* 1998 the courts had been specifically "charged by Parliament with delineating the boundaries of a rights-based democracy".

The concept of a "victim"

Section 7 of the 1998 Act (*ante*, § 16–22) provides that a person may rely on a Convention right only if he is or would be a "victim" for the purposes of Article 34 of the Convention. The Convention does not permit an *actio popularis*. Nor does it entitle an individual to claim *in abstracto* that a law is incompatible with the Convention. On the other hand, the Court has held that the concept of a "victim" includes any person who runs the risk of being directly affected by a law, even in the absence of a measure applying it to him, provided that the existence of the law interferes with his Convention rights: *Norris v. Ireland*, 13 E.H.R.R. 186 (applicant a victim of law criminalising homosexual activity, despite the fact that he had not been prosecuted); *Klass v. Germany*, 2 E.H.R.R. 214 (applicant could claim to be a victim of secret surveillance without the necessity to prove conclusively that his telephone conversation had been intercepted); see also *Bowman v. U.K.*, 26 E.H.R.R. 1 (person may be a victim by virtue of a prosecution resulting in an acquittal); *Halford v. U.K.*, 24 E.H.R.R. 523; *Marckx v. Belgium*, 2 E.H.R.R. 330. **16–31**

Where criminal proceedings have exceeded the reasonable time requirement, a reduction in sentence which has the express purpose of affording a remedy for the delay may deprive the defendant of his status as a "victim": *Eckle v. Germany*, 5 E.H.R.R. 1; *Bunkate v. The Netherlands*, 19 E.H.R.R. 477; *X v. Germany*, 25 D.R. 142; *Beck v. Norway*, unreported, June 26, 2001, ECtHR. See *post*, § 16–73.

Limitations on rights

16–32 The rights conferred by Articles 8 to 11 of the Convention contain limitations expressed in similar terms. Where there is a prima facie interference with one of these rights (as to which see *post*, §§ 16–106, 16–115, 16–121 and 16–134), it is for the state to show that any restriction on the exercise of the right concerned is justified according to the conditions set out under the second paragraph of each Article. Because the state may interfere with the exercise of rights where these conditions are satisfied, the rights themselves must be broadly and purposively construed (*Niemietz v. Germany*, 16 E.H.R.R. 97, at para. 31), but exceptions to the rights "must be narrowly interpreted" (*Sunday Times v. U.K.*, 2 E.H.R.R. 245, at para. 65). Regard should be had to the importance of the right in issue (*Dudgeon v. U.K.*, 4 E.H.R.R. 149, at para. 52).

16–33 For an interference to be permissible, the first condition which must be satisfied is that the measure taken was "prescribed by law" or "in accordance with law". This requires that the interference must have a basis in domestic law (*Silver v. U.K.*, 5 E.H.R.R. 347, at para. 86), and that the domestic law itself must be accessible and formulated with sufficient precision to be foreseeable in its consequences (*Sunday Times v. U.K.*, *ante*, at para. 49). The domestic law governing the power of a court to bind a defendant over for breach of the peace meets the requirement for reasonable legal certainty (*Steel v. U.K.*, 28 E.H.R.R. 603); but the power to bind a defendant over to be "of good behaviour" does not (*Hashman and Harrup v. U.K.*, 30 E.H.R.R. 241). See also *post* § 16–99.

16–34 Secondly, the interference must be "necessary in a democratic society" in pursuit of one of the legitimate aims set out in the text of the Article itself. The adjective "necessary" implies the existence of a "pressing social need" for the interference: *Sunday Times v. U.K.*, *ante*; *Handyside v. U.K.*, 1 E.H.R.R. 737; *Goodwin v. U.K.*, 22 E.H.R.R. 123. In addition, there must be a reasonable relationship of proportionality between the means employed and the aim pursued: *Handyside v. U.K.*, *ante*. The principle of proportionality involves the striking of a fair balance between the demands of the general interest of the community and the requirements of the protection of the individual's fundamental rights: *Sporrong and Lonroth v. Sweden*, 5 E.H.R.R. 35; *Soering v. U.K.*, 11 E.H.R.R. 439. Where it is alleged that criminal proceedings have interfered with one of the rights in Articles 8 to 11, the court should look to the combination of the prosecution, the conviction and the sentence to determine whether the measure taken was proportionate: *Laskey v. U.K.*, 24 E.H.R.R. 39; *Hoare v. U.K.* [1997] E.H.R.L.R. 678; and *Skalka v. Poland* (2004) 38 E.H.R.R. 1.

In *de Freitas v. Permanent Secretary of Ministry of Agriculture, Fisheries, Lands and Housing* [1999] 1 A.C. 69, PC, Lord Clyde identified (at p. 80) three criteria for determining the issue of proportionality in the context of statutory restrictions on a fundamental right. The court should ask (i) whether the legislative objective is sufficiently important to justify limiting a fundamental right; (ii) whether the measures designed to meet the legislative objective are rationally connected to it; and (iii) whether the means used to impair the right or freedom are no more than is necessary to accomplish that objective. This formulation was approved for application under the *Human Rights Act* 1998 in *R. v. A. (No. 2)* [2002] 1 A.C. 45, where the House of Lords considered the compatibility of section 41 of the *YJCEA* 1999 (*ante*, § 8–123m) with the requirements of Article 6. Lord Steyn (at [38]) observed that the critical question was embodied in the third criterion identified in *de Freitas*. Given the centrality of the right to a fair trial in the scheme of the Convention, and giving due weight to the intention of Parliament, the question would be whether the legislation in issue made an "excessive inroad" into the guarantee of a fair trial. In *R. v. Shayler* [2003] 1 A.C. 247, HL, Lord Hope observed (at [59]) that an authority seeking to justify a restriction on a fundamental right must discharge the burden of showing that the legislative means adopted were no greater than necessary.

Other principles

16–35 Articles 17 and 18 of the Convention contain additional principles governing the interpretation of the rights guaranteed and the restrictions thereto (see s.1(1) of the 1998 Act, *ante*, § 16–10).

Articles 17 and 18

Prohibition of abuse of rights

17. Nothing in this Convention may be interpreted as implying for any State, group or person any right to engage in any activity or perform any act aimed at the destruction of any of the rights and freedoms set forth herein or at their limitation to a greater extent than is provided for in the Convention.

Limitations on use of restrictions on rights

18. The restrictions permitted under this Convention to the said rights and freedoms shall not be applied for any purpose other than those for which they have been prescribed.

IV. THE RIGHTS GUARANTEED

A. Right to Life

Article 2

16–36 **2.**—(1) Everyone's right to life shall be protected by law. No one shall be deprived of his life intentionally save in the execution of a sentence of a court following his conviction of a crime for which this penalty is provided by law.

(2) Deprivation of life shall not be regarded as inflicted in contravention of this Article when it results from the use of force which is no more than absolutely necessary:

(a) in defence of any person from unlawful violence;

(b) in order to effect a lawful arrest or to prevent the escape of a person lawfully detained;

(c) in action lawfully taken for the purpose of quelling a riot or insurrection.

Scope

16–37 Article 2 ranks as one of the most fundamental provisions of the Convention from which no derogation is permitted, even in times of national emergency. Its provisions must be strictly construed, and any deprivation of life must be subjected to "the most careful scrutiny" (*McCann, Savage and Farrell v. U.K.*, 21 E.H.R.R. 97, at paras 147–150). It requires not only that the state must refrain from taking life intentionally, but also that appropriate steps must be taken to safeguard life (*Osman v. U.K.*, 29 E.H.R.R. 245). These include the establishment and implementation of an effective system of criminal law: *Öneryildiz v. Turkey* (2005) 41 E.H.R.R. 20.

Permissible exceptions

16–38 Article 2(2) is exhaustive and must be narrowly interpreted (*Stewart v. U.K.*, 7 E.H.R.R. 453). The term "absolutely necessary" establishes a test of "strict proportionality" (*ibid.*), which is arguably higher than the reasonable force standard applied in domestic law (*McCann*, *ante*; *Brady v. U.K.*, unreported, April 3, 2001, ECtHR). It does not follow, however, that the common law test of reasonable force is incompatible with Article 2: *R. (Bennett) v. H.M. Coroner for Inner South London*, 170 JP. 109, QBD (Collins J.). Article 2 is not confined to intentional killing, but includes deliberate use of force which has the unintended consequence of causing loss of life (*Stewart v. U.K.*, *ante*; *McCann v. U.K.*, *ante*; *McShane v. U.K.* (2002) 35 E.H.R.R. 23). See also *Ogur v. Turkey* (2001) 31 E.H.R.R. 40 (a finding of a violation of Article 2 in circumstances where a warning shot was fired in a manner that amounted to gross negligence); *Gul v. Turkey* (2002) 34 E.H.R.R. 28 (suspect believed to be armed shot 50 times behind a closed door); and *Kakoulli v. Turkey* (2007) 45 E.H.R.R. 12 (suspect, believed to be armed, shot while he was lying wounded on the floor). Article 2 may be engaged by the use of life threatening force even where the victim survives: *Makaratzis v. Greece* (2005) 41 E.H.R.R 49 (applicant shot in the foot by police during the course of a car chase). As to firearms operations that are negligently planned or carried out, see *McCann v. U.K.*, *ante*; *Andronicou and Constantinou v. Cyprus*, 25 E.H.R.R. 491; and *Makaratzis*, *ante*. See also *Bubbins v. U.K.* (2005) 41 E.H.R.R. 24. Insofar as criminal proceedings would cause a risk to the life of a defendant (for example by disclosing his status as an informant) the prosecution are under an obligation to carry out a thorough examination of the risk before continuing with the prosecution: *R. (D.) v. Central Criminal Court* [2004] 1 Cr.App.R. 41, DC.

The withdrawal of medical treatment for patients in a persistent vegetative state, where continued treatment is not considered to be in the patient's best interests, is not incompatible with Article 2: *N.H.S. Trust A. v. M.*; *N.H.S. Trust B. v. H.* [2001] 1 All E.R. 801, Fam D. See also *Re A. (Children) (Conjoined Twins: Surgical Separation)* [2001] Fam. 147, CA (Civ. Div.); and *R. (Burke) v. General Medical Council* [2006] Q.B. 273, CA (Civ. Div.). As to the deportation of terminally ill persons to countries where it is known that they will not receive adequate medical treatment, see *D. v. U.K.*, 24 E.H.R.R. 423. As to assisted suicide, see *post*, § 18–6.

Positive obligations

16–38a Article 2 imposes a positive obligation on the police to take reasonable steps to protect potential victims from a real and immediate threat to their lives which is attributable to the actual or threatened criminal acts of a third party: *Osman v. U.K.*, 29 E.H.R.R. 245. *Cf. W. v. U.K.*, 32 D.R. 190; *M. v. U.K.*, 47 D.R. 27. See also *Edwards v. U.K* (2002) 35 E.H.R.R. 19; and *Van Colle v. Chief Constable of Hertfordshire Police*; *Smith v. Chief Constable of Sussex Police* [2008] 3 All E.R. 977, HL. As to the duty on a court to ensure that it does not expose a witness to the real possibility of a risk to his life, see *R. (A.) v. Lord Saville of Newdigate* [2002] 1 W.L.R. 1249, CA (Civ. Div.); *R. (A.) v. Inner South London Coroner*, *The Times*, November 11, 2004, CA (Civ. Div.); and *Re Officer L.* [2007] 1 W.L.R. 2135, HL. In exceptional circumstances, the courts have the power to issue injunctions to prevent publication of information concerning the identity or whereabouts of individuals where this would put them at risk of serious injury or death: *Venables v. News Group Newspapers Ltd* [2001] Fam. 430, Fam. D.

Procedural obligations

16–38b Article 2 also implies that the state is under an obligation to conduct an effective official investigation into alleged breaches of the right to life. The authorities must act of their own motion and cannot leave it to the next-of-kin to initiate a complaint or take proceedings. The investigation must be independent, thorough and prompt, and must be capable of leading to the identification and, where appropriate, the punishment of those responsible. There must be a sufficient element of public scrutiny of the investigation or its results to ensure accountability and the next-of-kin must be involved to an extent necessary to safeguard their legitimate interests: *McKerr v. U.K.* (2002) 34 E.H.R.R. 20; *Jordan v. U.K.* (2003) 37 E.H.R.R. 2; *Edwards v. U.K*, *ante*; and *Ramsahai v. Netherlands*, May 15, 2007, ECtHR (Grand Chamber). The absence of any direct state responsibility for a death will not remove the duty to carry out an effective investigation: *Menson v. U.K.* (2003) 27 E.H.R.R. CD220. As to the application of these principles in the domestic courts, see *R. (Amin) v. Secretary of State for the Home Department* [2004] 1 A.C. 653, HL; *R. (Middleton) v. West Somerset Coroner* [2004] 2 A.C. 182, HL; and *R. (Scholes) v. Secretary of State for the Home Department*, *The Times*, November 10, 2006, CA (Civ. Div.). In conducting an investigation the state has an additional duty to establish whether a killing was racially motivated: *Nachova v. Bulgaria* (2006) 42 E.H.R.R. 43 (*post*, § 16–140). As to the relevance of Article 2 to the duty of the Crown Prosecution Service to give reasons for a decision not to prosecute in connection with a death in custody, see *R. v. DPP, ex p. Manning* [2001] Q.B. 330, DC. As to the circumstances in which a failure to prosecute an offence of gross negligence manslaughter may give rise to a breach of Article 2, see *Öneryildiz v. Turkey*, *ante*, § 16–37. As to the compatibility of the evidential test in the Code for Crown Prosecutors (Appendix E–6) with Article 2, see *R. (Da Silva) v. DPP*, 157 N.L.J. 31, DC.

B. PROHIBITION OF TORTURE

Article 3

3. No one shall be subjected to torture or to inhuman or degrading treatment or punishment. **16–39**

Scope

In order to constitute a violation of Article 3, the treatment or punishment complained of "must attain a minimum level of severity": *Ireland v. U.K.*, 2 E.H.R.R. 25. The threshold is relative and will depend on the "sex, age and state of health" of the victim: *ibid.*; *Campbell and Cosans v. U.K.*, 4 E.H.R.R. 293. **16–40**

More recent decisions have indicated that certain acts which were classified in the past as "inhuman and degrading treatment" as opposed to "torture" could be classified differently in the future: *Selmouni v. France*, 29 E.H.R.R. 403. Bearing this guidance in mind, in *A. (No. 2) v. Secretary of State for the Home Department* [2006] 2 A.C. 221, HL, Lord Bingham (at [53]), and Lord Hoffmann (at [97]) held that the conduct previously characterised by the European Court as inhuman and degrading in *Ireland v. U.K.*, *ante*, would now be characterised as torture.

Both the Commission and the Court have previously indicated that the overall length of a custodial sentence could, in principle, amount to inhuman punishment. Although such a finding is unlikely in practice (see, *e.g. Treholt v. Norway*, 71 D.R. 168 at 191; *X. v. Germany*, 6 D.R. 127), the Court has on occasion raised doubts about the length of sentences imposed: see *Weeks v. U.K.*, 10 E.H.R.R. 293; *Hussain v. U.K.*, 22 E.H.R.R. 1. In the context of extradition, the Court has held that a sentence may violate Article 3 if it is wholly unjustified or disproportionate to the gravity of the crime committed: *Soering v. U.K.*, 11 E.H.R.R. 439. See also *R. (Wellington) v. Secretary of State for the Home Department* [2008] 3 All E.R. 248, DC; and *Bader v. Sweden* (2008) 46 E.H.R.R. 13. However, the fact that the penalty is more severe than would apply in other European states is not sufficient: *C. v. Germany*, 46 D.R. 179. The detention of a sick or otherwise vulnerable person may "raise issues under Article 3": see *Bonnechaux v. Switzerland*, 3 E.H.R.R. 259; *De Varga-Hirsch v. France*, 33 D.R. 158; *B. v. Germany*, 55 D.R. 271; *Mouisel v. France* (2004) 38 E.H.R.R. 34; *Gelfman v. France* (2006) 42 E.H.R.R. 4; *Matthew v. Netherlands* (2006) 43 E.H.R.R. 23; and *Paladi v. Moldova* (2008) 47 E.H.R.R. 15.

The mandatory life sentence for murder under the *Murder (Abolition of Death Penalty) Act* 1965, s.1(1) (*post*, § 19–93) does not constitute a violation of Article 3, although other mandatory or minimum sentences may operate in a disproportionate and arbitrary manner in particular cases: *R. v. Lichniak* [2003] 1 A.C. 903, HL; and this is so even in the case of a "whole-life" tariff: *R. v. Bieber*, *The Times*, August 11, 2008, CA (such a sentence is not to be regarded as irreducible on account of Secretary of State's power to release the prisoner on compassionate grounds under the *C(S)A* 1997, s.30(1)). See also *R. v. Offen* [2001] 1 Cr.App.R. 24, CA; *Reyes v. R.* [2002] 2 A.C. 235, PC; and *Kafkaris v. Cyprus*, unreported, February 12, 2008, ECtHR (Grand Chamber) (no breach of Art. 3 where a prisoner serving a whole life tariff had the right to petition for early release). As to the imposition of an automatic life sentence under the *PCC(S)A* 2000, s.109, on an offender who fulfilled the criteria for the making of a hospital order, see *R. v. Drew* [2003] 2 Cr.App.R. 24.

As to the circumstances in which conditions of detention may amount to a breach of Article 3, see *McFeeley v. U.K.*, 3 E.H.R.R. 161; *Price v. U.K.* (2002) 34 E.H.R.R. 53; *Peers v. Greece* (2001) 33 E.H.R.R. 51; *Kalashnikov v. Russia* (2003) 36 E.H.R.R. 34. See also *Napier v. Scottish Ministers*, *The Times*, November 15, 2001, Court of Session; *R v. Governor of Frankland Prison, ex. p. Russell* [2000] 1 W.L.R. 2027, DC; *Rohde v. Denmark* (2006) 43 E.H.R.R. 17; and *Jalloh v. Germany*, *post*, § 16–67. As to the need to provide appropriate medical or psychiatric treatment to prisoners, see *Keenan v. U.K.* (2001) 33 E.H.R.R. 38; and *McGlinchey v. U.K.* (2003) 37 E.H.R.R. 41.

As to the use of handcuffs on an unconvicted prisoner, see *ante*, § 3–200a; *Raninen v. Finland*, 26 E.H.R.R. 563; and *D.G. v. Ireland* (2002) 35 E.H.R.R. 33. As to the conduct of strip searches, see *Iwańczuk v. Poland* (2004) 38 E.H.R.R. 8; and *Wieser v. Austria* (2007) 45 E.H.R.R. 44.

Positive obligations

16–40a Article 3 imposes positive obligations which have important implications for the rights of victims of crime. The criminal law must provide adequate protection for individuals against the infliction of inhuman or degrading treatment by other private individuals. The provision of civil remedies alone is insufficient: see *X. and Y. v. Netherlands*, 8 E.H.R.R. 235. In *A. v. U.K.*, 27 E.H.R.R. 611, the court held that the defence of lawful correction available on a charge of assault against a person *in loco parentis* affords insufficient protection to the rights of the child victim. The common law defence was subsequently refined in *R. v. H.* [2002] 1 Cr.App.R. 7, CA (*post*, § 19–185) in order to bring it into line with the requirements of Article 3. See also *R. (Williamson) v. Secretary of State for Education* [2005] 2 A.C. 246, HL.

Vulnerable individuals are entitled to "protection by way of effective deterrence" against serious breaches of their personal integrity; and the authorities are under an obligation to take reasonable steps to prevent ill treatment of which they had or ought to have had knowledge: *Z. v. U.K.* (2002) 34 E.H.R.R. 3; and *E. v. U.K.* (2003) 36 E.H.R.R. 31.

In *Aydin v. Turkey*, 25 E.H.R.R. 251, the applicant alleged that she had been raped and assaulted. The Court held that Article 3 (taken in conjunction with Article 13) imposes a positive obligation on the state to carry out a thorough and effective investigation capable of leading to the identification and punishment of those responsible for alleged violations. An inadequate response by the investigating or prosecuting authorities will amount to a violation. See also *Assenov v. Bulgaria*, 28 E.H.R.R. 652; *M.C. v. Bulgaria* (2005) 40 E.H.R.R. 20; *Krastanov v. Bulgaria* (2005) 41 E.H.R.R. 50; *Bekos v. Greece* (2006) 43 E.H.R.R. 2; and *Yavuz v. Turkey* (2007) 45 E.H.R.R. 16. For the application of these principles to domestic law, see *R. (D.) v. Secretary of State for the Home Department (Inquest Intervening)* [2006] 3 All E.R. 946, CA (Civ. Div.); and *R. (L.) (a Patient) (by the Official Solicitor as litigation friend) v. Secretary of State for the Home Department* [2008] 1 W.L.R. 158, CA (Civ. Div.). The life, liberty and security of victims and witnesses must also be adequately protected within the criminal justice system itself: *Doorson v. Netherlands*, 22 E.H.R.R. 330 (*post* § 16–68).

C. PROHIBITION OF SLAVERY AND FORCED LABOUR

Article 4

16–41 **4.**—(1) No one shall be held in slavery or servitude.

(2) No one shall be required to perform forced or compulsory labour.

(3) For the purpose of this Article the term "forced or compulsory labour" shall not include:

(a) any work required to be done in the ordinary course of detention imposed according to the provisions of Article 5 of this Convention or during conditional release from such detention;

(b) any service of a military character or, in case of conscientious objectors in countries where they are recognised, service exacted instead of compulsory military service;

(c) any service exacted in case of an emergency or calamity threatening the life or well-being of the community;

(d) any work or service which forms part of normal civic obligations.

16–42 Compulsory labour is work exacted under the menace of a penalty and performed against the will of the person concerned: *Van der Mussele v. Belgium*, 6 E.H.R.R. 163. The categories established in Article 4(3) are not limitations on the right in Article 4(2). Rather, they delimit the content of the right and aid its interpretation: *Schmidt v. Germany*, 18 E.H.R.R. 513; *Van der Mussele, ante*.

16–42a Article 4 has to be read as imposing positive obligations on the state to enact provisions of criminal law punishing the practices prohibited therein and to apply those provisions in practice: *Siliadin v. France* (2006) 43 E.H.R.R. 16.

D. RIGHT TO LIBERTY AND SECURITY

Article 5

5.—(1) Everyone has the right to liberty and security of the person. No one shall be deprived of his liberty save in the following cases and in accordance with a procedure prescribed by law: **16–43**

(a) the lawful detention of a person after conviction by a competent court;

(b) the lawful arrest or detention of a person for non-compliance with the lawful order of a court or in order to secure the fulfilment of any obligation prescribed by law;

(c) the lawful arrest or detention of a person effected for the purpose of bringing him before the competent legal authority on reasonable suspicion of having committed an offence or when it is reasonably considered necessary to prevent his committing an offence or fleeing after having done so;

(d) the detention of a minor by lawful order for the purpose of educational supervision or his lawful detention for the purpose of bringing him before the competent legal authority;

(e) the lawful detention of persons for the prevention of the spreading of infectious diseases, of persons of unsound mind, alcoholics or drug addicts or vagrants;

(f) the lawful arrest or detention of a person to prevent his effecting an unauthorised entry into the country or of a person against whom action is being taken with a view to deportation or extradition.

(2) Everyone who is arrested shall be informed promptly, in a language which he understands, of the reasons for his arrest and of any charge against him.

(3) Everyone arrested or detained in accordance with the provisions of paragraph (1)(c) of this Article shall be brought promptly before a judge or other officer authorised by law to exercise judicial power and shall be entitled to trial within a reasonable time or to release pending trial. Release may be conditioned by guarantees to appear for trial.

(4) Everyone who is deprived of his liberty by arrest or detention shall be entitled to take proceedings by which the lawfulness of his detention shall be decided speedily by a court and his release ordered if the detention is not lawful.

(5) Everyone who has been the victim of arrest or detention in contravention of the provisions of this Article shall have an enforceable right to compensation.

General

Article 5(1)(a) to (f) provides an exhaustive definition of the circumstances in which a person may be lawfully deprived of his liberty and is to be given a narrow construction: *Winterwerp v. Netherlands*, 2 E.H.R.R. 387, at para. 37. **16–44**

In addition to falling within sub-paragraphs (a) to (f), any detention must be: (a) "lawful"; and (b) carried out "in accordance with a procedure prescribed by law". These terms refer to conformity with national law and procedure, and it is therefore in the first place for the national authorities, notably the courts, to interpret and apply the law: *ibid.*; *Wassink v. Netherlands* (1990) Series A/185–A (at para. 24). Nevertheless, it remains the function of the European Court of Human Rights to determine whether Article 5 has been violated, and it therefore has the ultimate power to interpret and apply national law: *Bozano v. France*, 9 E.H.R.R. 297, at para. 58; *Van der Leer v. Netherlands*, 12 E.H.R.R. 567; *Benham v. U.K.*, 22 E.H.R.R. 293; *Loukanov v. Bulgaria*, 24 E.H.R.R. 121. In particular the term "lawful" has been held to require that the domestic law on which the detention is based must be accessible and precise: *Zamir v. U.K.*, 40 D.R. 42, at paras 90–91; *Amuur v. U.K.*, 22 E.H.R.R. 533, at para. 50. In *Steel v. U.K.*, 28 E.H.R.R. 602, the Court held that domestic law governing arrest and detention for breach of the peace was "formulated with the degree of precision required by the Convention". *Cf. Hashman and Harrup v. U.K.*, 30 E.H.R.R. 241 (bind over to be "of good behaviour" failed to give any reliable indication of what would constitute a breach of the order). **16–45**

As to whether executive action against an individual amounts to a "deprivation of liberty" so as to engage Article 5, or a mere restriction of movement, see *Engel v. Netherlands*, 1 E.H.R.R. 647; *Guzzardi v. Italy*, 3 E.H.R.R. 333; *Raimondo v. Italy*, 18 E.H.R.R. 237; and *Labita v. Italy* (2008) 46 E.H.R.R. 50. For a consideration of the same issue under domestic law, see *R. (Gillan) v. Commr of Police of the Metropolis*; *R. (Quinton) v. Same* [2006] 2 A.C. 307, HL; *R. (Laporte) v. Chief Constable of Gloucestershire Constabulary* [2005] Q.B. 678, CA (Civ. Div.) (Art. 5 not considered on appeal to the House of Lords ([2007] 2 A.C. 105), see *post*, § 16–129a); *Austin v.*

Commr of Police of the Metropolis [2008] Q.B. 660, CA (Civ. Div.); and *Secretary of State for the Home Department v. J.J.* [2008] 1 A.C. 385, HL.

Arbitrary detention

16–46 Article 5(1) also requires that a detention is not arbitrary: *Van Droogenbroeck v. Belgium*, 4 E.H.R.R. 443, at para. 40; *Weeks v. U.K.*, 10 E.H.R.R. 293, at para. 49; *Loukanov v. Bulgaria, ante*. See also the general principles outlined by Lord Hope in *R. v. Governor of H.M.P. Brockhill, ex p. Evans (No. 2)* [2001] 2 A.C. 19, HL; *R. (Abbasi) v. Secretary of State for Foreign and Commonwealth Affairs, The Times*, November 8, 2002, CA (Civ. Div.); and *A. v. Secretary of State for the Home Department* [2005] 2 A.C. 68, HL.

The fact that time spent in custody abroad awaiting extradition is not taken into account in computing the length of a prison sentence does not render the additional period of detention arbitrary: *C. v. U.K.*, 43 D.R. 177. Nor does the fact that the detention results from a "loss of time" order by the Court of Appeal (under the *CAA* 1968, s.29(1), *ante*, § 7–225): *Monnell and Morris v. U.K.*, 10 E.H.R.R. 205.

As to the safeguards against arbitrariness which are required when imposing a sentence of life imprisonment, see *R. v. Drew* [2003] 2 Cr.App.R. 24, HL; *R. v. Lichniak* [2003] 1 A.C. 903, HL; and *R. v. Offen* [2001] 1 Cr.App.R. 24, CA.

Detention following conviction

16–47 Article 5(1)(a) does not permit a challenge to the fairness of a trial (as to which see Article 6) or the length of a sentence (as to which see Article 3): *Krzycki v. Germany*, 13 D.R. 57; *Weeks v. U.K., ante*. Nor is a detention rendered retroactively unlawful because the conviction or sentence is overturned on appeal: *Krzycki v. Germany, ante*. *Aliter*, if the court of first instance had no power to order detention: *Van der Leer v. Netherlands, ante*; *Wassink v. Netherlands* (1990) Series A/185–A (at para. 27); *Benham v. U.K., ante*. See also *Grauslys v. Lithuania* (2002) 34 E.H.R.R. 46. The right of a serving prisoner to seek early release from his sentence falls within the ambit of Article 5, and thus differential treatment of one prisoner compared with another, otherwise than on the merits of their respective cases, will give rise to a potential complaint under Article 14 (*post*, § 16–139): *R. (Clift) v. Secretary of State for the Home Department*; *R. (Hindawi) v. Same*; *R. (Headley) v. Same* [2007] 1 A.C. 484, HL. A decision by the Secretary of State to recall a serving prisoner while released on a home detention curfew under the *CJA* 2003, s. 246 (*ante*, § 5–374), does not give rise to an entitlement to an independent assessment of the legality of the decision in accordance with Article 5(4), it being the case that the curfew is no more than a continuation of the original deprivation of liberty by an alternative means: *R. (Benson) v. Secretary of State for Justice* [2008] A.C.D. 15, Q.B.D. (Collins J) (approved in *Mason v. Ministry of Justice*, unreported, July 28, 2008, QBD (Cranston J.) ([2008] EWHC 1787 (QB))).

Detention for non-compliance with court order/ to secure compliance with legal obligation

16–48 The first limb of Article 5(1)(b) encompasses certain forms of contempt proceedings, but is not relevant to criminal contempt which falls within Article 5(1)(a). The second limb is the legal basis for powers of temporary detention exercisable by the police without reasonable suspicion: *Filip-Reyntjens v. Belgium* (1992) 73 D.R. 136 (detention for the purpose of establishing identification). As to the requirement to hold a person in detention for no longer than necessary to fulfil the obligation, see *Vasileva v. Denmark* (2005) 40 E.H.R.R. 27. Detention for a short period to enable a power of stop and search to be exercised would normally fall outside the ambit of Article 5: *R. (Gillan) v. Commr of Police for the Metropolis*; *R. (Quinton) v. Same, ante*, § 16–45. See also *Laporte, ante*, § 16–45 (both Art. 5 and the common law prohibited the detention of a group of protesters in circumstances where there was not an immediately apprehended breach of the peace). *Cf. R. (H.) v. Wood Green Crown Court* [2007] 2 All E.R. 259, DC (*ante*, § 8–14).

Arrest on reasonable suspicion

Article 5(1)(c) authorises arrest on reasonable suspicion of having committed a criminal offence. The arrest must be for the purpose of bringing the person concerned before the "competent legal authority" which in England and Wales is a magistrates' court. The detention of a person because of an anticipated breach of the peace, in circumstances where there was no intention to bring him before the magistrates, would not, therefore, fall within Article 5(1)(c): see *Laporte*, *ante*, § 16–45. The words "reasonable suspicion" mean the existence of facts or information which would satisfy an objective observer that the person concerned may have committed the offence: *Fox, Campbell and Hartley v. U.K.*, 13 E.H.R.R. 157, at para. 32. See also *Murray v. U.K.*, 19 E.H.R.R. 193; *O'Hara v. U.K.* (2002) 34 E.H.R.R. 32; and *Al Fayed v. Metropolitan Police Commr* (2004) 148 S.J. 1405, CA (Civ. Div.). **16–49**

Reasons for arrest

Article 5(2) requires that an arrested person be provided with the reasons for an arrest. The detained person must be told "in simple, non-technical language that he can understand, the essential legal and factual grounds for his arrest so as to be able, if he sees fit, to apply to a court to challenge its lawfulness": *Fox, Campbell and Hartley v. U.K.*, *ante*, at para. 40. See also *Taylor v. Chief Constable of Thames Valley* [2004] 1 W.L.R. 3155, CA (Civ. Div.). **16–50**

Detention in a police station

Article 5(3) guarantees the right of an arrested person to be brought before a judge or other judicial officer "promptly" after an arrest. Although the Commission and Court have refrained from setting abstract time limits, it seems certain that the general regime established by sections 41 to 46 of the *PACE Act* 1984 would be found to comply with Article 5(3). By contrast, detention for four days and six hours under the *Prevention of Terrorism (Temporary Provisions) Act* 1984 (*rep.*) was found to breach Article 5(3) in *Brogan v. U.K.*, 11 E.H.R.R. 117. **16–51**

Bail

Article 5(3) also limits pre-trial detention. A person charged with an offence must be released pending trial unless the state can show that there are "relevant and sufficient" reasons to justify his continued detention: *Wemhoff v. Germany*, 1 E.H.R.R. 55. This requires the exercise of a judicial discretion. In *Caballero v. U.K.* [2000] Crim.L.R. 587, the Government conceded that section 25 of the *CJPOA* 1994 (*ante*, § 3–55) was in breach of Article 5(3). As enacted, section 25 imposed an absolute prohibition on the grant of bail on a charge of certain serious offences where the accused had a prior conviction for any such offence. Section 25 has since been amended so as to restore an element of judicial discretion. A strong presumption against the grant of bail for offences of a specified level of seriousness may be incompatible with Article 5(3) since it is for the state to satisfy the court that there are relevant and sufficient reasons for withholding bail: *Ilijokov v. Bulgaria* [2001] 7 *Archbold News* 1, ECtHR. See also *Hurnam v. State of Mauritius* [2006] 1 W.L.R. 857, PC (*ante*, § 3–53); and *R. (O.) v. Crown Court at Harrow* [2007] 1 A.C. 249, HL (*ante*, § 3–55). The fact that a trial will occur promptly is not a justification for pre-trial detention: *Gault v. U.K.* (2008) 46 E.H.R.R. 48. **16–52**

Article 5(3) requires the consideration of bail by a "judge or other officer authorised by law to exercise judicial power". The detention of service personnel pending a court martial by order of the commanding officer does not meet this requirement: *Hood v. U.K.* 29 E.H.R.R. 365; *Jordan v. U.K.* (2001) 31 E.H.R.R. 6.

The Court has held that the "equality of arms" principle inherent in Article 6 (*post*, § 16–64) also applies to bail hearings: *Woukam Moudefo v. France*, 13 E.H.R.R. 549. This includes a right to disclosure of prosecution evidence for the purposes of making a bail application: *Lamy v. Belgium*, 11 E.H.R.R. 529; *Wloch v. Poland* (2002) 34 E.H.R.R. 9. See also *R. v. DPP, ex. p. Lee* [1999] 2 Cr.App.R. 304, DC. Where there is evidence which prima facie appears to have a bearing on the issue of the continuing lawfulness of the detention, it is essential that a court examines and assesses it: *Becciev v. Moldova* (2007) 45 E.H.R.R. 11. As to the application of the procedural guarantees in Articles 5 and 6 to bail hearings, see *R. (DPP) v. Havering Magistrates' Court*; *R. (McKeown) v. Wirral Borough Magistrates' Court* [2001] 2 Cr.App.R. 2, DC (defendant arrested under the *Bail Act* 1976, s.7); and *Wildman v. DPP*, 165 J.P. 453 (application to extend custody time limits); and see also *Garcia Alva v. Germany* (2003) 37 E.H.R.R. 12. A court should give reasons for a refusal of bail: *Tomasi v. France*, 15 E.H.R.R. 1; *Smirnova v. Russia* (2004) 39 E.H.R.R. 22; and should permit renewed applications at reasonable intervals: *Bezicheri v. Italy*, 12 E.H.R.R. 210. As to the extent of the duty to hear bail applications in public, see *ante*, § 3–16.

Acceptable reasons for a refusal of bail fall into four categories.

(i) *Risk that the accused will fail to appear at trial*

Refusal of bail on this ground requires "a whole set of circumstances ... which give reason to suppose that the consequences and hazards of flight will seem to him to be a lesser evil than continued imprisonment": *Stögmüller v. Austria*, 1 E.H.R.R. 155, at para. 15. Relevant considerations are those "relating to the character of the person involved, his morals, his home, his occupation, his assets, his family ties, and all kinds of links with the country in which he is being prosecuted": *Neumeister v. Austria*, 1 E.H.R.R. 91. The severity of the potential sentence, though important, is not an independent ground, and cannot itself justify the refusal of bail: *ibid.*; *Letellier v. France*, 14 E.H.R.R. 83. See also *W. v. Switzerland*, 17 E.H.R.R. 60; and *Mansur v. Turkey*, 20 E.H.R.R. 535.

(ii) *Interference with the course of justice*

Bail may be refused where there is a well-founded risk that the accused, if released, would take action to prejudice the administration of justice: *Wemhoff v. Germany*, *ante*. The risk may involve interference with witnesses, warning other suspects, or the destruction of relevant evidence: *Letellier v. France*, *ante*; *Wemhoff v. Germany*, *ante*. A generalised risk is insufficient; the risk must be identifiable and there must be evidence in support: *Clooth v. Belgium*, 14 E.H.R.R. 717.

(iii) *Prevention of further offences*

The public interest in the prevention of crime may justify detention on remand where there are good reasons to believe that the accused, if released, would be likely to commit further offences: *Matznetter v. Austria*, 1 E.H.R.R. 198; *Toth v. Austria*, 14 E.H.R.R. 551.

(iv) *The preservation of public order*

Where the nature of the crime alleged and the likely public reaction are such that the release of the accused may give rise to public disorder, then temporary detention on remand may be justified: *Letellier v. France*, *ante*. The court emphasised that this was confined to offences of particular gravity.

Conditions of bail

16–53 Permissible conditions of bail under Article 5(3) include a requirement to surrender travel documents and driving documents (*Stögmüller v. Austria*, *ante*; *Schmid v. Austria*, 44 D.R. 195), the imposition of a residence requirement (*Schmid*, *ante*), and the provision of a sum of money as a surety or security (*Wemhoff v. Germany*, *ante*). Where a financial condition is imposed, the figure must be assessed by reference to the means of the accused, if it is a security, or of the person standing surety, and must take account of the relationship between the two: *Neumeister v. Austria*, *ante*; *Schertenleib v. Switzerland*, 23 D.R. 137. Insofar as the amount of any surety or security will effectively determine whether the person is released, the courts must take as much care in choosing the appropriate sum as in deciding whether or not the accused's continued detention is indispensable: *Iwańczuk v. Poland* (2004) 38 E.H.R.R. 8. See also *R. (CPS) v. Chorley JJ.*, 166 J.P. 764, DC; and *McDonald v. Procurator Fiscal, Elgin*, *The Times*, April 17, 2003, High Court of Justiciary, *ante*, § 3–11a.

Trial within a reasonable time

In this requirement, Article 5(3) overlaps with Article 6(1) (see *post* § 16–73). However, the reasonable time guarantee in Article 5(3) is to be distinguished from that contained in Article 6(1). The fact that there has been a lack of special diligence on the part of the authorities so as to violate Article 5(3) does not necessarily lead to the conclusion that there has also been a violation of the reasonable time guarantee in Article 6(1): *Punzelt v. Czech Republic* (2001) 33 E.H.R.R. 49. See also *Smirnova v. Russia* (2004) 39 E.H.R.R. 22 (requirement to give detailed reasons for any decision to extend any pre-trial remand into custody). **16–54**

Habeas corpus

Article 5(4) guarantees the right to *habeas corpus* in order to challenge the legality of detention. The burden of proving the legality of the detention rests with the state: *Zamir v. U.K.*, 40 D.R. 42, at para. 102. **16–55**

In *R. (Kashamu) v. Governor of Brixton Prison*; *R. (Makhlulif) v. Bow Street Magistrates' Court* [2002] Q.B. 887, DC, it was held that in order to comply with the requirements of Article 5(4), a magistrates' court hearing committal proceedings in an extradition case must have jurisdiction to entertain an application for discharge on grounds of abuse of process. Any such inquiry was, however, to be confined to allegations of bad faith or deliberate abuse of the court's process.

Life sentence and extended sentence prisoners

Article 5(4) has also been interpreted as requiring regular periodic access to a judicial tribunal in the case of preventative detention: *Van Droogenbroeck v. Belgium*, 4 E.H.R.R. 443. As to the significance of this to persons subject to discretionary life sentences, see *Weeks v. U.K.*, 10 E.H.R.R. 293; *Thynne, Wilson and Gunnell v. U.K.*, 13 E.H.R.R. 666; and to juveniles convicted of murder and detained at Her Majesty's pleasure under section 90 of the *PCC(S)A* 2000, see *Hussain v. U.K.*, 22 E.H.R.R. 1; *Curley v. U.K.* (2001) 31 E.H.R.R. 14; and *V. v. U.K.*, 30 E.H.R.R. 121. As to discretionary life sentence prisoners who have been transferred to mental hospital pursuant to sections 47 and 49 of the *MHA* 1983, see *Benjamin and Wilson v. U.K.* (2003) 36 E.H.R.R. 1; and *R. (D) v. Secretary of State for the Home Department* [2003] 1 W.L.R. 1315, QBD (Stanley Burnton J.). As to those subject to mandatory life sentences, see *Stafford v. U.K.* (2002) 35 E.H.R.R. 32; *R. (Anderson) v. Secretary of State for the Home Department* [2003] 1 A.C. 837, HL; *Waite v. U.K.* (2003) 36 E.H.R.R. 54; and *Easterbrook v. U.K.* (2003) 37 E.H.R.R. 40. Any significant delay in affording a parole hearing once the tariff has expired will give rise to a breach of Article 5(4): *R. (Noorkoiv) v. Secretary of State for the Home Department* [2002] 1 W.L.R. 3284, CA (Civ. Div.); *R. (Johnson) v. Secretary of State for the Home Department* [2007] 1 W.L.R. 1990, CA (Civ. Div.); and *R. (Cooper) v. Parole Board*, *The Times*, June 6, 2007, QBD (Collins J.). See also *Blackstock v. U.K.* (2006) 42 E.H.R.R. 2 (22 month delay between Parole Board hearings). However, the appropriate length of time to be set between each parole review will depend on the facts of the case: *R. (Spence) v. Secretary of State for the Home Department* (2003) 147 S.J. 660, CA (Civ. Div.). See also *Murray v. Parole Board*, *The Times*, November 12, 2003, CA (Civ. Div.); and *R. (Day) v. Secretary of State for the Home Department* [2004] A.C.D. 78, QBD (Gibbs J.). Where a determinate sentence prisoner, released on licence, seeks to resist subsequent revocation of his licence, the common law requirements of procedural fairness, read in conjunction with Article 5(4), may require an oral hearing before the Parole Board, especially where a factual dispute arises: *R. (West) v. Parole Board*; *R. (Smith) v. Parole Board (No. 2)* [2005] 1 W.L.R. 350, HL. **16–56**

As to Article 5(4) and extended sentences under the *PCC(S)A* 2000, s.85, see *R. (Sim) v. Parole Board* [2004] Q.B. 1288, CA (Civ. Div.); and as to Article 5(4) and longer than commensurate sentences under section 80(2)(b) of the 2000 Act, see *R. (Giles) v. Parole Board* [2004] 1 A.C. 1, HL.

E. RIGHT TO A FAIR TRIAL

Article 6

16–57 **6.**—(1) In the determination of his civil rights and obligations or of any criminal charge against him, everyone is entitled to a fair and public hearing within a reasonable time by an independent and impartial tribunal established by law. Judgment shall be pronounced publicly but the press and public may be excluded from all or part of the trial in the interest of morals, public order or national security in a democratic society, where the interests of juveniles or the protection of the private lives of the parties so require, or to the extent strictly necessary in the opinion of the court in special circumstances where publicity would prejudice the interests of justice.

(2) Everyone charged with a criminal offence shall be presumed innocent until proved guilty according to law.

(3) Everyone charged with a criminal offence has the following minimum rights:

(a) to be informed promptly, in a language which he understands and in detail, of the nature and cause of the accusation against him;

(b) to have adequate time and facilities for the preparation of his defence;

(c) to defend himself in person or through legal assistance of his own choosing or, if he has not sufficient means to pay for legal assistance, to be given it free when the interests of justice so require;

(d) to examine or have examined witnesses against him and to obtain the attendance and examination of witnesses on his behalf under the same conditions as witnesses against him;

(e) to have the free assistance of an interpreter if he cannot understand or speak the language used in court.

Application

16–58 Article 6(1) guarantees the general right to a fair trial and is to be given a broad and purposive interpretation: *Moreiva de Azvedo v. Portugal*, 13 E.H.R.R. 721; *Delcourt v. Belgium*, 1 E.H.R.R. 355; *De Cubber v. Belgium*, 7 E.H.R.R. 236. Fairness is a constantly evolving concept that may require the adequacy of procedures once deemed to be fair to be re-assessed: *R. v. H.* [2004] 2 A.C. 134, HL (at [11]). In considering whether the rights of the defence under Article 6 have been respected, the European Court of Human Rights will have regard to the proceedings as a whole, including appellate proceedings, and may consider whether or not the appellate proceedings have rectified any defect which arose at the first instance hearing: *Adolf v. Austria*, 4 E.H.R.R. 313; *De Cubber v. Belgium*, 7 E.H.R.R. 236; *Andersson v. Sweden*, 15 E.H.R.R. 218; *Helmers v. Sweden*, 15 E.H.R.R. 285; *Edwards v. U.K.*, 15 E.H.R.R. 417.

16–59 The minimum guarantees set out in Article 6(3)(a) to (e) are specific aspects of the general right to a fair trial and are not therefore exhaustive: *Artico v. Italy*, 3 E.H.R.R. 1; *T. v. Italy* (1992) Series A/245–C (at para. 25); *Edwards v. U.K.*, *ante*; *Foucher v. France*, 25 E.H.R.R. 234. The relationship between Article 6(1) and (3) "is that of the general to the particular"; accordingly, a trial could fail to fulfil the general conditions of Article 6(1), even though the minimum rights guaranteed by Article 6(3) are respected: *Jespers v. Belgium*, 27 D.R. 61. In *Brown v. Stott* [2003] 1 A.C. 681, PC, Lord Bingham observed that whilst the overall fairness of a criminal trial cannot be compromised, the constituent rights comprised, whether expressly or implicitly, within Article 6 are not themselves absolute. Limited qualification of those rights would be acceptable if reasonably directed towards "a clear and proper public objective" and if representing no greater qualification than the situation called for. The Strasbourg case law had consistently eschewed the formulation of hard-edged and inflexible statements of principle from which no departure could be sanctioned whatever the background or circumstances. Instead the Court had "paid very close attention to the facts of particular cases coming before it, giving effect to factual differences and recognising differences of degree." In *R. v. A. (No. 2)* [2002] 1 A.C. 45, HL, Lord Steyn observed (at [38]) that it was well-established that the right to a fair trial in Article 6 was absolute in the sense that a conviction obtained in breach of it cannot stand. The only balancing permitted was in respect of what the concept of a fair trial entails; account could be taken of the familiar triangulation of interests of the accused, the victim and society. In that context proportionality (*ante*, § 16–34) had a role to play. See also *R. v. Forbes* [2001] 1 A.C. 473, HL; and *Att. Gen.'s Reference (No. 2 of 2001)* [2004] 2 A.C. 72, HL; and

O'Halloran and Francis v. U.K. (2008) 46 E.H.R.R. 21 (the constituent elements of fairness cannot be the subject of a single unvarying rule and must depend on the circumstances of the particular case).

The guarantees under Article 6 apply equally to proceedings concerning all types of offence from the most straightforward to the most complex. The point has been made a number of times by the European Court in relation to serious fraud (*Saunders v. U.K.*, 23 E.H.R.R. 313); drug trafficking (*Teixeira de Castro v. Portugal*, 28 E.H.R.R. 101; and *Jalloh v. Germany*, *post*, § 16–67); and terrorism (*Heaney and McGuiness v. Ireland* (2001) 33 E.H.R.R. 12; *Shannon v. U.K.* (2006) 42 E.H.R.R. 31; and *Hulki Güneş v. Turkey* (2006) 43 E.H.R.R. 15). For recognition of these principles in domestic law, see *R. v. Looseley*; *Att.-Gen.'s Reference (No. 3 of 2000)* [2002] 1 Cr.App.R. 29, HL (*per* Lord Hoffmann at [59]); *Montgomery v. H.M. Advocate* [2003] 1 A.C. 641, PC (*per* Lord Hope at 673D); *R. v. Lambert* [2002] 2 A.C. 545, HL (*per* Lord Steyn at [40]); *R. v. Jones* [2003] 1 A.C. 1, HL (*per* Lord Bingham at [14]); *Mills v. H.M. Advocate* [2004] 1 A.C. 441, PC (*per* Lord Steyn at [10], and *per* Lord Hope at [49]); and *Sheldrake v. DPP*; *Att.-Gen.'s Reference (No. 4 of 2002)* [2005] 1 A.C. 264, HL (*per* Lord Bingham at [21] and [51]).

Scope

The application of Article 6(1) to criminal proceedings is confined to proceedings **16–60**
which involve a "criminal charge". In considering whether proceedings are "criminal" for the purposes of Article 6, three criteria are to be applied, namely (a) the classification of the proceedings in domestic law, (b) the nature of the offence itself, and (c) the severity of the penalty which may be imposed: *Engel v. Netherlands*, 1 E.H.R.R. 647, at para. 82. If the applicable domestic law classifies the proceeding as criminal, this will be decisive. But where the domestic law classifies the proceeding as non-criminal, the domestic classification will be no more than a "starting point": *ibid*. The European Court of Human Rights will conduct an independent assessment of the true nature of the proceedings, taking into account in particular the severity of the penalty which may be imposed. If a domestic court has power to impose imprisonment, this will generally be sufficient to define the proceedings as "criminal", unless the "nature, duration or manner of execution of the imprisonment" is such that it could not be "appreciably detrimental": *ibid*; see also *Demicoli v. Malta*, 14 E.H.R.R. 47, at para. 31. The following have been held to be criminal proceedings: prison disciplinary proceedings (*Campbell and Fell v. U.K.*, 7 E.H.R.R. 165; *Ezeh and Connors v. U.K.* (2004) 39 E.H.R.R. 1; *Black v. U.K.* (2007) 45 E.H.R.R. 25; and *Young v. U.K.* (2007) 45 E.H.R.R. 29 (*cf.* prison disciplinary proceedings against a life sentence prisoner where a punishment of "additional days" could not be in issue: *R. (Tangney) v. Secretary of State for the Home Department*, *The Times*, August 30, 2005, CA (Civ. Div.)); proceedings in respect of tax evasion leading to the imposition of large financial penalties (*Bendenoun v. France*, 18 E.H.R.R. 54); commitment to prison for non-payment of the community charge (*Benham v. U.K.*, 22 E.H.R.R. 293); imprisonment for refusal to be bound over to keep the peace (*Steel v. U.K.*, 28 E.H.R.R. 603; *Hooper v. U.K.* (2005) 41 E.H.R.R. 1), or to be of good behaviour (*Hashman and Harrup v. U.K.*, 30 E.H.R.R. 241); proceedings in connection with an assessment to a penalty under the *Finance Act* 1985, s.13, the *Finance Act* 1994, s.8, and the *Value Added Tax Act* 1994, s.60, in respect of dishonest evasion of V.A.T. or excise duty (*Georgiou (t/a Marios Chippery) v. U.K.* [2001] S.T.C. 80, ECtHR; *Han v. Customs and Excise Commrs* [2001] 1 W.L.R. 2253, CA (Civ. Div.)); the system governing the imposition of penalties for the delivery of fraudulent or negligent income tax returns (*King v. Walden* [2001] S.T.C. 822, Ch D; *Janosevic v. Sweden* (2004) 38 E.H.R.R. 22; and *King v. U.K. (No. 2)* [2004] S.T.C. 911, ECtHR); and the imposition of a penalty under section 32 of the *Immigration and Asylum Act* 1999, and the *Carriers' Liability (Clandestine Entrants and Sale of Transporters) Regulations* 2000 (S.I. 2000 No. 685) (*International Transport Roth Gmbh v. Secretary of State for the Home Department* [2003] Q.B. 728, CA (Civ. Div.)). As to contempt proceedings, see *Harman v. U.K.*, 38 D.R. 53 (admissibility); *Weber v. Switzerland*, 12 E.H.R.R. 508; *Kyprianou v. Cyprus* (2007) 44 E.H.R.R. 28; *R. v.*

MacLeod [2001] Crim.L.R. 589, CA; and *R. v. Dodds* [2003] 1 Cr.App.R. 60, CA. See also *Newman v. Modern Bookbinders Ltd* [2000] 1 W.L.R. 2559, CA (Civ. Div.); *Wilkinson v. S.* [2003] 1 W.L.R. 1254, CA (Civ. Div.); and *Raja v. Van Hoogstraten* [2004] 4 All E.R. 793, CA (Civ. Div.). *Cf. Ravnsborg v. Sweden*, 18 E.H.R.R. 38.

The criminal provisions of Article 6 have no application to proceedings under either section 1 (anti-social behaviour orders) or 2 (sex offender orders) of the *CDA* 1998: *R. (McCann) v. Crown Court at Manchester* [2003] 1 A.C. 787, HL (s.1); *B. v. Chief Constable of Avon and Somerset Constabulary* [2001] 1 W.L.R. 340, DC; *Jones v. Greater Manchester Police Authority* [2002] A.C.D. 4, DC (s.2 (repealed by the *SOA* 2003; see now s.104 thereof)); or to football banning orders under section 14B(4) of the *Football Spectators Act* 1989: *Gough v. Chief Constable of Derbyshire* [2002] Q.B. 1213, CA (Civ. Div.). Nor do they apply to proceedings relating to deportation, save where a recommendation for deportation is made in criminal proceedings (*Maaouia v. France* (2001) 33 E.H.R.R. 42, *per* Sir Nicolas Bratza); to proceedings for a civil recovery order under Part 5 of the *PCA* 2002 (*R. (Director of the Assets Recovery Agency) v. He and Chen*, unreported, December 7, 2004, QBD (Collins J.) ([2004] EWHC 3021 Admin)); to proceedings under Schedule 3 to the *Customs and Excise Management Act* 1979 for the condemnation of goods as liable to forfeiture (*Goldsmith v. Customs and Excise Commrs* [2001] 1 W.L.R. 1673, DC; *R. (Mudie) v. Dover Magistrates Court* [2003] Q.B. 1238, CA (Civ. Div.)); to disciplinary proceedings instituted by the Financial Services Authority (*R. (Fleurose) v. Securities and Futures Authority*, *The Times*, January 15, 2002, CA (Civ. Div.)); to proceedings under section 6(1) of the *CDDA* 1986 (*Official Receiver v. Stern* [2000] 1 W.L.R. 2230, CA (Civ. Div.)); to a declaration made in civil proceedings that, on the balance of probabilities, the defendant had contravened sections 3 and 35 of the *Banking Act* 1987 (*Financial Services Authority v. Rourke*, *The Times*, November 12, 2001, Ch D); or to proceedings against a company under section 242A of the *Companies Act* 1985 for failure to comply with the requirements as to the delivery of accounts and directors' reports to the registrar (*R. (POW Trust) v. Chief Executive and Registrar of Companies* [2004] B.C.C. 268, QBD); or to proceedings under the *Prevention of Terrorism Act* 2005, s.3 (*Secretary of State for the Home Department v. M.B.*; *Same v. A.F.* [2008] 1 A.C. 440, HL) .

16–61 Article 6 does not necessarily apply to preliminary hearings concerning trial arrangements and matters of procedure: *X v. U.K.*, 5 E.H.R.R. 273; nor to civil proceedings brought by a third party to recover goods declared forfeit in earlier criminal proceedings: *AGOSI v. U.K.*, 9 E.H.R.R. 1; nor to the classification of a prisoner as category A: *X. v. U.K.*, 20 D.R. 202; nor to a determination by the Parole Board as to whether a prisoner's release on licence should be revoked: *R. (West) v. Parole Board*; *R. (Smith) v. Parole Board (No. 2)* [2005] 1 W.L.R. 350, HL. Proceedings leading to the making of a confiscation order under the *DTA* 1994 or the *CJA* 1988 do not involve the determination of a criminal charge; rather, they are to be regarded as part of the sentencing procedure following conviction: *Phillips v. U.K.*, 11 B.H.R.C. 280; *R. v. Benjafield*; *R. v. Rezvi* [2003] 1 A.C. 1099, HL. It has been emphasised on a number of occasions that it is unnecessary to prove the criminal conduct of a person in possession of unlawfully obtained property as a pre-requisite for a forfeiture order: *Air Canada v. U.K.*, 20 E.H.R.R. 150. See also *Butler v. U.K.*, unreported, June 27, 2002, ECtHR (forfeiture order pursuant to the *DTA* 1994, s.43(1)). In *R. v. H.* [2003] 1 W.L.R. 411, HL, it was held that proceedings under section 4 or 4A of the *Criminal Procedure (Insanity) Act* 1964, to determine whether the accused is unfit to plead and if so, whether he did the act or made the omission charged against him, do not involve the determination of a criminal charge for the purposes of Article 6 since they cannot result in a conviction or in any punishment or order that could be seen as retributive or deterrent. This analysis was endorsed in *Antoine v. U.K.*, unreported, May 13, 2003, ECtHR.

16–62 As to extradition proceedings, see *Soering v. U.K.*, 11 E.H.R.R. 439 (Article 6 does not generally apply, but see para. 113); and *Drozd and Janousek v. France and Spain*, 14 E.H.R.R. 745, at para. 110.

16–63 To the extent that Article 6(1) relates to criminal proceedings, it is confined to the rights of the defendant. Nothing in the language of the provision suggests that it is directed in any way to the position of a prosecutor; and "it would stand the Convention on its head" to interpret it as strengthening the rights of the prosecutor: *R. v. Weir* [2001] 1 W.L.R. 421, HL (*per* Lord Bingham at [17]). Neither does it afford a general right to bring a private prosecution: *Helmers v. Sweden*, 15 E.H.R.R. 285. However, where domestic law does permit a private prosecution, the proceedings must comply with Article 6: *ibid*.

"Equality of arms"

The right to a fair trial involves observance of the principle of "equality of arms" **16–64**
under which the defendant in criminal proceedings must have "a reasonable opportunity of presenting his case to the court under conditions which do not place him at a substantial disadvantage *vis-à-vis* his opponent": *Kaufman v. Belgium*, 50 D.R. 98 at 115; *Neumeister v. Austria*, 1 E.H.R.R. 91; *Delcourt v. Belgium*, 1 E.H.R.R. 355; *Borgers v. Belgium*, 15 E.H.R.R. 92, at paras 26–28; *Jespers v. Belgium*, 27 D.R. 61; *Bendenoun v. France*, *ante*; and see generally *R. v. H.* [2004] 2 A.C. 134, HL. The principle of equality of arms under Article 6(1) overlaps with the specific guarantees in Article 6(3), though it is not confined to those aspects of the proceedings. For example, it will be a breach of the principle where an expert witness appointed by the defence is not afforded equal treatment with one appointed by the prosecution or the court (*Bosnisch v. Austria*, 9 E.H.R.R. 191); or where the defence are given insufficient opportunity to instruct an expert (*G.B. v. France* (2002) 35 E.H.R.R. 36); or where an expert relies upon material that has not been made available to the defence (*Mantonvanelli v. France*, 24 E.H.R.R. 370). See also *Foucher v. France*, 25 E.H.R.R. 234 (non-disclosure to the defence), *post*, § 16–83.

In *McLean v. Buchanan* [2001] 1 W.L.R. 2425, the Privy Council held that the system of fixed fees for an accused's legal representative, irrespective of the work done, as provided for by the *Criminal Legal Aid (Fixed Payments) (Scotland) Regulations* 1999 (S.I. 1999 No. 491), did not *per se* involve a violation of Article 6. Whilst there was the potential for a conflict of interest between the accused and his lawyer, the question whether the accused had been afforded effective representation would depend on the facts. As to the position of a defendant who has chosen to represent himself, see *R. v. Walton* [2001] 8 *Archbold News* 2, CA (*post*, § 16–86). As to whether the "equality of arms" principle requires representation that matches the representation of the prosecution, see *Att.-Gen.'s Reference (No. 82a of 2000)*; *R. v. Lea*; *R. v. Shatwell* [2002] 2 Cr.App.R. 24, CA (*ante*, § 6–167). As to the extent to which the statutory provision of special measures in relation to juvenile witnesses, but not in relation to juvenile defendants, engages the principle of equality of arms, see *R. (D.) v. Camberwell Green Youth Court*; *R. (G.) v. Same* [2005] 1 W.L.R. 393, HL.

Jury trial

Where the trial is conducted with a jury, particular requirements may arise. The **16–65**
right to a fair trial will be violated if the judge's summing up is not fair, balanced and accurate: *X. v. U.K.* (1973) 45 C.D. 1; *X. v. U.K.*, 3 D.R. 10. A "virulent press campaign against the accused" is capable of violating the right to a fair trial: *X. v. Austria* (1963) 11 C.D. 31 at 43; *Ensslin, Baader and Raspe v. Germany*, 14 D.R. 64. The Court will take account of the fact that some press comment on a trial involving a matter of public interest is inevitable: *X. v. Norway* (1970) 35 C.D. 37. The Court will also consider whether the effect of prejudicial comment has been effectively countered by the judge's direction to the jury to ignore it: *X. v. U.K.* (1978) App. No. 7542/76, 2 Digest 688. See also *Noye v. U.K.* (2003) 36 E.H.R.R. CD 231. In the event of a conflict between the right of an accused to a fair trial, and the right of the media to report on matters of public interest primacy must be accorded to the right to a fair trial: *Montgomery and Coulter v. H.M. Advocate* [2003] 1 A.C. 641, PC (considered in *R. v. Abu Hamza*, *ante*, § 4–72a). As to prejudicial statements by public officials, see Article 6(2); *Allenet de Ribemont v. France*, 20 E.H.R.R. 557 (*post*, 16–79). As to contempt of court, see *post*, § 16–131a.

The common law rule on the inadmissibility of evidence relating to jury deliberations is compatible with Article 6, notwithstanding that it would prevent a court from considering material that would indicate that the defendant was denied an impartial hearing: *R. v. Mirza*; *R. v. Connor and Rollock* [2004] 1 A.C. 1118, HL. *Aliter*, where evidence of impartiality emerges prior to the returning of the verdict and it is not adequately investigated and/or remedied by the judge: *Remli v. France*, 22 E.H.R.R. 253; *Gregory v. U.K.*, 25 E.H.R.R. 577, and *Sander v. U.K.* (2001) 31 E.H.R.R. 1003. See also *R. v. Smith*; *R. v. Mercieca* [2005] 1 W.L.R. 704, HL (failure of judge to give sufficiently strong warning to jury). *Cf. Practice Direction (Guidance to Jurors)* [2004] 1 W.L.R. 665 (*ante*, § 4–254), issued as a response to the decision in *R. v. Mirza*; *R. v. Connor and Rollock*, *ante*.

Evidence

16–66 In general, the assessment of evidence is within the appreciation of the domestic courts, and it is not open to the European Court of Human Rights to substitute its own view of the facts for an assessment which has been fairly reached by an independent and impartial court. The Court may only interfere where there is an indication that the domestic court has drawn unfair or arbitrary conclusions from the evidence before it: *Edwards v. U.K.*, 15 E.H.R.R. 417; *Van Mechelen v. Netherlands*, 25 E.H.R.R. 647. In an exceptional case, however, the Court will be prepared to assess the weight of the evidence before a national court: *Barbera, Messegue and Jabardo v. Spain*, 11 E.H.R.R. 360. See, for example, *Telfner v. Austria* (2002) 34 E.H.R.R. 7.

16–67 Article 6(1) does not require the adoption of any particular rules of evidence, since this is in principle a matter for domestic law. However, the admission of certain types of evidence may render the trial as a whole unfair. There is no absolute requirement to exclude illegally obtained evidence, but the use of such evidence may give rise to unfairness on the facts of a particular case: *Schenck v. Switzerland*, 13 E.H.R.R. 242; *X. v. Germany*, 11 E.H.R.R. 84. In *Khan v. U.K.* (2001) 31 E.H.R.R. 45, the Court held that the admission of evidence obtained by means of a listening device in breach of Article 8 did not automatically render the proceedings unfair. Where unlawfully obtained evidence was relied upon to secure a conviction, the compatibility of the proceedings with Article 6 would depend upon an examination of the nature of the unlawful activity alleged and, if it involved a violation of another Convention right, the nature of the violation found. The Court noted that the use of a listening device was not unlawful under domestic law since there was, at the time, no legally enforceable right to privacy in English law; that the police had acted compatibly with Home Office guidelines; that the incriminating statements had been made voluntarily and without inducements; and that the "unlawfulness" in issue related solely to the absence of a statutory basis for the surveillance. Whilst the Court in *Schenck*, *ante*, had attached weight to the existence of other evidence implicating the accused, the relevance of independent evidence depended on the circumstances. Where the contested evidence was compelling, and there was no challenge to its reliability, the need for supporting evidence would be correspondingly weaker. The applicant had had the opportunity to challenge both the authenticity and the admissibility of the tape recording. After it was ruled admissible, he pleaded guilty. At each stage of the domestic proceedings the courts had assessed the impact of the admission of the evidence on the fairness of the proceedings and it was clear that if they had concluded that its admission would have led to substantive unfairness, they would have had a discretion to exclude it. In those circumstances, the proceedings as a whole were fair. Nevertheless, Article 13 of the Convention required an effective remedy before a national authority for the alleged violation of Article 8. The discretion to exclude evidence under section 78 of the *PACE Act* 1984 was inadequate to meet this requirement because, prior to the enactment of the *Human Rights Act* 1998, the national courts had not had jurisdiction to rule on the substance of the applicant's Article 8 complaint or to grant appropriate relief if the complaint was well-founded (see *R. v. Khan (Sultan)* [1997] A.C. 558, HL).

Khan was followed in *P.G. v. U.K.* (2008) 46 E.H.R.R. 51, where the court found breaches of Article 8 in relation to the use of a covert listening device under the Home Office guidelines, and in relation to the covert recording of suspects' conversations in the police station for the purpose of voice pattern comparison, but nonetheless held that the admission of the resulting evidence at trial was compatible with Article 6. The voice samples, which in themselves contained no incriminating admissions, were to be regarded as analogous to bodily samples or other items of real evidence. However, different considerations apply to evidence obtained in violation of Article 3. In *Jalloh v. Germany* (2007) 44 E.H.R.R. 32, the Grand Chamber distinguished *Khan* and *P.G.* (*ante*), holding that evidence obtained by torture, whether a confession or real evidence, should never be relied on as proof of the victim's guilt, irrespective of its probative value. The general question of whether the use of evidence not obtained by torture but by an act which qualified as inhuman or degrading treatment would automatically render a trial unfair was left open. However, on the facts, the Court made such a finding where a suspect had been pinned down by four police officers and an emetic had been administered in order to force him to regurgitate a swallowed bag of drugs. See also *Harutyunyan v. Armenia*, unreported, June 28, 2007, ECtHR, where the Court found that the admission in evidence of statements obtained from the applicant and other witnesses, all of which were obtained by torture in police custody, violated Article 6 notwithstanding that they were subsequently confirmed by their makers before an investigating prosecutor.

The principles of the common law standing alone, and also when applied in accordance with international law (including, *inter alia*, Article 6) compel the conclusion that evidence obtained by torture may not be admitted against a party in a British court, irrespective of where, or by whom, or on whose authority the torture was inflicted: *A. v. Secretary of State for the Home Department (No. 2)* [2006] 2 A.C. 221, HL. See also *Montgomery v. H.M. Advocate* [2003] 1 A.C. 641, PC, *per* Lord Hoffmann (at p. 649D–E); *Jalloh v. Germany, ante*; and *Harutyunyan v. Armenia, ante*.

In *R. v. X, Y and Z, The Times*, May 23, 2000, the Court of Appeal held that the domestic courts should attach "considerable importance" to any breach of Article 8 in determining an application to exclude evidence, but that it would remain necessary to engage in the exercise of reviewing and balancing all the circumstances of the case. In *R. v. P.* [2002] 1 A.C. 146, HL, Lord Hobhouse observed that the decision in *Khan v. U.K., ante*, was consistent with the House of Lords' judgment in *R. v. Khan (Sultan)*, and that the admissibility of unlawfully obtained evidence was to be determined by reference to Article 6 and section 78 rather than Article 8. This approach is reflected in *R. v. Loveridge (William), Lee (Charles) and Loveridge (Christine)* [2001] 2 Cr.App.R. 29, where the Court of Appeal held that although the police had acted unlawfully and in breach of Article 8 in obtaining video footage of the suspects in a magistrates' court for the purpose of comparison with closed circuit television of a robbery, the evidence could nonetheless be admitted compatibly with Article 6. See also *R. v. Mason* [2002] 2 Cr.App.R. 38, CA (covert tape recordings made in the police station in breach of Article 8 nevertheless properly admitted) (affirmed in *Wood v. U.K., The Times*, November 23, 2004); and *R. v. Rosenberg, post*, § 16–109 (admission of evidence of drug dealing obtained by a neighbour who placed a video camera on his property).

The admission of hearsay evidence, without an opportunity to cross-examine, may render the trial as a whole unfair if the conviction is based wholly or mainly on such evidence: *Unterpertinger v. Austria*, 13 E.H.R.R. 175 (see Article 6(3)(d), *post*, §§ 16–91 *et seq.*). The evidence of an accomplice who has been promised immunity from prosecution may be admitted without violating Article 6, provided the jury are made fully aware of the circumstances: *X. v. U.K.*, 7 D.R. 115. Nor is it a breach of Article 6 to admit the evidence of an undercover agent placed in a prison to eavesdrop on conversations involving the accused: *X. v. Germany, ante*. The position may be different if the undercover officer takes an active role in eliciting the evidence (*Allan v. U.K.* (2003) 36 E.H.R.R. 12; *R. v. Allan* [2005] Crim.L.R. 716, CA; see also *R. v. Swaffield*; *Pavic v. R.* (1980) 192 C.L.R. 159); or if communications between prisoners and their lawyers are monitored (see *R. v. Grant* [2005] 2 Cr.App.R. 29, CA; *R. v. Mason* (*ante*), and *ante*, § 15–532). In *Grant, ante*, the Court of Appeal held that deliberate acts carried out by the police which are designed to violate a suspected person's right to privileged communications with his lawyer constitute such an affront to the integrity of the justice system and the rule of law that they will invariably lead to a stay of the proceedings, notwithstanding the absence of prejudice to the defence. The Commission has held that the admission of a co-defendant's plea of guilty pursuant to the *PACE Act* 1984, s.74, did not violate Article 6: *M.H. v. U.K.* [1997] E.H.R.L.R. 279.

Anonymity of witnesses

16–68 If the defence are deprived of the information necessary to challenge a witness's credibility, then this will amount to an insurmountable obstacle to a fair trial. Ignorance as to the identity of a witness may deprive the defence of the particulars which would enable it to demonstrate that he is prejudiced, hostile or unreliable: *Kostovski v. Netherlands*, 12 E.H.R.R. 434. In *Doorson v. Netherlands*, 22 E.H.R.R. 330, however, the Court emphasised the need to balance the interests of the accused against any risk to the life, liberty or security of a witness. Where there is an identifiable threat to the safety of a witness, arrangements to preserve anonymity can in principle be justified, providing adequate safeguards are in place to counter-balance the resulting unfairness to the defence. In particular, the judge should be made aware of the witness's identity; the defence should have an opportunity to question the witness; the evidence should be treated with "extreme care"; and a conviction should not be based "solely or to a decisive extent" on evidence given anonymously. In addition, the Court should always consider alternative methods of protecting a witness, and should adopt the least intrusive method available: *Van Mechelen v. Netherlands*, 25 E.H.R.R. 647. As to the position of undercover police officers, see *Van Mechelen v. Netherlands, ante*; *Lüdi v. Switzerland*, 15 E.H.R.R. 201. As to the use of screens see *X. v. U.K.*, 15 E.H.R.R. CD 113. As to public interest immunity, see *post*, § 16–85.

As to the approach of the House of Lords to anonymous witnesses, see *R. v. Davis* [2008] 3 W.L.R. 125 (*ante*, § 8–70); and see now the *Criminal Evidence (Witness Anonymity) Act* 2008 (*ante*, §§ 8–71 *et seq.*).

Entrapment and agents provocateurs

16–68a The right to a fair trial will be violated where police officers have stepped beyond an "essentially passive" investigation of a suspect's criminal activities and have "exercised an influence such as to incite the commission of the offence": *Teixeira de Castro v. Portugal*, 28 E.H.R.R. 101, ECtHR. See also *Lüdi v. Switzerland, ante*; and *Eurofinacom v. France* [2005] Crim.L.R. 134, ECtHR. As to the application of this principle to domestic law, see *R. v. Looseley*; *Att.-Gen's Reference (No. 2 of 2000)* [2002] 1 Cr.App.R. 29, HL (*ante*, § 4–63). As to the approach in the Commonwealth, see *Mack v. R.*, 44 C.C.C. 3(d) 513; *Ridgeway v. R.* (1995) 184 C.L.R. 19; and *R. v. Pethig* (1977) 1 N.Z.L.R. 448.

As to entrapment and public interest immunity, see *Edwards and Lewis v. U.K.* (2005) 40 E.H.R.R. 24, *ante*, § 12–80a.

The protection against self-incrimination

16–69 The right to a fair trial includes "the right of anyone charged with a criminal offence ... to remain silent and not to contribute to incriminating himself": *Funke v. France*, 16 E.H.R.R. 297. In *Saunders v. U.K.*, 23 E.H.R.R. 313, the Court considered that the admission in evidence at the applicant's trial of transcripts of interviews with inspectors of the Department of Trade and Industry violated Article 6(1) since at the time of the interrogation the applicant was under a duty to answer the inspectors' questions, a duty which was enforceable by proceedings for contempt. The Court described the right to silence and the right not to incriminate oneself as generally recognised international standards which lay at the heart of a notion of a fair procedure under Article 6. The latter right presupposed that the prosecution in a criminal case must prove its case without resort to evidence obtained through methods of coercion and oppression in defiance of the will of the accused. In this sense the privilege against self-incrimination was "closely linked" to the presumption of innocence (see *post*, § 16–77). See also *I.J.L., G.M.R. and A.K.P. v. U.K.* (2001) 33 E.H.R.R. 11; and *Serves v. France*, 28 E.H.R.R. 265 (breach of Article 6 where the applicant was fined after refusing to give evidence against two co-accused). It is incompatible with the privilege against self incrimination for a judge to direct a jury that they may rely upon a confession that they are sure is true even if it was, or may have been, made as a result of oppression or other improper circumstances: *R. v. Mushtaq* [2005] 1 W.L.R. 1513, HL; as was a requirement imposed on a person who had been charged with criminal offences, to attend an interview with financial investigators to answer questions in connection with events forming the basis of the charges, on pain of penalty for non-compliance: *Shannon v. U.K.* (2006) 42 E.H.R.R. 31.

The House of Lords considered the implications of the earlier decisions in *R. v. Hertfordshire C.C., ex p. Green Environmental Industries Ltd* [2000] 2 A.C. 412. The protection against self-incrimination, as it was understood in *Saunders*, was relevant only where the prosecution sought to introduce evidence obtained by powers of compulsory questioning in the course of a criminal trial. Under the *Human Rights Act* 1998, it would be incumbent on a judge to consider whether Article 6(1) required the exclusion of such evidence. Article 6 did not, however, prevent the use of compulsory questioning powers during the investigative phase of an inquiry. Notwithstanding the decision in *Funke*, the Court had drawn a clear distinction in *Saunders* between questioning during the course of "extra-judicial inquiries" and the use of the material thereby obtained in a subsequent criminal prosecution. See *Weh v. Austria* (2005) 40 E.H.R.R. 37. There is, however, no principle which prohibits statements obtained under compulsory powers being passed from one law enforcement authority to another. Neither is there any obligation to provide the maker of the statement with notice that this has been done: *R. v. Brady* [2005] 1 Cr.App.R. 5, CA; and *R. (Kent Pharmaceuticals Ltd) v. Director of Serious Fraud Office* [2005] 1 W.L.R. 1302, CA (Civ. Div.).

In *Brown v. Stott* [2003] 1 A.C. 681, PC, it was held that the admission of answers obtained pursuant to powers of compulsory questioning under section 172 of the *RTA* 1988 (*post*, § 32–133) was compatible with Article 6 as interpreted in *Saunders*. In contrast to the position in *Saunders*, section 172 provided for the putting of a single simple question rather than prolonged interrogation and the penalty for non-compliance was moderate and non-custodial. Section 172 was a proportionate response to the problem of maintaining road safety, which did not involve improper coercion or oppression. The reasoning of the Privy Council was endorsed by the Grand Chamber in *O'Halloran and Francis v. U.K.* (2008) 46 E.H.R.R. 21. In particular, the court emphasised that those who chose to keep and drive motor cars could be taken to have accepted certain responsibilities and obligations as part of the regulatory regime relating to motor vehicles, and, in the legal framework of the United Kingdom, those responsibilities included the obligation, in the event of the suspected commission of road traffic offences, to inform the authorities of the identity of the driver. *Cf. Telfner v. Austria* (2002) 34 E.H.R.R. 7. In *Att.-Gen's Reference (No. 7 of 2000)* [2001] 2 Cr.App.R. 19, the Court of Appeal held that Article 6 did not prohibit the admission in evidence of documents delivered up to the Official Receiver or produced under compulsion pursuant to section 291 of the *Insolvency Act* 1986 (*post*, § 30–64). Insofar as *Funke* supported the proposition that the protection against self-incrimination extended to documents which had an existence independent of the will of the accused, the decision was inconsistent with *Saunders*, and the reasoning in the latter case was to be preferred. See also *R. v. Hundal and Dhaliwal* [2004] 2 Cr.App.R. 19, CA (documentary evidence obtained through a compulsory search under the *Terrorism Act* 2000, Sched. 7); and *Office of Fair Trading v. X.* [2004] I.C.R. 105, QBD (Morrison J.) (warrant issued under the *Competition Act* 1998, s.28). *Cf. J.B. v. Switzerland* [2001] Crim.L.R. 748, where the European Court followed *Funke*, finding a breach of Article 6 in a case where the applicant had been fined for failing to surrender financial documents to the tax authorities; and *Jalloh v. Germany*, *ante*, § 16–67, where it was said that to the extent that the effect of *Saunders* was that the privilege did not cover material obtained from the suspect through the use of compulsory powers where that material had an existence independent of the will of the suspect, this would be distinguishable in a case where the evidence sought required the forcible introduction of a tube through the nose and the administration of an emetic so as to produce a pathological reaction in the body, *viz.* vomiting; in such a case, the privilege would be engaged; whether it had been violated would depend on the nature and degree of compulsion used, the weight of the public interest in the investigation and punishment of the offence in issue, the existence of any relevant safeguards, and the use to which any material obtained was put. See also, *Heaney and McGuinness v. Ireland* (2001) 33 E.H.R.R. 12, in which it was held that a criminal prosecution for withholding information in connection with an alleged act of terrorism was incompatible with Article 6 since it destroyed the "very essence" of the privilege against self-incrimination.

16–69a In *R. v. Allen* [2002] 1 A.C. 509, the House of Lords held that the prosecution of a taxpayer for furnishing a false declaration of assets, which had been provided under compulsion pursuant to section 20 of the *Taxes Management Act* 1970, and the "*Hansard*" procedure, did not violate Article 6. The position would be otherwise if the defendant had given true and accurate information to the effect that he had earlier cheated the revenue and had then been prosecuted for that earlier dishonesty on the basis of the statement. He would then have a strong argument that the proceedings were unfair and an even stronger one that the evidence should be excluded.

This reasoning was upheld in *Allen v. U.K.* [2003] Crim L.R. 280, ECtHR, on the basis that the prosecution for making a false declaration "was not an example of forced self-incrimination about an offence which had previously been committed; it was the offence itself". See also *R. v. Gill* [2004] 1 Cr.App.R. 20, CA; and *Weh v. Austria* (2005) 40 E.H.R.R. 37 (conviction for providing false details as to who was driving a vehicle in response to a statutory notice compelling provision of the relevant information).

16–69b In *Allan v. U.K.* (2003) 36 E.H.R.R. 12, a detained suspect who had previously exercised his right to silence during police station interviews was placed in a cell with a police informant, whose purpose was to elicit information from the suspect. The Court held that the right to silence was not confined to cases where duress has been brought to bear on the accused or where the will of the accused has been directly overborne. The role of the informant in asking questions amounted to the functional equivalent of an interrogation without the attendant safeguards of a police interview. The information gained was obtained in defiance of the will of the applicant in so far as his comments were not voluntary, spontaneous and unprompted, but were induced by persistent questioning carried out at the behest of the police. In those circumstances the use of the evidence at trial impinged on the applicant's right to silence and privilege against self-incrimination. *Cf. R. v. Allan* [2005] Crim.L.R. 716, CA.

16–70 Different considerations apply to rules permitting the drawing of adverse inferences from the silence of the accused under interrogation or at trial. In *Murray v. U.K.*, 22 E.H.R.R. 29, the Court found that the provisions of the *Criminal Evidence (Northern Ireland) Order* 1988 (S.I. 1988 No. 1987), as applied to the facts of that case, did not constitute a violation of Article 6(1). The Court emphasised that the independent evidence of guilt was strong, and that the Northern Ireland legislation incorporated a number of safeguards: in particular, the adverse inferences had been drawn by a judge, sitting without a jury, whose decision was recorded in a reasoned judgment which was susceptible to scrutiny on appeal. In *R. v. Birchall* [1999] Crim.L.R. 311, the Court of Appeal recognised that the application of sections 34 and 35 of the *CJPOA* 1994 (*ante*, §§ 15–414 *et seq.*, 4–305 respectively) in a jury trial could lead to violations of Article 6(1) and (2) unless the provisions were the subject of carefully framed directions. In *Condron v. U.K.* (2001) 31 E.H.R.R. 1, the European Court of Human Rights held that the direction given to the jury had failed to strike the balance required by Article 6. In particular, the jury should have been directed, as a matter of fairness, that if the applicants' silence at interview could not be attributed to their having no answer, or none that would stand up to cross-examination, then no adverse inference should be drawn. The unfairness which resulted from such a misdirection could not be cured on appeal. Whilst it was possible, in some cases, for a defect at trial to be remedied at the appellate level (see *Edwards v. U.K.*, 15 E.H.R.R. 417) that was not the position in the present case, since the Court of Appeal had no means of knowing whether the applicants' silence played a significant role in the jury's decision to convict them. See also *Averill v. U.K.* (2001) 31 E.H.R.R. 36; *Beckles v. U.K.* (2003) 36 E.H.R.R. 13; and *R. v. Beckles* [2005] 1 Cr.App.R. 23, CA.

As to the approach adopted by the domestic courts in giving effect to these principles, see *ante*, §§ 15–415 *et seq.*

Hearings in camera

The right to a hearing in public is intended to protect litigants "against the administration of justice in secret with no public scrutiny", and to maintain public confidence in the administration of justice: *Pretto v. Italy*, 6 E.H.R.R. 182. Access by the press is of particular importance: *Axen v. Germany*, 6 E.H.R.R. 195. The right is subject to the express restrictions set out in the second sentence of Article 6(1). Applying these restrictions, the Commission has upheld the exclusion of the public from the trial of an accused for sexual offences against children: *X. v. Austria* (1965) App. No. 1913/63, 2 Digest 438; and the screening of the accused from a witness in a terrorist case: *X. v. U.K.*, 15 E.H.R.R. CD 113. See also *R. v. Shayler* [2003] A.C.D. 79, CA (order for closed proceedings at certain stages during a prosecution under the *Official Secrets Act* 1989 where there were grounds to believe that the defendant would use the proceedings to introduce irrelevant material in a public forum that would constitute a risk to national security); and *Re A.* [2006] 1 W.L.R. 1361, CA (where the exceptional facility of *in camera* proceedings was held to be necessary in order to enable the defendant to be provided with material which might advance an abuse of process application without obliging the prosecution to discontinue proceedings). As to contempt of court, see *Worm v. Austria*, 25 E.H.R.R. 454. As to *ex parte* public interest immunity hearings, see *post*, § 16–85. **16–71**

Trial in the absence of the accused

The right to a fair trial implies the right of an accused to be present so that he may participate effectively in the conduct of his case: *Ekbatani v. Sweden*, 13 E.H.R.R. 504; *Stanford v. U.K.* (1994) Series A/282–A. A defendant may, however, waive his right to be present either expressly or impliedly by failing to attend a hearing having been given effective notice of it: *C. v. Italy*, 56 D.R. 40. The waiver must be clear and unequivocal: *Colozza v. Italy*, 7 E.H.R.R. 516; *Brozicek v. Italy*, 12 E.H.R.R. 371; *Poitrimol v. France*, 18 E.H.R.R. 130; *Lala v. Netherlands*, 18 E.H.R.R. 586; *Pelladoah v. Netherlands*, 19 E.H.R.R. 81. In addition, a court may proceed in the absence of the accused where the state has acted diligently but unsuccessfully to give him effective notice of the hearing: *Colozza v. Italy*, *ante*. Where this occurs, however, the accused must be able to obtain "a fresh determination of the merits of the charge" when he later learns of the proceedings which took place in his absence: *ibid*. Exceptionally, a court may proceed where the accused is absent through illness, provided the accused's interests are fully protected: *Ensslin, Baader and Raspe v. Germany*, 14 D.R. 64. *Cf. Romanov v. Russia* (2007) 44 E.H.R.R. 23 (*ante*, § 3–206). As to the presence of the accused at an appeal hearing, see *post*, § 16–96. **16–72**

In *R. v. Jones (Anthony)* [2003] 1 A.C. 1 (affirmed in *Jones v. U.K.* (2003) 37 E.H.R.R. CD 269), the House of Lords held that there was nothing in the Strasbourg case law to suggest that a trial of a criminal defendant held in his absence, where he had been fully informed of the forthcoming trial and had chosen not to attend, was incompatible with Article 6. As to this, see also *ante*, § 3–197.

Trial of vulnerable defendants in the Crown Court

See *ante*, §§ 4–96a *et seq*. **16–72a**

As to the use of special measures protecting child witnesses who give evidence against child defendants, see *ante*, § 8–55c. As to special measures for vulnerable defendants, see *ante*, § 8–52a.

Trial within a reasonable time

Article 6(1) guarantees the right to trial within a reasonable time. The provision is designed to prevent a person charged from remaining "too long in a state of uncertainty about his fate" (*Stögmüller v. Austria*, 1 E.H.R.R. 155; *Dyer v. Watson* [2004] 1 A.C. 379, PC (*per* Lord Bingham at [50]); and *Mills v. H.M. Advocate* [2004] 1 A.C. 441, PC (*per* Lord Steyn at [14])). It is therefore directed primarily towards excessive procedural delays in the conduct of a prosecution, including any appeal. The reasonable time guarantee runs from the moment that an individual is subject to a "charge" **16–73** within the meaning of the Convention. This is taken to be the time when the defendant is "officially notified" or "substantially affected" by proceedings taken against him: *Deweer v. Belgium*, 2 E.H.R.R. 439; *Eckle v. Germany*, 5 E.H.R.R. 1; *Coriaglano v. Italy*, 5 E.H.R.R. 334; *Foti v. Italy*, 5 E.H.R.R. 313. This will usually be the date of charge by the police (*Ewing v. U.K.*, 10 E.H.R.R. 141); but in a case where the charge is delayed, or subsequent charges are added it may be the date of a person's initial arrest, or the date on which the defendant becomes aware that he is being "seriously investigated" and that "immediate consideration" is being given to the possibility of a prosecution (*X. v. U.K.*, 14 D.R. 26; *X. v. U.K.*, 17 D.R. 122). In certain situations, the operative date will be the date of the first interview (*Howarth v. U.K.* (2005) 41 E.H.R.R. 2; *Massey v. U.K.*, *The Times*, November 24, 2004, ECtHR); or of an initial search of the premises (*Neubeck v. Germany*, 41 D.R. 13). See also *King v. U.K. (No. 2)* [2004] S.T.C. 911, and *King v. U.K.* (2005) 41 E.H.R.R. 2 (date of "Hansard" warning).

The period to be considered under Article 6(1) continues from the date of "official notification" until the conclusion of any appeal: *Eckle v. Germany*, *ante*; and see also *Neumeister v. Austria*, 1 E.H.R.R. 91 at para. 19. For examples of unreasonable delay in the appellate stages of proceedings, see *Mellors v. U.K.* (2004) 38 E.H.R.R. 11; and *Massey v. U.K.*, *ante*. Where an accused is not finally brought to trial, Article 6 ceases to apply as at the date of discontinuance: *Orchin v. U.K.*, 6 E.H.R.R. 391 (entering of *nolle prosequi*). Where charges have been left to lie on the file, Article 6 ceases to apply if the prosecution undertake not to proceed with them (*X. v. U.K.*, 17 D.R. 122); or if it is established practice not to do so (*X. v. U.K.*, 5 E.H.R.R. 508). Factors to be taken into account are the complexity of the case, the conduct of the defendant, and the conduct of the prosecuting authorities. A more rigorous standard applies when the defendant is in custody: *Abdoella v. Netherlands*, 20 E.H.R.R. 585. Complexity may arise from the number of defendants or charges, from the difficulty of the legal issues involved, or from the need to obtain evidence from abroad: *Neumeister v. Austria*, *ante*; or from the volume of evidence: *Wemhoff v. Germany*, 1 E.H.R.R. 55. The state is not responsible for delays attributable to the applicant or his lawyers: *König v. Germany*, 2 E.H.R.R. 170; and periods spent unlawfully at large are to be disregarded in determining the overall length of the proceedings: *Girolami v. Italy* (1991) Series A/196–E. The state is however responsible for delays attributable to the prosecution or the court: *Orchin v. U.K.*, *ante* (delay in entering of a *nolle prosequi*); *Eckle v. Germany*, *ante* (delay in commencement of trial). Neither the workload of the court, nor a shortage of resources, is a sufficient justification for delay in a trial. The Convention places a duty on contracting parties, regardless of cost, "to organise their legal systems so as to allow the courts to comply with the requirements of Article 6(1)": *Zimmerman and Steiner v. Switzerland*, 6 E.H.R.R. 17; *Abdoella*, *ante*.

In *Porter v. Magill*; *Weeks v. Magill* [2002] 2 A.C. 357, the House of Lords confirmed that there was no requirement to demonstrate specific prejudice in order to establish a breach of the right to trial within a reasonable time. In *Dyer v. Watson* [2004] 1 A.C. 379, the Privy Council gave the following general guidance as to the application of the reasonable time guarantee. The first step was to consider the time that had elapsed. Unless that period was one which, on its face and without more, gave grounds for real concern, it was almost certainly unnecessary to go further since the Convention was directed not to departures from the ideal but to infringements of basic rights. The threshold was a high one. If, however, the period that had elapsed was one that gave ground for real concern, two consequences followed. First, it was necessary for the court to look at the detailed facts and circumstances. Secondly, it was necessary for the state to explain and justify the apparently excessive lapse of time. The relevant factors were the complexity of the case, the conduct of the defendant, and the manner in which the case had been dealt with by the administrative and judicial authorities. As to the latter, the state could not blame unacceptable delays on a general want of prosecutors or judges or courthouses or on chronic underfunding of the legal system. But the courts were not required to shut their eyes to the practical reality of litigious life even in a reasonably well-organised legal system. Thus it was not objectionable for a prosecutor to deal with cases according to what he reasonably regarded as their priority, so as to achieve an orderly dispatch of business; and it had to be accepted that a prosecutor could not ordinarily devote his whole time to a single case. Courts were entitled to draw up their lists of cases for trial some time in advance. It might be necessary to wait for the availability of a judge possessing a special expertise or of a courthouse with special facilities or security; plans might be disrupted by unexpected illness, or the pressure on a court might be increased by a sudden and unforeseen surge in business. Whilst there was no general obligation on a prosecutor to act with all due diligence and expedition, a marked lack of expedition, if unjustified, would point towards a breach of the reasonable time requirement, and whilst time ran from the date of charge, the passage of any considerable time before charge might call for greater than normal expedition.

In *Att.-Gen's Reference (No. 2 of 2001)* [2004] 2 A.C. 72, HL, it was held that (i) in cases where there has been a breach of the reasonable time requirement, a stay would only be appropriate if a fair trial was no longer possible or if it was for any compelling reason unfair to try the defendant; and (ii) time ran for this purpose from the earliest time when the defendant was officially alerted to the likelihood of criminal proceedings being taken against him, which would normally be when he was charged or served with a summons; as to (i) where there was a breach, there had to be an appropriate remedy; what that was would depend on the nature of the breach and all the circumstances, including particularly the stage at which the breach was established; if established before the hearing, the appropriate remedy might be a public acknowledgement of the breach, action to expedite the hearing to the greatest extent practicable, and, perhaps, if the defendant was in custody, release on bail; neither the prosecutor nor the court would act incompatibly with the defendant's right under Article 6 within section 6(1) of the *Human Rights Act* 1998 by continuing with the prosecution since the breach consisted of the delay which had accrued, and not the prospective hearing; if the breach were only established after the hearing, the remedy might be a public acknowledgement, a reduction in sentence or the payment of compensation to an acquitted defendant; cases where it might be unfair to try the defendant include cases of bad faith, executive manipulation and abuse of process, and also where the delay was of such an order, or where a prosecutor's breach of professional duty was such as to make it unfair that the proceedings should continue; but such cases would be exceptional, and a stay would never be an appropriate remedy if any lesser remedy would adequately vindicate the defendant's Convention right. These principles were analysed and applied in *R. v. S.*, 170 J.P. 434, CA, *ante*, § 4–66.

See also *Spiers (Procurator Fiscal) v. Ruddy* [2008] 2 W.L.R. 608, PC (not following *H.M. Advocate v. R.* [2004] 1 A.C. 462, PC which was in conflict with the decision in *Att.-Gen's Reference (No. 2 of 2001)*, *ante*).

As to the remedy for unreasonable delay in appellate proceedings where there was no unreasonable delay at first instance, see *ante*, § 7–46a. For delays brought about by ordering retrials see *Henworth v. U.K.* (2005) 40 E.H.R.R. 33. *Cf. R. v. Henworth* [2001] 2 Cr.App.R. 4, CA. For unacceptable delays in the enforcement of a confiscation order, see *Crowther v. U.K.*, *The Times*, February 11, 2005; and *Lloyd v. Bow Street Magistrates' Court* [2004] 1 Cr.App.R. 11, DC.

Independence of the judiciary

Article 6 requires a tribunal which is independent of the parties, the executive and **16–73a** the legislature. In determining whether this requirement has been met, "regard must be had, *inter alia*, to the manner of appointment of [the tribunal's] members and their term of office, the existence of guarantees against outside pressures, and the question whether the body presents an appearance of independence": *Findlay v. U.K.*, 24 E.H.R.R. 221, at para. 73. Any direct involvement in the passage of legislation or executive rules is likely to be sufficient to cast doubt on the judicial impartiality of a person subsequently called upon to determine a dispute as to the existence of reasons for permitting a variation from the legislation or rules in issue: *McGonnell v. U.K.*, 30 E.H.R.R. 289. See also *Davidson v. Scottish Ministers*, *The Times*, July 16, 2004, HL. The fixing of a tariff period to be served by a juvenile convicted of murder and sentenced to detention at Her Majesty's pleasure under section 90 of the *PCC(S)A* 2000 is a sentencing exercise which attracts the guarantees of Article 6. Accordingly, it is a breach of the independence requirement in Article 6(1) for the tariff period to be set by a member of the executive: *V. v. U.K.*, 30 E.H.R.R. 122. The same principle was recognised in relation to mandatory life sentences in *Stafford v. U.K.* (2002) 35 E.H.R.R. 32; and *Easterbrook v. U.K.* (2003) 37 E.H.R.R. 40. In *Starrs v. Procurator Fiscal*, 8 B.H.R.C. 1, the High Court of Justiciary held that the post of temporary sheriff was incompatible with Article 6 since the appointment was for a fixed period of 12 months, and its renewal was within the unfettered discretion of the executive. The court considered that security of tenure was the cornerstone of judicial independence, and that such independence could be threatened not only by interference, but also by a judge being influenced, consciously or unconsciously, by his hopes and fears about possible treatment by the executive in the future. As to the role of the clerk in a magistrates' court, see *Mort v. U.K.* [2002] Crim.L.R. 920, ECtHR; *Clark v. Kelly* [2004] 1 A.C. 681, PC; and *Practice Direction (Criminal Proceedings: Consolidation)*, para. V.55 [2002] 1 W.L.R. 2870.

In *Millar v. Dickson*; *Payne v. Heywood*; *Stewart v. Same*; *Tracey v. Same* [2002] 1 W.L.R. 1615, PC, it was held that the right to trial by an independent and impartial tribunal is one which cannot be eroded or compromised. It is not appropriate to take into account that there has been no unfairness or injustice as a result, nor to weigh the infringement of the rights of the defendant against the general public interest. As to disqualification being automatic, see *AWG Group Ltd v. Morrison* [2006] 1 W.L.R. 1163, CA (Civ. Div.) (*ante*, § 4–32). See also *R. v. Dundon* [2004] 4 *Archbold News* 2, Ct-MAC.

In determining an application to stay proceedings or to exclude evidence, it may be incompatible with Article 6 for a judge to be shown material which is wholly adverse to the interests of a defendant during an *ex parte* public interest immunity application, without the defendant's legal representatives (or in exceptional cases, a special advocate) having the opportunity to comment upon the material: *Edwards and Lewis v. U.K.* (2005) 40 E.H.R.R. 24; and *R. v. H and C* [2004] 2 A.C. 134, HL. *Cf. R. v. May* [2005] 3 All E.R. 523, CA (judge in confiscation proceedings expressly indicating that he had ignored any material revealed to him in the PII hearings during the trial); and *R. v. Dawson* [2007] 4 *Archbold News* 3, CA (judge deciding entrapment argument in circumstances where he made it plain that his decision was not based upon material which had been shown to him during an *ex parte* hearing).

As to the position of courts-martial, see *R. v. Spear* [2003] 1 A.C. 734, HL; *R. v. Skuse, The Independent (C.S.)*, June 17, 2002, Ct-MAC ([2002] EWCA Crim. 991); *Grieves v. U.K.* (2004) 39 E.H.R.R. 2; *Cooper v. U.K.*, *ibid.*, 8; *Thompson v. U.K.* (2005) 40 E.H.R.R. 11; and *Martin v. U.K.* (2007) 44 E.H.R.R. 31 (expressing "considerable doubt" as to the outcome of *R. v. Martin (Alan)* [1998] A.C. 917, HL). As to prison disciplinary proceedings, see *Whitfield v. U.K.* (2005) 41 E.H.R.R. 44; and *R. (Al-Hassan) v. Secretary of State for the Home Department*; *R. (Carroll) v. Same* [2005] 1 W.L.R. 688, HL.

Impartiality

16–74 The requirement for trial by an "impartial tribunal" embodies the protection against actual and presumed bias, and applies equally to the judge and to the jury. The Court has adopted a dual test, examining first the evidence of actual bias, and then making an objective assessment of the circumstances alleged to give rise to a risk of bias: *Piersack v. Belgium*, 5 E.H.R.R. 160, at para. 30. The onus of establishing actual bias on the subjective test is a heavy one. There is a presumption that the court has acted impartially, which must be displaced by evidence to the contrary: *Le Compte, Van Leuren and De Meyer v. Belgium*, 4 E.H.R.R. 1, at para. 58; *Hauschildt v. Denmark*, 12 E.H.R.R. 266. This applies equally to juries: *Sander v. U.K.* (2001) 31 E.H.R.R. 44; *Rojas v. Bellaque (Att.-Gen. for Gibraltar intervening)* [2004] 1 W.L.R. 201; and *R. v. Mirza*; *R. v. Connor and Rollock* [2004] 1 A.C. 1118, HL. In applying the objective test, the question is whether a legitimate doubt as to the impartiality of the tribunal can be "objectively justified": *Hauschildt v. Denmark*, *ante*. For examples see *X. v. Norway*

(1970) 35 C.D. 37; *X. v. Austria*, 13 D.R. 36; *Holm v. Sweden*, 18 E.H.R.R. 79; *Pullar v. U.K.*, 22 E.H.R.R. 391; *Gregory v. U.K.*, 25 E.H.R.R. 577; *Remli v. France*, 22 E.H.R.R. 253; *Findlay v. U.K.*, 24 E.H.R.R. 221; *Sander v. U.K.* (2001) 31 E.H.R.R. 44 (*ante*, § 4–256); and *Crummock (Scotland) Ltd v. H.M. Advocate*, *The Times*, May 9, 2000, JC (*ante*, § 4–256). See also *Locabail (U.K.) Ltd v. Bayfield Properties Ltd* [2000] Q.B. 451, CA (Civ.Div.) (*ante*, § 4–32) (guidance on judicial impartiality).

In *Porter v. Magill*; *Weeks v. Magill* [2002] 2 A.C. 357, the House of Lords held that the test to be adopted was that put forward in *Re Medicaments and Related Classes of Goods (No. 2)* [2001] 1 W.L.R. 700, CA (Civ. Div.). The court should first ascertain all the relevant circumstances and then ask whether those circumstances would lead a fair-minded and informed observer to conclude that there was a real possibility that the tribunal was biased. For applications of this principle, see *R. v. Cromer* [2002] 1 Cr.App.R.(S) 34, CA; *Taylor v. Lawrence* [2003] Q.B. 528, CA (Civ. Div.); *R. v. Mason* [2002] 2 Cr.App.R. 38, CA; *R. v. Brown (Robert Clifford)* [2002] Crim.L.R. 409, CA; and *R. v. George* [2006] 1 Cr.App.R.(S.) 119, CA (*ante*, § 5–73) (*Newton* hearings). As to the issues that may arise where a crown prosecutor, police or prison officer is a juror, see *ante*, §§ 4–233a, 4–233b. As to the summary procedure in cases of alleged contempt, see *Wilkinson v. S.* [2003] 1 W.L.R. 1254, CA (Civ. Div.); and *Kyprianou v. Cyprus* (2007) 44 E.H.R.R. 28. See also *Chmelíř v. Czech Republic* (2007) 44 E.H.R.R. 20.

Reasoned judgment

The right to a fair hearing presumes that the court will give reasons for its judgment: *Hadjianastassiou v. Greece*, 16 E.H.R.R. 219. Where a submission to the judge in the course of a trial would, if accepted, be decisive of the outcome of the case, it must be specifically and expressly addressed in a ruling: *Hiro Balani v. Spain*, 19 E.H.R.R. 566, at para. 27. The fact that a jury gives no reasons for their decision to convict is not, however, incompatible with Article 6: *Saric v. Denmark*, unreported, February 2, 1999 ECtHR. **16–75**

A magistrates' court does not have to state its reasons for convicting a defendant in the form of a judgment reciting the charges, the evidence and all their findings of fact. The essence of the exercise is to inform the defendant why he has been found guilty and this could usually be done in a few simple sentences. If an aggrieved party sought to obtain more detailed reasons then a request could be made for the statement of a case for the High Court: *R. (McGowan) v. Brent JJ.*, 166 J.P. 29, DC. See also *Cedeno v. Logan* [2001] 1 W.L.R. 86, PC. Article 6 imposes no obligation on a magistrates' court to give reasons when rejecting a submission of no case to answer (*Moran v. DPP*, 166 J.P. 467, DC), and very limited reasons will suffice when a magistrates court is called upon to decide which of two linked cases should be heard first (*R. (Pace) v. West Wiltshire JJ.* [2002] 2 *Archbold News* 2, DC).

Other issues

The physical arrangements in the courtroom may raise issues under Article 6: see *X. v. U.K.*, 15 E.H.R.R. 113, CD (use of screen to conceal witness); *Stanford v. U.K.* (1994) Series A/282–A (accused unable to hear); and *Campbell v. U.K.*, 57 D.R. 148. **16–76**

In *C.G. v. U.K.* (2002) 34 E.H.R.R. 31, the court found no violation of Article 6 despite "excessive and undesirable" interventions by the trial judge during cross-examination and during the defendant's evidence. Although the judge's behaviour had disconcerted defence counsel, he had not been prevented from pursuing any lines of defence, and had been able to make his closing speech to the jury without unnecessary interruption. *Cf. R. v. Cordingley* [2008] Crim. L.R. 299, CA. See also *Ranson v. U.K.* (2004) 38 E.H.R.R. CD 25. As to the circumstances in which improper and inflammatory conduct by prosecution counsel may render a trial unfair, see *Randall v. R.* [2002] 2 Cr.App.R. 17, PC; *Benedetto v. R.*; *Labrador v. R.* [2003] 1 W.L.R. 1545, PC. As to the circumstances in which a breach of Article 6 will arise where undertakings are given by the prosecution which are not subsequently complied with, see *Marpa Zeeland B.V. and Metal Welding B.V. v. Netherlands* (2005) 40 E.H.R.R. 34; and *ante*, § 4–62.

The presumption of innocence

16–77 Article 6(2) guarantees the presumption of innocence in criminal proceedings. It applies only to a person who is subject to a criminal charge (*ante*, §§ 16–60 *et seq.*) and does not therefore apply at the investigation stage: *X. v. Germany* (1962) 5 Y.B. 192; *X. v. Netherlands*, 16 D.R. 184. Nor does it govern extradition proceedings: *X. v. Austria* (1963) 6 Y.B. 484. It has limited application to sentencing and orders made following a conviction: *Engel v. Netherlands*, 1 E.H.R.R. 647; *Phillips v. U.K.*, 11 B.H.R.C. 280; and *Böhmer v. Germany* (2004) 38 E.H.R.R. 19. The refusal of costs to an acquitted defendant on grounds which reflect an opinion that he was, in reality, guilty of the offence may involve a breach of the presumption of innocence: *Minelli v. Switzerland*, 5 E.H.R.R. 554; *Baars v. Netherlands* (2004) 39 E.H.R.R. 25; *Del Latte v. Netherlands* (2005) 41 E.H.R.R. 12; and *Hussain v. U.K.*, *The Times*, April 5, 2006, ECtHR. *Cf. Leutscher v. Netherlands*, 24 E.H.R.R. 181. The revised costs practice direction reflects this principle (see paras II.1.1, II.2.1, *ante*, §§ 6–105, 6–106). It will generally be incompatible with Article 6(2) if the defendant's guilt is put in issue during compensation proceedings subsequent to an acquittal: *Sekanina v. Austria*, 17 E.H.R.R. 221; *Weixelbraun v. Austria* (2003) 36 E.H.R.R. 45; and *Capeau v. Belgium* (2008) 46 E.H.R.R. 25; but see *R. (Harris) v. Secretary of State for the Home Department*, unreported, July 15, 2008, CA (Civ. Div.) ([2008] EWCA Civ. 808) (denial of compensation to a defendant whose conviction has been quashed but who does not fall within the *CJA* 1988, s.133, does not infringe the presumption of innocence). There is, however, nothing wrong in principle with separate civil proceedings against an acquitted defendant provided that the language employed in the judgment does not directly cast doubt on the correctness of the acquittal: *Y. v. Norway* (2005) 41 E.H.R.R. 7. See also *Raja v. Van Hoogstraten*, *The Independent*, February 6, 2006, Ch D (Lightman J.); and *Ashley v. Chief Constable of Sussex Police (Sherwood intervening)*; *Ashley v. Same* [2008] 2 W.L.R. 975, HL.

16–78 Article 6(2) does not prohibit rules which transfer an evidential burden to the accused, provided the overall burden of proving guilt remains with the prosecution: *Lingens and Leitgens v. Austria*, 4 E.H.R.R. 373, at para. 4. Neither does Article 6(2) necessarily prohibit the operation of presumptions of law or fact. However, any rule which shifts the burden of proof, or which applies a presumption operating against the accused must be confined within reasonable limits: *Salabiaku v. France*, 13 E.H.R.R. 379, at para. 28 (consideration of French customs code); *Pham Hoang v. France*, 16 E.H.R.R. 53. In *X. v. U.K.* (1972) 42 C.D. 135, the Commission upheld a rebuttable presumption that a man proved to be living with, or controlling a prostitute was living off immoral earnings. Offences of strict liability do not violate Article 6(2), provided the prosecution retains the burden of proving the commission of the offence: *Salabiaku v. France*, *ante*; *Bates v. U.K.* [1996] E.H.R.L.R. 312 (*Dangerous Dogs Act* 1991). The application of these principles to statutory reverse onus provisions in England and Wales was considered by Lord Hope in *R. v. DPP, ex p. Kebilene* [2000] 2 A.C. 326, HL. The first stage in any inquiry as to whether such a provision is vulnerable to challenge under Article 6(2) is to identify the nature of the provision which is said to transfer a burden of proof. Some provisions would be more objectionable than others. A merely evidential burden, requiring the accused to do no more than raise a reasonable doubt on the issue to which it related, would not breach the presumption of innocence. However, a statute which imposed a persuasive burden, requiring the accused to prove, on a balance of probabilities, a fact which is essential to his guilt or innocence, required further examination. The court should determine whether the legislative technique which had been adopted was mandatory or discretionary, and whether it related to an essential element of the offence, or merely to an exemption or proviso. A mandatory presumption of guilt on an important essential element of the offence would be inconsistent with the presumption of innocence. It did not necessarily follow, however, that such a provision would violate Article 6(2). The Convention case law showed that although Article 6(2) is framed in absolute terms, it was not regarded in Strasbourg as imposing an absolute prohibition on reverse onus clauses. In each case the question would be whether the presumption was confined within reasonable limits. In determining that issue a court might usefully consider three questions. (1) What do the prosecution have to prove in order to transfer the onus to the defence? (2) Does the burden imposed on the accused relate to something which is likely to be difficult for him to prove, or does it relate to something which is likely to be within his knowledge or to which he has ready access? (3) What is the nature of the threat faced by society which the provision is designed to combat? *Cf. McIntosh v. H.M. Advocate* [2003] 1 A.C. 1078, PC, where Lord Hope emphasised (at [46]) that the questions were not presented as a set of rules and were no more than an indication of an approach which it might be useful to adopt when the interests of the individual are being balanced against those of society.

In *R. v. Lambert* [2002] 2 A.C. 545, the House of Lords applied these principles to section 28(2) and (3) of the *Misuse of Drugs Act* 1971 (specific "knowledge" defences available on a charge of possession, *post*, § 27–123). Read according to orthodox cannons of construction, the provisions imposed a legal or persuasive burden on the accused to disprove the requisite knowledge. Whilst there was an objective justification for some interference with the burden of proof in drugs cases, the imposition of a persuasive burden meant that an accused could be convicted notwithstanding that the jury entertained a reasonable doubt on the issue of knowledge. That was incompatible with Article 6(2). However, applying section 3 of the *Human Rights Act* 1998 (*ante*, § 16–15), the proper balance could be achieved by reading the provisions as imposing an evidential burden only. Once the accused adduced sufficient evidence to raise the issue, it would then be for the prosecution to prove the requisite knowledge beyond reasonable doubt. The requirement under section 2 of the *Homicide Act* 1957 for an accused to establish the defence of diminished responsibility on a charge of murder (*post*, § 19–66) is not, however, incompatible with Article 6(2): *R. v. Lambert*; *R. v. Ali*; *R. v. Jordan* [2001] 2 W.L.R. 211, CA.

Subsequent to *Lambert*, provisions imposing a persuasive burden of proof on the accused were recast as evidential burdens in *R. v. Carass* [2002] 1 W.L.R. 1714, CA (*Insolvency Act* 1986, s.206(4), *post*, § 30–160); *R. v. Daniel* [2003] 1 Cr.App.R. 6, CA (*Insolvency Act* 1986, s.352, *post*, § 30–171); *Sheldrake v. DPP*; *Att.-Gen.'s Reference (No. 4 of 2002)* [2005] 1 A.C. 264, HL (*Terrorism Act* 2000, s.11(1) and (2), *post*, § 25–60); and *R. v. Keogh* [2007] 1 W.L.R. 1500, CA (*Official Secrets Act* 1989, ss. 2 and 3, *post*, §§ 25–327, 25–328). *Carass* was, however, disapproved, and *Daniel* was effectively overtaken by *Att.-Gen.'s Reference (No. 1 of 2004)*; *R. v. Edwards*; *R. v. Denton*; *R. v. Hendley*; *R. v. Crowley* [2004] 2 Cr.App.R. 27, CA, in which it was held that section 352 of the 1986 Act, when applied to section 357 (fraudulent disposal of property (*post*, § 30–182)) had to be interpreted as imposing merely an evidential burden, but when applied to section 353 (non-disclosure (*post*, § 30–176)) was to be taken as imposing a legal burden which was compatible with the presumption of innocence.

Similar challenges have, however, been rejected in *L. v. DPP* [2002] 1 Cr.App.R. 32, DC, and *R. v. Matthews* [2003] 3 W.L.R. 693, CA (*CJA* 1991, s.139, *post*, § 24–125); *R. v. Davies* [2003] 1 *Archbold News* 3, CA (*Health and Safety at Work etc. Act* 1974, s.40); *R. v. Drummond* [2002] 2 Cr.App.R. 25, CA (*RTA* 1988, s.15(3), *post*, § 32–162); *Sheldrake v. DPP*; *Att.-Gen.'s Reference (No. 4 of 2002)*, *ante* (*RTA* 1988, s.5(1)(b), *post*, §§ 32–75, 32–85); *R. v. Navabi*; *R. v. Embaye*, *The Times*, December 5, 2005, CA (*Asylum and Immigration (Treatment of Claimants, etc.) Act* 2004, s.2(1)); *R. v. Makuwa* [2006] 2 Cr.App.R. 11, CA (*Immigration and Asylum Act* 1999, s.31, *post*, § 25–228d); and *R. (Griffin) v. Richmond Magistrates' Court* [2008] 1 Cr.App.R. 37, DC (*Insolvency Act* 1986, s.208(4) (not following *R. v. Carass*, *ante*)).

As to the compatibility of strict liability offences with Article 6, see *R. (Barnfather) v. Islington L.B.C.* [2003] 1 W.L.R. 2318, DC (*Education Act* 1996, s.444(1)); *R. v. Muhamad* [2003] Q.B. 1031, CA (*Insolvency Act* 1986, s.362(1)(a)); *Att.-Gen.'s Reference (No. 1 of 2004)*; *R. v. Edwards*; *R. v. Denton*; *R. v. Hendley*; *R. v. Crowley*, *ante* (*Protection from Eviction Act* 1977, s.1(2) (*post*, § 29–61); *Homicide Act* 1957, s.4(1) (*post*, § 19–83); and *CJPOA* 1994, s.51(7) (*post*, § 28–143)); and *R. v. G (Secretary of State for the Home Department intervening)* [2008] 1 W.L.R. 1379, HL (*SOA* 2003, s.5 (*post*, § 20–56)).

In *R. v. Johnstone* [2003] 1 W.L.R. 1736, the House of Lords held that the imposition of a legal burden of proof on a defendant by section 92(5) of the *Trade Marks Act* 1994 to show that he believed on reasonable grounds that the use of a sign was not an infringement of a registered trade mark was compatible with Article 6(2). In reviewing the case law since *Lambert*, Lord Nicholls (at [49–50]) indicated that the striking of a balance between the interests of society and the interests of the defendant was not as easy as it might seem. A sound starting point is that if an accused is required to prove a fact on the balance of probability to avoid conviction, this permits a conviction in spite of the fact-finding tribunal having a reasonable doubt as to the guilt of the accused: see Dickson C.J. in *R. v. Whyte* (1988) 51 D.L.R. (4th) 481, 493. This consequence of a reverse burden of proof should colour the court's approach. The more serious the punishment which may flow from conviction, the more compelling must be the justification for imposing a persuasive burden of proof on the accused. The extent and nature of the factual matters required to be proved by the accused, and their importance relative to the matters required to be proved by the prosecution, have to be taken into account. So also does the extent to which the burden on the accused relates to facts which, if they exist, are readily provable by him as matters within his own knowledge or to which he has ready access.

In *Att.-Gen.'s Reference (No. 1 of 2004)*; *R. v. Edwards*; *R. v. Denton*; *R. v. Hendley*; *R. v. Crowley*, *ante*, the Court of Appeal observed (at [38]) that a legal burden was much more likely to have to be reduced to an evidential burden on Lord Steyn's approach in *Lambert* than it was on Lord Nicholls' approach in *Johnstone* and to the extent that there was a difference of approach in the two speeches the latter was to be preferred. This view was not followed by the House of Lords in *Sheldrake v. DPP*; *Att.-Gen.'s Reference (No. 4 of 2002)*, *ante*, where it was held that both *Lambert* and *Johnstone* were recent decisions of the House, binding on all lower courts. Nothing said in *Johnstone* suggested an intention to depart from or modify the earlier decision, which should not be treated as superseded or implicitly overruled. Differences of emphasis (and Lord Steyn was not a lone voice in *Lambert*) were explicable by the difference in the subject matter of the two cases. In conducting an exercise of statutory interpretation in accordance with the *Human Rights Act* 1998, the task of the court was never to decide whether a reverse burden should be imposed on a defendant, but always to assess whether a burden enacted by Parliament unjustifiably infringed the presumption of innocence. The courts should not proceed on the assumption that Parliament would not have made an exception without good reason. Such an approach might give too much weight to the enactment under review and too little to the presumption of innocence and the obligation imposed by section 3 of the 1998 Act. The justifiability and fairness of provisions which imposed a burden of proof on a defendant in a criminal trial had to be judged in the particular context of each case. The Convention did not prohibit presumptions of fact or law but required that they should be kept within reasonable limits and should not be arbitrary. The substance and effect of any presumption adverse to a defendant had to be examined on all the facts and circumstances relevant to the particular provision. Material considerations would include the opportunity given to the defendant to rebut the presumption, the extent to which the subject matter of his defence was so closely conditioned by his knowledge and state of mind at the material time as to make it relatively easy for him to discharge the burden of proof, the maintenance of the rights of the defence generally, flexibility in the application of the presumption, the retention by the court of a power to assess the evidence, the importance of what was at stake and the difficulty which a prosecutor might find in the absence of a presumption. See further, *post*, §§ 25–60 and 32–85.

As to the compatibility of Article 6(2) with the statutory assumptions in the legislation providing for the confiscation of the proceeds of crime and drug trafficking, see *Phillips v. U.K.* [2001] Crim.L.R. 817, ECtHR; *R. v. Benjafield*; *R. v. Rezvi* [2003] 1 A.C. 1099, HL; and *R. v. Barnham* (2005) 149 S.J. 576, CA. *Cf. Geerings v. Netherlands*, (2008) 46 E.H.R.R. 49.

16–79 Pre-trial publicity involving statements by police officers or other public officials to the effect that an accused person is guilty of the offence with which he is charged may amount to a violation of Article 6(2): *Allenet de Ribemont v. France*, 20 E.H.R.R. 557.

See also *Daktaras v. Lithuania* (2002) 34 E.H.R.R. 60. *C.f. Geerings v. Netherlands*, (2008) 46 E.H.R.R.49.

Right to be informed of the charge

16–80 Article 6(3)(a) is aimed at the information required to be given at the time of charge or the commencement of proceedings, rather than the disclosure of evidence necessary to enable the accused to prepare for trial (which is governed by Article 6(3)(b), *post*, §§ 16–81 *et seq.*). Under Article 6(3)(a) a defendant will be entitled to detailed particulars of the acts which he is alleged to have committed and the legal characterisation given to those acts: *Pélissier and Sassi v. France* 30 E.H.R.R. 716; *Sadak v. Turkey* (2003) 36 E.H.R.R. 26; *Mattocia v. Italy* (2003) 36 E.H.R.R. 47; and *Brozicek v. Italy*, 12 E.H.R.R. 371 (*ante*, § 1–132). *Cf. R. v. Mercer* [2004] 4 *Archbold News* 1, CA (the precise role attributed to each defendant need not ordinarily be specified when the allegation is one of joint enterprise).

Adequate time and facilities for the preparation of the defence

16–81 Article 6(3)(b) guarantees the right to adequate time and facilities for the preparation of the defence. The adequacy of the time allowed will depend upon the complexity of the case: see generally *Albert and Le Compte v. Belgium*, 5 E.H.R.R. 533. The defence lawyer must be appointed in sufficient time to allow proper preparation: *X. and Y. v. Austria*, 15 D.R. 160; *Goddi v. Italy*, 6 E.H.R.R. 457 (change of lawyer). Furthermore, it is not sufficient to make prosecution papers available to the lawyers without giving the accused sufficient time to see them: *Öcalan v. Turkey* (2005) 41 E.H.R.R. 45. Although it was formerly the practice of the Commission to examine a case to determine if the late appointment of the defence lawyer had actually prejudiced the accused (*X. v. U.K.* (1970) 13 Y.B. 690; *Murphy v. U.K.* (1972) 43 C.D. 1), the current emphasis is upon the appearance of fairness, and upon "the increased sensitivity of the public to the fair administration of justice": *Borgers v. Belgium*, 15 E.H.R.R. 92, at para. 24. To expect the accused to prove that an inadequate defence had caused actual prejudice would be "asking for the impossible": *Artico v. Italy*, 3 E.H.R.R. 1, at para. 35. See also *P., C. and S. v. U.K.* (2002) 35 E.H.R.R. 31.

A persistent failure of the defendant to prepare a case over a period of time may justify proceeding to trial without further adjournment: *R. (Lappin) v. H.M. Customs and Excise* [2004] A.C.D. 48, DC.

In *Brennan v. U.K.* (2002) 34 E.H.R.R 18, the court found a violation of Article 6 where the accused had been required to consult with his solicitor in the immediate presence of a police officer, and subject to restrictions on the content of their discussions. The fact that the accused was inhibited in his ability to speak frankly with his lawyer was sufficient to establish that he had been directly affected by the restrictions and that his rights to an effective defence had thereby been infringed. It was not necessary for him to prove that the restrictions had a prejudicial impact on his subsequent trial. See also *S. v. Switzerland*, 14 E.H.R.R. 670; and *Öcalan* (*ante*). However, in the absence of any real (as opposed to fanciful) possibility of prejudice in the preparation of the defence, the mere fact that a solicitor has to take instructions in a cell with the possibility of being overheard through a wicket, or that a detainee consulting a solicitor over the telephone is required to do so in the presence of a police officer, has been held insufficient to amount to a breach of Article 6(3)(b): *R. (M.) v. Commr of Police of the Metropolis*; *R. (La Rose) v. Same* [2002] Crim.L.R. 215, DC.

16–82 The requirement to afford adequate facilities for the preparation of the defence creates more than a negative obligation to refrain from interference. There is a positive obligation on the state to adopt appropriate measures to place the defence in a position of parity with the prosecution: see *Patanki and Dunshirn v. Austria* (1963) 6 Y.B. 714; *Jespers v. Belgium*, 27 D.R. 61. As to the late changes to the way in which the prosecution put their case, see *Mattocia v. Italy* (2003) 36 E.H.R.R. 47 (*ante*, § 1–132).

The prosecution's duty of disclosure

16–83 In *Jespers v. Belgium*, *ante*, the Commission held that the "equality of arms" principle imposes on prosecuting and investigating authorities an obligation to disclose any material in their possession, or to which they could gain access, which may assist the accused in exonerating himself or in obtaining a reduction in sentence. This principle extends to material which might undermine the credibility of a prosecution witness (*ibid.*, para. 58). Non disclosure of evidence relevant to credibility may also raise an issue under Article 6(3)(d): *Edwards v. U.K.*, 15 E.H.R.R. 417, Op. Comm., para. 50). See also *Foucher v. France*, 25 E.H.R.R. 234. As to the disclosure of a prison psychiatric report prepared on a co-defendant, see *Hardiman v. U.K.* [1996] E.H.R.L.R. 425; and of the defence statement of a co-defendant, see *R. v. Cairns, Zaidi and Chaudhary* [2003] 1 Cr.App.R. 38, CA (*ante*, § 12–58). See also *Sofri v. Italy* [2004] Crim. L.R. 846, ECtHR (approach to be adopted where items of evidence are destroyed by the police prior to the trial) (*ante*, § 4–65).

16–84 In *Edwards v. U.K.*, *ante*, undisclosed evidence was discovered in time for the appeal hearing, and the Court of Appeal was able to assess its impact on the safety of the conviction. This assessment was held to have rectified the shortcoming in the original trial. See also *Botmeh and Alami v. U.K.* (2008) 46 E.H.R.R. 31. Where unused material appears to be *prima facie* irrelevant, it is not incompatible with Article 6 for a defendant to be required to give, if only briefly, specific reasons as to why material should be disclosed: *Bendenoun v. France*, 18 E.H.R.R. 54.

Public interest immunity

16–85 The Court in *Edwards*, *ante*, specifically left open the question whether the rules of public interest immunity in England and Wales conform to the requirements of Article 6 (see, in particular, the observations of Judge Pettiti at p. 433). In *Rowe and Davis v. U.K.*, 30 E.H.R.R. 1, the Court held that whilst Article 6(1) generally requires the prosecution to disclose to the defence all material evidence for or against the accused, considerations of national security or the protection of vulnerable witnesses may, in certain circumstances, justify an exception to this rule. Any departure from the principles of open adversarial justice must however be strictly necessary, and the consequent handicap imposed on the defence must be adequately counterbalanced by procedural safeguards to protect the rights of the accused. Where the prosecution had withheld relevant evidence on public interest immunity grounds, without first submitting the material to the trial judge, the requirements of Article 6 were not met; and the resulting defect could not be cured by submitting the material to the Court of Appeal in the course of an appeal against conviction. See also *Atlan v. U.K.* (2002) 34 E.H.R.R. 33; and *Dowsett v. U.K.* (2004) 38 E.H.R.R. 41. *Cf. Fitt v. U.K.*, 30 E.H.R.R. 480, and *Jasper v. U.K.*, 30 E.H.R.R. 441, where the Court held, by a majority of nine to eight, that there was no violation of Article 6 where the material in question had been submitted to the trial judge under the *ex parte* procedure established in *R. v. Davis, Johnson and Rowe*, 97 Cr.App.R. 110. *Jasper* was, however, distinguished in *Edwards and Lewis v. U.K.* (2005) 40 E.H.R.R. 24 (*ante*, § 12–80a); and *Rowe and Davis* was distinguished on the issue of the matter being capable of remedy in the Court of Appeal in *Botmeh and Alami v. U.K.*, *ante*.

Where a judge, considering the admissibility of certain evidence held an *ex parte* hearing during which he put questions to a witness that the witness had previously declined to answer in open court on grounds of public interest immunity, the procedure adopted did not violate Article 6: *P.G. v. U.K.* (2008) 46 E.H.R.R. 51. See also *Mansell v. U.K.* (2003) 36 E.H.R.R. CD 221.

The implications of the European jurisprudence for domestic criminal practice were considered by the House of Lords in *R. v. H.* [2004] 2 A.C. 134: see *ante*, § 12–80d.

The right to legal representation and legal aid

16–86 The rights guaranteed by Article 6(3)(c) are not unqualified. The court may place reasonable restrictions on the right of an accused to appear without a lawyer in a complex case: *Croissant v. Germany*, 16 E.H.R.R. 135; *Philis v. Greece*, 66 D.R. 260. Moreover, a defendant who chooses to exercise his right under Article 6(3)(c) to represent himself cannot ordinarily complain of the shortcomings in his ability to present his own defence in support of an argument that there was such inequality of arms as to render his conviction unsafe: *R. v. Walton* [2001] 8 *Archbold News* 2, CA. See also *Jahree v. State of Mauritius* [2005] 1 W.L.R. 1952, PC. *Cf. Mitchell (John) v. R.* [1999] 1 W.L.R. 1679, PC. Similarly, the right of the accused to counsel of his choice is not absolute (see *R. (Howe) v. South Durham Magistrates' Court*, 168 J.P. 424, DC: interests of justice required that a defendant's lawyer could be summoned to give evidence at his trial for driving whilst disqualified, where no other means of proving disqualification was available, even if this meant that the defendant would have to find other legal representation). See also *Eurofinacom v. France* [2005] Crim.L.R. 134, ECtHR (company lawyer who otherwise would have represented the corporate defendant also charged). As a general rule, the accused's choice of lawyer should be respected: *Goddi v. Italy*, 6 E.H.R.R. 457. An appointment made against the wishes of the accused will be "incompatible with the notion of a fair trial ... if it lacks relevant and sufficient justification": *Croissant v. Germany*, *ante*. Article 6(3)(c) does not, however, guarantee the accused the right to choose a court-appointed lawyer: *X. v. U.K.*, 5 E.H.R.R. 273; *X. v. Germany*, 6 D.R. 114. A lawyer may be excluded by the court for good reason: *X. v. U.K.* (1975) App. No. 6298/73, 2 Digest 831 (disrespect to the court); *Ensslin, Baader and Raspe v. Germany*, 14 D.R. 64 (breach of professional ethics). As to equality of arms, see *ante*, § 16–64.

Article 6(3)(c) has been interpreted as requiring confidentiality of communications between an accused person and his lawyer: see *S. v. Switzerland*, 14 E.H.R.R. 670, where the Court held that eavesdropping or interception by the police violated "one of the basic requirements of a fair trial in a democratic society" (at para. 48). See also *Campbell v. U.K.*, 15 E.H.R.R. 137; *Niemietz v. Germany*, 16 E.H.R.R. 97; *Foxley v. U.K.* (2001) 31 E.H.R.R. 25; *Schönenberger and Durmaz v. Switzerland*, 11 E.H.R.R. 202; and *Öcalan v. Turkey* (2005) 41 E.H.R.R. 45. For judicial recognition of the inviolability of the right to confidential lawyer-client relations, and that there will inevitably be a stay of proceedings if that right is deliberately interfered with, see *R. v. Grant* [2005] 2 Cr.App.R. 29, CA. Denial of access to a solicitor during police detention may violate Article 6(3)(c) in conjunction with Article 6(1), particularly if adverse inferences are subsequently drawn from the defendant's failure to answer questions in interview: *Murray v. U.K.*, 22 E.H.R.R. 29. *Cf. Kennedy v. DPP* [2004] R.T.R. 6, DC (the procedure for taking samples to determine whether a suspect has driven with excess alcohol need not be postponed for any significant time to enable the suspect to take legal advice). See also *Bowman v. Fels* [2005] 2 Cr.App.R. 19, CA (Civ. Div.), *post*, § 26–12; and *Ordre des barreaux francophones et germanophones v. Conseil des Ministres (Conseil des barreaux de l'Union europeénne and Ordre des avocats du barreau de Liège, interveners) (Case C-305/05)*, *The Times*, July 2, 2007, ECJ (*post*, § 26–14). **16–87**

The second limb of Article 6(3)(c) imposes a requirement to provide legal aid in criminal cases. This is not, however, confined to proceedings recognised as criminal by domestic law, since the term "criminal charge" has an autonomous Convention meaning (*ante*, § 16–60). **16–88**

The obligation to provide legal aid is subject to the means of the defendant, and is confined to cases where the interests of justice require it. The "interests of justice" criterion will take account of the capacity of the individual defendant to represent himself, the complexity of the case, and the severity of the potential sentence: *Granger v. U.K.*, 12 E.H.R.R. 469; *Quaranta v. Switzerland* (1991) Series A/205. Where the accused faces imprisonment, this will usually be sufficient in itself to require the grant of legal aid: *Benham v. U.K.*, 22 E.H.R.R. 293; *Quaranta v. Switzerland*, *ante*; *Beet v. U.K.* (2005) 41 E.H.R.R. 23; *Perks v. U.K.* 30 E.H.R.R. 33. As to the approach of the Privy Council to this issue, see *Hinds v. Att.-Gen. of Barbados* [2002] 1 A.C. 854. **16–89**

In order to meet the requirements of Article 6(3)(c), representation provided by the state must be effective. The state will not generally be responsible for shortcomings in the way a legal aid lawyer performs his duties: *Artico v. Italy*, 3 E.H.R.R. 1. But the relevant authorities may be required to intervene where the failure to provide effective representation is manifest or has been brought to their attention: *Artico v. Italy*, *ante*; *Kamasinski v. Austria*, 13 E.H.R.R. 36. In assessing the impact of errors allegedly **16–90** made by trial counsel, it may no longer be appropriate to apply the "flagrant incompetence" test approved in *R. v. Donnelly* [1998] Crim.L.R. 131, CA. If the conduct of legal advisers has been such as to render the trial unfair for the purposes of Article 6, then the court may be compelled to intervene: *R. v. Nangle* [2001] Crim.L.R. 506, CA. See also *Boodram v. State of Trinidad and Tobago* [2002] 1 Cr.App.R. 12, PC.

The prohibition on hearsay evidence

16–91 The term "witness" in Article 6(3)(d) includes a person whose statements are produced in evidence before a court, but who is not called to give oral evidence: *Kostovski v. Netherlands*, 12 E.H.R.R. 434. Article 6(3)(d) gives the accused the right to have such a "witness" called to give oral evidence, and subjected to cross-examination. The right to cross-examine need not be available at the trial itself, provided the witness has been cross-examined at an earlier stage, such as a full committal: *Kostovski v. Netherlands*, *ante*. In the absence of an opportunity to cross-examine, the admission of disputed hearsay (*e.g.* under the *CJA* 2003, ss.114–116) is prima facie inconsistent with the requirements of Article 6(3)(d); see *Luca v. Italy* (2003) 36 E.H.R.R. 46; but section 114 of the 2003 Act (*ante*, § 11–3) is not inherently incompatible with Article 6(3)(d): see *R. v. Xhabri* [2006] 1 Cr.App.R. 26, CA; and *R. v. Cole*; *R. v. Keet* [2008] 1 Cr. App. R. 5, CA, which deals with section 116 of the 2003 Act to the same effect (*ante*, §§ 11–15, 11–18a). See generally, *Grant v. State* [2007] 1 A.C. 1, PC (*ante*, § 11–25).

16–92 However, it does not follow that the admission of documentary hearsay pursuant to these provisions will necessarily amount to a violation of Article 6: *Trivedi v. U.K.*, 89 A D.R. 136. In keeping with its approach to the interpretation of Article 6(1), the European Court of Human Rights will examine the importance of the prohibited hearsay in the context of the proceedings as a whole: see *Unterpertinger v. Austria*, 13 E.H.R.R. 175; *Kostovski v. Netherlands*, *ante*; *Windisch v. Austria*, 13 E.H.R.R. 281; *Lüdi v. Switzerland*, 15 E.H.R.R. 173; *Barbera Messegue and Jabardo v. Spain*, 11 E.H.R.R. 360; *Bricmont v. Belgium*, 12 E.H.R.R. 217; *Delta v. France*, 16 E.H.R.R. 574; *Saidi v. France*, 17 E.H.R.R. 251; *P.S. v. Germany* (2003) 36 E.H.R.R. 61; *Sadak v. Turkey* (2003) 36 E.H.R.R. 26; and *Hulki Güneş v. Turkey* (2006) 43 E.H.R.R. 15. For cases on the other side of the line, see *Asch v. Austria*, 15 E.H.R.R. 597; *Artner v. Austria* (1992) Series A/242–A; *Isgro v. Italy* (1990) Series A/194; *S.N. v. Sweden* (2004) 39 E.H.R.R. 13; and *Magnusson v. Sweden* [2004] Crim.L.R. 847. The seriousness of the alleged offence is not a factor which of itself could ever justify the admission of hearsay: see *Saidi v. France*, *ante*, and *Hulki Güneş v. Turkey*, *ante*.

As to the approach of the Court of Appeal to Article 6(3)(d), see *ante*, §§ 11–24 *et seq.* As to the application of Article 6(3)(d) to video testimony, see *R. v. D.* [2002] 2 Cr.App.R. 36, CA.

16–93 The prohibition embodied in Article 6(3)(d) is worded so as to apply only to witnesses who give evidence against the accused. There is no equivalent rule against the introduction of hearsay evidence by the defence. On the other hand, there is no obligation under Article 6 to admit hearsay evidence which purports to exonerate the accused: *Blastland v. U.K.*, 10 E.H.R.R. 528. See also *Perna v. Italy* (2004) 39 E.H.R.R. 28.

The right to free interpretation

16–94 The right to be provided with a free interpreter is unqualified. It is part of the state's obligation to run its judicial system fairly. A convicted person cannot therefore be ordered to pay the costs of an interpreter since Article 6(3)(e) provides "neither a conditional remission, nor a temporary exemption, nor a suspension, but a once and for all exemption or exoneration": *Luedicke, Belkacem and Koç v. Germany*, 2 E.H.R.R. 149. See also *Cuscani v. U.K.* (2003) 36 E.H.R.R. 2, *ante*, § 4–37.

In *Wei Hai Restaurant Ltd v. Kingston upon Hull City Council*, 166 J.P. 185, DC, the refusal of a magistrates' court to appoint an interpreter during the course of the defence case was held not to render the trial unfair where there had been no prior indication of the need for an interpreter, and there was no evidence that the defence had in fact been prejudiced.

Application of Article 6 to appellate proceedings

16–95 Article 6 does not guarantee a right of appeal. Where, however, domestic law provides for an appeal against conviction or sentence, whether on grounds of fact or law, then the appeal proceedings will be treated as an "extension of the trial process" and accordingly will be subject to Article 6: *Delcourt v. Belgium*, 1 E.H.R.R. 355, at para. 25; *Edwards v. U.K.*, 15 E.H.R.R. 417, at para. 34. This has been held to include the hearing of a renewed application for leave to appeal: *Monnell and Morris v. U.K.*, 10 E.H.R.R. 205; and a reference to the Court of Appeal by the Home Secretary under the *CAA* 1968, s.17 (*rep.*): *Callaghan v. U.K.*, 60 D.R. 296. However, the requirements of fairness will not necessarily be the same on appeal as at first instance; the manner of application of Article 6 to appellate proceedings depends upon the special features of the proceedings involved, seen in their domestic law context, and taking account of the role and functions of the appeal court: *Ekbatani v. Sweden*, 13 E.H.R.R. 504; *Andersson v. Sweden*, 15 E.H.R.R. 218; *Helmers v. Sweden*, 15 E.H.R.R. 285; *Edwards v. U.K.*, *ante*. In general, where an appeal involves an assessment of disputed questions of fact, the requirements of fairness are more akin to those of a criminal trial.

The procedure whereby the Court of Appeal may determine an application for leave to appeal without the accused being present or represented by counsel is not incompatible with Article 6(1) providing the prosecution are unrepresented; nor is the absence of legal aid for the hearing of a renewed application for leave to appeal: *Monnell and Morris v. U.K.*, *ante*. See also *Hermi v. Italy* (2008) 46 E.H.R.R. 46. In *R. v. Oates* [2002] 1 W.L.R. 2833, the Court of Appeal held there was nothing in the Strasbourg case law to suggest that justice required that legal aid be extended, absent exceptional circumstances, to cover legal representation to present oral argument to the full court on a renewed application for leave to appeal against conviction. It was sufficient for the purposes of Article 6(3)(c) that the defendant was provided with publicly funded representation at trial which extended to the provision of advice on appeal and the drafting of grounds for consideration by the single judge under section 31 of the *CAA* 1968. Legal aid must, however, be available for the hearing of a substantive appeal: *Granger v. U.K.*, 12 E.H.R.R. 469; *Boner v. U.K.*, 19 E.H.R.R. 246; *Maxwell v. U.K.*, 19 E.H.R.R. 97; *Twalib v. Greece* (2001) 33 E.H.R.R. 24. A rule which requires an appellant in criminal proceedings to surrender to custody, in accordance with an order made by a lower court, before he can be heard on an appeal against the decision, may be incompatible with the right of access to court in Article 6: *Omar v. France*, 29 E.H.R.R. 210; and *Khalfaoui v. France* (2001) 31 E.H.R.R. 42. Accordingly, it is no longer appropriate for the Registrar of Criminal Appeals to treat an application for leave to appeal on behalf of a defendant who has absconded as ineffective: *R. v. Charles*; *R. v. Tucker* [2001] 2 Cr.App.R. 15, CA. **16–96**

Since the Convention regards appeal proceedings as an extension of the trial process (*Delcourt v. Belgium*, 1 E.H.R.R. 355 at para. 25) it follows that a breach of Article 6 at trial can, in some circumstances, be rectified on appeal: *Edwards v. U.K.*, 15 E.H.R.R. 417 (relevant evidence withheld at trial but disclosed prior to appeal). However, in *Findlay v. U.K.*, 24 E.H.R.R. 221, the court held that a person charged with a serious offence was "entitled to a first instance tribunal which fully met the requirements of Article 6(1)". Accordingly, a defect which went directly to the independence of the trial court could not be corrected by appeal proceedings which met the requirements of Article 6. See also *Riepan v. Austria* [2001] Crim.L.R. 230 (failure to hold a first instance trial in public cannot be corrected by a *de novo* hearing on appeal). Similarly, in *Condron v. U.K.* (2001) 31 E.H.R.R. 1, the Court held that a serious misdirection to the jury concerning the defendants' silence in interview was not capable of being cured by a review of the applicants' convictions on appeal. The Court of Appeal had no means of knowing how significant a role the applicants' silence had played in the jury's decision to convict them; and there was, in any event, a difference between the "fairness" of criminal proceedings and the "safety" of any resulting conviction. See also *Rowe and Davis v. U.K.*, 30 E.H.R.R. 1 (*ex parte* hearing on appeal incapable of remedying procedural defect at trial). **16–96a**

As to the effect of a breach of the right to a fair trial on the safety of a conviction, see *ante*, § 7–51c. In *R. v. Lyons* [2003] 1 A.C. 976, the House of Lords held that where the European Court of Human Rights had declared the appellant's trial to have been unfair by reason of the admission of evidence pursuant to an express statutory provision, the domestic courts had no jurisdiction to quash the conviction since this would amount to the partial repeal of legislation enacted by Parliament. See also *Lyons v. U.K.* (2003) 37 E.H.R.R. CD 183. The position is otherwise, however, where an appellant relies on an Article 6 judgment of the European Court in order to advance a ground of appeal which was available to him under the common law in any event: *R. v. Allan* [2005] Crim.L.R. 716, CA; *R. v. Beckles* [2005] 1 Cr.App.R. 24, CA; and *R. v. Lewis* [2005] Crim.L.R. 796, CA.

F. NO PUNISHMENT WITHOUT LAW

Article 7

16–97 **7.**—(1) No one shall be held guilty of any criminal offence on account of any act or omission which did not constitute a criminal offence under national or international law at the time when it was committed. Nor shall a heavier penalty be imposed than the one that was applicable at the time the criminal offence was committed.

(2) This Article shall not prejudice the trial and punishment of any person for any act or omission which, at the time it was committed, was criminal according to the general principles of law recognised by civilised nations.

Retroactive offences

16–98 The first limb of Article 7(1) prohibits the retroactive application of criminal offences so as to penalise conduct which was not criminal at the time when the relevant act or omission occurred. This corresponds to the general prohibition on retroactivity in English criminal law: see *Waddington v. Miah* [1974] 1 W.L.R. 683, HL. As to the application of the principle to section 11 of the *Terrorism Act* 2000 (*post*, § 25–60), see *R. v. Hundal and Dhaliwal* [2004] 2 Cr.App.R. 19, CA. Article 7 prohibits not only the creation of retroactive offences by legislation, but also the retroactive application of existing criminal offences through the development of the common law, so as to encompass conduct which would not previously have been regarded as a crime: *X. Ltd and Y. v. U.K.*, 28 D.R. 77. Thus, Article 7 requires that the criminal law should be sufficiently accessible and precise to enable an individual to know in advance whether his conduct is criminal: *Handyside v. U.K.* (1974) 17 Y.B. 228 at 290, Op. Comm. (concerning the definition of obscenity in the *Obscene Publications Acts* 1959 to 1964). In *Handyside*, the Commission held that Article 7 "includes the requirement that the offence should be clearly described by law", but held that it was sufficient if the legislation provided a general description which was then interpreted and applied by the courts.

16–99 In *S.W. and C.R. v. U.K.*, 21 E.H.R.R. 363, the Court held that the removal of the marital rape exemption by the House of Lords (see *R. v. R.* [1992] A.C. 599) did not amount to a retrospective change in the elements of the offence. Article 7 allows for "gradual clarification" of the rules of criminal liability through judicial interpretation from case to case, provided the resultant development is consistent with the essence of the offence and could reasonably be foreseen. See also *R. v. C.* [2004] 2 Cr.App.R. 15, CA.

In relation to statutory offences, however clearly drafted a provision may be, there is an inevitable element of judicial interpretation, and there will always be the need for elucidation of doubtful points and for adaptation to changing circumstances: *E.K. v. Turkey* (2002) 35 E.H.R.R. 41.

The requirements of legal certainty were found to be met in *R. v. Pattni* [2001] Crim.L.R. 570, CA (cheating the public revenue); *R. v. Cotter, Clair and Wynn* [2002] 2 Cr.App.R. 29, CA (perverting the course of justice); *R. v. Muhamad* [2003] Q.B. 1031, CA (materially contributing to, or increasing the extent of, insolvency by gambling contrary to the *Insolvency Act* 1986, s.362(1)(a)); *R. v. Misra and Srivastava* [2005] 1 Cr.App.R. 21, CA (gross negligence manslaughter); *R. v. Rimmington*; *R. v. Goldstein* [2006] 1 A.C. 459, HL (causing a public nuisance); *O'Carroll v. U.K.* (2005) 41 E.H.R.R. SE1 (importation of indecent material contrary to *CEMA* 1979, s.170(2)(b)). The House of Lords did, however, apply the principle of legal certainty to exclude certain price fixing and cartel arrangements from the scope of the common law offence of conspiracy to defraud in *Norris v. Government of United States of America* [2008] 2 W.L.R. 673, HL.

In addition to the prohibition on retrospectivity, Article 7 "embodies, more generally, the principle that only law can define a crime and prescribe a penalty ... and the principle that criminal law must not be extensively construed to an accused's detriment, for instance by analogy": *Kokkinakis v. Greece*, 17 E.H.R.R. 397. **16–99a**

Retroactive penalties

The second limb of Article 7(1) prohibits a retroactive increase in the penalty applicable to an offence. The term "penalty" has an autonomous meaning, defined by reference to criteria analogous to those which apply to the term "criminal charge" in Article 6: *Welch v. U.K.*, 20 E.H.R.R. 247, at paras 27–35. The measure must be one that is imposed following conviction for a criminal offence. Other factors to be taken into account are the nature and purpose of the measure; its characterisation under national law; the procedures involved in the making and implementation of the measure; and its severity. Thus, in *Welch* a confiscation order was made under the *Drug Trafficking Offences Act* 1986 in respect of an offence committed before the Act entered into force. In deciding that the confiscation order was an additional penalty, and therefore in violation of Article 7(1), the Court noted that the measure had punitive as well as preventative and reparative aims; that the order was calculated by reference to "proceeds" rather than profits; that the amount of the order could take account of culpability; and that the order was enforceable by a term of imprisonment in default. In *Ibbotson v. U.K.* [1999] Crim.L.R. 153, by contrast, the Commission held that the registration requirements of the *Sex Offenders Act* 1997 (which have a partially retrospective operation, see s.1(3)) were preventative rather than punitive in character and did not therefore constitute a "penalty" for the purposes of Article 7. See, to the same effect, *Gough v. Chief Constable of the Derbyshire Constabulary* [2002] Q.B. 459, CA (Civ. Div.) (football banning orders under the *Football Spectators Act* 1989, ss.14A and 14B do not amount to a penalty for the purposes of Article 7); *R. v. Field*; *R. v. Young* [2003] 2 Cr.App.R. 3, CA (disqualification from working with children, *ante*, § 5–854); and *Director of the Assets Recovery Agency v. Ashton*, unreported, March 31, 2006, QBD (Newman J.) ([2006] EWHC 1064 (Admin.)) (civil recovery order under the *PCA* 2002, s.243). **16–100**

A judge's obligation (under the *CJA* 2003, s.172 (*ante*, § 5–100)) to have regard to relevant sentencing guidelines if they apply at the date of sentence, even if they did not apply at the time the defendant pleaded guilty, does not infringe Article 7(1), notwithstanding that the defendant would have received a more lenient sentence under pre-guideline sentencing authorities, since sentencing guidelines are reflections of current sentencing policy and practice and not rules of law: *R. v. Bao* [2008] 2 Cr.App.R.(S.) 10, CA.

In *R. v. Offen* [2001] 1 Cr.App.R. 24, the Court of Appeal rejected an argument that the imposition of a mandatory life sentence under section 109 of the *PCC(S)A* 2000 (§ 5–251j in the supplement) was incompatible with Article 7. See also *Achour v France* (2007) 45 E.H.R.R. 2; and *Kafkaris v. Cyprus*, *ante*, § 16–40. As to continuing offences, increases in maximum penalties and Article 7, see *R. v. Hobbs* [2002] 2 Cr.App.R. 22, CA, and *Ecer and Zeyrek v. Turkey* (2002) 35 E.H.R.R. 26 (*ante*, § 5–286).

Where as a consequence of a person having attained a certain age at the date of conviction, he receives a sentence which is harsher than he would have been eligible to receive at the date of the commission of the offence, there will be no violation of Article 7: *Taylor v. U.K.* (2003) 36 E.H.R.R. CD 104; and *ante*, § 5–279. See also *R. (Uttley) v. Secretary of State for the Home Department* [2004] 1 W.L.R. 2478, HL (a change in the parole provisions does not constitute a "heavier penalty" provided that the overall sentence served is not longer than the maximum sentence that was available prior to the change in the law).

G. RIGHT TO RESPECT FOR PRIVATE AND FAMILY LIFE

Article 8

8.—(1) Everyone has the right to respect for his private and family life, his home and his correspondence. **16–101**

(2) There shall be no interference by a public authority with the exercise of this right

except such as is in accordance with the law and is necessary in a democratic society in the interests of national security, public safety or the economic well-being of the country, for the prevention of disorder or crime, for the protection of health or morals, or for the protection of the rights and freedoms of others.

Scope

16–102 "Private life" is a concept that has been broadly defined to cover the moral, psychological and physical integrity of the person: *Niemietz v. Germany*, 16 E.H.R.R. 97; *Stubbings v. U.K.*, 23 E.H.R.R. 213; *Botta v. Italy*, 26 E.H.R.R. 241; and *Von Hannover v. Germany* (2005) 40 E.H.R.R. 1. In *Botta v. Italy*, the Court held the "the guarantee afforded by Article 8 is primarily intended to ensure the development, without outside interference, of the personality of each individual in his relations with other human beings". "Private life" therefore extends "to those features which are integral to a person's identity or ability to function socially as a person": *R. (Razgar) v. Secretary of State for the Home Department* [2004] 2 A.C. 368, HL (*per* Lord Bingham at [9]). As to the application of the concept of private life to business relationships, see *Niemietz* (*ante*); to the work place, see *Halford v. U.K.*, 24 E.H.R.R. 523; and *Copeland v. U.K.* (2008) 45 E.H.R.R. 47; and to public places in general, see *Von Hannover* (*ante*); and *Sciacca v. Italy* (2006) 43 E.H.R.R. 20. The quality and dignity of a person's life are protected under Article 8: *Pretty v. U.K.* (2002) 35 E.H.R.R. 1. Thus, treatment which does not violate Article 3 (*ante*, § 16–39) may nonetheless breach Article 8 where there are sufficiently adverse effects on the physical and moral integrity of the individual: *Bensaid v. U.K.* (2001) 33 E.H.R.R. 10; and *Wainwright v. U.K.* (2007) 44 E.H.R.R. 40. See also *D. v. Secretary of State for the Home Department*, *The Times*, December 27, 2004, QBD (Stanley Burnton J.) (unreasonable delay in transferring a prisoner to hospital). A compulsory medical intervention, even if it is of minor importance, constitutes an interference with Article 8: *Y.F. v. Turkey* (2004) 39 E.H.R.R. 34. As to consensual sexual relationships, see *Dudgeon v. U.K.*, 4 E.H.R.R. 149; *Norris v. Ireland*, 13 E.H.R.R. 186; *Modinos v. Cyprus*, 16 E.H.R.R. 485; and *A.D.T. v. U.K.*, (2001) 31 E.H.R.R. 33. *Cf. Laskey v. U.K.* 24 E.H.R.R. 39.

16–103 Family life extends beyond the formal relationships created by marriage, and includes relationships between a parent and an illegitimate child (*Marckx v. Belgium*, 2 E.H.R.R. 330); siblings (*Moustaquim v. Belgium*, 13 E.H.R.R. 802); uncle and nephew (*Boyle v. U.K.*, 19 E.H.R.R. 179, Op. Comm.); grandparents and grandchildren (*Marckx v. Belgium*, *ante*, at para. 45); an unmarried couple in a stable relationship who are not living together (*Kroon v. Netherlands*, 19 E.H.R.R. 263); an engaged couple (*Wakefield v. U.K.*, 66 D.R. 251); children and foster parents or adopters (*Gaskin v. U.K.*, 12 E.H.R.R. 36; *X v. France*, 31 D.R. 241; *M.G. v. U.K.* (2003) 36 E.H.R.R. 3). See also *Fitzpatrick v. Sterling Housing Association Ltd* [2001] 1 A.C. 27, HL, and *Ghaidan v. Mendoza* [2004] 3 W.L.R. 113, HL.

16–104 The right to respect for a person's home includes the right to peaceful enjoyment free from intrusion: *López-Ostra v. Spain*, 20 E.H.R.R. 277; *Arrondelle v. U.K.*, 26 D.R. 5. The concepts of a person's home and private life may, in some circumstances, extend to professional or business activities or premises: *Niemietz v. Germany*, *ante*; *Chappell v. U.K.*, 12 E.H.R.R. 1, Op. Comm. In *R. v. Broadcasting Standards Commission, ex p. BBC* [2001] Q.B. 885, CA (Civ. Div.), it was held that corporations do not enjoy a right to privacy. Subsequently, however, the European Court has held that the rights guaranteed by Article 8 may include the right to respect for a company's office, branches, or other business premises: *Société Colas Est v. France* (2004) 39 E.H.R.R. 17. See also *Office of Fair Trading v. X.* [2004] I.C.R. 105, QBD (Morrison J.). Article 8 has no application to the question of whether a criminal confiscation order ought to be made, but would clearly be engaged in subsequent enforcement proceedings where the sale of a property occupied by a third party is sought by the prosecution: *R. v. Ahmed*; *R. v. Qureshi* [2005] 1 W.L.R. 122, CA.

16–105 Correspondence includes both written communications and telephone calls: *Klass v. Germany*, 2 E.H.R.R. 214; *Malone v. U.K.*, 7 E.H.R.R. 14. It will also extend to modern means of electronic communication provided the person concerned can reasonably expect that his communications will be private.

Interference

A criminal prosecution constitutes an "interference by a public authority" for the purposes of Article 8(2): *Dudgeon v. U.K.*, *ante*; *Modinos v. Cyprus*, 16 E.H.R.R. 485. The mere threat of a prosecution may be sufficient if it directly interferes with private life: *Norris v. Ireland*, 13 E.H.R.R. 186. The following have all been held to constitute interferences with the right protected by Article 8: searches of private or business premises (*Funke v. France*, 16 E.H.R.R. 297; *Chappell v. U.K.*, *ante*); searches of motor vehicles (*X. v. Belgium*, 45 C.D. 20); temporary seizure of personal papers (*X. v. Germany*, 3 D.R. 104); intrusive surveillance (*Klass v. Germany*, *ante*; *Khan v. U.K.* [2000] Crim.L.R. 684; see also *post*, § 16–109); security vetting (*Hilton v. U.K.*, 57 D.R. 108 at 117); the compilation and disclosure of criminal records (*Leander v. Sweden*, 9 E.H.R.R. 433); photographing suspects or detainees (*Murray v. U.K.*, 19 E.H.R.R. 193; *McVeigh, O'Neill and Evans v. U.K.*, 5 E.H.R.R. 71), unless carried out in a public place, such as during the course of a demonstration (*Friedl v. Austria*, 21 E.H.R.R. 83, Op. Comm., at paras 48–51; *R. (Wood) v. Commr of Police of the Metropolis*, *The Times*, June 13, 2008, QBD (McCombe J.)); the publication of a photograph taken by the authorities during the course of a criminal investigation (*Sciacca v. Italy* (2006) 43 E.H.R.R. 20); a refusal to permit a detained person to contact his family (*McVeigh, O'Neill and Evans v. U.K.*, *ante*); the disclosure of confidential information about the medical condition of a witness (*Z. v. Finland*, 25 E.H.R.R. 371); the disclosure by police or social services to a third party of an allegation concerning the sexual abuse of children (*R. v. Local Authority and Police Authority in the Midlands, ex p. L.M.* [2000] 1 F.L.R. 612, QBD, *post* § 16–110a). See also *R. (Ellis) v. Chief Constable of Essex Police* [2003] 2 F.L.R. 566, DC (recidivist offender naming scheme); *X. (formerly known as Mary Bell) v. S.*, *The Daily Telegraph*, May 29, 2003, QBD (Dame Elizabeth Butler-Sloss P.) (life time injunction preventing press reporting true identity of rehabilitated adult convicted of notorious crime when a child). **16–106**

The keeping of a dossier on an individual, albeit only for the purpose of access by law enforcement agents will constitute a prima facie interference with Article 8: *Roturu v. Romania*, unreported, May 4, 2000, ECtHR. See also *Amann v. Switzerland*, 30 E.H.R.R. 843. In *R. (S.) v. Chief Constable of South Yorkshire*; *R. (Marper) v. Same* [2004] 1 W.L.R. 2196, HL, it was accepted that the retention of an acquitted person's DNA was capable of being an interference for the purpose of Article 8, which therefore required justification under Article 8(2).

Justification

As to Article 8(2), see *ante*, §§ 16–32 *et seq.* **16–107**

In *R. (S.) v. Chief Constable of South Yorkshire*; *R. (Marper) v. Same*, *ante*, it was held that the provision in section 64(1A) of the *PACE Act* 1984, which permits the retention of fingerprints or samples following acquittal or discontinuance was not incompatible with Article 8. To the extent that Article 8(1) was engaged, the interference was modest, and was objectively justified under Article 8(2) as being for the prevention of crime and the protection of the rights of others to be free from crime. In *R. v. Pearce* [2002] 1 Cr.App.R. 39, CA, it was held that the principle that children and unmarried partners were compellable witnesses, whilst spouses were not, involved no breach of Article 8. Insofar as compulsion to give evidence was an interference with the right to respect for private and family life, it was justified under Article 8(2) as necessary for the prevention of crime. See also *R. (Stanley, Marshall and Kelly) v. Metropolitan Police Commr and London Borough of Brent*, 168 J.P. 623, DC (publicity given to anti-social behaviour orders). *Cf. Wainwright v. U.K.* (2007) 44 E.H.R.R. 40 (conduct of strip searches during prison visits).

Police powers of entry

In *McLeod v. U.K.*, 27 E.H.R.R. 493, the Court held that the common law power of entry to prevent or deal with a breach of the peace (which is expressly preserved by section 17(6) of the *PACE Act* 1984), was "defined with sufficient precision for the **16–107a** forseeability criterion to be satisfied". The Court nevertheless found a violation of Article 8, where two police officers had entered the applicant's home in her absence to assist her ex-husband to remove items of property. There was no risk of a breach of the peace in fact and the officers had failed to take adequate steps to establish that the husband had a lawful right of entry. See also *Keegan v. U.K.* (2007) 44 E.H.R.R. 33 (search warrant obtained on the basis of a mistake as to fact, that could reasonably have been verified, held to be a disproportionate interference).

A failure by justices to give reasons for issuing a warrant would not necessarily violate Article 8, where it was reasonable to assume that the information requesting the warrant formed the basis for their decision, and anyone wishing to challenge the legality of the warrant was given access to the information: *Cronin v. U.K.* (2004) 38 E.H.R.R. CD 233 (considering *R. (Cronin) v. Sheffield JJ.* [2003] 1 W.L.R. 752, DC). *Cf. Ernst v. Belgium* (2004) 39 E.H.R.R. 35.

Positive obligations

16–107b In *X and Y v. Netherlands*, 8 E.H.R.R. 235, the Court held that Article 8 imposed a positive obligation on the state to ensure that its criminal law provided effective deterrence against sexual abuse of a mentally handicapped 16-year-old.

Consensual sexual offences

16–108 "Particularly serious reasons" are required to justify interference with the right to private enjoyment of consensual sexual relations: *Dudgeon v. U.K., ante*. Criminalisation of consensual homosexual activity between adults in private is disproportionate to the protection of morals or of the rights and freedoms of others: *ibid.*; *Norris v. Ireland, ante*; *Modinos v. Cyprus*, 16 E.H.R.R. 485; and *A.D.T. v. U.K.* (2001) 31 E.H.R.R. 33. Article 8 does not, however, prohibit the criminalisation of sexual activity in public places: *X. v. Y. (Employment: Sex Offender)*, *The Times*, June 16, 2004, CA (Civ. Div). In *Sutherland v. U.K.*, 24 E.H.R.R. 22 CD, the Commission held that the enforcement of a different age of consent for homosexual and heterosexual activity was in breach of Article 8 in conjunction with Article 14. See also *L. v. Austria* (2003) 36 E.H.R.R. 55; and *B. v. U.K.* (2004) 39 E.H.R.R. 30. As to the prosecution of a male aged under 18 in respect of consensual sexual activity with a female child, see *R. v. G. (Secretary of State for the Home Department intervening)* [2008] 1 W.L.R. 1379, HL (*post*, § 20–56), and *E. v. DPP*, *The Times*, February 9, 2005, DC. A prosecution for consensual sado-masochistic assault has been held to be proportionate to the protection of health, although the fact that the prosecution involved an interference with a Convention right may entitle the defendant to receive a discount in any sentence, if convicted: *Laskey v. U.K.*, 24 E.H.R.R. 39. As to discounting the sentence, see also *R. v. G. (Secretary of State for the Home Department intervening), ante*.

Intrusive surveillance and interception of communications

16–109 Intrusive surveillance constitutes an interference with the rights protected by Article 8: *Klass v. Germany*, 2 E.H.R.R. 214; *Malone v. U.K.*, 7 E.H.R.R. 14; *Huvig v. France*, 12 E.H.R.R. 528. It can in principle be justified in the interests of national security or for the prevention of crime, and provided it is "in accordance with law". The term "in accordance with law" has a special meaning in this context. The law must give an adequate indication of the circumstances in which, and the conditions under which, such surveillance can occur: *Malone v. U.K., ante*. The rules must define with clarity the categories of citizens liable to be the subject of such techniques, the offences which might give rise to such an order, the permitted duration of the interception, and the circumstances in which recordings are to be destroyed: *Huvig v. France, ante*; *Kruslin v. France*, 12 E.H.R.R. 547. There must, in addition, be adequate and effective safeguards against abuse: *Klass v. Germany, ante*; *Malone v. U.K., ante*. Whilst it is desirable that the machinery of supervision should be in the hands of a judge, this is not essential providing the supervisory body enjoys sufficient independence to give an objective ruling: *Klass v. Germany, ante*. The machinery of Commissioners and Tribunals established under the *Interception of Communications Act* 1985 and the *Intelligence Services Act* 1994 complies with the requirements of Article 8: *Christie v. U.K.*, 78A D.R. 119; *Esbester v. U.K.*, 18 E.H.R.R. 72 CD; *Hewitt and Harman v. U.K. (No. 2)* (1993) No. 20317/92 (unreported). In *Khan v. U.K.* (2001) 31 E.H.R.R. 45, the Court held that the use of a covert listening device prior to the coming into force of the *Police Act* 1997 was in breach of Article 8. The relevant Home Office guidelines were neither legally binding nor publicly accessible and the interference was therefore inadequately regulated by law. Moreover, the Court held that there was no effective remedy for the violation, as required by Article 13 of the Convention. The discretion to exclude evidence under section 78 of the *PACE Act* 1984 was inadequate because, prior to the enactment of the *Human Rights Act* 1998, the national courts did not have jurisdiction under section 78 to determine the substance of the applicant's complaint under Article 8 (see *R. v. Khan (Sultan)* [1997] A.C. 558, HL), nor did they have power to grant appropriate relief for the violation. The system for investigating complaints against the police established in Part IX of the 1984 Act failed to meet the requisite standards of independence necessary to constitute sufficient protection against abuse of authority, and thus to provide an effective remedy within the meaning of Article 13. See also *Govell v. U.K.* [2000] E.H.R.L.R. 121, since affirmed by the Committee of Ministers (Resolution DH (98) 212). Similarly, in the absence of statutory authority, the covert recording of suspects at a police station for the purposes of voice pattern comparison has been held to amount to a breach of Article 8: *P.G. v. U.K.* (2008) 46 E.H.R.R. 51; as has the covert filming of suspects in the cell area of a court building for the purpose of having the film compared with closed circuit television footage of a robbery: *R. v. Loveridge (William), Lee (Charles) and Loveridge (Christine)* [2001] 2 Cr.App.R. 29, CA. See also *R. v. Mason* [2002] 2 Cr.App.R. 38, CA (affirmed in *Wood v. U.K.*, *The Times*, November 23, 2004); and *Perry v. U.K.* (2004) 39 E.H.R.R. 3.

Investigating authorities cannot evade their Convention responsibilities by the use of private agents: *M.M. v. Netherlands* (2004) 39 E.H.R.R. 19 (police encouraged complainant to tape record telephone conversations with the suspect). See also *A. v. France*, 17 E.H.R.R. 462. *Cf. Ludi v. Switzerland*, 15 E.H.R.R. 201 (use of an undercover agent to buy drugs in circumstances in which the suspect must have known that he was engaging in criminal activity, was not an interference with private life within the meaning of Article 8(1)). In *R. v. Rosenberg* [2006] Crim L.R. 540, CA, it was held that a video camera "of the most ostentatious type", used by a neighbour in order to film drug offences on an adjacent property, did not amount to a breach of Article 8 and/or require an authorisation pursuant to Part II of the *RIPA* 2000, *ante*, § 15–253. In so far as the filming of the offences involved an interference with Article 8(1), which was doubted, the conduct of the neighbour was held to be justified under paragraph (2) on the basis that the surveillance was necessary for the prevention of serious crime.

Whilst intrusive surveillance carried out without appropriate safeguards may violate **16–110** the right to privacy in Article 8, it is not necessarily a requirement of a fair trial in Article 6 that such evidence be excluded (see *ante* § 16–67). The Court will examine the nature of the breach and the importance of the disputed evidence in the context of the proceedings as a whole: *Schenk v. Switzerland*, 13 E.H.R.R. 242; *Smith v. U.K.* [1997] E.H.R.L.R. 277 (consent of one party to the call); *Khan v. U.K.*, *ante*; *P.G. and J.H. v. U.K.*, *ante*; *Chalkley v. U.K.* [2003] Crim.L.R. 51; and *Perry v. U.K.* [2003] Crim.L.R. 281, ECtHR. Following the enactment of the *Human Rights Act* 1998, the domestic courts should attach "considerable importance" to any breach of Article 8 in determining an application to exclude evidence, but it remains necessary to engage in the exercise of reviewing and balancing all the circumstances of the case: *R. v. X, Y and Z*, *The Times*, May 23, 2000, CA; *R. v. P.* [2002] 1 A.C. 146, HL. The fact that covert surveillance evidence has been obtained in breach of Article 8 does not lead to the conclusion that it would be a further breach of Article 8 for a court to admit the evidence. The fairness of admitting such evidence is to be determined by reference to Article 6: *R. v. Button* [2005] Crim. L.R. 571, CA.

The disclosure by police or social services of an allegation concerning the sexual **16–110a** abuse of children is apt to interfere with the private life of the individual subject of the allegations, and can only be justified by a pressing social need. It was incumbent on the authorities concerned to carry out a balancing exercise, weighing the public interest in the need to protect vulnerable children against the need to safeguard the right of an individual to respect for his private life. Relevant factors would be the apparent reliability of the allegations; the interest of the third party in obtaining the information; and the degree of risk posed by the person if the disclosure is not made: *R. v. A Local Authority and a Police Authority in the Midlands, ex p. L.M.* [2000] 1 F.L.R. 612, QBD. See also *R. (Dr. D.) v. Secretary of State for Health, The Times*, August 28, 2006, CA (Civ. Div.).

As to the requirement to maintain the anonymity of a witness whose confidential medical records have been disclosed in a trial, see *Z. v. Finland*, 25 E.H.R.R. 371; and *Craxi (No. 2) v. Italy* (2004) 38 E.H.R.R. 47. In limited circumstances, Article 8 may require an order protecting the anonymity of a defendant in criminal proceedings, where publication of his identity would seriously harm the interests of a child: *Re S (a child) (identification: restrictions on publication)* [2005] 1 A.C. 593, HL (*ante*, § 4–17); applied in *A Local Authority v. W., L., W., T. and R. (by the children's guardian)* [2006] 1 F.L.R. 1, Fam D (Sir Mark Potter P.) (anonymity order granted for a mother of two children charged with knowingly infecting her partner with HIV); but see *Re Trinity Mirror plc* [2008] 2 Cr.App.R. 1, CA (*ante*, § 4–17). *Cf. Ex p. Gazette Media Company Ltd* [2005] E.M.L.R. 34, CA (*ante*, § 4–27). See also *R. (Ellis) v. Chief Constable of Essex Police* [2003] 2 F.L.R. 566, DC (offender naming scheme, on its current level of appraisal, was disproportionate). *Cf. R. (Stanley, Marshall and Kelly) v. Metropolitan Police Commr and London Borough of Brent, ante*, § 16–107.

Legal professional privilege

16–111 A high level of protection is to be accorded to communications between a detained person and his lawyer. It is a matter of general importance that consultations with lawyers should take place under conditions which favour full and uninhibited discussion: *Campbell v. U.K.*, 15 E.H.R.R. 137, at para. 47; *Foxley v. U.K.* (2001) 31 E.H.R.R. 25. A breach of privilege may give rise to violation of Article 8 and Article 6 (*ante*, § 16–87). Search of a lawyer's offices requires particularly compelling justification. In *Niemietz v. Germany*, 16 E.H.R.R. 97, at para. 37, the Court noted that "where a lawyer is involved, an encroachment on professional secrecy may have repercussions on the proper administration of justice and hence on the rights guaranteed by Article 6 of the Convention". See also *Bowman v. Fels* [2005] 2 Cr.App.R. 19, CA (Civ. Div.). As to the proper procedure for executing search warrants in a solicitor's office, see *Tamosius v. U.K.* [2002] S.T.C. 1307, ECtHR (considering *R. v. Middlesex Guildhall Crown Court, ex. p. Tamosius & Partners (a firm)* [2000] 1 W.L.R. 435, DC); *R. v. Chesterfield JJ., ex p. Bramley* [2000] Q.B. 576, DC; and *Wieser and Bicos Beteiligungen GmbH v. Austria* (2008) 46 E.H.R.R. 54 (safeguards relating to the search of a computer in a lawyer's office).

Recommendation for deportation

16–112 See *ante*, § 5–919.

Other issues

16–112a As to assisted suicide, see *Pretty v. U.K.* (2002) 35 E.H.R.R. 1 (*post*, § 18–6). As to the use of cannabis for medical necessity, see *R. v. Quayle*; *R. v. Wales*; *R. v. Kenny*; *R. v. Taylor and Lee*; *Att.-Gen.'s Reference (No. 2 of 2004)* [2005] 2 Cr.App.R. 34, CA (*post*, § 17–131).

H. FREEDOM OF THOUGHT, CONSCIENCE AND RELIGION

Article 9

16–113 **9.**—(1) Everyone has the right to freedom of thought, conscience and religion; this right includes freedom to change his religion or belief and freedom, either alone or in community with others and in public or private, to manifest his religion or belief, in worship, teaching, practice and observance.

(2) Freedom to manifest one's religion or beliefs shall be subject only to such limitations

as are prescribed by law and are necessary in a democratic society in the interests of public safety, for the protection of public order, health or morals, or for the protection of the rights and freedoms of others.

Scope

Article 9 applies not only to religious beliefs, but also to the conscientious beliefs of "atheists, agnostics, sceptics and the unconcerned": *Kokkinakis v. Greece*, 17 E.H.R.R. 397. For a detailed consideration of the scope of Article 9 in the context of the prohibition of corporal punishment under section 548 of the *Education Act* 1996, see *R. (Williamson) v. Secretary of State for Eduction* [2005] 2 A.C. 246, HL. **16–114**

Limitations

The private practice of a person's religion or beliefs is absolutely protected under Article 9. The permissible grounds for limitation under Article 9(2) apply only to the freedom to "manifest" one's religion or belief. This term refers to public "worship, teaching, practice and observance": *Arrowsmith v. U.K.*, 19 D.R. 5. In *Arrowsmith*, the applicant, who was a pacifist, had been convicted of incitement to disaffection for distributing leaflets to soldiers urging them to refuse to serve in Northern Ireland. The Commission accepted that pacifism, as a belief, fell within the ambit of Article 9, but nevertheless concluded that there had been no interference with the applicant's right since the distribution of the leaflets did not constitute the practice of her belief. In *Mohisin Khan v. Royal Air Force Summary Appeals Court*, *The Times*, October 28, 2004, the Divisional Court held that a prosecution of a volunteer Muslim serviceman for being absent without leave pending a tour of duty in Iraq did not constitute an interference with his freedom of conscience or religion, because he had failed to manifest his objection to service on those grounds by way of available procedures prior to absenting himself. **16–115**

The fact that the English law of blasphemy does not apply to publications which offend against the beliefs of non-Christian religions does not give rise to a violation of Article 9: *Choudhury v. U.K.* (1991) 12 H.R.L.J. 172; *R. v. Chief Metropolitan Stipendiary Magistrate, ex p. Choudhury* [1991] 1 Q.B. 429, 91 Cr.App.R. 393, DC. **16–116**

Justification

As to Article 9(2) generally, see *ante*, §§ 16–32 *et seq.* **16–117**

The protection of health criterion in Article 9(2) has been held to justify the requirement of the criminal law that a sikh motorcyclist should wear a crash helmet (*X. v. U.K.*, 14 D.R. 234); and the prosecution of a farmer for refusing, on religious grounds, to take part in a compulsory government scheme to prevent disease among farm animals (*X. v. Netherlands*, 5 Y.B. 278). **16–118**

As to the prosecution of a Rastafarian for possession of cannabis with intent to supply, where the supply was intended to be to other Rastafarians for use in connection with religious worship, see *R. v. Taylor* [2002] 1 Cr.App.R. 37, CA (*post*, § 27–49).

I. FREEDOM OF EXPRESSION

Article 10

10.—(1) Everyone has the right to freedom of expression. This right shall include freedom to hold opinions and to receive and impart information and ideas without interference by public authority and regardless of frontiers. This Article shall not prevent States from requiring the licensing of broadcasting, television or cinema enterprises. **16–119**

(2) The exercise of these freedoms, since it carries with it duties and responsibilities, may be subject to such formalities, conditions, restrictions or penalties as are prescribed by law and are necessary in a democratic society, in the interests of national security, territorial integrity or public safety, for the prevention of disorder or crime, for the protection of health or morals, for the protection of the reputation or rights of others, for preventing the disclosure of information received in confidence, or for maintaining the authority and impartiality of the judiciary.

Scope

Freedom of expression "constitutes one of the essential foundations" of a democratic **16–120** society, and applies "not only to information or ideas that are favourably received, or regarded as inoffensive or as a matter of indifference, but also to those that offend, shock or disturb the State or any sector of the population": *Handyside v. U.K.*, 1 E.H.R.R. 737, at para. 49.

Interference

16–121 Criminal prosecution for an offence committed through the medium of speech, publication or broadcasting will generally give rise to an interference with the right to freedom of expression: *Handyside v. U.K.*, *ante*; *X. Ltd and Y. v. U.K.*, 28 D.R. 77; *Lingens v. Austria*, 8 E.H.R.R. 407; *Müller v. Switzerland*, 13 E.H.R.R. 212; *Barford v. Denmark*, 13 E.H.R.R. 493; *Scherer v. Switzerland*, 18 E.H.R.R. 276, Op. Comm.; *Jersild v. Denmark*, 19 E.H.R.R. 1; *Otto-Premiger-Institut v. Austria*, 19 E.H.R.R. 34; *Prager and Oberschlick v. Austria*, 21 E.H.R.R. 1; *Incal v. Turkey*, 29 E.H.R.R. 449 (incitement). See also *Goodwin v. U.K.*, 22 E.H.R.R. 123 (order under the *Contempt of Court Act* 1981, s.10); *Oberschlick v. Austria (No. 2)*, 25 E.H.R.R. 357; *Worm v. Austria*, 25 E.H.R.R. 454.

Justification

16–122 As to Article 10(2) generally, see *ante*, §§ 16–32 *et seq*. Where Article 10 rights are engaged, the justification for any criminal sanction must be "convincingly established": *Sunday Times v. U.K. (No. 2)*, 14 E.H.R.R. 229; *Goodwin v. U.K.*, *ante*; *Jersild v. Denmark*, 19 E.H.R.R. 1; *Worm v. Austria*, *ante*.

Article 10(2) affords limited scope for criminal prosecution in relation to political speech or debate on questions of public interest, see *Sener v. Turkey* (2003) 37 E.H.R.R. 34; *Ibrahim Askoy v. Turkey* (2002) 34 E.H.R.R. 57; and *Erdogdu v. Turkey* (2002) 34 E.H.R.R. 50. See also *R. v. Shayler* [2003] 1 A.C. 247, HL (*post*, § 25–326). Even where criminal prosecution is justified in principle, a disproportionate sentence may give rise to a breach of Article 10: *Skalka v. Poland* (2004) 38 E.H.R.R. 1 (eight months' imprisonment for insulting the judiciary held to be a violation of Article 10). See also *Kyprianou v. Cyprus* (2007) 44 E.H.R.R. 28 (five days' imprisonment for a comment made by an advocate to judges during his cross-examination of a witness).

Obscenity

16–123 Potentially obscene material is within the scope of Article 10. Criminal prosecution may be justified for the prevention of crime or the protection of morals, providing it meets the requirements of Article 10(2) (*ante*, §§ 16–32 *et seq.*). The definition of obscenity in the *Obscene Publications Acts* 1959 to 1964 is sufficiently precise to satisfy the requirement that any restriction must be prescribed by law: *Handyside*, *ante*. The question of proportionality is to be determined primarily by the likely audience (*cf.* the *Obscene Publications Act* 1959, s.1, *post*, § 31–63). In *Handyside*, the Court held that there was no violation where the applicant was prosecuted for publishing a book which contained factually accurate but sexually explicit information aimed at children. See also *Muller v. Switzerland*, 13 E.H.R.R. 212 (sexually explicit paintings displayed without warnings in a public gallery); *Hoare v. U.K.* [1997] E.H.R.L.R. 678 (videotapes distributed by post with insufficient safeguards to ensure that only intended purchasers would have access to the material). By contrast, in *Scherer v. Switzerland*, 18 E.H.R.R. 276, the applicant's prosecution for publishing an obscene film did violate Article 10 because the film had been shown in a small projection room at the back of a sex shop. Since it was unlikely that any member of the public would be confronted with the material unintentionally or against his will, there would have to be "particularly compelling reasons" to justify the interference. See also *R. v. Perrin* [2002] 4 *Archbold News* 2, CA (*post*, § 31–73).

Race hatred

16–124 The Commission has held (in reliance on Article 17 (*ante*, § 16–35)) that extreme racist speech is outside the protection of Article 10 because of its potential to undermine public order and the rights of the targeted minority: *Kühnen v. Germany*, 56 D.R. 205; *Glimmerveen and Haagenback v. Netherlands*, 18 D.R. 187.

In *Jersild v. Denmark*, *ante*, the applicant was a journalist convicted of aiding and abetting the dissemination of racial insults. He had produced a short documentary which included an interview with three youths who expressed extreme racist views. The programme was broadcast without comment or disclaimer. Nevertheless, it was common ground that it consisted of good faith reporting and was not intended to promote racist attitudes but to expose them. The youths were prosecuted and convicted of making racist statements, and the journalist of aiding and abetting them. The Court accepted unreservedly that the convictions of the youths were justified and that their speech was outside the protection of Article 10. But it nevertheless held that the conviction of the journalist was disproportionate to the protection of the rights of the targeted minorities. News reports based on interviews constituted one of the most important means by which the press was able to perform its "vital role as public watchdog". The punishment of a journalist for disseminating the statements of others in an interview would seriously hamper press freedom and "should not be envisaged unless there are particularly strong reasons for doing so". In *Gündüz v. Turkey* (2005) 41 E.H.R.R. 5, the prosecution of a leader of an Islamist sect for inciting hatred on grounds of religion after taking part in a live television debate in which he described Turkish society as "impious", fiercely criticised secularism and democracy and called for the introduction of a regime based on Sharia, was held to be a breach of Article 10, having regard in particular to the fact that the applicant's comments were made in the context of a balanced debate and he did not incite violence as a means of achieving his aims. The mere fact of defending the Sharia could not be described as "hate speech". As to holocaust denial offences see *Lehideux and Isorni v. France*, 30 E.H.R.R. 665; *Witzsch v. Germany*, unreported, April 20, 1999. As to racially aggravated public order offences, see *Norwood v. DPP* [2003] Crim.L.R. 888, DC (affirmed in *Norwood v. U.K.* (2005) 40 E.H.R.R. SE11); and *DPP v. Hammond* [2004] Crim.L.R. 851, DC. *Cf. Percy v. DPP*, 166 J.P. 93, DC. The standards of an open, multi-racial society render it justifiable under Article 10(2) to prosecute a person for using the public telecommunications system to leave racist messages: *DPP v. Collins* [2007] 1 Cr.App.R. 5, HL. In that context, racist language may be "grossly offensive", even if the person to whom the racist comments are made is not a member of the racial group to which the language refers: *ibid*. 16–125

Blasphemy

The prohibition of blasphemy through the criminal law does not violate Article 10: *X. Ltd and Y. v. U.K.*, 28 D.R. 77; *Otto-Premiger-Institut v. Austria*, 19 E.H.R.R. 34; *Wingrove v. U.K.*, 24 E.H.R.R. 1. 16–126

Defamatory libel

Criminal prosecutions for libel are not necessarily in breach of Article 10. In *Lingens and Leitgens v. Austria*, 4 E.H.R.R. 373 at 394, the Commission emphasised that each case must be judged on its facts and that it is "of the utmost importance that these restrictive regulations should only be applied where it is really necessary in the particular case". Public figures must be prepared to accept even harsh criticisms of their public activities and statements, and such criticism could not be characteristed as defamatory unless it threw considerable doubt on their character and integrity. In *Lingens v. Austria*, 8 E.H.R.R. 407, the Court distinguished between assertions of fact and expressions of opinion, and emphasised that the limits of acceptable criticism were wider as regards politicians than for private individuals. See also *Oberschlick v. Austria (No. 2)*, 25 E.H.R.R. 357. In *Gleaves v. Deakin* [1980] A.C. 477, HL, Lord Diplock expressed the view that the English offence of defamatory libel was "difficult to reconcile" with Article 10. *Cf. Worme v. Commr of Police of Grenada* [2004] 2 A.C. 430, PC. 16–127

Defamation of the judiciary

It remains a common law contempt of court to publish matter so defamatory of a 16–128 judge or court as to be likely to interfere with the due administration of justice by seriously lowering the authority of the judge or the court (see *post*, § 28–52). Such a prosecution would not involve a violation of Article 10 provided it was based on assertions of fact which amount to a serious personal attack on the integrity of the individual judge and was strictly proportionate to the need to maintain the authority and impartiality of the judiciary: *Barford v. Denmark*, 13 E.H.R.R. 493; *Prager and Oberschlick v. Austria*, 21 E.H.R.R. 1. *Cf. De Haes and Gijsels v. Belgium*, 25 E.H.R.R. 1. See also *Skalka v. Poland* (2004) 38 E.H.R.R. 1. As to the extent to which the right of lawyers to comment on the administration of justice both in and outside court can be subject to limitation, see *Schopfer v. Switzerland* (2001) 33 E.H.R.R. 34; *Nikula v. Finland* (2004) 38 E.H.R.R. 45; *Steur v. Netherlands* (2004) 39 E.H.R.R. 33; *Amihalachioaie v. Moldova* (2005) 40 E.H.R.R. 35; and *Kyprianou v. Cyprus* (2007) 44 E.H.R.R. 28.

Incitement to disaffection

16–129 Prosecutions for incitement to disaffection may be permissible under Article 10(2) as being necessary for the prevention of disorder: *Arrowsmith v. U.K.*, 19 D.R. 5. The term "disorder" is not limited to public order but encompasses the order required by membership of a specified group such as the military or the police: *Engel v. Netherlands*, 1 E.H.R.R. 647. However, the prosecution and penalty must be proportionate to the nature of the incitement and to the manner of its publication: *Panayiotis Grigoriades v. Greece* [1997] E.H.R.L.R. 89 (prosecution and imprisonment for "insulting the military" disproportionate on the facts).

Public order

16–129a Participation in a political protest or demonstration constitutes an act of expression attracting the protection of Article 10. The arrest and detention of a person for breach of the peace in the course of such a protest will be compatible with Article 10(2) only to the extent that it is proportionate to the need to maintain public order or to protect the rights and freedoms of others: *Steel v. U.K.*, 28 E.H.R.R. 603. In *Steel*, the arrest and detention of two applicants for physical obstruction was held compatible with Article 10(2). However, the arrest and detention of three other applicants, for handing out leaflets and holding up banners during a demonstration, was held to be in breach of Article 10. In *Hashman and Harrup v. U.K.*, 30 E.H.R.R. 241, an order imposed on two hunt saboteurs, requiring them to be "of good behaviour", was held to be in breach of Article 10 since it was not "prescribed by law" within the meaning of Article 10(2). In the Court's view, the concept of behaviour *contra bonos mores* was too vague to qualify as law, and failed to provide any objective criteria by which the applicants' past and future actions could be judged. See also *Percy v. DPP*, 166 J.P. 93, DC (*post*, § 29–34a); *Redmond-Bate v. DPP*, 163 J.P. 789, DC; and the approach of the Supreme Court of New Zealand in *Brooker v. Police* [2007] NZSC 30.

In *R. (Laporte) v. Chief Constable of Gloucestershire Constabulary* [2007] 2 A.C. 105, HL, protesters were prevented from attending a demonstration by coach and detained in the vehicle for a number of hours while they were escorted back to London by the police. It was held that since there had been no indication of any imminent breach of the peace when the coaches were intercepted and searched and since the defendant had not considered that such a breach was then likely to occur, the action taken in preventing the claimant from continuing to the demonstration had been an interference with her right to demonstrate at a lawful assembly which was not prescribed by domestic law; further, that, in any event, the police action had been premature and indiscriminate and represented a disproportionate restriction on the claimant's rights under Articles 10 and 11.

Election offences

16–130 In *Bowman v. U.K.*, 26 E.H.R.R. 1, the applicant, an anti-abortion campaigner, had been prosecuted under section 75 of the *Representation of the People Act* 1983 for incurring unauthorised expenditure during an election campaign, by printing and distributing leaflets setting out the candidates' voting record on abortion. The Court accepted that the legislation pursued the legitimate aim of controlling the expenditure of individual candidates so as to ensure that they were on an equal footing as regards the financing of their personal campaigns. Nevertheless, the prosecution was found to violate Article 10. Since the allegation related to the communication of factually accurate information concerning candidates' views on important legal and moral issues during an election campaign, it was disproportionate to the aim which the legislation sought to achieve.

Official secrets

See *R. v. Shayler* [2003] 1 A.C. 247, HL (*post*, § 25–326); and *Att.-Gen. v. Punch Ltd* [2003] 1 A.C. 1046, HL. **16–130a**

Unlicensed broadcasting

The Commission has held that since Article 10 expressly permits the licensing of broadcasting enterprises, it also permits states to prosecute those engaged in the promotion of unlicensed broadcasting: *X. v. U.K.*, 16 D.R. 190 (prosecution for displaying a sticker advertising a pirate radio station not in breach of Article 10). **16–131**

Contempt of court

Media reporting of criminal proceedings plays an important part in the public administration of justice: *Pretto v. Italy*, 6 E.H.R.R. 182, at para. 21; *Axen v. Germany*, 6 E.H.R.R. 195, at para. 25. However, the limits of permissible comment may not extend to statements which are likely to prejudice a fair trial or undermine the confidence of the public in the administration of justice: *Worm v. Austria*, 25 E.H.R.R. 454; *Hodgson, Woolf Productions and the N.U.J. v. U.K.*, 10 E.H.R.R. 503; and *Crociani v. Italy*, 22 D.R. 147. See also *Ex p. Telegraph Group plc* [2001] 1 W.L.R. 1983, CA; and *Montgomery v. H.M. Advocate* [2003] 1 A.C. 641, PC, *per* Lord Hope at p. 670. As to the compatibility of the *Contempt of Court Act* 1981, s.8 (*post*, § 28–90) with Article 10, see *Att.-Gen. v. Scotcher* [2005] 2 Cr.App.R. 35, HL. **16–131a**

J. FREEDOM OF ASSEMBLY AND ASSOCIATION

Article 11

11.—(1) Everyone has the right to freedom of peaceful assembly and to freedom of association with others, including the right to form and to join trade unions for the protection of his interests. **16–132**

(2) No restrictions shall be placed on the exercise of these rights other than such as are prescribed by law and are necessary in a democratic society in the interests of national security or public safety, for the prevention of disorder or crime, for the protection of health or morals or for the protection of the rights and freedoms of others. This Article shall not prevent the imposition of lawful restrictions on the exercise of these rights by members of the armed forces, of the police or of the administration of the State.

Scope

The first limb of Article 11 protects the right to organise and participate in peaceful public demonstrations (*Rassemblement Jurassien and Unité Jurassienne v. Switzerland*, 17 D.R. 93) and marches (*Christians Against Racism and Fascism v. U.K.*, 21 D.R. 138). The right extends to meetings which cause an obstruction on public thoroughfares, provided they are peaceful: *Rassemblement Jurassien*, *ante*; *G. v. Germany*, 60 D.R. 256. The right to freedom of peaceful assembly (*lex specialis*) may be regarded as one means whereby the right to freedom of expression (*lex generalis*) is afforded: *Laporte*, *ante*, § 16–129a. **16–133**

Interference

A ban, or the imposition of legally enforceable conditions on a peaceful demonstration will clearly amount to a "restriction", and thus require justification under Article **16–134**

11(2). But requirements to notify the authorities in advance (see the *Public Order Act* 1986, s.11) or to seek permission, will not generally constitute an interference in themselves: *Rassemblement Jurassien, ante*. Criminal prosecution after the event also amounts to a "restriction" requiring justification: *Ezelin v. France*, 14 E.H.R.R. 362, at para. 39.

Justification

16–135 As to Article 11(2) generally, see *ante*, §§ 16–32 *et seq.*

16–136 The permissible grounds of restriction most likely to be relied upon in this context are the prevention of disorder or crime and the protection of the rights and freedoms of others. In *Christians Against Racism and Fascism v. U.K.*, 21 D.R. 138, a blanket ban which was intended to prevent violent marches by the National Front was held by the Commission to be justified, even though it had the incidental effect of preventing peaceful demonstrations. However, in *Plattform Ärtze für das Leben v. Austria*, 13 E.H.R.R. 204, the Court held that there is a positive obligation on the police to protect a peaceful demonstration from violent disturbance by counter-demonstrators, so that a threat of violent disruption could not of itself justify banning a peaceful demonstration if disorder could be prevented by less far-reaching methods. An individual does not, therefore, cease to enjoy the right to peaceful assembly as a result of sporadic violence or other punishable acts committed by others in the course of the demonstration, if the individual in question remains peaceful in his own intentions or behaviour: *Ouranio Toxo v. Greece* (2007) 45 E.H.R.R. 8; *Ziliberberg v. Moldova*, unreported, May 4, 2004, ECtHR; and *Ezelin v. France*, 14 E.H.R.R. 362, Comm. Dec., para 34. See also *Laporte, ante*, § 16–129a; and *R. (Brehony) v. Chief Constable of Greater Manchester, The Times*, April 15, 2005, QBD (Bean J.).

K. RIGHT TO MARRY

Article 12

16–137 **12.** Men and women of marriageable age have the right to marry and to found a family, according to the national laws governing the exercise of this right.

16–138 Article 12 protects the right to marry "according to national laws governing the exercise of this right". It follows that there is no question of a defendant successfully invoking Article 12 in connection with a prosecution for bigamy (*post*, §§ 31–1 *et seq.*) or perjury under section 3(1)(a) and (b) of the *Perjury Act* 1911 in relation to false declarations to the Registrar of Births, Deaths and Marriages (*post*, §§ 28–176 *et seq.*). Convention case law under Article 12 establishes that it is for the state to decide on the content of its marriage laws: *X. v. Germany*, 1 D.R. 64.

L. PROHIBITION OF DISCRIMINATION

Article 14

16–139 **14.** The enjoyment of the rights and freedoms set forth in this Convention shall be secured without discrimination on any ground such as sex, race, colour, language, religion, political or other opinion, national or social origin, association with a national minority, property, birth or other status.

16–140 Article 14 safeguards individuals who are "placed in analogous situations" against discriminatory differences of treatment. For the purposes of Article 14, a difference of treatment is discriminatory if it "has no objective and reasonable justification", that is, if it does not pursue a "legitimate aim" or if there is not a "reasonable relationship of proportionality between the means employed and the aim sought to be realised": *Marckx v. Belgium*, 2 E.H.R.R. 330. Discrimination may also arise when the state, without an objective and reasonable justification, fails to treat differently persons whose situations are significantly different: *Thlimminos v. Greece* (2001) 31 E.H.R.R. 15. Article 14 is designed to complement the other Convention rights, even in circumstances where the substantive right is not violated, but in which a personal interest close to the core of such a right is infringed: *R. (Clift) v. Secretary of State for the Home Department*; *R. (Hindawi) v. Same*; *R. (Headley) v. Same* [2007] 1 A.C. 484, HL. The prohibition of discrimination has therefore been held to extend beyond the enjoyment of the specific

Convention rights, and to apply to those additional rights, falling within the general scope of any Convention article, for which the state has voluntarily decided to provide: see *ibid.*, and *Stec v. U.K.* (2005) 41 E.H.R.R. SE 295.

As to the relevance of Article 14 to the length of a sentence, see *R.M. v. U.K.*, 77 A D.R. 98 (concerning the refusal of the Court of Appeal to recognise reduced life expectancy as a result of AIDS as a mitigating factor for the purposes of sentence); in the context of sentencing powers, see *R. (W.) v. Thetford Youth Court*; *R. (M.) v. Waltham Forest Youth Court* [2003] 1 Cr.App.R.(S.) 67, DC (youth court declining jurisdiction in relation to defendant under 12 because of limitation on sentencing powers which did not apply to children over 12); and, in the context of parole, see *R. (Clift) v. Secretary of State for the Home Department*; *R. (Hindawi) v. Same*; *R. (Headley) v. Same*, *ante*, § 16–47 (discrimination in relation to different offences (justifiable) and nationality (not justifiable)). As to the relevance of Article 14 to the offence of gross indecency, see *Sutherland v. U.K.*, 24 E.H.R.R. 22 CD; and to the offence of unlawful sexual intercourse with a girl under 16 (*SOA* 1956, s.6 (*rep.*)), where the defendant was under 16 at the time, see *E. v. DPP*, *The Times*, February 9, 2005, DC.

The retention of fingerprint and DNA samples of people who are acquitted, or not proceeded against does not amount to a breach of Article 14: *R. (S.) v. Chief Constable of South Yorkshire*; *R. (Marper) v. Same* [2004] 1 W.L.R. 2196, HL.

A failure of the State to investigate whether a killing was racially motivated may give rise to a violation of Article 14 taken together with Article 2: *Nachova v. Bulgaria* (2006) 42 E.H.R.R. 43 (see *ante*, § 16–38b). See also *Bekos v. Greece* (2006) 43 E.H.R.R. 2.

CHAPTER 17

THE MENTAL ELEMENT IN CRIME

I. MENS REA

A. ACTUS NON FACIT REUM NISI MENS SIT REA

17–1 (a) "The deed does not make a man guilty unless his mind be guilty." This maxim of the common law applies, though not invariably, to statutory as well as to common law offences, and is of fundamental importance in upholding the rule of law. The maxim, which does not apply to the common law offences of public nuisance, libel or contempt, was disliked by Stephen J. In *R. v. Tolson* (1889) 23 Q.B.D. 168, he said (at p. 185) that it was misleading because it suggests that, apart from all particular definitions of crimes, such a thing exists as a "*mens rea*" or "guilty mind" which is always expressly or by implication involved in every definition. This, he said was obviously not the case, for the mental elements of different crimes differ widely. He thought it confusing to call so many dissimilar states of mind by one name.

> "The principle involved appears to me, when fully considered, to amount to no more than this. The full definition of every crime contains expressly or by implication a proposition as to a state of mind. Therefore, if the mental element of any conduct alleged to be a crime is proved to have been absent in any given case, the crime so defined is not committed; or, again, if a crime is fully defined nothing amounts to that crime which does not satisfy that definition" (at p. 187).

Smith and Hogan, *Criminal Law*, 12th ed., are to the same effect:

> "*Mens rea* is a term which has no single meaning. Every crime has its own *mens rea* which can be ascertained only by reference to its statutory definition or the case law. The most we can do is to state a general principle, or presumption, which governs its definition. ... The result is that the best we can do by way of a general definition of *mens rea* is as follows: 'Intention, knowledge or recklessness with respect to all the elements of the offence *together with any ulterior intent which the definition of the crime requires*'" (at pp. 123–126).

17–2 (b) To make a man liable to imprisonment for an offence which he does not know that he is committing and is unable to prevent is repugnant to the ordinary man's conception of justice and brings the law into contempt; see *The Mental Element in Crime* (Law Com. Working Paper No. 31), p. 4, and the observations of Lord Reid in *Sweet v. Parsley* [1970] A.C. 132 at 149, HL, and his dissenting opinion in *Warner v. Metropolitan Police Commr* [1969] 2 A.C. 256 at 271–283, HL. Yet, in the relatively recent past, there have been several decisions where the appellate courts have so interpreted Acts of Parliament as to achieve just this result. See, *e.g. Warner*, *ante*, and Lord Reid in *per Sweet v. Parsley*, *ante*, at p. 150.

17–3 (c) It is difficult to reconcile the decision of the House of Lords in *Sweet v. Parsley* with their earlier decision in *Warner* (although four out of five of their Lordships sat on both appeals). Lord Reid said in *Sweet v. Parsley*, *ante*:

> "It is firmly established by a host of authorities that *mens rea* is an essential ingredient of every offence unless some reason can be found for holding that that is not necessary. It is also firmly established that the fact that other sections of the Act expressly require *mens rea*, for example because they contain the word 'knowingly', is not in itself sufficient to justify a decision that a section which is silent as to *mens rea* creates an absolute offence. In the absence of a clear indication in the Act that an offence is intended to be an absolute offence, it is necessary to go outside the Act and examine all relevant circumstances in order to establish that this must have been the intention of Parliament. I say 'must have been', because it is a universal principle that if a penal provision is reasonably capable of two interpretations, that interpretation which is most favourable to the accused must be adopted" (at p. 149).

After referring to a class of acts which "are not criminal in any real sense, but ... which in the public interest are prohibited under penalty", he said:

> "It does not in the least follow that, when one is dealing with a truly criminal act, it is sufficient merely to have regard to the subject-matter of the enactment. One must put oneself in the position of a legislator. It has long been the practice to recognise absolute offences in this class of quasi-criminal acts, and one can safely assume that, when Parliament is passing new legislation dealing with this class of offences, its silence as to *mens rea* means that the old practice is to apply. But when one comes to acts of a truly criminal character, it appears to me that there are at least two other factors which any reasonable legislator would have in mind. In the first place, a stigma still attaches to any person convicted of a truly criminal offence, and the more serious or disgraceful the offence, the greater the stigma. So he would have to

consider whether, in a case of this gravity, the public interest really requires that an innocent person should be prevented from proving his innocence in order that fewer guilty men may escape. And equally important is the fact that, fortunately, the Press in this country are vigilant to expose injustice, and every manifestly unjust conviction made known to the public tends to injure the body politic by undermining public confidence in the justice of the law and of its administration. But I regret to observe that, in some recent cases where serious offences have been held to be absolute offences, the court has taken into account no more than the wording of the Act and the character and seriousness of the mischief which constitutes the offence" (at pp. 149–150).

In determining whether a statutory offence is an offence of strict liability or whether it is an offence requiring proof of *mens rea* as to its essential facts, regard should be had, in particular, to *Sherras v. De Rutzen* [1895] 1 Q.B. 918 at 921; *Lim Chin Aik v. R.* [1963] A.C. 160 at 172–175, PC; and *Sweet v. Parsley*, *ante*.

In *Gammon (Hong Kong) Ltd v. Att.-Gen. of Hong Kong* [1985] A.C. 1, PC, Lord Scarman stated that these decisions founded the following propositions: (i) there is a presumption of law that *mens rea* is required before a person can be convicted of a criminal offence; (ii) the presumption is particularly strong where the offence is "truly criminal" in character; (iii) the presumption applies to statutory offences and can be displaced only if this is clearly or by necessary implication the effect of the statute; (iv) the only situation in which the presumption can be displaced is where the statute is concerned with an issue of social concern, *e.g.* public safety; (v) even where a statute is concerned with such an issue, the presumption of *mens rea* stands unless it can also be shown that the creation of strict liability will be effective to promote the objects of the statute by encouraging greater vigilance to prevent the commission of the prohibited act. *Gammon* was considered and applied in *Wings Ltd v. Ellis* [1985] A.C. 272, HL (trade descriptions); *R. v. Wells Street Metropolitan Stipendiary Magistrate, ex p. Westminster City Council* [1986] 1 W.L.R. 1046, DC (planning); *R. v. Brockley*, 99 Cr.App.R. 385, CA (undischarged bankrupt acting as company director); *R. v. Bezzina*, 99 Cr.App.R. 356, CA (dangerous dogs, *post*, § 31–37); and *R. v. Jackson* [2007] 1 Cr.App.R. 28, CA (low flying). **17–4**

(d) The so-called defences of insanity, automatism, drunkenness and duress, discussed *post*, §§ 17–74 *et seq.*, are developments of the doctrine of *mens rea* as applied to particular situations. Until the decision of the House of Lords in *Woolmington v. DPP* [1935] A.C. 462, there was a body of opinion which held that the onus was on the defendant to negative *mens rea*, both generally and when the issues of insanity, etc., arose, *e.g.* *R. v. Tolson* (1889) 23 Q.B.D. 168 at 181. Since *Woolmington*, it has been firmly established that the onus is on the prosecution to establish *mens rea* beyond all reasonable doubt, whether generally or when such particular issues arise, in all cases other than insanity or where it is otherwise laid down by statute, *e.g.* diminished responsibility in murder. In the case of insanity, anomalously, the burden is on the defence to prove insanity on a balance of probabilities. This has given rise to difficult and indeed somewhat absurd situations where the issues of insanity and automatism have arisen on the same facts. **17–5**

(e) The "act" which the *mens rea* must accompany must be voluntary in the sense that it is the product of the will of the defendant, however reluctant he may be to do it: see *Lynch v. DPP for Northern Ireland* [1975] A.C. 653, HL. This does not apply where the defendant was senseless owing to self-induced intoxication and the *mens rea* of the offence is "recklessness": see *post*, § 17–105. **17–6**

(f) In general, the *mens rea* must exist at the time of the act or omission, but on this, see *post*, § 17–113, as to the position where voluntary drunkenness supervenes upon a mind already intent upon a crime. **17–7**

(g) Article 6 of the ECHR (*ante*, § 16–57) does not restrict the power of the legislature to create offences of strict liability; it being concerned exclusively with procedural and evidential matters going to the fairness of a trial, there was no scope for reading into a provision creating an offence of strict liability a defence where Parliament had not done so: *Barnfather v. Islington Education Authority* [2003] 1 W.L.R. 2318, DC.

B. Mental Element Included in Definition of Offence

Where the definition of a statutory offence or an offence at common law, *e.g.* murder **17–8** (*post*, § 19–1), includes a particular requirement or requirements as to the state of mind of the offender, there is, as a general rule, no need to import any additional such requirement. These requirements are often explained in general terms, *e.g.* "maliciously" or "wilfully": see *post*, §§ 17–45, 17–47.

17–9 It is in the case of offences, the definitions of which are silent as to any mental element, that questions of importation of *mens rea* arise. These are usually statutory offences, the mental elements of common law offences having been developed by the courts over many years.

C. MISTAKE OF FACT

Introduction

17–10 It has long been recognised that mistake of fact, in the sense of a belief in circumstances which, if true, would make the defendant's conduct innocent, is a "defence" to some, but not all, criminal charges. For many years the leading authority was widely recognised to be *R. v. Tolson* (1889) 23 Q.B.D. 168, in which it was held that it was a good defence to a charge of bigamy that the accused believed, on reasonable grounds, that the first spouse was dead. This was said to be an exemplification of the common law principle that an honest and reasonable belief in the existence of circumstances, which, if true, would make the act for which the defendant is indicted an innocent act had always been a good defence; and that it applied equally to statutory offences unless excluded expressly or by necessary implication.

This principle was intended to be of general application, and was accepted as such by the Privy Council in *Bank of New South Wales v. Piper* [1897] A.C. 383 at 389, by Lord Reid in his dissenting speech in *Warner v. Metropolitan Police Commr* [1969] 2 A.C. 256 at 276, by Lord Diplock in *Sweet v. Parsley* [1970] A.C. 132 at 163–164, and by the Court of Appeal in *R. v. Gould* [1968] 2 Q.B. 65, 52 Cr.App.R. 152. The decision of the House of Lords in *DPP v. Morgan* [1976] A.C. 182, is commonly thought of as being a turning point in the development of the law, and is frequently cited as authority for the proposition that a defence based on mistake of fact may succeed though it is not based on reasonable grounds, so long as it was honestly held. *Morgan* was indeed a landmark case, but it is an over-simplification of the decision to describe its effect as being the removal of the requirement of reasonableness.

The real importance of *Morgan* was that it emphasised that the first requirement in relation to any offence, common law or statutory, was to have regard to the definition of the offence. It then served to underline that some mistakes of fact have the effect of negativing an element of the offence required to be proved by the prosecution. In such cases, it is misleading to speak in terms of a defence. The defendant is not guilty because the prosecution have not proved an element of the offence. In other cases, however, the prosecution may prove all the elements in the definition of the offence. In these cases, the mistake of the defendant does not negative any of these elements: the issue may therefore be genuinely referred to as one as to whether or not the mistake affords a defence.

Mistake negativing ingredient of offence

17–11 In *Morgan*, *ante*, the charge was rape. It was held that since the then definition of rape included an intention to have sexual intercourse without the consent of the woman, or being reckless, not caring whether she consented or not, it would be inconsistent with such definition to direct the jury that the accused would be entitled to be acquitted only if he believed on reasonable grounds that the woman was consenting. If he believed that she was consenting, whether reasonably or not, he did not have an intention to have sexual intercourse without her consent, or recklessly, not caring whether or not she consented. If such was, or may have been his belief, the prosecution had failed to prove one of the ingredients of the offence, and he was entitled to be acquitted.

Morgan was applied to an allegation of assault occasioning actual bodily harm in *R. v. Williams (G.)*, 78 Cr.App.R. 276, CA. One of the elements of the latter offence is that the accused was acting unlawfully (*i.e.* he was not acting in self-defence, or in the defence of others or for the prevention of crime), and a successful prosecution depends upon proof of an awareness of the circumstances rendering the attack unlawful. It follows that if the defendant believes in facts which would have rendered his use of force lawful, the prosecution have failed to prove the case. Accordingly, it was held that the jury should have been directed that, first, the prosecution had the burden of proving the unlawfulness of the defendant's actions; secondly, if the defendant might have been labouring under a mistake as to the facts, he was to be judged according to his mistaken view of the facts, whether or not that mistake was, on an objective view, reasonable or not. The reasonableness or unreasonableness of the belief was material only to the question whether the belief was in fact held by him.

Williams was approved by the Privy Council in *R. v. Beckford* [1988] A.C. 130, and has subsequently been applied in *R. v. Jones (Terence)*, 83 Cr.App.R. 375, CA, and *Blackburn v. Bowering* [1994] 1 W.L.R. 1324, CA (Civ. Div.).

Morgan was applied to the offence of indecent assault (contrary to the *SOA* 1956, s.14 (*rep.*)) in *R. v. Kimber*, 77 Cr.App.R. 225, CA. The alleged victim had been an adult, and it was held that, an essential ingredient of the offence being an assault, if the defendant had believed that the complainant was consenting, the *mens rea* of an assault would not have existed. *Kimber* was itself applied (together with *B. (A Minor) v. DPP*, *post*, § 17–13) to an offence of indecent assault where the complainant was under 16 at the time of the alleged offence, and thus incapable as a matter of law, of giving a consent which would otherwise prevent an act from being an indecent assault (see s.14(2) of the 1956 Act), in *R. v. K.* [2002] 1 A.C. 462, HL. If the defendant believed that the complainant was consenting and was at least 16 years of age he would not have had the *mens rea* of an assault, and, therefore of an indecent assault.

Mistake not negativing ingredient of offence

R. v. Tolson was such a case. The charge was bigamy, contrary to section 57 of the *Offences against the Person Act* 1861 (*post*, § 31–1). The material part of the definition of the offence was: "Whosoever, being married, shall marry any other person, during the life of the former husband or wife … shall be guilty of an offence". The defendant had done just that. Her belief that her first husband was dead did not negative any element of the definition of the offence, but it was held that it did provide her with a defence, based as it had been found to be, on reasonable grounds. **17–12**

In *Morgan*, the majority were quite specific about the fact that they were not overruling *Tolson*. On the contrary, Lord Cross said that he could see no objection to the inclusion of the element of reasonableness in such a case. Further, it is manifest that he would have held that the rule in *Tolson* would have operated were a statute to provide simply that it is an offence "to have sexual intercourse with a woman without her consent", being silent as to intention, knowledge or belief.

In *Albert v. Lavin*, 72 Cr.App.R. 178, DC, the *Tolson* rule was applied to a charge of assault on a constable in the execution of his duty, the court ruling that a mistaken belief that the victim was not a constable would not avail the defendant if there were no reasonable grounds for the belief. The decision was affirmed by the House of Lords on other grounds ([1982] A.C. 546). The reasoning of the Divisional Court was, however, subsequently disapproved in both *Kimber* and *Williams*, *ante*.

In *R. v. Barrett and Barrett*, 72 Cr.App.R. 212, CA, the court proceeded on the basis that *Tolson* was still good law.

> "The case of *Tolson* and the cases preceding and following *Tolson* correctly affirm the principle that an honest belief in a certain state of things does afford a defence, including an honest though mistaken belief about legal rights. But these cases were never intended to extend, and do not extend, to the situation where the rights in question have been the subject of litigation between the parties and a court of competent jurisdiction has stated what the rights are but the losing party simply refuses, through obstinacy, to accept the order of the court" (at p. 216).

In *R. v. Phekoo*, 73 Cr.App.R. 107, CA, it was held that the offence under section 1(3) of the *Protection from Eviction Act* 1977 (*post*, § 29–61) was not an absolute offence, in that it had to be proved that the defendant intended to harass someone known or believed to be a person who, in effect, was not just a "squatter". The court went on to say, *obiter*, in reliance on *Tolson*, that where the issue arose, the defendant would only be entitled to be acquitted if the belief that the person was not a residential occupier was based on reasonable grounds. This, however, was directly contrary to what was said in *Morgan*. The court dealt with *Morgan* by saying that it was intended to be confined to rape. This view of *Morgan* was unsustainable, and was rejected in *Kimber*, and by Lord Bridge in *Westminster City Council v. Croyalgrange Ltd*, 83 Cr.App.R. 155 at 164, HL.

17–13 The distinction between mistakes which negative an element of the offence and those which do not was blurred by the decision of the House of Lords in *B. (A Minor) v. DPP* [2000] 2 A.C. 428. The offence in question was that contrary to section 1 of the *Indecency with Children Act* 1960 (*rep.*). This provided that a person "who commits an act of gross indecency with or towards a child under the age of fourteen" was guilty of an offence. It was held that if the defendant honestly believed the child was 14 or over, he would not be guilty of the offence, however unreasonable his belief. What is not clear from the decision is whether their Lordships were holding that, notwithstanding the absence of any reference to knowledge or belief as to the child's age, the provision was to be construed as requiring proof of knowledge of, or recklessness as to, the child's age, or whether they were holding that it was a *Tolson* case, and were now rejecting the requirement of reasonableness. If it was the former, then the principle in *Morgan* would plainly apply.

Lord Nicholls, with whom Lord Irvine L.C. agreed, said at p. 463G:

> "If a man genuinely believes that the girl with whom he is committing a grossly indecent act is over 14, he is not intending to commit such an act with a girl under 14. Whether such an intention is an essential ingredient of the offence depends upon a proper construction of section 1 ...."

His Lordship said he would turn to that question. Unfortunately, he never answers it. Over the next two pages of the judgment, he sets out his reasons for holding that *mens rea* should attach to the age element of the offence. These reasons have nothing to do with the wording of the statute, but relate to the general presumption in favour of *mens rea* in the case of serious criminal offences. As has been stated, his Lordship never says that the prosecution have to prove knowledge or recklessness in relation to age, the question he posed for himself. Instead, he merely concludes that "the necessary mental element regarding the age ingredient ... is the absence of a genuine belief that the victim was 14 years of age or above" (at p. 466B).

This is a remarkable way of describing the mental element of any offence. Expressing it in negative terms is never done. Did his Lordship envisage that the indictment would include such a negative allegation? The truth appears to be that his Lordship muddled the two principles—*Morgan* and *Tolson*. He starts with *Morgan*, asking the appropriate question as to what it is the prosecution have to prove, but he never answers it. Instead, he refers back to Lord Diplock's statement in *Sweet v. Parsley* [1970] A.C. 132 at 163:

> "a general principle of construction of any enactment, which creates a criminal offence, [is] that, even where the words used to describe the prohibited conduct would not in any other context connote the necessity for any particular mental element, they are nevertheless to be read as subject to the implication that a necessary element in the offence is the absence of belief, held honestly and upon reasonable grounds, in the existence of facts which, if true, would make the act innocent"

but he removes the requirement of reasonableness. In effect, it may perhaps be said that he applied *Morgan* to a *Tolson* situation.

17–14 Lord Steyn referred to the first certified question, namely whether a defendant is entitled to be acquitted if he holds or may hold an honest belief that the child was 14 years or over, adding that the "question of statutory interpretation ... is whether *mens rea* is an ingredient of the offence or whether the subsection creates an offence of strict liability" (at p. 466G). Having concluded that there had been no intention to create an offence of strict liability, he then referred to the second question which was whether the belief had to be based on reasonable grounds. The prosecution had not argued this point: this seems surprising in view of the long line of authority in favour of it. His Lordship indicated that he had initially thought this to be an acceptable solution (at p. 477D). He rejected it, however, saying that it is now settled as a matter of general principle that mistake, whether reasonable or not, is a defence where it prevents the defendant from having the *mens rea* which the law requires for the crime with which he is charged. This was, of course, the decision in *Morgan*: it begs the question, however, as to what *mens rea* the law required in the case of the offence in question. His Lordship did not answer it any more than Lord Nicholls did. He contented himself with saying that it would be in disharmony with "this development" now to rule that in respect of a defence under section 1(1) the belief must be based on reasonable grounds.

Lord Hutton concluded that it was not a necessary implication of the statute that it was intended to create strict liability. Accordingly, a mistake as to age should afford a defence, and as to whether such mistake had to be reasonable, his Lordship agreed with Lord Steyn. Lord Mackay appears to have agreed with Lords Nicholls, Steyn and Hutton.

Offences of strict liability (absolute offences)

In respect of those offences in relation to which there is no requirement of *mens rea*, a mistake of fact, whether based on reasonable grounds or not, will not provide a defence. Thus, it was held in *R. v. Howells* [1977] Q.B. 614, 65 Cr.App.R. 86, CA, that an honest and reasonable belief that a firearm was an antique, and therefore exempt from section 1 of the *Firearms Act* 1968, was no defence. **17–15**

Mistake of fact induced by drink

A defendant is not entitled to rely, so far as self-defence is concerned, upon a mistake of fact which has been induced by voluntary intoxication: see *R. v. Lipman* [1970] 1 Q.B. 152, 53 Cr.App.R. 600, CA; *DPP v. Majewski* [1977] A.C. 443, HL; *R. v. O'Grady* [1987] Q.B. 995, 85 Cr.App.R. 315, CA; and *R. v. Hatton* [2006] 1 Cr.App.R. 16, CA. Where the charge is murder the jury clearly have to be directed that before they can convict of murder they must be sure that the act which caused death was unlawful. That ingredient will not have been proved if the defendant was or may have been acting in self-defence, nor will it have been proved if the defendant was or may have been acting in the honest though mistaken belief that it was necessary to defend himself: see *Williams (G.)* and *Beckford*, *ante*. Where that honest though mistaken belief is attributable to the voluntary taking of drink, the act *will* be unlawful (see *Majewski* cited *post*, §§ 17–107 *et seq.*) and the defendant will be guilty at least of manslaughter. The common law position has now been codified in section 76(5) of the *CJIA* 2008, *post*, § 19–39a. Whilst self-defence may not be open to the defendant who mistakes the situation as a result of his consumption of drink, it will still, of course, be necessary to prove that he had the necessary intent. **17–16**

As to the position when: (a) an accused as a result of drink mistakenly thought an alleged rape victim was consenting, see *R. v. Woods (W.)*, 74 Cr.App.R. 312, *post*, § 17–116; (b) an accused may have thought, as a result of drink that "the thing" which he knew he had was not a controlled drug, see *R. v. Young (Robert)*, 78 Cr.App.R. 288, Ct-MAC, *post*, § 27–124.

Conclusion

Notwithstanding the formidable bank of authority to support the rule in *Tolson*, the decision of the House of Lords in *B. (A Minor) v. DPP* has been accepted as the leading authority (see *R. v. Kumar* [2005] 1 Cr.App.R. 34, CA), despite the unsatisfactory nature of the reasoning and the uncertainty as to what it actually decided. It seems probable, however, that it will be taken to have decided that in the case of all offences other than those involving strict liability, a mistaken belief in circumstances which, if true, would render the act of the accused an innocent act will afford a defence (*Kumar*, *ante*). The reasonableness of the belief will go only to the issue of whether it was genuinely held. Where the issue is raised, it is for the prosecution to prove that no such belief was held. The rule in *Tolson* is probably to be taken to be confined to the particular offence with which that case was concerned. **17–17**

[The next paragraph is § 17–22.]

D. MISTAKE OF LAW

17–22 (a) Although there is not and never has been a presumption that everyone knows the law, there is a rule of law that ignorance of the law does not excuse—a maxim of different scope and application, see *Evans v. Bartlam* [1937] A.C. 473 at 479, *per* Lord Atkin. An honest and reasonable belief that an action is not criminal is no defence, though it may afford considerable mitigation, see *e.g. Johnson v. Youden* [1950] 1 K.B. 544 at 546, DC. This is so even where the offender is a foreigner and the offence is not criminal in his own country: *R. v. Esop* (1836) 7 C. & P. 456; *R. v. Barronet and Allain* (1852) Dears. 51. A belief by the defendant that he will not be prosecuted affords no defence: *R. v. Arrowsmith* [1975] Q.B. 678, 60 Cr.App.R. 211, CA.

17–23 (b) It should be observed that the law in question is the criminal law. A mistake as to the civil law may have the effect of negativing *mens rea*. This principle has received statutory recognition in section 2(1)(a) of the *Theft Act* 1968 (claim of right) (*post*, § 21–23). Apart from statute, see, for example, *R. v. Smith (David Raymond)* [1974] Q.B. 354, 58 Cr.App.R. 320, CA (mistaken belief as to ownership of property as defence to charge of criminal damage, *post*, § 23–8); *R. v. Gould* [1969] 2 Q.B. 65, 52 Cr.App.R. 152, CA (honest and reasonable mistake as to previous marriage having been ended by valid divorce negatives *mens rea* of bigamy, *post*, § 31–9); and *R. v. Barrett and Barrett* (mistaken belief as to legal rights may afford defence, *ante*, § 17–12).

(c) In the case of an alleged contravention of a statutory instrument, section 3(2) of the *Statutory Instruments Act* 1946 provides a limited defence: see *ante*, § 9–28.

(d) As to the relevance of "mistake of law" where the offence alleged is conspiracy, see *Churchill v. Walton* [1967] 2 A.C. 224, HL (*post*, § 33–16).

E. "TRANSFERRED MALICE"

17–24 It is well established that if a man by mistake, or, *e.g.* by bad aim, causes injury to a person or property other than the person or property which he intended to attack, he is guilty of a crime of the same degree as if he had achieved his object. For example, if a man shoots at A with intent to kill him, and kills B by mistake, it is murder: Fost. 261; Hale (1) 438 at 441. The harm done however must be of the same kind as the harm intended, *e.g.* a man who throws a stone at another and by mistake breaks a window without realising that this is a probable consequence of his action is guilty of no offence: see *R. v. Pembliton* (1874) L.R. 2 C.C.R. 119. As suicide is no longer a crime, it is submitted that killing another by mistake for oneself is no longer murder, and that *R. v. Hopwood*, 8 Cr.App.R. 143, CCA, and *R. v. Spence*, 41 Cr.App.R. 80, CCA, should not be followed.

Similarly, if a man shoots in lawful self-defence and by mistake kills an innocent bystander he is not guilty of murder or manslaughter: see Fost. 299.

Where a person attacks a pregnant woman intending to do her grievous bodily harm and in consequence of that attack, she goes into premature labour with the child being born alive but subsequently dying as a result of being born prematurely, the doctrine of transferred malice has no application: *Att.-Gen.'s Reference (No. 3 of 1994)* [1998] A.C. 245, HL. (See also *post*, § 19–16.)

F. VICARIOUS LIABILITY

17–25 (a) Apart from the criminal liability of corporations, dealt with at §§ 17–30 *et seq.*, vicarious liability rarely arises in trials on indictment, as it is usually confined to summary offences.

(b) Where an offence has been held to be an absolute offence, in that *mens rea* as defined above is not required, "the person on whom a duty is thrown is responsible, whether he has delegated or whether he has acted through a servant": *R. v. Winson* [1969] 1 Q.B. 371, CA (*per curiam*). See also *Barker v. Levinson* [1951] 1 K.B. 342, DC; *C. Gabriel Ltd v. Enfield L.B.C.* [1971] R.T.R. 265, DC; *R. v. British Steel plc* [1995] 1 W.L.R. 1356, CA; *R. v. Associated Octel Co. Ltd* [1996] 1 W.L.R. 1543, HL; and *R. v. Gateway Foodmarkets Ltd* [1997] 2 Cr.App.R. 40, CA; and contrast *Reynolds v. G.H. Austin and Sons Ltd* [1951] 2 K.B. 135, DC.

(c) The mere fact that the offence is one which requires some degree of *mens rea* does not preclude the possibility of vicarious liability. In *Mousell Bros Ltd v. London and North Western Ry Co.* [1917] 2 K.B. 836, DC, a company was convicted of the offence of having given a false account of goods to be carried on the railway with intent to avoid the payment of the correct tolls, contrary to section 99 of the *Railway Clauses Consolidation Act* 1845. The magistrates had found that the goods had been falsely described by a servant of the company on the instruction of their manager with intent to avoid payment of the correct tolls. The conviction was upheld. Viscount Reading C.J. quoted the following passage from the judgment of Channell J. in *Pearks, Gunston and Tee v. Ward* [1902] 2 K.B. 1 at 11, as stating the true principle of law: **17–26**

"By the general principles of the criminal law, if a matter is made a criminal offence, it is essential that there should be something in the nature of *mens rea*, and, therefore, in ordinary cases a corporation cannot be guilty of a criminal offence, nor can a master be liable criminally for an offence committed by his servant. But there are exceptions to this rule in the case of quasi-criminal offences, as they may be termed, that is to say, where certain acts are forbidden by law under a penalty, possibly even under a personal penalty, such as imprisonment, at any rate in default of a fine."

The Lord Chief Justice then referred to *Coppen v. Moore (No. 2)* [1898] 2 Q.B. 306 and continued:

"Prima facie, then, a master is not to be made criminally responsible for the acts of his servant to which the master is not a party. But it may be the intention of the legislature, in order to guard against the happening of the forbidden thing, to impose a liability upon a principal even though he does not know of, and is not a party to, the forbidden act done by his servant. Many statutes are passed with this object. Acts done by the servant of the licensed holder of licensed premises render the licensed holder in some instances liable, even though the act was done by his servant without the knowledge of the master. Under the Food and Drugs Acts there are again instances well known in these courts where the master is made responsible, even though he knows nothing of the act done by his servant, and he may be fined or rendered amenable to the penalty enjoined by the law. In those cases the legislature absolutely forbids the act and makes the principal liable without a *mens rea*" (at p. 844).

This citation was quoted with approval by Lord Morris in *Tesco Supermarkets Ltd v. Nattrass* [1972] A.C. 153 at 176. Delivering a concurring judgment in *Mousell Bros Ltd*, Atkin J. said:

"I think that the authorities cited by my Lord make it plain that while prima facie a principal is not to be made criminally responsible for the acts of his servants, yet the legislature may prohibit an act or enforce a duty in such words as to make the prohibition or the duty absolute; in which case the principal is liable if the act is in fact done by his servants. To ascertain whether a particular Act of Parliament has that effect or not, regard must be had to the object of the statute, the words used, the nature of the duty laid down, the person upon whom it is imposed, the person by whom it would in ordinary circumstances be performed, and the person upon whom the penalty is imposed. ... When a penalty is imposed for the breach of the duty, it is reasonable to infer that the penalty is imposed for a default of the person by whom the duty would ordinarily be performed. If the servant is to prepare the account, then it is the fault of the servant in not preparing the account that makes the owner liable to the penalty ... I see no difficulty in the fact that an intent to avoid payment is necessary to constitute the offence. That is an intent which the servant might well have, inasmuch as he is the person who has to deal with the particular matter. The penalty is imposed upon the owner for the act of the servant, if the servant commits the default provided for in the statute in the state of mind provided for in the statute" (at pp. 845–846).

See also *Mullins v. Collins* (1874) L.R. 9 Q.B. 292, *Bosley v. Davies* (1875) 1 Q.B.D. 84, and *Meridian Global Funds Management Asia Ltd v. Securities Commission* [1995] 2 A.C. 500, PC (*post*, § 17–31).

(d) It is clear from the authorities cited, *ante*, that in deciding who may be liable under a penal statute, close regard must be paid to the words used. Sometimes, the verb used which constitutes the essence of the offence will be peculiarly apposite to the principal. The examples most frequently given are "sells", "possesses" and "uses": thus, where a shop assistant makes a sale, it will equally be a sale by the principal, as in *Coppen v. Moore (No. 2)*, *ante*. Where the offence is one of strict liability, there is no issue of vicarious liability in such cases: the act of the employee is the act of the employer. Where some form of *mens rea* is required to be proved, provided the employee is **17–27** acting within the scope, or in the course of his employment, his state of mind will be attributed to the employer: *Coppen v. Moore (No. 2)*, *ante*, and see the citation from the speech of Atkin J. in *Mousell Bros Ltd*, *ante*.

17–28 (e) In the class of cases, where a duty is thrown on a particular category of persons, *e.g.* licence holders, it has been held that if that person has delegated his responsibilities to another, the *mens rea* of the delegate will be imputed to the principal so as to make the latter criminally liable. This form of liability has been termed "vicarious liability". The leading case appears to be *Linnett v. Metropolitan Police Commr* [1946] K.B. 290, DC. A licensee of a public house was held to have been rightly convicted of "knowingly permitting disorderly conduct" where he had absented himself from the premises and had left control to another man who himself had knowingly permitted the disorderly conduct, though the licensee defendant was unaware of it.

Lord Goddard C.J. said:

> "The point does not, as I say, depend merely on the fact that the relationship of master and servant exists; it depends on the fact that the person who is responsible in law as the ... licensee of the house has chosen to delegate his duties, powers and authority to somebody else. ... I do not wish it to be thought that I am saying that where a statute provides that in any business a certain act permitted by the manager shall be an offence on the part of the manager if it is done with his knowledge, that if the act takes place whilst the manager himself is carrying on that business and is in charge of the business but without his knowledge, so that he was powerless to prevent it, that person necessarily commits the offence. But if the manager chooses to delegate the carrying on of the business to another, whether or not that other is his servant, then what that other does or what he knows must be imputed to the person who put the other into that position" (at pp. 295–296).

17–29 (f) Considerable doubt was cast upon the doctrine of "vicarious liability by delegation" in *Vane v. Yiannopoullos* [1965] A.C. 486, HL. It was reaffirmed, however, by the Court of Appeal in *R. v. Winson* [1969] 1 Q.B. 371, where *Vane v. Yiannopoullos* was considered. In *R. v. Winson*, the licensee was absent from the premises, and the knowledge of the manager was imputed to the absent licensee. In *Howker v. Robinson* [1973] 1 Q.B. 178, DC, the doctrine was extended to the case where the licensee was on the premises but had delegated the control of a particular bar to the barman. The barman's knowledge was imputed to the licensee. It is submitted that it is at least doubtful whether the House of Lords would approve of any extension of this doctrine to offences where it had not already been applied before the decision in *Vane v. Yiannopoullos*.

G. OFFENCES BY CORPORATIONS

17–30 (a) The question of which offences can be charged against corporations is considered in Chapter 1 (§§ 1–78 *et seq.*), *ante*. It is proposed now to consider for whose acts, intention, knowledge, etc., a corporation is held responsible. The authorities are mainly concerned with limited companies, but it is submitted that they will apply to all bodies corporate.

Where vicarious liability exists, the same principles apply as to the liability of a personal defendant for the acts of its servants, or its agents: see *ante*, §§ 17–25 *et seq.*

(b) The conventional view is that a company will have imputed to it the acts and state of mind of those of its directors and managers who represent its "directing mind and will": *Lennard's Carrying Co. v. Asiatic Petroleum Co.* [1915] A.C. 705; *Bolton (Engineering) Co. v. Graham* [1957] 1 Q.B. 159 (*per* Lord Denning M.R. at p. 172); *Tesco Supermarkets Ltd v. Nattrass* [1972] A.C. 153, HL. In *R. v. Andrews Weatherfoil Ltd*, 56 Cr.App.R. 31, CA, it was stated that it was not every "responsible agent" or "high executive" or "agent acting on behalf of the company" who could by his actions make the company criminally responsible; and that it was necessary for the judge to invite the jury to consider whether or not there were established those facts which the judge decided as a matter of law were necessary to identify the person concerned with the company.

17–31 (c) In *Meridian Global Funds Management Asia Ltd v. Securities Commission* [1995] 2 A.C. 500, PC, it was said that the question was one of construction rather than metaphysics. A company's rights and obligations are determined by rules whereby the acts of natural persons are attributed to the company; such rules are normally to be determined by reference to the primary rules of attribution generally contained in the company's constitution and implied by company law, and to general rules of agency. The company will appoint servants and agents whose acts, by a combination of the general principles of agency and the company's primary rules of attribution, count as the acts of the company. Having done so, it will also make itself subject to the general rules by which liability for the acts of others can be attributed to natural persons, such as vicarious liability in tort. The company's primary rules of attribution together with the general principles of agency and vicarious liability are usually sufficient to determine its rights and obligations. Exceptionally, they will not provide an answer: this will be the case when a rule of law excludes attribution on the basis of the general principles of agency or vicarious liability. Assuming that the rule of law is intended to apply to companies, one possibility is that the court might interpret the law as meaning that it could apply to a company only on the basis of its primary rules of attribution, *i.e.* if the act giving rise to liability was specifically authorised by a resolution of the board or unanimous agreement of the shareholders. But there will be many cases in which the court concludes that the law was intended to apply to companies and that, although it excludes ordinary vicarious liability, insistence on the primary rules of attribution would in practice defeat that intention. The court must, therefore, fashion a special rule of attribution for the particular substantive rule. This is a matter of interpretation: given that it was intended to apply, whose act (or knowledge or state of mind) was for this purpose intended to count as the act, etc., of the company? The answer is to be found by applying the usual canons of interpretation, taking into account the language of the rule (if it is a statute) and its content and policy. Often, the phrase "the directing mind and will" will be the most appropriate description of the person designated by the relevant attribution rule, but not every such rule had to be forced into the same formula.

The statute in question imposed a duty on any person acquiring a substantial shareholding in a "public issuer" to give certain notices; it was held on the true construction of the statute that the appropriate rule of attribution to be implied was that a corporate security holder knew that it was a substantial security holder in a public issuer when that was known to the person who had acquired the relevant interest with the company's authority, whereupon the company was obliged to give the relevant notice.

It is submitted that the principle expounded by the Privy Council coincides exactly **17–32**
with the statements of principle in *Mousell Bros Ltd v. London and North West Ry Co.* (*ante*, § 17–26), especially in the extract from the judgment of Atkin J. The only difference seems to be that the Divisional Court appears to have regarded the liability of the company as a form of vicarious liability, whereas the Privy Council clearly did not (no doubt because there was no primary liability in the employee). The result is the same.

(d) In the case of an offence involving proof of *mens rea*, it may be possible to combine **17–32a**
proof of the *actus reus* on the part of an employee of the corporation who would not form part of the controlling mind with proof of *mens rea* on the part of a person who does form part of the controlling mind. Thus, in *Information Commissioner v. Islington L.B.C.* [2003] L.G.R. 38, DC, it was held that on a prosecution of a local authority for an offence, contrary to section 5(5) of the *Data Protection Act* 1984 (*rep.*), of recklessly using data for a purpose other than the purpose or purposes described in the entry in the data protection register relating to the authority (the registration for that purpose having lapsed), the act of one of its employees in using data for an unauthorised purpose could be combined with the recklessness of the controlling minds of the authority as to the lack of registration, where there was evidence of such an act (but no evidence that the actor knew or was reckless as to the lapse of the registration) and of such recklessness (but no evidence that the controlling minds had any individual knowledge of the particular act).

(e) There is authority for the proposition that a corporation may be liable for the act **17–33**
of its servant even though that act was done in fraud of the corporation itself. Thus, in *Moore v. I. Bresler Ltd* [1944] 2 All E.R. 515, DC, the submission by officers of a company of false returns of goods sold (required for assessment of purchase tax) was held sufficient to render the company liable, although the returns had been made to

conceal from the company the fact that sales in fraud of the company had been made. The decision was cited with approval in *Meridian Global Funds Management Asia Ltd v. Securities Commission* (*ante*, *per* Lord Hoffman at p. 512); it provided "an example of an attribution rule for a particular purpose, tailored as it always must be to the terms and policies of the substantive rule". See also *R. v. St Margaret's Trust Ltd*, 42 Cr.App.R. 183, CCA.

II. SPECIFIC REQUIREMENTS AS TO STATE OF MIND

A. "WITH INTENT TO"

(1) General

17–34 The leading cases arise out of convictions for murder; the discussion of the law is in the context of the particular ingredients of that offence, but it is submitted that there is nothing in the decisions to suggest that the principles to be derived therefrom are not of general application. The cases in question are *R. v. Moloney* [1985] A.C. 905, HL, *R. v. Hancock and Shankland* [1986] A.C. 455, HL, *R. v. Nedrick*, 83 Cr.App.R. 267, CA, and *R. v. Woollin* [1999] 1 A.C. 82, HL (which must now be taken to be the leading authority). The following is a distillation of the essence of these authorities.

17–35 (a) When a judge is directing a jury upon the mental element necessary in a crime of specific intent (such as murder), he should avoid any elaboration or paraphrase of what is meant by intent, and leave it to the jury's good sense to decide whether the accused acted with the necessary intent.

(b) Foresight of the consequences which it must be proved that the accused intended (in murder, death or really serious bodily injury), is no more than evidence of the existence of the intent; it must be considered, and its weight assessed, together with all the evidence in the case. Foresight of consequences may be a fact from which the jury may think it right to infer the necessary intent.

(c) The probability of the result is an important matter for the jury to consider and can be critical in their determining whether the result was intended. It will only be necessary to direct the jury by reference to foresight of consequences if the judge is convinced that, on the facts and having regard to the way the case has been presented to the jury in evidence and argument, some further explanation is necessary to avoid misunderstanding.

(d) Where, exceptionally, it is insufficient to give the jury the simple direction that it is for them to decide whether the defendant intended to kill or do serious bodily harm, they should be told that they are not entitled to find the necessary intention, unless they feel sure that death or serious bodily harm was a virtual certainty (barring some unforeseen intervention) as a result of the defendant's actions and that the defendant appreciated that such was the case; they should always be told that the decision is theirs to be made on a consideration of the whole of the evidence.

(e) In appropriate cases, it will be necessary to explain to the jury that intent is something quite different from motive or desire.

If, in a case falling within paragraph (d), there is evidence that the defendant was under the influence of alcohol at the relevant time, the judge should deal with the question of the effect of the defendant's consumption of alcohol by telling the jury that this is relevant to the question whether the defendant appreciated that his actions were virtually certain to have the specified result: *R. v. Hayes* [2003] Crim.L.R. 48, CA.

(2) Proof of criminal intent

Criminal Justice Act 1967, s.8

Proof of criminal intent

17–36 **8.** A court or jury, in determining whether a person has committed an offence,

(a) shall not be bound in law to infer that he intended or foresaw a result of his actions by reason only of its being a natural and probable result of those actions; but

(b) shall decide whether he did intend or foresee that result by reference to all the evidence drawing such inferences from the evidence as appears proper in the circumstances.

All that this section did was to enact what many had thought to be the law before the decision of the House of Lords in *DPP v. Smith* [1961] A.C. 290, namely that there was no presumption of law that a man intended or foresaw the natural consequences of his acts. It has nothing to do with the substantive law, not laying down in what cases the establishment of guilt is dependent on proof of intention or foresight or any other mental state: see *DPP v. Majewski* [1977] A.C. 443, HL (*per* Lord Elwyn-Jones L.C. at p. 475, and Lord Edmund-Davies at p. 497).

(3) Particular offences

As a general proposition, it is submitted that wherever the definition of an offence requires proof of a specific intent, the approach of the court should be exactly as in murder (*ante*, §§ 17–34, 17–35) (reference should, however, be made to the treatment of particular offences for consideration of any authorities concerning the application of these principles to those offences). It is possible, however, that in a particular statutory provision the context may lead to a narrow interpretation of "intends", *e.g.* desires. This seems to be the explanation given by Lord Simon in *Lynch v. DPP for Northern Ireland* [1975] A.C. 653 at 699, HL, of the judgment in *R. v. Steane* [1947] K.B. 997, 32 Cr.App.R. 61, CCA. It is submitted, however, that the real issue in *R. v. Steane* should have been duress, and that some of the observations in the judgment are better explained by the maxim "hard cases make bad law". **17–37**

(4) Future and conditional intent

In *R. v. Bentham* [1973] Q.B. 357, 56 Cr.App.R. 618, the Court of Appeal held that on a charge of possessing a firearm with intent to endanger life contrary to section 16 of the *Firearms Act* 1968 (*post*, § 24–36), the prosecution are not required to prove an immediate or unconditional intention to endanger life. The mischief at which the section was aimed must be that of a person possessing a firearm ready for use, if and when the occasion arises, in a manner which endangers life. See also *R. v. Buckingham*, 63 Cr.App.R. 159, CA (having custody of an article intending to use it to damage property). **17–38**

In *Att.-Gen.'s References (Nos 1 and 2 of 1979)* [1980] Q.B. 180, 69 Cr.App.R. 266, CA, it was held, following *R. v. Walkington*, 68 Cr.App.R. 427, CA, and explaining *R. v. Hussein*, 67 Cr.App.R. 131, CA, that: (a) on a charge of burglary with intent to steal the accused is guilty if he intended to steal only if he found something in the building worth stealing; (b) on a charge of stealing or attempting to steal specific items the Crown must prove an intent to steal one or more of the items specified; (c) an intention to steal can exist even if, unknown to the accused, there is nothing to steal; and (d) the same principles apply whether the charge is burglary or attempted burglary, theft or attempted theft. See also *post*, §§ 21–80 *et seq.* **17–39**

It is submitted that the above principles apply in any case where intent has to be proved, but the case against the accused is that he was an accessory. This is implicit in the judgment of the Court of Appeal in *R. v. Becerra and Cooper*, 62 Cr.App.R. 212, a case of murder where the facts were that B supplied C with the weapon used. At page 216, the court made it clear that if B had supplied the weapon to C in order that, *if the necessity arose*, it could be used for the purpose of inflicting serious injury, B as well as C would be guilty of murder. As to the mental element in secondary parties generally, see *post*, §§ 17–67 *et seq.*; as to the liability of secondary parties in homicide, see also *post*, §§ 19–23 *et seq.*

(5) Crimes of "basic" intent

Where the definition of a crime relates intention not to a particular result of the proscribed conduct ("with intent to cause grievous bodily harm") or to a generalised purpose in the mind of the person doing the proscribed acts ("with intent to steal", "with intent to endanger life"), but to the *actus reus* itself ("intentionally touches" - see *SOA* 2003, s.3, *post*, § 20–29), this requires that the prohibited act be done deliberately; doing the **17–39a** act recklessly (let alone, accidentally) will not suffice: *R. v. Heard* [2007] 1 Cr.App.R. 37, CA. As to this case, see also *post*, § 20–34a. As to whether voluntary intoxication may serve to negative the *mens rea* of a crime of basic intent, see *post*, §§ 17–105 *et seq*.

(6) Jurisdiction

17–40 In general, it is immaterial whether the intention is to do something within or without the jurisdiction providing the intention existed at a time when the defendant was within the jurisdiction: see *ante*, §§ 2–34 *et seq*.

(7) Alternative intents: aiders and abettors

17–41 See *post*, §§ 17–71 *et seq*.

B. "ATTEMPTS TO"

17–42 As to what amounts to an attempt in the criminal law, see *post*, §§ 33–119 *et seq*. The mental element required to make a man guilty of an attempt to commit an offence is often, if not invariably, greater than that required for the full offence: see, for example, *R. v. Whybrow*, 35 Cr.App.R. 141, CCA (intent to kill necessary for attempted murder); *R. v. Mohan* [1976] Q.B. 1, 60 Cr.App.R. 272, CA (intent to cause bodily harm necessary for attempting to cause bodily harm by wanton driving).

C. "NEGLIGENTLY"

17–43 This standard is not found often in indictable offences without qualifying words. It occurs in manslaughter, but with such qualifications that it is clear that the standard of negligence required for manslaughter is peculiar to that crime: see *post*, §§ 19–108 *et seq*.

Manslaughter apart, the definition proposed in the Law Commission Working Paper No. 31 (*ante*, § 17–2), at p. 7, probably represents the existing law: "A person is negligent if he fails to exercise such care, skill or foresight as a reasonable man in his situation would exercise." It will be noted that the test is objective.

In indictable offences, the more usual provision is "by wilful neglect" or the like, *cf. CYPA* 1933, s.1 and *MHA* 1983, s.127. For "wilfully", see *post*, § 17–47.

D. "UNLAWFULLY"

17–44 This means without lawful justification or excuse, *e.g.* self-defence. Generations of judges have so directed juries upon a charge of murder (see *post*, §§ 19–1, 19–3), and upon charges of statutory offences where the word occurs. It is submitted that the observation of Hodgson J. in *Albert v. Lavin*, 72 Cr.App.R. 178, DC, that, "In defining a criminal offence the word 'unlawful' is tautologous and adds nothing to its essential ingredients", though following dicta in other cases, is misleading. It is, for example, an essential ingredient of the crime of murder that the killing, albeit accompanied by the necessary intent, was not, *e.g.* done in the course of reasonable self-defence. Hodgson J.'s dictum has since been disapproved in *R. v. Kimber*, 77 Cr.App.R. 225 at 229–230, CA, and *R. v. Williams (G.)*, 78 Cr.App.R. 276, CA, *ante*, §§ 17–13 *et seq.*

E. "MALICIOUSLY"

17–45 This word frequently occurs as part of the definition of a statutory offence. It means an actual intention to do the particular kind of harm that was in fact done, or recklessness as to whether such harm should occur (*i.e.* the accused has foreseen that the particular kind of harm might be done and yet has gone on to take the risk of it): it is neither limited to nor does it require any ill will towards the person injured: *R. v. Cunningham* [1957] 2 Q.B. 396, 41 Cr.App.R. 155, CCA. The harm foreseen need not be of the same degree as that prohibited: *R. v. Mowatt* [1968] 1 Q.B. 421, 51 Cr.App.R. 402, CA. Thus, on a charge of wounding, or inflicting grievous bodily harm, contrary to section 20 of the *Offences against the Person Act* 1861 (*post*, § 19–200), it is enough that the accused foresaw that some physical harm to some person, albeit of a minor character, might result from his action: *ibid.*; *R. v. Savage*; *DPP v. Parmenter* [1992] 1 A.C. 699, HL.

Where the word "maliciously" is combined with words requiring a specific intent, *e.g.* maliciously wounding with intent to cause grievous bodily harm, it will often be unnecessary to direct the jury as to the meaning of the word "maliciously", because it will be included in the words defining the specific intent. See *post*, § 19–211, as to circumstances in which a separate direction on "maliciously" may be required. **17–46**

Even where no specific intent is required, as in section 20 of the *Offences against the Person Act* 1861, it will often be unnecessary and perhaps confusing to direct the jury as to the meaning of the word "maliciously", *e.g.* where it is indisputable that the act, if done by the defendant, was done maliciously: see *Mowatt*, *ante*.

F. "WILFULLY"

The leading case is *R. v. Sheppard* [1981] A.C. 394, HL, in which the majority held that a man "wilfully" fails to provide adequate medical attention for a child if he *either* (a) deliberately does so, knowing that there is some risk that the child's health may suffer unless he receives such attention; *or* (b) does so because he does not care whether the child may be in need of medical treatment or not. **17–47**

The charge had been brought under section 1(1) of the *CYPA* 1933 (*post*, § 19–291). That section makes it an offence for certain persons "wilfully" to assault, ill-treat, neglect, abandon or expose a child under the age of 16 years, in a manner likely to cause him unnecessary suffering or injury to health. Subsection (2)(a) provides that certain persons (*e.g.* the child's parents) shall be deemed to have neglected the child in a manner likely to cause injury to his health if they have failed to provide adequate food, clothing, medical aid or lodging for him. Lord Diplock said:

> "The presence of the adverb 'wilfully' qualifying all five verbs 'assaults, ill-treats, neglects, abandons or exposes', makes it clear that any offence under section 1 requires *mens rea*, a state of mind on the part of the offender directed to the particular act or failure to act that constitutes the *actus reus* and warrants the description 'wilful'. The other four verbs refer to positive acts, 'neglect' refers to failure to act, and the judicial explanation of the state of mind denoted by the statutory expression 'wilfully' in relation to the doing of a positive act, is not necessarily wholly apt in relation to a failure to act at all" (at p. 403).

His Lordship then said that he would confine his observations to cases in the latter category. He did not, however, do so. He said:

> "In the context of doing to a child a positive act (assault, ill-treat, abandon or expose) that is likely to have specified consequences (to cause him unnecessary suffering or injury to health), 'wilfully', which must describe the state of mind of the actual doer of the act, may be capable of bearing the narrow meaning that the wilfulness required extends only to the doing of the physical act itself which in fact results in the consequences described, even though the doer thought that it would not and would not have acted as he did had he foreseen a risk that those consequences might follow. Although this is a possible meaning of 'wilfully', it is not the natural meaning even in relation to positive acts defined by reference to the consequences to which they are likely to give rise and, in the context of the section, if this were all the adverb 'wilfully' meant it would be otiose. Section 1(1) would have the same effect if it were omitted; for even in absolute offences (unless vicarious liability is involved) the physical act relied upon as constituting the offence, must be wilful in this limited sense, for which the synonym in the field of criminal liability that has now become the common term of legal art is 'voluntary'" (at p. 404).

Lord Keith, who was also in the majority, said that "wilfully" is a word which ordinarily carries a pejorative sense. **17–48**

> "It is used here to describe the mental element, which, in addition to the fact of neglect, must be proved. ... The primary meaning of 'wilful' is 'deliberate'. So a parent who knows that his child needs medical care and deliberately, that is by conscious decision, refrains from calling a doctor, is guilty under the subsection. As a matter of general principle, recklessness is to be equiparated with deliberation. A parent who fails to provide medical care which his child needs because he does not care whether it is needed or not is reckless of his child's welfare. He too is guilty of an offence. But a parent who has genuinely failed to appreciate that his child needs medical care, through personal inadequacy or stupidity or both, is not guilty" (at p. 418).

The majority, accordingly, equated "wilfully" with common law recklessness. In the absence of a specific decision on a specific statutory provision to the contrary, it is submitted that any provision containing the word "wilfully" in the definition of a crime should be construed in accordance with the approach in *Sheppard*.

Sheppard was applied by the Court of Appeal in *R. v. Gittins* [1982] R.T.R. 363 on a prosecution under section 36 of the *Malicious Damage Act* 1861 (wilful obstruction of railway): see further, *post*, § 23–60.

See also *Att.-Gen.'s Reference (No. 3 of 2003)* [2004] 2 Cr.App.R. 23, CA, where it was said that there was no material difference between *Sheppard* and *R. v. G.* [2004] 1 A.C. 1034, HL (now the leading case on recklessness), and in which it was said that "wilful" misconduct means deliberately doing something that is wrong, knowing it to be wrong, or with reckless indifference as to whether it is wrong or not; and *Willmott v. Atack* [1977] Q.B. 498, 63 Cr.App.R. 207, DC, in which it was held that in order to establish an offence against section 89(2) of the *Police Act* 1996 (wilful obstruction of a police officer in the execution of his duty), it is necessary to prove that the defendant so acted as to obstruct the constable in the execution of his duty and that he intended to do so. There must be something in the nature of a criminal intention and hostility towards the officer. It is not enough merely to show that the defendant intended to do what he did and that it did in fact have the result of the police being obstructed.

G. "KNOWINGLY"

17–49 Where this word is included in the definition of an offence it makes it plain that the doctrine of *mens rea* applies to that offence. However, its absence is no indication that the doctrine does not apply: see, *per* Lord Reid in *Sweet v. Parsley* [1970] A.C. 132 at 149, HL. It follows, therefore, that the Crown has to prove knowledge on the part of the offender of all the material circumstances of the offence. For example, on a charge of "knowingly having in his possession an explosive substance", the Crown must prove that the accused knew both that he had it in his possession and that it was an explosive substance: *R. v. Hallam* [1957] 1 Q.B. 569, 41 Cr.App.R. 111, CCA. The courts, however, have refused to apply this rule in relation to matters of exception from the definition of an offence. See *Brooks v. Mason* [1902] 2 K.B. 743, DC (knowingly selling liquors to minors except such as are sold in corked and sealed vessels: no defence though defendant genuinely thought vessels were corked and sealed).

There is some authority for the view that in the criminal law "knowledge" includes "wilfully shutting one's eyes to the truth": see, *e.g. per* Lord Reid in *Warner v. Metropolitan Police Commr* [1969] 2 A.C. 256 at 279, HL; *Atwal v. Massey*, 56 Cr.App.R. 6, DC; and *Flintshire C.C. Reynolds*, 170 J.P. 73, DC (constructive knowledge, *i.e.* having the means of knowledge, as where a person signed a form containing false information after it had been completed by another, is insufficient, but wilful blindness, *i.e.* deliberately refraining from making inquiries the results of which a person might not care to have, does equate to knowledge). However, such a proposition must be treated with caution. The alternative view is that this is a matter of evidence, and that nothing short of actual knowledge (or, in the case of dishonest handling, belief) will suffice. See the dictum of Lord Bridge in *Westminster City Council v. Croyalgrange Ltd*, 83 Cr.App.R. 155 at 164, HL ("… it is always open to the tribunal of fact … to base a finding of knowledge on evidence that the defendant had deliberately shut his eyes to the obvious or refrained from inquiry because he suspected the truth but did not wish to have his suspicion confirmed"), and the cases cited, *post*, §§ 21–310 *et seq*.

Where an Australian statutory offence of destroying evidence described the *mens rea* in terms of "knowing that any book, document or other thing … is or may be required in evidence", the use of the word "may" in the particular context indicated that "knowing" meant "believing": see *R. v. Ensbey* [2005] 1 Qd R. 159, Queensland Court of Appeal.

H. "SUSPECTS"

17–49a In *R. v. Da Silva* [2006] 2 Cr.App.R. 35, CA, it was held (i) that where the *mens rea* of an offence required suspicion on the part of the defendant as to the existence of a particular fact, a judge could not be criticised if he declined to define "suspicion" other than by saying that it was an ordinary English word and that the jury should apply their own understanding of it; but (ii) that the mere fact that a word is an "ordinary English word" within *Brutus v. Cozens* [1973] A.C. 854, HL, does not prevent a judge from providing assistance to the jury as to its meaning (*R. v. Gillard*, 87 Cr.App.R. 189, CA); (iii) that where such assistance is provided, in the absence of judicial authority, the dictionary definition would be likely to be an appropriate starting place; (iv) that in the context of the money laundering offences created by the *CJA* 1988, what was required was that the defendant had to have thought that there was a possibility, which was more than fanciful, that the relevant fact existed; and whilst a vague feeling of unease would not suffice, there was no requirement for the suspicion to be "clear" or "firmly grounded and targeted on specific facts", or based upon "reasonable grounds" (other than where there was a specific requirement of "reasonable grounds"); (v) that if a judge felt it appropriate to assist the jury with the word "suspecting", a direction along these lines would ordinarily be adequate; (vi) that a more careful direction may be required where there was reason to suppose that the defendant's suspicion was not of a settled nature, such as where he had entertained a suspicion (as defined) but, on further thought, had dismissed it from his mind as being outweighed by other considerations; and (vii) that use of words such as "inkling" or "fleeting thought" to explain the meaning of suspicion was liable to mislead; if they were to be used, they should ordinarily be combined with the more careful direction referred to in (vi).

I. "RECKLESSLY"

(1) Background

Prior to the decisions of the House of Lords in *R. v. Caldwell* [1982] A.C. 341 (criminal damage) and *R. v. Lawrence* [1982] A.C. 510 (reckless driving) the concept of recklessness in the criminal law was largely reflected in the judgment of the Court of Criminal Appeal in *Cunningham*, *ante*, § 17–45. **17–50**

In *Caldwell*, *Cunningham* was approved but distinguished on the basis that it was concerned with the word "maliciously" when used as a term of art in the description of an offence in the *Offences against the Person Act* 1861, and consequently had no bearing on the meaning of the word "reckless" in section 1 of the *Criminal Damage Act* 1971. In *Lawrence*, a case of causing death by reckless driving, the House followed their own decision in *Caldwell*, holding that *Caldwell* established that the adjective "reckless" when used in a criminal statute had not acquired a special meaning as a legal term of art, but bore its popular meaning of careless, regardless or heedless of the possible consequences of one's acts. The critical feature of these decisions was that a person could be held to be reckless with regard to a consequence even though he himself never foresaw the risk of it occurring, if the tribunal of fact concluded that the risk would have been obvious to the ordinary and prudent bystander.

The opinions expressed in both *Caldwell* (by the majority) and *Lawrence* on the meaning of "reckless" and "recklessly" were clearly intended to be of general application, save for its meaning in the definition of the word "maliciously" (*ante*, § 17–45), and were initially taken as such: see, in particular, *per* Lord Roskill in *R. v. Seymour (E.)* [1983] 2 A.C. 493 at 506, HL. The decisions were, however, the subject of intense criticism, both academic and judicial: see in particular, the dissenting speech of Lord Edmund-Davies in *Caldwell*. As the years passed, the Court of Appeal became increasingly resourceful in limiting their effect. The culmination of this process was the decision of the House of Lords in *R. v. G.* [2004] 1 A.C. 1034, when their Lordships had another opportunity to consider recklessness in the context of an allegation of criminal damage. The upshot was not only the unanimous overruling of *Caldwell*, but also the establishment of a fresh approach to recklessness, which reinstates *Cunningham*, and which may safely be taken to be a formulation of general application to the criminal law of England and Wales.

(2) Principle

In *R. v. G.*, *ante*, it was held that a person acts recklessly with respect to (i) a circumstance when he is aware of a risk that it exists or will exist, and (ii) a result when he is aware of a risk that it will occur, and it is in the circumstances known to him, **17–51** unreasonable to take the risk. *Caldwell*, *ante*, should not be followed, despite the fact that it had constituted the leading authority for over 20 years and had been applied on countless occasions; first, it was a salutary principle that conviction of serious crime should depend on proof not simply that the defendant caused, by act or omission, an injurious result to another but that his state of mind when so acting was culpable; whilst the most obvious culpable state of mind was an intention to cause an injurious result, knowing disregard of an appreciated and unacceptable risk of causing an injurious result or a deliberate closing of the mind to such a risk would be readily accepted as culpable also; but it was not clearly blameworthy to do something involving a risk of injury to another if, for reasons other than self-induced intoxication, one genuinely did not perceive the risk; secondly, the *Caldwell* formulation was capable of leading to injustice; thirdly, the criticism by academics, judges and practitioners of *Caldwell* was not to be ignored; and, fourthly, it was clear that the majority's interpretation of "reckless" in *Caldwell* had been a misinterpretation of Parliament's intention which had been to leave the essential law unchanged, whilst doing away with the outmoded and misleading use of the word "maliciously".

Whilst their Lordships' decision was in the context of a charge of criminal damage, there is no doubt about the fact that it will be taken to be of general application: see, for example, the decision of the Court of Appeal, considering "recklessness" in the offence of misconduct in a public office, in *Att.-Gen.'s Reference (No. 3 of 2003)* [2004] 2 Cr.App.R. 23.

R. v. G., *ante*, does not require the prosecution to prove that the defendant had foreseen an "obvious and significant" risk of the occurrence of a particular result as a consequence of his actions in order to establish recklessness in relation thereto; what was required was proof that he was aware of the risk and, in the circumstances known to him, it was unreasonable to take the risk; in directing a jury, there was no need for a judge to qualify the word "risk": *R. v. Brady* [2007] Crim.L.R. 564, CA.

(3) Recklessness and alcohol/ drugs

17–52 Notwithstanding the generality of the formulation of the test of recklessness in *R. v. G.*, *ante*, it is apparent that there was no intention to undermine the decision in *DPP v. Majewski* [1977] A.C. 443, HL, to the effect that failure to foresee a risk provides no defence where the failure results from self-induced intoxication. The basis of criminal liability in such cases was explained by Lord Elwyn-Jones L.C.:

> "If a man of his own volition takes a substance which causes him to cast off the restraints of reason and conscience, no wrong is done to him by holding him answerable criminally for any injury he may do while in that condition. His course of conduct in reducing himself by drugs and drink to that condition in my view supplies the evidence of *mens rea*, of guilty mind certainly sufficient for crimes of basic intent. It is a reckless course of conduct and recklessness is enough to constitute the necessary *mens rea* [in such cases]" (at pp. 474–475).

The application of the *Majewski* principle will be affected, however, by *R. v. G.* in that the question for the court in such a case will no longer be as to whether the risk would have been obvious to a sober and reasonable man in the position of the accused (*per* Lord Diplock in *Caldwell*, *ante*, at p.355); it will now be whether the accused would have been aware of the risk had he been sober. See also *R. v. Aitken*, 95 Cr.App.R. 304, Ct-MAC; *R. v. Richardson and Irwin* [1999] 1 Cr.App.R. 392, CA (cases decided after *Caldwell*, but prior to *G.*, but in which the objectivist approach of *Caldwell* had been rejected in respect of particular offences).

Where "the substance" taken is alcohol or a drug well known for being liable to cause unpredictability or aggressiveness, no problem arises. However, in cases where criminal damage or criminal violence to the person is alleged, it is wrong to proceed on the basis that the taking of *any* drug, which in fact brought about the behaviour complained of, itself establishes the ingredient of recklessness, see *R. v. Bailey*, 77 Cr.App.R. 76, CA, *post*, § 17–90, and *R. v. Hardie*, 80 Cr.App.R. 157, CA, *post*, § 17–105.

[The next paragraph is § 17–62.]

J. "WITH INTENT TO DEFRAUD" OR "FRAUDULENTLY"

17–62 (a) "To defraud" or to act "fraudulently" is dishonestly to prejudice or to take the risk of prejudicing another's right, knowing that you have no right to do so: *Welham v. DPP* [1961] A.C. 103, HL (and see now the ambit of the offence of fraud under the *Fraud Act* 2006, ss.1–4, *post*, §§ 21–356 *et seq.*). The word "dishonestly" is inserted in deference to opinions, mostly *obiter*, expressed in several cases (*e.g. R. v. Sinclair*, 52 Cr.App.R. 618, CA; *Wai Yu Tsang v. R.* [1992] 1 A.C. 269, PC). In the leading case of *Welham*, however, there is no mention of any need to tell the jury that they must be satisfied that the accused was acting dishonestly. It is submitted that the reason for this is that their Lordships considered it beyond argument that intentionally to take the risk of prejudicing another's right, knowing that there is no right to do so, is dishonest. In *Scott v. Metropolitan Police Commr* [1975] A.C. 819, HL, Lord Diplock suggested, *obiter*, that where the intended victim of a conspiracy to defraud is a private individual, the *purpose* of the conspirators must be to cause economic loss; this view is inconsistent with *Welham* and has been rejected by the Court of Appeal (*R. v. Alsop*, 64 Cr.App.R. 29) and the Privy Council (*Wai Yu Tsang v. R., ante*). In general, fraudulent conspirators neither desire nor foresee loss or injury to another; the fraud consists in taking the risk of injuring another's right which the accused know they have no right to take.

(b) It is not confined to a risk of possible injury resulting in economic loss, though **17–63** most cases do involve this: *Welham v. DPP*, *ante*; *Adams v. R.* [1995] 2 Cr.App.R. 295, PC. In *Scott*, *ante*, Lord Diplock also suggested, *obiter*, that where the intended victim of a conspiracy to defraud is a private individual, the risk must be of economic loss. It is submitted, however, that this is wrong as being inconsistent with *Welham* (see *per* Lord Radcliffe at p. 124, and *per* Lord Denning at p. 131) and with the *obiter* opinion of the remainder of their Lordships in *Scott* (see *per* Viscount Dilhorne at p. 839). Where, however, an allegation of conspiracy to defraud is based on economic loss, it is necessary for the prosecution to prove that the victim had a right or interest which was capable of being prejudiced either by actual loss or by being put at risk: *Adams v. R., ante*.

(c) Dishonestly to induce a person performing a public duty to act in a way which **17–64** would be contrary to his duty if he had known the true position is to risk injury to the right of the state, or the public authority as the case may be, to have that duty properly performed and amounts to an intent to defraud: *Welham v. DPP, ante*. For the practical application of this aspect of the principle, see *R. v. Terry* [1984] A.C. 374, HL (fraudulent use of vehicle excise licence contrary to the forerunner of the *Vehicle Excise and Registration Act* 1994, s.45) and *R. v. Moses and Ansbro* [1991] Crim.L.R. 617, CA (conspiracy to defraud).

(d) "Deceit" is not an essential ingredient of fraud *per se*: *Scott v. Metropolitan Police Commr, ante*.

(e) The fact that the accused put forward false evidence in order to substantiate a genuine claim does not negative an intent to defraud: *R. v. de Courcy*, July 10, 1964, CCA (unreported on this point). The court said that uttering to a court, or to any person, of a false document with intent that it be acted on as if it were true is extremely strong evidence of intent to defraud; the fact that it is done with the purpose of supporting a genuine claim is irrelevant.

K. "DISHONESTLY"

See *post*, §§ 21–2b, 21–2c, 21–23 and 21–24. **17–65**

L. "CAUSES"

The general rule applicable to a statutory offence of causing another person to do a **17–66** prohibited act is that the offence is only committed if the accused contemplated or desired that the act would ensue and it was done on his express or implied authority or as a result of him exercising control or influence over the other person: *Att.-Gen. of Hong Kong v. Tse Hung-lit* [1986] A.C. 876, PC.

Where a statute prohibits the causing of a particular result, the word "causes" imports neither knowledge nor negligence; it is to be given a common sense meaning: *Alphacell Ltd v. Woodward* [1972] A.C. 824, HL. Whether the defendant caused the prohibited result is a question of fact, the determination of which is dependent on the application of common sense. Refinements such as *causa causans*, effective cause or *novus actus* are to be avoided: *ibid*. It is clear that the act of the defendant need not be the only operative cause, but "mere tacit standing by and looking on" are insufficient to amount to causing: *ibid.*; *Price v. Cromack* [1975] 1 W.L.R. 988, DC; *Att.-Gen.'s Reference (No. 1 of 1994)* [1995] 1 W.L.R. 599, CA.

Where the defendant produced a situation in which there was the potential for the prohibited result to occur (the escape of noxious liquid from a tank maintained by him into controlled waters), but its actual occurrence depended on the act of a third party or a natural event, the question for the court was whether or not the act or event was in the general run of things a matter of ordinary occurrence, even if it was not foreseeable that it would happen to that particular defendant or take that particular form; the defendant's liability would only be negatived if the act or event could be regarded as something extraordinary; the distinction was one of fact and degree, to which common sense and local knowledge had to be applied; vandalism and terrorism provided examples of acts on either side of the line: *Environment Agency v. Empress Car Company (Abertillery) Ltd* [1999] 2 A.C. 22, HL. As to a burst tyre being an event in the ordinary run of things, see *Express Ltd (t/a Express Dairies Distribution) v. Environment Agency* [2003] 2 All E.R. 778, DC.

M. "PERMITS"

17–66a The meaning given to "permits" depends on its context. It may be confined to "allows" or "authorises", or it may be wider and embrace "fails to take reasonable steps to prevent". The narrow meaning will usually import knowledge, in the sense of knowledge of what is being allowed or authorised. In the normal way, a person cannot be said to allow a particular activity, still less authorise it, unless he is aware of the activity being carried on or expected to be carried on. Where the word is to be given its broader meaning, however, what has to be proved is a failure to match up to an objective standard, plus a causal link between that failure and the prohibited result; provided that the failure was deliberate in the sense that the omissions were deliberate and not due to honest mistake or accident, there is no need to prove subjective foresight of the prospect, or risk, of a contravention occurring: *Vehicle Inspectorate v. Nuttall* [1999] 1 W.L.R. 629, HL (considering *Roper v. Taylor's Central Garages (Exeter) Ltd* [1951] 2 T.L.R. 284, DC, *Browning v. J.W.H. Watson (Rochester) Ltd* [1953] 1 W.L.R. 1172, DC, *James & Son Ltd v. Smee* [1955] 1 Q.B. 78, DC, and *Grays Haulage Co. Ltd v. Arnold* [1966] 1 W.L.R. 534, DC). *Vehicle Inspectorate v. Nuttall* was followed and applied in *Yorkshire Traction Co. Ltd v. Vehicle Inspectorate* [2001] R.T.R. 34, DC.

III. MENTAL ELEMENT IN ACCESSORIES

A. INTENTION

17–67 The law in relation to the *mens rea* of accessories has developed considerably in recent years. The development has occurred particularly in the context of offences against the person: see *post*, §§ 19–23 *et seq*. It is clear now that no additional mental element beyond what is required for a principal is necessary to make a person guilty as an accessory (*Lynch v. DPP for Northern Ireland* [1975] A.C. 653, HL), and that, in one respect, a lesser mental element may suffice for an accessory than for a principal.

In *R. v. Powell*; *R. v. English* [1999] 1 A.C. 1, HL, it was held (following *Chan Wing-Siu v. R.* [1985] A.C. 168, PC), that a secondary party is guilty of murder if he participates in a joint venture realising (but without agreeing thereto) that in the course thereof the principal might use force with intent to kill or to cause grievous bodily harm, and the principal does so. The secondary party has lent himself to the enterprise and, by doing so, he has given assistance and encouragement to the principal in carrying out an enterprise which the secondary party realises may involve murder.

It is submitted that this should be the approach whenever it is alleged that the defendant is guilty as an aider and abettor (*i.e.* someone who assists the commission of the crime whether by the supply of the instrument by means of which the crime is facilitated or committed, by keeping watch at a distance from the actual commission of the crime, by active encouragement at the scene, or in any other way), whatever the crime alleged. To realise something might happen is to contemplate it as a real not a fanciful possibility: see *R. v. Roberts*, 96 Cr.App.R. 291, CA, *post*, § 19–29. Thus, if A supplies B with a jemmy realising that B may use it for the purposes of burglary, and B so uses it, A will be guilty of burglary, even though he had no idea what premises B intended to burgle. If B also uses it to inflict lethal violence on the occupier of the premises and does so with an intent to kill, A will only be guilty of murder if he contemplated such use of the jemmy as a real possibility.

On the basis of this analysis, it can be seen that it is somewhat misleading to say that the mental element required of an aider and abettor may be a lesser one than that required of the principal. It is by definition a different one; the aider and abettor in murder is never going to have an intention to kill. He may, of course, hope or desire that the principal does kill but what needs to be proved is an intention to render assistance to another in the realisation that that other may kill and do so deliberately or intending to inflict serious injury.

It is not necessary that, at the time of any act of assistance, the principal should have formed a settled intention to commit the crime; all that was necessary was that at the time of the act of assistance, the defendant foresaw as a real possibility that the principal would commit the crime: *R. v. Bryce* [2004] 2 Cr.App.R. 35, CA. Where the act of assistance was done in advance of the crime, which was committed in the defendant's absence, it must be proved that the act in fact assisted the later commission of the crime, that it was done deliberately, that the defendant realised that it was capable of assisting the commission of the offence, and foresaw its commission as a real possibility, and that when doing the act he intended to assist the principal in what he was doing: *ibid*. As to the avoidance of liability where this much is proved, see *post*, § 18–26.

In *R. v. Jefferson*, 99 Cr.App.R. 13, CA, it was held that the phrase "only if he **17–68**
intends ..." in section 6 of the *Public Order Act* 1986 (*post*, § 29–35) relates only to the *mens rea* that must be proved in a principal offender and does not exclude the existence of a common law offence of aiding and abetting an offence created by the 1986 Act.

Where the allegation is that the defendant "counselled" or "procured" the offence (giving those words their strict meaning), it seems that it is necessary to prove that the defendant intended that the offence or an offence of the same type should be committed: see *Ferguson v. Weaving* [1951] 1 K.B. 814 at 819, DC (*per* Lord Goddard C.J.); *Att.-Gen.'s Reference (No. 1 of 1975)* [1975] Q.B. 773, 61 Cr.App.R. 118, CA (*per* Lord Widgery C.J.); and *Blakely v. DPP* [1991] R.T.R. 405 at 415H, DC (*per* McCullough J.).

B. Knowledge of Circumstances

In *Johnson v. Youden* [1950] 1 K.B. 544, DC, Lord Goddard C.J. said: **17–69**

> "Before a person can be convicted of aiding and abetting the commission of an offence he must at least know the essential matters which constitute that offence. He need not actually know that an offence has been committed, because he may not know that the facts constitute an offence and ignorance of the law is not a defence. If a person knows all the facts and is assisting another person to do certain things, and it turns out that the doing of those things constitutes an offence, the person who is assisting is guilty of aiding and abetting that offence ..." (at pp. 546–547).

This statement was approved by the House of Lords in *Churchill v. Walton* [1967] 2 A.C. 224, and in *Maxwell v. DPP for Northern Ireland*, 68 Cr.App.R. 128, HL. It was also referred to in *Mok Wei Tak v. R.* [1990] 2 A.C. 333, PC, where a conviction was upheld for aiding and abetting an offence consisting of a course of conduct over a period of time. As a general proposition, any criminal offence may be the subject of aiding and abetting if the alleged aider and abettor knew the facts which constitute the principal offence and actively assisted or encouraged the principal offender: *ibid.*, at p. 344E.

C. Motive

The motive which the secondary party has for participating in the crime is irrelevant, **17–70** unless some special defence, such as duress, applies: *DPP for Northern Ireland v. Lynch* [1975] A.C. 653, HL. Similarly, it was held in *National Coal Board v. Gamble* [1959] 1 Q.B. 11, DC, that whilst evidence of an interest in the crime or of an express purpose to assist it may greatly strengthen the hand of the prosecution, an indifference to the result of the crime does not negative aiding and abetting. To hold otherwise would be to negative the rule that *mens rea* is a matter of intent only and does not depend on desire or motive.

As to a possible defence available to a police informer or police officer who participates in an offence which is already "laid on" for the sole purpose of bringing the principal offenders to justice, see *post*, § 18–25.

D. ALTERNATIVE INTENTS

(1) Principle

17–71 It is not necessary that an aider and abettor should know the precise crime that was intended and which in the event was committed. If he "realises" (see *R. v. Powell*; *R. v. English*, *ante*, § 17–67) or "contemplates" (see *Maxwell*, *post*, § 17–73) that one of a number of crimes may be committed, and one of those crimes is committed, his intention to assist the commission of any one of those crimes is sufficient *mens rea* for the crime actually committed. Similarly, where a person counsels or procures another to commit a particular type of offence and the other commits an offence of that type, the first person may be guilty of counselling or procuring its commission though he had no knowledge of the actual crime committed and no intention that the other should commit a particular offence, *e.g.* burgle a particular house.

(2) Target or victim unknown

17–72 Where a person supplies equipment to be used in the course of committing an offence of a particular type, he is guilty of aiding and abetting the commission of any such offence committed by the person to whom he supplies the equipment, providing (a) he knows the purpose to which the equipment is to be put or realises that there is a real possibility that the equipment will be used for that purpose, and (b) the equipment is actually used for the purpose; it matters not, however, that he has no knowledge of the particular premises to be burgled, victim to be murdered, etc.: *R. v. Bullock*, 38 Cr.App.R. 151, CCA; *R. v. Bainbridge* [1960] 1 Q.B. 129, 43 Cr.App.R. 194, CCA. In *Bullock*, the court left open the question whether a mere suspicion of the use to which the equipment is to be put would be sufficient to make the supplier liable: it is submitted that it would not and that the test is whether he foresaw the unlawful use as a real possibility: see *ante*, § 17–67, and *Blakely v. DPP* [1991] R.T.R. 405, DC.

See also *Thambiah v. R.* [1966] A.C. 37, PC, from which it is plain that one person may aid and abet another in the commission of an offence by helping to set the stage even before the victim has been found. If he helps the other in preparation for crimes of a certain nature, with the intention that the other shall commit crimes of that nature (or appreciating that there is a real possibility that he will do so), he may be said to aid and abet those crimes when they come to be committed.

(3) Offence unknown

17–73 In the leading case on this topic, *Maxwell v. DPP for Northern Ireland*, 68 Cr.App.R. 128, the House of Lords answered in the affirmative the question certified:

> "If the crime committed by the principal, and actually assisted by the accused, was one of a number of offences which the accused knew the principal would probably commit, was the guilty mind which must be proved against an accomplice thereby proved against the accused?"

Their Lordships approved *Bainbridge*, *ante*, and *Johnson v. Youden* [1950] 1 K.B. 544 (*ante*, § 17–69). The guilt of an accessory springs from the fact that he contemplates the commission of one or more of a number of crimes by the principal and he intentionally lends his assistance in order that such a crime will be committed. The relevant crime must be within the contemplation of the accomplice; only exceptionally would evidence be found to support an allegation that the accomplice had given the principal a complete blank cheque (see *per* Lord Scarman at p. 152).

IV. INSANITY AT TIME OF OFFENCE

A. Introduction

Every person of the age of discretion is, unless the contrary is proved, presumed by law to be sane, and to be accountable for his actions: *R. v. Layton* (1849) 4 Cox 149. Insanity at the time of the commission of the alleged offence is merely a particular situation where *mens rea* is lacking. It differs from other such situations in two respects (ignoring the defence of diminished responsibility which is peculiar to murder, see *post*, §§ 19–66 *et seq.*). **17–74**

(a) The onus is on the defence to establish such insanity on a balance of probabilities: *R. v. Smith (Oliver)*, 6 Cr.App.R. 19, CCA; *R. v. Carr-Briant* [1943] K.B. 607, 29 Cr.App.R. 76, CCA.

(b) The *Trial of Lunatics Act* 1883, s.2(1) (*ante*, § 4–468) provides for a special verdict of not guilty by reason of insanity. As to the powers of the court where there is such a verdict, see the *Criminal Procedure (Insanity) Act* 1964, s.5, *ante*, § 4–175. (The 1883 Act does not exclude the defence of insanity in summary proceedings: it is available as a defence, with no special verdict, to any offence where *mens rea* is an issue: *R. v. Horseferry Road Magistrates' Court, ex p. K.* [1996] 2 Cr.App.R. 574, DC; and *R. (Surat Singh) v. Stratford Magistrates' Court* [2008] 1 Cr.App.R. 2, DC (but see *ante*, § 5–897a as to the procedure to be followed where there is a possibility of a disposal under the *MHA* 1983, s.37(3))).

As the defence of insanity is based on the absence of *mens rea*, the mental condition recognised by the law as insanity for this purpose is not the same as insanity, or mental illness as recognised by medical science.

B. Hysterical Amnesia

The contention that hysterical amnesia covering the period of the events which are the subject of the indictment renders a man unfit to be tried was rejected in *R. v. Podola* [1960] 1 Q.B. 325, 43 Cr.App.R. 220, CCA. **17–75**

C. Who May Raise the Issue

In exceptional circumstances, a judge can of his own volition raise an issue of insanity and leave the issue to the jury provided there is evidence embracing all the relevant considerations in the *M'Naghten Rules* (see *post*). If a judge is minded to take such a course he must give counsel for the defence and for the prosecution the opportunity to call such evidence as they think necessary, even if that involves an adjournment of the trial. There is no precedent acknowledging the right of the prosecution to raise the issue of insanity, but where, on a charge of murder, the accused contends that at the time of the alleged offence he was suffering from diminished responsibility, the prosecution may adduce evidence tending to show that he was insane at the time so as not to be responsible according to law for his actions (*Criminal Procedure (Insanity) Act* 1964, s.6, *post*, § 19–79). If the prosecution have evidence of insanity they are obliged to make the evidence available to the defence: *R. v. Dickie*, 79 Cr.App.R. 213, CA. **17–76**

D. The Act or Omission Charged

Before the jury can return the special verdict, the prosecution must first prove beyond reasonable doubt that the defendant "did the act or made the omission charged" (see s.2(1) of the 1883 Act, *ante*, § 4–468). If they fail to prove this, the defendant is entitled to be acquitted *simpliciter* whether or not he was insane at the time of the alleged offence. The words "act or omission charged" refer only to the *actus reus* of the crime: *Att.-Gen.'s Reference (No. 3 of 1998)* [1999] 3 All E.R. 40, CA. **17–77**

E. M'NAGHTEN'S CASE (1843) 10 CL. & F. 200

(1) The answers of the judges

17–78 Owing to the difficulty in obtaining reports of this case, set out below are the questions to, and answers of, the judges. They have repeatedly been accepted as laying down the law of England as to insanity at the time of the alleged offence: *R. v. Holt*, 15 Cr.App.R. 10, CCA; *R. v. True*, 16 Cr.App.R. 164, CCA; *R. v. Windle* [1952] 2 Q.B. 826, 36 Cr.App.R. 85, CCA; *R. v. Sullivan* [1984] A.C. 156, HL; and see *Att.-Gen. (S. Australia) v. Brown* [1960] A.C. 432 at 449, PC.

Question 1

17–79 "What is the law respecting alleged crimes committed by persons afflicted with insane delusion in respect of one or more particular subjects or persons: as, for instance, where at the time of the commission of the alleged crime the accused knew he was acting contrary to law, but did the act complained of with a view, under the influence of insane delusion, of redressing or revenging some supposed grievance or injury, or of producing some public benefit?"

Answer

"Assuming that your lordships' inquiries are confined to those persons who labour under such partial delusions only, and are not in other respects insane, we are of opinion, that, notwithstanding the party did the act complained of with a view, under the influence of insane delusion, of redressing or revenging some supposed grievance or injury, or of producing some public benefit, he is nevertheless punishable, according to the nature of the crime committed, if he knew, at the time of committing such crime, that he was acting contrary to law, by which expression we understand your lordships to mean the law of the land."

Question 2

17–80 "What are the proper questions to be submitted to the jury when a person alleged to be afflicted with insane delusion respecting one or more particular subjects or persons, is charged with the commission of a crime (murder, for example), and insanity is set up as a defence?"

Question 3

"In what terms ought the question to be left to the jury as to the prisoner's state of mind at the time when the act was committed?"

Answers—to the second and third questions

"That the jury ought to be told in all cases that every man is presumed to be sane, and to possess a sufficient degree of reason to be responsible for his crimes, until the contrary be proved to their satisfaction; and that, *to establish a defence on the ground of insanity, it must be clearly proved that, at the time of the committing of the act, the party accused was labouring under such a defect of reason, from disease of the mind, as not to know the nature and quality of the act he was doing, or, if he did know it, that he did not know he was doing what was wrong*. The mode of putting the latter part of the question to the jury on these occasions has generally been, whether the accused, at the time *of doing the act, knew the difference between right and wrong*, which mode, though rarely, if ever, leading to any mistake with the jury, is not, as we conceive, so accurate when put generally, and in the abstract, as when put as to the party's knowledge of right and wrong in respect to the very act with which he is charged. If the question were to be put as to the knowledge of the accused, solely and exclusively with reference to the law of the land, it might tend to confound the jury, by inducing them to believe that an actual knowledge of the law of the land was essential in order to lead to a conviction, whereas the law is administered upon the principle that every one must be taken conclusively to know it without proof that he does know it. If the accused was conscious that the act was one which he ought not to do, and if that act was at the same time contrary to the law of the land, he is punishable; and the usual course, therefore, has been to leave the question to the jury, whether the party accused had a sufficient degree of reason to know that he was doing an act that was wrong: and this course, we think, is correct, accompanied with such observations and explanations as the circumstances of each particular case may require."

The answer to questions 2 and 3 (*i.e.* the answer which contains the "insanity test") was considered by the House of Lords in *R. v. Sullivan* [1984] A.C. 156, HL (*post*, § 17–91).

Question 4

17–81 "If a person under an insane delusion as to the existing facts commits an offence in consequence thereof, is he thereby excused?"

Answer

"The answer must, of course, depend on the nature of the delusion; but making the same assumption as we did before, that he labours under such partial delusion only, and is not in other respects insane, we think he must be considered in the same situation as to responsibility as if the facts with respect to which the delusion exists were real. For example, if, under the influence of his delusion, he supposes another man to be in the act of attempting to take away his life, and he kills that man, as he supposes in self-defence, he would be exempted from punishment. If his delusion was that the deceased had inflicted a serious injury to his character and fortune, and he killed him in revenge for such supposed injury, he would be liable to punishment." (See *R. v. Townley* (1863) 3 F. & F. 839.)

Question 5

"Can a medical man, conversant with the disease of insanity, who never saw the prisoner previously to the trial, but who was present during the whole trial, and the examination of all the witnesses, be asked his opinion as to the state of the prisoner's mind at the time of the commission of the alleged crime, or his opinion whether the prisoner was conscious, at the time of doing the act, that he was acting contrary to law, or whether he was labouring under any and what delusion at the time?" **17–82**

Answer

"We think the medical man, under the circumstances supposed, cannot in strictness be asked his opinion in the terms above stated, because each of those questions involves the determination of the truth of the facts deposed to, which it is for the jury to decide: and the questions are not mere questions upon a matter of science, in which case such evidence is admissible. But where the facts are admitted or not disputed, and the question becomes substantially one of science only, it may be convenient to allow the question to be put in that general form, though the same cannot be insisted on as a matter of right."

(2) Delusions

Although questions 1 and 2 are concerned with persons suffering from insane delusions, it is clear that the answer to questions 2 and 3 applies whenever the defence of insanity at the time of the alleged offence is raised, whether or not the evidence indicates that the defendant suffered from delusions: *R. v. Windle* [1952] 2 Q.B. 826, 36 Cr.App.R. 85, CCA; *R. v. Sullivan* [1984] A.C. 156, HL (*post*, § 17–91). **17–83**

(3) The "nature and quality of the act"

These words (answer to questions 2 and 3) refer to the physical, not the moral, character of the act: *R. v. Codere*, 12 Cr.App.R. 21, CCA. **17–83a**

(4) Knowledge that act was wrong

The defence must establish that the defendant did not know that his act was unlawful: see the answer to the second and third questions and *R. v. Windle* [1952] 2 Q.B. 826, 36 Cr.App.R. 85, CCA; and *R. v. Johnson* [2008] Crim.L.R. 132, CA. The judgment in *Windle* is in terms which suggest that knowledge of illegality is the sole criterion. This would mean that a defendant who proved that he did not know that his act was unlawful, but who knew that his act was regarded as morally wrong by the bulk of mankind was entitled to succeed in his defence. This was not the point that fell for decision in *Windle*, and it is submitted that such conclusion is inconsistent with the tenor of the answer to the second and third questions and with observations of the court in *Codere*, *ante*. It is submitted that the defence should fail if the defendant knew either that his act was unlawful or that it was morally wrong according to the standards of ordinary people. **17–83b**

(5) "Disease of the mind"

See *post*, §§ 17–84 *et seq.* **17–83c**

F. INSANITY OR AUTOMATISM?

(1) Principle

The phrase "disease of the mind" has given rise to difficulties in interpretation where **17–84** the defence of "automatism" is raised, *i.e.* lack of *mens rea* due to some failure of the mind *not* due to disease. Before the question of "automatism" can be left to the jury, a proper foundation for such a defence must have been laid: *Hill v. Baxter* [1958] 1 Q.B. 277, 42 Cr.App.R. 51, DC; *Broome v. Perkins*, 85 Cr.App.R. 321, DC; *R. v. Burgess* [1991] 2 Q.B. 92, 93 Cr.App.R. 41, CA. Once such evidence exists, it is for the prosecution to negative it by proving that the defendant's acts were voluntary in the sense that they were committed when he was fully conscious: *R. v. Stripp*, 69 Cr.App.R. 318, CA (the words "fully conscious" must be read in the light of *R. v. Sullivan, post*, § 17–91). See also *Bratty v. Att.-Gen. for Northern Ireland*: *post*, § 17–86. The position is the same as when the issue of self-defence is raised: see *post*, § 19–43. There must be evidence, whether from the prosecution or the defence, fit to be considered by the jury on that issue.

The question of "automatism" is often raised in driving cases—see *Hill v. Baxter, ante*; *Watmore v. Jenkins* [1962] 2 Q.B. 572, DC; *Broome v. Perkins, ante*; and *Att.-Gen.'s Reference (No. 2 of 1992)*, 97 Cr.App.R. 429, CA: *post*, § 17–95. The term "automatism" connotes no wider or looser a concept than an involuntary movement of the body or limbs of a person. Whether there is evidence of a state of automatism is a question of law. If there is such evidence, the prosecution must exclude it as an explanation for what was done beyond any reasonable doubt—see the authorities cited, *ante*. "I do not doubt that there are genuine cases of automatism, but I do not see how the layman can safely attempt without the help of some medical or scientific evidence to distinguish the genuine from the fraudulent", *per* Devlin J. in *Hill v. Baxter, ante*.

(2) Authorities

(a) *R. v. Kemp [1957] 1 Q.B. 399, 40 Cr.App.R. 121, Assizes (Devlin J.) (insanity: arteriosclerosis)*

17–85 The defendant was indicted with causing grievous bodily harm with intent. He suffered from arteriosclerosis. It was common ground that by reason of the disease he lacked *mens rea*, though the medical witnesses differed as to whether the illness could properly be called a disease of the mind. The defendant raised the defence of "automatism", asking for a simple acquittal on the grounds that he was not suffering from a disease of the mind. Devlin J. ruled as a matter of law that whichever medical evidence was accepted by the jury it would still show that the defendant had a disease of the mind for the purposes of the criminal law.

> "In my judgment, the words ... are not to be construed as if they were put in for the purpose of distinguishing between diseases which have a mental origin and diseases which have a physical origin .... They were put in for the purpose of limiting the effect of the words 'defect of reason'. A defect of reason is by itself enough to make the act irrational and therefore normally to exclude responsibility in law. But the Rule was not intended to apply to defects of reason caused simply by brutish stupidity without rational power... . The words ensure that unless the defect is due to a diseased mind and not simply to an untrained one there is insanity within the meaning of the Rule. Hardening of the arteries is a disease which is shown on the evidence to be capable of affecting the mind in such a way as to cause a defect, temporarily or permanently, of its reasoning, understanding and so on ... and so is a disease of the mind ... within the meaning of the Rules" (at pp. 408, 127).

This ruling was approved by Lord Denning in *Bratty's case, post*. He disapproved of the ruling of Barry J. in *R. v. Charlson*, 39 Cr.App.R. 37, Assizes, to the effect that epilepsy or brain tumour were not diseases of the mind, even though they led to violent and irrational action.

(b) *Bratty v. Att.-Gen. for Northern Ireland [1963] A.C. 386, HL (insanity: psychomotor epilepsy)*

17–86 The charge was murder. The defence called medical evidence to the effect that the appellant suffered at the time from psychomotor epilepsy, and hence lacked *mens rea*. The judge's ruling that this was a defence of insanity and that there was no evidence to go to the jury of automatism due to some cause other than a disease of the mind was upheld by the House of Lords. The majority of their Lordships expressed the view *obiter*, that sleepwalking (but see *R. v. Burgess*, *post*, § 17–94) and concussion were examples of automatism and were not due to disease of the mind. The majority also expressed the *obiter* opinion that, while in relation to the issue of insanity the onus is on the defence to prove insanity on a balance of probabilities, where the issue is automatism not due to a disease of the mind, the onus is on the prosecution to negative automatism beyond reasonable doubt. This view has been accepted by the Court of Appeal in later cases, see, *e.g. R. v. Burns*, *post*, § 17–89.

(c) *R. v. Quick [1973] Q.B. 910, 57 Cr.App.R. 722, CA (automatism: hypoglycaemia)*

The accused raised the defence of automatism by reason of an imbalance of insulin which as a diabetic he was taking on prescription. The trial judge, purporting to follow *Bratty*, *ante*, ruled that this amounted to a defence of insanity, whereupon the appellant pleaded guilty. The Court of Appeal held that the alternative of automatism should have been left to the jury. **17–87**

The court reviewed a number of English and Commonwealth authorities.

> "In this quagmire of law, seldom entered nowadays save by those in desperate need of some kind of defence, *Bratty* … provides the only firm ground. Is there any discernible path? We think there is. Judges should follow in a common-sense way their sense of fairness. This seems to have been the approach … in *Cottle* [1958] N.Z.L.R. 999 and … *Carter* (1959) Vict. R. 105 [each reviewed in *Quick* at pp. 920–921, 731–732]. In our judgment, no help can be obtained by speculating … as to what the judges who answered the House of Lords questions in 1843 meant by disease of the mind…. Our task has been to decide what the law means now by the words 'disease of the mind'. In our judgment, the fundamental concept is of a malfunctioning of the mind caused by disease. A malfunctioning of the mind of transitory effect caused by the application to the body of some external factor such as violence, drugs, including anaesthetics, alcohol and hypnotic influences cannot fairly be said to be due to disease. Such malfunctioning, unlike that caused by a defect of reason from disease of the mind, will not always relieve an accused from criminal responsibility. A self induced incapacity will not excuse (see *Lipman* [1970] 1 Q.B. 152, (1969) 53 Cr.App.R. 600), nor will one which could have been reasonably foreseen as a result of either doing, or omitting to do something, as, for example, taking alcohol against medical advice after using certain prescribed drugs, or failing to have regular meals whilst taking insulin. From time to time difficult border line cases are likely to arise. When they do, the test suggested … in *Cottle* (*supra*) is likely to give the correct result, *viz.* can this mental condition be fairly regarded as amounting to or producing a defect of reason from disease of the mind?" (at pp. 922, 734–735).

Dealing with the instant case, the court held:

> "Quick's alleged mental condition, if it ever existed, was not caused by his diabetes, but by his use of the insulin prescribed by his doctor. Such malfunctioning of his mind as there was was caused by an external factor and not by a bodily disorder in the nature of a disease which disturbed the working of his mind. It follows, in our judgment, that Quick was entitled to have his defence of automatism left to the jury … ."

As to self-induced incapacity, see *post*, §§ 17–105 *et seq*. As to the limitations on the defence where a diabetic claims to have been driving in a state of automatism, see also *R. v. C.*, unreported, May 23, 2007, CA ([2007] EWCA Crim. 1862) (*post*, § 32–22).

(d) *R. v. Clarke, 56 Cr.App.R. 225, CA*

In this case, decided before *R. v. Quick* (*ante*), but not referred to in the judgment therein, though cited to the court, the appellant was charged with shoplifting. She said that she put the goods into her bag in a fit of absent-mindedness when suffering from a depression, which a doctor described as a "minor mental illness". The judge ruled that this must be treated as a defence of insanity, whereupon she changed her plea to "guilty". The Court of Appeal in quashing the conviction said that the *M'Naghten Rules* did not apply to a momentary failure to concentrate. **17–88**

(e) *R. v. Burns, 58 Cr.App.R. 364, CA*

The appellant was convicted of indecent assault. A psychiatrist gave evidence that the appellant had a history of clinical alcoholism and periods of amnesia, both in the **17–89** ordinary sense of not remembering past events, and "in the sense that the thing does not register at the time because the brain function is impaired at the time". Asked about the appellant's probable condition at the time of the alleged offence, he said that he had probably taken a quantity of alcohol, possibly made much worse by a quantity of Mandrax, and his state was such that he was not aware of himself. He later said that he thought that the appellant was not able to have knowledge of what he was doing or that it was wrong. Later still, he said that the appellant had brain damage which needed in addition drink or drugs to cause him to "act in that way".

The Court of Appeal delivered a reserved judgment which appears to say that the trial judge did not leave the issue of automatism to the jury as a separate issue from insanity, because he considered that, as in *Bratty's case*, *ante*, the doctor's evidence showed that automatism, if it had occurred, must have been due to a disease of the mind. The court considered that in view of *R. v. Quick*, *ante*, automatism should have been left as a separate issue, because there was some evidence "of other factors operating upon a disease of the appellant's mind" (apparently the consumption of alcohol or Mandrax) "and of the possibility that the appellant did not appreciate the effect which they might have had".

While recognising that the onus was on the defence to prove insanity on a balance of probabilities, and on the prosecution to negative automatism not due to disease of the mind beyond reasonable doubt, the court dismissed the appeal on the ground that as the jury must have rejected the doctor's evidence on the issue of insanity they would have rejected it as readily on the issue of automatism if that issue had been left to them. It is submitted that this conclusion fails to take into account the difference in onus and standard of proof on the two issues.

(f) *R. v. Bailey, 77 Cr.App.R. 76, CA (automatism: hypoglycaemia)*

17–90 The extent to which the defence of automatism is available where the conduct in question occurred at a time when the defendant was suffering from hypoglycaemia resulting from a failure to take food after taking insulin, was further considered in this case. B was charged with wounding with intent and unlawful wounding in the alternative. He was convicted of wounding with intent, the judge having directed the jury that automatism was not available as a defence because his incapacity was self-induced. In holding that direction to be wrong, the court observed (applying *DPP v. Majewski* [1977] A.C. 443, *post*, § 17–107) that even if the incapacity of mind is self-induced by the voluntary taking of drugs or alcohol, in offences (such as this), involving a specific intent, the intent may thereby be negatived. In considering the position under section 20 (unlawful wounding), a crime of basic intent, the court observed that automatism resulting from intoxication due to voluntary ingestion of alcohol or dangerous drugs does not negative the *mens rea* necessary because the conduct of the accused is reckless and recklessness is enough to constitute the necessary *mens rea* in assault cases where no specific intent is involved: see *Majewski*. However, self-induced automatism *other than* that due to intoxication from alcohol or drugs may provide a defence to crimes of basic intent. The question in each case will be whether the prosecution has proved the necessary element of recklessness. In cases of assault, if the accused knows that his actions or inaction are likely to make him aggressive, unpredictable or uncontrolled with the result that he may cause some injury to others and he persists in the action or takes no remedial action when he knows it is required, it will be open to the jury to find that he was reckless. Accordingly, if a diabetic who fails to take food after insulin does appreciate the risk that such a failure may lead to aggressive, unpredictable and uncontrollable conduct and he nevertheless deliberately runs the risk or otherwise disregards it, that will amount to recklessness.

(g) *R. v. Sullivan [1984] A.C. 156, HL (insanity: psychomotor epilepsy)*

17–91 This establishes a number of points.

(a) As to the application of the *M'Naghten Rules* to all cases of alleged insanity, see *ante*, § 17–83.

(b) Although the nomenclature adopted by the medical profession may change from time to time, the meaning of the expression "disease of the mind" as the cause of a defect of reason remains unchanged for the purposes of the application of the *M'Naghten Rules*. The word "mind" is used in the ordinary sense of the mental faculties of reason, memory and understanding: see *R. v. Kemp*, *ante*, § 17–85 (at pp. 407, 128). If the effect of a disease is to impair those faculties so severely as to have either of the consequences referred to in the latter part of the answer, it matters not whether the aetiology of the impairment is organic (as in epilepsy) or functional or whether the impairment itself is permanent or is transient and intermittent, provided that it subsisted at the time of the commission of the act. The purpose of the legislation relating to the defence of insanity has been to protect society against a recurrence of dangerous conduct. Accordingly, the duration of a temporary suspension of the mental faculties of reason, memory and understanding (particularly if it is recurrent) cannot be relevant to the application by the courts of the *M'Naghten Rules*, though it may be relevant to the course adopted by the Secretary of State.

(c) Devlin J.'s ruling in *Kemp* should not be regarded (as it was in *Quick*) as exclud- **17–92** ing the possibility of non-insane automatism (for which the proper verdict would be a verdict of not guilty) in cases where temporary impairment, not being self-induced by consuming drink or drugs, results from some external physical factor such as a blow on the head causing concussion or the administration of an anaesthetic for therapeutic purposes. As to this, see also *R. v. Bailey*, *ante*, § 17–90.

(d) The *ratio decidendi* of the dismissal of the appeal in *Bratty* was that the jury having negatived the explanation that *Bratty* might have been acting unconsciously in the course of an attack of psychomotor epilepsy, there was no evidential foundation for the suggestion that he was acting unconsciously from any other cause. Accordingly, once the jury had rejected insanity, the judge was correct in refusing to leave automatism to them—the suggested basis of the automatism being the same as for the defence of insanity, namely psychomotor epilepsy. The House of Lords rejected the suggestion that *Sullivan* could be distinguished from *Bratty* on the ground that the medical evidence in *Sullivan* was that epilepsy was not regarded as a disease of the mind, whereas in *Bratty* the point was not argued, it being accepted by all the doctors that it was—see further, proposition (b) above.

(h) *R. v. Hennessy, 89 Cr.App.R. 10, CA (automatism: hyperglycaemia)*

The appellant was an insulin-dependent diabetic: the offences with which he was **17–93** charged were committed at a time when he had not taken insulin and had not eaten for several days. He was in a hyperglycaemic state (high blood sugar, in contrast to *Quick*, *ante*, § 17–87, where the low blood sugar level was caused by the injection of insulin), therefore, which it was said was caused or, at least, contributed to by stress, anxiety and depression. The trial judge ruled that the appellant's alleged state of mind was caused by disease, namely, diabetes, that he had no defence of automatism and that it was a case of legal "insanity" within the *M'Naghten Rules*. The Court of Appeal considered various authorities, including, in particular *R. v. Quick* and *R. v. Sullivan*, *ante*. It dismissed the appeal on the basis that external factors could result in stress, anxiety and depression, but that they were not in themselves, separately or together, external factors of the kind capable in law of causing or contributing to a state of automatism, for they constituted a state of mind prone to recur and lacking the features of novelty or accident which were the basis of the distinction drawn by Lord Diplock in *Sullivan*: *ante*, § 17–92(c). See also the observations of Devlin J. in *Hill v. Baxter* [1958] 1 Q.B. 277 at 285, 42 Cr.App.R. 51 at 60, DC.

(i) *R. v. Burgess, 93 Cr.App.R. 41, CA (sleepwalking)*

The defence to a charge contrary to section 18 of the *Offences against the Person* **17–94** *Act* 1861 was non-insane automatism, in that the violence was committed whilst sleepwalking. Expert medical evidence was called by both sides. The trial judge ruled that the medical evidence adduced concerning automatism amounted to evidence of insanity within the *M'Naghten Rules*. On appeal, it was held that, on a defence of automatism, the judge had to decide, first, whether a proper evidential foundation had been laid for the defence and, secondly, whether the evidence showed the case to be one of insane automatism within the *M'Naghten Rules*, or one of non-insane automatism. It was further held that the judge had undertaken that task and had correctly concluded that the appellant's state was an abnormality or disorder which, albeit transitory and unlikely to recur in the form of serious violence, was due to an internal factor, whether functional or organic, which had manifested itself in violence and might recur, and, therefore, amounted to a "disease of the mind". The court said that a danger of recurrence of a mental disorder manifesting itself in violence may be an added reason for categorising the condition as a disease of the mind but the absence of such danger is not a reason for saying that it cannot be such a disease.

(j) *Att.-Gen.'s Reference (No. 2 of 1992), 97 Cr.App.R. 429, CA ("driving without awareness")*

17–95 The respondent to the reference had been charged with causing death by reckless driving. His defence was non-insane automatism. In support thereof, an expert psychologist was called. He described a condition known as "driving without awareness". The expert acknowledged that this was not a scientific term, but a provisional or interim descriptive phrase coined at a conference he had attended. He said that there were two essential components to the act of driving, namely collision avoidance and steering within highway lanes. In a state of driving without awareness, the driver's capacity to avoid a collision ceased to exist because repetitive stimuli experienced on long journeys on straight, flat and featureless motorways could induce a trance-like state in which the focal point for forward vision gradually came nearer and nearer until the driver was focusing just ahead of his windscreen. He, therefore, failed to see further ahead in the central field of vision. However, peripheral vision continued to send signals which were dealt with subconsciously and enabled the driver to steer within highway lanes. The condition could occur insidiously without the driver being aware that it was happening. A driver would usually "snap out" of the condition in response to major stimuli, such as flashing lights, appearing in front of him.

The Court of Appeal said that the reference raised the first of the two issues identified in *Burgess*, *ante*, namely whether a proper evidential foundation had been laid for the defence of automatism. It was held that it had not been, and that, therefore, the judge had been wrong to leave it to the jury as an issue. The authorities showed that the defence of automatism required that there was a total destruction of voluntary control on the defendant's part. Impaired or reduced control was not enough. As the witness had accepted, someone driving without awareness within his description retained some control. He would be able to steer the vehicle and usually to react and return to full awareness when confronted by significant stimuli.

(k) *R. v. Roach [2002] 3 Archbold News 1, CA*

17–96 Here, it was held, in reliance on *Quick*, *ante*, § 17–87, and *Burns*, *ante*, § 17–89, that the legal definition of automatism allows that if external factors (taking of prescription drugs and drink) are operative on an underlying condition ("mixed personality disorder"), which would not otherwise produce a state of automatism, then the defence should be left to the jury.

[The next paragraph is § 17–98.]

G. UNCONTROLLABLE IMPULSE

17–98 If the defence fail to prove insanity as laid down by the answers of the judges in *M'Naghten's case*, proof of insanity short of this will not suffice. In particular, evidence that the defendant acted under uncontrollable impulse will not suffice: *R. v. Kopsch*, 19 Cr.App.R. 50, CCA; *Sodeman v. R.* [1936] 2 All E.R. 1138, PC; *Att.-Gen. for South*

Australia v. Brown [1960] A.C. 432. In the last case, the Privy Council said that it was wrong to direct a jury that evidence of uncontrollable impulse may afford strong grounds for the inference that the defendant was labouring under such a defect of reason from disease of the mind as not to know that he was doing what was wrong, regardless of the medical evidence or the absence of such evidence.

H. MEDICAL AND OTHER EVIDENCE

The opinion of an expert is admissible to furnish the court with scientific information which is likely to be outside the experience and knowledge of a judge or jury: *R. v. Turner (T.)* [1975] Q.B. 834, 60 Cr.App.R. 80, CA. It follows that whenever there is an issue as to the sanity of the accused, expert evidence will be admissible. Indeed, such evidence is now a pre-requisite of an acquittal on the ground of insanity. Section 1(1) of the *Criminal Procedure (Insanity and Unfitness to Plead) Act* 1991 (*ante*, § 4–469) stipulates that such a verdict shall not be returned except on the evidence of two registered medical practitioners, at least one of whom is "duly approved": see section 6(1) of the 1991 Act, *ante*, § 4–177. As to the admissibility of evidence of an expert who has not examined the accused, see the answer to the fifth question in *M'Naghten's case* (*ante*, § 17–82). The rule prohibiting an expert from giving his opinion on the ultimate issue (long honoured more in the breach than in the observance) was finally laid to rest in *R. v. Stockwell*, 97 Cr.App.R. 260, CA. **17–99**

The cases which give rise to difficulty are those in which the defence seek to call an expert not to establish insanity (or diminished responsibility), but to raise a doubt about the accused having had the necessary *mens rea* of the offence charged, or about his ability to form the necessary *mens rea*, usually an intention to do something or to bring about a result. The test of admissibility is the same, but its application in practice may lead to fine distinctions. The authorities are considered at §§ 4–326 *et seq.*, *ante*. A suggestion (based on *R. v. Toner*, 93 Cr.App.R. 382, *ante*, § 4–327) in the 2005 edition of this work that the attitude of the Court of Appeal had been somewhat relaxed over the last 25 years was rejected in *R. v. Henry* [2006] 1 Cr.App.R. 6, CA, save in relation to confession evidence. The court pointed out that *Toner* concerned the possible effect of hypoglycaemia on the formation of intention, and not of mental defects *per se*. Accordingly, it was held that evidence that the appellant was "borderline mental defective" with an I.Q. of 71 had not been admissible at his trial for murder on the issue of intent.

Medical evidence apart, the words and actions of the defendant, both contemporary to the alleged offence and prior thereto, will be relevant to this issue: see *Att.-Gen. for South Australia v. Brown* (*ante*), at pp. 452 and 454 (the suggestion that such evidence alone may suffice has been overtaken by the 1991 Act, *ante*). It is submitted that, in principle, subsequent acts and words should also be relevant for this purpose. See also *R. v. Dart* (1878) 14 Cox 143; *R. v. Rivett*, 34 Cr.App.R. 87, CCA. **17–100**

Counsel will not be allowed, upon a question of insanity, to quote in his address to the jury the opinions of medical writers as expressed in their books: *R. v. Taylor* (1874) 13 Cox 77. *Aliter*, if the writings have been adopted by an expert who has given evidence.

The onus of establishing insanity on the balance of probabilities lies upon the defendant (*ante*, § 17–74). The procedure that the defence should call any witness whose evidence is directed to that issue should be strictly followed, the duty of the prosecution being limited to supplying the defence with a copy of any report or statement of any prison medical officer who can give evidence on that issue and to making such person available as a witness for the defence: *R. v. Casey*, 32 Cr.App.R. 91, CCA. Where evidence to establish insanity has been called for the defence, the prosecution may call rebutting evidence: *R. v. Smith (Gilbert)*, 8 Cr.App.R. 72, CCA. And where it is clear from the cross-examination of witnesses for the prosecution that the defence of insanity will be raised, and it is ascertained that no evidence will be called to establish this defence, the Crown may, before closing its own case, call evidence to negative insanity: *R. v. Abramovitch*, 7 Cr.App.R. 145, CCA. Where the defence have raised the issue of diminished responsibility, the prosecution may raise the issue of insanity: see *post*, § 19–79. **17–101**

As to "unfitness to plead", see *ante*, §§ 4–166 *et seq.*

V. *DRINK AND DRUGS*

A. INTRODUCTION

17–102 Although most of the authorities are concerned with the effect of alcohol, it is submitted that what is said as to the responsibility of a man whose mind is impaired by alcohol at the time of the alleged offence, will apply equally to the case of a man whose mind is impaired by drugs: *R. v. Lipman* [1970] 1 Q.B. 152, 53 Cr.App.R. 600, CA. However, before the principles which apply in the case of impairment resulting from the voluntary taking of alcohol can apply to impairment resulting from the voluntary taking of a drug the *caveat* emphasised in *R. v. Hardie, post*, § 17–105, must be borne in mind.

[The next paragraph is § 17–104.]

B. INVOLUNTARY INTOXICATION

17–104 Where the necessary mental element for an offence existed at the time of the commission of the *actus reus* thereof, it is no defence that it only existed as a result of involuntary intoxication, for which the defendant bore no blame; the absence of moral fault does not suffice to negative the mental element of an offence: *R. v. Kingston* [1995] 2 A.C. 355, HL.

Ignorance of the strength of a drink that a person is voluntarily taking does not make his subsequent intoxication other than voluntary: *R. v. Allen (K.)* [1988] Crim.L.R. 698, CA.

C. SELF-INDUCED INTOXICATION

(1) Principle

17–105 (a) Where the prosecution have to prove recklessness (*ante*, § 17–51) as an element of the offence, if due to self-induced intoxication the accused was unaware of a risk of which he would have been aware had he been sober, he is to be treated as if he had been aware of that risk (*ante*, § 17–52).

(b) This applies whether the intoxication has been induced by alcohol or drugs providing, in the case of a drug, there had been an element of recklessness in self-administering it, such as would ordinarily be the case when the drug was well known for being liable to cause unpredictability or aggressiveness. Where, however, there is no evidence that the defendant knew, or that it was generally known, that the taking of a particular drug in the quantity taken by the defendant would be liable to render a person aggressive or incapable of appreciating risks to others or to have other side effects such that its taking would itself contain an element of recklessness, the jury should be directed that if they concluded that as a result of the defendant taking the drug in question he was unable to appreciate the risks to persons and property resulting from his actions, they should then consider whether the taking of the drug was itself reckless: see *R. v. Hardie*, 80 Cr.App.R. 157, CA; and *R. v. Bailey, ante*, § 17–90. If they find against the defendant on this issue, then, pursuant to *R. v. G., ante*, § 17–52, they will still have to go on to decide whether the defendant would have aware of the relevant risk had he not taken the drug.

17–106 (c) Where, however, the prosecution have to prove any other mental element, such as a specific intent or knowledge, the jury must consider any evidence of intoxication in determining whether the necessary mental element has been proved.

> "(I)n cases where drunkenness and its possible effect upon the defendant's *mens rea* is in issue, ... the proper direction to a jury is, first, to warn them that the mere fact that the defendant's mind was affected by drink so that he acted in a way in which he would not have done had he been sober does not assist him at all, provided that the necessary intention was there. A drunken intent is nevertheless an intent. Secondly, and subject to this, the jury should merely be instructed to have regard to all the evidence, including that relating to drink, to draw such inferences as they think proper from the evidence, and on that basis to

ask themselves whether they feel sure that at the material time the defendant had the requisite intent" (*R. v. Sheehan and Moore*, 60 Cr.App.R. 308 at 312, CA).

See also *R. v. Pordage* [1975] Crim.L.R. 575, CA; *R. v. Bennett* [1995] Crim.L.R. 877, CA; *R. v. Brown and Stratton* [1998] Crim.L.R. 485, CA (jury should be directed that in deciding whether the defendant had the intent alleged they must take into account the evidence in relation to the consumption of alcohol and the defendant's condition and, if they considered that because of drink he did not or might not have had the requisite intent, he should be acquitted; insufficient simply to direct them that a drunken intent was still an intent for the purposes of the law); and *R. v. Hayes* [2003] Crim.L.R. 48, CA (*ante*, § 17–35).

In *R. v. McKnight*, *The Times*, May 5, 2000, CA, it was held that the JSB specimen direction on voluntary intoxication in cases of specific intent, based on *R. v. Sheehan and Moore*, need not be given where there is no factual basis for such direction; neither evidence that the defendant was drunk nor that he could not remember what he had been doing as a result of being drunk was sufficient; the essence of the defence was that the defendant did not have the necessary guilty intent because his mind was so affected by drink that he did not know what he was doing at the time when he did the act in question, and the degree of intoxication must have been such that it had prevented him from foreseeing or knowing what he would have foreseen or known had he been sober.

The court relied, in large part, for its conclusions on *Sooklal v. The State* [1999] 1 W.L.R. 2011, PC. As in that case, the court seems to have erred in suggesting that drunkenness is a defence. It is not, and it is certainly not a special defence with some burden on the accused. Intent is for the prosecution to prove and in deciding whether it has been proved a court or jury is to do so by reference to "all the evidence drawing such inferences ... as appear proper in the circumstances" (*CJA* 1967, s.8 (*ante*, § 17–36)). Where intent is in issue and there is evidence of drunkenness, it is submitted that a *Sheehan and Moore* direction should routinely be given. Where intent is not in issue (*e.g.* the defence to murder is self-defence or provocation), then the giving of a *Sheehan and Moore* direction is inappropriate and liable to confuse.

In *R. v. Alden and Jones* [2001] 5 *Archbold News* 3, Ct-MAC, the court rejected a suggestion that there were two inconsistent lines of authority, *Sheehan and Moore* and *Bennett*, *ante*, on the one hand, and *Sooklal* and *McKnight*, on the other. The court said that so far as alcohol and specific intent are concerned, the crucial question where there is evidence of the consumption by the defendant of a substantial quantity of drink, is whether there is an issue as to the defendant's formation of specific intent by reason of the alcohol which he has taken; and that the necessary pre-requisite to a direction of the kind identified in *Sheehan and Moore*, is that there must be an issue as to the effect of drunkenness upon the defendant's state of mind.

Where, on a charge requiring proof of specific intent, there is evidence of the consumption of a large quantity of alcohol by the defendant, but it is not part of his case that he was unable to form the necessary intent, it is open to the judge to enquire of counsel whether ability to form the intent is in issue; and if it is made clear that it is not, it is open to the judge not to give the normal direction along the lines that a drunken intent is nevertheless an intent, and simply to direct the jury that they had to be sure, having regard to all the evidence, that the defendant did in fact have the necessary intent: *R. v. Groark* [1999] Crim.L.R. 669, CA.

(d) When the question of drunkenness arises, it is not a question of the *capacity* of the defendant to form the particular intent which is in issue; what is in issue is simply whether he did form such an intent: *R. v. Garlick*, 72 Cr.App.R. 291, CA.

(2) Authorities

(a) *DPP v. Majewski [1977] A.C. 443, HL*

The appeal was heard by seven Lords of Appeal, all of whom were agreed that the answer to the question "Whether a defendant may properly be convicted of assault notwithstanding that, by reason of his self-intoxication, he did not intend to do the act alleged to constitute the assault" was "Yes". **17–107**

The leading opinion was delivered by Lord Elwyn-Jones L.C. Lords Diplock, Simon, and Kilbrandon agreed with his opinion. The appellant had been convicted of assaults occasioning actual bodily harm and assaults on police officers in the execution of their duty. His defence was that by reason of drugs voluntarily taken he did not know what he was doing.

17–108 It was clear that the only mental element in these offences appeared in the definition of assault. On this, the Lord Chancellor adopted the words of Lord Simon in *DPP v. Morgan* [1976] A.C. 182 at 216, HL, to the effect that crimes of "basic intent", of which assault was an example, were crimes where the *mens rea* did not extend beyond the act and its consequences, however remote, as defined in the *actus reus*. He went on to say that in the crime of assault "the *actus reus* is an act which causes another person to apprehend immediate and unlawful violence. The *mens rea* corresponds exactly. The prosecution must prove that the accused foresaw that his act would probably cause another person to have apprehension of immediate and unlawful violence or would possibly have that consequence, such being the purpose of the act, or that he was reckless as to whether or not his act caused such apprehension." Holding that it was no defence that the accused, by reason of self-induced intoxication, was senseless and therefore had neither intent nor recklessness with regard to the *actus reus*, the Lord Chancellor ended his opinion as follows:

> "My noble and learned friends and I think it may be helpful if we give the following indications of the general lines on which in our view the jury should be directed as to the effect upon criminal responsibility of the accused of drink or drugs or both, whenever death or bodily injury to another person results from something done by the accused for which there is no legal justification and the offence with which the accused is charged is manslaughter or assault at common law or the statutory offence of unlawful wounding under section 20, or of assault occasioning actual bodily harm under section 47 of the *Offences against the Person Act* 1861. In the case of these offences it is no excuse in law that, because of drink or drugs which the accused himself had taken knowingly and willingly, he had deprived himself of the ability to exercise self-control, to realise the possible consequences of what he was doing, or even to be conscious that he was doing it. As in the instant case, the jury may be properly instructed that they 'can ignore the subject of drink or drugs as being in any way a defence' to charges of this character" (at p. 476).

17–109 What judges and practitioners will want to know is what other charges are "of this character". It is clear that the Lord Chancellor had in mind crimes of "basic intent" as opposed to crimes of "specific intent", where the Crown has to prove the "specific intent" and the jury must take into account evidence of intoxication, even though self-induced, in deciding whether in fact the Crown has proved that intent. This appears from the reason he gave for his decision:

> "If a man of his own volition takes a substance which causes him to cast off the restraints of reason and conscience, no wrong is done to him by holding him answerable criminally for any injury he may do while in that condition. His course of conduct in reducing himself by drugs and drink to that condition in my view supplies the evidence of *mens rea*, of guilty mind certainly sufficient for crimes of basic intent. It is a reckless course of conduct and recklessness is enough to constitute the necessary *mens rea* in assault cases. ... The drunkenness is itself an intrinsic, an integral part of the crime, the other part being the evidence of the unlawful use of force against the victim. Together they add up to criminal recklessness. On this I adopt the conclusion of Stroud in 1920, 36 L.Q.R. 273. '... By allowing himself to get drunk and thereby putting himself in such a condition as to be no longer amenable to the law's commands, a man shows such regardlessness as amounts to *mens rea* for the purpose of all ordinary crimes'" (at p. 475).

17–110 In the light of *R. v. Caldwell* (*post*, § 17–112), it is submitted, therefore, that despite the use of the expression "basic intent" (as to which, see also *post*, § 7–112a) what the Lord Chancellor, and the House, had in mind were "offences where recklessness is sufficient *mens rea*". This would seem to include the following offences:

(a) common assault (*ante*, § 17–108);
(b) assault occasioning actual bodily harm (*ante*, § 17–108);
(c) manslaughter (*ante*, § 17–108);
(d) assault on a police officer in the execution of his duty (one of the charges of which *Majewski* was convicted);
(e) both offences against section 20 of the *Offences against the Person Act* 1861 (*ante*, § 17–108—the two offences cannot be distinguished in this regard);

(f) taking a conveyance without the owner's authority, contrary to section 12(1) of the *Theft Act* 1968: *R. v. MacPherson* [1973] R.T.R. 157, CA;

(g) arson or criminal damage contrary to section 1(1) of the *Criminal Damage Act* 1971 if recklessness is charged: *R. v. O'Driscoll*, 65 Cr.App.R. 50, CA; *R. v. Stephenson* [1979] Q.B. 695, 69 Cr.App.R. 213, CA; and

(h) arson or criminal damage contrary to section 1(2) of that Act if recklessness is charged (see *R. v. Caldwell*, *post*).

In view of the passage set out in § 17–108, *ante*, it is perhaps necessary to point out that even where the prosecution have to prove "intent" as opposed to "recklessness" the mere fact that self-induced intoxication has deprived the accused of the ability to exercise self-control can never be an answer to the charge, see *Sheehan and Moore*, *ante*, § 17–106. **17–111**

The trial judge in *Majewski* had told the jury that for the purposes of that case an assault meant some kick or blow, not something which was purely accidental. It is possible, however, to read the Lord Chancellor's opinion as saying that whether the assault was accidental or not is irrelevant. Moreover, Lords Simon, at page 477, Salmon, at page 484, and Edmund-Davies, at page 494, appear to have approved the decision of the Court of Appeal in *R. v. Lipman* [1970] 1 Q.B. 152, 53 Cr.App.R. 600, where it was held that the appellant had been guilty of an unlawful and dangerous act causing death, and therefore guilty of manslaughter, when he was completely hallucinated due to drugs and thought that he was wrestling with serpents.

There is, however, a palliative to this harsh doctrine, which is sometimes overlooked and which, it is submitted, would exclude from criminal liability the person whose act was purely accidental, however drunk he was. The tribunal of fact still has to be satisfied that the defendant would have foreseen the relevant risk had he been sober. See the last three lines of the extract from Lord Diplock's speech in *Caldwell*, quoted at § 17–112, *post*.

(b) *R. v. Caldwell [1982] A.C. 341, HL*

The House of Lords extended the *Majewski* doctrine to the element of recklessness wherever it occurs in the definition of an offence and whether it relates to the act and its consequences as defined in the *actus reus* or not. The House applied it to "being reckless as to whether the life of another would be endangered" under section 1(2) of the *Criminal Damage Act* 1971: see *post* § 23–13. Here the *mens rea* required was over and above intent or recklessness as to the act and its consequences, as defined in the *actus reus*. **17–112**

Lord Diplock, delivering the leading opinion with which Lords Keith and Roskill agreed, said:

> "The speech of Lord Elwyn-Jones L.C. in *Majewski* is authority … that self-induced intoxication is no defence to a crime in which recklessness is enough to constitute the necessary *mens rea* …. Reducing oneself by drink or drugs to a condition in which the restraints of reason and conscience are cast off was held to be a reckless course of conduct and an integral part of the crime. Lord Elwyn-Jones accepted as correctly stating English law the provision in para. 2.08(2) of the American Model Penal Code: 'When recklessness establishes an element of the offence, if the actor, due to self-induced intoxication, is unaware of a risk of which he would have been aware if sober, such unawareness is immaterial'.
>
> So, in the instant case, the fact that the respondent was unaware of the risk of endangering the lives of residents in the hotel owing to his self-induced intoxication would be no defence if that risk would have been obvious to him had he been sober" (at p. 355).

(c) *R. v. Heard [2007] 1 Cr.App.R. 37, CA*

The Court of Appeal held that voluntary intoxication can only be relied on as negativing *mens rea* in the case of crimes an ingredient of which is a specific or purposive intent; and that sexual assault, contrary to section 3 of the *SOA* 2003 (*post*, § 20–29) is not such a crime, notwithstanding that one element of the offence which has to be proved is an "intentional" touching of the complainant by the defendant (see s.3(1)(a)). The court said that whilst this means that the touching must be deliberate, and not accidental or even reckless, in those exceptional cases where the defendant's mind did not **17–112a** go with his physical act on account of his self-induced intoxication, this will not avail him. The use of the adverb "intentionally" in conjunction with the *actus reus* of the offence is a new phenomenon in the statutory definitions of offences, but it occurs throughout the 2003 Act, and such offences may perhaps be more readily described as crimes "of basic intent" than the offences listed at § 17–110, *ante*, for which recklessness as to the prohibited consequences will suffice. Whilst the court stressed that a drunken intent was a sufficient intent and that doing something in drink did not mean that it was not done deliberately, it not only said that the corollary was that a drunken accident was still an accident, but also that an act of sexual touching which might be categorised as reckless in a sober person would still only be reckless in the drunk.

D. THE MATERIAL TIME

17–113 In *Att.-Gen. for Northern Ireland v. Gallagher* [1963] A.C. 349 at 382, HL, Lord Denning considered that the question arose whether, if a man forms an intent to kill or do grievous bodily harm and drinks a quantity of alcohol in order to give himself "Dutch courage" to carry out his intention, the crime of murder is reduced to manslaughter if at the time he kills he is so affected by drink that he does not possess the necessary intent for murder. His Lordship considered that he was guilty of murder.

Although, at first sight, this view seems inconsistent with the fact that in general the mental element of a crime must exist at the time of the physical act, it can perhaps be justified by extending the maxim *"qui facit per alium facit per se"*.

E. RELATIONSHIP TO PARTICULAR DEFENCES

(1) Insanity

17–113a Where insanity has been caused by drunkenness, the supervening insanity, though it be but temporary, is just as much a defence as insanity produced by other causes: *DPP v. Beard* [1920] A.C. 479, HL. The same principle applies to *delirium tremens* if it produces insanity, albeit temporary: *R. v. Davis* (1881) 14 Cox 563.

(2) Diminished responsibility

17–113b See *post*, §§ 19–70 *et seq*.

(3) Automatism

17–113c In Scotland, the High Court of Justiciary has held that automatism cannot be established as a defence to a charge of driving with excess alcohol upon proof of a transitory state of parasomnia (sleep-walking) resulting from, and induced by deliberate and self-induced intoxication: *Finegan v. Heywood*, *The Times*, May 10, 2000.

(4) Provocation

17–114 See *post*, § 19–62.

(5) Self-defence

17–115 See *ante*, § 17–16.

F. DRUNKENNESS AND PARTICULAR OFFENCES

(1) Sexual offences

17–116 As to drunkenness and intention under the *SOA* 2003, see *R. v. Heard*, *ante*, § 17–112a, and *post*, § 20–34a. A separate issue under the 2003 Act relates to the ingredient of the new offences under sections 1 to 4 (rape, assault by penetration, sexual assault, causing a person to engage in sexual activity without consent (*post*, §§ 20–19 *et seq.*)) that the defendant did not "reasonably believe" that the complainant consented. Two cases on the former sexual offences legislation (*i.e.* the *SOA* 1956, and the *Sexual Offences (Amendment) Act* 1976, s.1(2)) strongly suggest the courts will not even entertain the possibility that a belief resulting from self-induced intoxication could be a "reasonable" belief: see *R. v. Woods (W.)*, 74 Cr.App.R. 312, CA; and *R. v. Fotheringham*,

88 Cr.App.R. 206, CA. It is submitted, however, that it is a matter for the jury alone to decide whether a belief is reasonable; and that any rule to the effect that a person who is affected by alcohol or drugs could never make a "reasonable" mistake would be an unwarranted intrusion into the province of the jury, and calculated to lead to harsh results where there are factors other than the defendant's inebriation that caused him to have the mistaken belief.

(2) Possession of controlled drugs

See *R. v. Young (R.)*, 78 Cr.App.R. 288, Ct-MAC: *post*, § 27–124. **17–117**

[The next paragraph is § 17–119.]

VI. DURESS

A. AVAILABILITY

Duress is a defence to all crimes except murder, attempted murder and *semble*, treason involving the death of the sovereign. The defence is not available to a person charged with murder whether as principal or as an aider, abettor, counsellor or procurer: *R. v. Howe* [1987] A.C. 417, HL, overruling *Lynch v. DPP for Northern Ireland* [1975] A.C. 653, HL. And the rule applies to a child of the age of criminal responsibility no matter how susceptible he might be to the duress: *R. v. Wilson* [2007] 2 Cr.App.R. 31, CA. **17–119**

Duress is not available as a defence to a charge of attempted murder: *R. v. Gotts* [1992] 2 A.C. 412, HL.

Duress is capable of constituting a defence to an allegation of contempt: *R. v. K.*, 78 Cr.App.R. 82, CA; and see *R. v. Lewis (James)*, 96 Cr.App.R. 412, CA. It is also a possible defence to a charge of perjury: *R. v. Hudson and Taylor* [1971] 2 Q.B. 202, 56 Cr.App.R. 1, CA.

In *R. v. Fisher* [2004] Crim.L.R. 938, CA, it was held that where a person is charged with an offence of having a firearm with intent to commit an indictable offence while having the firearm with him (*Firearms Act* 1968, s.18(2), *post*, § 24–51), duress is a potential defence though there was no duress in relation to the firearm, but only in relation to the intended offence. *Sed quaere*, see the commentary in *Criminal Law Week* 2004/41/7.

As to the availability of the defence to those who voluntarily join criminal organisations, see *post*, § 17–126.

B. PRINCIPLE

A definitive statement of the scope of the defence is not to be found in the authorities. In *Lynch v. DPP for Northern Ireland*, *ante*, Lord Simon said that a number of questions remained unanswered. **17–120**

> "(I)t is convenient to have a working definition of duress—even though it is actually an extremely vague and elusive juristic concept. I take it for present purposes to denote such [well grounded] fear, produced by threats, of death or grievous bodily harm [or unjustified imprisonment] if a certain act is not done, as overbears the wish not to perform the act, and is effective, at the time of the act, in constraining him to perform it. I am quite uncertain whether the words which I have put in square brackets should be included in any such definition. It is arguable that the test should be purely subjective, and that it is contrary to principle to require the fear to be a reasonable one. Moreover, I have assumed, on the basis of *Hudson* that threat of future injury may suffice, although Stephen, *Digest of the Criminal Law*, Art. 10 is to the contrary. Then the law leaves it also quite uncertain whether the fear induced by threats must be of death or grievous bodily harm, or whether loss of liberty suffices: cases of duress in the law of contract suggest that duress may extend to unjustified imprisonment; but the criminal law returns no clear answer. It also leaves entirely unanswered whether, to constitute such a general criminal defence, the threat must be of harm to the person required to perform the act, or extends to the immediate family of the actor (and how immediate?), or to any person. Such questions are not academic, in these

> days when hostages are so frequently seized. Is it worse to have a pistol thrust into your back and a grenade into your hand, or to have your child (or a neighbour's child) seized by terrorists and held at peril until you have placed in a public building a parcel which you believe to contain a bomb?" (at p. 686).

This extract from Lord Simon's speech was quoted with approval by Lord Mackay in *Howe, ante*, at pp. 453–454.

17–121 Lord Simon then said that, where so little is clear, "this at least seems to be established: that the type of threat which affords a defence must be one of human physical harm (including possibly, imprisonment), so that threat of injury to property is not enough". The threat may relate to a person for whose safety the defendant would reasonably regard himself as responsible: *R. v. Wright* [2000] Crim.L.R. 510, CA; *R. v. Ortiz*, 83 Cr.App.R. 173, CA (where this was assumed).

In *Howe, ante*, the House of Lords approved the judgments of the Court of Appeal in that case and also in *R. v. Graham*, 74 Cr.App.R. 235. Both judgments had been given by Lord Lane C.J. From these sources, the following test can be advanced: was a threat of physical harm to the person (including, possibly, of imprisonment) made, which was of such gravity that it might well have caused a sober person of reasonable firmness sharing the defendant's characteristics and placed in the same situation to act in the same way as the defendant acted? The Court of Appeal in *Graham* had said that consistency of approach in defences to criminal liability was desirable.

> "In provocation the words or actions of one person break the self-control of another. In duress, the words or actions of one person break the will of another. The law requires a defendant to have the self-control reasonably to be expected of the ordinary citizen in his situation. It should likewise require him to have the steadfastness reasonably to be expected of the ordinary citizen in his situation" (*per* Lord Lane C.J., at p. 241).

17–122 In one respect, this dictum is misleading. His Lordship speaks of the will of the defendant having been broken. However, in *Lynch, ante*, Lords Morris, Simon and Edmund-Davies considered the true basis of the plea of duress. They rejected the notion that duress was inconsistent with act and will as a matter of legal definition. "An infraction of the criminal code under duress does not involve that the conduct is either involuntary or unintentional" (*per* Lord Simon at p. 696). Lord Edmund-Davies said (at p. 710) that duress is to be regarded as a plea in confession and avoidance.

The question of what are the relevant characteristics to which the court should have regard was considered in *R. v. Bowen* [1996] 2 Cr.App.R. 157, CA. The mere fact that the accused was more timid than the ordinary person is irrelevant. It would be relevant that the accused belonged to a category of persons less able to resist pressure than people not within that category: obvious examples were youth, pregnancy, physical disability, recognised mental illness or psychiatric condition, such as post-traumatic stress disorder leading to learnt helplessness. A low intelligence quotient, short of mental impairment or defectiveness, was irrelevant, since it did not make a person less able to withstand threats than an ordinary person. Characteristics due to self-imposed abuse were also irrelevant. If it is the defence case that the accused had some peculiar characteristic which was relevant, there is a duty to raise it with the judge. Furthermore, it was the court's view that the direction to the jury should go further than suggested in *Graham*, and should point out what characteristics were capable of being regarded as relevant; in most cases, it would only be the age and sex of the offender that were relevant, and the jury should be so informed. Asperger's Syndrome (a developmental disorder of autistic personality, characterised by vulnerability) is a mental illness or psychiatric condition of a kind relevant to the issue of duress and is a characteristic to which the court may have regard: *R. v. Rogers* [1999] 9 *Archbold News* 1, CA.

It is essential that the threat should have been effective at the time when the crime was committed. Furthermore, it is always open to the prosecution to prove that the defendant failed to avail himself of an opportunity which was reasonably open to him to render the threat ineffective; upon that being proved, the threat in question can no longer be relied upon: see *R. v. Bianco* [2002] 1 *Archbold News* 2, CA. In deciding whether such an opportunity was reasonably open to the defendant, the jury should have regard to his age and circumstances, and to any risks to him which may be involved in the course of action relied upon: *ibid.*, and see *R. v. Sharp (D.)* [1987] Q.B. 853,

85 Cr.App.R. 207, CA; and *R. v. Baker and Ward* [1999] 2 Cr.App.R. 355, CA. In *R. v. Hudson and Taylor* [1971] 2 Q.B. 202, 56 Cr.App.R. 1, CA, it was said that the fact that the threat may not be of immediate injury in the event of non-compliance is not fatal to the defence; but this was doubted in *R. v. Z.* [2005] 2 A.C. 467, HL, where it was said that it should be made clear to juries that if the retribution threatened against the defendant or his family or a person for whom he feels responsible is not such as he reasonably expects to follow immediately or almost immediately on his failure to comply with the threat, there may be little room for doubt that he could have taken evasive action, whether by going to the police or in some other way, to avoid committing the crime with which he is charged.

If, as a result of duress, a person embarks on a course of conduct, which would otherwise constitute a continuing offence, it will be for the tribunal of fact to determine whether he continued the conduct when his will was no longer overborne by terror: *DPP v. Bell* [1992] Crim.L.R. 176, DC.

Liability of secondary party where principal subject to duress

A secondary party is liable to conviction of the full offence, although the principal has **17–123** the defence of duress: *R. v. Bourne*, 36 Cr.App.R. 125, CCA; *R. v. Howe* [1987] A.C. 417, HL.

Duress of circumstances

There has in recent years developed the expression "duress of circumstances". The **17–124** use of the word "duress" in this context is misleading. Duress, whether in criminal law or civil law, suggests pressure being brought to bear by one person on another person to persuade that other person to do something which he is unwilling to do. "Duress of circumstances" has nothing to do with one person being told to commit a crime "or else": it relates to a situation where a person is driven to commit a crime by force of circumstances. Accordingly, despite the nomenclature, duress of circumstances is more conveniently dealt with under the heading of "necessity", *post*, §§ 17–127 *et seq.* Indeed, it may be that duress, strictly so called, should itself be regarded as a form of the defence of necessity: see, *per* Lord Hailsham L.C. in *R. v. Howe*, *post*, § 17–129.

C. ONUS OF PROOF AND EVIDENCE

Once the judge has ruled that there is evidence of duress fit to be left to the jury, it is **17–125** for the Crown to prove beyond reasonable doubt that the defendant was not acting under duress: *R. v. Bone*, 52 Cr.App.R. 546, CA. And it is for the judge to direct the jury as to the requirements of the defence, even though prosecution counsel has cross-examined the accused only as to whether the alleged duress occurred at all: *R. v. Ward* [1998] 8 *Archbold News* 3, CA (97 05223 X5). By so doing, he is not introducing a new issue into the case, as in cases such as *R. v. Cristini* [1987] Crim.L.R. 504, CA, and the other cases referred to at § 4–378, *ante*: *ibid.*

In *R. v. Bianco* (*ante*, § 17–122), it was said that where no reasonable jury properly directed as to the law could fail to find duress disproved, no legitimate purpose is served by leaving it to the jury; and that there must at least be some evidence upon which a jury could properly conclude that the defence of duress had not been negatived in order to require the defence to be left to the jury. It is submitted that this formulation gets the emphasis the wrong way round. If there is evidence of duress, then the judge is duty bound to leave the issue to the jury. The fact that the judge may think that no reasonable jury could fail to find the defence disproved provides no justification for not leaving the issue to the jury.

In *R. v. Jaquith and Emode* [1989] Crim.L.R. 508, CA, one of three defendants gave evidence. His defence was duress and he gave evidence of threats being made against him. His evidence on this issue had not been challenged by the Crown. On a submission made immediately before the commencement of closing speeches, counsel for this defendant submitted that there was no case to answer because the Crown, not having challenged the evidence of duress, had not made out its case. The submission was upheld but, according to the Court of Appeal on the appeal against conviction of the other two defendants, was wrongly upheld. The submission contained a fallacy. It might have been that the defendant was under threat but that, as a matter of law, was not sufficient to make out the defence of duress. The matter was still for the jury to decide.

Since the standard by which a person's reaction to duress is to be judged contains an objective element, namely, whether in all the circumstances a person of reasonable firmness, sharing the appellant's characteristics, could not be reasonably expected to resist (*ante*, § 17–121), it follows that expert evidence that the defendant's personality lacked reasonable firmness is irrelevant to any issue a jury would have to determine: *R. v. Hurst* [1995] 1 Cr.App.R. 82, CA. But psychiatric evidence might be admissible to show that the accused was suffering from mental illness or impairment or recognised psychiatric condition provided that persons generally suffering from such condition might be more susceptible to pressure and threats, and thus to assist the jury in deciding whether a reasonable person suffering from such condition might have been compelled to act as the defendant did: *R. v. Bowen* [1996] 2 Cr.App.R. 157, CA.

In *R. v. Nethercott* [2002] 2 Cr.App.R. 7, CA, it was held that where the defence to a charge was duress consisting of a series of threats of violence made by a co-defendant, evidence to the effect that the appellant had been stabbed by the co-defendant was relevant to that defence albeit that the stabbing had occurred three months after the offence; such evidence was of particular relevance where the defence of duress had never been mentioned in interview.

As to cross-examination as to the convictions of a person who is not a witness and who is alleged to have been responsible for the duress (whether in the form of threats or not), see *R. v. Murray* [1995] R.T.R. 239, *ante*, § 13–21.

D. VOLUNTARY EXPOSURE TO RISK OF DURESS

17–126 If a person, by joining an illegal organisation or a similar group of men with criminal objectives and coercive methods, voluntarily exposes and submits himself to illegal compulsion, he cannot rely on the duress to which he has voluntarily exposed himself as an excuse either in respect of the crimes he commits against his will or in respect of his continued but unwilling association with those capable of exercising upon him the duress which he calls in aid: *R. v. Fitzpatrick* [1977] N.I.L.R. 20.

In *R. v. Sharp (D.)* [1987] Q.B. 853, 85 Cr.App.R. 207, Lord Lane C.J., delivering the judgment of the Court of Appeal, cited *Fitzpatrick* with approval. His Lordship said (at pp. 857, 210):

> "No one could question that if a person can avoid the effects of duress by escaping from the threats, without damage to himself, he must do so .... It seems to us to be part of the same argument, or at least to be so close to the same argument as to be practically indistinguishable from it, to say that a man must not voluntarily put himself in a position where he is likely to be subjected to such compulsion."

The conclusion of the court was that where a person has voluntarily, and with knowledge of its nature, joined a criminal organisation or gang which he knew might bring pressure to bear on him to commit an offence, and was an active member when he was put under such pressure, he cannot avail himself of the defence.

In *R. v. Z.* [2005] 2 A.C. 467, the House of Lords reviewed this limitation on the defence in detail. Their Lordships said that the policy of the law must be to discourage association with known criminals, and it should be slow to excuse the criminal conduct of those who do so. It was held that the defence of duress is unavailable when as a result of the accused's voluntary association with others engaged in criminal activity he foresaw or ought reasonably to have foreseen the risk of being subjected to any compulsion by threats of violence; nothing should turn on foresight of the manner in which, in the event, the dominant party chooses to exploit the defendant's subservience; there need not be foresight of coercion to commit crimes, although it was not easy to envisage circumstances in which a party might be coerced to act lawfully; to the extent that *R. v. Baker and Ward* [1999] 2 Cr.App.R. 335, CA, suggested that there must be foresight of coercion to commit crimes of the kind with which the defendant is charged, it misstated the law; and the test in relation to the defendant's foresight should be an objective one.

VII. NECESSITY

Introduction

English courts have never defined "necessity" as a defence in such terms as would lay down a general principle: *Russell*, 12th ed., Vol. I, 93; but most textbook writers appear to recognise the existence of such a defence within an extremely limited sphere. Stephen, *Digest of the Criminal Law*, p. 9, says that an act which would otherwise be a crime may in some cases be excused if the defendant can show that: (a) it was done only in order to avoid consequences which could not otherwise be avoided and which, if they had followed, would have inflicted upon him, or upon others whom he was bound to protect, inevitable and irreparable evil; (b) that no more was done than was reasonably necessary for that purpose; and (c) that the evil inflicted by it was not disproportionate to the evil avoided. **17–127**

Availability and scope

Until recently, it was thought that necessity could never be a defence to a charge of murder (*R. v. Dudley and Stephens* (1884) 14 Q.B.D. 273), or to attempted murder or some forms of treason (*R. v. Pommell* [1995] 2 Cr.App.R. 607, CA). In *Re A. (Children) (Conjoined Twins: Surgical Separation)* [2001] Fam. 147 at 224, 225, CA (Civ. Div.), however, it was held that *Dudley and Stephens* was not decisive of the issue, and that necessity may in the rarest of circumstances provide a defence even to a charge or murder. It would seem that it would only succeed where the inevitable consequence of taking no action would have been the death of two individuals, whereas the consequence of the defendant taking action was to save the life of one of those individuals, albeit at the cost of accelerating the death of the other. The defendant might be one of the two individuals, as in the example of a rock climber who has fallen and is dangling at the end of a rope held by the defendant who has the choice of dying with his companion or of cutting the rope and saving himself, or he may be a third party, as in the case of a surgeon who can operate to separate conjoined twins, with the prospect of saving one, but the certainty of killing the other. **17–128**

It is clear that the Court of Appeal in *Re A.* had no intention of allowing necessity to operate as a defence to murder where the deceased and the defendant could not both survive but had an equal (or approximately equal) chance of doing so; nor even to the situation where the sacrifice of one would save the lives of several (as by throwing one person overboard from an overcrowded lifeboat). If, however, such situations are to be excluded from the defence, it would seem that some modification of Stephen's three requirements of the defence will be necessary, for it is arguable that such situations (certainly that of the lifeboat) meet those requirements. The fundamental objection is that which was articulated by the judges in *Dudley and Stephens*. Who is to be the judge of this sort of necessity? And what is to be the measure of the comparative value of lives?

Prior to *Re A.*, it had been held that necessity is a potential defence to hijacking an aircraft: *R. v. Abdul-Hussain* [1999] Crim.L.R. 570, CA; and to allegations of dangerous driving or driving without due care and attention: *R. v. Symonds* [1998] Crim.L.R. 280, CA; *R. v. Backshall* [1999] 1 Cr.App.R. 35, CA; but the tenor of the judgments of the Court of Appeal in the earlier cases of *R. v. Willer*, 83 Cr.App.R. 225, and *R. v. Denton*, 85 Cr.App.R. 246, is to the effect that it would only be in the most extreme circumstances that a defendant would be entitled to succeed on this ground. Where the driver of an emergency vehicle is charged with either such offence as a result of driving through a red light, the defence will not avail him if he has contravened regulation 36 of the *Traffic Signs Regulations and General Directions* 2002 (S.I. 2002 No. 3113) (which provides a limited dispensation for such drivers): *DPP v. Harris* [1995] 1 Cr.App.R. 170, DC.

In *R. v. Conway* [1989] Q.B. 290, 88 Cr.App.R. 159, the Court of Appeal, after examining the authorities, concluded that: **17–129**

> "necessity can only be a defence to a charge of reckless driving where the facts establish 'duress of circumstances', ... *i.e.* where the defendant was constrained by circumstances to

drive as he did to avoid death or serious bodily harm to himself or some other person ... (T)o admit a defence of 'duress of circumstances' is a logical consequence of the existence of the defence of duress as that term is ordinarily understood, *i.e.* 'do this or else'. This approach does no more than recognise that duress is an example of necessity. Whether 'duress of circumstances' is called 'duress' or 'necessity' does not matter. What is important is that ... it is subject to the same limitation as the 'do this or else' species of duress. As Lord Hailsham said in ... *R. v. Howe* [1987] A.C. 417, 429:

'There is, of course, no obvious distinction between duress and necessity as potential defences: duress arises from the wrongful threats or violence of another human being and necessity arises from any other objective dangers threatening the accused. This ... is ... a distinction without a relevant difference, since ... duress is only that species of the genus of necessity which is caused by wrongful threats. I cannot see that there is any way in which a person of ordinary fortitude can be excused from the one type of pressure on his will rather than the other.'

...

It follows that a defence of 'duress of circumstances' is available only if *from an objective standpoint* the defendant can be said to be acting in order to avoid death or serious injury. The approach must be that indicated by Lord Lane C.J. in *Graham*, 74 Cr.App.R. 235, 241 ... in a passage of his judgment approved by the House of Lords in *R. v. Howe* [1987] A.C. 417, 459" (at pp. 297–298, 164–165).

As to the passage in *Graham* which is being referred to, see *ante*, § 17–121.

17–130 *Conway*, *ante*, was applied in *R. v. Martin*, 88 Cr.App.R. 343, CA, in which Simon Brown J., giving the court's judgment, restated the relevant principles as follows:

"First, English law does, in extreme circumstances, recognise a defence of necessity. Most commonly this defence arises as duress, that is pressure upon the accused's will from the wrongful threats or violence of another. Equally, however, it can arise from other objective dangers threatening the accused or others. Arising thus it is conveniently called 'duress of circumstances'. Secondly, the defence is available only if, from an objective standpoint, the accused can be said to be acting reasonably and proportionately in order to avoid a threat of death or serious injury. Thirdly, assuming the defence to be open to the accused on his account of the facts, the issue should be left to the jury, who should be directed to determine these two questions: first, was the accused, or may he have been, impelled to act as he did because as a result of what he reasonably believed to be the situation he had good cause to fear that otherwise death or serious physical injury would result? Second, if so, may a sober person of reasonable firmness, sharing the characteristics of the accused, have responded to the situation as the accused acted? If the answer to both these questions was yes then the ... defence of necessity would have been established" (at pp. 345–346).

In *DPP v. Rogers* [1998] Crim.L.R. 202, the Divisional Court said that the principles relating to the defence of necessity were accurately stated by the Court of Appeal in *Martin*. Inconsistently with this observation, however, the court also said that there was no requirement of reasonableness in relation to the defendant's belief as to the facts. In *R. v. Martin (David Paul)* [2000] 2 Cr.App.R. 42, there is an *obiter* observation to the same effect. The reasoning is unconvincing as the court relied on *R. v. Cairns* [1999] 2 Cr.App.R. 137, CA; but the point in *Cairns* was a different one (*viz.* whether there had to be an actual risk of death or injury), whereas on this issue, *Cairns* seems to have assumed that there is a requirement of reasonableness. On general principles relating to mistake of fact (*ante*, §§ 17–10 *et seq.*), it is submitted that there should be no requirement of reasonableness, but the first of the two questions to be put to the jury (as stated in *Martin*, *ante*) clearly imports such a requirement, and must be taken to represent the law at least at the level of the Court of Appeal.

In *R. v. Abdul-Hussain* [1999] Crim.L.R. 570, CA, it was said (in reliance on *R. v. Hudson and Taylor*, *ante*, § 17–122) that the fact that the death or serious injury would not have immediately occurred if the accused had not acted as he did is not necessarily fatal to the defence. Though neither *Hudson and Taylor* nor *Abdul-Hussain* were formally overruled by the House of Lords in *Z.* (*ante*, § 17–122), grave reservations about them were expressed. The important point, it is submitted, is simply that the more distant the perceived threat, the easier it will be for the prosecution to demonstrate that it was not necessary to commit the offence charged in order to avoid it. Would it have occurred at all? Could it have been avoided in another way?

17–131 In *DPP v. Bell* [1992] R.T.R. 335, DC, the prosecution contended that the defence was not available to someone whose actions would have been the same if the threatening circumstances had not occurred. Mann L.J. appears to have accepted this argument in principle, saying that it would have been relevant that the threats were not the *sine qua non* of his doing the prohibited act. On the findings of fact made by the lower court, however, his Lordship said that it was too late to debate this point. It is submitted, however, that it would be extremely surprising if the fact that the threats were not the *sine qua non* was not relevant: see the extract from the speech of Lord Simon in *Lynch*, cited at § 17–120, *ante*.

Where a person charged with a continuing offence, such as driving with excess alcohol, relies on a defence of necessity (driving off to escape serious physical injury), it will be open to the prosecution to defeat the defence by showing that, even if driving off in the first place was reasonable (so as to satisfy the objective element of the defence), there came a point when continuing to drive ceased to be reasonable; and, where they had shown that the police, to the knowledge of the defendant, were readily to hand and capable of affording the defendant adequate protection against the perceived risk of injury, they had discharged that burden; once the threat was removed, the necessity to continue the criminal action ceased; that the defendant might have been embarrassed (by virtue of being in her nightclothes) at having to give herself up to the protection of the police was irrelevant: *DPP v. Mullally*, unreported, November 6, 2006, DC ([2006] EWHC 3448 (Admin.)).

In *R. v. Quayle*; *R. v. Wales*; *R. v. Kenny*; *R. v. Taylor and Lee*; *Att.-Gen.'s Reference (No. 2 of 2004)* [2005] 2 Cr.App.R. 34, the Court of Appeal excluded the possibility of a defence of medical necessity (for purposes of pain relief) in relation to charges relating to the production, importation, possession, supply, prescription and use of cannabis, and its derivatives. Permitting such a defence would create a conflict with the purpose and effect of the current legislative scheme relating to drugs; first, no such use was permitted under the present legislation, even on a doctor's prescription except in the context of trials for medical research purposes; secondly, the suggested defence involved the proposition that it was lawful for unqualified individuals to prescribe cannabis to themselves as patients or to assume the role of unqualified doctors by obtaining it, prescribing and supplying it to other individual "patients". Furthermore, it was held that a defence of necessity could not be made out in such circumstances because, (i) there must be an objectively ascertainable extraneous influence, (ii) the defence is confined to cases where there is an imminent danger of physical injury, rather than continuing pain, and (iii) the defence required imminence and immediacy, whereas the conduct under consideration involved a deliberately considered course of action over a substantial period of time, involving continuous or regular breaches of the law. See also *R. v. Altham* [2006] 2 Cr.App.R. 8, CA.

As to necessity as a defence to charges under sections 1 and 4 of the *Official Secrets Act* 1989, see *R. v. Shayler* [2001] 1 W.L.R. 2206, CA, *post*, § 25–326.

Conclusions

It is submitted that this much emerges from the authorities. A person will have a defence to a charge of crime if: (a) the commission of the crime was necessary, or reasonably believed to have been necessary (see *R. v. Cairns* [1999] 2 Cr.App.R. 137, CA; and *R. v. Safi (Ali Ahmed)* [2004] 1 Cr.App.R. 14, CA), for the purpose of avoiding or preventing death or serious injury to himself or another; (b) that necessity was the *sine qua non* of the commission of the crime; and (c) the commission of the crime, viewed objectively, was reasonable and proportionate having regard to the evil to be avoided or prevented. It will not avail the defendant that he believed what he did to have been necessary to avoid the evil if, viewed objectively, it was unnecessary, or, though necessary, was disproportionate. This formula may require modification in its application to the offence of murder, so as to confine it to cases of acceleration of death of an individual having no chance of survival. **17–132**

VIII. COERCION BY HUSBAND

Criminal Justice Act 1925, s.47

17–133 **47.** Any presumption of law that an offence committed by a wife in the presence of her husband is committed under the coercion of the husband is hereby abolished, but on a charge against a wife for any offence other than treason or murder it shall be a good defence to prove that the offence was committed in the presence of and under the coercion of, the husband.

The onus is on the defendant to prove the statutory defence of coercion by her husband on a balance of probabilities.

In *DPP for Northern Ireland v. Lynch* [1975] A.C. 653, HL, Lord Simon said (at p. 693) that "coercion" in its popular sense denotes an external force which cannot be resisted and which impels its subject to act otherwise than he would wish. His Lordship said that in this popular sense it came into the law of probate as invalidating a testamentary instrument.

> "Though threats are not necessary to constitute coercion in the law of probate, it will be noted that the state of mind is precisely that produced by duress. It was this state of mind which was presumed by the law to be that of a wife performing certain acts prohibited by the law in the presence of her husband; and the law held her to be thereby excused."

See also, *per* Lords Morris, at p. 676, Wilberforce, at p. 684, and Edmund-Davies, at pp. 712–713.

In *R. v. Shortland* [1996] 1 Cr.App.R. 116, the Court of Appeal held that coercion went beyond persuasion out of loyalty, but it need not involve physical force or the threat thereof. To succeed, the woman has to prove that her will was overborne by the wishes of her husband, whether this was as a result of physical force, or the threat thereof, or of moral force.

In *R. v. Ditta, Hussain and Kara* [1988] Crim.L.R. 42, CA, it was held that before a woman can bring herself within the terms of section 47 of the 1925 Act, it must be shown that she is a wife in the strict sense of theterm and that the person who coerced her was her husband in the strict sense of the term. The fact that she may have believed, even on reasonable grounds, that she was married when she was not is not sufficient. The court considered but left open the question whether a polygamous Islamic marriage was a proper foundation for a defence under section 47.

IX. SUPERIOR ORDERS

17–134 The common law of England, Australia and the United States of America does not recognise a general defence of superior orders or of Crown or executive *fiat*: see *Lewis v. Dickson* [1976] R.T.R. 476, DC; *R. v. Howe* [1987] A.C. 417, HL, *per* Lord Hailsham, at p. 427; *A. v. Hayden (No. 2)* (1984) 156 C.L.R. 532, High Court of Australia; and *Yip Chiu-Cheung v. R.* [1995] 1 A.C. 111, PC.

Chapter 18

PRINCIPALS AND SECONDARY PARTIES

I. INTRODUCTION

A. Categories of Offender

When the law relating to principals and accessories as such is under consideration there is only one crime, although there may be more than one person criminally liable in respect of it: *Russell on Crime* (11th ed.), approved in *Surujpaul v. R.*, 42 Cr.App.R. 266 at 269, PC. Those liable may be categorised as either principals or secondary parties. Secondary parties are those who either aid, abet, counsel or procure the party who most immediately causes the *actus reus* of the crime. Some overlap may be discerned between the various categories. Furthermore, it should be borne in mind, when reading some of the older authorities, that at common law, in relation to felonies, a person who most immediately caused the *actus reus* of the crime was referred to as "a principal in the first degree", a secondary party who participated at the time when the felony was actually perpetrated was referred to as "a principal in the second degree" and a person who participated at some earlier time was "an accessory before the fact". The law relating to a further category of offenders known as "accessories after the fact" was replaced by the *CLA* 1967, s.4, *post*, § 18–34. **18–1**

B. Liability to Trial as Principal Offender

Accessories and Abettors Act 1861, s.8

8. Whosoever shall aid, abet, counsel or procure the commission of any indictable offence, whether the same be an offence at common law or by virtue of any Act passed or to be passed, shall be liable to be tried, indicted and punished as a principal offender. **18–2**

[This section is printed as amended by the *CLA* 1977, Sched. 12.]

As to the meaning of "indictable offence", see Appendix B–28. **18–3**

As to the particulars to be included in an indictment, see *post*, §§ 18–32, 18–33.

Section 8 reflects the common law rule in relation to misdemeanours: see *Du Cros v. Lambourne* [1907] 1 K.B. 40, DC.

Liability as a secondary party is a common law notion, not a creation of statute; it is of general application to all offences, unless expressly or impliedly excluded by statute: *R. v. Jefferson*, 99 Cr.App.R. 13, CA. Section 8 is a deeming provision as to how secondary parties are to be dealt with at trial: *ibid*. As to the liability of secondary parties for manslaughter, see *post*, § 19–112.

C. SUMMARY OFFENCES

Magistrates' Courts Act 1980, s.44

18–4 **44.**—(1) A person who aids, abets, counsels or procures the commission by another person of a summary offence shall be guilty of the like offence and may be tried (whether or not he is charged as a principal) either by a court having jurisdiction to try that other person or by a court having by virtue of his own offence jurisdiction to try him.

(2) Any offence consisting in aiding, abetting, counselling or procuring the commission of an offence triable either way (other than an offence listed in Schedule 1 to this Act) shall by virtue of this subsection be triable either way.

As to the meaning of "summary offence" and "offence triable either way", see Appendix B–28.

D. SPECIFIC STATUTORY PROVISIONS

18–5 Notwithstanding the unrestricted ambit of section 8 of the 1861 Act, there remain on the statute book various provisions specifically stipulating it to be an offence to be an accessory to the commission of an offence under the statute in question: see, for example, the *Official Secrets Act* 1920, s.7 (*post*, § 25–318) and the *Perjury Act* 1911, s.7 (*post*, § 28–185).

In addition, the *Suicide Act* 1961, s.2 makes it an offence to aid, abet, counsel or procure another to commit suicide, or attempt to do so, although suicide is no longer a crime.

Suicide Act 1961, s.2

Criminal liability for complicity in another's suicide

18–6 **2.**—(1) A person who aids, abets, counsels or procures the suicide of another, or an attempt by another to commit suicide, shall be liable on conviction on indictment to imprisonment for a term not exceeding fourteen years.

(2) If on the trial of an indictment for murder or manslaughter it is proved that the accused aided, abetted, counselled or procured the suicide of the person in question, the jury may find him guilty of that offence.

(3) [*Gives effect to Sched. 1 (amendments).*]

(4) ... no proceedings shall be instituted for an offence under this section except by or with the consent of the Director of Public Prosecutions.

[This section is printed as repealed in part by the *CLA* 1967, s.10(2) and Sched. 3, Pt II; and the *Criminal Jurisdiction Act* 1975, s.14(5) and Sched. 6.]

See generally, *R. v. McShane*, 66 Cr.App.R. 97, CA.

In *R. (Pretty) v. DPP, Secretary of State for the Home Department intervening* [2002] 1 A.C. 800, HL, it was held that there is no incompatibility between section 2(1) of the 1961 Act and the provisions of Article 2 (right to life) (*ante*, § 16–36), Article 3 (prohibition on inhuman or degrading treatment) (*ante*, § 16–39), Article 8 (right to respect for private and family life) (*ante*, § 16–101), Article 9 (freedom of thought, conscience and religion) (*ante*, § 6–113) or Article 14 (prohibition of discrimination) (*ante*, § 16–139) of the ECHR. On the appellant's application to the European Court of Human Rights, it was held in *Pretty v. U.K.* (2002) 35 E.H.R.R. 1, that on the assumption that the prohibition on assisted suicide in section 2(1) of the 1961 Act constituted an interference with the right to respect for the applicant's private life, as guaranteed by Article 8(1), she being physically incapable of taking her own life, the interference conformed to the requirements of Article 8(2); there being no dispute that the interference was prescribed by law and served a legitimate aim, the only question was whether it was "necessary in a democratic society" for the purpose of achieving that aim; states were entitled to regulate, through the operation of the general criminal law, activities detrimental to the life and safety of other individuals, and the more serious the harm involved, the more heavily would weigh considerations of public health and safety against the countervailing principle of personal autonomy; section 2 was designed to safeguard life by protecting the weak and the vulnerable and especially those not in a condition to take informed decisions against acts intended to end life or to assist in ending life; it was primarily for states to assess the risk and the likely incidence of abuse if the general prohibition on assisted suicides were relaxed, but there was a clear risk of abuse; and in those circumstances, the blanket nature of the ban could not be considered disproportionate; flexibility was provided by the requirement that any prosecution should have the consent of the Director of Public Prosecutions and in the provision of a maximum punishment, so allowing any lesser punishment to be imposed according the needs of the particular case; and nor was there anything disproportionate about the Director's refusal to give an advance undertaking that there would be no prosecution of the applicant's husband were he to assist her suicide; strong arguments based on the rule of law could be mounted against any claim by the executive to exempt individuals or classes of individuals from the operation of the law; and as to Article 14, there was objective and reasonable justification for not distinguishing between those who were and those who were not physically capable of committing suicide; to create an exception for the latter would seriously undermine the protection of life which the 1961 Act was intended to safeguard and greatly increase the risk of abuse.

In *Dunbar v. Plant* [1998] Ch. 412, CA (Civ. Div.), Phillips L.J., in the course of considering the application of the civil forfeiture rule to the survivor of a suicide pact, expressed the view that where two people are driven to attempting to take their own lives and one survives, the survivor would normally attract public sympathy, and that, whether the pact was rational or irrational, the public interest would not normally call for a prosecution under section 2.

The circumstances in which the distributors of a booklet published by the Voluntary Euthanasia Society might be guilty of aiding and abetting, etc., the suicide of those to whom the booklet had been sent were considered by Woolf J. in *Att.-Gen. v. Able* [1984] Q.B. 795, 78 Cr.App.R. 197, QBD.

Offences under section 2 are class 3 offences: see *ante*, § 2–17.

See also *post*, § 19–83, as to suicide pacts.

II. PRINCIPALS

A principal is one who is the actor or actual perpetrator of the fact: 1 Hale 233, 615. **18–7** It is possible for two or more persons to be principals in the same crime, but the distinction between a joint principal and an abettor is sometimes difficult, and unnecessary, to draw. Certain of the authorities disclose a tendency to use the expression "parties to a joint enterprise" without distinguishing between principals and secondary parties: *e.g. R. v. Williams and Davis*, 95 Cr.App.R. 1, CA. See further *post*, §§ 18–15 *et seq.* as to joint enterprise generally.

It is not necessary that a principal should be actually present when the offence is committed: *R. v. Harley* (1830) 4 C. & P. 369. Nor is it necessary that the act should have been perpetrated with his own hands; for if an offence is committed through the medium of an innocent agent, the employer, though absent when the act is done, is answerable as a principal: *R. v. Manley* (1844) 1 Cox 104; *R. v. Bull and Schmidt* (1845) 1 Cox 281; *R. v. Butt* (1884) 15 Cox 564, CCR; 1 Russ.Cr., 12th ed., 129. Thus, if a child under the age of discretion, or any other person who is not criminally responsible (whether by reason of defect of understanding, ignorance of the facts, absence of *mens rea* or other cause) is incited to the commission of any crime, the inciter, though absent when the act constituting the crime is committed, is liable for the act of his agent, and is a principal: Fost. 349; 1 Hawk. c. 31, s.7; *R. v. Butcher* (1858) Bell 6; *R. v. Tyler* (1838) 8 C. & P. 616 (liability for acts of insane man). The same principle will apply where the crime is committed through the agency of an animal.

Where, however, the agent acts with full knowledge of the facts, but not in concert **18–8** with the principal, but for his own purposes, his conduct will fall within the general principle of causation that the free, deliberate and informed intervention of a second person, intending to exploit a situation created by the first but not acting in concert with him, relieves the first of criminal responsibility: *R. v. Latif and Shahzad* [1996] 2 Cr.App.R. 92, HL. (See further as to this case, *post*, § 25–461.)

III. SECONDARY PARTIES

A. GENERAL

18–9 The words "aid, abet, counsel or procure" should be given their ordinary meaning, if possible; the use of four words suggests that there is a difference between the words, for, if there were none, Parliament would be wasting time in using four words where two or three would do: *Att.-Gen.'s Reference (No. 1 of 1975)* [1975] Q.B. 773, 61 Cr.App.R. 118, CA.

The courts have tended to construe these words so as to coincide with the common law in relation to felonies; thus aiders and abettors have been equated with principals in the second degree, and counsellors and procurers with accessories before the fact (*ante*, § 18–1). This is unsatisfactory because it produces results which do not reflect the natural meaning of the words. It is submitted that the better approach is to give the words their natural meaning; thus an aider and abettor may be present giving active assistance to the principal; he may be some distance away (as in the case of a look-out who watches the householder whilst the principal, with whom he is in contact via a mobile telephone burgles the house); or his act of assistance could be far removed in time and place (as in the case of the supplier of a gun who knows that it is required for the purpose of committing murder). Counselling and procuring inevitably takes place before the offence itself, but it need not be long before and there is no reason why the counsellor and procurer should not be present (although this is unlikely).

B. AIDERS AND ABETTORS

(1) Definition

18–10 In *Ferguson v. Weaving* [1951] 1 K.B. 814, DC, it was said that the words "aid and abet" are apt to describe the action of a person who is present at the time of the commission of an offence and takes some part therein. In some subsequent authorities, such as *National Coal Board v. Gamble* [1959] 1 Q.B. 11, 42 Cr.App.R. 240, DC (*post*, § 18–14), and *Thambiah v. R.* [1966] A.C. 37, PC (*ante*, § 17–72), the words "aiding and abetting" have been used in a wider sense, so as to include acts committed before the perpetration of the *actus reus*. In *Blakely v. DPP* [1991] R.T.R. 405, DC, McCullough J. said, at p. 411, that there are many accessories before the fact of whose activity none of the words "counselling, procuring and commanding" would seem to be apt; for example, the man who supplies the equipment for use in a robbery which has already been determined upon by others and at which he will not be present. The words "aiding and abetting" would seem more appropriate to describe such activity. For the reasons given at § 18–9, *ante*, it is submitted that the latter is the better view.

(2) Mens rea

18–11 See generally, *ante*, §§ 17–67 *et seq.*

(3) Capacity

18–12 A person may be an aider and abettor even if from sex or age incapable of being a principal: *R. v. Eldershaw* (1828) 3 C. & P. 396 (boy under 14 abetting rape); *R. v. Ram* (1893) 17 Cox 609 (woman abetting rape). But a person for whose protection an enactment has been passed cannot be convicted of aiding and abetting the person who commits the offence against him or her: *R. v. Tyrell* [1894] 1 Q.B. 710, CCR (unlawful sexual intercourse with a girl under 16); *R. v. Whitehouse* [1977] Q.B. 868, 65 Cr.App.R. 33, CA (girl under 16 could not aid and abet incest by her father).

(4) Presence

18–13 For the reasons given at § 18–9, *ante*, it is submitted that presence at the commission of the offence is unnecessary to guilt as an aider and abettor; under the common law relating to liability as a secondary party for felony, presence was the vital distinction between a principal in the second degree and an accessory before the fact.

Where presence may be entirely accidental, it is not even evidence of aiding and abetting; where presence is prima facie not accidental, it is evidence, but no more than evidence, for the jury: *per* Cave J. in *R. v. Coney* (1882) 8 Q.B.D. 534 at 540; and see *Wilcox v. Jeffery* [1951] 1 All E.R. 464, DC; *R. v. Allan* [1965] 1 Q.B. 130 at 135, 138, 47 Cr.App.R. 243 at 246, 249, CCA; and *R. v. Clarkson*, 55 Cr.App.R. 445, Ct-MAC. See further *post*, §§ 18–18 *et seq.*

(5) Participation

There must also be a participation in the act: *R. v. Borthwick* (1779) 1 Doug. 207; for even if a man is present whilst an offence is committed, if he takes no part in it and does not act in concert with those who commit it, he does not become an aider and abettor merely because he does not endeavour to prevent the offence, or fails to apprehend the offender: 1 Hale 439; Fost. 350; *R. v. Fretwell* (1862) L. & C. 161; and *R. v. Atkinson* (1869) 11 Cox C.C. 330. See also *Smith v. Baker* [1971] R.T.R. 350, DC; *R. v. Searle* [1971] Crim.L.R. 592, CA; and *R. v. Bland*, 151 J.P. 857, CA. See, however, *post*, §§ 18–18, 18–19, as to participation by encouragement. **18–14**

In *National Coal Board v. Gamble* [1959] 1 Q.B. 11, 42 Cr.App.R. 240, DC, the defendant's conviction for aiding and abetting the driving of an overweight lorry was upheld when the servant of the defendant had loaded coal onto the lorry of the principal offender and, with knowledge that the load had rendered the lorry overweight and that the driver intended to take it on the highway in that state, had completed the sale of coal, thereby facilitating the commission of the principal offence. Devlin J. said:

> "A person who supplies the instrument for a crime or anything essential to its commission aids in the commission of it; and if he does so knowingly and with intent to aid, he abets it as well and is therefore guilty of aiding and abetting. I use the word 'supplies' to comprehend giving, lending, selling or any other transfer of the right of property. In a sense a man who gives up to a criminal a weapon which the latter has a right to demand from him aids in the commission of the crime as much as if he sold or lent the article. But this has never been held to be aiding in law ... In the transfer of property there must be either a physical delivery or a positive act of assenting to the taking" (at pp. 20, 247).

See also *Blakely v. DPP* [1991] R.T.R. 405, DC, *ante*, § 18–10, and see *R. v. Bainbridge* [1960] 1 Q.B. 129, 43 Cr.App.R. 194, CCA, *ante*, § 17–72.

(6) Joint enterprise/ common design

See *ante*, § 18–7 as to the use of the expression "joint enterprise" generally. **18–15**

Where two or more persons embark on a joint enterprise each is liable for the acts done in pursuance of that joint enterprise. That includes liability for unusual consequences if they arise from the execution of the agreed joint enterprise. However, if a participant in the venture goes beyond what has been tacitly agreed as part of the common enterprise the other participants are not liable for the consequences of that unauthorised act. It is for the jury to decide whether what was done was part of the joint enterprise or was or may have been an unauthorised act and therefore outside the scope of the joint enterprise: *R. v. Anderson and Morris* [1966] 1 Q.B. 110, 50 Cr.App.R. 216, CCA; *R. v. Lovesey and Peterson* [1970] 1 Q.B. 352, 53 Cr.App.R. 461, CA; *R. v. Powell*; *R. v. English* [1999] A.C. 1, HL. Where, however, the principal does the very act contemplated by an accessory, but with an intent outside the contemplation of the accessory, it has been held by the Northern Ireland Court of Appeal in *R. v. Gilmour* [2000] 2 Cr.App.R. 407, that the accessory is not absolved of all responsibility; in such circumstances, he may be found guilty of the degree of offence appropriate to the intention with which he acted; where, therefore, the principal had done an act with the *mens rea* of murder (throwing a petrol bomb into a house), but the accessory intended only to start a fire, the latter could be convincted of manslaughter. As to this, see also *post*, § 19–26.

If three persons amuse themselves by shooting with a rifle at a target, without taking proper precautions to prevent injury to others, and one of the shots kills a man, all three are guilty of manslaughter, although there is no proof which of the three fired the **18–16** fatal shot: *R. v. Salmon* (1880) 6 Q.B.D. 79. Again, if two persons incite each other to drive furiously, and one of them runs over and kills a man, it is manslaughter by both: *R. v. Swindall and Osborne* (1846) 2 C. & K. 230; *cf. R. v. Baldessare*, 22 Cr.App.R. 70, CCA. See also *post*, §§ 18–18, 18–19 as to participation by encouragement.

The act must be the result of the confederacy; for, if several are out for the purpose of committing an offence and, upon alarm and pursuit, run different ways, and one of them kills a pursuer to avoid being taken, the others are not to be considered as aiders and abettors in *that* offence: *R. v. White and Richardson* (1806) R. & R. 99.

18–17 The principles relating to joint enterprise remain the same whatever the offence. For further explanation, and examples, of the application of these principles, see:

(a) *ante*, §§ 17–67 *et seq.* (*mens rea*);

(b) *post*, §§ 19–23 *et seq.* (homicide and generally);

(c) *R. v. Grundy*, 89 Cr.App.R. 333, CA (inflicting grievous bodily harm with intent); and *R. v. Percival, The Times*, May 23, 2003, CA (wounding), *post*, § 19–212;

(d) *post*, §§ 21–168 *et seq.* (abstracting electricity).

See also *post*, § 18–24.

(7) Encouragement

18–18 To establish aiding and abetting on the basis of encouragement, it must be proved that the defendant intended to encourage and *wilfully* did encourage the crime committed. Mere continued voluntary presence at the scene of a crime, even though it was not accidental, does not of itself necessarily amount to encouragement; but the fact that a person was voluntarily and purposely present witnessing the commission of a crime and offered no opposition, though he might reasonably be expected to prevent it and had the power to do so, or at least express his dissent, might in some circumstances afford cogent evidence upon which a jury would be justified in finding that he wilfully encouraged and so aided and abetted, but it would be purely a question of fact for the jury whether he did so or not: *R. v. Clarkson*, 55 Cr.App.R. 445, Ct-MAC.

18–19 In *R. v. Jones and Mirrless*, 65 Cr.App.R. 250, CA, it was emphasised (following *R. v. Allan* [1965] 1 Q.B. 130, 47 Cr.App.R. 243, CCA) that mere voluntary presence which in fact encouraged the principal was not enough; nor was mere voluntary presence coupled with a secret intention to assist, if required. What none of the cases make absolutely clear is whether mere voluntary presence, which in fact encourages the principal, and which is intended to do so, is sufficient. In principle, it is submitted that it should be; the act is the voluntary act of being present. This conclusion is consistent, it is submitted, with the leading case of *R. v. Coney* (1882) 8 Q.B.D. 534, CCR (non-accidental presence at an unlawful prize-fight capable of being encouragement); and with *Wilcox v. Jeffrey* [1951] 1 All E.R. 464, DC (intentional encouragement in fact by voluntary attendance at a concert performance known to be unlawful).

The voluntary presence of a defendant as part of a crowd engaged in threatening behaviour over a period of time and/or distance is sufficient to raise a prima facie case against him on a charge of threatening behaviour, notwithstanding the absence of evidence of any act done by himself: *Allan v. Ireland*, 79 Cr.App.R. 206, DC, applying *R. v. Allan*, *ante*. The same principle plainly applies, for example, to affray.

Knowledge of the principal's offence, plus an ability to control his actions, coupled with a deliberate decision not to exercise such control, may constitute aiding and abetting: *R. v. J.F. Alford Transport Ltd* [1997] 2 Cr.App.R. 326, CA (allegation against employer in relation to falsification of tachograph records by employees). See also *Du Cros v. Lambourne* [1907] 1 K.B. 40; *Rubie v. Faulkner* [1940] 1 K.B. 571, DC; *R. v. Harris* [1964] Crim.L.R. 54, CCA; *R. v. Hands and Plant*, unreported, 1966, Staffordshire Assizes; and *R. v. Webster* [2006] 2 Cr.App.R. 6, CA (all cases involving allegations of aiding and abetting motoring offences committed by another, in the defendant's presence, in circumstances where he had a right of, or opportunity to take, control over the vehicle (see *post*, § 32–19)); *Tuck v. Robson* [1970] 1 W.L.R. 741, DC (licensee convicted of aiding and abetting customers who consumed alcohol after permitted hours); and *R. v. Turner* [1991] Crim.L.R. 57, CA (driver racing another car, convicted of aiding and abetting offence of causing death by reckless driving committed by driver of other car; *cf. R. v. Swindall and Osborne, ante*, § 18–16).

C. COUNSELLORS AND PROCURERS

(1) Definitions

General

As to the general approach to the meaning of these words, see *ante*, § 18–9. As to the *mens rea* of accessories, see generally, *ante*, §§ 17–67 *et seq*. **18–20**

Counselling

The ordinary meaning of the word "counsel" is "advise" or "solicit". There is no implication in the word itself that there should be any causal connection between the counselling and the offence. However, one who counsels or commands (as well as procures) is liable and, by implication liable only, for an offence which is committed in consequence of such counselling (or commandment or procurement), but it is not necessary to prove that the counselling was a substantial cause of the commission of the offence: *R. v. Calhaem* [1985] Q.B. 808, 81 Cr.App.R. 131, CA; *Stephen's Digest* (4th ed.), Art. 39. A person who counsels an offence which is actually committed will not be liable for the offence if the principal in committing the act, acts outside the scope of his authority and advice: *Calhaem, ante* (see the unlikely example given at pp. 813, 135). **18–21**

Where the offence that is solicited is not in fact committed, the person doing the soliciting will be liable for one of the offences created by the *SCA* 2007, Pt 2, *post*, §§ 33–92 *et seq*.

Procuring

In *Att.-Gen.'s Reference (No. 1 of 1975)* [1975] Q.B. 773, 61 Cr.App.R. 118, CA, it was said that: **18–22**

> "To procure means to produce by endeavour. You procure a thing by setting out to see that it happens and taking the appropriate steps to produce that happening. We think that there are plenty of instances in which a person may be said to procure the commission of a crime by another even though there is no sort of conspiracy between the two, even though there is no attempt at agreement or discussion as to the form which the offence should take" (at pp. 779, 121).

An offence cannot, however, be said to have been procured unless there is a causal link between what the alleged procurer did and the commission of the offence. Accordingly, when A surreptitiously laces the drink of B with additional alcohol and, thereafter, B, unaware of what has happened, commits the offence of driving a motor vehicle with an alcohol concentration above the prescribed limit (an absolute offence), A may be convicted of having procured B to commit that offence. The Crown must prove beyond reasonable doubt (a) that A knew that B was going to drive, and (b) that he knew that the ordinary and natural result of lacing B's drink would be to bring his alcohol concentration above the prescribed limit: *ibid. Cf. Blakely v. DPP* [1991] R.T.R. 405, DC, where the intention of the persons lacing the drinks was said to have been to prevent the drinker from driving. For observations on the position of the "generous host" (as opposed to the "surreptitious lacer"), see *Att.-Gen.'s Reference (No. 1 of 1975) ante*, at pp. 780, 122. Should such a case arise, "the basis on which the case will be put against the host is bound to be on the footing that he has supplied the tool with which the offence is committed".

The procurement may be personal, or through the intervention of a third person: Fost. 125; *R. v. Earl of Somerset* (1616) 2 St.Tr. 965; 19 St. Tr. 804; *R. v. Cooper* (1833) 5 C. & P. 535. It may also be direct, by hire, counsel, command, or conspiracy; or indirect, by evincing an express liking, approbation, or assent to another's criminal design of committing an offence: 2 Hawk. c. 29, s.16; but the bare concealment of an offence contemplated by another will not make the party concealing it liable: 2 Hawk. c. 29, s.23; nor will a tacit acquiescence, or words which amount to a bare permission, be sufficient to constitute an offence: 1 Hale 616. **18–23**

As to the meaning of the word "procure", see also *R. v. Broadfoot*, 64 Cr.App.R. 71, CA (considering the use of the word in the *SOA* 1956 (*rep.*)).

(2) Commission of crime different from the one commanded

18–24 If the counsellor or procurer orders or advises one crime, and the principal intentionally commits another; as, for instance, if he was ordered or advised to burn a house, and instead thereof committed theft, the counsellor or procurer would not be liable. If, however, the counsellor or procurer ordered the principal to commit a crime against A, and instead of so doing the principal by mistake committed the same against B, it seems that the counsellor or procurer would be liable: Fost. 270 *et seq.*; but see 1 Hale 617; 3 Co.Inst. 51; 1 Russ.Cr., 12th ed., 160. If, however, the principal deliberately committed the crime, which had been counselled or procured, against B, instead of against A, Hale's view is that the counsellor or procurer would not be liable: 1 Hale 617. But it is clear that the counsellor or procurer would still be liable for all that ensued upon the execution of the unlawful act commanded: as, for instance, if A commands B to beat C, and he beats him so that he dies, A is liable for the death: 4 Bl. Com. 37; 1 Hale 617. Or if A commands B to burn the house of C, and in doing so the house of D is also burnt, A is liable for the burning of D's house: *R. v. Saunders and Archer* (1573) Plowd. 473. So, if the offence commanded is in fact committed, although by different means from those commanded: as for instance, if JW hires JS to poison A, and instead of poisoning him, he shoots him, JW is, nevertheless, liable: Fost. 369, 370.

D. AGENTS PROVOCATEURS

18–25 The fact that the defendant would not have committed the offence if it were not for the activity of an *agent provocateur* is no defence in English law: *R. v. Sang* [1980] A.C. 402, HL. See generally, *ante*, §§ 15–514 *et seq.*, as to the position of the defendant whose offence resulted from the conduct of an *agent provocateur*.

The issue here is whether the *agent provocateur* may himself be prosecuted. The authorities seem to support the following propositions: it is unlawful for a police officer or police informer to counsel or procure the commission of an offence which would not otherwise take place, but it may be proper for a police officer to take part in, or to encourage an informer to take part in, an offence which is already "laid on" solely for the purpose of apprehending the offenders; it is for the jury to decide whether any given case is within this exceptional category: see *R. v. Birtles*, 53 Cr.App.R. 469, CA; *R. v. McCann*, 56 Cr.App.R. 359, CA; *R. v. Clarke (D.G.)*, 80 Cr.App.R. 344, CA. The cases make clear that it should only be in rare circumstances that such a defence should succeed. It is submitted that not only is this correct but also that claims that the offence was already "laid on" should be scrutinised with the greatest care; even if the offence was already planned, the defence should fail unless it is clear that the assistance given by the undercover officer or informer made no difference to the commission of the offence. For example, a person may supply a gun knowing that the recipient intends to use it to commit murder; a person may drive a burglar to a particular house knowing it is his intention to burgle it. If the offences are committed, neither the supplier of the gun, nor the driver should be exonerated from guilt on account of an intention to frustrate the offences by bringing the offender to justice before the act is done; the fact that he did his best to achieve this by informing the police should make no difference. The true principle is that motive for rendering assistance is irrelevant (except to sentence), as is the fact that the *agent provocateur* did not have the *mens rea* required of a principal. Thus, in *Clarke*, *ante*, it should have been regarded as irrelevant that the defendant, in assisting burglars, had no intention permanently to deprive: the *mens rea* of a secondary party is different, being an intention *to assist* (see generally, *ante*, §§ 17–67 *et seq.*).

E. COUNTERMAND AND WITHDRAWAL

18–26 A secondary party may be able to escape liability for aiding, abetting, counselling or procuring an offence if he makes an effective withdrawal before the offence is actually committed: see 1 Hale 618; 1 Russ.Cr., 12th ed., 162. In *R. v. Whitehouse* [1941] 1 W.W.R. 112 (Court of Appeal of British Columbia), Sloan J.A. said:

"After a crime has been committed and before a prior abandonment of the common enterprise may be found by a jury there must be, in my view, in the absence of exceptional circumstances, something more than a mere mental change of intention and physical change of place by those associates who wish to dissociate themselves from the consequences attendant upon their willing assistance up to the moment of the actual commission of that crime. I would not attempt to define too closely what must be done in criminal matters involving participation in a common unlawful purpose to break the chain of causation and responsibility. That must depend on the circumstances of each case but it seems to me that one essential element ought to be established in a case of this kind: where practicable and reasonable there must be timely communication of the intention to abandon the common purpose from those who wish to dissociate from the contemplated crime to those who desire to continue in it. What is 'timely communication' must be determined by the facts of each case but where practicable and reasonable it ought to be such communication, verbal or otherwise, that it will serve unequivocal notice upon the other party to the common unlawful cause that if he proceeds upon it he does so without the further aid and assistance of those who withdraw."

This dictum, as approved in *R. v. Becerra and Cooper*, 62 Cr.App.R. 212, CA, and *R. v. Grundy* [1977] Crim.L.R. 543, CA, was applied in *R. v. Whitefield*, 79 Cr.App.R. 36, CA, where it was said that if participation has been confined to advice or encouragement there must at least be communication of the change of mind such as to give unequivocal notice to the effect mentioned in the dictum of Sloan J.A. In *R. v. Perman* [1996] 1 Cr.App.R. 24, the Court of Appeal doubted whether it is possible for a party to a joint enterprise to withdraw therefrom once the contemplated criminal activity has commenced. In *R. v. Robinson* [2000] 5 *Archbold News* 2, CA, it was said that only exceptionally can a person withdraw from a crime he has initiated. To do so, he must communicate his withdrawal in order to give the principal(s) the opportunity to desist rather than complete the crime, and this is so even in cases of spontaneous violence, unless it is not practicable or reasonable so to communicate, as in the exceptional circumstances pertaining in *R. v. Mitchell and King*, 163 J.P. 75, CA, where the accused had thrown down his weapon and moved away before the final and fatal blows were struck. And in *R. v. Bryce* [2004] 2 Cr.App.R. 35, CA, it was said that where an act of assistance or encouragement, accompanied by the necessary *mens rea* (as to which, see *ante*, § 17–67), was proved, the defendant would only avoid liability if he did a further act that amounted to a countermanding of the earlier assistance and a withdrawal from the common purpose; repentance alone would not suffice; the fact that his mind was innocent when the crime was committed was no defence.

In *R. v. O'Flaherty, Ryan and Toussaint* [2004] 2 Cr.App.R. 20, CA, it was said that a person who effectively disengages or withdraws before the fatal injury is, or injuries are, inflicted is not guilty of murder because he was not party to and did not participate in any unlawful violence which caused death; to disengage from an incident a person must do enough to demonstrate that he is withdrawing from the joint enterprise; ultimately, this is a question of fact and degree, account being taken, *inter alia*, of the nature of the assistance and encouragement already given and how imminent the infliction of the fatal injury or injuries is, as well as the action said to constitute the withdrawal; in a case of assistance, it is not an essential pre-requisite of an effective withdrawal that reasonable steps should have been taken to prevent the crime; and, in a case of spontaneous violence, it is possible, in principle, to withdraw by ceasing to fight, throwing down one's weapons and walking away (referring to *Mitchell and King*, but not to *Robinson*, *ante*). See the commentaries to this case, and to *Bryce*, *ante*, in *Criminal Law Week* 2004/14/10 and 2004/40/09, where it is suggested that the issue is not whether the alleged secondary party has withdrawn, but whether or not he has effectively neutralised the encouragement or assistance already given (see also *post*).

Where there is evidence of withdrawal by a secondary party, that evidence should be **18–27**
left to the jury to decide whether it amounts to an effective withdrawal in the particular circumstances. In *R. v. Whitefield*, *ante*, it was held to be an error of law for a judge to rule that in failing to communicate with the police, or take any other steps to prevent the burglary for which he had provided information, the defendant remained liable in law for the burglary even if he had, as asserted, communicated to the other parties his withdrawal from the matter before the offence was committed. A similar situation had arisen in *R. v. Grundy*, *ante*.

18–28 In *Becerra and Cooper*, *ante*, the appellants had been convicted of murder committed during the course of a burglary. B had provided the knife to C shortly before the killing. It was held that B's sudden departure from the scene with the words "Let's go" when surprised by the victim was an insufficient communication of withdrawal. A valid withdrawal could only have been effected in some manner "vastly different and vastly more effective". The court left open the question whether the circumstances were such that physical action with a view to preventing the crime was required if B's prior assistance was to be effectively neutralised. The point was again left open in *R. v. Rook*, 97 Cr.App.R. 327, CA. In principle, it seems clear that the measures necessary to absolve a person from liability as an accessory will vary according to what assistance, encouragement, etc., he has given. If, for example, a party provides the gun for a murder, it is submitted that even the plainest spoken communication to the principal would be insufficient on its own to absolve him from liability; but in each case it should be for the jury to decide whether there has been an effective neutralisation: see *Whitefield*, *ante*.

18–29 An effective withdrawal prior to the commission of the substantive offence will not, it is submitted, provide a defence to a charge of conspiracy to commit that offence, because the offence of conspiracy will already be complete by the time of the withdrawal: see *post*, § 33–5. By the same reasoning, withdrawal could not provide a defence to a charge of incitement to commit an offence or to a charge of attempt to commit an offence when an act that is more than preparatory has been done before communication of the withdrawal.

F. ACQUITTAL OF PRINCIPAL, ETC.

18–30 There can be no conviction for aiding, abetting, counselling or procuring an offence unless the *actus reus* of the substantive offence is shown to have occurred: *R. v. Assistant Recorder of Kingston-upon-Hull, ex p. Morgan* [1969] 2 Q.B. 58, 53 Cr.App.R. 96, DC; *R. v. Loukes* [1996] 1 Cr.App.R. 444, CA; *R. v. Roberts and George* [1997] R.T.R. 462, CA (but for a criticism of the application of this principle in the latter case, see *Criminal Law Week* 1997/08/27). However, a secondary party may, in certain circumstances, be convicted when the actual perpetrator of the *actus reus* of the substantive offence is either acquitted or is convicted of a lesser offence.

The secondary party may be convicted and the "principal" acquitted where there is evidence against the secondary party that is not admissible against the "principal": see *R. v. Humphreys and Turner* [1965] 3 All E.R. 689, Liverpool Crown Court (H.H.J. Chapman); or where there is insufficient evidence that the person charged as principal was in fact involved in the offence: *R. v. Davis* [1977] Crim.L.R. 542, CA. See also *R. v. Burton* (1875) 13 Cox 71, CCR. The acquittal of the alleged principal at an earlier trial is not only no bar to the subsequent conviction of an accessory, but is inadmissible at the trial of the accessory, since it is irrelevant as being merely evidence of the opinion of the first jury: *Hui Chi-Ming v. R.* [1992] 1 A.C. 34, PC.

18–31 As to the inadmissibility of the acts of the alleged principal as against the secondary party, where the case against the principal is withdrawn for lack of evidence, see *R. v. Fuller* [1998] Crim.L.R. 61, CA (but it is submitted that such acts would be admissible if it could be established against the secondary party, *e.g.* by his admission, that there was a common enterprise with the alleged principal).

The secondary party may also be convicted where the "principal" has some defence that does not benefit the secondary party. Thus, in *R. v. Bourne*, 36 Cr.App.R. 125, CCA, the appellant was convicted of aiding and abetting his wife to commit buggery with a dog in circumstances where the wife, if charged, would have been entitled to an acquittal on the basis of duress. Similarly, in *R. v. Cogan and Leak* [1976] 1 Q.B. 217, 61 Cr.App.R. 217, CA, where the appellant's conviction for aiding and abetting the rape of his wife was held not to be vitiated by the quashing of the conviction of the "principal", who contended that he believed the woman consented. And in *DPP v. K. and B.* [1997] 1 Cr.App.R. 36, DC, it was held that the fact that the presumption that a child aged over 10 but under 14 was *doli incapax* had not been rebutted in the case of the principal did not preclude the conviction of others as accessories. In *R. v. Pickford* [1995] 1 Cr.App.R. 420, CA, it was said, *obiter*, that the decisions in *R. v. Bourne* and

R. v. Cogan and Leak do not support the proposition that where the principal offender lacks all legal capacity to commit the crime in question, another may nevertheless be guilty of aiding and abetting him. These were cases in which the person who had committed the acts said to constitute the principal offence was fully capable in law of committing that offence, but had a complete defence on the facts.

In *R. v. Howe* [1987] 1 A.C. 417, HL, it was held that where a person has been killed and that result is the result intended by another participant, the mere fact that the actual killer may be convicted only of the reduced charge of manslaughter for some reason special to himself does not result in a compulsory reduction for the other participant (*R. v. Richards* [1974] Q.B. 776, 58 Cr.App.R. 60, CA, overruled).

G. INDICTMENT

It is usual to indict secondary parties, within the *Accessories and Abettors Act* 1861, s.8 (*ante*, § 18–2), as principals. No objection could be taken to an indictment in such form, but it is desirable that the particulars should bear some relation to the realities, making it clear, if it be the case, that the defendant is alleged to be an accessory: see *DPP for Northern Ireland v. Maxwell*, 68 Cr.App.R. 128 (*per* Viscount Dilhorne at p. 143; *per* Lord Hailsham at p. 147; *per* Lord Edmund Davies at p. 150); *R. v. Gaughan*, 155 J.P. 235, CA; and *R. v. Taylor, Harrison and Taylor* [1998] Crim.L.R. 582, CA. But there is nothing to prevent the indictment alleging participation as a principal where the prosecution case is advanced on alternative bases of participation as a principal or as an accessory: *Gaughan*, *ante*. In certain cases, *e.g.* where the principal offence is that of a person holding a special status, such as that of a bankrupt under the *Insolvency Act* 1986, it is necessary to indict the abettor in the following form. **18–32**

IN THE CROWN COURT AT.......... .... [OR: IN THE CENTRAL CRIMINAL COURT]

THE QUEEN
v.
A B AND C D

A B and C D are charged as follows:—[OR: *A B and C D are charged with the following offence*:]

STATEMENT OF OFFENCE

A B, a bankrupt obtaining credit, contrary to section 360(1)(a) of the Insolvency Act *1986.*

C D, being aider and abettor to same offence.

PARTICULARS OF OFFENCE

A B, being an undischarged bankrupt, obtained credit, which by about —— 20— amounted to £——, from —— Bank plc. without informing the said bank that he was then an undischarged bankrupt.

C D, at the same time and place did aid and abet, counsel and procure A B to commit the said offence.

The wording of the particulars of the principal offence in this example is based on the suggestion of the Court of Appeal in *R. v. Hartley* [1972] 2 Q.B. 1, 56 Cr.App.R. 189 (*post*, § 30–187).

The words "aid and abet, counsel and procure" may all be used together to charge a person who is alleged to have participated in the offence otherwise than as a principal: *Re Smith* (1858) 3 H. & N. 227; *Ferguson v. Weaving* [1951] 1 K.B. 814, DC. **18–33**

IV. ASSISTING OFFENDERS

A. STATUTE

Criminal Law Act 1967, s.4

Penalties for assisting offenders

4.—(1) Where a person has committed a relevant offence, any other person who, knowing or **18–34**

believing him to be guilty of the offence or of some other relevant offence, does without lawful authority or reasonable excuse any act with intent to impede his apprehension or prosecution shall be guilty of an offence.

(1A) In this section and section 5 below, "relevant offence" means—

(a) an offence for which the sentence is fixed by law,

(b) an offence for which a person of 18 years or over (not previously convicted) may be sentenced to imprisonment for a term of five years (or might be so sentenced but for the restrictions imposed by section 33 of the *Magistrates' Courts Act* 1980).

(2) If on the trial of an indictment for a relevant offence the jury are satisfied that the offence charged (or some other offence of which the accused might on that charge be found guilty) was committed, but find the accused not guilty of it, they may find him guilty of any offence under subsection (1) above of which they are satisfied that he is guilty in relation to the offence charged (or that other offence).

(3) A person committing an offence under subsection (1) above with intent to impede another person's apprehension or prosecution shall on conviction on indictment be liable to imprisonment according to the gravity of the other person's offence, as follows:—

(a) if that offence is one for which the sentence is fixed by law, he shall be liable to imprisonment for not more than ten years;

(b) if it is one for which a person (not previously convicted) may be sentenced to imprisonment for a term of fourteen years, he shall be liable to imprisonment for not more than seven years;

(c) if it is not one included above but is one for which a person (not previously convicted) may be sentenced to imprisonment for a term of ten years, he shall be liable to imprisonment for not more than five years;

(d) in any other case, he shall be liable to imprisonment for not more than three years.

(4) No proceedings shall be instituted for an offence under subsection (1) above except by or with the consent of the Director of Public Prosecutions: ....

[This section is printed as amended and repealed in part by the *PACE Act* 1984, s.119(1), and Sched. 6, Pt I, para. 17; the *Theft Act* 1968, s.33(3), and Sched. 3, Pt III; the *Criminal Jurisdiction Act* 1975, Sched. 6, Pt I; the *CLA* 1977, Sched. 13; the *Extradition Act* 1989, Sched. 2; and the *SOCPA* 2005, s.111, and Sched. 7, para. 40(1) and (2).]

As to alternative verdicts under subsection (2), see *post*, § 18–36.

As to the offence of perverting the course of justice, see *post*, §§ 28–1 *et seq*. As to concealment of evidence, see section 5 of the 1967 Act, *post*, § 28–29.

B. INDICTMENT

STATEMENT OF OFFENCE

18–35 *Assisting offender, contrary to section 4(1) of the* Criminal Law Act *1967.*

PARTICULARS OF OFFENCE

C D having committed an arrestable [a relevant] offence, namely the theft of an overcoat belonging to E F; A B on the —— day of —— 20—, knowing or believing that the said C D had committed the said offence or some other arrestable [relevant] offence, without lawful authority or reasonable excuse removed from the said overcoat the name of the said E F, with intent to impede the apprehension or prosecution of the said C D.

This offence is triable either way: *MCA* 1980, s.17(1), and Sched. 1, *ante*, § 1–75af.

18–36 The indictment must specify the principal offence alleged, but it is possible to apply section 6(3) of the 1967 Act (*ante*, § 4–455) to this ingredient of the offence; thus, if the principal offence alleged is murder, it would be open to the jury to convict if satisfied only that the principal offender committed manslaughter: *R. v. Morgan (M.M.)*, 56 Cr.App.R. 181, CA. Where such a course is left open to the jury, it would be necessary to ascertain from the jury whether they were satisfied of the principal offence alleged or of the alternative only, because the maximum penalty varies according to the gravity of the principal offence: see section 4(3) and *R. v. Morgan, ante*.

Where the prosecution propose to rely on the possibility of a conviction contrary to section 4(1), there should be a specific count if this possibility is foreseen before trial; if section 4(2) is to be relied upon, the issue should be raised as early as possible during the trial: *R. v. Cross and Channon*, 55 Cr.App.R. 540, CA; *R. v. Vincent*, 56 Cr.App.R. 281, CA.

The wording of section 4(2) appears to require that before a conviction may be returned pursuant to that provision, the jury must return a verdict of not guilty of the charge specified in the indictment: see *R. v. Collison*, 71 Cr.App.R. 249, CA (considering similar wording in section 6(3) of the 1967 Act, *ante*, § 4–455); and *R. v. Griffiths* [1998] Crim.L.R. 348, CA (considering similar wording in section 24(1) of the *RTOA* 1988, *post*, § 32–165).

As to alternative verdicts generally, see *ante*, §§ 4–453 *et seq*.

C. INGREDIENTS OF THE OFFENCE

Whereas it is not necessary that the defendant be proved to have known the nature of the principal offence, his state of mind may be a material factor in mitigation and, in an exceptional case, it might be appropriate to invite the jury to return a special verdict on the point: *R. v. Morgan (M.M.), ante*. The policy of the Act, however, is that those who assist offenders do so at their peril, the punishment being directly related to the nature of the principal offence, not to the knowledge of the defendant. **18–37**

It is unnecessary to prove that the defendant knew the identity of the principal offender: *R. v. Brindley and Long* [1971] 2 Q.B. 300, 55 Cr.App.R. 258, CA. Nor is it necessary that the principal offender has been convicted: *R. v. Donald and Donald*, 83 Cr.App.R. 49, CA.

Where admissible evidence of the principal offence is lacking, it may be possible to pursue a charge of perverting the course of justice: see *post*, §§ 28–1 *et seq*. Where the principal offender has been convicted, his commission of the offence may be proved by proving his conviction under sections 73 and 74 of the *PACE Act* 1984 (*ante*, §§ 9–80, 9–82).

V. MISPRISION OF TREASON

Misprision of treason consists of failing with due diligence to inform of treasons committed or threatened by others without the assent of the prisoner, or any active part in rescuing traitors from justice: Fourth Report Crim. Law Commissioners, 1848, p. 79. As to misprisions generally, see 3 Co. Inst. 140; 1 Hawk. c. 20; 2 Hawk. c. 29, s.23. **18–38**

The offence is a misdemeanour at common law, punishable by imprisonment for life.

The procedure on a prosecution for misprision of treason is the same as for treason. See the statutes collected under that title, *post*, §§ 25–1 *et seq*.

13-38 Misprision of treason consists of failing, with due diligence, to inform of treason committed or intended by others without the assent of the prospect of any active part in treating treason: Report of the Criminal Law Commissioners 1843, p. 79. As to misprision generally, see 1 Hale c. 29; 1 Hawk. c. 20, s. 23.

Chapter 19

OFFENCES AGAINST THE PERSON

I. HOMICIDE

A. MURDER

(1) Definition

19–1 The following definition is based on that contained in *Coke's Institutes* (Co. Inst. Pt III (1797 ed.), ch. 7, p. 47), modified to conform with changes made by statute and decisions of the courts:

"Subject to three exceptions, the crime of murder is committed where a person of sound mind and discretion (*post*, § 19–2)—unlawfully (*post*, § 19–3)—kills (*post*, §§ 19–4 *et seq.*)—any reasonable creature (*post*, § 19–15)—in being (*post*, § 19–16)—and under the Queen's peace (*post*, § 19–18)—with intent to kill or cause grievous bodily harm (*post*, §§ 19–19 *et seq.*)."

At common law there was a further requirement, *viz.* that the death followed within a year and a day. This rule continues to apply where the act or omission (or the last of the acts or omissions) which caused death occurred before June 16, 1996; otherwise it has been abolished: *Law Reform (Year and a Day Rule) Act* 1996, ss.1, 3(2). See further, *post*, § 19–22.

An offence which would otherwise be murder is reduced to manslaughter if the accused:

(a) was provoked (*post*, § 19–50); or
(b) suffered from diminished responsibility (*post*, § 19–66); or
(c) was acting in pursuance of a suicide pact (*post*, § 19–83).

As to (a) the onus remains throughout upon the Crown to negative provocation beyond any reasonable doubt. As to (b) and (c) the onus is cast upon the accused to prove the facts reducing the offence to manslaughter on a balance of probabilities.

Apart from these three exceptions, the elements of manslaughter are the same as those of murder save for the requirement that there should be an intent to kill or cause grievous bodily harm. Some of the authorities cited below were cases of manslaughter where the principles laid down apply equally to murder.

"Of sound mind and discretion"

19–2 This means anyone who is not insane or under 10 years old. The restriction is not peculiar to homicide (see *ante*, §§ 1–90, 17–74 *et seq.*).

If any person procures a person who is not of sound mind and discretion to kill another, the procurer is guilty of the murder as principal, even if absent at the time: 1 Hawk. c. 31, s.37.

"Unlawfully"

19–3 This means without legal justification or excuse, *e.g.* self-defence or bona fide surgical treatment: see *post*, §§ 19–37 *et seq.* The onus is on the Crown to prove that the killing was unlawful.

"Kills"

(i) *Principle*

19–4 With one exception, any act which is a substantial cause of death renders the doer responsible for that death if the other elements of murder are proved. The exception is the taking away of a man's life by perjury, which is not, in law, murder or, *semble*, manslaughter: *R. v. Daniel* (1754) 1 Leach 44; 1 East P.C. 333; and see Bl.Com. 196n.

(ii) *The act*

With this exception, it is not necessary that there should be any contact between the killer and his victim, or any weapon used. **19–5**

If a man does any act of which the consequence is death, such killing may be murder although no stroke were struck by himself; as was the case of a gaoler, who caused the death of a prisoner by imprisoning him in unwholesome air: *R. v. Huggins* (1730) 17 St.Tr. 309 at 376; *cf. R. v. Acton* (1729) 17 St.Tr. 462 at 511, 526, 546; *R. v. Bambridge, ibid.*, 397. So, for a mother to throw her child onto a heap of ashes and leave it there in the open air exposed to the cold whereby it dies, may amount to murder: *R. v. Waters* (1848) 1 Den. 356, and see *R. v. Pinhorn* (1844) 1 Cox 70; *R. v. Phillpot* (1853) Dears. 179.

If a person knowingly gives poison to A to administer as a medicine to B, but A neglecting to do so, it is accidentally given to B by a child or other unconscious agent, this is in law a poisoning by the party himself, as much as if he had administered it with his own hands: *R. v. Michael* (1840) 2 Mood. 120.

(iii) *"Substantial cause"*

In homicide cases, it is rarely necessary to give the jury any direction on causation as such. When such direction is needed, they should be told that in law it is enough that the accused's act contributed significantly to the death; it need not be the sole or principal cause thereof (see *R. v. Pitts* (1842) C. & Mar. 248; *R. v. Curley*, 2 Cr.App.R. 96, 109, CCA). A proper direction on a charge of causing death by dangerous driving is that the driving, if dangerous, must be "*a* substantial cause" of death, as indicating that it must be something more than *de minimis* (and as avoiding the necessity to go into details of legal causation and remoteness): *R. v. Henningan*, 55 Cr.App.R. 262, CA. A similar direction has been given in other cases of homicide (*e.g. R. v. Cato*, 62 Cr.App.R. 41 at 46, where the Court of Appeal approved such a direction in a case of manslaughter resulting from an injection of heroin). **19–6**

Where there is an issue as to whether death was caused by some supervening event (*e.g.* medical negligence), there is no onus on the prosecution to prove that the supervening event was not a significant cause of death; their duty is to prove that the accused's act contributed significantly to the death and the direction to the jury should be so confined: *R. v. Mellor*, *The Times*, February 29, 1996, CA.

(iv) *Novus actus interveniens*

Occasionally a specific issue of causation arises. One such case is where, although an act of the accused constitutes a *causa sine qua non* of the death of the victim, nevertheless the intervention of a third person may be regarded as the sole cause of the victim's death (or *novus actus interveniens*) thereby relieving the accused of criminal liability. However, a reasonable act performed for the purpose of self-preservation, including a reasonable act of self-defence, does not operate as a *novus actus* nor does an act done in the execution of legal duty: *R. v. Pagett*, 76 Cr.App.R. 279, CA (conviction for manslaughter upheld; appellant used deceased as shield whilst firing at police; deceased killed by retaliatory shot fired by police). **19–7**

As to causation in the context of fear of violence, see *post*, § 19–10, and of medical treatment, see *post*, §§ 19–12 *et seq.*

(v) *Acceleration of death*

If a man is suffering from a disease, which in all likelihood would terminate his life in a short time, and another gives him a wound or hurt which hastens his death, this is such a killing as constitutes murder: 1 Hale 427, or at the very least manslaughter: *R. v. Martin* (1832) 5 C. & P. 128; *R. v. Murton* (1862) 3 F. & F. 492; *R. v. Dyson* [1908] 2 K.B. 454, 1 Cr.App.R. 13, CCA; and see *R. v. Cato, ante*, at p.45. **19–8**

See also *R. v. Hayward* (1908) 21 Cox C.C. 692 (victim with abnormal heart condition, such that any combination of physical exertion and fright or strong emotion might cause death); and *R. v. Wall* (1802) 28 St.Tr. 51 at 145 (victim's action aggravating condition caused by accused); 1 Russ.Cr., 12th ed., 425.

As to medical treatment being a factor in causation, see *post*, §§ 19–12 *et seq.*

(vi) *Absence of body*

19–9 Evidence afforded by the accused himself is sufficient: *R. v. Davidson*, 25 Cr.App.R. 21, CCA. The fact of death is also provable by circumstantial evidence, notwithstanding that neither the body nor any trace of the body has been found: *R. v. Onufrejczyk* [1955] 2 Q.B. 388, 39 Cr.App.R. 1, CCA. Before the defendant can be convicted, the fact of death should be proved by such circumstances as render the commission of the crime certain and leave no ground for reasonable doubt. The circumstantial evidence should be so cogent and compelling as to convince a jury that on no rational hypothesis other than murder can the facts be accounted for: *ibid.*

If a person was killed by one or other of two or more acts by an assailant, each of which was sufficient to establish manslaughter if it caused the death, then it is unnecessary in order to found such a conviction for the Crown to prove which act caused the death. It follows that the absence of a body and/or a post mortem report revealing the cause of death, is immaterial: *Att.-Gen.'s Reference (No. 4 of 1980)*, 73 Cr.App.R. 40, CA.

(vii) *Fear of violence*

19–10 To constitute the essential ingredients of a charge of manslaughter, laid upon the basis that a person has sustained fatal injuries while trying to escape from assault by the accused, it must be proved:

(a) that the victim immediately before he sustained the injuries was in fear of being hurt physically;
(b) that this fear was such that it caused him to try to escape;
(c) that while he was trying to escape, and because he was trying to escape, he met his death;
(d) that his fear of being hurt there and then was reasonable and was caused by the conduct of the accused;
(e) that the accused's conduct which caused the fear was unlawful; and
(f) that his conduct was such that any sober and reasonable person would recognise it as likely to subject the victim to at least the risk of some harm resulting from it, albeit not serious harm.

It is unnecessary to prove the accused's knowledge that his conduct was unlawful. It is sufficient to prove that the accused's act was intentional, and that it was dangerous on an objective test: *DPP (Jamaica) v. Daley* [1980] A.C. 237, PC, following *DPP v. Newbury* [1977] A.C. 500, HL, and, except on the point of knowledge that the act was unlawful, *R. v. Mackie*, 57 Cr.App.R. 453, CA (*post*, § 19–103). Dangerous in this context means "likely to subject the victim to at least the risk of some harm albeit not serious harm".

The test is not whether the accused himself foresaw the conduct of the victim, but whether that conduct could reasonably have been foreseen as the consequence of what the accused was saying or doing: *R. v. Roberts*, 56 Cr.App.R. 95, CA (assault occasioning actual bodily harm). See also *R. v. Beech*, 7 Cr.App.R. 197, CCA; and *R. v. Marjoram* [2000] Crim.L.R. 372, CA, where it was said that whilst the question is purely objective it should be answered by reference to what could reasonably have been foreseen by a responsible person finding himself in the circumstances of the accused. Such formulation is, however, liable to confuse, and to lead to submissions such as that the jury should have regard to the age and sex of the offender. There is ample authority for saying that the test is to be applied by reference only to the reasonable man observing the situation.

Although a direction in the above terms is sufficient in most cases, it is inadequate where there is a real issue as to causation: *R. v. Williams and Davis*, 95 Cr.App.R. 1, CA. The deceased had been given a lift by the appellants. Later, he had jumped from the car while it was travelling at about 30 miles per hour, sustaining fatal injuries. What had happened in the car was unclear, although there was some evidence of threats and an attempt to rob the deceased. The conviction was quashed, despite a

direction exactly in accordance with *DPP (Jamaica) v. Daley*, *ante*, on the ground that it was inadequate in circumstances where there was a real issue as to causation and the unlawful act relied on was merely a threat, unaccompanied by, and not preceded by any actual violence. Where there was an almost total lack of evidence as to the nature of the threat, it was impermissible for the Crown to invite the jury to infer the gravity of the threat from the reaction of the deceased. In such circumstances, the jury should consider two additional questions: (a) whether it was reasonably foreseeable that some harm, albeit not serious harm, was likely to result from the threat itself; (b) whether the deceased's reaction in jumping from the moving car was within the range of responses which might be expected from a victim placed in the situation in which he was. The jury should bear in mind any particular characteristic of the victim and the fact that in the agony of the moment he may act without thought and deliberation (at pp. 8, 9). See also *R. v. Evans* [1992] Crim.L.R. 659, CA, where a conviction for manslaughter was quashed because the Crown could not point to any unlawful act by the appellant which caused the deceased to jump out of the window.

(viii) *Aggravated assault*

The same principles as those set out in (vii), *ante*, apply where death does not result: see *R. v. Roberts*, *ante*; *R. v. Beech*, *ante*; *R. v. Martin* (1881) 8 Q.B.D. 54 (intentionally causing terror amongst audience leaving theatre by blocking exit and extinguishing lights); *R. v. Halliday* (1889) 61 L.T. 701 (victim threatened by accused tried to escape via a window but was restrained by her daughter, whereupon accused threatened daughter who then let go of the victim so that she fell to the ground); and *R. v. Lewis* [1970] Crim.L.R. 647, CA (immaterial that the accused had not approached within reach of the victim when she jumped from a window). **19–11**

(ix) *Medical treatment: causation*

Where a blow was given which in the opinion of a surgeon rendered a restorative necessary, and the injured person being unable to swallow was choked in administering the restorative, it was held that the death was caused by the blow: *R. v. McIntyre* (1847) 2 Cox 379. **19–12**

If a man is wounded, and the wound turns to a gangrene or fever for want of proper applications, or from neglect, or leads to septic pneumonia or meningitis, and the man dies from the gangrene, fever, etc. (*Brintons Ltd v. Turvey* [1905] A.C. 230 at 235; *R. v. Dyson* [1908] 2 K.B. 454, 1 Cr.App.R. 13, CCA); or if it becomes fatal from the refusal of the party to undergo a surgical operation (*R. v. Holland* (1841) 2 M. & Rob. 351); or if death results from an operation rendered advisable by the act of the defendant (*R. v. Davis* (1883) 15 Cox 174); this is homicide, and whether it be murder or manslaughter will depend upon the circumstances under which the wound is given: 1 Hale 428.

Where it is alleged that death resulted from negligence in the treatment of injuries caused by the accused, the jury should be told that such negligence does not exclude the responsibility of the accused unless the negligent treatment was so independent of his acts, and in itself so potent in causing death, that they regard the contribution made by the acts of the accused as insignificant: *R. v. Cheshire*, 93 Cr.App.R. 251, CA (considering *R. v. Jordan*, 40 Cr.App.R. 152, CCA, and *R. v. Smith (T. J.)* [1959] 2 Q.B. 35, 43 Cr.App.R. 121, CCA). It is not the function of the jury to evaluate competing causes or to choose which is the dominant provided they are satisfied that the accused's acts can fairly be said to have made a contribution to the victim's death, "significant" meaning a contribution which is more then negligible: *ibid*. **19–13**

Where life support apparatus is switched off after brain death has occurred, this does not prevent the original assailant from being responsible for the death: *R. v. Malcherek and Steel*, 73 Cr.App.R. 173, CA (in such circumstances issue of causation may properly be withdrawn from jury). **19–14**

See also *R. v. Blaue*, 61 Cr.App.R. 271, CA (victim refused blood transfusion as being contrary to religious belief; conviction upheld).

Where it is alleged that death resulted from a lack of medical treatment which it was

the defendant's duty to administer, or cause to be administered or to seek on behalf of the deceased, it would have to be proved that medical aid, or prompt medical aid, would have prolonged the life of the deceased: *R. v. Morby* (1882) 15 Cox 35.

(x) *Alternative acts*

19–14a Where the prosecution rely on alternative acts as the cause of death, the jury should be directed as to the need for unanimity (subject to the possibility of a majority verdict) as to at least one of the acts: *R. v. Carr* [2000] 2 Cr.App.R. 149, CA; *R. v. Boreman* [2000] 1 All E.R. 307, CA; or, alternatively, that they must all be sure that if it was not the one act, then it was the other: *R. v. Giannetto* [1997] 1 Cr.App.R. 1, CA (*post* § 19–35a).

As to the need for unanimity generally, see *ante*, §§ 4–391 *et seq.*

"Any reasonable creature"

19–15 "Reasonable", it is submitted, relates to the appearance rather than the mental capacity of the victim and is apt to exclude monstrous births. This submission was considered in *Re A. (Children) (Conjoined Twins: Surgical Separation)* [2001] Fam. 147 at 212–214, CA (Civ. Div.).

"In being"—unborn and newly born children

19–16 To kill a child in its mother's womb is neither murder nor manslaughter: *Att.-Gen.'s Reference (No. 3 of 1994)* [1998] A.C. 245, HL; although it is an offence under the *Infant Life (Preservation) Act* 1929, see *post*, § 19–130.

Where a person attacks a pregnant woman intending to do her grievous bodily harm and in consequence of that attack, she goes into premature labour with the child being born alive but subsequently dying as a result of being born prematurely, the attacker would be guilty of manslaughter in relation to the death of the child but could not be guilty of murder: *Att.-Gen.'s Reference (No. 3 of 1994)*, *ante*.

The House of Lords declined to consider the liability of a person whose intent was to kill or do serious harm to the child, rather than the mother, but the decision of the Court of Appeal ([1996] 1 Cr.App.R. 351), together with the ancient authorities of *R. v. Senior* (1832) 1 Mood. 346 and *R. v. West* (1848) 2 C. & K. 784, suggest that he would be liable to conviction for murder. In so far as the decision of the Court of Appeal depended on the doctrine of transferred malice, it must, however, be regarded as open to doubt in view of the unwillingness of the House of Lords to apply that doctrine where the attacker's intent was directed against the mother. For further consideration of this aspect of the decision of the Court of Appeal; see the third and fourth supplements to the 1996 edition of this work.

19–17 For murder or manslaughter, it must be proved that the entire child has actually been born into the world in a living state: *R. v. Poulton* (1832) 5 C. & P. 329; and the fact of its having breathed is not conclusive proof thereof: *R. v. Sellis* (1837) 7 C. & P. 850; *R. v. Crutchley* (1837) 7 C. & P. 814. There must be an independent circulation in the child before it can be accounted alive: *R. v. Enoch* (1833) 5 C. & P. 539; *R. v. Wright* (1841) 9 C. & P. 754. A child is born alive when it exists as a live child, breathing and living by reason of its breathing through its own lungs alone, without deriving any of its living or power of living by or through any connection with its mother: *R. v. Handley* (1874) 13 Cox 79. But the fact of the child's being still connected with the mother by the umbilical cord will not prevent the killing from being murder: *R. v. Crutchley ante*; *R. v. Reeves* (1839) 9 C. & P. 25; *R. v. Trilloe* (1842) 2 Mood. 260; *R. v. Pritchard* (1901) 17 T.L.R. 310.

"Under the Queen's peace"

19–18 The person killed must be "under the Queen's peace". This includes even persons under sentence of death. The inclusion of these words in the definition of murder (*ante*, § 19–1) is meant only to except from murder killing in the course of war and possibly rebellion: *R. v. Page* [1954] 1 Q.B. 170, 37 Cr.App.R. 189, Ct-MAC.

If the deceased were an alien enemy, and killed in the actual heat and exercise of war, this is a matter of justification, as the alien is not in the Queen's peace: see 1 Hale 433; 3 Co.Inst. 50.

But killing even an alien enemy within the kingdom, unless in the actual exercise of war, would be murder: 1 Hale 433. The same rule applies where an alien enemy is charged with killing a British subject: *R. v. Depardo* (1807) R. & R. 134; and if the crime be committed in England, it is no defence that the alien did not know English law: *R. v. Esop* (1836) 7 C. & P. 456.

As to the jurisdiction to try murder by British subjects abroad, see *ante*, § 2–51.

"With intent to kill or cause grievous bodily harm"

(i) *"With intent to"*

See *ante*, §§ 17–34 *et seq.* **19–19**

(ii) *"Grievous bodily harm"*

This means injury which is really serious but not necessarily dangerous to life: *R. v. Cunningham* [1982] A.C. 566, HL. It is for the judge to decide whether the facts require the use of the word "really" before "serious bodily harm": *R. v. Janjua and Choudhury* [1999] 1 Cr.App.R. 91, CA.

(iii) *"Constructive malice"*

The *Homicide Act* 1957, s.1, abolished the doctrine of constructive malice (whereunder a killing in certain circumstances, *e.g.* during the course of a violent felony, might be murder in the absence of an intent to kill or do serious bodily harm). **19–20**

(iv) *Killing person believed to be dead*

The defendant inflicted serious injuries on a woman and soon afterwards, while she was still alive, flung her into a river. She continued to breathe for an appreciable time afterwards and the eventual cause of her death was drowning. His defence to a charge of murder was that he had believed her to be dead when he threw her into the river. It was said by the Court of Criminal Appeal, following *Meli (Thabo) v. R.* [1954] 1 W.L.R. 228, PC, that the proper direction to the jury was that, if they regarded his behaviour from the moment when he first struck her to the moment when he threw her into the river as a series of acts designed to cause her death or grievous bodily harm, it was open to them to convict of murder, even though the defendant believed she was dead when he threw her in the river: *R. v. Church* [1966] 1 Q.B. 59, 49 Cr.App.R. 206, CCA. What was said was strictly *obiter* as the defendant was acquitted of murder, but convicted of manslaughter; as to this case and manslaughter, see *post*, § 19–105. See too *R. v. Moore and Dorn* [1975] Crim.L.R. 239, CA (conviction for murder upheld). **19–21**

(v) *"Killing the wrong person"*

For "transferred malice", where the actual victim is unintended, see *ante*, § 17–24.

"Within a year and a day"

The common law required that death ensued within a year and a day of the act or omission of the defendant which caused the death (see *R. v. Dyson* [1908] 2 K.B. 454, 1 Cr.App.R. 13, CCA); this rule applied to murder, manslaughter, and, it seems, any other offence involving the death of another person. The basis of the rule was a presumption that after such a time it would be impossible to say whether cause of death was the act of the defendant or some natural cause. This rule continues to apply where the act or omission (or the last of the acts or omissions) which caused death occurred before June 16, 1996; otherwise it has been abolished for all purposes: *Law Reform (Year and a Day Rule) Act* 1996, ss.1, 3(2). As to certain restrictions on the institution of proceedings where the injury alleged to have caused the death was sustained more than three years before the death occurred, see *post*, § 19–88a. **19–22**

(2) Liability of secondary parties

Introduction

19–23 There are no special principles relating to the liability of secondary parties to murder. The subject warrants separate treatment only because of the large number of cases in which the principles have been considered in the context of offences against the person. It is no longer necessary to refer to the majority of the decisions of the Court of Appeal, as the law was clarified by the House of Lords in *R. v. Powell*; *R. v. English* [1999] 1 A.C. 1.

Principle

19–24 A secondary party is guilty of murder if he participates in a joint venture realising that in the course thereof the principal might use force with intent to kill or to cause grievous bodily harm, and the principal does kill with such intent; but if he goes beyond the scope of the joint venture (*i.e.* does an act not foreseen as a possibility), the secondary party is not guilty of murder or manslaughter; thus, if there is a joint enterprise to cause grievous bodily harm by the use of non-deadly weapons (*e.g.* wooden stakes), the unsuspected production by one participant of a deadly weapon (*e.g.* a knife or gun), with which he kills the victim, would take him outside the scope of the joint enterprise and the other participant would be liable for neither murder nor manslaughter; *aliter*, if the use of a deadly weapon was foreseen, but the principal used a deadly weapon of a different type to the one contemplated: *R. v. Powell*; *R. v. English*, *ante*. For their conclusion on the first issue, their Lordships relied principally on *Chan Wing-Siu v. R.* [1985] A.C. 168, PC; and for their conclusion on the second issue, on *R. v. Anderson and Morris* [1966] 2 Q.B. 110, 50 Cr.App.R. 216, CCA.

19–25 In both appeals before the House of Lords in *R. v. Powell*; *R. v. English*, the persons whose liability was in issue had been present at the time of the killing. It is plain, however, that the same principles apply when the liability of a person not present at the time is under consideration: see *R. v. Rook*, 97 Cr.App.R. 327, CA.

19–26 Following on from *R. v. Powell*; *R. v. English*, the House of Lords held in *R. v. Rahman* [2008] 3 W.L.R. 264, HL, that where, in the course of a joint enterprise to inflict unlawful violence, the principal killed the victim intending to do so, but the secondary party only foresaw that the principal might use force with an intent to cause serious injury, the secondary party was still guilty of murder as the principal's intention was not relevant to (i) whether the killing was within the scope of the joint enterprise or (ii) whether the principal's act was fundamentally different from the act or acts which the secondary party foresaw as part of the joint enterprise. This effectively laid to rest the *obiter* observation in *Att.-Gen.'s Reference (No. 3 of 2004)* [2006] Crim.L.R. 63, CA, that an act could, as a matter of law, be outside the scope of a joint enterprise, even though the only difference between the act, the possibility of which was foreseen, and the act which occurred was the state of mind of the primary party. See also the decisions of the Northern Ireland Court of Appeal in *R. v. Gilmour* [2000] 2 Cr.App.R. 407 (*ante*, § 18–15) and of the High Court of Australia in *Gillard v. R.* (2003) 202 A.L.R. 202, which suggest that where the secondary party foresees the act of the principal, but not the murderous intent (*i.e.* to kill or cause serious harm), he may nevertheless be found guilty of manslaughter.

19–27 Mere foresight is not enough; the secondary party, in order to be guilty, must have foreseen the relevant act of the principal as a possible incident of the common unlawful enterprise and must, with such foresight, have participated in the enterprise: *Hui Chi-Ming v. R.* [1992] 1 A.C. 34, PC.

19–28 In *Chan Wing-Siu*, *ante*, the Privy Council said that in cases where an issue of remoteness arises, it is for the jury to decide whether the risk as recognised by the accused was sufficient to make him a party to the crime committed by the principal. No one of various available formulae is exclusively preferable, *e.g.* a substantial risk, a real risk, a risk that something might well happen. The question is not one of semantics. What has to be brought home to the jury is that occasionally a risk may have occurred to an accused's mind, fleetingly or even causing him some deliberation, but may

genuinely have been dismissed by him as altogether negligible. If the jury think there is a reasonable possibility that the case is in that class, taking the risk in such circumstances should not make the accused a party to such a crime of intention as murder or wounding with intent. The judge is entitled to warn the jury to be cautious before reaching that conclusion.

In *R. v. Roberts*, 96 Cr.App.R. 291, CA, the court said with regard to *Chan Wing-Siu* that it was doubtful whether a defendant, who fleetingly thought of the risk of the principal using violence with murderous intent in the course of a joint enterprise, only to dismiss it from his mind and go on to lend himself to the venture, could truly be said, at the time when he so lent himself, to "foresee" or "realise" that the principal might commit murder. To realise something might happen was to contemplate it as a real not a fanciful possibility. Accordingly, to seek to distinguish between a fleeting but rejected consideration of a risk and a continuing realisation of a real risk would, in most cases, be unnecessary. It would also over-complicate directions to juries and possibly lead to confusion. **19–29**

If a person participates with others in an attack, and anticipates that one of the others may use a deadly weapon with the necessary intent for murder, and one of the others does so, with fatal consequences, the first person will also be guilty of murder though he had no particular person in mind as being likely to use such weapon: *R. v. Nelson* [1999] 6 *Archbold News* 2, CA (9801747 Z5). And as to the liability of the members of an armed gang where an unidentified member of the gang, upon their being confronted by a doorman, produced a firearm and shot the doorman dead, having been encouraged by at least some of the others to do so, see *R. v. Smith* [2008] 7 *Archbold News* 2, CA (it was sufficient to prove against any one of them that he participated in a gang whose common objective was to be achieved with the aid of loaded guns if necessary, and that he knew of the presence of guns and realised that there was a possibility that one or more of their number would use a gun with a murderous intent if they were thwarted). **19–30**

Where a person lends another a weapon anticipating that the other will use it to commit one murder and realising that he may use it to commit a second murder, the lender of the weapon will be guilty of both murders if the other does in fact use it to kill twice: *R. v. Reardon* [1999] Crim.L.R. 392, CA.

Guidance

In both *R. v. Uddin* [1999] 1 Cr.App.R. 319, and in *Rahman*, *ante* (see [2007] 2 Cr.App.R. 16), the Court of Appeal offered guidance as to the application of the principle established in *R. v. Powell*; *R. v. English*. In *Rahman*, the court went as far as to set out a series of elaborate questions for the jury. When *Rahman* reached the House of Lords, however, Lord Bingham (at [27]) said that there can be no prescriptive formula for directing juries, and that it is for trial judges, having made clear the governing principle, to choose the terms most apt to enable juries to reach a just decision in the particular case. His Lordship then added that he preferred the directions of the trial judge to the series of questions that the Court of Appeal had suggested should be asked. Lord Neuberger (at [104]) expressly agreed with Lord Bingham on this point. **19–31**

Lords Scott, Rodger and Brown did not directly address the issue of how to direct a jury, but Lord Brown did advance a restatement of the governing principle, which he derived from *R. v. Hyde*, 92 Cr.App.R. 131, and *R. v. Powell*; *R. v. English*. Lords Scott, Rodger and Neuberger concurred in this restatement. His Lordship stated: **19–32**

> "If B realises (without agreeing to such conduct being used) that A may kill or intentionally inflict serious injury, but nevertheless continues to participate with A in the venture, that will amount to a sufficient mental element for B to be guilty of murder if A, with the requisite intent, kills in the course of the venture unless (i) A suddenly produces and uses a weapon of which B knows nothing and which is more lethal than any weapon which B contemplates that A or any other participant may be carrying and (ii) for that reason A's act is to be regarded as fundamentally different from anything foreseen by B" (at [68]).

Whilst this may strictly have been *obiter*, it is a relatively simple restatement in an area which has been bedevilled by over-elaboration and confusion. It has ample authority to support it and trial judges are likely to latch onto it in preference to the complex series of questions suggested by the Court of Appeal.

Withdrawal

19–33 As to the position of a person who withdraws from a spontaneous attack before the fatal blow is delivered by another, see *R. v. Mitchell and King*, 163 J.P. 75, CA, and *R. v. O'Flaherty, Ryan and Toussaint* [2004] 2 Cr.App.R. 20, CA (*ante*, § 18–26).

The indictment

19–34 As to the drafting of the indictment in such cases, see *R. v. Greatrex and Bates* [1999] 1 Cr.App.R. 126, CA (*post*, § 19–86).

Parents

19–35 At common law, the parents of a child were in no different position from any other person charged with crime, save that one parent may have a duty to intervene in the ill-treatment of their child by the other parent, whereas a stranger would have no such duty: *per* Lord Lane C.J. in *R. v. Russell and Russell*, 85 Cr.App.R. 388 at 393, CA. Breach of such duty may give rise to liability in manslaughter: see *post*, §§ 19–108 *et seq.* As to the extent of such duty when it arises, see *R. v. Beard (S.D.)*, 85 Cr.App.R. 395 at 399–400, CA. Where it was clear that the injuries inflicted on a child which caused its death were inflicted by one or other parent, but there was no evidence as to who was responsible and no basis for an inference that there was a joint enterprise between them, it followed on ordinary principles of criminal liability that both should be acquitted: *R. v. Abbott* [1955] 2 Q.B. 497, 39 Cr.App.R. 141, CCA; *R. v. Lane and Lane*, 82 Cr.App.R. 5, CA; and *R. v. Russell and Russell*, *ante*. In such a case, the deficiency of evidence could not be made good by proof of lies told by the defendants in answer to questions put by persons investigating the cause of death: *R. v. Strudwick and Merry*, 99 Cr.App.R. 326, CA.

The common law has been supplemented now by the offence created by section 5 of the *Domestic Violence, Crime and Victims Act* 2004 (*post*, § 19–118a). This was designed to cater for the situation where a child has died at the hands of one or other, or both parents, but it is likely to be difficult to prove whether it was the mother, the father or both. In such cases, it is likely that the parents will be charged with both murder or manslaughter and an offence contrary to section 5. This will trigger the important procedural provisions in subsections (2) to (4) of section 6 (*post*, § 19–118f). It should be noted that these provisions apply not only to the death of a child, but also to the death of a vulnerable adult.

As to basing a prosecution of a parent (or other carer) for murder on expert evidence alone, see *R. v. Cannings* [2004] 2 Cr.App.R. 7, CA, and *R. v. Holdsworth* [2008] 5 *Archbold News* 1, CA (*ante*, § 10–67).

Alternative allegations

19–35a Where the prosecution are unable to say whether the accused was the principal or a secondary party, it is legitimate to advance the case in the alternative; the basis on which the jury must be agreed is that the accused, having the necessary *mens rea*, by whatever means caused the result which was criminalised by the law: *R. v. Giannetto* [1997] 1 Cr.App.R. 1, CA; *R. v. Tirnaveanu* [2007] 2 Cr.App.R. 23, CA.

See also the *Domestic Violence, Crime and Victims Act* 2004, ss.5 and 6 (causing or allowing death of child or vulnerable adult) (*post*, §§ 19–118a *et seq.*).

Attempts

19–36 As against an accessory, it is enough to prove that he knew the principal might attempt to kill: *R. v. O'Brien* [1995] 2 Cr.App.R. 649, CA (*Chan Wing-Siu*, *ante*, applied).

(3) Lawful homicide

Execution of sentence

19–37 The execution of a prisoner in strict conformity with the sentence of a court is lawful.

Medical or surgical treatment

Bona fide medical or surgical treatment is not "unlawful" and therefore death resulting therefrom does not amount to murder, even though death or serious injury is foreseen as a probable consequence. Nor does it amount to manslaughter, unless the person giving the treatment has been guilty of "gross negligence", as to which see §§ 19–108 *et seq.*, *post*. **19–38**

Use of force in prevention of crime

Criminal Law Act 1967, s.3

Use of force in making arrest, etc.

3.—(1) A person may use such force as is reasonable in the circumstances in the prevention of crime, or in effecting or assisting in the lawful arrest of offenders or suspected offenders or of persons unlawfully at large. **19–39**

(2) Subsection (1) above shall replace the rules of the common law on the question when force used for a purpose mentioned in the subsection is justified by that purpose.

Criminal Justice and Immigration Act 2008, s.76

Reasonable force for purposes of self-defence etc.

76.—(1) This section applies where in proceedings for an offence— **19–39a**

(a) an issue arises as to whether a person charged with the offence ("D") is entitled to rely on a defence within subsection (2), and

(b) the question arises whether the degree of force used by D against a person ("V") was reasonable in the circumstances.

(2) The defences are—

(a) the common law defence of self-defence; and

(b) the defences provided by section 3(1) of the *Criminal Law Act* 1967 or section 3(1) of the *Criminal Law Act (Northern Ireland)* 1967 (use of force in prevention of crime or making arrest).

(3) The question whether the degree of force used by D was reasonable in the circumstances is to be decided by reference to the circumstances as D believed them to be, and subsections (4) to (8) also apply in connection with deciding that question.

(4) If D claims to have held a particular belief as regards the existence of any circumstances—

(a) the reasonableness or otherwise of that belief is relevant to the question whether D genuinely held it; but

(b) if it is determined that D did genuinely hold it, D is entitled to rely on it for the purposes of subsection (3), whether or not—

(i) it was mistaken, or

(ii) (if it was mistaken) the mistake was a reasonable one to have made.

(5) But subsection (4)(b) does not enable D to rely on any mistaken belief attributable to intoxication that was voluntarily induced.

(6) The degree of force used by D is not to be regarded as having been reasonable in the circumstances as D believed them to be if it was disproportionate in those circumstances.

(7) In deciding the question mentioned in subsection (3) the following considerations are to be taken into account (so far as relevant in the circumstances of the case)—

(a) that a person acting for a legitimate purpose may not be able to weigh to a nicety the exact measure of any necessary action; and

(b) that evidence of a person's having only done what the person honestly and instinctively thought was necessary for a legitimate purpose constitutes strong evidence that only reasonable action was taken by that person for that purpose.

(8) Subsection (7) is not to be read as preventing other matters from being taken into account where they are relevant to deciding the question mentioned in subsection (3).

(9) This section is intended to clarify the operation of the existing defences mentioned in subsection (2).

(10) In this section—

(a) "legitimate purpose" means—

(i) the purpose of self-defence under the common law, or

(ii) the prevention of crime or effecting or assisting in the lawful arrest of persons mentioned in the provisions referred to in subsection (2)(b);

(b) references to self-defence include acting in defence of another person; and

(c) references to the degree of force used are to the type and amount of force used.

Section 76 came into force on July 14, 2008 (*Criminal Justice and Immigration Act 2008 (Commencement No. 2 and Transitional and Saving Provisions) Order* 2008 (S.I. 2008 No. 1586)). It applies whenever the alleged offence took place: 2008 Act, s.148(2), and Sched. 27, para. 27(1); but it does not apply in relation to (a) any trial on indictment where the arraignment took place before the commencement date or (b) any summary trial which began before that date, and nor does it apply in relation to any proceedings in respect of any such trial: *ibid*., para. 27(2).

19–39b As subsection (9) declares, the provisions of this section are not intended to change the law, but to clarify it; and, as the following paragraphs reveal, it does indeed do nothing other than restate the common law principles, in particular as to (i) a defendant being entitled to be judged on the facts as he believed them to be even if he made an unreasonable mistake, (ii) the defendant not being entitled to rely on a mistake as to the facts that was induced by his own voluntary intoxication, (iii) the reasonableness or otherwise of any claimed mistake going only to the issue of whether or not the claim was genuine, (iv) the force used having to be proportionate, (v) there being no expectation that in an emergency a person should weigh to a nicety the force required, and (vi) a person doing only what he instinctively and honestly thought was necessary being strong evidence that only reasonable force was used.

19–39c As to the lawful use of reasonable force by a police officer, see *post*, §§ 19–188, 19–268 *et seq*., 19–343 *et seq*.

The provisions of section 3 of the 1967 Act will, in fact, cover the great majority of cases of self-defence and defence of others and many cases of defence of property for in these cases the person who uses lawful force will be doing so for the purpose of preventing crime (although it is unlikely that the person involved will think of it in those terms). In practice, however, judges and practitioners rarely make reference to section 3 in the context of such cases; this is because at common law a person was entitled to use such force as was reasonably necessary to protect himself or another or property (see *R. v. Duffy* [1967] 1 Q.B. 63, 50 Cr.App.R. 68, CCA), and, despite the enactment of the 1967 Act, the courts continued to talk in terms of the common law rules. It is submitted that this is of no practical consequence as section 3 reflects the common law.

Section 3 does not cover all cases of defence of property and it may not cover all cases of defence of the person. If a person were attacked by someone who was insane so as not to be responsible in law for his acts, the common law justification of the use of force in defence of oneself or another would apply.

The word "crime" in section 3 is to be construed as referring to an offence committed against a domestic common law or statutory rule, and not to an offence recognised only in customary international law; and the crime of aggression, whilst it had been defined with sufficient clarity as a matter of customary international law, had not been assimilated into domestic criminal law: *R. v. Jones*; *Ayliffe v. DPP*; *Swain v. Same* [2007] 1 A.C. 136, HL.

19–39d In *R. v. Jones*; *Ayliffe v. DPP*; *Swain v. Same*, *ante*, Lord Hoffmann made the following *obiter* observations with regard to section 3. His Lordship said that whilst a defendant had to be judged on the basis of the facts as he believed them to be, it was not sufficient to excuse him that he honestly believed that the force used was reasonable, as the force used must actually have been reasonable on an objective assessment; and as to what is reasonable force for the purposes of protecting the interests of a third party or of the community at large, in a moment of emergency, when individual action is necessary to prevent some imminent crime or to apprehend an escaping criminal, it may be legitimate, even praiseworthy, for the citizen to use force of his own initiative, but when law enforcement officers, if called upon, would be in a position to do whatever is necessary, the citizen must leave the use of force to them; if the law enforcement authorities will not assist (as for operational reasons), a citizen whose person or property is under threat may take reasonable steps to protect himself; but the right of the citizen to use force is more closely circumscribed when he is not defending his own interests, but simply wishes to see the law enforced in the interests of the community at large; the law

will not tolerate vigilantes; if the citizen cannot get the courts to order the law enforcement authorities to intervene, then he must use the democratic process to seek to have the law changed; the rule of law requires that disputes over whether action is lawful be resolved in the courts. His Lordship said that the practical implications for the conduct of trials of direct action protesters are that if an issue is raised as to whether their conduct in doing acts which would otherwise be criminal was somehow justified, the burden is on the prosecution to negative the defence, but the issue must first be raised by evidence on which a court could find that the acts were justified; where it is a requirement that the conduct of the accused should in all the circumstances have been reasonable, his acts must be considered in the context of a functioning state in which legal disputes can be peacefully submitted to the courts and disputes over what should be law or government policy can be submitted to the democratic process; the apprehension, however honest or reasonable, of acts which are thought to be unlawful or contrary to the public interest, cannot justify the commission of criminal acts, and the issue of justification should be withdrawn from the jury; evidence to support the opinions of the defendants as to the legality of the acts in question is irrelevant and inadmissible and disclosure going to such issue should not be ordered. Lord Bingham did not touch on the issues raised by Lord Hoffmann, but Lords Rodger, Carswell and Mance expressly agreed with him.

Use of force at schools, etc.

Section 93(1) of the *Education and Inspections Act* 2006 enables a member of school staff to use reasonable force to prevent a pupil from committing an offence, causing personal injury, damaging property or doing something that prejudices discipline at the school. It does not authorise the doing of anything amounting to corporal punishment within the meaning of section 548 of the *Education Act* 1996 (s.93(4)); and "offence" includes anything that would be an offence but for the operation of any presumption that a person under a particular age is incapable of committing an offence (s.93(6)). Section 85C of the *Further and Higher Education Act* 1992 (inserted by s.165 of the 2006 Act) creates a corresponding power in relation to institutions in the further education sector. **19–40**

Section 45 of the *VCRA* 2006 inserted a new section 550AA in the 1996 Act, conferring a power on head teachers or persons authorised by them to search (using force if necessary) pupils and their possessions for knives and offensive weapons. A search may only be carried out on school premises, or elsewhere where the member of staff has lawful control or charge of the pupil to be searched; and where such items are found, they may be seized and retained and then delivered to a constable. Section 46 inserted a corresponding new section 85B in the 1992 Act; and section 47 is a corresponding provision in relation to attendance centres.

Self-defence

(i) *Common law and statute*

As to the significance of section 76 of the *CJIA* 2008, see *ante*, § 19–39b; as to the relationship of the common law defence to the defence provided by section 3 of the *CLA* 1967, see *ante*, § 19–39c. **19–41**

(ii) *Principle*

The classic pronouncement upon the law relating to self-defence is that of the Privy Council in *Palmer v. R.* [1971] A.C. 814, approved and followed by the Court of Appeal in *R. v. McInnes*, 55 Cr.App.R. 551 (and now effectively reflected in the provisions of the *CJIA* 2008, s.76, *ante*, § 19–39a). **19–41a**

> "It is both good law and good sense that a man who is attacked may defend himself. It is both good law and common sense that he may do, but may only do, what is reasonably necessary. But everything will depend upon the particular facts and circumstances. ... It may in some cases be only sensible and clearly possible to take some simple avoiding action. Some attacks may be serious and dangerous. Others may not be. If there is some relatively minor

attack, it would not be common sense to permit some act of retaliation which was wholly out of proportion to the necessities of the situation. If an attack is serious so that it puts someone in immediate peril, then immediate defensive action may be necessary. If the moment is one of crisis for someone in immediate danger, he may have to avert the danger by some instant reaction. If the attack is over and no sort of peril remains, then the employment of force may be by way of revenge or punishment or by way of paying off an old score or may be pure aggression. There may be no longer any link with a necessity of defence. Of all these matters the good sense of the jury will be the arbiter. There are no prescribed words which must be employed ... in a summing up. All that is needed is a clear exposition, in relation to the particular facts of the case, of the concept of necessary self-defence. If there has been an attack so that defence is reasonably necessary, it will be recognised that a person defending himself cannot weigh to a nicety the exact measure of his defensive action. If the jury thought that in a moment of unexpected anguish a person attacked had only done what he honestly and instinctively thought necessary, that would be the most potent evidence that only reasonable defensive action had been taken. ... The defence of self-defence either succeeds so as to result in an acquittal or it is disproved, in which case as a defence it is rejected" (*per* Lord Morris, at pp. 831–832).

Palmer was applied in *R. v. Clegg* [1995] 1 A.C. 482, HL, in which it was held that where a person kills another with the requisite intent for murder in circumstances in which he would have been entitled to an acquittal on the ground of self-defence but for the use of excessive force, the defence fails altogether and he is guilty of murder, not of manslaughter; that there is no distinction to be drawn between the use of excessive force in self-defence and the use of excessive force in the prevention of crime or in arresting an offender; and that it makes no difference that the person using the force is a policeman or a soldier acting in the course of his duty.

19–42 The test of whether force used in self-defence was reasonable is not purely objective: *Palmer, ante*; *R. v. Shannon*, 71 Cr.App.R. 192, CA; and *R. v. Whyte*, 85 Cr.App.R. 283, CA; but in *R. v. Martin (Anthony)* [2002] 1 Cr.App.R. 27, CA, it was held that whilst a court is entitled to take account of the physical characteristics of the defendant in deciding what force was reasonable, it was not appropriate, absent exceptional circumstances which would make the evidence especially probative, to take account of whether the defendant was suffering from some psychiatric condition.

The old rule of law that a man attacked must retreat as far as he can has disappeared. Whether the accused did retreat is only one element for the jury to consider on the question of whether the force was reasonably necessary. Failure to demonstrate unwillingness to fight is merely a factor to be taken into consideration in determining whether the defendant was acting in self-defence, although evidence that he tried to call off a fight is likely to be the best evidence to cast doubt on a suggestion that he was the attacker, retaliator or acting in revenge and was thus not acting in self-defence: *R. v. Bird (D.)*, 81 Cr.App.R. 110, CA.

There is no rule of law that a man must wait until he is struck before striking in self-defence. If another strikes at him he is entitled to get his blow in first if it is reasonably necessary so to do in self-defence: *R. v. Deana*, 2 Cr.App.R. 75, CCA. And the mere fact that the defendant was the initial aggressor does not of itself render self-defence unavailable as a defence to what he does in any ensuing violence; availability must depend on all the circumstances, and allow for the possibility that the initial aggression may have resulted in a response by the victim which was so out of proportion as to give rise to an honest belief on the part of the defendant that it was necessary for him to defend himself, with the amount of force used for that purpose being reasonable: *R. v. Rashford* [2006] Crim.L.R. 547, CA.

(iii) *Burden of proof*

19–43 Where a defence of self-defence is raised, the burden of negativing it rests on the prosecution, but the prosecution are not obliged to give evidence-in-chief to rebut a suggestion of self-defence before that issue is raised, or indeed to give any evidence on that issue at all. If, on consideration of the whole of the evidence, the jury are either convinced of the innocence of the prisoner or are left in doubt whether he was acting in necessary self-defence, they should acquit: *R. v. Lobell* [1957] 1 Q.B. 547, 41 Cr.App.R. 100, CCA. Before the issue of self-defence is left to the jury, there

must be evidence, whether from the prosecution or the defence, which, if accepted, could raise a prima facie case of self-defence; if there is such evidence, the issue must be left to the jury, whether it is relied on by the defence or not: see *DPP (Jamaica) v. Bailey* [1995] 1 Cr.App.R. 257, PC, and *post*, § 19–55.

In *R. v. Wheeler*, 52 Cr.App.R. 28 at 30, the Court of Appeal said: **19–44**

> "Wherever ... the defendant puts forward a justification such as self-defence, such as provocation ..." [provocation only applies to murder so as to reduce the offence to manslaughter] "it is ... essential that the jury should understand ... that none of those issues of justification are properly to be regarded as defences. ... Where a judge does slip into the error ... of referring to such explanations as defences, it is particularly important that he should use language which suffices to make it clear to the jury that they are not defences in respect of which any onus rests upon the accused, but are matters which the prosecution must disprove as an essential part of their case before a verdict of guilty is justified."

In *R. v. Abraham*, 57 Cr.App.R. 799, the Court of Appeal repeated the above passage and suggested (at p. 803) that a judge should deal with such issues as follows: **19–45**

> "(G)ive a clear ... general direction as to onus and standard of proof; then immediately follow it with a direction that in the circumstances of the particular case there is a special reason for having in mind how the onus and standard of proof applies and go on to deal ... for example ... with the issue of self-defence by telling the jury something on these lines: 'Members of the jury, the general direction which I have just given to you in relation to onus and standard of proof has a particularly important operation in the circumstances of the present case. Here the accused has raised the issue that he acted in self-defence. A person who acts reasonably in his self-defence commits no unlawful act. By his plea of self-defence the accused is raising in a special form the plea of Not Guilty. Since it is for the Crown to show that the plea of Not Guilty is unacceptable, so the Crown must convince you beyond reasonable doubt that self-defence has no basis in the present case.' Having done that the trial judge can then proceed to deal with the facts of the particular case. The last thing I seek to do is to lend support to the misconception that any prescribed words have to be used in giving the direction (see *Palmer v. R.*)" (*ante*).

Defence of others

See the *CLA* 1967, s.3 (*ante*, § 19–39), and the *CJIA* 2008, s.76(10)(b) (*ante*, § 19–39a). Much of what was said in *Palmer* may be easily adapted to this situation (*e.g.* as to a person not being able to weigh to a nicety the exact measure of force needed). **19–46**

Defence of property, ejection of trespassers, etc.

This topic is dealt with at § 19–187, *post*. Reasonable force used for such purposes is lawful and it is submitted that the same principles apply as to self-defence. It should be pointed out that the common law rules as to this topic are only superseded by the *CLA* 1967, s.3 (*ante*, § 19–39) where force is used in the prevention of crime. Acts of trespass are often not criminal. Even when it was thought that to avail himself of the excuse of self-defence a man must have retreated as far as he could there was no duty to retreat in the face of a trespasser: see *R. v. Hussey*, 18 Cr.App.R. 160, CCA. **19–47**

Necessity

See *Re A. (Children) (Conjoined Twins: Surgical Separation)* [2001] Fam. 147 at 219–240, CA (Civ. Div.). As to necessity generally, see *ante*, §§ 17–127 *et seq.* **19–47a**

Corporal punishment

Reasonable chastisement of children by parents or others *in loco parentis* is lawful at common law: *Halliwell v. Counsell* (1878) 38 L.T. 176; *Cleary v. Booth* [1893] 1 Q.B. 465; and *R. v. H.* [2002] 1 Cr.App.R. 7, CA; but section 58 of the *Children Act* 2004 provides that in relation to an offence under section 18, 20 or 47 of the *Offences against the Person Act* 1861, battery of a child cannot be justified on the ground that it constituted reasonable punishment. *A fortiori* where death results. **19–48**

Mistake of fact

The ordinary doctrine of *mens rea* (*ante*, §§ 17–10 *et seq.*) applies to exculpate a person who acts, or who may have acted, under a genuine mistake of fact: see *R. v.* **19–49**

Williams (G.), 78 Cr.App.R. 276, CA, and *R. v. Beckford* [1988] A.C. 130, PC, *ante*, §§ 17–16, 17–17. The reasonableness or otherwise of the mistake is a factor to be taken into account when determining whether the mistake was or may have been a genuine one. Thus, where a defendant was neither under threatened nor actual attack, but honestly believed that he was, the jury should be directed to consider whether the degree of force used was commensurate with the degree of risk which he believed to be created by the attack under which he believed himself to be: *R. v. Oatridge*, 94 Cr.App.R. 367, CA.

A person's entitlement to use reasonable force to resist unlawful detention or restraint is not affected by his mistaken belief that he was in fact under lawful arrest and his knowledge that there was no entitlement to resist lawful arrest: *R. v. McKoy*, *The Times*, June 17, 2002, CA.

As to "mistake of fact" induced by the voluntary consumption of drink, see *R. v. Hatton* [2006] 1 Cr.App.R. 16, CA, *ante*, § 17–16.

(4) Defences

(a) *Provocation*

Introduction

19–50 Provocation reduces murder to manslaughter; and is available as a potential defence both for a principal and an accessory: *R. v. Marks* [1998] Crim.L.R. 676, CA. It is irrelevant on the issue of guilt in all other crimes.

The jury should be directed that before they have to consider the issue of provocation the Crown must have proved beyond reasonable doubt that all the other elements of murder were present, including the necessary intent: see *Lee Chun-Chuen v. R.* [1963] A.C. 220, PC; and *R. v. Martindale*, 50 Cr.App.R. 273, Ct-MAC.

Statute

19–51 The law as to provocation is governed by the *Homicide Act* 1957, s.3.

Homicide Act 1957, s.3

Provocation

19–52 **3.** Where on a charge of murder there is evidence on which the jury can find that the person charged was provoked (whether by things done or by things said or by both together) to lose his self-control, the question whether the provocation was enough to make a reasonable man do as he did shall be left to be determined by the jury; and in determining that question the jury shall take into account everything both done and said according to the effect which, in their opinion, it would have on a reasonable man.

This section altered as well as clarified the common law on this subject.

Duty of judge

19–53 Section 3 involves two questions: (a) is there any evidence of specific provoking conduct of the accused, and (b) is there any evidence that the provocation caused him to lose his self-control? If both questions are answered in the affirmative, the issue of provocation should be left to the jury notwithstanding the fact that in the opinion of the judge no reasonable jury could conclude on the evidence that a reasonable person would have been provoked to lose his self-control: *R. v. Gilbert*, 66 Cr.App.R. 237, CA; *Franco v. R.*, *The Times*, October 11, 2001, PC; notwithstanding that there may be circumstances suggesting that the accused acted in revenge, rather than as a result of a sudden and temporary loss of self-control: *R. v. Baillie* [1995] 2 Cr.App.R. 31, CA; and notwithstanding that the issue has not been raised by the defence: *Bullard v. R.* [1957] A.C. 635, PC; *DPP v. Camplin* [1978] A.C. 705, HL; *R. v. Rossiter*, 95 Cr.App.R. 326, CA; and would prefer it not to be left to the jury: *R. v. Dhillon* [1997] 2 Cr.App.R. 104, CA. The duty of the judge to leave all issues to the jury upon which there is evidence fit for their consideration, whether or not they have been adverted to during the course of the trial (*ante*, §§ 7–60, 7–62), is particularly important on a charge of murder, for

example, where the defence is mistaken identity and alibi and yet there may be evidence from witnesses for the Crown of self-defence or provocation.

Where, however, there is only a speculative possibility of the accused having acted as a result of provoking conduct, the issue should not be left to the jury: *R. v. Acott* [1997] 2 Cr.App.R. 94, HL (there must be some evidence of specific provoking conduct resulting in a loss of control by the accused; the source of such evidence is immaterial as is reliance thereon by the accused). Evidence of a loss of self-control is insufficient, for a loss of self-control might be brought on by fear, panic or sheer bad temper, as well as by provoking conduct: *ibid.* Questions put in cross-examination are not evidence: *ibid.* The observations in *Acott* are equally apt when considering whether there is sufficient evidence that a defendant was provoked, as they are when considering whether there was evidence of provoking conduct: *R. v. Miao, The Times*, November 26, 2003, CA. For the issue to be left to the jury, there has to be evidence from which a reasonable jury might conclude that the defendant was or may have been provoked: *R. v. Cambridge*, 99 Cr.App.R. 142, CA. See also *R. v. Jones (Robert James)* [2000] 3 *Archbold News* 2, CA (where the defence is self-defence, with no reliance by the defence on provocation, the judge should not leave provocation to the jury where the evidence of provoking conduct by the deceased, or the evidence that such conduct caused a loss of self-control by the defendant is minimal or fanciful).

Where a judge is obliged to leave provocation to the jury, he should indicate to them, unless it is obvious, what evidence might support the conclusion that the defendant had lost his self-control; this is particularly important where the defence have not raised the issue: *R. v. Stewart* [1996] 1 Cr.App.R. 229, CA. See also *R. v. Humphreys* [1995] 4 All E.R. 1008, CA (similar duty where there is a complex history with several distinct strands of potentially provocative conduct, building up over time until the final encounter).

Where provocation is not left to the jury when it should have been, a conviction for manslaughter will be substituted unless the court is sure that the jury would inevitably have convicted: *R. v. Dhillon*, *ante*, but an appellate court should be cautious in drawing inferences or making findings about how the jury would have resolved issues which were never before them; and that is particularly so in the context of section 3, since Parliament had gone out of its way, unusually, to stipulate that resolution of the objective issue should be exclusively reserved to the jury; to the extent that an appellate court took it upon itself to decide that issue, it was doing what Parliament had said that the jury should do, and section 3 could not be read as applying only to the trial court: *Franco v. R.*, *ante*.

In *R. v. Van Dongen and Van Dongen* [2005] 2 Cr.App.R. 38, CA, it was held that: (i) section 3 is concerned with provocative conduct, as opposed to merely causative conduct; yet a judgment that particular conduct was no more than causative risks straying into an evaluation of the objective element of the defence, which statute has left to the jury; accordingly, the prudent course for judges to take, in borderline cases, especially if the defence ask for a provocation direction to be given, is to leave the issue to the jury; (ii) where, therefore, in a case in which the defence had been self-defence and/or lack of intent and/or accident, but not provocation, there was evidence of conduct that was capable of being provoking conduct and there was evidence of a loss of self-control, the matter should have been left to the jury, more particularly as defence counsel had sought such a direction; but (iii) the failure to leave it did not mean that the conviction could not be upheld, notwithstanding that the Act specifically provides for the jury to determine the objective issue; *Franco v. R.*, *ante*, was not authority for the proposition that a conviction could not be upheld in such circumstances; whilst it was necessary to be cautious in drawing inferences or making findings about how the jury would have resolved issues which were never before them, the court must not overlook the matter of justice for those concerned with the victim, nor the requirements of a proportionate appellate system, which included that those who were surely and fairly shown to be guilty of murder, and were so found by a jury, should not escape the consequences on gossamer grounds; where, therefore, the unavoidable facts of the case and the necessary logic of the jury's verdict ruled out any possibility of a miscarriage of justice, the conviction should be upheld.

Duty of counsel

19–54 If there is evidence on which the jury could find provocation, counsel should regard it as their duty to point it out to the judge and to remind him, if he agrees, to leave it to the jury: *R. v. Cox (A.M.)* [1995] 2 Cr.App.R. 513, CA. It does not follow from this that an appeal will not succeed if defence counsel has not advanced the defence to the jury; but it does follow that if counsel has not raised the issue with the judge, an appeal based on the judge's failure to leave the issue to the jury is extremely unlikely to be entertained, let alone be successful.

Onus of proof

19–55 Once there is evidence from any source, sufficient to be left to the jury on the issue of provocation, the onus remains throughout upon the Crown to prove absence of provocation beyond reasonable doubt: *R. v. McPherson*, 41 Cr.App.R. 213, CCA. As to the necessity for a careful direction on onus of proof, see *R. v. Wheeler, ante*, § 19–44.

"Provoked ... to lose his self control"

(i) *Meaning of "provocation"*

19–56 In *R. v. Whitfield*, 63 Cr.App.R. 39 at 42, the Court of Appeal said that the meaning of provocation was still that given to it by Devlin J. in *R. v. Duffy* [1949] 1 All E.R. 932, as cited by Lord Goddard C.J. when giving the judgment of the Court of Criminal Appeal:

> "Provocation is some act, or series of acts, done [or words spoken] [by the dead man to the accused] which would cause in any reasonable person, and actually causes in the accused, a sudden and temporary loss of self-control, rendering the accused so subject to passion as to make him or her for the moment not master of his mind" (at p.932).

The words in the first pair of square brackets were not actually said by Devlin J. but appear in the quotation of him by Lord Lane C.J. as if spoken by him (presumably to take account of the express reference to "things said" in section 3 of the 1957 Act, *ante*, § 19–52); the words in the second pair of square brackets must be ignored in view of the wording of section 3. See also *post*, § 19–59.

(ii) *Loss of self-control must be associated with the act which causes death*

19–57 The point was considered in *R. v. Ibrams and Gregory*, 74 Cr.App.R. 154, CA. Provocation is available only in the case of a sudden and temporary loss of self-control of such a kind as to make the accused for the moment not master of his mind: see *R. v. Duffy* and *R. v. Whitfield, ante*. Circumstances which induce a desire for revenge are inconsistent with provocation, since the conscious formulation of a desire for revenge means that a person has had time to think, to reflect and that would negative a sudden temporary loss of self-control, which is the essence of provocation. But the mere existence of such circumstances does not mean that the judge should not leave the issue to the jury if there is evidence that the accused was in fact provoked; it is for the jury to decide: see *R. v. Baillie* [1995] 2 Cr.App.R. 31, CA.

(iii) *Cumulative provocation*

19–58 Although it is established that a temporary and sudden loss of self-control arising from an act of provocation is essential, it is less clear to what extent previous acts of provocation are admissible. Each case must be considered against the background of its own particular facts: *R. v. Thornton*, 96 Cr.App.R. 112, CA. In *R. v. Brown* [1972] 2 Q.B. 229, 56 Cr.App.R. 564, CA, a direction that the jury had to find provocation in something done on the morning of the killing was approved. In *R. v. Davies (P.)* [1975] Q.B. 691, 60 Cr.App.R. 253, the Court of Appeal described as "too generous" a direction that the jury could review the whole of the deceased's conduct throughout the years preceding death: and see *R. v. Ibrams and Gregory, ante*. In *R. v. Pearson* [1992] Crim.L.R. 193, the Court of Appeal substituted manslaughter for a conviction for murder on the grounds, *inter alia*, that the jury may have been left with the impression that an eight-year history of violent conduct by the deceased towards his

younger son was not to be taken into account when considering the case of the elder son, who had spent much of that time away from home.

A general approach can, however, be discerned from the authorities, namely that evidence of previous provocative acts or past conduct, particularly in cases of domestic violence, is admissible in order to place in its appropriate context the reaction of the accused to the alleged provocation on the occasion of the killing: see *R. v. Thornton*, *ante*, at p. 118. For the proper approach in relation to a history of provocation leading to a post-traumatic stress syndrome or "battered woman syndrome", see *R. v. Ahluwalia*, 96 Cr.App.R. 133, CA, and *R. v. Thornton (No. 2)* [1996] 2 Cr.App.R. 108, CA (a jury might more easily find that there was a sudden loss of self-control triggered even by a minor incident if the defendant had endured abuse over a period, on a last-straw basis).

"Things done or said"

The things done or said may be done or said by the deceased or anyone else: *R. v. Davies (P.)*, *ante*; *R. v. Doughty (S.)*, 83 Cr.App.R. 319, CA. **19–59**

"Reasonable man"

The "reasonable man" means "an ordinary person of either sex, not exceptionally excitable or pugnacious, but possessed of such powers of self-control as everyone is entitled to expect that his fellow citizens will exercise in society as it is today": *per* Lord Diplock in *DPP v. Camplin* [1978] A.C. 705 at 771, HL; means "a man of ordinary self-control": *ibid.*, *per* Lord Simon at p.726. Both formulations were approved by the majority in *Att.-Gen. for Jersey v. Holley* [2005] 2 A.C. 580, PC, in which an enlarged board of nine was assembled for the purpose of considering the conflict between *Camplin* and *Luc Thiet Thuan v. R.* [1997] A.C. 131, PC, on the one hand, and *R. v. Smith (Morgan)* [2001] 1 A.C. 146, HL, on the other, and to "clarify definitively the present state of English law". That it had done so was accepted by the Court of Appeal in *R. v. James*; *R. v. Karimi* [2006] 1 Cr.App.R. 29. **19–60**

The majority opinion in *Holley* was that the jury, in deciding whether the defendant lost his self-control and, if he did, whether he did so as a result of provocation, should take the defendant exactly as they find him ("warts and all" (including that he had a violent temperament: see *R. v. Mohammed (Faqir)* [2005] 9 *Archbold News* 3, CA)); but, having assessed the gravity of the provocation to the defendant (for which purpose they must, for example, take account of the fact that he is a homosexual if taunted for his homosexuality, that he is disabled if taunted for being a "cripple", *etc.*), the standard of self-control by which his conduct is to be evaluated is the external standard of a person having and exercising the ordinary powers of self-control to be expected of a person of the defendant's age and sex. The majority ruling in *Smith* was held to be wrong in that section 3 of the 1957 Act adopted a uniform, objective standard; whether the provocative act or words and the defendant's response met the "ordinary person" standard prescribed by the statute is the question the jury must consider, not the altogether looser question (suggested by *Smith*) of whether, having regard to all the circumstances, the jury consider the loss of self-control was sufficiently excusable; the statute, it was said, does not leave each jury free to set whatever standard they consider appropriate. Accordingly, it was held to follow that if the defendant had been taunted by reference to his being an alcoholic or a drug addict, his alcoholism or addiction might be relevant to the jury's consideration of the gravity of the taunt to the defendant, but it would not be relevant to the question whether he exercised ordinary self-control. **19–61**

Self-induced provocation

The mere fact that the defendant caused a reaction in others which in turn led him to lose his self-control does not preclude a successful defence of provocation: *R. v. Johnson (C.)*, 89 Cr.App.R. 148, CA. **19–62**

In *Edwards v. R.* [1973] A.C. 648, PC, the appellant's case was that the man whom he was blackmailing attacked him with a knife and he thereupon lost his temper and **19–63**

killed him. The relevant ordinance in Hong Kong was in the same terms as section 3 of the *Homicide Act* 1957, *ante*. The Board said (at p. 658):

> "No authority has been cited with regard to what may be called 'self-induced provocation'. On principle it seems reasonable to say that: (1) a blackmailer cannot rely on the predictable results of his own blackmailing conduct as constituting provocation sufficient to reduce his killing of the victim from murder to manslaughter, and the predictable results may include a considerable degree of hostile reaction by the person sought to be blackmailed, for instance vituperous words and even some hostile action such as blows with a fist; (2) but, if the hostile reaction by the person sought to be blackmailed goes to extreme lengths, it might constitute sufficient provocation even for a blackmailer; (3) there would in many cases be a question of degree to be decided by the jury."

Provocation and lies

19–64 Lies and attempts to cover up a killing are not necessarily inconsistent with provocation. In directions about lies, when the issue was murder or manslaughter, the jury should be alerted to the fact that, before they could treat lies as proof of guilt of the offence charged, they had to be sure that there was not some possible explanation which destroyed their potentially probative effect. A failure to give such a direction, coupled with an indication that the jury might regard lies as probative of murder rather than manslaughter, amounted to a material misdirection: *R. v. Richens*, 98 Cr.App.R. 43, CA; *R. v. Taylor* [1998] 7 *Archbold News* 3, CA.

Provocation and good character

19–64a Where there is evidence of the defendant's good character, the judge should direct the jury as to the relevance of that both to credibility and propensity; and, in particular, should reminded them that, as a man of good character, the defendant might have been unlikely to indulge in serious violence without first being provoked: *Paria v. R.* [2004] Crim.L.R. 228, PC.

Sentence

19–65 See the guideline issued by the Sentencing Guidelines Council (Appendix K–71 *et seq.*). Of the pre-guideline authorities, see, in particular, *Att.-Gen.'s References (Nos 74, 95 and 118 of 2002) (R. v. Suratan; R. v. Humes; R. v. Wilkinson)* [2003] 2 Cr.App.R.(S.) 42, CA, which is summarised at paragraph 2.1 of the guideline (Appendix K–74).

(b) *Diminished responsibility*

Homicide Act 1957, s.2

Persons suffering from diminished responsibility

19–66 **2.**—(1) Where a person kills or is a party to the killing of another, he shall not be convicted of murder if he was suffering from such abnormality of mind (whether arising from a condition of arrested or retarded development of mind or any inherent causes or induced by disease or injury) as substantially impaired his mental responsibility for his acts and omissions in doing or being a party to the killing.

(2) On a charge of murder, it shall be for the defence to prove that the person charged is by virtue of this section not liable to be convicted of murder.

(3) A person who but for this section would be liable, whether as principal or as accessory, to be convicted of murder shall be liable instead to be convicted of manslaughter.

(4) The fact that one party to a killing is by virtue of this section not liable to be convicted of murder shall not affect the question whether the killing amounted to murder in the case of any other party to it.

This defence is not available on a charge of attempted murder: *R. v. Campbell* [1997] Crim.L.R. 495, Crown Court (Sedley J.).

As to the taking of a plea to manslaughter on the ground of diminished responsibility, see *post*, § 19–88.

In *R. v. Sanderson*, 98 Cr.App.R. 325, CA, the court expressed the view, *obiter*, that the words "induced by disease or injury" refer to organic or physical injury or disease of the body including the brain; that this is the correct view was made more probable by

Parliament's deliberate omission of any reference to disease or injury to the mind, but its inclusion, as a permissible cause of "abnormality of mind", of "any inherent causes", which would cover functional mental illnesses (at p. 336).

Who may raise the issue?

In *R. v. Kooken*, 74 Cr.App.R. 30, the Court of Appeal "very much" doubted whether the trial judge has a discretion to call evidence of diminished responsibility. **19–67**

Kooken was referred to in *R. v. Campbell (C. F.)*, 84 Cr.App.R. 255, CA, in which the court expressed the view, *obiter*, that section 2(2) of the 1957 Act not only dictated which party shouldered the burden of proof once the issue was raised, but also left it to the defence to decide whether the issue should be raised at all. As the court indicated in *Kooken*, this was really an optional defence, and, at least in cases where the defendant was represented by counsel, it seemed that the most that a trial judge should do if he detected, or thought that he detected, evidence of diminished responsibility was to point this out to defence counsel, in the absence of the jury, so that the defence could decide whether they regarded the issue as one for the jury to consider. The judge's knowledge of the evidence available in relation to the issue of diminished responsibility would inevitably be limited, and if he did more than their Lordships had indicated, he might cause serious damage to a defence which had been put forward, without adding anything to the case.

As to the calling of evidence on this issue for the first time in the Court of Appeal, see *ante*, § 7–214.

As to the entitlement of the Crown to call evidence of diminished responsibility where the accused is contending he was insane at the material time and vice versa, see the *Criminal Procedure (Insanity) Act* 1964, s.6 (*post*, § 19–79).

Abnormality of mind—substantial impairment: s.2(1)

(i) *Abnormality of mind*

The authoritative interpretation of this element in the defence is to be found in the judgment of the Court of Criminal Appeal in *R. v. Byrne* [1960] 2 Q.B. 396, 44 Cr.App.R. 246 (followed in *Rose v. R.* [1961] A.C. 496, PC, *post*, § 19–73; *R. v. Terry* [1961] 2 Q.B. 314, 45 Cr.App.R. 180, CCA; and *R. v. Gomez*, 48 Cr.App.R. 310, CCA). The court said (the paragraphs below have been lettered for ease of reference): **19–68**

> (a) "'Abnormality of mind', ... means a state of mind so different from that of ordinary human beings that the reasonable man would term it abnormal. It appears to us to be wide enough to cover the mind's activities in all its aspects, not only the perception of physical acts and matters, and the ability to form a rational judgment whether an act is right or wrong, but also the ability to exercise will-power to control physical acts in accordance with that rational judgment. The expression 'mental responsibility for his acts' points to consideration of the extent to which the accused's mind is answerable for his physical acts, which must include a consideration of the extent of his ability to exercise will-power to control his physical acts."
>
> (b) "Whether the accused was at the time of the killing suffering from any 'abnormality of mind' ... is a question for the jury. On this question medical evidence is, no doubt, important, but the jury are entitled to take into consideration all the evidence including the acts or statements of the accused and his demeanour. They are not bound to accept the medical evidence, if there is other material before them which, in their good judgment, conflicts with it and outweighs it" (*post*, § 19–76). "The etiology of the abnormality of mind (namely, whether it arose from a condition of arrested or retarded development of mind or any inherent causes or was induced by disease or injury) does, however, seem to be a matter to be determined on expert evidence ..."
>
> (c) "Assuming that the jury are satisfied on a balance of probabilities, that the accused was suffering from 'abnormality of mind' from one of the causes specified in the parenthesis of the subsection the crucial question nevertheless arises: was the abnormality such as substantially impaired his mental responsibility for his acts in doing or being a party to the killing? This is a question of degree and essentially one for the jury. Medical evidence is of course relevant, but the question involves a decision not merely whether there was some impairment but whether such impairment can properly be called 'substantial' a matter upon which juries may quite properly differ from doctors" (*post*, § 19–69).

(d) "(T)he step between 'he did not resist his impulse' and 'he could not resist his impulse' … is one which is incapable of scientific proof. *A fortiori* there is no scientific measurement of the degree of difficulty which an abnormal person finds in controlling his impulses. These problems which in the present state of medical knowledge are scientifically insoluble the jury can only approach in a broad, common-sense way. This court has repeatedly approved directions to the jury which … indicate that such abnormality as 'substantially impairs his mental responsibility' involves a mental state which in popular language (not that of the *M'Naughten Rules*) a jury would regard as amounting to partial insanity or being on the borderline of insanity …" (see *post*, § 19–73).

(e) "Inability to exercise will-power to control physical acts, provided that it is due to abnormality of mind from one of the causes specified in the parenthesis of the subsection, is … sufficient to entitle the accused to the benefit of the section; difficulty in controlling his physical acts, depending on the degree of difficulty, may be sufficient" (at pp. 403–404, 252–254).

(ii) *The mental abnormality need not have existed from birth*

19–69 See *R. v. Gomez*, 48 Cr.App.R. 310, CCA.

(iii) "*Substantially*" (see (i)(c), *ante*).

In *R. v. Lloyd* [1967] 1 Q.B. 175, 50 Cr.App.R. 61, CCA, the court approved (at pp. 181, 66) the following direction on the words "substantially impaired" given by the trial judge:

"… your own common sense will tell you what it means. This far I will go. Substantial does not mean total, that is to say the mental responsibility need not be totally impaired, so to speak, destroyed altogether. At the other end of the scale substantial does not mean trivial or minimal. It is something in between and Parliament has left it to you … to say on the evidence: was the mental responsibility impaired, and, if so, was it substantially impaired?" (quoted at pp. 178–179, 64).

The Court of Appeal subsequently advised judges, at least where alcohol is a factor, that guidance as to the meaning of "substantial" should be explicitly provided to the jury by using one or other of the directions in *Lloyd*, *viz.* (a) to approach the word in a broad common sense way, or (b) that the word means "more than some trivial degree of impairment which does not make any appreciable difference to a person's ability to control himself, but it means less than total impairment": see *R. v. Egan*, 95 Cr.App.R. 278 at 284, 288.

(iv) *Drink and mental abnormality*

19–70 In a case where the defendant suffered from an abnormality of mind of the nature described in section 2(1), and had also taken alcohol before the killing, and where there was no evidence capable of establishing alcohol dependence syndrome as being an abnormality of mind within that subsection, the subsection meant that if the defendant satisfied the jury that, notwithstanding the effect of the alcohol he had consumed and its effect on him, his abnormality of mind substantially impaired his mental responsibility for his acts in doing the killing, the defence should succeed; this was because section 2(1) did not require the abnormality of mind to be the sole cause of the defendant's acts in doing the killing; even if the defendant would not have killed if he had not taken the drink, the causative effect of the drink did not necessarily prevent an abnormality of mind suffered by the defendant from substantially impairing his mental responsibility for the killing; a jury should, therefore, be directed along the following lines, "Assuming the defence have established that the defendant was suffering from mental abnormality … the important question is: did that abnormality substantially impair his mental responsibility for his acts in doing the killing? You know that … [he] had a lot to drink. Drink cannot be taken into account as something which contributed to his mental abnormality and to any impairment of mental responsibility arising from that abnormality. But you may take the view that both the defendant's mental abnormality and drink played a part in impairing his mental responsibility for the killing and that he might not have killed if he had not taken drink. If you take that view, then the question … to decide is this: has the defendant satisfied you that, despite the drink, his mental abnormality substantially impaired his mental

responsibility for his fatal acts … ?"; if the jury are so satisfied, then the defence is made out: *R. v. Dietschmann* [2003] 1 A.C. 1209, HL.

In *R. v. Hendy* [2006] 2 Cr.App.R. 33, CA, it was held that *Dietschmann* had done no more than re-state the law as set out in *R. v. Gittens* [1984] Q.B. 698, 79 Cr.App.R. 272, CA, before the Court of Appeal had taken a wrong turn in *R. v. Atkinson* [1985] Crim.L.R. 314, and *R. v. Egan*, 95 Cr.App.R. 278; that being so, if a conviction for murder obtained before the decision in *Dietschmann* was unsafe on the basis of the law as it is now understood to be, it was also unsafe as at the date on which it had been obtained (even though it was obtained on the basis of the law as it was erroneously understood to be at the time); appeals in such cases would not therefore be dismissed by reason of the rule, as expounded in *R. v. Bentley (Deceased)* [2001] 1 Cr.App.R. 307, CA, that the Court of Appeal must consider the appeal on the basis of the substantive law as at the date of the trial.

In *R. v. Tandy*, 87 Cr.App.R. 45, CA, it was held that, where alcoholism alone is relied on, an accused must establish: **19–71**

(a) that he was suffering from an abnormality of mind at the time of the killing;
(b) that the abnormality of mind was induced by disease, namely the disease of alcoholism; and
(c) that the abnormality of mind induced by alcoholism was such as substantially impaired his mental responsibility for the act which caused death.

Element (b) is not established unless the evidence shows that the abnormality of mind at the time was due to the fact that he was a chronic alcoholic. If the alcoholism had reached the level at which the brain had been injured by the repeated insult from intoxicants so that there was gross impairment of judgment and emotional responses, then "diminished responsibility" is available, provided element (c) is established. Alternatively, if the accused is able to establish that the alcoholism had reached a level where, although the brain had not been damaged to the extent identified above, but drinking had become involuntary (*i.e.* he was no longer able to resist the impulse to drink) "diminished responsibility" was available since if his drinking was involuntary then the abnormality of mind at the time of the act causing death was induced by the condition of alcoholism. The court held that the jury were correctly directed that if the taking of the first drink of the day was voluntary, then the whole of the drinking on the relevant day was voluntary. **19–72**

In *R. v. Wood* [2008] 3 All E.R. 898, CA, it was said that where alcohol dependency syndrome is relied on alone as being an illness or disease giving rise to an abnormality of mind, the sharp distinction drawn in *Tandy* between cases where brain damage has occurred as a result of the syndrome and those where it has not, is no longer appropriate; where it has occurred, the jury may be more likely to conclude that the defendant suffers from an abnormality of mind induced by disease or illness, but, whether it has occurred or not, the same question arises, *viz.* whether it has been established that the defendant's syndrome is of such an extent and nature that it constitutes an abnormality of mind induced by disease or illness; if it does, the jury must then be directed to address the question whether the defendant's mental responsibility for his actions at the time of the killing was substantially impaired as a result of the syndrome; and, in deciding that question, the jury should focus exclusively on the effect of alcohol consumed as a direct result of his illness or disease and ignore the effect of any alcohol consumed voluntarily. For a critique of this approach, see *Criminal Law Week* 2008/26/4.

In *R. v. Sanderson*, 98 Cr.App.R. 325, CA, the prosecution called evidence to the effect that whilst alcoholism may reach the stage where the brain itself is being injured, there was no medical science to indicate that such damage results from drugs as opposed to alcohol.

(v) *"Borderline of insanity" (see (i)(d), ante)*

It will sometimes be inappropriate to direct the jury that the test is the borderline of insanity, as where the abnormality of mind cannot readily be related to any of the generally recognised types of "insanity". If, however, insanity is to be referred to, as will usually be the case, the word must be used in its broad popular sense: **19–73**

Rose v. R. [1961] A.C. 496, PC; applied in *R. v. Seers*, 79 Cr.App.R. 261, CA (chronic reactive depression).

"Battered woman syndrome", having entered the standard British classification of mental diseases, is capable of founding a defence of diminished responsibility: *R. v. Hobson* [1998] 1 Cr.App.R. 31, CA.

Direction to jury

(i) *Proper explanation required*

19–74 A proper explanation of the terms of the section, as interpreted in *R. v. Byrne* (and subsequent authorities) should be given to the jury: *R. v. Terry* [1961] 2 Q.B. 314, 45 Cr.App.R. 180, CCA. It is submitted that in so far as the dicta in *R. v. Turnbull (L. G.)*, 65 Cr.App.R. 242 at 244, 245, CA, are inconsistent with this statement they should be disregarded, or should be regarded as being confined to the particular facts (the only element of the defence in issue was "substantial impairment"—the suggested direction on this issue was disapproved in *Gittens, ante*).

(ii) *Burden of proof*

The burden of proof is on the defence (s.2(2), *ante*, § 19–66); and this is not incompatible with the presumption of innocence, enshrined in common law and given effect in Article 6(2) of the ECHR (*ante*, § 16–57): *R. v. Lambert*; *R. v. Ali*; *R. v. Jordan* [2002] Q.B. 211, CA. The burden is discharged by establishing the contention on a balance of probabilities: *R. v. Dunbar* [1958] 1 Q.B. 1, 41 Cr.App.R. 182, CCA.

(iii) *Failure of defendant to give evidence*

19–75 While questions of diminished responsibility are largely matters of medical opinion, where there is any issue on the matter, it is for the defence to lay a foundation of fact upon which the experts can give their opinion. It will only rarely be appropriate for the defendant himself to be called: *R. v. Bathurst* [1968] 2 Q.B. 99, 52 Cr.App.R. 251, CA, explaining *R. v. Ahmed Din*, 46 Cr.App.R. 269, CCA. In *Bathurst*, it was said that it would be improper for the judge to comment on the failure of the defendant to give evidence in all except the rarest of cases; for example, where the defendant had recovered fully from any abnormality by the time of the trial (see *R. v. Bradshaw (C.)*, 82 Cr.App.R. 79, CA). Where any comment is justified, it should be limited to saying that the defendant is not bound to give evidence, that the burden of proof is on him, and that if he fails to give evidence, he runs the risk of being unable to prove his case: *Bathurst, ante*.

These decisions all pre-date section 35 of the *CJPOA* 1994 (*ante*, § 4–305). It seems probable that, save in those few cases where the defendant might reasonably be expected to give evidence (*i.e.* where limited comment would have previously been appropriate), judges will direct juries that it would be improper to draw any inference adverse to the defendant from his failure to give evidence; see section 35(3) as to the drawing of such inferences as appear proper from the failure of the accused to give evidence.

(iv) *Transcript of medical evidence*

It is inappropriate for the judge simply to provide the jury with a transcript of the medical evidence: *R. v. Terry, ante*.

Medical evidence (see § 19–68, ante, (i)(b))

19–76 (a) Medical evidence in support of a defence of diminished responsibility is a practical necessity if the defence is to succeed, as the onus is on the defendant: *R. v. Byrne, ante*, § 19–68; *R. v. Dix*, 74 Cr.App.R. 306, CA.

(b) Where the medical evidence in support of the defence is uncontradicted, and the jury return a verdict of "guilty of murder", if there are facts entitling the jury to reject or differ from the opinions of the medical men, the Court of Appeal will not interfere with the verdict. Evidence of the conduct of the defendant before, at the time of, and after

the killing may be a relevant consideration for the jury in determining this issue. Where, however, there was unchallenged medical evidence of abnormality of mind and consequent substantial impairment of mental responsibility, and no facts or circumstances appeared which could displace or throw a doubt on that evidence, a conviction for murder is liable to be quashed and a conviction for manslaughter substituted: *R. v. Matheson*, 42 Cr.App.R. 145, CCA. In *R. v. Bailey*, 66 Cr.App.R. 31, CCA, the court emphasised that although juries are not bound by what medical witnesses say, they must act on the evidence, and if there is nothing before them which throws doubt on the medical evidence, then that is all that they are left with and they must in such circumstances, accept it. And they should be so directed: *R. v. Sanders (L. J.)*, 93 Cr.App.R. 245, CA.

For a case where the Privy Council, distinguishing *R. v. Matheson*, held that the jury had been entitled not to follow the medical evidence, though uncontradicted by other medical evidence, see *Walton v. R.* [1978] A.C. 788. At page 793, the Board said: "It being recognised that the jury on occasion may properly refuse to accept medical evidence, it follows that they must be entitled to consider the quality and weight of that evidence."

(c) Where medical experts differ, it is for the jury alone to resolve the issue: *R. v. Jennion*, 46 Cr.App.R. 212, CCA.

(d) The jury must also form their own estimate of the truth of the facts on which this defence is based: *R. v. Ahmed Din*, 46 Cr.App.R. 269, CCA. The defence should establish the facts on which the medical evidence is based; the prosecution should investigate the basis of any such defence, including scrutiny of medical reports to see to what extent they depended on hearsay: *ibid*. **19–77**

(e) As a concession, doctors are sometimes allowed to base their opinion on what the defendant has told them without those matters being proved by admissible evidence. The strict (and correct) view is, however, that expressed in *Cross on Evidence*, 5th ed., p. 446 (11th ed., p. 579):

> "A doctor may not state what a patient told him about past symptoms as evidence of the existence of those symptoms because that would infringe the rule against hearsay, but he could give evidence of what the patient told him in order to explain the grounds on which he came to a conclusion with regard to the patient's condition."

Under the *CJA* 2003, s.114 (*ante*, § 11–3), it would be open to the court to admit such hearsay statements as being "in the interests of justice", but, where there was no other evidence on the matter, the judge would be entitled to direct the jury to bear in mind that there was but a flimsy foundation for the defendant's case: see *R. v. Bradshaw (C.)*, 82 Cr.App.R. 79, CA.

(f) As to whether the judge has a discretion to call medical evidence, see *R. v. Kooken*, 74 Cr.App.R. 30, CA, *ante*, § 19–67. **19–78**

(g) As to cross-examination of the accused upon statements he made to doctors who interviewed him with a view to preparing a written report for the authorities upon his mental state at the time of the offence, see *R. v. Smith (S.I.)*, 69 Cr.App.R. 378, CA.

Evidence for Crown on insanity or diminished responsibility

Criminal Procedure (Insanity) Act 1964, s.6

6. Where on a trial for murder the accused contends— **19–79**

(a) that at the time of the alleged offence he was insane so as not to be responsible according to law for his actions; or

(b) that at that time he was suffering from such abnormality of mind as is specified in subsection (1) of section 2 of the *Homicide Act* 1957 (diminished responsibility),

the court shall allow the prosecution to adduce or elicit evidence tending to prove the other of those contentions, and may give directions as to the stage of the proceedings at which the prosecution may adduce such evidence.

The onus on the prosecution to prove "the other of those contentions" is the usual one of proof beyond reasonable doubt: *per* Paull J. in *R. v. Grant* [1960] Crim.L.R. 424, Assizes.

Plea of guilty to manslaughter

As to the propriety of the Crown accepting a plea of guilty to manslaughter on the grounds of diminished responsibility, see *R. v. Cox (M.)*, *post*, § 19–88. **19–80**

Sentence

19–81 Manslaughter is a "specified offence" and a "serious offence" for the purposes of Chapter 5 of Part 12 of the *CJA* 2003 (*ante*, §§ 5–292 *et seq.*). Where a defendant is convicted of manslaughter on the ground of diminished responsibility, if the psychiatric reports recommend and justify it, and there are no contrary indications, a hospital order is the likely disposal: see *R. v. Chambers*, 5 Cr.App.R.(S.) 190, CA. Where this is not appropriate, the sentence will, in accordance with the provisions of Chapter 5 of Part 12 of that Act, be one of imprisonment for life or of imprisonment for public protection where the court is of the opinion that there is a significant risk to members of the public of serious harm occasioned by the commission of further offences by the defendant (see s.225). If the case is not one for a hospital order nor for a sentence under section 225, then the sentence should reflect the offender's degree of responsibility for his acts, with it being possible to give him his freedom, possibly with some supervision, where his responsibility was so grossly impaired as to make his culpability minimal: see *Chambers*, *ante*. As to the need to reflect the offender's diminished responsibility in the punitive element of any sentence imposed, see also *R. v. Bryan* [2006] 2 Cr.App.R.(S.) 66, CA.

(c) *Quarrels and "chance medley"*

19–82 The old doctrine of "chance medley" no longer has any place in the law of homicide: *R. v. Semini* [1949] 1 K.B. 405, 33 Cr.App.R. 51, CCA.

(d) *Killing by the survivor of a suicide pact*

Homicide Act 1957, s.4

19–83 **4.**—(1) It shall be manslaughter, and shall not be murder, for a person acting in pursuance of a suicide pact between him and another to kill the other or be a party to the other ... being killed by a third person.

(2) Where it is shown that a person charged with the murder of another killed the other or was a party to his ... being killed, it shall be for the defence to prove that the person charged was acting in pursuance of a suicide pact between him and the other.

(3) For the purposes of this section "suicide pact" means a common agreement between two or more persons having for its object the death of all of them, whether or not each is to take his own life, but nothing done by a person who enters into a suicide pact shall be treated as done by him in pursuance of the pact unless it is done while he has the settled intention of dying in pursuance of the pact.

[This section is printed as amended by the *Suicide Act* 1961, Sched. 3.]

The *Suicide Act* 1961, s.1, abrogated the rule of law whereby it is a crime for a person to commit suicide.

As to criminal liability for complicity in another person's suicide, see the *Suicide Act* 1961, s.2, *ante*, § 18–6.

Section 4(2) imposes a legal burden on the accused, which is compatible with the presumption of innocence in Article 6(2) of the ECHR: *Att.-Gen.'s Reference (No.1 of 2004)*; *R. v. Edwards*; *R. v. Denton*; *R. v. Hendley*; *R. v. Crowley* [2004] 1 W.L.R. 2111, CA.

Sentence

19–84 For decisions of the Court of Appeal, see CSP B1–5.3B. In *R. v. Sweeney*, 8 Cr.App.R.(S.) 419, CA, Watkins L.J. said that it was the policy of the law that even desperate people must be deterred from taking life, and that those who contemplated suicide and did not achieve it in a suicide pact would be punished if the other party died. Sentences of two or three years' imprisonment have been upheld.

(5) Indictment

STATEMENT OF OFFENCE

Murder. 19–85

PARTICULARS OF OFFENCE

A B, on the —— day of ——, 20—, murdered J N.

The date specified is the date of death, the offence not being complete until such date.

As to sentence, see *post*, § 19–92.

Murder is a class 1 offence: *ante*, § 2–17.

Joinder of offences and offenders

As to the general principles relating to the joinder of offenders and offences, see *ante*, §§ 1–164 *et seq.* Subject to those principles, there is nothing to prevent the joinder of a count of murder with a count charging another offence of murder (*R. v. Kray* [1970] 1 Q.B. 125, 53 Cr.App.R. 569, CA), or with a count charging a different offence (*Connelly v. DPP* [1964] A.C. 1254, HL), such as causing or allowing the death of a child or vulnerable adult, contrary to section 5 of the *Domestic Violence, Crime and Victims Act* 2004 (*post*, § 19–118a), in which case the evidence and procedure provisions of section 6 (*post*, § 19–118f) of that Act will apply. 19–86

A count of conspiracy to murder may be joined with a count alleging aiding and abetting murder: *R. v. Schepke*, *The Times*, May 4, 1995, CA.

As to the need, in cases where death results from an attack by two or more persons, for the indictment to contain appropriate alternative counts to cater for the possibility that the jury find, in the case of one or more defendants, that there was participation with intent to cause grievous bodily harm but, because of the unforeseen production and use of a lethal weapon by one of the attackers, there is no liability to conviction for murder or manslaughter, see *R. v. Greatrex and Bates* [1999] 1 Cr.App.R. 126, CA, and *Att.-Gen.'s Reference (No. 3 of 2004)* [2006] Crim.L.R. 63, CA.

Plea to manslaughter by one or more of several co-accused

Where two or more persons are jointly charged with murder, and the prosecution regard the evidence as pointing more strongly in the direction of one defendant as the author of the fatal blows, the prosecution are at liberty to indicate a willingness to accept pleas of guilty to manslaughter by the other(s) if the defendant in question admits his guilt on the murder charge. If he does not do so, then it is open to the prosecution to insist that the jury resolve the evidence on the murder charge against all defendants: *R. v. Richards and Stober*, 96 Cr.App.R. 258, CA. 19–87

Plea to manslaughter on ground of diminished responsibility

Where on an indictment for murder, the medical evidence plainly points to substantially diminished responsibility, it is proper to accept a plea of guilty to manslaughter based on that ground: *R. v. Cox (M.)*, 52 Cr.App.R. 130, CA. In *R. v. Vinagre*, 69 Cr.App.R. 104, CA, the court observed *obiter* that such pleas should only be accepted when there is clear evidence of mental imbalance. 19–88

(6) Restriction on prosecution

Proceedings against a person for a "fatal offence" may only be instituted by or with the consent of the Attorney-General if the injury alleged to have caused the death was sustained more than three years before the death occurred or the person has previously been convicted of an offence committed in circumstances alleged to be connected to the death: *Law Reform (Year and a Day Rule) Act* 1996, s.2(1), (2). A "fatal offence" means murder, manslaughter, infanticide or any other offence of which one of the elements is causing a person's death, an offence of aiding, abetting, counselling or procuring a person's suicide, or an offence contrary to section 5 of the *Domestic Violence, Crime and Victims Act* 2004: *ibid.* s.2(3). No provision that proceedings may be instituted only by or with the consent of the DPP shall apply to any such proceedings: *ibid.* s.2(4). 19–88a

The 1996 Act was passed on June 16, 1996. Section 2 came into force on August 16, 1996; but it applies to the institution of proceedings on or after the latter date in a case where the death occurred during the period between the two dates, as well as in any case where the death occurred after the latter date: *ibid.*, s.3(2).

(7) Alternative verdicts

General

19–89 See the *CLA* 1967, s.6(2) (*ante*, § 4–459) for the available alternatives.

As to when an available alternative verdict should be left to the jury for their consideration, see *ante*, §§ 4–463, 4–464.

Questioning the jury as to basis of verdict

19–90 When the defence ask for a verdict of manslaughter on the ground of diminished responsibility and also on some other ground, such as provocation, and the jury return a verdict of guilty of manslaughter, the judge may, and generally should, ask them whether the verdict is based on diminished responsibility or on the other ground or on both: *R. v. Matheson*, 42 Cr.App.R. 145, CCA. This dictum is contrary to what was said by the Court of Criminal Appeal in *R. v. Larkin* [1943] K.B. 174 at 177, 29 Cr.App.R. 18 at 27, 28; and in *R. v. Byrne* [2003] 1 Cr.App.R.(S.) 68, CA, where the defence was lack of intent, and the judge left the issue of provocation to the jury, it was held that he had had a discretion to decline to ask the jury the basis of their verdict.

If the jury are to be asked upon what basis a verdict of manslaughter was returned, they should be told during the course of the summing up that the question will be put to them: see *R. v. Jones (Douglas)*, *The Times*, February 17, 1999, CA, in which it was pointed out that the jury are under no obligation to answer. In *Jones*, the court also said that if the jury were satisfied that the defendant had committed an unlawful act which caused death, they could convict though there was no unanimity as to the basis of their verdict, and that *R. v. Brown (Kevin)*, 79 Cr.App.R. 115, CA (*ante*, § 4–391), has no application where a verdict of manslaughter is returned as an alternative to murder.

As to the imposition of sentence where there were two possible bases for a verdict of manslaughter, see *post*, § 19–117.

(8) Attempted murder

19–91 The intention which the prosecution have to prove on a charge of attempted murder is an intention to kill: *R. v. Whybrow*, 35 Cr.App.R. 141, CCA. As to the appropriate direction on "intent", see *ante*, §§ 17–34 *et seq.* In the great majority of cases, it will be unnecessary to direct the jury by reference to foresight of consequences; the simple direction on intention will suffice: *R. v. Walker and Hayles*, 90 Cr.App.R. 226, CA. Where the expanded ("foresight") direction is appropriate, the jury should be directed to use "virtual certainty" as the test rather than "high probability": *ibid.*; and *R. v. Woollin* [1999] 1 A.C. 82, HL.

(9) Sentence

19–92 In all cases of murder, the sentence is mandatory. Offenders aged 21 or over must be sentenced to imprisonment for life. Offenders under 18 at the time of the offence must be detained during Her Majesty's pleasure. For offenders aged 18 when the offence was committed and under 21 on the date of conviction, the sentence is custody for life. For full details, see *ante*, §§ 5–235 *et seq.*

As to the sentence for attempted murder, see *post*, § 33–138.

[The next paragraph is § 19–97.]

B. MANSLAUGHTER

(1) Voluntary manslaughter

19–97 Voluntary manslaughter occurs when all the elements of murder are present, including an intent to kill or cause grievous bodily harm, but the crime is reduced to

manslaughter by reason of (a) provocation (*ante*, § 19–50); (b) diminished responsibility (*ante*, § 19–66); or (c) death being caused in pursuance of a suicide pact (*ante*, § 19–83).

(2) Involuntary manslaughter

(a) *Introduction*

Involuntary manslaughter is unlawful killing without intent to kill or cause grievous bodily harm: *R. v. Taylor* (1834) 2 Lew. 215; and see Stephen Dig.Cr.L., 9th ed., p. 221. Apart from intent, the elements of the offence are the same as in murder (see *ante*, §§ 19–1 to 19–18, 19–21, 19–22, 19–37 to 19–49). The rules as to causation, self-defence, etc., therefore apply: see, *e.g. R. v. Pagett, ante*, § 19–7; *R. v. Mitchell, post*, § 19–101. **19–98**

The difficulty is to identify the elements which may make the killing unlawful: *Andrews v. DPP* [1937] A.C. 576, HL, *per* Lord Atkin at p. 581. The law was, however, considerably clarified by the House of Lords in *R. v. Adomako* [1995] 1 A.C. 171 (*post*, §§ 19–108, 19–109). There are two classes of involuntary manslaughter, namely "unlawful act" manslaughter and manslaughter by gross negligence involving breach of duty.

(b) *"Unlawful act" manslaughter*

In respect of manslaughter arising from the unlawful act of the accused, the following propositions appear to be established: **19–99**

(a) the killing must be the result of the accused's unlawful act (though not his unlawful omission): see *post*, §§ 19–100 *et seq.*;

(b) the unlawful act must be one, such as an assault, which all sober and reasonable people would inevitably realise must subject the victim to, at least, the risk of some harm resulting therefrom, albeit not serious harm: see *post*, § 19–105;

(c) it is immaterial whether or not the accused knew that the act was unlawful and dangerous, and whether or not he intended harm; the *mens rea* required is that appropriate to the unlawful act in question: see *post*, §§ 19–100, 19–105; and

(d) "harm" means physical harm: see *post*, § 19–107.

Unlawful acts

In *DPP v. Newbury* [1977] A.C. 500 at 506, 507, the House of Lords approved the following dictum in *R. v. Larkin*, 29 Cr.App.R. 18 at 23 (unreported on this point at [1943] K.B. 174): **19–100**

> "Where the act which a person is engaged in performing is unlawful, then if at the same time it is a dangerous act, that is, an act which is likely to injure another person, and quite inadvertently the doer of the act causes the death of that other person by that act, then he is guilty of manslaughter."

The act must be unlawful. However, an act which is otherwise lawful (such as driving a vehicle) does not become an unlawful act for these purposes if it contravenes the criminal law merely by the manner of its execution, *e.g.* by driving carelessly: see *Andrews v. DPP, ante*. Similarly, a clear distinction should be drawn between an act of omission and an act of commission likely to cause harm. If the latter act is unlawful and death results, an accused may be charged with manslaughter. If death results from an act of omission, a charge of manslaughter will not inevitably follow: *R. v. Lowe* [1973] Q.B. 702 at 709, 57 Cr.App.R. 365 at 371, CA. (Nevertheless a charge of manslaughter may arise by way of gross negligence involving breach of duty: see *post*, § 19–108.)

In *R. v. Lamb* [1967] 2 Q.B. 981, 51 Cr.App.R. 417, CA, the accused had pulled the trigger of a revolver in jest. The court pointed out that this was not an unlawful act and therefore the prosecution could only establish manslaughter by proving gross negligence. Injecting another person with heroin which the defendant had unlawfully taken into his possession for that purpose, is an unlawful act and if death results the offence is manslaughter notwithstanding that the victim consented and the heroin is only one of the causes of death, *i.e.* a cause of death outside the *de minimis* range: *R. v. Cato*, 62 Cr.App.R. 41, CA (*ante*, § 19–6).

In *R. v. Kennedy (No. 2)* [2008] 1 A.C. 269, HL, it was held that a person is not guilty of unlawful act manslaughter if he is involved in the supply of a class A controlled

drug to a fully informed and responsible adult, which drug is then freely and voluntarily self-administered by the person to whom it was supplied, and the administration of the drug then causes that person's death, since the act of supplying the drug, without more, cannot harm the person supplied in any physical way, and so cannot form the foundation of a charge of unlawful act manslaughter, and, in any event, the act of supplying cannot be said to cause death because the informed voluntary choice of the person supplied to administer the drug to himself breaks the chain of causation. As to section 23 of the *Offences Against the Person Act* 1861 (*post*, § 19–223), any allegation that the defendant had caused the victim to take the substance within that section would similarly fail by virtue of the informed, voluntary choice of the deceased to self-administer the substance. *R. v. Rogers* [2003] 2 Cr.App.R. 10, CA, was overruled. As to whether facts such as these may found an allegation of manslaughter by gross negligence, see *post*, § 19–111.

Death resulting from an unlawful attempt to procure an abortion is manslaughter at the least: *R. v. Buck and Buck*, 44 Cr.App.R. 213, Assizes (Edmund Davies J.); *R. v. Creamer* [1966] 1 Q.B. 72, 49 Cr.App.R. 368, CCA.

In *R. v. P.* [2005] 10 *Archbold News* 2, CA, where the prosecution case had been that the appellant and another youth had, following post-exam drinking, thrown a 16-year-old non-swimmer off a bridge into a river below, causing him to drown, and that they had done so in the course of horseplay or as a practical joke, but that the appellant must have known that the deceased was not consenting (albeit it was not suggested that he knew that the deceased had been a non-swimmer), it had been sufficient for the judge to direct the jury that the prosecution had to prove, (i) that the appellant had taken some part in causing the deceased to fall from the bridge, (ii) that, in doing so, he had applied pressure to the deceased without his consent, (iii) that he had not held a genuine but mistaken belief, whether held reasonably or not, that the deceased was in fact consenting, (iv) that the deceased falling from the bridge was not an accident, and (v) that all sober and reasonable people would inevitably have realised that what the defendant did, in taking some part in causing the deceased to fall from the bridge, must have subjected the deceased to the risk of harm, albeit not serious harm, whether the defendant realised it or not; neither *R. v. Brown (A.)* [1994] 1 A.C. 212, HL (in which Lord Mustill said that as a matter of public policy, the courts have decided that criminal law does not concern itself with such activities as "rough horseplay"), nor *R. v. Barnes* (*post*, § 19–181), required the judge to have asked the jury a further question as to whether, absent consent, they regarded the conduct as "truly criminal".

An offence of affray may constitute the unlawful act: see *R. v. Carey* [2006] Crim.L.R. 842, CA; but see the commentaries thereto in both the *Criminal Law Review* and *Criminal Law Week* 2006/33/13, especially in relation to the uncertainty as to the manner in which the prosecution put their case. Where the deceased was the victim of the affray (see the definition thereof in section 3(1) of the *Public Order Act* 1986, *post*, § 29–17), the prudent and straightforward course will be to found an allegation of manslaughter on the assault on the victim.

19–101 An act calculated to harm A is manslaughter if it kills B and it is immaterial that there was no physical contact between the assailant and B: *R. v. Mitchell* [1983] Q.B. 741, 76 Cr.App.R. 293, CA (X, having been assaulted, fell against Y, an elderly person, who fell over, suffering injury which led to her death). See also *R. v. Pagett, ante*, § 19–7.

The unlawful act need not be directed at the victim so long as there is no fresh and intervening cause between the act and the death: *R. v. Goodfellow*, 83 Cr.App.R. 23, CA (considering *Dalby*, *Pagett* and *Mitchell*) (arson at own home committed with view to obtaining re-housing; intention to rescue family, but fire got out of hand).

Joint enterprise and unlawful acts

19–102 For joint enterprise in homicide cases generally, see *ante*, §§ 19–23 *et seq.*

Killing of children by correction

19–103 At common law, the reasonable correction of a child by a person *in loco parentis* was not unlawful, but the effect of section 58 of the *Children Act* 2004 would seem to be

that any battery of a child that causes actual bodily harm or worse will not be capable of being justified as reasonable chastisement. In *R. v. Griffin* (1869) 11 Cox 402, the trial judge observed that the law as to correction had reference only to a child capable of appreciating correction, and not to an infant, and that although a slight slap might be lawfully given to an infant by her mother, more violent treatment by her father would not be justifiable. An elder brother has no right to strike a younger who is cheeky to him, and if he does so, he must take the risk of the physical condition of his brother. If death ensues, he may be guilty of manslaughter: *R. v. Woods*, 85 J.P. 272.

In *R. v. Mackie*, 57 Cr.App.R. 453, CA, the appellant was convicted of the manslaughter of a boy aged three, to whom he was *in loco parentis*, by putting him in fear of excessive punishment so that he ran away and fell downstairs, dislocating his neck (for the proper directions to be given as to whether death was caused by fear of violence on the part of the accused, see *ante*, § 19–10). The court approved the question posed for the jury by the judge "Had the defendant passed from lawful chastisement to unlawful violence?" It also upheld the decision of the judge to admit evidence of excessive violence by the accused upon the child on previous occasions, not to prove violence or threat of violence at the time of the incident resulting in death, but to prove that the child's fear of being hurt, which caused him to try to escape, was reasonable.

Sporting contests

All struggles in anger are unlawful and death occasioned by them is manslaughter at the least: *R. v. Canniff* (1840) 9 C. & P. 359. However, contact sports, fairly conducted, are not unlawful. Thus it is not manslaughter where death occurs from an injury received during a gloved sparring match, fairly conducted. Such a match may become unlawful if the fight continues unreasonably and the parties are placed in danger thereby: see *R. v. Coney* (1882) 8 Q.B.D. 534, and the cases discussed therein. In *R. v. Turner* (1864) F. & F. 339, it was held that however "fair" a contest might be, if it took place with swords or other dangerous weapons, those taking part and all who were parties to it would be guilty of manslaughter. As to injuries caused during contact sports, such as football, see *R. v. Barnes* [2005] 1 Cr.App.R. 30, CA, *post*, § 19–181. **19–104**

Recognising the risk of the unlawful act

Mens rea is essential to manslaughter, but it is limited to the *mens rea* appropriate to the unlawful act: *R. v. Lamb* [1967] 2 Q.B. 981, 51 Cr.App.R. 417, CA; *R. v. Lowe* [1973] Q.B. 702, 57 Cr.App.R. 365, CA. Accordingly, it is unnecessary to prove that the accused knew that the act was unlawful or dangerous: *DPP v. Newbury* [1977] A.C. 500, HL. **19–105**

The test to be applied was stated in *R. v. Church* [1966] 1 Q.B. 59, 49 Cr.App.R. 206, CCA (approved in *DPP v. Newbury*, at p. 510):

> "... an unlawful act causing the death of another cannot, simply because it is an unlawful act, render a manslaughter verdict inevitable. For such a verdict inexorably to follow, the unlawful act must be such as all sober and reasonable people would inevitably recognise must subject the other person to, at least, the risk of some harm resulting therefrom, albeit not serious harm" (at pp. 70, 213).

The practice of directing juries other than in accordance with the principles set out above should cease: *Newbury*, at p. 509.

Where a series of events culminate in death with no break in the chain of causation between the first event and the death, the act which causes the death and the necessary mental element need not coincide in point of time: *R. v. Le Brun* [1992] 1 Q.B. 61, 94 Cr.App.R. 101, CA, following *Church, ante*. For the facts of *Church*, see *ante*, § 19–21; the Court of Criminal Appeal said that if a killing by the first act would have been manslaughter, a later disposal of the supposed corpse would also be manslaughter.

In assessing the risk of harm, the jury are entitled to ascribe to the hypothetical bystander knowledge which the accused would have gained during the commission of the offence: see *R. v. Watson (C.)*, 89 Cr.App.R. 211, CA (during course of burglary accused confronted by sole occupant, an 87-year-old man, who died of heart failure within **19–106**

90 minutes of the entry; the unlawful act comprised the whole of the burglarious intrusion, during which the accused must have become aware of the victim's approximate age and frailty).

Harm

19–107 In *R. v. Dawson*, 81 Cr.App.R. 150, CA, the court expressed the *obiter* view that whilst "harm" means physical harm, in the context of manslaughter this includes injury to the person through the operation of shock emanating from fright. This is consistent with *Watson*, *ante*. Neither *Dawson* nor *Watson* were referred to in *R. v. Perman* [1996] 1 Cr.App.R. 24, CA, in which the court said that robbery with an unloaded gun, used for the purpose of causing fright or hysteria, would not found a conviction for manslaughter; *aliter*, if the intention were the same but the gun, being loaded, went off accidentally. It should be noted, however, that *Perman* was actually concerned with the liability of an accessory where the principal went outside the scope of a joint enterprise by intentionally shooting the victim.

(c) *Manslaughter by gross negligence*

Introduction

19–108 The law relating to manslaughter by gross negligence was clarified by the decision of the House of Lords in *R. v. Adomako* [1995] 1 A.C. 171.There is a mass of authority on this topic which pre-dates *Adomako*; it is submitted that whilst the test as set out in *Adomako* may prove difficult in its practical application, there is no warrant for referring back to the old cases, save: (a) in relation to two authorities specifically approved by the House of Lords and which may prove useful in formulating directions to juries (*post*, § 19–110); and (b) in relation to the few special points referred to in § 19–111, *post*.

The test

19–109 The ordinary principles of the law of negligence apply to determine whether the defendant was in breach of a duty of care towards the victim; on the establishment of such breach of duty the next question is whether it caused the death of the victim, and if so, whether it should be characterised as gross negligence and therefore a crime; it is eminently a jury question to decide whether, having regard to the risk of death involved, the defendant's conduct was so bad in all the circumstances as to amount to a criminal act or omission: *R. v. Adomako, ante*, following *R. v. Bateman*, 19 Cr.App.R. 8, CCA, and *Andrews v. DPP* [1937] A.C. 576, HL. Evidence as to the defendant's state of mind is not a pre-requisite of a conviction: *Att.-Gen's Reference (No. 2 of 1999)* [2000] 2 Cr.App.R. 207, CA. As to the need to direct a jury in accordance with *Adomako*, see *R. v. Watts* [1998] Crim.L.R. 833, CA.

In *R. v. Misra and Srivastava* [2005] 1 Cr.App.R. 21, CA, it was held that the ingredients of the offence were sufficiently clearly defined in *R. v. Adomako*, and involved no incompatibility with the certainty requirements of Article 7 of the ECHR (*ante*, § 16–97); as to the suggested circularity in the definition (*viz.* it was for the jury to decide whether the defendant's conduct was so bad in all the circumstances as to amount to a crime), the question for the jury was not whether the defendant's negligence was gross and whether, additionally, it was a crime, but whether his behaviour was grossly negligent and consequently criminal.

The direction to the jury should refer to the fact that it is the risk of death, not merely of serious injury that is relevant: *R. v. Misra and Srivastava, ante*. Whether a direction complied with this requirement had to be examined in its context, however; where, therefore, the only risk engaged was the risk of death (as in the case of travelling fast with a defective tyre), a direction that equated gross negligence with "such disregard for the life and safety of others that you, the jury, conclude that it amounts to a crime" could only have been referable to the risk of death: *R. v. Yaqoob* [2005] 9 *Archbold News* 2, CA.

Where the matter was properly left to the jury, there would need to be compelling grounds indeed before it would be proper for the Court of Appeal to say that the jury had set the standard impermissibly high: *R. v. Litchfield* [1998] Crim.L.R. 507, CA.

In a speech with which the remainder of their Lordships agreed, Lord Mackay L.C. said (in *Adomako*) that a judge is free to use the word "reckless" in its ordinary meaning as part of his exposition of the law if he deems it appropriate in the circumstances of the particular case. His Lordship said that the ordinary connotation of recklessness was expressed with complete accuracy in *R. v. Stone and Dobinson* [1977] Q.B. 354, 64 Cr.App.R. 186, CA, and *R. v. West London Coroner, ex p. Gray* [1988] Q.B. 467, DC.

In *Stone and Dobinson, ante*, Lane L.J., giving the judgment of the court, quoted from the speech of Lord Atkin in *Andrews* (*ante*, at p. 583) and continued: **19–110**

> "It is clear from that passage that indifference to an obvious risk and appreciation of such risk, coupled with a determination nevertheless to run it, are both examples of recklessness. ... What the prosecution have to prove is a breach of ... duty in circumstances that the jury feel convinced that the defendant's conduct can properly be described as reckless. That is to say a reckless disregard of danger to the health and welfare of the infirm person. Mere inadvertence is not enough. The defendant must have been proved to have been indifferent to an obvious risk of injury to health, or actually to have foreseen the risk but to have determined nevertheless to run it" (at pp. 363, 193).

In *R. v. West London Coroner, ex p. Gray, ante*, Watkins L.J. said:

> "It should be explained that to act recklessly means that there was an obvious and serious risk to the health and welfare of M to which that police officer, having regard to his duty, was indifferent or that, recognising that risk to be present, he deliberately chose to run the risk by doing nothing about it. It should be emphasised, however, that a failure to appreciate that there was such a risk would not by itself be sufficient to amount to recklessness" (at p. 477).

In *R. v. Lidar* [2000] 4 *Archbold News* 3, CA, it was said that in a case of conscious risk-taking, it is appropriate to direct the jury by reference to recklessness; and that what has to be proved is an obvious risk of serious harm from the defendant's conduct, objectively assessed, and an indifference to that risk on the part of the defendant, or foresight thereof plus a determination nevertheless to run it. It was further said that self-defence and defence of another may be an issue to be left to the jury where the case is put on the basis of recklessness, whereas if it is put on the basis of gross negligence such issues are inevitably wrapped up in the issue of negligence itself.

Where an allegation of manslaughter is based on an omission to act (not itself being unlawful), the issues to be left to the jury are whether a duty of care was owed to the deceased; whether there had been a breach of that duty; whether the breach had caused death; and whether it should be characterised as gross negligence and, therefore, as a criminal act: *R. v. Khan and Khan* [1998] Crim.L.R. 830, CA.

The existence of the duty of care

The duty of care belongs more to the fields of contract and tort than to this work. However, the following should be noted. **19–111**

(a) It is in general for the judge to decide whether there is evidence capable of giving rise to a duty of care, and, if there is, it is for the judge to give the jury appropriate directions, but it is for the jury to decide, in the light of those directions, whether the defendant in fact owed the deceased a duty of care; but there might be exceptional cases where a duty of care obviously existed, as between doctor and patient or where Parliament had imposed a statutory duty, and, in such cases, the judge could properly direct the jury as to the existence of the duty: *R. v. Willoughby* [2005] 1 Cr.App.R. 29, CA.

(b) A person may become liable for manslaughter by neglect of a positive duty arising from the nature of his occupation: *R. v. Lowe* (1850) 3 C. & K. 123 (an engineer in charge of the lift in a mine left it in the care of an ignorant boy); *R. v. Markus* (1864) 4 F. & F. 356 (a doctor absenting himself for the purpose of sport or some similar activity left unattended a patient whom he knew to be in a precarious condition); *R. v. Curtis* (1885) 15 Cox 746 (a local authority officer neglected to provide medical assistance to a destitute person). To hold that a person who supplied controlled drugs to another, owed the other a duty of care when the other, having consumed the drugs in his presence, was in obvious need of medical attention, would undoubtedly enlarge the class of persons to whom a duty of care was owed: *R. v. Khan and Khan, ante*. *Cf. R. v. Sinclair*, 148 N.L.J. 1353, CA (97 8400/2/4 Y4): whilst there is no authority holding that a medically unqualified person is under a duty to render assistance to a stranger or could

come under such duty by virtue of the passage of time, a person who had been instrumental in his friend obtaining a fatal overdose of drugs, and who remained with him throughout the period of unconsciousness might come under such duty; and *R. v. Ruffell* [2003] 2 Cr.App.R.(S.) 53, CA: where the appellant, an experienced drug user, and the deceased, a friend who had been clean for some time, went to the appellant's family home, after an evening's drinking and there injected themselves with heroin, following which the deceased became ill, whereupon the appellant took steps to revive him, it had been open to the jury to find that the appellant had assumed a duty of care towards the deceased.

(c) There is old authority which suggests that liability for manslaughter does not arise where the death is not the direct and immediate result of the personal neglect or default of the defendant: see *R. v. Pocock* (1851) 17 Q.B. 34; *R. v. Ledger* (1862) 2 F. & F. 857; *R. v. Haines* (1847) 2 C. & K. 368; and *R. v. Bennett* (1858) Bell 1. It is doubtful whether, in the light of the broad approach of the House of Lords in *Adomako*, *ante*, the courts would now recognise any such artificial limitation to the general principle; the modern approach is likely to regard the lack of a direct link between the breach of duty and the death as relevant only to the question whether the death was caused by the breach.

(d) It is no defence, where the death of the deceased is shown to have been caused in part by the negligence of the defendant, that the deceased was also guilty of negligence and so contributed to his own death: *R. v. Swindall and Osbourne* (1846) 2 C. & K. 230; 1 Russ. Cr., 12th ed., 418; and see the summing up of Pollock C.B. in that case. See also *R. v. Dant* (1865) L. & C. 567; *R. v. Hutchinson* (1864) 9 Cox 555; *R. v. Jones* (1870) 11 Cox 544; and *R. v. Kew and Jackson* (1872) 12 Cox 355. But evidence which in a civil case might be given to prove contributory negligence may in a criminal case be relevant to show that the death of the deceased was not due to the *culpable* negligence of the defendant. If gross negligence is shown, then it is sufficient if it was a substantial cause of the death: see *ante*, § 19–6.

(e) For the purposes of the criminal law, the courts will not decline to hold that one person owes a duty of care to another because they are jointly involved in a criminal enterprise: *R. v. Wacker* [2003] 1 Cr.App.R. 22, CA.

(3) Liability of secondary parties, attempt and conspiracy

Liability of secondary parties

19–112 There may be secondary parties to involuntary manslaughter: *R. v. Creamer* [1966] 1 Q.B. 72, 49 Cr.App.R. 368, CCA.

> "A man is guilty of involuntary manslaughter when he intends an unlawful act and one likely to do harm to the person and death results which was neither foreseen nor intended. It is the accident of death resulting which makes him guilty of manslaughter ... Bearing that in mind, it is quite consistent that a man who has counselled and procured such an illegal and dangerous act from which death, unintended, results should be guilty of being accessory before the fact to manslaughter" (at pp. 82, 378).

As to whether a person alleged to be a secondary party to murder may be convicted of manslaughter where the jury convict the principal of murder on the basis that in killing the victim he went outside the scope of the joint enterprise, see *ante*, §§ 19–23 *et seq*.

As to voluntary manslaughter, it is obviously unreal to speak of secondary parties to voluntary manslaughter. In relation to diminished responsibility, a person alleged to be a secondary party may rely on the defence regardless of the position of the principal; equally, a secondary party to a killing may be convicted of murder where the principal successfully raises the defence of diminished responsibility: see the terms of section 2 of the *Homicide Act* 1957 (*ante*, § 19–66).

Where the principal successfully relies on the defence of provocation (*ante*, § 19–50), there seems to be no reason in principle why a person alleged to be an accessory—who was not provoked—should not be convicted of murder. Such conclusion would be consistent with the decision of the House of Lords in *R. v. Howe* [1987] A.C. 417 (secondary party liable to conviction of full offence, although principal has defence of duress).

Similarly, where there is a suicide pact between A and B, and C assists A to kill B, A will be guilty of manslaughter, but C will be guilty of murder; see section 4 of the *Homicide Act* 1957 (*ante*, § 19–83).

Attempt and conspiracy

In *R. v. Creamer*, *ante*, at pp. 81, 378, the court said *obiter* that attempted manslaughter and conspiracy to commit manslaughter are offences unknown to the law. It is submitted that from the context the court were confining their attention to involuntary manslaughter. There seems no reason why a person who conspired or attempted to kill another in pursuance of a suicide pact should not be guilty of conspiracy or attempt to commit manslaughter. **19–113**

(4) Indictment

STATEMENT OF OFFENCE

Manslaughter. **19–114**

PARTICULARS OF OFFENCE

A B, on the —— day of ——, 20—, unlawfully killed J N.

The date specified is the date of death, the offence not being complete until such date.

Where the defendant is also charged with an offence of causing or allowing the death of a child or vulnerable adult contrary to section 5 of the *Domestic Violence, Crime and Victims Act* 2004 (*post*, § 19–118a) in respect of the same death, the evidence and procedure provisions in section 6 of that Act (*post*, § 19–118f) will apply.

(5) Class of offence and mode of trial

This offence is a class 1 offence, *ante*, § 2–17, triable only on indictment. **19–115**

(6) Restriction on prosecution

As to the restriction on prosecutions in certain circumstances, see *ante*, § 19–88a. **19–115a**

(7) Alternative verdicts

On a trial for manslaughter of a child, the jury may convict of child destruction: *Infant Life (Preservation) Act* 1929, s.2(2) (*post*, § 19–131). **19–115b**

(8) Sentence

Maximum

Imprisonment for life: *Offences against the Person Act* 1861, s.5. **19–116**

Manslaughter is a specified violent offence within Schedule 15 to the *CJA* 2003 (*ante*, § 5–299).

Where manslaughter is committed by the driver of a motor vehicle, disqualification from driving for a minimum period of two years and endorsement are compulsory; the disqualification must also be until the offender passes a driving test; and the offence carries 3 to 11 penalty points: *RTOA* 1988, ss.28, 34, 36 and 44 and Sched. 2, Pt II (*post*, §§ 32–175, 32–181, 32–198, 32–210, 32–222). As to the power to deprive the offender of the vehicle used, see the *PCC(S)A* 2000, s.143 (*ante*, § 5–439).

Basis of sentence

As to questioning a jury as to the basis of a verdict of guilty of manslaughter, see *ante*, § 19–90. **19–116a**

In *R. v. Byrne* [2003] 1 Cr.App.R.(S.) 68, CA, where it was held that the judge had been justified in declining to ask the jury for the basis of their verdict even in a case where the defence to murder had been lack of intent and it had been the judge who had raised and left the issue of provocation to the jury, it was further held that in

passing sentence, the judge had not been bound to adopt the defence case. Provided he explained his reasoning, it was open to him to form his own conclusion, but this did not oblige him to undertake a detailed review of the evidence.

Involuntary manslaughter

19–116b The Court of Appeal has said that sentences for involuntary manslaughter cover the widest band of sentences of any offence: *R. v. Boyer*, 3 Cr.App.R.(S.) 35.

In *Att.-Gen.'s References (Nos 19, 20 and 21 of 2001) (R. v. Byrne, Field and Cuthbert)* [2002] 1 Cr.App.R.(S.) 33, CA, it was said that in considering the appropriate sentence for manslaughter, the court would look at a number of factors; first, it would examine the context in which death was caused; if it was particularly reprehensible conduct, or conduct which called for deterrence, the court would be bound to impose a sentence longer than otherwise might be the case; examples were domestic burglary and street robbery; public concern and the need for deterrence must be reflected in the sentences passed by the courts; this would inevitably mean longer sentences than might have been considered appropriate some years ago; the second factor that had to be considered was whether any violence of any kind was contemplated or intended by the offender; having established the extent of any violence contemplated or intended, the court must then consider the risk inherent in what was being done of really serious injury or death, and the extent to which this must have been apparent to those involved.

In cases where death has been caused in the course of a serious robbery by armed men, sentences of up to 18 years have been upheld: see *R. v. Tominey*, 8 Cr.App.R.(S.) 161, CA. As to the need for caution before relating the sentence for manslaughter committed in the course of a burglary or robbery to the 30-year starting point for murder in such circumstances (see the *CJA* 2003, Sched. 21, para. 5, *ante*, § 5–246), see *Att.-Gen.'s References (Nos 90 and 91 of 2006) (R. v. Richards and Botchett)* [2007] 2 Cr.App.R.(S.) 31, CA (there was no doubt that the fact that the offence was committed in the course of a criminal venture had to be reflected in the sentence imposed, but the critical feature, when sentencing in manslaughter cases, was the absence of an intent to cause really serious harm or to kill).

Where death has been caused by a blow in the course of a fist fight which was not intended or likely to result in death or serious injury, as a result of the deceased falling and striking his head on the ground, the range (on a plea) will be from 12 to 48 months: see *R. v. Coleman*, 95 Cr.App.R. 159, CA; *R. v. Furby* [2006] 2 Cr.App.R.(S.) 8, CA; and *R. v. Warwood* [2006] 2 Cr.App.R.(S.) 113, CA. In *Att.-Gen.'s Reference (No. 9 of 2005) (R. v. Uddin)* [2005] 2 Cr.App.R.(S.) 105, the Court of Appeal said that it was not realistic to treat what was described as "one-punch manslaughter" as comprising a single identical set of circumstances; cases involving death resulting from a single blow varied greatly in their seriousness and a lengthy debate about individual features arising in the reported cases rarely assisted. The court said that those who were violent had to face up to the consequences of their actions, even if they were unintended.

In *R. v. Case* [2007] 1 Cr.App.R.(S.) 57, CA, sentences of 12 years' detention in a young offender institution on conviction of an offence that came close to the top of the scale of seriousness for offences of manslaughter were upheld.

In *Att.-Gen.'s Reference (No. 111 of 2006) (R. v. Hussain)* [2007] 2 Cr.App.R.(S.) 26, it was said (i) that cases of motor manslaughter can vary considerably in their characteristics; whether there was any animosity shown by the defendant towards the victim will be relevant (as to which, see also *R. v. Mitchell (K.S.)*, 89 Cr.App.R. 169, CA), as will be the questions whether the gross negligence was prolonged or short-lived and whether it took place in the context of some other offence; and the number of deaths caused will also be relevant; (ii) that the guidance on cases of causing death by dangerous driving (*post*, §§ 32–7 *et seq.*) may be of some assistance because the aggravating and mitigating factors may sometimes apply; and (iii) that the cases, none of which purport to be guideline cases, and the facts of which vary hugely, suggest a bracket of four to seven years' imprisonment on a plea of guilty, with most sentences tending to be in the upper half of that range. In *R. v. Dudley* [2006] 2 Cr.App.R.(S.) 77, CA, a sentence of 14 years' imprisonment on a late plea of guilty was upheld for

what the court described as one of the gravest cases of motor manslaughter. The court commented that, whilst an awareness on the part of the offender that his act was dangerous was not an ingredient of the offence, it could amount to a matter of aggravation for sentencing purposes.

For examples of sentences upheld in cases of involuntary manslaughter in various circumstances, see CSP B1–3.

Voluntary manslaughter

As to sentence in cases of voluntary manslaughter, see *ante*, § 19–65 (provocation), § 19–81 (diminished responsibility), § 19–84 (killing in pursuance of a suicide pact). **19–116c**

C. CORPORATE MANSLAUGHTER

(1) The offence

Corporate Manslaughter and Corporate Homicide Act 2007, s.1

The offence

1.—(1) An organisation to which this section applies is guilty of an offence if the way in which its activities are managed or organised— **19–117**

(a) causes a person's death, and

(b) amounts to a gross breach of a relevant duty of care owed by the organisation to the deceased.

(2) The organisations to which this section applies are—

(a) a corporation;

(b) a department or other body listed in Schedule 1;

(c) a police force;

(d) a partnership, or a trade union or employers' association, that is an employer.

(3) An organisation is guilty of an offence under this section only if the way in which its activities are managed or organised by its senior management is a substantial element in the breach referred to in subsection (1).

(4) For the purposes of this Act—

(a) "relevant duty of care" has the meaning given by section 2, read with sections 3 to 7;

(b) a breach of a duty of care by an organisation is a "gross" breach if the conduct alleged to amount to a breach of that duty falls far below what can reasonably be expected of the organisation in the circumstances;

(c) "senior management", in relation to an organisation, means the persons who play significant roles in—

(i) the making of decisions about how the whole or a substantial part of its activities are to be managed or organised, or

(ii) the actual managing or organising of the whole or a substantial part of those activities.

(5) The offence under this section is called—

(a) corporate manslaughter, in so far as it is an offence under the law of England and Wales or Northern Ireland;

(b) [*Scotland*].

(6) An organisation that is guilty of corporate manslaughter or corporate homicide is liable on conviction on indictment to a fine.

(7) [*Scotland*.]

As to the commencement of sections 1 to 26 of this Act, see section 27, *post*, § 19–117v.

The departments and bodies listed in Schedule 1 (as amended by the *SCA* 2007, ss.74(2) and 92, Sched. 8, para. 145, and Sched. 14, and the *Corporate Manslaughter and Corporate Homicide Act 2007 (Amendment of Schedule 1) Order* 2008 (S.I. 2008 No. 396)) are as follows: the Attorney-General's Office, the Cabinet Office, the Central Office of Information, the Crown Office and Procurator Fiscal Service, the Crown Prosecution Service, the Department for Business, Enterprise and Regulatory Reform, the Department for Children, Schools and Families, the Department for Communities and Local Government, the Department for Culture, Media and Sport, the

Department for Environment, Food and Rural Affairs, the Department for Innovation, Universities and Skills, the Department for International Development, the Department for Transport, the Department for Work and Pensions, the Department of Health, the Export Credits Guarantee Department, the Foreign and Commonwealth Office, the Forestry Commission, the General Register Office for Scotland, the Government Actuary's Department, Her Majesty's Land Registry, Her Majesty's Revenue and Customs, Her Majesty's Treasury, the Home Office, the Ministry of Defence, the Ministry of Justice, the National Archives, the National Archives of Scotland, the National Audit Office, National Savings and Investments, the National School of Government, the Northern Ireland Audit Office, the Northern Ireland Court Service, the Northern Ireland Office, the Office for National Statistics, the Office of Her Majesty's Chief Inspector of Education and Training in Wales, the Ordnance Survey, the Public Prosecution Service for Northern Ireland, the Registers of Scotland Executive Agency, the Revenue and Customs Prosecutions Office, the Royal Mint, the Scottish Executive, the Serious Fraud Office, the Treasury Solicitor's Department, UK Trade and Investment and the Welsh Assembly Government.

For the purposes of this Act, whether a particular organisation owes a duty of care to a particular individual is a question of law: s.2(5) (*post*, § 19–117a).

Any rule of the common law that has the effect of preventing a duty of care from being owed by one person to another by reason of the fact that they are jointly engaged in unlawful conduct and any such rule that has the effect of preventing a duty of care from being owed to a person by reason of his acceptance of a risk of harm is to be disregarded for the purposes of this Act: s.2(6) (*post*, § 19–117a).

As to the factors a jury must consider, and the factors they may consider, when deciding whether there has been a gross breach of a duty of care, see section 8 (*post*, § 19–117g).

As to the power of a court to make an order (failure to comply with which is an offence) that an organisation convicted of corporate manslaughter must take remedial steps (including steps to remedy a breach mentioned in subs. (1) of this section), see section 9 (*post*, § 19–117h).

As to the power of a court to make an order (failure to comply with which is an offence) that an organisation convicted of corporate manslaughter must publicise the conviction, and various connected matters, see section 10 (*post*, § 19–117i).

As to the application of this Act to Crown bodies, see section 11 (*post*, § 19–117j), and, in particular, note that an organisation that is a servant or agent of the Crown is not immune from prosecution under this Act for that reason (s.11(1)).

As to the application of this Act to the armed forces, police forces and partnerships, see sections 12 to 14 respectively (*post*, §§ 19–117k *et seq.*).

Any statutory provision about criminal proceedings applies (subject to any prescribed adaptation or modification) in relation to proceedings under this Act against departments or bodies listed in Schedule 1, police forces, partnerships, trade unions, or employers' associations, as it applies in relation to proceedings against a corporation: s.15 (*post*, § 19–117n).

As to the procedure where an organisation liable to be charged with an offence under this section has transferred its functions, see section 16 (*post*, § 19–117o).

Proceedings for an offence under this section may not be instituted without the consent of the DPP: s.17 (*post*, § 19–117p).

An individual cannot be guilty of aiding, abetting, counselling or procuring the commission of an offence of corporate manslaughter: s.18 (*post*, § 19–117q).

As to a conviction for an offence under health and safety legislation at the same time as proceedings, or subsequent to a conviction, for an offence of corporate manslaughter against the same defendant in respect of the same, or partially the same, set of circumstances, see section 19 (*post*, § 19–117r).

As to the abolition of liability of corporations (and other organisations to which this section applies) for manslaughter by gross negligence at common law, see section 20 (*post*, § 19–117s).

(2) Relevant duty of care

Corporate Manslaughter and Corporate Homicide Act 2007, ss.2–7

Meaning of "relevant duty of care"

2.—(1) A "relevant duty of care", in relation to an organisation, means any of the following duties owed by it under the law of negligence— **19–117a**

(a) a duty owed to its employees or to other persons working for the organisation or performing services for it;

(b) a duty owed as occupier of premises;

(c) a duty owed in connection with—

(i) the supply by the organisation of goods or services (whether for consideration or not),

(ii) the carrying on by the organisation of any construction or maintenance operations,

(iii) the carrying on by the organisation of any other activity on a commercial basis, or

(iv) the use or keeping by the organisation of any plant, vehicle or other thing;

[(d) a duty owed to a person who, by reason of being a person within subsection (2), is someone for whose safety the organisation is responsible].

(2) A person is within this subsection if—

(a) he is detained at a custodial institution or in a custody area at a court or police station;

(b) he is detained at a removal centre or short-term holding facility;

(c) he is being transported in a vehicle, or being held in any premises, in pursuance of prison escort arrangements or immigration escort arrangements;

(d) he is living in secure accommodation in which he has been placed;

(e) he is a detained patient.

(3) Subsection (1) is subject to sections 3 to 7.

(4) A reference in subsection (1) to a duty owed under the law of negligence includes a reference to a duty that would be owed under the law of negligence but for any statutory provision under which liability is imposed in place of liability under that law.

(5) For the purposes of this Act, whether a particular organisation owes a duty of care to a particular individual is a question of law.

The judge must make any findings of fact necessary to decide that question.

(6) For the purposes of this Act there is to be disregarded—

(a) any rule of the common law that has the effect of preventing a duty of care from being owed by one person to another by reason of the fact that they are jointly engaged in unlawful conduct;

(b) any such rule that has the effect of preventing a duty of care from being owed to a person by reason of his acceptance of a risk of harm.

(7) In this section—

"construction or maintenance operations" means operations of any of the following descriptions—

(a) construction, installation, alteration, extension, improvement, repair, maintenance, decoration, cleaning, demolition or dismantling of—

(i) any building or structure,

(ii) anything else that forms, or is to form, part of the land, or

(iii) any plant, vehicle or other thing;

(b) operations that form an integral part of, or are preparatory to, or are for rendering complete, any operations within paragraph (a);

"custodial institution" means a prison, a young offender institution, a secure training centre, a young offenders institution, a young offenders centre, a juvenile justice centre or a remand centre;

"detained patient" means —

(a) a person who is detained in any premises under—

(i) Part 2 or 3 of the *Mental Health Act* 1983 ("the 1983 Act"), or

(ii) [*Northern Ireland*];

(b) a person who (otherwise than by reason of being detained as mentioned in paragraph (a)) is deemed to be in legal custody by—

(i) section 137 of the 1983 Act,

(ii) [*Northern Ireland*], or

(iii) [*Scotland*];

(c) [*Scotland*];

"immigration escort arrangements" means arrangements made under section 156 of the *Immigration and Asylum Act* 1999;

"the law of negligence" includes —

(a) in relation to England and Wales, the *Occupiers' Liability Act* 1957, the *Defective Premises Act* 1972 and the *Occupiers' Liability Act* 1984;

(b) [*Scotland*];

(c) [*Northern Ireland*];

"prison escort arrangements" means arrangements made under section 80 of the *Criminal Justice Act* 1991 or under section 102 or 118 of the *Criminal Justice and Public Order Act* 1994;

"removal centre" and "short-term holding facility" have the meaning given by section 147 of the *Immigration and Asylum Act* 1999;

"secure accommodation" means accommodation, not consisting of or forming part of a custodial institution, provided for the purpose of restricting the liberty of persons under the age of 18.

As to the commencement of subsection (1)(d), see *post*, § 19–117z.

Public policy decisions, exclusively public functions and statutory inspections

19–117b **3.**—(1) Any duty of care owed by a public authority in respect of a decision as to matters of public policy (including in particular the allocation of public resources or the weighing of competing public interests) is not a "relevant duty of care".

(2) Any duty of care owed in respect of things done in the exercise of an exclusively public function is not a "relevant duty of care" unless it falls within section 2(1)(a), (b) or (d).

(3) Any duty of care owed by a public authority in respect of inspections carried out in the exercise of a statutory function is not a "relevant duty of care" unless it falls within section 2(1)(a) or (b).

(4) In this section—

"exclusively public function" means a function that falls within the prerogative of the Crown or is, by its nature, exercisable only with authority conferred—

(a) by the exercise of that prerogative, or

(b) by or under a statutory provision;

"statutory function" means a function conferred by or under a statutory provision.

Military activities

19–117c **4.**—(1) Any duty of care owed by the Ministry of Defence in respect of—

(a) operations within subsection (2),

(b) activities carried on in preparation for, or directly in support of, such operations, or

(c) training of a hazardous nature, or training carried out in a hazardous way, which it is considered needs to be carried out, or carried out in that way, in order to improve or maintain the effectiveness of the armed forces with respect to such operations,

is not a "relevant duty of care".

(2) The operations within this subsection are operations, including peacekeeping operations and operations for dealing with terrorism, civil unrest or serious public disorder, in the course of which members of the armed forces come under attack or face the threat of attack or violent resistance.

(3) Any duty of care owed by the Ministry of Defence in respect of activities carried on by members of the special forces is not a "relevant duty of care".

(4) In this section "the special forces" means those units of the armed forces the maintenance of whose capabilities is the responsibility of the Director of Special Forces or which are for the time being subject to the operational command of that Director.

Policing and law enforcement

19–117d **5.**—(1) Any duty of care owed by a public authority in respect of—

(a), (b) [*identical to s.4(1)(a), (b)*, ante, *§ 19–117c*],

(c) training of a hazardous nature, or training carried out in a hazardous way, which it is considered needs to be carried out, or carried out in that way, in order to improve or maintain the effectiveness of officers or employees of the public authority with respect to such operations,

is not a "relevant duty of care".

(2) Operations are within this subsection if—

(a) they are operations for dealing with terrorism, civil unrest or serious disorder,

(b) they involve the carrying on of policing or law-enforcement activities, and

(c) officers or employees of the public authority in question come under attack, or face the threat of attack or violent resistance, in the course of the operations.

(3) Any duty of care owed by a public authority in respect of other policing or law enforcement activities is not a "relevant duty of care" unless it falls within section 2(1)(a), (b) or (d).

(4) In this section "policing or law-enforcement activities" includes—

(a) activities carried on in the exercise of functions that are—

(i) functions of police forces, or

(ii) functions of the same or a similar nature exercisable by public authorities other than police forces;

(b) activities carried on in the exercise of functions of constables employed by a public authority;

(c) activities carried on in the exercise of functions exercisable under Chapter 4 of Part 2 of the *Serious Organised Crime and Police Act* 2005 (protection of witnesses and other persons);

(d) activities carried on to enforce any provision contained in or made under the *Immigration Acts*.

Emergencies

6.—(1) Any duty of care owed by an organisation within subsection (2) in respect of the way in which it responds to emergency circumstances is not a "relevant duty of care" unless it falls within section 2(1)(a) or (b). **19–117e**

(2) The organisations within this subsection are—

(a) a fire and rescue authority in England and Wales;

(b), (c) [*Scotland and Northern Ireland*];

(d) any other organisation providing a service of responding to emergency circumstances either—

(i) in pursuance of arrangements made with an organisation within paragraph (a), (b) or (c), or

(ii) (if not in pursuance of such arrangements) otherwise than on a commercial basis;

(e) a relevant NHS body;

(f) an organisation providing ambulance services in pursuance of arrangements—

(i) made by, or at the request of, a relevant NHS body, or

(ii) made with the Secretary of State or with the Welsh Ministers;

(g) an organisation providing services for the transport of organs, blood, equipment or personnel in pursuance of arrangements of the kind mentioned in paragraph (f);

(h) an organisation providing a rescue service;

(i) the armed forces.

(3) For the purposes of subsection (1), the way in which an organisation responds to emergency circumstances does not include the way in which—

(a) medical treatment is carried out, or

(b) decisions within subsection (4) are made.

(4) The decisions within this subsection are decisions as to the carrying out of medical treatment, other than decisions as to the order in which persons are to be given such treatment.

(5) Any duty of care owed in respect of the carrying out, or attempted carrying out, of a rescue operation at sea in emergency circumstances is not a "relevant duty of care" unless it falls within section 2(1)(a) or (b).

(6) Any duty of care owed in respect of action taken—

(a) in order to comply with a direction under Schedule 3A to the *Merchant Shipping Act* 1995 (safety directions), or

(b) by virtue of paragraph 4 of that Schedule (action in lieu of direction),

is not a "relevant duty of care" unless it falls within section 2(1)(a) or (b).

(7) In this section—

"emergency circumstances" means circumstances that are present or imminent and—

(a) are causing, or are likely to cause, serious harm or a worsening of such harm, or

(b) are likely to cause the death of a person;

"medical treatment" includes any treatment or procedure of a medical or similar nature;

"relevant NHS body" means —

(a) a Strategic Health Authority, Primary Care Trust, NHS trust, Special Health Authority or NHS foundation trust in England;

(b) a Local Health Board, NHS trust or Special Health Authority in Wales;

(c), (d) [*Scotland and Northern Ireland*];

"serious harm" means —

(a) serious injury to or the serious illness (including mental illness) of a person;

(b) serious harm to the environment (including the life and health of plants and animals);

(c) serious harm to any building or other property.

(8) A reference in this section to emergency circumstances includes a reference to circumstances that are believed to be emergency circumstances.

Child-protection and probation functions

19–117f **7.**—(1) A duty of care to which this section applies is not a "relevant duty of care" unless it falls within section 2(1)(a), (b) or (d).

(2) This section applies to any duty of care that a local authority or other public authority owes in respect of the exercise by it of functions conferred by or under—

(a) Parts 4 and 5 of the *Children Act* 1989,

(b), (c) [*Scotland and Northern Ireland*].

(3) This section also applies to any duty of care that a local probation board, a provider or probation services or other public authority owes in respect of the exercise by it of functions conferred by or under—

(a) Chapter 1 of Part 1 of the *Criminal Justice and Court Services Act* 2000,

(aa) section 13 of the *Offender Management Act* 2007,

(b), (c) [*Scotland and Northern Ireland*].

(4) This section also applies to any duty of care that a provider of probation services owes in respect of the carrying out by it of activities in pursuance of arrangements under section 3 of the *Offender Management Act* 2007.

[This section is printed as amended by the *Offender Management Act 2007 (Consequential Amendments) Order* 2008 (S.I. 2008 No. 912), art. 3, and Sched. 1, para. 25.]

(3) Gross breach

Corporate Manslaughter and Corporate Homicide Act 2007, s.8

Factors for jury

19–117g **8.**—(1) This section applies where—

(a) it is established that an organisation owed a relevant duty of care to a person, and

(b) it falls to the jury to decide whether there was a gross breach of that duty.

(2) The jury must consider whether the evidence shows that the organisation failed to comply with any health and safety legislation that relates to the alleged breach, and if so—

(a) how serious that failure was;

(b) how much of a risk of death it posed.

(3) The jury may also—

(a) consider the extent to which the evidence shows that there were attitudes, policies, systems or accepted practices within the organisation that were likely to have encouraged any such failure as is mentioned in subsection (2), or to have produced tolerance of it;

(b) have regard to any health and safety guidance that relates to the alleged breach.

(4) This section does not prevent the jury from having regard to any other matters they consider relevant.

(5) In this section "health and safety guidance" means any code, guidance, manual or similar publication that is concerned with health and safety matters and is made or issued

(under a statutory provision or otherwise) by an authority responsible for the enforcement of any health and safety legislation.

(4) Remedial orders and publicity orders

Corporate Manslaughter and Corporate Homicide Act 2007, ss.9, 10

Power to order breach etc to be remedied

9.—(1) A court before which an organisation is convicted of corporate manslaughter or corporate homicide may make an order (a "remedial order") requiring the organisation to take specified steps to remedy— **19–117h**

(a) the breach mentioned in section 1(1) ("the relevant breach");

(b) any matter that appears to the court to have resulted from the relevant breach and to have been a cause of the death;

(c) any deficiency, as regards health and safety matters, in the organisation's policies, systems or practices of which the relevant breach appears to the court to be an indication.

(2) A remedial order may be made only on an application by the prosecution specifying the terms of the proposed order.

Any such order must be on such terms (whether those proposed or others) as the court considers appropriate having regard to any representations made, and any evidence adduced, in relation to that matter by the prosecution or on behalf of the organisation.

(3) Before making an application for a remedial order the prosecution must consult such enforcement authority or authorities as it considers appropriate having regard to the nature of the relevant breach.

(4) A remedial order—

(a) must specify a period within which the steps referred to in subsection (1) are to be taken;

(b) may require the organisation to supply to an enforcement authority consulted under subsection (3), within a specified period, evidence that those steps have been taken.

A period specified under this subsection may be extended or further extended by order of the court on an application made before the end of that period or extended period.

(5) An organisation that fails to comply with a remedial order is guilty of an offence, and liable on conviction on indictment to a fine.

[Power to order conviction etc to be publicised

10.—(1) A court before which an organisation is convicted of corporate manslaughter or corporate homicide may make an order (a "publicity order") requiring the organisation to publicise in a specified manner— **19–117i**

(a) the fact that it has been convicted of the offence;

(b) specified particulars of the offence;

(c) the amount of any fine imposed;

(d) the terms of any remedial order made.

(2) In deciding on the terms of a publicity order that it is proposing to make, the court must—

(a) ascertain the views of such enforcement authority or authorities (if any) as it considers appropriate, and

(b) have regard to any representations made by the prosecution or on behalf of the organisation.

(3) A publicity order—

(a) must specify a period within which the requirements referred to in subsection (1) are to be complied with;

(b) may require the organisation to supply to any enforcement authority whose views have been ascertained under subsection (2), within a specified period, evidence that those requirements have been complied with.

(4) An organisation that fails to comply with a publicity order is guilty of an offence, and liable on conviction on indictment to a fine.]

As to the commencement of this section, see *post*, § 19–117z.

(5) Application to particular categories of organisation

Corporate Manslaughter and Corporate Homicide Act 2007, ss.11–14

Application to Crown bodies

19–117j **11.**—(1) An organisation that is a servant or agent of the Crown is not immune from prosecution under this Act for that reason.

(2) For the purposes of this Act—

(a) a department or other body listed in Schedule 1, or

(b) a corporation that is a servant or agent of the Crown,

is to be treated as owing whatever duties of care it would owe if it were a corporation that was not a servant or agent of the Crown.

(3) For the purposes of section 2—

(a) a person who is—

(i) employed by or under the Crown for the purposes of a department or other body listed in Schedule 1, or

(ii) employed by a person whose staff constitute a body listed in that Schedule,

is to be treated as employed by that department or body;

(b) any premises occupied for the purposes of—

(i) a department or other body listed in Schedule 1, or

(ii) a person whose staff constitute a body listed in that Schedule,

are to be treated as occupied by that department or body.

(4) For the purposes of sections 2 to 7 anything done purportedly by a department or other body listed in Schedule 1, although in law by the Crown or by the holder of a particular office, is to be treated as done by the department or other body itself.

(5) [*Northern Ireland.*]

Application to armed forces

19–117k **12.**—(1) In this Act "the armed forces" means any of the naval, military or air forces of the Crown raised under the law of the United Kingdom.

(2) For the purposes of section 2 a person who is a member of the armed forces is to be treated as employed by the Ministry of Defence.

(3) A reference in this Act to members of the armed forces includes a reference to—

(a) members of the reserve forces (within the meaning given by section 1(2) of the *Reserve Forces Act* 1996) when in service or undertaking training or duties;

(b) persons serving on Her Majesty's vessels (within the meaning given by section 132(1) of the *Naval Discipline Act* 1957).

Application to police forces

19–117l **13.**—(1) In this Act "police force" means—

(a) a police force within the meaning of—

(i) the *Police Act* 1996, or

(ii) the *Police (Scotland) Act* 1967;

(b), (c) [*Northern Ireland*];

(d) the British Transport Police Force;

(e) the Civil Nuclear Constabulary;

(f) the Ministry of Defence Police.

(2) For the purposes of this Act a police force is to be treated as owing whatever duties of care it would owe if it were a body corporate.

(3) For the purposes of section 2—

(a) a member of a police force is to be treated as employed by that force;

(b) a special constable appointed for a police area in England and Wales is to be treated as employed by the police force maintained by the police authority for that area;

(c) a special constable appointed for a police force mentioned in paragraph (d) or (f) of subsection (1) is to be treated as employed by that force;

(d) a police cadet undergoing training with a view to becoming a member of a police force mentioned in paragraph (a) or (d) of subsection (1) is to be treated as employed by that force;

(e), (f) [*Northern Ireland*];

(g) a member of a police force seconded to the Serious Organised Crime Agency or the National Policing Improvement Agency to serve as a member of its staff is to be treated as employed by that Agency.

(4) A reference in subsection (3) to a member of a police force is to be read, in the case of a force mentioned in paragraph (a)(ii) of subsection (1), as a reference to a constable of that force.

(5) For the purposes of section 2 any premises occupied for the purposes of a police force are to be treated as occupied by that force.

(6) For the purposes of sections 2 to 7 anything that would be regarded as done by a police force if the force were a body corporate is to be so regarded.

(7) Where—

(a) by virtue of subsection (3) a person is treated for the purposes of section 2 as employed by a police force, and

(b) by virtue of any other statutory provision (whenever made) he is, or is treated as, employed by another organisation,

the person is to be treated for those purposes as employed by both the force and the other organisation.

Application to partnerships

14.—(1) For the purposes of this Act a partnership is to be treated as owing whatever duties of care it would owe if it were a body corporate. **19–117m**

(2) Proceedings for an offence under this Act alleged to have been committed by a partnership are to be brought in the name of the partnership (and not in that of any of its members).

(3) A fine imposed on a partnership on its conviction of an offence under this Act is to be paid out of the funds of the partnership.

(4) This section does not apply to a partnership that is a legal person under the law by which it is governed.

(6) Miscellaneous

Corporate Manslaughter and Corporate Homicide Act 2007, ss.15–20

Procedure, evidence and sentencing

15.—(1) Any statutory provision (whenever made) about criminal proceedings applies, subject to any prescribed adaptations or modifications, in relation to proceedings under this Act against— **19–117n**

(a) a department or other body listed in Schedule 1,

(b) a police force,

(c) a partnership,

(d) a trade union, or

(e) an employers' association that is not a corporation,

as it applies in relation to proceedings against a corporation.

(2) In this section—

"prescribed" means prescribed by an order made by the Secretary of State;

"provision about criminal proceedings" includes—

(a) provision about procedure in or in connection with criminal proceedings;

(b) provision about evidence in such proceedings;

(c) provision about sentencing, or otherwise dealing with, persons convicted of offences;

"statutory" means contained in, or in an instrument made under, any Act or any Northern Ireland legislation.

(3) A reference in this section to proceedings is to proceedings in England and Wales or Northern Ireland.

(4) An order under this section is subject to negative resolution procedure.

Transfer of functions

16.—(1) This section applies where— **19–117o**

(a) a person's death has occurred, or is alleged to have occurred, in connection with the carrying out of functions by a relevant public organisation, and

(b) subsequently there is a transfer of those functions, with the result that they are still carried out but no longer by that organisation.

(2) In this section "relevant public organisation" means—

(a) a department or other body listed in Schedule 1;

(b) a corporation that is a servant or agent of the Crown;

(c) a police force.

(3) Any proceedings instituted against a relevant public organisation after the transfer for an offence under this Act in respect of the person's death are to be instituted against—

(a) the relevant public organisation, if any, by which the functions mentioned in subsection (1) are currently carried out;

(b) if no such organisation currently carries out the functions, the relevant public organisation by which the functions were last carried out.

This is subject to subsection (4).

(4) If an order made by the Secretary of State so provides in relation to a particular transfer of functions, the proceedings referred to in subsection (3) may be instituted, or (if they have already been instituted) may be continued, against—

(a) the organisation mentioned in subsection (1), or

(b) such relevant public organisation (other than the one mentioned in subsection (1) or the one mentioned in subsection (3)(a) or (b)) as may be specified in the order.

(5) If the transfer occurs while proceedings for an offence under this Act in respect of the person's death are in progress against a relevant public organisation, the proceedings are to be continued against—

(a) the relevant public organisation, if any, by which the functions mentioned in subsection (1) are carried out as a result of the transfer;

(b) if as a result of the transfer no such organisation carries out the functions, the same organisation as before.

This is subject to subsection (6).

(6) If an order made by the Secretary of State so provides in relation to a particular transfer of functions, the proceedings referred to in subsection (5) may be continued against—

(a) the organisation mentioned in subsection (1), or

(b) such relevant public organisation (other than the one mentioned in subsection (1) or the one mentioned in subsection (5)(a) or (b)) as may be specified in the order.

(7) An order under subsection (4) or (6) is subject to negative resolution procedure.

DPP's consent required for proceedings

19–117p **17.** Proceedings for an offence of corporate manslaughter—

(a) may not be instituted in England and Wales without the consent of the Director of Public Prosecutions;

(b) [*Northern Ireland*].

No individual liability

19–117q **18.**—(1) An individual cannot be guilty of aiding, abetting, counselling or procuring the commission of an offence of corporate manslaughter.

(1A) An individual cannot be guilty of an offence under Part 2 of the *Serious Crime Act* 2007 (encouraging or assisting crime) by reference to an offence of corporate manslaughter.

(2) [*Scotland.*]

[Subs. (1A) was inserted by the *SCA* 2007, s.62. As to this amendment, see the saving provision in Sched. 13, para. 5, to the 2007 Act: *post*, § 33–118.]

Convictions under this Act and under health and safety legislation

19–117r **19.**—(1) Where in the same proceedings there is—

(a) a charge of corporate manslaughter or corporate homicide arising out of a particular set of circumstances, and

(b) a charge against the same defendant of a health and safety offence arising out of some or all of those circumstances, the jury may, if the interests of justice so require, be invited to return a verdict on each charge.

(2) An organisation that has been convicted of corporate manslaughter or corporate homicide arising out of a particular set of circumstances may, if the interests of justice so require, be charged with a health and safety offence arising out of some or all of those circumstances.

(3) In this section "health and safety offence" means an offence under any health and safety legislation.

Abolition of liability of corporations for manslaughter at common law

19–117s **20.** The common law offence of manslaughter by gross negligence is abolished in its application to corporations, and in any application it has to other organisations to which section 1 applies.

(7) General and supplemental

Corporate Manslaughter and Corporate Homicide Act 2007, ss.21–28

21. [*Power to extend section 1 to other organisations.*] **19–117t**

22. [*Power to amend Schedule 1.*] **19–117u**

23. [*Power to extend section 2(2).*] **19–117v**

24. [*Orders.*] **19–117w**

Interpretation

25. In this Act— **19–117x**

"armed forces" has the meaning given by section 12(1);

"corporation" does not include a corporation sole but includes any body corporate wherever incorporated;

"employee" means an individual who works under a contract of employment or apprenticeship (whether express or implied and, if express, whether oral or in writing), and related expressions are to be construed accordingly; see also sections 11(3)(a), 12(2) and 13(3) (which apply for the purposes of section 2);

"employers' association" has the meaning given by section 122 of the *Trade Union and Labour Relations (Consolidation) Act* 1992 or Article 4 of the *Industrial Relations (Northern Ireland) Order* 1992 (S.I. 1992/807 (N.I. 5));

"enforcement authority" means an authority responsible for the enforcement of any health and safety legislation;

"health and safety legislation" means any statutory provision dealing with health and safety matters, including in particular provision contained in the *Health and Safety at Work etc. Act* 1974 or the *Health and Safety at Work (Northern Ireland) Order* 1978 (S.I. 1978/1039 (N.I. 9));

"member", in relation to the armed forces, is to be read in accordance with section 12(3);

"partnership" means —

(a) a partnership within the *Partnership Act* 1890, or

(b) a limited partnership registered under the *Limited Partnerships Act* 1907, or a firm or entity of a similar character formed under the law of a country or territory outside the United Kingdom;

"police force" has the meaning given by section 13(1);

"premises" includes land, buildings and moveable structures;

"public authority" has the same meaning as in section 6 of the *Human Rights Act* 1998 (disregarding subsections (3)(a) and (4) of that section);

"publicity order" means an order under section 10(1);

"remedial order" means an order under section 9(1);

"statutory provision", except in section 15, means provision contained in, or in an instrument made under, any Act, any Act of the Scottish Parliament or any Northern Ireland legislation;

"trade union" has the meaning given by section 1 of the *Trade Union and Labour Relations (Consolidation) Act* 1992 or Article 3 of the *Industrial Relations (Northern Ireland) Order* 1992 (S.I. 1992/807 (N.I. 5)).

26. [*Minor and consequential amendments.*] **19–117y**

Commencement and savings

27.—(1) The preceding provisions of this Act come into force in accordance with provision made by order by the Secretary of State. **19–117z**

(2) An order bringing into force paragraph (d) of section 2(1) is subject to affirmative resolution procedure.

(3) Section 1 does not apply in relation to anything done or omitted before the commencement of that section.

(4) Section 20 does not affect any liability, investigation, legal proceeding or penalty for or in respect of an offence committed wholly or partly before the commencement of that section.

(5) For the purposes of subsection (4) an offence is committed wholly or partly before the commencement of section 20 if any of the conduct or events alleged to constitute the offence occurred before that commencement.

The *Corporate Manslaughter and Corporate Homicide Act 2007 (Commencement*

No. 1) Order 2008 (S.I. 2008 No. 401) brought the Act into force, to the extent that it was not already in force, on April 6, 2008, except for sections 2(1)(d) and 10. While section 2(1)(d) is not in force, the common law offence of gross negligence manslaughter by corporations (abolished by s.20) will continue to apply in respect of a duty referred to in that paragraph: art. 2(3).

Extent and territorial application

19–118 **28.**—(1) Subject to subsection (2), this Act extends to England and Wales, Scotland and Northern Ireland.

(2) [*Extent of amendments.*]

(3) Section 1 applies if the harm resulting in death is sustained in the United Kingdom or—

- (a) within the seaward limits of the territorial sea adjacent to the United Kingdom;
- (b) on a ship registered under Part 2 of the *Merchant Shipping Act* 1995;
- (c) on a British-controlled aircraft as defined in section 92 of the *Civil Aviation Act* 1982;
- (d) on a British-controlled hovercraft within the meaning of that section as applied in relation to hovercraft by virtue of provision made under the *Hovercraft Act* 1968;
- (e) in any place to which an Order in Council under section 10(1) of the *Petroleum Act* 1998 applies (criminal jurisdiction in relation to offshore activities).

(4) For the purposes of subsection (3)(b) to (d) harm sustained on a ship, aircraft or hovercraft includes harm sustained by a person who—

- (a) is then no longer on board the ship, aircraft or hovercraft in consequence of the wrecking of it or of some other mishap affecting it or occurring on it, and
- (b) sustains the harm in consequence of that event.

D. CAUSING OR ALLOWING THE DEATH OF A CHILD OR VULNERABLE ADULT

(1) Statute

Domestic Violence, Crime and Victims Act 2004, s.5

The offence

19–118a **5.**—(1) A person ("D") is guilty of an offence if—

- (a) a child or vulnerable adult ("V") dies as a result of the unlawful act of a person who—
  - (i) was a member of the same household as V, and
  - (ii) had frequent contact with him,
- (b) D was such a person at the time of that act,
- (c) at that time there was a significant risk of serious physical harm being caused to V by the unlawful act of such a person, and
- (d) either D was the person whose act caused V's death or—
  - (i) D was, or ought to have been, aware of the risk mentioned in paragraph (c),
  - (ii) D failed to take such steps as he could reasonably have been expected to take to protect V from the risk, and
  - (iii) the act occurred in circumstances of the kind that D foresaw or ought to have foreseen.

(2) The prosecution does not have to prove whether it is the first alternative in subsection (1)(d) or the second (sub-paragraphs (i) to (iii)) that applies.

(3) If D was not the mother or father of V—

- (a) D may not be charged with an offence under this section if he was under the age of 16 at the time of the act that caused V's death;
- (b) for the purposes of subsection (1)(d)(ii) D could not have been expected to take any such step as is referred to there before attaining that age.

(4) For the purposes of this section—

- (a) a person is to be regarded as a "member" of a particular household, even if he does not live in that household, if he visits it so often and for such periods of time that it is reasonable to regard him as a member of it;
- (b) where V lived in different households at different times, "the same household as V" refers to the household in which V was living at the time of the act that caused V's death.

(5) For the purposes of this section an "unlawful" act is one that—

(a) constitutes an offence, or

(b) would constitute an offence but for being the act of—

(i) a person under the age of ten, or

(ii) a person entitled to rely on a defence of insanity.

Paragraph (b) does not apply to an act of D.

(6) In this section—

"act" includes a course of conduct and also includes omission;

"child" means a person under the age of 16;

"serious" harm means harm that amounts to grievous bodily harm for the purposes of the *Offences against the Person Act* 1861;

"vulnerable adult" means a person aged 16 or over whose ability to protect himself from violence, abuse or neglect is significantly impaired through physical or mental disability or illness, through old age or otherwise.

(7) A person guilty of an offence under this section is liable on conviction on indictment to imprisonment for a term not exceeding 14 years or to a fine, or to both.

The reference to an unlawful act in subsection (1) does not include an act that (or so much of an act as) occurs before the commencement of this section (*i.e.* March 21, 2005: *Domestic Violence, Crime and Victims Act 2004 (Commencement No. 1) Order* 2005 (S.I. 2005 No. 579)): s.59 of the 2004 Act, and Sched. 12, para. 2.

(2) Indictment

STATEMENT OF OFFENCE

Causing or allowing the death of a child, contrary to section 5 of the Domestic Violence, Crime and Victims Act *2004*. **19–118b**

PARTICULARS OF OFFENCE

CD, a child, having died on or about the —— day of ——, 20—, as a result of the unlawful act of a person who was a member of the same household as him and who had frequent contact with him, and there having been at that time a significant risk of serious physical harm being caused to him by the unlawful act of such a person, AB, having been such a person at the time of the act, either (a) caused CD's death by his own unlawful act or (b) was, or ought to have been, aware of the aforesaid risk, and failed to take such steps as he could reasonably have been expected to take to protect CD from the risk, the unlawful act having occurred in circumstances of the kind that he foresaw or ought to have foreseen.

(3) Class of offence and mode of trial

This offence is a class 3 offence, *ante*, § 2–17, triable only on indictment. **19–118c**

(4) Sentence

14 years' imprisonment: 2004 Act, s.5(7), *ante*. An offence contrary to section 5 is a specified violent offence within Schedule 15 to the *CJA* 2003 (*ante*, § 5–299). **19–118d**

It was held in *R. v. Ikram and Parveen* [2008] 2 Cr.App.R. 24, CA, that the range of culpability for an offence under section 5 is wide. Encompassing, as it does, circumstances which amount to murder through all levels of manslaughter, a conviction under section 5 nonetheless means that it has at the least been established that the defendant failed to protect the victim and that he appreciated or ought to have appreciated that the victim would endure serious harm at the hands of the ultimate perpetrator in circumstances which he foresaw or ought to have foreseen. It was said that the general approach to sentencing in manslaughter cases will provide useful assistance. Here, where at least one of either parent inflicted grievous bodily harm in a brutal attack on the 16-month-old victim and where there had been repetitive inflicted trauma over a period of weeks, whilst the other, knowing of the risk that grievous bodily harm would be inflicted, failed to take any preventative steps, but where the identity of the defendant responsible for causing the death was never established, a sentence of nine years' imprisonment on conviction was severe but not manifestly excessive nor wrong in principle; the judge was right not to approach sentencing on the basis that since one or other of them had caused the fatal injury, they were both to be sentenced as if they had; the correct approach was that while neither defendant was to be sentenced as a perpetrator, both were to be sentenced for allowing the perpetrator to act as he did.

(5) Restriction on prosecution

19–118e As to the restriction on prosecutions in certain circumstances, see *ante*, § 19–88a.

(6) Evidence and procedure

Domestic Violence, Crime and Victims Act 2004, s.6

Evidence and procedure: England and Wales

19–118f **6.**—(1) Subsections (2) to (4) apply where a person ("the defendant") is charged in the same proceedings with an offence of murder or manslaughter and with an offence under section 5 in respect of the same death ("the section 5 offence").

(2) Where by virtue of section 35(3) of the *Criminal Justice and Public Order Act* 1994 a court or jury is permitted, in relation to the section 5 offence, to draw such inferences as appear proper from the defendant's failure to give evidence or refusal to answer a question, the court or jury may also draw such inferences in determining whether he is guilty—

(a) of murder or manslaughter, or

(b) of any other offence of which he could lawfully be convicted on the charge of murder or manslaughter,

even if there would otherwise be no case for him to answer in relation to that offence.

(3) The charge of murder or manslaughter is not to be dismissed under paragraph 2 of Schedule 3 to the *Crime and Disorder Act* 1998 (unless the section 5 offence is dismissed).

(4) At the defendant's trial the question whether there is a case for the defendant to answer on the charge of murder or manslaughter is not to be considered before the close of all the evidence (or, if at some earlier time he ceases to be charged with the section 5 offence, before that earlier time).

(5) An offence under section 5 is an offence of homicide for the purposes of the following enactments—

sections 24 and 25 of the *Magistrates' Courts Act* 1980 (mode of trial of child or young person for indictable offence);

section 51A of the *Crime and Disorder Act* 1998 (sending cases to the Crown Court: children and young persons);

section 8 of the *Powers of Criminal Courts (Sentencing) Act* 2000 (power and duty to remit young offenders to youth courts for sentence).

Paragraph 3 of Schedule 12 to the 2004 Act provides that if, in committal proceedings, a magistrates' court is considering whether to commit the accused for trial for an offence of murder or manslaughter, and the accused is also charged with an offence under section 5 in respect of the same death, then, if there is sufficient evidence to warrant committal for trial on the section 5 charge, there shall be deemed to be sufficient evidence to commit for trial on the charge of murder or manslaughter.

(7) Elements of the offence

19–118g Nothing in the Act suggested that the word "significant" in section 5(1)(c) should bear anything other than its ordinary meaning (applying *Brutus v. Cozens* [1973] A.C. 854, HL); when directing the jury, a judge should not seek to define the word (as here, by saying that it means "more than minimal"); and, if they ask for a definition, they should be directed that the word should be given its ordinary meaning: *R. v. Stephens and Mujuru* [2007] 2 Cr.App.R. 26, CA.

E. SOLICITING TO MURDER

(1) Statute

Offences against the Person Act 1861, s.4

19–119 **4.** Whosoever shall solicit, encourage, persuade or endeavour to persuade, or shall propose to any person, to murder any other person, whether he be a subject of her Majesty or not, and whether he be within the Queen's dominions or not, shall be guilty of a misdemeanour, and being convicted thereof shall be liable to imprisonment for life.

[This section is printed as amended by the *CLA* 1977, s.5(10).]

(2) Indictment

STATEMENT OF OFFENCE

Soliciting to murder, contrary to section 4 of the Offences against the Person Act *1861.* 19–120

PARTICULARS OF OFFENCE

A B, on the —— day of ——, 20—, solicited [encouraged, persuaded, endeavoured to persuade or proposed to] C D to murder J N.

(3) Class of offence and mode of trial

This offence is a class 1 offence, *ante*, § 2–17, triable only on indictment. 19–121

(4) Sentence

Imprisonment for life: *Offences against the Person Act* 1861, s.4 (*ante*). 19–122

An offence contrary to section 4 is a specified violent offence within Schedule 15 to the *CJA* 2003 (*ante*, § 5–299).

There are no guidelines on sentencing in cases of soliciting to murder. For illustrative decisions of the Court of Appeal, see CSP B2–1.3B. In *R. v. Hunter* [2008] 2 Cr.App.R.(S.) 40, CA, it was held that the judge had not erred in taking into account the change in approach to the most serious offences of murder since the coming into force of the *CJA* 2003, Sched. 21 (*ante*, § 5–245), and the need for a corresponding increase in sentences for cases involving soliciting to murder. *Cf.* the similar approach to attempted murder, *post*, § 33–138.

(5) Ingredients of the offence

The publication and circulation of an article in a newspaper may be an encouragement, or endeavour to persuade to murder, although not addressed to any person in particular: *R. v. Most* (1881) 7 Q.B.D. 244. The jury were directed that if they thought that by the publication of the article, M intended to, and did, encourage or endeavour to persuade any person to murder any other person, whether a subject of Her Majesty or not, and whether within the Queen's dominions or not, and that such encouragement and endeavouring to persuade was the natural and reasonable effect of the article, they should find him guilty. It was held that such direction was correct. *Cf. R. v. Bourtzeff* (1898) 127 C.C.C.Sess.Pap. 284; *R. v. Antonelli and Barberi*, 70 J.P. 4. 19–123

Section 4 bears its natural meaning and encompasses the soliciting of a foreign national in England and Wales to commit murder abroad, and it is not restricted to intended murders of British subjects: *R. v. Abu Hamza* [2007] 1 Cr.App.R. 27, CA. It also encompasses the soliciting of another to commit murder as a secondary party: *R. v. Winter*, *The Times*, December 20, 2007, CA.

As to the evidence necessary to prove solicitation or incitement to murder, see *R. v. Ransford* (1874) 13 Cox 9, CCR, and *R. v. Fox*, 19 W.R. 109 (Ir.).

There must be actual communication between the defendant and the person solicited; but it is not necessary to show that the latter's mind was affected by the communication: *R. v. Krause*, 66 J.P. 121. See also *R. v. McCarthy* [1903] 2 I.R. 146 at 154. In the absence of actual communication, there may be a conviction for an attempt: *R. v. Krause*, *ante*; *R. v. Banks* (1873) 12 Cox 393.

Where A solicited B, who was at the time pregnant, to murder her child at birth and subsequently the child was born alive, it was held that there was a soliciting to murder "a person" within the meaning of this section: *R. v. Shephard* [1919] 2 K.B. 125, 14 Cr.App.R. 26, CCA.

Where the prosecution case was that the appellant had exhorted his audience to kill Americans and others on an indiscriminate basis, and his defence had been that, properly understood, what he had said had been limited to killing in the battlefield, properly so-called, that that is what he had intended and that is what would have been understood, it had been sufficient for the judge to direct the jury in general terms as to when, in English law, killing would not be unlawful by reason of being done in self-defence or in defence of others, although it would have been preferable if there had been an additional direction linking the general law to the specific factual way in which the defence was advanced (*i.e.* that what was being exhorted was killing in specific areas of world conflict ("the battlefield") when done in self-defence in the face of attack): *R. v. El-Faisal* [2004] 3 *Archbold News* 3, CA.

As to the mental element required, it is submitted that the same principles apply as in "attempts", see *ante*, § 17–42.

F. THREATS TO KILL

(1) Statute

Offences against the Person Act 1861, s.16

19–124 **16.** A person who without lawful excuse makes to another a threat, intending that that other would fear it would be carried out, to kill that other or a third person shall be guilty of an offence and liable on conviction on indictment to imprisonment for a term not exceeding ten years.

[This section is printed as substituted by the *CLA* 1977, Sched. 12.]

(2) Indictment

STATEMENT OF OFFENCE

19–125 *Making a threat to kill, contrary to section 16 of the* Offences against the Person Act *1861.*

PARTICULARS OF OFFENCE

A B, on the —— day of ——, 20—, without lawful excuse made to C D a threat to kill E F intending that C D would fear that the said threat would be carried out.

(3) Class of offence and mode of trial

19–126 This offence is a class 3 offence, *ante*, § 2–17, triable either way: *MCA* 1980, s.17(1) and Sched. 1 (*ante*, § 1–75af).

(4) Sentence

19–127 Imprisonment not exceeding 10 years: s.16, *ante*.

An offence contrary to section 16 is a specified violent offence within Schedule 15 to the *CJA* 2003 (*ante*, § 5–299).

In *R. v. Fletcher* [2002] 2 Cr.App.R.(S.) 127, the Court of Appeal upheld consecutive sentences for offences of indecent assault and threats to kill arising from the same incident; the gravamen of the former offence was the indecency, whereas the gravamen of the latter offence was the extreme terror which such threats engendered.

(5) Ingredients of the offence

19–128 It is for the jury to say whether a letter amounts to a threat to kill: *R. v. Boucher* (1831) 4 C. & P. 562; *R. v. Tyler* (1835) 1 Mood. 428.

A foetus *in utero* is not "a third person" distinct from its mother within section 16: *R. v. Tait* [1990] Q.B. 290, 90 Cr.App.R. 44, CA. But it would seem that a threat to kill a child after its birth made at a time when it was still a foetus is capable of being an offence within the section: *ibid.*

A lawful excuse could exist if the threat was made for the prevention of crime (see *CLA* 1967, s.3, *ante*, § 19–39) or for self-defence, provided that it was reasonable in the circumstances to make such a threat; what was reasonable is a question for the jury: *R. v. Cousins* [1982] Q.B. 526; 74 Cr.App.R. 363, CA. The onus is on the prosecution to prove that there was no lawful excuse; if there is evidence of facts which could give rise to lawful excuse, the jury must be directed to those facts and reminded of the onus on the prosecution to prove absence of lawful excuse: *ibid.*

(6) Evidence

Evidence of previous history between the parties is admissible as tending to prove that the defendant intended his words to be taken seriously: *R. v. Williams (C.I.)*, 84 Cr.App.R. 299, CA. (See also *ante*, §§ 13–29 *et seq.*) **19–129**

II. CHILD DESTRUCTION, INFANTICIDE AND ENDEAVOURING TO CONCEAL THE BIRTH OF CHILDREN

A. CHILD DESTRUCTION

(1) Statute

Infant Life (Preservation) Act 1929, ss.1, 2

Punishment for child destruction

1.—(1) Subject as hereinafter in this subsection provided, any person who, with intent to destroy the life of a child capable of being born alive, by any wilful act causes a child to die before it has an existence independent of its mother, shall be guilty of an offence, to wit, of child destruction, and shall be liable on conviction thereof on indictment to imprisonment for life: Provided that no person shall be found guilty of an offence under this section unless it is proved that the act which caused the death of the child was not done in good faith for the purpose only of preserving the life of the mother. **19–130**

(2) For the purposes of this Act, evidence that a woman had at any material time been pregnant for a period of twenty-eight weeks or more shall be prima facie proof that she was at that time pregnant of a child capable of being born alive.

Prosecution of offences

2.—(2) Where upon the trial of any person for the murder or manslaughter of any child, or for infanticide, or for an offence under section fifty-eight of the *Offences against the Person Act* 1861 (which relates to administering drugs or using instruments to procure abortion), the jury are of opinion that the person charged is not guilty of murder, manslaughter or infanticide, or of an offence under the said section fifty-eight, as the case may be, but that he is shown by the evidence to be guilty of the offence of child destruction, the jury may find him guilty of that offence, and thereupon the person convicted shall be liable to be punished as if he had been convicted upon an indictment for child destruction. **19–131**

(3) Where upon the trial of any person for the offence of child destruction the jury are of opinion that the person charged is not guilty of that offence, but that he is shown by the evidence to be guilty of an offence under the said section fifty-eight of the *Offences against the Person Act* 1861, the jury may find him guilty of that offence, and thereupon the person convicted shall be liable to be punished as if he had been convicted upon an indictment under that section.

[Subss. (1) and (4) were repealed by the *CLA* 1967, s.10 and Sched. 3, Pts II and III. Subs. (5) was repealed by the *PACE Act* 1984, s.119(7) and Sched. 7, Pt V.]

(2) Indictment

STATEMENT OF OFFENCE

Child destruction, contrary to section 1(1) of the Infant Life (Preservation) Act *1929.* **19–132**

PARTICULARS OF OFFENCE

A B, on the —— day of ——, 20—, with intent to destroy the life of a child capable of being born alive, wilfully inserted an instrument into the womb of J N and thereby caused the death of her child before it had an existence independent of her.

(3) Class of offence and mode of trial

This offence is a class 1 offence, *ante*, § 2–17, triable only on indictment. **19–133**

(4) Alternative verdicts

On a count of child destruction, the accused may be convicted of an offence under section 58 of the *Offences against the Person Act* 1861 (procuring abortion, *post*, § 19–149): s.2(3) of the 1929 Act, *ante*. **19–134**

(5) Sentence

19–135 Imprisonment for life: s.1(1) of the 1929 Act, *ante*.

An offence contrary to section 1 of the 1929 Act is a specified violent offence within Schedule 15 to the *CJA* 2003 (*ante*, § 5–299).

(6) Child destruction and abortion

19–136 There is an overlap between the provisions of the *Infant Life (Preservation) Act* 1929, s.1 and those of the *Offences against the Person Act* 1861, s.58 (*post*, § 19–149). The latter section prohibits attempts to procure a miscarriage at any time between conception and the birth of the child alive, while the former prohibits the killing of any child capable of being born alive. The *Abortion Act* 1967 renders lawful, abortions effected in certain circumstances and subject to certain formalities (*post*, § 19–151). Section 5(1) of the 1967 Act (*post*, § 19–153) provides that no offence under the 1929 Act shall be committed by a registered medical practitioner who terminates a pregnancy in accordance with the provisions of the Act. If the case does not come within the 1967 Act, a person otherwise coming within the terms of section 1(1) of the 1929 Act will have a defence, if the act which caused the death of the child was done in good faith for the purpose of preserving the life of the mother (see the proviso to s.1(1)) or, possibly her health: *R. v. Bourne* [1939] 1 K.B. 687, CCA; *R. v. Newton and Stungo* [1958] Crim.L.R. 469. Although *Bourne* (and *Newton and Stungo*, which followed *Bourne*) was decided under section 58 of the 1861 Act, it purports to be declaratory of the common law and to interpret the proviso to section 1(1).

Although a foetus of a gestational age of between 18 and 21 weeks could be said to demonstrate real and discernible signs of life, if the medical evidence is such that the foetus would be incapable of breathing either naturally or with the aid of a ventilator, then such a foetus cannot properly be described as being "capable of being born alive" within section 1(1) of the 1929 Act. Accordingly, the termination of a pregnancy of that length does not constitute an offence under the 1929 Act: *C. v. S.* [1988] Q.B. 135, CA (Civ. Div.). In *Rance v. Mid-Downs Health Authority* [1991] 1 Q.B. 587, QBD (Brooke J.) it was held that "a child capable of being born alive" meant capable of existing as a live child, breathing and living by reason of its breathing through its own lungs alone, without deriving any of its living, or power of living, by or through any connection with its mother.

B. INFANTICIDE

(1) Statute

Infanticide Act 1938, s.1

Offence of infanticide

19–137 **1.**—(1) Where a woman by any wilful act or omission causes the death of her child being a child under the age of twelve months, but at the time of the act or omission the balance of her mind was disturbed by reason of her not having fully recovered from the effect of giving birth to the child or by reason of the effect of lactation consequent upon the birth of the child, then, notwithstanding that the circumstances were such that but for this Act the offence would have amounted to murder, she shall be guilty of an offence, to wit of infanticide, and may for such offence be dealt with and punished as if she had been guilty of the offence of manslaughter of the child.

(2) Where upon the trial of a woman for the murder of her child, being a child under the age of twelve months, the jury are of opinion that she by any wilful act or omission caused its death, but that at the time of the act or omission the balance of her mind was disturbed by reason of her not having fully recovered from the effect of giving birth to the child or by reason of the effect of lactation consequent upon the birth of the child, then the jury may, notwithstanding that the circumstances were such that but for the provisions of this Act they might have returned a verdict of murder, return in lieu thereof a verdict of infanticide.

(3) Nothing in this Act shall affect the power of the jury upon an indictment for the murder of a child to return a verdict of manslaughter, or a verdict of guilty but insane, ...

[The remainder of subs. (3) and the whole of subs. (4) were repealed by the *CLA* 1967, s.10(3) and Sched. 3, Pt III.]

(2) Indictment

STATEMENT OF OFFENCE

Infanticide, contrary to section 1(1) of the Infanticide Act *1938.* 19–138

PARTICULARS OF OFFENCE

A B, on the —— day of ——, 20—, caused the death of her child under the age of twelve months, by a wilful act [omission], *that is to say, by stabbing him with a knife* [by wilfully neglecting to ...], *but at the time of the act* [omission] *she had not fully recovered from the effect of giving birth to such child* [or *from the effect of lactation consequent upon the birth of the child*] *and by reason thereof the balance of her mind was then disturbed.*

(3) Class of offence and mode of trial

This offence is a class 1 offence, *ante*, § 2–17, triable only on indictment. 19–139

(4) Restriction on prosecution

As to the restriction on prosecutions in certain circumstances, see *ante* § 19–88a. 19–139a

(5) Alternative verdicts

On a count of infanticide, the accused may be convicted of an offence of child destruction: *Infant Life (Preservation) Act* 1929, s.2(2) (*ante*, § 19–131). 19–140

(6) Sentence

Imprisonment for life, "as if she had been guilty of the offence of manslaughter of such child": see s.1(1), *ante*, § 19–137. 19–141

An offence of infanticide is a specified violent offence within Schedule 15 to the *CJA* 2003 (*ante*, § 5–299).

For cases of infanticide and related offences, see CSP B1–6.3. Custodial sentences are extremely rare.

(7) Ingredients of the offence

It is not necessary for all the elements of murder (in particular, an intention to kill or to cause grievous bodily harm) to be proved: *R. v. Gore* [2008] Crim.L.R. 388, CA. 19–141a

C. CONCEALMENT OF BIRTH

(1) Statute

Offences against the Person Act 1861, s.60

60. If any woman shall be delivered of a child, every person who shall, by any secret disposition of the dead body of the said child, whether such child died before, at, or after its birth, endeavour to conceal the birth thereof, shall be guilty of a misdemeanour, and being convicted thereof shall be liable, at the discretion of the court, to be imprisoned for any term not exceeding two years, ... 19–142

[The proviso to section 60 was repealed by the *CLA* 1967, s.10(2), Sched. 3.]

(2) Indictment

STATEMENT OF OFFENCE

Endeavouring to conceal birth, contrary to section 60 of the Offences against the Person Act *1861.* 19–143

PARTICULARS OF OFFENCE

A B, on the —— day of ——, 20—, endeavoured to conceal the birth of a child, of which she had been delivered, by secretly disposing of the dead body of the child.

(3) Class of offence and mode of trial

This offence is a class 3 offence, *ante*, § 2–17, triable either way: *MCA* 1980, s.17(1), and Sched. 1 (*ante*, § 1–75af). 19–144

(4) Sentence

19–145 Imprisonment not exceeding two years: *Offences against the Person Act* 1861, s.60 (*ante*). See *R. v. English*, 52 Cr.App.R. 119, CA.

(5) Ingredients of the offence

"A child"

19–146 In *R. v. Berriman* (1854) 6 Cox 388, Erle J., at p. 390, said that on a charge of endeavouring to conceal the birth of a child it must appear that the child had "arrived at that stage of maturity at the time of birth that it might have been a living child". See also *R. v. Hewitt and Smith* (1866) 4 F. & F. 1101, although in *R. v. Colmer* (1864) 9 Cox 506, a foetus no bigger than a man's finger, but having the shape of a child, was held to be a child within the statute; *quaere* whether this is still good law.

Identification

19–147 It has been said that, in order to convict an accused of endeavouring to conceal the birth of a child, a dead body must be found and identified as the child of which the mother is said to have been delivered: *R. v. Williams* (1871) 11 Cox 684; and see *R. v. Bell* (1874) Ir.Rep. 8 C.L. 542; or that at least a confession should have been made by the accused: *R. v. Kersey*, 1 Cr.App.R. 260, CCA; but it is difficult to see why the principles laid down in *R. v. Onufrejczyk* [1955] 2 Q.B. 388, 39 Cr.App.R. 1, CCA (*ante*, § 19–9), should not apply in such a case: see also *R. v. Davidson*, 25 Cr.App.R. 21, CCA.

Concealment—secret disposition

19–148 Mere denial of the birth is not sufficient to support a conviction for this offence, without some actual and secret disposition of the body: *R. v. Turner* (1839) 8 C. & P. 755; see also *R. v. Farnham* (1845) 1 Cox 349 and *R. v. Opie* (1860) 8 Cox 332. What amounts to a secret disposition will depend upon the particular facts of the case: *R. v. Brown* (1870) L.R. 1 C.C.R. 244. In that case, Bovill C.J. seems to indicate that the test of a "secret disposition" is the likelihood or probability of the body being found. There may, therefore, be a secret disposition where the body is put in a secluded place, even though it is not actually concealed from view, as in *R. v. Brown*, *ante*, while conversely, there may be no secret disposition even where the body is concealed from view, as in *R. v. George* (1868) 11 Cox 41: see also *R. v. Rosenberg*, 70 J.P. 264; *R. v. Sleep* (1864) 9 Cox 559; *R. v. Cook* (1870) 11 Cox 542; *R. v. Clarke* (1866) 4 F. & F.1040; *R. v. Nixon*, *ibid.* at 1040 n.

It must be proved that the accused performed the act of secret disposition after the death of the child: *R. v. Coxhead* (1845) Car. & Kir. 623; *R. v. May* (1867) 10 Cox 448. Where, however, a woman placed a living child in a place of concealment and, returning to find it dead, left it where it lay, replacing the materials by which the concealment was effected, this was held to be a concealment within the statute (9 Geo. 4, c.31, s.14) which preceded the 1861 Act: *R. v. Hughes* (1850) 4 Cox 447.

The fact that the mother had previously allowed the fact of the birth to be known to some persons is not *conclusive* evidence negativing an endeavour to conceal: *R. v. Douglas* (1836) 1 Mood. 480; *R. v. Cornwall* (1817) R. & R. 336.

III. ABORTION

(1) Statute

Offences against the Person Act 1861, ss.58, 59

Use of poison or instruments to cause miscarriage

19–149 **58.** Every woman being with child who, with intent to procure her own miscarriage, shall unlawfully administer to herself any poison or other noxious thing, or shall unlawfully use any instrument or other means whatsoever with the like intent, and whosoever, with intent to procure the miscarriage of any woman whether she be or be not with child, shall unlawfully administer to her or cause to be taken by her any poison or other noxious thing, or shall unlawfully use any instrument or other means whatsoever with the like intent, shall be ... liable ... to *imprisonment* for life. ...

[This section is printed as amended by the *CJA* 1948, s.1(1); and as repealed in part by the *Statute Law Revision Act* 1892; and the *Statute Law Revision (No. 2) Act* 1893.]

Supplying or procuring poison or instruments with like intent

59. Whosoever shall unlawfully supply or procure any poison or other noxious thing, or any instrument or thing whatsoever, knowing that the same is intended to be unlawfully used or employed with intent to procure the miscarriage of any woman, whether she be or be not with child, shall be guilty of a misdemeanour, and being convicted thereof shall be liable ... to imprisonment ... [for any term not exceeding five years]. ... **19–150**

[This section is printed as amended or repealed in part by the *Penal Servitude Act* 1891, s.1(1); the *Statute Law Revision Act* 1892; and the *CJA* 1948, s.1(1).]

Abortion Act 1967, s.1

Medical termination of pregnancy

1.—(1) Subject to the provisions of this section, a person shall not be guilty of an offence under the law relating to abortion when a pregnancy is terminated by a registered medical practitioner if two registered medical practitioners are of the opinion, formed in good faith— **19–151**

(a) that the pregnancy has not exceeded its twenty-fourth week and that the continuance of the pregnancy would involve risk, greater than if the pregnancy were terminated, of injury to the physical or mental health of the pregnant woman or any existing children of her family; or

(b) that the termination is necessary to prevent grave permanent injury to the physical or mental health of the pregnant woman; or

(c) that the continuance of the pregnancy would involve risk to the life of the pregnant woman, greater than if the pregnancy were terminated; or

(d) that there is a substantial risk that if the child were born it would suffer from such physical or mental abnormalities as to be seriously handicapped.

(2) In determining whether the continuance of a pregnancy would involve such risk of injury to health as is mentioned in paragraph (a) or (b) of subsection (1) of this section, account may be taken of the pregnant woman's actual or reasonably foreseeable environment.

(3) Except as provided by subsection (4) of this section, any treatment for the termination of pregnancy must be carried out in a hospital vested in the Secretary of State for the purposes of his functions under the *National Health Service Act* 2006 or the *National Health Service (Scotland) Act* 1978 or in a hospital vested in a Primary Care Trust or a National Health Service Trust or an NHS foundation trust or in a place approved for the purposes of this section by the Secretary of State.

(3A) The power under subsection (3) of this section to approve a place includes power, in relation to treatment consisting primarily in the use of such medicines as may be specified in the approval and carried out in such manner as may be so specified, to approve a class of places.

(4) Subsection (3) of this section, and so much of subsection (1) as relates to the opinion of two registered medical practitioners, shall not apply to the termination of a pregnancy by a registered medical practitioner in a case where he is of the opinion, formed in good faith, that the termination is immediately necessary to save the life or to prevent grave permanent injury to the physical or mental health of the pregnant woman.

[This section is printed as amended by the *Health Services Act* 1980, ss.1, 2 and Sched. 1, para. 17(1); the *Human Fertilisation and Embryology Act* 1990, s.37(1)–(3); the *National Health Service Care and Community Act* 1990, s.66(1) and Sched. 9, para. 8; the *Health Act 1999 (Supplementary, Consequential, etc. Provisions) Order* 2000 (S.I. 2000 No. 90); the *Health and Social Care (Community Health and Standards) Act* 2003, s.34, and Sched. 4, para. 10; and the *National Health Service (Consequential Provisions) Act* 2006, s.2, and Sched. 1, para. 30.]

Section 2 authorises the making of regulations for requiring, *inter alia*, (a) any such opinion as is referred to in section 1 to be certified by the practitioners or practitioner concerned in such form and at such time as may be prescribed, and (b) any registered **19–152** medical practitioner who terminates a pregnancy to give notice of the termination and such other information relating thereto as may be prescribed. The current regulations are the *Abortion Regulations* 1991 (S.I. 1991 No. 499), as amended by the *Abortion (Amendment) (England) Regulations* 2002 (S.I. 2002 No. 887) and the *Abortion (Amendment) Regulations* 2008 (S.I. 2008 No. 735).

Section 3 applies the Act to any force which is a visiting force within the meaning of any of the provisions of Part I of the *Visiting Forces Act* 1952 and any headquarters within the meaning of the Schedule to the *International Headquarters and Defence Organisations Act* 1964.

Abortion Act 1967, ss.5, 6

Supplementary provisions

19–153 **5.**—(1) No offence under the *Infant Life (Preservation) Act* 1929 shall be committed by a registered medical practitioner who terminates a pregnancy in accordance with the provisions of this Act.

(2) For the purposes of the law relating to abortion, anything done with intent to procure a woman's miscarriage (or, in the case of a woman carrying more than one foetus, her miscarriage of any foetus) is unlawfully done unless authorised by section 1 of this Act and, in the case of a woman carrying more than one foetus, anything done with intent to procure her miscarriage of any foetus is authorised by that section if—

(a) the ground for termination of the pregnancy specified in subsection (1)(d) of that section applies in relation to any foetus and the thing is done for the purpose of procuring the miscarriage of that foetus, or

(b) any of the other grounds for termination of the pregnancy specified in that section applies.

[This section is printed as amended by the *Human Fertilisation and Embryology Act* 1990, s.37(4).]

Interpretation

19–154 **6.** In this Act, the following expressions have meanings hereby assigned to them:—

"law relating to abortion" means sections 58 and 59 of the *Offences against the Person Act* 1861, and any rule of law relating to the procurement of abortion.

[This section is printed as repealed in part by the *Health Services Act* 1980, s.25(4) and Sched. 7.]

(2) Indictment

COUNT 1

STATEMENT OF OFFENCE

19–155 *Administering poison* [*Using an instrument*] *with intent to procure miscarriage, contrary to section 58 of the* Offences against the Person Act *1861*.

PARTICULARS OF OFFENCE

A B, on the —— day of ——, 20—, with intent to procure the miscarriage of a woman named J N, unlawfully administered to [or *caused to be taken by*] *her a poison or other noxious thing called ——*, [or *the nature of which is unknown*, as the case may be] [*used an instrument or some other unknown means*].

COUNT 2

STATEMENT OF OFFENCE

19–156 *Procuring* [or *Supplying*] *poison to be used with intent to procure abortion, contrary to section 59 of the* Offences against the Person Act *1861*.

PARTICULARS OF OFFENCE

A B, on the —— day of ——, 20—, supplied [or *procured*] *a poison or other noxious thing called ——*, [or *the nature of which is unknown*, as the case may be], *knowing that it was intended to be unlawfully used or employed with intent to procure the miscarriage of a woman named J N*.

(3) Class of offence and mode of trial

The offence contrary to section 58 is a class 1 offence, *ante*, § 2–17, triable only on indictment; the offence contrary to section 59 is also triable only on indictment and is a class 3 offence, *ante*, § 2–17. **19–157**

(4) Alternative verdicts

As to the power to find a verdict of guilty of an offence of child destruction on an indictment for an offence under section 58 and vice versa, see the *Infant Life (Preservation) Act* 1929, s.2(2), (3) (*ante*, § 19–131). **19–158**

(5) Sentence

Count 1: imprisonment for life, s.58, *ante*. **19–159**

Count 2: imprisonment not exceeding five years, s.59, *ante*.

(6) Ingredients of the offences

Section 58

(i) *The administration*

Where the accused gave the prosecutrix a drug for the purpose of procuring an abortion, and she took it for that purpose in the absence of the accused, this was held to be "causing it to be taken" within 7 Will. 4 & 1 Vict. c. 85, s.6 (*rep.*) of which section 58 of the 1861 Act is a re-enactment: *R. v. Wilson* (1856) Dears. & B. 127; see also *R. v. Farrow* (1857) Dears. & B. 164. It is not necessary that there should be an actual delivery by the hand of the accused: *R. v. Harley* (1830) 4 C. & P. 369. **19–160**

It is not sufficient to prove merely that the accused imagined that the substance administered would have the effect intended; but it must be shown that it was in fact either a "poison" or a "noxious thing": *R. v. Isaacs* (1862) L.J.M.C. 52; *R. v. Hollis* (1873) 12 Cox 463 at 467. (A sleeping pill has been held not to be noxious: *R. v. Weatherall* [1968] Crim.L.R. 115, CA.) It is not, however, essential that the substance should be an abortifacient: *R. v. Marlow*, 49 Cr.App.R. 49, CCC (Brabin J.); *R. v. Douglas* [1966] N.Z.L.R. 45. The Act distinguishes between a "poison" and a "noxious thing". Where the substance is a recognised poison then it may be that, although the quantity administered by the accused is so small as to be incapable of doing harm, it is still sufficient to bring him within the section: *R. v. Cramp* (1880) 5 Q.B.D. 307. Where the substance is not a recognised poison then, although when administered in small quantities it may be innocuous and even useful, yet if the quantity administered by the accused is in fact noxious, the substance becomes a "noxious thing" within the statute: *ibid*. If a substance produces a miscarriage it is clearly a "noxious thing": *Hollis*, *ante*; and even if it does not, and cannot, it may still be such: *Marlow*, *ante* (although *Hollis* suggested the contrary); provided that in the quantities administered it can have some harmful effect on the human system: *R. v. Brown* (1870) L.R. 1 C.C.R. 244; *R. v. Hennah* (1877) 13 Cox 547. *Hennah* was applied in *R. v. Marcus*, 73 Cr.App.R. 49, CA (an offence under s.24 of the *Offences against the Person Act* 1861, *post*, § 19–223). It is, of course, otherwise where the substance, although noxious if administered in large quantities, is innocuous in the quantity administered by the accused: *Hennah*, *ante*; *R. v. Perry* (1845) 2 Cox 223.

As to evidence of similar acts by the accused, see *R. v. Bond* [1906] 2 K.B. 389; *R. v. Palm*, 4 Cr.App.R. 253, CCA; *R. v. Sanders*, 46 Cr.App.R. 60, Ct-MAC.

(ii) *"instrument or other means"*

The words "other means" include manual interference, even though no instrument is employed, and even though the medical evidence is such that the act could not, in the circumstances, have caused a miscarriage: *R. v. Spicer*, 39 Cr.App.R. 189, Assizes (Finnemore J.). Where the instrument alleged to have been used may be used for an innocent purpose, evidence may be given, in order to prove the criminal intent, **19–161** that the accused had at other times caused miscarriages by similar means: *R. v. Dale* (1889) 16 Cox 703. Evidence of the administration of drugs to other women for the purpose of procuring abortions may be admissible on a charge of using an *instrument*, and vice versa in order to rebut a defence of innocent use: *R. v. Starkie*, 16 Cr.App.R. 61, CCA.

(iii) *The intent*

19–162 Provided that an intent to procure a miscarriage is proved, it is immaterial that no miscarriage was in fact produced: *R. v. Cramp, ante*; *R. v. Spicer, ante*.

If a woman, with intent to procure her own miscarriage, does any of the acts specified in the section, she commits an offence only where she is in fact with child. Where the offence is completed, she may be indicted for aiding and abetting another to produce her miscarriage: *R. v. Sockett*, 1 Cr.App.R. 101, CCA. Similarly, where two or more persons are involved, it may be that she could be indicted for conspiracy with the others to procure her own miscarriage: see *R. v. Whitchurch* (1890) 24 Q.B.D. 420. But this will not be so if the woman is properly described as "the victim" of the offence: see s.2(1) of the *CLA* 1977, *post*, § 33–26. It is submitted that this is the better view. Even if the primary purpose of the legislation is the protection of the unborn child, it is the woman to whom the poison, etc., is administered. Though she may consent, she can nevertheless be sensibly regarded as a victim of the offence.

The word "miscarriage" in sections 58 and 59 relates to the spontaneous exclusion of the products of pregnancy, and, on the basis that a pregnancy does not come into existence until the fertilised ovum has become implanted in the womb, it follows that anything done, such as the supply and/ or use of the morning-after pill, before a pregnancy has become established, with the intention of preventing the successful implantation in the uterine wall of any fertilised ovum that may result from a prior act of sexual intercourse, will not amount to an offence under either section: *R. (Smeaton on behalf of SPUC) v. Secretary of State for Health (Schering Health Care Ltd and FPA as interested parties)* [2002] 2 F.L.R. 146, QBD (Munby J.).

(iv) *"unlawfully"*

19–163 In view of sections 5(2) and 6 of the *Abortion Act* 1967 (*ante*, §§ 19–153, 19–154), section 1 of the Act is the sole criterion of lawfulness. An abortion is unlawful, therefore, unless it complies with the conditions prescribed by the Act.

Where a charge of abortion is brought against a doctor, which calls in question his good faith within the meaning of section 1(1) of the 1967 Act, the question of good faith must be decided not by the evidence of any member or members of the medical profession, but by the jury on the totality of the evidence. Without evidence in relation to professional practice and medical probabilities, a verdict of guilty against a doctor is often likely to be unsafe, but such evidence does not determine the question: *R. v. Smith (John Anthony James)*, 58 Cr.App.R. 106, CA. A doctor giving expert evidence is entitled to support his opinion by referring to a professional practice with which he is familiar: *ibid*.

Provided a doctor prescribes the treatment for the termination of a pregnancy, remains in charge and accepts responsibility throughout and the treatment is carried out in accordance with his directions, the pregnancy is "terminated by a registered medical practitioner" for the purposes of the Act and any person taking part in the termination is entitled to the protection afforded by section 1(1) of the Act: *Royal College of Nursing of the U.K. v. DHSS* [1981] A.C. 800, HL.

Section 59

(i) *"procure"*

19–164 This means to get possession from another person of something which the defendant has not already got: *R. v. Mills* [1963] 1 Q.B. 522, 47 Cr.App.R. 49, CCA.

(ii) *"noxious thing"*

19–165 In order to constitute the offence of "procuring" or "supplying" a noxious thing, knowing that the same was intended to be used with intent to procure a miscarriage, the substance must be of a noxious character in the quantity in which it was supplied: *R. v. Cramp*, *ante*; *R. v. Hennah*, *ante*; and see *ante*, § 19–160. If the drug administered produces a miscarriage, even though there is no other evidence of its character, this is sufficient evidence of its being a noxious thing: *R. v. Hollis*; *ante*, § 19–160. It is not necessary that the substance should have been in fact an abortifacient: *R. v. Marlow*, 49 Cr.App.R. 49, CCC (Brabin J.).

(iii) *Knowledge*

As to the meaning of "miscarriage", see *R. (Smeaton) v. Secretary of State for Health*, *ante*, § 19–162.

In *R. v. Hillman* (1863) 9 Cox 386, it was held that it was sufficient knowledge on the part of the accused if "he believed that the noxious thing was to be used for the purpose of procuring a miscarriage, although no person other than the accused may have intended that it should be used for such purpose and although the woman herself may not have intended to use the drug"; see also *R. v. Titley* (1880) 14 Cox 502 (where the woman was not, and had never been, pregnant). It is questionable whether these authorities would be followed today.

IV. COMMON ASSAULT AND BATTERY

A. DEFINITIONS

Assault

The term "assault" is frequently used to include both an assault and a battery (as to "battery" see also, *post*, § 19–174). This can lead to confusion between the two offences: *R. v. Rolfe*, 36 Cr.App.R. 4, CCA. Strictly, "assault" is an independent offence and should be treated as such: *Fagan v. Metropolitan Police Commr* [1969] 1 Q.B. 439, 52 Cr.App.R. 700, DC. An assault is any act—and not a mere omission to act—by which a person intentionally—or recklessly—causes another to apprehend immediate unlawful violence: *ibid.*; *R. v. Venna* [1976] Q.B. 421 at 429, 61 Cr.App.R. 310 at 314, CA; *Smith v. Chief Superintendent Woking Police Station*, 76 Cr.App.R. 234, DC; *R. v. Ireland*; *R. v. Burstow* [1998] A.C. 147, HL. As to an omission to act founding liability, see the dubious authority of *DPP v. Santa-Bermudez*, 168 J.P. 373, DC (*post*, § 19–195). **19–166**

The act must be accompanied by a hostile intent calculated to cause apprehension in the mind of the victim. Where the hostile intent is not present, there will be no assault (see *R. v. Lamb* [1967] 2 Q.B. 981, 51 Cr.App.R. 417, CA, *ante*, § 19–100) unless, of course, it is proved that the alleged assailant was reckless as to whether the complainant would apprehend immediate and unlawful violence.

Battery

When the term "assault" is used to include a battery, it may be defined as an act by which a person intentionally or recklessly causes the complainant to apprehend immediate unlawful personal violence or to sustain unlawful personal violence: see *R. v. Kimber*, 77 Cr.App.R. 225 at 228, CA. When, as is usually the case, the word "assault" is used to mean a battery it simply means an act by which a person intentionally or recklessly applies unlawful force to the complainant: *R. v. Williams (G.)*, 78 Cr.App.R. 276 at 279, CA; *DPP v. Morgan* [1976] A.C. 182, HL (*per* Lord Simon at pp. 216, 217); *Haystead v. DPP*, 164 J.P. 396, DC. Provided those ingredients are proved, the offence will have been committed however slight the force (see 1 Hawk. c. 62, s.2). **19–166a**

Recklessness in assault and battery

The test of recklessness in assault and battery is that propounded in *R. v. Cunningham* [1957] 2 Q.B. 396, 41 Cr.App.R. 155, CCA: *R. v. Spratt*, 91 Cr.App.R. 362, CA; and see *R. v. Savage*; *DPP v. Parmenter* [1992] 1 A.C. 699, HL. Recklessness in common assault, therefore, involves foresight of the possibility that the complainant would **19–167** apprehend immediate and unlawful violence and taking that risk; in battery, it involves foresight of the possibility that the complainant will be subjected to unlawful force, however slight, and taking that risk. For an example of a reckless bite, see *D. v. DPP* [2005] Crim.L.R. 962, DC (where, during struggle to avoid recapture, defendant had brought police officer's hand to his mouth, justices had been entitled to find that there was a clearly foreseeable risk, taken by the defendant, of contact with his teeth as he shouted and struggled).

Voluntary intoxication

19–168 Assault and battery being crimes of "basic intent", self-induced intoxication provides no defence and is irrelevant. The same principle applies to the voluntary taking of drugs: *DPP v. Majewski* [1977] A.C. 443, HL. See *ante*, §§ 17–107 *et seq.*

Mistake of fact

19–169 If the defendant may have been labouring under a mistake as to the facts, he must be judged according to his mistaken view of the facts: *R. v. Kimber, ante*; *R. v. Williams (G.), ante*; *R. v. Beckford* [1988] A.C. 130, PC (*ante*, §§ 17–15 *et seq.*).

In *R. v. Scarlett*, 98 Cr.App.R. 290, CA, there is a suggestion in the judgment (at pp. 295–296) that not only is the accused entitled to be acquitted if he used no more force than would be reasonable in the circumstances as he believed them to be, but he would also be so entitled if he used no more force than he himself genuinely thought necessary in the circumstances as he believed them to be, even though excessive on an objective assessment. The customary view is that it is for the tribunal of fact to say what degree of force is reasonable in the circumstances as the accused believed them to be. *Scarlett* was considered in *R. v. Owino* [1996] 2 Cr.App.R. 128, CA, but the customary view was upheld.

One type of mistake will not avail a defendant, however, even if genuinely held and, it seems, even if held on reasonable grounds. If the defendant mistakenly believes that an arrest which is in fact lawful is unlawful, whether of himself or another, he is not entitled to use force to resist it: *R. v. Fennell* [1971] 1 Q.B. 428, 54 Cr.App.R. 451, CA. The mistake here is not purely of fact; it is one of mixed law and fact. It is the "They're not allowed to do that" mistake. In *R. v. Ball (S.L.)*, 90 Cr.App.R. 378, the Court of Appeal, relying on *Fennell*, held, strictly *obiter*, that an honest but mistaken belief that the police were using too much force in effecting an arrest is no defence to a charge of assault; nor, it was said, would an honest belief that the person being arrested was "in danger" be a defence, even if he was in fact in danger, provided no more force was being used than was reasonably necessary. Here, again, the mistake may be one of mixed law and fact: the defendant may be under no mistake about how much force is in fact being used, but he may think that the police are not entitled to use such force. Such a belief will not and should not avail him. There may, however, be a genuine mistake of fact as to the amount of force being used. A person may genuinely believe that an amount of force is being used which would clearly be unjustifiable, *e.g.* because it would be life-threatening. What is he to do? According to *Ball*, he intervenes at his peril. On general principle, however, it is submitted he should be judged on the basis of his mistaken belief.

Mistake of fact induced by voluntary intoxication

19–170 A defendant is not entitled to rely on a mistake of fact which has been induced by his voluntary taking of alcohol or drugs: *R. v. O'Grady* [1987] Q.B. 995, 85 Cr.App.R. 315, CA; and *R. v. Hatton* [2006] 1 Cr.App.R. 16, CA. See also *DPP v. Majewski* [1977] A.C. 443, HL, and *R. v. Lipman* [1970] 1 Q.B. 152, 53 Cr.App.R. 600, CA (*ante*, § 17–16).

As to mistake of fact generally, see *ante*, §§ 17–10 *et seq.*; as to the effect of drink and drugs generally, see *ante*, §§ 17–102 *et seq.*

Hostile intent

As to the requirement of a "hostile intent", see also *Collins v. Wilcock*, 79 Cr.App.R. 229, DC. For a helpful review of the principles when applied in the context of a civil claim for trespass, see *Wilson v. Pringle* [1986] 2 All E.R. 440, CA (Civ. Div.). **19–171**

Examples—assault

Striking at a person with a stick or a fist is an assault, even though the person striking misses his aim; drawing a weapon such as a knife or throwing a bottle with intent to wound or strike, will constitute an assault; as will any other like act indicating an intention to use violence against the person of another: 1 Hawk. c. 62, s.1; *Martin v. Shoppee* (1837) 3 C. & P. 373. To incite a dog to bite a horse, or to strike a horse causing the rider to fall, would be assaults: *Dodwell v. Burford* (1669) 1 Mod. 24. An act may cause grievous harm or other injury, yet not constitute an assault. Causing a deleterious drug to be taken by another is not an assault: *R. v. Walkden* (1845) 1 Cox 282. **19–172**

An unlawful imprisonment is also an assault: see *Hunter v. Johnson* (1884) 13 Q.B.D. 225 (detention of a child after school hours by the master, without lawful authority); and see *R. v. Linsberg and Leies*, 69 J.P. 107. As to the common law offence of false imprisonment, see *post*, § 19–331. **19–173**

Words alone may constitute an assault, as may mere silence (as in a silent telephone call): *R. v. Ireland*; *R. v. Burstow* [1998] A.C. 147, HL. Because of the requirement that the victim is caused to fear immediate unlawful violence, a silent telephone call is unlikely ever to constitute an assault in practice.

Examples—battery

Where an assault involves a battery, it is immaterial whether the battery is inflicted directly by the body of the offender or through the medium of some weapon or instrument controlled by his actions. For an obiter expression of opinion that the force may be indirect, see *Haystead v. DPP*, *ante*, § 19–166a. The *actus reus* and the *mens rea* must be present at the same time, but it is not necessary that the *mens rea* should be present at the inception of the *actus reus*; it may be superimposed upon it. Once, however, an act has been completed without *mens rea*, the subsequent inception of *mens rea* cannot convert it into an assault: *Fagan v. Metropolitan Police Commr* [1969] 1 Q.B. 439, 52 Cr.App.R. 700, DC (wheel of a car driven onto, and allowed to remain on, a person's foot; this was held to be an assault because although the act was initially unintentional, it was a continuing act which became unlawful when F, knowing the wheel was on the person's foot, allowed it to remain there). **19–174**

In relation to the offence of "battery", the fundamental principle is that every person's body is inviolate. The effect is that everybody is protected not only against physical injury but against any form of physical molestation: *Collins v. Wilcock*, 79 Cr.App.R. 229, DC. There are exceptions, for example, the correction of children, the lawful exercise of the power of arrest, the use of reasonable force when the necessity to act in self-defence arises. Further, a broader exception exists which caters for the exigencies of everyday life such as jostling in crowded places and touching a person for the purpose of engaging his attention. The approach to the facts of any particular case where there is an element of persistence in the touching should not be unreal. In each case, the test must be whether the physical contact so persisted in has in the circumstances gone beyond generally acceptable standards of conduct: *ibid*. Where the person causing the physical contact is a police officer who is not lawfully exercising a power (for example a power of arrest or a power to stop and search), the officer has no greater rights than ordinary citizens have. See further as to this, *post*, §§ 19–269 *et seq*. **19–175**

B. MODE OF TRIAL, PUNISHMENT, ETC.

(1) Mode of trial and penalty

Common assault and battery are summary offences with a maximum penalty for either offence of a fine not exceeding level 5 on the standard scale, or imprisonment for a term not exceeding six months (increased to 51 weeks as from a day to be appointed (but only in relation to offences committed on or after the day on which the amendment takes effect): *CJA* 2003, s.281(4)–(6)) or both: *CJA* 1988, s.39. (As to "the standard **19–176** scale", see *ante*, § 5–403.) See Appendix K–113 *et seq.* for the Sentencing Guidelines Council's definitive guideline on assault and other offences against the person.

19–177 An offence of "common assault" (to be construed as including battery—*R. v. Lynsey* [1995] 2 Cr.App.R. 667, CA) may in certain circumstances be tried on indictment: see the *CJA* 1988, s.40 (*ante*, § 1–75ai).

As to racially aggravated assaults, see *post*, §§ 19–214a *et seq.*

(2) Indictment

COUNT 1

STATEMENT OF OFFENCE

19–178 *Battery, contrary to section 39 of the* Criminal Justice Act *1988.*

PARTICULARS OF OFFENCE

A B, on the —— day of ——, 20—, assaulted J N by beating him.

COUNT 2

STATEMENT OF OFFENCE

Common assault, contrary to section 39 of the Criminal Justice Act *1988.*

PARTICULARS OF OFFENCE

A B, on the —— day of ——, 20—, assaulted J N.

The specimen indictment given above charges the offences as being contrary to section 39 of the 1988 Act. This is in deference to the decision of the Divisional Court in *DPP v. Taylor*; *DPP v. Little* [1992] 1 Q.B. 645, 95 Cr.App.R. 28, in which it was held that they are statutory offences. For criticism of this decision, see the 1993 supplements to this work; the 1994 and 1996 editions thereof; Smith and Hogan, *Criminal Law*, 12th ed., p. 584, and the commentary by Professor J. C. Smith at [1991] Crim.L.R. 900. And in *Haystead v. DPP*, *ante*, § 19–166, the Divisional Court expressed the *obiter* opinion that common assault and battery remain common law offences.

Notwithstanding *Haystead v. DPP*, the safe course is to allege the offences as being contrary to the statute. The court further decided that as there are in law two distinct offences, a charge which alleged that the defendant "assaulted and battered" the victim was bad for duplicity. It did not decide that "assaulted and beat" would also be bad for duplicity, acknowledging that this was the phrase by reference to which many thousands of people had been convicted over many years. However, there does not seem to be any logical difference and the court said that adoption of the expression "assaulted by beating" would be immune from argument. Despite the long-standing practice on indictment of charging "common assault" in cases where the allegation includes actual violence, the safer course would appear to be to charge such cases as "battery".

(3) Alternative verdict

19–179 A verdict of guilty of common assault may be returned as an alternative verdict under section 6 of the *CLA* 1967, *ante*, § 4–455: see section 6(3A), the effect of which is to reverse *R. v. Mearns* [1991] 1 Q.B. 82, 91 Cr.App.R. 312, CA.

C. DEFENCES

Consent

19–180 On a charge of common assault, it is necessary for the prosecution to prove absence of consent: see *R. v. Brown (A.)* [1994] 1 A.C. 212, HL. Where actual or grievous bodily harm or a wound is caused, however, consent will be no defence in the absence of good reason: *ibid.* As to what constitutes such good reason, the Court of Appeal in *Att.-Gen.'s Reference (No. 6 of 1980)* [1981] Q.B. 715, 73 Cr.App.R. 63, instanced "properly conducted lawful games and sports, lawful chastisement or correction, reasonable surgical interference, dangerous exhibitions, etc." (at pp. 719, 66). In reliance on the "etc." and certain dicta in *R. v. Donovan* [1934] 2 K.B. 498, 25 Cr.App.R. 1, CCA, the Court of Appeal in *R. v. Jones (T.)*, 83 Cr.App.R. 375, added rough and undisciplined horseplay to the list, provided there was no intention to injure. Furthermore, the court pointed out that even if consent was absent, a genuine belief that it was present would constitute a defence.

R. v. Jones (T.) was applied in the context of RAF officers taking part in "mess games" in *R. v. Aitken*, 95 Cr.App.R. 304, Ct-MAC (convictions contrary to section 20 of the *Offences against the Person Act* 1861 (*post*, § 19–200) quashed because of a misdirection on consent and belief in consent, it having been accepted that there had been no intention to cause injury).

As to injuries caused in the course of sporting events, it was held in *R. v. Barnes* [2005] 1 Cr.App.R. 30, CA, that: (i) in determining what the approach of the courts should be as to when it is appropriate for criminal proceedings to be instituted in respect of such injuries, the starting point is the fact that most organised sports have their own disciplinary procedures for enforcing their particular rules and standards of conduct; as a result, in the majority of situations there is not only no need for criminal proceedings, but it is undesirable that there should be any; prosecution should be reserved for those situations where the conduct is sufficiently grave to be properly categorised as criminal; (ii) although consent is generally irrelevant when bodily harm is caused, as a matter of public policy there are certain exceptions, which include physical injury sustained in the course of contact sports; if what occurs goes beyond what a player can reasonably be regarded as having accepted by taking part in the sport, this indicates that the conduct will not be covered by the defence; though what is implicitly accepted in one sport will not necessarily be covered by the defence in another sport; (iii) the fact that play is within the rules and practice of the game, will be a firm indication that what has happened is not criminal; in making a judgment as to whether conduct is criminal or not, it has to be borne in mind that, in highly competitive sports, conduct outside the rules can be expected to occur in the heat of the moment, and even if the conduct justifies not only being penalised but also a warning or even a sending off, it still may not reach the threshold level required for it to be criminal; that level is an objective one, and does not depend upon the views of individual players; the type of sport, the level at which it is played, the nature of the act, the degree of force used, the extent of the risk of injury, and the state of mind of the defendant are all likely to be relevant in determining whether the defendant's actions go beyond the threshold; and (iv) where a judge used the concept of "legitimate sport" in his summing up, but failed to identify what was and what was not "legitimate" in the context of the relevant sport, and failed generally to give the jury the assistance required in order to determine the issues, the conviction was unsafe. As to the directions to the jury on a prosecution under section 20 of the 1861 Act, see *post*, § 19–211. **19–181**

The satisfaction of sado-masochistic desires does not constitute good reason for the infliction of bodily harm or a wound: *R. v. Brown (A.)*, *ante*; and see *Laskey, Jaggard and Brown v. U.K.*, 24 E.H.R.R. 39, ECtHR (the prosecution and conviction of the appellants (men of full age) for offences contrary to sections 20 and 47 of the 1861 Act (*post*, §§ 19–190, 19–200) in respect of their consensual sado-masochistic activities involved no violation of Article 8 of the ECHR). **19–182**

Brown was distinguished in *R. v. Wilson (A.)* [1996] 2 Cr.App.R. 241, CA, in which the accused, at his wife's instigation, had branded his initials on her buttocks with a hot knife. There was no evidence that what he did was any more dangerous or painful than tattooing, which, if carried out with the consent of an adult, did not involve an offence contrary to section 47 of the 1861 Act, albeit that actual bodily harm was deliberately inflicted; further, there was no aggressive intent. It was not in the public interest that such consensual activity between husband and wife in private should be made the subject of a criminal prosecution; accordingly, in the circumstances, the wife's consent afforded a defence.

Wilson was itself distinguished in *R. v. Emmett*, *The Independent (C.S.)*, July 19, 1999, CA, in which it was held that consent is no defence where the harm caused to the "victim" consists of a more than transient or trivial injury. As in *Wilson*, the prosecution was concerned with injuries caused during the course of consensual sexual activity. Whilst the injuries were certainly not trifling, there was no intention on the part of either participant that they should be suffered. They were the unintended consequences of the consensual participation of both parties in high-risk activity. The court regarded itself as bound by *Brown*, but it must be doubtful that the decision in *Brown* would have been the same had their Lordships been concerned with the unintended consequences of consensual activity.

19–182a It is a criminal assault to perform physically invasive treatment without a patient's consent; a mentally competent patient has an absolute right to refuse consent to medical treatment for any reason, rational or irrational, or for no reason at all, even where that decision will lead to his or her own death: *Re J.T. (Adult: Refusal of Medical Treatment)* [1998] 1 F.L.R. 48, Fam D (Wall J.); and *Re B. (adult: refusal of medical treatment)* [2002] 2 All E.R. 449, Fam D (Dame Elizabeth Butler-Sloss P.).

Apparent consent

19–183 A patient's ignorance of the fact that the dentist who treated him was suspended from practice did not vitiate the patient's consent to treatment so as to make the dentist guilty of assault; there would be an assault only where there was consent to the actions of another in the mistaken belief that they or he were other than they truly were (the common law not being concerned as to the reason for the mistake); the concept of the identity of the person was not to be extended to cover the qualifications or attributes of the person; to do so would be to extend the everyday meaning of identity: *R. v. Richardson* [1998] 2 Cr.App.R. 200, CA.

19–184 In *Burrell v. Harmer* [1967] Crim.L.R. 169, DC, a conviction for assault followed the tattooing of two boys aged 12 and 13. The court observed that if a child of the age of understanding was unable to appreciate the nature of an act, apparent consent to it was no consent at all. (Tattooing is now regulated by the *Tattooing of Minors Act* 1969: it is a summary offence to tattoo a person under the age of 18, subject to an exception for doctors tattooing for medical reasons.)

Lawful correction

19–185 It is a good defence that the alleged battery was merely the correcting of a child by its parents, provided that the correction be moderate in the manner, the instrument and the quantity of it: 1 Hawk. c. 60, s.23; c. 62, s.2; *R. v. Hopley* (1860) 2 F. & F. 202; and section 58 of the *Children Act* 2004 provides that in relation to an offence under section 18, 20 or 47 of the *Offences against the Person Act* 1861, battery of a child cannot be justified on the ground that it constituted reasonable chastisement.

The relationship of teacher and pupil formerly carried with it the right of reasonable chastisement: *Cleary v. Booth* [1893] 1 Q.B. 465. See also *Mansell v. Griffin* [1908] 1 K.B. 160, and *R. v. Newport (Salop) JJ., ex p. Wright* [1929] 2 K.B. 416 at 427, 428. Section 548 of the *Education Act* 1996 provides, however, that corporal punishment given by, or on the authority of, a member of staff to a child (*i.e.* a person under 18) for whom education is provided at any school or under arrangements made by a local authority or for whom specified nursery education is provided otherwise than at a school, cannot be justified in any proceedings on the ground that it was given in pursuance of a right exercisable by the member of staff by virtue of his position as such; and this applies whether the punishment is administered at the school or elsewhere.

As to the general permission granted to any member of the staff of a school to use reasonable force to prevent offences, etc., see *ante*, § 19–40.

Corporal punishment in prisons was abolished by the *CJA* 1967, s.65.

Self-defence

19–186 See generally, *ante*, §§ 19–40 *et seq.*

Defence of property

19–187 It is a good defence that the battery was committed by the defendant in defence of his possession; as, for instance, to remove the prosecutor out of the prisoner's close or house; or to prevent him from entering it: 2 Rolle Abr. 548, l. 25; to restrain him from taking or destroying his goods, etc.: 2 Rolle Abr. 549, l. 7; from taking or rescuing cattle, etc., in his custody upon a distress: *ibid*. l. 16; or the like. In the case of a trespass in law merely, without actual force, the owner of the close, etc., must first request the trespasser to depart, before he can justify laying his hand on him for the purpose of removing him; and, even if he refuses, he can justify so much force only as is necessary to remove him: *Weaver v. Bush* (1798) 8 T.R. 78. But if the trespasser uses force, then the owner may oppose force to force: *Weaver v. Bush, ante*; *Tullay v. Reed* (1823) 1 C. & P. 6; and in such case, if he is assaulted or beaten, he may justify even a wounding. In answer, however, to a justification in defence of his possession, the other party may prove that the battery was excessive: *King v. Tebbart* (1693) Skin. 387; or justify the alleged trespass on the defendant's possession by proving that he had a right of way over the close, or the like. See also *R. v. Hussey*, 18 Cr.App.R. 160, CCA, *R. v. Faraj, post*, § 19–339, and *Taylor v. Mucklow* [1973] Crim.L.R. 750, DC, *post*, § 24–60.

Prevention of crime, effecting lawful arrest, etc.

See the *CLA* 1967, s.3, *ante*, § 19–39. **19–188**

See also the *PACE Act* 1984, s.117 (*ante*, § 15–26) which provides that a constable may use reasonable force, if necessary, in the exercise of any power conferred on him by the Act except such powers as may only be exercised with the consent of some other person, other than a police officer.

Execution of process

It is a good defence that the defendant, as an officer of justice, arrested the prosecutor by virtue of a certain writ of process, if that is the alleged battery complained of: 2 Rolle Abr. 547 (A.). A sheriff's officer, however, can only justify laying his hand upon a man, in order to arrest him upon a writ of process: *Harrison v. Hodgson* (1830) 10 B. & C. 445; unless he resist, or an attempt be made to rescue him, or to prevent or hinder the arrest: *Truscott v. Carpenter and Man* (1697) 1 Ld.Raym. 229 at 232; and even then he can justify no greater degree of force than was necessary in order to secure the prisoner: *Levy v. Edwards* (1823) 1 C. & P. 40. A man may justify laying his hand upon another to prevent him from fighting, or committing a breach of the peace: Com.Dig.Pleader, 3 M. 16; or to prevent him from rescuing goods taken in execution: *Bridgwater v. Bythway* (1683) 3 Lev. 113; or the like. Yet, even in these cases, he must not use more force than is requisite to restrain the other party, otherwise he cannot avail himself of the threatened breach of the peace, etc., as a justification. Serving process by thrusting a document into the fold of a man's coat is not necessarily an assault: *Rose v. Kempthorne*, 75 J.P. 71. As to the right of a person to resist officers executing civil process, see *Southam v. Smout* [1964] 1 Q.B. 308, and *Vaughan v. McKenzie* [1969] 1 Q.B. 557, and the authorities considered there. **19–189**

V. ASSAULT OCCASIONING ACTUAL BODILY HARM

(1) Statute

Offences against the Person Act 1861, s.47

Punishment of assaults

47. Whosoever shall be convicted on indictment of any assault occasioning actual bodily harm shall be liable … to imprisonment for not more than five years. **19–190**

[This section is printed as amended and repealed in part by the *Penal Servitude Act* 1891, s.1(1); the *CJA* 1948, s.1(1); and the *CJA* 1988, s.170(2) and Sched. 16.]

As to racially aggravated assault occasioning actual bodily harm, see *post*, §§ 19–214a *et seq*.

(2) Indictment

STATEMENT OF OFFENCE

Assault occasioning actual bodily harm, contrary to section 47 of the Offences against the Person Act *1861*. **19–191**

PARTICULARS OF OFFENCE

A B, on the —— day of ——, 20—, assaulted J N, thereby occasioning him actual bodily harm.

As to the necessity to lay the offence as being contrary to section 47 of the 1861 Act, see *R. v. Harrow JJ., ex p. Osaseri* [1986] Q.B. 589, 81 Cr.App.R., DC.

(3) Class of offence and mode of trial

19–192 This offence is a class 3 offence, *ante*, § 2–17, triable either way: *MCA* 1980, s.17(1), and Sched. 1 (*ante*, § 1–75af).

(4) Sentence

Maximum

19–193 Imprisonment not exceeding five years, s.47, *ante*.

An offence contrary to section 47 is a specified violent offence within Schedule 15 to the *CJA* 2003 (*ante*, § 5–299).

Guidelines

19–194 See Appendix K–113 *et seq.* for the Sentencing Guidelines Council's definitive guideline on assault and other offences against the person.

Whilst "road rage" incidents will fall within the guideline as much as any other assault, there is no shortage of pre-guideline examples of the Court of Appeal viewing such cases with particular seriousness: see *R. v. Robertson*, 12 Cr.App.R.(S.) 278, CA (assault on a traffic warden); *Att.-Gen.'s Reference (No. 60 of 1996) (R. v. Hartnett)* [1997] 2 Cr.App.R.(S.) 198, CA; *R. v. Doyle* [1999] 1 Cr.App.R.(S.) 383, CA; and *R. v. Clarke* [2007] 1 Cr.App.R.(S.) 15. And an order disqualifying the offender from driving under the *PCC(S)A* 2000, s.146 (*ante*, § 5–844), may well be appropriate: see *R. v. Aylett* [2006] 1 Cr.App.R.(S.) 34, CA.

(5) Ingredients of the offence

The assault

19–195 As to what constitutes an "assault" generally, see *ante*, §§ 19–166 *et seq.* Whether or not there was an assault cannot depend on whether or not bodily harm was suffered by the alleged victim, yet in *DPP v. Santa-Bermudez*, 168 J.P. 373, DC, it was held that where someone (by act or word or a combination of the two) creates a danger and thereby exposes another to a reasonably foreseeable risk of injury which materialises, there is an evidential basis for the *actus reus* of an assault occasioning actual bodily harm. The case concerned a police officer who pricked her finger on a needle whilst conducting a search of the defendant's pockets, having been told by him that there was nothing sharp therein. The court did not address the issue as to what constituted the assault. A second difficulty with the court's formulation is that it is well-established (*post*, § 19–196) that proof of this offence has never required that the harm should have been foreseen or foreseeable. The court did not have the benefit of full argument.

It must be proved that the assault (which includes "battery") "occasioned" or caused the bodily harm. Where the harm is not the direct result of the defendant's act, as, for example, where his conduct was such as to provoke the victim to jump from a moving car, the test is whether the victim's act was the natural result of the defendant's action or words, in the sense that it was something that could reasonably have been foreseen as the consequence of what he was saying or doing: *R. v. Roberts*, 56 Cr.App.R. 95, CA.

Mens rea

19–196 The *mens rea* of assault occasioning actual bodily harm is the same as for common assault (*ante*, §§ 19–166 *et seq.*). The only extra ingredient which has to be proved is that the assault in fact occasioned actual bodily harm: *R. v. Roberts*, *ante*; *R. v. Venna* [1976] Q.B. 421, 61 Cr.App.R. 310, CA; *R. v. Savage*; *DPP v. Parmenter* [1992] 1 A.C. 699, HL.

Actual bodily harm

"Bodily harm" has its ordinary meaning and includes any hurt or injury calculated to interfere with the health or comfort of the victim; such hurt or injury need not be permanent, but must be more than merely transient or trifling: *R. v. Donovan* [1934] 2 K.B. 498, 25 Cr.App.R. 1, CCA, cited with approval by Lords Templeman and Jauncey in *R. v. Brown (A.)* [1994] 1 A.C. 212, HL, at pp. 230 and 242 respectively. It may include the cutting off of a substantial part of a person's hair: *DPP v. Smith* [2006] 2 Cr.App.R. 1, DC; or a momentary loss of consciousness; where there is injurious impairment to the victim's sensory functions, "it is axiomatic that the bodily harm was actual": *R. (T.) v. DPP* [2003] Crim.L.R. 622, QBD (Maurice Kay J.). **19–197**

Actual bodily harm is capable of including psychiatric injury but it does not include mere emotions, such as fear, distress or panic: *R. v. Chan-Fook*, 99 Cr.App.R. 147, CA; *R. v. Ireland*; *R. v. Burstow* [1998] A.C. 147, HL; or psychological injury: *R. v. Dhaliwal* [2006] 2 Cr.App.R. 24, CA. Without appropriate expert evidence, the question whether an assault had occasioned psychiatric injury should not be left to the jury: *R. v. Chan-Fook*, *ante*.

In a case of "non-physical assault" ("stalking"), if the prosecution rely on symptoms described by the victim (fright/anxiety/physical aches and pains) as evidence of bodily harm, there should be expert evidence to prove that the symptoms other than pain amounted to psychological illness or injury and that the pains experienced were the result of the conduct complained of: *R. v. Morris (Clarence Barrington)* [1998] 1 Cr.App.R. 386, CA.

(6) Defences

See *ante*, §§ 19–180 *et seq.* **19–198**

VI. WOUNDING, CAUSING GRIEVOUS BODILY HARM

(1) Statute

Offences against the Person Act 1861, ss.18, 20

Wounding with intent to do grievous bodily harm

18. Whosoever shall unlawfully and maliciously by any means whatsoever wound or cause any grievous bodily harm to any person, ... with intent, ... to do some ... grievous bodily harm to any person, or with intent to resist or prevent the lawful apprehension or detainer of any person, shall be guilty of an offence, and being convicted thereof shall be liable ... to *imprisonment* for life.... **19–199**

[This section is printed as amended or repealed in part by the *Statute Law Repeals Act* 1892; the *Statute Law Repeals (No. 2) Act* 1893; the *CJA* 1948, s.1(1); and the *CLA* 1967, ss.10(2) and 12(5)(a) and Sched. 3.]

Inflicting bodily injury, with or without weapon

20. Whosoever shall unlawfully and maliciously wound or inflict any grievous bodily harm upon any other person, either with or without any weapon or instrument, shall be guilty of a misdemeanor, and being convicted thereof shall be liable ... to *imprisonment* ... for not more than five years. **19–200**

[This section is printed as amended or repealed in part by the *Penal Servitude Act* 1891, s.1(1); the *Statute Law Revision Act* 1892; and the *CJA* 1948, s.1(1).]

As to the racially aggravated version of the offence contrary to section 20, see *post*, §§ 19–214a *et seq.*

(2) Indictment

COUNT 1

STATEMENT OF OFFENCE

Wounding [Causing grievous bodily harm] with intent, contrary to section 18 of the Offences against the Person Act *1861*. **19–201**

PARTICULARS OF OFFENCE

A B, on the —— day of ——, 20—, unlawfully and maliciously wounded [caused grievous bodily harm to] J N, with intent to do him grievous bodily harm, or to resist the lawful apprehension of him, the said A B.

COUNT 2

STATEMENT OF OFFENCE

Unlawful wounding [Inflicting grievous bodily harm], contrary to section 20 of the Offences against the Person Act *1861.*

PARTICULARS OF OFFENCE

A B, on the —— day of ——, 20—, unlawfully and maliciously wounded [inflicted grievous bodily harm on] J N.

Section 18 created three offences (wounding, causing grievous bodily harm and shooting), any of which could be committed with any of the intents specified; the intents may be laid in the alternative: *R. v. Naismith* [1961] 2 All E.R. 735, Ct-MAC. The reference to shooting was repealed by the *CLA* 1967, s.10(2), and Sched. 3.

An indictment, of which the statement of offence read "Inflicting grievous bodily harm, contrary to section 18 of the *Offences against the Person Act* 1861", and of which the particulars alleged that the defendants "unlawfully inflicted grievous bodily harm" on the victim, was defective, but not a nullity: *R. v. Hodgson and Pollin* [2008] 2 Cr.App.R. 35, CA (as to which, see *ante*, § 1–117).

As to whether an indictment should routinely contain a count under section 20 as an alternative allegation to one under section 20, see *R. v. Lahaye*, *post*, § 19–203.

(3) Class of offence and mode of trial

19–202 Offences contrary to sections 18 and 20 are class 3 offences, *ante*, § 2–17. Offences contrary to section 18 are indictable only, whereas those contrary to section 20 are triable either way: *MCA* 1980, s.17(1), and Sched. 1 (*ante*, § 1–75af).

(4) Alternative verdicts

19–203 As to alternative verdicts generally, see *ante*, §§ 4–453 *et seq*.

On a charge of wounding with intent, "unlawful wounding" contrary to section 20 and assault occasioning actual bodily harm contrary to section 47 of the 1861 Act (*ante*, § 19–190) are alternatives, as will be the section 47 offence on a charge of unlawful wounding contrary to section 20: see *R. v. Savage*; *DPP v. Parmenter* [1992] 1 A.C. 699, HL. Common assault will be a further alternative wherever assault occasioning actual bodily harm is an alternative: see section 6(3A) of the *CLA* 1967, *ante*, § 4–455.

On a charge of causing grievous bodily harm with intent, contrary to section 18, verdicts of wounding or inflicting grievous bodily harm, contrary to section 20, or of assault occasioning actual bodily harm, contrary to section 47 (or common assault), are available alternatives: see *R. v. Mandair* [1995] 1 A.C. 208, HL (in which it was held that where a jury returned a verdict of "causing grievous bodily harm contrary to section 20" of the 1861 Act as an alternative to a count alleging an offence contrary to s.18, it had not convicted him of an offence unknown to law; the causing of the grievous bodily harm was contrary to s.20 in that it had consisted of inflicting grievous bodily harm upon another person). On a charge of an offence of wounding or inflicting grievous bodily harm, contrary to section 20, a verdict of assault occasioning actual bodily harm (or common assault) is an available alternative: *R. v. Wilson*; *R. v. Jenkins* [1984] A.C. 242, HL.

In *R. v. Lahaye* [2006] 1 Cr.App.R. 11, the Court of Appeal suggested that good practice should dictate that where there is an allegation of an offence contrary to section 18, a count under section 20 should routinely be included in the indictment from the outset. Where the ulterior intent may be in issue (even though not the primary issue), such a course has obvious practical advantages; but it is submitted that there should be no such universal rule. What good practice dictates will ultimately depend on the facts of the particular case, and there are many cases where the inclusion of a count under section 20 will serve only to distract the attention of the jury.

(5) Sentence

Maximum

Count 1: imprisonment for life, s.18, *ante*. **19–204**

Count 2: imprisonment not exceeding five years, s.20, *ante*.

Offences contrary to sections 18 and 20 are specified violent offences within Schedule 15 to the *CJA* 2003 (*ante*, § 5–299).

Guideline

The Sentencing Guidelines Council has issued definitive guidelines on assault and other offences against the person and on assaults on children and cruelty to a child: see Appendix K–113 *et seq.*, K–131 *et seq.* **19–205**

Pre-guideline cases are going to be of strictly limited value, but practitioners and judges may derive assistance from decisions such as *R. v. Jones (D.G.)*, 93 Cr.App.R. 169, CA (sentencing considerations in relation to wounding by use of a motor car); *R. v. Cotterill* [2007] 2 Cr.App.R.(S.) 64, CA (sentencing considerations where offence committed by one professional sportsman against another during a match); and *Att.-Gen.'s Reference (No. 55 of 2007) (R. v. Dunning)* [2008] 1 Cr.App.R.(S.) 39, CA (attacks on police officers are particularly grave, as are knife attacks).

(6) Ingredients of the offences

(a) *Grievous bodily harm*

Meaning

"Grievous bodily harm" should be given its ordinary and natural meaning of really serious bodily harm, and it is undesirable to attempt any further definition of it: *DPP v. Smith* [1961] A.C. 290, HL; *R. v. Cunningham* [1982] A.C. 566, HL; *R. v. Brown (A.)* [1994] 1 A.C. 212, HL; *R. v. Brown and Stratton* [1998] Crim.L.R. 485, CA. It is not necessary that grievous bodily harm should be either permanent or dangerous: *R. v. Ashman* (1858) 1 F. & F. 88. Nor is it a pre-condition that the victim should require treatment or that the harm would have lasting consequences; in assessing whether particular harm was "grievous", account had to be taken of the effect on, and the circumstances of, the particular victim: *R. v. Bollom*, *The Times*, December 15, 2003, CA. Bodily harm includes psychiatric injury: *R. v. Ireland*; *R. v. Burstow* [1998] A.C. 147, HL; but not psychological injury: *R. v. Dhaliwal* [2006] 2 Cr.App.R. 24, CA. **19–206**

Cases of joint enterprise

Where several persons inflict injuries on a victim, it is the totality of the injuries which are to be considered in relation to a charge of causing grievous bodily harm with intent contrary to section 18. It is immaterial that one person joins in the attack slightly after the others have begun to inflict injuries, which may have included the most serious single injury. He is aiding the commission of the offence and participating in it as soon as he joins in: *R. v. Grundy*, 89 Cr.App.R. 333, CA. *Cf. R. v. Percival*, *post*, § 19–212, in relation to an allegation of wounding. **19–207**

(b) *"Cause" or "inflict"*

It was formerly accepted that "causing" was wider than "inflicting" and that where the allegation was of causing grievous bodily harm, the issue was a straightforward one of causation. Did the injury result from the act of the accused? There is no requirement of physical contact between the defendant and the victim. The distinction has, however, been reduced to vanishing point by the decision of the House of Lords in *R. v. Ireland*; *R. v. Burstow*, *ante*, to the effect that grievous bodily harm could be "inflicted" without an assault and without the direct or indirect application of force to the victim's person (psychiatric injury caused by persistent harassment). **19–208**

[The next paragraph is § 19–210.]

(c) *"Unlawfully and maliciously"*

19–210 The requirement in both sections that the wounding or grievous bodily harm be unlawful imports no more than that self-defence, defence of others, defence of property, force used for the purpose of prevention of crime (see the *CLA* 1967, s.3, *ante*, § 19–39) are all potential "defences": see also *ante*, § 17–44. If raised, the burden of negativing self-defence, defence of others, etc., is on the prosecution. The general principles relating to these defences are set out at §§ 19–40 *et seq.*, *ante*. As to the exclusion of reasonable chastisement as a defence to a charge under section 18 or 20, see section 58 of the *Children Act* 2004 (*ante*, § 19–185). As to consent as a defence where the injury was caused in the course of a lawful sporting contest, see *R. v. Barnes*, *ante*, § 19–181.

As to "maliciously" generally, see *ante*, § 17–45.

In *R. v. Dica* [2004] 2 Cr.App.R. 28, CA, it was held that where a person, at a time when he knows that he is suffering from serious sexual disease, infects another with that disease as a result of consensual sexual activity, but not having deliberately set out to do so with the intention of passing on the infection, he will be liable to conviction of inflicting grievous bodily harm, contrary to section 20, where the infected person did not consent to the risk of contracting the infection; and that where the person infected knew of the other person's condition at the time of the sexual activity that resulted in the infection, he may be said to have consented to the risk. The court observed, *obiter*, that in the case of intentional spreading of serious disease, the consent of the infected party will provide no defence (on the principle in *R. v. Brown (A.)*, *ante*, § 19–180). In *R. v. Konzani* [2005] 2 Cr.App.R. 14, CA, it was said that the consent of the infected person must be "informed" for it to avail the defendant. There is a critical distinction between taking a risk of the various, potentially adverse and possibly problematic consequences of sexual intercourse, and giving informed consent to the risk of infection with a fatal disease; silence in such circumstances is incongruous with honesty, or with a genuine belief in informed consent. The court added, however, that there may be circumstances in which it would be open to a jury to infer that, notwithstanding that the defendant was reckless and concealed his condition from the complainant, she may nevertheless have given an informed consent to the risk of contracting the HIV virus; for example, an individual may develop a sexual relationship with someone who knew him while he was in hospital receiving treatment for the condition, or he may honestly believe that his new sexual partner was told of his condition by someone else; even if in such circumstances she did not in fact consent, there would be the basis for an argument that the defendant honestly believed in her informed consent. For the defendant's honest belief to afford a defence, however, it must be concomitant with the consent which would provide a defence, *i.e.* it must be an honest belief in informed consent to the risk of contracting the disease from which the defendant was suffering.

19–211 In *R. v. Mowatt* [1968] 1 Q.B. 421, 51 Cr.App.R. 402, CA, Diplock L.J. observed that on a charge contrary to section 18, "maliciously" adds nothing, because the ulterior intent required by the section is more specific than such element of foresight of consequences as is implicit in the word "maliciously". This will be the case where the allegation is causing grievous bodily harm with intent to do grievous bodily harm. Where the charge is wounding with intent to do grievous bodily harm, it is at least theoretically possible that the defendant intended to do grievous bodily harm, but did not intend to wound. In such a case the word "maliciously" would theoretically come into play, but since "malicious wounding" requires proof only of foresight of some physical harm, the point is likely to remain theoretical only. Anyone who intends to do grievous bodily harm may safely be taken to foresee some physical harm resulting from his actions. It is respectfully submitted, therefore, that, in these two cases, judges, directing juries, can safely ignore the word "maliciously" as was suggested in *Mowatt*.

Where, however, the ulterior intent alleged is an intent "to resist or prevent the lawful apprehension or detainer of any person" it is submitted that "maliciously" plainly does add something. The wounding or causing of grievous bodily harm may be committed recklessly. The test of recklessness will be that prescribed by *R. v. Cunningham* [1957] 2 Q.B. 396, 41 Cr.App.R. 155, CCA (*ante*, § 17–45), and *R. v. G.* [2004] 1 A.C. 1034, HL (*ante*, 17–51). See also *R. v. Morrison (L. A.)*, 89 Cr.App.R. 17, CA.

In *R. v. Barnes* [2005] 1 Cr.App.R. 30, CA, it was said that where a prosecution for an offence contrary to section 20 arises out of injury sustained during the course of a lawful sporting contest, such as a football match, in the great majority of cases, the existence of malicious intent is not likely to be an issue. "Maliciously" includes "recklessly", which in the context means no more than that the defendant foresaw the risk that some bodily harm (however slight) might result from what he was going to do and yet, ignoring that risk, he went on to commit the offending act. The court said that in a sport like football, anyone going to tackle another player in possession of the ball can be expected to have the necessary malicious intent according to that approach. The court said that in many cases, therefore, it would only confuse the jury to make unnecessary reference to the word "maliciously" and to invite them to consider the improbability that the defendant did not foresee the risk. As to *Barnes*, see also *ante*, § 19–181.

(d) *Wound*

The word "wound" in section 18 includes incised wounds, punctured wounds, lacerated wounds, contused wounds and gun-shot wounds. See *Shea v. R.* (1848) 3 Cox 141 (Ir.). But to constitute a wound within the statute, the continuity of the skin must be broken: *R. v. Wood* (1830) 1 Mood. 278; or, in other words, the outer covering of the body (that is, the *whole skin*, not the mere cuticle or upper skin) must be divided: *R. v. M'Loughlin* (1838) 8 C. &. P. 635; *R. v. Beckett* (1836) 1 M. & Rob. 526. But a division of the *internal* skin, *e.g.* within the cheek or lip, is sufficient to constitute a wound within the statute: *R. v. Smith (L.)* (1837) 8 C. & P. 173; *R. v. Warman* (1846) 1 Den. 183. The rupture of blood vessels internally is not sufficient to constitute a wound—there must be a break in the continuity of the whole skin: *J. J. C. (a Minor) v. Eisenhower* [1983] 3 All E.R. 230, DC, applying *Wood* and *M'Loughlin, ante*. In *R. v. Shadbolt* (1835) 5 C. & P. 504, the skin broken had been that inside the mouth and in *R. v. Waltham* (1849) 3 Cox 442, there had been a rupture of the lining membrane of the urethra, which had caused blood to issue. In each case the injury had been held to constitute a wound. **19–212**

In *R. v. Percival, The Times*, May 23, 2003, CA, it was held (distinguishing *Grundy*, *ante*, § 19–207) that where an offence of wounding has been committed by one or more persons, if another person then attacks the victim, without having previously formed any intention to be a party to the wounding offence and without causing a fresh wound, he would be guilty of assault (or assault occasioning actual bodily harm), but he would not be guilty of the wounding.

(e) *With intent, etc.*

On an allegation of an intent to cause grievous bodily harm, the jury should be directed in the following or very similar terms: "You must feel sure that the defendant intended to cause serious bodily harm to the victim. You can only decide what his intention was by considering all the relevant circumstances and in particular what he did and what he said about it": *R. v. Purcell*, 83 Cr.App.R. 45, CA. As to intention generally, see *ante*, § 17–34. As to alcohol and intention, see *ante*, § 17–106. **19–213**

As to "intent" in the context of attempting to cause grievous bodily harm with intent, see *R. v. Mohan* [1976] Q.B. 1, 60 Cr.App.R. 272, CA, and *R. v. Pearman*, 80 Cr.App.R. 259, CA.

If an indictment alleges an intent to do some grievous bodily harm, it will not be supported by proof of an intention to prevent a lawful apprehension: *R. v. Duffin and Marshall* (1818) R. & R. 365; *R. v. Boyce* (1824) 1 Mood. 29; unless, for the purpose of effecting his escape, the prisoner also harboured the intent stated in the indictment: *R. v. Gillow* (1825) 1 Mood. 85; for where both intents exist, it is immaterial which is the principal and which the subordinate: see also *R. v. Cox* (1818) R. & R. 362.

Where the defendant is charged with wounding A with intent to cause him grievous bodily harm, but the evidence establishes that whilst he wounded A, the blow had been aimed at B, he cannot be convicted of the offence charged: *R. v. Monger* [1973] Crim.L.R. 301, Crown Court (Mocatta J.); and *R. v. Slimmings* [1998] 8 *Archbold News* 1, CA. Note, however, that a count may be drafted under section 18 of wounding **19–214**

A with intent to cause grievous bodily harm to B; on the facts of *Monger*, there was no dispute that the defendant would be guilty of a section 20 offence in respect of A (see also *R. v. Latimer* (1886) 17 Q.B.D. 359); and the defendant would undoubtedly be guilty of the section 18 offence where he wounded A intending to do so, but mistakenly thought he was B, the person whom he desired (had been paid) to wound (*R. v. Stopford* (1870) 11 Cox 643; *R. v. Smith* (1855) Dears. 559). But if a person who, in legitimate self-defence, shoots at A with the necessary intent, misses and hits B who poses him no threat, he will not be guilty of the offence in respect of B. As to "transferred malice", see *ante*, § 17–24. Where there is a generalised intent to do grievous bodily harm, though not directed at any individual, but merely at a crowd, this is sufficient: *R. v. Fretwell* (1864) L. & C. 443.

Where the intent laid is an intent to prevent a lawful apprehension, it must be shown that the arrest would have been lawful and where the circumstances are not such that the party must know why he is about to be apprehended (*R. v. Howarth* (1828) 1 Mood. 207), it must be proved that he was appraised of the intention to apprehend him: *R. v. Ricketts* (1811) 3 Camp. 68; but see *R. v. Bentley* (1850) 4 Cox 406.

VII. RACIALLY OR RELIGIOUSLY AGGRAVATED OFFENCES

(1) Statute

Crime and Disorder Act 1998, s.29

Racially or religiously aggravated assaults

19–214a **29.**—(1) A person is guilty of an offence under this section if he commits—

(a) an offence under section 20 of the *Offences Against the Person Act* 1861 (malicious wounding or grievous bodily harm);

(b) an offence under section 47 of that Act (actual bodily harm); or

(c) common assault,

which is racially or religiously aggravated for the purposes of this section.

(2) A person guilty of an offence falling within subsection (1)(a) or (b) above shall be liable—

(a) on summary conviction, to imprisonment for a term not exceeding *six* [12] months or to a fine not exceeding the statutory maximum, or to both;

(b) on conviction on indictment, to imprisonment for a term not exceeding seven years or to a fine, or to both.

(3) A person guilty of an offence falling within subsection (1)(c) above shall be liable—

(a) on summary conviction, to imprisonment for a term not exceeding *six* [12] months or to a fine not exceeding the statutory maximum, or to both;

(b) on conviction on indictment, to imprisonment for a term not exceeding two years or to a fine, or to both.

[This section came into force on September 30, 1998: *Crime and Disorder Act 1998 (Commencement No. 2 and Transitional Provisions) Order* 1998 (S.I. 1998 No. 2327). The words "or religiously" were inserted by the *Anti-terrorism, Crime and Security Act* 2001, s.39(5) and (6)(a). In subss. (2)(a) and (3)(a), "12" is substituted for "six", as from a day to be appointed, by the *CJA* 2003, s.282(2) and (3). The increase has no application to offences committed before the substitutions take effect: s.282(4).]

As to the meaning of "racially or religiously aggravated" for the purposes of this section, see section 28 of the *CDA* 1998, *ante*, § 5–84.

(2) Indictment

Statement of Offence

19–214b *Racially aggravated assault occasioning actual bodily harm, contrary to section 29(1)(b) of the* Crime and Disorder Act *1998.*

Particulars of Offence

A B, on the —— day of ——, 20—, assaulted J N thereby occasioning him actual bodily harm, and at the time of doing so, or immediately before doing so, demonstrated towards J N hostility based on J N's membership or presumed membership of a particular racial group, namely —— [or *and was wholly or partly motivated to do so by hostility towards members of a particular racial group, namely ——, based on their membership of such racial group*].

(3) Class of offence and mode of trial

Offences contrary to section 29 are class 3 offences triable either way: see *ante*, § 2–17, and s.29(2), (3), *ante*. **19–214c**

(4) Sentence

On conviction on indictment: racially or religiously aggravated wounding or infliction of grievous bodily harm or assault occasioning actual bodily harm, seven years' imprisonment, or a fine, or both; racially or religiously aggravated common assault, two years' imprisonment, or a fine, or both (s.29(2), (3)). **19–214d**

On summary conviction: six months' imprisonment (increased to 12 months as from a day to be appointed), or a fine not exceeding the statutory maximum, or both (*ibid.*).

An offence contrary to section 29 is a specified violent offence within Schedule 15 to the *CJA* 2003 (*ante*, § 5–299).

In *R. v. Saunders* [2000] 1 Cr.App.R. 458, CA, it was said that those guilty of offences contrary to section 29 must expect a further term of up to two years to be added to their sentence; particular matters to take into account are the nature of the hostility as manifested in the language used, the use of a weapon, whether the location was public or private, whether it was one where the conduct would be likely to give special offence, and the numbers involved.

VIII. MISCELLANEOUS OFFENCES UNDER THE OFFENCES AGAINST THE PERSON ACT 1861

A. ATTEMPTING TO CHOKE, SUFFOCATE OR STRANGLE, ETC., WITH INTENT

(1) Statute

Offences against the Person Act 1861, s.21

21. Whosoever shall, by any means whatsoever, attempt to choke, suffocate, or strangle any other person, or shall, by any means calculated to choke, suffocate, or strangle, attempt to render any other person insensible, unconscious, or incapable of resistance, with intent in any of such cases thereby to enable himself or any other person to commit, or with intent in any of such cases thereby to assist any other person in committing any indictable offence, shall be guilty of an offence, and being convicted thereof shall be liable ... to *imprisonment* for life.... **19–215**

[This section is printed as repealed in part by the *Statute Law Revision Act* 1892; and as amended by the *CJA* 1948, s.1(1); and the *CLA* 1967, s.12(5)(a).]

(2) Indictment

STATEMENT OF OFFENCE

Attempting to choke, contrary to section 21 of the Offences against the Person Act *1861*. **19–216**

PARTICULARS OF OFFENCE

A B, on the —— day of ——, 20—, attempted to choke, suffocate, or strangle J N, with intent to enable himself [or *E F*] *to rob* [or *assist E F to rob*] *the said J N.*

(3) Class of offence and mode of trial

This offence is a class 3 offence, *ante*, § 2–17, triable only on indictment. **19–217**

(4) Sentence

Imprisonment for life: s.21, *ante*. **19–218**

An offence contrary to section 21 is a specified violent offence within Schedule 15 to the *CJA* 2003 (*ante*, § 5–299).

B. ADMINISTERING, ETC., CHLOROFORM, ETC., TO COMMIT INDICTABLE OFFENCES

(1) Statute

Offences against the Person Act 1861, s.22

19–219 **22.** Whosoever shall unlawfully apply or administer to, or cause to be taken by, or attempt to apply or administer to, or attempt to cause to be administered to or taken by, any person, any chloroform, laudanum, or other stupefying or overpowering drug, matter, or thing, with intent in any of such cases thereby to enable himself or any other person to commit, or with intent in any of such cases thereby to assist any other person in committing, any indictable offence, shall be guilty of an offence, and being convicted thereof shall be liable ... to *imprisonment* for life ....

[This section is printed as repealed in part by the *Statute Law Revision Act* 1892; and as amended by the *CJA* 1948, s.1(1); and the *CLA* 1967, s.12(5)(a).]

(2) Indictment

STATEMENT OF OFFENCE

19–220 *Administering chloroform, contrary to section 22 of the* Offences against the Person Act *1861.*

PARTICULARS OF OFFENCE

A B, on the —— day of ——, 20—, unlawfully applied or administered to [or *caused to be taken by*] [or *attempted to apply or administer to* or *attempted to cause to be administered to or taken by*] *J N chloroform* [*laudanum or other stupefying or overpowering drug, matter, or thing*] *with intent to enable himself* [or *E F*] *to steal a watch from the person of J N*, [or *with intent to assist E F to steal a watch from the person of the said J N*.]

(3) Class of offence and mode of trial

19–221 This offence is a class 3 offence, *ante*, § 2–17, triable only on indictment.

(4) Sentence

19–222 Imprisonment for life: s.22, *ante*.

An offence contrary to section 22 is a specified violent offence within Schedule 15 to the *CJA* 2003 (*ante*, § 5–299).

C. ADMINISTERING, ETC., POISON, ETC., SO AS TO ENDANGER LIFE, ETC., OR WITH INTENT TO INJURE, ETC.

(1) Statute

Offences against the Person Act 1861 ss.23, 24, 25

19–223 **23.** Whosoever shall unlawfully and maliciously administer to, or cause to be administered to or taken by any other person any poison, or other destructive or noxious thing, so as thereby to endanger the life of such person, or so as thereby to inflict upon such person any grievous bodily harm, shall be guilty of an offence, and being convicted thereof shall be liable ... to *imprisonment* for any term not exceeding ten years.

24. Whosoever shall unlawfully and maliciously administer to, or cause to be administered to or taken by any other person, any poison or other destructive or noxious thing, with intent to injure, aggrieve, or annoy such person, shall be guilty of a misdemeanor, and being convicted thereof shall be liable ... to *imprisonment* ... for not more than five years.

25. If, upon the trial of any person for any felony in the last but one preceding section mentioned, the jury shall not be satisfied that such person is guilty thereof, but shall be satisfied that he is guilty of any misdemeanor in the last preceding section mentioned, then and in every such case the jury may acquit the accused of such felony, and find him guilty of such misdemeanor, and thereupon he shall be liable to be punished in the same manner as if convicted upon an indictment for such misdemeanor.

[Sections 23 and 24 are printed as repealed in part by the *Statute Law Revision Act* 1892; and the *Statute Law Revision (No. 2) Act* 1893 (s.24 only); and as amended by the *CJA* 1948, s.1(1); and the *CLA* 1967, s.12(5)(a) (s.23); and by the *Penal Servitude Act* 1891, s.1(1); and the *CJA* 1948, s.1(1) (s.24).]

As to the reference to "felony" in section 25, see section 12(5)(a) of the *CLA* 1967 (*ante*, § 1–12).

(2) Indictment

COUNT 1

STATEMENT OF OFFENCE

Administering poison, so as to endanger life, contrary to section 23 of the Offences against the Person Act *1861*. **19–224**

PARTICULARS OF OFFENCE

A B, on the —— day of ——, 20—, unlawfully and maliciously administered to [or *caused to be administered to or taken by*] *J N a poison or other destructive or noxious thing so as thereby to endanger the life of J N or to inflict grievous bodily harm upon him.*

COUNT 2

STATEMENT OF OFFENCE

Administering poison, contrary to section 24 of the Offences against the Person Act *1861*.

PARTICULARS OF OFFENCE

As in count one down to "noxious thing", then "*with intent to injure, aggrieve, or annoy J N*".

(3) Class of offence and mode of trial

Both offences are class 3 offences, *ante*, § 2–17, triable only on indictment. **19–225**

(4) Alternative verdict

On a count alleging an offence contrary to section 23, the jury, if not satisfied that the accused is guilty thereof, may convict of an offence contrary to section 24: s.25, *ante*. **19–226**

(5) Sentence

Maximum

Count 1: imprisonment not exceeding 10 years, s.23, *ante*. **19–227**
Count 2: imprisonment not exceeding five years, s.24, *ante*.
An offence contrary to section 23 is a specified violent offence within Schedule 15 to the *CJA* 2003 (*ante*, § 5–299).

Relevant considerations

The correct approach to a section 24 offence is to equate it with either a section 20 offence of inflicting bodily injury, or perhaps with a fairly serious offence of assault occasioning actual bodily harm (s.47): *R. v. Jones (R. G.)*, 12 Cr.App.R.(S.) 233, CA. See also CSP B2–3.3C. **19–228**

(6) Ingredients of the offences

Mens rea

As to "maliciously", see *R. v. Cunningham* [1957] 2 Q.B. 396, 41 Cr.App.R. 155, CCA, *ante*, § 17–45. The court said, in respect of a charge under section 23, that it has to be proved that the defendant foresaw that the gas which he caused to escape, when he broke open a meter in order to steal its contents, might injure someone. It is submitted, however, that on a strict construction of the section, what the defendant has to be proved to have foreseen (or intended) is that his action might cause another person to take poison, etc. No doubt if he does foresee that, he equally foresees that he might cause injury, but it is clear that whilst the endangerment of life or the infliction of grievous bodily harm has to be proved, there is no requirement that the defendant intended or foresaw such result: see *R. v. Cato*, 62 Cr.App.R. 41, CA. **19–229**

If the poison, etc., is administered merely with intent "to injure, aggrieve, or annoy", which in itself would only amount to an offence under section 24, yet if it does in fact "inflict grievous bodily harm", this amounts to an offence under section 23: *Tulley v. Corrie* (1867) 10 Cox 640.

Administration

19–229a The word "administer" includes conduct which, albeit without the application of direct force, brings the noxious thing into contact with the victim's body, and it is for the judge to direct the jury as to the meaning of the word: *R. v. Gillard*, 87 Cr.App.R. 189, CA.

In *R. v. Kennedy (No. 2)* [2008] 1 A.C. 269, HL, it was held that a person would not be guilty of an offence under section 23 if he was involved in the supply of a class A controlled drug to a fully informed and responsible adult, which drug was then freely and voluntarily self-administered by the person to whom it was supplied. *R. v. Rogers* [2003] 2 Cr.App.R. 10, CA, in which the supplier had assisted in raising a vein into which the person supplied could inject himself and where the conviction was upheld on the basis that this made him a participant in the administration, was overruled. The House of Lords held that whilst he may have facilitated or contributed to the administration of the drug, it was the person supplied who had administered it as a result of his voluntary and informed decision. See also *ante*, § 19–100.

"noxious thing"

19–230 The jury has to consider the evidence of what was administered both in quality and quantity and to decide as a question of fact and degree in all the circumstances whether that thing was noxious. A substance which may be harmless in small quantities may yet be noxious in the quantity administered: *R. v. Marcus*, 73 Cr.App.R. 49, CA. The court further held that "noxious" did not mean harmful in the sense of injury to bodily health. The meaning of the word is clearly very wide—see the *Shorter Oxford English Dictionary* definition: "injurious, hurtful, harmful, unwholesome". In the opinion of the court, if a person were to put an unwholesome thing into an article of food or drink with intent to annoy any person who might consume it, an offence would be committed. They gave the example of the snail in the ginger beer bottle.

Heroin is a "noxious thing": the fact that it is administered to a person with a high degree of tolerance to whom it is unlikely to do particular harm is irrelevant: *R. v. Cato, ante*.

Intent to "injure"

19–231 Whether there was an intent to injure may depend on the purpose for which the noxious substance was administered: see *R. v. Hill (F.)*, 83 Cr.App.R. 386, HL. Stimulants had been given to boys by the accused with the object either of ingratiating himself with them or of rendering them more susceptible to homosexual advances; it was held that he had an intent to injure in the sense of causing harm to the metabolism of their bodies by overstimulation. But it was also said that an intention to keep a child awake for some entirely benevolent purpose could not amount to an intent to injure. It is submitted that a more satisfactory way of distinguishing the two cases might be to say that in one the administration is unlawful, whereas in the other, it is lawful.

D. INJURING OR ATTEMPTING TO INJURE PERSONS BY EXPLOSIVE OR CORROSIVE SUBSTANCES, ETC.

(1) Statute

Offences against the Person Act 1861, ss.28, 29, 30, 64

Causing bodily injury by explosives

19–232 **28.** Whosoever shall unlawfully and maliciously, by the explosion of gunpowder or other explosive substance, burn, maim, disfigure, disable, or do any grievous bodily harm to any person, shall be guilty of an offence, and being convicted thereof shall be liable, at the discretion of the court, to *imprisonment* for life.…

[This section is printed as repealed in part by the *Statute Law Revision Act* 1892; the *Statute Law Revision (No. 2) Act* 1893; and the *CJA* 1948, s.83(3), Sched. 10, Pt I; and as amended by the *CJA* 1948, s.1(1); and the *CLA* 1967, s.12(5)(a).]

Using explosives or corrosives with intent to do grievous bodily harm

29. Whosoever shall unlawfully and maliciously cause any gunpowder or other explosive substance to explode, or send or deliver to, or cause to be taken or received by any person, any explosive substance or any other dangerous or noxious thing, or put or lay at any place, or cast or throw at or upon or otherwise apply to any person, any corrosive fluid or any destructive or explosive substance, with intent in any of the cases aforesaid to burn, maim, disfigure, or disable any person, or to do some grievous bodily harm to any person shall, whether any bodily injury be effected or not, be guilty of an offence, and being convicted thereof shall be liable, at the discretion of the court, to *imprisonment* for life....

[This section is printed as repealed in part by the *Statute Law Revision Act* 1893; the *Statute Law Revision (No. 2) Act* 1893; and the *CJA* 1948, s.83(3), Sched. 10, Pt I; and as amended by the *CJA* 1948, s.1(1); and the *CLA* 1967, s.12(5)(a).]

Placing explosives near buildings or ships with intent to do grievous bodily harm

30. Whosoever shall unlawfully and maliciously place or throw in, into, upon, against, or **19–233**
near any building, ship, or vessel, any gunpowder or other explosive substance, with intent to do any bodily injury to any person shall, whether or not any explosion take place, and whether or not any bodily injury be effected, be guilty of an offence, and being convicted thereof shall be liable at the discretion of the court, to *imprisonment* for any term not exceeding fourteen years....

[This section is printed as repealed in part by the *Statute Law Revision Act* 1892; the *Statute Law Revision Act* 1893; the *Statute Law Revision (No. 2) Act* 1893; and the *CJA* 1948, s.83(3), Sched. 10, Pt I; and as amended by the *CJA* 1948, s.1(1); and the *CLA* 1967, s.12(5)(a).]

Making gunpowder, etc., to commit offences against the Act

64. Whosoever shall knowingly have in his possession, or make or manufacture, any **19–234**
gunpowder, explosive substance or any dangerous or noxious thing, or any machine, engine, instrument, or thing, with intent by means thereof to commit, or for the purpose of enabling any other person to commit, any of the felonies in this Act mentioned shall be guilty of a misdemeanor and being convicted thereof shall be liable at the discretion of the court, to be imprisoned for any term not exceeding two years....

[This section is printed as repealed in part by the *Statute Law Revision (No. 2) Act* 1893; and the *CJA* 1948, s.83(3) and Sched. 10, Pt I.]

In connection with the reference to "felonies", see the *CLA* 1967, s.12(5)(a) (*ante*, § 1–12). Further, the reference to felonies is to be construed as including any offence mentioned in the Act for which a person (not previously convicted) may be tried on indictment otherwise than at his own instance: *ibid.* s.10(1) and Sched. 2, para. 8.

An offence contrary to section 28, 29 or 30 is a "Convention offence" within the *Terrorism Act* 2006: see *post*, §§ 25–142k, 25–142l.

See also the *Explosive Substances Act* 1883, s.2 (causing explosion likely to endanger life or property); s.3 (attempt to cause explosion, or making or keeping explosive with intent to endanger life or property); and s.4 (making or possessing explosives under suspicious circumstances), *post*, §§ 23–62 *et seq.*

(2) Indictment

COUNT 1

STATEMENT OF OFFENCE

Causing bodily injury by explosives, contrary to section 28 of the Offences against the Person Act *1861*. **19–235**

PARTICULARS OF OFFENCE

A B, on the —— day of ——, 20—, by the explosion of gunpowder or other explosive substance, maliciously burned [or *did grievous bodily harm to*] *J N.*

COUNT 2

STATEMENT OF OFFENCE

19–236 *Sending explosive substance with intent, contrary to section 29 of the* Offences against the Person Act *1861*.

PARTICULARS OF OFFENCE

A B, on the —— day of ——, 20—, maliciously sent [or *delivered to*] [or *caused to be taken or received by*] *J N an explosive substance or other dangerous or noxious thing called ——, with intent to do grievous bodily harm to J N.*

(3) Class of offence and mode of trial

19–237 Offences contrary to sections 28, 29, 30 and 64 are class 3 offences, *ante*, § 2–17, triable on indictment only.

(4) Sentence

Maximum

19–238 Counts 1 and 2: imprisonment for life, ss.28 and 29, *ante*.

The offences contrary to sections 30 and 64 carry 14 years and two years' imprisonment respectively (as provided by the sections themselves).

Offences contrary to sections 28, 29 and 30 are specified violent offences within Schedule 15 to the *CJA* 2003 (*ante*, § 5–299).

Practice

19–239 In relation to offences contrary to section 29, see CSP B2–2.3D. Sentences where acid is thrown are generally within the range of five to 14 years' imprisonment. Shorter sentences have occasionally been substituted in cases of extreme provocation or where no substantial injury has been caused.

(5) Ingredients of the offences

19–240 As to "maliciously", see *ante*, § 17–45. As to "explosive substance", see *R. v. Howard* [1993] Crim.L.R. 213, CA (*post*, § 23–85).

On an allegation of an intent to disable (ss.28, 29), it is not necessary to prove an intent to disable permanently: *R. v. James*, 70 Cr.App.R. 215, CA.

Boiling water was held to be "destructive matter" within 7 Will. 4 & 1 Vict. c.85, s.5 (*rep.*): *R. v. Crawford* (1845) 1 Den. 100.

Self-defence is an available defence to a charge under section 64: see *Att.-Gen.'s Reference (No. 2 of 1983)* [1984] Q.B. 456, 78 Cr.App.R. 183, CA.

E. SETTING SPRING-GUNS, ETC., WITH INTENT, ETC.

Offences against the Person Act 1861, s.31

19–241 **31.** Whosoever shall set or place, or cause to be set or placed, any spring-gun, man-trap, or other engine calculated to destroy human life or inflict grievous bodily harm, with intent that the same or whereby the same may destroy or inflict grievous bodily harm upon a trespasser or other person coming in contact therewith, shall be guilty of a misdemeanor, and being convicted thereof shall be liable ... to *imprisonment* for any term not exceeding five years ...; and whosoever shall knowingly and wilfully permit any such spring-gun, man-trap, or other engine which may have been set or placed in any place then being in or afterwards coming into his possession or occupation by some other person to continue so set or placed, shall be deemed to have set and placed such gun, trap, or engine with such intent as aforesaid: Provided that nothing in this section contained shall extend to make it illegal to set or place any gin or trap such as may have been or may be usually set or placed with the intent of destroying vermin: Provided also, that nothing in thissection shall be deemed to make it unlawful to set or place, or cause to be set or placed, or to be continued set or placed, from sunset to sunrise, any spring-gun, man-trap, or other engine which shall be set or placed, or caused or continued to be set or placed in a dwelling-house for the protection thereof.

[This section is printed as repealed in part by the *Statute Law Revision Act* 1892; and as amended by the *Penal Servitude Act* 1891, s.1(1); and the *CJA* 1948, s.1(1).]

Indictment

For a specimen indictment, see the 1996 edition of this work. **19–242**

Imprisonment for not more than five years: s.31, *ante*.

An offence contrary to section 31 is a specified violent offence within Schedule 15 to the *CJA* 2003 (*ante*, § 5–299).

Evidence

This statute applies only to instruments set with an intention to do grievous bodily harm thereby to human beings, or whereby grievous bodily harm may be done to a human being. If death is caused by setting a spring-gun, the setter is guilty of manslaughter: *R. v. Heaton*, 60 J.P. 508. **19–243**

In *R. v. Munks* [1964] 1 Q.B. 304, 48 Cr.App.R. 56, CCA, the court held that an "engine" meant a mechanical contrivance and therefore did not include an arrangement of electrical wires designed to administer a shock to any intruder into the appellant's house. In *R. v. Cockburn* [2008] 2 Cr.App.R. 4, CA, however, it was held that the words "mechanical contrivance" should not be used so as to lead to the exclusion of a contraption which falls within the ambit of the statute. The object itself as well as the manner, if any, in which it was to be activated should be examined pragmatically to see whether, looked at overall, it fell within the statutory language. Accordingly, it was held that a spiked metal object made from two pieces of heavy steel plate, and which was connected to the roof of a shed by a wire and to the door of the shed by another wire in such a way that opening the door would release it, whereupon the force of gravity would cause it to swing down towards a person entering the shed, could properly be described as a mechanical contrivance or machine, and it was unquestionably an "other engine" for the purposes of the section.

F. Endangering the Safety of Railway Passengers

(1) Statute

Offences against the Person Act 1861, ss.32, 33, 34

32. Whosoever shall unlawfully and maliciously put or throw upon or across any railway, any wood, stone, or other matter or thing, or shall unlawfully and maliciously take up, remove, or displace any rail, sleeper, or other matter or thing belonging to any railway, or shall unlawfully and maliciously turn, move, or divert any points or other machinery belonging to any railway, or shall unlawfully and maliciously make or show, hide or remove, any signal or light upon or near to any railway, or shall unlawfully and maliciously do or cause to be done any other matter or thing, with intent, in any of the cases aforesaid, to endanger the safety of any person travelling or being upon such railway, shall be guilty of an offence, and being convicted thereof shall be liable, at the discretion of the court, to *imprisonment* for life… . **19–244**

33. Whosoever shall unlawfully and maliciously throw, or cause to fall or strike, at, against, into, or upon any engine, tender, carriage, or truck used upon any railway, any wood, stone, or other matter or thing, with intent to injure or endanger the safety of any person being in or upon such engine, tender, carriage or truck, or in or upon any other engine, tender, carriage, or truck of any train of which such first-mentioned engine, tender, carriage, or truck shall form part, shall be guilty of an offence, and being convicted thereof shall be liable … to *imprisonment* for life… .

[Section 32 is printed as repealed in part by the *Statute Law Revision Act* 1892; and the *CJA* 1948, s.83(3) and Sched. 10, Pt I. Section 33 is printed as repealed in part by the former Act. Both sections are printed as amended by the *CJA* 1948, s.1(1); and the *CLA* 1967, s.12(5)(a).]

34. Whosoever, by any unlawful act or by any wilful omission or neglect, shall endanger or cause to be endangered the safety of any person conveyed or being in or upon a railway, or shall aid or assist therein, shall be guilty of a misdemeanor, and being convicted thereof shall be liable at the discretion of the court, to be imprisoned for any term not exceeding two years, …

(2) Indictment

STATEMENT OF OFFENCE

Endangering safety of railway passengers, contrary to section 32 of the Offences against the Person Act *1861*. **19–245**

PARTICULARS OF OFFENCE

A B, on the —— day of ——, 20—, unlawfully and maliciously put or threw upon or across the railway lines between London and ——, a stone [*wood or other matter or thing*] *with intent to endanger the safety of persons travelling or being upon the said railway.*

An acquittal on this indictment is no bar to a subsequent indictment on the same facts for an offence under section 34: *R. v. Gilmore* (1882) 15 Cox 85.

(3) Class of offence and mode of trial

19–246 The offences contrary to sections 32 and 33 are class 3 offences, *ante*, § 2–17, triable only on indictment. The offence contrary to section 34 is a class 3 offence, *ante*, § 2–17, triable either way: *MCA* 1980, s.17(1), and Sched. 1 (*ante*, § 1–75af).

(4) Sentence

19–247 The offences contrary to sections 32 and 33 carry life imprisonment; the offence contrary to section 34 carries two years' imprisonment on conviction on indictment: see the terms of each of those sections, respectively.

An offence contrary to section 32 is a specified violent offence within Schedule 15 to the *CJA* 2003 (*ante*, § 5–299).

(5) Ingredients of the offences

19–248 As to "maliciously", see *ante*, § 17–45.

As to the meaning of "wilful", see *R. v. Holroyd* (1841) 2 M. & Rob. 339; *R. v. Senior* [1899] 1 Q.B. 283; and *R. v. Sheppard* [1981] A.C. 394, HL (*ante*, § 17–47).

Throwing a stone at engines or carriages appears to be an offence within section 34, *ante*: *R. v. Bowray* (1846) 10 Jur. 211. So is playing with a cart on railway premises with the result of letting it run within a dangerous distance of the track: *R. v. Monaghan and Granger* (1870) 11 Cox 608. Neglect by an engine driver to keep a good look-out for signals appears to be within the words of section 34, *ante*.

Potential danger or a lowering of the standards of safety which would lead to the endangering of the safety of a passenger is sufficient to constitute the offence under section 34 and proof of actual danger is not required: *R. v. Pearce* [1967] 1 Q.B. 150, 50 Cr.App.R. 305, CA.

G. CAUSING BODILY HARM BY WANTON OR FURIOUS DRIVING

(1) Statute

Offences against the Person Act 1861, s.35

19–248a **35.** Whosoever having the charge of any carriage or vehicle, shall, by wanton or furious driving or racing, or other wilful misconduct, or by wilful neglect, do or cause to be done any bodily harm to any person whatsoever, shall be guilty of an offence and being convicted thereof shall be liable, at the discretion of the court, to be imprisoned for any term not exceeding two years… .

[This section is printed as amended by the *CJA* 1948, s.1(2).]

(2) Indictment

STATEMENT OF OFFENCE

19–248b *Causing bodily harm, contrary to section 35 of the* Offences against the Person Act *1861.*

PARTICULARS OF OFFENCE

A B, on the —— day of ——, 20—, having the charge of a public omnibus, by wanton or furious driving [*or by wilful neglect*] *caused bodily harm to J N.*

The offence contrary to section 35 is used today to deal with horse-drawn carriages and vehicles, and with motorists and cyclists who cannot be prosecuted for dangerous driving or cycling because their conduct did not take place on a road or (in the case of motorists) on a public place, or because they were not given a warning of intended prosecution (see s.1 of the *RTOA* 1988, *post*, § 32–152). For the offence of dangerous driving, see *post*, § 32–27.

(3) Class of offence and mode of trial

This offence is a class 3 offence, *ante*, § 2–17, triable only on indictment. **19–248c**

(4) Sentence

Imprisonment not exceeding two years: s.35, *ante*. **19–248d**

An offence contrary to section 35 is a specified violent offence within Schedule 15 to the *CJA* 2003 (*ante*, § 5–299); and it carries discretionary disqualification and obligatory endorsement (3 to 9 penalty points): *RTOA* 1988, ss.28, 34 and 44, and Sched. 2, Pt II (*post*, §§ 32–175, 32–181, 32–210, 32–222); but only if it was committed on or after September 24, 2007 (*Road Safety Act 2006 (Commencement No. 2) Order* 2007 (S.I. 2007 No. 2462)): *RSA* 2006, s.61(3).

As to the power to deprive the offender of the vehicle used, see the *PCC(S)A* 2000, s.143 (*ante*, § 5–439).

(5) Ingredients of the offence

As to "cause", see *ante*, §§ 19–6 *et seq*. (causation generally), and *ante*, § 19–208 (causing grievous bodily harm). It is clear that the offence may be committed although there is no direct contact between the defendant's vehicle and the victim. **19–248e**

As to "bodily harm", see *ante*, § 19–197.

The section applies to all carriages and vehicles, public or private; also to bicycles: *R. v. Parker*, 59 J.P. 793. A bicycle is a "carriage": *Taylor v. Goodwin* (1879) 4 Q.B.D. 228; *cf*. *Cannan v. Earl of Abingdon* [1900] 2 Q.B. 66. It is not restricted to driving on a road: see *R. v. Cooke* [1971] Crim.L.R. 44, Nottingham Q.S., where a van was driven in a recreation ground.

On a charge of "wilful misconduct" it is not necessary for the prosecution to prove an intention to cause bodily harm; it is sufficient if they show that the driving was intentional and that it fell below the normal standard so as to amount to "misconduct": *R. v. Cooke*, *ante*. In *R. v. Okosi* [1996] Crim.L.R. 666, CA, it was assumed, without deciding the point, that the *mens rea* for wanton and furious driving involved recklessness of a subjective, rather than an objective, character. If this is correct, it must cast doubt on *Cooke*, *ante*; it cannot be right that one way of committing an offence requires proof of foresight of consequence, whereas another requires proof of no such foresight.

H. Obstructing, etc., Ministers of Religion in Discharge of Their Duties

Offences against the Person Act 1861, s.36

36. Whosoever shall by threats or force, obstruct or prevent or endeavour to obstruct or prevent, any clergyman or other minister in or from celebrating divine service or otherwise officiating in any church, chapel, meeting-house, or other place of divine worship, or in or from the performance of his duty in the lawful burial of the dead in any churchyard or other burial place, or shall strike or offer any violence to, or shall, upon any civil process, or under the pretence of executing any civil process, arrest any clergyman or other minister who is engaged in, or to the knowledge of the offender is about to engage in, any of the rites or duties in this section aforesaid, or who to the knowledge of the offender shall be going to perform the same or returning from the performance thereof, shall be guilty of a misdemeanor and being convicted thereof shall be liable, at the discretion of the court, to be imprisoned for any term not exceeding two years… . **19–249**

Indictment

For a specimen indictment, see the 1992 edition of this work. **19–250**

Imprisonment not exceeding two years: s.36, *ante*. This offence is triable either way: *MCA* 1980, s.17(1), and Sched. 1, *ante*, § 1–75af.

As to the meaning of "divine service", see *Matthews v. King* [1934] 1 K.B. 505.

I. ASSAULTS ON OFFICERS, ETC., SAVING WRECK

Offences against the Person Act 1861, s.37

19–251 **37.** Whosoever shall assault and strike or wound any magistrate, officer, or other person whatsoever lawfully authorized, in or on account of the exercise of his duty in or concerning the preservation of any vessel in distress, or of any vessel, goods, or effects wrecked, stranded, or cast on shore, or lying under water, shall be guilty of a misdemeanor and being convicted thereof shall be liable ... to *imprisonment* for any term not exceeding seven years....

[This section is printed as repealed in part by the *Statute Law Revision Act* 1892; and as amended by the *CJA* 1948, s.1(1).]

Indictment

19–252 For a specimen indictment, see the 1992 edition of this work.

An offence contrary to section 37 is a specified violent offence within Schedule 15 to the *CJA* 2003 (*ante*, § 5–299).

As to the meaning of "assault", see *ante*, §§ 19–166 *et seq.*; as to the meaning of "wound", see *ante*, § 19–212.

J. IMPEDING PERSONS ENDEAVOURING TO ESCAPE FROM WRECKS

Offences against the Person Act 1861, s.17

19–253 **17.** Whosoever shall unlawfully and maliciously prevent or impede any person, being on board of or having quitted any ship or vessel which shall be in distress, or wrecked, stranded, or cast on shore, in his endeavour to save his life, or shall unlawfully and maliciously prevent or impede any person in his endeavour to save the life of any such person as in this section first aforesaid, shall be guilty of an offence, and being convicted thereof shall be liable ... to *imprisonment* for life....

[This section is printed as repealed in part by the *Statute Law Revision Act* 1892; and the *Statute Law Revision (No. 2) Act* 1893; and as amended by the *CJA* 1948, s.1(1).]

Indictment

19–254 For a specimen indictment, see the 1996 edition of this work.

K. ASSAULTS WITH INTENT TO RESIST ARREST

Offences against the Person Act 1861, s.38

Assault with intent to resist arrest, etc.

19–255 **38.** Whosoever ... shall assault any person with intent to resist or prevent the lawful apprehension or detainer of himself or of any other person for any offence, shall be guilty of a misdemeanor, and being convicted thereof shall be liable, at the discretion of the court, to be imprisoned for any term not exceeding two years....

[This section is printed as repealed in part by the *Police Act* 1964, s.64(3) and Sched. 10, Pt I; and the *CLA* 1967, s.10(2) and Sched. 3, Pt III.]

This offence is triable either way: *MCA* 1980, s.17(1), and Sched. 1, *ante*, § 1–75af.

An offence contrary to section 38 is a specified violent offence within Schedule 15 to the *CJA* 2003 (*ante*, § 5–299).

As to sentence, see the guideline of the Sentencing Guidelines Council on assault (Appendix K–113 *et seq.*).

Assault

19–256 As to what constitutes an "assault", see *ante*, §§ 19–166 *et seq.*

The ulterior intent

19–257 The intent must be to resist or prevent the lawful apprehension or detainer of the defendant or another person for any offence.

Lawful apprehension or detainer for any offence

19–258 It must be proved that the person assaulted had the right to apprehend or detain the defendant for any offence: see *R. v. Self*, 95 Cr.App.R. 42, CA. The words "for any offence" would seem to exclude arrest on civil process and arrest in respect of breach of the peace. Conduct constituting a breach of the peace or giving rise to a fear that a breach of the peace will ensue does not constitute an offence as such. Contempt of court, it is submitted, is an offence for these purposes, whether the contempt is "criminal" or "civil": see *Att.-Gen. v. Newspaper Publishing plc.* [1988] Ch. 333, CA (Civ. Div.), and *Dean v. Dean* [1987] 1 F.L.R. 517, CA (Civ. Div.); but see *Cobra Golf Ltd v. Rata* [1998] Ch. 109, Ch D (Rimer J.) ("civil" contempt is not a criminal offence).

The words "or detainer" add nothing to "lawful apprehension". It is trite law that there is no power of detention short of arrest for an offence: see *Kenlin v. Gardiner* [1967] 2 Q.B. 510, DC. Whilst there are statutory powers of stop and search (*PACE Act* 1984, s.1 (*ante*, § 15–49); *Terrorism Act* 2006, s.44 (*post*, § 25–88)), and whilst the exercise of such powers may lead to an arrest "for any offence", it cannot be said that when a constable exercises the power of stop and search, he is detaining the person searched "for any offence".

(i) *Powers of arrest*

The general powers of arrest for offences without a warrant of both constables and ordinary citizens are contained in sections 24 and 24A of the *PACE Act* 1984: *ante*, §§ 15–161 *et seq.* In addition, certain special powers of arrest were preserved by section 26(2) of, and Schedule 2 to, the 1984 Act: *ante*, § 15–171. **19–259**

As to the information to be given upon making an arrest without a warrant, see section 28 of the 1984 Act: *ante*, § 15–176.

As to arrest on a warrant, see *post*, § 19–341.

(ii) *Mistake of fact*

It has been seen that on a charge under section 38 it must be proved that the defendant assaulted someone intending to resist or prevent what was, or would have been, a lawful arrest for an offence. It clearly does not have to be proved that he was aware of the circumstances which made the arrest lawful, although, in practice, he often will be. He could, however, be the totally innocent victim of a case of mistaken identity: the arrest could be lawful, yet he would not know that. If he assaulted the person endeavouring to arrest him he would be guilty of the offence. **19–260**

What is the position if the person to be arrested genuinely believes in the existence of circumstances that would make the arrest unlawful or that the persons seeking to make the arrest were not in fact police officers? General principle suggests that where a defendant has made a mistake of fact his criminality should be judged on the basis of his mistaken view of the facts: *R. v. Kimber*, 77 Cr.App.R. 225, CA; *R. v. Williams (G.)*, 78 Cr.App.R. 276, CA; and *R. v. Beckford* [1988] A.C. 130, PC. The reasonableness or unreasonableness of the defendant's belief is material only to the question of whether the belief was held by the defendant at all: *ibid.*

There appears to be no reason why these principles should not apply to an allegation of an offence contrary to section 38. The decision of the Court of Appeal in *R. v. Ball (S.L.)*, 90 Cr.App.R. 378, suggests, however, that they have extremely limited application: see *ante*, § 19–169. **19–261**

See also *R. v. Browne* [1973] N.I. 96; Smith and Hogan, *Criminal Law*, 12th ed., 2008, pp. 138–140; and *ante*, §§ 17–10 *et seq.*

L. NEGLECTING TO PROVIDE FOOD, ETC., FOR, OR ASSAULTING, ETC., APPRENTICES OR SERVANTS

Offences against the Person Act 1861, s.26

26. Whosoever, being legally liable, either as a master or mistress, to provide for any apprentice or servant necessary food, clothing, or lodging, shall wilfully and without lawful excuse refuse or neglect to provide the same, or shall unlawfully and maliciously do, or cause to be done, any bodily harm to any such apprentice or servant, so that the life of such apprentice or servant shall be endangered, or the health of such apprentice or servant shall have been or shall be likely to be permanently injured, shall be guilty of a misdemeanor, and being convicted thereof shall be liable ... to *imprisonment* ... for any term not exceeding five years. **19–262**

[This section is printed as amended or repealed in part by the *Penal Servitude Act*

1891, s.1(1); the *Statute Law Revision Act* 1892; the *Statute Law Revision (No. 2) Act* 1893; and the *CJA* 1948, s.1(1).]

Indictment

19–263 For a specimen indictment, see the 1992 edition of this work.

This offence is triable either way: *MCA* 1980, s.17(1), and Sched. 1, *ante*, § 1–75af.

Imprisonment not exceeding five years: s.26, *ante*.

Ingredients of the offence

19–264 It is not clear whether or not the words "so that the life of such apprentice or servant be endangered", etc., apply to all the preceding part of the section or refer only to the doing of some bodily harm. Until there has been some decision on the subject, it will be safer to regard them as applying to the whole of the section, and to be prepared with evidence to support them. It would seem, indeed, to be the better opinion, that the words "so that the life of such person shall be endangered", etc., override all the preceding matter, otherwise a mere single wilful refusal to provide a dinner would be within the clause.

IX. OFFENCES IN RELATION TO POLICE OFFICERS

A. ASSAULTS

Introduction

19–265 Section 89(1) of the *Police Act* 1996 makes it a summary offence to assault a constable in the execution of his duty, a person assisting a constable in the execution of his duty or a person who is a "member of an international joint investigation team" (as to which see subss. (4) and (5)) carrying out his functions as a member of that team. The maximum penalty is six months' imprisonment (increased to 51 weeks as from a day to be appointed (but only in relation to offences committed on or after the day on which the amendment takes effect): *CJA* 2003, s.281(4)–(6)) or a fine not exceeding level 5 on the standard scale, or both. Subsection (2) creates summary offences of resisting or wilfully obstructing a constable in the execution of his duty (as to which, see *post*, § 19–272).

Section 89 applies to a member of a police force maintained in Scotland or Northern Ireland when he is executing a warrant or otherwise acting in England or Wales by virtue of any enactment conferring powers on him in England and Wales: s.89(3). For the purposes of section 89, any person who is carrying out surveillance in England and Wales under section 76A of the *RIPA* 2000 is to be treated as if he were acting as a constable in the execution of his duty: *Crime (International Co-operation) Act* 2003, s.84(1).

As the offence created by section 89(1) is summary only, it prima facie falls outside the scope of this work. However, section 89(1) calls for consideration on two grounds. First, it has been held (*R. v. Baker* [1962] 2 Q.B. 530, 46 Cr.App.R. 47, CCA) that to prove an offence contrary to section 17(2) of the *Firearms Act* 1968 of having possession of a firearm at the time of committing or being arrested for certain specified offences (including the offence contrary to section 89(1)), it has to be proved that the defendant was in fact guilty of the relevant offence. Secondly, questions relating to the nature and extent of a constable's duty frequently arise on prosecutions for offences other than those created by section 89. In relation to the first of these points, it should be noted that *Baker* was not followed in *R. v. Nelson* [2000] 2 Cr.App.R. 160, CA.

Assault

19–266 As to what constitutes an assault, see *ante*, §§ 19–166 *et seq.*

Constables

19–267 Every police officer in England and Wales holds the office of constable: *Lewis v. Cattle* [1938] 2 K.B. 454 at 457.

Prison officers, while acting as such, have by virtue of their appointment all the powers, authorities, protection and privileges of a constable: *Prison Act* 1952, s.8. Section 8 does not apply to prisoner custody officers employed at contracted out prisons: *CJA* 1991, s.87(2).

In the execution of duty

Statute

The powers, duties and responsibilities of police officers are in general governed by the *Police Act* 1996. Their powers in relation to the stopping and searching of persons and vehicles, the seizure of articles, entering premises with and without search warrants, and the arrest and detention of persons are largely determined by the *PACE Act* 1984. Where any provision of the 1984 Act confers a power on a constable and does not provide that the power may only be exercised with the consent of some person, other than a police officer, the officer may use reasonable force, if necessary, in the exercise of the power: *ibid.*, s.117. **19–268**

Apart from the general provisions of the *Police Act* 1996 and the *PACE Act* 1984, many statutes confer specific powers or duties on police constables. If an officer acts in accordance with the terms of a statute he will clearly be acting in the execution of his duty. The legislature, in an effort to keep pace and to deal with the complexity of modern society, has often made enactments regulating many different aspects of society. Road traffic is an obvious example. Such statutes cannot be considered as totally determining a constable's powers or obligations: see *Johnson v. Phillips* [1975] 3 All E.R. 682, DC, *post*.

Common law

It is part of the obligations and duties of a police constable to take all steps which appear to him necessary for keeping the peace, for preventing crime, or for protecting property from criminal injury. There is no exhaustive definition of the powers and obligations of the police, but they are at least these, and would further include the duty to detect crime and bring an offender to justice: *Rice v. Connolly* [1966] 2 Q.B. 414, *per* Lord Parker C.J. See also *R. v. Waterfield and Lynn* [1964] 1 Q.B. 164 at 170, 171, 48 Cr.App.R. 42 at 47, CCA, and *Coffin v. Smith*, 72 Cr.App.R. 221, DC. Stemming from the constable's duty to give adequate protection to all persons and their property, is his duty to control traffic on public roads: *Johnson v. Phillips*, *ante* (a constable has the right to disobey a traffic regulation or direct another to do so if acting in the execution of his duty to protect life and property). **19–269**

A constable, like any other member of the public, has implied leave and licence from a house-holder to enter land and approach the door of a house for the purpose of making inquiries; if requested to leave by the occupier, the lapse of a reasonable time must be deemed necessary to enable him to leave: *Robson v. Hallett* [1967] 2 Q.B. 939, 51 Cr.App.R. 307, DC. Where a constable is off private premises, it would be his duty to enter such premises to prevent a breach of the peace: *ibid.* See also *Kay v. Hibbert* [1977] Crim.L.R. 226, DC, and *R. v. Lamb* [1990] Crim.L.R. 58, DC, in which it was held that there was no obligation on a police officer who was a trespasser to nullify his unlawful act by leaving the land before taking steps to prevent a breach of the peace which he reasonably anticipated was about to occur on the land. **19–270**

As to the duty of a constable to prevent breaches of the peace which he reasonably apprehends, see also *Duncan v. Jones* [1936] 1 K.B. 218, DC; *Thomas v. Sawkins* [1935] 2 K.B. 249; *McGowan v. Chief Constable of Kingston-upon-Hull* [1968] Crim.L.R. 34, DC; *King v. Hodges* [1974] Crim.L.R. 424, DC; *Moss v. McLachlan*, 149 J.P. 167, DC; and *post*, §§ 19–343, 19–344. As to what constitutes a breach of the peace, see *post*, § 29–55.

In *DPP v. Morrison*, 167 J.P. 577, DC, it was held that, provided that they acted reasonably, the police had power to cordon off an area of land in private ownership but to which there was access by public right of way, if their purpose was to preserve evidence subsequent to the commission of an offence; on the assumption that the owner of the land would have the right to refuse consent, the police were nevertheless entitled to proceed on the assumption that consent would be given.

19–271 It is not every interference with a citizen's liberty that will amount to a course of conduct sufficient to take the officer out of the execution of his duty: *Donnelly v. Jackman*, 54 Cr.App.R. 229, DC (touching a person on the shoulder to attract his attention); but *cf. Kenlin v. Gardiner* [1967] 2 Q.B. 510, DC (an unjustified though technical assault); *Bentley v. Brudzinski*, 75 Cr.App.R. 217, DC (unlawfully preventing citizen from walking away after he had answered officer's questions was held to be more than just a "trivial interference with a citizen's liberty"—see *Donnelly v. Jackman*); *Ludlow v. Burgess*, 75 Cr.App.R. 227, DC (taking hold of a person's arm but without proceeding to arrest); and *Wood v. DPP, The Times*, May 23, 2008, DC (where a police officer restrains a person, but does not at that time intend or purport to arrest him, he commits an assault, even if an arrest would have been justified). The cases which concern the distinction between unlawful restraint and a lawfully acceptable degree of physical contact between a police officer and another were considered in *Collins v. Wilcock*, 79 Cr.App.R. 229, DC.

19–272 A police officer is not acting in the execution of his duty if he attempts to prevent a breach of the peace by trying to restrain a person who is using force to prevent an unlawful search by another officer: *McBean v. Parker* [1983] Crim.L.R. 399, DC. Nor if he restrains someone in the mistaken belief that that person has been lawfully arrested by another officer: *Kerr v. DPP* [1995] Crim.L.R. 394, DC.

A police officer is entitled to use force to restrain a person from leaving a police station provided it has been made clear to him that he is under arrest: *R. v. Inwood*, 57 Cr.App.R. 529, CA (see also *ante*, § 15–159). Where an issue arises upon this question, it is a question of fact for the tribunal of fact to decide: *ibid*.

Where a police officer, acting reasonably on a genuine inquiry into the suspected commission of a crime, required a motor vehicle to stop, pursuant to his power at common law or under [what is now] the *RTA* 1988, s.163 (*post*, § 32–136), he was entitled to detain it for such reasonable time as to enable him, if he suspected it to have been stolen, to effect an arrest and explain to the driver the reason for the arrest: *Lodwick v. Saunders*, 80 Cr.App.R. 304, DC. In connection with section 163, see also the *PACE Act* 1984, s.4, *ante*, § 15–57, and *Leach v. DPP* [1993] R.T.R. 161, DC.

Whilst the citizen is under no legal duty to assist the police, the offence created by the *Police Act* 1996, s.89(2) (*ante*, § 19–265), limits his freedom of action once he is approached by a police officer who seeks to question him about the commission of an offence, and who identifies himself as such; the citizen would be entitled not to answer any questions put to him; he would be entitled to say that he had no intention of answering any questions and that he did intend to go on his way; and he would be entitled to refuse to accompany the police officer (unless arrested) to any place to which he might be requested to go; but running away with the intention of impeding apprehension would be wilfully to obstruct the officer in the execution of his duty: *Sekfali, Banamira and Ouham v. DPP*, 170 J.P. 393, DC.

19–273 There is old authority for the proposition that a police officer is not in the execution of his duty if he is doing something that he is not compelled by law to do: *R. v. Prebble* (1858) 1 F. & F. 325; *R. v. Roxburgh* (1871) 12 Cox 8. These two cases were disapproved of by the Divisional Court in *Coffin v. Smith*, 72 Cr.App.R. 221 (officers acting in execution of their duty in assisting to eject persons from youth club; they thought their presence would assist in keeping the peace).

19–274 See also *R. v. Chief Constable of Devon and Cornwall, ex p. Central Electricity Generating Board* [1982] Q.B. 458, CA (Civ. Div.), in which it was held that there must be either a breach of the peace or reasonable cause for suspecting that there is a real and imminent risk of one occurring before the police would be bound to assist in the removal of protestors from a site from which the board had the right to eject them. But, according to Templeman L.J., they would be entitled to assist at an earlier stage:

> "In addition to other powers possessed by the police, they are entitled to enter on private land at the invitation of the owner or ... of any person who himself has a right to be on the land. The board are entitled to enter on the site and to complete the survey and they are entitled to invite the police to enter on the site to assist the board to establish conditions

under which the board will be able to complete the survey without any outbreak of violence taking place" (at p. 479).

Lawton L.J. did not go so far: he said that in the event that the protestors did allow themselves to be removed without struggling or causing uproar the police would have no reason for taking action and should not do so (see p. 476). *Coffin v. Smith*, *ante*, was not referred to.

Mens rea

Knowledge that the person assaulted was a police officer is not necessary to sustain a charge contrary to section 89(1) of the 1996 Act: *R. v. Forbes and Webb* (1865) 10 Cox 362; *R. v. Maxwell and Clanchy*, 2 Cr.App.R. 26, CCA. See also *McBride v. Turnock* [1964] Crim.L.R. 456, DC. Nor is it necessary to prove that the accused knew that the officer was in the execution of his duty; the offence is not assaulting an officer *knowing* him to be in the execution of his duty, but assaulting him *being* in the execution of his duty: *ibid.*; and see Russ.Cr., 12th ed., p. 687. **19–275**

If the defendant had a genuine belief either that the victim was not a police officer or in the existence of circumstances which would mean the officer was not acting in the course of his duty, it is submitted that the general principle relating to *mens rea* and mistake of fact should apply and his liability should be judged on the basis of that belief: see *R. v. Kimber*, 77 Cr.App.R. 225, CA; *R. v. Williams (G.)*, 78 Cr.App.R. 276, CA; *R. v. Beckford* [1988] A.C 130, PC; and see *ante*, §§ 19–169, 19–260. There is first instance authority in support of this proposition: *R. v. Mark, Brown and Mark* [1961] Crim.L.R. 173, CCC (Judge Maxwell Turner). However, the direction to the jury there was that the mistaken belief must be reasonably held. It is submitted that if mistake of fact is available to a defendant then the authorities now clearly establish that the mistake does not have to be reasonable: *Kimber*, *Williams (G.)*, *Beckford*, *ante*.

In *Kenlin v. Gardiner* [1967] 2 Q.B. 510, DC, Winn L.J., said, *obiter*, that whilst knowledge that the man attacked is a police officer is unnecessary, a genuine mistake of fact as to the character of the person concerned, *e.g.* genuine and reasonable belief that he was a thug and not a police officer, would be highly material in judging the reasonableness of resistance exerted and the degree of force falling within the liberty or justification of self-defence. This appears to be saying that such a mistake will not avail a defendant except where he is in law entitled to use some force because the officer is using excessive force or should not be using force at all. This appears to beg the question because if the officer should not be using force or is using excessive force he has presumably gone beyond the scope of his duty. **19–276**

See also *Albert v. Lavin* [1982] A.C. 546, HL, *post*, § 19–343.

As to a mistake as to the powers and duties of a constable, see *R. v. Fennell* [1971] 1 Q.B. 428, 54 Cr.App.R. 451, CA, and *R. v. Ball (S.L.)* 90 Cr.App.R. 378, CA, *ante*, § 19–169.

B. REFUSAL TO AID CONSTABLE

Refusing to aid and assist a constable in the execution of his duty, in order to preserve the peace, is an indictable misdemeanor at common law. In order to support such indictment, it must be proved that the constable saw a breach of the peace committed; that there was a reasonable necessity for calling upon the defendant for his assistance; and that when duly called on to do so, the defendant, without any physical impossibility or lawful excuse, refused to do so. And it is no defence that the single aid of the defendant could have been of no avail: *R. v. Brown* (1841) C. & Mar. 314. An indictment for refusing to assist a constable in the execution of his duty, and to prevent an assault made upon him by persons in his custody on a charge of an offence made with intent to resist their lawful apprehension, is sufficient without stating how the apprehension became lawful; and it is sufficient if it states a refusal to assist, without the further allegation that the prisoner did not, in fact, assist: *R. v. Sherlock* (1866) L.R. 1 CCR 20. **19–277**

X. *HARASSMENT*

A. INTRODUCTION

The *Protection from Harassment Act* 1997 describes itself as an Act "to make provision for protecting persons from harassment and similar conduct". It was passed for the **19–277a** purpose of dealing with the phenomenon of "stalking". There is, however, no attempt at a definition of harassment, although section 7(2) provides that references to harassing a person include alarming the person or causing the person distress. In *Huntingdon Life Sciences Ltd v. Curtin, The Times*, December 11, 1997, QBD, Eady J. said that the Act was not intended to clamp down on the discussion of matters of public interest or upon the rights of political protest and public demonstration, being a part of the democratic tradition; his Lordship added that the courts would resist any wide interpretation of the Act. In *DPP v. Dziurzynski*, 166 J.P. 545, DC, it was held that on a proper construction of the Act, only human beings may be victims of harassment within the Act (but it is "tolerably clear" that the perpetrator may be a corporate body: *per* Lord Nicholls in *Majrowski v. Guy's and St Thomas's NHS Trust* [2007] 1 A.C. 224, HL (at [19])); where, therefore, a charge alleged harassment of "the employees" of a particular corporation, but there was no evidence of any individual employee being present at the time of the allegedly harassing conduct on more than one occasion, the charge could not be sustained on the basis that the corporation was being harassed on more than one occasion through conduct directed at different employees on different days (see also *Daiichi Pharmaceuticals U.K. Ltd v. Stop Huntingdon Animal Cruelty*, *post*, § 19–277b). In *Tuppen v. Microsoft Corporation Ltd, The Times*, November 15, 2000, QBD, Douglas Brown J. held that there being no definition of "harassment" in the Act, it was legitimate to have recourse to the proceedings in Parliament as an aid to construction because of the wide potential and far-reaching meaning that might be attributed to the word; such reference made clear that the behaviour sought to be controlled was conduct such as stalking, anti-social behaviour by neighbours and racial harassment; the conduct of oppressive litigation could not, however, amount to harassment within the Act. But in *Thomas v. News Group Newspapers Ltd, The Times*, July 25, 2001, CA (Civ. Div.), it was held that the Act is concerned with conduct targeted at an individual, which was calculated to produce alarm or distress and which was oppressive and unreasonable; and that a series of articles in a newspaper was capable of amounting to such conduct where they were calculated to incite racial hatred.

As to the inter-relationship between parallel jurisdictions and remedies in cases of domestic violence, see *Lomas v. Parle (Practice Note)* [2004] 1 W.L.R. 1642, CA (Civ. Div.), where it was said that it is not difficult for a persistent course of domestic violence to generate concurrent proceedings in three courts, and that, however effectively the proceedings were managed, a perpetrator might face sentence for the same act which amounted to both a breach of an injunction made in family proceedings and a crime under the 1997 Act. It was said that the first court to sentence must not anticipate or allow for a future sentence; it is for the second court to sentence to reflect the prior sentence, in order to ensure the offender is not punished twice; and it is thus essential that the second court should be fully informed of the factors and circumstances reflected in the first sentence; to this end, there was an obligation on the first court to ensure that the basis of its sentence was fully expressed and that a transcript of its judgment was made available.

B. STATUTE

Protection from Harassment Act 1997, ss.1, 2

Prohibition of harassment

19–277b **1.**—(1) A person must not pursue a course of conduct—

(a) which amounts to harassment of another, and

(b) which he knows or ought to know amounts to harassment of the other.

(1A) A person must not pursue a course of conduct—

(a) which involves harassment of two or more persons, and

(b) which he knows or ought to know involves harassment of those persons, and

(c) by which he intends to persuade any person (whether or not one of those mentioned above)—

(i) not to do something that he is entitled or required to do, or

(ii) to do something that he is not under any obligation to do.

(2) For the purposes of this section, the person whose course of conduct is in question ought to know that it amounts to or involves harassment of another if a reasonable person in possession of the same information would think the course of conduct amounted to harassment of the other.

(3) Subsection (1) or (1A) does not apply to a course of conduct if the person who pursued it shows—

(a) that it was pursued for the purpose of preventing or detecting crime,

(b) that it was pursued under any enactment or rule of law or to comply with any condition or requirement imposed by any person under any enactment, or

(c) that in the particular circumstances the pursuit of the course of conduct was reasonable.

[This section is printed as amended by the *SOCPA* 2005, s.125(1) and (2).]

Two incidents can constitute a "course of conduct" (see s.7(3), *post*, § 19–277g), but the fewer the incidents and the greater their separation in time, the less likely it is that they could be described as a "course of conduct": *Lau v. DPP* [2000] 1 F.L.R. 799, DC.

In *Pratt v. DPP*, 165 J.P. 800, DC, it was said that the concern which the 1997 Act had been intended to meet was that persons should not be put in a state of alarm or distress by the behaviour of others; and that purpose had to be borne in mind when deciding whether to prosecute where there was only a small number of incidents relied upon. On the facts, it was held that two incidents, three months apart, in the first of which the defendant threw a beaker of water at his wife, and in the second of which he chased her round their house, swearing and repeatedly questioning her, were close to the line, but the conviction could be sustained where the incidents took place against a background of an undertaking having been given in civil proceedings by the defendant not to use or threaten violence against his wife, nor to harass or pester her.

The word "person", as it appears in section 1(1) does not on its proper construction embrace a corporate entity as the potential victim: *Daiichi Pharmaceuticals U.K. Ltd v. Stop Huntingdon Animal Cruelty* [2004] 1 W.L.R. 1503, QBD (Owen J.) (as to which, see also *ante*, § 19–277a). The use of the singular, however, includes the plural; where, therefore, a person pursues a course of conduct against two (or more) people which amounts to harassment of them, a single offence is committed, and it matters not that individual acts forming part of that course of conduct are directed at one only of the victims: *DPP v. Dunn*, 165 J.P. 130, DC.

Under section 1(2), the test is entirely objective; the reasonable man is not to be imbued with the peculiar characteristics of the offender, such as his mental illness; and the test in section 1(3)(c) is even more clearly objective: *R. v. Colohan*, 165 J.P. 594, CA.

Offence of harassment

2.—(1) A person who pursues a course of conduct in breach of section 1(1) or (1A) is guilty of an offence. **19–277c**

(2) A person guilty of an offence under this section is liable on summary conviction to imprisonment for a term not exceeding *six months* [51 weeks], or a fine not exceeding level 5 on the standard scale, or both.

(3) [*Repealed by* Police Reform Act *2002, s.107 and Sched. 8*.]

[This section is printed as amended by the *SOCPA* 2005, s.125(1) and (3). The words in square brackets are substituted for the italicised words as from a day to be appointed: *CJA* 2003, s.281(4) and (5), but this substitution has no effect in relation to offences committed before the day on which it takes effect: *ibid.*, s.281(6).]

As to a conviction for an offence contrary to section 2 as an alternative verdict on a prosecution for an offence under section 4, see section 4(5), *post*, § 19–277e. In *R. v. Patel* [2005] 1 Cr.App.R. 27, CA, it was held that when directing a jury in relation to the offence of harassment as a possible alternative verdict in respect of a count under section 4, if the incidents upon which the principal charge was based were few in number and widely spaced in time, a cautious approach needed to be adopted; it was necessary for the jury to be given guidance in order for them to address the question whether there was a sufficient nexus between the incidents to have given rise to a "course of conduct"; and this was particularly so where there was a possibility that the jury, if they acquitted of the principal offence, would do so on the basis that they rejected the evidence of one or more of the incidents altogether, thus leaving an even smaller number of incidents more widely spread as the possible basis for finding that there was a course of conduct.

Where a defendant was charged with harassment contrary to section 2, and the course of conduct which was the subject of the charge lasted for two years and eight months, the provisions of section 127 of the *MCA* 1980 would not be violated so long as at least one of the incidents relied on occurred within the six month limitation period for summary proceedings; the offence was a continuing offence and was only complete when the last act was committed; and, in any event, the evidence prior to the six month limitation period could be admitted as "highly relevant" background evidence, subject to any arguments as to fairness under section 78 of the *PACE Act* 1984: *DPP v. Baker*, 169 J.P. 140, DC.

As to the "racially or religiously aggravated" version of this offence, see *post*, § 19–277j.

Protection from Harassment Act 1997, ss.3–5

Civil remedy

19–277d 3.—(1) An actual or apprehended breach of section 1(1) may be the subject of a claim in civil proceedings by the person who is or may be the victim of the course of conduct in question.

(2) [*Award of damages*.]

(3) Where—

(a) in such proceedings the High Court or a county court grants an injunction for the purpose of restraining the defendant from pursuing any conduct which amounts to harassment, and

(b) the plaintiff considers that the defendant has done anything which he is prohibited from doing by the injunction,

the plaintiff may apply for the issue of a warrant for the arrest of the defendant.

(4) An application under subsection (3) may be made—

(a) where the injunction was granted by the High Court, to a judge of that court, and

(b) where the injunction was granted by a county court, to a judge or district judge of that or any other county court.

(5) The judge or district judge to whom an application under subsection (3) is made may only issue a warrant if—

(a) the application is substantiated on oath, and

(b) the judge or district judge has reasonable grounds for believing that the defendant has done anything which he is prohibited from doing by the injunction.

(6) Where—

(a) the High Court or a county court grants an injunction for the purpose mentioned in subsection (3)(a), and

(b) without reasonable excuse the defendant does anything which he is prohibited from doing by the injunction,

he is guilty of an offence.

(7) Where a person is convicted of an offence under subsection (6) in respect of any conduct, that conduct is not punishable as a contempt of court.

(8) A person cannot be convicted of an offence under subsection (6) in respect of any conduct which has been punished as a contempt of court.

(9) A person guilty of an offence under subsection (6) is liable—

(a) on conviction on indictment, to imprisonment for a term not exceeding five years, or a fine, or both, or

(b) on summary conviction, to imprisonment for a term not exceeding *six* [12] months, or a fine not exceeding the statutory maximum, or both.

[This section is printed as amended by the *SOCPA* 2005, s.125(1) and (4). In subs. (9)(b), "12" is substituted for "six", as from a day to be appointed, by the *CJA* 2003, s.282(2) and (3). The increase has no application to offences committed before the substitution takes effect: s.282(4).]

Section 3A (inserted by the *SOCPA* 2005, s.125(1) and (5)) provides for the grant of an injunction where there is an actual or apprehended breach of section 1(1A). Subsection (3) provides that subsections (3) to (9) of section 3 apply in relation to an injunction granted under this section as they apply in relation to an injunction granted as mentioned in section 3(3)(a).

Putting people in fear of violence

4.—(1) A person whose course of conduct causes another to fear, on at least two occasions, that violence will be used against him is guilty of an offence if he knows or ought to know that his course of conduct will cause the other so to fear on each of those occasions. **19–277e**

(2) For the purposes of this section, the person whose course of conduct is in question ought to know that it will cause another to fear that violence will be used against him on any occasion if a reasonable person in possession of the same information would think the course of conduct would cause the other so to fear on that occasion.

(3) It is a defence for a person charged with an offence under this section to show that—

(a) his course of conduct was pursued for the purpose of preventing or detecting crime,

(b) his course of conduct was pursued under any enactment or rule of law or to comply with any condition or requirement imposed by any person under any enactment, or

(c) the pursuit of his course of conduct was reasonable for the protection of himself or another or for the protection of his or another's property.

(4) A person guilty of an offence under this section is liable—

(a), (b) [*identical to s.3(9)(a), (b) (including the prospective amendment)*, ante].

(5) If on the trial on indictment of a person charged with an offence under this section the jury find him not guilty of the offence charged, they may find him guilty of an offence under section 2.

(6) The Crown Court has the same powers and duties in relation to a person who is by virtue of subsection (5) convicted before it of an offence under section 2 as a magistrates' court would have on convicting him of the offence.

As to the "racially or religiously aggravated" version of this offence, see *post*, § 19–277. As to section 4(5), see *R. v. Livesey* [2007] 1 Cr.App.R. 35, in which the Court of Appeal followed *R. v. Carson*, 92 Cr.App.R. 236, CA (*post*, § 29–37).

There is no reason, in directing the jury as to the ingredients of the offence under this section, not to use the words of the subsection, and, on such a prosecution, a direction as to the effect of subsection (2) ought to be routine: *R. v. Henley* [2000] 3 *Archbold News* 3, CA.

It is not necessary that the defendant's conduct is directed at the complainant; nor is it necessary that there be direct evidence from the complainant as to having feared that violence would be used against him, but such evidence should be elicited where possible; in its absence, however, it was open to the court to draw appropriate inferences: *R. v. DPP*, 165 J.P. 349, DC.

In *Caurti v. DPP* [2002] Crim.L.R. 131, DC, it was held that on a prosecution under section 4, it must be proved that at least one person feared violence would be used against himself on at least two occasions; it is not permissible to invoke section 6 of the *Interpretation Act* 1978 (singular includes plural (Appendix B–6)) so as to re-draft section 4 in order to allow of a conviction where on at least two occasions any member of a group (such as a household) was caused to fear for the safety of any other member of the group.

In *R. v. Hills* [2001] 1 F.L.R. 580, CA, a prosecution under section 4(1), which was based on two incidents six months apart between two people who were partners and lived together, was said to have been "miles away" from the stalking type of offence for which the Act was intended.

Restraining orders [on conviction]

5.—(1) A court sentencing or otherwise dealing with a person ("the defendant") convicted of an offence *under section 2 or 4* may (as well as sentencing him or dealing with him in any other way) make an order under this section. **19–277f**

(2) The order may, for the purpose of protecting the victim or victims of the offence, or any other person mentioned in the order, from *further* conduct which—

(a) amounts to harassment, or
(b) will cause a fear of violence,

prohibit the defendant from doing anything described in the order.

(3) The order may have effect for a specified period or until further order.

[(3A) In proceedings under this section both the prosecution and the defence may lead, as further evidence, any evidence that would be admissible in proceedings for an injunction under section 3.]

(4) The prosecutor, the defendant or any other person mentioned in the order may apply to the court which made the order for it to be varied or discharged by a further order.

[(4A) Any person mentioned in the order is entitled to be heard on the hearing of an application under subsection (4).]

(5) If without reasonable excuse the defendant does anything which he is prohibited from doing by an order under this section, he is guilty of an offence.

(6) [*Identical to s.4(4) (including the prospective amendment)*, ante.]

[(7) A court dealing with a person for an offence under this section may vary or discharge the order in question by a further order.]

[This section is printed as amended by the *SOCPA* 2005, s.125(1) and (6); and, as further amended, as from a day to be appointed, by the *Domestic Violence, Crime and Victims Act* 2004, ss.12(1) to (4), and 58(1), and Sched. 10, para. 43 (omission of italicised words, insertion of words in square brackets). The amendments made by the 2004 Act do not apply where the conviction occurs before the commencement of the amendment: 2004 Act, s.59, and Sched. 12, para. 43.]

In *R. v. Debnath* [2006] 2 Cr.App.R.(S.) 25, CA, it was held that since an offence of harassment may be committed by publishing the truth about someone, a restraining order under this section, which prohibited the offender from publishing true information, did not of necessity amount to a violation of the offender's right to freedom of expression under Article 10 of the ECHR (*ante*, § 16–119); in exceptional circumstances (here, the offender had shown that she was incapable of distinguishing between what was true and what was false, and, if permitted to publish any information about the victims, she would continue to harass them), the wide terms of the order were necessary for the prevention of crime and were justified under Article 10(2) (being (i) prescribed by law, (ii) in furtherance of a legitimate aim, (iii) necessary in a democratic society, and (iv) proportionate).

In *R. v. Mann* [2000] L.S. Gazette, April 6, 41, CA, it was held that an order under section 5 must identify the person intended to be protected. The order made by the Crown Court was further varied from one which provided that the defendant must not "contact or communicate with any member of staff" at a hostel, to one that prohibited "conduct which amounts to harassment, or which would cause a fear of violence". Such a formula, however, defeats the purpose of the legislation. Harassment and causing a fear of violence are proscribed and punishable under the preceding provisions of the Act. The purpose of a restraining order is to prohibit particular conduct with a view to preventing offences under section 2 or 4. For example, if the victim is a nurse, it would be a legitimate use of section 5 to make an order prohibiting the defendant from entering the grounds of the hospital. If he does so, then he will commit a separate offence, enabling the law to intervene at an earlier stage than that of actual harassment of the victim. *Cf.* the case law on the making of anti-social behaviour orders and the terms thereof, *ante*, §§ 5–884 *et seq.*

The only question on an application, under section 5(4), to discharge a restraining order, was whether something had changed so that the continuance of the order was neither necessary nor appropriate; otherwise an applicant would be entitled to have the merits of an earlier decision re-determined without appealing against it, and it would in any case be contrary to the principle of finality in litigation and potentially wasteful of scarce judicial resources, and, accordingly, contrary to the public interest: *Shaw v. DPP* [2005] 7 *Archbold News* 2, DC.

The duration of a restraining order may be extended (with or without limit of time) under subsection (4) where something has changed so as to make such a course necessary or appropriate (applying *Shaw v. DPP*, *ante*); there being no express provision to the contrary, and the duration of the order (whether for a specified period or without limit of time) being just as much a term as any specific provision, section 5(4) should be construed so as to enable the court to protect a victim, or potential victim, from harassment in the most expeditious way: *DPP v. Hall* [2006] 1 W.L.R. 1000, DC.

Where a restraining order is varied, it is desirable that the order as varied should be drawn up as a fresh document containing all its terms: *R. v. Liddle* [2002] 1 *Archbold News* 2, CA.

Protection from Harassment Act 1997, s.5A

[Restraining orders on acquittal

5A.—(1) A court before which a person ("the defendant") is acquitted of an offence may, if it considers it necessary to do so to protect a person from harassment by the defendant, make an order prohibiting the defendant from doing anything described in the order. **19–277fa**

(2) Subsections (3) to (7) of section 5 apply to an order under this section as they apply to an order under that one.

(3) Where the Court of Appeal allow an appeal against conviction they may remit the case to the Crown Court to consider whether to proceed under this section.

(4) Where—

(a) the Crown Court allows an appeal against conviction, or

(b) a case is remitted to the Crown Court under subsection (3),

the reference in subsection (1) to a court before which a person is acquitted of an offence is to be read as referring to that court.

(5) A person made subject to an order under this section has the same right of appeal against the order as if—

(a) he had been convicted of the offence in question before the court which made the order, and

(b) the order had been made under section 5.]

[This section is inserted as from a day to be appointed by the *Domestic Violence, Crime and Victims Act* 2004, s.12(5).]

Protection from Harassment Act 1997, ss.7, 12

Interpretation of this group of sections

7.—(1) This section applies for the interpretation of sections *1 to 5* [1 to 5A]. **19–277g**

(2) References to harassing a person include alarming the person or causing the person distress.

(3) A "course of conduct" must involve—

(a) in the case of conduct in relation to a single person (see section 1(1)), conduct on at least two occasions in relation to that person, or

(b) in the case of conduct in relation to two or more persons (see section 1(1A)), conduct on at least one occasion in relation to each of those persons.

(3A) A person's conduct on any occasion shall be taken, if aided, abetted, counselled or procured by another—

(a) to be conduct on that occasion of the other (as well as conduct of the person whose conduct it is); and

(b) to be conduct in relation to which the other's knowledge and purpose, and what he ought to have known, are the same as they were in relation to what was contemplated or reasonably foreseeable at the time of the aiding, abetting, counselling or procuring.

(4) "Conduct" includes speech.

(5) References to a person, in the context of the harassment of a person, are references to a person who is an individual.

[This section is printed as amended by the *CJPA* 2001, s.44(1); and the *SOCPA* 2005, s.125(1) and (7); and as amended, as from a day to be appointed, by the *Domestic Violence, Crime and Victims Act* 2004, s.58(1), and Sched. 10, para. 44 (substitution of words in square brackets for italicised words). The amendment made by the 2004 Act does not apply where the acquittal (or, where s.5A(5) applies, the allowing of the appeal) occurs before the commencement of the amendment: 2004 Act, s.59, and Sched. 12, para. 5(3).]

In *Kelly v. DPP*, 166 J.P. 621, QBD (Burton J.), the making of three telephone calls within five minutes of each other was held to be capable of constituting a "course of conduct" for the purposes of this Act, since it involved conduct on "at least two occasions"; and the fact that the recipient heard them all on the same occasion (when she accessed her voicemail) was irrelevant to this issue. *Kelly* and *Pratt v. DPP*, *ante*, § 19–277b, were considered in *Buckley and Smith v. DPP* [2008] A.C.D. 39, DC, where it was held that a series of four closely related incidents on the same day were sufficiently distinct, at least as to two of them, to amount to a course of conduct.

National security, etc.

19–277h **12.**—(1) If the Secretary of State certifies that in his opinion anything done by a specified person on a specified occasion related to—

(a) national security,

(b) the economic well-being of the United Kingdom, or

(c) the prevention or detection of serious crime,

and was done on behalf of the Crown, the certificate is conclusive evidence that this Act does not apply to any conduct of that person on that occasion.

(2) In subsection (1), "specified" means specified in the certificate in question.

(3) A document purporting to be a certificate under subsection (1) is to be received in evidence and, unless the contrary is proved, be treated as being such a certificate.

Sentencing considerations

19–277i *R. v. Liddle*; *R. v. Hayes* [1999] 3 All E.R. 816, CA, was formerly regarded as the leading case in relation to sentencing for offences under the 1997 Act. It has, however, been removed from the compendium of cases regarded by the Sentencing Guidelines Council as considered guidance. This was presumably on the basis that it has been overtaken by the council's definitive guidelines on breach of a protective order and on domestic violence (Appendix K–81, K–82).

C. RACIAL OR RELIGIOUS AGGRAVATION

Crime and Disorder Act 1998, s.32

Racially or religiously aggravated harassment etc.

19–277j **32.**—(1) A person is guilty of an offence under this section if he commits—

(a) an offence under section 2 of the *Protection from Harassment Act* 1997 (offence of harassment); or

(b) an offence under section 4 of that Act (putting people in fear of violence),

which is racially or religiously aggravated for the purposes of this section.

(2) [*Repealed by* Police Reform Act *2002, s.108 and Sched. 8.*]

(3) A person guilty of an offence falling within subsection (1)(a) above shall be liable—

(a) on summary conviction, to imprisonment for a term not exceeding *six* [12] months or to a fine not exceeding the statutory maximum, or to both;

(b) on conviction on indictment, to imprisonment for a term not exceeding two years or to a fine, or to both.

(4) A person guilty of an offence falling within subsection (1)(b) above shall be liable—

(a) on summary conviction, to imprisonment for a term not exceeding *six* [12] months or to a fine not exceeding the statutory maximum, or to both;

(b) on conviction on indictment, to imprisonment for a term not exceeding seven years or to a fine, or to both.

(5) If, on the trial on indictment of a person charged with an offence falling within subsection (1)(a) above, the jury find him not guilty of the offence charged, they may find him guilty of the basic offence mentioned in that provision.

(6) If, on the trial on indictment of a person charged with an offence falling within subsection (1)(b) above, the jury find him not guilty of the offence charged, they may find him guilty of an offence falling within subsection (1)(a) above.

(7) *Section 5 of the* Protection from Harassment Act *1997 (restraining orders) shall have effect in relation to a person convicted of an offence under this section as if the reference in subsection (1) of that section to an offence under section 2 or 4 included a reference to an offence under this section.*

[The words "or religiously" were inserted by the *Anti-terrorism, Crime and Security*

Act 2001, s.39(5) and (6)(d). In subss. (3)(a) and (4)(a), "12" is substituted for "six", as from a day to be appointed, by the *CJA* 2003, s.282(2) and (3). The increase has no application to offences committed before the substitutions take effect: s.282(4). Subs. (7) is repealed as from a day to be appointed: *Domestic Violence, Crime and Victims Act* 2004, s.58(1), and Sched. 10, para. 48; but this repeal does not apply where the conviction occurs before it takes effect: *ibid.*, s.59, and Sched. 12, para. 5(1).]

As to the meaning of "racially or religiously aggravated" for the purposes of this section, see section 28 of the 1998 Act, *ante*, § 5–227.

As to the framing of an indictment, see *ante*, § 19–214.

XI. ILL-TREATMENT OF PERSONS OF UNSOUND MIND

(1) Statute

Mental Health Act 1983, s.127

Ill-treatment of patients

127.—(1) It shall be an offence for any person who is an officer on the staff of or otherwise employed in, or who is one of the managers of, a hospital, independent hospital or care home— **19–278**

(a) to ill-treat or wilfully to neglect a patient for the time being receiving treatment for mental disorder as an in-patient in that hospital or home; or

(b) to ill-treat or wilfully to neglect, on the premises of which the hospital or home forms part, a patient for the time being receiving such treatment there as an out-patient.

(2A) [*Repealed by* Mental Health Act *2007, s.55, and Sched. 11, Pt 5.*]

(2) It shall be an offence for any individual to ill-treat or wilfully to neglect a mentally disordered patient who is for the time being subject to his guardianship under this Act or otherwise in his custody or care (whether by virtue of any legal or moral obligation or otherwise).

(3) Any person guilty of an offence under this section shall be liable—

(a) on summary conviction, to imprisonment for a term not exceeding *six* [12] months or to a fine not exceeding the statutory maximum or to both;

(b) on conviction on indictment, to imprisonment for a term not exceeding five years or to a fine, or to both.

(4) No proceedings shall be instituted for an offence under this section except by or with the consent of the Director of Public Prosecutions.

[This section is printed as amended by the *Mental Health (Patients in the Community) Act* 1995, s.1(2), and Sched. 1, para. 18; the *Care Standards Act* 2000, s.116 and Sched. 4, para. 9(1), (8); and the *MHA* 2007, s.42 (substituting "five" for "two" in subs. (3), with effect from October 1, 2007 (*Mental Health Act 2007 (Commencement No. 3) Order* 2007 (S.I. 2007 No. 2798))). In subs. (3)(a), "12" is substituted for "six", as from a day to be appointed, by the *CJA* 2003, s.282(2) and (3). The increase has no application to offences committed before the substitution takes effect: s.282(4).]

"Statutory maximum" means the prescribed sum within the meaning of section 32 of the *MCA* 1980 (*ante*, § 1–75aa): *Interpretation Act* 1978, Sched. 1 (Appendix B–28).

(2) Indictment

STATEMENT OF OFFENCE

Ill-treating [or *Wilfully neglecting*] *a patient, contrary to section 127(1) of the* Mental Health Act *1983*. **19–279**

PARTICULARS OF OFFENCE

A B, between the —— day of —— and the —— day of ——, 20—, then being an officer [or *manager, nurse, attendant, servant* or *employee*] *of a certain institution for patients, to wit the X Y Mental Hospital at ——, ill-treated* [or *wilfully neglected*] *J N, a patient in the said institution.*

Offences of ill-treatment and wilful neglect are continuing offences: see *R. v. Hayles* [1969] 1 Q.B. 364, 53 Cr.App.R. 36, CA.

(3) Class of offence and mode of trial

19–280 This offence is a class 3 offence, *ante*, § 2–17, triable either way (s.127(3)).

(4) Sentence

19–281 Imprisonment not exceeding two years, or a fine, or both, s.127(3), *ante*.

(5) Ingredients of the offence

19–282 Section 127 was considered in *R. v. Newington*, 91 Cr.App.R. 247, CA. The court advised that allegations of neglect and of ill-treatment of a patient should be set out in separate counts, but did not rule as to whether a count containing both allegations would be bad for duplicity. It set out a model direction in respect of matters which have to be proved for a conviction of ill-treatment as follows: "1. deliberate conduct by the defendant which could properly be described as ill-treatment whether or not that ill-treatment damaged or threatened to damage the health of the victim; and 2. a guilty mind, involving either an appreciation by the defendant at the time that he was inexcusably ill-treating a patient, or that he was reckless as to whether he was inexcusably acting in that way."

In *R. v. Davies and Poolton* [2000] Crim.L.R. 297, CA, it was held that the question whether a particular institution was a "hospital or mental nursing home" is a question of fact; if this is in issue, the judge should direct the jury by reference to the statutory definition in the *Registered Homes Act* 1984, s.22(1), and should assist them by referring, as appropriate to the statutory definitions of alternative possibilities (*e.g.* "residential care home" (s.1 of the 1984 Act) or "children's home" (*Children Act* 1989, s.1)); registration or non-registration as a particular form of home is not decisive; and as to the mental element of the offence, it is not necessary to prove an awareness on the part of the accused of the facts which constitute the institution a "hospital" or "mental nursing home", nor of the facts which constitute the person ill-treated or neglected a "patient" (*i.e.* "a person suffering or appearing to be suffering from mental disorder") or of the facts which constitute "treatment for mental disorder".

As to wilful neglect, see *R. v. Sheppard* [1981] A.C. 394, *ante*, § 17–47 and *post*, §§ 19–300, 19–303.

XII. FEMALE GENITAL MUTILATION

Female Genital Mutilation Act 2003, ss.1–3

Offence of female genital mutilation

19–283 **1.**—(1) A person is guilty of an offence if he excises, infibulates or otherwise mutilates the whole or any part of a girl's labia majora, labia minora or clitoris.

(2) But no offence is committed by an approved person who performs—

(a) a surgical operation on a girl which is necessary for her physical or mental health, or

(b) a surgical operation on a girl who is in any stage of labour, or has just given birth, for purposes connected with the labour or birth.

(3) The following are approved persons—

(a) in relation to an operation falling within subsection (2)(a), a registered medical practitioner,

(b) in relation to an operation falling within subsection (2)(b), a registered medical practitioner, a registered midwife or a person undergoing a course of training with a view to becoming such a practitioner or midwife.

(4) There is also no offence committed by a person who—

(a) performs a surgical operation falling within subsection (2)(a) or (b) outside the United Kingdom, and

(b) in relation to such an operation exercises functions corresponding to those of an approved person.

(5) For the purpose of determining whether an operation is necessary for the mental health of a girl it is immaterial whether she or any other person believes that the operation is required as a matter of custom or ritual.

Offence of assisting a girl to mutilate her own genitals

2. A person is guilty of an offence if he aids, abets, counsels or procures a girl to excise, infibulate or otherwise mutilate the whole or any part of her own labia majora, labia minora or clitoris. **19–284**

Offence of assisting a non-UK person to mutilate overseas a girl's genitalia

3.—(1) A person is guilty of an offence if he aids, abets, counsels or procures a person who is not a United Kingdom national or permanent United Kingdom resident to do a relevant act of female genital mutilation outside the United Kingdom. **19–285**

(2) An act is a relevant act of female genital mutilation if—

(a) it is done in relation to a United Kingdom national or permanent United Kingdom resident, and

(b) it would, if done by such a person, constitute an offence under section 1.

(3) But no offence is committed if the relevant act of female genital mutilation—

(a) is a surgical operation falling within section 1(2)(a) or (b), and

(b) is performed by a person who, in relation to such an operation, is an approved person or exercises functions corresponding to those of an approved person.

Extra-territorial acts

Section 4(1) extends sections 1 to 3 to any act done outside the United Kingdom by a United Kingdom national or permanent United Kingdom resident. If an offence under the Act is committed outside the United Kingdom, proceedings may be taken, and the offence may for incidental purposes be treated as having been committed, anywhere in England, Wales or Northern Ireland (s.4(2)). **19–285a**

Mode of trial and penalties

All offences under the Act are triable either way and are punishable on conviction on indictment with 14 years' imprisonment or a fine, or both; and, on summary conviction, with six months' imprisonment (12 months as from a day to be appointed: *CJA* 2003, s.282(2) and (3); but not in relation to offences committed before the increase takes effect: s.282(4)), or a fine not exceeding the statutory maximum, or both: s.5. **19–285b**

Definitions

"Girl" includes "woman": s.6(1). A "United Kingdom national" is an individual who is a British citizen, a British overseas territories citizen, a British National (Overseas) citizen, a person who under the *British Nationality Act* 1981 is a British subject, or a British protected person within the meaning of that Act: s.6(2); and a "permanent United Kingdom resident" is an individual who is settled in the United Kingdom, within the meaning of the *Immigration Act* 1971: s.6(3). **19–285c**

XIII. OFFENCES RELATING TO CHILDREN AND YOUNG PERSONS

A. OFFENCES RELATING TO THE TREATMENT, CONTROL AND MAINTENANCE OF CHILDREN AND YOUNG PERSONS

(1) Abandonment of children under two

Offences against the Person Act 1861, s.27

Abandoning or exposing children under two years of age whereby life is endangered

27. Whosoever shall unlawfully abandon or expose any child, being under the age of two years, whereby the life of such child shall be endangered, or the health of such child shall have been or shall be likely to be permanently injured, shall be guilty of a misdemeanor, and being convicted thereof shall be liable ... to *imprisonment* ... for any term not exceeding five years. **19–286**

[This section is printed as repealed in part by the *Statute Law Revision Act* 1892; and the *Statute Law Revision (No. 2) Act* 1893; and as amended by the *Penal Servitude Act* 1891, s.1(1); and the *CJA* 1948, s.1(1).]

In practice this section is superseded by the *CYPA* 1933, s.1, *post*, § 19–291.

As to evidence and procedure, see also the *CYPA* 1933, ss.41 (*post*, § 19–325), 42 **19–287** (*ante*, § 10–26) and 43 (*ante*, § 10–47). As to presumption of age, see *CYPA* 1933, s.99, *post*, § 19–326.

Indictment

19–287a For a specimen indictment, see the 1996 edition of this work. "Abandoning" is a continuous offence: *R. v. White* (1871) L.R. 1 C.C.R. 311.

Sentence

19–288 Imprisonment for not more than five years: s.27, *ante*.

An offence contrary to section 27 is a specified violent offence within Schedule 15 to the *CJA* 2003 (*ante*, § 5–299).

Mode of trial

19–289 This offence is triable either way: *MCA* 1980, s.17(1) and Sched. 1, *ante*, § 1–75af.

Ingredients of the offence

19–290 In order to sustain an indictment under this section it is only necessary to prove that the defendant wilfully abandoned or exposed the child mentioned in the indictment; that the child was then under two years of age; and that its life was thereby endangered or its health had been or then was likely to be permanently injured. "Abandonment" means leaving a child to its fate: *R. v. Boulden*, 41 Cr.App.R. 105, CCA; and see *post*, § 19–304.

A woman who was living apart from her husband, and who had the actual custody of their child, under two years of age, left it outside the father's door, telling him she had done so. He knowingly allowed it to remain lying outside his door from 7 p.m. until 1 a.m., when it was removed by a constable, being then cold and stiff. Upon this state of facts, it was held, that although the father had not the actual custody and possession of the child, yet, as he was by law bound to provide for it, his allowing it to remain where he did was an abandonment and exposure of the child by him, whereby its life was endangered, within the meaning of section 27: *R. v. White*, *ante*.

(2) Cruelty

(a) *Statute*

Children and Young Persons Act 1933, s.1

Cruelty to persons under sixteen

19–291 **1.**—(1) If any person who has attained the age of sixteen years and has responsibility for any child or young person under that age, wilfully assaults, ill-treats, neglects, abandons, or exposes him, or causes or procures him to be assaulted, ill-treated, neglected, abandoned, or exposed, in a manner likely to cause him unnecessary suffering or injury to health (including injury to or loss of sight, or hearing, or limb, or organ of the body, and any mental derangement), that person shall be guilty of an offence, and shall be liable—

(a) on conviction on indictment, to a fine … or alternatively, … or in addition thereto, to imprisonment for any term not exceeding ten years;

(b) on summary conviction, to a fine not exceeding the prescribed sum or alternatively, … or in addition thereto, to imprisonment for any term not exceeding *six* [12] months.

(2) For the purposes of this section—

(a) a parent or other person legally liable to maintain a child or young person, or the legal guardian of a child or young person shall be deemed to have neglected him in a manner likely to cause injury to his health if he has failed to provide adequate food, clothing, medical aid or lodging for him, or if, having been unable otherwise to provide such food, clothing, medical aid or lodging, he has failed to take steps to procure it to be provided under the enactments applicable in that behalf;

(b) where it is proved that the death of an infant under three years of age was caused by suffocation (not being suffocation caused by disease or the presence of any foreign body in the throat or air passages of the infant) while the infant was in bed with some other person who has attained the age of sixteen years, that other person shall, if he was, when he went to bed, under the influence of drink, be deemed to have neglected the infant in a manner likely to cause injury to its health.

(3) A person may be convicted of an offence under this section— **19–292**

(a) notwithstanding that actual suffering or injury to health, or the likelihood of actual suffering or injury to health, was obviated by the action of another person;

(b) notwithstanding the death of the child or young person in question.

[This section is printed as repealed in part by the *CYPA* 1963, s.64(1), (3), Sched. 3, para. 1, and Sched. 5; the *CLA* 1967, s.10(2) and Sched. 3; the *Children Act* 1975, s.108(1)(b), and Sched. 4, Pt III; and the *CJA* 1988, s.170(2), and Sched. 16; and as amended by the *National Assistance (Adaptation of Enactments) Regulations* 1950 (S.I. 1951 No. 174); the *MCA* 1980, s.32(2); the *CJA* 1988, s.45(1); the *Children Act* 1989, s.108(4), (5), and Sched. 12, para. 2, and Sched. 13, para. 2; and the *Children Act* 2004, s.64, and Sched. 5, Pt 5. In subs. (1)(b), "12" is substituted for "six", as from a day to be appointed, by the *CJA* 2003, s.282(2) and (3). The increase has no application to offences committed before the substitution takes effect: s.282(4).]

(b) *Indictment*

STATEMENT OF OFFENCE

Cruelty to a person under 16, contrary to section 1(1) of the Children and Young Persons Act *1933*. **19–293**

PARTICULARS OF OFFENCE

A B, between the —— day of —— and the —— day of ——, 20—, being a person who had attained the age of 16 years, and having the responsibility for J N a child under that age, wilfully ill-treated the said child, in a manner likely to cause unnecessary suffering to the said child or injury to its health.

As to the inclusion of other counts in the indictment, see *R. v. Roe*, 51 Cr.App.R. 10, CA. **19–294**

The word "wilfully" governs the words "assaults, ill-treats, neglects", etc. It should be inserted in the count: *R. v. Walker*, 24 Cr.App.R. 117, CCA. As to the meaning of "wilfully", see *post*, § 19–300.

A count alleging "neglect" or "abandonment and exposure" may be added where applicable.

Section 1(1) is not divided into watertight compartments constituting five distinct offences, but creates a single offence dealing with various forms of cruelty. Where the indictment charges ill-treating and the evidence shows conduct which comes within that word, there may be a conviction, even though another word (*e.g.* neglecting) might have been more appropriate: *R. v. Hayles* [1969] 1 Q.B. 364, 53 Cr.App.R. 36, CA. *Hayles* was applied (with evident reluctance) in *R. v. Beard (S. D.)*, 85 Cr.App.R. 395, CA. Having cited a passage in the *Hayles* judgment (at pp. 369, 40), the court in *Beard* stated:

> "All of that is clearly binding upon us. That we must accept although the consequences of having to do so may in some circumstances lead, so we think, to the giving of directions which may cause a jury to convict upon an uncertain basis and moreover, present to a judge, following conviction, a difficult problem of sentencing. That problem can ... be overcome by asking the jury to explain the basis upon which a conviction has been made, but that is the sort of request to a jury which ought if possible to be avoided. It is, in our experience, very seldom resorted to.... (W)e take this opportunity to say that the decision in *Hayles*, in our opinion, imposes a burden upon a prosecutor when drafting an indictment under section 1(1) to choose with care that word which appears in the subsection which more precisely and appropriately than any other describes the conduct complained of. If that had been done in the present case we think the word 'neglect' and not 'ill-treatment' would have been chosen.... There was sufficient evidence of neglect to found the conviction recorded. In any event, following *Hayles*, the conviction must stand because neglect amounts to ill-treatment" (at pp. 401–402).

In *R. v. Young*, 97 Cr.App.R. 280, CA, the particulars of offence had alleged that the appellant had assaulted, ill-treated or neglected the child. The court approved this course: on the basis that the section creates only one offence which can be committed in a number of ways, this would appear to be correct as a matter of law. It corresponds with the almost invariable practice in relation to the second part of section 22(1) of the *Theft Act* 1968: see *post*, §§ 21–272 *et seq*. However, it does not appear to accord with the spirit of the observations of the court in *Beard*, *ante*, which was not referred to in the judgment. A disadvantage to having alternatives in the same count is that the judge will not know on what basis the jury have convicted unless he asks them: such questioning of a jury is a practice which has been disapproved of by the Court of Appeal, as in *Beard*. The better course, it is submitted, when there is good reason for alleging alternatives, is to have two or more counts. The particular point in *Young* concerned a submission on behalf of the appellant that the jury should have been directed that they had to be unanimous as to the set of facts alleged to constitute the offence. This submission was based on *R. v. Brown (K.)*, 79 Cr.App.R. 115: *ante*, §§ 4–391 *et seq*. It was held that, whilst the members of the jury might well differ as to the emphasis to place on different incidents, as long as they were unanimous that cruelty in the sense alleged by the prosecution had been established, that was sufficient.

(c) *Class of offence and mode of trial*

19–295 This offence is a class 3 offence, *ante*, § 2–17, triable either way (s.1(1), *ante*).

(d) *Sentence*

19–296 Imprisonment not exceeding 10 years, or a fine, or both (s.1(1), *ante*).

An offence contrary to section 1 is a specified violent offence within Schedule 15 to the *CJA* 2003 (*ante*, § 5–299).

The Sentencing Guidelines Council has issued a definitive guideline on assaults on children and cruelty to a child: see Appendix K–131 *et seq.*

(e) *Basis of joint liability of parents*

19–296a If two people are jointly indicted for the commission of a crime and the evidence does not point to one rather than the other, and there is no evidence that they were acting in concert, the jury ought to acquit both: *R. v. Abbott* [1955] 2 Q.B. 497 at 503, 39 Cr.App.R. 141 at 148, CCA, *per* Lord Goddard C.J. This statement of the general principle has been considered in the context of acts of violence committed upon a child within the privacy of the home by one or other or both "parents". The basis of joint liability in such cases was considered in *R. v. Gibson and Gibson*, 80 Cr.App.R. 24, CA; *R. v. Lane and Lane*, 82 Cr.App.R. 5, CA; *R. v. Russell and Russell*, 85 Cr.App.R. 388, CA; and *R. v. Beard (S.D.)*, 85 Cr.App.R. 395, CA: see *ante*, § 19–35.

(f) *Ingredients of the offence*

"Age of sixteen"

19–297 Strict proof of age is not necessary when the court can judge from appearances or from the circumstances of the case: *R. v. Cox* [1898] 1 Q.B. 179; see also *R. v. Viasani*, 31 J.P. 260 and *R. v. Turner* [1910] 1 K.B. 346, 3 Cr.App.R. 103, CCA. A birth certificate, coupled with evidence of identity, is legal evidence of the age of the child mentioned in the certificate, but the age may be proved by any other admissible evidence: *Cox*, *ante*. As to presumption and determination of age, see the *CYPA* 1933, s.99, *post*, § 19–326.

"Responsibility for"

19–298 See section 17 of the 1933 Act, as substituted by the *Children Act* 1989, *post*, § 19–324. In *Liverpool Society for the Prevention of Cruelty to Children v. Jones* [1914] 3 K.B. 813, DC, it was said that whether or not a person has the "custody, charge or care" of a child may often be a question of fact for the jury. This would appear to apply equally to the expression "responsibility for" which was introduced by the 1989 Act to replace the "custody, charge or care" formula.

Child or young person

19–299 A child is a person under 14 years of age and a young person is a person who has attained the age of 14 years but is under 18: *CYPA* 1933, s.107(1) (*post*, § 19–328). The offence, however, is restricted to the ill-treatment, etc., of persons under 16.

As to proof of age, see *ante*, § 19–297.

Wilfully

19–300 This word qualifies all five verbs (assaults, ill-treats, neglects, abandons or exposes), and makes it clear that any offence under section 1 requires *mens rea*, a state of mind on the part of the offender directed to the particular act or failure to act that constitutes the *actus reus* and warrants the description "wilful": *R. v. Sheppard* [1981] A.C. 394, HL. *Sheppard* is the leading authority on the interpretation of "wilful" in a criminal statute and is considered in more detail in § 17–47, *ante*.

Assault

19–301 It is clear from *R. v. Hatton* [1925] 2 K.B. 322, 19 Cr.App.R. 29, CCA, that in order for an assault to fall within this section, there must be something more than a mere common assault. The section provides that not only must there be a "wilful assault" but it must also be committed "in a manner likely to cause him unnecessary suffering or injury to his health".

Section 58 of the *Children Act* 2004 provides that in relation to an offence under this section, battery of a child cannot be justified on the ground that it constituted reasonable punishment.

Ill-treat

19–302 There is no definition of this word in the Act, but one may assume that it is intended to cover a course of wilful ill-treatment, and that bullying or frightening will suffice, or any course of conduct calculated to cause unnecessary suffering or injury to health. There is no need to prove an assault or battery (as to which see *ante*, §§ 19–166 *et seq.*) but clearly a series of assaults, even though not coming within the scope of the assaults envisaged by the section, might amount to wilful ill-treatment.

Neglect

19–303 In giving the leading judgment in *Sheppard* (*ante*, § 19–300, at p. 400G), Lord Diplock said: "The *actus reus* of the offence with which the accused were charged in the instant case does not involve construing the verb 'neglect' for the offence fell within the deeming provision;" (s.1(2)(a)) "and the only question as respects the *actus reus* was: did the parents fail to provide ... medical aid that was in fact adequate in view of his actual state of health at the relevant time? This ... is a pure question of objective fact to be determined in the light of what has become known by the date of the trial to have been the child's actual state of health at the relevant time." If the answer was, "Yes", then, by virtue of the deeming provision, the *actus reus*, namely neglect in a manner likely to cause injury to health, was established, but it still had to be proved that the neglect was wilful; as to that, see *ante*, §§ 17–47, 19–300.

It was held in *R. v. Ryland* (1867) L.R. 1 C.C.R. 99, that the word "neglect" sufficiently alleged the ability of the parents to provide for the child and that it was not necessary for the indictment to allege specifically that the parents had means. A failure to resort to the assistance authorities for the means of maintaining a child where a parent cannot do so out of his own pocket would presumably amount to neglect: see s.1(2), *ante*, § 19–291. Refusal to permit an operation may be, but is not necessarily, such a failure to provide medical aid as to amount to wilful neglect causing injury to health. The question is one of fact to be decided in each case upon the evidence: *Oakey v. Jackson* [1914] 1 K.B. 216, DC. As to a deliberate omission to supply medical or surgical aid on conscientious grounds, see *R. v. Senior* [1899] 1 Q.B. 283, which is fully explained in *Sheppard*, *ante*.

Where a father who earned a sufficient wage did not pay over to his wife enough to clothe and feed the children properly, it was held to be no defence for the father, when charged with neglect, to say that by resort to the assistance authorities the mother might have obviated the effects of the father's neglect: *Cole v. Pendleton*, 60 J.P. 359. Evidence of the possession by the accused of such means at a date before the neglect as would presumably not be exhausted at the date of the neglect is some evidence of the possession of means at the date of the neglect: *R. v. Jones* (1901) 19 Cox 678.

Expose or abandon

19–304 "Abandonment" means leaving a child to its fate: *R. v. Boulden*, 41 Cr.App.R. 105, CCA. *Cf. R. v. Whibley*, 26 Cr.App.R. 184, CCA. As to the evidence necessary to prove exposure, see *R. v. Williams (John)*, 4 Cr.App.R. 89, CCA, where it was held that the exposure need not necessarily consist of physically placing the child somewhere with intent to injure him.

See also *ante*, § 19–290, as to exposure and abandonment under section 27 of the *Offences against the Person Act* 1861.

In a manner likely to cause unnecessary suffering or injury to health

19–305 These words qualify all the preceding words "assaults", "ill-treats", "neglects", etc.: *R. v. Hatton* [1925] 2 K.B. 322, 19 Cr.App.R. 29, CCA. The suffering or injury must be something more than a slight fright or some small mental anxiety: *R. v. Whibley*, *ante*.

Direct proof that the neglect, ill-treatment, etc., did in fact, or was likely to, cause unnecessary suffering or injury to health is not required. It may be proved from the evidence of the ill-treatment or neglect, etc.: *R. v. Brenton* (1890) 111 C.C.C. Sess.Pap. 309; and see *Cole v. Pendleton*, 60 J.P. 359.

It is no defence that the actual injury was caused by the act of a third party: *R. v. Connor* [1908] 2 K.B. 26.

(g) *Evidence of child and parent*

19–306 As to the giving of evidence by children generally, see *ante*, §§ 8–32 *et seq.* See also the *CYPA* 1933, ss.41 (*post*, § 19–325), 42 (*ante*, § 10–26) and 43 (*ante*, § 10–47).

As to the compellability and competence of the defendant's spouse, see the *PACE Act* 1984, s.80, *ante*, § 8–46, and the *YJCEA* 1999, s.53, *ante*, § 8–36, respectively.

(h) *Direction to jury*

19–307 In *R. v. Bowditch* [1991] Crim.L.R. 831, CA, it was said to be essential, in cases involving injuries to a small child, that a very clear direction as to the burden of proof should be given to counteract any temptation on the part of the jury, albeit subconsciously, to succumb to emotional feelings about such things being done to a child.

B. ABDUCTION OF CHILDREN

Introduction

19–308 The *Child Abduction Act* 1984 amended the criminal law relating to the abduction of children. The Act was extensively amended, and partly repealed, by the *Children Act* 1989, s.108(4), (7) and Sched. 12, paras 37 to 40, and Sched. 15.

Section 11(1) amends the definition of "offence against the person" in the Schedule to the *Visiting Forces Act* 1952 so as to include a reference to this Act.

Restrictions on prosecutions for kidnapping

19–309 No prosecution for an offence of kidnapping a child under 16 by a person connected with the child, within the meaning of section 1, shall be instituted except by or with the consent of the DPP: *Child Abduction Act* 1984, s.5. As to kidnapping, see *post*, § 19–333.

See also *R. v. C.* [1991] 2 F.L.R. 252, CA, *post*, § 19–336.

Special evidential and procedural provisions

19–310 References in the *CYPA* 1933 to the offences mentioned in Schedule 1 to that Act shall include offences under Part I of the 1984 Act: *CJA* 1988, s.170(1), and Sched. 15, para. 9. See *post*, §§ 19–322 *et seq*.

Child Abduction Act 1984, s.1

Offence of abduction of child by parent, etc.

1.—(1) Subject to subsections (5) and (8) below, a person connected with a child under the age of sixteen commits an offence if he takes or sends the child out of the United Kingdom without the appropriate consent. **19–311**

(2) A person is connected with a child for the purposes of this section if—

(a) he is a parent of the child; or

(b) in the case of a child whose parents were not married to each other at the time of his birth, there are reasonable grounds for believing that he is the father of the child; or

(c) he is a guardian of the child; or

(ca) he is a special guardian of the child; or

(d) he is a person in whose favour a residence order is in force with respect to the child; or

(e) he has custody of the child.

(3) In this section "the appropriate consent", in relation to a child, means—

(a) the consent of each of the following—

(i) the child's mother;

(ii) the child's father, if he has parental responsibility for him;

(iii) any guardian of the child;

(iiia) any special guardian of the child;

(iv) any person in whose favour a residence order is in force with respect to the child;

(v) any person who has custody of the child; or

(b) the leave of the court granted under or by virtue of any provision of Part II of the *Children Act* 1989; or

(c) if any person has custody of the child, the leave of the court which awarded custody to him.

(4) A person does not commit an offence under this section by taking or sending a child out of the United Kingdom without obtaining the appropriate consent if—

(a) he is a person in whose favour there is a residence order in force with respect to the child, and he takes or sends the child out of the United Kingdom for a period of less than one month; or

(b) he is a special guardian of the child and he takes or sends the child out of the United Kingdom for a period of less than three months.

(4A) Subsection (4) above does not apply if the person taking or sending the child out of the United Kingdom does so in breach of an order under Part II of the *Children Act* 1989.

(5) A person does not commit an offence under this section by doing anything without the consent of another person whose consent is required under the foregoing provisions if— **19–312**

(a) he does it in the belief that the other person—

(i) has consented;

(ia) who is a special guardian of the child; or

(ii) would consent if he was aware of all the relevant circumstances; or

(b) he has taken all reasonable steps to communicate with the other person but has been unable to communicate with him; or

(c) the other person has unreasonably refused to consent.

(5A) Subsection (5)(c) above does not apply if—

(a) the person who refused to consent is a person—

(i) in whose favour there is a residence order in force with respect to the child, or

(ii) who has custody of the child; or

(b) the person taking or sending the child out of the United Kingdom is, by so acting, in breach of an order made by a court in the United Kingdom.

(6) Where, in proceedings for an offence under this section, there is sufficient evidence to raise an issue as to the application of subsection (5) above, it shall be for the prosecution to prove that that subsection does not apply.

(7) For the purposes of this section—
(a) "guardian of a child", "special guardian", "residence order" and "parental responsibility" have the same meaning as in the *Children Act* 1989; and
(b) a person shall be treated as having custody of a child if there is in force an order of a court in the United Kingdom awarding him (whether solely or jointly with another person) custody, legal custody or care and control of the child.

(8) This section shall have effect subject to the provisions of the Schedule to this Act in relation to a child who is in the care of a local authority detained in a place of safety, remanded to a local authority accommodation or the subject of proceedings or an order relating to adoption.

[This section is printed as amended by the *Children Act* 1989, s.108(4), and Sched. 12, para. 37; and the *Adoption and Children Act* 2002, s.139, and Sched. 3, para. 42.]

As to the meaning of "guardian of a child", see the *Children Act* 1989, s.105(1); as to the meaning of "residence order", see *ibid.*, s.8(1); as to the meaning of "parental responsibility", see *ibid.*, s.3.

In *R. v. C.* [1991] 2 F.L.R. 252, CA, the provision to the jury of a copy of section 1 of the 1984 Act was deplored by the Court of Appeal. Section 1 was complicated and it was unsafe to provide such a copy unless the legislation was relatively short and straightforward.

As to the liability of a person who is not "connected with" the child abducted to be convicted of conspiracy to contravene section 1, or possibly of the substantive offence (as a secondary party), see *R. v. Sherry and El Yamani* [1993] Crim.L.R. 536, CA.

Child Abduction Act 1984, s.2

Offence of abduction of child by other persons

19–313 **2.**—(1) Subject to subsection (3) below, a person, other than one mentioned in subsection (2) below commits an offence if, without lawful authority or reasonable excuse, he takes or detains a child under the age of sixteen—
(a) so as to remove him from the lawful control of any person having lawful control of the child; or
(b) so as to keep him out of the lawful control of any person entitled to lawful control of the child.

(2) The persons are—
(a) where the father and mother of the child in question were married to each other at the time of his birth, the child's father and mother;
(b) where the father and mother of the child in question were not married to each other at the time of his birth, the child's mother; and
(c) any other person mentioned in section 1(2)(c) to (e) above.

(3) In proceedings against any person for an offence under this section, it shall be a defence for that person to prove—
(a) where the father and mother of the child in question were not married to each other at the time of his birth—
(i) that he is the child's father; or
(ii) that, at the time of the alleged offence, he believed, on reasonable grounds, that he was the child's father; or
(b) that, at the time of the alleged offence, he believed that the child had attained the age of sixteen.

[This section is printed as amended by the *Children Act* 1989, s.108(4), and Sched. 12, para. 38.]

19–314 Section 2 is disapplied to persons providing refuges for children at risk in certain circumstances: see the *Children Act* 1989, s.51.

In *Foster v. DPP* [2005] 1 W.L.R. 1400, DC, it was held that where a child was no longer in the lawful control of her foster parents when she was detained by the defendants, the offence of abduction of a child so as to remove her from a person having lawful control of her could not be proved; where, therefore, one defendant had removed a child from the control of her foster parents, and the other had been complicit in removing her or keeping her from such control, but neither was guilty of abduction since each believed the child to be over 16 at that time, the defendants were not guilty of an offence contrary to section 2(1)(a) where they continued to keep the child in their home having discovered she was under 16; the distinction between removal from a person having control, and keeping from a person entitled to control, was intended to reflect materially different states of affairs; the first required the child there and then to be in the lawful control of someone when taken or detained; the second required only that the child was kept out of the lawful control of someone entitled to it when taken or detained; by the time the defendants knew that their inducements in respect of the child were unlawful, she was no longer in the lawful custody of her foster parents.

The words "so as to", at the beginning of subsection (1)(a) and (b), refer to the objective effect of the defendant's actions, not to his intention: *R. v. Mousir* [1987] Crim.L.R. 562, CA; and *Foster v. DPP*, *ante*, in which the court rejected the alternative approach adopted in *Re Owens* [2000] 1 Cr.App.R. 195, DC.

In *R. v. A.* [2000] 1 Cr.App.R. 418, CA, it was held that the offence of taking a child may be committed though the child consents to the taking; the issue is whether the accused caused "the child to accompany him" (see s.3(a), *post*). If the jury are satisfied that he did so, it is immaterial that he was not the sole cause or even the main cause for the child doing so, provided that his actions were something more than merely peripheral or inconsequential.

In *R. v. Leather*, 98 Cr.App.R. 179, CA, the appellant had on three occasions approached small groups of children aged about 11 years. Each time, the appellant pretended to be looking for a bicycle and asked for help as to where a stolen bicycle might be hidden. Each time, he managed to induce at least two of the children to go with him away from where they were, supposedly to help look for the bicycle. It was submitted on behalf of the appellant that, although there was a taking in each case, the taking was not such as to remove the child from the lawful control of any person having lawful control of the child. It was held that there was no necessary spatial element in the concept of "control". Section 3 (*post*) simply required some movement sufficient to amount to an accompanying; subject to that, no geographical removal was contemplated by the words "so as to remove him from the lawful control of the person having lawful control of the child". Who has control of a child is a question of fact. Being an ordinary English word, there is no need for any complicated definition. What has to be proved is not the removal of the child, but the removal of the control of the child from the parent or other person having lawful control to the accused. Owen J., giving the judgment of the court, said that a relevant question in each case would have been:

> "Was the child concerned, without any lawful authority or reasonable excuse, deflected by some action of the accused from that which with the consent of his parents, or other person at the time having lawful control, he would otherwise have been doing into some activity induced by the accused? If ... the answer to that question was 'Yes', then it was open to the jury to say that the offence was made out" (at p. 184).

If, as a result of a case of mistaken identity, a man takes child X believing him to be child Y, and believing himself to be the father of child Y (not having been married to child Y's mother at the time of birth), the case does not come within section 2(3) as the words "child in question" refer back to the child taken: *R. v. Berry* [1996] Crim.L.R. 574, CA. In such a case, the accused is to be judged on the facts as he believed them to be and the issue is one of reasonable excuse: *ibid*.

Child Abduction Act 1984, ss.3, 4

Construction of references to taking, sending and detaining

3. For the purposes of this Part of this Act— **19–315**

(a) a person shall be regarded as taking a child if he causes or induces the child to accompany him or any other person or causes the child to be taken;

(b) a person shall be regarded as sending a child if he causes the child to be sent;

(c) a person shall be regarded as detaining a child if he causes the child to be detained or induces the child to remain with him or any other person; and

(d) references to a child's parents and to a child whose parents were (or were not) married to each other at the time of his birth shall be construed in accordance with section 1 of the *Family Law Reform Act* 1987 (which extends their meaning).

[This section is printed as amended and repealed in part by the *Children Act* 1989, s.108(4), (7), and Sched. 12, para. 39, and Sched. 15.]

Penalties and prosecutions

19–316 **4.**—(1) A person guilty of an offence under this Part of this Act shall be liable—

(a) on summary conviction, to imprisonment for a term not exceeding *six* [12] months or to a fine not exceeding the statutory maximum, ... or to both such imprisonment and fine;

(b) on conviction on indictment, to imprisonment for a term not exceeding seven years.

(2) No prosecution for an offence under section 1 above shall be instituted except by or with the consent of the Director of Public Prosecutions.

[The words omitted were repealed by the *Statute Law (Repeals) Act* 1993, Sched. 1, Pt XIV. For the meaning of "statutory maximum", see Schedule 1 to the *Interpretation Act* 1978 (Appendix B–28). The effect is that it means the prescribed sum within the meaning of section 32 of the *MCA* 1980, *ante*, § 1–33. In subs. (1)(a), "12" is substituted for "six", as from a day to be appointed, by the *CJA* 2003, s.282(2) and (3). The increase has no application to offences committed before the substitution takes effect: s.282(4).]

Child Abduction Act 1984, Sched.

SCHEDULE

MODIFICATIONS OF SECTION 1 FOR CHILDREN IN CERTAIN CASES

Children in care of local authorities and voluntary organisations

19–317 1.—(1) This paragraph applies where—

(a) a child is placed for adoption by an adoption agency under section 19 of the *Adoption and Children Act* 2002, or an adoption agency is authorised to place the child for adoption under that section; or

(b) a placement order is in force in respect of the child; or

(c) an application for such an order has been made in respect of the child and has not been disposed of; or

(d) an application for an adoption order has been made in respect of the child and has not been disposed of; or

(e) an order under section 84 of the *Adoption and Children Act* 2002 (giving parental responsibility prior to adoption abroad) has been made in respect of the child, or an application for such an order in respect of him has been made and has not been disposed of.

(2) Where this paragraph applies, section 1 of this Act shall have effect as if—

(a) the reference in subsection (1) to the appropriate consent were—

(i) in a case within sub-paragraph (1)(a) above, a reference to the consent of each person who has parental responsibility for the child or to the leave of the High Court;

(ii) in a case within sub-paragraph (1)(b) above, a reference to the leave of the court which made the placement order;

(iii) in a case within sub-paragraph (1)(c) or (d) above, a reference to the leave of the court to which the application was made;

(iv) in a case within sub-paragraph (1)(e) above, a reference to the leave of the court which made the order or, as the case may be, to which the application was made;

(b) subsection (3) were omitted;

(c) in subsection (4), in paragraph (a), for the words from "in whose favour" to the first mention of "child" there were substituted "who provides the child's home in a case falling within sub-paragraph (1)(a) or (b) of paragraph (3) of the Schedule to this Act"; and

(d) subsections (4A), (5), (5A) and (6) were omitted.

Children in places of safety

2.—(1) This paragraph applies in the case of a child who is—

(a) detained in a place of safety under [[paragraph 4(1)(a) of Schedule 1 or paragraph 6(4)(a) of Schedule 8 to the *Powers of Criminal Courts (Sentencing)*

Act 2000 or]] paragraph *7(4)* [21(2)] of Schedule 7 [2] to the Powers of Criminal Courts (Sentencing) Act *2000* [*Criminal Justice and Immigration Act* 2008]; or

(b) remanded to local authority accommodation under section 23 of the *Children and Young Persons Act* 1969[[, paragraph 4 of Schedule 1 or paragraph 6 of Schedule 8 to the *Powers of Criminal Courts (Sentencing) Act* 2000]] [or paragraph 21 of Schedule 2 to the *Criminal Justice and Immigration Act* 2008].

(2) Where this paragraph applies, section 1 of this Act shall have effect as if—

(a) the reference in subsection (1) to the appropriate consent were a reference to the leave of any magistrates' court acting for the area in which the place of safety is; and

(b) subsections (3) to (6) were omitted.

Adoption and custodianship

3.—(1) This paragraph applies in the case of a child— **19–318**

(a) who is the subject of an order under section 18 of the *Adoption Act* 1976 freeing him for adoption; or

(b) who is the subject of a pending application for such an order; or

(c) who is the subject of a pending application for an adoption order; or

(d) who is the subject of an order under section 55 of the *Adoption Act* 1976 relating to adoption abroad or of a pending application for such an order; or

… .

(2) Where this paragraph applies, section 1 of this Act shall have effect as if—

(a) the reference in subsection (1) to the appropriate consent were a reference—

(i) in a case within sub-paragraph (1)(a) above, to the consent of the adoption agency which made the application for the section 18 order or, if the section 18 order has been varied under section 21 of that Act so as to give parental responsibility to another agency to the consent of that other agency;

(ii) in a case within sub-paragraph (1)(b), or (c) above, to the leave of the court to which the application was made; and

(iii) in a case within sub-paragraph (1)(d) above, to the leave of the court which made the order or, as the case may be, to which the application was made; and

(b) subsections (3) to (6) were omitted.

Cases within paragraphs 1 and 3

4. In the case of a child falling within both paragraph 1 and paragraph 3 above, the provisions of paragraph 3 shall apply to the exclusion of those in paragraph 1. **19–319**

Interpretation

5. In this Schedule— **19–320**

(a) "adoption agency", "adoption order", "placed for adoption by an adoption agency" and "placement order" have the same meaning as in the *Adoption and Children Act* 2002; and

(b) "area" in relation to a magistrates' court, means the petty sessions area … for which the court is appointed.

[This schedule is printed as amended and repealed in part by the *Children Act* 1989, s.108(4), (7), and Sched. 12, para. 40, and Sched. 15; the *Access to Justice Act* 1999, Sched. 15, Pt V(1); the *PCC(S)A* 2000, s.165(1), and Sched. 9, para. 93; and the *Adoption and Children Act* 2002, s.139, and Sched. 3, para. 43; and as amended, as from a day to be appointed, by the *CJIA* 2008, s.6(2) and (3), and Sched. 4, paras 31 (insertion in para. 2(1) of material in single square brackets, omission of "7(4)", "7" and "Powers of Criminal Courts Act *2000*") and 104 (insertion in para. 2(1) of material in double square brackets). In connection with these amendments, see the 2008 Act, Sched. 27, para. 1 (transitory, transitional and saving provisions).]

As to the meaning of "child who is in the care of a local authority", see the *Children Act* 1989, ss.31(1) and (11), and 105(1). As to the meaning of "adoption agency", "adoption order", "placed for adoption by an adoption agency" and "placement order", see the *Adoption and Children Act* 2002, ss.2(1), 46(1), 18(5) and 21(1) respectively.

C. GENERAL STATUTORY PROVISIONS RELATING TO CHILDREN IN CRIMINAL PROCEEDINGS

Protection of children

19–321 Section 44 of the *Children Act* 1989 makes provision for the making of orders for the emergency protection of children. The powers conferred by such an order are supplemented by section 48, the provisions of which are intended to ensure that the whereabouts of children in need of protection are discovered. These include the issuing of a warrant authorising a constable to assist a person attempting to exercise powers under an emergency protection order, using force if necessary.

Section 49 makes the abduction of children in care, the subject of an emergency protection order or in police protection, a summary offence. Section 50 makes provision for the making of a "recovery order" in relation to a child in respect of whom there is reason to believe that he or she has been abducted contrary to section 49. *Inter alia*, a recovery order authorises a constable to enter any premises specified in the order and search for the child, using reasonable force if necessary. This section supplements the power contained in section 32 of the *CYPA* 1969 to arrest without a warrant a child who is absent from care.

Offences to which special provisions apply

Children and Young Persons Act 1933, Sched. 1

19–322 The murder or manslaughter of a child or young person.

Infanticide.

An offence under section 5 of the *Domestic Violence, Crime and Victims Act* 2004, in respect of a child or young person.

Any offence under sections twenty-seven or fifty-six of the *Offences against the Person Act* 1861, and any offence against a child or young person under sections 5, ... of that Act.

Any offence under section one, three, four, eleven or twenty-three of this Act.

Any offence against a child or young person under any of sections 1 to 41, 47 to 53, 57 to 61, 66 and 67 of the *Sexual Offences Act* 2003, or any attempt to commit such an offence.

Any offence under section 62 or 63 of the *Sexual Offences Act* 2003 where the intended offence was an offence against a child or young person, or any attempt to commit such an offence.

Any other offence involving bodily injury to a child or young person.

[This Schedule is printed as amended and repealed in part by the *SOA* 1956, ss.48, 51, Sched. 3 and Sched. 4; the *CJA* 1988, s.170(2), and Sched. 16; the *SOA* 2003, s.139, and Sched. 6, para. 7; and the *Domestic Violence, Crime and Victims Act* 2004, s.58(1), and Sched. 10, para. 2.]

By the *Suicide Act* 1961, Sched. 1, the reference to the murder or manslaughter of a child or young person shall apply also to aiding, abetting, counselling or procuring the suicide of a child or young person.

References in the 1933 Act to the offences mentioned in the first schedule to that Act shall include offences under section 1(1)(a) of the *Protection of Children Act* 1978 (s.1(5) of the 1978 Act) (*post*, § 31–107), and offences under Part I of the *Child Abduction Act* 1984 (*CJA* 1988, s.170(1), and Sched. 15, para. 9) (*ante*, §§ 19–311 *et seq.*).

The extant provisions of the Act referring to Schedule 1 are: section 14 (*post*, § 19–323); section 41 (*post*, § 19–325); section 42 (*ante*, § 10–26); and section 99 (*post*, § 19–326).

Mode of charging offences and limitation of time

Children and Young Persons Act 1933, s.14

19–323 **14.**—(1) Where a person is charged with committing any of the offences mentioned in the First Schedule to this Act in respect of two or more children or young persons, the same information or summons may charge the offence in respect of all or any of them, but the person charged shall not, if he is summarily convicted, be liable to a separate penalty in respect of each child or young person except upon separate informations.

(2) The same information or summons ... may charge him with the offences of assault, ill-treatment, neglect, abandonment, or exposure, together or separately, and may charge him with committing all or any of those offences in a manner likely to cause unnecessary suffering or injury to health, alternatively or together, but when those offences are charged together the person charged shall not, if he is summarily convicted, be liable to a separate penalty for each.

(4) When any offence mentioned in the first Schedule to this Act charged against any person is a continuous offence, it shall not be necessary to specify in the information, summons, or indictment, the date of the acts constituting the offence.

[The words omitted from subs. (2) were repealed by the *Children Act* 1989, s.108(7), and Sched. 15. Subs. (3) was repealed by the *CYPA* 1963, ss.21, 64(3) and Sched. 5.]

Interpretation of Part I

Children and Young Persons Act 1933, s.17

17.—(1) For the purposes of this Act, the following shall be presumed to have responsibility for a child or young person— **19–324**

(a) any person who—

(i) has parental responsibility for him (within the meaning of the *Children Act* 1989), or

(ii) is otherwise legally liable to maintain him; and

(b) any person who has care of him.

(2) A person who is presumed to be responsible for a child or young person by virtue of subsection (1)(a) shall not be taken to have ceased to be responsible for him by reason only that he does not have care of him.

[This section is printed as substituted by the *Children Act* 1989, s.108(5), and Sched. 13, para. 5.]

As to the meaning of "parental responsibility", see the *Children Act* 1989, s.3.

Power to proceed with case in absence of child or young person

Children and Young Persons Act 1933, s.41

41. Where in any proceedings with relation to any of the offences mentioned in the First Schedule to this Act, the court is satisfied that the attendance before the court of any child or young person in respect of whom the offence is alleged to have been committed is not essential to the just hearing of the case, the case may be proceeded with and determined in the absence of the child or young person. **19–325**

See *R. v. Hale* [1905] 1 K.B. 126, as to the effect of this section.

Presumption and determination of age

Children and Young Persons Act 1933, s.99

99.—(1) Where a person, whether charged with an offence or not, is brought before any court otherwise than for the purpose of giving evidence, and it appears to the court that he is a child or young person, the court shall make due inquiry as to the age of that person, and for that purpose shall take such evidence as may be forthcoming at the hearing of the case, but an order or judgment of the court shall not be invalidated by any subsequent proof that the age of that person has not been correctly stated to the court, and the age presumed or declared by the court to be the age of the person so brought before it shall, for the purposes of this Act, be deemed to be the true age of that person, and, where it appears to the court that the person so brought before it has attained the age of eighteen years, that person shall for the purposes of this Act be deemed not to be a child or young person. **19–326**

(2) Where in any charge or indictment for any offence under this Act or any of the offences mentioned in the First Schedule to this Act, except as provided in that Schedule, it is alleged that the person by or in respect of whom the offence was committed was a child or young person or was under or had attained any specified age, and he appears to the court to have been at the date of the commission of the alleged offence a child or young person, or to have been under or to have attained the specified age, as the case may be, he shall for the purposes of this Act be presumed at that date to have been a child or young person or to have been under or to have attained that age, as the case may be, unless the contrary is proved.

(3) Where, in any charge or indictment for any offence under this Act or any of the offences mentioned in the First Schedule to this Act, it is alleged that the person in respect of whom the offence was committed was a child or was a young person, it shall not be a defence to prove that the person alleged to have been a child was a young person or the person alleged to have been a young person was a child in any case where the acts constituting the alleged offence would equally have been an offence if committed in respect of a young person or child respectively.

(4) Where a person is charged with an offence under this Act in respect of a person apparently under a specified age it shall be a defence to prove that the person was actually of or over that age.

[This section is printed as amended by the *SOA* 1956, s.48, and Sched. 3; and the *CJA* 1991, s.68, and Sched. 8, para. 1(2).]

References in subsection (1) to the 1933 Act are to be construed as including references to the *CYPA* 1969: *CYPA* 1969, s.70(3).

As to Schedule 1 to the 1933 Act, see *ante*, § 19–322.

General interpretation provisions

19–327 The interpretation provisions for Part I of the 1933 Act (prevention of cruelty and exposure to moral and physical danger) are contained in section 17 (see *ante*, § 19–324). Section 107 contains the general interpretation provisions.

Children and Young Persons Act 1933, s.107

19–328 **107.**—(1) In this Act, unless the context otherwise requires, the following expressions have the meanings hereby respectively assigned to them, that is to say,—

…

"Chief officer of police" …, as regards Scotland has the same meaning as in the *Police (Scotland) Act* 1967, and as regards Northern Ireland means a district inspector of the Royal Ulster Constabulary;

"Child" means a person under the age of fourteen years;

"Guardian", in relation to a child or young person, includes any person who, in the opinion of the court having cognisance of any case in relation to the child or young person or in which the child or young person is concerned, has for the time being the care of the child or young person;

"Intoxicating liquor" has the same meaning as in the *Licensing Act* 1964;

"Legal guardian", in relation to a child or young person, means a guardian of a child as defined in the *Children Act* 1989;

["Legal representative" means a person who, for the purposes of the *Legal Services Act* 2007, is an authorised person in relation to an activity which constitutes the exercise of a right of audience or the conduct of litigation (within the meaning of that Act);]

"Place of safety" means a community home provided by a local authority or a controlled community home, any police station, or any hospital, surgery, or any other suitable place, the occupier of which is willing temporarily to receive a child or young person;

"Prescribed" means prescribed by regulations made by the Secretary of State;

"Public place" includes any public park, garden, sea beach or railway station, and any ground to which the public for the time being have or are permitted to have access, whether on payment or otherwise;

"Street" includes any highway and any public bridge, road, lane, footway, square, court, alley or passage, whether a thoroughfare or not;

"Young person" means a person who has attained the age of fourteen and is under the age of eighteen years.

[This section is printed as amended by the *CYPA* 1963, s.64(1) and Sched. 3, para. 24; the *Police Act* 1964, s.63 and Sched. 9; the *Police (Scotland) Act* 1967, ss.52, 53 and Sched. 4; the *Finance Act* 1967, s.5(1)(e); the *CYPA* 1969, s.72(3) and Sched. 5, para. 12; the *Children Act* 1989, s.108(5) and Sched. 13, para. 7; and the *CJA* 1991, s.68 and Sched. 8, para. 1(3) (see *post*); and as repealed in part by the *National Assistance Act* 1948, s.62 and Sched. 7, Pt III; the *CYPA* 1963, s.64(3) and Sched. 5; the *Police Act* 1964, s.64(3) and Sched. 10; the *CYPA* 1969, s.72(3), (4), Sched. 5, para. 12, and Sched. 6; the *Child Care Act* 1980, s.89(3), and Sched. 6; the *Statute Law (Repeals) Act* 1986; the *Children Act* 1989, s.108(7), and Sched. 15; and the *Police Act* 1996,

Sched. 9; and as amended, as from a day to be appointed, by the *Legal Services Act* 2007, s.208(1), and Sched. 21, paras 15 and 20 (insertion of words in square brackets).]

NOTE: the definition of "young person" was amended by the *CJA* 1991, s.68, and Sched. 8, para. 1(3). The amendment came into force on October 1, 1992, save to the extent that it would otherwise apply to the interpretation of section 34 of the 1933 Act: *Criminal Justice Act 1991 (Commencement No. 3) Order* 1992 (S.I. 1992 No. 333), art. 2(2) and (4). As to this saving, see *ante*, § 15–209. **19–329**

For the meaning of "chief officer of police", in relation to England and Wales, see the *Police Act* 1996, s.101(1): *Interpretation Act* 1978, Sched. 1 (Appendix B–28).

As to the meaning of "guardian of a child", see the *Children Act* 1989, s.105(1).

Summary of miscellaneous provisions relating to giving evidence, publicity, etc.

The *CYPA* 1933 contains a range of other provisions which may be relevant to any proceedings in which a child or young person is concerned. Section 36 (*ante*, § 4–12) prohibits children being in court during the trial of other persons. Section 37 (*ante*, § 4–13) provides for a court being cleared while a child or young person is giving evidence in certain cases. Section 39 (*ante*, § 4–27) contains a power to prohibit publication of certain matters in newspapers or in sound or television broadcasts. Section 49 (*ante*, § 4–29) restricts the reporting of proceedings in youth courts, proceedings on appeal from a youth court, proceedings under sections 15 or 16 of the *CYPA* 1969 (variation or revocation of supervision orders) and proceedings on appeal from a magistrates' court arising out of proceedings under either of those sections. **19–330**

Section 42 of the 1933 Act (*ante*, § 10–26) extends the power to take a deposition from a child or young person. Section 43 (*ante*, § 10–47) provides for the admission in evidence of the deposition of a child or young person.

See also sections 53 (competence of witnesses to give evidence) (*ante*, § 8–36a) and 55 (determining whether witness is to be sworn) (*ante*, § 8–26) of the *YJCEA* 1999.

XIV. FALSE IMPRISONMENT AND KIDNAPPING

(1) Offences

False imprisonment

False imprisonment consists in the unlawful and intentional or reckless restraint of a victim's freedom of movement from a particular place—it is unlawful detention which stops the victim from moving away as he or she would wish to move. A parent will seldom be guilty of this offence in relation to his or her child because the sort of restrictions imposed upon children are usually well within the realm of reasonable parental discipline and are therefore not unlawful. However, there are many ways in which the prosecution might prove "unlawfulness"—*e.g.* (a) the existence of a court order and detention by the parent contrary to that order; (b) detention for such a period or in such circumstances as to take it out of the realm of reasonable parental discipline—whether that stage had been reached is a matter for the jury to decide provided that there is evidence fit for them to consider: *R. v. Rahman*, 81 Cr.App.R. 349, CA (considering *R. v. D.* [1984] A.C. 778, HL). Thus, it is false imprisonment to detain a defendant after his acquittal or after his term of imprisonment has expired: *Mee v. Cruickshank* (1902) 20 Cox 210; *Migotti v. Colvill* (1879) 4 CPD 233. So, the detention of a man upon warrant or process which is regular in form is unlawful if the warrant be executed at an unlawful time, *e.g.* in the case of civil process, on a Sunday, or in a privileged place, such as a royal palace or a court of justice, or on a person privileged from arrest. **19–331**

Every confinement of the person is an imprisonment, whether it is in a common prison or in a private house, or even by forcibly detaining a person in the public streets: 2 Co.Inst. 482 at 589. Merely preventing a man from proceeding along a particular way, when, without going along that way, he may still get to his desired destination, is not an imprisonment: *Bird v. Jones* (1845) 7 Q.B. 742.

19–332 Detention in obedience to a specific order of a court is not actionable if the exigency of the order or warrant is obeyed (*Greaves v. Keene* (1879) 4 Ex.D. 73) and the order is valid on the face of it: *Henderson v. Preston* (1888) 21 Q.B.D. 362. Where a warrant is issued, but it is used merely as a summons, and no arrest is made on it, and the party goes voluntarily before the magistrate, this is not an imprisonment: *Arrowsmith v. Le Mesurier* (1806) 2 B. & P. (N.R.) 211; *Berry v. Adamson* (1827) 6 B. & C. 528.

An act of false imprisonment may amount in itself to an assault: see *ante*, § 19–173, but the offence may be committed by mere detention without violence: *R. v. Linsberg and Leies*, 69 J.P. 107; *Hunter v. Johnson* (1884) 13 Q.B.D. 225.

Kidnapping

19–333 Kidnapping has long been a criminal offence. In *R. v. D.* [1984] A.C. 778, the House of Lords, for the first time, had to consider the nature, ingredients and scope of the offence. The offence was held to comprise the following four ingredients:

(a) the taking or carrying away of one person by another;
(b) by force or fraud;
(c) without the consent of the person so taken or carried away; and
(d) without lawful excuse.

Their Lordships rejected the two limitations placed upon the scope of the offence by the Court of Appeal and held: (a) the offence *can* be committed by anyone against a child under the age of 14; and (b) the offence *can* be committed by a parent against an unmarried child who is still a minor.

R. v. D. was considered in *R. v. Rahman, ante*, § 19–331.

Consent: children

19–334 In relation to the kidnapping of a child, in all cases it is the absence of the child's consent which is material—whatever the child's age. In the case of a young child, the child will not have the understanding or intelligence to give its consent, so that absence of consent will be a necessary inference from the child's age. In the case of an older child, it must be a question of fact for the jury whether the child concerned has sufficient understanding and intelligence to give its consent—while the matter will always be for the jury alone to decide, "I should not expect a jury to find at all frequently that a child under 14 had sufficient understanding and intelligence to give its consent" (*per* Lord Brandon in *R. v. D., ante*, at p. 806). While the absence of the consent of the person having custody or care and control of a child is not material to the third ingredient of the common law offence, the giving of consent by such a person may be very relevant to the fourth ingredient, in that, depending on all the circumstances, it might well support a defence of lawful excuse: *ibid*.

19–335 The offence of kidnapping may be committed by a husband on his wife if he treats her with hostile force and that force results in carrying her away from the place where she wishes to remain: *R. v. Reid* [1973] Q.B. 299, 56 Cr.App.R. 703, CA. The fact that at the time of the offence they were cohabiting is immaterial: *ibid*. The offence is complete when the victim is seized and carried away against his will, *i.e.* it is not a continuing offence involving the concealment of the person seized: *ibid*.

On a charge of kidnapping, the prosecution do not have to prove that the kidnapper carried the victim to the place he intended. All that has to be proved is a deprivation of liberty and carrying away from the place where the victim wished to be: *R. v. Wellard*, 67 Cr.App.R. 364, CA.

As to the abduction of children under 16 years of age, see the *Child Abduction Act* 1984, *ante*, § 19–308.

Consent: fraud

19–335a In *R. v. Hendy-Freegard* [2007] 2 Cr.App.R. 27, CA, it was said to be implicit in that element of the offence that consists of the "taking or carrying away of one person by another" that there must be some deprivation of the liberty of the person taken or carried away (explaining *R. v. D., ante*); to the extent that *R. v. Cort* [2004] 1 Cr.App.R. 18, CA, suggested that the offence would be committed by a person who by fraudulent means induced another person to accompany him from one place to another in circumstances in which there was no deprivation of liberty of that person, it represented an unjustified departure from established principle; but it may be that there would be a deprivation of liberty where one person acquiesced in accompanying another because he believed he was under compulsion. The court added that, whether or not *Cort* was correct, there was no basis for extending the offence further, so that it would be committed by a person who by fraudulent means induced another to go unaccompanied from one place to another.

(2) Indictment

COUNT 1

Statement of Offence

Kidnapping. **19–336**

Particulars of Offence

A B, on the —— day of ——, 20—, unlawfully and by force or by fraud took or carried away J N against her will.

COUNT 2

Statement of Offence

False imprisonment.

Particulars of Offence

A B, on divers days between the —— day of —— and the —— day of ——, 20—, [assaulted J N and] unlawfully and injuriously imprisoned J N and detained her against her will.

Where a count alleging abduction of a child contrary to section 1(1) of the 1984 Act encompassed the allegation made by the prosecution against a defendant, the inclusion of a count alleging kidnapping was to be deprecated: *R. v. C.* [1991] 2 F.L.R. 252, CA.

(3) Sentence

Both kidnapping and false imprisonment are common law offences, punishable by fine or imprisonment, or both. Both are specified violent offences within Schedule 15 to the *CJA* 2003 (*ante*, § 5–299). **19–337**

General guidance on sentencing in cases of kidnapping and false imprisonment was given in *R. v. Spence and Thomas*, 5 Cr.App.R.(S.) 413, CA, where Lord Lane C.J. said that in cases at the top of the scale, where abductions were planned and the victim was used as a hostage or where ransom money was demanded, sentences would seldom be less than eight years. Much longer sentences would be proper in such cases where violence or firearms were used or the victim was detained over a long period of time. At the other end of the scale, cases arising out of family tiffs or lovers disputes would seldom require anything more than 18 months.

Sentences in cases of kidnapping for ransom generally fall within the bracket of five years to about 15 years, the shorter sentences being employed where the offender has kidnapped the victim with a view to enforcing payment of a debt owed to him. For other cases of kidnapping and abduction of a child, see CSP B3–4.

(4) Restriction on prosecutions for kidnapping

Section 5 of the *Child Abduction Act* 1984 provides that, except by or with the consent of the Director of Public Prosecutions, no prosecution shall be instituted for an offence of kidnapping if it was committed against a child under the age of 16 by a person "connected with" the child within the meaning of section 1 of that Act. As to the 1984 Act, see *ante*, §§ 19–308 *et seq.* **19–338**

(5) Defences

General

An imprisonment or detention will be lawful if it is in pursuance of the sentence of a **19–339** court, if it is an exercise of lawful restraint, or if it results from the exercise of a power of arrest conferred by law. In addition to these general justifications, there may be specific statutory justification for a particular restraint upon an individual's liberty, such as the *MHA* 1983 or the *Merchant Shipping Act* 1995, s.105. Of all the heads of justification, that which is likely to be most significant in practice is the exercise of a lawful power of arrest (as to which, see *post*).

As to lawful restraint other than by way of arrest, a parent may restrain a child (*ante*, § 19–331), and a householder is entitled to use reasonable force to defend his property, and for this purpose he is entitled to be judged on the basis of the facts as he believed them to be, however unreasonably: *R. v. Faraj* [2007] 2 Cr.App.R. 25) (holding that a householder would be entitled to use reasonable force to detain a person believed to be a burglar).

Arrest under civil process

19–340 Arrest under civil process is now abolished, except (a) for contempt of court of a civil nature; and (b) in the circumstances and subject to the restrictions set out in the *Debtors Act* 1869, ss.4–6, and the *Administration of Justice Act* 1970, s.11. See also the *Family Law Act* 1996, s.47.

Arrest under criminal process

(i) *By warrant*

19–341 A warrant from a magistrate having general cognizance of the matter of it will justify the officer in executing it, whether there be any grounds in fact for granting it, or not (*Shergold v. Holloway* (1734) 2 St.Tr. 1002); but if the magistrate had not cognizance of the matter of the warrant; if, for instance, he granted a warrant to take up J N, to answer a plea of debt, the constable would not be justified in arresting: *ibid*. A conviction by a magistrate having competent jurisdiction over the subject matter of it, upon which the party has been arrested, is, until reversed or quashed, conclusive evidence in favour of the magistrate, in a prosecution against him for false imprisonment: 7 T.R. 633n. As to gaolers, see *Henderson v. Preston* (1888) 21 Q.B.D. 362 and the *Prison Act* 1952, ss.12, 13. As to judges of the superior courts, see *Taaffe v. Downes* (1812) 3 St.Tr.(n.s.) 1317.

The issue of warrants by a magistrates' court is governed by the *MCA* 1980. The issue of warrants by the Crown Court is governed by the *Supreme Court Act* 1981, ss.80, 81 (renamed the *Senior Courts Act* 1981 as from a day to be appointed: *Constitutional Reform Act* 2005, s.59(5), and Sched. 11, para. 1(1)). The death of the issuing magistrate does not affect a warrant issued by him: *MCA* 1980, s.124.

Section 125(2) of the 1980 Act (as amended) provides that a warrant of arrest issued by a justice of the peace may be executed anywhere in England and Wales by any person to whom it is directed or by any constable acting within his police area.

As to the execution of English warrants in Scotland, see the *Summary Jurisdiction (Process) Act* 1881.

Section 125A(1) of the 1980 Act provides that a warrant to which that subsection applies may be executed anywhere in England and Wales by a civilian enforcement officer. A "civilian enforcement officer" is a person employed by an authority of a prescribed class which performs functions in relation to any area specified in the warrant and who is authorised in the prescribed manner to execute warrants (subs. (2)). Subsection (1) applies to, *inter alia*, warrants of arrest, commitment or detention issued by a justice of the peace under any provision specified for the purposes of the subsection by order, or for the enforcement of a court order of any descripton so specified (subs. (3)). For orders under this subsection, see the *Magistrates' Courts Warrants (Specification of Provisions) Order* 2000 (S.I. 2000 No. 3278), the *Magistrates' Courts Warrants (Specification of Provisions) (Amendment) Order* 2004 (S.I. 2004 No. 1835) and the *Magistrates' Courts Warrants (Specifications of Provisions) (Amendment) Order* 2007 (S.I. 2007 No. 3011). Section 125B provides for the execution of warrants, to which section 125A(1) applies, by an approved enforcement agency. As to "civilian enforcement officers", see the *Magistrates' Courts (Civilian Enforcement Officers) Rules* 1990 (S.I. 1990 No. 2260), as amended and renamed by the *Magistrates' Courts (Civilian Enforcement Officers) Rules* 2001 (S.I. 2001 No. 164).

Section 125D governs the execution of warrants by persons not in possession of the warrant. A warrant to which section 125A(1) applies may be executed by any person entitled to execute it even though not in possession of it (subs. (1)). A warrant to which section 125D(2) applies, and which is not a warrant to which section 125A(1) applies, may be executed by a constable even though it is not in his possession at the time (subs. (2)). Subsection (3) provides that subsection (2) applies to, *inter alia*, warrants—

(a) to arrest a person in connection with an offence;
(b) under the *Army Act* 1955, s.186(3), the *Air Force Act* 1955, s.186(3), the *Naval Discipline Act* 1957, s.105(3) or the *Reserve Forces Act* 1996, Sched. 2 (as from a day to be appointed, the *AFA* 2006, s.378(1), and Sched. 16, para. 89, substitute a reference to "a warrant under section 313, 314 or 317" of the 2006 Act);
(c) under the *Family Law Act* 1996, s.47(8);
(d) under the *CDA* 1998, Sched. 3, para. 4;
(e) under the *PCC(S)A* 2000, Sched. 1, para. 3(2); and
(f) under the 1980 Act, ss.55, 76, 93, 97 or 97A.

Section 125D(4) provides that where, by virtue of that section, a warrant is executed by a person not in possession of it, it shall, on the demand of the person arrested, committed or detained, be shown to him as soon as practicable. As to this, see *R. v. Purdy* [1975] Q.B. 288, 60 Cr.App.R. 30, CA, *post*, and *De Costa Small v. Kirkpatrick*, 68 Cr.App.R. 186, DC.

Where a person was arrested upon a warrant issued under paragraph 3 of Schedule 3 to the *PCC(S)A* 2000 (§ 5–123r in the supplement), he was being arrested "in connection with an offence" within the meaning of section 125(4): accordingly, the fact that the constable making the arrest was not in possession of the warrant at the time did not mean that he was not acting "in the execution of his duty": *Jones v. Kelsey*, 85 Cr.App.R. 226, DC. **19–342**

Where a person is arrested on a warrant otherwise than for a criminal offence, it is essential that he should be able to know for what he is being arrested and whether he is being arrested for such a matter as non-payment of a fine, arrears of maintenance, etc. He can "buy" his freedom from arrest by instant payment of the sum stated in the warrant. This is the basis of the common law rule that unless an officer making an arrest has the warrant with him, ready to be produced if required, the arrest will be unlawful: see *Galliard v. Laxton* (1862) B. & S. 363 at 372–373. Where an officer left the warrant in the police car some 50 or 60 yards away the court held that the common law requirement was satisfied: *R. v. Purdy*, *ante*.

(ii) *Without warrant*

Common law powers. A justice of the peace may apprehend, or cause to be apprehended by a verbal order merely, any person committing a serious offence or breach of the peace in his presence: 2 Hale 86. **19–343**

There is a common law power of arrest vested in both the police and ordinary citizens where (a) a breach of the peace is committed in the presence of the person making the arrest, or (b) the arrestor reasonably believes that such a breach will be committed in the immediate future by the person arrested though he has not yet committed any breach, or (c) where a breach has been committed and it is reasonably believed that a renewal of it is threatened: *R. v. Howell* [1982] Q.B. 416, 73 Cr.App.R. 31, CA. In the instances where the power is exercised in the belief that a breach of the peace is imminent, it must be established that it is not only an honest albeit mistaken belief, but a belief which is founded on reasonable grounds: *ibid.*, pp. 426, 36; and *Foulkes v. Chief Constable of the Merseyside Police* [1998] 3 All E.R. 705, CA (Civ. Div.).

The test of reasonableness is objective in the sense that it is for the court to decide whether, in the light of what the constable knew and perceived at the time, it was satisfied that it was reasonable to fear an imminent breach of the peace; and the reasonableness of the belief was, therefore, to be evaluated without the qualification of hindsight: *Redmond-Bate v. DPP*, 163 J.P. 789, DC. Allowance must be made for circumstances in which a constable has to make a spur of the moment decision in an emergency: *G. v. Chief Superintendent of Police, Stroud*, 86 Cr.App.R. 92, DC. Where, however, the only threat to the peace came from the response of others to a public speech which may have been irritating, contentious, eccentric, heretical and/or provocative (provided it did not tend to provoke violence), there would be no basis for arresting the speaker; the law extends tolerance to opinion of every kind and expects it in the conduct of those who disagree, even strongly, with what they hear: *Redmond-Bate v. DPP, ante*.

Every citizen (whether policeman or not) in whose presence a breach of the peace is being, or reasonably appears to be about to be, committed has the right to take reasonable steps to make the person who is breaking or threatening to break the peace refrain from doing so; and those reasonable steps in appropriate cases will include detaining him against his will short of arresting him: *Albert v. Lavin* [1982] A.C. 546, HL. It followed, therefore, that an assailant's honestly mistaken belief that the person detaining him was not a police officer was immaterial to the issue of guilt upon a charge of assault on a police officer in the execution of his duty: *ibid*. See also *Joyce v. Hertfordshire Constabulary*, 80 Cr.App.R. 298, DC.

19–344 In *McConnell v. Chief Constable of Greater Manchester Police* [1990] 1 W.L.R. 364, CA (Civ. Div.), it was held that a breach of the peace could take place on private premises even though the disturbance was confined only to the persons immediately involved; the absence of third parties is legally irrelevant. *McConnell* was followed in *McQuade v. Chief Constable of Humberside Police* [2002] 1 W.L.R. 1347, CA (Civ. Div.). Police officers are entitled in the execution of their duty to prevent a breach of the peace, to enter and remain on private premises, and this is so even where the person threatening the breach was threatening to commit it otherwise than on those premises; the officers would not have to wait for him to cross his boundary before being entitled to arrest him: *Addison v. Chief Constable of West Midlands Police (Note)* [2004] 1 W.L.R. 29, CA (Civ. Div.).

In *Chief Constable of Cleveland Police v. McGrogan* [2002] 1 F.L.R. 707, CA (Civ. Div.), it was held that: (i) where a person has been arrested for breach of the peace, the power to detain to prevent a further breach of the peace is limited to circumstances where there is a real (rather than fanciful) apprehension based on all the circumstances that if released the arrestee will renew his breach of the peace within a short time; the officer making the decision for continued detention must have an honest belief that further detention is necessary to prevent a breach of the peace, and there must be reasonable grounds for such belief; continued detention cannot be justified on the ground that sooner or later the arrestee, if released, is likely to breach the peace; (ii) the police practice of treating any person detained for breach of the peace as if the *PACE Act* 1984 applied is correct, involving as it does the need for regular review of the question whether continued detention is justified.

In *R. (Laporte) v. Chief Constable of Gloucestershire Constabulary* [2007] 2 A.C. 105, HL, it was held that whereas at common law every constable, and also every citizen, enjoys the power, and is subject to a duty, to seek, by taking reasonable steps, to prevent, *inter alia*, any breach of the peace (*i.e.* actual violence) which is about to occur (*Albert v. Lavin, ante*), no power (or duty) will arise to take preventive action unless and until the constable (or citizen) reasonably apprehends that an actual breach of the peace is imminent (about to happen); and even when a breach of the peace is reasonably judged to be imminent, no more intrusive action should be taken than appears necessary to prevent it; the test was the same whether the intervention was by arrest or by action short of arrest, and there was nothing to support the proposition that action short of arrest may be taken when a breach of the peace was not so imminent as to justify an arrest.

Where the lawfulness of a police officer's (or, presumably, an ordinary citizen's) conduct depends upon the existence of a breach of the peace, there need not be express evidence that there was a breach of the peace going on if the circumstances were such that this is self-evident: *Joyce v. Hertfordshire Constabulary*, 80 Cr.App.R. 298, DC. See also *Percy v. DPP* [1995] 1 W.L.R. 1382, DC; and *Nicol and Selvanayagam v. DPP* [1966] Crim.L.R. 318, DC.

See also Glanville Williams, "Arrest for Breach of the Peace" [1954] Crim.L.R. 578, and *R. v. Kelbie* [1996] Crim.L.R. 802, CA.

As to what constitutes a breach of the peace, see *post*, § 29–55.

Statutory powers. See, in particular, the *PACE Act* 1984, Pt III (*ante*, §§ 15–153 *et seq.*). Note that the general repeal of statutory powers of arrest contained in section 26 of the 1984 Act (*ante*, § 15–171), (a) only applies to the powers of constables, and (b) only applies to powers of arrest "for an offence". Thus statutory powers conferred on private citizens are preserved, as are a constable's statutory powers of arrest otherwise than for an offence (*e.g.* the *Family Law Act* 1996, s.47). **19–345**

Where any provision of the 1984 Act confers a power on a constable and does not provide that the power may only be exercised with the consent of some person other than a police officer, the officer may use reasonable force, if necessary, in the exercise of the power: s.117, *ante*, § 15–26. The use of excessive force does not *per se* render an arrest unlawful, although it might be the basis of some other remedy: *Simpson v. Chief Constable of South Yorkshire Police*, *The Times*, March 7, 1991, CA (Civ. Div.).

What constitutes arrest. See *ante*, § 15–159. **19–346**

Information to be given on arrest. See *ante*, §§ 15–176 *et seq.* **19–347**

Consequences of arrest. See *ante*, § 15–160. **19–348**

XV. TORTURE

Criminal Justice Act 1988, ss.134, 135

Torture

134.—(1) A public official or person acting in an official capacity, whatever his nationality, commits the offence of torture if in the United Kingdom or elsewhere he intentionally inflicts severe pain or suffering on another in the performance or purported performance of his official duties. **19–349**

(2) A person not falling within subsection (1) above commits the offence of torture, whatever his nationality, if—

(a) in the United Kingdom or elsewhere he intentionally inflicts severe pain or suffering on another at the instigation or with the consent or acquiescence—

(i) of a public official; or

(ii) of a person acting in an official capacity; and

(b) the official or other person is performing or purporting to perform his official duties when he instigates the commission of the offence or consents to or acquiesces in it.

(3) It is immaterial whether the pain or suffering is physical or mental and whether it is caused by an act or an omission.

(4) It shall be a defence for a person charged with an offence under this section in respect of any conduct of his to prove that he had lawful authority, justification or excuse for that conduct.

(5) For the purposes of this section "lawful authority, justification or excuse" means—

(a) in relation to pain or suffering inflicted in the United Kingdom, lawful authority, justification or excuse under the law of the part of the United Kingdom where it was inflicted;

(b) in relation to pain or suffering inflicted outside the United Kingdom—

(i) if it was inflicted by a United Kingdom official acting under the law of the United Kingdom or by a person acting in an official capacity under that law, lawful authority, justification or excuse under that law;

(ii) if it was inflicted by a United Kingdom official acting under the law of any part of the United Kingdom or by a person acting in an official capacity under such law, lawful authority, justification or excuse under the law of the part of the United Kingdom under whose law he was acting; and

(iii) in any other case, lawful authority, justification or excuse under the law of the place where it was inflicted.

(6) A person who commits the offence of torture shall be liable on conviction on indictment to imprisonment for life.

Requirement of Attorney-General's consent for prosecutions

19–350 **135.** Proceedings for an offence under section 134 above shall not be begun—

(a) in England and Wales, except by, or with the consent of, the Attorney- General; or

(b) [*Northern Ireland*].

Chapter 20

SEXUAL OFFENCES

I. INTRODUCTION

Sexual Offences Acts 1956 to 1992

The *SOA* 1956 consolidated the statutory law with regard to sexual offences. The *SOA* 1967 amended the law relating to homosexual acts. It provided, *inter alia*, that consensual buggery or acts of gross indecency between men over the age of 21 years (reduced to 18 years in 1994, *post*, § 20–3, and to 16 in 2000, *post*, § 20–8) and in private would no longer amount to offences. **20–1**

The *Sexual Offences (Amendment) Act* 1976 enacted a statutory definition of rape, provided for the anonymity of complainants and defendants in rape cases, and restricted the ambit of permissible cross-examination of the complainant in a case of rape. The provisions relating to anonymity of defendants were repealed by the *CJA* 1988, s.158. The *Sexual Offences (Amendment) Act* 1992 extended the existing anonymity provisions in order to cover victims of various sexual offences from the time an allegation is made. The *YJCEA* 1999 repeals the anonymity provisions in the 1976 Act and amends the 1992 Act so as to extend its operation to cover offences previously covered only by the 1976 Act.

The 1956, 1967, 1976 and 1992 Acts may be cited together as the *Sexual Offences Acts* 1956 to 1992 (see s.8(2) of the 1992 Act).

All but a few provisions of the 1956 and 1967 Acts have now been repealed by the

SOA 2003 (*post*, § 20–9). The 2003 Act came into force on May 1, 2004 (*Sexual Offences Act 2003 (Commencement) Order* 2004 (S.I. 2004 No. 874)), but neither the Act itself nor the commencement order contains any provision for saving the repealed legislation in relation to offences committed before that date (*cf. Theft Act* 1968, s.32(1), *Public Order Act* 1986, s.41(2)). Liability for pre-commencement conduct will, therefore, depend on the application of the general provisions of section 16(1)(c) and (e) of the *Interpretation Act* 1978 (Appendix B–16). Having regard to the lengthy delays that are a common feature of prosecutions for sexual offences, the 1956 Act will continue to be the applicable law in some cases for many years to come. Practitioners concerned with such prosecutions should make reference to the 2004 edition of this work; and to the supplement, where new decisions in relation to the former law will be collected.

Violent Crime Reduction Act 2006, s.55

Continuity of sexual offences law

20–1a **55.**—(1) This section applies where, in any proceedings—

(a) a person ("the defendant") is charged in respect of the same conduct both with an offence under the *Sexual Offences Act* 2003 ("the 2003 Act offence") and with an offence specified in subsection (2) ("the pre-commencement offence");

(b) the only thing preventing the defendant from being found guilty of the 2003 Act offence is the fact that it has not been proved beyond a reasonable doubt that the time when the conduct took place was after the coming into force of the enactment providing for the offence; and

(c) the only thing preventing the defendant from being found guilty of the pre-commencement offence is the fact that it has not been proved beyond a reasonable doubt that that time was before the coming into force of the repeal of the enactment providing for the offence.

(2) The offences referred to in subsection (1)(a) are—

(a) any offence under the *Sexual Offences Act* 1956;

(b) an offence under section 4 of the *Vagrancy Act* 1824 (obscene exposure);

(c) an offence under section 28 of the *Town Police Clauses Act* 1847 (indecent exposure);

(d) an offence under section 61 or 62 of the *Offences against the Person Act* 1861 (buggery etc.);

(e) an offence under section 128 of the *Mental Health Act* 1959 (sexual intercourse with patients);

(f) an offence under section 1 of the *Indecency with Children Act* 1960 (indecency with children);

(g) an offence under section 4 or 5 of the *Sexual Offences Act* 1967 (procuring an man to commit buggery and living on the earnings of male prostitution);

(h) an offence under section 9 of the *Theft Act* 1968 (burglary, including entering premises with intent to commit rape);

(i) an offence under section 54 of the *Criminal Law Act* 1977 (incitement of girl under 16 to commit incest);

(j) an offence under section 1 of the *Protection of Children Act* 1978 (indecent photographs of children);

(k) an offence under section 3 of the *Sexual Offences (Amendment) Act* 2000 (abuse of position of trust);

(l) an offence under section 145 of the *Nationality, Immigration and Asylum Act* 2002 (traffic in prostitution).

(3) For the purpose of determining the guilt of the defendant it shall be conclusively presumed that the time when the conduct took place was—

(a) if the maximum penalty for the pre-commencement offence is less than the maximum penalty for the 2003 Act offence, a time before the coming into force of the repeal of the enactment providing for the precommencement offence; and

(b) in any other case, a time after the coming into force of the enactment providing for the 2003 Act offence.

(4) In subsection (3) the reference, in relation an offence [*sic*], to the maximum penalty is a reference to the maximum penalty by way imprisonment or other detention that could be imposed on the defendant on conviction of the offence in the proceedings in question.

(5) A reference in this section to an offence under the *Sexual Offences Act* 2003 or to an offence specified in subsection (2) includes a reference to—

(a) inciting the commission of that offence;

(b) conspiracy to commit that offence; and

(c) attempting to commit that offence;

and, in relation to an offence falling within paragraphs (a) to (c), a reference in this section to the enactment providing for the offence so falling has effect as a reference to the enactment providing for the offence under that Act or, as the case may be, for the offence so specified.

(6) This section applies to any proceedings, whenever commenced, other than proceedings in which the defendant has been convicted or acquitted of the 2003 Act offence or the pre-commencement offence before the commencement of this section.

This provision was enacted as a response to *R. v. Newbon* [2005] 4 *Archbold News* 6, Crown Court (at Stoke-on-Trent) (Judge Glenn), in which it was held that where there were two counts of rape, one contrary to the 1956 Act and one contrary to the 2003 Act, because the complainant was unable to say whether the incident occurred before or after the commencement of the 2003 Act, both counts must fail; and *R. v. A. (Prosecutor's appeal)* [2006] 1 Cr.App.R. 28, CA, in which it was held that where the prosecution were unable to prove whether an indecent assault had been committed before or after midnight on April 30, 2004, albeit the date on which an offence was committed was not generally a material averment, if there were alternative counts, one alleging an offence under the 1956 Act and one alleging an offence under the 2003 Act, then there would have to be acquittals on both counts. As to why the enactment of section 55 was unnecessary, and as to why all that was needed was a single count alleging conduct that was contrary to both the 1956 Act and the 2003 Act (the statement of offence identifying both provisions), see the 2007 edition of this work. **20–1b**

Sexual Offences Acts 1985 and 1993

The *SOA* 1985 increased the penalties for attempted rape and indecent assault on a woman. It also created two summary offences relating to the soliciting of women by men for the purposes of prostitution (*post*, § 20–237). The *SOA* 1993 abolished the common law presumption that a boy under 14 years was incapable of sexual intercourse. **20–2**

Criminal Justice and Public Order Act 1994

This Act effected further substantial changes to the law. It redefined the offence of rape to include non-consensual anal intercourse with a man or a woman. It made lawful the buggery of a woman in private where the woman consented and both parties were over 18. It legalised homosexual acts in private where both parties consented and were over 18; the previous minimum age had been 21. It extended the *SOA* 1967 to the armed forces and the merchant navy. It revised the penalties for the various circumstances in which buggery remained unlawful despite the consent of both parties. It further extended the anonymity provisions to cover allegations of inchoate offences. All of these changes, except the last, took effect upon Royal Assent, *viz.* November 3, 1994; the exception came into force on February 3, 1995. **20–3**

Sexual Offences (Conspiracy and Incitement) Act 1996

As to the extended jurisdiction of the courts of England and Wales in relation to offences of incitement to commit certain sexual offences against children, see section 2 of the 1996 Act, *ante*, § 2–36b. Section 1 (dealing with conspiracy) was repealed by the *Criminal Justice (Terrorism and Conspiracy) Act* 1998: see now the more general section 1A of the *CLA* 1977, inserted therein by the 1998 Act (*post*, § 33–22). **20–4**

Sex Offenders Act 1997

This Act imposed requirements as to the notification of information to the police by persons who have committed certain sexual offences, and to make provision with respect to the commission of certain sexual acts outside the United Kingdom. The whole Act (which came into force on September 1, 1997 (*Sex Offenders Act 1997* **20–5**

(Commencement) Order 1997 (S.I. 1997 No. 1920))) was repealed as from May 1, 2004 (*ante*, § 20–1) by the *SOA* 2003. Part I (notification requirements, other than section 5A) has been replaced by sections 80 to 92 of the 2003 Act. Section 5A (inserted by the *CJCSA* 2000) made provision for the making of a restraining order on conviction. "Restraining orders" have been replaced by "sexual offences prevention orders" (s.104 of the 2003 Act), and they may be made in respect of an offence committed before the commencement date (see s.106(4)), and the notification requirements are little more than a continuation of the former provisions, which in any event had retrospective effect (*Ibbotson v. U.K.* [1999] Crim.L.R. 153, European Commission on Human Rights). There will thus be no further need to refer to Part I of this Act after May 1, 2004.

Part II (ss.7 and 8) extended the jurisdiction of the courts of the United Kingdom (section 8 relating to Scotland). Section 7 has been replaced by section 72 of the 2003 Act (*ante*, §§ 2–36b *et seq.*)), but it will continue to apply in relation to acts done prior to the commencement date (*ante*, § 20–1).

Sexual Offences (Protected Material) Act 1997

20–6 See *ante*, §§ 12–111 *et seq.*

Youth Justice and Criminal Evidence Act 1999

20–7 This Act further restricted the cross-examination of complainants. First, it prohibited cross-examination by the accused in person (see *ante*, § 8–123b). Secondly, it tightened up the rules as to cross-examination of the complainant about previous sexual experience (*ante*, §§ 8–123h *et seq.*). Thirdly, it extended the latter restrictions to complainants of all sexual offences, whereas they were formerly confined to allegations of "a rape offence".

Sexual Offences (Amendment) Act 2000

20–8 This Act amended the Acts of 1956 and 1967 so as to reduce the age at which consensual homosexual activity in private is lawful from 18 years to 16 years. It also created a new offence consisting of a person aged 18 or over having sexual intercourse or engaging "in any other form of sexual activity with or directed towards" a person under that age if he is in a position of trust in relation to that person. Section 3, which created this offence, has been repealed and replaced by the more extensive provisions of sections 16 to 24 of the *SOA* 2003. This repeal took effect on May 1, 2004, but the repealed provision will continue to apply in relation to conduct occurring before that date, but on or after January 8, 2001 (*Sexual Offences (Amendment) Act 2000 (Commencement No. 1) Order* 2000 (S.I. 2000 No. 3303)): see generally, *ante*, § 20–1.

Sexual Offences Act 2003

20–9 The long title describes it as making "new provision about sexual offences, their prevention and the protection of children from harm from other sexual acts". It came into force on May 1, 2004 (as to which, see *ante*, § 20–1). It re-defines some offences (*e.g.* rape), creates a range of new offences (varying from assault by penetration to voyeurism), provides a definition of "sexual", makes express provision in relation to the key issue of consent, re-enacts, with amendments, the provisions of the *Sex Offenders Act* 1997 (*ante*, § 20–5), and establishes a range of new measures intended to guard against the commission of further offences by sex offenders (notification orders, foreign travel orders, risk of sexual harm orders).

For further discussion of the Act, see Temkin & Ashworth, "Rape, Sexual Assaults and the Problems of Consent" [2004] Crim.L.R. 328, and J.R. Spencer, "Child and Family Offences" [2004] Crim.L.R. 347.

Delay and the prosecution of sexual offences

20–9a It is a common feature of prosecutions for sexual offences that many years have passed between the alleged offence and the institution of proceedings. The usual reason for this is that the complainant has delayed making any form of allegation of impropriety such as would trigger a formal investigation. Apart from giving rise to issues as to which legislation is the appropriate legislation in respect of any prosecution (as to which, see *ante*, §§ 20–1, 20–1a), and as to what penalties are available in the event of a conviction, this phenomenon frequently gives rise to an application for the proceedings to be stayed as an abuse of process, on the ground that it would be impossible for the defendant to receive a fair trial. As to this, see *ante*, § 4–70; as to appropriate directions to the jury, see *ante*, § 4–71; and, as to the attitude of the Court of Appeal, see *ante*, § 7–48.

Sentencing guidelines

In May, 2007, the Sentencing Guidelines Council issued a definitive guideline on sexual offences, which applies to offenders sentenced on or after May 14, 2007. Although its title refers only to the *SOA* 2003, it also deals with offences concerning indecent photographs of children (*Protection of Children Act* 1978, s.1, *CJA* 1988, s.160 (*post*, §§ 31–107 *et seq.*)) and keeping a brothel used for prostitution (*SOA* 1956, s.33A (*post*, § 20–229)). For details thereof, see Appendix K–83 *et seq.* **20–9b**

II. OFFENCES

A. GENERAL INTERPRETATION

(1) Consent

Sexual Offences Act 2003, s.74

"Consent"

74. For the purposes of this Part, a person consents if he agrees by choice, and has the freedom and capacity to make that choice. **20–10**

The reference to "this Part" is to Part 1 of the Act, comprising sections 1 to 79.

The fact that a defendant had not disclosed that he was suffering from a serious sexually transmitted disease is not relevant to the issue of whether a person with whom he engaged in sexual intercourse had consented to it within the meaning of section 74; in such a case, no issues arose under the presumptions in relation to consent under sections 75 and 76 (*post*, §§ 20–14, 20–15), since they made reference only to two particular deceptions, and made no reference at all to implied deceptions: *R. v. B.* [2007] 1 Cr.App.R. 29, CA (observing that no defence of consent would be available if the defendant were to be charged with an offence contrary to the *Offences against the Person Act* 1861, s.20 (*ante*, § 19–200) where the complainant contracted the disease through the sexual intercourse).

(i) As to the effect of excessive but voluntary consumption of alcohol on the ability of a person to consent to sexual activity, the proper construction of section 74 is that consent can only be said to have been absent if the effect of the alcohol was such that the complainant had temporarily lost the capacity to choose whether to engage in the sexual activity; this stage may be reached before unconsciousness; whether or not it had was a question of fact, which would depend on the actual state of mind of the parties involved; the question of capacity was not dependent on (a) whether the alcohol had made either or both parties less inhibited than they would otherwise have been, (b) whether either or both might afterwards have regretted what happened, and wished that it had not, (c) whether either or both may have had a poor recollection of what happened, or (d) whether either or both had behaved irresponsibly; the essential question for decision would be whether the evidence proved that the complainant had not consented; (ii) as to how juries should be directed in such cases, it would not be sufficient merely to read the statutory definition of consent in section 74 without further elucidation; assistance would be necessary as to the meaning of "capacity"; and it may, in some cases, be necessary to direct the jury as to the distinction between an allegation that the complainant was unconscious, and an allegation that although she was capable of consenting, despite her state, she was not in fact consenting and was giving clear indications that she was rejecting the defendant: *R. v. Bree* [2007] 2 Cr.App.R. 13, CA.

In *R. v. H.*, unreported, July 10, 2007, CA ([2007] EWCA Crim. 2056), the Court of Appeal further considered the issue of a complainant's capacity to consent to intercourse where she (or he) has voluntarily consumed excessive quantities of alcohol or drugs, or both. The court held that: (i) the jury would be entitled, as a matter of law, to bear in mind any lies, if that is what the jury found them to be, told by the defendant as to whether or not he had intercourse with the complainant on the occasion in question, when considering not only whether the defendant had a reasonable belief in consent, but also whether the complainant did in fact consent; (ii) it was for the jury, not the judge, to decide, on the basis of the evidence called, whether or not the complainant had the capacity to consent or whether or not she did in fact consent; and (iii) any supposed principle to the effect that a complainant's inability to remember whether or not she consented must prove fatal to the prosecution case had been expressly disavowed by the court in *R. v. Bree*.

There is Canadian authority to the effect that there is no defence of "prior" consent to sexual activity; consent must be given to a particular activity, and at the time of that activity, and is a continuing state of mind, which does not remain operative after a person has become unconscious and incapable of consenting: see *R. v. Ashlee*, 212 C.C.C. (3d) 477, Alberta Court of Appeal.

Evidence as to complainant's sexual history

20–11 Evidence about the lack of sexual experience of a complainant, and about her attitudes and religious beliefs that intercourse before marriage was wrong, is capable of relating to the issue of consent: *R. v. Amado-Taylor* [2001] 8 *Archbold News* 1, CA. Where, therefore, the defence to a charge of rape was not just consent, but enthusiastic participation with a person who was "very nearly a stranger" to the complainant, evidence as to her previous virginity, as to her objection to intercourse before marriage and as to her religious beliefs on that topic was admissible from her, as was evidence from her boyfriend of six weeks as to her steadfast objection to intercourse before marriage: *ibid. Amado-Taylor* was followed in *R. v. Tobin* [2003] Crim.L.R. 408, CA (a case of indecent assault), but the court acknowledged that the case was less strong and that the evidence (of the mother of the 16-year-old complainant to the effect that she was a good girl at home) was of little value. It is submitted that, at best, it should be regarded as confined to its particular facts; and that it should not be regarded as laying down any principle for the reasons given in the commentary in *Criminal Law Week* 2003/20/2.

Evidence of, or cross-examination, as to the complainant's prior sexual behaviour for the purposes of showing consent is severely restricted: see the *YJCEA* 1999, s.41, *ante*, §§ 8–123k *et seq.*

Recent complaint

20–12 As to the admissibility at common law, in cases of rape and kindred offences, of the fact that a complaint was made by the victim shortly after the alleged offence and of the details thereof, see §§ 8–103 *et seq.* in the 2005 edition of this work. As to the admissibility of "recent complaint" statements under the *CJA* 2003, see section 120(1), (4), (7) and (8), *ante*, § 11–34. It should be noted that whereas at common law, recent complaint evidence was admissible only as evidence of the consistency of the conduct of the complainant, and as tending to negative consent, under the 2003 Act, such evidence is evidence of the truth of the matter stated. Whilst it remains to be seen how the courts will interpret the 2003 Act, one thing seems clear, and one thing seems likely. First, there can be no doubting that where, at common law, such statements were admitted to show consistency, they will continue to be admissible for the same purpose. Secondly, it is probable that the courts will stick to the long-standing rule of common law (and common-sense) that a complainant's previous consistent statement is incapable of amounting to corroboration (the rule against self-corroboration).

Distress of complainant

20–13 The weight to be given to evidence of the complainant's apparent distress varies infinitely, and a jury should be directed that although such evidence may amount to corroboration, they should be satisfied that there is no question of it having been feigned before they treat it as such; it should not be routine to direct the jury that little weight should be accorded to such evidence, although in an appropriate case, they should be alerted to the sometimes real risk that such evidence might have been feigned: *R. v. Romeo* [2004] Crim.L.R. 302, CA; and see also *R. v. Knight*, 50 Cr.App.R. 122, CA; *R. v. Wilson (T.)*, 58 Cr.App.R. 304, CA; *R. v. Chauhan*, 73 Cr.App.R. 232, CA; and *R. v. Venn*, unreported, February 14, 2003, CA ([2003] EWCA Crim. 236). Key considerations going to the weight to be attached to such evidence will be, first, as to whether it was genuine or feigned, and, secondly, if genuine, was it referable to being the victim of an offence or, for example, to having consented to conduct subsequently regretted? As to the first issue, the court will want to consider whether the distress manifested itself as part and parcel of the complaint or independently thereof, and, if the latter, whether the complainant had any reason to suppose that he or she was being observed.

General evidence of the demeanour of the victim of an alleged offence after the occasion of the alleged offence is inadmissible for the purpose of supporting the veracity of his or her account of the offence: *R. v. Keast* [1998] Crim.L.R. 748, CA. Such evidence should only be admitted where there was some concrete basis for regarding the demeanour and state of mind described by the witness as confirming or disproving that sexual abuse had occurred: *R. v. Venn, ante*.

Sexual Offences Act 2003, ss.75, 76

Evidential presumptions about consent

75.—(1) If in proceedings for an offence to which this section applies it is proved— **20–14**

(a) that the defendant did the relevant act,

(b) that any of the circumstances specified in subsection (2) existed, and

(c) that the defendant knew that those circumstances existed,

the complainant is to be taken not to have consented to the relevant act unless sufficient evidence is adduced to raise an issue as to whether he consented, and the defendant is to be taken not to have reasonably believed that the complainant consented unless sufficient evidence is adduced to raise an issue as to whether he reasonably believed it.

(2) The circumstances are that—

(a) any person was, at the time of the relevant act or immediately before it began, using violence against the complainant or causing the complainant to fear that immediate violence would be used against him;

(b) any person was, at the time of the relevant act or immediately before it began, causing the complainant to fear that violence was being used, or that immediate violence would be used, against another person;

(c) the complainant was, and the defendant was not, unlawfully detained at the time of the relevant act;

(d) the complainant was asleep or otherwise unconscious at the time of the relevant act;

(e) because of the complainant's physical disability, the complainant would not have been able at the time of the relevant act to communicate to the defendant whether the complainant consented;

(f) any person had administered to or caused to be taken by the complainant, without the complainant's consent, a substance which, having regard to when it was administered or taken, was capable of causing or enabling the complainant to be stupefied or overpowered at the time of the relevant act.

(3) In subsection (2)(a) and (b), the reference to the time immediately before the relevant act began is, in the case of an act which is one of a continuous series of sexual activities, a reference to the time immediately before the first sexual activity began.

As to the offences to which this section applies, this is specified in the sections concerned, *e.g.* section 1(3), *post*, § 20–19.

Conclusive presumptions about consent

76.—(1) If in proceedings for an offence to which this section applies it is proved that the defendant did the relevant act and that any of the circumstances specified in subsection (2) existed, it is to be conclusively presumed— **20–15**

(a) that the complainant did not consent to the relevant act, and
(b) that the defendant did not believe that the complainant consented to the relevant act.

(2) The circumstances are that—
(a) the defendant intentionally deceived the complainant as to the nature or purpose of the relevant act;
(b) the defendant intentionally induced the complainant to consent to the relevant act by impersonating a person known personally to the complainant.

As to the application of this section, see the note to section 75, *ante*.

In *R. v. Jheeta* [2007] 2 Cr.App.R. 34, CA, it was held that the ambit of the presumptions in section 76 is limited to the "relevant act" involved in the offence alleged (*e.g.*, on a charge of rape, penetration of the complainant by the defendant with his penis (see s.77, *post*)); therefore, the conclusive presumption stemming from the defendant having intentionally deceived the complainant as to the nature or purpose of the relevant act (s.76(2)(a)) will rarely arise, and will not arise merely because the complainant was deceived by disingenuous blandishments; examples of deceptions as to the nature of the act which would fall within section 76(2)(a) were *R. v. Flattery* [1877] 2 Q.B.D. 410, and *R. v. Williams* [1923] 1 K.B. 340, CCA (what was being done was some form of medical procedure); and examples of deceptions as to the purpose of the act were *R. v. Tabassum* [2000] 2 Cr.App.R. 328, CA (women submitting to breast examinations by non-medically qualified person pretending to be qualified and to be conducting breast cancer survey), and *R. v. Green*, unreported, May 20, 2002, CA ([2002] EWCA Crim. 1501) (bogus experiment whereby complainants were asked to masturbate to assess their potential for impotence); but an example falling outside section 76(2)(a) would be *R. v. Linekar* [1995] 2 Cr.App.R. 49, CA (deception as to an intention to pay for intercourse). As to *Tabassum*, it should be noted that it is possible to read the judgment of the court in *Jheeta*, *ante* (at [26]), as not being categorical about the situation in that case being within section 76(2)(a).

In *R. v. Devonald*, 72 J.C.L. 280, CA ([2008] EWCA Crim. 527), a teenage boy had been tricked into masturbating in front of a webcam by the applicant who had been pretending, over the internet, to be a 20-year-old girl, and whose purpose had been to teach the boy a lesson for some supposed slight upon the applicant's daughter and to embarrass him. On a prosecution for causing the boy to engage in sexual activity without consent, it was held that it had been open to the jury to conclude that he had been deceived as to the purpose of the act of masturbation within section 76; he was deceived into believing that he was indulging in a sexual act with, and for the gratification of, a girl with whom he was having an online relationship and that is why he agreed to do what he did; whilst the "nature" of the act was undoubtedly sexual, its "purpose" encompassed rather more than the specific purpose of sexual gratification by the defendant in the act of masturbation. For the suggestion that the court went too far, see the commentary of Jonathan Rogers (in the Journal of Criminal Law) and Smith and Hogan, *Criminal Law* (12th ed., 2008, by David Ormerod, at pp.688, 689).

For further discussion, see Temkin & Ashworth, "Rape, Sexual Assaults and the Problems of Consent" [2004] Crim.L.R. 328.

Sexual Offences Act 2003, s.77

Sections 75 and 76: relevant acts

20–16 **77.** In relation to an offence to which sections 75 and 76 apply, references in those sections to the relevant act and to the complainant are to be read as follows—

Offence	*Relevant Act*
An offence under section 1 (rape).	The defendant intentionally penetrating, with his penis, the vagina, anus or mouth of another person ("the complainant").

Offence	*Relevant Act*
An offence under section 2 (assault by penetration).	The defendant intentionally penetrating, with a part of his body or anything else, the vagina or anus of another person ("the complainant"), where the penetration is sexual.
An offence under section 3 (sexual assault).	The defendant intentionally touching another person ("the complainant"), where the touching is sexual.
An offence under section 4 (causing a person to engage in sexual activity without consent).	The defendant intentionally causing another person ("the complainant") to engage in an activity, where the activity is sexual.

(2) "Sexual"

Sexual Offences Act 2003, s.78

"Sexual"

78. For the purposes of this Part (except section 71), penetration, touching or any other activity is sexual if a reasonable person would consider that— 20–17

(a) whatever its circumstances or any person's purpose in relation to it, it is because of its nature sexual, or

(b) because of its nature it may be sexual and because of its circumstances or the purpose of any person in relation to it (or both) it is sexual.

As to the need for a two-stage approach to the application of this section, see *R. v. H., post*, § 20–36.

(3) "Penetration", "touching" and other words and expressions

Sexual Offences Act 2003, s.79

Part 1: general interpretation

79.—(1) The following apply for the purposes of this Part. 20–18

(2) Penetration is a continuing act from entry to withdrawal.

(3) References to a part of the body include references to a part surgically constructed (in particular, through gender reassignment surgery).

(4) "Image" means a moving or still image and includes an image produced by any means and, where the context permits, a three-dimensional image.

(5) References to an image of a person include references to an image of an imaginary person.

(6) "Mental disorder" has the meaning given by section 1 of the *Mental Health Act* 1983.

(7) References to observation (however expressed) are to observation whether direct or by looking at an image.

(8) Touching includes touching—

(a) with any part of the body,

(b) with anything else,

(c) through anything,

and in particular includes touching amounting to penetration.

(9) "Vagina" includes vulva.

(10) In relation to an animal, references to the vagina or anus include references to any similar part.

The reference to "this Part" is to Part 1 of the Act, *i.e.* sections 1 to 79.

For section 1 of the *MHA* 1983, see *ante*, § 5–887.

B. RAPE

(1) Statute

Sexual Offences Act 2003, s.1

Rape

1.—(1) A person (A) commits an offence if— 20–19

(a) he intentionally penetrates the vagina, anus or mouth of another person (B) with his penis,
(b) B does not consent to the penetration, and
(c) A does not reasonably believe that B consents.

(2) Whether a belief is reasonable is to be determined having regard to all the circumstances, including any steps A has taken to ascertain whether B consents.

(3) Sections 75 and 76 apply to an offence under this section.

(4) A person guilty of an offence under this section is liable, on conviction on indictment, to imprisonment for life.

For sections 75 and 76, see, *ante*, §§ 20–14, 20–15.

(2) Indictment

STATEMENT OF OFFENCE

20–20 *Rape, contrary to section 1(1) of the* Sexual Offences Act *2003*.

PARTICULARS OF OFFENCE

A B on the —— day of ——, 20—, intentionally penetrated the vagina [*or "anus" or "mouth"*] *of C D who did not consent to the penetration, the said A B not reasonably believing that C D consented.*

It is submitted that where there is non-consensual penetration of both the vagina and the anus or the mouth, two offences will have been committed, provided all the other ingredients are present, and there should be separate counts to reflect this. Where there is repeated penetration of, for example, the vagina, common sense should dictate whether there should be more than one count.

(3) Class of offence and mode of trial

20–21 This offence is a class 2 offence, *ante*, § 2–17, triable on indictment only: s.1(4), *ante*.

(4) Sentence

Maximum

20–22 Life imprisonment: s.1(4), *ante*.

Guidelines

20–23 See now the Sentencing Guidelines Council's definitive guideline for sentencing in cases involving sexual offences (Appendix K–83 *et seq.*). The guideline applies to offenders sentenced on or after May 14, 2007.

(5) Elements of the offence

Penetration

20–24 Penetration is a continuing act from entry to withdrawal: see s.79(1), (2), *ante*, § 20–18. It follows that consensual intercourse will become rape if the woman (or man) ceases to consent during the intercourse, and the man (other man), with the necessary *mens rea*, continues the intercourse; and similarly, non-consensual intercourse will become rape if the man continues the intercourse after ceasing to believe on reasonable grounds that the complainant was consenting: see *Kaitamaki v. R.* [1985] A.C. 147, PC.

Where vaginal rape is alleged, it is not necessary to prove penetration of the vagina, properly so-called; it is sufficient that there was any degree of penetration by the penis within the labia of the pudendum of the complainant: *R. v. J.F.*, unreported, December 16, 2002, CA ([2002] EWCA Crim. 2936); and see section 79(1), (9), *ante*, § 20–18 ("'Vagina' includes vulva.").

Intention

20–24a See *R. v. Heard* [2007] 1 Cr.App.R. 37, CA (*post*, § 20–34a).

Lack of consent

See *ante*, §§ 20–10 *et seq*. **20–25**

Absence of reasonable belief in consent

Whether a belief is reasonable is to be determined having regard to all the circumstances, including any steps the defendant has taken to ascertain whether the complainant in fact consented: s.1(2), *ante*, § 20–19. As to the relevance of alcohol or drugs taken by the defendant, see *ante*, § 17–116. **20–25a**

(6) Liability of accessories

A woman may be convicted as a secondary party: *R. v. Ram* (1893) 17 Cox 609 at 610n. **20–26**

A person may be convicted as an aider and abettor, though the principal is acquitted on the ground that he believed the complainant was consenting: *R. v. Cogan and Leak* [1976] Q.B. 217, 61 Cr.App.R. 217, CA.

(7) Attempt

An attempt to commit rape will be charged as contrary to the *Criminal Attempts Act* 1981 and the general law of attempt will apply thereto. The test, therefore, will be whether the defendant did an act with the requisite intent which was more than merely preparatory to the commission of the full offence: see section 1(1) of the 1981 Act (*post*, § 33–120). Where there is evidence sufficient in law to support a finding that he did such an act, the question whether or not his act fell within section 1(1) is a question of fact: *ibid*., s.4(3) (*post*, § 33–124). Accordingly, it is not necessary that the defendant should have done an act of an unequivocally sexual nature: *R. v. Patnaik* [2000] 3 *Archbold News* 2, CA. It is sufficient if there is evidence from which the intent can be inferred and there are proved acts which a jury could properly regard as more than merely preparatory to the commission of the full offence: *Att.-Gen.'s Reference (No. 1 of 1992)*, 96 Cr.App.R. 298, CA. **20–27**

Where an indictment charged H with rape, and W as an aider and abettor, and the jury found H guilty of attempting to commit a rape and W of aiding H in the attempt, and it was contended that this finding amounted to an acquittal of W, the objection was overruled and the conviction of W was affirmed: *R. v. Hapgood* (1870) L.R. 1 C.C.R. 221.

C. ASSAULTS

(1) Statute

Sexual Offences Act 2003, ss.2, 3

Assault by penetration

2.—(1) A person (A) commits an offence if— **20–28**

(a) he intentionally penetrates the vagina or anus of another person (B) with a part of his body or anything else,

(b) the penetration is sexual,

(c) B does not consent to the penetration, and

(d) A does not reasonably believe that B consents.

(2), (3) [*Identical to s.1(2), (3),* ante, *§ 20–19.*]

(4) A person guilty of an offence under this section is liable, on conviction on indictment, to imprisonment for life.

Sexual assault

3.—(1) A person (A) commits an offence if— **20–29**

(a) he intentionally touches another person (B),

(b) the touching is sexual,

(c) B does not consent to the touching, and

(d) A does not reasonably believe that B consents.

(2), (3) [*Identical to s.1(2), (3),* ante, *§ 20–19.*]

(4) A person guilty of an offence under this section is liable—

(a) on summary conviction, to imprisonment for a term not exceeding *6* [12] months or a fine not exceeding the statutory maximum or both;

(b) on conviction on indictment, to imprisonment for a term not exceeding 10 years.

[In subs. (4)(a), "12" is substituted for "6", as from a day to be appointed, by the *CJA* 2003, s.282(2) and (3). The increase has no application to offences committed before the substitution takes effect: s.282(4).]

(2) Indictments

(a) *Assault by penetration*

STATEMENT OF OFFENCE

20–30 *Assault by penetration, contrary to section 2(1) of the* Sexual Offences Act *2003.*

PARTICULARS OF OFFENCE

A B, on the —— day of ——, 20—, intentionally penetrated sexually the vagina [or *anus*] *of C D with a part of his body, namely …* [or *with a …*], *the circumstances being that the penetration was sexual, CD did not consent to the penetration, and the said A B did not reasonably believe that CD consented.*

(b) *Sexual assault*

STATEMENT OF OFFENCE

20–31 *Sexual assault, contrary to section 3(1) of the* Sexual Offences Act *2003.*

PARTICULARS OF OFFENCE

A B, on the —— day of ——, 20—, intentionally touched C D, the circumstances being that the touching was sexual, CD did not consent to the touching, and the said A B did not reasonably believe that C D consented to the touching.

(3) Class of offence and mode of trial

20–32 The offence contrary to section 2 is indictable only (s.2(4), *ante*), and that contrary to section 3 is triable either way (s.3(4), *ante*). The offence contrary to section 2 is a class 2 offence, and that contrary to section 3 is a class 3 offence: *ante*, § 2–17.

(4) Sentence

20–33 The offence contrary to section 2, life imprisonment: s.2(4), *ante*.

The offence contrary to section 3, on conviction on indictment, 10 years' imprisonment, and on summary conviction, six (12, as from a day to be appointed) months' imprisonment, or a fine not exceeding the statutory maximum, or both: s.3(4), *ante*.

For guidance, see now the Sentencing Guidelines Council's definitive guideline for sentencing in cases involving sexual offences (Appendix K–83 *et seq.*). The guideline applies to offenders sentenced on or after May 14, 2007.

(5) Elements of the offences

Penetration

20–34 See *ante*, § 20–24.

Intention

20–34a In *R. v. Heard* [2007] 1 Cr.App.R. 37, CA, it was said that voluntary intoxication can only be relied on as negativing *mens rea* in the case of crimes an ingredient of which is a specific or purposive intent; and it was held that sexual assault, contrary to section 3 of the 2003 Act, is not such a crime, notwithstanding that one element of the offence which has to be proved is an "intentional" touching of the complainant by the defendant (see s.3(1)(a)); whilst this means that the touching must be deliberate, and not accidental or even reckless, in those exceptional cases where the defendant's mind did not go with his physical act on account of his self-induced intoxication, this will not avail him. Whilst the case was concerned with section 3, the reasoning must apply equally to the offence under section 2 (and, indeed, section 1), however unlikely it may be that there would ever be a live issue as to the intentional nature of an act of penetration.

Any part of the body

See, in particular, section 79(3), *ante*, § 20–18. **20–35**

"Sexual"

See section 78, *ante*, § 20–17. **20–36**

In *R. v. H.* [2005] 2 Cr.App.R. 9, CA, it was held, (i) that where a person was charged with an offence under section 3, in determining whether the touching was sexual within the meaning of section 78 (*ante*, § 20–17), a two-stage approach was required; the first question was whether the touching, because of its nature, might be sexual, and the second was whether the touching, because of its circumstances or the purpose of any person in relation to it, was sexual; the nature of the touching referred to the actual touching that took place and, therefore, in considering whether the touching, because of its nature, might be sexual, the jury were not concerned with the circumstances before or after the touching, or the purpose of the defendant in relation to the touching; and (ii) that where the complainant had left her house during the evening, and had encountered a young man who had asked her for the time and had then said, "Do you fancy a shag?", before grabbing her tracksuit bottoms by the fabric in the area of one of the side-pockets and trying to pull her towards him, whereupon she managed to escape, there had been a "touching" for the purposes of section 3 (touching includes a touching of the clothing), and, although the judge had not adopted the two-stage approach (having taken the view that the circumstances alone (including what was said) could make the touching sexual), the conviction was not unsafe, looking at the case as a whole.

Assault/ touching

Although both offences have the word "assault" as part of their statutory name, it is **20–37** clear that this is intended as no more than a convenient label. Any attempt to introduce the common law notion of an assault in relation to either offence would clearly be inappropriate.

As to "touching", see, in particular, section 79(8), *ante*, § 20–18; and *R. v. H.*, *ante*.

Lack of consent

See *ante*, §§ 20–10 *et seq*. **20–38**

Absence of reasonable belief in consent

Whether a belief is reasonable is to be determined having regard to all the circum- **20–39** stances, including any steps the defendant has taken to ascertain whether the complainant in fact consented: ss.2(2), 3(2), *ante*, §§ 20–19, 20–28, 20–29. As to the relevance of alcohol or drugs taken by the defendant, see *ante*, § 17–116.

D. Causing Sexual Activity without Consent

(1) Statute

Sexual Offences Act 2003, s.4

Causing a person to engage in sexual activity without consent

4.—(1) A person (A) commits an offence if— **20–40**

(a) he intentionally causes another person (B) to engage in an activity,

(b) the activity is sexual,

(c) B does not consent to engaging in the activity, and

(d) A does not reasonably believe that B consents.

(2), (3) [*Identical to s.1(2), (3),* ante, *§ 20–19.*]

(4) A person guilty of an offence under this section, if the activity caused involved—

(a) penetration of B's anus or vagina,

(b) penetration of B's mouth with a person's penis,

(c) penetration of a person's anus or vagina with a part of B's body or by B with anything else, or

(d) penetration of a person's mouth with B's penis,

is liable, on conviction on indictment, to imprisonment for life.

(5) Unless subsection (4) applies, a person guilty of an offence under this section is liable—

(a) on summary conviction, to imprisonment for a term not exceeding *6* [12] months or to a fine not exceeding the statutory maximum or both;

(b) on conviction on indictment, to imprisonment for a term not exceeding 10 years.

[In subs. (5)(a), "12" is substituted for "6", as from a day to be appointed, by the *CJA* 2003, s.282(2) and (3). The increase has no application to offences committed before the substitution takes effect: s.282(4).]

(2) Indictment

STATEMENT OF OFFENCE

20–41 *Causing a person to engage in sexual activity without consent, contrary to section 4(1) of the* Sexual Offences Act *2003*.

PARTICULARS OF OFFENCE

A B, on the —— day of ——, 20—, intentionally caused C D to engage in an activity, namely ..., the circumstances being such that the activity was sexual, CD did not consent to engage in the activity and the said A B did not reasonably believe that C D consented.

It is essential that if the activity alleged falls within the various activities specified in subsection (4), this should be particularised in the indictment.

(3) Class of offence and mode of trial

20–42 If the particulars allege an activity falling within subsection (4), the offence will be triable only on indictment; otherwise, it will be triable either way: s.4(4), (5), *ante*. According to whether it is triable only on indictment, or either way, it will be a class 2 or class 3 offence, *ante*, § 2–17.

(4) Sentence

20–43 Upon conviction of the aggravated offence, life imprisonment: s.4(4); otherwise, on conviction on indictment, 10 years' imprisonment, or on summary conviction, six (12, as from a day to be appointed) months' imprisonment, or a fine not exceeding the statutory maximum, or both: s.4(5).

For guidance, see the Sentencing Guidelines Council's definitive guideline for sentencing in cases involving sexual offences (Appendix K–83 *et seq.*). The guideline applies to offenders sentenced on or after May 14, 2007.

(5) Elements of the offence

Penetration

20–44 See *ante*, § 20–24.

Any part of the body

20–45 See, in particular, section 79(3), *ante*, § 20–18.

"Sexual"

20–46 See section 78, *ante*, § 20–17.

Lack of consent

See *ante*, §§ 20–10 *et seq.* **20–47**

Absence of reasonable belief in consent

Whether a belief is reasonable is to be determined having regard to all the circumstances, including any steps the defendant has taken to ascertain whether the complainant in fact consented: s.4(2), *ante*, §§ 20–19, 20–40. As to the relevance of alcohol or drugs taken by the defendant, see *ante*, § 17–116. **20–48**

E. RAPE AND OTHER OFFENCES AGAINST CHILDREN UNDER 13

(1) Statute

Sexual Offences Act 2003, ss.5–8

Rape of a child under 13

5.—(1) A person commits an offence if— **20–49**

(a) he intentionally penetrates the vagina, anus or mouth of another person with his penis, and

(b) the other person is under 13.

(2) [*Identical to s.2(4)* ante, *§ 20–28.*]

Assault of a child under 13 by penetration

6.—(1) A person commits an offence if— **20–50**

(a) he intentionally penetrates the vagina or anus of another person with a part of his body or anything else,

(b) the penetration is sexual, and

(c) the other person is under 13.

(2) [*Identical to s.2(4)* ante, *§ 20–28.*]

Sexual assault of a child under 13

7.—(1) A person commits an offence if— **20–51**

(a) he intentionally touches another person,

(b) the touching is sexual, and

(c) the other person is under 13.

(2) A person guilty of an offence under this section is liable—

(a) on summary conviction, to imprisonment for a term not exceeding *6* [12] months or a fine not exceeding the statutory maximum or both;

(b) on conviction on indictment, to imprisonment for a term not exceeding 14 years.

[In subs. (3)(a), "12" is substituted for "6", as from a day to be appointed, by the *CJA* 2003, s.282(2) and (3). The increase has no application to offences committed before the substitution takes effect: s.282(4).]

Causing or inciting a child under 13 to engage in sexual activity

8.—(1) A person commits an offence if— **20–52**

(a) he intentionally causes or incites another person (B) to engage in an activity,

(b) the activity is sexual, and

(c) B is under 13.

(2) A person guilty of an offence under this section, if the activity caused or incited involved—

(a) penetration of B's anus or vagina,

(b) penetration of B's mouth with a person's penis,

(c) penetration of a person's anus or vagina with a part of B's body or by B with anything else, or

(d) penetration of a person's mouth with B's penis,

is liable, on conviction on indictment, to imprisonment for life.

(3) Unless subsection (2) applies, a person guilty of an offence under this section is liable—

(a) on summary conviction, to imprisonment for a term not exceeding *6* [12] months or to a fine not exceeding the statutory maximum or both;

(b) on conviction on indictment, to imprisonment for a term not exceeding 14 years.

[In subs. (3)(a), "12" is substituted for "6", as from a day to be appointed, by the *CJA* 2003, s.282(2) and (3). The increase has no application to offences committed before the substitution takes effect: s.282(4).]

(2) Indictments

STATEMENT OF OFFENCE

20–53 *Rape of a child under 13, contrary to section 5(1) of the* Sexual Offences Act *2003*.

PARTICULARS OF OFFENCE

A B, on the —— day of ——, 20—, intentionally penetrated the vagina [or *anus* or *mouth*] *of C D, a person under the age of 13 years, with his penis.*

Indictments for offences contrary to sections 6 to 8 can easily be modelled on a combination of this indictment and the corresponding offences contrary to sections 2 to 4.

As to whether there should be one count or several, see *ante*, § 20–20.

(3) Class of offence and mode of trial

20–54 Offences contrary to sections 5 and 6, and the aggravated version of the offence contrary to section 8 are triable only on indictment (ss.5(2), 6(2), 8(2), *ante*), and are class 2 offences: *ante*, § 2–17. An offence contrary to section 7, and the non-aggravated version of the offence contrary to section 8 are triable either way (ss.7(2), 8(3), *ante*), and are class 3 offences: *ante*, § 2–17.

(4) Sentence

20–55 Offences contrary to sections 5 and 6, and the aggravated version of the offence contrary to section 8, life imprisonment: ss.5(2), 6(2), and 8(2). An offence contrary to section 7, and the non-aggravated version of the offence contrary to section 8, 14 years' imprisonment on conviction on indictment, or, on summary conviction, six (12, as from a day to be appointed) months' imprisonment, or a fine not exceeding the statutory maximum, or both: ss.7(2) and 8(3).

For guidance, see now the Sentencing Guidelines Council's definitive guideline for sentencing in cases involving sexual offences (K–83 *et seq.*). The guideline applies to offenders sentenced on or after May 14, 2007.

The circumstances in which a non-custodial sentence can possibly be appropriate when an adult man, even if young and immature, starts or continues serious sexual activity with a child known to be aged 11, must be vanishingly rare, even where there is no element of corruption and the child is an enthusiastic participant: *Att.-Gen.'s Reference (No. 29 of 2008) (R. v. Dixon)*, *The Times*, August 29, 2008, CA (ruling that such a sentence did not meet the essential fact that the law was there not only to protect children from the baleful influence of adults with an inappropriate interest in children but was also designed to protect them from themselves).

(5) Elements of the offences

20–56 The elements of the offences contrary to sections 5 to 8 correspond to those of the offences contrary to sections 1 to 4, *ante*, §§ 20–19 *et seq.*, save that (i) for an offence under any of these sections it has to be proved that the complainant was under the age of 13 years at the time of the offence, (ii) there is no need to prove either a lack of consent on the part of the complainant or an absence of reasonable belief in consent on the part of the defendant; and (iii) section 8, unlike section 4, includes "inciting" as well as "causing" sexual activity to be engaged in without consent.

It is plain from the manner in which the next group of sections are worded (see, in particular, sections 9(1)(c), 10(1)(c), 11(1)(d) and 12(1)(c)) that even a reasonable mistake as to the complainant's age will not avail a defendant. That section 5 creates an offence of strict liability involves no incompatibility with the ECHR: *R. v. G. (Secretary of State for the Home Department intervening)* [2008] 1 W.L.R. 1379, HL; and the prosecution of a child under section 5, rather than section 13 (child sex offences committed by children or young persons (*post*, § 20–79)), in relation to consensual sexual intercourse, does not engage Article 8: *ibid*.

As to proof of the child's age, section 99(2) of the *CYPA* 1933, taken together with Schedule 1 to that Act (*ante*, §§ 19–326, 19–328) make provision for a court to presume that the child was under the specified age where he "appears to the court" to have been under that age at the material time, unless the contrary is proved. It is submitted that a court should only proceed on the basis of appearance where it is sure that so to do is correct, and that a jury should be so directed. Where there is any possibility, therefore, that the court will not be sure about this, the prosecution ought to tender strict proof of the matter. The best way of doing this is to produce a duly certified copy of the certificate of birth, coupled with evidence of identity; but age may be proved by any other legal means: *R. v. Cox* [1898] 1 Q.B. 179 (age could be proved by persons who had seen the child and by a teacher at an elementary school which the child attended). Where a certificate of birth is put in, there must be evidence of identity as well: see *R. v. Nicholls* (1867) 10 Cox 476; *R. v. Bellis*, 6 Cr.App.R. 283, CCA; *R. v. Rogers*, 10 Cr.App.R. 276, CCA.

In the case of an adopted child, the date of birth may be proved by a certified copy of an entry in the Adopted Child Register: *Adoption and Children Act* 2002, s.77(5).

An offence of inciting a child to engage in sexual activity, contrary to section 8(1), may be committed (subject to the other elements of the offence being satisfied) by the making of a statement which is addressed to the world at large (here, by writing graffiti saying, "Girl 8-13 wanted for sex"), as opposed to being addressed to any specific or identifiable person; the gravamen of the offence is the incitement, rather than the actual effect on a particular child; and it is not significant that the term "another" is used in the section as opposed to the term "any other": *R. v. Jones (Ian)* [2007] 2 Cr.App.R. 21, CA (applying *R. v. Most* (1881) 7 Q.B.D. 244 (*ante*, § 19–123)).

(6) Secondary parties

Sexual Offences Act 2003, s.73

Exceptions to aiding, abetting and counselling

73.—(1) A person is not guilty of aiding, abetting or counselling the commission against a child of an offence to which this section applies if he acts for the purpose of— **20–57**

(a) protecting the child from sexually transmitted infection,

(b) protecting the physical safety of the child,

(c) preventing the child from becoming pregnant, or

(d) promoting the child's emotional well-being by the giving of advice,

and not for the purpose of obtaining sexual gratification or for the purpose of causing or encouraging the activity constituting the offence or the child's participation in it.

(2) This section applies to—

(a) an offence under any of sections 5 to 7 (offences against children under 13);

(b) an offence under section 9 (sexual activity with a child);

(c) an offence under section 13 which would be an offence under section 9 if the offender were aged 18;

(d) an offence under any of sections 16, 25, 30, 34 and 38 (sexual activity) against a person under 16.

(3) This section does not affect any other enactment or any rule of law restricting the circumstances in which a person is guilty of aiding, abetting or counselling an offence under this Part.

F. CHILD SEX OFFENCES

(1) Sexual activity with a child

(a) *Statute*

Sexual Offences Act 2003, s.9

Sexual activity with a child

9.—(1) A person aged 18 or over (A) commits an offence if— **20–58**

(a) he intentionally touches another person (B),
(b) the touching is sexual, and
(c) either—
(i) B is under 16 and A does not reasonably believe that B is 16 or over, or
(ii) B is under 13.

(2) A person guilty of an offence under this section, if the touching involved—
(a) penetration of B's anus or vagina with a part of A's body or anything else,
(b) penetration of B's mouth with A's penis,
(c) penetration of A's anus or vagina with a part of B's body, or
(d) penetration of A's mouth with B's penis,

is liable, on conviction on indictment, to imprisonment for a term not exceeding 14 years.

(3) [*Identical to s.8(3) (including the prospective amendment),* ante, *§ 20–52.*]

(b) *Indictment*

STATEMENT OF OFFENCE

20–59 *Sexual activity with a child, contrary to section 9(1) of the* Sexual Offences Act *2003.*

PARTICULARS OF OFFENCE

A B, a person of [or *over*] *the age of 18 years, on the —— day of ——, 20—, intentionally touched C D, in circumstances where the touching was sexual, C D was aged under 16 years,* [*and*] *the said A B did not reasonably believe that she was of or over the age of 16 years* [*and the touching involved penetration of C D's mouth with A B's penis*].

Where the complainant was under the age of 13, if the touching does not fall within subsection (2), then this provision adds nothing to section 7 (*ante*, § 20–51). Where the complainant was under the age of 13, if the touching falls within subsection (2)(a) or (b), then the appropriate charge will be under section 5 or 6 (*ante*, §§ 20–49, 20–50). The only circumstances, therefore, in which it would be appropriate to proceed under this section in the case of a complainant under the age of 13 will be where the touching falls within subsection (c) or (d). Such cases will also fall within section 7, but Parliament has indicated in this section an intention that such offences should be tried on indictment only, and it is only by charging them under this section that effect can be given to that intention. For further discussion of the inter-relationship between the offences, see J.R. Spencer, "Child and Family Offences" [2004] Crim.L.R. 347.

Whatever the age of the complainant, if it is alleged that the touching falls within subsection (2), this must be averred in the particulars.

(c) *Class of offence and mode of trial*

20–60 Where the charge is laid as falling within subsection (2), the offence is triable only on indictment; otherwise it is triable either way. Offences contrary to this section fall within class 3: *ante*, § 2–17.

(d) *Sentence*

20–61 On conviction on indictment, 14 years' imprisonment; on summary conviction, six (12, as from a day to be appointed) months' imprisonment, or a fine not exceeding the statutory maximum, or both: s.9(2), (3).

As to sentencing guidance, see now the Sentencing Guidelines Council's definitive guideline for sentencing in cases involving sexual offences (K–83 *et seq.*). The guideline applies to offenders sentenced on or after May 14, 2007.

(e) *Elements of the offence*

20–62 As to "penetration", see *ante*, § 20–24. As to "touching", see *ante*, § 20–37. As to "sexual", see *ante*, § 20–17. As to "intentionally", see *ante*, § 20–34a.

(f) *Secondary parties*

20–63 See section 73 of the 2003 Act, *ante*, § 20–57.

(2) Causing or inciting a child to engage in sexual activity

(a) *Statute*

Sexual Offences Act 2003, s.10

Causing or inciting a child to engage in sexual activity

10.—(1) A person aged 18 or over (A) commits an offence if— **20–64**

(a) he intentionally causes or incites another person (B) to engage in an activity,

(b) the activity is sexual, and

(c) either—

(i) B is under 16 and A does not reasonably believe that B is 16 or over, or

(ii) B is under 13.

(2) A person guilty of an offence under this section, if the activity caused or incited involved—

(a) penetration of B's anus or vagina,

(b) penetration of B's mouth with a person's penis,

(c) penetration of a person's anus or vagina with a part of B's body or by B with anything else, or

(d) penetration of a person's mouth with B's penis,

is liable, on conviction on indictment, to imprisonment for a term not exceeding 14 years.

(3) [*Identical to s.8(3) (including the prospective amendment),* ante, *§ 20–52.*]

(b) *Indictment*

STATEMENT OF OFFENCE

Causing [or *inciting*] *a child to engage in sexual activity, contrary to section 10 of the* Sexual Offences Act *2003.* **20–65**

PARTICULARS OF OFFENCE

A B, a person of [or *over*] *the age of 18 years, on the —— day of ——, 20—, intentionally caused* [or *incited*] *C D to engage in an activity, namely …, the circumstances being such that the activity was sexual, C D was aged under 16 years and the said A B did not reasonably believe that she was of or over the age of 16 years.*

Where the complainant was under the age of 13, there appears to be no scope for the operation of this section. The entirety of the ground seems to be covered by section 8 (*ante*, § 20–52). If the activity caused or incited does not fall within subsection (2), then the mode of trial and penalty provisions are identical (ss.8(3) and 10(3)). If, however, the activity caused or incited does fall within subsection (2), then the maximum penalty under this section is lower than the maximum penalty under section 8. The curious, and surely unintended result, is that identical offences are created, but with different maximum penalties. The statement that the offences are identical is subject to the qualification that the offence under section 10 can only be committed by a person aged 18 or over. This underlines the anomaly, as it means that a 17-year-old can only be prosecuted for the offence with the higher maximum penalty. And the anomaly is further compounded by section 13 (*post*, § 20–79), which specifically addresses the case of a person under 18 doing anything that would be an offence under any of sections 9 to 12. This stipulates that in such a case, the offender is guilty of a distinct offence with a significantly lower maximum penalty (five years). This appears to overlook the fact where the complainant was under 13, the offending conduct will frequently fall within section 5, 6, 7 or 8, as well as section 9 or 10.

If it is alleged that the touching falls within subsection (2), this must be averred in the particulars.

(c) *Class of offence and mode of trial*

Where the charge is laid as falling within subsection (2), the offence is triable only on indictment; otherwise it is triable either way. Offences contrary to this section fall within class 3, but it would seem that if ever a case involving a child under 13 and falling within subsection (2) were to be prosecuted under this section (as to which, see *ante*, § 20–65), then it would properly be regarded as a class 2 offence: *ante*, § 2–17. **20–66**

(d) *Sentence*

20–67 On conviction on indictment, 14 years' imprisonment; on summary conviction, six (12, as from a day to be appointed) months' imprisonment, or a fine not exceeding the statutory maximum, or both: s.10(2), (3).

As to sentencing guidance, see now the Sentencing Guidelines Council's definitive guideline for sentencing in cases involving sexual offences (K–83 *et seq.*). The guideline applies to offenders sentenced on or after May 14, 2007.

(e) *Elements of the offence*

20–68 As to "penetration", see *ante*, § 20–24. As to "sexual", see *ante*, § 20–17.

(3) Engaging in sexual activity in the presence of a child

(a) *Statute*

Sexual Offences Act 2003, s.11

Engaging in sexual activity in the presence of a child

20–69 **11.**—(1) A person aged 18 or over (A) commits an offence if—

(a) he intentionally engages in an activity,

(b) the activity is sexual,

(c) for the purpose of obtaining sexual gratification, he engages in it—

(i) when another person (B) is present or is in a place from which A can be observed, and

(ii) knowing or believing that B is aware, or intending that B should be aware, that he is engaging in it, and

(d) either—

(i) B is under 16 and A does not reasonably believe that B is 16 or over, or

(ii) B is under 13.

(2) A person guilty of an offence under this section is liable—

(a) on summary conviction, to imprisonment for a term not exceeding *6* [12] months or a fine not exceeding the statutory maximum or both;

(b) on conviction on indictment, to imprisonment for a term not exceeding 10 years.

[In subs. (2)(a), "12" is substituted for "6", as from a day to be appointed, by the *CJA* 2003, s.282(2) and (3). The increase has no application to offences committed before the substitution takes effect: s.282(4).]

(b) *Indictment*

STATEMENT OF OFFENCE

20–70 *Engaging in sexual activity in the presence of a child, contrary to section 11(1) of the* Sexual Offences Act *2003*.

PARTICULARS OF OFFENCE

A B, a person of [or *over*] *the age of 18 years, on the —— day of ——, 20—, for the purpose of obtaining sexual gratification, intentionally engaged in sexual activity when C D, a person under the age of 16 years, was present* [or *in a place from which A B could be observed*], *A B knowing or believing that C D was aware, or intending that C D should be aware, that he was engaging in such activity, and not reasonably believing that C D was aged 16 years or over.*

(c) *Class of offence and mode of trial*

20–71 This offence is triable either way: s.11(2); and falls within class 3: *ante*, § 2–17.

(d) *Sentence*

20–72 On conviction on indictment, 10 years' imprisonment; on summary conviction, six (12, as from a day to be appointed) months' imprisonment, or a fine not exceeding the statutory maximum, or both: s.11(2).

As to sentencing guidance, see now the Sentencing Guidelines Council's definitive guideline for sentencing in cases involving sexual offences (K–83 *et seq.*). The guideline applies to offenders sentenced on or after May 14, 2007.

(e) *Elements of the offence*

As to "sexual", see *ante*, § 20–17. As to "observed", see section 79(1), (7), *ante*, § 20–18. **20–73**

(4) Causing a child to watch a sexual act

(a) *Statute*

Sexual Offences Act 2003, s.12

Causing a child to watch a sexual act

12.—(1) A person aged 18 or over (A) commits an offence if— **20–74**

(a) for the purpose of obtaining sexual gratification, he intentionally causes another person (B) to watch a third person engaging in an activity, or to look at an image of any person engaging in an activity,

(b) the activity is sexual, and

(c) either—

(i) B is under 16 and A does not reasonably believe that B is 16 or over, or

(ii) B is under 13.

(2) [*Identical to s.11(2) (including the prospective amendment),* ante, *§ 20–69.*]

(b) *Indictment*

STATEMENT OF OFFENCE

Causing a child to watch a sexual act, contrary to section 12(1) of the Sexual Offences Act *2003.* **20–75**

PARTICULARS OF OFFENCE

A B, a person of [or *over*] *the age of 18 years, on the —— day of ——, 20—, for the purpose of obtaining sexual gratification, intentionally caused C D, a person under the age of 16 years, to watch E F engaging in a sexual activity* [or *to look at an image of a person engaging in a sexual activity*], *the said A B not reasonably believing that C D was aged 16 years or over.*

(c) *Class of offence and mode of trial*

This offence is triable either way: s.12(2); and falls within class 3: *ante*, § 2–17. **20–76**

(d) *Sentence*

On conviction on indictment, 10 years' imprisonment; on summary conviction, six (12, as from a day to be appointed) months' imprisonment, or a fine not exceeding the statutory maximum, or both: s.12(2). **20–77**

As to sentencing guidance, see now the Sentencing Guidelines Council's definitive guideline for sentencing in cases involving sexual offences (K–83 *et seq.*). The guideline applies to offenders sentenced on or after May 14, 2007.

(e) *Elements of the offence*

As to "sexual", see *ante*, § 20–17. As to "image", see section 79(1), (4), (5), *ante*, § 20–18. **20–78**

Whereas it is an element of this offence that the defendant acted "for the purpose of obtaining sexual gratification", there is nothing to suggest that the offence would only be committed if the sexual gratification and the causing of the child to watch the sexual act are simultaneous, contemporaneous, or synchronised; the defendant's purpose may involve both short-term and long-term sexual gratification, or immediate or deferred, or immediate and deferred gratification: *R. v. Abdullahi* [2007] 1 Cr.App.R. 14, CA.

(5) Child sex offences committed by persons aged under 18

(a) *Statute*

Sexual Offences Act 2003, s.13

Child sex offences committed by children or young persons

20–79 **13.**—(1) A person under 18 commits an offence if he does anything which would be an offence under any of sections 9 to 12 if he were aged 18.

(2) A person guilty of an offence under this section is liable—

(a) on summary conviction, to imprisonment for a term not exceeding *6* [12] months or a fine not exceeding the statutory maximum or both;

(b) on conviction on indictment, to imprisonment for a term not exceeding 5 years.

[In subs. (2)(a), "12" is substituted for "6", as from a day to be appointed, by the *CJA* 2003, s.282(2) and (3). The increase has no application to offences committed before the substitution takes effect: s.282(4).]

(b) *Indictment*

20–80 Appropriate particulars may be framed from the specimens set out, *ante*, for sections 9 to 12, but the particulars should allege that the defendant was under the age of 18 at the time of the offence.

(c) *Class of offence and mode of trial*

20–81 This offence is triable either way: s.13(2); and falls within class 3: *ante*, § 2–17.

In *R. (G.) v. Burnley Magistrates' Court*, 171 J.P. 445, DC, a decision to commit the claimant for trial under the *MCA* 1980, s.24 (*ante*, § 1–75m) on an offence under this section was quashed, the court pointing out that since the maximum sentence on conviction on indictment is five years' detention, there would be a range of sentences for offences against this section some way below the maximum, particularly in the case of persons of previous good character.

(d) *Sentence*

20–82 On conviction on indictment, five years' imprisonment; on summary conviction, six (12, as from a day to be appointed) months' imprisonment, or a fine not exceeding the statutory maximum, or both: s.13(2).

An offence contrary to section 13 is not a "serious" specified offence for the purposes of the dangerous offender provisions of the *CJA* 2003 (*ante*, §§ 5–292 *et seq.*): *R. v. B.* [2008] Crim.L.R. 730, CA.

For guidance, see the Sentencing Guidelines Council's definitive guideline for sentencing in cases involving sexual offences (K–83 *et seq.*). The guideline applies to offenders sentenced on or after May 14, 2007.

(e) *Elements of the offence*

20–83 As to the elements of the offences contrary to sections 9 to 12, see *ante*, §§ 20–58 *et seq.*

As to the anomaly created by this section, see *ante*, § 20–65.

(f) *Secondary parties*

20–84 See section 73 of the 2003 Act, *ante*, § 20–57.

(6) Arranging or facilitating commission of a child sex offence

(a) *Statute*

Sexual Offences Act 2003, s.14

Arranging or facilitating commission of a child sex offence

20–85 **14.**—(1) A person commits an offence if—

(a) he intentionally arranges or facilitates something that he intends to do, intends another person to do, or believes that another person will do, in any part of the world, and

(b) doing it will involve the commission of an offence under any of sections 9 to 13.

(2) A person does not commit an offence under this section if—

(a) he arranges or facilitates something that he believes another person will do, but that he does not intend to do or intend another person to do, and

(b) any offence within subsection (1)(b) would be an offence against a child for whose protection he acts.

(3) For the purposes of subsection (2), a person acts for the protection of a child if he acts for the purpose of—

(a) protecting the child from sexually transmitted infection,

(b) protecting the physical safety of the child,

(c) preventing the child from becoming pregnant, or

(d) promoting the child's emotional well-being by the giving of advice,

and not for the purpose of obtaining sexual gratification or for the purpose of causing or encouraging the activity constituting the offence within subsection (1)(b) or the child's participation in it.

(4) A person guilty of an offence under this section is liable—

(a) on summary conviction, to imprisonment for a term not exceeding *6* [12] months or a fine not exceeding the statutory maximum or both;

(b) on conviction on indictment, to imprisonment for a term not exceeding 14 years.

[In subs. (4)(a), "12" is substituted for "6", as from a day to be appointed, by the *CJA* 2003, s.282(2) and (3). The increase has no application to offences committed before the substitution takes effect: s.282(4).]

(b) *Indictment*

STATEMENT OF OFFENCE

Arranging or facilitating commission of a child sex offence, contrary to section 14(1) of the Sexual Offences Act *2003*. **20–86**

PARTICULARS OF OFFENCE

A B, on the —— day of ——, 20—, intentionally arranged or facilitated the doing of an act, which he intended to do [or *intended E F to do or believed E F would do*] *and the doing of which would involve the commission of an offence of sexual activity with a child, contrary to section 9 of the* Sexual Offences Act *2003, in that he* [give brief particulars of the act of arrangement or facilitation].

(c) *Class of offence and mode of trial*

This offence is triable either way: s.14(4); and falls within class 3: *ante*, § 2–17. **20–87**

(d) *Sentence*

On conviction on indictment, 14 years' imprisonment; on summary conviction, six (12, as from a day to be appointed) months' imprisonment, or a fine not exceeding the statutory maximum, or both: s.14(4). **20–88**

An offence contrary to section 14 is a "lifestyle offence" within the *PCA* 2002, Sched. 2 (*ante*, § 5–660), in respect of which a financial reporting order may be made under the *SOCPA* 2005, s.76 (*ante*, § 5–886a).

For guidance, see the Sentencing Guidelines Council's definitive guideline for sentencing in cases involving sexual offences (K–83 *et seq.*). The guideline applies to offenders sentenced on or after May 14, 2007.

(e) *Elements of the offence*

As to the elements of the offences contrary to sections 9 to 13, see *ante*, §§ 20–58 *et seq.* **20–89**

Whilst this offence criminalises acts that are preparatory to the commission of another offence, a person may properly be convicted of an attempt to commit it, contrary to the *Criminal Attempts Act* 1981, s.1 (*post*, § 33–120): *R. v. Robson* [2008] 2 Cr.App.R. 38, CA.

(f) *Defence*

20–90 The explanatory notes accompanying the statute give as an example of the operation of the defence under subsection (2), the case of a health worker who, believing that a person is having sex with a child under 16, advises that person that it is unlawful to have sex with a child under 16, but supplies him with condoms because he believes that the person will otherwise have unprotected sex with the child.

(7) Meeting a child following sexual grooming

(a) *Statute*

Sexual Offences Act 2003, s.15

Meeting a child following sexual grooming etc.

20–91 **15.**—(1) A person aged 18 or over (A) commits an offence if—

(a) A has met or communicated with another person (B) on at least two occasions and subsequently—

(i) A intentionally meets B,

(ii) A travels with the intention of meeting B in any part of the world or arranges to meet B in any part of the world, or

(iii) B travels with the intention of meeting A in any part of the world,

(b) A intends to do anything to or in respect of B, during or after the meeting mentioned in paragraph (a)(i) to (iii) and in any part of the world, which if done will involve the commission by A of a relevant offence,

(c) B is under 16, and

(d) A does not reasonably believe that B is 16 or over.

(2) In subsection (1)—

(a) the reference to A having met or communicated with B is a reference to A having met B in any part of the world or having communicated with B by any means from, to or in any part of the world;

(b) "relevant offence" means—

(i) an offence under this Part,

(ii) *an offence within any of paragraphs 61 to 92 of Schedule 3*, or

(iii) anything done outside England and Wales *and Northern Ireland* which is not an offence within sub-paragraph (i) *or (ii)* but would be an offence within sub-paragraph (i) if done in England and Wales.

(3) [*Application to Northern Ireland.*]

(4) [*Identical to s.11(2) (including the prospective amendment),* ante, *§ 20–69.*]

[This section is printed as amended by the *CJIA* 2008, s.73, and Sched. 15, para. 1; and as amended, as from a day to be appointed, by the *Sexual Offences (Northern Ireland Consequential Amendments) Order* 2008 (S.I. 2008 No. 1779), arts 3 and 4 (omission of italicised words and subs. (3)).]

(b) *Indictment*

STATEMENT OF OFFENCE

20–92 *Meeting a child following sexual grooming, contrary to section 15(1) of the* Sexual Offences Act *2003.*

PARTICULARS OF OFFENCE

A B, a person of [or *over*] *the age of 18 years, having met or communicated with C D on two previous occasions, on the —— day of ——, 20—, intentionally met* [or *travelled with the intention of meeting*] *C D, a person under the age of 16 years, A B not reasonably believing that C D was aged 16 years, and intending to do anything to or in respect of C D, during or after the meeting, which, if done, would involve the commission by him of a relevant offence.*

(c) *Class of offence and mode of trial*

20–93 This offence is triable either way: s.15(4); and falls within class 3: *ante*, § 2–17.

(d) *Sentence*

20–94 On conviction on indictment, 10 years' imprisonment; on summary conviction, six

(12, as from a day to be appointed) months' imprisonment, or a fine not exceeding the statutory maximum, or both: s.15(2).

For guidance, see the Sentencing Guidelines Council's definitive guideline for sentencing in cases involving sexual offences (K–83 *et seq.*). The guideline applies to offenders sentenced on or after May 14, 2007.

(e) *Elements of the offence*

As to the definition of "relevant offence" in subsection (2)(b), "this Part" comprises sections 1 to 79, and paragraphs 61 to 92 of Schedule 3 (not set out in this work) list various sexual offences under the law of Northern Ireland. **20–95**

G. Abuse of Position of Trust

(1) Statute

Sexual Offences Act 2003, ss.16–24

Abuse of position of trust: sexual activity with a child

16.—(1) A person aged 18 or over (A) commits an offence if— **20–96**

(a) he intentionally touches another person (B),

(b) the touching is sexual,

(c) A is in a position of trust in relation to B,

(d) where subsection (2) applies, A knows or could reasonably be expected to know of the circumstances by virtue of which he is in a position of trust in relation to B, and

(e) either—

(i) B is under 18 and A does not reasonably believe that B is 18 or over, or

(ii) B is under 13.

(2) This subsection applies where A—

(a) is in a position of trust in relation to B by virtue of circumstances within section 21(2), (3), (4) or (5), and

(b) is not in such a position of trust by virtue of other circumstances.

(3) Where in proceedings for an offence under this section it is proved that the other person was under 18, the defendant is to be taken not to have reasonably believed that that person was 18 or over unless sufficient evidence is adduced to raise an issue as to whether he reasonably believed it.

(4) Where in proceedings for an offence under this section—

(a) it is proved that the defendant was in a position of trust in relation to the other person by virtue of circumstances within section 21(2), (3), (4) or (5), and

(b) it is not proved that he was in such a position of trust by virtue of other circumstances,

it is to be taken that the defendant knew or could reasonably have been expected to know of the circumstances by virtue of which he was in such a position of trust unless sufficient evidence is adduced to raise an issue as to whether he knew or could reasonably have been expected to know of those circumstances.

(5) A person guilty of an offence under this section is liable—

(a) on summary conviction, to imprisonment for a term not exceeding *6* [12] months or a fine not exceeding the statutory maximum or both;

(b) on conviction on indictment, to imprisonment for a term not exceeding 5 years.

[In subs. (5)(a), "12" is substituted for "6", as from a day to be appointed, by the *CJA* 2003, s.282(2) and (3). The increase has no application to offences committed before the substitution takes effect: s.282(4).]

Abuse of position of trust: causing or inciting a child to engage in sexual activity

17.—(1) A person aged 18 or over (A) commits an offence if— **20–97**

(a) he intentionally causes or incites another person (B) to engage in an activity,

(b) the activity is sexual,

(c) A is in a position of trust in relation to B,

(d), (e) [*identical to s.16(1)(d), (e),* ante, *§ 20–96*].

(2)–(5) [*Identical to s.16(2)–(5) (including the prospective amendment of subs. (5)),* ante, *§ 20–96*].

Abuse of position of trust: sexual activity in the presence of a child

18.—(1) A person aged 18 or over (A) commits an offence if— **20–98**

(a) he intentionally engages in an activity,

(b) the activity is sexual,

(c) for the purpose of obtaining sexual gratification, he engages in it—

(i) when another person (B) is present or is in a place from which A can be observed, and

(ii) knowing or believing that B is aware, or intending that B should be aware, that he is engaging in it,

(d) A is in a position of trust in relation to B,

(e), (f) [*identical to s.16(1)(d), (e),* ante, *§ 20–96*].

(2)–(5) [*Identical to s.16(2)–(5) (including the prospective amendment of subs. (5)),* ante, *§ 20–96*].

Abuse of position of trust: causing a child to watch a sexual act

20–99 **19.**—(1) A person aged 18 or over (A) commits an offence if—

(a) for the purpose of obtaining sexual gratification, he intentionally causes another person (B) to watch a third person engaging in an activity, or to look at an image of any person engaging in an activity,

(b) the activity is sexual,

(c) A is in a position of trust in relation to B,

(d), (e) [*identical to s.16(1)(d), (e),* ante, *§ 20–96*].

(2)–(5) [*Identical to s.16(2)–(5) (including the prospective amendment of subs. (5)),* ante, *§ 20–96*].

Abuse of position of trust: acts done in Scotland

20–100 **20.** Anything which, if done in England and Wales *or Northern Ireland*, would constitute an offence under any of sections 16 to 19 also constitutes that offence if done in Scotland [or Northern Ireland].

[This section is printed as amended, as from a day to be appointed, by S.I. 2008 No. 1779 (*ante*, § 20–91), arts 3 and 5 (omission of italicised words, insertion of words in square brackets).]

Positions of trust

20–101 **21.**—(1) For the purposes of sections 16 to 19, a person (A) is in a position of trust in relation to another person (B) if—

(a) any of the following subsections applies, or

(b) any condition specified in an order made by the Secretary of State is met.

(2) This subsection applies if A looks after persons under 18 who are detained in an institution by virtue of a court order or under an enactment, and B is so detained in that institution.

(3) This subsection applies if A looks after persons under 18 who are resident in a home or other place in which—

(a) accommodation and maintenance are provided by an authority under section 23(2) of the *Children Act* 1989 *or Article 27(2) of the* Children (Northern Ireland) Order *1995 (S.I. 1995/755 (N.I. 2))*, or

(b) accommodation is provided by a voluntary organisation under section 59(1) of that Act *or Article 75(1) of that Order*,

and B is resident, and is so provided with accommodation and maintenance or accommodation, in that place.

(4) This subsection applies if A looks after persons under 18 who are accommodated and cared for in one of the following institutions—

(a) a hospital,

(b) an independent clinic,

(c) a care home, *residential care home or private hospital,*

(d) a community home, voluntary home or children's home, [or]

(e) a home provided under section 82(5) of the *Children Act* 1989, *or*

(f) *a residential family centre,*

and B is accommodated and cared for in that institution.

(5) This subsection applies if A looks after persons under 18 who are receiving education at an educational institution and B is receiving, and A is not receiving, education at that institution.

(6) *This subsection applies if A is appointed to be the guardian of B under Article 159 or 160 of the* Children (Northern Ireland) Order *1995 (S.I. 1995/755 (N.I. 2)).*

(7) This subsection applies if A is engaged in the provision of services under, or pursuant to anything done under—

(a) sections 8 to 10 of the *Employment and Training Act* 1973, or

(b) section 114 of the *Learning and Skills Act* 2000,

and, in that capacity, looks after B on an individual basis.

(8) This subsection applies if A regularly has unsupervised contact with B (whether face to face or by any other means)—

(a) in the exercise of functions of a local authority under section 20 or 21 of the *Children Act* 1989, *or*

(b) *in the exercise of functions of an authority under Article 21 or 23 of the* Children (Northern Ireland) Order *1995*.

(9) This subsection applies if A, as a person who is to report to the court under section 7 of the *Children Act* 1989 *or Article 4 of the* Children (Northern Ireland) Order *1995* on matters relating to the welfare of B, regularly has unsupervised contact with B (whether face to face or by any other means).

(10) This subsection applies if A is a personal adviser appointed for B under—

(a) section 23B(2) of, or paragraph 19C of Schedule 2 to, the *Children Act* 1989, *or*

(b) *Article 34A(10) or 34C(2) of the* Children (Northern Ireland) Order *1995*,

and, in that capacity, looks after B on an individual basis.

(11) This subsection applies if—

(a) B is subject to a care order, a supervision order or an education supervision order, and

(b) in the exercise of functions conferred by virtue of the order on an authorised person or the authority designated by the order, A looks after B on an individual basis.

(12) This subsection applies if A—

(a) is an officer of the Service or Welsh family proceedings officer (within the meaning given by section 35 of the *Children Act* 2004) appointed for B under section 41(1) of the *Children Act* 1989,

(b) is appointed a children's guardian of B under rule 6 or rule 18 of the *Adoption Rules* 1984 (S.I. 1984/265), or

(c) is appointed to be the guardian ad litem of B under rule 9.5 of the *Family Proceedings Rules* 1991 (S.I. 1991/1247) *or under Article 60(1) of the* Children (Northern Ireland) Order *1995*,

and, in that capacity, regularly has unsupervised contact with B (whether face to face or by any other means).

(13) This subsection applies if—

(a) B is subject to requirements imposed by or under an enactment on his release from detention for a criminal offence, or is subject to requirements imposed by a court order made in criminal proceedings, and

(b) A looks after B on an individual basis in pursuance of the requirements.

[This section is printed as amended by the *Children Act* 2004, s.40, and Sched. 3, para. 18; and as amended, as from a day to be appointed, by S.I. 2008 No. 1779 (*ante*, § 20–91), arts 3 and 6 (omission of italicised words (other than names of Acts), insertion of word in square brackets).]

Positions of trust: interpretation

22.—(1) The following provisions apply for the purposes of section 21. **20–102**

(2) Subject to subsection (3), a person looks after persons under 18 if he is regularly involved in caring for, training, supervising or being in sole charge of such persons.

(3) A person (A) looks after another person (B) on an individual basis if—

(a) A is regularly involved in caring for, training or supervising B, and

(b) in the course of his involvement, A regularly has unsupervised contact with B (whether face to face or by any other means).

(4) A person receives education at an educational institution if—

(a) he is registered or otherwise enrolled as a pupil or student at the institution, or

(b) he receives education at the institution under arrangements with another educational institution at which he is so registered or otherwise enrolled.

(5) In section 21—

"authority" —

(a) in relation to England and Wales, means a local authority; …

"care home" means an establishment which is a care home for the purposes of the *Care Standards Act* 2000;

"care order" has—

(a) in relation to England and Wales, the same meaning as in the *Children Act* 1989, …

"children's home" has—

(a) in relation to England and Wales, the meaning given by section 1 of the *Care Standards Act* 2000, …

"community home" has the meaning given by section 53 of the *Children Act* 1989;

"education supervision order" has—

(a) in relation to England and Wales, the meaning given by section 36 of the *Children Act* 1989, …

"hospital"—

(a) in relation to England and Wales, means a hospital within the meaning given by section 275(1) of the *National Health Service Act* 2006 or section 206(1) of the *National Health Service Act* 2006, or any other establishment which is a hospital within the meaning given by section 2(3) of the *Care Standards Act* 2000; …

"independent clinic" has—

(a) in relation to England and Wales, the meaning given by section 2 of the *Care Standards Act* 2000; …

"supervision order" has—

(a) in relation to England and Wales, the meaning given by section 31(11) of the *Children Act* 1989, …

"voluntary home" has—

(a) in relation to England and Wales, the meaning given by section 60(3) of the *Children Act* 1989, … .

[This section is printed as amended by the *National Health Service (Consequential Provisions) Act* 2006, s.2, and Sched. 1, para. 238. Definitions which relate to Northern Ireland and which are repealed as from a day to be appointed by S.I. 2008 No. 1779 (*ante*, § 20–91), arts 3 and 7, have been omitted.]

Sections 16 to 19: exception for spouses and civil partners

20–103 **23.**—(1) Conduct by a person (A) which would otherwise be an offence under any of sections 16 to 19 against another person (B) is not an offence under that section if at the time—

(a) B is 16 or over, and

(b) A and B are lawfully married or civil partners of each other.

(2) In proceedings for such an offence it is for the defendant to prove that A and B were at the time lawfully married or civil partners of each other.

[This section is printed as amended by the *Civil Partnership Act* 2004, s.261(1), and Sched. 27, para. 173.]

Sections 16 to 19: sexual relationships which pre-date position of trust

20–104 **24.**—(1) Conduct by a person (A) which would otherwise be an offence under any of sections 16 to 19 against another person (B) is not an offence under that section if, immediately before the position of trust arose, a sexual relationship existed between A and B.

(2) Subsection (1) does not apply if at that time sexual intercourse between A and B would have been unlawful.

(3) In proceedings for an offence under any of sections 16 to 19 it is for the defendant to prove that such a relationship existed at that time.

(2) Indictment

STATEMENT OF OFFENCE

20–105 *Sexual activity with a child by a person in a position of trust, contrary to section 16(1) of the* Sexual Offences Act *2003*.

PARTICULARS OF OFFENCE

A B, a person of [or over] *the age of 18 years, on the —— day of ——, 20—, intentionally touched C D, in circumstances where the touching was sexual, C D was aged under 18 years and the said A B did not reasonably believe that she was of or over the age of 18 years, the said A B being in a position of trust in relation to C D at the time by virtue of the fact that the said A B looked after persons under 18 who were receiving education at an educational institution, and C D was receiving, whilst A B was not receiving, education at that institution, and the said A B knew or could reasonably be expected to know of the circumstances by virtue of which he was in a position of trust in relation to C D.*

The circumstances by virtue of which it is said that the defendant was in a position of trust in relation to the child should be particularised. Where, however, they do not fall within subsections (2) to (5) of section 21, it is unnecessary to aver that the defendant knew of, or could reasonably be expected to know of, those circumstances.

Indictments for offences contrary to sections 17 to 19 may be framed from the above indictment and the specimen counts in relation to sections 10 to 12, *ante*, §§ 20–65, 20–70, 20–75.

(3) Class of offence and mode of trial

Offences contrary to sections 16 to 19 are triable either way (subs. (5) of each section), and fall within class 3: *ante*, § 2–17. **20–106**

(4) Sentence

On conviction on indictment, five years' imprisonment; on summary conviction, six (12, as from a day to be appointed) months' imprisonment, or a fine not exceeding the statutory maximum, or both: ss.16(5), 17(5), 18(5), 19(5). **20–107**

In *R. v. Hubbard* [2002] 2 Cr.App.R.(S.) 101, CA, it was held, in relation to the predecessor provision, that the setting out of various positions of trust in various subsections was not to be taken as indicating a descending order of seriousness.

For guidance, see the Sentencing Guidelines Council's definitive guideline for sentencing in cases involving sexual offences (K–83 *et seq.*). The guideline applies to offenders sentenced on or after May 14, 2007.

(5) Elements of the offences

Apart from the additional element of abuse of a position of trust, the offences under sections 16 to 19 cover the same ground as the offences under sections 9 to 12 (*ante*, §§ 20–58 *et seq.*). As to "sexual", see *ante*, § 20–17. As to "image", "observed" and "touching", see *ante*, § 20–18. **20–108**

In relation to the issues of knowledge of the age of the child and knowledge of the circumstances by virtue of which the defendant was in a position of trust in relation to the child, subsections (3) and (4) of each of sections 16 to 19 make provision for a rebuttable presumption. It is for the defendant to adduce sufficient evidence to raise an issue in respect of either or both matters. Once that burden is discharged, the prosecution will then assume the burden of proving knowledge to the normal standard.

(6) Secondary parties

Section 73 (*ante*, § 20–57) applies to an offence under section 16 against a person under 16. **20–109**

H. FAMILIAL CHILD SEX OFFENCES

(1) Statute

Sexual Offences Act 2003, ss.25–29

Sexual activity with a child family member

25.—(1) A person (A) commits an offence if— **20–110**

(a) he intentionally touches another person (B),

(b) the touching is sexual,

(c) the relation of A to B is within section 27,

(d) A knows or could reasonably be expected to know that his relation to B is of a description falling within that section, and

(e) either—
(i) B is under 18 and A does not reasonably believe that B is 18 or over, or
(ii) B is under 13.

(2) Where in proceedings for an offence under this section it is proved that the other person was under 18, the defendant is to be taken not to have reasonably believed that that person was 18 or over unless sufficient evidence is adduced to raise an issue as to whether he reasonably believed it.

(3) Where in proceedings for an offence under this section it is proved that the relation of the defendant to the other person was of a description falling within section 27, it is to be taken that the defendant knew or could reasonably have been expected to know that his relation to the other person was of that description unless sufficient evidence is adduced to raise an issue as to whether he knew or could reasonably have been expected to know that it was.

(4) A person guilty of an offence under this section, if aged 18 or over at the time of the offence, is liable—
(a) where subsection (6) applies, on conviction on indictment to imprisonment for a term not exceeding 14 years;
(b) in any other case—
(i) on summary conviction, to imprisonment for a term not exceeding *6* [12] months or a fine not exceeding the statutory maximum or both;
(ii) on conviction on indictment, to imprisonment for a term not exceeding 14 years.

(5) Unless subsection (4) applies, a person guilty of an offence under this section is liable—
(a) on summary conviction, to imprisonment for a term not exceeding *6* [12] months or a fine not exceeding the statutory maximum or both;
(b) on conviction on indictment, to imprisonment for a term not exceeding 5 years.

(6) This subsection applies where the touching involved—
(a) penetration of B's anus or vagina with a part of A's body or anything else,
(b) penetration of B's mouth with A's penis,
(c) penetration of A's anus or vagina with a part of B's body, or
(d) penetration of A's mouth with B's penis.

[In subss. (4)(a) and (5)(a), "12" is substituted for "6", as from a day to be appointed, by the *CJA* 2003, s.282(2) and (3). The increase has no application to offences committed before the substitution takes effect: s.282(4).]

Inciting a child family member to engage in sexual activity

20–111 **26.**—(1) A person (A) commits an offence if—
(a) he intentionally incites another person (B) to touch, or allow himself to be touched by, A,
(b)–(e) [*identical to s.25(1)(b)–(e)*, ante, *§ 20–110*].

(2), (3) [*Identical to s.25(2), (3)* ante, *§ 20–110.*]

(4) A person guilty of an offence under this section, if he was aged 18 or over at the time of the offence, is liable—
(a) where subsection (6) applies, on conviction on indictment to imprisonment for a term not exceeding 14 years;
(b) in any other case—
(i) on summary conviction, to imprisonment for a term not exceeding *6* [12] months or a fine not exceeding the statutory maximum or both;
(ii) on conviction on indictment, to imprisonment for a term not exceeding 14 years.

(5), (6) [*Identical to s.25(5) (including the prospective amendment), (6),* ante, *§ 20–110.*]

[In subss. (4)(b) and (5)(a), "12" is substituted for "6", as from a day to be appointed, by the *CJA* 2003, s.282(2) and (3). The increase has no application to offences committed before the substitution takes effect: s.282(4).]

Family relationships

20–112 **27.**—(1) The relation of one person (A) to another (B) is within this section if—
(a) it is within any of subsections (2) to (4), or
(b) it would be within one of those subsections but for section 39 of the *Adoption*

Act 1976 or section 67 of the *Adoption and Children Act* 2002 (status conferred by adoption).

(2) The relation of A to B is within this subsection if—

(a) one of them is the other's parent, grandparent, brother, sister, half-brother, half-sister, aunt or uncle, or

(b) A is or has been B's foster parent.

(3) The relation of A to B is within this subsection if A and B live or have lived in the same household, or A is or has been regularly involved in caring for, training, supervising or being in sole charge of B, and—

(a) one of them is or has been the other's step-parent,

(b) A and B are cousins,

(c) one of them is or has been the other's stepbrother or stepsister, or

(d) the parent or present or former foster parent of one of them is or has been the other's foster parent.

(4) The relation of A to B is within this subsection if—

(a) A and B live in the same household, and

(b) A is regularly involved in caring for, training, supervising or being in sole charge of B.

(5) For the purposes of this section—

(a) "aunt" means the sister or half-sister of a person's parent, and "uncle" has a corresponding meaning;

(b) "cousin" means the child of an aunt or uncle;

(c) a person is a child's foster parent if—

(i) he is a person with whom the child has been placed under section 23(2)(a) or 59(1)(a) of the *Children Act* 1989 (fostering for local authority or voluntary organisation), or

(ii) he fosters the child privately, within the meaning given by section 66(1)(b) of that Act;

(d) a person is another's partner (whether they are of different sexes or the same sex) if they live together as partners in an enduring family relationship;

(e) "step-parent" includes a parent's partner and "stepbrother" and "stepsister" include the child of a parent's partner.

[This section is printed as amended by the *CJIA* 2008, s.73, and Sched. 15, paras 2 and 3.]

Sections 25 and 26: exception for spouses and civil partners

28.—(1) Conduct by a person (A) which would otherwise be an offence under section 25 or 26 against another person (B) is not an offence under that section if at the time— **20–113**

(a) B is 16 or over, and

(b) A and B are lawfully married or civil partners of each other.

(2) In proceedings for such an offence it is for the defendant to prove that A and B were at the time lawfully married or civil partners of each other.

[This section is printed as amended by the *Civil Partnership Act* 2004, s.261(1), and Sched. 27, para. 174.]

Sections 25 and 26: sexual relationships which pre-date family relationships

29.—(1) Conduct by a person (A) which would otherwise be an offence under section 25 or 26 against another person (B) is not an offence under that section if— **20–114**

(a) the relation of A to B is not within subsection (2) of section 27,

(b) it would not be within that subsection if section 39 of the *Adoption Act* 1976 or section 67 of the *Adoption and Children Act* 2002 did not apply, and

(c) immediately before the relation of A to B first became such as to fall within section 27, a sexual relationship existed between A and B.

(2) Subsection (1) does not apply if at the time referred to in subsection (1)(c) sexual intercourse between A and B would have been unlawful.

(3) In proceedings for an offence under section 25 or 26 it is for the defendant to prove the matters mentioned in subsection (1)(a) to (c).

[This section is printed as amended by the *CJIA* 2008, s.73, and Sched. 15, paras 2 and 4.]

(2) Indictment

STATEMENT OF OFFENCE

20–115 *Sexual activity with a child family member, contrary to section 25(1) of the* Sexual Offences Act *2003.*

PARTICULARS OF OFFENCE

A B, on the —— day of ——, 20—, a person of [or over] *the age of 18 years, intentionally touched his daughter C D, a person under the age of 18 years, by penetrating her mouth with his penis, in circumstances where the touching was sexual, where the said A B knew or could reasonably be expected to have known that the said C D was his daughter, and where the said A B did not reasonable believe that the said C D was aged 18 or over.*

Where the defendant is alleged to have been 18 or over at the time of the offence, this should be alleged in the indictment, as the section effectively creates separate offences (with differing maximum penalties) according to the age of the defendant at the time of the offence. Equally, where the circumstances are alleged to fall within subsection (6), a charge should particularise these circumstances so as to ensure that the case is tried on indictment, and it is submitted that good practice would dictate that such particulars should be set out in the indictment.

An indictment for an offence contrary to section 26 may be framed from the above specimen.

(3) Class of offence and mode of trial

20–116 In the case of an offence contrary to either section 25 or section 26, where the defendant was aged 18 or over at the time of the offence, and the circumstances fall within subsection (6), the offence will be triable only on indictment. In the case of any other offence contrary to either section, the offence will be triable either way. Whatever the mode of trial, offences contrary to either section fall within class 3: *ante*, § 2–17.

(4) Sentence

Maximum

20–117 Section 25 or section 26: where the defendant was aged 18 or over at the time of the offence, 14 years' imprisonment on conviction on indictment; or, on summary conviction (where the offence is triable either way, *ante*), six (12, as from a day to be appointed) months' imprisonment, or a fine not exceeding the statutory maximum, or both.

Guidelines

20–118 See now the Sentencing Guidelines Council's definitive guideline for sentencing in cases involving sexual offences (K–83 *et seq.*). The guideline applies to offenders sentenced on or after May 14, 2007.

[The next paragraph is § 20–123.]

(5) Elements of the offences

20–123 Apart from the additional element of familial relationship, the offence under section 25 covers the same ground as the offence under section 9 (*ante*, § 20–58). The offence under section 26 is significantly narrower, however, than the offence under section 10 (*ante*, § 20–64), in that it applies to the "incitement" of certain activity, but not "causing" such activity; and the range of activity covered is narrower.

As to "sexual", see *ante*, § 20–17. As to "touching", see *ante*, § 20–18.

As to knowledge of age, and of the relationship with the child being one falling within section 27, see *ante*, § 20–108.

(6) Secondary parties

20–124 Section 73 (*ante*, § 20–57) applies to an offence under section 25 against a person under 16.

I. OFFENCES AGAINST PERSONS WITH A MENTAL DISORDER IMPEDING CHOICE

(1) Statute

Sexual Offences Act 2003, ss.30–33

Sexual activity with a person with a mental disorder impeding choice

30.—(1) A person (A) commits an offence if— **20–125**

(a) he intentionally touches another person (B),

(b) the touching is sexual,

(c) B is unable to refuse because of or for a reason related to a mental disorder, and

(d) A knows or could reasonably be expected to know that B has a mental disorder and that because of it or for a reason related to it B is likely to be unable to refuse.

(2) B is unable to refuse if—

(a) he lacks the capacity to choose whether to agree to the touching (whether because he lacks sufficient understanding of the nature or reasonably foreseeable consequences of what is being done, or for any other reason), or

(b) he is unable to communicate such a choice to A.

(3) A person guilty of an offence under this section, if the touching involved—

(a) penetration of B's anus or vagina with a part of A's body or anything else,

(b) penetration of B's mouth with A's penis,

(c) penetration of A's anus or vagina with a part of B's body, or

(d) penetration of A's mouth with B's penis,

is liable, on conviction on indictment, to imprisonment for life.

(4) Unless subsection (3) applies, a person guilty of an offence under this section is liable—

(a) on summary conviction, to imprisonment for a term not exceeding 6 [12] months or to a fine not exceeding the statutory maximum or both;

(b) on conviction on indictment, to imprisonment for a term not exceeding 14 years.

[In subs. (4)(a), "12" is substituted for "6", as from a day to be appointed, by the *CJA* 2003, s.282(2) and (3). The increase has no application to offences committed before the substitution takes effect: s.282(4).]

Causing or inciting a person, with a mental disorder impeding choice, to engage in sexual activity

31.—(1) A person (A) commits an offence if— **20–126**

(a) he intentionally causes or incites another person (B) to engage in an activity,

(b) the activity is sexual,

(c), (d) [*identical to s.30(1)(c), (d),* ante, *§ 20–125*].

(2) B is unable to refuse if—

(a) he lacks the capacity to choose whether to agree to engaging in the activity caused or incited (whether because he lacks sufficient understanding of the nature or reasonably foreseeable consequences of the activity, or for any other reason), or

(b) he is unable to communicate such a choice to A.

(3) A person guilty of an offence under this section, if the activity caused or incited involved—

(a) penetration of B's anus or vagina,

(b) penetration of B's mouth with a person's penis,

(c) penetration of a person's anus or vagina with a part of B's body or by B with anything else, or

(d) penetration of a person's mouth with B's penis,

is liable, on conviction on indictment, to imprisonment for life.

(4) [*Identical to s.30(4) (including the prospective amendment),* ante, *§ 20–125.*]

Engaging in sexual activity in the presence of a person with a mental disorder impeding choice

32.—(1) A person (A) commits an offence if— **20–127**

(a) he intentionally engages in an activity,
(b) the activity is sexual,
(c) for the purpose of obtaining sexual gratification, he engages in it—
(i) when another person (B) is present or is in a place from which A can be observed, and
(ii) knowing or believing that B is aware, or intending that B should be aware, that he is engaging in it,
(d), (e) [*identical to s.30(1)(c), (d),* ante, *§ 20–125*].

(2) B is unable to refuse if—
(a) he lacks the capacity to choose whether to agree to being present (whether because he lacks sufficient understanding of the nature of the activity, or for any other reason), or
(b) he is unable to communicate such a choice to A.

(3) A person guilty of an offence under this section is liable—
(a) on summary conviction, to imprisonment for a term not exceeding *6* [12] months or a fine not exceeding the statutory maximum or both;
(b) on conviction on indictment, to imprisonment for a term not exceeding 10 years.

[In subs. (3)(a), "12" is substituted for "6", as from a day to be appointed, by the *CJA* 2003, s.282(2) and (3). The increase has no application to offences committed before the substitution takes effect: s.282(4).]

Causing a person, with a mental disorder impeding choice, to watch a sexual act

20–128 **33.**—(1) A person (A) commits an offence if—
(a) for the purpose of obtaining sexual gratification, he intentionally causes another person (B) to watch a third person engaging in an activity, or to look at an image of any person engaging in an activity,
(b) the activity is sexual,
(c), (d) [*identical to s.30(1)(c), (d),* ante, *§ 20–125*].

(2) B is unable to refuse if—
(a) he lacks the capacity to choose whether to agree to watching or looking (whether because he lacks sufficient understanding of the nature of the activity, or for any other reason), or
(b) he is unable to communicate such a choice to A.

(3) [*Identical to s.32(3) (including the prospective amendment),* ante, *§ 20–127*.]

(2) Indictment

STATEMENT OF OFFENCE

20–129 *Sexual activity with a person with a mental disorder impeding choice, contrary to section 30(1) of the* Sexual Offences Act *2003*.

PARTICULARS OF OFFENCE

A B, on the —— day of ——, 20—, intentionally touched C D, by penetrating her mouth with his penis, in circumstances where the touching was sexual, where C D was unable to refuse because of or for a reason related to a mental disorder, and A B knew or could reasonably have been expected to know that C D had a mental disorder and that because of it or for a reason related to it C D was likely to be unable to refuse.

Where the circumstances are alleged to fall within subsection (3), this should be particularised in any charge and in the indictment.

Indictments in respect of offences contrary to sections 31 to 33 may be framed from the above indictment and the specimen indictments for the corresponding offences under sections 10 to 12 (*ante*, §§ 20–65 *et seq.*).

(3) Class of offence and mode of trial

20–130 Section 30(1): if the offence falls within subsection (3), it is triable only on indictment, and is a class 2 offence; otherwise, it is triable either way, and falls within class 3: *ante*, § 2–17.

Section 31(1): as for section 30(1), save that all offences under this section fall within class 3: *ante*, § 2–17.

Offences contrary to section 32(1) and 33(1) are triable either way, and fall within class 3: *ante*, § 2–17.

(4) Sentence

The indictable only offences contrary to section 30(1) and 31(1) are punishable with imprisonment for life. Otherwise, offences contrary to those provisions carry a maximum of 14 years' imprisonment on conviction on indictment, or six (12, as from a day to be appointed) months' imprisonment, or a fine not exceeding the statutory maximum, or both, on summary conviction: ss.30(3), (4), 31(3), (4). **20–131**

Offences contrary to sections 32(1) and 33(1), 10 years' imprisonment on conviction on indictment, or six (12, as from a day to be appointed) months' imprisonment, or a fine not exceeding the statutory maximum, or both, on summary conviction: ss.32(3), 33(3).

For guidance, see the Sentencing Guidelines Council's definitive guideline for sentencing in cases involving sexual offences (K–83 *et seq.*). The guideline applies to offenders sentenced on or after May 14, 2007.

(5) Elements of the offences

Apart from the additional elements of the victim's mental disorder and the defendant's mens rea in relation thereto, the offences under sections 30 to 33 broadly correspond to the offences contrary to sections 9 to 12 (*ante*, §§ 20–58 *et seq.*). **20–132**

As to the meaning of "or for any other reason" in section 30(2)(a), the effect of a mental disorder would have to be severe for it to be such as to render the person unable to choose to submit to sexual activity, notwithstanding that he understood the nature of the activity; an acute episode of a mental disorder that resulted in an inability to make a rational decision might do so, but an irrational fear that prevented the exercise of choice could not be equated to a lack of capacity to choose, which could not be "person specific" or even "situation specific": *R. v. C. (Mental disorder: Sexual activity)*, *The Times*, June 9, 2008, CA.

Where a woman with cerebral palsy, and having a mental age well below her chronological age of 27 years, was physically able to speak but was unable effectively to communicate her wishes in the way that any woman of her age, not suffering from such disabilities, would have done in similar circumstances, she was "unable to communicate" her choice of whether to agree to sexual touching within the meaning of section 30(2)(b) and, therefore, "unable to refuse" the sexual touching "because of or for a reason related to a mental disorder" within subsection (1): *Hulme v. DPP*, 170 J.P. 598, DC.

(6) Secondary parties

Section 73 (*ante*, § 20–57) applies to an offence under section 30 against a person under 16. **20–133**

J. INDUCEMENTS ETC. TO PERSONS WITH A MENTAL DISORDER

(1) Statute

Sexual Offences Act 2003, ss.34–37

Inducement, threat or deception to procure sexual activity with a person with a mental disorder

34.—(1) A person (A) commits an offence if— **20–134**

(a) with the agreement of another person (B) he intentionally touches that person,

(b) the touching is sexual,

(c) A obtains B's agreement by means of an inducement offered or given, a threat made or a deception practised by A for that purpose,

(d) B has a mental disorder, and

(e) A knows or could reasonably be expected to know that B has a mental disorder.

(2) [*Identical to s.30(3)*, ante, *§ 20–125*.]

(3) Unless subsection (2) applies, a person guilty of an offence under this section is liable—

(a) on summary conviction, to imprisonment for a term not exceeding *6* [12] months or a fine not exceeding the statutory maximum or both;

(b) on conviction on indictment, to imprisonment for a term not exceeding 14 years.

[In subs. (3)(a), "12" is substituted for "6", as from a day to be appointed, by the *CJA* 2003, s.282(2) and (3). The increase has no application to offences committed before the substitution takes effect: s.282(4).]

Causing a person with a mental disorder to engage in or agree to engage in sexual activity by inducement, threat or deception

20–135 **35.**—(1) A person (A) commits an offence if—

(a) by means of an inducement offered or given, a threat made or a deception practised by him for this purpose, he intentionally causes another person (B) to engage in, or to agree to engage in, an activity,

(b) the activity is sexual,

(c), (d) [*identical to s.34(1)(d), (e),* ante, *§ 20–134*].

(2) A person guilty of an offence under this section, if the activity caused or agreed to involved—

(a) penetration of B's anus or vagina,

(b) penetration of B's mouth with a person's penis,

(c) penetration of a person's anus or vagina with a part of B's body or by B with anything else, or

(d) penetration of a person's mouth with B's penis,

is liable, on conviction on indictment, to imprisonment for life.

(3) [*Identical to s.34(3) (including the prospective amendment),* ante, *§ 20–134.*]

Engaging in sexual activity in the presence, procured by inducement, threat or deception, of a person with a mental disorder

20–136 **36.**—(1) A person (A) commits an offence if—

(a) he intentionally engages in an activity,

(b) the activity is sexual,

(c) for the purpose of obtaining sexual gratification, he engages in it—

(i) when another person (B) is present or is in a place from which A can be observed, and

(ii) knowing or believing that B is aware, or intending that B should be aware, that he is engaging in it,

(d) B agrees to be present or in the place referred to in paragraph (c)(i) because of an inducement offered or given, a threat made or a deception practised by A for the purpose of obtaining that agreement,

(e), (f) [*identical to s.34(1)(d), (e),* ante, *§ 20–134*].

(2) [*Identical to s.32(3) (including the prospective amendment),* ante, *§ 20–127.*]

Causing a person with a mental disorder to watch a sexual act by inducement, threat or deception

20–137 **37.**—(1) A person (A) commits an offence if—

(a) for the purpose of obtaining sexual gratification, he intentionally causes another person (B) to watch a third person engaging in an activity, or to look at an image of any person engaging in an activity,

(b) the activity is sexual,

(c) B agrees to watch or look because of an inducement offered or given, a threat made or a deception practised by A for the purpose of obtaining that agreement,

(d), (e) [*identical to s.34(1)(d), (e),* ante, *§ 20–134*].

(2) [*Identical to s.32(3) (including the prospective amendment),* ante, *§ 20–127.*]

(2) Indictment

STATEMENT OF OFFENCE

20–138 *Sexual activity with a person with a mental disorder whose agreement thereto is procured by inducement, threat or deception, contrary to section 34(1) of the* Sexual Offences Act *2003.*

PARTICULARS OF OFFENCE

A B, on the —— day of ——, 20—, intentionally touched C D, a person with a mental disorder, by penetrating her mouth with his penis, in circumstances where the touching was sexual, where C D agreed to the touching, where A B had obtained her agreement by giving her an inducement [or *making a threat*] [or *practising a deception*], *namely …, and where A B knew or could reasonably have been expected to know that C D had a mental disorder.*

Where the circumstances are alleged to fall within subsection (2), this should be particularised in any charge and in the indictment.

Indictments in respect of offences contrary to sections 35 to 37 may be framed from the above indictment and the specimen indictments for the corresponding offences under sections 10 to 12 (*ante*, §§ 20–65 *et seq.*).

(3) Class of offence and mode of trial

Section 34(1): if the offence falls within subsection (2), it is triable only on indictment, and is a class 2 offence; otherwise, it is triable either way, and falls within class 3: *ante*, § 2–17. **20–139**

Section 35(1): as for section 34(1), save that all offences under this section fall within class 3: *ante*, § 2–17.

Offences contrary to sections 36(1) and 37(1) are triable either way, and fall within class 3: *ante*, § 2–17.

(4) Sentence

The indictable only offences contrary to section 34(1) and 35(1) are punishable with imprisonment for life. Otherwise, offences contrary to those provisions carry a maximum of 14 years' imprisonment on conviction on indictment, or six (12, as from a day to be appointed) months' imprisonment, or a fine not exceeding the statutory maximum, or both, on summary conviction: ss.34(2), (3), 35(2), (3). **20–140**

Offences contrary to sections 36(1) and 37(1), 10 years' imprisonment on conviction on indictment, or six (12, as from a day to be appointed) months' imprisonment, or a fine not exceeding the statutory maximum, or both, on summary conviction: ss.36(3), 37(3).

For guidance, see the Sentencing Guidelines Council's definitive guideline for sentencing in cases involving sexual offences (K–83 *et seq.*). The guideline applies to offenders sentenced on or after May 14, 2007.

(5) Elements of the offences

Apart from the additional elements of the victim's mental disorder, the defendant's *mens rea* in relation thereto, and the obtaining of the victim's agreement by offering or giving an inducement, making a threat or practising a deception, the offences under sections 34 to 37 broadly correspond to the offences contrary to sections 9 to 12 (*ante*, §§ 20–58 *et seq.*). It may be noted, however, that the offence under section 35 extends to "causing", but not "inciting". **20–141**

(6) Secondary parties

Section 73 (*ante*, § 20–57) applies to an offence under section 34 against a person under 16. **20–142**

K. OFFENCES BY CARE WORKERS FOR PERSONS WITH A MENTAL DISORDER

(1) Statute

Sexual Offences Act 2003, ss.38–44

Care workers: sexual activity with a person with a mental disorder

38.—(1) A person (A) commits an offence if— **20–143**

(a) he intentionally touches another person (B),

(b) the touching is sexual,

(c) B has a mental disorder,

(d) A knows or could reasonably be expected to know that B has a mental disorder, and

(e) A is involved in B's care in a way that falls within section 42.

(2) Where in proceedings for an offence under this section it is proved that the other person had a mental disorder, it is to be taken that the defendant knew or could reasonably have been expected to know that that person had a mental disorder unless sufficient evidence is adduced to raise an issue as to whether he knew or could reasonably have been expected to know it.

(3) A person guilty of an offence under this section, if the touching involved—

(a) penetration of B's anus or vagina with a part of A's body or anything else,

(b) penetration of B's mouth with A's penis,

(c) penetration of A's anus or vagina with a part of B's body, or

(d) penetration of A's mouth with B's penis,

is liable, on conviction on indictment, to imprisonment for a term not exceeding 14 years.

(4) Unless subsection (3) applies, a person guilty of an offence under this section is liable—

(a) on summary conviction, to imprisonment for a term not exceeding *6* [12] months or a fine not exceeding the statutory maximum or both;

(b) on conviction on indictment, to imprisonment for a term not exceeding 10 years.

[In subs. (4)(a), "12" is substituted for "6", as from a day to be appointed, by the *CJA* 2003, s.282(2) and (3). The increase has no application to offences committed before the substitution takes effect: s.282(4).]

Care workers: causing or inciting sexual activity

20–144 **39.**—(1) A person (A) commits an offence if—

(a) he intentionally causes or incites another person (B) to engage in an activity,

(b) the activity is sexual,

(c)–(e) [*identical to s.38(1)(c)–(e),* ante, *§ 20–143*].

(2) [*Identical to s.38(2),* ante, *§ 20–143*.]

(3) A person guilty of an offence under this section, if the activity caused or incited involved—

(a) penetration of B's anus or vagina,

(b) penetration of B's mouth with a person's penis,

(c) penetration of a person's anus or vagina with a part of B's body or by B with anything else, or

(d) penetration of a person's mouth with B's penis,

is liable, on conviction on indictment, to imprisonment for a term not exceeding 14 years.

(4) [*Identical to s.38(4) (including the prospective amendment),* ante, *§ 20–143*.]

Care workers: sexual activity in the presence of a person with a mental disorder

20–145 **40.**—(1) A person (A) commits an offence if—

(a) he intentionally engages in an activity,

(b) the activity is sexual,

(c) for the purpose of obtaining sexual gratification, he engages in it—

(i) when another person (B) is present or is in a place from which A can be observed, and

(ii) knowing or believing that B is aware, or intending that B should be aware, that he is engaging in it,

(d)–(f) [*identical to s.38(1)(c)–(e),* ante, *§ 20–143*].

(2) [*Identical to s.38(2),* ante, *§ 20–143*.]

(3) A person guilty of an offence under this section is liable—

(a) on summary conviction, to imprisonment for a term not exceeding *6* [12] months or a fine not exceeding the statutory maximum or both;

(b) on conviction on indictment, to imprisonment for a term not exceeding 7 years.

[In subs. (3)(a), "12" is substituted for "6", as from a day to be appointed, by the *CJA* 2003, s.282(2) and (3). The increase has no application to offences committed before the substitution takes effect: s.282(4).]

Care workers: causing a person with a mental disorder to watch a sexual act

20–146 **41.**—(1) A person (A) commits an offence if—

(a) for the purpose of obtaining sexual gratification, he intentionally causes another person (B) to watch a third person engaging in an activity, or to look at an image of any person engaging in an activity,

(b) the activity is sexual,

(c)–(e) [*identical to s.38(1)(c)–(e),* ante, *§ 20–143*].

(2) [*Identical to s.38(2),* ante, *§ 20–143*.]

(3) [*Identical to s.40(3) (including the prospective amendment),* ante, *§ 20–145*.]

Care workers: interpretation

42.—(1) For the purposes of sections 38 to 41, a person (A) is involved in the care of another person (B) in a way that falls within this section if any of subsections (2) to (4) applies. **20–147**

(2) This subsection applies if—

(a) B is accommodated and cared for in a care home, community home, voluntary home or children's home, and

(b) A has functions to perform in the home in the course of employment which have brought him or are likely to bring him into regular face to face contact with B.

(3) This subsection applies if B is a patient for whom services are provided—

(a) by a National Health Service body or an independent medical agency, or

(b) in an independent clinic or an independent hospital,

and A has functions to perform for the body or agency or in the clinic or hospital in the course of employment which have brought him or are likely to bring him into regular face to face contact with B.

(4) This subsection applies if A—

(a) is, whether or not in the course of employment, a provider of care, assistance or services to B in connection with B's mental disorder, and

(b) as such, has had or is likely to have regular face to face contact with B.

(5) In this section—

"care home" means an establishment which is a care home for the purposes of the *Care Standards Act* 2000;

"children's home" has the meaning given by section 1 of that Act;

"community home" has the meaning given by section 53 of the *Children Act* 1989;

"employment" means any employment, whether paid or unpaid and whether under a contract of service or apprenticeship, under a contract for services, or otherwise than under a contract;

"independent clinic", "independent hospital" and "independent medical agency" have the meaning given by section 2 of the *Care Standards Act* 2000;

"National Health Service body" means —

(a) a Health Authority,

(b) a National Health Service trust,

(c) a Primary Care Trust, or

(d) a Special Health Authority;

"voluntary home" has the meaning given by section 60(3) of the *Children Act* 1989.

Sections 38 to 41: exception for spouses and civil partners

43.—(1) Conduct by a person (A) which would otherwise be an offence under any of sections 38 to 41 against another person (B) is not an offence under that section if at the time— **20–148**

(a) B is 16 or over, and

(b) A and B are lawfully married or civil partners of each other.

(2) In proceedings for such an offence it is for the defendant to prove that A and B were at the time lawfully married or civil partners of each other.

[This section is printed as amended by the *Civil Partnership Act* 2004, s.261(1), and Sched. 27, para. 175.]

Sections 38 to 41: sexual relationships which pre-date care relationships

44.—(1) Conduct by a person (A) which would otherwise be an offence under any of sections 38 to 41 against another person (B) is not an offence under that section if, immediately before A became involved in B's care in a way that falls within section 42, a sexual relationship existed between A and B. **20–149**

(2) Subsection (1) does not apply if at that time sexual intercourse between A and B would have been unlawful.

(3) In proceedings for an offence under any of sections 38 to 41 it is for the defendant to prove that such a relationship existed at that time.

(2) Indictment

STATEMENT OF OFFENCE

20–150 *Sexual activity with a person with a mental disorder by a care worker, contrary to section 38(1) of the* Sexual Offences Act *2003*.

PARTICULARS OF OFFENCE

A B, on the —— day of ——, 20—, intentionally touched C D, a person with a mental disorder, by penetrating her mouth with his penis, in circumstances where the touching was sexual, where A B knew or could reasonably have been expected to know that C D had a mental disorder, and where A B was a person involved in C D's care in a way falling within section 42 of the Sexual Offences Act *2003*.

Where the circumstances are alleged to fall within subsection (3), this should be particularised in any charge and in the indictment.

Indictments in respect of offences contrary to sections 39 to 41 may be framed from the above indictment and the specimen indictments for the corresponding offences under sections 10 to 12 (*ante*, §§ 20–65 *et seq.*).

(3) Class of offence and mode of trial

20–151 Section 38(1): if the offence falls within subsection (3), it is triable only on indictment, and is a class 2 offence; otherwise, it is triable either way, and falls within class 3: *ante*, § 2–17.

Section 39(1): as for section 38(1), save that all offences under this section fall within class 3: *ante*, § 2–17.

Offences contrary to section 40(1) and 41(1) are triable either way, and fall within class 3: *ante*, § 2–17.

(4) Sentence

20–152 The indictable only offences contrary to section 38(1) and 39(1) are punishable with imprisonment not exceeding 14 years. Otherwise, offences contrary to those provisions carry a maximum of 10 years' imprisonment on conviction on indictment, or six (12, as from a day to be appointed) months' imprisonment, or a fine not exceeding the statutory maximum, or both, on summary conviction: ss.38(3), (4), 39(3), (4).

Offences contrary to sections 40(1) and 41(1), seven years' imprisonment on conviction on indictment, or six (12, as from a day to be appointed) months' imprisonment, or a fine not exceeding the statutory maximum, or both, on summary conviction: ss.40(3), 41(3).

For guidance, see the Sentencing Guidelines Council's definitive guideline for sentencing in cases involving sexual offences (K–83 *et seq.*). The guideline applies to offenders sentenced on or after May 14, 2007.

(5) Elements of the offences

20–153 Apart from the additional elements of the victim's mental disorder, the defendant's *mens rea* in relation thereto, and the involvement of the defendant in the care of the victim in a way that falls within section 42, the offences under sections 38 to 41 broadly correspond to the offences contrary to sections 9 to 12 (*ante*, §§ 20–58 *et seq.*). It may be noted, however, that the offence under section 41 extends to "causing", but not "inciting".

(6) Secondary parties

20–154 Section 73 (*ante*, § 20–57) applies to an offence under section 38 against a person under 16.

L. ABUSE OF CHILDREN THROUGH PROSTITUTION AND PORNOGRAPHY

(1) Paying for sexual services of a child

(a) *Statute*

Sexual Offences Act 2003, s.47

Paying for sexual services of a child

47.—(1) A person (A) commits an offence if— **20–155**

(a) he intentionally obtains for himself the sexual services of another person (B),

(b) before obtaining those services, he has made or promised payment for those services to B or a third person, or knows that another person has made or promised such a payment, and

(c) either—

(i) B is under 18, and A does not reasonably believe that B is 18 or over, or

(ii) B is under 13.

(2) In this section, "payment" means any financial advantage, including the discharge of an obligation to pay or the provision of goods or services (including sexual services) gratuitously or at a discount.

(3) A person guilty of an offence under this section against a person under 13, where subsection (6) applies, is liable on conviction on indictment to imprisonment for life.

(4) Unless subsection (3) applies, a person guilty of an offence under this section against a person under 16 is liable—

(a) where subsection (6) applies, on conviction on indictment, to imprisonment for a term not exceeding 14 years;

(b) in any other case—

(i) on summary conviction, to imprisonment for a term not exceeding *6* [12] months or a fine not exceeding the statutory maximum or both;

(ii) on conviction on indictment, to imprisonment for a term not exceeding 14 years.

(5) Unless subsection (3) or (4) applies, a person guilty of an offence under this section is liable—

(a) on summary conviction, to imprisonment for a term not exceeding *6* [12] months or a fine not exceeding the statutory maximum or both;

(b) on conviction on indictment, to imprisonment for a term not exceeding 7 years.

(6) This subsection applies where the offence involved—

(a) penetration of B's anus or vagina with a part of A's body or anything else,

(b) penetration of B's mouth with A's penis,

(c) penetration of A's anus or vagina with a part of B's body or by B with anything else, or

(d) penetration of A's mouth with B's penis.

(7) [*Northern Ireland (repealed, as from a day to be appointed, by S.I. 2008 No. 1779* (ante, *§ 20–91*).]

[In subss. (4)(b) and (5)(a), "12" is substituted for "6", as from a day to be appointed, by the *CJA* 2003, s.282(2) and (3). The increase has no application to offences committed before the substitution takes effect: s.282(4).]

(b) *Indictment*

STATEMENT OF OFFENCE

Paying for sexual services of a child, contrary to section 47(1) of the Sexual Offences Act *2003*. **20–156**

PARTICULARS OF OFFENCE

A B, on the —— day of ——, 20—, intentionally obtained for himself the sexual services of C D, the said C D being aged under 18 years and the said A B not reasonably believing that she was of or over the age of 18 years, and, before obtaining those services, the said A B promised payment for those services to C D [or *E F*] [or *knew that G H had made payment for those services to the said C D* [or *E F*]].

Where the victim is under 13, the defendant's conduct is almost certain to fall within section 5, 6 or 7 (*ante*, §§ 20–49 *et seq.*), and where the victim is under 16, the defendant's conduct is almost certain to fall within section 9 (*ante*, § 20–58). Those sections carry similar maximum penalties, and have the advantage that there is no necessity to prove payment or a promise thereof. It is possible, however, that the legislative intent was that where the defendant's conduct falls within one of the earlier sections and also within this section, the prosecution should be under this section, as an aggravated form of the offence (the aggravating feature being the encouragement of the child's prostitution).

Where a prosecution is brought under this section in respect of a child under 16 or under 13, and it is alleged that the offence involved conduct falling within subsection (6), the particulars of offence should allege the age of the child as being either "under 16 years" or "under 13 years" and should specify the conduct within subsection (6).

(c) *Class of offence and mode of trial*

20–157 Where the charge alleges an offence against a child under 16, and circumstances falling within subsection (6), the charge will be triable only on indictment (see subss. (3) and (4)(a)); any other allegation of an offence under this section will be an allegation of an offence triable either way. Where the charge alleges an offence against a child under 13, and circumstances falling within subsection (6), it will fall within class 2; all other offences contrary to this section will fall within class 3: *ante*, § 2–17.

(d) *Sentence*

20–158 Where the child was under 13 and the offence involved conduct falling within subsection (6): life imprisonment (see subs. (3)); where the child was aged 13 to 15, and the offence involved conduct falling within subsection (6): 14 years' imprisonment (see subs. (4)(a)); where the child was under 16, but the offence did not involve conduct falling within subsection (6), 14 years' imprisonment on conviction on indictment, or, on summary conviction six (12, as from a day to be appointed) months' imprisonment or a fine not exceeding the statutory maximum, or both (see subs. (4)(b)); in any other case, seven years' imprisonment on conviction on indictment, or, on summary conviction, six (12, as from a day to be appointed) months' imprisonment or a fine not exceeding the statutory maximum, or both (see subs. (5)).

For guidance, see the Sentencing Guidelines Council's definitive guideline for sentencing in cases involving sexual offences (K–83 *et seq.*). The guideline applies to offenders sentenced on or after May 14, 2007.

(e) *Elements of the offence*

20–159 As to the obvious overlap between the offences created by this section, and those created by sections 5 to 7 and 9, see *ante*, § 20–156; but this section has the potential to cover much conduct not included within those sections. There is no definition of "services", but "sexual" is defined in section 78, *ante*, § 20–17. Apart from the fact that the definition of the offence refers to "sexual services", which has the potential for being extremely broadly construed, it also applies to persons aged 16 and 17. Thus, conduct which is lawful if done with the consent of a 16- or 17-year-old without payment or reward becomes criminal if done for payment. "Payment" is defined in subsection (2). This includes not just the payment of money, but the discharge of an obligation and the provision of services free or at a discount. The definition even includes the provision of "sexual" services free or at a discount. The offence, therefore, covers an obtaining of sexual services which are to be paid for by other sexual services. Quite what the draftsman had in mind by this is difficult to fathom.

The principal focus of attention is bound to be in relation to the ambit of "services" (stripping? lap dancing? posing nude, topless, suggestively? participating in a love/ sex scene for mainstream film, theatre or television?) and "payment" (does an 18-year-old boy who makes an extravagant promise to his 17-year-old girlfriend as part of the seduction process commit an offence under this section?), but there will be secondary issues. One of these is bound to relate to the position of a defendant who honestly and reasonably believed the girl, whose sexual services he paid for, to have been 16 or 17, when in fact she was 15. He will be guilty of the offence, but is the maximum offence to be regarded as 14 years' imprisonment, or as seven years? There appears to be no means of obtaining the verdict of the jury on this issue, which will, therefore, have to be decided by the judge. It is submitted that, whilst as a matter of law, the maximum sentence is to be regarded as 14 years, as a matter of principle, the judge, unless satisfied to the criminal standard, that the defendant had no such belief, should sentence on the basis that the maximum is seven years' imprisonment.

As to the definition of "payment", *cf.* the definition of "gain" in section 54(1), *post*, § 20–174.

(2) Causing, inciting, facilitating, etc., child prostitution or pornography

(a) *Statute*

Sexual Offences Act 2003, ss.48, 50, 51

Causing or inciting child prostitution or pornography

48.—(1) A person (A) commits an offence if— **20–160**

(a) he intentionally causes or incites another person (B) to become a prostitute, or to be involved in pornography, in any part of the world, and

(b) either—

(i) B is under 18, and A does not reasonably believe that B is 18 or over, or

(ii) B is under 13.

(2) A person guilty of an offence under this section is liable—

(a) on summary conviction, to imprisonment for a term not exceeding 6 [12] months or a fine not exceeding the statutory maximum or both;

(b) on conviction on indictment, to imprisonment for a term not exceeding 14 years.

[In subs. (2)(a), "12" is substituted for "6", as from a day to be appointed, by the *CJA* 2003, s.282(2) and (3). The increase has no application to offences committed before the substitution takes effect: s.282(4).]

Arranging or facilitating child prostitution or pornography

50.—(1) A person (A) commits an offence if— **20–161**

(a) he intentionally arranges or facilitates the prostitution or involvement in pornography in any part of the world of another person (B), and

(b) [*identical to s.48(1)(b),* ante, *§ 20–160*].

(2) [*Identical to s.48(2) (including the prospective amendment),* ante, *§ 20–160.*]

Sections 48 to 50: interpretation

51.—(1) For the purposes of sections 48 to 50, a person is involved in pornography if an indecent image of that person is recorded; and similar expressions, and "pornography", are to be interpreted accordingly. **20–162**

(2) In those sections "prostitute" means a person (A) who, on at least one occasion and whether or not compelled to do so, offers or provides sexual services to another person in return for payment or a promise of payment to A or a third person; and "prostitution" is to be interpreted accordingly.

(3) In subsection (2), "payment" means any financial advantage, including the discharge of an obligation to pay or the provision of goods or services (including sexual services) gratuitously or at a discount.

(b) *Indictment*

STATEMENT OF OFFENCE

Causing [or *inciting*] *child prostitution or pornography, contrary to section 48(1) of the* Sexual Offences Act *2003*. **20–163**

PARTICULARS OF OFFENCE

A B, on the —— day of ——, 20—, intentionally incited C D, a person under the age of

18 years, to become a prostitute, the said A B not reasonably believing that C D was aged 18 years or over.

An indictment for an offence contrary to section 50 may easily be framed from the above indictment.

(c) *Class of offence and mode of trial*

20–164 Offences under either section are triable either way, and fall within class 3: *ante*, § 2–17.

(d) *Sentence*

20–165 On conviction on indictment, 14 years' imprisonment, or, on summary conviction, six (12, as from a day to be appointed) months' imprisonment, or a fine not exceeding the statutory maximum, or both: ss.48(2), 50(2).

Offences contrary to section 48 and 50 are "lifestyle offences" within the *PCA* 2002, Sched. 2 (*ante*, § 5–660), in respect of which a financial reporting order may be made under the *SOCPA* 2005, s.76 (*ante*, § 5–886a).

For guidance, see the Sentencing Guidelines Council's definitive guideline for sentencing in cases involving sexual offences (K–83 *et seq.*). The guideline applies to offenders sentenced on or after May 14, 2007.

(e) *Elements of the offences*

20–166 As to "causing" generally, see *ante*, § 17–66. As to "pornography", and "prostitute", see section 51 of the 2003 Act, *ante*, § 20–162. As to "sexual services" and "payment", see *ante*, § 20–159. As to "image", see *ante*, § 20–18.

(3) Controlling a child prostitute or a child involved in pornography

(a) *Statute*

Sexual Offences Act 2003, s.49

Controlling a child prostitute or a child involved in pornography

20–167 **49.**—(1) A person (A) commits an offence if—

(a) he intentionally controls any of the activities of another person (B) relating to B's prostitution or involvement in pornography in any part of the world, and

(b) [*identical to s.48(1)(b),* ante, *§ 20–160*].

(2) [*Identical to s.48(2) (including the prospective amendment),* ante, *§ 20–160.*]

(b) *Indictment*

STATEMENT OF OFFENCE

20–168 *Causing* [or *inciting*] *child prostitution* [or *pornography*], *contrary to section 49(1) of the* Sexual Offences Act *2003*.

PARTICULARS OF OFFENCE

A B, between the —— day of ——, 20—, and the —— day of ——, 20—, intentionally controlled the activities of C D relating to the said C D's prostitution [or *involvement in pornography*], *the said C D being a person under the age of 18 years, and the said A B not reasonably believing that the said C D was aged 18 years or over.*

(c) *Class of offence and mode of trial*

20–169 This offence is triable either way, and falls within class 3: *ante*, § 2–17.

(d) *Sentence*

20–170 On conviction on indictment, 14 years' imprisonment, or, on summary conviction, six (12, as from a day to be appointed) months' imprisonment, or a fine not exceeding the statutory maximum, or both: s.49(2).

An offence contrary to section 49 is a "lifestyle offence" within the *PCA* 2002, Sched. 2 (*ante*, § 5–660), in respect of which a financial reporting order may be made under the *SOCPA* 2005, s.76 (*ante*, § 5–886a).

For guidance, see the Sentencing Guidelines Council's definitive guideline for sentencing in cases involving sexual offences (K–83 *et seq.*). The guideline applies to offenders sentenced on or after May 14, 2007.

(e) *Elements of the offence*

As to "pornography", and "prostitute", see section 51 of the 2003 Act, *ante*, § 20–162. As to "control", see *R. v. Massey*, *post*, § 20–178. **20–171**

M. EXPLOITATION OF PROSTITUTION

(1) Statute

Sexual Offences Act 2003, ss.52–54

Causing or inciting prostitution for gain

52.—(1) A person commits an offence if— **20–172**

(a) he intentionally causes or incites another person to become a prostitute in any part of the world, and

(b) he does so for or in the expectation of gain for himself or a third person.

(2) A person guilty of an offence under this section is liable—

(a) on summary conviction, to imprisonment for a term not exceeding *6* [12] months or a fine not exceeding the statutory maximum or both;

(b) on conviction on indictment, to imprisonment for a term not exceeding 7 years.

[In subs. (2)(a), "12" is substituted for "6", as from a day to be appointed, by the *CJA* 2003, s.282(2) and (3). The increase has no application to offences committed before the substitution takes effect: s.282(4).]

Controlling prostitution for gain

53.—(1) A person commits an offence if— **20–173**

(a) he intentionally controls any of the activities of another person relating to that person's prostitution in any part of the world, and

(b) he does so for or in the expectation of gain for himself or a third person.

(2) [*Identical to s.52(2) (including the prospective amendment),* ante, *§ 20–172.*]

Sections 52 and 53: interpretation

54.—(1) In sections 52 and 53, "gain" means— **20–174**

(a) any financial advantage, including the discharge of an obligation to pay or the provision of goods or services (including sexual services) gratuitously or at a discount; or

(b) the goodwill of any person which is or appears likely, in time, to bring financial advantage.

(2) In those sections "prostitute" and "prostitution" have the meaning given by section 51(2).

(2) Indictment

STATEMENT OF OFFENCE

Causing [or *inciting*] *prostitution for gain, contrary to section 52(1) of the* Sexual Offences Act *2003*. **20–175**

PARTICULARS OF OFFENCE

A B, on the —— day of ——, 20—, intentionally incited C D to become a prostitute, and did so for or in the expectation of gain for himself or of a third person.

An indictment for an offence contrary to section 53 may easily be framed from the above indictment.

(3) Class of offence and mode of trial

Offences under either section are triable either way, and fall within class 3: *ante*, § 2–17. **20–176**

(4) Sentence

On conviction on indictment, seven years' imprisonment, or, on summary conviction, **20–177** six (12, as from a day to be appointed) months' imprisonment, or a fine not exceeding the statutory maximum, or both: ss.52(2), 53(2).

Offences contrary to section 52 and 53 are "lifestyle offences" within the *PCA* 2002, Sched. 2 (*ante*, § 5–660), in respect of which a financial reporting order may be made under the *SOCPA* 2005, s.76 (*ante*, § 5–886a).

For guidance, see the Sentencing Guidelines Council's definitive guideline for sentencing in cases involving sexual offences (K–83 *et seq.*). The guideline applies to offenders sentenced on or after May 14, 2007.

(5) Elements of the offences

20–178 As to "causing" generally, see *ante*, § 17–66. As to "pornography", and "prostitute", see section 51 of the 2003 Act, *ante*, § 20–162. As to "sexual services" and "payment", see *ante*, § 20–159.

The definition of "gain" is identical to the definition of "payment" in section 47(2), but here the reference to "sexual services" makes considerably more sense. The man who controls the activities of a prostitute, and does so only in the expectation that she will herself provide him with sexual services free, will fall within the section.

In *R. v. Massey* [2008] 1 Cr.App.R. 28, CA, it was held that "control" in section 53(1) (and, *obiter*, in s.49(1), *ante*, § 20–167) includes, but is not limited to, "compulsion", "coercion" and "force". Whilst it was neither necessary nor appropriate to seek to lay down a comprehensive definition of what was an ordinary English word, it would certainly be enough that the other person acted under the instructions or directions of the defendant (for whatever reason).

N. TRAFFICKING

(1) Statute

Sexual Offences Act 2003, ss.57–60C

Trafficking into the UK for sexual exploitation

20–179 **57.**—(1) A person commits an offence if he intentionally arranges or facilitates the arrival, or the entry into, in the United Kingdom of another person (B) and either—

(a) he intends to do anything to or in respect of B, after B's arrival but in any part of the world, which if done will involve the commission of a relevant offence, or

(b) he believes that another person is likely to do something to or in respect of B, after B's arrival but in any part of the world, which if done will involve the commission of a relevant offence.

(2) A person guilty of an offence under this section is liable—

(a) on summary conviction, to imprisonment for a term not exceeding 6 [12] months or a fine not exceeding the statutory maximum or both;

(b) on conviction on indictment, to imprisonment for a term not exceeding 14 years.

[This section is printed as amended by the *UK Borders Act* 2007, s.31(3). In subs. (2)(a), "12" is substituted for "6", as from a day to be appointed, by the *CJA* 2003, s.282(2) and (3). The increase has no application to offences committed before the substitution takes effect: s.282(4).]

Trafficking within the UK for sexual exploitation

20–180 **58.**—(1) A person commits an offence if he intentionally arranges or facilitates travel within the United Kingdom by another person (B) and either—

(a) he intends to do anything to or in respect of B, during or after the journey and in any part of the world, which if done will involve the commission of a relevant offence, or

(b) he believes that another person is likely to do something to or in respect of B, during or after the journey and in any part of the world, which if done will involve the commission of a relevant offence.

(2) [*Identical to s.57(2) (including the prospective amendment),* ante, *§ 20–179.*]

Trafficking out of the UK for sexual exploitation

20–181 **59.**—(1) A person commits an offence if he intentionally arranges or facilitates the departure from the United Kingdom of another person (B) and either—

(a) he intends to do anything to or in respect of B, after B's departure but in any part of the world, which if done will involve the commission of a relevant offence, or

(b) he believes that another person is likely to do something to or in respect of B, after B's departure but in any part of the world, which if done will involve the commission of a relevant offence.

(2) [*Identical to s.57(2) (including the prospective amendment),* ante, *§ 20–179.*]

Sections 57 to 59: interpretation and jurisdiction

60.—(1) In sections 57 to 59, "relevant offence" means— **20–182**

(a) an offence under this Part,

(b) an offence under section 1(1)(a) of the *Protection of Children Act* 1978,

(ba) an offence under any provision of the *Sexual Offences (Northern Ireland) Order* 2008;

(c) an offence listed in Schedule 1 to the *Criminal Justice (Children) (Northern Ireland) Order* 1998 (S.I. 1998/1504 (N.I. 9)),

(d) an offence under Article 3(1)(a) of the *Protection of Children (Northern Ireland) Order* 1978 (S.I. 1978/1047 (N.I. 17)), or

(e) anything done outside England and Wales and Northern Ireland which is not an offence within any of paragraphs (a) to (d) but would be if done in England and Wales or Northern Ireland.

(2) Sections 57 to 59 apply to anything done whether inside or outside the United Kingdom.

[This section is printed as amended by the *UK Borders Act* 2007, s.31(4); and S.I. 2008 No. 1779 (*ante*, § 20–91), arts 3 and 9.]

Forfeiture of land vehicle, ship or aircraft

60A.—(1) This section applies if a person is convicted on indictment of an offence under sections 57 to 59. **20–182a**

(2) The court may order the forfeiture of a land vehicle used or intended to be used in connection with the offence if the convicted person—

(a) owned the vehicle at the time the offence was committed;

(b) was at that time a director, secretary or manager of a company which owned the vehicle;

(c) was at that time in possession of the vehicle under a hire-purchase agreement;

(d) was at that time a director, secretary or manager of a company which was in possession of the vehicle under a hire-purchase agreement; or

(e) was driving the vehicle in the course of the commission of the offence.

(3) The court may order the forfeiture of a ship or aircraft used or intended to be used in connection with the offence if the convicted person—

(a) owned the ship or aircraft at the time the offence was committed;

(b) was at that time a director, secretary or manager of a company which owned the ship or aircraft;

(c) was at that time in possession of the ship or aircraft under a hire-purchase agreement;

(d) was at that time a director, secretary or manager of a company which was in possession of the ship or aircraft under a hire-purchase agreement;

(e) was at that time a charterer of the ship or aircraft; or

(f) committed the offence while acting as captain of the ship or aircraft.

(4) But in a case to which subsection (3)(a) or (b) does not apply, forfeiture may be ordered only—

(a) in the case of a ship, if subsection (5) or (6) applies;

(b) in the case of an aircraft, if subsection (5) or (7) applies.

(5) This subsection applies where a person who, at the time the offence was committed, owned the ship or aircraft or was a director, secretary or manager of a company which owned it, knew or ought to have known of the intention to use it in the course of the commission of an offence under sections 57 to 59.

(6) This subsection applies where a ship's gross tonnage is less than 500 tons.

(7) This subsection applies where the maximum weight at which an aircraft (which is not a hovercraft) may take off in accordance with its certificate of airworthiness is less than 5,700 kilogrammes.

(8) Where a person who claims to have an interest in a land vehicle, ship or aircraft applies to a court to make representations on the question of forfeiture, the court may not make an order under this section in respect of the vehicle, ship or aircraft unless the person has been given an opportunity to make representations.

Detention of land vehicle, ship or aircraft

20–182b **60B.**—(1) If a person has been arrested for an offence under sections 57 to 59, a constable or a senior immigration officer may detain a relevant vehicle, ship or aircraft—

(a) until a decision is taken as to whether or not to charge the arrested person with that offence;

(b) if the arrested person has been charged, until he is acquitted, the charge against him is dismissed or the proceedings are discontinued; or

(c) if he has been charged and convicted, until the court decides whether or not to order forfeiture of the vehicle, ship or aircraft.

(2) A vehicle, ship or aircraft is a relevant vehicle, ship or aircraft, in relation to an arrested person if it is a land vehicle, ship or aircraft which the constable or officer concerned has reasonable grounds for believing could, on conviction of the arrested person for the offence for which he was arrested, be the subject of an order for forfeiture made under section 60A.

(3) A person (other than the arrested person) may apply to the court for the release of a land vehicle, ship or aircraft on the grounds that—

(a) he owns the vehicle, ship or aircraft;

(b) he was, immediately before the detention of the vehicle, ship or aircraft, in possession of it under a hire-purchase agreement; or

(c) he is a charterer of the ship or aircraft.

(4) The court to which an application is made under subsection (3) may, on such security or surety being tendered as it considers satisfactory, release the vehicle, ship or aircraft on condition that it is made available to the court if—

(a) the arrested person is convicted; and

(b) an order for its forfeiture is made under section 60A.

(5) In this section, "court" means—

(a) in relation to England and Wales—

(i) if the arrested person has not been charged, or he has been charged but proceedings for the offence have not begun to be heard, a magistrates' court;

(ii) if he has been charged and proceedings for the offence are being heard, the court hearing the proceedings;

(b) [*Northern Ireland*].

(6) In this section, "senior immigration officer" means an immigration officer (appointed or employed as such under the *Immigration Act* 1971) not below the rank of chief immigration officer.

Sections 60A and 60B: interpretation

20–182c **60C.**—(1) In this section and sections 60A and 60B, unless the contrary intention appears—

"aircraft" includes hovercraft;

"captain" means master (of a ship) or commander (of an aircraft);

"land vehicle" means any vehicle other than a ship or aircraft;

"ship" includes every description of vessel used in navigation.

(2) In sections 60A and 60B, a reference to being an owner of a vehicle, ship or aircraft includes a reference to being any of a number of persons who jointly own it.

[Sections 60A to 60C were inserted by the *VCRA* 2006, s.54, and Sched. 4, paras 1 and 2.]

(2) Indictment

STATEMENT OF OFFENCE

20–183 *Trafficking into the United Kingdom for sexual exploitation, contrary to section 57(1) of the* Sexual Offences Act *2003.*

PARTICULARS OF OFFENCE

A B, on the —— day of ——, 20—, intentionally arranged [or *facilitated*] *the arrival in the United Kingdom of C D, the said A B intending to do anything to or in respect of the said C D, after C D's arrival but in any part of the world which would involve the commission of a relevant offence.*

Indictments alleging offences contrary to section 58 or 59 may readily be framed from the above indictment.

(3) Class of offence and mode of trial

Offences under any of these sections are triable either way, and fall within class 3: *ante*, § 2–17. **20–184**

(4) Sentence

On conviction on indictment, 14 years' imprisonment, or, on summary conviction, six (12, as from a day to be appointed) months' imprisonment, or a fine not exceeding the statutory maximum, or both: ss.57(2), 58(2), 59(2). **20–185**

For guidance, see now the Sentencing Guidelines Council's definitive guideline for sentencing in cases involving sexual offences (K–83 *et seq.*). The guideline applies to offenders sentenced on or after May 14, 2007.

(5) Elements of the offences

As to the definition of "relevant offence" in section 60(1), "this Part" comprises sections 1 to 79 of the 2003 Act. For section 1 of the *Protection of Children Act* 1978, see *post*, § 31–107. **20–186**

It should be noted that whilst the conduct constituting the "relevant offence" may take place, or be intended to take place, anywhere in the world, the conduct constituting the arrangement or facilitation may take place outside the United Kingdom only where the person doing the arranging or facilitating is an individual falling within section 60(3), or a body incorporated under the law of a part of the United Kingdom.

O. PREPARATORY OFFENCES

(1) Administering a substance with intent

(a) *Statute*

Sexual Offences Act 2003, s.61

Administering a substance with intent

61.—(1) A person commits an offence if he intentionally administers a substance to, or causes a substance to be taken by, another person (B)— **20–187**

(a) knowing that B does not consent, and

(b) with the intention of stupefying or overpowering B, so as to enable any person to engage in a sexual activity that involves B.

(2) A person guilty of an offence under this section is liable—

(a) on summary conviction, to imprisonment for a term not exceeding *6* [12] months or a fine not exceeding the statutory maximum or both;

(b) on conviction on indictment, to imprisonment for a term not exceeding 10 years.

[In subs. (2)(a), "12" is substituted for "6", as from a day to be appointed, by the *CJA* 2003, s.282(2) and (3). The increase has no application to offences committed before the substitution takes effect: s.282(4).]

(b) *Indictment*

STATEMENT OF OFFENCE

Administering a substance with intent, contrary to section 61(1) of the Sexual Offences Act *2003.* **20–188**

PARTICULARS OF OFFENCE

A B, on the —— day of ——, 20—, intentionally administered a substance [or *caused a substance to be taken by*] *C D, knowing that C D did not consent and with the intention of stupefying or overpowering C D, so as to enable A B* [or *EF*] *to engage in sexual activity that involved C D.*

(c) *Class of offence and mode of trial*

20–189 This offence is triable either way, and falls within class 3: *ante*, § 2–17.

(d) *Sentence*

20–190 On conviction on indictment, 10 years' imprisonment, or, on summary conviction, six (12, as from a day to be appointed) months' imprisonment, or a fine not exceeding the statutory maximum, or both: s.61(2).

For guidance, see the Sentencing Guidelines Council's definitive guideline for sentencing in cases involving sexual offences (K–83 *et seq.*). The guideline applies to offenders sentenced on or after May 14, 2007.

(e) *Elements of the offences*

20–191 As to "consent", see section 74 of the 2003 Act, *ante*, § 20–10. As to "sexual", see section 78 of the 2003 Act, *ante*, § 20–17.

(2) Committing an offence with intent to commit a sexual offence

(a) *Statute*

Sexual Offences Act 2003, s.62

Committing an offence with intent to commit a sexual offence

20–192 **62.**—(1) A person commits an offence under this section if he commits any offence with the intention of committing a relevant sexual offence.

(2) In this section, "relevant sexual offence" means any offence under this Part (including an offence of aiding, abetting, counselling or procuring such an offence).

(3) A person guilty of an offence under this section is liable on conviction on indictment, where the offence is committed by kidnapping or false imprisonment, to imprisonment for life.

(4) Unless subsection (3) applies, a person guilty of an offence under this section is liable—

(a) on summary conviction, to imprisonment for a term not exceeding *6* [12] months or a fine not exceeding the statutory maximum or both;

(b) on conviction on indictment, to imprisonment for a term not exceeding 10 years.

[In subs. (4)(a), "12" is substituted for "6", as from a day to be appointed, by the *CJA* 2003, s.282(2) and (3). The increase has no application to offences committed before the substitution takes effect: s.282(4).]

(b) *Indictment*

STATEMENT OF OFFENCE

20–193 *Committing an offence with intent to commit a sexual offence, contrary to section 62(1) of the* Sexual Offences Act *2003*.

PARTICULARS OF OFFENCE

A B, on the —— day of ——, 20—, committed the offence of kidnapping particularised in count one above, and did so with the intention of committing a relevant sexual offence.

It is submitted that good practice will dictate that there should be two counts, the first alleging the base offence, and the second alleging that that offence was committed with the specified intention. This obviates any need to set out the particulars of the base offence in the count under section 62, and will forestall any difficulties which might arise if there were only one count, and all members of the jury were satisfied about the base offence, but there was no sufficient agreement about the ulterior intention.

(c) *Class of offence and mode of trial*

20–194 Where the base offence is kidnapping or false imprisonment, the offence is triable only on indictment, and is a class 2 offence: *ante*, § 2–17; otherwise it is triable either way, and is a class 3 offence: *ibid*.

(d) *Sentence*

Where the base offence is kidnapping or false imprisonment, life imprisonment; otherwise, on conviction on indictment, 10 years' imprisonment, or, on summary conviction six (12, as from a day to be appointed) months' imprisonment, or a fine not exceeding the statutory maximum, or both: s.62(3), (4). **20–195**

For guidance, see now the Sentencing Guidelines Council's definitive guideline for sentencing in cases involving sexual offences (K–83 *et seq.*). The guideline applies to offenders sentenced on or after May 14, 2007.

(e) *Elements of the offence*

The reference to "this Part" (in subs. (2)) is a reference to sections 1 to 79 of the Act. **20–196**

It is submitted that whilst it will not normally be necessary for the prosecution to aver a particular sexual offence as having been intended in the indictment, they must nevertheless satisfy the jury that the defendant intended a course of conduct which would involve the commission of a relevant offence. It would not matter that some of the jury were sure that he intended to rape the victim, whereas others only were sure that he intended a sexual assault. An offence under section 1 or 2 of the 2003 Act would necessarily involve an assault contrary to section 3; and if it were the case that the jury as a whole were entirely satisfied that he intended to commit either offence A or offence B, but were not satisfied that it was one or the other, then it is submitted that that would warrant a conviction. Where the defendant commits the base offence, hoping that the victim will consent to having sex with him, but intending to rape her if she does not consent, that, it is submitted, would be a sufficient intent.

(3) Trespass with intent

(a) *Statute*

Sexual Offences Act 2003, s.63

Trespass with intent to commit a sexual offence

63.—(1) A person commits an offence if— **20–197**

(a) he is a trespasser on any premises,

(b) he intends to commit a relevant sexual offence on the premises, and

(c) he knows that, or is reckless as to whether, he is a trespasser.

(2) In this section—

"premises" includes a structure or part of a structure;

"relevant sexual offence" has the same meaning as in section 62;

"structure" includes a tent, vehicle or vessel or other temporary or movable structure.

(3) [*Identical to s.61(2)(including the prospective amendment),* ante, *§ 20–187*.]

(b) *Indictment*

STATEMENT OF OFFENCE

Trespassing with intent to commit a sexual offence, contrary to section 63(1) of the Sexual Offences Act *2003*. **20–198**

PARTICULARS OF OFFENCE

A B, on the —— day of ——, 20—, whilst trespassing on premises, namely ——, knowing that he was a trespasser therein, or being reckless as to whether he was a trespasser, intended to commit a relevant sexual offence on those premises.

(c) *Class of offence and mode of trial*

This offence is triable either way, and is a class 3 offence: *ante*, § 2–17. **20–199**

(d) *Sentence*

On conviction on indictment, 10 years' imprisonment, or, on summary conviction six **20–200**

(12, as from a day to be appointed) months' imprisonment, or a fine not exceeding the statutory maximum, or both: s.63(2).

For guidance, see the Sentencing Guidelines Council's definitive guideline for sentencing in cases involving sexual offences (K–83 *et seq.*). The guideline applies to offenders sentenced on or after May 14, 2007.

(e) *Elements of the offences*

20–201 As to the intent to commit a relevant sexual offence, see *ante*, § 20–196. As to the definition of trespass, see *post*, §§ 21–116, 21–117. As to recklessness, it is submitted on the basis of *R. v. G.* [2004] 1 A.C. 1034, HL, that the defendant will be reckless as to whether he is a trespasser when he is aware that there is a risk that he is in a building in the possession of another who does not consent to his entry, and it is unreasonable in all the circumstances known to him to take that risk.

P. SEX WITH AN ADULT RELATIVE

(1) Statute

Sexual Offences Act 2003, ss.64, 65

Sex with an adult relative: penetration

20–202 **64.**—(1) A person aged 16 or over (A) (subject to subsection (3A)) commits an offence if—

(a) he intentionally penetrates another person's vagina or anus with a part of his body or anything else, or penetrates another person's mouth with his penis,

(b) the penetration is sexual,

(c) the other person (B) is aged 18 or over,

(d) A is related to B in a way mentioned in subsection (2), and

(e) A knows or could reasonably be expected to know that he is related to B in that way.

(2) The ways that A may be related to B are as parent, grandparent, child, grandchild, brother, sister, half-brother, half-sister, uncle, aunt, nephew or niece.

(3) In subsection (2)—

(za) "parent" includes an adoptive parent;

(zb) child includes an adopted person within the meaning of Chapter 4 of Part 1 of the *Adoption and Children Act* 2002;

(a) "uncle" means the brother of a person's parent, and "aunt" has a corresponding meaning;

(b) "nephew" means the child of a person's brother or sister, and "niece" has a corresponding meaning.

(3A) Where subsection (1) applies in a case where A is related to B as B's child by virtue of subsection (3)(zb), A does not commit an offence under this section unless A is 18 or over.

(4) Where in proceedings for an offence under this section it is proved that the defendant was related to the other person in any of those ways, it is to be taken that the defendant knew or could reasonably have been expected to know that he was related in that way unless sufficient evidence is adduced to raise an issue as to whether he knew or could reasonably have been expected to know that he was.

(5) A person guilty of an offence under this section is liable—

(a) on summary conviction, to imprisonment for a term not exceeding *6* [12] months or a fine not exceeding the statutory maximum or both;

(b) on conviction on indictment, to imprisonment for a term not exceeding 2 years.

(6) Nothing in—

(a) section 47 of the *Adoption Act* 1976 (which disapplies the status provisions in section 39 of that Act for the purposes of this section in relation to adoptions before 30 December 2005), or

(b) section 74 of the *Adoption and Children Act* 2002 (which disapplies the status provisions in section 67 of that Act for those purposes in relation to adoptions on or after that date),

is to be read as preventing the application of section 39 of the *Adoption Act* 1976 or section 67 of the *Adoption and Children Act* 2002 for the purposes of subsection (3)(za) and (zb) above.

[This section is printed as amended by the *CJIA* 2008, s.73, and Sched. 15, paras 2 and 5. In subs. (5)(a), "12" is substituted for "6", as from a day to be appointed, by the *CJA* 2003, s.282(2) and (3). The increase has no application to offences committed before the substitution takes effect: s.282(4).]

Sex with an adult relative: consenting to penetration

65.—(1) A person aged 16 or over (A) (subject to subsection (3A)) commits an offence if— **20–203**

(a) another person (B) penetrates A's vagina or anus with a part of B's body or anything else, or penetrates A's mouth with B's penis,

(b) A consents to the penetration,

(c) the penetration is sexual,

(d) B is aged 18 or over,

(e), (f) [*identical to s.64(1)(d), (e),* ante, *§ 20–202*].

(2)–(6) [*Identical to s.64(2)–(6),* ante, *§ 20–202.*]

[See the note to s.64, *ante* (but substituting a reference to "Sched. 15, paras 2 and 6" for the reference to "Sched. 15, paras 2 and 5").]

(2) Indictment

COUNT 1

STATEMENT OF OFFENCE

Sex with an adult relative, contrary to section 64(1) of the Sexual Offences Act *2003.* **20–204**

PARTICULARS OF OFFENCE

A B, a person of [or *over*] *the age of 16 years, on the —— day of ——, 20—, intentionally penetrated the vagina of C D with a part of his body, in circumstances where the penetration was sexual, the said C D was aged 18 years or over, the relationship of A B to C D was that of brother and sister, and the said A B knew or could reasonably have been expected to know that he was so related to C D.*

COUNT 2

STATEMENT OF OFFENCE

Sex with an adult relative, contrary to section 65(1) of the Sexual Offences Act *2003.*

PARTICULARS OF OFFENCE

C D, a person of [or *over*] *the age of 16 years, on the —— day of ——, 20—, consented to the penetration of her vagina by A B with a part of his body, in circumstances where the penetration was sexual, the said A B was aged 18 years or over, the relationship of C D to A B was that of sister and brother, and the said C D knew or could reasonably have been expected to know that she was so related to A B.*

(3) Class of offence and mode of trial

An offence under either section is triable either way, and falls within class 3: *ante*, § 2–17. **20–205**

(4) Sentence

On conviction on indictment, two years' imprisonment, or, on summary conviction, six (12, as from a day to be appointed) months' imprisonment, or a fine not exceeding the statutory maximum, or both: ss.64(5), 65(5). **20–206**

For guidance, see the Sentencing Guidelines Council's definitive guideline for sentencing in cases involving sexual offences (K–83 *et seq.*). The guideline applies to offenders sentenced on or after May 14, 2007.

(5) Elements of the offences

As to "penetration", to references to "a part of the body", and "vagina", see section 79, *ante*, §§ 20–18, 20–24. As to "sexual", see section 78, *ante*, § 20–17. **20–207**

In relation to the issue of the defendant's knowledge of the prohibited relationship, subsection (4) of each section makes provision for a rebuttable presumption. It is for the defendant to adduce sufficient evidence to raise an issue in respect of this matter. Once that burden is discharged, the prosecution will then assume the burden of proving knowledge to the normal standard.

Q. OTHER STATUTORY OFFENCES

(1) Exposure

(a) *Statute*

Sexual Offences Act 2003, s.66

Exposure

20–208 **66.**—(1) A person commits an offence if—

(a) he intentionally exposes his genitals, and

(b) he intends that someone will see them and be caused alarm or distress.

(2) [*Identical to s.64(5) (including the prospective amendment),* ante, *§ 20–202.*]

(b) *Indictment*

STATEMENT OF OFFENCE

20–209 *Exposure, contrary to section 66(1) of the* Sexual Offences Act *2003.*

PARTICULARS OF OFFENCE

A B, on the —— day of ——, 20—, intentionally exposed his genitals, intending that someone would see them and be caused alarm or distress.

(c) *Class of offence and mode of trial*

20–210 This offence is triable either way, and falls within class 3: *ante*, § 2–17.

(d) *Sentence*

20–211 On conviction on indictment, two years' imprisonment, or, on summary conviction, six (12, as from a day to be appointed) months' imprisonment, or a fine not exceeding the statutory maximum, or both: s.66(2).

For guidance, see now the Sentencing Guidelines Council's definitive guideline for sentencing in cases involving sexual offences (K–83 *et seq.*). The guideline applies to offenders sentenced on or after May 14, 2007.

(2) Voyeurism

(a) *Statute*

Sexual Offences Act 2003, ss.67, 68

Voyeurism

20–212 **67.**—(1) A person commits an offence if—

(a) for the purpose of obtaining sexual gratification, he observes another person doing a private act, and

(b) he knows that the other person does not consent to being observed for his sexual gratification.

(2) A person commits an offence if—

(a) he operates equipment with the intention of enabling another person to observe, for the purpose of obtaining sexual gratification, a third person (B) doing a private act, and

(b) he knows that B does not consent to his operating equipment with that intention.

(3) A person commits an offence if—

(a) he records another person (B) doing a private act,

(b) he does so with the intention that he or a third person will, for the purpose of obtaining sexual gratification, look at an image of B doing the act, and

(c) he knows that B does not consent to his recording the act with that intention.

(4) A person commits an offence if he instals equipment, or constructs or adapts a

structure or part of a structure, with the intention of enabling himself or another person to commit an offence under subsection (1).

(5) [*Identical to s.64(5) (including the prospective amendment),* ante, *§ 20–202.*]

Voyeurism: interpretation

68.—(1) For the purposes of section 67, a person is doing a private act if the person is in a place which, in the circumstances, would reasonably be expected to provide privacy, and— **20–213**

(a) the person's genitals, buttocks or breasts are exposed or covered only with underwear,

(b) the person is using a lavatory, or

(c) the person is doing a sexual act that is not of a kind ordinarily done in public.

(2) In section 67, "structure" includes a tent, vehicle or vessel or other temporary or movable structure.

(b) *Indictment*

STATEMENT OF OFFENCE

Voyeurism, contrary to section 67(1) of the Sexual Offences Act *2003.* **20–214**

PARTICULARS OF OFFENCE

A B, on the —— day of ——, 20—, for the purpose of obtaining sexual gratification, observed C D doing a private act, C D being in a place which, in the circumstances, would reasonably be expected to provide privacy, and her breasts being exposed at the time, the said A B knowing that C D did not consent to being observed for A B's sexual gratification.

Indictments alleging offences contrary to subsections (2) to (4) may readily be framed from the above indictment and the terms of the subsections.

(c) *Class of offence and mode of trial*

All offences under this section are triable either way, and fall within class 3: *ante*, § 2–17. **20–215**

(d) *Sentence*

On conviction on indictment, two years' imprisonment, or, on summary conviction, six (12, as from a day to be appointed) months' imprisonment, or a fine not exceeding the statutory maximum, or both: s.67(5). **20–216**

For guidance, see now the Sentencing Guidelines Council's definitive guideline for sentencing in cases involving sexual offences (K–83 *et seq.*). The guideline applies to offenders sentenced on or after May 14, 2007.

(e) *Elements of the offence*

As to "consent", see section 74 of the 2003 Act, *ante*, § 20–10. As to references to observation and an "image", see section 79 of the 2003 Act, *ante*, § 20–18. **20–217**

The reference to "breasts" in section 68(1) does not include a man's breasts: *R. v. Bassett*, 172 J.P. 491, CA.

(3) Intercourse with an animal

(a) *Statute*

Sexual Offences Act 2003, s.69

Intercourse with an animal

69.—(1) A person commits an offence if— **20–218**

(a) he intentionally performs an act of penetration with his penis,

(b) what is penetrated is the vagina or anus of a living animal, and

(c) he knows that, or is reckless as to whether, that is what is penetrated.

(2) A person (A) commits an offence if—

(a) A intentionally causes, or allows, A's vagina or anus to be penetrated,

(b) the penetration is by the penis of a living animal, and

(c) A knows that, or is reckless as to whether, that is what A is being penetrated by.

(3) [*Identical to s.64(5) (including the prospective amendment),* ante, *§ 20–202.*]

(b) *Indictment*

STATEMENT OF OFFENCE

20–219 *Intercourse with an animal, contrary to section 69(1) of the* Sexual Offences Act *2003*.

PARTICULARS OF OFFENCE

A B, on the —— day of ——, 20—, intentionally performed an act of penetration of the vagina or anus of a living animal, namely a cow, the said A B knowing that, or being reckless as to whether, that is what was penetrated.

(c) *Class of offence and mode of trial*

20–220 Offences under this section are triable either way, and fall within class 3: *ante*, § 2–17.

(d) *Sentence*

20–221 On conviction on indictment, two years' imprisonment, or, on summary conviction, six (12, as from a day to be appointed) months' imprisonment, or a fine not exceeding the statutory maximum, or both: s.69(3).

For guidance, see the Sentencing Guidelines Council's definitive guideline for sentencing in cases involving sexual offences (K–83 *et seq.*). The guideline applies to offenders sentenced on or after May 14, 2007.

(e) *Elements of the offence*

20–222 As to "penetration" and references to the vagina or anus of an animal, see section 79 of the 2003 Act, *ante*, §§ 20–18, 20–24. As to "intentionally", see *ante*, § 20–34a. As to recklessness, see *ante*, § 20–201.

(4) Sexual penetration of a corpse

(a) *Statute*

Sexual Offences Act 2003, s.70

Sexual penetration of a corpse

20–223 **70.**—(1) A person commits an offence if—

(a) he intentionally performs an act of penetration with a part of his body or anything else,

(b) what is penetrated is a part of the body of a dead person,

(c) he knows that, or is reckless as to whether, that is what is penetrated, and

(d) the penetration is sexual.

(2) [*Identical to s.64(5) (including the prospective amendment),* ante, *§ 20–202.*]

(b) *Indictment*

STATEMENT OF OFFENCE

20–224 *Sexual penetration of a corpse, contrary to section 70(1) of the* Sexual Offences Act *2003*.

PARTICULARS OF OFFENCE

A B, on the —— day of ——, 20—, intentionally performed an act of penetration of a part of the body of a dead person with a part of his body in circumstances where the penetration was sexual and the said A B knew that that is what was being penetrated, or was reckless in relation thereto.

(c) *Class of offence and mode of trial*

20–225 Offences under this section are triable either way, and fall within class 3: *ante*, § 2–17.

(d) *Sentence*

20–226 On conviction on indictment, two years' imprisonment, or, on summary conviction, six (12, as from a day to be appointed) months' imprisonment, or a fine not exceeding the statutory maximum, or both: s.70(2).

(e) *Elements of the offence*

20–227 As to "penetration" and references to "a part of the body", see section 79 of the 2003 Act, *ante*, §§ 20–18, 20–24. As to "intentionally", see *ante*, § 20–34a. As to "sexual", see *ante*, § 20–17.

As to recklessness, see *ante*, § 20–201.

(5) Sexual activity in a public lavatory

20–228 Section 71 of the *SOA* 2003 creates a summary offence of intentionally engaging in sexual activity in a public lavatory. The offence is punishable with six months' imprisonment (51 weeks as from a day to be appointed, but only in relation to offences committed on or after that day (*CJA* 2003, s.281(4)–(6))), or a fine not exceeding level 5 on the standard scale, or both. For guidance, see the Sentencing Guidelines Council's definitive guideline for sentencing in cases involving sexual offences (K–83 *et seq.*). The guideline applies to offenders sentenced on or after May 14, 2007.

(6) Suppression of brothels

(a) *Statute*

Sexual Offences Act 1956, s.33A

Keeping a brothel used for prostitution

20–229 **33A.**—(1) It is an offence for a person to keep, or to manage, or act or assist in the management of, a brothel to which people resort for practices involving prostitution (whether or not also for other practices).

(2) In this section "prostitution" has the meaning given by section 51(2) of the *Sexual Offences Act* 2003.

[This section was inserted, as from May 1, 2004, by the *SOA* 2003, s.55(1) and (2).]

Sections 33, and 34 to 36 of the 1956 Act create summary offences for the suppression of brothels. Section 6 of the *SOA* 1967 provides that for the purposes of these sections, premises shall be treated as a brothel if people resort there for the purpose of lewd homosexual practices in circumstances in which resort thereto for lewd heterosexual practices would have led to them being treated as a brothel for the purposes of those sections.

Section 33 makes it an offence to keep a brothel or to manage, or act in the management of a brothel. Section 34 makes it an offence to let premises for use as a brothel. Sections 35 and 36 respectively make it an offence for a tenant to permit premises to be used as a brothel or for the purposes of prostitution (whether any prostitute involved is male or female). For guidance, see the Sentencing Guidelines Council's definitive guideline for sentencing in cases involving sexual offences (K–83 *et seq.*). The guideline applies to offenders sentenced on or after May 14, 2007.

(b) *Indictment*

STATEMENT OF OFFENCE

20–230 *Keeping a brothel used for prostitution, contrary to section 33A(1) of the* Sexual Offences Act *1956.*

PARTICULARS OF OFFENCE

A B, between the —— day of ——, 20—, and the —— day of ——, 20—, kept [or *managed*] [or *acted or assisted in the management of*] *a brothel to which people resorted for practices involving prostitution.*

(c) *Class of offence and mode of trial*

20–231 The offence contrary to section 33A is triable either way (*SOA* 1956, s.37, and Sched. 2, para. 33A), and falls within class 3: *ante*, § 2–17. The offences contrary to sections 33 and 34 to 36 are summary only (s.37, and Sched. 2, paras 33 and 34 to 36).

(d) *Sentence*

20–232 On conviction on indictment, an offence contrary to section 33A is punishable with seven years' imprisonment, and on summary conviction, it is punishable with six months' imprisonment (12 months as from a day to be appointed, but only in relation to offences committed on or after that day (*CJA* 2003, s.282(2)–(4))), or a fine not exceeding the statutory maximum, or both: *SOA* 1956, s.37, and Sched. 2, para. 33A.

Offences contrary to sections 33 and 34 to 36 carry a maximum sentence of three months' imprisonment, or a fine not exceeding level 3 on the standard scale, or both. For offences committed after a conviction under any of the four sections, the maximum penalty is six months (51 weeks as from a day to be appointed, but only in relation to offences committed on or after that day (*CJA* 2003, s.281(4)–(6))), or a fine not exceeding level 4 on the standard scale, or both: *SOA* 1956, s.37 and Sched. 2, paras 33 and 34 to 36. For the standard scale of fines, see *ante*, § 5–403.

Offences contrary to section 33 and 34 are "lifestyle offences" within the *PCA* 2002, Sched. 2 (*ante*, § 5–660), in respect of which a financial reporting order may be made under the *SOCPA* 2005, s.76 (*ante*, § 5–886a).

For guidance, see the Sentencing Guidelines Council's definitive guideline for sentencing in cases involving sexual offences (K–83 *et seq.*). The guideline applies to offenders sentenced on or after May 14, 2007.

(e) *Elements of the offence*

"Brothel"

20–233 Whether premises constitute a brothel is a question of fact and degree: they are not precluded from being a brothel by the fact that, on any one day, only one prostitute is present. Where there is a joint use of premises by a team of women (albeit involving only one of them using the premises on any particular day) for the purposes of prostitution, the premises constitute a brothel: *Stevens v. Christy*, 85 Cr.App.R. 249, DC. Conversely, premises which are used by only one woman for prostitution are not a brothel: *ibid.*, and *Gorman v. Standen*; *Palace-Clark v. Standen* [1964] 1 Q.B. 294, 48 Cr.App.R. 30, DC.

It is not essential to show that the premises are in fact used for the purpose of prostitution (which involves payment for services rendered), since a brothel exists where women offer sexual intercourse without charging; nor is it necessary to prove that the women are known to police as prostitutes: see *Winter v. Woolfe* [1931] 1 K.B. 549, DC, and *Kelly v. Purvis* [1983] Q.B. 663, 76 Cr.App.R. 165, DC.

The fact that one of the women is the tenant and occupier is immaterial: see *Gorman v. Standen*; *Palace-Clark v. Standen*, *ante*.

It is not necessary that there should be evidence of any indecency or disorderly conduct being perceptible from the exterior of the house: *R. v. Rice and Wilton* (1866) L.R. 1 C.C.R. 21; *J'Anson v. Stuart* (1787) 1 T.R. 748.

Where rooms or flats in one building are separately let to women who use them for purposes of prostitution, it is a question of fact whether the whole premises constitutes a brothel. It may be that in some cases the evidence will show that the separate lettings are a subterfuge: *Strath v. Foxon* [1956] 1 Q.B. 67, 39 Cr.App.R. 162, DC (dismissal of information upheld). For a case on the other side of the line, see *Abbott v. Smith* [1965] 2 Q.B. 662, DC.

20–234 Where a porter was employed to look after a block of 18 flats, among the tenants of which were 12 women who were in the habit of bringing different men nightly to the premises for the purpose of prostitution, it was held that he could be convicted under the *Criminal Law Amendment Act* 1885, s.13(3) (s.34 of the 1956 Act) of being wilfully a party to the continued use of the premises or part thereof as a brothel: *Durose v. Wilson*, 71 J.P. 263.

The mere fact that individual rooms in the house or the relevant part of it were originally let under separate tenancies to separate women with their own keys does not of itself prevent the whole or part of the house from being a brothel, nor is it necessary in every case to prove that the original independent lettings were effected as a subterfuge to escape the consequences of section 34 of the Act of 1956. Where the landlord of the premises is charged with being a party to the continuing use of part of the premises as a brothel, and where in a single house the individual rooms occupied by prostitutes and used by them for their trade are in sufficient proximity to constitute a "nest" of prostitutes, the fact that the rooms were originally the subject of independent lettings for exclusive occupation may be of no weight at all, and the user of the rooms must be the dominant consideration: *Donovan v. Gavin* [1965] 2 Q.B. 648, DC.

Evidence of visits to premises by two women each described as "a prostitute known to me as 'X' [or 'Y']", each accompanied on different occasions by a different man, is admissible to prove that the premises are a brothel provided that the fact of the women being prostitutes is within the personal knowledge of the witness: *R. v. Korie* [1966] 1 All E.R. 50, Liverpool Crown Court (H.H.J. Chapman). *Cf. R. v. Rothwell*, 99 Cr.App.R. 388 (*post*, § 27–78) (proof of persons being heroin users). **20–235**

In *Woodhouse v. Hall*, 72 Cr.App.R. 39, DC, it was held that, on a prosecution for acting in the management of a brothel, contrary to section 33 of the 1956 Act, evidence by police officers of conversations in the absence of the defendant in which immoral services were offered to them by women employed at the premises, was admissible to show the purpose for which the premises were used. The relevance of the evidence lay in the fact that such offers were being made.

"Management", "assists in the management"

See the following cases, decided in relation to section 33 of the 1956 Act ("assisting in the management of a brothel"): *Abbott v. Smith* [1965] 2 Q.B. 662, DC (meaning of "management"); *Gorman v. Standen*; *Palace-Clark v. Standen*, *ante*; *Jones and Wood v. DPP*, 96 Cr.App.R. 130, DC; and *Elliott v. DPP*; *Dublides v. DPP*, *The Times*, January 19, 1989, DC ("assisting in the management"). In the last of these cases, the court appears to have accepted a distinction between assisting in the management of premises and assisting the management of premises. **20–236**

(7) Soliciting, kerb-crawling, etc.

Under the *Street Offences Act* 1959, s.1, it is an offence for a common prostitute (male or female) to loiter or solicit in a street or public place for the purpose of prostitution. Such offence is punishable with a fine not exceeding level 2 on the standard scale, or level 3 in the case of a second or subsequent conviction. Under the *SOA* 1985, s.1, it is a summary offence punishable with a fine not exceeding level 3 on the standard scale for a person to solicit another person or persons for the purpose of prostitution from a motor vehicle while it is in a street or public place, or in a street or public place while in the immediate vicinity of a motor vehicle that the person has just got out of, and to do so persistently or in such manner or in such circumstances as to be likely to cause annoyance to the person being solicited (or any of them), or nuisance to other persons in the neighbourhood. Section 2 creates a summary offence (similarly punishable) of persistent solicitation in a street or public place for the purpose of prostitution. All three sections were amended by the *SOA* 2003, s.56, and Sched. 1, so as to make them no longer gender-specific. **20–237**

R. COMMON LAW OFFENCES

(1) Acts outraging public decency

Common law

In general, all open lewdness, grossly scandalous behaviour, and whatever openly outrages decency or is offensive and disgusting, or is injurious to public morals by tending to corrupt the mind and destroy the love of decency, morality and good order, is an offence indictable at common law. See 2 Russ.Cr., 12th ed., 1423. **20–238**

Where the facts of a case may be covered by a particular statute, that does not make any the less appropriate the common law offence of committing an act of a lewd, obscene and disgusting nature and outraging public decency: *R. v. May (John)*, 91 Cr.App.R. 157, CA; but see *R. v. Rimmington*; *R. v. Goldstein* [2006] 1 A.C. 459, HL (*post*, § 31–33).

Indictment

STATEMENT OF OFFENCE

20–239 *Committing an act outraging public decency.*

PARTICULARS OF OFFENCE

A B, on the —— day of ——, 20—, committed an act of a lewd, obscene and disgusting nature and outraging public decency, by behaving in an indecent manner with a dog.

As to the form of the indictment, see *R. v. Mayling* [1963] 2 Q.B. 717, 47 Cr.App.R. 102, CCA.

Class of offence and mode of trial

20–239a This offence is a class 3 offence (*ante*, § 2–17), and is triable either way: see Sched. 1 to the *MCA* 1980 (*ante*, § 1–75af).

Sentence

20–240 On conviction on indictment, the punishment for this offence, which is a common law offence, is a fine or imprisonment or both. It would seem that there is no limit to the amount of either the fine or the imprisonment that may be imposed provided the sentence is not inordinate: *R. v. Morris* [1951] 1 K.B. 394, 34 Cr.App.R. 210, CCA.

Juxtaposition with offences under the Obscene Publications Act 1959

20–241 The Court of Appeal considered the juxtaposition of offences of outraging public decency at common law and offences under the *Obscene Publications Act* 1959 (*post* §§ 31–62 *et seq.*), in *R. v. Gibson and Sylveire* [1990] 2 Q.B. 619, 91 Cr.App.R. 341, CA. G had sculpted a human head, to each ear of which he had attached an earring made from a freeze-dried human foetus of three to four months' gestation. The sculpture was displayed in S's gallery. They were indicted at common law.

The first question was whether the common law offence of outraging public decency still existed. Applying the dicta of Lord Simon in *Knuller (Publishing, Printing and Promotions) Ltd v. DPP* [1973] A.C. 435 at 493, HL, the Court of Appeal held that it did.

Secondly, were the prosecution precluded from proceeding at common law by section 2(4) of the 1959 Act (*post*, § 31–74)? That depended on the meaning of the word "obscene". Did it carry the broad definition as something which constitutes a serious breach of recognised standards of propriety on account of its tendency to corrupt, or on account of its indecent appearance, or its tendency to engender revulsion or disgust or outrage? Their Lordships thought not. There were, or had been, two broad types of offence involving obscenity: (a) those involving corruption of public morals, and (b) those which involved an outrage on public decency, whether or not public morals were involved. These two types of offence were factually and morally distinct. In their Lordships' opinion, it was clear that "obscene" in the 1959 Act bore the restricted meaning of offences involving corruption of public morals. It followed that prosecution for the common law offence was not precluded by section 2(4).

20–242 In their Lordships' judgment, the requirements with regard to *mens rea* should be the same in outraging public decency as they were in the common law offence of obscene libel. Accordingly, applying *Whitehouse v. Gay News Ltd* [1979] A.C. 617, HL (*post*, § 27–5), the prosecution did not have to prove an intention to outrage or recklessness. They merely had to prove an intent to publish an article which was in fact obscene, whatever the author himself might think its likely effect might be.

Evidence

20–243 It must first be proved that the act complained of was committed in public which means that it must be committed in a place, public or private, where at least two people were able to witness (which could be by means other than sight, such as hearing: *R. v. Hamilton* [2008] 1 Cr.App.R. 13, CA) the act and where there existed a real possibility that members of the general public might witness it: *R. v. Walker (S.)* [1996] 1 Cr.App.R. 111, CA. If the act was capable of being witnessed by one person only, then no offence is committed: *R. v. Mayling* [1963] 2 Q.B. 717, 47 Cr.App.R. 102, CCA (approved in *Knuller (Publishing, Printing and Promotions) Ltd v. DPP* [1973] A.C. 435, HL, *post*); but nobody need actually have seen the act: *R. v. Hamilton, ante*. Secondly, it must be proved that the act was of such a lewd, obscene or disgusting character as constitutes an outrage on public decency. It is not necessary for the prosecution further to prove that the act in fact disgusted or annoyed the persons within whose purview it was committed: *R. v. Mayling, ante*. But if the prosecution do choose to call evidence to this effect, positive evidence of disgust or annoyance may properly be given by a police officer: *ibid*.

As to the first requirement, it was held in *Rose v. DPP* [2006] 2 Cr.App.R. 29, QBD (Stanley Burnton J.), that this would not be established where an unidentified person had performed an act of oral sex upon the defendant in a public place, where the defendant did not deny knowledge of the existence of closed-circuit television cameras or the possibility that the act could have been seen by people passing by, but where the act was in fact seen only by one person when subsequently viewing the footage from the camera.

As to the second requirement, it is not necessary that the act itself is of a sexual nature or is inherently lewd, obscene or disgusting; whether an act is obscene, lewd or disgusting is a question of fact in respect of which the Court of Appeal would not intervene unless it was unarguable that the act was not of such character; where, therefore, the act consisted of filming women as they used the lavatory in a supermarket, it would have been open to a jury to find such act to be of the requisite nature: *R. v. Choi* [1999] 8 *Archbold News* 3, CA. Where, however, the act does not have the requisite quality of lewdness or obscenity, evidence of intention or motive could not make good that deficiency: *R. v. Rowley*, 94 Cr.App.R. 95, CA. **20–244**

In *Knuller (Publishing, Printing and Promotions) Ltd v. DPP, ante*, the House of Lords confirmed that there was such an offence as a conspiracy to outrage public decency (as well as a conspiracy to corrupt public morals, as to which their Lordships followed their own decision in *Shaw v. DPP* [1962] A.C. 220). The House emphasised, however, that the requirement of "public" outrage applied as much to a conspiracy as to the substantive offence, and that the word "outrage" (like "corrupt") was a strong word. Outraging public decency, it was said, goes considerably further than offending the susceptibilities of, or even shocking, reasonable people. The offence is concerned with minimum standards which are likely to vary from time to time, and the jury should be reminded where appropriate that in a plural society with a tradition of toleration towards minorities, this atmosphere is itself part of public decency. As to this, see also *R. v. Labaye, post*, § 20–246. **20–245**

In connection with allegations of conspiracy to corrupt public morals or to outrage public decency, see also the *CLA* 1977, s.5(3), *post*, § 33–34.

(2) Keeping a disorderly house

Definition

A disorderly house is one which is not regulated by the restraints of morality and which is so conducted as to violate law and good order. There must be an element of "open house" but it does not need to be open to the public at large: *R. v. Berg*, 20 Cr.App.R. 38, CCA. A disorderly house may amount to a common nuisance but it is not an essential ingredient of the offence of keeping a disorderly house. Where indecent performances or exhibitions are alleged as rendering the premises a disorderly house, it must be proved that matters are there performed or exhibited of such a character that their performance or exhibition in a place of common resort (a) amounts to an outrage of public decency, or (b) tends to corrupt or deprave, or (c) is otherwise calculated to injure the public interest so as to call for condemnation and punishment. These ingredients should not, however, be regarded as mutually exclusive and a performance **20–246** may well offend in all three respects: *R. v. Quinn and Bloom* [1962] 2 Q.B. 245, 45 Cr.App.R. 279, CCA.

In *R. v. Tan* [1983] Q.B. 1053, 76 Cr.App.R. 300, CA (in which the cases cited above were considered), the court observed that many forms of conduct may fall within the scope of the offence of keeping a disorderly house. Establishing a universal definition with precision is both undesirable and impossible. Where the ground on which the charge is based is that premises are being used for the provision of sexual services, a jury should be directed that they must be sure that the services provided are open to those members of the public who wish to partake of them and are of such a character and are conducted in such a manner (whether by advertisement or otherwise) that their provision amounts to an outrage of public decency or is otherwise calculated to injure the public interest to such an extent as to call for condemnation and punishment. The jury should further be directed, that the fact that the services are provided by a single prostitute to one client at a time and without spectators does not prevent the house being a disorderly house.

Practitioners may derive assistance from the more modern approach of the Supreme Court of Canada in *R. v. Labaye* [2005] 3 S.C.R. 728. The court was concerned with the test of indecency in the context of a prosecution of the owner of a "swingers' club" for keeping a "common bawdy-house" for the practice of acts of indecency, contrary to the Criminal Code of Canada, a "common bawdy-house" being defined as "... a place that is (a) kept or occupied, or (b) resorted to by one or more persons, for the purpose of prostitution or the practice of acts of indecency ...". It was held that to establish that conduct was "indecent", two matters must be proved on an objective basis; first, that by its *nature* the conduct at issue caused harm or presented a significant risk of harm to individuals or society in a way that undermined or threatened to undermine a value reflected in law (*i.e.* one not based on individual notions of harm or on the teachings of a particular ideology, but on what society, through its laws and institutions, has recognised as essential to its proper functioning); examples of harm falling within this limb of the test are (a) confronting members of the public with conduct that significantly interferes with their autonomy and liberty, (b) predisposing others to anti-social behaviour, or (c) physically or psychologically harming persons involved in the conduct; the categories of harm are not closed and the examples given are not integral to the definition of harm; secondly, it must be shown that the harm or risk of harm was of a *degree* that was incompatible with the proper functioning of society; formulated in this way, the test satisfies the basic requirements of the criminal law of fair notice to potential offenders and clear enforcement standards to the police.

In *Moores v. DPP* [1992] 1 Q.B. 125, 94 Cr.App.R. 173, DC, it was held that in order to establish the offence of keeping a disorderly house it had to be proved that the defendant habitually or persistently kept such a house and did so with knowledge of the use to which the premises were put, and that a house did not become disorderly for this purpose because disorder occurred there on a single occasion. See also *R. v. Brady and Ram*, 47 Cr.App.R. 196, CCA.

Evidence

20–247 In *R. v. Quinn and Bloom*, *ante*, the rejection of an application for a film taken three months after the events complained of, but alleged to portray what three of the performers actually did in the course of their acts, to be exhibited, was upheld by the Court of Criminal Appeal; evidence consisting of the reconstruction of an entire scene which had been brought into existence in private for the purpose of constituting evidence at a trial could never be admissible.

The prosecution are entitled to call evidence to show that what happened during the period covered by the indictment was merely a continuation of a prior user: *R. v. Brady and Ram*, *ante*; such evidence is relevant to the issue of persistence and it may tend to rebut any suggestion of unintentional or casual excess.

Mode of trial

20–248 In *Moores v. DPP*, *ante*, the defendant was convicted after a summary trial, but there is no indication as to why it was thought that the offence was triable summarily. If the allegation is that the offence caused a public nuisance or outraged public decency, then it will be triable summarily (see the *MCA* 1980, s.17(1), and Sched. 1, paras 1 and 1A (*ante*, § 1–75af)), but neither such allegation is essential to an allegation of keeping a disorderly house (see *R. v. Quinn and Bloom*, *ante*, and *R. v. Tan*, *ante*). Where there is no such allegation, the offence will be triable only on indictment. As to *Moores*, it seems likely that the lower court was led into error by the reference (since repealed) to the *Disorderly Houses Act* 1751 in paragraph 2 of Schedule 1 to the 1980 Act. The Divisional Court was concerned exclusively with the ingredients of the offence. Mode of trial was not an issue before that court.

Sentence

See *ante*, § 20–240. For cases of brothels, disorderly houses and "massage parlours", see CSP B5–1.3A. **20–249**

[The next paragraph is § 20–257.]

III. ANONYMITY OF VICTIMS

Sexual Offences (Amendment) Act 1992, ss.1–4

Anonymity of victims of certain offences

1.—(1) Where an allegation has been made that an offence to which this Act applies has been committed against a person, no matter relating to that person shall during that person's lifetime be included in any publication if it is likely to lead members of the public to identify that person as the person against whom the offence is alleged to have been committed. **20–257**

(2) Where a person is accused of an offence to which this Act applies, no matter likely to lead members of the public to identify a person as the person against whom the offence is alleged to have been committed ("the complainant") shall during the complainant's lifetime be included in any publication.

(3) This section—

(a) does not apply in relation to a person by virtue of subsection (1) at any time after a person has been accused of the offence, and

(b) in its application in relation to a person by virtue of subsection (2), has effect subject to any direction given under section 3.

(3A) The matters relating to a person in relation to which the restrictions imposed by subsection (1) or (2) apply (if their inclusion in any publication is likely to have the result mentioned in that subsection) include in particular—

(a) the person's name,

(b) the person's address,

(c) the identity of any school or other educational establishment attended by the person,

(d) the identity of any place of work, and

(e) any still or moving picture of the person.

(4) Nothing in this section prohibits the inclusion in a publication of matter consisting only of a report of criminal proceedings other than proceedings at, or intended to lead to, or on an appeal arising out of, a trial at which the accused is charged with the offence.

[This section is printed as amended by the *YJCEA* 1999, s.48 and Sched. 2, para. 7.]

Offences to which this Act applies

2.—(1) This Act applies to the following offences against the law of England and Wales— **20–258**

(aa) rape;

(ab) burglary with intent to commit rape;

(a) any offence under any of the provisions of the *Sexual Offences Act* 1956 mentioned in subsection (2);

(b) any offence under section 128 of the *Mental Health Act* 1959 (intercourse with mentally handicapped person by hospital staff etc.);

(c) any offence under section 1 of the *Indecency with Children Act* 1960 (indecent conduct towards young child);

(d) any offence under section 54 of the *Criminal Law Act* 1977 (incitement by man of his grand-daughter, daughter or sister under the age of 16 to commit incest with him);

(da) any offence under any of the provisions of Part 1 of the *Sexual Offences Act* 2003 except section 64, 65, 69 or 71;

(e) any attempt to commit any of the offences mentioned in paragraphs (aa) to (da);

(f) any conspiracy to commit any of those offences;

(g) any incitement of another to commit any of those offences;

(h) aiding, abetting, counselling or procuring the commission of any of the offences mentioned in paragraphs (aa) to (e) and (g).

(2) [*Offences under 1956 Act to which 1992 Act applies, viz. offences contrary to ss.2 to 7, 9 to 12 and 14 to 17.*]

(3) [*Northern Ireland.*]

(4) [*Service offences/ offences contrary to the* Armed Forces Act *2006, s.42, to which the Act applies.*]

[This section is printed as amended by the *CJPOA* 1994, s.168(1) and Sched. 9, para. 52(1), (2); the *YJCEA* 1999, s.48, and Sched. 2, para. 8; and the *SOA* 2003, s.139, and Sched. 6, para. 31. Subs. (4) is substituted, as from a day to be appointed, by the *AFA* 2006, s.378(1), and Sched. 16, para. 124.]

The reference to the common law offence of incitement in section 2(1)(g) has effect as a reference to the offences under Part 2 of the *SCA* 2007: 2007 Act, s.63(1), and Sched. 6, para. 20(a).

Power to displace section 1

20–259 **3.**—(1) If, before the commencement of a trial at which a person is charged with an offence to which this Act applies, he or another person against whom the complainant may be expected to give evidence at the trial, applies to the judge for a direction under this subsection and satisfies the judge—

(a) that the direction is required for the purpose of inducing persons who are likely to be needed as witnesses at the trial to come forward; and

(b) that the conduct of the applicant's defence at the trial is likely to be substantially prejudiced if the direction is not given,

the judge shall direct that section 1 shall not, by virtue of the accusation alleging the offence in question, apply in relation to the complainant.

(2) If at a trial the judge is satisfied—

(a) that the effect of section 1 is to impose a substantial and unreasonable restriction upon the reporting of proceedings at the trial, and

(b) that it is in the public interest to remove or relax the restriction,

he shall direct that that section shall not apply to such matter as is specified in the direction.

(3) A direction shall not be given under subsection (2) by reason only of the outcome of the trial.

(4) If a person who has been convicted of an offence and has given notice of appeal against the conviction, or notice of an application for leave so to appeal, applies to the appellate court for a direction under this subsection and satisfies the court—

(a) that the direction is required for the purpose of obtaining evidence in support of the appeal; and

(b) that the applicant is likely to suffer substantial injustice if the direction is not given,

the court shall direct that section 1 shall not, by virtue of an accusation which alleges an offence to which this Act applies and is specified in the direction, apply in relation to a complainant so specified.

(5) A direction given under any provision of this section does not affect the operation of section 1 at any time before the direction is given.

(6) In subsections (1) and (2), "judge" means—

(a) in the case of an offence, which is to be tried summarily or for which the mode of trial has not been determined, any justice of the peace acting for the petty sessions area concerned; and

(b) in any other case, any judge of the Crown Court in England and Wales.

(6A) [*Northern Ireland.*]

[(6B) [*Application of this section where person charged with an offence within s.2(4).*]]

(7) If, after the commencement of a trial at which a person is charged with an offence to which this Act applies, a new trial of the person for that offence is ordered, the commencement of any previous trial shall be disregarded for the purposes of subsection (1).

[This section is printed as amended by the *YJCEA* 1999, s.48 and Sched. 2, para. 9. Subs. (6B) is inserted, as from a day to be appointed, by the *AFA* 2006, s.378(1), and Sched. 16, para. 125.]

Special rules for cases of incest or buggery

4.—(1) In this section— **20–260**

"section 10 offence" means an offence under section 10 of the *Sexual Offences Act* 1956 (incest by a man) or an attempt to commit that offence;

"section 11 offence" means an offence under section 11 of that Act (incest by a woman) or an attempt to commit that offence;

"section 12 offence" means an offence under section 12 of that Act (buggery) or an attempt to commit that offence.

(2) Section 1 does not apply to a woman against whom a section 10 offence is alleged to have been committed if she is accused of having committed a section 11 offence against the man who is alleged to have committed the section 10 offence against her.

(3) Section 1 does not apply to a man against whom a section 11 offence is alleged to have been committed if he is accused of having committed a section 10 offence against the woman who is alleged to have committed the section 11 offence against him.

(4) Section 1 does not apply to a person against whom a section 12 offence is alleged to have been committed if that person is accused of having committed a section 12 offence against the person who is alleged to have committed the section 12 offence against him.

(5) Subsection (2) does not affect the operation of this Act in relation to anything done at any time before the woman is accused.

(6) Subsection (3) does not affect the operation of this Act in relation to anything done at any time before the man is accused.

(7) Subsection (4) does not affect the operation of this Act in relation to anything done at any time before the person mentioned first in that subsection is accused.

(8) [*Northern Ireland*.]

(9) [*Service offences*.]

[Subs. (8) was inserted by the *YJCEA* 1999, s.48, and Sched. 2, para. 10. Subs. (9) was inserted by the *AFA* 2001, s.34, and Sched. 6, Pt 1, para. 2. It is repealed, as from a day to be appointed, by the *AFA* 2006, s.378(1) and (2), Sched. 16, para. 126, and Sched. 17.]

Section 5 creates a summary offence consisting of the publication of any matter in contravention of section 1. The offence is punishable by a fine not exceeding level 5 on the standard scale. In connection with this offence, see *Brown v. DPP*, 162 J.P. 333, DC (decided in relation to the corresponding offence contrary to section 4(5) of the *Sexual Offences (Amendment) Act* 1976); and *O'Riordan v. DPP*, *The Times*, May 31, 2005, DC (compatibility of statutory scheme in sections 1 and 5 of this Act with Article 10 of the ECHR (*ante*, § 16–119)).

Sexual Offences (Amendment) Act 1992, s.6

Interpretation

6.—(1) In this Act— **20–261**

"complainant" has the meaning given in section 1(2);

"corresponding civil offence" in relation to a service offence, means the civil offence (within the meaning of the Army Act *1955, the* Air Force Act *1955 or the* Naval Discipline Act *1957) the commission of which constitutes the service offence*;

"picture" includes a likeness however produced;

"publication" includes any speech, writing, relevant programme or other communication in whatever form, which is addressed to the public at large or any section of the public (and for this purpose every relevant programme shall be taken to be so addressed), but does not include an indictment or other document prepared for use in particular legal proceedings;

"relevant programme" means a programme included in a programme service, within the meaning of the *Broadcasting Act* 1990;

"service offence" means an offence against section 70 of the Army Act *1955, section 70 of the* Air Force Act *1955 or section 42 of the* Naval Discipline Act *1957.*

[(1A) Section 48 of the *Armed Forces Act* 2006 (attempts, conspiracy, encouragement and assistance and aiding and abetting outside England and Wales) applies for the purposes of this Act as if the reference in subsection (3)(b) of that section to any of the following provisions of that Act were a reference to any provision of this Act.]

(2) For the purposes of this Act—

(a) where it is alleged that an offence to which this Act applies has been committed, the fact that any person has consented to an act which, on any prosecution for that offence, would fall to be proved by the prosecution, does not prevent that person from being regarded as a person against whom the alleged offence was committed; and

(b) where a person is accused of an offence of incest or buggery, the other party to the act in question shall be taken to be a person against whom the offence was committed even though he consented to that act.

(2A) For the purposes of this Act, where it is alleged or there is an accusation—

(a) that an offence of conspiracy or incitement to commit an offence mentioned in section 2(1)(aa) to (d) or (3)(a) to (h) has been committed, or

(b) that an offence of aiding, abetting, counselling or procuring the commission of an offence of incitement of another to commit an offence mentioned in section 2(1)(aa) to (d) or (3)(a) to (h) has been commited,

the person against whom the substantive offence is alleged to have been intended to be committed shall be regarded as the person against whom the conspiracy or incitement is alleged to have been committed.

In this subsection, "the substantive offence" means the offence to which the alleged conspiracy or incitement related.

(3) For the purposes of this Act, a person is accused of an offence, other than *a service offence* [an offence under section 42 of the *Armed Forces Act* 2006], if—

(a) an information is laid, or (in Northern Ireland) a complaint is made alleging that he has committed the offence,

(b) he appears before a court charged with the offence,

(c) a court before which he is appearing commits him for trial on a new charge alleging the offence, or

(d) a bill of indictment charging him with the offence is preferred before a court in which he may lawfully be indicted for the offence,

and references in subsection (2A) and in section 3 to an accusation alleging an offence shall be construed accordingly.

(3A) For the purposes of this Act, a person is accused of *a service offence if he is treated by section 75(4) of the* Army Act *1955, section 75(4) of the* Air Force Act *1955 or section 47A (4) of the* Naval Discipline Act *1957 as charged* [an offence under section 42 of the *Armed Forces Act* 2006 if he is charged (under Part 5 of that Act)] with the offence, and references in section 3 to an accusation alleging an offence shall be construed accordingly.

(4) Nothing in this Act affects any prohibition or restriction imposed by virtue of any other enactment upon a publication or upon matter included in a relevant programme.

[This section is printed as amended by the *CJPOA* 1994, s.168(1), and Sched. 9, para. 52(1), (3)(b); the *YJCEA* 1999, s.48, and Sched. 2, para. 12; and the *AFA* 2001, s.34, Sched. 6, Pt 1, para. 3; and as amended, as from a day to be appointed by the *AFA* 2006, s.378(1) and (2), Sched. 16, para. 127, and Sched. 17 (omission of definitions of "corresponding civil offence" and "service offence" in subs. (1), insertion of subs. (1A), omission of italicised words, insertion of words in square brackets in subss. (3) and (3A)). Subs. (1A) is itself printed as amended by the *SCA* 2007, s.60, and Sched. 5, para. 2.]

The reference to the common law offence of incitement in subsection (2A) has effect as a reference to the offences under Part 2 of the *SCA* 2007: 2007 Act, s.63(1), and Sched. 6, para. 20(b).

Miscellaneous provisions

20–262 Section 7 of the Act applies it to courts-martial, subject to specified modifications. Section 8 provides for the short title, commencement and extent of the Act.

IV. NOTIFICATION AND ORDERS

A. NOTIFICATION REQUIREMENTS

(1) Summary

Part I of the *Sex Offenders Act* 1997 imposed "notification requirements" on certain sex offenders. That Act came into force on September 1, 1997. These provisions were repealed and replaced, as from May 1, 2004, by the provisions of sections 80 to 92 of the *SOA* 2003. **20–263**

Section 80 deals with the persons becoming subject to notification requirements. A person is subject to notification requirements (for the period set out in section 82) if he is convicted of an offence listed in Schedule 3, is found not guilty of such an offence by reason of insanity, is found to be under a disability having done such an act or is cautioned in respect of such an offence. Such a person is a "relevant offender" (s.80(2)). Persons formerly subject to Part 1 of the 1997 Act are dealt with in section 81. The notification period for persons falling within section 80 or 81 is provided for in section 82. The initial notification must be made within three days of the relevant date: s.83(1). The offender must notify the police of the information set out in subsection (5), such as his date of birth, and his home address. The requirement to inform the police of any changes to the information provided is set out in section 84. Section 85 provides that the information must be updated periodically (intervals of not more than one year). The Secretary of State may make regulations requiring relevant offenders who leave the United Kingdom to disclose to the police the date on which they leave, the country to be visited, information about their return, and any other information prescribed by the regulations (s.86). The method of notification is outlined in section 87. The interpretation of section 87 is provided for in section 88. Section 89 provides that where a relevant offender is under 18, the obligations which would be imposed on the offender by sections 83 to 86 are to be treated instead as obligations on the person having parental responsibility for him (s.89(2)), but this depends on a direction of the court applying subsection (2) to the person with parental responsibility. Variations, renewals and discharges of parental directions are provided for in section 90. The offences relating to notification are set out in section 91, and the provision of certificates for the purposes of Part 2 is dealt with in section 92.

(2) The function of the criminal court

An offender's notification obligations under the 1997 and the 2003 Acts do not depend on any order of a court, and a criminal court before which an offender is convicted of a sexual offence has no power to order anything: *R. v. Longworth* [2006] 1 W.L.R. 313, HL. Courts should, however, continue to follow the practice of informing offenders of any notification requirements which apply to them, but this should not be done in such a way as to make such information part of the sentence or so as to clothe it with the authority of a further order of the court: *ibid*. **20–264**

The court has just two functions under the legislation itself. First, it may issue a certificate under section 92. Such a certificate constitutes evidence of the facts stated therein for the purposes of Part 2 of the 2003 Act. Secondly, it may make a direction under section 89, in the case of a defendant under the age of 18 at the date of conviction or finding, that the obligations that would be imposed on the defendant under sections 83 to 86 should be treated as obligations on the individual having parental responsibility for him.

(3) Legislation

Sexual Offences Act 2003, s.80

Persons becoming subject to notification requirements

80.—(1) A person is subject to the notification requirements of this Part for the period set out in section 82 ("the notification period") if— **20–265**

(a) he is convicted of an offence listed in Schedule 3;

(b) he is found not guilty of such an offence by reason of insanity;

(c) he is found to be under a disability and to have done the act charged against him in respect of such an offence; or

(d) in England and Wales or Northern Ireland, he is cautioned in respect of such an offence.

(2) A person for the time being subject to the notification requirements of this Part is referred to in this Part as a "relevant offender".

The obligation on a person convicted and sentenced before the commencement of the 1997 Act (*ante*, § 20–263) to comply with its requirements does not constitute a penalty within Article 7 of the ECHR (*ante*, § 16–97)); whether a measure amounted to a penalty for this purpose depended on whether it was conditional on a criminal conviction (this was), on its nature and purpose (this was preventative, not punitive), its characterisation in national law (non-criminal) and its severity (it required mere registration): *Ibbotson v. U.K.* [1999] Crim.L.R. 153, European Commission of Human Rights.

Sexual Offences Act 2003, ss.81, 82

20–266 **81.** [*Persons formerly subject to Part I of the* Sex Offenders Act *1997*.]

The notification period

20–267 **82.**—(1) The notification period for a person within section 80(1) or 81(1) is the period in the second column of the following Table opposite the description that applies to him.

TABLE

Description of relevant offender	*Notification period*
A person who, in respect of the offence, is or has been sentenced to imprisonment for life, to imprisonment for public protection under section 225 of the *Criminal Justice Act* 2003 or to imprisonment for a term of 30 months or more	An indefinite period beginning with the relevant date
A person who, in respect of the offence, has been made the subject of an order under section 210F(1) of the *Criminal Procedure (Scotland) Act* 1995 (order for lifelong restriction)	An indefinite period beginning with that date
A person who, in respect of the offence or finding, is or has been admitted to a hospital subject to a restriction order	An indefinite period beginning with that date
A person who, in respect of the offence, is or has been sentenced to imprisonment for a term of more than 6 months but less than 30 months	10 years beginning with that date
A person who, in respect of the offence, is or has been sentenced to imprisonment for a term of 6 months or less	7 years beginning with that date
A person who, in respect of the offence or finding, is or has been admitted to a hospital without being subject to a restriction order	7 years beginning with that date
A person within section 80(1)(d)	2 years beginning with that date
A person in whose case an order for conditional discharge or, in Scotland, a probation order, is made in respect of the offence	The period of conditional discharge or, in Scotland, the probation period
A person of any other description	5 years beginning with the relevant date

(2) Where a person is under 18 on the relevant date, subsection (1) has effect as if for any reference to a period of 10 years, 7 years, 5 years or 2 years there were substituted a reference to one-half of that period.

(3) Subsection (4) applies where a relevant offender within section 80(1)(a) or 81(1)(a) is or has been sentenced, in respect of two or more offences listed in Schedule 3—

(a) to consecutive terms of imprisonment; or

(b) to terms of imprisonment which are partly concurrent.

(4) Where this subsection applies, subsection (1) has effect as if the relevant offender were or had been sentenced, in respect of each of the offences, to a term of imprisonment which—

(a) in the case of consecutive terms, is equal to the aggregate of those terms;

(b) in the case of partly concurrent terms (X and Y, which overlap for a period Z), is equal to X plus Y minus Z.

(5) Where a relevant offender the subject of a finding within section 80(1)(c) or 81(1)(c) is subsequently tried for the offence, the notification period relating to the finding ends at the conclusion of the trial.

(6) In this Part, "relevant date" means—

(a) in the case of a person within section 80(1)(a) or 81(1)(a), the date of the conviction;

(b) in the case of a person within section 80(1)(b) or (c) or 81(1)(b) or (c), the date of the finding;

(c) in the case of a person within section 80(1)(d) or 81(1)(d), the date of the caution;

(d) in the case of a person within section 81(7), the date which, for the purposes of Part 1 of the *Sex Offenders Act* 1997, was the relevant date in relation to that person.

[This section is printed as amended by the *VCRA* 2006, s.57(1).]

Where an offender is made the subject of an extended sentence under section 85 of the *PCC(S)A* 2000, the term for which he was to be taken to have been "sentenced to imprisonment" for the purposes of Part I of the 1997 Act (and the corresponding provisions of the 2003 Act) was the "custodial term" element of the extended sentence and not the whole length of the extended sentence: *R. v. S. (Graham)* [2001] 1 Cr.App.R. 7, CA. Doubts about the correctness of this view were, however, expressed in *R. v. Wiles* [2004] 2 Cr.App.R.(S.) 88, CA (*ante*, § 5–865); and the wording of the provisions for extended sentences under sections 227 and 228 of the *CJA* 2003 (*ante*, §§ 5–295, 5–296) makes clear that in the case of such sentences it will be the whole term that matters for the purposes of these provisions.

As to the application of section 82(1) to a person sentenced to a detention and training order, see *R. v. Slocombe*, *post*, § 20–339.

A person who was conditionally discharged did not fall within the provisions of the *Sex Offenders Act* 1997: *R. v. Longworth* [2006] 1 W.L.R. 313, HL.

Sexual Offences Act 2003, ss.83–86

Notification requirements: initial notification

83.—(1) A relevant offender must, within the period of 3 days beginning with the relevant date (or, if later, the commencement of this Part), notify to the police the information set out in subsection (5). **20–268**

(2) Subsection (1) does not apply to a relevant offender in respect of a conviction, finding or caution within section 80(1) if—

(a) immediately before the conviction, finding or caution, he was subject to the notification requirements of this Part as a result of another conviction, finding or caution or an order of a court ("the earlier event"),

(b) at that time, he had made a notification under subsection (1) in respect of the earlier event, and

(c) throughout the period referred to in subsection (1), he remains subject to the notification requirements as a result of the earlier event.

(3) Subsection (1) does not apply to a relevant offender in respect of a conviction, finding or caution within section 81(1) or an order within section 81(7) if the offender complied with section 2(1) of the *Sex Offenders Act* 1997 in respect of the conviction, finding, caution or order.

(4) Where a notification order is made in respect of a conviction, finding or caution, subsection (1) does not apply to the relevant offender in respect of the conviction, finding or caution if—

(a) immediately before the order was made, he was subject to the notification requirements of this Part as a result of another conviction, finding or caution or an order of a court ("the earlier event"),

(b) at that time, he had made a notification under subsection (1) in respect of the earlier event, and

(c) throughout the period referred to in subsection (1), he remains subject to the notification requirements as a result of the earlier event.

(5) The information is—

(a) the relevant offender's date of birth;

(b) his national insurance number;

(c) his name on the relevant date and, where he used one or more other names on that date, each of those names;

(d) his home address on the relevant date;

(e) his name on the date on which notification is given and, where he uses one or more other names on that date, each of those names;

(f) his home address on the date on which notification is given;

(g) the address of any other premises in the United Kingdom at which, at the time the notification is given, he regularly resides or stays;

(h) any prescribed information.

(5A) In subsection (5)(h) "prescribed" means prescribed by regulations made by the Secretary of State.

(6) When determining the period for the purpose of subsection (1), there is to be disregarded any time when the relevant offender is—

(a) remanded in or committed to custody by an order of a court [or kept in service custody];

(b) serving a sentence of imprisonment or a term of service detention;

(c) detained in a hospital; or

(d) outside the United Kingdom.

(7) In this Part, "home address" means, in relation to any person—

(a) the address of his sole or main residence in the United Kingdom, or

(b) where he has no such residence, the address or location of a place in the United Kingdom where he can regularly be found and, if there is more than one such place, such one of those places as the person may select.

[This section is printed as amended by the *CJIA* 2008, s.142(1); and as amended, as from a day to be appointed, by *ibid.*, s.148(1), and Sched. 26, paras. 53 and 54(1) (insertion of words in square brackets).]

Notification requirements: changes

20–269 **84.**—(1) A relevant offender must, within the period of 3 days beginning with—

(a) his using a name which has not been notified to the police under section 83(1), this subsection, or section 2 of the *Sex Offenders Act* 1997,

(b) any change of his home address,

(c) his having resided or stayed, for a qualifying period, at any premises in the United Kingdom the address of which has not been notified to the police under section 83(1), this subsection, or section 2 of the *Sex Offenders Act* 1997,

(ca) any prescribed change of circumstances; or

(d) his release from custody pursuant to an order of a court or from imprisonment, service detention or detention in a hospital,

notify to the police that name, the new home address, the address of those premises, the prescribed details or (as the case may be) the fact that he has been released, and (in addition) the information set out in section 83(5).

(2) A notification under subsection (1) may be given before the name is used, the change of home address or the prescribed change of circumstances occurs or the qualifying period ends, but in that case the relevant offender must also specify the date when the event is expected to occur.

(3) If a notification is given in accordance with subsection (2) and the event to which it relates occurs more than 2 days before the date specified, the notification does not affect the duty imposed by subsection (1).

(4) If a notification is given in accordance with subsection (2) and the event to which it relates has not occurred by the end of the period of 3 days beginning with the date specified—

(a) the notification does not affect the duty imposed by subsection (1), and

(b) the relevant offender must, within the period of 6 days beginning with the date specified, notify to the police the fact that the event did not occur within the period of 3 days beginning with the date specified.

(5) Section 83(6) applies to the determination of the period of 3 days mentioned in subsection (1) and the period of 6 days mentioned in subsection (4)(b), as it applies to the determination of the period mentioned in section 83(1).

(5A) In this section—

(a) "prescribed change of circumstances" means any change—

(i) occurring in relation to any matter in respect of which information is required to be notified by virtue of section 83(5)(h), and

(ii) of a description prescribed by regulations made by the Secretary of State;

(b) "the prescribed details", in relation to a prescribed change of circumstances, means such details of the change as may be so prescribed.

(6) In this section, "qualifying period" means—

(a) a period of 7 days, or

(b) two or more periods, in any period of 12 months, which taken together amount to 7 days.

[This section is printed as amended by the *CJIA* 2008, s.142(2)–(5).]

Notification requirements: periodic notification

85.—(1) A relevant offender must, within the applicable period after each event within subsection (2), notify to the police the information set out in section 83(5), unless within that period he has given a notification under section 84(1). **20–270**

(2) The events are—

(a) the commencement of this Part (but only in the case of a person who is a relevant offender from that commencement);

(b) any notification given by the relevant offender under section 83(1) or 84(1); and

(c) any notification given by him under subsection (1).

(3) Where the applicable period would (apart from this subsection) end whilst subsection (4) applies to the relevant offender, that period is to be treated as continuing until the end of the period of 3 days beginning when subsection (4) first ceases to apply to him.

(4) This subsection applies to the relevant offender if he is—

(a) remanded in or committed to custody by an order of a court [or kept in service custody],

(b) serving a sentence of imprisonment or a term of service detention,

(c) detained in a hospital, or

(d) outside the United Kingdom.

[This section is printed as amended by the *CJIA* 2008, s.142(6)-(8); and as amended, as from a day to be appointed, by *ibid.*, s.148(1), and Sched. 26, paras. 53 and 55(1) (insertion of words in square brackets).]

Notification requirements: travel outside the United Kingdom

86.—(1) The Secretary of State may by regulations make provision requiring relevant offenders who leave the United Kingdom, or any description of such offenders— **20–271**

(a) to give in accordance with the regulations, before they leave, a notification under subsection (2);

(b) if they subsequently return to the United Kingdom, to give in accordance with the regulations a notification under subsection (3).

(2) A notification under this subsection must disclose—

(a) the date on which the offender will leave the United Kingdom;

(b) the country (or, if there is more than one, the first country) to which he will travel and his point of arrival (determined in accordance with the regulations) in that country;

(c) any other information prescribed by the regulations which the offender holds about his departure from or return to the United Kingdom or his movements while outside the United Kingdom.

(3) A notification under this subsection must disclose any information prescribed by the regulations about the offender's return to the United Kingdom.

(4) [*Repealed by* CJIA *2008, s.149, and Sched. 28, Pt 4.*]

For regulations made under this section, see the *Sexual Offences Act 2003 (Travel Notification Requirements) Regulations* 2004 (S.I. 2004 No. 1220).

Sexual Offences Act 2003, ss.87–91

Method of notification and related matters

87.—(1) A person gives a notification under section 83(1), 84(1) or 85(1) by— **20–272**

(a) attending at such police station in his local police area as the Secretary of State may by regulations prescribe or, if there is more than one, at any of them, and
(b) giving an oral notification to any police officer, or to any person authorised for the purpose by the officer in charge of the station.

(2) A person giving a notification under section 84(1)—
(a) in relation to a prospective change of home address, or
(b) in relation to premises referred to in subsection (1)(c) of that section,

may give the notification at a police station that would fall within subsection (1) above if the change in home address had already occurred or (as the case may be) if the address of those premises were his home address.

(3) Any notification under this section must be acknowledged; and an acknowledgment under this subsection must be in writing, and in such form as the Secretary of State may direct.

(4) Where a notification is given under section 83(1), 84(1) or 85(1), the relevant offender must, if requested to do so by the police officer or person referred to in subsection (1)(b), allow the officer or person to—
(a) take his fingerprints,
(b) photograph any part of him, or
(c) do both these things.

(5) The power in subsection (4) is exercisable for the purpose of verifying the identity of the relevant offender.

(6) [*Identical to s.86(4)*, ante, *§ 20–271*.]

[Subs. (6) is repealed as from a day to be appointed: *CJIA* 2008, s.149, and Sched. 28, Pt 4.]

For regulations made under this section, see the *Sexual Offences Act 2003 (Prescribed Police Stations) Regulations* 2005 (S.I. 2005 No. 210).

Section 87: interpretation

20–273 **88.**—(1) Subsections (2) to (4) apply for the purposes of section 87.

(2) "Photograph" includes any process by means of which an image may be produced.

(3) "Local police area" means, in relation to a person—
(a) the police area in which his home address is situated;
(b) in the absence of a home address, the police area in which the home address last notified is situated;
(c) in the absence of a home address and of any such notification, the police area in which the court which last dealt with the person in a way mentioned in subsection (4) is situated.

(4) The ways are—
(a) dealing with a person in respect of an offence listed in Schedule 3 or a finding in relation to such an offence;
(b) dealing with a person in respect of an offence under section 128 or a finding in relation to such an offence;
(c) making, in respect of a person, a notification order, interim notification order, sexual offences prevention order or interim sexual offences prevention order;
(d) making, in respect of a person, an order under section 2, 2A or 20 of the *Crime and Disorder Act* 1998 (sex offender orders and interim orders made in England and Wales or Scotland) or Article 6 or 6A of the *Criminal Justice (Northern Ireland) Order* 1998 (S.I. 1998/2839 (N.I. 20)) (sex offender orders and interim orders made in Northern Ireland);

and in paragraphs (a) and (b), "finding" in relation to an offence means a finding of not guilty of the offence by reason of insanity or a finding that the person was under a disability and did the act or omission charged against him in respect of the offence.

(5) Subsection (3) applies as if Northern Ireland were a police area.

Young offenders: parental directions

20–274 **89.**—(1) Where a person within the first column of the following Table ("the young offender") is under 18 (or, in Scotland, 16) when he is before the court referred to in the second column of the Table opposite the description that applies to him, that court may direct that subsection (2) applies in respect of an individual ("the parent") having parental responsibility for (or, in Scotland, parental responsibilities in relation to) the young offender.

TABLE

Description of person	*Court which may make the direction*
A relevant offender within section 80(1)(a) to (c) or 81(1)(a) to (c)	The court which deals with the offender in respect of the offence or finding
A relevant offender within section 129(1)(a) to (c)	The court which deals with the offender in respect of the offence or finding
A person who is the subject of a notification order, interim notification order, sexual offences prevention order or interim sexual offences prevention order	The court which makes the order
A relevant offender who is the defendant to an application under subsection (4) (or, in Scotland, the subject of an application under subsection (5))	The court which hears the application

(2) Where this subsection applies—

(a) the obligations that would (apart from this subsection) be imposed by or under sections 83 to 86 on the young offender are to be treated instead as obligations on the parent, and

(b) the parent must ensure that the young offender attends at the police station with him, when a notification is being given.

(3) A direction under subsection (1) takes immediate effect and applies—

(a) until the young offender attains the age of 18 (or, where a court in Scotland gives the direction, 16); or

(b) for such shorter period as the court may, at the time the direction is given, direct.

(4) A chief officer of police may, by complaint to any magistrates' court whose commission area includes any part of his police area, apply for a direction under subsection (1) in respect of a relevant offender ("the defendant")—

(a) who resides in his police area, or who the chief officer believes is in or is intending to come to his police area, and

(b) who the chief officer believes is under 18.

(5) [*Scotland.*]

Parental directions: variations, renewals and discharges

90.—(1) A person within subsection (2) may apply to the appropriate court for an order varying, renewing or discharging a direction under section 89(1). **20–275**

(2) The persons are—

(a) the young offender;

(b) the parent;

(c) the chief officer of police for the area in which the young offender resides;

(d) a chief officer of police who believes that the young offender is in, or is intending to come to, his police area;

(e) [*Scotland*];

(f) where the direction was made on an application under section 89(4), the chief officer of police who made the application;

(g) where the direction was made on an application under section 89(5), the chief constable who made the application.

(3) An application under subsection (1) may be made—

(a) where the appropriate court is the Crown Court (or in Scotland a criminal court), in accordance with rules of court;

(b) in any other case, by complaint (or, in Scotland, by summary application).

(4) On the application the court, after hearing the person making the application and (if they wish to be heard) the other persons mentioned in subsection (2), may make any order, varying, renewing or discharging the direction, that the court considers appropriate.

(5) In this section, the "appropriate court" means—

(a) where the Court of Appeal made the order, the Crown Court;

(b) in any other case, the court that made the direction under section 89(1).

Offences relating to notification

91.—(1) A person commits an offence if he— **20–276**

(a) fails, without reasonable excuse, to comply with section 83(1), 84(1), 84(4)(b), 85(1), 87(4) or 89(2)(b) or any requirement imposed by regulations made under section 86(1); or

(b) notifies to the police, in purported compliance with section 83(1), 84(1) or 85(1) or any requirement imposed by regulations made under section 86(1), any information which he knows to be false.

(2) A person guilty of an offence under this section is liable—

(a) on summary conviction, to imprisonment for a term not exceeding *6* [12] months or a fine not exceeding the statutory maximum or both;

(b) on conviction on indictment, to imprisonment for a term not exceeding 5 years.

(3) A person commits an offence under paragraph (a) of subsection (1) on the day on which he first fails, without reasonable excuse, to comply with section 83(1), 84(1) or 85(1) or a requirement imposed by regulations made under section 86(1), and continues to commit it throughout any period during which the failure continues; but a person must not be prosecuted under subsection (1) more than once in respect of the same failure.

(4) Proceedings for an offence under this section may be commenced in any court having jurisdiction in any place where the person charged with the offence resides or is found.

[In subs. (2)(a), "12" is substituted for "6", as from a day to be appointed, by the *CJA* 2003, s.282(2) and (3). The increase has no application to offences committed before the substitution takes effect: s.282(4).]

As to sentencing for an offence contrary to this section or its predecessor, see *R. v. Clark* [2003] 1 Cr.App.R.(S.) 2, CA; and *R. v. Bowman (Maximus John)* [2006] 2 Cr.App.R.(S.) 40, CA, in which the court acknowledged the complexities that could arise where an offender, who was subject to notification requirements, was not of fixed abode and at times had been homeless.

Sexual Offences Act 2003, s.92

Certificates for purposes of Part 2

20–277 **92.**—(1) Subsection (2) applies where on any date a person is—

(a) convicted of an offence listed in Schedule 3;

(b) found not guilty of such an offence by reason of insanity; or

(c) found to be under a disability and to have done the act charged against him in respect of such an offence.

(2) If the court by or before which the person is so convicted or found—

(a) states in open court—

(i) that on that date he has been convicted, found not guilty by reason of insanity or found to be under a disability and to have done the act charged against him, and

(ii) that the offence in question is an offence listed in Schedule 3, and

(b) certifies those facts, whether at the time or subsequently,

the certificate is, for the purposes of this Part, evidence (or, in Scotland, sufficient evidence) of those facts.

(3) Subsection (4) applies where on any date a person is, in England and Wales or Northern Ireland, cautioned in respect of an offence listed in Schedule 3.

(4) If the constable—

(a) informs the person that he has been cautioned on that date and that the offence in question is an offence listed in Schedule 3, and

(b) certifies those facts, whether at the time or subsequently, in such form as the Secretary of State may by order prescribe,

the certificate is, for the purposes of this Part, evidence (or, in Scotland, sufficient evidence) of those facts.

Sexual Offences Act 2003, Sched. 3

Section 80 SCHEDULE 3

SEXUAL OFFENCES FOR PURPOSES OF PART 2

England and Wales

20–278 1. An offence under section 1 of the *Sexual Offences Act* 1956 (rape).

2. An offence under section 5 of that Act (intercourse with girl under 13). **20–279**

3. An offence under section 6 of that Act (intercourse with girl under 16), if the offender was 20 or over. **20–280**

4. An offence under section 10 of that Act (incest by a man), if the victim or (as the case may be) other party was under 18. **20–281**

5. An offence under section 12 of that Act (buggery) if— **20–282**

(a) the offender was 20 or over, and

(b) the victim or (as the case may be) other party was under 18.

6. An offence under section 13 of that Act (indecency between men) if— **20–283**

(a), (b) [*identical to para. 5(a), (b),* ante, § *20–282*].

7. An offence under section 14 of that Act (indecent assault on a woman) if— **20–284**

(a) the victim or (as the case may be) other party was under 18, or

(b) the offender, in respect of the offence or finding, is or has been—

(i) sentenced to imprisonment for a term of at least 30 months; or

(ii) admitted to a hospital subject to a restriction order.

8. An offence under section 15 of that Act (indecent assault on a man) if— **20–285**

(a), (b) [*identical to para. 7(a), (b),* ante, § *20–284*].

9. An offence under section 16 of that Act (assault with intent to commit buggery), if the victim or (as the case may be) other party was under 18. **20–286**

10. An offence under section 28 of that Act (causing or encouraging the prostitution of, intercourse with or indecent assault on girl under 16). **20–287**

11. An offence under section 1 of the *Indecency with Children Act* 1960 (indecent conduct towards young child). **20–288**

12. An offence under section 54 of the *Criminal Law Act* 1977 (inciting girl under 16 to have incestuous sexual intercourse). **20–289**

13. An offence under section 1 of the *Protection of Children Act* 1978 (indecent photographs of children), if the indecent photographs or pseudo-photographs showed persons under 16 and— **20–290**

(a) the conviction, finding or caution was before the commencement of this Part, or

(b) the offender—

(i) was 18 or over, or

(ii) is sentenced in respect of the offence to imprisonment for a term of at least 12 months.

14. An offence under section 170 of the *Customs and Excise Management Act* 1979 (penalty for fraudulent evasion of duty etc.) in relation to goods prohibited to be imported under section 42 of the *Customs Consolidation Act* 1876 (indecent or obscene articles), if the prohibited goods included indecent photographs of persons under 16 and— **20–291**

(a), (b) [*identical to para. 13(a), (b),* ante, § *20–290*].

15. An offence under section 160 of the *Criminal Justice Act* 1988 (possession of indecent photograph of a child), if the indecent photographs or pseudo-photographs showed persons under 16 and— **20–292**

(a), (b) [*identical to para. 13(a), (b),* ante, § *20–290*].

16. An offence under section 3 of the *Sexual Offences (Amendment) Act* 2000 (abuse of position of trust), if the offender was 20 or over. **20–293**

17. An offence under section 1 or 2 of this Act (rape, assault by penetration). **20–294**

18. An offence under section 3 of this Act (sexual assault) if— **20–295**

(a) where the offender was under 18, he is or has been sentenced, in respect of the offence, to imprisonment for a term of at least 12 months;

(b) in any other case—

(i) the victim was under 18, or

(ii) the offender, in respect of the offence or finding, is or has been—

(a) sentenced to a term of imprisonment,

(b) detained in a hospital, or

(c) made the subject of a community sentence of at least 12 months.

19. An offence under any of sections 4 to 6 of this Act (causing sexual activity without consent, rape of a child under 13, assault of a child under 13 by penetration). **20–296**

20. An offence under section 7 of this Act (sexual assault of a child under 13) if the offender— **20–297**

(a) was 18 or over, or

(b) is or has been sentenced in respect of the offence to imprisonment for a term of at least 12 months.

20–298 21. An offence under any of sections 8 to 12 of this Act (causing or inciting a child under 13 to engage in sexual activity, child sex offences committed by adults).

20–299 22. An offence under section 13 of this Act (child sex offences committed by children or young persons), if the offender is or has been sentenced, in respect of the offence, to imprisonment for a term of at least 12 months.

20–300 23. An offence under section 14 of this Act (arranging or facilitating the commission of a child sex offence) if the offender—

(a), (b) [*identical to para. 20(a), (b),* ante, *§ 20–297*].

20–301 24. An offence under section 15 of this Act (meeting a child following sexual grooming etc).

20–302 25. An offence under any of sections 16 to 19 of this Act (abuse of a position of trust) if the offender, in respect of the offence, is or has been—

(a) sentenced to a term of imprisonment,
(b) detained in a hospital, or
(c) made the subject of a community sentence of at least 12 months.

20–303 26. An offence under section 25 or 26 of this Act (familial child sex offences) if the offender—

(a), (b) [*identical to para. 20(a), (b),* ante, *§ 20–297*].

20–304 27. An offence under any of sections 30 to 37 of this Act (offences against persons with a mental disorder impeding choice, inducements etc. to persons with mental disorder).

20–305 28. An offence under any of sections 38 to 41 of this Act (care workers for persons with mental disorder) if—

(a) where the offender was under 18, he is or has been sentenced in respect of the offence to imprisonment for a term of at least 12 months;
(b) in any other case, the offender, in respect of the offence or finding, is or has been—
 (i) sentenced to a term of imprisonment,
 (ii) detained in a hospital, or
 (iii) made the subject of a community sentence of at least 12 months.

20–306 29. An offence under section 47 of this Act (paying for sexual services of a child) if the victim or (as the case may be) other party was under 16, and the offender—

(a), (b) [*identical to para. 20(a), (b),* ante, *§ 20–297*].

20–306a 29A. An offence under section 48 of this Act (causing or inciting child prostitution or pornography) if the offender—

(a), (b) [*identical to para. 20(a), (b),* ante, *§ 20–297*].

29B. An offence under section 49 of this Act (controlling a child prostitute or a child involved in pornography) if the offender—

(a), (b) [*identical to para. 20(a), (b),* ante, *§ 20–297*].

29C. An offence under section 50 of this Act (arranging or facilitating child prostitution or pornography) if the offender—

(a), (b) [*identical to para. 20(a), (b),* ante, *§ 20–297*].

20–307 30. An offence under section 61 of this Act (administering a substance with intent).

20–308 31. An offence under section 62 or 63 of this Act (committing an offence or trespassing, with intent to commit a sexual offence) if—

(a) where the offender was under 18, he is or has been sentenced in respect of the offence to imprisonment for a term of at least 12 months;
(b) in any other case—
 (i) the intended offence was an offence against a person under 18, or
 (ii) the offender, in respect of the offence or finding, is or has been—
  (a) sentenced to a term of imprisonment,
  (b) detained in a hospital, or
  (c) made the subject of a community sentence of at least 12 months.

20–309 32. An offence under section 64 or 65 of this Act (sex with an adult relative) if—

(a) where the offender was under 18, he is or has been sentenced in respect of the offence to imprisonment for a term of at least 12 months;
(b) in any other case, the offender, in respect of the offence or finding, is or has been—
 (i) sentenced to a term of imprisonment, or

(ii) detained in a hospital.

33. An offence under section 66 of this Act (exposure) if— 20–310

(a), (b) [*identical to para. 18(a), (b),* ante, *§ 20–295*].

34. An offence under section 67 of this Act (voyeurism) if— 20–311

(a), (b) [*identical to para. 18(a), (b),* ante, *§ 20–295*].

35. An offence under section 69 or 70 of this Act (intercourse with an animal, sexual penetration of a corpse) if— 20–312

(a), (b) [*identical to para. 32(a), (b),* ante, *§ 20–309*].

[35A. An offence under section 63 of the *Criminal Justice and Immigration Act* 2008 (possession of extreme pornographic images) if the offender— 20–312a

(a) was 18 or over, and
(b) is sentenced in respect of the offence to imprisonment for a term of at least 2 years.]

Scotland

36.–60. [*Scotland.*] 20–313

61.–92V. [*Northern Ireland.*] 20–314

93. [*Service offences.*] 20–315

General

94. A reference in a preceding paragraph to an offence includes— 20–316

(a) a reference to an attempt, conspiracy or incitement to commit that offence, and
(b) except in paragraphs 36 to 43, a reference to aiding, abetting, counselling or procuring the commission of that offence.

94A. A reference in a preceding paragraph to an offence ("offence A") includes a reference to an offence under Part 2 of the *Serious Crime Act* 2007 in relation to which offence A is the offence (or one of the offences) which the person intended or believed would be committed. 20–316a

95. A reference in a preceding paragraph to a person's age is— 20–317

(a) in the case of an indecent photograph, a reference to the person's age when the photograph was taken;
(b) in any other case, a reference to his age at the time of the offence.

96. In this Schedule "community sentence" has— 20–318

(a) in relation to England and Wales, the same meaning as in the *Powers of Criminal Courts (Sentencing) Act* 2000, and
(b) in relation to Northern Ireland, the same meaning as in the *Criminal Justice (Northern Ireland) Order* 1996 (S.I. 1996/3160 (N.I. 24)).

97. For the purposes of paragraphs 14, 44 and 78— 20–319

(a) a person is to be taken to have been under 16 at any time if it appears from the evidence as a whole that he was under that age at that time;
(b) section 7 of the *Protection of Children Act* 1978 (interpretation), subsections (2) to (2C) and (8) of section 52 of the *Civic Government (Scotland) Act* 1982 (c. 45), and Article 2(2) and (3) of the *Protection of Children (Northern Ireland) Order* 1978 (S.I. 1978/1047 (N.I. 17)) (interpretation) (respectively) apply as each provision applies for the purposes of the Act or Order of which it forms part.

98. [*Scotland.*] 20–320

[Schedule 3 is printed as amended by the *Sexual Offences Act 2003 (Amendment of Schedules 3 and 5) Order* 2007 (S.I. 2007 No. 296); and the *SCA* 2007, s.63(2), and Sched. 6, para. 63(1) and (2); and as amended, as from a day to be appointed, by the *CJIA* 2008, s.148(1), and Sched. 26, paras 53 and 58(1) and (2).]

Interpretation of Schedule 3

See, in particular, section 132 of the 2003 Act, *post*, § 20–340. 20–321

B. ENTRY AND SEARCH OF HOME ADDRESS

Sexual Offences Act 2003, s.96B

Power of entry and search of relevant offender's home address

96B.—(1) If on an application made by a senior police officer of the relevant force a justice of 20–321a the peace is satisfied that the requirements in subsection (2) are met in relation to any premises, he may issue a warrant authorising a constable of that force—

(a) to enter the premises for the purpose of assessing the risks posed by the relevant offender to which the warrant relates; and

(b) to search the premises for that purpose.

(2) The requirements are—

(a) that the address of each set of premises specified in the application is an address falling within subsection (3);

(b) that the relevant offender is not one to whom subsection (4) applies;

(c) that it is necessary for a constable to enter and search the premises for the purpose mentioned in subsection (1)(a); and

(d) that on at least two occasions a constable has sought entry to the premises in order to search them for that purpose and has been unable to obtain entry for that purpose.

(3) An address falls within this subsection if—

(a) it is the address which was last notified in accordance with this Part by a relevant offender to the police as his home address; or

(b) there are reasonable grounds to believe that a relevant offender resides there or may regularly be found there.

(4) This subsection applies to a relevant offender if he is—

(a) remanded in or committed to custody by order of a court;

(b) serving a sentence of imprisonment or a term of service detention;

(c) detained in a hospital; or

(d) outside the United Kingdom.

(5) A warrant issued under this section must specify the one or more sets of premises to which it relates.

(6) The warrant may authorise the constable executing it to use reasonable force if necessary to enter and search the premises.

(7) The warrant may authorise entry to and search of premises on more than one occasion if, on the application, the justice of the peace is satisfied that it is necessary to authorise multiple entries in order to achieve the purpose mentioned in subsection (1)(a).

(8) Where a warrant issued under this section authorises multiple entries, the number of entries authorised may be unlimited or limited to a maximum.

(9) In this section a reference to the relevant offender to whom the warrant relates is a reference to the relevant offender—

(a) who has in accordance with this Part notified the police that the premises specified in the warrant are his home address; or

(b) in respect of whom there are reasonable grounds to believe that he resides there or may regularly be found there.

(10) In this section—

"the relevant force" means the police force maintained for the police area in which the premises in respect of which the application is made or the warrant is issued are situated;

"senior police officer" means a constable of the rank of superintendent or above.

[This section was inserted by the the *VCRA* 2006, s.58(1).]

C. NOTIFICATION ORDERS

20–322 Sections 97 to 103 of the *SOA* 2003 make provision for "notification orders". Section 97 provides that a chief officer of police may apply for such an order to any magistrates' court within his police area if he believes that a person (the "defendant" to the application) is intending to come into his police area and under the law in force in a country outside the United Kingdom he has been convicted or cautioned of a relevant offence, he has been found not guilty by reason of insanity or he has been found to be under a disability. The court must make an order if the conditions set out in section 96 are met. The effect of such an order is set out in section 98 (the defendant becomes liable to the notification requirements in Part 2 of the Act, subject to specified modifications). "Relevant offence" for the purposes of sections 97 and 98 is defined in section 99 as an offence under the law in force in the country concerned which would have constituted an offence listed in Schedule 3 if it had been committed in any part of the United Kingdom.

The ability to apply for an interim notification order is set out in section 100. Provision is made for an appeal to the Crown Court against the making of a notification order or interim notification order (s.101). Sections 102 and 103 apply to Scotland.

D. SEXUAL OFFENCES PREVENTION ORDERS

(1) Introduction

Sections 104 to 113 make provision for sexual offences prevention orders. They replace "restraining orders" under section 5A of the *Sex Offenders Act* 1997 (first introduced by way of amendment effected by the *CJCSA* 2000), and sex offender orders under the *CDA* 1998, s.2. Such orders may be made not only on conviction, or upon a finding of not guilty by reason of insanity or a finding that the defendant is under a disability and that he did the act charged against him, but also on an application made to a magistrates' court; and they may be made on the basis of a range of offences which are not sexual offences, if the court is satisfied that it is necessary to make such an order for the purpose of protecting the public or any particular members of the public from serious sexual harm from the defendant. **20–323**

(2) Legislation

Sexual Offences Act 2003, ss.104–113

Sexual offences prevention orders

Sexual offences prevention orders: applications and grounds

104.—(1) A court may make an order under this section in respect of a person ("the defendant") where any of subsections (2) to (4) applies to the defendant and— **20–324**

(a) where subsection (4) applies, it is satisfied that the defendant's behaviour since the appropriate date makes it necessary to make such an order, for the purpose of protecting the public or any particular members of the public from serious sexual harm from the defendant;

(b) in any other case, it is satisfied that it is necessary to make such an order, for the purpose of protecting the public or any particular members of the public from serious sexual harm from the defendant.

(2) This subsection applies to the defendant where the court deals with him in respect of an offence listed in Schedule 3 or 5.

(3) This subsection applies to the defendant where the court deals with him in respect of a finding—

(a) that he is not guilty of an offence listed in Schedule 3 or 5 by reason of insanity, or

(b) that he is under a disability and has done the act charged against him in respect of such an offence.

(4) This subsection applies to the defendant where—

(a) an application under subsection (5) has been made to the court in respect of him, and

(b) on the application, it is proved that he is a qualifying offender.

(5) A chief officer of police may by complaint to a magistrates' court apply for an order under this section in respect of a person who resides in his police area or who the chief officer believes is in, or is intending to come to, his police area if it appears to the chief officer that—

(a) the person is a qualifying offender, and

(b) the person has since the appropriate date acted in such a way as to give reasonable cause to believe that it is necessary for such an order to be made.

(6) An application under subsection (5) may be made to any magistrates' court whose commission area includes—

(a) any part of the applicant's police area, or

(b) any place where it is alleged that the person acted in a way mentioned in subsection (5)(b).

Where an offender did not pose a risk of "serious harm" such as would render him liable to the imposition of a sentence under the dangerous offender provisions in Chapter 5 of Part 12 of the *CJA* 2003 (*ante*, §§ 5–292 *et seq.*), this did not preclude a **20–324a** finding that a sexual offences prevention order was necessary for the purpose of protecting the public from "serious sexual harm" from the defendant; though it was a fine one, there was a distinction between the two tests in that (i) the element of risk for the purposes of the dangerous offender provisions had to be shown to be significant, whereas there was no equivalent before a sexual offences prevention order could be made, (ii) a sentence under the dangerous offender provisions could be a life sentence, whereas a sexual offences prevention order would last for not less than five years, and (iii) the dangerous offender provisions defined serious harm to mean death or serious personal injury, whether physical or psychological, whereas "serious sexual harm" for the purposes of section 104 was defined by reference to "serious physical or psychological harm" (as opposed to "injury"): *R. v. Rampley* [2007] 1 Cr.App.R.(S.) 87, CA (followed in *R. v. Richards* [2007] 1 Cr.App.R.(S.) 120, CA).

As to the need to consider whether the restrictions that could be imposed on an offender by means of a sexual offences prevention order would sufficiently reduce the risk posed by him as to mean that the criteria for an indeterminate sentence under the dangerous offender provisions would not be met, see *R. v. Terrell* [2008] 2 Cr.App.R. (S.) 49, CA, where it was held that those provisions do not apply where, simply as a matter of generalisation, a small, uncertain and indirect contribution to harm may be made by repetition of an offender's offending. Where, therefore, the appellant, who had a previous conviction for a serious specified sexual offence, pleaded guilty to four offences of making indecent photographs of a child (*Protection of Children Act* 1978, s.1 (*post*, § 31–107) and asked for 36 similar offences to be taken into consideration which involved, for the most part, single images at the lowest level, the judge should not have concluded that the offender was liable to a sentence of imprisonment for public protection on the ground that there was a significant risk that he would commit such offences again in the future and that there was a reasonable inference that such offences would be likely to cause serious harm of a psychological nature to the victims of the abuse. There was no suggestion that he would progress to commit graver offences in the future and the serious harm relied on was, therefore, the perpetuation of the market or distribution networks for indecent images. It could not reasonably be said that there was a significant risk of the appellant's re-offending occasioning harm to a child or children whether through perpetuating the market, through further indecent images being taken, or through a child becoming aware of the indecent purposes to which photographs might be put. The link between the offending act and the possible harm which might be done to children was too remote to satisfy the requirement that it would be this appellant's re-offending which would cause the serious harm. As to a sexual offences prevention order, the court said that the potential utility of such an order in a case such as this did not mean that the test in section 104 would necessarily be satisfied; but, as had been indicated in *R. v. Beaney* [2004] 2 Cr.App.R.(S.) 82, CA, and *R. v. Collard* [2005] 1 Cr.App.R.(S.) 34, CA, the indirect and uncertain harm which any downloading of indecent images may cause may suffice for the purposes of section 104.

Where an order is made under section 104 for the particular purpose of protecting a child of the defendant, but it is wished to provide for a measure of flexibility in case the child should in the future wish to have contact with the defendant, this could be achieved by invoking the jurisdiction of the family court and framing an order along the following lines, "shall not, without the order of a judge exercising jurisdiction under the *Children Act* 1989, communicate or seek to communicate, whether directly or indirectly with [the child in question] whilst he remains under 16 years of age": *R. v. D. (Sexual offences prevention order)* [2006] 1 W.L.R. 1088, CA.

SOPOs: further provision as respects Scotland

20–325 **105.** [*Scotland.*]

Section 104: supplemental

20–326 **106.**—(1) In this Part, "sexual offences prevention order" means an order under section 104 or 105.

(2) Subsections (3) to (8) apply for the purposes of section 104.

(3) "Protecting the public or any particular members of the public from serious sexual harm from the defendant" means protecting the public in the United Kingdom or any

particular members of that public from serious physical or psychological harm, caused by the defendant committing one or more offences listed in Schedule 3.

(4) Acts, behaviour, convictions and findings include those occurring before the commencement of this Part.

(5) "Qualifying offender" means a person within subsection (6) or (7).

(6) A person is within this subsection if, whether before or after the commencement of this Part, he—

(a) has been convicted of an offence listed in Schedule 3 (other than at paragraph 60) or in Schedule 5,

(b) has been found not guilty of such an offence by reason of insanity,

(c) has been found to be under a disability and to have done the act charged against him in respect of such an offence, or

(d) in England and Wales or Northern Ireland, has been cautioned in respect of such an offence.

(7) A person is within this subsection if, under the law in force in a country outside the United Kingdom and whether before or after the commencement of this Part—

(a) he has been convicted of a relevant offence (whether or not he has been punished for it),

(b) a court exercising jurisdiction under that law has made in respect of a relevant offence a finding equivalent to a finding that he is not guilty by reason of insanity,

(c) such a court has made in respect of a relevant offence a finding equivalent to a finding that he is under a disability and did the act charged against him in respect of the offence, or

(d) he has been cautioned in respect of a relevant offence.

(8) "Appropriate date", in relation to a qualifying offender, means the date or (as the case may be) the first date on which he was convicted, found or cautioned as mentioned in subsection (6) or (7).

(9) In subsection (7), "relevant offence" means an act which—

(a) constituted an offence under the law in force in the country concerned, and

(b) would have constituted an offence listed in Schedule 3 (other than at paragraph 60) or in Schedule 5 if it had been done in any part of the United Kingdom.

(10) An act punishable under the law in force in a country outside the United Kingdom constitutes an offence under that law for the purposes of subsection (9), however it is described in that law.

(11) Subject to subsection (12), on an application under section 104(5) the condition in subsection (9)(b) (where relevant) is to be taken as met unless, not later than rules of court may provide, the defendant serves on the applicant a notice—

(a) stating that, on the facts as alleged with respect to the act concerned, the condition is not in his opinion met,

(b) showing his grounds for that opinion, and

(c) requiring the applicant to prove that the condition is met.

(12) The court, if it thinks fit, may permit the defendant to require the applicant to prove that the condition is met without service of a notice under subsection (11).

(13) Subsection (14) applies for the purposes of section 104 and this section in their application in relation to England and Wales or Northern Ireland.

(14) In construing any reference to an offence listed in Schedule 3, any condition subject to which an offence is so listed that relates—

(a) to the way in which the defendant is dealt with in respect of an offence so listed or a relevant finding (as defined by section 132(9)), or

(b) to the age of any person,

is to be disregarded.

[This section is printed as amended by the *CJIA* 2008, s.141(1).]

SOPOs: effect

107.—(1) A sexual offences prevention order— **20–327**

(a) prohibits the defendant from doing anything described in the order, and

(b) has effect for a fixed period (not less than 5 years) specified in the order or until further order.

(2) The only prohibitions that may be included in the order are those necessary for the purpose of protecting the public or any particular members of the public from serious sexual harm from the defendant.

(3) Where—

(a) an order is made in respect of a defendant who was a relevant offender immediately before the making of the order, and

(b) the defendant would (apart from this subsection) cease to be subject to the notification requirements of this Part while the order (as renewed from time to time) has effect,

the defendant remains subject to the notification requirements.

(4) Where an order is made in respect of a defendant who was not a relevant offender immediately before the making of the order—

(a) the order causes the defendant to become subject to the notification requirements of this Part from the making of the order until the order (as renewed from time to time) ceases to have effect, and

(b) this Part applies to the defendant, subject to the modification set out in subsection (5).

(5) The "relevant date" is the date of service of the order.

(6) Where a court makes a sexual offences prevention order in relation to a person already subject to such an order (whether made by that court or another), the earlier order ceases to have effect.

(7) Section 106(3) applies for the purposes of this section and section 108.

SOPOs: variations, renewals and discharges

20–328 **108.**—(1) A person within subsection (2) may apply to the appropriate court for an order varying, renewing or discharging a sexual offences prevention order.

(2) The persons are—

(a) the defendant;

(b) the chief officer of police for the area in which the defendant resides;

(c) a chief officer of police who believes that the defendant is in, or is intending to come to, his police area;

(d) where the order was made on an application under section 104(5), the chief officer of police who made the application.

(3) An application under subsection (1) may be made—

(a) where the appropriate court is the Crown Court, in accordance with rules of court;

(b) in any other case, by complaint.

(4) Subject to subsections (5) and (6), on the application the court, after hearing the person making the application and (if they wish to be heard) the other persons mentioned in subsection (2), may make any order, varying, renewing or discharging the sexual offences prevention order, that the court considers appropriate.

(5) An order may be renewed, or varied so as to impose additional prohibitions on the defendant, only if it is necessary to do so for the purpose of protecting the public or any particular members of the public from serious sexual harm from the defendant (and any renewed or varied order may contain only such prohibitions as are necessary for this purpose).

(6) The court must not discharge an order before the end of 5 years beginning with the day on which the order was made, without the consent of the defendant and —

(a) where the application is made by a chief officer of police, that chief officer, or

(b) in any other case, the chief officer of police for the area in which the defendant resides.

(7) In this section "the appropriate court" means—

(a) where the Crown Court or the Court of Appeal made the sexual offences prevention order, the Crown Court;

(b) where a magistrates' court made the order, that court, a magistrates' court for the area in which the defendant resides or, where the application is made by a chief officer of police, any magistrates' court whose commission area includes any part of the chief officer's police area;

(c) where a youth court made the order, that court, a youth court for the area in which the defendant resides or, where the application is made by a chief officer of police, any youth court whose commission area includes any part of the chief officer's police area.

(8) This section applies to orders under—

(a) section 5A of the *Sex Offenders Act* 1997 (restraining orders),

(b) section 2 or 20 of the *Crime and Disorder Act* 1998 (sex offender orders made in England and Wales or Scotland), and

(c) Article 6 of the *Criminal Justice (Northern Ireland) Order* 1998 (S.I. 1998/2839 (N.I. 20)) (sex offender orders made in Northern Ireland),

as it applies to sexual offences prevention orders.

Interim SOPOs

109.—(1) This section applies where an application under section 104(5) or 105(1) ("the main application") has not been determined. **20–329**

(2) An application for an order under this section ("an interim sexual offences prevention order")—

(a) may be made by the complaint by which the main application is made, or

(b) if the main application has been made, may be made by the person who has made that application, by complaint to the court to which that application has been made.

(3) The court may, if it considers it just to do so, make an interim sexual offences prevention order, prohibiting the defendant from doing anything described in the order.

(4) Such an order—

(a) has effect only for a fixed period, specified in the order;

(b) ceases to have effect, if it has not already done so, on the determination of the main application.

(5) Section 107(3) to (5) apply to an interim sexual offences prevention order as if references to an order were references to such an order, and with the omission of "as renewed from time to time" in both places.

(6) The applicant or the defendant may by complaint apply to the court that made the interim sexual offences prevention order for the order to be varied, renewed or discharged.

(7) Subsection (6) applies to orders under—

(a) section 2A or 20(4)(a) of the *Crime and Disorder Act* 1998 (interim orders made in England and Wales or Scotland), and

(b) Article 6A of the *Criminal Justice (Northern Ireland) Order* 1998 (S.I. 1998/2839 (N.I. 20)) (interim orders made in Northern Ireland),

as it applies to interim sexual offences prevention orders.

SOPOs and interim SOPOs: appeals

110.—(1) A defendant may appeal against the making of a sexual offences prevention order— **20–330**

(a) where section 104(2) applied to him, as if the order were a sentence passed on him for the offence;

(b) where section 104(3) (but not section 104(2)) applied to him, as if he had been convicted of the offence and the order were a sentence passed on him for that offence;

(c) where the order was made on an application under section 104(5), to the Crown Court.

(2) A defendant may appeal to the Crown Court against the making of an interim sexual offences prevention order.

(3) A defendant may appeal against the making of an order under section 108, or the refusal to make such an order—

(a) where the application for such an order was made to the Crown Court, to the Court of Appeal;

(b) in any other case, to the Crown Court.

(4) On an appeal under subsection (1)(c), (2) or (3)(b), the Crown Court may make such orders as may be necessary to give effect to its determination of the appeal, and may also make such incidental or consequential orders as appear to it to be just.

(5) Any order made by the Crown Court on an appeal under subsection (1)(c) or (2) (other than an order directing that an application be re-heard by a magistrates' court) is for the purpose of section 108(7) or 109(7) (respectively) to be treated as if it were an order of the court from which the appeal was brought (and not an order of the Crown Court).

111. [*Scotland.*] **20–331**

20–332 **112.** [*Scotland.*]

Offence: breach of SOPO or interim SOPO

20–333 **113.**—(1) A person commits an offence if, without reasonable excuse, he does anything which he is prohibited from doing by—

(a) a sexual offences prevention order;

(b) an interim sexual offences prevention order;

(c) an order under section 5A of the *Sex Offenders Act* 1997 (restraining orders);

(d) an order under section 2, 2A or 20 of the *Crime and Disorder Act* 1998 (sex offender orders and interim orders made in England and Wales and in Scotland);

(e) an order under Article 6 or 6A of the *Criminal Justice (Northern Ireland) Order* 1998 (S.I. 1998/2839 (N.I. 20)) (sex offender orders and interim orders made in Northern Ireland).

(2) A person guilty of an offence under this section is liable—

(a) on summary conviction, to imprisonment for a term not exceeding *6* [12] months or a fine not exceeding the statutory maximum or both;

(b) on conviction on indictment, to imprisonment for a term not exceeding 5 years.

(3) Where a person is convicted of an offence under this section, it is not open to the court by or before which he is convicted to make, in respect of the offence, an order for conditional discharge or, in Scotland, a probation order.

[In subs. (2)(a), "12" is substituted for "6", as from a day to be appointed, by the *CJA* 2003, s.282(2) and (3). The increase has no application to offences committed before the substitution takes effect: s.282(4).]

20–334 For sentencing cases involving offences under section 5A of the *Sex Offenders Act* 1997 (which carried a like maximum penalty), see *R. v. Brown (Graham)* [2002] 1 Cr.App.R.(S.) 1, CA; *R. v. Beech* [2002] 1 Cr.App.R.(S.) 3, CA; *R. v. Clark* [2003] 1 Cr.App.R.(S.) 2, CA; *R. v. Wilcox* [2003] 1 Cr.App.R.(S.) 43, CA; and *R. v. Munday* [2003] 2 Cr.App.R.(S.) 23, CA.

In *R. v. Fenton* [2007] 1 Cr.App.R.(S.) 97, CA, it was said that where a breach involves no real or obvious risk to the section of the public whom the order was intended to protect, the appropriate sentence may well be a community penalty which assists the offender to live within the terms of the order; but repeated breaches will necessarily require a custodial sentence if only to demonstrate that orders of the court are not to be ignored and cannot be breached with impunity; any breach which does cause a real or obvious risk to those whom the order was intended to protect must be treated more seriously, and multiple or repeated breaches may well justify sentences that might otherwise have been considered far higher than any specific criminal offence or misconduct would have attracted (applying to sex offender orders, the approach to breaches of anti-social behaviour orders to be found in *R. v. Braxton*, *R. v. Boness*, *R. v. Lamb*, and *R. v. H., Stevens and Lovegrove* (*ante*, §§ 5–884a, 5–884b)).

Sexual offences for purposes of Part 2

20–335 These are listed in Schedule 3, as to which, see *ante*, §§ 20–278 *et seq*.

Other offences for purposes of Part 2

20–336 These are listed in Schedule 5. They are as follows: murder, manslaughter, kidnapping, false imprisonment, outraging public decency, an offence under section 4, 16, 18, 20 to 23, 27 to 32, 35, 37, 38 or 47 of the *Offences against the Person Act* 1861, an offence under section 2 or 3 of the *Explosive Substances Act* 1883, under the *Infant Life (Preservation) Act* 1929, s.1, under the *CYPA* 1933, s.1, under the *Infanticide Act* 1938, s.1, under section 16, 16A, 17(1), 17(2) or 18 of the *Firearms Act* 1968, under section 1, 8, 9(1)(a) or 10 of the *Theft Act* 1968, an offence of aggravated vehicle-taking under section 12A of that Act involving an accident which caused the death of any person, an offence of arson under section 1 of the *Criminal Damage Act* 1971, an offence other than arson under section 1(2) of that Act, an offence under the *Taking of Hostages Act* 1982, s.1, under sections 1 to 4 of the *Aviation Security Act* 1982, under the *MHA* 1983, s.127, under section 1 or 2 of the *Child Abduction Act* 1984, under the *Prohibition of Female Circumcision Act* 1985, s.1, under sections 1 to 3 of the *Public Order Act* 1986, under the *CJA* 1988, s.134, under section 1 or 3A of the *RTA* 1988, under section 1, 9, 10, 11, 12 or 13 of the *Aviation and Maritime Security Act* 1990, under Part II of the *Channel Tunnel (Security) Order* 1994 (S.I. 1994 No. 570), under section 2 or 4 of the *Protection from Harassment Act* 1997, under the *CDA* 1998, s.29, or falling within section 31(1)(a) or (b) of that Act, under the *Postal Services Act* 2000, s.85(3) or (4), under section 51 or 52 of the *International Criminal Court Act* 2001 (other than one involving murder), under the *Communications Act* 2003, s.127(1), under sections 51 to 53, 57 to 59 of the 2003 Act itself, under section 47 of that Act (where the victim, or (as the case may be) other party, was 16 or over), an offence under section 5 of the *Domestic Violence, Crime and Victims Act* 2004, an offence of aiding, abetting, counselling or procuring the commission of any of the above offences, and an offence of attempt, conspiracy or incitement to commit any such offence.

Paragraphs 64 to 171B list Scottish and Northern Irish offences, and paragraphs 172 and 172A (inserted as from a day to be appointed by the *AFA* 2006, s.378(1), and Sched. 16, para. 213) provides for service offences.

Paragraph 173A (inserted by the *SCA* 2007, s.63(2), and Sched. 6, para. 63(1) and (3)) is in identical terms to paragraph 94A of Schedule 3 (*ante*, § 20–316a).

Paragraph 174 provides that a reference in a preceding paragraph to a person's age is a reference to his age at the time of the offence.

E. FOREIGN TRAVEL ORDERS

Section 114 of the *SOA* 2003 makes provision for an application to a magistrates' court by a chief officer of police for a "foreign travel order". The defendant must be a qualifying offender (as to which, see s.116) and must have acted in such a way as to give reasonable cause to believe that it is necessary for such an order to be made. The court may make such order if satisfied that the offender is a qualifying offender and that his behaviour since the appropriate date makes it necessary to make such order, for the purpose of protecting children generally or any child from serious sexual harm from the defendant outside the United Kingdom. Section 115 makes provision as to the interpretation of section 114. Section 116 provides for the interpretation of "qualifying offender". The effect of such an order is provided for by section 117. It has effect for a fixed period of not more than six months and prohibits foreign travel as specified in the order. Variation, renewal and discharge are regulated by section 118, and appeals by section 119. Sections 120 and 121 apply to Scotland. Section 122 creates an either way offence consisting of breach, without reasonable excuse, of such an order (maximum penalty on conviction on indictment, five years' imprisonment). **20–337**

F. RISK OF SEXUAL HARM ORDERS

A chief officer of police may apply for an order in respect of a person who he believes is in, or intending to come into his police area, where it appears that the person has on at least two occasions done an act within subsection (3), which includes engaging in sexual activity involving a child or in the presence of a child, giving a child anything that relates to sexual activity or contains a reference to such activity, and communicating with a child, where any part of the communication is sexual. The court may make the order if satisfied of these matters and that it is necessary to make such an order, for the purpose of protecting children generally or any child from harm from the defendant. Such an order prohibits the defendant from doing anything described in the order, but the only prohibitions that may be imposed are those necessary for the purpose of protecting children generally or any child from harm from the defendant. Section 124 provides for the interpretation of section 123. Variations, renewals and discharges of such orders are dealt with in section 125, interim orders in section 126 and appeals in section 127. It is an offence triable either way to breach such an order (maximum penalty on conviction on indictment, five years' imprisonment) (s.128). The effect of a conviction under section 128 is set out in section 129. **20–338**

G. INTERPRETATION, ETC. OF PART 2

Sexual Offences Act 2003, ss.131–136

General

Young offenders: application

20–339 **131.** This Part applies to—

(a) a period of detention which a person is liable to serve under a detention and training order [(including an order under section 211 of the *Armed Forces Act* 2006)], or a secure training order,

(b) a period for which a person is ordered to be detained in residential accommodation under section 44(1) of the *Criminal Procedure (Scotland) Act* 1995,

(c) a period of training in a training school, or of custody in a remand centre, which a person is liable to undergo or serve by virtue of an order under section 74(1)(a) or (e) of the *Children and Young Persons Act (Northern Ireland)* 1968,

(d) a period for which a person is ordered to be detained in a juvenile justice centre under Article 39 of the *Criminal Justice (Children) (Northern Ireland) Order* 1998 (S.I. 1998/1504 (N.I. 9)),

(e) a period for which a person is ordered to be kept in secure accommodation under Article 44A of the Order referred to in paragraph (d),

(f) a sentence of detention in a young offender institution, a young offenders institution or a young offenders centre,

(g) a sentence under a custodial order within the meaning of section 71AA of, or paragraph 10(1) of Schedule 5A to, the *Army Act* 1955 or the *Air Force Act* 1955 or section 43AA of, or paragraph 10(1) of Schedule 4A to, the *Naval Discipline Act* 1957,

(h) a sentence of detention under section 90 or 91 of the *Powers of Criminal Courts (Sentencing) Act* 2000, [section 209 or 218 of the *Armed Forces Act* 2006,] section 208 of the *Criminal Procedure (Scotland) Act* 1995 or Article 45 of the *Criminal Justice (Children) (Northern Ireland) Order* 1998,

(i) a sentence of custody for life under section 93 or 94 of the *Powers of Criminal Courts (Sentencing) Act* 2000,

(j) a sentence of detention, or custody for life, under section 71A of the *Army Act* 1955 or the *Air Force Act* 1955 or section 43A of the *Naval Discipline Act* 1957,

(k) a sentence of detention for public protection under section 226 of the *Criminal Justice Act* 2003 [(including one passed as a result of section 221 of the *Armed Forces Act* 2006)],

(l) an extended sentence under section 228 of *that* Act [the *Criminal Justice Act* 2003 (including one passed as a result of section 222 of the *Armed Forces Act* 2006)],

as it applies to an equivalent sentence of imprisonment; and references in this Part to prison or imprisonment are to be interpreted accordingly.

[This section is printed as amended by the *CJA* 2003, s.304, and Sched. 32, paras 142 and 143; and as amended, as from a day to be appointed, by the *AFA* 2006, s.378(1), and Sched. 16, para. 208 (omission of italicised words, insertion of words in square brackets).]

For the purposes of section 131(a), the period of detention which a person sentenced to a detention and training order is liable to serve is the period of detention itself, and not the entire term of the detention and training order; accordingly, a person sentenced to a 12-month detention and training order is to be treated, for the purposes of section 82(1) of the 2003 Act (*ante*, § 20–267), as if he had been sentenced to six months' imprisonment: *R. v. Slocombe* [2006] 1 W.L.R. 328, CA.

Offences with thresholds

20–340 **132.**—(1) This sectionapplies to an offence which in Schedule 3 is listed subject to a condition relating to the way in which the defendant is dealt with in respect of the offence or (where a relevant finding has been made in respect of him) in respect of the finding (a "sentencing condition").

(2) Where an offence is listed if either a sentencing condition or a condition of another description is met, this section applies only to the offence as listed subject to the sentencing condition.

(3) For the purposes of this Part (including in particular section 82(6))—

(a) a person is to be regarded as convicted of an offence to which this section applies, or

(b) (as the case may be) a relevant finding in relation to such an offence is to be regarded as made,

at the time when the sentencing condition is met.

(4) In the following subsections, references to a foreign offence are references to an act which—

(a) constituted an offence under the law in force in a country outside the United Kingdom ("the relevant foreign law"), and

(b) would have constituted an offence to which this section applies (but not an offence, listed in Schedule 3, to which this section does not apply) if it had been done in any part of the United Kingdom.

(5) In relation to a foreign offence, references to the corresponding UK offence are references to the offence (or any offence) to which subsection (4)(b) applies in the case of that foreign offence.

(6) For the purposes of this Part, a person is to be regarded as convicted under the relevant foreign law of a foreign offence at the time when he is, in respect of the offence, dealt with under that law in a way equivalent to that mentioned in Schedule 3 as it applies to the corresponding UK offence.

(7) Where in the case of any person a court exercising jurisdiction under the relevant foreign law makes in respect of a foreign offence a finding equivalent to a relevant finding, the court's finding is, for the purposes of this Part, to be regarded as made at the time when the person is, in respect of the finding, dealt with under that law in a way equivalent to that mentioned in Schedule 3 as it applies to the corresponding UK offence.

(8) Where (by virtue of an order under section 130 or otherwise) an offence is listed in Schedule 5 subject to a sentencing condition, this section applies to that offence as if references to Schedule 3 were references to Schedule 5.

(9) In this section, "relevant finding", in relation to an offence, means—

(a) a finding that a person is not guilty of the offence by reason of insanity, or

(b) a finding that a person is under a disability and did the act charged against him in respect of the offence.

Part 2: general interpretation

133.—(1) In this Part— **20-341**

"admitted to a hospital" means admitted to a hospital under—

(a) section 37 of the *Mental Health Act* 1983, section 57(2)(a) or 58 of the *Criminal Procedure (Scotland) Act* 1995 or Article 44 or 50A(2) of the *Mental Health (Northern Ireland) Order* 1986 (S.I. 1986/595 (N.I. 4));

(b) Schedule 1 to the *Criminal Procedure (Insanity and Unfitness to Plead) Act* 1991; or

(c) section 46 of the *Mental Health Act* 1983, section 69 of the *Mental Health (Scotland) Act* 1984 or Article 52 of the *Mental Health (Northern Ireland) Order* 1986;

"cautioned" means —

(a) cautioned (or, in Northern Ireland, cautioned by a police officer) after the person concerned has admitted the offence, or

(b) reprimanded or warned within the meaning given by section 65 of the *Crime and Disorder Act* 1998, and "caution" is to be interpreted accordingly;

"community order" means —

(a) a community order within the meaning of the *Powers of Criminal Courts (Sentencing) Act* 2000;

(b) a probation order or community service order under the *Criminal Procedure (Scotland) Act* 1995 or a supervised attendance order made in pursuance of section 235 of that Act;

(c) a community order within the meaning of the *Criminal Justice (Northern Ireland) Order* 1996 (S.I. 1996/3160 (N.I. 24)), a probation order under section 1 of the *Probation Act (Northern Ireland)* 1950) or a community service order under Article 7 of the *Treatment of Offenders (Northern Ireland) Order* 1976 (S.I. 1976/226 (N.I. 40)); or

(d) a community supervision order;

"community supervision order" means an order under paragraph 4 of Schedule 5A to the *Army Act* 1955 or the *Air Force Act* 1955 or Schedule 4A to the *Naval Discipline Act* 1957;

"country" includes territory;

"detained in a hospital" means detained in a hospital under—

(a) Part 3 of the *Mental Health Act* 1983, section 71 of the *Mental Health (Scotland) Act* 1984, Part 6 of the *Criminal Procedure (Scotland) Act* 1995 or Part III of the *Mental Health (Northern Ireland) Order* 1986;

(b) Schedule 1 to the *Criminal Procedure (Insanity and Unfitness to Plead) Act* 1991; or

(c) section 46 of the *Mental Health Act* 1983, section 69 of the *Mental Health (Scotland) Act* 1984 or Article 52 of the *Mental Health (Northern Ireland) Order* 1986;

"guardianship order" means a guardianship order under section 37 of the *Mental Health Act* 1983, section 58 of the *Criminal Procedure (Scotland) Act* 1995 or Article 44 of the *Mental Health (Northern Ireland) Order* 1986 (S.I. 1986/595 (N.I. 4));

"home address" has the meaning given by section 83(7);

"interim notification order" has the meaning given by section 100(2);

"interim risk of sexual harm order" has the meaning given by section 126(2);

"interim sexual offences prevention order" has the meaning given by section 109(2);

["kept in service custody" means kept in service custody by virtue of an order under section 105(2) of the *Armed Forces Act* 2006 (but see also subsection (3));]

"local police area" has the meaning given by section 88(3);

"local probation board" has the same meaning as in the *Criminal Justice and Court Services Act* 2000;

"notification order" has the meaning given by section 97(1);

"notification period" has the meaning given by section 80(1);

"order for conditional discharge" has the meaning given by each of the following—

(a) *section 12(3) of the* Powers of Criminal Courts (Sentencing) Act *2000;*

(b) *Article 2(2) of the* Criminal Justice (Northern Ireland) Order *1996 (S.I. 1996/3160 (N.I. 24));*

(c) *paragraph 2(1) of Schedule 5A to the* Army Act *1955;*

(d) *paragraph 2(1) of Schedule 5A to the* Air Force Act *1955;*

(e) *paragraph 2(1) of Schedule 4A to the* Naval Discipline Act *1957;*

["order for conditional discharge" means an order under any of the following provisions discharging the offender conditionally—

(a) section 12 of the *Powers of Criminal Courts (Sentencing) Act* 2000;

(b) Article 4 of the *Criminal Justice (Northern Ireland) Order* 1996;

(c) section 185 of the *Armed Forces Act* 2006;

(d) paragraph 3 of Schedule 5A to the *Army Act* 1955 or *Air Force Act* 1955 or Schedule 4A to the *Naval Discipline Act* 1957;]

"parental responsibility" has the same meaning as in the *Children Act* 1989 or the *Children (Northern Ireland) Order* 1995 (S.I. 1995/755 (N.I. 2)), and "parental responsibilities" has the same meaning as in Part 1 of the *Children (Scotland) Act* 1995;

"the period of conditional discharge" has the meaning given by each of the following—

(a) section 12(3) of the *Powers of Criminal Courts (Sentencing) Act* 2000;

(b) Article 2(2) of the *Criminal Justice (Northern Ireland) Order* 1996 (S.I. 1996/3160 (N.I. 24));

(c) *paragraph 2(1) of Schedule 5A to the* Army Act *1955* [section 185(2) of the *Armed Forces Act* 2006];

(d) *paragraph 2(1) of Schedule 5A to the* Army Act *1955;*

(e) *paragraph 2(1) of Schedule 4A to the* Naval Discipline Act *1957;*

"probation order" has the meaning given by section 228(1) of the *Criminal Procedure (Scotland) Act* 1995;

"probation period" has the meaning given by section 307(1) of the *Criminal Procedure (Scotland) Act* 1995;

"relevant date" has the meaning given by section 82(6) (save in the circumstances mentioned in sections 98, 100, 107, 109 and 129);

"relevant offender" has the meaning given by section 80(2);

"restriction order" means —

(a) an order under section 41 of the *Mental Health Act* 1983, section 57(2)(b) or 59 of the *Criminal Procedure (Scotland) Act* 1995 or Article 47(1) of the *Mental Health (Northern Ireland) Order* 1986;

(b) a direction under paragraph 2(1)(b) of Schedule 1 to the *Criminal Procedure (Insanity and Unfitness to Plead) Act* 1991 or Article 50A(3)(b) of the *Mental Health (Northern Ireland) Order* 1986 (S.I. 1986/595 (N.I. 4)); or

(c) a direction under section 46 of the *Mental Health Act* 1983, section 69 of the *Mental Health (Scotland) Act* 1984 or Article 52 of the *Mental Health (Northern Ireland) Order* 1986;

"risk of sexual harm order" has the meaning given by section 123(1);

["service detention" has the meaning given by section 374 of the *Armed Forces Act* 2006;]

"sexual offences prevention order" has the meaning given by section 106(1);

"supervision" means supervision in pursuance of an order made for the purpose or, in the case of a person released from prison on licence, in pursuance of a condition contained in his licence;

"term of service detention" means a term of detention awarded under section 71(1)(e) of the Army Act *1955 or the* Air Force Act *1955 or section 43(1)(e) of the* Naval Discipline Act *1957.*

(1A) A reference to a provision specified in paragraph (a) of the definition of "admitted to a hospital", "detained in a hospital" or "restriction order" includes a reference to the provision as it applies by virtue of—

(a) section 5 of the *Criminal Procedure (Insanity) Act* 1964,

(b) section 6 or 14 of the *Criminal Appeal Act* 1968,

[(ba) Schedule 4 to the *Armed Forces Act* 2006 (including as applied by section 16(2) of the *Court-Martial Appeals Act* 1968),]

(c) section 116A of the *Army Act* 1955 or the *Air Force Act* 1955 or section 63A of the *Naval Discipline Act* 1957, or

(d) section 16 or 23 of the *Courts-Martial (Appeals) Act* 1968.

(2) Where under section 141 different days are appointed for the commencement of different provisions of this Part, a reference in any such provision to the commencement of this Part is to be read (subject to section 98(4)) as a reference to the commencement of that provision.

(3) In relation to any time before the commencement of section 105(2) of the *Armed Forces Act* 2006, "kept in service custody" means being kept in military, air-force or naval custody by virtue of an order made under section 75A(2) of the *Army Act* 1955 or of the *Air Force Act* 1955 or section 47G(2) of the *Naval Discipline Act* 1957 (as the case may be).

[This section is printed as amended by the *Domestic Violence, Crime and Victims Act* 2004, s.58(1), and Sched. 10, para. 57; and the *CJIA* 2008, s.148(1), and Sched. 26, paras 53 and 56(1), (2)(a) and (4); and as amended and repealed in part, as from a day to be appointed, by the *AFA* 2006, s.378(1) and (2), Sched. 16, para. 209, and Sched. 17 (substitution of definition of "order for conditional discharge" in square brackets for italicised definition, substitution of words in square brackets for italicised words in para. (c) of the definition of "the period of conditional discharge" and omission of paras (d) and (e) in that definition, insertion of definition of "service detention", omission of definition of "term of service detention" and insertion of subs. (1A)(ba)); and the *CJIA* 2008, s.148(1), and Sched. 26, paras 53 and 56(2)(b), (3) and (4) (insertion of definition of "kept in service custody" and of subs. (3)).]

Conditional discharges and probation orders

134.—(1) The following provisions do not apply for the purposes of this Part to a conviction for an offence in respect of which an order for conditional discharge or, in Scotland, a probation order is made— **20-342**

(a) section 14(1) of the *Powers of Criminal Courts (Sentencing) Act* 2000 (conviction with absolute or conditional discharge deemed not to be a conviction);

(b) Article 6(1) of the *Criminal Justice (Northern Ireland) Order* 1996 (S.I. 1996/3160 (N.I. 24)) (conviction with absolute or conditional discharge deemed not to be a conviction);

(c) section 247(1) of the *Criminal Procedure (Scotland) Act* 1995 (conviction with probation order or absolute discharge deemed not to be a conviction);

[(ca) section 187(1) of the *Armed Forces Act* 2006 (conviction with absolute or conditional discharge deemed not to be a conviction),]

(d) paragraph 5(1) of Schedule 5A to the *Army Act* 1955 or the *Air Force Act* 1955 or Schedule 4A to the *Naval Discipline Act* 1957 (conviction with absolute or conditional discharge or community supervision order deemed not to be a conviction).

(2) Subsection (1) applies only to convictions after the commencement of this Part.

(3) The provisions listed in subsection (1)(d) do not apply for the purposes of this Part to a conviction for an offence in respect of which a community supervision order is or has (before or after the commencement of this Part) been made.

[This section is printed as amended, as from a day to be appointed, by the *AFA* 2006, s.378(1), and Sched. 16, para. 210 (insertion of subs. (1)(ca)).]

Interpretation: mentally disordered offenders

20–343 **135.**—(1) In this Part, a reference to a conviction includes a reference to a finding of a court in summary proceedings, where the court makes an order under an enactment within subsection (2), that the accused did the act charged; and similar references are to be interpreted accordingly.

(2) The enactments are—

(a) section 37(3) of the *Mental Health Act* 1983;

(b) section 58(3) of the *Criminal Procedure (Scotland) Act* 1995;

(c) Article 44(4) of the *Mental Health (Northern Ireland) Order* 1986 (S.I. 1986/595 (N.I. 4)).

(3) In this Part, a reference to a person being or having been found to be under a disability and to have done the act charged against him in respect of an offence includes a reference to his being or having been found—

(a) unfit to be tried for the offence;

(b) to be insane so that his trial for the offence cannot or could not proceed; or

(c) unfit to be tried and to have done the act charged against him in respect of the offence.

(4) In section 133—

(a) a reference to admission or detention under Schedule 1 to the *Criminal Procedure (Insanity and Unfitness to Plead) Act* 1991, and the reference to a direction under paragraph 2(1)(b) of that Schedule, include respectively—

(i) a reference to admission or detention under Schedule 1 to the *Criminal Procedure (Insanity) Act* 1964; and

(ii) a reference to a restriction order treated as made by paragraph 2(1) of that Schedule;

(b) a reference to admission or detention under any provision of Part 6 of the *Criminal Procedure (Scotland) Act* 1995, and the reference to an order under section 57(2)(b) or 59 of that Act, include respectively—

(i) a reference to admission or detention under section 174(3) or 376(2) of the *Criminal Procedure (Scotland) Act 1975*; and

(ii) a reference to a restriction order made under section 178(1) or 379(1) of that Act;

(c) [*repealed by* Domestic Violence, Crime and Victims Act *2004, s.58(1), and Sched. 10, para. 58*].

Part 2: Northern Ireland

20–344 **136.** [*Northern Ireland.*]

CHAPTER 21

OFFENCES UNDER THE THEFT AND FRAUD ACTS

I. INTRODUCTION

Background

The *Theft Act* 1968 was based on "a fundamental reconsideration of the principles underlying this branch of the law" (Criminal Law Revision Committee: 8th Report, Cmnd. 2977). The 1978 Act was intended to remedy perceived defects in the 1968 legislation, but much of it was repealed by the *Fraud Act* 2006, which resulted from the Law Commission's Report on *Fraud* (Law. Com. No. 276, Cm 5560, 2002) and the Home Office consultation paper, *Fraud Law Reform* (May, 2004). With effect from January 15, 2007, the 2006 Act abolished all the deception offences in the *Theft Acts*, **21–1** replacing them with an offence of fraud which can be committed in three different ways and an offence of obtaining services dishonestly; it also replaced the offence of going equipped to cheat with much wider offences of possessing and making articles for use in fraud. For offences committed, or partly committed, before this date, see the 2007 edition of this work, at §§ 21–172 *et seq.*; for the transitional provisions, and the definition of "partly committed", see *post*, § 21–414.

21–2 The charging of deception offences has been simplified considerably by the *Fraud Act* 2006, since offences of fraud by false representation (in breach of section 2, *post*, § 21–357) do not depend upon any property actually being obtained; thus the false representation does not require a person actually to have been deceived, the issue of whether what was obtained had belonged to the victim (central to the decision in *R. v. Preddy and Slade*; *R. v Dhillon* [1996] A.C. 815, HL) does not arise, and the same charge is appropriate whether the intended gain is in the form of cash, a credit to a bank account, or the execution of a valuable security.

Overlap between offences

21–2a The various offences created by these three Acts are not mutually exclusive. In particular, the offence of fraud by abuse of position will include offences of theft committed in breach of trust; and the majority decision in *R. v. Gomez* [1993] A.C. 442, HL (*post*, § 21–32) means that there is a considerable degree of overlap between theft and fraud by false representation. It does not follow, however, that charges may be equally preferred under either Act. First, it is submitted that to charge a true fraud by false representation as theft is an unnecessary complication. The lay view that theft is taking without permission, as opposed to tricking an owner into parting with possession, should be reflected in the charges where possible. Secondly, it is submitted that it is important that the charge or charges preferred reflect the true criminality involved. There will be borderline cases, but where a case is obviously a case of fraud it should, it is submitted, be charged as such, even though it may also, as a matter of law, be a case of theft; furthermore, where a theft is truly an abuse of position within the terms of section 4 of the 2006 Act, it is submitted that it should be charged as such. Thirdly, the choice of the appropriate offence, in respect of which proceedings ought to be brought, may also be influenced by the available penalties: as to this, see *post*, § 21–4a.

Dishonesty

21–2b Most of the offences created by the *Theft Acts* and the *Fraud Act* involve dishonesty as a specific ingredient. The same test of dishonesty applies for each; the leading authority is *R. v. Ghosh* [1982] Q.B. 1053, 75 Cr.App.R. 154, CA.

Having reviewed many of the earlier (difficult to reconcile) authorities, Lord Lane concluded that there were two aspects to dishonesty, the objective and the subjective, and that the tribunal of fact, in determining the issue, would have to go through a two-stage process before it could convict the defendant.

> "In determining whether the prosecution has proved that the defendant was acting dishonestly, a jury must first of all decide whether according to the ordinary standards of reasonable and honest people what was done was dishonest. If it was not dishonest by those standards, that is the end of the matter and the prosecution fails.
>
> If it was dishonest by those standards, then the jury must consider whether the defendant himself must have realised that what he was doing was by those standards dishonest. In most cases, where the actions are obviously dishonest by ordinary standards, there will be no doubt about it. It will be obvious that the defendant himself knew that he was acting dishonestly. It is dishonest for a defendant to act in a way which he knows ordinary people consider to be dishonest, even if he asserts or genuinely believes that he is morally justified in acting as he did. For example, Robin Hood or those ardent anti-vivisectionists who remove animals from vivisection laboratories are acting dishonestly, even though they may consider themselves to be morally justified in doing what they do, because they know that ordinary people would consider these actions to be dishonest" (pp. 1064, 162–163).

21–2c There is no need to give a *Ghosh*-based direction unless the defendant has raised the issue that he did not know that anybody would regard what he did as dishonest: *R. v. Roberts (W.)*, 84 Cr.App.R. 117, CA. See also *R. v. Price (R.W.)*, 90 Cr.App.R. 409,

CA (*Ghosh* direction need only be given where the defendant might have believed that what he was alleged to have done was in accordance with the ordinary person's idea of honesty). When a *Ghosh* direction is to be given it is wise to use the actual words of Lord Lane C.J.: *R. v. Vosper*, *The Times*, February 26, 1990, CA; *R. v. Ravenshead* [1990] Crim.L.R. 398, CA; *R. v. Green* [1992] Crim.L.R. 292, CA; *R. v. Hyam* [1997] Crim.L.R. 440, CA.

Ignorance of the law

The fact that a defendant did not know what was criminal and what was not, or that he did not understand the relevant principles of the civil law, could not save him from conviction if what he did, coupled with his state of mind, satisfied the elements of the offence of which he was accused. However, where the defence is that no dishonesty had been involved, it may be necessary to explain to the jury the clear distinction between a defendant's lack of knowledge of the law, and his appreciation that he was doing something which, by the ordinary standards of reasonable and honest people, was regarded as dishonest: *R. v. Lightfoot*, 97 Cr.App.R. 24, CA. **21–3**

Jurisdiction

The offences created by sections 1 (theft), 17 (false accounting), 19 (false statements by company directors, etc., *post*, § 30–267), 21 (blackmail) and 22 (handling stolen goods) of the *Theft Act* 1968, and sections 1 (fraud), 6 (possession, etc., of articles for use in frauds), 7 (making or supplying articles for use in frauds), 9 (participating in fraudulent business carried on by sole trader, etc., *post*, § 30–126) and 11 (obtaining services dishonestly) of the *Fraud Act* are "Group A" offences within Part I of the *CJA* 1993. As to the effect of this, see *ante*, §§ 2–37 *et seq.* **21–4**

Maximum sentences

The maximum terms of imprisonment for offences under the *Theft Acts* and the *Fraud Act* that may be tried on indictment are as follows: **21–4a**

Life:	robbery, assault with intent to rob, aggravated burglary;
14 years:	burglary of a dwelling, blackmail, handling stolen property;
10 years:	burglary other than of a dwelling, retaining a wrongful credit, fraud, making or supplying articles for use in frauds;
7 years:	theft, false accounting, suppression of documents;
5 years:	removal of articles from places open to the public, abstraction of electricity, possession etc. of articles for use in frauds, obtaining services dishonestly;
3 years:	going equipped to steal, making off without payment;
2 years:	aggravated vehicle taking;
6 months:	taking a conveyance without authority (increased, from a day to be appointed, to 51 weeks by the *Criminal Justice Act* 2003, s.281(4)–(6)).

Financial reporting orders and serious crime prevention orders

A financial reporting order may be made in respect of a person convicted of an offence under section 17 (false accounting) or 21 (blackmail) of the *Theft Act* 1968, or section 1 (fraud) or 11 (obtaining services dishonestly) of the *Fraud Act*: *SOCPA* 2005, s.76 (*ante*, § 5–886a). **21–4b**

A serious crime prevention order may be made by the Crown Court in respect of a person convicted of an offence under section 8 (robbery or assault with intent to rob, but only where the use or threat of force involves a firearm, an imitation firearm or an offensive weapon), 17 or 21 of the 1968 Act, or section 1, 6 (possession of an article for use in fraud), 7 (making or supplying an article for use in fraud) or 11 of the 2006 Act: *SCA* 2007, s.19, and Sched. 1 (*ante*, §§ 5–875c, 5–878).

Sentencing guidelines

As to "guideline cases" being only guidelines, see *R. v. Nicholas*, *The Times*, April **21–4c**

23, 1986, CA, *ante*, § 7–142. For illustrative decisions, see *CSP*, B6–12002 to B6–13112 and B6–33A05 to B6–33F22.

In March, 2008, the Sentencing Guidelines Council issued a consultation guideline on theft in breach of trust, theft from the person, theft in a dwelling and theft from a shop. Whilst the guideline does not purport to deal with dwelling house burglaries, in the "theft in a dwelling" section it describes circumstances which undoubtedly would constitute burglary in law, most particularly where entry is gained by a trick. For details of any definitive guideline, see Appendix K.

Theft in breach of trust

21–4d In *R. v. Barrick*, 81 Cr.App.R. 78, CA, Lord Lane C.J. said that the case provided an opportunity to make some observations on the proper sentence to be passed in respect of certain types of theft and fraud. The types of cases were where, for example, an accountant, solicitor, bank employee or postman had used his position to defraud. He would usually be a person of hitherto impeccable character. It was practically certain that he would never again offend and, in the nature of things, he would never again be able to secure similar employment with all that that meant in terms of disgrace for himself and hardship both for himself and for his family. There was no proper basis for distinguishing between such cases simply on the basis of the offender's occupation. Professional men should expect to be punished as severely as the others, in some cases more severely.

Immediate imprisonment was inevitable, save in very exceptional circumstances or where the amount of money obtained was small. The court should pass a sufficiently substantial term of imprisonment to mark publicly the gravity of the offence. The sum involved was obviously not the only factor to be considered but it might provide a useful guide.

21–4e The guideline figures that follow are as modified in *R. v. Clark* [1998] 2 Cr.App.R. 137, CA, so as to take account of (a) changes in the rules as to the proportion of a custodial sentence that must be served, (b) inflation, and (c) the reduction in the maximum sentence for theft to seven years' imprisonment. Where the amount stolen was not small, but was less than £17,500, prison terms ranging from the very short up to 21 months were appropriate. Cases involving sums of between about £17,500 and £100,000 would merit a term of two to three years' imprisonment. Cases involving sums between £100,000 and £250,000 would merit a term of three to four years. Cases involving £250,000 to £1 million would merit between five and nine years, with cases involving more than £1 million attracting a sentence of 10 years or more.

The suggested terms are appropriate to contested cases and take into account the possibility of consecutive sentences, where appropriate. A plea of guilty should attract an appropriate discount.

The sentencing court would, doubtless, wish to pay regard to the following matters, *inter alia*, in determining the proper level of sentence:

(a) the quality and degree of trust reposed in the offender, including his rank;
(b) the period over which the fraud or the thefts had been perpetrated;
(c) the use to which the money or property taken was put;
(d) the effect on the victim;
(e) the impact of the offences on the public and public confidence;
(f) the effect on fellow employees or partners;
(g) the effect on the offender himself;
(h) his own history; and
(i) those matters of mitigation special to the offender, such as illness, being placed under great strain by excessive responsibility or the like, where, as sometimes happened, there had been a long delay, say, over two years, between his being confronted with his dishonesty and the start of his trial and any help given by him to the police.

In *R. v. Whitehouse and Morrison* [1999] 2 Cr.App.R.(S.) 259, the Court of Appeal reiterated that *Clark* provided guidelines only. A sentence outside the guidelines was justified by the aggravating feature that the principal defendant had stolen from his employers out of revenge. In *R. v. Roach* [2002] 1 Cr.App.R.(S.) 12, CA, it was said that reliance on the *Clark* guidelines was inappropriate in cases of breach of trust of an elderly and vulnerable victim. *Roach* is included in the Sentencing Guidelines Council's compendium of guideline cases (Appendix K–500), and was followed in *R. v. Hooper* [2003] 2 Cr.App.R.(S.) 96, CA, which drew a distinction between the *Barrick* and *Clark* types of case which relate to theft in breach of trust from employers, charitable bodies or similar organisations, and cases like *Roach* which involve the exploitation of pitiful and vulnerable people, whether due to age or infirmity, or a combination of both.

It should also be noted that all these cases predate the introduction of the maximum sentence of 10 years' imprisonment for fraud by abuse of position (*Fraud Act* 2006, ss.1 and 4 (*post*, § 21–359)).

Mortgage frauds

The relevant factors in sentencing for mortgage fraud were considered in *R. v. Stevens*, 96 Cr.App.R. 303, CA. Among the factors to be taken into account are the degree of sophistication of the fraud, the use of false names, properties and values, and the obtaining of loans for commercial purposes under the guise of domestic mortgages. The part played by the accused is important. If he recruited others to participate, that is an aggravating feature. If a professional or semi-professional person was involved, there was necessarily a breach of trust. The length of involvement and the extent of any personal benefit were also relevant. It was also of consequence whether there was any genuine intention to repay the loans. Regard should be had to the amount loaned as well as to any losses sustained. **21–4f**

Delay might also be a relevant feature. It was important to consider what had happened to a defendant during any period of such delay. In this context, however, any stress and anxiety which might be occasioned by the delay was of little value in mitigation, as these were the effects, not the causes of the offending. Finally, the nature and the timing of any guilty plea is relevant where there has been delay. In all cases, the court must pay particular regard to the character and age of the perpetrator.

Theft by airport baggage handlers

In *R. v. Dhunay*, 8 Cr.App.R.(S.) 107, CA, the court was concerned with sentencing for persistent pilfering committed by baggage handlers at airports. *Barrick* was said not to be fully applicable. Three years' imprisonment was the starting point: the imposition of more severe or less severe punishment than that should be considered with regard to the particular circumstances in each case and to any individual mitigation. **21–4g**

Fraudulent obtaining of welfare benefits

See *R. v. Stewart*, 85 Cr.App.R. 66, CA, in which guidance was given in relation to both the average offender and the "professional fraudsmen ... [who] have selected the welfare departments as an easy target for their depredations and have made a profitable business out of defrauding the public" (*per* Lord Lane C.J. at p. 69). This guidance was affirmed by *R. v. Graham*; *R. v. Whatley* [2005] 1 Cr.App.R.(S.) 115, CA, and updated to make allowance for the effect of inflation. Where imprisonment is necessary, terms of up to about nine to 12 months will usually be sufficient in a contested case where the over-payment is less than £20,000. **21–4h**

"Ringing" stolen cars

A ringleader pleading not guilty to offences of theft, handling or fraud in relation to the "ringing" of stolen cars might expect a prison sentence of four to five years' imprisonment; for a lieutenant, a sentence of three years on a plea of not guilty might be appropriate: *R. v. Evans* [1996] 1 Cr.App.R.(S.) 105, CA. See also *R. v. Dennard and Draper* [2000] 1 Cr.App.R.(S.) 232, CA. **21–4i**

"Shoplifting"

In *R. v. Page* [2005] 2 Cr.App.R.(S.) 37, the Court of Appeal said that in dealing with isolated individual adult shoplifters, the following principles should be borne in **21–4j** mind: (i) custody would be the sentence of last resort and would almost never be appropriate for a first offence; though it might be merited where the offence was aggravated by the use of a child; a community penalty might be appropriate on a plea by a first-time offender even where other adults were involved and the offence was organised; (ii) when the offending was attributable to drug addiction, a drug treatment and testing order would often be appropriate; (iii) custody not exceeding one month might be appropriate for an offender who persistently stole on a small scale; where the offending was aggravated by the use of equipment designed to facilitate the offending, up to two months might be appropriate; (iv) even where the defendant was to be sentenced for a large number of offences or had a history of persistent similar offending on a significant scale, the comparative lack of seriousness and the need for proportionality between the sentence and the particular offence would, on a plea of guilty, rarely require a sentence of more than two years, and would often merit no more than 12 to 18 months; (v) young offenders would usually be dealt with appropriately by non-custodial penalties; (vi) in the case of repeated, or large-scale offending by organised gangs, sentences of the order of four years might well be appropriate; (vii) if violence was used to a shopkeeper after the theft, so that robbery was inappropriate as a charge, then a sentence in excess of four years was likely to be appropriate.

II. THEFT

(1) Definition

Theft Act 1968, ss.1–6

Basic definition of "theft"

21–5 **1.**—(1) A person is guilty of theft if he dishonestly appropriates property belonging to another with the intention of permanently depriving the other of it; and "thief" and "steal" shall be construed accordingly.

(2) It is immaterial whether the appropriation is made with a view to gain, or is made for the thief's own benefit.

(3) The five following sections of this Act shall have effect as regards the interpretation and operation of this section (and, except as otherwise provided by this Act, shall apply only for purposes of this section).

2. [*"Dishonesty." See* post, *§ 21–23.*]
3. [*"Appropriates." See* post, *§ 21–31.*]
4. [*"Property." See* post, *§ 21–48.*]
5. [*"Belonging to another." See* post, *§ 21–58.*]
6. [*"With the intention of permanently depriving the other of it." See* post, *§ 21–76.*]

(2) Indictment

(a) *General*

STATEMENT OF OFFENCE

21–6 *Theft, contrary to section 1(1) of the* Theft Act *1968.*

PARTICULARS OF OFFENCE

A B on the —— day of ——, 20—, stole a bag belonging to J N.

Itemising the property

21–7 Where it is possible to itemise the property stolen, this should be done and expressions such as "and other goods" should be avoided: *R. v. Yates*, 15 Cr.App.R. 15, CCA; *R. v. Young*, 17 Cr.App.R. 131, CCA. Vague expressions such as "a quantity of money" or "a quantity of watches" may fall foul of the *Criminal Procedure Rules* 2005 (S.I. 2005 No. 384), r.14.2 (*ante*, § 1–115), as not making clear "what the prosecutor alleges against the defendant", and, in any event, it is undesirable that upon a conviction, the record should provide no indication of whether the defendant stole, for example, £5 or £5,000. If the exact amount stolen is unknown, then suitable words can be used (*e.g.*

"approximately" or "valued together at between £500 and £750"). Where out of necessity, a less precise form of wording is used, but the evidence subsequently clarifies the issue, the indictment should be amended to accord with the evidence. Particular care is needed in respect of thefts from bank accounts: see *post*, § 21–50.

It is not necessary to prove all the articles mentioned in the indictment to have been stolen; if it is proved that the defendant stole any one of them, it is sufficient: *Machent v. Quinn* [1970] 2 All E.R. 255, DC; *R. v. Parker*, 53 Cr.App.R. 289, CA (*per* Donaldson J. at p. 289). It is submitted that the jury must be agreed on which particular article was stolen (see *R. v. Brown (K.)*, 79 Cr.App.R. 115, CA, *ante*, §§ 4–391 *et seq.*). The sentence should relate only to the articles proved to have been stolen.

Charge distinct takings

As to the general rule that only one offence should be charged in a single count, see *ante*, §§ 1–135 *et seq.*; however, where multiple incidents of theft amount to a course of conduct they may be included in a single count (*Criminal Procedure Rules* 2005 (S.I. 2005 No. 384) r.14.2(2), *ante*, § 1–115). This encompasses the "general deficiency" exception to the rule against duplicity (*ante*, § 1–143). Paragraph IV.34.8 (*ante*, § 1–140) of the consolidated criminal practice direction makes clear that a single count covering multiple incidents is inappropriate where different issues arise in respect of different incidents; in this regard, therefore, rule 14.2(2) maintains the principle set out in cases such as *R. v. Jackson*, *The Guardian*, November 20, 1991, CA (91 05435 X3) (separate counts required where it was apparent to the prosecution that various items stolen from an employer were taken on different occasions and that different defences might be advanced in relation to different items). **21–8**

As to the possibility of a jury, trying a single count including a number of incidents of theft, returning a partial verdict in relation to some but not all of the incidents included in the count, see paragraph IV.34.13 of the consolidated criminal practice direction, *ante* § 1–140; however, this gives no indication as to how this should be achieved in practice, and such a jury would have to be carefully directed as to the degree of unanimity required (see *ante*, § 4–393). As to the potential problems to which such a count may give rise, see *ante*, §§ 1–141 *et seq.*

Amendment

Where the evidence discloses that multiple incidents of theft have been included inappropriately in a single count, the count should be amended to restrict it to a single offence, or to such a smaller group of incidents as can appropriately be included in a single count (such as where it transpires that there is a common defence to some but not all of the incidents originally included in the single count). Ordinarily, there could be no objection to a further amendment by way of adding one or more counts which would relate to the other thefts: *R. v. Radley*, 58 Cr.App.R. 394, CA, *ante*, § 1–152. As to the principles which govern the amendment of an indictment, see *ante*, §§ 1–147 *et seq.* **21–9**

(b) *Alternative counts*

(i) *Alternative counts of theft*

In *R. v. Dowdall and Smith*, 13 Cr.App.R.(S.) 441, CA (following *R. v. Young*, 12 Cr.App.R.(S.) 279, CA), it was held to have been inappropriate to have alternative counts with varying particulars to cater for different possibilities as to how the defendant stole the property in question. One count had alleged theft of a purse from the victim's handbag (reflecting the prosecution's case), with a second count alleging theft by finding (the defendant's version). The court rejected a suggestion in *R. v. Devall* [1984] Crim.L.R. 429, CA, that this was appropriate. Alternative averments which particularise different methods of appropriation are immaterial averments, and in effect leave to the jury questions which are not for them to determine. If sentence turns on which version is right, a judge can either accept the defence account or try an issue as to the circumstances, in accordance with *R. v. Newton*, 77 Cr.App.R. 13 (*ante*, § 5–74). **21–10**

Notwithstanding *Dowdall and Smith,* the Court of Appeal appear to have reopened the issue. In *R. v. Bossom* [1999] Crim.L.R. 596, it was apparently said that, where alternative appropriations are alleged, it may sometimes be appropriate to have separate counts. There is, however, no indication in this report as to the circumstances in which the court thought that such course would be appropriate. Sir John Smith Q.C.'s commentary to the report sets out cogent reasons why it is undesirable to have separate counts.

(ii) *Theft and handling*

21–10a See *post*, §§ 21–280 *et seq.*

(c) *Alternative verdicts*

21–11 On an indictment for theft, the defendant may be convicted where appropriate of an offence under section 12 of the *Theft Act* 1968 (taking a motor vehicle or other conveyance without authority): see s.12(4), *post*, § 21–141.

For alternative verdicts generally, see the *CLA* 1967, s.6(3), (4), *ante*, § 4–455. There is no power under section 6(3) to convict of handling stolen goods on a count alleging theft of the goods: *R. v. Woods* [1969] 1 Q.B. 447, 53 Cr.App.R. 30, CA.

(3) Class of offence and mode of trial

21–12 Theft is triable either way (*MCA* 1980, s.17(1), and Sched. 1, *ante*, § 1–75af). It is a class 3 offence, *ante*, § 2–17.

(4) Sentence

21–13 The maximum sentence upon conviction on indictment is seven years' imprisonment: *Theft Act* 1968, s.7. For the maximum sentence upon summary conviction, see the *MCA* 1980, s.32(1), *ante*, § 1–75aa.

An offence of theft or attempted theft of a motor vehicle carries discretionary disqualification: *RTOA* 1988, ss.34 and 97 and Sched. 2, Pt II. Disqualification should generally be restricted to cases involving bad driving, persistent motoring offences or the use of vehicles for the purpose of crime: *R. v. Callister* [1993] R.T.R. 70, CA.

Guidelines for sentences in theft cases are set out at §§ 21–4c *et seq.*, *ante*.

[The next paragraph is § 21–22.]

(5) Elements of the offence of theft

(a) *Four elements*

21–22 "Theft ... involves four elements: (a) a dishonest (b) appropriation (c) of property belonging to another (d) with the intention of permanently depriving the owner of it": *per* Megaw L.J. in *R. v. Lawrence*, 55 Cr.App.R. 73 at 78, CA. The House of Lords specifically approved this and added that there is not to be implied a further requirement that the dishonest appropriation must be without the consent of the owner: *Lawrence v. Metropolitan Police Commr* [1972] A.C. 626, HL; *R. v. Gomez* [1993] A.C. 442, HL (*post*, § 21–33).

(b) *Dishonesty*

Theft Act 1968, s.2

21–23 **2.**—(1) A person's appropriation of property belonging to another is not to be regarded as dishonest—

(a) if he appropriates the property in the belief that he has in law the right to deprive the other of it, on behalf of himself or of a third person;

(b) if he appropriates the property in the belief that he would have the other's consent if the other knew of the appropriation and the circumstances of it; or

(c) (except where the property came to him as trustee or personal representative) if he appropriates the property in the belief that the person to whom the property belongs cannot be discovered by taking reasonable steps.

(2) A person's appropriation of property belonging to another may be dishonest notwithstanding that he is willing to pay for the property.

The leading authority on dishonesty, *R. v. Ghosh* [1982] Q.B. 1053, 75 Cr.App.R. 154, CA, applies to theft as to other *Theft Act* offences (see *ante*, § 21–2b). Section 2(1), however, only applies to theft; its significance in the context of *Ghosh* is submitted to be as follows: if the jury conclude that the defendant had, or may have had, one of the beliefs set out in paragraphs (a), (b) and (c) of section 2(1), then they must as a matter of law answer the first of the two questions in *Ghosh* in favour of the defendant. See also *R. v. Woolven*, *post*, § 21–28. **21–24**

[The next paragraph is § 21–28.]

Claim of right

To come within the terms of section 2(1)(a), the defendant must believe that in law he has the right to deprive the other of his property: *R. v. Bernhard*, 26 Cr.App.R. 137, CCA; *Harris v. Harrison* [1963] Crim.L.R. 497, DC. It is immaterial that there exists no basis in law for such belief: *Bernhard*, *ante*; *R. v. Turner (No. 2)*, 55 Cr.App.R. 336, CA. Belief in moral right is no defence: *Harris v. Harrison*, *ante*. In *Bernhard*, the court approved the following passage in Stephen's *History of the Criminal Law of England*: **21–28**

"Fraud is inconsistent with a claim of right made in good faith to do the act complained of. A man who takes possession of property which he really believes to be his own does not take it fraudulently, however unfounded his claim may be. This, if not the only, is nearly the only case in which ignorance of the law affects the legal character of acts done under its influence" (Vol. III, p. 124).

As to the importance of referring to section 2(1)(a) where a claim of right is raised: see *R. v. Falconer-Atlee*, 58 Cr.App.R. 348, CA. In *R. v. Woolven*, 77 Cr.App.R. 231, CA, it was said that a direction on dishonesty based on *Ghosh* (*ante*, § 21–24) would be likely to cover all occasions where a section 2(1)(a) type direction might otherwise have been desirable. *Woolven*, however, was a case on section 15 of the Act (since repealed) to which section 2 did not apply. In cases involving an allegation of theft *simpliciter*, burglary or robbery, it is submitted that it would still be necessary to give a section 2(1)(a) direction because, if the case comes within that provision, the jury must as a matter of law determine the first of the two questions in *Ghosh* in the defendant's favour. See also *R. v. Wootton* [1990] Crim.L.R. 201, CA, and *R. v. Wood* [1999] 5 *Archbold News* 2, CA.

Belief in consent

A defendant's "belief that he would have the other's consent" must be an honest belief in a true consent, honestly obtained: *per* Megaw L.J. in *R. v. Lawrence*, 55 Cr.App.R. 73 at 80, CA. As to the situation where the other is a company of which the defendant is in total control, see *post*, § 21–35. **21–29**

Belief that property has been abandoned

Property that has been abandoned cannot be stolen (see *post*, § 21–64). If property had not been abandoned, but the defendant believed that it had, he cannot be convicted of theft, whether his belief was reasonable or unreasonable. He would not be acting dishonestly: *R. v. Small*, 86 Cr.App.R. 170. The relevance of reasonableness of the belief is as to whether it was actually held: *ibid*. Where the prosecution case is that it was patently unreasonable for the defendant to have believed the property to have been abandoned, the jury should be specifically reminded that even an unreasonable belief may nevertheless be an honest one: *R. v. Wood* [2002] 4 *Archbold News* 3, CA; and where the sole question for the jury was as to the genuineness of the defendant's belief as to the factual situation, not as to the ordinary person's idea of honesty, the giving of a *Ghosh* direction (*ante*) was inappropriate and liable to confuse the jury: *ibid*. **21–30**

(c) *"Appropriates"*

Theft Act 1968, s.3

3.—(1) Any assumption by a person of the rights of an owner amounts to an appropriation, **21–31**

and this includes, where he has come by the property (innocently or not) without stealing it, any later assumption of a right to it by keeping or dealing with it as owner.

(2) Where property or a right or interest in property is or purports to be transferred for value to a person acting in good faith, no later assumption by him of rights which he believed himself to be acquiring shall, by reason of any defect in the transferor's title amount to theft of the property.

Any assumption of the rights of the owner

21–32 In order to constitute an "appropriation" within section 3(1) of the *Theft Act* 1968, it is not necessary to demonstrate an assumption by the accused of *all* the owner's rights; it is enough for the prosecution to show the assumption of *any* of the rights of the owner of the goods in question: *R. v. Morris* [1984] A.C. 320, HL, *per* Lord Roskill at 331. That dictum was specifically approved by the House of Lords in the majority opinion delivered by Lord Keith in *R. v. Gomez* [1993] A.C. 442 at 458.

In *R. v. Pitham and Hehl*, 65 Cr.App.R. 45, CA, it was held that the definition of theft in section 1(1) of the *Theft Act* 1968 comprised a dishonest appropriation, "appropriation" being defined in section 3(1), the final words of that subsection being words of inclusion, and the general words at the beginning of that subsection being wide enough to cover *any* assumption by a person of the rights of an owner. In that case, M, who knew that a particular householder was in prison, took P and H to the house in order to sell them some of the furniture. P and H, having been convicted of handling stolen goods, appealed on the ground that their handling was "in the course of the stealing", and that, therefore, they could not be guilty of the offence contrary to section 22(1) of the *Theft Act* 1968 (*post*, § 21–270). It was held that M had assumed the rights of the owner within section 3(1) when he took P and H to the house and showed them the furniture and invited them to buy what they wanted, and at that moment he appropriated the goods to himself; thus there was no question of P and H dealing with the goods "in the course of the stealing".

21–32a Although assumption of *any* of the rights of an owner amounts to appropriation, there must still be a taking or assumption of one or more of such rights. The word appropriation in isolation is an objective description of the act done, irrespective of the mental state of either the owner or the accused: *R. v. Gomez*, *ante*, at 495, *per* Lord Browne-Wilkinson.

21–32b This dictum was referred to approvingly in *R. v. Gallasso*, 98 Cr.App.R. 284, CA, in which it was said that whilst it is no answer that the owner consented (*post*), neither does a dishonest motive turn an action which is not an appropriation into an appropriation. However, it is difficult to reconcile the actual decision in *Gallasso* with *Gomez*. The appellant was a nurse who had been in charge of the finances of a number of her severely mentally handicapped patients. She was the sole signatory on their trust accounts. In the case of one patient, she had opened a second bank account in his name. When a substantial cheque arrived, she paid it into that account. Thereafter she withdrew money therefrom on a regular basis. She was charged, *inter alia*, with theft of the cheque. The conviction was quashed because her conduct did not constitute an appropriation of the cheque. It is submitted with respect that this overlooks the essence of the decision in *Gomez*, which was to underline that the 1968 Act refers to an "appropriation" not a "misappropriation"; the protection for the defendant lies in the overriding requirement that the appropriation is dishonest. It was because of a series of decisions of the courts in the years following *Lawrence* (*post*) which approached the interpretation of the Act as if the word was "misappropriation" that there was so much confusion, which, it was to be hoped, had been eliminated by the decision in *Gomez*. *Gallasso* threatens to reintroduce the former muddle. As to the significance of use of the word "appropriation" as opposed to "misappropriation", see the speech of Lord Browne-Wilkinson in *Gomez* (*ante*, at p. 495).

Appropriation and consent

21–33 Section 1(1) of the 1968 Act is not to be construed as though it contained the words "without the consent of the owner", and accordingly it is not necessary for the prosecution to prove that the appropriation was without the owner's consent: *Lawrence v. Metropolitan Police Commr* [1972] A.C. 626, HL. *Lawrence* must be regarded as authoritative and correct, and there is no question of it now being right to depart from it: *R. v. Gomez*, *ante*.

In *Lawrence*, the House of Lords considered the question of the extent to which consent was relevant to the issue of whether or not there had been an appropriation within the meaning of section 3. Viscount Dilhorne, delivering an opinion in which the other Law Lords concurred, said:

> "Section 3(1) states that any assumption by a person of the rights of an owner amounts to an appropriation. ... Section 2(1) provides, *inter alia*, that a person's appropriation of property belonging to another is not to be regarded as dishonest if he appropriates the property in the belief that he would have the other's consent if the other knew of the appropriation and the circumstances of it. *A fortiori*, a person is not to be regarded as acting dishonestly if he appropriates another's property believing that with full knowledge of the circumstances that other person has in fact agreed to the appropriation. ... When Megaw L.J. said that if there was true consent, the essential element of dishonesty was not established, I understand him to have meant this. Belief or the absence of belief that the owner had with such knowledge consented to the appropriation is relevant to the issue of dishonesty, not to the question whether or not there has been an appropriation. That may occur even though the owner has permitted or consented to the property being taken" (at p. 632).

In consequence of the subsequent decision of the House of Lords in *R. v. Morris* **21–34**
[1984] A.C. 320, there was for several years confusion as to the status of the decision in *Lawrence*. In *Morris*, the House of Lords acknowledged that there could be theft although the owner of the property in question had consented to the acts done by the defendant, but decided that to be within the *Theft Act* 1968 an appropriation had to be an unauthorised appropriation.

In *R. v. Gomez*, *ante*, the House of Lords reviewed its two earlier decisions and concluded that *Lawrence* must be regarded as authoritative and correct, and that there is no question of it now being right to depart from it. Lord Keith stated (at p. 464) that *R. v. Skipp* [1975] Crim.L.R. 114, CA, and *R. v. Fritschy* [1985] Crim.L.R. 745, CA, were inconsistent with *Lawrence* and were wrongly decided. However, *Gomez* effectively overrules all of those cases which proceeded upon the basis that appropriation required an act not authorised by or consented to by the owner. These include *R. v. Meech* [1974] Q.B. 549, 58 Cr.App.R. 74, CA; *Kaur v. Chief Constable of Hampshire*, 72 Cr.App.R. 359, DC; and *Eddy v. Niman*, 73 Cr.App.R. 237, DC.

Consequences of the approach in R. v. Gomez

Gifts

Appropriation includes acquisition as a gift; belief or lack of belief that the owner **21–34a**
consented to the appropriation is relevant only to the issue of dishonesty: *R. v. Hinks* [2001] 2 A.C. 241, HL, where the relevant question for the jury was whether the donor was so mentally incapable that the defendant herself realised that ordinary and decent people would regard it as dishonest to accept the gift from him. The House of Lords rejected the argument that the word "appropriates" should be interpreted as if the word "unlawfully" preceded it so that only an act which is unlawful under the general law can be an appropriation:

> "If the law is restated by adopting a narrower definition of appropriation, the outcome is likely to place beyond the reach of the criminal law dishonest persons who should be found guilty of theft. The suggested revisions would unwarrantably restrict the scope of the law of theft and complicate the fair and effective prosecution of theft. In my view the law as settled in *Lawrence* and *Gomez* does not demand the suggested revision. Those decisions can be applied by judges and juries in a way which, absent human error, does not result in injustice. ... In practice the mental requirements of theft are an adequate protection against injustice" (*per* Lord Steyn at pp. 1600, 1601).

Appropriation of company assets

In *Gomez*, Lord Browne-Wilkinson, in a speech with which the majority concurred, **21–35**
said:

"Where a company is accused of a crime, the acts and intentions of those who are the directing minds and will of the company are to be attributed to the company. That is not the law where the charge is that those who are the directing minds and will have themselves committed a crime against the company: see *Attorney-General's Reference (No. 2 of 1982)*, 78 Cr.App.R. 131, applying *Belmont Finance Corporation Ltd v. Williams Furniture Ltd* [1979] Ch. 250.

In any event, your Lordships' decision in this case, re-establishing as it does the decision in *Lawrence*, renders the whole question of consent by the company irrelevant. Whether or not those controlling the company consented or purported to consent to the abstraction of the company's property by the accused, he will have appropriated the property of the company. The question will be whether the other necessary elements are present, *viz.*, was such appropriation dishonest and was it done with the necessary intention of permanently depriving the company of such property?" (at p. 496).

Lord Browne-Wilkinson went on to approve the concession made by counsel (that there had been an appropriation) in *Att.-Gen.'s Reference (No. 2 of 1982)*, *ante*, and the decision in both that case and *R. v. Phillipou*, 89 Cr.App.R. 290, CA; *R. v. Roffel* [1985] V.R. 511, and *R. v. McHugh and Tringham*, 88 Cr.App.R. 385, CA, were specifically disapproved.

Loss unnecessary

21–35a Where an official in control of government building contracts awarded a contract to a company in which he had an undisclosed interest, the fact that there was no evidence that the price paid under the contract was excessive was no answer to a charge of theft under the British Virgin Islands criminal code (modelled on the *Theft Act* 1968, ss.1–6); the disbursement of funds held to the order of the government constituted an appropriation of those funds, and the only question was whether the official had acted dishonestly: *Wheatley v. Commr of Police of the British Virgin Islands* [2006] 1 W.L.R. 1683, PC.

Later assumptions of a right of the owner

21–36 There may be an "appropriation" within section 3(1) not only by a bailee (see *Rogers v. Arnott* [1960] 2 Q.B. 244, DC), but also by an innocent finder or by a person who acquires property through the mistake of another. Similarly, the dishonest appropriation by a parent of property brought home by a child under the age of criminal responsibility (see *post*, § 21–301) will amount to theft. As to appropriation by handlers of stolen goods, see *post*, § 21–283.

Where an agent in purported exercise of his authority dishonestly sells the principal's property to a third party at an undervalue, he clearly exceeds his authority and thereby assumes the rights of the owner in a way which amounts to an appropriation: *Att.-Gen. of Hong Kong v. Nai-Keung* [1987] 1 W.L.R. 1339, PC.

21–37 The possession of goods for a period may give rise to an inference that the possessor has assumed the rights of an owner: *Broom v. Crowther, The Times*, May 15, 1984, DC. The appellant was convicted of theft of property which had been previously stolen and which he had bought at a considerable undervalue. The justices found as a fact that when he bought it, he suspected it was stolen, and therefore concluded he was not a bona fide purchaser in good faith and that section 3(2) did not protect him. Subsequently, he found out that the property was stolen and a week after that, he was arrested. The justices found that during that week he had simply kept the property, he had not used it and had not made up his mind what to do with it. Goff L.J., delivering a judgment with which Mann J. agreed, said:

"I have no doubt that there may be cases in which having regard to all the circumstances of the case and the fact that an accused person has kept goods which have been stolen for a period of time after he has discovered that they are stolen, the inference by the court will properly be that he was keeping them as owner."

On the facts found, however, the court concluded that during the week since he found out that the property was stolen he had not assumed a right to keep it as owner. (*NOTE: The Times* report is inaccurate in that it suggests that the appellant had bought the property in good faith.)

Innocent purchasers

By virtue of section 3(2) of the Act (*ante*, § 21–31), a bona fide purchaser for value of stolen goods, who subsequently discovers them to be stolen, does not commit theft if he keeps them for himself, sells them or otherwise deals with them: *R. v. Wheeler*, 92 Cr.App.R. 279, CA. But see section 24A of the *Theft Act* 1968, *post*, §§ 21–323a *et seq.*: there is no exemption for the bona fide purchaser who dishonestly retains a wrongful credit, although the prosecution still has to prove dishonesty. **21–38**

[The next paragraph is § 21–42.]

Appropriation as a continuing act

Before *R. v. Gomez*, *ante*, §§ 21–32a, 21–34, the authorities indicated that an act of appropriation did not suddenly cease; it may be a continuous act and it is for the jury to decide whether or not the act of appropriation has finished: *R. v. Hale*, 68 Cr.App.R. 415, CA (*post*, § 21–100). In *R. v. Gregory*, 77 Cr.App.R. 41, CA, which was in a sense a mirror image of the situation in *R. v. Pitham and Hehl* (*ante*, § 21–32), the defendant was convicted of burglary upon the basis that someone else had originally burgled the premises and he had gone there as a receiver. It was argued, relying on *Pitham and Hehl*, that the appropriation was complete and therefore he could only have been convicted of handling stolen goods. The Court of Appeal rejected this argument, saying that not only may an "appropriation" be a continuous act but there may be more than one appropriation. **21–42**

The effect of *Gomez* on the question whether appropriation was a continuing act was considered in *R. v. Atakpu*, 98 Cr.App.R. 254, CA. The court stated that on a strict reading of *Gomez*, any dishonest assumption of the rights of the owner made with the necessary intention constituted theft, which left little room for a continuous course of action. However, such restriction and rigidity might lead to technical anomalies and injustice, and the court preferred to leave it to the common sense of the jury to decide that an appropriation could continue for so long as the thief could sensibly be regarded as in the act of stealing, or, in more understandable words, so long as he was "on the job". As the matter was not strictly necessary for their decision, the court specifically left the question open for further argument. For a case in which *Atakpu* was considered in relation to theft of money by means of a computer, see *R. v. Governor of Brixton Prison, ex p. Levin* [1997] 1 Cr.App.R. 335, DC: *post*, § 21–45a.

What the court did decide in *Atakpu* was that, once goods have been stolen, they cannot be appropriated again within section 3(1) by the same thief exercising the same or other rights of ownership over them. *Aliter*, if the goods have been restored to lawful possession or custody (see *Metropolitan Police Commr v. Streeter*, 71 Cr.App.R. 113, DC, *per* Ackner L.J. at p. 119). Similarly, if the goods are stolen from the original thief, it is submitted that a re-taking of the goods by him would be a second offence by him.

Appropriation through the act of an innocent agent

Property may be appropriated through the acts of an innocent agent: *R. v. Stringer*, 94 Cr.App.R. 13, CA. As to appropriation by children under the age of 10, see *post*, § 21–301. **21–43**

Deceiving an owner into doing something with his own property does not in itself amount to an appropriation of the property: *R. v. Briggs* [2004] 1 Cr.App.R. 34, CA.

Where appropriation takes place

Where property is appropriated outside the jurisdiction no offence is committed within the jurisdiction: *R. v. Atakpu*, *ante*, § 21–42. There is a conflict of authority as between *R. v. Tomsett* [1985] Crim.L.R. 369, CA, and *R. v. Governor of Pentonville Prison, ex p. Osman*, 90 Cr.App.R. 281, DC (followed in *R. v. Ngan* [1998] 1 Cr.App.R. 331, CA) as to whether the courts of England and Wales would have jurisdiction where the property appropriated was outside the jurisdiction, but the act constituting the appropriation was done within the jurisdiction. It is submitted that, having **21–44** regard to *R. v. Smith (Wallace Duncan) (No. 4)* [2004] 2 Cr.App.R. 17, CA, in which it was held that where a substantial measure of the activities constituting a crime takes place within the jurisdiction, then the courts of England and Wales have jurisdiction to try the crime, save only where it can seriously be argued on a reasonable view that these activities should, on the basis of international comity, be dealt with by another country, the courts are now likely to take the view that it would be sufficient to found jurisdiction that either the property is situated in, or the act assuming the rights of the owner is done within, the jurisdiction. See also *R. v. Governor of Brixton Prison, ex p. Levin*, *post*, § 21–45a.

As to jurisdiction generally, see *ante*, §§ 2–33 *et seq*. Theft is a "Group A" offence within Part I of the *CJA* 1993; as to the effect of this on the jurisdiction of the courts in England and Wales, see *ante*, §§ 2–37 *et seq*.

Appropriation of choses in action

21–45 As to choses in action generally, see *post*, § 21–49.

Where a person steals monies held in a bank account or an agreed overdraft facility by means of appropriating a cheque, then that person may be charged with theft of a chose in action, namely, the monies held in the account or the overdraft facility: *R. v. Kohn*, 69 Cr.App.R. 395, CA. Similarly, where a person receives a cheque from another which he then presents and which is honoured, he causes the other's credit balance to be diminished and thereby appropriates it; and if he is acting dishonestly he may be convicted of theft: *R. v. Williams (Roy)* [2001] 1 Cr.App.R. 23, CA (following *Kohn*).

It is inappropriate to charge a person with theft of the cheque form, for there will be no intention permanently to deprive the drawer of the cheque form, which would on presentation for payment be returned to the drawer via his bank: *R. v. Preddy and Slade*; *R. v. Dhillon* [1996] A.C. 815, HL, *post*, § 21–78.

In *ex p. Osman*, *ante*, it was held that a theft of funds in a bank account is complete when a cheque is dishonestly drawn on the account without authority. The theft is complete in law even though it might not be complete in fact until the account has been debited. It would not matter if the account was never in fact debited. The court preferred the direction of the trial judge in *R. v. Wille*, 86 Cr.App.R. 296, which was approved by the Court of Appeal (to the effect that if a person drew a cheque on an account on which he had no authority to draw, the act of drawing the cheque and issuing it constituted an appropriation of the debt owed by the bank to the account holder) to the contrary view expressed, *obiter*, in *Kohn*, *ante*. In *R. v. Hilton* [1997] 2 Cr.App.R. 445, CA, it was held that appropriation takes place when a person does an act, such as faxing instructions or signing a cheque, which causes a transfer to be made and the offence of theft could be committed even though the appropriation had the effect of destroying the property. *Hilton* was distinguished in *R. v. Briggs* (*ante*, § 21–43), where the defendant did not have any direct control of the bank account and had instead deceived the victim into giving instructions for a payment to be made.

In *R. v. Ngan*, *ante*, it was held that where a person, knowing that his bank account in England had been mistakenly credited with a large sum of money, signs a blank cheque and sends it to his accomplice in Scotland who is aware of the amount of the mistaken credit and completes the cheque, as the account holder anticipates, in an amount which can only be paid by reference to the mistaken credit, and "presents" the cheque for payment in Scotland, the account holder is not guilty of theft because the appropriation has taken place outside the jurisdiction. (For a criticism of this decision as being out of line with both *R. v. Wille* and *ex p. Osman*, see *Criminal Law Week* 1997/28/21; and as to whether it now matters that the appropriation occurred outside the jurisdiction if the property was within the jurisdiction, see *ante*.)

It is immaterial that the end result of the transaction may be a legal nullity, for it is not possible to read into section 3(1) any requirement that the assumption of rights there envisaged should have a legally efficacious result: *Chan Man-sin v. Att.-Gen. of Hong Kong* [1988] 1 W.L.R. 196, PC.

Where a person writes a cheque supported by a cheque guarantee card, knowing that there are insufficient funds in the account to meet the cheque and no overdraft arrangement, he is not guilty of theft of the funds of the bank, either when the cheque is handed to the payee or when it is presented for payment, because he has not assumed the rights of an owner over the bank's funds: *R. v. Navvabi*, 83 Cr.App.R. 271, CA. Delivery of the cheque and use of the guarantee card did no more than give the payee a contractual right to be paid a specified sum from the bank's funds on presentation of the cheque. That was not itself an assumption of the rights of the bank to that part of the bank's funds to which the sum specified in the cheque corresponded.

Theft of a credit by means of a computer

In *R. v. Governor of Brixton Prison, ex p. Levin* [1997] 1 Cr.App.R. 335, DC, the court held, distinguishing *ex p. Osman, ante* (telexing of instructions), that where a person by using a computer terminal in one country operates a computer in another country, he may be said to be acting in the second country. (This aspect of the court's decision was not subject of appeal to the House of Lords ([1997] A.C. 741).) **21–46**

Other examples of appropriation

Mere forcible tugging at a handbag in an effort to release it from its owner's grasp is an act of appropriation: *Corcoran v. Anderton*, 71 Cr.App.R. 104, DC. **21–47**

(d) *"Property"*

Theft Act 1968, s.4

4.—(1) "Property" includes money and all other property, real or personal, including things in action and other intangible property. **21–48**

(2) A person cannot steal land, or things forming part of land and severed from it by him or by his directions, except in the following cases, that is to say—

(a) when he is a trustee or personal representative, or is authorised by power of attorney, or as liquidator of a company, or otherwise, to sell or dispose of land belonging to another, and he appropriates the land or anything forming part of it by dealing with it in breach of the confidence reposed in him; or

(b) when he is not in possession of the land and appropriates anything forming part of the land by severing it or causing it to be severed, or after it has been severed; or

(c) when, being in possession of the land under a tenancy, he appropriates the whole or part of any fixture or structure let to be used with the land.

For purposes of this subsection "land" does not include incorporeal hereditaments; "tenancy" means a tenancy for years or any less period and includes an agreement for such a tenancy, but a person who after the end of a tenancy remains in possession as statutory tenant or otherwise is to be treated as having possession under the tenancy, and "let" shall be construed accordingly.

(3) A person who picks mushrooms growing wild on any land, or who picks flowers, fruit or foliage from a plant growing wild on any land, does not (although not in possession of the land) steal what he picks, unless he does it for reward or for sale or other commercial purpose.

For purposes of this subsection "mushroom" includes any fungus, and "plant" includes any shrub or tree.

(4) Wild creatures, tamed or untamed, shall be regarded as property; but a person cannot steal a wild creature not tamed nor ordinarily kept in captivity, or the carcase of any such creature, unless either it has been reduced into possession by or on behalf of another person and possession of it has not since been lost or abandoned, or another person is in course of reducing it into possession.

Things or choses in action

A chose in action is a legal expression used to describe all personal rights over property which can only be claimed or enforced by action, and not by taking physical possession: *per* Channel J. in *Torkington v. Magee* [1902] 2 K.B. 427 at 429, DC. It does not include a right of action such as a right to recover damages for breach of contract or a legal right to recover damages arising out of an assault: *per* Rigby L.J. in *May v. Lane* (1894) 64 L.J.Q.B. 236 at 238, CA. A debt is a chose in action. In respect of bank and **21–49** similar accounts, monies paid into the account belong to the bank, but the bank owes a debt (a chose in action) to the crediting customer, which it undertakes to repay on demand: *Joachimson v. Swiss Bank Corporation* [1921] 3 K.B. 110 at 127.

21–50 In *R. v. Kohn*, 69 Cr.App.R. 395, CA, K drew cheques on the bank account of P. Ltd, of which he was a director, in favour of various third parties. The cheques, however, were intended for the benefit of K rather than the company and he accordingly was charged, in relation to each of a number of such payments, with theft of a chose in action, namely a debt owed to P. Ltd by the bank. Some of the drawings occurred when the account was in credit, some when it was overdrawn but within the agreed facility, and one drawing when the account was over the agreed limit. It was held that where the account was either in credit or overdrawn within the agreed limit, the bank had an obligation to meet cheques drawn on it which could be enforced by action. The customer therefore had a right of property, a chose in action. As to the count which related to the period when the agreed overdraft limit was exceeded, there was then no relationship of debtor and creditor, even notionally, and so the bank had no duty to the customer to meet the cheque: even if it did so as a matter of grace, that did not retrospectively create any personal right of property in the customer and did not create any duty retrospectively in the bank. The conviction on that count was quashed. The need to establish an existing, as opposed to a contingent, liability was emphasised in *R. v. Doole* [1985] Crim.L.R. 450, CA.

Where an apparent credit balance on a bank account is created by fraud this will not be property within section 4(1) because it is not a thing in action: any action to enforce the apparent liability would be capable of immediate defeasance as soon as the fraud is pleaded: *R. v. Thompson (Michael)*, 79 Cr.App.R. 191, CA. This situation is now covered by section 1 of the *Fraud Act* 2006 (*post*, § 21–356).

Intangible property

21–51 Confidential information *per se* does not come within the definition of "property" in section 4: *Oxford v. Moss*, 68 Cr.App.R. 183, DC. In *Att.-Gen. of Hong Kong v. Nai-Keung* [1987] 1 W.L.R. 1339, PC, it was held that export quotas which were transferable for value on a temporary or permanent basis were "property". Although they were not things in action, they did come within the words "other intangible property".

Gas, water and electricity

21–52 At common law a thing could not be larcenable unless (a) it was tangible, (b) it was movable, (c) it was of some value, and (d) it had an owner (Russ. Cr., 12th ed., 1964, pp. 887–891). However, even under common law, it was held that there was nothing in the nature of gas to prevent it being the subject of larceny: *R. v. White* (1853) 3 C. & K. 363. See also *R. v. Firth* (1869) 11 Cox 234 (*ante*, § 1–143a). Water supplied by a water company and standing in the consumer's pipes, could also be the subject of larceny at common law: *Ferens v. O'Brien* (1883) 11 Q.B.D. 21.

Electricity is subject to specific statutory provisions: see section 13 of the *Theft Act* 1968, *post*, § 21–164. It is not appropriated by switching on a current and could not be described as "property" within the meaning of section 4: *Low v. Blease* [1975] Crim.L.R. 513, DC. As to the dishonest obtaining of electronic communications services, see the *Communications Act* 2003, s.125 (*post*, § 25–363).

Plants

21–53 Although section 4(3) excludes flowers, fruits, foliage or mushrooms, growing wild on any land, from the definition of property which may be stolen, unless done for reward or sale or other commercial purpose, the complete uprooting of a plant other than a mushroom will amount to theft.

Wild creatures

21–54 The exemption in section 4(4) of the *Theft Act* 1968 will not apply to any creature which has been tamed or which is ordinarily kept in captivity. The taking or destroying of fish are made offences punishable on summary conviction only: s.32 and Sched. 1. The poaching of deer and related offences are covered by the *Deer Act* 1991: see s.1 thereof.

Wild creatures can only be stolen if there is sufficient evidence of a reduction into possession: *R. v. Howlett* [1968] Crim.L.R. 222, CA.

Corpses

At common law there is no property in a corpse: 2 East P.C. 652; *Dobson v. North Tyneside Health Authority* [1997] 1 W.L.R. 596, CA (Civ. Div.). Larceny could only be committed in respect of things which were the subject of property, and, therefore, there could be no larceny of a corpse. In *R. v. Kelly and Lindsay* [1999] Q.B. 621, CA, the common law rule was confirmed, subject to the exception (following *Doodeward v. Spence* (1908) 6 C.L.R. 406) that if a corpse or part thereof had undergone a process of skill with the object of preserving it, for example for the purpose of medical or scientific examination, it thereby acquired a usefulness or value and was capable of becoming property and of being stolen. The court said the common law did not stand still and it might be that in the future a court would hold that body parts were property even without the acquisition of different attributes, if, for example, they were required for use in an organ transplant. **21–55**

Identifying property

There must be some specific property which is alleged to have been stolen. It is sufficient, however, to allege the appropriation of an unascertained part of an ascertained whole. In *R. v. Tideswell* [1905] 2 K.B. 273, CCR, D was in the habit of buying from a company portions of the accumulated ashes from its works. The only agreement between the company's managing director and D was as to the price per ton, D being free to take as much as he wanted, upon the understanding that the amount of the purchase in each case should be determined as ascertained by the company's weigher. It was the latter's duty to enter in a book a record of the weights of the ashes purchased: he fraudulently, and in collusion with D, delivered to D 32 tons 13 cwt of the ashes and entered the weight in the book as being 31 tons 3 cwt only. It was held that D had been rightly indicted for larceny of 1 ton 10 cwt. **21–56**

> "It was contended that what took place was an arrangement whereby the property passed to [D]. If there had been a completed contract … covering all the goods in the trucks, then no doubt the property would have passed, and no subsequent fraud would make the receipt of the goods larceny. The offence in such a case would be only a conspiracy to defraud the sellers of part of the price. But here there was no intention to pass the property except in such goods as should be ascertained by the weighing—that is to say, in the smaller quantity. Consequently there was a larceny of the balance" (*per* Kennedy J. at p. 278).

Tideswell was applied in *Pilgram v. Rice-Smith*, 65 Cr.App.R. 142, DC, in which a shop assistant (A) and a customer (B) had pursued a fraudulent scheme whereunder A, who worked at the meat counter in a supermarket, purported to sell B a quantity of sliced meat. The price A marked on the wrapper was 83½p less than the true price. B eventually paid one sum at the checkout for all the articles including the meat. A and B were charged with the theft of meat valued at 83½p. The court held that since A had no authority from her employers to sell the meat at an undervalue, and since the fraud had operated from before the meat had been handed over the counter to B, the purported sale was a nullity. Since no contract of sale had been entered into in respect of the meat, it would have been unobjectionable if the defendants had been charged and convicted in respect of the theft of the whole of the meat. **21–57**

(e) *"Belonging to another"*

Theft Act 1968, s.5

5.—(1) Property shall be regarded as belonging to any person having possession or control of it, or having in it any proprietary right or interest (not being an equitable interest arising only from an agreement to transfer or grant an interest). **21–58**

(2) Where property is subject to a trust, the persons to whom it belongs shall be regarded

as including any person having a right to enforce the trust, and an intention to defeat the trust shall be regarded accordingly as an intention to deprive of the property any person having that right.

(3) Where a person receives property from or on account of another, and is under an obligation to the other to retain and deal with that property or its proceeds in a particular way, the property or proceeds shall be regarded (as against him) as belonging to the other.

(4) Where a person gets property by another's mistake, and is under an obligation to make restoration (in whole or in part) of the property or its proceeds or of the value thereof, then to the extent of that obligation the property or proceeds shall be regarded (as against him) as belonging to the person entitled to restoration, and an intention not to make restoration shall be regarded accordingly as an intention to deprive that person of the property or proceeds.

(5) Property of a corporation sole shall be regarded as belonging to the corporation notwithstanding a vacancy in the corporation.

Property belonging to any person

21–59 In *Lawrence v. Metropolitan Police Commr* [1972] A.C. 626, HL, Viscount Dilhorne said that the words "belonging to another" in section 1(1) signify no more than that, at the time of the appropriation or the obtaining, the property belonged to another with the words "belonging to another" having the extended meaning given by section 5. Considerations as to whether ownership passed from the victim to the defendant as a result of the transaction were therefore irrelevant.

21–60 Where property has already passed to the defendant at the time of the alleged act of appropriation, there can be no question of its theft: see *Edwards v. Ddin* [1976] 1 W.L.R. 942, DC (driving away from petrol station without paying for petrol where attendant had filled up tank after being asked to do so by motorist); and *Corcoran v. Whent* [1977] Crim.L.R. 52, DC (making off from restaurant without paying for meal). Such conduct is now covered by section 3 of the *Theft Act* 1978, *post*, § 21–349. In the case of a self-service petrol station, provided that the dishonest intent has been formed at the time the petrol is put in the tank, the facts will plainly amount to theft: *R. v. McHugh*, 64 Cr.App.R. 92, CA.

21–61 In *Davies v. Leighton*, 68 Cr.App.R. 4, DC, it was held that a customer who, in a self-service store, had acquired possession of fruit from an assistant who had weighed and bagged it at the customer's request, did not acquire the property in it before paying the price for it at the check-out. Giving the leading judgment, Ackner J. said that the law is well settled in relation to purchases in supermarkets (referring to *Lacis v. Cashmarts* [1969] 2 Q.B. 400, DC). The intention of the parties is the fundamental issue, and, in the case of a supermarket, the intention of the parties is clearly that the property shall not pass until the price is paid.

His Lordship also referred approvingly to a dictum of Winn L.J. in *Martin v. Puttick* [1968] 1 Q.B. 82, DC, to the effect that the counter assistant's authority is limited to wrapping and handing over the goods and does not extend to dealing with any transfer of property in the goods from the shop to the customer. Ackner J. pointed out that there was no reference to the assistant being in a managerial or other special category "where a special situation might possibly arise" (at p. 8).

21–62 In *R. v. Walker* [1984] Crim.L.R. 112, CA, the defendant sold a video recorder. Because it did not work satisfactorily it was returned to him for repair. The purchaser subsequently issued a summons claiming the price of the recorder, as the "return of money paid for defective goods". Two days later the defendant sold the recorder. He was charged with theft. The Court of Appeal held that it was incumbent on the judge in such a case to give a careful direction as to the law relating to the passing of property and rejection of goods under the *Sale of Goods Act* 1979.

In *Att.-Gen.'s Reference (No. 2 of 1982)* [1984] Q.B. 624, 78 Cr.App.R. 131, CA, the court held that a person in total control of a limited liability company, by reason of his shareholding and directorship, or two or more such persons acting in concert, were capable in law of stealing the property of the company. The court rejected a submission that since they were the sole owners of the company and, through their shareholding, the sole owners of all its property, they could not in effect be charged with stealing from themselves: see also *ante*, § 21–35.

It has been held that a bribe received by an employee does not "belong to" his employer: *Powell v. MacRae* [1977] Crim.L.R. 571, DC (turnstile operator bribed to allow entry to stadium to person without ticket); but this must now be regarded as doubtful, see *Att.-Gen. of Hong Kong v. Reid* [1994] 1 A.C. 324, PC (dissapproving *Lister and Co. v. Stubbs* (1890) 45 Ch.D. 1, CA). **21–63**

In *R. v. Gilks*, 56 Cr.App.R. 734, CA, D placed a bet on several horses in a betting shop. His winnings amounted to £10.62. The bookmaker, believing that D had backed a certain successful horse when he had not, handed D £117.25. D was aware of the bookmaker's mistake but accepted the money and kept it. He was charged with stealing £106.63 from the bookmaker. It was held that property in the £106.63 never passed to D. Where a mistake resulted in the overpayment of a sum of money, the person accepting the overpayment with knowledge of the mistake was guilty of theft. For the proposition that property never passed, the court seemed to rely on *R. v. Middleton* (1893) L.R. 2 C.C.R. 38. It has been suggested (see the commentary on *Gilks* in [1972] Crim.L.R. 585, and Ormerod & Williams, *Smith's Law of Theft*, 9th ed., p. 102), that *Middleton*, a case itself the subject of much criticism, ought not to have been relied upon in *Gilks*, and that, in any event, its *ratio* was inapplicable because in that case the mistake was one of identity, either of the payee or of what was being paid, and that, whilst under the civil law such a mistake as to identity may prevent ownership from passing, there was no such mistake involved in *Gilks*. Therefore, there was nothing to prevent ownership from passing as it was undoubtedly the bookmaker's intention that property should pass. In any event, on the authority of *Lawrence v. Metropolitan Police Commr*, *ante*, § 21–59, and *R. v. Gomez*, *ante*, § 21–33, such a taking plainly constitutes an "appropriation". See also the *Theft Act* 1968, s.24A (dishonestly retaining a wrongful credit) (*post*, §§ 21–323b *et seq.*).

Abandoned property

Things of which the ownership has been abandoned are not capable of being stolen: *R. v. White*, 7 Cr.App.R. 266, CCA. **21–64**

In *Williams v. Phillips*, 41 Cr.App.R. 5, DC, dustmen employed by a corporation were convicted by justices of stealing goods from dustbins collected in the course of their duties. It was held that refuse put in a bin was not abandoned: it was the householder's property until it was taken away, when it became the corporation's property.

Treasure

The *Treasure Act* 1996 abolished treasure trove and replaced it with statutory provisions in relation to the ownership of treasure (s.4). Appropriation of treasure (defined in s.1) may amount to theft, provided all the ingredients are present. **21–65**

Owner unknown

There may be a conviction of theft of property belonging to a person unknown, provided it can be proved that the property must have belonged to someone and that the defendant knew it belonged to someone other than himself. That the property is stolen may be proved from circumstantial evidence: *R. v. Burton* (1854) Dears. 282; *R. v. Mockford* (1868) 11 Cox 16; *Noon v. Smith*, 49 Cr.App.R. 55, DC; *Sturrock v. DPP*, *The Times*, February 9, 1995, DC (a prosecution under section 12(5), *post*, § 21–141). See also *R. v. Sbarra*, 13 Cr.App.R. 118, CCA, and *R. v. Fuschillo*, 27 Cr.App.R. 193, CCA, both cases on receiving stolen goods (*post*, § 21–294). **21–66**

For a convincing argument that property which has not been abandoned, but which cannot be shown to have belonged to a particular person, certainly belongs to the Crown as *bona vacantia*, see the commentary by Sir John Smith Q.C. to *R. v. Sullivan and Ballion* [2002] Crim.L.R. 758, Crown Court (at Maidstone) (Aikens J.). See also the commentary at *Criminal Law Week* 2002/35/6.

"Possession or control"

See section 5(1), *ante*, § 21–58. **21–67**

There is no ground for qualifying the words "possession or control" in any way. It is sufficient if it is found that the person from whom the property is appropriated was at the time in fact in possession or control: *R. v. Turner (No. 2)*, 55 Cr.App.R. 336, CA. It is not necessary to prove that the person's possession or control was lawful: *R. v. Kelly and Lindsay* [1999] Q.B. 621, CA (at p. 631) (*ante*, § 21–55).

A person in control of a site, by excluding others from it, is prima facie also in control of articles on that site, it being immaterial that he was unconscious of their existence: *R. v. Woodman* [1974] Q.B. 754, 59 Cr.App.R. 200, CA.

"Any proprietary right or interest"

21–68 See section 5(1), *ante*, § 21–58.

Partners have a proprietary right in partnership property: *R. v. Bonner*, 54 Cr.App.R. 257, CA. Accordingly, provided all the other ingredients of theft are present, one partner can steal partnership property from another: *ibid*. The same applies to co-owners who are not partners.

Secret profits

21–69 A public house manager employed by brewers contracted with them to sell on their premises only goods supplied by them and to retain and deal with such sales for the brewers' benefit. He bought beer from a wholesaler and intended, by selling it to customers on the brewers' premises, to make a secret profit, as he had done for some time past. He was charged with stealing sums of money belonging to the brewers in respect of the secret profit from beer sales. The trial judge ruled that there was no case to answer. On a reference by the Attorney-General, it was held: (a) that the property in the form of money from beer sales over the counter was received by the manager not on account of the brewers but on his own account as a result of his private venture; so that while the manager was doubtless under a civil obligation to account to the brewers at least for the profit from beer sales, the argument for the Attorney-General based on section 5(3) (see *post*, §§ 21–71 *et seq.*) was misconceived; (b) that a person in a fiduciary position who uses that position to make a secret profit for which he will be held accountable is not a trustee of that secret profit and, therefore, does not come within section 5; and (c) that since the brewers would not have been able to sue the customers for the price of the beer, they could not be said to have a "proprietary interest" in the proceeds of sale or any part of it: *Att.-Gen.'s Reference (No. 1 of 1985)* [1986] Q.B. 491, 83 Cr.App.R. 70, CA.

21–70 The Court of Appeal further held that if, contrary to their view, section 5(1) does import the constructive trust into the *Theft Act* 1968, on the facts of the case the brewers still obtained no proprietary right or interest in any of the money. The reason for this particular ruling was that no trust will come into existence until the trust property is identifiable as a particular fund: here the secret profit element for which the manager would have been liable to account never had any identifiable separate existence.

In delivering the court's judgment, Lord Lane C.J. referred, among other authorities, to *Lister and Co. v. Stubbs*, *ante*, § 21–63, and to *R. v. Governor of Pentonville Prison, ex p. Tarling*, 70 Cr.App.R. 77, DC and HL, in which Lord Wilberforce said:

> "The transactions would ... appear, prima facie, to amount to cases of persons in a fiduciary capacity making a secret profit at the expense of their companies—conduct for which there exist classical remedies in equity. ... Breach of fiduciary duty, exorbitant profit-making, secrecy, failure to comply with the law as to company accounts ... are one thing: theft and fraud are others" (*per* Lord Lane C.J. at p. 110).

Lord Lane also said that the concept of theft, by importing the equitable doctrine of the constructive trust, is so abstruse and so far from ordinary people's understanding of what constitutes stealing that it should not amount to stealing.

This situation is now covered by sections 1 and 4 of the *Fraud Act* 2006 (fraud by abuse of position, *post*, § 21–359).

An obligation to retain and deal with property in a particular way

21–71 See section 5(3), *ante*, § 21–58.

The "obligation" must be a legal one, as opposed to a social or moral obligation: *R.*

v. Gilks, 56 Cr.App.R. 734, CA; *R. v. Hall (G.)* [1973] Q.B. 126, 56 Cr.App.R. 547, CA; *Wakeman v. Farrar* [1974] Crim.L.R. 136, DC; *R. v. Klineberg and Marsden* [1999] 1 Cr.App.R. 427, CA; and see also *Floyd v. DPP* [2000] Crim.L.R. 411, DC. The obligation of the defendant must be one of which he was aware: knowledge of an agent cannot be imputed to the principal for the purposes of the criminal law, whatever may be the position in civil law: *R. v. Wills*, 92 Cr.App.R. 297, CA.

The obligation can arise because the defendant has obtained the property by fraud, and holds it as constructive trustee for the person defrauded: *Re Holmes* [2005] 1 Cr.App.R. 16, DC, in which the remarks of Lord Lane C.J. in *Att.-Gen.'s Reference (No. 1 of 1985)*, *ante*, § 21–70, as to the undesirability of importing the concept of constructive trust into the law of theft were distinguished on the basis that the conduct in *Holmes* was far closer to the misappropriation of specific property entrusted to an accused than to the making of a secret profit in breach of a contract of employment, with which Lord Lane C.J. had been concerned.

The issue is frequently whether the accused in receiving money from a client, did so under an obligation to retain the money in a separate client account and not to mix it with his own money or that of his business. For cases on either side of the line, see *R. v. Hall*, *ante* (no evidence that travel agent expected by his clients to retain and deal with their money in a particular way), and *R. v. McHugh*, 97 Cr.App.R. 335, CA (investment money). In *McHugh*, the court said that a jury should be directed that section 5(3) only applies, where there is no written agreement, if both parties clearly understood that the investment or its proceeds was to be kept separate. In *Hall*, the court emphasised a number of general points.

(a) Each case turns on its own facts.
(b) Dishonesty should be present at the time of the appropriation.
(c) The judge's direction to the jury should contain a careful exposition of the subsection.
(d) Mixed questions of law and fact may call for consideration in deciding whether, in a particular case, the Crown has succeeded in establishing an "obligation" of the kind coming within section 5(3).

If the transaction is wholly in writing, it will be for the judge to direct the jury as to **21–72** the legal effect thereof: *ibid*. In any other case, if the facts relied upon by the prosecution are in dispute, the judge should direct the jury to make their findings as to the facts and should add that if they find certain facts, then, as a matter of law, the defendant was under a legal obligation to which section 5(3) applies: *R. v. Dubar* [1995] 1 Cr.App.R. 280, Ct-MAC, following *R. v. Mainwaring and Madders*, 74 Cr.App.R. 79, CA, and disapproving (on this point) *R. v. Hall*, *ante*, and *R. v. Hayes*, 64 Cr.App.R. 82, CA.

See also *Wakeman v. Farrar* [1974] Crim.L.R. 136, DC, *R. v. Brewster*, 69 Cr.App.R. 375, CA, *Davidge v. Bunnett* [1984] Crim.L.R. 297, DC, *R. v. Breaks and Huggan* [1998] Crim.L.R. 349, CA, and *Re Kumar* [2000] Crim.L.R. 504, DC. In *Brewster*, it appears that, despite the references to section 5(3), the decision that the property in question, insurance premiums, "belonged to another" did not depend upon the application of that subsection.

Although there must be a legal obligation, there need not be a legally enforceable one. That the obligation might have become impossible of performance or of enforcement on grounds of illegality or of public policy is irrelevant: *R. v. Meech* [1974] Q.B. 549, 58 Cr.App.R. 74, CA. The obligee would not have been able to enforce performance because of his own fraud. However, at the time of entering into the obligation, the defendant was unaware of the fraud; it seems the court regarded this feature as important and that the conclusion may, therefore, have been different had the defendant been aware from the outset of the fraud.

A person who collects money for charity is subject to an obligation in respect of the **21–73** money or its proceeds by reason of the donor's intention to give money to the charity which is sufficient to impose a trust; accordingly the property or proceeds is to be regarded as belonging to the beneficiaries: *R. v. Wain* [1995] 2 Cr.App.R. 660, CA, overruling *Lewis v. Lethridge* [1987] Crim.L.R. 59, DC.

The subsection may be applied, even where the recipient is throughout the legal owner of the property, if by agreement he recognises a legal obligation to retain and deal with the property in the interest and/or for the benefit of the transferor: *R. v. Arnold* [1997] 4 All E.R. 1, CA (for the facts, see *post*, § 21–78).

In *DPP v. Huskinson* (1988) 20 H.L.R. 562, DC, it was held that there was no legal obligation upon a recipient of housing benefit to use that benefit directly for payment for rent. It was given in the expectation that the recipient would use it to pay his rent as he had a legal obligation to his landlord to pay the rent, but there was not an obligation upon him to apply the cheque directly for the rent.

Property got by another's mistake

21–74 See section 5(4), *ante*, § 21–58.

The "obligation" to make restoration must be a legal one: *R. v. Gilks, ante*; *R. v. Hall (G.), ante*; *Att.-Gen.'s Reference (No. 1 of 1983)* [1985] Q.B. 182, 79 Cr.App.R. 288, CA. See also *ante*, § 21–71.

In *Att.-Gen.'s Reference (No. 1 of 1983), ante*, an overpayment had been made through the direct debiting system, thereby crediting the respondent's bank account with an extra £74 which her employer had mistakenly believed was due to her in respect of overtime. In the Crown Court and in the Court of Appeal it was assumed that her bank account was in credit. The Court of Appeal accordingly held that she had "got" property by another's mistake, the property being the debt owed to her by her bank, and that she had been under an obligation to make restoration, which was to be taken to mean the same as "make restitution", of the value thereof.

21–75 "Generally speaking the respondent, in these circumstances, is obliged to pay for a benefit received when the benefit has been given under a mistake on the part of the giver as to a material fact. The mistake must be as to a fundamental or essential fact and the payment must have been due to that fundamental or essential fact. The mistake here was that this [respondent] had been working on a day when she had been at home and not working at all. The authority for that proposition is to be found in *Norwich Union Fire Insurance Society Ltd v. Wm H. Price Ltd* [1934] A.C. 455" (*per* Lord Lane C.J., at pp. 189, 291–292).

Where the payee of a cheque exchanges that cheque with a third party for cash before the cheque is presented, the cash received represents the "proceeds" of the cheque for the purposes of section 5(4): *R. v. Davis (G.)*, 88 Cr.App.R. 346, CA. Where a person who is entitled to one cheque is sent two cheques by mistake, the prosecution, on a charge of theft of the proceeds of one cheque, is not obliged to identify the cheque to which the charge relates: *ibid*. See also the *Theft Act* 1968, s.24A (dishonestly retaining a wrongful credit) (*post*, §§ 21–323a *et seq.*).

(f) *"With the intention of permanently depriving the other of it"*

Theft Act 1968, s.6

21–76 **6.**—(1) A person appropriating property belonging to another without meaning the other permanently to lose the thing itself is nevertheless to be regarded as having the intention of permanently depriving the other of it if his intention is to treat the thing as his own to dispose of regardless of the other's rights; and a borrowing or lending of it may amount to so treating it if, but only if, the borrowing or lending is for a period and in circumstances making it equivalent to an outright taking or disposal.

(2) Without prejudice to the generality of subsection (1) above, where a person, having possession or control (lawfully or not) of property belonging to another, parts with the property under a condition as to its return which he may not be able to perform, this (if done for purposes of his own and without the other's authority) amounts to treating the property as his own to dispose of regardless of the other's rights.

21–77 In *R. v. Fernandez* [1996] 1 Cr.App.R. 175, CA, the appellant was a solicitor who had transferred funds from his clients' account to his book-keeper, R., for investment in a firm of licensed backstreet money lenders of which R. was a partner. The money disappeared. The appellant contended that he did not intend permanently to deprive the owner of the money. The judge had directed the jury in accordance with the words of the first part of section 6(1) of the Act, that he could be regarded as having the requisite intention if his intention was to treat the thing as his own to dispose of, regardless of the other's rights. The Court of Appeal, considering the effect of section 6(1), held:

> "The critical notion, stated expressly in the first limb and incorporated by reference in the second, is whether a defendant intended 'to treat the thing as his own to dispose of regardless of the other's rights'. The second limb of subsection (1), and also subsection (2), are merely specific illustrations of the application of that notion. We consider that section 6 may apply to a person in possession or control of another's property who, dishonestly and for his own purpose, deals with that property in such a manner that he knows he is risking its loss.
>
> In the circumstances alleged here, an alleged dishonest disposal of someone else's money on an obviously insecure investment, we consider that the judge was justified in referring to section 6" (*per* Auld L.J., at p. 188).

Where a person obtains a cheque dishonestly from another intending to present the cheque for payment, a charge of theft of the cheque form will not succeed, for there will be no intention permanently to deprive the drawer of the cheque form, which would on presentation for payment be returned to the drawer via his bank: *R. v. Preddy and Slade*; *R. v. Dhillon* [1996] A.C. 815, HL. Where, however, unlike in *Preddy*, there are identifiable rights belonging to another in a piece of paper, section 6(1) enables an intention permanently to deprive to be found notwithstanding the ultimate return to the owner of the, by then valueless, piece of paper (*e.g. R. v. Downes*, 77 Cr.App.R. 260, CA, vouchers belonging to the Inland Revenue, *R. v. Arnold* [1997] 4 All E.R. 1, CA, a bill of exchange drawn by A, accepted by B, redelivered by A to B on the understanding that it was to be retained by A as security for B's obligations under a franchising agreement, but discounted by A as against whom the bill was to be regarded as belonging to B by virtue of section 5(3), *ante*, § 21–58, and *R. v. Marshall, Coombes and Eren* [1998] 2 Cr.App.R. 282, CA, unexpired travel tickets issued on terms that they could only be used by the purchaser, acquired from the purchasers and sold on regardless of the issuer's rights). **21–78**

In *R. v. Coffey* [1987] Crim.L.R. 498, CA, the appellant had decided to exert pressure on the victim, with whom he had been in dispute and who had refused to negotiate, by obtaining machinery from him by use of a worthless cheque and keeping it until he got what he wanted. His conviction for obtaining property by deception was quashed because of an inadequate direction on intention. The court said that the culpability of the appellant's act depended upon the quality of the intended detention, considered in all its aspects, including in particular the appellant's own assessment at the time as to the likelihood of the victim coming to terms and of the time for which the machinery would have to be retained. This reasoning would have been equally apposite had he seized the machinery and been charged with theft. **21–79**

Conditional appropriation

A conditional appropriation will not suffice to constitute the offence of theft. If the appropriator has it in mind merely to deprive the owner of such of his property as, on examination, proves worth taking and then, finding that the booty is valueless to him, leaves it ready to hand to be repossessed by the owner, he has not committed theft: *R. v. Easom* [1971] 2 Q.B. 315, 55 Cr.App.R. 410, CA (where the allegation was of theft of a list of specified property). *Easom* was applied in *R. v. Hussein*, 67 Cr.App.R. 131, CA, and *R. v. Hector*, 67 Cr.App.R. 224, CA. In both cases the allegation had been one of attempted theft of specific articles. **21–80**

In such cases, an allegation of attempting to steal unspecified property will be unobjectionable, as the prosecution need only prove a general intent to steal, the same intent as is required on a charge of burglary under section 9(1)(a) of the *Theft Act* 1968 (*post*, § 21–108): *Att.-Gen.'s References (Nos 1 and 2 of 1979)* [1980] Q.B. 180, 69 Cr.App.R. 266, CA. **21–81**

Giving the judgment on the references, Roskill L.J. said:

> "... we see no reason in principle why what was described in argument as a more imprecise method of criminal pleading should not be adopted, if the justice of the case requires it, as for example, attempting to steal some or all the contents of a car or some or all of the contents of a handbag" (at pp. 194, 276).

See also *R. v. Smith and Smith* [1986] Crim.L.R. 166, CA, in which the Court of Appeal appears to have been hinting at a form of wording such as that suggested by **21–82**

Professor J.C. Smith in his commentary on this case in the *Criminal Law Review* (at p. 167). The suggestion is that any difficulties as to what has to be proved could be avoided by simply charging the defendant with "attempting to steal from a handbag".

(6) Attempted theft

21–83 The effect of section 1(2) of the *Criminal Attempts Act* 1981 (*post*, § 33–120) was to reverse *Haughton v. Smith* [1975] A.C. 476, HL, and *Partington v. Williams*, 62 Cr.App.R. 220, DC: it is no longer necessary for the prosecution to prove that there did, in fact, exist property capable of being stolen. For the law relating to attempts generally, see *post*, §§ 33–119 *et seq*.

III. ROBBERY AND ASSAULT WITH INTENT TO ROB

A. ROBBERY

(1) Statute

Theft Act 1968, s.8

Robbery

21–84 **8.**—(1) A person is guilty of robbery if he steals, and immediately before or at the time of doing so, and in order to do so, he uses force on any person or puts or seeks to put any person in fear of being then and there subjected to force.

(2) A person guilty of robbery, or of an assault with intent to rob, shall on conviction on indictment be liable to imprisonment for life.

(2) Indictment

STATEMENT OF OFFENCE

21–85 *Robbery, contrary to section 8(1) of the* Theft Act *1968.*

PARTICULARS OF OFFENCE

A B, on the —— day of ——, 20—, robbed J N of £10,000 in money.

21–86 Where for example a bank cashier is robbed of the bank's money, or a lorry driver of his load or a shop manager of his takings, it is unnecessary to name the actual owner since property is regarded as belonging to any person having possession or control of it: s.5(1), *ante*, § 21–58.

21–87 As to the inclusion of a count under the *Firearms Act* 1968 where the use of a firearm is an incident of an offence of robbery, see *post*, § 24–49.

(3) Class of offence and mode of trial

21–88 Robbery is a class 3 offence (*ante*, § 2–17), triable only on indictment.

(4) Sentence

Maximum

21–89 Imprisonment for life: *Theft Act* 1968, s.8(2), *ante*, § 21–84.

An offence under section 8(1) is a specified violent offence within Schedule 15 to the *CJA* 2003 (*ante*, § 5–299). As to the application of the dangerous offender provisions of the 2003 Act to street robberies, see *post*, § 21–94.

Where the use or threat of force involves a firearm, an imitation firearm or an offensive weapon, offences under section 8(1) are specified serious offences within Schedule 1 to the *SCA* 2007, enabling the court to make a serious crime prevention order under section 19 on conviction (*ante*, § 5–875c).

Guideline cases

21–90 As to guideline cases generally, see *ante*, § 21–16. For illustrative decisions, see CSP, B6–22001 to B6–23D38.

Armed robbery

21–91 In *R. v. Turner (B.J.)*, 61 Cr.App.R. 67, the Court of Appeal said that the normal sentence for anyone taking part in a single offence of armed robbery was 15 years and the maximum total sentence for those who committed more than one robbery was 18 years. In *R. v. Adams and Harding* [2000] 2 Cr.App.R.(S.) 274, CA, the Court of Appeal said that although *Turner* provided the starting point, the guidelines now had to be revised upwards in today's sentencing climate. A sentence of 25 years may be appropriate for a person found guilty of more than one offence and a sentence of more than 15 years may be appropriate for a person with a previous conviction for armed robbery who is found guilty of a single offence.

Robbery in the course of burglary

21–92 In *Att.-Gen.'s References (Nos 32 and 33 of 1995) (R. v. Pegg and Martin)* [1996] 2 Cr.App.R.(S.) 346, the Court of Appeal said that where an elderly victim, living alone, is violently attacked by intruders within the home and is injured, the likely sentence will be in double figures. See also *Att.-Gen.'s Reference (No. 89 of 1999) (R. v. Farrow)* [2000] 2 Cr.App.R.(S.) 382, CA.

Where, apart from the fact that it was committed in the victim's home, a robbery would fall within the guideline issued by the Sentencing Guidelines Council, *post*, two years, or possibly a little more, in addition to the sentence under the guideline would reflect this fact: *Att.-Gen.'s Reference (Nos 38, 39 and 40 of 2007) (R. v. Crummack, Stell and Campbell)* [2008] 1 Cr.App.R. 56, CA (in which entry had been gained by subterfuge rather than force).

Street robberies, robberies of small businesses, and "less sophisticated commercial robberies"

21–93 In July, 2006, the Sentencing Guidelines Council issued a final guideline in relation to such offences. For the details thereof, see Appendix K–80 *et seq.* As to the importance of maintaining a differential in sentencing between a single offence or just a few offences, and a campaign of multiple robberies, see *Att.-Gen.'s References (Nos 24, 25, 26, 27, 28 and 41 of 2006) (R. v. Blackwood)* [2007] 1 Cr.App.R.(S.) 50, CA (such a campaign against small shops and similar premises committed by adults with knives, crowbars and other weapons being carried, and sometimes used, would merit sentences of the order of 15 years' imprisonment on conviction of offenders of previous good character).

21–94 For examples of the application of the dangerous offender provisions in sections 224 to 229 of the *CJA* 2003 (*ante*, §§ 5–292 *et seq.*) to cases of street robbery, see *R. v. Davies* [2006] 2 Cr.App.R. (S.) 73, CA; *R. v. Johnson* [2006] 2 Cr.App.R.(S.) 54, CA; and *R. v. Folkes*, *ibid.*, 55, CA (all decided prior to the modifications effected by the *CJIA* 2008).

Hijacking of cars

21–94a See *R. v. Snowden*, *The Times*, November 11, 2002, CA (pre-planned hijacking of a car would usually involve ramming from behind and would almost always involve at least two offenders, thereby increasing victim's fear and sense of helplessness, which would be even greater if the impact from behind was followed by violence and/ or the use of a weapon or the threat of such use; when the car stolen was particularly valuable the proceeds might well equate to robbing a bank or building society and the penalty should reflect that; a defendant, even where he had no prior convictions, convicted of several such offences, aggravated by the use or threat of additional violence, could expect at least 10 years' imprisonment on conviction). *Snowden* was applied in *R. v. Gbedje and Owoola* [2007] 2 Cr.App.R.(S.) 89, CA, and *R. v. Khan and Khan* [2007] 2 Cr.App.R.(S.) 95, CA.

(5) Alternative verdicts

21–95 On a charge of robbery, the defendant may be convicted of theft pursuant to the *CLA* 1967, s.6(3) (*ante*, § 4–455): *R. v. Shendley* [1970] Crim.L.R. 49, CA.

21–96 In *R. v. Barnard*, 70 Cr.App.R. 28, CA, it was held that a conspiracy to steal was not a lesser form of a conspiracy to rob: it was a different agreement. Accordingly, section 6 of the 1967 Act had no application.

(6) Elements of the offence of robbery

(a) *"Steals"*

21–97 Prove a theft. Appropriation of the property is sufficient whether it has been taken away or not. As to what constitutes "appropriation", see *ante*, §§ 21–31 *et seq.*

Claim of right

21–98 Claim of right negatives theft and, therefore, it may negative robbery: *R. v. Skivington* [1968] 1 Q.B. 166, 51 Cr.App.R. 167, CA; *R. v. Robinson* [1977] Crim.L.R. 173, CA.

(b) *"Immediately before or at the time of doing so and in order to steal"*

21–99 The force or threat of the use of force must be immediately before or at the time of the stealing and for the purpose of stealing.

Force used after a theft is complete will not amount to a robbery, although that force may constitute a separate criminal act. The offence of theft will be complete as soon as there is an assumption of the rights of an owner which is dishonest and which is accompanied by an intention permanently to deprive.

So, where A picked B's pocket and B did not realise the fact until he saw the purse in A's hand and upon his remonstrating with A he was threatened this was not, and would not now be, robbery since the threats were not used in order to steal and the theft was complete: *R. v. Harman* (1620) 1 Hale 534. See also Criminal Law Revision Committee, 8th Report, Cmnd. 2977, para. 65.

21–100 Difficult questions may arise as to when the theft is complete. In *R. v. Hale*, 68 Cr.App.R. 415, CA, where the offenders had forced their way into the victim's house, and where it was objected on appeal that the judge had left it open to the jury to convict of robbery on the basis of force used (tying the victim up) after the theft itself was complete, it was held that an appropriation does not suddenly cease; it was for the jury to say whether any force used or threatened was "at the time of" the theft, and in order to effect it. See also *ante*, § 21–42.

The force must be used or threatened in order to steal; thus it would seem that where a man attempted to rape a woman and she, in order to get him to stop, gave him money which he pocketed (*cf. R. v. Blackham* (1787) 2 East P.C. 711), this would not now be robbery since the force was not used in order to steal.

(c) *Use or threat of force*

21–101 It must be proved that the defendant used force on any person or put or sought to put any person in fear of being then and there subjected to force. In *R. v. Dawson and James*, 64 Cr.App.R. 170 (a case of jostling the victim so as to cause him to lose his balance), the Court of Appeal said that in directing a jury where the charge is robbery the judge should direct his attention to the words of the statute. Whether the defendant used force on any person in order to steal is an issue that should be left to the jury.

Where threats are used they must amount to threats of *then and there* subjecting the victim or some other person to force. A less immediate threat of force might constitute blackmail under section 21 of the *Theft Act* 1968: see *post*, § 21–256. If the defendant by his words or conduct has sought to make the victim or some other person apprehend that he would be subjected to force, it is not necessary that he actually be afraid that the force will be used (see *B. and R. v. DPP*, 171 J.P. 404, DC).

In *R. v. Harris, The Times*, March 4, 1988, CA, it was held to be a misdirection to tell the jury that the defendant was guilty of robbery if she had taken advantage of the victim by stealing, when the victim had been rendered powerless by others without the complicity of the defendant.

(d) *On any person*

21–102 The force or threats of force must be directed to the person. Hence a threat of "£100 or I will burn your house" may not amount to robbery but may be blackmail under section 21 of the *Theft Act* 1968. The force may be directed at a person who is not the victim of the theft if such force is used in order to effect the theft.

B. ASSAULT WITH INTENT TO ROB

(1) Indictment

STATEMENT OF OFFENCE

Assault with intent to rob, contrary to section 8(2) of the Theft Act *1968*. **21–103**

PARTICULARS OF OFFENCE

A B, on the —— day of ——, 20—, assaulted J N with intent to rob him.

The better view is that this is a common law offence, the penalty only being provided by the statute; but the safer course is to include a reference to section 8(2) in the statement of offence: see *R. v. Harrow JJ., ex p. Osaseri* [1986] Q.B. 589, DC.

(2) Class of offence and mode of trial

Assault with intent to rob is a class 3 offence (*ante*, § 2–17), triable only on indictment. **21–104**

(3) Alternative verdict

Common assault: *CLA* 1967, s.6(3), (3A), *ante*, § 4–458. **21–105**

(4) Sentence

Imprisonment for life: *Theft Act* 1968, s.8(2), *ante*, § 21–84. **21–106**

An offence under section 8(2) is a specified violent offence within Schedule 15 to the *CJA* 2003 (*ante*, § 5–299).

Where the assault involves a firearm, an imitation firearm or an offensive weapon, assault with intent to rob is a specified serious offence within Schedule 1 to the *SCA* 2007, enabling the court to make a serious crime prevention order under section 19 on conviction (*ante*, § 5–875c).

Guidance as to the appropriate sentence may be gained from the authorities in relation to robbery, *ante*, §§ 21–89 *et seq.*

(5) Evidence

To support this indictment, the prosecution must prove the assault, and that it was coupled with an intent to rob. As to what constitutes an assault, see *ante*, §§ 19–166 *et seq.* **21–107**

The intent to rob must be proved from the surrounding circumstances and any admission or confession made by the defendant. No actual demand of money, etc., is necessary to support this indictment: *R. v. Trusty and Howard* (1783) 1 East P.C. 418; *R. v. Sharwin* (1785) 1 East P.C. 421.

IV. BURGLARY AND AGGRAVATED BURGLARY

A. BURGLARY

(1) Statute

Theft Act 1968, s.9

9.—(1) A person is guilty of burglary if— **21–108**

(a) he enters any building or part of a building as a trespasser and with intent to commit any such offence as is mentioned in subsection (2) below; or

(b) having entered any building or part of a building as a trespasser he steals or attempts to steal anything in the building or that part of it or inflicts or attempts to inflict on any person therein any grievous bodily harm.

(2) The offences referred to in subsection (1)(a) above are offences of stealing anything in the building or part of a building in question, of inflicting on any person therein any

grievous bodily harm ... therein, and of doing unlawful damage to the building or anything therein.

(3) A person guilty of burglary shall on conviction on indictment be liable to imprisonment for a term not exceeding—

(a) where the offence was committed in respect of a building or part of a building which is a dwelling, fourteen years;

(b) in any other case, ten years.

(4) References in subsections (1) and (2) above to a building, and the reference in subsection (3) above to a building which is a dwelling, shall apply also to an inhabited vehicle or vessel, and shall apply to any such vehicle or vessel at times when the person having a habitation in it is not there as well as at times when he is.

[This section is printed as amended, and repealed in part, by the *CJA* 1991, s.26(2); the *CJPOA* 1994, s.168(2) and Sched. 10; and the *SOA* 2003, s.140, and Sched. 7.]

For the offence of trespass with intent to commit a sexual offence, see *post*, § 20–197.

(2) Indictments

Indictment for burglary (entering with intent)

STATEMENT OF OFFENCE

21–109 *Burglary, contrary to section 9(1)(a) of the* Theft Act *1968.*

PARTICULARS OF OFFENCE

A B, on the —— day of ——, 20—, entered as a trespasser a building [or *"part of a building"*], *being a dwelling, known as ——, with intent to steal therein* [or *"to inflict grievous bodily harm on C D, a person therein"*] [or *"to do unlawful damage to the said building by fire"*].

Indictment for burglary after having entered a building

STATEMENT OF OFFENCE

21–110 *Burglary, contrary to section 9(1)(b) of the* Theft Act *1968.*

PARTICULARS OF OFFENCE

A B, on the —— day of ——, 20—, having entered as a trespasser a building [or *"part of a building"*], *being a dwelling known as ——, stole therein a diamond ring and £—— in money* [or *"attempted to steal therein"*] [or *"inflicted grievous bodily harm upon C D, a person therein"*].

It appears not to be necessary or desirable to specify any person as owner of the building. Where the offence is committed in relation to a dwelling, this should be specified in the particulars because of the higher maximum penalty.

(3) Class of offence and mode of trial

21–111 Burglary is triable either way unless it comprises the commission of, or an intention to commit, an offence which is triable only on indictment or it is committed in a dwelling and any person in the dwelling was subjected to violence or the threat of violence: *MCA* 1980, s.17(1) and Sched. 1, para. 28, *ante*, § 1–75af. Whatever the mode of trial, it is a class 3 offence: see *ante*, § 2–17.

(4) Alternative verdict

21–112 Upon a charge of burglary contrary to section 9(1)(b) the jury may acquit of burglary but convict of the relevant offence in paragraph (b) of section 9(1): *R. v. Lillis* [1972] 2 Q.B. 236, 56 Cr.App.R. 373, CA. Upon a charge contrary to section 9(1)(b) alleging entry as a trespasser plus the infliction of grievous bodily harm, the jury may convict of assault occasioning actual bodily harm: *R. v. Wilson*; *R. v. Jenkins* [1984] A.C. 242, HL. Upon a charge contrary to section 9(1)(b) of having "entered and stolen" the jury may convict of "entering with intent to steal" contrary to section 9(1)(a): *R. v. Whiting*, 85 Cr.App.R. 78, CA.

(5) Sentence

Maximum

Where the offence is committed in respect of a building or part of a building which is a dwelling, 14 years' imprisonment; otherwise 10 years: s.9(3), *ante*. For illustrative decisions, see CSP, B6–42001 to B6–43F12. For section 111 of the *PCC(S)A* 2000 (minimum sentence for third domestic burglary), see *ante*, § 5–253. **21–113**

An offence under section 9(1)(a), other than one committed by reason only of an intent to steal, is a specified violent offence within Schedule 15 to the *CJA* 2003 (*ante*, § 5–299).

Authorities (dwellings)

In *R. v. McInerney*; *R. v. Keating* [2003] 1 Cr.App.R. 36, CA, specific guidance was given in respect of the sentencing principles set out in *R. v. Brewster*; *R. v. Thorpe*; *R. v. Ishmael*; *R. v. Blanchard*; *R. v. Woodhouse*; *R. v. H. (R.)* [1998] 1 Cr.App.R. 220. This takes account of the advice of the Sentencing Advisory Panel. A "standard burglary" would have some at least of the following features; it would be committed by a repeat offender, would involve the theft of electrical goods or personal items, damage would be caused by the break-in, some turmoil would be caused inside, but there would be no injury or violence although there would be some trauma to the victim. High-level aggravating features include force used or threatened, a victim injured, an especially traumatic effect on the victim, professional planning, etc., vandalism, racial aggravation, a vulnerable victim deliberately targeted. Medium-level aggravating features include a vulnerable victim not deliberately targeted, the victim being at home, high-value goods stolen (economic or sentimental), and offenders working as a group. Other aggravating factors include the number of offences committed and an offence committed whilst on bail. In all cases, the court should have regard to the harm done. Mitigating features include a first offence, little or nothing stolen, the playing of a minor role, no damage being done, the crime being committed on impulse. As to the offender's criminal record, it was necessary to take into account the number and type of offences previously committed; and the efforts which an offender had made to rehabilitate himself were important. **21–114**

As to the panel's suggested starting points, for a low-level domestic burglary by a first offender, and for some second offenders, where there was no damage and only low-value property stolen, the starting point should be a community sentence; for a domestic burglary showing most of the features of the standard burglary but committed by a first offender, the starting point should be nine months' custody; for a second offender, it should be 18 months, and for an offender with two or more domestic burglary convictions, the starting point was a custodial sentence of three years (the presumptive minimum prescribed by the *PCC(S)A* 2000, s.111); in the case of a standard burglary with one of the medium-level aggravating features, the starting point should be 12 months in the case of a first offender; for a second offender, it should be two years, and for an offender with two or more previous convictions, it should be three-and-a-half years; for a standard burglary with one of the high-level aggravating features, the starting point for a first time burglar, should be 18 months; for a second offender it should be three years, and for an offender with two or more convictions, it should be four-and-a-half years; the presence of more than one high-level aggravating factor could take the sentence to a significantly higher level. As to the court's starting points, the panel's recommendations were to be adopted, save that in any case where the panel recommended a starting point of up to 18 months, the initial approach should be to impose a community sentence subject to conditions that ensured that the sentence was effective punishment and one which offered action on the part of the probation service to tackle the offender's criminal behaviour and any underlying problems such as addiction; the fact that an offender had not complied with a community sentence would be a strong indicator that a custodial sentence was necessary, but any such sentence should be no longer than necessary; incremental increases for second and subsequent offences should slow significantly after the third qualifying conviction as it was necessary to retain a degree of proportionality between the level of sentence for burglary and other serious offences. As to section 111 of the 2000 Act, this created a presumption that the sentence should be at least three years for a third domestic burglary, but the sentencer was given a substantial degree of discretion as to the categories of situations where the presumption might be rebutted; for example, the third offence might be committed many years after the first two, or the offender might have made a real effort to reform or conquer an addiction, with some personal tragedy triggering the third offence, or the first two offences might have been committed when the offender was not yet 16. As to young offenders, it was particularly important that they were dealt with by youth courts and not the Crown Court, where appropriate, and that community disposals were adopted wherever possible. As to compensation and restitution, these important powers should always be exercised when appropriate.

In *R. v. Kempster*, unreported, December 11, 2003, CA ([2003] EWCA Crim. 3555), it was said that the above guidelines were not principally directed to a case such as this, where the offender, with a history of similar offending, had deliberately targeted the homes of elderly and vulnerable people by night. And in *R. v. Cawley and Cawley* [2008] 1 Cr.App.R.(S.) 59, CA, sentences of seven and eight years' imprisonment were upheld in the case of offenders with substantial criminal records, including convictions for similar offences, on their conviction of a sophisticated distraction burglary of a 91-year-old widower, the court observing that *R. v. McInerney*; *R. v. Keating* did not demonstrate any intention that the courts should take a more lenient approach towards this kind of offence.

As to the appropriate level of sentence where a robbery is committed in the course of a burglary, see *ante*, § 21–92. As to guideline cases generally, see *ante*, § 21–4c.

In *R. v. Stratton*, *The Times*, January 15, 1988, CA, it was said that where a car was used for the purposes of facilitating the commission of offences of burglary it was appropriate for the court to take advantage of the powers under section 143 of the *PCC(S)A* 2000 (*ante*, § 5–439) to bring home to the offender the serious consequences of his conduct.

Non-dwellings

21–114a In March, 2008, the Sentencing Guidelines Council issued a consultation guideline in relation to burglaries of premises other than dwellings. For details of any definitive guideline, see Appendix K.

(6) Elements of offence of burglary

(a) *The building*

21–115 Any building or part of a building may be the subject of burglary; also an inhabited vehicle or vessel, whether the occupier is there or not at the time of the offence (s.9(3)). This includes houseboats and caravans which are regularly inhabited even if empty at times.

The word "building" being an ordinary word of the English language and the context not being such as to show that the word is used in an unusual sense, its meaning is a question of fact not law: see *Brutus v. Cozens* [1973] A.C. 854, HL. It is for the tribunal of fact to decide whether in the whole circumstances the words of the statute do or do not as a matter of ordinary usage of the English language apply to the facts which have been proved: *ibid*. For a further discussion on this matter, see Ormerod & Williams, *Smith's Law of Theft*, 9th ed., p. 258, in which the view is taken that an unfinished building may in some circumstances be a "building": see also *R. v. Manning* (1871) L.R. 1 C.C.R. 338, where an unfinished house of which all the walls, external and internal, had been built, the roof was on, a considerable part of the flooring laid, etc., was held to be "a building" under the *Malicious Damage Act* 1861, s.6 (*rep.*). It was held that the issue had been properly left to jury, and that their finding upon the issue was conclusive. "Such words as those in the section must be interpreted in their ordinary sense. And it would certainly not have been a departure from ordinary language to have asked, 'Who built that structure?'" (*per* Byles J. at p. 340). "I do not think four walls erected a foot high would be a building" (*per* Lush J. at p. 341).

(b) *Entry as a trespasser*

The definition of trespass comes from the law of tort, *i.e.* any intentional, reckless or negligent entry into a building will constitute a trespass if the building is in the possession of another person who does not consent to the entry. However, such an entry must be accompanied by *mens rea*: the defendant must know or be reckless as to the facts which make the entry a trespass: *R. v. Collins* [1973] Q.B. 100, 56 Cr.App.R. 554, CA. In *R. v. Smith and Jones*, 63 Cr.App.R. 47, CA, James L.J. cited *Collins* and *Hillen and Pettigrew v. I.C.I. (Alkali) Ltd* [1936] A.C. 65, as authority for the proposition that: **21–116**

> "a person is a trespasser for the purpose of section 9(1)(b) ... if he enters premises of another knowing that he is entering in excess of the permission that has been given to him, or being reckless as to whether he is entering in excess of the permission that has been given to him to enter, providing the facts are known to the accused which enable him to realise that he is acting in excess of the permission given or that he is acting recklessly as to whether he exceeds that permission, then that is sufficient for the jury to decide that he is in fact a trespasser" (at p. 52).

The occupier's son had a general permission to enter the house. However, he exceeded that permission when he entered with an accomplice and with an intent to steal, and, accordingly, he committed burglary.

In *Collins*, *ante*, it was argued that it was not open to a person, other than the owner, tenant or occupier of premises to extend an effective invitation to enter. The argument was dealt with summarily by Edmund-Davies L.J.: "Whatever be the position in the law of tort, to regard such a proposition as acceptable in the criminal law would be unthinkable" (at pp. 107, 563). However, it is submitted that it would be trespass for a person to enter in response to an invitation which the person entering knew was extended without any authority or in excess of a limited authority.

The common law doctrine of trespass *ab initio* has no application to burglary under the *Theft Act* 1968: *R. v. Collins*, *ante*. A prima facie case of trespass may be established without direct evidence from the occupier: *R. v. Maccuish* [1996] 6 *Archbold News* 2, CA.

Entry for a purpose alien to a licence to enter, or under false pretences

There is abundant authority for the proposition that a person who has the right of entry on the land of another for a specific purpose commits a trespass if he enters for any other purpose: *Taylor v. Jackson* (1898) 78 L.T. 555; *Hillen and Pettigrew v. I.C.I. (Alkali) Ltd* [1936] A.C. 65; *Farrington v. Thomson and Bridgland* [1959] V.R. 286; *Strong v. Russell* (1904) 24 N.Z.L.R. 916. *A fortiori*, it would seem that where a consent to entry is obtained by fraud, the entry will be trespassory; whether or not the consent can be said to be vitiated by the fraud, situations such as that where a person gains entry by falsely pretending he has come to read the gas meter can clearly be brought within the principle for which the foregoing cases are authority. **21–117**

(c) *The entry*

The Court of Appeal in *R. v. Collins* [1973] Q.B. 100, 56 Cr.App.R. 554, said that what had to be proved was that the defendant made an "effective and substantial" entry into the building (*per* Edmund-Davies L.J. at p. 562). **21–118**

In *R. v. Brown (V.)* [1985] Crim.L.R. 212, CA, the court said that the word "substantial" in Edmund-Davies L.J.'s dictum in *Collins* did not assist. The court thought it perfectly sensible to say that a man who had both feet on the ground outside a shop "entered" the shop when he leaned through a broken window with the upper half of his body, including, of course, his arms and hands.

(d) *The ulterior intent: section 9(1)(a)*

21–119 The intention must be to commit one of the offences specified in section 9(2). The intent laid in the indictment must be proved as laid: *R. v. Pearson*, 4 Cr.App.R. 40, CCA. Where the intent is at all doubtful, it may be laid in the alternative—either in the same count (*ante*, § 1–120), or in different counts.

Where a person attempts to enter premises as a trespasser intending to commit one or other of the offences set out in section 9(2), that is sufficient to constitute the offence of attempted burglary. It is not necessary to prove an attempt to carry out the ulterior offence: *R. v. Toothill* [1998] Crim.L.R. 876, CA. As to what constitutes an attempt, see *post* §§ 33–119 *et seq.*

Stealing, contrary to section 1(1)

21–120 Where a person enters a building as a trespasser with an intention to steal it is no defence that he only intends to steal if he finds anything worth stealing, or that in the building or part of a building which he enters there is, in fact, nothing to steal: *R. v. Walkington*, 68 Cr.App.R. 427, CA; *Att.-Gen.'s References (Nos 1 and 2 of 1979)* [1980] Q.B. 180, 69 Cr.App.R. 266, CA.

Inflicting grievous bodily harm

21–121 If a person enters a building intending to inflict grievous bodily harm on a person inside the building, then he has done so with the intention of committing therein an offence contrary to section 18 of the *Offences against the Person Act* 1861: *ante*, § 19–199.

Unlawful damage

21–122 Offences of damaging property are now contained in the *Criminal Damage Act* 1971: see *post*, §§ 23–1 *et seq.*

(e) *The ulterior offence: section 9(1)(b)*

Theft or attempted theft

21–123 This must be proved in the manner directed: *ante*, §§ 21–22 *et seq.*

Inflicting or attempting to inflict grievous bodily harm

21–124 The statute does not expressly say that the infliction of grievous bodily harm must constitute an offence, but it is submitted that this is in fact a requirement. The minimum, therefore, that the prosecution must prove is the commission of an offence contrary to section 20 of the *Offences against the Person Act* 1861 (*ante*, § 19–200), or an attempt to commit such an offence.

(7) Recent possession

21–125 There has been widespread misunderstanding of the so called doctrine of recent possession. The "rule" (for it is no more than the application of common sense) is that where it is proved that premises have been entered and property stolen therefrom and that soon after the entry the defendant was found in possession of the property, it is open to the jury to convict him of burglary, and the jury should be so directed: see *R. v. Loughlin*, 35 Cr.App.R. 69, CCA; *R. v. Seymour*, 38 Cr.App.R. 68, CCA. This, of course, applies equally to thefts other than in the course of a burglary, whether a pick-pocketing or an armed robbery.

In *R. v. Smythe*, 72 Cr.App.R. 8, CA, the court stressed that it is a misconception to think that recent possession is a material consideration only in cases of handling. It adopted the following passage from *Cross on Evidence*, 5th ed., p. 49 (11th ed., p. 45):

> "If someone is found in possession of goods soon after they have been missed, and he fails to give a credible explanation of the manner in which he came by them, the jury are justified in inferring that he was either the thief or else guilty of dishonestly handling the goods, knowing or believing them to have been stolen. ... The absence of an explanation is equally signif-

icant whether the case is being considered as one of theft or handling, but it has come into particular prominence in connection with the latter because persons found in possession of stolen goods are apt to say that they acquired them innocently from someone else. Where the only evidence is that the defendant on a charge of handling was in possession of stolen goods, a jury may infer guilty knowledge or belief (a) if he offers no explanation to account for his possession, or (b) if the jury are satisfied that the explanation he does offer is untrue."

Every case depends on its own facts. There is no magic in any given length of time. However, it is submitted that in many cases where the *only* evidence is that of recent possession, it will be impossible to exclude the possibility that the defendant was merely a receiver of the stolen property: in such cases, a count of burglary ought not to be left to the jury. However, that applies where recent possession is literally the only evidence. The reality is, that in the great majority of cases there are other pieces of evidence which tend to point the case one way or the other. It would be impossible to compile a definitive list of circumstances which might be relevant. They will include, however, the time and place of the theft, the type of property stolen, the likelihood of it being sold on quickly, the circumstances of the defendant, whether he has any connection with the victim or with the place where the theft occurred, anything said by the defendant and how that fits in or does not fit in with the other available evidence. **21–126**

In *R. v. Greaves, The Times*, July 11, 1987, the Court of Appeal rejected an argument to the effect that because the Court of Appeal had said in *R. v. Cash* [1985] Q.B. 801, 80 Cr.App.R. 314 (*post*, §§ 21–290 *et seq.*) that it would be impossible to infer participation in a burglary from possession of some of the stolen property nine days later, it was automatically wrong for the trial judge to have left it open to the jury to convict of burglary where the time lapse was 17 days. This, it is submitted, was plainly correct. On the particular facts of the case, however, the Court of Appeal quashed the conviction for burglary on the basis that the case should not have been left to the jury and substituted a verdict of guilty of handling. **21–127**

There is, however, a difficulty with the decision in *Greaves* to substitute a conviction for handling. The point is closely connected with the discussion at §§ 21–280 *et seq.*, *post*, as to the relationship between the offences of theft and handling stolen goods. The indictment contained an alternative allegation of handling stolen goods to which the defendant pleaded guilty. The plea was not acceptable. The jury were not put in charge in respect of that matter and, there having been a conviction of burglary, no sentence was passed upon it. The Court of Appeal, however, substituted a verdict of guilty of handling under section 3 of the *CAA* 1968: see *ante*, § 7–106. But that section applies only where (a) "the jury could on the indictment have found him guilty of some other offence", and (b) "on the finding of the jury it appears to the Court of Appeal that the jury must have been satisfied of facts which proved him guilty of the other offence". As to the first requirement, it is difficult to see how the jury could on the indictment have found him guilty of handling if they were never put in charge on that count. That may be technical: more substantial is the fact that the jury—by convicting of burglary—were clearly *not* satisfied of facts which proved him guilty of handling. *R. v. Dolan*, 62 Cr.App.R. 36, CA, suggests that the Court of Appeal could simply have sentenced the appellant under section 4 of the *CAA* 1968 (*ante*, § 7–108) on the basis of his plea of guilty to handling; but section 4 depends on there being a conviction, and a plea of guilty without sentence being passed is not a conviction (*R. v. Cole* [1965] 2 Q.B. 388, 49 Cr.App.R. 199, CCA, *ante*, § 4–109). **21–128**

As to the proper course when the evidence is as consistent with handling as with burglary, see *post*, §§ 21–280 *et seq.*

B. AGGRAVATED BURGLARY

(1) Statute

Theft Act 1968, s.10

10.—(1) A person is guilty of aggravated burglary if he commits any burglary and at the time has with him any firearm or imitation firearm, any weapon of offence, or any explosive; and for this purpose— **21–129**

(a) "firearm" includes an airgun or air pistol, and "imitation firearm" means anything which has the appearance of being a firearm, whether capable of being discharged or not; and

(b) "weapon of offence" means any article made or adapted for use for causing injury to or incapacitating a person, or intended by the person having it with him for such use; and

(c) "explosive" means any article manufactured for the purpose of producing a practical effect by explosion, or intended by the person having it with him for that purpose.

(2) A person guilty of aggravated burglary shall on conviction on indictment be liable to imprisonment for life.

(2) Indictment

STATEMENT OF OFFENCE

21–130 *Aggravated burglary, contrary to section 10(1) of the* Theft Act *1968*.

PARTICULARS OF OFFENCE

A B, on the —— day of ——, 20—, entered as a trespasser a building [or *"part of a building"*] *known as —— with intent to steal therein* [or *"to inflict grievous bodily harm on C D, a person therein"*] [or *"to do unlawful damage to the said building by fire"*] *and at the time of the said entry had with him a firearm* [or *"weapon of offence"*] [or *"explosive"*], *namely a ——.*

Where the burglary consists in having committed an offence after entry as under section 9(1)(b) of the *Theft Act* 1968 (*ante*, § 21–108), the particulars of offence should follow the precedent set out at § 21–110, *ante*, and conclude *"and at the time of the said offence had with him"*, etc.

It appears not to be necessary or desirable to specify any person as the owner of the building.

(3) Class of offence and mode of trial

21–131 Aggravated burglary is triable only on indictment: see the *Magistrates' Courts Act* 1980, s.17(1) and Sched. 1, para. 28, *ante*, § 1–75af. It is a class 3 offence, *ante*, § 2–17.

(4) Alternative verdict

21–132 See *ante*, § 21–112.

(5) Sentence

21–133 Imprisonment for life: s.10(2), *ante*. See the cases cited at § 21–92, *ante*.

An offence under section 10 is a specified violent offence within Schedule 15 to the *CJA* 2003 (*ante*, § 5–299).

(6) Evidence

21–134 Prove the burglary as directed (*ante*, §§ 21–115 *et seq.*) and prove that at the time thereof the defendant had with him the firearm, weapon of offence or explosive particularised in the indictment. Where the burglary arises under section 9(1)(a) the "time thereof" will clearly be the time of entry: under section 9(1)(b) it will be the time of commission of the ulterior offence: *R. v. Francis* [1982] Crim.L.R. 363, CA; *R. v. O'Leary*, 82 Cr.App.R. 341, CA (defendant armed himself with a knife from within burgled premises but before committing ulterior offence).

It is not necessary to prove that the defendant intended to use the article alleged to be a "weapon of offence" as a weapon before the occasion to use it as such arose: *R. v. Kelly (R.P.)*, 97 Cr.App.R. 245, CA (defendant disturbed in course of a burglary whereupon he produced a screwdriver which he then used as a weapon).

Where the principal in an offence of burglary does not have with him at the time of commission of the offence a firearm, weapon of offence, etc., but a secondary party (*i.e.* not a joint principal) does, neither party is guilty of the offence of aggravated burglary: *R. v. Klass* [1998] 1 Cr.App.R. 453, CA.

The expression "firearm" is given a wide meaning in section 57 of the *Firearms Act* 1968 (*post*, § 24–85), which will afford useful guidance to a court in construing the meaning of "firearm" in section 10(1)(a) of the 1968 Act. However, it is submitted that the definition in section 57 should be taken as providing no more than guidance: to give the word "firearm" in this context a meaning wider than that which it naturally bears would be contrary to the general rule that criminal statutes are to be construed restrictively. It may be that articles which only fall within the extended definition in section 57 will nevertheless come within the definition of "weapon of offence". The definition of this term is more extensive than that of the expression "offensive weapon" in the *Prevention of Crime Act* 1953 (*post*, §§ 24–106a, 24–115), since it refers to incapacitation.

In the case of articles made or adapted for use for causing injury to or incapacitating a person, the prosecution need prove no more than that the article was so made or adapted. In the case of any other article it must be proved that the defendant had it with him intending to use it for the purpose of causing injury to or incapacitating a person. It is submitted that it would be wholly irrelevant that the defendant hopes he will not have to use the article at all because he hopes he will not be disturbed; if he intends to use it for either of the stated purposes if the need arises, that is sufficient. To hold otherwise would, it is submitted, be contrary to both the plain meaning of the statute and its intent, and would be inconsistent with the decisions of the Court of Appeal in *R. v. Walkington*, 68 Cr.App.R. 427, and *Att.-Gen.'s References (Nos 1 and 2 of 1979)* [1980] Q.B. 180, 69 Cr.App.R. 266, CA, *ante*, § 21–119a. **21–135**

It is sufficient that the defendant was carrying a weapon of offence during the burglary with the intention of using it on some person, albeit that person might be unconnected with the premises burgled: *R. v. Stones*, 89 Cr.App.R. 26, CA.

On the analogy of *R. v. Cugullere*, 45 Cr.App.R. 108, CCA (*post*, § 24–110), it would appear that the prosecution must prove that the defendant *knowingly* had with him the article which was in fact a weapon of offence.

V. REMOVAL OF ARTICLES FROM PLACES OPEN TO THE PUBLIC

(1) Statute

Theft Act 1968, s.11

11.—(1) Subject to subsections (2) and (3) below, where the public have access to a building in order to view the building or part of it, or a collection or part of a collection housed in it, any person who without lawful authority removes from the building or its grounds the whole or part of any article displayed or kept for display to the public in the building or that part of it or in its grounds shall be guilty of an offence. **21–136**

For this purpose "collection" includes a collection got together for a temporary purpose, but references in this section to a collection do not apply to a collection made or exhibited for the purpose of effecting sales or other commercial dealings.

(2) It is immaterial for purposes of subsection (1) above that the public's access to a building is limited to a particular period or particular occasion; but where anything removed from a building or its grounds is there otherwise than as forming part of, or being on loan for exhibition with, a collection intended for permanent exhibition to the public, the person removing it does not thereby commit an offence under this section unless he removes it on a day when the public have access to the building as mentioned in subsection (1) above.

(3) A person does not commit an offence under this section if he believes that he has lawful authority for the removal of the thing in question or that he would have it if the person entitled to give it knew of the removal and the circumstances of it.

(4) A person guilty of an offence under this section shall, on conviction on indictment, be liable to imprisonment for a term not exceeding five years.

(2) Indictment

STATEMENT OF OFFENCE

Removing article from place open to public, contrary to section 11(1) of the Theft Act *1968*. **21–137**

PARTICULARS OF OFFENCE

A B, on the —— day of —— 20—, without lawful authority removed from the —— Art Gallery, a building to which the public had access in order to view a collection of paintings housed therein, a painting displayed to the public therein, intituled —— by——.

Where the article removed was in the building otherwise than as forming part of, or being on loan for exhibition with, a collection intended for permanent exhibition to the public there should be added the words "on the said day" after the word "public" where it first appears in the above precedent.

(3) Class of offence and mode of trial

21–138 This offence is triable either way: *MCA* 1980, s.17(1) and Sched. 1, para. 28, *ante*, § 1–75af. It is a class 3 offence, *ante*, § 2–17.

(4) Sentence

21–139 Imprisonment not exceeding five years: s.11(4), *ante*.

(5) Evidence

21–140 Prove (a) the removal, (b) from a building or the grounds of a building, (c) to which building the public have access, (d) in order to view it or part of it or a collection or part of a collection housed in it, (e) of the whole or part of any article, (f) displayed or kept for display to the public, (g) in the building or that part of it or the grounds of the building.

A collection which is made or exhibited for the purpose of effecting sales or other commercial dealings is not within the ambit of this provision. However, it seems that where items are collected principally for exhibition but also for "sale" the collection will be covered.

A local authority owned an art gallery which was open to the public on weekdays but closed on Sundays. Only part of the collection of pictures owned by the authority was on view at any one time but the pictures were all shown at least once a year, sections of the collection being exhibited at various times of the year for short periods. Early one Sunday morning D removed a painting from the collection then on view at the gallery. It was submitted that the picture did not form part of "a collection intended for permanent exhibition to the public", since each picture in the collection was only seldom exhibited. It was held that the words "a collection intended for permanent exhibition to the public", meant simply a collection intended to be permanently available for exhibition to the public. That intention was sufficiently manifested by the local authority's settled practice of periodically displaying to the public at the gallery the pictures in their permanent collection: *R. v. Durkin* [1973] 1 Q.B. 786, 57 Cr.App.R. 637, CA.

Where the issue has been raised whether the defendant believed that he had lawful authority for the removal, or that he would have had it if the person entitled to authorise the removal had known of the removal and its attendant circumstances, the burden is on the prosecution to prove lack of bona fides on the part of the defendant.

VI. TAKING CONVEYANCES WITHOUT AUTHORITY

A. THE SIMPLE OFFENCE

(1) Statute

Theft Act 1968, s.12

21–141 **12.**—(1) Subject to subsections (5) and (6) below, a person shall be guilty of an offence if, without having the consent of the owner or other lawful authority, he takes any conveyance for his own or another's use or, knowing that any conveyance has been taken without such authority, drives it or allows himself to be carried in or on it.

(2) A person guilty of an offence under subsection (1) above shall be liable on summary conviction to a fine not exceeding level 5 on the standard scale, to imprisonment for a term not exceeding *six months* [51 weeks] or to both.

(3) [*Repealed by* Police and Criminal Evidence Act *1984, Sched.* 7.]

(4) If on the trial of an indictment for theft the jury are not satisfied that the accused committed theft, but it is proved that the accused committed an offence under subsection (1) above, the jury may find him guilty of the offence under subsection (1) and if he is found guilty of it, he shall be liable as he would have been liable under subsection (2) above on summary conviction.

(4A) Proceedings for an offence under subsection (1) above (but not proceedings of a kind falling within subsection (4) above) in relation to a mechanically propelled vehicle—

(a) shall not be commenced after the end of the period of three years beginning with the day on which the offence was committed; but

(b) subject to that, may be commenced at any time within the period of six months beginning with the relevant day.

(4B) In subsection (4A)(b) above "the relevant day" means—

(a) in the case of a prosecution for an offence under subsection (1) above by a public prosecutor, the day on which sufficient evidence to justify the proceedings came to the knowledge of any person responsible for deciding whether to commence any such prosecution;

(b) in the case of a prosecution for an offence under subsection (1) above which is commenced by a person other than a public prosecutor after the discontinuance of a prosecution falling within paragraph (a) above which relates to the same facts, the day on which sufficient evidence to justify the proceedings came to the knowledge of the person who has decided to commence the prosecution or (if later) the discontinuance of the other prosecution;

(c) in the case of any other prosecution for an offence under subsection (1) above, the day on which sufficient evidence to justify the proceedings came to the knowledge of the person who has decided to commence the prosecution.

(4C) For the purposes of subsection (4A)(b) above a certificate of a person responsible for deciding whether to commence a prosecution of a kind mentioned in subsection (4B)(a) above as to the date on which such evidence as is mentioned in the certificate came to the knowledge of any person responsible for deciding whether to commence any such prosecution shall be conclusive evidence of that fact.

(5) Subsection (1) above shall not apply in relation to pedal cycles; but, subject to subsection (6) below, a person who, without having the consent of the owner or other lawful authority, takes a pedal cycle for his own or another's use, or rides a pedal cycle knowing it to have been taken without such authority, shall on summary conviction be liable to a fine not exceeding level 3 on the standard scale.

(6) A person does not commit an offence under this section by anything done in the belief that he has lawful authority to do it or that he would have the owner's consent if the owner knew of his doing it and the circumstances of it.

(7) For purposes of this section—

(a) "conveyance" means any conveyance constructed or adapted for the carriage of a person or persons whether by land, water or air, except that it does not include a conveyance constructed or adapted for use only under the control of a person not carried in or on it, and "drive" shall be construed accordingly; and

(b) "owner", in relation to a conveyance which is the subject of a hiring agreement or hire-purchase agreement, means the person in possession of the conveyance under that agreement.

[This section is printed as amended by the *CJA* 1982, ss.37, 38; the *CJA* 1988, s.37(1); and the *Vehicles (Crime) Act* 2001, s.37(1). In subs. (2), "51 weeks" is substituted for "six months", as from a day to be appointed, by the *CJA* 2003, s.281(4) and (5). The increase has no application to offences committed before the substitution takes effect: s.281(6).]

(2) Indictment

COUNT 1

STATEMENT OF OFFENCE

Taking conveyance without authority, contrary to section 12(1) of the Theft Act *1968.* **21–142**

PARTICULARS OF OFFENCE

A B, on the —— day of ——, 20—, without the consent of the owner or other lawful authority, took a conveyance, namely a Ford motor car registration number —— for the use of himself [or *the use of C D*].

COUNT 2

STATEMENT OF OFFENCE

21–143 *Driving conveyance taken without authority, contrary to section 12(1) of the* Theft Act *1968*.

PARTICULARS OF OFFENCE

A B, on the —— day of ——, 20—, knowing that a conveyance, namely a Ford motor car, registration number ——, had been taken without the consent of the owner or other lawful authority, drove the said conveyance [or *allowed himself to be carried in or on the said conveyance*].

(3) Mode of trial

21–144 Offences contrary to section 12 are summary offences. An allegation of an offence contrary to subsection (1) may, however, be included as a count in an indictment in the circumstances provided for by section 40 of the *CJA* 1988 (*ante*, § 1–75ai). Such an offence may also be committed for trial in conjunction with an either way offence pursuant to section 41 of the 1988 Act (*ante*, § 1–75am).

(4) Alternative verdict

21–145 Conviction of an offence contrary to section 12(1) is a possible alternative verdict to an allegation of theft: s.12(4).

(5) Sentence

21–146 Whatever the mode of trial, the maximum penalty is a fine not exceeding level 5 on the standard scale or imprisonment for a term not exceeding six months (51 weeks, as from a day to be appointed), or both: see subs. (2) and (4), and s.40(2) of the 1988 Act. As to "the standard scale", see *ante*, § 5–403.

In addition, an offence or attempt to commit an offence in respect of a motor vehicle under section 12 carries discretionary disqualification: *RTOA* 1988, ss.34, 97, and Sched. 2, Pt II.

21–147 In *R. v. Simpson*, *The Times*, December 14, 1989, CA, it was said to be wrong to impose a substantial period of disqualification on defendants found guilty and imprisoned for taking and driving away a vehicle in the course of a burglary, where there was no suggestion that the vehicle had been driven dangerously and the disqualification could only be regarded as part of the overall penalty. Once the prison sentences had been served, it was important that the defendants were able to find employment. That might be easier if they were in possession of current valid driving licences. See also *R. v. Callister* [1993] R.T.R. 70, CA (*ante*, § 21–15).

(6) Elements of the offence of taking a vehicle

General

21–148 Prove that the defendant took the conveyance named in the indictment for his own use or for the use of another person. A taking *only* has to be proved and not a taking and driving away as under the *RTA* 1960, s.217 (*rep.*).

Prove also that the owner did not consent to the taking of the vehicle by the defendant. "Owner" includes a person in possession of the conveyance under a hiring or hire-purchase agreement (s.12(7)(b)).

"Conveyance"

21–149 See section 12(7)(a) *ante*, § 21–141. As to pedal cycles, see section 12(5), *ante*, § 21–141. In *Neal v. Gribble*, 68 Cr.App.R. 9, DC, it was held (a) that giving "conveyance" its ordinary meaning, it did not include a horse; and (b) that even if it did, putting a halter on a horse did not "adapt" it for the purposes of section 12(7)(a).

Mens rea

Self-induced intoxication is no defence to a charge of taking a conveyance without authority: *R. v. MacPherson* [1973] R.T.R. 157, CA. 21–150

Where an issue has been raised as to whether the defendant took the conveyance in the belief that he had lawful authority to take it, or that he would have had the owner's consent if the owner had known of the taking and its attendant circumstances, the burden rests on the prosecution to prove that the defendant did not have such belief: *ibid.*

MacPherson was considered in *R. v. Gannon*, 87 Cr.App.R. 254, CA. The trial judge had ruled that if a belief in lawful authority arises as a result of self-induced intoxication it is not a belief that affords a defence under section 12(6). The Court of Appeal found it unnecessary to rule on this issue. The decision in *Jaggard v. Dickinson* [1981] Q.B. 527, 72 Cr.App.R. 33, DC, on a similar provision in the *Criminal Damage Act* 1971 (*post*, § 23–48) (to which the court was referred in argument), would suggest that the ruling of the judge in the instant case was wrong. It is questionable, however, whether section 12(6) had any relevance at all: the belief that the defendant was supposed to have had was a belief that the car he took was his own. It is submitted that where someone innocently takes the wrong car he is not guilty of an offence contrary to section 12 because he lacks basic *mens rea*, *i.e.* knowledge that he is taking a car without the consent of the owner or recklessness as to the fact that it is being taken without the owner's consent. It is artificial to say that he believes he has lawful authority because he thinks it is his own: lawful authority relates to situations where the taker knows it is not his own but for one reason or another nevertheless believes he has lawful authority to take it.

Consent

There is no general principle that fraud vitiates consent. Section 12 was intended to deal with the situation where vehicles are taken without any attempt to obtain the owner's consent and where, in the majority of cases, the owner was not consulted at all. The commission of an offence does not depend on whether the possession of the vehicle had been obtained by fraud, but upon whether the effect of the fraud was such that it precluded the existence of objective agreement to part with possession of it: *Whittaker v. Campbell* [1984] Q.B. 318, 77 Cr.App.R. 267, DC (dictum of Sachs L.J. in *R. v. Peart* [1970] 2 Q.B. 672 at 676, 54 Cr.App.R. 374 at 378, 379, CA, applied). In *Whittaker v. Campbell*, the appellants had hired a van using a stolen driving licence; their convictions were quashed. 21–151

Where a person borrowed a vehicle subject to an implied limitation, of which he knew, as to the purpose for which it was to be driven, he did not have "the consent of the owner" to drive it for a purpose outside the implied limitation: *Singh v. Rathour (Northern Star Insurance Co. Ltd, Third Party)* [1988] 1 W.L.R. 422, CA (Civ. Div.), distinguishing *Whittaker v. Campbell* and *Peart*, *ante*.

In the trial of a passenger for allowing himself to be carried, the fact that the vehicle had been taken without consent can be proved by proving the driver's conviction for so taking the vehicle: *DPP v. Parker* [2006] R.T.R. 26, DC.

"takes"

Evidence that there has merely been an unauthorised taking of possession or control adverse to the rights of the owner is not sufficient to found a conviction for the full offence. Some element of movement is implicit in the word "take" and *semble*, the movement must be caused by a voluntary act done with the intention of putting the vehicle in motion, see *Blayney v. Knight*, 60 Cr.App.R. 269, DC. In the absence of any evidence of movement there may nonetheless be sufficient evidence to found a conviction for attempt: *R. v. Bogacki* [1973] 1 Q.B. 832, 57 Cr.App.R. 593, CA. *Cf. R. v. Pearce* [1973] Crim.L.R. 321, CA, where P took an inflatable rubber dinghy, put it on a trailer and drove it away—conviction upheld. However, merely being on board a moored motor launch does not amount to being carried on it for the purposes of the 21–152 section: *R. v. Miller* [1976] Crim.L.R. 147, CA, applied in *R. v. Diggin*, 72 Cr.App.R. 204, CA. Getting into the driving seat of a car with the intention of taking it may constitute an attempt to take the vehicle. It is for the judge to say whether it is capable of constituting an attempt and for the jury to decide whether they are satisfied that there was an attempt: *R. v. Cook*, 48 Cr.App.R. 98, CCA.

21–153 Where the defendant borrowed a motor vehicle with the owner's consent for a specific purpose, but failed to return it on completion of that purpose, and used it thereafter for a wholly different purpose without the owner's consent and without a reasonable belief that the owner would have given his consent to the further use, if asked, it was held on appeal that the subsequent use after the termination of the specific purpose constituted an offence. His passenger who had knowledge of the facts was guilty of allowing himself to be carried in the vehicle: *R. v. Phipps and McGill*, 54 Cr.App.R. 300, CA.

In considering *R. v. Phipps and McGill* and two cases decided under the previous law (*Mowe v. Perraton*, 35 Cr.App.R. 194, DC, and *R. v. Wibberley* [1966] 2 Q.B. 214, 50 Cr.App.R. 51, CCA), the Divisional Court observed in *McKnight v. Davies* [1974] R.T.R. 4, that it is difficult to define the kind of unauthorised activity by a driver, originally in lawful control of the vehicle, which amounted to an unlawful taking under section 12. Not every brief, unauthorised diversion from his proper route by an employed driver in the course of his working day would necessarily involve a "taking". If, however (as in *R. v. Wibberley*), he returned to the vehicle after he had parked it for the night and drove it off on an unauthorised errand, he was clearly guilty. Similarly, if in the course of his working day or otherwise while his authority to use the vehicle was unexpired, he appropriated it to his own use in a manner which repudiated the rights of the true owner and showed that he had assumed control of the vehicle for his own purpose he could properly be regarded as having taken the vehicle (preferring *R. v. Phipps and McGill* to *Mowe v. Perraton*). The same test applies where the person who had originally been authorised to drive the vehicle is alleged to have taken it by letting someone else drive it, who, to his knowledge or belief, would not have had the owner's permission to drive it: *McMinn v. McMinn* [2006] 3 All E.R. 87, QBD (Keith J.). See also *Singh v. Rathour (Northern Star Insurance Co. Ltd, Third Party)*, *ante*, § 21–151.

21–154 Where a vehicle is unlawfully taken and then abandoned, if it is subsequently taken without authority a further offence is committed: *DPP v. Spriggs* [1994] R.T.R. 1, DC.

"for his own or another's use"

21–155 In *R. v. Bow*, 64 Cr.App.R. 54, CA, B and others were approached by a gamekeeper who, suspecting they were poachers, asked for their names and addresses which they refused to give. The gamekeeper then parked his Land-Rover so as to block the exit of their car from the lane in which it was then parked. B (the gamekeeper having refused to move the Land-Rover), then got into it, released the handbrake and coasted 200 yards down the lane to enable his vehicle to be driven away. In rejecting B's appeal against conviction (the ground of the appeal being that he had not taken the vehicle for his own use), the court held that although the phrase "for his own or another's use" involved something more than the mere movement of the vehicle, namely that it should be used as a conveyance, *i.e.* as a means of transport, it did not follow that the moving of an obstructing vehicle so that it ceased to be an obstruction could not involve the use of the vehicle as a conveyance. The vehicle was, in the ordinary sense of the English language, driven 200 yards (no point being taken as to the fact that the engine was not used) and that inevitably involved using it as a conveyance—B's motive for so using it was immaterial. *Aliter*, had the vehicle been pushed out of the way for a yard or two. The facts of the removal must be examined in each case.

It is not essential that the vehicle taken has actually been used as a conveyance: *R. v. Pearce* [1973] Crim.L.R. 321, CA; *R. v. Marchant and McAllister*, 80 Cr.App.R. 361, CA.

(7) Attempt

As to proof of an attempt to commit this offence, see *Jones v. Brooks*, 52 Cr.App.R. 614, DC. As to the distinction between the full offence and an attempt to commit it, see *R. v. Marchant and McCallister*, *ante*. **21–156**

For the summary offence of "vehicle interference", see the *Criminal Attempts Act* 1981, s.9 (outside the scope of this work).

(8) Driving vehicle taken without consent

A person cannot be said to be the driver of a vehicle unless he is in the driving seat or in control of the steering wheel and also has something to do with the propulsion: *R. v. Roberts* [1965] 1 Q.B. 85, 48 Cr.App.R. 296, CCA. An activity is not to be described as "driving" (see *post*, § 32–14) if the activity is something which could not be accepted as driving in any ordinary use of the word in the English language: *R. v. MacDonagh* [1974] Q.B. 448, 59 Cr.App.R. 55, CA (a decision in relation to the offence of driving whilst disqualified); *Blayney v. Knight*, 60 Cr.App.R. 269, DC. **21–157**

B. THE AGGRAVATED OFFENCE

(1) Statute

Theft Act 1968, s.12A

Aggravated vehicle-taking

12A.—(1) Subject to subsection (3) below, a person is guilty of aggravated taking of a vehicle if— **21–158**

(a) he commits an offence under section 12(1) above (in this section referred to as a "basic offence") in relation to a mechanically propelled vehicle; and

(b) it is proved that, at any time after the vehicle was unlawfully taken (whether by him or another) and before it was recovered, the vehicle was driven, or injury or damage was caused, in one or more of the circumstances set out in paragraphs (a) to (d) of subsection (2) below.

(2) The circumstances referred to in subsection (1)(b) above are—

(a) that the vehicle was driven dangerously on a road or other public place;

(b) that, owing to the driving of the vehicle, an accident occurred by which injury was caused to any person;

(c) that, owing to the driving of the vehicle, an accident occurred by which damage was caused to any property, other than the vehicle;

(d) that damage was caused to the vehicle.

(3) A person is not guilty of an offence under this section if he proves that, as regards any such proven driving, injury or damage as is referred to in subsection (1)(b) above, either—

(a) the driving, accident or damage referred to in subsection (2) above occurred before he committed the basic offence; or

(b) he was neither in nor on nor in the immediate vicinity of the vehicle when that driving, accident or damage occurred.

(4) A person guilty of an offence under this section shall be liable on conviction on indictment to imprisonment for a term not exceeding two years or, if it is proved that, in circumstances falling within subsection (2)(b) above, the accident caused the death of the person concerned, fourteen years.

(5) If a person who is charged with an offence under this section is found not guilty of that offence but it is proved that he committed a basic offence, he may be convicted of the basic offence.

(6) If by virtue of subsection (5) above a person is convicted of a basic offence before the Crown Court, that court shall have the same powers and duties as a magistrates' court would have had on convicting him of such an offence.

(7) For the purposes of this section a vehicle is driven dangerously if—

(a) it is driven in a way which falls far below what would be expected of a competent and careful driver, and

(b) it would be obvious to a competent and careful driver that driving the vehicle in that way would be dangerous.

(8) For the purposes of this section a vehicle is recovered when it is restored to its owner or to other lawful possession or custody; and in this subsection "owner" has the same meaning as in section 12 above.

[This section was inserted by the *Aggravated Vehicle-Taking Act* 1992, s.1(1). Subs. (4) is printed as amended by the *CJA* 2003, s.285(1) (substitution of "fourteen" for "five").]

As to subsection (7), see section 2A of the *RTA* 1988, *post*, § 32–17. As to the definition of owner in subsection (8), see *ante*, § 21–141.

(2) Indictment

COUNT 1

STATEMENT OF OFFENCE

21–159 *Aggravated vehicle-taking involving a fatal accident, contrary to section 12A of the* Theft Act *1968*.

PARTICULARS OF OFFENCE

A B, on the —— day of ——, 20—, without the consent of the owner or other lawful authority, took a mechanically propelled vehicle, namely a Ford motor car, registration number ——, for the use of himself [or *the use of C D*], *and thereafter, and before the vehicle was recovered, and owing to the driving of the vehicle, an accident occurred which caused the death of E F.*

COUNT 2

STATEMENT OF OFFENCE

21–159a *Aggravated vehicle-taking, contrary to section 12A of the* Theft Act *1968*.

PARTICULARS OF OFFENCE

A B, on the —— day of ——, 20—, without the consent of the owner or other lawful authority, took a mechanically propelled vehicle, namely a Ford motor car, registration number ——, for the use of himself [or *the use of C D*], *and thereafter, and before the vehicle was recovered, the vehicle was driven dangerously on the M25* [or *damage was caused to the vehicle*] [or *and owing to the driving of the vehicle, an accident occurred by which injury was caused to E F/damage was caused to a Vauxhall motor car registration number ——*].

(3) Class of offence and mode of trial

21–159b The offence is triable either way (and is a class 3 offence, *ante*, § 2–17): *MCA* 1980, s.17 and Sched. 1, and the *Aggravated Vehicle-Taking Act* 1992, s.1(2)(b). However, if the allegation is that the vehicle was merely damaged and the value of the damage is small, the offence is triable summarily only: *MCA* 1980, s.22 and Sched. 2 (*ante*, §§ 1–75i *et seq.*). The current relevant sum is £5,000. The criteria by which the value of the damage is to be established are set out in Schedule 2 to the 1980 Act.

Where one person is charged with taking a vehicle and a second person is charged in a separate information with allowing himself to be carried in it, they are to be regarded as being jointly charged for the purposes of section 24 of the *MCA* 1980 (*ante*, § 1–75m): *Ex p. Allgood, The Times*, November 25, 1994, DC. The court said that the situation in relation to vehicles was separate and distinct because only one person could drive a car at one time.

(4) Alternative verdict

21–159c Section 12A(5) applies to trial in a magistrates' court as much as to trial in the Crown Court; where, therefore, a magistrates' court upheld a submission of no case in relation to the aggravated offence, it had been open to the court to continue the hearing in relation to the basic offence: *R. (H.) v. Liverpool City Youth Court* [2001] Crim.L.R. 487, DC.

(5) Sentence

Maximum

21–160 See section 12A(4), *ante*, which is without prejudice to section 127 of the *PCC(S)A* 2000, under which the Crown Court has a general power to fine an offender convicted on indictment: *Aggravated Vehicle-Taking Act* 1992, s.1(2)(a). For illustrative decisions, see CSP, B12–13D01 to B12–13D07.

An offence under this section which involves an accident which caused the death of any person is a specified violent offence within Schedule 15 to the *CJA* 2003 (*ante*, § 5–299).

Disqualification and endorsement

This offence carries obligatory disqualification and endorsement (3 to 11 points): *RTOA* 1988, ss.28, 34, 44, 96 and 97 and Sched. 2, Pt II. The fact that the person convicted did not drive the vehicle in question at any particular time or at all shall not be regarded as a special reason for the purposes of section 34(1) of the 1988 Act (disqualification for certain offences): *ibid.* s.34(1A) (*post*, § 32–181). **21–161**

In the case of a passenger, it is inappropriate to order him to take an extended driving test at the end of a period of disqualification: *R. v. Bradshaw*, *The Times*, December 31, 1994, CA.

(6) Elements of the offence

Two offences created

Section 12A creates two offences: one with a maximum penalty of two years' imprisonment and, where additional facts under section 12A(2)(b) are proved and death results, one with a maximum penalty of 14 (formerly five, *ante*, § 21–158) years' imprisonment. It is essential that the indictment makes it clear which offence is being charged: *R. v. Button*, *The Times*, October 21, 1994, CA (applying *R. v. Courtie* [1984] A.C. 463, HL). **21–162**

"Owing to the driving of the vehicle"

In *R. v. Marsh* [1997] 1 Cr.App.R. 67, CA, it was held that the words "owing to the driving of the vehicle" were plain and simple and it was unhelpful to gloss the statute by referring to the manner or mode of driving (p. 70). There is no requirement of fault in the driving of the vehicle. **21–163**

"Accident"

The word "accident" can include a situation where a person has deliberately caused injury: *R. v. Branchflower* [2005] 1 Cr.App.R. 10, CA, where it was held that the word means "something which happens" but it does not have to be unintended or fortuitous; section 12A is intended to have regard to the consequences of what occurred and is not really concerned with the way in which they came about. **21–163a**

Damage to the vehicle

Where the accused took a vehicle which had been specially adapted so as to cut out the engine and to lock the doors after only a few yards and, in an attempt to escape before the arrival of the police, broke a window, it was held that he fell within the section: *Dawes v. DPP* [1994] R.T.R. 209, DC. **21–163b**

VII. ABSTRACTION OF ELECTRICITY

(1) Statute

Theft Act 1968, s.13

13. A person who dishonestly uses without due authority, or dishonestly causes to be wasted or diverted, any electricity shall on conviction on indictment be liable to imprisonment for a term not exceeding five years. **21–164**

(2) Indictment

STATEMENT OF OFFENCE

Abstracting electricity, contrary to section 13 of the Theft Act *1968.* **21–165**

PARTICULARS OF OFFENCE

A B, on the —— day of ——, 20—, dishonestly used without due authority [or *dishonestly caused to be wasted or diverted*] *a quantity of electricity.*

(3) Class of offence and mode of trial

21–166 This offence is triable either way: *MCA* 1980, s.17(1) and Sched. 1, para. 28, *ante*, § 1–75af. It is a class 3 offence, *ante*, § 2–17.

(4) Sentence

21–167 Imprisonment not exceeding five years: s.13, *ante*. For illustrative decisions, see CSP, B6–82001 to B6–83A02.

(5) Elements of the offence

21–168 Prove that the defendant dishonestly used a quantity of electricity and that he did so without due authority; or that he dishonestly caused to be wasted or diverted a quantity of electricity. As to the requirement of dishonesty, see generally, *ante*, §§ 21–23 *et seq.* Where it was discovered that a meter in a house had been tampered with so as not to record the electricity being consumed and the two occupants had been convicted of dishonestly using electricity, the Court of Appeal held in *R. v. Hoar and Hoar* [1982] Crim.L.R. 606, that their convictions should be quashed because of an insufficient direction on joint enterprise. Watkins L.J., delivering the judgment of the court, said:

> "The jury ... should have been specially directed that in order to convict this husband and wife of theft [*sic*] on the basis that they stole [*sic*] electricity as the result of participating in a joint enterprise, they should be satisfied that (1) each of them agreed to obtain for use in their home electricity for which neither of them would pay, (2) each of them knew the means to be adopted to achieve that end ..., (3) one of them, to the knowledge of the other, who was ready to assist if needed, tampered with the meter so that electricity could be obtained without payment and (4) each of them knew that thereafter electricity which had not been paid for and which neither of them intended to pay for was being used in their home" (p. 6 of transcript 4168/B2/81, 4169/B2/81).

Assuming that the reference to theft was just a slip, it is nevertheless difficult to disagree with the commentary in the *Criminal Law Review* that on a charge of "using" this direction is far more elaborate than is necessary.

21–169 *Hoar and Hoar* was considered in *Collins and Fox v. Chief Constable of Merseyside* [1988] Crim.L.R. 247, DC. The facts were similar and the appellants were jointly charged with dishonestly using electricity without due authority. Bingham L.J., giving a judgment with which Mann J. agreed, stated that the elaborate direction suggested in *Hoar and Hoar* need only be resorted to where the case is put forward as one of joint enterprise. His Lordship said that complications would perhaps be avoided if more attention were directed to the simple ingredients of the offence and less to the more complicated concept of joint enterprise. It is submitted that this is plainly correct: where "use" is charged, as opposed to "causing to be wasted or diverted", joint enterprise has little relevance. On the facts, the court held that it was not enough to convict one appellant, who was the registered consumer, merely because she was the registered consumer and, therefore, a beneficiary of the unlawful interference with the meter. It was possible, the court thought, for her co-habitee to have interfered with the meter without her being aware of it. Equally, the court held that the other appellant, the co-habitee, ought not to have been convicted purely on the basis that he lived with the registered consumer as man and wife and, therefore, must have known what had been done. Clearly one appellant was guilty; quite possibly, both were, but it was impossible to be sure which version was correct: accordingly, both appellants ought to have been acquitted.

In *R. v. McCreadie and Tume*, 96 Cr.App.R. 143, CA, it was held that the offence of dishonestly using electricity without authority did not necessarily involve tampering with the meter. It is sufficient to prove that electricity was used without the authority of the electricity supplier by persons who had no intention of paying for it.

As to the dishonest obtaining of an electronic communications service, see the *Communications Act* 2003, s.125 (*post*, § 25–363).

In *Att.-Gen.'s Reference (No. 1 of 1980)*, 72 Cr.App.R. 60, the Court of Appeal held that the words "made or required" in section 17(1)(a) indicated that a distinction should be drawn between documents made specifically for accounting purposes and those made for some other purpose but required for accounting purposes. Thus documents such as the personal loan proposal forms with which the court was concerned would fall within section 17 if they were merely required for accounting purposes as a subsidiary consideration and the fact that the falsified information was contained in a different part from that required for accounting purposes was irrelevant, for the document must be examined as a whole.

A form claiming entitlement to housing benefit is a "document made or required for an accounting purpose": *Osinuga v. DPP*, 162 J.P. 120, DC.

In *R. v. Manning* [1998] 2 Cr.App.R. 461, CA, it was held that it is open to a court to find that a document is a document required for an accounting purpose without evidence to explain the actual use made of the document; in the circumstances, it had been open to the jury to find that false insurance cover notes provided to the insured were such documents, in that they set out the rate of, and dates on which, premiums were to be paid. By contrast, in *R. v. Sundhers* [1998] Crim.L.R. 497, CA, convictions for false accounting based on dishonest insurance claim forms were quashed where there was no evidence as to how the documents were "required for [an] accounting purpose"; although only a little evidence as to the use made of the claim forms once submitted would probably have sufficed for this purpose, it was not a matter which could simply be left to the jury for them to draw their own conclusions.

(b) *Falsification*

Section 17(2), which applies to "an account or other document" but not to a record, is not a definition section but a deeming provision, so that if there was a conflict between section 17(2) and section 17(1)(a) the court would have no hesitation in ignoring the former and construing the words of the latter as they appeared: *Edwards v. Toombs* [1983] Crim.L.R. 43, DC. **21–233**

In *R. v. Shama*, 91 Cr.App.R. 138, CA, the appellant, an international telephone operator, was required to record details of each call to an overseas subscriber on one of a number of identical printed forms, which were later used for accounting purposes. At his trial, on counts of contravening section 17(1)(a) by failing to complete the appropriate form, thereby omitting material particulars from a document required for an accounting purpose, a submission that false accounting could not take place unless an account had actually been brought into existence was rejected. It was held that as soon as the defendant's duty to complete a form arose, one of the standard forms became a "document ... required for (an) accounting purpose" so that an identifiable document existed for the purposes of the section. The prosecution merely had to prove that the appellant had dishonestly, and for the required purpose, omitted material particulars from such a document.

(c) *With a view to gain, or with intent to cause loss*

Theft Act 1968, s.34(2)(a)

(2) For purposes of this Act— **21–234**

(a) "gain" and "loss" are to be construed as extending only to gain or loss in money or other property, but as extending to any such gain or loss whether temporary or permanent; and—

(i) "gain" includes a gain by keeping what one has, as well as a gain by getting what one has not; and

(ii) "loss" includes a loss by not getting what one might get, as well as a loss by parting with what one has;

In *R. v. Golechha and Choraria*, 90 Cr.App.R. 241, CA, it was held that where a debtor falsifies documents required for an accounting purpose and does so dishonestly, intending thereby to induce his creditor to forebear from suing on the debt, he does not have "a view to gain" within section 34(2). A debtor was not possessed of any proprietary rights; he did not have money and the chose in action represented by the debt was owned by the creditor. **21–235**

In *R. v. Eden*, 55 Cr.App.R. 193, CA, the court held that there were various forms of temporary gain which could result in a verdict of guilty on a charge under section 17, including (on the facts of the case) a gain constituted "by putting off the evil day of having to sort out the muddle and pay up what may have been in error kept within the sub-post office when it ought to have been sent to head office" (at p. 197).

21–236 "Gain" or "loss" must relate to money or other property; but there is no necessity to prove that the defendant had no legal entitlement to the property in question: *Att.-Gen.'s Reference (No. 1 of 2001)* [2002] 3 All E.R. 840, CA. In *R. v. Masterton*, unreported, April 30, 1996, CA (94 02221 X5), a company director was charged with obtaining property by deception and false accounting. The deception counts were described as being the springboard for the false accounting counts. The defendant was acquitted of the deception counts at the close of the prosecution's case, on the direction of the judge. The false accounting counts were left to the jury. They related to two false invoices which purported to show sales or services for large sums of money by two companies which had been recently acquired by the company of which the defendant was a director. The effect of the invoices was to improve the apparent financial status of the acquired companies. The prosecution contended that the defendant was seeking to mollify his co-directors, who were dissatisfied with the acquisitions. This was said to remove any chance of his having to use his own financial resources to placate them, even though there was no legal obligation on him to do so. It was argued that this was done "with a view to gain for himself" because it would enable him to "keep what he had", namely his own financial resources. The Court of Appeal quashed the convictions and held that a desire to improve relations with business partners did not involve monetary gain and an intent to retain his own resources was an artificial concept when he was never at risk *vis-à-vis* his co-directors.

In *Lee Cheung Wing v. R.*, 94 Cr.App.R. 355, PC, the appellants were employees of a company dealing in futures contracts. As such, they were not allowed to operate an account on their own behalf. They opened an account in a friend's name and were charged with false accounting by falsifying withdrawal slips to authorise the release of the funds. It was argued that the admitted dishonest falsification of the withdrawal slips was not done with a view to gain, as defined by section 8(2) of the *Theft Ordinance of Hong Kong* (which is in the same terms as section 34(2)(a) of the *Theft Act* 1968). It was contended that no gain resulted from the falsification of the slips but only from the sale of the futures contracts and the company suffered no loss since the money had always been that of the appellants. It was held that a servant who uses his position of employment to make a personal profit is bound to account to his master for such profit, regardless of whether the master had suffered any loss as a result. The falsification of the withdrawal slips enabled them to recover from the company funds to which they were not entitled and was done "with a view to gain".

See also *R. v. Bevans*, 87 Cr.App.R. 64, CA, *post*, § 21–267.

(d) *Dishonesty*

21–237 See generally *ante*, §§ 21–2b, 21–24 *et seq.* In *R. v. Eden*, *ante*, the appellant's convictions were quashed, although he had acted "with a view to gain", because the jury had said after the verdicts had been returned that they found him "not dishonest, but muddled".

(6) Theft and false accounting

21–238 In *R. v. Eden*, *ante*, Sachs L.J. said:

> "It seems to this Court to be rather odd that two counts, theft and false accounting, should be put in parallel setting, if it is the object of the prosecution to secure a conviction on the first only if the second is proved, or on the second only if the first is proved. ... It would be better in future that the prosecution should make up its mind as to whether or not it really wants a conviction on a count for false accounting only if theft is proved: if so, reliance should be placed on one count only. On the other hand, there may be cases when it is wise to have a count for false accounting; where, for instance, a temporary gain could be the object of the dishonest act" (at pp. 198–199).

(7) Jurisdiction

Statute

As to the effect of the *CJA* 1993, Pt I (an offence contrary to section 17 is a "Group A" offence), see *ante*, §§ 2–37 *et seq.* **21–239**

Common law

As to jurisdiction generally, see *R. v. Smith (Wallace Duncan) (No. 4)* [2004] 2 Cr.App.R. 17, CA (*ante*, § 21–210), and *ante*, §§ 2–33 *et seq.* As to jurisdiction and a charge of false accounting, see, in particular, *R. v. Governor of Pentonville Prison, ex p. Osman*, 90 Cr.App.R. 281, DC, but it is submitted that the tentative views advanced therein as to the possible places of commission of such an offence must now be regarded as subordinated to the considered, and more generalised opinion of the Court of Appeal in *Smith, ante*, §§ 2–33 *et seq.* **21–240**

X. OFFENCES RELATING TO COMPANIES AND COMPANY DIRECTORS

For (a) the liability of company officers for certain offences by a company, see the *Theft Act* 1968, s.18, *post*, § 30–265, and (b) false statements by company directors, see the *Theft Act* 1968, s.19, *post*, §§ 30–267 *et seq.* **21–241**

XI. SUPPRESSION OF DOCUMENTS

(1) Introduction

Section 20(2) of the *Theft Act* 1968 (procuring the execution of a valuable security by deception) was repealed by the *Fraud Act* 2006 with effect from January 15, 2007. The separate offence under section 20(1) (destroying, etc., a valuable security) remains, and introduces the element of a view to gain to the offender or another, or an intent to cause loss to another. "Gain" and "loss" are defined in section 34(2)(a): *ante*, § 21–234. Dishonesty is a separate requirement: see *ante*, §§ 21–2b *et seq.* Subsection (3) defines "valuable security". **21–242**

(2) Statute

Theft Act 1968, s.20

20.—(1) A person who dishonestly, with a view to gain for himself or another or with intent to cause loss to another, destroys, defaces or conceals any valuable security, any will or other testamentary document or any original document of or belonging to, or filed or deposited in, any court of justice or any government department shall on conviction on indictment be liable to imprisonment for a term not exceeding seven years. **21–243**

(2) [*Repealed by* Fraud Act *2006, s.14(1) and (3), Sched. 1, para. 1, and Sched. 3.*]

(3) For purposes of this section "valuable security" means any document creating, transferring, surrendering or releasing any right to, in or over property, or authorising the payment of money or delivery of any property, or evidencing the creation, transfer, surrender or release of any such right, or the payment of money or delivery of any property, or the satisfaction of any obligation.

[Subs. (3) is printed as amended by the *Fraud Act* 2006, s.14(1) and (3), Sched. 1, para. 5, and Sched. 3.]

As to the saving of the former law in relation to an offence partly committed before the commencement of the 2006 Act, see *post*, § 21–414.

(3) Indictment for destroying a will

STATEMENT OF OFFENCE

Destroying a will, contrary to section 20(1) of the Theft Act *1968.* **21–244**

PARTICULARS OF OFFENCE

A B, on the —— day of ——, 20—, dishonestly and with a view to gain for himself or another or with intent to cause loss to another destroyed the will of one J N.

(4) Class of offence and mode of trial

21–245 This offence is triable either way: *MCA* 1980, s.17(1) and Sched. 1, para. 28, *ante*, § 1–75af. It is a class 3 offence, *ante*, § 2–17.

(5) Sentence

21–246 Imprisonment not exceeding seven years: s.20(1), *ante*.

(6) Elements of the offence

21–247 Prove the destruction of the will by the defendant as stated in the indictment, and also that he did it dishonestly for the purpose of gain for himself or another or of causing loss to another as alleged. The purpose can, in most cases, be only a matter of inference not capable of direct proof (see *R. v. Morris* (1839) 9 C. & P. 89); but the mere destruction, unexplained by the defendant, is evidence from which the purpose of the defendant may fairly be presumed.

[The next paragraph is § 21–256.]

XII. BLACKMAIL

(1) Statute

Theft Act 1968, s.21

21–256 **21.**—(1) A person is guilty of blackmail if, with a view to gain for himself or another or with intent to cause loss to another, he makes any unwarranted demand with menaces; and for this purpose a demand with menaces is unwarranted unless the person making it does so in the belief—

(a) that he has reasonable grounds for making the demand; and

(b) that the use of the menaces is a proper means of reinforcing the demand.

(2) The nature of the act or omission demanded is immaterial, and it is also immaterial whether the menaces relate to action to be taken by the person making the demand.

(3) A person guilty of blackmail shall on conviction on indictment be liable to imprisonment for a term not exceeding fourteen years.

"Gain" and "loss" are defined in the *Theft Act* 1968, s.34(2)(a): *ante*, § 21–234.

(2) Indictment

STATEMENT OF OFFENCE

21–257 *Blackmail, contrary to section 21(1) of the* Theft Act *1968.*

PARTICULARS OF OFFENCE

A B on the —— day of ——, 20—, with a view to gain for himself in a letter dated —— and addressed to C D at ——, made an unwarranted demand of £100 from C D with menaces.

(3) Class of offence and mode of trial

21–258 This offence is indictable only: see the *MCA* 1980, s.17(1), and Sched. 1, para. 28, *ante*, § 1–75af. It is a class 3 offence, *ante*, § 2–17.

(4) Sentence

21–259 Imprisonment not exceeding 14 years: s.21(3), *ante*. For illustrative decisions, see CSP, B6–63A01 to B6–63B15.

In giving the judgment of the Court of Appeal in *R. v. Hadjou*, 11 Cr.App.R.(S.) 29, Lord Lane C.J. said that in the calendar of criminal offences blackmail was one of the ugliest and most vicious because it involved what one found so often, attempted murder of the soul. Perhaps because courts always imposed severe sentences for such a crime, one so seldom found a person convicted for the second time of blackmail. Deterrence was perhaps the most important part of the sentence in such a case.

Blackmail is a "lifestyle offence" within the *PCA* 2002, Sched. 2 (*ante*, § 5–661), and, as such, is an offence in respect of which a financial reporting order may be made under section 76 of the *SOCPA* 2005 (*ante*, § 5–886a).

It is also a specified serious offence within Schedule 1 to the *SCA* 2007, enabling the court to make a serious crime prevention order under section 19 on conviction (*ante*, § 5–875c).

(5) Elements of the offence

Prove that (a) a demand with (b) menaces was made; (c) that it was unwarranted; and (d) that at the time of making the demand the defendant made it with a view to gain for himself or another or with intent to cause loss to another. **21–260**

(a) *The demand*

The demand may be made in writing or by speech or by conduct. It need not be explicit provided that if implicit, the demand was such that "the demeanour of the accused and the circumstances of the case were such that an ordinary reasonable man would understand that a demand ... was being made of him ...": *R. v. Collister and Warhurst*, 39 Cr.App.R. 100 at 102, CCA. The demand does not have to be communicated to the person of whom it is made: *Treacy v. DPP* [1971] A.C. 537, HL. **21–261**

(b) *Menaces*

The demand must be made with menaces. In *R. v. Clear* [1968] 1 Q.B. 670, 52 Cr.App.R. 58, CA, a decision under the former law, Sellers L.J. reviewed the authorities as to the meaning of the word "menaces". Having done so, his Lordship continued: **21–262**

> "Words or conduct which would not intimidate or influence anyone to respond to the demand would not be menaces ..., but threats and conduct of such a nature and extent that the mind of an ordinary person of normal stability and courage might be influenced or made apprehensive so as to accede unwillingly to the demand would be sufficient for a jury's consideration. ... There may be special circumstances unknown to the accused which would make the threats innocuous and unavailing for the accused's demand, but such circumstances would have no bearing on the accused's state of mind and of his intention. If an accused knew that what he threatened would have no effect on the victim it might be different" (at pp. 679–680, 69).

In *Thorne v. Motor Trade Association* [1937] A.C. 797, HL, Lord Wright also thought that the word "menace" is to be "liberally construed and not as limited to threats of violence but as including threats of any action detrimental to or unpleasant to the person addressed. It may also include a warning that in certain events such action is intended" (at p. 817). Lord Atkin said:

> "The ordinary blackmailer normally threatens to do what he has a perfect right to do namely, communicate some compromising conduct to a person whose knowledge is likely to affect the person threatened. Often indeed he has not only the right but also the duty to make the disclosure, as of a felony, to the competent authorities. What he has to justify is not the threat, but the demand of money. The *gravamen* of the charge is the demand without reasonable or probable cause: and I cannot think that the mere fact that the threat is to do something a person is entitled to do either causes the threat not to be a 'menace' ... or in itself provides a reasonable or probable cause for the demand" (at pp. 806–807).

Their Lordships were concerned with section 29(1) of the *Larceny Act* 1916, which provided: "Every person who—(1) utters, knowing the contents thereof, any letter or writing demanding of any person with menaces, and without any reasonable or probable cause, any property or valuable thing ... shall be guilty of felony. ..."

In *R. v. Lawrence and Pomroy*, 57 Cr.App.R. 64, it was argued before the Court of Appeal that the trial judge had wrongly failed to give the jury a definition of what constitutes a menace in accordance with *Clear*, *ante*: **21–263**

> "The word 'menaces' is an ordinary English word which any jury can be expected to understand. In exceptional cases where because of special knowledge in special circumstances what would be a menace to an ordinary person is not a menace to the person to whom it is

addressed, or where the converse may be true, it is no doubt necessary to spell out the meaning of the word" (*per* Cairns L.J. at p. 72).

Clear and *Lawrence and Pomroy* were referred to approvingly in *R. v. Garwood*, 85 Cr.App.R. 85, CA. There were two possible situations where some elaboration of the word "menaces" might be required. The first was where the threats might affect the mind of an ordinary person of normal stability but did not affect the person actually addressed. Such circumstances would amount to a sufficient menace. The second was where the threats in fact affected the victim's mind although they would not have affected the mind of a person of ordinary stability: in such a case the existence of menaces was proved, provided that the accused was aware of the likely effect of his actions on the victim.

(c) *Unwarranted*

21–264 Any demand with menaces is unwarranted unless the defendant is able to bring himself within both paragraphs (a) and (b) of section 21(1). Thus the essential nature of the offence is that the accused demands with menaces when he believes he is not entitled to the thing demanded or when he believes the use of menaces is improper notwithstanding his genuine claim. It appears to follow from this that a claim of right cannot be a defence as such to a charge of blackmail. The fact that dishonesty is not an ingredient of the offence adds weight to this contention. In *R. v. Lawrence and Pomroy*, *ante*, one of the defendants apparently had a genuine belief that the money demanded was lawfully due to him: no point was taken on this, however, and it certainly did not occur to the Court of Appeal that there might be anything in the point. It is true that the Court of Criminal Appeal in *R. v. Bernhard* [1938] 2 K.B. 264, 26 Cr.App.R. 137, held that a claim of right was a good defence to a charge under section 30 of the *Larceny Act* 1916, one of the old group of offences commonly referred to as "blackmail". However, it is submitted, that *Bernhard* is not authority for suggesting that a claim of right as such is a defence under section 21 of the *Theft Act* 1968. This is because the rationale of that decision has now disappeared: under section 30, it had to be proved that the defendant intended to steal the property he demanded. If he had a claim of right, clearly he could not be said to have the requisite intention.

21–265 Each case will turn on its own facts. A threat to do some harm disproportionate to the sum or property legally claimed would be strong evidence of the absence of any belief in the propriety of the threat. That it is the defendant's own belief that matters was emphasised in *R. v. Harvey*, 72 Cr.App.R. 139, CA. Bingham J., giving the court's judgment, said: "It matters not what the reasonable man, or any other man than the defendant, would believe save in so far as that may throw light on what the defendant in fact believed" (at p. 141). This applies to both paragraphs (a) and (b). In relation to paragraph (b), the court considered the question of what or whose standards were to be applied in relation to the issue of the defendant's belief that the use of the menaces was a "proper" means of reinforcing the demand. The Crown submitted that a threat to perform a criminal act can never as a matter of law be a proper means within the subsection. Bingham J. said (at p. 142) that the word "proper" is:

> "plainly a word of wide meaning, certainly wider than (for example) 'lawful'. But the greater includes the less and no act which was not believed to be lawful could be believed to be proper within the meaning of the subsection. ... The test is not what (the defendant) regards as justified, but what he believed to be proper. And where ... the threats were to do acts which any sane man knows to be against the laws of every civilised country no jury would hesitate long before dismissing the contention that the defendant genuinely believed the threats to be a proper means of reinforcing even a legitimate demand."

21–266 In *Harvey*, the menaces were to kill or to maim or to rape. The court held that a proper direction would have been as follows: the demand with menaces was not to be regarded as unwarranted unless the Crown satisfied the jury that the defendant did not make the demand with menaces in the genuine belief both (a) that he had reasonable grounds for making a demand, and (b) that the use of the menaces was in the circumstances a proper (meaning for present purposes a lawful, and not a criminal) means of reinforcing the demand.

It is for the defence to raise the issues contained in both paragraphs if they so wish and establish the defendant's belief in the grounds and the means. Once the issue is raised, it is for the prosecution to negative so that a jury can be sure that the defendant did not have the beliefs he alleges in relation to either the grounds of the demand or the means of reinforcing it. In *R. v. Lawrence and Pomroy*, *ante*, neither defendant suggested in evidence that, if menaces were used by them, it was a proper means of reinforcing the demand for payment of the debt. They contended on appeal that the judge should have directed the jury on proviso (b) to section 21(1). It was held that where on the face of it the means adopted to obtain payment of a debt are not the proper way of enforcing it and where the accused does not at his trial set up the case that he believed it to be, there is no need for any direction to be given on proviso (b). The same principle will apply to (a): if, on the face of it, there are no reasonable grounds for the demand and the defence do not raise the issue, there will be no need for the judge to direct the jury on proviso (a). See also *R. v. Harvey*, *ante*, at p. 142.

(d) *With a view to gain for himself or another or with intent to cause loss to another*

The demand must be accompanied by either a view to gain or an intention to cause loss. Gain or loss is to be construed as extending only to money or other property: see s.34(2)(a), *ante*, § 21–234. **21–267**

There is no requirement of economic interest: *R. v. Bevans*, 87 Cr.App.R. 64, CA (doctor threatened patient in severe pain who wanted an injection of morphine).

Since the definition of "gain" includes "getting what one has not", there is no justification for any argument that "gain" should be limited to "gain" in the sense of "profit". If a person makes a demand for a debt lawfully owed to him, it may be that he does not do so with a view to profit, but he certainly does so with a view to getting what he has not. It has been held at first instance that by demanding money lawfully owing to him the defendant did have a view to "gain": by obtaining hard cash as opposed to a mere right of action in respect of the debt the defendant was getting more than he already had: *R. v. Parkes* [1973] Crim.L.R. 358, Crown Court (H.H.J. Dean Q.C.). *Parkes* was specifically approved by the Court of Appeal in *Att.-Gen.'s Reference (No. 1 of 2001)* [2002] 3 All E.R. 840. See also *R. v. Lawrence and Pomroy*, *ante*.

(6) Jurisdiction

Statute

As to the effect of the *CJA* 1993, Pt I (blackmail is a "Group A" offence), see *ante*, §§ 2–37 *et seq.* **21–268**

Common law

The courts in England and Wales have jurisdiction to try a defendant on a charge of blackmail when a defendant writes and posts a letter in England and the letter (which contains an unwarranted demand with menaces) is addressed to and received by a person outside the jurisdiction: *Treacy v. DPP* [1971] A.C. 537, HL. As to whether the English courts have jurisdiction where a letter is sent from outside the jurisdiction to an address in England or Wales, see *Treacy v. DPP*, *ante*, *R. v. Baxter (R.)* [1972] 1 Q.B. 1, 55 Cr.App.R. 214, CA, *R. v. Smith (Wallace Duncan) (No. 4)* [2004] 2 Cr.App.R. 17, CA (not a blackmail case); and *ante*, §§ 2–33 *et seq.* **21–269**

XIII. HANDLING STOLEN PROPERTY

(1) Statute

Theft Act 1968, s.22

Handling stolen goods

22.—(1) A person handles stolen goods if (otherwise than in the course of the stealing) knowing or believing them to be stolen goods he dishonestly receives the goods, or dishonestly undertakes or assists in their retention, removal, disposal or realisation by or for the benefit of another person, or if he arranges to do so. **21–270**

(2) A person guilty of handling stolen goods shall on conviction on indictment be liable to imprisonment for a term not exceeding fourteen years.

Theft Act 1968, s.34(2)(b)

21–270a (2) For purposes of this Act—

(a) [ante, *§ 21–234*];

(b) "goods", except in so far as the context otherwise requires, includes money and every other description of property except land, and includes things severed from land by stealing.

As to the scope of the term "stolen goods", see section 24, *post*, § 21–297.

(2) Indictment

STATEMENT OF OFFENCE

21–271 *Handling stolen goods, contrary to section 22(1) of the* Theft Act *1968.*

PARTICULARS OF OFFENCE

A B, on the —— day of ——, 20—, dishonestly received certain stolen goods, namely a bag [belonging to C D] knowing or believing the same to be stolen goods.

The above count will suffice where there is clear evidence of possession by the defendant of the goods alleged to have been stolen. Where, however, the prosecution desire to rely also on the other limbs of the offence of handling, a second count should be added.

STATEMENT OF OFFENCE

Handling stolen goods, contrary to section 22(1) of the Theft Act *1968.*

PARTICULARS OF OFFENCE

A B, on the —— day of ——, 20—, dishonestly undertook or assisted in the retention, removal, disposal or realisation of certain stolen goods namely a bag[belonging to C D] by or for the benefit of another, or dishonestly arranged so to do, knowing or believing the same to be stolen goods.

For observations upon a compendious count for handling when property is discovered in the context of an "Aladdin's cave", see *R. v. Smythe*, 72 Cr.App.R. 8, CA, *post*, § 21–282. As to the application of the "continuous offence", "general deficiency" principle to an allegation of handling, see *R. v. Cain* [1983] Crim.L.R. 802, CA, *post*, § 21–276.

Form of the indictment

21–272 In *Griffiths v. Freeman* [1970] 1 All E.R. 1117, DC, it was held that section 22(1) constitutes a single offence of handling stolen goods. Accordingly an information preferred in a magistrates' court simply alleging handling of goods contrary to the section was not bad for duplicity.

> "It seems to me ... that it is sufficient to allege a handling of goods contrary to the section, but that in the ordinary way particulars should be given in order to enable the accused to understand the ingredients of the charge which he has to face. ... In a case where there is likely to be any embarrassment it is quite clear to me that the information should set out particulars, and that if it does not, an application for particulars should be acceded to. ... I would like to confine this judgment to proceedings in magistrates' courts. It may be, whatever be the true position in law, that when one comes to deal with indictments, the better practice may be of having ... separate counts describing the different methods of handling" (*per* Lord Parker C.J., at pp. 1118–1119).

In *R. v. Sloggett* [1972] 1 Q.B. 430, 55 Cr.App.R. 532, the Court of Appeal expressed its agreement with these observations. It was held that no count for an offence of handling stolen goods by dishonestly undertaking or assisting in the retention, removal, disposal or realisation of stolen goods by or for the benefit of another person should omit the words "by or for the benefit of another person", since on the true construction of section 22(1) the nouns retention, removal, disposal and realisation are all governed by those words which form an essential part of the offence: see also *R. v. Bloxham* [1983] 1 A.C. 109, HL, *post*, § 21–306; and *R. v. Gingell* [2000] 1 Cr.App.R. 88, CA (on a charge of second limb handling, the other person cannot be a co-accused in the same count).

There then followed a series of further cases in which the proper form of an indictment for handling stolen goods was considered: *R. v. Ikpong* [1972] Crim.L.R. 432, CA; *R. v. Alt*, 56 Cr.App.R. 457, CA; *R. v. Willis and Syme*, 57 Cr.App.R. 1, CA; *R. v. Deakin*, 56 Cr.App.R. 841, CA; *R. v. Pitchley*, 57 Cr.App.R. 30, CA. **21–273**

All of the foregoing authorities were considered in *R. v. Nicklin*, 64 Cr.App.R. 205, CA. D was charged with handling stolen lead by dishonestly receiving it. He admitted assisting the thief in the removal of the lead. The prosecution did not seek leave to amend the indictment and the jury were directed that they could return a verdict of "not guilty as charged but guilty of handling stolen goods in dishonestly assisting in the removal or disposal of them". The jury brought in a verdict as directed. D's appeal was allowed on the ground that, the prosecution having charged handling by receiving with no alternative count, he could not be convicted of a form of handling with which he had not been charged.

> "... the effect of those cases is this. An indictment which alleges an offence of handling *simpliciter* unparticularised is not a defective indictment ... and convictions of a particular type of handling can be upheld where allowing the charge in that generalised form has led to no injustice or confusion; but the better practice is to particularise the form of handling for which the defendant is blamed. If the prosecution were to consider and provide for all possible forms of handling ... some 18 counts might be necessary. That would be absurd but the prosecution ought, generally speaking, to nail its colours to the mast of a particular form of handling. If there is any uncertainty about which form of handling, two counts will generally cover every form: one count for the first limb, dishonestly receiving, and a second for the second limb, dishonestly undertaking or assisting in the retention, removal, disposal or realisation, with arrangement to do those things if need be. The second count, covering all those alternatives, would not be bad for duplicity and might be advisable. It is quite clear that in many cases a second count would be advisable but a second count alleging only one or two of the alternatives set out in the section, perhaps assisting in the retention or removal, something of that kind. ... If there is any doubt about what form of handling is being charged ..., particulars of the charge or charges should figure clearly in the indictment. In other words the handling should be particularised and, if necessary, particularised in more than one way, but as a general rule certainly not in more than two counts" (*per* Stephenson L.J. at pp. 208–209).

The words "... or if he arranges to do so" at the end of section 22(1) apply to both limbs of the provision. The 18 possible forms of handling referred to by Stephenson L.J. in *Nicklin*, *ante*, can only be calculated on the basis that "arranging to receive" is a form of handling: see also *Ikpong*, *ante*. Furthermore, section 27(3) of the *Theft Act* 1968, supports this interpretation by providing that where a person is being proceeded against for handling stolen goods "... if evidence has been given of his having or arranging to have in his possession the goods the subject of the charge" evidence of previous possession can be admitted to prove that he had guilty knowledge. **21–274**

Averment of ownership

In *R. v. Gregory*, 56 Cr.App.R. 441, the Court of Appeal held that where on a receiving charge the property in question was of a common and undistinctive type it might well be necessary to name the owner in the particulars of the charge since cases could arise, where, unless the ownership was so assigned in the particulars, the accused might be unable to understand fully the nature of the case he had to meet. For a case where the Court of Appeal took the view that the attribution of ownership did not constitute a material averment, see *R. v. Deakin*, 56 Cr.App.R. 841: the court stressed that it was "impossible to dispute" that the property in question was stolen. It was immaterial from whom it was stolen. See generally *ante*, § 1–122. **21–275**

General deficiency and handling

Rule 14.2(2) of the *Criminal Procedure Rules* 2005 (S.I. 2005 No. 384) (*ante*, § 1–115) allows multiple incidents of receiving stolen goods to be included in a single count **21–276** where they amount to a course of conduct, thus maintaining the "general deficiency" principle illustrated by cases such as *R. v. Cain* [1983] Crim.L.R. 802, CA (in which the allegation was that the defendant had over a period of several years received a total of £20,000 from a co-defendant).

Joinder, etc.: evidence disclosing separate offences

Theft Act 1968, s.27(1), (2)

21–277 **27.**—(1) Any number of persons may be charged in one indictment, with reference to the same theft, with having at different times or at the same time handled all or any of the stolen goods, and the persons so charged may be tried together.

(2) On the trial of two or more persons indicted for jointly handling any stolen goods the jury may find any of the accused guilty if the jury are satisfied that he handled all or any of the stolen goods, whether or not he did so jointly with the other accused or any of them.

For section 27(3), see *post*, § 21–313; for section 27(4), (5), see *post*, § 21–332.

Section 27(2) has its origins in section 14 of the *Criminal Procedure Act* 1851, passed apparently to counter the decision in *R. v. Dovey and Gray* (1851) 4 Cox 428, to the effect that where two persons are jointly indicted for receiving it is impossible for them both to be found guilty where the evidence discloses separate receipts by them. Because section 27(2) relates only to trial on indictment, *Dovey and Gray* will continue to apply to summary proceedings. It was considered by the House of Lords in *DPP v. Merriman* [1973] A.C. 584, but was neither overruled nor disapproved: see also *R. v. French* [1973] Crim.L.R. 632, CA.

(3) Class of offence and mode of trial

21–278 This offence is triable either way: *MCA* 1980, s.17(1), and Sched. 1, para. 28, *ante*, § 1–75af. It is a class 3 offence, *ante*, § 2–17.

(4) Sentence

21–279 Imprisonment not exceeding 14 years: s.22(2), *ante*.

As to compensation, see *R. v. Tyce*, 15 Cr.App.R.(S.) 415, CA (*ante*, § 5–415).

Guidelines

21–279a In *R. v. Webbe* [2002] 1 Cr.App.R.(S.) 22, the Court of Appeal issued guidelines on sentencing those convicted of handling stolen goods. Where the handler had knowledge of the original offence, the seriousness of the handling is inevitably linked to the seriousness of that offence. Other factors which significantly affect the seriousness of the offence are the level of sophistication of the handler, the ultimate destination of the goods, the criminal origin of the goods, the impact on the victim, the level of profit made or expected by the handler and the precise role played by the handler.

The court identified nine aggravating features:

1. the closeness of the handler to the primary offence (geographical or temporal);
2. particular seriousness in the primary offence;
3. high value of the goods, including sentimental value;
4. the fact that the goods were the proceeds of a domestic burglary;
5. sophistication in relation to the handling;
6. a high level of profit made or expected by the handler;
7. the provision by the handler of a regular outlet for stolen goods;
8. threats of violence or abuse of power by the handler over others; and
9. the commission of an offence while on bail.

The court identified the following mitigating features:

1. low monetary value of the goods;
2. the offence being a "one-off" offence committed by an otherwise honest defendant;

3. little or no benefit to the defendant; and
4. voluntary restitution to the victim.

Other factors to be taken into account were the personal mitigation of the defendant, ready co-operation with the police, previous convictions and a timely plea of guilty.

Where the property handled is of low monetary value (less than £1,000) and was acquired for the receiver's own use, the starting point should generally be a modest fine or, in some cases, a conditional discharge. Where any one of the aggravating features is present, this is likely to result in a community sentence. A defendant either with a record of offences of dishonesty or who engages in sophisticated law breaking, will attract a custodial sentence. Sentences in the range of 12 months to four years are likely to be appropriate where the value of the goods handled is up to around £100,000. Where the value is in excess of £100,000, or where the offence is highly organised and bears the hallmarks of a professional commercial operation, a sentence of four years and upwards is likely to be appropriate and it will be higher where the source of the handled property is known by the handler to be a serious violent offence such as armed robbery. These sentences are subject to discount in appropriate cases for a plea of guilty. Sentencers should always have in mind the power to make restitution, compensation and confiscation orders.

(5) Theft and handling

Practical issues

The legal issues which arise when considering alternative counts of theft and handling must be seen against the background of the practice and experience of the courts. Unnecessary complications, or unrealistic verdicts, may result from the inclusion of alternative counts in circumstances where they are wholly unnecessary on the facts: see *R. v. Christ*, 35 Cr.App.R. 76, CCA, and *R. v. Melvin and Eden* [1953] 1 Q.B. 481, 37 Cr.App.R. 1, CCA. **21-280**

R. v. Shelton, 83 Cr.App.R. 379, CA

In *R. v. Shelton*, Lawton L.J. made a number of points which his Lordship said were intended to give guidance to counsel in settling indictments and to judges as to how to act in order to produce sensible verdicts when dealing with alternative counts of theft and handling: **21-281**

> "the long established practice of charging theft and handling as alternatives should continue wherever there is a real possibility, not a fanciful one, that at trial the evidence might support one rather than the other. Secondly, ... there is a danger that juries may be confused by reference to second or later appropriations since the issue in every case is whether the defendant has in fact appropriated property belonging to another. If he has done so, it is irrelevant how he came to make the appropriation provided it was in the course of theft. Thirdly, ... a jury should be told that a handler can be a thief, but he cannot be convicted of being both a thief and a handler. Fourthly, ... handling is the more serious offence, carrying a heavier penalty because those who knowingly have dealings with thieves encourage stealing. Fifthly, in the unlikely event of the jury not agreeing amongst themselves whether theft or handling has been proved, they should be discharged. Finally, and perhaps most importantly, both judges and counsel when directing and addressing juries should avoid intellectual subtleties which some jurors may have difficulty in grasping: the golden rule should be 'Keep it short and simple' " (at p. 385).

Each of Lawton L.J.'s six points are examined below.

(i) *The inclusion of alternative counts*

It is perfectly proper in law to charge theft and handling in the alternative: *R. v. Shelton, ante*; *R. v. Bellman* [1989] A.C. 836, HL, *post*, § 21-289. In *Shelton*, Lawton L.J. made it clear that alternative counts of theft and handling should be included wherever there is a real possibility, not a fanciful one, that at trial the evidence might support one rather than the other. The most common situation faced by prosecutors was described by Lord Goddard in *R. v. Christ*, 35 Cr.App.R. 76, CCA: **21-282**

> "There are, of course, many cases in which, when a man is found in possession of property or

> has been seen to be associated with property, it is uncertain whether the evidence for the prosecution will ultimately satisfy the jury that he was guilty of stealing it or of receiving it, and, therefore, the indictment very properly, includes both counts, though they must necessarily be alternative counts. It may well be, even in a case such as the present case, that it is desirable that the two counts should be opened to the jury, because it is conceivable that the defence may take such a turn, or may raise such other facts as would make the count of receiving one which it would be desirable for the jury to consider ..." (at pp. 78–79).

Assuming the decision has been made to include alternative allegations, but the stolen property found in the defendant's possession comes from several thefts, burglaries or robberies with which the defendant is to be indicted, if it is the prosecution case that the property was received on a number of separate occasions, there should be a corresponding number of counts of receiving. It is only if the prosecution case is that all the property was received on one occasion that there should be one compendious count: *R. v. Smythe*, 72 Cr.App.R. 8, CA.

(ii) *First and second appropriations*

21–283 Because a handler is nearly always a thief, the inclusion of alternative counts may present a jury with three questions: (a) is the defendant the thief who originally appropriated the goods (the first appropriation); (b) did the defendant receive the goods knowing or believing them to be stolen; or (c) did the defendant steal the goods by acquiring them, other than in the course of the original stealing, and appropriate them by deciding to retain them with the intention of permanently depriving the owner of them (the second appropriation)? However, as Lawton L.J. observed in *Shelton*, *ante*, it is irrelevant how the defendant came to appropriate the goods provided it was in the course of theft. Accordingly, use of the phrases "first" and "second" appropriations is misleading and should be avoided.

The position is best illustrated by the facts of *Stapylton v. O'Callaghan* [1973] 2 All E.R. 782, DC, where the defendant was charged with the theft and handling of a driving licence in the alternative. The informations were dismissed because, although the magistrate found: (a) that the licence had been stolen; (b) that the defendant was found in possession of it; and (c) that he had come by it dishonestly and intended to keep it, he was unable to determine whether the defendant was guilty of theft or handling. On appeal it was held that as the defendant had been in dishonest possession of the licence and intended to keep it, it followed that whether he was the original thief or a subsequent receiver, he had dishonestly assumed a right to the licence "by keeping or dealing with it as owner" within section 3(1) of the *Theft Act* 1968 (*ante*, § 21–31). He had therefore dishonestly appropriated property belonging to another with the intention of permanently depriving the other of it within section 1(1). Accordingly, he was certainly guilty of theft, whether or not he was also guilty of receiving. As to the inappropriateness of alternative counts of theft with varying particulars, see *ante*, § 21–11.

(iii) *The distinction between handlers and thieves*

21–284 Lawton L.J.'s third point, that a jury should be told that a handler can be a thief, but that he cannot be convicted of being both a thief and a handler, refers both to the alternative nature of the counts and to the legal relationship between the offences.

21–285 **The legal relationship between the offences**. Because of the definition of the offence of theft and, in particular, the definition of "appropriates" in section 3 (*ante*, § 21–31), almost everyone who commits the offence of handling stolen goods contrary to section 22(1) of the Act will also commit the offence of theft. On the other hand, it will by no means be the case that every thief will also be guilty of handling. As a matter of law, however, it was said in *R. v. Dolan*, 62 Cr.App.R. 36, CA, that a person may steal and dishonestly handle the same goods.

21–286 **Theft and handling as mutually exclusive alternative counts**. In practice, the two offences are treated as alternatives, robbery, burglary or theft on the one hand and handling on the other. Where there are two such counts in the indictment, the prosecution invariably put the case on the basis that the jury should convict of one or other offence, but not of both. Where the prosecution so put their case, the Court of Appeal said in *Dolan* (*ante*, § 21–285) and again in *R. v. Smythe*, 72 Cr.App.R. 8, that the offences should be regarded as true alternatives and mutually exclusive.

The effect of mutually exclusive counts was considered in the House of Lords in *R. v. Bellman* [1989] A.C. 836, HL, where Lord Griffiths (at p. 851) rejected the respondent's argument that contradictory or mutually exclusive counts can never be joined in the same indictment, by pointing to the "long-established practice of charging counts of larceny and receiving as alternative and ... robbery or theft and handling as alternatives ...". Lord Griffiths had earlier observed that: **21–287**

> "it will only be comparatively rarely that the prosecution will wish to charge counts which are factually mutually contradictory in the sense that proof of one charge destroys the other. The very fact that offences are being charged in the alternative obviously weakens the prosecution case and enables the defence to invite the jury to say that as the prosecution cannot make up their mind which crime the accused committed they, the jury, cannot be sure of his guilt" (at p. 847).

Where there are alternative counts, the jury should be directed as to the relationship between the counts (including a direction that handling has to be otherwise than in the course of stealing), and they should be instructed to consider the theft (robbery, burglary) count first and that they will be asked to return their verdict in respect of that count first: *R. v. Fernandez* [1997] 1 Cr.App.R. 123, CA. **21–288**

In *Att.-Gen. of Hong Kong v. Yip Kai Foon* [1988] A.C. 642, PC, the defendant was charged with two counts of robbery: under Hong Kong law a verdict of handling stolen goods is a statutory alternative on a charge of robbery. He was convicted of handling on both counts. The Court of Appeal of Hong Kong allowed the appeal on the grounds, *inter alia*, that the judge had failed to direct the jury properly in relation to handling by not telling them that the prosecution had to prove that the receiving took place otherwise than in the course of robbery. The Privy Council overturned this decision, holding that the judge had properly directed the jury with regard to the alternative counts by telling them to consider first whether they were satisfied that the defendant was guilty of robbery and, if not, secondly whether he was guilty of handling stolen goods. On the assumption that the jury had obeyed this direction, it was held that once they acquitted the defendant of robbery, theft was no longer a live issue and therefore any receiving could not have been in the course of robbery. **21–289**

It appears that *Yip Kai Foon* was not cited to the Court of Appeal in *Fernandez*, *ante*. Although in *Yip Kai Foon* the Privy Council upheld the trial judge's direction, it is submitted that the better approach is to follow the recent guidance given in *Fernandez*, namely to direct the jury:

1. that the counts are alternatives and handling has to be otherwise than in the course of stealing;
2. to consider first the count of theft (robbery, burglary);
3. if they find the defendant guilty of theft, they will be discharged from returning a verdict on the handling count; but
4. if they find the defendant not guilty of theft, they should go on to consider the handling count.

In *R. v. Cash* [1985] Q.B. 801, 80 Cr.App.R. 314, CA, it was held that where the indictment charges only handling stolen goods, no direction to the jury is needed to the effect that they must be sure that the handling occurred otherwise than in the course of the stealing unless there was evidence to raise the issue; and the defendant's mere possession of stolen goods nine days after the theft was not such evidence. *Cf. R. v. Greaves*, *The Times*, July 11, 1987, CA, *ante*, §§ 21-127, 21-128. **21–290**

(iv) *Handling is the more serious offence*

In saying that handling was the more serious offence because those who knowingly deal with thieves encourage stealing, Lawton L.J. was reiterating Lord Widgery C.J.'s observation in *Stapylton v. O'Callaghan* [1973] 2 All E.R. 782 at 784, DC, that the offence of handling stolen goods was a more serious offence than theft in that it carried a heavier maximum penalty. These observations carry greater force in the light **21–291** of the reduction of the statutory maximum sentence for theft to seven years' imprisonment: *CJA* 1991, s.26(1) (see *ante*, § 21–15). Handling may be an alternative charge not only to theft, but also to burglary, which carries a maximum sentence similar to handling, and robbery, which carries a greater maximum sentence.

(v) *Leaving alternative counts to the jury*

21–292 Where alternative inconsistent allegations are included in the indictment, and the evidence establishes a prima facie case on both counts, the matter should be left to the jury to determine which, if either, count has been proved: *Bellman*, *ante*. See also *R. v. Seymour*, 38 Cr.App.R. 68, CCA; *R. v. Plain*, 51 Cr.App.R. 91, CA; *Shelton*, *ante*; and *R. v. Bosson* [1999] Crim.L.R. 596, CA. In *Plain*, Winn L.J. said:

> "I think it should be made perfectly clear that, where there are alternative charges of larceny and receiving ... the proper course in almost every case will be to allow both charges to proceed and be decided ultimately by the jury. Only in very rare cases would it be right to accede to a submission that there was no evidence on the larceny count or, on the other hand, no evidence upon the receiving count, at the end of the case for the prosecution. The reason for that is this, that very often it is only at the end of a trial that it can be seen, and made the subject of the proper direction to assist the jury, whether the facts of the particular case fall into the category of larceny or the category of receiving, or call for a verdict of not guilty of either" (at p. 93).

His Lordship then said that both counts might be withdrawn from the jury if there was insufficient evidence that the property in question had been stolen by anybody. Similarly in *R. v. Christ*, 35 Cr.App.R. 76, CCA, Lord Goddard observed:

> "but once it becomes apparent ... that the case is one of larceny or nothing, then it is, in our opinion, desirable that the trial judge, in his summing up, should put simply to the jury the count of larceny, and leave out altogether from their consideration the alternative count of receiving. ... It would, we think, much simplify matters for the consideration of a jury in this type of case if, as soon as it becomes apparent what is the real charge on which, if they are going to convict at all, they must convict, that charge alone is left to the jury ..." (at pp. 78–79).

If one or other count is to be withdrawn from the jury, this should not normally be done prior to the end of the evidence: *R. v. Bosson*, *ante*. In the unlikely event of the jury not agreeing amongst themselves whether theft or handling has been proved, they should be discharged: *R. v. Shelton*, *ante*.

(vi) *"Keep it simple"*

21–293 Lawton L.J.'s final exhortation in *Shelton*, *ante*, that judges and counsel when addressing juries should avoid intellectual subtleties, was undoubtedly a reflection of his earlier observation that the case was a striking example of what can happen if counsel, after studying the commentaries of academic writers, develop arguments which have the allure of legal logic but which, if taken too far, affront common sense.

(6) The elements of the offence

(a) *Stolen goods*

21–294 For the definition of "goods", see section 34(2)(b), *ante*, § 21–270a. Prove that the goods are stolen goods. This may be proved by the evidence of the thief: see *R. v. Reynolds*, 20 Cr.App.R. 125, CCA.

Where the thief has been convicted, his conviction may be proved pursuant to section 74 of the *PACE Act* 1984 (*ante*, § 9–82) in order to prove as against the alleged handler that the goods were stolen (this being a matter in issue within the *CJA* 2003, s.100(1), *ante*, § 13–11). As to its use in this situation, see dicta in *R. v. O'Connor*, 85 Cr.App.R. 298, CA, cited in *R. v. Robertson*; *R. v. Golder* [1987] Q.B. 920, 85 Cr.App.R. 304, CA.

That the goods are stolen may also be proved by circumstantial evidence although there may be no direct evidence, such as from the loser or the thief. For example, the circumstances in which the defendant handled the goods may of themselves be sufficient to prove that the goods were stolen and also, that at the time when the defendant handled them, he knew or believed that they were stolen. But each case depends on its own facts: see, for example, *R. v. Sbarra*, 13 Cr.App.R. 118, CCA; *R. v. Fuschillo*, 27 Cr.App.R. 193, CCA; *Cohen v. March* [1951] 2 T.L.R. 402, DC; *R. v. Young and Spiers*, 36 Cr.App.R. 200, CCA; and *Noon v. Smith*, 49 Cr.App.R. 55, DC.

Admission of belief that goods were stolen as evidence that they were

Where an accused, upon being questioned by the police about certain goods, admits that he had purchased them and that at the time he believed them to have been stolen, such an admission, in the absence of any other evidence, is not sufficient to permit an inference by the jury that the goods were stolen goods: *R. v. Porter* [1976] Crim.L.R. 58; *R. v. Marshall* [1977] Crim.L.R. 106; *Att.-Gen.'s Reference (No. 4 of 1979)*, 71 Cr.App.R. 341, CA. The general evidential principle upon which these decisions are based is that an accused person's admissions are only evidence against him where it appears that he had personal knowledge of the facts admitted: *Surujpaul v. R.*, 42 Cr.App.R. 266, PC; *Comptroller of Customs v. Western Lectric Co. Ltd* [1966] A.C. 367, PC. However, the circumstances in which the defendant received the property may be proved by his own admission, and on the basis of those circumstances an inference may properly be drawn that the property was stolen: *Bird v. Adams* [1972] Crim.L.R. 174, DC; *R. v. Hulbert*, 69 Cr.App.R. 243, CA; *R. v. MacDonald*, 70 Cr.App.R. 288. In *Hulbert* it was pointed out that the accused's statements may be admissible to prove, *inter alia*, the place in which the property was received, the amount paid, the circumstances in which it was offered, the state of the property and the personality of the seller. What the accused was told about the origin of the goods, while inadmissible for the purpose of proving the goods to be stolen, will of course be relevant to the question of dishonesty and whether or not the accused knew or believed the goods to be stolen. *Hulbert* was applied in *R. v. Korniak*, 76 Cr.App.R. 145, CA. **21–295**

Conviction for attempt where no proof that goods stolen

See *post*, § 21–322. **21–296**

Scope of offences relating to stolen goods

Theft Act 1968, s.24

24.—(1) The provisions of this Act relating to goods which have been stolen shall apply whether the stealing occurred in England or Wales or elsewhere, and whether it occurred before or after the commencement of this Act, provided that the stealing (if not an offence under this Act) amounted to an offence where and at the time when the goods were stolen; and references to stolen goods shall be construed accordingly. **21–297**

(2) For purposes of those provisions references to stolen goods shall include, in addition to the goods originally stolen and parts of them (whether in their original state or not),—

(a) any other goods which directly or indirectly represent or have at any time represented the stolen goods in the hands of the thief as being the proceeds of any disposal or realisation of the whole or part of the goods stolen or of goods so representing the stolen goods; and

(b) any other goods which directly or indirectly represent or have at any time represented the stolen goods in the hands of a handler of the stolen goods or any part of them as being the proceeds of any disposal or realisation of the whole or part of the stolen goods handled by him or of goods so representing them.

(3) But no goods shall be regarded as having continued to be stolen goods after they have been restored to the person from whom they were stolen or to other lawful possession or custody, or after that person and any other person claiming through him have otherwise ceased as regards those goods to have any right to restitution in respect of the theft.

(4) For purposes of the provisions of this Act relating to goods which have been stolen (including subsections (1) to (3) above) goods obtained in England or Wales or elsewhere either by blackmail or, subject to subsection (5) below, by fraud (within the meaning of the *Fraud Act* 2006) shall be regarded as stolen; and "steal", "theft" and "thief" shall be construed accordingly.

(5) Subsection (1) above applies in relation to goods obtained by fraud as if—

(a) the reference to the commencement of the Act were a reference to the commencement of the *Fraud Act* 2006, and

(b) the reference to an offence under this Act were a reference to an offence under section 1 of that Act.

[This section is printed as amended by the *Fraud Act* 2006, s.14(1), and Sched. 1, para. 6.]

Nothing in paragraph 6 of Schedule 1 to the 2006 Act affects the operation of section 24 of the 1968 Act in relation to goods obtained in the circumstances described in section 15(1) of that Act where the obtaining was the result of a deception made before the commencement of that paragraph (*i.e.* goods so obtained are to be regarded as stolen): *Fraud Act* 2006, s.14(2), and Sched. 2, para. 4.

As to references to stolen goods including money withdrawn from an account to which a wrongful credit has been made, see section 24A(8), *post*, § 21–323a.

Section 24(1)

21–298 Where the prosecution seek to rely on a theft committed abroad pursuant to section 24(1) they must prove that the behaviour complained of amounts to an offence under the relevant foreign jurisdiction. It is not open to the prosecution to rely on a rebuttable presumption that foreign law is the same as English law: *R. v. Ofori and Tackie (No. 2)*, 99 Cr.App.R. 223, CA.

Section 24(2)

21–299 In *Att.-Gen.'s Reference (No. 4 of 1979)*, 71 Cr.App.R. 341, CA, it was held that a balance in a bank account can be goods which directly or indirectly represent stolen goods for the purposes of section 24(2). The court was also of the opinion that a person who dishonestly accepts a transfer of stolen funds from another's account into his own account is receiving stolen goods within the meaning of section 22(1). The Law Commission, in its *Report on Offences of Dishonesty, Money Transfers* (Law Com. No. 243), thought that this opinion could not survive the reasoning in *R. v. Preddy and Slade*; *R. v. Dhillon* [1996] A.C. 815, HL.

This point was considered in *R. v. Forsyth* [1997] 2 Cr.App.R. 299, CA. It was alleged that N had stolen a chose in action, namely a credit balance of £400,000 in a bank in London. N ordered the transfer of the money to a bank in Switzerland. The appellant collected the money from the bank in Switzerland and transferred it to another bank in Switzerland. On the appellant's instructions, a proportion of the sum was then transferred to a bank in England and she brought back the balance in cash. The appellant was charged with handling the chose in action and the cash by assisting in the retention, etc., of the goods for the benefit of N. The appellant argued that, according to *Preddy*, the funds obtained by the transferee had never been in the hands of the thief at all, and the transferee in whose hands they were could not be regarded as a handler until it had first been determined that he had handled stolen goods. The court said the question was whether the total sum could be said directly or indirectly to represent the original stolen goods in the hands of the thief. It held that the words "in the hands of" meant in the possession or under the control of the thief. Accordingly the new credit balances remained under the control of N and could be handled by the appellant. (For commentaries on *Forsyth* by Sir John Smith Q.C., see [1997] Crim.L.R. 589, 755.)

In relation to money credits, it would now generally be appropriate to charge the defendant under section 24A of the *Theft Act* 1968 (dishonestly retaining a wrongful credit) (*post*, § 21–323a).

Section 24(3)

21–300 On an Attorney-General's reference to the Court of Appeal on the point of law as to whether stolen goods were restored to lawful custody when a police officer, suspecting them to be stolen, examined and kept observation on them with a view to tracing the thief or handler, the court was of the opinion that the issue as to whether goods had been reduced into the "lawful possession or custody" of a police officer was a question of fact which depended upon the intentions of the officer as to whether or not he had decided to take the goods into custody, reduce them into his possession or control, take charge of them so that they could not be removed and so that he would have the disposal of them. If he was of an entirely open mind as to whether the goods should be seized or not and was merely concerned to ensure that the driver did not get away without being questioned, then it could not be said that he had taken the goods into his possession or control: *Att.-Gen.'s Reference (No. 1 of 1974)* [1974] Q.B. 744, 59 Cr.App.R. 203, CA, applying *R. v. Villensky* [1892] 2 Q.B. 597.

In *Metropolitan Police Commr v. Streeter*, 71 Cr.App.R. 113, DC, the court held that section 24(3) did not apply in the following circumstances: a thief, having stolen four cartons of his employer's goods, loaded them on to his employer's lorry where they were seen by the security officer who initialled them for future identification and thereafter informed the police when he realised that they were stolen. The police followed the lorry and observed three of the marked cartons being delivered to S. S and later K (who had the fourth carton) were arrested and admitted receiving property they knew to be stolen. The court held that the property had not ceased to be stolen property at the time S and K received the cartons notwithstanding the actions of the security officer and the police. See also *R. v. Dolan* (1855) 6 Cox 449; *R. v. Schmidt* (1866) L.R. 1 C.C.R. 15; *Haughton v. Smith* [1975] A.C. 476, HL.

Goods received from child under 10

It is an irrebutable presumption of law that a child under 10 cannot be guilty of a **21–301** criminal offence. Where, therefore, a child under 10 has unlawfully acquired property and handed it to a person who receives it with guilty knowledge, since there can have been no theft of the property by the child, the person who receives the property from the child cannot be guilty of handling stolen property: *Walters v. Lunt*, 35 Cr.App.R. 94. The Divisional Court in *Walters v. Lunt* added that there was no reason why such a person should not be guilty of larceny as a bailee or larceny by finding provided he had the requisite intent. This will equally be the case under the *Theft Act* 1968: he will be guilty of theft if he dishonestly assumes a right to the property by keeping or dealing with it as owner (see s.3(1), *ante*, §§ 21–31, 21–36).

Evidence by statutory declaration

See *post*, § 21–332. **21–302**

(b) *The handling*

Having proved that the goods are stolen goods, it is necessary to prove that the de- **21–303** fendant handled them; that is, that he either (a) received them or arranged to do so, or (b) undertook or assisted in their retention, removal, disposal or realisation by or for the benefit of another person or arranged to do so.

Receiving

The words "by or for the benefit of another person" do not apply to receiving. **21–304**

There is no definition of receiving in the *Theft Act* 1968. Under the old authorities, to establish receiving it was necessary to establish possession in the sense of control by the defendant: *R. v. Wiley* (1850) 2 Den. 37; and see *R. v. Watson* [1916] 2 K.B. 385, 12 Cr.App.R. 62, CCA.

Such possession need not be exclusive but might be joint with another receiver: *R. v. Payne*, 3 Cr.App.R. 259, CCA; or joint with the thief himself: *R. v. Smith* (1855) Dears. 494; *R. v. Seiga*, 45 Cr.App.R. 26, CCA.

Since it is necessary to establish control of the goods by the defendant, proof that he has physically handled them is neither necessary nor sufficient. The defendant might have handled the goods physically without being in control of them or have been in control of the goods without physically handling them.

An example of the defendant having control of stolen goods without physically **21–305** handling them is provided where they were found on his premises; if he was absent when the goods arrived there, it must be proved that he became aware of their presence and exercised some control over them or that the goods came, albeit in his absence, at his invitation and by arrangement with him; if delivery has been taken by a servant in his master's absence, the master can be convicted only if there is evidence that he gave the servant authority or instructions to accept the goods: *R. v. Cavendish*, 45 Cr.App.R. 374, CCA. For other cases considering whether the defendant was in possession of property found on his premises, see *R. v. Savage*, 70 J.P. 36; *R. v. Lewis*, 4 Cr.App.R. 96, CCA. An example of a defendant physically handling the stolen goods without having control of them is afforded by *R. v. Court*, 44 Cr.App.R. 242, CCA.

Where receiving is alleged there must be a clear direction to the jury as to what constitutes possession: *R. v. Seiga*, 45 Cr.App.R. 26, CCA; *R. v. Frost and Hale*, 48 Cr.App.R. 284, CCA; *R. v. Comerford*, 49 Cr.App.R. 77, CCA.

Undertaking or assisting, etc.

21–306 Where a person is charged under this limb of section 22(1) there is no need to prove possession or control: *R. v. Shears* [1969] Crim.L.R. 319, CA; *R. v. Sanders*, 75 Cr.App.R. 84, CA. In *R. v. Bloxham* [1983] 1 A.C. 109, the House of Lords was called upon to determine the proper construction of the second limb of the subsection. Lord Bridge delivered a speech with which the remainder of their Lordships agreed. Having referred to the fact that the second half of the subsection creates a single offence which can be committed in various ways and having said that the words "or if he arranges to do so" could be ignored for present purposes, his Lordship said that four activities were contemplated: retention, removal, disposal and realisation.

> "The offence can be committed in relation to any one of these activities in one or other of two ways. First, the offender may himself undertake the activity *for the benefit of* another person. Secondly, the activity may be undertaken *by* another person and the offender may assist him. Of course, if the thief or an original receiver and his friend act together in, say, removing the stolen goods, the friend may be committing the offence in both ways. But this does not invalidate the analysis and if the analysis holds good, it must follow, I think, that the category of other persons contemplated by the subsection is subject to the same limitations in whichever way the offence is committed" (at pp. 113, 114).

The question certified by the Court of Appeal was: does a bona fide purchaser for value commit an offence of dishonestly undertaking the disposal or realisation of stolen property for the benefit of another if when he sells the goods on he knows or believes them to be stolen? The Court of Appeal had held that he does, the other person being the purchaser. Lord Bridge, however, said that according to his analysis of the subsection "a purchaser, as such, of stolen goods, cannot, in my opinion, be 'another person' within the subsection, since his act of purchase could not sensibly be described as a disposal or realisation of the stolen goods by him. Equally, therefore, even if the sale to him could be described as a disposal or realisation for his benefit" (about which his Lordship had expressed doubt on the ground that a natural use of language suggested the disposal or realisation is for the seller's benefit whereas it is the purchase that is for the benefit of the purchaser) "the transaction is not, in my view, within the ambit of the subsection".

In *R. v. Tokeley-Parry* [1999] Crim.L.R. 578, CA, it was held that where A commissioned B to travel abroad to collect what A knew, but B did not know, to be stolen antiquities, B knowing only that their exportation was prohibited, and B was paid by A for doing so, A was guilty of handling stolen goods, in that he assisted another to remove stolen goods; the fact that B may have been an innocent agent did not mean that he and A had to be treated as one person. *Sed quaere*.

21–307 Mere failure to reveal to the police the presence of stolen property on the defendant's premises does not amount to assisting in the retention of stolen property though it may be strong evidence of it: *R. v. Brown* [1970] 1 Q.B. 105, 53 Cr.App.R. 527, CA. In *R. v. Pitchley*, 57 Cr.App.R. 30, CA, P was held to have assisted in the retention of stolen money where, some 48 hours after innocently accepting it from his son for safe keeping and banking it, he discovered it was stolen and took no steps to have it returned to the owner before being visited by the police four days later. The court held that P's conduct in permitting the money to remain under his control in his bank was sufficient to constitute retention. The court adopted the dictionary meaning of the word "retain", *viz.*—keep possession of, not lose, continue to have. It was added that so far as any construction of the word "retain" is necessary, it is a question of law and when a defendant has admittedly kept possession of money it is not necessary to leave to the jury the question whether that amounted to retention.

In *R. v. Sanders*, *ante*, it was held that the mere use of goods known to be stolen could not amount to assisting in their retention. It must be proved that in some way the accused was assisting in the retention of the goods by concealing them or making them more difficult to identify or by hiding them pending their ultimate disposal, or by some other act that was part of the chain of dishonest handling. In *R. v. Kanwar*, 75 Cr.App.R. 87, CA, it was held that the requisite assistance need not be a physical act. Verbal representations, whether oral or in writing, for the purpose of concealing the identity of stolen goods may, if made dishonestly and for the benefit of another, amount to handling stolen goods by assisting in their retention. It was also held that the requisite assistance need not be successful in its object.

In *R. v. Coleman* [1986] Crim.L.R. 56, CA, it was held that where a person is charged with assisting in the disposal of stolen money, the *actus reus* of the offence is not made out by proof that he was getting the benefit of the disposal of the money. Such proof might, however, be evidence that he had assisted in the disposal, assisting meaning among other things helping or encouraging.

Arranging

The words "or if he arranges to do so" apply to both limbs of section 22(1): see *ante*, § 21–274. **21–308**

Where the prosecution allege an arrangement to receive, etc., stolen goods, it must be proved that the goods were stolen at the time the arrangement was made: where they were not stolen at that time, the proper charge will be one of conspiracy: *R. v. Park*, 87 Cr.App.R. 164, CA.

(c) *Dishonesty*

See generally *ante*, § 21–2b *et seq.* **21–309**

A "dishonest" handling must be established and the jury must be so directed: see *R. v. Sloggett* [1972] 1 Q.B. 430, 55 Cr.App.R. 532, CA. It is not sufficient to direct them that once it is proved that the goods have been stolen and have been handled by the defendant, and that the defendant knew they were stolen, that is sufficient to warrant a conviction for handling: *R. v. Dickson and Gray* [1955] Crim.L.R. 435, CCA. See, for example, *R. v. Matthews*, 34 Cr.App.R. 55, CCA, where the defence was that the accused handled the goods with the intention of returning them to the owner or of handing them to the police.

There is no special test of dishonesty on a charge of handling stolen goods: *R. v. Roberts*, 84 Cr.App.R. 117, CA (rejecting a suggestion that the dishonesty must relate to the owner of the property, but acknowledging that it would sometimes be necessary to consider whether the defendant had acted honestly or dishonestly *vis-à-vis* the loser).

(d) *Knowing or believing the goods to be stolen*

It must be proved by the prosecution (and the burden of establishing this remains on the Crown throughout), that the defendant, at the material time (when that was will depend upon the particular allegation being made, *e.g.* if the allegation is "receiving", the material time is the time when he received the goods) knew or believed the goods to be stolen: see *ante*, § 21–270. This is proved, either directly, by the evidence of the principal offender, or circumstantially. **21–310**

It is not sufficient to prove that the goods were "handled" in circumstances which would have put a reasonable man on inquiry. A summing-up is defective if in effect it leaves the jury with the impression that suspicious circumstances, irrespective of whether the accused himself appreciated they were suspicious, imposed a duty as a matter of law to act and inquire, and that a failure to do so was to be treated as knowledge or belief: *R. v. Grainge*, 59 Cr.App.R. 3, CA. The question is a subjective one, and it must be proved that the defendant knew, or believed the goods to be stolen. Suspicion that they were stolen, even coupled with the fact that he shut his eyes to the circumstances, is not enough, although those matters may be taken into account by a jury when deciding whether or not the necessary knowledge or belief existed: *R. v. Moys*, 79 Cr.App.R. 72, CA. See also *R. v. Ismail* [1977] Crim.L.R. 557, CA; *R. v. Reader*, 66 Cr.App.R. 33, CA; *R. v. Reeves*, 68 Cr.App.R. 334, CA.

21–311 In *R. v. Forsyth* [1997] 2 Cr.App.R. 299 (*ante*, § 21–299), the Court of Appeal doubted whether it is necessary or helpful to attempt an exposition of the meaning of the word "belief" by equating it with different and less easily understood states of mind, such as "unreasonable uncertainty" or "a refusal to believe the obvious". The court held that the trial judge ought to have followed the guidance given in *R. v. Moys*, *ante*, which is clear and readily understandable by a jury and avoids the potential confusion inherent in the direction suggested by the court in *R. v. Hall (E.)*, 81 Cr.App.R. 260 at 264.

In *R. v. Harris (M.)*, 84 Cr.App.R. 75, CA, it was submitted that it was insufficient for a judge simply to direct a jury that they must be satisfied that the defendant knew or believed the goods were stolen. The court was referred to *Moys* and *Hall*, *ante*. Lawton L.J. referred to what Lord Diplock had said in *Treacy v. DPP*, namely that the *Theft Act* 1968 had been deliberately drafted in simple language, avoiding as far as possible those terms of art which have acquired a special meaning understood only by lawyers. His Lordship said that "knowledge or belief" are words of ordinary usage and in many cases no elaboration at all was needed. It is submitted that where, on the facts of the case, some elaboration is needed, the judge ought to give a *Moys* direction, as approved in *Forsyth*.

21–312 It is sufficient that the defendant knew or believed that he was handling stolen goods, although he had no knowledge of the nature of the goods: *R. v. McCullum*, 57 Cr.App.R. 645, CA.

Proof of guilty knowledge by evidence of the possession of other stolen property or previous conviction

Theft Act 1968, s.27(3), (5)

21–313 **27.**—(3) Where a person is being proceeded against for handling stolen goods (but not for any offence other than handling stolen goods), then at any stage of the proceedings, if evidence has been given of his having or arranging to have in his possession the goods the subject of the charge, or of his undertaking or assisting in, or arranging to undertake or assist in, their retention, removal, disposal or realisation, the following evidence shall be admissible for the purpose of proving that he knew or believed the goods to be stolen goods:—

(a) evidence that he has had in his possession, or has undertaken or assisted in the retention, removal, disposal or realisation of, stolen goods from any theft taking place not earlier than twelve months before the offence charged; and

(b) (provided that seven days' notice in writing has been given to him of the intention to prove the conviction) evidence that he has within the five years preceding the date of the offence charged been convicted of theft or of handling stolen goods.

(5) This section is to be construed in accordance with section 24 of this Act; and in subsection 3(b) above the reference to handling stolen goods shall include any corresponding offence committed before the commencement of this Act.

For section 27(1), (2), see *ante*, § 21–277; for section 27(4), see *post*, § 21–332.

For section 24, see *ante*, § 21–297.

Evidence falling within section 27(3) falls within the definition of "bad character" evidence in section 98 of the *CJA* 2003 (*ante*, § 13–5). Section 101(1) of that Act (*ante*, § 13–25) stipulates that evidence of the defendant's bad character is admissible only in accordance with that section. On a literal interpretation this would appear to render the admissibility of evidence under section 27(3) subject to section 101. However, it is extremely doubtful that this is what was intended. First, it is apparent that Chapter 1 of Part 11 of the 2003 Act was intended only to replace the common law rules as to the admissibility of evidence of bad character (see s.99(1)). Had it been intended to subject existing statutory provisions to the new rules, it is inconceivable that those provisions would not have either been repealed or amended so as to make them expressly subject to the overriding provisions of the new Act. In any event, it may be observed that there has been no suggestion that the intent of the 2003 Act was to cut down on the admissibility of bad character evidence, and it may, therefore, be safely assumed that even if section 27(3) were to be subjected to section 101 of the 2003 Act, this would not narrow the ambit of its operation. The gateway through which section 27(3) evidence would pass under section 101 would be subsection (1)(d), "it is relevant to an important issue between the defendant and the prosecution". The issue is knowledge or belief that the goods were stolen, and is provided for by the terms of section 27(3) itself. This would be the safety first route to admissibility, but it is so cumbersome that it merely serves to underline that there can have been no intention that the new provisions should have any impact on existing statutory provisions.

Great care should be taken, where evidence is admitted under section 27(3), to direct the jury that the purpose of the evidence is restricted to assisting them to determine the issue of guilty knowledge. Such evidence has no relevance to the question of possession. Accordingly, where an accused is charged with several counts of handling, in some of which guilty knowledge is in issue and in others possession, particular care should be exercised by the judge before admitting such evidence. If it is admitted, equal care should be exercised to ensure that the jury realise to which issue the evidence relates: *R. v. Wilkins*, 60 Cr.App.R. 300, CA.

Evidence of other stolen property in defendant's possession

Under section 27(3)(a) evidence may be given that other property stolen within the period of 12 months preceding the date of the offence charged was found or had been in the possession of the defendant, or that he had otherwise "handled" it, although such other property is the subject of another indictment against him: see *R. v. Jones*, 14 Cox 3. There is no authority for the introduction of evidence which goes beyond what the subsection specifically describes. Accordingly, details of the transactions as a result of which the earlier property had come into the defendant's possession may not be given: *R. v. Bradley*, 70 Cr.App.R. 200, CA. *Bradley* was followed in *R. v. Wood (W.D.)*, 85 Cr.App.R. 287, CA, where Mustill L.J., giving the judgment of the court, said that: **21–314**

> "if section 27(3)(a) ... is to be given a literal interpretation, the consequence will be that the jury is to be told simply that the defendant was on a previous occasion found to be in possession of stolen goods, without being furnished with any facts upon which they could base a conclusion as to whether on that occasion the possession was guilty or innocent; and they might well be tempted to assume that since they had been told about the incident, this must be because some guilty knowledge attending it could properly be inferred. The task of conveying to the jury that the only relevance of the fact is that the previous occasion would have served as a warning to be more careful in future (if indeed this is the rationale of paragraph (a)) will not be easily performed. On the other hand to let in evidence of circumstances from which the existence of guilty knowledge on the prior occasion could be inferred would be such a striking inroad into the general rule which excludes evidence of prior unconnected offences that one would need clear words in the statute to justify it, and section 27(3) is quite silent" (at p. 292).

Notwithstanding their view as to the proper ambit of section 27(3)(a), the court upheld a ruling by the trial judge admitting a statement made by the defendant at the time of the earlier possession which, albeit edited, revealed some of the detail of how he came to be in possession of the stolen goods. The justification for this, according to the Court of Appeal, was that it was necessary to prove that the defendant had indeed been in possession of the goods. This object could have been achieved however, by the defence making an admission. It seems that the unarticulated reason for admitting the statement was the virtually identical circumstances of the two receipts, but that fact, it is submitted, would have been admissible at common law: see *Cross & Tapper on Evidence*, 11th ed., p. 446. **21–315**

It is essential, in order to admit such evidence, that the property which is found is stolen property; if the prosecution fails to prove this, then the evidence admitted under this section ought to be withdrawn by the judge from the consideration of the jury: *R. v. Girod and Girod* (1906) 22 T.L.R. 720. Similarly, where evidence in relation to other property is admitted under this provision but there is no evidence at the end of the prosecution case that the defendant personally had come into possession of it, the jury **21–316** should then be told to ignore this evidence: *R. v. Garside*, 52 Cr.App.R. 85, CA (a decision under the old law where only possession was relevant).

Evidence by the thief to prove that he had sold stolen property to the handler at any previous time is admissible against the handler at common law, and is not excluded by the time limitation in the statute: *R. v. Powell*, 3 Cr.App.R. 1, CCA.

The material words in the statute are "not earlier than twelve months before the offence charged"; as, therefore, the statute does not read "within the period of twelve months before the offence charged" evidence is admissible under this provision of the possession of other stolen goods at a date after the date of the offence charged: *R. v. Davis* [1972] Crim.L.R. 431, CA.

Evidence of previous conviction

21–317 A notice in pursuance of section 27(3)(b) is not defective because it does not state that it is given under or for the purpose of the section: *R. v. Airlie* [1973] Crim.L.R. 310, CA.

In *R. v. Hacker* [1995] 1 Cr.App.R. 332, the House of Lords held that, on the true construction of section of 27(3)(b), when read together with section 73 of the *PACE Act* 1984 (*ante*, § 9–80), a certificate of previous conviction should, where the conviction was on indictment, state the substance and effect, omitting the formal parts, of the indictment and conviction; reference therein to the nature of the property stolen or handled was not a formal part, but was the substance of the indictment and conviction; if the conviction was in summary proceedings, the certificate should record the nature of the property stolen or handled, and the whole of the certificate was admissible.

It was held under section 43(1) of the *Larceny Act* 1916 (*rep.*), that a judge has a discretion to exclude the evidence if its prejudicial effect greatly outweighs its probative value: *R. v. List*, 50 Cr.App.R. 81, Assizes (Roskill J.); *R. v. Herron* [1967] 1 Q.B. 107, 50 Cr.App.R. 132, CCA. The reasoning in these cases has been applied to section 27(3): *R. v. Knott* [1973] Crim.L.R. 36, CA. See also *R. v. Rasini*, *The Times*, March 20, 1986, CA: where the only issue in the trial of a defendant charged with handling stolen goods was whether he had guilty knowledge, evidence of previous offences should only be introduced under this provision where the interests of justice so demanded: it should not be adduced as a matter of course.

21–318 It is no answer to an application under this provision that "system" cannot be spelt out of the previous conviction(s) and the instant allegation; the section is concerned with the question of general disposition to be dishonest in connection with the theft or handling of stolen goods: *R. v. Perry* [1984] Crim.L.R. 680, CA. If the judge concludes that the evidence could be of only minimal assistance to the jury, then it is his duty to exclude it: *ibid*.

Evidence of previous convictions for handling should not be admitted under section 27(3) where the defendant admits knowing that the goods were stolen but denies dishonesty: *R. v. Duffas*, *The Times*, October 19, 1993, CA.

Recent possession as evidence of guilty knowledge

21–319 The onus of proving guilty knowledge or belief always remains upon the prosecution. Where the only evidence against the defendant is that he was in possession of recently stolen property, the jury should be directed that they may infer guilty knowledge (a) if the defendant has offered no explanation to account for his possession of the property, or (b) if they are satisfied that any explanation consistent with innocence which has been given is untrue. They should also be told that if an explanation has been offered which leaves them in reasonable doubt as to the knowledge of the defendant that the property had been stolen, the offence has not been proved, and the verdict should be not guilty: *R. v. Aves*, 34 Cr.App.R. 159, CCA. See also *R. v. Garth*, 33 Cr.App.R. 100, CCA; *R. v. Norris*, 12 Cr.App.R. 156, CCA; *R. v. Badash*, 13 Cr.App.R. 17, CCA; *R. v. Bailey*, 13 Cr.App.R. 27, CCA; *R. v. Brain*, 13 Cr.App.R. 197, CCA; *R. v. Currell*, 25 Cr.App.R. 116, CCA; *R. v. Hepworth and Fearnley* [1955] 2 Q.B. 600, 39 Cr.App.R. 152, CCA; *R. v. Smythe*, 72 Cr.App.R. 8, CA; *R. v. Cash* [1985] Q.B. 801, 80 Cr.App.R. 314, CA.

In *R. v. Bradley*, 70 Cr.App.R. 200, CA, it was said *obiter* that where there is direct evidence of the circumstances in which the defendant came into possession of the stolen goods the doctrine of recent possession has no application. In *R. v. Raviraj*, 85 Cr.App.R. 93, CA, the court said that it did not think that the decision in *Bradley* warranted a general statement of the law in those terms. The court said that whilst clearly, in that case, a direction on recent possession was an embarrassment to the jury, that was no ground for saying that where something is known of the circumstances in which stolen goods are received, the doctrine of recent possession does not apply.

> "The doctrine is only a particular aspect of the general proposition that where suspicious circumstances appear to demand an explanation, and no explanation or an entirely incredible explanation is given, the lack of explanation may warrant an inference of guilty knowledge in the defendant. This again is only part of a wider proposition that guilt may be inferred from unreasonable behaviour of a defendant when confronted with facts which seem to accuse" (*per* Stocker L.J. at p. 103).

Prior to the *CJPOA* 1994, a failure to give an explanation could not be relied upon for these purposes if the accused had been cautioned (*Raviraj*, *ante*), but this can no longer be the law: in appropriate cases, an inference of guilty knowledge may be drawn pursuant to the provisions of section 34 of the 1994 Act (*ante*, § 15–414).

In *R. v. Ball and Winning*, 77 Cr.App.R. 131, CA, it was held that the so-called doctrine of recent possession applied not only to cases of receiving but also to cases brought under the second limb of section 22. **21–320**

What constitutes "recent possession" depends upon the nature of the property and the circumstances of the particular case: *cf. R. v. Adams* (1829) 3 C. & P. 600; *R. v. Partridge* (1836) 7 C. & P. 551; *R. v. Langmead* (1864) L. & C. 427; *R. v. McMahon* (1875) 13 Cox 275, C.C.R. (Ir.); *R. v. Deer* (1862) L. & C. 240. In *R. v. Smythe*, 72 Cr.App.R. 8, Kilner Brown J., giving the Court of Appeal's judgment, said: "Nearly every reported case is merely a decision of fact as an example of what is no more than a rule of evidence" (at p. 11).

See also generally *ante*, §§ 21–125 *et seq.*

(7) Jurisdiction

An offence contrary to section 22(1) is a "Group A" offence within Part I of the *CJA* 1993: see generally, *ante*, §§ 2–37 *et seq.* **21–321**

(8) Attempt

In *Haughton v. Smith* [1975] A.C. 476, HL, it was decided that a person who dishonestly handles goods which he believes to be stolen goods but which, in fact, are not stolen goods cannot be convicted of an attempt to handle stolen goods. The decision was reversed by the *Criminal Attempts Act* 1981, s.1. In *Anderton v. Ryan* [1985] A.C. 567, the House of Lords appeared to rule that the law was still as laid down in *Haughton v. Smith*. However, in *R. v. Shivpuri* [1987] A.C. 1, the House of Lords applied the *Practice Statement (Judicial Precedent)* [1966] 1 W.L.R. 1234, HL, and overruled its own decision in *Anderton v. Ryan*. As to attempts generally, see *post*, §§ 33–119 *et seq.* **21–322**

(9) Advertisements offering rewards for the return of stolen goods

See the summary offence created by section 23 of the *Theft Act* 1968. It is an offence of strict liability (*Denham v. Scott*, 77 Cr.App.R. 210, DC), punishable with a fine not exceeding level 3 on the standard scale. As to the "standard scale", see *ante*, § 5–403. **21–323**

XIV. RETAINING A WRONGFUL CREDIT

(1) Statute

Theft Act 1968, s.24A

Dishonestly retaining a wrongful credit

24A.—(1) A person is guilty of an offence if— **21–323a**

(a) a wrongful credit has been made to an account kept by him or in respect of which he has any right or interest;

(b) he knows or believes that the credit is wrongful; and

(c) he dishonestly fails to take such steps as are reasonable in the circumstances to secure that the credit is cancelled.

(2) References to a credit are to a credit of an amount of money.

(2A) A credit to an account is wrongful to the extent that it derives from—

(a) theft;

(b) blackmail;

(c) fraud (contrary to section 1 of the *Fraud Act* 2006);

(d) stolen goods.

(3), (4) [*Repealed by* Fraud Act *2006, s.14(1) and (3), Sched. 1, para. 7(1), and Sched. 3.*]

(5) In determining whether a credit to an account is wrongful, it is immaterial (in particular) whether the account is overdrawn before or after the credit is made.

(6) A person guilty of an offence under this section shall be liable on conviction on indictment to imprisonment for a term not exceeding ten years.

(7) Subsection (8) below applies for the purposes of the provisions of this Act relating to stolen goods (including subsection (2A) above).

(8) References to stolen goods include money which is dishonestly withdrawn from an account to which a wrongful credit has been made, but only to the extent that the money derives from that credit.

(9) "Account" means an account kept with—

(a) a bank;

(b) a person carrying on a business which falls within subsection (10); or

(c) an issuer of electronic money (as defined for the purposes of Part 2 of the *Financial Services and Markets Act* 2000).

(10) A business falls within this subsection if—

(a) in the course of the business money received by way of deposit is lent to others; or

(b) any other activity of the business is financed, wholly or to any material extent, out of the capital of or the interest on money received by way of deposit.

(11) References in subsection (10) to a deposit must be read with—

(a) section 22 of the *Financial Services and Markets Act* 2000;

(b) any relevant order under that section; and

(c) Schedule 2 to that Act;

but any restriction on the meaning of deposit which arises from the identity of the person making it is to be disregarded.

(12) For the purposes of subsection (10)—

(a) all the activities which a person carries on by way of business shall be regarded as a single business carried on by him; and

(b) "money" includes money expressed in a currency other than sterling.

[This section was inserted as from December 18, 1996 by the *Theft (Amendment) Act* 1996, s.2(1); and it is printed as amended by the *Fraud Act* 2006, s.14(1), and Sched. 1, para. 7.]

Nothing in paragraph 7 of Schedule 1 to the 2006 Act affects the operation of section 24A(7) and (8) of the 1968 Act in relation to credits falling within section 24A(3) or (4) and made before the commencement of that paragraph (*i.e.* a wrongful credit within subs. (8) will include the credit side of a money transfer obtained contrary to section 15A of the 1968 Act and a credit that derives from such an offence): *Fraud Act* 2006, s.14(2), and Sched. 2, para. 5.

(2) Indictment

STATEMENT OF OFFENCE

21–323b *Dishonestly retaining a wrongful credit, contrary to section 24A of the* Theft Act *1968*

PARTICULARS OF OFFENCE

A B, on the —— day of ——, 20—, knowing or believing that a wrongful credit in the sum of £10,000 made to an account kept by him [or *in respect of which he had a right or interest*] *at X Bank plc was wrongful, dishonestly failed to take such steps as were reasonable in the circumstances to secure that the credit was cancelled.*

(3) Class of offence and mode of trial

This offence is triable either way: *MCA* 1980, s.17(1), and Sched. 1, para. 28 (*ante*, § 1–75af). It is a class 3 offence (*ante*, § 2–17). **21–323c**

(4) Sentence

Imprisonment not exceeding 10 years: s.24A(6) (*ante*, § 21–323b). **21–323d**

(5) Jurisdiction

The offence of dishonestly retaining a wrongful credit contrary to section 24A is a "Group A" offence within Part I of the *CJA* 1993 (set out at §§ 2–37 *et seq.*, *ante*). **21–323e**

(6) The elements of the offence

The elements of the offence under section 24A differ in two important respects from other offences under the *Theft Act* 1968. **21–323f**

1. There is no exemption for the bona fide purchaser, such as is to be found in section 3 of the Act (*ante*, § 21–38). For example, A innocently sells his car to B, who pays A with stolen money. A pays the money into his bank account and then learns that it derives from theft. A will be guilty of an offence under section 24A if he dishonestly fails to take such steps as are reasonable in the circumstances to secure that the credit is cancelled.
2. The rule that a person cannot be guilty of handling stolen goods in the course of stealing them does not apply to the offence of dishonestly retaining a wrongful credit. The offence under section 24A can be committed at the same time as the offences of theft, blackmail or fraud (for the relationship between theft and handling stolen goods generally, see *ante*, § 21–284).

The word "cancelled", as used in subsection(1)(c), means cancelling the original credit so as to achieve the same effect as if it had not been made in the first place; it does not include removing the funds for the recipient's own purposes: *R. v. Lee*, unreported, January 12, 2006, CA ([2006] EWCA Crim. 156). **21–323g**

XV. GOING EQUIPPED TO STEAL

(1) Statute

Theft Act 1968, s.25

Going equipped for stealing, etc.

25.—(1) A person shall be guilty of an offence if, when not at his place of abode, he has with him any article for use in the course of or in connection with any burglary or theft. **21–324**

(2) A person guilty of an offence under this section shall on conviction on indictment be liable to imprisonment for a term not exceeding three years.

(3) Where a person is charged with an offence under this section, proof that he had with him any article made or adapted for use in committing a burglary or theft shall be evidence that he had it with him for such use.

(4) [*Repealed by* Serious Organised Crime and Police Act *2005, s.174(2), and Sched. 17, Pt 2.*]

(5) For purposes of this section an offence under section 12(1) of this Act of taking a conveyance shall be treated as theft.

[This section is printed as amended by the *Fraud Act* 2006, s.14(1) and (3), Sched. 1, para. 8, and Sched. 3.]

The offence of going equipped to cheat has been replaced by section 6 of the *Fraud Act* 2006 (possession, etc., of articles for use in frauds (*post*, § 21–390)), which applies equally to articles at the offender's place of abode, and has a maximum sentence of five years imprisonment.

(2) Indictment

STATEMENT OF OFFENCE

21–325 *Going equipped for burglary* [or *theft*], *contrary to section 25(1) of the* Theft Act *1968*.

PARTICULARS OF OFFENCE

A B, on the —— day of ——, 20—, not being at his place of abode, had with him articles for use in the course of or in connection with burglary [or *theft*] *namely a screwdriver and a bunch of skeleton keys*.

(3) Class of offence and mode of trial

21–326 This offence is triable either way: *MCA* 1980, s.17(1), and Sched. 1, para. 28, *ante*, §§ 1–75af *et seq.* It is a class 3 offence, *ante*, § 2–17.

(4) Sentence

21–327 Imprisonment not exceeding three years: s.25(2), *ante*. An offence under this section committed with reference to the theft or taking of a motor vehicle involves discretionary disqualification: see the *RTOA* 1988, ss.34 and 97, and Sched. 2, Pt II.

(5) Elements of the offence

21–328 Prove that the defendant at the time of the alleged offence was not at his place of abode and that he had with him the articles named in the indictment, and that they were articles for use in the course of or in connection with burglary or theft. Where a person lives and drives around in a car in which he keeps burglary tools, the car is his place of abode for the purpose of section 25(1) only when it is on a site where he intends to abide: *R. v. Bundy*, 65 Cr.App.R. 239, CA.

If the article is made or adapted for use in committing burglary or theft, proof that the accused had it with him is evidence that he had it with him for such use. If the article is not so made or adapted it is a matter of inference for the jury to draw from its nature and the circumstances in which the accused was in possession of it, what his intent was see *R. v. Harrison* [1970] Crim.L.R. 415, CA.

It must be proved that the defendant had the article in question for the purpose, or with the intention, of using it in the course of or in connection with some burglary or theft to be committed in the future. But it is not necessary to prove that the defendant intended the article to be used in the course of or in connection with any specific burglary or theft; it is enough to prove a general intention so to use it. Nor is it necessary to prove that the defendant intended to use it himself; it will be enough to prove that he had it with him with the intention that it should be used by someone else: *R. v. Ellames*, 60 Cr.App.R. 7, CA. In *R. v. Mansfield* [1975] Crim.L.R. 101, CA, it was held that the tendering of certain employment and driving documents to a potential employer in the hope of securing a driving job which in turn would enable the accused to steal a load, was too remote an act to sustain a charge of having articles (the documents) with him for use in connection with theft.

[The next paragraph is § 21–331.]

XVI. THEFT ACT 1968: GENERAL PROVISIONS

A. SEARCH FOR STOLEN GOODS

Theft Act 1968, s.26

21–331 **26.**—(1) If it is made to appear by information on oath before a justice of the peace that there is reasonable cause to believe that any person has in his custody or possession or on his premises any stolen goods, the justice may grant a warrant to search for and seize the same; but no warrant to search for stolen goods shall be addressed to a person other than a constable except under the authority of an enactment expressly so providing.

(2) [*Repealed by* PACE Act *1984*, *Sched. 7*, *Pt I*.]

(3) Where under this section a person is authorised to search premises for stolen goods, he may enter and search the premises accordingly, and may seize any goods he believes to be stolen goods.

(4) [*Repealed by* CJA *1972, Sched. 6, Pt II.*]

(5) This section is to be construed in accordance with section 24 of this Act; and in subsection (2) above the references to handling stolen goods shall include any corresponding offence committed before the commencement of this Act.

Subsection (3) preserves the law as laid down in *Chic Fashions (West Wales) Ltd v. Jones* [1968] 2 Q.B. 299, CA (Civ. Div.).

As to applications for, and the execution of, search warrants, see the *PACE Act* 1984, ss.15 and 16 respectively, *ante*, §§ 15–101 *et seq.*

B. EVIDENCE BY STATUTORY DECLARATION

Theft Act 1968, s.27

27.—(1), (2) [*See* ante, *§ 21–277.*] 21–332

(3) [*See* ante, *§ 21–313.*]

(4) ... In any proceedings for the theft of anything in the course of transmission (whether by post or otherwise), or for handling stolen goods from such a theft, a statutory declaration made by any person that he despatched or received or failed to receive any goods or postal packet, or that any goods or postal packet when despatched or received by him were in a particular state or condition, shall be admissible as evidence of the facts stated in the declaration, subject to the following conditions:—

(a) a statutory declaration shall only be admissible where and to the extent to which oral evidence to the like effect would have been admissible in the proceedings; and

(b) a statutory declaration shall only be admissible if at least seven days before the hearing or trial a copy of it has been given to the person charged, and he has not, at least three days before the hearing or trial or within such further time as the court may in special circumstances allow, given the prosecutor written notice requiring the attendance at the hearing or trial of the person making the declaration.

(4A) *Where the proceedings mentioned in subsection (4) above are proceedings before a magistrates' court inquiring into an offence as examining justices that subsection shall have effect with the omission of the words from "subject to the following conditions" to the end of the subsection.*

(5) This section is to be construed in accordance with section 24 of this Act; and in subsection (3)(b) above the reference to handling stolen goods shall include any corresponding offence committed before the commencement of this Act.

[Subs. (4A) was inserted by the *CPIA* 1996, s.47 and Sched. 1, para. 20. It is repealed as from a day to be appointed: *CJA* 2003, s.332, and Sched. 7, Pt 4.]

For section 24, see *ante*, § 21–297.

C. ORDERS FOR RESTITUTION

See the *PCC(S)A* 2000, s.148, *ante*, §§ 5–431 *et seq.* 21–333

D. SPOUSES AND CIVIL PARTNERS

Theft Act 1968, s.30

30.—(1) This Act shall apply in relation to the parties to a marriage, and to property belonging to the wife or husband whether or not by reason of an interest derived from the marriage, as it would apply if they were not married and any such interest subsisted independently of the marriage. 21–334

(2) Subject to subsection (4) below, a person shall have the same right to bring proceedings against that person's wife or husband for any offence (whether under this Act or otherwise) as if they were not married, *and a person bringing any such proceedings shall be competent to give evidence for the prosecution at every stage of the proceedings.*

(3) [*Repealed by* Police and Criminal Evidence Act *1984, Sched. 7.*]

(4) Proceedings shall not be instituted against a person for any offence of stealing or doing unlawful damage to property which at the time of the offence belongs to that person's wife or husband or civil partner, or for any attempt, incitement or conspiracy to commit

such an offence, unless the proceedings are instituted by or with the consent of the Director of Public Prosecutions:

Provided that—

(a) this subsection shall not apply to proceedings against a person for an offence—

(i) if that person is charged with committing the offence jointly with the wife or husband or civil partner;

(ii) if by virtue of any judicial decree or order (wherever made) that person and the wife or husband are at the time of the offence under no obligation to cohabit; or

(iii) an order (wherever made) is in force providing for the separation of that person and his or her civil partner;

(b) [*repealed by* Criminal Jurisdiction Act *1975, Sched. 6*].

(5) Notwithstanding section 6 of the *Prosecution of Offences Act* 1979, subsection (4) of this section shall apply—

(a) to an arrest (if without warrant) made by the wife or husband or civil partner, and

(b) to a warrant of arrest issued on an information laid by the wife or husband or civil partner.

[This section is printed as amended by the *Civil Partnership Act* 2004, s.261(1), and Sched. 27, para. 27. The italicised words in subs. (2) are repealed, as from a day to be appointed, by the *YJCEA*, s.67(3) and Sched. 6. Subs. (5) was added by the *Criminal Jurisdiction Act* 1975, Sched. 5; and subsequently amended by the *Prosecution of Offences Act* 1979, Sched. 1. The whole of the 1979 Act was repealed by the *Prosecution of Offences Act* 1985, s.31(6) and Sched. 2. Section 6 of the 1979 Act is re-enacted in section 25 of the 1985 Act (*ante*, § 1–278a) and the reference to section 6 should be construed as a reference to section 25: *Interpretation Act* 1978, s.17(2)(a) (Appendix B–17). The reference in subs. (4) to incitement has effect as a reference to the offences under the *SCA* 2007, Pt 2: 2007 Act, s.63(1), and Sched. 6, para. 1.]

21–335 In *Woodley v. Woodley* [1978] Crim.L.R. 629, DC, the court held that where at the material time the husband, who was alleging criminal damage by his wife, was the subject of an order committing him to prison which was suspended on terms that he did not molest his wife or approach within 200 yards of her home, the protection offered by subsection (4) did not extend to the wife because the judicial order debarred the husband from the matrimonial home and accordingly the obligation to cohabit was not in existence at the time of the alleged offence.

E. EFFECT ON CIVIL PROCEEDINGS AND RIGHTS

Theft Act 1968, s.31

21–336 **31.**—(1) A person shall not be excused, by reason that to do so may incriminate that person or the spouse or civil partner of that person of an offence under this Act—

(a) from answering any question put to that person in proceedings for the recovery or administration of any property, for the execution of any trust or for an account of any property or dealings with property; or

(b) from complying with any order made in any such proceedings;

but no statement or admission made by a person in answering a question put or complying with an order made as aforesaid shall, in proceedings for an offence under this Act, be admissible in evidence against that person or (unless they married or became civil partners after the making of the statement or admission) against the spouse or civil partner of that person.

(2) Notwithstanding any enactment to the contrary, where property has been stolen or obtained by fraud or other wrongful means, the title to that or any other property shall not be affected by reason only of the conviction of the offender.

[This section is printed as amended by the *Civil Partnership Act* 2004, s.261(1), and Sched. 27, para. 28.]

Conspiracy to commit an offence under the *Theft Act* 1968 is not an "offence under" that Act: *Sociedade Nacional de Combustiveis de Angola U.E.E. v. Lundqvist* [1991] 2 Q.B. 310, CA (Civ. Div.).

F. EFFECT ON EXISTING LAW AND CONSTRUCTION OF REFERENCES TO OFFENCES

Theft Act 1968, s.32

32.—(1) The following offences are hereby abolished for all purposes not relating to offences committed before the commencement of this Act, that is to say— **21–337**

(a) any offence at common law of larceny, robbery, burglary, receiving stolen property, obtaining property by threats, extortion by colour of office or franchise, false accounting by public officers, concealment of treasure trove and, except as regards offences relating to the public revenue, cheating; and

(b) [*repeal of statutory offences listed in Sched. 3, Pt I*];

but so that the provisions in Schedule 1 to this Act (which preserve with modifications certain offences under the *Larceny Act* 1861 of taking or killing deer and taking or destroying fish) shall have effect as there set out.

(2) Except as regards offences committed before the commencement of this Act, and except in so far as the context otherwise requires,—

(a) references in any enactment passed before this Act to an offence abolished by this Act shall, subject to any express amendment or repeal made by this Act, have effect as references to the corresponding offence under this Act, and in any such enactment the expression "receive" (when it relates to an offence of receiving) shall mean handle, and "receiver" shall be construed accordingly; and

(b) without prejudice to paragraph (a) above, references in any enactment, whenever passed, to theft or stealing (including references to stolen goods), and references to robbery, blackmail, burglary, aggravated burglary or handling stolen goods, shall be construed in accordance with the provisions of this Act, including those of section 24.

Cheating the public revenue

The words of section 32 should be given their plain meaning: if there was an offence of common law cheating which related to the public revenue, the offence was still indictable, whatever statutory offences might have been available on the facts: *R. v. Redford*, 89 Cr.App.R. 1, CA (*post*, § 25–385a). **21–338**

G. INTERPRETATION

Theft Act 1968, s.34

34.—(1) Sections 4(1) and 5(1) of this Act shall apply generally for purposes of this Act as they apply for purposes of section 1. **21–339**

(2) For purposes of this Act—

(a) ["gain" and "loss": *see* ante, *§ 21–234*];

(b) ["goods": *see* ante, *§ 21–270a*];

(c) ["mail bag" and "postal packet": *see* ante, *§ 21–171*].

XVII. THEFT ACT 1978

A. INTRODUCTION

The *Theft Act* 1978 implemented, with some modifications, the recommendations of the Criminal Law Revision Committee in their Thirteenth Report (Cmnd. 6733). Sections 1 and 2 of the 1978 Act have been repealed by the *Fraud Act* 2006, s.14(3), and Sched. 3. Section 1 (obtaining services by deception) has been replaced by section 11 of the 2006 Act (obtaining services dishonestly, *post*, § 21–403). The conduct to which section 2 (evasion of a liability by deception) related will now be covered by sections 1 and 2 of the 2006 Act (fraud by false representation (*post*, §§ 21–356 *et seq.*)) if the defendant intended, by means of the false representation, to make a gain or cause a loss, etc., within the terms of section 5 of that Act (*post*, § 21–360). **21–340**

[The next paragraph is § 21–349.]

B. MAKING OFF WITHOUT PAYMENT

(1) Statute

Theft Act 1978, s.3

Making off without payment

21–349 **3.**—(1) Subject to subsection (3) below, a person who, knowing that payment on the spot for any goods supplied or service done is required or expected from him, dishonestly makes off without having paid as required or expected and with intent to avoid payment of the amount due shall be guilty of an offence.

(2) For purposes of this section "payment on the spot" includes payment at the time of collecting goods on which work has been done or in respect of which service has been provided.

(3) Subsection (1) above shall not apply where the supply of the goods or the doing of the service is contrary to law, or where the service done is such that payment is not legally enforceable.

(4) [*Repealed by* Serious Organised Crime and Police Act *2005, s.174(2), and Sched. 17, Pt 2*.]

(2) Indictment

STATEMENT OF OFFENCE

21–350 *Making off without payment, contrary to section 3(1) of the* Theft Act *1978.*

PARTICULARS OF OFFENCE

A B on the —— day of ——, 20—, knowing that payment on the spot for a meal costing £45 was required or expected from him, dishonestly made off from the X Y restaurant without having paid as required or expected.

For punishment and mode of trial, see *post*, § 21–354.

(3) The elements of the offence

21–351 In *R. v. Brooks*, 76 Cr.App.R. 66, CA, the court observed that the words "dishonestly makes off" were easily understandable by any jury, and in the majority of cases required no elaboration in a summing-up. The jury should be told to apply the words in their natural meaning and relate them to the facts of the case. "Making off" involved a departure from the spot where payment was required. If the accused is stopped before passing that spot, the jury should be directed that that may constitute an attempt to commit the offence, provided the other ingredients are established.

21–352 In *R. v. Allen* [1985] A.C. 1029, HL, it was held that the following must be proved to secure a conviction under section 3: that the defendant in fact made off without making payment on the spot; knowledge that payment on the spot was required or expected of him; dishonesty; and an intent permanently to avoid payment of the amount due. An intention to delay or defer payment does not suffice. The wording "on the spot" does not require payment to be made at any particular spot: it means "there and then" and relates to the knowledge which the customer had to have of when the payment was to be made: *R. v. Aziz* [1993] Crim.L.R. 708, CA.

Where a person enters into an agreement with the supplier of goods or services that "payment on the spot" need not be made, his subsequent making off without payment on the spot does not constitute the offence, even though he had no intention of paying, and the supplier's agreement was obtained by deception; as a matter of fact, when the customer makes off, payment on the spot is neither expected, nor required: *R. v. Vincent* [2001] 2 Cr.App.R. 10, CA.

21–353 In *Troughton v. Metropolitan Police* [1987] Crim.L.R. 138, DC, a taxi driver agreed to take the appellant to his home address. The appellant, having had a great deal to drink, had not told the driver his address. The driver had to stop to obtain directions from the appellant at some point. There was an argument, the appellant accusing the driver of making an unnecessary diversion. The driver, being unable to get an address from the appellant, drove to the nearest police station to see if someone else could help. The appellant was convicted of making off without payment. The conviction was quashed on the basis that the journey had not been completed and the consequence of that was a breach of contract by the driver. Instead of resolving the argument about further instructions during the journey, the driver broke away from the route which would have taken the appellant home in order to go to the police station. The driver, being in breach of contract, was not lawfully able to demand the fare at any time thereafter. For that reason, among others, the appellant was never in a situation in which he was bound to pay or even tender the money for the journey, and thus it could not be contended that he made off without payment.

C. MODE OF TRIAL AND PENALTIES

Theft Act 1978, s.4

Punishments

4.—(1) Offences under this Act shall be punishable either on conviction on indictment or on summary conviction. **21–354**

(2) A person convicted on indictment shall be liable—

(a) ...

(b) for an offence under section 3 of this Act, to imprisonment for a term not exceeding two years.

(3) A person convicted summarily of any offence under this Act shall be liable—

(a) to imprisonment for a term not exceeding *six* [12] months; or

(b) to a fine not exceeding the prescribed sum for the purposes of section 32 of the *Magistrates' Courts Act* 1980 (punishment on summary conviction of offences triable either way: £2,000 or other sum substituted by order under that Act),

or to both.

[This section is printed as amended by the *MCA* 1980, s.154(1), and Sched. 7, para. 170; and the *Fraud Act* 2006, s.14(1) and (3), Sched. 1, para.14, and Sched. 3. In subs. (3)(a), "12" is substituted for "six"as from a day to be appointed: *CJA* 2003, s.282(2) and (3). The increase has no application to offences committed before the substitution takes effect: s.282(4).]

For section 32 of the 1980 Act, see *ante*, § 1–75aa.

D. SUPPLEMENTARY

Section 5(1) was repealed by the *Fraud Act* 2006, s.14(1) and (3), Sched. 1, para. 15 and Sched. 3; section 5(2) provides that section 30(1) (spouse or civil partner, *ante*, § 21–334), section 31(1) (effect on civil proceedings, *ante*, § 21–336) and section 34 (interpretation, *ante*, § 21–339) of the 1968 Act, shall apply (so far as they are applicable) in relation to the 1978 Act. **21–355**

XVIII. FRAUD ACT 2006

A. FRAUD

(1) Statute

Fraud Act 2006, ss.1–4

Fraud

1.—(1) A person is guilty of fraud if he is in breach of any of the sections listed in subsection (2) (which provide for different ways of committing the offence). **21–356**

(2) The sections are—

(a) section 2 (fraud by false representation),

(b) section 3 (fraud by failing to disclose information), and

(c) section 4 (fraud by abuse of position).

(3) A person who is guilty of fraud is liable—

(a) on summary conviction, to imprisonment for a term not exceeding 12 months or to a fine not exceeding the statutory maximum (or to both);

(b) on conviction on indictment, to imprisonment for a term not exceeding 10 years or to a fine (or to both).

(4) [*Northern Ireland.*]

In relation to an offence committed before the commencement of section 154(1) of the *CJA* 2003, the reference to 12 months in section 1(3)(a) is to be read as a reference to six months: *Fraud Act* 2006, s.14(2), and Sched. 2, para. 1.

Fraud by false representation

21–357 **2.**—(1) A person is in breach of this section if he—

(a) dishonestly makes a false representation, and

(b) intends, by making the representation—

(i) to make a gain for himself or another, or

(ii) to cause loss to another or to expose another to a risk of loss.

(2) A representation is false if—

(a) it is untrue or misleading, and

(b) the person making it knows that it is, or might be, untrue or misleading.

(3) "Representation" means any representation as to fact or law, including a representation as to the state of mind of—

(a) the person making the representation, or

(b) any other person.

(4) A representation may be express or implied.

(5) For the purposes of this section a representation may be regarded as made if it (or anything implying it) is submitted in any form to any system or device designed to receive, convey or respond to communications (with or without human intervention).

Fraud by failing to disclose information

21–358 **3.** A person is in breach of this section if he—

(a) dishonestly fails to disclose to another person information which he is under a legal duty to disclose, and

(b) intends, by failing to disclose the information—

(i) to make a gain for himself or another, or

(ii) to cause loss to another or to expose another to a risk of loss.

Fraud by abuse of position

21–359 **4.**—(1) A person is in breach of this section if he—

(a) occupies a position in which he is expected to safeguard, or not to act against, the financial interests of another person,

(b) dishonestly abuses that position, and

(c) intends, by means of the abuse of that position—

(i) to make a gain for himself or another, or

(ii) to cause loss to another or to expose another to a risk of loss.

(2) A person may be regarded as having abused his position even though his conduct consisted of an omission rather than an act.

"Gain" and "loss"

21–360 **5.**—(1) The references to gain and loss in sections 2 to 4 are to be read in accordance with this section.

(2) "Gain" and "loss"—

(a) extend only to gain or loss in money or other property;

(b) include any such gain or loss whether temporary or permanent;

and "property" means any property whether real or personal (including things in action and other intangible property).

(3) "Gain" includes a gain by keeping what one has, as well as a gain by getting what one does not have.

(4) "Loss" includes a loss by not getting what one might get, as well as a loss by parting with what one has.

(2) Indictment

(a) *Fraud by false representation*

STATEMENT OF OFFENCE

21–361 *Fraud, contrary to section 1 of the* Fraud Act *2006*.

PARTICULARS OF OFFENCE

A B on the —— day of ——, 20—, dishonestly and intending thereby to make a gain for himself or another [or *to cause loss to another*] [or *to expose another to a risk of loss*], *made a representation to C D which was and which he knew was or might be untrue or misleading, namely that C D had won £1,000,000 in a lottery which A B was in a position to release to him upon receipt of an administration fee of £500, in breach of section 2 of the* Fraud Act *2006.*

Charge distinct representations

As to the general rule that only one offence should be charged in a single count, see *ante*, §§ 1–135 *et seq.*; as to the circumstances in which one count may charge multiple incidents, see *ante*, §§ 1–139 *et seq.* **21–362**

Where a person makes a number of different false representations on different occasions attempting to make the same gain, each occasion will constitute a different offence (albeit together amounting to a course of conduct), notwithstanding that under the repealed section 15 of the 1968 Act there would have been only one offence of obtaining by deception. Where, however, the person intends to make the gain (or cause the loss, etc.) by means of the cumulative effect of false representations made on different occasions, it is submitted that there is one offence committed over a period of time.

(b) *Fraud by failing to disclose information*

STATEMENT OF OFFENCE

Fraud, contrary to section 1 of the Fraud Act *2006.* **21–363**

PARTICULARS OF OFFENCE

A B, between the —— day of ——, 20— and the —— day of ——, 20—, dishonestly and intending thereby to make a gain for himself or another [or *to cause loss to another*] [or *to expose another to a risk of loss*], *failed to disclose to his insurance company information which he was under a legal duty to disclose, namely that since receiving payment of £1,000 in respect of his claim for the theft of an antique watch he had found the said watch and so discovered that it had been misplaced and not stolen, in breach of section 3 of the* Fraud Act *2006.*

(c) *Fraud by abuse of position*

STATEMENT OF OFFENCE

Fraud, contrary to section 1 of the Fraud Act *2006.* **21–364**

PARTICULARS OF OFFENCE

A B, on the —— day of ——, 20—, dishonestly and intending thereby to make a gain for himself or another [or *to cause loss to another*] [or *to expose another to a risk of loss*], *abused his position as employee of C D Ltd, in which he was expected to safeguard* [or *not to act against*] *the financial interests of C D Ltd, by providing a customer purchasing goods from C D Ltd with a staff discount to which the customer was not entitled, in breach of section 4 of the* Fraud Act *2006.*

(3) Class of offence and mode of trial

Fraud is triable either way: see s.1(3), *ante*, § 21–356. It is a class 3 offence, *ante*, § 2–17. **21–365**

(4) Sentence

Maximum

Imprisonment not exceeding 10 years: s.1(3)(b), *ante*, § 21–356. **21–366**

Financial reporting orders

A financial reporting order may be made in respect of a person convicted of an offence of fraud: *SOCPA* 2005, s.76 (*ante*, § 5–886a). **21–367**

Serious crime prevention orders

Fraud is a specified serious offence within Schedule 1 to the *SCA* 2007, enabling the **21–367a**

Crown Court to make a serious crime prevention order under section 19 on conviction (*ante*, § 5–875c).

Authorities

21–368 For guideline cases in respect of offences under the previous legislation, see, in particular, *R. v. Barrick*, 81 Cr.App.R. 78, CA, *R. v. Stewart*, 85 Cr.App.R. 66, CA, and *R. v. Graham*; *R. v. Whatley* [2005] 1 Cr.App.R.(S.) 115, CA, *ante*, §§ 21–4d, 21–4h. For illustrative decisions in such cases, see CSP, B6–33A05 to B6–33F22.

In *Att.-Gen.'s References (Nos 42, 43 and 44 of 2006) (R. v. Clemow)* [2007] 1 Cr.App.R.(S.) 80, the Court of Appeal said that offences of obtaining property by deception (under the *Theft Act* 1968, s.15), committed against elderly victims who were specifically targeted because of their vulnerability, fell to be treated as offences against the person where the lives of the victims had been "wrecked", with one particular victim having been targeted "month after month, mercilessly, relieving him of his last pennies under the hypocrisy of friendship"—a "cold-blooded crime", involving "despicable cruelty".

(5) The elements of the offence

(a) *General*

Dishonesty

21–369 All three ways of committing the offence of fraud require dishonesty. The Act contains no definition or qualification of the meaning of dishonesty; in particular, there is no reference to the provisions of the *Theft Act* 1968, and no express defence of a claim of right. The explanatory notes to the Act make it clear that it was envisaged that the test in *R. v. Ghosh* [1982] Q.B. 1053, 75 Cr.App.R. 154, CA, would apply: see generally *ante*, § 21–2b. In *Ghosh* (at pp.1060, 159) Lord Lane C.J. said, in respect of the now repealed offence of obtaining by deception, contrary to section 15 of the *Theft Act* 1968: "The difficulty ... is that dishonesty comes in twice. If a person knows that he is not telling the truth he is guilty of dishonesty. Indeed deliberate deception is one of the two most obvious forms of dishonesty. One wonders therefore whether 'dishonestly' in section 15(1) adds anything, except in the case of reckless deception." The element of dishonesty is likely, however, to be of considerably more significance under the *Fraud Act*, since, for example, the offence of fraud by false representation can be committed with knowledge merely that the representation might be untrue or misleading, and the other two methods of committing the offence can each be committed by omission.

Intention to make a gain or to cause a loss

21–370 The definitions of "gain" and "loss" in section 5 follow those in the *Theft Act* 1968, s.34(2), and thus authorities considering the latter section are equally applicable to offences of fraud (*ante*, §§ 21–234 *et seq.*). However, the application of the definition in the *Fraud Act* differs in two respects:

(i) in respect of "gain", the offence of fraud requires an intent, by means of the *actus reus*, "to make a gain", rather than the lesser requirement of acting "with a view to gain" in the *Theft Act* 1968, ss.17, 20 and 21; as a result, although none of the three ways of committing fraud has to be effective, each has to be intended to be; but

(ii) in respect of "loss", the necessary intent is less restrictive than under the *Theft Act* 1968, since it includes an intent merely to expose another to a risk of loss.

"Gain" and "loss" extend only to gain or loss in money or other property; "property" includes things in action. Relevant things in action, which might represent a gain, could arise from money transfers (covering the earlier offence under the *Theft Act* 1968, s.15A), or where a person is tricked into incurring a liability, such as under a contract or a guarantee.

"Gain" does not mean profit; there can be a gain where a person obtains money to which he is entitled (*Att.-Gen.'s Reference (No. 1 of 2001)* [2002] 3 All E.R. 840, CA, *ante*, § 21–267), and thus a person who uses a false representation to trick a debtor into paying money which he is owed will commit the offence if he acts dishonestly.

An intention permanently to deprive is not an element of fraud, since the intended gain or loss can be temporary or permanent; where property is gained which will later be returned to its owner (such as a voucher, bill of exchange, or cheque), the question of whether by then it will have lost its value (*cf.* the *Theft Act* 1968, s.6, *ante*, § 21–76) does not arise.

Inducing a creditor to forbear from suing on a debt is not a "gain": *R. v. Goleccha and Choraria*, 90 Cr.App.R. 241, CA, *ante*, § 21–234; consequently not all conduct previously caught by the offence of evading liability by deception (contrary to the *Theft Act* 1978, s.2) will constitute an offence under the *Fraud Act*.

Offences by companies

Where the "person" in breach of sections 2 to 4 is a body corporate, those involved in its management who have consented to or connived in the offence are also guilty of it by virtue of section 12 of the Act: see, *post*, § 21–412. **21–371**

(b) *Fraud by false representation*

Making a representation which is untrue or misleading

The offence is committed when the representation is made; it is not dependent on a result being achieved. The representation can be made to a machine (s.2(5), *ante*), but is only so made when "submitted"; by analogy, it is submitted that a representation to a person is only made when transmitted, so that a representation made by email will not be made until the email is sent. **21–372**

The representation must be untrue or misleading (s.2(2), *ante*). There is no express requirement of materiality in the respect in which it is untrue or misleading, either objectively or subjectively to the defendant. Thus a person who, intending to make a gain, knowingly makes a representation which is only peripherally false or misleading will be caught if and only if he is dishonest.

The representation may be as to fact or law, and includes a representation as to the state of mind of the person making the representation (such as his present intention) (s.2(3), *ante*). It is submitted that, as under the earlier legislation, "fact" means existing fact and does not extend to predictions as to the future.

Knowledge that the representation is or might be untrue or misleading

The definition of "false" incorporates the requirement that the person making the representation knows that the representation is, or might be, untrue or misleading. Whilst knowledge is a stricter requirement than suspicion, a person may know that a representation might be untrue without suspecting that it is - such as a defendant who has no idea one way or the other whether the representation he is making is true. **21–373**

The question of whether the defendant knew that the representation was or might be untrue or misleading is separate from the additional and essential requirement that the false representation be made dishonestly; applying the reasoning in *R. v. Feeny*, 94 Cr.App.R. 1, CA (considering reckless deception under the now repealed section 15 of the 1968 Act), it will be particularly important where the allegation is that the defendant knew merely that the representation might be untrue or misleading that there should be no risk that the jury might confuse this state of mind with dishonesty or conclude that dishonesty would inevitably follow.

Implied representations

A representation may be express or implied (s.2(4), *ante*). Authorities under earlier legislation as to the representations which can be inferred in common financial transactions will still apply. **21–374**

Payment by a cheque

The representations which may as a matter of law be inferred from the mere act **21–375** of drawing a cheque are: (a) that the drawer has an account with the bank upon which the cheque is drawn, and (b) that the existing state of facts is such that in ordinary course the cheque will be met, *i.e.* on first presentation (commonly expressed as "that the cheque is a good and valid order for the amount entered"). There is clear judicial authority supporting this as an accurate statement of principle: *Metropolitan Police Commr v. Charles* [1977] A.C. 177, HL; *R. v. Gilmartin* [1983] Q.B. 953, 76 Cr.App.R. 238, CA (*post*, § 21–376).

The decision of the Court of Appeal in *R. v. Greenstein and Green*, 61 Cr.App.R. 296, CA, appears to be authority for the proposition that it is open to a court to infer, from the act of drawing a cheque, a representation by the drawer that he is not relying, for the cheque to be met, on funds to be provided by the payee by way of a "return" cheque. The case was concerned with a "stagging" operation in shares: when new shares were issued, the defendants applied for more than they could pay for, knowing that only a small proportion of the shares applied for would be issued to them. The issuing houses required applications to be accompanied by a cheque for the full price of the shares applied for; they would send a "return" cheque for the price of shares not issued to the applicant.

Post-dated cheques

21–376 In *R. v. Gilmartin*, *ante*, Robert Goff L.J., giving the judgment of the Court of Appeal in a case under the 1968 Act, said that the act of drawing a post-dated cheque generally implies a representation that the drawer is a customer of the bank concerned, and referred to *R. v. Maytum-White*, 42 Cr.App.R. 165, CCA. His Lordship added that that was not the only representation which could be inferred.

> "We can see no reason why in the case of a post-dated cheque the drawer does not impliedly represent that the existing facts at the date when he gives the cheque to the payee or his agent are such that in the ordinary course the cheque will, on presentation on or after the date specified in the cheque, be met … . For the sake of clarity, we consider that in the generality of cases …, the courts should proceed on the basis that by the simple giving of a cheque, whether post-dated or not, the drawer impliedly represents that the state of facts existing at the date of handing over the cheque is such that in the ordinary course the cheque will, on presentation for payment on or after the date specified in the cheque, be met" (at pp. 961, 245).

Cheque cards

21–377 Where the holder of a cheque card presented the card together with a cheque made out in accordance with the conditions of the card, it was open to the court to infer that a representation had been made by the drawer that he had authority as between himself and the bank to use the card in order to oblige the bank to honour the cheque: *Metropolitan Police Commr v. Charles*, *ante*; but the authority given to the cheque card holder is not unlimited, in that it does not extend to the use of the card to secure acceptance of a cheque which he knows would not be met if the cheque card had not been used: *ibid.*, *per* Viscount Dilhorne (at p. 186); and *per* Lord Diplock (at pp.182-183).

Credit cards

21–378 In *R. v. Lambie* [1982] A.C. 449, HL, the issue was whether the reasoning of the House of Lords in *Charles*, *ante*, as to the representations to be inferred from the use of a cheque backed by a cheque card applied to the use of a credit card. It was held that it did, and that where a person presented a credit card in payment for goods or services, that person represented that he had actual authority to make the contract with the supplier on the bank's behalf and that the bank would honour the voucher on presentation.

Withdrawal slips

21–379 Where a person withdraws or seeks to withdraw money from a bank account (or building society account) the presentation of the withdrawal slip is a representation that the bank is indebted (*i.e.* lawfully owes) to him in the amount shown: *R. v. Harrison*, 92 Cr.App.R. 54, CA. The facts concerned withdrawals of money from accounts funded by means of forged cheques. No cheques were involved in the obtaining or attempt at obtaining the money.

Quotations

In *R. v. Silverman*, 86 Cr.App.R. 213, CA, it was said that it could not be right to say that someone who was asked for a quotation for work or services would inevitably come into conflict with the criminal law if he pitched his quotation very high. Whether or not he had made a false representation that the amount was a fair and reasonable price had to depend upon the particular circumstances. Where there was a relationship of trust between customers and tradesmen, so that the customers relied upon the tradesmen to act fairly and reasonably towards them at all times, a false representation might be made if a grossly excessive price was quoted and charged for work or services, even if, apart from mentioning the price, nothing more was said and no pressure was applied to encourage the acceptance of the quotation. **21–380**

"Phishing"

The explanatory notes to the Act state that the offence of fraud by false representation would be committed by someone who engaged in "phishing" by disseminating an email to a large group of people falsely representing that it had been sent by a legitimate financial institution and prompting the reader to provide information such as credit card and bank account numbers so that the "phisher" could gain access to others' assets (*sed quaere* whether the "phisher" would intend, by that representation, to make a gain in money or other property, or whether that intention would instead accompany a subsequent representation made to the financial institution using the information provided). **21–381**

Representations which were true when first made

In *DPP v. Ray* [1974] A.C. 370, HL, which concerned the now repealed section 15 of the 1968 Act, Lord Morris said (at p. 386) that a continuing representation which is true initially but subsequently becomes false becomes a deliberate deception. This can only be so under section 2 of the *Fraud Act* if the representation is made again, expressly or impliedly, once the person making it knows that it has or might have become untrue or misleading. Accepting benefits flowing from a representation after it has ceased to be true may involve an implied representation that it is still true: for an example under the earlier legislation, see *R. v. Rai* [2000] 1 Cr.App.R. 242, CA (home improvements for the benefit of the defendant's mother, applied for when she was still alive, but accepted after her death). **21–382**

Where a person is under a legal duty to disclose the fact that the representation has become false, section 3 will apply (*post*).

(c) *Fraud by failing to disclose information*

Legal duty to disclose

The defendant must be under a legal duty to disclose the undisclosed information. Examples given in the explanatory notes to the Act are duties of disclosure in applications for insurance, company prospectuses, and as between agent and principal. Section 3(a), *ante*, § 21–358, does not state expressly that the legal duty must be to disclose to the person to whom the defendant has failed to disclose the information, but it is submitted that this is implicit in the definition of the offence. **21–383**

There is no requirement that the defendant must know that he is under a legal duty to disclose the information, although his knowledge on this issue will be relevant to dishonesty. On the other hand, he must know that the information is material, for otherwise he could not intend, by failing to disclose the information, to make the gain, etc.

Failure to disclose

The requirements of dishonesty and the necessary intent (*ante*, §§ 21–369 *et seq.*) ensure that the failure must be deliberate. The offence will be committed at the point when the defendant first has the necessary *mens rea* and is under the duty, and will continue so long as both subsist without disclosure being made. A defendant who, upon **21–384** specific enquiry, provides information which he had been under a legal duty to provide earlier will have committed the offence if he had intended dishonestly to make the gain or cause the loss without the enquiry being made.

(d) *Fraud by abuse of position*

Position

21–385 The offence requires a person to occupy a position in which he is expected to safeguard, or not to act against, the financial interests of another person: s.4(1)(a), *ante*, § 21–359. The Act does not specify by whose expectation the position is to be judged; it must thus be by the reasonable member of the public as personified by the jury. Examples given in the explanatory notes to the Act include the relationship between trustee and beneficiary, director and company, employee and employer, between partners, and within the family.

A person who did not occupy such a position could nonetheless be guilty of the offence as a secondary party, such as the beneficiary of a dishonestly awarded contract.

Abuse of the position

21–386 Abuse is not defined in the Act; it is submitted, however, that it must involve acting contrary to the expectation by which the position is defined (*viz.* to safeguard, or not to act against, the financial interests of another person) and in a way which is made possible because of the position. Abuse of position will include theft in breach of trust; and the offence can be committed by omission: s.4(2), *ante*.

As with the other ways of committing the offence of fraud, the abuse of position need not result in actual gain or loss.

Mens rea

21–387 The abuse must be dishonest and must be accompanied by the requisite intent as to gain and loss (*ante*, § 21–370). There is no express requirement that the defendant must know that he is expected to safeguard or not to act against the financial interests of the other person, or to know that his act (or failure to act) constitutes an abuse of his position. However, he must intend that the act (or failure to act) which constitutes the abuse of the position will make a gain or cause loss, etc., to another (not necessarily the person whose interests he is expected to safeguard).

(6) Jurisdiction

Statute

21–388 The offence of fraud is a "Group A" offence within Part 1 of the *CJA* 1993. Part 1 is set out at §§ 2–37 *et seq.*, *ante*, where the effect is considered in detail. Jurisdiction is conferred if a "relevant event", defined by section 2 of that Act, occurred in England and Wales. In respect of an offence of fraud, relevant events include the occurrence of a gain, if the fraud involved an intention to make that gain, and the occurrence of a loss, if the fraud involved an intention to cause or to expose another to the risk of that loss (see s.2(1A)).

Common law

21–389 The common law rules governing jurisdiction do not apply to offences of fraud, since any such offence must have been committed after January 15, 2007, and thus after the commencement of Part 1 of the *CJA* 1993.

B. ARTICLES FOR USE IN FRAUDS

(1) Statute

Fraud Act 2006, ss.6–8

Possession etc. of articles for use in frauds

21–390 6.—(1) A person is guilty of an offence if he has in his possession or under his control any article for use in the course of or in connection with any fraud.

(2) A person guilty of an offence under this section is liable—

(a) on summary conviction, to imprisonment for a term not exceeding 12 months or to a fine not exceeding the statutory maximum (or to both);

(b) on conviction on indictment, to imprisonment for a term not exceeding 5 years or to a fine (or to both).

(3) [*Northern Ireland.*]

Making or supplying articles for use in frauds

7.—(1) A person is guilty of an offence if he makes, adapts, supplies or offers to supply any article— **21–391**

(a) knowing that it is designed or adapted for use in the course of or in connection with fraud, or

(b) intending it to be used to commit, or assist in the commission of, fraud.

(2) A person guilty of an offence under this section is liable—

(a) [*identical to s.6(2)(a)*, ante, *§ 21–390*];

(b) on conviction on indictment, to imprisonment for a term not exceeding 10 years or to a fine (or to both).

(3) [*Northern Ireland.*]

"Article"

8.—(1) For the purposes of— **21–392**

(a) sections 6 and 7, and

(b) the provisions listed in subsection (2), so far as they relate to articles for use in the course of or in connection with fraud,

"article" includes any program or data held in electronic form.

(2) The provisions are—

(a) section 1(7)(b) of the *Police and Criminal Evidence Act* 1984,

(b) section 2(8)(b) of the *Armed Forces Act* 2001, and

(c) [*Northern Ireland*];

(meaning of "prohibited articles" for the purposes of stop and search powers).

In relation to an offence committed before the commencement of section 154(1) of the *CJA* 2003, the reference to 12 months in sections 6(2)(a) and 7(2)(a) is to be read as a reference to six months: *Fraud Act* 2006, s.14(2), and Sched. 2, para. 1. For section 1(7)(b) of the 1984 Act, see *ante*, § 15–50.

(2) Indictment

(a) *Possession of an article for use in fraud*

STATEMENT OF OFFENCE

Possession, etc., of an article for use in fraud, contrary to section 6(1) of the Fraud Act *2006.* **21–393**

PARTICULARS OF OFFENCE

A B, on the —— day of ——, 20—, had in his possession or under his control an article for use in the course of or in connection with a fraud, namely a credit card in the name of C D.

(b) *Making or supplying an article for use in fraud*

STATEMENT OF OFFENCE

Making [or *Adapting*] [or *Supplying*] [or *Offering to supply*] *an article for use in fraud, contrary to section 7(1) of the* Fraud Act *2006.* **21–394**

PARTICULARS OF OFFENCE

A B, on the —— day of ——, 20—, made [or *adapted*] [or *supplied to C D*] [or *offered to supply to C D*] *an article, namely a device designed to be attached to an electricity meter so as to cause the meter to malfunction, knowing that it was designed* [or *adapted*] *for use in the course of or in connection with* [or *intending it to be used to commit, or to assist in the commission of,*] *fraud.*

(3) Class of offence and mode of trial

21–395 Offences under sections 6 and 7 are triable either way: see ss.6(2) and 7(2), *ante*, §§21–390, 21–391. They are class 3 offences, *ante*, § 2–17.

(4) Sentence

21–396 For possession of articles for use in frauds, imprisonment not exceeding five years: s.6(2) (*ante*, § 21–390); for making or supplying such articles, imprisonment not exceeding 10 years: s.7(2) (*ante*, § 21–391).

Both offences are specified serious offences within Schedule 1 to the *SCA* 2007, enabling the Crown Court to make a serious crime prevention order under section 19 on conviction (*ante*, § 5–875c).

(5) The elements of the offences

(a) *Possession of an article for use in fraud*

21–397 Prove simply that the defendant had the article in his possession or under his control and that it was an article for use in the course of or in connection with any fraud, *i.e.* any fraud falling within section 1 of the Act (*ante*, § 21–356). It is submitted that if Parliament had intended to include other fraudulent conduct then language such as that in section 13 ("or a related offence", *post*, § 21–413) would have been used. Unlike the offence of going equipped, contrary to section 25 of the *Theft Act* 1968 (*ante*, § 21–324), there is no requirement that the defendant not be at his place of abode.

Article

21–398 An article includes any program or data held in electronic form: s.8(1), *ante*. If such an article were on the defendant's computer completely unbeknown to him, he would not be guilty of the offence, since possession requires some degree of knowledge; and where the file has been deleted, possession also requires the know-how and the software to retrieve it: see *Atkins v. DPP*; *Goodland v. DPP* [2000] 2 Cr.App.R. 248, DC, and *R. v. Porter* [2006] 2 Cr.App.R. 25, CA, respectively (*post*, § 31–118). For possession generally, see, *post*, §§ 27–54 *et seq.*

For use in fraud

21–399 By analogy with the offence of going equipped to steal (*ante*, §§ 21–324 *et seq.*), it is not necessary to prove that the defendant intended the article to be used in the course of or in connection with any specific fraud; it will be enough to prove a general intention that it be so used, whether by himself or by someone else: *R. v. Ellames*, 60 Cr.App.R. 7, CA (for cases on the *Theft Act* 1968, s.25, see *ante*, § 21–328).

(b) *Making or supplying an article for use in fraud*

21–400 Prove that the defendant did one of the four specified acts in relation to the article, *viz.* making it, adapting it, supplying it or offering to supply it, and that he did so with one of the two specified states of mind, *viz.* knowing that it was designed (not necessarily by him) or adapted for use in the course of or in connection with fraud, or intending it to be used (not necessarily by him or by the person to whom he supplied it) to commit, or assist in the commission of, fraud.

Knowledge

21–401 Proof of knowledge also requires proof that the article was in fact designed or adapted for use in the course of or in connection with fraud (*cf. R. v. Montila* [2005] 1 Cr.App.R. 26, HL, *post*, § 33–4). As with the offence of possession, this need not be in the course of or in connection with any specific fraud: *Ellames*, *ante*.

Intent

21–402 Where the *actus reus* is supplying, or offering to supply, and the *mens rea* is intent rather than knowledge, the article need not be designed or adapted for use in the course of or in connection with fraud. The intention, *viz.* that it be used to commit, or assist in the commission of, fraud, is differently worded and suggests a closer connection to the commission of a particular, intended, fraud.

C. OBTAINING SERVICES DISHONESTLY

(1) Statute

Fraud Act 2006, s.11

Obtaining services dishonestly

11.—(1) A person is guilty of an offence under this section if he obtains services for himself or another— **21–403**

(a) by a dishonest act, and

(b) in breach of subsection (2).

(2) A person obtains services in breach of this subsection if—

(a) they are made available on the basis that payment has been, is being or will be made for or in respect of them,

(b) he obtains them without any payment having been made for or in respect of them or without payment having been made in full, and

(c) when he obtains them, he knows—

(i) that they are being made available on the basis described in paragraph (a), or

(ii) that they might be,

but intends that payment will not be made, or will not be made in full.

(3) A person guilty of an offence under this section is liable—

(a) on summary conviction, to imprisonment for a term not exceeding 12 months or to a fine not exceeding the statutory maximum (or to both);

(b) on conviction on indictment, to imprisonment for a term not exceeding 5 years or to a fine (or to both).

(4) [*Northern Ireland.*]

(2) Indictment

STATEMENT OF OFFENCE

Obtaining services dishonestly, contrary to section 11(1) of the Fraud Act *2006.* **21–404**

PARTICULARS OF OFFENCE

A B, on the —— day of ——, 20—, obtained services for himself [or *another*], *namely the performance of a play at the —— Theatre, knowing that they were made available on the basis that payment had been* [or *was being*] [or *would be*] *made, when in fact no payment had been made for them and intending that payment would not be made, by a dishonest act, namely by gaining access to the auditorium without a ticket via a fire exit.*

(3) Class of offence and mode of trial

This offence is triable either way: see s.11(3). It is a class 3 offence, *ante*, § 2–17. **21–405**

(4) Sentence

Maximum

Imprisonment not exceeding five years: s.11(3), *ante*. **21–406**

Financial reporting orders

A financial reporting order may be made in respect of a person convicted of an offence of obtaining services dishonestly: *SOCPA* 2005, s.76 (*ante*, § 5–886a). **21–407**

Serious crime prevention orders

Obtaining services dishonestly is a specified serious offence within Schedule 1 to the *SCA* 2007, enabling the Crown Court to make a serious crime prevention order under section 19 on conviction (*ante*, § 5–875c). **21–407a**

(5) The elements of the offence

Obtaining services

21–408 The services must actually have been obtained; in this respect, the offence differs from the offence of fraud. They must also be services which were made available on the basis that they had been, were being or would be paid for, and for which payment had not been made, or had not been made in full, at the time they were obtained: s.11(2)(a) and (b), *ante*. Thus a person who dishonestly obtains and pays for services to which he knows he is not entitled does not commit the offence.

Unlike its predecessor, the Act does not define "services"; it is likely that it will embrace at least all those benefits which had been said to fall within the definition which was provided under the *Theft Act* 1978, s.1, such as a loan, or the provision of banking or credit card services (*R. v. Sofroniou* [2004] 1 Cr.App.R. 35, CA), professional, commercial or financial services (*R. v. Graham (H.K.)*; *R. v. Kansal*; *R. v. Ali (Sajid)*; *R. v. Marsh* [1997] 1 Cr.App.R. 302, CA), or a hire-purchase agreement (*R. v. Widdowson*, 82 Cr.App.R. 314, CA).

Knowledge

21–409 The defendant must obtain the services knowing that they are, or might be, being made available on the basis that they had been, were being or would be paid for: s.11(2)(c), *ante*.

Intent not to pay

21–410 The defendant must intend that payment will not be made, or will not be made in full: s.11(2)(c), *ante*.

Dishonest act

21–411 The services must be obtained by an act (and thus not by omission), and that act must be dishonest; this is in addition to the requirement that they be obtained knowing that payment is or might be required and intending not to pay. The dishonest act could be, but is not limited to, the making of a false representation. As to dishonesty, see, *ante*, § 21–2b.

D. SUPPLEMENTARY PROVISIONS

Liability of company officers

21–412 Section 12 of the *Fraud Act* 2006 relates to offences under the Act which are committed by a body corporate and is in materially identical terms to section 18 of the *Theft Act* 1968 (*post*, § 30–265).

Fraud Act 2006, s.13

Evidence

21–413 **13.**—(1) A person is not to be excused from—

(a) answering any question put to him in proceedings relating to property, or

(b) complying with any order made in proceedings relating to property,

on the ground that doing so may incriminate him or his spouse or civil partner of an offence under this Act or a related offence.

(2) But, in proceedings for an offence under this Act or a related offence, a statement or admission made by the person in—

(a) answering such a question, or

(b) complying with such an order,

is not admissible in evidence against him or (unless they married or became civil partners after the making of the statement or admission) his spouse or civil partner.

(3) "Proceedings relating to property" means any proceedings for—

(a) the recovery or administration of any property,

(b) the execution of a trust, or

(c) an account of any property or dealings with property,

and "property" means money or other property whether real or personal (including things in action and other intangible property).

(4) "Related offence" means—

(a) conspiracy to defraud;

(b) any other offence involving any form of fraudulent conduct or purpose.

This section is to the same effect as section 31(1) of the *Theft Act* 1968 (*ante*, § 21–336), which formerly applied to the offences repealed and replaced by the *Fraud Act*, save that it extends the ambit of the provision to conspiracy to defraud and other offences involving fraudulent conduct or purpose. The distinguishing feature of such other offences was held in *Kensington International Ltd v. Republic of Congo (formerly People's Republic of Congo) (Vitol Services Ltd, third parties)* [2008] 1 W.L.R. 1144, CA (Civ. Div.), to be that they involve some element of deception or, *per* Carnwath L.J., surreptitious dealing (deciding that bribery was such an offence). To come within subsection (3), the proceedings need not relate to the property which is the subject matter of the offence, and can include an action for recovery of a debt: *ibid*.

Transitional provisions

Section 14(2) gives effect to the transitional provisions in Schedule 2. **21–414**

Fraud Act 2006, Sched. 2, para. 3

Abolition of deception offences

3.—(1) Paragraph 1 of Schedule 1 [*abolition of offences under* Theft Act *1968, ss.15, 15A, 16 and 20(2), and* Theft Act *1978, ss.1 and 2*] does not affect any liability, investigation, legal proceeding or penalty for or in respect of any offence partly committed before the commencement of that paragraph.

(2) An offence is partly committed before the commencement of paragraph 1 of Schedule 1 if—

(a) a relevant event occurs before its commencement, and

(b) another relevant event occurs on or after its commencement.

(3) "Relevant event", in relation to an offence, means any act, omission or other event (including any result of one or more acts or omissions) proof of which is required for conviction of the offence.

As to the commencement date for paragraph 1 of Schedule 1, see *post*, § 21–415. As to offences completed before the commencement date, see the *Interpretation Act* 1978, s.16 (Appendix B–16).

These provisions do not restrict section 13 (*ante*) to questions which might incriminate a person of an offence committed after commencement of that section: *Kensington International Ltd v. Republic of Congo (formerly People's Republic of Congo) (Vitol Services Ltd, third parties), ante*.

Commencement

Section 15(1) provides that sections 1 to 14 were to come into force on a day to be appointed. The appointed day was January 15, 2007: *Fraud Act 2006 (Commencement) Order* 2006 (S.I. 2006 No. 3200). **21–415**

CHAPTER 22

FORGERY, PERSONATION AND CHEATING

I. FORGERY

A. FORGERY AND COUNTERFEITING ACT 1981

(1) Introduction

The *Forgery and Counterfeiting Act* 1981 was a codifying measure based largely on the Law Commission's Report on Forgery and Counterfeit Currency (Law Com. No. 55). The *Forgery Act* 1913 and the *Coinage Offences Act* 1936 were repealed in their entirety, together with such sections of the *Forgery Act* 1861 as remained unrepealed, with the exception of sections 34, 36, 37 and 55. Further, by section 13, the offence of forgery at common law was abolished. **22–1**

As to counterfeiting, see *post*, §§ 25–241 *et seq.*

Prior to the publication of their report, the Law Commission had issued a Working Paper (No. 26). In paragraph 13 of the report, they state: "Our Working Paper ... proceeded on the basis that the main aim was to simplify the existing law and it did not question the basic concept of forgery or examine the necessity for the retention of such an offence." In paragraph 17, the report continues: "[W]e think that the most useful course at the present time is to recommend a rationalisation and simplification of the law of forgery which will lead to the elimination of the many specific offences not only in the Forgery Act but also in the many statutes which create such offences." **22–2**

Moving the third reading of the Bill in the House of Commons, Mr Norman Miscampbell said that the Bill dealt with the recommendations of the Law Commission. He referred to the complications which had existed under the previous law and said that radical simplification was required, and that this was the objective of the legislation (*Hansard*, H.C., June 19, 1981, col. 1292).

(2) The scheme of the Act

Parts I (ss.1–13), II (ss.14–28) and III (ss.29–34) are respectively entitled *Forgery and Kindred Offences*, *Counterfeiting and Kindred Offences* and *Miscellaneous and General*. For Part II, see *post*, §§ 25–241 *et seq.* **22–3**

(3) Jurisdiction

Offences contrary to sections 1, 2, 3, 4 and 5 of the 1981 Act are Group A offences within the meaning of Part I of the *CJA* 1993 (*ante*, §§ 2–37 *et seq.*). **22–4**

(4) Forgery

(a) *Statute*

Forgery and Counterfeiting Act 1981, s.1

1. A person is guilty of forgery if he makes a false instrument, with the intention that he or **22–5**

another shall use it to induce somebody to accept it as genuine, and by reason of so accepting it to do or not to do some act to his own or any other person's prejudice.

As to the meaning of "instrument", see *post*, § 22–10; of "makes" and "false", see *post*, § 22–17; of "induce" and "prejudice", see *post*, § 22–22.

(b) *Indictment*

STATEMENT OF OFFENCE

22–6 *Forgery, contrary to section 1 of the* Forgery and Counterfeiting Act *1981*.

PARTICULARS OF OFFENCE

A B, on the —— day of ——, 20—, made an instrument, namely a cheque numbered 123456, which was false in that it purported to be made in the form in which it was made by a person who did not in fact make it in that form, with the intention that he, A B, or another, should use it to induce C D [or *somebody*] *to accept it as genuine and, by reason of so accepting it, to do some act, or not to do some act, to his own or any other person's prejudice.*

(c) *Mode of trial and sentence*

22–7 The mode of trial and maximum sentences for offences under the 1981 Act are provided for by section 6 (*post*, § 22–37). All offences in Part I are triable either way; and they are all class 3 offences, *ante*, § 2–17.

(d) *Elements of the offence*

Concept and rationale

22–8 This section, creating the main offence of forgery, follows almost exactly the definition in the Law Commission's draft Bill. As has been seen (*ante*, § 22–2), the Law Commission did not question the basic concept of forgery. Section 1, taken together with the interpretative provisions in sections 8 to 10, and, in particular, section 9 (*post*, §§ 22–17 *et seq.*), is clearly intended to give effect to this approach.

The concept of forgery and the rationale of the offence were summarised in paragraphs 41 to 43 of the Law Commission report:

> "By the middle of the nineteenth century it was established that for the purpose of the law of forgery the fact that determined whether a document was false was not that it contained lies, but that it told a lie about itself. It was in *R. v. Windsor* (1865) 10 Cox 118, 123 that Blackburn J. said: 'Forgery is the false making of an instrument purporting to be that which it is not, it is not the making of an instrument which purports to be what it really is, but which contains false statements. Telling a lie does not become a forgery because it is reduced into writing.' This test was applied in the Court of Appeal in *R. v. Dodge and Harris* [1972] 1 Q.B. 416. ... As we have said ... the primary reason for retaining a law of forgery is to penalise the making of documents which, because of the spurious air of authenticity given to them are likely to lead to their acceptance as true statements of the facts related in them. We do not think that there is any need for the extension of forgery to cover falsehoods that are reduced to writing. ... The essential feature of a false instrument in relation to forgery is that it is an instrument which 'tells a lie about itself' in the sense that it purports to be made by a person who did not make it (or altered by a person who did not alter it) or otherwise purports to be made or altered in circumstances in which it was not made or altered."

In *R. v. More*, 86 Cr.App.R. 234, the House of Lords construed the 1981 Act in accordance with the concept of forgery set out in the Law Commission report. See further *post*, §§ 22–18 *et seq.*

Double intention

22–8a The intention which section 1 requires to be proved is two-fold: (a) the intention that the false instrument shall be used to induce somebody to accept it as genuine, and (b) the intention to induce somebody, by reason of so accepting it, to do or not do some act to his own or any other person's prejudice: *R. v. Campbell*, 80 Cr.App.R. 47, CA. See further *post*, § 22–29.

A person who makes a false instrument, intending to copy it and to induce another person to accept the copy as a copy of a genuine instrument and by reason of so accepting it to do an act to his prejudice, is guilty of forgery; such an intention equates to an intention to induce somebody to accept the instrument itself as genuine: *R. v. Ondhia* [1998] 2 Cr.App.R. 150, CA.

"any other person"

The words "any other person" cannot refer to the forger himself: *R. v. Utting*, 86 Cr.App.R. 164, CA. It is unnecessary to prove the identity of the person intended to be prejudiced as a result of the acceptance by that person or another of the false instrument as genuine: *R. v. Johnson* [1997] 8 *Archbold News* 1, CA. It is submitted that the same principle must apply to the identity of the person who is intended to be induced to accept the instrument as genuine. **22–9**

"instrument"

Forgery and Counterfeiting Act 1981, s.8

Meaning of "instrument"

8.—(1) Subject to subsection (2) below, in this Part of this Act "instrument" means— **22–10**

(a) any document, whether of a formal or informal character;

(b) any stamp issued or sold by a postal operator;

(c) any Inland Revenue stamp; and

(d) any disc, tape, sound track or other device on or in which information is recorded or stored by mechanical, electronic or other means.

(2) A currency note within the meaning of Part II of this Act is not an instrument for the purposes of this Part of this Act.

(3) A mark denoting payment of postage which a postal operator authorises to be used instead of an adhesive stamp is to be treated for the purposes of this Part of this Act as if it were a stamp issued by the postal operator concerned.

(3A) In this section "postal operator" has the same meaning as in the *Postal Services Act* 2000.

(4) In this Part of this Act "Inland Revenue Stamp" means a stamp as defined in section 27 of the *Stamp Duties Management Act* 1891.

[This section is printed as amended by the *Postal Services Act 2000 (Consequential Modifications No. 1) Order* 2001 (S.I. 2001 No. 1149), art. 3(1) and Sched. 1, para. 50.]

"any document"

Section 8(1)(a), by defining the primary subject matter of forgery (*i.e.* an "instrument") as "any document, whether of a formal or informal character", has failed to introduce that clarity into the law which was the object of the legislation. **22–11**

Although the courts will no doubt be reluctant to look at authorities under the old law in determining the scope of the 1981 Act it is necessary to go behind the Act if only to appreciate the difficulty. In *R. v. Closs* (1858) Dears. & B. 460, it was held that at common law a forgery must be of some document or writing and that, therefore, the painting of an artist's name in the corner of a picture in order to pass it off as an original picture by that artist was not a forgery. The painting of the name in the corner "was merely in the nature of a mark put upon the painting with a view to identifying it, and was no more than if the painter put any other arbitrary mark as a recognition of the picture being his" (*per* Cockburn C.J. at p. 466).

In *R. v. Smith* (1858) Dears. & B. 566, the complainant, B, sold powders called "B's Baking Powders" and "B's Egg Powders", which he invariably sold in packets wrapped up in printed papers. The defendant procured 10,000 wrappers to be printed and in these he enclosed powders of his own. In the case of the baking powders the wrappers were very similar to B's and in the case of the egg powders the wrappers were identical. The defendant's conviction for forgery was quashed. Pollock C.B. said he doubted whether the wrappers "in their present shape ... are anything like a document or instrument which is the subject of forgery at common law. To say that they belong to that class of instruments seems to me to be confounding things together as alike which are essentially different. It might as well be said, that if one tradesman used brown paper for his wrappers, and another tradesman had his brown paper wrappers made in the same way, he could be accused of forging the brown paper" (at p. 574). Willes J. agreed with this reasoning: "This is not one of the different kinds of instrument which may be made the subject of forgery. It is not made the subject of forgery simply by reason of the assertion of that which is false" (*ibid.*). Bramwell B. and Byles J. seemed to prefer to rest their decision that the conviction should be quashed on the ground that the wrappers did not tell a lie about themselves.

22–12 By the *Forgery Act* 1913 the subject matter of forgery was a document, but no definition was provided. In paragraph 19 of their report the Law Commission pointed out that among text-book writers there were two main schools of thought as to the ambit of the word "document".

> "The one school, while accepting the proposition that a document is a writing, contends that if the thing alleged to be forged is intended to have utility apart from the fact that its contents convey information or record a promise, it is not a document."

(See, in particular, Smith and Hogan, *Criminal Law*, 4th ed., pp. 626–628, and Glanville Williams (1948) 11 M.L.R. 150–162.) The Law Commission state that this view is based on a common rationalisation of the decisions in *R. v. Closs*, *ante*, and *R. v. Smith*, *ante*, and continue:

> "Smith and Hogan and Glanville Williams also suggest as an alternative test that the writing must be an instrument, that is to say, a document made for the purpose of creating or modifying or terminating a right. The editor of *Kenny*, *Outline of Criminal Law*, 19th ed., pp. 383 *et seq.*, on the other hand, suggests that a document is a writing in any form on any material which communicates to some person or persons a human statement whether of fact or fiction. He maintains that *Closs* was wrongly decided, not because the picture with the false signature was a document, but because the signature was a writing intended to convey the information that the apparent signatory had painted the picture, just as if there were a certificate to that effect signed by him posted on the back."

22–13 Having stated the problem, the Law Commission then set out their objective at paragraph 22:

> "The essence of forgery, in our view, is the making of a false document intending that it be used to induce a person to accept and act upon the message contained in it, as if it were contained in a genuine document. In the straightforward case a document usually contains messages of two distinct kinds—first a message about the document itself (such as the message that the document is a cheque or a will) and secondly a message to be found in the words of the document that is to be accepted and acted upon (such as the message that a banker is to pay a specified sum or that property is to be distributed in a particular way). In our view it is only documents which convey not only the first type of message but also the second type that need to be protected by the law of forgery. Forgery should not be concerned, for example, with the false making of the autograph of a celebrity on a plain piece of paper but it should be concerned with the false making of a signature as an endorsement on the back of a promissory note."

The Commission concluded that the word "instrument" best reflected "the underlying distinguishing feature of the type of document to which forgery should apply" (para. 23). In their draft Bill, "instrument" was defined as "any instrument in writing whether of a formal or informal character, with 'writing' including for this purpose not only words and letters but also figures and other symbols". In an explanatory note, the Commission say: "An instrument in writing, whether of a formal or informal character embraces all those documents, the contents of which are to be acted upon." In paragraph 23 they maintain that the definition "will serve to exclude such things as a painting purporting to bear the signature of the artist, the false autograph and any writing on manufactured articles indicating the name of the manufacturer or the country of origin".

22–14 By failing to adopt the Law Commission proposal on this point Parliament seems to have opened the door to all the former problems as to the meaning of the word "document", so that it will be open to argument that the picture with a false signature is a "document", although this was clearly not the intention of the Law Commission and apparently not the intention of Parliament. In the third reading debate in the House of Commons, Mr Patrick Mayhew, then Minister of State at the Home Office, said the intention was that fake paintings or photographs and their passing off as genuine could be dealt with under the *Theft Act* 1968. "The joint characteristics of paintings and of photographs is that they do not seek to communicate any message such as one would normally expect to find in a document" (*Hansard*, H.C., June 19, 1981, col. 1310). The whole point of the argument put forward by the editor of *Kenny* (*ante*), and which apparently found favour in *R. v. Douce* [1972] Crim.L.R. 105, Quarter Sessions, is that the signature in the corner is intended to communicate a message just as much as if there were a certificate on the back.

What approach the courts will take is still not clear, but it may be that even if items of the type discussed in the preceding paragraph are indeed documents they will not be "false" in the sense required by section 9 of the 1981 Act (*post*, § 22–17) and explained in *R. v. More* (*post*, § 22–18). See also Smith and Hogan, *Criminal Law*, 12th ed., pp. 960 *et seq.* **22–15**

"recorded or stored"

The words "recorded or stored" in section 8(1)(d) should be given their ordinary and natural meaning; this connotes the preservation of the thing which is the subject-matter of them for an appreciable time with the object of subsequent retrieval or recovery: *R. v. Gold and Schifreen* [1988] A.C. 1063, HL (a "computer hacking" case; see now the *Computer Misuse Act* 1990, *post*, §§ 23–86 *et seq.*). See also *R. v. Governor of Brixton Prison, ex p. Levin* [1997] 1 Cr.App.R. 335, DC. **22–16**

"false"; "making"

Forgery and Counterfeiting Act 1981, s.9

Meaning of "false" and "making" in section 1

9.—(1) An instrument is false for the purposes of this Part of this Act— **22–17**

(a) if it purports to have been made in the form in which it is made by a person who did not in fact make it in that form, or

(b) if it purports to have been made in the form in which it is made on the authority of a person who did not in fact authorise its making in that form; or

(c) if it purports to have been made in the terms in which it is made by a person who did not in fact make it in those terms; or

(d) if it purports to have been made in the terms in which it is made on the authority of a person who did not in fact authorise its making in those terms; or

(e) if it purports to have been altered in any respect by a person who did not in fact alter it in that respect; or

(f) if it purports to have been altered in any respect on the authority of a person who did not in fact authorise the alteration in that respect; or

(g) if it purports to have been made or altered on a date on which, or at a place at which, or otherwise in circumstances in which, it was not in fact made or altered; or

(h) if it purports to have been made or altered by an existing person but he did not in fact exist.

(2) A person is to be treated for the purposes of this Part of this Act as making a false instrument if he alters an instrument so as to make it false in any respect (whether or not it is false in some other respect apart from that alteration).

In *R. v. More*, 86 Cr.App.R. 234, CA and HL, Lord Ackner, with whom the remainder of their Lordships agreed, said that it was common ground that the consistent use of the word "purports" in each of the paragraphs (a) to (h), imports a requirement that for an instrument to be false it must tell a lie about itself, in the sense that it purports to be made by a person who did not make it (or altered by a person who did not alter it) or otherwise purports to be made or altered in circumstances in which it was not made or altered (at p. 253). **22–18**

The facts in *More*, were that the defendant, having stolen a cheque payable to M.R.J., opened a building society account in the name M.R.J. He waited for the cheque to be cleared and then returned to the building society where he completed a withdrawal form for the amount of the cheque. He signed the form "M.R.J.". The form was said to be a forgery. The trial judge accepted the Crown's contention that the form came within section 9(1)(a) and section 9(1)(c). The Court of Appeal held that the form fell rather within section 9(1)(h). "The document was undoubtedly made by [M] and it was undoubtedly made in the form of a withdrawal form. It was undoubtedly signed by the person making it and that signature was undoubtedly the signature of the holder of the account in the name 'Mark Richard Jessel'." The document thus did not purport to have been made by the Mr Jessel in whose name the cheque used to open the account had been drawn, since the form made no mention on the face of it of that cheque. The House of Lords, however, while upholding the Court of Appeal's rejection of section 9(1)(a) and (c) rejected too the Court of Appeal's category—section 9(1)(h). M, after all, was a real person. It was he who was the holder of the account and in that capacity had signed the withdrawal form. The form clearly purported to be signed by the person who originally opened the account and in this respect it was wholly accurate. It could not therefore be contended that the document told a lie about itself.

The Court of Appeal in *More* said that whether or not an instrument is false is, on any given facts, a question of law for the judge to decide. Where the facts are in dispute it is, of course, for the jury to determine what the facts are, but the judge will direct the jury that if they find certain facts proved then the instrument in question is to be regarded as false.

22–19 In the earlier case of *R. v. Donnelly*, 79 Cr.App.R. 76, CA, the appellant was the manager of a jeweller's shop owned by a well-known company. He made out and signed what purported to be a written valuation of six scheduled items of jewellery. The certificate was on a printed form issued by the National Association of Goldsmiths and it also contained a statement that the appellant had examined the scheduled items and the figures given represented their insurance value. He signed that document and stamped the shop owner's name and address below his signature. The valuation was intended to defraud an insurance company, for in fact there was no jewellery to be valued. In the Court of Appeal the prosecution conceded that the valuation would not have been a forgery at common law nor under the *Forgery Act* 1913. Lawton L.J., delivering the brief judgment of the court, in which no reference was made to any authorities, said that the 1981 Act was intended to make new law, and referred to the opening words of the long title: "An Act to make fresh provision ... with respect to forgery and kindred offences." His Lordship then read the terms of section 9(1)(g) and concluded:

> "In our judgment the words coming at the end of paragraph (g) 'otherwise in circumstances ...' expand its ambit beyond dates and places to *any* case in which an instrument purports to be made when it was not in fact made. This valuation purported to be made *after* the appellant had examined the items of jewellery set out in the schedule. He did not make it after examining these items because they did not exist. That which purported to be a valuation after examination of items was nothing of the kind: it was a worthless piece of paper. ... This purported valuation was a forgery (at p. 78)."

22–20 In *R. v. Lack*, 84 Cr.App.R. 342, CA, submissions were apparently made to the effect that it was still a requirement of forgery that the document must not simply tell a lie but must tell a lie about itself. Counsel referred to *R. v. Dodge and Harris* [1972] 1 Q.B. 416, 55 Cr.App.R. 440, CA. Lawton L.J., giving the court's judgment, pointed out that that case was decided before the 1981 Act and its *ratio* might have to be re-examined in the light of the 1981 Act and of the decision in *Donnelly*. It appears, therefore, that the court in *Lack* regarded *Donnelly* as having been decided on the basis that the 1981 Act had made a fundamental change in the essential features of forgery. The question now arises whether this stance is inconsistent with the view of the House of Lords in *R. v. More*, *ante*, § 22–18. Reference was made to *Donnelly* in argument, but it was not specifically mentioned in the decision. The point did not, in the event, affect the result in *R. v. Lack* because the relevant documents were held to tell lies about themselves.

22–21 In two subsequent decisions, the Court of Appeal reached inconsistent conclusions. In *R. v. Jeraj* [1994] Crim.L.R. 595, the court said that it remained bound by *Donnelly* unless it was plainly wrong, but it was not plainly wrong; it was right. It was not undermined by *More*. In *R. v. Warneford and Gibbs* [1994] Crim.L.R. 753, a differently constituted court, not having been referred to *Jeraj*, held that to come within section 9(1), a lie told in a document must relate to the actual circumstances of the document's making and that a lie told about facts extraneous to the document will not suffice. Section 9(1) was mistakenly construed in *Donnelly*. The court held that an employment reference given by someone who had not employed the person to whom the reference related did not fall within section 9(1)(g).

In *Att.-Gen.'s Reference (No. 1 of 2000)* [2001] 1 Cr.App.R. 15, CA, it was held that the decision in *Donnelly* was still binding. However, both *Donnelly* and *Jeraj* should be restricted in their application so that they only applied where circumstances needed to exist before the document could be properly made or altered. If those circumstances did not exist, there would then be a false instrument for the purposes of section 9(1)(g). If the circumstances did not exist, the document would be telling a lie about itself because it was saying that it was made in circumstances which did not exist. *Warneford and Gibbs* was to be regarded as wrongly decided on its facts, although the court agreed that the lie in the document must relate to the actual circumstances of the document's making and not to facts extraneous to the document. Where, therefore, a tachograph record purported to show that during a particular period the vehicle to which it was connected had been in motion and that the defendant was resting, whereas he had in fact been driving the vehicle, the record was false in that it purported to have been made in circumstances where another person was driving. The court said that in *Warneford and Gibbs* there had to have been the relationship of master and servant before the employer could make the reference relating to the employee. The need for the existence of such circumstances prior to the making of the instrument explained why, if the circumstances did not exist, the document would be telling a lie about itself.

"prejudice"; "induce"

Forgery and Counterfeiting Act 1981, s.10

Meaning of "prejudice" and "induce" in section 1

10.—(1) Subject to subsections (2) and (4) below, for the purposes of this Part of this Act an act or omission intended to be induced is to a person's prejudice if, and only if, it is one which, if it occurs— **22–22**

(a) will result—

(i) in his temporary or permanent loss of property; or

(ii) in his being deprived of an opportunity to earn remuneration or greater remuneration; or

(iii) in his being deprived of an opportunity to gain a financial advantage otherwise than by way of remuneration; or

(b) will result in somebody being given an opportunity—

(i) to earn remuneration or greater remuneration from him; or

(ii) to gain a financial advantage from him otherwise than by way of remuneration; or

(c) will be the result of his having accepted a false instrument as genuine, or a copy of a false instrument as a copy of a genuine one, in connection with his performance of any duty.

(2) An act which a person has an enforceable duty to do and an omission to do an act which a person is not entitled to do shall be disregarded for the purposes of this Part of this Act.

(3) In this Part of this Act references to inducing somebody to accept a false instrument as genuine, or a copy of a false instrument as a copy of a genuine one, include references to inducing a machine to respond to the instrument or copy as if it were a genuine instrument or, as the case may be, a copy of a genuine one.

(4) Where subsection (3) above applies, the act or omission intended to be induced by the machine responding to the instrument or copy shall be treated as an act or omission to a person's prejudice.

(5) In this section "loss" includes not getting what one might get as well as parting with what one has.

22–23 The Act gives "prejudice" a slightly wider meaning than did the Law Commission's draft Bill. The extended definition was introduced by way of amendment in the House of Commons. The new part of the definition is in subsection (1) at (a)(ii) and (iii), and at (b)(i). When the Bill returned to the House of Lords, Viscount Colville of Culross, who had originally piloted the Bill through the House of Lords, said of this amendment, that it had become apparent during discussion in the House of Commons:

> "that the definition was not sufficiently wide to cover circumstances in which a person could be prejudiced by being deprived of an opportunity to gain financial advantage or earn remuneration, and also it did not cover circumstances in which a person obtains an opportunity to gain a financial advantage from another thus prejudicing another person; gaining a financial advantage from person A to the prejudice of person B. It was thought ... that circumstances of this sort needed to be catered for. The classic example was quoted of a person who resorts to forgery in order to obtain a contract for which he and others had been bidding by forging testimonials or something of that sort, and thereby depriving the genuine tenderer of what would have been his contract if it had not been for the forgery" (*Hansard*, HL, July 16, 1981, col. 1439).

22–24 In an explanatory note to the draft Bill, the Law Commission said, of the provision now contained in section 10(1)(c), it:

> "covers, for example, the case where a doorkeeper is to be induced by a false instrument, such as a door pass, to admit an unauthorised person to premises. It also covers the type of case of which *Welham v. DPP* [1961] A.C. 103 is an example, where the intention in the making or using of the false instrument is to induce someone responsible for a duty to behave in a way in which he would not have behaved in relation to that duty had he not accepted the instrument as genuine."

In relation to section 10(2) it was the Law Commission's view that it should not be forgery to make a false instrument to induce another to do what he is obliged to do or refrain from doing what he is not entitled to do. The offence of blackmail would provide an adequate remedy if the false instrument contained improper menaces designed to reinforce the demand: see para. 34 of the Law Commission report.

Potential prejudice is not enough. The words "will result" in section 10 mean that the intended act or omission, if it occurs, must result in one of the consequences in section 10(1)(a) or (b), or be the result of the induced person accepting a false instrument as genuine, or a copy of a false instrument as a copy of a genuine one, in connection with his performance of any duty (s.10(1)(c)): *R. v. Garcia*, 87 Cr.App.R. 175, CA. However, section 1 focuses on the intention of the maker of the false document, and whether he succeeds as he intends, and whether prejudice within the meaning of section 10 in fact occurs, are immaterial: *R. v. Ondhia* [1998] 2 Cr.App.R. 150, CA.

In order to prove "prejudice" within section 10(1)(a)(i), it is not necessary for the prosecution to prove that the defendant had no legal entitlement to the property: *Att.-Gen.'s Reference (No. 1 of 2001)* [2002] 3 All E.R. 840, CA.

Where a person who qualified for housing benefit submitted in support of his application for such benefit a false document which he had made (a letter, accurate in itself, but purporting to have been written by his landlord), he committed forgery in that he intended the false document to be accepted as genuine by the council to whom the application was made, and by reason of so accepting it to do an act to their prejudice, *i.e.* pay benefit in accordance with their duty; and section 10(2) did not avail him as, upon consideration of the relevant legislation (the *Social Security Administration Act* 1992, s.1 and the *Housing Benefit (General) Regulations* 1987 (S.I. 1987 No. 1971), reg. 73), the council had no duty to pay benefit unless and until the regulations had been complied with, and they could not be complied with by the provision of false documentation as evidence in support of the application: *R. v. Winston* [1999] 1 Cr.App.R. 337, CA.

(5) Copying a false instrument

Forgery and Counterfeiting Act 1981, s.2

22–25 **2.** It is an offence for a person to make a copy of an instrument which is, and which he knows or believes to be, a false instrument, with the intention that he or another shall use it to induce somebody to accept it as a copy of a genuine instrument, and by reason of so accepting it to do or not to do some act to his own or any other person's prejudice.

As to the meaning of "instrument", see section 8, *ante*, §§ 22–10 *et seq.*; of "false", see section 9, *ante*, §§ 22–17 *et seq.*; of "prejudice" and "induce", see section 10, *ante*, §§ 22–22 *et seq.*

As to penalties and other powers, see sections 6 and 7, *post*, §§ 22–37, 22–38.

As to the words "any other person", see *ante*, § 22–9. As to the necessary intent, see *post*, § 22–29.

The reference to a "false" instrument as opposed to a "forged" instrument is deliberate and is designed to obviate the necessity which there was under the old law of establishing that the offending instrument was made with the requisite intention. Accordingly, a person who, with the necessary intent, uses a false instrument will be liable, although the instrument may have been made innocently: see para. 48 of the Law Commission report.

(6) Using a false instrument

Forgery and Counterfeiting Act 1981, s.3

3. It is an offence for a person to use an instrument which is, and which he knows or believes to be, false, with the intention of inducing somebody to accept it as genuine, and by reason of so accepting it to do or not to do some act to his own or any other person's prejudice. **22–26**

As to the meaning of "instrument", see section 8, *ante*, §§ 22–10 *et seq.*; of "false", see section 9, *ante*, §§ 22–17 *et seq.*; of "prejudice" and "induce", see section 10, *ante*, §§ 22–22 *et seq.*

As to the reference to a "false" instrument, see *ante*, § 22–25.

As to the words "any other person", see *ante*, § 22–9.

Indictment

STATEMENT OF OFFENCE

Using a false instrument, contrary to section 3 of the Forgery and Counterfeiting Act *1981.* **22–27**

PARTICULARS OF OFFENCE

A B on the —— day of ——, 20—, used an instrument, namely a cheque number 123456, which was and which he knew or believed to be false, with the intention of inducing C D to accept it as genuine and, by reason of so accepting it, to do or not to do some act to his own or any other person's prejudice.

Class of offence, mode of trial and sentence

The mode of trial and maximum sentences for offences under the 1981 Act are provided for by section 6 (*post*, § 22–37). All offences in Part I are triable either way; and they are all class 3 offences, *ante*, § 2–17. **22–28**

Double intention

Section 3 requires proof of an intention to induce someone to accept the instrument as genuine *and* an intention that the other should act to his own or someone else's prejudice: *R. v. Tobierre*, 82 Cr.App.R. 212, CA. The reasoning of the court would appear to apply equally to the offences under sections 1, 2, 4, 5(1) and 5(3) of the Act, all of which have similarly worded provisions as to intention: see *R. v. Campbell*, 80 Cr.App.R. 47, CA, *ante*, § 22–8. The principle was reaffirmed in *R. v. Garcia*, 87 Cr.App.R. 175, CA. **22–29**

(7) Using a copy of a false instrument

Forgery and Counterfeiting Act 1981, s.4

4. It is an offence for a person to use a copy of an instrument which is, and which he knows or believes to be, a false instrument, with the intention of inducing somebody to accept it as a copy of a genuine instrument, and by reason of so accepting it to do or not to do some act to his own or any other person's prejudice. **22–30**

As to the meaning of "instrument", see section 8, *ante*, §§ 22–10 *et seq.*; of "false", see section 9, *ante*, §§ 22–17 *et seq.*; of "prejudice" and "induce", see section 10, *ante*, §§ 22–22 *et seq.* See *ante*, § 22–29, as to the necessary intent.

As to penalties and other powers, see sections 6 and 7, *post*, §§ 22–37, 22–38.

As to the words "any other person", see *ante*, § 22–9.

As with the offence of copying a false instrument contrary to section 2, *ante*, § 22–25, section 4 refers to a "false" instrument not a "forged" instrument. It follows, therefore, that there may be an offence contrary to this section even though the instrument and indeed the copy of it were themselves made innocently.

(8) Custody or control of certain false instruments and manufacture, custody or control of equipment or materials with which such instruments may be made

Forgery and Counterfeiting Act 1981, s.5

Offences relating to money orders, share certificates, passports, etc.

22–31 **5.**—(1) It is an offence for a person to have in his custody or under his control an instrument to which this section applies which is, and which he knows or believes to be, false, with the intention that he or another shall use it to induce somebody to accept it as genuine, and by reason of so accepting it to do or not to do some act to his own or any other person's prejudice.

(2) It is an offence for a person to have in his custody or under his control, without lawful authority or excuse, an instrument to which this section applies which is, and which he knows or believes to be, false.

(3) It is an offence for a person to make or to have in his custody or under his control a machine or implement, or paper or any other material, which to his knowledge is or has been specially designed or adapted for the making of an instrument to which this section applies, with the intention that he or another shall make an instrument to which this section applies which is false and that he or another shall use the instrument to induce somebody to accept it as genuine, and by reason of so accepting it to do or not to do some act to his own or any other person's prejudice.

(4) It is an offence for a person to make or to have in his custody or under his control any such machine, implement, paper or material, without lawful authority or excuse.

(5) The instruments to which this section applies are—

(a) money orders;
(b) postal orders;
(c) United Kingdom postage stamps;
(d) Inland Revenue stamps;
(e) share certificates;
(g) cheques and other bills of exchange;
(h) travellers' cheques;
(ha) bankers' drafts;
(hb) promissory notes;
(j) cheque cards;
(ja) debit cards;
(k) credit cards;
(l) certified copies relating to an entry in a register of births, adoptions, marriages, civil partnerships or deaths and issued by the Registrar General, the Registrar General for Northern Ireland, a registration officer or a person lawfully authorised to issue certified copies relating to such entries; and
(m) certificates relating to entries in such registers.

(6) In subsection (5)(e) above "share certificate" means an instrument entitling or evidencing the title of a person to a share or interest—

(a) in any public stock, annuity, fund or debt of any government or state, including a state which forms part of another state; or
(b) in any stock, fund or debt of a body (whether corporate or unincorporated) established in the United Kingdom or elsewhere.

(7), (8) [*Power of Secretary of State to specify other monetary instruments as instruments to which this section applies; power exercisable by statutory instrument.*]

[This section is printed as amended, and repealed in part, by the *Crime (International*

Co-operation) Act 2003, s.88; the *Asylum and Immigration (Treatment of Claimants, etc.) Act* 2004, s.3; the *Civil Partnership Act* 2004, s.261(1), and Sched. 27, para. 67; and the *Identity Cards Act* 2006, s.44(2), and Sched. 2.]

As to the meaning of "instrument" and "Inland Revenue stamp", see also section 8, *ante*, § 22–10; of "false", see section 9, *ante*, §§ 22–17 *et seq.*; of "prejudice" and "induce", see section 10, *ante*, §§ 22–22 *et seq.* See *ante*, § 22–29, as to the intent required by section 5(1) and (3).

As with the offences under sections 2 to 4 of the Act, this section refers to "false" instruments not "forged" instruments. This obviates any need to prove that when the instrument was originally made it was made with the requisite intention of forgery: see *ante*, § 22–25.

Section 5 again follows closely the proposals of the Law Commission. Subsections (3) and (4) are new and the list of specified instruments in subsection (5) is more extensive. **22–32**

As to the words "any other person" (in subss. (1) and (3)), see *ante*, § 22–9.

As to penalties and other powers, see sections 6 and 7, *post*, §§ 22–37, 22–38.

In *R. v. Fitzgerald* [2003] 2 Cr.App.R. 17, CA, the court expressed the view, *obiter*, that an allegation of an offence contrary to section 5(1) amounts to or includes (expressly or by implication) an allegation of an offence contrary to section 5(2) for the purposes of section 6(3) of the *CLA* 1967 (*ante*, § 4–455).

Custody or control

In an explanatory note to clause 4 of their draft Bill, the Law Commission give their reasons for the use of this expression. **22–33**

> "'Custody' means physical custody and 'control' imports the notion of the power to direct what shall be done with the things in question. The words provide a simpler concept than 'possession', which is a technical term of some difficulty."

Any other material

See *R. v. Maltman* [1995] 1 Cr.App.R. 239, CA, *post*, § 25–251, where the words "any thing" in section 17 of the 1981 Act were considered. **22–34**

Lawful authority or excuse

The *Forgery Act* 1913 prohibited the possession of certain forged documents without lawful authority or excuse, the proof whereof was expressly placed upon the accused. The Law Commission referred to the proposal of the Criminal Law Revision Committee (*Eleventh Report*, 1972, Cmnd. 4911), that the general rule applicable to the burden of proof on an accused at common law should be made the general rule in statutory offences as well. Thus, if there is sufficient evidence to raise an issue on the matter, the prosecution must satisfy the jury of the accused's guilt in the ordinary way, beyond reasonable doubt. "In our view the situation now under consideration is a suitable one for the application of the rule proposed" (para. 70). The drafting of the Act so as to omit any reference to the burden of proof is clearly designed to achieve the effect intended by the Commission. **22–35**

Limited guidance as to what may constitute lawful authority or excuse may be gained from *Dickins v. Gill* [1896] 2 Q.B. 310, DC, and *R. v. Wuyts* [1969] 2 Q.B. 476, 53 Cr.App.R. 417, CA. In *Dickins v. Gill*, the prosecution was brought under the *Post Office (Protection) Act* 1884, s.7, which provided that "a person shall not ... unless he shows a lawful excuse, have in his possession any die ... for making any fictitious stamp". The proprietor of a newspaper circulating among stamp collectors caused a die to be made for him abroad, from which imitations or representations of a current colonial postage-stamp could be produced. The only purpose for which the die was ordered by him, and was subsequently kept in his possession, was for making illustrations in a stamp catalogue of the stamp in question: the illustrations were in black and white and not in the actual colours of the stamp. *Held*, that the possession of a die for making a false stamp, known to be such to its possessor, was, however innocent the use that he intended to make of it, a possession without lawful excuse. Neither Grantham J. nor Collins J. gave any real clue as to what might constitute a lawful excuse, except that the **22–36** former gave an example of a person accused of having a fictitious stamp in his possession who would be able to establish a lawful excuse if he could show he believed it was genuine. However, this seems to be no more than to say that if the defendant showed a lack of *mens rea* he would establish a lawful excuse. Whatever the precise position under the former law, it is clear that under the 1981 Act, the prosecution must prove *mens rea*, in the sense of knowledge or belief, before the issue of lawful authority or excuse arises at all. This is spelt out in section 5(2) and it is submitted that the reference in section 5(4) to "any such machine", etc., refers to a machine, etc., which "to his knowledge is or has been specially designed or adapted", etc. That this is the correct interpretation of section 5(4) is, it is submitted, confirmed by a consideration of section 17(2) which creates the corresponding offence in Part II of the Act relating to counterfeiting. In that provision the requirement is spelt out and it would be quite inconsistent for knowledge to be an ingredient of the one offence but not of the other.

In *R. v. Wuyts*, *ante*, the prosecution related to the possession without lawful excuse of a forged banknote. Without laying down any general principles, the Court of Appeal held that if a person retained possession of a forged note solely in order to hand it over to the police, he had a lawful excuse. *Wuyts* was applied in *R. v. Sunman* [1995] Crim.L.R. 569, CA (possession of counterfeit currency) (*post*, § 25–249).

(9) Penalties for offences under Part I

Forgery and Counterfeiting Act 1981 s.6

22–37 **6.**—(1) A person guilty of an offence under this Part of this Act shall be liable on summary conviction—

(a) to a fine not exceeding the statutory maximum; or

(b) to imprisonment for a term not exceeding *six* [12] months; or

(c) to both.

(2) A person guilty of an offence to which this subsection applies shall be liable on conviction on indictment to imprisonment for a term not exceeding ten years.

(3) [*Subs. (2) applies to offences under ss.1 to 4, 5(1) and 5(3).*]

(4) A person guilty of an offence under section 5(2) or (4) above shall be liable on conviction on indictment to imprisonment for a term not exceeding two years.

(5) [*Repealed by* Statute Law (Repeals) Act *1993, Sched. 1, Pt XIV.*]

[In subs. (1)(b), "12" is substituted for "six", as from a day to be appointed, by the *CJA* 2003, s.282(2) and (3). The increase has no application to offences committed before the substitution takes effect: s.282(4).]

The "statutory maximum" means the prescribed sum within the meaning of section 32 of the *MCA* 1980 (*ante*, §§ 1–75aa *et seq.*): *Interpretation Act* 1978, Sched. 1 (Appendix B–28).

(10) Powers of search, forfeiture, etc.

Forgery and Counterfeiting Act 1981, s.7

22–38 **7.**—(1) If it appears to a justice of the peace from information given him on oath, that there is reasonable cause to believe that a person has in his custody or under his control—

(a) any thing which he or another has used, whether before or after the coming into force of this Act, or intends to use, for the making of any false instrument or copy of a false instrument, in contravention of section 1 or 2 above; or

(b) any false instrument or copy of a false instrument which he or another has used, whether before or after the coming into force of this Act, or intends to use, in contravention of section 3 or 4 above; or

(c) any thing custody or control of which without lawful authority or excuse is an offence under section 5 above,

the justice may issue a warrant authorising a constable to search for and seize the object in question, and for that purpose to enter any premises specified in the warrant.

(2) A constable may at any time after the seizure of any object suspected of falling within paragraph (a), (b) or (c) of subsection (1) above (whether the seizure was effected by virtue of a warrant under that subsection or otherwise) apply to a magistrates' court for an order under this subsection with respect to the object; and the court, if it is satisfied both that the object in fact falls within any of those paragraphs and that it is conducive to the public interest to do so, may make such order as it thinks fit for the forfeiture of the object and its subsequent destruction or disposal.

(3) Subject to subsection (4) below, the court by or before which a person is convicted of an offence under this Part of this Act may order any object shown to the satisfaction of the court to relate to the offence to be forfeited and either destroyed or dealt with in such other manner as the court may order.

(4) The court shall not order any object to be forfeited under subsection (2) or (3) above where a person claiming to be the owner of or otherwise interested in it applies to be heard by the court, unless an opportunity has been given to him to show cause why the order should not be made.

As to "custody or control", see *ante*, § 22–33.

The provisions of section 7(2) apply in relation to an item seized under section 50 of the *CJPA* 2001 as if the item had been seized under the power of seizure in reliance on which it was seized: *CJPA* 2001, s.70 and Sched. 2, Pt 1, para. 10. For this purpose an item is seized under section 50 of the 2001 Act in reliance on a power of seizure if the item is seized in exercise of so much of any power conferred by that section as is exercisable by reference to that power of seizure: *ibid.*, s.70 and Sched. 2, Pt 1, para. 12.

(11) Defence

Section 31 of the *Immigration and Asylum Act* 1999 (*post*, § 25–228d) provides a special defence, based on the Convention relating to the Status of Refugees done at Geneva on July 28, 1951, and the Protocol to the Convention, for a person charged with an offence under Part I of the 1981 Act. **22–38a**

B. MISCELLANEOUS OFFENCES AKIN TO FORGERY

(1) Registers of births, etc.

Non-parochial Registers Act 1840, s.8

Wilful injury or forgery of registers

8. Every person who ... shall wilfully insert or cause to be inserted in any of such registers or records any false entry of any birth or baptism, naming or dedication, death or burial, or marriage, or shall wilfully give any false certificate, or shall certify any writing to be an extract from any register or record knowing the same register or record to be false in any part thereof, ... shall be guilty of an offence. **22–39**

[This section is printed as repealed in part by the *Forgery Act* 1913, s.20 and Sched., Pt I; and the *Criminal Damage Act* 1971, s.11(8) and Sched., Pt I. The reference to "an offence" is substituted for "felony" by reason of the *CLA* 1967, s.12(5)(a).]

The words repealed included reference to "any register or record of birth or baptism, naming or dedication, death or burial deposited with the Registrar-General by virtue of this Act". The words "any of such registers or records" should be construed accordingly: see *Att.-Gen. v. Lamplough* (1878) 3 Ex. D. 214 at 233, *per* Kelly C.B., as to the principle of statutory construction involved.

This section was extended by the *Births and Deaths Registration Act* 1858, s.3, to non-parochial registers deposited under that Act with the Registrar-General.

The statute provides no specific penalty for the commission of an offence under this section. It is submitted, however, that by a combination of common law rules and statute, an offence under this section is punishable by way of fine and/or imprisonment not exceeding two years: see *Castro v. R.* (1880) 5 Q.B.D. 490 at 508, the *PCC(S)A* 2000, s.77 and the *CJA* 2003, s.163, *ante*, §§ 5–280, 5–393 respectively. **22–40**

Forgery Act 1861, ss.36, 37

Destruction of registers of births, etc.

36. Whosoever shall unlawfully destroy, deface, or injure, or cause or permit to be destroyed, defaced, or injured, any register of births, baptisms, marriages, deaths, or burials which now is or hereafter shall be by law authorised or required to be kept in England or Ireland, or any part of any such register, or any certified copy of any such register, or any part thereof, ... or shall knowingly and unlawfully insert or cause or permit to be inserted in any such register, or in any certified copy thereof, any false entry of any matter relating to any birth, baptism, marriage, death, or burial, or shall knowingly and unlawfully give any false certificate relating to any birth, baptism, marriage, death, or burial, or shall certify any writing to be a copy or extract from any **22–41**

such register, knowing such writing, or the part of such register whereof such copy or extract shall be so given, to be false in any material particular, ... or shall offer, utter, dispose of, or put off any such register, entry, certified copy, certificate, ... knowing the same to be false, ... or shall offer, utter, dispose of, or put off any copy of any entry in any such register, knowing such entry to be false, ... shall be guilty of an offence, and being convicted thereof, shall be liable ... to imprisonment for life.

[This section is printed as repealed in part by the *Statute Law Revision Act* 1892; the *Statute Law Revision (No. 2) Act* 1893; and the *Forgery Act* 1913, s.20 and Sched., Pt I. As to the substitution of "an offence" for "felony", see *ante*, § 22–39. The reference to "imprisonment" is substituted by reason of the *CJA* 1948, s.1.]

The reference to Ireland is to be construed as exclusive of the Republic of Ireland: *Irish Free State (Consequential Adaptation of Enactments) Order* 1923 (S.R. & O. 1923 No. 405).

Making false entries in copies of registers sent to registrar

22–42 **37.** Whosoever shall knowingly and wilfully insert or cause or permit to be inserted in any copy of any register directed or required by law to be transmitted to any registrar or other officer any false entry of any matter relating to any baptism, marriage, or burial, ... or shall knowingly and wilfully sign or verify any copy of any register so directed or required to be transmitted as aforesaid, which copy shall be false in any part thereof, knowing the same to be false, or shall unlawfully destroy, deface, or injure, or shall for any fraudulent purpose take from its place of deposit, or conceal, any such copy of any register, shall be guilty of an offence, and being convicted thereof shall be liable, at the discretion of the court, ... to imprisonment for life ....

[See the note to s.36, *ante*.]

Evidence and authorities

22–43 Upon an indictment for making a false entry in a marriage register, it is not necessary that the entry should be made with intent to defraud; and it is no defence that the marriage, being bigamous, was void. If a person, knowing his name to be A, signs another name as a witness to a marriage in the register, he is guilty of inserting a false entry in the register and it is immaterial that he is a third witness, the Marriage Act requiring only two: *R. v. Asplin* (1873) 12 Cox 391.

Where a false entry had actually been made in a register of births, etc., on the information of the defendant, he was held to be guilty thereby of the offence mentioned in the *Births and Deaths Registration Act* 1836, s.43 (re-enacted in the *Forgery Act* 1861, s.36), and not merely of the offence of making a false statement for the same purpose, within section 41 of that Act: *R. v. Mason* (1848) 2 C. & K. 622; *R. v. Dewitt*, *ibid.*, at 905.

Defacing

22–44 It is no less a "destroying, defacing, or injuring" of a register, within the meaning of the statute, because the register, when produced in evidence, has the torn part pasted in, and is as legible as before: *R. v. Bowen* (1844) 1 Den. 22.

Uttering

22–45 As to uttering, see *R. v. Heywood* (1847) 2 C. & K. 352.

(2) Identity documents

(a) *Offences*

Identity Cards Act 2006, ss.25, 26

Possession of false identity documents etc.

22–45a **25.**—(1) It is an offence for a person with the requisite intention to have in his possession or under his control—

(a) an identity document that is false and that he knows or believes to be false;

(b) an identity document that was improperly obtained and that he knows or believes to have been improperly obtained; or

(c) an identity document that relates to someone else.

(2) The requisite intention for the purposes of subsection (1) is—

(a) the intention of using the document for establishing registrable facts about himself; or

(b) the intention of allowing or inducing another to use it for establishing, ascertaining or verifying registrable facts about himself or about any other person (with the exception, in the case of a document within paragraph (c) of that subsection, of the individual to whom it relates).

(3) It is an offence for a person with the requisite intention to make, or to have in his possession or under his control—

(a) any apparatus which, to his knowledge, is or has been specially designed or adapted for the making of false identity documents; or

(b) any article or material which, to his knowledge, is or has been specially designed or adapted to be used in the making of false identity documents.

(4) The requisite intention for the purposes of subsection (3) is the intention—

(a) that he or another will make a false identity document; and

(b) that the document will be used by somebody for establishing, ascertaining or verifying registrable facts about a person.

(5) It is an offence for a person to have in his possession or under his control, without reasonable excuse—

(a) an identity document that is false;

(b) an identity document that was improperly obtained;

(c) an identity document that relates to someone else; or

(d) any apparatus, article or material which, to his knowledge, is or has been specially designed or adapted for the making of false identity documents or to be used in the making of such documents.

(6) A person guilty of an offence under subsection (1) or (3) shall be liable, on conviction on indictment, to imprisonment for a term not exceeding ten years or to a fine, or to both.

(7) A person guilty of an offence under subsection (5) shall be liable—

(a) on conviction on indictment, to imprisonment for a term not exceeding two years or to a fine, or to both;

(b) on summary conviction in England and Wales, to imprisonment for a term not exceeding twelve months or to a fine not exceeding the statutory maximum, or to both;

(c) [*Scotland and Northern Ireland*];

but, in relation to an offence committed before the commencement of section 154(1) of the *Criminal Justice Act* 2003, the reference in paragraph (b) to twelve months is to be read as a reference to six months.

(8) For the purposes of this section—

(a) an identity document is false only if it is false within the meaning of Part 1 of the *Forgery and Counterfeiting Act* 1981 (see section 9(1) of that Act); and

(b) an identity document was improperly obtained if false information was provided, in or in connection with the application for its issue or an application for its modification, to the person who issued it or (as the case may be) to a person entitled to modify it;

and references to the making of a false identity document include references to the modification of an identity document so that it becomes false.

(9) [*Scotland.*]

(10) In this section "identity document" has the meaning given by section 26.

Identity documents for the purposes of s.25

26.—(1) In section 25 "identity document" means any document that is, or purports to be— **22–45b**

(a) an ID card;

(b) a designated document;

(c) an immigration document;

(d) a United Kingdom passport (within the meaning of the *Immigration Act* 1971);

(e) a passport issued by or on behalf of the authorities of a country or territory outside the United Kingdom or by or on behalf of an international organisation;

(f) a document that can be used (in some or all circumstances) instead of a passport;

(g) a UK driving licence; or

(h) a driving licence issued by or on behalf of the authorities of a country or territory outside the United Kingdom.

(2) In subsection (1) "immigration document" means—

(a) a document used for confirming the right of a person under the Community Treaties in respect of entry or residence in the United Kingdom;

(b) a document which is given in exercise of immigration functions and records information about leave granted to a person to enter or to remain in the United Kingdom; or

(c) a registration card (within the meaning of section 26A of the *Immigration Act* 1971);

and in paragraph (b) "immigration functions" means functions under the *Immigration Acts* (within the meaning of the *Asylum and Immigration (Treatment of Claimants, etc.) Act* 2004).

(3) In that subsection "UK driving licence" means—

(a) a licence to drive a motor vehicle granted under Part 3 of the *Road Traffic Act* 1988; or

(b) a licence to drive a motor vehicle granted under Part 2 of the *Road Traffic (Northern Ireland) Order* 1981 (S.I. 1981/154 (N.I. 1)).

(4), (5) [*Amendment of list of documents in subs. (1) by order.*]

For section 9 of the 1981 Act, see *ante*, § 22–17.

(b) *Interpretation*

Identity Cards Act 2006, ss.1(5)–(8), 42

22–45c **1.**—(5) In this Act "registrable fact", in relation to an individual, means—

(a) his identity;

(b) the address of his principal place of residence in the United Kingdom;

(c) the address of every other place in the United Kingdom or elsewhere where he has a place of residence;

(d) where in the United Kingdom and elsewhere he has previously been resident;

(e) the times at which he was resident at different places in the United Kingdom or elsewhere;

(f) his current residential status;

(g) residential statuses previously held by him;

(h) information about numbers allocated to him for identification purposes and about the documents to which they relate;

(i) information about occasions on which information recorded about him in the Register has been provided to any person; and

(j) information recorded in the Register at his request.

(6) But the registrable facts falling within subsection (5)(h) do not include any sensitive personal data (within the meaning of the *Data Protection Act* 1998) or anything the disclosure of which would tend to reveal such data.

(7) In this section references to an individual's identity are references to—

(a) his full name;

(b) other names by which he is or has previously been known;

(c) his gender;

(d) his date and place of birth and, if he has died, the date of his death; and

(e) external characteristics of his that are capable of being used for identifying him.

(8) In this section "residential status", in relation to an individual, means—

(a) his nationality;

(b) his entitlement to remain in the United Kingdom; and

(c) where that entitlement derives from a grant of leave to enter or remain in the United Kingdom, the terms and conditions of that leave.

Interpretation

22–45d **42.**—(1) In this Act—

"apparatus" includes any equipment, machinery or device and any wire or cable, together with any software used with it;

"card" includes a document or other article, or a combination of a document and an article, in or on which information is or may be recorded;

"designated document" means a document of a description designated for the purposes of this Act by an order under section 4;

"document" includes a stamp or label;

"false", in relation to information, includes containing any inaccuracy or omission that results in a tendency to mislead (and is to be construed subject to section 3(5));

"ID card" is to be construed in accordance with section 6(1);

"information" includes documents and records;

"issue", in relation to a document or card, and cognate expressions are to be construed in accordance with subsection (5);

"modification" includes omission, addition or alteration, and cognate expressions are to be construed accordingly;

"place of residence" and "resides" and cognate expressions are to be construed subject to any regulations under subsection (10);

"the Register" means the National Identity Register established and maintained under section 1;

"registrable fact" has the meaning given by section 1(5) and (6);

(5) References in this Act to the issue of a document or card include references to its renewal, replacement or re-issue (with or without modifications).

(6) References in this Act to a designated document being issued together with an ID card include references to the ID card and the designated document being comprised in the same card.

(10) The Secretary of State may by regulations make provision for the purposes of this Act as to the circumstances in which a place is to be regarded, in relation to an individual—

(a) as a place where he resides; or

(b) as his principal place of residence in the United Kingdom.

This section is in force only so far as necessary for the interpretation of sections 25 and 26, *ante*. Provisions of this section that are not relevant to those sections have been omitted.

(c) *Mode of trial and sentence*

It should be noted that, unlike their predecessor offences under the *Forgery and Counterfeiting Act* 1981, the offences contrary to section 25(1) and (3) are triable only on indictment. It seems unlikely that this is what would have been intended. **22–45e**

The maximum penalties on conviction on indictment are the same as for the corresponding offences under the 1981 Act. Particular regard must be had to whether a charge is under section 25(1) or (5), which carries a much lower maximum term; it does not, however, follow that sentences for offences under subsection (1) will invariably be at a higher level than for any offence under subsection (5) (as to which, see also *R. v. Carneiro* [2008] 1 Cr.App.R.(S.) 95, CA); possession of false identity documents being a serious matter, an immediate custodial sentence will usually be justified even for simple possession, and notwithstanding a plea of guilty; and a sentencer may take into account the fact that no innocent explanation for possession of a forged document has been volunteered, even where specific intent is not an ingredient of the offence, the purpose of the defendant being in possession of the document being material to sentence: *R. v. Zenasni* [2008] 1 Cr.App.R. (S.) 94, CA.

For sentencing under the 1981 Act in the case of the use or possession of false passports, see *R. v. Olurunnibe* [1998] 2 Cr.App.R.(S.) 260, CA; *R. v. Osman* [1999] 1 Cr.App.R.(S.) 230, CA; *R. v. Cheema* [2002] 2 Cr.App.R.(S.) 79, CA; and *R. v. Kolawole* [2005] 2 Cr.App.R.(S.) 14, CA (appropriate sentence for using, contrary to section 3, or having with the intention of use, contrary to section 5(1), one false passport, even on a guilty plea by a defendant of previous good character, should usually be in the range of 12 to 18 months' imprisonment). As to this guidance carrying across to the 2006 Act, see *R. v. Juma* [2008] 1 Cr.App.R.(S.) 5, CA.

In *R. v. De Oliveira* [2006] 2 Cr.App.R.(S.) 17, CA, it was said that *Kolawole* had no application to cases of simple possession of a false passport; and in *R. v. Mutede* [2006] 2 Cr.App.R.(S.) 22, CA, it was said that *Kolawole* was principally concerned with offences of using false passports, or having the same with the intent; and that it was necessary to distinguish between a case of using a false passport to gain entry to this country, from the situation where the defendant was lawfully in the country, but used false documentation to procure work. Since *Mutede*, the Court of Appeal has adopted divergent paths. In *R. v. Adebayo* [2008] 1 Cr.App.R.(S.) 7, CA, it was said that *Kolawole* applied with full force where it was a passport that was used to obtain work. In *R. v. Omotade*, *The Times*, September 10, 2008, CA, however, it was said that the use to which a passport was put was significant and could take the case outside the range recommended in *Kolawole*; and in *Att.-Gen.'s References (Nos 1 and 6 of 2008) (R. v. Dziruni and Laby)* [2008] Crim.L.R. 577, CA, it was said that *Kolawole* was of limited application to a case that did not concern activities designed to undermine immigration control; and a suspended sentence was held not to have been unduly lenient even where it was a passport that had been used. Importantly, it may be noted that it is the latter case and *Mutede* (and not *Adebayo*) that have now been added to the Sentencing Guidelines Council's compendium of guidance cases (Appendix K-500).

(d) *Ingredients of the offences*

22–45f The fact that the "National Identity Register" under section 1 of the 2006 Act has not yet been created does not mean that it is impossible to commit an offence contrary to section 25; whilst the requisite intention for the purposes of the offences under section 25 is concerned with the establishment, etc., of "registrable facts", there is nothing in the definition of that term in sections 1(5) and 42 (*ante*, §§ 22–45c, 22–45d) to suggest that there must be a register in existence or that a person must be on the register before a fact about him can be described as "registrable": *R. v. Soule Ali and Bonbatu* [2007] 2 Cr.App.R. 2, CA.

(3) False statement for purpose of procuring passport

Criminal Justice Act 1925, s.36

Forgery of passport

22–46 **36.**—(1) ... the making by any person of a statement which is to his knowledge untrue for the purpose of procuring a passport, whether for himself or any other person, shall be an offence punishable with imprisonment not exceeding two years or a fine ... or both such imprisonment and fine.

(2) [*Not printed in this work.*]

[This section is printed as repealed in part by the *CJA* 1967, s.92(8); and by the *Forgery and Counterfeiting Act* 1981, s.30 and Sched., Pt I.]

This offence is triable either way: *MCA* 1980, s.17(1), and Sched. 1, para. 19 (*ante*, §§ 1–75af *et seq.*).

Where an attempt has been made to obtain a passport by deception, the prosecution have a discretion whether to proceed under section 36 or under section 1(1) of the *Criminal Attempts Act* 1981 (attempting to obtain property by deception). However, it is more appropriate to charge the lesser offence under section 36 where the defendant has not succeeded in obtaining a passport: *R. v. Bunche*, 96 Cr.App.R. 274, CA.

22–47 On a charge of conspiracy to obtain passports by deception (*i.e.* a conspiracy to commit the offence created by section 15 of the *Theft Act* 1968), the sentence is not limited to the maximum sentence prescribed for the substantive offence created by section 36(1) of the 1925 Act; a greater sentence may be appropriate where passports have actually been obtained and used: *R. v. Ashbee*, 88 Cr.App.R. 357, CA.

As to sentence, see *R. v. Walker (D.M.)* [1999] 1 Cr.App.R.(S.) 42, CA.

(4) Judicial documents

County Courts Act 1984, s.133

False certificate of service

22–48 **133.**—(1) Where any summons or other process issued from a county court is served by an officer of a court, the service may be proved by a certificate in a prescribed form ... showing the fact and mode of the service.

(2) Any officer of a court wilfully and corruptly giving a false certificate under subsection (1) above in respect of the service of a summons or other process shall be guilty of an offence, and, on conviction thereof, shall be removed from office and shall be liable—

(a) on conviction on indictment, to imprisonment for any term not exceeding two years; or

(b) on summary conviction, to imprisonment for any term not exceeding *six* [12] months or to a fine not exceeding the statutory maximum or to both such imprisonment and fine.

[The words omitted from subs. (1) were repealed by the *Civil Procedure (Modification of Enactments) Order* 1998 (S.I. 1998 No. 2940). In subs. (2)(b), "12" is substituted for "six", as from a day to be appointed, by the *CJA* 2003, s.282(2) and (3). The increase has no application to offences committed before the substitution takes effect: s.282(4).]

The "statutory maximum" means the prescribed sum within section 32 of the *MCA* 1980: *Interpretation Act* 1978, Sched. 1 (Appendix B–28). For details of that sum, see *ante*, § 1–75aa.

A notice to produce was held not to be a process in *R. v. Castle* (1837) Dears & B. 363.

County Courts Act 1984, s.135

Penalty for falsely pretending to act under authority of court

135. Any person who— **22–49**

(a) delivers or causes to be delivered to any other person any paper falsely purporting to be a copy of any summons or other process of a county court, knowing it to be false; or

(b) acts or professes to act under any false colour or pretence of the process or authority of a county court;

shall be guilty of an offence and shall for each offence be liable on conviction on indictment to imprisonment for a term not exceeding 7 years.

As to the power to impose a fine, see *ante*, § 5–393.

(5) Dies and stamps

Stamp Duties Management Act 1891, s.13

Offences in relation to dies and stamps

13.—(1) A person commits an offence who does, or causes or procures to be done, or knowingly aids, abets, or assists in doing any of the acts following, that is to say,— **22–50**

(1), (2)…

(3) Fraudulently prints or makes an impression upon any material from a genuine die;

(4) Fraudulently cuts, tears, or in any way removes from any material any stamp, with intent that any use should be made of such stamp or of any part thereof;

(5) Fraudulently mutilates any stamp, with intent that any use should be made of any part of such stamp;

(6) Fraudulently fixes or places upon any material or upon any stamp, any stamp or part of a stamp which, whether fraudulently or not, has been cut, torn, or in any way removed from any other material, or out of or from any other stamp;

(7) Fraudulently erases or otherwise either really or apparently removes from any stamped material any name, sum, date, or other matter or thing whatsoever thereon written, with the intent that any use should be made of the stamp upon such material;

(8) Knowingly sells or exposes for sale or utters or uses … any stamp which has been fraudulently printed or impressed from a genuine die;

(9) Knowingly, and without lawful excuse (the proof whereof shall lie on the person accused), has in his possession … any stamp which has been fraudulently printed or impressed from a genuine die, or any stamp or part of a stamp which has been fraudulently cut, torn, or otherwise removed from any material, or any stamp which has been fraudulently mutilated, or any stamped material out of which any name, sum, date, or other matter or thing has been fraudulently erased or otherwise either really or apparently removed,

…

(2) A person guilty of an offence under this section is liable—

(a) on summary conviction, to imprisonment for a term not exceeding *six* [12] months or a fine not exceeding the statutory maximum, or both;

(b) on conviction on indictment, to imprisonment for a term not exceeding ten years or a fine, or both.

[This section is printed as repealed in part by the *Forgery Act* 1913, s.20 and Sched., Pt I; and as amended by the *Finance Act* 1999, s.115 and Sched. 18, para. 5 (insertion of subs. (2)). In subs. (2)(a), "12" is substituted for "six", as from a day to be appointed, by the *CJA* 2003, s.282(2) and (3). The increase has no application to offences committed before the substitution takes effect: s.282(4).]

22–51 For regulations applying this section with modifications, see the *National Savings Stamps Regulations* 1969 (S.I. 1969 No. 1343), and the *Social Security (Contributions) Regulations* 1979 (S.I. 1979 No. 591), *post*, § 22–55.

As to the power to impose a fine, see *ante*, § 5–393.

For definitions of "die" and "stamp", see *post*, §§ 22–53, 22–54.

As to subsection (1), para. (4), see *R. v. Smith* (1831) 5 C. & P. 107; *R. v. Field* (1785) 1 Leach 383; *R. v. Allday* (1837) 8 C. & P. 136.

22–52 A person who sells a forged stamp commits an offence against subsection (8) even if the stamp when sold bears a cancellation mark: *R. v. Lowden* [1914] 1 K.B. 144, 9 Cr.App.R. 195, CCA.

22–53 In the *Stamp Duties Management Act* 1891, unless the context otherwise requires, the expression "Commissioners" means Commissioners for Her Majesty's Revenue and Customs; the expression "die" includes any plate, type, tool, or implement whatever used under the direction of the Commissioners for expressing or denoting any duty or rate of duty, or the fact that any duty or rate of duty or penalty has been paid, or that an instrument is duly stamped, or is not chargeable with any duty or for denoting any fee, and also any part of any such plate, type, tool or implement; the expression "stamp" means as well a stamp impressed by means of a die as an adhesive stamp for denoting any duty or fee: s.27 (as amended by the *Commissioners for Revenue and Customs Act* 2005, s.50(1)). See also *post*, § 22–54.

Stamp Duties Management Act 1891, s.23

Application of Act to excise labels

22–54 **23.** The provisions of this Act in reference to offences relating to stamps shall apply to any label now or hereafter provided by the Commissioners for denoting any duty of excise other than a duty of excise chargeable on goods imported into the United Kingdom and any label so provided shall be deemed to be included in the term "stamp" as defined by this Act.

[This section is printed as amended by the *Customs and Excise Management Act* 1979, s.177(1) and Sched. 4, para. 12, Table, Pt I.]

Extension of Act to national savings, social security stamps

22–55 Section 13(3), (8) and (9) (down to the words "from a genuine die") apply to national savings stamps: *Post Office Act* 1969, s.122 (*rep.*); *National Debt Act* 1972, ss.10(1) and 17(2); and the *National Savings Stamps Regulations* 1969 (S.I. 1969 No. 1343).

Section 13(3) to (9) were applied to national insurance stamps by the *Social Security (Contributions) Regulations* 1979, reg. 57, Sched. 2, Pt I (S.I. 1979 No. 591). These regulations were made pursuant to the power given by the *Social Security Act* 1975. The 1975 Act has been repealed and a power to make regulations applying, *inter alia*, the provisions of the 1891 Act to national insurance stamps is now contained in the *Social Security Contributions and Benefits Act* 1992, Sched. 1, para. 8(3). As at October 1, 2008, no such regulations had been made pursuant to the 1992 Act but, by virtue of section 2(2) of the *Social Security (Consequential Provisions) Act* 1992, the 1979 regulations continued to have effect. Regulation 57 and Schedule 2 were themselves revoked as from April 11, 1993, by the *Social Security (Contributions) Amendment Regulations* 1993 (S.I. 1993 No. 260), reg. 7, but they continue to apply to any stamps prepared or issued in respect of any period before that date.

(6) Hallmarks

Hallmarking Act 1973, s.6(1)–(3)

Counterfeiting, etc. of dies and marks

22–56 **6.**—(1) Any person who—

(a) with intent to defraud or deceive, makes a counterfeit of any die or mark; or

(b) removes any mark from an article of precious metal with intent to transpose it to any other article (whether of precious metal or not) or affixes to any article (whether of precious metal or not) any mark which has been removed from an article of precious metal; or

(c) utters any counterfeit of a die or any article bearing a counterfeit of a mark; or

(d) without lawful authority or excuse, has in his custody or under his control anything which is, and which he knows or believes to be, a counterfeit of a die or an article (whether of precious metal or not) which bears a counterfeit of any mark,

shall be guilty of an offence and liable on summary conviction to a fine not exceeding the prescribed sum, or on conviction on indictment to a fine or imprisonment for a term not exceeding ten years.

(2) In subsection (1) above—

"die" means the whole or part of any plate, tool or instrument by means whereof any mark of the nature of a sponsor's mark or a hallmark is struck on any metal; and

"mark" means any mark of the nature of a sponsor's mark or hallmark.

(3) For the purposes of subsection (1) above, a person utters any counterfeit die or article bearing a counterfeit of a mark if, knowing or believing the die or mark, as the case may be, to be a counterfeit, he supplies, offers to supply, or delivers the die or article.

[The reference to "the prescribed sum" is substituted by virtue of the *Magistrates' Courts Act* 1980, s.32(2).]

For details of "the prescribed sum", see *ante*, §§ 1–75aa *et seq.*

As to the treatment of articles following conviction, see section 10. Schedule 3 to the Act contains further provisions relating to offences created by the Act.

(7) Road transport

See *post*, §§ 32–218 *et seq.* **22–57**

(8) Mental health

Mental Health Act 1983, s.126

Forgery, false statements, etc.

126.—(1) Any person who without lawful authority or excuse has in his custody or under his control any document to which this subsection applies, which is, and which he knows or believes to be, false within the meaning of Part I of the *Forgery and Counterfeiting Act* 1981, shall be guilty of an offence. **22–58**

(2) Any person who without lawful authority or excuse makes or has in his custody or under his control, any document so closely resembling a document to which subsection (1) above applies as to be calculated to deceive shall be guilty of an offence.

(3) The documents to which subsection (1) above applies are any documents purporting to be—

(a) an application under Part II of this Act;

(b) a medical recommendation or report under this Act; and

(c) any other document required or authorised to be made for any of the purposes of this Act.

(4) Any person who—

(a) wilfully makes a false entry or statement in any application, recommendation, report, record or other document required or authorised to be made for any of the purposes of this Act; or

(b) with intent to deceive, makes use of any such entry or statement which he knows to be false,

shall be guilty of an offence.

(5) Any person guilty of an offence under this section shall be liable—

(a) on summary conviction, to imprisonment for a term not exceeding *six* [12] months or to a fine not exceeding the statutory maximum, or to both;

(b) on conviction on indictment, to imprisonment for a term not exceeding two years or to a fine of any amount, or to both.

[In subs. (5)(a), "12" is substituted for "six", as from a day to be appointed, by the

CJA 2003, s.282(2) and (3). The increase has no application to offences committed before the substitution takes effect: s.282(4).]

"Statutory maximum" means the prescribed sum within the meaning of section 32 of the *Magistrates' Courts Act* 1980, *ante*, § 1–75aa: *Interpretation Act* 1978, Sched. 1 (Appendix B–28).

A local social services authority may institute proceedings for an offence under this section: *MHA* 1983, s.130.

(9) Gun barrels

22–59 All commercially produced gun barrels are required to be proved by either the Worshipful Company of the Gunmakers of the City of London Proof House or the Guardians of the Birmingham Proof House ("the two Companies"): *Gun Barrel Proof Act* 1868. Section 121 of that Act creates a range of offences, punishable on conviction on indictment with a term of imprisonment not exceeding two years. There are 14 heads of offence in subsection (1). They include forging or counterfeiting any stamp or any part of any stamp provided or used by either of the two Companies for marking any barrel; selling or parting with possession of any such forged or counterfeit stamp or part thereof; marking any barrel with any such forged or counterfeit stamp or part thereof; making up any barrel so marked; possessing, selling or parting with possession of any barrel so marked; and forging or counterfeiting or producing by any means upon any barrel an imitation of any mark of any stamp or any part of any stamp provided or used by either of the two Companies for marking any barrel.

Section 121(2) effectively extends the offences to stamps and marks used by an official proof house of a foreign state.

22–60 Section 122(6) makes it an offence fraudulently to erase, obliterate, deface or cause to be erased, obliterated or defaced from any barrel any mark of any stamp or part of a stamp provided or used by either of the two Companies for marking any barrel. This offence is triable either way. On conviction on indictment the maximum penalty is a fine; on summary conviction the maximum penalty is a fine not exceeding the statutory maximum: see the *Gun Barrel Proof Act* 1868, as amended by the *Gun Barrel Proof Act* 1978, s.8 and Sched. 3. The "statutory maximum" means the prescribed sum within section 32 of the *MCA* 1980, *ante*, § 1–75aa: *Interpretation Act* 1978, Sched. 1 (Appendix B–28).

II. PERSONATION

A. AT COMMON LAW

22–61 Personation was an indictable misdemeanor if it amounted to a common law cheat. The common law offence of cheating has been abolished (*Theft Act* 1968, s.32(1)) except as regards offences relating to the public revenue: see *ante*, § 21–338.

It is a common law offence to personate a juror, and it is not necessary to prove that the personator had any corrupt motive or anything to gain by his conduct or any specific intention to deceive other than that which is involved in his going into the jury box and taking the oath in the name of another: *R. v. Clark* (1918) 26 Cox 138, CCC (Avory J.). It is no answer that he did not know he was doing wrong. See also *R. v. Wakefield* [1918] 1 K.B. 216, 13 Cr.App.R. 56, CCA.

B. BY STATUTE

(1) Personating police officers

22–62 By section 90(1) of the *Police Act* 1996 it is an offence to impersonate a police officer. It is punishable with six months' imprisonment (increased to 51 weeks as from a day to be appointed by the *CJA* 2003, s.281(4) and (5); but the increase has no application to offences committed before the amendment takes effect: *ibid.*, s.281(6)), or a fine not exceeding level 5 on the standard scale, or both. Subsections (2) and (3) create further summary offences in relation to the wearing and possession of articles of police uniform. The wearing of an article of uniform must be in circumstances where it gives the person wearing it an appearance so nearly resembling that of a member of a police force as to be "calculated to deceive": subs. (2). These words mean "likely to deceive" and, therefore, the fact that there was no intent to deceive is immaterial: *Turner v. Shearer* [1972] 1 W.L.R. 1387, DC.

(2) Personating for purpose of bail, etc.

Forgery Act 1861, s.34

34. Whosoever, without lawful authority or excuse (the proof whereof shall lie on the party accused), shall, in the name of any other person, acknowledge any recognizance or bail, or any *cognovit actionem*, or judgment, or any deed or other instrument, before any court, judge, or other person lawfully authorised in that behalf, shall be guilty of an offence, and being convicted thereof shall be liable … to imprisonment for any term not exceeding seven years. … **22–63**

[This section is printed as repealed in part by the *Statute Law Revision Act* 1892; and the *Statute Law Revision (No. 2) Act* 1893. The reference to "an offence" is substituted for "felony" by reason of the *CLA* 1967, s.12(5)(a). The reference to "imprisonment" is substituted by reason of the *CJA* 1948, s.1.]

"Other person lawfully authorised" includes a commissioner for oaths: *Commissioners for Oaths Act* 1889, s.1(2). This provides that a commissioner for oaths may, in England or elsewhere, take any bail or recognizance in or for the purpose of any civil proceeding in the Supreme Court [Senior Courts].

As to bail in criminal cases, see *ante*, §§ 3–1 *et seq*.

The recognizance must be a valid recognizance into which a person may lawfully be required to enter: *R. v. McKenzie*, 55 Cr.App.R. 294, Assizes (Cantley J.).

(3) Pretending to be a Commissioner or officer of Revenue and Customs

It is a summary offence (51 weeks, level 5 fine, or both) to pretend to be a Commissioner for Her Majesty's Revenue and Customs or an officer of Revenue and Customs with a view to obtaining admission to premises, information or any other benefit: *Commissioners for Revenue and Customs Act* 2005, s.30(1) and (2). **22–64**

In relation to an offence committed before the commencement of section 281(4) and (5) of the *CJA* 2003, the maximum term of imprisonment is six months: s.55(4) of the 2005 Act. **22–65**

(4) Personation for purpose of providing bodily sample

If, for the purpose of providing a bodily sample for a test required to give effect to a direction under section 20 of the *Family Law Reform Act* 1969 (power of court to require use of scientific tests), any person personates another, or proffers a child knowing that it is not the child named in the direction, he shall be liable (a) on conviction on indictment, to imprisonment for a term not exceeding two years, or (b) on summary conviction, to a fine not exceeding the "prescribed sum" within the meaning of section 32 of the *MCA* 1980 (*ante*, §§ 1–75aa *et seq.*): *Family Law Reform Act* 1969, s.24. **22–66**

(5) Personation of voters

Representation of the People Act 1983, s.60

60.—(1) A person shall be guilty of a corrupt practice if he commits, or aids, abets, counsels or procures the commission of, the offence of personation. **22–67**

(2) A person shall be deemed to be guilty of personation at a parliamentary or local government election if he—

(a) votes in person or by post as some other person, whether as an elector or as proxy, and whether that other person is living or dead or is a fictitious person; or

(b) votes in person or by post as proxy—

(i) for a person whom he knows or has reasonable grounds for supposing to be dead or to be a fictitious person; or

(ii) when he knows or has reasonable grounds for supposing that his appointment as proxy is no longer in force.

(3) For the purposes of this section, a person who has applied for a ballot paper for the purpose of voting in person or who has marked, whether validly or not, and returned a ballot paper issued for the purpose of voting by post, shall be deemed to have voted.

22–68 A corrupt practice is punishable on conviction on indictment or on summary conviction: *Representation of the People Act* 1983, s.168, as amended and repealed in part by the *Representation of the People Act* 1985, Scheds 3, 4 and 5. A person who commits the offence of personation or of aiding, abetting, counselling or procuring the commission of the offence of personation is liable on conviction on indictment to imprisonment for a term not exceeding two years, or to a fine, or to both, and on summary conviction to a term of imprisonment not exceeding six months (increased to 12 months as from a day to be appointed by the *CJA* 2003, s.282(2) and (3), but the increase has no application to offences committed before the amendment takes effect: *ibid.*, s.282(4)), or to a fine not exceeding the statutory maximum or both: *ibid.* By the *Interpretation Act* 1978, Sched. 1 (Appendix B–28), the "statutory maximum" means the prescribed sum within the meaning of the *MCA* 1980, s.32: *ante*, § 1–75aa.

III. CHEATING

A. AT COMMON LAW

22–69 Cheating as a common law offence was abolished by the *Theft Act* 1968, s.32(1), except in relation to revenue offences (*ante*, § 21–337). See also *Scott v. Metropolitan Police Commr* [1975] A.C. 819, HL.

B. BY STATUTE

Gambling Act 2005, s.42

Cheating

22–70 **42.**—(1) A person commits an offence if he—

(a) cheats at gambling, or

(b) does anything for the purpose of enabling or assisting another person to cheat at gambling.

(2) For the purposes of subsection (1) it is immaterial whether a person who cheats—

(a) improves his chances of winning anything, or

(b) wins anything.

(3) Without prejudice to the generality of subsection (1) cheating at gambling may, in particular, consist of actual or attempted deception or interference in connection with—

(a) the process by which gambling is conducted, or

(b) a real or virtual game, race or other event or process to which gambling relates.

(4) A person guilty of an offence under this section shall be liable—

(a) on conviction on indictment, to imprisonment for a term not exceeding two years, to a fine or to both, or

(b) on summary conviction, to imprisonment for a term not exceeding 51 weeks, to a fine not exceeding the statutory maximum or to both.

(5) [*Scotland.*]

(6) Section 17 of the *Gaming Act* 1845 (winning by cheating) shall cease to have effect.

22–71 This section came into force on September 1, 2007: *Gambling Act 2005 (Commencement No. 6 and Transitional Provisions) Order* 2006 (S.I. 2006 No. 3272).

The penalty provisions in relation to summary conviction are flawed in two respects. First, the offence being triable either way, the maximum penalty on summary conviction should have been expressed to be "12 months", in line with section 154(1) of the *CJA* 2003 (*ante*, § 5–268). "51 weeks" would be appropriate to a summary offence: see section 281 of the 2003 Act. Secondly, and more importantly, there is a serious flaw in the commencement arrangements, in that there is no transitional provision in relation to the maximum penalty. It is standard practice in legislation since 2003 to include provision to the effect that pending the commencement of section 154(1) or of section 281(5) of the 2003 Act (as the case may be), the reference to "12 months" or to "51 weeks" should be read as a reference to "six months" (see, for example, the *Domestic Violence,*

Crime and Victims Act 2004, Sched. 12, para. 1(2) (s.154(1)) and the *UK Borders Act* 2007, s.3(5) (s.281(5)). There is no such provision in the 2005 Act (although many other offences under the Act provide for a maximum on summary conviction of 51 weeks' imprisonment) and there is no such provision in the commencement order or in any of the other subordinate legislation made under the Act.

As to the meaning of "gambling", see section 3. As to the interpretation of "real" and "virtual game, race or other event or process", see section 353(1).

CHAPTER 23

CRIMINAL DAMAGE AND KINDRED OFFENCES

I. CRIMINAL DAMAGE ACT 1971

A. DESTROYING OR DAMAGING PROPERTY

(1) Simple offence

Criminal Damage Act 1971, s.1(1)

1.—(1) A person who without lawful excuse destroys or damages any property belonging to another intending to destroy or damage any such property or being reckless as to whether any such property would be destroyed or damaged shall be guilty of an offence. **23–1**

As to the meaning of "lawful excuse", see section 5, *post*, §§ 23–47 *et seq.*; of "damage", see *post*, §§ 23–6 *et seq.*; of "property" and "belonging to another", see section 10, *post*, §§ 23–54 *et seq.*; and of "reckless", see *post*, § 23–9.

Indictment

STATEMENT OF OFFENCE

Destroying [or *Damaging*] *property, contrary to section 1(1) of the* Criminal Damage Act *1971.* **23–2**

PARTICULARS OF OFFENCE

A B, on the —— day of ——, 20—, without lawful excuse, destroyed [or *damaged*] *a bungalow belonging to J N, intending to destroy* [or *damage*] *such property or being reckless as to whether such property would be destroyed* [or *damaged*].

Class of offence and mode of trial

This offence is a class 3 offence, *ante*, § 2–17. **23–3**

As to the mode of trial of offences of criminal damage, see *post*, §§ 23–41 *et seq.*

Sentence

Imprisonment for 10 years: *Criminal Damage Act* 1971, s.4, *post*, § 23–46. **23–4**

There are no Crown Court sentencing guidelines for criminal damage. For illustrative decisions, see CSP, B7–2.3.

Consent

As to the need to obtain the Director of Public Prosecution's consent before instituting proceedings against a person for an offence of doing unlawful damage to property belonging to that person's spouse, see the *Theft Act* 1968, s.30(4), *ante*, § 21–334. **23–5**

"Damage"

23–6 "Damage" is interpreted widely to include not only permanent or temporary physical harm, but also permanent or temporary impairment of value or usefulness: *Morphitis v. Salmon* [1990] Crim. L.R. 48, DC; *R. v. Whiteley*, 93 Cr.App.R. 25, CA (where the authorities are usefully reviewed); and *R. v. Fiak* [2005] 10 *Archbold News* 1, CA.

It is not necessary to prove that the damage itself is tangible, although by section 10 of the 1971 Act (*post*, § 23–54) the property which is damaged must be tangible: *Whiteley, ante*.

A modification of the contents of a computer shall not be regarded as damaging any computer or computer storage medium unless its effect on that computer or computer storage medium impairs its physical condition: see the *Computer Misuse Act* 1990, s.3(6) (*post*, § 23–89), which is repealed and replaced, as from a day to be appointed, by section 10(5) of the 1971 Act (*post*, § 23–54).

23–7 Examples of damage include the following: taking away a part of a machine or other structure so as to make the whole useless (*R. v. Tacey* (1821) Russ. and Ry. 452), although if the removed part is not damaged it is essential to charge damage to the whole rather than to the part (*Morphitis v. Salmon, ante*); disabling a steam engine so as to make it temporarily useless (*R. v. Fisher* (1865) L.R. 1 C.C.R. 7); diluting milk with water (*Roper v. Knott* [1898] 1 Q.B. 868); dumping rubbish onto land (*Henderson and Batley*, unreported, November 27, 1984, CA); applying water-soluble paint to a pavement (*Hardman v. Chief Constable of Somerset* [1986] Crim.L.R. 330, DC); smearing mud on the wall of a police cell (*Roe v. Kingerlee* [1986] Crim.L.R. 735, DC); and flooding a police cell with clean water by blocking a lavatory with a blanket, thus requiring both the cell and the blanket to be cleaned and the blanket to be dried (*R. v. Fiak, ante*). But applying a wheelclamp to a car does not intrude into the car's integrity and thus cannot constitute damage to the car under the *RTA* 1988, s.5(3) (*post*, § 32–75): *Drake v. DPP* [1994] R.T.R. 411, DC.

Mens rea

23–8 In *R. v. Smith (D.R.)* [1974] Q.B. 354, 58 Cr.App.R. 320, CA, it was held that the intention, recklessness and absence of lawful excuse required to constitute the offence refer to property belonging to another. No offence is committed, therefore, if a person destroys or damages property belonging to another if he does so in the honest though mistaken belief that the property is his own, and, provided that the belief is honestly held, it is irrelevant to consider whether it is justifiable. See also *post*, §§ 23–48 *et seq.*

Recklessness

23–9 In *R. v. G.* [2004] 1 A.C. 1034, HL, "recklessness" for the purposes of the 1971 Act was defined as follows:

> "A person acts recklessly within the meaning of section 1 of the *Criminal Damage Act* 1971 with respect to—
>
> (i) a circumstance when he is aware of a risk that it exists or will exist;
>
> (ii) result when he is aware of a risk that it will occur;
>
> and it is, in the circumstances known to him, unreasonable to take the risk."

The earlier definition of recklessness propounded by the majority in *R. v. Caldwell* [1982] A.C. 341, HL (see the 2004 edition of this work), was founded on a misinterpretation of section 1 and is no longer good law: *ibid*. It follows that the acquittal in cases such as *Elliott v. C.*, 77 Cr.App.R. 103, DC, would now be upheld on appeal (risk would not have been obvious to 14-year-old of low intelligence).

If a defendant closes his mind to a risk, he must be aware that there is a risk, which will usually be decisive on the issue of recklessness: *R. v. Caldwell, ante* (*per* Lord Edmund-Davies at p.358D); *R. v. G., ante* (*per* Lord Steyn at [58], and see also Lord Bingham at [32]); and *Booth v. CPS*, 170 J.P. 305, DC.

23–10 It is submitted that, where a defendant omits to act after accidentally causing a fire, the combined effect of *R. v. Miller* [1983] 2 A.C. 161, HL, and *R. v. G., ante*, is that he would be guilty under section 1(1), in respect of damage to property resulting from the subsequent spread of the fire and occurring after he has realised that he was responsible for starting the fire, if he does not try to prevent or reduce the risk of damage by his own efforts or, if necessary, by sending for the fire brigade, and the reason why he does not is because, having recognised that there is a risk of damage to the property in question, he has decided unreasonably not to try to prevent or reduce it.

Effect of drink and drugs

See generally, *ante*, §§ 17–102 *et seq.* **23–11**

Where the allegation is that the destruction or damage was intentional, then self-induced intoxication such as to prevent the defendant from forming the necessary intent will constitute a defence: *R. v. Caldwell, ante*. Where recklessness is relied on, then notwithstanding the generality of the formulation of the test in *R. v. G., ante*, it is apparent that their Lordships had no intention of undermining the decision in *DPP v. Majewski* (*ante*, §§ 17–107 *et seq.*), to the effect that failure to foresee a risk provides no defence where the failure results from self-induced intoxication. However, the application of the *Majewski* principle will be affected, in that the question for the court in such a case will no longer be as to whether the risk would have been obvious to a sober and reasonable man in the position of the accused; it will be whether the accused would have been aware of the risk had he been sober. It is submitted that similarly there would be no defence where a person mistakenly makes a positive decision that there is no risk, but would not have so decided had he been sober: see *ante*, § 17–16. *Cf. Jaggard v. Dickinson, post*, § 23–48.

It makes no difference whether the intoxication was induced by drugs or drink save that, where the drug is a sedative or soporific, as opposed to dangerous, the question for the jury is whether the taking of the drug was itself reckless: *R. v. Hardie*, 80 Cr.App.R. 157, CA (valium) (*ante*, § 17–105).

Attempts

Mere recklessness as to whether criminal damage is caused, as opposed to an intent to cause such damage, is insufficient where the charge is attempting to cause damage: *R. v. Millard and Vernon* [1987] Crim.L.R. 393, CA. See also *post*, § 23–23. **23–12**

(2) Aggravated offence

Criminal Damage Act 1971, s.1(2)

1.—(2) A person who without lawful excuse destroys or damages any property, whether belonging to himself or another— **23–13**

(a) intending to destroy or damage any property or being reckless as to whether any property would be destroyed or damaged; and

(b) intending by the destruction or damage to endanger the life of another or being reckless as to whether the life of another would be thereby endangered;

shall be guilty of an offence.

As to the meaning of "damage", see *ante*, §§ 23–6 *et seq.*; of "property", see section 10, *post*, §§ 23–54 *et seq.*; and of "reckless", see *ante*, § 23–9.

Indictment

COUNT 1

STATEMENT OF OFFENCE

Destroying [or *Damaging*] *property with intent to endanger life, contrary to section 1(2) of the* Criminal Damage Act *1971*. **23–14**

PARTICULARS OF OFFENCE

A B, on the —— day of ——, 20—, without lawful excuse, destroyed [or *damaged*] *a bungalow belonging to him the said A B, intending to destroy* [or *damage*] *property or being reckless as to whether property would be destroyed* [or *damaged*], *and intending by the said destruction* [or *damage*] *to endanger the life of J N.*

COUNT 2

STATEMENT OF OFFENCE

Destroying [or *Damaging*] *property being reckless as to whether life would be endangered, contrary to section 1(2) of the* Criminal Damage Act *1971*.

PARTICULARS OF OFFENCE

A B, on the —— day of ——, 20—, without lawful excuse, destroyed [or *damaged*] *a bungalow belonging to him the said A B, intending to destroy* [or *damage*] *property or being reckless as to whether property would be destroyed* [or *damaged*], *and being reckless as to whether the life of another would thereby be endangered.*

Where the aggravated offence is charged and the prosecution rely on the alternatives of intention and recklessness, there should be two counts, one charging an intent to endanger life, and the other recklessness as to whether life is endangered (as *ante*): *R. v. Hoof*, 72 Cr.App.R. 126, CA; *R. v. Hardie*, 80 Cr.App.R. 157, CA. If an indictment is drawn so as to embody the alternatives in one count, the judge should direct that it be amended: *Hardie*, *ante*.

Where there are alternative counts, and the jury convict on the more serious charge, the jury should be discharged from giving a verdict on the lesser charge. It is wrong to allow convictions to be recorded in respect of two offences arising out of the same act if one is a lesser form of the other: *R. v. Haddock* [1976] Crim.L.R. 374, CA.

It is open to a jury to convict of criminal damage contrary to section 1(1) of the 1971 Act (the simple offence) as an alternative verdict under section 6(3) of the *CLA* 1967 (*ante*, § 4–455), notwithstanding that the value of the damage caused is under £5,000 (see *post*, § 23–43, as to the significance of this sum); the *MCA* 1980, s.22 (*ante*, § 1–75i), affects mode of trial but has no effect on the classification of criminal damage as an "offence triable either way": *R. v. Fennell* [2000] 2 Cr.App.R. 318, CA (not following *R. v. Burt*, 161 J.P. 77, CA), and approved in *R. v. Alden* [2002] 2 Cr.App.R.(S.) 74, CA (see *post*, § 23–44).

Sentence

23–15 Imprisonment for life: *Criminal Damage Act* 1971, s.4, *post*, § 23–46.

An offence contrary to section 1(2) is a "specified violent offence" within Chapter 5 of Part 12 of the *CJA* 2003 (life sentences, sentences for public protection and extended sentences): see s.224, and Sched. 15, *ante*, §§ 5–292, 5–299.

There are no sentencing guidelines for this offence.

Class of offence and mode of trial

23–16 This offence is a class 3 offence, *ante*, § 2–17. It is triable only on indictment (*post*, §§ 23–41 *et seq.*).

Consent

23–17 See *ante*, § 23–5.

"Without lawful excuse"

23–18 For the purposes of section 1(2), this phrase is wholly undefined: the partial definition in section 5 (*post*, § 23–47) does not apply to the aggravated offence.

Danger to life must result from destruction or damage intended

23–19 In *R. v. Steer* [1988] A.C. 111, HL, it was held that under section 1(2) the danger to life must result from the destruction of, or damage to, the property. It is not sufficient that the danger resulted from the act which caused the destruction or damage. In *Steer*, the defendant fired a rifle at a bungalow and caused trivial damage. Although in firing the shots he was reckless as to whether the occupants' lives would be endangered, that danger was not caused by the damage done by the bullets, and thus he had not committed the offence under section 1(2). By contrast, in *R. v. Dudley* [1989] Crim.L.R. 57, CA, the defendant was held guilty under section 1(2) where he threw a fire-bomb at a house which the occupants were able to extinguish before it caused more than trivial damage. Distinguishing *Steer*, the court held that the words "destruction or damage" in section 1(2)(b) refer back to the destruction or damage intended, or as to which there was recklessness, in section 1(2)(a). Although the actual damage caused in *Dudley* was trivial, the defendant's recklessness related to potentially much more serious damage.

Steer and *Dudley* were applied in *R. v. Asquith*; *R. v. Warwick* [1995] 1 Cr.App.R. 492, CA. In approving *Dudley*, the court stated that the true construction of section 1(2) is that the *actus reus* is defined in the first two lines of the subsection, while paragraphs (a) and (b) deal with *mens rea*: **23–20**

> "Otherwise, the gravamen of an offence involving damage by a missile would depend not on the defendant's intention but on whether he was a good shot in seeking to carry it out. Thus, if a defendant throws a brick at the windscreen of a moving vehicle, given that he causes *some* damage to the vehicle, whether he is guilty under section 1(2) does not depend on whether the brick hits or misses the windscreen, but whether he intended to hit it and intended that the damage therefrom should endanger life or whether he was reckless as to that outcome" (at pp. 496G–497A).

Mens rea of aggravated offence

In *R. v. Caldwell* [1982] A.C. 341, HL (*ante*, § 23–9), Lord Diplock said: **23–21**

> "Where the charge is under section 1(2) the question of the state of mind of the accused must be approached in stages, corresponding to paragraphs (a) and (b). The jury must be satisfied that what the accused did amounted to an offence under section 1(1), either because he actually intended to destroy or damage the property or because he was reckless ... as to whether it might be destroyed or damaged. Only if they are so satisfied must the jury go on to consider whether the accused also either actually intended that the destruction or damage of the property should endanger someone's life or was reckless ... as to whether a human life might be endangered" (at pp. 354–355).

It is submitted that this passage remains good law provided that "reckless" is defined in accordance with *R. v. G.* [2004] 1 A.C. 1034, HL (*ante*, § 23–9). It is also subject to the qualification that there are defences to section 1(1) which do not apply to section 1(2), *i.e.* in respect of the latter, it is irrelevant that the property is one's own, and section 5 does not apply: see § 23–18, *ante*.

Effect of drink and drugs

See § 23–11, *ante*. **23–22**

Attempts

On a charge of attempted criminal damage in the aggravated form, in addition to establishing a specific intent to cause criminal damage, it is sufficient to prove that the defendant was reckless as to whether life would thereby be endangered: *Att.-Gen.'s Reference (No. 3 of 1992)*, 98 Cr.App.R. 383, CA. (See the commentary at [1994] Crim.L.R. 350.) **23–23**

(3) By fire

Criminal Damage Act 1971, s.1(3)

1.—(3) An offence committed under this section by destroying or damaging property by fire shall be charged as arson. **23–24**

It is unclear whether this provision means that, in the Crown Court, it is mandatory to use the word "arson", or whether it is sufficient to allege that the destruction or damage was by fire: see *R. v. Drayton* [2006] Crim.L.R. 243, CA, where the position in the Crown Court was left open, notwithstanding the apparently mandatory approach taken in *R. v. Booth* [1999] Crim. L.R. 144, CA. In a magistrates' court, the use of the word "arson" is not mandatory, although it might be helpful if it were employed: *Drayton*, *ante*.

Indictment: simple offence

STATEMENT OF OFFENCE

23–25 *Arson, contrary to section 1(1) and (3) of the* Criminal Damage Act *1971.*

PARTICULARS OF OFFENCE

A B, on the —— day of ——, 20—, without lawful excuse, destroyed [or *damaged*] *by fire a shop belonging to J N, intending to destroy* [or *damage*] *such property or being reckless as to whether such property would be destroyed* [or *damaged*].

Sentence

23–26 Imprisonment for life: *Criminal Damage Act* 1971, s.4, *post*, § 23–46.

For sentencing, see *post*, § 23–29.

Class of offence and mode of trial

23–27 This offence is a class 3 offence, *ante*, § 2–17. As to mode of trial, see *post*, §§ 23–41 *et seq.*

Indictment: aggravated offence

COUNT 1

STATEMENT OF OFFENCE

23–28 *Arson with intent to endanger life, contrary to section 1(2) and (3) of the* Criminal Damage Act *1971.*

PARTICULARS OF OFFENCE

A B, on the —— day of ——, 20—, without lawful excuse, destroyed [or *damaged*] *by fire a bungalow belonging to him the said A B, intending to destroy* [or *damage*] *property or being reckless as to whether property would be destroyed* [or *damaged*], *and intending thereby to endanger the life of J N.*

COUNT 2

STATEMENT OF OFFENCE

Arson being reckless as to whether life would be endangered, contrary to section 1(2) and (3) of the Criminal Damage Act *1971.*

PARTICULARS OF OFFENCE

A B, on the —— day of ——, 20—, without lawful excuse, destroyed [or *damaged*] *by fire a bungalow belonging to him the said A B, intending to destroy* [or *damage*] *property or being reckless as to whether property would be destroyed* [or *damaged*], *and being reckless as to whether the life of another would thereby be endangered.*

As to the desirability of having two counts, see *ante*, § 23–14.

Sentence

23–29 Imprisonment for life: *Criminal Damage Act* 1971, s.4, *post*, § 23–46.

It is unwise to sentence in a case of arson without a psychiatric report: see *R. v. Calladine*, *The Times*, December 3, 1975, CA.

Arson is a "specified violent offence" within Chapter 5 of Part 12 of the *CJA* 2003 (life sentences, sentences for public protection and extended sentences): see s.224, and Sched. 15, *ante*, §§ 5–292, 5–299.

There are no Crown Court sentencing guidelines for arson. However, in *R. v. Frankham* [2008] 1 Cr.App.R.(S.) 27, CA, it was said that a range of eight to 10 years' imprisonment was the starting point for cases of arson with intent to endanger life. For illustrative decisions, see CSP, B7–1.3.

Class of offence and mode of trial

23–30 This offence is a class 3 offence, *ante*, § 2–17. It is triable only on indictment.

Omission to act after accidentally causing fire

See *R. v. Miller*, *ante*, § 23–10. 23–31

(4) Racially or religiously aggravated criminal damage

Crime and Disorder Act 1998, s.30

30.—(1) A person is guilty of an offence under this section if he commits an offence under section 1(1) of the *Criminal Damage Act* 1971 (destroying or damaging property belonging to another) which is racially or religiously aggravated for the purposes of this section. 23–31a

(2) A person guilty of an offence under this section shall be liable—

(a) on summary conviction, to imprisonment for a term not exceeding *six* [12] months or to a fine not exceeding the statutory maximum, or to both;

(b) on conviction on indictment, to imprisonment for a term not exceeding fourteen years or to a fine, or to both.

(3) For the purposes of this section, 28(1)(a) above shall have effect as if the person to whom the property belongs or is treated as belonging for the purposes of that Act were the victim of the offence.

[Subs. (1) is printed as amended by the *Anti-terrorism, Crime and Security Act* 2001, s.39(5)(b) and (6)(b). In subs. (2)(a), "12" is substituted for "six", as from a day to be appointed, by the *CJA* 2003, s.282(2) and (3). The increase has no application to offences committed before the substitution takes effect: s.282(4).]

Section 28 of the 1998 Act, which defines "racially or religiously aggravated", is set out at § 5–84, *ante*.

Indictment

An indictment for the racially or religiously aggravated version of the offence may be adapted from the specimen indictment for an offence contrary to section 29(1)(b) of the 1998 Act, *ante*, § 19–214b. 23–31b

Sentence

Imprisonment for 14 years: s.30(2)(b), *ante*. 23–31c

There are no Crown Court sentencing guidelines for this offence. For an illustrative decision, see CSP, B7–2.3C. As to sentencing for racially aggravated offences generally, see *R. v. Saunders* [2000] 1 Cr.App.R. 458, CA, and *R. v. Morrison* [2001] 1 Cr.App.R.(S.) 5, CA.

Class of offence and mode of trial

This offence is a class 3 offence, *ante*, § 2–17. It is triable either way: see subs. (2). For the Sentencing Guidelines Council's guideline on mode of trial, see Appendix K-183. The guideline in relation to arson (Appendix K-183) does not apply to the racially or religiously aggravated version of the offence, but it may nevertheless be used as a starting point in making a mode of trial decision. 23–31d

B. THREATS TO DESTROY OR DAMAGE PROPERTY

Criminal Damage Act 1971, s.2

2. A person who without lawful excuse makes to another a threat, intending that that other would fear it would be carried out,— 23–32

(a) to destroy or damage any property belonging to that other or a third person; or

(b) to destroy or damage his own property in a way which he knows is likely to endanger the life of that other or a third person;

shall be guilty of an offence.

As to the meaning of "lawful excuse", see section 5, *post*, §§ 23–47 *et seq.*; of "damage", see *ante*, §§ 23–6 *et seq.*; of "property" and "belonging to that other", see section 10, *post*, §§ 23–54 *et seq.*

Indictment

STATEMENT OF OFFENCE

23–33 *Threatening to destroy* [or *damage*] *property, contrary to section 2 of the* Criminal Damage Act *1971*.

PARTICULARS OF OFFENCE

A B, on the —— day of ——, 20—, without lawful excuse, threatened J N that he would burn the said J N's house, intending that the said J N would fear that the said threat would be carried out.

Sentence

23–34 Imprisonment for 10 years: *Criminal Damage Act* 1971, s.4, *post*, § 23–46.

There are no sentencing guidelines for this offence.

Class of offence and mode of trial

23–35 This offence is a class 3 offence, *ante*, § 2–17. It is triable either way: *MCA* 1980, s.17(1), and Sched. 1, *ante*, § 1–75af.

Mens rea

23–35a Section 2 was examined in *R. v. Cakmak* [2002] 2 Cr.App.R. 10, CA. Whether an offence under section 2(a) or 2(b) is charged, the jury must be satisfied that the defendant made a threat to another with the intention (recklessness is not enough) that the other would fear that it would be carried out; the nature of the threat must be considered objectively (the actual thoughts and fears of the person threatened are irrelevant); whether the threat is capable of coming within paragraph (a) or (b) is a matter of law; and if so capable, whether it did amount to such a threat is a question of fact. Paragraph (a) deals exclusively with the property of a person other than the defendant, whereas paragraph (b) deals with the defendant's property. It is only in relation to the latter paragraph that the prosecution must prove that the defendant knew that the damage or destruction threatened was likely, if carried out, to endanger the life of a person other than the defendant.

C. POSSESSING ANYTHING WITH INTENT TO DESTROY OR DAMAGE PROPERTY

Criminal Damage Act 1971, s.3

Possessing anything with intent to destroy or damage property

23–36 **3.** A person who has anything in his custody or under his control intending without lawful excuse to use it or cause or permit another to use it—

(a) to destroy or damage any property belonging to some other person; or

(b) to destroy or damage his own or the user's property in a way which he knows is likely to endanger the life of some other person;

shall be guilty of an offence.

As to the meaning of "lawful excuse", see section 5, *post*, §§ 23–47 *et seq.*; of "damage", see *ante*, §§ 23–6 *et seq.*; of "property" and "belonging to some other person", see section 10, *post*, §§ 23–54 *et seq.*

Indictment

STATEMENT OF OFFENCE

23–37 *Possessing articles with intent to destroy* [or *damage*] *property, contrary to section 3 of the* Criminal Damage Act *1971*.

PARTICULARS OF OFFENCE

A B, on the —— day of ——, 20—, had in his custody or under his control a hacksaw and an iron bar intending without lawful excuse to use the said articles or cause or permit another to use them to destroy [or *damage*] *a box belonging to J N* [or *destroy* [or *damage*) *the roof of his own house in a way which he knew was likely to endanger the life of his wife and members of his family*].

Sentence

Imprisonment for 10 years: *Criminal Damage Act* 1971, s.4, *post*, § 23–46. There are no sentencing guidelines for this offence. **23–38**

Class of offence and mode of trial

This offence is a class 3 offence, *ante*, § 2–17. It is triable either way: *MCA* 1980, s.17(1) and Sched. 1, *ante*, § 1–75af. **23–39**

Mens rea

An offence under section 3(a) may be committed only where the defendant intends to use, or cause or permit another to use, the thing to destroy or damage property. It is not enough that the defendant realises that the thing may be so used. It is unnecessary that the defendant should intend an immediate use of the thing; it is enough that he possesses it with the necessary intent even though he contemplates actual use of it at some future time. A conditional intent (an intent to use the thing to cause damage if necessary) will suffice: *R. v. Buckingham*, 63 Cr.App.R. 159, CA. **23–40**

D. Mode of Trial of Offences Under 1971 Act

Offences triable on indictment only

The only offences under the 1971 Act triable on indictment only are the aggravated offences contrary to section 1(2) and (3). **23–41**

Offences triable either way

Offences under sections 1(1), 1(1) and (3), 2 and 3 are triable either way: *MCA* 1980, s.17(1), and Sched. 1, *ante*, §§ 1–75af *et seq.* As to the maximum penalty on summary conviction, see *ibid.*, s.32(1), *ante* § 1–75aa. As to the mode of trial guidelines of the Sentencing Guidelines Council, see Appendix K–182, K–183. **23–42**

Certain offences triable either way to be tried summarily if value involved is small

Where a person is charged with an offence contrary to section 1(1) (other than an offence charged as arson), or with aiding, abetting, counselling or procuring such an offence, or with attempting to commit, or inciting, such an offence, and the value involved is less than £5,000, he must be tried summarily: *MCA* 1980, s.22, and Sched. 2 (*ante*, §§ 1–75i *et seq.*), and see *R. v. Bristol Magistrates' Court, ex p. E.* [1999] 1 Cr.App.R. 144, DC (attempting to commit low-value criminal damage triable summarily). This does not apply if: (a) the offence charged is one of two or more such offences which constitute or form part of a series of two or more offences of the same or a similar character and the aggregate of the values involved exceeds £5,000; or (b) the offence charged consists in inciting two or more such offences and the aggregate of the values involved exceeds £5,000: *ibid.*, s.22(11). **23–43**

As to sentence, where a person is convicted following summary trial in pursuance of section 22, see *ibid.*, s.33, *ante*, § 1–75ab (maximum term of imprisonment three months, increased to 51 weeks as from a day to be appointed). The *PCC(S)A* 2000, s.101(2) (*ante*, § 5–349), precludes the imposition of a detention and training order in the case of an offender aged under 18 convicted of an offence which would be subject to a maximum of three months' imprisonment if committed by an adult: *Pye v. Leeds Youth Court*, *The Independent (C.S.)*, October 6, 2006, DC ([2006] EWHC 2527 (Admin.)).

Power to join in indictment certain summary offences

An offence which would otherwise be triable only summarily by virtue of section 22 of **23–44** the 1980 Act, *ante*, may in certain circumstances be included as a count in an indictment: see the *CJA* 1988, s.40(1), (3) (*ante*, § 1–75ai). In the event of conviction, the powers of the Crown Court are limited to those of a magistrates' court: *ibid.*, s.40(2). This is so even where a defendant charged, *inter alia*, with criminal damage is sent to the Crown Court for trial pursuant to the *CDA* 1998, s.51 (§ 1–17, *ante*): *R. v. Gwynn* [2003] 2 Cr.App.R. (S.) 41, CA. But where there has been no committal or sending for trial on a charge of criminal damage, and the indictment is amended to add a count of criminal damage, the maximum sentence is 10 years' imprisonment even though the value involved is less than £5,000: *R. v. Alden* [2002] 2 Cr.App.R.(S.) 74, CA (see also *ante*, § 23–14), not following *R. v. McKechnie*, 94 Cr.App.R. 51, CA. For criticism of *Alden*, and a submission that it is inconsistent with *R. v. Walker* [1996] 1 Cr.App.R.(S.) 447, CA (court in no doubt that maximum sentence for low-value criminal damage is three months), see *Criminal Law Week* 2002/15/06.

[The next paragraph is § 23–46.]

E. MISCELLANEOUS PROVISIONS

Criminal Damage Act 1971, ss.4, 5

Punishment of offences

23–46 **4.**—(1) A person guilty of arson under section 1 above or of an offence under section 1(2) above (whether arson or not) shall on conviction on indictment be liable to imprisonment for life.

(2) A person guilty of any other offence under this Act shall on conviction on indictment be liable to imprisonment for a term not exceeding ten years.

"Without lawful excuse"

23–47 **5.**—(1) This section applies to any offence under section 1(1) above and any offence under section 2 or 3 above other than one involving a threat by the person charged to destroy or damage property in a way which he knows is likely to endanger the life of another or involving an intent by the person charged to use or cause or permit the use of something in his custody or under his control so to destroy or damage property.

(2) A person charged with an offence to which this section applies shall, whether or not he would be treated for the purposes of this Act as having a lawful excuse apart from this subsection, be treated for those purposes as having a lawful excuse—

(a) if at the time of the act or acts alleged to constitute the offence he believed that the person or persons whom he believed to be entitled to consent to the destruction of or damage to the property in question had so consented, or would have consented to it if he or they had known of the destruction or damage and its circumstances; or

(b) if he destroyed or damaged or threatened to destroy or damage the property in question or, in the case of a charge of an offence under section 3 above, intended to use or cause or permit the use of something to destroy or damage it, in order to protect property belonging to himself or another or a right or interest in property which was or which he believed to be vested in himself or another, and at the time of the act or acts alleged to constitute the offence he believed—

(i) that the property, right or interest was in immediate need of protection; and

(ii) that the means of protection adopted or proposed to be adopted were or would be reasonable having regard to all the circumstances.

(3) For the purposes of this section it is immaterial whether a belief is justified or not if it is honestly held.

(4) For the purposes of subsection (2) above a right or interest in property includes any right or privilege in or over land, whether created by grant, licence or otherwise.

(5) This section shall not be construed as casting doubt on any defence recognised by law as a defence to criminal charges.

23–48 The fact that a person was suffering from self-induced intoxication at the time of an alleged contravention of section 1(1) does not preclude reliance on the defence afforded by section 5(2) and (3): *Jaggard v. Dickinson*, 72 Cr.App.R. 33, DC, where a drunken defendant mistakenly but honestly believed that the house into which she was breaking belonged to a friend.

Where company property is destroyed or damaged, the individual committing the destruction or damage will have a defence if the company consents to his act. If the destruction or damage is *ultra vires* the company (*e.g.* with a view to making a fraudulent insurance claim) there is no actual consent, but there would still be a defence under section 5(2)(a) if the individual believes (a) that the company is entitled to consent, or that another person (such as the company proprietor) is entitled to consent (see *R. v. Denton*, 74 Cr.App.R. 81, CA), and (b) that such consent exists or would exist if the company or person entitled to consent were to know of the destruction or damage and its circumstances.

Where the defence raise an issue under section 5(2)(b), the judge is only entitled to withdraw the defence from the jury if there is no evidence of lawful excuse; if there is some evidence, however tenuous or nebulous, the question should be left to the jury; on no account should there be a direction to convict: *R. v. Wang* [2005] 2 Cr.App.R. 8, HL, disapproving the course taken in *R. v. Hill*; *R. v. Hall*, 89 Cr.App.R. 74, CA. **23–49**

The question whether or not a particular act of destruction or damage or threat of destruction or damage was done or made "in order to protect property" is not conclusively answered by a defendant's genuine beliefs; the test is objective: *R. v. Hunt*, 66 Cr.App.R. 105, CA (setting fire to bed in old people's home in order to demonstrate inadequacy of fire alarm—conviction upheld); *R. v. Ashford and Smith* [1988] Crim.L.R. 682, CA; *R. v. Hill*; *R. v. Hall*, *ante* (campaign of minor criminal damage against United States bases with intent to bring about their closure, and thus lead to reduced risk of the area being target for nuclear attack, with consequent reduced risk of damage to homes in the vicinity); *Johnson v. DPP* [1994] Crim.L.R. 673, DC (squatter damaging door frame in changing locks to secure his belongings when he moved them in); and *R. v. Kelleher* (2003) 147 S.J. 1395, CA. Similarly, a defendant's genuine belief that property was "in immediate need of protection" (s.5(2)(b)(i)) is not conclusive. There is an objective aspect to the word "immediate"; the defence is only made out where there is evidence on which it could be said that the defendant believed that immediate action had to be taken to do something which would otherwise be a crime in order to prevent the immediate risk of something worse happening: *R. v. Hill*; *R. v. Hall*, *ante*, at pp. 79–80. See also *Johnson v. DPP*, *ante*: the squatter's belief that a lock was necessary to secure his belongings was not a belief that they were in "immediate need of protection".

There is no basis under section 5(2)(b) for requiring the defendant to show that the threat is of *unlawful* damage to his or another's property: *R. v. Jones and Milling*; *R. v. Olditch and Pritchard*; *R. v. Richards* [2005] 1 Cr.App.R. 12, CA (legality of Iraq war irrelevant to s.5(2)(b) defence). This ruling, in the defendants' favour and not appealed by the prosecution, was not examined in the House of Lords, where the defendants' appeals on other grounds were dismissed (*R. v. Jones and Milling*; *R. v. Olditch and Pritchard*; *R. v. Richards*; *Ayliffe v. DPP*; *Swain v. Same* [2007] 1 A.C. 136): see *ante*, § 19–39; but Lord Hoffmann's observations in relation to the unavailability of a defence under section 3 of the *CLA* 1967 (reasonable force for the prevention of crime) in the case of direct action protesters leaves little, if any, scope for a successful defence under section 5 where a defence under section 3 of the 1967 Act would fail. Although he left the position under section 5 open (see [73]), it seems clear that his Lordship would have held that property could not be said to be "in immediate need of protection" where the state authorities could have, if they had so chosen, taken action to avoid what the defendant asserted to be the greater evil. In one respect, however, the defence under section 5 does differ from that under section 3. Under section 5, there is no requirement that the steps actually taken should be reasonable. It is enough that the defendant believed that they were reasonable (the fact that they may have been totally unreasonable going only to the question whether the defendant genuinely held any such belief).

In *Chamberlain v. Lindon* [1998] 1 W.L.R. 1252, DC, the respondent demolished a wall erected on the appellant's land some nine months previously. The respondent's defence to a charge of criminal damage was that he had demolished the wall to protect his right of way over the land. It was held in the magistrates' court that he came within the section 5(2)(b) defence in that he honestly believed that his right or interest was in **23–49a** immediate need of protection and that the means adopted were reasonable having regard to all the circumstances. The appeal against the respondent's acquittal was dismissed. It was held: (1) that the fact that the respondent damaged the wall in the hope of avoiding civil litigation did not prevent his purpose being to protect his right of way (which qualified as a right or interest in property by virtue of section 5(4)); and (2) that the right of way was in immediate need of protection within the meaning of section 5(2)(b)(i), because there was a present need to remove the wall, and the longer it remained the more urgent the need to remove it so as to avoid any suggestion of acquiescence in the obstruction.

23–50 A motorist parking in a private car park displaying clear warnings that unauthorised vehicles would be wheel clamped, consented to the risk of his car being clamped. He had no lawful excuse for damaging the clamp. Causing damage in such circumstances can only be contemplated when there is no reasonable alternative: *Lloyd v. DPP* [1992] 1 All E.R. 982, DC; *R. v. Mitchell* [2004] R.T.R. 14, CA.

23–51 A defendant's genuine belief that he was carrying out God's instructions does not provide a defence of lawful excuse to a charge of criminal damage: *Blake v. DPP* [1993] Crim.L.R. 586, DC.

The defence of damaging property to protect property (s.5(2)(b)) does not extend to the protection of the person: *R. v. Baker and Wilkins* [1997] Crim.L.R. 497, CA.

The words "property belonging to himself or another" (section 5(2)(b)) specify two requirements of the thing sought to be protected. It must be "property" and it must belong to the person charged or another: *Cresswell v. DPP*; *Currie v. DPP*, 171 J.P. 233, DC. Keene L.J. was of the opinion that the section 5(2)(b) defence cannot apply where both the destroyed property and the thing to be protected are in the ownership of the same person, whereas Walker J. left this point open. As to this case, see also *post*, § 23–55.

Section 5(2) and (5) make it clear that the common law defence of protection of property remains, but it has always been an ingredient of that defence that what is being experienced or feared by the defendant is an unlawful or criminal act: *Cresswell v. DPP*; *Currie v. DPP*, *ante* (in contrast to the position under section 5: see *R. v. Jones and Milling*, *ante*, § 23–49).

Criminal Damage Act 1971, ss.6, 9, 10

Search for things intended for use in committing offences of criminal damage

23–52 **6.**—(1) If it is made to appear by information on oath before a justice of the peace that there is reasonable cause to believe that any person has in his custody or under his control or on his premises anything which there is reasonable cause to believe has been used or is intended for use without lawful excuse—

(a) to destroy or damage property belonging to another; or

(b) to destroy or damage any property in a way likely to endanger the life of another,

the justice may grant a warrant authorising any constable to search for and seize that thing.

(2) A constable who is authorised under this section to search premises for anything, may enter (if need be by force) and search the premises accordingly and may seize anything which he believes to have been used or to be intended to be used as aforesaid.

(3) [*Application of* Police (Property) Act *1897*.]

Effect on civil proceedings

23–53 **9.** [*Identical to s.31(1) of the* Theft Act *1968*, ante, *§ 21–336 (including the amendments).*]

Interpretation

23–54 **10.**—(1) In this Act "property" means property of a tangible nature, whether real or personal, including money and—

(a) including wild creatures which have been tamed or are ordinarily kept in captivity, and any other wild creatures or their carcasses if, but only if, they have been reduced into possession which has not been lost or abandoned or are in the course of being reduced into possession; but

(b) not including mushrooms growing wild on any land or flowers, fruit or foliage of a plant growing wild on any land.

For the purposes of this subsection "mushroom" includes any fungus and "plant" includes any shrub or tree.

(2) Property shall be treated for the purposes of this Act as belonging to any person—

(a) having the custody or control of it;

(b) having in it any proprietary right or interest (not being an equitable interest arising only from an agreement to transfer or grant an interest); or

(c) having a charge on it.

(3) Where property is subject to a trust, the person to whom it belongs shall be so treated as including any person having a right to enforce that trust.

(4) Property of a corporation sole shall be so treated as belonging to the corporation notwithstanding a vacancy in the corporation.

[(5) For the purposes of this Act a modification of the contents of a computer shall not be regarded as damaging any computer or computer storage medium unless its effect on that computer or computer storage medium impairs its physical condition.]

[This section is printed as amended, as from a day to be appointed, by the *PJA* 2006, s.52, and Sched. 14, para. 2 (insertion of subs. (5)).]

Cf. sections 4 and 5 of the *Theft Act* 1968, *ante*, §§ 21–48, 21–58. **23–55**

As to the relationship between *mens rea* and "property belonging to another", see *R. v. Smith (D.R.)*, 58 Cr.App.R. 320, CA (*ante*, § 23–8).

In *Cresswell v. DPP*; *Currie v. DPP*, *ante*, § 23–51, Keene L.J. held that badgers for which traps had been set, but which had not yet been trapped, were not "property" as defined by section 10(1)(a) ("wild creatures ... if, but only if, ... they are in the course of being reduced into possession"), even if particular badgers had entered a trap prior to it being set. Walker J. expressed no concluded view on this point. However, both judges agreed that the badgers did not belong to anybody, as nobody had custody or control of them, nor any proprietary right or interest in them (see s.10(2)); so the defendants who destroyed the traps could not rely on the section 5(2)(b) defence: see *ante*, § 23–51.

II. MALICIOUS DAMAGE ACT 1861

Malicious Damage Act 1861, ss.35, 36

Placing wood, etc. on railway, etc.

35. Whosoever shall unlawfully and maliciously put, place, cast, or throw upon or across any railway any wood, stone, or other matter or thing, or shall unlawfully and maliciously take up, remove, or displace any rail, sleeper, or other matter or thing, belonging to any railway, or shall unlawfully and maliciously turn, move, or divert any points or other machinery belonging to any railway, or shall unlawfully and maliciously make or show, hide, or remove, any signal or light upon or near to any railway, or shall unlawfully and maliciously do or cause to be done any other matter or thing, with intent, in any of the cases aforesaid, to obstruct, upset, overthrow, injure, or destroy any engine, tender, carriage, or truck using such railway, shall be ... liable, at the discretion of the court, to imprisonment for life **23–56**

Obstructing engines or carriages on railways

36. Whosoever, by any unlawful act, or by any wilful omission or neglect, shall obstruct or cause to be obstructed, any engine or carriage using any railway, or shall aid or assist therein, shall be guilty of an offence, and being convicted thereof shall be liable, at the discretion of the court, to be imprisoned for any term not exceeding two years **23–57**

Indictment

Specimen counts under both sections 35 and 36 are contained in the repealed Schedule to the *Indictments Act* 1915. **23–58**

An acquittal on an indictment framed under section 35 is no bar to a subsequent indictment upon the same facts for an offence under section 36: *R. v. Gilmore* (1882) 15 Cox 85.

Class of offence and mode of trial

The offences contrary to sections 35 and 36 are class 3 offences, *ante*, § 2–17. The latter is triable either way: *MCA* 1980, s.17(1), and Sched. 1, *ante*, § 1–75af. The penalty on summary conviction is six months' imprisonment (increased to 12 months, as from a **23–59** day to be appointed, by the *CJA* 2003, s.282(2) and (3), but not in relation to any offence committed before the date of commencement: s.282(4)), a fine not exceeding £5,000, or both: *ibid.*, s.32(1), *ante*, §§ 1–75aa *et seq.*

Mens rea

23–60 As to the meaning of "maliciously", see generally, *ante*, §§ 17–45 *et seq.* and, in particular, *R. v. Cunningham* [1957] 2 Q.B. 396, 41 Cr.App.R. 155, CCA. Section 58 of the Act provides that where malice is an ingredient of an offence under the Act it is immaterial whether the offence is committed "from malice conceived against the owner of the property in respect of which it shall be committed, or otherwise".

As to the meaning of "wilful", see *R. v. Holroyd* (1841) 2 M. & Rob. 339, *R. v. Senior* [1899] 1 Q.B. 283 and *R. v. Sheppard* [1981] A.C. 394, HL, *ante*, § 17–47.

In *R. v. Gittins* [1982] R.T.R. 363, CA, it was held (applying *R. v. Sheppard*, *ante*) that in order to be guilty of wilful neglect (s.36), the accused must know that his conduct involves the risk of an obstruction to the railway unless he takes reasonable care and yet, knowing that, he deliberately falls short of exercising it.

Actus reus

23–61 On a prosecution under section 36, it would seem not to be necessary to prove that any train was obstructed in fact: see *R. v. Bradford* (1860) 8 Cox 309; *R. v. Gatenby* [1960] Crim.L.R. 195, Assizes (Thesiger J.).

Where a defendant unlawfully causes a train to slow down or stop, whether by altering some railway signals (*R. v. Hadfield* (1870) L.R. 1 C.C.R. 253) or imitating an inspector's hand signals (*R. v. Hardy* (1870) L.R. 1 C.C.R. 278), he is guilty of "obstructing" a train within the meaning of section 36. "Any unlawful act" in section 36 includes each of the acts mentioned in section 35: *Hadfield* and *Hardy*, *ibid.*

It does not matter whether the railway is public or private: *O'Gorman v. Sweet*, 54 J.P. 663.

III. EXPLOSIVE SUBSTANCES ACT 1883

Explosive Substances Act 1883, s.2

Causing explosion likely to endanger life or property

23–62 **2.** A person who in the United Kingdom or (being a citizen of the United Kingdom and Colonies) in the Republic of Ireland unlawfully and maliciously causes by any explosive substance an explosion of a nature likely to endanger life or to cause serious injury to property shall, whether any injury to person or property has been actually caused or not, be guilty of an offence and on conviction on indictment shall be liable to imprisonment for life.

[This section is printed as substituted by the *Criminal Jurisdiction Act* 1975, s.7.]

An offence contrary to section 2 is a "Convention offence" for the purposes of Part 1 of the *Terrorism Act* 2006: see s.20(2) and Sched. 1, para. 1(2)(a).

Indictment

STATEMENT OF OFFENCE

23–63 *Causing an explosion, contrary to section 2 of the* Explosive Substances Act *1883*.

PARTICULARS OF OFFENCE

A B, on the —— day of ——, 20—, maliciously caused by gunpowder or other explosive substance an explosion of a nature likely to endanger life or to cause serious injury to property.

Sentence

23–64 Imprisonment for life: s.2 (*ante*).

This offence is a "specified violent offence"within Chapter 5 of Part 12 of the *CJA*

2003 (life sentences, sentences for public protection and extended sentences): see s.224, and Sched. 15, *ante*, §§ 5–292, 5–299.

For sentencing guidelines, see CSP, B7–3.2; and *R. v. Martin (P.H.S.)* [1999] 1 Cr.App.R.(S.) 477, CA (although the guidelines in this case were said to "require review" in *R. v. Barot*, *ante*, § 5–239m).

Class of offence and mode of trial

This offence is a class 3 offence, *ante*, § 2–17. It is triable only on indictment: s.2, *ante*. **23–65**

Ingredients

"Maliciously"

See *ante*, §§ 17–45 *et seq*., and, in particular, *R. v. Cunningham* [1957] 2 Q.B. 396, 41 Cr.App.R. 155, CCA. **23–65a**

"Who in the United Kingdom"

In *R. v. Ellis*, 95 Cr.App.R. 52 at 66, CCC, Swinton Thomas J. observed *obiter* that it "would be quite extraordinary if, in the circumstances prevailing in 1975, Parliament when enacting the new section 2 intended to limit the crime so as to require the physical presence of the offender as opposed to defining the place where the damage occurred".

Explosive Substances Act 1883, s.3

Attempt to cause explosion, or making or keeping explosive with intent to endanger life or property

3.—(1) A person who in the United Kingdom or a dependency or (being a citizen of the United Kingdom and Colonies) elsewhere unlawfully and maliciously— **23–66**

(a) does any act with intent to cause, or conspires to cause, by an explosive substance an explosion of a nature likely to endanger life, or cause serious injury to property, whether in the United Kingdom or elsewhere, or

(b) makes or has in his possession or under his control an explosive substance with intent by means thereof to endanger life, or cause serious injury to property, whether in the United Kingdom or elsewhere, or to enable any other person so to do,

shall, whether any explosion does or does not take place, and whether any injury to person or property is actually caused or not, be guilty of an offence and on conviction on indictment shall be liable to imprisonment for life, and the explosive substance shall be forfeited.

(2) In this section "dependency" means the Channel Islands, the Isle of Man and any colony, other than a colony for whose external relations a country other than the United Kingdom is responsible.

[This section is printed as substituted by the *Criminal Jurisdiction Act* 1975, s.7; and as subsequently amended by the *CLA* 1977, s.65(4) and Sched. 12; and the *Terrorism Act* 2006, s.17(5).]

An offence contrary to section 3 is a "Convention offence" for the purposes of Part 1 of the *Terrorism Act* 2006: see s.20(2) and Sched. 1, para. 1(2)(b).

Indictment

COUNT 1

STATEMENT OF OFFENCE

Conspiracy to cause an explosion, contrary to section 3(1)(a) of the Explosive Substances Act 1883. **23–67**

PARTICULARS OF OFFENCE

A B, on the —— day of ——, 20—, unlawfully and maliciously conspired with J N to cause by an explosive substance an explosion of a nature likely to endanger life or cause serious injury to property in the United Kingdom or the Republic of Ireland.

COUNT 2

STATEMENT OF OFFENCE

Possession of an explosive substance with intent, contrary to section 3(1)(b) of the Explosive Substances Act *1883.*

PARTICULARS OF OFFENCE

A B, on the —— day of ——, 20—, unlawfully and maliciously made or had in his possession or under his control an explosive substance with intent by means thereof to endanger life or cause serious injury to property in the United Kingdom or the Republic of Ireland.

Sentence

23–68 Imprisonment for life and forfeiture of the explosive substance: s.3 (*ante*).

This offence is a "specified violent offence" within Chapter 5 of Part 12 of the *CJA* 2003 (life sentences, sentences for public protection and extended sentences): see s.224, and Sched. 15, *ante*, §§ 5–292, 5–299.

For sentencing guidelines, see CSP, B7–3.2; and *R. v. Martin (P.H.S.)* [1999] 1 Cr.App.R.(S.) 477, CA (although the guidelines in this case were said to "require review" in *R. v. Barot*, *ante*, § 5–239m).

Class of offence and mode of trial

23–69 This offence is a class 3 offence, *ante*, § 2–17. It is triable only on indictment: s.3, *ante*.

Ingredients

"Maliciously"

23–70 See *ante*, § 23–65a.

"Who in the United Kingdom"

23–71 In *R. v. Ellis*, *ante*, it was held that the word "who" in section 3 governs the acts described in the section rather than the person. If the intended explosions were planned to take place in the United Kingdom, therefore, it would be no defence to show that the defendant had not been in the United Kingdom at the relevant time.

Explosive Substances Act 1883, s.4

Making or possession of explosive under suspicious circumstances

23–72 **4.**—(1) Any person who makes or knowingly has in his possession or under his control any explosive substance, under such circumstances as to give rise to a reasonable suspicion that he is not making it or does not have it in his possession or under his control for a lawful object, shall, unless he can show that he made it or had it in his possession or under his control for a lawful object, be guilty of [an offence] and liable to imprisonment for a term not exceeding fourteen years, and the explosive substance shall be forfeited.

(2) [*Repealed by* PACE Act *1984, s.119(2) and Sched. 7, Pt V.*]

Indictment

STATEMENT OF OFFENCE

23–73 *Making* [or *Possessing*] *explosives, contrary to section 4 of the* Explosive Substances Act *1883.*

PARTICULARS OF OFFENCE

A B, on the —— day of ——, 20—, made [or *knowingly had in his possession or under his control*] *a certain explosive substance, to wit* [describe the explosive substance] *in such circumstances as to give rise to a reasonable suspicion that he had not made it* [or *that it was not in his possession or under his control*] *for a lawful object.*

Where the charge is that of possessing explosives, the omission of the word "knowingly" from the indictment renders the indictment defective (*R. v. Stewart and Harris*, 44 Cr.App.R. 29, CCA), but not a nullity (*R. v. McVitie*, 44 Cr.App.R. 201, CCA).

Sentence

23–74 Imprisonment not exceeding 14 years and forfeiture of the explosive substance: s.4 (*ante*).

There are no sentencing guidelines for this offence. For an illustrative decision, see CSP, B7–3.3B.

Class of offence and mode of trial

This offence is a class 3 offence, *ante*, § 2–17. It is triable only on indictment. **23–75**

Ingredients

Possessing explosives

The prosecution must prove: **23–76**

(a) that the defendant was knowingly in possession of a substance which is an explosive substance as defined by section 9 (*post*, § 23–84), and

(b) that the possession was in such circumstances as to give rise to a reasonable suspicion that he did not have it in his possession for a lawful object.

The prosecution must prove both that the defendant knew that he was in possession of the substance and also that he knew that it was an explosive substance; though, if the prosecution establish (b) as set out above, the jury may easily infer knowledge that the substance was explosive: *R. v. Hallam*, 41 Cr.App.R. 111, CCA. It then lies on the defendant to show that he had it in his possession for a lawful object.

Making explosives

The prosecution must prove: **23–77**

(a) that the defendant knew that the substance he made was an explosive substance as defined by section 9 (*post*, § 23–84), and

(b) that he made it in such circumstances as to give rise to a reasonable suspicion that he did not make it for a lawful object.

Mens rea is a specific ingredient of the offence of making explosives, even though the word "knowingly" in section 4(1) qualifies only "has in his possession or under his control": *R. v. Berry*, 99 Cr.App.R. 88, CA.

Lawful object

Self-defence is a defence to a charge under section 4. The defendant must satisfy the jury on the balance of probabilities that his object was to protect himself or his family or his property against imminent apprehended attack and to do so by means which he believed were no more than reasonably necessary to meet the force used by the attackers: *Att.-Gen's. Reference (No. 2 of 1983)* [1984] Q.B. 456, 78 Cr.App.R. 183, CA (petrol bombs). The court observed, applying *R. v. Fegan*, 78 Cr.App.R. 189, CCA (N.I.), that the object or purpose or end for which the explosive substance was made was not in itself rendered unlawful by the fact that it could not be fulfilled without the commission of another offence (in *Fegan*, possession of a firearm without a certificate). Further, an explosive substance may be made with a lawful object, but if it is retained after the threat has passed which justified the making of it, the continued retention will be an offence under section 4. **23–78**

In *R. v. Berry* [1985] A.C. 246, HL, it was held that the "lawful object" specified in section 4(1) is not confined to a purpose which takes place in the United Kingdom and the lawfulness of which is to be defined by English law. Accordingly, if the evidence is that the accused manufactured an explosive substance for use abroad and he cannot show, on the balance of probabilities, that such use was lawful outside the United Kingdom, he is liable to conviction.

Common design

If several persons are concerned in a common design to have articles amounting to an explosive substance made for an unlawful purpose, each is responsible in respect of such articles as are in the possession of others connected in the carrying out of their common design: *R. v. Charles* (1892) 17 Cox 499. **23–79**

Aiding and abetting

The aiding and abetting of an offence contrary to section 4 is an offence known to the law and is established where it is proved that the defendant: **23–79a**

(a) knew that the principal offender had the explosive substance in his possession or under his control;
(b) knew facts giving rise to a reasonable suspicion that the principal offender did not have the substance in his possession or under his control for a lawful object; and
(c) was present actively encouraging or in some way helping the principal offender in the commission of the offence: *R. v. McCarthy*, 48 Cr.App.R. 111, CCA (applied in *Mok Wei Tak v. R.* [1990] 2 A.C. 333, PC).

Explosive Substances Act 1883, ss.5, 7

Punishment of accessories

23–80 **5.** Any person who within or (being a subject of Her Majesty) without Her Majesty's dominions by the supply of or solicitation for money, the providing of premises, the supply of materials, or in any manner whatsoever, procures, counsels, aids, abets, or is accessory to, the commission of any crime under this Act, shall be guilty of [an offence] and shall be liable to be tried and punished for that crime, as if he had been guilty as a principal.

An offence contrary to section 5 is a "Convention offence" for the purposes of Part 1 of the *Terrorism Act* 2006: see s.20(2) and Sched. 1, para. 1(2)(c).

No prosecution except by leave of Attorney-General

23–81 **7.**—(1) Proceedings for a crime under this Act shall not be instituted except by or with the consent of the Attorney-General.

(2) [*Repealed by* Indictments Act *1915, s.9 and Sched. 2.*]

(3) [*Repealed by* Criminal Law Act *1967, s.10(2) and Sched. 3, Pt III.*]

(4) [*Repealed by* Statute Law (Repeals) Act *1989, s.1(1) and Sched. 1, Pt I.*]

[Subs. (1) is printed as substituted by the *Administration of Justice Act* 1982, s.63(1).]

23–82 Section 7(1) does not prevent the arrest without warrant, or the issue or execution of a warrant for the arrest, of a person for any offence, or the remand in custody or on bail of a person charged with any offence: *Prosecution of Offences Act* 1985, s.25(2), *ante*, § 1–278.

For authorities on the form of, and time for, the Attorney-General's consent to the institution of proceedings, see *ante*, § 1–245.

Search for and seizure of explosive substances

23–83 Section 8(1) of the 1883 Act provides that sections 73, 74, 75, 89 and 96 of the *Explosives Act* 1875 (which sections relate to the search for, seizure and detention of explosive substances, and the forfeiture thereof, and the disposal of explosive substances seized or forfeited), shall apply as if a crime or forfeiture under the 1883 Act were an offence or forfeiture under the 1875 Act.

Explosive Substances Act 1883, s.9

Definitions

23–84 **9.**—(1) In this Act, unless the context otherwise requires—

The expression "explosive substance" shall be deemed to include any materials for making any explosive substance; also any apparatus, machine, implement, or materials used, or intended to be used, or adapted for causing, or aiding in causing, any explosion in or with any explosive substance; also any part of any such apparatus, machine, or implement.

The expression "Attorney-General" means Her Majesty's Attorney-General for England or Ireland, ...

(2) [*Scotland.*]

[This section is printed as amended by the *Law Officers Act* 1997, s.3(2), and Sched.]

The 1883 Act does not define "explosive". In *R. v. Wheatley*, 68 Cr.App.R. 287, CA, it was held that the Act should be construed in the light of the definition of "explosive" in section 3 of the *Explosives Act* 1875, *viz.*:

"This Act shall apply to gunpowder and other explosives as defined by this section. The term 'explosive' in this Act—(1) Means gunpowder, nitroglycerine, dynamite, gun-cotton, blasting powders, fulminate of mercury or of other metals, coloured fires and every other substance, whether similar to those above mentioned or not, used or manufactured with a view to producing a practical effect by explosion or a pyrotechnic effect; and (2) includes fog-signals, fireworks, fuzes, rockets, percussion caps, detonators, cartridges, ammunition of all description, and every adaptation or preparation of an explosive as above defined."

Wheatley was applied in *R. v. Bouch*, 76 Cr.App.R. 11, CA (petrol bomb consisting of some petrol in a bottle with a rag rammed into its neck to form a wick is an "explosive substance" within the 1883 Act). *Bouch* was followed in *R. v. Howard* [1993] Crim.L.R. 213, CA, in respect of the *Offences against the Person Act* 1861, s.29 (*ante*, § 19–232). **23–85**

The term "explosive substance" has been held to include a shot gun (*R. v. Downey* [1971] N.I. 224) and a part of a vessel which itself is filled with an explosive substance (*R. v. Charles* (1892) 17 Cox 499). **23–86**

IV. COMPUTER MISUSE ACT 1990

A. COMPUTER MISUSE OFFENCES

Computer Misuse Act 1990, s.1

Unauthorised access to computer material

1.—(1) A person is guilty of an offence if— **23–87**

(a) he causes a computer to perform any function with intent to secure access to any program or data held in any computer;

(b) the access he intends to secure is unauthorised; and

(c) he knows at the time when he causes the computer to perform the function that that is the case.

(2) The intent a person has to have to commit an offence under this section need not be directed at—

(a) any particular program or data;

(b) a program or data of any particular kind; or

(c) a program or data held in any particular computer.

(3) A person guilty of an offence under this section shall be liable—

(a) on summary conviction in England and Wales, to imprisonment for a term not exceeding 12 months or to a fine not exceeding the statutory maximum or to both;

(b) [*Scotland.*]

(c) on conviction on indictment, to imprisonment for a term not exceeding two years or to a fine or to both.

[This section is printed as amended by the *PJA* 2006, s.35(1) and (3). Subs. (2) (which effected further prospective amendments) was itself repealed without ever having been brought into force by the *SCA* 2007, ss.61(1) and (2), and 92, and Sched. 14.]

The amendments effected by the 2006 Act are subject to transitional provisions. By section 38(2)(a), the substitution of section 1(3) does not apply in relation to an offence committed before the substitution took effect (*viz.* October 1, 2008: *Police and Justice Act 2006 (Commencement No. 9) Order* 2008 (S.I. 2008 No. 2503)). By section 38(6), in the case of an offence committed before the *CJA* 2003, s.154(1), comes into force, the new subsection (3) has effect as if for "12 months", there were substituted "six months".

The words of section 1(1)(a) should be given their plain and ordinary meaning: *Att.-Gen.'s Reference (No. 1 of 1991)* [1993] Q.B. 94, CA. An offence under the section need not involve the use of one computer to secure access to another; the section is also contravened where a person causes a computer to perform a function with intent to gain unauthorised access to any program or data held in the same computer: *ibid*.

It is unclear whether an offence is committed under section 1 by a person who is authorised to secure access to computer material, but does so for unauthorised purposes. In *DPP v. Bignell* [1998] 1 Cr.App.R. 1, DC (police officers for undisclosed private purposes procuring innocent computer operator to extract details of cars from Police

National Computer), it was held that the offence was not committed in such circumstances, but some of the court's reasoning in relation to section 17(5), albeit not the result, was disapproved in *R. v. Bow Street Metropolitan Stipendiary Magistrate, ex p. Government of the United States of America* [2000] 2 A.C. 216, HL (an extradition case: see *post*, § 23–101). See the commentaries at [1999] Crim.L.R. 971 and *Criminal Law Week* 1999/32/16.

Computer Misuse Act 1990, ss.2, 3, 3A

Unauthorised access with intent to commit or facilitate commission of further offences

23–88 **2.**—(1) A person is guilty of an offence under this section if he commits an offence under section 1 above ("the unauthorised access offence") with intent—

(a) to commit an offence to which this section applies; or

(b) to facilitate the commission of such an offence (whether by himself or by any other person);

and the offence he intends to commit or facilitate is referred to below in this section as the further offence.

(2) This section applies to offences—

(a) for which the sentence is fixed by law; or

(b) for which a person *of twenty-one years of age or over (not previously convicted)* [who has attained the age of twenty-one years (eighteen in relation to England and Wales) and has no previous convictions] may be sentenced to imprisonment for a term of five years (or, in England and Wales, might be so sentenced but for the restrictions imposed by section 33 of the *Magistrates' Courts Act* 1980).

(3) It is immaterial for the purposes of this section whether the further offence is to be committed on the same occasion as the unauthorised access offence or on any future occasion.

(4) A person may be guilty of an offence under this section even though the facts are such that the commission of the further offence is impossible.

(5) A person guilty of an offence under this section shall be liable—

(a) on summary conviction in England and Wales, to imprisonment for a term not exceeding 12 months or to a fine not exceeding the statutory maximum or to both;

(b) [*Scotland.*];

(c) on conviction on indictment, to imprisonment for a term not exceeding five years or to a fine or to both.

[This section is printed as amended by the *PJA* 2006, s.52, and Sched. 14, para. 17; and as amended, as from a day to be appointed, by the *CJCSA* 2000, s.74 and Sched. 7, para. 98 (substitution of words in square brackets for italicised words in subs. (2)). The reference to "12 months" in subs. (5) should be read as "six months" in relation to any offence committed before the commencement of the *CJA* 2003, s.154(1): 2006 Act, s.38(6)).]

Unauthorised acts with intent to impair, or with recklessness as to impairing, operation of computer, etc.

23–89 **3.**—(1) A person is guilty of an offence if—

(a) he does any unauthorised act in relation to a computer;

(b) at the time when he does the act he knows that it is unauthorised; and

(c) either subsection (2) or subsection (3) below applies.

(2) This subsection applies if the person intends by doing the act—

(a) to impair the operation of any computer;

(b) to prevent or hinder access to any program or data held in any computer; or

(c) to impair the operation of any such program or the reliability of any such data.

(3) This subsection applies if the person is reckless as to whether the act will do any of the things mentioned in paragraphs (a) to (c) of subsection (2) above.

(4) The intention referred to in subsection (2) above, or the recklessness referred to in subsection (3) above, need not relate to—

(a) any particular computer;

(b) any particular program or data; or

(c) a program or data of any particular kind.

(5) In this section—

(a) a reference to doing an act includes a reference to causing an act to be done;

(b) "act" includes a series of acts;

(c) a reference to impairing, preventing or hindering something includes a reference to doing so temporarily.

(6) A person guilty of an offence under this section shall be liable—

(a) on summary conviction in England and Wales, to imprisonment for a term not exceeding 12 months or to a fine not exceeding the statutory maximum or to both;

(b) [*Scotland*];

(c) on conviction on indictment, to imprisonment for a term not exceeding ten years or to a fine or to both.

[This section is printed as substituted by the *PJA* 2006, s.36; and as subsequently amended by the *SCA* 2007, ss.61(1) and (3), and 92, and Sched. 14.]

An offence is not committed under the new section 3 unless every act or other event proof of which is required for conviction of the offence takes place after the substitution took effect (*viz.* October 1, 2008: *Police and Justice Act 2006 (Commencement No. 9) Order* 2008 (S.I. 2008 No. 2503)): 2006 Act, s.38(3). Where, by reason of section 38(3), an offence is not committed under the new section 3, the old section 3 has effect: *ibid.*, s.38(4). In the case of an offence committed before the *CJA* 2003, s.154(1), comes into force, the new section 3(6)(a) has effect as if for "12 months" there were substituted "six months": *ibid.*, s.38(6).

If a computer is caused to record information which shows that it came from one person, when it in fact came from someone else, that manifestly affects its reliability, and thus the reliability of the data in the computer is impaired within the meaning of section 3(2)(c): *Zezev and Yarimaka v. Governor of H.M. Prison Brixton* [2002] 2 Cr.App.R. 33, DC.

In *DPP v. Lennon*, 170 J.P. 532, DC, it was held that a person causing a substantial number of e-mail messages to be sent to a computer server committed the *actus reus* of the offence contrary to the original section 3(1), where the addition of the data from the e-mail messages was "unauthorised" within the meaning of section 17(8): see *post*, § 23–101.

Making, supplying or obtaining articles for use in offence under section 1 or 3

3A.—(1) A person is guilty of an offence if he makes, adapts, supplies or offers to supply any article intending it to be used to commit, or to assist in the commission of, an offence under section 1 or 3. **23–89a**

(2) A person is guilty of an offence if he supplies or offers to supply any article believing that it is likely to be used to commit, or to assist in the commission of, an offence under section 1 or 3.

(3) A person is guilty of an offence if he obtains any article with a view to its being supplied for use to commit, or to assist in the commission of, an offence under section 1 or 3.

(4) In this section "article" includes any program or data held in electronic form.

(5) [*Identical to s.1(3)*, ante, *§ 23–87*.]

[This section was inserted by the *PJA* 2006, s.37.]

An offence is not committed under section 3A unless every act or other event proof of which is required for conviction of the offence takes place after section 37 of the 2006 Act came into force (as to which, see *ante*, § 23–89): 2006 Act. s.38(5). As to the effect of section 38(6), see *ante*, § 23–89.

B. JURISDICTION

Computer Misuse Act 1990, ss.4–9

Territorial scope of offences under sections 1 to 3

4.—(1) Except as provided below in this section, it is immaterial for the purposes of any offence under section 1 or 3 above— **23–90**

(a) whether any act or other event proof of which is required for conviction of the offence occurred in the home country concerned; or

(b) whether the accused was in the home country concerned at the time of any such act or event.

(2) Subject to subsection (3) below, in the case of such an offence at least one significant link with domestic jurisdiction must exist in the circumstances of the case for the offence to be committed.

(3) There is no need for any such link to exist for the commission of an offence under section 1 above to be established in proof of an allegation to that effect in proceedings for an offence under section 2 above.

(4) Subject to section 8 below, where—

(a) any such link does in fact exist in the case of an offence under section 1 above; and

(b) commission of that offence is alleged in proceedings for an offence under section 2 above;

section 2 above shall apply as if anything the accused intended to do or facilitate in any place outside the home country concerned which would be an offence to which section 2 applies if it took place in the home country concerned were the offence in question.

(5) [*Scotland.*]

(6) References in this Act to the home country concerned are references—

(a) in the application of this Act to England and Wales, to England and Wales;

(b) in the application of this Act to Scotland, to Scotland; and

(c) in the application of this Act to Northern Ireland, to Northern Ireland.

[The heading to this section is printed as amended by the *PJA* 2006, s.52, and Sched. 14, para. 18.]

Significant links with domestic jurisdiction

23–91 **5.**—(1) The following provisions of this section apply for the interpretation of section 4 above.

(2) In relation to an offence under section 1, either of the following is a significant link with domestic jurisdiction—

(a) that the accused was in the home country concerned at the time when he did the act which caused the computer to perform the function; or

(b) that any computer containing any program or data to which the accused secured or intended to secure unauthorised access by doing that act was in the home country concerned at that time.

(3) In relation to an offence under section 3, either of the following is a significant link with domestic jurisdiction—

(a) that the accused was in the home country concerned at the time when he did the unauthorised act (or caused it to be done); or

(b) that the unauthorised act was done in relation to a computer in the home country concerned.

[Subs. (3) is printed as amended by the *PJA* 2006, s.52, and Sched. 14, para. 19(1) and (3).]

Where, by reason of section 38(3) of the 2006 Act (as to which, see *ante*, § 23–89), an offence is not committed under the new section 3 of the 1990 Act, the amendments to section 5(3) do not apply: *ibid.*, s.38(4).

Territorial scope of inchoate offences related to offences under sections 1 to 3

23–92 **6.**—(1) On a charge of conspiracy to commit an offence under section 1, 2 or 3 above the following questions are immaterial to the accused's guilt—

(a) the question where any person became a party to the conspiracy; and

(b) the question whether any act, omission or other event occurred in the home country concerned.

(2) On a charge of attempting to commit an offence under section 3 above the following questions are immaterial to the accused's guilt—

(a) the question where the attempt was made; and

(b) the question whether it had an effect in the home country concerned.

(3) [*Repealed by* SCA *2007, ss.63(2) and 92, Sched. 6, para. 59(1) and (2), and Sched. 14.*]

(4) This section does not extend to Scotland.

[This section is printed as amended by the *PJA* 2006, s.52, and Sched. 14, para. 20.]

Territorial scope of inchoate offences related to offences under external law corresponding to offences under this Act [sections 1 to 3]

7.—(1), (2) [*Repealed by* Criminal Justice (Terrorism and Conspiracy) Act *1998, s.9(2) and Sched. 2, Pt II.*] **23–93**

(3) [*See* post, *§ 33–120.*]

(4) [*Repealed by* SCA *2007, ss.63(2) and 92, Sched. 6, para. 59(1) and (3), and Sched. 14.*]

Relevance of external law

8.—(1) A person is guilty of an offence triable by virtue of section 4(4) above only if what he intended to do or facilitate would involve the commission of an offence under the law in force where the whole or any part of it was intended to take place. **23–94**

(3) A person is guilty of an offence triable by virtue of section 1(1A) of the *Criminal Attempts Act* 1981 ... only if what he had in view would involve the commission of an offence under the law in force where the whole or any part of it was intended to take place.

(4) Conduct punishable under the law in force in any place is an offence under that law for the purposes of this section, however it is described in that law.

(5) Subject to subsection (7) below, a condition specified in subsection (1) or (3) above shall be taken to be satisfied unless not later than rules of court may provide the defence serve on the prosecution a notice—

(a) stating that, on the facts as alleged with respect to the relevant conduct, the condition is not in their opinion satisfied;

(b) showing their grounds for that opinion; and

(c) requiring the prosecution to show that it is satisfied.

(6) In subsection (5) above "the relevant conduct" means—

(a) where the condition in subsection (1) above is in question, what the accused intended to do or facilitate; ...

(c) where the condition in subsection (3) above is in question, what the accused had in view.

(7) The court, if it thinks fit, may permit the defence to require the prosecution to show that the condition is satisfied without the prior service of a notice under subsection (5) above.

(8) [*Scotland.*]

(9) In the Crown Court the question whether the condition is satisfied shall be decided by the judge alone.

(10) [*Scotland.*]

[This section is printed as amended by the *Criminal Justice (Terrorism and Conspiracy) Act* 1998, s.9(1), (2), and Scheds 1, Pt II, and 2, Pt II; and the *SCA* 2007, ss.63(2) and 92, Sched. 6, para. 59(1) and (4), and Sched. 14.]

British citizenship immaterial

9.—(1) In any proceedings brought in England and Wales in respect of any offence to which this section applies it is immaterial to guilt whether or not the accused was a British citizen at the time of any act, omission or other event proof of which is required for conviction of the offence. **23–95**

(2) This section applies to the following offences—

(a) any offence under section 1, 2 or 3 above;

(b) [*repealed by* Criminal Justice (Terrorism and Conspiracy) Act *1998, s.9(1), (2), and Sched. 1, Pt II, and Sched. 2, Pt II*];

(c) any attempt to commit an offence under section 3 above; and ... .

[This section is printed as amended by the *PJA* 2006, s.52, and Sched. 14, para. 22; and the *SCA* 2007, ss.63(2) and 92, Sched. 6, para. 59(1) and (5), and Sched. 14.]

C. MISCELLANEOUS AND GENERAL

Computer Misuse Act 1990, ss.10, 17

Saving for certain law enforcement powers

10. Section 1(1) above has effect without prejudice to the operation— **23–96**

(a) in England and Wales of any enactment relating to powers of inspection, search and seizure; and

(b) [*Scotland*]

and nothing designed to indicate a withholding of consent to access to any program or data from persons as enforcement officers shall have effect to make access unauthorised for the purposes of the said section 1(1).

In this section "enforcement officer" means a constable or other person charged with the duty of investigating offences; and withholding consent from a person "as" an enforcement officer of any description includes the operation, by the person entitled to control access, of rules whereby enforcement officers of that description are, as such, disqualified from membership of a class of persons who are authorised to have access.

[This section is printed as amended by the *CJPOA* 1994, s.162(1).]

[The next paragraph is § 23–100.]

Computer Misuse Act 1990, s.17

Interpretation

23–100 **17.**—(1) The following provisions of this section apply for the interpretation of this Act.

(2) A person secures access to any program or data held in a computer if by causing a computer to perform any function he—

(a) alters or erases the program or data;

(b) copies or moves it to any storage medium other than that in which it is held or to a different location in the storage medium in which it is held;

(c) uses it; or

(d) has it output from the computer in which it is held (whether by having it displayed or in any other manner);

and references to access to a program or data (and to an intent to secure such access) shall be read accordingly.

(3) For the purposes of subsection (2)(c) above a person uses a program if the function he causes the computer to perform—

(a) causes the program to be executed; or

(b) is itself a function of the program.

(4) For the purposes of subsection (2)(d) above—

(a) a program is output if the instructions of which it consists are output; and

(b) the form in which any such instructions or any other data is output (and in particular whether or not it represents a form in which, in the case of instructions, they are capable of being executed or, in the case of data, it is capable of being processed by a computer) is immaterial.

(5) Access of any kind by any person to any program or data held in a computer is unauthorised if—

(a) he is not himself entitled to control access of the kind in question to the program or data; and

(b) he does not have consent to access by him of the kind in question to the program or data from any person who is so entitled;

but this subsection is subject to section 10.

(6) References to any program or data held in a computer include references to any program or data held in any removable storage medium which is for the time being in the computer; and a computer is to be regarded as containing any program or data held in any such medium.

(8) An act done in relation to a computer is unauthorised if the person doing the act (or causing it to be done)—

(a) is not himself a person who has responsibility for the computer and is entitled to determine whether the act may be done; and

(b) does not have consent to the act from any such person.

In this subsection "act" includes a series of acts.

(9) References to the home country concerned shall be read in accordance with section 4(6) above.

(10) References to a program include references to part of a program.

[This section is printed as amended by the *CJPOA* 1994, s.162(2); and the *PJA* 2006, s.52, Sched. 14, para. 29, and Sched. 15, Pt 4 (but see *post*, for transitional provisions).]

Where, by reason of section 38(3) of the 2006 Act (as to which, see *ante*, § 23–89), an offence is not committed under the new section 3 of the 1990 Act, the repeal of section 17(7), and the substitution of a new section 17(8), do not apply: *PJA* 2006, s.38(4).

Section 17(5) was examined in *R. v. Bow Street Metropolitan Stipendiary Magistrate, ex p. Government of the United States of America* [2000] 2 A.C. 216, HL (an extradition case): access by any person to any program or data held in a computer is unauthorised if that person is neither entitled to control, in the sense of authorising or forbidding, access to the program or data involved, nor has the consent of a person entitled to exercise such control. Authority to view data may not extend to authority to alter or copy that data. Authorised access to certain data cannot be construed as including authority to access other data of the same kind (*dicta* in *DPP v. Bignell* [1998] 1 Cr.App.R. 1, DC, *ante*, § 23–87, disapproved). **23–101**

The original subsection (8)(b) (modification is unauthorised if person making the modification "does not have consent to the modification" from any person entitled to determine whether modification should be made) was considered in *DPP v. Lennon*, 170 J.P. 532, DC (see also *ante*, § 23–89), where it was held that, although a computer owner is ordinarily to be taken to consent to the sending of e-mails to his computer, such consent is not unlimited and plainly does not cover e-mails which are not sent for the purpose of communication with the owner, but are sent for the purpose of interrupting the proper operation and use of his system; where many e-mails are sent, for example by way of a continuous "mail-bombing" program, the defendant's conduct is not to be judged on an e-mail by e-mail basis, but as a whole; (*obiter*) the mere sending of an e-mail purporting to come from someone other than its actual sender is not, however, necessarily to be treated as unauthorised if, for example, the e-mail is sent as a joke and without malicious intent.

CHAPTER 24

FIREARMS AND OFFENSIVE WEAPONS

I. FIREARMS

A. FIREARMS ACT 1968

(1) Introduction

Statutory framework

The possession and use of firearms are controlled by the *Firearms Acts* 1968 to 1997. **24–1**
These comprise seven statutes: the *Firearms Act* 1968, the *Firearms Act* 1982, the *Firearms (Amendment) Act* 1988, the *Firearms (Amendment) Act* 1992, the *Firearms (Amendment) Act* 1994, the *Firearms (Amendment) Act* 1997 and the *Firearms (Amendment) (No. 2) Act* 1997 (referred to in this chapter as "the 1968 Act", etc.; the two 1997 statutes are "the 1997 Act" and "the 1997 (No. 2) Act"). In this work, offences triable summarily only have been omitted or summarised.

Subordinate legislation

As from September 1, 1998, the *Firearms Rules* 1998 (S.I. 1998 No. 1941) (as **24–2**
amended by the *Firearms (Amendment) Rules* 2007 (S.I. 2007 No. 2605)) prescribe the forms to be used in connection with the grant of certificates and permits for the purposes of the *Firearms Acts* 1968 to 1988, and the registration of firearms dealers, and also the form of the register of transactions to be kept by such dealers.

The *Firearms Acts (Amendment) Regulations* 1992 (S.I. 1992 No. 2823), made under section 2(2) of the *European Communities Act* 1972, were brought into force on January 1, 1993, to implement Council Directive No. 91/477/EEC (the European Weapons Directive). The regulations amend the *Firearms Act* 1968 and the *Firearms (Amendment) Act* 1988 and, *inter alia*, create new offences relating to breaches of the Directive.

Prosecution and punishment of offences

For the prosecution and punishment of offences under the 1968 Act, see generally **24–2a**
post, § 24–82a.

(2) Offences relating to firearms certificates

Firearms Act 1968, s.1

Requirement of firearm certificate

1.—(1) Subject to any exemption under this Act, it is an offence for a person— **24–3**

(a) to have in his possession, or to purchase or acquire, a firearm to which this section applies without holding a firearm certificate in force at the time, or otherwise than as authorised by such a certificate;

(b) to have in his possession, or to purchase or acquire, any ammunition to which this section applies without holding a firearm certificate in force at the time, or, otherwise than as authorised by such a certificate, or in quantities in excess of those so authorised.

(2) [*Summary offence: failure to comply with condition on firearm certificate.*]

(3) This section applies to every firearm except—

(a) a shot gun within the meaning of this Act, that is to say a smooth-bore gun (not being an air gun) which—

(i) has a barrel not less than 24 inches in length and does not have any barrel with a bore exceeding 2 inches in diameter;

(ii) either has no magazine or has a non-detachable magazine incapable of holding more than two cartridges; and

(iii) is not a revolver gun; and

(b) an air weapon (that is to say, an air rifle, air gun or air pistol which does not fall within section 5(1) and which is not of a type declared by rules made by the Secretary of State under section 53 of this Act to be specially dangerous).

(3A) A gun which has been adapted to have such a magazine as is mentioned in subsection (3)(a)(ii) above shall not be regarded as falling within that provision unless the magazine bears a mark approved by the Secretary of State for denoting the fact and that mark has been made, and the adaptation has been certified in writing as having been carried out in a manner approved by him, either by one of the two companies mentioned in section 58(1) of this Act or by such other person as may be approved by him for that purpose.

(4) This section applies to any ammunition for a firearm, except the following articles, namely:—

(a) cartridges containing five or more shot, none of which exceeds .36 inch in diameter;

(b) ammunition for an air gun, air rifle or air pistol; and

(c) blank cartridges not more than one inch in diameter measured immediately in front of the rim or cannelure of the base of the cartridge.

[This section is printed as amended by the 1988 Act, s.2(2); and the *Anti-social Behaviour Act* 2003, s.39(2).]

The exemptions referred to above are contained in sections 7 to 13 and 15 of the 1968 Act (*post*, §§ 24–28 *et seq.*) and, by virtue of section 25(4) of the 1988 Act (*post*, § 24–105), sections 15 to 19 of, and the Schedule to, the 1988 Act: *post*, §§ 24–97 *et seq.*

For the meaning of "acquire" and "firearm certificate", see section 57(4); for "firearm", see section 57(1); for "ammunition", see section 57(2); for "length", see section 57(6)(a); for "revolver", see section 57(2B). Section 57 is set out in full with commentary *post*, §§ 24–85 *et seq.*

The two companies mentioned in section 58(1) (*post*, § 24–89) are the Society of the Mystery of Gunmakers of the City of London and the Birmingham proof house.

Class of offence and mode of trial

24–4 This offence is a class 3 offence, *ante*, § 2–17, and is triable either way: 1968 Act, s.51 and Sched. 6.

Sentence

24–5 On summary conviction, six months (increased to 12 months, as from a day to be appointed, by the *CJA* 2003, s.282(2) and (3), but not in relation to any offence committed before the date of commencement: *ibid.*, s.282(4)), or a fine of the prescribed sum, or both. On indictment, when committed in an aggravated form within the meaning of section 4(4) (*post*, § 24–16), seven years, or a fine, or both; otherwise, five years, or a fine, or both: 1968 Act, s.51 and Sched. 6.

For sentencing guidance, see *R. v. Avis* [1998] 1 Cr.App.R. 420, CA, *post*, § 24–82a.

For illustrative decisions, see CSP, B3–3.3A; but note the effect of *R. v. Clarke (T.)* [1997] 1 Cr.App.R.(S.) 323, CA, *post*, § 24–82a.

Possession

Section 1(1) creates absolute offences. In *R. v. Hussain*, 72 Cr.App.R. 143, CA (a case concerning s.1(1)(a)), the court held (applying *Warner v. Metropolitan Police Commr* [1969] 2 A.C. 256, HL, a drugs case) that if the prosecution prove that the defendant knowingly had in his possession an article which in fact was a firearm as defined in the 1968 Act (see s.57(1), *post*, § 24–85), then the offence is committed, and the defendant's ignorance that the article in his possession was a firearm for which a certificate was required is immaterial. *Hussain* was followed in *R. v. Waller* [1991] Crim.L.R. 381, CA (conviction upheld where defendant in possession of friend's bag did not realise it contained firearm as opposed to crowbar), and *R. v. Steele* [1993] Crim.L.R. 298, CA (defendant guilty even though he could not reasonably have been expected to know that bag contained firearm). In *R. v. Vann and Davis* [1996] Crim.L.R. 52, CA (see also *post*, § 24–59), it was held that this line of authority should not be re-opened even after having consulted Hansard. **24–6**

Accordingly, an honest and reasonable belief that a modern reproduction is an antique firearm (see s.58(2) of the 1968 Act, *post*, § 24–89), is no defence to a charge of possessing a firearm without a certificate contrary to section 1(1)(a): *R. v. Howells* [1977] Q.B. 614, 65 Cr.App.R. 86, CA. See further, § 17–15, *ante*.

The purpose of section 1 is to regulate and license not only those who keep firearms where they live but also those who have them under their control; for example, where an owner keeps his firearm(s) at the home of a relative for safe custody. An owner might not have physical possession of the firearms, but may still possess them for the purposes of section 1: *Sullivan v. Earl of Caithness* [1976] Q.B. 966, 62 Cr.App.R. 105, DC; *Hall v. Cotton and Treadwell* [1987] Q.B. 504, 83 Cr.App.R. 257, DC. In the latter case, the court held that the concept of possession embraced both proprietary and custodial possession, and so on the particular facts of that case (see *post*, § 24–88) both the owner and the temporary recipient of the shot guns were held to be in possession for the purposes of the Act.

See also *Woodage v. Moss* [1974] 1 W.L.R. 411, DC (*post*, § 24–29), where the defendant was held to be in possession of a revolver when he was in the process of delivering it to a firearms dealer as a favour for someone else.

Construction of certificate

The construction of a firearms certificate is a matter of law, not fact, and thus must be determined by a judge and not a jury: *R. v. Paul* [1999] Crim.L.R. 79, CA (see also *post*, §§ 24–15a, 24–87). **24–6a**

"Shot gun"

This is defined in section 57(4) (*post*, § 24–85) as having the meaning assigned to it by section 1(3)(a), *ante*. **24–7**

If a rifle with a barrel more than 24 inches long has its rifling removed so that the bore is smooth, it qualifies as a shot gun within the meaning of the Act and no longer requires a firearms certificate under section 1(1): *R. v. Hucklebridge*, 71 Cr.App.R. 171, CA.

If a rifle with a barrel less than 24 inches long is converted into a shot gun (or an air weapon), it remains a firearm for the purposes of section 1: 1988 Act, s.7(2), *post*, § 24–94 (but note the exception in s.7(3)).

"Air weapon"

This is defined in section 57(4) (*post*, § 24–85) as having the meaning assigned to it by section 1(3)(b), *ante*. On its true construction, paragraph (b) is not limited to air weapons which are also firearms (*i.e.* not limited to lethal air weapons: see s.57(1), *post*, § 24–85): *DPP v. Street*, *The Times*, January 23, 2004, DC. **24–8**

The *Firearms (Dangerous Air Weapons) Rules* 1969 (S.I. 1969 No. 47) and the *Firearms (Dangerous Air Weapons) (Amendment) Rules* 1993 (S.I. 1993 No. 1490) have been made under section 53 in pursuance of section 1(3)(b).

Firearms (Dangerous Air Weapons) Rules 1969 (S.I. 1969 No. 47), rr.2, 3

24–8a **2.**—(1) Subject to paragraph (2) below, rule 3 of these Rules applies to an air weapon (that is to say, an air rifle, air gun or air pistol)—

(a) which is capable of discharging a missile so that the missile has, on being discharged from the muzzle of the weapon, kinetic energy in excess, in the case of an air pistol, of 6ft. lb, or, in the case of an air weapon other than an air pistol, of 12ft. lb., or

(b) which is disguised as another object.

(2) Rule 3 of these Rules does not apply to a weapon which only falls within paragraph 1(a) above and which is designed for use only when submerged in water.

3. An air weapon to which this Rule applies is hereby declared to be specially dangerous.

[These rules are printed as amended by S.I. 1993 No. 1490. The effect of the 1993 Rules is to include, as specially dangerous, air weapons which have been disguised as other objects.]

Any reference to an air rifle, air pistol or an air gun in the *Firearms Acts* "shall include a reference to a rifle, pistol or gun powered by compressed carbon dioxide": 1997 Act, s.48.

Firearms Act 1968, s.2

Shotguns

24–9 **2.**—(1) Subject to any exemption under this Act, it is an offence for a person to have in his possession, or to purchase or acquire, a shot gun without holding a certificate under this Act authorising him to possess shot guns.

(2) [*Summary offence: failure to comply with condition of shot gun certificate.*]

The exemptions referred to above are contained in sections 7 to 13 and 15 of the 1968 Act (*post*, §§ 24–28 *et seq.*) and, by virtue of section 25(4) of the 1988 Act (*post*, § 24–105), sections 17 to 19 of, and the Schedule to, the 1988 Act: *post*, §§ 24–100 *et seq.*

For the meaning of "acquire" and "shot gun certificate", see section 57(4) (*post*, § 24–85); for "shot gun", see section 1(3)(a) (*ante*, § 24–3); for "possession", see *ante*, § 24–6.

Class of offence and mode of trial

24–10 This offence is a class 3 offence, *ante*, § 2–17, and is triable either way: 1968 Act, s.51 and Sched. 6.

Sentence

24–11 On summary conviction, six months (increased to 12 months, as from a day to be appointed, by the *CJA* 2003, s.282(2) and (3), but not in relation to any offence committed before the date of commencement: *ibid.*, s.282(4)), or a fine of the prescribed sum, or both. On indictment, five years, or a fine, or both: 1968 Act, s.51 and Sched. 6.

For sentencing guidance, see *R. v. Avis* [1998] 1 Cr.App.R. 420, CA, *post*, § 24–82a.

Firearms Act 1968, s.3

Dealing in firearms

24–12 **3.**—(1) A person commits an offence if, by way of trade or business, he—

(a) manufactures, sells, transfers, repairs, tests or proves any firearm or ammunition to which section 1 of this Act applies, or a shot gun;

(b) exposes for sale or transfer, or has in his possession for sale, transfer, repair, test or proof any such firearm or ammunition, or a shot gun, or

(c) sells or transfers an air weapon, exposes such a weapon for sale or transfer or has such a weapon in his possession for sale or transfer,

without being registered under this Act as a firearms dealer.

(2) It is an offence for a person to sell or transfer to any other person in the United Kingdom, other than a registered firearms dealer, any firearm or ammunition to which section 1 of this Act applies, or a shot gun, unless that other produces a firearm certificate authorising him to purchase or acquire it or, as the case may be, his shot gun certificate, or shows that he is by virtue of this Act entitled to purchase or acquire it without holding a certificate.

(3) It is an offence for a person to undertake the repair, test or proof of a firearm or ammunition to which section 1 of this Act applies, or of a shot gun, for any other person in the United Kingdom other than a registered firearms dealer as such unless that other produces or causes to be produced a firearm certificate authorising him to have possession of the firearm or ammunition or, as the case may be, his shot gun certificate, or shows that he is by virtue of this Act entitled to have possession of it without holding a certificate.

(4) Subsections (1) to (3) above have effect subject to any exemption under subsequent provisions of this Part of this Act.

(5) A person commits an offence if, with a view to purchasing or acquiring, or procuring the repair, test or proof of, any firearm or ammunition to which section 1 of this Act applies, or a shot gun, he produces a false certificate or a certificate in which any false entry has been made, or personates a person to whom a certificate has been granted, or knowingly or recklessly makes a statement false in any material particular.

(6) [*Summary offence relating to pawnbrokers.*]

[This section is printed as amended by the 1997 Act, s.52, and Sched. 2, para. 2(1); and the *VCRA* 2006, ss.31(1) and 65, and Sched. 5.]

The exemptions referred to above are, by virtue of section 3(4), contained in sections 7 to 13 and 15 of the 1968 Act (*post*, §§ 24–28 *et seq.*) and, by virtue of section 25(4) of the 1988 Act (*post*, §§ 24–105), sections 15 to 19 of, and the Schedule to, the 1988 Act (*post*, §§ 24–97 *et seq.*). See particularly sections 8(2) (*post*, § 24–29) and 9(2) and (4) (*post*, § 24–30).

For the meaning of "transfer", "registered", "firearms dealer" and "firearm certificate", see section 57(4); for "firearm", see section 57(1); for "ammunition", see section 57(2); for "shot gun", see section 1(3)(a) (*ante*, §§ 24–3 *et seq.*) and also, in relation to section 3(1), section 57(4); for "possession", see *ante*, § 24–6. Section 57 is set out in full, *post*, §§ 24–85 *et seq.*

As to the meaning of "sells", see *DPP v. Holmes*, *The Times*, April 7, 1988, DC, a **24–13**
case on the *Copyright Act* 1956, s.21(1)(b); as to "transfer", see *Hall v. Cotton and Treadwell* [1987] Q.B. 504, 83 Cr.App.R. 257, DC, *post*, § 24–88; as to subsection (2) generally, see *Wilson v. Coombe* [1989] 1 W.L.R. 78, DC.

Class of offence and mode of trial

These offences are class 3 offences, *ante*, § 2–17, and are triable either way: 1968 Act, **24–14**
s.51 and Sched. 6.

Sentence

On summary conviction, six months (increased to 12 months, as from a day to be ap- **24–15**
pointed, by the *CJA* 2003, s.282(2) and (3), but not in relation to any offence committed before the date of commencement: *ibid.*, s.282(4)), or a fine of the prescribed sum, or both. On indictment, five years, or a fine, or both: 1968 Act, s.51 and Sched. 6.

For sentencing guidance, see *R. v. Avis* [1998] 1 Cr.App.R. 420, CA, *post*, § 24–82a.

This offence is a lifestyle offence (*PCA* 2002, s.75, Sched. 2, para. 5(2), *ante*, § 5–657); accordingly, a person convicted under section 3 will be liable to a financial reporting order (*SOCPA* 2005, s.76, *ante*, § 5–886a).

Nature of offence

The offence under section 3(2) is an absolute offence in that the transferee's intended **24–15a**
use of the firearm and the transferor's understanding of that use are both irrelevant. The test is objective, namely whether the firearm in question corresponds with the description relied on in any certificate produced by the transferee: *R. v. Paul* [1999] Crim.L.R. 79, CA (see *ante*, § 24–6a, and *post*, § 24–87).

(3) Conversion of weapons

Firearms Act 1968, s.4

4.—(1) Subject to this section, it is an offence to shorten the barrel of a shot gun to a length **24–16**
less than 24 inches.

(2) It is not an offence under subsection (1) above for a registered firearms dealer to

shorten the barrel of a shot gun for the sole purpose of replacing a defective part of the barrel so as to produce a barrel not less than 24 inches in length.

(3) It is an offence for a person other than a registered firearms dealer to convert into a firearm anything which, though having the appearance of being a firearm, is so constructed as to be incapable of discharging any missile through its barrel.

(4) A person who commits an offence under section 1 of this Act by having in his possession, or purchasing or acquiring, a shot gun which has been shortened contrary to subsection (1) above or a firearm which has been converted as mentioned in subsection (3) above (whether by a registered firearms dealer or not), without holding a firearm certificate authorising him to have it in his possession, or to purchase or acquire it, shall be treated for the purposes of provisions of this Act relating to the punishment of offences as committing that offence in an aggravated form.

[Subs. (4) is printed as amended by the 1988 Act, s.23(1).]

For the meaning of "registered firearms dealer", "acquire" and "firearm certificate", see section 57(4); for "firearm", see section 57(1); for "shot gun", see section 1(3)(a) (*ante*, § 24–3); for "length", see section 57(6)(a); for "possession", see *ante*, § 24–6. Section 57 is set out in full, *post*, §§ 24–85 *et seq.*

For the offence of shortening the barrel of a smooth-bore gun, see the 1988 Act, s.6(1) (*post*, § 24–93).

Class of offence and mode of trial

24–17 These offences are class 3 offences, *ante*, § 2–17, and are triable either way: 1968 Act, s.51 and Sched. 6.

Sentence

24–18 On summary conviction for the offences created by section 4(1) and (3), six months (increased to 12 months, as from a day to be appointed, by the *CJA* 2003, s.282(2) and (3), but not in relation to any offence committed before the date of commencement: *ibid.*, s.282(4)), or a fine of the prescribed sum, or both. On indictment, seven years, or a fine, or both: 1968 Act, s.51 and Sched. 6.

For sentencing guidance, see *R. v. Avis* [1998] 1 Cr.App.R. 420, CA, *post*, § 24–82a.

(4) Prohibited weapons and ammunition

Firearms Act 1968, s.5

24–19 **5.**—(1) A person commits an offence if, without the authority of the Defence Council, he has in his possession, or purchases or acquires, or manufactures, sells or transfers—

(a) any firearm which is so designed or adapted that two or more missiles can be successively discharged without repeated pressure on the trigger;

(ab) any self-loading or pump-action rifled gun other than one which is chambered for .22 rim-fire cartridges;

(aba) any firearm which either has a barrel less than 30 centimetres in length or is less than 60 centimetres in length overall, other than an air weapon, a muzzle-loading gun or a firearm designed as signalling apparatus;

(ac) any self-loading or pump-action smooth-bore gun which is not an air weapon or chambered for .22 rim-fire cartridges and either has a barrel less than 24 inches in length or is less than 40 inches in length overall;

(ad) any smooth-bore revolver gun other than one which is chambered for 9mm rim-fire cartridges or a muzzle-loading gun;

(ae) any rocket launcher, or any mortar, for projecting a stabilised missile, other than a launcher or mortar designed for line-throwing or pyrotechnic purposes or as signalling apparatus;

(af) any air rifle, air gun or air pistol which uses, or is designed or adapted for use with, a self-contained gas cartridge system;

(b) any weapon of whatever description designed or adapted for the discharge of any noxious liquid, gas or other thing; and

(c) any cartridge with a bullet designed to explode on or immediately before impact, any ammunition containing or designed or adapted to contain any such noxious thing as is mentioned in paragraph (b) above and, if capable of being used with a firearm of any description, any grenade, bomb (or other like missile), or rocket or shell designed to explode as aforesaid.

(1A) Subject to section 5A of this Act, a person commits an offence if, without the authority of the Secretary of State, he has in his possession, or purchases or acquires, or sells or transfers— **24–20**

(a) any firearm which is disguised as another object;

(b) any rocket or ammunition not falling within paragraph (c) of subsection (1) of this section which consists in or incorporates a missile designed to explode on or immediately before impact and is for military use;

(c) any launcher or other projecting apparatus not falling with paragraph (ae) of that subsection which is designed to be used with any rocket or ammunition falling within paragraph (b) above or with ammunition which would fall within that paragraph but for its being ammunition falling within paragraph (c) of that subsection;

(d) any ammunition for military use which consists in or incorporates a missile designed so that a substance contained in the missile will ignite on or immediately before impact;

(e) any ammunition for military use which consists in or incorporates a missile designed, on account of its having a jacket and hard-core, to penetrate armour plating, armour screening or body armour;

(f) any ammunition which incorporates a missile designed or adapted to expand on impact;

(g) anything which is designed to be projected as a missile from any weapon and is designed to be, or has been, incorporated in—

(i) any ammunition falling within any of the preceding paragraphs; or

(ii) any ammunition which would fall within any of those paragraphs but for its being specified in subsection (1) of this section.

(2) The weapons and ammunition specified in subsections (1) and (1A) of this section (including, in the case of ammunition, any missiles falling within subsection (1A)(g) of this section) are referred to in this Act as "prohibited weapons" and "prohibited ammunition" respectively.

(3)–(6) [*Not printed.*]

(7) For the purposes of this section and section 5A of this Act—

(a) any rocket or ammunition which is designed to be capable of being used with a military weapon shall be taken to be for military use;

(b) references to a missile designed so that a substance contained in the missile will ignite or immediately before impact include references to any missile containing a substance that ignites on exposure to air; and

(c) references to a missile's expanding on impact include references to its deforming in any predictable manner on or immediately after impact.

(8) For the purposes of subsection (1)(aba) and (ac) above, any detachable, folding, retractable or other movable butt-stock shall be disregarded in measuring the length of any firearm.

(9) Any reference in this section to a muzzle-loading gun is a reference to a gun which is designed to be loaded at the muzzle end of the barrel or chamber with a loose charge and a separate ball (or other missile).

[This section is printed as amended and repealed in part by the 1988 Act, s.1(2), (3); the *Firearms Acts (Amendment) Regulations* 1992 (S.I. 1992 No. 2823), reg. 3; the 1997 Act, ss.1, 9 and 52, and Sched. 3, although the amendment effected by section 1(3) of that Act (substituting "rifled gun" for "rifle" in subs. (1)(ab)) does not have effect in relation to weapons prohibited by section 5(1)(aba) (*Firearms (Amendment) Act 1997 (Commencement) (No. 2) Order* 1997 (S.I. 1997 No. 1535), art. 5); the 1997 (No. 2) Act, ss.1 and 2(7) and Sched.; and the *Anti-social Behaviour Act* 2003, s.39(3) (insertion of subs. (1)(af)—in force with effect from January 20, 2004, in so far as it relates to the purchase, acquisition, manufacture, sale or transfer of the prohibited weapon, and from April 30, 2004, for all other purposes (*Anti-Social Behaviour Act 2003 (Commencement No. 1 and Transitional Provisions) Order* 2003 (S.I. 2003 No. 3300)), but see *post*, § 24–20a).]

The insertion of section 5(1)(af), *ante*, into the 1968 Act, is subject to the 2003 Act, **24–20a** s.39(4) and (5) (in force as of January 20, 2004 (S.I. 2003 No. 3300, *ante*)). As to the transitional regime, see *R. v. Mehmet* [2006] 1 Cr.App.R.(S.) 75, CA, where it appears that the effect of subsections (4) and (5) may have been overlooked.

Anti-social Behaviour Act 2003, s.39(4), (5)

24–20b (4) If at the time when subsection (3) comes into force a person has in his possession an air rifle, air gun or air pistol of the kind described in section 5(1)(af) of the *Firearms Act* 1968 (inserted by subsection (3) above)—

(a) section 5(1) of that Act shall not prevent the person's continued possession of the air rifle, air gun or air pistol,

(b) section 1 of that Act shall apply, and

(c) a chief officer of police may not refuse to grant or renew, and may not revoke or partially revoke, a firearm certificate under Part II of that Act on the ground that the person does not have a good reason for having the air rifle, air gun or air pistol in his possession.

(5) But subsection (4)(a) to (c) shall not apply to possession in the circumstances described in section 8 of that Act (authorised dealing).

24–21 For the meaning of "acquire", "rifle" and "transfer", see section 57(4); for "firearm", see section 57(1); for "self-loading" and "pump-action", see section 57(2A); for "ammunition", see section 57(2); for "length", see section 57(6)(a); for "revolver", see section 57(2B); for "possession", see *ante*, § 24–6; for "sells", see *ante*, § 24–13. Section 57 is set out in full, *post*, §§ 24–85 *et seq*.

Conversion of a weapon described in section 5(1) or (1A) into a different kind of weapon does not affect its classification: 1988 Act, s.7 (*post*, § 24–94).

By the *Transfer of Functions (Prohibited Weapons) Order* 1968 (S.I. 1968 No. 1200) the functions of the Defence Council under sections 5 and 12(1) were transferred to the Secretary of State, and those provisions and sections 31, 34(3) and 38(2) and Schedule 6, Pt I, are to have effect as if for any reference to the Defence Council there were substituted a reference to the Secretary of State.

By section 5(3), an authority given by the Secretary of State under this section must be in writing and may be subject to conditions imposed under subsection (4). Subsection (6) allows the Secretary of State to revoke the authority. Subsections (5) and (6) create summary offences.

Class of offence and mode of trial

24–22 As from January 22, 2004 (*Criminal Justice Act 2003 (Commencement No. 2 and Saving Provisions) Order* 2004 (S.I. 2004 No. 81)), the offences under section 5(1)(a), (ab), (aba), (ac), (ad), (ae), (af) and (c), and section 5(1A)(a), are triable only on indictment, and are class 3 offences, *ante*, § 2–17; the offences under section 5(1)(b) and section 5(1A)(b), (c), (d), (e), (f) and (g) are triable either way and are class 3 offences, *ante*, § 2–17: 1968 Act, s.51, and Sched. 6, as amended by the *CJA* 2003, s.288.

Sentence

24–23 Offences contrary to section 5(1) and (1A) attract a maximum sentence on indictment of 10 years' imprisonment: s.51, and Sched. 6. Offences contrary to section 5(1)(a), (ab), (aba), (ac), (ad), (ae), (af) and (c), and section 5(1A)(a), if committed on or after January 22, 2004, attract the minimum sentence provisions in section 51A of the 1968 Act (*ante*, § 5–258) if, but only if, the indictment has a specific count alleging the relevant offence under section 5: *Att.-Gen.'s Reference (No. 114 of 2004) (R. v. McDowell)* [2005] 2 Cr.App.R.(S.) 6, CA. The remaining offences, *i.e.* under section 5(1)(b) and section 5(1A)(b)–(g), attract a maximum sentence, on summary conviction, of six months' imprisonment (increased to 12 months, as from a day to be appointed, by the *CJA* 2003, s.282(2) and (3), but not in relation to any offence committed before the date of commencement: *ibid.*, s.282(4)), or a fine not exceeding the statutory maximum, or both, and on indictment, 10 years' imprisonment, or a fine, or both: s.51, and Sched. 6.

For sentencing guidance, see *R. v. Avis* [1998] 1 Cr.App.R. 420, CA, *post* § 24–82a.

Mens rea

24–24 Section 5 creates offences of strict liability: *R. v. Bradish* [1990] Q.B. 981, 90 Cr.App.R. 271, CA (no defence where defendant in possession of CS gas canister did not know or suspect that it was a prohibited weapon); and *R. v. Deyemi and Edwards* [2008] 1 Cr.App.R. 25, CA. See *ante*, § 24–6, for authorities on possession.

Prohibited weapon

The component parts of a prohibited weapon are themselves prohibited weapons: *R. v. Clarke (F.)*, 82 Cr.App.R. 308, CA, and see section 57(1)(b) (*post*, § 24–85). A sub-machine gun therefore comes within section 5(1)(a) even though it is missing an essential component such as a trigger. **24–25**

Section 5(1)(a) does not import any intention on the part of the designer or adapter. The correct test is the weapon's objective capability: *R. v. Law* [1999] Crim.L.R. 837, CA (gun capable of burst fire, albeit only in expert hands, prohibited).

A hand-held device (sometimes called a stun gun) designed to stun a victim by way of electric shock is a prohibited weapon within section 5(1)(b) (*Flack v. Baldry*, 87 Cr.App.R. 130, HL), even if it does not work properly because of some unknown fault (*Brown v. DPP*, *The Times*, March 27, 1992, DC).

A "Fairy Liquid" bottle filled with hydrochloric acid is not a weapon designed or adapted for the discharge of any noxious liquid within the meaning of section 5(1)(b): *R. v. Formosa and Upton*, 92 Cr.App.R. 11, CA. The word "adapted" means that the object itself must be altered for the use in question, whereas the addition of acid does not change the bottle in any way. See also *R. v. Titus* [1971] Crim.L.R. 279, CCC (H.H. Judge Price Q.C.) (water pistol filled with ammonia outwith s.5(1)(b)).

Special exemptions from prohibition of small firearms

The general prohibition of small firearms contained in section 5(1)(aba) of the 1968 Act (*ante*, § 24–19) is, by section 1(7) of the 1997 Act, subject to the exemptions contained in sections 2 to 8 of the 1997 Act. By section 1(8) of the 1997 Act, any reference in these sections to a firearms certificate shall include a reference to a visitor's firearm permit. **24–25a**

Firearms (Amendment) Act 1997, ss.2–8

Slaughtering instruments

2. The authority of the Secretary of State is not required by virtue of subsection (1)(aba) of section 5 of the 1968 Act— **24–25b**

(a) for a person to have in his possession, or to purchase or acquire, or to sell or transfer, a slaughtering instrument if he is authorised by a firearm certificate to have the instrument in his possession, or to purchase or acquire it;

(b) for a person to have a slaughtering instrument in his possession if he is entitled, under section 10 of the 1968 Act, to have it in his possession without a firearm certificate.

Firearms used for humane killing of animals

3. The authority of the Secretary of State is not required by virtue of subsection (1)(aba) of section 5 of the 1968 Act for a person to have in his possession, or to purchase or acquire, or to sell or transfer, a firearm if he is authorised by a firearm certificate to have the firearm in his possession, or to purchase or acquire it, subject to a condition that it is only for use in connection with the humane killing of animals. **24–25c**

Shot pistols used for killing vermin

4.—(1) The authority of the Secretary of State is not required by virtue of subsection (1)(aba) of section 5 of the 1968 Act for a person to have in his possession, or to purchase or acquire, or to sell or transfer, a shot pistol if he is authorised by a firearm certificate to have the shot pistol in his possession, or to purchase or acquire it, subject to a condition that it is only for use in connection with the shooting of vermin. **24–25d**

(2) For the purposes of this section, "shot pistol" means a smooth-bored gun which is chambered for .410 cartridges or 9mm rim-fire cartridges.

Races at athletic meetings

5. The authority of the Secretary of State is not required by virtue of subsection (1)(aba) of section 5 of the 1968 Act— **24–25e**

(a) for a person to have a firearm in his possession at an athletic meeting for the purpose of starting races at that meeting; or

(b) for a person to have in his possession, or to purchase or acquire, or to sell or transfer, a firearm if he is authorised by a firearm certificate to have the firearm in his possession, or to purchase or acquire it, subject to a condition that it is only for use in connection with starting races at athletic meetings.

Trophies of war

24–25f **6.** The authority of the Secretary of State is not required by virtue of subsection (1)(aba) of section 5 of the 1968 Act for a person to have in his possession a firearm which was acquired as a trophy of war before 1st January 1946 if he is authorised by a firearm certificate to have it in his possession.

Firearms of historic interest

24–25g **7.**—(1) The authority of the Secretary of State is not required by virtue of subsection (1)(aba) of section 5 of the 1968 Act for a person to have in his possession, or to purchase or acquire, or to sell or transfer, a firearm which—

(a) was manufactured before 1st January 1919; and

(b) is of a description specified under subsection (2) below,

if he is authorised by a firearm certificate to have the firearm in his possession, or to purchase or acquire it, subject to a condition that he does so only for the purpose of its being kept or exhibited as part of a collection.

(2) The Secretary of State may by order made by statutory instrument specify a description of firearm for the purposes of subsection (1) above if it appears to him that—

(a) firearms of that description were manufactured before 1st January 1919; and

(b) ammunition for firearms of that type is not readily available.

(3) The authority of the Secretary of State is not required by virtue of subsection (1)(aba) of section 5 of the 1968 Act for a person to have in his possession, or to purchase or acquire, or to sell or transfer, a firearm which—

(a) is of particular rarity, aesthetic quality or technical interest, or

(b) is of historical importance,

if he is authorised by a firearm certificate to have the firearm in his possession subject to a condition requiring it to be kept and used only at a place designated for the purposes of this subsection by the Secretary of State.

(4) This section has effect without prejudice to section 58(2) of the 1968 Act (antique firearms).

The *Firearms (Amendment) Act 1997 (Firearms of Historic Interest) Order* 1997 (S.I. 1997 No. 1537) has been made under section 7(2).

Weapons and ammunition used for treating animals

24–25h **8.** The authority of the Secretary of State is not required by virtue of subsection (1)(aba), (b) or (c) of section 5 of the 1968 Act for a person to have in his possession, or to purchase or acquire, or to sell or transfer, any firearm, weapon or ammunition designed or adapted for the purpose of tranquillising or otherwise treating any animal, if he is authorised by a firearm certificate to possess, or to purchase or acquire, the firearm, weapon or ammunition subject to a condition restricting its use to use in connection with the treatment of animals.

Firearms Act 1968, s.5A

Exemptions from requirement of authority under s.5

24–26 **5A.**—(1) Subject to subsection (2) below, the authority of the Secretary of State shall not be required by virtue of subsection (1A) of section 5 of this Act for any person to have in his possession, or to purchase, acquire, sell or transfer, any prohibited weapon or ammunition if he is authorised by a certificate under this Act to possess, purchase or acquire that weapon or ammunition subject to a condition that he does so only for the purpose of its being kept or exhibited as part of a collection.

(2) No sale or transfer may be made under subsection (1) above except to a person who—

(a) produces the authority of the Secretary of State under section 5 of this Act for his purchase or acquisition; or

(b) shows that he is, under this section or a licence under the Schedule to the *Firearms (Amendment) Act* 1988 (museums etc.), entitled to make the purchase or acquisition without the authority of the Secretary of State.

(3) The authority of the Secretary of State shall not be required by virtue of subsection (1A) of section 5 of this Act for any person to have in his possession, or to purchase or

acquire, any prohibited weapon or ammunition if his possession, purchase or acquisition is exclusively in connection with the carrying on of activities in respect of which—

(a) that person; or

(b) the person on whose behalf he has possession, or makes the purchase or acquisition,

is recognised, for the purposes of the law of another member State relating to firearms, as a collector of firearms or a body concerned in the cultural or historical aspects of weapons.

(4) The authority of the Secretary of State shall not be required by virtue of subsection (1A) of section 5 of this Act for any person to have in his possession, or to purchase or acquire, or to sell or transfer, any expanding ammunition or the missile for any such ammunition if—

(a) he is authorised by a firearm certificate or visitor's firearm permit to possess, or purchase or acquire, any expanding ammunition; and

(b) the certificate or permit is subject to a condition restricting the use of any expanding ammunition to use in connection with any one or more of the following, namely—

(i) the lawful shooting of deer;

(ii) the shooting of vermin or, in the course of carrying on activities in connection with the management of any estate, other wildlife;

(iii) the humane killing of animals;

(iv) the shooting of animals for the protection of other animals or humans.

(5) The authority of the Secretary of State shall not be required by virtue of subsection (1A) of section 5 of this Act for any person to have in his possession any expanding ammunition or the missile for any such ammunition if—

(a) he is entitled, under section 10 of this Act, to have a slaughtering instrument and the ammunition for it in his possession; and

(b) the ammunition or missile in question is designed to be capable of being used with a slaughtering instrument.

(6) The authority of the Secretary of State shall not be required by virtue of subsection (1A) of section 5 of this Act for the sale or transfer of any expanding ammunition or the missile for any such ammunition to any person who produces a certificate by virtue of which he is authorised under subsection (4) above to purchase or acquire it without the authority of the Secretary of State.

(7) The authority of the Secretary of State shall not be required by virtue of subsection (1A) of section 5 of this Act for a person carrying on the business of a firearms dealer, or any servant of his, to have in his possession, or to purchase, acquire, sell or transfer, any expanding ammunition or the missile for any such ammunition in the ordinary course of that business.

(8) In this section—

(a) references to expanding ammunition are references to any ammunition which incorporates a missile which is designed to expand on impact; and

(b) references to the missile for any such ammunition are references to anything which, in relation to any such ammunition, falls within section 5(1A)(g) of this Act.

[This section was inserted by the *Firearms Acts (Amendment) Regulations* 1992 (S.I. 1992 No. 2823), reg. 3. It is printed as amended by the 1997 Act, ss.10 and 52 and Sched. 3.]

For definitions, see *ante*, § 24–21.

In *Lacey v. Commr of Police for the Metropolitan Police* [2000] Crim.L.R. 853, DC, it was held that section 5A(4) should be construed as follows: the word "any", as in "any expanding ammunition" in paragraphs (a) and (b), means "such"; and "the management of any estate" in paragraph (b)(ii) relates to estates in Great Britain only. **24–27**

(5) Special exemptions from sections 1 to 5

Firearms Act 1968, ss.7, 8

Police permit

7.—(1) A person who has obtained from the chief officer of police for the area in which he resides a permit for the purpose in the prescribed form may, without holding a certificate under this Act, have in his possession a firearm and ammunition in accordance with the terms of the permit. **24–28**

(2) [*Summary offence: false statements.*]

Authorised dealing with firearms

24–29 **8.**—(1) A person carrying on the business of a firearms dealer and registered as such under this Act, or a servant of such a person may, without holding a certificate, have in his possession, or purchase or acquire, a firearm or ammunition in the ordinary course of that business.

(1A) Subsection (1) above applies to the possession, purchase or acquisition of a firearm or ammunition in the ordinary course of the business of a firearms dealer notwithstanding that the firearm or ammunition is in the possession of, or purchased or acquired by, the dealer or his servant at a place which is not a place of business of the dealer or which he has not registered as a place of business under section 33 or 37 of this Act.

(2) It is not an offence under section 3(2) of this Act for a person—

(a) to part with the possession of any firearm or ammunition, otherwise than in pursuance of a contract of sale or hire or by way of gift or loan, to a person who shows that he is by virtue of this Act entitled to have possession of the firearm or ammunition without holding a certificate; or

(b) to return to another person a shot gun which he has lawfully undertaken to repair, test or prove for the other.

[Subs. (1A) was inserted by the 1997 Act, s.42(1).]

In *R. v. Bull*, 99 Cr.App.R. 193 at 202, CA, it was held that the special exemption in section 8 applies to:

"(i) a person carrying on the business of a firearms dealer;

(ii) who is registered as such under section 33 [see *post*, § 24–72];

(iii) who in order to be registered under section 33 has furnished the chief officer of police with the prescribed particulars (including particulars of *every place of business* at which he proposes to carry on business in the area as a firearms dealer);

(iv) who has in his possession or purchases or acquires a firearm or ammunition in the ordinary course of *that* business."

The court went on to say that "the special exemption does not apply to the possession of a firearm or ammunition at a place of business whose address has not been furnished in accordance with (iii) above". The conviction of a firearms dealer who kept ammunition in a barn which he had not registered as a place of business was accordingly upheld.

See also *Woodage v. Moss* [1974] 1 W.L.R. 411, DC (*ante*, § 24–6)—master and servant relationship held not to have existed where the defendant was taking the firearm to a dealer at the latter's request without obligation or remuneration. However, the defendant might have been acquitted if he had argued necessity: see *R. v. Pommell* [1995] 2 Cr.App.R. 607, CA.

Firearms Act 1968, ss.9–13

Carriers, auctioneers, etc.

24–30 **9.**—(1) A person carrying on the business of an auctioneer, carrier or warehouseman, or a servant of such a person, may, without holding a certificate, have in his possession a firearm or ammunition in the ordinary course of that business.

(2) It is not an offence under section 3(1) of this Act for an auctioneer to sell by auction, expose for sale by auction or have in his possession for sale by auction a firearm or ammunition without being registered as a firearms dealer, if he has obtained from the chief officer of police for the area in which the auction is held a permit for that purpose in the prescribed form and complies with the terms of the permit.

(3) [*Summary offence: false statement.*]

(4) It is not an offence under section 3(2) of this Act for a carrier or warehouseman, or a servant of a carrier or warehouseman, to deliver any firearm or ammunition in the ordinary course of his business or employment as such.

Slaughter of animals

24–31 **10.**—(1) A person licensed under the *Welfare of Animals (Slaughter or Killing) Regulations* 1995 to slaughter horses, cattle, sheep, swine or goats may, without holding a certificate, have in his possession a slaughtering instrument and ammunition therefor in any slaughterhouse or knacker's yard in which he is employed.

(2) The proprietor of a slaughterhouse or knacker's yard or a person appointed by him

to take charge of slaughtering instruments and ammunition therefore for the purpose of storing them in safe custody at that slaughterhouse or knacker's yard may, without holding a certificate, have in his possession a slaughtering instrument or ammunition therefor for that purpose.

[This section is printed as amended by the *Slaughterhouses Act* 1974, Sched. 3; the *Slaughter of Animals (Scotland) Act* 1980, Sched. 1; and the *Welfare of Animals (Slaughter or Killing) Regulations* 1995 (S.I. 1995 No. 731), reg. 28(2) and Sched. 14, para. 1.]

Sports, athletics and other approved activities

11.—(1) A person carrying a firearm or ammunition belonging to another person holding a certificate under this Act may, without himself holding such a certificate, have in his possession that firearm or ammunition under instructions from and for the use of, that other person for sporting purposes only. **24–32**

(2) A person may, without holding a certificate, have a firearm in his possession at an athletic meeting for the purpose of starting races at that meeting.

(3) [*Repealed by* Armed Forces Act *1996, s.35(2) and Sched. 7, Pt III.*]

(4) A person conducting or carrying on a miniature rifle range (whether for a rifle club or otherwise) or shooting gallery at which no firearms are used other than air weapons or miniature rifles not exceeding ·23 inch calibre may, without holding a certificate, have in his possession, or purchase or acquire, such miniature rifles and ammunition suitable therefor; and any person may, without holding a certificate, use any such rifle and ammunition at such a range or gallery.

(5) A person may, without holding a shot gun certificate, borrow a shot gun from the occupier of private premises and use it on those premises in the occupier's presence.

(6) A person may, without holding a shot gun certificate, use a shot gun at a time and place approved for shooting at artificial targets by the chief officer of police for the area in which that place is situated.

[This section is printed as amended by the 1988 Act, s.15(7).]

Theatre and cinema

12.—(1) A person taking part in a theatrical performance or a rehearsal thereof, or in the production of a cinematography film, may, without holding a certificate, have a firearm in his possession during and for the purpose of the performance, rehearsal or production. **24–33**

(2) Where the Defence Council are satisfied, on the application of a person in charge of a theatrical performance, a rehearsal of such a performance or the production of a cinematography film, that a prohibited weapon is required for the purpose of the performance, rehearsal or production, they may under section 5 of this Act, if they think fit, not only authorise that person to have possession of the weapon but also authorise such other persons as he may select to have possession of it while taking part in the performance, rehearsal or production.

[This section is printed as amended by the 1988 Act, s.23(2).]

For "Defence Council", read "Secretary of State": see *ante*, § 24–21.

Equipment for ships and aircraft

13.—(1) A person may, without holding a certificate— **24–34**

(a) have in his possession a firearm or ammunition on board a ship, or a signalling apparatus or ammunition therefor on board an aircraft or at an aerodrome, as part of the equipment of the ship, aircraft or aerodrome;

(b) remove a signalling apparatus or ammunition therefor, being part of the equipment of an aircraft, from one aircraft to another at an aerodrome, or from or to an aircraft at an aerodrome to or from a place appointed for the storage thereof in safe custody at that aerodrome, and keep any such apparatus or ammunition at such a place; and

(c) if he has obtained from a constable a permit for the purpose in the prescribed form, remove a firearm from or to a ship, or a signalling apparatus from or to an aircraft or aerodrome, to or from such place and for such purpose as may be specified in the permit.

(2) [*Summary offence relating to procuring permit.*]

[This section is printed as amended by the 1988 Act, s.23(3).]

References in whatever terms in the 1968 Act to ships, vessels, or boats or activities or places connected therewith, are extended to include hovercraft or activities or places connected with hovercraft by the *Hovercraft (Application of Enactments) Order* 1972 (S.I. 1972 No. 971).

Section 14 was repealed by the 1988 Act, s.23(8). See now section 17 of the 1988 Act, dealing with visitors' permits, *post*, §§ 24–100 *et seq*.

Firearms Act 1968, s.15

Holder of Northern Ireland certificate

24–35 **15.** Section 2(1) of this Act does not apply to a person holding a firearm certificate issued in Northern Ireland authorising him to possess a shot gun.

(6) Prevention of crime and preservation of public safety

(a) *Possession with intent to endanger life*

Firearms Act 1968, s.16

24–36 **16.** It is an offence for a person to have in his possession any firearm or ammunition with intent by means thereof to endanger life ... or to enable another person by means thereof to endanger life ..., whether any injury ... has been caused or not.

[This section is printed as repealed in part by the *Criminal Damage Act* 1971, s.11, and Sched., Pt I.]

For the meaning of "firearm", see section 57(1); for "ammunition", see section 57(2); for "possession", see *ante*, § 24–6. Section 57 is set out in full, *post*, §§ 24–85 *et seq*.

As to adding a firearms count to an indictment charging other offences, see *post*, § 24–49.

Class of offence and mode of trial

24–37 This offence is a class 3 offence, *ante*, § 2–17, and is triable on indictment only: 1968 Act, s.51 and Sched. 6.

Sentence

24–38 On indictment, life imprisonment, or a fine, or both: 1968 Act, s.51 and Sched. 6.

As to offences under this section committed on or after April 6, 2007, in relation to certain firearms or ammunition, being subject to a minimum sentence, see section 51A of the 1968 Act (*ante*, § 5–258).

This offence is a "specified violent offence" within Chapter 5 of Part 12 of the *CJA* 2003 (life sentences, sentences for public protection and extended sentences): see s.224, and Sched. 15, *ante*, §§ 5–292, 5–299.

For sentencing guidance, see *R. v. Avis* [1998] 1 Cr.App.R. 420, CA, *post*, § 24–82a. In a contested case, simple possession of a firearm, together with ammunition, with intent to endanger life, merits a sentence of between seven and eight years: *Att.-Gen.'s References (Nos. 58–66 of 2002)* (2003) 147 S.J. 296, CA, following *Att.-Gen.'s Reference (No. 49 of 1998) (R. v. Chevelleau)* [1999] 1 Cr.App.R.(S.) 396, CA, and *Att.-Gen.'s Reference (No. 2 of 2000) (R. v. Hinds)* [2001] 1 Cr.App.R.(S.) 27, CA.

For sentencing practice on conviction of other offences, see *post*, § 24–49. For illustrative decisions, see CSP, B3–3.3D; but note the effect of *R. v. Clarke (T.)* [1997] 1 Cr.App.R.(S.) 323, CA, *post*, § 24–82a.

Ingredients

24–38a The mischief at which section 16 is aimed is that of a person possessing a firearm ready for use, if and when occasion arises, in a manner which endangers life. The prosecution are not required to prove an immediate or unconditional intention to endanger life: *R. v. Bentham* [1973] Q.B. 357, 56 Cr.App.R. 618, CA.

A charge under the first limb of section 16 requires proof of two elements: (a) possession of a firearm in the United Kingdom, and (b) at the time of possession, an intent by means thereof to endanger life. The offence is not limited to an intention to endanger life in the United Kingdom: *R. v. El-Hakkaoui*, 60 Cr.App.R. 281, CA.

It was decided at first instance that the provision only applies to the life of another: *R. v. Norton* [1977] Crim.L.R. 478, Crown Court at Norwich (Gibson J.). It is a defence to show that the possession with intent to endanger life had a lawful purpose, *i.e.* self-defence, but only where the defendant fears immediate attack and has not armed himself before he is in fear: *R. v. Georgiades*, 89 Cr.App.R. 206, CA; and *R. v. Salih* [2008] 2 All.E.R. 319, CA.

As to intent, see *R. v. Brown and Ciarla* [1995] Crim.L.R. 328, CA. What is required is an intention to behave in such a way as will, in fact, to the defendant's knowledge, endanger life. An intention to kill is not necessary (*dicta* in *R. v. East* [1990] Crim.L.R. 413, CA, disapproved).

The second limb of section 16 ("... to enable another person by means thereof to endanger life ...") was considered in *R. v. Jones (I. F.)* [1997] 1 Cr.App.R. 46, CA. To "enable" means more than "to give the opportunity", because otherwise the offence would almost be one of strict liability. The section requires proof that the possessor intends life to be endangered, although it is unnecessary to prove an immediate or unconditional intent that life should be endangered. It is sufficient if the intent is that the firearm or ammunition should be used in a manner which endangers life as and when the occasion requires. The trial judge wrongly gave the jury the impression that the offence was made out if the appellants were in possession of firearms intending to supply them to persons who were in fact criminals.

(b) *Possession of firearm with intent to cause fear of violence*

Firearms Act 1968, s.16A

16A. It is an offence for a person to have in his possession any firearm or imitation firearm with intent— **24–39**

(a) by means thereof to cause, or

(b) to enable another person by means thereof to cause,

any person to believe that unlawful violence will be used against him or another person.

[This section was inserted by the 1994 Act, s.1(1).]

For the meaning of "firearm", see section 57(1); for "imitation firearm", see section 57(4), and *post*, § 24–87; for "possession", see *ante*, § 24–6. Section 57 is set out in full, *post*, §§ 24–85 *et seq.*

As to adding a firearms count to an indictment charging other offences, see *post*, § 24–49.

Class of offence and mode of trial

This offence is a class 3 offence, *ante*, § 2–17, and is triable on indictment only: 1968 Act, s.51 and Sched. 6. **24–40**

Sentence

On indictment, 10 years, or a fine, or both: 1968 Act, s.51 and Sched. 6. **24–41**

As to offences under this section committed on or after April 6, 2007, in relation to certain firearms or ammunition, being subject to a minimum sentence, see section 51A of the 1968 Act (*ante*, § 5–258).

This offence is a "specified violent offence" within Chapter 5 of Part 12 of the *CJA* 2003 (life sentences, sentences for public protection and extended sentences): see s.224, and Sched. 15, *ante*, §§ 5–292, 5–299.

For sentencing guidance, see *R. v. Avis* [1998] 1 Cr.App.R. 420, CA, *post*, § 24–82a. For illustrative decisions, see CSP, B3–3.3E.

(c) *Use of firearms to resist arrest*

Firearms Act 1968, s.17

17.—(1) It is an offence for a person to make or attempt to make any use whatsoever of a firearm or imitation firearm with intent to resist or prevent the lawful arrest or detention of himself or another person. **24–42**

(2) If a person, at the time of his committing or being arrested for an offence specified

in Schedule 1 to this Act has in his possession a firearm or imitation firearm, he shall be guilty of an offence under this subsection unless he shows that he had it in his possession for a lawful object.

(3) [*Repealed by* Theft Act *1968, s.33(3) and Sched. 3.*]

(4) For purposes of this section, the definition of "firearm" in section 57(1) of this Act shall apply without paragraphs (b) and (c) of that subsection, and "imitation firearm" shall be construed accordingly.

For the purposes of this section, "imitation firearm" is to be construed as provided by subsection (4) and is defined in section 57(4), *post*, § 24–85.

Firearms Act 1968, Sched. 1

SCHEDULE 1

OFFENCES TO WHICH SECTION 17(2) APPLIES

24–43 1. Offences under section 1 of the *Criminal Damage Act* 1971.

2. Offences under any of the following provisions of the *Offences against the Person Act* 1861:

sections 20 to 22 (inflicting bodily injury; garrotting; criminal use of stupefying drugs);

section 30 (laying explosive to building etc.);

section 32 (endangering railway passengers by tampering with track);

section 38 (assault with intent to commit felony or resist arrest);

section 47 (criminal assaults).

2A. Offences under Part I of the *Child Abduction Act* 1984 (abduction of children).

3. [*Repealed by Schedule (Pt II) to the* Criminal Attempts Act *1981.*]

4. Theft, robbery, burglary, blackmail and any offence under section 12(1) of the *Theft Act* 1968 (taking of motor vehicle or other conveyance without owner's consent).

5. Offences under section 89(1) of the *Police Act* 1996 or section 41 of the *Police (Scotland) Act* 1967 (assaulting constable in execution of his duty).

5A. An offence under section 90(1) of the *Criminal Justice Act* 1991 (assaulting prison custody officer).

5B. An offence under section 13(1) of the *Criminal Justice and Public Order Act* 1994 (assaulting secure training centre custody officer).

[5C. An offence under paragraph 4 of Schedule 11 to the *Immigration and Asylum Act* 1999 (assaulting a detainee custody officer).]

6. Offences under any of the following provisions of the *Sexual Offences Act* 2003—

(a) section 1 (rape);

(b) section 2 (assault by penetration);

(c) section 4 (causing a person to engage in sexual activity without consent), where the activity caused involved penetration within subsection (4)(a) to (d) of that section;

(d) section 5 (rape of a child under 13);

(e) section 6 (assault of a child under 13 by penetration);

(f) section 8 (causing or inciting a child under 13 to engage in sexual activity), where an activity involving penetration within subsection (3)(a) to (d) of that section was caused;

(g) section 30 (sexual activity with a person with a mental disorder impeding choice), where the touching involved penetration within subsection (3)(a) to (d) of that section;

(h) section 31 (causing or inciting a person, with a mental disorder impeding choice, to engage in sexual activity), where an activity involving penetration within subsection (3)(a) to (d) of that section was caused.

7. Aiding or abetting the commission of any offence specified in paragraphs 1 to 6 of the Schedule.

8. Attempting to commit any offence so specified.

[This Schedule is printed as amended or repealed in part by the *Theft Act* 1968, s.33(2) and Sched. 2; the *Criminal Damage Act* 1971, s.11(7); the *Child Abduction Act* 1984, s.11(2), (5)(c); the *Criminal Attempts Act* 1981, s.10 and Sched.; the *CJPOA* 1994, s.168(1) and Sched. 9, para. 8; the *Police Act* 1996, s.103(1) and Sched. 7, para. 16; and the *SOA* 2003, s.139, and Sched. 6, para. 16 (substituting a new para. 6); and, as from a day to be appointed, the *Immigration and Asylum Act* 1999, s.169(1) and Sched. 14, paras 34 and 35 (insertion of para. 5C).]

Supplementary provisions as to trial and punishment of offences

Firearms Act 1968, Sched. 6, Pt II, paras 3–6

3.—(1) *Where in England or Wales a person who has attained the age of seventeen is charged before a magistrates' court with an offence triable either way listed in Schedule 1 to the* Magistrates' Courts Act *1980 ("the listed offence") and is also charged before that court with an offence under section 17(1) or (2), of this Act the following provisions of this paragraph shall apply.* 24–44

(2) *Subject to the following sub-paragraph the court shall proceed as if the listed offence were triable only on indictment and sections 18 to 23 of the said Act of 1980 (procedure for determining mode of trial of offences triable either way) shall not apply in relation to that offence.*

(3) *If the court determines not to commit the accused for trial in respect of the offence under section 17(1) or (2), or if the proceedings before the court for that offence are otherwise discontinued, the preceding sub-paragraph shall cease to apply as from the time when this occurs and—*

(a) *if at that time the court has not yet begun to inquire into the listed offence as examining justices the court shall, in the case of the listed offence, proceed in the ordinary way in accordance with the said sections 18 to 23; but*

(b) *if at that time the court has begun so to inquire into the listed offence, those sections shall continue not to apply and the court shall proceed with its inquiry into that offence as examining justices, but shall have power in accordance with section 25(3) and (4) of the said Act of 1980 to change to summary trial with the accused's consent.*

4. Where a person commits an offence under section 17(1) of this Act in respect of the lawful arrest or detention of himself for any other offence committed by him, he shall be liable to the penalty provided by Part I of this Schedule in addition to any penalty to which he may be sentenced for the other offence.

5. If on the trial of a person for an offence under section 17(1) of this Act the jury are not satisfied that he is guilty of that offence but are satisfied that he is guilty of an offence under section 17(2), the jury may find him guilty of the offence under section 17(2) and he shall then be punishable accordingly.

6. The punishment to which a person is liable for an offence under section 17 (2) of this Act shall be in addition to any punishment to which he may be liable for the offence first referred to in section 17(2).

[Para. 3 is printed as substituted by the *CLA* 1977, s.65(4) and Sched. 12; and as amended by the *MCA* 1980, s.154, and Sched. 7. It is repealed, as from a day to be appointed, by the *CJA* 2003, ss.41 and 332, Sched. 3, para. 45, and Sched. 37, Pt 4.]

Schedule 1 to the 1980 Act is set out *ante*, at §§ 1–75af *et seq*. The reference in paragraph 3(1) above to "an offence triable either way listed in Schedule 1" to the 1980 Act includes a reference to an offence under section 1 of the *Criminal Attempts Act* 1981 of attempting to commit the offence so listed: *Criminal Attempts Act* 1981, s.7(2). 24–45

[The next paragraph is § 24–47.]

Class of offence and mode of trial

These offences are class 3 offences, *ante*, § 2–17, and are triable on indictment only: 1968 Act, s.51 and Sched. 6. 24–47

Alternative verdicts

On a count alleging an offence contrary to section 17(1), the jury, if not satisfied that the accused is guilty thereof, may convict of an offence contrary to section 17(2): 1968 Act, Sched. 6, para. 5, *ante*, § 24–44. 24–47a

Sentence

On indictment, life imprisonment, or a fine, or both: 1968 Act, s.51 and Sched. 6. 24–48

As to offences under this section committed on or after April 6, 2007, in relation to certain firearms or ammunition, being subject to a minimum sentence, see section 51A of the 1968 Act (*ante*, § 5–258).

The offences under section 17(1) and (2) are "specified violent offences" within Chapter 5 of Part 12 of the *CJA* 2003 (life sentences, sentences for public protection and extended sentences): see s.224, and Sched. 15, *ante*, §§ 5–292, 5–299.

For sentencing guidance, see *R. v. Avis* [1998] 1 Cr.App.R. 420, CA, *post*, § 24–82a.

For illustrative decisions, see CSP, B3–3; but note the effect of *R. v. Clarke (T.)* [1997] 1 Cr.App.R.(S.) 323, CA, *post*, § 24–82a.

Indicting and sentencing practice

24–49 Where using a firearm is an incident of another offence, such as robbery, cases such as *R. v. Guy*, 93 Cr.App.R. 108, CA, show that a firearms count should be included in the indictment for two reasons (despite a suggestion in *R. v. Benfield* [2004] 1 Cr.App.R. 8, CA (at [14]), that an indictment might be cluttered where there is no issue as to the use of a firearm). First, it resolves the issue of whether or not a firearm was used. Secondly, it allows for the imposition of a consecutive sentence, which will convey the message that those who carry firearms when committing other offences are liable to an additional penalty: see *R. v. McGrath*, 8 Cr.App.R.(S.) 372, CA; and *R. v. Greaves and Jaffier* [2004] 2 Cr.App.R.(S.) 10, CA; although consecutive sentences are not mandatory: *Att.-Gen.'s References (Nos 21 and 22 of 2003) (R. v. Hahn and Webster)* [2004] 2 Cr.App.R.(S.) 13, CA.

Where there is an issue as to whether a firearm was used, it should be determined by a jury, not by way of a *Newton* hearing: *R. v. Eubank* [2002] 2 Cr.App.R.(S.) 4, CA; *R. v. Murphy* [2003] 1 Cr.App.R.(S.) 39, CA.

Ingredients

24–50 The issue under section 17(1) is whether the firearm was being used intentionally for the purpose prohibited under the Act. Whether the police intended an arrest is irrelevant: *R. v. Mather* [1998] Crim.L.R. 821, CA.

An offence under section 17(2) is committed when, in possession of a firearm or imitation firearm, a defendant is lawfully arrested for one of the scheduled offences, whether or not that offence has been committed: *R. v. Nelson* [2000] 2 Cr.App.R. 160, CA, not following *R. v. Baker* [1962] Q.B. 530, 46 Cr.App.R. 47, CCA. For criticism of *Nelson*, see *Criminal Law Week* 2000/09/9 and [2000] Crim.L.R. 591.

"Possession" in section 17(2) bears the same meaning as in section 1 and is to be construed as in *Sullivan v. Earl of Caithness* and *Hall v. Cotton and Treadwell* (both cited at § 24–6, *ante*): *R. v. North* [2001] Crim.L.R. 746, CA.

(d) *Carrying firearm with criminal intent*

Firearms Act 1968, s.18

24–51 **18.**—(1) It is an offence for a person to have with him a firearm or imitation firearm with intent to commit an indictable offence, or to resist arrest or prevent the arrest of another, in either case while he has the firearm or imitation firearm with him.

(2) In proceedings for an offence under this section proof that the accused had a firearm or imitation firearm with him and intended to commit an offence, or to resist or prevent arrest, is evidence that he intended to have it with him while doing so.

(3) [*Scotland.*]

For the meaning of "firearm", see section 57(1); for "imitation firearm", see section 57(4), and *post*, § 24–87. Section 57 is set out in full, *post*, §§ 24–85 *et seq.*

As to adding a firearms count to an indictment charging other offences, see *ante*, § 24–49.

Class of offence and mode of trial

24–52 This offence is a class 3 offence, *ante*, § 2–17, and is triable on indictment only: 1968 Act, s.51 and Sched. 6.

Sentence

On indictment, life imprisonment, or a fine, or both: 1968 Act, s.51 and Sched. 6. **24–53**

As to offences under this section committed on or after April 6, 2007, in relation to certain firearms or ammunition, being subject to a minimum sentence, see section 51A of the 1968 Act (*ante*, § 5–258).

This offence is a "specified violent offence" within Chapter 5 of Part 12 of the *CJA* 2003 (life sentences, sentences for public protection and extended sentences): see s.224, and Sched. 15, *ante*, §§ 5–292, 5–299.

For sentencing guidance, see *R. v. Avis* [1998] 1 Cr.App.R. 420, CA, *post*, § 24–82a.

For sentencing practice on conviction of other offences, see *ante*, § 24–49. For illustrative decisions, see CSP, B3–3.3C; but note the effect of *R. v. Clarke (T.)* [1997] 1 Cr.App.R.(S.) 323, CA, *post*, § 24–82a.

Ingredients

The ingredients of the offence under section 18(1) are made out if it is proved that: (a) the defendant had with him a firearm; (b) he intended to have it with him; and (c) at the same time he had the intention to commit an indictable offence or to resist or prevent arrest: *R. v. Stoddart* [1998] 2 Cr.App.R. 25, CA. The court, referring to section 18(2), said that the requisite intents under (b) and (c) are distinct rather than composite elements of the offence, and held that the prosecution do not have to prove an intention to use or carry the firearm in furtherance of the indictable offence. **24–53a**

In *R. v. Houghton* [1982] Crim.L.R. 112, CA, it was held that it was not essential for the required intent to have been formed before the firearm was used. Authorities such as *Ohlson v. Hylton* [1975] 1 W.L.R. 724 (*post*, § 24–112) were distinguished. They were authorities on the *Prevention of Crime Act* 1953 (*post*, §§ 24–106 *et seq.*), the purpose of which is different to that of the 1968 Act.

"Have with him"

R. v. Kelt, 65 Cr.App.R. 74, CA, establishes two propositions. First, in directing a jury, it is necessary to distinguish between "having a firearm" and "possession"—mere possession is not enough. As Steyn L.J. said in *R. v. Pawlicki and Swindell*, 95 Cr.App.R. 246, CA: **24–54**

> "A man who leaves a shotgun at home while he proceeds to the next town to rob a bank is still in possession of the shotgun but he does not 'have it with him' when he commits the robbery at the bank. Under section 18 the words 'have it' import an element of propinquity which is not required for possession" (at p. 250).

The second proposition is that "having with him a firearm" is a wider concept than merely carrying one, notwithstanding the marginal note to the section. In *Kelt*, it was held that, subject to a proper direction, the words "have with him" were capable of covering the situation where the firearm was found in the defendant robber's kitchen, in which he was arrested. In *Pawlicki and Swindell*, convictions were upheld where at the critical time the guns were in a locked car 50 yards away from the intended site of a robbery: **24–55**

> "... the emphasis must be not so much on exact distances between criminals and their guns but rather on the accessibility of those guns, judged in a common sense way in the context of criminals embarking on a joint enterprise to commit an indictable offence" (*per* Steyn L.J. at p. 251).

A person cannot have a firearm with him when it is two or three miles away: *R. v. Bradish and Hall* [2004] 6 *Archbold News* 3, CA.

(e) *Carrying firearm in a public place*

Firearms Act 1968, s.19

19. A person commits an offence if, without lawful authority or reasonable excuse (the proof whereof lies on him) he has with him in a public place— **24–56**

(a) a loaded shot gun,

(b) an air weapon (whether loaded or not),

(c) any other firearm (whether loaded or not) together with ammunition suitable for use in that firearm, or
(d) an imitation firearm.

[This section is printed as amended by the *Anti-social Behaviour Act* 2003, s.37(1).]

For the meaning of "firearm", see section 57(1); for "has with him", see *ante*, § 24–54; for "public place", see *post*, § 24–61, and section 57(4); for "loaded", see section 57(6)(b); for "shot gun", see section 1(3)(a) (*ante*, § 24–3); for "air weapon", see section 1(3)(b) (*ante*, § 24–3); for "ammunition", see section 57(2); for "imitation firearm", see section 57(4), and *post*, § 24–87. Section 57 is set out in full, *post*, §§ 24–85 *et seq.*

As to adding a firearms count to an indictment charging other offences, see *ante*, § 24–49.

Class of offence and mode of trial

24–57 This offence is a class 3 offence, *ante*, § 2–17, and is triable either way, but an offence contrary to this section committed on or after April 6, 2007 (*VCRA* 2006, s.30(5), and the *Violent Crime Reduction Act 2006 (Commencement No. 2) Order* 2007 (S.I. 2007 No. 858)), in respect of a firearm or ammunition specified in section 5(1)(a), (ab), (aba), (ac), (ad), (ae), (af) or (c) or section 5(1A)(a) of the 1968 Act, is triable only on indictment, and an offence relating to an imitation firearm or an air weapon is triable only summarily: 1968 Act, Sched. 6 (as amended by the 2006 Act, s.30(4)). As from October 1, 2007 (*Violent Crime Reduction Act 2006 (Commencement No. 4) Order* 2007 (S.I. 2007 No. 2518)), however, if the weapon is an imitation firearm, the offence is triable either way: 1968 Act, Sched. 6 (as amended by the 2006 Act, s.41(1)(a)) (but only in relation to offences committed after the amendment takes effect: 2006 Act, s.41(3)(a)).

Sentence

24–58 On summary conviction, six months (increased to 12 months, as from a day to be appointed, by the *CJA* 2003, s.282(2) and (3), but not in relation to an offence committed before the date of commencement: *ibid.*, s.282(4)), or a fine of the prescribed sum, or both. On indictment, seven years (12 months where the weapon is an imitation firearm), or a fine, or both: 1968 Act, s.51, and Sched. 6 (as amended by the *VCRA* 2006, s.41(1)(b)). Section 41(2) of the 2006 Act provides that an offence under section 19 in respect of an imitation firearm which is triable either way by virtue of section 41(1) is to be treated as an offence to which section 282(3) of the *CJA* 2003 (increase in maximum sentence on conviction of an either way offence) applies, and as not being an offence to which section 281(5) of that Act (increase of maximum sentence on conviction of summary only offence) applies; and, so far as this subsection relates to section 282(3) of the 2003 Act, it does so only in respect of offences committed after the commencement of that subsection (s.41(3)(b)).

As to offences under this section committed on or after April 6, 2007, in relation to certain firearms or ammunition, being subject to a minimum sentence, see section 51A of the 1968 Act (*ante*, § 5–258).

For sentencing guidance, see *R. v. Avis* [1998] 1 Cr.App.R. 420, CA, *post*, § 24–82a.

For sentencing practice on conviction of other offences, see *ante*, § 24–49.

Mens rea

24–59 Subject to the statutory defence of lawful authority or reasonable excuse, section 19 creates an absolute offence: *R. v. Vann and Davis* [1996] Crim.L.R. 52, CA (prosecution not required to prove that defendant knew that the article she had was a gun, although the position might have been different if she genuinely believed that the item was not a gun or had had no opportunity of discovering what it was); *R. v. Harrison* [1996] 1 Cr.App.R. 138, CA (prosecution not required to prove that defendant knew that the gun he had was loaded). See *ante*, § 24–6, for authorities on possession.

"Without lawful authority or reasonable excuse"

24–60 These concepts were considered in *R. v. Jones (T.)* [1995] 1 Cr.App.R. 262, CA, where the court considered three points of law. First, it was held that the possession of a valid firearm certificate is not lawful authority for having the firearm and the ammunition to which it relates in a public place: the holding of a certificate merely saves the possessor of a firearm or shotgun, wherever he has it, from committing an offence under sections 1 and 2 of the 1968 Act. Auld J., giving the judgment of the court, added:

> "The question whether a person is in lawful possession of a firearm and ammunition in a public place must depend upon the circumstances. Whilst being the holder of a valid certificate would not of itself amount to lawful authority, its existence and compliance with its conditions may be a pre-requisite of, or, when considered with other matters, at least relevant to, such a defence" (at p. 267B).

The second issue in *Jones* was whether, if holding a firearm certificate is lawful authority for having it in a public place, a mistaken belief by the holder of an invalid certificate that the certificate is valid is capable of being a reasonable excuse. This was academic given the court's ruling on the first point, but the court said that, where there is an honest but mistaken belief in facts which, if true, would constitute lawful authority, it is capable of being a reasonable excuse within the section and the judge should so direct the jury, leaving them to determine whether the defendant has proved the requisite facts and whether in the circumstances his belief in them amounts to a reasonable excuse. The third point of law was whether the appellant's mistaken belief both that his certificate was valid and that it constituted lawful authority was capable of being a reasonable excuse. The court held that a belief in lawful authority based on facts which, if true, would not amount to lawful authority, is not capable of being a reasonable excuse. The court approved *Ross v. Collins* [1982] Crim.L.R. 368, DC (duck-shooting shot gun certificate holder's belief that holding a valid certificate was lawful authority for having with him a loaded shot gun, and that the River Thames was not a public place, not a defence) and stated that the general approach to reasonable excuse under section 19 was of a piece with the courts' approach to reasonable excuse under the *Prevention of Crime Act* 1953, s.1: see *post*, §§ 24–106a *et seq*.

In *Taylor v. Mucklow* [1973] Crim.L.R. 750, DC, the court upheld a conviction where the defendant stood in the roadway pointing a loaded air weapon and threatening to shoot a builder who had begun to demolish part of an extension (then under construction) to the defendant's house because the defendant had refused to pay the labour charges. The defendant's claim that he had a reasonable excuse for use of the gun in the circumstances, in that he was taking steps to safeguard his house, was rejected. The court, in approving the justices' view that at no time was his house or home genuinely in any danger (the demolition affected the newly erected brickwork of the extension), observed that the question for the justices was whether the use of the loaded air gun was a reasonable use of force in all the circumstances carried out by the defendant in the protection of his home—for anyone to argue nowadays that a loaded firearm was a suitable way of restraining the kind of bad temper exhibited by the builder was to show a lack of appreciation of modern trends and dangers.

"Public place"

See section 57(4), *post*, § 24–85. Where the public have access to one part of premises but not the other (*e.g.* behind the counter in a shop), the right approach to the question whether the latter part is a "public place" for the purposes of section 19 is to consider whether the whole of the premises form an entire unit (see *Cawley v. Frost* [1976] 1 W.L.R. 1207, DC, a public order case): *Anderson v. Miller*, 64 Cr.App.R. 178, DC (loaded revolver kept under counter of shop for use, if necessary, to defend persons or property in shop—*held*: s.19 contravened). See further *post*, §§ 24–113 *et seq.* and § 25–293. **24–61**

(f) *Trespassing with a firearm*

Firearms Act 1968, s.20

20.—(1) A person commits an offence if, while he has a firearm or imitation firearm with him, he enters or is in any building or part of a building as a trespasser and without reasonable excuse (the proof whereof lies on him). **24–62**

(2) [*Summary offence: entry on land.*]

(3) [*Interpretation of "land".*]

[This section is printed as amended by the 1994 Act, s.2(1).]

For the meaning of "firearm", see section 57(1); for "imitation firearm", see section 57(4), and § 24–87, *post*. Section 57 is set out in full, *post*, § 24–85.

Class of offence and mode of trial

24–63 This offence is a class 3 offence, *ante*, § 2–17, and is triable either way, but an offence relating to an imitation firearm or an air weapon is triable only summarily, and an offence committed on or after April 6, 2007 (*VCRA* 2006, s.30(5), and S.I. 2007 No. 858 (*ante*, § 24–57)), in respect of a firearm or ammunition specified in section 5(1)(a), (ab), (aba), (ac), (ad), (ae), (af) or (c) or section 5(1A)(a) of the 1968 Act, is triable only on indictment: 1968 Act, Sched. 6 (as amended by the 2006 Act, s.30(4)).

Sentence

24–64 On summary conviction, six months (increased to 12 months, as from a day to be appointed, by the *CJA* 2003, s.282(2) and (3), but not in relation to any offence committed before the date of commencement: *ibid.*, s.282(4)), or a fine of the prescribed sum, or both. On indictment, seven years, or a fine, or both: 1968 Act, s.51 and Sched. 6.

As to offences under this section committed on or after April 6, 2007, in relation to certain firearms or ammunition, being subject to a minimum sentence, see section 51A of the 1968 Act (*ante*, § 5–258).

For sentencing practice on conviction of other offences, see *ante*, § 24–49.

(g) *Possession of firearms by persons previously convicted of crime*

Firearms Act 1968, s.21

24–65 **21.**—(1) A person who has been sentenced to custody for life or to imprisonment for a term of three years or more or to youth custody or detention in a young offender institution for such a term, shall not at any time have a firearm or ammunition in his possession.

(2) A person who has been sentenced to imprisonment for a term of three months or more but less than three years or to youth custody or detention in a young offender institution for such a term, or who has been sentenced to be detained for such a term in a detention centre or [*Scotland*] or who has been subject to a secure training order or a detention and training order, shall not at any time before the expiration of the period of five years from the date of his release have a firearm or ammunition in his possession.

(2A) For the purposes of subsection (2) above, "the date of his release" means—

(a) in the case of a person sentenced to imprisonment with an order under section 47(1) of the *Criminal Law Act* 1977 (prison sentence partly served and partly suspended), the date on which he completes service of so much of the sentence as was by that order required to be served in prison;

(b) in the case of a person who has been subject to a secure training order—

(i) the date on which he is released from detention under the order;

(ii) the date on which he is released from detention ordered under section 4 of the *Criminal Justice and Public Order Act* 1994; or

(iii) the date halfway through the total period specified by the court in making the order,

whichever is the later;

(c) in the case of a person who has been subject to a detention and training order—

(i) the date on which he is released from detention under the order;

(ii) the date on which he is released from detention ordered under section 104 of the *Powers of Criminal Courts (Sentencing) Act* 2000; or

(iii) the date of the half-way point of the term of the order,

whichever is the later;

(d) in the case of a person who has been subject to a sentence of imprisonment to which an intermittent custody order under section 183(1)(b) of the *Criminal Justice Act* 2003 relates, the date of his final release.

(2B) A person who is serving a sentence of imprisonment to which an intermittent custody order under section 183 of the *Criminal Justice Act* 2003 relates shall not during any licence period specified for the purposes of subsection (1)(b)(i) of that section have a firearm or ammunition in his possession.

(3) A person who—

(a) is the holder of a licence issued under section 53 of the *Children and Young Persons Act* 1933 (which section provides for the detention of children and young persons convicted of serious crime, but enables them to be discharged on licence by the Secretary of State); or

(b) is subject to a recognizance to keep the peace or to be of good behaviour, a condition of which is that he shall not possess, use or carry a firearm, or is subject to a community order containing a requirement that he shall not possess, use or carry a firearm; or

(c) [*Scotland*]

shall not, at any time during which he holds the licence or is so subject or has been so ordained, have a firearm or ammunition in his possession.

(3ZA) In subsection (3)(b) above, "community order" means—

(a) a community order within the meaning of Part 12 of the *Criminal Justice Act* 2003[, or a youth rehabilitation order within the meaning of Part 1 of the *Criminal Justice and Immigration Act* 2008,] made in England and Wales, or

(b) a probation order made in Scotland.

(3A) Where by section 19 of the *Firearms Act (Northern Ireland) 1969*, or by any other enactment for the time being in force in Northern Ireland and corresponding to this section, a person is prohibited in Northern Ireland from having a firearm or ammunition in his possession, he shall also be so prohibited in Great Britain at any time when to have it in his possession in Northern Ireland would be a contravention of the said section 19 or corresponding enactment.

(4) It is an offence for a person to contravene any of the foregoing provisions of this section. **24-66**

(5) It is an offence for a person to sell or transfer a firearm or ammunition to, or to repair, test or prove a firearm or ammunition for, a person whom he knows or has reasonable ground for believing to be prohibited by this section from having a firearm or ammunition in his possession.

(6) A person prohibited under subsection (1), (2), (2B), (3) or (3A) of this section from having in his possession a firearm or ammunition may apply to the Crown Court or [*Scotland*] for a removal of the prohibition; and if the application is granted that prohibition shall not then apply to him.

(7) Schedule 3 to this Act shall have effect with respect to the courts with jurisdiction to entertain an application under this section and to the procedure appertaining thereto.

[This section is printed as amended or repealed in part by the *Courts Act* 1971, s.56(2) and Sched. 9; the *CJA* 1972, s.29; the *CLA* 1977, s.47 and Sched. 9; the *CJA* 1982, s.77 and Sched. 14; the *CJA* 1988, ss.123(6), 170(2) and Scheds 8, Pt I, and 16; the *CJPOA* 1994, s.168(2) and Sched. 10, para. 24(2); the *CDA* 1998, s.119 and Sched. 8, para. 14(1), (2); the *PCC(S)A* 2000, s.165(1) and Sched. 9, para. 31; and the *CJA* 2003, s.304, and Sched. 32, paras 11 and 12; and as amended, as from a day to be appointed (as to which, see *ante*, § 5–1), by the *CJIA* 2008, s.6(2), and Sched. 4, paras 5 and 6 (insertion of words in square brackets in subs. (3ZA)).]

For the meaning of "firearm", see section 57(1); for "ammunition", see section 57(2); for "possession", see *ante*, § 24–6; for "sell", see *ante*, § 24–13; for "transfer", see section 57(4). Section 57 is set out in full, *post*, § 24–85.

Class of offence and mode of trial

These offences are class 3 offences, *ante*, § 2–17, and are triable either way: 1968 Act, s.51 and Sched. 6. **24-67**

Sentence

On summary conviction, six months (increased to 12 months, as from a day to be appointed, by the *CJA* 2003, s.282(2) and (3), but not in relation to any offence committed before the date of commencement: *ibid.*, s.282(4)), or a fine of the prescribed sum, or both. On indictment, five years, or a fine, or both: 1968 Act, s.51 and Sched. 6. **24-68**

For sentencing guidance, see *R. v. Avis* [1998] 1 Cr.App.R. 420, CA, *post*, § 24–82a, and *R. v. Hill (N.D.W.)* [1999] 2 Cr.App.R.(S.) 388, CA (offence rightly classified in *Avis* as among those likely to attract custodial term of considerable length).

For illustrative decisions, see CSP, B3–3.3G; but note the effect of *R. v. Clarke (T.)* [1997] 1 Cr.App.R.(S.) 323, CA, *post*, § 24–82a.

Indictment

24–68a A count alleging an offence contrary to section 21 should not be included in an indictment unless there is a real purpose to be served, because otherwise a jury may be prejudiced by knowing that the defendant has served a substantial prison sentence: *R. v. Laycock* [2003] Crim. L.R. 803, CA.

Ingredients

24–69 The words "a term of three years or more" in section 21(1) apply to a term of three years or more consisting of separate shorter sentences (including the implementation of a suspended sentence) ordered to run consecutively: *Davies v. Tomlinson*, 71 Cr.App.R. 279, DC.

The prohibition in section 21(2) does not apply to a person who has received a suspended sentence: *R. v. Fordham* [1970] 1 Q.B. 77, Assizes (Mocatta J.).

(h) *Firing an air weapon beyond premises*

24–69a The *VCRA* 2006, s.34(1) and (2), inserted section 21A into the 1968 Act, thereby creating a summary offence. The offence is committed if a person (a) has an air weapon on premises, and (b) uses it for firing a missile beyond the premises. It is a defence to show that the occupier of the only premises into or across which the missile was fired had consented to the firing of the missile.

(7) Acquisition and possession of firearms by minors, etc.

24–70 Sections 22, 23 and 24 deal with the acquisition and possession of firearms by minors and with the supplying of firearms to minors. Sections 22 and 24 were amended by the *VCRA* 2006, s.33, so as to increase the various age limits. Section 24A (inserted by the 2006 Act, s.40) prohibits the buying and selling of an imitation firearm from or to a person under 18. Section 25 prohibits the supply of firearms to persons who are drunk or insane. The offences created by these sections are only triable summarily.

(8) Firearm and shot gun certificates

24–70a The 1997 Act, s.37, substituted, for section 26 of the 1968 Act, sections 26A and 26B.

Firearms Act 1968, ss.26A, 26B

Applications for firearm certificates

24–70b **26A.**—(1) An application for the grant of a firearm certificate shall be made in the prescribed form to the chief officer of police for the area in which the applicant resides and shall state such particulars as may be required by the form.

(2), (3) [*Matters for which rules made by the Secretary of State under section 53 may provide.*]

Applications for shot gun certificates

24–70c **26B.**—(1) [*Identical to section 26A(1),* ante, *save that "shot gun" is substituted for "firearm".*]

(2) [*Matters for which rules made by the Secretary of State under section 53 may provide.*]

24–70d As to the meaning of "resides", see *Burditt v. Joslin* [1981] 3 All E.R. 203, DC.

On appeal to the Crown Court against the refusal of a chief constable to grant a shot gun certificate, the Crown Court is not bound by the ordinary rules of evidence. Subject to the rules of natural justice, it can take into account all the matters which the chief constable is at liberty to consider: *Kavanagh v. Chief Constable of Devon and Cornwall* [1974] Q.B. 624, DC, CA (Civ. Div.) (considered in *R. v. Aylesbury Crown Court, ex p. Farrer, The Times*, March 9, 1988, CA (Civ. Div.)).

Firearms Act 1968, ss.27, 28

Special provisions about firearms certificates

27.—(1) A firearm certificate shall be granted where the chief officer of police is satisfied— **24–70e**

(a) that the applicant is fit to be entrusted with a firearm to which section 1 of this Act applies and is not a person prohibited by this Act from possessing such a firearm;

(b) that he has a good reason for having in his possession, or for purchasing or acquiring, the firearm or ammunition in respect of which the application is made; and

(c) that in all the circumstances the applicant can be permitted to have the firearm or ammunition in his possession without danger to the public safety or to the peace.

(1A) For the purposes of subsection (1) above a person under the age of eighteen shall be capable of having a good reason for having a firearm or ammunition in his possession, or for purchasing or acquiring it, only if he has no intention of using the firearm or ammunition, at any time before he attains the age of eighteen, for a purpose not authorised by the European weapons directive.

(2) A firearm certificate shall be in the prescribed form and shall specify the conditions (if any) subject to which it is held, the nature and number of the firearms to which it relates, including if known their identification numbers, and, as respects ammunition, the quantities authorised to be purchased or acquired and to be held at any one time thereunder.

(3) This section applies to the renewal of a firearm certificate as it applies to a grant.

[This section is printed as amended by the 1988 Act, s.23(5); the *Firearms Acts (Amendment) Regulations* 1992 (S.I. 1992 No. 2823), reg. 4; and the 1997 Act, s.38.]

Special provisions about shot gun certificates

28.—(1) Subject to subsection (1A) below, a shot gun certificate shall be granted or, as the case may be, renewed by the chief officer of police if he is satisfied that the applicant can be permitted to possess a shot gun without danger to the public safety or to the peace. **24–70f**

(1A) No such certificate shall be granted or renewed if the chief officer of police—

(a) has reason to believe that the applicant is prohibited by this Act from possessing a shot gun; or

(b) is satisfied that the applicant does not have a good reason for possessing, purchasing or acquiring one.

(1B) For the purposes of paragraph (b) of subsection (1A) above an applicant shall, in particular, be regarded as having a good reason if the gun is intended to be used for sporting or competition purposes or for shooting vermin; and an application shall not be refused by virtue of that paragraph merely because the applicant intends neither to use the gun himself nor to lend it for anyone else to use.

(1C) A person under the age of eighteen shall be regarded for the purposes of paragraph (b) of subsection (1A) above as not having a good reason for possessing, purchasing or acquiring a shot gun if it is his intention to use the shot gun, at any time before he attains the age of eighteen, for a purpose not authorised by the European weapons directive.

(2) A shot gun certificate shall be in the prescribed form and shall—

(a) be granted or renewed subject to any prescribed conditions and no others; and

(b) specify the conditions, if any, subject to which it is granted or renewed.

(2A) A shot gun certificate shall specify the description of the shot guns to which it relates including, if known, the identification numbers of the guns.

(3) [*Repealed by 1997 Act, s.52 and Sched. 3.*]

[This section is printed as amended by the 1988 Act, s.3(1), (2), and the *Firearms Acts (Amendment) Regulations* 1992 (S.I. 1992 No. 2823), reg. 4.]

Firearms Act 1968, s.29

Variation of firearm certificates

29.—(1) The chief officer of police for the area in which the holder of a firearm certificate resides may at any time by notice in writing vary the conditions subject to which the certificate is held, except such of them as may be prescribed, and may by the notice require the holder to deliver up the certificate to him within twenty-one days from the date of the notice for the purpose of amending the conditions specified therein. **24–70g**

(2) A firearm certificate may also, on the application of the holder, be varied from time to time by the chief officer of police for the area in which the holder for the time being resides; and a person aggrieved by the refusal of a chief officer to vary a firearm certificate may in accordance with section 44 of this Act appeal against the refusal.

(3) [*Summary offence: false statements.*]

24–70h The holder of a firearms certificate cannot purchase or acquire a replacement firearm for one which he already possesses and to which the certificate relates, albeit the proposed replacement is of the same description as that authorised by the certificate, without first applying for, and obtaining, a variation of the certificate under section 29(2). A firearms certificate is not merely a certificate to possess a type of weapon. It is a certificate permitting the holder to have a specified weapon in his possession: *Wilson v. Coombe* [1989] 1 W.L.R. 78, DC.

A decision by a chief officer of police under section 29(1) of the Act to vary the conditions subject to which a certificate is held cannot be appealed to the Crown Court. If the holder wishes to challenge the decision, he must do so by way of judicial review: *R. v. Cambridge Crown Court, ex p. Buckland, The Times*, September 17, 1998, DC.

The 1997 Act, s.40, substituted for section 30 of the 1968 Act, sections 30A, 30B, 30C and 30D.

Firearms Act 1968, ss.30A–30D

Revocation of firearm certificates

24–70i **30A.**—(1) A firearm certificate may be revoked by the chief officer of police for the area in which the holder resides on any of the grounds mentioned in subsections (2) to (5) below.

(2) The certificate may be revoked if the chief officer of police has reason to believe—

(a) that the holder is of intemperate habits or unsound mind or is otherwise unfitted to be entrusted with a firearm; or

(b) that the holder can no longer be permitted to have the firearm or ammunition to which the certificate relates in his possession without danger to the public safety or to the peace.

(3) The certificate may be revoked if the chief officer of police is satisfied that the holder is prohibited by this Act from possessing a firearm to which section 1 of this Act applies.

(4) The certificate may be revoked if the chief officer of police is satisfied that the holder no longer has a good reason for having in his possession, or for purchasing or acquiring, the firearm or ammunition which he is authorised by virtue of the certificate to have in his possession or to purchase or acquire.

(5) A firearm certificate may be revoked if the holder fails to comply with a notice under section 29(1) of this Act requiring him to deliver up the certificate.

(6) A person aggrieved by the revocation of a certificate under subsection (2), (3) or (4) of this section may in accordance with section 44 of this Act appeal against the revocation.

Partial revocation of firearm certificates

24–70j **30B.**—(1) The chief officer of police for the area in which the holder of a firearm certificate resides may partially revoke the certificate, that is to say, he may revoke the certificate in relation to any firearm or ammunition which the holder is authorised by virtue of the certificate to have in his possession or to purchase or acquire.

(2) A firearm certificate may be partially revoked only if the chief officer of police is satisfied that the holder no longer has a good reason for having in his possession, or for purchasing or acquiring, the firearm or ammunition to which the partial revocation relates.

(3) A person aggrieved by the partial revocation of a certificate may in accordance with section 44 of this Act appeal against the partial revocation.

Revocation of shot gun certificates

24–70k **30C.**—(1) A shot gun certificate may be revoked by the chief officer of police for the area in which the holder resides if he is satisfied that the holder is prohibited by this Act from possessing a shot gun or cannot be permitted to possess a shot gun without danger to the public safety or to the peace.

(2) A person aggrieved by the revocation of a shot gun certificate may in accordance with section 44 of this Act appeal against the revocation.

Revocation of certificates: supplementary

24–70l **30D.**—(1) Where a certificate is revoked under section 30A or 30C of this Act the chief officer of police shall by notice in writing require the holder to surrender the certificate.

(2) Where a certificate is partially revoked under section 30B of this Act the chief officer of police shall by notice in writing require the holder to deliver up the certificate for the purpose of amending it.

(3) It is an offence for the holder of a certificate to fail to comply with a notice under subsection (1) or (2) above within twenty-one days from the date of the notice.

(4) If an appeal is brought against a revocation or partial revocation—

(a) this section shall not apply to that revocation or partial revocation unless the appeal is abandoned or dismissed; and

(b) it shall then apply with the substitution, for the reference to the date of the notice, of a reference to the date on which the appeal was abandoned or dismissed.

(5) This section shall not apply in relation to—

(a) the revocation of a firearm certificate on any ground mentioned in section 30A(2), (3) or (4) of this Act;

(b) the revocation of a shot gun certificate,

if the chief officer of police serves a notice on the holder under section 12 of the *Firearms Act* 1988 requiring him to surrender forthwith his certificate and any firearms and ammunition in his possession by virtue of the certificate.

The provisions of sections 30A to 30D are supplemented by section 12 of the 1988 Act (*post*, § 24–96). **24–70m**

On an appeal under section 44 of the 1968 Act against the decision of a chief officer of police to revoke a firearm certificate under section 30(1) of the 1968 Act, the Crown Court must apply its own discretion. It is not enough for the Crown Court to ask itself whether the chief officer was entitled to revoke the certificate: *R. v. Acton Crown Court, ex p. Varney* [1984] Crim.L.R. 683, DC. **24–70n**

"Without danger ... to the peace" (s.30A(2)(b))

In the leading case of *Ackers v. Taylor* [1974] 1 W.L.R. 405, DC (poachers' certificates held to be rightly revoked), Ashworth J. said that the chief officer of police: **24–70o**

"... should consider, when he is deciding whether a certificate should be revoked on the ground of danger to the public peace, whether there is a danger that the gun may be misused in such a way that good order is disturbed or that there is a risk of that happening" (p. 410H).

It must be danger to the peace arising out of the possession, or use, or misuse of the shot gun which the police officer must consider: *ibid.* This does not mean, however, that the officer can only take into account conduct arising out of the misuse or abuse of a shot gun: *Chief Constable of Essex v. Germain*, 156 J.P. 109, DC (chief constable was entitled, in revoking a shot gun licence, to take into account the licence-holder's drink-driving convictions; by reason of his irresponsibility and lack of self-control as demonstrated by the drink-driving convictions, there was a future risk of danger to the peace involving the shot gun). By contrast, in *Spencer-Stewart v. Chief Constable of Kent*, 89 Cr.App.R. 307, DC, the licence-holder's handling conviction was considered not to pose any future risk in relation to his possession of a shot gun, and thus the revocation of his licence was not justified.

The fact that the licence-holder is innocent of any misconduct herself may not prevent a revocation: *Dabek v. Chief Constable of Devon and Cornwall*, *The Times*, June 25, 1990, DC (holder's certificate rightly revoked where her husband had two ancient drug convictions and still associated with drug users).

Firearms Act 1968, s.31

Certificate for prohibited weapon

31.—(1) A chief officer of police shall not refuse to grant or renew, and shall not revoke, a firearm certificate in respect of a prohibited weapon or prohibited ammunition if the applicant for the certificate is for the time being authorised by the Defence Council under section 5 of this Act to have possession of that weapon or ammunition. **24–70p**

(2) Where an authority of the Defence Council under that section to have possession of, or to purchase or acquire, a prohibited weapon or prohibited ammunition is revoked, the firearm certificate relating to that weapon or ammunition shall be revoked or varied accordingly by the chief officer of police by whom it was granted.

(9) Issue of documents for European purposes

24–71 Section 32A deals with documents issued in Great Britain for European purposes; section 32B with renewing European firearms passes; and section 32C with the variation and endorsement of European documents.

(10) Registration of dealers

24–72 Sections 33 to 39 deal with the registration of firearms dealers, section 39 creating summary offences. Section 33 is printed here in full in view of the decision in *R. v. Bull*, 99 Cr.App.R. 193, CA, *ante*, § 24–29.

Firearms Act 1968, s.33

Registration of firearms dealers

24–72a **33.**—(1) For purposes of this Act, the chief officer of police for every area shall keep in the prescribed form a register of firearms dealers.

(2) Except as provided by section 34 of this Act, the chief officer of police shall enter in the register the name of any person who, having or proposing to have a place of business in the area, applies to be registered as a firearms dealer.

(3) An applicant for registration as a firearms dealer must furnish the chief officer of police with the prescribed particulars, which shall include particulars of every place of business at which he proposes to carry on business in the area as a firearms dealer and, except as provided by this Act, the chief officer of police shall (if he registers the applicant as a firearms dealer) enter every such place of business in the register.

(4) When a person is registered, the chief officer of police shall grant or cause to be granted to him a certificate of registration.

(5) A person for the time being registered shall, on or before the expiration of the period of three years from the grant of the certificate of registration for the time being held by him—

(a) surrender his certificate to the chief officer of police; and

(b) apply in the prescribed form for a new certificate;

and thereupon the chief officer of police shall, subject to sections 35(3) and 38(1) below, grant him a new certificate of registration.

[This section is printed as amended by the 1988 Act, s.13(1); and by the 1997 Act, s.42(2).]

(11) Supplementary

24–73 Sections 40 and 41 relate to a compulsory register of transactions in firearms.

(12) Appeals

24–74 Section 44, as substituted by the 1997 Act, s.41(1), deals with appeals to the Crown Court under sections 26, 29, 30, 34, 36, 37 and 38 of the 1968 Act and under the 1988 Act, s.12. By subsection (1), an appeal lies to the Crown Court against a decision of a chief officer of police under sections 28A, 29, 30A, 30B, 30C, 34, 36, 37 or 38. By subsection (2), an appeal shall be determined on the merits and not by way of review. By subsection (3), the court may consider any evidence or other matter, whether or not it was available when the decision of the chief officer was taken.

24–75 Schedule 5, Pt II, to the 1968 Act contains procedural provisions in relation to appeals.

Firearms Act 1968, Sched. 5, Pt II

Procedural provisions for appeal to Crown Court

24–76 1. Notice of an appeal, signed by the appellant or by his agent on his behalf and stating the general grounds of the appeal, shall be given by him to the clerk of the peace and also to the chief officer of police by whose decision the appellant is aggrieved.

2. A notice of appeal shall be given within twenty-one days after the date on which the appellant has received notice of the decision of the chief officer of police by which he is aggrieved.

3. On receiving notice of an appeal the clerk of the peace shall enter the appeal and

give notice to the appellant and to the chief officer of police to whom the notice of the appeal is required by paragraph 1 of this Part of this Schedule to be given, of the date, time and place fixed for the hearing.

4. An appellant may at any time, not less than two clear days before the date fixed for the hearing, abandon his appeal by giving notice in writing to the clerk of the peace and to the chief officer of police; ...

5. The chief officer of police may appear and be heard on the hearing of an appeal.

6. [*Repealed by* Crown Court Rules *1971 (S.I. 1971 No. 1292).*]

7. On the hearing of an appeal the court may either dismiss the appeal or give the chief officer of police such directions as it thinks fit as respects the certificate or register which is the subject of the appeal.

8. [*Repealed by* Crown Court Rules *1971 (S.I. 1971 No. 1292).*]

Firearms Act 1968, s.45

Consequences of conviction of registered dealer

45.—(1) Where a registered firearms dealer is convicted of an offence relevant for the purposes of this section the court may order— **24–77**

(a) that the name of the dealer be removed from the register; and

(b) that neither the dealer nor any person who acquires his business, nor any person who took part in the management of the business and was knowingly a party to the offence, shall be registered as a firearms dealer; and

(c) that any person who, after the date of the order, knowingly employs in the management of his business the dealer convicted of the offence or any person who was knowingly a party to the offence, shall not be registered as a firearms dealer or, if so registered, shall be liable to be removed from the register; and

(d) that any stock-in-hand of the business shall be disposed of by sale or otherwise in accordance with such directions as may be contained in the order.

(2) The offences relevant for the purposes of this section are:—

(a) all offences under this Act, except an offence under section 2, 22(3) or 24(3) or an offence relating specifically to air weapons; and

(b) offences against the enactments relating to customs in respect of the import or export of firearms or ammunition to which section 1 of this Act applies, or of shot guns.

(3) A person aggrieved by an order made under this section may appeal against the order in the same manner as against the conviction, and the court may, if it thinks fit, suspend the operation of the order pending the appeal.

(13) Law enforcement and punishment of offences

Firearms Act 1968, ss.46–48

Power of search with warrant

46.—(1) If a justice of the peace or, in Scotland, the sheriff, is satisfied by information on oath that there is reasonable ground for suspecting— **24–78**

(a) that an offence relevant for the purposes of this section has been, is being, or is about to be committed; or

(b) that, in connection with a firearm or ammunition, there is a danger to the public safety or to the peace,

he may grant a warrant for any of the purposes mentioned in subsection (2) below.

(2) A warrant under this section may authorise a constable or civilian officer—

(a) to enter at any time any premises or place named in the warrant, if necessary by force, and to search the premises or place and every person found there;

(b) to seize and detain anything which he may find on the premises or place, or on any such person, in respect of which or in connection with which he has reasonable ground for suspecting—

(i) that an offence relevant for the purposes of this section has been, is being or is about to be committed; or

(ii) that in connection with a firearm, imitation firearm or ammunition there is a danger to the public safety or to the peace.

(3) The power of a constable or civilian officer under subsection (2)(b) above to seize and detain anything found on any premises or place shall include power to require any information which is stored in any electronic form and is accessible from the premises or

place to be produced in a form in which it is visible and legible or from which it can readily be produced in a visible and legible form and can be taken away.

(4) The offences relevant for the purposes of this section are all offences under this Act except an offence under section 22(3) or an offence relating specifically to air weapons.

(5) It is an offence for any person intentionally to obstruct a constable or civilian officer in the exercise of his powers under this section.

[This section was substituted by the 1997 Act, s.43(1). It is printed as amended by the *CJPA* 2001, s.70, and Sched. 2, para. 15.]

As from April 1, 2003 (*Criminal Justice and Police Act 2001 (Commencement No. 9) Order* 2003 (S.I. 2003 No. 708)), the additional powers of seizure conferred by the *CJPA* 2001, ss.50 and 51 (*ante*, §§ 15–124 *et seq.*), and the obligation to return excluded and special procedure material pursuant to section 55 of that Act (*ante*, § 15–132), apply to the power of seizure under section 46: *CJPA* 2001, ss.50(5), 51(5), 55(4), and Sched. 1, paras 8, 76 and 91.

A constable executing a warrant under section 46 has the power to detain persons in the premises for the purpose of searching them and to use reasonable force for the purpose: *Connor v. Chief Constable of Merseyside Police* [2007] H.R.L.R. 6, CA (Civ. Div.), following *DPP v. Meaden* [2004] 1 W.L.R. 955, DC (*post*, § 27–104), in relation to analogous powers under the *Misuse of Drugs Act* 1971, s.23(3).

As to the application of section 46 in relation to certain sections of the *VCRA* 2006, see *post*, § 24–146.

Power of constables to stop and search

24–79 **47.**—(1) A constable may require any person whom he has reasonable cause to suspect—

(a) of having a firearm, with or without ammunition, with him in a public place; or

(b) to be committing or about to commit, elsewhere than in a public place, an offence relevant for the purposes of this section,

to hand over the firearm or any ammunition for examination by the constable.

(2) It is an offence for a person having a firearm or ammunition with him to fail to hand it over when required to do so by a constable under subsection (1) of this section.

(3) If a constable has reasonable cause to suspect a person of having a firearm with him in a public place, or to be committing or about to commit, elsewhere than in a public place, an offence relevant for the purposes of this section, the constable may search that person and may detain him for the purpose of doing so.

(4) If a constable has reasonable cause to suspect that there is a firearm in a vehicle in a public place, or that a vehicle is being or is about to be used in connection with the commission of an offence relevant for the purposes of this section elsewhere than in a public place, he may search the vehicle and for that purpose require the person driving or in control of it to stop it.

(5) For the purpose of exercising the powers conferred by this section a constable may enter any place.

(6) The offences relevant for the purpose of this section are those under sections 18(1) and (2) and 20 of this Act.

Production of certificates

24–80 **48.**—(1) A constable may demand, from any person whom he believes to be in possession of a firearm or ammunition to which section 1 of this Act applies, or of a shot gun, the production of his firearm certificate or, as the case may be, his shot gun certificate.

(1A) Where a person upon whom a demand has been made by a constable under subsection (1) above and whom the constable believes to be in possession of a firearm fails—

(a) to produce a firearm certificate or, as the case may be, a shot gun certificate;

(b) to show that he is a person who, by reason of his place of residence or any other circumstances, is not entitled to be issued with a document identifying that firearm under any of the provisions which in the other member States correspond to the provisions of this Act for the issue of European firearms passes; or

(c) to show that he is in possession of the firearm exclusively in connection with the carrying on of activities in respect of which, he or the person on whose behalf he has possession of the firearm, is recognised, for the purposes of the law of another member State relating to firearms, as a collector of firearms or a body concerned in the cultural or historical aspects of weapons,

the constable may demand from that person the production of a document which has been issued to that person in another member State under any such corresponding provisions, identifies that firearm as a firearm to which it relates and is for the time being valid.

(2) If a person upon whom a demand is made under this section fails to produce the certificate or document or to permit the constable to read it, or to show that he is entitled by virtue of this Act to have the firearm, ammunition or shot gun in his possession without holding a certificate, the constable may seize and detain the firearm, ammunition or shot gun and may require the person to declare to him immediately his name and address.

(3) If under this section a person is required to declare to a constable his name and address, it is an offence for him to refuse to declare it or to fail to give his true name and address.

(4) [*Summary offence: failure to comply with demand under (1A).*]

[This section is printed as amended by the *Firearms (Amendment) Regulations* 1992 (S.I. 1992 No. 2823), reg. 7(2)–(4).]

Firearms Act 1968, ss.49, 51, 51A, 52

Police powers in relation to arms traffic

49.—(1) A constable may search for and seize any firearms or ammunition which he has reason to believe are being removed, or to have been removed, in contravention of an order made under section 6 of this Act or of a corresponding Northern Irish order within the meaning of subsection (3)(c) of that section. **24–81**

(2) A person having the control or custody of any firearms or ammunition in course of transit shall, on demand by a constable, allow him all reasonable facilities for the examination and inspection thereof and shall produce any documents in his possession relating thereto.

(3) [*Summary offence: failure to comply with subsection (2) of this section.*]

[This section is printed as amended by the 1988 Act, s.23(3).]

Prosecution and punishment of offences

51.—(1) Part I of Schedule 6 to this Act shall have effect with respect to the way in which offences under this Act are punishable on conviction. **24–82**

(2) In relation to an offence under a provision of this Act specified in the first column of the Schedule (the general nature of the offence being described in the second column),—

(a) the third column shows whether the offence is punishable on summary conviction or on indictment or either in one way or the other; and

(b) the fourth column shows the maximum punishment by way of fine or imprisonment under this Act which may be imposed on a person convicted of the offence in the way specified in relation thereto in the third column (that is to say, summarily or on indictment), any reference in the fourth column to a period of years or months being construed as a reference to a term of imprisonment of that duration.

(3) The provisions contained in Part II of Schedule 6 to this Act (being provisions as to the inclusion in an indictment in Scotland of certain summary offences, the punishments which may be imposed when a person is convicted of more than one offence arising out of the same set of circumstances, alternative verdicts and the orders which, in certain cases, a court may make when a person is convicted by or before it) shall have effect in relation to such of the offences specified in Part I of that Schedule as are indicated by entries against those offences in the fifth column of that Part.

(4) Notwithstanding section 127(1) of the *Magistrates' Courts Act* 1980 or section 23 of the *Summary Jurisdiction (Scotland) Act* 1954 (limitation of time for taking proceedings) summary proceedings for an offence under this Act, other than an offence under section 22(3) or an offence relating specifically to air weapons, may be instituted at any time within four years after the commission of the offence:

Provided that no such proceedings shall be instituted in England after the expiration of six months after the commission of the offence unless they are instituted by, or by the direction of, the Director of Public Prosecutions.

[This section is printed as amended by the *MCA* 1980, s.154(1) and Sched. 7.]

For Schedule 6, Part II, paras 3 to 6, see *ante*, § 24–44. Schedule 6, Pt I (table of offences with mode of trial and maximum sentence) is not printed in this work: the relevant details are given in the context of the individual offences.

As to "the prescribed sum" (the maximum fine on summary conviction for all the offences triable either way), see the *MCA* 1980, s.32 (*ante*, § 1–75aa).

As to the application of section 51(4) in relation to certain sections of the *VCRA* 2006, see *post*, § 24–146.

24–82a In *R. v. Avis* [1998] 1 Cr.App.R. 420, CA, it was said that some of the sentences imposed in the past for firearms offences had been too lenient (see also *R. v. Clarke (T.)* [1997] 1 Cr.App.R.(S.) 323, CA: cases decided before February 3, 1995, *i.e.* before the increase in maximum sentences effected by the *CJPOA* 1994, are no longer authoritative). The sentencing court should usually ask itself four questions:

1. What sort of weapon is involved? Genuine weapons are more dangerous than imitations, loaded firearms than unloaded, unloaded for which ammunition is available than those for which none is available. Possession of a firearm which has no lawful use, such as a sawn-off shot gun, is more serious than possessing a firearm capable of lawful use.
2. What use, if any, was made of the firearm? The more prolonged, premeditated and violent the use, the more serious the offence is likely to be.
3. With what intention, if any, did the defendant possess the firearm? The most serious offences under the Act are generally those requiring proof of a specific intent. The more serious the act intended, the more serious the offence.
4. What is the defendant's record? The seriousness of any firearms offence is increased if there is an established record of committing such offences or crimes of violence.

Save for minor infringements, offences committed under sections 1(1), 2(1), 3, 4, 5(1A), 16, 16A, 17(1) and (2), 18(1), 19 and 21(4) generally merit custodial sentences, even on a plea of guilty and where the offender has no previous record. On breaches of sections 4, 5, 16, 16A, 17(1) and (2), 18(1), 19 and 21(4), the custodial term is likely to be considerable and, where the answers to the four questions, *ante*, are adverse to the offender, at or approaching the maximum in a contested case. However, an indeterminate sentence should only be imposed where the established criteria for such a sentence are met. *Avis* is subject to the qualification that, as from January 22, 2004, the offences under section 5(1)(a), (ab), (aba), (ac), (ad), (ae), (af) and (c), and section 5(1A)(a), are subject to a minimum sentence under section 51A: see *ante*, § 5–258.

Shooting an air gun across a street or public place where people are likely to be passing should, in a contested case, attract an immediate custodial sentence in the region of 12 to 15 months: *Att.-Gen.'s Reference (No. 47 of 2006) (R. v. Hadavi)* [2007] 1 Cr.App.R.(S.) 63, CA.

For an example of "minor infringements", for which a non-custodial sentence could be justified, see *R. v. Southwark Crown Court, ex p. Smith* [2001] 2 Cr.App.R.(S.) 35, DC (uncertificated possession of rifle, sound moderators and ammunition where failure to renew certificates had been an oversight by person of exemplary character, distracted by other matters, and who had no intention of putting the weapon to any nefarious use or of concealing it from the police).

24–82b **51A.** [*Minimum sentence for certain offences under s.5: see* ante, *§ 5–258.*]

Forfeiture and disposal of firearms and cancellation of certificate on conviction

24–83 **52.**—(1) Where a person—

(a) is convicted of an offence under this Act (other than an offence under section 22(3) or an offence relating specifically to air weapons) or is convicted of a crime for which he is sentenced to imprisonment, or detention *in a young offender institution or* [*Scotland*] or is subject to a detention and training order; or

(b) has been ordered to enter into a recognizance to keep the peace or to be of good behaviour, a condition of which is that he shall not possess, use or carry a firearm; or

(c) is subject to a community order containing a requirement that he shall not possess, use or carry a firearm; or

(d) [*Scotland*],

the court by or before which he is convicted, or by which the order is made, may make such order as to the forfeiture or disposal of any firearm or ammunition found in his possession as the court thinks fit and may cancel any firearm certificate or shot gun certificate held by him.

(1A) In subsection (1)(c) "community order" means—

(a) a community order within the meaning of Part 12 of the *Criminal Justice Act* 2003[, or a youth rehabilitation order within the meaning of Part 1 of the *Criminal Justice and Immigration Act* 2008,] made in England and Wales, or

(b) a probation order made in Scotland.

(2) Where the court cancels a certificate under this section—

(a) the court shall cause notice to be sent to the chief officer of police by whom the certificate was granted; and

(b) the chief officer of police shall by notice in writing require the holder of the certificate to surrender it; and

(c) it is an offence for the holder to fail to surrender the certificate within twenty-one days from the date of the notice given him by the chief officer of police.

(3) A constable may seize and detain any firearm or ammunition which may be the subject of an order for forfeiture under this section.

(4) A court of summary jurisdiction or [*Scotland*] ... may, on the application of the chief officer of police, order any firearm or ammunition seized and detained by a constable under this Act to be destroyed or otherwise disposed of.

(5) In this section references to ammunition include references to a primer to which section 35 of the *Violent Crime Reduction Act* 2006 applies and to an empty cartridge case incorporating such a primer.

[This section is printed as amended and repealed in part by the *CJA* 1988, ss.123(6), 170(2), and Scheds 8, paras l and 2, and 16; the *CJPOA* 1994, s.168(2), and Sched. 10, para. 24(1), (3); the *CDA* 1998, s.119, and Sched. 8, para. 15; the *CJA* 2003, s.304, and Sched. 36, paras 11 and 13; and the *VCRA* 2006, s.50(5); and, as from a day to be appointed, by the *CJCSA* 2000, s.75, and Sched. 8 (omission of italicised words in subs. (1)(a)); and the *CJIA* 2008, s.6(2), and Sched. 4, paras 5 and 7 (insertion of words in square brackets in subs. (1A)). For the transitional provision in relation to the latter amendment, see *ante*, § 5–1.]

As to the *VCRA* 2006, s.35, see *post*, § 24–105l. As to the application of section 52 of the 1968 Act to certain sections of the 2006 Act, see *post*, § 24–146.

(14) General provisions

Section 53 empowers the Secretary of State to make rules which may, by section 55, relate to the exercise of police functions. Section 54 (as amended by various enactments) deals with the application of Parts I and II of the Act to Crown servants. Section 56 deals with the service of notices by registered post or recorded delivery to a person's last or usual place of abode or, in the case of a registered firearms dealer, to any place of business in respect of which he is registered. **24–84**

(15) Definitions

Firearms Act 1968, s.57

57.—(1) In this Act, the expression "firearm" means a lethal barrelled weapon of any description from which any shot, bullet or other missile can be discharged and includes— **24–85**

(a) any prohibited weapon, whether it is such a lethal weapon as aforesaid or not; and

(b) any component part of such a lethal or prohibited weapon; and

(c) any accessory to any such weapon designed or adapted to diminish the noise or flash caused by firing the weapon;

and so much of section 1 of this Act as excludes any description of firearm from the category of firearms to which that section applies shall be construed as also excluding component parts of, and accessories to, firearms of that description.

(2) In this Act, the expression "ammunition" means ammunition for any firearm and includes grenades, bombs and other like missiles, whether capable of use with a firearm or not, and also includes prohibited ammunition.

(2A) In this Act "self-loading" and "pump action" in relation to any weapon mean respectively that it is designed or adapted (otherwise than as mentioned in section 5(1)(a)) so that it is automatically re-loaded or that it is so designed or adapted that it is re-loaded by the manual operation of the fore-end or forestock of the weapon.

(2B) In this Act "revolver", in relation to a smooth-bore gun, means a gun containing a series of chambers which revolve when the gun is fired.

(3) For purposes of sections 45, 46, 50, 51(4) and 52 of this Act, the offences under this Act relating specifically to air weapons are those under sections 22(4), 22(5), 23(1) and 24(4).

(4) In this Act—

"acquire" means hire, accept as a gift or borrow and "acquisition" shall be construed accordingly;

"air weapon" has the meaning assigned to it by section 1(3)(b) of this Act;

"another member State" means a member State other than the United Kingdom, and "other member States" shall be construed accordingly;

"area" means a police area;

"Article 7 authority" means a document issued by virtue of section 32A(1)(b) or (2) of this Act;

"certificate"(except in a context relating to the registration of firearms dealers) and "certificate under this Act" means a firearm certificate or a shot gun certificate and—

(a) "firearm certificate" means a certificate granted by a chief officer of police under this Act in respect of any firearm or ammunition to which section 1 of this Act applies and includes a certificate granted in Northern Ireland under section 1 of the *Firearms Act* 1920, or under an enactment of the Parliament of Northern Ireland amending or substituted for that section; and

(b) "shot gun certificate" means a certificate granted by a chief officer of police under this Act and authorising a person to possess shot guns;

"civilian officer" means—

(a) a person employed by a police authority or the Corporation of the City of London who is under the direction and control of a chief officer of police;

(b) . . .

"European firearms pass" means a document to which the holder of a certificate under this Act is entitled by virtue of section 32A(1)(a) of this Act;

"European weapons directive" means the directive of the Council of the European Communities No. 91/477/EEC (directive on the control of the acquisition and possession of weapons);

"firearms dealer" means a person who, by way of trade or business—

(a) manufactures, sells, transfers, repairs, tests or proves firearms or ammunition to which section 1 of this Act applies or shot guns; or

(b) sells or transfers air weapons;

"imitation firearm" means any thing which has the appearance of being a firearm (other than such a weapon as is mentioned in section 5(1)(b) of this Act) whether or not it is capable of discharging any shot, bullet or other missile;

"premises" includes any land;

"prescribed" means prescribed by rules made by the Secretary of State under section 53 of this Act;

"prohibited weapon" and "prohibited ammunition" have the meanings assigned to them by section 5(2) of this Act;

"public place" includes any highway and any other premises or place to which at the material time the public have or are permitted to have access, whether on payment or otherwise;

"registered", in relation to a firearms dealer, means registered either—

(a) in Great Britain, under section 33 of this Act, or

(b) in Northern Ireland, under section 8 of the *Firearms Act* 1920, or any enactment of the Parliament of Northern Ireland amending or substituted for that section,

and references to "the register", "registration" and a "certificate of registration" shall be construed accordingly, except in section 40;

"rifle" includes carbine;

"shot gun" has the meaning assigned to it by section 1(3)(a) of this Act and, in sections 3(1) and 45(2) of this Act and in the definition of "firearms dealer", includes any competent part of a shot gun and any accessory to a shot gun designed or adapted to diminish the noise or flash caused by firing the gun;

"slaughtering instrument" means a firearm which is specially designed or adapted for the instantaneous slaughter of animals or for the instantaneous stunning of animals with a view to slaughtering them; and

"transfer" includes let on hire, give, lend and part with possession, and "transferee" and "transferor" shall be construed accordingly.

(4A) For the purposes of any reference in this Act to the use of any firearm or ammunition for a purpose not authorised by the European weapons directive, the directive shall be taken to authorise the use of a firearm or ammunition as or with a slaughtering instrument and the use of a firearm and ammunition—

(a) for sporting purposes;
(b) for the shooting of vermin, or, in the course of carrying on activities in connection with the management of any estate, of other wildlife; and
(c) for competition purposes and target shooting outside competitions.

(5) The definitions in subsections (1) to (3) above apply to the provisions of this Act except where the context otherwise requires.

(6) For purposes of this Act—

(a) the length of the barrel of a firearm shall be measured from the muzzle to the point at which the charge is exploded on firing; and
(b) a shot gun or an air weapon shall be deemed to be loaded if there is ammunition in the chamber or barrel or in any magazine or other device which is in such a position that the ammunition can be fed into the chamber or barrel by the manual or automatic operation of some part of the gun or weapon.

[Subss. (2A) and (2B) were inserted by the 1988 Act, s.25(2). Subs. (4) is printed as amended by the 1988 Act, s.25(3); the *Firearms Acts (Amendment) Regulations* 1992 (S.I. 1992 No. 2823), reg. 5(2); the 1997 Act, s.43(2); the *Anti-Terrorism, Crime and Security Act* 2001, s.101, and Sched. 7, paras 8 and 10; the *Railways and Transport Safety Act* 2003, s.73(1), and Sched. 5, para. 4(1) and (2)(b); and the *VCRA* 2006, s.31(3); and as repealed in part by the *CLA* 1977, s.65(3), and Sched. 13; and the *Greater London Authority Act* 1999, s.325, and Sched. 27, para. 22. Subs. (4A) was inserted by S.I. 1992 No. 2823 (*ante*).]

"Firearm"

Whether a weapon is a firearm is a question of fact. Accordingly, the reported cases do not establish as a matter of law that a particular type of weapon is a firearm: see *Grace v. DPP* [1989] Crim.L.R. 365, DC, where the court declined to treat *Moore v. Gooderham* (*post*) as authority for the proposition that all air guns are lethal weapons. **24–86**

"Lethal"

A lethal weapon is one which, when misused, is capable of causing injury from which death may result: *R. v. Thorpe*, 85 Cr.App.R. 107, CA, approving the test laid down in *Moore v. Gooderham* [1960] 1 W.L.R. 1308, DC. If it is capable of causing more than trifling and trivial injury, it is capable of causing death if discharged point-blank into a vulnerable part of the body, such as an eye, and whether or not it was designed to cause injury is irrelevant: *Moore v. Gooderham*, *ante*.

"Barrelled"

See *R. v. Singh* [1989] Crim.L.R. 724, CA, where there was an evidential dispute as to whether a flare launcher was barrelled.

"From which any ... missile can be discharged"

This phrase includes weapons which, although incapable of being fired, can be adapted or altered to discharge a missile: *R. v. Freeman*, 54 Cr.App.R. 251, CA (starting pistol which could fire bullets if barrel drilled), following *Cafferata v. Wilson* [1936] 3 All E.R. 149, DC. See also the 1982 Act, s.1, *post*, §§ 24–91 *et seq*.

To prove that a weapon is a firearm, it is essential to call evidence that it is one from which any missile can be discharged or which can be adapted to discharge any missile: *Grace v. DPP*, *ante*, where the conviction was quashed in the absence of evidence that an air rifle had been fired or was capable of being fired. Such evidence need not necessarily come from an expert—it could also come from somebody who had seen the weapon being fired or who was familiar with the weapon and could indicate that it did work and what its observed effect was when fired (*ibid.*), although the absence of any evidence as to the firing's effect was not fatal to conviction in *Castle (J.) v. DPP*, *The Times*, April 3, 1998, DC.

"Accessory"

Something which is an integral part of a firearm is not an accessory under section 57, even if it increases the firearm's lethal qualities: *Broome v. Walter* [1989] Crim.L.R. 725, DC (justices entitled to conclude that detachable muzzle not an accessory). However, a silencer which is not an integral part of the firearm can be an accessory thereto if it can be used with the firearm and the defendant had it for that purpose, even though it might in fact have been made for a different weapon: *R. v. Buckfield* [1998] Crim.L.R. 673, CA.

"Ammunition"

24–87 In deciding whether something is "ammunition", the test seems to be whether it is capable of producing an explosive effect when the firearm is operated: see *R. v. Stubbings* [1990] Crim.L.R. 811, CA. "Ammunition" has been held to include blank cartridges (*Burfitt v. A. & E. Kille* [1939] 2 K.B. 473, KBD), primed cartridges (*Stubbings*, *ante*) and flares (*R. v. Singh* [1989] Crim.L.R. 724, CA).

"Public place"

See *ante*, § 24–61.

"Imitation firearm"

In considering whether a thing has an appearance of being a firearm, the jury should focus on its appearance at the time of the offence rather than at any other time, having regard to the evidence of witnesses who saw the thing at the relevant time, together with the jury's own observation of the thing itself (if available): *R. v. Morris and King*, 79 Cr.App.R. 104, CA. A person's finger is not capable of being an "imitation firearm" within the 1968 Act; the reference to "any thing" contemplates something other than a part of the offender's body: *R. v. Bentham* [2005] 1 W.L.R. 1057, HL.

"Slaughtering instrument"

The words "humane killer" in a firearms certificate should be given the same meaning as "slaughtering instrument": *R. v. Paul* [1999] Crim.L.R. 79, CA (see also *ante*, §§ 24–6a, 24–15a).

"Transfer"

24–88 In *Hall v. Cotton and Treadwell* [1987] Q.B. 504, 83 Cr.App.R. 257, DC, the owner's leaving of shot guns at another's house for safekeeping while both parties were on holiday and for cleaning by the recipient after their return from holiday was held to be a transfer within section 57(4). Accordingly, because the recipient did not have a shot gun certificate, the owner was guilty of an offence under section 3(2) of the Act: see *ante*, § 24–12. In construing section 57(4), the court said that, although on the authority of *Sullivan v. Earl of Caithness* (*ante*, § 24–6), the owner had retained proprietary possession of the shot guns, he had transferred custodial possession to the recipient. This was so whether the phrase "lend and part with possession" is disjunctive, as the court thought, or conjunctive.

(16) Particular savings

Firearms Act 1968, s.58

24–89 **58.**—(1) Nothing in this Act shall apply to the proof houses of the Master, Wardens and Society of the Mystery of Gunmakers of the City of London and the guardians of the Birmingham proof house or the rifle range at Small Heath in Birmingham where firearms are sighted and tested, so as to interfere in any way with the operations of those two companies in proving firearms under the provisions of the *Gun Barrel Proof Act* 1868 or any other Acts for the time being in force, or to any person carrying firearms to or from any such proof house when being taken to such proof house for the purposes of proof or being removed therefrom after proof.

(2) Nothing in this Act relating to arms shall apply to an antique firearm which is sold, transferred, purchased, acquired or possessed as a curiosity or ornament.

(3) The provisions of this Act relating to ammunition shall be in addition to and not in derogation of any enactment relating to the keeping and sale of explosives.

(4) The powers of arrest and entry conferred by Part III of this Act shall be without prejudice to any power of arrest or entry which may exist apart from this Act; and section 52(3) of this Act is not to be taken as prejudicing the power of a constable, when arresting a person for an offence, to seize property found in his possession or any other power of a constable to seize firearms, ammunition or other property, being a power exercisable apart from that subsection.

(5) Nothing in this Act relieves any person using or carrying a firearm from his obligation to take out a licence to kill game under the enactments requiring such a licence.

As to the application of section 58 to certain sections of the *VCRA* 2006, see *post*, § 24–146.

Antiques

Once there is some evidence that a firearm is capable of being within section 58(2), it is for the prosecution to prove that the firearm is not and it is for the jury, not the judge, to resolve the matter: *R. v. Burke*, 67 Cr.App.R. 220, CA. **24–89a**

The question whether a gun is within section 58(2) is one of fact and degree in each case: *Richards v. Curwen*, 65 Cr.App.R. 95, DC (prosecutor's appeal dismissed—defendant was a genuine collector and had two revolvers as ornaments which were approximately 100 years old—one was capable of being fired, the other could be rendered capable of being fired). However, although the "over 100 years old" test was rejected by the court in *Richards v. Curwen*, *ante*, in *Bennett v. Brown*, 71 Cr.App.R. 109, DC, Eveleigh L.J. stated "... it would be quite impossible to say that any weapon that could reasonably be envisaged as available for use in a war in this [20th] century could properly be regarded as an antique", and Watkins J. stated "... I am prepared to say that no reasonable bench of justices could conclude, regardless of whether or not a firearm could be used in a war at any time, that a firearm which has been manufactured during this century is an antique". An honest and reasonable belief that a modern reproduction is an antique firearm is no defence to a charge of possessing a firearm without a certificate contrary to section 1(1)(a) of the 1968 Act: *R. v. Howells* [1977] Q.B. 614, 65 Cr.App.R. 86, and see *ante*, § 17–15.

B. FIREARMS ACT 1982

This Act applies the provisions of the 1968 Act (with certain exceptions) to imitation firearms which are readily convertible into firearms to which section 1 of the 1968 Act applies. **24–90**

Firearms Act 1982, ss.1, 2

Control of imitation firearms readily convertible into firearms to which section 1 of the 1968 Act applies

1.—(1) This Act applies to an imitation firearm if— **24–91**

(a) it has the appearance of being a firearm to which section 1 of the 1968 Act (firearms requiring a firearm certificate) applies; and

(b) it is so constructed or adapted as to be readily convertible into a firearm to which that section applies.

(2) Subject to section 2(2) of this Act and the following provisions of this section, the 1968 Act shall apply in relation to an imitation firearm to which this Act applies as it applies in relation to a firearm to which section 1 of that Act applies.

(3) Subject to the modifications in subsection (4) below, any expression given a meaning for the purposes of the 1968 Act has the same meaning in this Act.

(4) For the purposes of this section and the 1968 Act, as it applies by virtue of this section—

(a) the definition of air weapon in section 1(3)(b) of that Act (air weapons excepted from requirement of firearm certificate) shall have effect without the exclusion of any type declared by rules made by the Secretary of State under section 53 of that Act to be specially dangerous; and

(b) the definition of firearm in section 57(1) of that Act shall have effect without paragraphs (b) and (c) of that subsection (component parts and accessories).

(5) In any proceedings brought by virtue of this section for an offence under the 1968 Act involving an imitation firearm to which this Act applies, it shall be a defence for the accused to show that he did not know and had no reason to suspect that the imitation firearm was so constructed or adapted as to be readily convertible into a firearm to which section 1 of that Act applies.

(6) For the purposes of this section an imitation firearm shall be regarded as readily convertible into a firearm to which section 1 of the 1968 Act applies if—

(a) it can be so converted without any special skill on the part of the person converting it in the construction or adaptation of firearms of any description; and

(b) the work involved in converting it does not require equipment or tools other than such as are in common use by persons carrying out works of construction and maintenance in their own homes.

Provisions supplementary to section 1

2.—(1) Subject to subsection (2) below, references in the 1968 Act, and in any order made under section 6 of that Act (orders prohibiting movement of firearms or ammunition) before this Act comes into force—

(a) to firearms (without qualification); or

(b) to firearms to which section 1 of that Act applies;

shall be read as including imitation firearms to which this Act applies.

(2) The following provisions of the 1968 Act do not apply by virtue of this Act to an imitation firearm to which this Act applies, that is to say—

(a) section 4(3) and (4) (offence to convert anything having appearance of firearm into a firearm and aggravated offence under section 1 involving a converted firearm); and

(b) the provisions of that Act which relate to, or to the enforcement of control over, the manner in which a firearm is used or the circumstances in which it is carried;

but without prejudice, in the case of the provisions mentioned in paragraph (b) above, to the application to such an imitation firearm of such of those provisions as apply to imitation firearms apart from this Act.

(3) The provisions referred to in subsection (2)(b) above are sections 16 to 20 and section 47.

C. FIREARMS (AMENDMENT) ACT 1988

(1) Introduction

24–92 Sections 6 to 8 (converted and de-activated weapons);section 12 (revocation of certificates); sections 15 to 19 (exemptions); section 25 (interpretation) and the Schedule to the 1988 Act are set out in this section or summarised. Purely summary offences are omitted. Amendments effected by the Act to the 1968 Act are incorporated into the 1968 Act as printed, *ante*, §§ 24–3 *et seq*.

(2) Converted and de-activated weapons

Firearms (Amendment) Act 1988, ss.6–8

Shortening of barrels

24–93 **6.**—(1) Subject to subsection (2) below, it is an offence to shorten to a length less than 24 inches the barrel of any smooth-bore gun to which section 1 of the principal Act applies other than one which has a barrel with a bore exceeding 2 inches in diameter; and that offence shall be punishable—

(a) on summary conviction, with imprisonment for a term not exceeding six months or a fine not exceeding the statutory maximum or both;

(b) on indictment, with imprisonment for a term not exceeding five years or a fine or both.

(2) It is not an offence under this section for a registered firearms dealer to shorten the

barrel of a gun for the sole purpose of replacing a defective part of the barrel so as to produce a barrel not less than 24 inches in length.

Conversion not to affect classification

7.—(1) Any weapon which— 24–94

(a) has at any time (whether before or after the passing of the *Firearms (Amendment) Act* 1997) been a weapon of a kind described in section 5(1) or (1A) of the principal Act (including any amendments to section 5(1) made under section 1(4) of this Act); and

(b) is not a self-loading or pump-action smooth-bore gun which has at any such time been such a weapon by reason only of having had a barrel less than 24 inches in length,

shall be treated as a prohibited weapon notwithstanding anything done for the purpose of converting it into a weapon of a different kind.

(2) Any weapon which—

(a) has at any time since the coming into force of section 2 above been a weapon to which section 1 of the principal Act applies; or

(b) would at any previous time have been such a weapon if those sections had then been in force,

shall, if it has, or at any time has had, a rifled barrel less than 24 inches in length, be treated as a weapon to which section 1 of the principal Act applies notwithstanding anything done for the purpose of converting it into a shot gun or an air weapon.

(3) For the purposes of subsection (2) above there shall be disregarded the shortening of a barrel by a registered firearms dealer for the sole purpose of replacing part of it so as to produce a barrel not less than 24 inches in length.

[This section is printed as amended by the 1997 Act, s.52(1) and Sched. 2, para. 16.]

De-activated weapons

8. For the purposes of the principal Act and this Act it shall be presumed, unless the contrary is shown, that a firearm has been rendered incapable of discharging any shot, bullet or other missile, and has consequently ceased to be a firearm within the meaning of those Acts, if— 24–95

(a) it bears a mark which has been approved by the Secretary of State for denoting that fact and which has been made either by one of the two companies mentioned in section 58(1) of the principal Act or by such other person as may be approved by the Secretary of State for the purposes of this section; and

(b) that company or person has certified in writing that work has been carried out on the firearm in a manner approved by the Secretary of State for rendering it incapable of discharging any shot, bullet or other missile.

(3) Firearm and shot gun certificates

Where a certificate is revoked pursuant to section 30 of the 1968 Act, section 12 of the 1988 Act gives the chief officer of police the power to require the certificate holder to surrender the certificate and the relevant firearms and ammunition. 24–96

(4) Exemptions

Firearms (Amendment) Act 1988, s.15

Approved rifle clubs and muzzle-loading pistol clubs

15.—(1) Subject to subsection (4) below, a member of a rifle club approved by the Secretary of State may, without holding a firearm certificate, have in his possession a rifle and ammunition when engaged as a member of the club in connection with target shooting. 24–97

(2) Any rifle club may apply for approval, whether or not it is intended that any club members will, by virtue of subsection (1) above, have rifles or ammunition in their possession without holding firearm certificates.

(3) The Secretary of State may publish such guidance as he considers appropriate for the purpose of informing those seeking approval for a club of criteria that must be met before any application for such approval will be considered.

(4) The application of subsection (1) above to members of an approved rifle club may—

(a) be excluded in relation to the club, or

(b) be restricted to target shooting with specified types of rifle,

by limitations contained in the approval.

(5) An approval—

(a) may be granted subject to such conditions specified in it as the Secretary of State thinks fit;

(b) may at any time be varied or withdrawn by the Secretary of State; and

(c) shall (unless withdrawn) continue in force for six years from the date on which it is granted or last renewed.

(6) [*Fees.*]

(7) A constable or civilian officer authorised in writing in that behalf may, on producing if required his authority, enter any premises occupied or used by an approved rifle club and inspect those premises, and anything on them, for the purpose of ascertaining whether the provisions of this section, and any limitations or conditions in the approval, are being complied with.

(8) The power of a constable or civilian officer under subsection (7) above to inspect anything on club premises shall include power to require any information which is kept by means of a computer and is accessible from the premises to be made available for inspection in a visible and legible form.

(9) [*Summary offence: obstruction of constable.*]

(10) In this section and section 15A below—

"approval", means an approval under this section; and "approved" shall be construed accordingly;

"civilian officer" has the same meaning as in the principal Act; and

"rifle club" includes a miniature rifle club.

(11) This section applies in relation to a muzzle-loading pistol club and its members as it applies to a rifle club and its members with the substitution for any reference to a rifle of a reference to a muzzle-loading pistol.

(12) In subsection (11) above—

"muzzle-loading pistol club" means a club where muzzle-loading pistols are used for target shooting; and

"muzzle-loading pistol" means a pistol designed to be loaded at the muzzle end of the barrel or chamber with a loose charge and a separate ball (or other missile).

[This section is printed as substituted by the 1997 Act, s.45(1).]

24–98 W, a member of a rifle club, had arranged a private shoot. In connection with this he had acquired ammunition in excess of the amount authorised by his firearm certificate. The shoot did not take place because of bad weather and the ammunition was found in his home when searched by the police a month later. The judge's ruling that section 11(3) of the 1968 Act (see now section 15(1) of the 1988 Act) could have no application to the case was upheld. Whatever might be the situation with regard to shorter lengths of time, after one month it could not possibly be said that W was "engaged as a member of a club in connection with target practice", namely the day's shoot: *R. v. Wilson (M.)* [1989] Crim.L.R. 901, CA.

Firearms (Amendment) Act 1988, ss.16, 16A, 16B

Borrowed rifles on private premises

24–99 **16.**—(1) A person of or over the age of seventeen may, without holding a firearm certificate, borrow a rifle from the occupier of private premises and use it on those premises in the presence either of the occupier or of a servant of the occupier if—

(a) the occupier or servant in whose presence it is used holds a firearm certificate in respect of that rifle; and

(b) the borrower's possession and use of it complies with any conditions as to those matters specified in the certificate.

(2) A person who by virtue of subsection (1) above is entitled without holding a firearm certificate to borrow and use a rifle in another person's presence may also without holding such a certificate, purchase or acquire ammunition for use in the rifle and have it in his possession during the period for which the rifle is borrowed if—

(a) the firearm certificate held by that other person authorises the holder to have in his possession at that time ammunition for the rifle of a quantity not less than that purchased or acquired by, and in the possession of, the borrower; and

(b) the borrower's possession and use of the ammunition complies with any conditions as to those matters specified in the certificate.

Possession of firearms on service premises

16A.—(1) A person under the supervision of a member of the armed forces may, without holding a certificate or obtaining the authority of the Secretary of State under section 5 of the principal Act, have in his possession a firearm and ammunition on service premises.

(2) Subsection (1) above does not apply to a person while engaged in providing security protection on service premises.

(3) In this section—

"armed forces" means any of the naval, military or air forces of Her Majesty; and

"service premises" means premises, including any ship or aircraft, used for any purpose of the armed forces.

[This section was inserted by the *AFA* 1996, s.28(2).]

Possession of firearms on Ministry of Defence Police premises

16B.—(1) A person who is being trained or assessed in the use of firearms under the supervision of a member of the Ministry of Defence Police may, without holding a certificate or obtaining the authority of the Secretary of State under section 5 of the principal Act, have in his possession a firearm and ammunition on relevant premises for the purposes of the training or assessment. **24–99a**

(2) In this section "relevant premises" means premises used for any purpose of the Ministry of Defence Police.

[This section was inserted by the *Police Reform Act* 2002, s.81.]

Firearms (Amendment) Act 1988, s.17(1), (1A)

Visitors' permits

17.—(1) The holder of a visitor's firearm permit may, without holding a firearm certificate, have in his possession any firearm, and have in his possession, purchase or acquire any ammunition, to which section 1 of the principal Act applies; and (subject to subsection (1A) below) the holder of a visitor's shot gun permit may, without holding a shot gun certificate, have shot guns in his possession and purchase or acquire shot guns. **24–100**

(1A) A visitor's shot gun permit shall not authorise the purchase or acquisition by any person of any shot gun with a magazine except where—

(a) that person is for the time being the holder of a licence granted, for the purposes of any order made under section 1 of the *Import, Export and Customs Powers (Defence) Act* 1939, in respect of the exportation of that shot gun;

(b) the shot gun is to be exported from Great Britain to a place outside the member States without first being taken to another member State;

(c) the shot gun is acquired on terms which restrict that person's possession of the gun to the whole or a part of the period of his visit to Great Britain and preclude the removal of the gun from Great Britain; or

(d) the shot gun is purchased or acquired by that person exclusively in connection with the carrying on of activities in respect of which—

(i) that person; or

(ii) the person on whose behalf he makes the purchase or acquisition,

is recognised, for the purposes of the law of another member State relating to firearms, as a collector of firearms or a body concerned in the cultural or historical aspects of weapons.

[This section is printed as amended by the *Firearms Acts (Amendment) Regulations* 1992 (S.I. 1992 No. 2823), regs. 6(1) and 7(1).]

Section 17(2) deals with the circumstances in which a visitor's permit can be granted where the application is made on the visitor's behalf by a person resident in the relevant area. Subsections (3) and (3A) set out restrictions on the granting of visitors' permits. Subsection (4) deals with the form of the permit. Subsection (5) gives the chief officer of police the power to vary the permit. Subsection (6) provides that the permit comes into force on the date that is specified in it and shall continue in force for the specified period (not to exceed 12 months). Subsection (7) provides for a group application for up to 20 permits. Subsections (8) and (9) deal with fees. Subsection (10) creates two summary offences.

Firearms (Amendment) Act 1988, ss.18(1), (1A), 19

Firearms acquired for export

24–101 **18.**—(1) A person may, without holding a firearm or shot gun certificate, purchase a firearm from a registered firearms dealer if—

(a) that person has not been in Great Britain for more than thirty days in the preceding twelve months; and

(b) the firearm is purchased for the purpose only of being exported from Great Britain without first coming into that person's possession.

(1A) A person shall not be entitled under subsection (1) above to purchase any firearm which falls within category B for the purposes of Annex I to the European weapons directive unless he—

(a) produces to the dealer from whom he purchases it a document which—

(i) has been issued under provisions which, in the member State where he resides, correspond to the provisions of the principal Act for the issue of Article 7 authorities; and

(ii) contains the prior agreement to the purchase of that firearm which is required by Article 7 of the European weapons directive;

(b) shows that he is purchasing the firearm exclusively in connection with the carrying on of activities in respect of which he, or the person on whose behalf he is purchasing the firearm, is recognised, for the purposes of the law of another member State relating to firearms, as a collector of firearms or a body concerned in the cultural or historical aspects of weapons; or

(c) shows that he resides in the United Kingdom or outside the member States.

[This section is printed as amended by the *Firearms Acts (Amendment) Regulations* 1992 (S.I. 1992 No. 2823), reg. 8.]

Section 18(2) requires the dealer selling the firearm to send notice of the transaction within 48 hours to the relevant chief officer of police. Subsection (3) deals with the form of the notice and subsection (4) with the details to be entered in the register. Subsections (5) and (6) relate to a summary offence. Section 18A deals with the purchase or acquisition of firearms in other Member States and creates a summary offence for failure to comply with its requirements.

Firearms and ammunition in museums

24–102 **19.** The Schedule to this Act shall have effect for exempting firearms and ammunition in museums from certain provisions of the principal Act.

Firearms (Amendment) Act 1988, Sched., paras 1(1), (2), (4), 6

Section 19

SCHEDULE

FIREARMS AND AMMUNITION IN MUSEUMS

Museum firearms licences

24–103 1.—(1) The Secretary of State may, on an application in writing made on behalf of a museum to which this Schedule applies, grant a museum firearms licence in respect of that museum.

(2) While a museum firearms licence (in this Schedule referred to as a "licence") is in force in respect of a museum the persons responsible for its management and their servants—

(a) may, without holding a firearm certificate or shot gun certificate, have in their possession, and purchase or acquire, for the purposes of the museum firearms and ammunition which are or are to be normally exhibited or kept on its premises or on such of them as are specified in the licence; and

(b) if the licence so provides, may, without the authority of the Secretary of State under section 5 of the principal Act, have in their possession, purchase or acquire for those purposes any prohibited weapons and ammunition which are or are to be normally exhibited or kept as aforesaid.

(4) Where a licence is revoked the Secretary of State shall by notice in writing require the persons responsible for the management of the museum in question to surrender the licence to him.

Interpretation

6. In this Schedule references to the persons responsible for the management of a

museum are to the board of trustees, governing body or other person or persons (whether or not incorporated) exercising corresponding functions.

Paragraph 1(3) of the Schedule requires the Secretary of State, before granting a licence, to consult the relevant chief officer of police and satisfy himself of the arrangements for keeping the firearms and ammunition in question. Sub-paragraph (4) deals with the form of the licence and sub-paragraphs (5), (6) and (7) with its duration. Paragraph 2 of the Schedule entitles the Secretary of State to vary or revoke the licence. Paragraph 3 deals with fees. Paragraph 4 creates summary offences relating to the provisions of the Schedule. Paragraph 5 (which is amended by the 1997 Act, s.47) lists the museums to which the Schedule applies. **24–104**

(5) Interpretation

Firearms (Amendment) Act 1988, s.25

Interpretation and supplementary provisions

25.—(1) In this Act "the principal Act" means the *Firearms Act* 1968 and any expression which is also used in that Act has the same meaning as in that Act. **24–105**

(2), (3) [*Amend* Firearms Act *1968, s.57*.]

(4) Any reference in the principal Act to a person who is by virtue of that Act entitled to possess, purchase or acquire any weapon or ammunition without holding a certificate shall include a reference to a person who is so entitled by virtue of any provision of this Act.

(5) Sections 46, 51(4) and 52 of the principal Act (powers of search, time limit for prosecutions and forfeiture and cancellation orders on conviction) shall apply also to offences under this Act except that on the conviction of a person for an offence under the Schedule to this Act no order shall be made for the forfeiture of anything in his possession for the purpose of the museum in question.

(6) Sections 53 to 56 and section 58 of the principal Act (rules, Crown application, service of notices and savings) shall have effect as if this Act were contained in that Act.

(7) The provisions of this Act other than sections 15 and 17 shall be treated as contained in the principal Act for the purposes of the *Firearms Act* 1982 (imitation firearms readily convertible into firearms to which section 1 of the principal Act applies).

D. FIREARMS (AMENDMENT) ACT 1997

(1) Introduction

Sections 2 to 8 of the 1997 Act are set out *ante*, §§ 24–25b *et seq*. Sections 32 to 36 are set out in full, *post*, §§ 24–105e *et seq.*; other relevant sections are summarised. Amendments effected by the Act to the 1968 or1988 Acts are incorporated *ante*, §§ 24–3 *et seq*. **24–105a**

[The next paragraph is § 24–105d.]

(2) Surrender of firearms and compensation

Sections 15 to 18, as amended by the 1997 (No. 2) Act, s.2, deal with the surrender of firearms and ammunition and the payment of compensation. **24–105d**

(3) Regulation of firearms and ammunition

Firearms (Amendment) Act 1997, ss.32–36

Transfers of firearms etc. to be in person

32.—(1) This section applies where, in Great Britain— **24–105e**

(a) a firearm or ammunition to which section 1 of the 1968 Act applies is sold, let on hire, lent or given by any person, or

(b) a shot gun is sold, let on hire or given, or lent for a period of more than 72 hours by any person,

to another person who is neither a registered firearms dealer nor a person who is entitled to purchase or acquire the firearm or ammunition without holding a firearm or shot gun certificate or a visitor's firearm or shot gun permit.

(2) Where a transfer to which this section applies takes place—

(a) the transferee must produce to the transferor the certificate or permit entitling him to purchase or acquire the firearm or ammunition being transferred;

(b) the transferor must comply with any instructions contained in the certificate or permit produced by the transferee;

(c) the transferor must hand the firearm or ammunition to the transferee, and the transferee must receive it, in person.

(3) A failure by the transferor or transferee to comply with subsection (2) above shall be an offence.

Notification of transfers involving firearms

24–105f **33.**—(1) This section applies where in Great Britain—

(a) any firearm to which section 1 of the 1968 Act applies is sold, let on hire, lent or given;

(b) any shot gun is sold, let on hire or given, or lent for a period of more than 72 hours.

(2) Any party to a transfer to which this section applies who is the holder of a firearm or shot gun certificate or, as the case may be, a visitor's firearm or shot gun permit which relates to the firearm in question shall within seven days of the transfer give notice to the chief officer of police who granted his certificate or permit.

(3) A notice required by subsection (2) above shall—

(a) contain a description of the firearm in question (giving its identification number if any); and

(b) state the nature of the transaction and the name and address of the other party;

and any such notice shall be sent by registered post or the recorded delivery service.

(4) A failure by a party to a transaction to which this section applies to give the notice required by this section shall be an offence.

Notification of de-activation, destruction or loss of firearms etc.

24–105g **34.**—(1) Where, in Great Britain—

(a) a firearm to which a firearm or shot gun certificate relates; or

(b) a firearm to which a visitor's firearm or shot gun permit relates,

is de-activated, destroyed or lost (whether by theft or otherwise), the certificate holder who was last in possession of the firearm before that event shall within seven days of that event give notice of it to the chief officer of police who granted the certificate or permit.

(2) Where, in Great Britain, any ammunition to which section 1 of the 1968 Act applies, and a firearm certificate or a visitor's firearm permit relates, is lost (whether by theft or otherwise), the certificate or permit holder who was last in possession of the ammunition before that event shall within seven days of the loss give notice of it to the chief officer of police who granted the certificate or permit.

(3) A notice required by this section shall—

(a) describe the firearm or ammunition in question (giving the identification number of the firearm if any);

(b) state the nature of the event;

and any such notice shall be sent by registered post or the recorded delivery service.

(4) A failure, without reasonable excuse, to give a notice required by this section shall be an offence.

(5) For the purposes of this section and section 35 below a firearm is de-activated if it would, by virtue of section 8 of the 1988 Act be presumed to be rendered incapable of discharging any shot, bullet or other missile.

Notification of events taking place outside Great Britain involving firearms etc.

24–105h **35.**—(1) Where, outside Great Britain, any firearm or shot gun is sold or otherwise disposed of by a transferor whose acquisition or purchase of the firearm or shot gun was authorised by a firearm certificate or shot gun certificate, the transferor shall within 14 days of the disposal give notice of it to the chief officer of police who granted his certificate.

(2) A failure to give a notice required by subsection (1) above shall be an offence.

(3) Where, outside Great Britain—

(a) a firearm to which a firearm or shot gun certificate relates is de-activated, destroyed or lost (whether by theft or otherwise); or

(b) any ammunition to which section 1 of the 1968 Act applies, and a firearm certificate relates, is lost (whether by theft or otherwise),

the certificate holder who was last in possession of the firearm or ammunition before that event shall within 14 days of the event give notice of it to the chief officer of police who granted the certificate.

(4) A failure, without reasonable excuse, to give a notice required by subsection (3) above shall be an offence.

(5) A notice required by this section shall—

(a) contain a description of the firearm or ammunition in question (including any identification number); and

(b) state the nature of the event and, in the case of a disposal, the name and address of the other party.

(6) A notice required by this section shall be sent within 14 days of the disposal or other event—

(a) if it is sent from a place in the United Kingdom, by registered post or by the recorded delivery service; and

(b) in any other case, in such manner as most closely corresponds to the use of registered post or the recorded delivery service.

Penalty for offences under ss.32 to 35

36. An offence under section 32, 33, 34 or 35 above shall— **24–105i**

(a) if committed in relation to a transfer or other event involving a firearm or ammunition to which section 1 of the 1968 Act applies be punishable—

(i) on summary conviction with imprisonment for a term not exceeding *six* [12] months or a fine not exceeding the statutory maximum or both;

(ii) on conviction on indictment with imprisonment for a term not exceeding five years or a fine or both;

(b) if committed in relation to a transfer or other event involving a shot gun be punishable on summary conviction with imprisonment for a term not exceeding six months or a fine not exceeding level 5 on the standard scale or both.

[In para. (a)(i), "12" is substituted for "six", as from a day to be appointed, by the *CJA* 2003, s.282(2) and (3). The increase has no application to offences committed before the substitution takes effect: s.282(4).]

Section 39 of the 1997 Act creates a central register of all persons who have applied for a firearm or shot gun certificate or who hold such a certificate. Section 44 provides for special conditions for firearms certificates for certain firearms used for target shooting. For section 48, see *ante*, § 24–80. **24–105j**

(4) Interpretation

Firearms (Amendment) Act 1997, s.50

Interpretation and supplementary provisions

50.—(1) In this Act— **24–105k**

"small-calibre pistol" means—

(a) a pistol chambered for .22 or smaller rim-fire cartridges; or

(b) an air pistol to which section 1 of the 1968 Act applies and which is designed to fire .22 or smaller diameter ammunition;

"the 1968 Act" means the *Firearms Act* 1968;

"the 1988 Act" means the *Firearms (Amendment) Act* 1988.

(2) Any expression used in this Act which is also used in the 1968 Act or the 1988 Act has the same meaning as in that Act.

(3) Any reference in the 1968 Act to a person who is by virtue of that Act entitled to possess, purchase or acquire any weapon or ammunition without holding a certificate shall include a reference to a person who is so entitled by virtue of any provision of this Act.

(4) Sections 46, 51(4) and 52 of the 1968 Act (powers of search, time-limit for prosecutions and forfeiture and cancellation orders on conviction) shall apply also to offences under this Act.

(5) Sections 53 to 56 and section 58 of the 1968 Act (rules, Crown application, services of notices and savings) shall have effect as if this Act were contained in that Act.

(6) The provisions of this Act shall be treated as contained in the 1968 Act for the purposes of the *Firearms Act* 1982 (imitation firearms readily convertible into firearms to which section 1 of the 1968 Act applies).

[This section is printed as repealed in part by the 1997 (No. 2) Act, s.2(7) and Sched.]

E. VIOLENT CRIME REDUCTION ACT 2006

24–105l Sections 32, 35 and 36 to 39 of the *VCRA* 2006 relate respectively to the sale of air weapons by way of trade or business, the sale and purchase of primers and the manufacture, import and sale of realistic imitation firearms. Section 35 came into force on April 6, 2007 (*Violent Crime Reduction Act 2006 (Commencement No. 2) Order* 2007 (S.I. 2007 No. 858)). Sections 32 and 36 to 39 came into force on October 1, 2007 (*Violent Crime Reduction Act 2006 (Commencement No. 3) Order* 2007 (S.I. 2007 No. 2180)). The following provisions create summary offences: sections 32(2) (where, in the course of the sale of an air weapon by way of a trade or business to an individual in Great Britain, who is not registered as a firearms dealer, the seller or his representative transfers possession of the weapon to the buyer when both parties are not present in person); 35(2) (selling, except in specified circumstances, a cap-type primer (*i.e.* components of ammunition which contain a chemical compound that detonates on impact) designed for use in metallic ammunition for a firearm, or an empty cartridge case incorporating such a primer); 35(4) (corresponding offence of buying or attempting to buy the same, specified circumstances apart); 36(1) (manufacture, sale or importation of "realistic imitation firearms" as defined in section 38, subject to the defences set out in section 37); and 39(3) (manufacturing or importing an imitation firearm which does not comply with any specifications prescribed pursuant to regulations made under subsection (2)). The *Violent Crime Reduction Act 2006 (Realistic Imitation Firearms) Regulations* 2007 (S.I. 2007 No. 2606) sets out defences to the section 36 offence and specifies sizes and colours which are to be regarded as unrealistic for the purposes of section 38. All these offences are punishable by 51 weeks' imprisonment, or a level 5 fine, or both (subject to a transitional provision in relation to the commencement of the *CJA* 2003, s.281(5)). As to certain sections of the *Firearms Act* 1968 applying as if these sections were contained in that Act, see *post*, § 24–146.

II. OFFENSIVE WEAPONS

A. INTRODUCTION

24–106 The rest of this chapter is concerned with the *Prevention of Crime Act* 1953, the *CJA* 1988 (in so far as it creates indictable offences), the *Knives Act* 1997 and the *VCRA* 2006. The *Restriction of Offensive Weapons Act* 1959 creates summary offences and is outside the scope of this work (but see *post*, § 24–132c).

B. PREVENTION OF CRIME ACT 1953

(1) Statute

Prevention of Crime Act 1953, s.1

24–106a **1.**—(1) Any person who without lawful authority or reasonable excuse, the proof whereof shall lie on him, has with him in any public place any offensive weapon shall be guilty of an offence, and shall be liable—

(a) on summary conviction, to imprisonment for a term not exceeding *six* [12] months or a fine not exceeding the prescribed sum or both;

(b) on conviction on indictment, to imprisonment for a term not exceeding four years or a fine, or both.

(2) Where any person is convicted of an offence under subsection (1) of this section the court may make an order for the forfeiture or disposal of any weapon in respect of which the offence was committed.

(3) [*Repealed by* PACE Act *1984, Sched.* 7.]

(4) In this section "public place" includes any highway and any other premises or place to which at the material time the public have or are permitted to have access, whether on payment or otherwise; and "offensive weapon" means any article made or adapted for use for causing injury to the person, or intended by the person having it with him for such use by him or by some other person.

[This section is printed as amended by the *Public Order Act* 1986, s.40(2), and Sched. 2; the *CJA* 1988, s.46(1); the *Offensive Weapons Act* 1996, s.2(1); and as repealed in part by the *CLA* 1977, s.32(1); and the *PACE Act* 1984, ss.26(1), 119(2) and Sched. 7. In subs. (1)(a), the reference to "the prescribed sum" is substituted by virtue of the *MCA* 1980, s.32(2); for the current value thereof, see s.32(9), *ante*, § 1–75aa; and "12" is substituted for "six", as from a day to be appointed, by the *CJA* 2003, s.282(2) and (3) (but the increase has no application to offences committed before the substitution takes effect: s.282(4)).]

(2) Indictment

STATEMENT OF OFFENCE

24–107 *Having an offence weapon, contrary to section 1 of the* Prevention of Crime Act *1953.*

PARTICULARS OF OFFENCE

A B, on the —— day of ——, 20—, without lawful authority or reasonable excuse, had with him in a public place, namely—, an offensive weapon, namely a flick-knife.

"Time" and "place" are material averments. Where on day one, two defendants travelled by car from Reading to Cornwall taking with them three domestic knives which were to be used to threaten a third person in Cornwall, it was held that a count charging a contravention of section 1 on day two during the return journey (the defendants having been stopped by the police in Wiltshire on their way back to Reading) restricted the Crown to the date and place averred. Accordingly, it was a misdirection to tell the jury that it was sufficient for the Crown to prove that the necessary intention was present at any time during the period between leaving Reading and their apprehension in Wiltshire: *R. v. Allamby and Medford*, 59 Cr.App.R. 189, CA.

Even if there may be an issue as to whether an article is offensive *per se* or whether it is offensive because the defendant had it with the necessary intent, it is not necessary to include two counts in the indictment: *R. v. Flynn*, 82 Cr.App.R. 319, CA.

However, the jury must be unanimous as to which category of offensive weapon a particular weapon belongs to, see *Flynn*, *ante*, and *R. v. Rowe* [1990] Crim.L.R. 344, CA: see further §§ 4–391 *et seq.*, *ante*.

(3) Class of offence and mode of trial

24–108 This offence is a class 3 offence, *ante*, § 2–17, and is triable either way: s.1(1), *ante*. For the Sentencing Guidelines Council's guideline on mode of trial, see Appendix K-161 (but note the effect of *R. v. Povey*, *post*, § 24–109).

(4) Sentence

24–109 On summary conviction, six months (increased to 12 months, as from a day to be appointed (*ante*)), or a fine of the prescribed sum, or both: s.1(1)(a), *ante*. On indictment, four years, or a fine, or both: s.1(1)(b), *ante*.

In *R. v. Poulton*; *R. v. Celaire* [2003] 1 Cr.App.R.(S.) 116, CA, the court issued sentencing guidelines for the offence under the 1953 Act. Where it is committed in conjunction with another offence, the usual considerations in relation to totality apply; a concurrent sentence will usually be appropriate if the weapons offence is ancillary to another more serious offence; where the weapons offence is distinct and independent of another offence, a consecutive sentence will usually be called for; a balance must be struck between the offence not in itself involving physical injury and the public's legitimate concern that a culture of carrying weapons encourages violence and may lead to more serious criminal behaviour; in assessing the seriousness of an offence, it is necessary to consider the offender's intention, the circumstances of the offence and the nature of the weapon involved; and it may be helpful for the sentencer to ask the questions posed in *R. v. Avis* [1998] 1 Cr.App.R. 420, CA (*ante*, § 24–82a).

As to intention, there are three specific aggravating factors:

(1) specifically planned use of the weapon to commit violence or threaten violence or intimidate others;

(2) hostility towards a minority individual or group, which may give rise to an aggravating feature, such as racial motivation within the *CDA* 1998, s.28; and

(3) acting under the influence of alcohol or drugs.

The circumstances of the offence may be aggravated if its commission takes place at premises such as a school, a hospital or other place where vulnerable people may be present; or at a large public gathering, especially one where there may be a risk of disorder; or on public transport or licensed premises or premises where people are carrying out public services, such as in a doctor's surgery or at a social security office; or if committed while on bail.

Although some weapons are more dangerous than others, the nature of the weapon will not be the primary determinant of the offence's seriousness, because a less dangerous weapon may be used to create fear, whereas a more obviously dangerous weapon may be carried for self-defence or no actual attempt may have been made by the offender to use it. But the nature of the weapon may shed light on an offender's intention, if he is carrying a weapon which is offensive *per se*, such as a flick-knife or a butterfly knife, or a weapon designed or adapted to cause serious injury.

Mitigating factors include the weapon being carried only on a temporary basis. A defendant, with previous convictions for violence or carrying weapons, who is convicted of carrying a particularly dangerous weapon, in circumstances including any of the above aggravating factors and with the clear intention of causing injury or fear, can expect to receive a sentence at or near the statutory maximum. In relation to an adult offender of previous good character, the custody threshold will almost invariably be passed where there is a combination of dangerous circumstances and actual use of the weapon to threaten or cause fear. The nature of the weapon and other aggravating or mitigating factors will bear on the length of the custodial term. Custody may still be appropriate, depending on the circumstances, where no threatening use was made of the weapon. Alternatively, absent any aggravating features and where no threat has been made and where the weapon is not particularly dangerous, the custody threshold may not be passed and a community sentence towards the top end of the available range may be appropriate. It will almost invariably be appropriate, in the case of young offenders, to obtain a pre-sentence report before proceeding to sentence. A forfeiture order should almost always be made.

In *R. v. Povey* [2008] Crim.L.R. 816, CA, the court referred to the escalation in the number of offences of carrying a knife or other weapon, and observed that sentencers should focus on the reduction of crime, including its reduction by deterrence, and the protection of the public; and the guidance in *Poulton and Celaire*, *ante*, decided when conditions were far less grave, should be applied with these considerations in mind.

The Magistrates' Court Sentencing Guidelines cover, amongst other offences, the possession of an offensive weapon or a knife (see Appendix K–161), and are based on *Poulton and Celaire*, *ante*. In *Povey*, *ante*, the court said that the guidance should normally be applied at the most severe end of the appropriate range.

(5) Ingredients of the offence

(a) *"has with him"*

Knowledge

24–110 The words "has with him in any public place" mean "knowingly has with him in any public place", and it is for the prosecution to prove knowledge: *R. v. Cugullere*, 45 Cr.App.R. 108, CCA.

In *R. v. McCalla*, 87 Cr.App.R. 372, CA, it was held that once a person has something knowingly, he continues to have it until he does something to rid himself of it. Merely forgetting that he has it is not enough to prevent him from continuing to have it. The decision to the contrary in *R. v. Russell (R.)*, 81 Cr.App.R. 315, CA, was held to be *per incuriam*. When the forgetfulness is coupled with the particular circumstances relating to the original acquisition of the article, that combination could, given sufficient facts, be a reasonable excuse for having the offensive weapon: *ibid.*; and *R. v. Glidewell*, 163 J.P. 557, CA (forgetfulness potentially a reasonable excuse where defendant taxi-driver had not introduced the items into his car and had intended to clear them out, but forgot).

"Has with him" distinguished from possession

The words "has with him" require proof of closer contact with the article than mere possession. "Every case of having is one of possessing, but it does not necessarily follow that every case of possessing is one of having ...": *McCalla*, *ante*, and followed in *R. v. Daubney*, 164 J.P. 519, CA. **24–110a**

Joint enterprise

Where several persons are charged jointly with having offensive weapons, and the evidence shows that each was carrying a weapon not made or adapted for use for causing injury to the person, particularly if the carrying took place by day and in a place where the oddity of the articles carried was not itself manifest, the jury should be directed to consider whether they are sure that the defendant whose case they are considering intended himself to use the article which he was carrying to injure someone, or, in the alternative, whether he was a party to a common purpose with one or more of the others of using some or all of the articles which they were severally carrying for the purpose of inflicting injury on some person; and in considering the latter alternative, that it is an essential pre-condition that they should be sure that he knew that the others or one of the others had with him the article that the other one was shown to have been carrying: *R. v. Edmonds* [1963] 2 Q.B. 142, 47 Cr.App.R. 114, CCA. **24–111**

The principle in R. v. Jura

Where a person uses an article offensively in a public place, the offensive use of the article is not conclusive of the question whether he had it with him as an offensive weapon within section 1(1): *R. v. Jura* [1954] 1 Q.B. 503, 38 Cr.App.R. 53, CCA; *Ohlson v. Hylton* [1975] 1 W.L.R. 724, DC; *R. v. Humphreys* [1977] Crim.L.R. 225, CA; *R. v. Veasey* [1999] Crim.L.R. 158, CA (motorist assaulting horsewoman with Krooklock not necessarily guilty under section 1(1)); and *C. v. DPP* [2002] Crim.L.R. 322, QBD (Elias J.) (dog lead not an offensive weapon where its use on police officers was immediately preceded by detaching the lead from the dog). This is so both in the case of an article made or adapted for use for causing injury where the person having the article has lawful authority or reasonable excuse for having it (as in *Jura*—rifle at rifle range), and in the case of an ordinary article used on the spur of the moment (as in *Ohlson v. Hylton*—a hammer). Having an article innocently will be converted into having the article guiltily if an intent to use the article offensively is formed before the actual occasion to use violence has arisen: *Ohlson v. Hylton*, *ante*. The unlawful use of the article as a weapon can be appropriately dealt with under the *Offences against the Person Act* 1861: *per* Lord Goddard C.J. in *Jura* (at pp. 506, 56). **24–112**

See also *Bates v. Bulman*, 68 Cr.App.R. 21, DC (the principle in *Jura* applies equally to the case of a person who in the course of an altercation asks to be handed an article which he then proceeds to use offensively); and *R. v. Dayle*, 58 Cr.App.R. 100, CA, where it was said that section 1 of the 1953 Act applies not just to the person who goes out with an offensive weapon without lawful authority or reasonable excuse, but also to the person who, while out, deliberately selects an article with the intention of using it without such authority or excuse.

(b) *"public place"*

The definition in subsection (4) (*ante*, § 24–106a) is the same as that in the *Firearms Act* 1968 (*ante*, §§ 24–61, 24–85), the *Public Order Act* 1936 (*post*, § 25–292), and the *CLA* 1967, s.91(4). In a case on the latter section (*Williams v. DPP*, 95 Cr.App.R. 415, DC), the court quoted with approval the following passage from Barry J.'s summing up to the jury in *R. v. Kane* [1965] 1 All E.R. 705, on whether a place is a public place: **24–113**

> "The real question is whether [the place] is open to the public, whether on payment or not, or whether, on the other hand, access to it is so restricted to a particular class, or even to particular classes of the public, such, for example, as the members of an ordinary householder's family and his relations and friends, and the plumber or other tradesmen who come to do various repairs about the house. If it is restricted to that sort of class of person then, of course, it is not a public place, it is a private place" (at p. 709).

In *DPP v. Vivier* [1991] 4 All E.R. 18, DC, a decision on the *RTA* 1988 (where the phrase "public place" is not defined), Simon Brown J. gave the following guidance:

> "How then, in cases where some particular road or place is used by an identifiable category of people, should justices decide whether that category is 'special' or 'restricted' or 'particular' such as to distinguish it from the public at large? What, in short, is the touchstone by which to recognise a special class of people from members of the general public? ... [O]ne asks whether there is about those who obtain permission to enter 'some reason personal to them for their admittance'. If people come to a private house as guests, postmen or meter readers, they come for reasons personal to themselves, to serve the purposes of the occupier.
>
> But what of the rather different type of case such as the present where those seeking entry are doing so for their own, rather than the occupier's purposes and yet are screened in the sense of having to satisfy certain conditions for admission. Does the screening process operate or endow those passing through with some special characteristic whereby they lose their identity as members of the general public and become instead a special class?
>
> Our approach would be as follows. By the same token that one asks in the earlier type of case whether permission is being granted for a reason personal to the user, in these screening cases one must ask: do those admitted pass through the screening process for a reason, or on account of some characteristic, personal to themselves? Or are they in truth merely members of the public who are being admitted as such and processed simply so as to make them subject to payment and whatever other conditions the landowner chooses to impose" (at p. 24).

Before land can be said to be public, the onus is on the prosecution to prove that the public had access to it, and the best way of doing so is to prove that they actually use it: *Pugh v. Knipe* [1972] R.T.R. 286, DC. Where a place is a "public place", before it can become a private place there must be evidence which shows that after a certain hour or at a particular point of time there is some physical obstruction to be overcome, so that anyone entering does so in defiance of the prohibition, express or implied: *R. v. Waters*, 47 Cr.App.R. 149, CCA. In *Sandy v. Martin* [1974] Crim.L.R. 258, DC, the defendant parked his car in a car park bearing a notice that it was for the use of patrons of the inn only. The defendant remained in the inn until closing time and an hour later was found by the police leaning against his van in the car park, drunk. The court, upholding the justices' decision to dismiss the information as they were not satisfied that the car park was a public place at the time of the incident, observed that an otherwise private place is public if and so long as the public have access at the invitation of the landowner. Here, there was no evidence that the licensee's invitation continued an hour after closing time.

24–114 The following have been held to be a public place: a field where point-to-point races are held (*R. v. Collinson*, 23 Cr.App.R. 49, CCA); a football stadium (*Cawley v. Frost* [1976] 1 W.L.R. 1207, DC); hospital grounds where visitors to the hospital and their friends were permitted to enter (*R. v. Powell* [1963] Crim.L.R. 511, CCA); a public house car park (*Elkins v. Cartlidge* [1947] 1 All E.R. 289, but *cf. Sandy v. Martin*, *ante*, and *Havell v. DPP* [1993] Crim.L.R. 621, DC—community centre car park not a public place); a caravan park (*DPP v. Vivier*, *ante*); a multi-storey car park (*Bowman v. DPP* [1991] R.T.R. 263, DC); a ferry lane (*DPP v. Coulman* [1993] R.T.R. 230, DC); and the upper landing of a block of flats in respect of which there were no notices, doors or barriers to restrain the public walking in off the street (*Knox v. Anderton*, 76 Cr.App.R. 156, DC, but *cf. Williams v. DPP*, *ante*—block of flats held not to be a public place where access to it controlled and restricted by security doors, intercom systems and a caretaker).

A person's garden cannot be a public place, notwithstanding the possibility that from there he might be able to inflict injury with a weapon on a passer-by on adjacent land to which the public has access: *R. v. Roberts (Leroy)* [2004] 1 Cr.App.R. 16, CA. See also *Harriot v. DPP*, 170 J.P. 494, DC (bail hostel forecourt not a public place).

(c) *"offensive weapon"*

Three categories

24–115 In *R. v. Simpson (C.)*, 78 Cr.App.R. 115, CA, Lord Lane C.J. (considering the definition in s.1(4), *ante*, § 24–106a) identified three categories of offensive weapon: those made for use for causing injury to the person, *i.e.* offensive *per se*; those adapted for such a purpose; and those not so made or adapted, but carried with the intention of causing injury to the person. In the first two categories, the prosecution do not have to prove that the defendant had the weapon with him for the purpose of inflicting injury (see *Davis v. Alexander*, 54 Cr.App.R. 398, DC): if the jury are sure that the weapon is offensive *per se*, the defendant will only be acquitted if he establishes lawful authority or reasonable excuse (see *post*).

Offensive per se

In *Simpson*, *ante*, Lord Lane C.J. gave as instances of weapons offensive *per se* a bayonet, a stiletto or a handgun. A police truncheon has been held to be offensive *per se*: *Houghton v. Chief Constable of Greater Manchester*, 84 Cr.App.R. 319, CA (Civ. Div.). So have a swordstick (*Davis v. Alexander*, 54 Cr.App.R. 398, DC; *R. v. Butler* [1988] Crim.L.R. 696, CA), "sand gloves" advertised as suitable for self-defence (*R. v. R. (Offensive weapon)* [2008] 1 Cr.App.R. 26, CA), and a rice-flail (*Copus v. DPP* [1989] Crim.L.R. 577, DC, but it does not appear that there was full argument on this issue; a genuine rice-flail is not made for causing injury; see the commentary of Sir John Smith Q.C.). **24–116**

Weapons which are manufactured for an innocent purpose are not offensive *per se*, *e.g.* a razor (*R. v. Petrie*, 45 Cr.App.R. 72, CA); a penknife (*R. v. Humphreys* [1977] Crim.L.R. 225, CA); some types of sheath knife (see *R. v. Williamson*, 67 Cr.App.R. 35, CA, and observations thereon in *Simpson*, *ante*); a lock-knife (*Patterson v. Block* (1984) 81 L.S.Gaz. 2458, DC); and a machete and catapult (*Southwell v. Chadwick*, 85 Cr.App.R. 235, DC).

In general, unless the weapon is a flick-knife or butterfly knife (see *post*) or, perhaps, a swordstick (the Court of Appeal in *Butler*, *ante*, thought that the trial judge had been generous in leaving the issue to the jury), the question of whether a weapon is offensive *per se* is for the jury to decide. To take the issue from the jury may result in an appeal being allowed: *Williamson*, *ante*.

Flick-knives and butterfly knives

As a matter of law, not fact, flick-knives (see the definition in the *Restriction of Offensive Weapons Act* 1959, s.1(1)—not printed in this work) are offensive *per se*: *R. v. Simpson (C.)*, *ante*, following *Gibson v. Wales*, 76 Cr.App.R. 60, DC. *Simpson* was applied to a butterfly knife in *DPP v. Hynde* [1998] 1 Cr.App.R. 288, DC. "Butterfly knife" is defined in the *Criminal Justice Act 1988 (Offensive Weapons) Order* 1988 (S.I. 1988 No. 2019) (not printed in this work).

"adapted for use"

This is treated in many cases as being another instance of weapons offensive *per se*. The example given in *Simpson*, *ante*, was a bottle broken deliberately: see *Bryan v. Mott*, *post*. **24–117**

"for causing injury to the person"

In *Bryan v. Mott*, 62 Cr.App.R. 71, DC, the Crown Court's finding that an article adapted to commit suicide was adapted "for causing injury to the person" was not challenged. For a Crown Court decision to the opposite effect, see *R. v. Fleming* [1989] Crim.L.R. 71. **24–118**

"intended by the person having it with him for use for causing injury to the person"

This means intended for such use, if necessary, either offensively or defensively. Thus in *Patterson v. Block* (1984) 81 L.S.Gaz. 2458, DC, where a defendant had with him a lock-knife (not an offensive weapon *per se*), and the only evidence against him was his statement to the police that he carried it for self defence, the court held that justices could properly draw the inference that for the purposes of defending himself he would, if necessary, use the knife to cause injury to the person. **24–119**

Recklessness as to the causing of injury is insufficient: *R. v. Byrne* [2004] Crim.L.R. 582, CA.

Intention to frighten/ cause injury by shock

24–120 In *R. v. Edmonds* [1963] 2 Q.B. 142, 47 Cr.App.R. 114, CCA, it was held that an intention to frighten is not enough unless it is "intimidation" and of a sort which is capable of producing injury through the operation of shock (*Woodward v. Koessler* [1958] 1 W.L.R. 1255, DC, considered). Indeed, the use of the words "frighten" or "intimidate" should be avoided unless the evidence discloses that the intention of the person having with him the article alleged to be an offensive weapon, was to cause injury by shock and hence injury to the person: *R. v. Rapier*, 70 Cr.App.R. 17, CA.

(d) *"without lawful authority or reasonable excuse"*

Lawful authority

24–121 In *Bryan v. Mott*, 62 Cr.App.R. 71, DC, Lord Widgery C.J. said *obiter*:

> "The reference to lawful authority in the section is a reference to those people who from time to time carry an offensive weapon as a matter of duty—the soldier and his rifle and the police officer with his truncheon. They are all carrying offensive weapons, but they do so normally under lawful authority" (at p. 73).

Security guards at dance halls do not have lawful authority to carry a truncheon: *R. v. Spanner* [1973] Crim.L.R. 704, CA. See also "reasonable excuse", *post*.

Reasonable excuse

Self-defence

24–122 In *Evans v. Hughes*, 56 Cr.App.R. 813, DC, Lord Widgery C.J. made the following statement of principle:

> "... it may be a reasonable excuse for the carrying of an offensive weapon that the carrier is in anticipation of imminent attack and is carrying it for his own personal defence, but what is abundantly clear to my mind is that this Act never intended to sanction the permanent or constant carriage of an offensive weapon merely because of some constant or enduring supposed or actual threat or danger to the carrier" (at p. 817).

So it is not a reasonable excuse for a "greaser" to carry a knife in case he is attacked by a "skinhead" (*R. v. Peacock* [1973] Crim.L.R. 639, CA); for a taxi-driver to carry a weapon in case he meets violent passengers (*Grieve v. Macleod* [1967] Crim.L.R. 424 (Scotland)); or for an employer to keep weapons in his car in case he is attacked when collecting wages (*Evans v. Wright* [1964] Crim.L.R. 466, DC), although the position might have been otherwise had the employer only carried the weapons on his way to and from the bank.

The position of security guards is unclear. In *R. v. Spanner*, *ante*, it was held that dance hall security guards did not have a reasonable excuse for carrying truncheons, but Bingham L.J. appeared to suggest in *Malnik v. DPP* [1989] Crim.L.R. 451, DC, that those concerned with security could reasonably arm themselves to repel unlawful violence.

Where the defendant carries the weapon as a result of a recent attack which he fears might be repeated, it is a question of degree whether he has a reasonable excuse. Carrying the weapon for a day or two after the attack is probably reasonable, but for eight days is borderline (*Evans v. Hughes, ante*); for 16 days (*Bradley v. Moss* [1974] Crim.L.R. 430, DC) or four weeks (*Pittard v. Mahoney* [1977] Crim.L.R. 169, DC) is excessive.

If the defendant arms himself to repel unlawful violence which he himself is about to create (*e.g.* by visiting somebody whom he knows is likely to greet him with violence) he does not establish a reasonable excuse: *Malnik v. DPP*, *ante*. However, in *R. v. Archbold*, 171 J.P. 664, CA, it was held that that the issue as to whether the defendant had a reasonable excuse on the ground that he was anticipating imminent attack and was carrying a weapon for his own personal defence should have been left to the jury even where he had knowingly put himself into a position where he might come under attack, by leaving home with a knife and seeking out the complainant (who had been throwing stones at his car and the windows of his house).

Other excuses

An innocent motive for carrying an offensive weapon can sometimes amount to a reasonable excuse: see *Houghton v. Chief Constable of Greater Manchester*, 84 Cr.App.R. 319, CA (reasonable excuse to carry truncheon as part of police uniform for fancy dress party), and *Southwell v. Chadwick*, 85 Cr.App.R. 235, DC (reasonable to carry machete and catapult for killing grey squirrels). By contrast, it was held not to be reasonable in *Bryan v. Mott*, 62 Cr.App.R. 71, DC, to carry a broken milk bottle for the purpose of committing suicide. The fact that the accused did not know that an article was made or adapted for causing injury to the person cannot amount to a reasonable excuse for having it in a public place: *R. v. Densu* [1998] 1 Cr.App.R. 400, CA. As for forgetfulness as a reasonable excuse, see *ante*, § 24–110. **24–123**

Burden and standard of proof

The standard of proof (on the defendant) is the balance of probabilities: *R. v. Brown*, 55 Cr.App.R. 478, CA. **24–124**

C. Criminal Justice Act 1988

(1) Having article with blade or point in public place

Criminal Justice Act 1988, s.139

139.—(1) Subject to subsections (4) and (5) below, any person who has an article to which this section applies with him in a public place shall be guilty of an offence. **24–125**

(2) Subject to subsection (3) below, this section applies to any article which has a blade or is sharply pointed except a folding pocketknife.

(3) This section applies to a folding pocketknife if the cutting edge of its blade exceeds 3 inches.

(4) It shall be a defence for a person charged with an offence under this section to prove that he had good reason or lawful authority for having the article with him in a public place.

(5) Without prejudice to the generality of subsection (4) above, it shall be a defence for a person charged with an offence under this section to prove that he had the article with him—

(a) for use at work;

(b) for religious reasons; or

(c) as part of any national costume.

(6) A person guilty of an offence under subsection (1) above shall be liable

(a) on summary conviction, to imprisonment for a term not exceeding *six* [12] months, or a fine not exceeding the statutory maximum, or both;

(b) on conviction on indictment, to imprisonment for a term not exceeding four years, or a fine, or both.

(7) In this section "public place" includes any place to which at the material time the public have or are permitted access, whether on payment or otherwise.

(8) This section shall not have effect in relation to anything done before it comes into force.

[This section is printed as amended by the *Offensive Weapons Act* 1996, s.3(1); and, as from February 12, 2007 (*Violent Crime Reduction Act 2006 (Commencement No. 1) Order* 2007 (S.I. 2007 No. 74)), by the *VCRA* 2006, s.42(1) (increase in maximum penalty from two to four years, but only in relation to offences committed on or after that date: s.42(2)). In subs. (6)(a), "12" is substituted for "six", as from a day to be appointed, by the *CJA* 2003, s.282(2) and (3). The increase has no application to offences committed before the substitution takes effect: s.282(4).]

Class of offence and mode of trial

This offence is a class 3 offence, *ante*, § 2–17, and is triable either way: s.139(6), *ante*. **24–126**

For the Sentencing Guidelines Council's guideline on mode of trial, see Appendix K–161 (but note the effect of *R. v. Povey*, *ante*, § 24–109).

Sentence

24–127 On summary conviction, six months (increased to 12 months, as from a day to be appointed (*ante*)), or a fine of the prescribed sum, or both: s.139(6)(a), *ante*. On indictment, four years (subject to the transitional provision, *ante*), or a fine, or both: s.139(6)(b), *ante*.

As for sentencing guidelines, see *ante*, § 24–109. It seems that for sentencing purposes the possession of a knife is to be treated in a similar way to the possession of other offensive weapons.

Ingredients

24–128 For the meaning of "has ... with him", see *ante*, §§ 24–110 *et seq*. For "public place", see *ante*, §§ 24–113, 24–114.

A butter knife, with no cutting edge and no point, is a bladed article within the meaning of section 139(2): *Brooker v. DPP*, 169 J.P. 368, DC; but a screwdriver is not: *R. v. Davis* [1998] Crim.L.R. 564, CA.

A "lock-knife" does not come into the category of "folding pocketknife" excluded from the section because it is not immediately foldable at all times. A further process is required, namely the pressing of a button: *R. v. Deegan* [1998] 2 Cr.App.R. 121, CA, following *Harris v. DPP*; *Fehmi v. DPP*, 96 Cr.App.R. 235, DC.

The reverse burden provisions in section 139(4) and (5) do not contravene Article 6 of the ECHR (*ante*, § 16–57) in placing a persuasive burden on the accused: *R. v. Matthews* [2003] 2 Cr.App.R. 19, CA, following *L. v. DPP* [2002] 1 Cr.App.R. 32, DC.

A judge is only entitled to withdraw from the jury a defence under subsection (4) or (5) if there is *no* evidence to support it; if there is some evidence, however tenuous or nebulous, the question should be left to the jury; on no account should there be a direction to convict: *R. v. Wang* [2005] 2 Cr.App.R. 8, HL (impliedly disapproving *R. v. Bown* [2004] 1 Cr.App.R. 13, CA).

A defendant does not discharge the burden of showing "good reason" (s.139(4)) for having the article with him merely by providing an explanation which is uncontradicted by any prosecution evidence: *Godwin v. DPP*, 96 Cr.App.R. 244, DC.

The meaning of the phrases "good reason" (s.139(4)) and "for use at work" (s.139(5)(a)) are for the jury to determine in the context of the case and do not require judicial definition: *R. v. Manning* [1998] Crim.L.R. 198, CA.

Forgetfulness alone cannot amount to a good reason, but forgetfulness combined with another reason might (such as a parent buying a knife, putting it in the car's glove compartment to keep it out of a child's reach, and then forgetting to retrieve the knife on arrival home): *R. v. Jolie*, 167 J.P. 313, CA, following *McCalla* and *Glidewell* (*ante*, § 24–110), there being no significant difference between "reasonable excuse" under the 1953 Act and "good reason" under the 1988 Act, and disapproving *DPP v. Gregson*, 96 Cr.App.R. 240, DC, and the reasoning in *R. v. Hargreaves* [2000] 1 *Archbold News* 2, CA. But carrying a "multi-purpose utility tool", which includes a blade, out of habit is not a good reason: *R. v. Giles* [2003] 5 *Archbold News* 3, CA.

The defence of having the article for religious reasons (s.139(5)(b)) is only established if the reason proffered is the predominant motivation for having the bladed article at the material time, *i.e.* the reason specifically motivated the accused to have the article on the occasion in question: *R. v. Wang*, 168 J.P. 224, CA (this aspect of the decision was not challenged in the House of Lords, *ante*).

(2) Having article with blade or point (or offensive weapon) on school premises

Criminal Justice Act 1988, s.139A

24–129 **139A.**—(1) Any person who has an article to which section 139 of this Act applies with him on school premises shall be guilty of an offence.

(2) Any person who has an offensive weapon within the meaning of section 1 of the *Prevention of Crime Act* 1953 with him on school premises shall be guilty of an offence.

(3) It shall be a defence for a person charged with an offence under subsection (1) or (2) above to prove that he had good reason or lawful authority for having the article or weapon with him on the premises in question.

(4) Without prejudice to the generality of subsection (3) above, it shall be a defence for a person charged with an offence under subsection (1) or (2) above to prove that he had the article or weapon in question with him—

(a) for use at work;
(b) for educational purposes,
(c) for religious reasons; or
(d) as part of any national costume.

(5) A person guilty of an offence—

(a) under subsection (1) above shall be liable—
(i) on summary conviction to imprisonment for a term not exceeding *six* [12] months, or a fine not exceeding the statutory maximum, or both;
(ii) on conviction on indictment, to imprisonment for a term not exceeding four years, or a fine, or both.
(b) under subsection (2) above shall be liable—
(i) [*identical to para. (a)(i),* ante];
(ii) on conviction on indictment, to imprisonment for a term not exceeding four years, or a fine, or both.

(6) In this section and section 139B, "school premises" means land used for the purposes of a school excluding any land occupied solely as a dwelling by a person employed at the school; and "school" has the meaning given by section 4(1) of the *Education Act* 1996.

(7) [*Northern Ireland.*]

[This section was inserted by the *Offensive Weapons Act* 1996, s.4(4). It is printed as amended by the *Education Act* 1996, s.582(1), and Sched. 37, para. 69; and, as from February 12, 2007 (S.I. 2007 No. 74 (*ante*, § 24–125)), by the *VCRA* 2006, s.42(1) (increase in maximum penalty for offence contrary to subs. (1) from two to four years, but only in relation to offences committed on or after that date: s.42(2)). In subs. (5)(a)(i), "12" is substituted for "six", as from a day to be appointed, by the *CJA* 2003, s.282(2) and (3). The increase has no application to offences committed before the substitution takes effect: s.282(4).]

Class of offence and mode of trial

These offences are class 3 offences, *ante*, § 2–17, and are triable either way: s.139(5), *ante*. For the Sentencing Guidelines Council's guideline on mode of trial, see Appendix K–161 (but note the effect of *R. v. Povey*, *ante*, § 24–109). **24–130**

Sentence

On summary conviction, six months (increased to 12 months, as from a day to be appointed (*ante*)), or a fine of the prescribed sum, or both: s.139A(5), *ante*. On indictment, four years (subject to the transitional provision, *ante*), or a fine, or both: *ibid*. **24–131**

As for sentencing guidelines, see *ante*, § 24–109. It seems that for sentencing purposes the possession of a knife is to be treated in a similar way to the possession of other offensive weapons.

Ingredients

For the meaning of "has ... with him", see *ante*, §§ 24–110 *et seq*. For "public place", see *ante*, § 24–113. **24–131a**

For the meaning of "good reason" and "for use at work", see *ante*, § 24–128.

(3) Entry and search provisions

Criminal Justice Act 1988, s.139B

139B.—(1) A constable may enter school premises and search those premises and any person on those premises for— **24–132**

(a) any article to which section 139 of this Act applies, or
(b) any offensive weapon within the meaning of section 1 of the *Prevention of Crime Act* 1953,

if he has reasonable grounds for suspecting that an offence under section 139A of this Act is being, or has been, committed.

(2) If in the course of a search under this section a constable discovers an article or weapon which he has reasonable grounds for suspecting to be an article or weapon of a kind described in subsection (1) above, he may seize and retain it.

(3) The constable may use reasonable force, if necessary, in the exercise of the power of entry conferred by this section.

(4) [*Northern Ireland.*]

[This section was inserted by the *Offensive Weapons Act* 1996, s.4(4). It is printed as amended by the *VCRA* 2006, s.48.]

(4) Summary offences

24–132a Section 141(1) of the *CJA* 1988 makes it a summary offence to manufacture, sell or hire or offer for sale or hire, to expose or have possession for the purpose of sale or hire, or lend or give to any other person, a weapon to which the section applies. Subsection (2) empowers the Secretary of State to direct that the section applies to any description of weapon except (a) any weapon subject to the *Firearms Act* 1968, and (b) crossbows. Subsection (4) prohibits importation of a weapon to which the section applies. As amended by the *VCRA* 2006, s.43(1), (3) and (4), particular defences are provided by subsections (5), (8), (9) and (11B) (in relation to all of which, see subs. (11C)).

24–132b The *Criminal Justice Act 1988 (Offensive Weapons) Order* 1988 (S.I. 1988 No. 2019), as amended by S.I. 2002 No. 1668, S.I. 2004 No. 1271 and S.I. 2008 No. 973 (itself amended by S.I. 2008 No. 2039), brings the following weapons (all of which are more fully described in the order) within section 141: (a) "knuckleduster"; (b) "swordstick"; (c) "handclaw"; (d) "belt buckle knife"; (e) "push dagger"; (f) "hollow kubotan"; (g) "footclaw"; (h) "shuriken" or "shaken" or "death star"; (i) "balisong" or "butterfly knife"; (j) "telescopic truncheon"; (k) "blowpipe" or "blowgun"; (l) "kusari gama"; (m) "kyoketsu shoge"; (n) "manrikigusari" or "kusari"; (o) "disguised knife"; (p) "stealth knife"; (q) "straight, side-handled or friction-lock truncheon" or "baton"; and (r) (subject to specified defences) a sword with a curved blade of 50 centimetres or over in length (commonly known as a "samurai sword").

24–132c Section 141A was inserted into the 1988 Act by the *Offensive Weapons Act* 1996, s.6(1). As amended by the *VCRA* 2006, s.43(2), it creates a summary offence of selling knives and certain other articles with a blade or point to a person under the age of 18 years. By section 141A(2), the section applies to any knife, knife blade or razor blade, any axe, and any other article which has a blade or which is sharply pointed and which is made or adapted for use for causing injury to the person. However, this is subject to subsection (3), which provides that the section does not apply to any article described in (a) the *Restriction of Offensive Weapons Act* 1959, s.1 ("flick knife" or "flick gun", and "gravity knife"); (b) any order made under the 1988 Act, s.141(2) (*ante*, § 24–132b); and (c) any order made under section 141A (see the *Criminal Justice Act 1988 (Offensive Weapons) (Exemption) Order* 1996 (S.I. 1996 No. 3064), which exempts a folding pocket-knife if the cutting edge of its blade does not exceed 7.62 centimetres (three inches), and razor blades permanently enclosed in a cartridge or housing where less than two millimetres of any blade is exposed beyond the plane which intersects the highest point of the surfaces preceding and following such blades).

24–132d In connection with the weapons to which sections 141 and 141A apply, see also the offence, under the *VCRA* 2006, s.28 (*post*, § 24–143), of using someone to mind a weapon.

D. KNIVES ACT 1997

(1) The offences

Knives Act 1997, ss.1–4

Unlawful marketing of knives

24–133 **1.**—(1) A person is guilty of an offence if he markets a knife in a way which—

(a) indicates, or suggests, that it is suitable for combat; or

(b) is otherwise likely to stimulate or encourage violent behaviour involving the use of the knife as a weapon.

(2) "Suitable for combat" and "violent behaviour" are defined in section 10.

(3) For the purposes of this Act, an indication or suggestion that a knife is suitable for combat may, in particular, be given or made by a name or description—

(a) applied to the knife;

(b) on the knife or on any packaging in which it is contained; or

(c) included in any advertisement which, expressly or by implication, relates to the knife.

(4) For the purposes of this Act, a person markets a knife if—

(a) he sells or hires it;

(b) he offers, or exposes, it for sale or hire; or

(c) he has it in his possession for the purpose of sale or hire.

(5) A person who is guilty of an offence under this section is liable—

(a) on summary conviction to imprisonment for a term not exceeding *six* [12] months or to a fine not exceeding the statutory maximum, or to both;

(b) on conviction on indictment to imprisonment for a term not exceeding two years or to a fine, or to both.

[This section is printed as amended, as from a day to be appointed, by the *CJA* 2003, s.282(2) and (3) (substitution of "12" for "six", but not in relation to any offence committed before the date of commencement: *ibid.*, s.282(4)).]

Publications

2.—(1) A person is guilty of an offence if he publishes any written, pictorial or other material in connection with the marketing of any knife and that material— **24–134**

(a) indicates, or suggests, that the knife is suitable for combat; or

(b) is otherwise likely to stimulate or encourage violent behaviour involving the use of the knife as a weapon.

(2) [*Identical to s.1(5),* ante, *§ 24–133.*]

(2) The defences

Exempt trades

3.—(1) It is a defence for a person charged with an offence under section 1 to prove that— **24–135**

(a) the knife was marketed—

(i) for use by the armed forces of any country;

(ii) as an antique or curio; or

(iii) as falling within such other category (if any) as may be prescribed;

(b) it was reasonable for the knife to be marketed in that way; and

(c) there were no reasonable grounds for suspecting that a person into whose possession the knife might come in consequence of the way in which it was marketed would use it for an unlawful purpose.

(2) It is a defence for a person charged with an offence under section 2 to prove that—

(a) the material was published in connection with marketing a knife—

(i) for use by the armed forces of any country;

(ii) as an antique or curio; or

(iii) as falling within such other category (if any) as may be prescribed;

(b) it was reasonable for the knife to be marketed in that way; and

(c) there were no reasonable grounds for suspecting that a person into whose possession the knife might come in consequence of the publishing of the material would use it for an unlawful purpose.

(3) In this section "prescribed" means prescribed by regulations made by the Secretary of State.

Other defences

4.—(1) It is a defence for a person charged with an offence under section 1 to prove that he did not know or suspect, and had no reasonable grounds for suspecting, that the way in which the knife was marketed— **24–136**

(a) amounted to an indication or suggestion that the knife was suitable for combat; or

(b) was likely to stimulate or encourage violent behaviour involving the use of the knife as a weapon.

(2) It is a defence for a person charged with an offence under section 2 to prove that he did not know or suspect, and had no reasonable grounds for suspecting, that the material—

(a) amounted to an indication or suggestion that the knife was suitable for combat; or

(b) was likely to stimulate or encourage violent behaviour involving the use of the knife as a weapon.

(3) It is a defence for a person charged with an offence under section 1 or 2 to prove that he took all reasonable precautions and exercised all due diligence to avoid committing the offence.

(3) Supplementary powers

24–137 Section 5 of the 1997 Act contains supplementary powers of entry, seizure and retention. The additional powers of seizure conferred by the *CJPA* 2001, s.50 (*ante*, § 15–124), apply to the power of seizure under this section. Section 6 provides on conviction for the forfeiture of knives and publications seized under a warrant issued under section 5 or in the offender's possession or under his control at the relevant time which, by subsection (5), means the time of his arrest or the issue of a summons in respect of it. By subsection (4), in considering whether to make a forfeiture order, the court must have regard to the value of the property and the likely financial and other effects on the offender of making the order (taken together with any other order that the court contemplates making). Section 7 deals with the effect of a forfeiture order and permits the court to make a recovery order in favour of an applicant other than the offender from whom it was ordered if it appears to the court that the applicant owns the property in question. By subsections (8) and (9), the Secretary of State may make regulations in relation to the disposal of and dealings with forfeited property and in relation to investing money and auditing accounts. The *Knives (Forfeited Property) Regulations* 1997 (S.I. 1997 No. 1907) have been made pursuant to these subsections. For the text of sections 5, 6 and 7, see the 2001 edition of this work.

[The next paragraph is § 24–141.]

(4) Miscellaneous

Knives Act 1997, ss.9, 10

Offences by bodies corporate

24–141 **9.**—(1) If an offence under this Act committed by a body corporate is proved—

(a) to have been committed with the consent or connivance of an officer, or

(b) to be attributable to any neglect on his part,

he as well as the body corporate is guilty of the offence and liable to be proceeded against and punished accordingly.

(2) In subsection (1) "officer", in relation to a body corporate, means a director, manager, secretary or other similar officer of the body, or a person purporting to act in any such capacity.

(3) If the affairs of a body corporate are managed by its members, subsection (1) applies in relation to the acts and defaults of a member in connection with his functions of management as if he were a director of the body corporate.

(4) [*Scotland.*]

Interpretation

24–142 **10.** In this Act—

"the court" means—

(a) in relation to England and Wales or Northern Ireland, the Crown Court or a magistrate's court;

(b) [*Scotland*];

"knife" means an instrument which has a blade or is sharply pointed;

"marketing" and related expressions are to be read with section 1(4);

"publication" includes a publication in electronic form and, in the case of a publication which is, or may be, produced from electronic data, any medium on which the data are stored;

"suitable for combat" means suitable for use as a weapon for inflicting injury on a person or causing a person to fear injury;

"violent behaviour" means an unlawful act inflicting injury on a person or causing a person to fear injury.

E. VIOLENT CRIME REDUCTION ACT 2006

(1) The offence

Violent Crime Reduction Act 2006, s.28

Using someone to mind a weapon

28.—(1) A person is guilty of an offence if— **24–143**

(a) he uses another to look after, hide or transport a dangerous weapon for him; and

(b) he does so under arrangements or in circumstances that facilitate, or are intended to facilitate, the weapon's being available to him for an unlawful purpose.

(2) For the purposes of this section the cases in which a dangerous weapon is to be regarded as available to a person for an unlawful purpose include any case where—

(a) the weapon is available for him to take possession of it at a time and place; and

(b) his possession of the weapon at that time and place would constitute, or be likely to involve or to lead to, the commission by him of an offence.

(3) In this section "dangerous weapon" means—

(a) a firearm other than an air weapon or a component part of, or accessory to, an air weapon; or

(b) a weapon to which section 141 or 141A of the *Criminal Justice Act* 1988 applies (specified offensive weapons, knives and bladed weapons).

(4) [*Scotland.*]

This section came into force on April 6, 2007: *Violent Crime Reduction Act 2006 (Commencement No. 2) Order* 2007 (S.I. 2007 No. 858).

For the meaning of "firearm", see the *Firearms Act* 1968, s.57(1) (*ante*, §§ 24–85 *et seq.*); of "air weapon", see the 1968 Act, ss.1(3)(b) (*ante*, §§ 24–3, 24–8) and 57(4) (*ante*, § 24–85); and for the 1988 Act, ss.141 and 141A, see *ante*, §§ 24–132a *et seq.* **24–144**

(2) Sentence and mode of trial

Violent Crime Reduction Act 2006, s.29

Penalties etc. for offence under s.28

29.—(1) This section applies where a person ("the offender") is guilty of an offence under section 28. **24–145**

(2) Where the dangerous weapon in respect of which the offence was committed is a weapon to which section 141 or 141A of the *Criminal Justice Act* 1988 (specified offensive weapons, knives and bladed weapons) applies, the offender shall be liable, on conviction on indictment, to imprisonment for a term not exceeding 4 years or to a fine, or to both.

(3) Where—

(a) at the time of the offence, the offender was aged 16 or over, and

(b) the dangerous weapon in respect of which the offence was committed was a firearm mentioned in section 5(1)(a) to (af) or (c) or section 5(1A)(a) of the 1968 Act (firearms possession of which attracts a minimum sentence),

the offender shall be liable, on conviction on indictment, to imprisonment for a term not exceeding 10 years or to a fine, or to both.

(4) On a conviction in England and Wales, where—

(a) subsection (3) applies, and

(b) the offender is aged 18 or over at the time of conviction,

the court must impose (with or without a fine) a term of imprisonment of not less than 5 years, unless it is of the opinion that there are exceptional circumstances relating to the offence or to the offender which justify its not doing so.

(5) In relation to times before the commencement of paragraph 180 of Schedule 7 to the *Criminal Justice and Court Services Act* 2000, the reference in subsection (4) to a sentence

of imprisonment, in relation to an offender aged under 21 at the time of conviction, is to be read as a reference to a sentence of detention in a young offender institution.

(6) On a conviction in England and Wales, where—

(a) subsection (3) applies, and

(b) the offender is aged under 18 at the time of conviction,

the court must impose (with or without a fine) a term of detention under section 91 of the *Powers of Criminal Courts (Sentencing) Act* 2000 of not less than 3 years, unless it is of the opinion that there are exceptional circumstances relating to the offence or to the offender which justify its not doing so.

(7)–(9) [*Scotland*.]

(10) In any case not mentioned in subsection (2) or (3), the offender shall be liable, on conviction on indictment, to imprisonment for a term not exceeding 5 years or to a fine, or to both.

(11) Where—

(a) a court is considering for the purposes of sentencing the seriousness of an offence under section 28, and

(b) at the time of the offence the offender was aged 18 or over and the person used to look after, hide or transport the weapon was not,

the court must treat the fact that that person was under the age of 18 at that time as an aggravating factor (that is to say, a factor increasing the seriousness of the offence).

(12) Where a court treats a person's age as an aggravating factor in accordance with subsection (11), it must state in open court that the offence was aggravated as mentioned in that subsection.

(13) Where—

(a) an offence under section 28 of using another person for a particular purpose is found to have involved that other person's having possession of a weapon, or being able to make it available, over a period of two or more days, or at some time during a period of two or more days, and

(b) on any day in that period, an age requirement was satisfied,

the question whether subsection (3) applies or (as the case may be) the question whether the offence was aggravated under this section is to be determined as if the offence had been committed on that day.

(14) In subsection (13) the reference to an age requirement is a reference to either of the following—

(a) the requirement of subsection (3) that the offender was aged 16 or over at the time of the offence;

(b) the requirement of subsection (11) that the offender was aged 18 or over at that time and that the other person was not.

(15) [*Scotland*.]

This section came into force on April 6, 2007: S.I. 2007 No. 858 (*ante*, § 24–143).

(3) Supplemental provisions

24–146 The *VCRA* 2006, s.50(3), provides that the *Firearms Act* 1968, ss.46 (*ante*, § 24–78), 51(4) (*ante*, § 24–82), 52 (*ante*, § 24–83) and 58 (*ante*, § 24–89) apply as if sections 28, 29, 32, and 35 to 39, of the 2006 Act were contained in the 1968 Act. Section 50(3) came into force on April 6, 2007 (S.I. 2007 No. 858 (*ante*, § 24–143)), to the extent that it makes provision those provisions of the 1968 Act to apply as if sections 28, 29 and 35 of the 2006 Act were contained in that Act. Sections 32 and 35 to 39 of the 2006 Act are summarised at § 24–105l, *ante*.

CHAPTER 25

OFFENCES AGAINST THE CROWN AND GOVERNMENT

I. HIGH TREASON

Treason Act 1351

Declaration of Treasons

Item, whereas divers opinions have been before this time in what case treason shall be said, and in what not; the King, at the request of the lords and of the commons, hath made a **25–1** declaration in the manner as hereafter followeth; that is to say, when a man doth compass or imagine the death of our lord the King, or of our lady his Queen, or of their eldest son and heir; or if a man do violate the King's companion, or the King's eldest daughter unmarried or the wife of the King's eldest son and heir; or if a man do levy war against our lord the King in his realm, or be adherent to the King's enemies in his realm, giving to them aid and comfort in the realm, or elsewhere, and thereof be provably ["*provalement*"] attainted of open deed by the people of their condition ... and if a man slea [*sic*] the chancellor, treasurer, or the King's justices of the one bench, or the other, justices in eyre, or justices of assize, and all other justices assigned to hear and determine, being in their places doing their offices. And it is to be understood, that in the cases above rehearsed, that ought to be judged treason which extends to our lord the King, and his royal majesty. ...

This statute was passed after petition by the Commons to the King representing that certain justices had lately given judgment in their courts for treason and accroachment of royal power, and praying that it might be declared in Parliament to what cases this accroachment of royal power extended (2 Rot.Parl. 166, n.15; Rot.Parl. 25 Edw. 3, p. 2, n.17; 1 Hale 86, 87; 1 East P.C. 37). It is said to be declaratory of the common law (3 Co.Inst. 1; *Sindercombe's case* (1657) 5 St.Tr. 848; *Bellew's case* (1672) 1 Vent. 254n.; *O'Brien v. R.* (1849) 7 St.Tr.(N.S.) 1): *R. v. Casement* [1917] 1 K.B. 98 at 124.

"Elsewhere"

25–2 That is, out of the realm of England. The realm of England comprehends the narrow seas and Wales, but not Ireland (*Lord MacGuire's case* (1645) 4 St.Tr. 653), nor Scotland, nor the Channel Islands (1 Hale 153, 154).

11 Hen. 7, c. 1, s.1.—Service in war under the King *de facto* for the time being not to be deemed treason against the King *de jure*. See *Sir Harry Vane's Case* (1662) 6 St.Tr. 120.

Treason Act 1695, ss.5, 6

Limitation of prosecution

25–3 **5.** ... no person or persons whatsoever shall be indicted tried or prosecuted for any such treason as aforesaid or for misprision of such treason that shall be committed or done within the kingdom of England dominion of Wales or town of Berwick upon Tweed ... unless the same indictment be [found by a grand jury] within three years next after the treason or offence done and committed. ...

Grand juries were abolished by the *Administration of Justice (Miscellaneous Provisions) Act* 1933, s.1, and now by section 2(8) of, and Schedule 2, paragraph 1 to, that Act the indictment must be signed within three years.

Exceptions to section 5

25–4 **6.** Always provided and excepted that if any person or persons whatsoever shall be guilty of designing endeavouring or attempting any assassination on the body of the king by poison or otherwise such person or persons may be prosecuted at any time notwithstanding the aforesaid limitation.

Treason Act 1702, s.3

25–5 [*High treason to attempt by overt acts to hinder the succession to the Crown as limited by the* Act of Settlement *1700*.]

Penalties, procedure, etc.

25–6 The punishment for treason is life imprisonment: *Treason Act* 1702, s.3 (as amended by the *CDA* 1998, s.36(2)); *Treason Act* 1814, s.1 (as amended by *ibid.*, s.36(4)). Forfeiture on conviction for treason was abolished by section 1 of the *Forfeiture Act* 1870 (*rep.*): see also *CLA* 1967, s.7(5) (*rep.*). A conviction for treason disqualifies a person from holding any military, air force or naval office, or any civil office under the Crown or any other public employment and from being elected, sitting or voting as a member of either House of Parliament and from exercising any right to vote. If he holds any such office or any office in any university or corporation or is entitled to any pension or superannuation allowance payable out of public funds at the time of conviction the office or employment will become vacant and any such pension or allowance will cease to be payable upon conviction: *Forfeiture Act* 1870, s.2.

The procedure on trials for treason or misprision of treason is the same as that on trials for murder: *CLA* 1967, s.12(6).

Indictment for compassing the Queen's death

For a specimen indictment, see earlier editions of this work. 25–7

The overt acts of the alleged treason must be set out separately from the particulars of offence.

Any number of overt acts may be laid in the same count, but proof of any one overt act will maintain the count provided the overt act so proved is a sufficient overt act of the species of treason charged in the indictment: Kel.(J.) 8; 1 Hale 122; Fost. 194.

Venue

Most of the cases cited *post*, § 25–26, from the State Trials—(except where otherwise 25–8
stated, the references to the State Trials in the present edition of this work are to Howell's State Trials and to State Trials (New Series); for a table showing references to Hargreave's State Trials, see Vol. 34 of Howell)—as containing counts for adhering to the King's enemies contain also counts for compassing the King's death in this country. In the following cases, the offence of "compassing, etc.", is charged as having been committed "in parts beyond the seas", *viz. R. v. Hesketh* (1582) K.B.Roll. 1592; *R. v. Asheton* (1592) K.B.Roll. 1592; *R. v. Skinner* (1592) K.B.Roll. 1592.

Allegiance

"High treason, being an offence committed against the duty of allegiance, it may be proper 25–9
... to consider from whom and to whom allegiance is due. With regard to natural born subjects, there can be no doubt. They owe allegiance to the Crown at all times and in all places. This is what we call natural allegiance, in contradistinction to that which is local. ... Natural allegiance is founded on the relation every man standeth in to the Crown considered as the head of that society whereof he is born a member: and on the peculiar privileges he deriveth from that relation which are with great propriety called his birthright; this birthright nothing but his own demerit can deprive him of; it is indefeasible and perpetual; and consequently the duty of allegiance which ariseth out of it and is inseparably connected with it, is in consideration of law likewise unalienable and perpetual": Fost.C.L. 183, quoted with approval in *R. v. Casement* [1917] 1 K.B. 98 at 130.

"The subjects of the King owe him allegiance and the allegiance follows the person of the subject. He is the King's liege wherever he may be and he may violate his allegiance in a foreign country just as well as he may violate it in this country": *R. v. Casement*, *ante*, at p. 137.

Note that the liability of British subjects who are not also citizens of the United Kingdom and colonies for offences against the law of the United Kingdom committed elsewhere is limited by the *British Nationality Act* 1948, s.3.

Liability of aliens

Alien friends may be convicted of high treason (*R. v. De la Motte* (1781) 21 St.Tr. 25–10
687 at 814), but alien enemies cannot (*Calvin's case* (1608) 7 Co.Rep. 1 at 6 b; and see 4 St.Tr. 1182); unless they accept British protection during the war (Fost. 185). A British subject is not exempt from the penalties of treason because he holds a commission in the enemy's forces, *Napper Tandy's case* (1800) 27 St.Tr. 1191; *Macdonald's case* (1747) Fost. 59, 183, 18 St.Tr. 857; *Townley's case* (1746) Fost. 7, 18 St.Tr. 1329; *R. v. Lynch* [1903] 1 K.B. 444. An alien resident within British Territory owes allegiance to the Crown, and if he assists invaders while Her Majesty's forces, for strategical or other reasons, are temporarily withdrawn, he is liable to conviction of high treason: *De Jager v. Att.-Gen. of Natal* [1907] A.C. 326; and see 3 Co.Inst. 4; 1 Hale 94; Fost. 185.

An alien who has been resident in but has left the Queen's dominions may be 25–11
convicted of high treason in respect of an act done by him outside the realm if at the time of the commission of the act he was still enjoying such protection from the Crown as to require of him continuance of his allegiance, *e.g* by being in possession of a British passport: *Joyce v. DPP* [1946] A.C. 347, HL. So long as the appellant held a passport

which was capable of affording him the protection of the Crown, he was enjoying that protection so as to raise a corresponding duty of allegiance, and there being no suggestion that he had surrendered his passport or taken any step to withdraw from his allegiance, he remained under the duty of allegiance at the material time and was, accordingly, properly convicted of treason: *ibid*.

Evidence

(i) *Overt acts*

25–12 The evidence must be applied to the proof of the overt act, and not to the proof of the principal treason: for the overt act is the charge to which the defendant must apply his defence. And whether the overt act proved is a sufficient overt act of the principal treason laid in the indictment is a matter of law to be determined by the court. No evidence may be admitted of any overt act not laid in the indictment: that is to say, no overt act amounting to a distinct independent charge, although it be an overt act of the species of treason charged, shall be admitted in evidence, unless it be expressly laid in the indictment; but if an overt act not laid amounts to a direct proof of any overt act which is laid, it may be given in evidence to prove such overt act: *R. v. Deacon* (1746) 18 St.Tr. 365 at 369; *R. v. Layer* (1722) 16 St.Tr. 94.

The defendant is not bound to show what was the object or meaning of the acts done by him; it is for the Crown to make out that they amount to the treason charged in the indictment: *R. v. Frost* (1839) 9 C. & P. 129.

(ii) *Examples of overt acts*

25–13 The following acts have been decided or have been deemed by writers upon the subject to be sufficient overt acts of compassing the death of the Sovereign within the *Treason Act* 1351 (*ante*, § 25–1). That statute is declaratory of the common law; but all the law of treason now rests on statute, and the doctrine of constructive treason is discouraged, if not exploded.

Everything wilfully or deliberately done or attempted, whereby the Queen's life may be endangered, is an overt act of compassing her death: Fost. 195. Killing the Queen is an overt act of compassing her death; see Kel.(J.) 8. So, going armed for the purpose of killing the Queen: *Somervile's case*, 1 Anderson 104; providing arms, ammunition, poison, or the like, for the purpose of killing the Queen: 1 Hale 108, 3 Co.Inst. 12; conspirators meeting and consulting on the means of killing the Queen: Fost. 195; *Sir Harry Vane's Case* (1662) 6 St.Tr. 120; *R. v. Tonge* (1662) 6 St.Tr. 225; and see Kel.(J.) 81; or of deposing her, or of usurping the powers of government: *R. v. Hardy* (1794) 1 East P.C. 60, 24 St.Tr. 199; or resolving to do it: *R. v. Rookwood* (1696) 13 St.Tr. 139; *R. v. Charnock* (1696) 12 St.Tr. 1377; acting as counsel against the Queen in order to take away her life: *R. v. Cook* (1660) 5 St.Tr. 1077; and see *R. v. Harrison* (1660) 5 St.Tr. 1008: all these, and the like, are sufficient overt acts of compassing the Queen's death.

So, other species of high treason, which are distinct heads of treason in themselves, may be laid as overt acts of compassing the Queen's death. Thus, the following have been held to be sufficient overt acts of compassing the Queen's death: levying war *directly* against the Queen: Fost. 197, 210, 211; 1 Hale 122, 123, 151; 3 Co.Inst. 12; 13 St.Tr. 110, 113; *R. v. Hensey* (1758) 19 St.Tr. 1341 (but not a mere constructive levying of war, such as pulling down all inclosures, or the like, 1 Hale 123, see *post*, § 25–23); or even a conspiracy to levy war directly against the Queen, for the purpose of dethroning her, or of obliging her to change her measures, or the like: Fost. 197, 211; 1 Hale 119, 121; *R. v. Layer* (1722) 16 St.Tr. 94; *R. v. Lord Russell* (1683) 9 St.Tr. 577; *R. v. Sidney* (1683) 9 St.Tr. 817 (but not a conspiracy to effect a rising for the purpose of throwing down all inclosures, or any other species of constructive levying of war: Fost. 213; Holt 682; *per curiam*, 10 Mod. 322); adhering to the Queen's enemies: Fost. 196, 197; *R. v. Stone* (1796) 25 St.Tr. 1155; inciting foreigners to invade the realm. Fost. 196; 1 Hale 120; 3 Co.Inst. 14; *R. v. Story* (1571) 1 St.Tr. 1087 (where the indictment is incorrectly set out (see K.B. Rolls, (1571)); *R. v. Parkyns* (1696) 13 St.Tr.63.

levied, and not merely of a conspiracy to levy it: 1 Hale 141–8; 1 Hawk. c. 17, s.27. But, according to Foster, the conspiracy may be dealt with as an overt act in compassing the Sovereign's death: Fost. 195.

In the case of war levied directly against the Sovereign, all persons assembled and marching with the rebels are guilty of treason, whether they are aware of the purpose of the assembly, or aid and assist in committing acts of violence, or not: *R. v. Earls of Essex and Southampton* (1600) 1 St.Tr. 1334; unless compelled to join and continue with them *pro timore mortis*: Fost. 216, 217; 3 Co.Inst. 10; 1 Hale 49, 51, 139; and actual compulsion is an excuse for adhering to rebels, but mere apprehension of loss of property or injury not endangering the person is not an excuse: *M'Growther's Case* (1746) 18 St.Tr. 391, Fost. 13, 217, 1 East P.C. 71; *R. v. Gordon* (1746) 1 East P. C. 71; and see *ante*, § 17–119. But in the case of a constructive levying of war, those only of the rabble who actually aid and assist in doing those acts of violence which form the constructive treason are traitors; the rest are merely rioters: *R. v. Messenger* (1668) 6 St.Tr. 879.

Indictment for adhering to the King's enemies abroad

For a specimen indictment, see *Joyce v. DPP* [1946] A.C. 347, HL (the relevant count in the indictment is set out in full at p. 348). **25–24**

The special acts of adherence must be set forth in the indictment as overt acts; but it is not necessary in this or in any other case of treason, that in laying the overt acts the details of the evidence intended to be given at the trial should be stated; it is sufficient if the charge be reduced to a reasonable certainty, so that the defendant may be apprised of the nature of the offence with which he is charged: Fost. 194, 220.

Evidence

The count is proved by proving one or more of the overt acts laid. The fact of the persons adhered to being enemies may be proved by the production of the Gazette containing the proclamation, if war were formally proclaimed, or public notoriety is sufficient evidence of it: Y.B. 19 Edw. IV, f. 5; Fost. 219; 1 Hale 164. And whether they are enemies or not is a matter of fact to be determined by the jury: *ibid*. **25–25**

An actual adherence must be proved. A mere conspiracy or intention to adhere is not treason within this branch of the statute, although probably such a conspiracy might be laid as an overt act of compassing the Sovereign's death. But, if the prosecution can prove such a conspiracy, and connect the defendant with it by evidence, and can prove an act done by any one of the conspirators in furtherance of the common design, it may be given in evidence against the defendant, if it tends to prove any of the overt acts laid in the indictment; for the act of one, in such a case, is the act of all: *R. v. Stone* (1796) 25 St.Tr. 1155 (see *ante*, § 25–16).

(i) *"Giving aid and comfort, etc."*

The words in the *Treason Act* 1351 (*ante*, § 25–1), are "or be adherent to the King's enemies in his realm, giving to them aid and comfort in the realm or elsewhere". As to the words in the Parliament Roll and Statute Roll, see *R. v. Casement* [1917] 1 K.B. 98 at 134. The offence defined by these words is "adhering to the [Queen's] enemies within the land or without, and declaring the same by some overt act": 3 Co.Inst. 10, 11, 63; Co.Litt. 261 b; the offence being complete though both the adherence and the enemies adhered to are without the realm. As to the common law before the statute and as to the statute, see 1 Hale 91, 159, 165, 166, 169; 1 Hawk. c. 17, s.28; 1 East P.C. 60, 78; *R. v. Maclane* (1797) 26 St.Tr. 722 at 725; *Mulcahy v. R.* (1868) L. R. 3 H.L. 306 at 317; *R. v. Lynch* [1903] 1 K.B. 444. The words "giving aid and comfort to the [Queen's] enemies" are words in apposition; they are words to explain what is meant by being adherent to, so that a man may be adherent to the Queen's enemies in her realm by giving to them aid and comfort in her realm or he may be adherent to the Queen's enemies elsewhere by giving them aid and comfort elsewhere. In either case he is equally adherent to the Queen's enemies, and so commits this treason: *R. v. Casement*, *ante*, at p. 136. **25–26**

25–27 Records are preserved in the Public Record Office of the following cases, all of which contain indictments for adhering to, aiding, and assisting the Queen's enemies abroad, *viz.*: *R. v. Lord Wentworth* (1559) Queen's Bench Indictments (Baga de Secretis) K.B. 8/38; *R. v. Grymston*; *R. v. Chamberlayn* (1559): for the surrender of Calais, *ibid.* K.B. 8/38, 39; but as to this case, see *R. v. Casement, ante*, at p. 128; *R. v. Lord Middleton and John Stafford* (1713) K.B. Crown Rolls 28: for assisting the King of France in fighting against the British in France; *R. v. Duke of Wharton* (1729): for assisting the King of Spain in the siege of Gibraltar, Queen's Bench Indictments (Baga de Secretis), Trin. 2 Geo. 2, K.B. 8/67; *R. v. Cundell* (1812): for assisting "the French Government and the men of France under the said Government" in fighting against the British in the Isle of France, *ibid.* K.B. 8/89; followed in *R. v. Casement, ante.*

(ii) *Overt acts*

25–28 Every assistance given by the Queen's subjects to her enemies, unless given from a well-grounded apprehension of immediate death in case of a refusal, is high treason within this branch of the statute: 1 Hale 159. Any act done by a British subject which strengthens or tends to strengthen the enemies of the Queen in the conduct of a war against the Queen, or which weakens or tends to weaken the power of the Queen and of the country to resist or attack the enemies of the Queen and country, constitutes giving aid and comfort to her enemies within the meaning of this part of the Act of Edward III: *R. v. Casement* [1917] 1 K.B. 98. Therefore, if a British subject joins the Queen's enemies in acts of hostility against this country: Fost. 216; 1 Hawk. c. 17, s.28; or even against the Queen's allies: Fost. 220; *R. v. Vaughan* (1696) 13 St.Tr. 485; or raises troops for the enemy: *R. v. Harding* (1690) 2 Vent. 315 (where, after a special verdict, it was held that the indictment did not sufficiently charge an adherence to the King's enemies, as it did not state who those enemies were; but the defendant was convicted of compassing the King's death); or, whilst a state of war exists, endeavours in an enemy country to persuade British prisoners of war in that enemy country to join the armed forces of the enemy: *R. v. Casement, ante*; or takes part in an attempt to land arms and ammunition in any part of the United Kingdom for the use of the enemy: *ibid.*; or delivers up the Queen's castle, forts, or ships of war to the Queen's enemies through treachery or in combination with them: Fost. 219; 3 Col.Inst. 10; 1 Hale 168; or even detains the Queen's castles, etc., from her, if it is done in confederacy with the enemy: Fost. 219; 1 Hale 326; or sends money, arms, intelligence or the like to the Queen's enemies: Fost. 217; although such money, intelligence, etc., be intercepted and never reach them: *R. v. Gregg* (1708) 14 St.Tr. 1371 at 1376n.; Fost. 217, 218; *R. v. Hensey* (1758) 19 St.Tr.1341; *R. v. De La Motte* (1781) 21 St.Tr. 687; *R. v. Lord Preston* (1691) 12 St.Tr. 645; *R. v. Tyrie* (1782) 21 St.Tr. 815; he is guilty of treason.

25–29 It is not enough to prove that the defendant intentionally did acts which in fact assisted the enemy. His intention and purpose are relevant; it has to be shown that he had an evil intention and the purpose of aiding and comforting the King's enemies: *R. v. Ahlers* [1915] 1 K.B. 616, 11 Cr.App.R. 63, CCA.

The fact that intelligence transmitted to the enemy was calculated to dissuade them from invading this country and was sent with that intent is immaterial; if it were such as was likely to prove useful to them, in enabling them to annoy us, defend themselves, or shape their attacks, sending such intelligence with a view to its reaching the enemy was undoubtedly high treason: *R. v. Stone* (1796) 25 St.Tr. 1155.

If a British subject incites foreigners to invade this country, it is treason, whether the foreigners be enemies or not; if enemies, it is treason, within this branch of the statute; if not enemies, still it is an overt act of compassing the Sovereign's death: Fost. 196, 197; 1 Hale 167. But if a British subject is in a foreign country when war breaks out between that country and this, and continues to reside there, or if during a truce he goes to a foreign country, and returns before the truce expires, this is no treason, unless he actually conspires with the enemy, or aids him in forwarding his measures for hostility: 1 Hale 165, 166. Serving in war under the Sovereign *de facto* is not treason: 11 Hen. 7, c. 1 (*ante*, § 25–2).

Where letters, etc., have been intercepted, it is much better to charge them to have been sent from the place where the venue was laid, to be delivered in parts beyond the seas, to the enemy, according to the fact, than to state them to have been sent in *partes transmarinas*, to be delivered to the enemy: Fost. 218.

(iii) *Swearing fealty to a hostile power*

If an Englishman during war is taken by the enemy, and thereafter swears fealty to the enemy, if it is done voluntarily, it is an adhering to the Queen's enemies; but if it is done for fear of his life, and he returns, as soon as he may, to the allegiance of the crown of England, this is not such an adherence within the Act: 1 Hale 167. In *R. v. Lynch* [1903] 1 K.B. 444, it was held that the *Naturalisation Act* 1870 did not empower a British subject to become naturalised as a subject of a hostile State in time of war, and that the act of becoming naturalised in such circumstances was itself an act of treason. **25–30**

(iv) *Enemies*

The subjects of all States against which Her Majesty may have proclaimed or declared war are her enemies; so are the subjects of States in actual hostility with us, whether war has been solemnly proclaimed or not: Fost. 219; 1 Hale 162. Inciting the subjects of a State in amity with us to invade this country would not be treason within this branch of the statute, although it certainly would be an overt act of compassing the Queen's death: 1 Hale 167. But if the subjects of a State in amity with us were to invade the country in a hostile manner or otherwise commit hostilities against us, they would be enemies within the meaning of this statute, and adhering to them would be treason: Fost. 219; 1 Hale 164; 3 Co.Inst. 11; 4 Co.Inst. 162; *R. v. Vaughan* (1696) 13 St.Tr. 485. British subjects, however, can never be deemed the Queen's enemies within the meaning of this Act and therefore to give relief or assistance to a rebel would not be treason within this branch of the statute: 3 Co.Inst. 11; 1 Hale 159; 1 Hawk. c. 17, s.28. **25–31**

It must appear from the face of the indictment that the persons adhered to were enemies.

II. TREASON FELONY

Treason Felony Act 1848, ss.3, 6, 7

3. If any person whatsoever shall, within the United Kingdom or without, compass, imagine, invent, devise or intend to deprive or depose our most gracious Lady the Queen, … from the style, honour, or royal name of the imperial crown of the United Kingdom, or of any other of Her Majesty's dominions and countries, or to levy war against Her Majesty, … within any part of the United Kingdom, in order by force of constraint to compel Her … to change Her … measures or counsels, or in order to put any force or constraint upon, or in order to intimidate or overawe both houses or either house of parliament, or to move or stir any foreigner or stranger with force to invade the United Kingdom, or any other of Her Majesty's dominions or countries under the obeisance of Her Majesty, … and such compassings, imaginations, inventions, devices, or intentions, or any of them, shall express, utter, or declare by publishing any printing or writing, … or by any overt act or deed, every person so offending … shall be liable … to be imprisoned for the term of his or her natural life. … **25–32**

Saving as to 25 Edw. 3, st. 5, c. 2

6. Provided always, … that nothing herein contained shall lessen the force of or in any manner affect anything enacted by the *Treason Act* 1351. **25–33**

See *ante*, § 25–1.

Indictment for offence valid, though facts amount to treason

7. Provided also, … that if the facts or matters alleged in an indictment for any felony under this Act shall amount in law to treason, such indictment shall not by reason thereof be deemed void, erroneous, or defective; and if the facts or matters proved on the trial of any person indicted for any offence under this Act shall amount in law to treason, such person shall not by reason thereof be entitled to be acquitted of such offence; but no person tried for such offence shall be afterwards prosecuted for treason upon the same facts. **25–34**

[This section is printed as repealed in part by the *Statute Law Revision Act* 1891.]

Indictment

25–35 For a specimen indictment, see the 1992, and earlier, editions of this work.

Imprisonment for life: *Treason Felony Act* 1848, s.3.

This offence is a class 1 offence: *ante*, § 2–17.

As to the evidence, see *ante*, §§ 25–25 *et seq.*

The following seem to be all the reported cases on this statute: *R. v. Mitchel* (1848) 6 St.Tr. (n.s.) 599; *R. v. O'Doherty* (1848) 6 St.Tr.(N.S.) 831; *R. v. Dowling* (1848) 7 St.Tr.(N.S.) 381; *R. v. Cuffey* (1848) 7 St.Tr.(N.S.) 467; *R. v. Cumming* (1848) 7 St.Tr.(N.S.) 485; *R. v. Duffy* (1848) 7 St.Tr.(N.S.) 795; *R. v. Mullins* (1848) 7 St.Tr.(N.S.) 1110; *R. v. Constantine* (1848) 7 St.Tr.(N.S.) 1127; *R. v. Gallagher* (1883) 15 Cox 291; *R. v. Deasy* (1848) 15 Cox 334; and see the charge to a grand jury on the Act by Alderson B., 6 St.Tr.(N.S.) 1129. (In *R. v. Meany* (1867) Ir.Rep. 1 C.L. 500, C.C.R.Ir., tried at Dublin, where the indictment was under the *Treason Felony Act* 1848, and some of the overt acts charged in each count were conspiracies to effect the treasonable intent charged, it was held that overt acts done by some of the conspirators within the venue in furtherance of the conspiracies were acts for which the defendant, a fellow-conspirator, was responsible, though at the time the acts were done he was in America, and that therefore his offence was committed within the venue.)

As to whether section 3 criminalises advocacy of the deposition of the monarchy otherwise than by violence, see *R. (Rusbridger) v. Att.-Gen.* [2004] 1 A.C. 357, HL.

III. ATTEMPTS TO INJURE OR ALARM THE SOVEREIGN

Treason Act 1842, ss.2, 3

25–36 **2.** If any person shall wilfully discharge or attempt to discharge, or point, aim, or present at or near to the person of the Queen, any gun, pistol, or any other description of firearms or of other arms whatsoever, whether the same shall or shall not contain any explosive or destructive material, or shall discharge or cause to be discharged, or attempt to discharge or cause to be discharged, any explosive substance or material near to the person of the Queen, or if any person shall wilfully strike or strike at, or attempt to strike or to strike at, the person of the Queen, with any offensive weapon, or in any other manner whatsoever, or if any person shall wilfully throw or attempt to throw any substance, matter or thing whatsoever at or upon the person of the Queen, with intent in any of the cases aforesaid to injure the person of the Queen, or with intent in any of the cases aforesaid to break the public peace, or whereby the public peace may be endangered, or with intent in any of the cases aforesaid to alarm Her Majesty, or if any person shall, near to the person of the Queen, wilfully produce or have any gun, pistol, or any other description of firearms or other arms whatsoever, or any explosive, destructive, or dangerous matter or thing whatsoever, with intent to use the same to injure the person of the Queen, or to alarm Her Majesty, every such person so offending ... shall be liable, at the discretion of the court before which the said person shall be ... convicted, to be *imprisoned* for the term of seven years. ...

[This section is printed as repealed in part by the *Statute Law Revision (No. 2) Act* 1888; the *Statute Law Revision Act* 1892; the *Criminal Justice Administration Act* 1914; and the *CJA* 1948.]

For indictments and trials under this Act, see *R. v. Bean* (1842) 4 St.Tr.(N.S.) 1382; *R. v. Hamilton* (1849) 7 St.Tr.(N.S.) 1130; *R. v. Pate* (1850) 8 St.Tr.(N.S.) 1; *R. v. O'Connor* (1872) 8 St.Tr.(N.S.) 3n.

3. Provided, ... that nothing herein contained shall be deemed to alter in any respect the punishment which by law may now be inflicted upon persons guilty of high treason or misprision of treason.

[This section is printed as repealed in part by the *Statute Law Revision (No. 2) Act* 1888.]

See *ante*, § 25–6, and, as to misprision of treason, *ante*, § 18–38.

Indictment for presenting a pistol at the Queen

25–37 For a specimen indictment, see the 1992, and earlier, editions of this work.

Imprisonment for not more than seven years: *Treason Act* 1842, s.2 (*ante*).
This offence is a class 3 offence: *ante*, § 2–17.

IV. PIRACY

(1) Piracy jure gentium

Definition

Merchant Shipping and Maritime Security Act 1997, s.26(1), (2)

26.—(1) For the avoidance of doubt it is hereby declared that for the purposes of any proceedings before a court in the United Kingdom in respect of piracy, the provisions of the United Nations Convention on the Law of the Sea 1982 that are set out in Schedule 5 shall be treated as constituting part of the law of nations. **25–38**

(2) For the purposes of those provisions the high seas shall (in accordance with paragraph 2 of Article 58 of that Convention) be taken to include all waters beyond the territorial sea of the United Kingdom or any other state.

Merchant Shipping and Maritime Security Act 1997, Sched. 5

Section 26(1) SCHEDULE 5

PROVISIONS OF UNITED NATIONS CONVENTION ON THE LAW OF THE SEA TO BE TREATED AS PART OF THE LAW OF NATIONS

ARTICLE 101

Definition of piracy

Piracy consists of any of the following acts: **25–39**

(a) any illegal acts of violence or detention, or any act of depredation, committed for private ends by the crew or passengers of a private ship or a private aircraft, and directed—
   (i) on the high seas, against another ship or aircraft, or against persons or property on board such ship or aircraft;
   (ii) against a ship, aircraft, persons or property in a place outside the jurisdiction of any State;
(b) any act of voluntary participation in the operation of a ship or of an aircraft with knowledge of facts making it a pirate ship or aircraft;
(c) any act of inciting or of intentionally facilitating an act described in subparagraph (a) or (b).

ARTICLE 102

Piracy by a warship, government ship or government aircraft whose crew has mutinied

The acts of piracy, as defined in article 101, committed by a warship, government ship or government aircraft whose crew has mutinied and taken control of the ship or aircraft are assimilated to acts committed by a private ship or aircraft.

ARTICLE 103

Definition of a pirate ship or aircraft

A ship or aircraft is considered a pirate ship or aircraft if it is intended by the persons in dominant control to be used for the purpose of committing one of the acts referred to in article 101. The same applies if the ship or aircraft has been used to commit any such act so long as it remains under the control of the person guilty of that act.

This definition of piracy *iure gentium* (previously contained in the Schedule to the *Tokyo Convention Act* 1967) was drafted by the International Law Commission (*Yearbook of the ILC* [1956] Vol. 2, 282).

In *Cameron v. H.M. Advocate*, 1971 S.L.T. 333, the High Court of Justiciary took the view that the schedule (to the 1967 Act) supplemented the existing law and did not seek to redefine restrictively the offence of piracy *jure gentium*. In *Re Piracy Jure* **25–40**

Gentium [1934] A.C. 586, PC, Viscount Sankey L.C. drew attention to the fact that what had been held to be piracy *jure gentium* had changed over the years: "A careful examination of the subject shows a gradual widening of the earlier definition of piracy to bring it from time to time more in consonance with situations either not thought of or not in existence when the older jurisconsults were expressing their opinions" (at p. 600). His Lordship also pointed out that in determining a question of international law a wider range of sources had to be consulted than when the question for determination is one of municipal law. "The sources from which international law is derived include treaties between various States, State papers, municipal Acts of Parliament and the decisions of municipal Courts and last, but not least, opinions of jurisconsults or text-book writers. It is a process of inductive reasoning" (at p. 588). For these reasons, it is submitted that it is impossible to contend that the definition in the Schedule to the 1967 Act is a complete and final definition: in formulating a definition of piracy *jure gentium*, it will be a primary source but is not to be regarded as the only source. Courts would be slow to hold that anything outside the schedule constituted piracy *jure gentium*, not least because it is clear that the definition is sufficiently wide to embrace most acts considered to be piracy prior to the drawing up of the convention: see *Re Piracy Jure Gentium*, *ante*.

The Schedule does not define as piracy the violent taking possession of a ship by the crew or passengers of that ship: in the case of the crew this was deemed to be piracy by the *Piracy Act* 1698, s.8 (*rep.*), and, in the case of passengers, it was held to be piracy *jure gentium* in *Att.-Gen. of Hong Kong v. Kwok-a-Sing* (1873) L.R. 5 P.C. 179. Such conduct was certainly not intended to be included within their definition of piracy by the International Law Commission (*op. cit.*). It is submitted that since those responsible for the drafting of the Schedule had such conduct in mind and deliberately decided to exclude it from their definition, the decision in *Kwok-a-Sing* should no longer be regarded as good law. In this country, a prosecution under the *Aviation Security Act* 1982, s.1 (hijacking aircraft—*post*, § 25–178), or the *Aviation and Maritime Security Act* 1990, s.9 (hijacking ship—*post*, § 25–201) will almost certainly be more appropriate. For a contrary view as to the exhaustive nature of the definition, see Smith and Hogan, *Criminal Law*, 6th ed., pp. 816 *et seq.*

The definition preserves the essential feature of piracy, namely that the acts are done for private ends, that is not under the authority of any state. The accepted distinction between belligerency and piracy is the recognition of the existence of a regularly organised *de facto* government: 2 Russ.Cr., 12th ed., 1534. See also *Republic of Bolivia v. Indemnity Mutual Marine Assurance Co.* [1909] 1 K.B. 785.

Indictment

STATEMENT OF OFFENCE

25–41 *Piracy.*

PARTICULARS OF OFFENCE

A B, C D and E F, on the —— day of ——, 20—, upon the high seas, assaulted and put in fear of their lives certain mariners, unknown, in a ship called the Windsor Castle, and stole the apparel and tackle of the said ship and the cargo on board the said ship, namely: —.

The procedure as to arraignment, pleading, etc., on the trial of piracy is the same as in the case of other indictable offences. As to punishment, see *post*, § 25–46.

Jurisdiction, etc.

25–42 It seems that international law defines piracy as being piratical acts done upon the high seas, in the sense of outside the territorial waters of any state, or at a place outside the jurisdiction of any state: see the wording of Article 101 of the United Nations Convention, *ante*, § 25–39; Oppenheim's *International Law*, 9th ed., 1992, Vol. 1, para. 299; Colombos, *International Law of the Sea*, 6th ed., 1967, para. 368. The trial and punishment of crimes defined by international law is, however, left to the municipal law of individual states. So far as English municipal law is concerned, the *Offences at Sea Act* 1536 provided that acts of piracy committed within the jurisdiction of the Admiralty should be tried according to common law. The Admiralty jurisdiction extended over the "high seas" which phrase had no reference to territorial waters or any other concept of international law: see, *per* Scott L.J. in *The Tolten* [1946] P. 135, at p. 156. The limit that came to be set upon the Admiralty jurisdiction was that it extended no further than "where great ships go" or "where the tide flows, and below all bridges": *ibid*. The jurisdiction conferred on the Admiralty by the Act of 1536 was transferred to the Central Criminal Court in 1834 and was extended to all commissioners of assize in 1844. The 1536 Act was itself repealed by the *CLA* 1967: when assizes and quarter sessions were abolished, the jurisdiction was expressly conferred on the Crown Court: see now *Supreme Court [Senior Courts] Act* 1981, s.46(2) (renamed as from a day to be appointed: *Constitutional Reform Act* 2005, s.59(5), and Sched. 11, para. 1), *ante*, § 2–30.

The suggestion that acts which are piracy according to the law of nations are justiciable in this country even when committed by foreigners in respect of foreign ships so long as they are done at a place within the jurisdiction of the Admiralty, as defined above, received support in *The Magellan Pirates* (1853) 1 Sp. Ecc. & Ad. 81. The more modern view is that by the municipal law of England piracy may be committed within the territorial waters of a state, but may only be committed in respect of a ship when it is at sea in the ordinary meaning of that expression or in a geographical position where an attack on her could be described as a maritime offence: *Athens Maritime Enterprises Corporation v. Hellenic Mutual War Risks Association (Bermuda) Ltd* [1983] Q.B. 647, QBD. (Staughton J.); *Republic of Bolivia v. Indemnity Mutual Marine Assurance Co. Ltd* [1909] 1 K.B. 785, KBD and CA.

Section 6 of the *Territorial Waters Jurisdiction Act* 1878 provides that where any act of piracy as defined by the law of nations is also any such offence as is declared by that Act to be within the jurisdiction of the Admiralty (see section 2, *ante*, § 2–69), such offence may be tried in pursuance of the Act, or in pursuance of any other Act, law or custom relating thereto. This section, therefore, expressly saves the law of piracy in relation to "territorial waters of Her Majesty's dominions": see *Cameron v. H.M. Advocate*, 1971 S.L.T. 333. As to the meaning of that expression, see the *Territorial Sea Act* 1987, s.1(1) and (5), *ante*, § 2–70. **25–43**

Extension to aircraft

Aviation Security Act 1982, s.5

5.—(1) Any court in the United Kingdom having jurisdiction in respect of piracy committed on the high seas shall have jurisdiction in respect of piracy committed by or against an aircraft, wherever that piracy is committed. **25–44**

Section 5(2) stipulates that "aircraft" is to have the same meaning as in the *Civil Aviation Act* 1982, s.92 (*ante*, § 2–49) and that section 101 of that Act which contains a power to apply section 92 to Crown aircraft shall apply equally to this section.

(2) Piracy by statute

The *Piracy Act* 1698 and the *Piracy Act* 1721 were repealed by the *Statute Laws (Repeals) Act* 1993. These statutes deemed certain acts of the master or crew of a ship to be piracy; these included seizure of the ship by its crew and trading with pirates. **25–45**

(3) Punishment of piracy

Piracy Act 1837, s.2

Piracy with violence

2. Whosoever, with intent to commit or at the time of or immediately before or immediately after committing the crime of piracy in respect of any ship or vessel, shall assault, with intent to murder, any person being on board of or belonging to such ship or vessel, or shall stab, cut or wound any such person, or unlawfully do any act, by which the life of such person may be endangered, shall be guilty of an offence, and, being convicted thereof, shall be liable to imprisonment for life. ... **25–46**

[This section is printed as effectively amended by the *CLA* 1967, s.12(5)(a); and the *CDA* 1998, s.36(5); and as repealed in part by the *Statute Law Revision (No. 2) Act* 1888; and Sched. 3, Pt III to the 1967 Act.]

The "crime of piracy", it is submitted, should be taken to refer to the crime of piracy *jure gentium* as acts deemed to be piracy by statute were specifically dealt with in section 3. Where the facts are alleged to fall within this section the statement of offence should refer to it and the particulars should be framed accordingly, *e.g.* "*and at the time of or immediately before or immediately after such piracy stabbed, cut or wounded one J N on board the said ship*".

In the case of piracy *jure gentium* which falls short of this section, the penalty would appear to be governed by the *Offences at Sea Act* 1799, which provides that offences committed at sea shall be liable to the same penalty as if committed upon the shore, so that, for example, if the act of piracy would have amounted to the offence of robbery contrary to section 8 of the *Theft Act* 1968, the maximum penalty would be life imprisonment: see *ante*, § 21–84.

[The next paragraph is § 25–54.]

V. TERRORISM

A. TERRORISM ACT 2000

Introduction

25–54 This Act received Royal Assent, on July 20, 2000. The long title declares it to be an Act to make provision about terrorism, and to make temporary provision for Northern Ireland about the prosecution and punishment of certain offences, the preservation of peace and the maintenance of order. It is divided into eight parts, with 131 sections, and there are 16 schedules. It has been extensively amended by the *Anti-terrorism, Crime and Security Act* 2001, the *Crime (International Co-operation) Act* 2003, the *SOCPA* 2005 and the *Terrorism Act* 2006.

Management of terrorism cases

25–55 On January 30, 2007, Sir Igor Judge P. issued a revised protocol for the management of terrorism cases. For the details, see Appendix N–33 *et seq.*

Terrorism Act 2000, s.1

Terrorism: interpretation

25–56 **1.**—(1) In this Act "terrorism" means the use or threat of action where—

(a) the action falls within subsection (2)

(b) the use or threat is designed to influence the government or an international governmental organisation or to intimidate the public or a section of the public, and

(c) the use or threat is made for the purpose of advancing a political, religious or ideological cause.

(2) Action falls within this subsection if it—

(a) involves serious violence against a person,

(b) involves serious damage to property,

(c) endangers a person's life, other than that of the person committing the action,

(d) creates a serious risk to the health or safety of the public or a section of the public, or

(e) is designed seriously to interfere with or seriously to disrupt an electronic system.

(3) The use or threat of action falling within subsection (2) which involves the use of firearms or explosives is terrorism whether or not subsection (1)(b) is satisfied.

(4) In this section—

(a) "action" includes action outside the United Kingdom,

(b) a reference to any person or to property is a reference to any person, or to property, wherever situated,

(c) a reference to the public includes a reference to the public of a country other than the United Kingdom, and

(d) "the government" means the government of the United Kingdom, of a Part of the United Kingdom or of a country other than the United Kingdom.

(5) In this Act a reference to action taken for the purposes of terrorism includes a reference to action taken for the benefit of a proscribed organisation.

[This section is printed as amended by the *Terrorism Act* 2006, s.34.]

The reference to the government of a country other than the United Kingdom is not limited to countries governed by democratic or representative principles: *R. v. F.* [2007] 2 Cr.App.R. 3, CA. As to this case, see also *post*, § 25–98.

In *R. (Islamic Human Rights Commission) v. Civil Aviation Authority* [2007] A.C.D. 5, QBD, Ouseley J. said that the words of the definition of "terrorism" in this section, taken by themselves, were, by reason of subsection (3), wide enough to cover all lawful acts of war. However, he rejected a submission that they covered certain actions of Israel in Lebanon and Palestine. Beyond saying that it was "misconceived", he gave no reasons for this conclusion, save that it may perhaps be inferred that he took the view that lawful acts of war were impliedly excluded.

Terrorism Act 2000, s.3

PART II

PROSCRIBED ORGANISATIONS

Procedure

Proscription

3.—(1) For the purposes of this Act an organisation is proscribed if— **25–57**

(a) it is listed in Schedule 2, or

(b) it operates under the same name as an organisation listed in that Schedule.

(2) Subsection (1)(b) shall not apply in relation to an organisation listed in Schedule 2 if its entry is the subject of a note in that Schedule.

(3) The Secretary of State may by order—

(a) add an organisation to Schedule 2;

(b) remove an organisation from that Schedule;

(c) amend that Schedule in some other way.

(4) The Secretary of state may exercise his power under subsection (3)(a) in respect of an organisation only if he believes that it is concerned in terrorism.

(5) For the purposes of subsection (4) an organisation is concerned in terrorism if it—

(a) commits or participates in acts of terrorism,

(b) prepares for terrorism,

(c) promotes or encourages terrorism, or

(d) is otherwise concerned in terrorism.

(5A) The cases in which an organisation promotes or encourages terrorism for the purposes of subsection (5)(c) include any case in which activities of the organisation—

(a) include the unlawful glorification of the commission or preparation (whether in the past, in the future or generally) of acts of terrorism; or

(b) are carried out in a manner that ensures that the organisation is associated with statements containing any such glorification.

(5B) The glorification of any conduct is unlawful for the purposes of subsection (5A) if there are persons who may become aware of it who could reasonably be expected to infer that what is being glorified, is being glorified as—

(a) conduct that should be emulated in existing circumstances, or

(b) conduct that is illustrative of a type of conduct that should be so emulated.

(5C) In this section—

"glorification" includes any form of praise or celebration, and cognate expressions are to be construed accordingly;

"statement" includes a communication without words consisting of sounds or images or both.

(6) Where the Secretary of State believes—

(a) that an organisation listed in Schedule 2 is operating wholly or partly under a name that is not specified in that Schedule (whether as well as or instead of under the specified name), or

(b) that an organisation that is operating under a name that is not so specified is otherwise for all practical purposes the same as an organisation so listed,

he may, by order, provide that the name that is not specified in that Schedule is to be treated as another name for the listed organisation.

(7) Where an order under subsection (6) provides for a name to be treated as another name for an organisation, this Act shall have effect in relation to acts occurring while—

(a) the order is in force, and

(b) the organisation continues to be listed in Schedule 2,

as if the organisation were listed in that Schedule under the other name, as well as under the name specified in the Schedule.

(8) The Secretary of State may at any time by order revoke an order under subsection (6) or otherwise provide for a name specified in such an order to cease to be treated as a name for a particular organisation.

(9) Nothing in subsections (6) to (8) prevents any liability from being established in any proceedings by proof that an organisation is the same as an organisation listed in Schedule 2, even though it is or was operating under a name specified neither in Schedule 2 nor in an order under subsection (6).

[This section is printed as amended by the *Terrorism Act* 2006, ss.21 and 22(1) and (2).]

An organisation that has no capacity to carry on terrorist activities, that has taken no steps to acquire such capacity or otherwise to promote or encourage terrorist activities and that has decided to attempt to achieve its aims by other than violent means cannot be said to be "otherwise concerned in terrorism", within the meaning of section 3(5)(d) even if its leaders have the contingent intention to resort to terrorism in the future; the nexus between such an organisation and the commission of terrorist activities is too remote: *Lord Alton of Liverpool v. Secretary of State for the Home Department* [2008] 2 Cr.App.R. 31, CA (Civ. Div.) (contrasting such an organisation with one which has temporarily ceased terrorist activities for tactical reasons).

Terrorism Act 2000, ss.4–10

25–58 **4.** [*Deproscription: application.*]

5. [*Deproscription: appeal.*]

6. [*Further appeal.*]

Appeal: effect on conviction, etc.

7.—(1) This section applies where—

(a) an appeal under section 5 has been allowed in respect of an organisation.

(b) an order has been made under section 3(3)(b) in respect of the organisation in accordance with an order of the Commission under section 5(4) (and, if the order was made in reliance on section 123(5), a resolution has been passed by each House of Parliament under section 123(5)(b)),

(c) a person has been convicted of an offence in respect of the organisation under any of sections 11 to 13, 15 to 19 and 56, and

(d) the activity to which the charge referred took place on or after the date of the refusal to deproscribe against which the appeal under section 5 was brought.

(1A) This section also applies where—

(a) an appeal under section 5 has been allowed in respect of a name treated as the name for an organisation,

(b) an order has been made under section 3(8) in respect of the name in accordance with an order of the Commission under section 5(4),

(c) a person has been convicted of an offence in respect of the organisation under any of sections 11 to 13, 15 to 19 and 56, and

(d) the activity to which the charge referred took place on or after the date of the refusal, against which the appeal under section 5 was brought, to provide for a name to cease to be treated as a name for the organisation.

(2) If the person mentioned in subsection (1)(c) or (1A)(c) was convicted on indictment—

(a) he may appeal against the conviction to the Court of Appeal, and
(b) the Court of Appeal shall allow the appeal.

(3) A person may appeal against a conviction by virtue of subsection (2) whether or not he has already appealed against the conviction.

(4) An appeal by virtue of subsection (2)—

(a) must be brought within the period of 28 days beginning with the date on which the order mentioned in subsection (1)(b) or (1A)(b) comes into force, and
(b) shall be treated as an appeal under section 1 of the *Criminal Appeal Act* 1968 (but does not require leave).

(5) If the person mentioned in subsection (1)(c) or (1A)(c) was convicted by a magistrates' court—

(a) he may appeal against the conviction to the Crown Court, and
(b) the Crown Court shall allow the appeal.

(6) A person may appeal against a conviction by virtue of subsection (5)—

(a) whether or not he pleaded guilty,
(b) whether or not he has already appealed against the conviction, and
(c) whether or not he has made an application in respect of the conviction under section 111 of the *Magistrates' Courts Act* 1980 (case stated).

(7) An appeal by virtue of subsection (5)—

(a) must be brought within the period of 21 days beginning with the date on which the order mentioned in subsection (1)(b) or (1A)(b) comes into force, and
(b) shall be treated as an appeal under section 108(1)(b) of the *Magistrates' Courts Act* 1980.

(8) [*Amendment of* Criminal Justice Act *1988, s.133(5).*]

[This section is printed as amended by the *Terrorism Act* 2006, s.22(1), (7) and (8).]

The reference to "the Commission" is to the Proscribed Organisations Appeal Commission established by section 5(1).

8. [*Section 7: Scotland and Northern Ireland.*]

9. [Human Rights Act *1998*].

Immunity

10.—(1) The following shall not be admissible as evidence in proceedings for an offence under any of sections 11 to 13, 15 to 19 and 56— **25–59**

(a) evidence of anything done in relation to an application to the Secretary of State under section 4,
(b) evidence of anything done in relation to proceedings before the Proscribed Organisations Appeal Commission under section 5 above or section 7(1) of the *Human Rights Act* 1998,
(c) evidence of anything done in relation to proceedings under section 6 (including that section as applied bysection 9(2)), and
(d) any document submitted for the purposes of proceedings mentioned in any of paragraphs (a) to (c).

(2) But subsection (1) does not prevent evidence from being adduced on behalf of the accused.

Terrorism Act 2000, ss.11–13

Membership

11.—(1) A person commits an offence if he belongs or professes to belong to a proscribed organisation. **25–60**

(2) It is a defence for a person charged with an offence under subsection (1) to prove—

(a) that the organisation was not proscribed on the last (or only) occasion on which he became a member or began to profess to be a member, and
(b) that he has not taken part in the activities of the organisation at any time while it was proscribed.

(3) A person guilty of an offence under this section shall be liable—

(a) on conviction on indictment, to imprisonment for a term not exceeding ten years, to a fine or to both, or
(b) on summary conviction, to imprisonment for a term not exceeding *six* [12] months, to a fine not exceeding the statutory maximum or to both.

(4) In subsection (2) "proscribed" means proscribed for the purposes of any of the following—

(a) this Act
(b) the *Northern Ireland (Emergency Provisions) Act* 1996;
(c) the *Northern Ireland (Emergency Provisions) Act* 1991;
(d) the *Prevention of Terrorism (Temporary Provisions) Act* 1989;
(e) the *Prevention of Terrorism (Temporary Provisions) Act* 1984;
(f) the *Northern Ireland (Emergency Provisions) Act* 1978;
(g) the *Prevention of Terrorism (Temporary Provisions) Act* 1976;
(h) the *Prevention of Terrorism (Temporary Provisions) Act* 1974;
(i) the *Northern Ireland (Emergency Provisions) Act* 1973.

[In subs. (3)(b), "12" is substituted for "six", as from a day to be appointed, by the *CJA* 2003, s.282(2) and (3). The increase has no application to offences committed before the substitution takes effect: *ibid.*, s.282(4).]

As to the commission abroad of an offence under this section, see section 17 of the *Terrorism Act* 2006, *post*, § 25–142h.

In *Sheldrake v. DPP*; *Att.-Gen.'s Reference (No. 4 of 2002)* [2005] 1 A.C. 264, HL, it was held that section 11(2) should be read and given effect as imposing on the defendant an evidential burden only; a person who is innocent of any blameworthy or properly criminal conduct may fall within section 11(1); and there would be a clear breach of the presumption of innocence, and a real risk of unfair conviction, if such persons could exonerate themselves only by establishing the defence provided on the balance of probabilities; and this was particularly so given that (a) it might well be all but impossible for a defendant to satisfy subsection (2)(b) (such organisations do not produce minutes, others would not be willing to give evidence, etc.), (b) if the burden were a legal one, there would be no discretion if the defendant failed to prove the specified matters and the court would be obliged to convict, (c) the consequences of failing to establish the defence were severe (up to 10 years' imprisonment), and (d) while security considerations must always carry weight, they did not absolve states from their duty to ensure basic standards of fairness.

Support

25–61 **12.**—(1) A person commits an offence if—

(a) he invites support for a proscribed organisation, and
(b) the support is not, or is not restricted to, the provision of money or other property (within the meaning of section 15).

(2) A person commits an offence if he arranges, manages or assists in arranging or managing a meeting which he knows is—

(a) to support a proscribed organisation,
(b) to further the activities of a proscribed organisation, or
(c) to be addressed by a person who belongs or professes to belong to a proscribed organisation.

(3) A person commits an offence if he addresses a meeting and the purpose of his address is to encourage support for a proscribed organisation or to further its activities.

(4) Where a person is charged with an offence under subsection (2)(c) in respect of a private meeting it is a defence for him to prove that he had no reasonable cause to believe that the address mentioned in subsection (2)(c) would support a proscribed organisation or further its activities.

(5) In subsections (2) to (4)—

(a) "meeting" means a meeting of three or more persons, whether or not the public are admitted, and
(b) a meeting is private if the public are not admitted.

(6) [*Identical to s.11(3)*, ante, *§ 25–60*.]

In connection with the defence provided by section 12(4), see section 118, *post*, § 25–106.

Uniform

25–62 **13.**—(1) A person in a public place commits an offence if he—

(a) wears an item of clothing, or

(b) wears, carries or displays an article,

in such a way or in such circumstances as to arouse reasonable suspicion that he is a member or supporter of a proscribed organisation.

(2) [*Scotland: power of arrest.*]

(3) A person guilty of an offence under this section shall be liable on summary conviction to—

(a) imprisonment for a term not exceeding *six months* [51 weeks],

(b) a fine not exceeding level 5 on the standard scale, or

(c) both.

[In subs. (3)(a), "51 weeks" is substituted for "six months", as from a day to be appointed, by the *CJA* 2003, s.281(4) and (5). The increase has no application to offences committed before the substitution takes effect: *ibid*., s.281(6).]

Terrorism Act 2000, s.14

Part III

Terrorist Property

Interpretation

Terrorist property

14.—(1) In this Act "terrorist property" means— **25–63**

(a) money or other property which is likely to be used for the purposes of terrorism (including any resources of a proscribed organisation),

(b) proceeds of the commission of acts of terrorism, and

(c) proceeds of acts carried out for the purposes of terrorism.

(2) In subsection (1)—

(a) a reference to proceeds of an act includes a reference to any property which wholly or partly, and directly or indirectly, represents the proceeds of the act (including payments or other rewards in connection with its commission), and

(b) the reference to an organisation's resources includes a reference to any money or other property which is applied or made available, or is to be applied or made available, for use by the organisation.

Terrorism Act 2000, ss.15–23

Fund-raising

15.—(1) A person commits an offence if he— **25–64**

(a) invites another to provide money or other property, and

(b) intends that it should be used, or has reasonable cause to suspect that it may be used, for the purposes of terrorism.

(2) A person commits an offence if he—

(a) receives money or other property, and

(b) intends that it should be used, or has reasonable cause to suspect that it may be used, for the purposes of terrorism.

(3) A person commits an offence if he—

(a) provides money or other party, and

(b) knows or has reasonable cause to suspect that it will or may be used for the purposes of terrorism.

(4) In this section a reference to the provision of money or other property is a reference to its being given, lent or otherwise made available, whether or not for consideration.

Use and possession

16.—(1) A person commits an offence if he uses money or other property for the purposes of **25–65**
terrorism.

(2) A person commits an offence if he—

(a) possesses money or other property, and

(b) intends that it should be used, or has reasonable cause to suspect that it may be used, for the purpose of terrorism.

Funding arrangements

25–66 **17.** A person commits an offence if—

(a) he enters into or becomes concerned in an arrangement as a result of which money or other property is made available or is to be made available to another, and

(b) he knows or has reasonable cause to suspect that it will or may be used for the purposes of terrorism.

Money laundering

25–67 **18.**—(1) A person commits an offence if he enters into or becomes concerned in an arrangement which facilitates the retention or control by or on behalf of another person of terrorist property—

(a) by concealment,

(b) by removal from the jurisdiction,

(c) by transfer to nominees, or

(d) in any other way.

(2) It is a defence for a person charged with an offence under subsection (1) to prove that he did not know and had no reasonable cause to suspect that the arrangement related to terrorist property.

Offences contrary to sections 15 to 18 are "Convention offences" within the *Terrorism Act* 2006: see *post*, §§ 25–142k, 25–142l. They are also offences in respect of which a financial reporting order may be made under the *SOCPA* 2005, s.76 (*ante*, § 5–886a).

Disclosure of information: duty

25–68 **19.**—(1) This section applies where a person—

(a) believes or suspects that another person has committed an offence under any of sections 15 to 18, and

(b) bases his belief or suspicion on information which comes to his attention in the course of a trade, profession, business or employment.

(1A) But this section does not apply if the information came to the person in the course of a business in the regulated sector.

(2) The person commits an offence if he does not disclose to a constable as soon as is reasonably practicable—

(a) his belief or suspicion, and

(b) the information on which it is based.

(3) It is a defence for a person charged with an offence under subsection (2) to prove that he had a reasonable excuse for not making the disclosure.

(4) Where—

(a) a person is in employment,

(b) his employer has established a procedure for the making of disclosures of the matters specified in subsection (2), and

(c) he is charged with an offence under that subsection,

it is a defence for him to prove that he disclosed the matters specified in that subsection in accordance with the procedure.

(5) Subsection (2) does not require disclosure by a professional legal adviser of—

(a) information which he obtains in privileged circumstances, or

(b) a belief or suspicion based on information which he obtains in privileged circumstances.

(6) For the purpose of subsection (5) information is obtained by an adviser in privileged circumstances if it comes to him, otherwise than with a view to furthering a criminal purpose—

(a) from a client or a client's representative, in connection with the provision of legal advice by the adviser to the client,

(b) from a person seeking legal advice from the adviser, or from the person's representative, or

(c) from any person, for the purpose of actual or contemplated legal proceedings.

(7) For the purposes of subsection (1)(a) a person shall be treated as having committed an offence under one of sections 15 to 18 if—

(a) he has taken an action or been in possession of a thing, and

(b) he would have committed an offence under one of those sections if he had been in the United Kingdom at the time when he took the action or was in possession of the thing.

(7A) The reference to a business in the regulated sector must be construed in accordance with Schedule 3A.

(7B) The reference to a constable includes a reference to a member of the staff of the Serious Organised Crime Agency authorised for the purposes of this section by the Director General of that Agency.

(8) A person guilty of an offence under this section shall be liable—

(a) on conviction on indictment, to imprisonment for a term not exceeding five years, to a fine or to both, or

(b) on summary conviction, to imprisonment for a term not exceeding *six* [12] months, or to a fine not exceeding the statutory maximum or to both.

[This section is printed as amended by the *Anti-terrorism, Crime and Security Act* 2001, s.3, and Sched. 2, para. 5(3) and (4); and the *SOCPA* 2005, s.59, and Sched. 4, paras 125 and 126. In subs. (8)(b), "12" is substituted for "six", as from a day to be appointed, by the *CJA* 2003, s.282(2) and (3). The increase has no application to offences committed before the substitution takes effect: *ibid.*, s.282(4).]

Schedule 3A is not set out in this work. It was inserted by the *Anti-terrorism, Crime and Security Act* 2001, s.3, and Sched. 2, para. 5(6). It was then amended on a number of occasions prior to being substituted in its entirety by the *Terrorism Act 2000 (Business in the Regulated Sector and Supervisory Authorities) Order* 2007 (S.I. 2007 No. 3288).

In connection with sections 11 to 19, see *R. (Kurdistan Workers Party) v. Secretary of State for the Home Department* [2002] A.C.D. 99, QBD (Richards J.) (permission to apply for judicial review refused where the applicant organisations sought to challenge the regime of offences laid down by these sections and the lawfulness of the decision to proscribe them; but the grounds of claim were arguable, *viz.* that the proscription and the consequential criminal prohibitions gave rise to substantial interference with the rights to freedom of expression, to freedom of association and to enjoyment of property, they were not "prescribed by law" and were disproportionate, and no opportunity had been extended to the applicants to make representations as to why they should not be proscribed).

In *O'Driscoll v. Secretary of State for the Home Department* [2003] A.C.D. 35, DC, it was held that the offences created by section 16 are "prescribed by law"; to be so prescribed, the definition of the offence must be adequately accessible and formulated with sufficient care to enable the citizen to regulate his conduct, if need be with appropriate advice; when section 16 is read together with section 1(5) (*ante*, § 25–56) and the definition of "property" in section 121 (*post*, § 25–108), the citizen knows what he can and cannot do; it is important to recognise that in order to prove an offence contrary to section 16(2) it is necessary to prove that the defendant had a specific intent, or state of mind; and the same mental element is important in relation to the issue of proportionality; when deciding whether to proscribe an organisation, the Secretary of State, and on appeal the Proscribed Organisations Appeal Commission, have to balance the effects of proscription against the activities of the organisation under consideration; if, however, there is no question about the terrorist nature of the organisation it is difficult to see why section 16 should be regarded as disproportionate, having regard to the need for proof of a guilty mind and the extent of the criminal court's powers in relation to sentence; the section is not about freedom of expression (or restrictions thereon); it is about knowingly providing money or other property to support a proscribed organisation; so long as the organisation in question has been properly proscribed, the section cannot be regarded as disproportionate.

Disclosure of information: permission

20.—(1) A person may disclose to a constable— **25–69**

(a) a suspicion or belief that any money or other property is terrorist property or is derived from terrorist property;

(b) any matter on which the suspicion or belief is based.

(2) A person may make a disclosure to a constable in the circumstances mentioned in section 19(1) and (2).

(3) Subsections (1) and (2) shall have effect notwithstanding any restriction on the disclosure of information imposed by statute or otherwise.

(4) Where—

(a) a person is in employment, and

(b) his employer has established a procedure for the making of disclosures of the kinds mentioned in subsection (1) and section 19(2),

subsections (1) and (2) shall have effect in relation to that person as if any reference to disclosure to a constable included a reference to disclosure in accordance with the procedure.

(5) References to a constable include references to a member of the staff of the Serious Organised Crime Agency authorised for the purposes of this section by the Director General of that Agency.

[This section is printed as amended by the *Anti-terrorism, Crime and Security Act* 2001, s.3, and Sched. 2, para. 5(5); and the *SOCPA* 2005, s.59, and Sched. 4, paras 125 and 127.]

Cooperation with police

25–70 **21.**—(1) A person does not commit an offence under any of section 15 to 18 if he is acting with the express consent of a constable.

(2) Subject to subsections (3) and (4), a person does not commit an offence under any of sections 15 to 18 by involvement in a transaction or arrangement relating to money or other property if he discloses to a constable—

(a) his suspicion or belief that the money or other property is terrorist property, and

(b) the information on which his suspicion or belief is based.

(3) Subsection (2) applies only where a person makes a disclosure—

(a) after he becomes concerned in the transaction concerned,

(b) on his own initiative, and

(c) as soon as is reasonably practicable.

(4) Subsection (2) does not apply to a person if—

(a) a constable forbids him to continue his involvement in the transaction or arrangement to which the disclosure relates, and

(b) he continues his involvement.

(5) It is a defence for a person charged with an offence under any of sections 15(2) and (3) and 16 to 18 to prove that—

(a) he intended to make a disclosure of the kind mentioned in subsections (2) and (3), and

(b) there is reasonable excuse for his failure to do so.

(6) Where—

(a) a person is in employment, and

(b) his employer has established a procedure for the making of disclosures of the same kind as may be made to a constable under subsection (2),

this section shall have effect in relation to that person as if any reference to disclosure to a constable included a reference to disclosure in accordance with the procedure.

(7) A reference in this section to a transaction or arrangement relating to money or other property includes a reference to use or possession.

Arrangements with prior consent

25–70a **21ZA.**—(1) A person does not commit an offence under any of sections 15 to 18 by involvement in a transaction or an arrangement relating to money or other property if, before becoming involved, the person—

(a) discloses to an authorised officer the person's suspicion or belief that the money or other property is terrorist property and the information on which the suspicion or belief is based, and

(b) has the authorised officer's consent to becoming involved in the transaction or arrangement.

(2) A person is treated as having an authorised officer's consent if before the end of the notice period the person does not receive notice from an authorised officer that consent is refused.

(3) The notice period is the period of 7 working days starting with the first working day after the person makes the disclosure.

(4) A working day is a day other than a Saturday, a Sunday, Christmas Day, Good

Friday or a day that is a bank holiday under the *Banking and Financial Dealings Act* 1971 in the part of the United Kingdom in which the person is when making the disclosure.

(5) In this section "authorised officer" means a member of the staff of the Serious Organised Crime Agency authorised for the purposes of this section by the Director General of that Agency.

(6) The reference in this section to a transaction or arrangement relating to money or other property includes a reference to use or possession.

[Ss.21ZA–21ZC were inserted by the *Terrorism Act 2000 and Proceeds of Crime Act 2002 (Amendment) Regulations* 2007 (S.I. 2007 No. 3398) with effect from December 26, 2007.]

Disclosure after entering into arrangements

21ZB.—(1) A person does not commit an offence under any of sections 15 to 18 by involvement in a transaction or an arrangement relating to money or other property if, after becoming involved, the person discloses to an authorised officer— **25–70b**

(a) the person's suspicion or belief that the money or other property is terrorist property, and

(b) the information on which the suspicion or belief is based.

(2) This section applies only where—

(a) there is a reasonable excuse for the person's failure to make the disclosure before becoming involved in the transaction or arrangement, and

(b) the disclosure is made on the person's own initiative and as soon as it is reasonably practicable for the person to make it.

(3) This section does not apply to a person if—

(a) an authorised officer forbids the person to continue involvement in the transaction or arrangement to which the disclosure relates, and

(b) the person continues that involvement.

(4), (5) [*Identical to s.21ZA(5) and (6)*, ante, *§ 25–70a*.]

[See the note to s.21ZA, *ante*.]

Reasonable excuse for failure to disclose

21ZC. It is a defence for a person charged with an offence under any of sections 15 to 18 to prove that— **25–70c**

(a) the person intended to make a disclosure of the kind mentioned in section 21ZA or 21ZB, and

(b) there is a reasonable excuse for the person's failure to do so.

[See the note to s.21ZA, *ante*.]

Failure to disclose: regulated sector

21A.—(1) A person commits an offence if each of the following three conditions is satisfied. **25–71**

(2) The first condition is that he—

(a) knows or suspects, or

(b) has reasonable grounds for knowing or suspecting,

that another person has committed or attempted to commit an offence under any of sections 15 to 18.

(3) The second condition is that the information or other matter—

(a) on which his knowledge or suspicion is based, or

(b) which gives reasonable grounds for such knowledge or suspicion,

came to him in the course of a business in the regulated sector.

(4) The third condition is that he does not disclose the information or other matter to a constable or a nominated officer as soon as is practicable after it comes to him.

(5) But a person does not commit an offence under this section if—

(a) he has a reasonable excuse for not disclosing the information or other matter;

(b) he is a professional legal adviser or relevant professional adviser and the information or other matter came to him in privileged circumstances, or

(c) subsection (5A) applies to him.

(5A) This subsection applies to a person if—

(a) the person is employed by, or is in partnership with, a professional legal adviser or relevant professional adviser to provide the adviser with assistance or support,

(b) the information or other matter comes to the person in connection with the provision of such assistance or support, and

(c) the information or other matter came to the adviser in privileged circumstances.

(6) In deciding whether a person committed an offence under this section the court must consider whether he followed any relevant guidance which was at the time concerned—

(a) issued by a supervisory authority or any other appropriate body,

(b) approved by the Treasury, and

(c) published in a manner it approved as appropriate in its opinion to bring the guidance to the attention of persons likely to be affected by it.

(7) A disclosure to a nominated officer is a disclosure which—

(a) is made to a person nominated by the alleged offender's employer to receive disclosures under this section, and

(b) is made in the course of the alleged offender's employment and in accordance with the procedure established by the employer for the purpose.

(8) Information or other matter comes to a professional legal adviser or relevant professional adviser in privileged circumstances if it is communicated or given to him—

(a) by (or by a representative of) a client of his in connection with the giving by the adviser of legal advice to the client,

(b) by (or by a representative of) a person seeking legal advice from the adviser, or

(c) by a person in connection with legal proceedings or contemplated legal proceedings.

(9) But subsection (8) does not apply to information or other matter which is communicated or given with a view to furthering a criminal purpose.

(10) Schedule 3A has effect for the purpose of determining what is—

(a) a business in the regulated sector;

(b) a supervisory authority.

(11) For the purposes of subsection (2) a person is to be taken to have committed an offence there mentioned if—

(a) he has taken an action or been in possession of a thing, and

(b) he would have committed the offence if he had been in the United Kingdom at the time when he took the action or was in possession of the thing.

(12) A person guilty of an offence under this section is liable—

(a) on conviction on indictment, to imprisonment for a term not exceeding five years or to a fine or to both;

(b) on summary conviction, to imprisonment for a term not exceeding *six* [12] months or to a fine not exceeding the statutory maximum or to both.

(13) An appropriate body is any body which regulates or is representative of any trade, profession, business or employment carried on by the alleged offender.

(14) [*Identical to s.19(7B) (including the prospective amendment),* ante, *§ 25–68.*]

(15) In this section "relevant professional adviser" means an accountant, auditor or tax adviser who is a member of a professional body which is established for accountants, auditors or tax advisers (as the case may be) and which makes provision for—

(a) testing the competence of those seeking admission to membership of such a body as a condition for such admission; and

(b) imposing and maintaining professional and ethical standards for its members, as well as imposing sanctions for non-compliance with those standards.

[Ss.21A and 21B were inserted by the *Anti-terrorism, Crime and Security Act* 2001, s.3, and Sched. 2, para. 5(2). They are printed as amended by S.I. 2007 No. 3398 (*ante*, § 25–70a). In subs. (12)(b), "12" is substituted for "six", as from a day to be appointed, by the *CJA* 2003, s.282(2) and (3). The increase has no application to offences committed before the substitution takes effect: *ibid.*, s.282(4).]

Schedule 3A (as to which, see *ante*, § 25–68) is not set out in this work.

Protected disclosures

25–72 **21B.**—(1) A disclosure which satisfies the following three conditions is not to be taken to breach any restriction on the disclosure of information (however imposed).

(2) The first condition is that the information or other matter disclosed came to the person making the disclosure (the discloser) in the course of a business in the regulated sector.

(3) The second condition is that the information or other matter—

(a) causes the discloser to know or suspect, or

(b) gives him reasonable grounds for knowing or suspecting,

that another person has committed or attempted to commit an offence under any of sections 15 to 18.

(4) The third condition is that the disclosure is made to a constable or a nominated officer as soon as is practicable after the information or other matter comes to the discloser.

(5) A disclosure to a nominated officer is a disclosure which—

(a) is made to a person nominated by the discloser's employer to receive disclosures under this section, and

(b) is made in the course of the discloser's employment and in accordance with the procedure established by the employer for the purpose.

(6) The reference to a business in the regulated sector must be construed in accordance with Schedule 3A.

(7) [*Identical to s.19(7B) (including the prospective amendment),* ante, *§ 25–68.*]

[As to the insertion of this section, see the note to s.21A.]

Schedule 3A (as to which, see *ante*, § 25–68) is not set out in this work.

Disclosures to SOCA

21C.—(1) Where a disclosure is made under a provision of this Part to a constable, the constable must disclose it in full as soon as practicable after it has been made to a member of staff of the Serious Organised Crime Agency authorised for the purposes of that provision by the Director General of that Agency. **25–72a**

(2) Where a disclosure is made under section 21 (cooperation with police) to a constable, the constable must disclose it in full as soon as practicable after it has been made to a member of staff of the Serious Organised Crime Agency authorised for the purposes of this subsection by the Director General of that Agency.

[Ss.21C–21H were inserted by S.I. 2007 No. 3398 (*ante*, § 25–70a).]

Tipping off: regulated sector

21D.—(1) A person commits an offence if— **25–72b**

(a) the person discloses any matter within subsection (2);

(b) the disclosure is likely to prejudice any investigation that might be conducted following the disclosure referred to in that subsection; and

(c) the information on which the disclosure is based came to the person in the course of a business in the regulated sector.

(2) The matters are that the person or another person has made a disclosure under a provision of this Part—

(a) to a constable,

(b) in accordance with a procedure established by that person's employer for the making of disclosures under that provision,

(c) to a nominated officer, or

(d) to a member of staff of the Serious Organised Crime Agency authorised for the purposes of that provision by the Director General of that Agency,

of information that came to that person in the course of a business in the regulated sector.

(3) A person commits an offence if —

(a) the person discloses that an investigation into allegations that an offence under this Part has been committed is being contemplated or is being carried out;

(b) the disclosure is likely to prejudice that investigation; and

(c) the information on which the disclosure is based came to the person in the course of a business in the regulated sector.

(4) A person guilty of an offence under this section is liable—

(a) on summary conviction to imprisonment for a term not exceeding three months, or to a fine not exceeding level 5 on the standard scale, or to both;

(b) on conviction on indictment to imprisonment for a term not exceeding two years, or to a fine, or to both.

(5) This section is subject to—

(a) section 21E (disclosures within an undertaking or group etc),

(b) section 21F (other permitted disclosures between institutions etc), and
(c) section 21G (other permitted disclosures etc).

[See the note to s.21C, *ante*.]

Disclosures within an undertaking or group etc.

25–72c **21E.**—(1) An employee, officer or partner of an undertaking does not commit an offence under section 21D if the disclosure is to an employee, officer or partner of the same undertaking.

(2) A person does not commit an offence under section 21D in respect of a disclosure by a credit institution or a financial institution if—

(a) the disclosure is to a credit institution or a financial institution,
(b) the institution to whom the disclosure is made is situated in an EEA State or in a country or territory imposing equivalent money laundering requirements, and
(c) both the institution making the disclosure and the institution to whom it is made belong to the same group.

(3) In subsection (2) "group" has the same meaning as in Directive 2002/87/EC of the European Parliament and of the Council of 16th December 2002 on the supplementary supervision of credit institutions, insurance undertakings and investment firms in a financial conglomerate.

(4) A professional legal adviser or a relevant professional adviser does not commit an offence under section 21D if—

(a) the disclosure is to a professional legal adviser or a relevant professional adviser,
(b) both the person making the disclosure and the person to whom it is made carry on business in an EEA state or in a country or territory imposing equivalent money laundering requirements, and
(c) those persons perform their professional activities within different undertakings that share common ownership, management or control.

[See the note to s.21C, *ante*.]

Other permitted disclosures between institutions etc.

25–72d **21F.**—(1) This section applies to a disclosure—

(a) by a credit institution to another credit institution,
(b) by a financial institution to another financial institution,
(c) by a professional legal adviser to another professional legal adviser, or
(d) by a relevant professional adviser of a particular kind to another relevant professional adviser of the same kind.

(2) A person does not commit an offence under section 21D in respect of a disclosure to which this section applies if—

(a) the disclosure relates to—
 (i) a client or former client of the institution or adviser making the disclosure and the institution or adviser to whom it is made,
 (ii) a transaction involving them both, or
 (iii) the provision of a service involving them both;
(b) the disclosure is for the purpose only of preventing an offence under this Part of this Act;
(c) the institution or adviser to whom the disclosure is made is situated in an EEA State or in a country or territory imposing equivalent money laundering requirements; and
(d) the institution or adviser making the disclosure and the institution or adviser to whom it is made are subject to equivalent duties of professional confidentiality and the protection of personal data (within the meaning of section 1 of the *Data Protection Act* 1998).

[See the note to s.21C, *ante*.]

Other permitted disclosures etc.

25–72e **21G.**—(1) A person does not commit an offence under section 21D if the disclosure is—

(a) to the authority that is the supervisory authority for that person by virtue of the *Money Laundering Regulations* 2007 (S.I. 2007 No. 2157); or
(b) for the purpose of—
 (i) the detection, investigation or prosecution of a criminal offence (whether in the United Kingdom or elsewhere),
 (ii) an investigation under the *Proceeds of Crime Act* 2002, or

(iii) the enforcement of any order of a court under that Act.

(2) A professional legal adviser or a relevant professional adviser does not commit an offence under section 21D if the disclosure—

(a) is to the adviser's client, and

(b) is made for the purpose of dissuading the client from engaging in conduct amounting to an offence.

(3) A person does not commit an offence under section 21D(1) if the person does not know or suspect that the disclosure is likely to have the effect mentioned in section 21D(1)(b).

(4) A person does not commit an offence under section 21D(3) if the person does not know or suspect that the disclosure is likely to have the effect mentioned in section 21D(3)(b).

[See the note to s.21C, *ante*.]

Interpretation of sections 21D to 21G

21H.—(1) The references in sections 21D to 21G— **25–72f**

(a) to a business in the regulated sector, and

(b) to a supervisory authority,

are to be construed in accordance with Schedule 3A.

(2) In those sections—

"credit institution" has the same meaning as in Schedule 3A;

"financial institution" means an undertaking that carries on a business in the regulated sector by virtue of any of paragraphs (b) to (i) of paragraph 1(1) of that Schedule.

(3) References in those sections to a disclosure by or to a credit institution or a financial institution include disclosure by or to an employee, officer or partner of the institution acting on its behalf.

(4) For the purposes of those sections a country or territory imposes "equivalent money laundering requirements" if it imposes requirements equivalent to those laid down in Directive 2005/60/EC of the European Parliament and of the Council of 26th October 2005 on the prevention of the use of the financial system for the purpose of money laundering and terrorist financing.

(5) In those sections "relevant professional adviser" means an accountant, auditor or tax adviser who is a member of a professional body which is established for accountants, auditors or tax advisers (as the case may be) and which makes provision for—

(a) testing the competence of those seeking admission to membership of such a body as a condition for such admission; and

(b) imposing and maintaining professional and ethical standards for its members, as well as imposing sanctions for non-compliance with those standards.

[See the note to s.21C, *ante*.]

Schedule 3A (as to which, see *ante*, § 25–68) is not set out in this work.

Penalties

22. A person guilty of an offence under any of sections 15 to 18 shall be liable— **25–73**

(a) on conviction on indictment, to imprisonment for a term not exceeding 14 years, to a fine or to both, or

(b) on summary conviction, to imprisonment for a term not exceeding *six* [12] months, to a fine not exceeding the statutory maximum or to both.

[In para. (b), "12" is substituted for "six", as from a day to be appointed, by the *CJA* 2003, s.282(2) and (3). The increase has no application to offences committed before the substitution takes effect: *ibid.*, s.282(4).]

Forfeiture

23.—(1) The court by or before which a person is convicted of an offence under any of sections 15 to 18 may make a forfeiture order in accordance with the provisions of this section. **25–74**

(2) Where a person is convicted of an offence under section 15(1) or (2) or 16 the court may order the forfeiture of any money or other property—

(a) which, at the time of the offence, he had in his possession or under his control, and

(b) which, at that time, he intended should be used, or had reasonable cause to suspect might be used, for the purposes of terrorism.

(3) Where a person is convicted of an offence under section 15(3) the court may order the forfeiture of any money or other property—

(a) which, at the time of the offence, he had in his possession or under his control, and

(b) which, at that time, he knew or had reasonable casue to suspect would or might be used for the purposes of terrorism.

(4) Where a person is convicted of an offence under section 17 the court may order the forfeiture of the money or other property—

(a) to which the arrangement in question related, and

(b) which, at the time of the offence, he knew or had reasonable cause to suspect would or might be used for the purpose of terrorism.

(5) Where a person is convicted of an offence under section 18 the court may order the forfeiture of the money or other property to which the arrangement in question related.

(6) Where a person is convicted of an offence under any of sections 15 to 18, the court may order the forfeiture of any money or other property which wholly or partly, and directly or indirectly, is received by any person as a payment or other reward in connection with the commission of the offence.

(7) Where a person other than the convicted person claims to be the owner of or otherwise interested in anything which can be forfeited by an order under this section, the court shall give him an opportunity to be heard before making an order.

(8) [*Scotland.*]

(9) [*Gives effect to Schedule 4* (post).]

[The next paragraph is § 25–79.]

Terrorism Act 2000, s.32

PART IV

TERRORIST INVESTIGATIONS

Interpretation

Terrorist investigation

25–79 **32.** In this Act "terrorist investigation" means an investigation of—

(a) the commission, preparation or instigation of acts of terrorism,

(b) an act which appears to have been done for the purposes of terrorism,

(c) the resources of a proscribed organisation,

(d) the possibility of making an order under section 3(3), or

(e) the commission, preparation or instigation of an offence under this Act or under Part 1 of the *Terrorism Act* 2006 other than an offence under section 1 or 2 of that Act.

[This section is printed as amended by the *Terrorism Act* 2006, s.37(1).]

Cordons

25–80 Sections 33 and 34 confer on police officers, generally of at least the rank of superintendent, to designate an area as a cordoned area for the purposes of a terrorist investigation. Such an area is to be demarcated as such by the use of tape, or in such other manner as a constable considers appropriate. An order designating an area as a cordoned area may only be made where it is considered expedient for the purposes of a terrorist investigation. Section 35 provides for the duration of the designation, and section 36 sets out the powers of a constable in uniform in relation to a designated area. Failure to comply with an order of a constable is a summary offence, punishable with a maximum of three months' imprisonment (increased, as from a day to be appointed, to 51 weeks: *CJA* 2003, s.280(2), and Sched. 26, para. 55(1) and (2); but not in relation to any offence committed before the increase takes effect: *ibid.*, s.280(3)), or a fine, or both: s.36(4).

Terrorism Act 2000, ss.37–39

Information and evidence

37. [*Gives effect to Sched. 5 (power to obtain information, etc.)*: post, § *25–120*.] 25–81

Section 38 gives effect to Schedule 6 (financial information). Schedule 6 is not set out in this work. It enables a constable, for the purpose of a terrorist investigation, to apply to a judge for a customer information order: a financial institution must, by such an order, provide information identifying customers and their accounts. The purpose is to enable a constable to identify accounts in relation to terrorist investigations, and is intended for use at a stage earlier in an investigation than production and explanation orders under Schedule 5. 25–82

Section 38A (inserted by the *Anti-terrorism, Crime and Security Act* 2001, s.3, and Sched. 2, para. 1) gives effect to Schedule 6A (account monitoring orders) (*post*, §§ 25–126a *et seq.*).

Information about acts of terrorism

38B.—(1) This section applies where a person has information which he knows or believes might be of material assistance—

(a) in preventing the commission by another person of an act of terrorism, or

(b) in securing the apprehension, prosecution or conviction of another person, in the United Kingdom, for an offence involving the commission, preparation or instigation of an act of terrorism.

(2) The person commits an offence if he does not disclose the information as soon as reasonably practicable in accordance with subsection (3).

(3) Disclosure is in accordance with this subsection if it is made—

(a) in England and Wales, to a constable,

(b) in Scotland, to a constable, or

(c) in Northern Ireland, to a constable or a member of Her Majesty's forces.

(4) It is a defence for a person charged with an offence under subsection (2) to prove that he had a reasonable excuse for not making the disclosure.

(5) A person guilty of an offence under this section shall be liable—

(a) on conviction on indictment, to imprisonment for a term not exceeding five years, or to a fine or to both, or

(b) on summary conviction, to imprisonment for a term not exceeding *six* [12] months, or to a fine not exceeding the statutory maximum or to both.

(6) Proceedings for an offence under this section may be taken, and the offence may for the purposes of those proceedings be treated as having been committed, in any place where the person to be charged is or has at any time been since he first knew or believed that the information might be of material assistance as mentioned in subsection (1).

[This section was inserted by the *Anti-terrorism, Crime and Security Act* 2001, s.117(2). In subs. (5)(b), "12" is substituted for "six", as from a day to be appointed, by the *CJA* 2003, s.282(2) and (3). The increase has no application to offences committed before the substitution takes effect: *ibid.*, s.282(4).]

Disclosure of information, etc.

39.—(1) Subsection (2) applies where a person knows or has reasonable cause to suspect that a constable is conducting or proposes to conduct a terrorist investigation. 25–83

(2) The person commits an offence if he—

(a) discloses to another anything which is likely to prejudice the investigation, or

(b) interferes with material which is likely to be relevant to the investigation.

(3) Subsection (4) applies where a person knows or has reasonable cause to suspect that a disclosure has been or will be made under any of sections 19 to 21B or 38B.

(4) The person commits an offence if he—

(a) discloses to another anything which is likely to prejudice an investigation resulting from the disclosure under that section, or

(b) interferes with material which is likely to be relevant to an investigation resulting from the disclosure under that section.

(5) It is a defence for a person charged with an offence under subsection (2) or (4) to prove—

(a) that he did not know and had no reasonable cause to suspect that the disclosure or interference was likely to affect a terrorist investigation, or

(b) that he had a reasonable excuse for the disclosure or interference.

(6) Subsections (2) and (4) do not apply to a disclosure which is made by a professional legal adviser—

(a) to his client or to his client's representative in connection with the provision of legal advice by the adviser to the client and not with a view to furthering a criminal purpose, or

(b) to any person for the purpose of actual or contemplated legal proceedings and not with a view to furthering a criminal purpose.

(6A) Subsections (2) and (4) do not apply if—

(a) the disclosure is of a matter within section 21D(2) or (3)(a) (terrorist property: tipping off), and

(b) the information on which the disclosure is based came to the person in the course of a business in the regulated sector.

(7) [*Identical to s.38B(5),* ante, *§ 25–82.*]

(8) For the purposes of this section—

(a) a reference to conducting a terrorist investigation includes a reference to taking part in the conduct of, or assisting, a terrorist investigation, and

(b) a person interferes with material if he falsifies it, conceals it, destroys it or disposes of it, or if he causes or permits another to do any of those things.

(9) The reference in subsection (6A) to a business in the regulated sector is to be construed in accordance with Schedule 3A.

[This section is printed as amended by the *Anti-terrrorism, Crime and Security Act* 2001, s.117(3); and S.I. 2007 No. 3398 (*ante*, § 25–70a). In subs. (7)(b), "12" is substituted for "six", as from a day to be appointed, by the *CJA* 2003, s.282(2) and (3). The increase has no application to offences committed before the substitution takes effect: *ibid.*, s.282(4).]

In connection with the defence provided by section 39(5)(a), see section 118, *post*, § 25–106.

Schedule 3A (as to which, see *ante*, § 25–68) is not set out in this work.

Terrorism Act 2000, ss.40–43

PART V

COUNTER-TERRORIST POWERS

Suspected terrorists

Terrorist: interpretation

25–84 **40.**—(1) In this Part "terrorist" means a person who—

(a) has committed an offence under any of sections 11, 12, 15 to 18, 54 and 56 to 63, or

(b) is or has been concerned in the commission, preparation or instigation of acts of terrorism.

(2) The reference in subsection (1)(b) to a person who has been concerned in the commission, preparation or instigation of acts of terrorism includes a reference to a person who has been, whether before or after the passing of this Act, concerned in the commission, preparation or instigation of acts of terrorism within the meaning given by section 1.

Arrest without warrant

25–85 **41.**—(1) A constable may arrest without a warrant a person whom he reasonably suspects to be a terrorist.

(2) Where a person is arrested under this section the provisions of Schedule 8 (detention: treatment, review and extension) shall apply.

(3) Subject to subsections (4) to (7), a person detained under this section shall (unless detained under any other power) be released not later than the end of the period of 48 hours beginning—

(a) with the time of his arrest under this section, or

(b) if he was being detained under Schedule 7 when he was arrested under this section, with the time when his examination under that Schedule began.

(4) If on a review of a person's detention under Part II of Schedule 8 the review officer does not authorise continued detention, the person shall (unless detained in accordance with subsection (5) or (6)or under any other power) be released.

(5) Where a police officer intends to make an application for a warrant under paragraph 29 of Schedule 8 extending a person's detention, the person may be detained pending the making of the application.

(6) Where an application has been made under paragraph 29 or 36 of Schedule 8 in respect of a person's detention, he may be detained pending the conclusion of proceedings on the application.

(7) Where an application under paragraph 29 or 36 of Schedule 8 is granted in respect of a person's detention, he may be detained, subject to paragraph 37 of that Schedule, during the period specified in the warrant.

(8) The refusal of an application in respect of a person's detention under paragraph 29 or 36 of Schedule 8 shall not prevent his continued detention in accordance with this section.

(9) A person who has the powers of a constable in one Part of the United Kingdom may exercise the power under subsection (1) in any Part of the United Kingdom.

In connection with this section, see Code H issued under the *PACE Act* 1984, s.66 (Appendix A–213 *et seq.*).

Search of premises

42.—(1) A justice of the peace may on the application of a constable issue a warrant in relation to specified premises if he is satisfied that there are reasonable grounds for suspecting that a person whom the constable reasonably suspects to be a person falling within section 40(1)(b) is to be found there. **25–86**

(2) A warrant under this section shall authorise any constable to enter and search the specified premises for the purpose of arresting the person referred to in subsection (1) under section 41.

(3) [*Scotland.*]

Search of persons

43.—(1) A constable may stop and search a person whom he reasonably suspects to be a terrorist to discover whether he has in his possession anything which may constitute evidence that he is a terrorist. **25–87**

(2) A constable may search a person arrested under section 41 to discover whether he has in his possession anything which may constitute evidence that he is a terrorist.

(3) A search of a person under this section must be carried out by someone of the same sex.

(4) A constable may seize and retain anything which he discovers in the course of a search of a person under subsection (1) or (2) and which he reasonably suspects may constitute evidence that the person is a terrorist.

(5) A person who has the powers of a constable in one Part of the United Kingdom may exercise a power under this section in any Part of the United Kingdom.

Terrorism Act 2000, ss.44–47

Power to stop and search

Authorisations

44.—(1) An authorisation under this subsection authorises any constable in uniform to stop a vehicle in an area or at a place specified in the authorisation and to search— **25–88**

(a) the vehicle;

(b) the driver of the vehicle;

(c) a passenger in the vehicle;

(d) anything in or on the vehicle or carried by the driver or a passenger.

(2) An authorisation under this subsection authorises any constable in uniform to stop a pedestrian in an area or at a place specified in the authorisation and to search—

(a) the pedestrian;

(b) anything carried by him.

(3) An authorisation under subsection (1) or (2) may be given only if the person giving it considers it expedient for the prevention of acts of terrorism.

(4) An authorisation may be given—

(a) where the specified area or place is the whole or part of a police area outside Northern Ireland other than one mentioned in paragraph (b) or (c), by a police officer for the area who is of at least the rank of assistant chief constable;

(b) where the specified area or place is the whole or part of the metropolitan police district, by a police officer for the district who is of at least the rank of commander of the metropolitan police;

(c) where the specified area or place is the whole or part of the City of London, by a police officer for the City who is of at least the rank of commander in the City of London police force;

(d) where the specified area or place is the whole or part of Northern Ireland, by a member of the Royal Ulster Constabulary who is of at least the rank of assistant chief constable.

(4ZA) The power of a person mentioned in subsection (4) to give an authorisation specifying an area or place so mentioned includes power to give such an authorisation specifying such an area or place together with—

(a) the internal waters adjacent to that area or place; or

(b) such area of those internal waters as is specified in the authorisation.

(4A) In a case (within subsection (4)(a), (b) or (c)) in which the specified area or place is in a place described in section 34(1A), an authorisation may also be given by a member of the British Transport Police Force who is of at least the rank of assistant chief constable.

(4B) In a case in which the specified area or place is a place to which section 2(2) of the *Ministry of Defence Police Act* 1987 applies, an authorisation may also be given by a member of the Ministry of Defence Police Force who is of at least the rank of assistant chief constable.

(4BA) In a case in which the specified area or place is a place in which members of the Civil Nuclear Constabulary have the powers and privileges of a constable, an authorisation may also be given by a member of that constabulary who is of at least the rank of assistant chief constable.

(4C) But an authorisation may not be given by—

(a) a member of the British Transport Police Force, ...

(b) a member of the Ministry of Defence Police, or

(c) a member of the Civil Nuclear Constabulary.

in any other case.

(5) If an authorisation is given orally, the person giving it shall confirm it in writing as soon as is reasonably practicable.

(5A) In this section—

"driver", in relation to an aircraft, hovercraft or vessel, means the captain, pilot or other person with control of the aircraft, hovercraft or vessel or any member of its crew and, in relation to a train, includes any member of its crew;

"internal waters" means waters in the United Kingdom that are not comprised in any police area.

[This section is printed as amended by the *Anti-terrorism, Crime and Security Act* 2001, s.101, and Sched. 7, paras 29 and 31; the *British Transport Police (Transitional and Consequential Provisions) Order* 2004 (S.I. 2004 No. 1573), art. 12(6)(c); the *Energy Act* 2004, ss.57(1) and (2), and 197(9), and Sched. 23, Pt 1; and the *Terrorism Act* 2006, s.30(1)–(3).]

In *R. (Gillan) v. Commr of Police of the Metropolis* [2006] 2 A.C. 307, HL, it was held that sections 44 and 45 of the 2000 Act, did not, as a matter of construction, require that, for an authorisation to be given under section 44, there had to be reasonable grounds for considering that the powers were necessary and suitable for the prevention of terrorism, and, provided that the powers thereunder were properly exercised, they did not conflict with any of Articles 5 (right to liberty (*ante*, § 16–43)), 8 (private and family life (*ante*, § 16–101)), 10 (freedom of expression (*ante*, § 16–119)) or 11 (freedom of association (*ante*, § 16–132)) of the ECHR.

Exercise of power

25–89 **45.**—(1) The power conferred by an authorisation under section 44(1) or (2)—

(a) may be exercised only for the purpose of searching for articles of a kind which could be used in connection with terrorism, and

(b) may be exercised whether or not the constable has grounds for suspecting the presence of articles of that kind.

(2) A constable may seize and retain an article which he discovers in the course of a search by virtue of section 44(1) or (2) and which he reasonably suspects is intended to be used in connection with terrorism.

(3) A constable exercising the power conferred by an authorisation may not require a person to remove any clothing in public except for headgear, footwear, an outer coat, a jacket or gloves.

(4) Where a constable proposes to search a person or vehicle by virtue of section 44(1) or (2) he may detain the person or vehicle for such time as is reasonably required to permit the search to be carried out at or near the place where the person or vehicle is stopped.

(5) Where—

(a) a vehicle or pedestrian is stopped by virtue of section 44(1) or (2), and

(b) the driver of the vehicle or the pedestrian applies for a written statement that the vehicle was stopped, or that he was stopped, by virtue of section 44(1) or (2),

the written statement shall be provided.

(6) An application under subsection (5) must be made within the period of 12 months beginning with the date on which the vehicle or pedestrian was stopped.

(7) In this section "driver" has the same meaning as in section 44.

[This section is printed as amended by the *Terrorism Act* 2006, s.30(1) and (4).]

Duration of authorisation

46.—(1) An authorisation under section 44 has effect, subject to subsections (2) to (7), during the period— **25–90**

(a) beginning at the time when the authorisation is given, and

(b) ending with a date or at a time specified in the authorisation.

(2) The date or time specified under subsection (1)(b) must not occur after the end of the period of 28 days beginning with the day on which the authorisation is given.

(2A) An authorisation under section 44(4BA) does not have effect except in relation to times when the specified area or place is a place where members of the Civil Nuclear Constabulary have the powers and privileges of a constable.

(3) The person who gives an authorisation shall inform the Secretary of State as soon as is reasonably practicable.

(4) If an authorisation is not confirmed by the Secretary of State before the end of the period of 48 hours beginning with the time when it is given—

(a) it shall cease to have effect at the end of that period, but

(b) its ceasing to have effect shall not affect the lawfulness of anything done in reliance on it before the end of that period.

(5) Where the Secretary of State confirms an authorisation he may substitute an earlier date or time for the date or time specified under subsection (1)(b).

(6) The Secretary of State may cancel an authorisation with effect from a specified time.

(7) An authorisation may be renewed in writing by the person who gave it or by a person who could have given it; and subsections (1) to (6) shall apply as if a new authorisation were given on each occasion on which the authorisation is renewed.

[This section is printed as amended by the *Energy Act* 2004, s.57(1) and (3).]

Offences

47.—(1) A person commits an offence if he— **25–91**

(a) fails to stop a vehicle when required to do so by a constable in the exercise of the power conferred by an authorisation under section 44(1);

(b) fails to stop when required to do so by a constable in the exercise of the power conferred by an authorisation under section 44(2);

(c) wilfully obstructs a constable in the exercise of the power conferred by an authorisation under section 44(1) or (2).

(2) A person guilty of an offence under this section shall be liable on summary conviction to—

(a) imprisonment for a term not exceeding *six months* [51 weeks],

(b) a fine not exceeding level 5 on the standard scale, or

(c) both.

[In subs. (2)(a), "51 weeks" is substituted for "six months", as from a day to be appointed, by the *CJA* 2003, s.281(4) and (5). The increase has no application to offences committed before the substitution takes effect: *ibid.*, s.281(6).]

Parking restrictions and the removal of vehicles

25–92 Section 48 confers power on a police officer of or above the rank of commander (in the case of the Metropolitan or City of London police) or assistant chief constable (elsewhere) to give an authorisation for the purposes of the section where it appears expedient to do so in order to prevent acts of terrorism. The authorisation has effect in relation to specified roads for a specified period not exceeding 28 days: s.50(1), (2). It gives any constable power to prohibit or restrict the leaving of vehicles, or their remaining at rest, on any specified road, or part of a road: ss.48, 52. Failure to move a vehicle when ordered to do so by a constable is a summary offence, as is leaving vehicle or permitting a vehicle to remain at rest in contravention of a prohibition or restriction imposed under the section: s.51. There is provision for extension of the authorisation for further periods not exceeding 28 days: s.50(3).

Terrorism Act 2000, s.53

Port and border controls

Port and border controls

25–93 **53.**—(1) Schedule 7 (port and border controls) shall have effect.

(2) The Secretary of State may by order repeal paragraph 16 of Schedule 7.

(3) The powers conferred by Schedule 7 shall be exercisable notwithstanding the rights conferred by section 1 of the *Immigration Act* 1971 (general principles regulating entry into and staying in the United Kingdom).

Terrorism Act 2000, ss.54–58

PART VI

MISCELLANEOUS

Terrorist offences

Weapons training

25–94 **54.**—(1) A person commits an offence if he provides instruction or training in the making or use of—

(a) firearms,

(aa) radioactive material or weapons designed or adapted for discharge of any radioactive material,

(b) explosives, or

(c) chemical, biological or nuclear weapons.

(2) A person commits an offence if he receives instruction or training in the making or use of—

(a) firearms,

(aa) radioactive material or weapons designed or adapted for discharge of any radioactive material,

(b) explosives, or

(c) chemical, biological or nuclear weapons.

(3) A person commits an offence if he invites another to receive instruction or training and the receipt—

(a) would constitute an offence under subsection (2), or

(b) would constitute an offence under subsection (2) but for the fact that it is to take place outside the United Kingdom.

(4) For the purpose of subsections (1) and (3)—

(a) a reference to the provision of instruction includes a reference to making it available either generally or to one or more specific persons, and

(b) an invitation to receive instruction or training may be either general or addressed to one or more specific persons.

(5) It is a defence for a person charged with an offence under this section in relation to instruction or training to prove that his action or involvement was wholly for a purpose other than assisting, preparing for or participating in terrorism.

(6) A person guilty of an offence under this section shall be liable—

(a) on conviction on indictment, to imprisonment for a term not exceeding ten years, to a fine or to both, or

(b) on summary conviction, to imprisonment for a term not exceeding *six* [12] months, to a fine not exceeding the statutory maximum or to both.

(7) A court by or before which a person is convicted of an offence under this section may order the forfeiture of anything which the court considers to have been in the person's possession for purposes connected with the offence.

(8) Before making an order under subsection (7) a court must give an opportunity to be heard to any person, other than the convicted person, who claims to be the owner of or otherwise interested in anything which can be forfeited under that subsection.

(9) An order under subsection (7) shall not come into force until there is no further possibility of it being varied, or set aside, on appeal (disregarding any power of a court to grant leave to appeal out of time).

[This section is printed as amended by the *Anti-terrorism, Crime and Security Act* 2001, s.120(1). In subs. (6)(b), "12" is substituted for "six", as from a day to be appointed, by the *CJA* 2003, s.282(2) and (3). The increase has no application to offences committed before the substitution takes effect: *ibid.*, s.282(4).]

As to the commission abroad of an offence under this section, see section 17 of the *Terrorism Act* 2006, *post*, § 25–142h.

In connection with the defence provided by section 54(5), see section 118, *post*, § 25–106.

Weapons training: interpretation

55. In section 54— **25–95**

"biological weapon" means a biological agent or toxin (within the meaning of the *Biological Weapons Act* 1974) in a form capable of use for hostile purposes or anything to which section 1(1)(b) of that Act applies,

"chemical weapon" has the meaning given by section 1 of the *Chemical Weapons Act* 1996, and

...

"radioactive material" means radioactive material capable of endangering life or causing harm to human health.

[This section is printed as amended, and repealed in part, by the *Anti-terrorism, Crime and Security Act* 2001, s.120(2).]

Directing terrorist organisation

56.—(1) A person commits an offence if he directs, at any level, the activities of an organisation which is concerned in the commission of acts of terrorism. **25–96**

(2) A person guilty of an offence under this section is liable on conviction on indictment to imprisonment for life.

An offence contrary to section 56 is a "lifestyle offence" within the *PCA* 2002, Sched. 2 (*ante*, § 5–655), in respect of which a court may, as from April 1, 2006 (*Serious Organised Crime and Police Act 2005 (Commencement No. 5 and Transitional and Transitory Provisions and Savings) Order* 2006 (S.I. 2006 No. 378)), make a financial reporting order under section 76 of the *SOCPA* 2005 (*ante*, § 5–886a).

An offence contrary to section 56 is also a "Convention offence" within the *Terrorism Act* 2006: see *ante*, §§ 25–142k, 25–142l.

Possession for terrorist purposes

57.—(1) A person commits an offence if he possesses an article in circumstances which give rise to a reasonable suspicion that his possession is for a purpose connected with the commission, preparation or instigation of an act of terrorism. **25–97**

(2) It is a defence for a person charged with an offence under this section to prove that his possession of the article was not for a purpose connected with the commission, preparation or instigation of an act of terrorism.

(3) In proceedings for an offence under this section, if it is proved that an article—

(a) was on any premises at the same time as the accused, or

(b) was on premises of which the accused was the occupier or which he habitually used otherwise than as a member of the public,

the court may assume that the accused possessed the article, unless he proves that he did not know of its presence on the premises or that he had no control over it.

(4) A person guilty of an offence under this section shall be liable—

(a) on conviction on indictment, to imprisonment for a term not exceeding 15 years, to a fine or to both, or

(b) on summary conviction, to imprisonment for a term not exceeding six [12] months, to a fine not exceeding the statutory maximum or to both.

[This section is printed as amended by the *Terrorism Act* 2006, s.11(1) (increase in maximum penalty on conviction on indictment from 10 to 15 years, but only in respect of offences committed on or after April 13, 2006: s.11(2), and the *Terrorism Act 2006 (Commencement No. 1) Order* 2006 (S.I. 2006 No. 1013)).]

In connection with section 57(2) and (3), see section 118, *post*, § 25–106.

Documents or records in electronic or printed form may amount to "articles" for the purposes of this offence: *R. v. Rowe* [2007] Q.B. 975, CA (not following *R. v. M.* [2008] Crim.L.R. 71, CA, on the ground that it was decided *per incuriam*).

In *R. v. Zafar* [2008] 2 Cr.App.R. 8, CA, it was held (i) that the phrase "for a purpose connected with" in subsection (1) is so imprecise as to give rise to uncertainty unless defined in a manner that constrains it; that subsection must therefore be interpreted in a way that requires a direct connection between the object possessed and the act of terrorism, and as if it in fact read "A person commits an offence if he possesses an article in circumstances which give rise to a reasonable suspicion *that he intends it to be used for the purpose of* the commission, preparation or instigation of an act of terrorism"; and (ii) "instigation" must be construed having regard to its normal meaning, for which incitement is a synonym; possessing a document in circumstances which give rise to a reasonable suspicion that the possessor intends it to be used for the purpose of inciting an act of terrorism therefore falls within the ambit of the section, despite the fact that those responsible for it (including Parliament) did not apparently envisage that it would extend to possessing propaganda for the purpose of incitement to terrorist acts, the core purpose of the provision having been to criminalise the possession in suspicious circumstances of common or garden articles which could be used, for example, in the manufacture of bombs. The court added that the judgment should not be relied upon for the proposition that, for the purposes of this section, a general purpose article such as a computer, or a telephone, or a vehicle could be said to be "possessed for the purpose of" any single use that was intended to be made of the article.

As to sentencing considerations in cases under this section, see *R. v. Rowe*, *ante*.

Collection of information

25–98 **58.**—(1) A person commits an offence if—

(a) he collects or makes a record of information of a kind likely to be useful to a person committing or preparing an act of terrorism, or

(b) he possesses a document or record containing information of that kind.

(2) In this section "record" includes a photographic or electronic record.

(3) It is a defence for a person charged with an offence under this section to prove that he had a reasonable excuse for his action or possession.

(4) [*Identical to s.54(6) (including the amendment)*, ante, *§ 25–94*.]

(5) A court by or before which a person is convicted of an offence under this section may order the forfeiture of any document or record containing information of the kind mentioned in subsection (1)(a).

(6) Before making an order under subsection (5) a court must give an opportunity to be heard to any person, other than the convicted person, who claims to be the owner of or otherwise interested in anything which can be forfeited under that subsection.

(7) An order under subsection (5) shall not come into force until there is not further possibility of it being varied, or set aside, on appeal (disregarding any power of a court to grant leave to appeal out of time).

As to the overlap between sections 57 and 58, see *R. v. Rowe*, *ante*, § 25–97.

A document or record will only fall within this section if it is of a kind that is likely to provide practical assistance to a person committing or preparing an act of terrorism; it is insufficient that it simply encourages the commission of acts of terrorism; and the natural meaning of the section does not require the jury to have regard to the surrounding circumstances, and so, to infringe it, a document or record must contain information of such a nature as to raise a reasonable suspicion that it is intended to be used to assist in the preparation or commission of an act of terrorism; it must be information which calls for an explanation, hence the obligation on the person in possession to provide a reasonable excuse for possessing it; extrinsic evidence may be adduced to explain the nature of the information (*e.g.* evidence as to the nature of a substitution code in the possession of the defendant), but not to demonstrate that a document, innocuous on its face, was intended to be used for the purpose of committing or preparing a terrorist act (*e.g.* evidence that a map in the possession of the defendant was intended by him to be provided to a terrorist so that he could find his way to a place where a planned act of terrorism was to take place): *R. v. K.* [2008] 2 Cr.App.R. 7, CA.

In connection with the defence provided by section 58(3), see section 118, *post*, § 25–106.

A "reasonable excuse" within section 58(3) is an explanation that the document or record is possessed for a purpose other than to assist in the commission or preparation of an act of terrorism, and it is irrelevant whether that other purpose infringes some other provision of the criminal or civil law: *R. v. K.*, *ante*. Subsection (3) will not, however, apply where the facts relied on are to the effect that the documents or records had originated as part of an effort to change an illegal or undemocratic regime overseas; such a conclusion followed inexorably from the conclusion that the definition of "terrorism" in section 1 covered action designed to influence non-democratic or tyrannical governments: *R. v. F.* [2007] 2 Cr.App.R. 3, CA (as to which, see also *ante*, § 25–56).

Terrorism Act 2000, s.59

Inciting terrorism overseas

England and Wales

59.—(1) A person commits an offence if— **25–99**

(a) he incites another person to commit an act of terrorism wholly or partly outside the United Kingdom, and

(b) the act would, if committed in England and Wales, constitute one of the offences listed in subsection (2).

(2) Those offences are—

(a) murder,

(b) an offence under section 18 of the *Offences against the Person Act* 1861 (wounding with intent),

(c) an offence under section 23 or 24 of that Act (poison),

(d) an offence under section 28 or 29 of that Act (explosions), and

(e) an offence under section 1(2) of the *Criminal Damage Act* 1971 (endangering life by damaging property).

(3) A person guilty of an offence under this section shall be liable to any penalty to which he would be liable on conviction of the offence listed in subsection (2) which corresponds to the act which he incites.

(4) For the purposes of subsection (1) it is immaterial whether or not the person incited is in the United Kingdom at the time of the incitement.

(5) Nothing in this section imposes criminal liability on any person acting on behalf of, or holding office under, the Crown.

Terrorism Act 2000, ss.62, 63

Terrorist bombing and finance offences

Terrorist bombing: jurisdiction

62.—(1) If— **25–100**

(a) a person does anything outside the United Kingdom as an act of terrorism or for the purposes of terrorism, and

(b) his action would have constituted the commission of one of the offences listed in subsection (2) if it had been done in the United Kingdom,

he shall be guilty of the offence.

(2) The offences referred to in subsection (1)(b) are—

(a) an offence under section 2, 3 or 5 of the *Explosive Substances Act* 1883 (causing explosions, &c.),

(b) an offence under section 1 of the *Biological Weapons Act* 1974 (biological weapons), and

(c) an offence under section 2 of the *Chemical Weapons Act* 1996 (chemical weapons).

Terrorist finance: jurisdiction

25–101 **63.**—(1) If—

(a) a person does anything outside the United Kingdom, and

(b) his action would have constituted the commission of an offence under any of sections 15 to 18 if it had been done in the United Kingdom,

he shall be guilty of the offence.

(2) For the purposes of subsection (1)(b), section 18(1)(b) shall be read as if for "the jurisdiction" there were substituted "a jurisdiction".

Terrorism Act 2000, ss.63A–63E

Extra-territorial jurisdiction for other terrorist offences etc.

Other terrorist offences under this Act: jurisdiction

25–101a **63A.**—(1) If—

(a) a United Kingdom national or a United Kingdom resident does anything outside the United Kingdom, and

(b) his action, if done in any part of the United Kingdom, would have constituted an offence under … any of sections 56 to 61,

he shall be guilty in that part of the United Kingdom of the offence.

(2) For the purposes of this section and sections 63B and 63C a "United Kingdom national" means an individual who is—

(a) a British citizen, a British overseas territories citizen, a British National (Overseas) or a British Overseas citizen,

(b) a person who under the *British Nationality Act* 1981 is a British subject, or

(c) a British protected person within the meaning of that Act.

(3) For the purposes of this section and sections 63B and 63C a "United Kingdom resident" means an individual who is resident in the United Kingdom.

[As to the insertion of ss.63A to 63E, see *post*, § 25–101e. The words omitted from subs. (1) were repealed by the *Terrorism Act* 2006, s.37(5), and Sched. 3.]

Terrorist attacks abroad by UK nationals or residents: jurisdiction

25–101b **63B.**—(1) If—

(a) a United Kingdom national or a United Kingdom resident does anything outside the United Kingdom as an act of terrorism or for the purposes of terrorism, and

(b) his action, if done in any part of the United Kingdom, would have constituted an offence listed in subsection (2),

he shall be guilty in that part of the United Kingdom of the offence.

(2) These are the offences—

(a) murder, manslaughter, culpable homicide, rape, assault causing injury, assault to injury, kidnapping, abduction or false imprisonment,

(b) an offence under section 4, 16, 18, 20, 21, 22, 23, 24, 28, 29, 30 or 64 of the *Offences against the Person Act* 1861,

(c) an offence under any of sections 1 to 5 of the *Forgery and Counterfeiting Act* 1981,

(d) [*Scotland*],

(e) an offence under section 1 or 2 of the *Criminal Damage Act* 1971,

(f)–(h) [*Scotland and Northern Ireland*].

Terrorist attacks abroad on UK nationals, residents and diplomatic staff etc: jurisdiction

25–101c **63C.**—(1) If—

(a) a person does anything outside the United Kingdom as an act of terrorism or for the purposes of terrorism,

(b) his action is done to, or in relation to, a United Kingdom national, a United Kingdom resident or a protected person, and

(c) his action, if done in any part of the United Kingdom, would have constituted an offence listed in subsection (2), he shall be guilty in that part of the United Kingdom of the offence.

(2) These are the offences—

(a), (b) [*identical to s.63B(a), (b)*, ante],

(c) an offence under section 1, 2, 3, 4 or 5(1) or (3) of the *Forgery and Counterfeiting Act* 1981,

(d) the uttering of a forged document or an offence under section 46A(1) of the *Criminal Law (Consolidation) (Scotland) Act* 1995.

(3) For the purposes of this section and section 63D a person is a protected person if—

(a) he is a member of a United Kingdom diplomatic mission within the meaning of Article 1(b) of the Vienna Convention on Diplomatic Relations signed in 1961 (as that Article has effect in the United Kingdom by virtue of section 2 of and Schedule 1 to the *Diplomatic Privileges Act* 1964),

(b) he is a member of a United Kingdom consular post within the meaning of Article 1(g) of the Vienna Convention on Consular Relations signed in 1963 (as that Article has effect in the United Kingdom by virtue of section 1 of and Schedule 1 to the *Consular Relations Act* 1968),

(c) he carries out any functions for the purposes of the European Agency for the Evaluation of Medicinal Products, or

(d) he carries out any functions for the purposes of a body specified in an order made by the Secretary of State.

(4) The Secretary of State may specify a body under subsection (3)(d) only if—

(a) it is established by or under the Treaty establishing the European Community or the Treaty on European Union, and

(b) the principal place in which its functions are carried out is a place in the United Kingdom.

(5) If in any proceedings a question arises as to whether a person is or was a protected person, a certificate—

(a) issued by or under the authority of the Secretary of State, and

(b) stating any fact relating to the question,

is to be conclusive evidence of that fact.

Terrorist attacks or threats abroad in connection with UK diplomatic premises etc: jurisdiction

63D.—(1) If— **25–101d**

(a) a person does anything outside the United Kingdom as an act of terrorism or for the purposes of terrorism,

(b) his action is done in connection with an attack on relevant premises or on a vehicle ordinarily used by a protected person,

(c) the attack is made when a protected person is on or in the premises or vehicle, and

(d) his action, if done in any part of the United Kingdom, would have constituted an offence listed in subsection (2),

he shall be guilty in that part of the United Kingdom of the offence.

(2) These are the offences—

(a) an offence under section 1 of the *Criminal Damage Act* 1971,

(b) an offence under Article 3 of the *Criminal Damage (Northern Ireland) Order* 1977,

(c) malicious mischief,

(d) wilful fire-raising.

(3) If—

(a) a person does anything outside the United Kingdom as an act of terrorism or for the purposes of terrorism,

(b) his action consists of a threat of an attack on relevant premises or on a vehicle ordinarily used by a protected person,

(c) the attack is threatened to be made when a protected person is, or is likely to be, on or in the premises or vehicle, and

(d) his action, if done in any part of the United Kingdom, would have constituted an offence listed in subsection (4),

he shall be guilty in that part of the United Kingdom of the offence.

(4) These are the offences—

(a) an offence under section 2 of the *Criminal Damage Act* 1971,

(b) an offence under Article 4 of the *Criminal Damage (Northern Ireland) Order* 1977,

(c) breach of the peace (in relation to Scotland only).

(5) "Relevant premises" means—

(a) premises at which a protected person resides or is staying, or

(b) premises which a protected person uses for the purpose of carrying out his functions as such a person.

Sections 63B to 63D: supplementary

25–101e **63E.**—(1) Proceedings for an offence which (disregarding the Acts listed in subsection (2)) would not be an offence apart from section 63B, 63C or 63D are not to be started—

(a) in England and Wales, except by or with the consent of the Attorney General,

(b) in Northern Ireland, except by or with the consent of the Advocate General for Northern Ireland.

(2) These are the Acts—

(a) the *Internationally Protected Persons Act* 1978,

(b) the *Suppression of Terrorism Act* 1978,

(c) the *Nuclear Material (Offences) Act* 1983,

(d) the *United Nations Personnel Act* 1997.

(3) For the purposes of sections 63C and 63D it is immaterial whether a person knows that another person is a United Kingdom national, a United Kingdom resident or a protected person.

(4) [*Northern Ireland.*]

[Ss.63A to 63E were inserted by the *Crime (International Co-operation) Act* 2003, s.52, as from April 26, 2004 (*Crime (International Co-operation) Act 2003 (Commencement No. 1) Order* 2004 (S.I. 2004 No. 786)).]

Terrorism Act 2000, ss.114–131

PART VIII

GENERAL

Police powers

25–102 **114.**—(1) A power conferred by virtue of this Act on a constable—

(a) is additional to powers which he has at common law or by virtue of any other enactment, and

(b) shall not be taken to affect those powers.

(2) A constable may if necessary use reasonable force for the purpose of exercising a power conferred on him by virtue of this Act (apart from paragraphs 2 and 3 of Schedule 7).

(3) Where anything is seized by a constable under a power conferred by virtue of this Act, it may (unless the contrary intention appears) be retained for so long as is necessary in all the circumstances.

Officers' powers

25–103 **115.** Schedule 14 (which makes provision about the exercise of functions by authorised officers for the purposes of sections 25 to 31 and examining officers for the purposes of Schedule 7) shall have effect.

Powers to stop and search

25–104 **116.**—(1) A power to search premises conferred by virtue of this Act shall be taken to include power to search a container.

(2) A power conferred by virtue of this Act to stop a person includes power to stop a vehicle (other than an aircraft which is airborne).

(3) A person commits an offence if he fails to stop a vehicle when required to do so by virtue of this section.

(4) A person guilty of an offence under subsection (3) shall be liable on summary conviction to—

(a) imprisonment for a term not exceeding *six months* [51 weeks],

(b) a fine not exceeding level 5 on the standard scale, or
(c) both.

[In subs. (4)(a), "51 weeks" is substituted for "six months", as from a day to be appointed, by the *CJA* 2003, s.281(4) and (5). The increase has no application to offences committed before the substitution takes effect: *ibid.*, s.281(6).]

Consent to prosecution

117.—(1) This section applies to an offence under any provision of this Act other than an offence under— **25–105**

(a) section 36,
(b) section 51,
(c) paragraph 18 of Schedule 7,
(d) paragraph 12 of Schedule 12, or
(e) Schedule 13.

(2) Proceedings for an offence to which this section applies—

(a) shall not be instituted in England and Wales without the consent of the Director of Public Prosecutions, and
(b) [*Northern Ireland*].

(2A) But if it appears to the Director of Public Prosecutions or the Director of Public Prosecutions for Northern Ireland that an offence to which this section applies has been committed for a purpose wholly or partly connected with the affairs of a country other than the United Kingdom, his consent for the purposes of this section may be given only with the permission—

(a) in the case of the Director of Public Prosecutions, of the Attorney General; and
(b) [*Northern Ireland*].

(2B) [*Northern Ireland*.]

[This section is printed as amended by the *Terrorism Act* 2006, s.37(2).]

Defences

118.—(1) Subsection (2) applies where in accordance with a provision mentioned in subsection (5) it is a defence for a person charged with an offence to prove a particular matter. **25–106**

(2) If the person adduces evidence which is sufficient to raise an issue with respect to the matter the court or jury shall assume that the defence is satisfied unless the prosecution proves beyond reasonable doubt that it is not.

(3) Subsection (4) applies where in accordance with a provision mentioned in subsection (5) a court—

(a) may make an assumption in relation to a person charged with an offence unless a particular matter is proved, or
(b) may accept a fact as sufficient evidence unless a particular matter is proved.

(4) If evidence is adduced which is sufficient to raise an issue with respect to the matter mentioned in subsection (3)(a) or (b) the court shall treat it as proved unless the prosecution disproves it beyond reasonable doubt.

(5) The provisions in respect of which subsections (2) and (4) apply are—

(a) sections 12(4), 39(5)(a), 54, 57, 58, 77 and 103 of this Act, and
(b) sections 13, 32 and 33 of the *Northern Ireland (Emergency Provisions) Act* 1996 (possession and information offences) as they have effect by virtue of Schedule 1 to this Act.

119. [*Crown servants, regulators, etc.*]

Evidence

120.—(1) A document which purports to be— **25–107**

(a) a notice or direction given or order made by the Secretary of State for the purposes of a provision of this Act, and
(b) signed by him or on his behalf,

shall be received in evidence and shall, until the contrary is proved, be deemed to have been given or made by the Secretary of State.

(2) A document bearing a certificate which—

(a) purports to be signed by or on behalf of the Secretary of State, and
(b) states that the document is a true copy of a notice or direction given or order made by the Secretary of State for the purposes of a provision of this Act,

shall be evidence (or, in Scotland, sufficient evidence) of the document in legal proceedings.

(3) In subsections (1) and (2) a reference to an order does not include a reference to an order made by statutory instrument.

(4) The *Documentary Evidence Act* 1868 shall apply to an authorisation given in writing by the Secretary of State for the purposes of this Act as it applies to an order made by him.

Supplemental powers of court in respect of forfeiture orders

25–107a **120A.**—(1) Where court [*sic*] makes an order under section 54, 58 or 103 for the forfeiture of anything, it may also make such other provision as appears to it to be necessary for giving effect to the forfeiture.

(2) That provision may include, in particular, provision relating to the retention, handling, disposal or destruction of what is forfeited.

(3) Provision made by virtue of this section may be varied at any time by the court that made it.

[This section is inserted by the *Terrorism Act* 2006, s.37(3).]

Interpretation

25–108 **121.** In this Act—

"act" and "action" include omission,

"article" includes substance and any other thing,

"customs officer" means an officer of Revenue and Customs,

"dwelling" means a building or part of a building used as a dwelling, and a vehicle which is habitually stationary and which is used as a dwelling,

"explosive" means—

(a) an article or substance manufactured for the purpose of producing a practical effect by explosion,

(b) materials for making an article or substance within paragraph (a),

(c) anything used or intended to be used for causing or assisting in causing an explosion, and

(d) a part of anything within paragraph (a) or (c),

"firearm" includes an air gun or air pistol,

"immigration officer" means a person appointed as an immigration officer under paragraph 1 of Schedule 2 to the *Immigration Act* 1971,

"the Islands" means the Channel Islands and the Isle of Man,

"organisation" includes any assocation or combination of persons,

"premises", except in section 63D, includes any place and in particular includes—

(a) a vehicle,

(b) an offshore installation within the meaning given in section 44 of the *Petroleum Act* 1998, and

(c) a tent or moveable structure,

"property" includes property wherever situated and whether real or personal, heritable or moveable, and things in action and other intangible or incorporeal property,

"public place" means a place to which members of the public have or are permitted to have access, whether or not for payment,

"road" has the same meaning as in the *Road Traffic Act* 1988 (in relation to England and Wales), the *Roads (Scotland) Act* 1984 (in relation to Scotland) and the *Road Traffic Regulation (Northern Ireland) Order* 1997 (in relation to Northern Ireland), and includes part of a road, and

"vehicle", except in sections 48 to 52 and Schedule 7, includes an aircraft, hovercraft, train or vessel.

[This section is printed as amended by the *Crime (International Co-operation) Act* 2003, s.91, and Sched. 5, paras 75 and 76; and the *Commissioners for Revenue and Customs Act* 2005, s.50(6), and Sched. 4, para. 78.]

25–109 **122.** [*Index of defined expressions.*]

123. [*Orders and regulations.*]

124. [*Directions.*]

125. [*Amendments and repeals.*]

126. [*Repealed by* Terrorism Act *2006.*]

127. [*Money.*]

128. [*Commencement (see § 25–49,* ante).]

129. [*Transitional provisions.*]

Extent

130.—(1) Subject to subsections (2) to (6), this Act extends to the whole of the United Kingdom. **25–110**

(2) Section 59 shall extend to England and Wales only.

(3) The following shall extend to Northern Ireland only—

(a) section 60, and

(b) Part VII.

(4) Section 61 shall extend to Scotland only.

(5) In Schedule 5—

(a) Part I shall extend to England and Wales and Northern Ireland only, and

(b) Part II shall extend to Scotland only.

(6) The amendments and repeals in Schedules 15 and 16 shall have the same extent as the enactments to which they relate.

131. [*Short title.*]

Terrorism Act 2000, Sched. 2

Section 3

SCHEDULE 2

PROSCRIBED ORGANISATIONS

The Irish Republican Army. **25–111**
Cumann na mBan.
Fianna na hEireann.
The Red Hand Commando.
Saor Eire.
The Ulster Freedom Fighters.
The Ulster Volunteer Force.
The Irish National Liberation Army.
The Irish People's Liberation Organisation.
The Ulster Defence Association.
The Loyalist Volunteer Force.
The Continuity Army Council.
The Orange Volunteers.
The Red Hand Defenders.
Al-Qa'ida
Egyptian Islamic Jihad
Al-Gama'at al-Islamiya
Armed Islamic Group (Groupe Islamique Armée) (GIA)
Salafist Group for Call and Combat (Groupe Salafiste pour la Prédication et le Combat) (GSPC)
Babbar Khalsa
International Sikh Youth Federation
Harakat Mujahideen
Jaish e Mohammed
Lashkar e Tayyaba
Liberation Tigers of Tamil Eelam (LTTE)
The military wing of Hizballah, including the Jihad Council and all units reporting to it (including the Hizballah External Security Organisation)
Hamas-Izz al-Din al-Qassem Brigades
Palestinian Islamic Jihad—Shaqaqi
Abu Nidal Organisation
Islamic Army of Aden
Kurdistan Workers' Party (Partiya Karekeren Kurdistan) (PKK)
Revolutionary Peoples' Liberation Party-Front (Devrimci Halk Kurtulus Partisi-Cephesi) (DHKP-C)
Basque Homeland and Liberty (Euskadi ta Askatasuna) (ETA)
17 November Revolutionary Organisation (N17)

Abu Sayyaf Group
Asbat Al-Ansar
The Islamic Movement for Uzbekistan
Jemaah Islamiyah
Al Ittihad Al Islamia
Ansar Al Islam
Ansar Al Sunna
Groupe Islamique Combattant Marocain
Harakat-ul-Jihad-ul-Islami
Harakat-ul-Jihad-ul-Islami (Bangladesh)
Harakat-ul-Mujahideen/Alami
Hezb-e Islami Gulbuddin
Islamic Jihad Union
Jamaat ul-Furquan
Jundallah
Khuddam ul-Islam
Lashkar-e Jhangvi
Libyan Islamic Fighting Group
Sipah-e Sahaba Pakistan
Al-Ghurabaa
The Saved Sect
Baluchistan Liberation Army
Teyrebaz Azadiye Kurdistan
Jammat-ul Mujahideen Bangladesh
Tehrik Nefaz-e Shari'at Muhammadi

Note

The entry for The Orange Volunteers refers to the organisation which uses that name and in the name of which a statement described as a press release was published on 14th October 1998.

The entry for Jemaah Islamiyah refers to the organisation using that name that is based in south-east Asia, members of which were arrested by the Singapore authorities in December 2001 in connection with a plot to attack US and other Western targets in Singapore.

[This Schedule is printed as amended by the *Terrorism Act 2000 (Prescribed Organisations) (Amendment) Order* 2001 (S.I. 2001 No. 1261); the *Terrorism Act 2000 (Proscribed Organisations) (Amendment) Order* 2002 (S.I. 2002 No. 2724); the *Terrorism Act 2000 (Proscribed Organisations) (Amendment) Order* 2005 (S.I. 2005 No. 2892); the *Terrorism Act 2000 (Proscribed Organisations) (Amendment) Order* 2006 (S.I. 2006 No. 2016); the *Terrorism Act 2000 (Proscribed Organisations) (Amendment) Order* 2007 (S.I. 2007 No. 2184); the *Terrorism Act 2000 (Proscribed Organisations) (Amendment) Order* 2008 (S.I. 2008 No. 1645); and the *Terrorism Act 2000 (Proscribed Organisations) (Amendment) (No. 2) Order* 2008 (S.I. 2008 No. 1931).]

The *Proscribed Organisations (Name Changes) Order* 2006 (S.I. 2006 No. 1919) provides that the names "Kongra Gele Kurdistan", and "KADEK", not being names specified in Schedule 2, are to be treated as additional names for the organisation listed as the "Kurdistan Workers' Party (Partiya Karkeren Kurdistan) (PKK)".

Section 23

SCHEDULE 4

FORFEITURE ORDERS

PART I

England and Wales

Interpretation

25–112 1. In this Part of this Schedule—

"forfeiture order" means an order made by a court in England and Wales under section 23, and "forfeited property" means the money or other property to which a forfeiture order applies.

Implementation of forfeiture orders

2.—(1) Where a court in England and Wales makes a forfeiture order it may make such other provision as appears to it to be necessary for giving effect to the order, and in particular it may—

(a) require any of the forfeited property to be paid or handed over to the proper officer or to a constable designated for the purpose by the chief officer of police of a police force specified in the order;

(b) direct any of the forfeited property other than money or land to be sold or otherwise disposed of in such manner as the court may direct and the proceeds (if any) to be paid to the proper officer;

(c) appoint a receiver to take possession, subject to such conditions and exceptions as may be specified by the court, of any of the forfeited property, to realise it in such manner as the court may direct and to pay the proceeds to the proper officer;

(d) direct a specified part of any forfeited money, or of the proceeds of the sale, disposal or realisation of any forfeited property, to be paid by the proper officer to a specified person falling within section 23(7).

(2) A forfeiture order shall not come into force until there is no further possibility of it being varied, or set aside, on appeal (disregarding any power of a court to grant leave to appeal out of time).

(3) In sub-paragraph (1)(b) and (d) a reference to the proceeds of the sale, disposal or realisation of property is a reference to the proceeds after deduction of the costs of sale, disposal or realisation.

(4) Section 140 of the *Magistrates' Courts Act* 1980 (disposal of non-pecuniary forfeitures) shall not apply.

3. [*Receivers: appointment, etc.*]

4.—(1) In paragraphs 2 and 3 "the proper officer" means—

(a) where the forfeiture order is made by a magistrates' court, the designated officer for that court,

(b) where the forfeiture order is made by the Crown Court and the defendant was committed to the Crown Court by a magistrates' court, the justices' chief executive for the magistrates' court, and

(c) where the forfeiture order is made by the Crown Court and the proceedings were instituted by a bill of indictment preferred by virtue of section 2(2)(b) of the *Administration of Justice (Miscellaneous Provisions) Act* 1933, the justices' chief executive for the magistrates' court for the place where the trial took place.

(2) The proper officer shall issue a certificate in respect of a forfeiture order if an application is made by—

(a) the prosecutor in the proceedings in which the forfeiture order was made,

(b) the defendant in those proceedings, or

(c) a person whom the court heard under section 23(7) before making the order.

(3) The certificate shall state the extent (if any) to which, at the date of the certificate, effect has been given to the forfeiture order.

[Para. 4 is printed as amended by the *Courts Act* 2003, s.109(1), and Sched. 4, para. 388(1) and (2).]

Restraint orders

Paragraph 5 (as amended by the *Anti-terrorism, Crime and Security Act* 2001, **25-113**
Sched. 2, para. 2(1)–(4)) provides for the making by the High Court of a restraint order prohibiting any person from dealing with any property liable to forfeiture, that is any property in respect of which a forfeiture order has been made or in respect of which such an order could be made in current or prospective proceedings for an offence. Such an order may only be made on the application of the prosecutor; it may be made on a without notice application to a judge in chambers; any order made shall provide for notice to be given to the person affected by the order: para. 6(1).

Where an order is made a constable may, for the purpose of preventing any property subject to the order being removed from Great Britain, seize the property: para. 7.

There is provision for the discharge or variation of any order made; the order must be discharged if proceedings are not instituted within such time as the High Court considers reasonable or when proceedings for the offence are concluded: para. 6(3) and (4) (as amended by the *Anti-terrorism, Crime and Security Act* 2001, Sched. 2, para. 2(1) and (5)).

Compensation

25–114 Paragraphs 9 and 10 relate to the making of an order for compensation by the High Court where a restraint order or a forfeiture order has been made and the relevant proceedings result in an acquittal or any conviction is quashed on appeal or where the restraint order is discharged without any proceedings having been instituted.

Proceedings for an offence: timing

25–115 Paragraph 11 makes provision for the purposes of the schedule as to when proceedings are to be regarded as having been instituted and as having been concluded.

Enforcement of orders made elsewhere

25–115a As from a day to be appointed, the *Crime (International Co-operation) Act* 2003, s.90, and Sched. 4, para. 3, insert new paragraphs 11A to 11G in Schedule 4 to the 2000 Act. They have the effect of implementing, in relation to the proceeds and instrumentalities of terrorism, the Framework Decision on the execution in the European Union of orders freezing property adopted by the Council of the European Union on July 22, 2003. They provide a procedure for transmitting such orders abroad, and for giving effect to overseas freezing orders transmitted to the United Kingdom by another member state.

25–116 Paragraphs 12 to 14 relate to the enforcement of orders made elsewhere in the British Islands and in designated countries. As to the latter, see the *Prevention of Terrorism (Temporary Provisions) Act 1989 (Enforcement of External Orders) Order* 1995 (S.I. 1995 No. 760) (which has effect as if made under the 2000 Act by virtue of the *Interpretation Act* 1978, s.17(2)(b)): the sole designated country is India.

High Court proceedings

25–117 Applications for, and the making of, restraint and compensation orders are governed by *RSC*, Ord. 115, Pt III (rr.24–36) (as amended by the *Civil Procedure (Amendment) Rules* 2001 (S.I. 2001 No. 1388), the *Civil Procedure (Amendment No. 6) Rules* 2001 (S.I. 2001 No. 4016)) and the *Civil Procedure (Amendment No. 4) Rules* 2003 (S.I. 2003 No. 2113), as now set out in Schedule 1 to the *Civil Procedure Rules* 1998 (S.I. 1998 No. 3132).

Scotland and Northern Ireland

25–118 Parts II and III contain corresponding provisions for Scotland and Northern Ireland respectively.

Insolvency

25–119 Part IV governs the impact of a relevant insolvency on a forfeiture order.

Terrorism Act 2000, Sched. 5

Section 37 SCHEDULE 5

Terrorist Investigations: Information

Part I

England and Wales and Northern Ireland

Searches

25–120 1.—(1) A constable may apply to a justice of the peace for the issue of a warrant under this paragraph for the purposes of a terrorist investigation.

(2) A warrant under this paragraph shall authorise any constable—

(a) to enter premises mentioned in sub-paragraph (2A),

(b) to search the premises and any person found there, and

(c) to seize and retain any relevant material which is found on a search under paragraph (b).

(2A) The premises referred to in sub-paragraph (2)(a) are—

(a) one or more sets of premises specified in the application (in which case the application is for a "specific premises warrant"); or

(b) any premises occupied or controlled by a person specified in the application, including such sets of premises as are so specified (in which case the application is for an "all premises warrant").

(3) For the purpose of sub-paragraph (2)(c) material is relevant if the constable has reasonable grounds for believing that—

(a) it is likely to be of substantial value, whether by itself or together with other material, to a terrorist investigation, and

(b) it must be seized in order to prevent it from being concealed, lost, damaged, altered or destroyed.

(4) A warrant under this paragraph shall not authorise—

(a) the seizure and retention of items subject to legal privilege, or

(b) a constable to require a person to remove any clothing in public except for headgear, footwear, an outer coat, a jacket or gloves.

(5) Subject to paragraph 2, a justice may grant an application under this paragraph if satisfied—

(a) that the warrant is sought for the purposes of a terrorist investigation,

(b) that there are reasonable grounds for believing that there is material on premises to which the application relates which is likely to be of substantial value, whether by itself or together with other material, to a terrorist investigation and which does not consist of or include excepted material (within the meaning of paragraph 4 below), and

(c) that the issue of a warrant is likely to be necessary in the circumstances of the case, and

(d) in the case of an application for an all premises warrant, that it is not reasonably practicable to specify in the application all the premises which the person so specified occupies or controls and which might need to be searched.

[This paragraph is printed as amended by the *Terrorism Act* 2006, s.26(1)–(4).]

2.—(1) This paragraph applies where an application for a specific premises warrant is made under paragraph 1 and—

(a) the application is made by a police officer of at least the rank of superintendent,

(b) the application does not relate to residential premises, and

(c) the justice to whom the application is made is not satisfied of the matter referred to in paragraph 1(5) (c).

(2) The justice may grant the application if satisfied of the matters referred to in paragraph 1(5)(a) and (b).

(3) Where a warrant under paragraph 1 is issued by virtue of this paragraph, the powers under paragraph 1(2)(a) and (b) are exercisable only within the period of 24 hours beginning with the time when the warrant is issued.

(4) For the purpose of sub-paragraph (1) "residential premises" means any premises which the officer making the application has reasonable grounds for believing are used wholly or mainly as a dwelling.

[This paragraph is printed as amended by the *Terrorism Act* 2006, s.26(1) and (5).]

2A.—(1) This paragraph applies where an application for an all premises warrant is made under paragraph 1 and—

(a) the application is made by a police officer of at least the rank of superintendent, and

(b) the justice to whom the application is made is not satisfied of the matter referred to in paragraph 1(5)(c).

(2) The justice may grant the application if satisfied of the matters referred to in paragraph 1(5)(a), (b) and (d).

(3) Where a warrant under paragraph 1 is issued by virtue of this paragraph, the powers under paragraph 1(2)(a) and (b) are exercisable only—

(a) in respect of premises which are not residential premises, and

(b) within the period of 24 hours beginning with the time when the warrant is issued.

(4) For the purpose of sub-paragraph (3) "residential premises", in relation to a power under paragraph 1(2)(a) or (b), means any premises which the constable exercising the power has reasonable grounds for believing are used wholly or mainly as a dwelling.

[This paragraph is inserted by the *Terrorism Act* 2006, s.26(1) and (6).]

3.—(1) Subject to sub-paragraph (2), a police officer of at least the rank of superintendent may by a written authority signed by him authorise a search of specified premises which are wholly or partly within a cordoned area.

(2) A constable who is not of the rank required by sub-paragraph (1) may give an authorisation under this paragraph if he considers it necessary by reason of urgency.

(3) An authorisation under this paragraph shall authorise any constable—

(a) to enter the premises specified in the authority,

(b) to search the premises and any person found there, and

(c) to seize and retain any relevant material (within the meaning of paragraph 1(3)) which is found on a search under paragraph (b).

(4) The powers under sub-paragraph (3)(a) and (b) may be exercised—

(a) on one or more occasions, and

(b) at any time during the period when the designation of the cordoned area under section 33 has effect.

(5) An authorisation under this paragraph shall not authorise—

(a) the seizure and retention of items subject to legal privilege;

(b) a constable to require a person to remove any clothing in public except for headgear, footwear, an outer coat, or jacket or gloves.

(6) An authorisation under this paragraph shall not be given unless the person giving it has reasonable grounds for believing that there is material to be found on the premises which—

(a) is likely to be of substantial value, whether by itself or together with other material, to a terrorist investigation, and

(b) does not consist of or include excepted material.

(7) A person commits an offence if he wilfully obstructs a search under this paragraph.

(8) A person guilty of an offence under sub-paragraph (7) shall be liable on summary conviction to—

(a) imprisonment for a term not exceeding *three months* [51 weeks],

(b) a fine not exceeding level 4 on the standard scale, or

(c) both.

[In para. 3(8)(a), "51 weeks" is substituted for "three months", as from a day to be appointed, by the *CJA* 2003, s.280(2), and Sched. 26, para. 55(1) and (4)(a). The increase has no application to offences committed before the substitution takes effect: *ibid.*, s.280(3).]

Excepted material

25–121 4. In this Part—

(a) "excluded material" has the meaning given by section 11 of the *Police and Criminal Evidence Act* 1984,

(b) "items subject to legal privilege" has the meaning given by section 10 of that Act, and

(c) "special procedure material" has the meaning given by section 14 of that Act;

and material is "excepted material" if it falls within any of paragraphs (a) to (c).

Excluded and special procedure material: production & access

25–122 5.—(1) A constable may apply to a Circuit judge [or a District Judge (Magistrates' Courts)] for an order under this paragraph for the purposes of a terrorist investigation.

(2) An application for an order shall relate to particular material, or material of a particular description, which consists of or includes excluded material or special procedure material.

(3) An order under this paragraph may require a specified person—

(a) to produce to a constable within a specified period for seizure and retention any material which he has in his possession, custody or power and to which the application relates;

(b) to give a constable access to any material of the kind mentioned in paragraph (a) within a specified period;

(c) to state to the best of his knowledge and belief the location of material to which the application relates if it is not in, and it will not come into, his possession, custody or power within the period specified under paragraph (a) or (b).

(4) For the purposes of this paragraph—

(a) an order may specify a person only if he appears to the Circuit judge [or the District Judge (Magistrates' Courts)] to have in his possession, custody or power any of the material to which the application relates, and

(b) a period specified in an order shall be the period of seven days beginning with the date of the order unless it appears to the judge that a different period would be appropriate in the particular circumstances of the application.

(5) Where a Circuit judge [or a District Judge (Magistrates' Courts)] makes an order under sub-paragraph (3)(b) in relation to material on any premises, he may, on the application of a constable, order any person who appears to the judge to be entitled to grant entry to the premises to allow any constable to enter the premises to obtain access to the material.

[This paragraph is printed as amended, as from a day to be appointed, by the *Courts Act* 2003, s.65, and Sched. 4, para. 9 (insertion of words in square brackets).]

6.—(1) A Circuit judge [or a District Judge (Magistrates' Courts)] may grant an application under paragraph 5 if satisfied—

(a) that the material to which the application relates consists of or includes excluded material or specified procedure material,

(b) that it does not include items subject to legal privilege, and

(c) that the conditions in sub-paragraphs (2) and (3) are satisfied in respect of that material.

(2) The first condition is that—

(a) the order is sought for the purposes of a terrorist investigation, and

(b) there are reasonable grounds for believing that the material is likely to be of substantial value, whether by itself or together with other material, to a terrorist investigation.

(3) The second condition is that there are reasonable grounds for believing that it is in the public interest that the material should be produced or that access to it should be given having regard—

(a) to the benefit likely to accrue to a terrorist investigation if the material is obtained, and

(b) to the circumstances under which the person concerned has any of the material in his possession, custody or power.

[This paragraph is printed as amended, as from a day to be appointed, by the *Courts Act* 2003, s.65, and Sched. 4, para. 9(a) (insertion of words in square brackets).]

7.—(1) An order under paragraph 5 may be made in relation to—

(a) material consisting of or including excluded or special procedure material which is expected to come into existence within the period of 28 days beginning with the date of the order;

(b) a person who the Circuit judge [or the District Judge (Magistrates' Courts)] thinks is likely to have any of the material to which the application relates in his possession, custody or power within that period.

(2) Where an order is made under paragraph 5 by virtue of this paragraph, paragraph 5(3) shall apply with the following modifications—

(a) the order shall require the specified person to notify a named constable as soon as is reasonably practicable after any material to which the application relates comes into his possession, custody or power,

(b) the reference in paragraph 5(3)(a) to material which the specified person has in his possession, custody or power shall be taken as a reference to the material referred to in paragraph (a) above which comes into his possession, custody or power, and

(c) the reference in paragraph 5(3)(c) to the specified period shall be taken as a reference to the period of 28 days beginning with the date of the order.

(3) Where an order is made under paragraph 5 by virtue of this paragraph, paragraph 5(4) shall not apply and the order—

(a) may only specify a person falling within sub-paragraph (1)(b), and

(b) shall specify the period of seven days beginning with the date of notification required under sub-paragraph (2)(a) unless it appears to the judge that a different period would be appropriate in the particular circumstances of the application.

[This paragraph is printed as amended, as from a day to be appointed, by the *Courts Act* 2003, s.65, and Sched. 4, para. 9(b) (insertion of words in square brackets).]

8.—(1) An order under paragraph 5—

(a) shall not confer any rights to production of, or access to, items subject to legal privilege, and

(b) shall have effect notwithstanding any restriction on the disclosure of information imposed by statute or otherwise.

(2) Where the material to which an application under paragraph 5 relates consists of information contained in a computer—

(a) an order under paragraph 5(3)(a) shall have effect as an order to produce the material in a form in which it can be taken away and in which it is visible and legible, and

(b) an order under paragraph 5(3)(b) shall have effect as an order to give access to the material in a form in which it is visible and legible.

9.—(1) An order under paragraph 5 may be made in relation to material in the possession, custody or power of a government department.

(2) Where an order is made by virtue of sub-paragraph (1)—

(a) it shall be served as if the proceedings were civil proceedings against the department, and

(b) it may require any officer of the department, whether named in the order or not, who may for the time being have in his possession, custody or power the material concerned, to comply with the order.

(3) In this paragraph "government department" means an authorised government department for the purposes of the *Crown Proceedings Act* 1947.

10.—(1) An order of a Circuit judge [or a District Judge (Magistrates' Courts)] under paragraph 5 shall have effect as if it were an order of the Crown Court.

(2) Criminal Procedure Rules may make provision about proceedings relating to an order under paragraph 5.

(3) In particular, the rules may make provision about the variation or discharge of an order.

[This paragraph is printed as amended by the *Courts Act* 2003, s.109(1), and Sched. 8, para. 389(1) and (2); and, as from a day to be appointed, by *ibid*., s.65, and Sched. 4, para. 9(a) (insertion of words in square brackets).]

Excluded or special procedure material: search

25–123 11.—(1) A constable may apply to a Circuit judge [or a District Judge (Magistrates' Courts)] for the issue of a warrant under this paragraph for the purposes of a terrorist investigation.

(2) A warrant under this paragraph shall authorise any constable—

(a) to enter the premises mentioned in sub-paragraph (3A),

(b) to search the premises and any person found there, and

(c) to seize and retain any relevant material which is found on a search under paragraph (b).

(3) A warrant under this paragraph shall not authorise—

(a) the seizure and retention of items subject to legal privilege;

(b) a constable to require a person to remove any clothing in public except for headgear, footwear, an outer coat, a jacket or gloves.

(3A) [*Identical to para. 1(2A)*, ante, *§ 25–120*.]

(4) For the purpose of sub-paragraph (2)(c) material is relevant if the constable has reasonable grounds for believing that it is likely to be of substantial value, whether by itself or together with other material, to a terrorist investigation.

[This paragraph is printed as amended by the *Terrorism Act* 2006, s.26(1), (7) and (8); and as amended, as from a day to be appointed, by the *Courts Act* 2003, s.65, and Sched. 4, para. 9(a) (insertion of words in square brackets).]

12.—(1) A Circuit judge [or a District Judge (Magistrates' Courts)] may grant an application for a specific premises warrant under paragraph 11 if satisfied that an order made under paragraph 5 in relation to material on the premises specified in the application has not been complied with.

(2) A Circuit judge [or a District Judge (Magistrates' Courts)] may also grant an application for a specific premises warrant under paragraph 11 if satisfied that there are reasonable grounds for believing that—

(a) there is material on premises specified in the application which consists of or includes excluded material or special procedure material but does not include items subject to legal privilege, and

(b) the conditions in sub-paragraphs (3) and (4) are satisfied.

(2A) A Circuit judge or a District Judge (Magistrates' Courts) may grant an application for an all premises warrant under paragraph 11 if satisfied—

(a) that an order made under paragraph 5 has not been complied with, and

(b) that the person specified in the application is also specified in the order.

(2B) A Circuit judge or a District Judge (Magistrates' Courts) may also grant an application for an all premises warrant under paragraph 11 if satisfied that there are reasonable grounds for believing—

(a) that there is material on premises to which the application relates which consists of or includes excluded material or special procedure material but does not include items subject to legal privilege, and

(b) that the conditions in sub-paragraphs (3) and (4) are met.

(3) The first condition is that—

(a) the warrant is sought for the purposes of a terrorist investigation, and

(b) the material is likely to be of substantial value, whether by itself or together with other material, to a terrorist investigation.

(4) The second condition is that it is not appropriate to make an order under paragraph 5 in relation to the material because—

(a) it is not practicable to communicate with any person entitled to produce the material,

(b) it is not practicable to communicate with any person entitled to grant access to the material or entitled to grant entry to premises to which the application for the warrant relates, or

(c) a terrorist investigation may be seriously prejudiced unless a constable can secure immediate access to the material.

[This paragraph is printed as amended by the *Terrorism Act* 2006, s.26(1), (9)–(11); and as amended, as from a day to be appointed, by the *Courts Act* 2003, s.65, and Sched. 4, para. 9(a) (insertion of words in square brackets).]

Explanations

13.—(1) A constable may apply to a Circuit judge [or a District Judge (Magistrates' Courts)] for an order under this paragraph requiring any person specified in the order to provide an explanation of any material— **25–124**

(a) seized in pursuance of a warrant under paragraph 1 or 11, or

(b) produce or made available to a constable under paragraph 5.

(2) An order under this paragraph shall not require any person to disclose any information which he would be entitled to refuse to disclose on grounds of legal professional privilege in proceedings in the High Court.

(3) But a lawyer may be required to provide the name and address of his client.

(4) A statement by a person in response to a requirement imposed by an order under this paragraph—

(a) may be made orally or in writing, and

(b) may be used in evidence against him only on a prosecution for an offence under paragraph 14.

(5) Paragraph 10 shall apply to orders under this paragraph as it applies to orders under paragraph 5.

[This paragraph is printed as amended, as from a day to be appointed, by the *Courts Act* 2003, s.65, and Sched. 4, para. 9(a) (insertion of words in square brackets).]

14.—(1) A person commits an offence if, in purported compliance with an order under paragraph 13, he—

(a) makes a statement which he knows to be false or misleading in a material particular, or

(b) recklessly makes a statement which is false or misleading in a material particular.

(2) A person guilty of an offence under sub-paragraph (1) shall be liable—

(a) on conviction on indictment, to imprisonment for a term not exceeding two years, to a fine or to both, or

(b) on summary, conviction, to imprisonment for a term not exceeding *six* [12] months, to a fine not exceeding the statutory maximum or to both.

[In para. 14(2)(b), "12" is substituted for "six", as from a day to be appointed, by the *CJA* 2003, s.282(2) and (3). The increase has no application to offences committed before the substitution takes effect: *ibid.*, s.282(4).]

Urgent cases

25–125 15.—(1) A police officer of at least the rank of superintendent may by a written order signed by him give to any constable the authority which may be given by a search warrant under paragraph 1 or 11.

(2) An order shall not be made under this paragraph unless the officer has reasonable grounds for believing—

(a) that the case is one of great emergency, and

(b) that immediate action is necessary.

(3) Where an order is made under this paragraph particulars of the case shall be notified as soon as is reasonably practicable to the Secretary of State.

(4) A person commits an offence if he wilfully obstructs a search under this paragraph.

(5) A person guilty of an offence under sub-paragraph (4) shall be liable on summary conviction to—

(a) imprisonment for a term not exceeding *three months* [51 weeks],

(b) a fine not exceeding level 4 on the standard scale, or

(c) both.

[In para. 15(5)(a), "51 weeks" is substituted for "three months", as from a day to be appointed, by the *CJA* 2003, s.280(2), and Sched. 26, para. 55(1) and (4)(b). The increase has no application to offences committed before the substitution takes effect: *ibid.*, s.280(3).]

16.—(1) If a police officer of at least the rank of superintendent has reasonable grounds for believing that the case is one of great emergency he may by a written notice signed by him require any person specified in the notice to provide an explanation of any material seized in pursuance of an order under paragraph 15.

(2) Sub-paragraphs (2) to (4) of paragraph 13 and paragraph 14 shall apply to a notice under this paragraph as they apply to an order under paragraph 13.

(3) A person commits an offence if he fails to comply with a notice under this paragraph.

(4) It is a defence for a person charged with an offence under sub-paragraph (3) to show that he had a reasonable excuse for his failure.

(5) A person guilty of an offence under sub-paragraph (3) shall be liable on summary conviction to—

(a) imprisonment for a term not exceeding *six months* [51 weeks],

(b) a fine not exceeding level 5 on the standard scale, or

(c) both.

[In para. 16(5)(a), "51 weeks" is substituted for "six months", as from a day to be appointed, by the *CJA* 2003, s.281(4) and (5). The increase has no application to offences committed before the substitution takes effect: *ibid.*, s.281(6).]

Supplementary

17. For the purposes of sections 21 and 22 of the *Police and Criminal Evidence Act* 1984 (seized material: access, copying and retention) **25–126**

(a) a terrorist investigation shall be treated as an investigation of or in connection with an offence, and

(b) material produced in pursuance of an order under paragraph 5 shall be treated as if it were material seized by a constable.

18–21. [*Northern Ireland.*]

PART II

Scotland (paras 22–33)

Terrorism Act 2000, Sched. 6A

SCHEDULE 6A

ACCOUNT MONITORING ORDERS

Introduction

1.—(1) This paragraph applies for the purposes of this Schedule. **25–126a**

(2) A judge is—

(a) a Circuit judge [or a District Judge (Magistrates' Courts)], in England and Wales;

(b) the sheriff, in Scotland;

(c) a Crown Court judge, in Northern Ireland.

(3) The court is—

(a) the Crown Court, in England and Wales or Northern Ireland;

(b) the sheriff, in Scotland.

(4) An appropriate officer is—

(a) a police officer, in England and Wales or Northern Ireland;

(b) the procurator fiscal, in Scotland.

(5) "Financial institution" has the same meaning as in Schedule 6.

[This paragraph is printed as amended, as from a day to be appointed, by the *Courts Act* 2003, s.65, and Sched. 4, para. 11 (insertion of words in square brackets).]

Account monitoring orders

2.—(1) A judge may, on an application made to him by an appropriate officer, make an account monitoring order if he is satisfied that— **25–126b**

(a) the order is sought for the purposes of a terrorist investigation,

(b) the tracing of terrorist property is desirable for the purposes of the investigation, and

(c) the order will enhance the effectiveness of the investigation.

(2) The application for an account monitoring order must state that the order is sought against the financial institution specified in the application in relation to information which—

(a) relates to an account or accounts held at the institution by the person specified in the application (whether solely or jointly with another), and

(b) is of the description so specified.

(3) The application for an account monitoring order may specify information relating to—

(a) all accounts held by the person specified in the application for the order at the financial institution so specified,

(b) a particular description, or particular descriptions, of accounts so held, or

(c) a particular account, or particular accounts, so held.

(4) An account monitoring order is an order that the financial institution specified in the application for the order must—

(a) for the period specified in the order,

(b) in the manner so specified,

(c) at or by the time or times so specified, and

(d) at the place or places so specified,

provide information of the description specified in the application to an appropriate officer.

(5) The period stated in an account monitoring order must not exceed the period of 90 days beginning with the day on which the order is made.

Applications

25–126c 3.—(1) An application for an account monitoring order may be made *ex parte* to a judge in chambers.

(2) The description of information specified in an application for an account monitoring order may be varied by the person who made the application.

(3) If the application was made by a police officer, the description of information specified in it may be varied by a different police officer.

Discharge or variation

25–126d 4.—(1) An application to discharge or vary an account monitoring order may be made to the court by—

(a) the person who applied for the order;

(b) any person affected by the order.

(2) If the application for the account monitoring order was made by a police officer, an application to discharge or vary the order may be made by a different police officer.

(3) The court—

(a) may discharge the order;

(b) may vary the order.

Rules of court

25–126e 5.—(1) Rules of court may make provision as to the practice and procedure to be followed in connection with proceedings relating to account monitoring orders.

(2) [*Scotland.*]

Rule 62.1(1) of the *Criminal Procedure Rules* 2005 (S.I. 2005 No. 384) makes provision for the giving a copy of an account monitoring order to the financial institution specified in the order; and rule 62.1(2) requires a person other than a police officer, who proposes to make an application under paragraph 4(1), *ante*, to give a copy of the proposed application to a police officer at the police station specified in the account monitoring order not later than 48 hours before the application is to be made, together with notice of the time and place at which it is to be made.

Effect of orders

25–126f 6.—(1) In England and Wales and Northern Ireland, an account monitoring order has effect as if it were an order of the court.

(2) An account monitoring order has effect in spite of any restriction on the disclosure of information (however imposed).

Statements

25–126g 7.—(1) A statement made by a financial institution in response to an account monitoring order may not be used in evidence against it in criminal proceedings.

(2) But sub-paragraph (1) does not apply—

(a) in the case of proceedings for contempt of court;

(b) in the case of proceedings under section 23 where the financial institution has been convicted of an offence under any of sections 15 to 18;

(c) on a prosecution for an offence where, in giving evidence, the financial institution makes a statement inconsistent with the statement mentioned in sub-paragraph (1).

(3) A statement may not be used by virtue of sub-paragraph (2)(c) against a financial institution unless—

(a) evidence relating to it is adduced, or

(b) a question relating to it is asked,

by or on behalf of the financial institution in the proceedings arising out of the prosecution.

[This Schedule was inserted by the *Anti-terrorism, Crime and Security Act* 2001, s.3 and Sched. 2, para. 1.]

Terrorism Act 2000, Sched. 7

Section 53

SCHEDULE 7

PORT AND BORDER CONTROLS

Interpretation

25–127 1.—(1) In this Schedule "examining officer" means any of the following—

(a) a constable,

(b) an immigration officer, and

(c) a customs officer who is designated for the purpose of this Schedule by the Secretary of State and the Commissioners of Customs and Excise.

(2) In this Schedule—

"the border area" has the meaning given by paragraph 4,

"captain" means master of a ship or commander of an aircraft,

"port" includes an airport and a hoverport,

"ship" includes a hovercraft, and

"vehicle" includes a train.

(3) A place shall be treated as a port for the purposes of this Schedule in relation to a person if an examining officer believes that the person—

(a) has gone there for the purposes of embarking on a ship or aircraft, or

(b) has arrived there on disembarking from a ship or aircraft.

Power to stop, question and detain

2.—(1) An examining officer may question a person to whom this paragraph applies for the purpose of determining whether he appears to be a person falling within section 40(1)(b). **25–128**

(2) This paragraph applies to a person if—

(a) he is at a port or in the boarder area, and

(b) the examining officer believes that the person's presence at the port or in the area is connected with his entering or leaving Great Britain or Northern Ireland or his travelling by air within Great Britain or within Northern Ireland.

(3) This paragraph also applies to a person on a ship or aircraft which has arrived at any place in Great Britain or Northern Ireland (whether from within or outside Great Britain or Northern Ireland).

(4) An examining officer may exercise his powers under this paragraph whether or not he has grounds for suspecting that a person falls within section 40(1)(b).

[This paragraph is printed as amended by the *Anti-terrorism, Crime and Security Act* 2001, s.118(1)–(3).]

3. An examining officer may question a person who is in the border area for the purpose of determining whether his presence in the area is connected with his entering or leaving Northern Ireland.

4.—(1) A place in Northern Ireland is within the border area for the purposes of paragraphs 2 and 3 if it is no more than one mile from the border between Northern Ireland and the Republic of Ireland.

(2) If a train goes from the Republic of Ireland to Northern Ireland, the first place in Northern Ireland at which it stops for the purpose of allowing passengers to leave is within the border area for the purposes of paragraphs 2 and 3.

5. A person who is questioned under paragraph 2 or 3 must—

(a) give the examining officer any information in his possession which the officer requests;

(b) give the examining officer on request either a valid passport which includes a photograph or another document which establishes his identity;

(c) declare whether he has with him documents of a kind specified by the examining officer;

(d) give the examining officer on request any document which he has with him and which is of a kind specified by the officer.

6.—(1) For the purposes of exercising a power under paragraph 2 or 3 an examining officer may—

(a) stop a person or vehicle;

(b) detain a person.

(2) For the purpose of detaining a person under this paragraph, an examining officer may authorise the person's removal from a ship, aircraft or vehicle.

(3) Where a person is detained under this paragraph the provisions of Part I of Schedule 8 (treatment) shall apply.

(4) A person detained under this paragraph shall (unless detained under any other power) be released not later than the end of the period of nine hours beginning with the time when his examination begins.

Searches

25–129 7. For the purpose of satisfying himself whether there are any persons whom he may wish to question under paragraph 2 an examining officer may—

(a) search a ship or aircraft;

(b) search anything on a ship or aircraft;

(c) search anything which he reasonably believes has been, or is about to be, on a ship or aircraft.

8.—(1) An examining officer who questions a person under paragraph 2 may, for the purpose of determining whether he falls within section 40(1)(b)—

(a) search the person;

(b) search anything which he has with him, or which belongs to him, and which is on a ship or aircraft;

(c) search anything which he has with him, or which belongs to him, and which the examining officer reasonably believes has been, or is about to be, on a ship or aircraft;

(d) search a ship or aircraft for anything falling within paragraph (b);

(e) search a vehicle which is on a ship or aircraft;

(f) search a vehicle which the examining officer reasonably believes has been, or is about to be, on a ship or aircraft.

(2) Where an examining officer questions a person in the border area under paragraph 2 he may (in addition to the matters specified in sub-paragraph (1)), for the purpose of determining whether the person falls within section 40(1)(b)—

(a) search a vehicle;

(b) search anything in or on a vehicle;

(c) search anything which he reasonably believes has been, or is about to be, in or on a vehicle.

(3) A search of a person under this paragraph must be carried out by someone of the same sex.

[This paragraph is printed as amended by the *Terrorism Act* 2006, s.29.]

9.—(1) An examining officer may examine goods to which this paragraph applies for the purpose of determining whether they have been used in the commission, preparation or instigation of acts of terrorism.

(2) This paragraph applies to—

(a) goods which have arrived in or are about to leave Great Britain or Northern Ireland on a ship or a vehicle, and

(b) goods which have arrived at or are about to leave Great Britain or Northern Ireland on an aircraft (whether the place they have come from or are going to is within or outside Great Britain or Northern Ireland).

(3) In this paragraph "goods" includes—

(a) property of any description, and

(b) containers.

(4) An examining officer may board a ship or aircraft or enter a vehicle for the purpose of determining whether to exercise his power under this paragraph.

[This paragraph is printed as amended by the *Anti-terrrorism, Crime and Security Act* 2001, s.118(1)–(4).]

10.—(1) An examining officer may authorise a person to carry out on his behalf a search or examination under any of paragraphs 7 to 9.

(2) A person authorised under this paragraph shall be treated as an examining officer for the purposes of—

(a) paragraphs 9(4) and 11 of this Schedule, and

(b) paragraphs 2 and 3 of Schedule 14.

Detention of property

25–130 11.—(1) This paragraph applies to anything which—

(a) is given to an examining officer in accordance with paragraph 5(d),

(b) is searched or found on a search under paragraph 8, or

(c) is examined under paragraph 9.

(2) An examining officer may detain the thing—

(a) for the purpose of examination, for a period not exceeding seven days beginning with the day on which the detention commences,

(b) while he believes that it may be needed for use as evidence in criminal proceedings, or

(c) while he believes that it may be needed in connection with a decision by the Secretary of State whether to make a deportation order under the *Immigration Act* 1971.

Designated ports

12.—(1) This paragraph applies to a journey— **25–131**

(a) to Great Britain from the Republic of Ireland, Northern Ireland or any of the Islands,

(b) from Great Britain to any of those places,

(c) to Northern Ireland from Great Britain, the Republic of Ireland or any of the Islands, or

(d) from Northern Ireland to any of those places.

(2) Where a ship or aircraft is employed to carry passengers for reward on a journey to which this paragraph applies the owners or agents of the ship or aircraft shall not arrange for it to call at a port in Great Britain or Northern Ireland for the purpose of disembarking or embarking passengers unless—

(a) the port is a designated port, or

(b) an examining officer approves the arrangement.

(3) Where an aircraft is employed on a journey to which this paragraph applies otherwise than to carry passengers for reward, the captain of the aircraft shall not permit it to call at or leave a port in Great Britain or Northern Ireland unless—

(a) the port is a designated port, or

(b) he gives at least 12 hours' notice in writing to a constable for the police area in which the port is situated (or, where the port is in Northern Ireland, to a member of the Royal Ulster Constabulary).

(4) A designated port is a port which appears in the Table at the end of this Schedule.

(5) [*Power of Secretary of State to amend table by order.*]

Embarkation and disembarkation

13.—(1) The Secretary of State may by notice in writing to the owners or agents of ships or aircraft— **25–132**

(a) designate control areas in any port in the United Kingdom;

(b) specify conditions for or restrictions on the embarkation or disembarkation of passengers in a control area.

(2) Where owners or agents of a ship or aircraft receive notice under sub-paragraph (1) in relation to a port they shall take all reasonable steps to ensure, in respect of the ship or aircraft—

(a) that passengers do not embark or disembark at the port outside a control area, and

(b) that any specified conditions are met and any specified restrictions are complied with.

14.—(1) The Secretary of State may by notice in writing to persons concerned with the management of a port in the United Kingdom ("the port managers")—

(a) designate control areas in the port;

(b) require the port managers to provide at their own expense specified facilities in a control area for the purposes of the embarkation or disembarkation of passengers or their examining under this Schedule;

(c) require conditions to be met and restrictions to be complied with in relation to the embarkation or disembarkation of passengers in a control area;

(d) require the port managers to display, in specified locations in control areas, notices containing specified information about the provisions of this Schedule in such form as may be specified.

(2) Where port managers receive notice under sub-paragraph (1) they shall take all reasonable steps to comply with any requirement set out in the notice.

15.—(1) This paragraph applies to a ship employed to carry passengers for reward, or an aircraft, which—

(a) arrives in Great Britain from the Republic of Ireland, Northern Ireland or any of the Islands,

(b) arrives in Northern Ireland from Great Britain, the Republic of Ireland or any of the Islands,

(c) leaves Great Britain for the Republic of Ireland, Northern Ireland or any of the Islands, or

(d) leaves Northern Ireland for Great Britain, the Republic of Ireland or any of the Islands.

(2) The captain shall ensure—

(a) that passengers and members of the crew do not disembark at a port in Great Britain or Northern Ireland unless either they have been examined by an examining officer or they disembark in accordance with arrangements approved by an examining officer;

(b) that passengers and members of the crew do not embark at a port in Great Britain or Northern Ireland except in accordance with arrangements approved by an examining officer;

(c) where a person is to be examined under this Schedule on board the ship or aircraft, that he is presented for examination in an orderly manner.

(3) Where paragraph 27 of Schedule 2 to the *Immigration Act* 1971 (disembarkation requirements on arrival in the United Kingdom) applies, the requirements of sub-paragraph (2)(a) above are in addition to the requirements of paragraph 27 of that Schedule.

Carding

25–133 16.—(1) The Secretary of State may by order make provision requiring a person to whom this paragraph applies, if required to do so by an examining officer, to complete and produce to the officer a card containing such information in such form as the order may specify.

(2) An order under this paragraph may require the owners or agents of a ship or aircraft employed to carry passengers for reward to supply their passengers with cards in the form required by virtue of sub-paragraph (1).

(3) This paragraph applies to a person—

(a) who disembarks in Great Britain from a ship or aircraft which has come from the Republic of Ireland, Northern Ireland or any of the Islands,

(b) who disembarks in Northern Ireland from a ship or aircraft which has come from Great Britain, the Republic of Ireland, or any of the Islands,

(c) who embarks in Great Britain on a ship or aircraft which is going to the Republic of Ireland, Northern Ireland or any of the Islands, or

(d) who embarks in Northern Ireland on a ship or aircraft which is going to Great Britain, the Republic of Ireland, or any of the Islands.

Provision of passenger information

25–134 17.—(1) This paragraph applies to a ship or aircraft which—

(a) arrives or is expected to arrive in any place in the United Kingdom (whether from another place in the United Kingdom or from outside the United Kingdom), or

(b) leaves or is expected to leave the United Kingdom.

(2) If an examining officer gives the owners or agents of a ship or aircraft to which this paragraph applies a written request to provide specified information, the owners or agents shall comply with the request as soon as is reasonably practicable.

(3) A request to an owner or agent may relate—

(a) to a particular ship or aircraft,

(b) to all ships or aircraft of the owner or agent to which this paragraph applies, or

(c) to specified ships or aircraft.

(4) Information may be specified in a request only if it is of a kind which is prescribed by order of the Secretary of State and which relates—

(a) to passengers,

(b) to crew,

(c) to vehicles belonging to passengers or crew, or

(d) to goods.

(5) A passenger or member of the crew on a ship or aircraft shall give the captain any

information required for the purpose of enabling the owners or agents to comply with a request under this paragraph.

(6) Sub-paragraphs (2) and (5) shall not require the provision of information which is required to be provided under or by virtue of paragraph 27(2) or 27B of Schedule 2 to the *Immigration Act* 1971.

[This paragraph is printed as amended by the *Anti-terrrorism, Crime and Security Act* 2001, s.119.]

As to prescribed information, see Schedule 7 to the *Terrorism Act 2000 (Information) Order* 2002 (S.I. 2002 No. 1945).

Offences

18.—(1) A person commits an offence if he— 25–135

(a) wilfully fails to comply with a duty imposed under or by virtue of this Schedule,

(b) wilfully contravenes a prohibition imposed under or by virtue of this Schedule, or

(c) wilfully obstructs, or seeks to frustrate, a search or examination under or by virtue of this Schedule.

(2) A person guilty of an offence under this paragraph shall be liable on summary conviction to—

(a) imprisonment for a term not exceeding *three months* [51 weeks],

(b) a fine not exceeding level 4 on the standard scale, or

(c) both.

[In para. 18(2)(a), "51 weeks" is substituted for "three months", as from a day to be appointed, by the *CJA* 2003, s.280(2), and Sched. 26, para. 55(1) and (5). The increase has no application to offences committed before the substitution takes effect: *ibid.*, s.280(3).]

TABLE

Designated Ports

Great Britain

25–136

Seaports	*Airports*
Ardrossan	Aberdeen
Cairnryan	Biggin Hill
Campbeltown	Birmingham
Fishguard	Blackpool
Fleetwood	Bournemouth (Hurn)
Heysham	Bristol
Holyhead	Cambridge
Pembroke Dock	Cardiff
Plymouth	Carlisle
Poole Harbour	Coventry
Port of Liverpool	East Midlands
Portsmouth Continental Ferry Port	Edinburgh
Southampton	Exeter
Stranraer	Glasgow
Swansea	Gloucester/Cheltenham (Staverton)
Torquay	Humberside
Troon	Leeds/Bradford
Weymouth	Liverpool
	London-City
	London-Gatwick

Seaports	*Airports*
	London-Heathrow
	Luton
	Lydd
	Manchester
	Manston
	Newcastle
	Norwich
	Plymouth
	Prestwick
	Sheffield City
	Southampton
	Southend
	Stansted
	Teesside

Northern Ireland

Seaports	*Airports*
Ballycastle	Belfast City
Belfast	Belfast International
Larne	City of Derry
Port of Londonderry	
Warrenpoint	

Modifications in relation to the Channel Tunnel

25–136a As to the modification of Schedule 7 in its application to the Channel Tunnel, see the supplement.

Terrorism Act 2000, Sched. 8

SCHEDULE 8

DETENTION

PART I

Treatment of persons detained under section 41 or Schedule 7

Place of detention

25–137 1.—(1) The Secretary of State shall designate places at which persons may be detained under Schedule 7 or section 41.

(2) In this Schedule a reference to a police station includes a reference to any place which the Secretary of State has designated under sub-paragraph (1) as a place where a person may be detained under section 41.

(3) Where a person is detained under Schedule 7, he may be taken in the custody of an examining officer or of a person acting under an examining officer's authority to and from any place where his attendance is required for the purpose of—

(a) his examination under that Schedule,

(b) establishing his nationality or citizenship, or

(c) making arrangements for his admission to a country or territory outside the United Kingdom.

(4) A constable who arrests a person under section 41 shall take him as soon as is reasonably practicable to the police station which the constable considers the most appropriate.

(5) In this paragraph "examining officer" has the meaning given in Schedule 7.

(6) Where a person is arrested in one Part of the United Kingdom and all or part of his detention takes place in another Part, the provisions of this Schedule which apply to detention in a particular Part of the United Kingdom apply in relation to him while he is detained in that Part.

Identification

2.—(1) An authorised person may take any steps which are reasonably necessary for— 25–138
- (a) photographing the detained person,
- (b) measuring him, or
- (c) identifying him.

(2) In sub-paragraph (1) "authorised person" means any of the following—
- (a) a constable,
- (b) a prison officer,
- (c) a person authorised by the Secretary of State, and
- (d) in the case of a person detained in Schedule 7, an examining officer (within the meaning of that Schedule).

(3) This paragraph does not confer the power to take—
- (a) fingerprints, non-intimate samples or intimate samples (within the meaning given by paragraph 15 below), or
- (b) relevant physical data or samples as mentioned in section 18 of the *Criminal Procedure (Scotland) Act* 1995 as applied by paragraph 20 below.

Audio and video recording of interviews

3.—(1) The Secretary of State shall— 25–139
- (a) issue a code of practice about the audio recording of interviews to which this paragraph applies, and
- (b) make an order requiring the audio recording of interviews to which this paragraph applies in accordance with any relevant code of practice under paragraph (a).

(2) The Secretary of State may make an order requiring the video recording of—
- (a) interviews to which this paragraph applies;
- (b) interviews to which this paragraph applies which take place in a particular Part of the United Kingdom.

(3) An order under sub-paragraph (2) shall specify whether the video recording which it requires is to be silent or with sound.

(4) Where an order is made under sub-paragraph (2)—
- (a) the Secretary of State shall issue a code of practice about the video recording of interviews to which the order applies, and
- (b) the order shall require the interviews to be video recorded in accordance with any relevant code of practice under paragraph (a).

(5) Where the Secretary of State has made an order under sub-paragraph (2) requiring certain interviews to be video recorded with sound—
- (a) he need not make an order under sub-paragraph (1)(b) in relation to those interviews, but
- (b) he may do so.

(6) This paragraph applies to any interview by a constable of a person detained under Schedule 7 or section 41 if the interview takes place in a police station.

(7) A code of practice under this paragraph—
- (a) may make provision in relation to a particular Part of the United Kingdom;
- (b) may make different provision for different Parts of the United Kingdom.

4.—(1) This paragraph applies to a code of practice under paragraph 3.

(2)-(5) [*Procedure for issuing, revising code.*]

(6) The failure by a constable to observe a provision of a code shall not of itself make him liable to criminal or civil proceedings.

(7) A code—
- (a) shall be admissible in evidence in criminal and civil proceedings, and
- (b) shall be taken into account by a court or tribunal in any case in which it appears to the court or tribunal to be relevant.

Status

5. A detained person shall be deemed to be in legal custody throughout the period of his detention. 25–140

Rights: England, Wales and Northern Ireland

25–140a 6.—(1) Subject to paragraph 8, a person detained under Schedule 7 or section 41 at a police station in England, Wales or Northern Ireland shall be entitled, if he so requests, to have one named person informed as soon as is reasonably practicable that he is being detained there.

(2) The person named must be—

(a) a friend of the detained person,

(b) a relative, or

(c) a person who is known to the detained person or who is likely to take an interest in his welfare.

(3) Where a detained person is transferred from one police station to another, he shall be entitled to exercise the right under this paragraph in respect of the police station to which he is transferred.

7.—(1) Subject to paragraphs 8 and 9, a person detained under Schedule 7 or section 41 at a police station in England, Wales or Northern Ireland shall be entitled, if he so requests, to consult a solicitor as soon as is reasonably practicable, privately and at any time.

(2) Where a request is made under sub-paragraph (1), the request and the time at which it was made shall be recorded.

8.—(1) Subject to sub-paragraph (2), an officer of at least the rank of superintendent may authorise a delay—

(a) in informing the person named by a detained person under paragraph 6;

(b) in permitting a detained person to consult a solicitor under paragraph 7.

(2) But where a person is detained under section 41 he must be permitted to exercise his rights under paragraphs 6 and 7 before the end of the period mentioned in subsection (3) of that section.

(3) Subject to sub-paragraph (5), an officer may give an authorisation under sub-paragraph (1) only if he has reasonable grounds for believing—

(a) in the case of an authorisation under sub-paragraph (1)(a), that informing the named person of the detained person's detention will have any of the consequences specified in sub-paragraph (4), or

(b) in the case of an authorisation under sub-paragraph (1)(b), that the exercise of the right under paragraph 7 at the time when the detained person desires to exercise it will have any of the consequences specified in sub-paragraph (4).

(4) Those consequences are—

(a) interference with or harm to evidence of a serious … offence,

(b) interference with or physical injury to any person,

(c) the alerting of persons who are suspected of having committed a serious … offence but who have not been arrested for it,

(d) the hindering of the recovery of property obtained as a result of a serious … offence or in respect of which a forfeiture order could be made under section 23,

(e) interference with the gathering of information about the commission, preparation or instigation of acts of terrorism,

(f) the alerting of a person and thereby making it more difficult to prevent an act of terrorism, and

(g) the alerting of a person and thereby making it more difficult to secure a person's apprehension, prosecution or conviction in connection with the commission, preparation or instigation of an act of terrorism.

(5) An officer may also give an authorisation under sub-paragraph (1) if he has reasonable grounds for believing that—

(a) the detained person has benefited from his criminal conduct, and

(b) the recovery of the value of the property constituting the benefit will be hindered by—

(i) informing the named person of the detained person's detention (in the case of an authorisation under sub-paragraph (1)(a)), or

(ii) the exercise of the right under paragraph 7 (in the case of an authorisation under sub-paragraph (1)(b)).

(5A) For the purposes of sub-paragraph (5) the question whether a person has benefited from his criminal conduct is to be decided in accordance with Part 2 of the *Proceeds of Crime Act* 2002.

(6) If an authorisation under sub-paragraph (1) is given orally, the person giving it shall confirm it in writing as soon as is reasonably practicable.

(7) Where an authorisation under sub-paragraph (1) is given—

(a) the detained person shall be told the reason for the delay as soon as is reasonably practicable, and

(b) the reason shall be recorded as soon as is reasonably practicable.

(8) Where the reason for authorising delay ceases to subsist there may be no further delay in permitting the exercise of the right in the absence of a further authorisation under sub-paragraph (1).

(9) In this paragraph references to a "serious offence" are (in relation to England and Wales) to an indictable offence, and (in relation to Northern Ireland) to a serious arrestable offence within the meaning of Article 87 of the *Police and Criminal Evidence (Northern Ireland) Order* 1989; but also include—

(a) an offence under any of the provisions mentioned in section 40(1)(a) of this Act, and

(b) an attempt or conspiracy to commit an offence under any of the provisions mentioned in section 40(1)(a).

[This paragraph is printed as amended, and repealed in part, by the *PCA* 2002, s.456, and Sched. 11, para. 39(1) and (2); and the *SOCPA* 2005, s.111, and Sched. 7, para. 48.]

Where, pursuant to this paragraph, a police officer authorises a delay in permitting a person detained under section 41 to consult a solicitor, there is nothing in the legislative structure to preclude the admission in evidence of things said by the detainee at any interview that takes place whilst access to a solicitor is thus delayed; the admissibility of what is said depends on the ordinary rules relating to the admission of confessions, the exclusion of unfair evidence and the conduct of a fair trial; in applying section 78 of the *PACE Act* 1984 (*ante*, § 15–452), much would depend on the nature of the warning or caution, if any, given by the police to the detainee; much too would depend on whether the interview produced anything directly relevant to the charge which led to the detainee's original detention, or whether the first connection that the prosecution were able to establish between him and any offence arose directly out of what he said whilst co-operating in such an interview; and the fact that no adverse inference can be drawn against a defendant from his failure to mention, during such an interview, a fact subsequently relied on in his defence (*CJPOA* 1994, s.34(2A) (*ante*, § 15–414)) does not render what the detainee says during such an interview inadmissible even where he has been given a wrong and misleading caution to the effect that failure to reveal facts upon which he subsequently relies may harm his defence: *R. v. Ibrahim* [2008] 2 Cr.App.R. 23, CA.

9.—(1) A direction under this paragraph may provide that a detained person who wishes to exercise the right under paragraph 7 may consult a solicitor only in the sight and hearing of a qualified officer.

(2) A direction under this paragraph may be given—

(a) where the person is detained at a police station in England or Wales, by an officer of at least the rank of Commander or Assistant Chief Constable, or

(b) where the person is detained at a police station in Northern Ireland, by an officer of at least the rank of Assistant Chief Constable.

(3) A direction under this paragraph may be given only if the officer giving it has reasonable grounds for believing that, unless the direction is given, the exercise of the right by the detained person will have any of the consequences specified in paragraph 8(4) or the consequence specified in paragraph 8(5)(c).

(4) In this paragraph "a qualified officer" means a police officer who—

(a) is of at least the rank of inspector,

(b) is of the uniformed branch of the force of which the officer giving the direction is a member, and

(c) in the opinion of the officer giving the direction, has no connection with the detained person's case.

(5) A direction under this paragraph shall cease to have effect once the reason for giving it ceases to subsist.

10.—(1) This paragraph applies where a person is detained in England, Wales or Northern Ireland under Schedule 7 or section 41.

(2) Fingerprints may be taken from the detained person only if they are taken by a constable—

(a) with the appropriate consent given in writing, or
(b) without that consent under sub-paragraph (4).

(3) A non-intimate sample may be taken from the detained person only if it is taken by a constable—

(a) with the appropriate consent given in writing, or
(b) without that consent under sub-paragraph (4).

(4) Fingerprints or a non-intimate sample may be taken from the detained person without the appropriate consent only if—

(a) he is detained at a police station and a police officer of at least the rank of superintendent authorises the fingerprints or sample to be taken, or
(b) he has been convicted of a recordable offence and, where a non-intimate sample is to be taken, he was convicted of the offence on or after 10th April 1995 (or 29th July 1996 where the non-intimate sample is to be taken in Northern Ireland).

(5) An intimate sample may be taken from the detained person only if—

(a) he is detained at a police station,
(b) the appropriate consent is given in writing,
(c) a police officer of at least the rank of superintendent authorises the sample to be taken, and
(d) subject to paragraph 13(2) and (3), the sample is taken by a constable.

(6) Subject to sub-paragraph (6A), an officer may given an authorisation under sub-paragraph (4)(a) or (5)(c) only if—

(a) in the case of a person detained under section 41, the officer reasonably suspects that the person has been involved in an offence under any of the provisions mentioned in section 40(1)(a), and the officer reasonably believes that the fingerprints or sample will tend to confirm or disprove his involvement, or
(b) in any case, the officer is satisfied that the taking of the fingerprints or sample from the person is necessary in order to assist in determining whether he falls within section 40(1)(b).

(6A) An officer may also give an authorisation under sub-paragraph (4)(a) for the taking of fingerprints if—

(a) he is satisfied that the fingerprints of the detained person will facilitate the ascertainment of that person's identity; and
(b) that person has refused to identify himself or the officer has resonable grounds for suspecting that that person is not who he claims to be.

(6B) In this paragraph references to ascertaining a person's identity include references to showing that he is not a particular person.

(7) If an authorisation under sub-paragraph (4)(a) or (5)(c) is given orally, the person giving it shall confirm it in writing as soon as is reasonably practicable.

[This paragraph is printed as amended by the *Anti-terrorism, Crime and Security Act* 2001, s.89(1) and (2).]

11.—(1) Before fingerprints or a sample are taken from a person under paragraph 10, he shall be informed—

(a) that the fingerprints or sample may be used for the purposes of paragraph 14(4), section 63A(1) of the *Police and Criminal Evidence Act* 1984 and Article 63A(1) of the *Police and Criminal Evidence (Northern Ireland) Order* 1989 (checking of fingerprints and samples), and
(b) where the fingerprints or sample are to be taken under paragraph 10(2)(a), (3)(a) or (4)(b), of the reason for taking the fingerprints or sample.

(2) Before fingerprints or a sample are taken from a person upon an authorisation given under paragraph 10(4)(a) or (5)(c), he shall be informed—

(a) that the authorisation has been given,
(b) of the grounds upon which it has been given, and
(c) where relevant, of the nature of the offence in which it is suspected that he has been involved.

(3) After fingerprints or a sample are taken under paragraph 10, there shall be recorded as soon as is reasonably practicable any of the following which apply—

(a) the fact that the person has been informed in accordance with sub-paragraphs (1) and (2),

(b) the reason referred to in sub-paragraph (1)(b),

(c) the authorisation given under paragraph 10(4)(a) or (5)(c),

(d) the grounds upon which that authorisation has been given, and

(e) the fact that the appropriate consent has been given.

12.—(1) This paragraph applies where—

(a) two or more non-intimate samples suitable for the same means of analysis have been taken from a person under paragraph 10,

(b) those samples have proved insufficient, and

(c) the person has been released from detention.

(2) An intimate sample may be taken from the person if—

(a) the appropriate consent is given in writing,

(b) a police officer of at least the rank of superintendent authorises the same to be taken, and

(c) subject to paragraph 13(2) and (3), the sample is taken by a constable.

(3) Paragraphs 10(6) and (7) and 11 shall apply in relation to the taking of an intimate sample under this paragraph; and a reference to a person detained under section 41 shall be taken as a reference to a person who was detained under section 41 when the non-intimate samples mentioned in sub-paragraph (1)(a) were taken.

13.—(1) Where appropriate written consent to the taking of an intimate sample from a person under paragraph 10 or 12 is refused without good cause, in any proceedings against that person for an offence—

(a) the court, in determining whether to commit him for trial or whether there is a case to answer, may draw such inferences from the refusal as appear proper, and

(b) the court or jury, in determining whether that person is guilty of the offence charged, may draw such inferences from the refusal as appear proper.

(2) An intimate sample other than a sample of urine or a dental impression may be taken under paragraph 10 or 12 only by a registered medical practitioner acting on the authority of a constable.

(3) An intimate sample which is a dental impression may be taken under paragraph 10 or 12 only by a registered dentist acting on the authority of a constable.

(4) Where a sample of hair other than pubic hair is to be taken under paragraph 10 the sample may be taken either by cutting hairs or by plucking hairs with their roots so long as no more are plucked than the person taking the sample reasonably considers to be necessary for a sufficient sample.

14.—(1) This paragraph applies to—

(a) fingerprints or samples taken under paragraph 10 or 12, and

(b) information derived from those samples.

(2) The fingerprints and samples may be retained but shall not be used by any person except for the purposes of a terrorist investigation or for purposes related to the prevention or detection of crime, the investigation of an offence or the conduct of a prosecution.

(3) In particular, a check may not be made against them under—

(a) section 63A(1) of the *Police and Criminal Evidence Act* 1984 (checking of fingerprints and samples), or

(b) Article 63A(1) of the *Police and Criminal Evidence (Northern Ireland) Order* 1989 (checking of fingerprints and samples),

except for the purpose of a terrorist investigation or for purposes related to the prevention or detection of crime, the investigation of an offence or the conduct of a prosecution.

(4) The fingerprints, samples or information may be checked, subject to sub-paragraph (2), against—

(a) other fingerprints of samples taken under paragraph 10 or 12 or information derived from those samples,

(b) relevant physical data or samples taken by virtue of paragraph 20,

(c) any of the fingerprints, samples and information mentioned in section 63A(1)(a) and (b) of the *Police and Criminal Evidence Act* 1984 (checking of fingerprints and samples),

(d) any of the fingerprints, samples and information mentioned in Article 63A(1)(a) and (b) of the *Police and Criminal Evidence (Northern Ireland) Order* 1989 (checking of fingerprints and samples), and

(e) fingerprints or samples taken under section 15(9) of, or paragraph 7(5) of Schedule 5 to, the *Prevention of Terrorism (Temporary Provisions) Act* 1989 or information derived from those samples.

(4A) In this paragraph—

(a) a reference to crime includes a reference to any conduct which—

(i) constitutes one or more criminal offences (whether under the law of a part of the United Kingdom or of a country or territory outside the United Kingdom); or

(ii) is, or corresponds to, any conduct which, if it all took place in any one part of the United Kingdom, would constitute one or more criminal offences; and

(b) the references to an investigation and to a prosecution include references, respectively, to any investigation outside the United Kingdom of any crime or suspected crime and to a prosecution brought in respect of any crime in a country or territory outside the United Kingdom.

(5) This paragraph (other than sub-paragraph (4)) shall apply to fingerprints or samples taken under section 15(9) of, or paragraph 7(5) of Schedule 5 to, the *Prevention of Terrorism (Temporary Provisions) Act* 1989 and information derived from those samples as it applies to fingerprints or samples taken under paragraph 10 or 12 and the information derived from those samples.

[This paragraph is printed as amended by the *CJPA* 2001, s.84.]

15.—(1) In the application of paragraphs 10 to 14 in relation to a person detained in England or Wales the following expressions shall have the meaning given by section 65 of the *Police and Criminal Evidence Act* 1984 (Part V definitions)—

(a) "appropriate consent",

(b) "fingerprints",

(c) "insufficient",

(d) "intimate sample",

(e) "non-intimate sample",

(f) "registered dentist", and

(g) "sufficient".

(2) [*Northern Ireland.*]

(3) In paragraph 10 "recordable offence" shall have—

(a) in relation to a person detained in England or Wales, the meaning given by section 118(1) of the *Police and Criminal Evidence Act* 1984 (general interpretation), and

(b) [*Northern Ireland*].

Rights: Scotland (paras 16–20).

PART II

Review of detention under section 41

Requirement

25–140b 21.—(1) A person's detention shall be periodically reviewed by a review officer.

(2) The first review shall be carried out as soon as is reasonably practicably after the time of the person's arrest.

(3) Subsequent reviews shall, subject to paragraph 22, be carried out at intervals of not more than 12 hours.

(4) No review of a person's detention shall be carried out after a warrant extending his detention has been issued under Part III.

Postponement

25–140c 22.—(1) A review may be postponed if at the latest time at which it may be carried out in accordance with paragraph 21—

(a) the detained person is being questioned by a police officer and an officer is satisfied that an interpretation of the questioning to carry out the review would prejudice the investigation in connection with which the person is being detained,

(b) no review officer is readily available, or

(c) it is not practicable for any other reason to carry out the review.

(2) Where a review is postponed it shall be carried out as soon as is reasonably practicable.

(3) For the purposes of ascertaining the time within which the next review is to be carried out, a postponed review shall be deemed to have been carried out at the latest time at which it could have been carried out in accordance with paragraph 21.

Grounds for continued detention

23.—(1) A review officer may authorise a person's continued detention only if satisfied that it is necessary— **25–140d**

(a) to obtain relevant evidence whether by questioning him or otherwise,

(b) to preserve relevant evidence,

(ba) pending the result of an examination or analysis of any relevant evidence or of anything the examination or analysis of which is to be or is being carried out with a view to obtaining relevant evidence;

(c) pending a decision whether to apply to the Secretary of State for a deportation notice to be served on the detained person,

(d) pending the making of an application to the Secretary of State for a deportation notice to be served on the detained person,

(e) pending consideration by the Secretary of State whether to serve a deportation notice on the detained person, or

(f) pending a decision whether the detained person should be charged with an offence.

(2) The review officer shall not authorise continued detention by virtue of sub-paragraph (1)(a) or (b) unless he is satisfied that the investigation in connection with which the person is detained is being conducted diligently and expeditiously.

(3) The review officer shall not authorise continued detention by virtue of sub-paragraph (1)(c) to (f) unless he is satisfied that the process pending the completion of which detention is necessary is being conducted diligently and expeditiously.

(4) In this paragraph "relevant evidence" means evidence which—

(a) relates to the commission by the detained person of an offence under any of the provisions mentioned in section 40(1)(a), or

(b) indicates that the detained person falls within section 40(1)(b).

(5) In sub-paragraph (1) "deportation notice" means notice of a decision to make a deportation order under the *Immigration Act* 1971.

[This paragraph is printed as amended by the *Terrorism Act* 2006, s.24(1) and (4). The amendments do not apply to a case in which the arrest of the person detained under s.41, or his examination under Sched. 7, took place before the date of commencement of s.24 (s.24(6)), *i.e.* July 25, 2006 (*Terrorism Act 2006 (Commencement No. 2) Order* 2006 (S.I. 2006 No. 1936).]

Review officer

24.—(1) The review officer shall be an officer who has not been directly involved in the investigation in connection with which the person is detained. **25–140e**

(2) In the case of a review carried out within the period of 24 hours beginning with the time of arrest, the review officer shall be an officer of at least the rank of inspector.

(3) In the case of any other review, the review officer shall be an officer of at least the rank of superintendent.

25.—(1) This paragraph applies where—

(a) the review officer is of a rank lower than superintendent,

(b) an officer of higher rank than the review officer gives directions relating to the detained person, and

(c) those directions are at variance with the performance by the review officer of a duty imposed on him under this Schedule.

(2) The review officer shall refer the matter at once to an officer of at least the rank of superintendent.

Representations

25–140f 26.—(1) Before determining whether to authorise a person's continued detention, a review officer shall give either of the following persons an opportunity to make representations about the detention—

(a) the detained person, or

(b) a solicitor representing him who is available at the time of the review.

(2) Representations may be oral or written.

(3) A review officer may refuse to hear oral representations from the detained person if he considers that he is unfit to make representations because of his condition or behaviour.

Rights

25–140g 27.—(1) Where a review officer authorises continued detention he shall inform the detained person—

(a) of any of his rights under paragraphs 6 and 7 which he has not yet exercised, and

(b) if the exercise of any of his rights under either of those paragraphs is being delayed in accordance with the provisions of paragraph 8, of the fact that it is being so delayed.

(2) Where a review of a person's detention is being carried out at a time when his exercise of a right under either of those paragraphs is being delayed—

(a) the review officer shall consider whether the reason or reasons for which the delay was authorised continue to subsist, and

(b) if in his opinion the reason or reasons have ceased to subsist, he shall inform the officer who authorised the delay of his opinion (unless he was that officer).

(3)–(5) [*Scotland and Northern Ireland.*]

Record

25–140h 28.—(1) A review officer carrying out a review shall make a written record of the outcome of the review and of any of the following which apply—

(a) the grounds upon which continued detention is authorised,

(b) the reason for postponement of the review,

(c) the fact that the detained person has been informed as required under paragraph 27(1),

(d) the officer's conclusion on the matter considered under paragraph 27(2)(a),

(e) the fact that he has taken action under paragraph 27(2)(b), and

(f) the fact that the detained person is being detained by virtue of section 41(5) or (6).

(2) The review officer shall—

(a) make the record in the presence of the detained person, and

(b) inform him at that time whether the review officer is authorising continued detention, and if he is, of his grounds.

(3) Sub-paragraph (2) shall not apply where, at the time when the record is made, the detained person is—

(a) incapable of understanding what is said to him,

(b) violent or likely to become violent, or

(c) in urgent need of medical attention.

PART III

Extension of detention under section 41

Warrants of further detention

25–140i 29.—(1) Each of the following—

(a) in England and Wales, a Crown Prosecutor,

(b) in Scotland, the Lord Advocate or a procurator fiscal,

(c) in Northern Ireland, the Director of Public Prosecutions for Northern Ireland,

(d) in any part of the United Kingdom, a police officer of at least the rank of superintendent,

may apply to a judicial authority for the issue of a warrant of further detention under this Part.

(2) A warrant of further dentention—

(a) shall authorise the further detention under section 41 of a specified person for a specified period, and

(b) shall state the time at which it is issued.

(3) Subject to sub-paragraph (3A) and paragraph 36, the specified period in relation to a person shall be the period of seven days beginning—

(a) with the time of his arrest under section 41, or

(b) if he was being detained under Schedule 7 when he was arrested under section 41, with the time when his examination under that Schedule began.

(3A) A judicial authority may issue a warrant of further detention in relation to a person which specifies a shorter period as the period for which that person's further detention is authorised if—

(a) the application for the warrant is an application for a warrant specifying a shorter period; or

(b) the judicial authority is satisfied that there are circumstances that would make it inappropriate for the specified period to be as long as the period of seven days mentioned in sub-paragraph (3).

(4) In this Part "judicial authority" means—

(a) in England and Wales, ... a District Judge (Magistrates' Courts) who is designated for the purpose of this Part by the Lord Chief Justice of England and Wales after consulting the Lord Chancellor,

(b), (c) [*Scotland and Northern Ireland*].

(5) The Lord Chief Justice may nominate a judicial office holder (as defined in section 109(4) of the *Constitutional Reform Act* 2005) to exercise his functions under sub-paragraph (4)(a).

(6) [*Northern Ireland.*]

[This paragraph is printed as amended by the the *Courts Act* 2003, s.109(1), and Sched. 8, para. 391; the *Constitutional Reform Act* 2005, s.15(1), and Sched. 4, para. 290; and the *Terrorism Act* 2006, s.23(1)–(4); but the amendments made by the 2006 Act do not apply to a case in which the arrest of the person detained under s.41, or his examination under Sched. 7, took place before the commencement of s.23 (s.23(12)), as to which, see *post*, § 25–140qa.]

Time limit

30.—(1) An application for a warrant shall be made— **25–140j**

(a) during the period mentioned in section 41(3), or

(b) within six hours of the end of that period.

(2) The judicial authority hearing an application made by virtue of sub-paragraph (1)(b) shall dismiss the application if he considers that it would have been reasonably practicable to make it during the period mentioned in section 41(3).

(3) For the purposes of this Schedule, an application for a warrant is made when written or oral notice of an intention to make the application is given to a judicial authority.

Notice

31. An application for a warrant may not be heard unless the person to whom it relates **25–140k**
has been given a notice stating—

(a) that the application has been made,

(b) the time at which the application was made,

(c) the time at which it is to be heard, and

(d) the grounds upon which further detention is sought.

Grounds for extension

32.—(1) A judicial authority may issue a warrant of further detention only if satisfied **25–140l**
that—

(a) there are reasonable grounds for believing that the further detention of the person to whom the application relates is necessary as mentioned in sub-paragraph (1A), and

(b) the investigation in connection with which the person is detained is being conducted diligently and expeditiously.

(1A) The further detention of a person is necessary as mentioned in this sub-paragraph if it is necessary—

(a) to obtain relevant evidence whether by questioning him or otherwise;

(b) to preserve relevant evidence; or

(c) pending the result of an examination or analysis of any relevant evidence or of anything the examination or analysis of which is to be or is being carried out with a view to obtaining relevant evidence.

(2) In this paragraph "relevant evidence" means, in relation to the person to whom the application relates, evidence which—

(a) relates to his commission of an offence under any of the provisions mentioned in section 40(1)(a), or

(b) indicates that he is a person falling within section 40(1)(b).

[This paragraph is printed as amended by the *Terrorism Act* 2006, s.24(2), (3) and (5). The amendments do not apply to a case in which the arrest of the person detained under s.41, or his examination under Sched. 7, took place before date of commencement of s.24 (s.24(6)), as to which, see *ante*, § 25–140d.]

Representation

25–140m 33.—(1) The person to whom an application relates shall—

(a) be given an opportunity to make oral or written representations to the judicial authority about the application, and

(b) subject to sub-paragraph (3), be entitled to be legally represented at the hearing.

(2) A judicial authority shall adjourn the hearing of an application to enable the person to whom the application relates to obtain legal representation where—

(a) he is not legally represented,

(b) he is entitled to be legally represented, and

(c) he wishes to be so represented.

(3) A judicial authority may exclude any of the following persons from any part of the hearing—

(a) the person to whom the application relates;

(b) anyone representing him.

(4) A judicial authority may, after giving an opportunity for representations to be made by or on behalf of the applicant and the person to whom the application relates, direct—

(a) that the hearing of the application must be conducted, and

(b) that all representations by or on behalf of a person for the purposes of the hearing must be made,

by such means (whether a live television link or other means) falling within sub-paragraph (5) as may be specified in the direction and not in the presence (apart from by those means) of the applicant, of the person to whom the application relates or of any legal representative of that person.

(5) A means of conducting the hearing and of making representations falls within this sub-paragraph if it allows the person to whom the application relates and any legal representative of his (without being present at the hearing and to the extent that they are not excluded from it under sub-paragraph (3))—

(a) to see and hear the judicial authority and the making of representations to it by other persons; and

(b) to be seen and heard by the judicial authority.

(6) If the person to whom the application relates wishes to make representations about whether a direction should be given under sub-paragraph (4), he must do so by using the facilities that will be used if the judicial authority decides to give a direction under that sub-paragraph.

(7) Sub-paragraph (2) applies to the hearing of representations about whether a direction should be given under sub-paragraph (4) in the case of any application as it applies to a hearing of the application.

(8) A judicial authority shall not give a direction under sub-paragraph (4) unless—

(a) it has been notified by the Secretary of State that facilities are available at the place where the person to whom the application relates is held for the judicial authority to conduct a hearing by means falling within sub-paragraph (5); and

(b) that notification has not been withdrawn.

(9) If in a case where it has power to do so a judicial authority decides not to give a direction under sub-paragraph (4), it shall state its reasons for not giving it.

[Sub-paragraphs (4) to (9) were inserted by the *CJPA* 2001, s.75.]

In *Ward v. Police Service of Northern Ireland* [2007] 1 W.LR. 3013, HL, it was held that where an application for a warrant of further detention is made under Part III of Schedule 8, and where the ground on which the application is made is that there are reasonable grounds for believing that further detention of the person to whom the application relates is necessary in order to obtain relevant evidence by questioning him (see para. 32), the power to exclude that person and his legal representative under paragraph 33 may be exercised where the judge conducting the hearing wishes to be satisfied that the nature of any further questioning is on fresh topics, as opposed to on topics already covered in earlier questioning. Where the police are unwilling to disclose in advance the nature of the intended questioning, if the judge is satisfied by what is said in the detainee's absence, there is no obligation, when the hearing is resumed in his presence, to inform him of what was said in his absence. It is for the judge to scrutinise carefully the basis of the application to see if the exacting test for an extension is made out and where, in order to do that, it becomes necessary to exclude the detainee and his representative, he is entitled only to know the ground of the application (para. 31) and to make representations (para. 33(1)).

Information

34.—(1) The person who has made an application for a warrant may apply to the judicial authority for an order that specified information upon which he intends to rely be withheld from— **25–140n**

(a) the person to whom the application relates, and
(b) anyone representing him.

(2) Subject to sub-paragraph (3), a judicial authority may make an order under sub-paragraph (1) in relation to specified information only if satisfied that these are reasonable grounds for believing that if the information were disclosed—

(a) evidence of an offence under any of the provisions mentioned in section 40(1)(a) would be interfered with or harmed,
(b) the recovery of property obtained as a result of an offence under any of those provisions would be hindered,
(c) the recovery of property in respect of which a forfeiture order could be made under section 23 would be hindered,
(d) the apprehension, prosecution or conviction of a person who is suspected of falling within section 40(1)(a) or (b) would be made more difficult as a result of his being alerted.
(e) the prevention of an act of terrorism would be made more difficult as a result of a person being alerted,
(f) the gathering of information about the commission, preparation or instigation of an act of terrorism would be interfered with, or
(g) a person would be interfered with or physically injured.

(3) A judicial authority may also make an order under sub-paragraph (1) in relation to specified information if satisfied that there are reasonable grounds for believing that—

(a) the detained person has benefited from his criminal conduct, and
(b) the recovery of the value of the property constituting the benefit would be hindered if the information were disclosed.

(3A) For the purposes of sub-paragraph (3) the question whether a person has benefited from his criminal conduct is to be decided in accordance with Part 2 or 3 of the *Proceeds of Crime Act* 2002.

(4) The judicial authority shall direct that the following be excluded from the hearing of the application under this paragraph—

(a) the person to whom the application for a warrant relates, and
(b) anyone representing him.

[This paragraph is printed as amended by the *PCA* 2002, s.456, and Sched. 11, para. 39(1) and (5); and the *Terrorism Act* 2006, s.23(1) and (5). The amendments made by the 2006 Act do not apply to a case in which the arrest of the person detained under s.41, or his examination under Sched. 7, took place before the commencement of s.23 (s.23(12)) as to which, see *post*, § 25–140qa.]

Adjournments

25–140o 35.—(1) A judicial authority may adjourn the hearing of an application for a warrant only if the hearing is adjourned to a date before the expiry of the period mentioned in section 41(3).

(2) This paragraph shall not apply to an adjournment under paragraph 33(2).

Extensions of warrants

25–140p 36.—(1) Each of the following—

(a) in England and Wales, a Crown Prosecutor,

(b) in Scotland, the Lord Advocate or a procurator fiscal,

(c) in Northern Ireland, the Director of Public Prosecutions for Northern Ireland,

(d) in any part of the United Kingdom, a police officer of at least the rank of superintendent,

may apply for the extension or further extension of the period specified in a warrant of further detention.

(1A) The person to whom an application under sub-paragraph (1) may be made is—

(a) in the case of an application falling within sub-paragraph (1B), a judicial authority; and

(b) in any other case, a senior judge.

(1B) An application for the extension or further extension of a period falls within this sub-paragraph if—

(a) the grant of the application otherwise than in accordance with sub-paragraph (3AA)(b) would extend that period to a time that is no more than fourteen days after the relevant time; and

(b) no application has previously been made to a senior judge in respect of that period.

(2) Where the period specified is extended, the warrant shall be endorsed with a note stating the new specified period.

(3) Subject to sub-paragraph (3AA), the period by which the specified period is extended or further extended shall be the period which—

(a) begins with the time specified in sub-paragraph (3A); and

(b) ends with whichever is the earlier of—

(i) the end of the period of seven days beginning with that time; and

(ii) the end of the period of 28 days beginning with the relevant time.

(3A) The time referred to in sub-paragraph (3)(a) is—

(a) in the case of a warrant specifying a period which has not previously been extended under this paragraph, the end of the period specified in the warrant, and

(b) in any other case, the end of the period for which the period specified in the warrant was last extended under this paragraph.

(3AA) A judicial authority or senior judge may extend or further extend the period specified in a warrant by a shorter period than is required by sub-paragraph (3) if—

(a) the application for the extension is an application for an extension by a period that is shorter than is so required; or

(b) the judicial authority or senior judge is satisfied that there are circumstances that would make it inappropriate for the period of the extension to be as long as the period so required.

(3B) In this paragraph "the relevant time", in relation to a person, means—

(a) the time of his arrest under section 41, or

(b) if he was being detained under Schedule 7 when he was arrested under section 41, the time when his examination under that Schedule began.

(4) Paragraphs 30(3) and 31 to 34 shall apply to an application under this paragraph as they apply to an application for a warrant of further detention but, in relation to an application made by virtue of sub-paragraph (1A)(b) to a senior judge, as if—

(a) references to a judicial authority were references to a senior judge; and

(b) references to the judicial authority in question were references to the senior judge in question.

(5) A judicial authority or senior judge may adjourn the hearing of an application under sub-paragraph (1) only if the hearing is adjourned to a date before the expiry of the period specified in the warrant.

(6) Sub-paragraph (5) shall not apply to an adjournment under paragraph 33(2).

(7) In this paragraph and paragraph 37 "senior judge" means a judge of the High Court or the High Court of Justiciary.

[This paragraph is printed as amended and repealed in part by the *CJA* 2003, s.306(1) and (4); and the *Terrorism Act* 2006, ss.23(1), (2) and (6) to (10) and s.37(5), and Sched. 3. The amendments made by the 2006 Act do not apply to a case in which the arrest of the person detained under s.41, or his examination under Sched. 7, took place before the commencement of s.23 (s.23(12)), as to which, see *post*, § 25–140qa.]

As to the effect of section 25 of the 2006 Act, see *post*, § 25–140qa.

Detention—conditions

37. (1) This paragraph applies where— **25–140q**

(a) a person "the detained person" is detained by virtue of a warrant issued under this Part of this Schedule; and

(b) his detention is not authorised by virtue of section 41(5) or (6) or otherwise apart from the warrant.

(2) If it at any time appears to the police officer or other person in charge of the detained person's case that any of the matters mentioned in paragraph 32(1)(a) and (b) on which the judicial authority or senior judge last authorised his further detention no longer apply, he must—

(a) if he has custody of the detained person, release him immediately; and

(b) if he does not, immediately inform the person who does have custody of the detained person that those matters no longer apply in the detained person's case.

(3) A person with custody of the detained person who is informed in accordance with this paragraph that those matters no longer apply in his case must release that person immediately.

[This paragraph is printed as amended by the *Terrorism Act* 2006, s.23(1) and (11). The amendments do not apply to a case in which the arrest of the person detained under s.41, or his examination under Sched. 7, took place before the commencement of s.23 (s.23(12)), as to which, see *post*, § 25–140qa.]

As to the effect of section 25 of the 2006 Act, see *post*, § 25–140qa.

Expiry or renewal of extended detention maximum period

Section 25 of the *Terrorism Act* 2006 applies to any time which is more than one year after the date of commencement of section 23 (*viz.* July 25, 2006 (*Terrorism Act 2006 (Commencement No. 2) Order* 2006 (S.I. 2006 No. 1936))); and does not fall within a period in relation to which it is disapplied by an order under subsection (2) (s.25(1)). By subsection (2), the Secretary of State may disapply the section in relation to any period of not more than one year beginning with the coming into force of the order (see *post*). By subsection (3) it is provided that Schedule 8 has effect in relation to any further extension under paragraph 36 for a period beginning at a time to which section 25 applies, (a) as if in sub-paragraph (3)(b) of that paragraph, for "28 days" there were substituted "14 days"; and (b) as if that paragraph and paragraph 37 had effect with the further consequential modifications set out in subsection (4). Those further modifications are, (a) the substitution of the words "a judicial authority" for paragraphs (a) and (b) of paragraph 36(1A); (b) the omission of paragraph 36(1B) and (7); (c) the omission of the words "or senior judge" wherever occurring in paragraphs 36(3AA) and (5) and 37(2); and (d) the omission of the words from "but" onwards in paragraph 36(4). Subsection (5) provides that where, at a time to which section 25 applies, (a) a person is being detained by virtue of a further extension under paragraph 36, (b) his further detention was authorised (at a time to which section 25 did not apply) for a period ending more than 14 days after the relevant time, and (c) that 14 days has expired, the person with custody of that individual must release him immediately. Subsection (6) restricts the making of orders disapplying the section, and subsection (7) provides that in this section "the relevant time" has the same meaning as in paragraph 36 of Schedule 8. **25–140qa**

The *Terrorism Act 2006 (Disapplication of Section 25) Order* 2008 (S.I. 2008 No. 1745) was made under subsection (2) (*ante*); it disapplies section 25 until the end of July 24, 2009.

Code of practice

25–140qb In connection with Schedule 8, see Code H issued under the *PACE Act* 1984, s.66 (Appendix A–213 *et seq.*).

Terrorism Act 2000, Sched. 14

Section 115 SCHEDULE 14

EXERCISE OF OFFICERS' POWERS

General

25–140r 1. In this Schedule an "officer" means—

(a) an authorised officer within the meaning given by section 24, and
(b) an examining officer within the meaning of Schedule 7.

2. An officer may enter a vehicle (within the meaning of section 121) for the purpose of exercising any of the functions conferred on him by virtue of this Act.

3. An officer may if necessary use reasonable force for the purpose of exercising a power conferred on him by virtue of this Act (apart from paragraphs 2 and 3 of Schedule 7).

Information

25–140s 4.—(1) Information acquired by an officer may be supplied—

(a) to the Secretary of State for use in relation to immigration;
(b) to the Commissioners of Customs and Excise or a customs officer;
(c) to a constable;
(d) to the Serious Organised Crime Agency;
(e) to a person specified by order of the Secretary of State for use of a kind specified in the order.

(2) Information acquired by a customs officer or an immigration officer may be supplied to an examining officer within the meaning of Schedule 7.

Code of practice

25–141 5. An officer shall perform functions conferred on him by virtue of this Act in accordance with any relevant code of practice in operation under paragraph 6.

6.—(1) The Secretary of State shall issue codes of practice about the exercise by officers of functions conferred on them by virtue of this Act.

(2) The failure by an officer to observe a provision of a code shall not of itself make him liable to criminal or civil proceedings.

(3) A code—

(a) shall be admissible in evidence in criminal and civil proceedings, and
(b) shall be taken into account by a court or tribunal in any case in which it appears to the court or tribunal to be relevant.

(4) The Secretary of State may revise a code and issue the revised code.

7. [*Procedure for issuing code.*]

[This Schedule is printed as amended by the *SOCPA* 2005, s.59, and Sched. 4, paras 125 and 130.]

As to the modification of Schedule 14 in its application to the Channel Tunnel, see the supplement.

Information may be supplied in accordance with paragraph 4(2) only if the information has not been held solely in the exercise of functions relating to former Inland Revenue matters (within the *Commissioners for Revenue and Customs Act* 2005, s.7): see the 2005 Act, s.17, and Sched. 2, para. 19.

B. ANTI-TERRORISM, CRIME AND SECURITY ACT 2001

Anti-terrorism, Crime and Security Act 2001, ss.47–56

PART 6

WEAPONS OF MASS DESTRUCTION

Nuclear weapons

Use etc. of nuclear weapons

47.—(1) A person who— **25–141a**

(a) knowingly causes a nuclear weapon explosion;

(b) develops or produces, or participates in the development or production of, a nuclear weapon;

(c) has a nuclear weapon in his possession;

(d) participates in the transfer of a nuclear weapon; or

(e) engages in military preparations, or in preparations of a military nature, intending to use, or threaten to use, a nuclear weapon,

is guilty of an offence.

(2) Subsection (1) has effect subject to the exceptions and defences in sections 48 and 49.

(3) For the purposes of subsection (1)(b) a person participates in the development or production of a nuclear weapon if he does any act which—

(a) facilitates the development by another of the capability to produce or use a nuclear weapon, or

(b) facilitates the making by another of a nuclear weapon,

knowing or having reason to believe that his act has (or will have) that effect.

(4) For the purposes of subsection (1)(d) a person participates in the transfer of a nuclear weapon if—

(a) he buys or otherwise acquires it or agrees with another to do so;

(b) he sells or otherwise disposes of it or agrees with another to do so; or

(c) he makes arrangements under which another person either acquires or disposes of it or agrees with a third person to do so.

(5) A person guilty of an offence under this section is liable on conviction on indictment to imprisonment for life.

(6) In this section "nuclear weapon" includes a nuclear explosive device that is not intended for use as a weapon.

(7) This section applies to acts done outside the United Kingdom, but only if they are done by a United Kingdom person.

(8) Nothing in subsection (7) affects any criminal liability arising otherwise than under that subsection.

(9) Paragraph (a) of subsection (1) shall cease to have effect on the coming into force of the *Nuclear Explosions (Prohibition and Inspections) Act* 1998.

An offence contrary to this section is a "Convention offence" within the *Terrorism Act* 2006: see *post*, §§ 25–142k, 25–142l.

Exceptions

48.—(1) Nothing in section 47 applies— **25–141b**

(a) to an act which is authorised under subsection (2); or

(b) to an act done in the course of an armed conflict.

(2) The Secretary of State may—

(a) authorise any act which would otherwise contravene section 47 in such manner and on such terms as he thinks fit; and

(b) withdraw or vary any authorisation given under this subsection.

(3) Any question arising in proceedings for an offence under section 47 as to whether anything was done in the course of an armed conflict shall be determined by the Secretary of State.

(4) A certificate purporting to set out any such determination and to be signed by the Secretary of State shall be received in evidence in any such proceedings and shall be presumed to be so signed unless the contrary is shown.

Defences

49.—(1) In proceedings for an offence under section 47(1)(c) or (d) relating to an object it is a defence for the accused to show that he did not know and had no reason to believe that the object was a nuclear weapon. **25–141c**

(2) But he shall be taken to have shown that fact if—

(a) sufficient evidence is adduced to raise an issue with respect to it; and

(b) the contrary is not proved by the prosecution beyond reasonable doubt.

(3) In proceedings for such an offence it is also a defence for the accused to show that he knew or believed that the object was a nuclear weapon but, as soon as reasonably practicable after he first knew or believed that fact, he took all reasonable steps to inform the Secretary of State or a constable of his knowledge or belief.

Assisting or inducing weapons-related acts overseas

Assisting or inducing certain weapons-related acts overseas

25–141d **50.**—(1) A person who aids, abets, counsels or procures, or incites, a person who is not a United Kingdom person to do a relevant act outside the United Kingdom is guilty of an offence.

(2) For this purpose a relevant act is an act that, if done by a United Kingdom person, would contravene any of the following provisions—

(a) section 1 of the *Biological Weapons Act* 1974 (offences relating to biological agents and toxins);

(b) section 2 of the *Chemical Weapons Act* 1996 (offences relating to chemical weapons); or

(c) section 47 above (offences relating to nuclear weapons).

(3) Nothing in this section applies to an act mentioned in subsection (1) which—

(a) relates to a relevant act which would contravene section 47; and

(b) is authorised by the Secretary of State;

and section 48(2) applies for the purpose of authorising acts that would otherwise constitute an offence under this section.

(4) A person accused of an offence under this section in relation to a relevant act which would contravene a provision mentioned in subsection (2) may raise any defence which would be open to a person accused of the corresponding offence ancillary to an offence under that provision.

(5) A person convicted of an offence under this section is liable on conviction on indictment to imprisonment for life.

(6) This section applies to acts done outside the United Kingdom, but only if they are done by a United Kingdom person.

(7) Nothing in this section prejudices any criminal liability existing apart from this section.

Supplemental provisions relating to sections 47 and 50

Extra-territorial application

25–141e **51.**—(1) Proceedings for an offence committed under section 47 or 50 outside the United Kingdom may be taken, and the offence may for incidental purposes be treated as having been committed, in any part of the United Kingdom.

(2) Her Majesty may by Order in Council extend the application of section 47 or 50, so far as it applies to acts done outside the United Kingdom, to bodies incorporated under the law of any of the Channel Islands, the Isle of Man or any colony.

Powers of entry

25–141f **52.**—(1) If—

(a) a justice of the peace is satisfied on information on oath that there are reasonable grounds for suspecting that evidence of the commission of an offence under section 47 or 50 is to be found on any premises; or

(b) [*Scotland*],

he may issue a warrant authorising an authorised officer to enter the premises, if necessary by force, at any time within one month from the time of the issue of the warrant and to search them.

(2) The powers of a person who enters the premises under the authority of the warrant include power—

(a) to take with him such other persons and such equipment as appear to him to be necessary;

(b) to inspect, seize and retain any substance, equipment or document found on the premises;

(c) to require any document or other information which is held in electronic form and is accessible from the premises to be produced in a form—

(i) in which he can read and copy it; or
(ii) from which it can readily be produced in a form in which he can read and copy it;

(d) to copy any document which he has reasonable cause to believe may be required as evidence for the purposes of proceedings in respect of an offence under section 47 or 50.

(3) A constable who enters premises under the authority of a warrant or by virtue of subsection (2)(a) may—

(a) give such assistance as an authorised officer may request for the purpose of facilitating the exercise of any power under this section; and
(b) search or cause to be searched any person on the premises who the constable has reasonable cause to believe may have in his possession any document or other thing which may be required as evidence for the purposes of proceedings in respect of an offence under section 47 or 50.

(4) No constable shall search a person of the opposite sex.

(5) The powers conferred by a warrant under this section shall only be exercisable, if the warrant so provides, in the presence of a constable.

(6) A person who—

(a) wilfully obstructs an authorised officer in the exercise of a power conferred by a warrant under this section; or
(b) fails without reasonable excuse to comply with a reasonable request made by an authorised officer or a constable for the purpose of facilitating the exercise of such a power,

is guilty of an offence.

(7) A person guilty of an offence under subsection (6) is liable—

(a) on summary conviction, to a fine not exceeding the statutory maximum; and
(b) on conviction on indictment, to imprisonment for a term not exceeding two years or a fine (or both).

(8) In this section "authorised officer" means an authorised officer of the Secretary of State.

Revenue and Customs prosecutions

53.—(1) Proceedings for a nuclear weapons offence may be instituted by the Director of Revenue and Customs Prosecutions or by order of the Commissioners for Her Majesty's Revenue and Customs if it appears to the Director or to the Commissioners that the offence has involved— **25–141g**

(a) the development or production outside the United Kingdom of a nuclear weapon;
(b) the movement of a nuclear weapon into or out of any country or territory;
(c) any proposal or attempt to do anything falling within paragraph (a) or (b).

(2) In this section "nuclear weapons offence" means an offence under section 47 or 50 (including an offence of aiding, abetting, counselling, procuring or inciting the commission of, or attempting or conspiring to commit, such an offence).

(3) Any proceedings for an offence which are instituted by order of the Commissioners under subsection (1) shall be commenced in the name of an officer of Revenue and Customs, but may be continued by another officer.

(4) Where the Commissioners investigate, or propose to investigate, any matter with a view to determining—

(a) whether there are grounds for believing that a nuclear weapons offence has been committed, or
(b) whether a person should be prosecuted for such an offence,

that matter shall be treated as an assigned matter within the meaning of the *Customs and Excise Management Act* 1979.

(5) Nothing in this section affects any powers of any person (including any officer) apart from this section.

(7) This section does not apply to the institution of proceedings in Scotland.

[This section is printed as amended, and repealed in part, by the *Commissioners for Revenue and Customs Act* 2005, ss.50(6) and 52(2), Sched. 4, para. 87, and Sched. 5. The reference to the common law offence of incitement in subs. (2) has effect as a reference to the offences under the *SCA* 2007, Pt 2: 2007 Act, s.63(1), and Sched. 6, para. 43.]

Offences

25–141h **54.**—(1) A person who knowingly or recklessly makes a false or misleading statement for the purpose of obtaining (or opposing the variation or withdrawal of) authorisation for the purposes of section 47 or 50 is guilty of an offence.

(2) A person guilty of an offence under subsection (1) is liable—

(a) on summary conviction, to a fine of an amount not exceeding the statutory maximum;

(b) on conviction on indictment, to imprisonment for a term not exceeding two years or a fine (or both).

(3) Where an offence under section 47, 50 or subsection (1) above committed by a body corporate is proved to have been committed with the consent or connivance of, or to be attributable to any neglect on the part of—

(a) a director, manager, secretary or other similar officer of the body corporate; or

(b) any person who was purporting to act in any such capacity,

he as well as the body corporate shall be guilty of that offence and shall be liable to be proceeded against and punished accordingly.

(4) In subsection (3) "director", in relation to a body corporate whose affairs are managed by its members, means a member of the body corporate.

Consent to prosecutions

25–141i **55.** Proceedings for an offence under section 47 or 50 shall not be instituted—

(a) in England and Wales, except by or with the consent of the Attorney General;

(b) in Northern Ireland, except by or with the consent of the Attorney General for Northern Ireland.

Interpretation of Part 6

25–141j **56.**—(1) In this Part "United Kingdom person" means a United Kingdom national, a Scottish partnership or a body incorporated under the law of a part of the United Kingdom.

(2) For this purpose a United Kingdom national is an individual who is—

(a) a British citizen, a British overseas territories citizen, a British National (Overseas) or a British Overseas citizen;

(b) a person who under the *British Nationality Act* 1981 is a British subject; or

(c) a British protected person within the meaning of that Act.

[This section is printed as amended by the *British Overseas Territories Act* 2002, s.2.]

Anti-terrorism, Crime and Security Act 2001, ss.113–115

PART 13

MISCELLANEOUS

Dangerous substances

Use of noxious substances or things to cause harm and intimidate

25–141k **113.**—(1) A person who takes any action which—

(a) involves the use of a noxious substance or other noxious thing;

(b) has or is likely to have an effect falling within subsection (2); and

(c) is designed to influence the government or an international governmental organisation or to intimidate the public or a section of the public,

is guilty of an offence.

(2) Action has an effect falling within this subsection if it—

(a) causes serious violence against a person anywhere in the world;

(b) causes serious damage to real or personal property anywhere in the world;

(c) endangers human life or creates a serious risk to the health or safety of the public or a section of the public; or

(d) induces in members of the public the fear that the action is likely to endanger their lives or create a serious risk to their health or safety;

but any effect on the person taking the action is to be disregarded.

(3) A person who—

(a) makes a threat that he or another will take any action which constitutes an offence under subsection (1); and

(b) intends thereby to induce in a person anywhere in the world the fear that the threat is likely to be carried out,

is guilty of an offence.

(4) A person guilty of an offence under this section is liable—

(a) on summary conviction, to imprisonment for a term not exceeding *six* [12] months or a fine not exceeding the statutory maximum (or both); and

(b) on conviction on indictment, to imprisonment for a term not exceeding fourteen years or a fine (or both).

(5) In this section—

"the government" means the government of the United Kingdom, of a part of the United Kingdom or of a country other than the United Kingdom; and

"the public" includes the public of a country other than the United Kingdom.

[This section is printed as amended by the *Terrorism Act* 2006, s.34. In subs. (4)(a), "12" is substituted for "six", as from a day to be appointed, by the *CJA* 2003, s.282(2) and (3). The increase has no application to offences committed before the substitution takes effect: *ibid.*, s.282(4).]

Application of section 113

113A.—(1) Section 113 applies to conduct done— **25–141l**

(a) in the United Kingdom; or

(b) outside the United Kingdom which satisfies the following two conditions.

(2) The first condition is that the conduct is done for the purpose of advancing a political, religious or ideological cause.

(3) The second condition is that the conduct is—

(a) by a United Kingdom national or a United Kingdom resident;

(b) by any person done to, or in relation to, a United Kingdom national, a United Kingdom resident or a protected person; or

(c) by any person done in circumstances which fall within section 63D(1)(b) and (c) or (3)(b) and (c) of the *Terrorism Act* 2000.

(4) The following expressions have the same meaning as they have for the purposes of sections 63C and 63D of that Act—

(a) "United Kingdom national";

(b) "United Kingdom resident";

(c) "protected person".

(5) For the purposes of this section it is immaterial whether a person knows that another is a United Kingdom national, a United Kingdom resident or a protected person.

Consent to prosecution for offence under section 113

113B.—(1) Proceedings for an offence committed under section 113 outside the United Kingdom are not to be started— **25–141m**

(a) in England and Wales, except by or with the consent of the Attorney General;

(b) [*Northern Ireland*].

(2) Proceedings for an offence committed under section 113 outside the United Kingdom may be taken, and the offence may for incidental purposes be treated as having been committed, in any part of the United Kingdom.

(3) [*Northern Ireland.*]

[Ss.113A and 113B were inserted by the *Crime (International Co-operation) Act* 2003, s.53, as from April 26, 2004 (*Crime (International Co-operation) Act 2003 (Commencement No. 1) Order* 2004 (S.I. 2004 No. 786)).]

Hoaxes involving noxious substances or things

114.—(1) A person is guilty of an offence if he— **25–141n**

(a) places any substance or other thing in any place; or

(b) sends any substance or other thing from one place to another (by post, rail or any other means whatever);

with the intention of inducing in a person anywhere in the world a belief that it is likely to be (or contain) a noxious substance or other noxious thing and thereby endanger human life or create a serious risk to human health.

(2) A person is guilty of an offence if he communicates any information which he knows or believes to be false with the intention of inducing in a person anywhere in the world a

belief that a noxious substance or other noxious thing is likely to be present (whether at the time the information is communicated or later) in any place and thereby endanger human life or create a serious risk to human health.

(3) A person guilty of an offence under this section is liable—

(a) on summary conviction, to imprisonment for a term not exceeding *six* [12] months or a fine not exceeding the statutory maximum (or both); and

(b) on conviction on indictment, to imprisonment for a term not exceeding seven years or a fine (or both).

[In subs. (3)(a), "12" is substituted for "six", as from a day to be appointed, by the *CJA* 2003, s.282(2) and (3). The increase has no application to offences committed before the substitution takes effect: *ibid*., s.282(4).]

Sections 113 and 114: supplementary

25–141o **115.**—(1) For the purposes of sections 113 and 114 "substance" includes any biological agent and any other natural or artificial substance (whatever its form, origin or method of production).

(2) For a person to be guilty of an offence under section 113(3) or 114 it is not necessary for him to have any particular person in mind as the person in whom he intends to induce the belief in question.

C. TERRORISM ACT 2006

(1) Encouragement, etc. of terrorism

Terrorism Act 2006, ss.1, 2

Encouragement of terrorism

25–141p **1.**—(1) This section applies to a statement that is likely to be understood by some or all of the members of the public to whom it is published as a direct or indirect encouragement or other inducement to them to the commission, preparation or instigation of acts of terrorism or Convention offences.

(2) A person commits an offence if—

(a) he publishes a statement to which this section applies or causes another to publish such a statement; and

(b) at the time he publishes it or causes it to be published, he—

(i) intends members of the public to be directly or indirectly encouraged or otherwise induced by the statement to commit, prepare or instigate acts of terrorism or Convention offences; or

(ii) is reckless as to whether members of the public will be directly or indirectly encouraged or otherwise induced by the statement to commit, prepare or instigate such acts or offences.

(3) For the purposes of this section, the statements that are likely to be understood by members of the public as indirectly encouraging the commission or preparation of acts of terrorism or Convention offences include every statement which—

(a) glorifies the commission or preparation (whether in the past, in the future or generally) of such acts or offences; and

(b) is a statement from which those members of the public could reasonably be expected to infer that what is being glorified is being glorified as conduct that should be emulated by them in existing circumstances.

(4) For the purposes of this section the questions how a statement is likely to be understood and what members of the public could reasonably be expected to infer from it must be determined having regard both—

(a) to the contents of the statement as a whole; and

(b) to the circumstances and manner of its publication.

(5) It is irrelevant for the purposes of subsections (1) to (3)—

(a) whether anything mentioned in those subsections relates to the commission, preparation or instigation of one or more particular acts of terrorism or Convention offences, of acts of terrorism or Convention offences of a particular description or of acts of terrorism or Convention offences generally; and,

(b) whether any person is in fact encouraged or induced by the statement to commit, prepare or instigate any such act or offence.

(6) In proceedings for an offence under this section against a person in whose case it is not proved that he intended the statement directly or indirectly to encourage or otherwise

induce the commission, preparation or instigation of acts of terrorism or Convention offences, it is a defence for him to show—

(a) that the statement neither expressed his views nor had his endorsement (whether by virtue of section 3 or otherwise); and

(b) that it was clear, in all the circumstances of the statement's publication, that it did not express his views and (apart from the possibility of his having been given and failed to comply with a notice under subsection (3) of that section) did not have his endorsement.

(7) A person guilty of an offence under this section shall be liable—

(a) on conviction on indictment, to imprisonment for a term not exceeding 7 years or to a fine, or to both;

(b) on summary conviction in England and Wales, to imprisonment for a term not exceeding 12 months or to a fine not exceeding the statutory maximum, or to both;

(c) [*Scotland and Northern Ireland*].

(8) In relation to an offence committed before the commencement of section 154(1) of the *Criminal Justice Act* 2003, the reference in subsection (7)(b) to 12 months is to be read as a reference to 6 months.

As to the commission of offences abroad, see section 17, *post*, § 25–142i. As to the liability of company directors, etc., see section 18, *post*, § 25–142j. As to consents to prosecution, see section 19, *post*, § 25–142k. As to the interpretation of this section, and, in particular, what is referred to as a "Convention offence", see section 20, *post*, § 25–142l. **25–141q**

Dissemination of terrorist publications

2.—(1) A person commits an offence if he engages in conduct falling within subsection (2) and, at the time he does so— **25–141r**

(a) he intends an effect of his conduct to be a direct or indirect encouragement or other inducement to the commission, preparation or instigation of acts of terrorism;

(b) he intends an effect of his conduct to be the provision of assistance in the commission or preparation of such acts; or

(c) he is reckless as to whether his conduct has an effect mentioned in paragraph (a) or (b).

(2) For the purposes of this section a person engages in conduct falling within this subsection if he—

(a) distributes or circulates a terrorist publication;

(b) gives, sells or lends such a publication;

(c) offers such a publication for sale or loan;

(d) provides a service to others that enables them to obtain, read, listen to or look at such a publication, or to acquire it by means of a gift, sale or loan;

(e) transmits the contents of such a publication electronically; or

(f) has such a publication in his possession with a view to its becoming the subject of conduct falling within any of paragraphs (a) to (e).

(3) For the purposes of this section a publication is a terrorist publication, in relation to conduct falling within subsection (2), if matter contained in it is likely—

(a) to be understood, by some or all of the persons to whom it is or may become available as a consequence of that conduct, as a direct or indirect encouragement or other inducement to them to the commission, preparation or instigation of acts of terrorism; or

(b) to be useful in the commission or preparation of such acts and to be understood, by some or all of those persons, as contained in the publication, or made available to them, wholly or mainly for the purpose of being so useful to them.

(4) For the purposes of this section matter that is likely to be understood by a person as indirectly encouraging the commission or preparation of acts of terrorism includes any matter which—

(a) glorifies the commission or preparation (whether in the past, in the future or generally) of such acts; and

(b) is matter from which that person could reasonably be expected to infer that what is being glorified is being glorified as conduct that should be emulated by him in existing circumstances.

(5) For the purposes of this section the question whether a publication is a terrorist publication in relation to particular conduct must be determined—

(a) as at the time of that conduct; and

(b) having regard both to the contents of the publication as a whole and to the circumstances in which that conduct occurs.

(6) In subsection (1) references to the effect of a person's conduct in relation to a terrorist publication include references to an effect of the publication on one or more persons to whom it is or may become available as a consequence of that conduct.

(7) It is irrelevant for the purposes of this section whether anything mentioned in subsections (1) to (4) is in relation to the commission, preparation or instigation of one or more particular acts of terrorism, of acts of terrorism of a particular description or of acts of terrorism generally.

(8) For the purposes of this section it is also irrelevant, in relation to matter contained in any article whether any person—

(a) is in fact encouraged or induced by that matter to commit, prepare or instigate acts of terrorism; or

(b) in fact makes use of it in the commission or preparation of such acts.

(9) In proceedings for an offence under this section against a person in respect of conduct to which subsection (10) applies, it is a defence for him to show—

(a) that the matter by reference to which the publication in question was a terrorist publication neither expressed his views nor had his endorsement (whether by virtue of section 3 or otherwise); and

(b) that it was clear, in all the circumstances of the conduct, that that matter did not express his views and (apart from the possibility of his having been given and failed to comply with a notice under subsection (3) of that section) did not have his endorsement.

(10) This subsection applies to the conduct of a person to the extent that—

(a) the publication to which his conduct related contained matter by reference to which it was a terrorist publication by virtue of subsection (3)(a); and

(b) that person is not proved to have engaged in that conduct with the intention specified in subsection (1)(a).

(11), (12) [*Identical to s.1(7) and (8),* ante, *§ 25–141p.*]

(13) In this section—

"lend" includes let on hire, and "loan" is to be construed accordingly;

"publication" means an article or record of any description that contains any of the following, or any combination of them—

(a) matter to be read;

(b) matter to be listened to;

(c) matter to be looked at or watched.

25–141s As to the liability of company directors, etc., see section 18, *post*, § 25–142j. As to consents to prosecution, see section 19, *post*, §§ 25–142k. As to the interpretation of this section, see section 20, *post*, §§ 25–142l.

Section 28 applies to an article if it is likely to be the subject of conduct falling within subsection (2)(a) to (e), and it would fall for the purposes of this section to be treated, in the context of the conduct to which it is likely to be subject, as a terrorist publication. Subsection (1) of that section provides for the issue of a warrant where a justice of the peace is satisfied that there are reasonable grounds for suspecting that such articles are likely to be found on any premises, such warrant authorising a constable to enter and search the premises and to seize anything found there which the constable has reason to believe is such an article. The remainder of the section makes provision, *inter alia*, for the use of force, for the retention of articles seized and, together with Schedule 2, for the forfeiture of such articles.

Electronic commerce

25–141sa The *Electronic Commerce Directive (Terrorism Act 2006) Regulations* 2007 (S.I. 2007 No. 1550) give effect to European Parliament and Council Directive 2000/31/EC (on certain legal aspects of information society services, in particular electronic commerce, in the internal market) in relation to matters within the scope of sections 1 to 4 of the 2006 Act. Regulation 3(1) makes provision for an offence contrary to section 1 or 2 of the Act to be committed in the United Kingdom where, in the course of providing information society services, a service provider established in the United Kingdom does anything in an European Economic Area state (other than the United Kingdom) which if done in the United Kingdom would constitute the offence. Where the offence is committed only by virtue of that provision, the penalty on conviction on indictment is specified as being a term of imprisonment not exceeding two years: reg. 3(4). Regulation 4 prohibits the institution of proceedings for an offence contrary to section 1 or 2 against a non-United Kingdom service provider, or the service of a notice under section 3(3) (*post*) on the same, unless specified conditions are satisfied. Regulations 5, 6 and 7 respectively provide defences to a prosecution under section 1 or 2 where an information society services provider is a "mere conduit", or is "caching" or "hosting" the information in question.

Sentence

In *R. v. Rahman*; *R. v. Mohammed*, *The Times*, July 15, 2008, CA, it was said that **25–141sb** whether the defendant intended to encourage the commission, preparation or instigation of acts of terrorism or was merely reckless as to such consequences is likely to be significant when assessing culpability, and the volume and content of the material disseminated will be relevant to the harm caused, intended or foreseeable; although these are irrelevant considerations when determining whether the offence is made out, this does not make them irrelevant when sentencing, section 143(1) of the *CJA* 2003 (*ante*, § 5–54) applying as much to this offence as to any other; and, whilst it is true that terrorist acts are usually extremely serious and that sentences should reflect the need to deter others, care must be taken to ensure that the sentence is not disproportionate to the facts of the case, especially for an offence such as this where individual cases are capable of varying widely in seriousness; if sentences are imposed which are more serious than are warranted by the circumstances, this will be likely to inflame rather than deter extremism.

Terrorism Act 2006, ss. 3, 4

Application of ss.1 and 2 to internet activity etc.

3.—(1) This section applies for the purposes of sections 1 and 2 in relation to cases where— **25–141t**

(a) a statement is published or caused to be published in the course of, or in connection with, the provision or use of a service provided electronically; or

(b) conduct falling within section 2(2) was in the course of, or in connection with, the provision or use of such a service.

(2) The cases in which the statement, or the article or record to which the conduct relates, is to be regarded as having the endorsement of a person ("the relevant person") at any time include a case in which—

(a) a constable has given him a notice under subsection (3);

(b) that time falls more than 2 working days after the day on which the notice was given; and

(c) the relevant person has failed, without reasonable excuse, to comply with the notice.

(3) A notice under this subsection is a notice which—

(a) declares that, in the opinion of the constable giving it, the statement or the article or record is unlawfully terrorism-related;

(b) requires the relevant person to secure that the statement or the article or record, so far as it is so related, is not available to the public or is modified so as no longer to be so related;

(c) warns the relevant person that a failure to comply with the notice within 2 working days will result in the statement, or the article or record, being regarded as having his endorsement; and

(d) explains how, under subsection (4), he may become liable by virtue of the notice if the statement, or the article or record, becomes available to the public after he has complied with the notice.

(4) Where—

(a) a notice under subsection (3) has been given to the relevant person in respect of a statement, or an article or record, and he has complied with it, but

(b) he subsequently publishes or causes to be published a statement which is, or is for all practical purposes, the same or to the same effect as the statement to which the notice related, or to matter contained in the article or record to which it related, (a "repeat statement");

the requirements of subsection (2)(a) to (c) shall be regarded as satisfied in the case of the repeat statement in relation to the times of its subsequent publication by the relevant person.

(5) In proceedings against a person for an offence under section 1 or 2 the requirements of subsection (2)(a) to (c) are not, in his case, to be regarded as satisfied in relation to any time by virtue of subsection (4) if he shows that he—

(a) has, before that time, taken every step he reasonably could to prevent a repeat statement from becoming available to the public and to ascertain whether it does; and

(b) was, at that time, a person to whom subsection (6) applied.

(6) This subsection applies to a person at any time when he—

(a) is not aware of the publication of the repeat statement; or

(b) having become aware of its publication, has taken every step that he reasonably could to secure that it either ceased to be available to the public or was modified as mentioned in subsection (3)(b).

(7) For the purposes of this section a statement or an article or record is unlawfully terrorism-related if it constitutes, or if matter contained in the article or record constitutes—

(a) something that is likely to be understood, by any one or more of the persons to whom it has or may become available, as a direct or indirect encouragement or other inducement to the commission, preparation or instigation of acts of terrorism or Convention offences; or

(b) information which—

(i) is likely to be useful to any one or more of those persons in the commission or preparation of such acts; and

(ii) is in a form or context in which it is likely to be understood by any one or more of those persons as being wholly or mainly for the purpose of being so useful.

(8) The reference in subsection (7) to something that is likely to be understood as an indirect encouragement to the commission or preparation of acts of terrorism or Convention offences includes anything which is likely to be understood as—

(a) the glorification of the commission or preparation (whether in the past, in the future or generally) of such acts or such offences; and

(b) a suggestion that what is being glorified is being glorified as conduct that should be emulated in existing circumstances.

(9) In this section "working day" means any day other than—

(a) a Saturday or a Sunday;

(b) Christmas Day or Good Friday; or

(c) a day which is a bank holiday under the *Banking and Financial Dealings Act* 1971 in any part of the United Kingdom.

As to the restriction on the service of a notice under subsection (3) on a non-United Kingdom service provider, see *ante*, § 25–141sa.

Giving of notices under s.3

25–141u **4.**—(1) Except in a case to which any of subsections (2) to (4) applies, a notice under section 3(3) may be given to a person only—

(a) by delivering it to him in person; or

(b) by sending it to him, by means of a postal service providing for delivery to be recorded, at his last known address.

(2) Such a notice may be given to a body corporate only—

(a) by delivering it to the secretary of that body in person; or

(b) by sending it to the appropriate person, by means of a postal service providing for delivery to be recorded, at the address of the registered or principal office of the body.

(3) Such a notice may be given to a firm only—

(a) by delivering it to a partner of the firm in person;

(b) by so delivering it to a person having the control or management of the partnership business; or

(c) by sending it to the appropriate person, by means of a postal service providing for delivery to be recorded, at the address of the principal office of the partnership.

(4) Such a notice may be given to an unincorporated body or association only—

(a) by delivering it to a member of its governing body in person; or

(b) by sending it to the appropriate person, by means of a postal service providing for delivery to be recorded, at the address of the principal office of the body or association.

(5) In the case of—

(a) a company registered outside the United Kingdom,

(b) a firm carrying on business outside the United Kingdom, or

(c) an unincorporated body or association with offices outside the United Kingdom,

the references in this section to its principal office include references to its principal office within the United Kingdom (if any).

(6) In this section "the appropriate person" means—

(a) in the case of a body corporate, the body itself or its secretary;

(b) in the case of a firm, the firm itself or a partner of the firm or a person having the control or management of the partnership business; and

(c) in the case of an unincorporated body or association, the body or association itself or a member of its governing body.

(7) For the purposes of section 3 the time at which a notice under subsection (3) of that section is to be regarded as given is—

(a) where it is delivered to a person, the time at which it is so delivered; and

(b) where it is sent by a postal service providing for delivery to be recorded, the time recorded as the time of its delivery.

(8) In this section "secretary", in relation to a body corporate, means the secretary or other equivalent officer of the body.

As to the interpretation of sections 3 and 4, see section 20, *post*, § 25–142l. **25–141v**

(2) Preparation of terrorist acts and training

Terrorism Act 2006, ss.5–8

Preparation of terrorist acts

5.—(1) A person commits an offence if, with the intention of— **25–141w**

(a) committing acts of terrorism, or

(b) assisting another to commit such acts,

he engages in any conduct in preparation for giving effect to his intention.

(2) It is irrelevant for the purposes of subsection (1) whether the intention and preparations relate to one or more particular acts of terrorism, acts of terrorism of a particular description or acts of terrorism generally.

(3) A person guilty of an offence under this section shall be liable, on conviction on indictment, to imprisonment for life.

As to the liability of company directors, etc., see section 18, *post*, § 25–142j. As to consents to prosecution, see section 19, *post*, § 25–142k. As to the interpretation of this section, see section 20, *post*, § 25–142l. **25–141x**

Training for terrorism

6.—(1) A person commits an offence if— **25–141y**

(a) he provides instruction or training in any of the skills mentioned in subsection (3); and

(b) at the time he provides the instruction or training, he knows that a person receiving it intends to use the skills in which he is being instructed or trained—

(i) for or in connection with the commission or preparation of acts of terrorism or Convention offences; or

(ii) for assisting the commission or preparation by others of such acts or offences.

(2) A person commits an offence if—

(a) he receives instruction or training in any of the skills mentioned in subsection (3); and

(b) at the time of the instruction or training, he intends to use the skills in which he is being instructed or trained—

(i) for or in connection with the commission or preparation of acts of terrorism or Convention offences; or

(ii) for assisting the commission or preparation by others of such acts or offences.

(3) The skills are—

(a) the making, handling or use of a noxious substance, or of substances of a description of such substances;

(b) the use of any method or technique for doing anything else that is capable of being done for the purposes of terrorism, in connection with the commission or preparation of an act of terrorism or Convention offence or in connection with assisting the commission or preparation by another of such an act or offence; and

(c) the design or adaptation for the purposes of terrorism, or in connection with the commission or preparation of an act of terrorism or Convention offence, of any method or technique for doing anything.

(4) It is irrelevant for the purposes of subsections (1) and (2)—

(a) whether any instruction or training that is provided is provided to one or more particular persons or generally;

(b) whether the acts or offences in relation to which a person intends to use skills in which he is instructed or trained consist of one or more particular acts of terrorism or Convention offences, acts of terrorism or Convention offences of a particular description or acts of terrorism or Convention offences generally; and

(c) whether assistance that a person intends to provide to others is intended to be provided to one or more particular persons or to one or more persons whose identities are not yet known.

(5) A person guilty of an offence under this section shall be liable—

(a) on conviction on indictment, to imprisonment for a term not exceeding 10 years or to a fine, or to both;

(b) on summary conviction in England and Wales, to imprisonment for a term not exceeding 12 months or to a fine not exceeding the statutory maximum, or to both;

(c) [*Scotland and Northern Ireland*].

(6) [*Identical to s.1(8),* ante, *§ 25–141p.*]

(7) In this section—

"noxious substance" means—

(a) a dangerous substance within the meaning of Part 7 of the *Anti-terrorism, Crime and Security Act* 2001; or

(b) any other substance which is hazardous or noxious or which may be or become hazardous or noxious only in certain circumstances;

"substance" includes any natural or artificial substance (whatever its origin or method of production and whether in solid or liquid form or in the form of a gas or vapour) and any mixture of substances.

25–141z As to the commission of offences abroad, see section 17, *post*, § 25–142i. As to the liability of company directors, etc., see section 18, *post*, § 25–142j. As to consents to prosecution, see section 19, *post*, § 25–142k. As to the interpretation of this section, see section 20, *post*, § 25–142l. As to the definition of "noxious substance", section 58(1) of the 2001 Act defines "dangerous substance" as "(a) anything which consists of or includes a substance for the time being mentioned in Schedule 5; or (b) anything which is infected with or otherwise carries any such substance".

Powers of forfeiture in respect of offences under s.6

25–142 **7.**—(1) A court before which a person is convicted of an offence under section 6 may order the forfeiture of anything the court considers to have been in the person's possession for purposes connected with the offence.

(2) Before making an order under subsection (1) in relation to anything the court must give an opportunity of being heard to any person (in addition to the convicted person) who claims to be the owner of that thing or otherwise to have an interest in it.

(3) An order under subsection (1) may not be made so as to come into force at any time before there is no further possibility (disregarding any power to grant permission for the bringing of an appeal out of time) of the order's being varied or set aside on appeal.

(4) Where a court makes an order under subsection (1), it may also make such other provision as appears to it to be necessary for giving effect to the forfeiture.

(5) That provision may include, in particular, provision relating to the retention, handling, destruction or other disposal of what is forfeited.

(6) Provision made by virtue of this section may be varied at any time by the court that made it.

Attendance at a place used for terrorist training

8.—(1) A person commits an offence if— **25–142a**

(a) he attends at any place, whether in the United Kingdom or elsewhere;

(b) while he is at that place, instruction or training of the type mentioned in section 6(1) of this Act or section 54(1) of the *Terrorism Act* 2000 (weapons training) is provided there;

(c) that instruction or training is provided there wholly or partly for purposes connected with the commission or preparation of acts of terrorism or Convention offences; and

(d) the requirements of subsection (2) are satisfied in relation to that person.

(2) The requirements of this subsection are satisfied in relation to a person if—

(a) he knows or believes that instruction or training is being provided there wholly or partly for purposes connected with the commission or preparation of acts of terrorism or Convention offences; or

(b) a person attending at that place throughout the period of that person's attendance could not reasonably have failed to understand that instruction or training was being provided there wholly or partly for such purposes.

(3) It is immaterial for the purposes of this section—

(a) whether the person concerned receives the instruction or training himself; and

(b) whether the instruction or training is provided for purposes connected with one or more particular acts of terrorism or Convention offences, acts of terrorism or Convention offences of a particular description or acts of terrorism or Convention offences generally.

(4), (5) [*Identical to s.6(5) and (6),* ante, *§ 25–141x.*]

(6) References in this section to instruction or training being provided include references to its being made available.

As to the commission of offences abroad, see section 17, *post*, § 25–142i. As to the liability of company directors, etc., see section 18, *post*, § 25–142j. As to consents to prosecution, see section 19, *post*, § 25–142k. As to the interpretation of this section, see section 20, *post*, § 25–142l. **25–142b**

(3) Offences involving radioactive devices and material and nuclear facilities and sites

Terrorism Act 2006, ss.9–11

Making and possession of devices or materials

9.—(1) A person commits an offence if— **25–142c**

(a) he makes or has in his possession a radioactive device, or

(b) he has in his possession radioactive material,

with the intention of using the device or material in the course of or in connection with the commission or preparation of an act of terrorism or for the purposes of terrorism, or of making it available to be so used.

(2) It is irrelevant for the purposes of subsection (1) whether the act of terrorism to which an intention relates is a particular act of terrorism, an act of terrorism of a particular description or an act of terrorism generally.

(3) A person guilty of an offence under this section shall be liable, on conviction on indictment, to imprisonment for life.

(4) In this section—

"radioactive device" means —

(a) a nuclear weapon or other nuclear explosive device;

(b) a radioactive material dispersal device;

(c) a radiation-emitting device;

"radioactive material" means nuclear material or any other radioactive substance which—

(a) contains nuclides that undergo spontaneous disintegration in a process accompanied by the emission of one or more types of ionising radiation, such as alpha radiation, beta radiation, neutron particles or gamma rays; and

(b) is capable, owing to its radiological or fissile properties, of—

(i) causing serious bodily injury to a person;

(ii) causing serious damage to property;

(iii) endangering a person's life; or

(iv) creating a serious risk to the health or safety of the public.

(5) In subsection (4)—

"device" includes any of the following, whether or not fixed to land, namely, machinery, equipment, appliances, tanks, containers, pipes and conduits;

"nuclear material" has the same meaning as in the *Nuclear Material (Offences) Act* 1983 (see section 6 of that Act).

25–142d As to the commission of offences abroad, see section 17, *post*, § 25–142i. As to the liability of company directors, etc., see section 18, *post*, § 25–142j. As to consents to prosecution, see section 19, *post*, § 25–142k. As to the interpretation of this section, see section 20, *post*, § 25–142l. For section 6 of the 1983 Act, see *post*, § 25–174.

Misuse of devices or material and misuse and damage of facilities

25–142e **10.**—(1) A person commits an offence if he uses—

(a) a radioactive device, or

(b) radioactive material,

in the course of or in connection with the commission of an act of terrorism or for the purposes of terrorism.

(2) A person commits an offence if, in the course of or in connection with the commission of an act of terrorism or for the purposes of terrorism, he uses or damages a nuclear facility in a manner which—

(a) causes a release of radioactive material; or

(b) creates or increases a risk that such material will be released.

(3) A person guilty of an offence under this section shall be liable, on conviction on indictment, to imprisonment for life.

(4) In this section—

"nuclear facility" means—

(a) a nuclear reactor, including a reactor installed in or on any transportation device for use as an energy source in order to propel it or for any other purpose; or

(b) a plant or conveyance being used for the production, storage, processing or transport of radioactive material;

"radioactive device" and "radioactive material" have the same meanings as in section 9.

(5) In subsection (4)—

"nuclear reactor" has the same meaning as in the *Nuclear Installations Act* 1965 (see section 26 of that Act);

"transportation device" means any vehicle or any space object (within the meaning of the *Outer Space Act* 1986).

25–142f As to the commission of offences abroad, see section 17, *post*, § 25–142i. As to the liability of company directors, etc., see section 18, *post*, § 25–142j. As to consents to prosecution, see section 19, *post*, § 25–142k. As to the interpretation of this section, see section 20, *post*, § 25–142l.

Terrorist threats relating to devices, materials or facilities

25–142g **11.**—(1) A person commits an offence if, in the course of or in connection with the commission of an act of terrorism or for the purposes of terrorism—

(a) he makes a demand—

(i) for the supply to himself or to another of a radioactive device or of radioactive material;

(ii) for a nuclear facility to be made available to himself or to another; or

(iii) for access to such a facility to be given to himself or to another;

(b) he supports the demand with a threat that he or another will take action if the demand is not met; and

(c) the circumstances and manner of the threat are such that it is reasonable for the person to whom it is made to assume that there is real risk that the threat will be carried out if the demand is not met.

(2) A person also commits an offence if—

(a) he makes a threat falling within subsection (3) in the course of or in connection with the commission of an act of terrorism or for the purposes of terrorism; and

(b) the circumstances and manner of the threat are such that it is reasonable for the person to whom it is made to assume that there is real risk that the threat will be carried out, or would be carried out if demands made in association with the threat are not met.

(3) A threat falls within this subsection if it is—

(a) a threat to use radioactive material;

(b) a threat to use a radioactive device; or

(c) a threat to use or damage a nuclear facility in a manner that releases radioactive material or creates or increases a risk that such material will be released.

(4) A person guilty of an offence under this section shall be liable, on conviction on indictment, to imprisonment for life.

(5) In this section—

"nuclear facility" has the same meaning as in section 10;

"radioactive device" and "radioactive material" have the same meanings as in section 9.

As to the commission of offences abroad, see section 17, *post*, § 25–142i. As to the liability of company directors, etc., see section 18, *post*, § 25–142j. As to consents to prosecution, see section 19, *post*, § 25–142k. As to the interpretation of this section, see section 20, *post*, § 25–142l. **25–142h**

(4) Jurisdiction, procedure, etc.

Terrorism Act 2006, ss.17–19

Commission of offences abroad

17.—(1) If— **25–142i**

(a) a person does anything outside the United Kingdom, and

(b) his action, if done in a part of the United Kingdom, would constitute an offence falling within subsection (2),

he shall be guilty in that part of the United Kingdom of the offence.

(2) The offences falling within this subsection are—

(a) an offence under section 1 or 6 of this Act so far as it is committed in relation to any statement, instruction or training in relation to which that section has effect by reason of its relevance to the commission, preparation or instigation of one or more Convention offences;

(b) an offence under any of sections 8 to 11 of this Act;

(c) an offence under section 11(1) of the *Terrorism Act* 2000 (membership of proscribed organisations);

(d) an offence under section 54 of that Act (weapons training);

(e) conspiracy to commit an offence falling within this subsection;

(f) inciting a person to commit such an offence;

(g) attempting to commit such an offence;

(h) aiding, abetting, counselling or procuring the commission of such an offence.

(3) Subsection (1) applies irrespective of whether the person is a British citizen or, in the case of a company, a company incorporated in a part of the United Kingdom.

(4) In the case of an offence falling within subsection (2) which is committed wholly or partly outside the United Kingdom—

(a) proceedings for the offence may be taken at any place in the United Kingdom; and

(b) the offence may for all incidental purposes be treated as having been committed at any such place.

(5) [*Amends* Explosive Substances Act *1883, s.3*, ante, *§ 23–66*.]

(6) [*Scotland*.]

The reference to the common law offence of incitement in subsection (2)(f) has effect as a reference to the offences under the *SCA* 2007, Pt 2: 2007 Act, s.63(1), and Sched. 6, para. 52(a).

For sections 11 and 54 of the 2000 Act, see *ante*, §§ 25–60, 25–94.

Liability of company directors etc.

18.—(1) Where an offence under this Part is committed by a body corporate and is proved to have been committed with the consent or connivance of— **25–142j**

(a) a director, manager, secretary or other similar officer of the body corporate, or
(b) a person who was purporting to act in any such capacity,

he (as well as the body corporate) is guilty of that offence and shall be liable to be proceeded against and punished accordingly.

(2) [*Scottish firms.*]

(3) In this section "director", in relation to a body corporate whose affairs are managed by its members, means a member of the body corporate.

Consents to prosecutions

25–142k **19.**—(1) Proceedings for an offence under this Part—

(a) may be instituted in England and Wales only with the consent of the Director of Public Prosecutions; and
(b) [*Northern Ireland*].

(2) But if it appears to the Director of Public Prosecutions or the Director of Public Prosecutions for Northern Ireland that an offence under this Part has been committed for a purpose wholly or partly connected with the affairs of a country other than the United Kingdom, his consent for the purposes of this section may be given only with the permission—

(a) in the case of the Director of Public Prosecutions, of the Attorney General; and
(b) [*Northern Ireland*].

(3) [*Northern Ireland.*]

(5) Interpretation

Terrorism Act 2006, s.20

Interpretation of Part 1

25–142l **20.**—(1) Expressions used in this Part and in the *Terrorism Act* 2000 have the same meanings in this Part as in that Act.

(2) In this Part—

"act of terrorism" includes anything constituting an action taken for the purposes of terrorism, within the meaning of the *Terrorism Act* 2000 (see section 1(5) of that Act);

"article" includes anything for storing data;

"Convention offence" means an offence listed in Schedule 1 or an equivalent offence under the law of a country or territory outside the United Kingdom;

"glorification" includes any form of praise or celebration, and cognate expressions are to be construed accordingly;

"public" is to be construed in accordance with subsection (3);

"publish" and cognate expressions are to be construed in accordance with subsection (4);

"record" means a record so far as not comprised in an article, including a temporary record created electronically and existing solely in the course of, and for the purposes of, the transmission of the whole or a part of its contents;

"statement" is to be construed in accordance with subsection (6).

(3) In this Part references to the public—

(a) are references to the public of any part of the United Kingdom or of a country or territory outside the United Kingdom, or any section of the public; and
(b) except in section 9(4), also include references to a meeting or other group of persons which is open to the public (whether unconditionally or on the making of a payment or the satisfaction of other conditions).

(4) In this Part references to a person's publishing a statement are references to—

(a) his publishing it in any manner to the public;
(b) his providing electronically any service by means of which the public have access to the statement; or
(c) his using a service provided to him electronically by another so as to enable or to facilitate access by the public to the statement;

but this subsection does not apply to the references to a publication in section 2.

(5) In this Part references to providing a service include references to making a facility available; and references to a service provided to a person are to be construed accordingly.

(6) In this Part references to a statement are references to a communication of any description, including a communication without words consisting of sounds or images or both.

(7) In this Part references to conduct that should be emulated in existing circumstances

include references to conduct that is illustrative of a type of conduct that should be so emulated.

(8) In this Part references to what is contained in an article or record include references—

(a) to anything that is embodied or stored in or on it; and

(b) to anything that may be reproduced from it using apparatus designed or adapted for the purpose.

(9)–(11) [*Modification of Sched. 1 by order made by Secretary of State.*]

For section 1 of the Act of 2000, see *ante*, § 25–56. **25–142m**

Schedule 1 specifies as "Convention offences", offences contrary to the *Offences against the Person Act* 1861, ss.28 to 30 (*ante*, §§ 19–232 *et seq.*), the *Explosive Substances Act* 1883, ss.2, 3 and 5 (*ante*, §§ 23–62, 23–66 and 23–80), the *Biological Weapons Act* 1974, s.1 (development, *etc.*, of biological weapons), the *Internationally Protected Persons Act* 1978, s.1(1)(a) and (b) and (3) (*post*, § 25–143a), the *Taking of Hostages Act* 1982, s.1 (*post*, § 25–160), the *Aviation Security Act* 1982, ss.1 to 3 and 6(2) (*post*, §§ 25–178 *et seq.*), the *Nuclear Material (Offences) Act* 1983, ss.1(1) and 2 (amended, as from a day to be appointed, by the *CJIA* 2008, s.148(1) and Sched. 26, para. 79(1), (3) and (4), to "s.1(1)(a)–(d) (where committed in relation to or by means of nuclear material), s.1(a) or (b) (where the act making the person guilty of the offence is directed at a nuclear facility or interferes with the operation of such a facility and causes death, injury or damage resulting from the emission of ionising radiation or the release of radioactive material), s.1B, s.1C or s.2") (*post*, §§ 25–171 *et seq.*), the *Aviation and Maritime Security Act* 1990, ss.1 (*post*, § 25–199) and 9 to 14 (*post*, §§ 25–201 *et seq.*), the *Chemical Weapons Act* 1996, s.2 (use, development, etc., of chemical weapons), the *Terrorism Act* 2000, ss.15 to 18 (*ante*, §§ 25–64 *et seq.*) and 56 (*ante*, § 25–96), the *Anti-terrorism, Crime and Security Act* 2001, s.47 (*ante*, § 25–141a), and conspiracy to commit, inciting (to be construed as a reference to the offences under the *SCA* 2007, Pt 2: 2007 Act, s.63(1), and Sched. 6, para. 52(b)) the commission of, attempting to commit, and being an accessory to the commission of, a "Convention offence". As from a day to be appointed, a reference to offences under the *CEMA* 1979, ss.50(2) and (3), 68(2) and 170(1) and (2) (*post*, §§ 25–409 *et seq.*), if committed in connection with a prohibition or restriction relating to the importation, exportation or shipment as stores of nuclear material, is added to Schedule 1: *CJIA* 2008, s.148(1), and Sched. 26, para. 79(1) and (5).

The Act itself does not identify the convention that is referred to. The expression "Convention offence" was referred to, however, in paragraph 11 of the explanatory notes that accompanied the bill, as representing offences under United Kingdom law which parallel those referred to in the Council of Europe Convention on the Prevention of Terrorism (C.E.T.S. No. 196). The explanatory notes state (para. 20) that (what is now) section 1 of the Act was necessary to give effect to this convention (which requires state parties to criminalise "public provocation to commit a terrorist offence"), and that the new offence "supplements the existing common law offence of incitement to commit an offence".

D. Internationally Protected Persons Act 1978

This Act implements the Convention on the Prevention and Punishment of Crimes against Internationally Protected Persons adopted by the United Nations General Assembly in 1973. **25–143**

For the territories to which the provisions of the Act are applied by Order in Council under section 4, *post*, see *Halsburys Statutes*, 4th ed., Vol. 10 (2007 Reissue), p. 1059.

Internationally Protected Persons Act 1978, s.1

Attacks and threats of attacks on protected persons

1.—(1) If a person, whether a citizen of the United Kingdom and Colonies or not, does outside the United Kingdom— **25–143a**

(a) any act to or in relation to a protected person which, if he had done it in any part of the United Kingdom, would have made him guilty of the offence of murder, manslaughter, culpable homicide ... assault occasioning actual bodily harm or causing injury, kidnapping, abduction, false imprisonment or plagium or an offence under section 18, 20, 21, 22, 23, 24, 28, 29, 30 or 56 of the *Offences against the Person Act* 1861 or section 2 of the *Explosive Substances Act* 1883 or an offence listed in subsection (1A); or

(b) in connection with an attack on any relevant premises or on any vehicle ordinarily used by a protected person which is made when a protected person is on or in the premises or vehicle, any act which, if he had done it in any part of the United Kingdom, would have made him guilty of an offence under section 2 of the *Explosive Substances Act* 1883, section 1 of the *Criminal Damage Act* 1971 or article 3 of the *Criminal Damage (Northern Ireland) Order* 1977 or the offence of wilful fire-raising,

he shall in any part of the United Kingdom be guilty of the offences aforesaid of which the act would have made him guilty if he had done it there.

(1A) The offences mentioned in subsection (1)(a) are—

(a) in Scotland or Northern Ireland, rape;

(b) an offence under section 1 or 2 of the *Sexual Offences Act* 2003;

(c) an offence under section 4 of that Act, where the activity caused involved penetration within subsection (4)(a) to (d) of that section;

(d) an offence under section 5 or 6 of that Act;

(e) an offence under section 8 of that Act, where an activity involving penetration within subsection (3)(a) to (d) of that section was caused;

(f) an offence under section 30 of that Act, where the touching involved penetration within subsection (3)(a) to (d) of that section;

(g) an offence under section 31 of that Act, where an activity involving penetration within subsection (3)(a) to (d) of that section was caused.

(2) If a person in the United Kingdom or elsewhere, whether a citizen of the United Kingdom and Colonies or not—

(a) attempts to commit an offence which, by virtue of the preceding subsection or otherwise, is an offence mentioned in paragraph (a) of that subsection against a protected person or an offence mentioned in paragraph (b) of that subsection in connection with an attack so mentioned; or

(b) aids, abets, counsels or procures, or is art and part in, the commission of such an offence or of an attempt to commit such an offence,

he shall in any part of the United Kingdom be guilty of attempting to commit the offence in question or, as the case may be, of aiding, abetting, counselling or procuring, or being art and part in, the commission of the offence or attempt in question.

(3) If a person in the United Kingdom or elsewhere, whether a citizen of the United Kingdom and Colonies or not—

(a) makes to another person a threat that any person will do an act which is an offence mentioned in paragraph (a) of the preceding subsection; or

(b) attempts to make or aids, abets, counsels or procures or is art and part in the making of such a threat to another person,

with the intention that the other person shall fear that the threat will be carried out, the person who makes the threat or, as the case may be, who attempts to make it or aids, abets, counsels or procures or is art and part in the making of it, shall in any part of the United Kingdom be guilty of an offence and liable on conviction on indictment to imprisonment for a term not exceeding ten years and not exceeding the term of imprisonment to which a person would be liable for the offence constituted by doing the act threatened at the place where the conviction occurs and at the time of the offence to which the conviction relates.

(4) For the purposes of the preceding subsections it is immaterial whether a person knows that another person is a protected person.

(5) In this section—

"act" includes omission;

"a protected person" means, in relation to an alleged offence, any of the following, namely—

(a) a person who at the time of the alleged offence is a Head of State, a member of a body which performs the functions of Head of State under the constitution of the State, a Head of Government or a Minister for Foreign Affairs and is outside the territory of the State in which he holds office;

(b) a person who at the time of the alleged offence is a representative or an official of a State or an official or agent of an international organisation of an inter-governmental character, is entitled under international law to special protection from attack on his person, freedom or dignity and does not fall within the preceding paragraph;

(c) a person who at the time of the alleged offence is a member of the family of another person mentioned in either of the preceding paragraphs and—

(i) if the other person is mentioned in paragraph (a) above, is accompanying him,

(ii) if the other person is mentioned in paragraph (b) above, is a member of his household;

"relevant premises" means premises at which a protected person resides or is staying or which a protected person uses for the purpose of carrying out his functions as such a person; and

"vehicle" includes any means of conveyance;

and if in any proceedings a question arises as to whether a person is or was a protected person, a certificate issued by or under the authority of the Secretary of State and stating any fact relating to the question shall be conclusive evidence of that fact.

[This section is printed as amended by the *SOA* 2003, s.139, and Sched. 6, para. 22.]

The reference to "abduction" in section 1(1)(a) is to be construed as not including an offence under section 1 of the *Child Abduction Act* 1984 (*ante*, § 19–311): see s.11(3) of that Act. Further, section 56 of the *Offences against the Person Act* 1861 is repealed: *Child Abduction Act* 1984, s.11(5).

An offence contrary to subsection (1) or (3) is a "Convention offence" within the *Terrorism Act* 2006: see *ante*, §§ 25–142k, 25–142l.

Internationally Protected Persons Act 1978, s.2

Provisions supplementary to section 1

2.—(1) Proceedings for an offence which (disregarding the provisions of the *Suppression of Terrorism Act* 1978, the *Nuclear Material (Offences) Act* 1983, the *United Nations Personnel Act* 1997 and the *Terrorism Act* 2000) would not be an offence apart from the preceding section shall not be begun— **25–144**

(a) in Northern Ireland, except by or with the consent of the Attorney-General for Northern Ireland;

(b) in England and Wales, except by or with the consent of the Attorney General;

and references to a consent provision in article 7(3) to (5) of the *Prosecution of Offences (Northern Ireland) Order* 1972 (which relates to consents for prosecutions) shall include so much of this subsection as precedes paragraph (b).

(2) [*Scotland.*]

(3) Nothing in the preceding section shall prejudice the operation of any rule of law relating to attempts to commit offences, section 8 of the *Accessories and Abettors Act* 1861 or any rule of law in Scotland relating to art and part guilt.

(4) [*Amends Sched. to* Visiting Forces Act *1952.*]

[Subs. (1) is printed as amended by the *United Nations Personnel Act* 1997, Sched.; and the *Crime (International Co-operation) Act* 2003, s.91(1), and Sched. 5, paras 1 and 2.]

[The next paragraph is § 25–148.]

E. SUPPRESSION OF TERRORISM ACT 1978

This Act gave effect to the European Convention on the Suppression of Terrorism; it amended the law relating to extradition and the obtaining of evidence for criminal proceedings outside the United Kingdom. It also conferred jurisdiction in respect of certain offences committed outside the United Kingdom. The provisions of the Act pertaining to extradition have now been superseded by the *Extradition Act* 2003. **25–148**

Suppression of Terrorism Act 1978, s.4

Jurisdiction in respect of offences committed outside United Kingdom

4.—(1) If a person, whether a citizen of the United Kingdom and Colonies or not, does in a **25–149**

convention country any act which, if he had done it in a part of the United Kingdom, would have made him guilty in that part of the United Kingdom of—

(a) an offence mentioned in paragraph 1, 2, 4, 5, 10, 11, 11B, 12, 13, 14 or 15 of Schedule 1 to this Act; or

(b) an offence of attempting to commit any offence so mentioned,

he shall, in that part of the United Kingdom, be guilty of the offence or offences aforesaid of which the act would have made him guilty if he had done it there.

(2) [*Repealed by* Internationally Protected Persons Act *1978*.]

(3) If a person who is a national of a convention country but not a citizen of the United Kingdom and Colonies does outside the United Kingdom and that convention country any act which makes him in that convention country guilty of an offence and which, if he had been a citizen of the United Kingdom and Colonies, would have made him in any part of the United Kingdom guilty of an offence mentioned in paragraph 1, 2 or 13 of Schedule 1 to this Act, he shall, in any part of the United Kingdom, be guilty of the offence or offences aforesaid of which the act would have made him guilty if he had been such a citizen.

(4) Proceedings for an offence which (disregarding the provisions of the *Internationally Protected Persons Act* 1978, the *Nuclear Material (Offences) Act* 1983, the *United Nations Personnel Act* 1997 and the *Terrorism Act* 2000) would not be an offence apart from this section shall not be instituted—

(a) in Northern Ireland, except by or with the consent of the Attorney-General for Northern Ireland; or

(b) in England and Wales, except by or with the consent of the Attorney General;

and references to a consent provision in Article 7(3) to (5) of the *Prosecution of Offences (Northern Ireland) Order* 1972 (which relates to consents to prosecutions) shall include so much of this subsection as precedes paragraph (b).

(5) [*Scotland*.]

(6) [*Repealed by* Internationally Protected Persons Act *1978*.]

(7) For the purposes of this section any act done—

(a) on board a ship registered in a convention country, being an act which, if the ship had been registered in the United Kingdom, would have constituted an offence within the jurisdiction of the Admiralty; or

(b) on board an aircraft registered in a convention country while the aircraft is in flight elsewhere than in or over that country; or

(c) on board a hovercraft registered in a convention country while the hovercraft is in journey elsewhere than in or over that country,

shall be treated as done in that convention country; and subsection (4) of section 92 of the *Civil Aviation Act* 1982 (definition of "in flight" or, as applied to hovercraft, "in journey") shall apply for the purposes of this subsection as it applies for the purposes of that section.

[This section is printed as amended by the *Nuclear Material (Offences) Act* 1983, s.4(1); the *United Nations Personnel Act* 1997, Sched.; and the *Crime (International Co-operation) Act* 2003, s.91(1), and Sched. 5, paras 3 and 4.]

Suppression of Terrorism Act 1978, s.5

Power to apply section 4 to non-convention countries

25–150 **5.**—(1) The Secretary of State may by order direct that section 4 above shall apply in relation to a country falling within subsection (2) below as it applies in relation to a convention country, subject to the exceptions (if any) specified in the order.

(2) A country falls within this subsection if—

(a) it is not a convention country; and

(b) it is a category 1 territory or a category 2 territory within the meaning of the *Extradition Act* 2003.

[This section is printed as substituted by the *Extradition Act* 2003, s.219(1), and Sched. 3, para. 5.]

25–151 The *Suppression of Terrorism Act 1978 (United States of America) Order* 1986 (S.I. 1986 No. 2146) and the *Suppression of Terrorism Act 1978 (India) Order* 1993 (S.I. 1993 No. 2533) were made under section 5(1)(i) of the original enactment. To the extent that they apply section 4 to those countries, it is submitted that they will have effect as if made under the substituted section (see the *Interpretation Act* 1978, s.17(2)(b) (Appendix B–17)).

Suppression of Terrorism Act 1978, s.8

Provisions as to interpretation and orders

8.—(1) In this Act— 25–152

"act" includes omission;

"convention country" means a country for the time being designated in an order made by the Secretary of State as a party to the European Convention on the Suppression of Terrorism signed at Strasbourg on the 27th January, 1977;

"country" includes any territory;

"enactment" includes an enactment of the Parliament of Northern Ireland, a Measure of the Northern Ireland Assembly and an Order in Council under the *Northern Ireland (Temporary Provisions) Act* 1972 or the *Northern Ireland Act* 1974.

(2) Except so far as the context otherwise requires, any reference in this Act to an enactment is a reference to it as amended by or under any other enactment, including this Act.

(3) For the purpose of construing references in this Act to other Acts, section 38(1) of the *Interpretation Act* 1889 shall apply in cases of repeal and re-enactment by a Measure of the Northern Ireland Assembly or by an Order in Council under the *Northern Ireland Act* 1974 as it applies in cases of repeal and re-enactment by an Act.

(4)–(6) [*Procedure for exercising powers conferred on Secretary of State to make orders under Act.*]

The *Interpretation Act* 1889 was repealed and replaced by the *Interpretation Act* 1978 with effect from January 1, 1979.

For countries designated as convention countries, see the following statutory instruments, all of which are entitled the "*Suppression of Terrorism Act 1978 (Designation of Countries) Order*", S.I. 1978 No. 1245, S.I. 1979 No. 497, S.I. 1980 Nos 357 and 1392, S.I. 1981 Nos 1389 and 1507, S.I. 1986 Nos 271 and 1137, S.I. 1987 No. 2137, S.I. 1989 No. 2210, S.I. 1990 No. 1272 and S.I. 1994 No. 2978. The countries concerned are Austria, the Federal Republic of Germany and West Berlin, Sweden, the Republic of Cyprus, Norway, Iceland, Spain, the Republic of Turkey, Luxembourg, Belgium, the Netherlands, Portugal, Switzerland, Italy, Liechtenstein, France, the Republic of Ireland, Finland, Greece, the Czech Republic and Slovakia. 25–153

Scheduled offences

As amended by the *Firearms (Northern Ireland) Order* 1981 (S.I. 1981 No. 155), the *Aviation Security Act* 1982, s.40 and Sched. 2, the *Taking of Hostages Act* 1982, s.3(2), the *Child Abduction Act* 1984, s.11(4), the *CJA* 1988, s.22, the *Prevention of Terrorism (Temporary Provisions) Act* 1989, s.25(1) and Sched. 8, the *Aviation and Maritime Security Act* 1990, Sched. 3, the *Channel Tunnel (Security) Order* 1994 (S.I. 1994 No. 570), the *Terrorism Act* 2000, s.125(1) and Sched. 15, para. 3, and the *SOA* 2003, s.139, and Sched. 6, para. 23, Schedule 1 to the 1978 Act lists the following offences under the headings specified: 25–154

"*Common law offences*"—murder (para. 1), manslaughter or culpable homicide (2), rape under the law of Scotland or Northern Ireland (3), kidnapping, abduction or plagium (4), false imprisonment (5), assault occasioning actual bodily harm or causing injury (6), wilful fire-raising (7);

"*Offences against the person*"—offences contrary to sections 4, 18, 20 to 24 and 48 of the *Offences against the Person Act* 1861 (8), offences contrary to sections 1, 2, 4 (where the activity caused involved penetration within subsection (4)(a) to (d)), 5, 6, 8 (where an activity involving penetration within subsection (3)(a) to (d) was caused), 30 (where the touching involved penetration within subsection (3)(a) to (d)) and 31 (where an activity involving penetration within subsection (3)(a) to (d) was caused) of the *SOA* 2003 (9), an offence under section 134 of the *CJA* 1988 (9A);

"*Abduction*"—offences contrary to sections 55 and 56 of the *Offences against the Person Act* 1861 (10), an offence under section 20 of the *SOA* 1956 (11);

"*Taking of hostages*"—an offence under the *Taking of Hostages Act* 1982 (11A), an offence under section 2 of the *Child Abduction Act* 1984 (11B);

"*Explosives*"—offences contrary to sections 28 to 30 of the *Offences against the*

Person Act 1861 (12), offences contrary to sections 2 and 3 of the *Explosive Substances Act* 1883 (13);

"*Nuclear material*"—an offence under any provision of the *Nuclear Material (Offences) Act* 1983 (13A);

"*Firearms*"—offences contrary to sections 16 and 17(1) of the *Firearms Act* 1968 (14), offences contrary to Articles 17 and 18(1) of the *Firearms (Northern Ireland) Order* 1981 (15);

"*Offences against property*"—an offence under section 1(2) of the *Criminal Damage Act* 1971 (16), an offence under Article 3(2) of the *Criminal Damage (Northern Ireland) Order* 1977 (17);

"*Offences in relation to aircraft*"—an offence under Part I of the *Aviation Security Act* 1982 (other than an offence under section 4 or 7) (18); an offence under section 1 of the *Aviation and Maritime Security Act* 1990 (18A);

"*Offences relating to ships and fixed platforms*"—an offence under Part II of the *Aviation and Maritime Security Act* 1990 (other than an offence under section 15) (18B);

"*Offences relating to Channel Tunnel trains and the tunnel system*"—an offence under Part II of the *Channel Tunnel (Security) Order* 1994 (S.I. 1994 No. 570) (18C);

"*Financing terrorism*"—an offence under any of sections 15 to 18 of the *Terrorism Act* 2000 (19A);

"*Attempts*"—an offence of attempting to commit any offence mentioned in a preceding paragraph (20);

"*Conspiracy*"—an offence of conspiracy to commit any offence mentioned in a preceding paragraph (21).

F. UNITED NATIONS PERSONNEL ACT 1997

Introduction

25–155 This Act enables effect to be given to certain provisions of the Convention on the Safety of United Nations and Associated Personnel adopted by the General Assembly on December 9, 1994.

United Nations Personnel Act 1997, ss.1–5

Attacks on UN workers

25–156 **1.**—(1) If a person does outside the United Kingdom any act to or in relation to a UN worker which, if he had done it in any part of the United Kingdom, would have made him guilty of any of the offences mentioned in subsection (2), he shall in that part of the United Kingdom be guilty of that offence.

(2) The offences referred to in subsection (1) are—

(a) murder, manslaughter, culpable homicide, rape, assault causing injury, kidnapping, abduction and false imprisonment;

(b) an offence under section 18, 20, 21, 22, 23, 24, 28, 29, 30 or 47 of the *Offences against the Person Act* 1861; and

(c) an offence under section 2 of the *Explosive Substances Act* 1883.

Attacks in connection with premises and vehicles

2.—(1) If a person does outside the United Kingdom any act, in connection with an attack on relevant premises or on a vehicle ordinarily used by a UN worker which is made when a UN worker is on or in the premises or vehicle, which, if he had done it in any part of the United Kingdom, would have made him guilty of any of the offences mentioned in subsection (2), he shall in that part of the United Kingdom be guilty of that offence.

(2) The offences referred to in subsection (1) are—

(a) an offence under section 2 of the *Explosive Substances Act* 1883;

(b) an offence under section 1 of the *Criminal Damage Act* 1971;

(c) an offence under article 3 of the *Criminal Damage (Northern Ireland) Order* 1977; and

(d) wilful fire-raising.

(3) In this section—

"relevant premises" means premises at which a UN worker resides or is staying or which a UN worker uses for the purpose of carrying out his functions as such a worker; and

"vehicle" includes any means of conveyance.

Threats of attacks on UN workers

3.—(1) If a person in the United Kingdom or elsewhere contravenes subsection (2) he shall be guilty of an offence.

(2) A person contravenes this subsection if, in order to compel a person to do or abstain from doing any act, he—

(a) makes to a person a threat that any person will do an act which is—

(i) an offence mentioned in section 1(2) against a UN worker, or

(ii) an offence mentioned in subsection (2) of section 2 in connection with such an attack as is mentioned in subsection (1) of that section, and

(b) intends that the person to whom he makes the threat shall fear that it will be carried out.

(3) A person guilty of an offence under this section shall be liable on conviction on indictment to imprisonment for a term—

(a) not exceeding ten years, and

(b) not exceeding the term of imprisonment to which a person would be liable for the offence constituted by doing the act threatened at the place where the conviction occurs and at the time of the offence to which the conviction relates.

Meaning of UN worker

4.—(1) For the purposes of this Act a person is a UN worker, in relation to an alleged offence, if at the time of the alleged offence— **25–157**

(a) he is engaged or deployed by the Secretary-General of the United Nations as a member of the military, police or civilian component of a UN operation,

(b) he is, in his capacity as an official or expert on mission of the United Nations, a specialised agency of the United Nations or the International Atomic Energy Agency, present in an area where a UN operation is being conducted,

(c) he is assigned, with the agreement of an organ of the United Nations, by the Government of any State or by an international governmental organisation to carry out activities in support of the fulfilment of the mandate of a UN operation,

(d) he is engaged by the Secretary-General of the United Nations, a specialised agency or the International Atomic Energy Agency to carry out such activities, or

(e) he is deployed by a humanitarian non-governmental organisation or agency under an agreement with the Secretary-General of the United Nations, with a specialised agency or with the International Atomic Energy Agency to carry out such activities.

(2) Subject to subsection (3), in this section "UN operation" means an operation—

(a) which is established, in accordance with the Charter of the United Nations, by an organ of the United Nations,

(b) which is conducted under the authority and control of the United Nations, and

(c) which—

(i) has as its purpose the maintenance or restoration of international peace and security, or

(ii) has, for the purposes of the Convention, been declared by the Security Council or the General Assembly of the United Nations to be an operation where there exists an exceptional risk to the safety of the participating personnel.

(3) In this section "UN operation" does not include any operation—

(a) which is authorised by the Security Council of the United Nations as an enforcement action under Chapter VII of the Charter of the United Nations,

(b) in which UN workers are engaged as combatants against organised armed forces, and

(c) to which the law of international armed conflict applies.

(4) In this section—

"the Convention" means the Convention on the Safety of United Nations and Associated

Personnel adopted by the General Assembly of the United Nations on 9th December 1994; and

"specialised agency" has the meaning assigned to it by Article 57 of the Charter of the United Nations.

(5) If, in any proceedings, a question arises as to whether—

(a) a person is or was a UN worker, or

(b) an operation is or was a UN operation,

a certificate issued by or under the authority of the Secretary of State and stating any fact relating to the question shall be conclusive evidence of that fact.

Provisions supplementary to sections 1 to 3

5.—(1) Proceedings for an offence which (disregarding the provisions of the *Internationally Protected Persons Act* 1978, the *Suppression of Terrorism Act* 1978, the *Nuclear Material (Offences) Act* 1983 and the *Terrorism Act* 2000) would not be an offence apart from section 1, 2 or 3 above shall not be begun—

(a) in England and Wales, except by or with the consent of the Attorney General;

(b) [*Northern Ireland*].

(2) [*Scotland.*]

(3) A person is guilty of an offence under, or by virtue of, section 1, 2 or 3 regardless of his nationality.

(4) For the purposes of those sections, it is immaterial whether a person knows that another person is a UN worker.

[This section is printed as amended by the *Crime (International Co-operation) Act* 2003, s.91(1), and Sched. 5, paras 66 and 67.]

Miscellaneous

25–158 Section 7 gives effect to the Schedule (consequential amendments). Section 8 provides that in the Act, "act" includes "omission" and "UN worker" has the meaning given in section 4.

G. TAKING OF HOSTAGES ACT 1982

25–159 This Act implements the International Convention against the Taking of Hostages.

Taking of Hostages Act 1982, ss.1, 2

Hostage-taking

25–160 **1.**—(1) A person, whatever his nationality, who, in the United Kingdom or elsewhere,—

(a) detains any other person ("the hostage"), and

(b) in order to compel a State, international governmental organisation or person to do or abstain from doing any act, threatens to kill, injure or continue to detain the hostage,

commits an offence.

(2) A person guilty of an offence under this Act shall be liable, on conviction on indictment, to imprisonment for life.

An offence contrary to this section is a "Convention offence" within the *Terrorism Act* 2006: see *ante*, §§ 25–142k, 25–142l.

Prosecution of offences

25–161 **2.**—(1) Proceedings for an offence under this Act shall not be instituted—

(a) in England and Wales, except by or with the consent of the Attorney-General; and

(b) in Northern Ireland, except by or with the consent of the Attorney-General for Northern Ireland.

(2) [*Scotland.*]

(3) [*Repealed by* Northern Ireland (Emergency Provisions) Act *1991, Sched. 8.*]

[The next paragraph is § 25–170.]

H. NUCLEAR MATERIAL (OFFENCES) ACT 1983

25–170 The purpose of this Act is to implement the Convention on the Physical Protection of Nuclear Material.

Nuclear Material (Offences) Act 1983, ss.1–3A

Extended scope of certain offences

1.—(1) If a person, whatever his nationality, does outside the United Kingdom, in relation to or by means of nuclear material, any act which, had he done it in any part of the United Kingdom, would have made him guilty of— **25–171**

(a) the offence of murder, manslaughter, culpable homicide, assault to injury, malicious mischief or causing injury, or endangering the life of the lieges, by reckless conduct, or

(b) an offence under section 18 or 20 of the *Offences against the Person Act* 1861 or section 1 of the *Criminal Damage Act* 1971 or Article 3 of the *Criminal Damage (Northern Ireland) Order* 1977 or *section 78 of the* Criminal Justice (Scotland) Act *1980* [section 52 of the *Criminal Law (Consolidation) Act* 1995], or

(c) the offence of theft, embezzlement, robbery, assault with intent to rob, burglary or aggravated burglary, or

(d) the offence of fraud or extortion or an offence under section ... 21 of the *Theft Act* 1968 or section ... 20 of the *Theft Act (Northern Ireland)* 1969,

he shall in any part of the United Kingdom be guilty of such of the offences mentioned in paragraphs (a) to (d) above as are offences of which the act would have made him guilty had he done it in that part of the United Kingdom.

[(1A) If—

(a) a person, whatever his nationality, does outside the United Kingdom an act directed at a nuclear facility, or which interferes with the operation of such a facility,

(b) the act causes death, injury or damage resulting from the emission of ionising radiation or the release of radioactive material, and

(c) had he done that act in any part of the United Kingdom, it would have made him guilty of an offence mentioned in subsection (1)(a) or (b) above,

the person shall in any part of the United Kingdom be guilty of such of the offences mentioned in subsection (1)(a) and (b) as are offences of which the act would have made him guilty had he done it in that part of the United Kingdom.]

(2) *In this section and in section 2 below, "act" includes omission.*

[The words omitted were repealed by the *Fraud Act* 2006, s.14(1) and (3), Sched. 1, para. 20, and Sched. 3. As from a day to be appointed, the words in square brackets in subs. (1)(b) replace the italicised words that precede them, subs. (1A) is inserted and subs. (2) is omitted, by the *CJIA* 2008, s.75(1), and Sched. 17, paras 1 and 2.]

Certain offences contrary to this Act are "Convention offences" within the *Terrorism Act* 2006: see *ante*, §§ 25–142k, 25–142l.

[Increase in penalties for offences committed in relation to nuclear material etc.

1A.—(1) If— **25–171a**

(a) a person is guilty of an offence to which subsection (2), (3) or (4) applies, and

(b) the penalty provided by this subsection would not otherwise apply,

the person shall be liable, on conviction on indictment, to imprisonment for life.

(2) This subsection applies to an offence mentioned in section 1(1)(a) or (b) where the act making the person guilty of the offence was done in England and Wales or Northern Ireland and either—

(a) the act was done in relation to or by means of nuclear material, or

(b) the act—

(i) was directed at a nuclear facility, or interfered with the operation of such a facility, and

(ii) caused death, injury or damage resulting from the emission of ionising radiation or the release of radioactive material.

(3) This subsection applies to an offence mentioned in section 1(1)(c) or (d) where the act making the person guilty of the offence—

(a) was done in England and Wales or Northern Ireland, and

(b) was done in relation to or by means of nuclear material.

(4) This subsection applies to an offence mentioned in section 1(1)(a) to (d) where the offence is an offence in England and Wales or Northern Ireland by virtue of section 1(1) or (1A).]

[Offences relating to damage to environment

25–171b **1B.**—(1) If a person, whatever his nationality, in the United Kingdom or elsewhere contravenes subsection (2) or (3) he is guilty of an offence.

(2) A person contravenes this subsection if without lawful authority—

(a) he receives, holds or deals with nuclear material, and

(b) he does so either—

(i) intending to cause, or for the purpose of enabling another to cause, damage to the environment by means of that material, or

(ii) being reckless as to whether, as a result of his so receiving, holding or dealing with that material, damage would be caused to the environment by means of that material.

(3) A person contravenes this subsection if without lawful authority—

(a) he does an act directed at a nuclear facility, or which interferes with the operation of such a facility, and

(b) he does so either—

(i) intending to cause, or for the purpose of enabling another to cause, damage to the environment by means of the emission of ionising radiation or the release of radioactive material, or

(ii) being reckless as to whether, as a result of his act, damage would be caused to the environment by means of such an emission or release.

(4) A person guilty of an offence under this section shall be liable, on conviction on indictment, to imprisonment for life.]

[Offences of importing or exporting etc. nuclear material: extended jurisdiction

25–171c **1C.**—(1) If a person, whatever his nationality, outside the United Kingdom contravenes subsection (2) below he shall be guilty of an offence.

(2) A person contravenes this subsection if he is knowingly concerned in—

(a) the unlawful export or shipment as stores of nuclear material from one country to another, or

(b) the unlawful import of nuclear material into one country from another.

(3) For the purposes of subsection (2)—

(a) the export or shipment as stores of nuclear material from a country, or

(b) the import of nuclear material into a country,

is unlawful if it is contrary to any prohibition or restriction on the export, shipment as stores or import (as the case may be) of nuclear material having effect under or by virtue of the law of that country.

(4) A statement in a certificate issued by or on behalf of the government of a country outside the United Kingdom to the effect that a particular export, shipment as stores or import of nuclear material is contrary to such a prohibition or restriction having effect under or by virtue of the law of that country, shall be evidence (in Scotland, sufficient evidence) that the export, shipment or import was unlawful for the purposes of subsection (2).

(5) In any proceedings a document purporting to be a certificate of the kind mentioned in subsection (4) above shall be taken to be such a certificate unless the contrary is proved.

(6) A person guilty of an offence under this section shall be liable, on conviction on indictment, to imprisonment for a term not exceeding 14 years.

(7) In this section "country" includes territory.]

[Offences under section 1C: investigations and proceedings etc.

25–171d **1D.**—(1) Where the Commissioners for Her Majesty's Revenue and Customs investigate, or propose to investigate, any matter with a view to determining—

(a) whether there are grounds for believing that an offence under section 1C above has been committed, or

(b) whether a person should be prosecuted for such an offence,

the matter is to be treated as an assigned matter within the meaning of *CEMA* 1979 (see section 1(1) of that Act).

(2) Section 138 of *CEMA* 1979 (provisions as to arrest of persons) applies to a person who has committed, or whom there are reasonable grounds to suspect of having committed, an offence under section 1C above as it applies to a person who has committed, or whom there are reasonable grounds to suspect of having committed, an offence for which he is liable to be arrested under the customs and excise Acts.

(3) Sections 145 to 148 and 150 to 155 of *CEMA* 1979 (provisions as to legal proceedings) apply in relation to an offence under section 1C above, and to the penalty and proceedings for the offence, as they apply in relation to offences, penalties and proceedings under the customs and excise Acts.

(4) In this section—

" *CEMA 1979*" means the *Customs and Excise Management Act* 1979;

"the customs and excise Acts", "shipment" and "stores" have the same meanings as in *CEMA* 1979 (see section 1(1) of that Act).]

[Ss.1A to 1D are inserted, as from a day to be appointed, by the *CJIA* 2008, s.75(1), and Sched. 17, paras 1 and 3.]

Offences involving preparatory acts and threats

2.—(1) *If a person, whatever his nationality, in the United Kingdom or elsewhere contravenes subsection (2), (3) or (4) below he shall be guilty of an offence.* **25–172**

(2) *A person contravenes this subsection if he receives, holds or deals with nuclear material—*

(a) *intending, or for the purpose of enabling another, to do by means of that material an act which is an offence mentioned in paragraph (a) or (b) of subsection (1) of section 1 above; or*

(b) *being reckless as to whether another would so do such an act.*

(3) *A person contravenes this subsection if he—*

(a) *makes to another person a threat that he or any other person will do by means of nuclear material such an act as is mentioned in paragraph (a) of subsection (2) above; and*

(b) *intends that the person to whom the threat is made shall fear that it will be carried out.*

(4) *A person contravenes this subsection if, in order to compel a State, international governmental organisation or person to do, or abstain from doing, any act, he threatens that he or any other person will obtain nuclear material by an act which is an offence mentioned in paragraph (c) of subsection (1) of section 1 above.*

(5) *A person guilty of an offence under this section shall be liable, on conviction on indictment, to imprisonment for life.*

(6) *In subsection (5) above "contemplated act" means,—*

(a) *where the conviction relates to an offence under subsection (2) above, the act intended or as to the doing of which the person convicted was reckless, as the case may be; and*

(b) *where the conviction relates to an offence under subsection (3) or (4) above, the act threatened.*

(7) *In this section references to an act which is an offence mentioned in paragraph (a), (b) or (c) of subsection (1) of section 1 above are references to an act which, by virtue of that subsection or otherwise, is an offence so mentioned.*

(1) If a person, whatever his nationality, in the United Kingdom or elsewhere contravenes subsection (2), (3), (4) or (7) he shall be guilty of an offence.

(2) A person contravenes this subsection if without lawful authority—

(a) he receives, holds or deals with nuclear material, and

(b) he does so either—

(i) intending to cause, or for the purpose of enabling another to cause, relevant injury or damage by means of that material, or

(ii) being reckless as to whether, as a result of his so receiving, holding or dealing with that material, relevant injury or damage would be caused by means of that material.

(3) A person contravenes this subsection if without lawful authority—

(a) he does an act directed at a nuclear facility, or which interferes with the operation of such a facility, and

(b) he does so either—

(i) intending to cause, or for the purpose of enabling another to cause, relevant injury or damage by means of the emission of ionising radiation or the release of radioactive material, or

(ii) being reckless as to whether, as a result of his act, relevant injury or damage would be caused by means of such an emission or release.

(4) A person contravenes this subsection if he—

(a) makes a threat of a kind falling within subsection (5), and
(b) intends that the person to whom the threat is made shall fear that it will be carried out.

(5) A threat falls within this subsection if it is a threat that the person making it or any other person will cause any of the consequences set out in subsection (6) either—
(a) by means of nuclear material, or
(b) by means of the emission of ionising radiation or the release of radioactive material resulting from an act which is directed at a nuclear facility, or which interferes with the operation of such a facility.

(6) The consequences mentioned in subsection (5) are—
(a) relevant injury or damage, or
(b) damage to the environment.

(7) A person contravenes this subsection if, in order to compel a State, international organisation or person to do, or abstain from doing, any act, he threatens that he or any other person will obtain nuclear material by an act which, whether by virtue of section 1(1) above or otherwise, is an offence mentioned in section 1(1)(c) above.

(8) A person guilty of an offence under this section shall be liable, on conviction on indictment, to imprisonment for life.

(9) In this section references to relevant injury or damage are references to death or to injury or damage of a type which constitutes an element of any offence mentioned in section 1(1)(a) or (b) above.]

[Subss. (1)–(9) (in square brackets) are substituted for subss. (1)–(7) (in italics), as from a day to be appointed, by the *CJIA* 2008, s.75(1), and Sched. 17, paras 1 and 4. The original subs. (5) is printed as amended by the *Terrorism Act* 2006, s.14(1) (increase in maximum penalty, but only in relation to offences committed on or after April 13, 2006: s.14(2), and the *Terrorism Act 2006 (Commencement No. 1) Order* 2006 (S.I. 2006 No. 1013)).]

An offence contrary to section 2 is a "Convention offence" within the *Terrorism Act* 2006: see *ante*, §§ 25–142k, 25–142l.

[Inchoate and secondary offences: extended jurisdiction

25–172a **2A.**—(1) If a person, whatever his nationality—
(a) does an act outside the United Kingdom, and
(b) his act, if done in any part of the United Kingdom, would constitute an offence falling within subsection (2),

he shall be guilty in that part of the United Kingdom of the offence.

(2) The offences are—
(a) attempting to commit a nuclear offence;
(b) conspiring to commit a nuclear offence;
(c) inciting the commission of a nuclear offence;
(d) aiding, abetting, counselling or procuring the commission of a nuclear offence.

(3) In subsection (2) a "nuclear offence" means any of the following (wherever committed)—
(a) an offence mentioned in section 1(1)(a) to (d) above (other than a blackmail offence), the commission of which is (or would have been) in relation to or by means of nuclear material;
(b) an offence mentioned in section 1(1)(a) or (b) above, the commission of which involves (or would have involved) an act—
(i) directed at a nuclear facility, or which interferes with the operation of such a facility, and
(ii) which causes death, injury or damage resulting from the emission of ionising radiation or the release of radioactive material;
(c) an offence under section 1B, 1C or 2(1) and (2) or (3) above;
(d) an offence under section 50(2) or (3), 68(2) or 170(1) or (2) of the *Customs and Excise Management Act* 1979 the commission of which is (or would have been) in connection with a prohibition or restriction relating to the exportation, shipment as stores or importation of nuclear material;
(e) for the purposes of subsection (2)(b) to (d)—
(i) a blackmail offence, the commission of which is in relation to or by means of nuclear material;

(ii) an offence under section 2(1) and (4) or (7) above;

(iii) an offence of attempting to commit an offence mentioned in paragraphs (a) to (d).

(4) In subsection (3) "a blackmail offence" means—

(a) an offence under section 21 of the *Theft Act* 1968,

(b) an offence under section 20 of the *Theft Act (Northern Ireland)* 1969, or

(c) an offence of extortion.

(5) In subsection (2)(c) the reference to incitement is—

(a) a reference to incitement under the law of Scotland, or

(b) in relation to any time before the coming into force of Part 2 of the *Serious Crime Act* 2007 (encouraging or assisting crime) in relation to England and Wales or Northern Ireland, a reference to incitement under the common law of England and Wales or (as the case may be) of Northern Ireland.]

[S.2A is inserted, as from a day to be appointed, by the *CJIA* 2008, s.75(1), and Sched. 17, paras 1 and 4.]

Supplemental

3.—(1) Proceedings for an offence which (disregarding the provisions of the *Internationally Protected Persons Act* 1978, the *Suppression of Terrorism Act* 1978, the *United Nations Personnel Act* 1997 and the *Terrorism Act* 2000) would not be an offence apart from the preceding provisions of this Act shall not be begun— **25–173**

(a) in England and Wales, except by or with the consent of the Attorney General; or

(b) [*Northern Ireland*].

(2) [*Scotland.*]

[This section is printed as amended by the *United Nations Personnel Act* 1997, s.7 and Sched., para. 4; and the *Crime (International Co-operation) Act* 2003, s.91(1), and Sched. 5, paras 7 and 8.]

Nuclear Material (Offences) Act 1983, ss.3A, 6 and Sched.

3A. [*Exclusion of activities of armed forces (inserted, as from a day to be appointed, by* CJIA *2008*, s.75(1), *and Sched. 17, paras 1 and 5*.] **25–174**

Material to which the Act applies [Interpretation]

6.—[(A1) This section applies for the purposes of this Act.] **25–175**

(1) References *in this Act* to nuclear material are references to material which, within the meaning of the Convention, is nuclear material used for peaceful purposes.

[(1A) "A nuclear facility" means a facility (including associated buildings and equipment) used for peaceful purposes in which nuclear material is produced, processed, used, handled, stored or disposed of.

(1B) For the purposes of subsections (1) and (1A)—

(a) nuclear material is not used for peaceful purposes if it is used or retained for military purposes, and

(b) a facility is not used for peaceful purposes if it contains any nuclear material which is used or retained for military purposes.]

(2) If in any proceedings a question arises whether any material [or facility] was used for peaceful purposes, a certificate issued by or under the authority of the Secretary of State and stating that it was, or was not, so used at a time specified in the certificate shall be conclusive of that question.

(3) In any proceedings a document purporting to be such a certificate as is mentioned in subsection (2) above shall be taken to be such a certificate unless the contrary is proved.

(4) Paragraphs (a) and (b) of Article 1 of the Convention (which give the definition of "nuclear material" for the purposes of the Convention) are set out in the Schedule to this Act.

(5) *In this section "the Convention" means the Convention on the Physical Protection of Nuclear Material opened for signature at Vienna and New York on 3rd March 1980* ["Act" includes omission].

[(6) "The Convention" means the Convention on the Physical Protection of Nuclear Material and Nuclear Facilities (formerly the Convention on the Physical Protection of Nuclear Material and renamed by virtue of the Amendment adopted at Vienna on 8th July 2005).

(7) "The environment" includes land, air and water and living organisms supported by any of those media.

(8) "Radioactive material" means nuclear material or any other radioactive substance which—

(a) contains nuclides that undergo spontaneous disintegration in a process accompanied by the emission of one or more types of ionising radiation, such as alpha radiation, beta radiation, neutron particles or gamma rays, and

(b) is capable, owing to its radiological or fissile properties, of—

(i) causing bodily injury to a person,

(ii) causing damage or destruction to property,

(iii) endangering a person's life, or

(iv) causing damage to the environment.]

[This section is printed as amended by the *Extradition Act* 1989, s.36(9); and as amended, as from a day to be appointed, by the *CJIA* 2008, s.75(1), and Sched. 17, paras 1 and 6 (insertion of words in square brackets, omission of italicised words in subss. (2) and (5)).]

[The next paragraph is § 25–176.]

SCHEDULE

ARTICLE 1(A) AND (B) OF THE CONVENTION

ARTICLE 1

25–176 For the purposes of this Convention:

(a) "nuclear material" means plutonium except that with isotopic concentration exceeding 80% in the plutonium-238; uranium-233; uranium enriched in the isotopes 235 or 233; uranium containing the mixture of isotopes as occurring in nature other than in the form of ore or ore-residue; any material containing one or more of the foregoing;

(b) "uranium enriched in the isotope 235 or 233" means uranium containing the isotopes 235 or 233 or both in an amount such that the abundance ratio of the sum of these isotopes to the isotope 238 is greater than the ratio of the isotope 235 to the isotope 238 occurring in nature.

I. AVIATION SECURITY ACT 1982

(1) Introduction

25–177 This Act consolidated enactments relating to aviation security; the three most important such Acts were the *Hijacking Act* 1971, the *Protection of Aircraft Act* 1973 and the *Policing of Airports Act* 1974, all three of which were repealed in their entirety. Part I (ss.1–9) relates to offences against the safety of aircraft; Part II (ss.10–24A) contains provisions for the protection of aircraft, aerodromes and air navigation installations against acts of violence; Part III (ss.24B–31) relates to the policing of airports; Part IV (ss.32–36) relates to the aviation security fund; and Part V contains miscellaneous and general provisions.

(2) Offences against the safety of aircraft, etc.

Aviation Security Act 1982, s.1

Hijacking

25–178 **1.**—(1) A person on board an aircraft in flight who unlawfully, by the use of force or by threats of any kind, seizes the aircraft or exercises control of it commits the offence of hijacking, whatever his nationality, whatever the State in which the aircraft is registered and whether the aircraft is in the United Kingdom or elsewhere, but subject to subsection (2) below.

(2) If—

(a) the aircraft is used in military, customs or police service, or

(b) both the place of take-off and the place of landing are in the territory of the State in which the aircraft is registered, subsection (1) above shall not apply unless—

(i) the person seizing or exercising control of the aircraft is a United Kingdom national; or

(ii) his act is committed in the United Kingdom; or

(iii) the aircraft is registered in the United Kingdom or is used in the military or customs service of the United Kingdom or in the service of any police force in the United Kingdom.

(3) A person who commits the offence of hijacking shall be liable, on conviction on indictment, to imprisonment for life.

(4) If the Secretary of State by order made by statutory instrument declares—

(a) that any two or more States named in the order have established an organisation or agency which operates aircraft; and

(b) that one of those States has been designated as exercising, for aircraft so operated, the powers of the State of registration,

the State declared under paragraph (b) of this subsection shall be deemed for the purposes of this section to be the State in which any aircraft so operated is registered; but in relation to such an aircraft subsection (2)(b) above shall have effect as if it referred to the territory of any one of the States named in the order.

(5) For the purposes of this section the territorial waters of any State shall be treated as part of its territory.

An offence contrary to this section is a "Convention offence" within the *Terrorism Act* 2006: see *ante*, §§ 25–142k, 25–142l.

The fact that the commander of the aircraft may have been collaborating with the defendants does not preclude a conviction under this provision provided the defendants are proved to have threatened or used force on the remainder of the crew: *R. v. Membar* [1983] Crim.L.R. 618, CA.

Necessity may be a defence to hijacking: *R. v. Abdul-Hussain* [1999] Crim.L.R. 570, CA; *R. v. Safi (Ali Ahmed)* [2004] 1 Cr.App.R. 14, CA. For the defence of necessity generally, see *ante*, §§ 17–127 *et seq.* As to the suggestion in *R. v. Abdul-Hussain* that the defence should be left to the jury even though there was no immediate threat of the evil to be avoided (in the sense of "It's now or never"), see the doubts expressed by the House of Lords in *R. v. Z.* [2005] 2 A.C. 467 (*ante*, §§ 17–122, 17–126).

Aviation Security Act 1982, ss.2–4

Destroying, damaging or endangering safety of aircraft

2.—(1) It shall, subject to subsection (4) below, be an offence for any person unlawfully and intentionally— **25–179**

(a) to destroy an aircraft in service or so to damage such an aircraft as to render it incapable of flight or as to be likely to endanger its safety in flight; or

(b) to commit on board an aircraft in flight any act of violence which is likely to endanger the safety of the aircraft.

(2) It shall also, subject to subsection (4) below, be an offence for any person unlawfully and intentionally to place, or cause to be placed, on an aircraft in service any device or substance which is likely to destroy the aircraft, or is likely so to damage it, as to render it incapable of flight or as to be likely to endanger its safety in flight; but nothing in this subsection shall be construed as limiting the circumstances in which the commission of any act—

(a) may constitute an offence under subsection (1) above, or

(b) may constitute attempting or conspiring to commit, or aiding, abetting, counselling or procuring, or being art and part in, the commission of such an offence.

(3) Except as provided by subsection (4) below, subsections (1) and (2) above shall apply whether any such act as is therein mentioned is committed in the United Kingdom or elsewhere, whatever the nationality of the person committing the act and whatever the State in which the aircraft is registered.

(4) Subsections (1) and (2) above shall not apply to any act committed in relation to an aircraft used in military, customs or police service unless—

(a) the act is committed in the United Kingdom, or

(b) where the act is committed outside the United Kingdom, the person committing it is a United Kingdom national.

(5) A person who commits an offence under this section shall be liable, on conviction on indictment, to imprisonment for life.

(6) In this section "unlawfully"—

(a) in relation to the commission of an act in the United Kingdom, means so as (apart from this Act) to constitute an offence under the law of the part of the United Kingdom in which the act is committed, and

(b) in relation to the commission of an act outside the United Kingdom, means so that the commission of the act would (apart from this Act) have been an offence under the law of England and Wales if it had been committed in England and Wales or of Scotland if it had been committed in Scotland.

(7) In this section "act of violence" means—

(a) any act done in the United Kingdom which constitutes the offence of murder, attempted murder, manslaughter, culpable homicide or assault or an offence under section 18, 20, 21, 22, 23, 24, 28 or 29 of the *Offences against the Person Act* 1861 or under section 2 of the *Explosive Substances Act* 1883, and

(b) any act done outside the United Kingdom which, if done in the United Kingdom, would constitute such an offence as is mentioned in paragraph (a) above.

An offence contrary to this section is a "Convention offence" within the *Terrorism Act* 2006: see *ante*, §§ 25–142k, 25–142l.

Other acts endangering or likely to endanger safety of aircraft

25–180 **3.**—(1) It shall, subject to subsections (5) and (6) below, be an offence for any person unlawfully and intentionally to destroy or damage any property to which this subsection applies, or to interfere with the operation of any such property, where the destruction, damage or interference is likely to endanger the safety of aircraft in flight.

(2) Subsection (1) above applies to any property used for the provision of air navigation facilities, including any land, building or ship so used, and including any apparatus or equipment so used, whether it is on board an aircraft or elsewhere.

(3) It shall also, subject to subsections (4) and (5) below, be an offence for any person intentionally to communicate any information which is false, misleading or deceptive in a material particular, where the communication of the information endangers the safety of an aircraft in flight or is likely to endanger the safety of aircraft in flight.

(4) It shall be a defence for a person charged with an offence under subsection (3) above to prove—

(a) that he believed, and had reasonable grounds for believing, that the information was true; or

(b) that, when he communicated the information, he was lawfully employed to perform duties which consisted of or included the communication of information and that he communicated the information in good faith in the performance of those duties.

(5) Subsections (1) and (3) above shall not apply to the commission of any act unless either the act is committed in the United Kingdom, or, where it is committed outside the United Kingdom—

(a) the person committing it is a United Kingdom national; or

(b) the commission of the act endangers or is likely to endanger the safety in flight of a civil aircraft registered in the United Kingdom or chartered by demise to a lessee whose principal place of business, or (if he has no place of business) whose permanent residence, is in the United Kingdom; or

(c) the act is committed on board a civil aircraft which is so registered or so chartered; or

(d) the act is committed on board a civil aircraft which lands in the United Kingdom with the person who committed the act still on board.

(6) Subsection (1) above shall also not apply to any act committed outside the United Kingdom and so committed in relation to property which is situated outside the United Kingdom and is not used for the provision of air navigation facilities in connection with international air navigation, unless the person committing the act is a United Kingdom national.

(7) [*Identical to s.2(5), ante, § 25–179.*]

(8) In this section "civil aircraft" means any aircraft other than an aircraft used in military, customs or police service and "unlawfully" has the same meaning as in section 2 of this Act.

An offence contrary to this section is a "Convention offence" within the *Terrorism Act* 2006: see *ante*, §§ 25–142k, 25–142l.

Offences in relation to certain dangerous articles

4.—(1) It shall be an offence for any person without lawful authority or reasonable excuse (the proof of which shall lie on him) to have with him— **25–181**

(a) in any aircraft registered in the United Kingdom, whether at a time when the aircraft is in the United Kingdom or not, or

(b) in any other aircraft at a time when it is in, or in flight over, the United Kingdom, or

(c) in any part of an aerodrome in the United Kingdom, or

(d) in any air navigation installation in the United Kingdom which does not form part of an aerodrome,

any article to which this section applies.

(2) This section applies to the following articles, that is to say—

(a) any firearm, or any article having the appearance of being a firearm, whether capable of being discharged or not;

(b) any explosive, any article manufactured or adapted (whether in the form of a bomb, grenade or otherwise) so as to have the appearance of being an explosive, whether it is capable of producing a practical effect by explosion or not, or any article marked or labelled so as to indicate that it is or contains an explosive; and

(c) any article (not falling within either of the preceding paragraphs) made or adapted for use for causing injury to or incapacitating a person or for destroying or damaging property, or intended by the person having it with him for such use, whether by him or by any other person.

(3) For the purposes of this section a person who is for the time being in an aircraft, or in part of an aerodrome, shall be treated as having with him in the aircraft, or in that part of the aerodrome, as the case may be, an article to which this section applies if—

(a) where he is in an aircraft, the article, or an article in which it is contained, is in the aircraft and has been caused (whether by him or by any other person) to be brought there as being, or as forming part of, his baggage on a flight in the aircraft or has been caused by him to be brought there as being, or as forming part of, any other property to be carried on such a flight, or

(b) where he is in part of an aerodrome (otherwise than in an aircraft), the article, or an article in which it is contained, is in that or any other part of the aerodrome and has been caused (whether by him or by any other person) to be brought into the aerodrome as being, or as forming part of, his baggage on a flight from that aerodrome or has been caused by him to be brought there as being, or as forming part of, any other property to be carried on such a flight on which he is also to be carried,

notwithstanding that the circumstances may be such that (apart from this subsection) he would not be regarded as having the article with him in the aircraft or in a part of the aerodrome, as the case may be.

(4) A person guilty of an offence under this section shall be liable—

(a) on summary conviction, to a fine not exceeding the statutory maximum or to imprisonment for a term not exceeding three months or to both;

(b) on conviction on indictment, to a fine or to imprisonment for a term not exceeding five years or to both.

(5) Nothing in subsection (3) above shall be construed as limiting the circumstances in which a person would, apart from that subsection, be regarded as having an article with him as mentioned in subsection (1) above.

The "statutory maximum" means the prescribed sum within the meaning of section 32 of the *MCA* 1980, *ante*, § 1–75aa: *Interpretation Act* 1978, Sched. 1 (Appendix B–28).

Aviation Security Act 1982, ss.5–8

5. [*Jurisdiction of courts in respect of air piracy*: *see* ante, *§ 25–44*.] **25–182**

Ancillary offences

6.—(1) Without prejudice to section 92 of the *Civil Aviation Act* 1982 (application of criminal law to aircraft) or to section 2(1)(b) of this Act, where a person (of whatever nationality) does on board any aircraft (wherever registered) and while outside the United Kingdom any act which, if done in the United Kingdom would constitute the offence of murder, attempted murder, manslaughter, culpable homicide or assault or an offence under section 18, 20, 21, 22, 23, **25–183**

28 or 29 of the *Offences against the Person Act* 1861 or section 2 of the *Explosive Substances Act* 1883, his act shall constitute that offence if it is done in connection with the offence of hijacking committed or attempted by him on board that aircraft.

(2) It shall be an offence for any person in the United Kingdom to induce or assist the commission outside the United Kingdom of any act which—

(a) would, but for subsection (2) of section 1 of this Act, be an offence under that section; or

(b) would, but for subsection (4) of section 2 of this Act, be an offence under that section; or

(c) would, but for subsection (5) or (6) of section 3 of this Act, be an offence under that section.

(3) A person who commits an offence under subsection (2) above shall be liable, on conviction on indictment, to imprisonment for life.

(4) Subsection (2) above shall have effect without prejudice to the operation, in relation to any offence under section 1, 2 or 3 of this Act—

(a) in England and Wales, or in Northern Ireland, of section 8 of the *Accessories and Abettors Act* 1861; or

(b) in Scotland, of any rule of law relating to art and part guilt.

As to section 92 of the *Civil Aviation Act* 1982, see *ante*, § 2–49.

An offence contrary to section 6(2) is a "Convention offence" within the *Terrorism Act* 2006: see *ante*, §§ 25–142k, 25–142l.

Powers exercisable on suspicion of intended offence under Part I

25–184 **7.**—(1) Where a constable has reasonable cause to suspect that a person about to embark on an aircraft in the United Kingdom, or a person on board such an aircraft, intends to commit, in relation to the aircraft, an offence under any of the preceding provisions of this Part of this Act (other than section 4), the constable may prohibit him from travelling on board the aircraft, and for the purpose of enforcing that prohibition the constable—

(a) may prevent him from embarking on the aircraft or, as the case may be, may remove him from the aircraft, and

(b) may arrest him without warrant and detain him for so long as may be necessary for that purpose.

(2) Any person who intentionally obstructs ... a person acting in the exercise of a power conferred on him by subsection (1) above shall be guilty of an offence and liable—

(a) on summary conviction, to a fine not exceeding the statutory maximum;

(b) on conviction on indictment, to a fine or to imprisonment for a term not exceeding two years or to both.

(3) Subsection (1) above shall have effect without prejudice to the operation in relation to any offence under this Act—

(a) in England and Wales, of section 2 of the *Criminal Law Act* 1967 (which confers power to arrest without warrant) or of section 3 of that Act (use of force in making arrest etc.); or

(b) [*Scotland*]; or

(c) [*Northern Ireland*].

[This section is printed as amended and repealed in part by the *Aviation and Maritime Security Act* 1990, s.8 and Sched.1, para.1.]

Section 2 of the *CLA* 1967 has been repealed by the *PACE Act* 1984, s.119(2), and Sched. 7, and the power of arrest without warrant conferred by section 7(1) has ceased to have effect by virtue of section 26(1) of the 1984 Act. For the current powers of arrest without warrant, see sections 24 and 24A of the 1984 Act, *ante*, §§ 15–161 *et seq.*

As to the "statutory maximum", see *ante*, § 25–181.

Prosecution of offences and proceedings

25–185 **8.**—(1) Proceedings for an offence under any of the preceding provisions of this Part of this Act (other than sections 4 and 7) shall not be instituted—

(a) in England and Wales, except by, or with the consent of, the Attorney-General; and

(b) [*Northern Ireland*].

(2) [*Scotland.*]

As to when proceedings are "instituted", see *R. v. Elliott*, 81 Cr.App.R. 115, CA (*ante*, § 1–248), decided in relation to an almost identically worded provision in section 63(1) of the *Administration of Justice Act* 1982.

[The next paragraph is § 25–193.]

(3) Miscellaneous and general

Aviation Security Act 1982, ss.37, 38

Offences by bodies corporate

37.—(1) Where an offence under this Act (including any provision of Part II as applied by regulations made under section 21F of this Act) or under regulations made under section 21G of this Act has been committed by a body corporate and is proved to have been committed with the consent or connivance of, or to be attributable to any neglect on the part of, any director, manager, secretary or other similar officer of the body corporate, or any person who was purporting to act in any such capacity, he as well as the body corporate shall be guilty of that offence and shall be liable to be proceeded against and punished accordingly. **25–193**

(2) Where the affairs of a body corporate are managed by its members, subsection (1) above shall apply in relation to the acts and defaults of a member in connection with his functions of management as if he were a director of the body corporate.

[This section is printed as amended by the *Aviation and Maritime Security Act* 1990, s.8(1), and Sched. 1, para. 18.]

The only regulations to have been made under either section 21F or 21G by October 1, 2008, are the *Aviation Security (Air Cargo Agents) Regulations* 1993 (S.I. 1993 No. 1073), which were made under section 21F. Regulation 11 extends the provisions of Part II of the Act to air cargo agents on the list of security approved air cargo agents maintained by the Secretary of State pursuant to regulation 3.

In connection with subsection (1), see *R. v. Boal* [1992] 1 Q.B. 591, 95 Cr.App.R. 272, CA (*post*, § 30–103).

Interpretation, etc.

38.—(1) In this Act, except in so far as the context otherwise requires— **25–194**

"aerodrome" means the aggregate of the land, buildings and works comprised in an aerodrome within the meaning of the *Civil Aviation Act* 1982 and (if and so far as not comprised in an aerodrome as defined in that Act) any land, building or works situated within the boundaries of an area designated, by an order made by the Secretary of State which is for the time being in force, as constituting the area of an aerodrome for the purposes of this Act;

"air navigation installation" means any building, works, apparatus or equipment used wholly or mainly for the purpose of assisting air traffic control or as an aid to air navigation, together with any land contiguous or adjacent to any such building, works, apparatus or equipment and used wholly or mainly for purposes connected therewith;

"aircraft registered or operating in the United Kingdom" means any aircraft which is either—

(a) an aircraft registered in the United Kingdom, or

(b) an aircraft not so registered which is for the time being allocated for use on flights which (otherwise than in exceptional circumstances) include landing at or taking off from one or more aerodromes in the United Kingdom;

"article" includes any substance, whether in solid or liquid form or in the form of a gas or vapour;

"constable" includes any person having the powers and privileges of a constable;

"explosive" means any article manufactured for the purpose of producing a practical effect by explosion, or intended for that purpose by a person having the article with him;

"firearm" includes an airgun or air pistol;

"manager", in relation to an aerodrome, means the person (whether the Civil Aviation Authority, a local authority or any other person) by whom the aerodrome is managed;

"military service" includes naval and air force service;

"measures" (without prejudice to the generality of that expression) includes the construction, execution, alteration, demolition or removal of buildings or other works and also includes the institution or modification, and the supervision and enforcement, of any practice or procedure;

"operator" has the same meaning as in the *Civil Aviation Act* 1982;

"property" includes any land, buildings or works, any aircraft or vehicle and any baggage, cargo or other article of any description;

…

"United Kingdom national" means an individual who is—

(a) a British citizen, a British overseas territories citizen, a British National (Overseas) or a British Overseas citizen;

(b) a person who under the *British Nationality Act* 1981 is a British subject; or

(c) a British protected person (within the meaning of that Act).

25–195 (2) For the purposes of this Act—

(a) in the case of an air navigation installation provided by, or used wholly or mainly by, the Civil Aviation Authority, that Authority, and

(b) in the case of any other air navigation installation, the manager of an aerodrome by whom it is provided, or by whom it is wholly or mainly used,

shall be taken to be the authority responsible for that air navigation installation.

(3) For the purposes of this Act—

(a) the period during which an aircraft is in flight shall be deemed to include any period from the moment when all its external doors are closed following embarkation until the moment when any such door is opened for disembarkation, and, in the case of a forced landing, any period until the competent authorities take over responsibility for the aircraft and for persons and property on board; and

(b) an aircraft shall be taken to be in service during the whole of the period which begins with the pre-flight preparation of the aircraft for a flight and ends 24 hours after the aircraft lands having completed that flight, and also at any time (not falling within that period) while, in accordance with the preceding paragraph, the aircraft is in flight,

and anything done on board an aircraft while in flight over any part of the United Kingdom shall be treated as done in that part of the United Kingdom.

(4) For the purposes of this Act the territorial waters adjacent to any part of the United Kingdom shall be treated as included in that part of the United Kingdom.

(5) [*Order under subsection (1) to be made by statutory instrument.*]

(6) [*Revocation/ variation of directions under the Act.*]

(7) Subject to section 18 of the *Interpretation Act* 1978 (which relates to offences under two or more laws), Part I of this Act shall not be construed as—

(a) conferring a right of action in any civil proceedings in respect of any contravention of this Act, or

(b) derogating from any right of action or other remedy (whether civil or criminal) in proceedings instituted otherwise than under this Act.

(8) [*References to enactments to include Northern Ireland enactments.*]

25–196 [This section is printed as amended and repealed in part by the *Fines and Penalties (Northern Ireland) Order* 1984 (S.I. 1984 No. 703); the *Airports Act* 1986, Sched. 6; the *Hong Kong (British Nationality) Order* 1986 (S.I. 1986 No. 948); the *Aviation and Maritime Security Act* 1990, s.53(2) and Sched. 4; the *Statute Law (Repeals) Act* 1993, Sched. 1, Pt XIV; and the *British Overseas Territories Act* 2002, s.2.]

The prescribed sum is currently £5,000: see section 32(9) of the *MCA* 1980, *ante*, § 1–75aa. The interpretation section in the *Civil Aviation Act* 1982 (see the definitions of "aerodrome" and "operator") is section 105.

Aviation Security Act 1982, s.39

Extension of Act outside United Kingdom

25–197 **39.**—(2) Subsection 4 of the *Merchant Shipping and Maritime Security Act* 1997 (power to extend provisions about piracy to Isle of Man, Channel Islands and colonies) shall apply to section 5 of this Act as it applies to the provisions mentioned in that subsection.

(3) Her Majesty may by Order in Council make provision for extending any of the provisions of this Act (other than the provisions to which subsection (1) or (2) above applies and the provisions of Part III) with such exceptions, adaptations or modifications as may be specified in the Order, to any of the Channel Islands, the Isle of Man, any colony …

(4) Except in pursuance of subsection (1) … or (3) above, the provisions of this Act and, in particular, the repeal of the provisions which those subsections re-enact do not affect the law of any country or territory outside the United Kingdom.

[This section is printed as repealed in part by the *Extradition Act* 1989, s.37(1) and Sched. 2; the *Aviation and Maritime Security Act* 1990, s.53(2) and Sched. 4; and the *Merchant Shipping and Maritime Security Act* 1997, s.26(5) and Sched. 7.]

For a full list of Orders in Council made, or taking effect as if made (*Interpretation Act* 1978, s.17(2)(b), Appendix B–17), under this section, see *Halsbury's Statutes*, 4th ed., Vol. 4 (2004 reissue), p. 391.

J. AVIATION AND MARITIME SECURITY ACT 1990

(1) Introduction

The purpose of this Act was to give effect to the Protocol for the Suppression of Unlawful Acts of Violence at Airports Serving International Civil Aviation which supplements the Convention for the Suppression of Unlawful Acts against the Safety of Civil Aviation; to make further provision with respect to aviation security and civil aviation; to give effect to the Convention for the Suppression of Unlawful Acts against the Safety of Maritime Navigation and to the Protocol for the Suppression of Unlawful Acts against the Safety of Fixed Platforms Located on the Continental Shelf which supplements that Convention; and to make other provision for the protection of ships and harbour areas against acts of violence. **25–198**

Part I (ss.1–8) relates to aviation security. Apart from section 1 (*post*), it consists of a series of amendments to the *Aviation Security Act* 1982 (*ante*, §§ 25–177 *et seq*.). Part II (ss.9–17) creates a series of offences relating to the safety of ships and fixed platforms (*post*, §§ 25–201 *et seq*.). Part III (ss.18–46) mirrors Part II of the 1982 Act, and contains a range of provisions for the protection of ships and harbour areas against acts of violence.

(2) Aviation security

Aviation and Maritime Security Act 1990, s.1

Endangering safety at aerodromes

1.—(1) It is an offence for any person by means of any device, substance or weapon intentionally to commit at an aerodrome serving international civil aviation any act of violence which— **25–199**

(a) causes or is likely to cause death or serious personal injury, and

(b) endangers or is likely to endanger the safe operation of the aerodrome or the safety of persons at the aerodrome.

(2) It is also, subject to subsection (4) below, an offence for any person by means of any device, substance or weapon unlawfully and intentionally—

(a) to destroy or seriously to damage—

(i) property used for the provision of any facilities at an aerodrome serving international civil aviation (including any apparatus or equipment so used), or

(ii) any aircraft which is at such an aerodrome but is not in service, or

(b) to disrupt the services of such an aerodrome,

in such a way as to endanger or be likely to endanger the safe operation of the aerodrome or the safety of persons at the aerodrome.

(3) Except as provided by subsection (4) below, subsections (1) and (2) above apply whether any such act as is referred to in those subsections is committed in the United Kingdom or elsewhere and whatever the nationality of the person committing the act.

(4) Subsection (2)(a)(ii) above does not apply to any act committed in relation to an aircraft used in military, customs or police service unless—

(a) the act is committed in the United Kingdom, or

(b) where the act is committed outside the United Kingdom, the person committing it is a United Kingdom national.

(5) A person who commits an offence under this section is liable on conviction on indictment to imprisonment for life. **25–200**

(6) Sections 38(3)(b) (period during which aircraft in service) and 38(4) (territorial

waters) of the *Aviation Security Act* 1982 apply for the purposes of this section as they apply for the purposes of that Act; and the references in section 38(7) of that Act (other proceedings) to Part I of that Act and to that Act include references to this section.

(7) Proceedings for an offence under this section shall not be instituted—

(a) in England and Wales, except by, or with the consent of, the Attorney General, and

(b) in Northern Ireland, except by, or with the consent of, the Attorney General for Northern Ireland.

(8) [*Scotland.*]

(9) In this section—

"act of violence" means—

(a), (b) [*identical to paras (a), (b) of s.2(7) of the* Aviation Security Act *1982*, ante, *§ 25–179*];

"aerodrome" has the same meaning as in the *Civil Aviation Act* 1982;

"military service" and "United Kingdom national" have the same meaning as in the *Aviation Security Act* 1982; and

"unlawfully"—

(a) in relation to the commission of an act in the United Kingdom, means so as (apart from this section) to constitute an offence under the law of the part of the United Kingdom in which the act is committed, and

(b) in relation to the commission of an act outside the United Kingdom, means so that the commission of the act would (apart from this section) have been an offence under the law of England and Wales if it had been committed in England and Wales or of Scotland if it had been committed in Scotland.

For the definition of "aerodrome" in the *Civil Aviation Act* 1982, see s.105 thereof. The definitions of "military service" and "United Kingdom national" in the *Aviation Security Act* 1982 are contained in section 38(1) thereof. For section 38, see *ante*, §§ 25–194 *et seq.*

An offence contrary to this section is a "Convention offence" within the *Terrorism Act* 2006: see *ante*, §§ 25–142k, 25–142l.

For an example of a sentence imposed for an offence contrary to section 1(2)(b), see *R. v. Lees* [2003] 2 Cr.App.R.(S.) 47, CA.

(3) Offences against the safety of ships and fixed platforms

Aviation and Maritime Security Act 1990, ss.9–14

Hijacking of ships

25–201 **9.**—(1) A person who unlawfully, by the use of force or by threats of any kind, seizes a ship or exercises control of it, commits the offence of hijacking a ship, whatever his nationality and whether the ship is in the United Kingdom or elsewhere, but subject to subsection (2) below.

(2) Subsection (1) above does not apply in relation to a warship or any other ship used as a naval auxiliary or in customs or police service unless—

(a) the person seizing or exercising control of the ship is a United Kingdom national, or

(b) his act is committed in the United Kingdom, or

(c) the ship is used in the naval or customs service of the United Kingdom or in the service of any police force in the United Kingdom.

(3) A person guilty of the offence of hijacking a ship is liable on conviction on indictment to imprisonment for life.

Seizing or exercising control of fixed platforms

25–202 **10.**—(1) A person who unlawfully, by the use of force or by threats of any kind, seizes a fixed platform or exercises control of it, commits an offence, whatever his nationality and whether the fixed platform is in the United Kingdom or elsewhere.

(2) A person guilty of an offence under this section is liable on conviction on indictment to imprisonment for life.

Destroying ships or fixed platforms or endangering their safety

25–203 **11.**—(1) Subject to subsection (5) below, a person commits an offence if he unlawfully and intentionally—

(a) destroys a ship or a fixed platform,

(b) damages a ship, its cargo or a fixed platform so as to endanger, or to be likely to endanger, the safe navigation of the ship, or as the case may be, the safety of the platform, or

(c) commits on board a ship or on a fixed platform an act of violence which is likely to endanger the safe navigation of the ship, or as the case may be, the safety of the platform.

(2) Subject to subsection (5) below, a person commits an offence if he unlawfully and intentionally places, or causes to be placed, on a ship or fixed platform any device or substance which—

(a) in the case of a ship, is likely to destroy the ship or is likely so to damage it or its cargo as to endanger its safe navigation, or

(b) in the case of a fixed platform, is likely to destroy the fixed platform or so to damage it as to endanger its safety.

(3) Nothing in subsection (2) above is to be construed as limiting the circumstances in which the commission of any act—

(a) may constitute an offence under subsection (1) above, or

(b) may constitute attempting or conspiring to commit, or aiding, abetting, counselling, procuring or inciting, or being art and part in, the commission of such an offence.

(4) Except as provided by subsection (5) below, subsections (1) and (2) above apply whether any such act as is mentioned in those subsections is committed in the United Kingdom or elsewhere and whatever the nationality of the person committing the act.

(5) Subsections (1) and (2) above do not apply in relation to any act committed in relation to a warship or any other ship used as a naval auxiliary or in customs or police service unless—

(a) the person committing the act is a United Kingdom national, or

(b), (c) [*identical to paras (b), (c) of section 9(2)*, ante].

(6) [*Identical to s.10(2)*, ante.]

(7) [*Definitions for the purposes of the section of "act of violence" and "unlawfully" in identical terms to the definitions in s.2(6) and (7) of the* Aviation Security Act *1982*, ante, *§ 25–179*.]

The reference to the common law offence of incitement in subsection (3)(b) has effect as a reference to the offences under the *SCA* 2007, Pt 2: 2007 Act, s.63(1), and Sched. 6, para. 18(a).

Other acts endangering or likely to endanger safe navigation

12.—(1) Subject to subsection (6) below, it is an offence for any person unlawfully and intentionally— **25–204**

(a) to destroy or damage any property to which this subsection applies, or

(b) seriously to interfere with the operation of any such property,

where the destruction, damage or interference is likely to endanger the safe navigation of any ship.

(2) Subsection (1) above applies to any property used for the provision of maritime navigation facilities, including any land, building or ship so used, and including any apparatus or equipment so used, whether it is on board a ship or elsewhere.

(3) Subject to subsection (6) below, it is also an offence for any person intentionally to communicate any information which he knows to be false in a material particular, where the communication of the information endangers the safe navigation of any ship.

(4) It is a defence for a person charged with an offence under subsection (3) above to prove that, when he communicated the information, he was lawfully employed to perform duties which consisted of or included the communication of information and that he communicated the information in good faith in performance of those duties.

(5) [*Identical to s.11(4)*, ante, *save that "(6)" and "(3)" replace "(5)" and "(2)" respectively*.]

(6) For the purposes of subsections (1) and (3) above any danger, or likelihood of danger, to the safe navigation of a warship or any other ship used as a naval auxiliary or in customs or police service is to be disregarded unless—

(a)–(c) [*identical to paras (a)–(c) of s.11(5)*, ante].

(7) [*Identical to s.10(2)*, ante.]

(8) In this section "unlawfully" has the same meaning as in section 11 of this Act.

Offences involving threats

25–205 **13.**—(1) A person commits an offence if—

(a) in order to compel any other person to do or abstain from doing any act, he threatens that he or some other person will do in relation to any ship or fixed platform an act which is an offence by virtue of section 11(1) of this Act, and

(b) the making of that threat is likely to endanger the safe navigation of the ship or, as the case may be, the safety of the fixed platform.

(2) Subject to subsection (4) below, a person commits an offence if—

(a) in order to compel any other person to do or abstain from doing any act, he threatens that he or some other person will do an act which is an offence by virtue of section 12(1) of this Act, and

(b) the making of that threat is likely to endanger the safe navigation of any ship.

(3) [*Identical to s.11(4),* ante, *save that "(4)" replaces "(5)".*]

(4) Section 12(6) of this Act applies for the purposes of subsection (2)(b) above as it applies for the purposes of section 12(1) and (3) of this Act.

(5) [*Identical to s.10(2),* ante.]

Ancillary offences

25–206 **14.**—(1) Where a person (of whatever nationality) does outside the United Kingdom any act which, if done in the United Kingdom, would constitute an offence falling within subsection (2) below, his act shall constitute that offence if it is done in connection with an offence under section 9, 10, 11 or 12 of this Act committed or attempted by him.

(2) The offences falling within this subsection are murder, attempted murder, manslaughter, culpable homicide and assault and offences under sections 18, 20, 21, 22, 23, 28 and 29 of the *Offences against the Person Act* 1861 and section 2 of the *Explosive Substances Act* 1883.

(3) Subsection (1) above has effect without prejudice to section 281 or 282 of the *Merchant Shipping Act* 1995 (offences committed on board British ships or by British seamen) or section 10 of the *Petroleum Act* 1998 (application of criminal law to offshore installations).

(4) It is an offence for any person in the United Kingdom to induce or assist the commission outside the United Kingdom of any act which—

(a) would, but for subsection (2) of section 9 of this Act, be an offence under that section, or

(b) would, but for subsection (5) of section 11 of this Act, be an offence under that section, or

(c) would, but for subsection (6) of section 12 of this Act, be an offence under that section, or

(d) would, but for subsection (4) of section 13 of this Act, be an offence under that section.

(5) A person who commits an offence under subsection (4) above is liable on conviction on indictment to imprisonment for life.

(6) Subsection (4) above has effect without prejudice to the operation, in relation to any offence under section 9, 11, 12 or 13 of this Act—

(a) in England and Wales, or in Northern Ireland, of section 8 of the *Accessories and Abettors Act* 1861, or

(b) in Scotland, of any rule of law relating to art and part guilt.

[This section is printed as amended by the *Merchant Shipping Act* 1995, Sched. 14; and the *Petroleum Act* 1998, Sched. 4, para. 29.]

For sections 281 and 282 of the *Merchant Shipping Act* 1995, see *ante*, §§ 2–65, 2–68; for section 10 of the *Petroleum Act* 1998, see *ante*, § 2–77; and for section 8 of the *Accessories and Abettors Act* 1861, see *ante*, § 18–2.

Offences contrary to sections 9 to 14 are "Convention offences" within the *Terrorism Act* 2006: see *ante*, §§ 25–142k, 25–142l.

Aviation and Maritime Security Act 1990, s.15(1)–(5), (8)

Master's power of delivery

25–207 **15.**—(1) The provisions of this section shall have effect for the purposes of any proceedings before any court in the United Kingdom.

(2) If the master of a ship, wherever that ship may be, and whatever the State (if any) in which it may be registered, has reasonable grounds to believe that any person on board the ship has—

(a) committed any offence under section 9, 11, 12 or 13 of this Act,

(b) attempted to commit such an offence, or

(c) aided, abetted, counselled, procured or incited, or been art and part in, the commission of such an offence,

in relation to any ship other than a warship or other ship used as a naval auxiliary or in customs or police service, he may deliver that person to an appropriate officer in the United Kingdom or any other Convention country.

(3) Where the master of a ship intends to deliver any person in the United Kingdom or any other Convention country in accordance with subsection (2) above he shall give notification to an appropriate officer in that country—

(a) of his intention to deliver that person to an appropriate officer in that country; and

(b) of his reasons for intending to do so.

(4) Any notification under subsection (3) above must be given—

(a) before the ship in question has entered the territorial sea of the country concerned; or

(b) if in the circumstances it is not reasonably practicable to comply with paragraph (a) above, as soon as reasonably practicable after the ship has entered that territorial sea.

(5) Where the master of a ship delivers any person to an appropriate officer in any country under subsection (2) above he shall— **25–208**

(a) make to an appropriate officer in that country such oral or written statements relating to the alleged offence as that officer may reasonably require; and

(b) deliver to an appropriate officer in that country such other evidence relating to the alleged offence as is in the master's possession.

(8) In this section—

"appropriate officer" means—

(a) in relation to the United Kingdom, a constable or immigration officer, and

(b) in relation to any other Convention country, an officer having functions corresponding to the functions in the United Kingdom either of a constable or of an immigration officer,

"Convention country" means a country in which the Convention for the Suppression of Unlawful Acts against the Safety of Maritime Navigation, which was signed at Rome on 10th March 1988, is for the time being in force; and Her Majesty may by Order in Council certify that any country specified in the Order is for the time being a Convention country and any such Order in Council for the time being in force shall be conclusive evidence that the country in question is for the time being a Convention country, and

"master" has the same meaning as in the *Merchant Shipping Act* 1995.

[Subs. (8) is printed as amended by the *Merchant Shipping Act* 1995, Sched. 14. The reference to the common law offence of incitement in subs. (2)(c) has effect as a reference to the offences under the *SCA* 2007, Pt 2: 2007 Act, s.63(1), and Sched. 6, para. 18(b).]

Subsection (6) makes it a summary offence for the master of a ship to fail, without reasonable excuse, to comply with subsection (3) or (5). Subsection (7) provides a defence to a charge under subsection (6).

Prosecution of offences and proceedings

Section 16 corresponds to section 8 of the *Aviation Security Act* 1982 (*ante*, § 25–185) with respect to proceedings for an offence under Part II (ss.9–17) of the Act. **25–209**

Aviation and Maritime Security Act 1990, s.17

Interpretation of Part II

17.—(1) In this Part of this Act— **25–210**

"fixed platform" means—

(a) any offshore installation, within the meaning of the *Mineral Workings (Offshore Installations) Act* 1971, which is not a ship, and

(b) any other artificial island, installation or structure which—

(i) permanently rests on, or is permanently attached to, the seabed,

(ii) is maintained for the purposes of the exploration or exploitation of resources or for other economic purposes, and

(iii) is not connected with dry land by a permanent structure providing access at all times and for all purposes;

"naval service" includes military and air force service;

"ship" means any vessel (including hovercraft, submersible craft and other floating craft) other than one which—

(a) permanently rests on, or is permanently attached to, the seabed, or

(b) has been withdrawn from navigation or laid up; and

"United Kingdom national" means an individual who is—

(a) a British citizen, a British overseas territories citizen, a British National (Overseas) or a British Overseas citizen,

(b) a person who under the *British Nationality Act* 1981 is a British subject, or

(c) a British protected person (within the meaning of that Act).

(2) For the purposes of this Part of this Act the territorial waters adjacent to any part of the United Kingdom shall be treated as included in that part of the United Kingdom.

[This section is printed as amended by the *British Overseas Territories Act* 2002, s.2.]

As to the meaning of "offshore installation" within the *Mineral Workings (Offshore Installations) Act* 1971, see s.1(4) of that Act.

(4) Miscellaneous and general

Powers in relation to certain aircraft

25–211 Section 48 gives the Secretary of State power to act against foreign-registered aircraft that land in the United Kingdom from a state that has banned United Kingdom registered civil aircraft from its airspace in breach of an international agreement between that state and the United Kingdom. The Secretary of State may give certain directions to the manager of an aerodrome or the occupier of land where the aircraft has landed for the purpose of isolating it and ensuring that the only service it receives is such as to enable it to leave the United Kingdom.

Offences triable either way are created of failure to comply with a direction under the section, of intentionally obstructing anyone acting under such a direction and of entering the aircraft without lawful authority or reasonable excuse for some purpose other than as provided in the direction.

Offences by bodies corporate

25–212 Section 50 corresponds to section 37 of the *Aviation Security Act* 1982 (*ante*, § 25–193).

[The next paragraph is § 25–216.]

K. CHANNEL TUNNEL (SECURITY) ORDER 1994 (S.I. 1994 NO. 570)

(1) Introduction

25–216 This Order was made on March 4, 1994, by the Secretary of State for Transport under the *Channel Tunnel Act* 1987, s.11. By article 1, it came into force on the day after the day on which it was made.

The Order follows closely the structure and content of the *Aviation Security Act* 1982 (*ante*, §§ 25–178 *et seq.*) and the *Aviation and Maritime Security Act* 1990 (*ante*, §§ 25–198 *et seq.*). It is intended to provide for the security of the Channel Tunnel ("the tunnel system" which is defined in section 1(7) of the 1987 Act (Appendix F–3), subject to article 2(1) (*post*, § 25–218)) and of Channel Tunnel trains (defined in article 2(1)).

Part II (arts 4–9) creates various offences against the safety of the system and the trains. Part III (corresponding to Part II of the *Aviation Security Act* 1982 and Part III of the *Aviation and Maritime Security Act* 1990) provides for the protection of the trains and the system against acts of violence (defined in article 10(2)).

The Order applies outside the United Kingdom only to the extent specified in article 3, that is where articles 30 or 38 of the Protocol between the Government of the United Kingdom of Great Britain and Northern Ireland and the Government of the French Republic concerning Frontier Controls and Policing, Cooperation in Criminal Justice, Public Safety and Mutual Assistance Relating to the Channel Fixed Link (Cm. 1802) confer jurisdiction on the United Kingdom courts.

(2) Interpretation and extent

S.I. 1994 No. 570, arts 1–3

PART I

PRELIMINARY

1. [*Citation and commencement: see* ante.] **25–217**

Interpretation

2.—(1) In this Order, except where the context otherwise requires— **25–218**

"ammunition" has the same meaning as in the *Firearms Act* 1968,

"article" includes any substance, whether natural or artificial, in solid or liquid form or in the form of a gas or vapour,

"authorised person" means a person authorised in writing by the Secretary of State for the purposes of Part III of this Order,

"Channel Tunnel freight business" means the business of handling goods for delivery (by the person carrying on the business or by another person) for carriage by a Channel Tunnel train, in the case of a shuttle train, in a vehicle on that train, and "Channel Tunnel freight" shall be constructed [*sic*] accordingly;

"Channel Tunnel freight forwarder" means a person whose business includes Channel Tunnel freight business,

"Channel Tunnel train" means a train or any part of a train (including a shuttle train) which has been assigned for use (whether in the United Kingdom or elsewhere) for conveying passengers or goods through the tunnel system,

"constable" includes any person having the powers and privileges of a constable,

"employee", in relation to a body corporate includes officer,

"enforcement notice" has the meaning given by article 21(1) of this Order,

"explosive" means any article manufactured for the purpose of producing a practical effect by explosion, or intended for that purpose by a person having the article with him,

"firearm" has the same meaning as in the *Firearms Act* 1968,

"goods" means goods or burden of any description and includes baggage, stores and mail,

"measures" (without prejudice to the generality of that expression) includes the construction, execution, alteration, demolition or removal of any building or other works (whether on dry land or on the seabed or other land covered by water), and also includes the institution or modification, and the supervision and enforcement, of any practice or procedure,

"owner" includes a lessee,

"property" includes any land, building or works, any train or other vehicle and any goods or other article of any description,

"restricted zone", in relation to the tunnel system or any land, building or works, means any part of the tunnel system or the land, building or works designated under article 12 of this Order or, where the whole of the tunnel system or land, building or works is so designated, the tunnel system or the land, building or works,

"stores" means any goods intended for sale or use on a train, within the tunnel system or within a restricted zone, including fuel and spare parts and other articles of equipment, whether or not for immediate fitting,

"train manager" means in relation to a Channel Tunnel train, the person designated as train manager by the person operating the service on which the train is engaged or, in the absence of such designation, the driver of the train,

"United Kingdom national" means an individual who is—

(a) a British citizen, a British overseas territories citizen, a British National (Overseas) or a British Overseas citizen,

(b) a person who under the *British Nationality Act* 1981 is a British subject, or

(c) a British protected person (within the meaning of that Act),

"unlawfully", in relation to the commission of an act, means so that the commission of the act is (apart from this Order) an offence under the law of England and Wales, Scotland or Northern Ireland or would be if committed there, and

references to the tunnel system include references to the tunnel system or any part of it (whether in England or France), except the inland clearance depot at Ashford in Kent, for the accommodation, in connection with the application to them of customs and other controls, of freight vehicles which have been or are to be conveyed through the tunnels on shuttle services.

(2) In Part III of this Order "act of violence" shall be construed in accordance with article 10(2).

(3) Any power to give a direction under any provision of this Order includes power to revoke or vary any such direction by a further direction.

(4) For the purposes of this Order a person is permitted to have access to a restricted zone if he is permitted to enter that zone or if arrangements exist for permitting any of his employees or agents to enter that zone.

[This article is printed as amended by the *British Overseas Territories Act* 2002, s.2.]

Extraterritorial application and extent

25–219 **3.**—(1) This Order applies outside the United Kingdom only where jurisdiction is conferred by article 30 or 38 of the international articles.

(2) This Order extends to Northern Ireland.

(3) In this article "the international articles" has the same meaning as in the *Channel Tunnel (International Arrangements) Order* 1993 and in articles 30 and 38 of the international articles the expression "the Fixed Link" has for the purposes of this Order the meaning given in article 2(3) of that Order.

[The order referred to in article 3(3) is S.I. 1993 No. 1813 (Appendix F–12).]

(3) Offences

S.I. 1994 No. 570, arts 4–8

PART II

OFFENCES AGAINST THE SAFETY OF CHANNEL TUNNEL TRAINS AND THE TUNNEL SYSTEM

Hijacking of Channel Tunnel trains

25–220 **4.**—(1) A person who unlawfully, by the use of force or by threats of any kind, seizes a Channel Tunnel train or exercises control of it, commits the offence of hijacking a Channel Tunnel train.

(2) A person guilty of the offence of hijacking a Channel Tunnel train is liable on conviction on indictment to imprisonment for life.

Seizing or exercising control of the tunnel system

25–221 **5.**—(1) A person who unlawfully, by the use of force or by threats of any kind, seizes the tunnel system or exercises control of it, commits an offence.

(2) A person guilty of an offence under this article is liable on conviction on indictment to imprisonment for life.

Destroying a Channel Tunnel train or the tunnel system or endangering their safety

25–222 **6.**—(1) A person commits an offence if he unlawfully and intentionally—

(a) destroys a Channel Tunnel train or the tunnel system, or destroys any goods on the train or within the tunnel system so as to endanger or be likely to endanger, the safe operation of the train, or as the case may be, the safety of the tunnel system;

(b) damages a Channel Tunnel train or any goods on the train or the tunnel system or any goods within the system so as to endanger, or to be likely to endanger, the safe operation of the train, or as the case may be, the safety of the tunnel system; or

(c) commits on board a Channel Tunnel train or within the tunnel system an act of violence which is likely to endanger the safe operation of the train, or as the case may be, the safety of the tunnel system.

(2) A person commits an offence if he unlawfully and intentionally places, or causes to be placed, on a Channel Tunnel train or in the tunnel system any device or substance which—

(a) in the case of a Channel Tunnel train is likely to destroy the train, or is likely so to damage it or any goods on it as to endanger its safe operation, or

(b) in the case of the tunnel system, is likely to destroy the tunnel system or so to damage it as to endanger its safety.

(3) Nothing in paragraph (2) above shall be construed as limiting the circumstances in which the commission of any act—

(a) may constitute an offence under paragraph (1) above, or

(b) may constitute attempting or conspiring to commit, or aiding, abetting, counselling, procuring or inciting, or being art and part in, the commission of such an offence.

(4) [*Identical to art. 5(2)*, ante.]

(5) In this article "act of violence" means an act which constitutes—

(a) the offence of murder, attempted murder, manslaughter, culpable homicide or assault,

(b) an offence under section 18, 20, 21, 22, 23, 24, 28 or 29 of the *Offences against the Person Act* 1861 or

(c) an offence under section 2 of the *Explosive Substances Act* 1883,

or which if committed in England and Wales, Scotland or Northern Ireland would constitute such an offence.

Other acts endangering or likely to endanger the safe operation of a Channel Tunnel train or the safety of the tunnel system

7.—(1) It is an offence for any person unlawfully and intentionally— **25–223**

(a) to destroy or damage any property to which this paragraph applies, or

(b) to interfere with the operation of any such property,

where the destruction, damage or interference is likely to endanger the safe operation of any Channel Tunnel train or the safety of the tunnel system.

(2) Paragraph (1) above applies to any property used in connection with the operation of any Channel Tunnel train or the tunnel system, including any land, building or works, train, apparatus or equipment so used, whether it is on board a Channel Tunnel train or, as the case may be, within the tunnel system, or elsewhere.

(3) It is an offence for any person intentionally to communicate any information which he knows to be false in a material particular, where the communication of the information endangers the safe operation of any Channel Tunnel train or the safety of the tunnel system.

(4) [*Identical to s.12(4) of the* Aviation and Maritime Security Act *1990*, ante, *§ 25–204, save for a reference to "paragraph (3)" instead of "subsection (3)"*.]

(5) [*Identical to art. 5(2)*, ante.]

Offences involving threats

8.—(1) A person commits an offence if— **25–224**

(a) in order to compel any other person to do or abstain from doing any act, he threatens that he or some other person will do in relation to any Channel Tunnel train or the tunnel system an act which is an offence by virtue of article 6(1) of this Order, and

(b) the making of that threat is likely to endanger the safe operation of the train or, as the case may be, the safety of the tunnel system.

(2) A person commits an offence if—

(a) in order to compel any other person to do or abstain from doing any act, he threatens that he or some other person will do an act which is an offence by virtue of article 7(1) of this Order, and

(b) the making of the threat is likely to endanger the safe operation of any Channel Tunnel train or the safety of the tunnel system.

(3) [*Identical to art. 5(2)*, ante.]

Prosecution of offences

25–225 Article 9 corresponds to section 8 of the *Aviation Security Act* 1982 (*ante*, § 25–185) with respect to proceedings for an offence under Part II.

(4) Offences by bodies corporate

25–226 Article 37 corresponds to section 37 of the 1982 Act (*ante*, § 25–193).

[The next paragraph is § 25–228.]

VI. IMMIGRATION

25–228 The provisions of the *Immigration Act* 1971 relating to recommendations for deportation are set out *ante*, §§ 5–910 *et seq.* Part III (ss.24 to 28L) concerns criminal proceedings. Several offences are created by these sections, but all are triable only summarily save for those created by sections 24A, 25(1), 25A(1) and 25B(1) and (3), which are triable either way. Section 25 (*post*) makes it an offence to assist illegal entry or to harbour illegal entrants. Section 24 makes illegal entry itself an offence, but it is submitted that there is no necessity on a prosecution under section 25 to prove that the person or persons assisted or harboured were themselves guilty of an offence under section 24(1). Accordingly, neither section 24 nor sections 26 (general offences in connection with administration of Act) and 27 (offences by persons connected with ships or aircraft or with ports) are set out in this work.

Immigration Act 1971, s.24A

Deception

25–228a **24A.**—(1) A person who is not a British citizen is guilty of an offence if, by means which include deception by him—

(a) he obtains or seeks to obtain leave to enter or remain in the United Kingdom; or

(b) he secures or seeks to secure the avoidance, postponement or revocation of enforcement action against him.

(2) "Enforcement action", in relation to a person, means—

(a) the giving of directions for his removal from the United Kingdom ("directions") under Schedule 2 to this Act or section 10 of the *Immigration and Asylum Act* 1999;

(b) the making of a deportation order against him under section 5 of this Act; or

(c) his removal from the United Kingdom in consequence of directions or a deportation order.

(3) A person guilty of an offence under this section is liable—

(a) on summary conviction, to imprisonment for a term not exceeding *six* [12] months or to a fine not exceeding the statutory maximum, or to both; or

(b) on conviction on indictment, to imprisonment for a term not exceeding two years or to a fine, or to both.

(4) The extended time limit for prosecutions which is provided for by section 28 applies to an offence under this section.

25–228b [This section was inserted by the *Immigration and Asylum Act* 1999, s.28, as from February 14, 2000: *Immigration and Asylum Act 1999 (Commencement No. 2 and Transitional Provisions) Order* 2000 (S.I. 2000 No. 168). In subs. (3)(a), "12" is substituted for "six", as from a day to be appointed, by the *CJA* 2003, s.282(2) and (3). The increase has no application to offences committed before the substitution takes effect: *ibid.*, s.282(4).]

Defence

25–228c Section 31 of the *Immigration and Asylum Act* 1999 came into force on November 11, 1999. It provides for defences based on the Convention relating to the Status of Refugees done at Geneva on July 28, 1951, and the Protocol to the Convention ("the Refugee Convention"). These defences are available to persons charged with various offences, including the offence created by section 24A.

Immigration and Asylum Act 1999, s.31

Defences based on Article 31(1) of the Refugee Convention

31.—(1) It is a defence for a refugee charged with an offence to which this section applies to show that, having come to the United Kingdom directly from a country where his life or freedom was threatened (within the meaning of the Refugee Convention), he— **25–228d**

(a) presented himself to the authorities in the United Kingdom without delay;

(b) showed good cause for his illegal entry or presence; and

(c) made a claim for asylum as soon as was reasonably practicable after his arrival in the United Kingdom.

(2) If, in coming from the country where his life or freedom was threatened, the refugee stopped in another country outside the United Kingdom, subsection (1) applies only if he shows that he could not reasonably have expected to be given protection under the Refugee Convention in that other country.

(3) In England and Wales and Northern Ireland the offences to which this section applies are any offence, and any attempt to commit an offence, under—

(a) Part I of the *Forgery and Counterfeiting Act* 1981 (forgery and connected offences);

(aa) section 25(1) or (5) of the *Identity Cards Act* 2006;

(b) section 24A of the 1971 Act (deception); or

(c) section 26(1)(d) of the 1971 Act (falsification of documents).

(4) [*Scotland.*]

(5) A refugee who has made a claim for asylum is not entitled to the defence provided by subsection (1) in relation to any offence committed by him after making that claim.

(6) "Refugee" has the same meaning as it has for the purposes of the Refugee Convention.

(7) If the Secretary of State has refused to grant a claim for asylum made by a person who claims that he has a defence under subsection (1), that person is to be taken not to be a refugee unless he shows that he is.

(8) A person who—

(a) was convicted in England and Wales or Northern Ireland of an offence to which this section applies before the commencement of this section, but

(b) at no time during the proceedings for that offence argued that he had a defence based on Article 31(1),

may apply to the Criminal Cases Review Commission with a view to his case being referred to the Court of Appeal by the Commission on the ground that he would have had a defence under this section had it been in force at the material time.

(9) [*Scotland.*]

(10), (11) [*Amendment of subss. (3) and (4) by order.*]

[This section is printed as amended by the *Identity Cards Act* 2006, s.30(2)(a).]

Article 31(1) of the 1951 Convention provides: **25–228e**

> "The Contracting States shall not impose penalties, on account of their illegalentry or presence, on refugees who, coming directly from a territory where their life or freedom was threatened in the sense of Article 1, enter or are present in their territory without authorisation, provided they present themselves without delay to the authorities and show good cause for their illegal entry or presence."

Section 31 of the 1999 Act having been intended to give effect to Article 31, the defence provided by it should not be read as limited to offences attributable to a refugee's illegal entry into or presence in this country, but rather as providing immunity (if the conditions contained therein are fulfilled) from the imposition of criminal penalties for offences attributable to the attempt of a refugee to leave this country in the continuing course of a flight from persecution, even after a short stopover in transit: *R. v. Asfaw (United Nations High Commissioner for Refugees intervening)* [2008] 2 W.L.R. 1178, HL. Whereas the defence under section 31 applies only to certain offences, it is not an abuse of process for a defendant who has attempted to leave this country for another place of refuge using false documents to be charged both with an offence to which the defence applies and with an offence of dishonesty to which it does not, since the prosecution are entitled to question whether the defendant is a refugee, and, if he is not, then the defence will not avail him in respect of either count; however, if the two counts relate to identical conduct and the second count is included in the indictment in order to prevent the defendant from relying on the defence, there will be strong grounds for contending that prosecuting that count is an abuse of process, since it would be unfair and contrary to the intention of the Act to convict the defendant on that count if he has successfully raised the defence in respect of the first count; the appropriate course of action in such circumstances is for the court to stay the prosecution of the second count pending the determination of the first count by the jury, and to maintain the stay if the defendant is acquitted: *ibid*.

Their Lordships in *Asfaw* were not concerned with subsection (2), which is in narrower terms than Article 31, in that under section 31 a refugee who has stopped over in another country is protected only if he is able to show that he could not reasonably have been expected to be given protection under the Convention in that country, whereas under Article 31 a short-term stopover en route would not deprive the refugee of protection from prosecution. In *R. (Pepushi) v. CPS, The Times*, May 21, 2004, the Divisional Court held that where the scope of a section, which enacts an international treaty, is narrower than the terms of the treaty, the section takes precedence, and accordingly a refugee was not protected by Article 31 to the extent that it was broader than section 31(2). Even if the Court of Appeal and the House of Lords are not prepared to revisit subsection (2) in light of the purposive approach adopted in *Asfaw*, it is likely that the courts will adopt a generous approach to what refugees could "reasonably have expected" by way of protection in third countries.

In *R. v. Makuwa* [2006] 2 Cr.App.R. 11, CA, it was held that (i) where a defendant sought to rely on section 31, his "refugee" status was a matter to be determined by proof; but the burden on the defendant was a merely evidential burden, and provided that he adduced sufficient evidence to raise the issue, it was for the prosecution to show to the usual standard that he was not in fact a refugee; and (ii) as to the burden of proof in respect of the three matters set out in section 31(1)(a) to (c), this was clearly intended by Parliament to be on the defendant and to be a legal, not an evidential, burden; and as such, this was a justifiable infringement of the presumption of innocence guaranteed by Article 6(2) of the ECHR (*post*, § 16–57), notwithstanding the severity of the penalty should the defendant be convicted, since (a) the effect of section 31(1) was simply to provide a defence to a defined class of persons in prescribed circumstances rather than to require the defendant to disprove an essential element of the prosecution case, (b) the matters raised by the defence would be difficult for the Crown to prove in the negative, and (c) if the burden were no more than to raise the issue, the various offences to which the defence applied would be largely ineffective.

Immigration Act 1971, ss.25–25C

Assisting unlawful immigration to member State

25–229 **25.**—(1) Any person commits an offence if he—

(a) does an act which facilitates the commission of a breach of immigration law by an individual who is not a citizen of the European Union,

(b) knows or has reasonable cause for believing that the act facilitates the commission of a breach of immigration law by the individual, and

(c) knows or has reasonable cause for believing that the individual is not a citizen of the European Union.

(2) In subsection (1) "immigration law" means a law which has effect in a member State and which controls, in respect of some or all persons who are not nationals of the State, entitlement to—

(a) enter the State,

(b) transit across the State, or

(c) be in the State.

(3) A document issued by the government of a member State certifying a matter of law in that State—

(a) shall be admissible in proceedings for an offence under this section, and

(b) shall be conclusive as to the matter certified.

(4) Subsection (1) applies to things done inside or outside the United Kingdom.

(6) A person guilty of an offence under this section shall be liable—

(a) on conviction on indictment, to imprisonment for a term not exceeding 14 years, to a fine or to both, or

(b) on summary conviction, to imprisonment for a term not exceeding *six* [12] months, to a fine not exceeding the statutory maximum or to both.

(7) In this section—

(a) a reference to a member State includes a reference to a State on a list prescribed for the purposes of this section by order of the Secretary of State (to be known as the "Section 25 List of Schengen Acquis States"), and

(b) a reference to a citizen of the European Union includes a reference to a person who is a national of a State on that list.

(8) [*Making of orders under subs. (7)(a).*]

[Ss.25–25C were substituted for s.25 of the 1971 Act (as amended) by the *Nationality, Immigration and Asylum Act* 2002, s.143, as from February 10, 2003 (*Nationality, Immigration and Asylum Act 2002 (Commencement No. 2) Order* 2003 (S.I. 2003 No. 1)). S.25 is printed as subsequently amended by the *Asylum and Immigration (Treatment of Claimants, etc.) Act* 2004, s.1(1); and the *UK Borders Act* 2007, s.30(1). In subs. (6)(b), "12" is substituted for "six", as from a day to be appointed, by the *CJA* 2003, s.282(2) and (3). The increase has no application to offences committed before the substitution takes effect: *ibid.*, s.282(4).]

In connection with this section, see *R. v. Javaherifard and Miller*, *The Times*, January 20, 2006, CA (*post*, § 25–231).

Helping asylum-seeker to enter United Kingdom

25A.—(1) A person commits an offence if— **25–229a**

(a) he knowingly and for gain facilitates the arrival in, or the entry into, the United Kingdom of an individual, and

(b) he knows or has reasonable cause to believe that the individual is an asylum-seeker.

(2) In this section "asylum-seeker" means a person who intends to claim that to remove him from or require him to leave the United Kingdom would be contrary to the United Kingdom's obligations under—

(a) the Refugee Convention (within the meaning given by section 167(1) of the *Immigration and Asylum Act* 1999 interpretation)), or

(b) the Human Rights Convention (within the meaning given by that section).

(3) Subsection (1) does not apply to anything done by a person acting on behalf of an organisation which—

(a) aims to assist asylum-seekers, and

(b) does not charge for its services.

(4) Subsections (4) and (6) of section 25 apply for the purpose of the offence in subsection (1) of this section as they apply for the purpose of the offence in subsection (1) of that section.

[See the note to s.25, *ante*. S.25A is printed as amended by the *UK Borders Act* 2007, ss.29 and 30(2).]

Assisting entry to United Kingdom in breach of deportation or exclusion order

25B.—(1) A person commits an offence if he— **25–229b**

(a) does an act which facilitates a breach of a deportation order in force against an individual who is a citizen of the European Union, and

(b) knows or has reasonable cause for believing that the act facilitates a breach of the deportation order.

(2) Subsection (3) applies where the Secretary of State personally directs that the exclusion from the United Kingdom of an individual who is a citizen of the European Union is conducive to the public good.

(3) A person commits an offence if he—

(a) does an act which assists the individual to arrive in, enter or remain in the United Kingdom,

(b) knows or has reasonable cause for believing that the act assists the individual to arrive in, enter or remain in the United Kingdom, and

(c) knows or has reasonable cause for believing that the Secretary of State has personally directed that the individual's exclusion from the United Kingdom is conducive to the public good.

(4) Subsections (4) and (6) of section 25 apply for the purpose of an offence under this section as they apply for the purpose of an offence under that section.

[See the note to s.25, *ante*. S.25B is printed as amended by the *UK Borders Act* 2007, s.30(2).]

Forfeiture of vehicle, ship or aircraft

25–229c **25C.**—(1) This section applies where a person is convicted on indictment of an offence under section 25, 25A or 25B.

(2) The court may order the forfeiture of a vehicle used or intended to be used in connection with the offence if the convicted person—

(a) owned the vehicle at the time the offence was committed,

(b) was at that time a director, secretary or manager of a company which owned the vehicle,

(c) was at that time in possession of the vehicle under a hire-purchase agreement,

(d) was at that time a director, secretary or manager of a company which was in possession of the vehicle under a hire-purchase agreement, or

(e) was driving the vehicle in the course of the commission of the offence.

(3) The court may order the forfeiture of a ship or aircraft used or intended to be used in connection with the offence if the convicted person—

(a) owned the ship or aircraft at the time the offence was committed,

(b) was at that time a director, secretary or manager of a company which owned the ship or aircraft,

(c) was at that time in possession of the ship or aircraft under a hire-purchase agreement,

(d) was at that time a director, secretary or manager of a company which was in possession of the ship or aircraft under a hire-purchase agreement,

(e) was at that time a charterer of the ship or aircraft, or

(f) committed the offence while acting as captain of the ship or aircraft.

(4) But in a case to which subsection (3)(a) or (b) does not apply, forfeiture may be ordered only—

(a) in the case of a ship, if subsection (5) or (6) applies;

(b) in the case of an aircraft, if subsection (5) or (7) applies.

(5) This subsection applies where—

(a) in the course of the commission of the offence, the ship or aircraft carried more than 20 illegal entrants, and

(b) a person who, at the time the offence was committed, owned the ship or aircraft or was a director, secretary or manager of a company which owned it, knew or ought to have known of the intention to use it in the course of the commission of an offence under section 25, 25A or 25B.

(6) This subsection applies where a ship's gross tonnage is less than 500 tons.

(7) This subsection applies where the maximum weight at which an aircraft (which is not a hovercraft) may take off in accordance with its certificate of airworthiness is less than 5,700 kilogrammes.

(8) Where a person who claims to have an interest in a vehicle, ship or aircraft applies to a court to make representations on the question of forfeiture, the court may not make an order under this section in respect of the ship, aircraft or vehicle unless the person has been given an opportunity to make representations.

(9) In the case of an offence under section 25, the reference in subsection (5)(a) to an illegal entrant shall be taken to include a reference to—

(a) an individual who seeks to enter a member State in breach of immigration law (for which purpose "member State" and "immigration law" have the meanings given by section 25(2) and (7)), and

(b) an individual who is a passenger for the purpose of section 145 of the *Nationality, Immigration and Asylum Act* 2002 (traffic in prostitution).

(10) In the case of an offence under section 25A, the reference in subsection (5)(a) to an illegal entrant shall be taken to include a reference to—

(a) an asylum-seeker (within the meaning of that section), and

(b) an individual who is a passenger for the purpose of section 145(1) of the *Nationality, Immigration and Asylum Act* 2002.

(11) In the case of an offence under section 25B, the reference in subsection (5)(a) to an illegal entrant shall be taken to include a reference to an individual who is a passenger for the purpose of section 145(1) of the *Nationality, Immigration and Asylum Act* 2002.

[See the note to s.25, *ante*. S.25C is printed as subsequently amended (substitution of bracketed words in subs. (9)(a)) by the *Asylum and Immigration (Treatment of Claimants, etc.) Act* 2004, s.1(2), as from October 1, 2004 (*Asylum and Immigration (Treatment of Claimants, etc.) Act 2004 (Commencement No. 1) Order* 2004 (S.I. 2004 No. 2523)).]

For modification of the 1971 Act in relation to the Channel Tunnel, see *post*, § 25–233. **25–230**

An offence contrary to section 25, 25A or 25B is a "lifestyle offence" within the *PCA* 2002, Sched. 2 (*ante*, § 5–656), in respect of which a court may make a financial reporting order under section 76 of the *SOCPA* 2005 (*ante*, § 5–886a).

Section 25D of the 1971 Act (inserted by the *Immigration and Asylum Act* 1999, s.38(2), and renumbered and amended by s.143 of the *Nationality, Immigration and Asylum Act* 2002) provides for the detention of ships, aircraft and vehicles in connection with offences under section 25, 25A or 25B until a decision is made as to whether an arrested person should be charged, and, if he is charged, until he is acquitted, the proceedings are discontinued or dismissed, or, if he is convicted, until a decision is made by the court as to whether to order forfeiture under section 25C.

In *R. v. Javaherifard and Miller*, *The Times*, January 20, 2006, CA, it was held in relation to section 25(2) that: (i) where a person crosses the border by land from the Republic of Ireland into Northern Ireland before travelling by boat to mainland Britain, his point of "entry" into the United Kingdom is the point at which he crosses into Northern Ireland (there being no statutory provision, such as s.11, which deems otherwise); and acts done close to, but after, the actual entry has occurred, may still constitute the facilitating of "entry" where they are done to make the entry effective; (ii) "transit" covers those who do not enter the United Kingdom in the immigration sense but who are in transit through it, and to whom special rules apply even though they remain airside and do not pass through immigration control; and (iii) "to be in the State" covers all other aspects (than "enter" and "transit") of presence, including arrival pre-entry (as to which, see *R. v. Naillie*; *R. v. Kanesarajah* [1993] A.C. 674, HL), overstaying or breach of leave, or presence as an illegal immigrant who has no leave, and the fact that it is not an offence for an illegal immigrant to stay after illegal entry is immaterial since his staying involves a continuing breach of immigration law on his part. The court added that, since an offence under section 25 can only be committed with guilty knowledge, providing legal advice to an illegal immigrant with a view to regularising his position or to making an asylum claim (unless the claim is known to be false) or providing food or money to him as a human being (*e.g.* to avoid degradation or destitution) rather than to assist his presence as an illegal immigrant would not amount to an offence. **25–231**

In *R. v. Van Binh Le*; *R. v. Stark* [1999] 1 Cr.App.R.(S.) 422, the Court of Appeal held, in relation to the original section 25(1)(a) (facilitating entry of illegal entrant), that the appropriate penalty for all but the most minor offences would be one of immediate custody; the offence frequently calls for deterrent sentences, the problem of illegal entry being on the increase; in determining the seriousness of a particular case, it is necessary to have regard, in particular, to whether the offence was an isolated act or had been repeated or there were previous convictions for like offences, to the motivation (commercial/humanitarian), to the identity and number of the entrants (strangers/family), to the degree of organisation and to the role played. There can be no doubt about the thrust of this decision carrying across to the offences under sections 25 to 25B. At the time of this decision, the maximum penalty for an offence contrary to section 25 was seven years' imprisonment. That maximum was raised to 10 years' imprisonment in 2000 by the *Immigration and Asylum Act* 1999, and the new offences under sections 25 to 25B now carry a maximum of 14 years' imprisonment. **25–232**

The Channel Tunnel

For the purpose of enabling officers belonging to the United Kingdom to carry out **25–233** frontier controls, the 1971 Act extends to France and Belgium within a control zone: *Channel Tunnel (International Arrangements) Order* 1993 (S.I. 1993 No. 1813), art. 4(1). The Act was modified in its application to France and Belgium, and, in its application to the United Kingdom within the tunnel system, and elsewhere for the authorised purposes, by *ibid.*, Sched. 4, para. 1. For modifications of the original section 25, see para. 1(8). This provision has not (as at October 1, 2008) been amended to take account of the new provisions substituted by the 2002 Act. S.I. 1993 No. 1813 is set out *in extenso* in the supplement. As to "authorised purposes", see art. 2(2); as to "control zone", see art. 1 of the international articles (set out in Schedule 2 to the order). As to Belgium, see articles 4(1) and 7 of the *Channel Tunnel (Miscellaneous Provisions) Order* 1994 (S.I. 1994 No. 1405) (Appendix F–1, F–22).

Immigration Act 1971, s.28

Proceedings (time limits)

25–234 **28.**—(1) Where the offence is one to which, under section 24 ... or 26 above, an extended time limit for prosecutions is to apply, then—

(a) an information relating to the offence may in England and Wales be tried by a magistrates' court if it is laid within six months after the commission of the offence, or if it is laid within three years after the commission of the offence and not more than two months after the date certified by a chief officer of police to be the date on which evidence sufficient to justify proceedings came to the notice of an officer of his police force; and

(b) [*Scotland*]; and

(c) [*Northern Ireland*].

(2) [*Scotland*.]

(3) For the purposes of the trial of a person for an offence under this Part of this Act, the offence shall be deemed to have been committed either at the place at which it actually was committed or at any place at which he may be.

(4) Any powers exercisable under this Act in the case of any person may be exercised notwithstanding that proceedings for an offence under this Part of this Act have been taken against him.

[This section is printed as amended by the *Immigration Act* 1988, s.10 and Sched., para. 4; and the *Immigration and Asylum Act* 1999, s.169(1) and Sched. 14, para. 53; and as repealed in part by the *Nationality, Immigration and Asylum Act* 2002, s.161 and Sched. 9.]

25–235 In *Enaas v. Dovey*, *The Times*, November 25, 1986, DC, it was held that "evidence" in section 28(1)(a) meant something more than information given to a police officer over the telephone. Consequently, it was not appropriate for a police officer to conclude he had sufficient evidence to justify instituting proceedings under section 24(1)(b)(i) (remaining beyond time limited by leave) until he had written proof from the Home Office confirming the status of the potential defendant. The Act does not provide that the certificate should be absolute evidence of the facts stated in it. In appropriate circumstances it is permissible to go behind it. The question for the magistrate was whether on all the material before him the decision of the chief officer was reasonable or not: if it was not, the certificate could not be valid; if it was, then the certificate should be upheld: *ibid*.

The certificate need not be in existence when the information is laid. Provided that it is before the magistrates' court at the time of trial, the court has jurisdiction: *Quazi v. DPP* [1988] Crim.L.R. 529, DC. The entering of a plea of not guilty in a magistrates' court did not mark the commencement of a trial, but merely established the need for one.

Arrest, search and fingerprinting

25–236 Part VII (ss.128–139) of the *Immigration and Asylum Act* 1999 inserted a series of new sections at the end of Part III of the 1971 Act so as to confer on immigration officers increased powers of arrest, search and fingerprinting. Sections 28A to 28I relate respectively to arrest without warrant, search and arrest with a warrant, search and arrest without warrant, entry and search of premises, entry and search of premises following arrest, entry and search of premises following arrest for an offence under section 25, 25A or 25B of the 1971 Act, searching arrested persons, searching persons in police custody, access to, and copying of seized material, safeguards in relation to search warrants, execution of warrants and the interpretation of Part III (providing merely that "premises" and "items subject to legal privilege" have the same meanings as in the *PACE Act* 1984).

Sections 44 and 45 of the *UK Borders Act* 2007 give immigration officers and constables a power to search premises for documents relating to the nationality of a person arrested on suspicion of having committed an offence if they suspect he may not be a British citizen.

VII. OFFENCES AGAINST THE FOREIGN ENLISTMENT ACT 1870

(1) Purpose and application

The Act was designed to regulate the conduct of British subjects during the existence of hostilities between foreign states with which the United Kingdom is at peace. It applies to all Her Majesty's dominions and their territorial waters. **25–237**

(2) Principal offences

Section 4 makes it an offence for a British subject to enlist in the military or naval service of a foreign state at war with another foreign state with which Her Majesty is at peace ("a friendly state"). It is also an offence thereunder for anyone within Her Majesty's dominions to induce anyone so to enlist. In relation to this offence, see *R. v. Granatelli*, 7 St. Tr. (n.s.) 979, and *Burton v. Pinkerton* (1867) L.R. 2 Ex. 340. The Act does not extend to enlistment in the government or rebel forces during a civil war in a friendly state. **25–238**

Section 5 makes it an offence for a British subject to leave Her Majesty's dominions with intent to enlist in the military or naval service of a foreign state at war with a friendly state; it is also an offence for anyone to induce any other person to leave Her Majesty's dominions with such intent.

Section 6 makes it an offence to induce a person to leave Her Majesty's dominions or to go on board a ship by misrepresenting the service in which the person is to be engaged, with intent that such person may enlist in the military or naval service of a foreign state at war with a friendly state.

Section 7 makes it an offence to take illegally enlisted persons on board a ship. Section 8 creates offences in relation to illegal ship building and illegal expeditions. As to the latter, see *The Gauntlet* (1872) L.R. 4 P.C. 184, and *The International* (1871) L.R. 3 A. & E. 321.

Section 10 makes it an offence to aid the warlike equipment of foreign ships. Section 11 makes it an offence, without the licence of Her Majesty, to prepare or fit out any naval or military expedition to proceed against the dominions of a friendly state. It is not necessary that the expedition should be completely fitted out in this country; any act of preparation of the expedition in this country is within the section: *R. v. Sandoval* (1887) 16 Cox 206. If an expedition is unlawfully prepared within Her Majesty's dominions, a British subject who assists therein, even without such dominions, is liable under this section: *R. v. Jameson* [1896] 2 Q.B. 425, and see *The Salvador* (1870) L.R. 3 P.C. 218; *Att.-Gen. v. Sillem* (1863) 2 H. & C. 431 (decided on 59 Geo. 3, c.69, s.7 (*rep.*)).

(3) Procedure and penalties

Section 16 relates to jurisdiction (any offence against the Act is deemed to have been committed either where it was committed or at any place in Her Majesty's dominions that the offender may be). Section 17 relates to venue; as to the necessary statements in the indictment, see *R. v. Jameson*, *ante*, and *R. v. Sandoval*, *ante*. For a specimen indictment charging an offence contrary to section 11, see the 1992 and earlier editions of this work. **25–239**

Section 18 concerns the removal of offenders for trial.

The maximum penalty for any offence under the Act is two years' imprisonment: s.13 (all offences being triable only on indictment). There is express provision for the trial and punishment of accessories as if they were principals (s.12). The forfeiture of ships for offences against the Act is governed by section 19.

VIII. COINAGE OFFENCES

A. INTRODUCTION

25–240 The *Forgery and Counterfeiting Act* 1981 was based substantially on the Law Commission's Report on Forgery and Counterfeit Currency (No. 55), published in 1973. The forgery provisions are considered *ante*, §§ 22–1 *et seq.*

B. COUNTERFEITING NOTES AND COINS

Forgery and Counterfeiting Act 1981, s.14

Offences of counterfeiting notes and coins

25–241 **14.**—(1) It is an offence for a person to make a counterfeit of a currency note or of a protected coin, intending that he or another shall pass or tender it as genuine.

(2) It is an offence for a person to make a counterfeit of a currency note or of a protected coin without lawful authority or excuse.

The offences under both subsections (1) and (2) are triable either way: see section 22 of the Act (*post*, § 25–256) which also provides the penalties.

Forgery and Counterfeiting Act 1981, s.27

Meaning of "currency note" and "protected coin"

25–242 **27.**—(1) In this Part of this Act—

"currency note" means—

(a) any note which—

(i) has been lawfully issued in England and Wales, Scotland, Northern Ireland, any of the Channel Islands, the Isle of Man or the Republic of Ireland; and

(ii) is or has been customarily used as money in the country where it was issued; and

(iii) is payable on demand; or

(b) any note which—

(i) has been lawfully issued in some country other than those mentioned in paragraph (a)(i) above; and

(ii) is customarily used as money in that country, and

"protected coin" means any coin which—

(a) is customarily used as money in any country; or

(b) is specified in an order made by the Treasury for the purposes of this Part of this Act.

(2), (3) [*Making of orders under subs. (1).*]

25–243 The *Forgery and Counterfeiting (Protected Coins) Order* 1981 (S.I. 1981 No. 1505) specifies the following coins for the purposes of Part II of the Act:

Sovereign;

Half-sovereign;

Krugerrand;

Any coin denominated as a fraction of a Krugerrand;

Maria-Theresia thaler bearing the date of 1780.

The *Forgery and Counterfeiting (Protected Coins) Order* 1999 (S.I. 1999 No. 2095) specifies any euro coin produced in accordance with Council Regulation No. 975/98/EC by or at the instance of a member state which has adopted the single currency, for the purposes of Part II of the 1981 Act.

Forgery and Counterfeiting Act 1981, s.28

Meaning of "counterfeit"

28.—(1) For the purposes of this Part of this Act a thing is a counterfeit of a currency note or of a protected coin— **25–244**

(a) if it is not a currency note or a protected coin but resembles a currency note or protected coin (whether on one side only or on both) to such an extent that it is reasonably capable of passing for a currency note or protected coin of that description; or

(b) if it is a currency note or protected coin which has been so altered that it is reasonably capable of passing for a currency note or protected coin of some other description.

(2) For the purposes of this Part of this Act—

(a) a thing consisting of one side only of a currency note, with or without the addition of other material, is a counterfeit of such a note;

(b) a thing consisting—

(i) of parts of two or more currency notes; or

(ii) of parts of a currency note, or of parts of two or more currency notes, with the addition of other material,

is capable of being a counterfeit of a currency note.

(3) References in this Part of this Act to passing or tendering a counterfeit of a currency note or a protected coin are not to be construed as confined to passing or tendering it as legal tender.

In an explanatory note to their draft bill, the Law Commission said: **25–245**

> "A counterfeit is defined … as that which sufficiently resembles a note or coin to be reasonably capable of passing for it. It will be for the trier of fact in each case to decide whether, having regard to the thing counterfeited and the degree of resemblance, the test is satisfied. Accordingly, a thing may be a counterfeit notwithstanding that only one surface or face of it resembles a genuine note or coin, or that it bears words only discernible on a close examination, indicating that it is a copy or specimen only."

Section 14(2) does not correspond to any provision of the Law Commission's draft bill. It appears to have been inserted to cover the gap left by the requirement of an ulterior intention in the offence created by subsection (1) which, to that extent, is narrower than the corresponding offence in the *Coinage Offences Act* 1936 (*rep.*). As with the offences created by section 5(2) and (4) (*ante*, § 22–31) there is an evidential burden upon the accused in relation to lawful authority or excuse under section 14(2); once there is sufficient evidence to raise an issue upon the matter, the burden is discharged and the prosecution must prove lack of lawful authority or excuse in the ordinary way: see *ante*, § 22–35.

C. PASSING COUNTERFEIT NOTES AND COINS

Forgery and Counterfeiting Act 1981, s.15

Offences of passing etc. counterfeit notes and coins

15.—(1) It is an offence for a person— **25–246**

(a) to pass or tender as genuine any thing which is, and which he knows or believes to be, a counterfeit of a currency note or of a protected coin; or

(b) to deliver to another any thing which is, and which he knows or believes to be, such a counterfeit, intending that the person to whom it is delivered or another shall pass or tender it as genuine.

(2) It is an offence for a person to deliver to another, without lawful authority or excuse, any thing which is, and which he knows or believes to be, a counterfeit of a currency note or of a protected coin.

The offences under both subsections (1) and (2) are triable either way: see section 22 of the Act (*post*, § 25–256) which also provides the penalties.

As to the meaning of "currency note" and "protected coin", see section 27, *ante*, § 25–242. As to the meaning of "counterfeit", see section 28, *ante*, § 25–244.

The general comment made in relation to section 14(2) (*ante*, § 25–245) applies equally to section 15(2).

D. CUSTODY OR CONTROL OF COUNTERFEITS

Forgery and Counterfeiting Act 1981, s.16

Offences involving the custody or control of counterfeit notes and coins

25–247 **16.**—(1) It is an offence for a person to have in his custody or under his control any thing which is, and which he knows or believes to be, a counterfeit of a currency note or of a protected coin, intending either to pass or tender it as genuine or to deliver it to another with the intention that he or another shall pass or tender it as genuine.

(2) It is an offence for a person to have in his custody or under his control, without lawful authority or excuse, any thing which is, and which he knows or believes to be, a counterfeit of a currency note or of a protected coin.

(3) It is immaterial for the purposes of subsections (1) and (2) above that a coin or note is not in a fit state to be passed or tendered or that the making or counterfeiting of a coin or note has not been finished or perfected.

The offences under both subsections (1) and (2) are triable either way: see section 22 of the Act (*post*, § 25–256) which also provides the penalties.

As to the meaning of "currency note" and "protected coin", see section 27, *ante*, § 25–242. As to the meaning of "counterfeit", see section 28, *ante*, § 25–244. The definition given to "counterfeit" appears to be of particular importance having regard to subsection (3). The immateriality for the purposes of the offences contrary to subsections (1) and (2) of the note or coin not being in a fit state to be passed or tendered or being unfinished or imperfect must be read subject to the consideration that it will not be a "counterfeit" at all unless it is reasonably capable of passing as a genuine currency note or protected coin.

25–248 Apart from subsection (3), section 16 follows closely the Law Commission's draft bill. The Commission appeared to take the view that a provision such as that contained in subsection (3) was unnecessary. In paragraphs 98 and 99 of their report, they state:

> "We have given very full consideration to whether there should be a requirement of an intent to pass or tender the note or coin as genuine or to deliver it intending that it shall be passed or tendered as genuine, or whether it should be sufficient that there was no lawful authority or excuse for the custody or control. The law relating to coinage, which requires an intention to utter the coins has not so far as we are aware given rise to any difficulty in its administration, and in principle we prefer this requirement in the case of serious offences, to the penalising of possession unless the accused can discharge the evidential burden of proving lawful authority or excuse particularly because the scope of lawful authority or excuse is, on the authorities very limited. ... The creation of two offences will provide on the one hand for an offence with an adequate penalty for the case where circumstances establish that the accused had knowledge and the requisite intention; on the other hand a person who does not have this intention will not be put in jeopardy of conviction for a serious offence even where he cannot give any acceptable explanation of how he comes to have one or two notes or coins."

25–249 The authorities to which the Commission referred were *Dickins v. Gill* [1896] 2 Q.B. 310, DC, and *R. v. Wuyts* [1969] 2 Q.B. 476, 53 Cr.App.R. 417, CA: see *ante*, § 22–36.

Wuyts (mistakenly referred to as "*White*") was applied in *R. v. Sunman* [1995] Crim.L.R. 569, CA, in which it was said that a lawful excuse could only be based on a settled intention to hand in counterfeit currency to the appropriate authority. A state of indecision as to what to do with notes recently discovered to be counterfeit cannot constitute a lawful excuse.

"*Custody or control*". See *ante*, § 22–33.

Forgery and Counterfeiting Act 1981, s.17

Making, custody or control of counterfeiting materials and implements

25–250 **17.**—(1) It is an offence for a person to make, or to have in his custody or under his control, any thing which he intends to use, or to permit any other person to use, for the purpose of making a counterfeit of a currency note or of a protected coin with the intention that it be passed or tendered as genuine.

(2) It is an offence for a person without lawful authority or excuse—

(a) to make; or

(b) to have in his custody or under his control,

any thing which, to his knowledge, is or has been specially designed or adapted for the making of a counterfeit of a currency note.

(3) Subject to subsection (4) below, it is an offence for a person to make, or to have in

his custody or under his control, any implement which, to his knowledge, is capable of imparting to any thing a resemblance—

(a) to the whole or part of either side of a protected coin; or

(b) to the whole or part of the reverse of the image on either side of a protected coin.

(4) It shall be a defence for a person charged with an offence under subsection (3) above to show—

(a) that he made the implement or, as the case may be, had it in his custody or under his control, with the written consent of the Treasury; or

(b) that he had lawful authority otherwise than by virtue of paragraph (a) above, or a lawful excuse, for making it or having it in his custody or under his control.

The offences under subsections (1) to (3) are triable either way: see s.22 of the Act (*post*, § 25–256) which also provides the penalties. **25–251**

As to the meaning of "currency note" and "protected coin", see section 27, *ante*, § 25–242.

As to the meaning of "counterfeit", see section 28, *ante*, § 25–244.

As to "lawful authority or excuse", see *ante*, §§ 22–35, 25–248. As to "custody or control", see *ante*, § 22–33.

The words "any thing which he intends to use ... for the purpose of making a counterfeit" in subsection (1) are not confined to things to be used as a direct part of the process of making the counterfeit and which are essential thereto, but extend to cover non-essential things which are, in fact, intended to be so used, *e.g.* something to be used part way through the process as a check on quality: *R. v. Maltman* [1995] 1 Cr.App.R. 239, CA.

In paragraphs 104 and 105 of their report, the Law Commission pointed out that, because the offence created by section 17(1) is narrower in scope than the corresponding provision under the old law, there would be gaps in the law if there were no other offence created:

"For example, a plate specially designed to print, for advertising material for a magazine, the replica of a currency note is potentially a dangerous thing, yet possession of such a plate would not be an offence under [what is now section 17(1)] ...

We think, therefore, that there should be a further offence of making or having custody or control of, without lawful authority or excuse, any thing which, to the knowledge of the defendant, is specially designed or adapted for making a counterfeit of a currency note. ... The Treasury and the Mint are concerned at the weakening of the present law that would result in regard to making or possession of implements for making counterfeit coins if the offence [now in s.17(1)] were to be the only provision. It is not uncommon, they point out, for dies to be made which will be capable of impressing on metal the figure, stamp or apparent resemblance of one face of a current coin without there being any intention of using it to make counterfeits. It is dangerous for such dies to be in existence, because even if they are intended to make impression only on cardboard or such-like material, they may well be used by an unscrupulous person for counterfeiting."

Accordingly, the Commission recommended a third offence broadly corresponding with the offence created by subsection (3) of section 17.

E. Reproducing British Currency

Forgery and Counterfeiting Act 1981, ss.18, 19

The offence of reproducing British currency notes

18.—(1) It is an offence for any person, unless the relevant authority has previously consented in writing, to reproduce on any substance whatsoever, and whether or not on the correct scale, any British currency note or any part of a British currency note. **25–252**

(2) In this section—

"British currency note" means any note which—

(a) has been lawfully issued in England and Wales, Scotland or Northern Ireland; and

(b) is or has been customarily used as money in the country where it was issued; and

(c) is payable on demand; and

"the relevant authority", in relation to a British currency note of any particular description, means the authority empowered by law to issue notes of that description.

Offences of making etc. imitation British coins

25–253 **19.**—(1) It is an offence for a person—

(a) to make an imitation British coin in connection with a scheme intended to promote the sale of any product or the making of contracts for the supply of any service; or

(b) to sell or distribute imitation British coins in connection with any such scheme, or to have imitation British coins in his custody or under his control with a view to such sale or distribution,

unless the Treasury have previously consented in writing to the sale or distribution of such imitation British coins in connection with that scheme.

(2) In this section—

"British coin" means any coin which is legal tender in any part of the United Kingdom; and

"imitation British coin" means any thing which resembles a British coin in shape, size and the substance of which it is made.

The offences under both sections 18 and 19 are triable either way: see section 22 of the Act (*post*, § 25–256), which also provides the penalties. As to "custody or control", see *ante*, § 22–33. As to directors' liability where an offence under section 18 or 19 is committed by a body corporate, see *post*, § 25–259.

25–254 The mischiefs at which these two non-fraudulent offences were aimed were set out by the Law Commission at paragraphs 107 to 112 of their report.

"The Bank of England have drawn our attention to the dangers of allowing the reproduction of British currency notes even when there is no intention that they be tendered or passed as genuine. Such reproductions may appear in advertisements ..., or take the form of advertising vouchers or of properties for use in television or theatrical productions. The dangers are two-fold. In the first place people may be tempted to use the vouchers or stage properties or even reproductions cut from magazines as genuine notes; and in the second place the existence of accurate plates for the making of the reproductions may tempt persons to print copies for their own dishonest use. There is also a danger in the reproductions of notes or parts of notes on a scale larger than an actual note that this may provide useful assistance to a counterfeiter in the preparation of plates or reproductions to the correct scale. ... There is a related problem in regard to what may be called 'imitation' coins, which raise issues of a different nature. ... The main danger lies, we think, in the making and distribution of tokens of various sorts which, while not replicas of any current coin, yet from the appearance almost invite persons to use them as coins. This is a particular danger ... where the distribution is on a large scale and the tokens are likely to come into the possession of a wide range of people. ... We think that the right result will be achieved if it is made an offence to make, sell or distribute in connection with any scheme intended to promote the sale of any product any thing which resembles a current United Kingdom coin in shape, size and the substance of which it is made, unless the previous consent in writing of the Treasury has been obtained."

F. PROHIBITION OF IMPORTATION AND EXPORTATION OF COUNTERFEITS

Forgery and Counterfeiting Act 1981, ss.20, 21

Prohibition of importation of counterfeit notes and coins

25–255 **20.** The importation, landing or unloading of a counterfeit of a currency note or of a protected coin without the consent of the Treasury is hereby prohibited.

Prohibition of exportation of counterfeit notes and coins

21.—(1) The exportation of a counterfeit of a currency note or of a protected coin without the consent of the Treasury is hereby prohibited.

(2) A counterfeit of a currency note or of a protected coin which is removed to the Isle of Man from the United Kingdom shall be deemed to be exported from the United Kingdom—

(a) for the purposes of this section; and

(b) for the purposes of the customs and excise Acts, in their application to the prohibition imposed by this section.

(3) [*Amends* Isle of Man Act *1979, s.9(1)*.]

The general rule contained in section 9(1) of the *Isle of Man Act* 1979, is that goods removed to the Isle of Man from the United Kingdom shall be deemed for the purposes of the customs and excise Acts not to be exported from the United Kingdom. The combined effect of section 21(2) and (3) is to create an exception to the general rule.

G. PENALTIES, PROCEDURE, ETC., UNDER PART II

Forgery and Counterfeiting Act 1981, s.22

Penalties for offences under Part II

22.—(1) A person guilty of an offence to which this subsection applies shall be liable— **25–256**

(a) on summary conviction—

(i) to a fine not exceeding the statutory maximum; or

(ii) to imprisonment for a term not exceeding *six* [12] months; or

(iii) to both; and

(b) on conviction on indictment—

(i) to a fine; or

(ii) to imprisonment for a term not exceeding ten years; or

(iii) to both.

(2) [*Subs. (1) applies to offences under ss.14(1), 15(1), 16(1) and 17(1).*]

(3) A person guilty of an offence to which this subsection applies shall be liable—

(a) on summary conviction—

(i)–(iii) [*identical to subs. (1)(a)(i)–(iii),* ante]; and

(b) on conviction on indictment—

(i) to a fine, or

(ii) to imprisonment for a term not exceeding two years; or

(iii) to both.

(4) [*Subs. (3) applies to offences under ss.14(2), 15(2), 16(2), 17(2) and (3).*]

(5) A person guilty of an offence under section 18 or 19 above shall be liable—

(a) on summary conviction, to a fine not exceeding the statutory maximum; and

(b) on conviction on indictment, to a fine.

(6) [*Repealed by* Statute Law (Repeals) Act *1993, Sched. 1, Pt XIV.*]

[In subss. (1)(a) and (3)(a), "12" is substituted for "six", as from a day to be appointed, by the *CJA* 2003, s.282(2) and (3). The increase has no application to offences committed before the substitution takes effect: s.282(4).]

The "statutory maximum" means the prescribed sum within the meaning of section 32 of the *MCA* 1980 (*ante*, § 1–75aa): *Interpretation Act* 1978, Sched. 1 (Appendix B–28).

An offence contrary to section 14, 15, 16 or 17 of the 1981 Act is a "lifestyle offence" within the *PCA* 2002, Sched. 2 (*ante*, § 5–658), in respect of which a court may make a financial reporting order under section 76 of the *SOCPA* 2005 (*ante*, § 5–886a).

Guidelines

In *R. v. Howard (A.F.)*, 82 Cr.App.R. 262, CA, it was said that where a defendant is **25–257** convicted of passing counterfeit notes, the issue of which undermines the whole economy of the country, in nearly every case this requires a custodial sentence to punish the wrongdoer and deter him from committing the same sort of offence in the future and to act as a deterrent to others. The most important consideration is, perhaps, the quantity of counterfeit notes in the possession of the defendant, because that will demonstrate, with some degree of accuracy at least, the proximity to, or distance from, the source of the notes. A sentence of two years' imprisonment was upheld in respect of a man of previous good character who pleaded guilty to offences of having custody of counterfeit currency, namely £20 notes, and tendering one such note. It appears that he had had possession at one time or another of about £3,000 worth of such notes. (As to "guideline" cases generally, see *R. v. Nicholas*, *The Times*, April 23, 1986, CA, *ante*, § 7–142.)

For examples of sentences upheld in cases of counterfeiting banknotes, and of possession and tendering of counterfeit currency, see CSP, B9–3.

Forgery and Counterfeiting Act 1981, ss.24, 25

Powers of search, forfeiture, etc.

24.—(1) If it appears to a justice of the peace from information given him on oath, that there **25–258** is reasonable cause to believe that a person has in his custody or under his control—

(a) any thing which is a counterfeit of a currency note or of a protected coin, or which is a reproduction made in contravention of section 18 or 19 above; or

(b) any thing which he or another has used, whether before or after the coming into force of this Act, or intends to use, for the making of any such counterfeit, or the making of any reproduction in contravention of section 18 or 19 above,

the justice may issue a warrant authorising a constable to search for and seize the object in question, and for that purpose to enter any premises specified in the warrant.

(2) A constable may at any time after the seizure of any object suspected of falling within paragraph (a) or (b) of subsection (1) above (whether the seizure was effected by virtue of a warrant under that subsection or otherwise) apply to a magistrates' court for an order under this subsection with respect to the object; and the court, if it is satisfied both that the object in fact falls within one or other of those paragraphs and that it is conducive to the public interest to do so, may make such order as it thinks fit for the forfeiture of the object and its subsequent destruction or disposal.

(3) Subject to subsection (4) below, the court by or before which a person is convicted of an offence under this Part of this Act may order any thing shown to the satisfaction of the court to relate to the offence to be forfeited and either destroyed or dealt with in such other manner as the court may order.

(4) The court shall not order any thing to be forfeited under subsection (2) or (3) above where a person claiming to be the owner of or otherwise interested in it applies to be heard by the court, unless an opportunity has been given to him to show cause why the order should not be made.

(5) Without prejudice to the generality of subsections (2) and (3) above, the powers conferred on the court by those subsections include power to direct that any object shall be passed to an authority with power to issue notes or coins or to any person authorised by such an authority to receive the object.

(6) [*Scotland.*]

As to "custody or control", see *ante*, § 22–33.

Directors', etc. liability

25–259 **25.**—(1) Where an offence under section 18 or 19 of this Act which has been committed by a body corporate is proved to have been committed with the consent or connivance of, or to be attributable to any neglect on the part of, a director, manager, secretary or other similar officer of the body corporate, or any person who was purporting to act in any such capacity, he, as well as the body corporate, shall be guilty of that offence and be liable to be proceeded against and punished accordingly.

(2) Where the affairs of a body corporate are managed by its members, subsection (1) above shall apply in relation to the acts and defaults of a member in connection with his functions of management as if he were a director of the body corporate.

As to subsection (1), see *R. v. Boal* [1992] 1 Q.B. 591, 95 Cr.App.R. 272, CA (*post*, § 30–103).

As to sections 18 and 19, see *ante*, §§ 25–252 *et seq.*

IX. SEDITION (INCLUDING SEDITIOUS LIBEL)

(1) Definition

25–260 Sedition consists of any act done, or words spoken or written and published which (i) has or have a seditious tendency and (ii) is done or are spoken or written and published with a seditious intent. A person may be said to have a seditious intention if he has any of the following intentions, and acts or words may be said to have a seditious tendency if they have any of the following tendencies: an intention or tendency to bring into hatred or contempt, or to excite disaffection against the person of, Her Majesty, her heirs or successors, or the government and constitution of the United Kingdom, as by law established, or either House of Parliament, or the administration of justice, or to excite Her Majesty's subjects to attempt, otherwise than by lawful means, the alteration of any matter in Church or State by law established, [or to incite any person to commit any crime in disturbance of the peace] or to raise discontent or disaffection among Her Majesty's subjects, or to promote feelings of ill-will and hostility between different classes of such subjects.

This is the definition given by Stephen, *Digest of the Criminal Law*, 9th ed., Art. 114: the words in brackets were not included in some earlier editions, but in a footnote, Stephen makes clear that they are not intended to widen the definition but to clarify it.

Although the offence is a common law offence there is statutory authority for much of Stephen's definition: see the *Criminal Libel Act* 1819, s.1. The raising of discontent or disaffection among Her Majesty's subjects and the promotion of feelings of hostility between different classes of such subjects are not mentioned in the Act but there is authority to support that part of the definition: *R. v. Fussell* (1848) 6 St.Tr.(N.S) 723; *R. v. O'Brien* (1848) 6 St.Tr.(N.S.) 571 at 591n; *R. v. Sullivan*; *R. v. Pigott* (1868) 11 Cox 44; *R. v. Caunt* (1947), Birkett J. at Liverpool Assizes, noted in 64 L.Q.R. 203 and cited in Turner and Armitage, *Cases on Criminal Law*, 3rd ed., 624. In *R. v. Chief Metropolitan Stipendiary Magistrate, ex p. Choudhury* [1991] 1 Q.B. 429, 91 Cr.App.R. 393, DC, however, it was held that the mere intention to promote hostility and ill-will among different classes of Her Majesty's subjects did not amount to a seditious intention. What had to be proved was an intention thereby to incite violence against constituted authority. The argument on sedition was not the main point of the case, which principally concerned the law of blasphemy. The only authority referred to in the judgment on sedition was *Boucher v. R.* [1951] 2 D.L.R. 369, Supreme Court of Canada. Although none of the foregoing authorities were referred to, even in argument, they were (apart from *Caunt*) referred to in the judgments in *Boucher*. The court stated that, in its judgment, *Boucher* accurately reflected the law. Kellock J., to whose judgment Watkins L.J. specifically refers, said that one of the points in issue was whether an intention, "to promote feelings of ill-will and hostility between different classes of Her Majesty's subjects", taken literally and by itself, was sufficient. The conclusion was that it was not. **25–261**

There is authority to the effect that there is a further ingredient, namely that the act or words in question have a tendency to provoke disorder and violence: *R. v. Burdett* (1820) 1 St.Tr.(N.S.) 1; *R. v. Collins* (1839) 3 St.Tr.(N.S.) 1149; *R. v. Burns* (1886) 16 Cox 355; *R. v. Aldred* (1909) 22 Cox 1. See also *Boucher v. R.*, *ante* (approved on this point also by the Divisional Court in *ex p. Choudhury*), where the Supreme Court concluded that the offence of sedition required proof of an intention to incite to violence or to create public disorder.

Proof of the intention and the tendency

In determining whether the acts or words in question have a seditious tendency, all the circumstances including the nature of the audience addressed must be considered: *R. v. Burns*, *ante*; *R. v. Aldred*, *ante*. In determining whether the defendant had the requisite intention, there is some authority for the proposition that if his acts or words were calculated to have one or more of the proscribed effects then his intention will be presumed: *R. v. Burdett*, *ante*; *R. v. Harvey* (1823) 2 B. & C. 257; *R. v. Aldred*, *ante*; *R. v. Fussell*, *ante*; *R. v. Grant* (1848) 7 St.Tr.(N.S.) 507. The alternative view is that the natural tendency of the acts or words is not more than evidence of the intention of the person doing the acts or speaking or writing the words: see the dissenting judgment of Lord Cockburn in *Grant*, *ante*; *R. v. Burns*, *ante*; and *R. v. Caunt*, *ante*. If this point should ever arise for decision, it is submitted that the courts will uphold the latter view as being more restrictive of the scope of an offence which is liable to be abused at the expense of the liberty of the press and of liberty of expression: see, *per* Coleridge J. in *R. v. Aldred*. This would also be consistent with general principles relating to criminal liability and with section 8 of the *CJA* 1967 (*ante*, § 17–36), assuming that that section is not decisive of the issue. **25–262**

In order to prove the seditious intention, evidence is admissible of the defendant having published other copies of the same libel, *Plunkett v. Cobbett* (1804) 5 Esp. 136, or another libel, *R. v. Pearce* (1791) 1 Peake, 3rd ed., 106, provided they expressly refer to the subject of the libel set out in the indictment: see *Chubb v. Westley* (1834) 6 C. & P. 436.

On the other hand, the defendant may put in evidence other passages in the same speech, newspaper or publication, plainly referring to the subject in question, or fairly connected with it, in order to prove that his intention was not such as was imputed to him by the prosecution, or that the passage in question would not fairly bear the construction attempted to be given to it: *R. v. Lambert and Perry* (1810) 31 St.Tr. 335.

Lawful criticism

25–263 "An intention to show that Her Majesty has been misled or mistaken in her measures, or to point out errors or defects in the government or constitution as by law established, with a view to their reformation, or to excite Her Majesty's subjects to attempt by lawful means the alteration of any matter in Church or State by law established, or to point out, in order to their removal, matters which are producing or have a tendency to produce, feelings of hatred and ill-will between classes of Her Majesty's subjects, is not a seditious intention" (Cave J.'s direction to the jury in *R. v. Burns*, *ante*, adopting Stephen's *caveat* as to what was not sedition). See also *R. v. Sullivan*; *R. v. Pigott* (1868) 11 Cox 44. To impute corruption to judges has been said to be seditious: *R. v. Lord George Gordon* (1787) 22 St.Tr. 175; but it would seem to be properly punishable as contempt of court (*post*, § 28–52) or, possibly, as a defamatory libel (*post*, §§ 29–72 *et seq.*)

Truth is no defence

25–264 If the words spoken or written are seditious, evidence to prove their truth is inadmissible: *R. v. Aldred*, *ante*. The *Libel Act* 1843, s.6 (justification for the public benefit) does not apply to seditious libel: *R. v. Duffy* (1846) 2 Cox 45.

Indictment

STATEMENT OF OFFENCE

25–265 *Sedition.*

PARTICULARS OF OFFENCE

A B, on the —— day of ——, 20—, in the hearing of liege subjects of our lady the Queen, uttered a seditious speech, the purport of which was (state in ordinary language).

Fine or imprisonment, or both.

(2) Special rules relating to libels

25–266 The publication of any seditious matter in anything capable of being a libel will constitute a seditious libel; there must be something of a permanent nature about the publication: see *R. v. Sullivan*; *R. v. Pigott* (1868) 11 Cox 44 and *post*, § 29–73.

Publication

25–267 A publication must be proved. The publication may be by selling the libel, distributing it *gratis*, reading it to others (if the tendency of it was known beforehand) or by sending it and having it delivered to another person: 1 Hawk. c. 73, s.11. Evidence of the defendant's procuring another person to publish the libel is sufficient to maintain a count charging the defendant with having published it: and, therefore, evidence of the libel having been purchased in a bookseller's shop, or at a newspaper office, or the office of a newsvendor, from an employee there, in the course of business, will support a count charging the employer with having published it (*R. v. Almon* (1770) 20 St. Tr. 803 at 839), even although it be proved that the employer be not privy to it: *R. v. Gutch, Fisher and Alexander* (1829) M. & M. 433; *Att.-Gen. v. Siddon* (1830) 1 Cr. & J. 220.

Rebuttal of prima facie case of publication by agent

Libel Act 1843, s.7

25–268 **7.** Whensoever, upon the trial of any indictment or information for the publication of a libel, under the plea of not guilty, evidence shall have been given which shall establish a presumptive case of publication against the defendant by the act of any other person by his authority, it shall be competent to such defendant to prove that such publication was made without his authority, consent, or knowledge, and that the said publication did not arise from want of due care or caution on his part.

[This section is printed as repealed in part by the *Statute Law Revision Act* 1891.]

Evidence as to ownership of newspapers, identity of printers

See *post*, § 29–77. **25–269**

Function of judge and jury

Libel Act 1792 (Fox's Act), ss.1–4

Whereas doubts have arisen whether on the trial of an indictment or information for the making or publishing any libel, where an issue or issues are joined between the [Queen] and the defendant or defendants, on the plea of not guilty pleaded, it be competent to the jury empanelled to try the same to give their verdict upon the whole matter in issue: **25–270**

1. On every such trial the jury sworn to try the issue may give a general verdict of guilty upon the whole matter put in issue upon such indictment or information, and shall not be required or directed by the court or judge before whom such indictment or information shall be tried to find the defendant or defendants guilty merely on proof of the publication by such defendant or defendants of the paper charged to be a libel, and of the sense ascribed to the same in such indictment or information.

2. Provided always, that on every such trial the court or judge before whom such indictment or information shall be tried shall, according to their or his discretion, give their or his opinion and directions to the jury on the matter in issue between the [Queen] and the defendant or defendants, in like manner as in other criminal cases.

3. Provided also, that nothing herein contained shall extend or be construed to extend to prevent the jury from finding a special verdict, in their discretion, as in other criminal cases.

4. Provided also, that in case the jury shall find the defendant or defendants guilty it shall and may be lawful for the said defendant or defendants to move in arrest of judgment, on such ground and in such manner as by law he or they might have done before the passing of this Act, any thing herein contained to the contrary notwithstanding.

Indictment for seditious libel

STATEMENT OF OFFENCE

Seditious libel. **25–271**

PARTICULARS OF OFFENCE

A B, on the —— day of ——, 20—, seditiously wrote and published or caused or procured to be written and published a certain seditious libel concerning Her Majesty's Government, containing the following seditious matters:

[Set out the matter alleged to be seditious.]

Fine or imprisonment, or both. As to the seizure of copies of a seditious libel after conviction in respect thereof, and as to disposal of such copies, see the *Criminal Libel Act* 1819, ss.1, 2.

No prosecution against any person responsible for the publication of a newspaper, as defined by the *Newspaper Libel and Registration Act* 1881, s.1, for any libel published therein may be instituted without the order of a High Court judge: see *Law of Libel Amendment Act* 1888, ss.1, 8. A journalist is not such a person: *Gleaves v. Insall* [1999] 2 Cr.App.R. 466, DC.

Besides setting out the seditious passages of the publication, the indictment should also contain such averments and innuendoes as may be necessary to render it intelligible, and its application to the Sovereign or the Government, etc., evident: *R. v. Yates* (1872) 12 Cox 233.

If the libel is in a foreign language, and is set out in that language, together with a translation, the translation must be proved to be correct: *R. v. Peltier* (1803) 28 St. Tr. 529.

Privilege

See the *Defamation Act* 1996, ss.14 and 15. **25–272**

[The next paragraph is § 25–276.]

X. *INCITING TO DISAFFECTION*

Police Act 1996, s.91

Causing disaffection amongst members of police force

25–276 **91.**—(1) Any person who causes, or attempts to cause, or does any act calculated to cause, disaffection amongst the members of any police force, or induces or attempts to induce, or does any act calculated to induce, any member of a police force to withhold his services, shall be guilty of an offence and liable—

(a) on summary conviction, to imprisonment for a term not exceeding *six* [12] months or to a fine not exceeding the statutory maximum;

(b) on conviction on indictment, to imprisonment for a term not exceeding two years or to a fine or to both.

(2) This section applies to special constables appointed for a police area as it applies to members of a police force.

(3) Liability under subsection (1) for any behaviour is in addition to any civil liability for that behaviour.

[Subs. (3) was inserted by the *PJA* 2006, s.52, and Sched. 14, para. 30. In subs. (1)(a), "12" is substituted for "six", as from a day to be appointed, by the *CJA* 2003, s.282(2) and (3). The increase has no application to offences committed before the substitution takes effect: s.282(4).]

The "statutory maximum" means the prescribed sum within the meaning of section 32 of the *MCA* 1980 (*ante*, § 1–75aa): *Interpretation Act* 1978, Sched. 1 (Appendix B–28). As to the penalty on summary conviction, see the supplement.

Identically worded offences (with identical penalties) to those created by section 91(1) are created in relation to members of the Ministry of Defence police by section 6 of the *Ministry of Defence Police Act* 1987.

Aliens Restriction (Amendment) Act 1919, s.3

Incitement to sedition, etc.

25–277 **3.**—(1) If any alien attempts or does any act calculated or likely to cause sedition or disaffection amongst any of Her Majesty's Forces or the forces of Her Majesty's allies, or amongst the civilian population, he shall be liable on conviction on indictment to imprisonment for a term not exceeding ten years, or on summary conviction to imprisonment for a term not exceeding *three* [12] months.

(2) [*Summary offence relating to promotion of industrial unrest.*]

[In subs. (1), "12" is substituted for "three", as from a day to be appointed, by the *CJA* 2003, s.282(2) and (3). The increase has no application to offences committed before the substitution takes effect: s.282(4).]

The expression "alien" shall not include a British protected person: *British Nationality Act* 1948, s.3(3). "British protected person" has the same meaning as in the *British Nationality Act* 1981: *ibid.*, s.3(4). See sections 50(1) and 52(6) of, and Schedule 7 to, the *British Nationality Act* 1981.

Incitement to Disaffection Act 1934, s.1

25–278 **1.** If any person maliciously and advisedly endeavours to seduce any member of Her Majesty's forces from his duty or allegiance to Her Majesty, he shall be guilty of an offence under this Act.

Section 1 creates a single offence which is committed by anyone who endeavours to seduce members of the forces with a particular intent. The intent might either be to seduce them from their duty or from their allegiance or from both. The intent may be stated in the alternative in one count (see the *Indictment Rules* 1971, r.7, *ante*, § 1–120): *R. v. Arrowsmith* [1975] Q.B. 678, 60 Cr.App.R. 211, CA. As to who owes allegiance to the sovereign, see *Joyce v. DPP* [1946] A.C. 347 at 366, HL.

The word "maliciously" in section 1 means "something which is wilful or intentional: deliberate—wilfully and intentionally to do an unlawful act": *R. v. Arrowsmith, ante*.

Incitement to Disaffection Act 1934, ss.2, 3

25–279 **2.**—(1) If any person, with intent to commit or to aid, abet, counsel, or procure the commission of an offence under section one of this Act, has in his possession or under his control any document of such a nature that the dissemination of copies thereof among members of Her Majesty's forces would constitute such an offence, he shall be guilty of an offence under this Act.

(2) If a judge of the High Court is satisfied by information on oath that there is reasonable ground for suspecting that an offence under this Act has been committed, and that evidence of the commission thereof is to be found at any premises or place specified in the information, he may, on an application made by an officer of police of a rank not lower than that of inspector, grant a search warrant authorising any such officer as aforesaid named in the warrant together with any other persons named in the warrant and any other officers of police to enter the premises or place at any time within *one month* [three months] from the date of the warrant, if necessary by force, and to search the premises or place and every person found therein, and to seize anything found on the premises or place or on any such person which the officer has reasonable ground for suspecting to be evidence of the commission of such an offence as aforesaid:

Provided that—

(a) a search warrant shall only be issued in respect of an offence suspected to have been committed within the three months prior to the laying of the information thereof; and

(b) if a search warrant under this Act has been executed on any premises it shall be the duty of the officer of police who has conducted or directed the search to notify the occupier that the search has taken place, and to supply him with a list of any documents or other objects which have been removed from the premises, and where any documents have been removed from any other person to supply that person with a list of such documents.

(3) No woman shall, in pursuance of a warrant issued under the last foregoing subsection, be searched except by a woman.

(4) Anything seized under this section may be retained for a period not exceeding one **25–280** month, or if within that period proceedings are commenced for an offence under this Act until the conclusion of those proceedings, and, in relation to property which has come into the possession of the police under this section, the *Police Property Act* 1897 (which makes provision with respect to the disposal of property in possession of the police) shall have effect subject to the foregoing provisions of this subsection and to the provisions of this Act conferring powers on courts dealing with offences.

[This section is printed as amended by the *CJA* 1972, Sched. 5; and as amended, as from a day to be appointed, by the *SOCPA* 2005, s.174(1), and Sched. 16, para. 1 (substitution of words in square brackets for italicised words).]

3.—(1) A person guilty of an offence under this Act shall be liable, on conviction on indict- **25–281** ment to imprisonment for a term not exceeding two years or to a fine ..., or on summary conviction to imprisonment for a term not exceeding *four* [12] months or to a fine not exceeding the prescribed sum, or (whether on conviction on indictment or on summary conviction) to both such imprisonment and fine.

(2) No prosecution in England under this Act shall take place without the consent of the Director of Public Prosecutions.

(3) Where a prosecution under this Act is being carried on by the Director of Public Prosecutions, a court of summary jurisdiction shall not deal with the case summarily without the consent of the Director.

(4) Where any person is convicted of an offence under this Act, the court dealing with the case may order any documents connected with the offence to be destroyed or dealt with in such other manner as may be specified in the order, but no documents shall be destroyed before the expiration of the period within which an appeal may be lodged, and if an appeal is lodged no document shall be destroyed until after the appeal has been heard and decided.

[On conviction on indictment, the fine is at large by virtue of the *CLA* 1977, s.32, *ante*, § 5–391. The reference to "the prescribed sum" is substituted by virtue of the *MCA* 1980, s.32(2), *ante*, § 1–75aa. As to the amount thereof, see section 32(9), *ante*, § 1–75aa. In subs. (1), "12" is substituted for "four", as from a day to be appointed, by the *CJA* 2003, s.282(2) and (3). The increase has no application to offences committed before the substitution takes effect: s.282(4).]

Procuring or assisting desertion

As to the punishment of persons subject to military law who persuade or assist **25–282** soldiers, etc., to desert, see *Army Act* 1955, ss.37, 39; *Reserve Forces Act* 1996, s.98. Civilians guilty of these acts may be sentenced under section 192(2) of the *Army Act* 1955, on summary conviction to a fine not exceeding the prescribed sum (£5,000—*ante*, § 1–75aa) or to imprisonment for a term not exceeding three (12 as from a day to be appointed: *CJA* 2003, s.282(2) and (3); but only in relation to offences committed on or after the commencement date: s.282(4)) months, or to both such fine and imprisonment; or on conviction on indictment to a fine or to imprisonment for a term not exceeding two years or to both such fine and imprisonment. For corresponding provisions in the *Air Force Act* 1955 and the *Naval Discipline Act* 1957, see section 192 of the 1955 Act and section 97 of the 1957 Act. See also the *Reserve Forces Act* 1996, s.101.

The whole of the 1955 Acts and the 1957 Act are repealed as from a day to be appointed: *AFA* 2006, s.378(2), and Sched. 17. As to section 98 of the 1996 Act, as from a day to be appointed, subsection (5) is repealed: *ibid.*; and the remaining provisions are amended: *ibid.*, s.358, and Sched. 14, para. 92. Sections 8 and 10 of the 2006 Act correspond to sections 37 and 39 of the 1955 Act, and section 344 corresponds to section 192. Sections 345 and 346 punish the aiding and abetting of malingering, and the obstruction of persons subject to service law who are acting in the course of their duty. Section 347 supplements sections 344 to 346.

[The next paragraph is § 25–288.]

XI. PROHIBITION OF QUASI-MILITARY ORGANISATIONS

Uniforms

25–288 The *Public Order Act* 1936, s.1 makes it an offence for any person in any public place or at any public meeting to wear uniform signifying his association with any political organisation or with the promotion of any political object. There are restrictions on prosecutions and there is an exception in relation to ceremonial, anniversary or other special occasions. In connection with this offence, which is triable only summarily, see *O'Moran v. DPP* [1975] Q.B. 864, DC.

As to the penalty and the power of arrest, see section 7(2) and (3), *post*, § 25–291.

Public Order Act 1936, s.2

25–289 **2.**—(1) If the members or adherents of any association of persons, whether incorporated or not, are—

(a) organised or trained or equipped for the purpose of enabling them to be employed in usurping the functions of the police or of the armed forces of the Crown; or

(b) organised and trained or organised and equipped either for the purpose of enabling them to be employed for the use or display of physical force in promoting any political object, or in such manner as to arouse reasonable apprehension that they are organised and either trained or equipped for that purpose;

then any person who takes part in the control or management of the association, or in so organising or training as aforesaid any members or adherents thereof, shall be guilty of an offence under this section:

Provided that in any proceedings against a person charged with the offence of taking part in the control or management of such an association as aforesaid it shall be a defence to that charge to prove that he neither consented to nor connived at the organisation, training, or equipment of members or adherents of the association in contravention of the provisions of this section.

25–290 (2) No prosecution shall be instituted under this section without the consent of the Attorney-General.

(3) [*Application to High Court by Attorney-General for order preventing disposition of property of association, of which the members or adherents are organised, trained or equipped in contravention of this section.*]

(4) In any criminal or civil proceedings under this section proof of things done or of words written, spoken or published (whether or not in the presence of any party to the proceedings) by any person taking part in the control or management of an association or

in organising, training or equipping members or adherents of an association shall be admissible as evidence of the purposes for which, or the manner in which, members or adherents of the association (whether those persons or others) were organised, or trained, or equipped.

(5) If a judge of the High Court is satisfied by information on oath that there is reasonable ground for suspecting that an offence under this section has been committed, and that evidence of the commission thereof is to be found at any premises or place specified in the information, he may, on an application made by an officer of police of a rank not lower than that of inspector, grant a search warrant authorising any such officer as aforesaid named in the warrant together with any other persons named in the warrant and any other officers of police to enter the premises or place at any time within *one month* [three months] from the date of the warrant, if necessary by force, and to search the premises or place and every person found therein, and to seize anything found on the premises or place or on any such person which the officer has reasonable ground for suspecting to be evidence of the commission of such an offence as aforesaid:

Provided that no woman shall, in pursuance of a warrant issued under this subsection, be searched except by a woman.

(6) Nothing in this section shall be construed as prohibiting the employment of a reasonable number of persons as stewards to assist in the preservation of order at any public meeting held upon private premises or the making of arrangements for that purpose or the instruction of the persons to be so employed in their lawful duties as such stewards, or their being furnished with badges or other distinguishing signs.

[The words in square brackets in subs. (5) are substituted for the italicised words as from a day to be appointed: *SOCPA* 2005, s.174(1), and Sched. 16, para. 2.]

As to applications for search warrants, their execution and the powers of seizure thereunder, see sections 15, 16 and 19 of the *PACE Act* 1984, *ante*, §§ 15–101, 15–102, 15–112.

In *R. v. Jordan and Tyndall* [1963] Crim.L.R. 124, CCA, the applicants were convicted of organising and equipping an association of persons in such manner as to arouse reasonable apprehension that they were organised and equipped for the purpose of enabling them to be employed for the use or display of physical force in promoting a political object. They were sentenced to nine and six months' imprisonment respectively. It was held: (a) the fact that there was no evidence of actual attacks or plans for attacks on opponents did not necessarily remove grounds for "reasonable apprehension"; (b) the fact that these were the first convictions under subsection (1) made deterrent sentences appropriate.

Public Order Act 1936, s.7

7.—(1) Any person who commits an offence under section two of this Act shall be liable on summary conviction to imprisonment for a term not exceeding *six* [12] months or to a fine not exceeding the prescribed sum, or to both such imprisonment and fine, or, on conviction on indictment, to imprisonment for a term not exceeding two years or to a fine …, or to both such imprisonment and fine. **25–291**

(2) Any person guilty of any offence under this Act other than an offence under section 2 … shall be liable on summary conviction to imprisonment for a term not exceeding *three months* [51 weeks] or to a fine not exceeding level 4 on the standard scale or to both such imprisonment and fine.

(3) [*Repealed by* Serious Organised Crime and Police Act *2005, ss.111 and 174(2), Sched. 7, para. 13, and Sched. 17, Pt 2.*]

[This section is printed as amended by the *Public Order Act* 1963; the *MCA* 1980, s.32(2) (substitution of reference to "the prescribed sum", as to which, see *ante*, § 1–75aa); and the *CJA* 1982, ss.38, 46 (substitution of reference to "level 4 on the standard scale", as to which, see *ante*, § 5–403); and as repealed in part by the *CLA* 1977, s.32(1); and the *Public Order Act* 1986, s.40(3) and Sched. 3. In subs. (1), "12" is substituted for "six", as from a day to be appointed, by the *CJA* 2003, s.282(2) and (3). In subs. (2), "51 weeks" is substituted for "three months" as from a day to be appointed: *ibid.*, s.280(2), and Sched. 26, para. 8. Neither increase has any application to offences committed before the amendment takes effect: ss.280(3), 282(4).]

Public Order Act 1936, s.9

25–292 **9.**—(1) In this Act the following expressions have the meanings hereby respectively assigned to them, that is to say:—

"Meeting" means a meeting held for the purpose of the discussion of matters of public interest or for the purpose of the expression of views on such matters;

"Private premises" means premises to which the public have access (whether on payment or otherwise) only by permission of the owner, occupier, or lessee of the premises;

"Public meeting" includes any meeting in a public place and any meeting which the public or any section thereof are permitted to attend, whether on payment or otherwise;

"Public place" includes any highway and any other premises or place to which at the material time the public have or are permitted to have access, whether on payment or otherwise;

"Recognised corps" means a rifle club, miniature rifle club or cadet corps approved by a Secretary of State under the *Firearms Acts* 1920 to 1936, for the purposes of those Acts.

(2) [*Repealed by* Law Officers Act *1997, s.3(2) and Sched.*]

(3) Any order made under this Act … by a chief officer of police may be revoked or varied by a subsequent order made in like manner.

(4) The powers conferred by this Act on any chief officer of police may, in the event of a vacancy in the office or in the event of the chief officer of police being unable to act owing to illness or absence, be exercised by the person duly authorised in accordance with directions given by a Secretary of State to exercise those powers on behalf of the chief officer of police.

[This section is printed as amended by the *Police Act* 1964, s.64, and Sched. 10; the *CJA* 1972, ss.33, 66(7); and the *Public Order Act* 1986, s.40(3), and Sched. 3.]

25–293 In relation to the definition of "public place", see *Cawley v. Frost* [1976] 1 W.L.R. 1207, DC; *Anderson v. Miller*, 64 Cr.App.R. 178, DC; *R. v. Edwards and Roberts*, 67 Cr.App.R. 228, CA; *Marsh v. Arscott*, 75 Cr.App.R. 211, DC; *Lawrenson v. Oxford* [1982] Crim.L.R. 185, DC; and *Harriot v. DPP*, 170 J.P. 494, DC (*ante*, § 24–114). The definition of "public place" in section 9 accords with the definition in the *Firearms Act* 1968, *ante*, §§ 24–61, 24–85.

The reference to the *Firearms Acts* 1920 to 1936 in the definition of "recognised corps" should be construed as a reference to the *Firearms Act* 1968: see s.59(3) of the 1968 Act and the *Interpretation Act* 1978, s.17(2)(a) (Appendix B–17).

Indictment for managing a quasi-military organisation

STATEMENT OF OFFENCE

25–294 *Managing a quasi-military organisation, contrary to s.2(1)(b) of the* Public Order Act *1936*.

PARTICULARS OF OFFENCE

A B, between the —— day of —— and the —— day of ——, 20—, took part in the control and management of an association of persons called ——, which was organised and equipped for the purpose of enabling its members to be employed for the use or display of physical force in promoting a political object.

[The next paragraph is § 25–297.]

XII. DISCLOSURE, ETC., OF GOVERNMENT SECRETS

A. OFFICIAL SECRETS ACT 1911

Official Secrets Act 1911, s.1

25–297 **1.**—(1) If any person for any purpose prejudicial to the safety or interests of the State—

(a) approaches, inspects, passes over, or is in the neighbourhood of, or enters any prohibited place within the meaning of this Act; or

(b) makes any sketch, plan, model, or note which is calculated to be or might be or is intended to be directly or indirectly useful to an enemy; or

(c) obtains, collects, records, or publishes, or communicates to any other person any secret official code word, or pass word, or any sketch, plan, model, article, or note, or other document or information which is calculated to be or might be or is intended to be directly or indirectly useful to an enemy;

he shall be guilty of felony.

(2) On a prosecution under this section, it shall not be necessary to show that the accused person was guilty of any particular act tending to show a purpose prejudicial to the safety or interests of the State, and, notwithstanding that no such act is proved against him, he may be convicted if, from the circumstances of the case, or his conduct, or his known character as proved, it appears that his purpose was a purpose prejudicial to the safety or interests of the State; and if any sketch, plan, model, article, note, document, or information relating to or used in any prohibited place within the meaning of this Act, or anything in such a place, or any secret official code word or pass word, is made, obtained, collected, recorded, published, or communicated by any person other than a person acting under lawful authority, it shall be deemed to have been made, obtained, collected, recorded, published, or communicated for a purpose prejudicial to the safety or interests of the State unless the contrary is proved.

[This section is printed as amended by the *Official Secrets Act* 1920, s.10, and Sched. 1.]

The reference to being guilty of felony should be read as a reference to being guilty of an offence: *CLA* 1967, s.12(5)(a). **25–298**

In *Chandler v. DPP* [1964] A.C. 763, HL, the appellants intended and desired that a number of persons should enter an operational airfield (a "prohibited place" within s.3) and by obstruction prevent any aircraft taking off for a number of hours, their objective being to prevent nuclear war and to get the facts about it known to the public. They were convicted of conspiring to commit a breach of section 1, namely "for a purpose prejudicial to the safety or interests of the State" to enter the airfield. It was held that: (a) this section applies to sabotage as well as spying; (b) if the jury were satisfied that the defendants' "immediate purpose" in approaching a prohibited place was to obstruct its operation, they then had to consider whether the purpose was prejudicial to the interests of the State and disregard what the defendants' long-term purpose or motive might have been; and (c) the defendants were not entitled to adduce evidence on whether it was prejudicial to the interests of the State to have nuclear armaments since the disposition of the armed forces is within the discretion of the State and cannot be tried in a court of law.

In *R. v. M.*, 11 Cr.App.R. 207, CCA, upon a prosecution under the *Defence of the Realm (Consolidation) Regulations* 1914, which, *inter alia*, proscribed the communication of information "of such a nature as is calculated to be or might be directly or indirectly useful to an enemy", it was held that it was immaterial whether the information was true or false provided that the defendant intended to inform and not to mislead. The defendant takes the risk whether it is true or not.

In *R. v. Kent*, 28 Cr.App.R. 23, CCA, the appellant, who had been employed as a code clerk at the embassy of a foreign power in England, was on his dismissal arrested on charges of offences contrary to section 1 alleged to have been committed while he was a member of the diplomatic staff. He thereupon claimed diplomatic privilege, but any claim to such privilege was at once waived by the Ambassador, and subsequently by the Government of the foreign power. *Held*, assuming that diplomatic privilege can be claimed by a member of a diplomatic staff on a criminal charge, the privilege was that of the Ambassador and not of the individual and ceased from the moment of waiver (see *ante*, §§ 1–83 *et seq.*). It was further held that the Official Secrets Acts apply to acts done by a diplomatic agent in respect of the archives of the mission in which he is employed. **25–299**

The word "enemy" may be taken to mean a potential enemy with whom we might some day be at war: *R. v. Parrott*, 8 Cr.App.R. 186, CCA. **25–300**

As to punishment, see the *Official Secrets Act* 1920, s.8(1), *post*, § 25–319. As to "prohibited place", see section 3, *post*, § 25–302. As to "communicates", "obtains", "document", "model" and "sketch", see section 12, *post*, § 25–312. As to evidence of communications with a foreign agent being evidence of "purpose", see section 2 of the *Official Secrets Act* 1920, *post*, § 25–315.

Indictment for entering a prohibited place

STATEMENT OF OFFENCE

25–301 *Entering a prohibited place, contrary to section 1 of the* Official Secrets Act *1911.*

PARTICULARS OF OFFENCE

A B, on the —— day of ——, 20—entered a prohibited place, namely —— for a purpose prejudicial to the safety and interests of the State.

Imprisonment for not more than 14 years (*post*, § 25–319).

Official Secrets Act 1911, s.3

Definition of prohibited place

25–302 **3.** For the purposes of this Act, the expression "prohibited place" means—

(a) any work of defence, arsenal, naval or air force establishment or station, factory, dockyard, mine, minefield, camp, ship, or aircraft belonging to or occupied by or on behalf of [Her] Majesty, or any telegraph, telephone, wireless or signal station, or office so belonging or occupied, and any place belonging to or occupied by or on behalf of [Her] Majesty and used for the purpose of building, repairing, making, or storing any munitions of war, or any sketches, plans, models, or documents relating thereto, or for the purpose of getting any metals, oil, or minerals of use in time of war; and

(b) any place not belonging to [Her] Majesty where any munitions of war, or any sketches, models, plans, or documents relating thereto, are being made, repaired, gotten, or stored under contract with, or with any person on behalf of, [Her] Majesty, or otherwise on behalf of [Her] Majesty; and

(c) any place belonging to or used for the purposes of [Her] Majesty which is for the time being declared by order of a Secretary of State to be a prohibited place for the purposes of this section, on the ground that information with respect thereto, or damage thereto, would be useful to an enemy; and

(d) any railway, roadway, or channel, or other means of communication by land or water (including any works or structures being part thereof or connected therewith), or any place used for gas, water, or electricity works or other works for purposes of a public character, or any place where any munitions of war or any sketches, models, plans, or documents relating thereto, are being made, repaired, or stored otherwise than on behalf of [Her] Majesty, which is for the time being declared by order of a Secretary of State to be a prohibited place for the purposes of this section, on the ground that information with respect thereto, or the destruction or obstruction thereof, or interference therewith, would be useful to an enemy.

[This section is printed as amended by the *Official Secrets Act* 1920, s.10, and Sched. 1.]

25–303 Reference in whatever terms in this Act to ships, vessels or boats or activities or places connected therewith, are extended to include hovercraft or activities or places connected with hovercraft, by the *Hovercraft (Application of Enactments) Order* 1972 (S.I. 1972 No. 971).

For the purposes of section 3(c), *ante*, a place belonging to the Civil Aviation Authority shall be deemed to be a place belonging to Her Majesty: *Civil Aviation Act* 1982, s.18(2). Any electronic communications station or office belonging to, or occupied by, the provider of a public electronic communications service shall be a prohibited place for the purposes of the 1911 Act: *Communications Act* 2003, s.406, and Sched. 17, para. 2.

25–304 The *Atomic Energy Authority Act* 1954, s.6(3), enables the Secretary of State to declare places belonging to or used by the authority prohibited places for the purposes of the *Official Secrets Act* 1911. This includes a site to which a permit granted by the Secretary of State for Trade and Industry to a body corporate applies: see *Nuclear Installations Act* 1965, s.2, Sched. 1; *Atomic Energy Authority Act* 1971, s.17, Sched. The *Official Secrets (Prohibited Places) Order* 1994 (S.I. 1994 No. 968) declares the places specified in the Schedule to the Order to be prohibited places. Each of the places specified is, on the ground that information with respect thereto, or damage thereto, would be useful to an enemy, accordingly a prohibited place for the purposes of section 3 of the 1911 Act. Part I of the Schedule lists sites to which a permit applies within the meaning of Schedule 1, paragraph 1 to the *Nuclear Installations Act* 1965. Part II lists places belonging to or used for the purposes of the United Kingdom Atomic Energy Authority.

S.I. 1994 No. 968, Sched.

Article 3 SCHEDULE

PROHIBITED PLACES

PART I

The British Nuclear Fuels plc site at Sellafield, Seascale, Cumbria, CA20 1PG. **25–305**

The British Nuclear Fuels plc site at Capenhurst, near Chester, Cheshire, CH1 6ER.

The Urenco (Capenhurst) Limited site at Capenhurst, near Chester, Cheshire, CH1 6ER.

PART II

The United Kingdom Atomic Energy Authority site at Harwell, Didcot, Oxfordshire, OX11 0RA.

The United Kingdom Atomic Energy Authority site at Windscale, Seascale, Cumbria, CA20 1PF.

Official Secrets Act 1911, ss.6–12

Power to arrest

6. [*Repealed by* Serious Organised Crime and Police Act *2005, ss.111 and 174(2), Sched. 7, para. 12, and Sched. 17, Pt 2.*] **25–306**

Penalty for harbouring spies

7. If any person knowingly harbours any person whom he knows, or has reasonable grounds for supposing, to be a person who is about to commit or who has committed an offence under this Act, or knowingly permits to meet or assemble in any premises in his occupation or under his control any such persons, or if any person having harboured any such person or permitted to meet or assemble in any premises in his occupation or under his control any such persons, willingly omits or refuses to disclose to a superintendent of police any information which it is in his power to give in relation to any such person he shall be guilty of an offence. ... **25–307**

[This section is printed as amended by the *Official Secrets Act* 1920, s.10 and Sched. 1.]

As to punishment, see the *Official Secrets Act* 1920, s.8(2), *post*, § 25–319. As to "harbouring", see *ante*, § 25–232, and *post*, §§ 28–201 *et seq.*

Restriction on prosecution

8. A prosecution for an offence under this Act shall not be instituted except by or with the consent of the Attorney-General. **25–308**

[The proviso to section 8 was repealed by the *Criminal Jurisdiction Act* 1975.]

Search warrants

9.—(1) If a justice of the peace is satisfied by information on oath that there is reasonable ground for suspecting that an offence under this Act has been or is about to be committed, he may grant a search warrant authorising any constable ... to enter at any time any premises or place named in the warrant, if necessary, by force, and to search the premises or place and every person found therein, and to seize any sketch, plan, model, article, note, or document, or anything of a like nature or anything which is evidence of an offence under this Act having been or being about to be committed, which he may find on the premises or place or on any such person, and with regard to or in connection with which he has reasonable ground for suspecting that an offence under this Act has been or is about to be committed. **25–309**

(2) Where it appears to a superintendent of police that the case is one of great emergency and that in the interests of the State immediate action is necessary, he may by a written order under his hand give to any constable the like authority as may be given by the warrant of a justice under this section.

[The words omitted were repealed by the *PACE Act* 1984, s.119(2), and Sched. 7.]

Section 9 is extended by section 11(3) of the *Official Secrets Act* 1989, *post*, § 25–337.

Extent of Act and place of trial of offence

25–310 **10.**—(1) This Act shall apply to all acts which are offences under this Act when committed in any part of Her Majesty's dominions, or when committed by British officers or subjects elsewhere.

(2) An offence under this Act, if alleged to have been committed out of the United Kingdom, may be inquired of, heard, and determined, in any competent British court in the place where the offence was committed, or ... in England. ...

(3) An offence under this Act shall not be tried ... by the sheriff court in Scotland, nor by any court out of the United Kingdom which has not jurisdiction to try crimes which involve the greatest punishment allowed by law.

(4) [*Repealed by* Northern Ireland (Emergency Provisions) Act *1975, s.23(2) and Sched. 3*.]

[The words omitted in subs. (2) were repealed by the *Statute Law Revision Act* 1964, s.1, Sched. Subs. (2) is printed as amended by the *CJA* 1948, s.83 and Sched. 10. The words omitted in subs. (3) were repealed by the *CLA* 1967, s.10(2), Sched. 3.]

Saving for laws of British possessions

25–311 **11.** If by any law made before or after the passing of this Act by the legislature of any British possession provisions are made which appear to [Her] Majesty to be of the like effect as those contained in this Act, [Her] Majesty may, by Order in Council, suspend the operation within that British possession of this Act, or of any part thereof, so long as that law continues in force there, and no longer, ...:

Provided that the suspension of this Act, or of any part thereof, in any British possession shall not extend to the holder of an office under [Her] Majesty who is not appointed to that office by the Government of that possession.

[The words omitted were repealed by the *Statute Law (Repeals) Act* 1986.]

Interpretation

25–312 **12.** In this Act, unless the context otherwise requires,—

Any reference to a place belonging to [Her] Majesty includes a place belonging to any department of the Government of the United Kingdom or of any British possessions, whether the place is or is not actually vested in [Her] Majesty;

The expression "Attorney-General" means the Attorney- ... General for England; ... and, if the prosecution is instituted in any court out of the United Kingdom, means the person who in that court is Attorney-General, or exercises the like functions as the Attorney-General in England;

Expressions referring to communicating include any communicating, whether in whole or in part, and whether the sketch, plan, model, article, note, document, or information itself or the substance, effect, or description thereof only be communicated; expressions referring to obtaining or retaining any sketch, plan, model, article, note, or document, include the copying or causing to be copied the whole or any part of any sketch, plan, model, article, note, or document; and expressions referring to the communication of any sketch, plan, model, article, note or document include the transfer or transmission of the sketch, plan, model, article, note or document;

The expression "document" includes part of a document;

The expression "model" includes design, pattern, and specimen;

The expression "sketch" includes any photograph or other mode of representing any place or thing;

The expression "munitions of war" includes the whole or any part of any ship, submarine, aircraft, tank or similar engine, arms and ammunition, torpedo or mine, intended or adapted for use in war, and any other article, material, or device, whether actual or proposed, intended for such use;

The expression "superintendent of police" includes any police officer of a like or superior rank, and any person upon whom the powers of a superintendent of police are for the purpose of this Act conferred by a Secretary of State;

The expression "office under [Her] Majesty" includes any office or employment in or under any department of the Government of the United Kingdom, or of any British possession;

The expression "offence under this Act" includes any act, omission, or other thing which is punishable under this Act.

[This section is printed as amended by the *Official Secrets Act* 1920, ss.9, 10 and

Sched. 1; and the *Official Secrets Act* 1989, s.16(4), and Sched. 2; and as repealed in part by the *Law Officers Act* 1997, s.3(2) and Sched.]

As to the extended meaning to be given to "ship", see S.I. 1972 No. 971, *ante*, § 25–303.

B. OFFICIAL SECRETS ACT 1920

Official Secrets Act 1920, s.1

Unauthorised use of uniforms; falsification of reports, forgery, personation, and false documents

1.—(1) If any person for the purpose of gaining admission or of assisting any other person to gain admission, to a prohibited place, within the meaning of the *Official Secrets Act* 1911 (hereinafter referred to as "the principal Act"), or for any other purpose prejudicial to the safety or interests of the State within the meaning of the said Act— **25–313**

(a) uses or wears, without lawful authority, any naval, military, air-force, police, or other official uniform, or any uniform so nearly resembling the same as to be calculated to deceive, or falsely represents himself to be a person who is or has been entitled to use or wear any such uniform; or

(b) orally, or in writing in any declaration or application, or in any document signed by him or on his behalf, knowingly makes or connives at the making of any false statement or any omission; or

(c) … tampers with any passport or any naval, military, air-force, police, or official pass, permit, certificate, licence, or other document of a similar character (hereinafter in this section referred to as an official document), … or has in his possession any … forged, altered, or irregular official document; or

(d) personates, or falsely represents himself to be a person holding, or in the employment of a person holding office under [Her] Majesty, or to be or not to be a person to whom an official document or secret official code word or pass word has been duly issued or communicated, or with intent to obtain an official document, secret official code word or pass word, whether for himself or any other person, knowingly makes any false statement; or

(e) uses, or has in his possession or under his control, without the authority of the Government Department or the authority concerned, any die, seal, or stamp of or belonging to, or used, made or provided by any Government Department, or by any diplomatic, naval, military, or air-force authority appointed by or acting under the authority of [Her] Majesty, or any die, seal or stamp so nearly resembling any such die, seal or stamp as to be calculated to deceive, or counterfeits any such die, seal or stamp, or uses, or has in his possession, or under his control, any such counterfeited die, seal or stamp;

he shall be guilty of a misdemeanour.

(2) If any person— **25–314**

(a) retains for any purpose prejudicial to the safety or interests of the State any official document, whether or not completed or issued for use, when he has no right to retain it, or when it is contrary to his duty to retain it, or fails to comply with any directions issued by any Government Department or any person authorised by such department with regard to the return or disposal thereof; or

(b) allows any other person to have possession of any official document issued for his use alone, or communicates any secret official code word or pass word so issued, or, without lawful authority or excuse, has in his possession any official document or secret official code word or pass word issued for the use of some person other than himself, or on obtaining possession of any official document by finding or otherwise, neglects or fails to restore it to the person or authority by whom or for whose use it was issued, or to a police constable; or

(c) without lawful authority or excuse, manufactures or sells, or has in his possession for sale any such die, seal or stamp as aforesaid;

he shall be guilty of a misdemeanour.

(3) In the case of any prosecution under this section involving the proof of a purpose prejudicial to the safety or interests of the State, subsection (2) of section one of the principal Act shall apply in like manner as it applies to prosecutions under that section.

[The words omitted in section 1(1)(c) were repealed by the Schedule to the *Forgery and Counterfeiting Act* 1981.]

As to the meaning of "prohibited place", see *ante*, § 25–302.
As to punishment, see section 8(2), *post*, § 25–319.
For section 1(2) of the 1911 Act, see *ante*, § 25–297.

Official Secrets Act 1920, s.2

Communications with foreign agents to be evidence of commission of certain offences

25–315 **2.**—(1) In any proceedings against a person for an offence under section one of the principal Act, the fact that he has been in communication with, or attempted to communicate with, a foreign agent, whether within or without the United Kingdom, shall be evidence that he has, for a purpose prejudicial to the safety or interests of the State, obtained or attempted to obtain information which is calculated to be or might be or is intended to be directly or indirectly useful to an enemy.

(2) For the purpose of this section, but without prejudice to the generality of the foregoing provision—

(a) A person shall, unless he proves the contrary, be deemed to have been in communication with a foreign agent if—
  (i) He has, either within or without the United Kingdom, visited the address of a foreign agent or consorted or associated with a foreign agent; or
  (ii) Either, within or without the United Kingdom, the name or address of, or any other information regarding a foreign agent has been found in his possession, or has been supplied by him to any other person, or has been obtained by him from any other person:

(b) The expression "foreign agent" includes any person who is or has been or is reasonably suspected of being or having been employed by a foreign power either directly or indirectly for the purpose of committing an act, either within or without the United Kingdom, prejudicial to the safety or interests of the State, or who has or is reasonably suspected of having, either within or without the United Kingdom, committed, or attempted to commit, such an act in the interests of a foreign power:

(c) Any address, whether within or without the United Kingdom, reasonably suspected of being an address used for the receipt of communications intended for a foreign agent, or any address at which a foreign agent resides, or to which he resorts for the purpose of giving or receiving communications, or at which he carries on any business, shall be deemed to be the address of a foreign agent, and communications addressed to such an address to be communications with a foreign agent.

For section 1 of the 1911 Act, see *ante*, § 25–297.

The jury should consider the activities of the alleged foreign agent as evidence against the defendant only insofar as they showed that he was in communication with a foreign agent and that the alleged foreign agent was indeed a foreign agent: *R. v. Kent*, 28 Cr.App.R. 23, CCA.

Official Secrets Act 1920, s.3

Interfering with officers of the police or members of [Her] Majesty's forces

25–316 **3.** No person in the vicinity of any prohibited place shall obstruct, knowingly mislead or otherwise interfere with or impede, the chief officer or a superintendent or other officer of police, or any member of [Her] Majesty's forces engaged on guard, sentry, patrol, or other similar duty in relation to the prohibited place, and, if any person acts in contravention of, or fails to comply with, this provision, he shall be guilty of a misdemeanour.

In *Adler v. George* [1964] 2 Q.B. 7, DC, it was held that "in the vicinity of" meant "in or in the vicinity of".

For the meaning of "chief officer of police", see section 11(1A), *post*, § 25–324, and the *Police Act* 1996, s.101(1): *Interpretation Act* 1978, Sched. 1 (Appendix B–28). For the meaning of "prohibited place" and "superintendent of police", see sections 3 and 12 of the principal Act, *ante*, §§ 25–302, 25–312: s.11(1), *post*, § 25–324. As to punishment, see section 8(2), *post*, § 25–319.

Official Secrets Act 1920, s.6

Duty of giving information as to commission of offences

25–317 **6.**—(1) Where a chief officer of police is satisfied that there is reasonable ground for suspecting that an offence under section one of the principal Act has been committed and for believing that any person is able to furnish information as to the offence or suspected offence, he may apply to a Secretary of State for permission to exercise the powers conferred by this subsection and, if such permission is granted, he may authorise a superintendent of police, or any police officer not below the rank of inspector, to require the person believed to be able to furnish information to give any information in his power relating to the offence or suspected offence, and, if so required and on tender of his reasonable expenses, to attend at such reasonable time and place as may be specified by the superintendent or other officer; and if a person required in pursuance of such an authorisation to give information, or to attend as aforesaid, fails to comply with any such requirement or knowingly gives false information, he shall be guilty of a misdemeanour.

(2) Where a chief officer of police has reasonable grounds to believe that the case is one of great emergency and that in the interest of the State immediate action is necessary, he may exercise the powers conferred by the last foregoing subsection without applying for or being granted the permission of a Secretary of State, but if he does so shall forthwith report the circumstances to the Secretary of State.

(3) References in this section to a chief officer of police shall be construed as including references to any other officer of police expressly authorised by a chief officer of police to act on his behalf for the purposes of this section when by reason of illness, absence, or other cause he is unable to do so.

[This section is printed as substituted by the *Official Secrets Act* 1939, s.1.]

As to punishment, see section 8(2), *post*, § 25–319.

Official Secrets Act 1920, s.7

Attempts, incitements, etc.

7. Any person who attempts to commit any offence under the principal Act or this Act, or solicits or incites or endeavours to persuade another person to commit an offence, or aids or abets *and* does any act preparatory to the commission of an offence under the principal Act or this Act, shall be guilty of a felony or a misdemeanour or a summary offence, according as the offence in question is a felony, a misdemeanour or a summary offence, and on conviction shall be liable to the same punishment, and to be proceeded against in the same manner, as if he had committed the offence. **25–318**

In order to give intelligible meaning to this section, the word "and" where italicised must be read as "or": *R. v. Oakes* [1959] 2 Q.B. 350, 43 Cr.App.R. 114, CCA.

For a person to be convicted under section 7 of doing an act preparatory to the commission of an offence under the 1911 Act, it has to be shown that the act was done with the commission of an offence under the 1911 Act in mind. The prosecution only has to show that at the time of doing the act the accused realised that the transmission of prejudicial information was possible—it does not have to be proved that he realised it was probable: *R. v. Bingham* [1973] Q.B. 870, 57 Cr.App.R. 439, CA.

Official Secrets Act 1920, s.8

Provisions as to trial and punishment of offences

8.—(1) Any person who is guilty of a felony under the principal Act or this Act shall be liable to imprisonment for a term not exceeding fourteen years. **25–319**

(2) Any person who is guilty of a misdemeanour under the principal Act or this Act shall be liable on conviction on indictment to imprisonment, ... for a term not exceeding two years, or, on conviction under the *Summary Jurisdiction Acts*, to imprisonment ... for a term not exceeding *three* [12] months or to a fine not exceeding the prescribed sum, or both such imprisonment and fine:

Provided that no misdemeanour under the principal Act or this Act shall be dealt with summarily except with the consent of the Attorney-General.

(3) For the purposes of the trial of a person for an offence under the principal Act or this Act, the offence shall be deemed to have been committed either at the place in which the same actually was committed, or at any place in the United Kingdom in which the offender may be found.

(4) In addition and without prejudice to any powers which a court may possess to order the exclusion of the public from any proceedings, if in the course of proceedings before a court against any person for an offence under the principal Act or this Act or the proceedings on appeal, or in the course of the trial of a person for felony or misdemeanour under

the principal Act or this Act, application is made by the prosecution, on the ground that the publication of any evidence to be given or of any statement to be made in the course of the proceedings would be prejudicial to the national safety, that all or any portion of the public shall be excluded during any part of the hearing, the court may make an order to that effect, but the passing of sentence shall in any case take place in public.

(5) Where the person guilty of an offence under the principal Act or this Act is a company or corporation, every director and officer of the company or corporation shall be guilty of the like offence unless he proves that the act or omission constituting the offence took place without his knowledge or consent.

[This section is printed as amended by the *MCA* 1980, s.32(2), which substituted the reference to "the prescribed sum": as to this, see *ante*, § 1–75aa. In subs. (1), "12" is substituted for "three", as from a day to be appointed, by the *CJA* 2003, s.282(2) and (3). The increase has no application to offences committed before the substitution takes effect: s.282(4).]

25–320 The reference in subsection (2) to the *Summary Jurisdiction Acts* should be construed as a reference to the *MCA* 1980: *Interpretation Act* 1978, s.17(2)(a) (Appendix B–17).

Section 8(4) is extended by the *Official Secrets Act* 1989, s.11(4), *post*, § 25–324.

Consecutive sentences totalling 42 years' imprisonment for a series of offences against section 1(1)(c) of the principal Act were affirmed by the Court of Criminal Appeal in *R. v. Blake* [1962] 2 Q.B. 377, 45 Cr.App.R. 292.

25–321 In *Att.-Gen. v. Leveller Magazine Ltd* [1979] A.C. 440, HL, a witness at committal proceedings in respect of alleged offences contrary to the 1911 Act had been allowed, for reasons of national security, to write his name down. The court directed that his name should be shown only to the court, counsel and the defendants. Contempt proceedings were instituted in respect of the subsequent publication of the name of the witness in three separate magazines. In the House of Lords, none of their Lordships suggested that the magistrates' court had exceeded its jurisdiction in permitting the witness to write his name down. However, there were differences in the reasoning. Lord Diplock (at p. 451) appears to have taken the view that since the court could have acceded to an application under section 8(4) to hear the evidence of name and address *in camera* it had implied power to adopt the device which was adopted because it involved a lesser derogation from the general principle of open justice. Lord Russell agreed with Lord Diplock on this point (see p. 467). Lord Scarman (at pp. 470–471) thought that the justification for the device adopted had nothing to do with section 8(4). His Lordship, however, held that a court had power at common law to sit *in camera* if that was necessary for the protection of the administration of justice: if the Crown were to be deterred from prosecuting persons against whom there was evidence of the commission of an offence on the ground that national safety would be jeopardised by the conduct of the proceedings in public, then the court would be entitled to conclude that it was necessary for the protection of the administration of justice to conduct the proceedings *in camera*. His Lordship said that where the court had power to sit *in camera* it could also adopt the device adopted by the magistrates' court which was "a valuable and proper extension of the common law power to sit in private".

25–322 Viscount Dilhorne disagreed with Lords Diplock and Russell that the device adopted involved a lesser derogation from the principle of the open administration of justice than the giving of the witness's name *in camera* with the rest of the evidence being given in open court. He thought that section 8(4) could not be construed as giving power during a sitting in open court to permit or to direct that the name of a witness should not be disclosed. His Lordship also disagreed with Lord Scarman that the common law rule permitting a court to go into *camera* where a refusal to do so would render the administration of justice impracticable could be extended to permit a witness to write down his name and address. His Lordship said that a refusal to permit this device to be adopted could not render the administration of justice impracticable because the Crown rather than be deterred from instituting or continuing proceedings could apply for the proceedings to be held *in camera*.

The justification for the procedure, in Viscount Dilhorne's opinion, was that judges and justices have:

"a wide measure of control over the conduct of proceedings in their courts. On occasions for a variety of reasons witnesses are allowed to write down a piece of evidence instead of giving it orally and I know of a number of occasions when in Official Secrets Acts cases witnesses have been allowed to conceal their identity" (at p. 458).

His Lordship gave no clear indication, however, as to what criteria should govern a decision to permit such a course.

An application under section 8(4) does not need to be supported by evidence: the court is entitled in the exercise of its discretion to make an order under it in the light of the information given to it and the reasons advanced for taking that course: *ibid.*, *per* Viscount Dilhorne at p. 457. See also Lord Scarman, at p. 471.

In *R. v. Shayler (David Michael)* [2003] A.C.D. 79, CA, it was held that on a prose- **25–323**
cution under the *Official Secrets Act* 1989 (*post*, §§ 25–325 *et seq.*), where the defendant (a former security service officer) was representing himself, the judge had been entitled, (i) to order that certain members or former members of the security services should give evidence without being named, and screened in such a way as to be visible only to the judge, jury, counsel and the applicant, and (ii) to impose a "disclosure regime" whereunder the defendant was bound to give advance notice to the court if he wished to raise any matter relating, or purporting to relate, to security or intelligence; as to (i), the overall interests of justice required such order to be made where the prosecution had established that disclosure of the identity of the witnesses would give rise to a real risk to their safety and that their evidence was of such importance to the prosecution case that it would be unfair to make the prosecution proceed without it and where, therefore, failure to make the order would leave the prosecution with a stark choice between exposing them to the risk and abandoning the prosecution; as to potential prejudice to the defendant, the identity of the witnesses was known to the defendant, their credit-worthiness had been properly investigated and the result of that investigation had been disclosed to the defendant, and this was a case where some of the well-recognised advantages of open justice (*e.g.* increased pressure to tell the truth and the possibility that someone hearing or reading the evidence would know something relevant to the defence) were not significant factors; as to (ii) the defendant had failed to give any sort of assurance that he would not persist in attempting to raise "public interest" matters (contrary to the ruling of the judge that had been upheld in *R. v. Shayler* [2003] 1 A.C. 47, HL (*post*, § 25–326)); on the contrary, he had been maintaining his stance of wishing to raise matters that were irrelevant to the issues the jury had to decide. Where, therefore, the judge had been satisfied that mention in open court of any such matters would give rise to a risk to national safety within section 8(4), he was correct to impose a regime whereunder the defendant (on pain of being held in contempt) was obliged to raise the matter with the court first so that a ruling as to relevance could be made, and, if ruled relevant, a further ruling could be made as to whether the evidence should be given in open court or *in camera* pursuant to a prosecution application under that subsection.

Official Secrets Act 1920, s.11

Short title, construction, and repeal

11.—(1) This Act may be cited as the *Official Secrets Act* 1920, and shall be construed as one **25–324**
with the principal Act, and the principal Act and this Act may be cited together as the *Official Secrets Acts* 1911 and 1920:

Provided that—

(a) [*repealed by* Statute Law (Repeals) Act *1993, Sched. 1, Pt I*];

(b) [*Scotland*].

(1A) [*Northern Ireland.*]

(2) [*Repealed by* Statute Law Revision Act *1927.*]

(3) [*Repealed by* Statute Law (Repeals) Act *1993, Sched. 1, Pt I.*]

[Subs. (1A) was inserted by the *Statute Law (Repeals) Act* 1993, Sched. 2, para. 21.]

As to the extent of the 1911 Act, see section 10(1), *ante*, § 25–310.

C. OFFICIAL SECRETS ACT 1989

Official Secrets Act 1989, s.1

Security and intelligence

25–325 **1.**—(1) A person who is or has been—

(a) a member of the security and intelligence services, or

(b) a person notified that he is subject to the provisions of this subsection,

is guilty of an offence if without lawful authority he discloses any information, document or other article relating to security or intelligence which is or has been in his possession by virtue of his position as a member of any of those services or in the course of his work while the notification is or was in force.

(2) The reference in subsection (1) above to disclosing information relating to security or intelligence includes a reference to making any statement which purports to be a disclosure of such information or is intended to be taken by those to whom it is addressed as being such a disclosure.

(3) A person who is or has been a Crown servant or government contractor is guilty of an offence if without lawful authority he makes a damaging disclosure of any information, document or other article relating to security or intelligence which is or has been in his possession by virtue of his position as such but otherwise than as mentioned in subsection (1) above.

(4) For the purposes of subsection (3) above a disclosure is damaging if—

(a) it causes damage to the work of, or of any part of, the security and intelligence services; or

(b) it is of information or a document or other article which is such that its unauthorised disclosure would be likely to cause such damage or which falls within a class or description of information, documents or articles the unauthorised disclosure of which would be likely to have that effect.

(5) It is a defence for a person charged with an offence under this section to prove that at the time of the alleged offence he did not know, and had no reasonable cause to believe, that the information, document or articles in question related to security or intelligence or, in the case of an offence under subsection (3), that the disclosure would be damaging within the meaning of that subsection.

25–326 (6) Notification that a person is subject to subsection (1) above shall be effected by a notice in writing served on him by a Minister of the Crown; and such a notice may be served if, in the Minister's opinion, the work undertaken by the person in question is or includes work connected with the security and intelligence services and its nature is such that the interests of national security require that he should be subject to the provisions of that subsection.

(7) Subject to subsection (8) below, a notification for the purposes of subsection (1) above shall be in force for the period of five years beginning with the day on which it is served but may be renewed by further notices under subsection (6) above for periods of five years at a time.

(8) A notification for the purposes of subsection (1) above may at any time be revoked by a further notice in writing served by the Minister on the person concerned; and the Minister shall serve a further notice as soon as, in his opinion, the work undertaken by that person ceases to be such as is mentioned in subsection (6) above.

(9) In this section "security or intelligence" means the work of, or in support of, the security and intelligence services or any part of them, and references to information relating to security or intelligence include references to information held or transmitted by those services or by persons in support of, or of any part of, them.

In *R. v. Shayler* [2001] 1 W.L.R. 2206, CA, it was held that the defence of necessity is not excluded as a matter of law from being a defence to a charge under section 1 or 4 of the 1989 Act, but it would be available only where the defendant had committed an otherwise criminal act to avoid an imminent peril of danger to life or serious injury to himself or to somebody for whom he reasonably regarded himself as being responsible; and whilst such person might not be ascertained and identifiable, if it was not possible to name the individual(s) beforehand, it would have to be possible at least to describe the individuals by reference to the action which was threatened would be taken and which would make them victims absent avoiding action being taken by the defendant; secondly, the evil to be prevented must be greater than the evil done; thirdly, the act done should be no more than was reasonably necessary to avoid the harm feared and the harm resulting from the act should not be disproportionate to the harm avoided.

On the defendant's appeal to the House of Lords ([2003] 1 A.C. 247), their Lordships expressly declined to consider the availability of a defence of necessity, saying that it should never have been considered by the judge at first instance as it was not an issue that arose in the preparatory hearing and it should not therefore have been considered by the Court of Appeal. Their Lordships made clear, however, that their silence on this issue was not to be taken as acceptance of what the Court of Appeal had said in relation to it; but Lord Bingham did express the opinion that if necessity was available as a matter of law, the facts put forward by the defence did not come "within a measurable distance" of it.

The House of Lords held that sections 1(1)(a) and 4(1) and (3)(a) (*post*, § 25–329), given their ordinary and natural meaning, and read in the context of the Act as a whole, do not entitle a defendant prosecuted under those provisions to be acquitted if he showed that it was, or that he believed that it was, in the public or national interest to make the disclosure in question or if the jury concluded that it might have been or that the defendant might have believed it to have been in the public or national interest to make the disclosure in question. The prosecution were not required to prove that the disclosure was damaging or was not in the public interest, and, accordingly, the defendant was not entitled to argue that the disclosures he had made were in the public interest or that he thought that they were.

It was further held that the ban on the disclosure of information by members or former members of the security service was not absolute, but was confined to disclosure without lawful authority; that there were procedures available under the Act to enable them to make official complaints about malpractices in the service or to seek official authorisation before disclosing information or documents; such requests for authorisation should be considered bearing in mind the importance attached to the right of free expression and the need for any restriction to be necessary, responsive to a pressing social need and proportionate; if authorisation was refused it was open to the individual to apply for judicial review of the refusal, and, since such an application would involve an alleged violation of a human right, the court would be entiled to conduct a more rigorous and intrusive review than was normally permissible under its judicial review jurisdiction; and it followed, therefore, that to the extent that the restrictions in sections 1 and 4 constituted a restriction on freedom of expression, they were justified under Article 10(2) of the ECHR (*ante*, § 16–119) as being prescribed by law, in pursuit of one of the specified legitimate aims and necessary in a democratic society, in that they corresponded to a pressing social need and were proportionate.

It may be noted that whilst the House of Lords rejected a public interest defence, the White Paper that preceded the Act (Cm 408 (1988)) makes clear that the public interest is relevant when assessing whether any particular disclosure is damaging, and that the issue of prior publication will be relevant to the question whether a disclosure was damaging, but not decisive of it. That a disclosure is "damaging" is a requirement of all the offences under the Act except those under sections 1(1) and 4; and Lord Bingham in *Shayler*, *ante*, accepted that the recommendations in the White Paper bore "directly on the interpretation of the Act" (at [11]).

Official Secrets Act 1989, s.2

Defence

2.—(1) A person who is or has been a Crown servant or government contractor is guilty of an offence if without lawful authority he makes a damaging disclosure of any information, document or other article relating to defence which is or has been in his possession by virtue of his position as such. **25–327**

(2) For the purposes of subsection (1) above a disclosure is damaging if—

(a) it damages the capability of, or of any part of, the armed forces of the Crown to carry out their tasks or leads to loss of life or injury to members of those forces or serious damage to the equipment or installations of those forces; or

(b) otherwise than as mentioned in paragraph (a) above, it endangers the interests of the United Kingdom abroad, seriously obstructs the promotion or protection by the United Kingdom of those interests or endangers the safety of British citizens abroad; or

(c) it is of information or of a document or article which is such that its unauthorised disclosure would be likely to have any of those effects.

(3) It is a defence for a person charged with an offence under this section to prove that at the time of the alleged offence he did not know, and had no reasonable cause to believe, that the information, document or article in question related to defence or that its disclosure would be damaging within the meaning of subsection (1) above.

(4) In this section "defence" means—

(a) the size, shape, organisation, logistics, order of battle, deployment, operations, state of readiness and training of the armed forces of the Crown;

(b) the weapons, stores or other equipment of those forces and the invention, development, production and operation of such equipment and research relating to it;

(c) defence policy and strategy and military planning and intelligence;

(d) plans and measures for the maintenance of essential supplies and services that are or would be needed in time of war.

As to whether a disclosure is damaging, see *ante*, § 25–327.

Subsection (3) of this section and subsection (4) of section 3 (*post*) are to be construed as imposing an evidential burden only on the defendant: *R. v. Keogh* [2007] 2 Cr.App.R. 9, CA. Reversing the burden of proof would require the defendant to disprove a substantial ingredient of the offence, and such a significant infringement of the presumption of innocence under Article 6(2) of the ECHR (*ante*, § 16–57) was unnecessary for the Act to operate effectively; since the issue in relation to the mental element includes a question of objective fact, and not merely the subjective knowledge of the defendant, the prosecution would be able to prove that the defendant had reasonable cause to appreciate the relevant facts by reliance on natural inferences drawn from the subject matter disclosed, and from details of the defendant's service as a Crown servant or government contractor: *ibid*.

Official Secrets Act 1989, s.3

International relations

25–328 **3.**—(1) A person who is or has been a Crown servant or government contractor is guilty of an offence if without lawful authority he makes a damaging disclosure of—

(a) any information, document or other article relating to international relations; or

(b) any confidential information, document or other article which was obtained from a State other than the United Kingdom or an international organisation,

being information or a document or article which is or has been in his possession by virtue of his position as a Crown servant or government contractor.

(2) For the purposes of subsection (1) above a disclosure is damaging if—

(a) it endangers the interests of the United Kingdom abroad, seriously obstructs the promotion or protection by the United Kingdom of those interests or endangers the safety of British citizens abroad; or

(b) it is of information or of a document or article which is such that its unauthorised disclosure would be likely to have any of those effects.

(3) In the case of information or a document or article within subsection (1)(b) above—

(a) the fact that it is confidential, or

(b) its nature or contents,

may be sufficient to establish for the purposes of subsection (2)(b) above that the information, document or article is such that its unauthorised disclosure would be likely to have any of the effects there mentioned.

(4) It is a defence for a person charged with an offence under this section to prove that at the time of the alleged offence he did not know, and had no reasonable cause to believe, that the information, document or article in question was such as is mentioned in subsection (1) above or that its disclosure would be damaging within the meaning of that subsection.

(5) In this section "international relations" means the relations between States, between international organisations or between one or more States and one or more such organisations and includes any matter relating to a State other than the United Kingdom or to an international organisation which is capable of affecting the relations of the United Kingdom with another State or with an international organisation.

(6) For the purposes of this section any information, document or article obtained from a State or organisation is confidential at any time while the terms on which it was obtained require it to be held in confidence or while the circumstances in which it was obtained make it reasonable for the State or organisation to expect that it would be so held.

In connection with this section, see *R. v. Keogh*, *ante*, § 25–327.

Official Secrets Act 1989, s.4

Crime and special investigation powers

4.—(1) A person who is or has been a Crown servant or government contractor is guilty of an offence if without lawful authority he discloses any information, document or other article to which this section applies and which is or has been in his possession by virtue of his position as such. **25–329**

(2) This section applies to any information, document or other article—

(a) the disclosure of which—

(i) results in the commission of an offence; or

(ii) facilitates an escape from legal custody or the doing of any other act prejudicial to the safekeeping of persons in legal custody; or

(iii) impedes the prevention or detection of offences or the apprehension or prosecution of suspected offenders; or

(b) which is such that its unauthorised disclosure would be likely to have any of those effects.

(3) This section also applies to—

(a) any information obtained by reason of the interception of any communication in obedience to a warrant issued under section 2 of the *Interception of Communications Act* 1985 or under the authority of an interception warrant under section 5 of the *Regulation of Investigatory Powers Act* 2000, any information relating to the obtaining of information by reason of any such interception and any document or other article which is or has been used or held for use in, or has been obtained by reason of, any such interception; and

(b) any information obtained by reason of action authorised by a warrant issued under section 3 of the *Security Service Act* 1989 or under section 5 of the *Intelligence Services Act* 1994 or by an authorisation given under section 7 of that Act, any information relating to the obtaining of information by reason of any such action and any document or other article which is or has been used or held for use in, or has been obtained by reason of, any such action.

(4) It is a defence for a person charged with an offence under this section in respect of a disclosure falling within subsection (2)(a) above to prove that at the time of the alleged offence he did not know, and had no reasonable cause to believe, that the disclosure would have any of the effects there mentioned.

(5) It is a defence for a person charged with an offence under this section in respect of any other disclosure to prove that at the time of the alleged offence he did not know, and had no reasonable cause to believe, that the information, document or article in question was information or a document or article to which this section applies.

(6) In this section "legal custody" includes detention in pursuance of any enactment or any instrument made under an enactment.

[This section is printed as amended by the *Intelligence Services Act* 1994, Sched. 4, para. 4; and the *RIPA* 2000, s.82(1), and Sched. 4, para. 5.]

For section 5 of the *RIPA* 2000, see *post*, § 25–372.
In connection with this section, see *R. v. Shayler*, *ante*, § 25–326.

Official Secrets Act 1989, s.5

Information resulting from unauthorised disclosures or entrusted in confidence

5.—(1) Subsection (2) below applies where— **25–330**

(a) any information, document or other article protected against disclosure by the foregoing provisions of this Act has come into a person's possession as a result of having been—

(i) disclosed (whether to him or another) by a Crown servant or government contractor without lawful authority; or

(ii) entrusted to him by a Crown servant or government contractor on terms requiring it to be held in confidence or in circumstances in which the Crown servant or government contractor could reasonably expect that it would be so held; or

(iii) disclosed (whether to him or another) without lawful authority by a person to whom it was entrusted as mentioned in sub-paragraph (ii) above; and

(b) the disclosure without lawful authority of the information, document or article by the person into whose possession it has come is not an offence under any of those provisions.

(2) Subject to subsections (3) and (4) below, the person into whose possession the information, document or article has come is guilty of an offence if he discloses it without lawful authority knowing, or having reasonable cause to believe, that it is protected against disclosure by the foregoing provisions of this Act and that it has come into his possession as mentioned in subsection (1) above.

(3) In the case of information or a document or article protected against disclosure by sections 1 to 3 above, a person does not commit an offence under subsection (2) above unless—

(a) the disclosure by him is damaging; and

(b) he makes it knowing, or having reasonable cause to believe, that it would be damaging;

and the question whether a disclosure is damaging shall be determined for the purposes of this subsection as it would be in relation to a disclosure of that information, document or article by a Crown servant in contravention of section 1(3), 2(1) or 3(1) above.

(4) A person does not commit an offence under subsection (2) above in respect of information or a document or other article which has come into his possession as a result of having been disclosed—

(a) as mentioned in subsection (1)(a)(i) above by a government contractor; or

(b) as mentioned in subsection (1)(a)(iii) above,

unless that disclosure was by a British citizen or took place in the United Kingdom, in any of the Channel Islands or in the Isle of Man or a colony.

(5) For the purposes of this section information or a document or article is protected against disclosure by the foregoing provisions of this Act if—

(a) it relates to security or intelligence, defence or international relations within the meaning of section 1, 2 or 3 above or is such as is mentioned in section 3(1)(b) above; or

(b) it is information or a document or article to which section 4 above applies;

and information or a document or article is protected against disclosure by sections 1 to 3 above if it falls within paragraph (a) above.

(6) A person is guilty of an offence if without lawful authority he discloses any information, document or other article which he knows, or has reasonable cause to believe, to have come into his possession as a result of a contravention of section 1 of the *Official Secrets Act* 1911.

For section 1 of the 1911 Act, see *ante*, § 25–297. As to whether a disclosure is damaging, see *ante*, § 25–327.

Official Secrets Act 1989, s.6

Information entrusted in confidence to other States or international organisations

25–331 **6.**—(1) This section applies where—

(a) any information, document or other article which—

(i) relates to security or intelligence, defence or international relations; and

(ii) has been communicated in confidence by or on behalf of the United Kingdom to another State or to an international organisation,

has come into a person's possession as a result of having been disclosed (whether to him or another) without the authority of that State or organisation or, in the case of an organisation, of a member of it; and

(b) the disclosure without lawful authority of the information, document or article by the person into whose possession it has come is not an offence under any of the foregoing provisions of this Act.

(2) Subject to subsection (3) below, the person into whose possession the information, document or article has come is guilty of an offence if he makes a damaging disclosure of it knowing, or having reasonable cause to believe, that it is such as is mentioned in subsection (1) above, that it has come into his possession as there mentioned and that its disclosure would be damaging.

(3) A person does not commit an offence under subsection (2) above if the information,

[The Act is extended to Hong Kong subject to specified exceptions, adaptations and modifications by the *Official Secrets Act 1989 (Hong Kong) Order* 1992 (S.I. 1992 No. 1301).]

Short title, citation, consequential amendments, repeals, revocation and commencement

16.—(1) This Act may be cited as the *Official Secrets Act* 1989. **25–342**

(2) This Act and the *Official Secrets Acts* 1911 to 1939 may be cited together as the *Official Secrets Acts* 1911 to 1989.

(3) [*Consequential amendments: Schedule 1.*]

(4) [*Repeals and revocation: Schedule 2.*]

(5) Subject to any Order under subsection (3) of section 15 above the repeals in the *Official Secrets Act* 1911 and the *Official Secrets Act* 1920 do not extend to any of the territories mentioned in that subsection.

(6) [*Commencement.*]

The Act came into force on March 1, 1990: *Official Secrets Act 1989 (Commencement) Order* 1990 (S.I. 1990 No. 199).

"Prescribed" bodies or persons

The *Official Secrets Act 1989 (Prescription) Order* 1990 (S.I. 1990 No. 200) was made in exercise of the powers conferred on the Secretary of State by sections 7(5), 8(9), 12 and 13(1) of the 1989 Act. It has been amended by the *Official Secrets Act 1989 (Prescription) (Amendment) Order* 1993 (S.I. 1993 No. 847); the *Official Secrets Act 1989 (Prescription) (Amendment) Order* 2003 (S.I. 2003 No. 1918); and the *Official Secrets Act 1989 (Prescription) (Amendment) Order* 2007 (S.I. 2007 No. 2148). **25–343**

Article 2 provides that the bodies or classes of bodies set out in the first column of Schedule 1 to the Order and the classes of members or employees of those bodies which are set out in the second column of that Schedule are prescribed for the purposes of section 12(1)(f) of the Act. The bodies listed in the first column of Schedule 1 (as amended by S.I. 1993 No. 847, S.I. 2003 No. 1918 and S.I. 2007 No. 2148, *ante*) are as follows with the corresponding entry in the second column set out in brackets: British Nuclear Fuels plc. (the employees of the company); The Board of British Nuclear Fuels plc. (the members of the board); the United Kingdom Atomic Energy Authority (the members, officers and employees of the authority); Urenco Ltd (the employees of the company), the Board of Urenco Ltd (the members of the board); Urenco (Capenhurst) Ltd (the employees of the company); the Board of the above (the members of the Board); Enrichment Technology Company Ltd, Enrichment Technology U.K. Ltd and Urenco Enrichment Company Ltd (the members of the boards, and the employees, of those companies); the Nuclear Decommissioning Authority (the members and employees of the authority); any subsidiary of that authority (the employees of that subsidiary); the board of any subsidiary of that authority (the members of the board); and the Independent Police Complaints Commission (the members and employees of the commission).

Article 3 provides that the offices which are set out in the first column of Schedule 2 to the Order and the classes of employees of the holders of those offices which are set out in the second column of that Schedule are prescribed for the purposes of section 12(1)(g) of the Act. The offices listed in the first column of Schedule 2 are as follows with the corresponding entry (where there is one) in the second column set out in brackets: Comptroller and Auditor General; member of staff of the National Audit Office; Comptroller and Auditor General for Northern Ireland; member of staff of the Northern Ireland Audit Office; Parliamentary Commissioner for Administration (the officers of the Commissioner who are not otherwise Crown servants); officer of the Health Service Commissioner for England or Scotland or Wales being an officer who is authorised by the Parliamentary Commissioner for Administration to perform any of his functions and who is not otherwise a Crown servant; Northern Ireland Parliamentary Commissioner for Administration (the officers of the Commissioner who are not otherwise Crown servants); a private secretary to the Sovereign. **25–344**

Article 4, together with Schedule 3 (as amended by S.I. 2003 No. 1918, *ante*), provides that the Civil Aviation Authority is a prescribed body for the purposes of both section 7(5) and 8(9) of the Act and that the Investigatory Powers Tribunal established under the *RIPA* 2000, s.65, is a prescribed body for the purposes of section 7(5).

D. EUROPEAN COMMUNITIES ACT 1972

European Communities Act 1972, s.11(2)

25–345 **11.**—(2) Where a person (whether a British subject or not) owing either—

(a) to his duties as a member of any Euratom institution or committee, or as an officer or servant of Euratom; or

(b) to his dealings in any capacity (official or unofficial) with any Euratom institution or installation or with any Euratom joint enterprise;

has occasion to acquire, or obtain cognisance of, any classified information, he shall be guilty of a misdemeanour if, knowing or having reason to believe that it is classified information, he communicates it to any unauthorised person or makes any public disclosure of it, whether in the United Kingdom or elsewhere and whether before or after the termination of those duties or dealings; and for this purpose "classified information" means any facts, information, knowledge, documents or objects that are subject to the security rules of a member State or of any Euratom institution.

This subsection shall be construed, and the *Official Secrets Acts* 1911 to 1939 shall have effect, as if this subsection were contained in the *Official Secrets Act* 1911, but so that in that Act sections 10 and 11, except section 10(4), shall not apply.

For sections 10 and 11 of the 1911 Act, see *ante*, §§ 25–310, 25–311.

For the penalty, see section 8(2) of the 1920 Act, *ante*, § 25–319.

XIII. DISCLOSURE OF INFORMATION OBTAINED UNDER CERTAIN STATUTES RELATING TO TRADE, MAKING OF FALSE STATEMENTS IN INFORMATION REQUIRED FOR GOVERNMENT PURPOSE, ETC.

(1) Disclosure of information

25–346 Many statutes contain provisions for the compulsory obtaining of information in certain circumstances. The corollary of this is that there is invariably a duty of confidence imposed by the statute on persons who obtain information in consequence of such compulsory powers or who acquire information in the course of the exercise of other compulsory powers, such as a power of inspection. This duty of confidence is always subject to exceptions which operate so as not to restrict disclosure for defined purposes, one of the most commonly specified of which is disclosure "with a view to the institution of, or otherwise for the purposes of, criminal proceedings, whether under this Act or otherwise" (*e.g. Building Societies Act* 1986, s.53(2)(a)). Such exceptions apart, the statute makes it an offence to disclose information in contravention of the relevant provision. These offences are invariably triable either way, and typically carry a maximum penalty on conviction on indictment of two years' imprisonment or a fine, or both.

25–347 No enactment or rule of law prohibiting or restricting the disclosure of information shall preclude a person from furnishing the Data Protection Commissioner or the Data Protection Tribunal with any information necessary for the discharge of their functions under the *Data Protection Act* 1998: see section 58 thereof.

(2) Withholding information, furnishing false information, making false statements

25–348 Statutes providing for the compulsory obtaining of information (*ante*) frequently make the intentional withholding of information, or the furnishing of false information, or the making of false statements in the knowledge that it is, or they are, false, or being reckless as to the truth thereof, an offence.

These offences are invariably triable either way, and usually carry a maximum penalty on conviction on indictment of two years' imprisonment or a fine, or both. Sometimes, the only possible penalty is a fine.

An offence of making a false statement is committed at the place where it is received and at the time when it is received by the person or authority to whom it is addressed: *Lawrence v. Ministry of Agriculture, Fisheries and Food*, *The Times*, February 26, 1992, DC.

Recklessness involves "an indifference to, or disregard of, the feature of whether a statement is true or false": *per* James L.J. in *R. v. Staines*, 60 Cr.App.R. 160 at 162, CA (a decision in relation to "reckless" deceptions under the *Theft Act* 1968).

XIV. OFFENCES RELATING TO POSTS AND TELECOMMUNICATIONS

A. POSTAL SERVICES ACT 2000

Introduction

The long title to the Act describes it as an Act to establish the Postal Services Commission and the Consumer Council for Postal Services; to provide for the licensing of certain postal services and for a universal postal service; to provide for the vesting of the property, rights and liabilities of the Post Office in a company nominated by the Secretary of State and for the subsequent dissolution of the Post Office; to make further provision in relation to postal services; and for connected purposes. The *Post Office Act* 1953 was repealed in its entirety. **25–349**

Postal Services Act 2000, s.83

PART V

OFFENCES IN RELATION TO POSTAL SERVICES

Interfering with the mail: postal operators

83.—(1) A person who is engaged in the business of a postal operator commits an offence if, contrary to his duty and without reasonable excuse, he— **25–350**

(a) intentionally delays or opens a postal packet in the course of its transmission by post, or

(b) intentionally opens a mail-bag.

(2) Subsection (1) does not apply to the delaying or opening of a postal packet or the opening of a mail-bag under the authority of—

(a) this Act or any other enactment (including, in particular, in pursuance of a warrant issued under any other enactment), or

(b) any directly applicable Community provision.

(3) Subsection (1) does not apply to the delaying or opening of a postal packet in accordance with any terms and conditions applicable to its transmission by post.

(4) Subsection (1) does not apply to the delaying of postal packet as a result of industrial action in contemplation or furtherance of a trade dispute.

(5) In subsection (4) "trade dispute" has the meaning given by section 244 of the *Trade Union and Labour Regulations (Consolidation) Act* 1992 or Article 127 of the *Trade Union and Labour Relations (Northern Ireland) Order* 1995; and the reference to industrial action shall be construed in accordance with that Act or (as the case may be) that Order.

(6) A person who commits an offence under subsection (1) shall be liable—

(a) on summary conviction, to a fine not exceeding the statutory maximum or to imprisonment for a term not exceeding *six* [12] months or to both,

(b) on conviction on indictment, to a fine or to imprisonment for a term not exceeding two years or to both.

[In subs. (6)(a), "12" is substituted for "six", as from a day to be appointed, by the *CJA* 2003, s.282(2) and (3). The increase has no application to offences committed before the substitution takes effect: s.282(4).]

Section 84(1) creates corresponding summary offences which may be committed by any person. Subsections (2) to (5) of section 83 apply to those offences as they apply to section 83(1). Section 84(3) provides that a person commits an offence if, intending to **25–351** act to a person's detriment and without reasonable excuse, he opens a postal packet which he knows or reasonably suspects has been incorrectly delivered to him.

As to the application of the *Theft Act* 1968, s.27(4) (evidence by statutory declaration) (*ante*, § 21–332) to proceedings for an offence under either section 83 or 84, see section 109(2) of the 2000 Act.

Postal Services Act 2000, s.85

Prohibition on sending certain articles by post

25–352 **85.**—(1) A person commits an offence if he sends by post a postal packet which encloses any creature, article or thing of any kind which is likely to injure other postal packets in course of their transmission by post or any person engaged in the business of a postal operator.

(2) Subsection (1) does not apply to postal packets which enclose anything permitted (whether generally or specifically) by the postal operator concerned.

(3) A person commits an offence if he sends by post a postal packet which encloses—

(a) any indecent or obscene print, painting, photograph, lithograph, engraving, cinematograph film or other record of a picture or pictures, book, card or written communication, or

(b) any other indecent or obscene article (whether or not of a similar kind to those mentioned in paragraph (a)).

(4) A person commits an offence if he sends by post a postal packet which has on the packet, or on the cover of the packet, any words, marks or designs which are of an indecent or obscene character.

(5) A person who commits an offence under this section shall be liable—

(a) on summary conviction, to a fine not exceeding the statutory maximum,

(b) on conviction on indictment, to a fine or to imprisonment for a term not exceeding twelve months or to both.

25–353 This section is closely modelled on section 11 of the *Post Office Act* 1953, in relation to which the following authorities were decided. in *R. v. Anderson* [1972] 1 Q.B. 304, 56 Cr.App.R. 115, CA, it was held that the word "obscene" in the context of this provision does not bear the same meaning as in the *Obscene Publications Act* 1959 (*post*, §§ 31–63 *et seq.*). Here, it bears its ordinary dictionary meaning. "It includes things which are shocking and lewd and indecent and so on" (at pp. 311, 122). The test of indecency is objective and the character of the addressee is immaterial: *R. v. Straker* [1965] Crim.L.R. 229, CCA; *Kosmos Publications Ltd v. DPP* [1975] Crim.L.R. 345, DC. The effect on the recipient is irrelevant too. The issue of obscenity or indecency is for the jury and evidence cannot be called to assist them on that issue: *R. v. Stamford* [1972] 2 Q.B. 391, 56 Cr.App.R. 398, CA. See also *R. v. Kirk* [2006] Crim.L.R. 850, CA, in which it was said that the words were ordinary words of the English language which would be readily understood by a jury; and that it would be unnecessary and potentially misleading to direct them as to any narrower or enlarged meaning, and a simple direction using those words would suffice.

Where an indictment alleged that an article was "indecent and obscene", and the jury found that it was indecent but not obscene, the conviction was held to be good on the basis that the two words convey one idea, "obscene" being higher up the scale: *R. v. Stanley* [1965] 2 Q.B. 327, 49 Cr.App.R. 175, CCA. *Semble*, the appellant might have been charged in the disjunctive form, the article being alleged to be indecent or obscene.

As to sentence, see *R. v. Kirk, ante*, in which a short custodial sentence was held to be appropriate in the case of an anti-vivisectionist (with previous convictions for harassment type offences) who sent a package through the post, marked with the words "To the sons and daughters of Dr Joseph Mengele, @ Bloody Huntingdon Life Sciences, an Auschwitz Laboratory" and a large black swastika on the outside.

Postal Services Act 2000, s.125

Interpretation

25–354 **125.**—(1) In this Act, unless the context otherwise requires—

...

"letter" means any communication in written form on any kind of physical medium to be conveyed and delivered otherwise than electronically to the person or address indicated by the sender on the item itself or on its wrapping (excluding any book, catalogue, newspaper or periodical); and includes a postal packet containing any such communication,

"mail-bag" includes any form of container or covering in which postal packets in the course of transmission by post are enclosed by a postal operator in the United Kingdom or a foreign postal administration for the purpose of conveyance by post, whether or not it contains any such packets,

. . .

"post office" includes any house, building, room, vehicle or place used for the provision of any postal services,

"post office letter box" includes any pillar box, wall box, or other box or receptacle provided by a postal operator for the purpose of receiving postal packets, or any class of postal packets, for onwards transmission by post,

"postal operator" means a person who provides the service of conveying postal packets from one place to another by post or any of the incidental services of receiving, collecting, sorting and delivering such packets,

"postal packet" means a letter, parcel, packet or other article transmissible by post,

. . . .

(2) For the purposes of the definition of "letter" in subsection (1) the reference to a communication to be conveyed and delivered otherwise than electronically shall be construed as a reference to a communication to be conveyed and delivered otherwise than—

(a) by means of a telecommunication system (within the meaning of the *Telecommunications Act* 1984), or

(b) by other means but while in electronic form.

(3) For the purposes of this Act—

(a) a postal packet shall be taken to be in course of transmission by post from the time of its being delivered to any post office or post office letter box to the time of its being delivered to the addressee,

(b) the delivery of a postal packet of any description to a letter carrier or other person authorised to receive postal packets of that description for the post or to a person engaged in the business of a postal operator to be dealt with in the course of that business shall be a delivery to a post office, and

(c) the delivery of a postal packet—

(i) at the premises to which it is addressed or redirected, unless they are a post office from which it is to be collected,

(ii) to any box or receptacle to which the occupier of those premises has agreed that postal packets addressed to persons at those premises may be delivered, or

(iii) to the addressee's agent or to any other person considered to be authorised to receive the packet,

shall be a delivery to the addressee.

(4) [*Construction of references to "subsidiary".*]

Definitions that are immaterial to the provisions of the Act, set out *ante*, have been omitted from subsection (1). As to proof of an article being a postal packet, see section 109(1) of the Act (evidence that any article is in the course of transmission by post, or has been accepted by a postal operator for transmission by post, shall be sufficient evidence that the article is a postal packet).

As to subsection (3), see *Hood v. Smith* (1933) 30 Cox 82, DC (considering a like **25–355**
provision in the *Post Office Act* 1908). A letter posted in the ordinary way is a postal packet within the statute; therefore, where a fictitious letter is posted with money in it to try the honesty of the defendant, it is a postal packet: *R. v. Young* (1846) 1 Den. 194; *Hood v. Smith*, *ante*.

[The next paragraph is § 25–363.]

B. COMMUNICATIONS ACT 2003

Communications Act 2003, ss.125, 126

Dishonestly obtaining electronic communications services

125.—(1) A person who— **25–363**

(a) dishonestly obtains an electronic communications service, and

(b) does so with intent to avoid payment of a charge applicable to the provision of that service, is guilty of an offence.

(2) It is not an offence under this section to obtain a service mentioned in section 297(1) of the *Copyright, Designs and Patents Act* 1988 (dishonestly obtaining a broadcasting or cable programme service provided from a place in the UK).

(3) A person guilty of an offence under this section shall be liable—

(a) on summary conviction, to imprisonment for a term not exceeding *six* [12] months or to a fine not exceeding the statutory maximum, or to both;

(b) on conviction on indictment, to imprisonment for a term not exceeding five years or to a fine, or to both.

[In subs. (3)(a), "12" is substituted for "six", as from a day to be appointed, by the *CJA* 2003, s.282(2) and (3). The increase has no application to offences committed before the substitution takes effect: s.282(4).]

Possession or supply of apparatus etc. for contravening s.125

25–364 **126.**—(1) A person is guilty of an offence if, with an intention falling within subsection (3), he has in his possession or under his control anything that may be used—

(a) for obtaining an electronic communications service; or—

(b) in connection with obtaining such a service.

(2) A person is guilty of an offence if—

(a) he supplies or offers to supply anything which may be used as mentioned in subsection (1); and—

(b) he knows or believes that the intentions in relation to that thing of the person to whom it is supplied or offered fall within subsection (3).

(3) A person's intentions fall within this subsection if he intends—

(a) to use the thing to obtain an electronic communications service dishonestly;

(b) to use the thing for a purpose connected with the dishonest obtaining of such a service;

(c) dishonestly to allow the thing to be used to obtain such a service; or

(d) to allow the thing to be used for a purpose connected with the dishonest obtaining of such a service.

(4) An intention does not fall within subsection (3) if it relates exclusively to the obtaining of a service mentioned in section 297(1) of the *Copyright, Designs and Patents Act* 1988.

(5) [*Identical to s.125(3) (including the amendment)*, ante, *§ 25–363*.]

(6) In this section, references, in the case of a thing used for recording data, to the use of that thing include references to the use of data recorded by it.

[The next paragraph is § 25–367.]

C. REGULATION OF INVESTIGATORY POWERS ACT 2000

Introduction

25–367 The long title expresses it to be an Act to make provision for and about the interception of communications, the acquisition and disclosure of data relating to communications, the carrying out of surveillance, the use of covert human intelligence sources and the acquisition of the means by which electronic data protected by encryption or passwords may be decrypted or accessed; to provide for Commissioners and a tribunal with functions and jurisdiction in relation to those matters, to entries on and interferences with property or with wireless telegraphy and to the carrying out of their functions by the Security Service, the Secret Intelligence Service and the Government Communications Headquarters; and for connected purposes.

Part I (ss.1–25) is concerned with communications, and is divided into two chapters. Chapter I relates to interception and is in five groups of sections: 1–5 (unlawful and authorised interception), 6–11 (interception warrants), 12–14 (interception capability and costs), 15–19 (restrictions on use of intercepted material etc.) and 21 (interpretation). The majority of these provisions are set out, *post*.

For further details in relation to Part II (ss.26–48) of the Act ("Surveillance and covert human intelligence sources"), see *ante*, § 15–253 *et seq.*

Part III (ss.49–56) regulates the investigation of electronic data protected by encryption. Section 49 applies where protected information has come into the possession of a person in a variety of ways, such as by virtue of the exercise of a statutory power to seize, detain or inspect documents, or to intercept communications. A disclosure requirement may be imposed on any person suspected on reasonable grounds to be in possession of a key to that information. A disclosure requirement may only be imposed in the interests of national security, for the purpose of preventing or detecting crime or in the interests of the economic well-being of the United Kingdom. Section 50 sets out the effect of a notice imposing a disclosure requirement. Failure to make the disclosure required is an either way offence (maximum as in the case of s.1, *post*): s.53. Section 54 creates an offence of tipping-off, which may be committed where the section 49 notice contains a provision requiring the person to whom the notice is given and every other person who becomes aware of it or of its contents to keep secret the giving of the notice, its contents and things done in pursuance of it. Breach of this obligation of secrecy is an either way offence (maximum on conviction on indictment, five years, or a fine, or both). Various defences are provided (*e.g.* disclosure to a legal adviser). Section 55 contains safeguards, and section 56 provides for the interpretation of Part III.

Part IV (ss.57–72) makes provision in relation to the scrutiny of investigatory powers and of the functions of the intelligence services (commissioners and tribunal). Section 71 requires the Secretary of State to issue one or more codes of practice relating to the exercise and performance of the powers and duties that are conferred or imposed otherwise than on the Surveillance Commissioners by or under Parts I to III, the *Intelligence Services Act* 1994, s.5 and the *Police Act* 1997, Part III (authorisation by the police or revenue and customs of interference with property or wireless telegraphy). Section 72 provides for the effect of a code under section 71, including its admissibility in evidence in civil or criminal proceedings.

Part V (ss.73–83) contains miscellaneous and supplemental provisions. Section 79 is a standard provision for the liability of directors of a corporation guilty of an offence under the Act. Section 80 is a general saving for lawful conduct and section 81 is a general interpretation section.

Codes of practice

Codes of practice are provided for by sections 71 and 72 (*ante*, § 25–367). As at October 1, 2008, the codes of practice issued and in force in relation to Part I were those relating to the interception of communications under Chapter I and to the acquisition and disclosure of communications data (as defined by s.21(4)) under Chapter II. These were brought into force on July 1, 2002, by the *Regulation of Investigatory Powers (Interception of Communications: Code of Practice) Order* 2002 (S.I. 2002 No. 1693) and on October 1, 2007, by the *Regulation of Investigatory Powers (Acquisition and Disclosure of Communications Data: Code of Practice) Order* 2007 (S.I. 2007 No. 2197) respectively. **25–367a**

The *Regulation of Investigatory Powers (Investigation of Protected Electronic Information: Code of Practice) Order* 2007 (S.I. 2007 No. 2200) brought a code of practice relating to the investigation of protected electronic information under Part III of the Act into force on October 1, 2007.

A person exercising or performing a power or duty to which any of these codes applies shall, in doing so, have regard to the provisions of the code so far as they are applicable: s.72(1).

The codes of practice are available on the Home Office website (www.homeoffice.gov.uk).

Regulation of Investigatory Powers Act 2000, ss.1–5

PART I

COMMUNICATIONS

CHAPTER I

INTERCEPTION

Unlawful and authorised interception

Unlawful interception

25–368 **1.**—(1) It shall be an offence for a person intentionally and without lawful authority to intercept, at any place in the United Kingdom, any communication in the course of its transmission by means of—

(a) a public postal service; or
(b) a public telcommunication system.

(2) It shall be an offence for a person—

(a) intentionally and without lawful authority, and
(b) otherwise than in circumstances in which his conduct is excluded by subsection (6) from criminal liability under this subsection,

to intercept, at any place in the United Kingdom, any communication in the course of its transmission by means of a private telecommunication system.

(3) Any interception of a communication which is carried out at any place in the United Kingdom by, or with the express or implied consent of, a person having the right to control the operation or the use of a private telecommunication system shall be actionable at the suit or instance of the sender or recipient, or intended recipient, of the communication if it is without lawful authority and is either—

(a) an interception of that communication in the course of its transmission by means of that private system; or
(b) an interception of that communication in the course of its transmission, by means of a public telecommunication system, to or from apparatus comprised in that private telecommunication system.

(4) Where the United Kingdom is a party to an international agreement which—

(a) relates to the provision of mutual assistance in connection with, or in the form of, the interception of communications,
(b) requires the issue of a warrant, order or equivalent instrument in cases in which assistance is given, and
(c) is designated for the purposes of this subsection by an order made by the Secretary of State,

it shall be the duty of the Secretary of State to secure that no request for assistance in accordance with the agreement is made on behalf of a person in the United Kingdom to the competent authorities of a country or territory outside the United Kingdom except with lawful authority.

(5) Conduct has lawful authority for the purposes of this section if, and only if—

(a) it is authorised by or under section 3 or 4;
(b) it takes place in accordance with a warrant under section 5 ("an interception warrant"); or
(c) it is in exercise, in relation to any stored communication, of any statutory power that is exercised (apart from this section) for the purpose of obtaining information or of taking possession of any document or other property;

and conduct (whether or not prohibited by this section) which has lawful authority for the purposes of this section by virtue of paragraph (a) or (b) shall also be taken to be lawful for all other purposes.

(6) The circumstances in which a person makes an interception of a communication in the course of its transmission by means of a private telecommunication system are such that his conduct is excluded from the criminal liability under subsection (2) if—

(a) he is a person with a right to control the operation or the use of the system; or
(b) he has the express or implied consent of such a person to make the interception.

(7) A person who is guilty of an offence under subsection (1) or (2) shall be liable—

(a) on conviction on indictment, to imprisonment for a term not exceeding two years or to a fine, or to both;

(b) on summary conviction, to a fine not exceeding the statutory maximum.

(8) No proceedings for any offence which is an offence by virtue of this section shall be instituted—

(a) in England and Wales, except by or with the consent of the Director of Public Prosecutions;

(b) in Northern Ireland, except by or with the consent of the Director of Public Prosecutions for Northern Ireland.

The *Regulation of Investigatory Powers (Designation of an International Agreement) Order* 2004 (S.I. 2004 No. 158) designates the Convention on Mutual Assistance in Criminal Matters between the Member States of the European Union as a designated international agreement for the purposes of section 1(4).

A person would have "lawful authority" for the interception of a communication within section 1(5)(c) where the interception was done in order to comply with his obligation under paragraph 11 of Schedule 9 to the *PACE Act* 1984 (*ante*, § 15–77) not to destroy material to which an application for an order under paragraph 4 of that Schedule related; where, therefore, a telecommunications company served with notice of an application under Schedule 9 was only able to avoid destruction of the emails to which the application related by "intercepting" them within the meaning of the 2000 Act, it had lawful authority to do so: *R. (NTL Group Ltd) v. Crown Court at Ipswich* [2003] Q.B. 131, DC.

The exclusion from criminal liability for a person "with a right to control the operation or the use of the system" (subs. (6)(a)) does not extend to a person who merely has control in the physical sense of the ability to operate or manipulate the system; "control" in section 1(6)(a) means "authorise and forbid", *i.e.* controlling how the system is used and operated by others: *R. v. Stanford* [2006] 1 W.L.R. 1554, CA.

Meaning and location of "interception" etc.

2.—(1) In this Act— **25–369**

"postal service" means any service which—

(a) consists in the following, or in any one or more of them, namely, the collection, sorting, conveyance, distribution and delivery (whether in the United Kingdom or elsewhere) of postal items; and

(b) is offered or provided as a service the main purpose of which, or one of the main purposes of which, is to make available, or to facilitate, a means of transmission from place to place of postal items containing communications;

"private telecommunication system" means any telecommunication system which, without itself being a public telecommunication system, is a system in relation to which the following conditions are satisfied—

(a) it is attached, directly or indirectly and whether or not for the purposes of the communication in question, to a public telecommunication system; and

(b) there is apparatus comprised in the system which is both located in the United Kingdom and used (with or without other apparatus) for making the attachment to the public telecommunication system;

"public postal service" means any postal service which is offered or provided to, or to a substantial section of, the public in any one or more parts of the United Kingdom;

"public telecommunications service" means any telecommunications service which is offered or provided to, or to a substantial section of, the public in any one or more parts of the United Kingdom;

"public telecommunication system" means any such parts of a telecommunication system by means of which any public telecommunications service is provided as are located in the United Kingdom;

"telecommunications service" means any service that consists in the provision of access to, and of facilities for making use of, any telecommunication system (whether or not one provided by the person providing the service); and

"telecommunication system" means any system (including the apparatus comprised in it) which exists (whether wholly or partly in the United Kingdom or elsewhere) for the purpose of facilitating the transmission of communications by any means involving the use of electrical or electro-magnetic energy.

(2) For the purposes of this Act, but subject to the following provisions of this section, a person intercepts a communication in the course of its transmission by means of a telecommunication system if, and only if, he—

(a) so modifies or interferes with the system, or its operation,

(b) so monitors transmissions made by means of the system, or

(c) so monitors transmissions made by wireless telegraphy to or from apparatus comprised in the system,

as to make some or all of the contents of the communication available, while being transmitted, to a person other than the sender or intended recipient of the communication.

(3) References in this Act to the interception of the communication do not include references to the interception of any communication broadcast for general reception.

(4) For the purposes of this Act the interception of a communication takes place in the United Kingdom if, and only if, the modification, interference or monitoring or, in the case of a postal item, the interception is effected by conduct within the United Kingdom and the communication is either—

(a) intercepted in the course of its transmission by means of a public postal service or public telecommunication system; or

(b) intercepted in the course of its transmission by means of a private telecommunication system in a case in which the sender or intended recipient of the communication is in the United Kingdom.

(5) References in this Act to the interception of a communication in the course of its transmission by means of a postal service or telecommunication system do not include references to—

(a) any conduct that takes place in relation only to so much of the communication as consists in any traffic data comprised in or attached to a communication (whether by the sender or otherwise) for the purposes of any postal service or telecommunication system by means of which it is being or may be transmitted; or

(b) any such conduct, in connection with conduct falling within paragraph (a), as gives a person who is neither the sender nor the intended recipient only so much access to a communication as is necessary for the purpose of identifying traffic data so comprised or attached.

(6) For the purposes of this section references to the modification of a telecommunication system include references to the attachment of any apparatus to, or other modification of or interference with—

(a) any part of the system; or

(b) any wireless telegraphy apparatus used for making transmissions to or from apparatus comprised in the system.

(7) For the purposes of this section the times while a communication is being transmitted by means of a telecommunication system shall be taken to include any time when the system by means of which the communication is being, or has been, transmitted is used for storing it in a manner that enables the intended recipient to collect it or otherwise to have access to it.

(8) For the purposes of this section the cases in which any contents of a communication are to be taken to be made available to a person while being transmitted shall include any case in which any of the contents of the communication, while being transmitted, are diverted or recorded so as to be available to a person subsequently.

(9) In this section "traffic data", in relation to any communication, means—

(a) any data identifying, or purporting to identify, any person, apparatus or location to or from which the communication is or may be transmitted,

(b) any data identifying or selecting, or purporting to identify or select, apparatus through which, or by means of which, the communication is or may be transmitted,

(c) any data comprising signals for the actuation of apparatus used for the purposes of a telecommunication system for effecting (in whole or in part) the transmission of any communication, and

(d) any data identifying the data or other data as data comprised in or attached to a particular communication,

but that expression includes data identifying a computer file or computer program access to which is obtained, or which is run, by means of the communication to the extent only that the file or program is identified by reference to the apparatus in which it is stored.

(10) In this section—

(a) references, in relation to traffic data comprising signals for the actuation of apparatus, to a telecommunication system by means of which a communication is being or may be transmitted include references to any telecommunication system in which that apparatus is comprised; and

(b) references to traffic data being attached to a communication include references to the data and the communication being logically associated with each other;

and in this section "data", in relation to a postal item, means anything written on the outside of the item.

(11) In this section "postal item" means any letter, postcard or other such thing in writing as may be used by the sender for imparting information to the recipient, or any packet or parcel.

The tape recording of a telephone call by one party to it, without the knowledge of the other party, does not amount to interception of a communication within this section: *R. v. Hardy* [2003] 1 Cr.App.R. 30, CA.

In *R. v. E.* [2004] 2 Cr.App.R. 29, CA, it was held that a recording of what a person said on the telephone, picked up by a surveillance device placed in his car (which did not record any speech by the other party), was not an interception of a communication "in the course of its transmission" within section 2(2); the recording was made at the same time as being transmitted but the transmission was not recorded, just the voice from the sound waves in the car. It was further held that the 2000 Act complied with both Council Directive 97/66/EC on telecommunications data protection, which required member states to ensure the confidentiality of communications, and with Article 8 of the ECHR (right to respect for private and family life, *ante*, § 16–101).

Lawful interception without an interception warrant

3.—(1) Conduct by any person consisting in the interception of a communication is authorised by this section if the communication is one which, or which that person has reasonable grounds for believing, is both— **25–370**

(a) a communication sent by a person who has consented to the interception; and

(b) a communication the intended recipient of which has so consented.

(2) Conduct by any person consisting in the interception of a communication is authorised by this section if—

(a) the communication is one sent by, or intended for, a person who has consented to the interception; and

(b) surveillance by means of that interception has been authorised under Part II.

(3) Conduct consisting in the interception of a communication is authorised by this section if—

(a) it is conduct by or on behalf of a person who provides a postal service or a telecommunications service; and

(b) it takes place for purposes connected with the provision or operation of that service or with the enforcement, in relation to that service, of any enactment relating to the use of postal services or telecommunications services.

(4) Conduct by any person consisting in the interception of a communication in the course of its transmission by means of wireless telegraphy is authorised by this section if it takes place—

(a) with the authority of a designated person under section 5 of the *Wireless Telegraphy Act* 1949 (misleading messages and interception and disclosure of wireless telegraphy messages); and

(b) for purposes connected with anything falling within subsection (5).

(5) Each of the following falls within this subsection—

(a) the issue of licences under the *Wireless Telegraphy Act* 1949;

(b) the prevention or detection of anything which constitutes interference with wireless telegraphy; and

(c) the enforcement of any enactment contained in that Act or of any enactment not so contained that relates to such interference.

Power to provide for lawful interception

4.—(1) Conduct by any person ("the interceptor") consisting in the interception of a communication in the course of its transmission by means of a telecommunication system is authorised by this section if— **25–371**

(a) the interception is carried out for the purpose of obtaining information about the communications of a person who, or who the interceptor has reasonable grounds for believing, is in a country or territory outside the United Kingdom;

(b) the interception relates to the use of a telecommunications service provided to persons in that country or territory which is either—

(i) a public telecommunications service; or

(ii) a telecommunications service that would be a public telecommunications service if the persons to whom it is offered or provided were members of the public in a part of the United Kingdom;

(c) the person who provides that service (whether the interceptor or another person) is required by the law of that country or territory to carry out, secure or facilitate the interception in question;

(d) the situation is one in relation to which such further conditions as may be prescribed by regulations made by the Secretary of State are required to be satisfied before conduct may be treated as authorised by virtue of this subsection; and

(e) the conditions so prescribed are satisfied in relation to that situation.

(2) Subject to subsection (3), the Secretary of State may by regulations authorise any such conduct described in the regulations as appears to him to constitute a legitimate practice reasonably required for the purpose, in connection with the carrying on of any business, of monitoring or keeping a record of—

(a) communications by means of which transactions are entered into in the course of that business; or

(b) other communications relating to that business or taking place in the course of its being carried on.

(3) Nothing in any regulations under subsection (2) shall authorise the interception of any communication except in the course of its transmission using apparatus or services provided by or to the person carrying on the business for use wholly or partly in connection with that business.

(4) Conduct taking place in a prison is authorised by this section if it is conduct in exercise of any power conferred by or under any rules made under section 47 of the *Prison Act* 1952, section 39 of the *Prisons (Scotland) Act* 1989 or section 13 of the *Prison Act (Northern Ireland)* 1953 (prison rules).

(5) Conduct taking place in any hospital premises where high security psychiatric services are provided is authorised by this section if it is conduct in pursuance of, and in accordance with, any direction given under section 8 of the *National Health Service Act* 2006, or section 19 or 23 of the *National Health Service (Wales) Act* 2006 (directions as to the carrying out of their functions by health bodies) to the body providing those services at those premises.

(6) Conduct taking place in a state hospital is authorised by this section if it is conduct in pursuance of, and in accordance with, any direction given to the State Hospitals Board for Scotland under section 2(5) of the *National Health Service (Scotland) Act* 1978 (regulations and directions as to the exercise of their functions by health boards) as applied by Article 5(1) of and the Schedule to the *State Hospitals Board for Scotland Order* 1995 (which applies certain provisions of that Act of 1978 to the State Hospitals Board).

(7) In this section references to a business include references to any activities of a government department, of any public authority or of any person or office holder on whom functions are conferred by or under any enactment.

(8) In this section—

"government department" includes any part of the Scottish Administration, a Northern Ireland department and the Welsh Assembly Government;

"high security psychiatric services" has the same meaning as in section 4 of the *National Health Service Act* 2006;

"hospital premises" has the same meaning as in section 4(3) of that Act; and

"state hospital" has the same meaning as in the *National Health Service (Scotland) Act* 1978.

(9) In this section "prison" means—

(a) any prison, young offender institution, young offenders centre or remand centre which is under the general superintendence of, or is provided by, the Secretary of State under the *Prison Act* 1952 or the *Prison Act (Northern Ireland)* 1953, or

(b) any prison, young offenders institution or remand centre which is under the general superintendence of the Scottish Ministers under the *Prisons (Scotland) Act* 1989,

and includes any contracted out prison, within the meaning of Part IV of the *Criminal Justice Act* 1991 or section 106(4) of the *Criminal Justice and Public Order Act* 1994, and any legalised police cells within the meaning of section 14 of the *Prisons (Scotland) Act* 1989.

[This section is printed as amended by the *National Health Service (Consequential Provisions) Act* 2006, s.2, and Sched. 1, para. 208; and the *Government of Wales Act 2006 (Consequential Modifications and Transitional Provisions) Order* 2007 (S.I. 2007 No. 1388).]

The *Regulation of Investigatory Powers (Conditions for the Lawful Interception of Persons outside the United Kingdom) Regulations* 2004 (S.I. 2004 No. 157) prescribe the following conditions under section 4(1)(d): (a) the interception is carried out for the purposes of a criminal investigation; and (b) the criminal investigation is being carried out in a country or territory that is party to an international agreement designated for the purposes of section 1(4) of the Act. They come into force 90 days after the day on which the eighth member state ratifies the Convention on Mutual Assistance in Criminal Matters, if the United Kingdom is one of the first eight member states of the European Union to ratify; otherwise, 90 days after the day on which the United Kingdom ratifies the Convention.

Interception with a warrant

5.—(1) Subject to the following provisions of this Chapter, the Secretary of State may issue a warrant authorising or requiring the person to whom it is addressed, by any such conduct as may be described in the warrant, to secure any one or more of the following— **25–372**

(a) the interception in the course of their transmission by means of a postal service or telecommunication system of the communications described in the warrant;

(b) the making, in accordance with an international mutual assistance agreement, of a request for the provision of such assistance in connection with, or in the form of, an interception of communications as may be so described;

(c) the provision, in accordance with an international mutual assistance agreement, to the competent authorities of a country or territory outside the United Kingdom of any such assistance in connection with, or in the form of, an interception of communications as may be so described;

(d) the disclosure, in such manner as may be so described, of intercepted material obtained by any interception authorised or required by the warrant, and of related communications data.

(2) The Secretary of State shall not issue an interception warrant unless he believes—

(a) that the warrant is necessary on grounds falling within subsection (3); and

(b) that the conduct authorised by the warrant is proportionate to what is sought to be achieved by that conduct.

(3) Subject to the following provisions of this section, a warrant is necessary on grounds falling within this subsection if it is necessary—

(a) in the interests of national security;

(b) for the purpose of preventing or detecting serious crime;

(c) for the purpose of safeguarding the economic well-being of the United Kingdom; or

(d) for the purpose, in circumstances appearing to the Secretary of State to be equivalent to those in which he would issue a warrant by virtue ofparagraph (b), of giving effect to the provisions of any international mutual assistance agreement.

(4) The matters to be taken into account in considering whether the requirements of subsection (2) are satisfied in the case of any warrant shall include whether the information which it is thought necessary to obtain under the warrant could reasonably be obtained by other means.

(5) A warrant shall not be considered necessary on the ground falling within subsection (3)(c) unless the information which it is thought necessary to obtain is information relating to the acts or intentions of persons outside the British Islands.

(6) The conduct authorised by an interception warrant shall be taken to include—

(a) all such conduct (including the interception of communications not identified by the warrant) as it is necessary to undertake in order to do what is expressly authorised or required by the warrant;

(b) conduct for obtaining related communications data; and

(c) conduct by any person which is conduct in pursuance of a requirement imposed by or on behalf of the person to whom the warrant is addressed to be provided with assistance with giving effect to the warrant.

Interception warrants

25–373 Sections 6 to 11 (amended by the *Terrorism Act* 2006, s.32, the *Police, Public Order and Criminal Justice (Scotland) Act 2006 (Consequential Provisions and Modifications) Order* 2007 (S.I. 2007 No. 1098) and the *SCA* 2007, s.88, and Sched. 12, paras 5 and 6) provide for the making of an application for a warrant, the issue of a warrant, its contents, the duration, cancellation and renewal of a warrant, modification of the warrant or of a certificate issued by the Secretary of State under section 8(4) as to the descriptions of material the examination of which he considers necessary and the purpose of the examination, and the implementation of a warrant.

Regulation of Investigatory Powers Act 2000, s.11

Implementation of warrants

25–374 **11.**—(1) Effect may be given to an interception warrant either—

(a) by the person to whom it is addressed; or

(b) by that person acting through, or together with, such other persons as he may require (whether under subsection (2) or otherwise) to provide him with assistance with giving effect to the warrant.

(2) For the purpose of requiring any person to provide assistance in relation to an interception warrant the person to whom it is addressed may—

(a) serve a copy of the warrant on such persons as he considers may be able to provide such assistance; or

(b) make arrangements under which a copy of it is to be or may be so served.

(3) The copy of an interception warrant that is served on any person under subsection (2) may, to the extent authorised—

(a) by the person to whom the warrant is addressed, or

(b) by the arrangements made by him for the purposes of that subsection,

omit any one or more of the schedules to the warrant.

(4) Where a copy of an interception warrant has been served by or on behalf of the person to whom it is addressed on—

(a) a person who provides a postal service,

(b) a person who provides a public telecommunications service, or

(c) a person not falling within paragraph (b) who has control of the whole or any part of a telecommunication system located wholly or partly in the United Kingdom,

it shall (subject to subsection (5)) be the duty of that person to take all such steps for giving effect to the warrant as are notified to him by or on behalf of the person to whom the warrant is addressed.

(5) A person who is under a duty by virtue of subsection (4) to take steps for giving effect to a warrant shall not be required to take any steps which it is not reasonably practicable for him to take.

(6) For the purposes of subsection (5) the steps which it is reasonably practicable for a person to take in a case in which obligations have been imposed on him by or under section 12 shall include every step which it would have been reasonably practicable for him to take had he complied with all the obligations so imposed on him.

(7) A person who knowingly fails to comply with his duty under subsection (4) shall be guilty of an offence and liable—

(a) on conviction on indictment, to imprisonment for a term not exceeding two years or to a fine, or to both;

(b) on summary conviction, to imprisonment for a term not exceeding *six* [12] months or to a fine not exceeding the statutory maximum, or to both.

(8) [*Civil proceedings to enforce duty under subs. (4).*]

(9) For the purposes of this Act the provision of assistance with giving effect to an

interception warrant includes any disclosure to the person to whom the warrant is addressed, or to persons acting on his behalf, of intercepted material obtained by any interception authorised or required by the warrant, and of any related communications data.

[In subs. (7)(a), "12" is substituted for "six", as from a day to be appointed, by the *CJA* 2003, s.282(2) and (3). The increase has no application to offences committed before the substitution takes effect: s.282(4).]

Regulation of Investigatory Powers Act 2000, ss.15–19

Restrictions on use of intercepted material etc.

General safeguards

15.—(1) Subject to subsection (6), it shall be the duty of the Secretary of State to ensure, in relation to all interception warrants, that such arrangements are in force as he considers necessary for securing— **25–375**

(a) that the requirements of subsections (2) and (3) are satisfied in relation to the intercepted material and any related communications data; and

(b) in the case of warrants in relation to which there are section 8(4) certificates, that the requirements of section 16 are also satisfied.

(2) The requirements of this subsection are satisfied in relation to the intercepted material and any related communications data if each of the following—

(a) the number of persons to whom any of the material or data is disclosed or otherwise made available,

(b) the extent to which any of the material or data is disclosed or otherwise made available,

(c) the extent to which any of the material or data is copied, and

(d) the number of copies that are made,

is limited to the minimum that is necessary for the authorised purposes.

(3) The requirements of this subsection are satisfied in relation to the intercepted material and any related communications data if each copy made of any of the material or data (if not destroyed earlier) is destroyed as soon as there are no longer any grounds for retaining it as necessary for any of the authorised purposes.

(4) For the purposes of this section something is necessary for the authorised purposes if, and only if—

(a) it continues to be, or is likely to become, necessary as mentioned in section 5(3);

(b) it is necessary for facilitating the carrying out of any of the functions under this Chapter of the Secretary of State;

(c) it is necessary for facilitating the carrying out of any functions in relation to this Part of the Interception of Communications Commissioner or of the Tribunal;

(d) it is necessary to ensure that a person conducting a criminal prosecution has the information he needs to determine what is required of him by his duty to secure the fairness of the prosecution; or

(e) it is necessary for the performance of any duty imposed on any person by the *Public Records Act* 1958 or the *Public Records Act (Northern Ireland)* 1923.

(5) The arrangements for the time being in force under this section for securing that the requirements of subsection (2) are satisfied in relation to the intercepted material or any related communications data must include such arrangements as the Secretary of State considers necessary for securing that every copy of the material or data that is made is stored, for so long as it is retained, in a secure manner.

(6) Arrangements in relation to interception warrants which are made for the purposes of subsection (1)—

(a) shall not be required to secure that the requirements of subsections (2) and (3) are satisfied in so far as they relate to any of the intercepted material or related communications data, or any copy of any such material or data, possession of which has been surrendered to any authorities of a country or territory outside the United Kingdom; but

(b) shall be required to secure, in the case of every such warrant, that possession of the intercepted material and data and of copies of the material or data is surrendered to authorities of a country or territory outside the United Kingdom only if the requirements of subsection (7) are satisfied.

(7) The requirements of this subsection are satisfied in the case of a warrant if it appears to the Secretary of State—

(a) that requirements corresponding to those of subsections (2) and (3) will apply, to such extent (if any) as the Secretary of State thinks fit, in relation to any of the intercepted material or related communications data possession of which, or of any copy of which, is surrendered to the authorities in question; and

(b) that restrictions are in force which would prevent, to such extent (if any) as the Secretary of State thinks fit, the doing of anything in, for the purposes of or in connection with any proceedings outside the United Kingdom which would result in such a disclosure as, by virtue of section 17, could not be made in the United Kingdom.

(8) In this section "copy", in relation to intercepted material or related communications data, means any of the following (whether or not in documentary form)—

(a) any copy, extract or summary of the material or data which identifies itself as the product of an interception, and

(b) any record referring to an interception which is a record of the identities of the persons to or by whom the intercepted material was sent, or to whom the communications data relates,

and "copied" shall be construed accordingly.

Extra safeguards in the case of certificated warrants

25–376 **16.**—(1) For the purposes of section 15 the requirements of this section, in the case of a warrant in relation to which there is a section 8(4) certificate, are that the intercepted material is read, looked at or listened to by the persons to whom it becomes available by virtue of the warrant to the extent only that it—

(a) has been certified as material the examination of which is necessary as mentioned in section 5(3)(a), (b) or (c); and

(b) falls within subsection (2).

(2) Subject to subsections (3) and (4), intercepted material falls within this subsection so far only as it is selected to be read, looked at or listened to otherwise than according to a factor which—

(a) is referable to an individual who is known to be for the time being in the British Islands; and

(b) has as its purpose, or one of its purposes, the identification of material contained in communications sent by him, or intended for him.

(3) Intercepted material falls within subsection (2), notwithstanding that it is selected by reference to any such factor as is mentioned in paragraph (a) and (b) of that subsection, if—

(a) it is certified by the Secretary of State for the purposes of section 8(4) that the examination of material selected according to factors referable to the individual in question is necessary as mentioned in subsection 5(3)(a), (b) or (c); and

(b) the material relates only to communications sent during a period specified in the certificate that is no longer than the permitted maximum.

(3A) In subsection (3)(b) "the permitted maximum" means—

(a) in the case of material the examination of which is certified for the purposes of section 8(4) as necessary in the interests of national security, six months; and

(b) in any other case, three months.

(4) Intercepted material also falls within subsection (2), notwithstanding that it is selected by reference to any such factor as is mentioned in paragraph (a) and (b) of that subsection, if—

(a) the person to whom the warrant is addressed believes, on reasonable grounds, that the circumstances are such that the material would fall within that subsection; or

(b) the conditions set out in subsection (5) below are satisfied in relation to the selection of the material.

(5) Those conditions are satisfied in relation to the selection of intercepted material if—

(a) it has appeared to the person to whom the warrant is addressed that there has been such a relevant change of circumstances as, but for subsection (4)(b), would prevent the intercepted material from falling within subsection (2);

(b) since it first so appeared, a written authorisation to read, look at or listen to the material has been given by a senior official; and

(c) the selection is made before the end of the permitted period.

(5A) In subsection (5)(c) "the permitted period" means—

(a) in the case of material the examination of which is certified for the purposes of section 8(4) as necessary in the interests of national security, the period ending with the end of the fifth working day after it first appeared as mentioned in subsection (5)(a) to the person to whom the warrant is addressed; and

(b) in any other case, the period ending with the end of the first working day after it first so appeared to that person.

(6) References in this section to its appearing that there has been a relevant change of circumstances are references to its appearing either—

(a) that the individual in question has entered the British Islands; or

(b) that a belief by the person to whom the warrant is addressed in the individual's presence outside the British Islands was in fact mistaken.

[This section is printed as amended by the *Terrorism Act* 2006, s.32(1) and (5)–(7).]

Exclusion of matters from legal proceedings

17.—(1) Subject to section 18, no evidence shall be adduced, question asked, assertion or disclosure made or other thing done in, for the purposes of or in connection with any legal proceedings or *Inquiries Act* proceedings which (in any manner)— **25–377**

(a) discloses, in circumstances from which its origin in anything falling within subsection (2) may be inferred, any of the contents of an intercepted communication or any related communications data; or

(b) tends (apart from any such disclosure) to suggest that anything falling within subsection (2) has or may have occurred or be going to occur.

(2) The following fall within this subsection—

(a) conduct by a person falling within subsection (3) that was or would be an offence under section 1(1) or (2) of this Act or under section 1 of the *Interception of Communications Act* 1985;

(b) a breach by the Secretary of State of his duty under section 1(4) of this Act;

(c) the issue of an interception warrant or of a warrant under the *Interception of Communications Act* 1985;

(d) the making of an application by any person for an interception warrant, or for a warrant under that Act;

(e) the imposition of any requirement on any person to provide assistance with giving effect to an interception warrant.

(3) The persons referred to in subsection (2)(a) are—

(a) any person to whom a warrant under this Chapter may be addressed;

(b) any person holding office under the Crown;

(c) any member of the staff of the Serious Organised Crime Agency;

(ca) any member of the Scottish Crime and Drug Enforcement Agency;

(d) …;

(e) any person employed by or for the purposes of a police force;

(f) any person providing a postal service or employed for the purposes of any business of providing such a service; and

(g) any person providing a public telecommunications service or employed for the purposes of any business of providing such a service.

(4) In this section—

" *Inquiries Act* proceedings" means proceedings of an inquiry under the *Inquiries Act* 2005;

"intercepted communications" means any communication intercepted in the course of its transmission by means of a postal service or telecommunication system.

[This section is printed as amended, and repealed in part, by the *Inquiries Act* 2005, s.48(1), and Sched. 2, para. 20; the *SOCPA* 2005, s.59, and Sched. 4, paras 131 and 133; and S.I. 2007 No. 1098 (*ante*, § 25–373).]

Section 17(1) does not operate so as to prevent any evidence being adduced, question asked, assertion or disclosure made or other thing done so as to ascertain whether a telecommunication system is a public or private system; and the answer is the same if the evidence being adduced, question asked, etc., relates to events which took place before the 2000 Act came into force; where an interception of a communication took place on a private system before the commencement of the 2000 Act, it is permissible to ask questions or adduce evidence, etc., to establish that the interception was carried out by or on behalf of the person with the right to control the operation or use of the system (see s.1(6) (*ante*, § 25–368)); where the interception took place after the commencement of the 2000 Act, it is so permissible, subject to the facts of the particular case: *Att.-Gen.'s Reference (No. 5 of 2002)* [2005] 1 A.C. 167, HL. Their Lordships reasoned that, having regard to the provisions of sections 1(1), (2), (5) and (6), 3 to 5 and 17, it would be absurd that there could be no inquiry as to whether an interception was lawfully authorised or not, and as to whether or not the interceptor's conduct was excluded from criminal liability under section 1(6); given the obvious public interest in admitting probative evidence which satisfied the requirements of sections 1(6), 3 and 4, and the absence of any public interest in excluding it, a court might properly inquire whether an interception was of a public or private system and, if the latter, whether it was lawful; if the conclusion was that the system was public, then that would be the end of the inquiry, as it would be if it concluded that it was private, but the intercept was unlawful; if, however, it was private and the intercept was lawful, then the evidence could be admitted (subject to any other ground of objection).

Exceptions to section 17

25–378 **18.**—(1) Section 17(1) shall not apply in relation to—

(a) any proceedings for a relevant offence;

(b) any civil proceedings under section 11(8);

(c) any proceedings before the Tribunal;

(da) any control order proceedings (within the meaning of the *Prevention of Terrorism Act* 2005) or any proceedings arising out of such proceedings;

(d) any proceedings on an appeal or review for which provision is made by an order under section 67(8);

(e) any proceedings before the Special Immigration Appeals Commission or any proceedings arising out of proceedings before that Commission; or

(f) any proceedings before the Proscribed Organisations Appeal Commission or any proceedings arising out of proceedings before that Commission.

(2) Subsection (1) shall not, by virtue of paragraph (da) to (f), authorise the disclosure of anything—

(za) in the case of any proceedings falling within paragraph (da) to—

(i) a person who, within the meaning of the Schedule to the *Prevention of Terrorism Act* 2005, is or was a relevant party to the control order proceedings; or

(ii) any person who for the purposes of any proceedings so falling (but otherwise than by virtue of an appointment under paragraph 7 of that Schedule) represents a person falling within sub-paragraph (i);

(a) in the case of any proceedings falling within paragraph (e), to—

(i) the appellant to the Special Immigration Appeals Commission; or

(ii) any person who for the purposes of any proceedings so falling (but otherwise than by virtue of an appointment under section 6 of the *Special Immigration Appeals Commission Act* 1997) represents that appellant; or

(b) in the case of proceedings falling within paragraph (f), to—

(i) the applicant to the Proscribed Organisations Appeal Commission;

(ii) the organisation concerned (if different);

(iii) any person designated under paragraph 6 of Schedule 3 to the *Terrorism Act* 2000 to conduct proceedings so falling on behalf of that organisation; or

(iv) any person who for the purposes of any proceedings so falling (but otherwise than by virtue of an appointment under paragraph 7 of that Schedule) represents that applicant or that organisation.

(3) Section 17(1) shall not prohibit anything done in, for the purposes of, or in connection with, so much of any legal proceedings as relates to the fairness or unfairness of a dismissal on the grounds of any conduct constituting an offence under section 1(1) or (2), 11(7) or 19 of this Act, or section 1 of the *Interception of Communications Act* 1985.

(4) Section 17(1)(a) shall not prohibit the disclosure of any of the contents of a communication if the interception of that communication was lawful by virtue of section 1(5)(c), 3 or 4.

(5) Where any disclosure is proposed to be or has been made on the grounds that it is authorised by subsection (4), section 17(1) shall not prohibit the doing of anything in, or

for the purposes of, so much of any ... proceedings as relates to the question whether that disclosure is or was so authorised.

(6) Section 17(1)(b) shall not prohibit the doing of anything that discloses any conduct of a person for which he has been convicted of an offence under section 1(1) or (2), 11(7) or 19 of this Act, or section 1 of the *Interception of Communications Act* 1985.

(7) Nothing in section 17(1) shall prohibit any such disclosure of any information that continues to be available for disclosure as is confined to—

(a) a disclosure to a person conducting a criminal prosecution for the purpose only of enabling that person to determine what is required of him by his duty to secure the fairness of the prosecution; or

(b) a disclosure to a relevant judge in a case in which that judge has ordered the disclosure to be made to him alone; or

(c) a disclosure to the panel of an inquiry held under the *Inquiries Act* 2005 in the course of which the panel has ordered the disclosure to be made to the panel alone.

(8) A relevant judge shall not order a disclosure under subsection (7)(b) except where he is satisfied that the exceptional circumstances of the case make the disclosure essential in the interests of justice.

(8A) The panel of an inquiry shall not order a disclosure under subsection (7)(c) except where it is satisfied that the exceptional circumstances of the case make the disclosure essential to enable the inquiry to fulfil its terms of reference.

(9) Subject to subsection (10), where in any criminal proceedings—

(a) a relevant judge does order a disclosure under subsection (7)(b), and

(b) in consequence of that disclosure he is of the opinion that there are exceptional circumstances requiring him to do so,

he may direct the person conducting the prosecution to make for the purposes of the proceedings any such admission of fact as that judge thinks essential in the interests of justice.

(10) Nothing in any direction under subsection (9) shall authorise or require anything to be done in contravention of section 17(1).

(11) In this section "a relevant judge" means—

(a) any judge of the High Court or of the Crown Court or any Circuit judge;

(b) any judge of the High Court of Justiciary or any sheriff;

(c) in relation to *a court-martial, the judge advocate appointed in relation to that court-martial under section 84B of the* Army Act *1955, section 84B of the* Air Force Act *1955 or section 53B of the* Naval Discipline Act *1957* [proceedings before the Court Martial, the judge advocate for those proceedings]; or

(d) any person holding any such judicial office as entitles him to exercise the jurisdiciton of a judge falling within paragraph (a) or (b).

(12) In this section "relevant offence" means—

(a) an offence under any provision of this Act;

(b) an offence under section 1 of the *Interception of Communications Act* 1985;

(c) an offence under section 5 of the *Wireless Telegraphy Act* 1949;

(d) an offence under section 83 or 84 of the *Postal Services Act* 2000;

(e) an offence under section 45 of the *Telecommunications Act* 1984;

(f) an offence under section 4 of the *Official Secrets Act* 1989 relating to any such information, document or article as is mentioned in subsection (3)(a) of that section;

(g) an offence under section 1 or 2 of the *Official Secrets Act* 1911 relating to any sketch, plan, model, article, note, document or information which incorporates or relates to the contents of any intercepted communication or any related communications data or tends to suggest as mentioned in section 17(1)(b) of this Act;

(h) perjury committed in the course of any proceedings mentioned in subsection (1) or (3) of this section;

(i) attempting or conspiring to commit, or aiding, abetting, counselling or procuring the commission of, an offence falling within any of the preceding paragraphs; and

(j) contempt of court committed in the course of, or in relation to, any proceedings mentioned in subsection (1) or (3) of this section.

(13) In subsection (12) "intercepted communication" has the same meaning as in section 17.

[This section is printed as amended and repealed in part by the *Postal Services Act 2000 (Consequential Modifications No. 1) Order* 2001 (S.I. 2001 No. 1149); the

Inquiries Act 2005, s.48(1), and Sched. 2, para. 21; and the *Prevention of Terrorism Act* 2005, s.11(5), and Sched., para. 9; and as amended, as from a day to be appointed, by the *AFA* 2006, s.378(1), and Sched. 16, para. 169 (substitution of words in square brackets for italicised words in subs. (11)(c)).]

Offence for unauthorised disclosures

25–379 **19.**—(1) Where an interception warrant has been issued or renewed, it shall be the duty of every person falling within subsection (2) to keep secret all the matters mentioned in subsection (3).

(2) The persons falling within this subsection are—

(a) the persons specified in section 6(2);

(b) every person holding office under the Crown;

(c) every member of the staff of the Serious Organised Crime Agency;

(ca) every member of the Scottish Crime and Drug Enforcement Agency;

(d) …;

(e) every person employed by or for the purposes of a police force;

(f) persons providing postal services or employed for the purposes of any business of providing such a service;

(g) persons providing public telecommunications services or employed for the purposes of any business of providing such a service;

(h) persons having control of the whole or any part of a telecommunication system located wholly or partly in the United Kingdom.

(3) Those matters are—

(a) the existence and contents of the warrant and of any section 8(4) certificate in relation to the warrant;

(b) the details of the issue of the warrant and of any renewal or modification of the warrant or of any such certificate;

(c) the existence and contents of any requirement to provide assistance with giving effect to the warrant;

(d) the steps taken in pursuance of the warrant or of any such requirement; and

(e) everything in the intercepted material, together with any related communications data.

(4) A person who makes a disclosure to another of anything that he is required to keep secret under this section shall be guilty of an offence and liable—

(a) on conviction on indictment, to imprisonment for a term not exceeding five years or to a fine, or to both;

(b) on summary conviction, to imprisonment for a term not exceeding *six* [12] months or to a fine not exceeding the statutory maximum, or to both.

(5) In proceedings against any person for an offence under this section in respect of any disclosure, it shall be a defence for that person to show that he could not reasonably have been expected, after first becoming aware of the matter disclosed, to take steps to prevent the disclosure.

(6) In proceedings against any person for an offence under this section in respect of any disclosure, it shall be a defence for that person to show that—

(a) the disclosure was made by or to a professional legal adviser in connection with the giving, by the adviser to any client of his, of advice about the effect of provisions of this Chapter; and

(b) the person to whom or, as the case may be, by whom it was made was the client or a representative of the client.

(7) In proceedings against any person for an offence under this section in respect of any disclosure, it shall be a defence for that person to show that the disclosure was made by a legal adviser—

(a) in contemplation of, or in connection with, any legal proceedings; and

(b) for the purposes of those proceedings.

(8) Neither subsection (6) nor subsection (7) applies in the case of a disclosure made with a view to furthering any criminal purpose.

(9) In proceedings against any person for an offence under this section in respect of any disclosure, it shall be a defence for that person to show that the disclosure was confined to a disclosure made to the Interception of Communications Commissioner or authorised—

(a) by that Commissioner;

(3) Subject to subsection (5),the designated person may grant an authorisation for persons holding offices, ranks or positions with the same relevant public authority as the designated person to engage in any conduct to which this Chapter applies.

(4) Subject to subsection (5), where it appears to the designated person that a postal or telecommunications operator is or may be in possession of, or be capable of obtaining, any communications data, the designated person may, by notice to the postal or telecommunications operator, require the operator—

(a) if the operator is not already in possession of the data, to obtain the data; and

(b) in any case, to disclose all of the data in his possession or subsequently obtained by him.

(5) The designated person shall not grant an authorisation under subsection (3), or give a notice under subsection (4), unless he believes that obtaining the data in question by the conduct authorised or required by the authorisation or notice is proportionate to what is sought to be achieved by so obtaining the data.

(6) It shall be the duty of the postal or telecommunications operator to comply with the requirements of any notice given to him under subsection (4).

(7) A person who is under a duty by virtue of subsection (6) shall not be required to do anything in pursuance of that duty which it is not reasonably practicable for him to do.

(8) [*Civil proceedings to enforce duty under subs. (6).*]

(9) [*Procedure for order under subs. (2)(h).*]

Form and duration of authorisations and notices

23.—(1) An authorisation under section 22(3)— **25–380c**

(a) must be granted in writing or (if not in writing) in a manner that produces a record of its having been granted;

(b) must describe the conduct to which this Chapter applies that is authorised and the communications data in relation to which it is authorised;

(c) must specify the matters falling within section 22(2) by reference to which it is granted; and

(d) must specify the office, rank or position held by the person granting the authorisation.

(2) A notice under section 22(4) requiring communications data to be disclosed or to be obtained and disclosed—

(a) must be given in writing or (if not in writing) must be given in a manner that produces a record of its having been given;

(b) must describe the communications data to be obtained or disclosed under the notice;

(c) must specify the matters falling within section 22(2) by reference to which the notice is given;

(d) must specify the office, rank or position held by the person giving it; and

(e) must specify the manner in which any disclosure required by the notice is to be made.

(3) A notice under section 22(4) shall not require the disclosure of data to any person other than—

(a) the person giving the notice; or

(b) such other person as may be specified in or otherwise identified by, or in accordance with, the provisions of the notice;

but the provisions of the notice shall not specify or otherwise identify a person for the purposes of paragraph (b) unless he holds an office, rank or position with the same relevant public authority as the person giving the notice.

(4) An authorisation under section 22(3) or notice under section 22(4)—

(a) shall not authorise or require any data to be obtained after the end of the period of one month beginning with the date on which the authorisation is granted or the notice given; and

(b) in the case of a notice, shall not authorise or require any disclosure after the end of that period of any data not in the possession of, or obtained by, the postal or telecommunications operator at a time during that period.

(5) An authorisation under section 22(3) or notice under section 22(4) may be renewed at any time before the end of the period of one month applying (in accordance with subsection (4) or subsection (7)) to that authorisation or notice.

(6) A renewal of an authorisation under section 22(3) or of a notice under section 22(4)

shall be by the grant or giving, in accordance with this section, of a further authorisation or notice.

(7) Subsection (4) shall have effect in relation to a renewed authorisation or renewal notice as if the period of one month mentioned in that subsection did not begin until the end of the period of one month applicable to the authorisation or notice that is current at the time of the renewal.

(8) Where a person who has given a notice under subsection (4) of section 22 is satisfied—

(a) that it is no longer necessary on grounds falling within subsection (2) of that section for the requirements of the notice to be complied with, or

(b) that the conduct required by the notice is no longer proportionate to what is sought to be achieved by obtaining communications data to which the notice relates,

he shall cancel the notice.

(9) The Secretary of State may by regulations provide for the person by whom any duty imposed by subsection (8) is to be performed in a case in which it would otherwise fall on a person who is no longer available to perform it; and regulations under this subsection may provide for the person on whom the duty is to fall to be a person appointed in accordance with the regulations.

24. [*Arrangements for payments.*]

Interpretation of Part II

25–380d **25.**—(1) In this Chapter—

"communications data" has the meaning given by section 21(4);

"designated" shall be construed in accordance with subsection (2);

"postal or telecommunications operator" means a person who provides a postal service or telecommunications service;

"relevant public authority" means (subject to subsection (4)) any of the following—

(a) a police force;

(b) the Serious Organised Crime Agency; …

(ca) every member of the Scottish Crime and Drug Enforcement Agency;

(d) Her Majesty's Revenue and Customs; …

(f) any of the intelligence services;

(g) any such public authority not falling within paragraphs (a) to (f) as may be specified for the purposes of this subsection by an order made by the Secretary of State.

(2) Subject to subsection (3), the persons designated for the purposes of this Chapter are the individuals holding such offices, ranks or positions with relevant public authorities as are prescribed for the purposes of this subsection by an order made by the Secretary of State.

(3) The Secretary of State may by order impose restrictions—

(a) on the authorisations and notices under this Chapter that may be granted or given by any individual holding an office, rank or position with a specified public authority; and

(b) on the circumstances in which, or the purposes of which, such authorisations may be granted or notices given by any such individual.

(4) [*Removal of persons from list by order.*]

(5) [*Procedure for adding to list by order.*]

[This section is printed as amended, and repealed in part, by the *SOCPA* 2005, s.59, and Sched. 4, paras 131 and 135; S.I. 2007 No. 1098 (*ante*, § 25–373); and the *SCA* 2007, s.88, and Sched. 12, paras 5 and 8.]

For an order made under subsections (1)(g), (2) and (3), see the *Regulation of Investigatory Powers (Communications Data) Order* 2003 (S.I. 2003 No. 3172).

XV. MISCONDUCT IN JUDICIAL OR PUBLIC OFFICE

Misfeasance

25–381 In *Att.-Gen.'s Reference (No. 3 of 2003)* [2004] 2 Cr.App.R. 23, CA, it was held

Indictment

Statement of Offence

Making false statements tending to prejudice Her Majesty the Queen and the Public Revenue with intent to defraud her Majesty the Queen. 25–385a

Particulars of Offence

A B and C D, on the —— day of ——, 20—, being directors of X & Co. Ltd, did, with intent to defraud and to the prejudice of the Commissioners of Her Majesty's Revenue and Customs, deliver to or cause to be delivered to an inspector of taxes an account purporting to be a true trading and profit and loss account of the business of X & Co. Ltd, for the year 20—, which account falsely stated that the profits of the said business for the said year amounted to £——, whereas in truth and in fact the said profits largely exceeded the said sum of £——.

False statements in an employer's annual return under the PAYE system where the defendant was not the person required by statute to make the return; and false statements in a claim for allowances have also formed the subjects of similar indictments.

As to the need for a count alleging a cheat on the public revenue to be drafted with sufficient detail to inform the court and the defence of the exact nature of the factual allegation, and so as to eliminate the possibility of a conviction on either of two alternative bases, see *R. v. Litanzios* [1999] Crim.L.R. 667, CA.

For a review of sentencing in cases of cheating the public revenue, see *R. v. Regan*, 11 Cr.App.R.(S.) 15, CA. For recent examples, see *R. v. Rogers (Simon)* [2002] 1 Cr.App.R.(S.) 81, CA, *R. v. Gorasia* [2002] 1 Cr.App.R.(S.) 84, CA, *R. v. Ward* [2006] 1 Cr.App.R.(S.) 66, CA, *Att.-Gen.'s References (Nos 88, etc., of 2006) (R. v. Meehan)* [2007] 2 Cr.App.R.(S.) 28, CA (for the organisers of large-scale frauds involving a loss to the public revenue of well in excess of £1 million, sentences substantially in excess of the statutory maximum for the substantive offence of evasion of excise duty (*i.e.* "well into double figures") will be appropriate on conviction), *R. v. Youell* [2007] 2 Cr.App.R.(S.) 43, CA (guidelines in *R. v. Czyzewski*, *post*, § 25–481, were concerned with smuggling and did not provide the benchmark for sophisticated frauds on the public revenue), and *R. v. Namer* [2008] 2 Cr.App.R.(S.) 24, CA (consecutive sentence appropriate where offender organised several carousel frauds which resulted in losses to the public revenue of approximately £2.5m and where the last fraud occurred 18 months after the earlier frauds and thus represented a return to crime).

A financial reporting order may be made in respect of a person convicted of an offence of cheating the public revenue: *SOCPA* 2005, s.76 (*ante*, § 5–886a).

B. Customs and Excise Management Act 1979

(1) Introduction

The functions and powers of the Commissioners and officers of Her Majesty's Revenue and Customs

From April, 2005, the *Commissioners for Revenue and Customs Act* 2005 established a new government department, Her Majesty's Revenue and Customs, and a new prosecutions office, the Revenue and Customs Prosecutions Office. The Queen appoints Commissioners for Her Majesty's Revenue and Customs who are able to appoint officers of Revenue and Customs to exercise many of the Commissioners' functions. The Commissioners are responsible for all the functions, except prosecutions (which is the function of the Director of the Revenue and Customs Prosecutions Office: s.35 of the 2005 Act), which were previously the responsibility of the Commissioners of Inland Revenue and the Commissioners of Customs and Excise (s.5). Section 50(1) provides that, so far as appropriate in consequence of section 5, a "reference in an enactment, instrument or other document to the Commissioners for Customs and Excise, to customs and excise or to the Commissioners of Inland Revenue (however expressed) shall be taken as a reference to the Commissioners for Her Majesty's Revenue and Customs." Schedule 1 to the 2005 Act identifies all the functions previously carried out by the Inland Revenue. In order to prevent any inadvertent widening of powers, sections 6 and 7 of 25–386 the 2005 Act provide that powers previously available to the Commissioners of Customs and Excise and their officers may not be used for the former Inland Revenue functions, while powers previously available to the Commissioners of Inland Revenue and their officers may only be used for those functions. For example, customs officers had a power under section 289 of the *PCA* 2002 to search premises or persons for cash which may have been obtained through unlawful conduct. Although the power is restricted to cases where the unlawful conduct relates to a matter dealt with by Customs and Excise (s.289(5)), it is not explicitly limited to indirect taxes and duties. Were it not for sections 6 and 7 of the 2005 Act, the power could be used by officers of Revenue and Customs where the unlawful conduct related to income tax. In the same way, an officer of Revenue and Customs can use all the current Inland Revenue powers, but only in relation to former Inland Revenue matters. Section 50(2) of the 2005 Act provides that, so far as appropriate in consequence of sections 6 and 7, a "reference in an enactment, instrument or other document to any of the persons specified in section 6(2) or 7(3) (however expressed) shall be taken as a reference to an officer of Revenue and Customs." Those persons are, in summary, customs officers, officers of the Inland Revenue, an inspector of taxes, etc.

Many of the duties of the Commissioners under the *CEMA* 1979 are termed "assigned matters" (s.1), and every constable, coastguard and member of Her Majesty's armed forces is duty bound to assist in the enforcement of any assigned matter: s.11.

The Commissioners are required to co-operate with other customs services on matters of mutual concern: s.9.

Although the Commissioners control the movement of goods and substances transported by air (s.21); by hovercraft (s.23); by pipe-line (s.24); and by sea and the Channel Tunnel (numerous provisions), they are not limited in their activities to events at ports, docks and airports.

Principal powers

25–387 The *CEMA* 1979 remains the principal enactment under which the Revenue and Customs exercise their powers in relation to customs and excise matters. Although some powers provided by the 1979 Act have been repealed by the 2005 Act, those that remain include the power of officers to board and to rummage ships, aircraft or vehicles (s.27), to search premises (s.161), vessels (s.163) and persons (s.164); to inspect aircraft and goods therein (s.33); to make regulations in relation to small craft (s.81); to detain suspects (s.138); and to forfeit goods (ss.49 and 139), ships and aircraft (ss.88, 139 and 141). As to the power under section 141, see *Customs and Excise Commrs v. Air Canada* [1991] 2 Q.B. 446, CA (Civ. Div.)). The Commissioners also have powers in relation to customs and excise matters under other legislation. Important examples include powers under the *Value Added Tax Act* 1994 (see *post*, § 25–519); under the *Crime (International Co-operation) Act* 2003 (see s.27 thereof, together with the *Crime (International Co-operation) Act 2003 (Exercise of Functions) Order* 2005 (S.I. 2005 No. 425)); under the *PCA* 2002, s.289, in relation to the recovery of cash (*ante*, § 5–820); and under a number of *Finance Acts*.

Principal offences

25–388 Offences include improper importations (s.50) and exportations (s.68) and fraudulent evasions (s.170); counterfeiting documents (s.168); and the making of untrue declarations in relation to goods (s.167 and *cf*. s.78). Special penalties exist where smuggled goods are offered for sale (s.87). The hybrid offences of impersonating and obstructing a customs officer (ss.13 and 16) have been replaced by similar summary offences in respect of officers of Revenue and Customs (ss.30 to 32 of the 2005 Act).

Indicting "smuggling" offences

25–389 In respect of what may loosely be termed "smuggling offences" it will be seen that the *CEMA* 1979 creates offences in connection with the improper importation of goods (s.50) as well as specified offences in relation to the exportation of goods (s.68). However, it is not the usual practice for the prosecution to indict under either of those two sections. This is because offences under section 170 (fraudulent evasions of duty, etc.) are so all-embracing that it is difficult to see when it would be necessary, or tactically advantageous, to rely on section 50 or section 68. Accordingly, in a case involving the importation/exportation of prohibited, restricted or dutiable goods (being an investigation carried out by the Commissioners of Revenue and Customs) it is likely that the accused will face counts drafted under section 170. Where the goods imported are controlled drugs there is no reason why the prosecution cannot also draft counts under the provisions of the *Misuse of Drugs Act* 1971 (*e.g.* possession with intent to supply contrary to s.5(3)). However, in practice, the Commissioners prefer to use offences created under the 1979 Act rather than the offences created under the 1971 Act. Correspondingly, the police, if they are investigating the matter, prefer to bring charges under, say, the *Misuse of Drugs Act* 1971.

Drug smuggling-how the offence is created

The *CEMA* 1979 does not itself impose any prohibitions or restrictions on the importation or exportation of goods. This is because the Act serves as an "umbrella" under which a large number of enactments (which do impose such prohibitions or restrictions) are embraced. The *CEMA* 1979 "manages" those other enactments. Thus, section 170(2) provides, in blanket terms, that it is an offence to be "knowingly concerned in any fraudulent evasion of any prohibition" on the importation of goods. Controlled drugs are prohibited from exportation and importation by section 3(1) of the *Misuse of Drugs Act* 1971 (*post*, § 27–26). Accordingly, offences of unlawful exportation or importation of controlled drugs arise by a combination of section 3(1) of the 1971 Act and an offence under the *CEMA* 1979, s.170. **25–390**

Drafting different counts for different goods

Different penalties will often attach to different goods or categories of goods, the importation or exportation of which is either restricted, prohibited or subject to the payment of duty. In *R. v. Courtie* [1984] A.C. 463, HL, it was held that where different factual ingredients attracted different penalties then different offences were created. In the case of drug-related importations, three separate offences exist in relation to Class A, B and C drugs because each class attracts a different penalty: but note *R. v. Shivpuri* [1987] A.C. 1, HL. It is, therefore, essential to draft separate counts in respect of different goods imported. **25–391**

Care should also be taken to ensure that any substance described in a count as a "controlled drug" is in fact an accurate description of the substance in question. Thus, it is inappropriate to particularise the drug as "cannabis" when in fact the relevant drug is "cannabis resin". Both substances are separately controlled, being separately defined by the *Misuse of Drugs Act* 1971, and it is a mistake to regard terms such as "cannabis" as being generic: *Muir v. Smith* [1978] Crim.L.R. 293, DC. Where there is doubt as to the type of cannabis, "cannabis or cannabis resin" may be particularised without being bad for duplicity: *R. v. Best*, 70 Cr.App.R. 21, CA; *R. v. Mitchell* [1992] Crim.L.R. 723, CA.

When considering the provisions of the *CEMA* 1979, careful attention should be given to the distinction between *dutiable*, *restricted* and *prohibited* goods (see s.1, *post*, §§ 25–400 *et seq.*). A count should not refer to a certain commodity as being "prohibited" when in fact it is "restricted" or "dutiable". Similarly, an accused's account as to what he believed he was importing must be carefully analysed to determine whether, at the material time, his state of mind went to the category of goods which he, in fact, imported: see the authorities set out in the commentary to section 170, *post*, §§ 25–452 *et seq.*

Proving facts/presumptions

The burden of proving the fact of importation or exportation rests on the Crown. On at least one occasion, it has been suggested that there exists a presumption of importation, but grave doubts have been expressed by the Court of Appeal as to the **25–392** correctness of such an argument: see *R. v. Watts and Stack*, 70 Cr.App.R. 187, *post*, § 25–458. Once the fact of importation is proved, then it is undoubtedly correct that the importation is presumed to be unlawful unless the defence can prove the contrary on a balance of probabilities: s.154, *post*, § 25–437. One practical effect of the presumptions in section 154 is that all goods imported are presumed to be dutiable, or prohibited, or restricted (and indeed they are also presumed to have been unlawfully imported) unless the importer can establish the contrary. The presumptions can give rise to some startling results: see *Mizel v. Warren* [1973] 1 W.L.R. 899, DC.

Defining the moment of importation

25–393 The moment of importation or exportation is defined by statute: see s.5, *post*, § 25–406.

Time limits

25–394 On indictment, proceedings may be commenced up to 20 years from the date the offence was committed. In summary proceedings the period is up to three years: s.146A, *post*, § 25–430.

The history of the legislation is not straightforward. Under section 147(1) (now repealed) proceedings for an offence had to be commenced within three years of the date of the commission of the offence. Section 11(2) of the *Finance Act* 1988 amended section 147(1) so that the limitation period for commencing proceedings on indictment was extended to 20 years for offences committed on or after July 29, 1988. Section 16(2) of the *Finance Act* 1989 repealed section 147(1) and inserted section 146A in its place.

The net effect is that offences committed after July 28, 1988, are subject to a 20-year time limit for proceedings on indictment.

The forfeiture provisions of the CEMA 1979

25–395 Quite independently of provisions to be found in other enactments, the *CEMA* 1979 is peppered with an array of forfeiture provisions. Broadly speaking, those provisions affect two categories of objects. The first relates to goods which are prohibited, or restricted, or dutiable, or which have not been handled in accordance with the provisions of the Act. The second relates to vessels, aircraft and vehicles which have been used in contravention of various provisions of the customs and excise Acts.

(i) *Goods*

25–396 Goods which have been improperly imported, including those which have been unshipped or unloaded without payment of duty, or contrary to any prohibition or restriction are liable to forfeiture: s.49.

Goods shipped for exportation before entry has been duly made (s.53(4), (8) and *cf.* s.66(2)); or goods unloaded in breach of sections 69 to 71 (s.74(2)); or stores landed or unloaded without proper authority (s.61(5)), are similarly liable to forfeiture. Where any person is required to furnish information in relation to particular goods imported or exported and that person makes an untrue declaration (s.77) or fails to make an appropriate declaration (s.78), then the goods in question are liable to forfeiture. If goods which an officer has power to examine are, without authority, removed from customs and excise charge before they have been examined, they are liable to forfeiture (s.159(5)).

(ii) *Ships, aircraft, vehicles, etc.*

25–397 Certain vessels that are not "marked" as required by the Commissioners (s.81(7)); or vessels, aircraft and vehicles which have been constructed, adapted or fitted out for the purpose of concealing goods (s.88); or for the purpose of concealing or handling goods liable to forfeiture (s.141)—shall be liable to forfeiture.

(iii) *Cash*

25–398 See now Chapter 3 (ss.289–303) of Part 5 of the *PCA* 2002.

(iv) *Enforcement*

The power of seizure in relation to property liable to forfeiture is contained in section 139 of the *CEMA* 1979 (*post*, § 25–424). 25–399

(2) Definitions and application

Customs and Excise Management Act 1979, s.1

Interpretation

1.—(1) In this Act, unless the context otherwise requires— 25–400

…

"approved wharf" has the meaning given by section 20A below;

"armed forces" means the Royal Navy, the Royal Marines, the regular army and the regular air force, and any reserve or auxiliary force of any of those services which has been called out on permanent service, or called into actual service, or embodied;

"assigned matter" means any matter in relation to which the Commissioners, or officers of Revenue and Customs, have a power or duty;

…

As to whether investigations under the *DTOA* 1986 (and the *DTA* 1994) were "assigned matters", see *R. v. Stafford JJ., ex p. Customs and Excise Commrs* [1991] 2 Q.B. 339, DC.

"boundary" means the land boundary of Northern Ireland;

"British ship" means a British ship within the meaning of the *Merchant Shipping Act* 1995;

…

"commander", in relation to an aircraft, includes any person having or taking the charge or command of the aircraft;

"the Commissioners" means the Commissioners for Her Majesty's Revenue and Customs;

…

"container" includes any bundle or package and any box, cask or other receptacle whatsoever;

"the customs and excise Acts" means the *Customs and Excise Acts* 1979 and any other enactment for the time being in force relating to customs or excise;

"the *Customs and Excise Acts* 1979" means—

this Act,
the *Customs and Excise Duties (General Reliefs) Act* 1979,
the *Alcoholic Liquor Duties Act* 1979,
the *Hydrocarbon Oil Duties Act* 1979, and
the *Tobacco Products Duty Act* 1979;

"customs and excise airport" has the meaning given by section 21(7) below;

"customs and excise station" has the meaning given by section 26 below;

…

"dutiable goods", except in the expression "dutiable or restricted goods", means goods of a class or description subject to any duty of customs or excise, whether or not those goods are in fact chargeable with that duty, and whether or not that duty has been paid thereon;

"dutiable or restricted goods" has the meaning given by section 52 below;

"examination station" has the meaning given by section 22A below;

"excise warehouse" means a place of security approved by the Commissioners under subsection (1) (whether or not it is also approved under subsection (2)) of section 92 below, and, except in that section, also includes a distiller's warehouse;

"exporter", in relation to goods for exportation or for use as stores, includes the shipper of the goods and any person performing in relation to an aircraft functions corresponding with those of a shipper;

…

"goods" includes stores and baggage;

…

"importer", in relation to any goods at any time between their importation and the time when they are delivered out of charge, includes any owner or other person for the time being possessed of or beneficially interested in the goods, and, in relation to goods imported by means of a pipe-line, includes the owner of the pipe-line;

25–401 In *R. v. Collins* [1987] Crim.L.R. 256, CA, the defendant was the operator of a minibus service between London and Germany. On the return journey he acquired tobacco and alcohol for the maximum permitted duty-free allowance for all passengers. Before passing through customs he purported to make a declaration of gift to the passengers, but no genuine gift was intended. In giving the judgment of the court dismissing the defendant's appeal against his conviction of contravening section 170(2)(a) (*post*, § 25–452), McCowan J. said that it was a sham: the defendant evaded the duty intending to sell the goods and keep the profit to himself. He was the "owner", the "person ... possessed of ... the goods" and "beneficially interested" in them within the definition of "importer" in section 1(1) of the *CEMA* 1979.

...

"law officer of the Crown" means the Attorney General or in Scotland the Lord Advocate or in Northern Ireland the Attorney General for Northern Ireland;

"licence year", in relation to an excise licence issuable annually, means the period of 12 months ending on the date on which that licence expires in any year;

"master", in relation to a ship, includes any person having or taking the charge or command of the ship;

"night" means the period between 11 p.m. and 5 a.m.;

["nuclear material" has the same meaning as in the *Nuclear Material (Offences) Act* 1983 (see section 6 of that Act);]

"occupier", in relation to any bonded premises, includes any person who has given security to the Crown in respect of those premises;

"officer" means, subject to section 8(2) below, a person commissioned by the Commissioners;

"owner", in relation to an aircraft, includes the operator of the aircraft;

"owner", in relation to a pipe-line, means (except in the case of a pipe-line vested in the Crown which in pursuance of arrangements in that behalf is operated by another) the person in whom the line is vested and, in the said excepted case, means the person operating the line;

"pipe-line" has the meaning given by section 65 of the *Pipe-lines Act* 1962 (that Act being taken, for the purposes of this definition, to extend to Northern Ireland);

"port" means a port appointed by the Commissioners under section 19 below;

"prescribed area" means such an area in Northern Ireland adjoining the boundary as the Commissioners may by regulations prescribe;

"prescribed sum", in relation to the penalty provided for an offence, has the meaning given by section 171(2) below;

"prohibited or restricted goods" means goods of a class or description of which the importation, exportation or carriage coastwise is for the time being prohibited or restricted under or by virtue of any enactment;

"proper", in relation to the person by, with or to whom, or the place at which, any thing is to be done, means the person or place appointed or authorised in that behalf by the Commissioners;

"proprietor", in relation to any goods, includes any owner, importer, exporter, shipping or other person for the time being possessed of or beneficially interested in those goods;

"Queen's warehouse" means any place provided by the Crown or appointed by the Commissioners for the deposit of goods for security thereof and of the duties chargeable thereon;

...

"ship" and "vessel" include any boat or other vessel whatsoever (and, to the extent provided in section 2 below, any hovercraft);

"shipment" includes loading into an aircraft, and "shipped" and cognate expressions shall be construed accordingly;

"stores" means, subject to subsection (4) below, goods for use in a ship or aircraft and includes fuel and spare parts and other articles of equipment, whether or not for immediate fitting;

...

"transit shed" has the meaning given by section 25A below;

"vehicle" includes a railway vehicle;

...

"warehousing regulations" means regulations under section 93 below.

(2) This Act and the other Acts included in the *Customs and Excise Acts* 1979 shall be construed as one Act but where a provision of this Act refers to this Act that reference is not to be construed as including a reference to any of the others.

(3) [*Not printed.*]

(4) [*Goods for use in ship or aircraft as merchandise for sale by retail.*]

(5) [*Tobacco dealers deemed to be carrying on an excise licence trade.*]

(6) [*Computation of periods of days.*]

(7) The provisions of this Act in so far as they relate to customs duties apply, notwithstanding that any duties are imposed for the benefit of the Communities, as if the revenue from duties so imposed remained part of the revenues of the Crown.

[This section is printed as amended by the *Isle of Man Act* 1979, s.13 and Sched. 1; the *Betting and Gaming Duties Act* 1981, s.34(1) and Sched. 5, para. 5(a); the *Finance Act* 1981, s.11(1) and Sched. 8, Pt I, para. 1(1), (2); the *Finance Act* 1984, s.8 and Sched. 4, Pt II, para. 1; the *Finance (No. 2) Act* 1987, s.103(3); the *Territorial Sea Act* 1987, s.3(1), (4), Sched. 1, para. 4(1) and Sched. 2; the *Finance Act* 1991, s.11(1), (2); the *Customs Controls on Importation of Goods Regulations* 1991 (S.I. 1991 No. 2724), reg. 6(1) and (2); the *Finance (No. 2) Act* 1992, s.3 and Sched. 2; the *Finance Act* 1993, s.30; the *Merchant Shipping Act* 1995, Sched. 13; and the *Commissioners for Revenue and Customs Act* 2005, s.50(6), and Sched. 4, paras 20 and 22. The definition of "nuclear material" is inserted, as from a day to be appointed, by the *CJIA* 2008, s.75(2), and Sched. 17, para. 8(1) and (2). Immaterial definitions in subs. (1) have been omitted.]

Sections 20A ("approved wharf"), 21(7) ("customs and excise airport"), 22A ("examination station"), 25A ("transit shed"), 26 ("customs and excise station"), 52 ("dutiable or restricted goods") are not printed in this work.

[The next paragraph is § 25–406.]

Customs and Excise Management Act 1979, s.5

Time of importation, exportation, etc.

5.—(1) The provisions of this section shall have effect for the purposes of the customs and excise Acts. **25–406**

(2) Subject to subsections (3) and (6) below, the time of importation of any goods shall be deemed to be—

(a) where the goods are brought by sea, the time when the ship carrying them comes within the limits of a port;

(b) where the goods are brought by air, the time when the aircraft carrying them lands in the United Kingdom or the time when the goods are unloaded in the United Kingdom, whichever is the earlier;

(c) where the goods are brought by land, the time when the goods are brought across the boundary into Northern Ireland.

(3) In the case of goods brought by sea of which entry is not required under regulation 5 of the *Customs Controls on Importation of Goods Regulations* 1991, the time of importation shall be deemed to be the time when the ship carrying them came within the limits of the port at which the goods are discharged.

(4) Subject to subsections (5) and (7) below, the time of exportation of any goods from the United Kingdom shall be deemed to be—

(a) where the goods are exported by sea or air, the time when the goods are shipped for exportation;

(b) where the goods are exported by land, the time when they are cleared by the proper officer at the last customs and excise station on their way to the boundary.

(5) In the case of goods of a class or description with respect to the exportation of which any prohibition or restriction is for the time being in force under or by virtue of any enactment which are exported by sea or air, the time of exportation shall be deemed to be the time when the exporting ship or aircraft departs from the last port or customs and excise airport at which it is cleared before departing for a destination outside the United Kingdom.

(6) Goods imported by means of a pipe-line shall be treated as imported at the time when they are brought within the limits of a port or brought across the boundary into Northern Ireland.

(7) Goods exported by means of a pipe-line shall be treated as exported at the time when they are charged into that pipe-line for exportation.

(8) A ship shall be deemed to have arrived at or departed from a port at the time when the ship comes within or, as the case may be, leaves the limits of that port.

[This section is printed as amended by the *Customs and Excise (Single Market etc.) Regulations* 1992 (S.I. 1992 No. 3095), reg. 10(1), Sched. 1, para. 3.]

For time of importation through the Channel Tunnel, see *post*, § 25–413.

In *MacNeill v. H.M. Advocate*, 1986 S.C.C.R. 288, it was held that an "importation" occurs at any port where the goods are discovered and also at any port in the United Kingdom which has been entered *en route* to that port. The "limits of a port" are prescribed by statutory instruments which, collectively, cover the entire coastline of the United Kingdom.

(3) Offences in connection with Commissioners, officers, etc.

25–407 Sections 13 and 16 of the *CEMA* 1979, which created the hybrid offences of impersonating a Commissioner or an officer, and obstruction of an officer, were repealed by the *Commissioners for Revenue and Customs Act* 2005, s.52(2), and Sched. 5. They have been replaced by summary offences of impersonation or obstruction of, and assault on, a Commissioner or an officer of Revenue and Customs (ss.30 to 32 of the 2005 Act).

[The next paragraph is § 25–409.]

(4) Illegal importation

Customs and Excise Management Act 1979, s.50

Penalty for improper importation of goods

25–409 **50.**—(1) Subsection (2) below applies to goods of the following descriptions, that is to say—

(a) goods chargeable with a duty which has not been paid; and

(b) goods the importation, landing or unloading of which is for the time being prohibited or restricted by or under any enactment.

(2) If any person with intent to defraud Her Majesty of any such duty or to evade any such prohibition or restriction as is mentioned in subsection (1) above—

(a) unships or lands in any port or unloads from any aircraft in the United Kingdom or from any vehicle in Northern Ireland any goods to which this subsection applies, or assists or is otherwise concerned in such unshipping, landing or unloading; or

(b) removes from their place of importation or from any approved wharf, examination station, transit shed or customs and excise station any goods to which this subsection applies or assists or is otherwise concerned in such removal,

he shall be guilty of an offence under this subsection and may be arrested.

(3) If any person imports or is concerned in importing any goods contrary to any prohibition or restriction for the time being in force under or by virtue of any enactment with respect to those goods, whether or not the goods are unloaded, and does so with intent to evade the prohibition or restriction, he shall be guilty of an offence under this subsection and may be arrested.

(4) Subject to subsection (5), (5A) *or (5B)* [, (5B) or (5C)] below, a person guilty of an offence under subsection (2) or (3) above shall be liable—

(a) on summary conviction, to a penalty of the prescribed sum or of three times the value of the goods, whichever is the greater, or to imprisonment for a term not exceeding *6* [12] months, or to both; or

(b) on conviction on indictment, to a penalty of any amount, or to imprisonment for a term not exceeding 7 years, or to both.

25–410 (5) In the case of an offence under subsection (2) or (3) above in connection with a prohibition or restriction on importation having effect by virtue of section 3 of the *Misuse of*

Drugs Act 1971, subsection (4) above shall have effect subject to the modifications specified in Schedule 1 to this Act.

(5A) In the case of—

(a) an offence under subsection (2) or (3) above committed in Great Britain in connection with a prohibition or restriction on the importation of any weapon or ammunition that is of a kind mentioned in section 5(1)(a), (ab), (aba), (ac), (ad), (ae), (af) or (c) or (1A)(a) of the *Firearms Act* 1968,

(b) [*Northern Ireland*],

(c) any such offence committed in connection with the prohibition contained in section 20 of the *Forgery and Counterfeiting Act* 1981,

subsection (4)(b) above shall have effect as if for the words "7 years" there were substituted the words "10 years".

(5B) In the case of an offence under subsection (2) or (3) above in connection with the prohibition contained in regulation 2 of the *Import of Seal Skins Regulations* 1996, subsection (4) above shall have effect as if—

(a) for paragraph (a) there were substituted the following—

"(a) on summary conviction, to a fine not exceeding the statutory maximum or to imprisonment for a term not exceeding *three* [12] months, or to both"; and

(b) in paragraph (b) for the words "7 years" there were substituted the words "2 years".

[(5C) In the case of an offence under subsection (2) or (3) above in connection with a prohibition or restriction relating to the importation of nuclear material, subsection (4)(b) above shall have effect as if for the words "7 years" there were substituted the words "14 years".]

(6) If any person—

(a) imports or causes to be imported any goods concealed in a container holding goods of a different description; or

(b) directly or indirectly imports or causes to be imported or entered any goods found, whether before or after delivery, not to correspond with the entry made thereof,

he shall be liable on summary conviction to a penalty of three times the value of the goods or level 3 on the standard scale, whichever is the greater.

(7) In any case where a person would, apart from this subsection, be guilty of—

(a) an offence under this section in connection with the importation of goods contrary to a prohibition or restriction; and

(b) a corresponding offence under the enactment or other instrument imposing the prohibition or restriction, being an offence for which a fine or other penalty is expressly provided by that enactment or other instrument,

he shall not be guilty of the offence mentioned in paragraph (a) of this subsection.

[This section is printed as amended by the *Forgery and Counterfeiting Act* 1981, s.23(1); the *CJA* 1982, ss.37, 46; the *PACE Act* 1984, s.114(1); the *Finance Act* 1988, s.12(1)(a), (6); the *Import of Seal Skins Regulations* 1996 (S.I. 1996 No. 2686); and the *CJA* 2003, s.293(1) and (2) (substitution of subs. (5A)). The effect of the new subs. (5A) is to increase the maximum penalty for an offence falling within para. (a) with effect from January 22, 2004 (*Criminal Justice Act 2003 (Commencement No. 2 and Saving Provisions) Order* 2004 (S.I. 2004 No. 81)), but the increase has no effect in relation to an offence committed before that date (s.293(5)). In subs. (4)(a) and its modified version (see subs. (5B)), "12" is substituted for "6" and "three" respectively, as from a day to be appointed, by the *CJA* 2003, s.282(2) and (3). The increase has no application to offences committed before the substitution takes effect: s.282(4). As from a further day to be appointed, the words ", (5B) or (5C)" are substituted for the words "or (5B)" in subs. (4), and subs. (5C) is inserted, by the *CJIA* 2008, s.75(2), and Sched. 17, para. 8(1) and (3).]

The "prescribed sum", means the prescribed sum within the meaning of section 32 of the *MCA* 1980: *CEMA* 1979, s.171(2), *post*, § 25–480. For section 32, see *ante*, § 1–75aa. **25–411**

An offence contrary to section 50(2) or (3) is a "lifestyle offence" within the *PCA* 2002, Sched. 2 (*ante*, § 5–653), if committed in connection with a prohibition or restriction on importation which has effect by virtue of the *Misuse of Drugs Act* 1971, s.3, in respect of which a financial reporting order may be made under the *SOCPA* 2005, s.76 (*ante*, § 5–886a).

As to "prohibition or restriction", see *Superheater Co. Ltd v. Commrs of Customs and Excise* [1969] 1 W.L.R. 858.

For Schedule 1, see *post*, § 25–482. For section 20 of the *Forgery and Counterfeiting Act* 1981, see *ante*, § 25–255.

Section 50 contemplates that goods can be imported long before they are either "landed" or "unloaded" (and see s.5 of the Act, *ante*, § 25–406). Accordingly, there can be no goods which are merely "unloaded" or "landed" and not imported: see *R. v. Smith (Donald)* [1973] Q.B. 924, CA.

By "evade" Parliament meant no more than that there must be an intention on the part of the accused to "get around" the prohibition or restriction. "Evade", in this context, does not carry the connotation of fraud or dishonesty as it does in revenue laws: see *R. v. Hurford-Jones*, 65 Cr.App.R. 263, CA, and *post*, § 25–415. Evidence of an intention to take the imported goods elsewhere without landing them, or to keep the vessel, carrying the goods, in an anchorage only long enough to buy fuel for a voyage into international waters is irrelevant once it is proved that the accused knew that the goods were being imported contrary to a prohibition on importation: *MacNeill v. H.M Advocate*, 1986 S.C.C.R. 288.

Substances useful for manufacture

25–411a Regulation 7(1) of the *Controlled Drugs (Drug Precursors) (Community External Trade) Regulations* 2008 (S.I. 2008 No. 296) requires operators concerned in the import into the customs territory of the Community of certain drug precursors (*i.e.* a specified substance useful for the manufacture of controlled drugs and listed in Category 1 of the Annex to Council Regulation (EC) No. 111/2005) to have a valid import authorisation in accordance with that Regulation. Regulation 7(3) provides that for the purposes of section 50(2) and (3) of the 1979 Act, any scheduled substances shall be deemed to be imported contrary to a restriction for the time being in force with respect to it under the regulations if it is imported without the requisite authorisation. Regulation 7(4) modifies downwards the available penalties under section 50 for an offence that relates to a breach of this restriction. Section 50(4)(a) has effect as if (i) after the word "greater" there were added "but not exceeding the statutory maximum", and (ii) "3 months" were substituted for "6 months"; and section 50(4)(b) has effect as if "2 years" were substituted for "7 years".

Importation through the Channel Tunnel

Channel Tunnel (Customs and Excise) Order 1990 (S.I. 1990 No. 2167), Sched., para. 8

25–412 8. Section 50(2) (penalty for improper importation of goods) shall have effect as if—

(a) any person who unloads or assists or is otherwise concerned in the unloading of those goods mentioned in section 50(1) from any vehicle which has arrived from France through the tunnel, or who brings or assists or is otherwise concerned in the bringing of such goods into a control zone in France or Belgium, were a person who unships such goods in a port; and

(b) any person who removes or assists or is otherwise concerned in the removal of such goods from any customs approved area were a person who removes such goods from an approved wharf.

[Para. 8 is printed as amended by the *Channel Tunnel (International Arrangements) Order* 1993 (S.I. 1993 No. 1813), art. 8, and Sched. 5, para. 21; and the *Channel Tunnel (Miscellaneous Provisions) Order* 1994 (S.I. 1994 No. 1405), art. 8, and Sched. 4, para. 7.]

As to the Channel Tunnel legislation generally, see Appendix F. For the definition of "control zone", see Appendix F–15, F–16, F–24.

The Commissioners may approve, for such periods and subject to such conditions and restrictions as they think fit, places in the United Kingdom, and in France in a control zone within the tunnel system, for the customs and excise control of persons, goods or vehicles in relation to the construction, operation or use of the tunnel or any part of it, and may also so approve all or any through trains while they are within any area in the United Kingdom specified in the approval or while they constitute a control zone, and any place or train so approved is referred to as a "customs approved area": S.I. 1990 No. 2167, as amended by S.I. 1993 No. 1813, art. 8, Sched. 5, para. 9.

Time of importation

S.I. 1990 No. 2167, art. 5(1), (2)

5.—(1) The provisions of this article shall have effect for the purposes of the customs and excise Acts and of any enactment under or by virtue of which any prohibition or restriction with respect to the importation or exportation of any goods is for the time being in force. **25–413**

(2) Goods intended to be brought into the United Kingdom through the tunnel shall be treated as being imported into the United Kingdom—

(a) in the case of goods intended to be carried in a shuttle train, when they are taken into a control zone in France within the tunnel system,

(b) in the case of goods carried, while the train constitutes a control zone in France or Belgium, in a through train carrying passengers on a journey intended to end at a place in Great Britain other than London, at the time when officers become authorised under Article 12 of the international Articles or, as the case may be, under Article 5 of the Part II provisions, to begin to carry out controls, and

(c) in any other case, when they cross the frontier.

[Paras (1) and (2) are printed as amended by S.I. 1993 No. 1813, Sched. 5, Pt II, para. 10; and by S.I. 1994 No. 1405, Sched. 4, para. 6 (*ante*, § 25–412).]

The "international articles" has the same meaning as in the 1993 Order: S.I. 1990 No. 2167, art. 2(3) (as amended by the 1993 Order, Sched. 5, Pt II, para. 8 and by S.I. 1994 No. 1405, Sched. 4, para. 5(a)). For the meaning thereof, see S.I. 1993 No. 1813, art. 2(3) (Appendix F–13). For article 12, see Appendix F–16b.

The "Part II provisions" has the same meaning as in the 1994 Order: S.I. 1990 No. 2167, art. 2(4) (as inserted by the 1994 Order, Sched. 4, para. 5(b)). For the meaning thereof, see Schedule 1 to the 1994 Order (Appendix F–23). For article 5 thereof, see Appendix F–24a. (*NOTE*: Part I of Schedule 2 to the 1994 Order consists of the "Agreement" and Part II of Schedule 2 contains the "Protocol". The Agreement itself has a Part I and a Part II (which, in turn, contains an "article 5") but it is to article 5 in the Protocol in Part II of the Schedule that it is necessary to look for this purpose.)

(5) Illegal exportation

Customs and Excise Management Act 1979, s.68

Offences in relation to exportation of prohibited or restricted goods

68.—(1) If any goods are— **25–414**

(a) exported or shipped as stores; or

(b) brought to any place in the United Kingdom for the purpose of being exported or shipped as stores,

and the exportation or shipment is or would be contrary to any prohibition or restriction for the time being in force with respect to those goods under or by virtue of any enactment, the goods shall be liable to forfeiture and the exporter or intending exporter of the goods and any agent of his concerned in the exportation or shipment or intended exportation or shipment shall each be liable on summary conviction to a penalty of three times the value of the goods or level 3 on the standard scale, whichever is the greater.

(2) Any person knowingly concerned in the exportation or shipment as stores, or in the attempted exportation or shipment as stores, of any goods with intent to evade any such prohibition or restriction as is mentioned in subsection (1) above shall be guilty of an offence under this subsection and may be arrested.

(3) [*Identical to s.50(4) (including the prospective amendments),* ante, *§ 25–409, save that "(4) or (4A)" replaces "(5), (5A) or (5B)", and the words "or (3)" do not appear.*]

(4) In the case of an offence under subsection (2) above in connection with a prohibition on exportation having effect by virtue of section 3 of the *Misuse of Drugs Act* 1971, subsection (3) above shall have effect subject to the modifications specified in Schedule 1 to this Act.

(4A) [*Identical to s.50(5A),* ante, *§ 25–410, save that the references to "importation", "section 20" and "subsection (4)(b)" are replaced by references to "exportation", "section 21" and "subsection (3)(b)" respectively.*]

[(4B) In the case of an offence under subsection (2) above in connection with a prohibition or restriction relating to the exportation or shipment as stores of nuclear material, subsection (3)(b) above shall have effect as if for the words "7 years" there were substituted the words "14 years".]

(5) If by virtue of any such restriction as is mentioned in subsection (1) above any goods may be exported only when consigned to a particular place or person and any goods so consigned are delivered to some other place or person, the ship, aircraft or vehicle in which they were exported shall be liable to forfeiture unless it is proved to the satisfaction of the Commissioners that both the owner of the ship, aircraft or vehicle and the master of the ship, commander of the aircraft or person in charge of the vehicle—

(a) took all reasonable steps to secure that the goods were delivered to the particular place to which or person to whom they were consigned; and

(b) did not connive at or, except under duress, consent to the delivery of the goods to that other place or person.

(6) [*Corresponds to s.50(7),* ante, *§ 25–410.*]

[This section is printed as amended by the *Forgery and Counterfeiting Act* 1981, s.23(2); the *CJA* 1982, ss.38, 46; the *PACE Act* 1984, s.114(1); the *Finance Act* 1988, s.12(1)(a), (6); and the *CJA* 2003, s.293(1) and (3) (substitution of subs. (4A)). As to the effect of the latter amendment and as to the prospective amendment of subs. (3), see the note to s.50, *ante*, § 25–410. As from a day to be appointed, the words ", (4A) or (4B)" are substituted for the words "or (4A)" in subs. (3), and subs. (4B) is inserted, by the *CJIA* 2008, s.75(2), and Sched. 17, para. 8(1) and (4).]

25–415 As to forfeiture, see section 139, *post*, § 25–424.

An offence contrary to section 68(2) is a "lifestyle offence" within the *PCA* 2002, Sched. 2 (*ante*, §§ 5–653, 5–657), if committed in connection with a prohibition or restriction on exportation which has effect by virtue of the *Misuse of Drugs Act* 1971, s.3, or in connection with a firearm or ammunition, and in respect of which a financial reporting order may be made under the *SOCPA* 2005, s.76 (*ante*, § 5–886a).

As to "prohibition or restriction", see *Superheater Co. Ltd v. Commrs of Customs and Excise* [1969] 1 W.L.R. 858.

As to "any person knowingly concerned in the exportation", see *Garrett v. Arthur Churchill (Glass) Ltd* [1970] 1 Q.B. 92 DC, and *R. v. Redfern and Dunlop Ltd (Aircraft Division)*, 13 Cr.App.R.(S.) 704, CA. As to "intent to evade", see *R. v. Hurford-Jones*, 65 Cr.App.R. 263, CA.

The "prescribed sum" means the prescribed sum within the meaning of section 32 of the *MCA* 1980: *CEMA* 1979, s.171(2), *post*, § 25–480. For section 32, see *ante*, § 1–75aa.

For Schedule 1, see *post*, § 25–482. For section 21 of the *Forgery and Counterfeiting Act* 1981, see *ante*, § 25–255.

Section 68A (inserted by the *Finance Act* 1982, s.11(2), and amended by the *Finance Act* 1988, s.12(2), (6)) creates an offence of fraudulent evasion of agricultural levies chargeable on the export of goods.

Substances useful for manufacture

25–416 Regulation 6(1) of the *Controlled Drugs (Drug Precursors) (Community External Trade) Regulations* 2008 (S.I. 2008 No. 296) requires operators concerned in the export of a drug precursor (*i.e.* a specified substance useful for the manufacture of controlled drugs), to have a valid export authorisation, and regulation 6(3) provides that for the purposes of section 68 of the 1979 Act any drug precursor will be deemed to be exported contrary to a restriction on exportation if it is exported without such an authorisation. Regulation 6(4) modifies (downwards) the available penalties for an offence under section 68 that relates to a breach of this restriction. Section 68(1) has effect as if after the word "greater" there were added the words "but not exceeding level 5 on the standard scale"; section 68(3)(a) has effect as if (i) after the word "greater" there were added "but not exceeding the statutory maximum", and (ii) "3 months" were substituted for "6 months"; and section 68(3)(b) has effect as if "2 years" were substituted for "7 years".

For the 2008 regulations generally, see *post*, § 25–493.

Exportation through the Channel Tunnel

The *Channel Tunnel (Customs and Excise) Order* 1990 (S.I. 1990 No. 2167), art. 5(6) provides: **25–417**

> "In the case of goods of a class or description with respect to the exportation of which any prohibition or restriction is for the time being in force under or by virtue of any enactment and which are exported by vehicle through the tunnel, the time of exportation shall be deemed to be the time when the exporting vehicle departs from the last customs approved area at which goods were loaded onto it for exportation."

As to the meaning of "customs approved area", see *ante*, § 25–412.

(6) Control of persons entering or leaving the United Kingdom

Customs and Excise Management Act 1979, s.78

Customs and excise control of persons entering or leaving the United Kingdom

78.—(1) Any person entering the United Kingdom shall, at such place and in such manner as the Commissioners may direct, declare any thing contained in his baggage or carried with him which— **25–418**

(a) he has obtained outside the United Kingdom; or

(b) being dutiable goods or chargeable goods, he has obtained in the United Kingdom without payment of duty or tax,

and in respect of which he is not entitled to exemption from duty and tax by virtue of any order under section 13 of the *Customs and Excise Duties (General Reliefs) Act* 1979 (personal reliefs).

In this subsection "chargeable goods" means goods on the importation of which value added tax is chargeable or goods obtained in the United Kingdom before 1st April 1973 which are chargeable goods within the meaning of the *Purchase Tax Act* 1963; and "tax" means value added tax or purchase tax.

(1A) Subsection (1) above does not apply to a person entering the United Kingdom from the Isle of Man as respects anything obtained by him in the Island unless it is chargeable there with duty or value added tax and he has obtained it without payment of the duty or tax.

(1B) Subsection (1) above does not apply to a person entering the United Kingdom from another member State, except—

(a) where he arrives at a customs and excise airport in an aircraft in which he began his journey in a place outside the member States; or

(b) as respects such of his baggage as—

(i) is carried in the hold of the aircraft in which he arrives at a customs and excise airport, and

(ii) notwithstanding that it was transferred on one or more occasions from aircraft to aircraft at an airport in a member State, began its journey by air from a place outside the member States.

(2) Any person entering or leaving the United Kingdom shall answer such questions as the proper officer may put to him with respect to his baggage and any thing contained therein or carried with him, and shall, if required by the proper officer, produce that baggage and any such thing for examination at such place as the Commissioners may direct. **25–419**

(2A) Subject to subsection (1A) above, where the journey of a person arriving by air in the United Kingdom is continued or resumed by air to a destination in the United Kingdom which is not the place where he is regarded for the purposes of this section as entering the United Kingdom subsections (1) and (2) above shall apply in relation to that person on his arrival at that destination as they apply in relation to a person entering the United Kingdom.

(3) Any person failing to declare any thing or to produce any baggage or thing as required by this section shall be liable on summary conviction to a penalty of three times the value of the thing not declared or of the baggage or thing not produced, as the case may be, or level 3 on the standard scale whichever is the greater.

(4) Any thing chargeable with any duty or tax which is found concealed, or is not declared, and any thing which is being taken into or out of the United Kingdom contrary to any prohibition or restriction for the time being in force with respect thereto under or by virtue of any enactment, shall be liable to forfeiture.

[This section is printed as amended by the *Isle of Man Act* 1979, s.13, Sched. 1; the *CJA* 1982, ss.38, 46; the *Finance (No. 2) Act* 1992, s.5; and the *Customs and Excise (Single Market etc.) Regulations* 1992 (S.I. 1992 No. 3095), reg. 3(10).]

Section 78 can be distinguished from section 164 of the 1979 Act (*post*, § 25–446) in that: (a) it applies only to persons entering or leaving the United Kingdom; and (b) no reasonable grounds to suspect that the person entering or leaving is carrying a prohibited or restricted article or a dutiable article on which duty has not been paid need exist. However, the second distinction is qualified by the *Finance (No. 2) Act* 1992, s.4, see *post*, § 25–483.

Shoes being worn by the passenger may be a thing "carried with him" for the purposes of section 78(2): *R. v. Lucien* [1995] Crim.L.R. 807, CA. The court emphasised that section 78 did not provide an alternative basis for permitting customs officers to conduct rub-down, strip or intimate searches. That power existed only by virtue of section 164 of the 1979 Act.

The *Channel Tunnel (Customs and Excise) Order* 1990 (S.I. 1990 No. 2167), Sched., para. 17B (inserted by the *Channel Tunnel (International Arrangements) Order* 1993 (S.I. 1993 No. 1813), Sched. 5, para. 27), as amended by the *Channel Tunnel (Miscellaneous Provisions) Order* 1994 (S.I. 1994 No. 1405) provides that for the purposes of section 78 of the 1979 Act:

(a) a person intending to travel to the United Kingdom through the tunnel who has entered a control zone in France or Belgium shall be treated as a person entering the United Kingdom,

(b) a person who has travelled from the United Kingdom through the tunnel and is in such a control zone shall be treated as still being a person leaving the United Kingdom, and

(c) concealment shall be taken to include concealment in such a control zone.

For the definition of "control zone", see Appendix F–15, F–16, F–24.

(7) Prevention of smuggling

Customs and Excise Management Act 1979, s.85

Penalty for interfering with revenue vessels, etc.

25–420 **85.**—(1) Any person who save for just and sufficient cause interferes in any way with any ship, aircraft, vehicle, buoy, anchor, chain, rope or mark which is being used for the purposes of any functions of the Commissioners under Parts III to VII of this Act shall be liable on summary conviction to a penalty of level 1 on the standard scale.

(2) Any person who fires upon any vessel, aircraft or vehicle in the service of Her Majesty while that vessel, aircraft or vehicle is engaged in the prevention of smuggling shall be liable on conviction on indictment to imprisonment for a term not exceeding 5 years.

[This section is printed as amended by the *CJA* 1982, s.46.]

[The next paragraph is § 25–423.]

(8) Powers of arrest

Customs and Excise Management Act 1979, s.138

Provisions as to arrest of persons

25–423 **138.**—(1) Any person who has committed, or whom there are reasonable grounds to suspect of having committed, any offence for which he is liable to be arrested under the customs and excise Acts may be arrested by any officer or any member of Her Majesty's armed forces or coastguard at any time within 20 years from the date of the commission of the offence.

(2) Where it was not practicable to arrest any person so liable at the time of the commission of the offence, or where any such person having been then or subsequently arrested for that offence has escaped, he may be arrested by any officer or any member of Her Majesty's armed forces or coastguard at any time and may be proceeded against in like manner as if the offence had been committed at the date when he was finally arrested.

(3) Where any person who is a member of the crew of any ship in Her Majesty's employment or service is arrested by an officer for an offence under the customs and excise Acts,

the commanding officer of the ship shall, if so required by the arresting officer, keep that person secured on board that ship until he can be brought before a court and shall then deliver him up to the proper officer.

(4) Where any person has been arrested by a person who is not an officer—

(a) by virtue of this section; or

(b) by virtue of section 24 or 24A of the *Police and Criminal Evidence Act* 1984 in its application to the customs and excise Acts; or

(c) [*Northern Ireland*],

the person arresting him shall give notice of the arrest to an officer at the most convenient office of customs and excise.

[This section is printed as amended by the *PACE Act* 1984, ss.26(1), 114(1), 119(1), (2), 120 and Sched. 6, Pt II, para. 37; the *Finance Act* 1988, s.11(1), (3); the *Police and Criminal Evidence (Northern Ireland) Order* 1989 (S.I. 1989 No. 1341), art. 90(1), and Sched. 6, para. 9; and the *SOCPA* 2005, s.111, and Sched. 7, para. 54.]

For sections 24 and 24A of the 1984 Act, see *ante*, §§ 15–161 *et seq.*

For powers of arrest in a control zone in France or Belgium, see the *Channel Tunnel (International Arrangements) Order* 1993 (S.I. 1993 No. 1813), Sched. 3, Pt 1, and the *Channel Tunnel (Miscellaneous Provisions) Order* 1994 (S.I. 1994 No. 1405), Sched. 3 (Appendix F–17, F–25, F–26).

(9) Powers to seize and detain goods, etc.

Customs and Excise Management Act 1979, s.139

Provisions as to detention, seizure and condemnation of goods, etc.

139.—(1) Any thing liable to forfeiture under the customs and excise Acts may be seized or detained by any officer or constable or any member of Her Majesty's armed forces or coastguard. **25–424**

(2) Where any thing is seized or detained as liable to forfeiture under the customs and excise Acts by a person other than an officer, that person shall, subject to subsection (3) below, either—

(a) deliver that thing to the nearest convenient office of customs and excise; or

(b) if such delivery is not practicable, give to the Commissioners at the nearest convenient office of customs and excise notice in writing of the seizure or detention with full particulars of the thing seized or detained.

(3) Where the person seizing or detaining any thing as liable to forfeiture under the customs and excise Acts is a constable and that thing is or may be required for use in connection with any proceedings to be brought otherwise than under those Acts it may, subject to subsection (4) below, be retained in the custody of the police until either those proceedings are completed or it is decided that no such proceedings shall be brought.

(4) The following provisions apply in relation to things retained in the custody of the police by virtue of subsection (3) above, that is to say—

(a) notice in writing of the seizure or detention and of the intention to retain the thing in question in the custody of the police, together with full particulars as to that thing, shall be given to the Commissioners at the nearest convenient office of customs and excise;

(b) any officer shall be permitted to examine that thing and take account thereof at any time while it remains in the custody of the police;

(c) nothing in the *Police (Property) Act* 1897 shall apply in relation to that thing.

(5) Subject to subsections (3) and (4) above and to Schedule 3 to this Act, any thing seized or detained under the customs and excise Acts shall, pending the determination as to its forfeiture or disposal, be dealt with, and, if condemned or deemed to have been condemned or forfeited, shall be disposed of in such manner as the Commissioners may direct.

(6) Schedule 3 to this Act shall have effect for the purpose of forfeitures, and of proceedings for the condemnation of any thing as being forfeited, under the customs and excise Acts.

(7) If any person, not being an officer, by whom any thing is seized or detained or who has custody thereof after its seizure or detention, fails to comply with any requirement of this section or with any direction of the Commissioners given thereunder, he shall be liable on summary conviction to a penalty of level 2 on the standard scale.

(8) Subsections (2) to (7) above shall apply in relation to any dutiable goods seized or

detained by any person other than an officer notwithstanding that they were not so seized as liable to forfeiture under the customs and excise Acts.

[This section is printed as amended by the *CJA* 1982, s.46.]

25–425 The *Channel Tunnel (Customs and Excise) Order* 1990 (S.I. 1990 No. 2167), Sched., para. 20A (inserted by S.I. 1993 No. 1813, Sched. 5, para. 30) provides that the power conferred by section 139(1) to seize or detain any thing liable to forfeiture shall be taken to include a power for any officer or constable to seize or detain any such thing in a control zone in France. This was extended to a control zone in Belgium on December 1, 1997: see the *Channel Tunnel (Miscellaneous Provisions) Order* 1994 (S.I. 1994 No. 1405), art. 8, Sched. 4, para. 7. For a summary of the forfeiture provisions generally, see *ante*, §§ 25–395 *et seq*.

25–426 In *R. v. Uxbridge JJ., ex p. Sofaer*, 85 Cr.App.R. 367, DC, it was held that the destruction of goods by the Commissioners of Customs and Excise between the date of forfeiture of the goods and committal proceedings in respect of an alleged offence under the *CEMA* 1979 in relation to the goods, did not necessarily result in prejudice to the defendant or a breach of the rules of natural justice where secondary evidence in the form of photographs was available and could be put before a jury. There was no overriding duty on the prosecution to preserve evidence. Croom-Johnson L.J. said (at p. 377) that *R. v. Lushington, ex p. Otto* [1894] 1 Q.B. 420 (see *ante*, § 15–134) had been cited in support of such a proposition: his Lordship said that while that was no doubt a desirable standard, it was not always possible to apply. Exhibits sometimes went astray. Sometimes it was only by their destruction that one could get at the evidence. In those circumstances, it was customary to rely on secondary evidence. In this case, there were photographs and the commissioners contended that they constituted an adequate foundation upon which to base any decisions of fact: the justices had accepted that argument and it was impossible to say as a matter of law that they could not have reached the conclusion which they did. Peter Pain J. said (at p. 378) that the principle was stated too widely in *R. v. Lushington, ex p. Otto*. The decision could not square with the provisions of the 1979 Act.

Proceedings under section 139 and Schedule 3 are not criminal and thus not ones to which Article 6(2) of the ECHR (*ante*, § 16–57) applies: *Goldsmith v. Customs and Excise Commrs* [2001] 1 W.L.R. 1673, DC.

(10) General provisions as to legal proceedings

Customs and Excise Management Act 1979, s.145

Institution of proceedings

25–427 **145.**—(1) Subject to the following provisions of this section, no proceedings for an offence under the customs and excise Acts or for condemnation under Schedule 3 to this Act shall be instituted except—

(a) by or with the consent of the Director of Revenue and Customs Prosecutions, or

(b) by order of, or with the consent of, the Commissioners for Her Majesty's Revenue and Customs.

(2) Subject to the following provisions of this section, any proceedings under the customs and excise Acts instituted by order of the Commissioners in a magistrates' court, and any such proceedings instituted by order of the Commissioners in a court of summary jurisdiction in Northern Ireland, shall be commenced in the name of an officer of Revenue and Customs.

(3) [*Scotland.*]

(4) ...

(5) Nothing in the foregoing provisions of this section shall prevent the institution of proceedings for an offence under the customs and excise Acts by order and in the name of a law officer of the Crown in any case in which he thinks it proper that proceedings should be so instituted.

(6) Notwithstanding anything in the foregoing provisions of this section, where any person has been arrested for any offence for which he is liable to be arrested under the customs and excise Acts, any court before which he is brought may proceed to deal with the case although the proceedings have not been instituted in accordance with this section.

[This section is printed as amended by the *PACE Act* 1984, s.114(1); and the *Com-*

missioners for Revenue and Customs Act 2005, ss.50(6) and 52(2), Sched. 4, paras 20 and 23, and Sched. 5.]

In practice, few cases involving the prosecution of an offence under the customs and excise Acts would not meet the requirements of section 145(6), even if an order of the Commissioners had not been obtained under subsection (1). The section is chiefly designed to ensure that the Commissioners are aware of the existence of proceedings brought under those Acts. **25–428**

As to the interaction of section 145(1) and (6) with section 4(3) of the *CLA* 1977 (*post*, § 33–33), see *R. v. Whitehead and Nicholl* [1982] Q.B. 1272, 75 Cr.App.R. 389, CA (if a person is arrested for conspiracy to contravene the provisions of the customs and excise acts, an order of the Commissioners is unnecessary for the institution of proceedings); and *R. v. Keyes, Edjedewe and Chapman* [2000] 2 Cr.App.R. 181, CA.

Customs and Excise Management Act 1979, s.146

146. [*Service of process.*] **25–429**

Customs and Excise Management Act 1979, s.146A

Time limits for proceedings

146A.—(1) Except as otherwise provided in the customs and excise Acts, and notwithstanding anything in any other enactment, the following provisions shall apply in relation to proceedings for an offence under those Acts. **25–430**

(2) Proceedings for an indictable offence shall not be commenced after the end of the period of 20 years beginning with the day on which the offence was committed.

(3) Proceedings for a summary offence shall not be commenced after the end of the period of 3 years beginning with that day but, subject to that, may be commenced at any time within 6 months from the date on which sufficient evidence to warrant the proceedings came to the knowledge of the prosecuting authority.

(4) For the purposes of subsection (3) above, a certificate of the prosecuting authority as to the date on which such evidence as is there mentioned came to that authority's knowledge shall be conclusive evidence of that fact.

(5) [*Scotland.*]

(6) [*Northern Ireland.*]

(7) In this section, "prosecuting authority"—

(a) in England and Wales, means the Director of Revenue and Customs Prosecutions,

(b), (c) [*Scotland and Northern Ireland*].

[This section was inserted by the *Finance Act* 1989, s.16. It is printed as amended by the *Commissioners for Revenue and Customs Act* 2005, s.50(6), and Sched. 4, paras 20 and 24.]

For important considerations in relation to time limits, see *ante*, § 25–394.

Customs and Excise Management Act 1979, ss.147–149

Proceedings for offences

147.—(1) [*Repealed by* Finance Act *1989, s.16.*] **25–431**

(2) *Where, in England or Wales, a magistrates' court has begun to inquire into an information charging a person with an offence under the customs and excise Acts as examining justices the court shall not proceed under section 25(3) of the* Magistrates' Courts Act *1980 to try the information summarily without the consent of—*

(a) *the Attorney-General, in a case where the proceedings were instituted by his order and in his name; or*

(b) *the Commissioners, in any other case.*

(3) In the case of proceedings in England or Wales, without prejudice to any right to require the statement of a case for the opinion of the High Court, the prosecutor may appeal to the Crown Court against any decision of a magistrates' court in proceedings for an offence under the customs and excise Acts.

(4) In the case of proceedings in Northern Ireland, without prejudice to any right to require the statement of a case for the opinion of the High Court, the prosecutor may appeal to the county court against any decision of a court of summary jurisdiction in proceedings for an offence under the customs and excise Acts.

(5) [*Repealed by* Criminal Justice Act *1982, s.78 and Sched. 16.*]

[This section is printed as amended by the *MCA* 1980, s.154 and Sched. 7. Subs. (2) is repealed as from a day to be appointed: *CJA* 2003, ss.41 and 332, Sched. 3, para. 50, and Sched. 37, Pt 4.]

Place of trial for offences

25–432 **148.**—(1) Proceedings for an offence under the customs and excise Acts may be commenced—

(a) in any court having jurisdiction in the place where the person charged with the offence resides or is found; or
(b) if any thing was detained or seized in connection with the offence, in any court having jurisdiction in the place where that thing was so detained or seized or was found or condemned as forfeited; or
(c) in any court having jurisdiction anywhere in that part of the United Kingdom, namely—
 (i) England and Wales,
 (ii) Scotland, or
 (iii) Northern Ireland,

in which the place where the offence was committed is situated.

(2) Where any such offence was committed at some place outside the area of any commission of the peace, the place of the commission of the offence shall, for the purposes of the jurisdiction of any court, be deemed to be any place in the United Kingdom where the offender is found or to which he is first brought after the commission of the offence.

(3) The jurisdiction under subsection (2) above shall be in addition to and not in derogation of any jurisdiction or power of any court under any other enactment.

Non-payment of penalties, etc: maximum terms of imprisonment

25–433 **149.**—(1) Where, in any proceedings for an offence under the customs and excise Acts, a magistrates' court in England or Wales or a court of summary jurisdiction in Scotland, in addition to ordering the person convicted to pay a penalty for the offence—

(a) orders him to be imprisoned for a term in respect of the same offence; and
(b) further (whether at the same time or subsequently) orders him to be imprisoned for a term in respect of non-payment of that penalty or default of a sufficient distress to satisfy the amount of that penalty,

the aggregate of the terms for which he is so ordered to be imprisoned shall not exceed 15 months.

[(1A) In subsection (1)(b) as it applies to a magistrates' court in England or Wales the reference to default of sufficient distress to satisfy the amount of the penalty is a reference to want of sufficient goods to satisfy the amount, within the meaning given by section 79(4) of the *Magistrates' Courts Act* 1980.]

(2) [*Scotland.*]

(3) [*Northern Ireland.*]

[This section is printed as amended, as from a day to be appointed, by the *Tribunals, Courts and Enforcement Act* 2007, s.62(3), and Sched. 13, para. 44 (insertion of subs. (1A)).]

Customs and Excise Management Act 1979, ss.150, 152

Incidental provisions as to legal proceedings

25–434 **150.**—(1) Where liability for any offence under the customs and excise Acts is incurred by two or more persons jointly, those persons shall each be liable for the full amount of any pecuniary penalty and may be proceeded against jointly or severally as the Director of Revenue and Customs Prosecutions (in relation to proceedings instituted in England and Wales) or the Commissioners (in relation to proceedings instituted in Scotland or Northern Ireland) may see fit.

(2) In any proceedings for an offence under the customs and excise Acts instituted in England, Wales or Northern Ireland, any court by whom the matter is considered may mitigate any pecuniary penalty as they see fit.

(3) In any proceedings for an offence or for the condemnation of any thing as being forfeited under the customs and excise Acts, the fact that security has been given by bond or otherwise for the payment of any duty or for compliance with any condition in respect of the non-payment of which or non-compliance with which the proceedings are instituted shall not be a defence.

[This section is printed as amended by the *Commissioners for Revenue and Customs Act* 2005, s.50(6), and Sched. 4, paras 20 and 25.]

Power of Commissioners to mitigate penalties, etc.

152. The Commissioners may, as they see fit— 25–435

(a) compound an offence (whether or not proceedings have been instituted in respect of it) and compound proceedings or for [*sic*] the condemnation of any thing as being forfeited under the customs and excise Acts; or

(b) restore, subject to such conditions (if any) as they think proper, any thing forfeited or seized under those Acts; or

(c) …

(d) …

but paragraph (a) above shall not apply to proceedings on indictment in Scotland.

[This section is printed as amended, and repealed in part, by the *Commissioners for Revenue and Customs Act* 2005, ss.50(6) and 52(1)(a)(vi) and (vii), and (2), Sched. 4, paras 20 and 26, and Sched. 5.]

Commissioners for Revenue and Customs Act 2005, s.24

Evidence

24.—(1) A document that purports to have been issued or signed by or with the authority of the Commissioners— 25–436

(a) shall be treated as having been so issued or signed unless the contrary is proved, and

(b) shall be admissible in any legal proceedings.

(2) A document that purports to have been issued by the Commissioners and which certifies any of the matters specified in subsection (3) shall (in addition to the matters provided for by subsection (1)(a) and (b)) be treated as accurate unless the contrary is proved.

(3) The matters mentioned in subsection (2) are—

(a) that a specified person was appointed as a commissioner on a specified date,

(b) that a specified person was appointed as an officer of Revenue and Customs on a specified date,

(c) that at a specified time or for a specified purpose (or both) a function was delegated to a specified Commissioner,

(d) that at a specified time or for a specified purpose (or both) a function was delegated to a specified committee, and

(e) that at a specified time or for a specified purpose (or both) a function was delegated to another specified person.

(4) A photographic or other copy of a document acquired by the Commissioners shall, if certified by them to be an accurate copy, be admissible in any legal proceedings to the same extent as the document itself.

(5) Section 2 of the *Documentary Evidence Act* 1868 (proof of documents) shall apply to a Revenue and Customs document as it applies in relation to the documents mentioned in that section.

(6) In the application of that section to a Revenue and Customs document the Schedule to that Act shall be treated as if—

(a) the first column contained a reference to the Commissioners, and

(b) the second column contained a reference to a Commissioner or a person acting on his authority.

(7) In this section—

(a) "Revenue and Customs document" means a document issued by or on behalf of the Commissioners, and

(b) a reference to the Commissioners includes a reference to the Commissioners of Inland Revenue and to the Commissioners of Customs and Excise.

Customs and Excise Management Act 1979, s.154

Proof of certain other matters

154.—(1) An averment in any process in proceedings under the customs and excise Acts— 25–437

(a) that those proceedings were instituted by the order of the Commissioners; or

(b) that any person is or was a Commissioner, officer or constable, or a member of Her Majesty's armed forces or coastguard; or

(c) that any person is or was appointed or authorised by the Commissioners to discharge, or was engaged by the orders or with the concurrence of the Commissioners in the discharge of, any duty; or

(d) that the Commissioners have or have not been satisfied as to any matter as to which they are required by any provision of those Acts to be satisfied; or

(e) that any ship is a British ship; or

(f) that any goods thrown overboard, staved or destroyed were so dealt with in order to prevent or avoid the seizure of those goods,

shall, until the contrary is proved, be sufficient evidence of the matter in question.

(2) Where in any proceedings relating to customs or excise any question arises as to the place from which any goods have been brought or as to whether or not—

(a) any duty has been paid or secured in respect of any goods; or

(b) any goods or other things whatsoever are of the description or nature alleged in the information, writ or other process; or

(c) any goods have been lawfully imported or lawfully unloaded from any ship or aircraft; or

(d) any goods have been lawfully loaded into any ship or aircraft or lawfully exported or were lawfully waterborne; or

(e) any goods were lawfully brought to any place for the purpose of being loaded into any ship or aircraft or exported; or

(f) any goods are or were subject to any prohibition of or restriction on their importation or exportation,

then, where those proceedings are brought by or against the Commissioners, a law officer of the Crown or an officer, or against any other person in respect of anything purporting to have been done in pursuance of any power or duty conferred or imposed on him by or under the customs and excise Acts, the burden of proof shall lie upon the other party to the proceedings.

25–438 Section 154(2) has been modified by the *Channel Tunnel (Customs and Excise) Order* 1990 (S.I. 1990 No. 2167), art. 4, Sched., para. 23. This provides that any reference to goods loaded or to be loaded into or unloaded from an aircraft shall be construed respectively as including references to goods loaded or to be loaded on to or unloaded from a vehicle which is departing to or has arrived from France through the Channel Tunnel.

See *Garrett v. Arthur Churchill (Glass) Ltd* [1970] 1 Q.B. 92, DC. As to evidence relating to the place from which goods have been brought, see *Patel v. Comptroller of Customs* [1966] A.C. 356, PC, and *Comptroller of Customs v. Western Lectric Co. Ltd* [1966] A.C. 367, PC.

Establishing the country of origin, for the purposes of assessing the rate of import duty on imported goods, is the most likely explanation for the words "place from which any goods have been brought" in section 154(2). Accordingly, those words are probably not apt to describe a determination as to whether goods have in fact been imported or not: see *R. v. Watts and Stack*, 70 Cr.App.R. 187, CA, and see *Mizel v. Warren* [1973] 1 W.L.R. 899, DC ("description" in subs. (2)(b) may include place of manufacture).

Conduct of prosecutions

25–439 Sections 34 to 42 of the *Commissioners for Revenue and Customs Act* 2005 contain provision as to the conduct of prosecutions. An individual is to be appointed by the Attorney General as Director of Revenue and Customs Prosecutions, whose functions include the institution and conduct of criminal proceedings relating to a criminal investigation by the Revenue and Customs, and taking over the conduct of criminal proceedings instituted by the Revenue and Customs. The Director is accountable to the Attorney-General for the exercise of his functions. The Director and individuals designated under section 37 (prosecutors) or 39 (non-legal staff) are to have regard to the Code for Crown Prosecutors. Section 40 provides for the non-disclosure of information by the Revenue and Customs Prosecutions Office except in certain circumstances.

Customs and Excise Management Act 1979, s.156

Saving for outlying enactments of certain general provisions as to offences

25–440 **156.**—(1) In subsections (2), (3) and (4) below (which reproduce certain enactments not required as general provisions for the purposes of the enactments re-enacted in the *Customs and Excise Acts* 1979) "the outlying provisions of the customs and excise Acts" means the provisions of the customs and excise Acts, as for the time being amended, which were passed before the commencement of this Act and are not re-enacted in the *Customs and Excise Acts* 1979 or the *Betting and Gaming Duties Act* 1981.

(2) It is hereby declared that any act or omission in respect of which a pecuniary penalty (however described) is imposed by any of the outlying provisions of the customs and excise Acts is an offence under that provision; and accordingly in this Part of this Act any reference to an offence under the customs and excise Acts includes a reference to such an act or omission.

(3) Subject to any express provision made by the enactment in question, an offence under any of the outlying provisions of the customs and excise Acts—

(a) where it is punishable with imprisonment for a term of 2 years, with or without a pecuniary penalty, shall be punishable either on summary conviction or on conviction on indictment;

(b) in any other case, shall be punishable on summary conviction.

(4), (5) [*Scotland.*]

[This section is printed as amended by the *Betting and Gaming Duties Act* 1981, s.34(1) and Sched. 5, para. 5(b); and the *CJA* 1982, ss.77 and 78 and Sched. 14, para. 3.]

(11) General powers of examination and search

Customs and Excise Management Act 1979, s.159

Power to examine and take account of goods

159.—(1) Without prejudice to any other power conferred by the *Customs and Excise Acts* 1979, an officer may examine and take account of any goods— **25–441**

(a) which are imported; or

(b) which are in a warehouse or Queen's warehouse; or

(bb) which are in a free zone; or

(c) which have been loaded into any ship or aircraft at any place in the United Kingdom or the Isle of Man; or

(d) which are entered for exportation or for use as stores; or

(e) which are brought to any place in the United Kingdom for exportation or for shipment for exportation or as stores; or

(f) in the case of which any claim for drawback, allowance, rebate, remission or repayment of duty is made;

and may for that purpose require any container to be opened or unpacked.

(2) Any examination of goods by an officer under the *Customs and Excise Acts* 1979 shall be made at such place as the Commissioners appoint for the purpose.

(3) In the case of such goods as the Commissioners may direct, and subject to such conditions as they see fit to impose, an officer may permit goods to be skipped on the quay or bulked, sorted, lotted, packed or repacked before account is taken thereof.

(4) Any opening, unpacking, weighing, measuring, repacking, bulking, sorting, lotting, marking, numbering, loading, unloading, carrying or landing of goods or their containers for the purposes of, or incidental to, the examination by an officer, removal or warehousing thereof shall be done, and any facilities or assistance required for any such examination shall be provided, by or at the expense of the proprietor of the goods.

(5) If any imported goods which an officer has power under the *Customs and Excise Acts* 1979 to examine are without the authority of the proper officer removed from customs and excise charge before they have been examined, those goods shall be liable to forfeiture.

(6) If any goods falling within subsection (5) above are removed by a person with intent to defraud Her Majesty of any duty chargeable thereon or to evade any prohibition or restriction for the time being in force with respect thereto under or by virtue of any enactment, that person shall be guilty of an offence under this subsection and may be arrested.

(7) A person guilty of an offence under subsection (6) above shall be liable—

(a) on summary conviction, to a penalty of the prescribed sum or of three times the value of the goods, whichever is the greater, or to imprisonment for a term not exceeding *6* [12] months, or to both; or

(b) on conviction on indictment, to a penalty of any amount, or to imprisonment for a term not exceeding 7 years, or to both.

(8) Without prejudice to the foregoing provisions of this section, where by this section or by or under any other provision of the *Customs and Excise Acts* 1979 an account is authorised or required to be taken of any goods for any purpose by an officer, the Commissioners may, with the consent of the proprietor of the goods, accept as the account of those goods for that purpose an account taken by such other person as may be approved in that behalf by both the Commissioners and the proprietor of the goods.

[This section is printed as amended by the *Isle of Man Act* 1979, s.13 and Sched. 1; the *Finance Act* 1984, s.8 and Sched. 4; the *PACE Act* 1984, s.114(1); and the *Finance Act* 1988, s.12(1)(a). In subs. (7)(a), "12" is substituted for "6", as from a day to be appointed, by the *CJA* 2003, s.282(2) and (3). The increase has no application to offences committed before the substitution takes effect: s.282(4).]

25–442 Section 159(1) has been modified by the *Channel Tunnel (Customs and Excise) Order* 1990 (S.I. 1990 No. 2167), art. 4, Sched., para. 24. The reference in section 159(1)(c) to goods which have been loaded into a ship shall be construed as including a reference to goods which have been loaded onto a vehicle for exportation through the Channel Tunnel.

The "prescribed sum" means the prescribed sum within the meaning of section 32 of the *MCA* 1980: *CEMA* 1979, s.171(2), *post*, § 25–480. For section 32, see *ante*, § 1–75aa.

Customs and Excise Management Act 1979, ss.161–163A

Power to search premises: writ of assistance

25–443 **161.**—(1) The powers conferred by this section are exercisable by an officer having a writ of assistance if there are reasonable grounds to suspect that anything liable to forfeiture under the customs and excise Acts—

(a) is kept or concealed in any building or place, and

(b) is likely to be removed, destroyed or lost before a search warrant can be obtained and executed.

(2) The powers are—

(a) to enter the building or place at any time, whether by day or night, on any day, and search for, seize, and detain or remove any such thing, and

(b) so far as is necessary for the purpose of such entry, search, seizure, detention or removal, to break open any door, window or container and force and remove any other impediment or obstruction.

(3) An officer shall not exercise the power of entry conferred by this section by night unless accompanied by a constable.

(4) A writ of assistance shall continue in force during the reign in which it is issued and for six months thereafter.

[This section is printed as substituted by the *Finance Act* 2000, s.25.]

Power to search premises: search warrant.

25–443a **161A.**—(1) If a justice of the peace is satisfied by information upon oath given by an officer that there are reasonable grounds to suspect that anything liable to forfeiture under the customs and excise Acts is kept or concealed in any building or place, he may by warrant under his hand authorise any officer, and any person accompanying an officer, to enter and search the building or place named in the warrant.

(2) An officer or other person so authorised has power—

(a) to enter the building or place at any time, whether by day or night, on any day, and search for, seize, and detain or remove any such thing, and

(b) so far as is necessary for the purpose of such entry, search, seizure, detention or removal, to break open any door, window or container and force and remove any other impediment or obstruction.

(3) Where there are reasonable grounds to suspect that any still, vessel, utensil, spirits or materials for the manufacture of spirits is or are unlawfully kept or deposited in any building or place, subsections (1) and (2) above apply in relation to any constable as they would apply in relation to an officer.

(4) The powers conferred by a warrant under this section are exercisable until the end of the period of one month beginning with the day on which the warrant is issued.

(5) A person other than a constable shall not exercise the power of entry conferred by this section by night unless accompanied by a constable.

[This section was inserted by the *Finance Act* 2000, s.25.]

Power to enter land for or in connection with access to pipe-lines

162. Where any thing conveyed by a pipe-line is chargeable with a duty of customs or excise which has not been paid, an officer may enter any land adjacent to the pipe-line in order to get to the pipe-line for the purpose of exercising in relation to that thing any power conferred by or under the *Customs and Excise Acts* 1979 or to get from the pipe-line after an exercise of any such power. **25–444**

This section does not extend to Northern Ireland.

Power to search vehicles or vessels

163.—(1) Without prejudice to any other power conferred by the *Customs and Excise Acts* 1979, where there are reasonable grounds to suspect that any vehicle or vessel is or may be carrying any goods which are— **25–445**

(a) chargeable with any duty which has not been paid or secured; or

(b) in the course of being unlawfully removed from or to any place; or

(c) otherwise liable to forfeiture under the customs and excise Acts,

any officer or constable or member of Her Majesty's armed forces or coastguard may stop and search that vehicle or vessel.

(2) If when so required by any such officer, constable or member the person in charge of any such vehicle or vessel refuses to stop or to permit the vehicle or vessel to be searched, he shall be liable on summary conviction to a penalty of level 3 on the standard scale.

(3) This section shall apply in relation to aircraft as it applies in relation to vehicles or vessels but the power to stop and search in subsection (1) above shall not be available in respect of aircraft which are airborne.

[This section is printed as amended by the *CJA* 1982, ss.38 and 46; and the *Finance Act* 1992, s.10.]

Power to search articles

163A.—(1) Without prejudice to any other power conferred by the *Customs and Excise Acts* 1979, where there are reasonable grounds to suspect that a person in the United Kingdom (referred to in this section as "the suspect") has with him, or at the place where he is, any goods to which this section applies, an officer may— **25–445a**

(a) require the suspect to permit a search of any article that he has with him or at that place, and

(b) if the suspect is not under arrest, detain him (and any such article) for so long as may be necessary to carry out the search.

(2) The goods to which this section applies are dutiable alcoholic liquor, or tobacco products, which are—

(a) chargeable with any duty of excise, and

(b) liable to forfeiture under the customs and excise Acts.

(3) [*Scotland*.]

[This section was inserted by the *Finance Act* 1992, s.26.]

For "reasonable grounds to suspect" in sections 163 and 163A, see *R. (Hoverspeed Ltd) v. Customs and Excise Commrs* [2003] Q.B. 1041, CA (Civ. Div.).

Customs and Excise Management Act 1979, s.164

Power of search

164.—(1) Where there are reasonable grounds to suspect that any person to whom this section applies (referred to in this section as "the suspect") is carrying any article— **25–446**

(a) which is chargeable with any duty which has not been paid or secured; or

(b) with respect to the importation or exportation of which any prohibition or restriction is for the time being in force under or by virtue of any enactment,

an officer may exercise the powers conferred by subsection (2) below and, if the suspect is not under arrest, may detain him for so long as may be necessary for the exercise of those powers and (where applicable) the exercise of the rights conferred by subsection (3) below.

(2) The officer may require the suspect—

(a) to permit such a search of any article which he has with him; and

(b) subject to subsection (3) below, to submit to such searches of his person, whether rub-down, strip or intimate, as the officer may consider necessary or expedient; but no such requirement may be imposed under paragraph (b) above without the officer informing the suspect of the effect of subsection (3) below.

(3) If the suspect is required to submit to a search of his person, he may require to be taken—

(a) except in the case of a rub-down search, before a justice of the peace or a superior of the officer concerned; and

(b) in the excepted case, before such a superior;

and the justice or superior shall consider the grounds for suspicion and direct accordingly whether the suspect is to submit to the search.

(3A) A rub-down or strip search shall not be carried out except by a person of the same sex as the suspect; and an intimate search shall not be carried out except by a suitably qualified person.

(4) This section applies to the following persons, namely—

(a) any person who is on board or has landed from any ship or aircraft;

(b) any person entering or about to leave the United Kingdom;

(c) any person within the dock area of a port;

(d) any person at a customs and excise airport;

(e) any person in, entering or leaving any approved wharf or transit shed which is not in a port;

(ee) any person in, entering or leaving a free zone;

(f) in Northern Ireland, any person travelling from or to any place which is on or beyond the boundary.

(5) In this section—

"intimate search" means any search which involves a physical examination (that is, an examination which is more than simply a visual examination) of a person's body orifices;

"rub-down search" means any search which is neither an intimate search nor a strip search;

"strip search" means any search which is not an intimate search but which involves the removal of an article of clothing which—

(a) is being worn (wholly or partly) on the trunk; and

(b) is being so worn either next to the skin or next to an article of underwear;

"suitably qualified person" means a registered medical practitioner or a registered nurse.

(6) [*Scotland.*]

[This section is printed as amended by the *Finance Act* 1984, s.8, and Sched. 4, para. 6; and the *Finance Act* 1988, s.10.]

25–447 Section 114(3) of the *PACE Act* 1984 provides that nothing in any order under section 114(2) shall be taken to limit any powers exercisable under section 164. Section 114(2) provides for the making of orders by the Treasury directing that provisions of that Act relating to the investigation of offences by police officers and to persons detained by the police shall apply, with such modifications as may be specified in the order, to the investigation of offences relating to assigned matters by officers of Revenue and Customs or to persons detained by such officers. For section 114 and and the current order under section 114(2), see *ante*, §§ 15–40 *et seq.* As to "reasonable grounds to suspect", see *R. (Hoverspeed Ltd) v. Customs and Excise Commrs* [2003] Q.B. 1041, CA (Civ. Div.).

In relation to the Channel Tunnel, the persons to whom section 164 applies shall be taken to include any person who is (a) in the tunnel system in the United Kingdom; (b) in a through train in the United Kingdom; (c) in, entering or leaving a customs approved area in the United Kingdom; or (d) in a control zone in France: *Channel Tunnel (Customs and Excise) Order* 1990 (S.I. 1990 No. 2167), art. 4, Sched., para. 25, as substituted by the *Channel Tunnel (International Arrangements) Order* 1993 (S.I. 1993 No. 1813), art. 8, Sched. 5, para. 33. This was extended to a control zone in Belgium on December 1, 1997: see the *Channel Tunnel (Miscellaneous Provisions) Order* 1994 (S.I. 1994 No, 1405), art. 8, Sched. 4, para. 7. As to the meaning of "customs approved area", see *ante*, § 25–412. For the definitions of "control zone", see Appendix F–15, F–16, F–23, F–24.

(12) Untrue declarations and falsifying documents

Customs and Excise Management Act 1979, s.167

Untrue declarations, etc.

167.—(1) If any person either knowingly or recklessly— **25–448**

(a) makes or signs, or causes to be made or signed, or delivers or causes to be delivered to the Commissioners or an officer, any declaration, notice, certificate or other document whatsoever; or

(b) makes any statement in answer to any question put to him by an officer which he is required by or under any enactment to answer,

being a document or statement produced or made for any purpose of any assigned matter, which is untrue in any material particular, he shall be guilty of an offence under this subsection and may be arrested; and any goods in relation to which the document or statement was made shall be liable to forfeiture.

(2) Without prejudice to subsection (4) below, a person who commits an offence under subsection (1) above shall be liable—

(a) on summary conviction, to a penalty of the prescribed sum or to imprisonment for a term not exceeding *6* [12] months, or to both; or

(b) on conviction on indictment, to a penalty of any amount, or to imprisonment for a term not exceeding 2 years, or to both.

(3) If any person—

(a), (b) [*identical to paras (a), (b) of subs. (1)*],

being a document or statement produced or made for any purpose of any assigned matter, which is untrue in any material particular, then, without prejudice to subsection (4) below, he shall be liable on summary conviction to a penalty of level 4 on the standard scale.

(4), (5) [*Recoverability as civil debt of unpaid duty, overpayment of drawback, etc.*]

[Subss. (1)–(3) are printed as amended by the *CJA* 1982, ss.38 and 46; and the *PACE Act* 1984, s.114(1); subs. (5) was inserted by the *Finance Act* 1997, s.50 and Sched. 6, para. 5. In subs. (2)(a), "12" is substituted for "6", as from a day to be appointed, by the *CJA* 2003, s.282(2) and (3). The increase has no application to offences committed before the substitution takes effect: s.282(4).]

The "prescribed sum" means the prescribed sum within the meaning of section 32 of the *MCA* 1980: *CEMA* 1979, s.171(2), *post*, § 25–480. For section 32, see *ante*, § 1–75aa. As to the modification of the penalty where a person is convicted of an offence in connection with the "Intrastat" system, see *post*, § 25–451. **25–449**

Sections 167 and 168 (*post*) do not apply in relation to a declaration, document or statement in respect of a function relating to a matter to which section 7 of the 2005 Act (former Inland Revenue matters) applies: *Commissioners for Revenue and Customs Act* 2005, s.16, and Sched. 2, para. 6.

For decisions on similar offences in the Privy Council, see *Patel v. Comptroller of Customs* [1966] A.C. 356, and *Comptroller of Customs v. Western Lectric Co. Ltd* [1966] A.C. 367.

See generally on the predecessor of this section, *Att.-Gen.'s. Reference (No. 3 of 1975)*, 63 Cr.App.R. 87, CA.

In *R. v. Cross* [1987] Crim.L.R. 43, CA, the appellant had been convicted of an offence contrary to section 167(1) in relation to a document. The defence contended that the proper construction of the document itself as opposed to what the defendant may have meant or intended, was a question of law for the judge. This contention was upheld by the Court of Appeal: the principle in criminal cases is the same as in civil cases, namely that it is for the judge to construe a document.

Customs and Excise Management Act 1979, s.168

Counterfeiting documents, etc.

168.—(1) If any person— **25–450**

(a) counterfeits or falsifies any document which is required by or under any enactment relating to an assigned matter or which is used in the transaction of any business relating to an assigned matter; or

(b) knowingly accepts, receives or uses any such document so counterfeited or falsified; or

(c) alters any such document after it is officially issued; or

(d) counterfeits any seal, signature, initials or other mark of, or used by, any officer for the verification of such a document or for the security of goods or for any other purpose relating to an assigned matter,

he shall be guilty of an offence under this section and may be arrested.

(2) A person guilty of an offence under this section shall be liable—

(a), (b) [*identical to paras (a), (b) of s.167(2) (including the prospective amendment)*].

[This section is printed as amended by the *PACE Act* 1984, s.114(1). As to the amendment of subs. (2), see the note to s.167, *ante*.]

25–451 The "prescribed sum" means the prescribed sum within the meaning of section 32 of the *MCA* 1980: *CEMA* 1979, s.171(2), *post*, § 25–480. For section 32, see *ante*, § 1–75aa.

As to the application of this section to former Inland Revenue matters, see *ante*, § 25–449.

"Intrastat", a new statistical collection system relating to trading between E.C. Member States, was introduced by virtue of the *Statistics of Trade (Customs and Excise) Regulations* 1992 (S.I. 1992 No. 2790), as amended by S.I. 1993 No. 541 and S.I. 1993 No. 3015. The words "three months" should be substituted for the words "six months" in section 167(2)(a) and section 168(2)(a) where a person is convicted of an offence contrary to section 167(1) or section 168(1) in connection with the operation of the Intrastat system. When section 282(2) and (3) of the *CJA* 2003 come into force, their effect will be to neutralise this modification. They provide that in the case of offences triable either way under a "relevant enactment" (of which this is one), which are punishable with imprisonment on summary conviction, the maximum term of imprisonment to which a person is liable on summary conviction is increased to 12 months. The increase will not affect offences committed before it takes effect: s.282(4).

(13) Fraudulent evasion offences

Customs and Excise Management Act 1979, s.170

Penalty for fraudulent evasion of duty, etc.

25–452 **170.**—(1) Without prejudice to any other provision of the *Customs and Excise Acts* 1979, if any person—

(a) knowingly acquires possession of any of the following goods, that is to say—

(i) goods which have been unlawfully removed from a warehouse or Queen's warehouse;

(ii) goods which are chargeable with a duty which has not been paid;

(iii) goods with respect to the importation or exportation of which any prohibition or restriction is for the time being in force under or by virtue of any enactment; or

(b) is in any way knowingly concerned in carrying, removing, depositing, harbouring, keeping or concealing or in any manner dealing with any such goods,

and does so with intent to defraud Her Majesty of any duty payable on the goods or to evade any such prohibition or restriction with respect to the goods he shall be guilty of an offence under this section and may be arrested.

(2) Without prejudice to any other provision of the *Customs and Excise Acts* 1979, if any person is, in relation to any goods, in any way knowingly concerned in any fraudulent evasion or attempt at evasion—

(a) of any duty chargeable on the goods;

(b) of any prohibition or restriction for the time being in force with respect to the goods under or by virtue of any enactment; or

(c) of any provision of the *Customs and Excise Acts* 1979 applicable to the goods,

he shall be guilty of an offence under this section and may be arrested.

25–453 (3) Subject to subsection (4), (4A) *or (4B)* [, (4B) or (4C)] below, a person guilty of an offence under this section shall be liable—

(a) on summary conviction, to a penalty of the prescribed sum or of three times the value of the goods, whichever is the greater, or to imprisonment for a term not exceeding *6* [12] months, or to both; or

(b) on conviction on indictment, to a penalty of any amount, or to imprisonment for a term not exceeding 7 years, or to both.

(4) In the case of an offence under this section in connection with a prohibition or

restriction on importation or exportation having effect by virtue of section 3 of the *Misuse of Drugs Act* 1971, subsection (3) above shall have effect subject to the modifications specified in Schedule 1 to this Act.

(4A) In the case of—

(a) an offence under subsection (2) or (3) above committed in Great Britain in connection with a prohibition or restriction on the importation or exportation of any weapon or ammunition that is of a kind mentioned in section 5(1)(a), (ab), (aba), (ac), (ad), (ae), (af) or (c) or (1A)(a) of the *Firearms Act* 1968,

(b) [*Northern Ireland*], or

(c) any such offence committed in connection with the prohibitions contained in sections 20 and 21 of the *Forgery and Counterfeiting Act* 1981,

subsection (3)(b) above shall have effect as if for the words "7 years" there were substituted the words "10 years".

(4B) In the case of an offence under subsection (1) or (2) above in connection with the prohibition contained in regulation 2 of the *Import of Seal Skins Regulations* 1996, subsection (3) above shall have effect as if—

(a) for paragraph (a) there were substituted the following—

"(a) on summary conviction, to a fine not exceeding the statutory maximum or to imprisonment for a term not exceeding *three* [12] months, or to both"; and

(b) in paragraph (b) for the words "7 years" there were substituted the words "2 years".

[(4C) In the case of an offence under subsection (1) or (2) above in connection with a prohibition or restriction relating to the importation, exportation or shipment as stores of nuclear material, subsection (3)(b) above shall have effect as if for the words "7 years" there were substituted the words "14 years".]

(5) In any case where a person would, apart from this subsection, be guilty of—

(a) an offence under this section in connection with a prohibition or restriction; and

(b) a corresponding offence under the enactment or other instrument imposing the prohibition or restriction, being an offence for which a fine or other penalty is expressly provided by that enactment or other instrument,

he shall not be guilty of the offence mentioned in paragraph (a) of this subsection.

(6) Where any person is guilty of an offence under this section, the goods in respect of which the offence was committed shall be liable to forfeiture.

[This section is printed as amended by the *Forgery and Counterfeiting Act* 1981, s.23(3); the *PACE Act* 1984, s.114(1); the *Finance Act* 1988, s.12(1)(a); the *Finance (No. 2) Act* 1992, s.3, Sched. 2, para. 7; the *Import of Seal Skins Regulations* 1996 (S.I. 1996 No. 2686); and the *CJA* 2003, s.293(1) and (4) (substitution of subs. (4A)). As to the effect of the latter amendment, see the note to s.50, *ante*, § 25–410. In subs. (3)(a) and its modified version (see subs. (4B)), "12" is substituted for "6" and "three" respectively, as from a day to be appointed, by the *CJA* 2003, s.282(2) and (3). The increase has no application to offences committed before the substitution takes effect: s.282(4). As from a further day to be appointed, the words ", (4B) or (4C)" are substituted for the words "or (4B)" in subs. (3), and subs. (4C) is inserted, by the *CJIA* 2008, s.75(2), and Sched. 17, para. 8(1) and (5).]

The "prescribed sum" means the prescribed sum within the meaning of section 32 of the *MCA* 1980: *CEMA* 1979, s.171(2), *post*, § 25–480. For section 32, see *ante*, § 1–75aa.

A financial reporting order may be made in respect of a person convicted of an offence under section 170: *SOCPA* 2005, s.76 (*ante*, § 5–886a); and such an offence is a "lifestyle offence" within the *PCA* 2002, Sched. 2 (*ante*, §§ 5–653, 5–657), if committed in connection with a prohibition or restriction on importation or exportation which has effect by virtue of the *Misuse of Drugs Act* 1971, s.3, or in connection with a firearm or ammunition.

An offence under this section in relation to goods prohibited from importation by the *Customs Consolidation Act* 1876, s.42 (indecent or obscene articles) is a sexual offence for the purposes of Part 2 of the *SOA* 2003 (notification requirements, etc.), if the prohibited goods included indecent photographs of children under 16, and if the offender is 18 or over and sentenced to imprisonment for a term of at least 12 months: Sched. 3, para. 14, to the 2003 Act (*ante*, § 20–291).

For general provisions as to offences and penalties under this Act, see section 171, *post*, § 25–480.

For guideline cases, see *post*, § 25–481.

For Schedule 1, see *post*, § 25–482.

Sections 20 and 21 of the *Forgery and Counterfeiting Act* 1981 are set out at § 25–255, *ante*.

As to the meaning of "harbouring", see *R. v. Cohen*, 34 Cr.App.R. 239, CCA.

Ingredients to be proved under subsections (1) and (2)

25–454 On a charge under section 170(1) the prosecution must prove that:

(a) the accused either—
  (i) knowingly acquired possession of goods; or
  (ii) was "knowingly concerned" in carrying, removing, depositing, harbouring, keeping or concealing, "or in any other manner dealing" with goods; and

(b) the goods are subject to a prohibition or restriction on importation or exportation in force under or by virtue of any enactment, or have been unlawfully removed from any warehouse or Queen's warehouse, or are chargeable with a duty which has not been paid; and

(c) the accused intended to evade any such prohibition or restriction with respect to the goods or intended to defraud Her Majesty of any duty payable on the goods.

On a charge under section 170(2) the prosecution must prove that:

(a) there has been a fraudulent evasion or attempt at evasion in relation to any goods, of any duty chargeable thereon, of any prohibition or restriction in relation thereto or of any provision of the *Customs and Excise Acts* 1979 applicable thereto; and

(b) the accused was knowingly concerned therein.

Relationship between subsections (1) and (2)

25–455 In *R. v. Neal*, 77 Cr.App.R. 283, Griffiths L.J., giving the Court of Appeal's judgment, said that the language of subsection (1):

> "is so embracing and casts the net so wide that one is left to wonder what purpose is served by subsection (2), for it is difficult to think of any behaviour aimed at defrauding the Customs and Excise that would not be caught by subsection (1). However, subsection (2) has consistently appeared in a similar form in a succession of *Customs and Excise Acts* as the final and sweeping up provision. ... We are satisfied that it was inserted by the draftsman with the intention of casting his net as widely as words enabled him ..." (at p. 288).

However, whereas section 170(1)(a) requires proof that the accused acquired possession of the goods, and section 170(1)(b) requires proof that the accused performed any of the activities listed in subsection (1)(b), subsection (2) imposes no such limits on its application. For the purposes of subsection (2), the word "fraudulent" means dishonest conduct "deliberately intended to evade the prohibition or restriction with respect to, or the duty chargeable on, goods as the case may be": *per* Lord Lane C.J. in *Att.-Gen.'s Reference (No. 1 of 1981)* [1982] Q.B. 848.

Indictment for an offence under section 170(2)(b)

STATEMENT OF OFFENCE

25–456 *Being knowingly concerned in the fraudulent evasion of a prohibition on the importation of goods, contrary to section 170(2)(b) of the* Customs and Excise Management Act *1979*.

PARTICULARS OF OFFENCE

A B, on the —— day of —— 20—, in relation to a Class — controlled drug, namely — grams of —, was knowingly concerned in the fraudulent evasion of the prohibition on importation imposed by section 3(1) of the Misuse of Drugs Act *1971*.

Section 170(2) is an "activity" offence. Therefore, one count relating to a series of separately identifiable incidents over a period of months is not bad for duplicity unless the method of evasion is different: *R. v. Martin and White* [1998] 2 Cr.App.R. 385, CA.

Indictment for conspiracy to contravene section 170

STATEMENT OF OFFENCE

Conspiracy to contravene section 170 of the Customs and Excise Management Act *1979, contrary to section 1(1) of the* Criminal Law Act *1977.* 25–457

PARTICULARS OF OFFENCE

A B, between the —— day of —— 20—, and the —— day of —— 20—, conspired with CD, EF and other persons unknown fraudulently to evade the prohibition on the importation of a controlled drug of Class —, namely —— imposed by section 3(1) of the Misuse of Drugs Act *1971 in contravention of section 170 of the* Customs and Excise Management Act *1979.*

The actus reus

(i) *Proving the importation*

The burden of proving that the goods were imported into the United Kingdom rests with the prosecution and that burden is not displaced by any of the presumptions in section 154 of the *CEMA* 1979 (*ante*, § 25–437). In *R. v. Watts and Stack*, 70 Cr.App.R. 187, the defendants had been convicted of an offence under the forerunner to section 170(1). The Court of Appeal quashed the conviction on the ground that the trial judge had wrongly directed the jury that, on the "true" construction of the subsection, it was unnecessary to prove an actual importation. The court proceeded, however, to consider an alternative argument advanced on behalf of the Crown. This was to the effect that an importation may be presumed to have taken place by virtue of section 154(2), so that section 154(2) operates to place the burden of proving that there had been no importation on the defendant. The Court of Appeal accepted that once an importation was proved the onus of proof as to whether it was lawful or not lies upon the accused. However, Bridge L.J. said: 25–458

> "The court feels grave doubt as to whether the opening words of subsection (2) ... are ... apt to refer to an issue as to whether goods have been imported or not. We think it more probable that those words are directed to an issue, which may arise in determining at what rate import duty is to be levied, as to the country from which the imported goods have originated" (at pp. 191–192).

(ii) *"Evading" the prohibition or restriction*

Offences under section 170 are continuing offences because, by definition, the evasion of a prohibition or restriction often involves a continuing series of events and is rarely limited to the moment of importation itself (see s.5, *ante*, § 25–406). An illustration was given by Kenneth Jones J., in summing up to the jury in *R. v. Neal*, 77 Cr.App.R. 283: 25–459

> "Now, the words, 'the evasion of the prohibition on importation', ... are wider than simply the single word 'importation'. Let me give you a very simple example. A boat arrives in a port in this country and it has on board cannabis resin. One of the sailors ... actually carries that cannabis resin ashore. He hands it over to another man who is waiting, who loads it into a van. The van is driven off to some place where the drug is unloaded and is stored away in some building and there you have someone who helps in that unloading—perhaps the owner of the building in which it is stored. Maybe, at a later stage, it is transported to yet another building and is stored there and it may be ... that behind all this operation, controlling it and supervising it, is some organising person. Now you see, of all those men—the sailor, the van driver, the store keeper, the organiser—strictly speaking, only the sailor has imported the drugs into this country. He is the only person who carried it into this country, and that is what importation means, but he and each of those other persons ... have all taken a part in

> evading the prohibition on the importation of that drug and taken their part in getting round it, in setting at nought the ban which the law imposes on the importation of the drug" (at pp. 286–287).

Griffiths L.J., delivering the judgment of the Court of Appeal, said:

> "Subsection (1) clearly includes those who are not a part of the original smuggling team. For example, it includes anyone who acquires possession of goods unlawfully removed from a warehouse, or anyone who hides goods on which duty has not been paid, or anyone who carries goods the importation of which is forbidden; and there can be no warrant for reading into the language of the subsection the qualification 'provided they are part of the original smuggling team'" (at p. 288).

25–460 These remarks apply, with equal force, in respect of subsection (2).

Thus, in *R. v. Neal*, the provision of a barn in which six hundred-weight of cannabis was concealed, was sufficient evidence of being "knowingly concerned" in the fraudulent evasion of the prohibition on its importation for the purposes of section 170(2), despite the absence of any evidence as to how, or when, the drug had been imported.

In *R. v. Ardalan*, 56 Cr.App.R. 320, CA, it was held that the offence of acquiring possession of goods prohibited from importation may be committed at any time after the actual importation of the goods and at any place "provided always, of course, that the ... acquisition is done knowingly and with intent to evade that prohibition or restriction" (*per* Roskill L.J. at p. 327). And see, *post*, § 25–467.

Applying the same reasoning, acts done before the moment of importation with the requisite *mens rea*, are also punishable under section 170 even if the acts are performed abroad: *R. v. Wall*, 59 Cr.App.R. 58, CA; *R. v. Jakeman*, 76 Cr.App.R. 223, CA; *R. v. Smith (Donald)* [1973] Q.B. 924, 57 Cr.App.R. 737, CA.

The evasion continues until the goods cease to be prohibited or, possibly, until they are exported: *per* Ormrod L.J. in *R. v. Green (H.)* [1976] Q.B. 985, 62 Cr.App.R. 74, CA; and see *R. v. Berner*, 37 Cr.App.R. 113, CCA. It is no defence, therefore, that the defendant only acted fraudulently in relation to the goods after they had been imported innocently: *R. v. Coughlan* [1997] 8 *Archbold News* 2, CA (97/6721/W3).

The evasion does not cease merely because the drugs are seized by the authorities. This is because the *actus reus* of an offence under section 170 is not confined merely to successful evasions. So where, in *R. v. Green*, *ante*, customs officers removed cannabis from a crate shortly after it was imported and substituted a quantity of peat, the offence was complete when G subsequently stored the crate in a garage rented under a false name.

In *R. v. Ciaparra*, 87 Cr.App.R. 316, CA, two imported packets containing cocaine were intercepted by customs officers and the contents substituted with baking powder. There was no dispute that the importation was complete by the time the packages were intercepted, but even if they arrived unsolicited in C's hands, his subsequent conduct in relation to one packet—which he took to his place of work—was enough to bring him within section 170(2). See also *R. v. Mitchell* [1992] Crim.L.R. 594, CA.

Where restrictions are imposed by Council Regulations that restrict the introduction of listed species into the Community rather than to an individual Member State, an offence contrary to section 170(2)(b) is committed where the species is introduced to another Member State. There is jurisdiction in England and Wales to try such an offence where any part of the continuing sequence of acts of evasion occurs in England or Wales: *R. v. Sissen* [2001] 1 W.L.R. 902, CA (see commentary *Criminal Law Week* 2001/03/3).

(iii) *"Concerned"*

25–461 In *R. v. Ciaparra*, *ante*, May L.J. said (at p. 321): "We do not attempt any definition of the word 'concerned'. It is an ordinary English word with a well known and unspecialised meaning." Clearly some act of participation in the venture is required. In *MacNeill v. H.M. Advocate*, 1986 S.C.C.R. 288, it was held that to be concerned in the importation of goods, a person has to be involved in the enterprise in some way, if only in the sense of having accepted a role to be performed if circumstances so required. It is not enough for the Crown to show merely that the accused was being kept informed of what others were doing. There must be evidence that the accused played, or held himself available to play, some role in furtherance of the smuggling venture.

For guilt to be established, the importation must result as a consequence, if only in part, of the activity of the accused. An act of remorse, even if coupled with a desire not to pursue the venture, will not avoid conviction under section 170 if an importation in fact results: *R. v. Jakeman*, 76 Cr.App.R. 223, CA. Wood J. observed that "what matters is the state of mind at the time the relevant acts are done, *i.e.* at the time the defendant is concerned in bringing about the importation". This last statement should not be taken to apply literally in every case because it is clear that the court was considering what had to be established against a person whose part was played abroad in advance of the importation. His Lordship was careful to add that although "the importation takes place at one precise moment—when the aircraft lands—a person who is concerned in the importation may play his part before or after that moment" (at p. 228).

In *R. v. Latif and Shahzad* [1996] 2 Cr.App.R. 92, HL, a customs officer, under the orders of his superiors, brought drugs, obtained by S in Pakistan to England. S was persuaded to collect the drugs in London. It was held that, although the offence charged under section 170(2) could be committed through an innocent agent, the conduct of the customs officers who had acted not in concert with S, but deliberately for their own purposes, fell within the general principle of causation that the free, deliberate and informed intervention of a second person, intending to exploit a situation created by the first, but not acting in concert with him, relieved the first of criminal responsibility, and therefore, S had not been guilty of fraudulent evasion under section 170(2); but his acts did amount to attempts at evasion contrary to section 170(2), both in Pakistan and London. Since section 170(2) created one offence capable of being committed two different ways, rather than separate offences of evasion and attempted evasion, S was guilty of an offence under section 170(2). As to section 170(2) creating a single offence, see also *R. v. Isleworth Crown Court and Uxbridge Magistrates' Court, ex p. Buda* [2000] 1 Cr.App.R.(S.) 538, DC (after plea of guilty to full offence, but before sentence, discovered that attempt only committed).

A person who is not a party to the original smuggling operation will still commit an offence if he thereafter participates jointly with others to contravene section 170: see *R. v. Williams (H.L.)*, 55 Cr.App.R. 275, CA.

For examples of importation cases in which the Court of Appeal held that there was insufficient evidence of involvement to be left to the jury, see *R. v. Suurmeijer* [1991] Crim.L.R. 773, and *R. v. Berry* [1998] Crim.L.R. 487.

The mens rea

(i) *Knowledge that the goods are prohibited/restricted*

It must be noted that offences created by section 170(1) and 170(2) apply to two different categories of goods, namely *dutiable* goods and *prohibited or restricted* goods (for statutory definitions see s.1, *ante*, §§ 25–400 *et seq.*). Goods imported may be subject to the payment of duty but not prohibited or restricted from importation. Accordingly, an accused who imports cannabis (a prohibited substance) believing that he has imported brandy (a dutiable commodity) does not have the requisite *mens rea* for an offence under section 170(2)(b). **25–462**

To establish the offence under section 170(2)(b), the prosecution must prove that the defendant knew that the goods which were being imported were goods subject to a prohibition or restriction and that the operation with which he was concerned was an operation designed fraudulently to evade that prohibition or restriction, but they are not required further to prove that the defendant knew the precise category of the goods the importation of which had been prohibited or restricted: *R. v. Hussain* [1969] 2 Q.B. 567, 53 Cr.App.R. 448, CA. *Hussain* was applied in *R. v. Hennessey*, 68 Cr.App.R. 419, CA (claim of defendant caught smuggling drugs that he thought he was smuggling pornography of a type prohibited from importation held to be immaterial).

Both *Hussain* and *Hennessey* were distinguished by the House of Lords in *R. v. Taaffe* [1984] A.C. 539, where it was held that on the true construction of section **25–463**

170(2), the accused was to be judged on the facts as he believed them to be. Assuming T believed that the substance that he was importing was currency (which was not subject to a prohibition), he had not been knowingly concerned in the fraudulent evasion of the prohibition on the importation of cannabis (which was what he was in fact importing) and it made no difference that he thought that the importation of currency was subject to a prohibition. His error as to the law was irrelevant.

Hussain and *Hennessey* have been considered further in a series of subsequent decisions in the House of Lords and in the Court of Appeal. In *R. v. Shivpuri* [1987] A.C. 1, HL, *Hussain* was not only expressly approved but was also held to have been adopted by the legislature. The reasoning was that, as there was no provision in the legislation for applying section 28(3) of the *Misuse of Drugs Act* 1971 to importation offences, then the legislature must have taken the view that there was no necessity for it having regard to *Hussain*.

In *Shivpuri*, S was convicted of attempting to be knowingly concerned in dealing with (count 1) and in harbouring (count 2) diamorphine (heroin) with intent to evade the prohibition on its importation contrary to section 170(1)(b) of the *CEMA* 1979. A suitcase had been sent from India and delivered, in England, to S. Packages were found in the suitcase which S believed contained either heroin or cannabis. However, scientific analysis revealed the substance to be harmless vegetable matter. It was submitted on behalf of the appellant: (a) that section 170 created three separate offences in respect of Class A, B and C drugs; (b) that each offence required proof that goods of a particular category had been imported; and (c) that "knowingly" in section 170 required proof of a corresponding *mens rea*.

25–464 These submissions were founded on the decision in *R. v. Courtie* [1984] A.C. 463, HL: where a statute provides one maximum penalty on the basis that the prosecution can prove a particular factual ingredient and a different maximum penalty if the prosecution cannot prove that factual ingredient, then two distinct offences have been created. By Schedule 1 to the *CEMA* 1979 (as amended by the *Controlled Drugs (Penalties) Act* 1985) different maximum penalties now apply to Class A, B and C drugs. Whilst Lord Bridge recognised the force of this argument, he was clearly influenced by the practical argument that if this were the law, it would mean that if a defendant said that he thought he had been importing a class C drug when, in fact, he was importing a class A drug, the judge would be bound to direct the jury that if that might have been the case, they should acquit. Convictions would be difficult to obtain.

Where a prosecution is brought under the *Misuse of Drugs Act* 1971, in respect of an offence to which section 28 of that Act applies, then by section 28(3)(a) an accused shall not be acquitted of that offence by reason only of proving that he neither knew, nor suspected, nor had reason to suspect that the substance in question was the particular controlled drug alleged; but (by s.28(3)(b)) he shall be acquitted thereof if he proves: (a) that he neither believed nor suspected nor had reason to suspect that the substance or product in question was a controlled drug; or (b) that he believed the substance or product in question to be a controlled drug, or a controlled drug of a description, such that, if it had in fact been that controlled drug or a controlled drug of that description, he would not at the material time have been committing any offence to which section 28 applies.

Section 28 does not apply to offences under section 170 of the *CEMA* 1979 (taken together with section 3(1) of the *Misuse of Drugs Act* 1971) prohibiting the importation of controlled drugs. However, in *R. v. Shivpuri*, Lord Bridge concluded that the decision in *R. v. Hussain*, *ante*, § 25–462, made the application of section 28 unnecessary because:

> "Irrespective of the different penalties attached to offences in connection with the importation of different categories of prohibited goods, *R. v. Hussain* established that the only *mens rea* necessary for proof of any such offence was knowledge that the goods were subject to a prohibition on importation" (at p. 17).

In *R. v. Ellis and Street*; *R. v. Smith*, 84 Cr.App.R. 235, the Court of Appeal conducted an extensive review of the authorities; their conclusion was that in that court at least *R. v. Hennessey* remained good law and was binding.

Hussain was followed again in *R. v. Forbes (Giles)* [2002] 2 A.C. 512, HL. The appellant, who had imported prohibited obscene videos, pursued a "*Taaffe* defence" (*ante*) that he believed he was importing prohibited videos, but that they would not in fact have been prohibited had they contained what he thought they contained. The House of Lords rejected the argument that, having directed the jury on the *Taaffe* defence, the judge should also have directed them that the prosecution must prove that the defendant knew that the material contained in the videos was either obscene within the *Obscene Publications Act* 1959 (*post*, §§ 31–62 *et seq.*), or was material falling within the *Protection of Children Act* 1978 (*post*, § 31–107). The prosecution only had to establish that the defendant knew he was importing goods subject to a prohibition and that the operation on which he was engaged was an evasion of that prohibition. It was not necessary also to prove that he knew the precise nature of the goods he imported.

In relation to obscene articles, where the importer knows he is importing "blue movies" it is no defence to say that, until a jury have determined that the articles are obscene within section 1(1) of the 1959 Act (*post*, § 31–63), it is not possible for the importer to "know" that the articles are obscene: *R. v. Dunne*, 162 J.P. 399, CA.

(ii) *Meaning of "fraudulent"*

The presence of the word "fraudulent" in section 170(2) has the effect that, on a prosecution for fraudulent evasion or attempted evasion of a prohibition or restriction with respect to goods or duty chargeable thereon, the prosecution have to prove fraudulent, in the sense of dishonest, conduct deliberately intended to evade the prohibition or restriction with respect to the goods, or the duty chargeable on them. There is no necessity for the prosecution to prove acts of deceit practised on a customs officer in his presence: *Att.-Gen.'s Reference (No. 1 of 1981)* [1982] Q.B. 848, CA. **25–465**

See also *R. v. Latif and Shahzad* [1996] 2 Cr.App.R. 92, HL, *ante*, § 25–461.

(iii) *When must the guilty mind subsist?*

What matters is the defendant's state of mind at the time the relevant acts are done, that is, at the time the defendant is concerned in bringing about the importation. In order to convict it is not necessary that the guilty mind subsists at the precise moment of importation: *R. v. Jakeman*, 76 Cr.App.R. 223, CA (*ante*, § 25–461). **25–466**

(iv) *Proving mens rea after the moment of importation*

Given that an offence under section 170 is a continuing one—which may be committed at a time (or place) prior, or subsequent, to the moment of importation—it follows that, in theory, there can be no limit of time (or even place) before the offence ceases to run, provided always that the acts complained of are done with the requisite intent: see *R. v. Ardalan*, 56 Cr.App.R. 320, CA, *ante*, § 25–460. **25–467**

The further removed the accused is from the moment or place of importation the more difficult it may be for the prosecution to prove the necessary *mens rea*. In *R. v. Neal*, 77 Cr.App.R. 283, Griffiths L.J. remarked that:

> "If no more can be proved than that a piece of cannabis changed hands in Piccadilly Circus, no doubt it would be foolish of the prosecution to proceed under [s.170 of the *CEMA* 1979] for it would be far-fetched to suggest that the real intent of such a transaction is to evade the prohibition on the import of cannabis" (at p. 291 and see § 25–459, *ante*).

(v) *Proving mens rea by reference to the moment of importation*

In *R. v. Watts and Stack*, 70 Cr.App.R. 187, CA, the Crown sought to rely on what is now section 154 as establishing two presumptions in their favour, namely (a) a presumption of importation, and (b) that the importation was unlawful. Despite voicing grave doubts as to whether the words of the section were apt to apply to an issue as to whether goods had been imported or not, the court assumed that the argument of the Crown was correct and went on to consider whether the two presumptions "can ever be sufficient to justify a prosecution ... where there is nothing other than the presumptions to connect the activities of the defendant with the presumed importation" (*per* Bridge L.J. at p. 192). His Lordship referred to *R. v. Ardalan*, *ante*, and continued: **25–468**

> "But does it follow from that, that in establishing an intent to evade a prohibition on the importation of goods, it is sufficient for the Crown simply to rely on the presumptions which, for this purpose, we are assuming to be established by [s.154(2)]? In our judgment it clearly does not. It seems to us quite clear that, on the true construction of [s.170(1)], in order to establish that any particular dealing with goods was done with intent to evade the relevant prohibition on importation, the onus on the Crown to prove that intent must involve establishing a link or nexus between the *actus reus* of the offence and some prohibited importation. Merely to establish that there has been a dealing with the prohibited goods, and that by virtue of the presumptions they are presumed at some time in the indefinite past to have been unlawfully imported, would not, in our judgment, ever justify, without anything further, inviting a jury to conclude that the evidence established an intent to evade the prohibition on importation" (at p. 192).

The observations of Bridge L.J. have caused confusion due, in part, to extravagant arguments based on them, not least in *R. v. Neal, ante*. In *Neal*, the appellants, who had been convicted of an offence contrary to section 170(2), argued that the dicta of Bridge L.J. in *Watts and Stack* were authority for the proposition that, on a charge of being knowingly concerned in the fraudulent evasion of the prohibition on importation of a controlled drug, it had to be proved that the defendant was somehow involved in the importation itself. The court followed *Ardalan, ante*, and rejected this argument. The court doubted that Bridge L.J. had intended to advance any such proposition. This, with respect, seems to be right because Bridge L.J. expressly referred to *Ardalan*. However, Griffiths L.J., giving the court's judgment in *Neal*, said that if, contrary to their view, Bridge L.J. was intending to say that which was being argued on behalf of the appellants, then the court took the view that it was inconsistent with *Ardalan* and the dictum of Lord Salmon in *DPP v. Doot* [1973] A.C. 807 at p. 830).

It is plain that were Bridge L.J.'s observations applied to the facts of *Neal* there would, in any event, have been held to have been a sufficient nexus between the activities of the defendants and the prohibited importation: and see *R. v. Jakeman*, 76 Cr.App.R. 223, CA, and *R. v. Williams (H.L.)*, 55 Cr.App.R. 275, CA (*ante*, § 25–461).

(vi) *Recklessness not sufficient*

25–469 What is required, for the purposes of section 170, is proof of knowledge, *i.e.* a specific intent to be knowingly concerned in a fraudulent evasion of a prohibition. Recklessness is not enough. In *R. v. Panayi (No. 2) and Karte* [1989] 1 W.L.R. 187, CA, Bush J. said:

> "[T]hey cannot be knowingly concerned in the fraudulent evasion unless they intend dishonestly to evade the restriction. They cannot knowingly be involved in the evasion if one of the essential ingredients, namely the fact that they are within territorial waters, is unknown to them; provided of course that they never had any intention of entering the United Kingdom territorial waters.... Though it is possible in some cases to equate recklessness with knowledge or general intent, this cannot be done in this kind of case where the specific intent is required of being knowingly concerned in any fraudulent evasion" (at p. 192).

(vii) *Uncertainty*

25–469a Where a person agreed to look after an imported parcel, knowing that the parcel might contain drugs, he was knowingly concerned in the fraudulent evasion. The vice was being prepared to assist or participate in the enterprise if the circumstances arose: *Att.-Gen.'s Reference (No. 1 of 1998)*, 163 J.P. 390, CA.

(viii) *Mens rea of conspiracy*

25–470 See generally *post*, §§ 33–15 *et seq.*; see, in particular, *R. v. Siracusa*, 90 Cr.App.R. 340, CA, *R. v. Patel*, unreported, August 7, 1991, CA (89/4351/S1), and *R. v. Taylor (Robert John)* [2002] Crim.L.R. 205, *post*, §§ 33–18, 33–19.

(ix) *Proof of mens rea—use of documents and incriminating articles*

25–471 In prosecutions for being knowingly concerned in the evasion of the prohibition upon importation of controlled drugs, the real issue in many cases turns out to be whether it has been proved that the defendant knew of the existence of the drugs: the defence is frequently to the effect that the defendant was innocently helping a third party or that the drugs must have been "planted" on him, either for the purpose of getting them through customs using an unwitting courier or for the purpose of getting the courier into trouble.

For the purpose of proving knowledge and of rebutting the defence of innocent involvement, the prosecution were permitted in a number of cases which have been before the Court of Appeal, and which were decided at common law, to adduce evidence of matters having no immediate connection with the importation in question, but tending to show the defendant to have been otherwise involved in drugs. There were no special rules of evidence for drug cases or importation of drugs cases, as there were once thought to be for sexual cases. The general principles in *Makin v. Att.-Gen. for New South Wales* [1894] A.C. 57, PC; *DPP v. Boardman* [1975] A.C. 421, HL; and *DPP v. P.* [1991] 2 A.C. 447, HL (*ante*, §§ 13–39 *et seq.*), applied here as elsewhere. As in all cases, where the admission of this type of evidence was being considered, the most important feature to keep in mind was the issue to which the evidence was said to be relevant.

The overriding consideration was whether the evidence had sufficient probative force: the test was whether common sense made the combination of the direct evidence (*e.g.* finding of drugs in luggage) and the indirect evidence (*e.g.* finding of drugs at defendant's house) "inexplicable on the basis of coincidence" (see the extract from the speech of Lord Salmon in *Boardman* set out at § 13–42, *ante*), "against all the probabilities" on the basis of coincidence (see *per* Lord Morris at § 13–41, *ante*). (See also the reference to the relevance of coincidence in the extracts from the speeches of Lord Wilberforce, quoted at § 13–41, *ante*; of Lord Hailsham (would explanation on the basis of coincidence be an "affront to common sense"?), at § 13–41, *ante*; and of Lord Cross (would only an "ultra-cautious jury" not reject coincidence?), at § 13–42, *ante*.)

Under Chapter 1 of Part 11 of the *CJA* 2003 (*ante*, §§ 13–5 *et seq.*), such evidence will be admissible if it is "relevant to an important matter in issue between the prosecution and the defendant" (see s.101(1)(d)). In the cases under consideration, the matter in issue between prosecution and defendant is knowledge, but section 103(1)(a) deems another matter in issue to be whether the defendant has a propensity to commit offences of the kind with which he is charged, except where his having such a propensity makes it no more likely that he is guilty of the offence. Where it is said that the evidence of bad character is relevant to an issue in the case other than mere propensity, the Act establishes no standard of relevance. It is tentatively submitted, therefore, that where the evidence is tendered for a purpose for which it might have been tendered at common law (to prove identity or knowledge, or to rebut mistake, accident, etc.), the test should be unchanged. Where mere propensity is relied on, a lesser standard may be acceptable, but in turn the evidence should properly carry less significance. In cases such as those referred to in the ensuing paragraphs, the disputed evidence will be admissible under section 101(1)(d) as going to the issue of knowledge, not as going merely to the issue of propensity. For a more detailed consideration of the issues arising under section 101 of the 2003 Act, see *ante*, § 13–37 *et seq*.

In *R. v. Willis*, unreported, January 29, 1979, CA (2934/B/78), W arrived at Heathrow carrying her handbag and a suitcase. A photograph album found in her handbag contained 134.5 grammes of opium. Another album in her suitcase contained 75 grammes of heroin. From her home address was seized a spoon bearing traces of heroin and a box containing a folded piece of paper inside which was 80 milligrammes of heroin. W was charged with the unlawful importation of the drugs found in her luggage. In interview, she had denied knowledge of the drugs in her luggage. It was held that the items at her flat showed that W was connected with heroin inside the United Kingdom. That fact, in the ordinary way, would not have been relevant but it became relevant in the light of her defence disclosed in the interviews. The Court of Appeal stated as their reason that: **25–472**

> "... what the prosecution were doing was to show that her seeming possession in the United Kingdom of a small quantity of heroin was the odd coincidence in the case of a woman who was saying that she had no knowledge whatsoever that she was bringing dangerous drugs into the country. The jury were entitled to consider ... that coincidence."

In *R. v. Thrussell*, unreported, November 30, 1981, H and T travelled together on **25–473**

May 20, 1980 from London to Peru. On May 25, H returned to London. In a suitcase, which H carried, 2.93 kilogrammes of cocaine was discovered by customs officers. On May 26, T returned to London. T's home address was searched and the sum of $45,400 and a book entitled the *Cocaine Consumer's Handbook* were seized. The book described the methods of using cocaine; how to import it; the countries most suitable for export as well as data and advice on how the trade should be carried out. When asked about the cocaine in H's suitcase, T replied, "Where would I get that sort of stuff?" It was held that the book was relevant and admissible to prove knowledge by T of the importation of the drug.

The court said that the book showed knowledge by the appellant of the drug trade. It may be questioned how the book could be probative evidence against T that he knew of the importation. The answer to this question has to be seen in the light of the other evidence but, it is submitted, the decisive factor was the appellant's claim that he would not know where to get cocaine. The book was undoubtedly capable of rebutting that assertion. When coupled with the journey made by both defendants, and the circumstances in which the two men returned separately over two days, that was sufficient to render the book relevant, probative and admissible. See also *R. v. Sokialiois* [1993] Crim.L.R. 872, CA, in which evidence of drugs, not the subject of the charge, was admitted to rebut the defendant's assertion in interview that he was not a drug dealer, nor did he take drugs.

25–474 In *R. v. Alexiou*, unreported, November 14, 1983, CA, 24 boxes arrived at Heathrow airport. The boxes contained chandeliers but their false bottoms concealed a total of 107.45 kilogrammes of cannabis resin. The boxes were loaded onto a van and taken to an address where the appellant was waiting and he helped to carry the boxes into the house. The appellant's own home was searched. A suitcase and scales were found. Both items had traces of cannabis on them. Officers also seized £600 in cash from a bread bin, and a diary containing calculations said to relate to drug dealings. It was held, relying on *Willis*, *ante*, that the evidence was admissible to rebut the defence that his presence at the premises to which the drugs were delivered was innocent.

25–475 In *R. v. Bagga*, unreported, May 21, 1986, Mrs R arrived at Heathrow airport with a suitcase found to contain 12.3 kilogrammes of heroin. She was met by her husband and B. Officers searched B's house. They found a briefcase and electronic scales capable of weighing in grammes to an accuracy of two decimal points. Traces of heroin were found in the briefcase and on the scales. In interview, B asserted that his presence at the airport was innocent and that he had no knowledge of the presence of the heroin carried by Mrs R. It was held that the evidence of the traces found in the briefcase and on the scales was relevant and admissible.

The court concluded that it was open to the prosecution to invite the jury to consider whether the evidence of prior unexplained handling of heroin by the appellant destroyed his defence of innocent and ignorant presence. The presence of the traces of heroin *inside* the briefcase and on the scales (consistent arguably with the acts of a dealer) went, it was said, to that issue. See also *R. v. Barner-Rasmussen* [1996] Crim.L.R. 497, CA; and *R. v. Groves* [1998] Crim.L.R. 200, CA (see the commentary as to the need for caution when assessing probative value).

These principles are not restricted to cases where the drugs found were of the same kind as those to which the charge related: *R. v. Peters* [1995] 2 Cr.App.R. 77, CA.

Many of the foregoing authorities were considered in *R. v. Ilomuanya* [2006] Crim.L.R. 422, CA (a case decided under the common law), in which it was held that the critical considerations are the relevance (and hence probative value) of the evidence and the need to consider each case on its facts; that the facts that may be proved for this purpose are not limited to possession of drugs, or drugs paraphernalia, unconnected with the importation charged; and that *mens rea* might also be proved, for example, by evidence suggesting inexplicable coincidence in a pattern of meeting by arrangement drug couriers arriving at an airport. Where the issue is not knowledge, but whether or not the accused had any involvement in a particular importation, such evidence was held to have little or no probative force in *R. v. Balogun* [1997] Crim.L.R. 500, CA.

Attempt

25–476 Where a person does acts in relation to a substance which he believes to be a controlled drug, which would bring him within section 170(1) or (2) if the substance were a controlled drug, he may be convicted of an attempt contrary to section 1(1) of the *Criminal Attempts Act* 1981 if the substance was, in fact, harmless: *R. v. Shivpuri* [1987] A.C. 1, HL.

On a charge of being concerned in a fraudulent attempt at evasion of duty on goods, or of a prohibition or restriction with respect thereto, contrary to section 170(2), it is appropriate to direct the jury in relation to the allegation of attempt by reference to the definition of attempt in the *Criminal Attempts Act* 1981, s.1(1) (*post*, § 33–120): *R. v. Qadir and Khan* [1997] 9 *Archbold News* 1, CA (96/2311/X4).

Relevance of E.C. law

The issue whether a prohibition on importation imposed by United Kingdom legislation is ineffective on imports between Member States of the E.C. as being contrary to Article 28 (formerly 30) of the Treaty establishing the European Community, or "justified on grounds of ... public policy or public security or the protection of ... life" within Article 30 (formerly 36), is a question regarding the meaning or effect of the Treaty which, by virtue of the *European Communities Act* 1972, s.3(1), is to be treated as a question of law for the purposes of all legal proceedings. Accordingly, if that issue arises in a criminal trial it is an issue for the judge and not for the jury to decide and may be heard in the absence of the jury. If the prohibition comes within Article 28, it is for the prosecution to prove that it is justified under Article 30: *R. v. Goldstein* [1983] 1 W.L.R. 151, HL. **25–477**

The Channel Tunnel

Many of the provisions of the 1979 Act have had to be modified to reflect the opening of the Channel Tunnel (as referred to *ante* at the conclusion of each relevant section). Being a general provision, section 170 of the 1979 Act has required no specific modification. However, where the Channel Tunnel is used for importation or exportation, the provisions of the *Channel Tunnel Act* 1987 and subordinate legislation made under it may be relevant (see Appendix F). For powers of arrest and procedures following arrest, see S.I. 1993 No. 1813, Sched. 3, Pt 1, and S.I. 1994 No. 1405, Sched. 3 (Appendix F–17, F–25, F–26). For the provisions relating to the time of importation and exportation through the tunnel, see *ante*, §§ 25–413, 25–417 respectively. **25–478**

Evasion of excise duty

Evasion of excise duty has greatly increased since the introduction of the Single Market within the European Community on January 1, 1993, the increase of "own use" reliefs and the relaxation of intra E.C. border controls for excise matters pursuant to section 4 of the *Finance (No. 2) Act* 1992 (*post*, § 25–483). Sections 170 and 170B of the *CEMA* 1979 (*ante*, § 25–452, and *post*, § 25–479 respectively) are used to prosecute appropriate cases. Much of the case law on the *actus reus* and the *mens rea* of section 170 cases, relating primarily to drug importations (*ante*, §§ 25–458 *et seq.*), is relevant to evasion of excise duty prosecutions. "A person defrauds the Revenue if knowingly and consciously he acts with dutiable goods in such a way that the Customs are deprived of the duty": *Sayce v. Coupe* [1952] 2 All E.R. 715 at 717G, DC, *per* Lord Goddard C.J. **25–478a**

There are three excise regimes in operation, concerned with (i) dutiable goods manufactured in the U.K.; (ii) dutiable goods imported to the U.K. from within the Single Market; (iii) dutiable goods imported from elsewhere.

(i) *Dutiable goods manufactured in the U.K.*

The *Alcoholic Liquor Duties Act* 1979, the *Tobacco Products Duty Act* 1979 and the *Hydrocarbon Oil Duties Act* 1979 (not printed in this work) provide that duty is chargeable in relation to dutiable goods manufactured in the U.K. Numerous pieces of legislation provide for suspension of payment, in which case the duty is payable on release from "duty suspension" for consumption in the U.K. Duty is not payable when the goods are to be exported. Section 170 of the *CEMA* 1979 is sometimes used to prosecute "diversion" frauds where excise goods are manufactured in the U.K. on **25–478b** which no U.K. duty has been paid but which are held in duty suspension (in bond) prior to release for export. The goods are then diverted (*i.e.* not exported but sold inland) and false documentation is created which purports to show that they are destined for export or have been exported.

In *R. v. Hayward* [1999] Crim.L.R. 71, CA, it was held that where dutiable goods which had been held in a bonded warehouse under duty suspension arrangements pursuant to the *Excise Goods (Holding, Movement, Warehousing and REDS) Regulations* 1992 (S.I. 1992 No. 3135), were moved out of bond under the umbrella of continuing suspension arrangements for export purposes as a result of the use of fraudulent documentation, the suspension arrangements lapsed and the excise duty became payable immediately; to prove an offence of being knowingly concerned in the fraudulent evasion of duty chargeable on the goods, contrary to section 170(2), it was not necessary to prove that the goods were not in fact exported but were placed on the market in the United Kingdom.

As to the position of warehouse keepers under the 1992 regulations, see *Greenalls Management Ltd v. Customs and Excise Commrs* [2005] 1 W.L.R. 1754, HL.

(ii) *Dutiable goods imported to the U.K. from within the Single Market*

25–478c The introduction of the Single Market necessitated amending legislation for the purpose of implementing European Council Directive 92/12. This legislation includes the *Finance (No. 2) Act* 1992, S.I. 1992 No. 3135, *ante*, the *Beer Regulations* 1993 (S.I. 1993 No. 1228), the *Tobacco Products Regulations* 2001 (S.I. 2001 No. 1712) and the *Excise Goods, Beer and Tobacco Products (Amendment) Regulations* 2002 (S.I. 2002 No. 2692). The *Excise Duties (Personal Reliefs) Order* 1992 (S.I. 1992 No. 3155) was found to be incompatible with the Directive and revoked (*post*). For useful expositions of this legislation, together with the relevant Articles of the Treaty of Rome, see *R. v. Cousins* [1995] 3 C.M.L.R. 220, CA, and *R. v. Moore* [1995] 1 C.M.L.R. 654, Crown Court (H.H. Judge Watts).

Cross-border trading (commercial movement of dutiable goods). Duty on excise goods should be paid in the Member State in which the goods are placed on the market for retail sale (the "destination system"). Where the goods are bought for resale in another Member State (*i.e.* for commercial purposes), they would generally be transferred between Member States without payment of duty ("duty suspension") and the duty would be paid in the country of consumption at the local rates. S.I. 1992 No. 3135 (*ante*) creates a system of tax warehouses and Registered Excise Dealers and Shippers (REDS) for such commercial movements in duty suspension. If duty has already been paid in the Member State of origin there are arrangements for this to be refunded once the duty due in the Member State of destination has been paid. Frauds often involve a variation of "diversion" described at (i) above.

Cross-border shopping where goods are for "own use". If the excise goods are purchased for own use, *i.e.* for non-commercial purposes, the excise duty will have been paid in the member state where the goods were purchased and therefore no duty need be paid in the U.K. (the "origin system"). There is no limit to the quantity of excise goods a traveller may bring into the U.K. so long as it is for his own use. However, S.I. 1992 No. 3155 (*ante*) enacted a presumption that where goods in excess of prescribed quantities were imported they were being imported for a commercial purpose, and a burden was cast upon the importer to satisfy the Commissioners to the contrary.

The presumption as to commercial purpose provided for by S.I. 1992 No. 3155 was held to be incompatible with Council Directive 92/12/EC, and Article 28 of the E.C. Treaty (prohibition on quantitative restrictions on imports and all measures having equivalent effect as between member states) in *R. (Hoverspeed Ltd) v. Customs and Excise Commrs* [2003] Q.B. 1041, DC. It was held that under Articles 6 to 10 of the directive, excise duty was only chargeable on excise goods purchased by an individual in another member state when they were held in the United Kingdom for commercial purposes. In consequence of this decision, the order was revoked by the *Excise Duties (Personal Reliefs) (Revocation) Order* 2002 (S.I. 2002 No. 2691).

The relevant domestic legislation is now contained in S.I. 1992 No. 3135, S.I. 1993 No. 1228 and S.I. 2001 No. 1712 (*ante*). As amended by S.I. 2002 No. 2692 (*ante*), they implement the requirements of the directive in respect of the right of individuals to import goods which they have acquired duty-paid in another member state for their own use and which they have transported to the United Kingdom, by providing for an excise duty point (*i.e.* the time when a requirement to pay duty takes effect) where such goods are held or used in the United Kingdom for a commercial purpose. The regulations contain guidance, including a list of factors to be taken into consideration, as to when goods are to be regarded as held or used for a commercial purpose.

(iii) *Dutiable goods imported from outside the Single Market*

The *Alcoholic Liquor Duties Act* 1979, the *Tobacco Products Duty Act* 1979 and the *Hydrocarbon Oil Duties Act* 1979 provide that duty on goods imported from countries outside the Single Market is chargeable on importation. The goods are not released to the importer unless payment or arrangements to pay or secure the liability to pay the U.K. excise duty are made: *CEMA* 1979, ss.43–48 (not printed in this work). Import VAT (as well as excise duty) is payable on all such importations and is to be treated as a duty of excise (ss.1(1)(c) and 16(1) of the *VAT Act* 1994). There are reliefs from payment of such duty for travellers set out in the *Travellers' Allowances Order* 1994 (S.I. 1994 No. 955), amended by S.I. 1995 No. 3044. **25–478d**

For time of importation, see section 5 of the *CEMA* 1979, *ante*, §§ 25–406, 25–413.

Taking steps to evade excise duty

Customs and Excise Management Act 1979, s.170B

Offence of taking preparatory steps for evasion of excise duty

170B.—(1) If any person is knowingly concerned in the taking of any steps with a view to the fraudulent evasion, whether by himself or another, of any duty of excise on any goods he shall be liable— **25–479**

(a) on summary conviction, to a penalty of the prescribed sum or of three times the amount of the duty, whichever is the greater, or to imprisonment for a term not exceeding *six* [12] months or to both; and

(b) on conviction on indictment, to a penalty of any amount or to imprisonment for a term not exceeding seven years or to both.

(2) Where any person is guilty of an offence under this section, the goods in respect of which the offence was committed shall be liable to forfeiture.

[This section was inserted by the *Finance (No. 2) Act* 1992, s.3 and Sched. 2, para. 8. In subs. (1)(a), "12" is substituted for "six", as from a day to be appointed, by the *CJA* 2003, s.282(2) and (3). The increase has no application to offences committed before the substitution takes effect: s.282(4).]

For mode of trial, see *post*, § 25–513.

For "taking of steps with a view to" in section 72(1) of the *Value Added Tax Act* 1994, see *post*, § 25–515.

(14) Penalties and sentencing

Customs and Excise Management Act 1979, s.171

General provisions as to offences and penalties

171.—(1) Where— **25–480**

(a) by any provision of any enactment relating to an assigned matter a punishment is prescribed for any offence thereunder or for any contravention of or failure to comply with any regulation, direction, condition or requirement made, given or imposed thereunder; and

(b) any person is convicted in the same proceedings of more than one such offence, contravention or failure,

that person shall be liable to that punishment for each such offence, contravention or failure of which he is so convicted.

(2) In this Act the "prescribed sum", in relation to the penalty provided for an offence, means—

(a) if the offence was committed in England or Wales the prescribed sum within the meaning of section 32 of the *Magistrates' Courts Act* 1980 (£1,000 or other sum substituted by order under section 143(1) of that Act);

(b) [*Scotland*];

(c) [*Northern Ireland*];

and in subsection (1)(a) above, the reference to a provision by which a punishment is prescribed includes a reference to a provision which makes a person liable to a penalty of the prescribed sum within the meaning of this subsection.

(3) Where a penalty for an offence under any enactment relating to an assigned matter is required to be fixed by reference to the value of any goods, that value shall be taken as the price which those goods might reasonably be expected to have fetched, after payment of any duty or tax chargeable thereon, if they had been sold in the open market at or about the date of the commission of the offence for which the penalty is imposed.

(4) Where an offence under any enactment relating to an assigned matter which has been committed by a body corporate is proved to have been committed with the consent or connivance of, or to be attributable to any neglect on the part of any director, manager, secretary or other similar officer of the body corporate or any person purporting to act in any such capacity, he as well as the body corporate shall be guilty of that offence and shall be liable to be proceeded against and punished accordingly.

In this subsection "director," in relation to any body corporate established by or under any enactment for the purpose of carrying on under national ownership any industry or part of an industry or undertaking, being a body corporate whose affairs are managed by the members thereof, means a member of that body corporate.

(4A) Subsection (4) shall not apply to an offence which relates to a matter listed in Schedule 1 to the *Commissioners for Revenue and Customs Act* 2005 (former Inland Revenue matters).

(5) Where in any proceedings for an offence under the customs and excise Acts any question arises as to the duty or the rate thereof chargeable on any imported goods, and it is not possible to ascertain the relevant time specified in section 43 above or the relevant excise duty point, that duty or rate shall be determined as if the goods had been imported without entry at the time when the proceedings were commenced or, as the case may be, as if the time when the proceedings were commenced was the relevant excise duty point.

[This section is printed as amended and repealed in part by the *MCA* 1980, s.154 and Sched. 7, para. 178; the *Finance Act* 1984, s.9 and Sched. 5, para. 3; the *Fines and Penalties (Northern Ireland) Order* 1984 (S.I. 1984 No. 703), art. 19(1); the *Statute Law (Repeals) Act* 1986; the *Finance (No. 2) Act* 1992, s.3, Sched. 2, para. 9; the *Statute Law (Repeals) Act* 1993; and the *Commissioners for Revenue and Customs Act* 2005, s.50(6), and Sched. 4, paras 20 and 28.]

For section 32 of the *MCA* 1980, see *ante*, § 1–75aa.

As to the value of goods "in the open market", when the goods in question cannot be lawfully sold, see *Byrne v. Low* [1972] Crim.L.R. 551, DC.

Authorities

25–481 In *R. v. Czyzewski* [2004] 1 Cr.App.R.(S.) 49, it was held that the guidelines issued in respect of professional smuggling in *R. v. Dosanjh* [1999] 1 Cr.App.R. 371, CA, needed modification in the light of the suggestions of the Sentencing Advisory Panel. In assessing seriousness, the principal factors to be taken into account are the level of duty evaded, the complexity and sophistication of the organisation involved, the defendant's function within the organisation and the amount of personal profit; matters of aggravation (beyond what is implicit in the foregoing) were repeated importations (particularly after a warning), using a legitimate business front, abuse of a privileged position, using children or vulnerable adults, threatening violence to any law enforcement officer, dealing in goods with additional health risk of contamination, and disposal of goods to under-age purchasers. Appropriate starting points on conviction of a person with no relevant previous convictions would be a moderate fine, or, where there was strong personal mitigation, a conditional discharge where the duty evaded was less than £1,000; where the duty was up to £10,000, in the case of a first-time offender or an offender at a low level in an organisation or persistently as an individual, a community sentence, or higher level fine; for cases involving up to £100,000 where the defendant operated individually or at a low level in an organisation, up to nine months' custody; where the duty evaded exceeded £100,000, the custodial sentence would be determined by the degree of professionalism and the presence or absence of aggravating factors; for cases up to £500,000, the range would be nine months' to three years'; for cases up to £1m, up to five years'; and in excess of that amount, up to seven years'; it was to be stressed that the foregoing were guidelines not a straitjacket; and sentencers should also remember their powers of confiscation, compensation, and deprivation, and that the licensing authority should be notified where licensed premises had been used for the sale of smuggled goods. As to sentencing in cases involving a loss to the revenue of many millions of pounds, and charged as a cheat on the public revenue, see *ante*, § 25–385b.

In *R. v. Towers* [1999] 2 Cr.App.R.(S.) 110, CA, it was said that the original guidelines in *Dosanjh* could be applied to "diversion frauds" (see *ante*, § 25–478b), sentences for which should properly include a deterrent element. For those guidelines, see the previous edition of this work. It remains to be seen whether the Court of Appeal will decide that some downward adjustment should be made so as to correspond to the adjustment in relation to smuggling offences.

As to sentencing guidelines in cases involving the unlawful importation of controlled drugs, see *post*, §§ 27–107 *et seq.*

Customs and Excise Management Act 1979, Sched. 1

SCHEDULE 1

CONTROLLED DRUGS: VARIATION OF PUNISHMENTS FOR CERTAIN OFFENCES UNDER THIS ACT

1. Sections 50(4), 68(3) and 170(3) of this Act shall have effect in a case where the goods in respect of which the offence referred to in that subsection was committed were a Class A drug or a Class B drug as if for the words from "shall be liable" onwards there were substituted the following words, that is to say— **25–482**

"shall be liable—

(a) on summary conviction, to a penalty of the prescribed sum or of three times the value of the goods, whichever is the greater, or to imprisonment for a term not exceeding *6* [12] months, or to both;

(b) on conviction on indictment—

(i) where the goods were a Class A drug, to a penalty of any amount, or to imprisonment for life or to both; and

(ii) where they were a Class B drug, to a penalty of any amount, or to imprisonment for a term not exceeding 14 years, or to both".

2. Sections 50(4), 68(3) and 170(3) of this Act shall have effect in a case where the goods in respect of which the offence referred to in that subsection was committed were a Class C drug as if for the words from "shall be liable" onwards there were substituted the following words, that is to say—

"shall be liable—

(a) on summary conviction in Great Britain, to a penalty of three times the value of the goods or level 5 on the standard scale, whichever is the greater, or to imprisonment for a term not exceeding *3* [12] months, or to both;

(b) on summary conviction in Northern Ireland, to a penalty of three times the value of the goods or level 3 on the standard scale, whichever is the greater, or to imprisonment for a term not exceeding 6 months, or to both;

(c) on conviction on indictment, to a penalty of any amount, or to imprisonment for a term not exceeding 14 years, or to both".

3. In this Schedule "Class A drug", "Class B drug" and "Class C drug" have the same meanings as in the *Misuse of Drugs Act* 1971.

[This Schedule is printed as amended by the *Controlled Drugs (Penalties) Act* 1985, s.1(2); and the *CJA* 2003, s.284(1), and Sched. 28, para. 2 (substituting "14" for "5" in para. (c)). The references to levels on the standard scale are substituted by virtue of the *CJA* 1982, s.46. The amendment made by the 2003 Act took effect on January 29, 2004 (*Criminal Justice Act 2003 (Commencement No. 2 and Saving Provisions) Order* 2004 (S.I. 2004 No. 81)), but the increase has no effect in relation to an offence committed before that date (s.284(2)). In the substituted provisions set out in paras 1 and 2,

"12" is substituted for "6" and "3" respectively, as from a day to be appointed, by the *CJA* 2003, s.282(2) and (3). The increase has no application to offences committed before the substitution takes effect: s.282(4).]

As to "the prescribed sum", see the *MCA* 1980, s.32, *ante*, §§ 1–75aa *et seq.*

For section 50, see *ante*, § 25–409; for section 68, see *ante*, § 25–414; and for section 170, see *ante*, § 25–452.

(15) Qualification to certain powers under the 1979 Act

Finance (No. 2) Act 1992, s.4

Enforcement powers

25–483 **4.**—(1) Except in a case falling within subsection (2) below, the powers to which this section applies shall not be exercisable in relation to any person or thing entering or leaving the United Kingdom so as to prevent, restrict or delay the movement of that person or thing between different member States.

(2) The cases in which a power to which this section applies may be exercised as mentioned in subsection (1) above are those where it appears to the person on whom the power is conferred that there are reasonable grounds for believing that the movement in question is not in fact between different member States or that it is necessary to exercise the power for purposes connected with—

(a) securing the collection of any Community customs duty or giving effect to any Community legislation relating to any such duty;

(b) the enforcement of any prohibition or restriction for the time being in force by virtue of any Community legislation with respect to the movement of goods into or out of the member States; or

(c) the enforcement of any prohibition or restriction for the time being in force by virtue of any enactment with respect to the importation or exportation of goods into or out of the United Kingdom.

(3) Subject to subsection (4) below, this section applies to any power which is conferred on the Commissioners for Her Majesty's Revenue and Customs or any officer or constable under any of the following provisions of the *Customs and Excise Management Act* 1979, that is to say—

(a) section 21 (control of movement of aircraft into and out of the United Kingdom);

(b) section 26 (power to regulate movement by land into and out of Northern Ireland);

(c) section 27 (officers' powers of boarding);

(d) section 28 (officers' powers of access);

(e) section 29 (officers' powers to detain ships);

(f) section 34 (power to prevent flight of aircraft);

(g) section 78 (questions as to baggage of person entering or leaving the United Kingdom);

(h) section 164 (powers of search).

(4) [*Treasury power by statutory instrument to add to list in subs. (3).*]

(5) In this section—

"Community customs duty" includes any agricultural levy of the Economic Community; and

"the customs and excise Acts" and "goods" have the same meaning as in the *Customs and Excise Management Act* 1979;

and for the purposes of this section a power shall be taken to be exercised otherwise than in relation to a person or thing entering or leaving the United Kingdom in any case where the power is exercisable irrespective of whether the person or thing in question is entering or leaving the United Kingdom.

(6) This section shall come into force on January 1, 1993.

[This section is printed as amended by the *Commissioners for Revenue and Customs Act* 2005, s.50(1).]

By this provision the Revenue and Customs will not be entitled to use their powers listed in subsection (3) so as to prevent, restrict or delay the movement of goods or persons between the different Member States of the European Community. This is subject to reasonable exercise of powers to enforce Community rules or restrictions on importation into or exportation from the United Kingdom.

C. CRIMINAL JUSTICE (INTERNATIONAL CO-OPERATION) ACT 1990

(1) Introduction

The purpose of the Act was to enable the United Kingdom to co-operate with other countries in investigations and criminal proceedings, to implement the 1988 Vienna Convention against Illicit Traffic in Narcotic Drugs and Psychotropic Substances and to provide for the seizure, detention and forfeiture of drug trafficking money imported or exported in cash. Some of the provisions of the Act were repealed by, and re-enacted in, the *DTA* 1994, itself since repealed and replaced by the *PCA* 2002. **25–484**

(2) Manufacture and supply of scheduled substances

Criminal Justice (International Co-operation) Act 1990, s.12

Manufacture and supply of scheduled substances

12.—(1) It is an offence for a person— **25–485**

(a) to manufacture a scheduled substance; or

(b) to supply such a substance to another person,

knowing or suspecting that the substance is to be used in or for the unlawful production of a controlled drug.

(1A) A person does not commit an offence under subsection (1) above if he manufactures or, as the case may be, supplies the scheduled substance with the express consent of a constable.

(2) A person guilty of an offence under subsection (1) above is liable—

(a) on summary conviction, to imprisonment for a term not exceeding *six* [12] months or a fine not exceeding the statutory maximum or both;

(b) on conviction on indictment, to imprisonment for a term not exceeding fourteen years or a fine or both.

(3) In this section "a controlled drug" has the same meaning as in the *Misuse of Drugs Act* 1971 and "unlawful production of a controlled drug" means the production of such a drug which is unlawful by virtue of section 4(1)(a) of that Act.

(4) In this section and elsewhere in this Part of this Act "a scheduled substance" means a substance for the time being specified in Schedule 2 to this Act.

(5) [*Power to amend Schedule 2 by Order in Council.*]

[Subs. (1A) was inserted by the *Criminal Justice (International Co-operation) (Amendment) Act* 1998, s.1. In subs. (2)(a), "12" is substituted for "six", as from a day to be appointed, by the *CJA* 2003, s.282(2) and (3). The increase has no application to offences committed before the substitution takes effect: s.282(4).]

Sections 12 and 13 of the Act operate to regulate and control the manufacture, transportation and distribution of specified substances so as to prevent their diversion for the unlawful production of a controlled drug (see Arts 3, 12 and 13 of the Vienna Convention 1988).

The substances are particularised in Schedule 2 to the Act (*post*, § 25–492), and appear in one of two separate groups. Table I lists "precursors" (*e.g.* lysergic acid), essential chemicals used in the creation of certain controlled drugs (*e.g.* LSD). Table II specifies other chemicals which may be widely used in industry (*e.g.* acetone) but which are also used as re-agents or solvents in the process of manufacture of a drug.

Nothing in section 12 or 13 is intended to undermine the successful voluntary system of passing information to law enforcement agencies by manufacturers and distributors of such chemicals.

Regarding section 12(1A), see also Home Office Circular 33/1998, set out in full at 162 J.P.N. 769.

"To manufacture"

The term "manufacture" in subsection (1)(a) is to be contrasted with the broader term "production" as it appears in subsection (1). By subsection (3) "production" is to be **25–486** equated with the meaning employed in the *Misuse of Drugs Act* 1971 (see s.37(1) of that Act, *post*, § 27–127). To cultivate a drug is probably not a process of manufacture: *R. v. Goodchild (No. 2)*, 65 Cr.App.R. 165, CA.

"To supply"

25–487 This term is not defined by the Act, either by reference to the *Misuse of Drugs Act* 1971 or otherwise. However, it would be illogical to depart from the construction of "supply" and "supplying" as they appear in the *Misuse of Drugs Act* 1971 and as interpreted in section 37(1) of that Act. Accordingly, an act of "supply" includes "distribution" and need not be for a valuable consideration. As to the meaning of "supply" in the 1971 Act, see *post*, § 27–45; for section 37(1) thereof, see *post*, § 27–127.

"A person"

25–488 For liability of bodies corporate and officers of the company, see section 21 of the *Misuse of Drugs Act* 1971, *post*, § 27–100.

Sentence

25–489 See section 12(2), *ante*. Offences under section 12 are "lifestyle offences" within the *PCA* 2002, Sched. 2, para. 1 (*ante*, § 5–653), in respect of which a financial reporting order may be made under the *SOCPA* 2005, s.76 (*ante*, § 5–886a). The forfeiture provisions in section 27 of the *Misuse of Drugs Act* 1971 (*post*, § 27–118) also apply by virtue of the offence being a lifestyle offence within the 2002 Act.

Powers to search and obtain evidence under section 23 of the *Misuse of Drugs Act* 1971 (but not s.23(3)(a)) apply to an offence under section 12 (see s.23(3A) of the 1971 Act, *post*, § 27–103).

Criminal Justice (International Co-operation) Act 1990, s.13

Regulations about scheduled substances

25–490 **13.**—(1) The Secretary of State may by regulations make provision—

(a) imposing requirements as to the documentation of transactions involving scheduled substances;

(b) requiring the keeping of records and the furnishing of information with respect to such substances;

(c) for the inspection of records kept pursuant to the regulations;

(d) for the labelling of consignments of scheduled substances.

(2) Regulations made by virtue of subsection (1)(b) may, in particular, require—

(a) the notification of the proposed exportation of substances specified in Table I in Schedule 2 to this Act to such countries as may be specified in the regulations; and

(b) the production, in such circumstances as may be so specified, of evidence that the required notification has been given;

and for the purposes of section 68 of the *Customs and Excise Management Act* 1979 (offences relating to exportation of prohibited or restricted goods) any such substance shall be deemed to be exported contrary to a restriction for the time being in force with respect to it under this Act if it is exported without the requisite notification having been given.

(3) Regulations under this section may make different provision in relation to the substances specified in Table I and Table II in Schedule 2 to this Act respectively and in relation to different cases or circumstances.

(4) [*Procedure for making regulations.*]

(5) Any person who fails to comply with any requirement imposed by the regulations or, in purported compliance with any such requirement, furnishes information which he knows to be false in a material particular or recklessly furnishes information which is false in a material particular is guilty of an offence and liable—

(a) on summary conviction, to imprisonment for a term not exceeding *six* [12] months or a fine not exceeding the statutory maximum or both;

(b) on conviction on indictment, to imprisonment for a term not exceeding two years or a fine or both.

(6) No information obtained pursuant to the regulations shall be disclosed except for the purposes of criminal proceedings or of proceedings under the provisions relating to the confiscation of the proceeds of drug trafficking or corresponding provisions in force in Northern Ireland or of proceedings under Part 2, 3 or 4 of the *Proceeds of Crime Act* 2002.

[This section is printed as amended by the *DTA* 1994, s.65(1), Sched. 1, para. 26; and the *PCA* 2002, s.456 and Sched. 11, para. 21. In subs. (5)(a), "12" is substituted for "six", as from a day to be appointed, by the *CJA* 2003, s.282(2) and (3). The increase has no application to offences committed before the substitution takes effect: s.282(4).]

Section 13 implements Article 16 of the Vienna Convention 1988 for the purpose of assisting law enforcement agencies in gathering intelligence from legitimate chemical operations to detect illicit concerns (see *Hansard*, H.L., Vol. 513, col. 1220 (December 12, 1989)) and to monitor the movement of scheduled substances. **25–491**

Exportation of scheduled substances without proper notification falls within the ambit of section 68 of the *CEMA* 1979 (improper exportations): see *ante*, § 25–416).

Regulation 5(1) of the *Controlled Drugs (Drug Precursors) (Community External Trade) Regulations* 2008 (S.I. 2008 No. 296) provides that the obligations imposed under Articles 3 to 5, 8 and 9 of Council Regulation (EC) No. 111/2005 shall be treated as if they are requirements imposed by regulations made under section 13(1) of the 1990 Act, and as if references in those articles to scheduled substances were references to scheduled substances within the meaning of Part II of that Act; and regulation 5(2) stipulates that where a person is convicted of an offence contrary to section 13(5) as a result of the application of regulation 5(1), subsection (5)(a) shall have effect with the substitution of "3 months" for "six months". **25–492**

Similarly, regulation 6(1) of the *Controlled Drugs (Drug Precursors) (Intra-Community Trade) Regulations* 2008 (S.I. 2008 No. 295) provides that the obligations imposed on operators under Articles 5 (documentation), 7 (labelling) and 8 (notification of the competent authorities) of Council Regulation (EC) 273/2004 (which imposes obligations on operators who possess, or place on the market, drug precursors) shall be treated as if they are requirements imposed on them under section 13(1) of the 1990 Act, and as if references in those articles to scheduled substances were references to scheduled substances within the meaning of Part II of that Act; and regulation 6(2) stipulates that where a person is convicted of an offence contrary to section 13(5) as a result of the application of regulation 6(1), subsection (5)(a) shall have effect with the substitution of "3 months" for "six months".

Criminal Justice (International Co-operation) Act 1990, Sched. 2

Sections 12 and 13 SCHEDULE 2

SUBSTANCES USEFUL FOR MANUFACTURING CONTROLLED DRUGS

TABLE I

25–493

N-Acetylanthranilic Acid	Norephedrine
Ephedrine	1-Phenyl-2-Propanone
Ergometrine	Piperonal
Ergotamine	Pseudoephedrine
Isosafrole	Safrole
Lysergic Acid	
3, 4-Methylene-Dioxyphenyl-2-Propanone	

The salts of the substances listed in this Table whenever the existence of such salts is possible.

TABLE II

Acetic Anhydride	Phenylacetic Acid
Acetone	Piperidine
Anthranilic Acid	Potassium Permanganate
Ethyl Ether	Sulphuric Acid
Methyl Ethyl Ketone (also referred to as 2-Butanone or M.E.K.)	Toluene

The salts of the substances listed in this Table except hydrochloric acid and sulphuric acid whenever the existence of such salts is possible.

[This Schedule is printed as amended by the *Criminal Justice (International Co-operation) Act 1990 (Modification) Order* 1992 (S.I. 1992 No. 2873); and the *Criminal Justice (International Co-operation) Act 1990 (Modification) Order* 2001 (S.I. 2001 No. 3933).]

[The next paragraph is § 25–497.]

(3) Offences at sea

(a) *Offences*

Criminal Justice (International Co-operation) Act 1990, s.18

Offences on British ships

25–497 **18.** Anything which would constitute a drug trafficking offence if done on land in any part of the United Kingdom shall constitute that offence if done on a British ship.

Section 18 is designed to meet the United Kingdom's obligations under Article 17(2) and (3) of the Vienna Convention.

Proceedings under section 18 require the consent of the DPP or the Commissioners of Customs and Excise: s.21(2).

Criminal Justice (International Co-operation) Act 1990, s.19

Ships used for illicit traffic

25–498 **19.**—(1) This section applies to a British ship, a ship registered in a state other than the United Kingdom which is a party to the Vienna Convention (a "Convention state") and a ship not registered in any country or territory.

(2) A person is guilty of an offence if on a ship to which this section applies, wherever it may be, he—

(a) has a controlled drug in his possession; or

(b) is in any way knowingly concerned in the carrying or concealing of a controlled drug on the ship,

knowing or having reasonable grounds to suspect that the drug is intended to be imported or has been exported contrary to section 3(1) of the *Misuse of Drugs Act* 1971 or the law of any state other than the United Kingdom.

(3) A certificate purporting to be issued by or on behalf of the government of any state to the effect that the importation or export of a controlled drug is prohibited by the law of that state shall be evidence, and in Scotland sufficient evidence, of the matters stated.

(4) A person guilty of an offence under this section is liable—

(a) in a case where the controlled drug is a Class A drug—

(i) on summary conviction, to imprisonment for a term not exceeding *six* [12] months or a fine not exceeding the statutory maximum or both;

(ii) on conviction on indictment, to imprisonment for life or a fine or both;

(b) in a case where the controlled drug is a Class B drug—

(i) on summary conviction, to imprisonment for a term not exceeding *six* [12] months or a fine not exceeding the statutory maximum or both;

(ii) on conviction on indictment, to imprisonment for a term not exceeding fourteen years or a fine or both;

(c) in a case where the controlled drug is a Class C drug—

(i) on summary conviction, to imprisonment for a term not exceeding *three* [12] months or a fine not exceeding the statutory maximum or both;

(ii) on conviction on indictment, to imprisonment for a term not exceeding fourteen years or a fine or both.

(5) In this section "a controlled drug" and the references to controlled drugs of a specified Class have the same meaning as in the said Act of 1971; and an offence under this section shall be included in the offences to which section 28 of that Act (defences) applies.

[This section is printed as amended by the *CJA* 2003, s.284(1), and Sched. 28, para. 3 (substitution of "fourteen" for "five" in subs. (4)(c)(ii)). This amendment took effect on January 29, 2004 (*Criminal Justice Act 2003 (Commencement No. 2 and Saving Provisions) Order* 2004 (S.I. 2004 No. 81)), but the increase has no effect in relation to an offence committed before that date (s.284(2)). In subs. (4)(a)(i), (b)(i) and (c)(i), "12" is substituted for "six", "six" and "three" respectively, as from a day to be appointed, by the *CJA* 2003, s.282(2) and (3). The increase has no application to offences committed before the substitutions take effect: s.282(4).]

Article 17(1) of the Vienna Convention 1988 asks Member States for full co-operation to suppress illicit traffic by sea in conformity with the international law of the sea, including requesting the assistance of other Member States to suppress the use of a vessel (Art. 17(2)) by boarding or searching it (Art. 17(4)). **25–499**

Parliament saw no merit in such international assistance unless there were criminal sanctions attached "... to the carriage of the illicit drugs which may be found as a result" (*per* Minister of State, Home Office, *Hansard*, HL, Vol. 514, col. 890, January 20, 1990). Enforcement powers are contained in section 20 and Schedule 3, *post*, §§ 25–500 *et seq.*

For a prosecution under this section, see *R. v. Dean and Bolden* [1998] 2 Cr.App.R. 171, CA.

Offences under this section are subject to the defences available under section 28 of the *Misuse of Drugs Act* 1971: subs. (5), *ante*. For section 28, see *post*, § 27–123.

An offence under this section is specified in the *PCA* 2002, Sched. 2, para. 1 ("lifestyle offences"), and accordingly the forfeiture provisions of section 27 of the *Misuse of Drugs Act* 1971 apply. In addition, a financial reporting order may be made under section 76 of the *SOCPA* 2005 (*ante*, § 5–886a), by virtue of the offence being so specified.

The intended destination of the drugs is irrelevant to sentence. It was inevitable that there would be different consequences according to which jurisdiction defendants found themselves within: *R. v. Wagenaar and Pronk* [1997] 1 Cr.App.R.(S.) 178, CA (dismissing appeals against sentence based on the fact that persons closer to the centre of the organisation received sentences in Holland between one-third and half as long as those of the appellants); and *R. v. Maguire* [1997] 1 Cr.App.R.(S.) 130, CA.

(b) *Enforcement*

Criminal Justice (International Co-operation) Act 1990, s.20, Sched. 3

Enforcement powers

20.—(1) The powers conferred on an enforcement officer by Schedule 3 to this Act shall be exercisable in relation to any ship to which section 18 or 19 above applies for the purpose of detecting and the taking of appropriate action in respect of the offences mentioned in those sections. **25–500**

(2) Those powers shall not be exercised outside the landward limits of the territorial sea of the United Kingdom in relation to a ship registered in a Convention state except with the authority of the Commissioners of Customs and Excise; and they shall not give their authority unless that state has in relation to that ship—

(a) requested the assistance of the United Kingdom for the purpose mentioned in subsection (1) above; or

(b) authorised the United Kingdom to act for that purpose.

(3) In giving their authority pursuant to a request or authorisation from a Convention state the Commissioners of Customs and Excise shall impose such conditions or limitations on the exercise of the powers as may be necessary to give effect to any conditions or limitations imposed by that state.

(4) The Commissioners of Customs and Excise may, either of their own motion or in response to a request from a Convention state, authorise a Convention state to exercise, in relation to a British ship, powers corresponding to those conferred on enforcement officers by Schedule 3 to this Act but subject to such conditions or limitations, if any, as they may impose.

(5) Subsection (4) above is without prejudice to any agreement made, or which may be made, on behalf of the United Kingdom whereby the United Kingdom undertakes not to object to the exercise by any other state in relation to a British ship of powers corresponding to those conferred by that Schedule.

(6) The powers conferred by that Schedule shall not be exercised in the territorial sea of any state other than the United Kingdom without the authority of the Commissioners of Customs and Excise and they shall not give their authority unless that state has consented to the exercise of those powers.

[This section is printed as amended by the *CJA* 1993, s.23(2)(a).]

Section 20

SCHEDULE 3

ENFORCEMENT POWERS IN RESPECT OF SHIPS

Preliminary

25–501 1.—(1) In this Schedule "an enforcement officer" means—

(a) a constable;

(b) an officer commissioned by the Commissioners of Customs and Excise under section 6(3) of the *Customs and Excise Management Act* 1979; and

(c) any other person of a description specified in an order made for the purposes of this Schedule by the Secretary of State.

The *Criminal Justice (International Co-operation) Act 1990 (Enforcement Officers) Order* 1990 (S.I. 1992 No. 77) provides that the following descriptions of persons, in addition to those specified in paragraph 1(a) and (b) shall be enforcement officers under that Schedule—

(a) commissioned officers of any of Her Majesty's ships;

(b) officers of the sea-fishery inspectorate of the Minister of Agriculture, Fisheries and Food; and

(c) officers of the fishery protection service of the Secretary of State for Scotland holding the rank of commander, first officer or second officer.

(2) [*Procedure for making order under sub-para. (1)(c).*]

(3) In this Schedule "the ship" means the ship in relation to which the powers conferred by this Schedule are exercised.

Power to stop, board, divert and detain

25–502 2.—(1) An enforcement officer may stop the ship, board it and, if he thinks it necessary for the exercise of his functions, require it to be taken to a port in the United Kingdom and detain it there.

(2) Where an enforcement officer is exercising his powers with the authority of the Commissioners of Customs and Excise given under section 20(2) of this Act the officer may require the ship to be taken to a port in the Convention state in question or, if that state has so requested, in any other country or territory willing to receive it.

(3) For any of those purposes he may require the master or any member of the crew to take such action as may be necessary.

(4) If an enforcement officer detains a vessel he shall serve on the master a notice in writing stating that it is to be detained until the notice is withdrawn by the service on him of a further notice in writing signed by an enforcement officer.

Power to search and obtain information

3.—(1) An enforcement officer may search the ship, anyone on it and anything on it including its cargo.

(2) An enforcement officer may require any person on the ship to give information concerning himself or anything on the ship.

(3) Without prejudice to the generality of those powers an enforcement officer may—

(a) open any containers;

(b) make tests and take samples of anything on the ship;

(c) require the production of documents, books or records relating to the ship or anything on it;

(d) make photographs or copies of anything whose production he has power to require.

Powers in respect of suspected offence

4. If an enforcement officer has reasonable grounds to suspect that an offence mentioned in section 18 or 19 of this Act has been committed on a ship to which that section applies he may— **25–503**

(a) arrest without warrant anyone whom he has reasonable grounds for suspecting to be guilty of the offence; and

(b) seize and detain anything found on the ship which appears to him to be evidence of the offence.

Assistants

5.—(1) An enforcement officer may take with him, to assist him in exercising his powers—

(a) any other persons; and

(b) any equipment or materials.

(2) A person whom an enforcement officer takes with him to assist him may perform any of the officer's functions but only under the officer's supervision.

Use of reasonable force

6. An enforcement officer may use reasonable force, if necessary, in the performance of his functions.

Evidence of authority

7. An enforcement officer shall, if required, produce evidence of his authority.

Protection of officers

8. An enforcement officer shall not be liable in any civil or criminal proceedings for anything done in the purported performance of his functions under this Schedule if the court is satisfied that the act was done in good faith and that there were reasonable grounds for doing it.

Offences

9.—(1) A person is guilty of an offence if he— **25–504**

(a) intentionally obstructs an enforcement officer in the performance of any of his functions under this Schedule;

(b) fails without reasonable excuse to comply with a requirement made by an enforcement officer in the performance of those functions; or

(c) in purporting to give information required by an officer for the performance of those functions—

(i) makes a statement which he knows to be false in a material particular or recklessly makes a statement which is false in a material particular; or

(ii) intentionally fails to disclose any material particular.

(2) A person guilty of an offence under this paragraph is liable on summary conviction to a fine not exceeding level 5 on the standard scale.

[This Schedule is printed as amended by the *CJA* 1993, s.23(2)(c).]

(c) *Jurisdiction and interpretation*

Criminal Justice (International Co-operation) Act 1990, ss.21, 24

Jurisdiction and prosecutions

21.—(1) Proceedings under this Part of this Act or Schedule 3 in respect of an offence on a ship may be taken, and the offence may for all incidental purposes be treated as having been committed, in any place in the United Kingdom. **25–505**

(2) No such proceedings shall be instituted—

(a) in England or Wales except by or with the consent of the Director of Public Prosecutions or the Director of Revenue and Customs Prosecutions;

(b) [*Northern Ireland*].

(3) Without prejudice to subsection (2) above no proceedings for an offence under section 19 above alleged to have been committed outside the landward limits of the territorial sea of the United Kingdom on a ship registered in a Convention state shall be instituted except in pursuance of the exercise with the authority of the Commissioners for Her Majesty's Revenue and Customs of the powers conferred by Schedule 3 to this Act; and section 3 of the *Territorial Waters Jurisdiction Act* 1878 (consent of Secretary of State for certain prosecutions) shall not apply to those proceedings.

[This section is printed as amended by the *CJA* 1993, s.23(2)(b); and the *Commissioners for Revenue and Customs Act* 2005, s.50(1) and (6), and Sched. 4, para. 41.]

Interpretation of Part II

25–506 **24.**—(1) In this Part of this Act—

"British ship" means a ship registered in the United Kingdom or a colony;

"Convention state" has the meaning given in section 19(1) above;

"scheduled substance" has the meaning given in section 12(4) above;

"ship" includes any vessel used in navigation;

"the territorial sea of the United Kingdom" includes the territorial sea adjacent to any of the Channel Islands, the Isle of Man or any colony;

"the Vienna Convention" means the United Nations Convention against Illicit Traffic in Narcotic Drugs and Psychotropic Substances which was signed in Vienna on 20th December 1988.

(2) Any expression used in this Part of this Act which is also used in the *Drug Trafficking Act* 1994 has the same meaning as in that Act.

(3) [*Scotland.*]

(4) If in any proceedings under this Part of this Act any question arises whether any country or territory is a state or is a party to the Vienna Convention, a certificate issued by or under the authority of the Secretary of State shall be conclusive evidence on that question.

[This section is printed as amended by the *DTA* 1994, s.65(1), Sched. 1, para 28.]

D. VALUE ADDED TAX OFFENCES

(1) Introduction

25–507 The *Value Added Tax* 1994 consolidated the *Value Added Tax Act* 1983 and other enactments relating to value added tax. The offences and penalties most likely to be encountered by the criminal practitioner are to be found in section 72 which replaced section 39 of the 1983 Act. The 1994 Act came into force on September 1, 1994.

[The next paragraph is § 25–509.]

(2) Offences and penalties

Value Added Tax Act 1994, Sched. 13, paras 11–13

SCHEDULE 13

Offences and Penalties

25–509 11. Where an offence for the continuation of which a penalty was provided has been committed under an enactment repealed by this Act, proceedings may be taken under this Act in respect of the continuance of the offence after the commencement of this Act in the same manner as if the offence had been committed under the corresponding provision of this Act.

12. Part IV of this Act, except section 72, shall not apply in relation to any act done or omitted to be done before July 25, 1985, and the following provision of this Schedule shall have effect accordingly.

13.—(1) Section 72 shall have effect in relation to any offence committed or alleged to have been committed at any time ("the relevant time") before the commencement of this Act subject to the following provisions of this paragraph.

(2) Where the relevant time falls between July 25, 1983 and July 26, 1985 (the dates of passing of the 1983 and 1985 Finance Acts respectively), section 72 shall apply—

(a) with the substitution in subsection (1)(b), (3)(ii) and (8)(b) of "2 years" for "7 years";

(b) with the omission of subsections (2) and (4) to (7).

[*NOTE*: there is a drafting error in para. 13(2). The *Finance Act*s of 1983 and 1985 were passed on May 13, 1983 and July 25, 1985. The *Value Added Tax Act* 1983 was passed on July 26, 1983. *Semble*, the sub-para. should read "between July 26, 1983 and July 25, 1985 (the dates of passing of the 1983 Act and the *Finance Act* 1985 respectively)".]

Value Added Tax Act 1994, s.72

Offences

72.—(1) If any person is knowingly concerned in, or in the taking of steps with a view to, the fraudulent evasion of VAT by him or any other person, he shall be liable— **25-510**

(a) on summary conviction, to a penalty of the statutory maximum or of three times the amount of the VAT, whichever is the greater, or to imprisonment for a term not exceeding *6* [12] months or to both; or

(b) on conviction on indictment, to a penalty of any amount or to imprisonment for a term not exceeding 7 years or to both.

(2) Any reference in subsection (1) above or subsection (8) below to the evasion of VAT includes a reference to the obtaining of—

(a) the payment of a VAT credit; or

(b) a refund under section 35, 36 or 40 of this Act or section 22 of the 1983 Act; or

(c) a refund under any regulations made by virtue of section 13(5); or

(d) a repayment under section 39;

and any reference in those subsections to the amount of the VAT shall be construed—

(i) in relation to VAT itself or a VAT credit, as a reference to the aggregate of the amount (if any) falsely claimed by way of credit for input tax and the amount (if any) by which output tax was falsely understated, and

(ii) in relation to a refund or repayment falling within paragraph (b), (c) or (d) above, as a reference to the amount falsely claimed by way of refund or repayment.

(3) If any person— **25-511**

(a) with intent to deceive produces, furnishes or sends for the purposes of this Act or otherwise makes use for those purposes of any document which is false in a material particular; or

(b) in furnishing any information for the purposes of this Act makes any statement which he knows to be false in a material particular or recklessly makes a statement which is false in a material particular,

he shall be liable—

(i) on summary conviction, to a penalty of the statutory maximum or, where subsection (4) or (5) below applies, to the alternative penalty specified in that subsection if it is greater, or to imprisonment for a term not exceeding *6* [12] months or to both; or

(ii) on conviction on indictment, to a penalty of any amount or to imprisonment for a term not exceeding 7 years or to both.

(4) In any case where—

(a) the document referred to in subsection (3)(a) above is a return required under this Act, or

(b) the information referred to in subsection (3)(b) above is contained in or otherwise relevant to such a return;

the alternative penalty referred to in subsection (3)(i) above is a penalty equal to three times the aggregate of the amount (if any) falsely claimed by way of credit for input tax and the amount (if any) by which output tax was falsely understated.

(5) In any case where—

(a) the document referred to in subsection (3)(a) above is a claim for a refund under section 35, 36 or 40 of this Act or section 22 of the 1983 Act, for a refund under any regulations made by virtue of section 13(5) or for a repayment under section 39, or

(b) the information referred to in subsection (3)(b) above is contained in or otherwise relevant to such a claim, the alternative penalty referred to in subsection (3)(i) above is a penalty equal to 3 times the amount falsely claimed.

(6) The reference in subsection (3)(a) above to furnishing, sending or otherwise making use of a document which is false in a material particular, with intent to deceive, includes a reference to furnishing, sending or otherwise making use of such a document, with intent to secure that a machine will respond to the document as if it were a true document.

(7) Any reference in subsection (3)(a) or (6) above to producing, furnishing or sending a document includes a reference to causing a document to be produced, furnished or sent.

25–512 (8) Where a person's conduct during any specified period must have involved the commission by him of one or more offences under the preceding provisions of this section, then, whether or not the particulars of that offence or those offences are known, he shall, by virtue of this subsection, be guilty of an offence and liable—

(a) on summary conviction, to a penalty of the statutory maximum or, if greater, 3 times the amount of any VAT that was or was intended to be evaded by his conduct, or to imprisonment for a term not exceeding *6* [12] months or to both, or

(b) on conviction on indictment to a penalty of any amount or to imprisonment for a term not exceeding 7 years or to both.

(9) Where an authorised person has reasonable grounds for suspecting that an offence has been committed under the preceding provisions of this section, he may arrest anyone whom he has reasonable grounds for suspecting to be guilty of the offence.

(10) [*Summary offence: dealing, etc., with goods or services the VAT on which has been evaded.*]

(11) [*Summary offence: supplying goods or services in contravention of Sched. 11, para. 4(2).*]

(12) Subject to subsection (13) below, sections 145 to 155 of the *Management Act* (proceedings for offences, mitigation of penalties and certain other matters) shall apply in relation to offences under this Act (which include any act or omission in respect of which a penalty is imposed) and penalties imposed under this Act as they apply in relation to offences and penalties under the customs and excise Acts as defined in that Act; and accordingly in section 154(2) as it applies by virtue of this subsection the reference to duty shall be construed as a reference to VAT.

(13) In subsection (12) above the references to penalties do not include references to penalties under sections 60 to 70.

[In subss. (1)(a), (3)(i) and (8)(a), "12" is substituted for "six", as from a day to be appointed, by the *CJA* 2003, s.282(2) and (3). The increases have no application to offences committed before the substitutions take effect: s.282(4).]

25–513 The "*Management Act*" referred to in subsection (12) is the *CEMA* 1979: s.96. For sections 145 to 155 of the 1979 Act (except s.151), see *ante* §§ 25–427 *et seq.*

The offences created by section 72 are triable either way. In *R. v. Northamptonshire Magistrates' Court, ex p. Customs and Excise Commrs* [1994] Crim.L.R. 598, DC, the magistrates' decision to try summarily a case of fraudulent evasion contrary to section 39(1) of the 1983 Act where the amount of tax involved was £193,000 was held to be unreasonable.

Supplies of goods are subject to VAT unless they are subject to a total ban. The supply of counterfeit perfume is a taxable supply since its ban is not total in the sense that it would not be unlawful or subject to peremptory seizure in the hands of the final consumer and the user of it does not commit a criminal offence: *R. v. Goodwin and Unstead* [1997] S.T.C. 22, CA; *R. v. Goodwin* [1998] Q.B. 883, ECJ. See also *R. v. Citrone* [1999] S.T.C. 29, CA, in which it was held that the unlawful supply of anabolic steroids in contravention of the *Medicines Act* 1968 was chargeable to VAT; *Fisher v. Finanzamt Donaueschingen* [1998] Q.B. 883, ECJ; and *Staatssecrataris van Financiën v. Coffeshop "Siberië" vof* [1999] S.T.C. 742, ECJ.

A trader is entitled to credit for input VAT in respect of a transaction, not itself vitiated by fraud, which forms part of the chain of supply of a VAT "carousel fraud" in which another prior or subsequent transaction is fraudulent, provided that he has no knowledge of, nor means of knowledge of, the fraudulent nature of the other transaction; his transaction is a "supply of goods or services effected by a taxable person acting as such" and an "economic activity" for the purposes of Sixth Council Directive 77/388/

EEC where it fulfils the objective criteria on which the definitions of those terms are based, regardless of the intentions of a party to another transaction in the chain of which he had no knowledge and no means of knowledge: *Optigen Ltd v. Customs and Excise Commrs* [2006] Ch. 218, ECJ (rejecting the Commissioners' argument that, being devoid of economic substance, the entire chain of supply was outside the VAT regime). It followed that allegations of "carousel fraud" may properly be charged by reference to section 72 of the 1994 Act.

In *R. v. Hashash* [2008] S.T.C. 1158, CA, it was held that on the proper construction of Directive 77/388/EEC (*ante*), a transaction forming part of a "carousel fraud" is liable to VAT even where the trader is involved in the fraud, and though the goods the subject of the purported transaction may never have existed in fact; what matters is the objective character of the transaction (*Optigen Ltd v. Customs and Excise Commrs*, *ante*), as opposed to the intention with which it is carried out; where, therefore, there were invoices and delivery notes evidencing the sale and transfer of goods which were capable of being traded legitimately (computer parts (unlike the case of illicit drugs or counterfeit currency, in which there is no legitimate market)), and where money transfers had taken place as part of these transactions, on an objective appraisal, the transactions constituted supplies of goods by a taxable person acting as such, and economic activities within the meaning of the Directive, and were therefore subject to VAT; accordingly, an allegation of evasion of VAT was appropriate.

As to the compatibility of U.K. legislation with European Community legislation in the context of fraudulent evasion of VAT in respect of gaming machines, see *R. v. Ryan* [1994] S.T.C. 446, CA.

"evasion" and "knowingly concerned"

"Evasion" means a deliberate non-payment when payment is due. There is no need for the Crown to prove in addition an intention permanently to deprive: *R. v. Dealy* [1995] 2 Cr.App.R. 398, CA. **25–514**

For the offence of being "knowingly concerned in ... the fraudulent evasion of tax" (in cases where it is alleged that payment was due), the prosecution must prove that tax was in fact owing for the relevant period: see *R. v. Noble*, *Daily Telegraph*, June 10, 1988, CA.

"taking steps with a view to"

The words "taking steps with a view to" are clearly wider than the phrase being "knowingly concerned in" the fraudulent evasion of tax, and thus embrace conduct which could otherwise be described as being merely preparatory to the fraudulent evasion. Although, on a literal reading, the words "taking steps" suggest that omissions are excluded, this is not the law: *R. v. McCarthy* [1981] S.T.C. 298, CA. The appellant failed to register in circumstances where his taxable supplies exceeded the prescribed limit. **25–515**

Indictment for offences under section 72(1)

COUNT 1

STATEMENT OF OFFENCE

Being knowingly concerned in the fraudulent evasion of tax, contrary to section 72(1) of the Value Added Tax Act *1994*. **25–516**

PARTICULARS OF OFFENCE

A B, on or about the —— day of —— 20—, was knowingly concerned in the fraudulent evasion of Value Added Tax in respect of tax due from the said A B for the period from the —— day of —— 20— to the —— day of —— 20—.

COUNT 2

STATEMENT OF OFFENCE

Taking steps with a view to the fraudulent evasion of tax, contrary to section 72(1) of the Value Added Tax Act *1994*

PARTICULARS OF OFFENCE

A B, on or about the —— day of —— 20—, took steps with a view to the fraudulent evasion of Value Added Tax in respect of tax due from the said A B for the period from the —— day of —— 20— to the —— day of —— 20—, in that he [set out particulars] ...

Indictment for an offence under section 72(3)

STATEMENT OF OFFENCE

25–517 *Furnishing a false document, contrary to section 72(3)(a) of the* Value Added Tax Act *1994*

PARTICULARS OF OFFENCE

A B, on or about the —— day of —— 20—, with intent to deceive, furnished a Value Added Tax Return which was false in a material particular in that it stated that [particulars] ...

Where the statement of offence alleges conduct involving the commission of offences under what is now section 72(1) and (3) of the 1994 Act, contrary to section 72(8), and the particulars of offence specify numerous acts which fall within the ambit of both subsections (1) and (3), the indictment is not bad for duplicity: *R. v. Asif*, 82 Cr.App.R. 123, CA. If the facts permit, and the information is available, it is desirable to frame the indictment by giving the factual particulars that are relied on, which will constitute offences under section 72(1) and (3), thus avoiding the necessity of resorting to section 72(8): *R. v. Choudhury* [1996] 2 Cr.App.R. 484, CA.

A count charging an offence under section 72(8) in respect of two different aspects of the duty to account for VAT, one in relation to the understatement of output tax and the other relating to false claims in respect of input tax, was defective in so far as it did not properly allow the jury to determine whether the accused, if guilty at all, was guilty of one or both of the distinct allegations of fraudulent evasion: *R. v. Stanley*, *The Times*, December 8, 1998, CA.

When drafting a count for an offence contrary to section 72(8), the Court of Appeal has emphasised the importance of spelling out the necessary *mens rea* in the particular offence: *R. v. Ike* [1996] Crim.L.R. 515.

In serious and unusual cases of VAT fraud, the common law offence of cheating the public revenue may properly be charged notwithstanding the existence of the statutory offence of fraudulently evading the payment of VAT: *R. v. Mavji*, 84 Cr.App.R. 34, CA, and see *ante*, §§ 25–385a *et seq.*

Sentence

25–518 For sentencing in VAT frauds, see CSP, B9–2.3D.

In *R. v. Quigley* (2002) 146 S.J. (LB 229), CA, it was said that there is a significant difference between a case of evasion of excise duty by smuggling goods into the country, the only purpose of which is to make a dishonest profit, and the non-payment of VAT where the defendant's purpose is to keep afloat, albeit in a fraudulent way, a company that had previously traded honestly. The guidelines relating to the former (*ante*, § 25–481) do not apply to the latter type of case.

A financial reporting order may be made in respect of a person convicted of an offence under section 72: *SOCPA* 2005, s.76 (*ante*, § 5–886a).

(3) Enforcement

25–519 Schedule 11 to the 1994 Act (as amended by the *Commissioners for Revenue and Customs Act* 2005, s.50(6) and Sched. 4, para. 56) provides for administration, collection and enforcement of VAT. Under paragraph 10, Revenue and Customs are entitled to enter premises used in connection with the carrying on of a business and, with a warrant obtained on the basis that there is reasonable ground for suspecting that a serious fraud offence is being, has been, or is about to be committed, search them or persons found on the premises and seize material (see *R. (Paul da Costa and Co. (a firm)) v.*

Thames Magistrates' Court [2002] S.T.C. 267, DC). As to the seizure of material that might be the subject of a claim to legal privilege, see *R. v. Customs and Excise Commrs, ex p. Popely* [1999] S.T.C. 1016, DC, and *ante*, §§ 15–73, and 15–90 *et seq*. As to paragraph 10(5) and restrictions placed by the issuer of the warrant on the manner in which the powers conferred by it could be exercised (and for guidance on the use of paragraphs 7 and 11, *post*), see *Singh v. H.M. Advocate* [2001] S.T.C. 790, High Court of Justiciary. An argument that paragraph 10 is incompatible with European Council Directive 77/388 because it does not provide sufficient safeguards against the power to issue search warrants failed in *R. v. Customs and Excise Commrs, ex p. X Ltd*, *The Times*, June 12, 1997, DC.

Under paragraph 11, Revenue and Customs may obtain an order from a justice of the peace for the production of information, giving access to it and enabling it to be taken away. The use of this power has been criticised and the order set aside where the order was too wide: *R. v. Epsom JJ., ex p. Bell* [1989] S.T.C. 169, DC. Applications under paragraph 11 should normally be made *inter partes* unless there is real reason to believe that an application on notice might result in the loss of material valuable to the investigation. In such cases paragraph 11 enables an application to be made *ex parte*: *R. v. City of London Magistrates' Court, ex p. Asif* [1996] Crim.L.R. 725, DC. As to costs in respect of such an application, see *H.M. Commrs for Customs and Excise v. City of London Magistrates' Court* [2000] 2 Cr.App.R. 348, DC. See also *R. v. City of London Magistrates' Court, ex p. Peters* [1997] S.T.C. 141, DC. Paragraphs 12 and 13 provide for the procedure regarding the obtaining of a record and copies of what has been removed by the person from whom the material was removed.

Chapter 26

MONEY LAUNDERING OFFENCES

I. PROCEEDS OF CRIME ACT 2002

A. Introduction

(1) Background and sources

The explanatory notes to the *PCA* 2002 define "money laundering" as "the process by which the proceeds of crime are converted into assets which appear to have a legitimate origin, so that they can be retained permanently or recycled into further criminal enterprises". Money laundering was first criminalised in the United Kingdom in relation to the proceeds of drug trafficking (*DTOA* 1986). Further drug money laundering offences were subsequently created (*DTA* 1994), together with separate offences relating to the proceeds of other criminal conduct (*CJA* 1988) and terrorist funds (*Prevention of Terrorism (Temporary Provisions) Act* 1989). **26–1**

Part 7 (ss.327–340) of the 2002 Act (as amended by the *SOCPA* 2005) updates and reforms the money laundering provisions of the *DTA* 1994 and the *CJA* 1988. The money laundering provisions in the *Terrorism Act* 2000 (replacing the 1989 Act), *ante*, §§ 25–67 *et seq.*, are unaffected. The legislation designed to combat money laundering can be divided into three parts. First, the three principal money laundering offences in sections 327 to 329 of the 2002 Act criminalise money laundering and provide for sentences of up to 14 years' imprisonment. Secondly, there are provisions that are intended to encourage reporting of known or suspected money laundering and to discourage "tipping off" (principally ss.330–332 and 333A of the 2002 Act). Thirdly, the *Money Laundering Regulations* 2007 (S.I. 2007 No. 2157) (*post*, § 26–33) require the financial, accountancy, legal and other sectors to put in place systems to prevent the use of their services for money laundering or terrorist financing.

Guidance Notes on Money Laundering have been produced and issued since 1990 to regulated institutions by the financial services industry's Joint Money Laundering Steering Group ("JMLSG"), made up of leading United Kingdom trade associations in the financial services industry (www.jmlsg.org.uk). Guidance has also been produced by other bodies including the Law Society (www.lawsociety.org.uk), the Bar Council (www.barcouncil.org.uk), and the Institute of Chartered Accountants (www.icaew.co.uk). Such guidance may be regarded as relevant to all cases involving money laundering. Section 330(8) of the 2002 Act (*post*, § 26–14) and regulation 45(2) of the 2007 regulations (*post*, § 26–37) provide that it is mandatory to take such guidance into account where it has received Treasury approval and other conditions are met. The JMLSG guidance is the only guidance to have received such approval so far (*post*, § 26–34). As to money laundering and the legal profession, see *Bowman v. Fels* [2005] 2 Cr.App.R. 19, CA (Civ. Div.) (*post*, § 26–12).

The Financial Services Authority ("FSA") also produces a handbook of rules and guidance for the financial services sector (www.fsa.gov.uk). The FSA requires that all regulated firms must appoint a money laundering reporting officer ("MLRO"). The FSA and the JMLSG provide guidance as to the role of such officer, internal reporting of suspicious transactions, training for staff, compliance monitoring, record keeping, etc.

See also Sweet and Maxwell's *Anti-Money Laundering Guide* for information on the relevant law and practice and the latest available information and guidance on how money laundering is dealt with in key financial jurisdictions around the world.

(2) Commencement, transitional and saving provisions

Proceeds of Crime Act 2002 (Commencement No. 4, Transitional Provisions and Savings) Order 2003 (S.I. 2003 No. 120), arts 1–6

Citation and interpretation

26–2 **1.**—(1) [*Citation.*]

(2) In this Order—

(a) "the Act" means the *Proceeds of Crime Act* 2002;

(b) "the new failure to disclose offences" means sections 330, 331 and 332 of the Act;

(c) "the old failure to disclose offences" means—

(i) section 52 of the *Drug Trafficking Act* 1994;

(ii), (iii) [*Scotland and Northern Ireland*].

(d) "the new principal money laundering offences" means sections 327, 328 and 329 of the Act;

(e) "the old principal money laundering offences" means—

(i) sections 93A, 93B and 93C of the *Criminal Justice Act* 1988;

(ii) section 14 of the *Criminal Justice (International Co-operation) Act* 1990;

(iii) sections 49, 50 and 51 of the *Drug Trafficking Act* 1994;

(iv), (v) [*Scotland and Northern Ireland*].

Commencement of provisions

26–3 **2.**—(1) The provisions of the Act listed in column 1 of the Schedule to this Order shall come into force on 24th February 2003, subject to the transitional provisions and savings contained in this Order.

(2) But where a particular purpose is specified in relation to any such provision in column 2 of that Schedule, the provision concerned shall come into force only for that purpose.

[The listed provisions include the whole of Parts 7 (ss.327–340) and 8 (ss.341–416), together with Schedule 9.]

Transitional provisions and savings for the principal money laundering offences

26–4 **3.** The new principal money laundering offences shall not have effect where the conduct constituting an offence under those provisions began before 24th February 2003 and ended on or after that date and the old principal money laundering offences shall continue to have effect in such circumstances.

[This article is printed as amended by art.14 of the *Proceeds of Crime Act 2002 (Commencement No. 5, Transitional Provisions, Savings and Amendment) Order* 2003 (S.I. 2003 No. 333).]

For recent decisions concerning money laundering under the *CJA* 1988 and the *DTA* 1994, see the supplement.

Transitional provisions and savings for the failure to disclose offences

26–5 **4.** The new failure to disclose offences shall not have effect where the information or other matter on which knowledge or suspicion that another person is engaged in money laundering is based, or which gives reasonable grounds for such knowledge or suspicion, came to a person before 24th February 2003 and the old failure to disclose offences shall continue to have effect in such circumstances.

Transitional provisions and savings for the offences of tipping-off and prejudicing an investigation

26–6 **5.**—(1) Section 342 of the Act shall not have effect where the conduct constituting an offence under that section began before 24th February 2003 and ended on or after that date and the following provisions shall continue to have effect in such circumstances—

(a) sections 93D(1) of the *Criminal Justice Act* 1988;

(b) sections 53(1) and 58 of the *Drug Trafficking Act* 1994;

(c), (d) [*Scotland and Northern Ireland*].

(2) Section 93D(2) and (3) of the *Criminal Justice Act* 1988 shall continue to have effect where the disclosure mentioned in section 93D(2)(a) or 93D(3)(a), as the case may be, of that Act was made before 24th February 2003.

(3) Section 53(2) and (3) of the *Drug Trafficking Act* 1994 shall continue to have effect where the disclosure mentioned in section 53(2)(a) or 53(3)(a), as the case may be, of that Act was made before 24th February 2003.

(4), (5) [*Scotland and Northern Ireland.*]

[This article is printed as amended by art. 14 of S.I. 2003 No. 333 (*ante*).]

Savings in relation to prosecution by the Commissioners for Her Majesty's Revenue and Customs, application of offences to Crown servants and investigations

6. The following provisions shall continue to have effect in respect of offences committed before 24th February 2003 and offences committed by virtue of articles 3 to 5 of this Order— **26–7**

(a) sections 93F to 93J of the *Criminal Justice Act* 1988;

(b) sections 55 to 57 and 59 to 61 of the *Drug Trafficking Act* 1994;

(c), (d) [*Scotland and Northern Ireland*].

B. OFFENCES

(1) Summary

The three principal money laundering offences (ss.327–329) replace the parallel drug and non-drug crime money laundering offences with single offences that do not distinguish between the proceeds of drug trafficking and the proceeds of other crimes. They thereby resolve the problems caused by the dichotomy between the offences created by the *CJA* 1988 and the *DTA* 1994 where the prosecution could prove a conspiracy to launder the proceeds of illicit activity but could not prove whether they were the proceeds of drug trafficking or of other criminal activity (see § 25–520 in the 2003 edition of this work). **26–8**

The offences of failing to disclose possible money laundering (ss.330– 332), relate to those working in the business sector. Section 330 concerns a person who receives information in the course of a business in the regulated sector, as defined in Schedule 9 (*post*, § 26–15), and who thereby knows or suspects or has reasonable grounds for knowing or suspecting that another person is engaged in money laundering, and who fails to disclose to a nominated officer (see ss.338(5), 336(11) and 340(12)), or a person authorised for the purposes of Part 7 by the Director General of the Serious Organised Crime Agency, the information on which his knowledge or suspicion is based. Section 331 penalises a failure by a nominated officer working in the regulated sector, who receives a report under section 330, to disclose that report as soon as practicable where he has the requisite *mens rea* (which is same as that in section 330). Section 332 is in similar terms to section 331 save that it relates to nominated officers both inside and outside the regulated sector who receive reports under section 337 or 338 (a disclosure in relation to one of the principal money laundering offences or a voluntary disclosure). Section 330(2)(b) and section 331(3)(b) introduce a negligence test which means that an offence would be committed where a person has reasonable grounds for knowing or suspecting that another person is engaged in money laundering (as defined in s.340(11)), even if he did not actually have any such knowledge or suspicion. The basis for reporting suspicions that money laundering has occurred, or that funds derive from criminal conduct, is the criminal law of the United Kingdom. There is no duty to consider the law of any other country, but there is a duty to have regard to United Kingdom criminal law regardless of where the conduct in question occurred (see s.340(2) and (11)).

Section 333A creates an offence covering the regulated sector (as defined in Schedule 9), of disclosing to the customer concerned, or to other third persons, the fact that information about known or suspected money laundering has been disclosed or that a money laundering investigation is being, or may be, carried out ("tipping off"). Section

342 creates an offence of prejudicing a confiscation, civil recovery, detained cash or money laundering investigation where the person knows or suspects that there is or is likely to be an investigation. Although section 342 is included in Part 8 (investigations), it is dealt with in this chapter as an important offence-creating provison, which, together with section 333A, replaces section 93D of the *CJA* 1988 and section 53 of the *DTA* 1994.

(2) Mens rea

26–9 The interpretation section (s.340, *post*, § 26–29) is of crucial importance. Each of the principal money laundering offences (ss.327 to 329) requires proof that the conduct concerned "criminal property". Section 340(3) provides that property is criminal property if it constitutes a person's benefit from criminal conduct or it represents such a benefit (in whole or in part and whether directly or indirectly), and the alleged offender knows or suspects that it constitutes such a benefit. "Suspects" is also sufficient *mens rea* to prove the offences in sections 332, 333, 336(5) and 342. As to this, see *ante*, § 17–49a.

Where a conspiracy to commit any of the principal money laundering offences is charged, it is submitted that the effect of the decision of the House of Lords in *R. v. Saik* [2007] 1 A.C. 18 (a decision in relation to a charge of conspiring to contravene section 93C(2) of the *CJA* 1988) is that, by reason of section 1(2) of the *CLA* 1977 (*post*, § 33–3), an intention that the property to be laundered would be "criminal property" is required where the property had not been identified at the time of the agreement; and, where the property had been so identified, knowledge that the property was "criminal property" is required.

Sections 330 and 331 (offences that may only be committed by a person working in the regulated sector) introduce an objective or "negligence" test in that a person may be convicted if there were reasonable grounds for knowing or suspecting that another person was engaged in money laundering.

(3) Limitations to offences

26–10 The legislation replaced by Part 7 contained a series of "defence" provisions. Some of these would provide simply that, "It is a defence to a charge of committing an offence under this section that …" (*DTA* 1994, s.52), whereas others provided that, "In proceedings … under this section, it is a defence to prove that …" (*ibid.*, s.50). These provisions spawned a series of decisions on the nature of the burden on the accused: see *R. v. Butt* [1999] Crim.L.R. 414, CA; *R. v. Colle*, 95 Cr.App.R. 67, CA; and *R. v. Gibson* [2000] Crim.L.R. 479, CA.

It is submitted that neither these authorities, nor those in relation to similar provisions in other enactments, have any relevance to the interpretation of the 2002 legislation. A different drafting technique has been adopted throughout Part 7. The word "defence" does not appear therein. Instead, the draftsman has included a series of limitations on the scope of the various offences. These are contained in subsections beginning with the word "But" (ss.327(2), 328(2), 329(2), 330(6), etc.). It is manifest from the use of the word "But" at the beginning of a subsection that follows immediately upon the subsection that defines the positive aspects of the offence, that the two subsections are intended to be read together, as much as if their contents were in the same subsection, separated only by a comma or semi-colon. They are properly to be regarded as limitations on the ambit of the offences, rather than as "defences". It is submitted that the use of this drafting technique, including the avoidance of the word "defence", was deliberate and was intended to avoid argument as to burden and standard of proof.

Despite the fact that the *Criminal Procedure Rules* 2005 (S.I. 2005 No. 384), r.14.2 (*ante*, § 1–115), do not repeat the former express provision to this effect (see the *Indictment Rules* 1971 (S.I. 1971 No. 1253)), it is submitted that a count charging an offence under any of these provisions need not negative any of the limitations, and the prosecution are under no burden to adduce any evidence for the purposes of rebutting them unless and until an issue in relation to any such limitation is raised by the evidence. Once that is done, whether as a result of cross-examination of prosecution witnesses or evidence adduced by the defence, the onus is on the prosecution to prove the non-application of the limitation to the usual standard. That this is correct was confirmed in *Hogan v. DPP*, *post*, § 26–13.

(4) Legislation

Proceeds of Crime Act 2002, s.327

Concealing etc

327.—(1) A person commits an offence if he— 26–11

(a) conceals criminal property;

(b) disguises criminal property;

(c) converts criminal property;

(d) transfers criminal property;

(e) removes criminal property from England and Wales or from Scotland or from Northern Ireland.

(2) But a person does not commit such an offence if—

(a) he makes an authorised disclosure under section 338 and (if the disclosure is made before he does the act mentioned in subsection (1)) he has the appropriate consent;

(b) he intended to make such a disclosure but had a reasonable excuse for not doing so;

(c) the act he does is done in carrying out a function he has relating to the enforcement of any provision of this Act or of any other enactment relating to criminal conduct or benefit from criminal conduct.

(2A) Nor does a person commit an offence under subsection (1) if—

(a) he knows, or believes on reasonable grounds, that the relevant criminal conduct occurred in a particular country or territory outside the United Kingdom, and

(b) the relevant criminal conduct—

(i) was not, at the time it occurred, unlawful under the criminal law then applying in that country or territory, and

(ii) is not of a description prescribed by an order made by the Secretary of State.

(2B) In subsection (2A) "the relevant criminal conduct" is the criminal conduct by reference to which the property concerned is criminal property.

(2C) A deposit-taking body that does an act mentioned in paragraph (c) or (d) of subsection (1) does not commit an offence under that subsection if—

(a) it does the act in operating an account maintained with it, and

(b) the value of the criminal property concerned is less than the threshold amount determined under section 339A for the act.

(3) Concealing or disguising criminal property includes concealing or disguising its nature, source, location, disposition, movement or ownership or any rights with respect to it.

[This section is printed as amended by the *SOCPA* 2005, ss.102(1) and (2), and 103(1) and (2).]

"Criminal property" is defined in section 340(3) (*post*, § 26–29). As in the case of all the offences concerning "criminal property", the offence is only committed where a person knows or suspects that the property, the subject of the charge, constitutes or represents his own or another's benefit from criminal conduct (s.340(3)(b)). Even under the legislation replaced by the 2002 Act (see *ante*, § 26–1), the prosecution had to prove that the property, the subject of the charge, was in fact the proceeds of criminal conduct or of drug trafficking (see *R. v. Montila* [2005] 1 Cr.App.R. 26, HL), whether or not a substantive offence or a conspiracy was charged (*R. v. Harmer* [2005] 2 Cr.App.R. 2, CA). *A fortiori*, this is the case under the 2002 Act (see the definition of "criminal property", *ante*; and *R. v. Loizou* [2005] 2 Cr.App.R. 37, CA).

"Criminal conduct" is defined in section 340(2) (*post*, § 26–40) as "conduct which (a) constitutes an offence in any part of the United Kingdom, or (b) would constitute an offence in any part of the United Kingdom if it occurred there". The prosecution may prove that property is "criminal property" (a) by showing that it derived from conduct of a specific kind or kinds and that conduct of that kind was unlawful, or (b) by evidence that the circumstances in which the property was handled which were such as to give rise to an irresistible inference that it could only have been derived from crime: *R. v. Anwoir* [2008] 2 Cr.App.R. 36, CA. Such a conclusion, the court said, gave proper effect to *R. (Director of Assets Recovery Agency) v. Green, The Times*, February 27, 2006, QBD (Sullivan J.), and was in line with *R. v. Craig* [2008] 2 *Archbold News* 2, CA; to the extent that *Prosecution Appeal (No. 11 of 2007)*; *R. v. W.* [2008] 3 All E.R. 533, CA, appeared to suggest differently, this could be explained by the fact that in that case the prosecution's evidence was based essentially on the fact that the defendant had no other visible means of support, in contrast to the instant case, where there was clear evidence from which the jury could infer that the money in question came from drugs and/or VAT fraud and where the only innocent explanation for the money (*viz.* that it had emanated from legitimate trading) had evidently been roundly rejected by the jury. As to proving the defendant's involvement in unlawful conduct by reference to the bad character of his associates, see *R. v. Ross* [2008] Crim.L.R. 306, CA; but as to the suggested limitations of this case, see the commentary in *Criminal Law Week* 2008/11/2.

It is likely that section 327(1) will be construed as creating a single offence that can be committed in one of a number of ways (*cf.* the *Theft Act* 1968, s.22(1) (*ante*, §§ 21–271, 21–272)), thus permitting the different methods of commission to be alleged in a single count in the alternative (see *ante*, § 1–137)). This, however, should not be taken to be a licence to allege different methods of commission without discrimination. The prosecution should identify the possible methods of commission and should specify those methods and only those methods.

Where the prosecution case against the defendants was that they had been involved in a course of conduct, *viz.* laundering the proceeds of their own drug dealing over a number of years (by spending ("converting") it in thousands of different transactions, large and small, albeit intermingled with similar transactions representing some legitimate activity), but that it was largely impossible to untangle that activity, a single count charging them generally with converting criminal property between 2003 and 2005 was not bad for duplicity, as it was legitimate for the prosecution to allege a "general deficiency": *R. v. Middleton and Rourke*, unreported, January 31, 2008, CA ([2008] EWCA Crim. 233). As to this, see also *ante*, §§ 1–141, 1–142.

The *Proceeds of Crime Act 2002 (Money Laundering: Exceptions to Overseas Conduct Defence) Order* 2006 (S.I. 2006 No. 1070) prescribes conduct which would constitute an offence punishable with imprisonment for a maximum term in excess of 12 months in any part of the United Kingdom if it occurred there (other than offences contrary to the *Gaming Act* 1968, the *Lotteries and Amusements Act* 1976, or the *FSMA* 2000, ss.23 or 25) for the purposes of sections 327(2A), 328(3) (*post*, § 26–12) and 329(2A) (*post*, § 26–13) of the 2002 Act.

Proceeds of Crime Act 2002, s.328

Arrangements

26–12 **328.**—(1) A person commits an offence if he enters into or becomes concerned in an arrangement which he knows or suspects facilitates (by whatever means) the acquisition, retention, use or control of criminal property by or on behalf of another person.

(2) [*Identical to s.327(2)*, ante, *§ 26–11.*]

(3) [*Identical to s.327(2A)*, ante, *§ 26–11.*]

(4) In subsection (3) "the relevant criminal conduct" is the criminal conduct by reference to which the property concerned is criminal property.

(5) A deposit-taking body that does an act mentioned in subsection (1) does not commit an offence under that subsection if—

(a) it does the act in operating an account maintained with it, and

(b) the arrangement facilitates the acquisition, retention, use or control of criminal property of a value that is less than the threshold amount determined under section 339A for the act.

[This section is printed as amended by the *SOCPA* 2005, ss.102(1) and (3), and 103(1) and (3).]

As to "criminal property", see section 340(3) (*post*, § 26–29). As to subsection (3), see S.I. 2006 No. 1070, *ante*, § 26–11.

In *Bowman v. Fels* [2005] 2 Cr.App.R. 19, CA (Civ. Div.), it was held (i) that section 328 was not intended to cover or affect the ordinary conduct of litigation by legal professionals, which included any step taken in litigation from the issue of proceedings and the securing of injunctive relief or a freezing order up to its final disposal by judgment; Parliament could not have intended that proceedings or steps taken by lawyers in order to determine or secure legal rights and remedies for their clients should involve them in "becoming concerned in an arrangement which ... facilitates the acquisition, retention, use or control of criminal property", even if they suspected that the outcome of such proceedings might have such an effect; (ii) that even if section 328 did apply to the ordinary conduct of legal proceedings, it did not override legal professional privilege, since there was nothing in the language of the provision to suggest that Parliament expressly intended such an effect; it would require much clearer language than was contained in the section and its ancillary sections before a parliamentary intention could be gleaned to override legal professional privilege or to bring about a state of affairs in which a party's solicitor was obliged, in breach of an implied duty to the court to maintain the confidentiality of documents disclosed under compulsory process, and in breach of the duty of confidence owed to his client as his litigation solicitor, to disclose any suspicion he might have that any such documents disclosed by the other party evidenced one of the matters referred to in section 328; (iii) that as to a case where the parties agree to dispose of the whole or any aspect of legal proceedings on a consensual basis, the consensual resolution of issues is an integral part of the conduct of ordinary civil litigation; and (iv) that whilst this means that there is a distinction between consensual steps taken in an ordinary litigious context and consensual arrangements independent of litigation, this is a distinction that is inherent in recitals 17 and 18 to Directive 2001/97/EC of the European Parliament and of the Council (*post*, § 26–33), and in the 2002 Act. The legal profession's published guidance (*ante*, § 26–1) takes account of this decision, which reverses the relevant parts of *P. v. P. (Ancillary relief: Proceeds of crime)* [2004] Fam. 1, Fam D (Dame Elizabeth Butler-Sloss P.). As to the imposition of a duty to disclose facts indicative of money laundering on legal professionals, see also *Ordre des barreaux francophones et germanophones v. Conseil des Ministres (Conseil des barreaux de l'Union europeénne and Ordre des avocats du barreau de Liège, interveners) (Case C-305/05)*, *post*, § 26–14.

Once a bank suspected that a customer's account contained criminal property, it was obliged to report the matter to the relevant authority and not to carry out any transactions in relation to the account; if it did so, and the account held criminal property, it would commit an offence under section 328(1); that remained the position unless and until consent was given or the relevant time limit had expired (*post*, § 26–24); and if the bank told the customer why it had blocked the account it would breach the anti tip-off provisions (see ss.333 and 338 (*post*, §§ 26–21, 26–27)); the purpose of section 328(1) was to put pressure on (*e.g.* banks) to provide information to the relevant authorities to enable the latter to obtain information about possible criminal activity: *Squirrell Ltd v. National Westminster Bank plc (Customs and Excise Commrs intervening)* [2005] 2 All E.R. 784, Ch D (Laddie J.).

Since section 328 makes it an offence for a banker, who knows or suspects that money in a customer's account is criminal property, to proceed to process the customer's cheque into the account of another person without having made an authorised disclosure under section 338 and without having obtained appropriate consent under section 335 (*post*, § 26–24), and since it would be no defence to criminal proceedings that the bank was contractually obliged to obey its customer's instructions, there would be no basis upon which an injunction could be granted by a court during the periods prescribed by section 335 requiring the bank to act for the customer, unless it was shown that there was no basis upon which criminal liability would arise because there was no "suspicion" on the part of the bank; but, as to the practicality of a bank establishing that it had such a suspicion by way of defence to an allegation of breach of contract, the only certain way for it to ensure that it does not commit a tipping-off offence, contrary to section 333, would be for it to avail itself of subsections (2)(c) and (3)(b) of that section, by procuring its professional legal adviser to make the disclosure and then only to a person in connection with legal proceedings; and it would matter not how the disclosure was made because the solicitor could not be cross-examined as he would only be reporting the suspicion of another; and there was no provision under the Act that would enable the person who actually had the suspicion to give evidence in relation thereto; to the extent that there was scope for arbitrary and capricious exercise of power by the relevant public authorities, the remedy available to the customer would be judicial review: *K. Ltd v. National Westminster Bank plc (Revenue and Customs Commrs intervening) (Practice Note)* [2007] 1 W.L.R. 311, CA (Civ. Div.).

Where a bank was suspicious that funds received into a customer's account by way of CHAPS transfer were the proceeds of crime or a money laundering operation, the bank was not entitled to refuse to accept the transfer on the ground that it would commit a money laundering offence if it did; the bank did not commit an offence under section 93A of the *CJA* 1988 by accepting a transfer it was legally obliged to accept; however, the bank had to disclose the nature of its suspicions to the relevant authority: *Tayeb v. HSBC plc* [2004] 4 All E.R. 1024, QBD (Colman J.). It is submitted that the position would be the same under section 328(1) of the 2002 Act.

Proceeds of Crime Act 2002, s.329

Acquisition, use and possession

26–13 **329.**—(1) A person commits an offence if he—

(a) acquires criminal property;

(b) uses criminal property;

(c) has possession of criminal property.

(2) But a person does not commit such an offence if—

(a), (b) [*identical to s.327(2)(a), (b)*, ante, *§ 26–11*];

(c) he acquired or used or had possession of the property for adequate consideration;

(d) [*identical to s.327(2)(c)*, ante, *§ 26–11*].

(2A) [*Identical to s.327(2A)*, ante, *§ 26–11*.]

(2B) [*Identical* to *s.327(2B)*, ante, *§ 26–11*.]

(2C) A deposit-taking body that does an act mentioned in subsection (1) does not commit an offence under that subsection if—

(a) it does the act in operating an account maintained with it, and

(b) the value of the criminal property concerned is less than the threshold amount determined under section 339A for the act.

(3) For the purposes of this section—

(a) a person acquires property for inadequate consideration if the value of the consideration is significantly less than the value of the property;

(b) a person uses or has possession of property for inadequate consideration if the value of the consideration is significantly less than the value of the use or possession;

(c) the provision by a person of goods or services which he knows or suspects may help another to carry out criminal conduct is not consideration.

[This section is printed as amended by the *SOCPA* 2005, ss.102(1) and (4), and 103(1) and (4).]

As to "criminal property", see section 340(3) (*post*, § 26–29). As to subsection (2A), see S.I. 2006 No. 1070, *ante*, § 26–11.

A defendant bears no burden of proof if he seeks to rely on the exception under subsection (2)(c); the only burden is an evidential one, and once the defendant has done enough to raise the issue, the prosecution bear the burden of proving that there had been no consideration or that the consideration was inadequate; to place the legal burden on the defendant would involve too great an intrusion into the presumption of innocence: *Hogan v. DPP* [2007] 1 W.L.R. 2944, DC. As to this, see generally, *ante*, § 26–10.

Proceeds of Crime Act 2002, s.330

Failure to disclose: regulated sector

26–14 **330.**—(1) A person commits an offence if the conditions in subsections (2) to (4) are satisfied.

(2) The first condition is that he—

(a) knows or suspects, or

(b) has reasonable grounds for knowing or suspecting,

that another person is engaged in money laundering.

(3) The second condition is that the information or other matter—

(a) on which his knowledge or suspicion is based, or

(b) which gives reasonable grounds for such knowledge or suspicion,

came to him in the course of a business in the regulated sector.

(3A) The third condition is—

(a) that he can identify the other person mentioned in subsection (2) or the whereabouts of any of the laundered property, or

(b) that he believes, or it is reasonable to expect him to believe, that the information or other matter mentioned in subsection (3) will or may assist in identifying that other person or the whereabouts of any of the laundered property.

(4) The fourth condition is that he does not make the required disclosure to—

(a) a nominated officer, or

(b) a person authorised for the purposes of this Part by the Director General of SOCA,

as soon as is practicable after the information or other matter mentioned in subsection (3) comes to him.

(5) The required disclosure is a disclosure of—

(a) the identity of the other person mentioned in subsection (2), if he knows it,

(b) the whereabouts of the laundered property, so far as he knows it, and

(c) the information or other matter mentioned in subsection (3).

(5A) The laundered property is the property forming the subject-matter of the money laundering that he knows or suspects, or has reasonable grounds for knowing or suspecting, that other person to be engaged in.

(6) But he does not commit an offence under this section if—

(a) he has a reasonable excuse for not making the required disclosure,

(b) he is a professional legal adviser or relevant professional adviser and—

(i) if he knows either of the things mentioned in subsection (5)(a) and (b), he knows the thing because of information or other matter that came to him in privileged circumstances, or

(ii) the information or other matter mentioned in subsection (3) came to him in privileged circumstances, or

(c) subsection (7) or (7B) applies to him.

(7) This subsection applies to a person if—

(a) he does not know or suspect that another person is engaged in money laundering, and

(b) he has not been provided by his employer with such training as is specified by the Secretary of State by order for the purposes of this section.

(7A) Nor does a person commit an offence under this section if—

(a) he knows, or believes on reasonable grounds, that the money laundering is occurring in a particular country or territory outside the United Kingdom, and

(b) the money laundering—

(i) is not unlawful under the criminal law applying in that country or territory, and

(ii) is not of a description prescribed in an order made by the Secretary of State.

(7B) This subsection applies to a person if—

(a) he is employed by, or is in partnership with, a professional legal adviser or a relevant professional adviser to provide the adviser with assistance or support,

(b) the information or other matter mentioned in subsection (3) comes to the person in connection with the provision of such assistance or support, and

(c) the information or other matter came to the adviser in privileged circumstances.

(8) In deciding whether a person committed an offence under this section the court must consider whether he followed any relevant guidance which was at the time concerned—

(a) issued by a supervisory authority or any other appropriate body,

(b) approved by the Treasury, and

(c) published in a manner it approved as appropriate in its opinion to bring the guidance to the attention of persons likely to be affected by it.

(9) A disclosure to a nominated officer is a disclosure which—

(a) is made to a person nominated by the alleged offender's employer to receive disclosures under this section, and

(b) is made in the course of the alleged offender's employment … .

(9A) But a disclosure which satisfies paragraphs (a) and (b) of subsection (9) is not to be taken as a disclosure to a nominated officer if the person making the disclosure—

(a) is a professional legal adviser or relevant professional adviser,

(b) makes it for the purpose of obtaining advice about making a disclosure under this section, and

(c) does not intend it to be a disclosure under this section.

(10) Information or other matter comes to a professional legal adviser or relevant professional adviser in privileged circumstances if it is communicated or given to him—

(a) by (or by a representative of) a client of his in connection with the giving by the adviser of legal advice to the client,

(b) by (or by a representative of) a person seeking legal advice from the adviser, or

(c) by a person in connection with legal proceedings or contemplated legal proceedings.

(11) But subsection (10) does not apply to information or other matter which is communicated or given with the intention of furthering a criminal purpose.

(12) Schedule 9 has effect for the purpose of determining what is—

(a) a business in the regulated sector;

(b) a supervisory authority.

(13) An appropriate body is any body which regulates or is representative of any trade, profession, business or employment carried on by the alleged offender.

(14) A relevant professional adviser is an accountant, auditor or tax adviser who is a member of a professional body which is established for accountants, auditors or tax advisers (as the case may be) and which makes provision for—

(a) testing the competence of those seeking admission to membership of such a body as a condition for such admission; and

(b) imposing and maintaining professional and ethical standards for its members, as well as imposing sanctions for non-compliance with those standards.

[This section is printed as amended by the *SOCPA* 2005, ss.102(1) and (5), 104(1) to (3), 105(1) and (2), 106(1) and (2) and 174(2), and Sched. 17, Pt 2; the *Proceeds of Crime Act 2002 and Money Laundering Regulations 2003 (Amendment) Order* 2006 (S.I. 2006 No. 308), art. 2; the *SCA* 2007, s.74(2), and Sched. 8, paras 121 and 126; and the *Terrorism Act 2000 and Proceeds of Crime Act 2002 (Amendment) Regulations* 2007 (S.I. 2007 No. 3398).]

For Schedule 9, see *post*, § 26–16.

26–15 Subsection (2)(b) and section 331(3)(b) (*post*, § 26–19) introduce a negligence test. A failure to disclose offence will be committed where a person who receives information in the course of a "business in the regulated sector" has reasonable grounds for knowing or suspecting that another person is engaged in money laundering (as defined in s.340(11)), even if he did not actually know or suspect it. The section reflects the fact that persons carrying out activities in the regulated sector should be expected to exercise a higher level of diligence in handling transactions than those employed in other businesses. Where a business carries out some activities which are listed in Schedule 9 and some which are not, the explanatory note to section 330 states that only employees carrying out the listed activities will be caught by the provision. The offence is committed if the "required disclosure" (as to which, see subs. (5)) is not made to a nominated officer (as to which, see subs. (9) and s.340(12), *post*, § 26–29), or to a person authorised by the Director General of the Serious Organised Crime Agency, in the form and manner prescribed under section 339 (*post*, § 26–28), and as soon as practicable after the information or other matter mentioned in subsection (3) comes to the person's attention. This reflects the policy that disclosures in the regulated sector should be made directly to the Serious Organised Crime Agency, rather than through a constable or an officer of

Revenue and Customs. It gives those in the regulated sector the choice of either disclosing directly to the Serious Organised Crime Agency, which might be appropriate for sole practitioners, or disclosing to a nominated officer who will operate as a filter for disclosures to that agency.

Subsection (6) excludes from the ambit of the offence (a) a person who has a reasonable excuse for not disclosing the information and (b) a lawyer or other relevant professional adviser (*e.g.* accountant, auditor, tax adviser), where the information came to him in privileged circumstances (defined in subss. (10) and (11)). There is also an exclusion for staff in the regulated sector who have not had adequate training concerning the identification of transactions which may be indicative of money laundering. The training is that required to be provided under regulation 21 of the *Money Laundering Regulations* 2007 (S.I. 2007 No. 2157): *Proceeds of Crime Act 2002 (Failure to Disclose Money Laundering: Specified Training) Order* 2003 (S.I. 2003 No. 171) (as amended by S.I. 2007 No. 2157). The defendant would have to adduce evidence (see *ante*, § 26–10) that he did not know or suspect that another person was engaged in money laundering and that, in his case, his employer had not complied with requirements to provide employees with such training as is specified by the Secretary of State by order.

Section 330(8) provides that the court must take any guidance issued by a "supervisory authority" (listed in Part 2 of Schedule 9, *post*) or any other appropriate body (as defined in s.330(13)) that has been approved by the Treasury, into account when determining whether an offence has been committed. As to the guidance that has been issued, see *ante* § 26–1.

The imposition on independent legal professionals acting for clients in certain types of financial or real estate transactions of an obligation to disclose to the competent authorities any fact indicative of money laundering, and to furnish those authorities with all necessary information if requested to do so, does not give rise to incompatibility with the fundamental right of the lawyer's client to a fair trial guaranteed by Article 6 of the ECHR (*ante*, § 16–57); Article 6 only applies to judicial proceedings: *Ordre des barreaux francophones et germanophones v. Conseil des Ministres (Conseil des barreaux de l'Union europeénne and Ordre des avocats du barreau de Liège, interveners) (Case C-305/05)*, *The Times*, July 2, 2007, ECJ (considering the duty imposed by Article 6(1) of Council Directive 91/308/EEC (on prevention of the use of the financial system for the purposes of money laundering)). The court pointed out that where such legal representation of a client does amount to advice in connection with defending, instituting or avoiding judicial proceedings, then Article 6(3) of the directive exempted the lawyer from the obligations in paragraph (1), regardless of whether the information was received or obtained before, during or after the proceedings. The 1991 directive has been revoked and replaced by European Parliament and Council Directive 2005/60/EC (*post*, § 26–33), Article 23(2) of which corresponds to Article 6(3) of the 1991 directive.

The regulated sector and supervisory authorities

Schedule 9 to the 2002 Act (as substituted by the *Proceeds of Crime Act 2002 (Business in the Regulated Sector and Supervisory Authorities) Order* 2007 (S.I. 2007 No. 3287)) provides for the meaning of a business in the regulated sector and the meaning of a supervisory authority for the purposes of Part 7 of the 2002 Act. With one minor exception it is in identical terms to Schedule 3A to the *Terrorism Act* 2000. Neither schedule is set out in this work. **26–16**

Proceeds of Crime Act 2002, s.331

Failure to disclose: nominated officers in the regulated sector

331.—(1) A person nominated to receive disclosures under section 330 commits an offence if the conditions in subsections (2) to (4) are satisfied. **26–17**

(2) [*Identical to s.330(2)*, ante, *§ 26–14*.]

(3) The second condition is that the information or other matter—

(a) on which his knowledge or suspicion is based, or

(b) which gives reasonable grounds for such knowledge or suspicion,

came to him in consequence of a disclosure made under section 330.

(3A) The third condition is—

(a) that he knows the identity of the other person mentioned in subsection (2), or the whereabouts of any of the laundered property, in consequence of a disclosure made under section 330,

(b) that that other person, or the whereabouts of any of the laundered property, can be identified from the information or other matter mentioned in subsection (3), or

(c) that he believes, or it is reasonable to expect him to believe, that the information or other matter will or may assist in identifying that other person or the whereabouts of any of the laundered property.

(4) The fourth condition is that he does not make the required disclosure to a person authorised for the purposes of this Part by the Director General of SOCA as soon as is practicable after the information or other matter mentioned in subsection (3) comes to him.

(5) The required disclosure is a disclosure of—

(a) the identity of the other person mentioned in subsection (2), if disclosed to him under section 330,

(b) the whereabouts of the laundered property, so far as disclosed to him under section 330, and

(c) the information or other matter mentioned in subsection (3).

(5A) [*Identical to s.330(5A)*, ante, *§ 26–14*.]

(6) But he does not commit an offence under this section if he has a reasonable excuse for not making the required disclosure.

(6A) [*Identical to s.330(7A)*, ante, *§ 26–14*.]

(7) [*Identical to s.330(8)*, ante, *§ 26–14*.]

(8) Schedule 9 has effect for the purpose of determining what is a supervisory authority.

(9) An appropriate body is a body which regulates or is representative of a trade, profession, business or employment.

[This section is printed as amended by the *SOCPA* 2005, ss.102(1) and (6), and 104(1) and (4); and the *SCA* 2007, s.74(2), and Sched. 8, paras 121 and 127.]

26–18 Section 331 creates an offence where a nominated officer (see ss.338(5) and 340(12)) working in the regulated sector receives a disclosure under section 330 which causes him to know or suspect, or gives reasonable grounds for knowledge or suspicion, that money laundering is taking place, and does not disclose the information on which his knowledge or suspicion is based or which gives reasonable grounds for such knowledge or suspicion as soon as practicable after the information comes to him.

Subsection (5) specifies that the "required disclosure", which a nominated officer must make, has to be made to the Serious Organised Crime Agency in the form and manner (if any) prescribed by the order making power in section 339.

Proceeds of Crime Act 2002, s.332

Failure to disclose: other nominated officers

26–19 **332.**—(1) A person nominated to receive disclosures under section 337 or 338 commits an offence if the conditions in subsections (2) to (4) are satisfied.

(2) The first condition is that he knows or suspects that another person is engaged in money laundering.

(3) The second condition is that the information or other matter on which his knowledge or suspicion is based came to him in consequence of a disclosure made under the applicable section.

(3A) The third condition is—

(a) that he knows the identity of the other person mentioned in subsection (2), or the whereabouts of any of the laundered property, in consequence of a disclosure made under the applicable section,

(b) that that other person, or the whereabouts of any of the laundered property, can be identified from the information or other matter mentioned in subsection (3), or

(c) that he believes, or it is reasonable to expect him to believe, that the information or other matter will or may assist in identifying that other person or the whereabouts of any of the laundered property.

(4) [*Identical to s.331(4)*, ante, *§ 26–19*.]

(5) The required disclosure is a disclosure of—

(a) the identity of the other person mentioned in subsection (2), if disclosed to him under the applicable section,

(b) the whereabouts of the laundered property, so far as disclosed to him under the applicable section, and

(c) the information or other matter mentioned in subsection (3).

(5A) [*Identical to s.330(5A)*, ante, *§ 26–14*.]

(5B) The applicable section is section 337 or, as the case may be, section 338.

(6) [*Identical to s.331(6)*, ante, *§ 26–19*.]

(7) [*Identical to s.330(7A)*, ante, *§ 26–14*.]

[This section is printed as amended by the *SOCPA* 2005, ss.102(1) and (7), and 104(1), (5) and (6); and the *SCA* 2007, s.74(2), and Sched. 8, paras 121 and 128.]

Section 332 creates an offence where a nominated officer (see ss.330(9) and 340(12)) receives a report under section 337 or 338 which causes him to know or suspect that money laundering is taking place, where he knows the identity of the suspected money launderer or the whereabouts of the laundered property, or that identity or those whereabouts can be discovered from the information of which he is aware (see subs. (3A)), and he does not make the required disclosure as soon as practicable after the information or other matter comes to him. The nominated officer is required to make the disclosure to the Serious Organised Crime Agency in the form prescribed by section 339. This section applies to nominated officers both inside and outside the regulated sector. **26–20**

Proceeds of Crime Act 2002, ss.333A–333E

Tipping off: regulated sector

333A.—(1) A person commits an offence if— **26–21**

(a) the person discloses any matter within subsection (2);

(b) the disclosure is likely to prejudice any investigation that might be conducted following the disclosure referred to in that subsection; and

(c) the information on which the disclosure is based came to the person in the course of a business in the regulated sector.

(2) The matters are that the person or another person has made a disclosure under this Part—

(a) to a constable,

(b) to an officer of Revenue and Customs,

(c) to a nominated officer, or

(d) to a member of staff of the Serious Organised Crime Agency authorised for the purposes of this Part by the Director General of that Agency,

of information that came to that person in the course of a business in the regulated sector.

(3) A person commits an offence if—

(a) the person discloses that an investigation into allegations that an offence under this Part has been committed is being contemplated or is being carried out;

(b) the disclosure is likely to prejudice that investigation; and

(c) the information on which the disclosure is based came to the person in the course of a business in the regulated sector.

(4) A person guilty of an offence under this section is liable—

(a) on summary conviction to imprisonment for a term not exceeding three months, or to a fine not exceeding level 5 on the standard scale, or to both;

(b) on conviction on indictment to imprisonment for a term not exceeding two years, or to a fine, or to both.

(5) This section is subject to—

(a) section 333B (disclosures within an undertaking or group etc),

(b) section 333C (other permitted disclosures between institutions etc), and

(c) section 333D (other permitted disclosures etc).

Disclosures within an undertaking or group etc.

333B.—(1) An employee, officer or partner of an undertaking does not commit an offence **26–22**

under section 333A if the disclosure is to an employee, officer or partner of the same undertaking.

(2) A person does not commit an offence under section 333A in respect of a disclosure by a credit institution or a financial institution if—

(a) the disclosure is to a credit institution or a financial institution,

(b) the institution to whom the disclosure is made is situated in an EEA State or in a country or territory imposing equivalent money laundering requirements, and

(c) both the institution making the disclosure and the institution to whom it is made belong to the same group.

(3) In subsection (2) "group" has the same meaning as in Directive 2002/87/EC of the European Parliament and of the Council of 16th December 2002 on the supplementary supervision of credit institutions, insurance undertakings and investment firms in a financial conglomerate.

(4) A professional legal adviser or a relevant professional adviser does not commit an offence under section 333A if—

(a) the disclosure is to a professional legal adviser or a relevant professional adviser,

(b) both the person making the disclosure and the person to whom it is made carry on business in an EEA state or in a country or territory imposing equivalent money laundering requirements, and

(c) those persons perform their professional activities within different undertakings that share common ownership, management or control.

Other permitted disclosures between institutions etc.

26–23 **333C.**—(1) This section applies to a disclosure—

(a) by a credit institution to another credit institution,

(b) by a financial institution to another financial institution,

(c) by a professional legal adviser to another professional legal adviser, or

(d) by a relevant professional adviser of a particular kind to another relevant professional adviser of the same kind.

(2) A person does not commit an offence under section 333A in respect of a disclosure to which this section applies if—

(a) the disclosure relates to—

(i) a client or former client of the institution or adviser making the disclosure and the institution or adviser to whom it is made,

(ii) a transaction involving them both, or

(iii) the provision of a service involving them both;

(b) the disclosure is for the purpose only of preventing an offence under this Part of this Act;

(c) the institution or adviser to whom the disclosure is made is situated in an EEA State or in a country or territory imposing equivalent money laundering requirements; and

(d) the institution or adviser making the disclosure and the institution or adviser to whom it is made are subject to equivalent duties of professional confidentiality and the protection of personal data (within the meaning of section 1 of the *Data Protection Act* 1998).

Other permitted disclosures etc.

26–24 **333D.**—(1) A person does not commit an offence under section 333A if the disclosure is—

(a) to the authority that is the supervisory authority for that person by virtue of the *Money Laundering Regulations* 2007 (S.I. 2007 No. 2157); or

(b) for the purpose of—

(i) the detection, investigation or prosecution of a criminal offence (whether in the United Kingdom or elsewhere),

(ii) an investigation under this Act, or

(iii) the enforcement of any order of a court under this Act.

(2) A professional legal adviser or a relevant professional adviser does not commit an offence under section 333A if the disclosure—

(a) is to the adviser's client, and

(b) is made for the purpose of dissuading the client from engaging in conduct amounting to an offence.

(3) A person does not commit an offence under section 333A(1) if the person does not

know or suspect that the disclosure is likely to have the effect mentioned in section 333A(1)(b).

(4) A person does not commit an offence under section 333A(3) if the person does not know or suspect that the disclosure is likely to have the effect mentioned in section 333A(3)(b).

Interpretation of sections 333A to 333D

333E.—(1) For the purposes of sections 333A to 333D, Schedule 9 has effect for determining— **26–25**

(a) what is a business in the regulated sector, and

(b) what is a supervisory authority.

(2) In those sections—

"credit institution" has the same meaning as in Schedule 9;

"financial institution" means an undertaking that carries on a business in the regulated sector by virtue of any of paragraphs (b) to (i) of paragraph 1(1) of that Schedule.

(3) References in those sections to a disclosure by or to a credit institution or a financial institution include disclosure by or to an employee, officer or partner of the institution acting on its behalf.

(4) For the purposes of those sections a country or territory imposes "equivalent money laundering requirements" if it imposes requirements equivalent to those laid down in Directive 2005/60/EC of the European Parliament and of the Council of 26th October 2005 on the prevention of the use of the financial system for the purpose of money laundering and terrorist financing.

(5) In those sections "relevant professional adviser" means an accountant, auditor or tax adviser who is a member of a professional body which is established for accountants, auditors or tax advisers (as the case may be) and which makes provision for—

(a) testing the competence of those seeking admission to membership of such a body as a condition for such admission; and

(b) imposing and maintaining professional and ethical standards for its members, as well as imposing sanctions for non-compliance with those standards.

[Ss.333A to 333E were substituted for s.333 by S.I. 2007 No. 3398 (*ante*, § 26–14).]

Section 333A creates an offence covering the regulated sector (as defined in Schedule 9) of disclosing to the customer concerned or to other third persons the fact that information about known or suspected money laundering has been disclosed (s.333A(1)) or that a money laundering investigation is being, or may be, carried out (s.333A(3)); it must be proved that the disclosure was likely to be prejudicial. **26–26**

There is protection from the offence under section 333A for a person who may need to make a prohibited disclosure to another person in the same undertaking, or to a credit or financial institution within the same group; and for a legal professional or other relevant professional adviser who makes a disclosure to an equivalent person within a different undertaking that shares common ownership, management or control, provided that the other undertaking or institution or adviser is situated in an EEA state or in a country or territory imposing equivalent money laundering requirements; and there is also protection for a person where the disclosure is by one credit or financial institution to another, or by one legal professional or other relevant professional adviser to another, where the disclosure relates to a client or former client, or a transaction or provision of a service involving them both and the disclosure is for the purpose of preventing an offence under Part 7 of the Act and the institution or adviser to whom the disclosure is made is situated in an EEA State or in a country or territory imposing equivalent money laundering requirements and both parties are subject to equivalent duties of professional confidentiality and the protection of personal data (ss.333B and 333C).

As in sections 327(2)(c), 328(2)(c) and 329(2)(d), there is protection from an offence under section 333A for law enforcement officers who may need to make a prohibited disclosure in the course of their official duties (s.333D(1)(b)), and there is an additional exclusion for a person who did not know or suspect that the disclosure would prejudice an investigation (s.333D(3) and (4)). **26–27**

For guidance where conflict arises between the interest of the state in combating crime and the entitlement of private bodies to obtain redress from the courts, see

C. v. S. (Money Laundering: Discovery of Documents) (Practice Note) [1999] 1 W.L.R. 1551, CA (Civ. Div.). For guidance on action to be pursued by banks and the Serious Fraud Office where an account holder is known by the bank to be the subject of a police investigation, see *Governor and Company of the Bank of Scotland v. A. Ltd* [2001] 1 W.L.R. 751, CA (Civ. Div.); and *Amalgamated Metal Trading Ltd v. City of London Police Financial Investigation Unit* [2003] 1 W.L.R. 2711, QBD (Tomlinson J.).

Proceeds of Crime Act 2002, s.342

Offences of prejudicing investigation

26–28 **342.**—(1) This section applies if a person knows or suspects that an appropriate officer or (in Scotland) a proper person is acting (or proposing to act) in connection with a confiscation investigation, a civil recovery investigation, a detained cash investigation or a money laundering investigation which is being or is about to be conducted.

(2) The person commits an offence if—

(a) he makes a disclosure which is likely to prejudice the investigation, or

(b) he falsifies, conceals, destroys or otherwise disposes of, or causes or permits the falsification, concealment, destruction or disposal of, documents which are relevant to the investigation.

(3) A person does not commit an offence under subsection (2)(a) if—

(a) he does not know or suspect that the disclosure is likely to prejudice the investigation,

(b) the disclosure is made in the exercise of a function under this Act or any other enactment relating to criminal conduct or benefit from criminal conduct or in compliance with a requirement imposed under or by virtue of this Act, or

(ba) the disclosure is of a matter within section 333A(2) or (3)(a) (money laundering: tipping off) and the information on which the disclosure is based came to the person in the course of a business in the regulated sector,

(c) he is a professional legal adviser and the disclosure falls within subsection (4).

(4) [*Identical to s.333(3)*, ante, *§ 26–21*.]

(5) But a disclosure does not fall within subsection (4) if it is made with the intention of furthering a criminal purpose.

(6) A person does not commit an offence under subsection (2)(b) if—

(a) he does not know or suspect that the documents are relevant to the investigation, or

(b) he does not intend to conceal any facts disclosed by the documents from any appropriate officer or (in Scotland) proper person carrying out the investigation.

(7) A person guilty of an offence under subsection (2) is liable—

(a) on summary conviction, to imprisonment for a term not exceeding *six* [12] months or to a fine not exceeding the statutory maximum or to both, or

(b) on conviction on indictment, to imprisonment for a term not exceeding five years or to a fine or to both.

(8) For the purposes of this section—

(a) "appropriate officer" must be construed in accordance with section 378;

(b) "proper person" must be construed in accordance with section 412;

(c) Schedule 9 has effect for determining what is a business in the regulated sector.

[This section is printed as amended by the *SCA* 2007, s.77, and Sched. 10, paras 1 and 2; and S.I. 2007 No. 3398 (*ante*, § 26–14). In subs. (7)(a), "12" is substituted for "six", as from a day to be appointed, by the *CJA* 2003 , s.282(2) and (3). The increase has no application to offences committed before the substitution takes effect: *ibid.*, s.282(4).]

26–29 Section 342 creates offences triable either way where a person knows or suspects that a confiscation, civil recovery, detained cash or money laundering investigation is being or is about to be conducted and he makes a disclosure likely to prejudice the investigation (s.342(2)(a)); or he falsifies, conceals, destroys or otherwise disposes of documents which are relevant to the investigation (s.342(2)(b)). It replaces section 93D(1) of the *CJA* 1988 and section 53(1) of the *DTA* 1994.

For section 378, see *ante*, § 15–316.

C. APPROPRIATE CONSENT, PROTECTED AND AUTHORISED DISCLOSURES, FORM AND MANNER OF DISCLOSURES

(1) Summary

Section 335 makes provision in relation to "appropriate consent" for the doing of a prohibited act where there has been an authorised disclosure. Where "appropriate consent" to an otherwise prohibited act is to be given by a "nominated officer" (see ss.338(5), 336(11), and 340(12)), section 336 provides that he may not consent unless he has authorisation from the Serious Organised Crime Agency or he does not receive a notice granting or denying such authorisation within certain time limits. Section 336(5) makes it an offence for a nominated officer to give consent except as outlined above where he knows or suspects that the act is a prohibited act. **26–30**

Sections 337 to 339 provide for protected disclosures, authorised disclosures and the form and manner of disclosures. Section 337 protects a person making a disclosure who would otherwise be in breach of a restriction on the disclosure of information by virtue of his trade, profession, business or employment. Section 338 sets out the circumstances in which a disclosure will be authorised for the purposes of the limitations on the principal money laundering offences in sections 327(2)(a), 328(2)(a) and 329(2)(a). Section 339 provides for the Secretary of State to make an order prescribing the form and manner in which a disclosure must be made under section 330, 331, 332 or 338.

(2) Legislation

Proceeds of Crime Act 2002, s.335

Appropriate consent

335.—(1) The apropriate consent is— **26–31**

(a) the consent of a nominated officer to do a prohibited act if an authorised disclosure is made to the nominated officer;

(b) the consent of a constable to do a prohibited act if an authorised disclosure is made to a constable;

(c) the consent of an officer of Revenue and Customs to do a prohibited act if an authorised disclosure is made to a customs officer.

(2) A person must be treated as having the appropriate consent if—

(a) he makes an authorised disclosure to a constable or an officer of Revenue and Customs, and

(b) the condition in subsection (3) or the condition in subsection (4) is satisfied.

(3) The condition is that before the end of the notice period he does not receive notice from a constable or an officer of Revenue and Customs that consent to the doing of the act is refused.

(4) The condition is that—

(a) before the end of the notice period he receives notice from a constable or an officer of Revenue and Customs that consent to the doing of the act is refused, and

(b) the moratorium period has expired.

(5) The notice period is the period of seven working days starting with the first working day after the person makes the disclosure.

(6) The moratorium period is the period of 31 days starting with the day on which the person receives notice that consent to the doing of the act is refused.

(7) A working day is a day other than a Saturday, a Sunday, Christmas Day, Good Friday or a day which is a bank holiday under the *Banking and Financial Dealings Act* 1971 in the part of the United Kingdom in which the person is when he makes the disclosure.

(8) References to a prohibited act are to an act mentioned in section 327(1), 328(1) or 329(1) (as the case may be).

(9) A nominated officer is a person nominated to receive disclosures under section 338.

(10) Subsections (1) to (4) apply for the purposes of this Part.

[The references to "an officer of Revenue and Customs" are substituted for the references to a "customs officer" by virtue of the *Commissioners for Revenue and Customs Act* 2005, s.50(2).]

26–32 The section specifies time limits within which a constable (as to which, see s.340(13), *post*, § 26–29) or an officer of Revenue and Customs must respond to suspicious transaction reports in circumstances where a consent decision is required. Consent decisions must be made within seven "working days" (defined in s.335(7)). If nothing is heard within that time, then the discloser can go ahead with an otherwise prohibited act without an offence being committed. If consent is refused within the seven working days, then the constable or officer of Revenue and Customs has a further 31 calendar days in which to take further action such as seeking a restraint order. If no such steps are taken, then the discloser is to be treated as having "appropriate consent".

Where consent is refused, the Serious Organised Crime Agency must keep the matter under review throughout the moratorium period (s.335(6)), and give consent if there is no longer any good reason for withholding it; the obligation to review exists independently of a request from anybody affected by the withholding of consent; but any person so affected is entitled to ask the agency to review the refusal, whereupon it is obliged to do so: *R. (UMBS Online Ltd) v. Serious and Organised Crime Agency* [2008] 1 All E.R. 465, CA (Civ. Div.).

Proceeds of Crime Act 2002, s.336

Nominated officer: consent

26–33 **336.**—(1) A nominated officer must not give the appropriate consent to the doing of a prohibited act unless the condition in subsection (2), the condition in subsection (3) or the condition in subsection (4) is satisfied.

(2) The condition is that—

(a) he makes a disclosure that property is criminal property to a person authorised for the purposes of this Part by the Director General of SOCA, and

(b) such a person gives consent to the doing of the act.

(3) The condition is that—

(a) he makes a disclosure that property is criminal property to a person authorised for the purposes of this Part by the Director General of SOCA, and

(b) before the end of the notice period he does not receive notice from such a person that consent to the doing of the act is refused.

(4) The condition is that—

(a) he makes a disclosure that property is criminal property to a person authorised for the purposes of this Part by the Director General of SOCA,

(b) before the end of the notice period he receives notice from such a person that consent to the doing of the act is refused, and

(c) the moratorium period has expired.

(5) A person who is a nominated officer commits an offence if—

(a) he gives consent to a prohibited act in circumstances where none of the conditions in subsections (2), (3) and (4) is satisfied, and

(b) he knows or suspects that the act is a prohibited act.

(6) A person guilty of such an offence is liable—

(a) on summary conviction, to imprisonment for a term not exceeding *six* [12] months or to a fine not exceeding the statutory maximum or to both, or

(b) on conviction on indictment, to imprisonment for a term not exceeding five years or to a fine or to both.

(7) The notice period is the period of seven working days starting with the first working day after the nominated officer makes the disclosure.

(8) The moratorium period is the period of 31 days starting with the day on which the nominated officer is given notice that consent to the doing of the act is refused.

(9) [*Identical to s.335(7)*, ante, *§ 26–24, save for reference to* "nominated officer" *in lieu of* "person".]

(10), (11) [*Identical to s.335(8), (9)*, ante, *§ 26–24*.]

[This section is printed as amended by the *SOCPA* 2005, s.59, and Sched. 4, paras 168 and 173; and the *SCA* 2007, s.74(2), and Sched. 8, paras 121 and 129. In subs. (6)(a), "12" is substituted for "six", as from a day to be appointed, by the *CJA* 2003, s.282(2) and (3). The increase has no application to offences committed before the substitution takes effect: *ibid.*, s.282(4).]

Section 336 provides that a nominated officer (see s.336(11)) must not give appropriate consent unless he has authorisation from the Serious Organised Crime Agency or the time limits specified in subsections (7) and (8) have expired. Section 336(5) makes it an offence for a nominated officer to consent to an otherwise prohibited act except as outlined above; but he does not commit an offence unless he knows or suspects that the act is a prohibited act (*i.e.* one falling within section 327(1), 328(1) or 329(1)). **26–34**

Proceeds of Crime Act 2002, s.337

Protected disclosures

337.—(1) A disclosure which satisfies the following three conditions is not to be taken to breach any restriction on the disclosure of information (however imposed). **26–35**

(2) The first condition is that the information or other matter disclosed came to the person making the disclosure (the discloser) in the course of his trade, profession, business or employment.

(3) The second condition is that the information or other matter—

(a) causes the discloser to know or suspect, or

(b) gives him reasonable grounds for knowing or suspecting,

that another person is engaged in money laundering.

(4) The third condition is that the disclosure is made to a constable, an officer of Revenue and Customs or a nominated officer as soon as is practicable after the information or other matter comes to the discloser.

(4A) Where a disclosure consists of a disclosure protected under subsection (1) and a disclosure of either or both of—

(a) the identity of the other person mentioned in subsection (3), and

(b) the whereabouts of property forming the subject-matter of the money laundering that the discloser knows or suspects, or has reasonable grounds for knowing or suspecting, that other person to be engaged in,

the disclosure of the thing mentioned in paragraph (a) or (b) (as well as the disclosure protected under subsection (1)) is not to be taken to breach any restriction on the disclosure of information (however imposed).

(5) A disclosure to a nominated officer is a disclosure which—

(a) is made to a person nominated by the discloser's employer to receive disclosures under section 330 or this section, and

(b) is made in the course of the discloser's employment … .

[This section is printed as amended by the *SOCPA* 2005, ss.104(1) and (7), 105(1) and (2), 106(1) and (3), and 174(2), and Sched. 17, Pt 2. As to the effect of the *Commissioners for Revenue and Customs Act* 2005, s.50(2), see the note to s.335, *ante*, § 26–24.]

Section 337 exempts a person who receives information in the course of his trade, profession, business or employment from any legal or other obligations that would otherwise prevent him from making disclosures to the authorities. The protection extends not just to the regulated sector which is required to make disclosures in order to avoid committing an offence under section 330, but also to those carrying out any trade, profession, business or employment, even if this is not in the regulated sector, who voluntarily make disclosures about money laundering to the police. This includes those exercising a profession in a voluntary capacity such as accountants or solicitors giving free advice.

Proceeds of Crime Act 2002, s.338

Authorised disclosures

338.—(1) For the purposes of this Part a disclosure is authorised if— **26–36**

(a) it is a disclosure to a constable, an officer of Revenue and Customs or a nominated officer by the alleged offender that property is criminal property,

(b) …; and

(c) the first, second or third condition set out below is satisfied.

(2) The first condition is that the disclosure is made before the alleged offender does the prohibited act.

(2A) The second condition is that—

(a) the disclosure is made while the alleged offender is doing the prohibited act,
(b) he began to do the act at a time when, because he did not then know or suspect that the property constituted or represented a person's benefit from criminal conduct, the act was not a prohibited act, and
(c) the disclosure is made on his own initiative and as soon as is practicable after he first knows or suspects that the property constitutes or represents a person's benefit from criminal conduct.

(3) The third condition is that—
(a) the disclosure is made after the alleged offender does the prohibited act,
(b) he has a reasonable excuse for his failure to make the disclosure before he did the act, and
(c) the disclosure is made on his own initiative and as soon as it is practicable for him to make it.

(4) An authorised disclosure is not to be taken to breach any restriction on the disclosure of information (however imposed).

(5) A disclosure to a nominated officer is a disclosure which—
(a) is made to a person nominated by the alleged offender's employer to receive authorised disclosures, and
(b) is made in the course of the alleged offender's employment … .

(6) References to the prohibited act are to an act mentioned in section 327(1), 328(1) or 329(1) (as the case may be).

[This section is printed as amended by the *SOCPA* 2005, ss.105(1), (2) and (4), 106(1) and (4) to (6), and 174(2), and Sched. 17, Pt 2; and S.I. 2007 No. 3398 (*ante*, § 26–14). As to the effect of the *Commissioners for Revenue and Customs Act* 2005, s.50(2), see the note to s.335, *ante*, § 26–24.]

As to the meaning of "constable", see section 340(13), *post*, § 26–29.

Section 338 sets out the circumstances in which a disclosure will be "authorised" for the purposes of the limitations on the the principal money laundering offences in sections 327 to 329. Where a disclosure is "authorised" for these purposes, then it is not to be taken to breach any rule which would otherwise restrict that disclosure (s.338(4)). This is necessary because, in the course of their business, those working inside or outside the regulated sector may need to complete a transaction that they know or suspect could constitute one of the three principal money laundering offences.

Proceeds of Crime Act 2002, ss.339, 339ZA

Form and manner of disclosures

26–37 **339.**—(1) The Secretary of State may by order prescribe the form and manner in which a disclosure under section 330, 331, 332 or 338 must be made.

(1A) A person commits an offence if he makes a disclosure under section 330, 331, 332 or 338 otherwise than in the form prescribed under subsection (1) or otherwise than in the manner so prescribed.

(1B) But a person does not commit an offence under subsection (1A) if he has a reasonable excuse for making the disclosure otherwise than in the form prescribed under subsection (1) or (as the case may be) otherwise than in the manner so prescribed.

(2) The power under subsection (1) to prescribe the form in which a disclosure must be made includes power to provide for the form to include a request to a person making a disclosure that the person provide information specified or described in the form if he has not provided it in making the disclosure.

(3) Where under subsection (2) a request is included in a form prescribed under subsection (1), the form must—
(a) state that there is no obligation to comply with the request, and
(b) explain the protection conferred by subsection (4) on a person who complies with the request.

(4) A disclosure made in pursuance of a request under subsection (2) is not to be taken to breach any restriction on the disclosure of information (however imposed).

(7) Subsection (2) does not apply to a disclosure made to a nominated officer.

[This section is printed as amended by the *SOCPA* 2005, ss.105(1) and (5), and 174(2), and Sched. 17, Pt 2.]

By virtue of subsection (4) any information supplied under subsection (2) is given immunity from any restriction on the disclosure of information such as confidentiality clauses in contracts and the law of confidence. It is important to note that no offence is committed if the person making the disclosure does not supply the requested information referred to in subsection (2).

Disclosures to SOCA

339ZA. Where a disclosure is made under this Part to a constable or an officer of Revenue and Customs, the constable or officer of Revenue and Customs must disclose it in full to a person authorised for the purposes of this Part by the Director General of the Serious Organised Crime Agency as soon as practicable after it has been made. **26–38**

[This section was inserted by S.I. 2007 No. 3398 (*ante*, § 26–14).]

D. INTERPRETATION

Proceeds of Crime Act 2002, ss.339A, 340

Threshold amounts

339A.—(1) This section applies for the purposes of sections 327(2C), 328(5) and 329(2C). **26–39**

(2) The threshold amount for acts done by a deposit-taking body in operating an account is £250 unless a higher amount is specified under the following provisions of this section (in which event it is that higher amount).

(3) An officer of Revenue and Customs, or a constable, may specify the threshold amount for acts done by a deposit-taking body in operating an account—

(a) when he gives consent, or gives notice refusing consent, to the deposit-taking body's doing of an act mentioned in section 327(1), 328(1) or 329(1) in opening, or operating, the account or a related account, or

(b) on a request from the deposit-taking body.

(4) Where the threshold amount for acts done in operating an account is specified under subsection (3) or this subsection, an officer of Revenue and Customs, or a constable, may vary the amount (whether on a request from the deposit-taking body or otherwise) by specifying a different amount.

(5) Different threshold amounts may be specified under subsections (3) and (4) for different acts done in operating the same account.

(6) The amount specified under subsection (3) or (4) as the threshold amount for acts done in operating an account must, when specified, not be less than the amount specified in subsection (2).

(7) The Secretary of State may by order vary the amount for the time being specified in subsection (2).

(8) For the purposes of this section, an account is related to another if each is maintained with the same deposit-taking body and there is a person who, in relation to each account, is the person or one of the persons entitled to instruct the body as respects the operation of the account.

[This section was inserted by the *SOCPA* 2005, s.103(1) and (5).]

Interpretation

340.—(1) This section applies for the purposes of this Part. **26–40**

(2) Criminal conduct is conduct which—

(a) constitutes an offence in any part of the United Kingdom, or

(b) would constitute an offence in any part of the United Kingdom if it occurred there.

(3) Property is criminal property if—

(a) it constitutes a person's benefit from criminal conduct or it represents such a benefit (in whole or part and whether directly or indirectly), and

(b) the alleged offender knows or suspects that it constitutes or represents such a benefit.

(4) It is immaterial—

(a) who carried out the conduct;

(b) who benefited from it;

(c) whether the conduct occurred before or after the passing of this Act.

(5) A person benefits from conduct if he obtains property as a result of or in connection with the conduct.

(6) If a person obtains a pecuniary advantage as a result of or in connection with conduct, he is to be taken to obtain as a result of or in connection with the conduct a sum of money equal to the value of the pecuniary advantage.

(7) References to property or a pecuniary advantage obtained in connection with conduct include references to property or a pecuniary advantage obtained in both that connection and some other.

(8) If a person benefits from conduct his benefit is the property obtained as a result of or in connection with the conduct.

(9) Property is all property wherever situated and includes—

(a) money;

(b) all forms of property, real or personal, heritable or moveable;

(c) things in action and other intangible or incorporeal property.

(10) The following rules apply in relation to property—

(a) property is obtained by a person if he obtains an interest in it;

(b) references to an interest, in relation to land in England and Wales or Northern Ireland, are to any legal estate or equitable interest or power;

(c) references to an interest, in relation to land in Scotland, are to any estate, interest, servitude or other heritable right in or over land, including a heritable security;

(d) references to an interest, in relation to property other than land, include references to a right (including a right to possession).

(11) Money laundering is an act which—

(a) constitutes an offence under section 327, 328 or 329,

(b) constitutes an attempt, conspiracy or incitement to commit an offence specified in paragraph (a),

(c) constitutes aiding, abetting, counselling or procuring the commission of an offence specified in paragraph (a), or

(d) would constitute an offence specified in paragraph (a), (b) or (c) if done in the United Kingdom.

(12) For the purposes of a disclosure to a nominated officer—

(a) references to a person's employer include any body, association or organisation (including a voluntary organisation) in connection with whose activities the person exercises a function (whether or not for gain or reward), and

(b) references to employment must be construed accordingly.

(13) References to a constable include references to a person authorised for the purposes of this Part by the Director General of SOCA.

(14) "Deposit-taking body" means—

(a) a business which engages in the activity of accepting deposits, or

(b) the National Savings Bank.

[This section is printed as amended by the *SOCPA* 2005, ss.59 and 103(1) and (6), and Sched. 4, paras 168 and 174; and the *SCA* 2007, s.74(2), and Sched. 8, paras 121 and 130. The reference to the common law offence of incitement in subs. (11)(b) has effect as a reference to the offences under the *SCA* 2007, Pt 2: 2007 Act, s.63(1), and Sched. 6, para 44(a).]

26–41 Subsection (12) ensures that where Part 7 permits disclosure to a nominated officer, (under sections 330, 337 and 338) not only employees, but people exercising functions in relation to an organisation who are not technically employees, will also be able to disclose to a nominated officer, if the organisation has one. Directors, partners and volunteers, for example, will be able to make a report to a nominated officer. The liability for reporting to the Serious Organised Crime Agency or a constable, if appropriate, then falls on the nominated officer by virtue of sections 331 and 332.

As to the need to prove, on a prosecution under section 327, 328 or 329 (*ante* §§ 26–11 *et seq.*), that the property in question derives from criminal conduct, see *ante*, § 26–11.

In *R. v. Gabriel (Note)* [2007] 1 W.L.R. 2272, CA, it was held that where a person in receipt of state benefits failed to declare income from legitimate trade in goods to the Revenue and Customs and the Department of Work and Pensions, his profits from the trade itself could not be said to constitute criminal property within the meaning of section 340, so as to make him guilty of possessing criminal property contrary to section 329(1)(c) of the Act (*ante*, § 26–13); the failure to declare profits for the purposes of income tax may give rise to an offence, but that did not make the legitimate trading in goods an offence in itself (although state benefits obtained on the basis of a false declaration or a failure to disclose a change in circumstances may amount to obtaining a pecuniary advantage within section 340(6)). The court advised that where the prosecution allege that property is criminal property, it is sensible, by giving particulars either in advance or in opening, to set out the facts upon which they rely and the inferences which the jury will be invited to draw, and thus to define the ambit of their case.

Gabriel was considered in *R. v. K. (I.)* [2007] 2 Cr.App.R. 10, CA, in which it was held that where a person cheats the revenue by under-declaring the takings of a legitimate trade, he obtains a pecuniary advantage in the form of the tax avoided, and, by virtue of section 340(6), he is to be taken to have obtained, as a result of or in connection with his offence, a sum of money equal to the value of the pecuniary advantage; and it further followed from section 340(5) that he "benefited" from his conduct, and the value of his benefit was the value of the sum of money he was treated as having obtained. The court added that where a person with a legitimate business had engaged in such a cheat of the revenue and was found in possession of a large quantity of cash, it would have been open to the jury to infer that the cash represented the undeclared takings and (within section 340(3)(a)) represented the offender's "benefit" in part; and, if it did so, it would then be "criminal property", and thus could itself be the subject of one of the money laundering offences created by sections 327 to 329 (*ante*, §§ 26–11 *et seq.*).

In *R. v. Rose*; *R. v. Whitwam* [2008] 2 Cr.App.R. 15, CA, it was held that stolen goods in the hands of a thief or a receiver are "criminal property" for the purposes of the offence of acquiring criminal property, contrary to section 329(1)(a) (*ante*, § 26–13), since the offender obtains a right to possession of them in accordance with section 340(10)(a) and (d). The court further considered that whilst it was difficult to see why conduct which had the hallmarks of ordinary burglary/theft or handling stolen goods merited the charging of a money laundering offence, rather than appropriate charges under the *Theft Act* 1968, there was nothing wrong with the tenor of guidance given to crown prosecutors, nor did statistics show that section 329 was being used inappropriately by prosecutors. As to whether this decision will need to be reconsidered in light of the decisions of the House of Lords in *R. v. May* and *Jennings v. CPS*, see *ante*, § 5–774.

E. SENTENCE

Proceeds of Crime Act 2002, s.334

Penalties

334.—(1) A person guilty of an offence under section 327, 328 or 329 is liable— **26–42**

(a) on summary conviction, to imprisonment for a term not exceeding six months or to a fine not exceeding the statutory maximum or to both, or

(b) on conviction on indictment, to imprisonment for a term not exceeding 14 years or to a fine or to both.

(2) A person guilty of an offence under section 330, 331 or 332 is liable—

(a) on summary conviction, to imprisonment for a term not exceeding *six* [12] months or to a fine not exceeding the statutory maximum or to both, or

(b) on conviction on indictment, to imprisonment for a term not exceeding five years or to a fine or to both.

(3) A person guilty of an offence under section 339(1A) is liable on summary conviction to a fine not exceeding level 5 on the standard scale.

[This section is printed as amended by S.I. 2007 No. 3398 (*ante*, § 26–14). Subs. (3) was inserted by the *SOCPA* 2005, s.105(1) and (3). In subs. (2)(a), "12" is substituted for "six", as from a day to be appointed, by the *CJA* 2003, s.282(2) and (3). The increase has no application to offences committed before the substitution takes effect: s.282(4).]

See also ss.336(6) and 342(7), *ante*, §§ 26–25, 26–22. As to the "standard scale", see *ante*, § 5–403.

A financial reporting order under section 76 of the *SOCPA* 2005 (*ante*, § 5–886a) may be made in respect of a person convicted of an offence contrary to section 327, 328 or 329. In the case of sections 327 and 328, this is because they are "lifestyle offences" within Schedule 2 to the 2002 Act (*ante*, § 5–654) (see 76(3)(c) of the 2005 Act); in the case of section 329, this is because it is separately listed in section 76 (see subs. (3)(j)).

The argument that the sentence for money laundering offences should be linked to the maximum sentence for the antecedent offence (for example, fraudulent evasion of duty by smuggling) or set by reference to the guidelines for "bootlegging" cases has not found favour with the Court of Appeal, particularly in cases of conspiracy over a long period of time. There should nevertheless be an element of proportionality: see *R. v. Everson* [2002] 1 Cr.App.R.(S.) 132; and *R. v. Basra* [2002] 2 Cr.App.R.(S.) 100. See also *R. v. Gonzalez and Sarmiento* [2003] 2 Cr.App.R.(S.) 9, CA (observations along the lines that those who launder money are nearly as bad as those who commit the antecedent offences not apposite where the launderer has no knowledge of the antecedent offence); *R. v. El-Delbi* (2003) 147 S.J. 784, CA (there should be no direct arithmetical relationship between the sums shown to be involved and the length of sentence, but nonetheless sentences close to the maximum have to be reserved for cases where the evidence establishes laundering on a large scale); *R. v. Monfries* [2004] 2 Cr.App.R.(S.) 3, CA (regard should be had to nature of antecedent offence, the extent of the offender's knowledge of it, and the amount laundered); and *Att.-Gen.'s Reference (No. 48 of 2006) (R. v. Farrow)* [2007] 1 Cr.App.R.(S.) 90, CA (mathematical calculations based on the amount laundered in different cases are inappropriate).

In *R. v. Griffiths and Pattison* [2007] 1 Cr.App.R.(S.) 95, CA, it was said: (i) as to offences of entering into a money laundering arrangement (s.328, *ante* § 26–12) and acquiring criminal property (s.329, *ante*, § 26–13), being the organiser of the offence is always particularly serious (especially if an operation is set up) and custodial sentences will be absolutely inevitable in almost every case (if not every case); but a one-off attempt to conceal the assets of a person subject to confiscation proceedings does not fall within the same bracket as other forms of money laundering (considering *R. v. Gonzalez and Sarmiento* (*ante*), and *R. v. Yoonus* (*post*); and reducing from 36 to 27 months the sentence imposed on conviction of an estate agent who had approached a convicted drug dealer and purchased his home at an under market value); (ii) as to offences of failing to disclose a suspicion or knowledge of money laundering committed by a solicitor (s.330, *ante*, § 26–14), where the offence is no more than the product of a lapse of the high standards to be expected of a solicitor, rather than a desire to benefit from a money laundering offence, any penalty will be significantly enhanced because of the professional repercussions he will face (considering *R. v. Duff* [2003] 1 Cr.App.R.(S.) 88, CA; and reducing from 15 to six months a term of imprisonment imposed on a solicitor on conviction who had carried out the conveyance of a house at an undervalue).

For a case involving a person who, under the cover of a legitimate bureau de change, was prepared to launder substantial sums, which were not the proceeds of major crime, and from which he himself had limited financial benefit, see *R. v. Yoonus* [2005] 1 Cr.App.R.(S.) 46, CA.

F. MISCELLANEOUS

Proceeds of Crime Act 2002, ss.451, 452

Revenue and Customs prosecutions

26–43 **451.**—(1) Proceedings for a specified offence may be started by the Director of Revenue and Customs Prosecutions or by order of the Commissioners for Her Majesty's Revenue and Customs (the Commissioners).

(2) Where proceedings under subsection (1) are instituted by the Commissioners, the proceedings must be brought in the name of an officer of Revenue and Customs.

(4) If the Commissioners investigate, or propose to investigate, any matter to help them to decide—

(a) whether there are grounds for believing that a specified offence has been committed, or

(b) whether a person is to be prosecuted for such an offence,

the matter must be treated as an assigned matter within the meaning of the *Customs and Excise Management Act* 1979.

(5) This section—

(a) does not prevent any person (including an officer of Revenue and Customs) who has power to arrest, detain or prosecute a person for a specified offence from doing so;

(b) does not prevent a court from dealing with a person brought before it following his arrest by an officer of Revenue and Customs for a specified offence, even if the proceedings were not started by an order under subsection (1).

(6) The following are specified offences—

(a) an offence under Part 7;

(b) an offence under section 342;

(c) an attempt, conspiracy or incitement to commit an offence specified in paragraph (a) or (b);

(d) aiding, abetting, counselling or procuring the commission of an offence specified in paragraph (a) or (b).

(7) This section does not apply to proceedings on indictment in Scotland.

[This section is printed as amended, and repealed in part, by the *Commissioners for Revenue and Customs Act* 2005, ss.50(6) and 52(2), Sched. 4, para. 99, and Sched. 5.]

Crown servants

452.—(1) The Secretary of State may by regulations provide that any of the following provisions apply to persons in the public service of the Crown. **26–44**

(2) The provisions are—

(a) the provisions of Part 7;

(b) section 342.

The provisions listed in section 452(2) apply to the Director of Savings appointed under section 1 of the *National Debt Act* 1972 and any person employed or otherwise engaged in his service: *Proceeds of Crime Act 2002 (Crown Servants) Regulations* 2003 (S.I. 2003 No. 173).

II. MONEY LAUNDERING REGULATIONS 2007

With effect from December 15, 2007, the *Money Laundering Regulations* 2007 (S.I. 2007 No. 2157) (as amended by the *Money Laundering (Amendment) Regulations* 2007 (S.I. 2007 No. 3299)) revoke and replace the *Money Laundering Regulations* 2003 (S.I. 2003 No. 3075), so as to implement Directive 2005/60/EC of the European Parliament and of the Council on prevention of the use of the financial system for the purposes of money laundering and terrorist financing (the "Third Directive"), which repeals Council Directive 91/308/EEC (on prevention of the use of the financial system for the purposes of money laundering). The regulations require the financial, accountancy, legal and other sectors to apply risk-based customer due diligence measures (*post*, § 26–34), and to take other steps to prevent use of their services for money laundering or terrorist financing. The regulations are in six parts (51 regulations) and there are six schedules. Their nature is to set out a number of duties and prohibitions enforced by a system of civil penalties (regs 42– 44) and a single provision (reg. 45, *post*, § 26–37) making contravention of specified regulations an either way offence. The principal substantive change is the introduction of a requirement to vary the identification and monitoring of customers on a risk-sensitive basis, particularly in situations of high money laundering and terrorist financing risk. The explanatory memorandum states (para. 7.5) that in order to support this approach, "Government supervisors and law enforcement will ensure that firms have information on the threats and vulnerabilities they face. Guidance will be provided to industry on practical steps on implementing the risk-based approach." **26–45**

Part 1 (regs 1–4) deals with general matters. Regulation 3 stipulates that the regulations apply to the following persons acting in the course of business carried on by them in the United Kingdom ("relevant persons"), each of which is defined (reg. 3(3)–(13)): credit institutions, financial institutions, auditors, insolvency practitioners, external accountants and tax advisers, independent legal professionals, trust or company service providers, estate agents, high value dealers, and casinos. **26–46**

Part 2 (regs 5–18) introduces the principle of "customer due diligence". Regulation 5 provides a definition of "customer due diligence measures", the essence of which is a requirement to identify and verify the identity of a customer and any beneficial owner of the customer on the basis of documents, data or information from a reliable and independent source; and to obtain information on the purpose and intended nature of the business relationship. Regulation 6 defines "beneficial owner". Regulation 7(1) requires a relevant person to apply customer due diligence (a) when establishing a business relationship, (b) when carrying out an occasional transaction, (c) on suspecting money laundering or terrorist financing, or (d) when doubting the veracity or adequacy of documents, data, etc., previously obtained for the purposes of identification or verification. Regulation 7(2) requires relevant persons to apply customer due diligence measures at "other appropriate times". Regulation 7(3) requires a relevant person to determine the extent of customer due diligence measures necessary on a risk-sensitive basis depending on the customer and the business relationship, product or transaction, and to be in a position to demonstrate to his supervising authority (see Pt 4, *post*, § 26–36) the appropriateness of the measures chosen.

Regulation 8(1) requires a relevant person to conduct continuous monitoring of a business relationship; and regulation 8(3) applies the duty under regulation 7(3) to that duty. Regulation 9(2) imposes a general duty on relevant persons to verify the identity of a customer (and any beneficial owner) before establishing a business relationship or carrying out an occasional transaction; but this duty is subject to exceptions in paragraphs (3) to (5). Regulation 10(1) requires casinos to establish and verify the identity of all customers before entry to the casino or before access is given to remote gaming facilities, and where the customer seeks to pay more than 2,000 euros to the casino in connection with gaming facilities. Regulation 11(1) states that a relevant person who is unable to apply customer due diligence measures (a) must not carry out a transaction with, or for, the customer through a bank account, (b) must not establish a business relationship, or carry out an occasional transaction, with the customer, (c) must terminate any existing business relationship with the customer, and (d) must consider whether he is required to make a disclosure under Part 7 of the *PCA* 2002 or Part III of the *Terrorism Act* 2000. The duties in regulation 11(1) do not apply where a lawyer or other professional adviser is advising a client in connection with legal proceedings (including advice on the institution or avoidance of proceedings): reg. 11(2). Regulation 14(1) requires relevant persons to apply on a risk-sensitive basis enhanced customer due diligence measures and enhanced continuous monitoring where the customer has not been physically present for identification purposes, where a credit institution has or proposes to have a banking relationship with an institution from a non-EEA state, where it is proposed to establish a business relationship or to carry out an occasional transaction with a "politically exposed" person (as to which, see reg. 14(5), and Sched. 2, para 4), or in any other situation which by its nature can present a higher risk of money laundering or terrorist financing.

Regulation 15(1) requires credit institutions having branches and subsidiaries located in non-EEA states to apply (to the extent permitted by the law of the state) measures at least equivalent to those in these regulations. Regulation 15(2) requires any such institution to notify its supervising authority (*post*, reg. 23) if the law of the non-EEA state does not permit the application of such equivalent measures, and to take additional measures to handle effectively the risk of money laundering and terrorist financing. Regulation 16(1) prohibits credit institutions from entering into or continuing banking relationships with "shell banks" (i.e. a credit institution incorporated in a jurisdiction in which it has no physical presence, etc., and which is not part of a financial conglomerate). Regulation 16(2) requires such institutions to take appropriate measures to ensure that they do not enter into a relationship with a bank known to permit its accounts to be used by a shell bank. Regulation 16(3) prohibits credit or financial institutions from setting up anonymous accounts or passbooks for any new or existing customer; regulation 16(4) requires credit and financial institutions to apply customer due diligence measures to, and conduct continuous monitoring of, all existing anonymous accounts and passbooks in existence before the date of commencement of these regulations. This must be done as soon as reasonably practicable after that date, and in any event before such accounts or passbooks are used.

Regulation 17 entitles a relevant person to rely on certain specified others to apply any customer due diligence measures. Regulation 18 confers a power on the Treasury to direct any relevant person not to enter into a business relationship or carry out an occasional transaction (or to proceed further with the same) with a person who is situated in a non-EEA state to which the Financial Action Task Force (established by the G-7 in 1989) has decided to apply counter-measures.

Part 3 (regs 19–21) deals with record-keeping, procedures and training. Regulation 19(1) requires relevant persons to keep records of evidence of a customer's identity and supporting documents in respect of a business relationship or occasional transaction for a period of five years. Regulation 19(4) requires a relevant person who is relied on by another relevant person under regulation 17 to keep records of a customer's identity for the same period. There are detailed provisions as to when this period begins to run. Regulation 19(5) requires such persons to supply the records retained to the person relying on him as soon as reasonably practicable after being requested to do so; and regulation 19(6) requires a person who relies on another to ensure that the other person as soon as practicable makes available to him any information obtained about the customer and forwards to him any copies of any identification and verification data which that other person has obtained when applying due diligence measures. These requirements do not apply where a relevant person applies customer due diligence by means of an outsourcing service provider or agent: reg. 19(7). Regulation 20(1) requires relevant persons to establish and maintain appropriate and risk-sensitive policies and procedures relating to: customer due diligence measures and continuous monitoring; reporting; record-keeping; internal control; risk assessment and management; and the monitoring and management of compliance with, and internal communication of, such policies and procedures, in order to prevent activities related to money laundering and terrorist financing. Regulation 20(4) requires credit and financial institutions to establish and maintain systems enabling them to respond quickly and fully to enquiries from financial investigators, customs officers, constables, etc. Regulation 20(5) requires such institutions to communicate their policies and procedures to their subsidiaries located outside the United Kingdom. Regulation 21 requires relevant persons to take measures so that all relevant employees are made aware of the law concerning money laundering and terrorist financing, and are trained regularly to recognise and deal with suspicious transactions. **26–47**

Part 4 (regs 22–35) deals with supervision and registration. Regulations 23 and 24 allocate responsibility for supervision of the different sectors to which the regulations apply to various bodies (e.g. the Law Society, Bar Council) and set out the duties of such bodies (including a requirement to notify the Serious Organised Crime Agency of knowledge or suspicion that a person has engaged in money laundering or terrorist financing). Regulation 25 requires the Revenue and Customs Commissioners to maintain registers of high value dealers and money service businesses and trust or company service providers for which they are the supervisory body. Regulation 26 prohibits acting as such unless included in such a register. There is a transitional provision in connection with this requirement (see reg. 50, *post*, § 26–38). Regulation 27 makes provision for a person to be included in the register, with regulation 27(4) requiring a person who has provided information, etc., to the commissioners for that purpose to notify them of any change in the information provided or of any inaccuracy. Regulation 32 confers a discretionary power on certain supervisory bodies (not including the Law Society or Bar Council) to maintain their own registers. Where such registers are established, relevant persons must not carry on the business or profession to which the register relates for a period of more than six months after the register is established without being included in the register: reg. 33. **26–48**

Part 5 (regs 36–47) deals with enforcement. Regulation 36 designates various authorities for the purposes of enforcing the regulations (principally the Financial Services Authority, the Revenue and Customs Commissioners and the Office of Fair Trading). Regulations 37 to 41 make provision for the powers of officers of designated bodies including powers to require the provision of information from relevant persons (reg. 38) and to enter any premises used by a relevant person in connection with his business to inspect the premises and any recorded information found on the premises other than **26–49** that which the relevant person would be entitled to refuse to disclose on the grounds of legal professional privilege (reg. 38). Regulations 42 to 44 make provision for the imposition of civil penalties. Such penalties of a proportionate and dissuasive amount may be imposed by a designated authority on a relevant person who fails to comply with any requirement in regulation 7(1), (2) or (3), 8(1) or (3), 9(2), 10(1), 11(1), 14(1), 15(1) or (2), 16(1), (2), (3) or (4), 19(1), (4), (5) or (6), 20(1), (4) or (5), 21, 26, 27(4) or 33, or a direction made under regulation 18: reg. 42(1).

Regulation 45(1) makes it an either way offence (maximum penalty on conviction on indictment, two years' imprisonment, or a fine, or both) to fail to comply with any of the same requirements. In deciding whether such an offence has been committed, the court must consider any guidance which, at the time, had been issued by a supervisory or appropriate body, had the approval of the Treasury and had been published in a manner approved by the Treasury: reg. 45(2). The only Treasury approved guidance in relation to the 2007 regulations is the JMLSG Guidance Notes for the Financial Sector 2007, which received approval in December, 2007; and reference should be made to the JMLSG website, www.jmlsg.org.uk. The Law Society and the Bar Council, among others, have produced their own guidance (*ante*, § 26–1). There is a defence of taking all reasonable steps and exercising all due diligence to avoid committing the offence: reg. 45(4). Persons convicted of the offence are not also liable to a civil penalty: reg. 45(5).

Proceedings for an offence may be instituted by the Director of the Revenue and Customs Prosecution Office or by order of the Commissioners, the Office of Fair Trading, local weights and measures authorities, the Department of Enterprise, Trade and Investment, or the Director of Public Prosecutions: reg. 46(1). Such proceedings may only be instituted against relevant persons, or if the relevant person is a body corporate, a partnership or an unincorporated association, any person who is liable to be proceeded against under regulation 47 (*post*): reg. 46(2). Proceedings instituted by order of the Commissioners must be brought in the name of a revenue and customs officer; and investigations, etc., by the Commissioners in connection therewith are an assigned matter under the *CEMA* 1979, s.1(1) (*ante*, § 25–400): reg. 46(3), (7). There are special requirements in relation to prosecutions by local weights and measure authorities: reg. 46(4)–(6). Regulation 47 makes provision in standard form as to the liability of the officers of bodies corporate.

26–50 Part 6 (regs 48–51) contains miscellaneous provisions. Regulation 49 imposes an obligation on specified public authorities (including inspectors appointed under the *Companies Act* 1985) to inform the Serious Organised Crime Agency if it is known or suspected, or if there are reasonable grounds for knowing or suspecting, that a person has engaged in money laundering or terrorist financing. Regulation 50 sets out a transitional provision in connection with the requirement under regulation 26 (*ante*, § 26–36).

Chapter 27

HARMFUL OR DANGEROUS DRUGS

A. Introduction

(1) International obligations

The Single Convention on Narcotic Drugs, 1961, Cmnd. 2631, as amended by the Protocol (1972, Cmnd. 6487), provides a two-pronged attack in the international fight against narcotic abuse: first, the parties are encouraged to offer and to provide mutual co-operation incombatting narcotic abuse; secondly, each party undertakes (subject to its constitutional limitations) to make it a criminal offence (under their own domestic law), *inter alia*, to supply, manufacture, cultivate, produce, distribute, or to be in possession of those drugs which are set out in the schedules to the convention: see Art. 36 and *cf*. Art. 33. **27–1**

Following the 1961 convention, Parliament enacted the *Drugs (Prevention of Misuse) Act* 1964, the *Dangerous Drugs Act* 1965 and the *Dangerous Drugs Act* 1967. Major social changes at home and abroad, coupled with dissatisfaction with a piecemeal approach to the "drug problem", resulted in the passing of the *Misuse of Drugs Act* 1971 which repealed the three earlier Acts.

Sections 20 and 36(1) of the 1971 Act provide (broadly stated) that persons commit an offence in this country if they assist in or induce the commission of offences overseas which "correspond" with the provisions of the single convention or such other treaty, agreement or convention to which the United Kingdom is a party. However, the provisions of the Act fell short of some of the objectives stated in the convention. Furthermore, the Act did not go far enough to enable the United Kingdom to ratify the European Convention on Mutual Assistance 1959. Therefore, in great haste, following the signing of the Vienna Convention Against Illicit Traffic in Narcotic Drugs and Psychotropic Substances, 1988, Cmnd. 804, Parliament enacted the *Criminal Justice (International Co-operation) Act* 1990. That Act facilitated co-operation between states, endeavoured **27–2** to fill some of the loop-holes in the *DTOA* 1986, and created various new offences (as to which, see *ante*, §§ 25–484 *et seq.*). Some of its provisions were consolidated in the *DTA* 1994, and its mutual assistance provisions are largely superseded by the *Crime (International Co-operation) Act* 2003.

(2) The scope of the 1971 Act

27–3 The relevant drugs, for the purposes of the Act, are described as "controlled drugs" and are divided into three categories, Class A, Class B and Class C drugs (depending on the degree or type of harm involved): see section 2 of, and Schedule 2 to, the Act (*post*, §§ 27–6 *et seq.*). The mode of prosecution and the punishment of offences is determined by the category into which the drug falls: see Schedule 4 to the Act, *post*, § 27–130.

27–4 A large number of "controlled drugs" have a medicinal value. Accordingly, drugs are "controlled" in the sense that their distribution and use are regulated in such a fashion and for such period of time that any harmful effects related to their use or abuse are prevented, minimised or eliminated. To this end the Secretary of State is vested with wide statutory powers to make regulations affecting almost every facet of the Act although any amendments to Schedule 2 can only be made by Her Majesty by Order in Council (see s.2(2), (3)).

The powers of the Secretary of State to make regulations fall into two broad categories: first, to make such provision "as appears to him necessary or expedient for preventing the misuse of controlled drugs" (s.10); and secondly, he may except and/or authorise various activities which would otherwise be unlawful under the Act (s.7); see also section 31. The distinction between "excepting" and "authorising" is significant: *R. v. Hunt (R.)* [1987] A.C. 352, HL (*post*, §§ 27–20 *et seq.*).

The principal regulations are the *Misuse of Drugs Regulations* 2001 (S.I. 2001 No. 3998).

(3) Definition of a "controlled drug"

Misuse of Drugs Act 1971, s.2

Controlled drugs and their classification for purposes of this Act

27–5 **2.**—(1) In this Act—

(a) the expression "controlled drug" means any substance or product for the time being specified in Part I, II, or III of Schedule 2 to this Act, and

(b) the expressions "Class A drug", "Class B drug" and "Class C drug" mean any of the substances and products for the time being specified respectively in Part I, Part II and Part III of that Schedule;

and the provisions of Part IV of that Schedule shall have effect with respect to the meanings of expressions used in that Schedule.

(2)–(5) [*Power to amend Schedule 2 by Order in Council.*]

(4) Classification of controlled drugs

Misuse of Drugs Act 1971, Sched. 2

SCHEDULE 2

PART I

Class A Drugs

27–6 1. The following substances and products, namely—

(a) Acetorphine
Alfentanil
Allylprodine
Alphacetylmethadol
Alphameprodine
Alphamethadol
Alphaprodine
Anileridine
Benzethidine
Benzylmorphine (3-benzyl morphine)
Betacetylmethadol

Betameprodine
Betamethadol
Betaprodine
Bezitramide
Bufotenine
Carfentanil
Clonitazene
Coca leaf [see *post*, § 27–11]
Cocaine
Desomorphine
Dextromoramide
Diamorphine
Diampromide
Diethylthiambutene
Difenoxin (1-(3-cyano-3, 3-diphenyl propyl)-4-phenylpiperidine-4-carboxylic acid)
Dihydrocodeinone *O*-carboxymethyloxime
Dihydroetorphine
Dihydromorphine
Dimenoxadole
Dimepheptanol
Dimethylthiambutene
Dioxaphetyl butyrate
Diphenoxylate
Dipipanone
Drotebanol (3,4-dimethoxy-17-methylmorphinan-6β, 14-diol)
Ecgonine, and any derivative of ecgonine which is convertible to ecgonine or to cocaine
Ethylmethylthiambutene
Eticyclidine
Etonitazene
Etorphine
Etoxeridine
Etryptamine
Fentanyl
Fungus (of any kind) which contains psilocin or an ester of psilocin
Furethidine
Hydrocodone
Hydromorphinol
Hydromorphone
Hydroxypethidine
Isomethadone
Ketobemidone
Levomethorphan
Levomoramide
Levophenacylmorphan
Levorphanol
Lofentanil
Lysergamide
Lysergide and other *N*-alkyl derivatives of lysergamide
Mescaline
Metazocine
Methadone
Methadyl acetate
Methylamphetamine
Methyldesorphin
Methyldihydromorphine (6-methyldihydromorphine)
Metopon
Morpheridine
Morphine
Morphine methobromide, morphine *N*-oxide and other pentavalent nitrogen morphine derivatives
Myrophine
Nicomorphine (3,6-dinicotinoylmorphine)
Noracymethadol
Norlevorphanol
Normethadone
Normorphine
Norpipanone
Opium, whether raw, prepared or medicinal [see *post*, § 27–11]
Oxycodone
Oxymorphone
Pethidine
Phenadoxone
Phenampromide
Phenazocine
Phencyclidine
Phenomorphan
Phenoperidine
Piminodine
Piritramide
Poppy-straw and concentrate of poppy-straw [see *post*, § 27–11]
Proheptazine
Properidine (1-methyl-4-phenyl piperidine-4-carboxylic acid isopropyl ester)
Psilocin
Racemethorphan

Racemoramide
Racemorphan
Remifentanil
Rolicyclidine
Sufentanil
Tenocyclidine
Thebacon
Thebaine
Tilidate
Trimeperidine
4-Bromo-2,5-dimethoxy-α-methyl-phenethylamine
4-Cyano-2-dimethylamino-4,4-di-phenylbutane
4-Cyano-1-methyl-4-phenyl-piperidine
N,*N*-Diethyltryptamine
N,*N*-Dimenthyltryptamine
2,5-Dimethoxy-α,4-dimethylphenethylamine
N-Hydroxy-tenamphetamine
1-Methyl-4-phenylpiperidine-4-carboxylic acid
2-Methyl-3-morpholino-1,1 diphenylpropanecarboxylic acid
4-Methylaminorex
4-Phenylpiperidine-4-carboxylic acid ethylester

27–7 (b) any compound (not being a compound for the time being specified in sub-paragraph (a) above) structurally derived from tryptamine or from a ring-hydroxy tryptamine by substitution at the nitrogen atom of the sidechain with one or more alkyl substituents but no other substituent;

(ba) the following phenethylamine derivatives, namely:—
Allyl(α-methyl-3,4-methylenedioxyphenethyl)amine
2-Amino-1-(2,5-dimethoxy-4-methylphenyl)ethanol
2-Amino-1-(3,4-dimethoxyphenyl)ethanol
Benzyl(α-methyl-3,4-methylenedioxyphenethyl)amine
4-Bromo-β,2,5-trimethoxyphenethylamine
N-(4-*sec*-Butylthio-2,5-dimethoxyphenethyl)hydroxylamine
Cyclopropylmethyl(α-methyl-3,4-methylenedioxyphenethyl)amine
2-(4,7-Dimethoxy-2,3-dihydro-1*H*-indan-5-yl)ethylamine
2-(4,7-Dimethoxy-2,3-dihydro-1*H*-indan-5-yl)-1-methylethylamine
2-(2,5-Dimethoxy-4-methylphenyl)cyclopropylamine
2-(1,4-Dimethoxy-2-naphthyl)ethylamine
2-(1,4-Dimethoxy-2-naphthyl)-1-methylethylamine
N-(2,5-Dimethoxy-4-propylthiophenethyl)hydroxylamine
2-(1,4-Dimethoxy-5,6,7,8-tetrahydro-2-naphthyl)ethylamine
2-(1,4-Dimethoxy-5,6,7,8-tetrahydro-2-naphthyl)-1-methylethylamine
α,α-Dimethyl-3,4-methylenedioxyphenethylamine
α,α-Dimethyl-3,4-methylenedioxyphenethyl(methyl)amine
Dimethyl(α-methyl-3,4-methylenedioxyphenethyl)amine
N-(4-Ethylthio-2,5-dimethoxyphenethyl)hydroxylamine
4-Iodo-2,5-dimethoxy-α-methylphenethyl(dimethyl)amine
2-(1,4-Methano-5,8-dimethoxy-1,2,3,4-tetrahydro-6-naphthyl)ethylamine
2-(1,4-Methano-5,8-dimethoxy-1,2,3,4-tetrahydro-6-naphthyl)-1-methylethylamine
2-(5-Methoxy-2,2-dimethyl-2,3-dihydrobenzo[*b*]furan-6-yl)-1-methylethylamine
2-Methoxyethyl(α-methyl-3,4-methylenedioxyphenethyl)amine
2-(5-Methoxy-2-methyl-2,3-dihydrobenzo[*b*]furan-6-yl)-1-methylethylamine
β-Methoxy-3,4-methylenedioxyphenethylamine
1-(3,4-Methylenedioxybenzyl)butyl(ethyl)amine
1-(3,4-Methylenedioxybenzyl)butyl(methyl)amine
2-(α-Methyl-3,4-methylenedioxyphenethylamino)ethanol
α-Methyl-3,4-methylenedioxyphenethyl(prop-2-ynyl)amine
N-Methyl-*N*-(α-methyl-3,4-methylenedioxyphenethyl)hydroxylamine
O-Methyl-*N*-(α-methyl-3,4-methylenedioxyphenethyl)hydroxylamine
α-Methyl-4-(methylthio)phenethylamine

β,3,4,5-Tetramethoxyphenethylamine

β,2,5-Trimethoxy-4-methylphenethylamine;

(c) any compound (not being methoxyphenamine or a compound for the time being specified in sub-paragraph (a) above) structurally derived from phenethylamine, an *N*-alkylphenethylamine, α-methylphenethylamine, an *N*-alkyl-α-methylphenethylamine, α-ethylphenethylamine, or an *N*-alkyl-α-ethylphenethylamine by substitution in the ring to any extent with alkyl, alkoxy, alkyl-enedioxy or halide substituents, whether or not further substituted in the ring by one or more other univalent substituents.

(d) any compound (not being a compound for the time being specified in sub-paragraph (a) above) structurally derived from fentanyl by modification in any of the following ways, that is to say,

(i) by replacement of the phenyl portion of the phenethyl group by any heteromonocycle whether or not further substituted in the heterocycle;

(ii) by substitution in the phenethyl group with alkyl, alkenyl, alkoxy, hydroxy, halogeno, haloalkyl, amino or nitro groups;

(iii) by substitution in the piperidine ring with alkyl or alkenyl groups;

(iv) by substitution in the aniline ring with alkyl, alkoxy, alkylenedioxy, halogeno or haloalkyl groups;

(v) by substitution at the 4-position of the piperidine ring with any alkoxycarbonyl or alkoxyalkyl or acyloxy group;

(vi) by replacement of the *N*-propionyl group by another acyl group;

(e) any compound (not being a compound for the time being specified in sub-paragraph (a) above) structurally derived from pethidine by modification in any of the following ways, that is to say,

(i) by replacement of the l-methyl group by an acyl, alkyl whether or not unsaturated, benzyl or phenethyl group, whether or not further substituted;

(ii) by substitution in the piperidine ring with alkyl or alkenyl groups or with a propano bridge, whether or not further substituted;

(iii) by substitution in the 4-phenyl ring with alkyl, alkoxy, aryloxy, halogeno or haloalkyl group;

(iv) by replacement of the 4-ethoxycarbonyl by any other alkoxycarbonyl or any alkoxyalkyl or acyloxy group;

(v) by formation of an *N*-oxide or of a quaternary base.

2. Any stereoisomeric form of a substance for the time being specified in paragraph 1 above not being dextromethorphan or dextrorphan. **27–8**

3. Any ester or ether of a substance for the time being specified in paragraph 1 or 2 above not being a substance for the time being specified in Part II of this Schedule.

4. Any salt of a substance for the time being specified in any of paragraphs 1 to 3 above.

5. Any preparation or other product containing a substance or product for the time being specified in any of paragraphs 1 to 4 above.

6. Any preparation designed for administration by injection which includes a substance or product for the time being specified in any of paragraphs 1 to 3 of Part II of this Schedule.

PART II

Class B Drugs

1. The following substances and products, namely— **27–9**

(a) Acetyldihydrocodeine
Amphetamine
Codeine
Dihydrocodeine
Ethylmorphine (3-ethylmorphine)
Glutethimide
Lefetamine
Methaqualone
Methcathinone
α-Methylphenethylhydroxylamine
Methylphenidate
Methylphenobarbitone
Nicocodine
Nicodicodine (6-nicotinoyldihydrocodeine)

Norcodeine
Pentazocine
Phenmetrazine
Pholcodine
Propiram
Zipeprol

(b) any 5,5 disubstituted barbituric acid.

2. Any stereoisomeric form of a substance for the time being specified in paragraph 1 of this Part of this Schedule.

3. Any salt of a substance for the time being specified in paragraph 1 or 2 of this Part of this Schedule.

4. Any preparation or other product containing a substance for the time being specified in any of paragraphs 1 to 3 of this Part of this Schedule, not being a preparation falling within paragraph 6 of Part I of this Schedule.

PART III

Class C Drugs

27–10 1. The following substances, namely—

(a) Alprazolam
Aminorex
Benzphetamine
Bromazepam
Brotizolam
Buprenorphine
Camazepam
Cannabinol
Cannabinol derivatives [see *post*, § 27–11]
Cannabis and cannabis resin
Cathine
Cathinone
Chlordiazepoxide
Chlorphentermine
Clobazam
Clonazepam
Clorazepic acid
Clotiazepam
Cloxazolam
Delorazepam
Dextropropoxyphene
Diazepam
Diethylpropion
Estazolam
Ethchlorvynol
Ethinamate
Ethyl loflazepate
Fencamfamin
Fenethylline
Fenproporex
Fludiazepam
Flunitrazepam
Flurazepam
Halazepam
Haloxazolam
4-Hydroxy-n-butyric acid
Ketamine
Ketazolam
Loprazolam
Lorazepam
Lormetazepam
Mazindol
Medazepam
Mefenorex
Mephentermine
Meprobamate
Mesocarb
Methyprylone
Midazolam
Nimetazepam
Nitrazepam
Nordazepam
Oxazepam
Oxazolam
Pemoline
Phendimetrazine
Phentermine
Pinazepam
Pipadrol
Prazepam
Pyrovalerone
Temazepam
Tetrazepam
Triazolam
N-Ethylamphetamine
Zolpidem

(b) 4-Androstene-3, 17-dione
5-Androstene-3, 17-diol
Atamestane
Bolandiol
Bolasterone
Bolazine
Boldenone
Bolenol
Bolmantalate
Calusterone
4-Chloromethandienone
Clostebol
Drostanolone
Enestebol
Epitiostanol
Ethyloestrenol
Fluoxymesterone
Formebolone
Furazabol
Mebolazine
Mepitiostane
Mesabolone
Mestanolone
Mesterolone
Methandienone
Methandriol

Methenolone
Methyltestosterone
Metribolone
Mibolerone
Nandrolone
19-Nor-4-Androstene-3, 17-dione
19-Nor-5-Androstene-3, 17-diol
Norboletone
Norclostebol
Norethandrolone
Ovandrotone
Oxabolone
Oxandrolone
Oxymesterone
Oxymetholone
Prasterone
Propetandrol
Quinbolone
Roxibolone
Silandrone
Stanolone
Stanozolol
Stenbolone
Testosterone
Thiomesterone
Trenbolone

(c) any compound (not being Trilostane or a compound for the time being specified in sub-paragraph (b) above) structurally derived from 17-hydroxyandrostan-3-one or from 17-hydroxyestran-3-one by modification in any of the following ways, that is to say,
  (i) by further substitution at position 17 by a methyl or ethyl group;
  (ii) by substitution to any extent at one or more of positions 1, 2, 4, 6, 7, 9, 11, or 16, but at no other position;
  (iii) by unsaturation in the carbocyclic ring system to any extent, provided that there are no more than two ethylenic bonds in any one carbocyclic ring;
  (iv) by fusion of ring A with a heterocyclic system;

(d) any substance which is an ester or ether (or, where more than one hydroxyl function is available, both an ester and an ether) of a substance specified in sub-paragraph (b) or described insub-paragraph (c) above or of cannabinol or a cannabinol derivative;

Chorionic Gonadotrophin (HCG)
Clenbuterol
Non-human chorionic gonadotrophin
Somatrophin
Somatrem
Somatropin

2. Any stereoisomeric form of a substance for the time being specified in paragraph 1 of this Part of this Schedule not being phenylpropanolamine.

3. [*Identical to para. 3 of Pt II.*]

4. Any preparation or other product containing a substance for the time being specified in any of paragraphs 1 to 3 of this Part of this Schedule.

PART IV

Meaning of Certain Expressions used in this Schedule

For the purposes of this Schedule the following expressions (which are not among those defined in section 37(1) of this Act) have the meanings hereby assigned to them respectively, that is to say— **27–11**

"cannabinol derivatives" means the following substances, except where contained in cannabis or cannabis resin, namely tetrahydro derivatives of cannabinol and 3-alkyl homologues of cannabinol or of its tetrahydro derivatives;

"coca leaf" means the leaf of any plant of the genus *Erythroxylon* from whose leaves cocaine can be extracted either directly or by chemical transformation;

"concentrate of poppy-straw" means the material produced when poppy-straw has entered into a process for the concentration of its alkaloids;

"medicinal opium" means raw opium which has undergone the process necessary to adapt it for medicinal use in accordance with the requirements of the British Pharmacopoeia, whether it is in the form of powder or is granulated or is in any other form, and whether it is or is not mixed with neutral substances;

"opium poppy" means the plant of the species *Papaver somniferum L*;

"poppy straw" means all parts, except the seeds, of the opium poppy, after mowing;

"raw opium" includes powdered or granulated opium but does not include medicinal opium.

[This Schedule is printed as amended by the *Misuse of Drugs Act 1971 (Modification) Orders*: S.I. 1973 No. 771; S.I. 1975 No. 421; S.I. 1977 No. 1243; S.I. 1979 No. 299; S.I. 1983 No. 765; S.I. 1984 No. 859; S.I. 1985 No. 1995; S.I. 1986 No. 2230; S.I. 1989 No. 1340; S.I. 1990 No. 2589; S.I. 1995 No. 1966; S.I. 1996 No. 1300; S.I. 1998 No. 750; S.I. 2001 No. 3932; S.I. 2003 No. 1243; S.I. 2003 No. 3201; the *Misuse of Drugs Act 1971 (Amendment) Order* 2005 (S.I. 2005 No. 3178); the *Drugs Act* 2005, s.21; and the *Misuse of Drugs Act 1971 (Amendment) Order* 2006 (S.I. 2006 No. 3331).]

For section 37(1), see *post*, § 27–127.

(5) Interpretation

Particular drugs

(i) *"Cannabis"*

27–12 See section 37(1) of the *Misuse of Drugs Act* 1971, *post*, § 27–127.

(ii) *Cannabis resin*

27–13 See section 37(1) of the 1971 Act, *post*, § 27–127.

(iii) *"Cocaine"*

27–14 The word "cocaine" as used in Schedule 2 is a generic word which includes both the direct extracts of the coca leaf and whatever results from a chemical transformation of such extracts: *R. v. Greensmith*, 77 Cr.App.R. 202, CA. It had been contended that Schedule 2 distinguished between "natural" cocaine and its stereoisomeric forms, its esters and its salts, to the extent that it was necessary for the prosecution to prove that the substance possessed had been cocaine and not one of its stereoisomers, esters or salts. Lawton L.J. said that, when seen in the context of sections 2 and 5(3) and Part 4 of Schedule 2, it was clear that cocaine was a substance which had a number of forms and derivatives, all of which were "cocaine" for the purpose of the Act. It is not necessary to prove more than that the substance possessed had been cocaine in one or other of its forms or derivatives.

Greensmith was approved in *Att.-Gen. for the Cayman Islands v. Roberts* [2002] 1 W.L.R. 1842, PC, where it was held that, on a prosecution for possession of a "controlled drug, namely cocaine" with intent to supply, the fact that the prosecution's expert evidence, in the form of a certificate of analysis, referred to the substance seized from the defendant as "cocaine hydrochloride" provided no basis for challenging the conviction; the word "cocaine" in paragraph 1(a) of Part I of Schedule 1 to the 1971 Act is used in the generic sense, so that it includes the specific forms, derivatives or preparations of it which come within the wording of paragraphs 2 to 5; the reference in the definition of "coca leaf" in Part IV of the Schedule to the extraction of cocaine "either directly or by chemical transformation" makes it clear that "cocaine" includes the substance which is produced by extracting it from the leaves of the plant and converting it into powder form as cocaine hydrochloride; and, whilst paragraphs 2 to 5 deal separately with the various substances that can result from chemical transformations of the substances and products listed in paragraph 1, the generic word "cocaine" includes all such substances; furthermore, it is now within judicial knowledge that cocaine hydrochloride is a form of cocaine, being a "salt of" cocaine (see para. 4); as, therefore, the drug in question was cocaine which is a controlled drug in all its forms, it was not necessary for the certificate to state that the substance referred to in it as "cocaine hydrochloride" was a controlled drug.

(iv) *"Ecstasy" (methylenedioxymethylamphetamine—MDMA)*

27–15 "Ecstasy" (MDMA) is not specifically mentioned in Schedule 2, but it is a Class A controlled drug as being a compound falling within paragraph 1(c) of Part I; the words of that sub-paragraph simply serve to identify the drug; they do not involve the conclusion that MDMA produced by a process falling outside that sub-paragraph (as is possible) is outside the Act: *R. v. Couzens and Frankel* [1992] Crim.L.R. 822, CA.

Naturally subsisting drugs

It will be seen from the above that the term "controlled drug" is a term of art. Each drug that is controlled is identified in Schedule 2 by reference to its pharmaceutical description and not by a "brand name". Where there is a danger that a drug may be thought to be described in generic terms, then the legislature has been careful to provide further clarification. Thus "cannabis", "cannabis resin" and "cannabinol derivatives" are separately defined and they are therefore separately controlled. **27–16**

Accordingly, and subject to *Hodder and Matthews v. DPP* [1990] Crim.L.R. 261 (*post*), the offence of unlawful possession of any controlled drug described in Schedule 2 by its scientific name is not established by proof of possession of naturally occurring material of which the described drug is one of the constituents unseparated from the others. This is so whether or not the naturally occurring material is also included as another item in the list of controlled drugs: *DPP v. Goodchild*, 67 Cr.App.R. 56, HL.

The so-called "magic mushroom" (*Psilocybe Mexicana*) is specifically listed in Schedule 2 as a Class A controlled substance as a result of an amendment thereof effected by the *Drugs Act* 2005, s.21 (effective July 18, 2005: *Drugs Act 2005 (Commencement No. 1) Order* 2005 (S.I. 2005 No. 1650)).

Meaning of "product"

The Divisional Court in *Hodder and Matthews v. DPP*, *ante*, applied a "lay-man's" construction of the word "product", as it appears in Schedule 2 (Pt I, para. 5), so that where H picked, packaged and froze a quantity of "magic mushrooms" he was held to have been in possession of a "product" within paragraph 5. The court said, *obiter*, that the case could have been brought within paragraph 3 of Part I, and that prosecuting authorities' reluctance to rely on that paragraph seemed to be based on a misunderstanding of what had been said in *DPP v. Goodchild*, *ante*. It was said that that case was dealing with cannabis products rather than "magic mushrooms", where separation of the hallucinatory part was not necessary. Since Lord Diplock specifically mentioned "magic mushrooms" to illustrate the point being made (67 Cr.App.R. 56 at 59), the availability of paragraph 3 must remain open to question. For criticism of the decision, see the commentary in the *Criminal Law Review*. **27–17**

Meaning of "preparation"

The word "preparation", in the context of paragraph 5 of Part I, has no technical pharmaceutical meaning. In both *R. v. Stevens (R.)* [1981] Crim.L.R. 568, CA, and *R. v. Cunliffe* [1986] Crim.L.R. 547, CA, the defendants had deliberately subjected a quantity of the mushrooms to heat, so that they dried out. In *Stevens*, it was said that the mushrooms ceased to be in their natural growing state and were "altered by the hand of man". In *Cunliffe*, the court held that it was correctly left open to the jury to conclude that the appellant's conduct in subjecting a collection of psilocybin mushrooms, which he had picked, to a process of drying involved an act of "preparation". In *R. v. Walker* [1987] Crim.L.R. 565, CA, the court was disinclined to accept an argument that merely picking magic mushrooms amounted to "preparation", but left the point open; the conviction of possession of a preparation containing psilocybin was quashed because of an omission to direct the jury that it had to be proved that someone had deliberately brought about a change to the condition of the mushrooms. In *Hodder and Matthews v. DPP*, *ante*, the court held that freezing and packing "magic mushrooms" was not an act of "preparation". The argument is, perhaps, unlikely to recur, given that fungus containing psilocin or an ester of psilocin ("magic mushrooms") is now listed in Schedule 2 (*ante*, § 27–16). **27–18**

Intoxicating substances

The practice of "glue-sniffing" led to the passing of the *Intoxicating Substances (Supply) Act* 1985. Controlled drugs do not come within the ambit of that Act: s.1(1). **27–19**

(6) Proving that a drug is controlled

(a) *Analysts' reports*

(i) *Proof that the drug is in prohibited form*

27–20 It is for the Crown to prove that the substance in question is the controlled drug alleged and, in certain cases, it is also incumbent on the prosecution to prove that the drug had been in prohibited form at the material time. Thus, where (by virtue of the *Misuse of Drugs Act* 1971 and the regulations) it is an offence to have a controlled substance in one form but it is not an offence to have that substance in another form, then it is for the prosecution to prove that the substance is in the prohibited form for otherwise no offence is established: *R. v. Hunt (Richard)* [1987] A.C. 352, HL.

In *Hunt*, the appellant had been charged with the unlawful possession of morphine contrary to section 5(2) of the *Misuse of Drugs Act* 1971, after 154 milligrams of white powder was found at his home. The analyst's statement, which was read to the jury, stated that the powder contained morphine, but did not state the percentage of morphine therein.

27–21 By the *Misuse of Drugs Regulations* 1973 (S.I. 1973 No. 797) (now reg. 4(3) of, and Sched. 5 to, the *Misuse of Drugs Regulations* 2001 (S.I. 2001 No. 3998)), section 5(1) (possession) does not have effect in relation to any preparation of morphine containing not more than 0.2 per cent of morphine, being a preparation compounded with one or more other active or inert ingredients in such a way that the morphine cannot be recovered by readily applicable means.

It was held that, on its true construction, the particular regulation dealt not with an exception to what would otherwise be unlawful but with the definition of the essential ingredients of an offence; and that, as it was an offence to possess morphine in one form but not an offence to possess it in another form, it had been for the prosecution to prove that the morphine in the possession of the appellant had been in the prohibited form, which it had not done.

The regulation in question had been made pursuant to section 7(1)(a) (*post*, § 27–81); their Lordships drew attention to the significant difference between regulations made under that paragraph and those made under sub-paragraph (b). Under the former, a power is given to provide that it shall not be an offence to possess certain drugs; under the latter, a power is given to clothe certain persons with immunity for what would otherwise be unlawful acts. The latter regulations, providing special defences to what would otherwise be unlawful acts, place a burden upon the defendant to bring himself within them.

Hunt was distinguished in a case of possession of a controlled drug with intent to supply under legislation that is identical in all material respects to the 1971 Act. The fact that the prosecution's certificate of analysis referred to the substance seized from the defendant as "cocaine hydrochloride" and did not state that it was a controlled drug provided no basis for challenging the conviction: *Att-Gen. for the Cayman Islands v. Roberts* [2002] 1 W.L.R. 1842, PC. As to this, see also *ante*, § 27–14.

In *R. v. Leeson* [2000] 1 Cr.App.R. 233, CA, it was held that on a charge of possession of a specified drug, it is unnecessary to prove possession of that particular drug. All that is required is proof of possession of a controlled drug. For this reason, it was held to be irrelevant that a defendant charged with possession of cocaine with intent to supply thought that he was in possession of amphetamine. It is submitted that the court reached the correct result: see section 28(2) and (3), *post*, § 27–123. The reasoning, however, is flawed. It is elementary that on a charge of possession of cocaine, a conviction cannot be sustained by proof of possession of cannabis. The court's conclusion is inconsistent with the spirit of *Hunt*, with the decision in *R. v. Hill*, 96 Cr.App.R. 456, CA (*post*), and with the premise on which section 28(3) was drafted. See also the commentaries at [2000] Crim.L.R. 195, and in *Criminal Law Week* 1999/39/6.

As to the more general observations of their Lordships in *R. v. Hunt* in relation to the burden of proof in criminal proceedings, see *ante*, §§ 4–381, 4–389.

(ii) *The importance of a precise analyst's report*

27–22 In *Hunt*, Lord MacKay L.C. remarked (at p. 378 G–H):

"I consider that this case emphasises the need for absolute clarity in the terms of the analyst's certificate founded on by the prosecution in cases of this sort and, in my opinion, it would be wise where there is any possibility of one of the descriptions in the relevant Schedule applying ... that the analyst should state expressly whether or not the substance falls within that description as well as stating whether or not it is a controlled drug within the meaning of the Act of 1971."

It is, therefore, desirable that the analyst includes the level of purity (expressed as a percentage) of the controlled drug in the certificate. The need for clarity in the analyst's report was emphasised in *R. v. Jones (K.)*, 161 J.P. 597, CA.

Hunt was applied in *R. v. Hill, ante*. The appellant had been observed, on three occasions, to hand over to another for cash something which was described by the observing police officers as "small and very dark", "a small dark object" and "a dark substance". He had been charged with supplying cannabis resin. He appealed on the ground that, even if the jury were entitled to infer from the evidence that drug dealing had taken place, there was no evidence to identify the drug that had been supplied, since the prosecution had not produced any scientific evidence to prove that the dark substance was cannabis resin. *Held*, while scientific evidence was not required in every case to identify a drug, the prosecution must establish the identity of the drug that was the subject matter of the charge with sufficient certainty to achieve the standard of proof that was required in a criminal case. In the instant case, the evidence was insufficient to establish that what had changed hands was cannabis resin. *Semble*, the conclusion might have been different had the charge referred to "cannabis or cannabis resin": see p. 460 of the report, and *R. v. Best*, 70 Cr.App.R. 21, CA (*ante*, § 1–137).

(b) *Proof by admissions*

Written or oral statements of an accused may provide, having regard to the circumstances of the case, prima facie evidence as to the nature of a substance alleged to be a controlled drug: *R. v. Chatwood*, 70 Cr.App.R. 39, CA, approving *Bird v. Adams* [1972] Crim.L.R. 174, DC. In *Chatwood*, each of the appellants admitted that they had been in possession of the various drugs specified in the indictment (including heroin). Forbes J. said: **27–23**

"... these drug abusers were expressing an opinion, and an informed opinion, that, having so used the substance which they did use, it was indeed heroin, because they were experienced in the effects of heroin" (at p. 45).

The weight and probity of such opinions or admissions is central to this equation. In *Bird v. Adams*, *ante*, the appellant was found in possession of tablets which he claimed contained LSD and which he said he had been selling. The Divisional Court held that (a) where an accused was not an expert then an "admission" was in reality no admission at all; and (b) an admission may be valueless where an accused could not have the necessary knowledge; but (c), on the facts, the defendant had sufficient knowledge, having supplied the drug, to establish a prima facie case against him. **27–24**

(7) Principal prohibitions and offences under the Act

(a) The importation/exportation of a controlled drug is prohibited: s.3. **27–25**

(b) It is unlawful and an offence:

(i) to supply, to offer to supply, or to produce a controlled drug (or to be concerned in any of those activities): s.4;

(ii) to be in possession, or to possess with intent to supply, a controlled drug: s.5;

(iii) to cultivate cannabis: s.6;

(iv) for an occupier or manager of premises knowingly to permit certain drug related activities to take place on those premises: s.8;

(v) to perform certain activities, etc., relating to opium (s.9) or in connection with drug kits: s.9A;

(vi) to assist in or induce the commission abroad of an offence punishable under a corresponding law: s.20; and

(vii) to obstruct the exercise of powers of search and seizure, to conceal, or fail to produce, certain documents: s.23.

B. Restriction of Importation and Exportation of Drugs

Misuse of Drugs Act 1971, s.3

27–26 **3.**—(1) Subject to subsection (2) below—

(a) the importation of a controlled drug; and

(b) the exportation of a controlled drug,

are hereby prohibited.

(2) Subsection (1) above does not apply—

(a) to the importation or exportation of a controlled drug which is for the time being excepted from paragraph (a) or, as the case may be, paragraph (b) of subsection (1) above by regulations under section 7 of this Act; or

(b) to the importation or exportation of a controlled drug under and in accordance with the terms of a licence issued by the Secretary of State and in compliance with any conditions attached thereto.

As to exceptions under S.I. 2001 No. 3998, reg. 4, see *post*, § 27–135.

27–27 Any licence granted for the purpose of section 5 of the *Drugs (Prevention of Misuse) Act* 1964 or section 2, 3 or 10 of the *Dangerous Drugs Act* 1965 shall have effect as if granted for the purposes of section 3(2) of the 1971 Act: Sched. 5, para. 2.

Section 3 does not create an offence: the offence of evading the prohibitions imposed thereby arises from the combined effect of section 3 and section 170 of the *CEMA* 1979 (*ante*, § 25–452): *R. v. Whitehead* [1982] Q.B. 1272, 75 Cr.App.R. 389, CA. The court said that such an offence could be correctly described or charged as arising under either Act. However, it is desirable, and the court seems to have acknowledged this, that there should always be a reference to section 170 because that provision actually creates the offence. This is essential where a substantive offence is being charged, as opposed to conspiracy to evade the prohibition as charged in *Whitehead*.

It is an offence to contravene the conditions of a licence issued under section 3: s.18(2), *post*, § 27–94.

C. Restriction of Production and Supply of Controlled Drugs

(1) Statute

Misuse of Drugs Act 1971, s.4

27–28 **4.**—(1) Subject to any regulations under section 7 of this Act for the time being in force, it shall not be lawful for a person—

(a) to produce a controlled drug; or

(b) to supply or offer to supply a controlled drug to another.

(2) Subject to section 28 of this Act, it is an offence for a person—

(a) to produce a controlled drug in contravention of subsection (1) above; or

(b) to be concerned in the production of such a drug in contravention of that subsection by another.

(3) Subject to section 28 of this Act, it is an offence for a person—

(a) to supply or offer to supply a controlled drug to another in contravention of subsection (1) above; or

(b) to be concerned in the supplying of such a drug to another in contravention of that subsection; or

(c) to be concerned in the making to another in contravention of that subsection of an offer to supply such a drug.

As to section 28, see *post*, § 27–123.

Producing or supplying a controlled drug where the production or supply contravenes section 4(1) of the 1971 Act is drug trafficking for the purposes of sections 55 to 59 of the *DTA* 1994: section 59A of the 1994 Act, *ante*, § 15–268.

Misuse of Drugs Act 1971, s.4A

Aggravation of offence of supply of controlled drug

27–28a **4A.**—(1) This section applies if—

(a) a court is considering the seriousness of an offence under section 4(3) of this Act, and

(b) at the time the offence was committed the offender had attained the age of 18.

(2) If either of the following conditions is met the court—

(a) must treat the fact that the condition is met as an aggravating factor (that is to say, a factor that increases the seriousness of the offence), and

(b) must state in open court that the offence is so aggravated.

(3) The first condition is that the offence was committed on or in the vicinity of school premises at a relevant time.

(4) The second condition is that in connection with the commission of the offence the offender used a courier who, at the time the offence was committed, was under the age of 18.

(5) In subsection (3), a relevant time is—

(a) any time when the school premises are in use by persons under the age of 18;

(b) one hour before the start and one hour after the end of any such time.

(6) For the purposes of subsection (4), a person uses a courier in connection with an offence under section 4(3) of this Act if he causes or permits another person (the courier)—

(a) to deliver a controlled drug to a third person, or

(b) to deliver a drug related consideration to himself or a third person.

(7) For the purposes of subsection (6), a drug related consideration is a consideration of any description which—

(a) is obtained in connection with the supply of a controlled drug, or

(b) is intended to be used in connection with obtaining a controlled drug.

(8) In this section—

"school premises" means land used for the purposes of a school excluding any land occupied solely as a dwelling by a person employed at the school; and

"school" has the same meaning—

(a) in England and Wales, as in section 4 of the *Education Act* 1996;

(b) [*Scotland*];

(c) [*Northern Ireland*].

[This section was inserted by the *Drugs Act* 2005, s.1(1), with effect from January 1, 2006 (*Drugs Act 2005 (Commencement No. 3) Order* 2005 (S.I. 2005 No. 3053)). It does not apply to an offence committed before that day: *ibid.*, s.1(2).]

(2) Production

(a) *Indictment*

COUNT 1

STATEMENT OF OFFENCE

Producing a controlled drug, contrary to section 4(2)(a) of the Misuse of Drugs Act *1971.* **27–29**

PARTICULARS OF OFFENCE

A B, between the —— day of —— 20—, and the —— day of —— 20—, produced a controlled drug of Class —, namely ——, in contravention ofsection 4(1)(a) of the Misuse of Drugs Act *1971.*

COUNT 2

STATEMENT OF OFFENCE

Being concerned in the production of a controlled drug by another, contrary to section 4(2)(b) of the Misuse of Drugs Act *1971.* **27–30**

PARTICULARS OF OFFENCE

C D between the —— day of —— 20—, and the —— day of —— 20—, was concerned in the production of a controlled drug of Class —, namely ——, in contravention of section 4(1)(a) of the Misuse of Drugs Act *1971, by another, namely ——* [or *being a person unknown*].

(b) *Class of offence, mode of trial and sentence*

27–31 The mode of trial and maximum sentences for offences under the 1971 Act are provided for by section 25 (*post*, § 27–106) and Schedule 4 (*post*, § 27–130). Offences under this section are class 3 offences, *ante*, § 2–17.

An offence under section 4, if committed in respect of a specified Class A drug, is a "trigger offence" within Schedule 6 to the *CJCSA* 2000, as to which, see *ante*, §§ 15–245b and 15–245c; and, in the case of an offence committed prior to April 4, 2005, see also the *PCC(S)A* 2000, s.58A (§ 5–123l in the supplement).

Offences under section 4(2) and (3) are "lifestyle offences" within the *PCA* 2002, Sched. 2, *ante*, § 5–653. On conviction of such offence, a court may make a financial reporting order under section 76 of the *SOCPA* 2005, *ante*, § 5–886a.

As to sentencing generally, see *post*, §§ 27–107 *et seq.*

(c) *Ingredients of the offences*

Statutory definition of "production"

27–32 See section 37(1), *post*, § 27–127, which provides that production of a controlled drug means production of it by manufacture, cultivation or any other method; "any other method" includes the preparation of cannabis plants so as to discard those parts which are not usable and put together those parts which are: *R. v. Harris* [1996] 1 Cr.App.R. 369.

Conversion

27–33 The conversion of one form of a drug into another form of the same genus may be production. Thus, the conversion of cocaine hydrochloride (a salt falling within paragraph 4 of Part I of Schedule 2) into free base cocaine, "crack" (a substance falling within paragraph 5, but not paragraph 4), amounts to production of the free base cocaine. It is the production of a substance (not by manufacture or cultivation but by other method within section 37(1)) with physical and chemical features different from the salt from which it springs, albeit sharing the same generic term, cocaine: *R. v. Russell (P.A.)*, 94 Cr.App.R. 351, CA.

"Structurally derived" production

27–34 See the discussion of "Ecstasy", *ante*, § 27–15.

Participation

27–35 In *R. v. Farr* [1982] Crim.L.R. 745, the Court of Appeal held that there must be established some identifiable participation in the process of producing a controlled drug before a person can be convicted under section 4. What that decision does not make clear (as reported) is whether section 4(1) and (2) excludes the ordinary rules in respect of participation by secondary parties and thus restricts liability under section 4(2). It is submitted that this is not what either Parliament or the Court of Appeal intended. The full transcript of the judgment suggests that it is a case best seen as having been decided on its "unique" facts. Two men arrived unannounced at premises occupied by the appellant and were admitted. They asked to use the kitchen and the appellant knew that they were going to produce (as they did) pink heroin from morphine. In quashing the conviction, the court held that there was no evidence that "the appellant did anything that could amount to participation, or that could be interpreted as an act of participation, in the manufacture of a controlled drug": *per* Purchas J.

27–36 The court examined the relationship between section 8 (*post*, § 27–84) and section 4 and concluded that:

> "there must be some identifiable participation in the process of producing the drug, established before a person can be convicted as an aider and abettor under section 4. For example, if, by prior arrangement, the appellant had come to an agreement with [the men] that he would admit them to his premises and provide facilities, then another situation might well have arisen which would fall within section 4. In this case there is no doubt whatever that the facts established on the evidence would make this appellant liable to conviction under section 8. ... It is necessary ... to see whether any evidence can be spelt out of the interview

> between the police officers and this appellant which would indicate significant participation. This must involve both the intention to participate and some *actus reus* in that direction, before there would be evidence which could be left to the jury."

The court concluded that the appellant was doing no more than knowingly permitting or suffering the production of the drug, but added that there was no reason why someone who knowingly permitted or suffered production of a drug should not also be a participant in such production.

In the commentary to this case ([1982] Crim.L.R. 645), the question is posed why the appellant, in allowing his kitchen to be used for the production of pink heroin, did not aid and abet production for the purposes of section 4? One suggested answer was that section 4(2) excludes the application of the ordinary law of aiding and abetting and that support for such a construction may be found in section 4(2)(b) on the grounds that "concerned in" embraces many instances of aiding and abetting so that "section 4(2) has a narrowing effect on liability". It is plain, from the transcript, that the appellant had argued that the ordinary rules of aiding and abetting did not apply—not, however, on the basis of section 4(2)(b) but, rather on the grounds that section 8 covers the case of a person who permits or suffers production on premises and, therefore, such facts cannot fall under section 4. However, the court rejected that argument saying: **27–37**

> "There are sufficient areas upon which, taking various combinations of events, section 8 can impinge, without there being any conflict with an aiding and abetting under section 4 by making the premises available as a deliberate part of participation in the act of production of the controlled drug."

The case, therefore, seems to have been decided on a slender distinction. If the appellant had known that the men intended to produce heroin *before* he had admitted them, then this would have been some evidence of participation in the production by making the premises available for that purpose, but, sufferance of that activity *after* they had been admitted was held not to be enough. It would therefore seem that the court was not seeking to define the parameters of the offence under section 4 at all, but to decide whether the facts fell within the parameters of aiding and abetting in accordance with existing principles of law. *Farr* should therefore be applied with caution.

(3) Supply

(a) *Indictment*

COUNT 1

STATEMENT OF OFFENCE

Supplying a controlled drug to another, contrary to section 4(3)(a) of the Misuse of Drugs Act *1971*. **27–38**

PARTICULARS OF OFFENCE

A B, on the —— day of —— 20—, unlawfully supplied a controlled drug of Class —, namely ——, to another in contravention of section 4(1) of the Misuse of Drugs Act *1971*.

COUNT 2

STATEMENT OF OFFENCE

Being concerned in supplying a controlled drug to another, contrary to section 4(3)(b) of the Misuse of Drugs Act *1971*. **27–39**

PARTICULARS OF OFFENCE

A B on the —— day of —— 20—, was concerned in supplying a controlled drug of Class A, namely ——, to another in contravention of section 4(1) of the Misuse of Drugs Act *1971*.

The person whom the defendant is alleged to have supplied, or been concerned in the supply of, may be a defendant charged in another count of the indictment, but may not be a co-defendant in the same count: *R. v. Connelly*, 156 J.P. 406, CA (clarifying *R. v. Lubren and Adepoju* [1988] Crim.L.R. 378, CA).

(b) *Class of offence, mode of trial and sentence*

27–40 The mode of trial and maximum sentences for offences under the 1971 Act are provided for by section 25 (*post*, § 27–106) and Schedule 4 (*post*, § 27–130). Offences under this section are class 3 offences, *ante*, § 2–17.

As to certain offences under section 4 being "trigger offences" within Schedule 6 to the *CJCSA* 2000, see *ante*, § 27–31.

As to offences under section 4(3) being "lifestyle offences" within Schedule 2 to the *PCA* 2002 and the power to make a financial reporting order, see *ante*, § 27–31.

As to sentencing generally, see *post*, §§ 27–107 *et seq.*

(c) *Ingredients of the offences*

Being "concerned in"

27–41 For an offence to be shown to have been committed contrary to section 4(3)(b) (or (c)), the prosecution first has to prove the supply of a drug to another, or the making of an offer to supply a drug to another, in contravention of section 4(1) of the Act; secondly, participation by the defendant in an enterprise involving such supply, or such offer to supply; and thirdly, knowledge of the nature of the enterprise, *i.e.* that it involved supply of a drug, or offering to supply a drug: *R. v. Hughes (R.)*, 81 Cr.App.R. 344, CA. It is insufficient for the trial judge when directing the jury upon the law on this topic simply to read out the relevant provisions: *ibid*.

Section 4(3)(c) has been particularly widely drawn so as to involve people who may be at some distance from the actual making of the offer: *R. v. Blake*, 68 Cr.App.R. 1, CA; and see *R. v. Hughes (R.)*, *ante*.

Offer to supply

27–42 In deciding what constitutes an "offer", it is inappropriate to seek to introduce the rules of contract law relating to offer and acceptance (in particular that an offer, once accepted, can no longer be treated as an offer): *R. v. Dhillon* [2000] Crim.L.R. 760, CA.

Three situations often fall to be considered in respect of charges under section 4(3)(a) and (c). The first is where the accused makes an offer to supply a controlled drug of one description (*e.g.* cocaine) which in fact turns out to be a controlled drug of a wholly different description. On these facts there exists no difficulty and section 28(3) (*post*, § 27–123) affords no defence. The offence lies in the making of the offer to supply a controlled drug. The fact that a different controlled drug is involved is irrelevant.

The second situation is where a person offers to supply a controlled drug but the substance is in fact not controlled, albeit that he believes he is offering a controlled drug. *Haggard v. Mason* [1976] 1 W.L.R. 187, DC, makes it plain that he has no defence.

27–43 The third situation is where a person offers to supply a controlled drug, but the substance is, to the knowledge or belief of the accused, not controlled at all. As there is nothing in section 4(1)(b) which provides that the person who makes an offer to supply a controlled drug must intend to do so, the bogus nature of the offer is immaterial: *R. v. Goodard* [1992] Crim.L.R. 588, CA (where it appears that the offer was unrelated to any particular physical substance). The fact that there was no intention to supply a controlled drug is potential mitigation: *ibid.*

In *R. v. Mitchell* [1992] Crim.L.R. 723, CA, Staughton L.J. said, in delivering the judgment of the court:

> "An offer may be by words or conduct. If it is by words, one has to judge from the words whether it is an offer to supply a controlled drug. If a person knowingly makes an offer to supply in words which have that effect, that is the offence. Of course if the offer was by conduct, such as holding a packet in one's hand and in the other hand a placard saying '£20', it might be another question; there it might be relevant whether what was in the packet was a controlled drug or not."

Goodard was applied, and *Mitchell* was approved, in *R. v. Gill*, 97 Cr.App.R. 215, CA, where the defendants were guilty of a conspiracy to offer to supply controlled drugs, even though they intended to cheat their customers by supplying vitamin pills. *Cf. R. v. Kray* [1999] 2 *Archbold News* 3, CA, in which the court would not exclude the possibility that an offer could be made in such circumstances as to be so obviously a charade or joke that it could not properly be regarded as an offer in any real sense.

All of these authorities were considered in *R. v. Prior (Neil)* [2004] Crim.L.R. 849, CA, in which it was held that, when considering whether a person has offered to supply a drug, what is important is the effect of the words used, having regard to the way in which they were said and any other relevant circumstances apparent to the person to whom they were said at the time; whether the words uttered and the manner in which they were uttered had the appearance of an offer is essentially a matter for the tribunal of fact; the genuineness or otherwise of the offer, or indeed whether, notwithstanding appearances, it was meant as a joke, would be irrelevant; furthermore, there is no requirement that, although the prosecution need not prove the genuineness of the offer, they must prove that the defendant intended to make it look genuine (*i.e.* that the offeree should believe it was genuine); and, as to the effect of a withdrawal of an offer, it must follow from the conclusion that when an offer is made the offence is complete, that its subsequent withdrawal or revocation cannot have any effect; the only possible relevance of a later withdrawal of an offer in the same or closely connected conversations is whether, when looking at the conversation or conversations as a whole, it is not clear that an offer was made at all.

Section 28 of the Act (*post*, § 27–123) applies to offences under section 4(3). The question arises whether an accused falling within the third category, has a defence under section 28(3)(b)(i), *i.e.* that he neither believed nor suspected nor had reason to suspect that the substance was a controlled drug. However, section 28(3) only begins to come into play in cases where the prosecution are required to prove (and have proved) that the substance in question is a controlled drug. Section 28(3) therefore has no application where an offer to supply a controlled drug is made—at least by words: see *R. v. Mitchell*, *ante*. **27–44**

Meaning of the term "supply"

Section 37(1) (*post*, § 27–127) merely states that "supplying includes distributing". It would therefore seem that to pass a reefer cigarette from one person to another so that each smoker may take "a draw" amounts to an act of supply: *R. v. Moore* [1979] Crim.L.R. 789, Crown Court, declining to follow *R. v. King* [1978] Crim.L.R. 228. **27–45**

In *Holmes v. Chief Constable Merseyside Police* [1976] Crim.L.R. 125, the Divisional Court held that the word "supply" had to be given its ordinary everyday meaning so that if a person in physical possession of a controlled drug supplies it to others who prior to the supplying were in joint possession of the drug with him, that person *semble* commits an offence under section 5(3): and see *R. v. Buckley and Lane*, 69 Cr.App.R. 371, CA.

The offence does not require proof of payment or reward. Nor need a jury be unanimous as to whether an accused intended to supply on a commercial basis or to a friend: *R. v. Ibrahima* [2005] Crim.L.R. 887, CA.

In *R. v. Mills* [1963] 1 Q.B. 522, 47 Cr.App.R. 49, CCA, it was suggested that "supply" involves the passing of possession from one person to another, but this is manifestly too simplistic because, for example, a patron who hands his coat to a cloakroom attendant for safe-keeping does not (in ordinary speech) supply him with it and, conversely, the cloakroom attendant does not "supply" the depositor with his own coat when it is returned to him. However, this example creates practical difficulties in the context of the mischief which section 4 is endeavouring to tackle. Where a person deposits controlled drugs with another for "safe-keeping and return", the depositor often does not intend that the custodian should use the drug for his own purposes and the custodian often intends no more than that the depositor should resume actual possession.

This issue was considered in the leading case of *R. v. Maginnis* [1987] A.C. 303, HL. In the House of Lords the majority opinion was delivered by Lord Keith who (at p. 312) drew a distinction between the "custodier" who has the necessary intent to supply because his intention was to hand back the controlled drugs to the persons who had deposited them with him so as to enable those persons to apply the drugs to their own purposes and thus put them back in circulation (who would be guilty of supply), and **27–46** the "depositor" who places the drugs in the temporary custody of the "custodier" with no intention of enabling the "custodier" to use the drugs for his own purposes.

27–47 Their Lordships were unanimous in holding that an act of supply "connotes more than the mere transfer of physical control of some chattel or object from one person to another. No one would ordinarily say that to hand over something to a mere custodier was to supply him with it" (*per* Lord Keith at p. 309). By a majority (Lord Goff dissenting) their Lordships held that there was an "additional concept" namely, "that of enabling the recipient to apply the thing handed over to purposes for which he desires or has a duty to apply it". It was not a necessary element that the supply be made out of the provider's own resources: and see *R. v. Taylor* [1986] Crim.L.R. 680, approved in *Donnelly v. H.M. Advocate*, 1985 S.L.T. 243.

27–48 It is submitted that the vexed decision in *Maginnis* does not (*inter alia*) clarify the nature of the mental element which is required to be proved. Thus, is it enough merely to establish that the accused's conduct in fact enables the recipient to apply the drug for his desired purpose (or duty), or must it also be shown that the accused knew of the recipient's intentions? (*Cf. R. v. Carey* (1990) 20 N.S.W.L.R. 292, in which *Maginnis* was not followed.)

27–49 In *R. v. X.* [1994] Crim.L.R. 827, X was a registered police informant whose defence was that he had the drugs pursuant to an arrangement with police officers to pass them to R who would sell them to an undercover officer. The Court of Appeal, dismissing the appeal, held that if the jury accepted the defendant's evidence he would have intended to supply in the *Maginnis* sense. The supplier's motive is not relevant and should not be confused with his intention. The supplier's motive would be relevant to sentence and this is an issue which should be decided by the judge and not the jury: see commentary on *R. v. X.*

The *Maginnis* meaning of "supply" is to be applied regardless of whether the supplier was in voluntary or "involuntary" possession of the drugs supplied: *R. v. Panton*, *The Times*, March 27, 2001, CA.

Where two people agree to buy drugs for themselves, it is undesirable to charge the one who happens to take physical possession of the drugs with the supply of drugs when he distributes the other's share to him; although technically a supply, it was inevitable that a person convicted on the basis of such distribution would be dealt with as for simple possession: *R. v. Denslow* [1998] Crim.L.R. 566, CA.

If A injects B with a drug belonging to B, A is not supplying the drug in contravention of section 4(1): *R. v. Harris* [1968] 1 W.L.R. 769, CA.

The prosecution of a Rastafarian for possession of cannabis with intent to supply where the supply was to be to other Rastafarians for use in connection with religious worship, insofar as it interfered with his right to freedom of religion as guaranteed by Article 9(1) of the ECHR (*ante*, § 16–113), was justifiable under Article 9(2) as being prescribed by law and "necessary in a democratic society … for the protection of public order, health or morals"; there being no issue as to the restriction being "prescribed by law", the question was whether there was a pressing social need for the restriction and, if so, whether the means adopted constituted a proportionate response; as to this, the provisions of the Single Convention on Narcotic Drugs 1961, as amended by the Protocol of 1972 (*ante*, § 27–1), and of the Vienna Convention (*ante*, § 27–2), both of which require contracting parties to penalise the distribution or delivery "on any terms whatsoever" of any narcotic drug, constitute powerful evidence of an international consensus that an unqualified ban on the possession of cannabis with intent to supply is necessary to combat the dangers to public health and safety arising from such drugs; and the judge had been correct not to leave issues as to proportionality to the jury; as to compatibility of the legislation with the European Convention, a distinction is to be drawn between legislation prohibiting conduct because it relates to or is motivated by religious belief and legislation which is of general application but prohibits, for other reasons, conduct which happens to be encouraged or required by religious belief: *R. v. Taylor (Paul)* [2002] 1 Cr.App.R. 37, CA.

Conspiracy to supply

27–49a Where a conspiracy to supply "another" is alleged, that other must be taken to refer to someone other than a conspirator. It is, however, permissible to allege a conspiracy to supply one of the conspirators but that must be made clear in the particulars: *R. v. Drew* [2000] 1 Cr.App.R. 91, CA; *R. v. Jackson (Note)* [2000] 1 Cr.App.R. 97, CA.

D. RESTRICTION OF POSSESSION OF CONTROLLED DRUGS

(1) Statute

Misuse of Drugs Act 1971, s.5

Restriction of possession of controlled drugs

5.—(1) Subject to any regulations under section 7 of this Act for the time being in force, it shall not be lawful for a person to have a controlled drug in his possession. **27–50**

(2) Subject to section 28 of this Act and to subsection (4) below, it is an offence for a person to have a controlled drug in his possession in contravention of subsection (1) above.

(3) Subject to section 28 of this Act, it is an offence for a person to have a controlled drug in his possession, whether lawfully or not, with intent to supply it to another in contravention of section 4(1) of this Act.

(4) In any proceedings for an offence under subsection (2) above in which it is proved that the accused had a controlled drug in his possession, it shall be a defence for him to prove—

(a) that, knowing or suspecting it to be a controlled drug, he took possession of it for the purpose of preventing another from committing or continuing to commit an offence in connection with that drug and that as soon as possible after taking possession of it he took all such steps as were reasonably open to him to destroy the drug or to deliver it into the custody of a person lawfully entitled to take custody of it; or

(b) that, knowing or suspecting it to be a controlled drug, he took possession of it for the purpose of delivering it into the custody of a person lawfully entitled to take custody of it and that as soon as possible after taking possession of it he took all such steps as were reasonably open to him to deliver it into the custody of such a person.

[(4A) In any proceedings for an offence under subsection (3) above, if it is proved that the accused had an amount of a controlled drug in his possession which is not less than the prescribed amount, the court or jury must assume that he had the drug in his possession with the intent to supply it as mentioned in subsection (3).

(4B) Subsection (4A) above does not apply if evidence is adduced which is sufficient to raise an issue that the accused may not have had the drug in his possession with that intent.

(4C) Regulations under subsection (4A) above have effect only in relation to proceedings for an offence committed after the regulations come into force.]

(5) [*Repealed by* Criminal Attempts Act *1981*.]

(6) Nothing in subsection (4) above shall prejudice any defence which it is open to a person charged with an offence under this section to raise apart from that subsection.

[Subss. (4A) to (4C) are inserted, as from a day to be appointed, by the *Drugs Act* 2005, s.2.]

For section 28, see *post*, § 27–123.

Transporting or storing a controlled drug where possession of the drug contravenes section 5(1) of the 1971 Act is drug trafficking for the purposes of sections 55 to 59 of the *DTA* 1994: section 59A of the 1994 Act, *ante*, § 15–268.

(2) Indictment

COUNT 1

STATEMENT OF OFFENCE

Possessing a controlled drug with intent to supply, contrary to section 5(3) of the Misuse of Drugs Act *1971*. **27–51**

PARTICULARS OF OFFENCE

A B on the —— day of ——, 20—, had in his possession a controlled drug of Class — namely ——, with intent to supply it to another in contravention of section 4(1) of the Misuse of Drugs Act *1971*.

COUNT 2

STATEMENT OF OFFENCE

27–52 *Possessing a controlled drug, contrary to section 5(2) of the* Misuse of Drugs Act *1971*.

PARTICULARS OF OFFENCE

A B on the —— day of —— 20— unlawfully had in his possession a controlled drug of Class —, namely ——, in contravention of section 5(1) of the Misuse of Drugs Act *1971*.

(3) Class of offence, mode of trial and sentence

27–53 The mode of trial and maximum sentences for offences under the 1971 Act are provided for by section 25 (*post*, § 27–106) and Schedule 4 (*post*, § 27–130). Offences under this section are class 3 offences, *ante*, § 2–17.

Offences under section 5(2) and (3), if committed in respect of a specified Class A drug, are "trigger offences" within Schedule 6 to the *CJCSA* 2000, as to which, see *ante*, §§ 15–245b and 15–245c; and, in the case of an offence committed prior to April 4, 2005, see also the *PCC(S)A* 2000, s.58A (§ 5–123l in the supplement).

Offences under section 5(3) are "lifestyle offences" within Schedule 2 to the *PCA* 2002, *ante*, § 5–653. On conviction of such offence, a court may make a financial reporting order under section 76 of the *SOCPA* 2005, *ante*, § 5–886a.

As to sentencing generally, see *post*, §§ 27–107 *et seq*.

(4) The ingredients of the offences

The difficulty in defining "possession"

27–54 The *Misuse of Drugs Act* 1971 does not offer a definition of possession, save that section 37(3) (*post*, § 27–127) provides that for the purposes of the Act "the things which a person has in his possession shall be taken to include anything subject to his control which is in the custody of another".

In the ordinary way, a person has in his possession anything which is in his physical custody, or under his control: see *DPP v. Brooks* [1974] A.C. 862, PC. However, the concept of possession is far from straightforward. This is because, in the criminal law, every case of possession seems to involve a mental ingredient of some kind (but see Professor J. C. Smith's commentary to *R. v. Lewis (G.)*, 87 Cr.App.R. 270, at [1988] Crim.L.R. 517). Before the passing of the 1971 Act, offences of possession were charged under section 1(1) of the *Drugs (Prevention of Misuse) Act* 1964, which provided that "it shall not be lawful for a person to have in his possession a substance … specified in the Schedule to this Act". The House of Lords in the leading case of *Warner v. Metropolitan Police Commr* [1969] 2 A.C. 256 (*post*, §§ 27–55 *et seq*.), held that the offence was "absolute" but nonetheless went on to express lengthy opinions as to the nature of the mental element which the prosecution were required to prove in order to establish the fact of possession in various cases. By making section 5(2) and (3) of the 1971 Act subject to section 28 (*post*, § 27–123), Parliament has sought to ameliorate the harshness of the previous law.

27–55 Upon an initial reading of the speeches in *Warner*, *ante*, it may seem incongruous that an offence is declared to be "absolute" and yet explanations are then given as to the "mental ingredient" involved. However, it is suggested that this area of the criminal law is more clearly understood if the following points are borne in mind. First, the law separates the physical element of possession (the *corpus*) from the mental element (the *animus possidendi*), *i.e.* the intention to possess. It is this latter element which received much attention in *Warner*. Secondly, section 28 adds defences which were not previously available. Section 28 does not re-define the word "possession" so as to place the burden of proving a lack of an intention to possess on the accused: see *R. v. Wright*, 62 Cr.App.R. 169, CA, and *R. v. Ashton-Rickhardt*, 65 Cr.App.R. 67, CA. Thirdly, many cases of possession do no more than illustrate well-established propositions of law.

The following extracts from the speeches of their Lordships in *Warner*, *ante*, are designed to highlight the concept of "possession" and to provide guidance on the practical problems that are likely to arise. It is clear from the speeches of Lords Morris, Pearce and Wilberforce that there was for the purposes of the *Drugs (Prevention of Misuse) Act* 1964, a distinction to be made between mere physical custody of an object and its possession, and that possession connotes a mental element of some sort. **27–56**

Lord Morris said (p. 289):

"There can be no rigid formula to be used in directing a jury. Varying sets of facts and circumstances will call for guidance on particular matters. The conception to be explained, however, will be that of being knowingly in control of a thing in circumstances which have involved an opportunity (whether availed of or not) to learn or to discover at least in a general way what the thing is."

Lord Pearce, having reviewed the popular wide meaning of "possession" and related it to the Act, said (p. 305): **27–57**

"I think the term 'possession' is satisfied by a knowledge only of the existence of the thing itself and not its qualities and that ignorance or mistake as to its qualities will not excuse. This would comply with the general understanding of the word 'possess'. Though I reasonably believe the tablets which I possess to be aspirin, yet if they turn out to be heroin I am in possession of heroin tablets. This would be so, I think, even if I believed them to be sweets. It would be otherwise if I believed them to be something of a wholly different nature. At this point a question of degree arises as to when a difference in qualities amounts to a difference in kind. That is a matter for a jury who would probably decide it sensibly in favour of the genuinely innocent but against the guilty. The situation with regard to containers presents further problems. If a man is in possession of the contents of a package, prima facie his possession of the package leads to the strong inference that he is in possession of its contents. But can this be rebutted by evidence that he was mistaken as to its contents? As in the case of goods that have been 'planted' in his pocket without his knowledge, so I do not think that he is in possession of contents which are quite different in kind from what he believed."

Lord Wilberforce said (p. 310): **27–58**

"The question, to which an answer is required, and in the end a jury must answer it, is whether in the circumstances the accused should be held to have possession of the substance, rather than mere control. In order to decide between these two the jury should … be invited to consider all the circumstances—to use again the words of *Pollock & Wright* [*Possession in the Common Law, p. 119*]—the 'modes or events' by which the custody commences and the legal incident in which it is held. By these I mean, relating them to typical situations, that they must consider the manner and circumstances in which the substance, or something which contains it, has been received, what knowledge or means of knowledge or guilty knowledge as to the presence of the substance, or as to the nature of what has been received, the accused had at the time of receipt or thereafter up to the moment when he is found with it; his legal relation to the substance or package (including his right of access to it). On such matters as these (not exhaustively stated) they must make the decision whether, in addition to physical control, he has, or ought to have imputed to him, the intention to possess, or knowledge that he does possess, what is in fact a prohibited substance. If he has this intention or knowledge, it is not additionally necessary that he should know the nature of the substance."

This description of "possession" was adopted by Lord Scarman (with whose speech the other Lords of Appeal concurred) in *R. v. Boyesen* [1982] A.C. 768, HL.

What constitutes "possession"?

In *R. v. McNamara*, 87 Cr.App.R. 246, the Court of Appeal acknowledged the difficulty in expressing the concept of "possession" and in extracting the *ratio* from the speeches in *Warner*, *ante*. The following propositions, it was said, emerged from those speeches. **27–59**

(1) A man does not have possession of something which has been put into his pocket or house without his knowledge.

(2) A mere mistake as to the quality of a thing under the defendant's control is not enough to prevent him being in possession—for example, in possession of heroin believing it to be cannabis or aspirin: see *Searle v. Randolph* [1972] Crim.L.R. 779, DC.

(3) If the defendant believed that the thing was of a wholly different nature to that

which in fact it was, then, to use the words of Lord Pearce (in *Warner*), "the result would be otherwise".

(4) In the case of a package or box, the defendant's possession of it led to the strong inference that he was in possession of the contents. However, if the contents were quite different in kind from what he believed, he was not in possession of them.

To rebut the inference in proposition 4, the defendant must prove that (or raise a real doubt as to whether), either (a) he was a servant or bailee who had no right to open the package and no reason to suspect that its contents were illicit or were drugs, or (b) he had no knowledge of, or had made a genuine mistake as to, the nature of the contents, even though he was the owner, and that he had received the package innocently and had had no opportunity to acquaint himself with its actual contents: *per* Lord Pearce at p. 305D, *ante*, § 27–57.

The 1971 Act places the initial burden of proving that the defendant had, and knew that he had, a package in his control and that the package contained something, upon the prosecution. That establishes the necessary possession. The prosecution must also prove that the package contained the drug alleged. If any of those matters are unproved there is no case to go to the jury. Once those matters are proved, an evidential burden (see *post*, § 27–65) is cast on the defendant to bring himself within section 28(2) and (3): see Lord Lane C.J., at p. 252. In *R. v. Lambert* [2002] 2 A.C. 545, the House of Lords confirmed that the elements of the offence under section 5 had been correctly identified in *McNamara*.

27–60 *Warner* was applied in *R. v. Wright*, 62 Cr.App.R. 169, CA: where a person is handed a container and, at the moment he receives it, does not know or suspect or have reason to suspect that it contains drugs, and, before he has time to examine the contents, he is told to throw it away and does so, he could not be said to be in possession of the drugs which happened to be in the container. It makes no difference to this conclusion that what was said to induce him to throw the container away, made him suspicious about its contents.

As to the irrelevance of a person's mistaken belief as to type of drug which he is in possession of, to "intent to supply", see *R. v. Leeson* [2000] 1 Cr.App.R. 233, *ante*, § 27–21.

Drugs found in premises occupied by/ associated with defendant

27–61 In *R. v. Lewis (G.)*, 87 Cr.App.R. 270, CA, police officers discovered drugs during a search of a house in respect of which L was the sole tenant. L's case was that he rarely visited the house which was frequented by others. The drugs had apparently been found in a cassette case hidden under some clothing. The appellant submitted that the minimum that had to be proved was knowledge of the existence of the cassette case. The court rejected this, holding that the following is an adequate direction (conforming to *Warner*): a person is in possession of something when he has knowledge of its presence and some control over it; but he would not have possession unless he either knew, or the circumstances were such that he had the opportunity, whether he availed himself of it or not, to learn or to discover in a general way what the items were.

27–62 In *R. v. Peaston*, 69 Cr.App.R. 203, CA, P occupied a "bed-sit" in a building comprised entirely of such accommodation. An envelope containing a Class B drug arrived by post. It was placed with other letters for other people on the hall table. P had ordered the supplier to send the drug by post to his address. *Held*: P was properly to be regarded as in possession of the envelope containing the drug when it arrived through the letter box. The fact that at the time of arrival P was, for example, out or asleep was immaterial—see *R. v. Cavendish*, 45 Cr.App.R. 374 at 378 CCA.

27–63 In *R. v. Bland* [1988] Crim.L.R. 41, CA, the appellant had been living with her co-accused, R, in one room of a house which was occupied by others. The police had been observing the house and had seen a number of people calling. Some of the visitors were stopped and questioned and found to be in possession of drugs. A search warrant was executed and traces of drugs were found. The appellant denied knowledge of the presence of the drugs and said that she could not believe that R had either possessed or supplied drugs. She was charged with possession with intent to supply. The case against her rested solely on the fact that she was living with R at a time when he was undoubtedly dealing with drugs. The court ruled that the case should have been withdrawn from the jury. The fact that the appellant and R lived together in the same room was not sufficient evidence from which the jury could infer that she exercised custody or control. There was sufficient evidence to infer knowledge that R was drug dealing but no more. Assistance, though passive, required more than mere knowledge; for example, it required evidence of encouragement or some element of control; and see *R. v. Searle* [1971] Crim.L.R. 592, CA (*post*, § 27–69), and *R. v. Conway and Burkes* [1994] Crim.L.R. 826, CA. In *R. v. McNamara and McNamara* [1998] Crim.L.R. 278, CA, the convictions for possession of drugs found in the house of parents of a number of children who lived at, or regularly stayed at, home were upheld. *Bland* was a decision on its own facts and it was wrong to elevate it to a statement of principle. There was evidence to implicate the appellants in the location of the drugs and the appellants had been *in loco parentis* to the others in the house.

Possession is not dependent on memory

In *R. v. Martindale*, 84 Cr.App.R. 31, CA, it was held that while a person did not necessarily possess every article which he might have in his pockets, possession did not depend on the powers of memory of the alleged possessor and did not come and go as memory revived and faded. Since the applicant had himself placed the drug knowing it was cannabis in his wallet, he was then in possession of it and he remained in possession even though his memory of its presence had faded or gone. **27–64**

Compatibility of sections 5(4) and 28 with Article 6

In *R. v. Lambert* [2002] 2 A.C. 545, HL, it was held that in so far as section 28(2) and (3) (*post*, § 27–123) impose a persuasive burden on the defendant, they are incompatible with the presumption of innocence in Article 6(2) of the ECHR (*ante*, § 16–57), but it is permissible to invoke section 3 of the *Human Rights Act* 1998 (*ante*, § 16–15), as it is possible to read and give effect to those subsections in a manner compatible with Convention rights by construing them as imposing no more than an evidential burden on the accused; if sufficient evidence is adduced to raise the issue, it will be for the prosecution to show beyond reasonable doubt that the defence is not made out. **27–65**

Their Lordships did not deal with the issue arising under section 5(4) (*ante*, § 27–50), but it would seem likely that the same view would prevail. What was said on these issues in the House of Lords was strictly *obiter*, but it may safely be taken to be authoritative in relation to these particular statutory provisions.

In *R. v. Malinina*, unreported, December 20, 2007, CA ([2007] EWCA Crim. 3228), it was said that, in the absence of agreement that there was sufficient evidence to raise a "defence" under section 28, the judge would have to instruct the jury as to the difference between the evidential burden on the defendant and the legal burden on the prosecution. It was also said that the judge would have to explain that the evidential burden could be discharged by proof on a balance of probabilities. It is submitted that this is wrong. First, the suggestion that an evidential burden is discharged by proof on a balance of probabilities is contrary to all authority and is at odds with the essence of the decision in *Lambert*. Secondly, as with all defence evidential issues, such as self-defence (*ante*, § 19–43) or provocation (*ante*, § 19–55), it is for the judge to rule (in the absence of agreement) as to whether there is a sufficiency of evidence for the matter to be left to the jury. **27–66**

Relevance of quantity

In order to found a conviction for the offence of being in possession of a controlled drug contrary to section 5(2), the prosecution do not have to prove possession of a usable quantity of the drug, but merely possession of any quantity, however minute, providing it amounts to something. The question is one of fact for the common sense of **27–67** the tribunal. If it is visible, tangible and measurable it is certainly something. Quantity may also be relevant to the issue of knowledge. If knowledge cannot be proved, possession cannot be established. Possession denotes a physical control or custody of a thing plus knowledge that you have it in your custody or control. You may possess a thing without knowing or comprehending its nature, but you do not possess it unless you know you have it: *R. v. Boyesen* [1982] A.C. 768, HL. See also *DPP v. Brooks* [1974] A.C. 862, PC, *per* Lord Diplock at p. 866H.

Drugs consumed by the accused

27–68 Where traces of amphetamine powder had been found in urine samples, the Divisional Court upheld the decision of the magistrates' court to acquit the defendants, holding that the defendants were not in possession of the powder as it had been consumed and its character had altered: *Hambleton v. Callinan* [1968] 2 Q.B. 427.

Joint possession or aiding and abetting, etc.

27–69 As to the liability of secondary parties generally, see *ante*, Chapter 18.

In *R. v. Searle* [1971] Crim.L.R. 592, CA, the defendants were convicted of possessing a quantity of various dangerous drugs which had been found in a vehicle used by them for a touring holiday. It was alleged that they were all in joint possession of all the drugs. Possession of any particular drug could not be attributed to any particular defendant. The court held: (a) that mere knowledge of the presence of a forbidden article in the hands of a confederate was not enough, it being impossible to equate knowledge with possession; and (b) that an appropriate direction would be to invite the jury to consider whether the drugs formed a common pool from which all had the right to draw at will, and whether there was a joint enterprise to consume drugs together, because then the possession of drugs by one in pursuance of that common enterprise might well be possession on the part of all. See also, *R. v. Bland*, *ante*, § 27–63.

An allegation of joint possession of drugs, where they have not been found on the person of any of the alleged joint possessors, entails an allegation that each had the right to say what should be done with the drugs, a right shared with the other joint possessors. Knowledge is a *sine qua non* of possession, but it is not enough. A person in a car who is told of the presence of drugs in the car, is not thereby saddled with possession thereof: *R. v. Strong and Berry* [1989] L.S. Gazette, March 8, 41, CA. It appears clear from the tenor of the court's judgment, however, that their view was that evidence of a defendant's presence in a car where drugs are found combined with evidence of knowledge of the presence of the drugs would raise a prima facie case of possession against the defendant. If the defendant was the owner or the user of the car, then, depending on all the circumstances, knowledge might be inferred.

The ulterior intent

27–70 Where a possessor of drugs intends to supply them only when he arrives in a foreign country, it would appear that he commits no offence contrary to section 5(3) of the Act, given that the presumption against extra-territorial effect applies to the prohibition on supply in section 4(1): *Seymour v. The Queen* [2008] 1 A.C. 713, PC (although a decision in relation to the Bermudian legislation, it would seem to be equally applicable to the 1971 Act).

(5) Evidence

Of cash, extravagant lifestyle, etc.

27–71 The admissibility of evidence of an extravagant lifestyle in respect of a charge of possession with intent to supply was considered in a flurry of cases beginning in 1994. In spite of some early irreconcilable decisions (*R. v. Batt* [1994] Crim.L.R. 592, CA, and *R. v. Wright* [1994] Crim.L.R. 55, CA), the principles and the required directions to the jury are now clear.

27–72 In *R. v. Morris* [1995] 2 Cr.App.R. 69, CA, Morland J. said at p. 75G:

"In our judgment evidence of large amounts of money in the possession of a defendant or an extravagant lifestyle on his part, prima facie explicable only if derived from drug dealing, is admissible in cases of possession of drugs with intent to supply if it is of probative significance to an issue in the case. The fact that a defendant gives an explanation for the possession of large sums of money does not of itself render such evidence inadmissible; the Crown may be able to rebut such an explanation .... If a judge decides that such evidence is admissible in law he must then decide whether or not to admit it in his discretion, having regard to its probative value and its prejudicial effect. If such evidence is admitted, it is incumbent upon the judge to spell out to the jury what its probative significance can be while making it clear to the jury that it is for them to decide whether it has or has not that probative significance. The judge must then warn the jury that, if they reach the conclusion that the defendant is a drug dealer this is not of itself either evidence of possession of drugs on a particular occasion or a basis for disbelieving the defendant."

In *R. v. Gordon* [1995] 2 Cr.App.R. 61, the Court of Appeal stated that evidence of marginal relevance may be and should be excluded if it would lead to a multiplicity of subsidiary issues. It is the duty of the judge, whether objection is taken or not, to ensure that irrelevant evidence (particularly when it is prejudicial to the defence) is not received in court. By way of example, in *Gordon*, evidence of large sums of cash was admissible, as was the existence of active bank accounts with large credits which was relevant to forestall a defence argument as to the cash, that the accused did not trust banks. But it was not relevant or admissible to cross-examine as to past credits and withdrawals which could only found an inference of past drug dealing (as opposed to present and active drug dealing). When Gordon was arrested he was in possession of a mobile telephone and BMW car, both registered to third parties. The court held that the use of mobile telephones and BMW cars is the stereotype not only of drug dealers but also the young and upwardly mobile, and that registration of property in the name of another is equally consistent with a wish to frustrate creditors. As there was no evidence of the telephone or the car being used for drug dealing, they were matters which even if possibly relevant, were so much on the fringe of the inquiry that the evidence of them should not have been admitted. If it did go in, a careful direction was required. **27–73**

Where the issue is whether the accused was in possession of the drugs rather than the intent to supply, evidence of cash and lifestyle might only rarely be relevant, but it is not the law that such evidence has automatically to be excluded as irrelevant. It might be relevant and admissible not least to the issue of knowledge as an ingredient of possession: *R. v. Guney* [1998] 2 Cr.App.R. 242, CA (not following *R. v. Halpin* [1996] Crim.L.R. 112, CA, and *R. v. Scott* [1996] Crim.L.R. 652, CA); and see the *obiter* observations in *R. v. Edwards* [1998] Crim.L.R. 207, CA, and the principles at *ante*, §§ 25–471 *et seq. Guney* was followed in *R. v. Griffiths* [1998] Crim.L.R. 567, CA (ingredients of an offence are not to be artificially compartmentalised; defence cannot have evidence excluded on basis that intent to supply is not in issue). **27–74**

Where evidence of money, etc., is admitted, the jury should be directed: (a) that they should regard the finding of money as relevant only if they rejected any innocent explanation for it put forward by the accused; (b) that if there was any possibility of the money being in the accused's possession for reasons other than drug dealing, the evidence would not be probative; but (c) that if they concluded that the money indicated not merely past dealing but continuing dealing in drugs they could take into account the finding of the money, together with the drugs in question, in considering whether the necessary intention had been proved: *R. v. Grant* [1996] 1 Cr.App.R. 73, CA. As to the importance of this direction, see also *R. v. Smith (Ivor)* [1995] Crim.L.R. 940, CA, and *R. v. Malik* [2000] Crim.L.R. 197, CA, and the commentaries thereto. A similar direction should be given where the issue is intent to supply and documentary evidence, such as sheets of jottings, is admitted: *R. v. Lovelock* [1997] Crim.L.R. 821, CA. **27–75**

R. v. Grant was distinguished in *R. v. Graham* [2007] 7 *Archbold News* 2, CA, in which it was said that where a defendant's explanation for a large quantity of money was that he had come into possession of it recently, there was no requirement to direct the jury that if they rejected his explanation, they must also be satisfied that it did not relate merely to past dealing in drugs. The court also observed, *obiter*, that although evidence that showed that a defendant had supplied drugs in the past was now potentially admissible under the *CJA* 2003, s.101(1)(d) (*ante*, § 13–25), as evidence of a propensity **27–76** to supply drugs, the distinction between treating it as such and treating it as evidence of part of the current dealing in drugs was so fine that in many cases it would be a distinction without practical difference; accordingly, "as at present advised", it would generally be needlessly complicating for a judge to have to explore such a difference in giving directions to the jury and there would be something highly artificial in the prosecution having to make an application to admit the evidence on a propensity basis.

For other cases in which this topic has been considered, see *R. v. Simms* [1995] Crim.L.R. 304, CA; *R. v. Lucas* [1995] Crim.L.R. 400, CA; *R. v. Brown* [1995] Crim.L.R. 716, CA; *R. v. Okusanya* [1995] Crim.L.R. 941, CA; and *R. v. Nicholas* [1995] Crim.L.R. 942, CA.

Expert

Of street value of drugs and quantity that may be taken by users

27–77 In *R. v. Bryan*, unreported, November 8, 1984, CA, the court upheld a judge's decision to allow a police officer, with two years' experience in a drugs squad, to give evidence as to the usual quantity of cannabis "pushed" in a street deal, and as to the cost thereof. However, in *R. v. Edwards* [2001] 9 *Archbold News* 1, the Court of Appeal held that the judge was right to decline to admit the evidence of a police officer and a man employed for eight years by a drugs charity as to the quantity of a drug that might be taken by users, because the potential witnesses relied on experience rather than academic material. The experience was based on hearsay accounts by users of the quantity of the drug they ingested over a period.

Approving and following *Bryan*, and distinguishing *Edwards*, the Court of Appeal in *R. v. Hodges* [2003] 2 Cr.App.R. 15, held that a police officer with "an enormous body of knowledge after a long career in … drugs investigation …" had been properly allowed to give evidence as an expert as to the usual method of supplying heroin in a particular area, as to the price and as to whether a particular amount would have been more than for personal use. The "primary facts" (see *ante*, § 11–48) were the observed conduct of the appellants, and what had been found (drugs and paraphernalia), and these having been proved by first hand evidence, the officer had been shown to have sufficient expertise in the field to express an opinion in relation thereto. The officer's evidence met the twin test of admissibility of opinion evidence of an expert in *R. v. Bonython* (*ante*, § 10–65). Similarly, in *R. v. Ibrahima* [2005] Crim.L.R. 887, CA, the expert evidence of a deputy director of a national drug advice charity as to levels of consumption of ecstasy was held to be admissible. The witness had no medical qualifications but had visited many drug projects, researched drug use, produced papers on the subject, and considered the literature. Provided such a witness gave the categories of his sources of information, it was unnecessary for the people to whom he had spoken to give evidence.

Of argot of drug dealers

27–77a In *R. v. Nguyen*, unreported, August 22, 2007 ([2007] NSWCCA 249), the New South Wales Court of Criminal Appeal held that a police officer with considerable experience in investigating the supply of prohibited drugs, and who was a native speaker in the language in which a number of intercepted telephone calls had taken place between alleged drug dealers, could properly give evidence of considerable cogency that persons engaged in drug dealing often speak to each other in code, that certain particular words and expressions which are commonly used in such conversations are commonly used by drug dealers to refer to drugs and that these words and expressions, as used in the intercepted conversations, could refer to drugs, but he could not give opinion evidence that as a matter of fact the words used did refer to drugs.

As to expert evidence generally, see *ante*, §§ 10–66 *et seq*.

Application of rule against hearsay

27–78 See *R. v. Kearley* [1992] 2 A.C. 228, HL, and its effective reversal by the *CJA* 2003, *ante*, §§ 11–13, 11–14.

See also *R. v. Rothwell*, 99 Cr.App.R. 388, CA, in which it was held that a police officer could, depending on the source of his knowledge, give evidence that the recipients of packages from the accused were known to him as users of heroin. To the extent that such evidence is within the witness's own knowledge, no issue of hearsay arises; to the extent that it depends on statements made to the witness, it is hearsay and subject now to the provisions of the 2003 Act (*ante*, §§ 11–3 *et seq.*); and to the extent that it is evidence of the bad character of the person in question, it will also be subject to section 100 of that Act (*ante*, § 13–11) (as to which, see also *R. v. Warner and Jones*, 96 Cr.App.R. 324, CA (*ante*, § 13–18)).

(6) Defences

To succeed with the defence under section 5(4)(a) (*ante*, § 27–50) (having taken possession of drug to prevent commission of an offence by another, defendant took all such steps as were reasonably open to him to destroy the drug), the defendant must show that he did more than leave it to the forces of nature to destroy the drug (by burying it in a hole); what is contemplated is destruction of the drugs by the defendant's own act: *R. v. Murphy* [2003] 1 Cr.App.R. 17, CA. **27–78a**

As to the defence of medical necessity not being available to a defendant whose case is that his possession is for the alleviation of pain, see *R. v. Quayle*; *R. v. Wales*; *R. v. Kenny*; *R. v. Taylor and Lee*; *Att.-Gen's Reference (No. 2 of 2004)* [2005] 2 Cr.App.R. 34, CA, *ante*, § 17–131. In *R. v. Altham* [2006] 2 Cr.App.R. 8, CA, it was held that where the state had done nothing to exacerbate a pre-existing medical condition, which had arisen from circumstances unconnected with any act of the state, and where the sufferer of that condition had chosen to use cannabis to alleviate his pain, there was no reason to read the 1971 Act as if it were subject to a defence of medical necessity in order to ensure compatibility with Article 3 of the ECHR (prohibition on inhuman or degrading treatment (*ante*, § 16–39)); Article 3 did not require the state to take any steps to alleviate the condition; and as had been said in *R. v. Quayle*, *ante*, such a defence of medical necessity, if it existed in law, would enable individuals to undertake otherwise unlawful activities without medical intervention or prescription and would thus be in conflict with the purpose and effect of the legislative scheme.

E. RESTRICTION OF CULTIVATION OF CANNABIS PLANT

Misuse of Drugs Act 1971, s.6

6.—(1) Subject to any regulations under section 7 of this Act for the time being in force, it shall not be lawful for a person to cultivate any plant of the genus *Cannabis*. **27–79**

(2) Subject to section 28 of this Act, it is an offence to cultivate any such plant in contravention of subsection (1) above.

For section 28, see *post*, § 27–123.

For regulations under section 7, see S.I. 2001 No. 3998 (*post*, § 27–83).

Class of offence, mode of trial and sentence

The mode of trial and maximum sentences for offences under the 1971 Act are provided for by section 25 (*post*, § 27–106) and Schedule 4 (*post*, § 27–130). An offence under this section is triable either way, and is a class 3 offence, *ante*, § 2–17. **27–80**

As to sentencing generally, see *post*, §§ 27–107 *et seq.*

Once the prosecution have proved that the defendant cultivated a plant of the genus cannabis, there is an evidential burden on the defendant to prove, if he relies on section 28(2), that he did not know that the plant being cultivated was a plant of the genus cannabis: *R. v. Champ*, 73 Cr.App.R. 367, CA.

As to the limited value of this section in view of the definition of cannabis (as extended by the *CLA* 1977, s.52), and the definition of "production" as including production by cultivation (*ante*, § 27–32), see *Taylor v. Chief Constable of Kent*, 72 Cr.App.R. 318, DC.

F. AUTHORISATION OF ACTIVITIES OTHERWISE UNLAWFUL UNDER SECTIONS 3 TO 6

Misuse of Drugs Act 1971, s.7

27–81 **7.**—(1) The Secretary of State may by regulations—

(a) except from section 3(1)(a) or (b), 4(1)(a) or (b) or 5(1) of this Act such controlled drugs as may be specified in the regulations; and

(b) make such other provision as he thinks fit for the purpose of making it lawful for persons to do things which under any of the following provisions of this Act, that is to say sections 4(1), 5(1) and 6(1), it would otherwise be unlawful for them to do.

(2) Without prejudice to the generality of paragraph (b) of subsection (1) above, regulations under that subsection authorising the doing of any such thing as is mentioned in that paragraph may in particular provide for the doing of that thing to he lawful—

(a) if it is done under and in accordance with the terms of a licence or other authority issued by the Secretary of State and in compliance with any conditions attached thereto; or

(b) if it is done in compliance with such conditions as may be prescribed.

(3) Subject to subsection (4) below, the Secretary of State shall so exercise his power to make regulations under subsection (1) above as to secure—

(a) that is not unlawful under section 4(1) of this Act for a doctor, dentist, veterinary practitioner or veterinary surgeon, acting in his capacity as such, to prescribe, administer, manufacture, compound or supply a controlled drug, or for a pharmacist or a person lawfully conducting a retail pharmacy business, acting in either case in his capacity as such, to manufacture, compound or supply a controlled drug; and

(b) that it is not unlawful under section 5(1) of this Act for a doctor, dentist, veterinary practitioner, veterinary surgeon, pharmacist or person lawfully conducting a retail pharmacy business to have a controlled drug in his possession for the purpose of acting in his capacity as such.

27–82 (4) If in the case of any controlled drug the Secretary of State is of the opinion that it is in the public interest—

(a) for production, supply and possession of that drug to be either wholly unlawful or unlawful except for purposes of research or other special purposes; or

(b) for it to be unlawful for practitioners, pharmacists and persons lawfully conducting retail pharmacy businesses to do in relation to that drug any of the things mentioned in subsection (3) above except under a licence or other authority issued by the Secretary of State,

he may by order designate that drug as a drug to which this subsection applies; and while there is in force an order under this subsection designating a controlled drug as one to which this subsection applies, subsection (3) above shall not apply as regards that drug.

(5) [*Variation and revocation of orders.*]

(6) [*Procedure for making orders under this section.*]

(7) [*Duty to consult, or act on recommendation of, Advisory Council.*]

(8) References in this section to a person's "doing" things include references to his having things in his possession.

(9) [*Northern Ireland.*]

27–83 For regulations made under this section, see the *Misuse of Drugs Regulations* 2001 (S.I. 2001 No. 3998) (as most recently amended by the *Misuse of Drugs and Misuse of Drugs (Safe Custody) (Amendment) Regulations* 2007 (S.I. 2007 No. 2154)). The current order under section 7(4) is the *Misuse of Drugs (Designation) Order* 2001 (S.I. 2001 No. 3997).

As to the significant distinction between regulations made under section 7(1)(a) and (b), see *R. v. Hunt (Richard)* [1987] A.C. 352, HL, *ante*, § 27–21.

It is for a jury to decide whether, in the particular circumstances of the case, a doctor administering a prohibited drug to himself is acting in his capacity as a doctor within regulations made under this section: *R. v. Dunbar*, 74 Cr.App.R. 367, CA.

G. OCCUPIERS OF PREMISES

Misuse of Drugs Act 1971, s.8

27–84 **8.** A person commits an offence if, being the occupier or concerned in the management of any premises, he knowingly permits or suffers any of the following activities to take place on those premises, that is to say—

(a) producing or attempting to produce a controlled drug in contravention of section 4(1) of this Act;
(b) supplying or attempting to supply a controlled drug to another in contravention of section 4(1) of this Act, or offering to supply a controlled drug to another in contravention of section 4(1);
(c) preparing opium for smoking;
(d) smoking cannabis, cannabis resin or prepared opium.

Class of offence, mode of trial and sentence

The mode of trial and maximum sentences for offences under the 1971 Act are provided for by section 25 (*post*, § 27–106) and Schedule 4 (*post*, § 27–130). Offences under this section are class 3 offences, *ante*, § 2–17. **27–85**

Offences under section 8 are "lifestyle offences" within Schedule 2 to the *PCA* 2002, *ante*, § 5–653. On conviction of such offence, a court may make a financial reporting order under section 76 of the *SOCPA* 2005, *ante*, § 5–886a.

For examples of recent sentences, see: *R. v. Bradley* [1997] 1 Cr.App.R.(S.) 59, CA (permitting brothel to be used to supply class A drugs); *R. v. Coulson* [2001] 1 Cr.App.R.(S.) 418 (man allowing dealers to move into flat to supply class A drugs); *R. v. Brock and Wyner* [2001] 2 Cr.App.R. 3, CA (managers of a drop-in centre for the homeless permitting the supply of heroin); *R. v. Setchall* [2002] 1 Cr.App.R.(S.) 76, CA; and *R. v. Williams* [2002] 1 Cr.App.R.(S.) 125 (vulnerable mothers of young children); and *R. v. Kilby* [2002] 2 Cr.App.R.(S.) 6, CA; *R. v. Sykes* [2002] 2 Cr.App.R.(S.) 24, CA (addicts facilitating use and exchange of drugs without profit or corruption); and *R. v. Phillips* [2003] 2 Cr.App.R.(S.) 14, CA (permitting use of council flat by others as base for sale of cocaine, in exchange for payment in drugs).

As to sentencing generally, see *post*, §§ 27–107 *et seq.*

"being the occupier or concerned in the management of the premises"

For the purposes of section 8, the expression "occupier" cannot be limited to a person who has legal possession of the premises but includes anyone who has a licence which entitles him to exclusive possession, *i.e.* anyone who has the requisite degree of control over the premises to exclude from them those who might otherwise use them for the purposes forbidden by section 8. An undergraduate living in a furnished room at a hostel owned by his college, and for which he paid his college, is accordingly an "occupier" within the meaning of section 8: *R. v. Tao* [1977] Q.B. 141, 63 Cr.App.R. 163, CA, explaining *R. v. Mogford*, *post*, as being a correct decision on the facts. **27–86**

In *R. v. Mogford*, 63 Cr.App.R. 168, Assizes (Nield J.), two sisters aged 17 and 20, who lived at their parents' home, were charged with permitting the premises to be used for the purpose of smoking cannabis on an occasion when the parents were on holiday. The judge ruled that the defendants were not "occupiers". The mere power to invite guests to the house did not amount to the nature and measure of control required by the Act. A co-tenant of premises who knowingly permits another co-tenant to smoke cannabis may properly be convicted of permitting the premises to be used for smoking cannabis: *R. v. Ashdown*, 59 Cr.App.R. 193, CA. See also *R. v. Coid* [1998] Crim.L.R. 199, CA.

The accused does not have to have a legal right to be on the premises. If he is managing the premises in the sense of running them, organising them and planning them, then the fact that he is a mere squatter or trespasser does not prevent him from coming within the terms of section 8: *R. v. Josephs and Christie*, 65 Cr.App.R. 253, CA.

"Knowingly permits"

In *R. v. Souter*, 55 Cr.App.R. 403, CA, it was held that "permits" under the *Dangerous Drugs Act* 1965, s.5, meant actual knowledge that the premises were being so used, or knowledge of circumstances such that the defendant could be said to have shut his eyes to the obvious or allowed matters to go on without caring whether or not the smoking of cannabis had taken place. *R. v. Souter* was applied in *R. v. Thomas and Thompson*, 63 Cr.App.R. 65, CA, where it was held that the word "knowingly" does not **27–87** add anything to the offence created by the section. Suspicion is not knowledge but knowledge may be inferred from shutting one's eyes to suspicious circumstances. In other words, suspicion *per se* is not enough to constitute permission, but knowledge of one kind or another is essential to permission—*mens rea* in the offender personally is required. In *R. v. Brock and Wyner* [2001] 2 Cr.App.R. 3, CA, it was held that, apart from knowledge, "permits" involves an unwillingness to prevent the activity complained of, which can be inferred from failure to take reasonable steps readily available to prevent it. What is reasonable is to be judged objectively by the jury. The defendant's belief that the steps he had taken were reasonable was irrelevant.

See also *R. v. Farr* [1982] Crim.L.R. 745, CA, *ante*, § 27–35.

It is not necessary to prove more than knowledge of the supply of a controlled drug, even where the particular drug was specified: *R. v. Bett* [1999] 1 Cr.App.R. 361, CA.

The prohibited activity

27–88 The activity allegedly permitted or suffered must be proved to have taken place: *R. v. Auguste* [2004] 1 W.L.R. 917, CA.

H. OPIUM: PROHIBITED ACTIVITIES

Misuse of Drugs Act 1971 s.9

Prohibition of certain activities etc relating to opium

27–89 **9.** Subject to section 28 of this Act, it is an offence for a person—

(a) to smoke or otherwise use prepared opium; or

(b) to frequent a place used for the purpose of opium smoking; or

(c) to have in his possession—

(i) any pipes or other utensils made or adapted for use in connection with the smoking of opium, being pipes or utensils which have been used by him or with his knowledge and permission in that connection or which he intends to use or permit others to use in that connection; or

(ii) any utensils which have been used by him or with his knowledge and permission in connection with the preparation of opium for smoking.

For section 28, see *post*, § 27–123.

For the definition of "prepared opium", see section 37, *post*, § 27–127.

For mode of trial and penalties, see section 25 (*post*, § 27–106) and Schedule 4 (*post*, § 27–130).

I. SUPPLYING ARTICLES FOR ADMINISTERING OR PREPARING CONTROLLED DRUGS

27–90 Section 9A (inserted by the *DTOA* 1986, s.34) created two new summary offences: (a) supplying or offering to supply articles (other than a hypodermic syringe) for the purpose of administering a controlled drug, where the administration of the drug will be unlawful; and (b) supplying or offering to supply articles to be used in the preparation of a controlled drug for unlawful administration.

J. POWERS OF SECRETARY OF STATE FOR PREVENTING MISUSE OF CONTROLLED DRUGS

Misuse of Drugs Act 1971, s.10

27–91 **10.**—(1) Subject to the provisions of this Act, the Secretary of State may by regulations make such provision as appears to him necessary or expedient for preventing the misuse of controlled drugs.

(2) Without prejudice to the generality of subsection (1) above, regulations under this section may in particular make provision—

(a) for requiring precautions to be taken for the safe custody of controlled drugs;

(b) for imposing requirements as to the documentation of transactions involving controlled drugs, and for requiring copies of documents relating to such transactions to be furnished to the prescribed authority;

(c) for requiring the keeping of records and the furnishing of information with respect to controlled drugs in such circumstances and in such manner as may be prescribed;

(d) for the inspection of any precautions taken or records kept in pursuance of regulations under this section;

(e) as to the packaging and labelling of controlled drugs;

(f) for regulating the transport of controlled drugs and the methods used for destroying or otherwise disposing of such drugs when no longer required;

(g) for regulating the issue of prescriptions, containing controlled drugs and the supply of controlled drugs on prescriptions, and for requiring persons issuing or dispensing prescriptions containing such drugs to furnish to the prescribed authority such information relating to those prescriptions as may be prescribed;

(h) for requiring any doctor who attends a person who he considers, or has reasonable grounds to suspect, is addicted (within the meaning of the regulations) to controlled drugs of any description to furnish to the prescribed authority such particulars with respect to that person as may be prescribed;

(i) for prohibiting any doctor from administering, supplying and authorising the administration and supply to persons so addicted, and from prescribing for such persons, such controlled drugs as may be prescribed, except under and in accordance with the terms of a licence issued by the Secretary of State in pursuance of the regulations.

The *Misuse of Drugs (Safe Custody) Regulations* 1973 (S.I. 1973 No. 798, most recently amended by the *Misuse of Drugs and Misuse of Drugs (Safe Custody) (Amendment) Regulations* 2007 (S.I. 2007 No. 2154)) were made under section 10(2)(a). The *Misuse of Drugs (Notification of and Supply to Addicts) Regulations* 1973 (S.I. 1973 No. 799, most recently amended by S.I. 1997 No. 1001) were made under sections 10(2)(h) and (i) and 22(c). The *Misuse of Drugs Regulations* 2001 (S.I. 2001 No. 3998) were made under sections 7, 10, 22 and 31.

As to contravention of these regulations, see section 18, *post*, § 27–94.

K. Power to Direct Special Precautions at Certain Premises

Misuse of Drugs Act 1971, s.11

11.—(1) Without prejudice to any requirement imposed by regulations made in pursuance of section 10(2)(a) of this Act, the Secretary of State may by notice in writing served on the occupier of any premises on which controlled drugs are or are proposed to be kept give directions as to the taking of precautions or further precautions for the safe custody of any controlled drugs of a description specified in the notice which are kept on those premises. **27–92**

(2) It is an offence to contravene any directions given under subsection (1) above.

L. Directions Relating to Prescribing by Practitioners

Section 12 empowers the Secretary of State to give a direction to a practitioner or pharmacist who has been convicted of certain offences connected with controlled drugs prohibiting him from, *inter alia*, prescribing or supplying controlled drugs. Section 12(6) makes it an offence to contravene such a direction. Section 13(1) empowers the Secretary of State to give a direction to a doctor who has contravened regulations made pursuant to section 10(2)(h) or (i), or who has contravened a licence under section 10(2)(i) (see *ante*, § 27–91). Section 13(2) empowers him to give a direction to any practitioner if he considers that the practitioner is or has been prescribing, supplying, etc., controlled drugs in an irresponsible manner. Section 13(3) makes it an offence to contravene such directions. Section 14 provides for the investigation of any case where the Secretary of State considers that there are grounds for a direction under section 13(1) or (2). Section 15 provides for the giving of a direction under section 13(2) of a temporary nature in an emergency and section 16 contains provisions supplementary to sections 14 and 15. Section 17(1) empowers the Secretary of State to require a doctor, pharmacist or person carrying on a retail pharmacy business to furnish him with information concerning dangerous or otherwise harmful drugs in certain circumstances. Sections 17(3) and (4) create offences where a requirement under subsection (1) has not been complied with or where the information is known by the person giving it to be false in a material particular, or is false and recklessly given. **27–93**

For the mode of prosecution and punishment of offences created by sections 12(6), 13(3), 17(3) and 17(4), see Schedule 4 to the 1971 Act, *post*, § 27–130.

M. MISCELLANEOUS OFFENCES

Misuse of Drugs Act 1971, s.18

27–94 **18.**—(1) it is an offence for a person to contravene any regulations made under this Act other than regulations made in pursuance of section 10(2)(h) or (i).

(2) It is an offence for a person to contravene a condition or other term of a licence issued under section 3 of this Act or of a licence or other authority issued under regulations made under this Act, not being a licence issued under regulations made in pursuance of section 10(2)(i).

(3) A person commits an offence if, in purported compliance with any obligation to give information to which he is subject under or by virtue of regulations made under this Act, he gives any information which he knows to be false in a material particular or recklessly gives any information which is so false.

(4) A person commits an offence if, for the purpose of obtaining, whether for himself or another, the issue or renewal of a licence or other authority under this Act or under any regulations made under this Act, he—

(a) makes any statement or gives any information which he knows to be false in a material particular or recklessly gives any information which is so false; or

(b) produces or otherwise makes use of any book, record or other document which to his knowledge contains any statement or information which he knows to be false in a material particular.

The regulations which may be contravened under section 18(1) are the *Misuse of Drugs (Safe Custody) Regulations* 1973 (*ante* § 27–91), made under section 10(2)(a); and the *Misuse of Drugs Regulations* 2001 (S.I. 2001 No 3998), made under sections 7, 10, 22 and 31.

The *Misuse of Drugs (Notification of and Supply to Addicts) Regulations* 1973 (*ante*, § 27–91) were made under section 10(2)(h) and (i) and therefore contravention is not an offence. However, a doctor who contravenes those regulations may be given a direction by the Secretary of State, the contravention of which is an offence: s.13(1) and (3).

N. INCITEMENT

Misuse of Drugs Act 1971, s.19

27–95 **19.** It is an offence for a person to incite another to commit an offence under any other provision of this Act.

[This section is printed as amended, and repealed in part by the *Criminal Attempts Act* 1981, Sched., Pt I; and the *SCA* 2007, s.63(2), and Sched. 6, para. 53.]

As to mode of trial and punishment, see section 25(3) (*post*, § 27–106).

As to incitement generally, see *post*, §§ 33–78 *et seq*.

As to the need to read back into the section the words repealed by the 1981 Act, see *R. v. Marlow* [1997] Crim.L.R. 897, CA.

O. PARTICIPATING IN OFFENCES OUTSIDE THE UNITED KINGDOM

Misuse of Drugs Act 1971, s.20

27–96 **20.** A person commits an offence if in the United Kingdom he assists in or induces the commission in any place outside the United Kingdom of an offence punishable under the provisions of a corresponding law in force in that place.

As to "corresponding law", see section 36, *post*, § 27–126.

Class of offence, mode of trial and sentence

27–97 The mode of trial and maximum sentences for offences under the 1971 Act are provided for by section 25 (*post*, § 27–106) and Schedule 4 (*post*, § 27–130). Offences under this section are class 3 offences, *ante*, § 2–17.

Offences under section 20 are "lifestyle offences" within Schedule 2 to the *PCA* 2002, *ante*, § 5–653. On conviction of such offence, a court may make a financial reporting order under section 76 of the *SOCPA* 2005, *ante*, § 5–886a.

The maximum sentence under the corresponding law of the foreign country is irrelevant to sentence: *R. v. Faulkner and Thomas*, 63 Cr.App.R. 295, CA.

Ambit of offence

V agreed in England with J that he, V, would acquire a lorry, collect a number of speaker cabinets in London and transport them to Italy knowing that thereafter cannabis from a source unknown to V would be fitted into the cabinets and shipped by other persons to the United States in contravention of United States legislation. It was held that a charge of conspiring to contravene section 20 was well-founded. As a matter of everyday speech, what V agreed to do was to assist in the commission of the offence under United States law—there was no justification for placing an artificially restricted meaning (*e.g.* that the assistance had to take the form of acts directly concerned with the actual importation) on the plain English words used by the section: *R. v. Vickers*, 61 Cr.App.R. 48, CA, applied in *R. v. Evans*, 64 Cr.App.R. 237, CA. **27–98**

Section 20 is limited to assisting or inducing the commission of an offence overseas: *per* Scarman L.J. in *R. v. Vickers*, *ante*. Accordingly, a person cannot be guilty of an offence contrary to section 20, unless the offence outside the United Kingdom is in fact committed. Preparatory acts are therefore not embraced by section 20 if the "foreign" offence is not committed: *R. v. Panayi and Karte*, 86 Cr.App.R. 261, CA. **27–99**

Where A intended that drugs should be imported into Holland but assisted in a course of conduct which in fact resulted in the drug being shipped to Belgium (through the acts of an innocent third party), A's conduct brought him within section 20: *R. v. Ahmed* [1990] Crim.L.R. 648, CA.

P. Corporations

Misuse of Drugs Act 1971, s.21

21. Where any offence under this Act or Part II of the *Criminal Justice (International Co-operation) Act* 1990 ... committed by a body corporate is proved to have been committed with the consent or connivance of, or to be attributable to any neglect on the part of, any director, manager, secretary or other similar officer of the body corporate, or any person purporting to act in any such capacity, he as well as the body corporate shall be guilty of that offence and shall be liable to be proceeded against accordingly. **27–100**

[This section is printed as amended, and repealed in part, by the *Criminal Justice (International Co-operation) Act* 1990, s.23(3); the *DTA* 1994, s.65(1), and Sched. 1, para. 3; and the *PCA* 2002, s.457, and Sched. 12.]

See *R. v. Boal* [1992] 1 Q.B. 591, 95 Cr.App.R. 272, CA, *post*, § 30–103.

Q. Power of Secretary of State to Make Regulations

Misuse of Drugs Act 1971, s.22

22. The Secretary of State may by regulations make provision— **27–101**

(a) for excluding in such cases as may be prescribed—

(i) the application of any provision of this Act which creates an offence; or

(ii) the application of any of the following provisions of the *Customs and Excise Management Act* 1979, that is to say sections 50(1) to (4), 68(2) and (3) and 170, in so far as they apply in relation to a prohibition or restriction on importation or exportation having effect by virtue of section 3 of this Act;

(b) for applying any of the provisions of sections 14 to 16 of this Act and Schedule 3 thereto, with such modifications (if any) as may be prescribed—

(i) in relation to any proposal by the Secretary of State to give a direction under section 12(2) of this Act; or

(ii) for such purposes of regulations under this Act as may be prescribed;

(c) for the application of any of the provisions of this Act or regulations or orders thereunder to servants or agents of the Crown, subject to such exceptions, adaptations and modifications as may be prescribed.

[This section is printed as amended by the *Customs and Excise Management Act* 1979, s.177(1), and Sched. 4, para. 12.]

For regulations under this section, see the *Misuse of Drugs Regulations* 2001 (S.I. 2001 No. 3998) (as most recently amended by the *Misuse of Drugs and Misuse of Drugs (Safe Custody) (Amendment) Regulations* 2007 (S.I. 2007 No. 2154))

R. LAW ENFORCEMENT AND PUNISHMENT OF OFFENCES

(1) Search and seizure

Misuse of Drugs Act 1971, s.23

Powers to search and obtain evidence

27–102 **23.**—(1) A constable or other person authorised in that behalf by a general or special order of the Secretary of State (or in Northern Ireland either of the Secretary of State or the Ministry of Home Affairs for Northern Ireland) shall, for the purposes of the execution of this Act, have power to enter the premises of a person carrying on business as a producer or supplier of any controlled drugs and to demand the production of, and to inspect, any books or documents relating to dealings in any such drugs and to inspect any stocks of any such drugs.

(2) If a constable has reasonable grounds to suspect that any person is in possession of a controlled drug in contravention of this Act or of any regulations made thereunder, the constable may—

(a) search that person, and detain him for the purpose of searching him;

(b) search any vehicle or vessel in which the constable suspects that the drug may be found, and for that purpose require the person in control of the vehicle or vessel to stop it;

(c) seize and detain, for the purposes of proceedings under this Act, anything found in the course of the search which appears to the constable to be evidence of an offence under this Act.

In this subsection "vessel" includes a hovercraft within the meaning of the *Hovercraft Act* 1968; and nothing in this subsection shall prejudice any power of search or any power to seize or detain property which is exercisable by a constable apart from this subsection.

(3) If a justice of the peace (or in Scotland a justice of the peace, a magistrate or a sheriff) is satisfied by information on oath that there is reasonable ground for suspecting—

(a) that any controlled drugs are, in contravention of this Act or of any regulations made thereunder, in the possession of a person on any premises; or

(b) that a document directly or indirectly relating to, or connected with, a transaction or dealing which was, or an intended transaction or dealing which would if carried out be, an offence under this Act, or in the case of a transaction or dealing carried out or intended to be carried out in a place outside the United Kingdom, an offence against the provisions of a corresponding law in force in that place, is in the possession of a person on any premises,

he may grant a warrant authorising any constable acting for the police area in which the premises are situated at any time or times within one month from the date of the warrant, to enter, if need be by force, the premises named in the warrant, and to search the premises and any person found therein and, if there is reasonable ground for suspecting that an offence under this Act has been committed in relation to any controlled drugs found on the premises or in the possession of any such persons, or that a document so found is such a document as is mentioned in paragraph (b) above, to seize and detain those drugs or that document, as the case may be.

27–103 (3A) The powers conferred by subsection (1) above shall be exercisable also for the purposes of the execution of Part II of the *Criminal Justice (International Co-operation) Act* 1990 … and subsection (3) above (excluding paragraph (a)) shall apply also to offences under section 12 or 13 of that Act of 1990, taking references in those provisions to controlled drugs as references to scheduled substances within the meaning of that Part.

(4) A person commits an offence if he—

(a) intentionally obstructs a person in the exercise of his powers under this section; or

(b) conceals from a person acting in the exercise of his powers under subsection (1) above any such books, documents, stocks or drugs as are mentioned in that subsection; or

(c) without reasonable excuse (proof of which shall lie on him) fails to produce any such books or documents as are so mentioned where their production is demanded by a person in the exercise of his powers under that subsection.

(5) [*Northern Ireland.*]

[This section is printed as amended, and repealed in part, by the *Criminal Justice (International Co-operation) Act* 1990, s.23(1), (4); the *DTA* 1994, s.65(1), and Sched. 1, para. 4; and the *PCA* 2002, s.457, and Sched. 12.]

Regulation 8 of the *Controlled Drugs (Drug Precursors) (Intra-Community Trade) Regulations* 2008 (S.I. 2008 No. 295) applies the powers of entry and inspection under section 23(1) for the purposes of the execution of article 3 of Council Regulation (EC) 273/2004, which imposes requirements on operators who possess or place on the market drug precursors (*i.e.* specified substances useful for the manufacture of controlled drugs) and applies the provisions relating to warrants in section 23(3)(b) to the offence under regulation 7, which makes it an either-way offence (maximum penalty on conviction on indictment, two years' imprisonment or a fine, or both) to fail to comply with the requirements imposed by article 3.

As to powers to stop and search and powers of entry, search and seizure under the *PACE Act* 1984, see *ante*, §§ 15–48 *et seq.*, and §§ 15–84 *et seq.* respectively. As to the need for a constable carrying out a search under this section to comply with the requirements of the *PACE Act* 1984, s.2 (*ante*, § 15–52) and of Code A (in particular para. 3.2 (Appendix A–9)), see *R. (Bonner) v. DPP* [2005] A.C.D. 56, QBD (McCombe J.); *R. v. Bristol*, 172 J.P. 161, CA; and *B. v. DPP*, 172 J.P. 450, DC. **27–104**

A constable executing a warrant under subsection (3) had power to detain persons in the premises for the purpose of searching them and, by virtue of sections 15, 16 and 117 of the 1984 Act (*ante*, §§ 15–26, 15–101, 15–102), had power to use reasonable force for the purpose; although it was for the police to show, and the burden was a heavy one, that the use of force was necessary and reasonable, it was entirely reasonable that officers should seek by no more force than was necessary to restrict the movement of those in occupation of premises while they were being searched: *DPP v. Meaden* [2004] 1 W.L.R. 955, DC. Police officers who entered an unlicensed night cafe for the sole purpose of detecting offences under the *Misuse of Drugs Act* 1971 were held to be there lawfully because of their powers of entry under the *Greater London Council (General Powers) Act* 1968 and the *Gaming Act* 1845. In such circumstances, the fact that their entry had been effected without a warrant issued under section 23(3) was immaterial. Once a police officer was lawfully on the premises, no matter what power placed him in that position, he was lawfully there for all purposes: *Foster v. Attard*, 83 Cr.App.R. 214, DC.

Money seized under this section must be returned where the person entitled to possession of it is not convicted of a drug trafficking offence, even where it has been established in civil proceedings that it was the proceeds of drug trafficking: *Webb v. Chief Constable of Merseyside Police*; *Porter v. Same* [2000] Q.B. 427, CA (Civ. Div.).

Obstruction

The combined effect of subsections (2)(a) and (4)(a) is that an offence is committed if a person does any act which obstructs a constable who is lawfully detaining him or wishing to detain him for the purpose of searching him for illicit drugs. However, (a) the person must know that the constable is detaining him, or wishing to detain him, in order to search him for such drugs; and (b) the obstruction must be intentional, *i.e.* the act, viewed objectively, obstructed the constable's detention or search and viewed subjectively was intended so to obstruct: *R. v. Forde (J.)*, 81 Cr.App.R. 19, CA. **27–105**

Where there were no reasonable grounds for suspecting that the accused was in possession of drugs, his aggressive behaviour after being detained could not retrospectively provide reasonable grounds and there could be no conviction under section 23(4)(a): *Black v. DPP*, unreported, May 11, 1995, DC (CO 877–95). The searching constable himself must have reasonable grounds to suspect. He should not rely solely on what he is told by persons with no personal knowledge of the circumstances of the alleged possession: *French v. DPP* [1997] C.O.D. 174, DC.

(2) Procedure and penalties

Misuse of Drugs Act 1971, s.25

Prosecution and punishment of offences

25.—(1) Schedule 4 to this Act shall have effect, in accordance with subsection (2) below, with respect to the way in which offences under this Act are punishable on conviction. **27–106**

(2) In relation to an offence under a provision of this Act specified in the first column of the Schedule (the general nature of the offence being described in the second column)—

(a) the third column shows whether the offence is punishable on summary conviction or on indictment or in either way;

(b) the fourth, fifth and sixth columns show respectively the punishments which may be imposed on a person convicted of the offence in the way specified in relation thereto in the third column (that is to say, summarily or on indictment) according to whether the controlled drug in relation to which the offence was committed was a Class A drug, a Class B drug or a Class C drug; and

(c) the seventh column shows the punishments which may be imposed on a person convicted of the offence in the way specified in relation thereto in the third column (that is to say, summarily or on indictment), whether or not the offence was committed in relation to a controlled drug and, if it was so committed, irrespective of whether the drug was a Class A drug, or a Class B drug or a Class C drug;

and in the fourth, fifth, sixth and seventh columns a reference to a period gives the maximum term of imprisonment and a reference to a sum of money the maximum fine.

(3) An offence under section 19 of this Act shall be punishable on summary conviction, on indictment or in either way according to whether, under Schedule 4 to this Act, the substantive offence is punishable on summary conviction, on indictment or in either way; and the punishments which may be imposed on a person convicted of an offence under that section are the same as those which, under that Schedule, may be imposed on a person convicted of the substantive offence.

In this subsection "the substantive offence" means the offence under this Act to which the incitement mentioned in section 19 was directed.

(4) Notwithstanding anything in section 127(1) of the *Magistrates' Courts Act* 1980, a magistrates' court in England and Wales may try an information for an offence under this Act if the information was laid at any time within twelve months from the commission of the offence.

(5) [*Scotland.*]

(6) [*Northern Ireland.*]

[This section is printed as amended by the *MCA* 1980, s.154, and Sched. 7, para. 103; and as repealed in part by the *Criminal Attempts Act* 1981, s.10, and Sched.]

For Schedule 4, see *post*, § 27–130.

Sentencing guidelines

27–107 General sentencing guidelines for offences of importing or dealing in controlled substances were laid down by the Court of Appeal in *R. v. Aramah*, 76 Cr.App.R. 190. Subsequently, the maximum sentences for some of these offences were increased, and in the light of this increase, the guidelines relating to Class A substances were amended by the Court of Appeal in *R. v. Bilinski*, 9 Cr.App.R.(S.) 360, and *R. v. Satvir Singh*, 10 Cr.App.R.(S.) 402. In *R. v. Aranguren*, 99 Cr.App.R. 347, CA, the guidelines relating to Class A drugs were further amended so as to relate to the weight of pure drug involved in the consignment, rather than the street value.

27–107a The guidelines in relation to the importation of cannabis were modified and added to in *R. v. Ronchetti* [1998] 2 Cr.App.R.(S.) 100, CA. On January 29, 2004, two significant legislative amendments took effect. First, cannabinol and cannabinol derivatives (formerly Class A), and cannabis and cannabis resin (formerly Class B) were reclassified as Class C drugs (*Misuse of Drugs Act 1971 (Modification) (No. 2) Order* 2003 (S.I. 2003 No. 3201)); and, secondly, the maximum penalty on conviction on indictment of an offence contrary to section 4(2) or (3), 5(3), 8, 12(6) or 13(3), when committed in relation to a Class C drug was increased from five years' to 14 years' imprisonment (the same as Class B drugs) (*CJA* 2003, s.284, and Sched. 28). A similar increase was effected for importation and exportation offences under the *CEMA* 1979 committed in relation to Class C drugs. It is possible that the Court of Appeal will decide that the net effect of these amendments is "no change" when it comes to sentencing for cannabis offences. It is submitted, however, that some change must have been intended, and it would seem likely that the conclusion will be that what was intended was to provide for an extended range of sentences in the case of cannabis, and, in particular, that sentencing at the bottom of the range should be significantly more lenient, whereas there should be no change for the most serious cases, *i.e.* the lower bracket was to be extended downwards, whereas the upper bracket was to remain the same. As at October 1, 2008, there had been little guidance on the subject from the Court of Appeal beyond *R. v. Lappalainen* (2005) 149 S.J. 672 (level of sentencing for the supply and importation of cannabis has remained unchanged), *R. v. Herridge* [2006] 1 Cr.App.R.(S.) 45 (offence under s.6, *ante*, § 27–79, should attract a reduced sentence where cultivation solely for own use, in order to reflect significant reduction in penalty for simple possession), and *R. v. Vi To* [2006] 2 Cr.App.R.(S.) 38, CA (there was no prospect of the court reducing sentences for the commercial cultivation of cannabis as a result of its re-classification (as to the range for such offences, see *R. v. Xu*, *post*, § 27–111)).

Guidance on obtaining analysis of purity was given in *R. v. Morris* [2001] 1 Cr.App.R. 4. It is essential for sentencing purposes for cases of importation, or in other circumstances, where 500 grammes or more of cocaine, heroin or amphetamine are seized. Bearing in mind the cost and that analysis may cause delay, it will not generally be necessary or desirable on behalf of the prosecution or defence where a defendant is in possession of only a small quantity of cocaine, heroin or amphetamine, consistent with either personal use or only limited supply to others. In such a case the court can be expected to sentence only on the basis of a low level of retail dealing, but taking into account all the other circumstances of the particular case. But, as purity can indicate proximity to the primary source of supply, if there is reason for the prosecution to believe that the defendant in possession of a small quantity of drugs is close to the source of supply and is wholesaling rather than retailing, it will be necessary for purity analysis to be undertaken before a court can be invited to sentence on this more serious basis. In the absence of purity analysis or expert evidence, it is not open to a court to find or assume levels of purity, except in the case of Ecstasy and LSD [and opium] where the weight of drug can generally be assessed by reference to the number of tablets or doses (see *post*, §§ 27–112 *et seq.*). **27–107b**

The *Aramah* guidelines set out below have been edited to incorporate subsequent amendments and developments. **27–108**

Class "A" Drugs ... **27–109**

Importation of heroin, morphine, etc.: Large scale importation, that is where the weight of the drugs at 100 per cent purity is of the order of 500 grammes or more, sentences of 10 years and upwards are appropriate. Where the weight at 100 per cent purity is of the order of five kilogrammes or more, sentences of 14 years and upwards are appropriate. It will seldom be that an importer of any appreciable amount of the drug will deserve less than four years. [*In Att.-Gen.'s References (Nos 117 and 118 of 2005) (R. v. Byfield and Swaby)* [2007] 1 Cr.App.R.(S.) 22, CA, it was said that those prominently involved as organising spirits in a conspiracy to import cocaine that involved significant planning and a persistent series of importations by a number of couriers recruited by those organisers must expect sentences in excess of 20 years' imprisonment on conviction.]

This, however, is one area in which it is particularly important that offenders should be encouraged to give information to the police, and a confession of guilt, coupled with considerable assistance to the police can properly be marked by a substantial reduction in what would otherwise be the proper sentence.

Supplying heroin, morphine, etc.: It goes without saying that the sentence will largely depend on the degree of involvement, the amount of trafficking and the value of the drug being handled. It is seldom that a sentence of less than five years will be justified and the nearer the source of supply the defendant is shown to be, the heavier will be the sentence. There may well be cases where sentences similar to those appropriate to large scale importers may be necessary... **27–110**

Possession of heroin, morphine, etc. ... It is at this level that the circumstances of the individual offender become of much greater importance. Indeed the possible variety of considerations is so wide, including often those of a medical nature, that we feel it impossible to lay down any practical guidelines. On the other hand the maximum penalty for simple possession of Class "A" drugs is seven years' imprisonment and/or a fine, and there will be very many cases where deprivation of liberty is both proper and expedient.

Class "B" Drugs [but see *ante*, § 27–107a as to the re-classification of cannabis and the need for caution] ...

Importation of cannabis: Importation of very small amounts for personal use can be dealt with as if it were simple possession .... Otherwise importation of amounts up to about 20 kilogrammes of herbal cannabis or cannabis resin, or the equivalent in cannabis oil, will, save in the most exceptional cases, attract sentences of between 18 months and three years, with the lowest ranges reserved for pleas of guilty in cases where there has been small profit to the offender. The good character of the courier ... is of less importance than the good character of the defendant in other cases. The reason for this is, it is well known that the large scale operator looks for couriers of good character and for people of a sort which is likely to exercise the sympathy of the court if they are detected and arrested. Consequently one will frequently find students and sick and elderly people are used as couriers for two reasons: first ... they are vulnerable to suggestion and ... to the offer of quick profit, and secondly, it is felt that the courts may be moved to misplaced sympathy in their case. There are few, if any, occasions when anything other than an immediate custodial sentence is proper in this type of importation.

Medium quantities over 20 kilogrammes will attract sentences of three to six years' imprisonment, depending upon the amount involved, and all the other circumstances of the case.

Following a trial, the importation of 100 kilogrammes by persons playing more than a subordinate role, should attract a sentence of seven years to eight years. Ten years is the appropriate starting point, following a trial, for importations of 500 kilogrammes or more, by such persons. Larger importations would attract a higher starting point, which should rise according to the role played, the weight involved and all the other circumstances of the case, up to the statutory maximum of 14 years.

27–111 *Supply of cannabis*: Here again the supply of massive quantities will justify sentences in the region of 10 years for those playing anything more than a subordinate role. Otherwise the bracket should be between one to four years' imprisonment, depending upon the scale of the operation. Supplying a number of small sellers—wholesaling if you like—comes at the top of the bracket. At the lower end will be the retailer of a small amount to a consumer. Where there is no commercial motive (for example, where cannabis is supplied at a party), the offence may well be serious enough to justify a custodial sentence.

[*Production/cultivation of cannabis* (based on *R. v. Xu* [2008] 2 Cr.App.R.(S.) 50, CA): for those concerned in large scale commercial cultivation of cannabis, sentences with a starting point of three years are appropriate for those acting as "gardeners"; for those acting as "managers", sentences of three to seven years were to be expected depending on the level of involvement and the value of the drugs involved, and "organisers" should expect six to seven years. Longer sentences may be appropriate for those who control a large number of such operations. These suggestions make no allowance for a guilty plea or personal mitigation.]

Possession of cannabis: When only small amounts are involved being for personal use, the offence can often be met by a fine. If the history shows however a persisting flouting of the law, imprisonment may become necessary.

Ecstasy

27–112 In *R. v. Warren and Beeley* [1996] 1 Cr.App.R. 120, the Court of Appeal laid down further guidelines for cases involving the importation of Ecstasy. Lord Taylor C.J. said that Ecstasy was the collective and simple name given to three different Class A drugs, all being a complex including amphetamine; MDA, MDMA and MDEA. Five thousand tablets would be expected to contain a total of 500 grammes of the active constituent. As in the case of other Class A drugs, regard should be had to the weight of the drug, rather than to its street value. To maintain the tariff at about the same level as for other Class A drugs, in general for 5,000 tablets or more, the appropriate sentence would be of the order of 10 years and upwards: for 50,000 tablets or more, 14 years and upwards. That was on the basis that the tablets were of the average (or near average) content of 100 milligrammes of active constituent. If analysis showed a substantially different content in an individual case, then the weight of the constituent would be the determinative factor so far as this particular criterion was concerned. These criteria were by way of guidance only; the quantity of tablets or the weight of the constituent was only one factor to be considered in deciding the appropriate sentence. The role of the offender, his plea, any assistance he may have given to the authorities were some, but not all, of the other considerations which the court would have to weigh.

LSD

27–112a Where the dosage unit is about 50 micrograms pure LSD, the sentence on a plea of not guilty for possession with intent to supply 25,000 units should start at 10 years' imprisonment; for 250,000 units the sentence should start at 14 years; adjustment may be made where purity varied significantly; the suggested sentences were only guidelines and there has to be a measure of flexibility: *R. v. Hurley* [1998] 1 Cr.App.R.(S.) 299, CA.

Opium

The court should proceed on the assumption that any given consignment is of 100 per cent purity (as to which, see *post*), although the defence may call evidence to rebut that assumption. On the basis that the street value of opium is lower than that of heroin or cocaine, on a contested case the appropriate sentence for a consignment of 40 kilos or more of opium should be 14 years and upwards, and for a consignment of four kilos or more the sentence should be 10 years and upwards. If it were established that the importation was for the purpose of conversion into morphine or heroin the appropriate sentence should be based on the equivalent value of those drugs: *R. v. Mashaollahi* [2001] 1 Cr.App.R. 6, CA. As to longer sentences being justified where there have been multiple importations (of the same total amount), see *R. v. Degane* [2007] 1 Cr.App.R.(S.) 46, CA. In *R. v. Ghanbari-Monfared* [2008] 2 Cr.App.R.(S.) 47, the Court of Appeal explained that the reference to 100 per cent purity in *Mashaollahi* was to be taken to be a reference to the opium not being adulterated or contaminated, rather than as a reference to the percentage of the active ingredient; but that did not mean that the morphine concentration would be irrelevant; it would be important for the purposes of considering whether any given sentence was out of kilter with sentences that would be imposed for equivalent quantities of heroin or cocaine. **27–112b**

Amphetamine

For the reasons given in *R. v. Aranguren* (*ante*, § 27–107), levels of sentence should depend not on market value but on the quantity of amphetamine calculated on the basis of 100 per cent pure amphetamine base; that is the maximum theoretical purity of 73 per cent amphetamine base in amphetamine sulphate, the remaining 27 per cent being the sulphate. The penalty for importing a controlled drug would usually be higher than for possession with intent to supply. On conviction of importing amphetamine following a contested trial, a custodial sentence would almost invariably be called for, save in exceptional circumstances or where the quantity was so small as to be compatible only with personal consumption by the importer. The ordinary level of sentence on conviction following a contested trial, subject to all other considerations, should be: (i) up to 500 g, up to two years' imprisonment; (ii) more than 500 g but less than 2.5 kg, two to four years; (iii) more than 2.5 kg but less than 10 kg, four to seven years; (iv) more than 10 kg but less than 15 kg, seven to 10 years; (v) more than 15 kg, upwards of 10 years, subject to the statutory maximum of 14 years: *R. v. Wijs* [1998] 2 Cr.App.R. 436, CA. **27–112c**

Other decisions

Determining level of involvement/ "low level retailing". The amount of drugs found on the defendant is not necessarily decisive; what is important is the scale and nature of the dealing; where, as is often the case, there is only one count, the judge is not precluded from taking account of the admitted level of dealing as reflected by sums of money and drug paraphernalia found; but if there is a dispute and no conviction to indicate dealing over a period of time, the judge must exercise caution; to assist in deciding the correct sentence, it is sometimes helpful to look at the scale of sentences for importation; the appropriate sentence on conviction for a low-level retailer selling to finance his own addiction and a modest living is about six years; selling to the vulnerable, or the young or introducing a person to a Class A drug would aggravate the case; mitigation might be found in an early plea, personal circumstances and a determined attempt to break the habit: *R. v. Djahit* [1999] 2 Cr.App.R.(S.) 142, CA. Of offenders who were out-of-work drug addicts, whose motive was solely to finance their own addiction, who held no stock of drugs and who were shown only to have made a few retail supplies of Class A drugs to undercover police officers, there would be some for whom drug treatment and testing orders would be appropriate. In other such cases, generally **27–113** for a first drug-supply offence, adults, following a trial should be sentenced to less than four years' imprisonment, and, following a plea of guilty at the first reasonable opportunity, should be sentenced to a term of the order of two to two-and-a-half years' imprisonment: *R. v. Afonso*; *R. v. Sajid*; *R. v. Andrews* [2005] 1 Cr.App.R.(S.) 99, CA. Such sentences are intended for those with no criminal record: *R. v. Evans* (2005) 149 S.J. 1222, CA. For those with minor convictions for dishonesty or simple possession of drugs who have not previously served a custodial sentence, sentences between two and two-and-a-half years' imprisonment are appropriate. For those with more serious convictions of dishonesty, minor violence, simple possession of drugs, and who have served custodial sentences, three to three-and-a-half years is appropriate.Those with more serious previous convictions, including drug supply offences, are not within the category of offender identified in *Afonso*: *ibid.*

While a sentencer may, where the interests of justice require it, depart from the guidance expressed in *Afonso*, it is not open to him to ignore that guidance because he does not agree with it and does not feel bound by it: *R. v. Chambers* [2006] 1 Cr.App.R.(S.) 23, CA.

A drug dealer who is prepared to resort to violence and who keeps weapons for that purpose must expect that any sentence imposed on him will be significantly increased to reflect that fact and this should normally be emphasised by the imposition of consecutive sentences: *Att.-Gen.'s Reference (No. 68 of 2007) (R. v. Hawkes)*, *The Times*, December 11, 2007, CA.

Importation cases where personal use alone is claimed by defendant. The absence of a conviction for possession with intent to supply does not preclude the court from sentencing on the basis of an intent to supply. Smuggling prohibited drugs is a category of offence on its own, the gravity of which depends primarily on the quantity smuggled, and secondarily on all the other relevant circumstances. If a large quantity is imported, then irrespective of any specific intent to supply, it is a grave offence involving at the very least the risk that quantity imported will find its way on to the home market. A *Newton* hearing (*ante*, § 5–74) may be necessary to determine the truth of the defendant's claim that the drugs were for personal use: *R. v. Ribas*, 63 Cr.App.R. 147, CA.

Exportation. There is no difference in criminality between the importation and the exportation of controlled drugs: *R. v. Powell*, *The Times*, October 5, 2000, CA.

27–114 *Mistake over type of drug.* A mistaken belief on the part of the offender that the drug in his possession is a Class B drug rather than a Class A drug is a mitigating factor (*R. v. Bilinski*, 9 Cr.App.R.(S.) 360). Where the defendant advances such a claim, it may be necessary to hold a *Newton* hearing to determine the truth of the matter, although in appropriate circumstances if the defendant's assertion is manifestly implausible this may not be necessary.

27–115 *Drugs destined for another country.* It is no mitigation in a case of importation or production that the drugs concerned are destined for another country (see *R. v. Gasper*, 10 Cr.App.R.(S.) 173, CA; *R. v. Couzens and Frankel*, 14 Cr.App.R.(S.) 33, CA).

27–116 *Defendant believing relatively harmless substance to be of greater concentration than it actually is.* This was considered in *R. v. Patel and Varshney*, 16 Cr.App.R.(S.) 267. The Court of Appeal, having referred to *R. v. Aranguren*, *ante*, § 27–107, said that the appellants thought that they were importing heroin of normal strength. The argument that a man's belief as to what he had done should not be taken into account in considering the gravity of the offence and what should be his sentence had been rejected in earlier cases. The relevant factors were the quantity of pure drugs actually involved in the importation, the role of the individual defendant, and the element of *mens rea* on the part of the defendant. The appellants thought they were engaged in a major importation of a large quantity of commercially saleable heroin. An analogy could be drawn with cases of attempt, where the actual substantive offence is never committed, but there was nevertheless an important element of criminality. The sentences passed by the Crown Court were reduced by a modest amount.

27–117 *Supply to prisoners.* The Court of Appeal has always taken such offences particularly seriously: see, in particular, *R. v. Prince* [1996] 1 Cr.App.R.(S.) 335 (five years' imprisonment on pleas of guilty upheld in case of 59-year-old man of good character and who was in ill-health, who admitted possessing heroin with intent to supply it to his drug-addicted son in prison, and to having done so, at his son's entreaty, on two previous occasions). For more recent examples, see *R. v. Bentley* [2007] 1 Cr.App.R.(S.) 44, CA (prison officer), *R. v. Dooley* [2008] 1 Cr.App.R.(S.) 109, CA (trainee solicitor), and *R. v. Greaves* [2008] 2 Cr.App.R.(S.) 7, CA.

Examples. For examples of sentences upheld by the Court of Appeal in various types of drug cases, see CSP, B11. **27–117a**

Misuse of Drugs Act 1971, s.27

Forfeiture

27.—(1) Subject to subsection (2) below, the court by or before which a person is convicted of an offence under this Act or an offence falling within subsection (3) below or an offence to which section 1 of the *Criminal Justice (Scotland) Act* 1987 relates, may order anything shown to the satisfaction of the court to relate to the offence, to be forfeited and either destroyed or dealt with in such other manner as the court may order. **27–118**

(2) The court shall not order anything to be forfeited under this section, where a person claiming to be the owner of or otherwise interested in it applies to be heard by the court, unless an opportunity has been given to him to show cause why the order should not be made.

(3) An offence falls within this subsection if it is an offence which is specified in—

(a) paragraph 1 of Schedule 2 to the *Proceeds of Crime Act* 2002 (drug trafficking offences), or

(b) so far as it relates to that paragraph, paragraph 10 of that Schedule.

[This section is printed as amended by the *CJA* 1988, s.70; the *Criminal Justice (International Co-operation) Act* 1990, Sched. 4; the *DTA* 1994, s.65(1), and Sched. 1, para. 5; and the *PCA* 2002, s.456, and Sched. 11, para. 5.]

"Anything" in section 27(1) includes money: *R. v. Beard (G.)* [1975] Crim.L.R. 92, CCC (Caulfield J.). A judicial approach should be adopted in the manner in which anything ordered to be forfeited is to be dealt with. In *Beard*, the judge directed that part of the money was to be paid to Customs and Excise, and the balance was to be paid to the Sheriff of the City of London who in turn was to pay it as a reward to the investigating officer in accordance with the provisions of sections 28 and 29 of the *CLA* 1826. In *R. v. Morgan* [1977] Crim.L.R. 488, CA, it was held that where M had arranged to meet two others at a country cross-roads with the intention of selling them drugs, the money he had on him when arrested should not have been the subject of a forfeiture order under section 27 since, although no doubt it was part of his working capital for trading in drugs, there was no evidence that it related to the offence. **27–119**

The power of forfeiture applies only to tangible things capable of being physically destroyed and not to choses in action or other intangibles: *R. v. Cuthbertson* [1981] A.C. 470, HL. An English court has no jurisdiction to make an order which purports *ipso jure* to transfer movable property situated abroad into the jurisdiction: *ibid.* Section 27 cannot be used to order forfeiture of real property: *R. v. Khan (S.A.)*, 76 Cr.App.R. 29, CA; and *R. v. Pearce* [1996] Crim.L.R. 442, CA, where it was said that the problem could be mitigated by imposing a fine equal to or less than the value of the property in question, which could be enforced as a result of the sale of the property. **27–120**

In *R. v. Marland and Jones*, 82 Cr.App.R. 134, CA, the court emphasised that Cuthbertson was dealing with things which were tangible at the time when the defendant was arrested and had his property seized by the police. The fact that cash seized *in specie* (in the shape of coins and notes) is put into a bank account for safe custody to earn interest, rather than kept in the police station safe, does not put it beyond the reach of forfeiture. The moment to consider is the moment of seizure.

It is important to ensure that the property sought to be made the subject of forfeiture under section 27 should relate to the offence: see *Cuthbertson, ante*; *Haggard v. Mason* [1976] 1 W.L.R. 187, DC; *R. v. Simms* [1988] Crim.L.R. 186, CA; and *R. v. Askew* [1987] Crim.L.R. 584, CA.

Duty to hear evidence before making forfeiture order

The offender should have a proper opportunity to put before the court material to **27–121** establish that the requirements of the section are not satisfied: *R. v. Churcher*, 8 Cr.App.R.(S.) 94, CA.

Judicial review of forfeiture order against a third party

27–122 As to whether an order under section 27 is amenable to judicial review, see *R. v. Maidstone Crown Court, ex p. Gill*, 84 Cr.App.R. 96, DC. The court considered the principles relevant to making an order against a person who is not a defendant. The particular order concerned a car. Lord Lane C.J. said there might be cases where a person who lent his car should have been put on notice that the car was going to be used for some illegal purpose. In such circumstances it might be proper for the judge to make a forfeiture order.

S. LACK OF KNOWLEDGE A DEFENCE IN CERTAIN CASES

Misuse of Drugs Act 1971, s.28

Proof of lack of knowledge etc. to be a defence in proceedings for certain offences

27–123 **28.**—(1) This section applies to offences under any of the following provisions of this Act, that is to say section 4(2) and (3), section 5(2) and (3), section 6(2) and section 9.

(2) Subject to subsection (3) below, in any proceedings for an offence to which this section applies it shall be a defence for the accused to prove that he neither knew of nor suspected nor had reason to suspect the existence of some fact alleged by the prosecution which it is necessary for the prosecution to prove if he is to be convicted of the offence charged.

(3) Where in any proceedings for an offence to which this section applies it is necessary, if the accused is to be convicted of the offence charged, for the prosecution to prove that some substance or product involved in the alleged offence was the controlled drug which the prosecution alleges it to have been, and it is proved that the substance or product in question was that controlled drug, the accused—

(a) shall not be acquitted of the offence charged by reason only of proving that he neither knew nor suspected nor had reason to suspect that the substance or product in question was the particular controlled drug alleged; but

(b) shall be acquitted thereof—

(i) if he proves that he neither believed nor suspected nor had reason to suspect that the substance or product in question was a controlled drug; or

(ii) if he proves that he believed the substance or product in question to be a controlled drug, or a controlled drug of a description, such that, if it had in fact been that controlled drug or a controlled drug of that description, he would not at the material time have been committing any offence to which this section applies.

(4) Nothing in this section shall prejudice any defence which it is open to a person charged with an offence to which this section applies to raise apart from this section.

27–124 For consideration of section 28, see *R. v. McNamara*, 87 Cr.App.R. 246, CA (*ante*, § 27–59); *R. v. Ashton-Rickhardt*, 65 Cr.App.R. 67, CA (*ante*, § 27–55); and *R. v. Champ*, 73 Cr.App.R. 367, CA (*ante*, § 27–80). As to whether subsections (2) and (3) are compatible with Article 6(2) of the ECHR, see *R. v. Lambert* [2002] 2 A.C. 545, HL (*ante*, § 27–65). As to how the matter should be left to the jury, see *ante*, §§ 27–65, 27–66.

Section 28 does not apply to offences of conspiracy: *R. v. McGowan* [1990] Crim.L.R. 399, CA. Nor does it apply to an offence of offering to supply a controlled drug where the offer is made by words: see *R. v. Mitchell* [1992] Crim.L.R. 723, CA (*ante*, § 27–43).

Where a person's state of mind falls within section 28(3)(b)(i) only by virtue of his self-induced intoxication, he cannot avail himself of the defence provided thereby: *R. v. Young (R.)*, 78 Cr.App.R. 288, Ct-MAC.

T. MISCELLANEOUS AND INTERPRETATION PROVISIONS

Misuse of Drugs Act 1971, ss.30, 36, 37

27–125 **30.** [*Issue of licences and authorities.*]

Meaning of "corresponding law", and evidence of certain matters by certificate

27–126 **36.**—(1) In this Act the expression "corresponding law" means a law stated in a certificate purporting to be issued by or on behalf of the government of a country outside the United Kingdom to be a law providing for the control and regulation in that country of the production, supply, use, export and import of drugs and other substances in accordance with the provisions of the Single Convention on Narcotic Drugs signed at New York on March 30, 1961, or a law providing for the control and regulation in that country of the production, supply, use, export and import of dangerous or otherwise harmful drugs in pursuance of any treaty, convention or other agreement or arrangement to which the government of that country and Her Majesty's Government in the United Kingdom are for the time being parties.

(2) A statement in any such certificate as aforesaid to the effect that any facts constitute an offence against the law mentioned in the certificate shall be evidence, and in Scotland sufficient evidence, of the matters stated.

Interpretation

37.—(1) In this Act, except in so far as the context otherwise requires, the following expressions have the meanings hereby assigned to them respectively, that is to say— **27–127**

"the Advisory Council" means the Advisory Council on the Misuse of Drugs established under this Act;

"cannabis" (except in the expression "cannabis resin") means any plant of the genus *Cannabis* or any part of any such plant (by whatever name designated) except that it does not include cannabis resin or any of the following products after separation from the rest of the plant, namely—

(a) mature stalk of any such plant,

(b) fibre produced from mature stalk of any such plant, and

(c) seed of any such plant;

"cannabis resin" means the separated resin, whether crude or purified, obtained from any plant of the genus *Cannabis*;

"contravention" includes failure to comply, and "contravene" has a corresponding meaning;

"controlled drug" has the meaning assigned by section 2 of this Act;

"corresponding law" has the meaning assigned by section 36(1) of this Act;

"dentist" means a person registered in the dentists register under the *Dentists Act* 1984 or entered in the list of visiting EEA practitioners under Schedule 4 to that Act;

"doctor" means a registered medical practitioner within the meaning of Schedule 1 to the *Interpretation Act* 1978;

"enactment" includes an enactment of the Parliament of Northern Ireland;

"person lawfully conducting a retail pharmacy business" ... means a person lawfully conducting such a business in accordance with section 69 of the *Medicines Act* 1968;

"pharmacist" has the same meaning as in the *Medicines Act* 1968;

"practitioner" (except in the expression "veterinary practitioner") means a doctor, dentist, veterinary practitioner or veterinary surgeon;

"prepared opium" means opium prepared for smoking and includes dross and any other residues remaining after opium has been smoked;

"prescribed" means prescribed by regulations made by the Secretary of State under this Act;

"produce", where the reference is to producing a controlled drug, means producing it by manufacture, cultivation or any other method, and "production" has a corresponding meaning;

"supplying" includes distributing;

"veterinary practitioner" means a person registered in the supplementary veterinary register kept under section 8 of the *Veterinary Surgeons Act* 1966;

"veterinary surgeon" means a person registered in the register of veterinary surgeons kept under section 2 of the *Veterinary Surgeons Act* 1966.

(2) References in this Act to misusing a drug are references to misusing it by taking it; **27–128** and the reference in the foregoing provision to the taking of a drug is a reference to the taking of it by a human being by way of any form of self-administration, whether or not involving assistance by another.

(3) For the purposes of this Act the things which a person has in his possession shall be taken to include anything subject to his control which is in the custody of another.

(4) Except in so far as the context otherwise requires, any reference in this Act to an enactment shall be construed as a reference to that enactment as amended or extended by or under any other enactment.

(5) [*Repealed by* Statute Law (Repeals) Act *2004*, *Sched. 1, Pt 17.*]

[This section is printed as amended by the *CLA* 1977, s.52; the *Medical Act* 1983, s.56(1); the *Dentists Act* 1984, s.54(1); the *Dental Qualifications (Recognition) Regulations* 1996 (S.I. 1996 No. 1496); and as repealed in part by the *Pharmacy (Northern Ireland) Order* 1976 (S.I. 1976 No. 1213); and the *Statute Law (Repeals) Act* 2004, Sched. 1, Pt 17.]

As to "possession", see *ante*, §§ 27–54 *et seq.* As to "supplying", see *ante*, §§ 27–45 *et seq.* As to "production", see *ante*, §§ 27–32 *et seq.*

Cannabis and cannabis resin

27–129 Although "cannabis", "cannabis resin", "cannabinol" and "cannabinol derivatives" are types of cannabis, they are not generic for the purposes of drafting charges. Since each drug is separately controlled, they should be separately particularised: but see *Muir v. Smith* [1978] Crim.L.R. 293, DC, and *R. v. Best*, 70 Cr.App.R. 21, CA (legitimate to allege possession of "cannabis or cannabis resin").

"Cannabis resin" includes crude resin: *R. v. Thomas* [1981] Crim.L.R. 496, CA.

The kind of separation contemplated by section 37(1) in the definition of "cannabis resin" is a serious and deliberate removal of the resin of the plant by whatever process is available. Mere possession of some leaves and stalk from a plant of the genus cannabis, which have been separated from the plant, is not sufficient; nor does merely removing a stem or leaf or some other component of the plant constitute the kind of separation contemplated by section 37(1): *Att.-Gen.'s Reference (No. 1 of 1977)*, 65 Cr.App.R. 165, CA.

U. PENALTIES

27–130 The maximum penalties for offences under the *Misuse of Drugs Act* 1971 are set out in Schedule 4 to that Act, *post*. Only those provisions relating to offences triable "either way" have been printed. The summary offences have been omitted.

For section 110 of the *PCC(S)A* 2000, which sets out the circumstances in which a minimum sentence of seven years must be imposed for a third Class A drug trafficking offence, see *ante*, § 5–252.

As to sentencing generally, see *ante*, §§ 27–107 *et seq.*

SCHEDULE 4

Prosecution and Punishment of Offences

Section Creating Offence	General Nature of Offence	Mode of Prosecution	Punishment			
			Class A Drug Involved	Class B Drug Involved	Class C Drug Involved	General
s.4(2)	Production, or being concerned in the production, of a controlled drug.	(a) Summary	*6* [12] mths. or the prescribed sum, or both.	*6* [12] mths. or the prescribed sum, or both.	*3* [12] mths. or £2,500, or both.	
		(b) On indictment	Life or a fine, or both.	14 yrs. or a fine, or both.	14 yrs. or a fine, or both.	
s.4(3)	Supplying or offering to supply a controlled drug or being concerned in the doing of either activity by another.	(a) Summary	*6* [12] mths. or the prescribed sum, or both.	*6* [12] mths. or the prescribed sum, or both.	*3* [12] mths. or £2,500, or both.	
		(b) On indictment	Life or a fine, or both.	14 yrs. or a fine, or both.	14 yrs. or a fine, or both.	
s.5(2)	Having possession of a controlled drug.	(a) Summary	*6* [12] mths. or the prescribed sum, or both.	*3* [12] mths. or £2,500, or both.	*3* [12] mths. or £1,000, or both.	
		(b) On indictment	7 yrs. or a fine, or both.	5 yrs. or a fine, or both.	2 yrs. or a fine, or both.	
s.5(3)	Having possession of a controlled drug with intent to supply it to another.	(a) Summary	*6* [12] mths. or the prescribed sum, or both.	*6* [12] mths. or the prescribed sum, or both.	*3* [12] mths. or £2,500, or both.	
		(b) On indictment	Life or a fine, or both.	14 yrs. or a fine, or both.	14 yrs. or a fine, or both.	

Section Creating Offence	General Nature of Offence	Mode of Prosecution	Punishment: Class A Drug Involved	Punishment: Class B Drug Involved	Punishment: Class C Drug Involved	Punishment: General
s.6(2)	Cultivation of cannabis plant.	(a) Summary	—	—	—	*6* [12] mths. or the prescribed sum, or both.
		(b) On indictment	—	—	—	14 yrs. or a fine, or both.
s.8	Being the occupier, or concerned in the management, of premises and permitting or suffering certain activities to take place there.	(a) Summary	*6* [12] mths. or the prescribed sum, or both.	*6* [12] mths. or the prescribed sum, or both.	*3* [12] mths. or £2,500, or both.	
		(b) On indictment	14 yrs. or a fine, or both.	14 yrs. or a fine, or both.	14 yrs. or a fine, or both.	
s.9	Offences relating to opium.	(a) Summary	—	—	—	*6* [12] mths. or the prescribed sum, or both.
		(b) On indictment	—	—	—	14 yrs. or a fine, or both.

Section Creating Offence	General Nature of Offence	Mode of Prosecution	Punishment			
			Class A Drug Involved	Class B Drug Involved	Class C Drug Involved	General
s.11(2)	Contravention of directions relating to safe custody of controlled drugs.	(a) Summary	—	—	—	*6* [12] mths. or the prescribed sum or both.
		(b) On indictment	—	—	—	2 yrs. or a fine, or both.
s.12(6)	Contravention of direction prohibiting practitioner, etc., from possessing, supply, etc., controlled drugs.	(a) Summary	*6* [12] mths. or the prescribed sum, or both	*6* [12] mths. or the prescribed sum, or both.	*3* [12] mths. or £2,500, or both	
		(b) On indictment	14 yrs. or a fine, or both.	14 yrs. or a fine, or both.	14 yrs. or a fine, or both.	
s.13(3)	Contravention of direction prohibiting practitioner, etc., from prescribing, supplying, etc., controlled drugs.	(a) Summary	*6* [12] mths. or the prescribed sum, or both.	*6* [12] mths. or the prescribed sum, or both.	*3* [12] mths. or £2,500, or both.	
		(b) On indictment	14 yrs. or a fine, or both.	14 yrs. or a fine, or both.	14 yrs. or a fine, or both.	
s.17(4)	Giving false information in purported compliance with notice requiring information relating to prescribing, supply, etc., of drugs.	(a) Summary	—	—	—	*6* [12] mths. or the prescribed sum, or both.

Section Creating Offence	General Nature of Offence	Mode of Prosecution	Punishment			
			Class A Drug Involved	Class B Drug Involved	Class C Drug Involved	General
		(b) On indictment	—	—	—	2 yrs. or a fine, or both.
s.18(1)	Contravention of regulations (other than regulations relating to addicts).	(a) Summary	—	—	—	6 [12] mths. or the prescribed sum, or both.
		(b) On indictment	—	—	—	2 yrs. or a fine, or both.
s.18(2)	Contravention of terms of licence or other authority (other than licence issued under regulations relating to addicts).	(a) Summary	—	—	—	6 [12] mths. or the prescribed sum, or both.
		(b) On indictment	—	—	—	2 yrs. or a fine, or both.
s.18(3)	Giving false information in purported compliance with obligation to give information imposed under or by virtue of regulations.	(a) Summary	—	—	—	6 [12] mths. or the prescribed sum, or both.

Section Creating Offence	General Nature of Offence	Mode of Prosecution	Punishment			
			Class A Drug Involved	Class B Drug Involved	Class C Drug Involved	General
		(b) On indictment	—	—	—	2 yrs. or a fine, or both.
s.18(4)	Giving false information, or producing document, etc., containing false statement, etc., for purposes of obtaining issue or renewal of a licence or other authority.	(a) Summary	—	—	—	*6* [12] mths. or the prescribed sum, or both.
		(b) On indictment	—	—	—	2 yrs. or a fine, or both.
s.20	Assisting in or inducing commission outside United Kingdom of an offence punishable under a corresponding law	(a) Summary	—	—	—	*6* [12] mths. or the prescribed sum, or both
		(b) On indictment	—	—	—	14 yrs. or a fine, or both.
s.23(4)	Obstructing exercise of powers of search, etc., or concealing books, drugs, etc.	(a) Summary	—	—	—	*6* [12] mths. or the prescribed sum, or both.

Section Creating Offence	General Nature of Offence	Mode of Prosecution	Punishment			
			Class A Drug Involved	Class B Drug Involved	Class C Drug Involved	General
		(b) On indictment	—	—	—	2 yrs. or a fine, or both.

[This Schedule (entries relating to summary offences are omitted) is printed as amended by the *CLA* 1977, Sched. 5; the *MCA* 1980, Sched. 7; the *Controlled Drugs (Penalties) Act* 1985, s.1(1); the *CJPOA* 1994, s.157, Sched. 8, Pt II; and the *CJA* 2003, s.284(1), and Sched. 28, para. 1 (substituting all the references to "14" (instead of "5") in the column relating to Class C drugs, but such increase only applying to offences committed after January 28, 2004—see s.284(2), and the *Criminal Justice Act 2003 (Commencement No. 2 and Saving Provisions) Order* 2004 (S.I. 2004 No. 81)). The references to "the prescribed sum" are substituted by virtue of the *MCA* 1980, s.32(2). As to the maximum fines specified as a particular amount, see s.32(5) of the 1980 Act. As from a day to be appointed, the maximum term of imprisonment that may be imposed on summary conviction is increased from "3" or "6" months, according to the offence in question, to 12 months in all cases: *CJA* 2003, s.282(2) and (3), but these increases have no application to an offence committed before the date of commencement of the amendment: *ibid.*, s.282(4).]

Chapter 28

OFFENCES AGAINST PUBLIC JUSTICE

I. PERVERTING THE COURSE OF PUBLIC JUSTICE

A. The Elements of the Offence

It is a common law misdemeanour to pervert the course of public justice: *R. v. Vreones* [1891] 1 Q.B. 360, CCR; *R. v. Andrews* [1973] Q.B. 422, CA. The offence is committed where a person or persons: **28–1**

(a) acts or embarks upon a course of conduct,

(b) which has a tendency to, and

(c) is intended to pervert,

(d) the course of public justice: *R. v. Vreones*, *ante* (at p. 369).

A positive act, whether of concealment or distortion, is required. Inaction is insufficient: *R. v. Headley* [1996] R.T.R. 173, CA (failing to respond to a summons); *R. v. Clark* [2003] R.T.R. 27, CA; *R. v. Jabber* (*post*, § 28–5).

An attempt or incitement or conspiracy to pervert the course of justice is likewise indictable: *R. v. Andrews*, *ante*; *R. v. Sharpe and Stringer*, 26 Cr.App.R. 122, CCA; *R. v. Panayiotou and Antoniades*, 57 Cr.App.R. 762, CA.

In *R. v. Cotter* [2002] 2 Cr.App.R. 29, CA, it was held that the ambit of the offence was sufficiently well-defined for the purposes of Article 7 of the ECHR (*ante*, § 16–97); that article does not outlaw the gradual clarification of the rules of criminal liability through judicial interpretation from case to case, provided that the resultant development is consistent with the essence of the offence and could reasonably be foreseen; the offence in question had been through such a process of elucidation since *R. v. Vreones*, *ante*. But there is a need for caution if the ambit of the offence is to be enlarged; it had to be done on a step-by-step basis, not with one large leap: *R. v. Clark*, *ante* (at p. 369).

B. CONDUCT CAPABLE OF AMOUNTING TO THE OFFENCE

(1) Introduction

28–2 Any act or course of conduct tending and intended to interfere with the course of public justice will amount to the offence; but the offence should only be charged where there are serious aggravating features: *R. v. Sookoo*, *The Times*, April 10, 2002, CA. Such acts may also be contrary to specific statutory provisions or amount to contempt of court. The examples given below are not exhaustive, but represent those acts most frequently encountered in this area of the common law. See also *R. v. Selvage and Morgan* [1982] Q.B. 372 at 379, 380, 73 Cr.App.R. 333 at 339, 340, CA.

(2) Making false allegations

28–3 Conspiracy to charge a man falsely with any crime has long been indictable: *Macdaniel's case* (1755) 19 St.Tr. 745; and *R. v. Rispal* (1762) 3 Burr. 1320. It seems immaterial whether the conspiracy proceeds so far as actually indicting the person falsely accused; and if the object of the conspiracy is extortion, the truth or falsity of the charge is immaterial: *R. v. Hollingberry* (1825) 4 B. & C. 329.

The course of public justice includes the process of criminal investigation; to expose individuals, identified or not, to the risk of arrest, imprisonment pending trial and wrongful conviction and punishment by making a false allegation of crime is to prejudice the course of public justice; although the risk of an innocent person being subjected to wrongful arrest may be greater where the false allegation is capable of identifying individuals, it remains a risk even where it is not so capable if the alleged offence is described with sufficient particularity as to justify a significant police investigation; where, however, a false allegation is of such a generalised nature that there is no such risk, or no more than a theoretical risk, it may be more appropriate to prefer a charge of wasting police time, contrary to section 5(2) of the *CLA* 1967 (*post*, § 28–224): *R. v. Cotter, ante*, § 28–1. See also *R. v. Rowell*, 65 Cr.App.R. 174, CA (a charge of wasting police time is scarcely an appropriate way to deal with exposing individuals to the risk of arrest, imprisonment pending trial and possible wrongful conviction); and *R. v. C.* [2008] Crim.L.R. 394, CA (rarely appropriate merely to caution someone who made a false rape allegation). Where the false allegation is made against an individual who is in fact dead, the appropriate charge is attempting to pervert the course of justice: *R. v. Brown (V.J.)* [2004] Crim.L.R. 665, CA, approving *R. v. Bailey* [1956] N.I. 15 at 26.

As to intent, what has to be proved is that the person making the false allegation intended that it should be taken seriously by the police; it is not necessary to prove an intention that anybody should actually be arrested, etc.: *R. v. Cotter*, *ante*.

(3) Perjury

28–4 The fact that a person has either given false information to investigating officers or has committed perjury (denying on oath the truth of what he told the investigating officers) cannot of itself found a charge of attempting to pervert the course of public justice in relation to the prosecution he gave information about or evidence in. If perjury cannot be proved, the prosecution cannot be allowed to circumvent the statutory safeguard, as to the proof of falsity, by charging attempting to pervert: *Tsang Ping-Nam v. R.*, 74 Cr.App.R. 139, PC.

(4) Concealing the commission of an offence

The offence may be committed where acts are done with the intention of concealing the fact that a crime has been committed, although no proceedings in respect of it are pending or have commenced: *R. v. Sharpe and Stringer*, 26 Cr.App.R. 122, CCA; and see *R. v. Wilde* [1960] Crim.L.R. 116, Assizes (Slade J.) (agreement by two or more persons to conceal knowledge of criminal offence itself a criminal offence). See further *R. v. Rafique* [1993] Q.B. 843, 97 Cr.App.R. 395, CA, *post*, § 28–21. **28–5**

The offence is not wide enough to take in the conduct of a motorist who left the scene of an accident in order to avoid being breathalysed; it was difficult to characterise the mere removal of himself and his vehicle as the concealment of evidence: *R. v. Clark* [2003] R.T.R. 27, CA. See also *R. v. Jabber* [2006] 10 *Archbold News* 3, CA (mere escape from scene of crime and subsequent denial of involvement insufficient to prove concealment).

(5) Obstructing the police

Deliberate and intentional action taken with a view to frustrating statutory procedures required of the police (*e.g.* breath test procedures) can amount to the offence (*R. v. Britton* [1973] R.T.R. 502, CA), even where the initial arrest may have been unlawful (*R. v. Spratt* [2007] 3 N.Z.L.R. 810, NZCA). **28–6**

(6) Assisting others to evade arrest

A person who does an act intending to assist another to evade lawful arrest, with knowledge that the other is wanted by the police as a suspect, is guilty of attempting to pervert the course of justice: *R. v. Thomas and Ferguson*, 68 Cr.App.R. 275, CA. **28–7**

See also the offence contrary to section 4(1) of the *CLA* 1967 (*ante*, § 18–34) (a disadvantage of which is that it requires proof that the person assisted committed an arrestable offence).

(7) Failing to prosecute

Police officers who corruptly receive rewards to hinder prosecutions, by not bringing offenders before the courts or by warning persons of intended prosecutions, may be charged with "conspiracy to obstruct the course of public justice": *R. v. Hammersley*, 42 Cr.App.R. 207, CCA. However, mere failure on the part of a police officer to pursue a matter with a view to prosecution is not necessarily an offence. There is an undoubted discretion in a police officer not to pursue a matter although there is clear evidence of an offence having been committed. This is certainly so in trivial cases, such as riding a bicycle at night without lights or failing to sign a driving licence. However, whether a discretion existed in any particular case is eminently a matter for a jury to decide. For a police officer to be convicted of an offence of conduct tending and intended to pervert the course of justice, it must be proved not only that there was no room for the exercise of discretion on the particular facts, but also that the defendant knew that he had no discretion to act as he did: *R. v. Coxhead* [1986] R.T.R. 411, CA. See, to similar effect, *Beaudry v. The Queen*; *Att.-Gen. of Canada et alii, interveners*, 216 C.C.C. (3d) 353, Supreme Court of Canada. In *R. v. Ward and Hollister* [1995] Crim.L.R. 398, CA, it was held that where a police officer has a discretion, in the instant case administering a breath test, it might amount to an offence of perverting the course of public justice if the discretion was exercised perversely or for improper motives. **28–8**

(8) Procuring and indemnifying sureties

Agreeing to procure, indemnify or reward sureties amounts to perverting the course of public justice: *R. v. Head and Head* [1978] Crim.L.R. 427, CA. See also section 9 of the *Bail Act* 1976 for the offence of agreeing to indemnify sureties in criminal proceedings, *ante*, § 3–46. **28–9**

(9) Interfering with witnesses, evidence and jurors

Witnesses

28–10 A conspiracy to prevent a witness from giving evidence is indictable: *R. v. Steventon* [1802] 2 East 362. Similarly, a conspiracy by a witness bound over to attend a trial with others to absent himself from the trial is indictable, and if the necessary effect of the agreement is to defeat the ends of justice, that must be taken to be the object: *R. v. Hamp* (1852) 6 Cox 167. In *R. v. Bassi* [1985] Crim.L.R. 671, CA, it was held that if a person who has been summoned as a witness deliberately absents himself in return for payment he does an act which tends to pervert the course of justice. In this context, a witness is a person who has made a statement with a view to the provision of evidence in support of proceedings: *R. v. Panayiotou and Antoniades*, 57 Cr.App.R. 762 at 766–767, CA. The fact that no criminal proceedings have been instituted does not prevent a person from being described as a witness: *R. v. Sharpe and Stringer*, 26 Cr.App.R. 122, CCA.

28–11 In *R. v. Kellett* [1976] 1 Q.B. 372, 61 Cr.App.R. 240, the Court of Appeal, having considered the historical development of the offence and the previous case law, said:

28–12 "we would not consider that the offence of attempting to pervert the course of justice would necessarily be committed by a person who tried to persuade a false witness, or even a witness he believed to be false, to speak the truth or to refrain from giving false evidence.

> Secondly, … we think that however proper the end, the means must not be improper. Even if the intention of the meddler with a witness is to prevent perjury and injustice, he commits the offence if he meddles by unlawful means.
>
> Threats and bribery are the means used by offenders in the cases, and any pressure by those means—or by force, as for example by actually assaulting or detaining a witness—would, in our opinion, be an attempt to pervert the course of justice by unlawfully or wrongfully interfering with a witness. If he alters his evidence or will not give it 'through affection, fear, gain, reward or hope or promise thereof'…, the course of justice is perverted, whether his evidence is true or false and whether or not it is believed to be so by him who puts him in fear or hope" (at pp. 388, 249).
>
> "Where the attempt is to get a witness positively to give false evidence, the offence is an offence against section 7 of the *Perjury Act* 1911 [*post*, § 28–185]. Where the attempt is to restrain a witness from giving evidence, it may be necessary to indict for the offence charged in this case" (at pp. 391 to 392, 252).
>
> "There may be cases of interference with a witness in which it would be for the jury to decide whether what was done or said to the witness amounted to improper pressure, and so wrongfully interfered with the witness and attempted to pervert the course of justice, and it would be not only unnecessary and unhelpful but wrong for this court or the trial judge to usurp their function. The decision will depend on all the circumstances of the case, including not merely the method of interfering, but the time when it was done, the relationship between the person interfering and the witness and the nature of the proceedings in which the evidence is being given. Pressure which may be permissible at one stage may be improper at another. What may be proper for a friend or relation or a legal adviser may be oppressive and improper coming from a person in a position of influence or authority. But it is for the judge to direct the jury that some means of inducement are improper and, if proved, make the defendant guilty … . A jury should be directed that a threat (or promise) made to a witness is, like an assault on a witness, an attempt to pervert the course of justice, if made with the intention of persuading him to alter or withhold his evidence, whether or not what he threatens (or promises) is a lawful act, such as the exercise of a legal right, and whether or not he has any other intention or intends to do the act if the evidence is not altered or withheld" (at pp. 392–393, 252–253).

28–13 In *R. v. Toney*; *R. v. Ali*, 97 Cr.App.R. 176, CA, it was held that the offence may be committed even though the means of persuasion used against a potential witness is not in itself unlawful or improper, provided that the end in view is improper, as where the defendant has no genuine belief in the falsity of the witness's proposed evidence. The court, unable to envisage any form of bribery which would not amount to pressure, also held that if bribery is established on the facts, that would in law amount to unlawful means.

Exhibits, evidence, etc.

28–14 Interfering with exhibits or potential evidence is as much an offence as interfering with witnesses: *R. v. Murray (G. E.)*, 75 Cr.App.R. 58, CA; *R. v. Firetto* [1991] Crim.L.R. 208, CA (adulteration of blood sample supplied to motorist). As to the disposal of potential evidence, see *R. v. Rafique* [1993] Q.B. 843, 97 Cr.App.R. 395, CA, *post*, § 28–21.

Jurors

Any approach to a jury, or any member of it, to discuss a case, or express views about it, may amount to an attempt to pervert the course of justice. Solicitors who wish to take statements from jurors for the purposes of an appeal should only do so with the consent of the Court of Appeal: *R. v. Mickleburgh* [1995] 1 Cr.App.R. 297, CA; *R. v. Miah and Akhbar* [1997] 2 Cr.App.R. 12, CA. A trial judge is *functus officio* after verdict and sentence and therefore cannot embark on such inquiries: *R. v. McCluskey*, 98 Cr.App.R. 216, CA. **28–15**

Criminal Justice and Public Order Act 1994

An offence of intimidating witnesses, jurors or others, or taking reprisals against them, was created by section 51 of the *CJPOA* 1994, *post*, §§ 28–142 *et seq.* **28–16**

Criminal Procedure and Investigations Act 1996

Sections 54 and 55 of the *CPIA* 1996 created a procedure to quash an acquittal where there has been a conviction for an offence of perverting the course of justice arising from the same proceedings (see *ante*, §§ 4–128a *et seq.*). **28–16a**

(10) Publishing matters calculated to prejudice a fair trial

The publication of matter calculated to prejudice the fair trial of a pending case is an offence of perverting the course of public justice: *R. v. Fisher* (1811) 2 Camp. 563. Similarly, an agreement between an editor and a reporter to publish such matter is an indictable conspiracy: *R. v. Tibbits and Windust* [1902] 1 K.B. 77. **28–17**

C. TENDING TO PERVERT THE COURSE OF PUBLIC JUSTICE

"Tending" to pervert

In *R. v. Rowell*, 65 Cr.App.R. 174, the Court of Appeal cited with approval Pollock B.'s statement in *R. v. Vreones* [1891] 1 Q.B. 360 at 369, that: "The real offence … is the doing of some act which has a tendency and is intended to pervert the administration of public justice." See too *R. v. Britton* [1973] R.T.R. 502 at 506–507, CA. An act done with the intention of perverting the course of justice is not enough; the act must also have that tendency. To establish a tendency or a possibility, the prosecution do not have to prove that the tendency or possibility in fact materialised; there must be a possibility that what the accused has done "without more" might lead to injustice: *R. v. Murray (G. E.)*, 75 Cr.App.R. 58, CA; and see *R. v. Firetto* [1991] Crim.L.R. 208, CA. **28–18**

"Attempting" to pervert

The word "attempt" is sometimes used in this context, and can be misleading. An attempt to pervert the course of justice is a substantive common law offence and not an inchoate crime. As such it is not truly an attempt, and should not, therefore, be charged contrary to section 1(1) of the *Criminal Attempts Act* 1981: *R. v. Williams (K. J.)*, 92 Cr.App.R. 158, CA. However, the word "attempt" is convenient for use in a case where it cannot be proved that the course of justice was actually perverted. A jury should not be directed to assess the conduct of the accused in terms of proximity to an ultimate offence; they should be left to consider the tendency of the conduct and the intention of the accused: *R. v. Machin*, 71 Cr.App.R. 166, CA. See also *R. v. Brown (V.J.)*, *ante*, § 28–3 (the *Criminal Law Review* commentary suggests that the attempt charged was contrary to section 1(1) of the 1981 Act, rather than common law, but this is not clear from the transcript). **28–19**

D. INTENDING TO PERVERT THE COURSE OF PUBLIC JUSTICE

The prosecution must either prove an intent to pervert the course of justice or an **28–20** intent to do something which, if achieved, would pervert the course of justice: *R. v. Lalani* [1999] 1 Cr.App.R. 481, CA. It is not an intent to interfere with the course of public justice by unlawful means, but to interfere with the course of public justice *per se*: *R. v. Kellett, ante*, § 28–11; *R. v. Toney*; *R. v. Ali, ante*, § 28–13; *R. v. Rafique, post*. See also *R. v. Cotter, ante*, § 28–3.

The offence is concerned with the course of justice, and not merely with the ends of justice; where, therefore, a police officer made a false statement (as to her knowledge of the provenance of certain photographs of an offence of burglary being committed), persuaded the victim to make a false statement (as to the provenance of the photographs) and made a false statement to a suspect in interview (as to the provenance of the photographs), each one of those acts was capable of giving rise to an inference that there was the necessary intention to pervert the course of justice, notwithstanding that the officer may have had no intention of defeating what she believed to be the ends of justice or to procure what she believed to be a false verdict; whether or not her motive had been a laudable one of protecting the source of the photographs (too frightened of reprisals to become involved), and, if it had, whether or not that bore upon her intention in making the false statements or procuring them to be made, were pre-eminently matters for the jury: *Att.-Gen.'s Reference (No. 1 of 2002)* [2003] Crim.L.R. 410, CA.

To the extent that *Att.-Gen.'s Reference (No. 1 of 2002)* suggests that a laudable motive has potential relevance, it is submitted that it is in danger of being misleading. Proof of a person's motive for doing an act may found the basis for an inference as to the intent with which the act was done; but, in this context, it is submitted that all that is necessary is proof of knowledge of all the material circumstances and the intentional doing of an act having a tendency, when objectively considered, to pervert the course of justice: see *Att.-Gen.'s Application*; *Att.-Gen. v. Butterworth* [1963] 1 Q.B. 696, CA (*per* Donovan L.J., at p.726); *Connolly v. Dale* [1996] 1 Cr.App.R. 200, DC (*per* Balcombe L.J. at p.205); *R. v. Meissener* (1995) 130 A.L.R. 547, High Court of Australia (cited in *Lalani, ante*, at pp. 491–2); and Borrie and Lowe, *The Law of Contempt*, 3rd ed., pp. 64 *et seq.*, 410 *et seq.*

E. THE COURSE OF PUBLIC JUSTICE

28–21 In *R. v. Selvage and Morgan* [1982] Q.B. 372, 73 Cr.App.R. 333, CA, it was held that in order to lay a charge of attempting, or conspiring, to pervert the course of public justice, a course of justice must have been embarked upon in the sense that proceedings of some kind are in being or imminent or investigations which could or might bring proceedings about are in progress. Although this statement of the *sine qua non* of the offence seems to exclude cases where an offence has been committed and another or others do acts with the intention of concealing that fact, the judgment makes it clear that the Court of Appeal had well in mind:

> "... conduct which relates to judicial proceedings, civil or criminal, whether or not they have yet been instituted but which are within the contemplation of the wrong-doer whose conduct was designed to affect the outcome of them. That conduct includes giving false information to the police with the object of among other things putting the police on a false trail ..." (at pp. 379, 339).

In *R. v. Rafique* [1993] Q.B. 843, 97 Cr.App.R. 395, CA, it was held that the answer to the question of whether particular conduct had a tendency to pervert the course of justice could not depend on whether investigations of the matter, which might become court proceedings, had begun; if an intention to pervert the course of justice in relation to the matter was proved, the conduct had the same quality whether performed before the matter was investigated, or even discovered, as it would have had at a later stage. See also *ante*, § 28–5.

28–22 Even if a police investigation establishes that no offence has been committed, the inquiry is still part of the administration of justice. The concealment or destruction of evidence relevant to an investigation is clearly an act which has a tendency to pervert an investigation by turning it from its right course. To hold otherwise would mean that a person who destroyed the only evidence of a crime before an investigation began would not commit the offence: *R. v. Kiffin* [1994] Crim.L.R. 449, CA.

As to the course of public justice including the process of criminal investigation, see also *R. v. Cotter*, *ante*, § 28–3.

If a relevant act might mislead a court in any or all of the possible types of proceedings that might ensue, that is sufficient to justify a conviction: *R. v. Sinha* [1995] Crim.L.R. 68, CA.

[The next paragraph is § 28–26.]

F. INDICTMENT

STATEMENT OF OFFENCE

Doing an act [acts] tending and intended to pervert the course of public justice. **28–26**

PARTICULARS OF OFFENCE

A B, on a day between the —— and the —— days of —— 20—, with intent to pervert the course of public justice, did an act [a series of acts] which had a tendency to pervert the course of public justice in that he ….

28–27 This form of indictment avoids any confusion which might arise out of the fact that attempting to pervert the course of public justice is a common law offence and not a statutory attempt under the *Criminal Attempts Act* 1981. It was approved by the Court of Appeal in *R. v. Williams (K. J.), ante*, § 28–19.

G. SENTENCE

28–28 For cases of doing an act tending to pervert the course of justice, see CSP, B8–2.3. Custodial sentences are normally upheld: for threatening or otherwise interfering with witnesses, the usual bracket in the reported cases appears to be between about four months and 24 months, although in *R. v. Hall (A.M.)* [2007] 2 Cr.App.R.(S.) 42, CA, 10 years was said to be the starting point for a sustained attempt to intimidate a 15-year-old witness and her mother; for making a false allegation of crime, resulting in the arrest of an innocent person, from about four months to 12 months; for concealing evidence, from about four months to about 18 months, possibly longer where the evidence relates to serious crime: see *R. v. Walsh and Nightingale*, 14 Cr.App.R.(S.) 671, CA; *Att.-Gen.'s Reference (No. 19 of 1993)*, 15 Cr.App.R.(S.) 760, CA; *R. v. Myatt* [1996] 1 Cr.App.R.(S.) 306, CA; *R. v. Dowd and Huskins* [2000] 1 Cr.App.R.(S.) 349, CA; *R. v. Gosling* [2003] 1 Cr.App.R.(S.) 62, CA; and *R. v. Archer* [2003] 1 Cr.App.R.(S.) 86, CA. See also *R. v. Tunney* [2007] 1 Cr.App.R.(S.) 91, CA, where 30 months' imprisonment (on late plea) was held to be the correct sentence for making a witness statement providing a homicide suspect with a false alibi. A sentence for doing an act tending to pervert the course of justice should normally be consecutive to any sentence for the substantive offence in relation to which the act was committed: see *Att.-Gen.'s Reference (No. 1 of 1990)*, 12 Cr.App.R.(S.) 245, CA.

II. CONCEALMENT OF EVIDENCE

Criminal Law Act 1967, s.5

Penalties for concealing offences or giving false information

28–29 **5.**—(1) Where a person has committed a relevant offence, any other person who, knowing or believing that the offence or some other relevant offence has been committed, and that he has information which might be of material assistance in securing the prosecution or conviction of an offender for it, accepts or agrees to accept for not disclosing that information any consideration other than the making good of loss or injury caused by the offence, or the making of reasonable compensation for that loss or injury, shall be liable on conviction on indictment to imprisonment for not more than two years.

(2) [*See* post, *§ 28–224.*]

(3) No proceedings shall be instituted for an offence under this section except by or with the consent of the Director of Public Prosecutions.

(4) [*Repealed by* Criminal Law Act *1977, Sched. 13*.]

(5) The compounding of an offence other than treason shall not be an offence otherwise than under this section.

[This section is printed as amended by the *SOCPA* 2005, s.111, and Sched. 7, para. 40(1) and (3).]

Section 1 of the *Criminal Attempts Act* 1981 does not apply to section 5(1) of the 1967 Act: section 1(4) of the 1981 Act, *post*, § 33–120.

Offences under section 5(1) are triable either way: *MCA* 1980, Sched. 1, *ante*, §§ 1–75ae, 1–75af.

As to the offence of doing an act intended to impede the apprehension or prosecution of a person who has committed an arrestable offence, see section 4 of the *CLA* 1967, *ante*, §§ 18–34 *et seq*.

III. CONTEMPT OF COURT

A. INTRODUCTION

28–30 Contempt of court may arise in a myriad of ways and in a variety of forms. There is a substantial overlap between this offence and other offences against public justice and between the various species of contempt. Contempt of court may occur in relation to particular legal proceedings or the administration of justice as a continuing process.

The starting point in any attempt to identify what constitutes contempt of court is the common law; this is the primary source. It is important not to exaggerate the effect of the *Contempt of Court Act* 1981; this does not affect the basic concept of contempt as established by common law. The principal effects of the 1981 Act were:

(a) to limit liability for contempt under the "strict liability rule" (ss.1–7, together with Sched. 1);

(b) to deem specific conduct to be contempt of court (ss.8 and 9);

(c) to provide limited protection for a witness asked to reveal the source of information contained in a publication for which he is responsible (s.10);

(d) to allow a court to give directions restricting the publication of matters exempted from disclosure in court (s.11);

(e) to provide for offences of contempt of magistrates' courts (s.12); and

(f) to make provision for penalties for contempt (s.13).

28–31 Apart from the common law and the 1981 Act, various other statutory provisions stipulate that certain conduct is contempt of court, or is punishable "as if" it were criminal contempt of court: for examples of the former, see the *Criminal Procedure (Attendance of Witnesses) Act* 1965, s.3 (*ante*, § 8–12), the *CPIA* 1996, s.18(1) (*ante*, § 12–69) and the *Courts and Legal Services Act* 1990, s.70(6) (*post*, § 28–112); for examples of the latter, see the *Bail Act* 1976, s.6(5) (*ante*, § 3–27), and the *Juries Act* 1974, s.20(2) (*post*, § 28–46).

Contempt of the Crown Court will be dealt with either by the exercise of the court's summary power to punish for contempt (*post*, §§ 28–105 *et seq.*), or by way of application for committal under *RSC*, Ord. 52 (*post*, §§ 28–128 *et seq.*). The "almost ancient" way of proceeding by indictment should not be resurrected: *R. v. D.* [1984] A.C. 778, CA and HL (*per* Watkins L.J. at p. 792, giving the judgment of the Court of Appeal in a case of contempt consisting of disobedience of an order of a civil court); *Re Lonrho plc* [1990] 2 A.C. 154 at 177, HL.

Appeals against conviction and sentence in relation to findings of contempt are governed by the *Administration of Justice Act* 1960, s.13 (*post*, §§ 28–138 *et seq.*).

Civil contempt and criminal proceedings arising from the same facts

28–32 In *Harris v. Crisp*, *The Times*, August 12, 1992, CA (Civ. Div.), it was held that it was a matter for the judge in the civil contempt proceedings to decide on the facts of the case whether there was a real risk that a defendant would be seriously prejudiced in his criminal trial by hearing the contempt proceedings first. Although it is important to deal with contempt proceedings swiftly and decisively, a judge is not bound as a matter of law to go ahead with such proceedings notwithstanding the fact that criminal proceedings are pending. See also *RSC*, Ord. 52, rr.1–3 (*post*, §§ 28–128 *et seq.*), and *R. v. Green (B.)* [1993] Crim.L.R. 46, CA (*autrefois* defence unavailable in criminal case heard after civil contempt proceedings).

Third parties

A person who knowingly impedes or interferes with the administration of justice by the court in an action between two other parties is guilty of contempt of court notwithstanding that he is neither named in any order of the court nor has assisted a person against whom an order was made to breach it: *Att.-Gen. v. Times Newspapers Ltd* [1992] 1 A.C. 191, HL. A third party will be guilty of contempt, however, only if he acts so as to frustrate and set at naught the basis upon which the court has determined that justice should be administered, and acts with that intention; his conduct must be more than merely inconsistent with the order of the court; it must have had some significant adverse effect on the course of justice, although it is not necessary to show that it had been wholly frustrated or rendered utterly futile: *Att.-Gen. v. Newspaper Publishing plc* [1997] 1 W.L.R. 926, CA. The purpose of a court in issuing an interlocutory injunction is the preservation of the rights of the parties pending a final determination of the issues between them rather than the litigant's purpose in seeking the order; where, therefore, an injunction was issued restraining publication of information pending a decision as to whether it was entitled to protection on the ground of confidentiality, and the defendant, knowing of the injunction, published the material, the *actus reus* lay in the destruction of the confidentiality of the material which it had been the purpose of the injunction to protect; the fact that he had no intention to prejudice national security, the protection of which was the ultimate purpose of the claimant in seeking the injunction, was irrelevant: *Att.-Gen. v. Punch Ltd* [2003] 1 A.C. 1046, HL. **28–33**

Applicability of Article 6 of the European Convention on Human Rights

Contempt of court proceedings involve the determination of a criminal charge under Article 6: see, for example, *Kyprianou v. Cyprus* (2007) 44 E.H.R.R. 27, ECtHR, and the other cases cited at § 16–60, *ante*. **28–33a**

B. COMMON LAW

(1) Introduction

At common law, a contempt of court is an act or omission calculated to interfere with the due administration of justice: *Att.-Gen. v. Times Newspapers Ltd* [1992] 1 A.C. 191, HL; *Att.-Gen. v. Butterworth* [1963] 1 Q.B. 696; *The St James's Evening Post*, 2 Atk. 469 at 471; *Bahama Islands, re a special reference from* [1893] A.C. 138. Conduct is calculated to prejudice the due administration of justice if there is a real risk as opposed to a remote possibility that prejudice will result: *Att.-Gen. v. Times Newspapers Ltd* [1974] A.C. 273, HL. **28–34**

In the latter case, Lord Diplock outlined the various ways in which the due administration of justice might be prejudiced: **28–35**

> "The due administration of justice requires first that all citizens should have unhindered access to the constitutionally established courts of criminal or civil jurisdiction for the determination of disputes as to their legal rights and liabilities; secondly, that they should be able to rely upon obtaining in the courts the arbitrament of a tribunal which is free from bias against any party and whose decision will be based upon those facts only that have been proved in evidence adduced before it in accordance with the procedure adopted in courts of law; and thirdly that, once the dispute has been submitted to a court of law, they should be able to rely upon there being no usurpation by any other person of the function of that court to decide it according to law. Conduct which is calculated to prejudice any of these requirements or to undermine the public confidence that they will be observed is a contempt of court" (at p. 309).

The definition is wide enough to embrace improper interference with negotiations **28–36** between parties to a pending cause (*Att.-Gen. v. Times Newspapers Ltd, ante*) and improper interference with persons, who have been engaged in litigation, after it is concluded: *Att.-Gen. v. Butterworth, ante*, CA; and see *R. v. Socialist Worker Printers and Publishers, ex p. Att.-Gen.* [1975] Q.B. 637, DC.

(2) Civil and criminal contempts

28–37 Historically, there was a difference between civil and criminal contempt, but the modern approach is to treat the law relating to the two as substantively the same: see *Guildford B.C. v. Valler, The Times*, May 18, 1993, QBD (Sedley J.). Insofar as there is a difference, civil contempt often involves breaching an undertaking or court order and is brought to the court's attention by one of the litigants, whereas other forms of contempt are usually raised by the court itself, or are brought before the court by the Attorney-General: see *Home Office v. Harman* [1983] 1 A.C. 280 at 310, HL (*per* Lord Scarman); *Att.-Gen. v. Newspaper Publishing Plc* [1988] Ch. 333 at 362, CA (Civ. Div.) (*per* Sir John Donaldson M.R.).

[The next paragraph is § 28–39.]

(3) Nature of proceedings and standard of proof

28–39 Civil contempt is not a criminal offence: *Cobra Golf Ltd v. Rata* [1998] Ch. 109, Ch D (Rimer J.). Nonetheless, the standard of proof in all forms of contempt is the criminal standard: *Dean v. Dean* [1987] 1 F.L.R. 517, CA (Civ. Div.); *Att.-Gen. v. Newspaper Publishing plc, ante*.

(4) Mens rea

28–40 It was firmly established at common law that the publication of matter calculated to prejudice the fair trial of a pending cause was an absolute offence: see *R. v. Odhams Press Ltd, ex p. Att.-Gen.* [1957] 1 Q.B. 73, DC. This rule, known as the "strict liability rule", has been modified by the *Contempt of Court Act* 1981 (*post*, §§ 28–60 *et seq.*). The Act does not restrict liability for contempt in respect of conduct intended to impede or prejudice the administration of justice: s.6(c) (*post*, § 28–86).

Apart from cases to which the strict liability rule applies, the common law requires proof of an intent to impede or prejudice the administration of justice; this applies whether the case is one of publication contempt or any other conduct constituting a contempt of court: *Att.-Gen. v. Butterworth* [1963] 1 Q.B. 696, CA (hostile action against witness done with intent to punish him for giving evidence); *Att.-Gen. v. Judd* [1995] C.O.D. 15, DC (harassment of former juror); *R. v. Schot and Barclay* [1997] 2 Cr.App.R. 383, CA (jurors' refusal to return a verdict); *Att.-Gen. v. News Group Newspapers plc* [1989] Q.B. 110, DC; *Re Lonrho plc* [1990] 2 A.C. 154, HL; *Att.-Gen. v. Times Newspapers Ltd* [1992] 1 A.C. 191, HL; *Att.-Gen. v. Newspaper Publishing plc* (*ante*, § 28–33) (publications).

As to proving the necessary intent, in *Att.-Gen. v. Newspaper Publishing plc* [1988] Ch. 333, CA (Civ. Div.), Lloyd L.J. said:

> "I would therefore hold that the *mens rea* required in the present case is an intent to interfere with the course of justice. As in other branches of the criminal law, that intent may exist, even though there is no desire to interfere with the course of justice. Nor need it be the sole intent. It may be inferred, even though there is no overt proof. The more obvious the interference with the course of justice, the more readily will the requisite intent be inferred" (at p. 383).

28–41 Two matters must therefore be proved: (a) that the act created a real risk of prejudice to the administration of justice; and (b) that it was done with the specific intent of creating such a risk: *per* Bingham L.J. in *Att.-Gen. v. Sport Newspapers Ltd* [1991] 1 W.L.R. 1194 at 1200, CA (Civ. Div.).

(5) Unhindered access to the established courts

28–42 This principle, emphasised by the House of Lords in *Att.-Gen. v. Times Newspapers*

Ltd [1974] A.C. 273 (and see *Golder v. United Kingdom*, 1 E.H.R.R. 524, ECtHR, in which it was decided that access to a court was a right protected by Article 6 of the European Convention), was reasserted by the House of Lords in *Raymond v. Honey* [1983] 1 A.C. 1, as was the principle that a convicted prisoner retains all civil rights which are not taken away expressly or by necessary implication: see *R. v. Board of Visitors of Hull Prison, ex p. St. Germain* [1979] Q.B. 425 at 455, 68 Cr.App.R. 212 at 229, CA (Civ. Div.).

In *Re Martin (P.), The Times*, April 23, 1986, DC, it was held that a solicitor committed a contempt of court when, in correspondence with a barrister who had brought criminal proceedings against the solicitor's clients, he threatened to report the matter to the Inner Temple authorities. Glidewell L.J. accepted that there was a distinction between putting pressure on a witness and dissuasion of a litigant: the ambit of what was proper in relation to the latter was wider. A party could take proper steps to defeat his opponent but the pressure had to be fair, reasonable and moderate. **28–43**

His Lordship further pointed out that the reference to "unlawful threats" by Lord Diplock in *Att.-Gen. v. Times Newspapers Ltd, ante*, at p. 313, was used there to mean improper threats. The threats did not have to be unlawful or illegal. A threat to bring an action for malicious prosecution was near the boundary of what was or was not proper pressure but, in the circumstances, did not amount to contempt of court.

As regards a newspaper putting improper pressure on a party in proceedings to which it is a party, see *Att.-Gen. v. Hislop* [1991] 1 Q.B. 514, CA (Civ. Div.).

(6) Confidential information

A witness has no privilege which entitles him to refuse to disclose information obtained in confidence, but a court has a discretion to excuse a witness from answering a question which would involve a breach of confidence: *British Steel Corp. v. Granada Television* [1981] A.C. 1096, HL. See *ante*, § 12–24 as to how the discretion should be exercised. Apart from this discretion, section 10 of the *Contempt of Court Act* 1981 (*post*, § 28–94) gives limited protection for a witness in respect of the source of information contained in a publication for which he is responsible. **28–44**

It is of the utmost importance that whenever and wherever a journalist seeks in a criminal trial to claim the protection of confidentiality for his source of information the issue should be raised in full with the judge in the absence of the jury and a reasoned decision made upon the application: *Att.-Gen. v. Lundin*, 75 Cr.App.R. 90, DC. See also *Goodwin v. U.K.*, 22 E.H.R.R. 123, ECtHR, *post*, § 28–95.

(7) Contempt by jurors

It is a contempt for a juror or jury to refuse to deliver a verdict unless it be to state that he or they cannot agree: 2 Hawk.P.C. c. 22, s.17, or to refuse to deliver a verdict which the presiding judge directs them to return as a matter of law: *Bushell's case* (1670) Vaugh. 135 at 152. It is not a contempt for a jury to return a perverse verdict, but a contumacious refusal to reach a verdict because of a reluctance to judge another might establish the *actus reus* of contempt: *R. v. Schot and Barclay* [1997] 2 Cr.App.R. 383, CA. It is a contempt for a jury to reach their verdict capriciously as by tossing a coin: *Langedell v. Sutton* (1737) Barnes 32; *Foster v. Hawden* (1677) 2 Lev. 205. As to the confidentiality of a jury's deliberations, see the *Contempt of Court Act* 1981, s.8, *post*, § 28–90. **28–45**

Juries Act 1974, s.20

Offences

20.—(1) Subject to the provisions of subsections (2) to (4) below— **28–46**

(a) if a person duly summoned under this Act fails to attend (on the first or on any subsequent day on which he is required to attend by the summons or by the appropriate officer) in compliance with the summons, or

(b) if a person, after attending in pursuance of a summons, is not available when called on to serve as a juror, or is unfit for service by reason of drink or drugs,

he shall be liable to a fine not exceeding level 3 on the standard scale.

(2) An offence under subsection (1) above shall be punishable either on summary conviction or as if it were criminal contempt of court committed in the face of the court.

(3) Subsection (1)(a) above shall not apply to a person summoned otherwise than under section 6 of this Act, unless the summons was duly served on him on a date not later than fourteen days before the date fixed by the summons for his first attendance.

(4) A person shall not be liable to be punished under the preceding provisions of this section if he can show some reasonable cause for his failure to comply with the summons, or for not being available when called on to serve, and those provisions have effect subject to the provisions of this Act about the withdrawal or alteration of a summons, and about the granting of any excusal or deferral.

(5) [*Certain summary offences—see* ante, *§ 4–221.*]

[This section is printed as amended by the *CJA* 1988 s.170(1), and Sched. 15; and the *CJPOA* 1994, Sched. 10, para. 28. Subs. (5) is amended by the *CJA* 2003, s.321, and Sched. 33, paras 1 and 14.]

Where a judge proposes to proceed summarily under section 20(2), the essential conditions of a fair hearing are that, (a) the juror must understand what he is said to have done wrong, (b) the court must be satisfied that the juror, when he did wrong, had the means of knowing that it was wrong, (c) the juror must understand what defences (if any) are open to him, (d) he must have a reasonable opportunity to make representations, and (e) he must, if necessary, have an opportunity to consider what representations he wishes to make once he has understood the issues involved; legal representation is not obligatory (having regard to the maximum penalty), but if the juror were to apply for an adjournment in order to be represented, such application should be granted absent powerful reasons to the contrary: *R. v. Dodds* [2003] 1 Cr.App.R. 3, CA. A juror's objection to being subjected to compulsory security search procedures upon entering the building could not amount to "reasonable cause" within section 20(4); whilst there was no legislative provision authorising such security procedures, it was open to the Crown, like any owner of land, and within limits of reasonableness, to insist on a search as a condition of entry: *ibid.*

(8) Interference with persons concerned in litigation

28–47 It is a contempt knowingly to interfere with those who have duties to discharge in a court of justice: *Re Johnson* (1887) 20 Q.B.D. 68, CA (solicitor verbally abusing opposite number); *Garibaldo v. Cagnoni* (1704) 6 Mod. 90; *Purdin v. Roberts*, 74 J.P. 88; *Re de Court*, *The Times*, November 27, 1997, Ch D (assault on court official engaged in official business in administration of justice). Likewise, it is a contempt to seek to influence the outcome of a pending case by interfering with those involved in it, including the judge: *Martin's case* (1747) 2 Russ. & My. 674; *Ex p. Jones* (1806) 13 Ves. 237; *Re Ludlow Charities, Lechmere Charlton's case* (1837) 2 My. & Cr. 316 at 339. Improper interference with jurors is the offence of embracery (see *post*, § 28–151), though it may be treated as contempt or as an attempt to pervert the course of public justice: *Att.-Gen. v. Judd* [1995] C.O.D. 15, DC.

28–48 It is a contempt to endeavour to intimidate, bribe or improperly influence a person who is a potential witness in a pending cause with the intention of affecting that person's evidence when it is given in due course. That the attempt is unsuccessful is immaterial, the only question being whether the act complained of is calculated to interfere with the due administration of justice: *Shaw v. Shaw* (1861) 2 Sw. & Tr. 517; *Bromilow v. Phillips* (1891) 40 W.R. 220; *R. v. Greenberg* (1919) 121 L.T. 288; *Re B. (J. A.) (an Infant)* [1965] Ch. 1112. To prevent a witness duly summoned from attending court is punishable as a contempt: *R. v. Hall* (1776) 2 W.Bl. 1110; *R. v. Hamp* (1852) 6 Cox 167. As to the payment, or promise of payment, of witnesses by the media in advance of a trial, see *R. v. West* [1996] 2 Cr.App.R. 374 at 389, CA.

When interviewed as a murder suspect, C indicated that he spent the night of the murder at a hostel. His solicitor wished to interview potential alibi witnesses at the hostel but was prevented from doing so by the police who feared this might prejudice their inquiries. It was held that interference with witnesses, actual or potential, by threat, promise or subsequent punishment amounted to contempt of court; equally, interference with proper and reasonable attempts by a party's legal advisers to identify and interview potential witnesses was contempt; that the police had no right to stop an approach to potential witnesses, and attempts to identify potential alibi witnesses could not amount to wilful obstruction of a police officer in the execution of his duty; and that, accordingly, an implied threat to prosecute the solicitor for obstruction, with the intention deliberately to deny him unimpeded access to such witnesses, was a clear contempt of court: *Connolly v. Dale* [1996] 1 Cr.App.R. 200, DC.

Defendants, as well as witnesses and others, are entitled to go to and from court without being molested or assaulted or threatened with molestation: *R. v. Runting*, 89 Cr.App.R. 243, CA. **28–49**

See also the offence of interfering with witnesses, jurors and others under section 51 of the *CJPOA* 1994, *post*, §§ 28–142 *et seq.*

(9) Revenge on persons concerned in litigation

It is contempt to take or threaten revenge upon a person for what he has done in the discharge of his duty in the administration of justice. So it is a contempt to threaten a judge or juror with revenge (3 Co.Inst. 139), or to assault a man for what he has done in a court of law: *Re Johnson* (1887) 20 Q.B.D. 68; *Moore v. Clerk of Assize, Bristol* [1971] 1 W.L.R. 1669. Acts which are otherwise lawful may be a contempt if done with intent to punish a man for what he has done in court, as for an employer to dismiss a man who has given evidence against his interest (*Bowden v. The Universities Co-operative Association*, 25 S.J. 886); or for a landlord to punish a tenant for evidence he has given against him (*Chapman v. Honig* [1963] 2 Q.B. 502); or for an association or union to deprive a person of an honorary office as a punishment for evidence he has given which is considered against the interests of the association or union: *Att.-Gen. v. Butterworth* [1963] 1 Q.B. 696, CA. An intention to punish must be shown: *ibid.* **28–50**

See also section 51 of the *CJPOA* 1994, *post*, §§ 28–142 *et seq.*

(10) Abuse of the process of the court

It is a contempt fraudulently to abuse the process of the court, for instance by forging a writ or pleadings: *Finnerty v. Smith* (1835) 1 Bing.N.C. 649; *Bishop v. Willis* (1749) 5 Beav. 83n. To seek to mislead the court by commencing an action or pleading a defence known to be false is a contempt: *Lord v. Thornton* (1614) 2 Bulstr. 67; *R. v. Weisz, ex p. Hector Macdonald Ltd* [1951] 2 K.B. 611. **28–51**

(11) Publishing matter scandalising the court

It is a contempt to publish matter so defamatory of a judge or a court as to be likely to interfere with the due administration of justice, by seriously lowering the authority of the judge or court: *R. v. Gray* [1900] 2 Q.B. 36; *R. v. Editor of the New Statesman* (1928) 44 T.L.R. 301; and *Ahnee v. DPP* [1999] 2 A.C. 294, PC. It is only in a clear case that this jurisdiction will be exercised for any man may criticise a decision of a court even in an outspoken manner: *Ambard v. Att.-Gen. for Trinidad and Tobago* [1936] A.C. 322; *Bahama Islands, re A special reference from the* [1893] A.C. 138; *McLeod v. St. Aubyn* [1899] A.C. 549; *R. v. Metropolitan Police Commr, ex p. Blackburn* [1968] 2 Q.B. 150, CA (Civ. Div.). This species of contempt was described as "virtually obsolescent" by Lord Diplock in *Secretary of State for Defence v. Guardian Newspapers Ltd* [1985] A.C. 339, HL. **28–52**

Despite this, the Privy Council has said that the offence is reasonably justifiable in a democratic society bearing in mind its narrow scope; it exists solely to protect the administration of justice rather than the feelings of judges; there must be a real risk of undermining public confidence in the administration of justice; and there is a defence based on the "right of criticising, in good faith, in private or public, the public act done in the seat of justice" (*R. v. Gray, ante*, at p. 40, *per* Lord Russell C.J.); where, however, publication is intentional, the article is calculated to undermine the authority of the court, and the defence of fair criticism in good faith is inapplicable, the offence is made out, there being no further requirement of *mens rea*: *Ahnee v. DPP*, *ante*. See also *Harris v. Harris*; *Att.-Gen. v. Harris* [2001] 2 F.L.R. 895, Fam D (Munby J.) (where it was recognised (at p. 941) that in some circumstances restrictions on freedom of expression will be necessary in order to maintain the authority and impartiality of the judiciary within the meaning of Article 10(2) of the ECHR (*ante*, § 16–119)).

As to the effect of Convention jurisprudence, see *ante*, § 16–128.

(12) Publishing matter calculated to prejudice the fair trial of a pending or imminent cause

28–53 Liability under the strict liability rule is now regulated by the *Contempt of Court Act* 1981, ss.1–7. Liability at common law will now depend on proof of a specific intent to impede or prejudice the administration of justice (*ante*, § 28–40); such liability being specifically preserved by section 6(c) of the 1981 Act. At common law it must be established: (a) that publication of the material created a real risk of prejudice to the due administration of justice; and (b) that the material was published with the specific intent of causing such a risk: *per* Bingham L.J., *Att.-Gen. v. Sport Newspapers Ltd* [1991] 1 W.L.R. 1194 at 1200, DC (*post*, § 28–55).

It is always a serious matter to publish material which may prejudice a jury against an accused: *R. v. Bolam, ex p. Haigh* (1949) 93 S.J. 220, DC; *R. v. Odhams Press Ltd, ex p. Att.-Gen.* [1957] 1 Q.B. 73, DC. To publish a photograph of a person charged with an offence where it is reasonably clear that the identity of the accused has arisen or may arise, may also amount to a contempt: *R. v. Daily Mirror Newspapers, ex p. Smith* [1927] 1 K.B. 845, DC; *R. v. Evening Standard Co Ltd, ex p. Att.-Gen.*, *The Times*, November 3, 1976, DC.

28–54 It is contempt to publish statements which prejudice an issue in a pending cause: *Att.-Gen. v. Times Newspapers Ltd* [1974] A.C. 273, HL. In civil cases, a cause is pending as soon as it formally has been commenced (*Howitt v. Fagge* (1896) 12 T.L.R. 426 (writ); *Re Crown Bank* (1890) 44 Ch.D. 649 (petition)), but a retrial is not pending until it has been ordered: *Metzler v. Gounod* (1874) 30 L.T. 264; *Dallas v. Ledger*, 52 J.P. 328.

It has been held in criminal cases that a cause is pending until all possibilities of appeal have been exhausted: *R. v. Davies, ex p. Delbert-Evans* [1945] 1 K.B. 435, DC; *R. v. Duffy, ex p. Nash* [1960] 2 Q.B. 188, DC. Although the possibility of influencing appellate judges by publishing prejudicial matter after conviction is slight, there may be issues as to whether such publicity would prejudice a retrial: see *ex p. Delbert-Evans*, *ante*, at p. 442, and *R. v. Stone* [2001] Crim.L.R. 465, CA.

28–55 In *Att.-Gen. v. News Group Newspapers plc* [1989] Q.B. 110, 87 Cr.App.R. 323, DC, it was held that where a prosecution was virtually certain to be commenced, it was proper to describe such a prosecution as imminent. The court further held that a criminal contempt at common law could be committed even if the conduct did not relate to pending or imminent proceedings. In the instant case, the newspaper intended proceedings should be commenced at its expense as soon as possible and actively pursued that goal because it was determined to see the intended defendant charged, tried and convicted. Where, therefore, the newspaper published material about the person, whom it was intended should be prosecuted, which could only serve to and was intended to prejudice the fair trial of that person, the newspaper had engaged in conduct which amounted to contempt of court at common law. In *Att.-Gen. v. Sport Newspapers Ltd*, *ante*, § 28–53, two judges of the Divisional Court disagreed on the point when contempt at common law arose. Bingham L.J. said (at p. 1207) that the court would not be justified in departing from the recent and unambiguous decision in *Att.-Gen. v. News Group Newspapers*, *ante*, which had extended the boundaries of contempt as previously understood. If a publication created a real risk of prejudice to the due administration of justice and the alleged contemnor published with the specific intent of causing such risk, contempt might be committed even though proceedings were neither in existence nor imminent. Hodgson J. said that the *News Group* decision was wrong and the summary procedure for publication contempt should not be widened (at pp. 1229, 1230). It should only be a contempt when the relevant proceedings were pending.

In *Coe v. Central Television* [1994] E.M.L.R. 433, the Court of Appeal did not seek to resolve the above conflict, but did recognise that contempt at common law could occur where criminal proceedings "had not been begun". However, one of the reasons for holding that the necessary intent had not been proved was that no one had yet been charged with an offence. As to when proceedings are "active" under the *Contempt of Court Act* 1981, see *post*, §§ 28–62 *et seq.*

(13) Publication of matter relating to proceedings in private

As to the publication of information relating to proceedings before a court sitting in private, see the *Administration of Justice Act* 1960, s.12, which was considered in *Re R. (M. J.) (a Minor) (Publication of Transcript)* [1975] Fam. 89, a decision approved by the Court of Appeal in *Re F. (Minors) (Wardship: Police Investigation)* [1989] Fam. 18; *Re W. (Wards) (Publication of Information)* [1989] 1 F.L.R. 246 (Sir Stephen Brown P.); and *X. v. Dempster* [1999] 1 F.L.R. 894, Fam D (Wilson J.). The Act contains no express time-limit, but the best view is that once the reason for secrecy has disappeared then publication may occur, *e.g.* when a ward attains 21 years or secret matter is taken off the secret list: *cf.* Lord Shaw in *Scott v. Scott* [1913] A.C. 417 at 483. See generally *Re M. and N. (Minors) (Wardship: Publication of Information)* [1990] Fam. 211, CA (Civ. Div.); and *Hodgson v. Imperial Tobacco Ltd* [1998] 1 W.L.R. 1056, CA (Civ. Div.). Apart from cases falling within section 12(1), the disclosure of what occurs in chambers does not constitute contempt as long as any comment which is made does not substantially prejudice the administration of justice: *Hodgson v. Imperial Tobacco Ltd, ante*; *Clibbery v. Allan* [2002] Fam. 261, CA (Civ. Div.). **28–56**

As to publication of matter exempted from disclosure in court, see section 11 of the *Contempt of Court Act* 1981, *post*, § 28–96.

(14) Disobedience to an order of the court

To disobey an order of the court properly made is a contempt. In the following instances, orders have been held properly made and disobedience to them a contempt: (a) an order to a person hindering or interrupting proceedings to leave: *R. v. Webb, ex p. Hawker, The Times*, January 24, 1899; (b) an order to a person to desist from introducing matter ruled irrelevant into a trial or from acting in a manner offensive to the court: *R. v. Davison* [1821] 4 B. & Ald. 329; *Re Surrey (Sheriff)* [1860] 2 F. & F. 234; (c) an order that specified documents be not removed from court: *Watt v. Ligertwood* (1874) L.R. 2 Sc. & Div. 361, HL. **28–57**

There is no common law power to make an order postponing the publication of a report of proceedings conducted in open court; such a power can only be conferred by statute (*e.g. Contempt of Court Act* 1981, s.4(2), *post*, § 28–78); *R. v. Clement* (1821) 4 B. & Ald. 218, the only authority directly appearing to support the existence of such a common law power, gains little support from subsequent cases and provides too insecure a foundation on which to rest the existence of such a power: *Independent Publishing Co. Ltd v. Att.-Gen. of Trinidad and Tobago*; *Trinidad and Tobago News Centre Ltd v. Same, The Times*, June 24, 2004, PC.

There are additional powers to restrict the publication of part of proceedings in court, but the Acts granting these powers contain their own procedures to deal with breaches, *e.g. CYPA* 1933, s.39 (publication of details identifying children or young persons) (*ante*, § 4–27) (to be replaced, as from a day to be appointed, by the *YJCEA* 1999, ss.44–46, *ante*, §§ 4–29a *et seq.*). As to the desirability of proceeding under such provisions, rather than by way of proceedings for contempt, see *R. v. Tyne Tees Television Ltd, The Times*, October 20, 1997, CA (*ante*, § 4–27).

The offence of failing to surrender to custody contrary to the *Bail Act* 1976, s.6(1), is not a contempt of court: *R. v. Reader*, 84 Cr.App.R. 294, CA; *R. v. Lubega*, 163 J.P. 221, CA. Section 6(5) of the Act does not convert an offence under section 6(1) into a contempt of court but simply provides a speedy and effective alternative method for dealing with such an offence: *ibid.* **28–58**

Where a person was unaware of a summons issued in respect of his alleged breach of a community order and so failed to appear in the Crown Court in answer to it, he was not guilty of contempt, because he had neither knowledge of the summons nor an intention to fail to answer it: *R. v. Noble, The Times*, July 21, 2008, CA.

C. CONTEMPT OF COURT ACT 1981

(1) Introduction

The *Contempt of Court Act* 1981 implemented, with some modifications, the recommendations of the Phillimore Committee on Contempt of Court (1974, Cmnd. 5794) **28–59** and was also influenced by the decision of the European Court of Human Rights in *Sunday Times v. U.K.*, 2 E.H.R.R. 245. See also, *Hansard*, HL, Vol. 415, col. 660. According to Lord Diplock in *Att.-Gen. v. English* [1983] A.C. 116 at 139, HL, the Act had a twofold purpose: to remove liability for technical but venial contempts and to clarify the balance between a fair trial and a free press.

In relation to the concept of strict liability at common law, the Act sought to lessen the rigours thereof and confine it "within narrow limits": *per* Lloyd L.J. in *Att.-Gen. v. Newspaper Publishing plc* [1988] Ch. 333 at 381, CA (Civ. Div.). The strict liability rule, subject to certain defences, applies to publications (s.2(1)), which create a substantial risk that the course of public justice will be seriously impeded or prejudiced (s.2(2)), in particular legal proceedings which are "active" at the time of publication (s.2(3) and Sched. 1).

A literal interpretation of section 1 would exclude its application from publications which interfere with the course of justice as a continuing process and such publications would therefore fall to be considered in relation to the common law or other statutory provisions. Other offences under the Act, to which the strict liability rule does not apply, require proof of intention: *per* Lloyd L.J. in *Att.-Gen. v. Newspaper Publishing plc*, *ante*, at p. 383.

(2) The strict liability rule

Contempt of Court Act 1981, ss.1, 2

The strict liability rule

28–60 **1.** In this Act "the strict liability rule" means the rule of law whereby conduct may be treated as a contempt of court as tending to interfere with the course of justice in particular legal proceedings regardless of intent to do so.

Limitation of scope of strict liability

28–61 **2.**—(1) The strict liability rule applies only in relation to publications, and for this purpose "publication" includes any speech, writing, programme included in a programme service or other communication in whatever form, which is addressed to the public at large or any section of the public.

(2) The strict liability rule applies only to a publication which creates a substantial risk that the course of justice in the proceedings in question will be seriously impeded or prejudiced.

(3) The strict liability rule applies to a publication only if the proceedings in question are active within the meaning of this section at the time of the publication.

(4) Schedule 1 applies for determining the times at which proceedings are to be treated as active within the meaning of this section.

(5) In this section "programme service" has the same meaning as in the *Broadcasting Act* 1990.

[Section 2 is printed as amended by the *Broadcasting Act* 1990, s.203(1), and Sched. 20, para. 31(1).]

As to the definition of "programme service", see section 201 of the 1990 Act.

For a consideration of the definition of "publication", see *Secretary of State for Defence v. Guardian Newspapers Ltd* [1985] A.C. 339, HL.

The definition of "active" proceedings in Schedule 1 appears to be narrower in scope than the concept of "pending or imminent" proceedings at common law, see *ante*, §§ 28–54 *et seq.*

Contempt of Court Act 1981, Sched. 1

SCHEDULE 1

TIMES WHEN PROCEEDINGS ARE ACTIVE FOR PURPOSES OF SECTION 2

28–62 1. In this Schedule "criminal proceedings" means proceedings against a person in respect of an offence, not being appellate proceedings or proceedings commenced by motion for committal or attachment in England and Wales or Northern Ireland; and "appellate proceedings" means proceedings on appeal from or for the review of the decision of a court in any proceedings.

[1A. In paragraph 1 the reference to an offence includes a service offence within the meaning of the *Armed Forces Act* 2006.]

2. Criminal, appellate and other proceedings are active within the meaning of section 2 at the times respectively prescribed by the following paragraphs of this Schedule; and in relation to proceedings in which more than one of the steps described in any of those paragraphs is taken, the reference in that paragraph is a reference to the first of those steps.

3. Subject to the following provisions of this Schedule, criminal proceedings are active from the relevant initial step specified in paragraph 4 or 4A until concluded as described in paragraph 5.

4. The initial steps of criminal proceedings are—

(a) arrest without warrant;

(b) the issue, or in Scotland the grant, of a warrant for arrest;

(c) the issue of a summons to appear, or in Scotland the grant of a warrant to cite;

(d) the service of an indictment or other document specifying the charge;

(e) except in Scotland, oral charge.

4A. Where as a result of an order under section 54 of the *Criminal Procedure and Investigations Act* 1996 (acquittal tainted by an administration of justice offence) proceedings were brought against a person for an offence of which he has previously been acquitted, the initial step of the proceedings is a certification under subsection (2) of that section; and paragraph 4 has effect subject to this.

5. Criminal proceedings are concluded—

(a) by acquittal or, as the case may be, by sentence;

(b) by any other verdict, finding, order or decision which puts an end to the proceedings;

(c) by discontinuance or by operation of law.

6. The reference in paragraph 5(a) to sentence includes any order or decision consequent on conviction or finding of guilt which disposes of the case, either absolutely or subject to future events, and a deferment of sentence under section 1 of the *Powers of Criminal Courts (Sentencing) Act* 2000 ... [*Scotland, Northern Ireland*]. **28–63**

7. Proceedings are discontinued within the meaning of paragraph 5(c)—

(a) in England and Wales or Northern Ireland, if the charge or summons is withdrawn or a *nolle prosequi* entered;

(aa) in England and Wales, if they are discontinued by virtue of section 23 of the *Prosecution of Offences Act* 1985;

(b) [*Scotland*];

(c) in the case of proceedings in England and Wales or Northern Ireland commenced by arrest without warrant, if the person arrested is released, otherwise than on bail, without having been charged.

8. *Criminal proceedings before a court-martial or standing civilian court are not concluded until the completion of any review of finding or sentence.*

9. Criminal proceedings in England and Wales or Northern Ireland cease to be active if an order is made for the charge to lie on the file, but become active again if leave is later given for the proceedings to continue.

9A. Where proceedings in England and Wales have been discontinued by virtue of section 23 of the *Prosecution of Offences Act* 1985, but notice is given by the accused under subsection (7) of that section to the effect that he wants the proceedings to continue, they become active again with the giving of that notice.

10. Without prejudice to paragraph 5(b) above, criminal proceedings against a person cease to be active— **28–64**

(a) if the accused is found to be under a disability such as to render him unfit to be tried or unfit to plead or, in Scotland, is found to be insane in bar of trial; or

(b) if a hospital order is made in his case under section 51(5) of the *Mental Health Act* 1983 ... [*Northern Ireland, Scotland*],

but become active again if they are later resumed.

11. Criminal proceedings against a person which become active on the issue or the grant of a warrant for his arrest cease to be active at the end of the period of twelve months beginning with the date of the warrant unless he has been arrested within that period, but become active again if he is subsequently arrested.

12. Proceedings other than criminal proceedings and appellate proceedings are active

from the time when arrangements for the hearing are made or, if no such arrangements are previously made, from the time the hearing begins, until the proceedings are disposed of or discontinued or withdrawn; and for the purposes of this paragraph any motion or application made in or for the purposes of any proceedings, and any pre-trial review in the county court, is to be treated as a distinct proceeding.

28–65 13. In England and Wales or Northern Ireland arrangements for the hearing of proceedings to which paragraph 12 applies are made within the meaning of that paragraph—

(a) in the case of proceedings in the High Court for which provision is made by rules of court for setting down for trial, when the case is set down;

(b) in the case of any proceedings, when a date for the trial or hearing is fixed.

14. [*Scotland.*]

15. Appellate proceedings are active from the time when they are commenced—

(a) by application for leave to appeal or apply for review, or by notice of such an application;

(b) by notice of appeal or of application for review;

(c) by other originating process,

until disposed of or abandoned, discontinued or withdrawn.

16. Where, in appellate proceedings relating to criminal proceedings, the court—

(a) remits the case to the court below; or

(b) orders a new trial or a *venire de novo*, ... [*Scotland*]

any further or new proceedings which result shall be treated as active from the conclusion of the appellate proceedings.

[This Schedule is printed as amended by the *MHA* 1983, s.148, and Sched. 4, para. 57(c); the *Prosecution of Offences Act* 1985, s.31(5), and Sched. 1, Pt I, paras 4 and 5; the *CPIA* 1996, s.57(4); and the *PCC(S)A* 2000, s.165(1), and Sched. 9, para. 86; and as amended, as from a day to be appointed, by the *AFA* 2006, s.378(1) and (2), Sched. 16, para. 92, and Sched. 17 (insertion of para. 1A, omission of para. 8).]

Application of the rule

28–66 In *Att.-Gen. v. News Group Newspapers Ltd* [1987] Q.B. 1, CA (Civ. Div.), Sir John Donaldson M.R. said that the 1981 Act did nothing to create any new or wider offence of contempt than had previously existed. The most important provision of the Act for present purposes was section 2, which limited the application of the strict liability rule by reference to the nature of the conduct complained of, the risk of interference with the course of justice, the seriousness of the interference (if it were to occur) and the stage which had been reached in the proceedings which might be interfered with.

28–67 His Lordship said that there was a need for balance where: (a) there was an element of public interest in general discussion being permitted; and (b) there was an issue whether the proceedings sought to be protected were sufficiently proximate to the apprehended publication to require protection. The Act tackled proximity in two ways. First, it abrogated the strict liability rule in the period before the proceedings in need of protection became "active": s.2(3). Secondly, it abrogated the rule unless a strict test of need was satisfied: s.2(2). There had to be a substantial risk that the course of justice in the proceedings would be seriously impeded or prejudiced. That was a double test. "Substantial" as a qualification of "risk" did not have the meaning of "weighty" but meant rather "not insubstantial" or "not minimal".

The "risk" part of the test would usually be of importance in the context of the width of the publication. Proximity in time between the publication and the proceedings would probably have a greater bearing on the risk limb than on the seriousness limb, but it could go to both. For practical purposes, his Lordship said, those who were asked to make orders for prior restraint could, save in extraordinary circumstances, decide the matter solely by reference to the 1981 Act.

28–68 In *Re Lonrho plc* [1990] 2 A.C. 154, HL, an appellate committee of three Law Lords doubted the extent to which the approach of the House of Lords in *Att.-Gen. v. Times Newspapers* [1974] A.C. 273, HL, had survived the 1981 Act. The report of the appellate committee considered what should be the proper approach under the 1981 Act and continued:

> "The only safe course, we think, is to apply the test imposed by the statutory language according to its ordinary meaning, without any preconception derived from *Attorney-General v. Times Newspapers* as to what kind of publication is likely to impede or prejudice the course of justice. The question whether a particular publication, in relation to particular legal proceedings which are active, creates a substantial risk that the course of justice in those proceedings will be seriously impeded or prejudiced is ultimately one of fact. Whether the course of justice in particular proceedings will be impeded or prejudiced by a publication must depend primarily on whether the publication will bring influence to bear which is likely to divert the proceedings in some way from the course which they would otherwise have followed. The influence may affect the conduct of witnesses, the parties or the court. Before proceedings have come to trial and before the facts have been found, it is easy to see how critical public discussion of the issues and criticism of the conduct of the parties, particularly if a party is held up to public obloquy, may impede or prejudice the course of the proceedings by influencing the conduct of witnesses or parties in relation to those proceedings. If the trial is to be by jury, the possibility of prejudice by advance publicity directed to an issue which the jury will have to decide is obvious. The possibility that a professional judge will be influenced by anything he has read about the issues in a case which he has to try is very much more remote. He will not consciously allow himself to take account of anything other than the evidence and argument presented to him in court" (at p. 209). **28–69**

Their Lordships indicated that it was difficult to visualise circumstances in which an appellate court would be influenced by public discussion of the merits of the decision appealed against or of the parties' conduct in the proceedings.

[The next paragraph is § 28–74.]

Risk to be assessed by reference to time of publication

28–74 The risk that has to be assessed is that which was created by the publication of the allegedly offending matter at the time when it was published. That the risk that was created by the publication when it was actually published does not ultimately affect the outcome of the proceedings is immaterial: *Att.-Gen. v. English* [1983] A.C. 116 at 141, HL; *Att.-Gen. v. Guardian Newspapers Ltd (No. 3)* [1992] 1 W.L.R. 874, DC. The public policy underlying the strict liability rule is "deterrence": *Att.-Gen. v. English, ante*, at p. 141.

28–75 Section 2(2) creates two separate risks which might not always be mutually exclusive: *Att.-Gen. v. British Broadcasting Corporation* [1992] C.O.D. 264, DC. To "impede" is to retard, slow down, delay, hinder or obstruct. To "prejudice" something or someone is to say or do that which is detrimental or injurious to the interest of that thing or person. The BBC had broadcast an inaccurate report of a trial which had started that day. The next day, the judge and counsel watched a recording of the broadcast and discussed it. No application was made to discharge the jury and they were warned to ignore it. If the jury had been discharged, a retrial could not have started for four or five months. The trial proceeded and the defendants were acquitted.

The Divisional Court, in holding the BBC to be in contempt, stated that it was enough if the report, viewed objectively at the time of publication, could be said to create a substantial risk that the course of justice would be seriously impeded or prejudiced. The fact that the judge did not discharge the jury did not assist in deciding whether immediately following the broadcast there was a substantial risk. The risk was present at the relevant time.

The court must look at each publication separately as at the date of publication and consider the likelihood that it would be read by a potential juror, the likely impact of the article on an ordinary reader at the time of the publication and its residual impact on a notional juror at the time of the trial. The mere fact that there was already some risk of prejudice by reason of earlier publications did not preclude a finding that the latest publication had created a further risk: *Att.-Gen. v. M.G.N. Ltd* [1997] 1 All E.R. 456, DC.

28–76 In *Att.-Gen. v. Independent Television News Ltd* [1995] 1 Cr.App.R. 204, DC, the court took into account the limited circulation of the offending matter, particularly in the London area where the trial eventually took place, and the fact that it was common ground that a period of nine months was likely to elapse (and had elapsed) between publication and trial.

The fact that a trial judge had stayed criminal proceedings as an abuse of the process of the court due to prejudicial publicity was not necessarily determinative of whether a contempt had been committed, since the questions being considered in each case were not the same. Nevertheless, such a stay was highly likely to be a telling pointer on a contempt application: *Att.-Gen. v. Birmingham Post and Mail Ltd* [1999] 1 W.L.R. 361, DC. In *Att.-Gen. v. Guardian Newspapers Ltd* [1999] E.M.L.R. 904, DC, Sedley L.J., distinguishing *Birmingham Post and Mail*, said that the court should assume that jurors had read the publication, that an application to discharge the jury had been made and refused, that the judge had given the jury a proper direction to disregard anything they had read, that a conviction was not inevitable and that the jury had convicted. If, in such a situation, an appeal on the ground of prejudice would not succeed, no more should the publisher be guilty of contempt. By parity of reasoning, a case in which an appeal would in the assumed events succeed will ordinarily be a case where a contempt is made out.

Publication of material prejudicial to a defendant

28–76a Publication of certain material prejudicial to a defendant may amount to a contempt of court: *Solicitor General v. Henry and News Group Newspapers Ltd* [1990] C.O.D. 307, DC; *Att.-Gen. v. Associated Newspapers Ltd* [1998] E.M.L.R. 711, DC (previous convictions); *Att.-Gen. v. Times Newspapers Ltd, The Times*, February 12, 1983, DC (confessions); *Att.-Gen. v. News Group Newspapers plc* [1989] Q.B. 110, DC; *Att.-Gen. v. Morgan, ante* (assertions of guilt); and *Att.-Gen. v. News Group Newspapers Ltd*, 6 Cr.App.R.(S.) 418, DC (prejudicial photographs).

Defences and power to order postponement of reporting

Contempt of Court Act 1981, ss.3, 4

Defence of innocent publication or distribution

28–77 **3.**—(1) A person is not guilty of contempt of court under the strict liability rule as the publisher of any matter to which that rule applies if at the time of publication (having taken all reasonable care) he does not know and has no reason to suspect that relevant proceedings are active.

(2) A person is not guilty of contempt of court under the strict liability rule as the distributor of a publication containing any such matter if at the time of distribution (having taken all reasonable care) he does not know that it contains such matter and has no reason to suspect that it is likely to do so.

(3) The burden of proof of any fact tending to establish a defence afforded by this section to any person lies upon that person.

(4) [*Repealed by* Statute Law (Repeals) Act *2004, s.1(1), and Sched.1.*]

Contemporary reports of proceedings

28–78 **4.**—(1) Subject to this section a person is not guilty of contempt of court under the strict liability rule in respect of a fair and accurate report of legal proceedings held in public, published contemporaneously and in good faith.

(2) In any such proceedings the court may, where it appears to be necessary for avoiding a substantial risk of prejudice to the administration of justice in those proceedings, or in any other proceedings pending or imminent, order that the publication of any report of the proceedings, or any part of the proceedings, be postponed for such period as the court thinks necessary for that purpose.

(2A) Where in proceedings for any offence which is an administration of justice offence for the purposes of section 54 of the *Criminal Procedure and Investigations Act* 1996 (acquittal tainted by an administration of justice offence) it appears to the court that there is a possibility that (by virtue of that section) proceedings may be taken against a person for an offence of which he has been acquitted, subsection (2) of this section shall apply as if those proceedings were pending or imminent.

(3) For the purposes of subsection (1) of this section a report of proceedings shall be treated as published contemporaneously—

(a) in the case of a report of which publication is postponed pursuant to an order under subsection (2) of this section, if published as soon as practicable after that order expires;

(b) *in the case of a report of committal proceedings of which publication is permitted by virtue only of subsection (3) of section 8 of the* Magistrates' Courts Act *1980, if published as soon as practicable after publication is so permitted.*

[(b) in the case of a report of allocation or sending proceedings of which publication is permitted by virtue only of subsection (6) of section 52A of the *Crime and Disorder Act* 1998 ("the 1998 Act"), if published as soon as practicable after publication is so permitted;

(c) in the case of a report of an application of which publication is permitted by virtue only of sub-paragraph (5) or (7) of paragraph 3 of Schedule 3 to the 1998 Act, if published as soon as practicable after publication is so permitted.]

(4) [*Repealed by* Statute Law (Repeals) Act *2004, s.1(1) , and Sched. 1.*]

[This section is printed as amended by the *Defamation Act* 1996, s.16, and Sched. 2; and the *CPIA* 1996, s.57(3). As from a day to be appointed, subs. (3)(b) is replaced by new paras (b) and (c) (in square brackets): *CJA* 2003, s.41, and Sched. 3, para. 53.]

The defence under section 4(1) does not apply to a publication in breach of an order under section 4(2); such publication is a contempt on account of the disobedience of a court order (*ante*, § 28–57), not because of any tendency to interfere with the course of justice: see *R. v. Horsham JJ., ex p. Farquharson* [1982] 1 Q.B. 762, 76 Cr.App.R. 87, CA (Civ. Div.) (*per* Shaw L.J. at pp. 798, 101, and Ackner L.J. at pp. 805, 107; *cf.* Lord Denning M.R. at pp. 790, 94).

There is no express statutory provision as to who can make representations in respect of the making or continuance of an order under section 4(2). In *R. v. Clerkenwell Metropolitan Stipendiary Magistrate, ex p. The Daily Telegraph* [1993] Q.B. 462, 97 Cr.App.R. 18, DC, the court stated that any court had a discretionary power to hear representations from the press when deciding whether to make or continue an order. If there was no order, it was the press who would enjoy the right of reporting the proceedings and the interest which the making of an order would adversely affect was best represented by the news media serving in their capacity as the eyes and ears of the public. **28–79**

In any application under section 4(2) the prosecution should assist the court in an objective and unpartisan spirit in respect of the proper principles to be applied: *Ex p. News Group Newspapers Ltd, The Times*, May 21, 1999, CA.

As to appeals against orders made under section 4, see the *CJA* 1988, s.159, *ante*, §§ 7–308 *et seq.*

An arrest does not fall within the meaning of "legal proceedings held in public" in section 4(1); justices, therefore, have no power to make an order under section 4(2) prohibiting the broadcasting of a film of the defendant's arrest: *R. v. Rhuddlan JJ., ex p. HTV Ltd* [1986] Crim.L.R. 329, DC. Watkins L.J. drew attention to the possibility of applying to the High Court for injunctive relief (pursuant to the *Supreme Court Act* 1981 (to be cited, as from a day to be appointed, as the *Senior Courts Act* 1981: *Constitutional Reform Act* 2005, s.59, and Sched. 11, para. 1(1)), s.31(2)) where television companies or journalists sought to report matters which might prejudice a trial.

Practice Direction (Criminal Proceedings: Consolidation), para. I.3
[2002] 1 W.L.R. 2870

I.3.1 Under section 4(2) of the *Contempt of Court Act* 1981, a court may, where it appears necessary for avoiding a substantial risk of prejudice to the administration of justice in the proceedings before it or in any others pending or imminent, order that publication of any report of the proceedings or part thereof be postponed for such period as the court thinks necessary for that purpose. Section 11 of the Act provides that a court may prohibit the publication of any name or other matter in connection with the proceedings before it which it has allowed to be withheld from the public. **28–80**

I.3.2 When considering whether to make such an order there is nothing which precludes the court from hearing a representative of the press. Indeed it is likely that the court will wish to do so.

I.3.3 It is necessary to keep a permanent record of such orders for later reference. For this purpose all orders made under section 4(2) must be formulated in precise terms, having regard to the decision in *R. v. Horsham Justices, ex p. Farquharson* [*ante*], and orders under both sections must be committed to writing either by the judge personally or by the clerk of the court under the judge's directions. An order must state (a) its precise scope, (b) the time at which it shall cease to have effect, if appropriate, and (c) the specific purpose of making the order. Courts will normally give notice to the press in some form that an order has been made under either section of the Act and court staff should be prepared to answer any inquiry about a specific case, but it is, and will remain, the responsibility of those reporting cases, and their editors, to ensure that no breach of any orders occurs and the onus rests with them to make inquiry in any case of doubt.

28–81 Where an order is made under section 4(2) it might in some cases be appropriate for the judge to make clear whether and to what extent the terms of that order could be published: *Att.-Gen. v. Guardian Newspapers Ltd (No. 3)* [1992] 1 W.L.R. 874, DC. Such a report could cause the very mischief which the order was intended to prevent.

28–82 In *Re Central Television plc*, 92 Cr.App.R. 154, the Court of Appeal stressed the importance of following the practice direction; and added that, even where there was some slight risk of prejudice, judges would be well advised to bear in mind the words of Lord Denning M.R. in *R. v. Horsham JJ., ex p. Farquharson*, *ante*, at pp. 794, 98:

> "In considering whether to make an order under section 4(2), the sole consideration is the risk of prejudice to the administration of justice. Whoever has to consider it should remember that at a trial judges are not influenced by what they may have read in the newspapers. Nor are the ordinary folk who sit on juries. They are good, sensible people. They go by the evidence that is adduced before them and not by what they may have read in the newspapers. The risk of their being influenced is so slight that it can usually be disregarded as insubstantial—and therefore not the subject of an order under section 4(2)."

28–83 The provisions of section 4(2) are often invoked to avoid prejudicing a future trial. Where a defendant in a multi-handed trial pleads guilty before the trial of other defendants, and an issue arises as to whether to make an order under section 4, judges should bear in mind, (a) that a broadcaster or editor who fails to discharge his responsibility accurately to inform the public of court proceedings and to avoid publication of comment which might interfere with the administration of justice runs the risk of being held in contempt, and (b) that experience has shown that juries focus exclusively on the evidence given in court, not only because of the judge's direction, but also because the direction appeals to the jury's instinctive belief that the trial process must be fair: *R. v. B.* [2007] H.R.L.R. 1, CA.

In forming a view as to whether it is necessary to make an order under section 4(2), a court will inevitably have regard to the competing public interest considerations of ensuring a fair trial and of open justice. It is essential to keep distinct the two main requirements of the subsection, *viz.* (a) that publication would create a substantial risk of prejudice, and (b) that postponement of publication "appears to be necessary for avoiding" that risk. The second requirement is statutory recognition of the principle of open justice. If it is found that there is a substantial risk of prejudice to the administration of justice, the judge must still consider whether, in the light of the competing public interest of open justice, it is necessary to make an order and, if it is, in what terms: *R. v. Central Criminal Court, ex p. The Telegraph plc*, 98 Cr.App.R. 91, CA.

Where the court determines that there is a substantial risk of prejudice, it should first ask itself whether the risk can be avoided by some other means. If it can, then an order is not necessary. If it cannot, the court should still ask itself whether the degree of risk is tolerable in the sense of being the lesser of two evils: *Ex p. The Telegraph Group plc* [2001] 1 W.L.R. 1983, CA.

The fact that a defendant expects to face a second trial does not of itself justify the making of an order under section 4: *R. v. Beck, ex p. The Daily Telegraph*, 94 Cr.App.R. 376, CA; *R. v. Central Criminal Court, ex p. The Telegraph plc*, *ante*. Whether such an order is justified depends upon all the circumstances. If prejudice can be avoided by extending the period between the two trials or by transfer to another court, that should be done.

As to reporting restrictions in relation to children, young persons and others, see *ante*, §§ 4–28 *et seq.* As to the tension between the competing principles in such cases and the effect of international and European jurisprudence, see *McKerry v. Teesdale and Wear Valley JJ*, 164 J.P. 355, DC. See also, *ante*, §§ 16–119 *et seq.* Section 4(2) does not empower a criminal court to prohibit the publication of a defendant's name so as to avoid the identification of his children: *Re Trinity Mirror plc* [2008] 2 Cr.App.R. 1, CA; and it makes no difference that the defendant is himself a barrister: *C. v. CPS*, 172 J.P. 273, DC.

Contempt of Court Act 1981, s.5

Discussion of public affairs

5. A publication made as or as part of a discussion in good faith of public affairs or other matters of general public interest is not to be treated as a contempt of court under the strict liability rule if the risk of impediment or prejudice to particular legal proceedings is merely incidental to the discussion. **28–84**

Section 5 may be regarded as a defence: *Att.-Gen. v. English* [1983] 1 A.C. 116 at 123, HL; *Re Lonrho plc* [1990] 2 A.C. 154 at 213, HL. There is, however, no burden on the alleged contemnor to bring himself within its provisions. It does not take the form of a proviso or an exception to section 2(2). It stands on an equal footing with it, in that it states the sort of publication which will not amount to contempt, despite its tendency to interfere with the course of justice in particular proceedings. If the publication falls within section 5, it is for the Attorney-General to prove that the risk of prejudice was not merely incidental to the discussion. The section is intended to prevent the gagging of bona fide discussion in the press of controversial matters of general public interest, merely because there are in existence contemporaneous legal proceedings in which some particular instance of those controversial matters might be in issue. The test provided for in the section is not whether an article could have been written as effectively without the passages complained about or whether some phraseology might have been substituted for them that could have reduced the risk of prejudicing the proceedings: it is whether the risk created by the words actually chosen by the author was "merely incidental to the discussion", *i.e.* no more than an incidental consequence of expounding its main theme. The meaning of the word "discussion" is not confined to "the airing of views and the propounding and debating of principles and arguments". Discussion may involve accusation: *Att.-Gen. v. English*, *ante*. Humour is no shield for contempt: *Att.-Gen. v. British Broadcasting Corporation and Hat Trick Productions* [1997] E.M.L.R. 76, DC. **28–85**

Contempt of Court Act 1981, s.6

Savings

6. Nothing in the foregoing provisions of this Act— **28–86**

(a) prejudices any defence available at common law to a charge of contempt of court under the strict liability rule;

(b) implies that any publication is punishable as contempt of court under that rule which would not be so punishable apart from those provisions;

(c) restricts liability for contempt of court in respect of conduct intended to impede or prejudice the administration of justice.

Section 6(a) preserves any defences available at common law. Certain defences were peculiar to publication contempt; most of them are covered by sections 3 to 5 of the 1981 Act, but the following should be noted: (a) a fair and accurate report of proceedings of a public body: *R. v. Payne and Cooper* [1896] 1 Q.B. 577; (b) a temperate account of a pending cause to persons having a direct interest in its outcome, *e.g.* circulars to the trade in patent or trade mark cases: *Carl Zeiss Stiftung v. Rayner and Keeler Ltd* [1960] 1 W.L.R. 1145, Ch D; shareholders of a company subject to litigation: *Re London Flour Co.* (1868) 17 L.T. 636; *Re The New Gold Coast Exploration Co.* [1901] 1 Ch. 860. It may also be a defence that the publication merely repeats an earlier truthful assertion or is merely part of a general public discussion: *Att.-Gen. v. Times Newspapers Ltd* [1974] A.C. 273, HL. **28–87**

The effect of section 6(b) is that no one can be found guilty of contempt who would not have been found guilty under the common law prior to the 1981 Act: *R. v. Horsham JJ., ex p. Farquharson*, *ante*, § 28–82. As to liability at common law for contempt consisting of the publication of matter calculated to prejudice the fair trial of a pending or imminent cause, see *ante*, §§ 28–53 *et seq.*

Nothing in section 6(c) prevents the future development of the law of contempt of court: *Att.-Gen. v. Times Newspapers Ltd* [1992] 1 A.C. 191, HL (at p. 215).

Procedure

Contempt of Court Act 1981, s.7

Consent required for institution of proceedings

28–88 **7.** Proceedings for a contempt of court under the strict liability rule (other than Scottish proceedings) shall not be instituted except by or with the consent of the Attorney General or on the motion of a court having jurisdiction to deal with it.

28–89 Except in a fairly narrow range, Parliament intended proceedings for contempt under the strict liability rule to be commenced only by or with the consent of the Attorney-General. His decision is not subject to judicial review: *R. v. Solicitor-General, ex p. Taylor and Taylor* [1996] 1 F.C.R. 206, DC. A circuit judge has no jurisdiction to deal with a contempt in a book by a retired police officer which made a glancing reference to a defendant in a criminal trial: *Taylor v. Topping*, *The Times*, February 15, 1990, DC.

Section 7 only applies where a contempt has occurred; anyone with a sufficient interest in the proceedings may apply for a civil injunction to restrain future publication: *Peacock v. London Weekend Television*, 150 J.P. 71, CA (Civ. Div.).

(3) Miscellaneous offences

Contempt of Court Act 1981, s.8

Confidentiality of jury's deliberations

28–90 **8.**—(1) Subject to subsection (2) below, it is a contempt of court to obtain, disclose or solicit any particulars of statements made, opinions expressed, arguments advanced or votes cast by members of a jury in the course of their deliberations in any legal proceedings.

(2) This section does not apply to any disclosure of any particulars—

(a) in the proceedings in question for the purpose of enabling the jury to arrive at their verdict, or in connection with the delivery of that verdict, or

(b) in evidence in any subsequent proceedings for an offence alleged to have been committed in relation to the jury in the first mentioned proceedings,

or to the publication of any particulars so disclosed.

(3) [*Identical to s.7,* ante, *§ 28–88, save for reference to* "this section" *in lieu of* "the strict liability rule".]

28–91 In *Att.-Gen. v. Associated Newspapers Ltd* [1994] 2 A.C. 238, the House of Lords held that the word "disclose" in section 8 of the Act bore its plain and ordinary meaning and was apt to describe both the revelation of jury deliberations by an individual juror and the further disclosure of those same deliberations by publication in a newspaper, provided that such publication amounted to disclosure rather than republication of already known facts.

Section 8 was primarily intended to prevent disclosure by and to the press; it does not apply to the trial court or to an appellate court; a court cannot be in contempt of itself: *R. v. Mirza*; *R. v. Connor and Rollock* [2004] 1 A.C. 1118, HL (but see *ante*, §§ 4–254, 4–263, as to the common law rule that the court will not investigate or receive evidence about anything said in the course of the jury's deliberations while they were considering their verdict), disapproving *dicta* in *R. v. Young (S.A.)* [1995] 2 Cr.App.R. 379, CA.

Mirza, *ante*, was applied in *Att.-Gen. v. Scotcher* [2005] 2 Cr.App.R. 35, HL: "a juror who discloses to the court what is said or done during the jury's deliberations with the intention of prompting an investigation is not, without more, *e.g.* malice, dishonesty or improper motive, in contempt of court in terms of section 8(1). The subsection no more applies to the juror than to the court" (*per* Lord Rodger at [25]). But a juror who wrote to the mother of the defendants about the jury's deliberations was in breach of section 8(1); and it was no defence to claim that he was motivated by a desire to expose a miscarriage of justice: *ibid*.

Contempt of Court Act 1981, s.9

Use of tape recorders

9.—(1) Subject to subsection (4) below, it is a contempt of court— **28–92**

(a) to use in court, or bring into court for use, any tape recorder or other instrument for recording sound, except with the leave of court;

(b) to publish a recording of legal proceedings made by means of any such instrument, or any recording derived directly or indirectly from it, by playing it in the hearing of the public or any section of the public, or to dispose of it or any recording so derived, with a view to such publication;

(c) to use any such recording in contravention of any conditions of leave granted under paragraph (a).

(2) Leave under paragraph (a) of subsection (1) may be granted or refused at the discretion of the court, and if granted subject to such conditions as the court thinks proper with respect to the use of any recording made pursuant to the leave; and where leave has been granted the court may at the like discretion withdraw or amend it either generally or in relation to any particular part of the proceedings.

(3) Without prejudice to any other power to deal with an act of contempt under paragraph (a) of subsection (1), the court may order the instrument, or any recording made with it, or both, to be forfeited; and any object so forfeited shall (unless the court otherwise determines on application by a person appearing to be the owner) be sold or otherwise disposed of in such a manner as the court may direct.

(4) This section does not apply to the making or use of sound recordings for purposes of official transcripts of proceedings.

Practice Direction (Criminal Proceedings: Consolidation), para. I.2
[2002] 1 W.L.R. 2870

I.2.1 Section 9 of the *Contempt of Court Act* 1981 contains provisions governing the unofficial use of tape recorders in court. Section 9(1) provides that it is a contempt of court (a) to use in court, or bring into court for use, any tape recorder or other instrument for recording sound, except with the leave of the court; (b) to publish a recording of legal proceedings made by means of any such instrument, or any recording derived directly or indirectly from it, by playing it in the hearing of the public or any section of the public, or to dispose of it or any recording so derived, with a view to such publication; (c) to use any such recording in contravention of any conditions of leave granted under paragraph (a). These provisions do not apply to the making or use of sound recordings for purposes of official transcripts of the proceedings, on which the Act imposes no restriction whatever. **28–93**

I.2.2 The discretion given to the court to grant, withhold or withdraw leave to use tape recorders or to impose conditions as to the use of the recording is unlimited, but the following factors may be relevant to its exercise: (a) the existence of any reasonable need on the part of the applicant for leave, whether a litigant or a person connected with the press or broadcasting, for the recording to be made; (b) the risk that the recording could be used for the purpose of briefing witnesses out of court; (c) any possibility that the use of a recorder would disturb the proceedings or distract or worry any witnesses or other participants.

I.2.3 Consideration should always be given whether conditions as to the use of a recording made pursuant to leave should be imposed. The identity and role of the applicant for leave and the nature of the subject-matter of the proceedings may be relevant to this.

I.2.4 The particular restriction imposed by section 9(1)(b) applies in every case, but may not be present to the mind of every applicant to whom leave is given. It may, therefore, be desirable on occasion for this provision to be drawn to the attention of those to whom leave is given.

I.2.5 The transcript of a permitted recording is intended for the use of the person given leave to make it and is not intended to be used as, or to compete with, the official transcript mentioned in section 9(4).

As to taking photographs or making sketches in court, see the *CJA* 1925, s.41, *ante*, § 4–30.

(4) Protection of sources of information

Contempt of Court Act 1981, s.10

Sources of information

10. No court may require a person to disclose, nor is any person guilty of contempt of court **28–94**

for refusing to disclose, the source of information contained in a publication for which he is responsible, unless it be established to the satisfaction of the court that disclosure is necessary in the interests of justice or national security or for the prevention of disorder or crime.

28–95 The scope of section 10 was considered in *Secretary of State for Defence v. Guardian Newspapers Ltd* [1985] A.C. 339, HL; *Maxwell v. Pressdram Ltd* [1987] 1 W.L.R. 298, CA (Civ. Div.); *X. v. Y.* [1988] 2 All E.R. 648, QBD (Rose J.); *Re An Inquiry under the Company Securities (Insider Dealing) Act 1985* [1988] A.C. 660, HL; and *X. Ltd v. Morgan-Grampian (Publishers) Ltd* [1991] 1 A.C. 1, HL.

The burden of proof, on a balance of probabilities, is on the party seeking disclosure: *X v. Y, ante*. See also *Special Hospitals Service Authority v. Hyde* (1994) 20 B.M.L.R. 75, QBD (Pain J.).

In *X. Ltd v. Morgan-Grampian (Publishers) Ltd, ante*, in which a confidential document concerning the financial affairs of the plaintiffs, two private companies, was wrongfully removed from their premises and disclosed to a journalist, the House of Lords held, *inter alia*, that it was for the courts to interpret section 10 and to decide in the circumstances of any given case whether the protection of section 10 was to prevail. The journalist could not be left to be judge in his own cause and decide whether or not to make disclosure; there was no right of "conscientious objection" which entitled him to set himself above the law. It was too narrow to confine "justice" in section 10 to "the technical sense of the administration of justice in the course of legal proceedings in a court of law".

In *Goodwin v. U.K.*, 22 E.H.R.R. 123, the European Court of Human Rights held that the order requiring the journalist to reveal his source of information and the fine imposed for his refusal to do so in *X. Ltd v. Morgan-Grampian (Publishers) Ltd, ante*, breached the right of freedom of expression as contained in Article 10 of the ECHR. Such orders might be justified if necessity could be convincingly established but it had not been in the instant case. See also *Kelly v. BBC* [2001] Fam. 59, Fam D (Munby J.); *Lehideux and Isorni v. France*, 30 E.H.R.R. 665, ECtHR; *Janowski v. Poland*, 29 E.H.R.R. 705, ECtHR; *News Verlags GmbH & CoKG v. Austria* (2001) 31 E.H.R.R. 8, ECtHR; *Arslan v. Turkey* (2001) 31 E.H.R.R. 9, ECtHR, and *Buskaya and Okçuoglu v. Turkey* (2001) 31 E.H.R.R. 10, ECtHR. For Article 10, see *ante*, §§ 16–119 *et seq.*

In *Camelot Group plc v. Centaur Communications Ltd* [1999] Q.B. 124, CA (Civ. Div.), on a similar set of facts to those in the *Morgan-Grampian (Publishers) Ltd* litigation, an order for the delivery up of documents was upheld where compliance would necessarily reveal the source. There was no threat of further disclosure of confidential information (an injunction having been granted), but there was a continuing threat of damage in that there was unease and suspicion among the plaintiff's employees which inhibited good working relationships, and there was clearly a risk that an employee who had proved untrustworthy in one regard might be untrustworthy in a different respect and reveal other confidential information. The court said that in making its judgment a court should give great weight to any relevant judgment of the European Court of Human Rights (see now the *Human Rights Act* 1998, ss.2, 3 and 5, *ante*, §§ 16–13 *et seq.*). Having opened the door to the European jurisprudence, it is difficult to reconcile the court's own decision with that of the European Court in *Goodwin*. See further, *ante*, §§ 16–119 *et seq.* See also *Michael O'Mara Books Ltd v. Express Newspapers plc* [1998] E.M.L.R. 383, Ch D (Neuberger J.) (journalist ordered to disclose source of infringing copies of copyright work; until source identified, commercial reputations of two innocent companies at stake, and they would remain vulnerable to repetition). See also *Chief Constable of Leicestershire v. Garavelli* [1997] E.M.L.R. 543, DC.

In *Ashworth Hospital Authority v. MGN Ltd* [2002] 1 W.L.R. 2033, HL, it was said that the important protection that both section 10 of the 1981 Act and Article 10 provide for freedom of expression is that they require a court stringently to scrutinise any request for relief that would result in the court interfering with freedom of expression, including ordering the disclosure of a journalist's sources; a sufficiently strong positive case had to be made out; and it was held that such a case had been made out where the claimant authority sought an order against the defendant that it disclose such information as it had that might identify the source of a leak of the confidential medical records of a patient at the hospital who was detained on account of his dangerous, violent or criminal propensities. The authority's reason for seeking disclosure was so that it should be able to discipline the source; under section 10, an order for disclosure could be made as being "necessary in the interests of justice", even though the information was not required for the purpose of bringing an action against the informant; and the order was proportionate where it was necessary in order to deter repetition; the care of patients at special hospitals was fraught with difficulty, and disclosure of patients' records in breach of confidence increased the difficulties and dangers; the fact that the patient had himself put similar material into the public domain did not detract from the need to maintain confidentiality.

The need to protect legal professional privilege is not so great as to make it inevitable that, where privileged information has been disclosed, the balancing exercise under section 10 will come down in favour of disclosure: *Saunders v. Punch Ltd* [1998] 1 W.L.R. 986, Ch D (Lindsay J.) (refusing to order disclosure where an injunction would provide plaintiff with high degree of protection for the future and unlikely that he would suffer substantial foreseeable damage if order refused). Before making an order under section 10 it is a minimum requirement that the party seeking disclosure should have explored other means of ascertaining the source of the relevant material. If the court concludes that a compelling necessity has been established, the court then has to carry out a balancing exercise between the interests of vigorous journalism and the interests of justice. In conducting the balancing exercise, it should be remembered that an order for disclosure would not necessarily result in the identification of the source, which would have the effect of damaging one interest with no compensating advantage to the other: *John v. Express Newspapers Plc* [2000] 1 W.L.R. 1931, CA (Civ. Div.).

A claim under section 10 could be defeated where the source of information's evident purpose was a maleficent one or where the source had disclosed false information: *Interbrew S.A. v. Financial Times Ltd* [2002] E.M.L.R. 24, CA (Civ. Div.).

(5) Restriction of publication of matters exempted from disclosure

Contempt of Court Act 1981, s.11

Publication of matters exempted from disclosure in court

11. In any case where a court (having power to do so) allows a name or other matter to be withheld from the public in proceedings before the court, the court may give such directions prohibiting the publication of that name or matter in connection with the proceedings as appear to the court to be necessary for the purpose for which it was so withheld. **28–96**

As to the recording of orders made under section 11, see paragraph I.3.3 of the consolidated criminal practice direction, *ante*, § 28–80. As to appeals by "persons aggrieved" against orders made under section 11, see the *CJA* 1988, s.159, *ante*, §§ 7–308 *et seq.* As to the power to postpone publication, see *ante*, §§ 28–78 *et seq.* **28–97**

Section 11 can be contrasted with section 4(2) (*ante*, § 28–78) as it does not explicitly provide a power to make an order to restrict publication. The section was apparently intended to clarify the position that existed at common law: Lord Hailsham L.C., *Hansard*, H.L., Vol. 415, col. 664. The power to grant anonymity is, therefore, derived from common law (see *Att.-Gen. v. Leveller Magazine Ltd* [1979] A.C. 440 at 450, 458, 464, 471, HL), and may be supported by an appropriate order under section 11: *R. v. Westminster City Council, ex p. Castelli* [1996] 1 F.L.R. 534 at 536, QBD (Latham J.). As to the ambit of the common law power, see *ante*, §§ 4–3 *et seq.*

Once a reason for granting a witness anonymity is established on an objective basis, on the basis of a reasonable chance or a serious possibility, then a balancing exercise should still be performed: *R. v. Bedfordshire Coroner, ex p. Local Sunday Newspapers Ltd*, 164 J.P. 283, QBD (Burton J.).

A court can only exercise its powers under section 11 to give directions prohibiting the publication of a name in connection with court proceedings if the court first deliberately exercised its power to order that name to be withheld from the public in those proceedings: *R. v. Arundel JJ., ex p. Westminster Press Ltd* [1985] 1 W.L.R. 708, DC; *Re Trinity Mirror plc* [2008] 2 Cr.App.R. 1, CA (at [19]). The Court of Appeal has no power under section 11 to restrain publication of evidence given in open court and referred to openly in the judge's summing up: *R. v. Z.* [2005] 2 A.C. 467, HL.

In *R. v. Evesham JJ., ex p. McDonagh* [1988] Q.B. 553, 87 Cr.App.R. 19, 28, DC, the defendant, on a minor charge, having been harassed by his ex-wife at his previous address and not wishing her to find out where he was now living, applied to the justices not to reveal his address. The justices permitted him to write the address on a piece of paper and hand it to them. They also made an order under section 11 prohibiting publication of the address. On an application for judicial review by a journalist, it was held that notwithstanding the justices' power properly to control proceedings in their courts, such power was not to be exercised for the benefit of a defendant's feelings and comfort. The general principle of open justice has two aspects. As regards proceedings in the court itself, it requires that they should be held in open court to which the press and public are admitted, and that in criminal cases, at any rate, all evidence communicated to the court is communicated publicly. As respects the publication to a wider public of fair and accurate reports of proceedings that have taken place, the principle requires that nothing should be done to discourage this: see, *per* Lord Diplock in *Att.-Gen. v. Leveller Magazine Ltd*, *ante*, at 451, 452. This general rule may not be departed from save where the nature or the circumstances of the proceedings are such that the application of the general rule in its entirety would frustrate or render impracticable the administration of justice. The court concluded that the justices had misused the provisions of section 11 and had erred in not causing the defendant to give his home address publicly. See also *Birmingham Post and Mail Ltd v. Birmingham City Council*, 158 J.P. 307, DC; *R. v. Westminster City Council, ex p. Castelli*, *ante*. For two cases in which anonymity has been granted because of embarrassment arising out of a medical condition, see *H. v. Ministry of Defence* [1991] 2 Q.B. 103, CA (Civ. Div.); and *R. v. Criminal Injuries Compensation Board, ex p. A* [1992] C.O.D. 379, QBD (McCullough J.). For a case where anonymity was approved for witnesses who feared violence or reprisals, see *R. (A.) v. Lord Saville of Newdigate* [2002] 1 W.L.R. 1249, CA (Civ. Div.) (considering the impact of Article 2 of the ECHR (*ante*, § 16–36)). The modern practice, as approved by Lord Bingham C.J. in July 1996, is that witnesses should not be required to disclose their addresses in open court unless it is necessary: see (1997) 161 J.P.N. 351 at 353.

28–98 Financial damage or damage to reputation or goodwill which resulted from the institution of court proceedings concerning a person's business did not amount to the special circumstances envisaged as entitling the court to restrict or prevent press reporting: *R. v. Dover JJ., ex p. Dover District Council*, 156 J.P. 433, DC. Part of the order under review prevented any publicity at any time in respect of charges in relation to which there was an acquittal. This order was made at the outset of the proceedings. Neill L.J., with whom McCullough J. agreed, said that he could not imagine any circumstances in which there could be justifiable restrictions on reporting charges of which a person had been acquitted. As to the position of witnesses, see *R. v. Watford Magistrates' Court, ex p. Lenman* [1993] Crim.L.R. 388, CA; *R. v. Liverpool Magistrates' Court, ex p. DPP*, 161 J.P. 43, DC; *R. (A.) v. Lord Saville of Newdigate*, *ante*; *Re Officer L.* [2007] 1 W.L.R. 2135, HL; and *Z. v. Finland*, 25 E.H.R.R. 371, ECtHR, *ante* § 16–106. As to Article 8 of the ECHR, see *ante*, §§ 16–101 *et seq.* The legal profession is not in a special position in relation to applications under section 11: *R. v. Legal Aid Board, ex p. Kaim Todner (a firm)* [1999] Q.B. 966, CA (Civ. Div.).

Where evidence had been given in the presence of the public concerning a matter that, for reasons of protecting official secrets, the trial judge had ordered was to be heard *in camera*, it had been open to the judge to make an order under section 11 that embraced the evidence given: *Re Times Newspapers Ltd* [2008] 1 Cr.App.R. 16, CA. The jurisdiction under section 11 did not, however, permit the judge to make an order prohibiting publication of speculation as to the evidence that had been given *in camera*, but the publisher of any such (inaccurate) speculation risked himself being found to be in contempt as any such publication would be an attempt to flout the order of the court; the object of the restrictions on publication, the subject of the appeal, was to protect the administration of justice; they did not themselves prevent publication of the matter in question in publications that were not related to the legal proceedings in question, although there might be other legal inhibitions on publication of the information in question: *ibid*.

In *R. v. Tower Bridge JJ., ex p. Osborne*, 88 Cr.App.R. 28, DC, it was held that an application for a direction under section 11 of the Act that the proceedings be held *in camera* should itself be held *in camera*. It would frustrate the object of the application if the whole of the sensitive reasons had to be paraded in open court and put in danger of publication while the court decided whether or not to exercise its discretion.

As to reporting restrictions in respect of certain categories of witnesses, see *ante*, §§ 4–29a *et seq.*

(6) Magistrates' courts

The *Contempt of Court Act* 1981, s.12, deals with offences of contempt of magistrates' courts. For a summary of subsection (1), see *R. v. Powell*, *post*, § 28–108. For the text of section 12, cases thereon, and for the *MCA* 1980, s.97(4) (person refusing to be sworn or produce document or thing), see the 2004 edition of this work. **28–99**

Section 12(5) of the 1981 Act confers a right of appeal to the Crown Court against a finding of contempt under section 12, as well as against sentence: *Haw v. City of Westminster Magistrates' Court* [2008] 3 W.L.R. 465, DC (not following *obiter* observations to the contrary in *R. v. Havant JJ., ex p. Palmer*, 149 J.P. 609, DC).

[The next paragraph is § 28–102.]

(7) Sentencing

Contempt of Court Act 1981, s.14

Proceedings in England and Wales

14.—(1) In any case where a court has power to commit a person to prison for contempt of court and (apart from this provision) no limitation applies to the period of committal, the committal shall (without prejudice to the power of the court to order his earlier discharge) be for a fixed term, and that term shall not on any occasion exceed two years in the case of committal by a superior court, or one month in the case of committal by an inferior court. **28–102**

(2) In any case where an inferior court has power to fine a person for contempt of court and (apart from this provision) no limit applies to the amount of the fine, the fine shall not on any occasion exceed £2,500.

(2A) *In the case of jurisdiction to commit for contempt of court or any kindred offence the court shall not deal with the offender by making an order under section 60 of the* Powers of Criminal Courts (Sentencing) Act *2000 (an attendance centre order) if it appears to the court, after considering any available evidence, that he is under 17 years of age.*

(2A) A fine imposed under subsection (2) above shall be deemed, for the purposes of any enactment, to be a sum adjudged to be paid by a conviction.

(3) [*Repealed by* Criminal Justice Act *1982, s.78 and Sched. 16.*]

(4) Each of the superior courts shall have the like power to make a hospital order or guardianship order under section 37 of the *Mental Health Act* 1983 or an interim hospital order under section 38 of that Act in the case of a person suffering from mental disorder within the meaning of that Act who could otherwise be committed to prison for contempt of court as the Crown Court has under that section in the case of a person convicted of an offence.

(4A) Each of the superior courts shall have the like power to make an order under section 35 of the said Act of 1983 (remand for report on accused's mental condition) where there is reason to suspect that a person who could be committed to prison for contempt of court is suffering from mental disorder within the meaning of that Act as the Crown Court has under that section in the case of an accused person within the meaning of that section.

(4A) For the purposes of the preceding provisions of this section a county court shall be treated as a superior court and not as an inferior court.

(5) [*Gives effect to Sched. 2, Pt III (amendments).*]

[Subs. (2) is printed as amended by the *CJA* 1991, s.17(3), and Sched. 4, Pt I. The first subs. (2A) was inserted by the *CJA* 1982, s.77, and Sched. 14, para. 60, and is printed as amended by the *PCC(S)A* 2000, s.165(1), and Sched. 9, para. 84. As from a day to be appointed (as to which, see *ante*, § 5–1), it is repealed by the *CJIA* 2008, **28–103** ss.6(2) and 149, Sched. 4, para. 25, and Sched. 8, Pt 1. The second subs. (2A) was inserted by the *CJA* 1993, Sched. 3, para. 6, in substitution for a provision previously inserted by the *CJA* 1991. Subs. (4) is printed as amended by the *Mental Health (Amendment) Act* 1982, s.65(1), and Sched. 3, para. 59(a) and (b); the *MHA* 1983, s.148, and Sched. 4, para. 57(a); and the *MHA* 2007, s.1(4), and Sched. 1, para. 19. The first subs. (4A) was inserted by the 1982 Act, s.65(1), and Sched. 3, para. 60; and is printed as amended by the 1983 Act, s.148, and Sched. 4, para. 57(b); and the *MHA* 2007, s.1(4), and Sched. 1, para. 19. The second subs. (4A) was inserted by the *County Courts (Penalties for Contempt) Act* 1983, s.1.]

See also *post*, § 28–126, as to sentencing for contempt.

(8) Interpretation

Contempt of Court Act 1981, s.19

Interpretation

28–104 **19.** In this Act—

"court" includes any tribunal or body exercising the judicial power of the State, and "legal proceedings" shall be construed accordingly;

"publication" has the meaning assigned by subsection (1) of section 2, and "publish" (except in section 9) shall be construed accordingly;

"Scottish proceedings" [*definition omitted*];

"the strict liability rule" has the meaning assigned by section 1;

"superior court" means [the Supreme Court,] the Court of Appeal, the High Court, the Crown Court, the *Courts-Martial* [Court Martial] Appeal Court, the Restrictive Practices Court, the Employment Appeal Tribunal and any other court exercising in relation to its proceedings powers equivalent to those of the High Court, *and includes the House of Lords in the exercise of its appellate jurisdiction*.

[This section is printed as amended, as from a day to be appointed, by the *Constitutional Reform Act* 2005, ss.40(4) and 146, Sched. 9, para. 35(1) and (3), and Sched. 18, Pt 5 (insertion of reference to the Supreme Court, omission of italicised words at the end); and the *AFA* 2006, s.378(1), and Sched. 16, para. 92 (substitution of "Court Martial" for "Courts-Martial").]

A mental health review tribunal is a "court" for the purposes of the 1981 Act: *Pickering v. Liverpool Daily Post and Echo Newspapers plc* [1991] 2 A.C. 370, HL. An industrial tribunal is also a "court": *Peach Grey and Co. (a firm) v. Sommers* [1995] 2 All E.R. 513, DC. However, the Professional Conduct Committee of the General Medical Council is not a "court": *General Medical Council v. British Broadcasting Corporation* [1998] 1 W.L.R. 1573, CA (Civ. Div.).

D. SUMMARY POWERS TO DEAL WITH CONTEMPT

(1) The jurisdiction

28–105 Superior courts of record have jurisdiction to deal summarily with contempts both in the face of the court and out of court: 2 Hawk. P.C. b. 2, c. 22; *ex p. Fernandez* (1861) 10 C.B. (n.s.) 3. Inferior courts of record have jurisdiction to deal summarily only with contempts in the face of the court: *R. v. Brompton County Court, Judge of, and Vague* [1893] 2 Q.B. 195, DC.

By virtue of section 45(4) of the *Supreme Court Act* 1981 (*ante*, § 2–29) (to be cited, as from a day to be appointed, as the *Senior Courts Act* 1981: *Constitutional Reform Act* 2005, s.59, and Sched. 11, para. 1(1)), the Crown Court is a superior court of record. *RSC*, Ord. 52, r.5 (*post*, § 28–133), preserves the inherent power of the Crown Court to make an order of committal of its own motion, but Ord. 52, r.1(2) (*post*, § 28–129), restricts the circumstances in which such an order can be made by the Crown Court to contempt "in the face of the court", disobedience of a court order, or breach of an undertaking to the court: see *DPP v. Channel Four Television Co Ltd* [1993] 2 All E.R. 517 at 520, DC.

In *R. v. S.* [2008] Crim.L.R. 716, CA, the court drew a distinction between a "truly summary" procedure, being that described by Mustill L.J. in *R. v. Griffin*, *post*, § 28–108, and a more formal summary process, where the hearing of the contempt allegation is adjourned until after the trial, as in *R. v. Santiago*, *post*, § 28–115.

All other cases of contempt should be dealt with by the Divisional Court: *Balogh v. St Albans Crown Court* [1975] Q.B. 73, CA; *Re Lonrho plc* [1990] 2 A.C. 154, HL (referring to alleged contempt of court by the media). The expression "in the face of the court" has been interpreted broadly by the courts and is not restricted to contempts seen by the judge (see *post*, § 28–110). It is submitted that the above cases make it clear that this broadened definition applies only to superior courts of record.

Other superior courts of record comprise the House of Lords, the Court of Appeal, the several divisions of the High Court. The Queen's Bench Division of the High Court has a supervisory jurisdiction over all inferior courts and jurisdiction to deal with contempts affecting them. An alleged contempt of the House of Lords is determinable by the House of Lords alone: *Re Lonrho plc*, *ante*. Courts not of record, such as petty sessions, have power to eject those who interrupt their proceedings and a general power of binding over: *R. v. Webb, ex p. Hawker*, *The Times*, January 24, 1899. As to magistrates' courts, see *ante*, § 28–99. **28–106**

In general, one court may not punish a contempt of another court of equal rank, but the Divisional Court of the Queen's Bench Division has power to deal with certain contempts of the Crown Court under *RSC*, Ord. 52 (as now contained in Sched. 1 to the *Civil Procedure Rules* 1998 (S.I. 1998 No. 3132)) (see *post*, §§ 28–129 *et seq.*). As to one judge committing for contempt of another, see *post*, § 28–125. **28–107**

The Crown Court may deal with a contempt "in the face of the court" where the contempt is committed: (a) in the courtroom and witnessed by the court itself; (b) in the courtroom and reported to the court; (c) outside the courtroom and even beyond its precincts and is reported to the court and relates to proceedings then in progress or pending before the court: *Balogh*, *ante*. An employer who threatened to dismiss an employee summoned for jury service if he attended was dealt with by Melford Stevenson J. of his own motion: referred to at 130 J.P. 622, and approved by Lord Denning M.R. in *Balogh*, *ante* at pp. 84, 85.

Although it has been said that Article 6 of the EHCR adds nothing to domestic jurisprudence on summary powers to deal with contempt (*R. v. Dodds* [2003] 1 Cr.App.R. 3, CA), it was held in *Kyprianou v. Cyprus* (2007) 44 E.H.R.R. 27, ECtHR, that the use of the summary procedure involved, on the facts, a breach of Article 6(1) (right to an independent and impartial tribunal). The court did not regard it as necessary or desirable to review generally common law procedures for dealing with contempt in the face of the court.

(2) Contempt "in the face of the court"

(a) *General*

The summary procedure to deal with contempt is unique in English law. It is both substantive and procedural and has often raised concerns because of the lack of clearly defined principles. In *R. v. Griffin*, 88 Cr.App.R. 63, CA, Mustill L.J. said: **28–108**

> "[W]e are here concerned with the exercise of a jurisdiction which is *sui generis* so far as the English law is concerned. In proceedings for criminal contempt there is no prosecutor, or even a requirement that a representative of the Crown or of the injured party should initiate the proceedings. The judge is entitled to proceed of his own motion. There is no summons or indictment, nor is it mandatory for any written account of the accusation made against him to be furnished to the contemnor. ... Nor is the system adversarial in character. The judge himself enquires into the circumstances, so far as they are not within his personal knowledge. He identifies the grounds of complaint, selects the witnesses and investigates what they have to say (subject to a right of cross-examination), decides on guilt and pronounces sentence. This summary procedure, which by its nature is to be used quickly if it is to be used at all, omits many of the safeguards to which an accused is ordinarily entitled, and for this reason it has been repeatedly stated that the judge should choose to adopt it only in cases of real need" (at p. 67).

Activities falling within this category have in the past been collectively described as contempts "in the face of the court": see *R. v. Almon* (1765) Wilm. 243 at 254; *Blackstone*, 16th ed., 1825, Bk. 4, Ch. 20, p. 286, and *Oswald on Contempt*, 3rd ed., 1910.

The phrase "in the face of the court", has never been defined and its true meaning is to be ascertained from the practice of the judges over the centuries. It has never been confined to conduct which a judge saw with his own eyes.

In *R. v. Powell*, 98 Cr.App.R. 224, the Court of Appeal stated that the *Contempt of Court Act* 1981, s.12 (magistrates' courts' jurisdiction to try summarily those who wilfully (a) insult justices, witnesses, officers of the court, solicitors or counsel having business in the court, or (b) interrupt the proceedings or otherwise misbehave in court), gives a good indication of what type of behaviour amounts to contempt in the face of the court at common law.

28–109 It is treason to kill a judge of the High Court being in his place doing his office: *Treason Act* 1351. It is a contempt to assault a judge or any other person in court: *Re Cosgrave*, unreported; Seton, *Judgments and Orders*, 7th ed., p. 457; *Parashuram v. King Emperor* [1945] A.C. 264, PC, or to rescue or attempt by force to rescue a prisoner then being tried: *Earl of Thanet's case* (1799) 27 St.Tr. 821. It is likewise a contempt to interrupt or disturb the proceedings of a court which is sitting: *Morris v. Crown Office* [1970] 2 Q.B. 114, CA (Civ. Div.); *R. v. Aquarius*, 59 Cr.App.R. 165, CA. It is a contempt to disobey an order of the court made to regulate proceedings in a particular trial, as to remove a document contrary to the order of the court (*Watt v. Ligertwood* (1874) 2 Sc. & Div. 361), or to persist in introducing matter which the court has ruled irrelevant: *R. v. Davison* (1821) 4 B. & Ald. 329. To conduct a case in court in a manner calculated to bring the administration of justice into disrepute, as by insulting the judge or jury is also a contempt: *Parashuram v. King Emperor, ante*; *Ex p. Pater* (1834) 5 B. & S. 299.

Where a lawyer fails to co-operate with the court, *e.g.* by not attending a hearing, his conduct, however discourteous, may not necessarily amount to contempt: *R. v. Izoura* [1953] A.C. 237, PC; *Weston v. Central Criminal Courts Administrator* [1977] Q.B. 32, CA (Civ. Div.).

As to whether the summary procedure is compatible with the requirements of Article 6 of the EHCR, see *ante*, § 28–107.

(b) *In the sight of the court*

28–110 As to examples of this form of contempt, see *Morris v. Crown Office, ante*; *Ex p. Fernandez* (1861) 10 C.B. (N.S.) 3 (witness refusing to answer questions); *R. v. Aquarius, ante* (disruptive defendant); *R. v. Logan* [1974] Crim.L.R. 609, CA (outburst by defendant); and *R. v. Hill* [1986] Crim.L.R. 457, CA (outburst from the public gallery).

As to contempt by jurors, see *ante*, § 28–45.

Contempt by witnesses

28–111 A witness who without just cause disobeys a witness order or summons is guilty of contempt of court as if it were committed in the face of the court: *Criminal Procedure (Attendance of Witnesses) Act* 1965, s.3 (*ante*, § 8–12). However, where there is no witness summons or witness order, a witness is not in contempt if he deliberately fails to attend trial: *R. v. Wang* [2005] 4 *Archbold News* 1, CA. The position may be otherwise, both under section 3 and at common law, if, knowing that a witness summons is about to be issued, the witness evades service: *ibid*.

It is a contempt for a witness to remain in court after witnesses have been required to leave (*Roberts v. Garratt*, 6 J.P. 154), to refuse to be sworn or affirmed (*Hennegal v. Evance* (1806) 12 Ves. 201), to leave the court before his examination is completed (*Boyle v. Vivean* (1579) Cary 104), or to refuse to answer an admissible question unless he makes a claim of privilege which the court upholds (*Ex p. Fernandez, ante*; *Att.-Gen. v. Clough* [1963] 1 Q.B. 773, QBD; *Att.-Gen. v. Mulholland and Foster* [1963] 2 Q.B. 477, CA (Civ. Div.)). As to confidential information, see *ante*, §§ 28–44, 28–94. Perjury is a form of contempt and on occasions has been dealt with summarily: *Smith v. Bond* (1845) 13 M. & W. 594, *per* Alderson B.; *R. v. Royson* (1628) 1 Cro. Car. 146; *Apted v. Apted and Bliss* [1930] P. 246. It is submitted, however, that the better course is to proceed under the *Perjury Act* 1911, in view of section 13 thereof (*post*, § 28–164).

A mere conversation between a potential witness and a spectator at a trial is not a contempt; such behaviour is only a contempt if it is an attempt to pervert the course of justice or otherwise to interfere with the witness's freedom to give evidence, or has taken place in defiance of an express direction of the judge: *R. v. Jales* [2007] Crim.L.R. 800, CA.

Rights of audience, practice, etc., and contempt

The *Courts and Legal Services Act* 1990 creates a number of offences of acting in the purported exercise of a right of audience or a right to conduct litigation when not entitled to do so: s.70. A person guilty of an offence under section 70 is also guilty of contempt of court: s.70(6). **28–112**

(c) *Within the court but not seen by the judge*

In *Lecointe v. Courts Administrator of the Central Criminal Court*, unreported, February 8, 1973 (referred to in *Balogh v. St. Albans Crown Court* [1975] 1 Q.B. 73 at 90), a man distributed leaflets in the public gallery of one of the courts, inciting people to picket the building. A member of the public reported it to a police officer who reported it to the judge. The offender denied it. Melford Stevenson J. immediately heard the evidence on both sides, convicted the offender and sentenced him to seven days' imprisonment. His appeal was dismissed. **28–113**

(d) *At some distance from the court*

Contempts committed some distance from the court may also fall to be dealt with by the summary procedure: *Balogh, ante*, § 28–105. This includes the intimidation or bribery of witnesses (*Moore v. Clerk of Assize, Bristol* [1971] 1 W.L.R. 1669, CA (Civ. Div.)), or jurors (*Att.-Gen. v. Judd* [1995] C.O.D. 15, DC), the harassment of a defendant (*R. v. Runting*, 89 Cr.App.R. 243, CA), publication of a defendant's previous convictions during a trial and publication of material revealed during discussions between counsel and the judge in open court in the absence of the jury: *R. v. Border Television Ltd, ex p. Att.-Gen.*; *R. v. Newcastle Chronicle and Journal Ltd, ex p. Att.-Gen.*, 68 Cr.App.R. 375, DC. **28–114**

(3) Circumstances in which the summary power should be exercised

The power of summary punishment is a necessary power. It is given so as to maintain the dignity and authority of the judge and to ensure a fair trial. It is to be exercised by the judge of his own motion when "it is urgent and imperative to act immediately": *Balogh, ante*; *per* Lord Denning M.R. at p. 85. The summary procedure "should be used only in exceptional cases where a contempt is clearly proved, and it must never be invoked, except where nothing else will do to protect the ends of justice" (*per* McCowan L.J., in *R. v. Tamworth JJ., ex p. Walsh* [1994] C.O.D. 277, DC). However, the objections to the summary procedure have less force where the hearing of the contempt allegation is adjourned until after the trial, because, in those circumstances, the alleged contemnor will have a full opportunity to prepare his defence and make enquiries: *R. v. S.* [2008] Crim.L.R. 716, CA. **28–115**

The procedure, whilst draconian and not to be embarked upon lightly, is not limited to cases where it is necessary to preserve the integrity of a trial in progress: *Wilkinson v. S.* [2003] 1 W.L.R. 1254, CA (Civ. Div.); and a judge is entitled to defer until the close of a trial the issue of whether the defendant has committed a contempt during the trial, and any issue of punishment, even if the relevant conduct may also be a criminal offence: *R. v. Santiago* [2005] 2 Cr.App.R. 24, CA, and *R. v. S., ante*. Examples of urgency include where it is necessary to maintain the authority of the court, to prevent disorder, to enable witnesses to be free from fear and to protect jurors from being improperly influenced. However, "insults are best treated with disdain—save when they are gross and scandalous. Refusal to answer, with admonishment—save where it is vital to know the answer. But disruption of the court or threats to witnesses or to jurors should be visited with immediate arrest" (*per* Lord Denning M.R., in *Balogh, ante*, at p. 85, and see the two further instances listed by Lawton L.J. at p. 93). See also *Parashuram v. King Emperor* [1945] A.C. 264, PC, and *R. v. Owen*, 63 Cr.App.R. 199, CA, *post*, § 28–151.

"Contempts which are not likely to disturb the trial or affect the verdict or judgment can be dealt with by motion to commit under *RSC*, Ord. 52" (*per* Lawton L.J. in *Balogh*, at p. 93).

28–116 The above principles were reaffirmed in *Rooney v. Snaresbrook Crown Court*, 68 Cr.App.R. 78, CA (Civ. Div.), and in *DPP v. Channel Four Television Co Ltd* [1993] 2 All E.R. 517, DC. In *R. v. Goult*, 76 Cr.App.R. 140, CA, it was said that a judge had to make his own assessment as to the necessity or otherwise for immediate action on his own part to deal with a suggested contempt. Where, as in *Goult*, there was an allegation that attempts had been made in the court and immediately outside it to intimidate jurors, there was every reason for the judge to have an immediate and summary trial of his own motion by calling on the appellant for an explanation of his conduct. The judge had said that he was sure the appellant was guilty of contempt, but he gave no reasons. The Court of Appeal said that it would be better if, in such circumstances, the judge were to state what his findings of fact were, and, where appropriate, the process of reasoning by which he arrived at those findings.

An example of "just the sort of case in which it would have been better to proceed summarily for contempt" rather than reviving the obsolescent offence of embracery (see *post*, § 28–151) is *R. v. Owen*, 63 Cr.App.R. 199, CA (approach to juror in murder trial by relative of deceased).

Although a defendant can be held in contempt for refusing to attend for sentencing, in practice the power should probably not be exercised: *R. v. Santiago, ante*, § 28–115.

(4) Procedure, etc.

General

28–117 In *R. v. Moran*, 81 Cr.App.R. 51, CA, the court set out certain principles to be borne in mind in contempt cases.

(a) The decision to imprison a person for contempt should never be taken too quickly. There should always be time for reflection as to what is the best course to take.

(b) The judge should consider whether that time for reflection should extend overnight (see also *R. v. Huggins* [2007] 2 Cr.App.R. 8, CA).

(c) If it is possible for the contemnor to have legal advice he should be given an opportunity of having it, but justice does not require that in every circumstance of contempt the contemnor has a right to legal advice. Situations arise in court sometimes where a judge has to act quickly and to pass such sentence as he thinks proper at once. (See further, *post*.)

(d) Giving a contemnor an opportunity to apologise is one of the most important aspects of the summary procedure.

28–118 In the face of an outburst of protest from the public gallery, it is often wise for a judge to rise, leaving anyone intent on misbehaving to do so in his absence: *R. v. Lewis*, *The Times*, November 4, 1999, CA. Where, however, as in *R. v. Hill, ante*, § 28–110, a person disturbs the Crown Court by publicly abusing the judge in a way which cannot be overlooked, it is for the judge to take steps to safeguard the court's authority; steps additional to those indicated in *R. v. Moran, ante*, will, in appropriate cases, include:

(a) the immediate arrest and detention of the offender;

(b) telling the offender distinctly what the contempt is said to have been;

(c) entertaining counsel's submissions; and

(d) if satisfied that punishment is merited, imposing it within the limits fixed by statute.

Where circumstances dictate that a judge conducts an immediate inquiry into an allegation of intimidation of a prosecution witness by the defendant, the questioning of the witness should be undertaken by counsel for the prosecution, so as to avoid any impression of the judge acting as prosecutor; and, if the contempt is found proved, it might be better to postpone both the giving of reasons and the imposition of penalty to the end of the trial: *R. v. MacLeod* [2001] Crim.L.R. 589, CA. Delaying the giving of reasons would avoid the need to express a view about a witness who was still giving evidence, and the witness could be adequately protected by a withdrawal of bail. Moreover, the fact that the judge may have formed a favourable impression of the witness in the trial (as allegedly reflected in his summing up) did not compromise his position as an "independent and impartial" tribunal in relation to the allegation of contempt. It was not uncommon for a judge to hear a witness give evidence more than once, or in relation to different issues, and to accept the evidence of a witness in part only: *ibid*.

As to the necessity of making plain the nature of the alleged contempt, see also *Re Pollard* (1868) L.R. 2 P.C. 106; and *Maharaj v. Att.-Gen. for Trinidad* [1977] 1 All E.R. 411, PC.

In *Re Stevens and Holness, The Independent (C.S.),* June 9, 1997, DC (CO/1693/97), it was said that a Crown Court judge has no power to remand an alleged contemnor in custody before a contempt has been proved; and, in particular, that there is no power to remand in custody to the end of a trial or pending the decision of the Attorney-General as to whether to institute proceedings. But a judge must have, as ancillary to the power to deal summarily with contempt, a power to order the detention of the alleged contemnor for at least as long as is necessary for the judge to decide what course to take and to conduct summary proceedings if appropriate. Such power is recognised in the practice of the courts and in numerous decisions of the Court of Appeal (see, *e.g. R. v. Hill*, *ante*, § 28–110). If the arrangements for a summary trial mean that the alleged contemnor has to spend the night in custody, this is not unlawful. If the case cannot be heard the next day, the judge should ensure that the alleged contemnor is brought back to court, or if this is not possible, that the case is mentioned in open court, so that reasons for the delay are known and recorded and the question of bail considered: *Wilkinson v. S.* [2003] 1 W.L.R. 1254, CA (Civ. Div.); and see *R. v. Serumaga* [2005] 2 Cr.App.R. 12, CA (seven-day remand in custody to await judge's availability unjustifiable), and *R. v. Jales and Lawrence*, *ante*, § 28–111 (judge should have considered granting bail, rather than remanding alleged contemnors in custody over the weekend). But in *R. v. Yusuf* [2003] 2 Cr.App.R. 32, CA (*ante*, § 8–12; *post*, §§ 28–125, 28–127), it was held that a judge trying a murder case was justified in remanding a witness, who had failed to attend the trial in breach of a witness summons, in custody for 11 days before dealing with him for contempt.

In *R. v. Griffin*, 88 Cr.App.R. 63, CA, the alleged contempt consisted of improper **28–119** approaches made by the defendant in criminal proceedings to two prosecution witnesses, consisting of "a continuous process of intimidation which continued right up to the door of the court". The trial judge, upon being informed of these allegations, decided to proceed summarily before the start of the trial itself: he found the contempts proved, but postponed sentence until the end of the trial. The trial then took place, the witnesses giving evidence before the jury of the alleged approaches. The jury acquitted. The Court of Appeal, while not laying down any blueprint, quashed the conviction for contempt and said that the procedure adopted was inappropriate. The risks of postponing the summary process until after the trial were small since the events complained of had not prevented the witnesses from coming forward and any future intimidation was ruled out by a remand of the defendant to custody. On the other side of the balance was the risk that the jury might take one view and the judge another on essentially the same evidence.

Mustill L.J. said that the power to deal summarily with a contempt is a healthy one: **28–120** "If the offence is recent and clear the punitive and deterrent effect of the remedy is multiplied if it is exercised on the spot" (at p. 70).

In *R. v. Bromell, The Times*, February 9, 1995, CA, a defendant's brother allegedly attempted to bribe a witness at court. On the brother's appeal against the judge's finding of contempt, it was held that the judge was justified initially in proceeding summarily without the brother being legally represented, because of the incident's possible effect on the trial. However, once the judge adjourned the contempt issue to the end of the trial, without making any finding, he was wrong at the resumed contempt hearing to refuse to hear counsel except on the question of sentence.

Hearsay evidence is inadmissible where the Crown Court holds an inquiry into an apparent contempt: *R. v. Shokoya*, *The Times*, June 10, 1992, CA.

Witnesses who refuse to testify or answer questions

28–121 In *R. v. K.*, 78 Cr.App.R. 82, CA, it was said that a witness who, by refusing to give evidence, is liable to be found in contempt of court and thus risks committal to prison, should be given the opportunity of legal representation (as to which, see *post*, § 28–123):

> "This court is well aware of the difficulties confronting judges who from time to time are faced with an obdurate and stubborn person who refuses to give evidence when called upon to do so. There are many ways of dealing with a situation of that kind. Sometimes, inaction is as good a way as any and at other times stern measures are called for. It depends entirely upon the circumstances how best an incident of that kind is dealt with. What is always wise is that no action be taken in haste. Some reflection should be brought to bear upon the situation before a judge decides what he will do, if anything at all, to a witness who refuses to give evidence. This is quite unlike the situation with which a judge is confronted when suddenly protestors against one thing or another burst into his court and interrupt proceedings going on there. In that event, as is well known, the judge is called upon to take swift and sometimes punitive action, but none of that kind of necessity arises in a situation like this" (*per* Watkins L.J. at p. 87).

28–122 If a witness refuses, or appears to be disposed to refuse, to give evidence a judge is perfectly justified in making it clear to the witness that the consequences of his refusing might be serious and might involve punishment of the witness. In *R. v. Darby* [1989] Crim.L.R. 817, CA, it was said that it would be inappropriate, however, for the judge, at the preliminary stage, to ask the witness whether a witness statement was true: such inquiry is appropriate when, and if, the witness in the course of the trial proves hostile. In *R. v. Jones (K.M.)* [1998] Crim.L.R. 579, CA, the court distinguished *Darby*, saying that that was a case of a hostile witness, whereas the instant case was one of an unwilling witness, where it would be proper for the judge at the outset to ask the witness (not in front of the jury) whether a witness statement was true (so as to exclude unwillingness to give false evidence or to admit having made a false statement as the reason for being unwilling to give evidence). The ground for distinguishing *Darby* seems questionable as it appears that the case concerned two witnesses, one who was unwilling and one who was hostile. What the court said about the unwilling witness plainly did not relate to hostile witnesses only, as the unwilling witness was never in fact called and thus never had the opportunity to prove hostile. As to hostile witnesses generally, see *ante*, §§ 8–94 *et seq*.

In *R. v. Renshaw* [1989] Crim.L.R. 811, CA, a conviction for contempt was quashed on account of the manner in which the judge had conducted the proceedings. He had taken over the questioning of witnesses a number of times, had interrupted counsel to an extent which made examination in chief almost impossible and had generally shown himself to be conducting the proceedings with a view to making an example of the appellant so as to deter others who might "blow hot and cold". The Court of Appeal emphasised that the result of this case should not provide an excuse for people refusing without proper cause to give evidence, something which would normally be punishable with imprisonment. But in some cases inaction is the best policy: see *R. v. K.*, *ante*. See also *R. v. Lewis*, 96 Cr.App.R. 412, CA: the judge should have given the alleged contemnor an opportunity to give evidence in contempt proceedings, where the refusal to testify at an earlier trial was said to be due to fear of reprisals; the issue was whether the appellant's refusal was free and voluntary, putting him in contempt, or whether it was the result of a well-founded fear of attack, so real and compelling that he could not have been expected to act otherwise.

A witness may legitimately refuse to answer questions on a number of grounds. However, if a witness persists in refusing to answer proper questions he will be liable to be dealt with for contempt of court; but if it is necessary that he be arrested, this should be done in the absence of the jury: *R. v. Maguire* [1997] 1 Cr.App.R. 61, CA.

(5) Legal representation

28–123 In *Balogh v. St. Albans Crown Court* [1975] Q.B. 73, CA, Stephenson L.J.

expressed the view (at p. 90) that there should be few cases in which legal representation is not made available. See also *R. v. Moran*, *R. v. Hill*, *R. v. Bromell*, and *R. v. K.*, *ante*, §§ 28–117, 28–118, 28–120 and 28–121 respectively. It is generally desirable that an unrepresented alleged contemnor should be invited to consider whether he wants legal representation, having been warned, preferably by the judge, of the possible penalty if the alleged contempt is proved, and it is highly desirable that such a person, if he remains unrepresented, should be asked, after he has given evidence, whether he wishes to adduce any other evidence. As to the advisability of inviting the alleged contemnor to have legal representation, see also *R. v. Tyne Tees Television Ltd*, *The Times*, October 20, 1997, CA (judge thereby has advantage of assistance of counsel or solicitors when considering his powers), and *Togher v. Customs and Excise Commrs*, *The Independent (C.S.)*, May 21, 2001, CA (Civ. Div.) (as soon as there is an appreciable risk of imprisonment in contempt proceedings an unrepresented defendant should be asked by a judge whether he wishes to be represented).

The need for legal representation is strengthened by the right to legal representation guaranteed by Article 6(3)(c) of the ECHR: see *ante*, §§ 16–86 *et seq*. Section 83 of the *PCC(S)A* 2000 (*ante*, § 5–12), which restricts the imposition of sentences of imprisonment on persons who are not legally represented, does not apply to committals for contempt: see *R. v. Newbury JJ., ex p. Pont*, 78 Cr.App.R. 255, DC, and see the wording of the section. **28–124**

As to the availability of publicly funded legal representation, see the *Access to Justice Act* 1999, ss.12 to 14, and Sched. 3, *ante*, §§ 6–135 *et seq.*; and the *Criminal Defence Service (Funding) Order* 2007 (S.I. 2007 No. 1174), art. 13 (Appendix G–18).

(6) Consideration of the contempt by another judge

In *Wilkinson v. S., ante*, § 28–118, it was said that in many cases, where there had perforce to be delay between the alleged contempt and the summary trial, it would be wise to refer the matter to another judge if only to forestall arguments as to apparent bias. The court added that strictly speaking the procedure did not offend against the maxim *nemo iudex in causa sua* as it was aimed at the protection of the administration of justice, rather than the judge personally; where, therefore, there was no dispute as to the essential facts, it was open to the judge to deal with the matter himself, as a fair-minded observer would not conclude that there was a real possibility of bias. However, see *Kyprianou v. Cyprus*, *ante*, § 28–107, and *R v. Murray* (2006) 150 S.J. 1191, CA (judge can make findings of contempt where no dispute of fact, but should consider adjourning sentence to another judge to forestall arguments about bias). See also *DPP v. Channel Four Television Co Ltd* [1993] 2 All E.R. 517, DC; *R. v. Schot and Barclay* [1997] 2 Cr.App.R. 383, CA (judge should refer matter to another judge or to the Attorney-General if he prematurely expresses a view as to guilt); *Re Stevens and Holness*, *ante*, § 28–118 (if judge does not wish alleged contemnor to be at liberty during remainder of trial and unwilling to adjourn trial, he should refer matter to another judge); but contrast *R. v. Yusuf*, *ante*, § 28–118. **28–125**

(7) Sentence

Where a person is committed to prison or other custody for contempt of court, the committal must always be for a fixed term. In the case of a committal for contempt by a superior court, the maximum term is two years: *Contempt of Court Act* 1981, s.14, *ante*, § 28–102. **28–126**

An offender under the age of 21 may not be committed to prison (*PCC(S)A* 2000, s.89(1)(a)): *Mason v. Lawton* [1991] 1 W.L.R. 322, CA (Civ. Div.). An offender over the age of 18 and under the age of 21 may be ordered to be detained in a young offender institution for contempt of court under section 108 of the 2000 Act (*ante*, § 5–946). An offender aged under 18 may not be detained in custody (*R. v. Byas*, 16 Cr.App.R.(S.) 869, CA) and, if aged under 17, may not be ordered to attend an attendance centre: *Contempt of Court Act* 1981, s.14(2A), *ante*, § 28–102.

Neither a committal to prison for contempt of court nor a committal to custody under section 108 of the 2000 Act is a "custodial sentence" for the purposes of that Act:

see section 76 of that Act (*ante*, § 5–262). An imprisoned contemnor must be released unconditionally after serving half his sentence, and can be released earlier if the Secretary of State is satisfied that exceptional circumstances exist justifying release on compassionate grounds: *CJA* 2003, s.258(2), (4).

28–127 A committal to prison for contempt is not a sentence which may be suspended under the criminal sentencing legislation (see *Morris v. Crown Office* [1970] 2 Q.B. 114), but the Crown Court may suspend an order of committal by virtue of *RSC*, Ord. 52, r.7 (*post*, § 28–135), as applied by the *Supreme Court Act* 1981, s.45(4) (*ante*, § 2–29). The period of suspension, although usually for a fixed term, can be indefinite: *Griffin v. Griffin*, *The Times*, April 28, 2000, CA (Civ. Div.), not following *Pidduck v. Molloy* [1992] 2 F.L.R. 202 at 205, CA (Civ. Div.). See also *Villiers v. Villiers* [1994] 1 W.L.R. 493, CA (Civ. Div.) (total sentence cannot exceed two years on any one occasion, so consecutive sentences for contempt and breach of earlier suspended sentence imposed for contempt must not exceed two years in all); and *Phillips v. Symes (No. 3)* [2005] 1 W.L.R. 2986, CA (Civ. Div.) (where a party is in contempt in a number of respects, and as such is also in breach of a suspended sentence imposed for a previous contempt, wrong in principle to avoid overall two-year maximum by imposing the maximum in respect of some allegations, leaving others unresolved, and making no order on the suspended sentence so that it too continues to hang over him).

Once a finding of contempt is made, there is no general power to remand in custody pending sentence: *Delaney v. Delaney* [1996] Q.B. 387, CA (Civ. Div.). If the judge is uncertain what custodial term to fix, he can impose a term at the top end of the appropriate bracket, and direct that the matter be restored for a review (to be treated as an application to purge the contempt) after a particular period: *ibid*. However, there is a power to remand for a report on the contemnor's mental condition pursuant to the *MHA* 1983, s.35 (*ante* § 5–891), where there is reason to suspect that a person who could be committed to prison for contempt of court is suffering from mental illness or severe mental impairment: *Contempt of Court Act* 1981, s.14(4A), *ante*, § 28–102.

A person adjudged guilty of contempt may not be made the subject of a community order: see *R. v. Palmer*, 95 Cr.App.R. 170, CA (probation order); *Secretary of State for Defence v. Percy* [1999] 1 All E.R. 732 at 743, Ch D (community service order).

For examples of sentences imposed or upheld for contempt of court in various forms, see CSP, B8–3.3. For general guidance in the case of a witness refusing to give evidence, see *R. v. Montgomery* [1995] 2 Cr.App.R. 23, CA; *R. v. Bird and Holt*, 161 J.P. 96, CA; *R. v. Yusuf*, *ante*, §§ 8–12, 28–118, 28–125; and *R. v. Robinson* [2006] 2 Cr.App.R.(S.) 88, CA.

In *R. v. Phillips (P.A.)*, 78 Cr.App.R. 88, CA, the court emphasised that where there was a finding of contempt in such a case, sentence need not be passed immediately. The witness may change his mind. It is advisable to punish at the conclusion of the trial, or, at the soonest, at the close of the prosecution case. The court also said that in considering sentence in such a case, the effect on the trial is a relevant consideration. According to the nature of the evidence which the witness could have given, the contempt may constitute a serious interference with the administration of justice or may be such as can be very lightly punished or disregarded altogether.

Where a broadcaster, guilty of a serious contempt under the strict liability rule, immediately accepted liability to pay the substantial wasted costs of an aborted trial (*Prosecution of Offences Act* 1985, s.19B (*ante*, § 6–45a)), when those costs had not yet been quantified, this was a factor that had not been present in previous like cases and, being a form of punishment in itself, should be taken into account in subsequently fixing the amount of the fine: *Att.-Gen. v. ITV Central Ltd* [2008] L.S. Gazette, July 31, 16, DC ([2008] EWHC 1984 (Admin.)).

In *R. v. D. (Contempt of court: Illegal photography)*, *The Times*, May 13, 2004, CA, it was said that the taking of photographs using mobile phones in court has become a major problem; factors likely to influence sentence include the nature of the trial, the potential disruption of the trial as a result of the illegal photographs being taken, and the potential for misuse of the particular photographs; mitigating factors include a guilty plea, youthfulness, a genuine apology, and ignorance or innocence (*e.g.* on a tourist's part); in an appropriate case, immediate prison is likely; for less serious offences, a short sentence might be appropriate, in some instances the clang of the prison gates being enough (12 months' imprisonment upheld notwithstanding guilty plea).

E. Application to Divisional Court for Committal for Contempt

By virtue of section 45(4) of the *Supreme Court Act* 1981 (to be cited, as from a day to be appointed, as the *Senior Courts Act* 1981: *Constitutional Reform Act* 2005, s.59, and Sched. 11, para. 1(1)), the Crown Court has all the powers of the High Court in relation to contempt. The power to act of its own motion should normally only be used by the court when it is urgent and imperative to act immediately: see *ante*, §§ 28–115 *et seq*. In all other cases the court should refer the alleged contempt to the Attorney-General and let him or the aggrieved party apply to the Divisional Court for an order of committal under *RSC*, Ord. 52 (as now contained in Sched. 1 to the *Civil Procedure Rules* 1998 (S.I. 1998 No. 3132)): see *ante*, § 28–89; and *post*. The decision of the Attorney-General is not open to judicial review: *R. v. Solicitor-General, ex p. Taylor and Taylor*, *ante*, § 28–89. Order 52 is accompanied by a practice direction: *Practice Direction (Committal Applications)* [1999] 1 W.L.R. 1124, which deals with the procedures to be followed in relation to applications for orders of committal and specifically to orders in relation to a contempt in the face of the court. Although no such guidance is yet available in respect of contempt of court in the Crown Court, it is submitted that the practice direction is a useful starting point. **28–128**

Civil Procedure Rules 1998 (S.I. 1998 No. 3132), Sched. 1 (RSC, Ord. 52)

Committal for contempt of court

1.—(1) The power of the High Court or Court of Appeal to punish for contempt of court may be exercised by an order of committal. **28–129**

(2) Where contempt of court—

(a) is committed in connection with—

(i) any proceedings before a Divisional Court of the Queen's Bench Division; or

(ii) criminal proceedings, except where the contempt is committed in the face of the court or consists of disobedience to an order of the court or a breach of an undertaking to the court; or

(iii) proceedings in an inferior court; or

(b) is committed otherwise than in connection with any proceedings,

then, subject to paragraph (4), an order of committal may be made only by a Divisional Court of the Queen's Bench Division.

This paragraph shall not apply in relation to contempt of the Court of Appeal.

(3) [*Contempt in connection with High Court proceedings*.]

(4) [*Single High Court judge's jurisdiction in relation to contempts of other tribunals where statute so provides*.]

[This rule is printed as amended by the *Civil Procedure (Amendment) Rules* 2002 (S.I. 2002 No. 2058).]

As to contempt "in the face of the court", see *ante*, §§ 28–108 *et seq*.

As to "inferior court", see *Att.-Gen. v. British Broadcasting Corp.* [1981] A.C. 303, HL.

Rule 1 should be read in conjunction with rule 5, *post*, § 28–133.

Application to Divisional Court

2.—(1) No application to a Divisional Court for an order of committal against any person may be made unless permission to make such an application has been granted in accordance with this rule. **28–130**

(2) An application for such permission must be made without notice to a Divisional Court, except in vacation when it may be made to a judge in chambers, and must be supported by a statement setting out the name and description of the applicant, the name, description and address of the person sought to be committed and the grounds on which his committal is sought, and by an affidavit, to be filed before the application is made, verifying the facts relied on.

(3) The applicant must give notice of the application for permission not later than the preceding day to the Crown Office and must at the same time lodge in that office copies of the statement and affidavit.

(4) Where an application for permission under this rule is refused by a judge in chambers, the applicant may make a fresh application for such leave to a Divisional Court.

(5) An application made to a Divisional Court by virtue of paragraph (4) must be made within 8 days after the judge's refusal to give permission or, if a Divisional Court does not sit within that period, on the first day on which it sits thereafter.

Application for order after leave to apply granted

28–131 3.—(1) When permission has been granted under rule 2 to apply for an order of committal, the application for the order must be made by motion to a Divisional Court and, unless the Court or judge granting permission has otherwise directed, there must be at least 14 clear days between the service of the claim form and the day named therein for the hearing.

(2) Unless within 14 days after such permission was granted the claim form is issued the permission shall lapse.

(3) Subject to paragraph (4) the claim form, accompanied by a copy of the statement and affidavit in support of the application for permission, must be served personally on the person sought to be committed.

(4) Without prejudice to the powers of the Court or judge under Part 6 of the *CPR*, the Court or judge may dispense with service under this rule if it or he thinks it just to do so.

Application to Court other than Divisional Court

28–132 4.—(1)–(3) [*Procedural requirements for civil contempt application in High Court.*]

(4) This rule does not apply to committal applications which under rules 1(2) and 3(1) should be made to a Divisional Court but which, in vacation, have been properly made to a single judge in accordance with Order 64, rule 4.

Saving for power to commit without application for purpose

28–133 5. Nothing in the foregoing provisions of this Order shall be taken as affecting the power of the High Court or Court of Appeal to make an order of committal of its own initiative against a person guilty of contempt of court.

As to the power of the High Court and Court of Appeal to act of their own motion, see *Balogh v. St Albans Crown Court* [1975] Q.B. 75, CA, *ante*, §§ 28–105 *et seq.*

Provisions as to hearing

28–134 6.—(1) Subject to paragraph (2), the Court hearing an application for an order of committal may sit in private in the following cases, that is to say—

(a) where the application arises out of proceedings relating to the wardship or adoption of an infant or wholly or mainly to the guardianship, custody, maintenance or upbringing of an infant, or rights of access to an infant;

(b) where the application arises out of proceedings relating to a person suffering or appearing to be suffering from mental disorder within the meaning of the *Mental Health Act* 1983;

(c) where the application arises out of proceedings in which a secret process, discovery or invention was in issue;

(d) where it appears to the Court that in the interests of the administration of justice or for reasons of national security the application should be heard in private;

but, except as aforesaid, the application shall be heard in public.

(2) If the Court hearing an application in private by virtue of paragraph (1) decides to make an order of committal against the person sought to be committed, it shall in public state—

(a) the name of the person,

(b) in general terms the nature of the contempt of Court in respect of which an order of committal is being made, and

(c) the length of the period for which he is being committed.

(3) Except with the leave of the Court hearing an application for an order of committal, no grounds shall be relied upon at the hearing except the grounds set out in the statement under rule 2 or, as the case may be, in the claim form or application notice under rule 4.

(4) If on the hearing of the application the person sought to be committed expresses a wish to give oral evidence on his own behalf, he shall be entitled to do so.

[This rule is printed as amended by the *Civil Procedure (Amendment) Rules* 1999 (S.I. 1999 No. 1008).]

Power to suspend execution of committal order

28–135 7.—(1) The Court by whom an order of committal is made may by order direct that the execution of the order of committal shall be suspended for such period or on such terms or conditions as it may specify.

(2) Where execution of an order of committal is suspended by an order under paragraph (1), the applicant for the order of committal must, unless the Court otherwise directs, serve on the person against whom it was made a notice informing him of the making and terms of the order under that paragraph.

Warrant for arrest

7A. A warrant for the arrest of a person against whom an order of committal has been made shall not, without further order of the court, be enforced more than 2 years after the date on which the warrant is issued. **28–135a**

[This rule was inserted by the *Civil Procedure (Amendment No. 5) Rules* 2003 (S.I. 2003 No. 3361).]

Discharge of person committed

8.—(1) The Court may, on the application of any person committed to prison for any contempt of court, discharge him. **28–136**

(2) [*Irrelevant to criminal proceedings*.]

Saving for other powers

9. Nothing in the foregoing provisions of this Order shall be taken as affecting the power of the Court to make an order requiring a person guilty of contempt of court, or a person punishable by virtue of any enactment in the like manner as if he had been guilty of contempt of the High Court, to pay a fine or give security for his good behaviour, and those provisions, so far as applicable, and with the necessary modifications, shall apply in relation to an application for such an order as they apply in relation to an application for an order for committal. **28–137**

F. APPEALS

Administration of Justice Act 1960, s.13

13.—(1) Subject to the provisions of this section, an appeal shall lie under this section from any order or decision of a court in the exercise of jurisdiction to punish for contempt of court (including criminal contempt); and in relation to any such order or decision the provisions of this section shall have effect in substitution for any other enactment relating to appeals in civil or criminal proceedings. **28–138**

(2) An appeal under this section shall lie in any case at the instance of the defendant and, in the case of an application for committal or attachment, at the instance of the applicant and the appeal shall lie—

(a) from an order or decision of any inferior court not referred to in the next following paragraph to the High Court;

(b) from an order or decision of a county court or any other inferior court from which appeals generally lie to the Court of Appeal, and from an order or decision (other than a decision on an appeal under this section) of a single judge of the High Court, or of any court having the powers of the High Court or of a judge of that court to the Court of Appeal;

(bb) from an order or decision of the Crown Court to the Court of Appeal;

(c) from a decision of a single judge of the High Court on an appeal under this section, from an order or decision of a Divisional Court or the Court of Appeal (including a decision of either of those courts on an appeal under this section) and from an order or decision *of the Court of Criminal Appeal or the Courts-Martial Appeal Court* [(except one made in Scotland or Northern Ireland) of the Court Martial Appeal Court], to the *House of Lords* [Supreme Court].

(3) The court to which an appeal is brought under this section may reverse or vary the order or decision of the court below and make such other order as may be just; and without prejudice to the inherent powers of any court referred to in subsection (2) of this section, provision may be made by rules of court for authorising the release on bail of an appellant under this section. **28–139**

(4) Subsections (2) to (4) of section one and section two of this Act shall apply to an appeal to *the House of Lords* [the Supreme Court] under this section as they apply to an appeal to *that House* [the Supreme Court] under the said section one, except that so much of the said subsection (2) as restricts the grant of leave to appeal shall apply only where the decision of the court below is a decision on appeal to that court under this section.

(5) In this section "court" includes any tribunal or person having power to punish for

contempt; and references in this section to an order or decision of a court in the exercise of jurisdiction to punish for contempt of court include references—

(a) to an order or decision of the High Court, the Crown Court or county court under any enactment enabling that court to deal with an offence as if it were contempt of court;

(b) to an order or decision of a county court or of any court having the powers of a county court, under sections 14, 92 or 118 of the *County Courts Act* 1984;

(c) to an order or decision of a magistrates' court under subsection (3) of section 63 of the *Magistrates' Courts Act* 1980,

[(d) to an order or decision (except one made in Scotland or Northern Ireland) of the Court Martial, the Summary Appeal Court or the Service Civilian Court under section 309 of the *Armed Forces Act* 2006,]

but do not include references to orders under section five of the *Debtors Act* 1869, or under any provision of the *Magistrates' Courts Act* 1980, or the *County Courts Act* 1984, except those referred to in paragraphs (b) and (c) of this subsection and except sections 38 and 142 of the last mentioned Act so far as those sections confer jurisdiction in respect of contempt of court.

(6) This section does not apply to a conviction or sentence in respect of which an appeal lies under Part I of the *Criminal Appeal Act* 1968, or to a decision of the Criminal Division of the Court of Appeal under that Part of that Act.

[This section is printed as amended and repealed in part by the *CAA* 1968, s.52(1), Sched. 5; the *Courts Act* 1971, Sched. 11, Pt III, and Sched. 8; the *MCA* 1980, Sched. 7; the *Supreme Court Act* 1981, Sched. 7 (to be cited, as from a day to be appointed, as the *Senior Courts Act* 1981: *Constitutional Reform Act* 2005, s.59, and Sched. 11, para. 1(1)); the *County Courts Act* 1984, Sched. 2; and the *Access to Justice Act* 1999, s.64; and as amended, as from a day to be appointed, by the *Constitutional Reform Act* 2005, s.40(4), and Sched. 9, para. 13(1) and (7) (substitution of references to "Supreme Court" for references to "House of Lords"); and the *AFA* 2006, s.378(1), and Sched. 16, para. 45 (substitution of words in first pair of square brackets for italicised words that precede them, insertion of subs. (5)(d)).]

28–140 The reference to the Court of Criminal Appeal in section 13(2)(c) should be read as a reference to the criminal division of the Court of Appeal: *Supreme Court Act* 1981, s.151(5), and Sched. 4, para. 3 (to be cited, as from a day to be appointed, as the *Senior Courts Act* 1981: *Constitutional Reform Act* 2005, s.59, and Sched. 11, para. 1(1)).

For provisions as to procedure and bail on appeals to the Court of Appeal and the House of Lords, see *RSC*, Ord. 109, r.3 (as set out in Schedule 1 to the *Civil Procedure Rules* 1998 (S.I. 1998 No. 3132)), and r.4 (inserted by the *Civil Procedure (Amendment) Rules* 2000 (S.I. 2000 No. 221)).

Section 13(1) should be construed broadly to include all orders or decisions relating to contempt; it is not necessary, to trigger section 13, that there is a conviction for contempt: *R. v. Serumaga* [2005] 2 Cr.App.R. 12, CA (see also *ante*, § 28–118). However, section 13 does not confer any right of appeal against a finding of contempt by a magistrates' court under section 12 of the *Contempt of Court Act* 1981: *Haw v. City of Westminster Magistrates' Court* [2008] 3 W.L.R. 465, DC.

28–141 In *Linnett v. Coles* [1987] Q.B. 555, 84 Cr.App.R. 227, CA (Civ. Div.), it was held that section 13(3) gave the Court of Appeal wide powers to vary or reverse any order and to substitute that order with one thought to be just. This may include ordering a rehearing (*Duo v. Osborne* [1992] 1 W.L.R. 611, CA (Civ. Div.)) or granting bail (*R. v. Serumaga, ante*). The court should hesitate long before exercising its powers to increase a sentence: *Linnett v. Coles, ante*.

Save in exceptional circumstances, *habeas corpus* is not the appropriate remedy for appealing against committal orders: *Linnett v. Coles, ante*, p. 561, p. 232; *Rayne in the matter of S.* (2004) 148 S.J. 511, CA (Civ. Div.).

The power under section 13(3) to "make such other order as may be just" does not extend to making an order for costs out of central funds in favour of a successful appellant against a finding of contempt made by the Crown Court: *R. v. Moore* [2003] 1 W.L.R. 2170, CA.

Although not strictly a right of appeal, note also the sentencing court's power to discharge anyone committed for contempt: see the *Contempt of Court Act* 1981, s.14(1) (*ante*, § 28–102), and *RSC*, Ord. 52, r.8 (*ante*, § 28–136).

IV. INTIMIDATION OF WITNESSES, JURORS AND OTHERS

Criminal Justice and Public Order Act 1994, s.51

51.—(1) A person commits an offence if— **28–142**

(a) he does an act which intimidates, and is intended to intimidate, another person ("the victim"),

(b) he does the act knowing or believing that the victim is assisting in the investigation of an offence or is a witness or potential witness or a juror or potential juror in proceedings for an offence, and

(c) he does it intending thereby to cause the investigation or the course of justice to be obstructed, perverted or interfered with.

(2) A person commits an offence if—

(a) he does an act which harms, and is intended to harm, another person or, intending to cause another person to fear harm, he threatens to do an act which would harm that other person,

(b) he does or threatens to do the act knowing or believing that the person harmed or threatened to be harmed ("the victim"), or some other person, has assisted in an investigation into an offence or has given evidence or particular evidence in proceedings for an offence, or has acted as a juror or concurred in a particular verdict in proceedings for an offence, and

(c) he does or threatens to do it because of that knowledge or belief.

(3) For the purposes of subsections (1) and (2) it is immaterial that the act is or would be done, or that the threat is made—

(a) otherwise than in the presence of the victim, or

(b) to a person other than the victim.

(4) The harm that may be done or threatened may be financial as well as physical (whether to the person or a person's property) and similarly as respects an intimidatory act which consists of threats. **28–143**

(5) The intention required by subsection (1)(c) and the motive required by subsection (2)(c) above need not be the only or the predominating intention or motive with which the act is done or, in the case of subsection (2), threatened.

(6) A person guilty of an offence under this section shall be liable—

(a) on conviction on indictment, to imprisonment for a term not exceeding five years or a fine or both;

(b) on summary conviction, to imprisonment for a term not exceeding *six* [12] months or a fine not exceeding the statutory maximum or both.

(7) If, in proceedings against a person for an offence under subsection (1) above, it is proved that he did an act falling within paragraph (a) with the knowledge or belief required by paragraph (b), he shall be presumed, unless the contrary is proved, to have done the act with the intention required by paragraph (c) of that subsection.

(8) If, in proceedings against a person for an offence under subsection (2) above, it is proved that within the relevant period—

(a) he did an act which harmed, and was intended to harm, another person, or

(b) intending to cause another person fear or harm, he threatened to do an act which would harm that other person,

and that he did the act, or (as the case may be) threatened to do the act, with the knowledge or belief required by paragraph (b), he shall be presumed, unless the contrary is proved, to have done the act or (as the case may be) threatened to do the act with the motive required by paragraph (c) of that subsection.

(9) In this section— **28–144**

"investigation into an offence" means such an investigation by the police or other person charged with the duty of investigating offences or charging offenders;

"offence" includes an alleged or suspected offence;

"potential", in relation to a juror, means a person who has been summoned for jury service at the court at which proceedings for the offence are pending; *and*

["public prosecutor", "requisition" and "written charge" have the same meaning as in section 29 of the *Criminal Justice Act* 2003;]

"the relevant period" —

(a) in relation to a witness or juror in any proceedings for an offence, means the period beginning with the institution of the proceedings and ending with the first anniversary of the conclusion of the trial or, if there is an appeal or a reference under section 9 or 11 of the *Criminal Appeal Act* 1995, of the conclusion of the appeal;

(b) in relation to a person who has, or is believed by the accused to have, assisted in an investigation into an offence, but was not also a witness in proceedings for an offence, means the period of one year beginning with any act of his, or any act believed by the accused to be an act of his, assisting in the investigation; and

(c) in relation to a person who both has, or is believed by the accused to have, assisted in the investigation into an offence and was a witness in proceedings for the offence, means the period beginning with any act of his, or any act believed by the accused to be an act of his, assisting in the investigation and ending with the anniversary mentioned in paragraph (a) above.

28–145 (10) For the purposes of the definition of the relevant period in subsection (9) above—

(a) proceedings for an offence are instituted at the earliest of the following times—

(i) when a justice of the peace issues a summons or warrant under section 1 of the *Magistrates' Courts Act* 1980 in respect of the offence;

[(ia) when a public prosecutor issues a written charge and requisition in respect of the offence;]

(ii) when a person is charged with the offence after being taken into custody without a warrant;

(iii) when a bill of indictment is preferred by virtue of section 2(2)(b) of the *Administration of Justice (Miscellaneous Provisions) Act* 1933;

(b) proceedings at a trial of an offence are concluded with the occurrence of any of the following, the discontinuance of the prosecution, the discharge of the jury without a finding otherwise than in circumstances where the proceedings are continued without a jury, the acquittal of the accused or the sentencing of or other dealing with the accused for the offence of which he was convicted; and

(c) proceedings on an appeal are concluded on the determination of the appeal or the abandonment of the appeal.

(11) This section is in addition to, and not in derogation of, any offence subsisting at common law.

[This section is printed as amended by the *CAA* 1995, s.29(1), and Sched. 2, para. 19; the *YJCEA* 1999, s.67(1), and Sched. 4, para. 22; and the *CJA* 2003, s.331, and Sched. 36, paras 62 and 64; and, as from a day or days to be appointed, by the *CJA* 2003 as follows: by s.282(2) and (3) (substitution of "12" for "six" in subs. (6), but not in relation to an offence committed before the date of commencement: s.282(4)); and by s.331, and Sched. 36, para. 11 (omission of italicised word and insertion of words in square brackets in subs. (9)).]

Indictment

COUNT 1

STATEMENT OF OFFENCE

28–146 *Intimidation, contrary to section 51(1) of the* Criminal Justice and Public Order Act *1994*.

PARTICULARS OF OFFENCE

A B, on the —— day of ——, 20—, did an act namely, ——, which intimidated and was intended to intimidate CD, knowing or believing that CD was assisting in the investigation of an offence [was a witness/potential witness] [juror/potential juror] [in proceedings for an offence] and intended thereby to cause the investigation [course of justice] to be obstructed, perverted or interfered with.

COUNT 2

STATEMENT OF OFFENCE

28–147 *Taking [Threatening to take] revenge, contrary to section 51(2) of the* Criminal Justice and Public Order Act *1994*.

PARTICULARS OF OFFENCE

A B, on the —— day of ——, 20—, did an act, [threatened to do an act], namely ——, to J N, which harmed [would have harmed], and was intended to harm J N, knowing or believing that J N [or E F], had assisted in the investigation of an offence [had given evidence/particular evidence, in proceedings for an offence] [acted as a juror/concurred in a particular verdict in proceedings for an offence] and did the act [threatened to do the act] because of what he so knew or believed.

Section 51 creates two separate offences: intimidation of witnesses, jurors and those involved in the investigation of offences (s.51(1)); and taking revenge against these groups (s.51(2)). These offences appear to be wider in scope than the common law offences of contempt of court and perverting the course of justice and thus may become the preferred charge in such cases. **28–148**

See also the *Witnesses (Public Inquiries) Protection Act* 1892, ss.1–3, for the summary offence of obstructing or intimidating witnesses at any public "inquiry" (as defined in s.1); the *Inquiries Act* 2005, s.35(2)(b), for the summary offence of preventing any evidence, document or other thing from being given, produced or provided to an inquiry panel; and the *CJPA* 2001, ss.39–41, in respect of the intimidation and harming of witnesses in other proceedings. The latter provisions are closely modelled on section 51 of the 1994 Act.

Intimidation

In *R. v. Patrascu* [2005] 1 Cr.App.R. 35, CA, the court had to consider the correct interpretation of "an act which intimidates" in section 51(1)(a). May L.J. said (at [18]): **28–149**

> "In our judgment, a person does an act which intimidates another person within section 51(1)(a), if he puts the victim in fear. He also does so if he seeks to deter the victim from some relevant action by threat or violence. A threat unaccompanied by violence may be sufficient, and the threat need not necessarily be a threat of violence... The intimidation does not necessarily have to be successful in the sense that the victim does not have actually to be deterred or put in fear. But it will obviously be material evidence if the victim was not in fact deterred or put in fear. A person may intimidate another person without the victim being intimidated. This apparent contradiction arises from different shades of meaning of the active and passive use of the verb. An act may amount to intimidation and thus intimidate, even though the victim is sufficiently steadfast not to be intimidated."

For a criticism of this reasoning, and in particular for a submission that it would be better to rely on the law of attempt where the victim is not intimidated (the court acknowledging at [21] that, on its construction of section 51, attempt would rarely be an appropriate charge), see *Criminal Law Week* 2004/38/3.

There must be an investigation under way at the time of the alleged act; it is insufficient that the doer of the act believes this to be the case: *R. v. Singh (B.)* [1999] Crim.L.R. 681, CA.

The reverse burden provision in subsection (7) does not breach Article 6 of the ECHR if interpreted as imposing a legal burden on the defendant: *Att.-Gen.'s Reference (No. 1 of 2004)*; *R. v. Edwards*; *R. v. Denton*; *R. v. Hendley*; *R. v. Crowley* [2004] 1 W.L.R. 2111, CA.

Revenge

For the purposes of subsections (2) and (4), "harm" (financial harm aside) means physical harm and does not include assaults, such as spitting, which do not cause injury: *R. v. Normanton* [1998] Crim.L.R. 220, CA. **28–150**

Sentence

The fact that Parliament thought it necessary to enact section 51 is ample reason for holding that an offence contrary to it, that involves an assault, contains an extra element of criminality, above and beyond the assault: *R. v. Watmore* [1998] 2 Cr.App.R.(S.) 46, CA. For examples of sentences passed for intimidation, see CSP, B8–2.3AA. **28–150a**

V. EMBRACERY

In relation to this obsolescent offence, see the 2001 and earlier editions of this work. **28–151**

VI. PERJURY

A. STATUTE

Perjury Act 1911, s.1

Perjury

28–152 **1.**—(1) If any person lawfully sworn as a witness or as an interpreter in a judicial proceeding wilfully makes a statement material in that proceeding, which he knows to be false or does not believe to be true, he shall be guilty of perjury, and shall, on conviction thereof on indictment, be liable to imprisonment for a term not exceeding seven years, or to a fine or to both such imprisonment and fine.

(2) The expression "judicial proceeding" includes a proceeding before any court, tribunal, or person having by law power to hear, receive, and examine evidence on oath.

(3) Where a statement made for the purposes of a judicial proceeding is not made before the tribunal itself, but is made on oath before a person authorised by law to administer an oath to the person who makes the statement, and to record or authenticate the statement, it shall, for the purposes of this section, be treated as having been made in a judicial proceeding.

(4) A statement made by a person lawfully sworn in England for the purposes of a judicial proceeding—

(a) in another part of [Her] Majesty's dominions; or

(b) in a British tribunal lawfully constituted in any place by sea or land outside [Her] Majesty's dominions; or

(c) in a tribunal of any foreign state,

shall, for the purposes of this section, be treated as a statement made in a judicial proceeding in England.

28–153 (5) Where, for the purposes of a judicial proceeding in England, a person is lawfully sworn under the authority of an Act of Parliament—

(a) in any other part of [Her] Majesty's dominions; or

(b) before a British tribunal or a British officer in a foreign country, or within the jurisdiction of the Admiralty of England;

a statement made by such person so sworn as aforesaid (unless the Act of Parliament under which it was made otherwise specifically provides) shall be treated for the purposes of this section as having been made in the judicial proceeding in England for the purposes whereof it was made.

(6) The question whether a statement on which perjury is assigned was material is a question of law to be determined by the court of trial.

[In subs. (1), the first reference to "imprisonment" has been inserted, and references to "penal servitude" and "hard labour" have been omitted, by virtue of the *CJA* 1948, s.1.]

28–154 Section 1(1) is applied by the *European Communities Act* 1972, s.11(1)(a): *post*, § 28–190.

Section 1(4) has effect in relation to proceedings in the Court of Justice of the European Communities as it has effect in relation to a judicial proceeding in a tribunal of a foreign State: see the *Evidence (European Court) Order* 1976 (S.I. 1976 No.428).

Perjury Act 1911, s.1A

False unsworn statement under Evidence (Proceedings in Other Jurisdictions) Act 1975

28–155 **1A.** If any person in giving any testimony (either orally or in writing) otherwise than on oath, where required to do so by an order under section 2 of the *Evidence (Proceedings in Other Jurisdictions) Act* 1975, makes a statement—

(a) which he knows to be false in a material particular, or

(b) which is false in a material particular and which he does not believe to be true,

he shall be guilty of an offence and shall be liable on conviction on indictment to imprisonment for a term not exceeding two years or a fine or both.

[Section 1A was inserted by the *Evidence (Proceedings in Other Jurisdictions) Act* 1975, s.8(1), and Sched. 1.]

This offence is triable either way: *MCA* 1980, s.17(1), and Sched. 1, *ante*, §§ 1–75af *et seq.*

B. INDICTMENT

STATEMENT OF OFFENCE

Perjury, contrary to section 1(1) of the Perjury Act *1911.* 28–156

PARTICULARS OF OFFENCE

A B, on the —— day of ——, 20—, having been lawfully sworn as a witness in a judicial proceeding, namely the trial of an action in the Chancery Division of the High Court of Justice in England in which one —— was plaintiff and one —— was defendant, wilfully made a statement material in that proceeding which he knew to be false, namely that he saw one MN in the street called the Strand, London, on the —— day of ——, 20—.

See section 12 of the Act, *post*, § 28–183, as to the appropriate form of such an indictment.

Punishment: imprisonment for a term not exceeding seven years, or a fine, or both: s.1(1), *ante*. See also section 16(1), *post*, § 28–184. For cases of perjury, see CSP, B8–1.3; and *R. v. Archer* [2003] 1 Cr.App.R.(S.) 86, CA. In *R. v. Knight*, 6 Cr.App.R.(S.) 31, the Court of Appeal indicated that the punishment for perjury committed in trials relating to serious offences should be commensurate with the gravity of the offence for which the person in whose interest it was committed was on trial. Sentences of two to four years' imprisonment have been upheld in respect of perjury committed in the Crown Court: see, for example, *R. v. Cunningham* [2007] 2 Cr.App.R.(S.) 61, CA (four years' imprisonment where alleged kidnap victim gave false evidence that offence had not happened).

C. THE INGREDIENTS OF THE OFFENCE

In cases under section 1(1) the prosecution must prove the following: (a) that the witness was lawfully sworn as a witness; (b) in a judicial proceeding; (c) that the witness made a statement wilfully, that is to say deliberately and not inadvertently or by mistake (see *ante*, § 17–47, and *post*, § 28–178); (d) that that statement was false (as to which, see s.13, *post*, § 28–164); (e) that the witness knew it was false or did not believe it to be true; (f) that the statement was, viewed objectively, material in the judicial proceeding; by reason of section 1(6) this last requirement is a matter to be decided by the judge: *R. v. Millward* [1985] Q.B. 519, 80 Cr.App.R. 280, CA. Note, however, that (d) is not strictly a separate requirement; what the statute requires is proof that the witness made a statement known to be false or not believed to be true. 28–157

(1) Lawfully sworn

See section 15 of the 1911 Act, *post*, § 28–170. 28–158

As to making an affirmation instead of taking an oath, see the *Oaths Act* 1978, s.5 (*ante*, § 8–31).

Nothing in the Act of 1911 applies to the unsworn evidence of a child: s.16(2), *post*, § 28–184. As to the punishment of false statements made during the course of such evidence, see the *YJCEA* 1999, s.57 (*ante* § 8–34).

(2) Judicial proceeding

As to the meaning of "judicial proceeding", see section 1(2), *ante*, § 28–152. It should be noted that this subsection does not set out a comprehensive definition. 28–159

An income tax appeal tribunal consisting of two Commissioners is a legally constituted tribunal and a false statement made on oath before it amounts to perjury: *R. v. Hood-Barrs* [1943] K.B. 455, CCA.

Since the Act does not state that the court before which the false statement has been made must be a court of "competent jurisdiction", and having regard to the definition of "judicial proceeding" in section 1(2), it would seem that perjury may be committed though the court had no jurisdiction in the particular cause in which the statement was made.

(3) Materiality of statement

While the materiality of the truth, if told, might in some cases throw light on the 28–160 materiality of the false statement, it is the statement made which has to be material. This issue is for the judge to decide viewing the statement objectively: *R. v. Millward*, *ante*, § 28–157.

The requirement of materiality can be traced back to Coke: 3 Inst. 167. The rule has been narrowly construed and some of the authorities are less than consistent. Sworn evidence going solely to the question of punishment, even after conviction, may be material: *R. v. Wheeler*, 12 Cr.App.R. 159, CCA. Clearly, any evidence which has a direct bearing on the outcome of the case is also material. Where a defendant in a civil action falsely swore that his Christian name was "Edward", not "Bernard Edward" as appeared on the summons, and the judge struck out the action, this amounted to perjury: *R. v. Mullany* (1865) L. & C. 593.

Circumstantial lies which support the central untruth, for example a false alibi, are also material: *R. v. Tyson* (1867) L.R. 1 C.C.R. 107.

28–161 It is perjury to give false evidence, whereby the judge is induced to admit other material evidence—even though the latter evidence is afterwards withdrawn by counsel, or was legally inadmissible: *R. v. Phillpots* (1851) 2 Den. 302.

An answer that is only relevant to credit and not to the issue to be determined, may be material: *R. v. Griepe* (1697) 1 Ld. Raym. 256; *R. v. Overton* (1842) 2 Mood 263. Lord Russell C.J. in *R. v. Baker* [1895] 1 Q.B. 797, stated that:

> "the defendant's answers would affect his credit as a witness, and all false statements wilfully and corruptly made, as to matters which affect his credit, are material" (at p. 799).

28–162 It is submitted, however, that the lie must be capable of influencing the tribunal. In *R. v. Lavey* (1850) 3 C. & K. 26, Lord Campbell C.J. told a jury that the defendant's lie, that she had never been tried at the Old Bailey, was material if it might have influenced the county court judge in his approach to her other evidence. In *R. v. Sweet-Escott*, 55 Cr.App.R. 316, Assizes, Lawton J. held that a witness's false statement that he had no previous convictions was not material because the convictions were so old (20 years) that no reasonable tribunal could have taken an adverse view of the defendant's credit because of them. Lawton J. indicated that the matters about which a witness is questioned must relate to his likely standing after cross-examination.

Perjury may be assigned on a false statement which should have been excluded as inadmissible if in fact it was material: *R. v. Gibbons* (1862) 9 Cox 105.

(4) Falsity

28–163 The defendant must know the statement to be false or not believe it to be true. It follows that the statement need not necessarily be false.

Evidence of a confession that a sworn statement was false was evidence of the statement's falsity: *R. v. Peach*, 91 Cr.App.R. 379, CA. See further *post*, § 28–167.

Perjury Act 1911, s.13

28–164 **13.** A person shall not be liable to be convicted of any offence against this Act, or of any offence declared by any other Act to be perjury or subornation of perjury, or to be punishable as perjury or subornation of perjury solely upon the evidence of one witness as to the falsity of any statement alleged to be false.

28–165 In *R. v. Carroll*, 99 Cr.App.R. 381, CA, it was said that a judge is required in a summing up to refer to section 13 and the need for the jury to have before it the evidence which they accept of more than one witness; that is to say, either of one or more other witnesses or at least of some other supporting evidence by way of confession or otherwise, which supplements that of a single witness. The requirement of support in section 13 only goes to the issue of falsity and not to proving that the person charged knew what he was saying was false: *R. v. O'Connor* [1980] Crim.L.R. 43, CA.

28–166 The section means that falsity must be proved either by two witnesses, or by one witness and something else in addition: *R. v. Threlfall*, 10 Cr.App.R. 112 at 117; *R. v. Carroll*, *ante*. A letter or account written by the defendant contradicting his sworn evidence is sufficient: *R. v. Mayhew* (1834) 6 C. & P. 315, and see *R. v. Threlfall*, *ante*.

28–167 There are only two situations where the trial judge need not refer to section 13 in directing the jury. The first is the rare situation where the prosecution elects to proceed on the basis that the truth or falsehood of the statement forms no part of their case (*i.e.*

where it is alleged that the defendant made a statement which he did not believe to be true) and the second is where the falsity of the statement is not in issue: *R. v. Rider*, 83 Cr.App.R. 207, CA. *Cf. R. v. Stokes* [1988] Crim.L.R. 110, CA. In *R. v. Peach*, *ante*, § 28–163, it was held that evidence of a confession that a sworn statement was false was evidence of the statement's falsity and that, since two witnesses had testified to having heard the confession of falsity, the requirements of section 13 were satisfied.

D. JURISDICTION, PROOF OF EARLIER PROCEEDINGS AND INTERPRETATION

Perjury Act 1911, ss.8, 14, 15

Venue

8. Where an offence against this Act or any offence punishable as perjury or as subornation of perjury under any other Act of Parliament is committed in any place either on sea or land outside the United Kingdom, the offender may be proceeded against, indicted, tried, and punished in England. **28–168**

[This section is printed as repealed in part by the *CLA* 1967, s.10(2), Sched. 3.]

As to subornation of perjury, see *post*, § 28–185.

Proof of certain proceedings on which perjury is assigned

14. On a prosecution— **28–169**

(a) for perjury alleged to have been committed on the trial of an indictment; or

(b) for procuring or suborning the commission of perjury on any such trial,

the fact of the former trial shall be sufficiently proved by the production of a certificate containing the substance and effect (omitting the formal parts) of the indictment and trial purporting to be signed by the clerk of the court, or other person having the custody of the records of the court where the indictment was tried, or by the deputy of that clerk or other person, without proof of the signature or official character of the clerk or person appearing to have signed the certificate.

[This section is printed as repealed in part by the *CLA* 1967, Sched. 3, Pt III.]

Interpretation, etc.

15.—(1) For the purposes of this Act, the forms and ceremonies used in administering an oath are immaterial, if the court or person before whom the oath is taken has power to administer an oath for the purpose of verifying the statement in question, and if the oath has been administered in a form and with ceremonies which the person taking the oath has accepted without objection, or has declared to be binding on him. **28–170**

(2) In this Act—

The expression "oath" includes "affirmation" and "declaration", and the expression "swear" includes "affirm" and "declare"; and

The expression "statutory declaration" means a declaration made by virtue of the *Statutory Declarations Act* 1835, or of any Act, Order in Council, rule or regulation applying or extending the provisions thereof; and ...

[This section is printed as repealed in part by the *CLA* 1967, s.10(2), Sched. 3, Pt III; and the *Administration of Justice Act* 1977, ss.8(3), 32(4), Sched. 5, Pt III.]

For oaths and affirmations, see the *Oaths Act* 1978, *ante*, §§ 8–27 *et seq.*

Evidence of the earlier proceedings

The record of the trial at which the perjury is alleged to have taken place or a copy thereof, may be proved under the *Evidence Act* 1851, s.14, or the *CJA* 2003, s.117, *ante*, §§ 11–26 *et seq.* See also, the *Civil Procedure Rules* 1998 (S.I. 1998 No. 3132), r.5.4, as to the procedure for obtaining relevant documents. **28–171**

The evidence which the defendant gave upon the trial may be proved by the testimony of some person who was present at the trial. It is not necessary for a note to have been made or for the witness to recollect all that was said by a defendant, provided he can say what was said on the relevant issue: *R. v. Munton* (1829) 3 C. & P. 498; *R. v. Browne* (1829) 3 C. & P. 572. **28–172**

Tape recordings of evidence given at a hearing would, it is submitted, be primary evidence of what was said subject to proof of the tape recording and identification of the speaker. Notes of judges, clerks or shorthand writers may be used as memory refreshing documents: *R. v. Child* (1851) 5 Cox 197; *R. v. Newall* (1852) 6 Cox 21; but see *R. v. Morgan* (1852) 6 Cox 107 (advocate's notes admissible as primary, not secondary, evidence). As to not calling judges of superior courts as witnesses, see *R. v. Gazard* (1838) 8 C. & P. 595.

28–173 The substance of what is set out in the indictment must be proved substantially or literally: *R. v. Leefe* (1809) 2 Camp 134; and the evidence must be clear and precise: *R. v. Bird* (1891) 17 Cox 387.

If the materiality of the statement is in issue, then it will be necessary to prove the nature of the original charge: *R. v. Carr* (1867) 10 Cox 564, CCR. As to proof by secondary evidence, see *R. v. Dillon* (1877) 14 Cox 4. As to proof of records, judgments, etc., see *ante*, §§ 9–72 *et seq.*; *R. v. Scott* (1877) 2 Q.B.D. 415.

28–174 As to the evidential requirements of perjury in an affidavit, see *R. v. Barnes* (1867) 10 Cox 539; *R. v. Hailey* (1824) 1 C. & P. 258; and as to proof by secondary evidence where an affidavit has been lost or destroyed, see *R. v. Milnes* (1860) 2 F. & F. 10.

VII. OFFENCES AKIN TO PERJURY

A. FALSE STATEMENTS ON OATH AND DECLARATIONS

Perjury Act 1911, s.2

False statements on oath made otherwise than in a judicial proceeding

28–175 **2.** If any person—

(1) being required or authorised by law to make any statement on oath for any purpose, and being lawfully sworn (otherwise than in a judicial proceeding) wilfully makes a statement which is material for that purpose and which he knows to be false or does not believe to be true; or

(2) wilfully uses any false affidavit for the purposes of the *Bills of Sale Act* 1878, as amended by any subsequent enactment,

he shall be guilty of a misdemeanour, and, on conviction thereof on indictment, shall be liable to imprisonment for a term not exceeding seven years or to a fine or to both such imprisonment and fine.

[The details of penalty have been substituted by virtue of the *CJA* 1948, s.1.]

This offence is triable either way: *MCA* 1980, s.17(1), and Sched. 1, *ante*, §§ 1–75af *et seq.*

As to the meaning of "wilfully", see *ante*, § 17–47, and *post*, § 28–178; as to the need for "corroboration", see *ante*, § 28–164.

For oaths and affirmations, see generally the *Oaths Act* 1978, *ante*, §§ 8–27 *et seq.* For a decision under section 2, see *R. v. Stokes* [1988] Crim.L.R. 110, CA.

Perjury Act 1911, s.3

False statements, etc., with reference to marriage

28–176 **3.**—(1) If any person—

(a) for the purpose of procuring a marriage, or a certificate or licence for marriage, knowingly and wilfully makes a false oath, or makes or signs a false declaration, notice or certificate required under any Act of Parliament for the time being being in force relating to marriage; or

(b) knowingly and wilfully makes, or knowingly and wilfully causes to be made, for the purpose of being inserted in any register of marriage, a false statement as to any particular required by law to be known and registered relating to any marriage; or

(c) forbids the issue of any certificate or licence for marriage by falsely representing himself to be a person whose consent to the marriage is required by law knowing such representation to be false, or

(d) with respect to a declaration made under section 16(1A) or 27B(2) of the *Marriage Act* 1949—

(i) enters a caveat under subsection (2) of the said section 16, or

(ii) makes a statement mentioned in subsection (4) of the said section 27B,

which he knows to be false in a material particular,

he shall be guilty of a misdemeanour, and, on conviction thereof on indictment, shall be liable to imprisonment for a term not exceeding seven years or to a fine or to both such imprisonment and fine and on summary conviction thereof shall be liable to a penalty not exceeding the prescribed sum.

(2) No prosecution for knowingly and wilfully making a false declaration for the purpose of procuring any marriage out of the district in which the parties or one of them dwell shall take place after the expiration of eighteen months from the solemnization of the marriage to which the declaration refers.

[This section is printed as amended by the *CJA* 1925, s.28(1); the *MCA* 1980, s.32(2) (substitution of reference to "prescribed sum"); and the *Marriage (Prohibited Degrees of Relationship) Act* 1986, s.4. The details of penalty available on conviction on indictment have been substituted by virtue of the *CJA* 1948, s.1.]

As to "the prescribed sum", see *ante*, § 1–75aa.

See *post*, §§ 28–183, 28–184, as to the form of an indictment and certain miscellaneous provisions.

As to the meaning of "wilfully", see *ante*, § 17–47, and *post*, § 28–178; as to the need for "corroboration", see *ante*, § 28–164.

Perjury Act 1911, s.4

False statements, etc., as to births or deaths

4.—(1) If any person— **28–177**

(a) wilfully makes any false answer to any question put to him by any registrar of births or deaths relating to the particulars required to be registered concerning any birth or death, or wilfully gives to any such registrar any false information concerning any birth or death or the cause of any death; or

(b) wilfully makes any false certificate or declaration under or for the purposes of any Act relating to the registration of births or deaths, or, knowing any such certificate or declaration to be false, uses the same as true or gives or sends the same as true to any person; or

(c) wilfully makes, gives or uses any false statement or declaration as to a child born alive as having been still-born, or as to the body of a deceased person or a still-born child in any coffin, or falsely pretends that any child born alive was still-born; or

(d) makes any false statement with intent to have the same inserted in any register of births of deaths;

he shall be guilty of a misdemeanour and shall be liable—

(i) on conviction thereof on indictment, to imprisonment for a term not exceeding seven years, or to a fine;

(ii) on summary conviction thereof to a penalty not exceeding the prescribed sum.

(2) A prosecution on indictment for an offence against this section shall not be commenced more than three years after the commission of the offence.

[The details of penalty available on conviction on indictment have been substituted by virtue of the *CJA* 1948, s.1. The reference to "the prescribed sum" is substituted by virtue of the *MCA* 1980, s.32(2).]

As to "the prescribed sum", see *ante*, § 1–75aa.

See *post*, §§ 28–183, 28–184, as to the form of an indictment and certain miscellaneous provisions. As to the need for "corroboration", see *ante*, § 28–164.

Wilfully

"Wilfully" means "intentionally", that is, as applied to section 4(1)(b), knowing at the time of making the certificate that he was making false statements in relation to documents which purported to be made under the Act for the registration of births or deaths and could be used under the Act: *R. v. Ryan*, 10 Cr.App.R. 4, CCA. **28–178**

Perjury Act 1911, s.5

False statutory declarations and other false statements without oath

5. If any person knowingly and wilfully makes (otherwise than on oath) a statement false in a material particular, and the statement is made— **28–179**

(a) in a statutory declaration; or

(b) in an abstract, account, balance sheet, book, certificate, declaration, entry, estimate, inventory, notice, report, return, or other document which he is authorised or required to make, attest, or verify, by any public general Act of Parliament for the time being in force; or

(c) in any oral declaration or oral answer which he is required to make by, under, or in pursuance of any public general Act of Parliament for the time being in force;

he shall be guilty of a misdemeanour and shall be liable on conviction thereof on indictment to imprisonment for any term not exceeding two years, or to a fine or to both such imprisonment and fine.

[A reference to "hard labour" has been omitted by virtue of the *CJA* 1948, s.1.]

This offence is triable either way: *MCA* 1980, s.17(1), and Sched. 1, *ante*, §§ 1–75ae, 1–75af.

As to the meaning of "wilfully", see *ante*, §§ 17–47, 28–178. The motive for the statement and whether or not there was an active intention to deceive are irrelevant: *R. v. Sood* [1998] 2 Cr.App.R. 355, CA (the vice is the abuse of the occasion and the likely perpetuation of falsehood in relation to matters of public record).

Indictment

STATEMENT OF OFFENCE

28–180 *Making a false statutory declaration, contrary to section 5(a) of the* Perjury Act *1911.*

PARTICULARS OF OFFENCE

A B, on the —— day of ——, 20—, wilfully made a statement which was false in the following material particular(s) namely [state shortly the false statements alleged] *in a* [state the nature of the declaration] *made under* [quote the statute by virtue of which it was made].

Statutory declaration

28–181 As to the meaning of "statutory declaration", see section 15(2) of the *Perjury Act* 1911, *ante*, § 28–170.

It must be proved that the declaration was taken under the statute alleged, and the materiality and falsity of the statement impugned in the same manner as on a charge of perjury: *ante*, §§ 28–160 *et seq.*

Where the declaration confirms any writing, the latter must be produced or secondary evidence of it given after proof of proper notice to produce: *R. v. Cox* (1864) 4 F. & F. 42. On an indictment for a false declaration as to the occurrence of a fire in the defendant's house, it was held that, to prove the declaration to be wilfully false, evidence might be given that certificates sent to the insurers with the declaration were forged: *R. v. Boynes* (1843) 1 C. & K. 65.

Perjury Act 1911, ss.6, 12, 16

False declarations, etc., to obtain registration, etc., for carrying on a vocation

28–182 **6.** If any person—

(a) procures or attempts to procure himself to be registered on any register or roll kept under or in pursuance of any public general Act of Parliament for the time being in force of persons qualified by law to practise any vocation or calling; or

(b) procures or attempts to procure a certificate of the registration of any person on any such register or roll as aforesaid,

by wilfully making or producing or causing to be made or produced either verbally or in writing, any declaration, certificate or representation which he knows to be false or fraudulent, he shall be guilty of a misdemeanour and shall be liable on conviction thereof on indictment to imprisonment for any term not exceeding twelve months, or to a fine, or to both such imprisonment and fine.

This offence is triable either way: *MCA* 1980, s.17(1), and Sched. 1, *ante*, §§ 1–75ae, 1–75af.

As to the meaning of "wilfully", see *ante*, §§ 17–47, 28–178; as to the need for "corroboration", see *ante*, § 28–164.

Form of indictment

12.—(1) In an indictment— **28–183**

(a) for making any false statement or false representation punishable under this Act; or

(b) for unlawfully, wilfully, falsely, fraudulently, deceitfully, maliciously, or corruptly taking, making, signing, or subscribing any oath, affirmation, solemn declaration, statutory declaration, affidavit, deposition, notice, certificate, or other writing,

it is sufficient to set forth the substance of the offence charged, and before which court or person (if any) the offence was committed without setting forth the proceedings or any part of the proceedings in the course of which the offence was committed, and without setting forth the authority of any court or person before whom the offence was committed.

(2) In an indictment for aiding, abetting, counselling, suborning, or procuring any other person to commit any offence hereinbefore in this section mentioned, or for conspiring with any other person, to commit any such offence, it is sufficient—

(a) where such offence has been committed, to allege that offence, and then to allege that the defendant procured the commission of that offence; and

(b) where such offence has not been committed, to set forth the substance of the offence charged against the defendant without setting forth any matter or thing which it is unnecessary to aver in the case of an indictment for a false statement or false representation punishable under this Act.

[This section is printed as repealed in part by the *Criminal Attempts Act* 1981, s.10, Sched., Pt I.]

Savings

16.—(1) Where the making of a false statement is not only an offence under this Act, but also by virtue of some other Act is a corrupt practice or subjects the offender to any forfeiture or disqualification or to any penalty other than imprisonment, or fine, the liability of the offender under this Act shall be in addition to and not in substitution for his liability under such other Act. **28–184**

(2) Nothing in this Act shall apply to a statement made without oath by a child under the provisions of the *Children and Young Persons Act* 1933.

(3) Where the making of a false statement is by any other Act, whether passed before or after the commencement of this Act, made punishable on summary conviction, proceedings may be taken either under such other Act or under this Act: Provided that where such an offence is by any Act passed before the commencement of this Act, as originally enacted, made punishable only on summary conviction, it shall remain only so punishable.

[A reference to "penal servitude" has been omitted by virtue of the *CJA* 1948, s.1.]

As to false statements made in the unsworn evidence of a child, see the *YJCEA* 1999, s.57 (*ante*, § 8–34).

B. Subornation of Perjury

Perjury Act 1911, s.7

Aiders, abettors, suborners, etc.

7.—(1) Every person who aids, abets, counsels, procures, or suborns another person to commit an offence against this Act shall be liable to be proceeded against, indicted, tried and punished if he were a principal offender. **28–185**

(2) Every person who incites another person to commit an offence against this Act shall be guilty of a misdemeanour, and, on conviction thereof on indictment, shall be liable to imprisonment, or to a fine, or to both such imprisonment and fine.

[This section is printed as repealed in part by the *Criminal Attempts Act* 1981, s.10, Sched., Pt I.]

This offence is triable either way: *MCA* 1980, s.17(1), and Sched. 1, *ante*, §§ 1–75ae, 1–75af.

See *ante*, §§ 28–168 *et seq.* as to jurisdiction, proof of earlier proceedings and interpretation.

As to the form of an indictment, see *ante*, § 28–183.

C. FABRICATION OF FALSE EVIDENCE

28–186 It is an indictable offence to fabricate evidence with intent to mislead a judicial tribunal, even if the tribunal never sits and the evidence is not used: *R. v. Vreones* [1891] 1 Q.B. 360. The offence is punishable by fine and/or imprisonment.

The making use of a false instrument in order to pervert the course of justice is an offence: *O'Mealy v. Newell* (1807) 8 East 364.

This topic should be considered in the wider context of the offence of perverting the course of public justice, as to which see *ante*, §§ 28–1 *et seq.*

[The next paragraph is § 28–189.]

D. FALSE WRITTEN STATEMENTS TENDERED IN EVIDENCE

Criminal Justice Act 1967, s.89

28–189 **89.**—(1) If any person in a written statement tendered in evidence in criminal proceedings by virtue of section 9 of this Act, *or in proceedings before a court-martial by virtue of the said section 9 as extended by section 12 above or by section 99A of the* Army Act *1955* or *section 99A of the* Air Force Act *1955*, wilfully makes a statement material in those proceedings which he knows to be false or does not believe to be true, he shall be liable on conviction on indictment to imprisonment for a term not exceeding two years or a fine or both.

(2) The *Perjury Act* 1911 shall have effect as if this section were contained in that Act.

[This section is printed as amended by the *AFA* 1976, Sched. 9; and the *MCA* 1980, s.154(3), and Sched. 9; and as repealed in part, as from a day to be appointed, by the *AFA* 2006, s.378(2), and Sched. 17 (italicised words in subs. (1)).]

By virtue of subsection (2), this offence is triable either way: *MCA* 1980, s.17(1), and Sched. 1, *ante*, §§ 1–75ae, 1–75af.

A like offence is created by the *MCA* 1980, s.106 (repealed, as from a day to be appointed, by the *CJA* 2003, s.41, and Sched. 3, para. 51(1) and (6)), in relation to statements admitted in committal proceedings under section 5B.

E. FALSE EVIDENCE BEFORE EUROPEAN COURT

European Communities Act 1972, s.11(1)

28–190 **11.**—(1) A person who, in sworn evidence before the European Court or any court attached thereto, makes any statement which he knows to be false or does not believe to be true shall, whether he is a British subject or not, be guilty of an offence and may be proceeded against and punished—

(a) in England and Wales as for an offence against section 1(1) of the *Perjury Act* 1911; or
(b) [*Scotland*]; or
(c) [*Northern Ireland*].

[*Further provision relating to Northern Ireland.*]

[This section is printed as repealed in part by the *Prosecution of Offences Act* 1985, s.31(6), and Sched. 2; and the *European Communities (Amendment) Act* 1986, s.2.]

F. FALSE STATEMENTS ETC. WITH REFERENCE TO CIVIL PARTNERSHIPS

Civil Partnership Act 2004, s.80

28–190a **80.**—(1) A person commits an offence if—

(a) for the purpose of procuring the formation of a civil partnership, or a document mentioned in subsection (2), he—
  (i) makes or signs a declaration required under this Part or Part 5, or
  (ii) gives a notice or certificate so required,

  knowing that the declaration, notice or certificate is false,
(b) for the purpose of a record being made in any register relating to civil partnerships, he—

(i) makes a statement as to any information which is required to be registered under this Part or Part 5, or
(ii) causes such a statement to be made,

knowing that the statement is false,

(c) he forbids the issue of a document mentioned in subsection (2)(a) or (b) by representing himself to be a person whose consent to a civil partnership between a child and another person is required under this Part or Part 5, knowing the representation to be false, or
(d) with respect to a declaration made under paragraph 5(1) of Schedule 1 he makes a statement mentioned in paragraph 6 of that Schedule which he knows to be false in a material particular.

(2) The documents are—

(a) a civil partnership schedule or a Registrar General's licence under Chapter 1;
(b) a document required by an Order in Council under section 210 or 211 as an authority for two people to register as civil partners of each other;
(c) a certificate of no impediment under section 240.

(3) A person guilty of an offence under subsection (1) is liable—

(a) on conviction on indictment, to imprisonment for a term not exceeding 7 years or to a fine (or both);
(b) on summary conviction, to a fine not exceeding the statutory maximum.

(4) The *Perjury Act* 1911 has effect as if this section were contained in it.

VIII. PRISON SECURITY

A. ESCAPE

(1) Common law

It is an indictable offence at common law, punishable by fine and imprisonment, for a prisoner to escape without the use of force from lawful custody on a criminal charge or by civil process: 2 Hawk.C. 19; 1 Hale 590; *R. v. Allan* (1841) Car. & M. 295 (civil process); *R. v. Frascati*, 73 Cr.App.R. 28, CA. In *R. v. Dhillon* [2006] 1 Cr.App.R. 15, CA, it was held, after reviewing the authorities, that the prosecution must prove: **28–191**

(i) that the defendant was in custody;
(ii) that the defendant knew that he was in custody (or at least was reckless as to whether he was or not);
(iii) that the custody was lawful; and
(iv) that the defendant intentionally escaped from that lawful custody.

A prisoner in custody on a lawful charge includes a person in lawful custody following arrest: *R. v. Timmis* [1976] Crim.L.R. 129, Crown Court (H.H.J. Mynett Q.C.); or in custody awaiting trial, sentence, or serving a sentence: *R. v. Hinds*, 41 Cr.App.R. 143, CCA; or in transit to or from, or at, a prison, remand centre, court, etc.: *R. v. Moss and Harte*, 82 Cr.App.R. 116, CA. Whether a person could be said to be in custody at any given time was a question of fact. "Custody" is to be given its ordinary and natural meaning, *viz.* a person's immediate freedom of movement being under the direct control of another: *E. v. DPP* [2002] Crim.L.R. 737, DC; and *H. v. DPP* [2003] Crim.L.R. 560, QBD (Gage J.). Where a defendant on bail surrendered to the custody of the court, he was in the control of the court, regardless of whether he was subjected to physical restraint or had anyone physically present to restrain and control him: *R. v. Rumble*, 167 J.P. 205, CA.

A person who is on bail is not in lawful custody and, therefore, does not commit the offence of escape if he absconds: *R. v. Reader*, 84 Cr.App.R. 294, CA.

Where a prisoner, on temporary release from prison, failed to return to prison at the expiry of his release period, he could not be said to have escaped from custody and could not therefore be guilty of escape (although he might have committed the summary offence under the *Prisoners (Return to Custody) Act* 1995, s.1): *R. v. Montgomery* [2008] 1 Cr.App.R. 17, CA.

"Escape" also occurs where a person having a prisoner lawfully in his custody voluntarily or negligently suffers him to go at large. A custodian is guilty of an offence if he "voluntarily" or "negligently" allows his prisoner to escape from lawful custody; a custodian who "voluntarily" suffers the escape of a man in custody for treason, is guilty of treason: see 1 Hale 234–235, 570, 600. For specimen indictments, see *post*, §§ 28–203, 28–205, 28–207, 28–208. See *post*, §§ 28–204, 28–206, 28–209 as to the evidence required.

Persons who aid a prisoner to escape are at common law guilty as principals, or may be indicted for rescue: *post*, § 28–214; and see *R. v. Allan*, *ante*.

As to escape effected by the use of force, see *post*, § 28–211.

[The next paragraph is § 28–196.]

(2) Statute

Prison Act 1952 ss.13(2), 39

Legal custody of prisoner

28–196 **13.**—(2) A prisoner shall be deemed to be in legal custody while he is confined in or is being taken to or from any prison and while he is working, or is for any other reason, outside the prison in the custody or under the control of an officer of the prison and while he is being taken to any place to which he is required or authorised by or under this Act or *section 95, 98, 99 or 108(5) of the* Powers of Criminal Courts (Sentencing) Act *2000* [section 99 of the *Powers of Criminal Courts (Sentencing) Act* 2000 or section 61 of the *Criminal Justice and Court Services Act* 2000] to be taken, or is kept in custody in pursuance of any such requirement or authorisation.

[This subsection is printed as amended by the *PCC(S)A* 2000, s.165(1), and Sched. 9, para. 4; and as amended as from a day to be appointed (substitution of the words in square brackets for the italicised words) by the *CJCSA* 2000, s.74, and Sched. 7, paras 7 and 8.]

Assisting a prisoner to escape

28–197 **39.**—(1) A person who—

(a) assists a prisoner in escaping or attempting to escape from a prison, or

(b) intending to facilitate the escape of a prisoner—

 (i) brings, throws or otherwise conveys anything into a prison,

 (ii) causes another person to bring, throw or otherwise convey anything into a prison, or

 (iii) gives anything to a prisoner or leaves anything in any place (whether inside or outside a prison),

is guilty of an offence.

(2) A person guilty of an offence under this section is liable on conviction on indictment to imprisonment for a term not exceeding ten years.

[This section is printed as substituted by the *Offender Management Act* 2007, s.21.]

28–198 The phrase "an officer of the prison" in section 13 shall, in relation to a contracted out prison, be construed as a reference to a prisoner custody officer performing custodial duties at the prison or a prison officer who is temporarily attached to the prison: *CJA* 1991, s.87(1), (6), as amended by the *CJPOA* 1994, s.97(5). This phrase also applies to a prisoner custody officer at a directly managed prison performing custodial duties which have been contracted out: *CJA* 1991, s.88A(3)(a). Section 13(2) applies to a custody officer at a directly managed secure training centre performing custodial duties which have been contracted out: *CJPOA* 1994, s.11(3).

Section 43(5) of the 1952 Act provides that certain provisions thereof, including sections 13 and 39, shall apply to remand centres, detention centres, youth custody centres and secure training centres and to persons detained in them as they apply to prisons and prisoners, but subject to such adaptations and modifications as may be specified in rules made by the Secretary of State. Section 53(1) of the 1952 Act provides that in that Act "prison" does not include a naval, military or air force prison.

A person is guilty of assisting a prisoner to escape from prison even if the escape occurred while the prisoner was doing work outside the prison: *R. v. Abbott* [1956] Crim.L.R. 337, CCA.

See *post*, §§ 28–207, 28–208, for specimen indictments; and see *post*, § 28–209, as to the evidence required.

Prison Act 1952, s.8

Powers of prison officers

8. Every prison officer while acting as such shall have the powers, authority, protection and privileges of a constable. **28–199**

Section 8 is disapplied in relation to prisoner custody officers performing custodial duties at a contracted out prison: see section 87(3) of the *CJA* 1991 (as amended by the *CJPOA* 1994, s.97(3)). It appears that the intent was that section 8 should be taken to apply to an officer of a directly managed prison on attachment to a contracted out prison. This has, in any event, been made explicit by the *Offender Management Act* 2007, s.20(2), which substitutes a new subsection (3), which spells this out. The powers and duties of prisoner custody officers employed at contracted out prisons are provided for by the *CJA* 1991, s.86 (as amended by the *Offender Management Act* 2007, s.16). See also section 86A of the 1991 Act (inserted by s.17(1) of the 2007 Act) (power of prisoner custody officers to detain suspected offenders).

Criminal Justice Act 1961, s.22(2), (2A)

Harbouring escaped prisoners

22.—(2) If any person knowingly harbours a person who has escaped from a prison or other institution to which the said section 39 applies, or who, having been sentenced in any part of the United Kingdom or in any of the Channel Islands or the Isle of Man to imprisonment or detention, is otherwise unlawfully at large, or who gives to any such person any assistance with intent to prevent, hinder or interfere with his being taken into custody, he shall be liable— **28–200**

(a) on summary conviction, to imprisonment for a term not exceeding *six* [12] months, or to a fine not exceeding the prescribed sum, or to both;

(b) on conviction on indictment, to imprisonment for a term not exceeding ten years, or to a fine, or to both.

[(2A) The reference in subsection (2) to a person who has been sentenced as mentioned there includes—

(a) a person on whom a custodial sentence within the meaning of the *Armed Forces Act* 2006 has been passed (anywhere) in respect of a service offence within the meaning of that Act;

(b) a person in respect of whom an order under section 214 of that Act (detention for commission of offence during currency of order) has been made.]

[The reference to "the prescribed sum" is substituted by virtue of the *MCA* 1980, s.32(2): *ante*, § 1–75aa. For details of that sum, see s.32(9). The maximum sentence was increased to 10 years by the *Prison Security Act* 1992, s.2(2). In para. (b), "12" is substituted for "six", as from a day to be appointed, by the *CJA* 2003, s.282(2) and (3). The increase has no application to offences committed before the substitution takes effect: s.282(4). Subs. (2A) replaces subs. (3) (not printed) as from a day to be appointed: *AFA* 2006, s.378(1), and Sched. 16, para. 46.]

The reference to "the said section 39" is a reference to section 39 of the *Prison Act* 1952 (*ante*, § 28–197).

In this context "harbour" means to shelter a person, in the sense of giving or providing a refuge to that person. It is possible for a person to give shelter to a person within the category specified in section 22(2) even though the alleged harbourer has no interest in the relevant place and even if in fact he is a trespasser in that place: *Darch v. Weight*, 79 Cr.App.R. 40, DC; and see *R. v. Mistry*; *R. v. Asare* [1980] Crim.L.R. 177, CA (husband can harbour wife). **28–201**

Section 22(2) must be construed strictly according to its plain meaning and the provisions of section 13(2) of the 1952 Act should not be read into it: *Nicoll v. Catron*, 81 Cr.App.R. 339, DC (remand prisoner escaping from police van in police station—*Abbott*, *ante*, § 28–198, distinguished); *R. v. Moss and Harte*, 82 Cr.App.R. 116, CA (appellants assisted prisoner to escape from magistrates' court). **28–202**

Assisting patients to absent themselves without leave, etc.

It is an offence triable either way, punishable with up to two years' imprisonment or a **28–202a** fine or both, to induce or knowingly to assist a person who is liable to be detained in a hospital, or is subject to guardianship under the *MHA* 1983, or is a community patient, to absent himself: *MHA* 1983, s.128(1), as amended by the *MHA* 2007, s.32, and Sched. 3, para. 28. It is also an offence, similarly punishable, to induce or knowingly to assist a person in legal custody under section 137 of the Act to escape, or to harbour or assist a person unlawfully at large to remain at large: *MHA* 1983, s.128(2), (3).

(3) Indictments

(a) *Escape*

STATEMENT OF OFFENCE

28–203 *Escape.*

PARTICULARS OF OFFENCE

A B, on the —— day of ——, 20—, then being a prisoner in her Majesty's prison at ——, serving a sentence of twelve months' imprisonment passed on him at the Central Criminal Court on the —— day of ——, 20—, upon a conviction for theft, escaped.

Fine and (or) imprisonment: 2 Hawk, c.17, s.5; 1 Russ.Cr.12th ed., 322, 323.

Evidence

28–203a See *R. v. Dhillon, ante,* § 28–191. According to the old authorities, if AB is not lost sight of between the attempted escape and recapture, then no escape has occurred: 1 Hale 602; 2 Hawk. c.19, ss.6, 13; and see *R. v. Keane* [1921] N.Z.L.R. 581, NZCA. If the prisoner has not escaped, a conviction for attempt would be a possible alternative verdict in appropriate circumstances (*CLA* 1967, s.6(4)) (*ante,* § 4–455)). It is no defence that AB was not guilty of the offence for which he was in custody: *R. v. Frascati,* 73 Cr.App.R. 28, CA.

(b) *Against a constable for negligently permitting escape*

STATEMENT OF OFFENCE

28–203b *Permitting an escape.*

PARTICULARS OF OFFENCE

A B, being a police constable of the Metropolitan Police and having J N, a person arrested under a lawful warrant for theft, lawfully in his custody, on the —— day of ——, 20—, negligently permitted the said J N to escape out of his custody.

Where the escape is negligently permitted by an officer, the punishment has been said to be a fine only: 2 Hawk. c. 19; 1 Hale 600; 1 Russ.Cr., 12th ed., 327. This appears to be erroneous, and to arise from a misconception of the nature of a fine in medieval times. See 2 Pollock & Maitland, Hist. Eng. Law, p. 517.

Where a private person is guilty of negligently permitting an escape, the punishment is fine and/or imprisonment: 2 Hawk. c. 19, s.6 (*ante,* § 28–191). The offender must be restrained of his liberty for some criminal matter, otherwise the escape is not indictable at common law. Where the escape is due to the negligence of sheriffs or other officers, it may be dealt with under *Sheriffs Act* 1887, s.29, or by attachment.

Evidence

28–204 It must be proved that the arrest and detention were lawful (such facts cannot be presumed: *Dillon v. R.* [1982] A.C. 484, PC), that the defendant was a police constable and that he had J N in actual custody under a lawful warrant: see 2 Hawk. c. 19, ss.1, 4. The fact of the escape itself must also be proved. It is not necessary to prove negligence on the part of the constable; the law implies it, see 1 Hale 600; but if the escape were not in fact negligent, if J N by force rescued himself, or were rescued by others, and the constable made fresh pursuit after him, but without effect, all this must be proved by the defence. Also, it is immaterial whether J N was guilty of the offence for which he was arrested, provided that the warrant was such as would justify A B in detaining him.

(c) *Against a gaoler for a voluntary escape*

STATEMENT OF OFFENCE

Permitting an escape. 28–205

PARTICULARS OF OFFENCE

A B, then being the Governor of Her Majesty's Prison at ——, and having the lawful custody of J N, a prisoner undergoing a sentence of imprisonment in the said prison, on the —— day of ——, 20—, unlawfully permitted the said J N to escape.

Evidence

The conviction of J N must be proved and that, upon his conviction, he was remanded or committed to the custody of the defendant. It must further be proved that he was in the custody of the defendant, in pursuance of his sentence. Finally, the fact of the escape must be proved. An escape is voluntary where the keeper gives the prisoner his liberty with the object of saving him from trial and punishment. See 2 Hawk. c. 19, s.10; 1 Russ.Cr., 12th ed., 324. It does not seem to be necessary to prove that the escape was voluntary; the law, it would seem, will presume that until the contrary appears. 28–206

See *ante*, § 28–191, as to the relevant law.

(d) *Aiding escape*

STATEMENT OF OFFENCE

Aiding a prisoner to escape, contrary to section 39 of the Prison Act *1952.* 28–207

PARTICULARS OF OFFENCE

A B, on the —— day of ——, 20—, aided J N, a prisoner in Her Majesty's Prison at ——, in escaping [or *attempting to escape*] *from the said prison.*

See *ante*, §§ 28–196 *et seq.*, as to the relevant law.

(e) *Conveying an article*

STATEMENT OF OFFENCE

Assisting a prisoner to escape, contrary to section 39 of the Prison Act *1952.* 28–208

PARTICULARS OF OFFENCE

A B, on the —— day of ——, 20—, with intent to facilitate the escape of J N, a prisoner in Her Majesty's Prison at —— conveyed or caused to be conveyed unto the said prisoner two steel files.

See *ante*, §§ 28–196 *et seq.*, as to the relevant law.

Evidence

It must be proved that J N was in custody (see *Prison Act* 1952, s.13(2), *ante*, § 28–196), and a prisoner in the gaol mentioned in the indictment. The words of the statute are "any prisoner". It must then be proved that whilst J N was so in custody, the defendant conveyed to him one or more files; and proved that such files were intended to facilitate his escape by filing the window bars, or the like. The mere delivery of such instruments to the person in custody is a fact from which the jury may well infer the intent, and it is immaterial, upon this statute, whether an escape be actually made or not. 28–209

(4) Sentence

For cases of escape and related offences, see CSP, B8–5. For guidelines in such cases, see *R. v. Coughtrey* [1997] 2 Cr.App.R.(S.) 269, CA; *R. v. Golding* [2007] 28–210

2 Cr.App.R.(S.) 49, CA (absconding from open prison); and *R. v. Purchase* [2008] 1 Cr.App.R.(S.) 58, CA (where a prisoner escapes on his own due to some personal pressure, the sentence should be measured in months; where professional criminals are assisted to escape by confederates, the sentence should be measured in years; factors to consider include the degree of planning, whether violence was used or damage caused, the reason for the escape, whether the offender surrendered or made arrangements to surrender, how long he was at large, and what else he did whilst at large).

B. BREACH OF PRISON

(1) Common Law

28–211 It is an indictable offence at common law, punishable by fine and imprisonment, to breach prison. Breach of prison consists in the escape from lawful custody by the use of any force. It is immaterial whether the custody is criminal or civil and whether the prisoner is actually within a gaol, or is only in the constable's house or a lock-up, provided that he is lawfully imprisoned or restrained of his liberty: 2 Hawk. c. 18, s.21. As to escape without the use of force, see *ante*, § 28–191.

(2) Indictment

STATEMENT OF OFFENCE

28–212 *Breaking prison.*

PARTICULARS OF OFFENCE

A B, on the —— day of ——, 20—, then being a prisoner in Her Majesty's prison at ——, serving a sentence of twelve months' imprisonment passed on him at the Central Criminal Court on the —— day of ——, 20—, upon a conviction for theft, broke the said prison by cutting two iron bars of the prison by means whereof he escaped.

Fine and (or) imprisonment: 2 Hawk. c. 18, s.1; 1 Russ.Cr., 12th ed., 334.

(3) Evidence

28–213 It must be proved that the prisoner was in prison as alleged; and that, while in custody there, he broke the prison and escaped.

The breaking proved must be an actual breaking; merely getting over the walls, or passing out through a door, or the like, is an escape only (*ante*, § 28–191), and not a breach of prison: 1 Hale 611; *R. v. Burridge* (1735) 3 P.Wms. 439. For this reason, it would seem that the manner of the breaking should be stated in the indictment, as in the above precedent, in order that the court may see that it was such as is necessary in law to constitute a breach of prison. But the breaking need not be intentional; and therefore where a prisoner, in effecting his escape, by accident threw down some loose bricks at the top of the prison wall, placed there to impede escape and give alarm, it was held to be a prison breach: *R. v. Haswell* (1821) R. & R. 458.

The subsequent dismissal of the charge on which the prisoner was imprisoned is no defence to an indictment for breach of prison by the prisoner while in custody on that charge: *R. v. Frascati*, 73 Cr.App.R. 28, CA.

C. RESCUE

(1) Common Law

28–214 Rescue at common law is forcibly liberating a prisoner from lawful custody: 1 Co.Inst. 160; 1 Hale 606, 611; 2 Hawk. c. 21; 1 Russ.Cr., 12th ed., p. 335. If the prisoner is in private custody, the rescuer is not liable criminally unless he knew that the prisoner was in custody on a criminal charge: *ibid.* The offence is generally treason or misdemeanour according to the quality of the person rescued; but if the latter is not convicted of the offence for which he was in custody, the rescue is only a misdemeanour: *ibid.*

(2) Indictment

STATEMENT OF OFFENCE

28–215 *Rescuing a prisoner in custody.*

PARTICULARS OF OFFENCE

A B, on the —— day of ——, 20—, forcibly rescued J N, then in the lawful custody of E F, a police constable in the Metropolitan Police.

Fine and (or) imprisonment if the party rescued has not been convicted of the offence for which he was in custody: 2 Hawk. c. 21, s.8. If he has been convicted for high treason, the rescue is high treason; if for a misdemeanour, the rescue is a misdemeanour: 1 Hale 607.

(3) Evidence

It must be proved that J N was in the lawful custody of E F, a police constable. If the party was convicted, the conviction may be proved by a certificate of the proper officer: *PACE Act* 1984, s.73, *ante*, § 9–80. Further, that whilst so in custody the defendant forcibly rescued him. **28–216**

As to evidence for the defence, it may be observed that any circumstances that will excuse a breach of prison will excuse a rescue. See *ante*, § 28–213; 2 Hawk. c. 21, ss.1, 2.

D. PRISON MUTINY

(1) Statute

Prison Security Act 1992, s.1

Offence of prison mutiny

1.—(1) Any prisoner who takes part in a prison mutiny shall be guilty of an offence and liable, on conviction on indictment, to imprisonment for a term not exceeding ten years or to a fine or to both. **28–217**

(2) For the purposes of this section there is a prison mutiny where two or more prisoners, while on the premises of any prison, engage in conduct which is intended to further a common purpose of overthrowing lawful authority in that prison.

(3) For the purposes of this section the intentions and common purpose of prisoners may be inferred from the form and circumstances of their conduct and it shall be immaterial that conduct falling within subsection (2) above takes a different form in the case of different prisoners.

(4) Where there is a prison mutiny, a prisoner who has or is given a reasonable opportunity of submitting to lawful authority and fails, without reasonable excuse, to do so shall be regarded for the purposes of this section as taking part in the mutiny.

(5) Proceedings for an offence under this section shall not be brought except by or with the consent of the Director of Public Prosecutions.

(6) In this section— **28–218**

"conduct" includes acts and omissions;

"prison" means any prison, young offender institution or remand centre which is under the general superintendence of, or is provided by, the Secretary of State under the *Prison Act* 1952, including a contracted out prison within the meaning of Part IV of the *Criminal Justice Act* 1991;

"prisoner" means any person for the time being in a prison as a result of any requirement imposed by a court or otherwise that he be detained in legal custody.

(2) Indictment

COUNT 1

STATEMENT OF OFFENCE

Taking part in a prison mutiny, contrary to section 1(1) of the Prison Security Act *1992.* **28–219**

PARTICULARS OF OFFENCE

A B, being a person detained in legal custody, on the —— day of ——, 20—, while on the premises of a prison, namely ——, together with one or more other persons detained in legal custody, engaged in conduct intended to further a common purpose of overthrowing lawful authority in the aforesaid prison.

COUNT 2

STATEMENT OF OFFENCE

28–220 *Taking part in a prison mutiny, contrary to section 1(1) of the* Prison Security Act *1992.*

PARTICULARS OF OFFENCE

A B, being a person detained in legal custody, on the —— day of ——, 20—, while on the premises of a prison, namely ——, at which a prison mutiny was taking place, failed without reasonable excuse to submit to lawful authority when he had or was given a reasonable opportunity to do so.

(3) Evidence

28–221 In *R. v. Mason and Cummins* [2005] 1 Cr.App.R. 11, CA, the court considered the correct approach to section 1. A prisoner may commit the offence under the section in one of two ways: by conduct with the requisite common purpose as defined in subsection (2), *i.e.* of overthrowing lawful authority in that prison, or on a deemed basis pursuant to subsection (4). The former is more serious than the latter, and the indictment should make it clear upon which basis a person is charged (see *ante*, §§ 28–219 *et seq.*); where a person is charged in the alternative, there should be two counts. The deeming provision in subsection (4) does not require proof that the person failing to submit to lawful authority shared the common purpose as defined in subsection (2). However, subsection (4) does not apply unless the prosecution first prove the existence of a prison mutiny as defined in subsection (2). The following statement from the 2004 edition of this work was approved and adopted: "It is important to note that the common purpose is the 'overthrowing of lawful authority' in the prison and, it is submitted, this is a deliberately restrictive expression. It would not appear to cover a mere defiance of or challenge to lawful authority in prison." The court confirmed that "overthrowing" is more serious than disobeying orders or subverting order, and observed that in the course of the Bill's passage the Home Secretary stated that the provision was targeted on "the most serious disturbances".

Where the defendant is accused of actively participating in the mutiny, the jury do not have to agree on the nature of his participatory conduct, provided they are sure of his participation; in other words, a *Brown* direction (see *ante*, §§ 4–391 *et seq.*) is unnecessary: *R. v. Griffin and Kennedy* [2000] 1 *Archbold News* 3, CA.

(4) Sentence

28–222 See generally, *R. v. Mitchell and Pipes*, 16 Cr.App.R.(S.) 924, CA; and *R. v. Whiteman* [2004] 2 Cr.App.R.(S.) 59, CA. As to the appropriateness of making a sentence for prison mutiny consecutive to an existing sentence, see *R. v. Ali* [1998] 2 Cr.App.R.(S.) 123, CA; and *R. v. Whiteman*, *ante*.

E. SMUGGLING OF PROHIBITED ARTICLES INTO OR OUT OF PRISON

Prison Act 1952, ss.40A–40C

Sections 40B and 40C: classification of articles

28–222a **40A.**—(1) This section defines the categories of articles which are referred to in sections 40B and 40C.

(2) A List A article is any article or substance in the following list ("List A")—

(a) a controlled drug (as defined for the purposes of the *Misuse of Drugs Act* 1971);
(b) an explosive;
(c) any firearm or ammunition (as defined in section 57 of the *Firearms Act* 1968);
(d) any other offensive weapon (as defined in section 1(9) of the *Police and Criminal Evidence Act* 1984).

(3) A List B article is any article or substance in the following list ("List B")—

(a) alcohol (as defined for the purposes of the *Licensing Act* 2003);
(b) a mobile telephone;
(c) a camera;
(d) a sound-recording device.

(4) In List B—

"camera" includes any device by means of which a photograph (as defined in section 40E) can be produced;

"sound-recording device" includes any device by means of which a sound-recording (as defined in section 40E) can be made.

(5) The reference in paragraph (b), (c) or (d) of List B to a device of any description includes a reference to—

(a) a component part of a device of that description; or

(b) an article designed or adapted for use with a device of that description (including any disk, film or other separate article on which images, sounds or information may be recorded).

(6) A List C article is any article or substance prescribed for the purposes of this subsection by prison rules.

(7) [*Power of Secretary of State to amend lists by order.*]

Conveyance etc. of List A articles into or out of prison

40B.—(1) A person who, without authorisation— **28–222b**

(a) brings, throws or otherwise conveys a List A article into or out of a prison,

(b) causes another person to bring, throw or otherwise convey a List A article into or out of a prison,

(c) leaves a List A article in any place (whether inside or outside a prison) intending it to come into the possession of a prisoner, or

(d) knowing a person to be a prisoner, gives a List A article to him,

is guilty of an offence.

(2) In this section "authorisation" means authorisation given for the purposes of this section—

(a) in relation to all prisons or prisons of a specified description, by prison rules or by the Secretary of State; or

(b) in relation to a particular prison, by the Secretary of State or by the governor or director of the prison.

In paragraph (a) "specified" means specified in the authorisation.

(3) Authorisation may be given to specified persons or persons of a specified description—

(a) in relation to specified articles or articles of a specified description;

(b) in relation to specified acts or acts of a specified description; or

(c) on such other terms as may be specified.

In this subsection "specified" means specified in the authorisation.

(4) Authorisation given by the Secretary of State otherwise than in writing shall be recorded in writing as soon as is reasonably practicable after being given.

(5) Authorisation given by the governor or director of a prison shall—

(a) be given in writing; and

(b) specify the purpose for which it is given.

(6) A person guilty of an offence under this section is liable on conviction on indictment to imprisonment for a term not exceeding ten years or to a fine (or both).

Conveyance etc. of List B or C articles into or out of prison

40C.—(1) A person who, without authorisation— **28–222c**

(a) brings, throws or otherwise conveys a List B article into or out of a prison,

(b) causes another person to bring, throw or otherwise convey a List B article into or out of a prison,

(c) leaves a List B article in any place (whether inside or outside a prison) intending it to come into the possession of a prisoner, or

(d) knowing a person to be a prisoner, gives a List B article to him,

is guilty of an offence.

(2) A person who, without authorisation—

(a) brings, throws or otherwise conveys a List C article into a prison intending it to come into the possession of a prisoner,

(b) causes another person to bring, throw or otherwise convey a List C article into a prison intending it to come into the possession of a prisoner,

(c) brings, throws or otherwise conveys a List C article out of a prison on behalf of a prisoner,

(d) causes another person to bring, throw or otherwise convey a List C article out of a prison on behalf of a prisoner,

(e) leaves a List C article in any place (whether inside or outside a prison) intending it to come into the possession of a prisoner, or

(f) while inside a prison, gives a List C article to a prisoner,

is guilty of an offence.

(3) A person who attempts to commit an offence under subsection (2) is guilty of that offence.

(4) In proceedings for an offence under this section it is a defence for the accused to show that—

(a) he reasonably believed that he had authorisation to do the act in respect of which the proceedings are brought, or

(b) in all the circumstances there was an overriding public interest which justified the doing of that act.

(5) A person guilty of an offence under subsection (1) is liable—

(a) on conviction on indictment, to imprisonment for a term not exceeding two years or to a fine (or both);

(b) on summary conviction, to imprisonment for a term not exceeding 12 months or to a fine not exceeding the statutory maximum (or both).

(6) A person guilty of an offence under subsection (2) is liable on summary conviction to a fine not exceeding level 3 on the standard scale.

(7) In this section "authorisation" means authorisation given for the purposes of this section; and subsections (1) to (3) of section 40E apply in relation to authorisations so given as they apply to authorisations given for the purposes of section 40D.

Sections 40A to 40C were inserted, as from April 1, 2008 (*Offender Management Act 2007 (Commencement No. 2 and Transitional Provision) Order* 2008 (S.I. 2008 No. 504)), by the *Offender Management Act* 2007, s.22(1). In Schedule 4 to the 2007 Act, there is a standard transitional arrangement applying to the penalty provisions of the new sections 40C and 40D, pending the commencement of the *CJA* 2003, s.154(1) (*ante*, § 5–268).

The *Prison (Amendment) Rules* 2008 (S.I. 2008 No. 597) amend the *Prison Rules* 1999 (S.I. 1999 No. 728) so as to specify certain articles (*viz.* tobacco, money, clothing, food, drink, letters, paper, books, tools and information technology equipment (for which a definition is inserted)) as "List C" articles for the purposes of section 40C(2). The *Young Offender Institution (Amendment) Rules* 2008 (S.I. 2008 No. 599) make corresponding amendments to the *Young Offender Institution Rules* 2000 (S.I. 2000 No. 3371).

It should also be noted that section 40F (inserted by s.24 of the 2007 Act) extends Crown immunity in relation to offences under new sections 40B to 40D to designated persons working at a prison.

F. UNAUTHORISED PHOTOGRAPHY, RECORDINGS INSIDE PRISON

Prison Act 1952, ss.40D, 40E

Other offences relating to prison security

28–222d **40D.**—(1) A person who, without authorisation—

(a) takes a photograph, or makes a sound-recording, inside a prison, or

(b) transmits, or causes to be transmitted, any image or any sound from inside a prison by electronic communications for simultaneous reception outside the prison,

is guilty of an offence.

(2) It is immaterial for the purposes of subsection (1)(a) where the recording medium is located.

(3) A person who, without authorisation—

(a) brings or otherwise conveys a restricted document out of a prison or causes such a document to be brought or conveyed out of a prison, or

(b) transmits, or causes to be transmitted, a restricted document (or any information derived from a restricted document) from inside a prison by means of electronic communications,

is guilty of an offence.

(4) [*Identical to s.40C(4),* ante, *§ 28–222c.*]

(5) A person guilty of an offence under this section is liable—

(a) on conviction on indictment, to imprisonment for a term not exceeding two years or to a fine (or both); or

(b) on summary conviction, to imprisonment for a term not exceeding 12 months or to a fine not exceeding the statutory maximum (or both).

Section 40D: meaning of "authorisation" and other interpretation

40E.—(1) In section 40D (and the following provisions of this section) "authorisation" means authorisation given for the purposes of that section— **28–222e**

(a) in relation to all prisons or prisons of a specified description, by prison rules or by the Secretary of State;

(b) in relation to a particular prison—

(i) by the Secretary of State;

(ii) by the governor or director of the prison;

(iii) by a person working at the prison who is authorised by the governor or director to grant authorisation on his behalf.

In paragraph (a) "specified" means specified in the authorisation.

(2) Authorisation may be given—

(a) to persons generally or to specified persons or persons of a specified description; and

(b) on such terms as may be specified.

In this subsection "specified" means specified in the authorisation.

(3) Authorisation given by or on behalf of the governor or director of a prison must be in writing.

(4) In section 40D "restricted document" means the whole (or any part of)—

(a) a photograph taken inside the prison;

(b) a sound-recording made inside the prison;

(c) a personal record (or a document containing information derived from a personal record);

(d) any other document which contains—

(i) information relating to an identified or identifiable relevant individual, if the disclosure of that information would or might prejudicially affect the interests of that individual; or

(ii) information relating to any matter connected with the prison or its operation, if the disclosure of that information would or might prejudicially affect the security or operation of the prison.

(5) In subsection (4)—

"personal record" means any record which is required by prison rules to be prepared and maintained in relation to any prisoner (and it is immaterial whether or not the individual concerned is still a prisoner at the time of any alleged offence);

"relevant individual" means an individual who is or has at any time been—

(a) a prisoner or a person working at the prison; or

(b) a member of such a person's family or household.

(6) In section 40D and this section—

"document" means anything in which information is recorded (by whatever means);

"electronic communications" has the same meaning as in the *Electronic Communications Act* 2000;

"photograph" means a recording on any medium on which an image is produced or from which an image (including a moving image) may by any means be produced; and

"sound-recording" means a recording of sounds on any medium from which the sounds may by any means be reproduced.

Sections 40D and 40E were inserted as from April 1, 2008 (S.I. 2008 No. 504 (*ante*, § 28–222c)) by the *Offender Management Act* 2007, s.23(1). See *ante*, § 28–222c, as to the transitional provision in relation to the penalty on summary conviction.

As to the extension of Crown immunity to designated persons for the purposes of section 40D, see *ante*, § 28–224.

IX. EFFECTING A PUBLIC MISCHIEF

Common law

The common law offence of effecting a public mischief, if it ever existed, has certainly ceased to do so: see *R. v. Newland* [1954] 1 Q.B. 158, 37 Cr.App.R. 154, CCA. **28–223**

Furthermore, conspiracy to effect a public mischief, in the sense of an agreement to do an act which, although not unlawful in itself, is extremely injurious to the public, is not an offence known to law: *DPP v. Withers* [1975] A.C. 842, HL.

Criminal Law Act 1967, s.5(2), (3)

Wasteful employment of the police

28–224 **5.**—(2) Where a person causes any wasteful employment of the police by knowingly making to any person a false report tending to show that an offence has been committed, or to give rise to apprehension for the safety of any persons or property, or tending to show that he has information material to any police inquiry, he shall be liable on summary conviction to imprisonment for not more than *six months* [51 weeks] or to a fine of not more than level 4 on the standard scale or to both.

(3) No proceedings shall be instituted for an offence under this section except by or with the consent of the Director of Public Prosecutions.

[This section is printed as amended by the *CJA* 1982, ss.38 and 46. In subs. (2), "51 weeks" is substituted for "six months" as from a day to be appointed, but only in relation to offences committed on or after that day: *CJA* 2003, s.281(4)–(6).]

For subsections (1) and (5), see *ante*, § 28–29.

X. ADMINISTERING UNLAWFUL OATHS

Statutory Declarations Act 1835, ss.13 and 7

Justices not to administer oaths, etc., touching matters whereof they have no jurisdiction by statute

28–225 **13.** It shall not be lawful for any justice of the peace or other person to administer, or cause or allow to be administered, or to receive, or cause or allow to be received, any oath, affidavit, or solemn affirmation touching any matter or thing whereof such justice or other person hath not jurisdiction or cognisance by some statute in force at the time being: provided always, that nothing herein contained shall be construed to extend to any oath, affidavit, or solemn affirmation before any justice in any matter or thing touching the preservation of the peace, or the prosecution, trial, or punishment of offences, or touching any proceedings before either of the houses of parliament, or any committee thereof respectively, nor to any oath, affidavit, or affirmation which may be required by the laws of any foreign country to give validity to instruments in writing designed to be used in such foreign countries respectively.

Oaths in courts of justice, etc., still to be taken

28–226 **7.** Provided also that nothing in this Act contained shall extend or apply to any oath, solemn affirmation or affidavit, which now is or hereafter may be made or taken, or be required to be made or taken, in any judicial proceeding in any court of justice, or in any proceeding for or by way of summary conviction before any justice or justices of the peace, but all such oaths, affirmations and affidavits shall continue to be required, and to be administered, taken and made, as well and in the same manner as if this Act had not been passed.

Indictment

STATEMENT OF OFFENCE

28–227 *Administering an unlawful oath, contrary to section 13 of the* Statutory Declarations Act *1835*.

PARTICULARS OF OFFENCE

A B, being a justice of the peace for the county of ——, on the —— day of ——, 20— unlawfully administered an oath to J N in a matter in which he the said A B had no jurisdiction, namely [state the case in ordinary language].

Fine and/or imprisonment.

This offence is triable either way: *MCA* 1980, s.17(1), and Sched. 1, *ante*, § 1–75af.

Evidence

28–228 It must be proved that the defendant was, at the relevant time, a justice of the peace for the county mentioned in the indictment; evidence of his acting as such will, prima facie, be sufficient. Further, that he administered to J N an oath of the nature and touching the subject-matter mentioned in the indictment. It is not necessary to show that he acted wilfully in contravention of the statute; the doing so, even inadvertently is punishable: *R. v. Nott* (1843) 4 Q.B.D. 768.

Chapter 29

PUBLIC ORDER OFFENCES

I. PUBLIC ORDER ACT 1986

A. Introduction

Prior to the 1986 Act the law relating to public order consisted of a number of common law offences together with a range of miscellaneous statutory provisions. The 1986 Act was an attempt to clarify and rationalise the law. **29–1**

In view of the wholesale abolition of the old law (s.9), it is submitted, apart from one or two instances where words or expressions have plainly been taken from earlier legislation, there is no justification for referring to authorities on the old law: judges should direct their attention to the wording of the Act.

As to the background to the legislation, see, in particular, the Home Office and Scottish Office White Paper, *Review of Public Order Law* (1985) Cmnd. 9510 and the Law Commission's final report, *Offences Relating to Public Order* (1983) H.C. 85, Law Com. No. 123.

Scheme of 1986 Act

The Act has five parts: Part I (ss.1–10) is entitled "*New Offences*"; Part II (ss.11–16) is entitled "*Processions and Assemblies*"; Part III (ss.17–29) is entitled "*Racial Hatred*"; Part IV (ss.30–37) is entitled "*Exclusion Orders*"; and Part V (ss.38–43) is entitled "*Miscellaneous and General*". For what remains of Part IV, see, *ante*, § 5–840. **29–2**

The *CJPOA* 1994 effected significant amendments to the 1986 Act: in particular, it inserted new sections 4A (summary offence of intentional harassment, alarm or distress) and 14A to 14C (prohibition of trespassory assemblies). It also provides in Part V (ss.61–80) new powers to deal with trespassers (ss.61–62), raves (ss.63–66), persons guilty of aggravated trespass (ss.68–69), squatters (ss.72–76) and unauthorised campers (ss.77–80). See *post*, §§ 29–56 *et seq.* **29–3**

A new Part IIIA has been inserted by the *Racial and Religious Hatred Act* 2006.

B. New Offences (Pt I (ss.1–10))

(1) Riot

Public Order Act 1986, s.1

1.—(1) Where 12 or more persons who are present together use or threaten unlawful violence for a common purpose and the conduct of them (taken together) is such as would cause a **29–4**

person of reasonable firmness present at the scene to fear for his personal safety, each of the persons using unlawful violence for the common purpose is guilty of riot.

(2) It is immaterial whether or not the 12 or more use or threaten unlawful violence simultaneously.

(3) The common purpose may be inferred from conduct.

(4) No person of reasonable firmness need actually be, or be likely to be, present at the scene.

(5) Riot may be committed in private as well as in public places.

(6) A person guilty of riot is liable on conviction on indictment to imprisonment for a term not exceeding ten years or a fine or both.

As to the *mens rea* of the offence, see section 6(1), *post*, § 29–35.

As to the meaning of "violence", see section 8, *post*, § 29–38.

Indictment

STATEMENT OF OFFENCE

29–5 *Riot, contrary to section 1(1) of the* Public Order Act *1986.*

PARTICULARS OF OFFENCE

AB [CD and EF], on the —— day of ——, 20 ——, [each] being one of at least 12 persons who were present together and using or threatening unlawful violence for a common purpose, used unlawful violence for that common purpose, and the conduct of all of those who were present together using or threatening violence for that purpose, taken together, was such as would cause a person of reasonable firmness present at the scene to fear for his personal safety.

29–6 Where an indictment was defective because it alleged that the defendants "used or threatened unlawful violence", thereby widening the ambit of the offence to include threatening unlawful violence, the judge was right to allow the prosecution to amend the indictment at the close of its case so as to exclude the words "or threatened": *R. v. Tyler*, 96 Cr.App.R. 332, CA.

Class of offence and mode of trial

29–7 This offence is a class 3 offence, *ante*, § 2–17. It is triable only on indictment.

Consent of Director of Public Prosecutions

29–8 See section 7(1), *post*, § 29–36.

Sentence

29–9 Imprisonment not exceeding 10 years: s.1, *ante*.

For sentencing guidance in a case of inner-city riot, see *R. v. Najeeb* [2003] 2 Cr.App.R.(S.) 69, CA.

See CSP, B3–1.2 and B3–1.3D–E.

(2) Violent disorder

Public Order Act 1986, s.2

29–10 **2.**—(1) Where 3 or more persons who are present together use or threaten unlawful violence and the conduct of them (taken together) is such as would cause a person of reasonable firmness present at the scene to fear for his personal safety, each of the persons using or threatening unlawful violence is guilty of violent disorder.

(2) It is immaterial whether or not the 3 or more use or threaten unlawful violence simultaneously.

(3) No person of reasonable firmness need actually be, or be likely to be, present at the scene.

(4) Violent disorder may be committed in private as well as in public places.

(5) A person guilty of violent disorder is liable on conviction on indictment to imprisonment for a term not exceeding 5 years or a fine or both, or on summary conviction to imprisonment for a term not exceeding *6* [12] months or a fine not exceeding the statutory maximum or both.

[In subs. (5), "12" is substituted for "6", as from a day to be appointed, by the *CJA* 2003, s.282(2) and (3). The increase has no application to offences committed before the substitution takes effect: s.282(4).]

As to the *mens rea* of the offence, see section 6, *post*, § 29–35.

As to the meaning of "violence", see section 8, *post*, § 29–38.

The "statutory maximum" means the prescribed sum within the meaning of section 32 of the *MCA* 1980 (*ante*, § 1–75aa): *Interpretation Act* 1978, Sched. 1. The current amount is £5,000.

Indictment

STATEMENT OF OFFENCE

Violent disorder, contrary to section 2(1) of the Public Order Act *1986.* **29–11**

PARTICULARS OF OFFENCE

A B and B C, on the —— day of ——, 19—, being present together with each other and with C D, E F and other persons unknown, together with the said C D, E F and other persons unknown used or threatened unlawful violence and their conduct (taken together) was such as would cause a person of reasonable firmness present at the scene to fear for his personal safety.

See *R. v. Mahroof*, 88 Cr.App.R. 317, CA, *post*, as to the need to make it plain in the particulars if the conduct of persons other than the accused is being relied upon.

Class of offence and mode of trial

This offence is triable either way (subs. (5), *ante*), and is a class 3 offence, *ante*, § 2–17. **29–12**

Alternative verdict

As to the possibility of a conviction of an offence under section 4 (fear or provocation of violence) (*post*, § 29–25), see section 7(3), (4) (*post*, § 29–36). **29–13**

Alternative bases for finding of guilt

If, and only if, separate incidents are relied on in one count as truly alternative bases, the jury must be agreed on one or more of them: *R. v. Keeton* [1995] 2 Cr.App.R. 241, CA; *R. v. Houlden*, 99 Cr.App.R. 244, CA, considering *R. v. Brown (K.)*, 79 Cr.App.R. 115, *ante*, §§ 4–391 *et seq.* and *post*, §§ 29–21, 29–67. **29–14**

Sentence

See subsection (5), *ante*. It is not only the precise individual acts which matter but also the fact that the defendants have taken part in the violent disorder, threatening violence against other people and have been part of the whole threatening and alarming activity: *R. v. Hebron and Spencer*, 11 Cr.App.R.(S.) 226, CA; *R. v. Tomlinson*, 157 J.P. 695, CA; *R. v. Tyler*, 96 Cr.App.R. 332, CA (a "poll tax riot" case); *R. v. Green* [1997] 2 Cr.App.R.(S.) 191, CA; and *R. v. Rees* [2006] 2 Cr.App.R.(S.) 20, CA (alcohol fuelled violence following England loss in football match). For sentencing guidance in cases of serious disorder, see *R. v. Chapman* (2002) 146 S.J. (LB 242), CA. **29–14a**

Ingredients of the offence

"3 or more persons"

As to the requirement that there are three or more persons present together using or threatening unlawful violence before there can be a conviction of anyone, see *R. v. Mahroof*, *ante*. Where it is the prosecution's case that persons, whether their identities are known or unknown, other than the defendants were present together with the defendants and were using or threatening unlawful violence and that, therefore, **29–15** their conduct can be considered together with that of the defendants, this should be made plain in the particulars: *ibid*.

Mahroof was applied in *R. v. Fleming and Robinson* [1989] Crim.L.R. 658, CA. Where the only persons against whom there is evidence of using or threatening violence are those named in the indictment, the jury should be specifically directed that if they are not sure that three or more of the defendants were using or threatening violence they should acquit all the defendants, even if satisfied that one or more particular defendants were unlawfully fighting.

However, where it was held that absence of proof against at least three defendants was all that invalidated the convictions, and that all the elements of the offence of affray, contrary to section 3 (*post*), had been found proved by the jury, the Court of Appeal was empowered by section 3 of the *CAA* 1968 (*ante*, § 7–106) to substitute convictions of affray for those of violent disorder: *ibid*. In *R. v. McGuigan and Cameron* [1991] Crim.L.R. 719, the Court of Appeal declined to substitute convictions for affray since the evidence included violence to property and it would have been wrong to conclude that the jury must have been satisfied beyond reasonable doubt that the appellants had used or threatened unlawful violence towards another person.

"Use or threaten"

29–15a Being a member of a group which follows or "stalks" a man for three-quarters of a mile along a footpath in the middle of the night (to a point at which another murdered him with a baseball bat) (*R. v. Brodie* [2000] Crim.L.R. 775, CA), and running with a group, other members of which were armed and committed assaults (*R. v. Church* [2000] 4 *Archbold News* 3, CA), raised in each case a prima facie case of violent disorder. In *Brodie*, the conduct was held to be capable of involving a considerable implicit menace amounting to a threat, agreeing with the approach of the Divisional Court in *I. v. DPP*; *M. v. DPP*; *H. v. DPP* [2000] 1 Cr.App.R. 251 (not reversed on this point by the House of Lords (*post*, § 29–22)).

"Unlawful violence"

29–16 The word "unlawful" preserves the defences of self-defence and reasonable defence of others and permits actions which are no more than necessary to restore the peace: *R. v. Rothwell and Barton* [1993] Crim.L.R. 626, CA.

(3) Affray

Public Order Act 1986, s.3

29–17 **3.**—(1) A person is guilty of affray if he uses or threatens unlawful violence towards another and his conduct is such as would cause a person of reasonable firmness present at the scene to fear for his personal safety.

(2) Where 2 or more persons use or threaten the unlawful violence, it is the conduct of them taken together that must be considered for the purposes of subsection (1).

(3) For the purposes of this section a threat cannot be made by the use of words alone.

(4) No person of reasonable firmness need actually be, or be likely to be, present at the scene.

(5) Affray may be committed in private as well as public places.

(6) [*Repealed by* SOCPA *2005, ss.111 and 174(2), Sched. 7, para. 26(1) and (2), and Sched. 17, Pt 2.*]

(7) A person guilty of affray is liable on conviction on indictment to imprisonment for a term not exceeding 3 years or a fine or both, or on summary conviction to imprisonment for a term not exceeding *6* [12] months or a fine not exceeding the statutory maximum or both.

[In subs. (7), "12" is substituted for "6", as from a day to be appointed, by the *CJA* 2003, s.282(2) and (3). The increase has no application to offences committed before the substitution takes effect: s.282(4).]

As to the *mens rea* of the offence, see section 6, *post*, § 29–35.

As to the meaning of "violence", see section 8, *post*, § 29–38.

As to the "statutory maximum", see *ante*, § 29–10.

As to affray as the unlawful act for the purposes of a charge of manslaughter, see *R. v. Carey* [2006] Crim.L.R. 842, CA (*ante*, § 19–100).

Indictment

STATEMENT OF OFFENCE

Affray, contrary to section 3(1) of the Public Order Act *1986*. **29–18**

PARTICULARS OF OFFENCE

A B [and C D], on the —— day of ——, 19—, used or threatened unlawful violence towards J N [or *a person unknown*] *and his conduct* [*their conduct taken together*] *was such as would cause a person of reasonable firmness present at the scene to fear for his personal safety*.

Class of offence and mode of trial

This offence is triable either way (subs. (7), *ante*), and is a class 3 offence, *ante*, § 2–17. **29–19**

Alternative verdict

As to the possibility of a conviction of an offence under section 4 (fear or provocation of violence) (*post*, § 29–25), see section 7(3), (4) (*post*, § 29–36). **29–20**

Alternative bases for finding of guilt

An affray involves typically a continuous course of conduct, the criminal character of which depends on the general nature and effect of the conduct as a whole and not on particular incidents and events. Where the case is so presented it is not necessary to identify and prove particular incidents. Where, however, the prosecution case is advanced on the basis that there was one continuous affray, but that it had separate parts (*e.g.* it began inside certain premises, but was then continued outside) and that the jury should convict if satisfied that the defendant was involved in either part, the judge may so direct the jury, but he must also direct them that it is necessary for them to be agreed (subject to the majority verdict provisions) as to his involvement in one part or the other (or both); it is not enough that half the jury are satisfied that he is guilty because satisfied of his involvement in the first part (whilst not satisfied of his involvement in the second part) with the other half being satisfied about involvement in the second part, but not the first: *R. v. Smith (Christopher)* [1997] 1 Cr.App.R. 14, CA (applying *R. v. Brown (K.)*, 79 Cr.App.R. 115, CA (*ante* §§ 4–391 *et seq.*)). See also *ante*, § 29–14, and *post*, § 29–67. **29–21**

It is better to allege separate offences where there is an affray involving three distinct incidents and one defendant is involved in two of them and another defendant is involved in the third incident only: *R. v. Flounders and Alton* [2002] 6 *Archbold News* 1, CA.

Sentence

See subsection (7), *ante*; and CSP, B3–1.3. As to the need, in cases of affray and public order generally, to look at the whole picture, see *R. v. Fox and Hicks* [2006] 1 Cr.App.R.(S.) 17, CA (although what an individual had himself done was relevant, it was simply part of the whole to which he was contributing). **29–21a**

Ingredients of the offence

"threatens"

What amounts to a threat is essentially a question of fact in each case: *I. v. DPP*; *M. v. DPP*; *H. v. DPP* [2002] 1 A.C. 285, HL. The mere possession of a weapon, without threatening circumstances, for example where the weapon was concealed, would not be a sufficient threat. But carrying weapons, in this case petrol bombs, was clearly capable of being sufficient: *ibid*. Spoken words alone are insufficient: s.3(3). **29–22**

Making a threat in an aggressive tone of voice is not enough: *R. v. Robinson* [1993] Crim.L.R. 581, CA. But setting a dog on police officers with the words "Go on, go on" is sufficient: *R. v. Dixon* [1993] Crim.L.R. 579, CA; as is driving a car at another occupied vehicle: *R. v. Thind* [1999] Crim.L.R. 842, CA.

"unlawful"

29–23 The word "unlawful" (also in ss.1(1) and 2(1)) means that self-defence, defence of others, etc., are all potential "defences" (*ante*, § 19–39). For self-defence and affray, see, *e.g.*, *R. v. Pulham and Pulham* [1995] Crim.L.R. 296, CA, where an overloaded indictment caused difficulties.

"towards another"

29–23a The offence can only be committed where the threat is directed to another person or persons actually present at the scene: *I. v. DPP*; *M. v. DPP*; *H. v. DPP*, *ante*.

"a person of reasonable firmness"

29–24 The standard for the conduct is set by a hypothetical person of reasonable firmness who could be, but is not necessarily, at the scene: *R. v. Davison* [1992] Crim.L.R. 31, CA, considering the Law Commission's report, *Offences Relating to Public Order* (*ante*, § 29–1). The person of reasonable firmness must be someone other than the victim: *R. v. Sanchez* [1996] Crim.L.R. 572, CA; *R. v. Thind*, *ante*. A common assault on a particular individual, with no force or threat of force being directed at any other person, could not cause a person of reasonable firmness to fear for his safety: *R. v. Plavecz* [2002] Crim.L.R. 837, CA.

(4) Fear or provocation of violence

Public Order Act 1986, s.4

29–25 **4.**—(1) A person is guilty of an offence if he—

(a) uses towards another person threatening, abusive or insulting words or behaviour, or

(b) distributes or displays to another person any writing, sign or other visible representation which is threatening abusive or insulting,

with intent to cause that person to believe that immediate unlawful violence will be used against him or another by any person, or to provoke the immediate use of unlawful violence by that person or another, or whereby that person is likely to believe that such violence will be used or it is likely that such violence will be provoked.

(2) An offence under this section may be committed in a public or a private place, except that no offence is committed where the words or behaviour are used, or the writing, sign or other visible representation is distributed or displayed, by a person inside a dwelling and the other person is also inside that or another dwelling.

(3) [*Repealed by* SOCPA *2005, ss.111 and 174(2), Sched. 7, para. 26(1) and (3), and Sched. 17, Pt 2.*]

(4) A person guilty of an offence under this section is liable on summary conviction to imprisonment for a term not exceeding *6 months* [51 weeks] or a fine not exceeding level 5 on the standard scale or both.

[In subs. (4), "51 weeks" is substituted for "6 months", as from a day to be appointed, by the *CJA* 2003, s.281(4) and (5). The increase has no application to offences committed before the substitution takes effect: s.281(6).]

As to the *mens rea* of the offence, see section 6, *post*, § 29–35.

As to the meaning of "violence" and "dwelling", see section 8, *post*, § 29–38.

As to the "standard scale" (defined in Schedule 1 to the *Interpretation Act* 1978 (Appendix B–28)), see *ante*, § 5–403.

As to the correct wording of a charge, which should follow the statutory form, see *Loade v. DPP* [1990] 1 Q.B. 1052, 90 Cr.App.R. 162, DC.

As to compatibility with the right to freedom of expression, see *Dehal v. CPS* and *Percy v. DPP*, *post*, § 29–34a.

For the racially or religiously aggravated version of this offence (triable either way), see *post*, § 29–38a.

Alternative to sections 2 and 3

As to the possibility of a conviction of an offence under section 4 (but apparently not section 4A) as an alternative to a count alleging an offence contrary to either section 2 or 3, see section 7(3), (4) (*post*, § 29–36). Simply to read section 4 out to the jury is inadequate; what has to be done is to sort out from the words of the section those which are applicable to the instant case and either use only those words, or, better still, put them into the form of questions which the jury would have to answer if they are to find the ingredients of the offence proved: *R. v. Perrins* [1995] Crim.L.R. 432, CA. Where a jury was misdirected as to the ingredients of the offence under section 4, but correctly directed as to the ingredients of the offence charged and the jury convicted of the latter offence, the conviction was upheld: *R. v. Stanley and Knight* [1993] Crim.L.R. 618, CA. See also *R. v. Notman* [1994] Crim.L.R. 518, CA (plea to lesser offence not accepted). **29–26**

Background

This offence replaces the offence created by section 5 of the *Public Order Act* 1936. Because of the similarity of phrasing of the two sections, it is submitted that in this instance it is legitimate to look at authorities on the former offence in construing common expressions in the new section. **29–27**

Ingredients of the offence

"threatening, abusive or insulting"

In *Brutus v. Cozens* [1973] A.C. 854, the question was what was the proper meaning to be given to "insulting". The House of Lords held that this was not a question of law at all, but a question of fact. The meaning of an ordinary word of the English language, such as "insulting", is not a question of law. Although their Lordships were only concerned with the word "insulting", it is submitted that their reasoning applies equally to "abusive" and "threatening". **29–28**

See also *Simcock v. Rhodes*, 66 Cr.App.R. 192, DC; *Bryan v. Robinson* [1960] 1 W.L.R. 506, DC, in which it was said that words or behaviour might be annoying without being insulting; *R. v. Ambrose*, 57 Cr.App.R. 538, CA, in which it was said that words which are rude or offensive are not necessarily insulting; and *Parkin v. Norman* [1983] Q.B. 92, DC, in which it was said that insulting behaviour was not to be construed as offensive or disgusting behaviour. However, it should be emphasised that these decisions are no more than illustrative, being decisions on the facts of particular cases. As Lord Kilbrandon said in *Brutus v. Cozens*:

> "It would be unwise, in my opinion, to attempt to lay down any positive rules for the recognition of insulting behaviour as such, since the circumstances in which the application of the rules would be called for are almost infinitely variable; the most that can be done is to lay down limits, as was done in *Bryan v. Robinson* (*ante*), in order to ensure that the statute is not interpreted more widely than its terms will bear" (at pp. 866–867).

"likely to"

In *Parkin v. Norman*, *ante*, a conviction was quashed because the justices must have read "likely to" as if it read "liable to". **29–29**

It is the state of mind of the victim that is crucial, rather than the statistical risk of violence actually occurring within a short space of time: *DPP v. Ramos* [2000] Crim.L.R. 768, DC. This observation seems to be incomplete, in that it ignores that part of section 4(1) which sets out the intent of the suspect, in which the victim's belief is irrelevant save as evidence to prove intent.

"the other person", "another person"

The phrase "the other person" in section 4(2) is a reference to "another person" in section 4(1)(a): *Atkin v. DPP*, 89 Cr.App.R. 199, DC. **29–30** *"uses towards"*

29–31 "Uses towards" in section 4(1)(a) connotes present physical presence: if, for example, the "other person" is out of earshot, and the threatening words are communicated to him by an intermediary, no offence is committed under this section: *Atkin v. DPP*, *ante* (the suggestion in the headnote that the other person must perceive with his own senses the threatening, etc., words or behaviour goes further than is warranted by the judgment of the court). It is not essential that the victim is called to prove that he was present and perceived the conduct in question: *Swanston v. DPP*, 161 J.P. 203, DC.

"immediate unlawful violence"

29–32 In *R. v. Horseferry Road Magistrates' Court, ex p. Siadatan* [1991] 1 Q.B. 280, 92 Cr.App.R. 257, DC, it was held that "such violence" in section 4(1) referred back to "immediate unlawful violence": this did not mean instantaneous violence, but only a relatively short time interval might elapse between the act which was threatening, abusive or insulting and the unlawful violence. "Immediate" connoted proximity in time and in causation; that it was likely that violence would result within a relatively short period of time and without any other intervening occurrence.

It is an essential element of the offence created by section 4 that the violence threatened must be unlawful, that is that it did not amount to reasonable self-defence: *R. v. Afzal* [1993] Crim.L.R. 791, CA. See also *ante*, § 29–23.

Proof of identification and participation

29–33 See *Allan v. Ireland*, 79 Cr.App.R. 206, *ante*, §§ 14–69, 18–19 (persons appearing at court, and answering charges in their names, after they had been arrested, charged and bailed as part of a group said to have used threatening behaviour, had at least a prima facie case against them).

(5) Harassment, alarm or distress

Public Order Act 1986, s.4A

Intentional harassment, alarm or distress

29–34 **4A.**—(1) A person is guilty of an offence if, with intent to cause a person harassment, alarm or distress, he—

(a) uses threatening, abusive or insulting words or behaviour, or disorderly behaviour, or

(b) displays any writing, sign or other visible representation which is threatening, abusive or insulting,

thereby causing that or another person harassment, alarm or distress.

(2) An offence under this section may be committed in a public place or a private place, except that no offence is committed where the words or behaviour are used, or the writing, sign or other visible representation is displayed, by a person inside a dwelling and the person who is harassed, alarmed or distressed is also inside that or another dwelling.

(3) It is a defence for the accused to prove—

(a) that he was inside a dwelling and had no reason to believe that the words or behaviour used, or the writing, sign or other visible representation displayed, would be heard or seen by a person outside that or any other dwelling, or

(b) that his conduct was reasonable.

(4), (5) [*Identical to s.4(3), (4),* ante, *§ 29–25.*]

[This section was inserted by the *CJPOA* 1994, s.154. Subs. (4) is repealed, and subs. (5) is amended as in the case of the corresponding provisions in s.4, *ante*.]

Although the offences created by this section are summary only, see the racially or religiously aggravated versions in section 31 of the *CDA* 1998, *post*, § 29–38a, which are triable either way.

29–34a Section 5 of the 1986 Act creates lesser offences of a similar kind, with the maximum penalty being a fine not exceeding level 3 on the standard scale. Under section 5, there is no requirement to prove intent; it is sufficient that the words, behaviour or display are within the hearing or sight of a person likely to be caused harassment, alarm or distress. As with section 4A, there are racially or religiously aggravated versions of the offences: see *post*, § 29–38a. Unlike the racially or religiously aggravated versions of the section 4A offences, these offences are triable only summarily, but there is a higher maximum penalty (fine not exceeding level 4 on the standard scale).

The word "distress" takes its colour from its context. It is one of a trio of words "harassment, alarm or distress" which, in combination, give some idea of the mischief at which the legislation is aimed. They are relatively strong words as befits an offence which carries imprisonment or a fine. "Distress" requires real emotional disturbance or upset. While the degree of such disturbance or upset need not be grave, it should not be trivialised: *R. (R.) v. DPP*, 170 J.P. 661, DC (a case on s.4A). *R. (R.) v. DPP* was considered in *Southard v. DPP* [2007] A.C.D. 53, DC, where it was said that there was no requirement that the defendant's act was likely to lead to some kind of real emotional disturbance or upset; such a consequence would amount to "distress", but "harassment" (which need not be grave, but should also not be trivial) could be experienced without any real emotional disturbance or upset. The court also said that there was no rule of law that the offence could not be made out if the only person who saw or heard the defendant's conduct was a police officer.

As to the requisite public element of the offences contrary to sections 4A and 5, see *Chappell v. DPP*, 89 Cr.App.R. 82, DC. In relation to section 4A(1), it was held in *S. v. CPS* [2008] A.C.D. 46, DC, that where a person posts an image of a second person on a website that is available to the public with the necessary intent, the fact that the second person is unaware of it and does not see it until shown it by a third party does not break the chain of causation; and it would be equally immaterial that at the time the harassment, alarm or distress was caused the image was no longer displayed on the website.

In *Holloway v. DPP*, 169 J.P. 14, DC, it was held that for a person to be guilty of an offence contrary to section 5, the offending behaviour must actually have occurred within the sight or hearing of someone likely to be caused harassment, etc.; it is insufficient that someone might or could have seen or heard the offending behaviour; the court had to be able to infer that the defendant's behaviour was visible or audible to people in the vicinity at the time. See also *Taylor v DPP*, 170 J.P. 485, DC.

A "dwelling" for the purposes of the exception in section 4A(2) does not include a police cell: *R. v. Francis* [2007] 1 Cr.App.R. 36, CA.

As to whether a police officer can be a person caused "harassment, alarm or distress" within section 5, see *DPP v. Orum*, 88 Cr.App.R. 261, DC; *Cheeseman v. DPP*, 93 Cr.App.R. 145 at 152, DC; and *Lodge v. DPP*, *The Times*, October 26, 1988, DC (alarm for safety of third party). For the meaning of "disorderly behaviour", see *Chambers and Edwards v. DPP* [1995] Crim.L.R. 896, DC.

In *Dehal v. CPS*, 169 J.P. 581, QBD (Moses J.), it was held that where a prosecution engaged Article 10 of the ECHR (*ante*, § 16–119), the justification for a criminal sanction had to be convincingly established. Where, therefore, the appellant had been prosecuted under section 4A in respect of a notice he had displayed on the notice-board of a Sikh temple, such prosecution was unlawful as a result of section 3 of the *Human Rights Act* 1998 (*ante*, § 16–15) unless it could be established that prosecution, and nothing less, was necessary to prevent public disorder. See also *Percy v. DPP*, 166 J.P. 93, DC (conviction under s.5, in respect of defacement of American flag, quashed as being a disproportionate response to the defendant's Article 10 rights).

Section 5(3) makes it a defence for the defendant to prove that his conduct was reasonable: as to this, see *DPP v. Clarke*, 94 Cr.App.R. 359, DC; *Kwasi-Poku v. DPP* [1993] Crim.L.R. 703, DC; *Morrow v. DPP* [1994] Crim.L.R. 58, DC; and *Norwood v. DPP* [2003] Crim.L.R. 888, DC, in which the right to freedom of expression was limited to objectively reasonable conduct. See also *DPP v. Hammond*, 168 J.P. 601, DC.

For cases under section 5(4), see *R. v. Ball (S.L.)*, 90 Cr.App.R. 378, CA; *Groom v. DPP* [1991] Crim.L.R. 713, DC; and *Burrell v. CPS*, 69 J.C.L. 460, DC ([2005] EWHC 786 (Admin.)).

(6) Mental element: miscellaneous

Public Order Act 1986, s.6

29–35 **6.**—(1) A person is guilty of riot only if he intends to use violence or is aware that his conduct may be violent.

(2) A person is guilty of violent disorder or affray only if he intends to use or threaten violence or is aware that his conduct may be violent or threaten violence.

(3) A person is guilty of an offence under section 4 only if he intends his words or behaviour, or the writing, sign or other visible representation, to be threatening, abusive or insulting or is aware that it may be threatening, abusive or insulting.

(4) A person is guilty of an offence under section 5 only if he intends his words or behaviour, or the writing, sign or other visible representation, to be threatening, abusive or insulting, or is aware that it may be threatening, abusive or insulting or (as the case may be) he intends his behaviour to be or is aware that it may be disorderly.

(5) For the purposes of this section a person whose awareness is impaired by intoxication shall be taken to be aware of that of which he would be aware if not intoxicated, unless he shows either that his intoxication was not self-induced or that it was caused solely by the taking or administration of a substance in the course of medical treatment.

(6) In subsection (5) "intoxication" means any intoxication, whether caused by drink, drugs or other means, or by a combination of means.

(7) Subsections (1) and (2) do not affect the determination for the purposes of riot or violent disorder of the number of persons who use or threaten violence.

The offence of aiding and abetting an offence under the *Public Order Act* 1986 is not excluded by the words "only if he intends" in section 6: *R. v. Jefferson*, 99 Cr.App.R. 13, CA. See also *ante*, §§ 18–9 *et seq.*

Section 6(4) imputes a subjective awareness on the part of the defendant: *DPP v. Clarke*, *ante*, § 29–34.

(7) Procedure: miscellaneous

Public Order Act 1986, s.7

29–36 **7.**—(1) No prosecution for an offence of riot or incitement to riot may be instituted except by or with the consent of the Director of Public Prosecutions.

(2) For the purposes of the rules against charging more than one offence in the same count or information, each of sections 1 to 5 creates one offence.

(3) If on the trial on indictment of a person charged with violent disorder or affray the jury find him not guilty of the offence charged, they may (without prejudice to section 6(3) of the *Criminal Law Act* 1967) find him guilty of an offence under section 4.

(4) The Crown Court has the same powers and duties in relation to a person who is by virtue of subsection (3) convicted before it of an offence under section 4 as a magistrates' court would have on convicting him of the offence.

The reference to the common law offence of incitement in subsection (1) has effect as a reference to the offences under Part 2 of the *SCA* 2007: 2007 Act, s.63(1), and Sched. 6, para. 13.

A defendant indicted with an offence of violent disorder or affray may plead guilty to a lesser offence without it being necessary to empanel a jury: *R. v. O'Brien* [1993] Crim.L.R. 70, CA (see section 6(1)(b) of the *CLA* 1967, *ante*, § 4–115).

Where the judge decides to leave the alternative of a conviction under section 4 to the jury, defence counsel should be given an opportunity to address the jury thereon: *R. v. Perrins* [1995] Crim.L.R. 432, CA; *R. v. Stanley and Knight* [1993] Crim.L.R. 618, CA.

When considering whether to leave the offence under section 4 as an alternative, the impossibility of a conviction thereunder when the incident occurred within a dwelling should be borne in mind: *R. v. Va Kun Hau* [1990] Crim.L.R. 518, CA.

29–37 Where a judge directs a jury to return a verdict of not guilty of the offence charged, he is entitled under section 7(3) to leave for the jury's consideration the alternative offence under section 4: *R. v. Carson*, 92 Cr.App.R. 236.

For section 6(3) of the *CLA* 1967, see *ante*, § 4–455. Having regard to the definitions of the offences of riot in section 1 and violent disorder in section 2, it is submitted that a conviction of the latter offence would certainly be a possible alternative upon a charge of the former offence. In the light of the approach of the House of Lords to section 6(3) in *R. v. Wilson*; *R. v. Jenkins* [1984] A.C. 242 (*ante*, § 4–456) there may well be other possible alternatives where offences contrary to sections 1 to 3 of the 1986 Act are alleged.

(8) Interpretation

Public Order Act 1986, s.8

8. In this part— 29–38

"dwelling" means any structure or part of a structure occupied as a person's home or as other living accommodation (whether the occupation is separate or shared with others) but does not include any part not so occupied, and for this purpose "structure" includes a tent, caravan, vehicle, vessel or other temporary or movable structure;

"violence" means any violent conduct, so that—

(a) except in the context of affray, it includes violent conduct towards property as well as violent conduct towards persons, and

(b) it is not restricted to conduct causing or intended to cause injury or damage but includes any other violent conduct (for example, throwing at or towards a person a missile of a kind capable of causing injury which does not hit or falls short).

A communal landing in council flats is not a dwelling for the purposes of sections 4(2) and 8: *Rukwira v. DPP* [1993] Crim.L.R. 882, DC. The words "other living accommodation", in the definition of "dwelling", are associated with a person's home and do not include a police cell: *R. v. Francis*, *ante*, § 29–34a.

(9) Racially or religiously aggravated offences

Crime and Disorder Act 1998, s.31

Racially or religiously aggravated public order offences

31.—(1) A person is guilty of an offence under this section if he commits— 29–38a

(a) an offence under section 4 of the *Public Order Act* 1986 (fear or provocation of violence);

(b) an offence under section 4A of that Act (intentional harassment, alarm or distress); or

(c) an offence under section 5 of that Act (harassment, alarm or distress),

which is racially or religiously aggravated for the purposes of this section.

(2), (3) [*Repealed by* SOCPA *2005, ss.111 and 174(2), Sched. 7, para. 34, and Sched. 17, Pt 2.*]

(4) A person guilty of an offence falling within subsection (1)(a) or (b) above shall be liable—

(a) on summary conviction, to imprisonment for a term not exceeding *six* [12] months or to a fine not exceeding the statutory maximum, or to both;

(b) on conviction on indictment, to imprisonment for a term not exceeding two years or to a fine, or to both.

(5) A person guilty of an offence falling within subsection (1)(c) above shall be liable on summary conviction to a fine not exceeding level 4 on the standard scale.

(6) If, on the trial on indictment of a person charged with an offence falling within subsection (1)(a) or (b) above, the jury find him not guilty of the offence charged, they may find him guilty of the basic offence mentioned in that provision.

(7) For the purposes of subsection (1)(c) above, section 28(1)(a) above shall have effect as if the person likely to be caused harassment, alarm or distress were the victim of the offence.

[In subs. (4)(a), "12" is substituted for "six", as from a day to be appointed, by the *CJA* 2003, s.282(2) and (3). The increase has no application to offences committed before the substitution takes effect: s.282(4).]

For the meaning of "racially or religiously aggravated" for the purposes of this section, see section 28 of the 1998 Act, *ante*, § 5–84. "You're just a town full of Pakis", chanted at opposing supporters, were words "of a racialist nature" for the purposes of section 3(2)(b) of the *Football (Offences) Act* 1991: *DPP v. Stoke on Trent Magistrates' Court* [2004] 1 Cr.App.R. 4, DC. See also *Norwood v. DPP*, an anti-Muslim poster case (*ante*, § 29–34a); and *post*, § 29–40. 29–38b

An indictment may be framed from the specimen at § 19–214b, *ante*.

For sections 4, 4A and 5 of the 1986 Act, see *ante*, §§ 29–25, 29–34.

For an example of a custodial sentence in a case of anti-Muslim abuse, see *R. v. Barrie* [2006] 1 Cr.App.R. (S.) 40, CA.

C. PROCESSIONS AND ASSEMBLIES

General

29–39 Part II of the Act (as amended by the *CJPOA* 1994) requires advance notice of processions (s.11) and creates police powers to impose conditions on processions and assemblies (ss.12 and 14), to prohibit processions and trespassory assemblies (ss.13 and 14A), and to stop persons proceeding to trespassory assemblies (s.14C). Breaches of these provisions are offences which are summary only (and therefore outside the scope of this work).

D. RACIAL HATRED (PT III (ss.17–29))

(1) Meaning of "racial hatred"

Public Order Act 1986, s.17

Meaning of "racial hatred"

29–40 **17.** In this Part "racial hatred" means hatred against a group of persons ... defined by reference to colour, race, nationality (including citizenship) or ethnic or national origins.

[The words "in Great Britain" were repealed by the *Anti-terrorism, Crime and Security Act* 2001, s.125, and Sched. 8, Pt 4.]

This definition follows closely the definition of "racial group" in section 3(1) of the *Race Relations Act* 1976. In *Mandla v. Dowell Lee* [1983] 2 A.C. 548, HL, it was held that a group of persons defined by reference to "ethnic origins" in the context of that provision meant a group which was a segment of the population distinguished from others by a sufficient combination of shared customs, beliefs, traditions and characteristics derived from a common or presumed common past, even if not drawn from what in biological terms was a common racial stock, in that it was that combination which gave them an historically determined social identity in their own eyes, and those outside the group.

(2) Acts intended or likely to stir up racial hatred

Public Order Act 1986, s.18

Use of words or behaviour or display of written material

29–41 **18.**—(1) A person who uses threatening, abusive or insulting words or behaviour, or displays any written material which is threatening, abusive or insulting, is guilty of an offence if—

(a) he intends thereby to stir up racial hatred, or

(b) having regard to all the circumstances racial hatred is likely to be stirred up thereby.

(2) An offence under this section may be committed in a public or a private place, except that no offence is committed where the words or behaviour are used, or the written material is displayed, by a person inside a dwelling and are not heard or seen except by other persons in that or another dwelling.

(3) [*Repealed by* SOCPA *2005, ss.111 and 174(2), Sched. 7, para. 26(1) and (11), and Sched. 17, Pt 2.*]

(4) In proceedings for an offence under this section it is a defence for the accused to prove that he was inside a dwelling and had no reason to believe that the words or behaviour used, or the written material displayed, would be heard or seen by a person outside that or any other dwelling.

(5) A person who is not shown to have intended to stir up racial hatred is not guilty of an offence under this section if he did not intend his words or behaviour, or the written material, to be, and was not aware that it might be, threatening, abusive or insulting.

(6) This section does not apply to words or behaviour used, or written material displayed, solely for the purpose of being included in a programme included in a programme service.

[This section is printed as amended by the *Broadcasting Act* 1990, s.164(1), (2).]

As to the meaning of "programme service", "dwelling", "programme" and "written material", see section 29, *post*, § 29–53.

For the proper approach to the expressions "threatening, abusive or insulting" and "likely to", see *ante*, §§ 29–28, 29–29.

Public Order Act 1986, s.19

Publishing or distributing written material

19.—(1) A person who publishes or distributes written material which is threatening, abusive or insulting is guilty of an offence if— **29–42**

(a) he intends thereby to stir up racial hatred, or

(b) having regard to all the circumstances racial hatred is likely to be stirred up thereby.

(2) In proceedings for an offence under this section it is a defence for an accused who is not shown to have intended to stir up racial hatred to prove that he was not aware of the content of the material and did not suspect, and had no reason to suspect, that it was threatening, abusive or insulting.

(3) References in this Part to the publication or distribution of written material are to its publication or distribution to the public or a section of the public.

As to the meaning of "written material", see section 29, *post*, § 29–53.

For the proper approach to the expressions "threatening, abusive or insulting" and "likely to", see *ante*, §§ 29–28, 29–29.

Public Order Act 1986, s.20

Public performance of play

20.—(1) If a public performance of a play is given which involves the use of threatening, abusive or insulting words or behaviour, any person who presents or directs the performance is guilty of an offence if— **29–43**

(a) he intends thereby to stir up racial hatred, or

(b) having regard to all the circumstances (and, in particular, taking the performance as a whole) racial hatred is likely to be stirred up thereby.

(2) If a person presenting or directing the performance is not shown to have intended to stir up racial hatred, it is a defence for him to prove—

(a) that he did not know and had no reason to suspect that the performance would involve the use of the offending words or behaviour, or

(b) that he did not know and had no reason to suspect that the offending words or behaviour were threatening, abusive or insulting, or

(c) that he did not know and had no reason to suspect that the circumstances in which the performance would be given would be such that racial hatred would be likely to be stirred up.

(3) This section does not apply to a performance given solely or primarily for one or more of the following purposes—

(a) rehearsal,

(b) making a recording of the performance, or

(c) enabling the performance to be included in a programme service;

but if it is proved that the performance was attended by persons other than those directly connected with the giving of the performance or the doing in relation to it of the things mentioned in paragraph (b) or (c), the performance shall, unless the contrary is shown, be taken not to have been given solely or primarily for the purposes mentioned above.

(4) For the purposes of this section—

(a) a person shall not be treated as presenting a performance of a play by reason only of his taking part in it as a performer,

(b) a person taking part as a performer in a performance directed by another shall be treated as a person who directed the performance if without reasonable excuse he performs otherwise than in accordance with that person's direction, and

(c) a person shall be taken to have directed a performance of a play given under his direction notwithstanding that he was not present during the performance;

and a person shall not be treated as aiding or abetting the commission of an offence under this section by reason only of his taking part in a performance as a performer.

(5) In this section "play" and "public performance" have the same meaning as in the *Theatres Act* 1968.

(6) The following provisions of the *Theatres Act* 1968 apply in relation to an offence under this section as they apply to an offence under section 2 of that Act—

section 9 (script as evidence of what was performed),
section 10 (power to make copies of script),
section 15 (powers of entry and inspection).

[This section is printed as amended by the *Broadcasting Act* 1990, s.164(1), (2).]

As to the meaning of "recording", see section 21(2), *post*. As to the meaning of "play" and "public performance", see section 18(1) of the *Theatres Act* 1968, *post*, § 31–106. For sections 9 and 10 of the 1968 Act, see *post*, §§ 31–103, 31–104 respectively. Section 15 is not set out in this work.

For the proper approach to the expressions "threatening, abusive or insulting" and "likely to", see *ante*, §§ 29–28, 29–29.

Public Order Act 1986, s.21

Distributing, showing or playing a recording

29–44 **21.**—(1) A person who distributes, or shows or plays, a recording of visual images or sounds which are threatening, abusive or insulting is guilty of an offence if—

(a) he intends thereby to stir up racial hatred, or
(b) having regard to all the circumstances racial hatred is likely to be stirred up thereby.

(2) In this Part "recording" means any record from which visual images or sounds may, by any means, be reproduced; and references to the distribution, showing or playing of a recording are to its distribution, showing or playing to the public or a section of the public.

(3) [*Identical to s.19(2),* ante, *§ 29–42, save for reference to* "recording" *in lieu of* "material".]

(4) This section does not apply to the showing or playing of a recording solely for the purpose of enabling the recording to be included in a programme service.

[This section is printed as amended by the *Broadcasting Act* 1990, s.164(1), (2).]

As to the meaning of "programme service", see section 29, *post*, § 29–53.

For the proper approach to the expressions "threatening, abusive or insulting" and "likely to", see *ante*, §§ 29–28, 29–29.

Public Order Act 1986, s.22

Broadcasting or including programme in cable programme service

29–45 **22.**—(1) If a programme involving threatening, abusive or insulting visual images or sounds is included in a programme service, each of the persons mentioned in subsection (2) is guilty of an offence if—

(a) he intends thereby to stir up racial hatred, or
(b) having regard to all the circumstances racial hatred is likely to be stirred up thereby.

(2) The persons are—

(a) the person providing the programme service,
(b) any person by whom the programme is produced or directed, and
(c) any person by whom offending words or behaviour are used.

(3) If the person providing the service, or a person by whom the programme was produced or directed, is not shown to have intended to stir up racial hatred, it is a defence for him to prove that—

(a) he did not know and had no reason to suspect that the programme would involve the offending material, and
(b) having regard to the circumstances in which the programme was included in a programme service, it was not reasonably practicable for him to secure the removal of the material.

(4) It is a defence for a person by whom the programme was produced or directed who is not shown to have intended to stir up racial hatred to prove that he did not know and had no reason to suspect—

(a) that the programme would be included in a programme service, or
(b) that the circumstances in which the programme would be so included would be such that racial hatred would be likely to be stirred up.

(5) It is a defence for a person by whom offending words or behaviour were used and who is not shown to have intended to stir up racial hatred to prove that he did not know and had no reason to suspect— **29–46**

(a) that a programme involving the use of the offending material would be included in a programme service, or

(b) that the circumstances in which a programme involving the use of the offending material would be so included, or in which a programme broadcast or so included would involve the use of the offending material, would be such that racial hatred would be likely to be stirred up.

(6) A person who is not shown to have intended to stir up racial hatred is not guilty of an offence under this section if he did not know, and had no reason to suspect, that the offending material was threatening, abusive or insulting.

[This section is printed as amended and repealed in part by the *Broadcasting Act* 1990, s.164(3).]

As to the meaning of "programme service" and "programme", see section 29, *post*, § 29–53.

For the proper approach to the expressions "threatening, abusive or insulting" and "likely to", see *ante*, §§ 29–28, 29–29.

(3) Racially inflammatory material

Public Order Act 1986, s.23

Possession of racially inflammatory material

23.—(1) A person who has in his possession written material which is threatening, abusive or insulting, or a recording of visual images or sounds which are threatening, abusive or insulting, with a view to— **29–47**

(a) in the case of written material, its being displayed, published, distributed, or included in a programme service, whether by himself or another, or

(b) in the case of a recording, its being distributed, shown, played, or included in a programme service, whether by himself or another,

is guilty of an offence if he intends racial hatred to be stirred up thereby or, having regard to all the circumstances, racial hatred is likely to be stirred up thereby.

(2) For this purpose regard shall be had to such display, publication, distribution, showing, playing, or inclusion in a programme service as he has, or it may reasonably be inferred that he has, in view.

(3) [*Identical to s.19(2),* ante, *§ 29–42, save for reference to* "written material or recording" *in lieu of* "material".]

(4) [*Repealed by* Broadcasting Act *1990, s.164(4)(c).*]

[This section is printed as amended by the *Broadcasting Act* 1990, s.164(4).]

As to the meaning of "programme service" and "written material", see section 29, *post*, § 29–53. As to the meaning of "distribution" and "publication", see sections 19(3) and 21(2), *ante*, §§ 29–42, 29–44. As to the meaning of "recording", see section 21(2), *ante*, § 29–44.

For the proper approach to the expressions "threatening, abusive or insulting" and "likely to", see *ante*, §§ 29–28, 29–29.

For an up-to-date approach to sentencing, see *R. v. Gray* [1999] 1 Cr.App.R.(S.) 50, CA.

Public Order Act 1986, s.24

Powers of entry and search

24.—(1) If in England and Wales a justice of the peace is satisfied by information on oath laid by a constable that there are reasonable grounds for suspecting that a person has possession of written material or a recording in contravention of section 23, the justice may issue a warrant under his hand authorising any constable to enter and search the premises where it is suspected the material or recording is situated. **29–48**

(2) [*Scotland.*]

(3) A constable entering or searching premises in pursuance of a warrant issued under this section may use reasonable force if necessary.

(4) In this section "premises" means any place and, in particular, includes—

(a) any vehicle, vessel aircraft or hovercraft,
(b) any offshore installation as defined in section 1(3)(b) of the *Mineral Workings (Offshore Installations) Act* 1971, and
(c) any tent or movable structure.

As to the meaning of "recording", see section 21(2), *ante*, § 29–44. As to the meaning of "written material", see section 29, *post*, § 29–53.

As to applications for warrants, the execution thereof and the extent of the power of seizure thereunder, see the *PACE Act* 1984, ss.15, 16 and 19 respectively, *ante*, §§ 15–101, 15–102 and § 15–112 together with the *Code of Practice for Searches of Premises by Police Officers and the Seizure of Property found by Police Officers on Persons or Premises* (Appendix A–18).

Public Order Act 1986, s.25

Power to order forfeiture

29–49 **25.**—(1) A court by or before which a person is convicted of—
(a) an offence under section 18 relating to the display of written material, or
(b) an offence under section 19, 21 or 23,

shall order to be forfeited any written material or recording produced to the court and shown to its satisfaction to be written material or a recording to which the offence relates.

(2) An order made under this section shall not take effect—
(a) in the case of an order made in proceedings in England and Wales until the expiry of the ordinary time within which an appeal may be instituted or where an appeal is duly instituted, until it is finally decided or abandoned;
(b) in the case of an order made in proceedings in Scotland, until the expiration of the time within which, by virtue of any statute, an appeal may be instituted or, where such an appeal is duly instituted, until the appeal is finally decided or abandoned.

(3) For the purposes of subsection (2)(a)—
(a) an application for a case stated or for leave to appeal shall be treated as the institution of an appeal, and
(b) where a decision on appeal is subject to a further appeal, the appeal is not finally determined until the expiry of the ordinary time, within which a further appeal may be instituted or, where a further appeal is duly instituted, until the further appeal is finally decided or abandoned.

(4) For the purposes of subsection (2)(b) the lodging of an application for a stated case or note of appeal against sentence shall be treated as the institution of an appeal.

As to the meaning of "recording", see section 21(2), *ante*, § 29–44. As to the meaning of "written material", see section 29, *post*, § 29–53.

(4) Supplementary provisions

Public Order Act 1986, s.26

Savings for reports of parliamentary or judicial proceedings

29–50 **26.**—(1) Nothing in this Part applies to a fair and accurate report of proceedings in Parliament or in the National Assembly for Wales.

(2) Nothing in this Part applies to a fair and accurate report of proceedings publicly heard before a court or tribunal exercising judicial authority where the report is published contemporaneously with the proceedings or, if it is not reasonably practicable or would be unlawful to publish a report of them contemporaneously, as soon as publication is reasonably practicable and lawful.

[This section is printed as amended by the *Government of Wales Act* 2006, s.160(1), and Sched. 10, para. 19.]

Public Order Act 1986, s.27

Procedure and punishment

29–51 **27.**—(1) No proceedings for an offence under this Part may be instituted in England and Wales except by or with the consent of the Attorney General.

(2) For the purposes of the rules in England and Wales against charging more than one offence in the same count or information, each of sections 18 to 23 creates one offence.

(3) A person guilty of an offence under this Part is liable—

(a) on conviction on indictment to imprisonment for a term not exceeding seven years or a fine or both;

(b) on summary conviction to imprisonment for a term not exceeding *six* [12] months or a fine not exceeding the statutory maximum or both.

[This section is printed as amended by the *Anti-terrorism, Crime and Security Act* 2001, s.40 (substitution of "seven" for "two" in subs. (3)(a)). In subs. (3)(b), "12" is substituted for "six", as from a day to be appointed, by the *CJA* 2003, s.282(2) and (3). The increase has no application to offences committed before the substitution takes effect: s.282(4).]

As to the "statutory maximum", see *ante*, § 29–10.

In *R. v. Pearce*, 72 Cr.App.R. 295, CA, it was held in relation to section 5A(5) of the *Public Order Act* 1936, which was similar in its terms to section 27(1), that where the Attorney-General consents to a prosecution "for an offence or offences contrary to the provisions of the said section" that consent does not authorise a prosecution for conspiracy to contravene the section contrary to section 1(1) of the *CLA* 1977. Such a charge must be the subject of a further consent: see s.4(3) of the 1977 Act, *post*, § 33–33.

Public Order Act 1986, s.28

Offences by corporations

28.—(1) Where a body corporate is guilty of an offence under this Part and it is shown that the offence was committed with the consent or connivance of a director, manager, secretary or other similar officer of the body, or a person purporting to act in any such capacity, he as well as the body corporate is guilty of the offence and liable to be proceeded against and punished accordingly. **29–52**

(2) Where the affairs of a body corporate are managed by its members, subsection (1) applies in relation to the acts and defaults of a member in connection with his functions of management as it applies to a director.

As to subsection (1), see *R. v. Boal* [1992] 1 Q.B. 591, 95 Cr.App.R. 272, CA, *post*, § 30–103.

Public Order Act 1986, s.29

Interpretation

29. In this Part— **29–53**

"distribute", and related expressions, shall be construed in accordance with section 19(3) (written material) and section 21(2) (recordings);

"dwelling" means any structure or part of a structure occupied as a person's home or other living accommodation (whether the occupation is separate or shared with others) but does not include any part not so occupied, and for this purpose "structure" includes a tent, caravan, vehicle, vessel or other temporary or movable structure;

"programme" means any item which is included in a programme service;

"programme service" has the same meaning as in the *Broadcasting Act* 1990;

"publish" and related expressions, in relation to written material, shall be construed in accordance with section 19(3);

"racial hatred" has the meaning given by section 17;

"recording" has the meaning given by section 21(2), and "play" and "show", and related expressions, in relation to a recording, shall be construed in accordance with that provision;

"written material" includes any sign or other visible representation.

[This section is printed as amended and repealed in part by the *Broadcasting Act* 1990, s.164(5).]

As to the definition of "programme service", see section 201 of the 1990 Act (as amended by the *Broadcasting Act* 1996, Sched. 10, para. 11).

E. RELIGIOUS HATRED (PT 3A (SS.29A–29N))

Racial and Religious Hatred Act 2006

The long title proclaims it to be an Act to make provision about offences involving the **29–54** stirring up of hatred against persons on racial or religious grounds. The Act (save to the extent that it inserted a new s.29B(3) in the 1986 Act) came into force on October 1, 2007: *Racial and Religious Hatred Act 2006 (Commencement No. 1) Order* 2007 (S.I. 2007 No. 2490).

Section 1 inserts a new Part 3A ("Hatred against persons on religious grounds") (ss.29A–29N) in the *Public Order Act* 1986. The general structure of this new part corresponds closely to Part 3 ("Racial Hatred") (ss.17–29) of the 1986 Act (*ante*, §§ 29–40 *et seq.*), save that there is one additional section (29J). Section 29A defines "religious hatred" as "hatred against a group of persons defined by reference to religious belief or lack of religious belief". Sections 29B to 29F fall under the heading "Acts intended to stir up religious hatred", and are individually headed, "Use of words or behaviour or display of written material" (s.29B), "Publishing or distributing written material" (s.29C), "Public performance of play" (s.29D), "Distributing, showing or playing a recording" (s.29E), and "Broadcasting or including programme in programme service" (s.29F). Each of those sections corresponds to its equivalent in Part 3 (ss.18–22), with some differences. The principal difference relates to the offence created in subsection (1) of each new section. Whilst the *actus reus* of an offence in sections 18 to 22 encompasses acts which are abusive, threatening or insulting, an offence in sections 29B to 29F encompasses only acts which are threatening. Further, whilst the offences in sections 18 to 22 may be committed where the person doing the act intends thereby to stir up racial hatred, or where, having regard to all the circumstances, racial hatred is likely to be stirred up by the relevant act, the new offences in sections 29B to 29F are only committed where the relevant act is carried out with an intention to stir up religious hatred. Sections 29B to 29F correspond in all other respects to sections 18 to 22, save that it follows from the requirement that there should be a specific intent that there is no defence corresponding to that in sections 18(5), 19(2), 20(2), 21(3) and 22(3). Further, section 29B(3) provides a constable with a specific power of arrest without warrant, whereas the equivalent in section 18(3) was repealed by the *SOCPA* 2005.

29–55 Sections 29G to 29J fall under the heading "Inflammatory material", and are individually headed, "Possession of inflammatory material" (s.29G), "Powers of entry and search" (s.29H), "Power to order forfeiture" (s.29I), and "Protection of freedom of expression" (s.29J). Section 29G corresponds to section 23, save that it differs in the same respects as do sections 29B to 29F from their equivalents. Sections 29H and 29I correspond exactly to sections 24 and 25. Section 29J has no equivalent in Part 3. This section provides that nothing in Part 3A prohibits or restricts "discussion, criticism or expressions of antipathy, dislike, ridicule, insult or abuse of particular religions or the beliefs or practices of their adherents, or of any other belief system or the beliefs or practices of its adherents, or proselytising or urging adherents of a different religion or belief system to cease practising their religion or belief system."

29–56 Sections 29K to 29N fall under the heading "Supplementary provisions"; are individually headed, "Savings for reports of Parliamentary or judicial proceedings" (s.29K), "Procedure and punishment" (s.29L), "Offences by corporations" (s.29M), and "Interpretation" (s.29N); and correspond exactly to sections 26 to 29. In particular, it follows: (i) that no proceedings for an offence under Part 3A may be instituted in England and Wales except by or with the consent of the Attorney-General (s.29L(1)); (ii) that each of sections 29B to 29G creates one offence for the purposes of the rules against charging more than one offence in the same count or information (s.29L(2)); and (iii) that the offences in Part 3A are triable either way, the maximum penalty on conviction on indictment being seven years'imprisonment, or a fine, or both (s.29L(3)).

Criminal Justice and Immigration Act 2008

29–57 Part 3A of the 1986 Act is amended, and repealed in part, by the *CJIA* 2008, ss.74 and 149, and Scheds 16 and 28, Pt 5. The general effect is to extend the provisions of Part 3A, so that it encompasses hatred on the grounds of sexual orientation (*i.e.* hatred against a group of persons defined by reference to sexual orientation (whether towards persons of the same sex, the opposite sex or both)). To that end, amendments are made to the offences under sections 29B to 29G, so that they apply to hatred on the grounds of sexual orientation as they do to hatred on religious grounds. A new section 29AB (meaning of "hatred on the grounds of sexual orientation") is inserted, as is a new section 29JA, which provides that the discussion or criticism of sexual conduct or practices or the urging of persons to refrain from or modify such conduct or practices shall not be taken of itself to be threatening or intended to stir up hatred; and amendments are also made to sections 29H, 29I, 29K, 29L and 29N (in particular, increasing the maximum penalty on summary conviction of an offence under that part from six months' imprisonment to 12, subject to transitional provisions pending the commencement of the *CJA* 2003, s.282).

Some of these amendments and repeals took effect on Royal Assent (May 8, 2008); otherwise, they take effect as from a day to be appointed. In the former group are the repeal of section 29B(3) (which had never been given effect, having been excepted from the general commencement of the 2006 Act), the amendments to sections 29H, 29I, 29K and 29L and the insertion of new section 29JA.

Electronic commerce

The *Electronic Commerce Directive (Racial and Religious Hatred Act 2006) Regulations* 2007 (S.I. 2007 No. 2497) give effect to European Parliament and Council Directive 2000/31/EC (on certain legal aspects of information society services, in particular electronic commerce, in the internal market) in relation to matters within the scope of Part 3A of the 1986 Act. **29–58**

Regulation 3(1) makes provision for an offence contrary to Part 3A to be committed in the United Kingdom where, in the course of providing information society services, a service provider established in the United Kingdom does anything in an European Economic Area state (other than the United Kingdom) which if done in the United Kingdom would constitute the offence. Where the offence is committed only by virtue of this provision, the penalty on conviction on indictment is specified as being a term of imprisonment not exceeding two years (as against seven years: see s.29L): reg. 3(4). Regulation 4(1) prohibits the institution of proceedings for an offence contrary to the 1986 Act against a non-United Kingdom service provider unless the "derogation condition" is satisfied. The "derogation condition" is that the institution of proceedings (a) is necessary to pursue "the public interest objective" (*viz.* "public policy, in particular the prevention, investigation, detection and prosecution" of an offence under Part 3A (reg. 4(3)), (b) relates to an information society service that prejudices that objective or presents a serious and grave risk of prejudice to it, and (c) is proportionate to that objective: reg. 4(2). Regulations 5 to 7 respectively provide defences where an information society services provider is a "mere conduit", or is "caching" or "hosting" the information in question.

F. MISCELLANEOUS AND GENERAL (PT V (SS.38–43))

For section 38, see *post*, § 29–71. Section 39 was repealed by the *CJPOA* 1994, s.168(3) and Sched. 11. **29–59**

Breach of the peace

Section 40(4) of the *Public Order Act* 1986 provides that nothing therein affects the common law powers in England and Wales to deal with or prevent a breach of the peace. As to the powers of ordinary citizens as well as constables to take steps to prevent or restrain a breach of the peace, including the power of arrest, see *ante*, § 19–343. **29–60**

In *R. v. Howell* [1982] Q.B. 416, 73 Cr.App.R. 31, CA, it was held that there is a breach of the peace whenever harm is actually done or is likely to be done to a person or in his presence to his property or a person is in fear of being so harmed through an assault, an affray, a riot, unlawful assembly or other disturbance. Agitated or excited behaviour, not involving any injury or threat of injury, nor any verbal threat, is not capable of amounting to a breach of the peace: *Jarrett v. Chief Constable of West Midlands Police, The Times*, February 28, 2003, CA (Civ. Div.). And in *Hawkes v. DPP* [2006] 1 *Archbold News* 3, QBD (Newman J.) it was held that whilst language and an abusive and aggressive manner might justify an arrest on the ground of an apprehended breach of the peace, there had to be an incident of violence for an arrest to be justified on the ground that an actual breach of the peace had taken place; verbal abuse plus a refusal to get out of a police car did not amount to such an incident.

A breach of the peace is not an "offence" for the purposes of the detention provisions in section 34 of the *PACE Act* 1984 (*ante,* § 3–93): *Williamson v. Chief Constable of the West Midlands Police* [2004] 1 W.L.R. 14, CA (Civ. Div.); *Addison v. Chief Constable of West Midlands Police (Note)* [2004] 1 W.L.R. 29, CA (Civ. Div.).

II. UNLAWFUL EVICTION AND HARASSMENT OF OCCUPIER

Protection from Eviction Act 1977, s.1

Interim possession orders: false or misleading statements

29–61 **1.**—(1) In this section "residential occupier", in relation to any premises, means a person occupying the premises as a residence, whether under a contract or by virtue of any enactment or rule of law giving him the right to remain in occupation or restricting the right of any other person to recover possession of the premises.

(2) If any person unlawfully deprives the residential occupier of any premises of his occupation of the premises or any part thereof, or attempts to do so, he shall be guilty of an offence unless he proves that he believed, and had reasonable cause to believe, that the residential occupier had ceased to reside in the premises.

(3) If any person with intent to cause the residential occupier of any premises—

(a) to give up the occupation of the premises or any part thereof; or

(b) to refrain from exercising any right or pursuing any remedy in respect of the premises or part thereof;

does acts likely to interfere with the peace or comfort of the residential occupier or members of his household, or persistently withdraws or withholds services reasonably required for the occupation of the premises as a residence, he shall be guilty of an offence.

(3A) Subject to subsection (3B) below, the landlord of a residential occupier or an agent of the landlord shall be guilty of an offence if—

(a) he does acts likely to interfere with the peace or comfort of the residential occupier or members of his household, or

(b) he persistently withdraws or withholds services reasonably required for the occupation of the premises in question as a residence,

and (in either case) he knows, or has reasonable cause to believe, that that conduct is likely to cause the residential occupier to give up the occupation of the whole or part of the premises or to refrain from exercising any right or pursuing any remedy in respect of the whole or part of the premises.

(3B) A person shall not be guilty of an offence under subsection (3A) above if he proves that he had reasonable grounds for doing the acts or withdrawing or withholding the services in question.

(3C) In subsection (3A) above "landlord", in relation to a residential occupier of any premises, means the person who, but for—

(a) the residential occupier's right to remain in occupation of the premises, or

(b) a restriction on the person's right to recover possession of premises,

would be entitled to occupation of the premises and any superior landlord under whom that person derives title.

29–62 (4) A person guilty of an offence under this section shall be liable—

(a) on summary conviction, to a fine not exceeding the prescribed sum or to imprisonment for a term not exceeding *6* [12] months or to both;

(b) on conviction on indictment, to a fine or to imprisonment for a term not exceeding 2 years or to both.

(5) Nothing in this section shall be taken to prejudice any liability or remedy to which a person guilty of an offence thereunder may be subject in civil proceedings.

(6) Where an offence under this section committed by a body corporate is proved to have been committed with the consent or connivance of, or to be attributable to any neglect on the part of, any director, manager or secretary or other similar officer of the body corporate or any person who was purporting to act in any such capacity, he as well as the body corporate shall be guilty of that offence and shall be liable to be proceeded against and punished accordingly.

[This section is printed as amended by the *Housing Act* 1988, s.29(1), (2). The reference to "the prescribed sum" is substituted by virtue of the *MCA* 1980, s.32(2), *ante*, § 1–75aa; for the current value, see s.32(9). In subs. (4)(a), "12" is substituted for "6", as from a day to be appointed, by the *CJA* 2003, s.282(2) and (3). The increase has no application to offences committed before the substitution takes effect: s.282(4).]

In connection with this offence, see also section 42A of the *CJPA* 2001 (inserted therein by the *SOCPA* 2005, s.126) which creates a summary offence of harassment of a person in his home.

In connection with subsection (6), see *R. v. Boal* [1992] 1 Q.B. 591, 95 Cr.App.R. 272, CA, *post*, § 30–103.

Authorities

On a prosecution under section 1(2) it has been held that whether the defendant believed, and had reasonable cause to believe, that the residential occupier had ceased to reside in the premises are questions of fact for the jury to decide: *R. v. Davidson-Acres* [1980] Crim.L.R. 50, CA; and see *R. v. Phekoo*, 73 Cr.App.R. 107, CA. The burden cast on the defendant by this provision is a legal one and is compatible with Article 6(2) of the ECHR (*ante*, § 16–57); the defence is only available if the defendant can bring himself within a narrow class of exceptions, and it will be a rare case where a reverse burden is not justified in such circumstances: *Att.-Gen.'s Reference (No. 1 of 2004)*; *R. v. Edwards*; *R. v. Denton*; *R. v. Hendley*; *R. v. Crowley* [2004] 1 W.L.R. 2111, CA. **29–63**

On a prosecution under section 1(3) it must be proved that the defendant knew or believed that the person in question was a residential occupier: *R. v. Phekoo*, *ante*. The suggestion in the judgment, that if the defendant maintains that he believed the person in question to have not been a residential occupier then there must be reasonable grounds for that belief, is criticised in the commentary in the *Criminal Law Review* ([1981] Crim.L.R. 399) as being inconsistent with the primary ruling on the appeal, with the wording of the subsection and with general principles as to *mens rea*. See also *West Wiltshire D.C. v. Snelgrove* (1998) 30 H.L.R. 57, DC.

In *R. v. Yuthiwattana*, 80 Cr.App.R. 55, CA, it was held that for the purposes of an offence under subsection (2) the deprivation of occupation had to have the character of an "eviction". Permanency was not required but cases which were more appropriately described as "locking-out" cases, where a person was shut out of premises overnight or for a short period of time, but was allowed to remain in occupation of the premises, fell more appropriately under subsection (3).

In *Costelloe v. London Borough of Camden* [1986] Crim.L.R. 249, DC, Woolf J. drew attention to the fact that the Court of Appeal in *Yuthiwattana* had not, in fact, said that it was the period of exclusion that itself was critical, but rather the nature of the exclusion. If it was designed to evict the occupier it might come within the subsection, although, perhaps, it had lasted only a relatively short period because of, for example, a change of heart. **29–64**

Yuthiwattana was again considered by the Divisional Court in *Schon v. London Borough of Camden* (1987) 53 P.C.R. 361, in which it was held that "occupation" in the 1977 Act had the same meaning as in the *Rent Acts*. Glidewell L.J., giving a judgment with which Schiemann J. agreed, said:

> "there is a long line of authority for the proposition that, under the *Rent Acts*, a person may occupy premises as his residence although he is physically absent from the premises, provided that, to put it broadly, the absence is not, and is not intended to be, permanent and either his spouse or some other member of his family is physically in occupation or, at the very least, furniture and belongings remain in the premises" (at p. 366).

Accordingly, it was held that an intention to cause a residential occupier to leave premises for a temporary period so that certain works could be carried out did not constitute an intent coming within paragraph (a) of section 1(3), where an intent to cause the residential occupier to leave permanently would have to be proved. However, an intent to cause the residential occupier to leave for a temporary period could constitute an intent within section 1(3)(b), because it would be an intention to cause her to refrain from exercising her right to live in the premises and to be physically present in the premises. It was said *obiter* that where there is uncertainty whether to lay a charge under paragraph (a) or (b), it could be framed with alternative intents because section 1(3) creates only one offence.

29–65 If an act falls within subsection (3), it is immaterial that it does not constitute an actionable civil wrong: *R. v. Burke* [1991] 1 A.C. 135, HL.

In *R. v. A.M.K. (Property Management) Ltd* [1985] Crim.L.R. 600, CA, it was held, apparently *obiter*, that the "acts" with which section 1(3) was concerned were physical acts done. The Act was not designed to consider whether landlords made reasonable offers of compensation and it was not evidence of intention that insufficient compensation had been offered.

Omission to act not covered

29–66 Where a person has done an act which in fact interferes with the peace or comfort of the residential occupier but has done it without either of the intentions specified in section 1(3), and that person subsequently forms either of those intentions and realising that in order to achieve his intention it will suffice if he does nothing to rectify the damage done by the earlier act and accordingly does nothing, he will not be guilty of the offence created by section 1(3): *R. v. Ahmad (Zafar)*, 84 Cr.App.R. 64, CA.

Indictment alleging variety of acts: need for unanimity

29–67 In *R. v. Mitchell* [1994] Crim.L.R. 66, CA, it was held, applying *R. v. Brown (K.)*, 79 Cr.App.R. 115, CA (*ante*, §§ 4–391 *et seq.*), that where a number of different acts were alleged in a single count contrary to section 1(3), each of which was enough to found a conviction, and there was a realistic risk that the jury might think that, so long as they were unanimous that the defendant had committed one of the acts alleged, even though they did not all agree as to which, they could and should convict, they should be directed that they must be unanimous as to at least one particular act.

III. MAKING OF THREATS

A. GENERAL

29–68 A range of criminal offences have as an ingredient the making of threats or the use of threatening behaviour. Sections 1 to 3 of the *Public Order Act* 1986 refer to the threatening of unlawful violence; sections 4, 4A, 5, 18 and 20 refer to threatening words or behaviour; sections 19 and 23 refer to threatening written material; sections 21 and 23 refer to a threatening recording; section 22 refers to a programme involving threatening visual images or sounds. These sections are dealt with, *ante*, in this chapter.

Apart from these offences, the principal offences involving the making of threats are threats to kill, contrary to the *Offences against the Person Act* 1861 (*ante*, § 19–124), threats to destroy or damage property, contrary to the *Criminal Damage Act* 1971 (*ante*, § 23–32) and blackmail, contrary to section 21 of the *Theft Act* 1968 (*ante*, § 21–256).

B. BOMB HOAXES

Criminal Law Act 1977, s.51

29–69 **51.**—(1) A person who—

(a) places any article in any place whatever; or
(b) dispatches any article by post, rail or any other means whatever of sending things from one place to another,

with the intention (in either case) of inducing in some other person a belief that it is likely to explode or ignite and thereby cause personal injury or damage to property is guilty of an offence.

In this subsection "article" means substance.

(2) A person who communicates any information which he knows or believes to be false to another person with the intention of inducing in him or any other person a false belief that a bomb or other thing liable to explode or ignite is present in any place or location whatever is guilty of an offence.

(3) For a person to be guilty of an offence under subsection (1) or (2) above it is not necessary for him to have any particular person in mind as the person in whom he intends to induce the belief mentioned in that subsection.

(4) A person guilty of an offence under this section shall be liable—

(a) on summary conviction, to imprisonment for a term not exceeding *six* [12] months or to a fine not exceeding the prescribed sum or both;

(b) on conviction on indictment, to imprisonment for a term not exceeding seven years.

[Section 51(4) is printed as amended by the *CJA* 1991, s.26(4). The reference to "the prescribed sum" is substituted by virtue of the *MCA* 1980, s.32(2), *ante*, § 1–75aa; for the current value, see section 32(9). In subs. (4)(a), "12" is substituted for "six", as from a day to be appointed, by the *CJA* 2003, s.282(2) and (3). The increase has no application to offences committed before the substitution takes effect: s.282(4).]

The words "There is a bomb", said to the operator on a 999 call, were sufficient to give rise to an offence under section 51(2). It is not a necessary ingredient of the offence that the person communicating the false information should identify a "place or location": *R. v. Webb*, *The Times*, June 19, 1995, CA.

Sentencing

See CSP, B7–3.3A. Custodial sentences of between 12 months and two years have generally been approved by the Court of Appeal. See, for example, *R. v. Cook* [2006] 2 Cr.App.R. (S.) 106, CA. **29–70**

C. CONTAMINATION OF GOODS WITH INTENT

Public Order Act 1986, s.38

Contamination of or interference with goods with intention of causing public alarm or anxiety, etc.

38.—(1) It is an offence for a person, with the intention— **29–71**

(a) of causing public alarm or anxiety, or

(b) of causing injury to members of the public consuming or using the goods, or

(c) of causing economic loss to any person by reason of the goods being shunned by members of the public, or

(d) of causing economic loss to any person by reason of steps taken to avoid any such alarm or anxiety, injury or loss,

to contaminate or interfere with goods, or make it appear that goods have been contaminated or interfered with, or to place goods which have been contaminated or interfered with, or which appear to have been contaminated or interfered with, in a place where goods of that description are consumed, used, sold or otherwise supplied.

(2) It is also an offence for a person, with any such intention as is mentioned in paragraph (a), (c) or (d) of subsection (1), to threaten that he or another will do, or to claim that he or another has done, any of the acts mentioned in that subsection.

(3) It is an offence for a person to be in possession of any of the following articles with a view to the commission of an offence under subsection (1)—

(a) materials to be used for contaminating or interfering with goods or making it appear that goods have been contaminated or interfered with, or

(b) goods which have been contaminated or interfered with, or which appear to have been contaminated or interfered with.

(4) A person guilty of an offence under this section is liable—

(a) on conviction on indictment to imprisonment for a term not exceeding 10 years or a fine or both, or

(b) on summary conviction to imprisonment for a term not exceeding *six* [12] months or a fine not exceeding the statutory maximum or both.

(5) In this section "goods" includes substances whether natural or manufactured and whether or not incorporated in or mixed with other goods.

(6) The reference in subsection (2) to a person claiming that certain acts have been committed does not mean a person who in good faith reports or warns that such acts have been, or appear to have been committed.

[In subs. (4)(b), "12" is substituted for "six", as from a day to be appointed, by the *CJA* 2003, s.282(2) and (3). The increase has no application to offences committed before the substitution takes effect: s.282(4).]

The "statutory maximum" means the "prescribed sum" within the meaning of section 32 of the *MCA* 1980: *Interpretation Act* 1978, Sched. 1 (Appendix B–28). For the current value, see section 32(9), *ante*, § 1–75aa.

D. PROTECTION OF ANIMAL RESEARCH ORGANISATIONS

Serious Organised Crime and Police Act 2005, ss.145–148

Interference with contractual relationships so as to harm animal research organisation

29–71a **145.**—(1) A person (A) commits an offence if, with the intention of harming an animal research organisation, he—

(a) does a relevant act, or

(b) threatens that he or somebody else will do a relevant act,

in circumstances in which that act or threat is intended or likely to cause a second person (B) to take any of the steps in subsection (2).

(2) The steps are—

(a) not to perform any contractual obligation owed by B to a third person (C) (whether or not such non-performance amounts to a breach of contract);

(b) to terminate any contract B has with C;

(c) not to enter into a contract with C.

(3) For the purposes of this section, a "relevant act" is—

(a) an act amounting to a criminal offence, or

(b) a tortious act causing B to suffer loss or damage of any description;

but paragraph (b) does not include an act which is actionable on the ground only that it induces another person to break a contract with B.

(4) For the purposes of this section, "contract" includes any other arrangement (and "contractual" is to be read accordingly).

(5) For the purposes of this section, to "harm" an animal research organisation means—

(a) to cause the organisation to suffer loss or damage of any description, or

(b) to prevent or hinder the carrying out by the organisation of any of its activities.

(6) This section does not apply to any act done wholly or mainly in contemplation or furtherance of a trade dispute.

(7) In subsection (6) "trade dispute" has the same meaning as in Part 4 of the *Trade Union and Labour Relations (Consolidation) Act* 1992, except that section 218 of that Act shall be read as if—

(a) it made provision corresponding to section 244(4) of that Act, and

(b) in subsection (5), the definition of "worker" included any person falling within paragraph (b) of the definition of "worker" in section 244(5).

Intimidation of persons connected with animal research organisation

29–71b **146.**—(1) A person (A) commits an offence if, with the intention of causing a second person (B) to abstain from doing something which B is entitled to do (or to do something which B is entitled to abstain from doing)—

(a) A threatens B that A or somebody else will do a relevant act, and

(b) A does so wholly or mainly because B is a person falling within subsection (2).

(2) A person falls within this subsection if he is—

(a) an employee or officer of an animal research organisation;

(b) a student at an educational establishment that is an animal research organisation;

(c) a lessor or licensor of any premises occupied by an animal research organisation;

(d) a person with a financial interest in, or who provides financial assistance to, an animal research organisation;

(e) a customer or supplier of an animal research organisation;

(f) a person who is contemplating becoming someone within paragraph (c), (d) or (e);

(g) a person who is, or is contemplating becoming, a customer or supplier of someone within paragraph (c), (d), (e) or (f);

(h) an employee or officer of someone within paragraph (c), (d), (e), (f) or (g);

(i) a person with a financial interest in, or who provides financial assistance to, someone within paragraph (c), (d), (e), (f) or (g);

(j) a spouse, civil partner, friend or relative of, or a person who is known personally to, someone within any of paragraphs (a) to (i);

(k) a person who is, or is contemplating becoming, a customer or supplier of someone within paragraph (a), (b), (h), (i) or (j); or

(l) an employer of someone within paragraph (j).

(3) For the purposes of this section, an "officer" of an animal research organisation or a person includes—

(a) where the organisation or person is a body corporate, a director, manager or secretary;

(b) where the organisation or person is a charity, a charity trustee (within the meaning of the *Charities Act* 1993);

(c) where the organisation or person is a partnership, a partner.

(4) For the purposes of this section—

(a) a person is a customer or supplier of another person if he purchases goods, services or facilities from, or (as the case may be) supplies goods, services or facilities to, that other; and

(b) "supplier" includes a person who supplies services in pursuance of any enactment that requires or authorises such services to be provided.

(5) For the purposes of this section, a "relevant act" is—

(a) an act amounting to a criminal offence, or

(b) a tortious act causing B or another person to suffer loss or damage of any description.

(6) [*Secretary of State's power of amendment by order.*]

(7) This section does not apply to any act done wholly or mainly in contemplation or furtherance of a trade dispute.

(8) In subsection (7) "trade dispute" has the meaning given by section 145(7).

Penalty for offences under sections 145 and 146

147.—(1) A person guilty of an offence under section 145 or 146 is liable— **29–71c**

(a) on summary conviction, to imprisonment for a term not exceeding 12 months or to a fine not exceeding the statutory maximum, or to both;

(b) on conviction on indictment, to imprisonment for a term not exceeding five years or to a fine, or to both.

(2) No proceedings for an offence under either of those sections may be instituted except by or with the consent of the Director of Public Prosecutions.

In relation to an offence committed before the commencement of the *CJA* 2003, s.154, the reference to "12 months" in subsection (1)(a) should be read as a reference to "6 months": s.175(2) of the 2005 Act.

As to the focus of an offence contrary to section 145 being the interference with a contractual relationship, rather than the underlying criminal offence, see *R. v. Harris (Joseph)* [2007] 2 Cr.App.R.(S.) 37, CA. Where there is serious criminality involved in the base offence, it is submitted that it would be appropriate to have two counts, in order that the court should be able to reflect both aspects of the criminality, in the overall sentence imposed.

Animal research organisations

148.—(1) For the purposes of sections 145 and 146 "animal research organisation" means any person or organisation falling within subsection (2) or (3). **29–71d**

(2) A person or organisation falls within this subsection if he or it is the owner, lessee or licensee of premises constituting or including—

(a) a place specified in a licence granted under section 4 or 5 of the 1986 Act,

(b) a scientific procedure establishment designated under section 6 of that Act, or

(c) a breeding or supplying establishment designated under section 7 of that Act.

(3) A person or organisation falls within this subsection if he or it employs, or engages under a contract for services, any of the following in his capacity as such—

(a) the holder of a personal licence granted under section 4 of the 1986 Act,

(b) the holder of a project licence granted under section 5 of that Act,

(c) a person specified under section 6(5) of that Act, or
(d) a person specified under section 7(5) of that Act.

(4) [*Secretary of State's power of amendment by order.*]

(5) In this section—

"the 1986 Act" means the *Animals (Scientific Procedures) Act* 1986;
"organisation" includes any institution, trust, undertaking or association of persons;
"premises" includes any place within the meaning of the 1986 Act;
"regulated procedures" has the meaning given by section 2 of the 1986 Act.

Sections 145 to 148 came into force on July 1, 2005: *Serious Organised Crime and Police Act 2005 (Commencement No. 1, Transitional and Transitory Provisions) Order* 2005 (S.I. 2005 No. 1521).

IV. DEFAMATORY LIBEL

Introduction

29–72 For more detail in relation to this offence, see earlier editions of this work up to 1994. For seditious libel, see *ante*, §§ 25–266 *et seq.*; for libel affecting the administration of justice, see *ante*, § 28–52; for obscene libel, see *post*, § 31–60.

Definition

29–73 A defamatory libel is the expression or conveying of a defamatory statement by written or printed words or in some other permanent form. A defamatory statement is a statement which if published of and concerning a person is calculated to expose him to public hatred, contempt or ridicule, or to damage him in his trade, business, profession, calling or office.

The libel does not have to have been calculated to provoke a breach of the peace, as was once thought, but it must probably be serious, not trivial: *Gleaves v. Deakin* [1980] A.C. 477, HL; *Desmond v. Thorne* [1983] 1 W.L.R. 163, QBD (Taylor J.).

As to the compatibility of an offence of criminal libel with guarantees of freedom of expression, see *Worme v. Commr of Police of Grenada* [2004] 2 A.C. 430, PC. The publication must be in permanent form, which includes a broadcast (*Broadcasting Act* 1990, s.166(1)) and a play (*Theatres Act* 1968, s.4(1)).

Leave to commence prosecution

29–74 Defamatory libel is indictable only. Leave is required before commencing a prosecution against a proprietor, publisher, editor or any person responsible for publication of a newspaper: *Law of Libel Amendment Act* 1888, s.8. This does not include a journalist: *Gleaves v. Insall* [1999] 2 Cr.App.R. 467, DC. Leave of the Attorney-General is required for prosecution of material published in a play: *Theatres Act* 1968, s.8. For definitions of "newspaper" and "proprietor", see the *Newspaper Libel and Registration Act* 1881, s.1. Criminal prosecutions for defamatory libel are not necessarily in breach of Article 10 of the ECHR, see *ante*, § 16–127.

Defences

29–75 These mean absolute privilege, qualified privilege, fair comment (probably), justification for the public benefit (*Libel Act* 1843, s.6) and publication without authority, consent or knowledge (*Libel Act* 1843, s.7, *ante*, § 25–268). For further detail, see editions of this work up to 1994; and as to section 6, see *Worme*, *ante*, § 29–73.

As to the separate functions of judge and jury, see the *Libel Act* 1792 (*ante*, § 25–270).

Penalties

Libel Act 1843, ss.4, 5

False defamatory libel punishable by imprisonment and fine

29–76 **4.** If any person shall maliciously publish any defamatory libel, knowing the same to be false, every such person being convicted thereof, shall be liable to be imprisoned ... for any term not exceeding two years, and to pay such fine as the court shall award.

Malicious defamatory libel, by imprisonment or fine

5. If any person shall maliciously publish any defamatory libel, every such person, being convicted thereof, shall be liable to fine or imprisonment, or both, as the court may award, such imprisonment not to exceed the term of one year.

Section 5 neither creates nor defines an offence; it merely enjoins the punishment to be awarded for an existing common law offence: *R. v. Munslow* [1895] 1 Q.B. 758, CCR. Although both sections contain the word "maliciously", it is unnecessary to prove malice in the sense of an intention to defame, or even to aver it in the indictment: *ibid*.

Although neither an intention to defame nor knowledge of the falsity have to be proved at common law, knowledge of the libel itself as opposed to mere knowledge of the book or newspaper containing it does have to be proved: *Vizetelly v. Mudie's Select Library Ltd* [1900] 2 Q.B. 170, CA. But this principle will not operate to exonerate a defendant who did not know of the libel, but ought to have known of it, and it is for the defendant to prove that he was not negligent: *ibid*.

Where the more serious offence is charged but the Crown fail to prove knowledge, the jury may convict of the common law offence: *Boaler v. R.* (1888) 21 Q.B.D. 284.

Proof of certain matters

As to proof of the proprietorship of a newspaper, see the *Newspaper Libel and Registration Act* 1881, ss.8 and 15. **29–77**

As to the duty of printers (a) to print their name and address on papers and books printed by them, and (b) to keep at least one copy of any paper printed for hire, gain, reward or profit and to record thereon the name and address of the person or persons who employed them to print the paper, see the *Newspapers, Printers and Reading Rooms Repeal Act* 1869, Sched. 2, and the *Printers' Imprint Act* 1961, s.1, as amended by the *Patents, Designs and Marks Act* 1986, s.2 and Sched. 2.

Pleadings

For a specimen indictment, plea of justification and replication, see the editions of this work up to 1994. **29–78** convict such person being convicted thereof shall be liable to be imprisoned ... for any term not exceeding two years, and to pay such fine as the court shall award.

Maliciously publishing defamatory libel: penalty: imprisonment or fine

5. If any person shall maliciously publish any defamatory libel, every such person, being convicted thereof, shall be liable to fine or imprisonment, or both, as the court may award, such imprisonment not to exceed the term of one year.

29-[illegible] Section 5 neither creates nor defines an offence; it merely enlarges the punishment to be awarded for an existing common law offence: *R. v. Munslow* [1895] 1 Q.B. 758, CCR. Although both sections contain the word "maliciously", it is not necessary to prove malice in the sense of an intention to defame, or even to prove it in the sense of intent. [illegible] Although not, they are intended to define [illegible] knowledge of the libel may have to be proved at common law, knowledge of the libel itself as opposed to mere knowledge of the book or newspaper containing it does have to be proved: *R. v. Walter* ... *Vizetelly v. Mudie's Select Library Ltd* [1900] 2 Q.B. 170, CA. But this principle will not operate to exonerate a defendant who did not know of the libel but ought to have known of it, and it is for the defendant to prove that he was not negligent: *ibid*.

Where the more serious offence is charged but the Crown fail to prove knowledge the jury may convict of the common law offence: *Boaler v. R.* (1888) 21 Q.B.D. 284.

Proof of certain matters

29-77 As to proof of the proprietorship of a newspaper, see the *Newspaper Libel and Registration Act* 1881, ss.8 and 15.

As to the duty of printers (a) to print their name and address on papers and books printed by them and (b) to keep at least one copy of any paper printed for hire, reward or profit and to record thereon the name and address of the person or persons who employed them to print the paper, see the *Newspapers, Printers, and Reading Rooms Repeal Act* 1869, Sched. 2 and the *Printers' Imprint Act* 1961, s.2, as amended by the *Criminal Damage and Misc... Act* 1985, s.2 and Sched. 2.

Pleadings

29-78 For a specimen indictment, plea of justification and replication, see the editions of this work up to 1994.

Chapter 30

COMMERCE, FINANCIAL MARKETS AND INSOLVENCY

I. INVESTIGATIVE POWERS

A. Companies Acts 1985 and 2006

(1) Introduction

Part XIV of the 1985 Act is entitled "Investigation of Companies and their Affairs: Requisition of Documents". It comprises sections 431 to 453C and has been extensively amended by the 2006 Act. **30–1**

(2) Investigation of a company's affairs

The Secretary of State is empowered by section 431 of the *Companies Act* 1985 to appoint one or more inspectors to investigate and report on the affairs of a company. The appointment may be made on the application of the company or its members, provided that the application is supported by evidence to show that the applicant has good reason for requiring the investigation. As to the expression "the affairs of a company", see *R. v. Board of Trade, ex p. St Martin's Preserving Company Ltd* [1965] 1 Q.B. 603, DC. **30–2**

Under section 432(1), the Secretary of State shall appoint one or more inspectors to investigate the affairs of a company if the court orders an investigation. Section 432(2) of the *Companies Act* 1985 sets out the circumstances of fraud, prejudice or mismanagement in which the Secretary of State himself may make such an appointment. There is provision for reports under section 432(2) not to be published: s.432(2A). Inspectors appointed under either section 431 or 432 may, by virtue of section 433, also investigate the affairs of subsidiary or holding companies if they think it necessary. **30–3**

Companies Act 1985, ss.434, 437, 441

Production of documents and evidence to inspectors

434.—(1) When inspectors are appointed under section 431 or 432, it is the duty of all officers and agents of the company, and of all officers and agents of any other body corporate whose affairs are investigated under section 433(1)— **30–4**

(a) to produce to the inspectors all documents of or relating to the company or, as the case may be, the other body corporate which are in their custody or power,

(b) to attend before the inspectors when required to do so, and

(c) otherwise to give the inspectors all assistance in connection with the investigation which they are reasonably able to give.

(2) If the inspectors consider that an officer or agent of the company or other body corporate, or any other person, is or may be in possession of information relating to a matter which they believe to be relevant to the investigation, they may require him—

(a) to produce to them any documents in his custody or power relating to that matter,

(b) to attend before them, and

(c) otherwise to give them all assistance in connection with the investigation which he is reasonably able to give;

and it is that person's duty to comply with the requirement.

(3) An inspector may for the purposes of the investigation examine any person on oath, and may administer an oath accordingly.

(4) In this section a reference to officers or to agents includes past, as well as present, officers or agents (as the case may be); and "agents", in relation to a company or other body corporate, includes its bankers and solicitors and persons employed by it as auditors, whether these persons are or are not officers of the company or other body corporate.

(5) An answer given by a person to a question put to him in exercise of powers conferred by this section (whether as it has effect in relation to an investigation under any of sections 431 to 433, or as applied by any other section in this Part) may be used in evidence against him.

(5A) However, in criminal proceedings in which that person is charged with an offence to which this subsection applies—

(a) no evidence relating to the answer may be adduced, and

(b) no question relating to it may be asked,

by or on behalf of the prosecution, unless evidence relating to it is adduced, or a question relating to it is asked, in the proceedings by or on behalf of that person.

(5B) Subsection (5A) applies to any offence other than—

(a) an offence under section 2 or 5 of the *Perjury Act* 1911 (false statements made on oath otherwise than in judicial proceedings or made otherwise than on oath); or

(b) [*Scotland*].

(6) In this section "document" includes information recorded in any form.

(7) The power under this section to require production of a document includes power, in the case of a document not in hard copy form, to require the production of a copy of the document—

(a) in hard copy form, or

(b) in a form from which a hard copy can be readily obtained.

(8) An inspector may take copies of or extracts from a document produced in pursuance of this section.

[This section is printed as amended by the *Companies Act* 1989, s.56(1)–(5); the *YJCEA* 1999, s.59, and Sched. 3, para. 5; the *CJPA* 2001, s.70, and Sched. 2, para. 17; and the *Companies Act* 2006, s.1038(1).]

30–5 Where any person fails or refuses to produce to inspectors acting under section 434 all relevant documents or fails or refuses to attend before the inspectors, or provide all reasonable assistance to them, the inspectors may so certify to the court. For consideration of "reasonable assistance" see *Re an inquiry into Mirror Group Newspapers plc* [2000] Ch. 194, Ch D.

30–6 The court may then hear evidence, and if appropriate punish the offender as if he had been found guilty of contempt of the court: s.436.

Inspectors' reports

30–7 **437.**—(1) The inspectors may, and if so directed by the Secretary of State shall, make interim reports to the Secretary of State, and on the conclusion of their investigation shall make a final report to him.

(1A) Any persons who have been appointed under sections 431 or 432 may at any time and, if the Secretary of State directs them to do so, shall inform him of any matters coming to their knowledge as a result of their investigations.

(2) If the inspectors were appointed under section 432 in pursuance of an order of the court, the Secretary of State shall furnish a copy of any report of theirs to the court.

(3) In any case the Secretary of State may, if he thinks fit—

(a) forward a copy of any report made by the inspectors to the company's registered office,

(b) furnish a copy on request and on payment of the prescribed fee to—

(i) any member of the company or other body corporate which is the subject of the report,

(ii) any person whose conduct is referred to in the report,

(iii) the auditors of that company or body corporate,

(iv) the applicants for the investigation,

(v) any other person whose financial interests appear to the Secretary of State to be affected by the matters dealt with in the report, whether as a creditor of the company or body corporate, or otherwise, and

(c) cause any such report to be printed and published.

[This section is printed as amended by the *Financial Services Act* 1986, Sched. 13; the *Companies Act* 1989, s.57; and the *Companies Act* 2006, ss.1035(4) and 1295, and Sched. 16.]

Inspectors' report to be evidence

441.—(1) A copy of any report of inspectors appointed under this Part, certified by the Secretary of State to be a true copy, is admissible in any legal proceedings as evidence of the opinion of the inspectors in relation to any matter contained in the report and, in proceedings on an application under section 8 of the *Company Directors Disqualification Act* 1986, as evidence of any fact stated therein. **30–8**

(2) A document purporting to be such a certificate as is mentioned above shall be received in evidence and be deemed to be such a certificate, unless the contrary is proved.

[This section is printed as amended by the *Insolvency Act* 1985, Sched. 6; and the *Insolvency Act* 1986, Sched. 13.]

The powers of the inspectors must be exercised fairly, see *Re Pergamon Press Ltd* [1971] Ch. 388, CA (Civ. Div.), and the procedure must not be used oppressively, see *Re London United Investments plc* [1992] Ch. 578, CA (Civ. Div.). It is a question of fact in each case whether inspectors are "investigating offences" for the purposes of section 67(9) of the *PACE Act* 1984 (*ante*, § 15–5): *R. v. Seelig and Lord Spens*, 94 Cr.App.R. 17, CA. **30–9**

An examinee may claim legal professional privilege and may, in certain circumstances rely upon banking confidentiality, see section 452, *post*, § 30–28. The examinee is not entitled to rely on the common law privilege against self-incrimination to refuse to answer questions: see *Re London United Investments plc*, *ante*. Inspectors cannot themselves compel an examinee to answer questions. Their only power is to refer the matter to the court: *McClelland, Pope & Langley Ltd v. Howard* [1968] 1 All E.R. 569, HL. The court may then punish the examinee for contempt of court under section 436(3). Answers given by the examinee may only be given against him in evidence in criminal proceedings in the circumstances specified in section 434(5A) (inserted so as to give effect to *Saunders v. U.K.*, 23 E.H.R.R. 313, ECtHR). **30–10**

The Secretary of State has a discretion under section 451A to disclose information obtained by inspectors to prosecuting authorities, see *post*, § 30–27. It is generally accepted that a line should be drawn when a person has been charged with a criminal offence, and he should not thereafter be questioned by inspectors on matters relevant to that offence: *Re London United Investments plc*, *ante*. The Secretary of State has a discretion to delay publication of any report until after any criminal proceedings have finished: *R. v. Secretary of State for Trade and Industry, ex p. Lonrho plc* [1989] 1 W.L.R. 525, HL. **30–11**

As to the issue of a witness summons to procure the compulsory production of transcripts of evidence given to inspectors, see *R. v. Cheltenham JJ., ex p. Secretary of State for Trade* [1977] 1 W.L.R. 95, DC, and *R. v. Clowes*, 95 Cr.App.R. 440, CCC (Phillips J.), *ante*, § 8–6. There is a qualified duty of confidence attaching to the transcripts. Accordingly a person affected ought to be given notice of any application for disclosure or production, see *Soden v. Burns* [1996] 1 W.L.R. 1512, Ch D. **30–12**

(3) Investigation of company's ownership

The Secretary of State is empowered by section 442 of the *Companies Act* 1985 to **30–13** appoint inspectors to investigate and report on the membership of any company, provided that it appears to him that there is good reason to do so. This is for the purpose of determining the true persons who are or have been either financially interested in the (real or apparent) success or failure of the company, or able to control or materially to influence its policy.

30–14 Under section 442(3) members of the company may under certain circumstances require the Secretary of State to appoint inspectors to investigate unless he is satisfied that the members' application is vexatious. Further, there is power to exclude any matter, in so far as the Secretary of State is satisfied that it is unreasonable for it to be investigated: s.442(3A). The provisions in sections 451A and 452 apply to information obtained under this section: see *post*, §§ 30–27 *et seq*.

Companies Act 1985, s.443

Provisions applicable on investigation under section 442

30–15 **443.**—(1) For purposes of an investigation under section 442, sections 433(1), 434, 436 and 437 apply with the necessary modifications of references to the affairs of the company or to those of any other body corporate, subject however to the following subsections.

(2) Those sections apply to—

(a) all persons who are or have been, or whom the inspector has reasonable cause to believe to be or have been, financially interested in the success or failure or the apparent success or failure of the company or any other body corporate whose membership is investigated with that of the company, or able to control or materially influence its policy (including persons concerned only on behalf of others), and

(b) any other person whom the inspector has reasonable cause to believe possesses information relevant to the investigation,

as they apply in relation to officers and agents of the company or the other body corporate (as the case may be).

(3) If the Secretary of State is of opinion that there is good reason for not divulging any part of a report made by virtue of section 442 and this section, he may under section 437 disclose the report with the omission of that part; and he may cause to be kept by the registrar of companies a copy of the report with that part omitted or, in the case of any other such report, a copy of the whole report.

(4) [*Repealed by* C.A. *1989, Sched. 24*.]

30–16 By virtue of section 444 of the *Companies Act* 1985, the Secretary of State may, rather than appoint inspectors, require persons to give information about the ownership (past or present) of shares and debentures of a company, provided there is good reason to investigate such ownership.

30–17 Under section 444(3) and (4), a person failing to give the required information or making a statement knowing it to be false in a material particular, or being reckless as to its falsity, commits an offence and is liable to imprisonment and/or a fine. The provisions of sections 451A and 452 apply: see *post*, §§ 30–27 *et seq*.

(4) Powers of Secretary of State to give directions to inspectors

30–18 Where an inspector is appointed under section 431, 432(2) or 442(1), the Secretary of State may, by section 446A, give him directions including as to the subject matter of his investigation; as to the manner, form and timing of his report; and as to matters which should or should not be included. Such directions may be amended or revoked, and the inspector is required to comply with any direction given. The Secretary of State may also give a direction to terminate the investigation: s.446B.

30–19 Sections 446C to 446E contain provisions in relation to the resignation, removal and replacement of inspectors; and in relation to the obtaining of information from former inspectors.

(5) Examination of company's records

30–20 The groups of sections dealing with the requisition and seizure of the books and records of a company (ss.447–451), and containing supplementary provisions (ss.452–453C), have been substantially amended by the *Companies (Audit, Investigations and*

Community Enterprise) Act 2004, ss.21–25, and Sched. 2. The amendments came into force on April 6, 2005. Their stated purpose was to improve access to relevant information; reduce the possibility of delay or obstruction by companies under investigation; remove deterrents to individuals volunteering information when complaints are vetted for possible investigation; and introduce more effective sanctions. Guidelines have been issued on the conduct of investigations using these powers: see *Guide to the new investigations provisions introduced by the Companies (Audit, Investigations and Community Enterprise) Act 2004* (DTI, 2005). Further amendments were made by the *C.A.* 2006 (effective October 1, 2007). As to the production and inspection of documents where an offence is suspected, see section 1132 of the 2006 Act, *post*, § 30–107a.

Companies Act 1985, ss.447–451

Requisition and seizure of books and papers

Power to require production of documents

447.—(1) The Secretary of State may act under subsections (2) and (3) in relation to a company. **30–20a**

(2) The Secretary of State may give directions to the company requiring it—

(a) to produce such documents (or documents of such description) as may be specified in the directions;

(b) to provide such information (or information of such description) as may be so specified.

(3) The Secretary of State may authorise a person (an investigator) to require the company or any other person—

(a) to produce such documents (or documents of such description) as the investigator may specify;

(b) to provide such information (or information of such description) as the investigator may specify.

(4) A person on whom a requirement under subsection (3) is imposed may require the investigator to produce evidence of his authority.

(5) A requirement under subsection (2) or (3) must be complied with at such time and place as may be specified in the directions or by the investigator (as the case may be).

(6) The production of a document in pursuance of this section does not affect any lien which a person has on the document.

(7) The Secretary of State or the investigator (as the case may be) may take copies of or extracts from a document produced in pursuance of this section.

(8) A "document" includes information recorded in any form.

(9) [*Identical to s.434(7),* ante, *§ 30–4.*]

[This section is printed as substituted by the *Companies (Audit, Investigations and Community Enterprise) Act* 2004, s.21; and as subsequently amended by the *Companies Act* 2006, s.1038(2).]

Information provided: evidence

447A.—(1) A statement made by a person in compliance with a requirement under section 447 may be used in evidence against him. **30–21**

(2) But in criminal proceedings in which the person is charged with a relevant offence—

(a) no evidence relating to the statement may be adduced by or on behalf of the prosecution, and

(b) no question relating to it may be asked by or on behalf of the prosecution, unless evidence relating to it is adduced or a question relating to it is asked in the proceedings by or on behalf of that person.

(3) A relevant offence is any offence other than the following—

(a) an offence under section 451,

(b) an offence under section 5 of the *Perjury Act* 1911 (false statement made otherwise than on oath), or

(c) [*Scotland.*]

[This section was inserted by the *Companies (Audit, Investigations and Community Enterprise) Act* 2004, s.25(1), and Sched. 2, paras 16 and 17.]

Entry and search of premises

448.—(1) A justice of the peace may issue a warrant under this section if satisfied on information on oath given by or on behalf of the Secretary of State, or by a person appointed or **30–22**

authorised to exercise powers under this Part, that there are reasonable grounds for believing that there are on any premises documents whose production has been required under this Part and which have not been produced in compliance with the requirement.

(2) A justice of the peace may also issue a warrant under this section if satisfied on information on oath given by or on behalf of the Secretary of State, or by a person appointed or authorised to exercise powers under this Part—

(a) that there are reasonable grounds for believing that an offence has been committed for which the penalty on conviction on indictment is imprisonment for a term of not less than two years and that there are on any premises documents relating to whether the offence has been committed,

(b) that the Secretary of State, or the person so appointed or authorised, has power to require the production of the documents under this Part, and

(c) that there are reasonable grounds for believing that if production was so required the documents would not be produced but would be removed from the premises, hidden, tampered with or destroyed.

(3) A warrant under this section shall authorise a constable, together with any other person named in it and any other constables—

(a) to enter the premises specified in the information, using such force as is reasonably necessary for the purpose;

(b) to search the premises and take possession of any documents appearing to be such documents as are mentioned in subsection (1) or (2), as the case may be, or to take, in relation to any such documents, any other steps which may appear to be necessary for preserving them or preventing interference with them;

(c) to take copies of any such documents; and

(d) to require any person named in the warrant to provide an explanation of them or to state where they may be found.

30–23 (4) If in the case of a warrant under subsection (2) the justice of the peace is satisfied on information on oath that there are reasonable grounds for believing that there are also on the premises other documents relevant to the investigation, the warrant shall also authorise the actions mentioned in subsection (3) to be taken in relation to such documents.

(5) A warrant under this section shall continue in force until the end of the period of one month beginning with the day on which it is issued.

(6) Any documents of which possession is taken under this section may be retained—

(a) for a period of three months; or

(b) if within that period proceedings to which the documents are relevant are commenced against any person for any criminal offence, until the conclusion of those proceedings.

(7) Any person who intentionally obstructs the exercise of any rights conferred by a warrant issued under this section or fails without reasonable excuse to comply with any requirement imposed in accordance with subsection (3)(d) is guilty of an offence.

(7A) A person guilty of an offence under this section is liable—

(a) on conviction on indictment, to a fine;

(b) on summary conviction, to a fine not exceeding the statutory maximum.

(8) For the purposes of sections 449 and 451A (provision for security of information) documents obtained under this section shall be treated as if they had been obtained under the provision of this Part under which their production was or, as the case may be, could have been required.

(9) [*Scotland*.]

(10) In this section "document" includes information recorded in any form.

[This section is printed as amended by the *Companies Act* 1989, s.64(1); and the *Companies Act* 2006, ss.1124 and 1295, Sched. 3, para. 2, and Sched. 16.]

The additional powers of seizure conferred by the *CJPA* 2001, s.50 (*ante*, § 15–124) apply to the power of seizure under section 448(3): *CJPA* 2001, s.50(5), and Sched. 1, para. 35.

Protection in relation to certain disclosures: information provided to Secretary of State

30–23a **448A.**—(1) A person who makes a relevant disclosure is not liable by reason only of that disclosure in any proceedings relating to a breach of an obligation of confidence.

(2) A relevant disclosure is a disclosure which satisfies each of the following conditions—

(a) it is made to the Secretary of State otherwise than in compliance with a requirement under this Part;

(b) it is of a kind that the person making the disclosure could be required to make in pursuance of this Part;

(c) the person who makes the disclosure does so in good faith and in the reasonable belief that the disclosure is capable of assisting the Secretary of State for the purposes of the exercise of his functions under this Part;

(d) the information disclosed is not more than is reasonably necessary for the purpose of assisting the Secretary of State for the purposes of the exercise of those functions;

(e) the disclosure is not one falling within subsection (3) or (4).

(3) A disclosure falls within this subsection if the disclosure is prohibited by virtue of any enactment.

(4) A disclosure falls within this subsection if—

(a) it is made by a person carrying on the business of banking or by a lawyer, and

(b) it involves the disclosure of information in respect of which he owes an obligation of confidence in that capacity.

(5) An enactment includes an enactment—

(a) comprised in, or in an instrument made under, an Act of the Scottish Parliament;

(b) comprised in subordinate legislation (within the meaning of the *Interpretation Act* 1978);

(c) whenever passed or made.

[This section was inserted by the *Companies (Audit, Investigations and Community Enterprise) Act* 2004, s.22.]

Security of information obtained

Section 449 (as substituted by the *Companies (Audit, Investigations and Community Enterprise) Act* 2004, s.25(1), and Sched. 2, paras 16 and 18, and as subsequently amended by the *Companies Act* 2006, ss.1124 and 1295, Sched. 3, para. 3, and Sched. 16), provides for the security of information obtained in pursuance of a requirement imposed under section 447, by means of a relevant disclosure within the meaning of section 448A(2), or by an investigator in consequence of the exercise of his powers under section 453A (*post*, § 30–29a), and makes it an offence to contravene the prohibition on disclosure except in specified circumstances. **30–24**

Punishment for destroying, mutilating, etc., company documents

450.—(1) An officer of a company, ..., who— **30–25**

(a) destroys, mutilates or falsifies, or is privy to the destruction, mutilation or falsification of a document affecting or relating to the company's property or affairs, or

(b) makes, or is privy to the making of, a false entry in such a document,

is guilty of an offence, unless he proves that he had no intention to conceal the state of affairs of the company or to defeat the law.

(1A) Subsection (1) applies to an officer of an authorised insurance company which is not a body corporate as it applies to an officer of a company.

(2) Such a person as above mentioned who fraudulently either parts with, alters or makes an omission in any such document or is privy to fraudulent parting with, fraudulent altering or fraudulent making of an omission in, any such document, is guilty of an offence.

(3) A person guilty of an offence under this section is liable—

(a) on conviction on indictment, to imprisonment for a term not exceeding seven years or a fine (or both);

(b) on summary conviction—

(i) in England and Wales, to imprisonment for a term not exceeding twelve months or to a fine not exceeding the statutory maximum (or both);

(ii) [*Scotland and Northern Ireland*].

(5) In this section "document" includes information recorded in any form.

[This section is printed as amended by the *Companies Act* 1989, s.66; the *Financial Services and Markets Act 2000 (Consequential Amendments and Repeals) Order*

2001 (S.I. 2001 No. 3649), art. 23; and the *Companies Act* 2006, ss.1124 and 1295, Sched. 3, para. 4, and Sched. 16.]

Section 1131 of the *Companies Act* 2006 applies to any provision of "the *Companies Acts*" that provides that a person guilty of an offence is liable on summary conviction to imprisonment for a term not exceeding 12 months, and stipulates that in relation to offences committed before the commencement of the *CJA* 2003, s.154(1) (*ante*, § 5–268), the maximum penalty on summary conviction is six months' imprisonment. Section 2(1) of the 2006 Act defines "the *Companies Acts*" as the "the company law provisions of this Act", Part 2 of the *Companies (Audit, Investigations and Community Enterprise) Act* 2004, and the provisions of the 1985 Act that remain in force. The "company law provisions" of the 2006 Act are specified as being Parts 1 to 39 and Parts 45 to 47, so far as they apply for the purposes of those parts.

Punishment for furnishing false information

30–26 **451.**—(1) A person commits an offence if in purported compliance with a requirement under section 447 to provide information—

(a) he provides information which he knows to be false in a material particular;

(b) he recklessly provides information which is false in a material particular.

(2) A person guilty of an offence under this section is liable—

(a) on conviction on indictment, to imprisonment for a term not exceeding two years or a fine (or both);

(b) [*identical to s.450(3)(b)*, ante, *§ 30–25*].

[This section is printed as substituted by the *Companies (Audit, Investigations and Community Enterprise) Act* 2004, s.25(1), and Sched. 2, paras 16 and 19; and as subsequently amended by the *Companies Act* 2006, ss.1124 and 1295, Sched. 3, para. 5, and Sched. 16.]

As to the effect of section 1131 of the 2006 Act, see *ante*, § 30–25.

30–27 By virtue of section 451A of the *C.A.* 1985 (as amended by the *Companies (Audit, Investigations and Community Enterprise) Act* 2004, s.25(1), and Sched. 2, paras 16 and 20, and the *Companies Act* 2006, s.1037(2)), the Secretary of State may disclose, or authorise or require an inspector to disclose, information obtained under sections 434 to 446E or by an inspector in consequence of the exercise of his powers under section 453A (*post*, § 30–29a), to any person to whom, or for any purpose for which, disclosure is permitted under section 449: see *ante*, § 30–24. Section 451A(5) provides for disclosure of information obtained under section 444 to the company whose ownership was under investigation, and to any member, investigated person, auditor, or person whose financial interests appear to be affected by the investigated matters. Disclosure is also available in certain other limited circumstances.

Companies Act 1985, ss.452–453D

Supplementary

Privileged information

30–28 **452.**—(1) Nothing in sections 431 to 446E compels the disclosure by any person to the Secretary of State or to an inspector appointed by him of information in respect of which in an action in the High Court a claim to legal professional privilege, or in an action in the Court of Session a claim to confidentiality of communications, could be maintained.

(1A) Nothing in section 434, 443 or 446 requires a person (except as mentioned in subsection (1B) below) to disclose information or produce documents in respect of which he owes an obligation of confidence by virtue of carrying on the business of banking unless—

(a) the person to whom the obligation of confidence is owed is the company or other body corporate under investigation,

(b) the person to whom the obligation of confidence is owed consents to the disclosure or production, or

(c) the making of the requirement is authorised by the Secretary of State.

(1B) Subsection (1A) does not apply where the person owing the obligation of confidence is the company or other body corporate under investigation under section 431, 432 or 433.

(2) Nothing in sections 447 to 451—

(a) compels the production by any person of a document or the disclosure by any person of information in respect of which in an action in the High Court a claim to legal professional privilege, or in an action in the Court of Session a claim to confidentiality of communications, could be maintained;

(b) authorises the taking of possession of any such document which is in the person's possession.

(3) The Secretary of State must not under section 447 require, or authorise a person to require—

(a) the production by a person carrying on the business of banking of a document relating to the affairs of a customer of his, or

(b) the disclosure by him of information relating to those affairs, unless one of the conditions in subsection (4) is met.

(4) The conditions are—

(a) the Secretary of State thinks it is necessary to do so for the purpose of investigating the affairs of the person carrying on the business of banking;

(b) the customer is a person on whom a requirement has been imposed under section 447;

(c) the customer is a person on whom a requirement to produce information or documents has been imposed by an investigator appointed by the Secretary of State in pursuance of section 171 or 173 of the *Financial Services and Markets Act* 2000 (powers of persons appointed under section 167 or as a result of section 168(2) to conduct an investigation).

(5) Despite subsections (1) and (2) a person who is a lawyer may be compelled to disclose the name and address of his client.

[This section is printed as amended by the *Companies Act* 1989; the *Companies (Audit, Investigations and Community Enterprise) Act* 2004, s.25(1) and Sched. 2, paras 16 and 21; and the *Companies Act* 2006, s.1037(3).]

Investigation of overseas companies

453.—(1) The provisions of this Part apply to bodies corporate incorporated outside Great Britain which are carrying on business in Great Britain, or have at any time carried on business there, as they apply to companies under this Act; but subject to the following exceptions, adaptations and modifications. **30–29**

(1A) The following provisions do not apply to such bodies—

(a) section 431 (investigation on application of company or its members),

(b) ...

(c) sections 442 to 445 (investigation of company ownership and power to obtain information as to those interested in shares, &c.).

(1B) The other provisions of this Part apply to such bodies subject to such adaptations and modifications as may be specified by regulations made by the Secretary of State.

(2) [*Power to make regulations.*]

[This section is printed as amended, and as repealed in part, by the *Companies Act* 1989, s.70; and the *Companies Act* 2006, ss.1176(3) and 1295, and Sched. 16.]

Power to enter and remain on premises

453A.—(1) An inspector or investigator may act under subsection (2) in relation to a company if— **30–29a**

(a) he is authorised to do so by the Secretary of State, and

(b) he thinks that to do so will materially assist him in the exercise of his functions under this Part in relation to the company.

(2) An inspector or investigator may at all reasonable times—

(a) require entry to relevant premises, and

(b) remain there for such period as he thinks necessary for the purpose mentioned in subsection (1)(b).

(3) Relevant premises are premises which the inspector or investigator believes are used (wholly or partly) for the purposes of the company's business.

(4) In exercising his powers under subsection (2), an inspector or investigator may be accompanied by such other persons as he thinks appropriate.

(5) A person who intentionally obstructs a person lawfully acting under subsection (2) or (4) is guilty of an offence.

(5A) [*Identical to s.448(7A)*, ante, *§ 30–23*.]

(7) An inspector is a person appointed under section 431, 432 or 442.

(8) An investigator is a person authorised for the purposes of section 447.

[This section is printed as amended, and repealed in part, by the *Companies Act* 2006, ss.1124 and 1295, Sched. 3, para. 6, and Sched. 16.]

Power to enter and remain on premises: procedural

30–29b **453B.**—(1) This section applies for the purposes of section 453A.

(2) The requirements of subsection (3) must be complied with at the time an inspector or investigator seeks to enter relevant premises under section 453A(2)(a).

(3) The requirements are—

(a) the inspector or investigator must produce evidence of his identity and evidence of his appointment or authorisation (as the case may be);

(b) any person accompanying the inspector or investigator must produce evidence of his identity.

(4) The inspector or investigator must, as soon as practicable after obtaining entry, give to an appropriate recipient a written statement containing such information as to—

(a) the powers of the investigator or inspector (as the case may be) under section 453A;

(b) the rights and obligations of the company, occupier and the persons present on the premises, as may be prescribed by regulations.

(5) If during the time the inspector or investigator is on the premises there is no person present who appears to him to be an appropriate recipient for the purposes of subsection (8), the inspector or investigator must as soon as reasonably practicable send to the company—

(a) a notice of the fact and time that the visit took place, and

(b) the statement mentioned in subsection (4).

(6) As soon as reasonably practicable after exercising his powers under section 453A(2), the inspector or investigator must prepare a written record of the visit and—

(a) if requested to do so by the company he must give it a copy of the record;

(b) in a case where the company is not the sole occupier of the premises, if requested to do so by an occupier he must give the occupier a copy of the record.

(7) The written record must contain such information as may be prescribed by regulations.

(8) If the inspector or investigator thinks that the company is the sole occupier of the premises an appropriate recipient is a person who is present on the premises and who appears to the inspector or investigator to be—

(a) an officer of the company, or

(b) a person otherwise engaged in the business of the company if the inspector or investigator thinks that no officer of the company is present on the premises.

(9) If the inspector or investigator thinks that the company is not the occupier or sole occupier of the premises an appropriate recipient is—

(a) a person who is an appropriate recipient for the purposes of subsection (8), and (if different)

(b) a person who is present on the premises and who appears to the inspector or investigator to be an occupier of the premises or otherwise in charge of them.

(10) A statutory instrument containing regulations made under this section is subject to annulment in pursuance of a resolution of either House of Parliament.

Failure to comply with certain requirements

30–29c **453C.**—(1) This section applies if a person fails to comply with a requirement imposed by an inspector, the Secretary of State or an investigator in pursuance of either of the following provisions—

(a) section 447;

(b) section 453A.

(2) The inspector, Secretary of State or investigator (as the case may be) may certify the fact in writing to the court.

(3) If, after hearing—

(a) any witnesses who may be produced against or on behalf of the alleged offender;

(b) any statement which may be offered in defence,

the court is satisfied that the offender failed without reasonable excuse to comply with the requirement, it may deal with him as if he had been guilty of contempt of the court.

[Ss.453A to 453C were inserted by the *Companies (Audit, Investigations and Community Enterprise) Act* 2004, ss.23 and 24.]

Offences by body corporate

453D. Where an offence under any of sections 448, 449 to 451 and 453A is committed by a body corporate, every officer of the body who is in default also commits the offence. **29–29d**

For this purpose—

(a) any person who purports to act as director, manager or secretary of the body is treated as an officer of the body, and

(b) if the body is a company, any shadow director is treated as an officer of the company.

[S.453D was inserted by the *Companies Act 2006 (Consequential Amendments etc.) Order* 2008 (S.I. 2008 No. 948), art. 3(1), and Sched. 1, Pt 2, para. 82.]

The power to examine a company's records is the investigative power most frequently invoked by the Secretary of State. The power of investigation under section 447 is generally exercised on behalf of the Secretary of State by officials of the Companies Investigation Branch, part of the regulatory arm of the Department for Business, Enterprise and Regulatory Reform. Although the investigation branch is located within the Insolvency Service, an executive agency of the department, it is not limited to companies that have become insolvent. Most of its investigations are into companies that are actively trading. **30–30**

There is no obligation to produce documents that are subject to legal professional privilege or (in certain circumstances) banking documents. However, in the light of the reasoning of the civil division of the Court of Appeal in *Re London United Investments plc* [1992] Ch. 578, it is submitted that the common law privilege against self-incrimination cannot apply to investigations under section 447 and persons may not refuse to supply or to explain the records of a company on that ground. See also the *Fraud Act* 2006, s.13 (*ante*, § 21–413). **30–31**

Investigations carried out under section 447 are not announced; the information obtained is generally confidential and may be the subject of a claim to public interest immunity. **30–32**

In connection with section 453B, see the *Companies Act 1985 (Power to Enter and Remain on Premises: Procedural) Regulations* 2005 (S.I. 2005 No. 684).

B. INSOLVENCY ACT 1986

(1) Investigations by an administrator

Insolvency Act 1986, Sched. B1, paras 47, 48

Statement of company's affairs

47.—(1) As soon as is reasonably practicable after appointment the administrator of a company shall by notice in the prescribed form require one or more relevant persons to provide the administrator with a statement of the affairs of the company. **30–33**

(2) The statement must—

(a) be verified by a statement of truth in accordance with Civil Procedure Rules,

(b) be in the prescribed form,

(c) give particulars of the company's property, debts and liabilities,

(d) give the names and addresses of the company's creditors,

(e) specify the security held by each creditor,

(f) give the date on which each security was granted, and

(g) contain such other information as may be prescribed.

(3) In sub-paragraph (1) "relevant person" means—

(a) a person who is or has been an officer of the company,

(b) a person who took part in the formation of the company during the period of one year ending with the date on which the company enters administration,

(c) a person employed by the company during that period, and

(d) a person who is or has been during that period an officer or employee of a company which is or has been during that year an officer of the company.

(4) For the purpose of sub-paragraph (3) a reference to employment is a reference to employment through a contract of employment or a contract for services.

(5) [*Scotland*].

30–34 48.—(1) A person required to submit a statement of affairs must do so before the end of the period of 11 days beginning with the day on which he receives notice of the requirement.

(2) The administrator may—

(a) revoke a requirement under paragraph 47(1), or

(b) extend the period specified in sub-paragraph (1) (whether before or after expiry).

(3) If the administrator refuses a request to act under sub-paragraph (2)—

(a) the person whose request is refused may apply to the court, and

(b) the court may take action of a kind specified in sub-paragraph (2).

(4) A person commits an offence if he fails without reasonable excuse to comply with a requirement under paragraph 47(1).

[Sched. B1 was inserted by the *Enterprise Act* 2002, s.248, and Sched. 16 as from September 15, 2003 (*Enterprise Act 2002 (Commencement No. 4 and Transitional Provisions and Savings) Order* 2003 (S.I. 2003 No. 2093)).]

30–35 The administration order procedure was first introduced in the *Insolvency Act* 1985 as a result of one of the recommendations contained in the Report of the Insolvency Law Review Committee (the *Cork Report*), Cmnd. No. 8558 (1982). The process of administration was subject to substantial amendment in the *Enterprise Act* 2002. The Act streamlined the process of administration and restricted the use of administrative receivership. It introduced a single, clearly defined purpose for administration under paragraph 3 of Schedule B1. The administrator is to perform his functions with the primary objective of rescuing the company as a going concern, which should be taken to mean with as much as possible of its business. If this is not reasonably practicable, the administrator should pursue the objective of achieving a better result for the creditors as a whole than would be likely if the company were wound up, *e.g.* by allowing the company to trade for long enough to complete a large order. If this second objective would achieve a better result for the creditors as a whole than the first, then this objective may be pursued. Finally, where it is not reasonably practicable to achieve either of the first two, the objective will be to realise property to make a distribution to one or more secured or preferential creditors. Where an interim receiver has already been appointed under the *PCA* 2002, see *Re Q3 Media Ltd* (2006) 150 S.J. 705, Ch D (Rimer J.).

30–36 The first task of the administrator is to ascertain and investigate the state of the company's affairs. Paragraph 47 of Schedule B1 requires the administrator to obtain a statement as to the affairs of the company from those who are or have been connected with the company, such as officers or employees of the company or those who have taken part in the company's formation. The statement must be verified by affidavit and must show the company's assets, debts and liabilities, the names and addresses of the company's creditors, and provide details of the securities held by them. It is submitted that, in the light of the reasoning of the Court of Appeal in *Bishopsgate Investment Management Ltd v. Maxwell* [1993] Ch. 1, the common law privilege against self-incrimination cannot be invoked by those persons who are required to submit a statement of affairs. However, the statement of affairs may only be used in evidence in criminal proceedings in the circumstances specified in section 433(2) of the *Insolvency Act* 1986, *post*, § 30–74.

30–37 Paragraph 67 of Schedule B1 requires the administrator to take under his control all the property of the company. To this end he may invoke the assistance of the court by seeking an order of the court under section 234 (*post*, § 30–53) for the delivery up of any property, books, papers or records of the company. Further assistance for the administrator in investigating the company's affairs is to be found in sections 235 and 236 (*post*, §§ 30–54 *et seq.*), which impose duties on persons connected with the company to assist the administrator.

(2) Investigation by an administrative receiver

30–38 Typically when lending money to a company, a bank will take as security a charge over most or all of the assets of a company. The deed authorises the bank to appoint a receiver and manager of the company's undertaking, with power to carry on the company's business. Such a receiver is referred to in the *Insolvency Act* 1986 as an "administrative receiver", see *Re Atlantic Computer Systems plc* [1992] Ch. 505, Ch D. The provisions of this part of the *Insolvency Act* 1986 apply both to companies formed and registered under the *Companies Act* 1985 and to overseas companies liable to be wound up under Part V of the *Insolvency Act* 1986, see *Re International Bulk Commodities Ltd* [1993] Ch. 77, Ch D. It is questionable whether this part applies to unregistered companies, see *Re Devon & Somerset Farmers Ltd* [1994] Ch. 57, Ch D. As the result of changes made to the insolvency scheme in the *Enterprise Act* 2002 the ability of lenders to appoint an administrative receiver is restricted to the holders of pre-existing floating charges and financiers involved in certain capital market and other transactions where the ability to appoint an administrative receiver is fundamental to the effective operation of the market. The appointment of an administrative receiver effectively suspends the authority of the directors and places the company in the hands of the administrative receiver. The powers of the administrative receiver are set out in sections 42 and 43 of the *Insolvency Act* 1986.

An administrative receiver is under a duty to ascertain and investigate the state of the company's affairs. Section 47 of the *Insolvency Act* 1986 requires the administrative receiver to obtain a statement as to the affairs of the company from those who are or have been connected with the company. The detailed provisions thereof mirror those of paragraph 47 of Schedule B1 (*ante*, § 30–33). What was said in relation to a statement of affairs obtained by an administrator (*ante*, § 30–36) applies equally to a statement of affairs obtained by an administrative receiver. Furthermore, an administrative receiver may also take advantage of sections 234 to 236 of the 1986 Act (*post*, §§ 30–53 *et seq.*). **30–39**

(3) Investigation by a nominee or supervisor

Amendments made to the *Insolvency Act* 1986 by the *Insolvency Act* 2000 permit small companies in financial difficulty to make voluntary arrangements with their creditors by providing the option of a moratorium to give the firm's management time to put a rescue plan to creditors. The arrangement is subject to the oversight of a nominee or supervisor who is required to report suspected offences in connection with the moratorium or voluntary arrangement to the Secretary of State in England and Wales (see section 7A(2)). Where such a report is made, the Secretary of State may, for the purpose of investigating the matter reported to him and such other matters relating to the affairs of the company as appear to him to require investigation, exercise any of the powers which are exercisable by inspectors appointed under section 431 or 432 of the *Companies Act* 1985 to investigate a company's affairs. The obligation to assist the Secretary of State is identical to that under the 1985 Act. However, in criminal proceedings, evidence obtained from a defendant may only be used in a limited range of circumstances (see subs.7A(6)). **30–39a**

(4) Investigation in winding up

Insolvency Act 1986, ss.112, 131

CHAPTER V

PROVISIONS APPLYING TO BOTH KINDS OF VOLUNTARY WINDING UP

Reference of questions to the court

112.—(1) The liquidator or any contributory or creditor may apply to the court to determine any question arising in the winding up of a company, or to exercise as respects the enforcing of calls or any other matter, all or any of the powers which the court might exercise if the company were being wound up by the court. **30–40**

(2) The court, if satisfied that the determination of the question or the required exercise of power will be just and beneficial, may accede wholly or partially to the application on such terms and conditions as it thinks fit, or may make such other order on the application as it thinks just.

(3) [*Not printed in this work.*]

CHAPTER VI

WINDING UP BY THE COURT

Investigation procedures

Company's statement of affairs

30–41 **131.**—(1) Where the court has made a winding-up order or appointed a provisional liquidator, the official receiver may require some or all of the persons mentioned in subsection (3) below to make out and submit to him a statement in the prescribed form as to the affairs of the company.

(2)–(5) [*Identical in substance to Sched. B1, paras 47(2)–48(3)*, ante, *§§ 30–33, 30–34*.]

(6) In this section—

"employment" includes employment under a contract for services; and

"the relevant date" means—

(a) in a case where a provisional liquidator is appointed, the date of his appointment; and

(b) in a case where no such appointment is made, the date of the winding-up order.

(7) [*Identical to Sched. B1, para. 48(4)*, ante, *§ 30–34*.]

(8) [*Scotland*.]

As to circumstances in which the court will make a winding up order, see section 122. As to the appointment and powers of the provisional liquidator, see section 135.

Insolvency Act 1986, ss.132–134

Investigation by official receiver

30–42 **132.**—(1) Where a winding-up order is made by the court in England and Wales, it is the duty of the official receiver to investigate—

(a) if the company has failed, the causes of the failure; and

(b) generally, the promotion, formation, business, dealings and affairs of the company,

and to make such report (if any) to the court as he thinks fit.

(2) The report is, in any proceedings, prima facie evidence of the facts stated in it.

Public examination of officers

30–43 **133.**—(1) Where a company is being wound up by the court, the official receiver or, in Scotland, the liquidator may at any time before the dissolution of the company apply to the court for the public examination of any person who—

(a) is or has been an officer of the company; or

(b) has acted as liquidator or administrator of the company or as receiver or manager or, in Scotland, receiver of its property; or

(c) not being a person falling within paragraph (a) or (b), is or has been concerned, or has taken part, in the promotion, formation or management of the company.

(2) Unless the court otherwise orders, the official receiver or, in Scotland, the liquidator shall make an application under subsection (1) if he is requested in accordance with the rules to do so by—

(a) one-half, in value, of the company's creditors; or

(b) three-quarters, in value, of the company's contributories.

(3) On an application under subsection (1), the court shall direct that a public examination of the person to whom the application relates shall be held on a day appointed by the court; and that person shall attend on that day and be publicly examined as to the promotion, formation or management of the company or as to the conduct of its business and affairs, or his conduct or dealings in relation to the company.

(4) The following may take part in the public examination of a person under this section and may question that person concerning the matters mentioned in subsection (3), namely—

(a) the official receiver;

(b) the liquidator of the company;

(c) any person who has been appointed as special manager of the company's property or business;

(d) any creditor of the company who has tendered a proof or, in Scotland, submitted a claim in the winding up;

(e) any contributory of the company.

Enforcement of section 133

134.—(1) If a person without reasonable excuse fails at any time to attend his public examination under section 133, he is guilty of a contempt of court and liable to be punished accordingly. **30–44**

(2) In a case where a person without reasonable excuse fails at any time to attend his examination under section 133 or there are reasonable grounds for believing that a person has absconded, or is about to abscond, with a view to avoiding or delaying his examination under that section, the court may cause a warrant to be issued to a constable or prescribed officer of the court—

(a) for the arrest of that person; and

(b) for the seizure of any books, papers, records, money or goods in that person's possession.

(3) In such a case the court may authorise the person arrested under the warrant to be kept in custody, and anything seized under such a warrant to be held, in accordance with the rules, until such time as the court may order.

CHAPTER X

MALPRACTICE BEFORE AND DURING LIQUIDATION;
PENALISATION OF COMPANIES AND COMPANY OFFICERS;
INVESTIGATIONS AND PROSECUTIONS

Offences of fraud, deception, etc.

206.–211. [*See* post, *§§ 30–160* et seq.] **30–45**

Penalisation of directors and officers

212.–217. [*See* post, *§§ 30–166* et seq.] **30–46**

Insolvency Act 1986, ss.218, 219

Investigation and prosecution of malpractice

Prosecution of delinquent officers and members of company

218.—(1) If it appears to the court in the course of a winding up by the court that any past or present officer, or any member, of the company has been guilty of any offence in relation to the company for which he is criminally liable, the court may (either on the application of a person interested in the winding up or of its own motion) direct the liquidator to refer the matter— **30–47**

(a) in the case of a winding up in England and Wales, to the Secretary of State, and

(b) in the case of a winding up in Scotland, to the Lord Advocate.

(3) If in the case of a winding up by the court in England and Wales it appears to the liquidator, not being the official receiver, that any past or present officer of the company, or any member of it, has been guilty of an offence in relation to the company for which he is criminally liable, the liquidator shall report the matter to the official receiver.

(4) If it appears to the liquidator in the course of a voluntary winding up that any past or present officer of the company, or any member of it, has been guilty of an offence in relation to the company for which he is criminally liable, he shall forthwith report the matter—

(a) in the case of a winding up in England and Wales, to the Secretary of State, and

(b) in the case of a winding up in Scotland, to the Lord Advocate,

and shall furnish to the Secretary of State or (as the case may be), the Lord Advocate, such information and give to him such access to and facilities for inspecting and taking copies of documents (being information or documents in the possession or under the control of the liquidator and relating to the matter in question) as the Secretary of State or (as the case may be) the Lord Advocate requires.

(5) Where a report is made to the Secretary of State under subsection (4), he may, for **30–48**

the purpose of investigating the matter reported to him and such other matters relating to the affairs of the company as appear to him to require investigation, exercise any of the powers which are exercisable by inspectors appointed under section 431 or 432 of the *Companies Act* to investigate a company's affairs.

(6) If it appears to the court in the course of a voluntary winding up that—

(a) any past or present officer of the company, or any member of it, has been guilty as above-mentioned, and

(b) no report with respect to the matter has been made by the liquidator under subsection (4),

the court may (on the application of any person interested in the winding up or of its own motion) direct the liquidator to make such a report.

On the report being made accordingly, this section has effect as though the report has been made in pursuance of subsection (4).

[This section is printed as amended by the *Insolvency Act* 2000, s.10.]

Obligations arising under section 218

30–49 **219.**—(1) For the purpose of an investigation by the Secretary of State in consequence of a report made to him under section 218(4), any obligation imposed on a person by any provision of the *Companies Act* to produce documents or give information to, or otherwise to assist, inspectors appointed as mentioned in section 218(5) is to be regarded as an obligation similarly to assist the Secretary of State in his investigation.

(2) An answer given by a person to a question put to him in exercise of the powers conferred by section 218(5) may be used in evidence against him.

(2A) However, in criminal proceedings in which that person is charged with an offence to which this subsection applies—

(a) no evidence relating to the answer may be adduced, and

(b) no question relating to it may be asked,

by or on behalf of the prosecution, unless evidence relating to it is adduced, or a question relating to it is asked, in the proceedings by or on behalf of that person.

(2B) Subsection (2A) applies to any offence other than—

(a) an offence under section 2 or 5 of the *Perjury Act* 1911 (false statements made on oath otherwise than in judicial proceedings or made otherwise than on oath), or

(b) [*Scotland*].

(3) Where criminal proceedings are instituted by the Director of Public Prosecutions, the Lord Advocate or the Secretary of State following any report or reference under section 218, it is the duty of the liquidator and every officer and agent of the company past and present (other than the defendant or defender) to give to the Director of Public Prosecutions, the Lord Advocate or the Secretary of State (as the case may be) all assistance in connection with the prosecution which he is reasonably able to give.

For this purpose "agent" includes any banker or solicitor of the company and any person employed by the company as auditor, whether that person is or is not an officer of the company.

(4) If a person fails or neglects to give assistance in the manner required by subsection (3), the court may, on the application of the Director of Public Prosecutions, the Lord Advocate or the Secretary of State (as the case may be) direct the person to comply with that subsection; and if the application is made with respect to a liquidator, the court may (unless it appears that the failure or neglect to comply was due to the liquidator not having in his hands sufficient assets of the company to enable him to do so) direct that the costs shall be borne by the liquidator personally.

[This section is printed as amended by the *Insolvency Act* 2000, ss.10 and 11.]

30–50 There are two ways of winding up a company. The first is a compulsory winding up by the court. The second is a voluntary winding up, which may be either a members' voluntary winding up or a creditors' voluntary winding up. Under either mode the company ceases to carry on business save as may be required for the beneficial winding up, and the directors' powers cease. In a compulsory liquidation, the court has power under section 135 of the *Insolvency Act* 1986 to appoint a liquidator provisionally at any time after the presentation of a winding up petition. In practice, the provisional liquidator appointed is generally the official receiver. Under section 136, the official receiver becomes the liquidator after a winding up order has been made until such time as another person is appointed as liquidator. The court may, on an application by the liquidator or provisional liquidator, appoint a special manager: see section 177 of the

Insolvency Act 1986. By virtue of section 112 of that Act there is not necessarily any difference in the powers of investigation in a voluntary winding up as compared to a compulsory winding up save that, in a voluntary winding up, a court order is required before any of the statutory powers of investigation vested in the official receiver may be exercised.

Where a winding up order is made or a provisional liquidator is appointed, the official receiver has a discretion as to whether or not he will require certain officers or employees of the company to supply him with a statement of affairs. The statement must be verified by affidavit and must show the company's assets, debts and liabilities, the names and addresses of the company's creditors, and provide details of the securities held by them and any further information that may be required. In practice the official receiver supplies standard forms and guidance as to their completion to those persons selected to complete a statement of affairs. **30–51**

Sections 133 and 134 make provision for the public examination of officers and employees of a company which is being wound up, in a manner analogous to the public examination of individuals in bankruptcy cases. In view of the established principle of compulsion in bankruptcy cases, together with the clear legislative purpose of harmonising individual and corporate insolvency (as to which see *Bishopsgate Investment Management Ltd v. Maxwell* [1993] Ch. 1, CA (Civ. Div.)), it is submitted that a privilege against self-incrimination cannot be invoked in the course of a public examination under section 133. However, a statement made in a statement of affairs or made in the course of a public examination may only be used in evidence against the person making it in the circumstances specified in section 433(2) of the *Insolvency Act* 1986, *post*, § 30–74. The mandatory language of section 133 requires a court to make an order for public examination if the conditions in section 133(1) are satisfied, unless it appears that no useful purpose would be served thereby; for instance, because the examinee would be liable to such sanctions in a foreign jurisdiction as would make it unduly oppressive to require him to answer any questions. If, however, only some questions cannot be answered, those should be identified at the public examination: see *Re Casterbridge Properties Ltd (in liquidation)*; *Jeeves v. Official Receiver* [2004] 1 W.L.R. 602, CA (Civ. Div.). **30–52**

A provisional liquidator or a liquidator may also invoke the powers of the court under sections 234 and 236 of the *Insolvency Act* 1986: see *post*, §§ 30–53 *et seq.*

(5) General powers of office-holders

Insolvency Act 1986, ss.234–236

Getting in the company's property

234.—(1) This section applies in the case of a company where— **30–53**

(a) the company enters administration,

(b) an administrative receiver is appointed, or

(c) the company goes into liquidation, or

(d) a provisional liquidator is appointed;

and "the office-holder" means the administrator, the administrative receiver, the liquidator or the provisional liquidator, as the case may be.

(2) Where any person has in his possession or control any property, books, papers or records to which the company appears to be entitled, the court may require that person forthwith (or within such period as the court may direct) to pay, deliver, convey, surrender or transfer the property, books, papers or records to the office-holder.

(3)–(4) [*Not printed in this work.*]

[This section is printed as amended by the *Enterprise Act* 2002, s.248(3), and Sched. 17, paras 9 and 23.]

Duty to co-operate with office-holder

235.—(1) This section applies as does section 234; and it also applies, in the case of a company in respect of which a winding-up order has been made by the court in England and Wales, as if references to the office-holder included the official receiver, whether or not he is the liquidator. **30–54**

(2) Each of the persons mentioned in the next subsection shall—

(a) give to the office-holder such information concerning the company and its promotion, formation, business, dealings, affairs or property as the office-holder may at any time after the effective date reasonably require, and

(b) attend on the office-holder at such times as the latter may reasonably require.

(3) The persons referred to above are—

(a) those who are or have at any time been officers of the company,

(b) those who have taken part in the formation of the company at any time within one year before the effective date,

(c) those who are in the employment of the company, or have been in its employment (including employment under a contract for services) within that year, and are in the office-holder's opinion capable of giving information which he requires,

(d) those who are, or have within that year been, officers of, or in the employment (including employment under a contract for services) of, another company which is, or within that year was, an officer of the company in question, and

(e) in the case of a company being wound up by the court, any person who has acted as administrator, administrative receiver or liquidator of the company.

(4) For the purposes of subsections (2) and (3), "the effective date" is whichever is applicable of the following dates—

(a) the date on which the company entered administration,

(b) the date on which the administrative receiver was appointed or, if he was appointed in succession to another administrative receiver, the date on which the first of his predecessors was appointed,

(c) the date on which the provisional liquidator was appointed, and

(d) the date on which the company went into liquidation.

(5) If a person without reasonable excuse fails to comply with any obligation imposed by this section, he is liable to a fine and, for continued contravention, to a daily default fine.

[This section is printed as amended by the *Enterprise Act* 2002, s.248(3), and Sched. 17, paras 9 and 24.]

Inquiry into company's dealings, etc.

30–55 **236.**—(1) [*Identical to s.235(1)*, ante.]

(2) The court may, on the application of the office-holder, summon to appear before it—

(a) any officer of the company,

(b) any person known or suspected to have in his possession any property of the company or supposed to be indebted to the company, or

(c) any person whom the court think capable of giving information concerning the promotion, formation, business dealings, affairs or property of the company.

(3) The court may require any such person as is mentioned in subsection (2)(a) to (c) to submit an affidavit to the court containing an account of his dealings with the company or to produce any books, papers or other records in his possession or under his control relating to the company or the matters mentioned in paragraph (c) of the subsection.

(4) The following applies in a case where—

(a) a person without reasonable excuse fails to appear before the court when he is summoned to do so under this section, or

(b) there are reasonable grounds for believing that a person has absconded, or is about to abscond, with a view to avoiding his appearance before the court under this section.

(5) The court may for the purpose of bringing that person and anything in his possession before the court, cause a warrant to be issued to a constable or prescribed officer of the court—

(a) for the arrest of that person, and

(b) for the seizure of any books, papers or other records in that person's possession.

(6) The court may authorise a person arrested under such a warrant to be kept in custody, and anything seized under such a warrant to be held, in accordance with the rules, until that person is brought before the court under the warrant or until such other time as the court may order.

30–56 In the light of information gained by the investigative procedures under section 236, the court may order the delivery up of company property to the office holder by those persons found to be in possession of it (s.237(1)), and may order persons found to be indebted to the company to make full or partial payment to the office holder (s.237(2)). Section 237(3) makes provision for the examination of persons outside the jurisdiction of the court, and section 237(4) provides that any person who appears or is brought before the court under section 236 or section 237, may be examined on oath, either orally or by interrogatories concerning the company or the matters mentioned in section 236(2)(c).

Section 235 imposes a duty on officers, employees and office-holders of a company to co-operate with the office-holder or the official receiver of the company both by attending on them and also by giving them information concerning the company and its promotion, formation, business, dealings, affairs or property. Persons failing without reasonable excuse to comply with these obligations are liable to a fine. In addition, under rule 7.20(1)(c) of the *Insolvency Rules* 1986 (S.I. 1986 No. 1925) the court may make such orders as it thinks necessary for the enforcement of the obligations falling on any persons in accordance with section 235. The procedure adopted in relation to section 235 is generally informal. If a witness is unco-operative then the office-holder will normally have recourse to the formal procedures under section 236. In *Re Arrows Ltd (No. 4)* [1995] 2 A.C. 75, HL, Lord Browne-Wilkinson said that there was a substantial public interest in ensuring the free flow of informally obtained information under section 235. It is therefore possible that a claim of public interest immunity might arise in relation to information obtained under section 235. By way of contrast it was held that no question of public interest immunity arose in relation to information obtained under section 236. **30–57**

In *R. v. Brady* [2005] 1 Cr.App.R. 5, CA, it was held that once the Department of Trade and Industry or the official receiver is satisfied that material obtained under section 235 is required by another prosecuting authority for the purpose of investigating crime they should be free to disclose it without an order of the court or notice to the person who provided it.

Section 236 was described by Millett J. in *Re Barlow Clowes Gilt Managers Ltd* [1992] Ch. 208, Ch D, as "an extraordinary and secret mode of obtaining information". The purpose of the power is to enable the office-holder to get sufficient material to enable him to carry out his statutory function. In *Re British & Commonwealth Holdings plc (Nos 1 and 2)* [1993] A.C. 426, the House of Lords confirmed that the power was not limited to the obtaining of documents and information that could be said to be necessary to reconstitute the company's state of knowledge but extended to anything reasonably required by the office-holder to carry out his functions. However, the House of Lords also confirmed that the court must balance the reasonable requirements of the office-holder against the need to avoid making an order which was unreasonable, unnecessary or oppressive to the person concerned. See also *Re Cloverbay Ltd (No. 2)* [1991] 1 Ch. 90, Ch D. The different degrees of coercion involved may affect the judgment of the court on the question of oppression: *Official Receiver v. Stern* [2000] 1 W.L.R. 2230, Ch D. The court may order the production of information or of a document under section 236 even where it is in a foreign jurisdiction: see *Re Mid East Trading Ltd* [1997] 3 All E.R. 481, Ch D. The detailed provisions relating to applications for, and the conduct of, examinations under section 236 are contained in the *Insolvency Rules* 1986 (S.I. 1986 No. 1925). **30–58**

The examination takes place before a judge or registrar. The witness is entitled to legal representation and is entitled to advance notice, in general terms, of the topics on which he is to be examined. The record of such examination is subject to special statutory provisions relating to its custody and release which are designed to protect the witness from unauthorised disclosure, see *Macmillan Inc. v. Bishopsgate Investment Trust plc (No. 2)* [1993] 1 W.L.R. 837, Ch D. The witness has an obligation to give the best answer possible: *In re Richbell Strategic Holdings Ltd (No. 2)* [2000] 2 B.C.L.C. 794, Ch D.

A person subject to examination under section 236 may not refuse to answer questions on the ground that he may incriminate himself: *Bishopsgate Investment Management Ltd v. Maxwell* [1993] Ch. 1, CA (Civ. Div.). Further, in *Re Arrows Ltd (No. 2)* [1992] Ch. 545, CA (Civ. Div.), it was held that the fact that criminal proceedings have been commenced against an examinee was no bar to the making of an order under **30–59** section 236. A statement made by an examinee may not be used in evidence against him in criminal proceedings, save as provided by section 433(2), *post*, § 30–74. Section 433 does not, however, confer "derivative use immunity"; and a transcript obtained by prosecuting authorities may be used to construct a criminal case against the examinee. Access to the transcript is in the control of the courts: *Re RBG Resources plc*; *Shierson v. Rastogi* [2003] 1 W.L.R. 586, CA (Civ. Div.).

In *Re Pantmaenog Timber Co. Ltd* [2004] 1 A.C. 158, HL, it was held that a liquidator's functions in relation to a company that was being wound up are not limited to the recovery and distribution of assets, but extend to the investigations of the causes of the company's failure and the conduct of those concerned in its management, in the wider interest of appropriate action being taken against those engaged in commercially culpable conduct; and, accordingly, the powers conferred by section 236 could lawfully be exercised for the purpose only of obtaining evidence for use in disqualification proceedings.

30–60 Office-holders are entitled to seek orders under section 236 to compel statutory bodies (including the Serious Fraud Office) to produce documents relating to an insolvent company which have been obtained under the statutory bodies' compulsory powers. Those from whom the documents were originally seized are entitled to be heard by the court which is required to balance the competing interests: *Morris v. Director of the Serious Fraud Office* [1993] Ch. 372, Ch D. The Serious Fraud Office are in turn entitled to issue notices under section 2(3) of the *CJA* 1987 to compel office-holders to produce documents relating to an insolvent company which have been obtained under section 236 including transcripts of interviews, see *Re Arrows Ltd (No. 4)*, *ante* (and see *ante*, § 1–285). There is no equivalent right vested in defendants to obtain documents or transcripts from office-holders for the purposes of criminal proceedings, see *R. v. Maxwell*, unreported, February 9, 1995, CA, even if the defendant is a former director of the insolvent company, see *Re DPR Futures Ltd* [1989] 1 W.L.R. 778, Ch D.

(6) Investigation of a bankrupt's affairs

Insolvency Act 1986, ss.288–291

Investigation of bankrupt's affairs

Statement of affairs

30–61 **288.**—(1) Where a bankruptcy order has been made otherwise than on a debtor's petition, the bankrupt shall submit a statement of his affairs to the official receiver before the end of the period of 21 days beginning with the commencement of the bankruptcy.

(2) The statement of affairs shall contain—

(a) such particulars of the bankrupt's creditors and of his debts and other liabilities and of his assets as may be prescribed, and

(b) such other information as may be prescribed.

(3) The official receiver may, if he thinks fit—

(a) release the bankrupt from his duty under subsection (1), or

(b) extend the period specified in that subsection;

and where the official receiver has refused to exercise a power conferred by this section, the court, if it thinks fit, may exercise it.

(4) A bankrupt who—

(a) without reasonable excuse fails to comply with the obligation imposed under this section, or

(b) without reasonable excuse submits a statement of affairs that does not comply with the prescribed requirements,

is guilty of a contempt of court and is liable to be punished accordingly (in addition to any other punishment to which he may be subject).

Investigatory duties of official receiver

30–62 **289.**—(1) The official receiver shall—

(a) investigate the conduct and affairs of each bankrupt (including his conduct and affairs before the making of the bankruptcy order), and

(b) make such report (if any) to the court as the official receiver thinks fit.

(2) Subsection (1) shall not apply to a case in which the official receiver thinks an investigation under that subsection unnecessary.

(3) Where a bankrupt makes an application for discharge under section 280—

(a) the official receiver shall make a report to the court about such matters as may be prescribed, and

(b) the court shall consider the report before determining the application.

(4) A report by the official receiver under this section shall in any proceedings be prima facie evidence of the facts stated in it.

[This section is printed as substituted by the *Enterprise Act* 2002, s.258.]

Public examination of bankrupt

290.—(1) Where a bankruptcy order has been made, the official receiver may at any time before the discharge of the bankrupt apply to the court for the public examination of the bankrupt. **30–63**

(2) Unless the court otherwise orders, the official receiver shall make an application under subsection (1) if notice requiring him to do so is given to him, in accordance with the rules, by one of the bankrupt's creditors with the concurrence of not less than one-half, in value, of those creditors (including the creditor giving notice).

(3) On an application under subsection (1), the court shall direct a public examination of the bankrupt shall be held on a day appointed by the court; and the bankrupt shall attend on that day to be examined as to his affairs, dealings and property.

(4) The following may take part in the public examination of the bankrupt and may question him concerning his affairs, dealings and property and the causes of his failure, namely—

(a) the official receiver and, in the case of an individual adjudged bankrupt on a petition under section 264(1)(d), the Official Petitioner,

(b) the trustee of the bankrupt's estate, if his appointment has taken effect,

(c) any person who has been appointed as special manager of the bankrupt's estate or business,

(d) any creditor of the bankrupt who has tendered a proof in the bankruptcy.

(5) If a bankrupt without reasonable excuse fails at any time to attend his public examination under this section he is guilty of a contempt of court and is liable to be punished accordingly (in addition to any other punishment to which he may be subject).

Duties of bankrupt in relation to official receiver

291.—(1) Where a bankruptcy order has been made, the bankrupt is under a duty— **30–64**

(a) to deliver possession of his estate to the official receiver, and

(b) to deliver up to the official receiver all books, papers and other records of which he has possession or control and which relate to his estate and affairs (including any which would be privileged from disclosure in any proceedings).

(2) In the case of any part of the bankrupt's estate which consists of things possession of which cannot be delivered to the official receiver, and in the case of any property that may be claimed for the bankrupt's estate by the trustee, it is the bankrupt's duty to do all things as may reasonably be required by the official receiver for the protection of those things or that property.

(3) Subsections (1) and (2) do not apply where by virtue of section 297 below the bankrupt's estate vests in a trustee immediately on the making of the bankruptcy order.

(4) The bankrupt shall give the official receiver such inventory of his estate and such other information, and shall attend on the official receiver at such times, as the official receiver may reasonably require—

(a) for a purpose of this Chapter, or

(b) in connection with the making of a bankruptcy restrictions order.

(5) Subsection (4) applies to a bankrupt after his discharge.

(6) If a bankrupt without reasonable excuse fails to comply with any obligation imposed by this section, he is guilty of a contempt of court and liable to be punished accordingly (in addition to any other punishment to which he may be subject).

[This section is printed as amended by the *Enterprise Act* 2002, s.269, and Sched. 23, paras 1 and 5.]

Every bankruptcy is under the court's control and the bankrupt is obliged to obey the court's directions made for the purposes of his bankruptcy: see *Insolvency Act* 1986, s.263(2). At any time after a bankruptcy order has been made the official receiver or the trustee may seize, if necessary under warrant, the bankrupt's estate together with **30–65** any books, papers or records: see *Insolvency Act* 1986, ss.364, 365. This power is supplemental to the duty imposed on a bankrupt under section 291, *ante*.

Books, papers and other records delivered to the official receiver by a bankrupt pursuant to the latter's duty under section 291 are admissible in subsequent criminal proceedings and the use of such material does not contravene the bankrupt's right to a fair trial or breach his privilege against self-incrimination: *Att.-Gen.'s Reference (No. 7 of 2000)* [2001] 2 Cr.App.R. 19, CA, where attention was drawn to the distinction made in *Saunders v. U.K.* (*ante*, § 16–69) between statements made under compulsion and other material which existed independently of the will of the individual.

Insolvency Act 1986, s.366

Inquiry into bankrupt's dealings and property

30–66 **366.**—(1) At any time after a bankruptcy order has been made the court may, on the application of the official receiver or the trustee of the bankrupt's estate, summon to appear before it—

(a) the bankrupt or the bankrupt's spouse or former spouse or civil partner or former civil partner,

(b) any person known or believed to have any property comprised in the bankrupt's estate in his possession or to be indebted to the bankrupt,

(c) any person appearing to the court to be able to give information concerning the bankrupt or the bankrupt's dealings, affairs or property.

The court may require any such person as is mentioned in paragraphs (b) or (c) to submit an affidavit to the court containing an account of his dealings with the bankrupt or to produce any documents in his possession or under his control relating to the bankrupt or the bankrupt's dealings, affairs or property.

(2) Without prejudice to section 364, the following applies in a case where—

(a) a person without reasonable excuse fails to appear before the court when he is summoned to do so under this section, or

(b) there are reasonable grounds for believing that a person has absconded, or is about to abscond, with a view to avoiding his appearance before the court under this section.

(3) The court may, for the purpose of bringing that person and anything in his possession before the court, cause a warrant to be issued to a constable or prescribed officer of the court—

(a) for the arrest of that person, and

(b) for the seizure of any books, papers, records, money or goods in that person's possession.

(4) The court may authorise a person arrested under such a warrant to be kept in custody, and anything seized under such a warrant to be held, in accordance with the rules, until that person is brought before the court under the warrant or until such other time as the court may order.

[This section is printed as amended by the *Civil Partnership Act* 2004, s.261(1), and Sched. 27, para. 120.]

30–66a Section 366 gives a court power, on the application of the trustee in bankruptcy, to require any person who appears to the court to be able to give information concerning the bankrupt or the bankrupt's dealings, affairs or property, either to appear before the court for an oral examination, or to provide an affidavit containing an account of his dealings with the bankrupt, or to produce any documents, in his possession or control, relating to the bankrupt or the bankrupt's dealings, affairs or property. Even where the essential conditions for the exercise of the jurisdiction are satisfied, however, there is still a discretion to be exercised judicially, having regard to the circumstances of the case: *Buchler v. Al-Midani*, unreported, December 7, 2005, Ch D ([2005] EWHC 3183 (Ch.)).

30–67 Section 367 (court's enforcement powers under s.366) mirrors section 237 (*ante*, § 30–56). Section 368 provides that sections 366 and 367 apply where an interim receiver has been appointed under section 286 as they apply where a bankruptcy order has been made, as if references to the official receiver or the trustee were references to the interim receiver, and references to the bankrupt and to his estate were (respectively) to the debtor and his property.

Evidence and procedure

The detailed evidential and procedural provisions relating to the preparation of a statement of affairs and to both public and private examinations are contained in the *Insolvency Rules* 1986 (S.I. 1986 No. 1925). **30–68**

Statement of affairs

Where a debtor petitions for his own bankruptcy, the petition must be accompanied by a statement of affairs under the *Insolvency Rules* 1986, *ante*. Otherwise, where a bankruptcy order has been made, a bankrupt must submit a statement of his affairs within 21 days of the commencement of his bankruptcy: s.288, *ante*, § 30–61. **30–69**

Public examination

The bankrupt is not entitled to refuse to answer questions on the grounds that he may incriminate himself and he may be required to answer questions even after he has been charged with a criminal offence: see *R. v. Scott* (1856) Dears & B.C.C. 47; *R. v. Erdheim* [1896] 2 Q.B. 260; *Re Atherton* [1912] 2 K.B. 251; *Re Paget* [1927] 2 Ch. 85; and *R. v. Harris* [1970] 1 W.L.R. 1252, CCC (MacKenna J.). **30–70**

The *Insolvency Rules* 1986 (S.I. 1986 No. 1925) set out the detailed procedure for the conduct of all individual and corporate insolvency proceedings. Of particular interest to the criminal practitioner are rule 6.175, which deals with the conduct of a public examination of a bankrupt, rules 7.19 to 7.25, which deal with enforcement procedures (including the issue of warrants), and rules 9.1 to 9.6, which deal with the examination of persons concerned in company and individual insolvency. Provision is also made for the proof of certain matters under the rules: see rr.7.51, 12.6 (which regulates proof of documents issuing from the Secretary of State) and 12.20 (which regulates proof of facts stated in a notice in the *Gazette*). In *R. v. Kansal* [1993] Q.B. 244, 95 Cr.App.R. 348, CA, the court held that the terms of rule 6.175 made it clear that the privilege against self-incrimination was abrogated in any public examination of the bankrupt. Any statement made in such examination may not, however, be used in criminal proceedings, save in the circumstances set out in section 433(2) and (3), *post*, § 30–74. As to the court's discretion to suspend a public examination of a bankrupt, and to order a private examination, where section 433 might provide inadequate protection against self-incrimination in respect of foreign criminal proceedings, see *Re Rottmann (a Bankrupt), The Times*, July 16, 2008, Ch D (H.H. Judge Kaye Q.C.) **30–71**

Private examination

Private examinations are governed by sections 366 and 367 (*ante*). The purpose of such private examinations is to allow the trustee or the official receiver to investigate the bankrupt's affairs. However, it is submitted that, as with corporate insolvency examinations, the court will not allow an examination that is oppressive, vexatious and unfair. **30–72**

There is a strong line of authority to the effect that the bankrupt himself cannot invoke the privilege against self-incrimination when questioned in his own bankruptcy. This goes back before any distinction was drawn between public and private examination, *per* Dillon L.J. in *Bishopsgate Investment Management Ltd v. Maxwell* [1993] Ch. 1, CA (Civ. Div.). It is therefore submitted that the bankrupt is not entitled to rely on the privilege against self-incrimination, but any statement made may not be used against him in criminal proceedings, save in the circumstances specified in section 433(2), *post*, § 30–74. A person other than a bankrupt is, however, entitled to rely on the privilege: see *Ex p. Schofield*; *Re Firth* (1877) 6 Ch D 230. **30–73**

(7) General provisions of the Act applying to investigations

Insolvency Act 1986, s.433

Admissibility in evidence of statements of affairs, etc.

433.—(1) In any proceedings (whether or not under this Act)— **30–74**

(a) a statement of affairs prepared for the purposes of any provision of this Act which is derived from the *Insolvency Act* 1985, and

(b) any other statement made in pursuance of a requirement imposed by or under any such provision or by or under rules made under this Act,

may be used in evidence against any person making or concurring in making the statement.

(2) However, in criminal proceedings in which any such person is charged with an offence to which this subsection applies—

(a) no evidence relating to the statement may be adduced, and

(b) no question relating to it may be asked,

by or on behalf of the prosecution, unless evidence relating to it is adduced, or a question relating to it is asked, in the proceedings by or on behalf of that person.

(3) Subsection (2) applies to any offence other than—

(a) an offence under section 22(6), 47(6), 48(8), 66(6), 67(8), 95(8), 98(6), 99(3)(a), 131(7), 192(2), 208(1)(a) or (d) or (2), 210, 235(5), 353(1), 354(1)(b) or (3) or 356(1) or (2)(a) or (b) or paragraph 4(3)(a) of Schedule 7;

(b) an offence which is—

(i) created by rules made under this Act, and

(ii) designated for the purposes of this subsection by such rules or by regulations made by the Secretary of State;

(c) an offence which is—

(i) created by regulations made under any such rules, and

(ii) designated for the purposes of this subsection by such regulations;

(d) an offence under section 1, 2 or 5 of the *Perjury Act* 1911 (false statements made on oath or made otherwise than on oath); or

(e) [*Scotland*].

(4) [*Procedure for making regulations*.]

[This section is printed as amended by the *YJCEA* 1999, s.59, and Sched. 3, para. 7.]

In connection with this section, see *Re RBG Resources plc*; *Shierson v. Rastogi*, *ante*, § 30–59.

Legal professional privilege

30–75 Section 434C (inserted by the *Companies Act 2006 (Consequential Amendments etc.) Order* 2008 (S.I. 2008 No. 948), art. 3(1), and Sched. 1, Pt 2, para. 105) provides that in proceedings against a person for an offence under the Act, nothing in the Act is to be taken to require any person to disclose any information that he is entitled to refuse to disclose on grounds of legal professional privilege. This section applies, however, only for the purposes of the first group of parts (ss.1–251) and of sections 411 and 414 to 417: s.434A.

C. FINANCIAL SERVICES AND MARKETS ACT 2000

(1) Introduction

30–76 The *FSMA* 2000 received Royal Assent on June 14, 2000. The Act was intended to co-ordinate and modernise the regulation of financial services and provide for a single regulator of the financial services industry in the form of the Financial Services Authority ("the FSA") (referred to in the statute as "the Authority"). The FSA is responsible for regulating banks, building societies, insurance companies, friendly societies, credit unions, Lloyd's, investment and pensions advisers, stockbrokers, professional firms offering certain types of investment services, fund managers and derivative traders. The intention of the Act is to protect the integrity of financial markets and to reduce the prevalence of financial crime. It contains a number of distinct investigative powers vested in the FSA and the Secretary of State. It also creates a number of offences, as to which see *post*, §§ 30–202 *et seq*.

The *Financial Services and Markets Act 2000 (Commencement No. 7) Order* 2001 (S.I. 2001 No. 3538) appointed December 1, 2001, for the coming into force of all provisions of the Act, so far as not already in force, save that: (i) sections 104 and 347(1) and (2) came into force on that day for certain purposes only; (ii) the appointed day for section 416(3)(b) and (c) was March 2, 2002; and (iii) the appointed day for Part V of Schedule 18 and for the repeal of the provisions of the *Credit Union Act* 1979 effected by Schedule 22 was July 2, 2002.

The *Financial Services and Markets Act 2000 (Transitional Provisions and Savings) (Civil Remedies, Discipline, Criminal Offences, etc.) (No. 2) Order* 2001 (S.I. 2001 No. 3083) relates to the civil, prosecutorial and disciplinary powers of the FSA in relation to conduct that took place before the commencement of section 19 and related matters. Generally, these powers reflect the powers of the FSA before that commencement under the *Insurance Companies Act* 1982, the *Financial Services Act* 1986, the *Banking Act* 1987, and related enactments. In particular, article 13 provides that sections 401 (proceedings for offences) and 403 (jurisdiction and procedure in respect of offences) have effect as if each offence to which the article applies were an offence under the 2000 Act. The article applies to any offence committed before the commencement of section 19 under the 1982 Act, the 1986 Act, the 1987 Act, the *Banking Co-ordination (Second Council Directive) Regulations* 1992 (S.I. 1992 No. 3218), the *Investment Services Regulations* 1995 (S.I. 1995 No. 3375), section 9 or 43A of, or paragraph 3 of Schedule 3 to, the *Building Societies Act* 1986, or section 31 of the *Friendly Societies Act* 1992. Article 13(3) preserves the right to rely upon any defence or excuse that would have been available in relation to those offences prior to December 1, 2001. Articles 14 to 18 contain transitional modifications of sections 165 (*post*, § 30–81), 166 (*post*, § 30–82), 167 (*post*, § 30–83) and 168 (*post*, § 30–84). This order came into force on the day on which section 19 came into force (*i.e.* December 1, 2001).

(2) General inquiries by the Financial Services Authority

Financial Services and Markets Act 2000, ss.165–177

Authority's power to require information

165.—(1) The Authority may, by notice in writing given to an authorised person, require him— **30–77**

(a) to provide specified information or information of a specified description; or

(b) to produce specified documents or documents of a specified description.

(2) The information or documents must be provided or produced—

(a) before the end of such reasonable period as may be specified; and

(b) at such place as may be specified.

(3) An officer who has written authorisation from the Authority to do so may require an authorised person without delay—

(a) to provide the officer with specified information or information of a specified description; or

(b) to produce to him specified documents or documents of a specified description.

(4) This section applies only to information and documents reasonably required in connection with the exercise by the Authority of functions conferred on it by or under this Act.

(5) The Authority may require any information provided under this section to be provided in such form as it may reasonably require.

(6) The Authority may require—

(a) any information provided, whether in a document or otherwise, to be verified in such manner, or

(b) any document produced to be authenticated in such manner, as it may reasonably require.

(7) The powers conferred by subsections (1) and (3) may also be exercised to impose requirements on—

(a) a person who is connected with an authorised person;

(b) an operator, trustee or depositary of a scheme recognised under section 270 or 272 who is not an authorised person;

(c) a recognised investment exchange or recognised clearing house.

(8) "Authorised person" includes a person who was at any time an authorised person but who has ceased to be an authorised person.

(9) "Officer" means an officer of the Authority and includes a member of the Authority's staff or an agent of the Authority.

(10) "Specified" means—

(a) in subsections (1) and (2), specified in the notice; and

(b) in subsection (3), specified in the authorisation.

(11) For the purposes of this section, a person is connected with an authorised person ("A") if he is or has at any relevant time been—

(a) a member of A's group;
(b) a controller of A;
(c) any other member of a partnership of which A is a member; or
(d) in relation to A, a person mentioned in Part I of Schedule 15.

As to the transitional modification of section 165, see S.I. 2001 No. 3083, *ante*, § 30–75.

Reports by skilled persons

30–78 **166.**—(1) The Authority may, by notice in writing given to a person to whom subsection (2) applies, require him to provide the Authority with a report on any matter about which the Authority has required or could require the provision of information or production of documents under section 165.

(2) This subsection applies to—
(a) an authorised person ("A"),
(b) any other member of A's group,
(c) a partnership of which A is a member, or
(d) a person who has at any relevant time been a person falling within paragraph (a), (b) or (c), who is, or was at the relevant time, carrying on a business.

(3) The Authority may require the report to be in such form as may be specified in the notice.

(4) The person appointed to make a report required by subsection (1) must be a person—
(a) nominated or approved by the Authority; and
(b) appearing to the Authority to have the skills necessary to make a report on the matter concerned.

(5) It is the duty of any person who is providing (or who at any time has provided) services to a person to whom subsection (2) applies in relation to a matter on which a report is required under subsection (1) to give a person appointed to provide such a report all such assistance as the appointed person may reasonably require.

(6) The obligation imposed by subsection (5) is enforceable, on the application of the Authority, by an injunction or, [*procedure in Scotland*].

As to the transitional modification of section 166, see S.I. 2001 No. 3083, *ante*, § 30–75.

Appointment of investigators

Appointment of persons to carry out general investigations

30–79 **167.**—(1) If it appears to the Authority or the Secretary of State ("the investigating authority") that there is good reason for doing so, the investigating authority may appoint one or more competent persons to conduct an investigation on its behalf into—
(a) the nature, conduct or state of the business of a recognised investment exchange or an authorised person or of an appointed representative;
(b) a particular aspect of that business; or
(c) the ownership or control of a recognised investment exchange or an authorised person.

(2) If a person appointed under subsection (1) thinks it necessary for the purposes of his investigation, he may also investigate the business of a person who is or has at any relevant time been—
(a) a member of the group of which the person under investigation ("A") is part; or
(b) a partnership of which A is a member.

(3) If a person appointed under subsection (1) decides to investigate the business of any person under subsection (2) he must give that person written notice of his decision.

(4) The power conferred by this section may be exercised in relation to a former authorised person (or appointed representative) but only in relation to—
(a) business carried on at any time when he was an authorised person (or appointed representative); or
(b) the ownership or control of a former authorised person at any time when he was an authorised person.

(5) "Business" includes any part of a business even if it does not consist of carrying on regulated activities.

(6) References in subsection (1) to a recognised investment exchange do not include references to an overseas investment exchange (as defined by section 313(1)).

[This section is printed as amended by the *Financial Services and Markets Act 2000 (Markets in Financial Instruments) Regulations* 2007 (S.I. 2007 No. 126), reg. 3(5), and Sched. 5, para. 7.]

As to the transitional modification of section 167, see S.I. 2001 No. 3083, *ante*, § 30–75.

Appointment of persons to carry out investigations in particular cases

168.—(1) Subsection (3) applies if it appears to an investigating authority that there are circumstances suggesting that— **30–80**

(a) a person may have contravened any regulation made under section 142; or

(b) a person may be guilty of an offence under section 177, 191, 346 or 398(1) or under Schedule 4.

(2) Subsection (3) also applies if it appears to an investigating authority that there are circumstances suggesting that—

(a) an offence under section 24(1) or 397 or under Part V of the *Criminal Justice Act* 1993 may have been committed;

(b) there may have been a breach of the general prohibition;

(c) there may have been a contravention of section 21 or 238; or

(d) market abuse may have taken place.

(3) The investigating authority may appoint one or more competent persons to conduct an investigation on its behalf.

(4) Subsection (5) applies if it appears to the Authority that there are circumstances suggesting that—

(a) a person may have contravened section 20;

(b) a person may be guilty of an offence under prescribed regulations relating to money laundering;

(c) an authorised person may have contravened a rule made by the Authority;

(d) an individual may not be a fit and proper person to perform functions in relation to a regulated activity carried on by an authorised or exempt person;

(e) an individual may have performed or agreed to perform a function in breach of a prohibition order;

(f) an authorised or exempt person may have failed to comply with section 56(6);

(g) an authorised person may have failed to comply with section 59(1) or (2);

(h) a person in relation to whom the Authority has given its approval under section 59 may not be a fit and proper person to perform the function to which that approval relates;

(i) a person may be guilty of misconduct for the purposes of section 66; or

(j) a person may have contravened any provision made by or under this Act for the purpose of implementing the markets in financial instruments directive or by any directly applicable Community regulation made under that directive.

(5) The Authority may appoint one or more competent persons to conduct an investigation on its behalf.

(6) "Investigating authority" means the Authority or the Secretary of State.

[This section is printed as amended by S.I. 2007 No. 126 (*ante*, § 30–83), reg. 3(5), and Sched. 5, para. 8.]

The reference to the markets in financial instruments directive is a reference to Directive 2004/39/EC of the European Parliament and of the Council on markets in financial instruments: see reg. 2 of S.I. 2006 No. 127, though there is no definitional provision in the relevant part of the 2000 Act itself (but see para. 4C of Sched. 3).

As to the transitional modification of section 168, see S.I. 2001 No. 3083, *ante*, § 30–75.

Assistance to overseas regulators

Investigations etc. in support of overseas regulator

169.—(1) At the request of an overseas regulator, the Authority may— **30–81**

(a) exercise the power conferred by section 165; or

(b) appoint one or more competent persons to investigate any matter.

(2) An investigator has the same powers as an investigator appointed under section 168(3) (as a result of subsection (1) of that section).

(3) If the request has been made by a competent authority in pursuance of any Community obligation the Authority must, in deciding whether or not to exercise its investigative power, consider whether its exercise is necessary to comply with any such obligation.

(4) In deciding whether or not to exercise its investigative power, the Authority may take into account in particular—

(a) whether in the country or territory of the overseas regulator concerned, corresponding assistance would be given to a United Kingdom regulatory authority;

(b) whether the case concerns the breach of a law, or other requirement, which has no close parallel in the United Kingdom or involves the assertion of a jurisdiction not recognised by the United Kingdom;

(c) the seriousness of the case and its importance to persons in the United Kingdom;

(d) whether it is otherwise appropriate in the public interest to give the assistance sought.

(5) The Authority may decide that it will not exercise its investigative power unless the overseas regulator undertakes to make such contribution towards the cost of its exercise as the Authority considers appropriate.

(6) Subsections (4) and (5) do not apply if the Authority considers that the exercise of its investigative power is necessary to comply with a Community obligation.

(7) If the Authority has appointed an investigator in response to a request from an overseas regulator, it may direct the investigator to permit a representative of that regulator to attend, and take part in, any interview conducted for the purposes of the investigation.

(8) A direction under subsection (7) is not to be given unless the Authority is satisfied that any information obtained by an overseas regulator as a result of the interview will be subject to safeguards equivalent to those contained in Part XXIII.

(9)–(12) [*Policy to be applied in giving a subsection (7) direction.*]

(13) "Overseas regulator" has the same meaning as in section 195.

(14) "Investigative power" means one of the powers mentioned in subsection (1).

(15) "Investigator" means a person appointed under subsection (1)(b).

Conduct of investigations

Investigations: general

30–82 **170.**—(1) This section applies if an investigating authority appoints one or more competent persons ("investigators") under section 167 or 168(3) or (5) to conduct an investigation on its behalf.

(2) The investigating authority must give written notice of the appointment of an investigator to the person who is the subject of the investigation ("the person under investigation").

(3) Subsections (2) and (9) do not apply if—

(a) the investigator is appointed as a result of section 168(1) or (4) and the investigating authority believes that the notice required by subsection (2) or (9) would be likely to result in the investigation being frustrated; or

(b) the investigator is appointed as a result of subsection (2) of section 168.

(4) A notice under subsection (2) must—

(a) specify the provisions under which, and as a result of which, the investigator was appointed; and

(b) state the reason for his appointment.

(5) Nothing prevents the investigating authority from appointing a person who is a member of its staff as an investigator.

(6) An investigator must make a report of his investigation to the investigating authority.

(7) The investigating authority may, by a direction to an investigator, control—

(a) the scope of the investigation;

(b) the period during which the investigation is to be conducted;

(c) the conduct of the investigation; and

(d) the reporting of the investigation.

(8) A direction may, in particular—

(a) confine the investigation to particular matters;

(b) extend the investigation to additional matters;

(c) require the investigator to discontinue the investigation or to take only such steps as are specified in the direction;

(d) require the investigator to make such interim reports as are so specified.

(9) If there is a change in the scope or conduct of the investigation and, in the opinion of the investigating authority, the person subject to investigation is likely to be significantly prejudiced by not being made aware of it, that person must be given written notice of the change.

(10) "Investigating authority", in relation to an investigator, means—

(a) the Authority, if the Authority appointed him;

(b) the Secretary of State, if the Secretary of State appointed him.

Powers of persons appointed under section 167

171.—(1) An investigator may require the person who is the subject of the investigation ("the person under investigation") or any person connected with the person under investigation— **30–83**

(a) to attend before the investigator at a specified time and place and answer questions; or

(b) otherwise to provide such information as the investigator may require.

(2) An investigator may also require any person to produce at a specified time and place any specified documents or documents of a specified description.

(3) A requirement under subsection (1) or (2) may be imposed only so far as the investigator concerned reasonably considers the question, provision of information or production of the document to be relevant to the purposes of the investigation.

(3A) Where the investigation relates to a recognised investment exchange, an investigator has the additional powers conferred by sections 172 and 173 (and for this purpose references in those sections to an investigator are to be read accordingly).

(4) For the purposes of this section and section 172, a person is connected with the person under investigation ("A") if he is or has at any relevant time been—

(a) a member of A's group;

(b) a controller of A;

(c) a partnership of which A is a member; or

(d) in relation to A, a person mentioned in Part I or II of Schedule 15.

(5) "Investigator" means a person conducting an investigation under section 167.

(6) "Specified" means specified in a notice in writing.

(7) The reference in subsection (3A) to a recognised investment exchange does not include a reference to an overseas investment exchange (as defined by section 313(1)).

[This section is printed as amended by S.I. 2007 No. 126 (*ante*, § 30–83), reg. 3(5), and Sched. 5, para. 9.]

Additional power of persons appointed as a result of section 168(1) or (4)

172.—(1) An investigator has the powers conferred by section 171. **30–84**

(2) An investigator may also require a person who is neither the subject of the investigation ("the person under investigation") nor a person connected with the person under investigation—

(a) to attend before the investigator at a specified time and place and answer questions; or

(b) otherwise to provide such information as the investigator may require for the purposes of the investigation.

(3) A requirement may only be imposed under subsection (2) if the investigator is satisfied that the requirement is necessary or expedient for the purposes of the investigation.

(4) "Investigator" means a person appointed as a result of subsection (1) or (4) of section 168.

(5) "Specified" means specified in a notice in writing.

Powers of persons appointed as a result of section 168(2)

173.—(1) Subsections (2) to (4) apply if an investigator considers that any person ("A") is or may be able to give information which is or may be relevant to the investigation. **30–85**

(2) The investigator may require A—

(a) to attend before him at a specified time and place and answer questions; or

(b) otherwise to provide such information as he may require for the purposes of the investigation.

(3) The investigator may also require A to produce at a specified time and place any

specified documents or documents of a specified description which appear to the investigator to relate to any matter relevant to the investigation.

(4) The investigator may also otherwise require A to give him all assistance in connection with the investigation which A is reasonably able to give.

(5) "Investigator" means a person appointed under subsection (3) of section 168 (as a result of subsection (2) of that section).

Admissibility of statements made to investigators

30–86 **174.**—(1) A statement made to an investigator by a person in compliance with an information requirement is admissible in evidence in any proceedings, so long as it also complies with any requirements governing the admissibility of evidence in the circumstances in question.

(2) But in criminal proceedings in which that person is charged with an offence to which this subsection applies or in proceedings in relation to action to be taken against that person under section 123—

(a) no evidence relating to the statement may be adduced, and

(b) no question relating to it may be asked,

by or on behalf of the prosecution or (as the case may be) the Authority, unless evidence relating to it is adduced, or a question relating to it is asked, in the proceedings by or on behalf of that person.

(3) Subsection (2) applies to any offence other than one—

(a) under section 177(4) or 398;

(b) under section 5 of the *Perjury Act* 1911 (false statements made otherwise than on oath);

(c) [*Scotland*];

(d) [*Northern Ireland*].

(4) "Investigator" means a person appointed under section 167 or 168(3) or (5).

(5) "Information requirement" means a requirement imposed by an investigator under section 171, 172, 173 or 175.

Information and documents: supplemental provisions

30–87 **175.**—(1) If the Authority or an investigator has power under this Part to require a person to produce a document but it appears that the document is in the possession of a third person, that power may be exercised in relation to the third person.

(2) If a document is produced in response to a requirement imposed under this Part, the person to whom it is produced may—

(a) take copies or extracts from the document; or

(b) require the person producing the document, or any relevant person, to provide an explanation of the document.

(3) If a person who is required under this Part to produce a document fails to do so, the Authority or an investigator may require him to state, to the best of his knowledge and belief, where the document is.

(4) A lawyer may be required under this Part to furnish the name and address of his client.

(5) No person may be required under this Part to disclose information or produce a document in respect of which he owes an obligation of confidence by virtue of carrying on the business of banking unless—

(a) he is the person under investigation or a member of that person's group;

(b) the person to whom the obligation of confidence is owed is the person under investigation or a member of that person's group;

(c) the person to whom the obligation of confidence is owed consents to the disclosure or production; or

(d) the imposing on him of a requirement with respect to such information or document has been specifically authorised by the investigating authority.

(6) If a person claims a lien on a document, its production under this Part does not affect the lien.

(7) "Relevant person", in relation to a person who is required to produce a document, means a person who—

(a) has been or is or is proposed to be a director or controller of that person;

(b) has been or is an auditor of that person;

(c) has been or is an actuary, accountant or lawyer appointed or instructed by that person; or

(d) has been or is an employee of that person.

(8) "Investigator" means a person appointed under section 167 or 168(3) or (5).

Entry of premises under warrant

176.—(1) A justice of the peace may issue a warrant under this section if satisfied on information on oath given by or on behalf of the Secretary of State, the Authority or an investigator that there are reasonable grounds for believing that the first, second or third set of conditions is satisfied. **30–88**

(2) The first set of conditions is—

(a) that a person on whom an information requirement has been imposed has failed (wholly or in part) to comply with it; and

(b) that on the premises specified in the warrant—

(i) there are documents which have been required; or

(ii) there is information which has been required.

(3) The second set of conditions is—

(a) that the premises specified in the warrant are premises of an authorised person or an appointed representative;

(b) that there are on the premises documents or information in relation to which an information requirement could be imposed; and

(c) that if such a requirement were to be imposed—

(i) it would not be complied with; or

(ii) the documents or information to which it related would be removed, tampered with or destroyed.

(4) The third set of conditions is—

(a) that an offence mentioned in section 168 for which the maximum sentence on conviction on indictment is two years or more has been (or is being) committed by any person;

(b) that there are on the premises specified in the warrant documents or information relevant to whether that offence has been (or is being) committed;

(c) that an information requirement could be imposed in relation to those documents or information; and

(d) that if such a requirement were to be imposed—

(i) it would not be complied with; or

(ii) the documents or information to which it related would be removed, tampered with or destroyed.

(5) A warrant under this section shall authorise a constable—

(a) to enter the premises specified in the warrant;

(b) to search the premises and take possession of any documents or information appearing to be documents or information of a kind in respect of which a warrant under this section was issued ("the relevant kind") or to take, in relation to any such documents or information, any other steps which may appear to be necessary for preserving them or preventing interference with them;

(c) to take copies of, or extracts from, any documents or information appearing to be of the relevant kind;

(d) to require any person on the premises to provide an explanation of any document or information appearing to be of the relevant kind or to state where it may be found; and

(e) to use such force as may be reasonably necessary.

(6) In England and Wales, sections 15(5) to (8) and section 16 of the *Police and Criminal Evidence Act* 1984 (execution of search warrants and safeguards) apply to warrants issued under this section.

(7) [*Northern Ireland.*]

(8) Any document of which possession is taken under this section may be retained—

(a) for a period of three months; or

(b) if within that period proceedings to which the document is relevant are commenced against any person for any criminal offence, until the conclusion of those proceedings.

(9) [*Scotland.*]

(10) "Investigator" means a person appointed under section 167 or 168(3) or (5).

(11) "Information requirement" means a requirement imposed—

(a) by the Authority under section 165 or 175; or
(b) by an investigator under section 171, 172, 173 or 175.

Offences

30–88a **177.**—(1) If a person other than the investigator ("the defaulter") fails to comply with a requirement imposed on him under this Part the person imposing the requirement may certify that fact in writing to the court.

(2) If the court is satisfied that the defaulter failed without reasonable excuse to comply with the requirement, it may deal with the defaulter (and in the case of a body corporate, any director or officer) as if he were in contempt.

(3) A person who knows or suspects that an investigation is being or is likely to be conducted under this Part is guilty of an offence if—

(a) he falsifies, conceals, destroys or otherwise disposes of a document which he knows or suspects is or would be relevant to such an investigation, or
(b) he causes or permits the falsification, concealment, destruction or disposal of such a document, unless he shows that he had no intention of concealing facts disclosed by the documents from the investigator.

(4) A person who, in purported compliance with a requirement imposed on him under this Part—

(a) provides information which he knows to be false or misleading in a material particular, or
(b) recklessly provides information which is false or misleading in a material particular, is guilty of an offence.

(5) A person guilty of an offence under subsection (3) or (4) is liable—

(a) on summary conviction, to imprisonment for a term not exceeding *six* [12] months or a fine not exceeding the statutory maximum, or both;
(b) on conviction on indictment, to imprisonment for a term not exceeding two years or a fine, or both.

(6) Any person who intentionally obstructs the exercise of any rights conferred by a warrant under section 176 is guilty of an offence and liable on summary conviction to imprisonment for a term not exceeding *three months* [51 weeks] or a fine not exceeding level 5 on the standard scale, or both.

(7) "Court" means—

(a) the High Court;
(b) [*Scotland*].

[This section is printed as amended, as from a day to be appointed, by the *CJA* 2003, ss.280(2) and 282(2) and (3), and Sched. 26, para. 54 (substitution of words in square brackets for italicised words). The increases in penalty have no effect in relation to offences committed before the commencement of the amendments: *ibid.*, ss.280(3) and 282(4).]

30–88b This part of the *FSMA* 2000 (Pt XI) sets out the general powers of the FSA to require the production of information and documents, to require reports to be compiled, to conduct investigations and to obtain access to premises. Many of these powers are also held concurrently by the Secretary of State in recognition of his wider responsibilities in relation to company law. The powers provided for in this Part are in addition to the specific powers conferred on the FSA by other provisions of the *FSMA* 2000 to request information from unauthorised persons in particular circumstances, such as in connection with an application for authorisation or recognition. They enable the FSA to require information on an *ad hoc* basis and therefore supplement the FSA's ability to make rules requiring authorised persons to provide it with information on a routine basis under its general rule-making power (s.138). Under section 177, failure to comply with any requirement imposed using any of the powers in Part XI can be certified to the court and dealt with by the court as if the defaulter were in contempt. None of the powers in this part may be used to require the disclosure of material which is protected by section 413: see *post*, § 30–88f.

The *Money Laundering Regulations* 2007 (S.I. 2007 No. 2157) (*ante*, 26–45 *et seq.*) and the *Transfer of Funds (Information on the Payer) Regulations* 2007 (S.I. 2007 No. 3298) are prescribed for the purposes of section 168(4)(b) of the *FSMA* 2000. The effect of this is that the FSA may, under section 168(5), appoint a competent person to conduct an investigation on its behalf where it appears to it that a person may be guilty of an offence under the regulations. Both sets of regulations are also prescribed for the purposes of section 402(1)(b) of the Act. This will enable the FSA to institute proceedings for any offence under the regulations. In addition, under section 146 the FSA has power to make rules in relation to the prevention and detection of money laundering in connection with the carrying on of regulated activities by authorised persons.

(3) Investigation of listing and prospectus offences

Financial Services and Markets Act 2000, s.97

Appointment by competent authority of persons to carry out investigations

97.—(1) Subsection (2) applies if it appears to the competent authority that there are circumstances suggesting that— **30–88c**

(a) there may have been a contravention of—
  (i) a provision of this Part or of Part 6 rules, or
  (ii) a provision otherwise made in accordance with the prospectus directive or the transparency obligations directive;

(b) a person who was at the material time a director of a person mentioned in section 91(1), (1ZA)(a), (1A) or (1B) has been knowingly concerned in a contravention by that person of—
  (i) a provision of this Part or of Part 6 rules, or
  (ii) a provision otherwise made in accordance with the prospectus directive or the transparency obligations directive;

(c) ...

(d) there may have been a contravention of section 83, 85, 87G or 98.

(2) The competent authority may appoint one or more competent persons to conduct an investigation on its behalf.

(3) Part XI applies to an investigation under subsection (2) as if—

(a) the investigator were appointed under section 167(1);

(b) references to the investigating authority in relation to him were to the competent authority;

(c) references to the offences mentioned in section 168 were to those mentioned in subsection (1)(d);

(d) references to an authorised person were references to the person under investigation.

[This section is printed as amended by the *Financial Services and Markets Act 2000 (Market Abuse) Regulations* 2005 (S.I. 2005 No. 381), Sched. 1, para. 7; the *Prospectus Regulations* 2005 (S.I. 2005 No. 1433), reg. 2(1), and Sched. 1 para. 8(c); and the *Companies Act* 2006, s.1272, and Sched. 15, para. 8.]

The "prospectus directive" means Directive 2003/71/EC of the European Parliament and of the Council on the prospectus to be published when securities are offered to the public or admitted to trading, and the "transparency obligations directive" means Directive 2004/10/EC of the European Parliament and the Council relating to the harmonisation of transparency requirements in relation to information about issuers whose securities are admitted to trading on a regulated market: s.103(1).

Section 97 allows the competent authority to appoint investigators to carry out investigations. The section applies the provisions of Part XI (ss.165–177, *ante*) as if the investigator were appointed under section 167(1). This means that the procedures set out in section 170 must be followed and that the investigator will have the powers set out in section 171.

(4) Investigations into collective investment schemes

Under section 284 of the Act of 2000, the FSA or the Secretary of State can appoint a person to carry out an investigation into a collective investment scheme. The provisions do not generally extend to the investigation of open ended investment companies. Provisions concerning those investigations can be made in Treasury regulations under section 262. The person carrying out the investigation has powers to investigate other persons or matters where necessary or relevant. The provisions concerning the conduct **30–88d** of investigations set out in section 170 (*ante*, § 30–82) will generally apply and statements made to the investigator may be admissible in proceedings in the circumstances set out in section 174 (*ante*, § 30–86). Persons other than the managers, trustees, operators or depositaries of schemes, or directors of open ended investment companies, will not generally be required to disclose information subject to a banker's duty of confidentiality. The power of entry under section 176 (*ante*, § 30–88) will be available to back up information requirements imposed under this section. The provisions of section 177 (*ante*, § 30–88a) will also apply, so that failure to comply with a requirement imposed in connection with an investigation can be certified to a court and falsification or concealment will be an offence.

(5) Restrictions on disclosure of confidential information by Financial Services Authority

30–88e Part XXIII of the *FSMA* 2000 (ss.347–354) provides the framework for disclosure of confidential information under the Act. Section 348 defines confidential information, and sets out restrictions on its disclosure by the FSA (as to which, see *Real Estate Opportunities Ltd v. Aberdeen Asset Managers Jersey Ltd* [2007] 2 All E.R. 791, CA (Civ. Div.)). Section 349 provides for exceptions to those restrictions for the purposes of carrying out a public function (defined by s.349(5)) where permitted by regulations made under the Act. One purpose for which information may be disclosed is that of criminal proceedings (including proceedings under Parts 2 to 4 of the *PCA* 2002) or investigations: see reg. 4 of the *Financial Services and Markets Act 2000 (Disclosure of Confidential Information) Regulations* 2001 (S.I. 2001 No. 2188), as amended by the *Financial Services and Markets Act 2000 (Disclosure of Confidential Information) (Amendment) (No. 2) Regulations* 2003 (S.I. 2003 No. 2174). Sections 353 and 354 make provision for further exceptions to the restrictions.

Section 350 provides for disclosure of information by the Inland Revenue; and section 351 for disclosure of competition information, as defined by section 351(5).

Section 352 provides that disclosure in contravention of any restriction in the Act is an offence punishable on indictment by two years' imprisonment or a fine or both. The section also makes provision for a statutory defence.

(6) Limitation on powers to require documents

Financial Services and Markets Act 2000, s.413

Protected items

30–88f **413.**—(1) A person may not be required under this Act to produce, disclose or permit the inspection of protected items.

(2) "Protected items" means—

(a) communications between a professional legal adviser and his client or any person representing his client which fall within subsection (3);

(b) communications between a professional legal adviser, his client or any person representing his client and any other person which fall within subsection (3) (as a result of paragraph (b) of that subsection);

(c) items which—

(i) are enclosed with, or referred to in, such communications;

(ii) fall within subsection (3); and

(iii) are in the possession of a person entitled to possession of them.

(3) A communication or item falls within this subsection if it is made—

(a) in connection with the giving of legal advice to the client; or

(b) in connection with, or in contemplation of, legal proceedings and for the purposes of those proceedings.

(4) A communication or item is not a protected item if it is held with the intention of furthering a criminal purpose.

D. ENTERPRISE ACT 2002

(1) Introduction

30–89 The *Enterprise Act* 2002 received Royal Assent on November 7, 2002. The Act establishes the Office of Fair Trading (the "OFT") as a corporate body, with independent board members. This replaces the former statutory office of the Director General of Fair Trading. The Act replaces or amends legislation relating to the functions of the OFT, merger control, investigation of markets, enforcement of consumer legislation, appeals on points of competition law, Competition Commission procedures and handling of certain information by public authorities. The Act also introduces new provisions relating to criminalisation of cartels, disqualification of directors for breaches of competition law and super-complaints.

In order to investigate a cartel offence (as to which, see *post*, § 30–217), the 2002 Act provides the OFT with a wide range of investigative powers. These are in addition to its powers to investigate under the *Competition Act* 1998 and the market and merger investigative powers in the 2002 Act. The OFT has published guidance on the exercise of its investigative powers which is available on its website (www.oft.gov.uk).

(2) Investigation of cartel offences

Enterprise Act 2002, ss.192–202

Criminal investigations by OFT

Investigation of offences under section 188

192.—(1) The OFT may conduct an investigation if there are reasonable grounds for suspecting that an offence under section 188 has been committed. **30–90**

(2) The powers of the OFT under sections 193 and 194 are exercisable, but only for the purposes of an investigation under subsection (1), in any case where it appears to the OFT that there is good reason to exercise them for the purpose of investigating the affairs, or any aspect of the affairs, of any person ("the person under investigation").

Powers when conducting an investigation

193.—(1) The OFT may by notice in writing require the person under investigation, or any other person who it has reason to believe has relevant information, to answer questions, or otherwise provide information, with respect to any matter relevant to the investigation at a specified place and either at a specified time or forthwith. **30–91**

(2) The OFT may by notice in writing require the person under investigation, or any other person, to produce, at a specified place and either at a specified time or forthwith, specified documents, or documents of a specified description, which appear to the OFT to relate to any matter relevant to the investigation.

(3) If any such documents are produced, the OFT may—

(a) take copies or extracts from them;

(b) require the person producing them to provide an explanation of any of them.

(4) If any such documents are not produced, the OFT may require the person who was required to produce them to state, to the best of his knowledge and belief, where they are.

(5) A notice under subsection (1) or (2) must indicate—

(a) the subject matter and purpose of the investigation; and

(b) the nature of the offences created by section 201.

Power to enter premises under a warrant

194.—(1) On an application made by the OFT to the High Court, or, in Scotland, by the procurator fiscal to the sheriff, in accordance with rules of court, a judge or the sheriff may issue a warrant if he is satisfied that there are reasonable grounds for believing— **30–92**

(a) that there are on any premises documents which the OFT has power under section 193 to require to be produced for the purposes of an investigation; and

(b) that—

(i) a person has failed to comply with a requirement under that section to produce the documents;

(ii) it is not practicable to serve a notice under that section in relation to them; or

(iii) the service of such a notice in relation to them might seriously prejudice the investigation.

(2) A warrant under this section shall authorise a named officer of the OFT, and any other officers of the OFT whom the OFT has authorised in writing to accompany the named officer—

(a) to enter the premises, using such force as is reasonably necessary for the purpose;

(b) to search the premises and—

(i) take possession of any documents appearing to be of the relevant kind, or

(ii) take, in relation to any documents appearing to be of the relevant kind, any other steps which may appear to be necessary for preserving them or preventing interference with them;

(c) to require any person to provide an explanation of any document appearing to be of the relevant kind or to state, to the best of his knowledge and belief, where it may be found;

(d) to require any information which is stored in any electronic form and is accessible from the premises and which the named officer considers relates to any matter relevant to the investigation, to be produced in a form—

(i) in which it can be taken away, and

(ii) in which it is visible and legible or from which it can readily be produced in a visible and legible form.

(3) Documents are of the relevant kind if they are of a kind in respect of which the application under subsection (1) was granted.

(4) A warrant under this section may authorise persons specified in the warrant to accompany the named officer who is executing it.

(5) [*Amends Part 1 of Schedule 1 to the* Criminal Justice and Police Act *2001 to include OFT powers of seizure as a power to which section 50 of that Act applies.*]

Exercise of powers by authorised person

30–93 **195.**—(1) The OFT may authorise any competent person who is not an officer of the OFT to exercise on its behalf all or any of the powers conferred by section 193 or 194.

(2) No such authority may be granted except for the purpose of investigating the affairs, or any aspect of the affairs, of a person specified in the authority.

(3) No person is bound to comply with any requirement imposed by a person exercising powers by virtue of any authority granted under this section unless he has, if required to do so, produced evidence of his authority.

Privileged information etc.

30–94 **196.**—(1) A person may not under section 193 or 194 be required to disclose any information or produce any document which he would be entitled to refuse to disclose or produce on grounds of legal professional privilege in proceedings in the High Court, except that a lawyer may be required to provide the name and address of his client.

(2) A person may not under section 193 or 194 be required to disclose any information or produce any document in respect of which he owes an obligation of confidence by virtue of carrying on any banking business unless—

(a) the person to whom the obligation of confidence is owed consents to the disclosure or production; or

(b) the OFT has authorised the making of the requirement.

(3) [*Privilege in Scotland.*]

Restriction on use of statements in court

30–95 **197.**—(1) A statement by a person in response to a requirement imposed by virtue of section 193 or 194 may only be used in evidence against him—

(a) on a prosecution for an offence under section 201(2); or

(b) on a prosecution for some other offence where in giving evidence he makes a statement inconsistent with it.

(2) However, the statement may not be used against that person by virtue of paragraph (b) of subsection (1) unless evidence relating to it is adduced, or a question relating to it is asked, by or on behalf of that person in the proceedings arising out of the prosecution.

Use of statements obtained under Competition Act 1998

198. [*Inserts s.30A into the* Competition Act *1998 prohibiting use of statements made under sections 26 to 28 except in specified circumstances.*]

Surveillance powers

199. [*Amends ss.32–48 of the* Regulation of Investigatory Powers Act *2002 to permit the authorisation of intrusive surveillance by the Chairman of the OFT or a designated officer.*]

Authorisation of action in respect of property

200. [*Applies the* Police Act *1997, Pt III, to the Chairman of the OFT or a designated officer.*]

Offences

201.—(1) Any person who without reasonable excuse fails to comply with a requirement imposed on him under section 193 or 194 is guilty of an offence and liable on summary conviction to imprisonment for a term not exceeding *six months* [51 weeks] or to a fine not exceeding level 5 on the standard scale or to both. **30–96**

(2) A person who, in purported compliance with a requirement under section 193 or 194—

(a) makes a statement which he knows to be false or misleading in a material particular; or

(b) recklessly makes a statement which is false or misleading in a material particular,

is guilty of an offence.

(3) A person guilty of an offence under subsection (2) is liable—

(a) on conviction on indictment, to imprisonment for a term not exceeding two years or to a fine or to both; and

(b) on summary conviction, to imprisonment for a term not exceeding *six* [12] months or to a fine not exceeding the statutory maximum, or to both.

(4) Where any person—

(a) knows or suspects that an investigation by the Serious Fraud Office or the OFT into an offence under section 188 is being or is likely to be carried out; and

(b) falsifies, conceals, destroys or otherwise disposes of, or causes or permits the falsification, concealment, destruction or disposal of documents which he knows or suspects are or would be relevant to such an investigation,

he is guilty of an offence unless he proves that he had no intention of concealing the facts disclosed by the documents from the persons carrying out such an investigation.

(5) A person guilty of an offence under subsection (4) is liable—

(a) on conviction on indictment, to imprisonment for a term not exceeding 5 years or to a fine or to both; and

(b) on summary conviction, to imprisonment for a term not exceeding *six* [12] months or to a fine not exceeding the statutory maximum, or to both.

(6) A person who intentionally obstructs a person in the exercise of his powers under a warrant issued under section 194 is guilty of an offence and liable—

(a) on conviction on indictment, to imprisonment for a term not exceeding 2 years or to a fine or to both; and

(b) on summary conviction, to a fine not exceeding the statutory maximum.

[As from a day to be appointed, "51 weeks" is substituted for "six months" in subs. (1), and "12" is substituted for "six" in subss. (3) and (5): *CJA* 2003, ss.281(4) and (5), and 282(2) and (3); but the increases do not affect offences committed before the commencement of the amendments: *ibid.*, ss.281(6) and 282(4).]

Interpretation of sections 192 to 201

202. In sections 192 to 201— **30–97**

"documents" includes information recorded in any form and, in relation to information recorded otherwise than in a form in which it is visible and legible, references to its production include references to producing it in a form in which it is visible and legible or from which it can readily be produced in a visible and legible form;

"person under investigation" has the meaning given in section 192(2).

These comprehensive powers of investigation effectively place the OFT in a stronger position than the SFO to investigate cartel offences. The SFO and OFT have produced a memorandum of understanding as a framework for investigative co-operation (available on www.oft.gov.uk). **30–98**

Part 9 of the Act (ss.237– 247), as amended by the *Companies Act* 2006, s.1281, together with the *Enterprise Act 2002 (Part 9 Restrictions on Disclosure of Information) (Amendment and Specification) Order* 2003 (S.I. 2003 No. 1400), the *Enterprise Act 2002 (Part 9 Restrictions on Disclosure of Information) (Amendment and Specification) (No. 2) Order* 2003 (S.I. 2003 No. 2580), the *Enterprise Act 2002 (Part 9 Restriction and Disclosure of Information) (Specification) Order* 2004 (S.I. 2004 No. 693), the *Enterprise Act 2002 (Part 9 Restrictions on Disclosure of Information) (Amendment) Order* 2006 (S.I. 2006 No. 2909), and the *Enterprise Act 2002 (Part 9 Restrictions on Disclosure of Information) (Amendment and Specification) Order*

2007 (S.I. 2007 No. 2977) govern the disclosure of information obtained during the course of investigations.

Similar restrictions to those in section 197, *ante*, exist in relation to the use of statements made in response to a requirement imposed under section 62B or 63 of the *Competition Act* 1998, in a prosecution for an offence under section 188 of the 2002 Act: see s.65B of the 1998 Act.

[The next paragraph is § 30–101.]

II. OFFENCES IN RELATION TO COMMERCE, FINANCIAL MARKETS AND INSOLVENCY

A. COMPANIES ACTS 1985 AND 2006

(1) Company law reform

30–101 The *Companies Act* 2006 amends and restates many of the provisions of the *Companies Act* 1985. The reforms are based on the recommendations of the Company Law Review which reported in July, 2001. The proposals were dealt with in the White Papers "Modernising Company Law" (July 2002) and "Company Law Reform" (March 2005).

(2) General provisions as to offences

Companies Act 2006, ss.1121–1133

Liability of officer in default

30–102 **1121.**—(1) This section has effect for the purposes of any provision of the *Companies Acts* to the effect that, in the event of contravention of an enactment in relation to a company, an offence is committed by every officer of the company who is in default.

(2) For this purpose "officer" includes—

(a) any director, manager or secretary, and

(b) any person who is to be treated as an officer of the company for the purposes of the provision in question.

(3) An officer is "in default" for the purposes of the provision if he authorises or permits, participates in, or fails to take all reasonable steps to prevent, the contravention.

30–103 In *R. v. Boal* [1992] 1 Q.B. 591, 95 Cr.App.R. 272, CA (a case under s.23 of the *Fire Precautions Act* 1971, which contains the expression "any director, manager, secretary or other similar officer of the body corporate"), the conviction of an assistant general manager with day-to-day responsibility for running a shop, for offences under the Act, was quashed. Section 23 was intended to fix with criminal liability "only those who are in a position of real authority, the decision-makers within the company who have both the power and responsibility to decide corporate policy and strategy" (*per* Simon Brown J., at pp. 597–598, 276).

Liability of company as officer in default

30–104 **1122.**—(1) Where a company is an officer of another company, it does not commit an offence as an officer in default unless one of its officers is in default.

(2) Where any such offence is committed by a company the officer in question also commits the offence and is liable to be proceeded against and punished accordingly.

(3) In this section "officer" and "in default" have the meanings given by section 1121.

Application to bodies other than companies

1123.—(1) Section 1121 (liability of officers in default) applies to a body other than a company as it applies to a company.

(2) As it applies in relation to a body corporate other than a company—

(a) the reference to a director of the company shall be read as referring—

(i) where the body's affairs are managed by its members, to a member of the body,

(ii) in any other case, to any corresponding officer of the body, and

(b) the reference to a manager or secretary of the company shall be read as referring to any manager, secretary or similar officer of the body.

(3) As it applies in relation to a partnership—

(a) the reference to a director of the company shall be read as referring to a member of the partnership, and

(b) the reference to a manager or secretary of the company shall be read as referring to any manager, secretary or similar officer of the partnership.

(4) As it applies in relation to an unincorporated body other than a partnership—

(a) the reference to a director of the company shall be read as referring—

(i) where the body's affairs are managed by its members, to a member of the body,

(ii) in any other case, to a member of the governing body, and

(b) the reference to a manager or secretary of the company shall be read as referring to any manager, secretary or similar officer of the body.

1124. *[Amendments of* Companies Act *1985.]*

Meaning of "daily default fine"

1125.—(1) This section defines what is meant in the *Companies Acts* where it is provided that a person guilty of an offence is liable on summary conviction to a fine not exceeding a specified amount "and, for continued contravention, a daily default fine" not exceeding a specified amount. **30–105**

(2) This means that the person is liable on a second or subsequent summary conviction of the offence to a fine not exceeding the latter amount for each day on which the contravention is continued (instead of being liable to a fine not exceeding the former amount).

Consents required for certain prosecutions

1126.—(1) This section applies to proceedings for an offence under any of the following provisions— **30–106**

section 458, 460 or 949 of this Act (offences of unauthorised disclosure of information);

section 953 of this Act (failure to comply with rules about takeover bid documents);

section 448, 449, 450, 451 or 453A of the *Companies Act* 1985 (offences in connection with company investigations);

section 798 of this Act or section 455 of the *Companies Act* 1985 (offence of attempting to evade restrictions on shares).

(2) No such proceedings are to be brought in England and Wales except by or with the consent of—

(a) in the case of an offence under—

(i) section 458, 460 or 949 of this Act,

(ii) section 953 of this Act, or

(iii) section 448, 449, 450, 451 or 453A of the *Companies Act* 1985,

the Secretary of State or the Director of Public Prosecutions;

(b) in the case of an offence under section 798 of this Act or section 455 of the *Companies Act* 1985, the Secretary of State.

(3) [*Northern Ireland.*]

Summary proceedings: venue

1127.—(1) Summary proceedings for any offence under the *Companies Acts* may be taken—

(a) against a body corporate, at any place at which the body has a place of business, and

(b) against any other person, at any place at which he is for the time being.

(2) This is without prejudice to any jurisdiction exercisable apart from this section.

Summary proceedings: time limit for proceedings

1128.—(1) An information relating to an offence under the *Companies Acts* that is triable by a magistrates' court in England and Wales may be so tried if it is laid—

(a) at any time within three years after the commission of the offence, and

(b) within twelve months after the date on which evidence sufficient in the opinion of the Director of Public Prosecutions or the Secretary of State (as the case may be) to justify the proceedings comes to his knowledge.

(2), (3) [*Scotland*; *Northern Ireland.*]

(4) For the purposes of this section a certificate of the Director of Public Prosecutions, the Lord Advocate, the Director of Public Prosecutions for Northern Ireland or the Secretary of State (as the case may be) as to the date on which such evidence as is referred to above came to his notice is conclusive evidence.

Legal professional privilege

30–107 **1129.** In proceedings against a person for an offence under the *Companies Acts*, nothing in those Acts is to be taken to require any person to disclose any information that he is entitled to refuse to disclose on grounds of legal professional privilege (in Scotland, confidentiality of communications).

Proceedings against unincorporated bodies

1130.—(1) Proceedings for an offence under the *Companies Acts* alleged to have been committed by an unincorporated body must be brought in the name of the body (and not in that of any of its members).

(2) For the purposes of such proceedings—

(a) any rules of court relating to the service of documents have effect as if the body were a body corporate, and

(b) the following provisions apply as they apply in relation to a body corporate—

(i) in England and Wales, section 33 of the *Criminal Justice Act* 1925 and Schedule 3 to the *Magistrates' Courts Act* 1980,

(ii) [*Scotland*],

(iii) [*Northern Ireland*].

(3) A fine imposed on an unincorporated body on its conviction of an offence under the *Companies Acts* must be paid out of the funds of the body.

For section 33 of the 1925 Act, see *ante*, § 4–101. For Schedule 3 to the 1980 Act, see *ante*, § 1–242.

Imprisonment on summary conviction in England and Wales: transitory provision

1131. [*As to the effect of this section, see* ante, *§ 30–25.*]

Production and inspection of documents where offence suspected

30–107a **1132.**—(1) An application under this section may be made—

(a) in England and Wales, to a judge of the High Court by the Director of Public Prosecutions, the Secretary of State or a chief officer of police;

(b) [*Scotland*];

(c) [*Northern Ireland*].

(2) If on an application under this section there is shown to be reasonable cause to believe—

(a) that any person has, while an officer of a company, committed an offence in connection with the management of the company's affairs, and

(b) that evidence of the commission of the offence is to be found in any documents in the possession or control of the company,

an order under this section may be made.

(3) The order may—

(a) authorise any person named in it to inspect the documents in question, or any of them, for the purpose of investigating and obtaining evidence of the offence, or

(b) require the secretary of the company, or such other officer of it as may be named in the order, to produce the documents (or any of them) to a person named in the order at a place so named.

(4) This section applies also in relation to documents in the possession or control of a person carrying on the business of banking, so far as they relate to the company's affairs, as it applies to documents in the possession or control of the company, except that no such order as is referred to in subsection (3)(b) may be made by virtue of this subsection.

(5) The decision under this section of a judge of the High Court, any of the Lords Commissioners of Justiciary or the High Court is not appealable.

(6) In this section "document" includes information recorded in any form.

Transitional provision

1133. The provisions of this Part except section 1132 do not apply to offences committed before the commencement of the relevant provision.

The reference to "this Part" is a reference to Part 36 (*i.e.* ss.1121–1133).

(3) Interpretation

Schedule 8 to the *Companies Act* 2006 contains an index of provisions defining or otherwise explaining expressions used in the *Companies Acts*. The expressions "director" and "shadow director" are defined in sections 250 and 251 in terms that are materially identical to their predecessor provisions in section 741 of the *Companies Act* 1985. **30–108**

Companies Act 2006, ss.250, 251

"Director"

250. In the *Companies Acts* "director" includes any person occupying the position of director, by whatever name called. **30–108a**

"Shadow director"

251.—(1) In the *Companies Acts* "shadow director", in relation to a company, means a person in accordance with whose directions or instructions the directors of the company are accustomed to act. **30–108b**

(2) A person is not to be regarded as a shadow director by reason only that the directors act on advice given by him in a professional capacity.

(3) A body corporate is not to be regarded as a shadow director of any of its subsidiary companies for the purposes of—

Chapter 2 (general duties of directors),

Chapter 4 (transactions requiring members' approval), or

Chapter 6 (contract with sole member who is also a director),

by reason only that the directors of the subsidiary are accustomed to act in accordance with its directions or instructions.

The definition of "shadow director" in section 251 does not mean that it is necessary to prove any degree of compulsion by the shadow director over and above that implicit in the notion of the directors being accustomed to act in compliance with his directions. Whether a communication is a direction or instruction is to be objectively assessed. The definition of shadow director is intended to catch persons who have real influence over the affairs of the company, whether or not that influence is exercised over the whole range of corporate activity: *Secretary of State for Trade and Industry v. Deverell* [2001] Ch. 340, CA (Civ. Div.). **30–109**

(4) Table of indictable offences

The *Companies Act* 2006 contains no table of offences such as was contained in Schedule 24 to the *Companies Act* 1985. The following table is included to show the origins as well as the applicable maximum sentences of the offences under the Act which may be tried on indictment. The table is an abbreviated version of the table published in *Criminal Law Week* 2007/46/34, which also sets out the summary only offences. **30–110**

The key to the mode of trial and penalties column is as follows:—

E	1. On indictment	—fine.
	2. Summary	—fine not exceeding one tenth of statutory maximum for each day contravention continues.
F	1. On indictment	—fine.
	2. Summary	—fine not exceeding statutory maximum.
G	1. On indictment	—2 years' imprisonment, or a fine, or both.
	2. Summary	—12 months' imprisonment, or a fine not exceeding statutory maximum, or both.
H	1. On indictment	—7 years' imprisonment, or a fine, or both.
	2. Summary	—12 months' imprisonment, or a fine not exceeding statutory maximum, or both.

I	1. On indictment	—10 years' imprisonment, or a fine, or both.
	2. Summary	—12 months' imprisonment, or a fine not exceeding statutory maximum, or both.
J	1. On indictment	—2 years' imprisonment, or a fine, or both.
	2. Summary	—3 months' imprisonment, or a fine not exceeding statutory maximum, or both.
Y	Daily default fine of one tenth of the penalty on summary conviction.	
Z	Daily default fine of one fiftieth of the penalty on summary conviction.	

30–111 As to the maximum penalty on summary conviction of an offence committed before the commencement of section 154(1) of the *CJA* 2003, see the effect of section 1131, *ante*, § 30–25.

30–112 The table is printed to show all offences in the *Companies Act* 2006 that may be tried on indictment. The offence-creating sections which are in force, are sections 119, 183, 291, 293, 315, 336, 339, 350, 387, 389, 414, 415, 418, 419, 420, 422, 425, 450, 458, 460, 501, 507, 517 to 523, 530, 643, 644, 747, 767, 795, 798, 804, 806, 897, 949, 953, 980, 984, 993, 1213, 1215 and 1250.

30–113 In addition to the offences created by the sections set out in the table, other sections confer power on the Secretary of State to make regulations which create offences, some of which (*e.g.* those made under Parts 15 and 40) may be punishable on indictment.

Section of Act	General nature of offence	Mode of trial and penalties	Derivation (where applicable)
Part 8	**Part 8: A company's members**		
119(1)	Person making request containing false, *etc*. statement, to inspect company register or index of members' names	G	New offence
119(2)	Person provided with access to company register or index of members' names using or disclosing information obtained for an improper purpose	G	New offence
Part 10	**A company's directors**		
183(1)	Director failing to disclose interest in existing transaction or arrangement entered into by company	F	*C.A.* 1985, s.317(7)
Part 13	**Resolutions and meetings**		
291(5)	Officer of company in default by failing properly or at all to send written resolution proposed by directors to members of company	F	New offence
293(5)	Officer of company in default by failing properly or at all to send written resolution proposed by member of company to other members	F	New offence
315(3)	Officer of company in default by failing to circulate members' statement with respect to business to be dealt with at general meeting of company	F	*C.A.* 1985, s.376(7)
336(3)	Officer of company in default by failing to hold annual general meeting	F	*C.A.* 1985, s.366(4)
339(4)	Officer of public company in default by failing to circulate members' resolutions for company meetings	F	*C.A.* 1985, s.376(7)
350(3)	Person making false or misleading statement to independent assessor	G	New offence
Part 15	**Accounts and reports**		
387(1)	Officer of company in default by failing to keep accounting records	G	*C.A.* 1985, s.221(5)
389(1)	Officer of company failing to comply with requirements as to keeping of accounting records (where to be kept)	G	*C.A.* 1985, s.222(4)
389(3)	Officer of company failing to take steps for compliance by the company, *etc*., with requirements as to keeping of records (how long to be kept)	G	*C.A.* 1985, s.222(6)
414(4)	Directors approving and signing defective accounts	F	*C.A.* 1985, s.233(5)
415(4)	Directors failing to prepare directors' reports	F	*C.A.* 1985, s.234(5)

Section of Act	General nature of offence	Mode of trial and penalties	Derivation (where applicable)
418(5)	Directors approving report containing false statement as to disclosure to auditors	F	*C.A.* 1985, s.234ZA(6)
419(3)	Directors approving report which does not comply with requirements of the Act	F	*C.A.* 1985, s.234(5)
420(2)	Directors failing to prepare directors' remuneration report	F	*C.A.* 1985, s.234B(3)
422(2)	Directors knowingly or recklessly approving directors' remuneration report which does not comply with requirements of Act	F	*C.A.* 1985, s.234C(4)
425(1)	Company, and every officer in default, failing to send out copies of reports to those entitled to receive them	F	*C.A.* 1985, s.238(5)
450(4)	Directors approving abbreviated accounts which do not comply with prescribed requirements	F	*C.A.* 1985, s.233(5)
458(4)	Person contravening restrictions on disclosing or using information disclosed by Commissioners for Revenue and Customs	G	*C.A.* 1985, s.245E(3)
460(4)	Person contravening restrictions on disclosing information obtained under compulsory powers	G	*C.A.* 1985, s.245G(7)
Part 16	**Audit**		
501(1)	Person making false, misleading or deceptive statement to auditor	G	*C.A.* 1985, s.389B(1)
507(1)	Person knowingly or recklessly causing auditor's report on company's annual accounts to include misleading, false or deceptive matter	F	New offence
507(2)	Person knowingly or recklessly causing auditor's report on company's annual accounts to omit required statement	F	New offence
517(2)	Company, and every officer in default, failing send auditor's notice of resignation to registrar	F / Y	*C.A.* 1985, s.392(3)
518(6)	Directors failing to convene meeting requisitioned by resigning auditor	F	*C.A.* 1985, s.392A(5)
519(5)	Person ceasing to hold office as auditor failing to deposit statement at company's registered officer as to the circumstances connected with his ceasing to hold office	F	*C.A.* 1985, s.394A(1)
520(6)	Officer of company in default by failing to comply with requirements as to distribution, *etc.*, of statement of person ceasing to hold office as auditor	F	*C.A.* 1985, s.394A(4)
521(3)	Auditor ceasing to hold office, depositing statement under s.519, but failing to send copy to registrar	F	*C.A.* 1985, s.394A(1)

Section of Act	General nature of offence	Mode of trial and penalties	Derivation (where applicable)
522(5)	Person ceasing to hold office as auditor failing properly or at all to notify appropriate audit authority when ceasing to hold office	F	New offence
523(4)	Company, and every officer in default, failing to notify and give reasons to audit authority of auditor ceasing to hold office	F	New offence
530(1)	Officer of company in default by failing to comply with requirements as to website publication of members' statement of audit concerns	F	New offence
Part 17	**A company's share capital**		
542(4)	Officer of company in default by purporting to allot shares without fixed nominal value	F	New offence
549(4)	Directors exercising company's power to allot shares without authority	F	*C.A.* 1985, s.80(9)
557(1)	Officer of company in default by failing to make return of allotment of shares by limited company, or of new class of shares by unlimited company	F / Y	*C.A.* 1985, s.88(5)
572(2)	Person knowingly or recklessly authorising or permitting inclusion of misleading, false or deceptive material in directors' statement under s.571 (disapplication of pre-emption rights by special resolution)	G	*C.A.* 1985, s.95(6)
590(1)	Company, and every officer in default, contravening prohibitions (in Pt 17, Chap. 5) as to payment for shares	F	*C.A.* 1985, s.114
597(3)	Officer of company in default by failing properly or at all to deliver valuer's report under s.593 to registrar for registration	F / Y	*C.A.* 1985, s.111(3)
607(1)	Company, and every officer in default, contravening s.593 (public company allotting shares for non-cash consideration) or s.598 (public company entering into agreement for transfer of non-cash asset)	F	*C.A.* 1985, s.114
627(7)	Company, and every officer in default, passing resolution under s.626 (reduction of capital in connection with redomination) but failing properly or at all to give notice to registrar	F	*C.A.* 1985, s.122(2)
643(4)	Directors making solvency statement and delivering it to registrar without having reasonable grounds for opinions expressed in it	G	New offence
644(7)	Officer of company in default by delivering solvency statement to registrar without providing copy to members	F	New offence

Section of Act	General nature of offence	Mode of trial and penalties	Derivation (where applicable)
644(8)	Company, and every officer in default, failing properly or at all to deliver to registrar solvency statement and statement of capital and directors' statement as to the timing of the solvency statement and its provision to members	F	New offence
647(1)	Officer of company intentionally or recklessly concealing name of creditor or misrepresenting nature of debt	F	*C.A.* 1985, s.141
656(4)	Directors failing to convene general meeting of company on serious loss of capital	F	*C.A.* 1985, s.142(2)
Part 18	**Acquisition by limited company of its own shares**		
658(2)	Company, and every officer in default, contravening general rule against acquisition of its own shares	G	*C.A.* 1985, s.143(2)
680(1)	Company, and every officer in default, contravening prohibitions in s.678 or s.679 as to financial assistance	G	*C.A.* 1985, s.151(3)
707(6)	Officer of company in default by failing properly or at all to make return to registrar of purchase of shares by company	F / Y	*C.A.* 1985, s.169(6)
715(1)	Directors of private company making statement under s.714 (as to permissible capital for redemption or purchase of its own shares) without having reasonable grounds for opinions expressed in it	G	*C.A.* 1985, s.173(6)
728(4)	Officer of company failing properly or at all to deliver return to registrar where treasury shares sold or transferred for purposes of employees' share scheme	F / Y	*C.A.* 1985, s.169A(4)
732(1)	Company, and every officer in default, failing to comply with general requirements under Pt 18, Chap. 6, as to treasury shares	F	*C.A.* 1985, s.162G
Part 19	**Debentures**		
747(1)	Person making request containing false, *etc.* statement, to inspect company register of debenture or share holders	G	New offence
747(2)	Person provided with access to company register of debenture or share holders using or disclosing information obtained for an improper purpose	G	New offence
Part 20	**Private and public companies**		
767(1)	Company doing business or exercising borrowing power in contravention of s.761 (public company: requirement as to minimum share capital)	F	*C.A.* 1985, s.117(7)
Part 22	**Information about interests in a company's shares**		

Section of Act	General nature of offence	Mode of trial and penalties	Derivation (where applicable)
795(1)	Person failing to comply with notice under s.793 (notice requiring information about interests in company's shares) or making false statement in connection therewith	G	*C.A.* 1985, s.216(3)
798(2)	Person holding shares subject to restrictions imposed by order under s.794 (notice requiring information: order imposing restrictions on shares) seeking to exercise certain rights	F	*C.A.* 1985, s.455(1)
798(3)	Company, and every officer in default, issuing shares in contravention of restrictions imposed under s.794	F	*C.A.* 1985, s.455(2)
804(2)	Officer of company in default by failing to exercise powers under s.793 (notice requiring information about interests in company's shares) when requested to do so by members under s.803	F	*C.A.* 1985, s.214(5)
806(3)	Officers of company failing to comply with any other provision of s.805 (report to members on investigation under s.805)	F	*C.A.* 1985, s.215(8)
814(1)	Person making request containing false, *etc.* statement, to inspect company register or index of interests disclosed	G	New offence
814(2)	Person provided with access to company register or index of interests disclosed using or disclosing information obtained for an improper purpose	G	New offence
Part 25	**Company charges**		
860(4)	Company, and every officer in default, creating charge but failing properly or at all to deliver particulars and instrument to registrar	F	*C.A.* 1985, s.399(3)
862(4)	Company, and every officer in default, acquiring property subject to registrable charge and failing to deliver particulars and certified copy of instrument to registrar	F	*C.A.* 1985, s.400(4)
876(3)	Officer of company in default by knowingly and wilfully permitting omission of entry in company's register of charges	F	*C.A.* 1985, s.407(3)
Part 26	**Arrangements and reconstructions**		
897(5)	Company, and every officer in default, failing to make explanatory statement to creditors when giving notice summoning meeting of creditors for proposed compromise or arrangement	F	*C.A.* 1985, s.426(6)
Part 28	**Takeovers, *etc.***		

Section of Act	General nature of offence	Mode of trial and penalties	Derivation (where applicable)
949(1)	Unauthorised disclosure of information relating to the private affairs of individual, or any particular business, provided to the Takeovers Panel in connection with exercise of its functions	G	S.I. 2006 No. 1183, reg. 8
953(2)	Person making bid failing to comply with bid offer document rules	F	S.I. 2006 No. 1183, reg. 10(2)
953(4)	Directors and others officers of company failing to comply with bid response document rules	F	S.I. 2006 No. 1183, reg. 10(4)
980(6)	Person failing properly or at all to give notice of right to buy out minority shareholders ("squeeze out"); failure to accompany notice with statutory declaration that conditions satisfied; knowingly making false statement in such declaration	G / Z	S.I. 2006 No. 1183, Sched. 2
984(5)	Person failing properly or at all to give notice, *etc.*, of rights of minority shareholders to be bought out ("sell out")	F / Z	S.I. 2006 No. 1183, Sched. 2
Part 29	**Fraudulent trading**		
993(1)	Fraudulent trading	I	*C.A.* 1985, s.458
Part 31	**Dissolution and restoration to the register**		
1004(5)	Person making improper application under s.1003 (application for voluntary striking off of company name from register) on behalf of company when activities of company preclude striking off	F	*C.A.* 1985, s.652E(1)
1005(4)	Person making improper application under s.1003 (application for voluntary striking off of company name from register) on behalf of company when other proceedings not concluded	F	*C.A.* 1985, s.652E(1)
1006(4)	Person applying on behalf of company for its name to be struck off register failing to give copy of application to existing members, employees, *etc.*	F	*C.A.* 1985, s.652E(1)
1006(4)	Person applying on behalf of company for its name to be struck off register failing to give copy of application to existing members, employees, *etc.* (offence aggravated by intention to conceal making of application from person concerned)	H	*C.A.* 1985, s.652E(2)
1007(4)	Director of company failing to give copy of application for company name to be struck off register to person who becomes member, employee, *etc.*, after application was made	F	*C.A.* 1985, s.652E(1)

Section of Act	General nature of offence	Mode of trial and penalties	Derivation (where applicable)
1007(4)	Director of company failing to give copy of application for company name to be struck off register to person who becomes member, employee, *etc.*, after application was made (offence aggravated by intention to conceal making of application from person concerned)	H	*C.A.* 1985, s.652E(2)
1009(5)	Director of company failing to withdraw application for company name to be struck off register after company name changed, *etc.*	F	*C.A.* 1985, s.652E(1)
Part 35	**The registrar of companies**		
1112(1)	Person knowingly or recklessly delivering documents, or making statements, to register which are false or deceptive	G	New offence
Part 37	**Companies: supplementary provisions**		
1153(2)	Person knowingly or recklessly making misleading, false or deceptive statement to person carrying out valuation	G	New offence
Part 42	**Statutory auditors (this part does not fall under the umbrella of the "*Companies Acts*")**		
1213(3)	Person purporting to act as statutory auditor when ineligible to do so or without giving notice to audited person that he has resigned as a statutory auditor	F	*C.A.* 1989, s.28
1213(5)	Person convicted of offence under s.1212(3) (*ante*) through indelibility and continuing to act as statutory auditor	E	*C.A.* 1989, s.28
1213(6)	Person convicted of offence under s.1212(3) (*ante*) through failure to give notice and continuing to fail to give notice	E	*C.A.* 1989, s.28
1215(2)	Person continuing to act as statutory auditor when independence requirement no longer met, or failing to give notice to audited person that he has resigned by reason of his lack of independence	F	*C.A.* 1989, s.28
1215(4)	Person convicted of offence under s.1215(2) through acting when independence requirement no longer met yet continuing to act as statutory auditor	E	*C.A.* 1989, s.28
1215(5)	Person convicted of offence under s.1215(2) through failing to give notice yet continuing to fail to give notice	E	*C.A.* 1989, s.28
1224B	Person disclosing information in contravention of s.1224A	J	
1250(1)	Person knowingly or recklessly furnishing false, misleading or deceptive information in connection with application or requirement under this part	G	*C.A.* 1989, s.41(1)
1250(3)	Person whose name does not appear in register of auditors describing, *etc.*, himself to be a registered third country auditor	D	*C.A.* 1989, s.41(2)

(5) Fraudulent trading

Companies Act 2006, s.993

Offence of fraudulent trading

30–115 **993.**—(1) If any business of a company is carried on with intent to defraud creditors of the company or creditors of any other person, or for any fraudulent purpose, every person who is knowingly a party to the carrying on of the business in that manner commits an offence.

(2) This applies whether or not the company has been, or is in the course of being, wound up.

(3) A person guilty of an offence under this section is liable—

(a) on conviction on indictment, to imprisonment for a term not exceeding ten years or a fine (or both);

(b) on summary conviction—

(i) in England and Wales, to imprisonment for a term not exceeding twelve months or a fine not exceeding the statutory maximum (or both);

(ii) [*Scotland and Northern Ireland*].

Indictment

STATEMENT OF OFFENCE

30–116 *Fraudulent trading, contrary to section 993(1) of the* Companies Act *2006*

PARTICULARS OF OFFENCE

A B and CD, between the —— day of ——, 20—, and the —— day of ——, 20—, were knowingly party to the carrying on of the business of X Ltd for a fraudulent purpose, namely …

For an example of this indictment, see *R. v. Philippou*, 89 Cr.App.R. 290 at 300, CA.

Class of offence and mode of trial

30–117 This offence is triable either way. It is a class 3 offence, *ante*, § 2–17. It is in all essential respects identical to the offence of fraudulent trading under the *Companies Act* 1985, s.458, save that the maximum sentence on conviction on indictment is now 10 years' imprisonment (reflecting the increase brought about by the *Fraud Act* 2006, s.10, in relation to offences under the 1985 Act committed on or after January 15, 2007). Cases decided under section 458 will therefore continue to have relevance.

The nature of the offence

30–118 The section creates two different types of offence: *R. v. Inman* [1967] 1 Q.B. 140, 50 Cr.App.R. 247, CCA, namely (a) carrying on a business with intent to defraud creditors; and (b) carrying on a business for any fraudulent purpose.

A business may be "carried on" even where a company has ceased trading, save for the collection of debts and the payment of creditors: see *Re Sarflax Ltd* [1979] Ch. 592, Ch D. A single large transaction may constitute the carrying on of business for the purpose of the Act: *Re Gerald Cooper Chemicals Ltd* [1978] Ch. 262, Ch D, although the section is primarily aimed at the carrying on of a business and not at the execution of individual transactions. Misleading one creditor over a short period in relation to one debt was held not to be fraudulent trading under the similarly worded *Insolvency Act* 1986, s.213: *Morphitis v. Bernasconi* [2003] Ch. 552, CA (Civ. Div.).

30–119 A person must have taken some positive steps in the carrying on of the company's business; accordingly the mere failure of a secretary and financial adviser to advise the directors that the company was insolvent and should cease to trade did not constitute being a party to the carrying on of the company's business: *Re Maidstone Building Provisions Ltd* [1971] 1 W.L.R. 1085, Ch D. In *R. v. Miles* [1992] Crim.L.R. 657, the Court of Appeal approved the words of Lord Lane C.J. in *R. v. Grantham* [1984] 1 Q.B. 675, 79 Cr.App.R. 86, CA, that the section is intended to cover those who are "running the business", meaning exercising a controlling or managing function. It was held to have been a misdirection in *R. v. Miles* to direct the jury that the offence could be committed by "concurring in the trade which is involved in the business of the company". In *Re Augustus Barnett & Sons Ltd* [1986] B.C.L.C. 170, Ch D, Hoffman J. expressed the view that a person might be knowingly party to the carrying on of business for a fraudulent purpose even if he was an outsider who could not be said to have carried on the business or even assisted the carrying on of a business if he nevertheless in some way participated in the fraudulent acts. See also, *Morris v. Banque Arabe et Internationale d'Investissment SA (No. 2)* [2001] 1 B.C.L.C. 263, Ch D.

The section requires proof that an action which can be described as carrying on of some business of the company was done with intent to defraud or for a fraudulent purpose: *Re Augustus Barnett & Sons Ltd, ante*. "Dishonesty" is an essential ingredient of this offence: *R. v. Cox and Hodges*, 75 Cr.App.R. 291, CA, and for this purpose a *Ghosh* (*R. v. Ghosh* [1982] Q.B. 1053, 75 Cr.App.R. 154, CA, *ante*, §§ 21–2b, 21–2c) direction is appropriate; see *R. v. Lockwood* [1986] Crim.L.R. 244, CA. In *R. v. Smith (W.D.)* [1996] 2 Cr.App.R. 1, CA, the court confirmed that, in a case of a fraud on creditors, evidence of dishonesty directed towards the creditors was required. However, evidence of dishonesty in conducting the affairs of the company was admissible as evidence from which dishonesty directed towards creditors was capable of being inferred.

Knowledge in this context includes "blind-eye knowledge", *i.e.* a firmly grounded suspicion that relevant facts exist and a deliberate decision to avoid confirming their existence: *Re Bank of Credit and Commerce International S.A.*; *Morris v. State Bank of India* [2003] B.C.C. 735, Ch D (Patten J.).

If an offence of carrying on a business with intent to defraud creditors is charged it is **30–120** necessary to prove that the persons at whom the conduct was aimed were actual as opposed to potential creditors: see *R. v. Inman, ante*, at 146, 251, and *R. v. Burgess*, unreported, July 28, 1994 (94/1800/X4), CA. The word creditor takes its ordinary meaning of one to whom money is owed. Whether the debt can be presently sued for is immaterial: *R. v. Smith (W.D.) ante*. Accordingly, a supplier who has delivered goods to a company under a contract providing for deferred payment is a creditor of that company even if the contractual time for payment has not expired. The court said in *Smith* that there was no reason in principle why other kinds of creditors should not also be within the scope of section 458 (of the 1985 Act).

For the meaning of "intent to defraud", see *ante*, §§ 17–62 *et seq.*, and *Re Sarflax Ltd, ante*. A company which is carrying on business and incurring debts when, to the knowledge of the directors, there is no reasonable prospect of the debts being paid may be inferred to be carrying on the business of the company with intent to defraud creditors: *Re William C. Leitch Bros Ltd* [1932] 2 Ch. 71, Ch D. In the leading case of *Welham v. DPP* [1961] A.C. 103, HL (*ante* § 17–62), it was held that "to defraud" was to "act to the prejudice of another's right", which would include carrying on business (to the potential prejudice of the creditors) when the defendant knew there was a risk that the company would not be able to meet its debts as they fell due.

In *Grantham, ante*, the court emphasised that the speeches in *Welham* were directed **30–121** to the meaning of "intent to defraud" generally and were not limited to its meaning in the *Forgery Act* 1913 (*rep.*). It approved the following passage in the summing up:

> "Some fraudulent traders intend from the outset never to pay or never to pay more than a fraction of the debt. If that is true in your view in this case then the intent to defraud would be made out but a trader can intend to defraud if he obtains credit when there is a substantial risk of the creditor not getting his money or not getting the whole of his money and the defendant knows that that is the position and knows he is stepping beyond the bounds of what ordinary decent people engaged in business would regard as honest. ... [I]f a man honestly believes when he obtains credit that although funds are not immediately available he will be able to pay them when the debt becomes due or within a short time thereafter, no doubt you would say that is not dishonest and there is no intent to defraud but if he obtains or helps to obtain credit or further credit when he knows there is no good reason for thinking funds will become available to pay the debt when it becomes due or shortly thereafter then, though it is entirely a matter for you this question of dishonesty, you might well think that is dishonest and there is an intent to defraud" (at pp. 681, 90).

If an offence of carrying on a business "for any fraudulent purpose" is charged it is **30–122** not necessary to prove that there were any creditors in the contemplation of the wrongdoer. In *R. v. Kemp* [1988] 1 Q.B. 645, 87 Cr.App.R. 95, CA, the court held that, if a person carries on the business of a company with a fraudulent intent, namely the intent to defraud customers of the company, he commits the offence of fraudulent trading. Although customers are only potential creditors, the mischief aimed at is fraudulent trading and not fraudulent trading only in so far as it affects creditors; see *R. v. Seillon* [1982] Crim.L.R. 676, CA. Thus, for example, the concealment of transactions in order to maintain or renew licences issued by the Civil Aviation Authority and the Association of British Travel Agents was held to be capable of amounting to a fraudulent purpose within the meaning of the section: *R. v. Philippou*, 89 Cr.App.R. 290, CA.

The term "fraudulent purpose" connotes an intention to go "beyond the bounds of what ordinary decent people engaged in business would regard as honest", see *R. v. Grantham*, *ante*; or "involving, according to the current notions of fair trading among commercial men, real moral blame", see *Re Patrick & Lyon Ltd* [1933] Ch. 786, Ch D, *per* Maugham J. at p. 790.

Sentence

30–123 See *R. v. Richardson and George*, 14 Cr.App.R.(S.) 654, CA, *R. v. Cook*, 16 Cr.App.R.(S.) 917, CA, *R. v. Smith and Palk* [1997] 2 Cr.App.R.(S.) 167, CA (in broad terms a charge of fraudulent trading resulting in a deficiency of a given amount is less serious than a specific charge of theft or fraud to an equivalent amount), *R. v. Gibson* [1999] 2 Cr.App.R.(S.) 52, CA (in which caution was expressed about the appropriateness of using the guidelines in *R. v. Clark* [1998] 2 Cr.App.R. 137, CA (*ante*, § 21–4e), without some modification) and CSP, B13–5.3A; but it is important to note that, at the time these cases were decided, the maximum penalty was seven years' imprisonment.

(6) Other offences

30–124 Several new offences are created by the *Companies Act* 2006, amongst which are those contained in sections 119(1) and (2), 747(1) and (2), and 814(1) and (2). In each case, the offence contrary to subsection (1) is committed by a person who knowingly or recklessly makes a false, misleading or deceptive statement in a request to inspect, or for a copy of, a company's register of members (s.119), register of debentures (s.747), or register of disclosed interests (s.814). The offence contrary to subsection (2) is committed by a person who is in possession of information obtained through such a request, who does (or fails to do) anything that results in the information being disclosed to another person, knowing or having reason to suspect that that other person may use the information for a purpose that is not a proper purpose. There is no definition of a proper (or improper) purpose.

(7) Consequential and transitional provisions

30–125 Part 46 of the *Companies Act* 2006 (ss.1288–1297) contains general supplementary provisions, with sections 1294 to 1297 making consequential and transitional provision. See also the *Companies Act 2006 (Commencement No. 1, Transitional Provisions and Savings) Order* 2006 (S.I. 2006 No. 3428), the *Companies Act 2006 (Commencement No. 2, Consequential Amendments, Transitional Provisions and Savings) Order* 2007 (S.I. 2007 No. 1093), the *Companies Act 2006 (Commencement No. 3, Consequential Amendments, Transitional Provisions and Savings) Order* 2007 (S.I. 2007 No. 2194), the *Companies Act 2006 (Commencement No. 4 and Commencement No. 3 (Amendment)) Order* 2007 (S.I. 2007 No. 2607), the *Companies Act 2006 (Commencement No. 5, Transitional Provisions and Savings) Order* 2007 (S.I. 2007 No. 3495), the *Companies Act 2006 (Commencement No. 6, Savings and Commencement Nos 3 and 5 (Amendment)) Order* 2008 (S.I. 2008 No. 674) and the *Companies Act 2006 (Consequential Amendments etc.) Order* 2008 (S.I. 2008 No. 948).

B. FRAUD ACT 2006

30–126 The *Fraud Act* 2006 came into force on January 15, 2007. All the offences under the Act, bar that created by section 9 of participation in a fraudulent business carried on by a person outside the reach of section 993 of the *Companies Act* 2006, are dealt with in Chapter 21 (*ante*, §§ 21–356 *et seq.*).

Fraud Act 2006, s. 9

Participating in fraudulent business carried on by sole trader etc.

9.—(1) A person is guilty of an offence if he is knowingly a party to the carrying on of a business to which this section applies.

(2) This section applies to a business which is carried on—

(a) by a person who is outside the reach of section 993 of the *Companies Act* 2006 (offence of fraudulent trading), and

(b) with intent to defraud creditors of any person or for any other fraudulent purpose.

(3) The following are within the reach of that section—

(a) a company (within the meaning of that Act);

(b) a person to whom that section applies (with or without adaptations or modifications) as if the person were a company;

(c) a person exempted from the application of that section.

(5) "Fraudulent purpose" has the same meaning as in that section.

(6) A person guilty of an offence under this section is liable—

(a) on summary conviction, to imprisonment for a term not exceeding *6* [12] months or to a fine not exceeding the statutory maximum (or to both);

(b) on conviction on indictment, to imprisonment for a term not exceeding 10 years or to a fine (or to both).

[This section is printed as amended, and repealed in part, by the *Companies Act 2006 (Commencement No. 3, Consequential Amendments, Transitional Provisions and Savings) Order* 2007 (S.I. 2007 No. 2194). Pending the commencement of the *CJA* 2003, s.154, subs. (6)(a) has effect with the substitution of "6" for "12": 2006 Act, Sched. 2, para. 1.]

As to subsection (3)(b), see the *European Economic Interest Grouping Regulations* 1989 (S.I. 1989 No. 638), and the *Limited Liability Partnerships Regulations* 2001 (S.I. 2001 No. 1090). As to subsection (3)(c), see section 1043 of the *Companies Act* 2006.

Class of offence, mode of trial and sentence

This offence is triable either way. It is a class 3 offence, *ante*, § 2–17. The maximum sentence on conviction on indictment is 10 years' imprisonment, or a fine of any amount, or both; on summary conviction, the maximum is 12 months' imprisonment (but see *ante*), or a fine not exceeding the statutory maximum. **30–127**

The nature of the offence

Section 9 criminalises the carrying on of any business for a fraudulent purpose where the conduct is not made criminal by section 993 of the *Companies Act* 2006 (or its predecessor, section 458 of the 1985 Act). The approach of the courts to this offence of non-corporate fraudulent trading is likely to be heavily influenced by the approach adopted in relation to corporate fraudulent trading, as to which, see *ante*, §§ 30–115 *et seq.* **30–128**

[The next paragraph is § 30–144.]

C. INSOLVENCY ACT 1986

(1) General provisions as to offences and interpretation

The scheme of the Insolvency Act 1986

The first group of Parts (Pts I to VII inclusive) governs the insolvency and winding up of companies. The second group (Pts VIII to XI inclusive) governs the insolvency of individuals and bankruptcy. The third group (Pts XII to XIX inclusive) contains material relating to both company and individual insolvency as well as a number of general provisions. Part IV, Chap. X (ss.206 to 219) contains the principal corporate criminal of- **30–144** fences, dealing with malpractice before and during liquidation, either by companies or company officers, together with provisions as to prosecutions and investigations. Part IX, Chap. VI deals with offences committed by bankrupts. Rules made under sections 411 and 412 of the *Insolvency Act* 1986 also create criminal offences: see *post*, § 30–156. Both the corporate and the individual insolvency provisions have been extensively amended by Part 10 of the *Enterprise Act* 2002. Part 10 was brought into force (with minor exceptions) on September 15, 2003, and April 1, 2004, by the *Enterprise Act 2002 (Commencement No. 4 and Transitional Provisions and Savings) Order* 2003 (S.I. 2003 No. 2093).

There is no general definition of the term "insolvency" in the *Insolvency Act* 1986: however, section 122 provides the best guide to the general meaning of the word as it lists the circumstances in which a company may be wound up by the court. The list includes as one circumstance, amongst others, the fact that "the company is unable to pay its debts": see s.122(1)(f). Inability to pay debts is defined in section 123 as consisting of, *inter alia*, the fact that the company is unable to pay its debts as they fall due (see s.123(1)(e)) and the fact that the value of the company's assets is less than the amount of its liabilities taking into account its contingent and prospective liabilities: see s.123(2).

Insolvency Act 1986, ss.247, 249–251

PART VII

INTERPRETATION FOR FIRST GROUP OF PARTS

"Insolvency" and "go into liquidation"

30–145 **247.**—(1) In this Group of Parts, except in so far as the context otherwise requires, "insolvency", in relation to a company, includes the approval of a voluntary arrangement under Part I, or the appointment of an administrator or administrative receiver.

(2) For the purpose of any provision in this Group of Parts, a company goes into liquidation if it passes a resolution for voluntary winding up or an order for its winding up is made by the court at a time when it has not already gone into liquidation by passing such a resolution.

(3) The reference to a resolution for voluntary winding up in subsection (2) includes a reference to a resolution which is deemed to occur by virtue of—

(a) paragraph 83(6)(b) of Schedule B1, or

(b) an order made following conversion of administration or a voluntary arrangement into winding up by virtue of Article 37 of the EC Regulation.

[This section is printed as amended by the *Insolvency Act 1986 (Amendment) (No. 2) Regulations* 2002 (S.I. 2002 No. 1240), regs 3 and 12; and the *Enterprise Act* 2002, s.248(3), and Sched. 17, paras 9 and 33.]

"Connected" with a company

30–146 **249.** For the purpose of any provision in this Group of Parts, a person is connected with a company if—

(a) he is a director or a shadow director of the company or an associate of such a director or shadow director, or

(b) he is an associate of the company,

and "associate" has the meaning given in section 435 of Part XVIII of this Act.

"Member" of a company

30–147 **250.** For the purpose of any provision in this Group of Parts, a person who is not a member of a company but to whom shares in the company have been transferred or transmitted by operation of law, is to be regarded as a member of the company, and references to a member or members are to be read accordingly.

Expressions used generally

30–148 **251.** In this Group of Parts, except in so far as the context otherwise requires—

...

"director" includes any person occupying the position of director, by whatever name called;

...

"shadow director" in relation to a company, means a person in accordance with whose directions or instructions the directors of the company are accustomed to act (but so that a person is not deemed a shadow director by reason only that the directors act on advice given by him in a professional capacity);

…

and any expression for whose interpretation provision is made by Part XXVI of the *Companies Act*, other than an expression defined above in this section, is to be construed in accordance with that provision.

Summary proceedings

Summary proceedings for any offence under any of Parts I to VII of the Act may be taken against a body corporate at any place at which that body has a place of business, and against any other person at any place at which he is for the time being: *Insolvency Act* 1986, s.431(1). Notwithstanding anything in section 127(1) of the *MCA* 1980 (*ante*, § 1–200), an information relating to such an offence which is triable by a magistrates' court in England and Wales may be so tried if it is laid within three years after the commission of the offence and within 12 months after the date on which evidence sufficient in the opinion of the DPP or the Secretary of State to justify the proceedings comes to his knowledge: *ibid.*, s.431(2). A certificate of the DPP or the Secretary of State as to the date on which such evidence came to his knowledge is conclusive evidence: *ibid.*, s.431(4). **30–149**

Insolvency Act 1986, s.432

Offences by bodies corporate

432.—(1) This section applies to offences under this Act other than those excepted by subsection (4). **30–150**

(2) Where a body corporate is guilty of an offence to which this section applies and the offence is proved to have been committed with the consent or connivance of, or to be attributable to any neglect on the part of, any director, manager, secretary or other similar officer of the body corporate or any person who was purporting to act in any such capacity he, as well as the body corporate, is guilty of the offence and liable to be proceeded against and punished accordingly.

(3) Where the affairs of a body corporate are managed by its members, subsection (2) applies in relation to the acts and defaults of a member in connection with his functions of management as if he were a director of the body corporate.

(4) The offences excepted from this section are those under sections 30, 39, 51, 53, 54, 62, 64, 66, 85, 89, 164, 188, 201, 206, 207, 208, 209, 210 and 211 and those under paragraphs 16(2), 17(3)(a), 18(3)(a), 19(3)(a), 22(1) and 23(1)(a) of Schedule A1.

[This section is printed as amended by the *Insolvency Act* 2000, s.1 and Sched. 1, para. 11.]

See *R. v. Boal* [1992] 1 Q.B. 591, 95 Cr.App.R. 272, CA, *ante*, § 30–103.

Insolvency Act 1986, ss.433, 435

Admissibility in evidence of statement of affairs, etc.

433. [*Set out at § 30–74*, ante.] **30–151**

Meaning of "associate"

435.—(1) For the purposes of this Act any question whether a person is an associate of another person is to be determined in accordance with the following provisions of this section (any provision that a person is an associate of another person being taken to mean that they are associates of each other). **30–152**

(2) A person is an associate of an individual if that person is—

(a) the individual's husband or wife or civil partner,

(b) a relative of—

(i) the individual, or

(ii) the individual's husband or wife or civil partner, or

(c) the husband or wife or civil partner of a relative of—

(i) the individual, or

(ii) the individual's husband or wife or civil partner.

(3) A person is an associate of any person with whom he is in partnership, and of the husband or wife or civil partner or a relative of any individual with whom he is in partnership; and a Scottish firm is an associate of any person who is a member of the firm.

(4) A person is an associate of any person whom he employs or by whom he is employed.

(5) A person in his capacity as trustee of a trust other than—

(a) a trust arising under any of the second Group of Parts or the *Bankruptcy (Scotland) Act* 1985, or

(b) a pension scheme or an employees' share scheme (within the meaning of the *Companies Act*),

is an associate of another person if the beneficiaries of the trust include, or the terms of the trust confer a power that may be exercised for the benefit of, that other person or an associate of that other person.

(6) A company is an associate of another company—

(a) if the same person has control of both, or a person has control of one and persons who are his associates, or he and persons who are his associates, have control of the other, or

(b) if a group of two or more persons has control of each company, and the groups either consist of the same persons or could be regarded as consisting of the same persons by treating (in one or more cases) a member of either group as replaced by a person of whom he is an associate.

30–153 (7) A company is an associate of another person if that person has control of it or if that person and persons who are his associates together have control of it.

(8) For the purposes of this section a person is a relative of an individual if he is that individual's brother, sister, uncle, aunt, nephew, niece, lineal ancestor or lineal descendant, treating—

(a) any relationship of the half blood as a relationship of the whole blood and the stepchild or adopted child of any person as his child, and

(b) an illegitimate child as the legitimate child of his mother and reputed father;

and references in this section to a husband or wife include a former husband or wife and a reputed husband or wife [and references to a civil partner include a former civil partner].

(9) For the purposes of this section any director or other officer of a company is to be treated as employed by that company.

(10) For the purposes of this section a person is to be taken as having control of a company if—

(a) the directors of the company or of another company which has control of it (or any of them) are accustomed to act in accordance with his directions or instructions, or

(b) he is entitled to exercise, or control the exercise of, one third or more of the voting power at any general meeting of the company or of another company which has control of it;

and where two or more persons together satisfy either of the above conditions, they are to be taken as having control of the company.

(11) In this section "company" includes any body corporate (whether incorporated in Great Britain or elsewhere); and references to directors and other officers of a company and to voting power at any general meeting of a company have effect with any necessary modifications.

[This section is printed as amended by the *Civil Partnership Act* 2004, s.261(1), and Sched. 27, para. 122.]

Expressions used generally in the Act

30–154 Section 436 is a general interpretation section. *Inter alia*, it defines "property" as including "money, goods, things in action, land and every description of property wherever situated and also obligations and every description of interest, whether present or future or vested or contingent, arising out of, or incidental to, property"; and "transaction" as including "a gift, agreement or arrangement".

(2) Tables of indictable offences

Insolvency Act 1986, s.430

Provision introducing Schedule of punishments

30–155 **430.**—(1) Schedule 10 to this Act has effect with respect to the way in which offences under this Act are punishable on conviction.

(2) In relation to an offence under a provision of this Act specified in the first column of the Schedule (the general nature of the offence being described in the second column), the third column shows whether the offence is punishable on conviction on indictment, or on summary conviction, or either in the one way or the other.

(3) The fourth column of the Schedule shows, in relation to an offence, the maximum punishment by way of fine or imprisonment under this Act which may be imposed on a person convicted of the offence in the way specified in relation to it in the third column (that is to say, on indictment or summarily), a reference to a period of years or months being a term of imprisonment of that duration.

(4) The fifth column shows (in relation to an offence for which there is an entry in that column) that a person convicted of the offence after continued contravention is liable to a daily default fine; that is to say, he is liable on a second or subsequent conviction of the offence to the fine specified in that column for each day on which the contravention is continued (instead of the penalty specified for the offence in the fourth column of the Schedule).

(5) For the purpose of any enactment in this Act whereby an officer of a company who is in default is liable to a fine or penalty, the expression "officer who is in default" means any officer of the company who knowingly and wilfully authorises or permits the default, refusal or contravention mentioned in the enactment.

Insolvency Rules 1986, r.12.21

Punishment of offences

12.21.—(1) Schedule 5 to the Rules has effect with respect to the way in which contraventions of the Rules are punishable on conviction. **30–156**

(2) In relation to an offence under a provision of the Rules specified in the first column of the Schedule (the general nature of the offence being described in the second column), the third column shows whether the offence is punishable on conviction on indictment, or on summary conviction, or either in the one way or the other.

(3) The fourth column shows, in relation to an offence, the maximum punishment by way of fine or imprisonment which may be imposed on a person convicted of the offence in the way specified in relation to it in the third column (that is to say, on indictment or summarily), a reference to a period of years or months being to a term of imprisonment of that duration.

(4) [*Identical to s.430(4)*, ante.]

(5) Section 431 (summary proceedings), as it applies to England and Wales, has effect in relation to offences under the Rules as to offences under the Act.

Schedule 10 to the Act (*post*, § 30–158) and Schedule 5 to the Rules (*post*, § 30–159) set out the criminal offences, their mode of prosecution and punishment, under the Act and the Rules respectively. Summary only offences and offences having effect only in Scotland have been omitted from both tables. **30–157**

Insolvency Act 1986, Sched. 10

SCHEDULE 10

PUNISHMENT OF OFFENCES UNDER THIS ACT

Section of Act creating offence	General nature of offence	Mode of prosecution	Punishment	Daily default fine (where applicable)
6A(1)	False representation or fraud for purpose of obtaining members' or creditors' approval of proposed voluntary arrangement.	1. On indictment. 2. Summary.	7 years or a fine, or both. *6* [12] months or the statutory maximum, or both.	
		…		
30	Body corporate acting as receiver.	1. On indictment. 2. Summary.	A fine. The statutory maximum.	
31	Bankrupt [or person in respect of whom a debt relief order is made] acting as receiver or manager.	1. On indictment. 2. Summary.	2 years or a fine, or both. *6* [12] months or the statutory maximum, or both.	
		…		
47(6)	Failure to comply with provisions relating to statement of affairs, where administrative receiver appointed.	1. On indictment. 2. Summary.	A fine. The statutory maximum.	One-tenth of the statutory maximum.
		…		
89(4)	Director making statutory declaration of company's solvency without reasonable grounds for his opinion.	1. On indictment. 2. Summary.	2 years or a fine, or both. *6* [12] months or the statutory maximum, or both.	
		…		

Section of Act creating offence	General nature of offence	Mode of prosecution	Punishment	Daily default fine (where applicable)
98(6)	Company failing to comply with s.98 in respect of summoning and giving notice of creditors' meeting.	1. On indictment. 2. Summary.	A fine. The statutory maximum.	
99(3)	Directors failing to attend and lay statement in prescribed form before creditors' meeting.	1. On indictment. 2. Summary.	A fine. The statutory maximum.	
		…		
131(7)	Failing to comply with requirements as to statement of affairs, where liquidator appointed.	1. On indictment. 2. Summary.	A fine. The statutory maximum.	One-tenth of the statutory maximum.
164	Giving, offering etc. corrupt inducement affecting appointment of liquidator,	1. On indictment. 2. Summary.	A fine. The statutory maximum.	
		…		
206(1)	Fraud etc. in anticipation of winding up.	1. On indictment. 2. Summary.	7 years or a fine, or both. *6* [12] months or the statutory maximum, or both.	
206(2)	Privity to fraud in anticipation of winding up; fraud, or privity to fraud, after commencement of winding up.	1. On indictment. 2. Summary.	7 years or a fine, or both. *6* [12] months or the statutory maximum, or both.	
206(5)	Knowingly taking in pawn or pledge, or otherwise receiving, company property.	1. On indictment. 2. Summary.	7 years or a fine, or both. *6* [12] months or the statutory maximum, or both.	
207	Officer of company entering into transaction in fraud of company's creditors.	1. On indictment. 2. Summary.	2 years or a fine, or both. *6* [12] months or the statutory maximum, or both.	

Section of Act creating offence	General nature of offence	Mode of prosecution	Punishment	Daily default fine (where applicable)
208	Officer of company misconducting himself in course of winding up.	1. On indictment. 2. Summary.	7 years or a fine, or both. 6 [12] months or the statutory maximum, or both.	
209	Officer or contributory destroying, falsifying, etc., company books.	1. On indictment. 2. Summary.	7 years or a fine, or both. 6 [12] months or the statutory maximum, or both.	
210	Officer of company making material omission from statement relating to company's affairs.	1. On indictment. 2. Summary.	7 years or a fine, or both. 6 [12] months or the statutory maximum, or both.	
211	False representation or fraud for purpose of obtaining creditors' consent to an agreement in connection with winding up	1. On indictment. 2. Summary.	7 years or a fine, or both. 6 [12] months or the statutory maximum, or both.	
216(4)	Contravening restrictions on re-use of name of company in insolvent liquidation.	1. On indictment. 2. Summary.	2 years or a fine, or both. 6 [12] months or the statutory maximum, or both.	
235(5)	Failing to co-operate with office-holder.	1. On indictment. 2. Summary.	A fine. The statutory maximum.	One-tenth of the statutory maximum.
[251O(1)	False representations or omissions in making an application for a debt relief order.	1. On indictment. 2. Summary.	7 years or a fine, or both. 12 months or the statutory maximum, or both.]	
[251O(2)(a)	Failing to comply with duty in connection with an application for a debt relief order.	1. On indictment. 2. Summary.	2 years or a fine, or both. 12 months or the statutory maximum, or both.]	

Section of Act creating offence	General nature of offence	Mode of prosecution	Punishment	Daily default fine (where applicable)
[251O(2)(b)	False representations or omissions in connection with duty in relation to an application for a debt relief order.	1. On indictment. 2. Summary.	7 years or a fine, or both. 12 months or the statutory maximum, or both.]	
[251O(4)(a)	Failing to comply with duty in connection with with a debt relief order.	1. On indictment. 2. Summary.	2 years or a fine, or both. 12 months or the stautory maximum, or both.]	
[251O(4)(b)	False representations or omissions in connection with a duty in relation to a debt relief order.	1. On indictment. 2. Summary.	7 years or a fine, or both. 12 months or the statutory maximum, or both.]	
[251P(1)	Failing to deliver books, records and papers to official receiver, concealing or destroying them or making false entries in them by person in respect of whom a debt relief order is made.	1. On indictment. 2. Summary.	7 years or a fine, or both. 12 months or the statutory maximum, or both.]	
[251P(2)	Person in respect of whom debt relief order is made doing anything falling within paragraphs (c) to (e) of section 251P(1) during the period of 12 months ending with the application date or doing anything falling within paragraphs (b) to (e) of section 251P(1) after that date but before the effective date.	1. On indictment. 2. Summary.	7 years or a fine, or both. 12 months or the statutory maximum, or both.	
[251Q(1)	Fraudulent disposal of property by person in respect of whom a debt relief order is made.	1. On indictment. 2. Summary.	2 years or a fine, or both. 12 months or the statutory maximum, or both.]	

Section of Act creating offence	General nature of offence	Mode of prosecution	Punishment	Daily default fine (where applicable)
[251R(1)	Disposal of property that is not paid for by person in respect of whom a debt relief order is made.	1. On indictment. 2. Summary.	7 years or a fine, or both. 12 months or the statutory maximum, or both.]	
[251R(2)	Obtaining property in respect of which money is owed by a person in respect of whom a debt relief order is made.	1. On indictment. 2. Summary.	7 years or a fine, or both. 12 months or the stautory maximum, or both.]	
[251S(1)	Person in respect of whom a debt relief order is made obtaining credit or engaging in business without disclosing his status or name.	1. On indictment. 2. Summary.	2 years or a fine, or both. 12 months or the statutory maximum, or both.]	
262A(1)	False representation or fraud for purpose of obtaining creditors' approval of proposed voluntary arrangement.	1. On indictment. 2. Summary.	7 years or a fine, or both. *6* [12] months or the statutory maximum or both.	
353(1)	Bankrupt failing to disclose property or disposals to official receiver or trustee.	1. On indictment. 2. Summary.	7 years or a fine, or both. *6* [12] months or the statutory maximum, or both.	
354(1)	Bankrupt failing to deliver property to, or concealing property from, official receiver or trustee.	1. On indictment. 2. Summary.	7 years or a fine, or both. *6* [12] months or the statutory maximum, or both.	
354(2)	Bankrupt removing property which he is required to deliver to official receiver or trustee.	1. On indictment. 2. Summary.	7 years or a fine, or both. *6* [12] months or the statutory maximum, or both.	
354(3)	Bankrupt failing to account for loss of substantial part of property.	1. On indictment. 2. Summary.	2 years or a fine, or both. *6* [12] months or the statutory maximum, or both.	

Section of Act creating offence	General nature of offence	Mode of prosecution	Punishment	Daily default fine (where applicable)
355(1)	Bankrupt failing to deliver books, papers and records to official receiver or trustee.	1. On indictment. 2. Summary.	7 years or a fine, or both. *6* [12] months or the statutory maximum, or both.	
355(2)	Bankrupt concealing, destroying etc. books, papers or records, or making false entries in them.	1. On indictment. 2. Summary.	7 years or a fine, or both. *6* [12] months or the statutory maximum, or both.	
355(3)	Bankrupt disposing of, or altering, books, papers or records relating to his estate or affairs.	1. On indictment. 2. Summary.	7 years or a fine, or both. *6* [12] months or the statutory maximum, or both.	
356(1)	Bankrupt making material omission in statement relating to his affairs.	1. On indictment. 2. Summary.	7 years or a fine, or both. *6* [12] months or the statutory maximum, or both.	
356(2)	Bankrupt making false statement, or failing to inform trustee, where false debt proved.	1. On indictment. 2. Summary.	7 years or a fine, or both. *6* [12] months or the statutory maximum, or both.	
357	Bankrupt fraudulently disposing of property.	1. On indictment. 2. Summary.	2 years or a fine, or both. *6* [12] months or the statutory maximum, or both.	
358	Bankrupt absconding with property he is required to deliver to official receiver or trustee.	1. On indictment. 2. Summary.	2 years or a fine, or both. *6* [12] months or the statutory maximum, or both.	
359(1)	Bankrupt disposing of property obtained on credit and not paid for.	1. On indictment. 2. Summary.	7 years or a fine, or both. *6* [12] months or the statutory maximum, or both.	
359(2)	Obtaining property in respect of which money is owed by a bankrupt.	1. On indictment. 2. Summary.	7 years or a fine, or both. *6* [12] months or the statutory maximum, or both.	

Section of Act creating offence	General nature of offence	Mode of prosecution	Punishment	Daily default fine (where applicable)
360(1)	Bankrupt obtaining credit or engaging in business without disclosing his status or name in which he was made bankrupt.	1. On indictment. 2. Summary.	2 years or a fine, or both. *6* [12] months or the statutory maximum, or both.	
360(3)	Person made bankrupt in Scotland or Northern Ireland obtaining credit, etc. in England and Wales.	1. On indictment. 2. Summary.	2 years or a fine, or both. *6* [12] months or the statutory maximum, or both.	
389	Acting as insolvency practitioner when not qualified.	1. On indictment. 2. Summary.	2 years or a fine, or both. *6* [12] months or the statutory maximum, or both.	
429(5)	Contravening s.429 in respect of disabilities imposed by county court on revocation of administration order.	1. On indictment. 2. Summary.	2 years or a fine, or both. *6* [12] months or the statutory maximum, or both.	
Sch. A1, para. 9(2)	Directors failing to notify nominee of beginning of moratorium.	1. On indictment. 2. Summary.	2 years or a fine, or both. *6* [12] months or the statutory maximum, or both.	
Sch. A1, para. 17(3)(a)	Company obtaining credit without disclosing existence of moratorium.	1. On indictment. 2. Summary.	A fine. The statutory maximum.	
Sch. A1, para. 17(3)(b)	Obtaining credit for company without disclosing existence of moratorium	1. On indictment. 2. Summary.	2 years or a fine, or both. *6* [12] months or the statutory maximum, or both.	
Sch. A1, para. 18(3)(a)	Company disposing of property otherwise than in ordinary way of business.	1. On indictment. 2. Summary.	A fine. The statutory maximum.	
Sch. A1, para. 18(3)(b)	Authorising or permitting disposal of company property.	1. On indictment. 2. Summary.	2 years or a fine, or both. *6* [12] months or the statutory maximum, or both.	

Section of Act creating offence	General nature of offence	Mode of prosecution	Punishment	Daily default fine (where applicable)
Sch. A1, para. 19(3)(a)	Company making payments in respect of liabilities existing before beginning of moratorium	1. On indictment. 2. Summary.	A fine. The statutory maximum.	
Sch. A1, para. 19(3)(b)	Authorising or permitting such a payment.	1. On indictment. 2. Summary.	2 years or a fine, or both. 6 [12] months or the statutory maximum, or both.	
Sch. A1, para. 22(1)	Company disposing of charged property.	1. On indictment. 2. Summary.	A fine. The statutory maximum.	
Sch. A1, para. 22(2)	Authorising or permitting such a disposal.	1. On indictment. 2. Summary.	2 years or a fine, or both. 6 [12] months or the statutory maximum, or both.	
Sch. A1, para. 23(1)(a)	Company entering into market contract, etc.	1. On indictment. 2. Summary.	A fine. The statutory maximum.	
Sch. A1, para. 23(1)(b)	Authorising or permitting company to do so.	1. On indictment. 2. Summary.	2 years or a fine, or both. 6 [12] months or the statutory maximum, or both.	
Sch. A1, para. 41(2)	Fraud or privity to fraud in anticipation of moratorium	1. On indictment. 2. Summary.	7 years or a fine, or both. 6 [12] months or the statutory maximum, or both.	
Sch. A1, para. 41(3)	Fraud or privity to fraud during moratorium.	1. On indictment. 2. Summary.	7 years or a fine, or both. 6 [12] months or the statutory maximum, or both.	
Sch. A1, para. 41(7)	Knowingly taking in pawn or pledge, or otherwise receiving, company property.	1. On indictment. 2. Summary.	7 years or a fine, or both. 6 [12] months or the statutory maximum, or both.	

Section of Act creating offence	General nature of offence	Mode of prosecution	Punishment	Daily default fine (where applicable)
Sch. A1, para. 42(1)	False representation or fraud for purpose of obtaining or extending moratorium.	1. On indictment. 2. Summary.	7 years or a fine, or both. *6* [12] months or the statutory maximum, or both.	
Sch. B1, para. 18(7)	Making false statement in statutory declaration where administrator appointed by holder of floating charge.	1. On indictment. 2. Summary.	2 years, or a fine or both. *6* [12] months, or the statutory maximum or both.	
Sch. B1, para. 20	Holder of floating charge failing to notify administrator or others of commencement of appointment.	1. On indictment. 2. Summary.	2 years, or a fine or both. *6* [12] months, or the statutory maximum or both.	One-tenth of the statutory maximum.
Sch. B1, para. 27(4)	Making false statement in statutory declaration where appointment of administrator proposed by company or directors.	1. On indictment. 2. Summary.	2 years, or a fine or both. *6* [12] months, or the statutory maximum or both.	
Sch. B1, para. 29(7)	Making false statement in statutory declaration where administrator appointed by company or directors.	1. On indictment. 2. Summary.	2 years, or a fine or both. *6* [12] months, or the statutory maximum or both.	
Sch. B1, para. 32	Company or directors failing to notify administrator or others of commencement of appointment.	1. On indictment. 2. Summary.	2 years, or a fine or both. *6* [12] months, or the statutory maximum or both.	One-tenth of the statutory maximum.
Sch. B1, para. 48(4)	Failing to comply with provisions about statement of affairs where administrator appointed.	1. On indictment. 2. Summary.	A fine. The statutory maximum.	One-tenth of the statutory maximum.

[This Schedule is printed as amended by the *Insolvency Act* 2000, ss.1–3, and Sched. 1, para. 12 (insertion of entries relating to Sched. A1), Sched. 2, para. 12 (insertion of entry relating to s.6A), and Sched. 3, para. 16 (insertion of entry relating to s.262A); and the *Enterprise Act* 2002, s.248, and Sched. 17, para. 39 (insertion of entries relating to Sched. B1); and as repealed in part by *ibid.*, s.269, and Sched. 23, para. 17. The words in square brackets in the entry relating to section 31 and the entries relating to sections 251O to 251S are inserted, as from a day to be appointed, by the *Tribunals, Courts and Enforcement Act* 2007, s.108(3), and Sched. 20, paras 1 and 15(1)–(3). The references to "6" months as the maximum penalty on summary conviction are replaced by references to "12" months as from a day to be appointed: *CJA* 2003, s.282(2) and (3); but not in relation to any offence committed before the date of commencement of the increase: s.282(4). In the application of the entries relating to sections 251O to 251S to offences committed before the commencement of the *CJA* 2003, s.154(1), the references in the fourth column to "12 months" are to be read as references to "6 months": *Tribunals, Courts and Enforcement Act* 2007, s.108(3), and Sched. 20, paras 1 and 15(4).]

Insolvency Rules 1986, Sched. 5

SCHEDULE 5

PUNISHMENT OF OFFENCES UNDER THE RULES

Rule creating offence (where applicable)	General nature of offence	Mode of prosecution	Punishment	Daily default fine
In Part 1, Rule 1.30	False representation or fraud for purpose of obtaining members' or creditors' consent to proposal for voluntary arrangement.	1. On indictment 2. Summary	7 years or a fine, or both. *6* [12] months or the statutory maximum, or both.	
In Part 5, Rule 5.30	False representation or fraud for purpose of obtaining creditors' consent to proposal for voluntary arrangement.	1. On indictment 2. Summary	7 years or a fine, or both. *6* [12] months or the statutory maximum, or both.	
In Part 12, Rule 12.18	False representation of status for purpose of inspecting documents.	1. On indictment 2. Summary	2 years or a fine, or both. *6* [12] months or the statutory maximum, or both.	

[The references to "6" months as the maximum penalty on summary conviction are replaced by references to "12" months as from a day to be appointed: *CJA* 2003, s.282(2) and (3); but not in relation to any offence committed before the date of commencement of the increase: s.282(4).]

[The next paragraph is § 30–168.]

(3) Bankruptcy offences

(a) *General*

Part IX, Chapter VI of the *Insolvency Act* 1986 applies where a court has made a bankruptcy order on a bankruptcy petition; the bankrupt can however only be charged under this Chapter (ss.350 to 362) for an offence committed before his discharge: s.350(3), *post*. The intention of this part of the Act is to protect a bankrupt's property for later distribution amongst his creditors, and to punish any bankrupt who seeks to avoid these safeguards. Section 352 contains a statutory defence of innocent intention, applicable where specified. In the light of *R. v. Brockley*, 99 Cr.App.R. 385, CA (a case concerned with s.11 of the *CDDA* 1986, *post*, § 30–195), it is likely that the courts will hold that it is not a defence to any personal insolvency offence for the defendant to show that he did not believe he was a bankrupt at the material time. **30–168**

Insolvency Act 1986, ss.350–352

Scheme of this Chapter

350.—(1) Subject to section 360(3) below, this Chapter applies where the court has made a bankruptcy order on a bankruptcy petition. **30–169**

(2) This Chapter applies whether or not the bankruptcy order is annulled, but proceedings for an offence under this Chapter shall not be instituted after the annulment.

(3) Without prejudice to his liability in respect of a subsequent bankruptcy, the bankrupt is not guilty of an offence under this Chapter in respect of anything done after his discharge; but nothing in this Group of Parts prevents the institution of proceedings against a discharged bankrupt for an offence committed before his discharge.

(3A) Subsection (3) is without prejudice to any provision of this Chapter which applies to a person in respect of whom a bankruptcy restrictions order is in force.

(4) It is not a defence in proceedings for an offence under this Chapter that anything relied on, in whole or in part, as constituting that offence was done outside England and Wales.

(5) Proceedings for an offence under this Chapter or under the rules shall not be instituted except by the Secretary of State or by or with the consent of the Director of Public Prosecutions.

(6) A person guilty of any offence under this Chapter is liable to imprisonment or a fine, or both.

[This section is printed as amended by the *Enterprise Act* 2002, s.257 and Sched. 21, para. 2.]

Definitions

351. In the following provisions of this Chapter— **30–170**

(a) references to property comprised in the bankrupt's estate or to property possession of which is required to be delivered up to the official receiver or the trustee of the bankrupt's estate include any property which would be such property if a notice in respect of it were given under section 307 (after acquired property), section 308 (personal property and effects of bankrupt having more than replacement value) or section 308A (vesting in trustee of certain tenancies);

(b) "the initial period" means the period between the presentation of the bankruptcy petition and the commencement of the bankruptcy; and

(c) a reference to a number of months or years before petition is to that period ending with the presentation of the bankruptcy petition.

[This section is printed as amended by the *Housing Act* 1988, Sched. 17, para. 75.]

Defence of innocent intention

352. Where in the case of an offence under any provision of this Chapter it is stated that this section applies, a person is not guilty of the offence if he proves that, at the time of the conduct constituting the offence, he had no intent to defraud or to conceal the state of his affairs. **30–171**

When applied to section 357 (*post*, § 30–182), this section has to be interpreted as imposing merely an evidential burden (*i.e.* it has to be read down in accordance with the *Human Rights Act* 1998, s.3 (*ante*, § 16–15)), but when applied to section 353 (*post*, § 30–176), it is to be taken as imposing a legal burden which was compatible with the presumption of innocence: *Att.-Gen.'s Reference (No. 1 of 2004)*; *R. v. Edwards*; *R. v. Denton*; *R. v. Hendley*; *R. v. Crowley* [2004] 1 W.L.R. 2111, CA. The House of Lords in *Sheldrake v. DPP*; *Att.-Gen.'s Reference (No. 4 of 2002)* [2005] 1 A.C. 264, did not hear argument on the individual decisions of the Court of Appeal in these cases, but Lord Bingham (at [32]) indicated an inclination to agree with them. Lords Steyn and Phillips expressly concurred with Lord Bingham. Lords Rodger and Carswell did not address the issue. A court considering the application of section 352 to any of the other offences in this chapter of the 1986 Act should have regard to the guidance of the House of Lords in *Sheldrake v. DPP*; *Att.-Gen.'s Reference (No. 4 of 2002)*. For the details thereof, see *ante*, §§ 16–77 *et seq.*

Interpretation

30–172 Sections 381 to 385 are the interpretation provisions for the second group of Parts (*i.e.* Parts VIII to XI). Section 381 applies for the interpretation of "bankruptcy" and associated terminology; section 382 for the interpretation of "bankruptcy debt", etc., and section 383 for the interpretation of "creditor", etc.

Insolvency Act 1986, ss.384, 385

"Prescribed" and "the rules"

30–173 **384.**—(1) Subject to the next subsection "prescribed" means prescribed by the rules and "the rules" means rules made under section 412 in Part XV.

(2) References in this Group of Parts to the amount prescribed for the purposes of any of the following provisions—

[section 251S(4)];
section 273;
section 346(3);
section 354(1) and (2);
section 358;
section 360(1);
section 361(2); *and*
section 364(2)(d);
[paragraphs 6 to 8 of Schedule 4ZA];

and references in those provisions to the prescribed amount are to be read in accordance with section 418 in Part XV and orders made under this section.

[This section is printed as amended, as from a day to be appointed, by the *Tribunals, Courts and Enforcement Act* 2007, s.108(3), and Sched. 20, paras 1 and 4 (insertion of words in square brackets, omission of italicised word).]

30–174 Section 418(1) confers power on the Secretary of State by order to prescribe amounts for the purposes of the provisions listed in section 384(2) and provides that references in the second Group of Parts (*i.e.* Pts VIII to XI) to the amount prescribed for the purposes of any of those provisions, and references in those provisions to the prescribed amount are to be construed accordingly. The *Insolvency Proceedings (Monetary Limits) Order* 1986 (S.I. 1986 No. 1996), as amended by the *Insolvency Proceedings (Monetary Limits) (Amendment) Order* 2004 (S.I. 2004 No. 547), made under section 418, provides that the prescribed amount for the purposes of section 354(1) and (2) is £1,000, for the purposes of section 358 is £1,000, and for the purposes of section 360(1) is £500.

Miscellaneous definitions

30–175 **385.**—(1) The following definitions have effect—

"the court", in relation to any matter, means the court to which, in accordance with section 373 in Part X and the rules, proceedings with respect to that matter are allocated or transferred;

"creditor's petition" means a bankruptcy petition under section 264(1)(a);

"criminal bankruptcy order" means an order under section 39(1) of the *Powers of Criminal Courts Act* 1973;

"debt" is to be construed in accordance with section 382(3);

"the debtor" —

[(za) in relation to a debt relief order or an application for such an order, has the same meaning as in Part 7A,]

(a) in relation to a proposal for the purposes of Part VIII, means the individual making or intending to make that proposal, and

(b) in relation to a bankruptcy petition, means the individual to whom the petition relates;

"debtor's petition" means a bankruptcy petition presented by the debtor himself under section 264(1)(b);

["debt relief order" means an order made by the official receiver under Part 7A;]

"dwelling house" includes any building or part of a building which is occupied as a dwelling and any yard, garden, garage or outhouse belonging to the dwelling house and occupied with it;

"estate", in relation to a bankrupt is to be construed in accordance with section 283 in Chapter II of Part IX

"family", in relation to a bankrupt, means the persons (if any) who are living with him and are dependent on him;

"secured" and related expressions are to be construed in accordance with section 383; and

"the trustee", in relation to a bankruptcy and the bankrupt, means the trustee of the bankrupt's estate.

(2) Reference in this Group of Parts to a person's affairs include his business, if any.

[This section is printed as amended, as from a day to be appointed, by the *Tribunals, Courts and Enforcement Act* 2007, s.108(3), and Sched. 20, paras 1 and 5 (insertion of words in square brackets).]

(b) *Offences*

Insolvency Act 1986, s.353

Non-disclosure

353.—(1) The bankrupt is guilty of an offence if— **30–176**

(a) he does not to the best of his knowledge and belief disclose all the property comprised in his estate to the official receiver or the trustee, or

(b) he does not inform the official receiver or the trustee of any disposal of any property which but for the disposal would be so comprised, stating how, when, to whom and for what consideration the property was disposed of.

(2) Subsection (1)(b) does not apply to any disposal in the ordinary course of a business carried on by the bankrupt or to any payment of the ordinary expenses of the bankrupt or his family.

(3) Section 352 applies to this offence.

The offences created by this section broadly correspond to the offence created by section 154(1) of the *Bankruptcy Act* 1914. In that Act, the expression used was "in the ordinary way of his trade". Two old authorities, decided on similar wording in the *Debtors Act* 1869, s.11, paras 14 and 15 (*rep.*) may be of some assistance in approaching the 1986 Act: see *Ex p. Brett*; *Re Hodgson* (1875) 1 Ch D 151; *R. v. Thomas* (1870) 22 L.T. 138. **30–177**

As to the application of section 352 to this section, see *ante*, § 30–171.

Insolvency Act 1986, s.354

Concealment of property

354.—(1) The bankrupt is guilty of an offence, if— **30–178**

(a) he does not deliver up possession to the official receiver or trustee, or as the official receiver or trustee may direct, of such part of the property comprised in his estate as is in his possession or under his control, and possession of which he is required by law so to deliver up,

(b) he conceals any debt due to or from him or conceals any property the value of which is not less than the prescribed amount and possession of which he is required to deliver up to the official receiver or trustee, or

(c) in the 12 months before petition, or in the initial period, he did anything which would have been an offence under paragraph (b) above if the bankruptcy order had been made immediately before he did it.

Section 352 applies to this offence.

(2) The bankrupt is guilty of an offence if he removes, or in the initial period removed, any property the value of which was not less than the prescribed amount and possession of which he has or would have been required to deliver up to the official receiver or the trustee.

Section 352 applies to this offence.

(3) The bankrupt is guilty of an offence if he without reasonable excuse fails, on being required to do so by the official receiver, the trustee or the court—

(a) to account for the loss of any substantial part of his property incurred in the 12 months before petition or in the initial period, or

(b) to give a satisfactory explanation of the manner in which such a loss was incurred.

[This section is printed as amended by the *Enterprise Act* 2002, s.269, and Sched. 23, para. 12.]

30–179 As to the "prescribed amount", see *ante*, § 30–174. The offences created by section 354(1)(a), (b) and (c), section 354(2) and section 354(3) broadly correspond to the offences created by sections 154(2), (4), (5) and 157(1)(c) of the *Bankruptcy Act* 1914. In *R. v. Salter* [1968] 1 Q.B. 793, 52 Cr.App.R. 549, CA, it was held that the offence created by section 157(1)(c) was an absolute one. This clearly continues to be the case, by virtue of the fact that section 352 does not apply to the offence under section 354(3). In giving the judgment of the court in *Salter*, Sachs L.J. said:

> "A jury should be directed that if they are satisfied as regards the total sum of money constituting 'the loss of any substantial part of his estate' the bankrupt had not at the time of the alleged failure given with such reasonable detail as was appropriate in the circumstances an explanation which is both reasonably clear and true of how such sum was made up (for the loss may be composed of more than one component), of how it came to be lost, and of where the money has gone, then the offence has been committed. The degree of particularity required of the bankrupt may vary greatly according to the facts of the case: sums which are really small in relation to 'the substantial part of the estate' need not of course be traced, but an explanation unsupported by sufficient detail can be very unsatisfactory indeed. Section 157(1)(c) intends to and does, in the interests of the business community as a whole, put in peril the man who goes bankrupt without having so conducted his affairs as to be able satisfactorily to explain why some substantial loss has been incurred. It is as well to make it plain that, as the offence is absolute, it follows that, once a prosecution has been initiated, no issue arises before verdict as to the reasons why the failure has occurred or as to any motive which led to that failure" (at pp. 809, 563–4).

The offence created by section 354(3)(a) is not inconsistent with an individual's right not to incriminate himself; the demand for information was made in the course of an investigation into the bankrupt's estate and not as part of an inquiry into an offence, and however widely the word "charge" in Article 6 of the ECHR (*ante*, § 16–57) is construed there was no charge against the defendant in relation to which he could incriminate himself; furthermore, any information he provided could not be used to found any subsequent criminal proceedings because of the amendments to section 433 (*ante*, § 30–74), effected by the *YJCEA* 1999, following *Saunders v. U.K.*, 23 E.H.R.R. 313, ECtHR; and even if there was an element of infringement of the privilege against self-incrimination, the privilege was not absolute, and the interference with it was a proportionate legislative response to the problem of administering and investigating bankrupt estates, there being a public interest that a bankrupt's affairs should be investigated with a view to any assets being traced and distributed among any creditors: *R. v. Kearns* [2003] 1 Cr.App.R. 7, CA.

Insolvency Act 1986, ss.355–358

Concealment of books and papers; falsification

30–180 **355.**—(1) The bankrupt is guilty of an offence if he does not deliver up possession to the official receiver or the trustee, or as the official receiver or trustee may direct, of all books, papers and other records of which he has possession or control and which relate to his estate or his affairs. Section 352 applies to this offence.

(2) The bankrupt is guilty of an offence if—

(a) he prevents, or in the initial period prevented, the production of any books, papers or records relating to his estate or affairs;

(b) he conceals, destroys, mutilates or falsifies, or causes or permits the concealment, destruction, mutilation or falsification of, any books, papers or other records relating to his estate or affairs;

(c) he makes or causes or permits the making of, any false entries in any book, document or record relating to his estate or affairs; or

(d) in the 12 months before petition, or in the initial period, he did anything which would have been an offence, under paragraph (b) or (c) above if the bankruptcy order had been made before he did it.

Section 352 applies to this offence.

(3) The bankrupt is guilty of an offence if—

(a) he disposes of, or alters or makes any omission in, or causes or permits the disposal, altering or making of any omission in, any book, document or record relating to his estate or affairs, or

(b) in the 12 months before petition, or in the initial period, he did anything which would have been an offence under paragraph (a) if the bankruptcy order had been made before he did it.

Section 352 applies to this offence.

(4) In their application to a trading record subsections (2)(d) and (3)(b) shall have effect as if the reference to 12 months were a reference to two years.

(5) In subsection (4) "trading record" means a book, document or record which shows or explains the transactions or financial position of a person's business, including—

(a) a periodic record of cash paid;

(b) a statement of periodic stock-taking; and

(c) except in the case of goods sold by way of retail trade, a record of goods sold and purchased which identifies the buyer and seller or enables them to be identified.

[This section is printed as amended by the *Enterprise Act* 2002, s.269, and Sched. 23, para. 13.]

False statements

356.—(1) The bankrupt is guilty of an offence if he makes or has made any material omission in any statement made under any provision in this Group of Parts and relating to his affairs. **30–181**

Section 352 applies to this offence.

(2) The bankrupt is guilty of an offence if—

(a) knowing or believing that a false debt has been proved by any person under the bankruptcy, he fails to inform the trustee as soon as practicable; or

(b) he attempts to account for any part of his property by fictitious losses or expenses; or

(c) at any meeting of his creditors in the 12 months before petition or (whether or not at such a meeting) at any time in the initial period, he did anything which would have been an offence under paragraph (b) if the bankruptcy order had been made before he did it; or

(d) he is, or at any time has been, guilty of any false representation or other fraud for the purpose of obtaining the consent of his creditors, or any of them, to an agreement with reference to his affairs or to his bankruptcy.

Fraudulent disposal of property

357.—(1) The bankrupt is guilty of an offence if he makes or causes to be made, or has in the period of 5 years ending with the commencement of the bankruptcy made or caused to be made, any gift or transfer of, or any charge on, his property. **30–182**

Section 352 applies to this offence.

(2) The reference to making a transfer of or charge on any property includes causing or conniving at the levying of any execution against the property.

(3) The bankrupt is guilty of an offence if he conceals or removes, or has at any time before the commencement of the bankruptcy concealed or removed, any part of his property after, or within 2 months before, the date on which a judgment or order for the payment of money has been obtained against him, being a judgment or order which was not satisfied before the commencement of the bankruptcy.

Section 352 applies to this offence.

As to the application of section 352 to this section, see *ante*, § 30–171.

As to sentencing for an offence contrary to subsection (3), see *R. v. Mungroo*, *The*

Times, July 3, 1997, CA (immediate custodial sentence appropriate in respect of conduct which attacks the foundation of the bankruptcy legislation).

Absconding

30–183 **358.** The bankrupt is guilty of an offence if—

(a) he leaves, or attempts or makes preparations to leave, England and Wales with any property the value of which is not less than the prescribed amount and possession of which he is required to deliver up to the official receiver or the trustee, or

(b) in the 6 months before the petition, or in the initial period, he did anything which would have been an offence under paragraph (a) if the bankruptcy order had been made immediately before he did it.

Section 352 applies to this offence.

As to the "prescribed amount", see *ante*, §§ 30–173, 30–174.

Insolvency Act 1986, ss.359, 360

Fraudulent dealing with property obtained on credit

30–184 **359.**—(1) The bankrupt is guilty of an offence if, in the 12 months before petition, or in the initial period, he disposed of any property which he had obtained on credit and, at the time he disposed of it, had not paid for.

Section 352 applies to this offence.

(2) A person is guilty of an offence if, in the 12 months before petition or in the initial period, he acquired or received property from the bankrupt knowing or believing—

(a) that the bankrupt owed money in respect of the property, and

(b) that the bankrupt did not intend, or was unlikely to be able, to pay the money he so owed.

(3) A person is not guilty of an offence under subsection (1) or (2) if the disposal, acquisition or receipt of the property was in the ordinary course of a business carried on by the bankrupt at the time of the disposal, acquisition or receipt.

(4) In determining for the purposes of this section whether any property is disposed of, acquired or received in the ordinary course of a business carried on by the bankrupt, regard may be had, in particular, to the price paid for the property.

(5) In this section references to disposing of property include pawning or pledging it; and references to acquiring or receiving property shall be read accordingly.

As to "the ordinary course of a business", see *ante*, § 30–177.

Obtaining credit: engaging in business

30–185 **360.**—(1) The bankrupt is guilty of an offence if—

(a) either alone or jointly with any other person, he obtains credit to the extent of the prescribed amount or more without giving the person from whom he obtains it the relevant information about his status; or

(b) he engages (whether directly or indirectly) in any business under a name other than that in which he was adjudged bankrupt without disclosing to all persons with whom he enters into any business transaction the name in which he was so adjudged.

(2) The reference to the bankrupt obtaining credit includes the following cases—

(a) where goods are bailed to him under a hire-purchase agreement, or agreed to be sold to him under a conditional sale agreement, and

(b) where he is paid in advance (whether in money or otherwise) for the supply of goods or services.

(3) A person whose estate has been sequestrated in Scotland, or who has been adjudged bankrupt in Northern Ireland, is guilty of an offence if, before his discharge, he does anything in England and Wales which would be an offence under subsection (1) if he were an undischarged bankrupt and the sequestration of his estate or the adjudication in Northern Ireland were an adjudication under this Part.

(4) For the purposes of subsection (1)(a), the relevant information about the status of the person in question is the information that he is an undischarged bankrupt or, as the case may be, that his estate has been sequestrated in Scotland and that he has not been discharged.

(5) This section applies to the bankrupt after discharge while a bankruptcy restrictions order is in force in respect of him.

(6) For the purposes of subsection (1)(a) as it applies by virtue of subsection (5), the relevant information about the status of the person in question is the information that a bankruptcy restrictions order is in force in respect of him.

[This section is printed as amended by the *Enterprise Act* 2002, s.257, and Sched. 21, para. 3.]

As to the "prescribed amount", see *ante*, § 30–174. Offences under this section are absolute. In *R. v. Leinster (Duke of)* [1924] 1 K.B. 311, 17 Cr.App.R. 176, CCA (a case under the *Bankruptcy Act* 1914), it was held that a reasonable belief that information of the bankruptcy had been conveyed by an agent of the bankrupt to the person giving credit was no defence, and an intent to defraud was immaterial. This clearly remains the case and section 352 (*ante*, § 30–171) does not apply. In *R. v. Zeitlin*, 23 Cr.App.R. 163, CCA, it was held that the disclosure of bankruptcy need not be made at the very moment of obtaining the credit, it being sufficient if the information is given to the creditor a reasonable time before. **30–186**

The offence is committed when the relevant credit extends to the prescribed amount, although it may be made up by aggregating a series of smaller sums. **30–187**

Once the prescribed amount is reached, the offence is complete and any subsequent payments reducing the indebtedness, although they may go to mitigation, cannot provide a defence: *R. v. Hartley* [1972] 2 Q.B. 1, 56 Cr.App.R. 189, CA; *R. v. Juby* (1886) 16 Cox 160. It is not necessary that the goods in respect of which credit is obtained should all be supplied or ordered at the same time, provided that the total amount of credit is at least equal to the prescribed amount: *R. v. Juby*, *ante*, approved in *Hartley*.

In *R. v. Miller*, 65 Cr.App.R. 79, CA, it was held, in relation to the *Bankruptcy Act* 1914, s.155 (*rep.*), that where the hirer under a hire-purchase contract defaulted on one of the payments, there was no giving of credit by the finance company, who simply acquired an instant cause of action for the overdue instalment. That was the antithesis of giving credit. In giving the judgment of the court, Roskill L.J. said: **30–188**

> "The obtaining of credit, in our view, means obtaining some benefit from another, without immediately giving the consideration in return for which that benefit is confirmed [*sic*]. … As Sachs L.J. said … in *Hartley* [*ante*, at pp. 7, 194] there have to be words or conduct designed to secure that credit be given. … A mere allowing a default to occur does not, in our view, amount to words or conduct having that effect" (at p. 84). **30–189**

The defendant in *Miller* would now be guilty of an offence under section 360(1)(a) by virtue of subsection (2)(a). The principle underlying the decision survives, however, and was applied in *R. v. Ramzan* [1998] 2 Cr.App.R. 328, CA, where it was held that obtaining capital by falsely representing that the capital would be applied to a joint business venture was not obtaining credit within the meaning of section 360(1)(a). Rather the representee obtained an immediate right of action to avoid the agreement and recover his monies. **30–190**

In *R. v. Hayat*, 63 Cr.App.R. 181, CA, counsel for the appellant relied upon the words of Sachs L.J. in *Hartley*, in contending that there can be no "obtaining" without words or conduct on the part of the person who gets the credit; the offence is not committed merely by the fact that credit is received as distinct from being obtained. The defendant's current account had become overdrawn in consequence of certain cheques which he had paid into the account being returned unpaid by the banks upon which they were drawn. He had, in the meantime, drawn cheques on his own account which were paid. It was conceded on behalf of the appellant, on the authority of *R. v. Pryce*, 34 Cr.App.R. 21, CCA, that an overdraft at a bank was a credit for the purposes of section 155(a) of the 1914 Act. At trial, the judge had ruled on these facts that there was as a matter of law an obtaining of credit and, as a result, the appellant changed his plea to one of guilty. On appeal, the Court of Appeal did not rule that there had been no obtaining of credit, but simply held that the question whether there had been or not was a question of fact for the jury and that question having, in effect, been withdrawn from the jury, it quashed the conviction. James L.J. said, in the course of giving the judgment of the court, that: **30–191**

> "not only must the Crown prove that it is 'credit' which is obtained, but they must also prove

the 'obtaining' of the credit and in order to do that some conduct, either by words or otherwise, must be proved to have taken place on the part of the accused person which amounts to an obtaining. What amounts to an obtaining, in our judgment, must be a question of fact and not a question of law. There is, of course, as in many other fields in the criminal law the preliminary question of whether the evidence adduced by the Crown can amount to an obtaining. If it can amount to an obtaining as a matter of law it is a matter for the jury to determine whether the facts proved to their satisfaction do amount in fact to an obtaining of credit" (at p. 186).

However, see *Att.-Gen.'s Reference (No. 1 of 1988)* [1989] 1 A.C. 971, HL, where "obtained" in the *Company Securities (Insider Dealing) Act* 1985 was construed to include the coming into possession of a thing without effort on the part of the obtainer.

30–192 Where the facts disclose that credit was not obtained for the bankrupt but for another person, there is no offence. The critical question is always whether on the evidence the bankrupt holds himself out as the person for whom credit is sought; whether it is for a genuine and separate business or a charade to disguise the fact that he is the person seeking credit: *R. v. Godwin*, 71 Cr.App.R. 97, CA. Where there is an issue of fact as to whether the credit was extended to the bankrupt personally or was given to a business or the bankrupt's wife, the question must be decided by the jury: see *R. v. Goodall*, 43 Cr.App.R. 24, CCA.

(4) Offences in connection with debt relief orders

30–193 Section 108 of the *Tribunals, Courts and Enforcement Act* 2007 gives effect (as from a day to be appointed) to Schedules 17 to 20, and thereby inserts a new Part 7A (debt relief orders (ss.251A– 251X)) and Schedules 4ZA (conditions for making a debt relief order) and 4ZB (debt relief restrictions orders and undertakings) in the *Insolvency Act* 1986. Debt relief orders are a new form of personal insolvency made administratively by the official receiver on the application of an individual debtor who meets specified criteria in relation to his assets, income and liabilities (see Sched. 4ZA). Sections 251O to 251S create new offences in connection with debt relief orders. Those offences are as follows:

(i) false representations or omissions in making an application for a debt relief order (s.251O(1));

(ii) failing to comply with duty under section 251J(3) (providing assistance to official receiver, etc.), in connection with an application for a debt relief order, to inform the official receiver of errors, etc., in the application or of a change of circumstances (s.251O(2)(a));

(iii) false representations or omissions in connection with duty under section 251J(3) (s.251O(2)(b));

(iv) failing to comply with duty under section 251J(5), in connection with a debt relief order that has been made, to inform the official receiver of an increase in income or the acquisition of property (s.251O(4)(a));

(v) false representations or omissions in connection with duty under section 251J(5) (s.251O(4)(b));

(vi) failing to deliver books, records and papers to official receiver, concealing or destroying them or making false entries in them by person in respect of whom a debt relief order is made (s.251P(1));

(vii) person in respect of whom debt relief order is made doing anything falling within paragraphs (c) to (e) of section 251P(1) during the period of 12 months ending with the application date or doing anything falling within paragraphs (b) to (e) of section 251P(1) after that date but before the effective date (s.251P(2));

(viii) fraudulent disposal of property by person in respect of whom a debt relief order is made (s.251Q(1));

(ix) disposal of property that is not paid for by person in respect of whom a debt relief order is made (s.251R(1));

(x) obtaining property in respect of which money is owed by a person in respect of whom a debt relief order is made (s.251R(2)); and

(xi) person in respect of whom a debt relief order is made obtaining credit or engaging in business without disclosing his status or name (s.251S(1)).

The offences under Part 7A are all triable either way (see *ante*, § 30–158), and they broadly correspond to the offences under Chapter VI of Part IX (*ante*, §§ 30–168 *et seq.*). Section 251T requires the consent of the Secretary of State or the Director of Public Prosecutions for the institution of proceedings for any such offence. **30–194**

D. COMPANY DIRECTORS DISQUALIFICATION ACT 1986

Company Directors Disqualification Act 1986, s.11

Undischarged bankrupts

11.—(1) It is an offence for a person to act as a director of a company or directly or indirectly to take part in or be concerned in the promotion, formation or management of a company, without the leave of the court, at a time when— **30–195**

(a) he is an undischarged bankrupt,

[(aa) a moratorium period under a debt relief order applies in relation to him,] or

(b) a bankruptcy restrictions order [or a debt relief restrictions order] is in force in respect of him.

(2) "The court" for this purpose is the court by which the person was adjudged bankrupt or, in Scotland, sequestration of his estates was awarded.

(3) In England and Wales, the leave of the court shall not be given unless notice of intention to apply for it has been served on the official receiver; and it is the latter's duty, if he is of opinion that it is contrary to the public interest that the application should be granted, to attend on the hearing of the application and oppose it.

[This section is printed as amended by the *Enterprise Act* 2002, s.257, and Sched. 21, para. 5; and as amended, as from a day to be appointed, by the *Tribunals, Courts and Enforcement Act* 2007, s.108(3), and Sched. 20, para. 16.]

Section 11 creates an offence of absolute liability; it is no defence that the bankrupt did not believe that he was a bankrupt at the material time: *R. v. Brockley*, 99 Cr.App.R. 385, CA; nor that the bankruptcy order was subsequently annulled: *Commrs of Inland Revenue v. McEntaggart* [2007] B.C.C. 260, Ch D (Patten J.); and the defendant's own view as to whether he is acting as a director, etc., of the company is irrelevant; the sole question, once it is established that he was at the material time an undischarged bankrupt, is whether, as a matter of fact, his conduct fell within the activities proscribed by the statute: *R. v. Doring* [2003] 1 Cr.App.R. 9, CA. **30–196**

Company Directors Disqualification Act 1986, ss.13, 14

Criminal penalties

13. If a person acts in contravention of a disqualification order or disqualification undertaking or in contravention of section 12(2), 12A or 12B, or is guilty of an offence under section 11, he is liable— **30–197**

(a) on conviction on indictment, to imprisonment for not more than two years or a fine, or both, and

(b) on summary conviction, to imprisonment for not more than *six* [12] months or a fine not exceeding the statutory maximum, or both.

[This section is printed as amended by the *Insolvency Act* 2000, s.8 and Sched. 4, para. 8; and the *Insolvency Act 2000 (Company Directors Disqualification Undertakings) Order* 2004 (S.I. 2004 No. 1941), art. 2. In para. (b), "12" is substituted for "six", as from a day to be appointed, by the *CJA* 2003, s.282(2) and (3). The increase has no application to offences committed before the substitution takes effect: s.282(4).]

A "disqualification order" is an order against a person that he shall not, without the leave of the court, (a) be a director, liquidator or administrator of a company; (b) be a receiver or manager of a company's property; or (c) in any way, whether directly or indirectly, be concerned or take part in the promotion, formation or management of a company: see section 1 of the *CDDA* 1986, *ante*, § 5–851. The fact that the disqualification order requires amendment under the slip rule does not provide a defence against criminal liability: see *Re Cannonquest Ltd* [1997] B.C.C. 644, CA (Civ. Div.). **30–198**

Where a person is alleged to be in breach of a disqualification order, it is not an abuse for the Secretary of State to begin proceedings for civil disqualification rather than proceedings under section 13, the former being for the protection of the public while the latter is punitive: *Re Mea Corp. Ltd.*; *Secretary of State for Trade and Industry v. Aviss* [2007] B.C.C. 288, Ch D (Lewison J.).

Offences by body corporate

30–199 **14.**—(1) Where a body corporate is guilty of an offence of acting in contravention of a disqualification order or disqualification undertaking or in contravention of section 12A or 12B, and it is proved that the offence occurred with the consent or connivance of, or was attributable to any neglect on the part of any director, manager, secretary or other similar officer of the body corporate, or any person who was purporting to act in any such capacity he, as well as the body corporate, is guilty of the offence and liable to be proceeded against and punished accordingly.

(2) Where the affairs of a body corporate are managed by its members, subsection (1) applies in relation to the acts and defaults of a member in connection with his functions of management as if he were a director of the body corporate.

[This section is printed as amended by the *Insolvency Act* 2000, s.8, and Sched. 4, para. 9; and S.I. 2004 No. 1941 (*ante*), art. 2].

Company Directors Disqualification Act 1986, s.22

Interpretation

30–200 **22.**—(1) This section has effect with respect to the meaning of expressions used in this Act, and applies unless the context otherwise requires.

(2) The expression "company"—

(a) in section 11, includes an unregistered company and a company incorporated outside Great Britain which has an established place of business in Great Britain, and

(b) elsewhere, includes any company which may be wound up under Part V of the *Insolvency Act*.

(3) Section 247 in Part VII of the *Insolvency Act* (interpretation for first Group of Parts of that Act) applies as regards references to a company's insolvency and to its going into liquidation; and "administrative receiver" has the meaning given by section 251 of that Act and references to acting as an insolvency practitioner are to be read in accordance with section 388 of that Act.

(4) "Director" includes any person occupying the position of director, by what ever name called.

(5) "Shadow director", in relation to a company, means a person in accordance with whose directions or instructions the directors of the company are accustomed to act (but so that a person is not deemed a shadow director by reason only that the directors act on advice given by him in a professional capacity).

(6) Section 740 of the *Companies Act* applies as regards the meaning of "body corporate"; and "officer" has the meaning given by section 744 of that Act.

(7) In references to legislation other than this Act—

"the *Companies Act*" means the *Companies Act* 1985;

"the *Companies Acts*" has the meaning given by section 2 of the *Companies Act* 2006; and

"the *Insolvency Act*" means the *Insolvency Act* 1986;

and in sections 3(1) and 5(1) of this Act "the companies legislation" means the *Companies Acts*, Parts I to VII of the *Insolvency Act* and, in Part XV of that Act, sections 411, 413, 414, 416 and 417.

(8) Any reference to provisions, or a particular provision, of the *Companies Acts* or the *Insolvency Act* includes the corresponding provisions or provision of the former *Companies Acts* (as defined by section 1171 of the *Companies Act* 2006) or, as the case may be, the *Insolvency Act* 1985.

(9) Subject to the provisions of this section, expressions that are defined for the purposes of the *Companies Acts* have the same meaning in this Act.

(10) Any reference to acting as receiver—

(a) includes acting as manager or as both receiver and manager, but

(b) does not include acting as administrative receiver;

and "receivership" is to be read accordingly.

[This section is printed as amended by *Insolvency Act* 2000, ss.5(3) and (8), and Sched. 4, para. 15; and the *Companies Act 2006 (Consequential Amendments etc.) Order* 2008 (S.I. 2008 No. 948), art. 3(1), and Sched. 1, Pt 2, para. 106(1) and (4).]

Sections 22A, 22B and 22C (inserted by the *Companies Act* 1989, s.211(3), the *Friendly Societies Act* 1992, Sched. 21, and the *Health and Social Care (Community Health and Standards) Act* 2003, s.34, and Sched. 4, paras 67 and 68; and amended by S.I. 2008 No. 948 (*ante*), art. 3(1), and Sched. 1, Pt 2, para. 106(1) and (5) to (7)) apply the Act to building societies, incorporated friendly societies and NHS foundation trusts as it applies to companies. Section 23(1) gives effect to the transitional provisions and savings in Schedule 3 (without prejudice to anything in the *Interpretation Act* 1978 with regard to the effect of repeals). **30–201**

E. FINANCIAL SERVICES AND MARKETS ACT 2000

(1) Introduction

The *FSMA* 2000 received Royal Assent on June 14, 2000. For details of the commencement of the Act, and of various transitional provisions, see *ante*, § 30–75. **30–202**

This work does not cover offences connected with fair trading, consumer credit and the financial compensation and ombudsman schemes.

(2) General provisions as to offences and interpretation

Financial Services and Markets Act 2000, ss.400–403

Offences by bodies corporate etc.

400.—(1) If an offence under this Act committed by a body corporate is shown— **30–203**

(a) to have been committed with the consent or connivance of an officer, or

(b) to be attributable to any neglect on his part,

the officer as well as the body corporate is guilty of the offence and liable to be proceeded against and punished accordingly.

(2) If the affairs of a body corporate are managed by its members, subsection (1) applies in relation to the acts and defaults of a member in connection with his functions of management as if he were a director of the body.

(3) If an offence under this Act committed by a partnership is shown—

(a) to have been committed with the consent or connivance of a partner, or

(b) to be attributable to any neglect on his part,

the partner as well as the partnership is guilty of the offence and liable to be proceeded against and punished accordingly.

(4) In subsection (3) "partner" includes a person purporting to act as a partner.

(5) "Officer", in relation to a body corporate, means—

(a) a director, member of the committee of management, chief executive, manager, secretary or other similar officer of the body, or a person purporting to act in any such capacity; and

(b) an individual who is a controller of the body.

(6) If an offence under this Act committed by an unincorporated association (other than a partnership) is shown—

(a) to have been committed with the consent or connivance of an officer of the association or a member of its governing body, or

(b) to be attributable to any neglect on the part of such an officer or member,

that officer or member as well as the association is guilty of the offence and liable to be proceeded against and punished accordingly.

(7) Regulations may provide for the application of any provision of this section, with such modifications as the Treasury consider appropriate, to a body corporate or unincorporated association formed or recognised under the law of a territory outside the United Kingdom.

Institution of proceedings

Proceedings for offences

401.—(1) In this section "offence" means an offence under this Act or subordinate legislation made under this Act. **30–204**

(2) Proceedings for an offence may be instituted in England and Wales only—

(a) by the Authority or the Secretary of State; or

(b) by or with the consent of the Director of Public Prosecutions.

(3) [*Institution of proceedings in Northern Ireland.*]

(4) Except in Scotland, proceedings for an offence under section 203 may also be instituted by the Director General of Fair Trading.

(5) In exercising its power to institute proceedings for an offence, the Authority must comply with any conditions or restrictions imposed in writing by the Treasury.

(6) Conditions or restrictions may be imposed under subsection (5) in relation to—

(a) proceedings generally; or

(b) such proceedings, or categories of proceedings, as the Treasury may direct.

As to the extended application of section 401, see *ante*, § 30–75.

Power of the Authority to institute proceedings for certain other offences

402.—(1) Except in Scotland, the Authority may institute proceedings for an offence under—

(a) Part V of the *Criminal Justice Act* 1993 (insider dealing); or

(b) prescribed regulations relating to money laundering.

(2) In exercising its power to institute proceedings for any such offence, the Authority must comply with any conditions or restrictions imposed in writing by the Treasury.

(3) Conditions or restrictions may be imposed under subsection (2) in relation to—

(a) proceedings generally; or

(b) such proceedings, or categories of proceedings, as the Treasury may direct.

Jurisdiction and procedure in respect of offences

30–205 **403.**—(1) A fine imposed on an unincorporated association on its conviction of an offence is to be paid out of the funds of the association.

(2) Proceedings for an offence alleged to have been committed by an unincorporated association must be brought in the name of the association (and not in that of any of its members).

(3) Rules of court relating to the service of documents are to have effect as if the association were a body corporate.

(4) In proceedings for an offence brought against an unincorporated association—

(a) section 33 of the *Criminal Justice Act* 1925 and Schedule 3 to the *Magistrates' Courts Act* 1980 (procedure) apply as they do in relation to a body corporate;

(b)–(c) [*Scotland and Northern Ireland*].

(5) Summary proceedings for an offence may be taken—

(a) against a body corporate or unincorporated association at any place at which it has a place of business;

(b) against an individual at any place where he is for the time being.

(6) Subsection (5) does not affect any jurisdiction exercisable apart from this section.

(7) "Offence" means an offence under this Act.

30–206 As to the extended application of section 403, see *ante*, § 30–75.

The Secretary of State and the FSA can prosecute any offence under the *FSMA* 2000 in England or Wales. Others can only prosecute with the consent of the Director of Public Prosecutions. The FSA can also prosecute offences of insider dealing (Part V of the *CJA* 1993) and breaches of the *Money Laundering Regulations* 2007 (S.I. 2007 No. 2157), and the *Transfer of Funds (Information on the Payer) Regulations* 2007 (S.I. 2007 No. 3298) (see *ante*, § 30–88b).

(3) Carrying on unauthorised investment business

Financial Services and Markets Act 2000, ss.19, 21–25

The general prohibition

30–207 **19.**—(1) No person may carry on a regulated activity in the United Kingdom, or purport to do so, unless he is—

(a) an authorised person; or

(b) an exempt person.

(2) The prohibition is referred to in this Act as the general prohibition.

Restrictions on financial promotion

21.—(1) A person ("A") must not, in the course of business, communicate an invitation or inducement to engage in investment activity.

(2) But subsection (1) does not apply if—

(a) A is an authorised person; or
(b) the content of the communication is approved for the purposes of this section by an authorised person.

(3) In the case of a communication originating outside the United Kingdom, subsection (1) applies only if the communication is capable of having an effect in the United Kingdom.

(4) The Treasury may by order specify circumstances in which a person is to be regarded for the purposes of subsection (1) as—
(a) acting in the course of business;
(b) not acting in the course of business.

(5) The Treasury may by order specify circumstances (which may include compliance with financial promotion rules) in which subsection (1) does not apply.

(6) An order under subsection (5) may, in particular, provide that subsection (1) does not apply in relation to communications—
(a) of a specified description;
(b) originating in a specified country or territory outside the United Kingdom;
(c) originating in a country or territory which falls within a specified description of country or territory outside the United Kingdom; or
(d) originating outside the United Kingdom.

(7) The Treasury may by order repeal subsection (3).

(8) "Engaging in investment activity" means—
(a) entering or offering to enter into an agreement the making or performance of which by either party constitutes a controlled activity; or
(b) exercising any rights conferred by a controlled investment to acquire, dispose of, underwrite or convert a controlled investment.

(9) An activity is a controlled activity if—
(a) it is an activity of a specified kind or one which falls within a specified class of activity; and
(b) it relates to an investment of a specified kind, or to one which falls within a specified class of investment.

(10) An investment is a controlled investment if it is an investment of a specified kind or one which falls within a specified class of investment.

(11) Schedule 2 (except paragraph 26) applies for the purposes of subsections (9) and (10) with references to section 22 being read as references to each of those subsections.

(12) Nothing in Schedule 2, as applied by subsection (11), limits the powers conferred by subsection (9) or (10).

(13) "Communicate" includes causing a communication to be made.

(14) "Investment" includes any asset, right or interest.

(15) "Specified" means specified in an order made by the Treasury.

Regulated activities

The classes of activity and categories of investment

22.—(1) An activity is a regulated activity for the purposes of this Act if it is an activity of a specified kind which is carried on by way of business and— **30–208**
(a) relates to an investment of a specified kind; or
(b) in the case of an activity of a kind which is also specified for the purposes of this paragraph, is carried on in relation to property of any kind.

(2) Schedule 2 makes provision supplementing this section.

(3) Nothing in Schedule 2 limits the powers conferred by subsection (1).

(4) "Investment" includes any asset, right or interest.

(5) "Specified" means specified in an order made by the Treasury.

Offences

Contravention of the general prohibition

23.—(1) A person who contravenes the general prohibition is guilty of an offence and liable— **30–209**
(a) on summary conviction, to imprisonment for a term not exceeding *six* [12] months or a fine not exceeding the statutory maximum, or both;
(b) on conviction on indictment, to imprisonment for a term not exceeding two years or a fine, or both.

(2) In this Act "an authorisation offence" means an offence under this section.

(3) In proceedings for an authorisation offence it is a defence for the accused to show that he took all reasonable precautions and exercised all due diligence to avoid committing the offence.

[In subs. (1)(a), "12" is substituted for "six", as from a day to be appointed, by the *CJA* 2003, s.282(2) and (3). The increase has no application to offences committed before the substitution takes effect: s.282(4).]

False claims to be authorised or exempt

30–210 **24.**—(1) A person who is neither an authorised person nor, in relation to the regulated activity in question, an exempt person is guilty of an offence if he—

(a) describes himself (in whatever terms) as an authorised person;

(b) describes himself (in whatever terms) as an exempt person in relation to the regulated activity; or

(c) behaves, or otherwise holds himself out, in a manner which indicates (or which is reasonably likely to be understood as indicating) that he is—

(i) an authorised person; or

(ii) an exempt person in relation to the regulated activity.

(2) In proceedings for an offence under this section it is a defence for the accused to show that he took all reasonable precautions and exercised all due diligence to avoid committing the offence.

(3) A person guilty of an offence under this section is liable on summary conviction to imprisonment for a term not exceeding six months or a fine not exceeding level 5 on the standard scale, or both.

(4) But where the conduct constituting the offence involved or included the public display of any material, the maximum fine for the offence is level 5 on the standard scale multiplied by the number of days for which the display continued.

Contravention of section 21

30–211 **25.**—(1) A person who contravenes section 21(1) is guilty of an offence and liable—

(a) on summary conviction, to imprisonment for a term not exceeding *six* [12] months or a fine not exceeding the statutory maximum, or both;

(b) on conviction on indictment, to imprisonment for a term not exceeding two years or a fine, or both.

(2) In proceedings for an offence under this section it is a defence for the accused to show—

(a) that he believed on reasonable grounds that the content of the communication was prepared, or approved for the purposes of section 21, by an authorised person; or

(b) that he took all reasonable precautions and exercised all due diligence to avoid committing the offence.

[In subs. (1)(a), "12" is substituted for "six", as from a day to be appointed, by the *CJA* 2003, s.282(2) and (3). The increase has no application to offences committed before the substitution takes effect: s.282(4).]

30–212 Section 19 contains the general prohibition on unauthorised persons carrying on regulated activities in the United Kingdom. The *Financial Services and Markets Act 2000 (Exemption) Order* 2001 (S.I. 2001 No. 1201) exempts certain persons from the general prohibition imposed under section 19. The 2001 order has been subject to a series of amending orders, the most recent of which is the *Financial Services and Markets Act 2000 (Exemption) (Amendment) Order* 2008 (S.I. 2008 No. 682). See also the *Financial Services and Markets Act 2000 (Transitional Provisions) (Authorised Persons etc.) Order* 2001 (S.I. 2001 No. 2636), as amended by the *Financial Services and Markets Act 2000 (Miscellaneous Provisions) Order* 2001 (S.I. 2001 No. 3650). Section 23 (*ante*) contains the offence of contravening the general prohibition. Regulated activities include the operation of a "collective investment scheme", as to which, see *FSA v. Fradley*, *The Times*, December 1, 2005, CA (Civ. Div.).

Section 418 elaborates on when regulated activities will be considered to be carried out in the United Kingdom. The *Financial Services and Markets Act 2000 (Carrying on Regulated Activities by Way of Business) Order* 2001 (S.I. 2001 No. 1177) makes provision as to the circumstances in which a person is, or is not, to be regarded as carrying on a regulated activity by way of business for the purposes of section 19. The

Financial Services and Markets Act 2000 (Regulated Activities) Order 2001 (S.I. 2001 No. 544) specifies the kinds of activities and investments that may involve "regulated activity" for the purposes of the Act. The matters in respect of which provision may be made under section 22(1) in respect of activities and investments include those described in Schedule 2 to the Act. It is likely that the reasoning in *Securities and Investment Board v. Scandex Capital Management A/S* [1998] 1 W.L.R. 712, CA (Civ. Div.) in relation to the equivalent provisions in the *Financial Services Act* 1986 will be held to apply to the *FSMA* 2000 and a mistake of law as to the need for authorisation will therefore not give rise to a defence. Both S.I. 2001 No. 1177 and S.I. 2001 No. 544 have been subject to a series of amendments, the most recent of which are the *Financial Services and Markets Act 2000 (Regulated Activities) (Amendment No. 3) Order* 2006 (S.I. 2006 No. 3384) and the *Companies Act 2006 (Consequential Amendments etc.) Order* 2008 (S.I. 2008 No. 948) respectively.

The prohibition in section 21 applies to "invitations" or "inducements" to engage in investment activity, which are made in the course of business. The Treasury has power, if necessary, to determine the meaning of "in the course of business" since the prohibition would potentially catch communications whether they are made in the United Kingdom, into the United Kingdom from elsewhere, or from the United Kingdom to another country. The *Financial Services and Markets Act 2000 (Financial Promotion) Order* 2005 (S.I. 2005 No. 1529) sets out the activities and investments to which the restriction imposed by section 21 applies. Section 25 (*ante*) contains the offence of contravening section 21(1). For the most recent amendment to S.I. 2005 No. 1529, see the *Financial Services and Markets Act 2000 (Financial Promotion) (Amendment No. 2) Order* 2007 (S.I. 2007 No. 2615).

The *FSMA* 2000 provides for a single route to authorisation to operate in the financial services industry, replacing several sector-based regimes. Provisions relating to authorisation and exemption are contained in Part III (ss.31–39) which sets out those persons who are to be authorised for the purposes of the Act and gives the Treasury power to exempt certain persons from the requirement to be authorised. Authorised persons will also include those persons given permission under Part IV (ss.40–55) and certain persons from other Member States who are authorised in accordance with arrangements under the Treaty of Rome and the single market directives. Part XX (ss.325–333) exempts certain activities carried on by members of the professions. Section 333 creates a summary offence of falsely claiming exemption under Part XX. The FSA has power under section 56 to make a prohibition order prohibiting an authorised person from carrying on regulated activity. Breach of a prohibition order is a summary offence punishable by a fine not exceeding level 5: see s.56(4).

(4) Listing applications and prospectus offences

Financial Services and Markets Act 2000, s.85

Prohibition of dealing etc. in transferable securities without approved prospectus

85.—(1) It is unlawful for transferable securities to which this subsection applies to be offered to the public in the United Kingdom unless an approved prospectus has been made available to the public before the offer is made. **30–213**

(2) It is unlawful to request the admission of transferable securities to which this subsection applies to trading on a regulated market situated or operating in the United Kingdom unless an approved prospectus has been made available to the public before the request is made.

(3) A person who contravenes subsection (1) or (2) is guilty of an offence and liable—

(a) on summary conviction, to imprisonment for a term not exceeding *3* [12] months or a fine not exceeding the statutory maximum or both;

(b) on conviction on indictment, to imprisonment for a term not exceeding 2 years or a fine or both.

(4) [*Civil actions.*]

(5) Subsection (1) applies to all transferable securities other than—

(a) those listed in Schedule 11A;

(b) such other transferable securities as may be specified in prospectus rules.

(6) Subsection (2) applies to all transferable securities other than—

(a) those listed in Part 1 of Schedule 11A;

(b) such other transferable securities as may be specified in prospectus rules.

(7) "Approved prospectus" means, in relation to transferable securities to which this section applies, a prospectus approved by the competent authority of the home State in relation to the issuer of the securities.

[This section is printed as substituted by the *Prospectus Regulations* 2005 (S.I. 2005 No.1433). In subs. (3)(a), "12" is substituted for "three", as from a day to be appointed, by the *CJA* 2003, s.282(2) and (3), but the increase has no application to offences committed before the substitution takes effect: s.282(4).]

30–214 Section 86 (also substituted by S.I. 2005 No. 1453) provides for certain exemptions from the operation of section 85(1).

(5) Provision of false or misleading information to auditor or actuary

Financial Services and Markets Act 2000, s.346

Provision of false or misleading information to auditor or actuary

30–215 **346.**—(1) An authorised person who knowingly or recklessly gives an appointed auditor or actuary information which is false or misleading in a material particular is guilty of an offence and liable—

(a) on summary conviction, to imprisonment for a term not exceeding *six* [12] months or a fine not exceeding the statutory maximum, or both;

(b) on conviction on indictment to imprisonment for a term not exceeding two years or a fine, or both.

(2) Subsection (1) applies equally to an officer, controller or manager of an authorised person.

(3) "Appointed" means appointed under or as a result of this Act.

[In subs. (1)(a), "12" is substituted for "six", as from a day to be appointed, by the *CJA* 2003, s.282(2) and (3). The increase has no application to offences committed before the substitution takes effect: s.282(4).]

(6) Market rigging

Financial Services and Markets Act 2000, s.397

Misleading statements and practices

30–215a **397.**—(1) This subsection applies to a person who—

(a) makes a statement, promise or forecast which he knows to be misleading, false or deceptive in a material particular;

(b) dishonestly conceals any material facts whether in connection with a statement, promise or forecast made by him or otherwise; or

(c) recklessly makes (dishonestly or otherwise) a statement, promise or forecast which is misleading, false or deceptive in a material particular.

(2) A person to whom subsection (1) applies is guilty of an offence if he makes the statement, promise or forecast or conceals the facts for the purpose of inducing, or is reckless as to whether it may induce, another person (whether or not the person to whom the statement, promise or forecast is made)—

(a) to enter or offer to enter into, or to refrain from entering or offering to enter into, a relevant agreement; or

(b) to exercise, or refrain from exercising, any rights conferred by a relevant investment.

(3) Any person who does any act or engages in any course of conduct which creates a false or misleading impression as to the market in or the price or value of any relevant investments is guilty of an offence if he does so for the purpose of creating that impression and of thereby inducing another person to acquire, dispose of, subscribe for or underwrite those investments or to refrain from doing so or to exercise, or refrain from exercising, any rights conferred by those investments.

(4) In proceedings for an offence under subsection (2) brought against a person to whom subsection (1) applies as a result of paragraph (a) of that subsection, it is a defence for him to show that the statement, promise or forecast was made in conformity with—

(a) price stabilising rules;
(b) control of information rules; or
(c) the relevant provisions of Commission Regulation (EC) No 2273/2003 of 22 December 2003 implementing Directive 2003/6/EC of the European Parliament and of the Council as regards exemptions for buy-back programmes and stabilisation of financial instruments.

(5) In proceedings brought against any person for an offence under subsection (3) it is a defence for him to show—
(a) that he reasonably believed that his act or conduct would not create an impression that was false or misleading as to the matters mentioned in that subsection;
(b) that he acted or engaged in the conduct—
 (i) for the purpose of stabilising the price of investments; and
 (ii) in conformity with price stabilising rules;
(c) that he acted or engaged in the conduct in conformity with control of information rules; or
(a) [*sic*] that he acted or engaged in the conduct in conformity with the relevant provisions of Commission Regulation (EC) No 2273/2003 of 22 December 2003 implementing Directive 2003/6/EC of the European Parliament and of the Council as regards exemptions for buy-back programmes and stabilisation of financial instruments.

(6) Subsections (1) and (2) do not apply unless—
(a) the statement, promise or forecast is made in or from, or the facts are concealed in or from, the United Kingdom or arrangements are made in or from the United Kingdom for the statement, promise or forecast to be made or the facts to be concealed;
(b) the person on whom the inducement is intended to or may have effect is in the United Kingdom; or
(c) the agreement is or would be entered into or the rights are or would be exercised in the United Kingdom.

(7) Subsection (3) does not apply unless—
(a) the act is done, or the course of conduct is engaged in, in the United Kingdom; or
(b) the false or misleading impression is created there.

(8) A person guilty of an offence under this section is liable—
(a) on summary conviction, to imprisonment for a term not exceeding *six* [12] months or a fine not exceeding the statutory maximum, or both;
(b) on conviction on indictment, to imprisonment for a term not exceeding seven years or a fine, or both.

(9) "Relevant agreement" means an agreement—
(a) the entering into or performance of which by either party constitutes an activity of a specified kind or one which falls within a specified class of activity; and
(b) which relates to a relevant investment.

(10) "Relevant investment" means an investment of a specified kind or one which falls within a prescribed class of investment.

(11) Schedule 2 (except paragraphs 25 and 26) applies for the purposes of subsections (9) and (10) with references to section 22 being read as references to each of those subsections.

(12) Nothing in Schedule 2, as applied by subsection (11), limits the power conferred by subsection (9) or (10).

(13) "Investment" includes any asset, right or interest.

(14) "Specified" means specified in an order made by the Treasury.

[This section is printed as amended by the *Financial Services and Markets Act 2000 (Market Abuse) Regulations* 2005 (S.I. 2005 No. 381), reg. 8. In subs. (8)(a), "12" is substituted for "six", as from a day to be appointed, by the *CJA* 2003, s.282(2) and (3). The increase has no application to offences committed before the substitution takes effect: s.282(4).]

For orders made under subsection (14), see the *Financial Services and Markets Act 2000 (Misleading Statements and Practices) Order* 2001 (S.I. 2001 No. 3645), as amended by the *Financial Services and Markets Act 2000 (Misleading Statements and Practices) (Amendment) Order* 2003 (S.I. 2003 No. 1474).

30–215b These offences are based on the offences contained in sections 47 and 133 of the *Financial Services Act* 1986 and section 35 of the *Banking Act* 1987. Those offences were in turn shaped by section 13 of the *Prevention of Fraud (Investments) Act* 1958. The first offence, set out in subsections (1) and (2), applies where a person deliberately makes a misleading statement, promise or forecast, or dishonestly conceals facts from someone with the intention of inducing any other person to do or refrain from doing something in relation to an investment. A possible example of this offence would be someone lying about a company's financial position at a time when he was seeking to dispose of shares in that company. It is also an offence to make the misleading statement, promise or forecast recklessly and to be reckless as to whether another person was so induced. "Dishonestly" is only required to be proved in the case of concealment, and although not defined, it must bear the same meaning as in *R. v. Ghosh* [1982] Q.B. 1053, 75 Cr.App.R. 154, CA, *ante*, §§ 21–24 *et seq.* A number of different statements may be charged in a single count without violating the rule against duplicity: see *R. v. Linnell*, 53 Cr.App.R. 585, CA; although the jury must be directed that they should be agreed as to the particular statement they find proved: see *R. v. Brown (K.)*, 75 Cr.App.R. 115, CA. Where several statements are made together, it is the effect of them taken together that may be considered, see *Aaron's Reefs Ltd v. Twiss* [1896] A.C. 273, HL. Thus several statements taken together could be misleading even though each individually was true.

A person's present intention is a fact, and is therefore a fact that may be concealed within subsection (1)(b): *R. (Young) v. Central Criminal Court* [2002] 2 Cr.App.R. 12, DC (decided in relation to s.47 of the 1986 Act).

Subsection (2) specifies various activities in relation to a relevant agreement that must be intended to be induced or as to which the defendant must be reckless. Such activities are not confined to a single act which can only be done at a single point of time. Depending upon the nature of the agreement, they may include a whole variety of acts done over a period. Each act may constitute a separate offence but they are not mutually exclusive, see *R. v. Markus* [1976] A.C. 35, HL. Subsection (4) provides a defence against the offence in subsection (2) for a person if he can show that a statement, promise or forecast was made in compliance with price stabilising or control of information rules.

In *R. v. Page* [1996] Crim.L.R. 821, CA, the court approved a direction that a statement was reckless if it was a "rash statement ... with no real basis of fact to support it and not caring whether it was true or false".

The second offence, set out in subsection (3), is the creation of a misleading impression about an investment with the intention of inducing another person to do or not do something in relation to that investment. This covers such things as market manipulation, for example engaging in artificial trades in a particular investment in order to create the impression that there is more interest in the investment than really exists. Subsection (5) provides three defences against the offence in subsection (3). The first is that the person concerned reasonably believed that his conduct would not create a misleading impression. The second defence is where the person is engaged in price stabilisation in circumstances where this is permitted. The third defence is where the person acted in conformity with the control of information rules under section 147. The offence in subsection (3) is not committed unless the action done takes place in the United Kingdom, or the misleading impression this creates arises in the United Kingdom.

Sentence

30–215c Sentences of up to two years' imprisonment were held to be appropriate in relation to a conspiracy to defraud where the market was manipulated with a view to influencing the outcome of a takeover bid, see *R. v. Ward, Hendry and Howard*; *Att.-Gen.'s References (Nos 14, 15 and 16 of 1995)*, *The Times*, April 10, 1997, CA. For guidelines on sentencing under section 397(1)(c), see *R. v. Bailey and Rigby* [2006] 2 Cr.App.R.(S.) 36, CA. See also *R. v. Hipwell* [2006] 2 Cr.App.R.(S.) 98, CA (sentencing financial journalist).

In *R. v. Rigby and Bailey* [2007] 1 Cr.App.R.(S.) 73, CA, it was held that where an offender committed an offence contrary to section 397(1) by causing a false or misleading trading statement to be issued to the market, which statement had caused the share price of the company to which it related to rise before falling dramatically when a corrective statement was subsequently issued, there was no proper sense in which the offender could be said to have obtained a benefit or derived a pecuniary advantage for the purposes of section 71 of the *CJA* 1988 (see now the *PCA* 2002, s.76 (*ante*, § 5–637)) in respect of the unrealised increase to the value of his own shareholding in the company which had temporarily existed before the share price fell; the increase was neither the proceeds of the offence of which the offender was convicted nor the positive consequence of it (distinguishing *R. v. Wilkes* [2003] 2 Cr.App.R.(S.) 105, CA, and *R. v. Smith (David)* [2002] 1 W.L.R. 54, HL (*ante*, §§ 5–770, 5–772)); and as to a salary and other emoluments paid to the offender when the company had continued to employ him after the corrective statement had been issued for the purpose of assisting with the financial restructuring of the company, there was no basis upon which these could be said to have been a benefit or pecuniary advantage to the offender where there was no more than a narrative connection between the offence and the continued employment, and where the offender had been employed despite the offence rather than because of it.

(7) Provision of false or misleading information to the Financial Services Authority

Financial Services and Markets Act 2000, s.398

Misleading the Authority: residual cases

398.—(1) A person who, in purported compliance with any requirement imposed by or under this Act, knowingly or recklessly gives the authority information which is false or misleading in a material particular is guilty of an offence. **30–215d**

(2) Subsection (1) applies only to a requirement in relation to which no other provision of this Act creates an offence in connection with the giving of information.

(3) A person guilty of an offence, under this section is liable—

(a) on summary conviction, to a fine not exceeding the statutory maximum;

(b) on conviction on indictment, to a fine.

This section makes it an offence to give false or misleading information to the FSA in purported compliance with requirements under the *FSMA* 2000 in cases where this is not already an offence under other provisions (for example under section 177(4) regarding the provision of information to investigators).

F. ENTERPRISE ACT 2002

(1) Introduction

The *Enterprise Act* 2002 received Royal Assent on November 7, 2002. The Act introduces for the first time an offence in connection with the breach of competition law. The cartel offence will operate alongside the existing regime that imposes civil sanctions on undertakings that breach the *Competition Act* 1998 prohibition on anti-competitive agreements. **30–216**

(2) Cartel offence

Enterprise Act 2002, ss.188–190

Cartel offence

188.—(1) An individual is guilty of an offence if he dishonestly agrees with one or more other persons to make or implement, or to cause to be made or implemented, arrangements of the following kind relating to at least two undertakings (A and B). **30–217**

(2) The arrangements must be ones which, if operating as the parties to the agreement intend, would—

(a) directly or indirectly fix a price for the supply by A in the United Kingdom (otherwise than to B) of a product or service,

(b) limit or prevent supply by A in the United Kingdom of a product or service,

(c) limit or prevent production by A in the United Kingdom of a product,

(d) divide between A and B the supply in the United Kingdom of a product or service to a customer or customers,
(e) divide between A and B customers for the supply in the United Kingdom of a product or service, or
(f) be bid-rigging arrangements.

(3) Unless subsection (2)(d), (e) or (f) applies, the arrangements must also be ones which, if operating as the parties to the agreement intend, would—
(a) directly or indirectly fix a price for the supply by B in the United Kingdom (otherwise than to A) of a product or service,
(b) limit or prevent supply by B in the United Kingdom of a product or service, or
(c) limit or prevent production by B in the United Kingdom of a product.

(4) In subsections (2)(a) to (d) and (3), references to supply or production are to supply or production in the appropriate circumstances (for which see section 189).

(5) "Bid-rigging arrangements" are arrangements under which, in response to a request for bids for the supply of a product or service in the United Kingdom, or for the production of a product in the United Kingdom—
(a) A but not B may make a bid, or
(b) A and B may each make a bid but, in one case or both, only a bid arrived at in accordance with the arrangements.

(6) But arrangements are not bid-rigging arrangements if, under them, the person requesting bids would be informed of them at or before the time when a bid is made.

(7) "Undertaking" has the same meaning as in Part 1 of the 1998 Act.

As to subsection (7), see *post*, § 30–220.

Cartel offence: supplementary

30–218 **189.**—(1) For section 188(2)(a), the appropriate circumstances are that A's supply of the product or service would be at a level in the supply chain at which the product or service would at the same time be supplied by B in the United Kingdom.

(2) For section 188(2)(b), the appropriate circumstances are that A's supply of the product or service would be at a level in the supply chain—
(a) at which the product or service would at the same time be supplied by B in the United Kingdom, or
(b) at which supply by B in the United Kingdom of the product or service would be limited or prevented by the arrangements.

(3) For section 188(2)(c), the appropriate circumstances are that A's production of the product would be at a level in the production chain—
(a) at which the product would at the same time be produced by B in the United Kingdom, or
(b) at which production by B in the United Kingdom of the product would be limited or prevented by the arrangements.

(4) For section 188(2)(d), the appropriate circumstances are that A's supply of the product or service would be at the same level in the supply chain as B's.

(5) For section 188(3)(a), the appropriate circumstances are that B's supply of the product or service would be at a level in the supply chain at which the product or service would at the same time be supplied by A in the United Kingdom.

(6) For section 188(3)(b), the appropriate circumstances are that B's supply of the product or service would be at a level in the supply chain—
(a) at which the product or service would at the same time be supplied by A in the United Kingdom, or
(b) at which supply by A in the United Kingdom of the product or service would be limited or prevented by the arrangements.

(7) For section 188(3)(c), the appropriate circumstances are that B's production of the product would be at a level in the production chain
(a) at which the product would at the same time be produced by A in the United Kingdom, or
(b) at which production by A in the United Kingdom of the product would be limited or prevented by the arrangements.

Cartel offence: penalty and prosecution

30–219 **190.**—(1) A person guilty of an offence under section 188 is liable—
(a) on conviction on indictment, to imprisonment for a term not exceeding five years or to a fine, or to both;

(b) on summary conviction, to imprisonment for a term not exceeding *six* [12] months or to a fine not exceeding the statutory maximum, or to both.

(2) In England and Wales and Northern Ireland, proceedings for an offence under section 188 may be instituted only—

(a) by the Director of the Serious Fraud Office, or

(b) by or with the consent of the OFT.

(3) No proceedings may be brought for an offence under section 188 in respect of an agreement outside the United Kingdom, unless it has been implemented in whole or in part in the United Kingdom.

(4) Where, for the purpose of the investigation or prosecution of offences under section 188, the OFT gives a person written notice under this subsection, no proceedings for an offence under section 188 that falls within a description specified in the notice may be brought against that person in England and Wales or Northern Ireland except in circumstances specified in the notice.

[In subs. (1)(a), "12" is substituted for "six", as from a day to be appointed, by the *CJA* 2003, s.282(2) and (3). The increase has no application to offences committed before the substitution takes effect: s.282(4).]

An individual is liable to criminal prosecution if he or she dishonestly agrees with one **30–220**
or more other persons that undertakings will engage in one or more of the prohibited cartel activities. These are price-fixing, limitation of supply or production, market-sharing and bid-rigging. The offence only applies to agreements between undertakings at the same level in the supply chain, known as horizontal agreements. Vertical agreements will not fall within the scope of the offence. The offence does not therefore encompass monopoly abuse but may bite on collective dealing or other joint venture arrangements. If the agreement is made outside the U.K., proceedings may only be brought where some step has been taken to implement the agreement in the U.K. Part I of the 1998 Act (see s.188(7), *ante*) does not contain a definition of "undertaking". Its meaning, for the purposes of that Part, is to be derived from case law relating to Articles 81 and 82 of the E.C. Treaty. Thus, "undertaking" within the meaning of the Act includes any legal or natural person capable of carrying on commercial or economic activities relating to goods or services, irrespective of its legal status. It extends to companies, firms, businesses, partnerships, individuals operating as sole traders, trade associations and non-profit making organisations. A parent company and its subsidiaries will usually be treated as a single undertaking if they operate as a single economic unit, depending on the facts of each case. Neither central nor local government bodies are likely to be considered "undertakings" within the meaning of Articles 81 and 82; but where a local authority operates through a commercial body, that body will be an undertaking. An employee will not usually be considered as an "undertaking" although he acts on behalf of an undertaking.

The offence is committed only if the individual acts dishonestly, as to which, see *ante*, **30–221**
§§ 21–23 *et seq*. There is no requirement to prove that the agreement had any actual or intended anti-competitive effect and the agreement need not be unlawful *per se* under Article 81 of the E.C. Treaty or the *Competition Act* 1998, although a belief that an agreement had no anti-competitive effect or did not breach Article 81 might well be relevant to dishonesty and any defence based on a claim of right. The offence is committed irrespective of whether the agreement reached is actually implemented by the undertakings and irrespective of whether the individuals have the authority to act on behalf of the undertakings at the time of the agreement. It is not a defence to show that the agreement would have been exempt or that it serves the public interest. These issues are however liable to be raised in the context of "dishonesty".

The width of the offence will be mitigated by the stated policy of the OFT and the **30–222**
SFO to prosecute only in a limited category of cases. The general powers of the OFT are considerably enhanced by the existence of a wide range of parallel civil procedures, including a new power to seek disqualification under the *CDDA* 1986 for competition infringements. In addition, the OFT has power to issue "no action" letters (see s.190(4)), which will prevent a prosecution being brought against an individual in England, Wales or Northern Ireland for their participation in the cartel. Guidance on the issuance of "no action" letters is available on the OFT website (www.oft.gov.uk). The OFT stated

during the consultation period that it considers that it is in the interest of the economic well-being of the United Kingdom to grant leniency to individuals who inform competition authorities of cartels and who then co-operate in the process of investigation and prosecution. It is the secret nature of cartels and their damaging effects that are said to justify such a policy. The interests of customers and consumers in ensuring that such practices are detected and brought to an end outweigh the policy objectives of imposing penalties on those individuals who have committed an offence but who co-operate with the OFT and, where appropriate, any other competition authorities. The conditions for the grant of no action letters include a requirement that the person admits participation in the cartel offence; provides the OFT with full information on the existence and activities of the cartel; maintains complete co-operation throughout the investigation; and refrains from further participation in the cartel.

[The next paragraph is § 30–230.]

G. INSIDER DEALING

30–230 The *CJA* 1993 received Royal Assent on July 27, 1993; and Part V took effect on March 1, 1994 (*Criminal Justice Act 1993 (Commencement No. 5) Order* 1994 (S.I. 1994 No. 242)). The 1993 Act replaced the *Company Securities (Insider Dealing) Act* 1985 which in turn replaced similar provisions contained in sections 68 to 73 of the *Companies Act* 1980 which were based upon a preceding white paper, *The Conduct of Company Directors*, Cmnd. 7037 (1977). Part V amends and restates the law in conformity with the Council Directive 89/592/EEC requiring the harmonisation of the regulation of insider dealing throughout the Community.

Criminal Justice Act 1993, ss.52–64, Scheds 1, 2

PART V

INSIDER DEALING

The offence of insider dealing

The offence

30–231 **52.**—(1) An individual who has information as an insider is guilty of insider dealing if, in the circumstances mentioned in subsection (3), he deals in securities that are price-affected securities in relation to the information.

(2) An individual who has information as an insider is also guilty of insider dealing if—

(a) he encourages another person to deal in securities that are (whether or not that other knows it) price-affected securities in relation to the information, knowing or having reasonable cause to believe that the dealing would take place in the circumstances mentioned in subsection (3); or

(b) he discloses the information, otherwise than in the proper performance of the functions of his employment, office or profession, to another person.

(3) The circumstances referred to above are that the acquisition or disposal in question occurs on a regulated market, or that the person dealing relies on a professional intermediary or is himself acting as a professional intermediary.

(4) This section has effect subject to section 53.

Defences

30–232 **53.**—(1) An individual is not guilty of insider dealing by virtue of dealing in securities if he shows—

(a) that he did not at the time expect the dealing to result in a profit attributable to the fact that the information in question was price-sensitive information in relation to the securities; or

(b) that at the time he believed on reasonable grounds that the information had been disclosed widely enough to ensure that none of those taking part in the dealing would be prejudiced by not having the information; or

(c) that he would have done what he did even if he had not had the information.

(2) An individual is not guilty of insider dealing by virtue of encouraging another person to deal in securities if he shows—

(a) that he did not at the time expect the dealing to result in a profit attributable to the fact that the information in question was price-sensitive information in relation to the securities; or

(b) that at the time he believed on reasonable grounds that the information had been or would be disclosed widely enough to ensure that none of those taking part in the dealing would be prejudiced by not having the information; or

(c) that he would have done what he did even if he had not had the information.

(3) An individual is not guilty of insider dealing by virtue of a disclosure of information if he shows—

(a) that he did not at the time expect any person, because of the disclosure, to deal in securities in the circumstances mentioned in subsection (3) of section 52; or

(b) that, although he had such an expectation at the time, he did not expect the dealing to result in a profit attributable to the fact that the information was price-sensitive information in relation to the securities.

(4) Schedule 1 (special defences) shall have effect.

(5) The Treasury may by order amend Schedule 1.

(6) In this section references to a profit include references to the avoidance of loss.

Interpretation

Securities to which Part V applies

54.—(1) This Part applies to any security which— **30–233**

(a) falls within any paragraph of Schedule 2; and

(b) satisfies any conditions applying to it under an order made by the Treasury for the purposes of this subsection;

and in the provisions of this Part (other than that Schedule) any reference to a security is a reference to a security to which this Part applies.

(2) The Treasury may by order amend Schedule 2.

"Dealing" in securities

55.—(1) For the purposes of this Part, a person deals in securities if— **30–234**

(a) he acquires or disposes of the securities (whether as principal or agent); or

(b) he procures, directly or indirectly, an acquisition or disposal of the securities by any other person.

(2) For the purposes of this Part, "acquire", in relation to a security, includes—

(a) agreeing to acquire the security; and

(b) entering into a contract which creates the security.

(3) For the purposes of this Part, "dispose", in relation to a security, includes—

(a) agreeing to dispose of the security; and

(b) bringing to an end a contract which created the security.

(4) For the purposes of this subsection (1), a person procures an acquisition or disposal of a security if the security is acquired or disposed of by a person who is—

(a) his agent;

(b) his nominee; or

(c) a person who is acting at his direction,

in relation to the acquisition or disposal.

(5) Subsection (4) is not exhaustive as to the circumstances in which one person may be regarded as procuring an acquisition or disposal of securities by another.

"Inside information", etc.

56.—(1) For the purposes of this section and section 57, "inside information" means information which— **30–235**

(a) relates to particular securities or to a particular issuer of securities or to particular issuers of securities and not to securities generally or to issuers of securities generally;

(b) is specific or precise;

(c) has not been made public; and

(d) if it were made public would be likely to have significant effect on the price of any securities.

(2) For the purposes of this Part, securities are "price-affected securities" in relation to inside information, and inside information is "price-sensitive information" in relation to securities, if and only if the information would, if made public, be likely to have a significant effect on the price of the securities.

(3) For the purposes of this section "price" includes value.

"Insiders"

30–236 **57.**—(1) For the purposes of this Part, a person has information as an insider if and only if—

(a) it is, and he knows that it is, inside information; and

(b) he has it, and knows that he has it, from an inside source.

(2) For the purposes of subsection (1), a person has information from an inside source if and only if—

(a) he has it through—

(i) being a director, employee or shareholder of an issuer of securities; or

(ii) having access to the information by virtue of his employment, office or profession; or

(b) the direct or indirect source of his information is a person within paragraph (a).

Information "made public"

30–237 **58.**—(1) For the purposes of section 56, "made public", in relation to information, shall be construed in accordance with the following provisions of this section; but those provisions are not exhaustive as to the meaning of that expression.

(2) Information is made public if—

(a) it is published in accordance with the rules of a regulated market for the purpose of informing investors and their professional advisers;

(b) it is contained in records which by virtue of any enactment are open to inspection by the public;

(c) it can be readily acquired by those likely to deal in any securities—

(i) to which the information relates; or

(ii) of an issuer to which the information relates; or

(d) it is derived from information which has been made public.

(3) Information may be treated as made public even though—

(a) it can be acquired only by persons exercising diligence or expertise;

(b) it is communicated to a section of the public and not to the public at large;

(c) it can be acquired only by observation;

(d) it is communicated only on payment of a fee; or

(e) it is published only outside the United Kingdom.

"Professional intermediary"

30–238 **59.**—(1) For the purposes of this Part, a "professional intermediary" is a person—

(a) who carries on a business consisting of an activity mentioned in subsection (2) and who holds himself out to the public or any section of the public (including a section of the public constituted by persons such as himself) as willing to engage in any such business; or

(b) who is employed by a person falling within paragraph (a) to carry out any such activity.

(2) The activities referred to in subsection (1) are—

(a) acquiring or disposing of securities (whether as principal or agent); or

(b) acting as an intermediary between persons taking part in any dealings in securities.

(3) A person is not to be treated as carrying on a business consisting of an activity mentioned in subsection (2)—

(a) if the activity in question is merely incidental to some other activity not falling within subsection (2); or

(b) merely because he occasionally conducts one of those activities.

(4) For the purposes of section 52, a person dealing in securities relies on a professional intermediary if and only if a person who is acting as a professional intermediary carries out an activity mentioned in subsection (2) in relation to that dealing.

Other interpretation provisions

30–239 **60.**—(1) For the purposes of this Part, "regulated market" means any market however operated, which, by an order made by the Treasury, is identified (whether by name or by reference to criteria prescribed by the order) as a regulated market for the purposes of this Part.

(2) For the purposes of this Part an "issuer", in relation to any securities, means any company, public sector body or individual by which or by whom the securities have been or are to be issued.

(3) For the purposes of this Part—

(a) "company" means any body (whether or not incorporated and wherever incorporated or constituted) which is not a public sector body; and

(b) "public sector body" means—

(i) in the government of the United Kingdom, of Northern Ireland or of any country or territory outside the United Kingdom;

(ii) a local authority in the United Kingdom or elsewhere;

(iii) any international organisation the members of which include the United Kingdom or another member state;

(iv) the Bank of England; or

(v) the central bank of any sovereign State.

(4) For the purposes this Part, information shall be treated as relating to an issuer of securities which is a company not only where it is about the company but also where it may affect the company's business prospects.

Miscellaneous

Penalties and prosecution

61.—(1) An individual guilty of insider dealing shall be liable— **30–240**

(a) on summary conviction, to a fine not exceeding the statutory maximum or imprisonment for a term not exceeding *six* [12] months or to both; or

(b) on conviction on indictment, to a fine or imprisonment for a term not exceeding seven years or to both.

(2) Proceedings for offences under this Part shall not be instituted in England and Wales except by or with the consent of—

(a) the Secretary of State; or

(b) the Director of Public Prosecutions.

(3) [*Northern Ireland.*]

[In subs. (1)(a), "12" is substituted for "six", as from a day to be appointed, by the *CJA* 2003, s.282(2) and (3). The increase has no application to offences committed before the substitution takes effect: s.282(4).]

Territorial scope of offence of insider dealing

62.—(1) An individual is not guilty of an offence falling within subsection (1) of section 52 unless— **30–241**

(a) he was within the United Kingdom at the time when he is alleged to have done any act constituting or forming part of the alleged dealing;

(b) the regulated market on which the dealing is alleged to have occurred is one which, by an order made by the Treasury, is identified (whether by name or by reference to criteria prescribed by the order) as being, for the purposes of this Part, regulated in the United Kingdom; or

(c) the professional intermediary was within the United Kingdom at the time when he is alleged to have done anything by means of which the offence is alleged to have been committed.

(2) An individual is not guilty of an offence falling within subsection (2) of section 52 unless—

(a) he was within the United Kingdom at the time when he is alleged to have disclosed the information or encouraged the dealing; or

(b) the alleged recipient of the information or encouragement was within the United Kingdom at the time when he is alleged to have received the information or encouragement.

Limits on section 52

63.—(1) Section 52 does not apply to anything done by an individual acting on behalf of a public sector body in pursuit of monetary policies or policies with respect to exchange rates or the management of public debt or foreign exchange reserves. **30–242**

(2) No contract shall be void or unenforceable by reason only of section 52.

Orders

30–243 **64.** [*Procedure for making orders under Pt V; and permissible scope thereof.*]

For orders made pursuant to sections 54(1), 60(1), 62(1) and this section, see *post*, §§ 30–254 *et seq.*

Section 53(4)

SCHEDULE 1

SPECIAL DEFENCES

Market makers

30–244 1.—(1) An individual is not guilty of insider dealing by virtue of dealing in securities or encouraging another person to deal if he shows that he acted in good faith in the course of—

(a) his business as a market maker; or

(b) his employment in the business of a market maker.

(2) A market maker is a person who—

(a) holds himself out at all normal times in compliance with the rules of a regulated market or an approved organisation as willing to acquire or dispose of securities; and

(b) is recognised as doing so under those rules.

(3) In this paragraph "approved organisation" means an international securities self-regulating organisation approved by the Treasury under any relevant order under section 22 of the *Financial Services and Markets Act* 2000.

[This paragraph is printed as amended by the *Financial Services and Markets Act 2000 (Consequential Amendments and Repeals) Order* 2001 (S.I. 2001 No. 3649), art. 341.]

Market information

30–245 2.—(1) An individual is not guilt of insider dealing by virtue of dealing in securities or encouraging another person to deal if he shows that—

(a) the information which he had as an insider was market information; and

(b) it was reasonable for an individual in his position to have acted as he did despite having that information as an insider at the time.

(2) In determining whether it is reasonable for an individual to do any act despite having market information at the time, there shall, in particular, be taken into account—

(a) the content of the information;

(b) the circumstances in which he first had the information and in what capacity; and

(c) the capacity in which he now acts.

3. An individual is not guilty of insider dealing by virtue of dealing in securities or encouraging another person to deal if he shows—

(a) that he acted—

(i) in connection with an acquisition or disposal which was under consideration or the subject of negotiation, or in the course of a series of such acquisitions or disposals; and

(ii) with a view to facilitating the accomplishment of the acquisition or disposal or the series of acquisitions or disposals; and

(b) that the information which he had as an insider was market information arising directly out of his involvement in the acquisition or disposal or series of acquisitions or disposals.

4. For the purposes of paragraphs 2 and 3 market information is information consisting of one or more of the following facts—

(a) that securities of a particular kind have been or are to be acquired or disposed of, or that their acquisition or disposal is under consideration or the subject of negotiation;

(b) that securities of a particular kind have not been or are not to be acquired or disposed of;

(c) the number of securities acquired or disposed of or to be acquired or disposed of or whose acquisition or disposal is under consideration or the subject of negotiation;

(d) the price (or range of prices) at which securities have been or are to be acquired or disposed of or the price (or range of prices) at which securities whose acquisition or disposal is under consideration or the subject of negotiation may be acquired or disposed of;

(e) the identity of the person involved or likely to be involved in any capacity in an acquisition or disposal.

Price stabilisation

5.—(1) An individual is not guilty of insider dealing by virtue of dealing in securities or encouraging another person to deal if he shows that he acted in conformity with the price stabilisation rules or with the relevant provisions of Commission Regulation (EC) No 2273/2003 of 22 December 2003 implementing Directive 2003/6/EC of the European Parliament and of the Council as regards exemptions for buy-back programmes and stabilisation of financial instruments. **30–246**

(2) "Price stabilisation rules" means rules made under section 144(1) of the *Financial Services and Markets Act* 2000.

[This paragraph is printed as amended by S.I. 2001 No. 3649, art. 341 (*ante*, § 30–244); and the *Financial Services and Markets Act 2000 (Market Abuse) Regulations* 2005 (S.I. 2005 No. 381), reg. 3.]

Section 65(3) SCHEDULE 2

SECURITIES

Shares

1. Shares and stock in the share capital of a company ("shares"). **30–247**

Debt securities

2. Any instrument creating or acknowledging indebtedness which is issued by a company or public sector body, including, in particular, debentures, debentures stock, loan stock, bonds and certificates of deposit ("debt securities").

Warrants

3. Any right (whether conferred by warrant or otherwise) to subscribe for shares or debt securities ("warrants").

Depositary receipts

4.—(1) The rights under any depositary receipt.

(2) For the purposes of sub-paragraph (1) a "depositary receipt" means a certificate or other record (whether or not in the form of a document—

(a) which is issued by or on behalf of a person who holds any relevant securities of a particular issuer; and

(b) which acknowledges that another person is entitled to rights in relation to the relevant securities or relevant securities of the same kind.

(3) In sub-paragraph (2) "relevant securities" means shares, debt securities and warrants.

Options

5. Any option to acquire or dispose of any security falling within any other paragraph of this Schedule. **30–248**

Futures

6.—(1) Rights under a contract for the acquisition or disposal of relevant securities under which delivery is to be made at a future date and at a price agreed when the contract is made.

(2) In sub-paragraph (1)—

(a) the references to a future date and to a price agreed when the contract is made include references to a date and a price determined in accordance with terms of the contract; and

(b) "relevant securities" means any security falling within any other paragraph of this Schedule.

Contracts for differences

30–249 7.—(1) Rights under a contract which does not provide for the delivery of securities but whose purpose or pretended purpose is to secure a profit or avoid a loss by reference to fluctuations in—

(a) a share index or other similar factor connected with relevant securities;
(b) the price of particular relevant securities; or
(c) the interest rate offered on money placed on deposit.

(2) In sub-paragraph (1) "relevant securities" means any security falling within any other paragraph of this Schedule.

Indictment

COUNT 1

STATEMENT OF OFFENCE

30–250 *Insider dealing, contrary to section 52(1) of the* Criminal Justice Act *1993*

PARTICULARS OF OFFENCE

A B, on —— day of ——, 20—, having information contained in a confidential profit forecast relating to a particular issuer of securities, namely, X Ltd, as an insider through being a director of X Ltd, acquired on a regulated market, namely, the International Stock Exchange of the United Kingdom and the Republic of Ireland Limited, 1000 ordinary shares in X Ltd that were price affected securities in relation to that information.

COUNT 2

STATEMENT OF OFFENCE

Insider dealing, contrary to section 52(2)(a) of the Criminal Justice Act *1993*

PARTICULARS OF OFFENCE

A B, on —— day of ——, 20—, having information contained in a confidential profit forecast relating to a particular issuer of securities, namely, X Ltd, as an insider through being a director of X Ltd, encouraged CD to deal in the ordinary shares in X Ltd that were price affected securities in relation to the information knowing or having reasonable cause to believe that the dealing would take place on a regulated market.

COUNT 3

STATEMENT OF OFFENCE

Insider dealing, contrary to section 52(2)(b) of the Criminal Justice Act *1993*

PARTICULARS OF OFFENCE

A B, on —— day of ——, 20—, having information contained in a confidential profit forecast relating to a particular issuer of securities, namely, X Ltd, as an insider through being a director of X Ltd, disclosed the information to CD otherwise than in the proper performance of the functions of his employment, office or profession.

Class of offence, mode of trial and sentence

30–251 These offences are triable either way: s.61(1) of the Act, *ante*, § 30–240. They are class 3 offences, *ante* § 2–17. The maximum sentence on conviction on indictment is seven years' imprisonment or a fine of any amount, or both; on summary conviction, the maximum sentence is six months' imprisonment (12 months as from a day to be appointed, but only in relation to offences committed after the date on which the amendment takes effect) or a fine not exceeding the statutory maximum, or both: s.61(1) of the Act, *ante*, § 30–240. Some guidance as to sentencing levels may be gained from *R. v. Butt (Asif Nazir)* [2006] 2 Cr.App.R.(S.) 44, CA.

The scheme of the Act

The *CJA* 1993 widened the scope of the offence of insider dealing while at the same time extending the available defences. It retained the two stage approach seen in the *Company Securities (Insider Dealing) Act* 1985, in that the offences are defined both by reference to the status of the persons concerned ("insiders") and by reference to the type of information in their possession ("inside information"). The prosecution must prove that the person charged is an insider, and that the information he holds is price sensitive inside information in relation to securities. **30–252**

A purposive approach is to be taken to the language of the Act: see *Att.-Gen.'s Reference (No. 1 of 1988)* [1989] 1 A.C. 971, HL; and *R. v. Staines and Morrisey* [1997] 2 Cr.App.R. 426, CA (both cases under the 1985 Act). The white paper, *The Conduct of Company Directors*, *ante*, § 30–230, described the need for laws preventing "situations where a person buys and sells securities when he, but not the other party to the transaction, is in possession of confidential information which affects the value to be placed on those securities" (see para. 22). The preamble to the European Community Directive, *ante*, § 30–230, sets out the need for an "assurance afforded to investors that they are placed on an equal footing and that they will be protected against the improper use of inside information". The purpose of the 1993 Act is therefore clear. It is to prevent, so far as is practicable, transactions in securities where one party to the transaction is in possession of information that will affect the value to be placed on the securities and the other party is not.

Insiders

The distinction between "primary" and "secondary" insiders adopted by Lord Lowry in his speech in *Att.-Gen's Reference (No. 1 of 1988)*, *ante*, is a useful one. A primary insider in terms of section 57 of the 1993 Act is any person who has information through being a director, employee or shareholder of an issuer of securities; or any person who has information because of his employment, office or profession. Thus the ranks of primary insiders will consist of those individuals who have access to information rather than those individuals who are "connected with a company" (the definition adopted in the *Company Securities (Insider Dealing) Act* 1985). The definition in the 1993 Act increases the number of persons who are liable as primary insiders. It also increases the number of persons who are secondary insiders since any individual whose source of information is, directly or indirectly, a primary insider will be a secondary insider: see s.57(2)(b). However, by virtue of section 57(1) the insider (whether primary or secondary) must know that the information is inside information and that the source of the information was an inside source. This is likely to be easier to prove in the case of a primary insider than in the case of a secondary insider. **30–253**

Inside information

It is only if an insider is in possession of price sensitive inside information in relation to securities that the prohibitions in section 52 apply. Price sensitive inside information in relation to securities is defined in section 56. The fact that information would be likely to have a significant effect on the price of securities may be proved by reference to evidence of the conduct of the defendants themselves as well as by an expert witness, see *R. v. Gray* [1995] 2 Cr.App.R. 100, CA. **30–254**

Information may relate to a company where it is about a company or where it may affect the company's business prospects: see s.60(4). The approach of the court in *R. v. Staines and Morrisey*, *ante* (a case concerned with the 1985 Act) suggests that the definition of "inside information" should be approached with regard to the underlying rationale of the Act to ensure that the integrity of the market in securities is maintained by securing equality of knowledge. Accordingly, the fact that the identity of the relevant company is not expressly imparted to a defendant will not prevent the information from being "inside information" if the informant imparts such further information as is sufficient, without significant addition, to enable the defendant to identify the company concerned.

With regard to the question as to whether information has been "made public", it is submitted that the language of section 58 suggests that the test is broadly dependent on the general availability of information. This is to be contrasted with the approach of the 1985 Act which required that for information to be "unpublished price sensitive information", the information must not be generally known to those persons accustomed to or likely to deal in the relevant securities. A three stage approach is to be adopted to the question as to whether information has been "made public" within the meaning of the 1993 Act. (i) Has the information been disclosed in one of the four circumstances that the Act specifically states will amount to it having been made public (see s.58(2)(a)–(d))? (ii) If not, was the disclosure such that, within the ordinary meaning of the words "made public", the information has been made public? (iii) If the answer to (i) or (ii) above appears to be "no", do the deeming provisions in section 58(3) assist so as to lead to the conclusion that the information may be treated as having been made public?

The *Traded Securities (Disclosure) Regulations* 1994 (S.I. 1994 No. 188) give effect to Article 7 of the European Community Directive 89/592 [1989] O.J. L334/30 which requires all companies and undertakings whose shares are admitted to trading on any investment exchange to inform the public as soon as possible of any major new developments in the companies' sphere of activity which are not publicly known, and if known would lead to substantial movements in the share price. There is provision for exemption where disclosure would prejudice the company concerned.

Regulated markets

30–255 See the *Insider Dealing (Securities and Regulated Markets) Order* 1994 (S.I. 1994 No. 187), as amended by the *Insider Dealing (Securities and Regulated Markets) (Amendment) Order* 1996 (S.I. 1996 No. 1561); the *Insider Dealing (Securities and Regulated Markets) (Amendment) Order* 2000 (S.I. 2000 No. 1923); and the *Insider Dealing (Securities and Regulated Markets) (Amendment) Order* 2002 (S.I. 2002 No. 1874).

Securities

30–256 The definition of securities is contained in Schedule 2, *ante*, § 30–247. However, the Act only applies to such securities if they satisfy the conditions established by the Treasury in any order issued under section 54(1)(b).

S.I. 1994 No. 187 (as amended, *ante*) is the only order presently issued under section 54(1)(b). It provides that the Act will apply to securities falling within Schedule 2 if they are officially listed in a State within the European Economic Area or dealt with or quoted on a regulated market (see article 4). In addition, the Order specifies certain alternative conditions applying to warrants (article 5), depositary receipts (article 6), options, futures (article 7) and contracts for differences (article 8).

Prohibited activities

30–257 An insider in possession of price sensitive inside information in relation to securities is prohibited from dealing in those securities (s.52(1)) and from encouraging others to deal in those securities (s.52(2)(a)). The disclosure of the information other than in the proper performance of a duty is also prohibited by section 52(2)(c). These prohibitions apply only to individuals and not to bodies corporate. Individuals acting for a public sector body in pursuit of particular financial policies are exempted from the effect of section 52 by virtue of section 63(1).

Dealing

30–258 Insiders in possession of price sensitive inside information in relation to securities are prohibited from dealing in those securities on any regulated market or through any professional intermediary (such as a stockbroker), or as a professional intermediary. Private off-market dealing is still permitted. Dealing is widely defined by section 55. There is still no need to establish any causal link between the information and the dealing (see Lord Lane C.J. in *Att.-Gen.'s Reference (No. 1 of 1988)* [1989] 1 A.C. 971 at pp. 979–980, CA and HL), although it is now a defence if an insider can prove that he would have dealt even if he had not had the information: see s.53(1)(c).

Encouraging others to deal

The word "encourages" in section 52(2)(a) is clearly wider than the words "counsel or procure" used in the *Company Securities (Insider Dealing) Act* 1985, ss.1(7), 2(3)(b), 4(1)(b) and 5(1)(a). The courts may well regard the prohibition as extending to cover any act that is designed to have the effect of making it more likely that persons will deal in the relevant security. It is therefore possible that previously innocuous activities, such as issuing a favourable circular, will be treated as encouragement within the meaning of the section. **30–259**

Disclosing information

Insiders who are prohibited from dealing are also prohibited from disclosing that information to any other person if they know or have reasonable cause to believe that that person will deal in the securities on any regulated market or through any professional intermediary, or as a professional intermediary. **30–260**

As to the exception in section 52(2)(b), it has been held in relation to the provision of Council Directive 89/592/EEC (*ante*, § 30–230), upon which it is founded, that it is to be strictly construed; and that a disclosure would not fall within it unless there was a close link between the disclosure and the exercise of the person's employment, profession or duties, and the disclosure was strictly necessary for the exercise of that employment, etc.: *Criminal proceedings against Grongaard and Bang (Case C–384/02)*, unreported, November 22, 2005, ECJ. As part of its examination of these issues, the national court must take account of (i) the fact that the exception is to be interpreted strictly, (ii) the fact that each additional disclosure is liable to increase the risk of that information being exploited for a purpose contrary to the directive, and (iii) the sensitivity of the information; but what is to be regarded as coming within the normal ambit of the exercise of an employment, profession or duty depends, to a large extent, on the rules governing those questions in the national legal system: *ibid*.

Territorial scope

The territorial scope of the offence of insider dealing is limited by section 62. **30–261**

Defences

The prohibitions against dealing, encouraging dealing or disclosing information do not apply if an individual can bring himself within the terms of the general defences set out in section 53, or within the terms of the special defences in Schedule 1. In the light of the reasoning of the Court of Appeal in *R. v. Cross*, 91 Cr.App.R. 115, CA, it is likely that the courts will hold that the burden is on an insider to prove on the balance of probabilities any defence provided by section 53 or Schedule 1. **30–262**

There are four general areas of defence in section 53. First, it is a defence if the insider did not expect the dealing to result in a profit, or the avoidance of a loss, attributable to the fact that the information in question was price-sensitive information in relation to the securities: see s.53(1)(a), (2)(a), and (3)(b). Secondly, it is a defence that the insider believed on reasonable grounds that the information had been disclosed widely enough to ensure that none of those taking part in the dealing would be prejudiced by not having the information: see s.53(1)(b) and (2)(b). Thirdly, it is a defence if the insider would have done what he did even if he had not had the information: see s.53(1)(c), (2)(c). Fourthly, in a case involving the disclosure of inside information, it is a defence if the insider did not expect any person, because of the disclosure, to deal in the securities on any regulated market or through any professional intermediary, or as a professional intermediary: see s.53(3)(a). **30–263**

There are also four special areas of defence contained in Schedule 1, designed to ensure that the width of the offences created by section 52 does not affect activities that have always been treated as legitimate market activities. First, there is a defence that **30–264** protects market makers contained in paragraph 1. Secondly there is a "market information" defence contained in paragraph 2, by which an individual is not guilty of insider dealing by virtue of dealing in securities or encouraging another person to deal if he shows that the information that he had as an insider was market information and it was reasonable for him to have acted as he did despite having that information as an insider. Market information is defined in paragraph 4 and is, broadly, speaking, information relating to the acquisition or disposal of securities. Thirdly there is a defence for the benefit of individuals engaged in an acquisition or disposal. By virtue of paragraph 3 it is a defence to a charge under section 52(1), or a charge under section 52(2)(a), for an individual to show that he acted in connection with an acquisition or disposal, and with a view to facilitating the accomplishment of the acquisition or disposal, and that the information that he had as an insider was market information arising directly out of his involvement in the acquisition or disposal. Finally, there is a defence covering price stabilisation in paragraph 5.

H. THEFT ACT 1968

Theft Act 1968, s.18

Liability of company officers where a company has been guilty of obtaining property by deception, obtaining a pecuniary advantage by deception or false accounting

30–265 **18.**—(1) Where an offence committed by a body corporate under section 17 of this Act is proved to have been committed with the consent or connivance of any director, manager, secretary or other similar officer of the body corporate, or any person who was purporting to act in any such capacity, he as well as the body corporate shall be guilty of that offence, and shall be liable to be proceeded against and punished accordingly.

(2) Where the affairs of a body corporate are managed by its members, this section shall apply in relation to the acts and defaults of a member in connection with his functions of management as if he were a director of the body corporate.

[This section is printed as amended by the *Fraud Act* 2006, s.14(1) and (3), Sched. 1, para. 4, and Sched. 3.]

30–266 As to subsection (1), see *R. v. Boal*, *ante*, § 30–103.

Theft Act 1968, s.19

False statements by company directors, etc.

30–267 **19.**—(1) Where an officer of a body corporate or unincorporated association (or person purporting to act as such), with intent to deceive members or creditors of the body corporate or association about its affairs, publishes or concurs in publishing a written statement or account which to his knowledge is or may be misleading, false or deceptive in a material particular, he shall on conviction on indictment be liable to imprisonment for a term not exceeding seven years.

(2) For purposes of this section a person who has entered into a security for the benefit of a body corporate or association is to be treated as a creditor of it.

(3) Where the affairs of a body corporate or association are managed by its members, this section shall apply to any statement which a member publishes or concurs in publishing in connection with his functions of management as if he were an officer of the body corporate or association.

Indictment for publishing a false statement with intent to deceive

STATEMENT OF OFFENCE

30–268 *Publishing a false statement, contrary to section 19(1) of the* Theft Act *1968*.

PARTICULARS OF OFFENCE

A B, on the —— day of ——, 20—, being an of officer [or *purporting to act as an officer*] *of a body corporate* [or *unincorporated association*] *called* [name] *did publish* [or *concur in publishing*] *a certain written statement* [or *account*] *namely* [identify] *which to his knowledge was or might be misleading false or deceptive in certain material particulars* [state the particulars] *with intent thereby to deceive members* [or *creditors*] *of the said body corporate* [or *unincorporated association*] *about its affairs.*

Imprisonment not exceeding seven years: s.19(1) (*ante*). This offence is triable either way: *MCA* 1980, s.17(1), and Sched. 1, *ante*, §§ 1–75ae *et seq*.

In order to establish the offence it is necessary to prove that the defendant was an officer of a body corporate or unincorporated association (or person purporting to act as such). By the *Companies Act* 2006, s.1173(1) (and its statutory predecessor), "officer" in relation to a body corporate includes director, manager or secretary. An auditor of a company was held to be an officer within section 84 of the *Larceny Act* 1861 (*rep*.): *R. v. Shacter* [1960] 2 Q.B. 252, 44 Cr.App.R. 42, CCA. The articles or by-laws of a corporation frequently state who are to be officers of the company. **30–269**

It is also essential to prove that the defendant published or concurred in publishing a written statement or account which to his knowledge was or might be misleading, false or deceptive in a material particular. A statement or account may be false on account of what it omits although it is literally true: *R. v. Lord Kylsant* [1932] 1 K.B. 442, 23 Cr.App.R. 83, CCA; *R. v. Bishirgian*, 25 Cr.App.R. 176, CCA. It must also be proved that the defendant published the written statement or account with intent to deceive members or creditors of the body corporate or unincorporated association about its affairs.

III. FRAUDS UPON CREDITORS, WHETHER COMMITTED BY BANKRUPTS OR NOT

A. PREFERENTIAL PAYMENT TO CREDITOR BY TRUSTEE

Deeds of Arrangement Act 1914, s.17

17. If a trustee under a deed of arrangement pays to any creditor out of the debtor's property a sum larger in proportion to the creditor's claim than that paid to other creditors entitled to the benefit of the deed, then, unless the deed authorises him to do so, or unless such payments are either made to a creditor entitled to enforce his claim by distress or are such as would be lawful in a bankruptcy, he shall be guilty of a misdemeanor. **30–270**

Offences under this section are triable either way: *MCA* 1980, s.17(1), and Sched. 1, *ante*, §§ 1–75ae *et seq*. The statute provides no specific penalty in the case of conviction on indictment. It is submitted, however, that by a combination of common law rules and statute, an offence under this section is punishable on conviction on indictment by way of fine and/or imprisonment not exceeding two years: see *Castro v. R.* (1880) 5 Q.B.D. 490 at 508, the *PCC(S)A* 2000, s.77, and the *CJA* 2003, s.163, *ante*, §§ 5–280, 5–393 respectively. **30–271**

B. FRAUDULENT CONCEALMENT, REMOVAL, ETC., OF PROPERTY

Debtors Act 1869, s.13

13. Any person shall in each of the cases following be deemed guilty of a misdemeanor, and on conviction thereof shall be liable to be imprisoned for any time not exceeding one year ... that is to say: **30–272**

(1) [*Repealed by* Theft Act *1968, s.33(3) and Sched. 3.*]

(2) If he has, with intent to defraud his creditors, or any of them, made or caused to be made any gift, delivery, or transfer of or any charge on his property.

(3) If he has, with intent to defraud his creditors, concealed or removed any part of his property since or within two months before the date of any unsatisfied judgment or order for payment of money obtained against him.

Offences under this section are triable either way: *MCA* 1980, s.17(1), and Sched. 1, *ante*, §§ 1–75ae *et seq*.

Evidence

It is not necessary in order to render a person liable under the *Debtors Act* 1869, s.13(2) and (3), that he should be a bankrupt: *R. v. Rowlands* (1882) 8 Q.B.D. 530; but to fall within the section it would seem that the transfer, etc., must be fraudulent within the bankruptcy laws: *Re Cranston* (1892) 9 Morrell 160. A fictitious transfer seems to be within subsection (2): *R. v. Richman*, 4 Cr.App.R. 233, CCA. A plaintiff suing for unliquidated damages is not a creditor until judgment: *R. v. Hopkins* [1896] 1 Q.B. 652. **30–273**

CHAPTER 31

OFFENCES AGAINST PUBLIC MORALS AND POLICY

I. BIGAMY

(1) Statute

Offences against the Person Act 1861, s.57

57. Whosoever, being married, shall marry any other person, during the life of the former husband or wife, whether the second marriage shall have taken place in England or Ireland or elsewhere, shall be guilty of an offence and being convicted thereof shall be liable to be imprisoned for any term not exceeding seven years … . Provided that nothing in this section contained shall extend to any second marriage contracted elsewhere than in England and Ireland by any other than a subject of Her Majesty or to any person marrying a second time, whose husband or wife shall have been continually absent from such person for the space of seven years then last past, and shall not have been known by such person to be living within that time, or shall extend to any person who, at the time of such second marriage, shall have been divorced from the bond of the first marriage, or to any person whose former marriage shall have been declared void by the sentence of any court of competent jurisdiction. **31–1**

[This section is printed as amended by the *CJA* 1948, s.1(1); and as repealed in part by the *CJA* 1925, s.49, and Sched. 3; and the *CLA* 1967, s.10(2), and Sched. 3.]

(2) Indictment

STATEMENT OF OFFENCE

Bigamy, contrary to section 57 of the Offences against the Person Act *1861.* **31–2**

PARTICULARS OF OFFENCE

A B, on the —— day of ——, 20—married C D during the life of his wife, E F.

The word "married" has been commonly used in indictments and follows the language of the statute. It is submitted, however, that "went through a form of marriage with" would be more accurate.

(3) Class of offence and mode of trial

Bigamy is a class 3 offence, *ante*, § 2–17, triable either way: *MCA* 1980, s.17(1), and Sched. 1 (*ante*, § 1–75af). **31–3**

(4) Sentence

Imprisonment not exceeding seven years: *Offences against the Person Act* 1861, s.57 (*ante*). For the penalty on summary conviction, see the *MCA* 1980, s.32(1) (*ante*, § 1–75aa). **31–4**

For a recent example, see *R. v. Ballard* [2007] 2 Cr.App.R.(S.) 94, CA. A custodial sentence should be passed where the innocent party has been deceived and has suffered some injury in consequence: *R. v. Smith (James)*, 15 Cr.App.R.(S.) 407, CA. Where the offence was committed for money with a view to enabling the woman to evade immigration controls, 15 months' imprisonment on a plea of guilty was reduced to nine months: *R. v. Cairns* [1997] 1 Cr.App.R.(S.) 118, CA.

(5) Ingredients of the offence

"being married"

31–5 As to proof of the first marriage and its validity, see *post*, §§ 31–11 *et seq.*

The relevant time for determining whether an accused is within the meaning of the words "being married" in section 57 is the time of the alleged bigamous ceremony of marriage. Accordingly, although the marriage which is to be the foundation for a prosecution for bigamy must be a monogamous marriage, since a potentially polygamous marriage may in certain circumstances change its character and become monogamous (*e.g.* by a change in domicile to a country where monogamy is part of the law, or by a change in the law of the country where the marriage was celebrated), a charge of bigamy is well founded where such a change has occurred by the time of the alleged bigamous ceremony of marriage: *R. v. Sagoo* [1975] Q.B. 885, 61 Cr.App.R. 191, CA.

Ireland

31–6 This means exclusive of Eire: see the *Irish Free State (Consequential Adaptation of Enactments) Order* 1923 (S.R. & O. 1923 No. 405).

"or elsewhere"

31–7 The words "or elsewhere" mean "in any other part of the world": *Earl Russell's case* [1901] A.C. 446. A British subject resident in England is liable to be convicted of bigamy in England though both marriages were solemnised in Scotland: *R. v. Topping* (1856) Dears. 647.

"second marriage"

31–8 The "second marriage" with which the court is concerned is that which is the subject of the indictment; and if, on the hearing of that charge, it is proved that the lawful spouse had been absent for seven years, that defence is available to the person charged notwithstanding that that person has previously committed bigamy with some other person or persons: *R. v. Taylor* [1950] 2 K.B. 368, 34 Cr.App.R. 138, CCA.

Where a person already bound by an existing marriage goes through a form of marriage known to and recognised by the law as capable of producing a valid marriage the case is not the less within the statute by reason of any special circumstances, which independently of the bigamous character of the marriage may constitute a legal disability in the particular parties, or make the form of marriage resorted to specially inapplicable to their individual case: *R. v. Allen* (1872) L.R. 1 C.C.R. 367 (consanguinity); *R. v. Robinson*, 26 Cr.App.R. 129, CCA (residence qualification).

The offence will be complete though the defendant assumes a fictitious name at the second marriage: *R. v. Allison* (1806) R. & R. 109; or in his notice to the registrar: *R. v. Rea* (1872) L.R. 1 C.C.R. 365.

Mens rea

31–9 An honest and reasonable belief by the defendant in a fact which, if true, would make his second marriage lawful is a good defence; and no distinction is to be drawn between facts the result of which would be that he was innocent because he did not come within the enacting words at all (*e.g.* that his spouse had died, although known to have been alive within the last seven years), and facts the result of which would be that he was excluded from the enacting words by the proviso (*e.g.* that he was divorced): *R. v. Tolson* (1889) 23 Q.B.D. 168, CCR (belief that spouse dead); *R. v. King* [1964] 1 Q.B. 285, 48 Cr.App.R. 17, CCA (belief that first marriage void); *R. v. Gould* [1968] 2 Q.B. 65, 52 Cr.App.R. 152, CA (belief that first marriage dissolved).

Burden of proof

The primary burden on the prosecution is to prove: (a) the celebration of the first marriage and the identity of the parties; (b) the validity of the first marriage; (c) its subsistence at the date of the second marriage; and (d) celebration of the second "marriage". It has been suggested on the basis of *R. v. Thomson*, 70 J.P. 6, that if the defence contend that the first marriage was void, they have the burden of proving such facts as would render it void; but this is inconsistent with the rule that it is for the prosecution to prove all the elements of the offence, and with *R. v. Willshire* (1881) 6 Q.B.D. 366, CCR, and *R. v. Morrison*, 27 Cr.App.R. 1, CCA. **31–10**

Where the defence raise a mistake of fact (*ante*), it is clear that there is an evidential burden on them (*i.e.* to adduce evidence fit for consideration by the jury); but once that is done, it is submitted that the legal burden of proving guilt requires the prosecution to prove either that there were no reasonable grounds for the alleged mistaken belief or that it was not held at all. This is consistent with general principle (*ante*, §§ 4–380 *et seq.*) and with *R. v. Curgerwen* (1865) L.R. 1 C.C.R. 1 (followed in *R. v. Lund*, 16 Cr.App.R. 31, CCA, and *R. v. Peake*, 17 Cr.App.R. 22, CCA), in which it was held that once seven years' absence is proved, it is for the prosecution to prove that the defendant knew that the first spouse was still living during that period.

Curgerwen and *Lund* appear to have proceeded on the assumption that in relation to seven years' absence, the legal burden was on the defendant; this, it is submitted, is plainly correct, as this is a true exception to liability (see *per* Diplock L.J. in *Gould*, *ante*, at pp. 70, 154), to which the general rule in relation to exceptions should apply (*ante*, § 4–388). Any other construction of the statute would make little sense, for it would require the prosecution to prove knowledge that the spouse had been alive in the last seven years, though the defendant had not been able to establish on a balance of probabilities that he or she had even been absent for that period.

(6) Evidence

(a) *Of first marriage and identity of parties*

Celebration of the first marriage

It is immaterial when or where the first marriage was celebrated whether in England or elsewhere: 2 Hale 692; 1 Hawk. c. 42, s.7. **31–11**

There must be evidence of celebration, as evidence of acknowledgment, cohabitation or repute will not suffice: *Morris v. Miller* (1767) 4 Burr. 2057, 2058. It is not essential to prove that banns were published or a licence obtained or the marriage registered: *R. v. Allison* (1806) R. & R. 109; *R. v. Manwaring* (1856) 26 L.J.M.C. 10; and it is sufficient to call a person present at the ceremony, who can describe it so as to enable the judge to determine whether it would constitute a marriage in law: *R. v. Allison*, *ante*; *R. v. Millis* (1844) 10 Cl. & F. 534; and can identify the parties: *R. v. Manwaring*, *ante*; *R. v. Simpson* (1883) 15 Cox 323.

Proof by certified copy

The simplest means of proving the celebration of a marriage is by production of a certified copy of entries kept at the Family Records Centre at 1 Myddleton Street, London EC1R 1UW and at the General Register Office at Southport (Smedley Hydro, Trafalgar Road, Southport PR8 2HH). Section 65(3) of the *Marriage Act* 1949 provides that any certified copy of an entry purporting to be sealed or stamped with the seal of the General Register Office shall be received as evidence of the marriage to which it relates without any further or other proof of the entry. **31–12**

Copies of entries in marriage register books certified in accordance with section 63 or 64 of the *Marriage Act* 1949 are admissible in evidence under section 14 of the *Evidence Act* 1851, *ante*, § 9–24.

Identity of the parties

Evidence of the identity of the parties must also be given, and should be by persons **31–13** who were present at the ceremony, or have other adequate means of knowing the parties to the marriage. Identification by photograph has been allowed: *R. v. Tolson* (1864) 4 F. & F. 103. Proof from the register of marriages that a person of the same name as the defendant married R, and that the defendant had subsequently cohabited with R, and acknowledged and alluded to her as his wife, has been held to be sufficient evidence of identification: *R. v. Birtles*, 6 Cr.App.R. 177, CCA.

Marriage according to rites of Church of England

31–14 If celebrated in England, according to the rites of the Established Church, the marriage may be proved by the production of the original register of the marriage from the proper custody, that is, from the church itself, or from the custody of the "rector, vicar, curate, or other officiating minister": *Doe v. Fowler* (1850) 14 Q.B. 700; or by a copy thereof, or extract therefrom, provided it is proved to be an examined copy or extract or provided it purports to be signed and certified as a true copy or extract by the officer to whose custody the original is entrusted (*Evidence Act* 1851, s.14 (*ante*, § 9–24); *Sayer v. Glossop* (1848) 2 C. & K. 694), together with some proof either direct or presumptive of the identity of the parties.

Marriages in Naval, Military or Air Force Chapels

31–15 See the *Marriage Act* 1949, Pt V, ss.68 to 71.

Regular marriages in Scotland

31–16 Regular marriages in Scotland are best proved by certified extracts from the marriage register given under the *Registration of Births, Deaths and Marriages (Scotland) Act* 1965, s.41(3) and the *Marriage (Scotland) Act* 1977.

Marriages abroad

31–17 A marriage celebrated abroad may be proved by any person who was present at it; circumstances should also be proved from which the jury may infer that it was a valid marriage according to the laws of the country in which it was celebrated, or according to the national law of the parties if celebrated outside the State to which they belong. On this subject, evidence by experts is admissible: *Sussex Peerage Claim* (1844) 6 St.Tr.(N.S.) 79.

Marriages celebrated abroad by British officials under the *Foreign Marriage Act* 1892, are proved under that Act: see s.17.

A marriage of an officer or soldier serving abroad may be proved by a certified copy from the Registrar-General of an entry of the marriage in an Army Register Book of Marriages: *Registration of Births, Deaths and Marriages (Army) Act* 1879, s.3, and the *Registration of Births, Deaths and Marriages (Special Provisions) Act* 1957, s.3. Where an Order in Council under section 1 of the *Evidence (Foreign, Dominion and Colonial Documents) Act* 1933 or section 5(1) of the *Oaths and Evidence (Overseas Authorities and Countries) Act* 1963 has made the operation of the 1933 Act extend to any dominion, British colony or protectorate, foreign country, foreign colony or protectorate, or any mandated territory, an entry in a public register of that country is admissible in evidence in England, and may be proved by a certified copy, subject to any conditions specified in the order.

See generally Dicey & Morris, *The Conflict of Laws*, 13th ed., chapters 17 and 18.

(b) *Of validity of first marriage*

Proof of validity of first marriage

31–18 The second marriage is not bigamous unless the first marriage was valid; and the validity of the first marriage must be proved by the prosecution: *R. v. Kay* (1887) 16 Cox 292; for the law will not presume it in the case of bigamy, as it will in civil cases: *Smith v. Huson* (1811) 1 Phillimore 287. As to the requirement for marriages to be monogamous, and marriages which are void, see *post*, §§ 31–25 *et seq*.

In *R. v. Simmonite* (1843) 1 Cox 30, the defendant's admission of a prior marriage was held to be evidence that it was lawfully solemnised. But in *R. v. Savage* (1876) 13 Cox 178, the judge refused to act upon *R. v. Newton*, as being inconsistent with the *Sussex Peerage Claim* (1844) 11 Cl. & F. 85, 134; and held that the defendant's admission upon being apprehended that he had been married to his first wife in Scotland was no evidence that that marriage had been lawfully solemnised, and this view seems to be supported by *R. v. Truman* (1795) 1 East P.C. 470; *R. v. Flaherty* (1847) 2 C. & K. 782, and was adopted in *R. v. Lindsay*, 66 J.P. 505.

Marriages in England and abroad

To be valid, the marriage, if contracted in England, must have been celebrated in a manner recognised by the law of England and between persons capable of contracting marriage, and who might lawfully inter-marry (see *post*, § 31–25). If contracted elsewhere, it must have been according to the *lex loci contractus*, see *Nachimson v. Nachimson* [1930] P. 217; *Kenward v. Kenward* [1951] P. 124, or valid under English law under the provisions of the *Foreign Marriages Act* 1892, s.1. A marriage celebrated in England in a foreign embassy or embassy chapel between subjects of the ambassador's sovereign is treated as extra-territorial. See *Ruding v. Smith* 2 Hagg.Consist.Rep 371. **31–19**

A marriage is valid at common law if celebrated on a British ship at sea by an episcopally ordained minister: *Culling v. Culling* [1896] P. 116; see also *Du Moulin Druitt* (1860) 13 Ir.C.L.Rep. 212, or on a British ship in accordance with the *Foreign Marriage Act* 1892; or within the lines of the British army in a foreign country, if celebrated by an episcopally ordained minister and if one party is subject to military law: *Burn v. Farrar*, 2 Hagg.Consist.Rep. 369; *Ruding v. Smith, ibid.* 371; 1 St.Tr.(N.S.) 1053; *Waldegrave Peerage Claim* (1837) 4 Cl. & F. 649. Such a marriage is also valid if celebrated as prescribed by the *Foreign Marriage Act* 1892, s.22.

A marriage abroad between British subjects is not valid at common law if celebrated before a layman (*Catherwood v. Caslon* (1844) 13 M. & W. 261; but see *Catterall v. Catterall* (1845) 1 Rob.Eccl. 304; 3 *ibid.* 580; *Burt v. Burt* (1860) 29 L.J.(Matr.) 133); but may be validly celebrated by a marriage officer under the *Foreign Marriage Act* 1892.

If the marriage was celebrated in England, under English law, between foreigners not domiciled here, and in defiance of their national law, it would seem to be valid for purposes of a prosecution for bigamy. But this cannot be treated as absolutely settled. See *Sottomayer v. De Barros* (1879) 5 P.D. 94; *Scott v. Att.-Gen.* (1886) 11 P.D. 128; *Warter v. Warter* (1890) 15 P.D. 152; *Ogden v. Ogden* [1908] P. 46.

Validity in point of form

The validity of a marriage *in point of form* is substantially the same as due celebration, and in the case of a marriage in England no further proof is needed except that the persons married were not within the prohibited degrees of consanguinity or affinity, and were not already married. If the defence seeks to defeat the validity of the marriage by setting up an earlier and subsisting marriage of one of the parties, they must prove it: *Dalrymple v. Dalrymple* (1811) 2 Hagg.Consist.Rep. 54; *R. v. Millis* (1844) 10 Cl. & F. 534. **31–20**

As to marriages according to the rites of the Church of England, see the *Marriage Act* 1949, ss.5 to 25. As to other marriages, see sections 26 to 52 of the 1949 Act. As to void marriages, see sections 25 and 49. See also section 48 (proof of certain matters not necessary to validity of marriages).

Scottish marriages

As to what is necessary to constitute a valid marriage in Scots law, see *R. v. Povey* (1852) Dears. 32; *R. v. Topping* (1856) Dears. 647; *Lawford v. Davies* (1878) 4 P.D. 61; *Marriage (Scotland) Act* 1977. An irregular Scottish marriage, if fulfilling the conditions of the *Registration of Births, Deaths and Marriages (Scotland) Act* 1965, **31–21** is best proved by a certified extract from the marriage register given under that Act; if not fulfilling those conditions, it must be proved by an expert in Scots law.

Foreign (including Irish) and colonial marriages

31–22 Where an Order in Council has been made under the *Evidence (Foreign, Dominion and Colonial Documents) Act* 1933 or section 5 of the *Oaths and Evidence (Overseas Authorities and Countries) Act* 1963 (*ante*, § 31–17), the relevant entry will be admissible for the purpose of proof of the validity of the marriage: see *North v. North and Ogden* (1936) T.L.R. 380; *Motture v. Motture* [1955] 1 W.L.R. 1066. For a list of the relevant orders, see *Halsbury's Statutes*, 4th ed., Vol. 18 (2005 reissue), p. 195; and, for further detail, see Rayden and Jackson, *Divorce and Family Matters*, 18th ed., Vol. 2(2), p. 4253.

As to the *Foreign Marriage Act* 1892, see *ante*, § 31–19.

31–23 A marriage celebrated in a British colony, according to the rites and ceremonies of the Church of England, may be proved by the production of a certificate of the entry in the ecclesiastical register, signed by one of the clergy of the church in which the register is kept, without adducing expert evidence of the validity of the marriage or of the certificate according to local law: *Perry v. Perry* [1920] P. 361. It has been held, in reliance on the *Evidence (Colonial Statutes) Act* 1907 (*ante*, § 9–26) that a marriage in a Commonwealth country can be proved by the production of the marriage certificate, and of the local statute or ordinance making that certificate evidence of the marriage: *Gibson v. Gibson* (1920) 37 T.L.R. 124. The propriety of this method of proof has been doubted: see Rayden and Jackson, *ante*, Vol. 1(1), para. 7.24.

31–24 In all other cases, it will be necessary, in addition to proof of celebration, to call expert evidence as to the validity of the marriage: *R. v. Naguib*, 12 Cr.App.R. 187, CCA. This applies equally to the defendant who relies on the validity of a prior, subsisting foreign marriage as a defence to a charge of bigamy: *ibid*. The "expert" evidence required is either that of a professional lawyer or of one who is *peritus virtute officii*: *ibid.*; *R. v. Moscovitch*, 20 Cr.App.R. 121, CCA.

See generally Dicey & Morris, *The Conflict of Laws*, 13th ed., chapters 17 and 18.

Void and voidable marriages

31–25 Proof of a marriage which is merely *voidable* will support an indictment for bigamy: 3 Co.Inst. 88. But it is otherwise if the marriage is not voidable merely, but void. Section 11 of the *Matrimonial Causes Act* 1973 provides that marriages celebrated after July 31, 1971 shall only be void on one of the grounds in that section. See *Re Roberts (deceased)*; *Roberts v. Roberts* [1978] 1 W.L.R. 653, CA (Civ. Div.). The grounds are that (i) the parties are within the prohibited degrees of relationship (see also the *Marriage Act* 1949, s.1 and Sched. 1, and *post*, § 31–26), (ii) either party was under the age of 16 (*Marriage Act* 1949, s.2), (iii) the parties have married in disregard of the requirements as to the formation of marriage (*ante*, § 31–20), (iv) either party was already lawfully married, (v) the parties were of the same sex, or (vi) in the case of a polygamous marriage entered into outside England and Wales either party was at the time of the marriage domiciled in England and Wales. However, in the case of marriages governed by foreign law or celebrated abroad under English law, section 11 needs to be read in conjunction with section 14: see Rayden and Jackson, *ante*, Vol. 1(1), paras 8.30 *et seq.*

A marriage contracted outside England and Wales at any time is no longer void on the ground that it is "potentially polygamous", if it was not in fact polygamous when it was contracted: *Private International Law (Miscellaneous Provisions) Act* 1995, s.5, unless it is within the limited exceptions in section 6.

Section 11 of the 1973 Act re-enacted the relevant provisions of the *Nullity of Marriage Act* 1971 which was passed to re-state, with certain alterations, the grounds on which marriages contracted before August 1, 1971 are void, as to which see Rayden and Jackson, *ante*, Vol. 1(1), paras 5.1 *et seq.*

As to the grounds on which a marriage is voidable merely, see section 12 of the 1973 Act.

Prohibited degrees

31–26 A marriage between persons within the prohibited degrees of consanguinity or affinity is void under the *Marriage Act* 1949, s.1, if celebrated in England: *R. v. Chadwick*

(1847) 11 Q.B. 173 at 205; or if celebrated abroad between British subjects who at the time of celebration were domiciled in England: *Re De Wilton* [1900] 2 Ch. 481; *Brook v. Brook* (1861) 9 H.L.C. 193. It would seem that if a marriage was validly celebrated in the country of the husband's domicile between persons who are within the prohibited degrees of consanguinity or affinity according to English law, the parties would be indictable in England on a second marriage there, as the first marriage would be valid in England for succession to personalty (*Brook v. Brook, ante*); though not for succession to realty.

(c) *That the first marriage was subsisting*

The prosecution must prove that the first wife (or husband) was alive at the date of the second marriage. This may be done by someone who was acquainted with him or her, or saw him or her at the time of the second marriage or afterwards, or by his or her production in court and identification as the first husband or wife. The existence of the first husband or wife at a period *antecedent* to the second marriage may or may not afford a reasonable inference that he or she was living *at the time* of the second marriage. If, for example, it was proved that he or she was in good health on the day preceding the second marriage, the inference would be almost irresistible that he or she was living on the day of the second marriage. The question is entirely for the jury, and the law makes no presumption either way: *R. v. Lumley* (1869) L.R. 1 C.C.R. 196. **31–27**

It is equally a question for the jury where the defendant contends that the first marriage was void as itself being bigamous on account of the lawful spouse, by an earlier marriage, of himself or his "wife" being still alive: *R. v. Willshire* (1881) 6 Q.B.D. 366; *R. v. Morrison*, 27 Cr.App.R. 1, CCA. **31–28**

A marriage is a subsisting marriage even after a decree nisi for its dissolution and until the decree is made absolute: *Hulse v. Hulse and Tavenor* (1871) L.R. 2 P. & D. 259.

(d) *Of celebration of second "marriage"*

The celebration of the second marriage is proved in the same manner as that of the first (*ante*, §§ 31–11 *et seq.*). **31–29**

(7) Defences

Seven years' absence

See the *Offences against the Person Act* 1861, s.57 (*ante*, § 31–1). This means that the defendant must not have known at any period during the seven years the spouse to be alive: *R. v. Cullen* (1840) 9 C. & P. 681. Having the means of knowledge is irrelevant: *R. v. Briggs* (1856) Dears. & B. 98. **31–30**

As to the burden of proof, see *ante*, § 31–10

Belief, on reasonable grounds, in death of spouse

See *R. v. Tolson* (1889) 23 Q.B.D. 168, CCR (*ante*, §§ 17–10, 31–9). **31–31**

Dissolution or nullity of first marriage

Although referred to in the proviso to section 57 of the 1861 Act, neither of these matters are properly regarded as defences, as if the first marriage has been dissolved or was void *ab initio*, the case will not come within the first part of the section, as the first ingredient of the offence (*viz.* "being married") will not be made out. As to this, see *R. v. Gould* [1968] 2 Q.B. 65, 52 Cr.App.R. 152, CA. **31–32**

The recognition by the courts of England and Wales of divorces and annulments obtained within or without the United Kingdom is governed by the *Family Law Act* 1986, Pt II. For further detail, see Rayden and Jackson, *Divorce and Family Matters*, 18th ed., Chap. 13.

As to a mistaken belief that the first marriage was void or had been dissolved, see *ante*, § 31–9.

II. PUBLIC NUISANCE

A. STATUTE

(1) General

31–33 A wide range of conduct which has in the past been the subject of prosecution at common law for the offence of public nuisance is now regulated by statute. Thus, there are statutes concerned with the following matters: food, water, clean air, noise, vehicle and aircraft pollution, waste disposal, offensive trades, health and safety at work, highways, hygienic conditions in dwellings, trade premises and factories, cemeteries, animals, agriculture, medicines, transport, mines, the countryside and village greens and the protection of the environment generally. The statutes create many offences; in certain cases, the proscribed conduct is designated as a nuisance (*e.g.* the *Environmental Protection Act* 1990, s.79); in others, the definition of the statutory offence incorporates the common law notion of nuisance; and in others, there is no reference to nuisance, but the activity in question is nonetheless the type of activity which has formerly been held to be a nuisance.

As to the relationship between the various statutory offences and the common law offence, the House of Lords, in *R. v. Rimmington*; *R. v. Goldstein* [2006] 1 A.C. 459, held that where conduct fell within the ambit of a particular statutory offence, it was not possible to say that it would never be appropriate to prosecute for the common law offence of nuisance, but good practice and respect for the primacy of statute law required that the offence should be prosecuted under the relevant statutory provision unless there was good reason for doing otherwise; but the avoidance of a time limit, of a particular defence or of a maximum penalty that applied to the statutory offence could not ordinarily amount to a good reason. As to this case, see also *post*, §§ 31–40, 31–41.

Many of the offences created by statute are triable either way; the only statutory offences specifically dealt with in this work are those under the *Dangerous Dogs Act* 1991 (*post*), which have remained topical (and controversial) since their enactment. For offences under other statutes, reference will need to be made to other specialist works, in particular, in relation to environmental law.

(2) Dangerous Dogs Act 1991

Introduction

31–34 The Act was passed as a response to public outrage at the number of attacks on members of the public by uncontrolled dogs and, in particular, by dogs of particular types. It creates various offences: all are summary only, except for the aggravated form of the offences contrary to section 3(1) and (3). The *Dangerous Dogs (Amendment) Act* 1997 was intended to meet some of the criticisms of the 1991 Act, as originally enacted.

Dangerous Dogs Act 1991, s.3(1)–(4)

Keeping dogs under proper control

31–35 **3.**—(1) If a dog is dangerously out of control in a public place—

(a) the owner; and

(b) if different, the person for the time being in charge of the dog,

is guilty of an offence, or, if the dog while so out of control injures any person, an aggravated offence, under this subsection.

(2) In proceedings for an offence under subsection (1) above against a person who is the owner of a dog but was not at the material time in charge of it, it shall be a defence for the accused to prove that the dog was at the material time in the charge of a person whom he reasonably believed to be a fit and proper person to be in charge of it.

(3) If the owner or, if different, the person for the time being in charge of a dog allows it to enter a place which is not a public place but where it is not permitted to be and while it is there—

(a) it injures any person, or

(b) there are grounds for reasonable apprehension that it will do so,

he is guilty of an offence, or, if the dog injures any person, an aggravated offence, under this subsection.

(4) A person guilty of an offence under subsection (1) or (3) above other than an aggravated offence is liable on summary conviction to imprisonment for a term not exceeding six months or a fine not exceeding level 5 on the standard scale or both; and a person guilty of an aggravated offence under either of those subsections is liable—

(a) on summary conviction, to imprisonment for a term not exceeding *six* [12] months or a fine not exceeding the statutory maximum or both;

(b) on conviction on indictment, to imprisonment for a term not exceeding two years or a fine or both.

[In subs. (4)(a), "12" is substituted for "six", as from a day to be appointed, by the *CJA* 2003, s.282(2) and (3). The increase has no application to offences committed before the substitution takes effect: s.282(4).]

Subsections (5) to (7) relate to complaints and orders under section 2 of the *Dogs Act* 1871 (order on complaint that dog is dangerous and not kept under proper control).

Interpretation

Section 6 provides that where a dog is owned by a person less than 16 years old, a reference to its owner in section 3 includes a reference to the head of the household, if any, of which that person is a member. **31–36**

Section 10(2) defines "public place" as "any street, road or other place (whether or not enclosed) to which the public have or are permitted to have access whether for payment or otherwise and includes the common parts of a building containing two or more separate dwellings".

As to this provision, see *Bates v. DPP, The Times*, March 8, 1993, DC (interior of private car being driven on public road a "public place"); *Cummings v. DPP, The Times*, March 26, 1999, DC (public user of land in ownership of local council could be inferred); *R. (DPP) v. Zhao*, 167 J.P. 521, QBD (Owen J.) (evidence that children used to play in, and members of the public used to park their cars in, a cul-de-sac with bollards at the end and pathway beyond, unquestionably gave rise to prima facie case that the area was a "street to which the public have or are permitted to have access"); *Fellowes v. DPP, The Times*, February 1, 1993, DC (members of the public do not have access to a garden path *qua* members of the public, but *qua* lawful visitors under either implied or express terms); and *R. v. Bogdal*, 172 J.P. 178, CA (driveway shared between the defendant's home and a private care home was not a "public place"; members of the public were only entitled to use it as visitors to one of the premises to which it provided access and their right to use it remained *qua* visitors, not *qua* members of the public, whichever premises they happened to be visiting).

Section 10(3) provides that for the purposes of the Act a dog shall be regarded as dangerously out of control on any occasion on which there are grounds for reasonable apprehension that it will injure any person, whether or not it actually does so; but references to a dog injuring a person or there being grounds for reasonable apprehension that it will do so, do not include references to any case in which the dog is being used for a lawful purpose by a constable or person in the service of the Crown. This provision is not exclusive and does not read, as a matter of construction, "a dog shall only be regarded as dangerously out of control ..."; a court is entitled to have regard to the straightforward language of section 3(1); where, therefore, a dog had bitten a pedestrian in an unprovoked attack, this was sufficient evidence that the dog was out of control and was dangerous, even where the dog had been on a lead at the time, had never shown a propensity to attack people, and there had been no basis for a reasonable apprehension that it would injure anyone until the very moment of the attack: *R. v. Gedminintaite and Collier*, 172 J.P 413, CA. See also *Rafiq v. DPP*, 161 J.P. 412, DC (a finding that there were grounds for reasonable apprehension that a dog would injure a person may be based on the fact that it attacked one person without warning).

The word "allows" includes both taking and omitting to take a positive step. Accordingly, an offence under section 3(3) may be committed by omission, as by a failure to take adequate precautions to prevent a dog's escape: *Greener v. DPP, The Times*, February 15, 1996, DC.

Mens rea

The offences under subsections (1) and (3) are offences of strict liability: *R. v.* **31–37**

Bezzina, 99 Cr.App.R. 356, CA (s.3(1)); *Greener v. DPP*, *ante* (s.3(3)). In *Bezzina*, the court referred to *Gammon (Hong Kong) Ltd v. Att.-Gen. of Hong Kong* [1985] A.C. 1, PC (*ante*, § 17–4): the situation covered by section 3(1) is precisely that referred to in *Gammon*, where the presumption of *mens rea* is displaced because the statute is concerned with an issue of social concern such as public safety.

Statutory defence (s.3(2))

31–37a Where the defence under section 3(1) is non-ownership, it is nevertheless incumbent on the judge to direct the jury on the defence provided by section 3(2) if there is any evidence thereof: *R. v. Harter* [1998] Crim.L.R. 336, CA. Such defence should only succeed, however, where there is evidence that the owner had for the time being divested himself of responsibility in favour of an identifiable person: *R. v. Huddart* [1999] 2 *Archbold News* 1, CA.

Sentence

31–37b In *R. v. Cox (Jacqueline)* [2004] 2 Cr.App.R.(S.) 54, CA, it was said that the difference in maximum penalty between the basic and aggravated offences under section 3 demonstrated the clear intention of Parliament that courts in no small measure should look at the consequences of the offence when determining the penalty; and it was entirely appropriate to pass a custodial sentence to mark the nature and the extent of the obligation which owners of dogs owed to all those who might be affected if they roamed free. Where, however, a woman of good character pleaded guilty to the aggravated offence on the basis that she had failed to ensure that the five dogs living at her house were kept indoors, and those dogs had attacked a seven-year-old boy causing multiple puncture wounds and lacerations, nine months' imprisonment was too long; three months substituted. For a manifestation of a significantly different attitude, see *R. v. Haynes* [2004] 2 Cr.App.R.(S.) 9, CA.

Dangerous Dogs Act 1991, s.4(1)–(7)

Destruction and disqualification orders

31–38 **4.**—(1) Where a person is convicted of an offence under section 1 or 3(1) or (3) above or of an offence under an order made under section 2 above the court—

(a) may order the destruction of any dog in respect of which the offence was committed and, subject to subsection (1A) below, shall do so in the case of an offence under section 1 or an aggravated offence under section 3(1) or (3) above; and

(b) may order the offender to be disqualified, for such period as the court thinks fit, for having custody of a dog.

(1A) Nothing in subsection (1)(a) above shall require the court to order the destruction of a dog if the court is satisfied—

(a) that the dog would not constitute a danger to public safety; and

(b) where the dog was born before 30th November 1991 and is subject to the prohibition in section 1(3) above, that there is a good reason why the dog has not been exempted from that prohibition.

(2) Where a court makes an order under subsection (1)(a) above for the destruction of a dog owned by a person other than the offender, ... the owner may appeal to the Crown Court against the order.

(3) A dog shall not be destroyed pursuant to an order under subsection (1)(a) above—

(a) until the end of the period for giving notice of appeal against the conviction or, ... against the order; and

(b) if notice of appeal is given within that period, until the appeal is determined or withdrawn,

unless the offender and, in a case to which subsection (2) above applies, the owner of the dog give notice to the court that made the order that there is to be no appeal.

(4) Where a court makes an order under subsection (1)(a) above it may—

(a) appoint a person to undertake the destruction of the dog and require any person having custody of it to deliver it up for that purpose; and

(b) order the offender to pay such sum as the court may determine to be the reasonable expenses of destroying the dog and of keeping it pending its destruction.

(5) Any sum ordered to be paid under subsection (4)(b) above shall be treated for the purposes of enforcement as if it were a fine imposed on conviction.

(6) Any person who is disqualified for having custody of a dog by virtue of an order under subsection (1)(b) above may, at any time after the end of the period of one year beginning with the date of the order, apply to the court that made it (or a magistrates' court acting in the same local justice area as that court) for a direction terminating the disqualification.

(7) On an application under subsection (6) above the court may—

(a) having regard to the applicant's character, his conduct since the disqualification was imposed and any other circumstances of the case, grant or refuse the application; and

(b) order the applicant to pay all or any part of the costs of the application;

and where an application in respect of an order is refused no further application in respect of that order shall be entertained if made before the end of the period of one year beginning with the date of the refusal.

[This section is printed as amended and repealed in part by the *Dangerous Dogs (Amendment) Act* 1997, s.1; and the *Courts Act* 2003, s.109(1), and Sched. 8, para 353.]

Subsection (8) creates summary offences of having a dog in contravention of an order under subsection (1)(b) and of failure to comply with a requirement imposed under subsection (4)(a). Subsection (9) relates to the application of the section to Scotland.

A court should ordinarily consider, before ordering the immediate destruction of a dog, whether to exercise the power under section 4A(4) (*post*) to make a suspended order of destruction; if satisfied that the imposition of such a measure would mean the dog would not constitute a danger to public safety, a court should not order destruction; but, when deciding what order to make, the court must consider all the relevant circumstances, which include the dog's history of aggressive behaviour, the owner's history of controlling the dog concerned and the owner's character: *R. v. Flack* [2008] 2 Cr.App.R.(S.) 70, CA.

Whereas destruction of the dog is mandatory in the case of an aggravated offence under section 3, unless "the court is satisfied that the dog would not constitute a danger to public safety", the question for the court to determine is whether the dog, in the condition in which it actually is at the time of sentencing, and having regard to the circumstances in which it has lived, constitutes a danger to public safety; accordingly, evidence that the dog may not have been dangerous had it not been kept in the way that it had been kept is irrelevant: *R. v. Donnelly*, unreported, October 15, 2007, CA ([2007] EWCA Crim. 2548). As to disqualification, the principle of a disqualification order not being unnecessarily long and not impeding the pursuit of lawful activities is a proper matter to have in mind, as is the history of the owner's control of dogs, the owner's age and the seriousness of the offence leading to the proceedings: *ibid*.

Dangerous Dogs Act 1991, s.4A

Contingent destruction orders

4A.—(1) Where— **31–38a**

(a) a person is convicted of an offence under section 1 above or an aggravated offence under section 3(1) or (3) above;

(b) the court does not order the destruction of the dog under section 4(1)(a) above; and

(c) in the case of an offence under section 1 above, the dog is subject to the prohibition in section 1(3) above,

the court shall order that, unless the dog is exempted from that prohibition within the requisite period, the dog shall be destroyed.

(2) Where an order is made under subsection (1) above in respect of a dog, and the dog is not exempted from the prohibition in section 1(3) above within the requisite period, the court may extend that period.

(3) Subject to subsection (2) above, the requisite period for the purposes of such an order is the period of two months beginning with the date of the order.

(4) Where a person is convicted of an offence under section 3(1) or (3) above, the court

may order that, unless the owner of the dog keeps it under proper control, the dog shall be destroyed.

(5) An order under subsection (4) above—

(a) may specify the measures to be taken for keeping the dog under proper control, whether by muzzling, keeping on a lead, excluding it from specified places or otherwise; and

(b) if it appears to the court that the dog is a male and would be less dangerous if neutered, may require it to be neutered.

(6) Subsections (2) to (4) of section 4 above shall apply in relation to an order under subsection (1) or (4) above as they apply in relation to an order under subsection (1)(a) of that section.

[This section was inserted by the *Dangerous Dogs (Amendment) Act* 1997, s.2.]

31–38b Section 1 of the 1991 Act applies to certain types of dog bred for fighting. Section 1(3) prohibits any person from having such a dog in his possession after a day appointed by the Secretary of State (November 30, 1991). Subsection (5) provided for the making of an exemption scheme. The *Dangerous Dogs Compensation and Exemption Schemes Order* 1991 (S.I. 1991 No. 1744) provided for dogs born before the appointed day to be exempted from the prohibition subject to compliance with specified conditions. Section 4(1) of the 1997 Act provides that where an order is made under section 4A(1) of the 1991 Act, the exemption scheme provisions of the 1991 order shall have effect as if any reference to the appointed day were a reference to the end of the requisite period within the meaning of section 4A.

It appears that the intention behind section 4A(1) is that it should be possible to obtain an exemption for a dog even though it was born after the appointed day; and that, if this is done, the dog need not be destroyed. The drafting of section 4A gives rise to a number of questions, however. First, what does section 4A(1) require or permit a court to do in the event of a conviction of an aggravated offence under section 3(1) or (3)? A person may be convicted of such an offence in relation to a dog of a type which does not fall within section 1 at all. If the dog does not come within the prohibition, it can hardly be exempted from it. In relation to such cases, this subsection appears to be meaningless. Secondly, how is it to be determined whether an order under subsection (4) has been complied with? The legislation is silent as to this. It is inevitable that this is an issue which will be bitterly disputed in practice.

Search and seizure

31–39 Section 5 contains powers of seizure of dogs, including any appearing to be dangerously out of control in a public place. It also provides for the obtaining of a warrant to enter and search premises and to seize therein any dog or other thing found there which is evidence of the commission of an offence under the Act.

B. Common Law

(1) General

Introduction

31–40 Public nuisance is an offence at common law. A person is guilty of a public nuisance (also known as common nuisance), who (a) does an act not warranted by law, or (b) omits to discharge a legal duty, if the effect of the act or omission is to endanger the life, health, property or comfort of the public, or to obstruct the public in the exercise or enjoyment of rights common to all Her Majesty's subjects: 1 Hawk. c. 75; *Wilkes v. Hungerford Market Co.* (1835) 2 Bing.N.C. 281; *Barber v. Penley* [1893] 2 Ch. 447; *Stephen's Digest of the Criminal Law*, 8th ed., 1900, p. 184. This definition was approved in *R. v. Rimmington*; *R. v. Goldstein* [2006] 1 A.C. 459, in which the House of Lords held that the definition was clear, precise, adequate and based on a rational and discernible principle so that it had the certainty and predictability necessary to meet the requirements of the common law and of Article 7 of the ECHR (*ante*, § 16–97) that the citizen should be able to foresee, if need be with appropriate advice, the consequences which a given course of action might entail.

The common law remains important because of its flexibility in adapting to those areas not covered by special legislative schemes. Where, however, the conduct in question is criminalised by a particular statutory provision, the normal course will be to prosecute for the statutory offence: see *R. v. Rimmington*; *R. v. Goldstein*, *ante*, § 31–33. **31–41**

Actus reus

A public nuisance may be committed by an act or omission, as in *Att.-Gen. v. Tod Heatley* [1897] 1 Ch. 560 (allowing one's land to accumulate rubbish, even though it is deposited there by others for whom the defendant was not responsible), and *R. v. Watts* (1703) 1 Salk. 357 (allowing a house near the highway to become ruinous). **31–42**

Just how widely spread the effect of a nuisance must be for it to qualify as a public nuisance and to become the subject of a criminal prosecution or of a relator action by the Attorney-General was considered in *Att.-Gen. v. P.Y.A. Quarries Ltd* [1957] 2 Q.B. 169, CA. After considering the relevant, authorities Romer L.J. said (at p. 184):

> "It is clear in my opinion that any nuisance is 'public' which materially affects the reasonable comfort and convenience of life of a class of Her Majesty's subjects. The sphere of the nuisance may be described generally as the 'neighbourhood'; but the question whether the local community within that sphere comprises a sufficient number of persons to constitute a class of the public is a question of fact in every case. It is not necessary in my judgment to prove that every member of the class has been injuriously affected; it is sufficient to show that a representative cross-section of the class has been so affected for an injunction to issue."

Denning L.J. (at pp. 190–191) said:

> "I prefer to look to the reason of the thing and to say that a public nuisance is a nuisance which is so widespread in its range or so indiscriminate in its effect that it would not be reasonable to expect one person to take proceedings on his own responsibility to put a stop to it, but that it should be taken on the responsibility of the community at large."

If the effect of the act or omission is such as to affect injuriously, in any of the ways above stated, the public, the nuisance cannot be legalised by long continuance: see *Foster v. Warblington District Council* [1906] 1 K.B. 648 at 655. It is only in this respect, and in the *quantum* of annoyance, that public differs from private nuisance. *Semble*, a single act may give rise to both civil and criminal liability: see *R. v. Mutters* (1864) L. & C. 491; *Att.-Gen. v. P.Y.A. Quarries Ltd*, *ante*; *British Celanese Ltd v. A. H. Hunt (Capacitors) Ltd* [1961] 1 W.L.R. 959.

In *R. v. Rimmington*; *R. v. Goldstein*, *ante*, it was held (overruling *R. v. Johnson (A.T.)* [1996] 2 Cr.App.R. 434, CA) that an individual act of causing a private nuisance could not become a criminal public nuisance merely by reason of the fact that the act was one of a series, and that individual acts causing injury to several different people rather than to the community as a whole or a significant section of it could not amount to the offence of causing a public nuisance, however persistent or objectionable the acts might be.

It is no defence to say that the alleged nuisance has existed for a number of years, for no length of time will legalise a public nuisance: *Foster v. Warblington District Council* [1906] 1 K.B. 648 at 655; but proof of long continuance may justify a finding that it is not a nuisance in fact: *Hole v. Barlow* (1858) 27 L.J.C.P. 208 (Byles J.).

Mens rea

The object with which the act or omission is done or made is immaterial if the probable result is to affect injuriously the public (*R. v. Carlile* (1834) 6 C. & P. 636; *Barber v. Penley* [1893] 2 Ch. 447); or any appreciable part of it (*R. v. Lloyd* (1802) 4 Esp. 200). It is sufficient for the prosecution to show that the defendant knew or ought to have known, because the means of knowledge were available to him, that as a result of his action or omission a public nuisance would occur: *R. v. Shorrock* [1994] Q.B. 279, 98 Cr.App.R. 67, CA; *R. v. Rimmington*; *R. v. Goldstein*, *ante* (although, of course, he need have no knowledge of the legal label attaching to the circumstances constituting the nuisance). **31–43**

Vicarious liability

Where works are carried on in such a way as to be a nuisance, it is no answer to an **31–44** indictment for the nuisance against the employer, that he did not personally superintend the works, and that he had given express orders to the workmen that they should be carried on in a mode which, if followed, would have prevented their causing a nuisance: *R. v. Stephens* (1866) L.R. 1 Q.B. 702. Doubt was expressed about this decision by Field J. in *Chisholm v. Doulton* (1889) 22 Q.B.D. 736 at 740; his Lordship sought to distinguish it on the ground that the proceeding was civil. This is unconvincing as the proceedings in *Stephens* were by way of indictment and Blackburn J. (at p. 710) expressly dealt with the issue of vicarious liability in criminal proceedings. As to vicarious liability generally, see *ante*, §§ 17–25 *et seq.*

Conspiracy

31–45 Conspiracy to commit a public nuisance remains an offence and is contrary to section 1(1) of the *CLA* 1977 (*post*, § 33–2). That such an offence exists was recognised in *R. v. Soul*, 70 Cr.App.R. 295, CA. Whilst the House of Lords in *R. v. Rimmington*; *R. v. Goldstein*, *ante*, appeared to express some doubt about this decision, this was unrelated to the charge of conspiracy.

Statutory authorisation

31–46 A statute may authorise and legalise acts which would otherwise amount to a nuisance: *R. v. Pease* (1832) 4 B. & Ald. 30—confirmed in *Hammersmith etc., Ry v. Brand* (1869) L.R. 4 H.L. 171; *London, Brighton and South Coast Ry v. Truman* (1885) 11 App.Cas. 45; *Withington Local Board of Health v. Corporation of Manchester* [1893] 2 Ch. 19; *Att.-Gen. v. Mayor, etc., of Nottingham* [1904] 1 Ch. 673. But the statutory authorisation will not protect those relying on it unless: (a) it is given specifically or by necessary implication (*Metropolitan Asylum District Managers v. Hill* (1881) 6 App.Cas. 193; and cases above cited; *Canadian Pacific Ry v. Parke* [1899] A.C. 535); and (b) the manner of doing the act follows the authority of the statute, and avoids causing a nuisance if it can be avoided by reasonable care: *London, Brighton and South Coast Ry v. Truman, ante*; *Craies on Statute Law*, 7th ed., 1971, pp. 277–279. It is not unusual for a statute expressly to reserve liability to indictment for nuisance. See *Att.-Gen. v. Gas Light and Coke Co.* (1877) 7 Ch.D. 217; *Jordeson v. Sutton, Southcoates & Drypool Gas. Co.* [1899] 2 Ch. 217; *Colwell v. Mayor, etc., of St. Pancras* [1904] 1 Ch. 707.

(2) Indictment

STATEMENT OF OFFENCE

31–47 *Public nuisance.*

PARTICULARS OF OFFENCE

A B, on the —— day of —— 20—, and on other days between that date and the —— day of ——, 20—, caused a nuisance to the public by allowing [set out details of alleged nuisance].

(3) Class of offence and mode of trial

31–48 This offence is a class 3 offence, *ante*, § 2–17, triable either way: *MCA* 1980, s.17(1), and Sched. 1 (*ante*, § 1–75af).

(4) Sentence

31–49 Fine and (or) imprisonment, and judgment for "prostration" or abatement of the nuisance if it is alleged and proved to be then continuing. See *R. v. Incledon* (1810) 13 East 164. The penalty on summary conviction is governed by section 32 of the *MCA* 1980 (*ante*, § 1–75aa).

In *R. v. Bourgass* [2007] 2 Cr.App.R.(S.) 40, CA, 17 years' imprisonment was upheld in the case of an offender who was the prime mover in a conspiracy engaged in over several months to commit acts of terrorism (but charged as a conspiracy to cause a public nuisance) involving the use of poisons and explosives intended to destabilise the community by causing disruption, fear and injury.

(5) Classification of nuisances

In earlier editions of this work, public nuisances were grouped in four classes, being conduct which (i) interfered with comfort, enjoyment or health, (ii) was dangerous to public safety, (iii) was injurious to public morals, decency or order, or (iv) comprised the unlawful treatment of dead bodies. In view of the generality of the House of Lords' decision in *R. v. Rimmington*; *R. v. Goldstein*, *ante*, § 31–40, and their Lordships' discouragement of prosecutions for the common law offence where there was a statutory offence, such attempts at classification and reference to old authorities falling within the various classifications (apart from the fourth, as to which, see *post*) are no longer likely to be helpful. However, it should be noted, in deference to their Lordships' decision, that the reference to "morals" should in any event be struck out. As to outraging public decency, now treated as an offence in itself, rather than as a species of nuisance, see *ante*, §§ 20–238 *et seq.* As to keeping a disorderly house, see *ante*, §§ 20–246 *et seq.* **31–50**

[The next paragraph is § 31–54.]

(6) Unlawful treatment of dead bodies

Introduction

The offences dealt with in the ensuing paragraphs are particular common law offences, rather than species of the common law offence of nuisance, although conduct in relation to a dead body has been held to constitute a nuisance, as where a body was burnt in such a place and manner as to annoy persons passing along public roads or other places where they had a right to go: see *R. v. Price* (1884) 12 Q.B.D. 247; or where the naked body of a dead child was exposed in or near, and within view of, the highway: see *R. v. Clark* (1883) 15 Cox 171. They are collected here as a matter of convenience. **31–54**

Leaving corpse unburied

To leave unburied the corpse of a person for whom the defendant was bound to provide "Christian burial" (which probably means only "decent burial"), such as a wife or child, is an indictable offence, if he is shown to have had the ability to provide such burial: *R. v. Vann* (1851) 2 Den. 325; *R. v. Stewart* (1840) 12 A. & E. 773 at 778; *Jenkins v. Tucker* (1788) 1 H.Bl. 90. **31–55**

It is also an indictable offence to prevent the burial of a corpse: see Russ. Cr., 12th ed., pp. 1416, 1420; *R. v. Lynn* (1788) 2 T.R. 733; and *R. v. Hunter* [1974] Q.B. 95, where it was held that where persons agree to conceal a corpse and the concealment prevents burial, the offence of conspiracy to prevent the burial of a corpse is committed, notwithstanding that prevention of burial was not the object of the agreement.

Disposing of corpse

A person who, without lawful authority, disposes of a dead body for the purpose of dissection, is indictable at common law: *R. v. Lynn, ante*; *R. v. Gilles* (1820) K. & R. 366n. It appears to be immaterial whether the body was disposed of for gain or not: *R. v. Cundick* (1822) Dow. & Ry.N.P. 13. **31–56**

Removing corpse from grave

It is an offence at common law to remove, without lawful authority, a corpse from a grave, whether in a churchyard or in the burial-ground of a congregation of Protestant dissenters; and it is no defence to such a charge that the motives of the defendant were pious and laudable: *R. v. Sharpe* (1857) Dears. & B. 160. See also *R. v. Kenyon* (1901) 36 L.J.Newsp. 571 (unlawfully, wilfully and indecently digging open graves); and *R. v. Jacobson* (1880) 14 Cox 522 (for a precedent of an indictment). **31–57**

Obstructing coroner

Any disposition of a corpse with intent to obstruct or prevent a coroner's inquest, **31–58** when one ought to be held, is an offence at common law: *R. v. Stephenson* (1884) 13 Q.B.D. 331; *R. v. Price* (1884) 12 Q.B.D. 247. It must be established that there was a duty to hold an inquest. It is not sufficient to prove concealment of a corpse, the intent must be proved as stated: *R. v. Purcy*, 24 Cr.App.R. 70, CCA.

Indictment

STATEMENT OF OFFENCE

31–59 *Obstructing coroner in the execution of his duty.*

PARTICULARS OF OFFENCE

A B and G C, on the —— day of —— 20—, intending to prevent the Coroner of —— from holding an inquest in the execution of his duty upon view of the dead body of S C who died a violent or an unnatural death or a sudden death of which the cause was unknown or intending to obstruct the said Coroner in the holding of such inquest did bury the said body in a certain place called Hampstead Heath.

III. *OBSCENE OR INDECENT PUBLICATIONS AND DISPLAYS, ETC.*

A. COMMON LAW

Obscene libels

31–60 The publication of any obscene libel was an offence punishable at common law on indictment: 1 Hawk. c. 73, s.9; *R. v. Wilkes* (1770) 4 Burr. 2527 at 2574; *R. v. Hicklin* (1868) L.R. 3 Q.B. 360. But it is now provided by section 2(4) of the *Obscene Publications Act* 1959 (*post*, § 31–74) that a person publishing an article shall not be proceeded against for an offence at common law consisting of the publication of any matter contained or embodied in the article, where it is of the essence of the offence that the matter is obscene. Section 2(4) is extended to matter in sound and television programmes by the *Broadcasting Act* 1990, Sched. 15, para. 6, *post*, § 31–96.

However, the statutory definition of obscenity (see *post*, § 31–63) retained in substance the common law test, as defined by Lord Cockburn C.J. in *R. v. Hicklin*, *ante*, at p. 371 ("whether the tendency of the matter charged as obscenity is to deprave and corrupt those whose minds are open to such immoral influences, and into whose hands a publication of this sort may fall"). Thus, the following decisions at common law may still be usefully referred to for some purposes. A book is not necessarily obscene merely because it is in bad taste or undesirable: *R. v. Martin Secker and Warburg* [1954] 1 W.L.R. 1138. However, a publication is an obscene publication even if only part of it is obscene: *Paget Publications Ltd v. Watson* [1952] 1 All E.R. 1256.

Exhibitions

31–61 An obscene exhibition is an example of the offence of nuisance in the form of conduct which outrages public decency: see *R. v. Saunders* (1875) 1 Q.B.D. 15; and *R. v. Gibson and Sylveire* [1990] 2 Q.B. 619, 91 Cr.App.R. 341, CA (*ante*, § 20–241).

B. STATUTE

(1) Obscene Publications Acts 1959 and 1964

(a) *Introduction*

31–62 The law governing obscene publications is to be found principally in the *Obscene Publications Acts* 1959 and 1964. The test for obscenity is set out in section 1(1), and the offences are created by section 2, of the 1959 Act. Section 2(1) of that Act makes it an offence to publish an obscene article whether for gain or not; and, as amended by section 1(1) of the 1964 Act, makes it an offence to have an obscene article for publication for gain (whether gain to the defendant or to another). Possible defences are the "public good" (provided by s.4 of the 1959 Act) and, not having examined the article, having no reasonable cause to believe that the article is obscene (provided by s.2(5) of the 1959 Act and s.1(3) of the 1964 Act).

(b) *Definitions*

"obscene"

Obscene Publications Act 1959, s.1(1)

1.—(1) For the purposes of this Act an article shall be deemed to be obscene if its effect or (where the article comprises two or more distinct items) the effect of any one of its items is, if taken as a whole, such as to tend to deprave and corrupt persons who are likely, having regard to all relevant circumstances, to read, see or hear the matter contained or embodied in it. **31–63**

The test for obscenity depends on the article itself, and the purposes or intention of the author or publisher are immaterial, however noble or otherwise: see *Shaw v. DPP* [1962] A.C. 220 at 227, HL, and *R. v. Calder and Boyars Ltd* [1969] 1 Q.B. 151, 52 Cr.App.R. 706, CA. Obscenity is not confined to a tendency to depravity and corruption of a sexual nature. It includes material that advocates drug-taking by highlighting the favourable effects of drugs and so providing "a real danger that those into whose hands the book came might be tempted at any rate to experiment with drugs": *John Calder (Publications) Ltd v. Powell* [1965] 1 Q.B. 509. It also encompasses material that tends to induce violence. This proposition appears to have been taken for granted in *DPP v. A. and B.C. Chewing Gum Ltd* [1968] 1 Q.B. 159, DC, and *R. v. Calder and Boyars Ltd, ante.*

In *R. v. Anderson* [1972] 1 Q.B. 304, 56 Cr.App.R. 115, CA, the court emphasised that, as a specific test of obscenity is provided by the 1959 Act, it is that test alone which is to be applied; to refer a jury to the dictionary definition of "obscenity" in this context constitutes a misdirection. When applying the statutory test to novels, it is proper to judge the book as a whole rather than apply the test in isolation to selected passages: see *R. v. Penguin Books Ltd* [1961] Crim.L.R. 176 and *R. v. Calder and Boyars Ltd, ante*. In *R. v. Anderson, ante*, a direction that the jury should consider a magazine as a whole was held to be wrong. Where the court is considering an article comprising a number of distinct items (*e.g.* a magazine), the proper view of obscenity under section 1 of the 1959 Act is to apply the test to the individual items in question. If the test shows one item to be obscene, that is enough to make the whole article obscene. **31–64**

It is for the judge to decide as a matter of law whether an article is capable of being treated as distinct items: *R. v. Goring* [1999] Crim.L.R. 670, CA. Where, however, the entire case had been conducted on the basis that the article in question should be treated as a whole, it was too late for the judge to introduce the possibility of dividing it into distinct items when the jury, after retirement, asked for clarification of the phrase "taken as a whole": *ibid.*

"Deprave and corrupt"

The words "deprave" and "corrupt" have been widely interpreted in the past: see, *e.g. R. v. Hicklin* (1868) L.R. 3 Q.B. 360 at 371, and *R. v. Bradlaugh and Besant* (1877) 2 Q.B.D. 569 (reversed (1878) 3 Q.B.D. 607). They were defined by Byrne J. in the "Lady Chatterley" case as follows: **31–65**

> "To 'deprave' means to make morally bad, to pervert, to debase or corrupt morally. To 'corrupt' means to render morally unsound or rotten, to destroy the moral purity or chastity, to pervert or ruin a good quality, to debase, to defile": *R. v. Penguin Books Ltd* [1961] Crim.L.R. 176 at 177.

In *R. v. Calder and Boyars Ltd* [1969] 1 Q.B. 151, 52 Cr.App.R. 706, a similar definition was approved by the Court of Appeal (where a statute lays down a definition in plain English, it is rarely necessary for a judge to attempt to improve on it). The words "deprave" and "corrupt" refer, *inter alia*, to the effect of obscene articles on the mind. It is not necessary that any physical (or "overt") sexual activity should result: *DPP v. Whyte* [1972] A.C. 849, HL. The meaning of "deprave" and "corrupt" was also considered by the House of Lords in *Knuller (Publishing, Printing and Promotions) Ltd v. DPP* [1973] A.C. 435, *ante*, §§ 20–243 *et seq.*

Where the trial judge failed to remind the jury that the proposition central to the defence case was that certain illustrations could be so disgusting and filthy that they would not corrupt and deprave but rather would tend to cause people to revolt from activity of that kind, it was held that the omission was fatal to the conviction: *R. v. Calder and Boyars Ltd*, *ante*, and *R. v. Anderson*, *ante*.

"Persons"

31–66 In *R. v. Calder and Boyars Ltd*, *ante*, the Court of Appeal stated that the jury should have been directed to consider whether the effect of the book was to tend to deprave or corrupt a significant proportion of those persons likely to read it. However, in *DPP v. Whyte*, *ante*, Lord Pearson observed (at p. 865) that although such a direction had been suitable on the facts of the case, the phrase "significant proportion" cannot be safely transplanted to cases of a different character. The statutory definition of obscenity (*ante*) contains no requirement as to the number of persons or as to the proportion of its readers which the articles will tend to corrupt or deprave. The statutory definition:

> "... refers to 'persons', which means some persons, though I think in a suitable case, if the number of persons likely to be affected is so small as to be negligible—really negligible—the *de minimis* principle might be applied. But if a seller of pornographic books has a large number of customers who are not likely to be corrupted by such books, he does not thereby acquire a licence to expose for sale or sell such books to a small number of customers who are likely to be corrupted by them" (*ibid.*, at p. 866).

Lords Simon (at p. 868), Cross (at p. 869) and Salmon (at p. 873) accepted the "significant proportion" test, Lord Cross saying that a significant proportion of a class means a part which is not numerically negligible but which may be much less than half (at p. 870). Lord Wilberforce did not specifically consider this issue.

The justices had found that the class of likely customers for the defendant's pornographic publications was middle-aged men whose morals were already in a state of depravity and corruption, and they had not been satisfied, therefore, that the publications would have a tendency to deprave and corrupt a significant proportion (see *ante*) of likely readers. The House of Lords held that the Act was not merely concerned with the once and for all corruption of the wholly innocent; it equally protected the less innocent from further corruption and the addict from feeding or increasing his addiction and remitted the case with a direction to convict.

See also *R. v. O'Sullivan* [1995] 1 Cr.App.R. 455, CA.

In *R. v. Clayton and Halsey* [1963] 1 Q.B. 163, 46 Cr.App.R. 450, CCA, it was held that an article sold to a police officer could not be obscene where there was no chance of him being depraved or corrupted. This was, however, distinguished in *R. v. Perrin* [2002] 4 *Archbold News* 2, CA. It was held that where an allegation of publishing an obscene article was based on the publication of a single web page that acted as a sample of what was available to those willing to pay a subscription fee, the judge had correctly directed the jury in accordance with the terms of section 1(1) that the question of "obscenity" was to be decided according to whether or not the effect of the article was "such as to tend to deprave and corrupt persons who [were] likely, having regard to all the relevant circumstances, to ... see" it; who was likely to see it was for the jury to determine; and the fact that the only evidence of anyone having seen it was that of the police officer who saw it, did not bring the case within *R. v. Clayton and Halsey*. It was further held that in a case of "publication" (as opposed to one of having articles for publication), where there was no question of a defence of "public good", it had not been necessary to direct the jury to consider whether the effect of the article would have been to tend to deprave and corrupt "a significant proportion" of those likely to see it (*R. v. Calder and Boyars Ltd* and *R. v. O'Sullivan*, *ante*, distinguished).

Where publication is to be abroad

31–67 Where publication is to take place outside England and Wales, the question whether the article is obscene is to be decided according to the evidence that the article would or would not tend to deprave or corrupt likely readers in the country of destination. Although magistrates are not entitled simply to apply English standards of morality, they are entitled to form the opinion, from their own knowledge and without evidence, that having regard to the likely readers, the article was so clearly obscene as to be likely to deprave and corrupt: *Gold Star Publications Ltd v. DPP*, 73 Cr.App.R. 141, HL (proceedings for forfeiture under s.3 of the 1959 Act, *post*, § 31–84; but presumably the same reasoning would be applied to a prosecution under s.2 of the 1959 Act, *post*, § 31–74, for having an obscene article for publication for gain).

Expert evidence

Expert evidence is not limited to establishing or rebutting a defence of public good under section 4 of the 1959 Act (*post*, § 31–88). In *DPP v. A. and B.C. Chewing Gum Ltd* [1968] 1 Q.B. 159, DC, it was held that the evidence of psychiatrists was admissible to show the sort of effect bubble gum "battle cards" would have on the minds of children of different groups and what the cards would lead those children to do. However, this decision was described by the Court of Appeal in *R. v. Anderson* [1972] 1 Q.B. 304, 56 Cr.App.R. 115, as "highly exceptional and confined to its own circumstances, namely a case where the alleged obscene matter was directed at very young children and was itself of a somewhat unusual kind". Ordinarily, the issue "obscene or no" must be tried by the jury without the assistance of expert evidence on that issue: *R. v. Anderson*, *ante*; *R. v. Calder and Boyars Ltd* [1969] 1 Q.B. 151, 52 Cr.App.R. 706, CA; *R. v. Stamford* [1972] 2 Q.B. 391, 56 Cr.App.R. 398, CA; and *Att.-Gen.'s Reference (No. 3 of 1977)*, 67 Cr.App.R. 393, CA, *post*, § 31–90. In *DPP v. Whyte* [1972] A.C. 849, Lord Wilberforce (at p. 862) equated "expert" evidence in this context with "psychological, sociological or medical" evidence. **31–68**

The effect of cocaine and the various methods by which it is ingested are not within the experience of the ordinary person. Accordingly, in *R. v. Skirving* [1985] Q.B. 819, 81 Cr.App.R. 9, CA (authorities reviewed), the court held that expert evidence upon those topics had properly been admitted upon a charge of having an obscene article, namely a publication entitled "Attention Coke Lovers. Free Base. The Greatest Thing Since Sex" for publication for gain. To enable the jury to come to a proper conclusion on the main issue—whether the book had a tendency to deprave or corrupt—it was necessary for them, as a preliminary, to be informed about the effect of using cocaine. The evidence was called to enable the jury to have a scientific assessment of the characteristics of cocaine and the effect physically and mentally on the user and to explain the different effects of the various methods of ingesting the substance.

Non-expert evidence of effect

The appellant published a booklet entitled "The Ladies' Directory" with names, addresses and photographs of prostitutes, and abbreviations indicating practices in which these prostitutes were prepared to indulge. While the evidence of prostitutes as to the meaning of the abbreviations was admissible, their evidence as to the result of the advertisements, the age of those responding to them, and the practices indulged in by them, was not; nor was the evidence of police officers with regard to the premises advertised and what had been found therein: *Shaw v. DPP* [1962] A.C. 220, HL. **31–69**

Evidence of other publications

Evidence of other publications in circulation is inadmissible if designed to show that they are as obscene as, or are not materially different from, the articles in question: *R. v. Reiter* [1954] 2 Q.B. 16, 38 Cr.App.R. 62, CCA; *R. v. Elliott (C.J.)* [1996] 1 Cr.App.R. 432, CA. The position may be different where evidence of other publications is tendered under a defence of public good (see *post*, § 31–92). **31–70**

"article"

Obscene Publications Act 1959, s.1(2)

1.—(2) In this Act "article" means any description of article containing or embodying matter to be read or looked at or both, any sound record, and any film or other record of a picture or pictures. **31–71**

As to the extension of the 1959 Act to cover negatives, etc., had or kept for the reproduction or manufacture therefrom of articles for publication, see section 2 of the *Obscene Publications Act* 1964, *post*, § 31–77.

In *Att.-Gen.'s Reference (No. 5 of 1980)*, 72 Cr.App.R. 71, CA, it was held that the object of section 1(2) was to bring all articles which produced words or pictures or sounds within the compass of the Act, that the words "shows, plays or projects" in section 1(3)(b) (*post*) were sufficiently wide to cover pictures produced by a video cassette; and that, accordingly, a video cassette was an article within the meaning of section 1(2). So also is a computer disc: *R. v. Fellows and Arnold* [1997] 1 Cr.App.R. 244, CA.

"publishes"

Obscene Publications Act 1959, s.1(3)–(6)

31–72 **1.**—(3) For the purposes of this Act a person publishes an article who—

(a) distributes, circulates, sells, lets on hire, gives, or lends it, or who offers it for sale or for letting on hire; or

(b) in the case of an article containing or embodying matter to be looked at or a record, shows, plays or projects it, or, where the matter is data stored electronically, transmits that data.

(4) For the purposes of this Act a person also publishes an article to the extent that any matter recorded on it is included by him in a programme included in a programme service.

(5) Where the inclusion of any matter in a programme so included would, if that matter were recorded matter, constitute the publication of an obscene article for the purposes of this Act by virtue of subsection (4) above, this Act shall have effect in relation to the inclusion of that matter in that programme as if it were recorded matter.

(6) In this section "programme" and "programme service" have the same meaning as in the *Broadcasting Act* 1990.

[Subs. (3) is printed as amended by the *CLA* 1977, s.53; and the *CJPOA* 1994, s.168(1) and Sched. 9, para. 3; and as repealed in part by the *Broadcasting Act* 1990, ss.162 and 203(3) and Sched. 21. Subss. (4) to (6) were inserted by the 1990 Act, s.162(1)(b).]

For the definitions of "programme" and "programme service", see sections 202(1) and 201 of the 1990 Act, respectively.

Section 162(2) of the 1990 Act gives effect to Schedule 15 (*post*, § 31–94) for the purpose of supplementing the amendments to section 1 of the 1959 Act effected by subsection (1).

As to publication "for gain", see section 1(5) of the 1964 Act, *post*, § 31–76.

31–73 In *R. v. Barker*, 46 Cr.App.R. 227, CCA, it was said that the forms of publication included in the definition in section 1(3)(a) fall into three distinct groups, in one of which, comprising the words "sells, lets on hire, gives, or lends", the publication is to an individual; in the second group, comprising the words "distributes, circulates", publication is on a wider scale involving more than one person; in the third group, a mere offer for sale or letting on hire constitutes publication. In a case falling within the first group, assuming that publication is proved, the first issue for the jury is whether the effect of the article was such as to tend to deprave and corrupt the individual to whom it was published. The second issue is whether any other person or persons were likely to see the article. In this connection, the issue is not whether republication has or has not taken place, but whether it could reasonably have been expected. If the answer to the second issue is "yes", a third issue will arise, namely, whether the article is such as to tend to deprave and corrupt the person or persons to whom republication could reasonably have been expected. On the first issue, a jury should take into consideration both the article itself and the age or occupation of the person to whom it was published, if there is evidence on this. On the second issue, whether republication could reasonably have been expected, such age and occupation are relevant, but they are not the only relevant factors. On the third issue, considerations similar to those involved in the first are applicable. It was further held that the fact that the defendant was wholly unaware of the age or occupation of the person to whom the article has been published is irrelevant. A person who sells potentially obscene matter to an unknown applicant takes the risk that the latter is someone whom the article would tend to deprave and corrupt. On the other hand, if the unknown applicant is not of that type, the defendant's ignorance of the applicant's character cannot make the article obscene.

In *R. v. Taylor (Alan)* [1995] 1 Cr.App.R. 131, CA, it was held that the act of developing and printing obscene photographs which were then sold or passed back to the owners for gain was capable of amounting to an act of publication within the meaning of section 1(3). For the purposes of the Act, publication does not necessarily mean publication to a third party.

Where a person provides another with a password to enable him to access data stored on a computer, he may be said to be "showing" him the matter so stored: *R. v. Fellows and Arnold* [1997] 1 Cr.App.R. 244, CA.

The mere transmission of data electronically constituting "publication" within section 1(3)(b), it follows that the uploading or downloading of a web page constitutes publication: *R. v. Perrin* [2002] 4 *Archbold News* 2, CA.

(c) *Offences*

Obscene Publications Act 1959, s.2

Prohibition of publication of obscene matter

2.—(1) Subject as hereinafter provided, any person who, whether for gain or not, publishes an obscene article or who has an obscene article for publication for gain (whether gain to himself or gain to another) shall be liable— **31–74**

(a) on summary conviction to a fine not exceeding the prescribed sum or to imprisonment for a term not exceeding *six* [12] months;

(b) on conviction on indictment to a fine or to imprisonment for a term not exceeding *three* [five] years or both.

(2) [*Repealed by* Criminal Law Act *1977, Sched. 13*.]

(3) A prosecution ... for an offence against this section shall not be commenced more than two years after the commission of the offence.

(3A) Proceedings for an offence under this section shall not be instituted except by or with the consent of the Director of Public Prosecutions in any case where the article in question is a moving picture film of a width of not less than sixteen millimetres and the relevant publication or the only other publication which followed or could reasonably have been expected to follow from the relevant publication took place or (as the case may be) was to take place in the course of a film exhibition: and in this subsection "the relevant publication" means—

(a) in the case of any proceedings under this section for publishing an obscene article, the publication in respect of which the defendant would be charged if the proceedings were brought; and

(b) in the case of any proceedings under this section for having an obscene article for publication for gain, the publication which, if the proceedings were brought, the defendant would be alleged to have had in contemplation.

(4) A person publishing an article shall not be proceeded against for an offence at common law consisting of the publication of any matter contained or embodied in the article where it is of the essence of the offence that the matter is obscene.

(4A) Without prejudice to subsection (4) above, a person shall not be proceeded against for an offence at common law—

(a) in respect of a film exhibition or anything said or done in the course of a film exhibition, where it is of the essence of the common law offence that the exhibition or, as the case may be, what was said or done was obscene, indecent, offensive, disgusting or injurious to morality; or

(b) in respect of an agreement to give a film exhibition or to cause anything to be said or done in the course of such an exhibition where the common law offence consists of conspiring to corrupt public morals or to do any act contrary to public morals or decency.

(5) A person shall not be convicted of an offence against this section if he proves that he had not examined the article in respect of which he is charged and had no reasonable cause to suspect that it was such that his publication of it would make him liable to be convicted of an offence against this section.

(6) In any proceedings against a person under this section the question whether an article is obscene shall be determined without regard to any publication by another person

unless it could reasonably have been expected that the publication by the other person would follow from publication by the person charged.

(7) In this section "film exhibition" has the same meaning as in the *Cinemas Act* 1985.

[This section is printed as amended by the *Obscene Publications Act* 1964, s.1(1); the *CLA* 1977, s.53; the *MCA* 1980, s.32(2) (substitution of reference to "the prescribed sum"); and the *Cinemas Act* 1985, s.24(1) and Sched. 2, para. 6; and as repealed in part by the *CLA* 1977, s.65(5) and Sched. 13. In subs. (1)(a), "12" is substituted for "six", as from a day to be appointed, by the *CJA* 2003, s.282(2) and (3). The increase has no application to offences committed before the substitution takes effect: s.282(4). In subs. (1)(b), "five" is substituted for "three", as from a day to be appointed, by the *CJIA* 2008, s.71; but not in relation to offences committed before the commencement of that section: 2008 Act, s.148(2), and Sched. 27, para. 25.]

For the application of this section to matter in sound or television programmes or intended to be included therein, see Schedule 15 to the *Broadcasting Act* 1990, *post*, § 31–94.

31–75 For the definition of "film exhibition", see section 21 of the *Cinemas Act* 1985, as amended by the *Broadcasting Act* 1990, s.203(1) and Sched. 20, para. 40.

Section 1(2), (3) and (5) of the 1964 Act have effect for the purpose of elaborating the offence of having an obscene article for publication for gain: see *post*, § 31–76.

Obscene Publications Act 1964, s.1

Obscene articles intended for publication for gain

31–76 **1.**—(1) [*Amends section 2(1) of the 1959 Act:* ante, *§ 31–74.*]

(2) For the purpose of any proceedings for an offence against the said section 2 a person shall be deemed to have an article for publication for gain if with a view to such publication he has the article in his ownership, possession or control.

(3) In proceedings brought against a person under the said section 2 for having an obscene article for publication for gain the following provision shall apply in place of subsections (5) and (6) of that section that is to say—

(a) he shall not be convicted of that offence if he proves that he had not examined the article and had no reasonable cause to suspect that it was such that his having it would make him liable to be convicted of an offence against that section; and

(b) the question whether the article is obscene shall be determined by reference to such publication for gain of the article as in the circumstances it may reasonably be inferred he had in contemplation and to any further publication that could reasonably be expected to follow from it, but not to any other publication.

(4) When articles are seized under section 3 of the *Obscene Publications Act* 1959, and a person is convicted under section 2 of that Act of having them for publication for gain, the court on his conviction shall order the forfeiture of those articles:

Provided that an order made by virtue of this subsection (including an order so made on appeal) shall not take effect until the expiration of the ordinary time within which an appeal in the matter of the proceedings in which the order was made may be instituted or, where such an appeal is duly instituted, until the appeal is finally decided or abandoned; and for this purpose—

(a) an application for a case to be stated or for leave to appeal shall be treated as the institution of an appeal; and

(b) where a decision on appeal is subject to a further appeal, the appeal shall not be deemed to be finally decided until the expiration of the ordinary time within which a further appeal may be instituted or, where a further appeal is duly instituted, until the further appeal is finally decided or abandoned.

(5) References in section 3 of the *Obscene Publications Act* 1959, and this section to publication for gain shall apply to any publication with a view to gain, whether the gain is to accrue by way of consideration for the publication or in any other way.

For section 3 of the 1959 Act, see *post*, § 31–84.

Obscene Publications Act 1964, s.2

Negatives, etc., for production of obscene articles

31–77 **2.**—(1) The *Obscene Publications Act* 1959 (as amended by this Act) shall apply in relation to anything which is intended to be used, either alone or as one of a set, for the reproduction or manufacture therefrom of articles containing or embodying matter to be read, looked at or listened to as if it were an article containing or embodying that matter so far as that matter is to be derived from it or from the set.

(2) For the purposes of the *Obscene Publications Act* 1959 (as so amended) an article shall be deemed to be had or kept for publication if it is had or kept for the reproduction or manufacture therefrom of articles for publication; and the question, whether an article so had or kept is obscene shall—

(a) for purposes of section 2 of the Act be determined in accordance with section 1(3)(b) above as if any reference there to publication of the article were a reference to publication of articles reproduced or manufactured from it; and

(b) for purposes of section 3 of the Act be determined on the assumption that articles reproduced or manufactured from it would be published in any manner likely having regard to the circumstances in which it was found, but in no other manner.

Section 3 relates to powers of search and seizure: see *post*, §§ 31–84 *et seq.*

Freedom of expression

In *R. v. Perrin* [2002] 4 *Archbold News* 2, CA (see *ante*, § 31–66, 31–73), it was held that whilst Article 10 of the ECHR (*ante*, § 16–119) was engaged by section 2(1) of the 1959 Act, the restriction was justified under Article 10(2); the offence was sufficiently well-defined to be "prescribed by law", it served a legitimate purpose and was necessary in a democratic society, and there was nothing in the Convention to require that there should only be a prosecution in respect of alleged obscenity in the jurisdiction where the "major steps" in relation to publication took place. **31–77a**

Relationship between sections 1(3), 2(1) and 2(6) of the 1959 Act and section 1(3)(b) of the 1964 Act

In *Att.-Gen.'s Reference (No. 2 of 1975)*, 62 Cr.App.R. 255, the point referred to the Court of Appeal was as follows: **31–78**

> "Whether, for the purposes of section 2(1) of the 1959 Act (as amended), in relation to offences of having an obscene article for publication for gain and publishing an obscene article, the persons who are likely, having regard to all the relevant circumstances, to read, see or hear the matter contained or embodied in an allegedly obscene article, are to be or can be defined by reference to their opportunity to read, see or hear the matter otherwise than as a result of a publication of the article within section 1(3) of the 1959 Act and whether and if so, to what extent section 2(6) of the 1959 Act and section 1(3)(b) of the 1964 Act affect either the definition of the potential audience within section 1(1) or the publication of the article within section 1(3) of the 1959 Act."

Held: (a) The words "read, see or hear" in section 1(1) of the 1959 Act (*ante*, § 31–63) are to be defined as "read, see or hear as a result of a publication by a person who publishes within the meaning of section 1(3) of that Act and not otherwise". (b) The relationship between section 2(6) of the 1959 Act and section 1(3)(b) of the 1964 Act respectively and section 1(1) and (3) of the 1959 Act was that the sections must be read together as part of the whole Act of 1959. The effect was (i) that the publication referred to in section 2(6) and section 1(3)(b) was a publication resulting from publishing within the meaning of section 1(3) of the 1959 Act, and (ii) that the requirement that the court should have regard to the publication, or contemplated publication, for the purpose of determining obscenity restricted the person referred to in section 1(1) as "likely to read, see or hear" to those who read, saw or heard as the result of such publication.

Att.-Gen.'s Reference (No. 2 of 1975) was followed by the Court of Appeal in *R. v. O'Sullivan* [1995] 1 Cr.App.R. 455.

Time limit

In *R. v. Barton* [1976] Crim.L.R. 514, CA, B had acted in obscene films (made prior to May 1971) which were subsequently distributed for gain. A prosecution against him for having obscene articles for gain and publishing obscene articles was commenced in May 1973. Following his conviction, it was contended on appeal that the prosecution had been commenced out of time as once the films had been made he had no further **31–79** interest in them. In rejecting this approach, the court held that there was overwhelming evidence that B knew that the films were to be distributed for gain; he was an aider and abettor of a continuing offence and committed it upon the same dates as the principals.

Indictment

COUNT 1

STATEMENT OF OFFENCE

31–80 *Publishing an obscene article, contrary to section 2(1) of the* Obscene Publications Act *1959.*

PARTICULARS OF OFFENCE

A B, on the —— day of ——, 20—, sold [or *let on hire* or *gave* or *lent*] [or] [*distributed or circulated*] [or] [*offered for sale* or *for letting on hire*] *an obscene article, namely* —— [adding where necessary] *the particulars of which are deposited with this indictment.*

[Particulars to specify pages and lines complained of when necessary as in a book which may be in the following form:—]

PARTICULARS OF OBSCENE ARTICLES CONTAINED IN [BOOKS] ENTITLED ...

Count 1 of indictment. A book entitled the ——, beginning at p. ——, line ——, and ending at p. ——, line ——, with the words —— (and so on with other counts and passages).

COUNT 2

STATEMENT OF OFFENCE

31–81 *Having an obscene article for publication for gain, contrary to section 2(1) of the* Obscene Publications Act *1959.*

PARTICULARS OF OFFENCE

A B, on the —— day of —— 20—, had an obscene article, namely —— for publication for gain.

[Particulars may be required as in the last precedent.]

The particulars must be handed in with the indictment when it is delivered to the clerk of the court, unless they have already been deposited with him as an exhibit attached to the committal papers: *R. v. Barraclough* [1906] 1 K.B. 201 at 211.

It seems to be no defence that the article is in a foreign language: *R. v. Hirsch*, London County Sessions, March, 1899; 34 L.J.N. 132. But, if it is, a translation of the obscene words must be included in the particulars: see *R. v. Peltier* (1803) 28 St.Tr. 529.

Class of offence and mode of trial

31–82 Both offences contrary to section 2 are class 3 offences, *ante*, § 2–17, triable either way: s.2(1), *ante*, § 31–74.

Sentence

31–83 The maximum sentence for either offence on conviction on indictment is three [five, as from a day to be appointed] years' imprisonment or a fine or both, and on summary conviction is six (12, as from a day to be appointed) months' imprisonment or a fine not exceeding the prescribed sum or both: s.2(1), *ante*, § 31–74. As to the "prescribed sum", see the *MCA* 1980, s.32(2), (9) (*ante*, § 1–75aa).

See CSP, B10–1.3, and *R. v. Holloway*, 4 Cr.App.R.(S.) 128, CA; *R. v. Pace* [1998] 1 Cr.App.R.(S.) 121, CA; *R. v. Ibrahim* [1998] 1 Cr.App.R.(S.) 157, CA; and *R. v. Tunnicliffe and Greenwood* [1999] 2 Cr.App.R.(S.) 88, CA (all cases involving "front men" in video shops). In the last of these, it was said that a prison sentence would not always be necessary. For a case involving the shopkeeper himself, see *R. v. Singh (Jasjit)* [1999] 2 Cr.App.R.(S.) 160, CA.

As to the obligation to order forfeiture of articles seized under section 3 on conviction of an offence of having articles for publication for gain, see section 1(4) of the 1964 Act, *ante*, § 31–76.

(d) *Search, seizure and forfeiture*

Obscene Publications Act 1959, s.3

3.—(1) If a justice of the peace is satisfied by information on oath that there is reasonable ground for suspecting that, in any premises, or on any stall or vehicle, being premises or a stall or vehicle specified in the information, obscene articles are, or are from time to time, kept for publication for gain, the justice may issue a warrant under his hand empowering any constable to enter (if need be by force) and search the premises, or to search the stall or vehicle ... and to seize and remove any articles found therein or thereon which the constable has reason to believe to be obscene articles and to be kept for publication for gain. **31–84**

(2) A warrant under the foregoing subsection shall, if any obscene articles are seized under the warrant, also empower the seizure and removal of any documents found in the premises or, as the case may be, on the stall or vehicle which relate to a trade or business carried on at the premises or from the stall or vehicle.

(3) Subject to subsection (3A) of this section any articles seized under subsection (1) of this section shall be brought before a justice of the peace acting in the local justice area in which the articles were seized may thereupon issue a summons to the occupier of the premises or, as the case may be, the user of the stall or vehicle to appear on a day specified in the summons before a magistrates' court acting in that local justice area to show cause why the articles or any of them should not be forfeited; and if the court is satisfied, as respects any of the articles, that at the time when they were seized they were obscene articles kept for publication for gain, the court shall order those articles to be forfeited:

Provided that if the person summoned does not appear, the court shall not make an order unless service of the summons is proved.

Provided also that this subsection does not apply in relation to any article seized under subsection (1) of this section which is returned to the occupier of the premises or, as the case may be, to the user of the stall or vehicle in or on which it was found.

(3A) Without prejudice to the duty of a court to make an order for the forfeiture of an article where section 1(4) of the *Obscene Publications Act* 1964 applies (orders made on conviction), in a case where by virtue of subsection (3A) of section 2 of this Act proceedings under the said section 2 for having an article for publication for gain could not be instituted except by or with the consent of the Director of Public Prosecutions, no order for the forfeiture of the article shall be made under this section unless the warrant under which the article was seized was issued on an information laid by or on behalf of the Director of Public Prosecutions. **31–85**

(4) In addition to the person summoned, any other person being the owner, author or maker of any of the articles brought before the court, or any other person through whose hands they had passed before being seized, shall be entitled to appear before the court on the day specified in the summons to show cause why they should not be forfeited.

(5) Where an order is made under this section for the forfeiture of any articles, any person who appeared, or was entitled to appear, to show cause against the making of the order may appeal to the Crown Court, and no such order shall take effect until the expiration of the period within which notice of appeal to the Crown Court may be given against the order, or, if before the expiration thereof notice of appeal is duly given or application is made for the statement of a case for the opinion of the High Court, until the final determination or abandonment of the proceedings on the appeal or case.

(6) If as respects any articles brought before it the court does not order forfeiture, the court may if it thinks fit order the person on whose information the warrant for the seizure of the articles was issued to pay such costs as the court thinks reasonable to any person who has appeared before the court to show cause why those articles should not be forfeited; and costs ordered to be paid under this subsection shall be enforceable as a civil debt.

(7) For the purposes of this section the question whether an article is obscene shall be determined on the assumption that copies of it would be published in any manner likely having regard to the circumstances in which it was found, but in no other manner.

(8) [*Repeal of* Obscene Publications Act *1857*.]

[This section is printed as amended, and repealed in part, by the *Courts Act* 1971, s.56(2), Sched. 8, para. 37, and Sched. 9, Pt I; the *CLA* 1977, ss.53(5), 65(4), and Sched. 12; the *PACE Act* 1984, s.119(2) and Sched. 7, Pt I; and the *Courts Act* 2003, s.109(1), and Sched. 8, para. 106.]

Section 3(3) applies in relation to an item seized under section 50 of the *CJPA* 2001 (*ante*, § 15–124) as if the item had been seized under subsection (1): *CJPA* 2001, s.70 and Sched. 2, para. 10.

31–86 A justice of the peace shall not issue a warrant under section 3(1) of the 1959 Act except on an information laid by or on behalf of the Director of Public Prosecutions or by a constable: *CJA* 1967, s.25.

In *Darbo v. DPP, The Times*, July 11, 1991, DC, a warrant which purported to confer power to seize, *inter alia*, "any other material of a sexually explicit nature, also any material relating to the running of the business" was held to be bad in law as section 3 only referred to "obscene" articles; articles which were sexually explicit were not necessarily obscene.

A warrant under section 3 authorises only one entry, search and seizure; it is then spent: *R. v. Adams* [1980] Q.B. 575, 70 Cr.App.R. 149, CA.

Proper approach to forfeiture proceedings

31–87 It is not necessary for a justice to read every word of a book which is the subject of forfeiture proceedings. It is sufficient if he has made himself fully acquainted with the book as a whole so that he is in a position to pass judgment upon it. Accordingly, in proceedings presided over by six justices and involving 34 books, where, although not all the books had been read by all the justices (the books had been divided and each book had been read by at least two justices), all the books had been discussed and a collective opinion formed, the course taken by the justices was wholly proper: *Olympia Press Ltd v. Hollis* [1974] 1 All E.R. 108, DC. Where the defence of public good is raised, it is for the justices to conduct the proceedings in a manner which they think to be right and which will do justice to the prosecution and defence. Each case must depend on its own facts. In *Olympia Press Ltd*, *ante*, it was held that the justices had acted properly in first determining the issues of obscenity and then inviting the company to adduce its evidence and arguments upon the issue of public good.

On appeal under section 3(5) to the Crown Court against a forfeiture order under section 3(3), the judge is entitled to decline to inspect each article said to be obscene and to direct that the police divide the material into categories of pornographic behaviour or sexual perversions. From those categories, the judge can then take a number of articles at random to sample. They should be shown to the defence as an indication of the basis on which he has reached his decision: *R. v. Snaresbrook Crown Court, ex p. Commr of Police of the Metropolis*, 79 Cr.App.R. 184, DC.

As to forfeiture of articles intended for publication outside England and Wales, see *Gold Star Publications Ltd v. DPP*, 73 Cr.App.R. 141, HL, *ante*, § 31–67.

(e) *Defence of public good*

Obscene Publications Act 1959, s.4

31–88 **4.**—(1) Subject to subsection (1A) of this section a person shall not be convicted of an offence against section two of this Act, and an order for forfeiture shall not be made under the foregoing section, if it is proved that publication of the article in question is justified as being for the public good on the ground that it is in the interests of science, literature, art or learning, or of other objects of general concern.

(1A) Subsection (1) of this section shall not apply where the article in question is a moving picture film or soundtrack, but—

(a) a person shall not be convicted of an offence against section 2 of this Act in relation to any such film or soundtrack, and

(b) an order for forfeiture of any such film or soundtrack shall not be made under section 3 of this Act,

if it is proved that publication of the film or soundtrack is justified as being for the public good on the ground that it is in the interests of drama, opera, ballet or any other art, or of literature or learning.

(2) It is hereby declared that the opinion of experts as to the literary, artistic, scientific or other merits of an article may be admitted in any proceedings under this Act either to establish or to negative the said ground.

(3) In this section "moving picture soundtrack" means any sound record designed for playing with a moving picture film, whether incorporated with the film or not.

[This section is printed as amended by the *CLA* 1977, s.53(6), (7).]

Direction to jury

Where a defence is raised under section 4, the jury should be directed that they only consider the question of public good after they have come to the conclusion that the article is obscene. They must then consider, on the one hand, the number of readers they believe would tend to be depraved and corrupted by the book, the strength of the tendency to deprave and corrupt and the nature of the depravity or corruption. On the other hand, they should assess the strength of the literary, sociological or ethical merit which they consider the book to possess. They should then weigh up all these factors and decide whether on balance the publication is proved to be justified as being for the public good: *R. v. Calder and Boyars Ltd* [1969] 1 Q.B. 151, 52 Cr.App.R. 706, CA. It seems clear that the onus is on the accused to establish the defence on a balance of probabilities: *ibid*. See also *DPP v. Jordan* [1977] A.C. 699, HL, in which it was said that the proper course was to direct the jury to determine the issues (a) whether the article is obscene, and (b) whether it was published by the defendant, before considering whether the defendant had succeeded in establishing a defence under section 4. **31–89**

"other objects of general concern"

The structure of section 4 makes it clear that the words "or of other objects of general concern" fall within the same field or dimension as "science, literature, art or learning": *DPP v. Jordan*, *ante*. Accordingly, evidence to the effect that pornographic material is psychologically beneficial to persons with certain sexual tendencies in that it relieves their sexual tensions and may divert them from anti-social activities is inadmissible: *ibid*. **31–89a**

"learning"

Jordan, *ante*, was applied in *Att.-Gen.'s Reference (No. 3 of 1977)*, 67 Cr.App.R. 393, CA, where the judge had permitted the defence to call expert evidence in order to establish that certain magazines contained material which had merit in the field of sex education or had value in teaching about sexual matters or providing information about sexual matters, such evidence being called with a view to establishing the defence of "public good" on the ground of being in the interests of learning. *Held*: the word "learning" in section 4(1) is a noun, being the product of scholarship, something with inherent excellence gained by the work of a scholar; and expert evidence called under section 4 is not admissible on the issue of obscenity. As to the limited circumstances in which expert evidence may be called on the issue of obscenity, see *ante*, § 31–68. **31–90**

"other merits"

The words "other merits" in section 4(2) include ethical merits: *R. v. Penguin Books Ltd* [1961] Crim.L.R. 176, CCC; *R. v. Calder and Boyars Ltd*, *ante*. See too, observations in *DPP v. A. and B.C. Chewing Gum Ltd* [1968] 1 Q.B. 159, a decision described as "highly exceptional" by the Court of Appeal in *R. v. Anderson* [1972] 1 Q.B. 304, 56 Cr.App.R. 115, *ante*, § 31–68. **31–91**

Evidence of other books

In *R. v. Penguin Books Ltd*, *ante*, Byrne J. ruled that where a defence of public good is raised, evidence relating to other books and their literary merits may be admitted to establish the "climate of literature". But it is not permissible to prove that other books as obscene as the one in issue are in circulation and have not been the subject of a charge (*ante*, § 31–70). **31–92**

(f) *Television and sound programmes*

Section 162(1) of the *Broadcasting Act* 1990 amends the 1959 Act so as to extend the concept of "publication": see *ante*, § 31–72. Section 162(2) gives effect to Schedule 15 for the purpose of supplementing subsection (1). **31–93**

Broadcasting Act 1990, Sched. 15

Section 162

SCHEDULE 15

APPLICATION OF 1959 ACT TO TELEVISION AND SOUND PROGRAMMES

Interpretation

31–94 1. In this Schedule—

"the 1959 Act" means the *Obscene Publications Act* 1959;

"relevant programme" means a programme included in a programme service;

and other expressions used in this Schedule which are also used in the 1959 Act have the same meaning as in that Act.

Liability of person providing live programme material

2. Where—

(a) any matter is included by any person in a relevant programme in circumstances falling within section 1(5) of the 1959 Act, and

(b) that matter has been provided, for inclusion in that programme, by some other person,

the 1959 Act shall have effect as if that matter had been included in that programme by that other person (as well as by the person referred to in sub-paragraph (a)).

Obscene articles kept for inclusion in programmes

3. It is hereby declared that where a person has an obscene article in his ownership, possession or control with a view to the matter recorded on it being included in a relevant programme, the article shall be taken for purposes of the 1959 Act to be an obscene article had or kept by that person for publication for gain.

Requirement of consent of Director of Public Prosecutions

31–95 4.—(1) Proceedings for an offence under section 2 of the 1959 Act for publishing an obscene article shall not be instituted except by or with the consent of the Director of Public Prosecutions in any case where—

(a) the relevant publication, or

(b) the only other publication which followed from the relevant publication,

took place in the course of the inclusion of a programme in a programme service; and in this sub-paragraph "the relevant publication" means the publication in respect of which the defendant would be charged if the proceedings were brought.

(2) Proceedings for an offence under section 2 of the 1959 Act for having an obscene article for publication for gain shall not be instituted except by or with the consent of the Director of Public Prosecutions in any case where—

(a) the relevant publication, or

(b) the only other publication which could reasonably have been expected to follow from the relevant publication,

was to take place in the course of the inclusion of a programme in a programme service; and in this sub-paragraph "the relevant publication" means the publication which, if the proceedings were brought, the defendant would be alleged to have had in contemplation.

(3) [*Corresponds to s.3(3A) of 1959 Act*, ante, *§ 31–85, with substitution of reference to "sub-paragraph (2) above" for reference to "subsection (3A) of section 2 of this Act"*.]

Defences

31–96 5.—(1) A person shall not be convicted of an offence under section 2 of the 1959 Act in respect of the inclusion of any matter in a relevant programme if he proves that he did not know and had no reason to suspect that the programme would include matter rendering him liable to be convicted of such an offence.

(2) Where the publication in issue in any proceedings under that Act consists of the inclusion of any matter in a relevant programme, section 4(1) of that Act (general defence of public good) shall not apply; but—

(a) a person shall not be convicted of an offence under section 2 of that Act, and

(b) an order for forfeiture shall not be made under section 3 of that Act,

if it is proved that the inclusion of the matter in question in a relevant programme is justified as being for the public good on the ground that it is in the interests of—

(i) drama, opera, ballet or any other art,
(ii) science, literature or learning, or
(iii) any other objects of general concern.

(3) Section 4(2) of that Act (admissibility of opinions of experts) shall apply for the purposes of sub-paragraph (2) above as it applies for the purposes of section 4(1) and (1A) of that Act.

Exclusion of proceedings under common law

6. Without prejudice to section 2(4) of the 1959 Act, a person shall not be proceeded against for an offence at common law—

(a) in respect of a relevant programme or anything said or done in the course of such programme, where it is of the essence of the common law offence that the programme or (as the case may be) what was said or done was obscene, indecent, offensive, disgusting or injurious to morality; or

(b) in respect of an agreement to cause a programme to be included in a programme service or to cause anything to be said or done in the course of a programme which is to be so included, where the common law offence consists of conspiring to corrupt public morals or to do any act contrary to public morals or decency.

(2) Postal Services Act 2000

See section 85 of the 2000 Act, *ante*, § 25–352. **31–97**

[The next paragraph is § 31–99.]

(3) Theatres Act 1968

Theatres Act 1968, s.2

Prohibition of presentation of obscene performances of plays

2.—(1) For the purposes of this section a performance of a play shall be deemed to be obscene if, taken as a whole, its effect was such as to tend to deprave and corrupt persons who were likely, having regard to all relevant circumstances, to attend it. **31–99**

(2) Subject to sections 3 and 7 of this Act, if an obscene performance of a play is given, whether in public or private, any person who (whether for gain or not) presented or directed that performance shall be liable—

(a) on summary conviction, to a fine not exceeding the prescribed sum or to imprisonment for a term not exceeding *six* [12] months;

(b) on conviction on indictment, to a fine or to imprisonment for a term not exceeding three years or both.

(3) A prosecution on indictment for an offence under this section shall not be commenced more than two years after the commission of the offence.

(4) No persons shall be proceeded against in respect of a performance of a play or anything said or done in the course of such a performance—

(a) for an offence at common law where it is of the essence of the offence that the performance or, as the case may be, what was said or done was obscene, indecent, offensive, disgusting or injurious to morality; or

(b) [*repealed by* Indecent Displays (Control) Act *1981*];

(c) [*repealed by* Civic Government (Scotland) Act *1982*];

and no person shall be proceeded against for an offence at common law of conspiring to corrupt public morals, or to do any act contrary to public morals or decency, in respect of an agreement to present or give a performance of a play, or to cause anything to be said or done in the course of such a performance.

[This section is printed as amended by the *MCA* 1980, s.32(2) (substitution of reference to "the prescribed sum") (*ante*, § 1–30). In subs. (2)(a), "12" is substituted for "six", as from a day to be appointed, by the *CJA* 2003, s.282(2) and (3). The increase has no application to offences committed before the substitution takes effect: s.282(4).]

As to a script as evidence of what was performed, see section 9, *post*, § 31–103.

Sentences of 15 months' imprisonment were upheld in *R. v. Brownson* [1971] Crim.L.R. 551—the first prosecution under the Act.

Theatres Act 1968, s.3

Defence of public good

31–100 **3.**—(1) A person shall not be convicted of an offence under section 2 of this Act if it is proved that the giving of the performance in question was justified as being for the public good on the ground that it was in the interests of drama, opera, ballet or any other art, or of literature or learning.

(2) It is hereby declared that the opinion of experts as to the artistic, literary or other merits of a performance of a play may be admitted in any proceedings for an offence under section 2 of this Act either to establish or negative the said ground.

Authorities decided in the context of the *Obscene Publications Act* 1959 should be referred to when considering the effect of sections 2 and 3: see *ante*, §§ 31–63 *et seq.*

Theatres Act 1968, ss.7, 8

Exceptions for performances given in certain circumstances

31–101 **7.**—(1) Nothing in sections 2 to 4 of this Act shall apply in relation to a performance of a play given on a domestic occasion in a private dwelling.

(2) Nothing in sections 2 to 6 of this Act shall apply in relation to a performance of a play given solely or primarily for one or more of the following purposes, that is to say—

(a) rehearsal; or

(b) to enable—

(i) a record or cinematograph film to be made from or by means of the performance; or

(ii) the performance to be broadcast; or

(iii) the performance to be included in a programme service (within the meaning of the *Broadcasting Act* 1990) other than a sound or television broadcasting service;

but in any proceedings for an offence under section 2 ... or 6 of this Act alleged to have been committed in respect of a performance of a play or an offence at common law alleged to have been committed in England and Wales by the publication of defamatory matter in the course of a performance of a play, if it is proved that the performance was attended by persons other than persons directly connected with the giving of the performance or the doing in relation thereto of any of the things mentioned in paragraph (b) above, the performance shall be taken not to have been given solely or primarily for one or more of the said purposes unless the contrary is shown.

(3) In this section—

"broadcast" means broadcast by wireless telegraphy (within the meaning of the *Wireless Telegraphy Act* 1949), whether by way of sound broadcasting or television;

"cinematograph film" means any print, negative, tape or other article on which a performance of a play or any part of such a performance is recorded for the purposes of visual reproduction;

"record" means any record or similar contrivance for reproducing sound, including the sound-track of a cinematograph film; ...

[This section is printed as amended by the *Cable and Broadcasting Act* 1984, s.57(1) and Sched. 5, para. 21(2); the *Public Order Act* 1986, Sched. 3; and the *Broadcasting Act* 1990, s.203(1), Sched. 20, para. 13.]

Section 4 extends the law of defamation (*ante*, § 29–73); section 6 creates a summary offence relating to the public performance of a play involving the use of threatening or abusive words or behaviour.

Restriction on institution of proceedings

31–102 **8.** Proceedings for an offence under section 2 ... or 6 of this Act or an offence at common law committed by the publication of defamatory matter in the course of a performance of a play shall not be instituted in England and Wales except by or with the consent of the Attorney-General.

[This section is printed as amended by the *Public Order Act* 1986, Sched. 3.]

Theatres Act 1968, ss.9, 10

Script as evidence of what was performed

31–103 **9.**—(1) Where a performance of a play was based on a script, then, in any proceedings for an offence under section 2 ... or 6 of this Act alleged to have been committed in respect of that performance—

(a) an actual script on which that performance was based shall be admissible as evidence of what was performed and of the manner in which the performance or any part of it was given; and

(b) if such a script is given in evidence on behalf of any party to the proceedings then, except in so far as the contrary is shown, whether by evidence given on behalf of the same or any other party, the performance shall be taken to have been given in accordance with that script.

(2) In this Act "script", in relation to a performance of a play, means the text of the play (whether expressed in words or in musical or other notation) together with any stage or other directions for its performance, whether contained in a single document or not.

[This section is printed as amended by the *Public Order Act* 1986, Sched. 3.]

Power to make copies of scripts

10.—(1) If a police officer of or above the rank of superintendent has reasonable grounds for suspecting— **31–104**

(a) that an offence under section 2 ... or 6 of this Act has been committed by any person in respect of a performance of a play; or

(b) that a performance of a play is to be given and that an offence under the said section 2 ... or 6 is likely to be committed by any person in respect of that performance,

he may make an order in writing under this section relating to that person and that performance.

(2) Every order made under this section shall be signed by the police officer by whom it is made, shall name the person to whom it relates, and shall describe the performance to which it relates in a manner sufficient to enable that performance to be identified.

(3) Where an order under this section has been made, any police officer, on production if so required of the order—

(a) may require the person named in the order to produce, if such a thing exists, an actual script on which the performance was or, as the case may be, will be based; and

(b) if such a script is produced to him, may require the person so named to afford him an opportunity of causing a copy thereof to be made.

(4) Any person who without reasonable excuse fails to comply with a requirement under subsection (3) above shall be liable on summary conviction to a fine not exceeding level 3 on the standard scale.

(5) Where, in the case of a performance of a play based on a script a copy of an actual script on which that performance was based has been made by or on behalf of a police officer by virtue of an order under this section relating to that performance, section 9(1) of this Act shall apply in relation to that copy as it applies in relation to an actual script on which the performance was based.

[This section is printed as amended by the *CJA* 1982, ss.38 and 46; and the *Public Order Act* 1986, Sched. 3.]

As to "the standard scale", see *ante*, § 5–403.

Theatres Act 1968, ss.16, 18

Offences by bodies corporate

16. Where any offence under this Act committed by a body corporate is proved to have been committed with the consent or connivance of, or to be attributable to any neglect on the part of, any director, manager, secretary or other similar officer of the body corporate, or any person purporting to act in any such capacity, he as well as the body corporate shall be guilty of that offence and shall be liable to be proceeded against and punished accordingly. **31–105**

See *R. v. Boal* [1992] 1 Q.B. 591, 95 Cr.App.R. 272, CA (*ante*, § 30–103).

Interpretation

18.—(1) In this Act— **31–106**

"licensing authority" [*definition now applies only in relation to Scotland*]

"play" means—

(a) any dramatic piece, whether involving improvisation or not, which is given wholly or in part by one or more persons actually present and performing and in which the whole or a major proportion of what is done by the person or persons performing, whether by way of speech, singing or action, involves the playing of a role; and

(b) any ballet given wholly or in part by one or more persons actually present and performing, whether or not it falls within paragraph (a) of this definition;

"police officer" means a member ... of a police force;

"premises" includes any place;

"public performance" includes any performance in a public place within the meaning of the *Public Order Act* 1936, and any performance which the public or any section thereof are permitted to attend, whether on payment or otherwise;

"script" has the meaning assigned by section 9 (2) of this Act.

(2) For the purposes of this Act—

(a) a person shall not be treated as presenting a performance of a play by reason only of his taking part therein as a performer;

(b) a person taking part as a performer in a performance of a play directed by another person shall be treated as a person who directed the performance if without reasonable excuse he performs otherwise than in accordance with that person's direction; and

(c) a person shall be taken to have directed a performance of a play given under his direction notwithstanding that he was not present during the performance;

and a person shall not be treated as aiding or abetting the commission of an offence under section 2 ... or 6 of this Act in respect of a performance of a play by reason only of his taking part in that performance as a performer.

[This section is printed as amended, and repealed in part, by the *Local Government Act* 1972, s.204(6); the *Public Order Act* 1986, Sched. 3; the *Local Government (Wales) Act* 1994, Sched. 16; and the *Licensing Act* 2003, s.199, and Sched. 7.]

For the definition of "public place" in the *Public Order Act* 1936, see section 9 thereof, *ante*, § 25–292.

(4) Protection of Children Act 1978

Protection of Children Act 1978, ss.1–1B

Indecent photographs of children

31–107 **1.**—(1) Subject to sections 1A and 1B, it is an offence for a person—

(a) to take, or permit to be taken, or to make any indecent photograph or pseudo-photograph of a child; or

(b) to distribute or show such indecent photographs or pseudo-photographs; or

(c) to have in his possession such indecent photographs or pseudo-photographs, with a view to their being distributed or shown by himself or others; or

(d) to publish or cause to be published any advertisement likely to be understood as conveying that the advertiser distributes or shows such indecent photographs or pseudo-photographs, or intends to do so.

(2) For purposes of this Act, a person is to be regarded as distributing an indecent photograph or pseudo-photograph if he parts with possession of it to, or exposes or offers it for acquisition by, another person.

(3) Proceedings for an offence under this Act shall not be instituted except by or with the consent of the Director of Public Prosecutions.

(4) Where a person is charged with an offence under subsection (1)(b) or (c), it shall be a defence for him to prove—

(a) that he had a legitimate reason for distributing or showing the photographs or pseudo-photographs or (as the case may be) having them in his possession; or

(b) that he had not himself seen the photographs or pseudo-photographs and did not know, nor had any cause to suspect them to be indecent.

(5) References in the *Children and Young Persons Act* 1933 (except in sections 15 and 99) to the offences mentioned in Schedule 1 to that Act shall include an offence under subsection (1)(a) above.

(6) [*Repealed by* Extradition Act *1989, s.37(1) and Sched. 2.*]

(7) [*Amendment to* Visiting Forces Act *1952.*]

[This section is printed as amended and repealed in part by the *CJPOA* 1994, ss.84(2) and 168(3) and Sched. 11; and the *SOA* 2003, s.139, and Sched. 6, para. 24.]

Marriage and other relationships

31–107a **1A.**—(1) This section applies where, in proceedings for an offence under section 1(1)(a) of taking or making an indecent photograph of a child, or for an offence under section 1(1)(b) or (c) relating to an indecent photograph of a child, the defendant proves that the photograph was of the child aged 16 or over, and that at the time of the offence charged the child and he—

(a) were married or civil partners of each other, or

(b) lived together as partners in an enduring family relationship.

(2) Subsections (5) and (6) also apply where, in proceedings for an offence under section 1(1)(b) or (c) relating to an indecent photograph of a child, the defendant proves that the photograph was of the child aged 16 or over, and that at the time when he obtained it the child and he—

(a) were married or civil partners of each other, or

(b) lived together as partners in an enduring family relationship.

(3) This section applies whether the photograph showed the child alone or with the defendant, but not if it showed any other person.

(4) In the case of an offence under section 1(1)(a), if sufficient evidence is adduced to raise an issue as to whether the child consented to the photograph being taken or made, or as to whether the defendant reasonably believed that the child so consented, the defendant is not guilty of the offence unless it is proved that the child did not so consent and that the defendant did not reasonably believe that the child so consented.

(5) In the case of an offence under section 1(1)(b), the defendant is not guilty of the offence unless it is proved that the showing or distributing was to a person other than the child.

(6) In the case of an offence under section 1(1)(c), if sufficient evidence is adduced to raise an issue both—

(a) as to whether the child consented to the photograph being in the defendant's possession, or as to whether the defendant reasonably believed that the child so consented, and

(b) as to whether the defendant had the photograph in his possession with a view to its being distributed or shown to anyone other than the child,

the defendant is not guilty of the offence unless it is proved either that the child did not so consent and that the defendant did not reasonably believe that the child so consented, or that the defendant had the photograph in his possession with a view to its being distributed or shown to a person other than the child.

Exception for criminal proceedings, investigations etc.

1B.—(1) In proceedings for an offence under section 1(1)(a) of making an indecent photograph or pseudo-photograph of a child, the defendant is not guilty of the offence if he proves that— **31–107b**

(a) it was necessary for him to make the photograph or pseudo-photograph for the purposes of the prevention, detection or investigation of crime, or for the purposes of criminal proceedings, in any part of the world,

(b) at the time of the offence charged he was a member of the Security Service [or the Secret Intelligence Service], and it was necessary for him to make the photograph or pseudo-photograph for the exercise of any of the functions of *the* [that] Service, or

(c) at the time of the offence charged he was a member of GCHQ, and it was necessary for him to make the photograph or pseudo-photograph for the exercise of any of the functions of GCHQ.

(2) In this section "GCHQ" has the same meaning as in the *Intelligence Services Act* 1994.

[Ss.1A and 1B were inserted by the *SOA* 2003, ss.45(1) and (3), and 46(1). S.1A is printed as amended by the *Civil Partnership Act* 2004, s.261(1), and Sched. 27, para. 60. The words in square brackets in s.1B are inserted, and the italicised word is omitted, as from a day to be appointed, by the *CJIA* 2008, s.69(1) and (2).]

Drafting the indictment

See the guidance given in relation to section 160 of the *CJA* 1988 in *R. v. Thompson (Richard)* [2004] 2 Cr.App.R. 16, CA (*post*, § 31–117), which is likely to be carried across to the 1978 Act, although caution will be required as good practice in relation to offences the essence of which is "possession" may not be so readily applied to offences involving an activity such as "taking" or "making". **31–108**

Ingredients of the offences

31–108a The circumstances in which the alleged indecent photograph of a child was taken and the motives of the photographer are not relevant to the question whether the photograph is, in fact, indecent for the purposes of section 1(1)(a). In a case of "taking" the jury must consider two questions: (a) is it proved that the defendant deliberately and intentionally took the photograph of the subject as disclosed by the photograph produced; and (b) if so, is it indecent? In deciding (b), the jury have to apply the test as stated in *R. v. Stamford* [1972] 2 Q.B. 391 at 398, 56 Cr.App.R. 398 at 405, of applying the recognised standards of propriety. The circumstances and motivation of the taker of a photograph might be relevant to his *mens rea* as to whether his taking was intentional or accidental—they are not relevant to whether the photograph is indecent: *R. v. Graham-Kerr*, 88 Cr.App.R. 302, CA; and *R. v. Smethurst* [2002] 1 Cr.App.R. 6, CA (in which an argument to the effect that the conclusion in *Graham-Kerr* was incompatible with the right to freedom of expression as guaranteed by Article 10 of the ECHR (*ante*, § 16–119) was rejected). The word "indecent" in section 1(1) qualifies the words which follow it—"photograph of a child". Accordingly, since the jury must of necessity know the age of the child, they are entitled to have regard to that age when answering the question "is this an indecent photograph of a child?": *R. v. Owen (C. W.)*, 86 Cr.App.R. 291, CA.

In *R. v. Smith*; *R. v. Jayson* [2003] 1 Cr.App.R. 13, CA, it was held: (i) that where a person opens an attachment to an email that contains an indecent photograph or pseudo-photograph of a child, he may be said to "make" that photograph or pseudo-photograph within section 1(1)(a), and he will be guilty of an offence contrary to that provision if it is established that when he opened the attachment he did so intentionally and with knowledge that what he was making was, or was likely to be an indecent image of a child; (ii) that the mere act of downloading a photograph or pseudo-photograph from the internet to a computer screen could also be said to constitute the "making" of a photograph or pseudo-photograph, and that a person who did such an act intentionally and knowing that the image was, or was likely to be an indecent image of a child, would be guilty of an offence under section 1(1)(a); and (iii) that in neither case was it necessary to prove that the individual did any act with a view to saving the image on his computer. See also *R. v. Bowden* [2000] 1 Cr.App.R. 438, CA (*post*, § 31–114); *Atkins v. DPP*; *Goodland v. DPP* [2000] 2 Cr.App.R. 248, DC. These authorities were considered in *R. v. Harrison* [2008] 1 Cr.App.R. 29, CA, in which it was held that where the appellant had accessed legal pornograhic websites in which indecent photographs of children had appeared by way of an automatic "pop-up" mechanism, it was the appellant and not the web-designer who was the maker of the image. As to *mens rea*, the jury had to be sure that the appellant knew about the "pop-up" activity when he accessed the adult pornographic sites and that, in accessing those sites, there was a likelihood that the "pop-ups" would include illegal images: *ibid*.

A person who responded to an advertisement offering to supply indecent photographs of children by placing an order for the supply of such photographs could be charged with the common law offence of inciting the commission of an offence of distribution of indecent photographs of children, contrary to section 1(1)(b), or with an attempt at such incitement (depending on whether the order was received by the incitee); if the incitee supplied photographs pursuant to the order, that supply would constitute a separate and distinct offence of distribution from any offence that might have been committed by virtue of the publication of the advertisement itself: *R. v. Goldman* [2001] Crim.L.R. 822, CA. As to incitement to distribute at common law, see also *R. (O.) v. Coventry Magistrates' Court* [2004] Crim.L.R. 948, DC (§ 33–88 in the supplement). The common law offence of incitement has been abolished and replaced (in relation to acts done on or after October 1, 2008) by the statutory offences consisting of the doing of acts capable of encouraging or assisting crime under the *SCA* 2007, Pt 2 (*post*, §§ 33–92 *et seq.*).

To be guilty of an offence contrary to section 1(1)(c), a person must have a view to showing the photographs to another or others; a view only to show them to himself is insufficient: *R. v. E.T.*, 163 J.P. 349, CA. Where indecent images of which the defendant was in possession were left by him in a location where they were likely to be seen by others, his knowledge that this was so would be insufficient to bring him within the subsection; the prosecution would have to show that one of his reasons for keeping or leaving them in that particular location was to enable others to view them: *R. v. Dooley* [2006] 1 Cr.App.R. 21, CA.

Where a person provides another with a password to enable him to access data stored on a computer, he may be said to be "showing" him the matter so stored: *R. v. Fellows and Arnold* [1997] 1 Cr.App.R. 244, CA.

A conspiracy to distribute indecent photographs must relate to distribution to one or more persons outside the conspiracy: *R. v. Barker* [1998] 5 *Archbold News* 1, CA (97 05014 Z5).

If the defence of "legitimate reason" (subs. (4)(a)) is raised, the issue is one of fact; academic research might be such a reason, but a court would plainly be entitled to approach such a claim with a measure of scepticism: *Atkins v. DPP*; *Goodland v. DPP*, *ante*.

Protection of Children Act 1978, s.2

Evidence

2.—(1) [*Repealed by* Police and Criminal Evidence Act *1984, Sched.* 7.] **31–109**

(2) [*Repealed by* Magistrates' Courts Act *1980, Sched. 9*.]

(3) In proceedings under this Act relating to indecent photographs of children a person is to be taken as having been a child at any material time if it appears, from the evidence as a whole, that he was then under the age of 18.

[Subs. (3) is printed as amended by the *CJPOA* 1994, s.168(2), and Sched. 10, para. 37; and the *SOA* 2003, s.45(2) (substitution of "18" for "16" in subs. (3)).]

The purpose of expert evidence being to assist the court with information that is outside the normal experience of the court, expert paediatric evidence as to the age of a child shown in a photograph is inadmissible: *R. v. Land* [1998] 1 Cr.App.R. 301, CA.

Protection of Children Act 1978, ss.3–5

Offences by corporations

3.—(1) Where a body corporate is guilty of an offence under this Act and it is proved that the offence occurred with the consent or connivance of, or was attributable to any neglect on the part of, any director, manager, secretary or other officer of the body, or any person who was purporting to act in any such capacity he, as well as the body corporate, shall be deemed to be guilty of that offence and shall be liable to be proceeded against and punished accordingly. **31–110**

(2) Where the affairs of a body corporate are managed by its members, subsection (1) shall apply in relation to the acts and defaults of a member in connection with his functions of management as if he were a director of the body corporate.

See *R. v. Boal* [1992] 1 Q.B. 591, 95 Cr.App.R. 272, CA (*ante*, § 30–103).

Entry, search and seizure

4.—(1) The following applies where a justice of the peace is satisfied by information on oath, laid by or on behalf of the Director of Public Prosecutions or by a constable, that there is reasonable ground for suspecting that, in any premises, there is an indecent photograph or pseudo-photograph of a child. **31–111**

(2) The justice may issue a warrant under his hand authorising any constable to enter (if need be by force) and search the premises … and to seize and remove any articles which he believes (with reasonable cause) to be or include indecent photographs or pseudo-photographs of children.

(4) In this section "premises" has the same meaning as in the *Police and Criminal Evidence Act* 1984 (see section 23 of that Act).

[This section is printed as amended and repealed in part by the *CJA* 1988, s.170(1) and Sched. 15, para. 61; the *CJPOA* 1994, s.168(1), (2) and Scheds 9, para. 23, and 10, para. 37; the *Courts Act* 2003, s.109(1), and Sched. 8, para. 199; and the *PJA* 2006, ss.39(1) and (2), and 52, and Sched. 15, Pt 4.]

For section 23 of the 1984 Act, see *ante*, § 15–123.

Forfeiture

Section 5 of the 1978 Act (as substituted by the *PJA* 2006, s.39) gives effect to the **31–112** schedule to the Act. This provides for a revised procedure for the forfeiture of indecent photographs of children which are lawfully in the possession of the police, along with any other material that it is impossible to separate from the indecent photographs. The procedure applies irrespective of how the police came to be in possession of the photographs. It is similar to the procedure, under Schedule 3 to the *CEMA* 1979, for forfeiture, and for the bringing of proceedings in a magistrates' court for the condemnation of any thing as being forfeited, under the customs and excise Acts (as to which, see *ante*, §§ 25–424 *et seq.*). Court proceedings will only be required where a person claims the photographs or other property and the police dispute the claim. Any such proceedings will be initiated in a magistrates' court, and they are deemed by the schedule to be civil proceedings. There is a right of appeal to the Crown Court.

Unlike the original section 5, the schedule does not provide for an order for forfeiture by the court before which a person is convicted of an offence under the 1978 Act. It is anticipated, however, that a court before which such a conviction occurs will wish to consider the question of forfeiture. To that end, it may take advantage of the general power to make a "deprivation" order under section 143(2) of the *PCC(S)A* 2000 (*ante*, § 5–439), but it should be noted that that power only applies to offences consisting of the unlawful possession of property. It would, accordingly, be prudent, where it is desired to provide the court with a sound basis for making a deprivation order, to ensure that there is included in the indictment, assuming that it is otherwise appropriate, a count alleging "possession" of the photographs in question, whatever other allegations may be included. For this purpose, a count under section 1(1)(c) of the 1978 Act (*ante*, § 31–107), or under section 160 of the *CJA* 1988 (*post*, § 31–115), will suffice.

Protection of Children Act 1978, ss.6, 7

Punishments

31–113 **6.**—(1) Offences under this Act shall be punishable either on conviction on indictment or on summary conviction.

(2) A person convicted on indictment of any offence under this Act shall be liable to imprisonment for a term of not more than ten years, or to a fine or to both.

(3) A person convicted summarily of any offence under this Act shall be liable—

(a) to imprisonment for a term not exceeding *six* [12] months; or

(b) to a fine not exceeding the prescribed sum for the purposes of section 32 of the *Magistrates' Courts Act* 1980 (punishment on summary conviction of offences triable either way: £1,000 or other sum substituted by order under that Act), or to both.

[This section is printed as amended by the *MCA* 1980, s.154, and Sched. 7, para. 171; and the *CJCSA* 2000, s.41(1) (substitution of "ten" for "three" in subs. (2)). The latter amendment took effect on January 11, 2001: *Criminal Justice and Court Services Act 2000 (Commencement No. 1) Order* 2000 (S.I. 2000 No. 3302). In subs. (3)(a), "12" is substituted for "six", as from a day to be appointed, by the *CJA* 2003, s.282(2) and (3). The increase has no application to offences committed before the substitution takes effect: s.282(4).]

An offence contrary to section 1 of the 1978 Act is a specified sexual offence within Schedule 15 to the *CJA* 2003 (*ante*, § 5–299).

As to the current value of "the prescribed sum", see *ante*, § 1–75aa.

Guidelines for the sentencing of offenders who fell to be sentenced before May 14, 2007, were to be found in the decision of the Court of Appeal in *R. v. Oliver*; *R. v. Hartrey*; *R. v. Baldwin* [2003] 1 Cr.App.R. 28, CA. For offenders falling to be sentenced on or after that date, see Part 6A of the Sentencing Guidelines Council's definitive guideline for sentencing for sexual offences (Appendix K–101).

In a case of downloading child pornography from the internet, it makes no difference to culpability whether the material was paid for or not; and downloading for research purposes would provide only minimal mitigation: *R. v. Langham* [2007] L.S. Gazette, November 29, 27, CA ([2007] EWCA Crim. 3004).

As to the making of a sexual offences prevention order under section 104 of the *SOA* 2003 in respect of offences under section 1, see *R. v. Terrell* [2008] 2 Cr.App.R.(S.) 49, CA, *ante*, § 20–324.

Interpretation

7.—(1) The following subsections apply for the interpretation of this Act. **31–114**

(2) References to an indecent photograph include an indecent film, a copy of an indecent photograph or film, and an indecent photograph comprised in a film.

(3) Photographs (including those comprised in a film) shall, if they show children and are indecent, be treated for all purposes of this Act as indecent photographs of children and so as respects pseudo-photographs.

(4) References to a photograph include—

(a) the negative as well as the positive version; and

(b) data stored on a computer disc or by other electronic means which is capable of conversion into a photograph.

[(4A) References to a photograph also include—

(a) a tracing or other image, whether made by electronic or other means (of whatever nature)—

(i) which is not itself a photograph or pseudo-photograph, but

(ii) which is derived from the whole or part of a photograph or pseudo-photograph (or a combination of either or both); and

(b) data stored on a computer disc or by other electronic means which is capable of conversion into an image within paragraph (a);

and subsection (8) applies in relation to such an image as it applies in relation to a pseudo-photograph.]

(5) "Film" includes any form of video-recording.

(6) "Child", subject to subsection (8), means a person under the age of 18.

(7) "Pseudo-photograph" means an image, whether made by computer-graphics or otherwise howsoever, which appears to be a photograph.

(8) If the impression conveyed by a pseudo-photograph is that the person shown is a child, the pseudo-photograph shall be treated for all purposes of this Act as showing a child and so shall a pseudo-photograph where the predominant impression conveyed is that the person shown is a child notwithstanding that some of the physical characteristics shown are those of an adult.

(9) References to an indecent pseudo-photograph include—

(a) a copy of an indecent pseudo-photograph; and

(b) data stored on a computer disc or by other electronic means which is capable of conversion into *a* [an indecent] pseudo-photograph.

[This section is printed as amended by the *CJPOA* 1994, s.84(1), (3); and the *SOA* 2003, s.45(2) (substitution of "18" for "16"); and as amended, as from a day to be appointed, by the *CJIA* 2008, s.69(1), (3) and (4) (omission of italicised word, insertion of words in square brackets). The insertion of subs. (4A) applies only in relation to things done after it takes effect: 2008 Act, s.148(2), and Sched. 27, para. 24(1).]

It follows from the provisions of subsections (2) and (4)(b) that to download or print out images from the internet is to "make" a photograph within section 1(1)(a): *R. v. Bowden* [2000] 1 Cr.App.R. 438, CA.

An image made by an item which obviously consisted of parts of two different photographs could not be said to appear to be a photograph, and thus a "pseudo-photograph" within section 7(7): *Atkins v. DPP*; *Goodland v. DPP* [2000] 2 Cr.App.R. 248, DC.

A video which consisted of two parts, the first part being a recording of a television programme showing scenes of a doctor examining the genitalia of a naked boy who suffered from a genital defect, together with commentary which explained what the doctor was doing, and the second part being some of the previous pictures, without the commentary, slowed down and focusing in particular on the manipulation by the doctor of the boy's penis, was capable of being an indecent photograph; the jury were entitled to look at the second part as being a quite separate set of images to those which constituted the programme, and to determine whether the images were, objectively speaking, indecent, applying what they considered to be recognised standards of propriety: *R. v. Murray* [2005] Crim.L.R. 387, CA.

(5) Criminal Justice Act 1988

Criminal Justice Act 1988, ss.160, 160A

Possession of indecent photograph of child

31–115 **160.**—(1) Subject to section 160A, it is an offence for a person to have any indecent photograph or pseudo-photograph of a child in his possession.

(2) Where a person is charged with an offence under subsection (1) above, it shall be a defence for him to prove—

(a) that he had a legitimate reason for having the photograph or pseudo-photograph in his possession; or
(b) that he had not himself seen the photograph or pseudo-photograph and did not know, nor had any cause to suspect, it to be indecent; or
(c) that the photograph or pseudo-photograph was sent to him without any prior request made by him or on his behalf and he did not keep it for an unreasonable time.

(2A) A person shall be liable on conviction on indictment of an offence under this section to imprisonment for a term not exceeding five years or a fine, or both.

(3) A person shall be liable on summary conviction of an offence under this section to imprisonment for a term not exceeding *six* [12] months or a fine not exceeding level 5 on the standard scale, or both.

(4) Sections 1(3), 2(3), 3 and 7 of the *Protection of Children Act* 1978 shall have effect as if any reference in them to that Act included a reference to this section.

[This section is printed as amended and repealed in part by the *CJPOA* 1994, ss.84(4)(a) and (b), 86(1) and 168(3), and Sched. 11; the *CJCSA* 2000, s.41(3) (insertion of subs. (2A)); the *SOA* 2003, s.139, and Sched. 6, para. 29(1) and (3); and the *CJIA* 2008, s.148(1), and Sched. 26, paras 22 and 24. In subs. (3)(a), "12" is substituted for "six", as from a day to be appointed, by the *CJA* 2003, s.282(2) and (3). The increase has no application to offences committed before the substitution takes effect: s.282(4).]

An offence contrary to this section is a specified sexual offence within Schedule 15 to the *CJA* 2003 (*ante*, § 5–299).

Marriage and other relationships

31–116 **160A.**—(1) This section applies where, in proceedings for an offence under section 160 relating to an indecent photograph of a child, the defendant proves that the photograph was of the child aged 16 or over, and that at the time of the offence charged the child and he—

(a) were married or civil partners of each other, or
(b) lived together as partners in an enduring family relationship.

(2) This section also applies where, in proceedings for an offence under section 160 relating to an indecent photograph of a child, the defendant proves that the photograph was of the child aged 16 or over, and that at the time when he obtained it the child and he—

(a) were married or civil partners of each other, or
(b) lived together as partners in an enduring family relationship.

(3) This section applies whether the photograph showed the child alone or with the defendant, but not if it showed any other person.

(4) If sufficient evidence is adduced to raise an issue as to whether the child consented to the photograph being in the defendant's possession, or as to whether the defendant reasonably believed that the child so consented, the defendant is not guilty of the offence unless it is proved that the child did not so consent and that the defendant did not reasonably believe that the child so consented.

[Section 160A was inserted by the *SOA* 2003, s.45(4). It is printed as amended by the *Civil Partnership Act* 2004, s.261(1), and Sched. 27, para. 127.]

Drafting the indictment

31–117 In *R. v. Thompson (Richard)* [2004] 2 Cr.App.R. 16, CA, it was said that in cases where there are significant numbers of photographs, the following practice should be adopted in the drafting of indictments, and could be used in selecting the images for presentation in summary proceedings: (i) in addition to specific counts, there should be a comprehensive count covering the remainder; (ii) the photographs used in the specific counts should, if it is practicable, be selected so as to be broadly representative of the images in the comprehensive count; if agreement can be reached between the parties as to the number of images at each level (as identified in *R. v. Oliver*; *R. v. Hartrey*; *R. v. Baldwin*, *ante*, § 31–113), the need for the judge to view the entirety of the offending material may be avoided; (iii) where it is impracticable to present the court with specific counts that are agreed to be representative of the comprehensive count there must be available to the court an approximate breakdown of the number of images at each of the levels; this may best be achieved by the prosecution providing the defence with a schedule setting out the information and ensuring that the defence have ample opportunity of viewing the images and checking the accuracy of the schedule; (iv) specific counts should make it clear whether the image in question is a real image or a pseudo-image; the same count should not charge both; where there is a dispute there should be alternative counts; (v) each image charged in a specific count should be identified by reference to its "jpg" or other reference so that it is clear with which image the specific count is dealing; and (vi) the estimated age range of the child shown in each of the images should, where possible, be provided to the court.

As to the advisability of including a count of possession (whether contrary to the 1978 Act, s.1(1)(c) (*ante*, § 31–107), or contrary to section 160 of the 1988 Act), see *ante*, § 31–112.

Possession

Where a person views an indecent image of a child on the internet and his computer automatically caches the image, unbeknown to him, he could not be said to be in possession of the photograph in the cache for possession requires some degree of knowledge: *Atkins v. DPP*; *Goodland v. DPP*, *ante*, § 31–108a. The court referred to *R. v. Steele* [1993] Crim.L.R. 298, CA (firearm in holdall, *ante*, § 24–6), but said that it was not the computer that was to be regarded as analogous to the holdall; it was the computer's cache that was to be equated to the holdall for this purpose. **31–118**

In *R. v. Porter* [2006] 2 Cr.App.R. 25, CA, it was held that a person would have possession of indecent images if he had custody or control of them. Where, therefore, the images had been deleted from a person's computer, whether or not he had possession of them would depend on whether or not he had the know-how and the software to allow him to retrieve them, so that it could be said, as a matter of fact, that he had control over them.

Defence

The defence under section 160(2) is available to a defendant, notwithstanding that the prosecution prove possession of an indecent photograph of a child with the mental element identified in *Atkins v. DPP*; *Goodland v. DPP*, *ante*, § 31–108a (*viz.* knowing possession of the article containing the image); it is irrelevant whether the defendant had cause to suspect that the photograph was indecent *per se*, the issue is whether the defendant had cause to suspect it was an indecent photograph of a child: *R. v. Collier* [2005] 1 Cr.App.R. 9, CA. **31–119**

(6) Criminal Justice and Immigration Act 2008

Criminal Justice and Immigration Act 2008, ss.63–68

[Possession of extreme pornographic images

63.—(1) It is an offence for a person to be in possession of an extreme pornographic image. **31–120**

(2) An "extreme pornographic image" is an image which is both—

(a) pornographic, and

(b) an extreme image.

(3) An image is "pornographic" if it is of such a nature that it must reasonably be assumed to have been produced solely or principally for the purpose of sexual arousal.

(4) Where (as found in the person's possession) an image forms part of a series of images, the question whether the image is of such a nature as is mentioned in subsection (3) is to be determined by reference to—

(a) the image itself, and

(b) (if the series of images is such as to be capable of providing a context for the image) the context in which it occurs in the series of images.

(5) So, for example, where—

(a) an image forms an integral part of a narrative constituted by a series of images, and

(b) having regard to those images as a whole, they are not of such a nature that they must reasonably be assumed to have been produced solely or principally for the purpose of sexual arousal,

the image may, by virtue of being part of that narrative, be found not to be pornographic, even though it might have been found to be pornographic if taken by itself.

(6) An "extreme image" is an image which—

(a) falls within subsection (7), and

(b) is grossly offensive, disgusting or otherwise of an obscene character.

(7) An image falls within this subsection if it portrays, in an explicit and realistic way, any of the following—

(a) an act which threatens a person's life,

(b) an act which results, or is likely to result, in serious injury to a person's anus, breasts or genitals,

(c) an act which involves sexual interference with a human corpse, or

(d) a person performing an act of intercourse or oral sex with an animal (whether dead or alive),

and a reasonable person looking at the image would think that any such person or animal was real.

(8) In this section "image" means—

(a) a moving or still image (produced by any means); or

(b) data (stored by any means) which is capable of conversion into an image within paragraph (a).

(9) In this section references to a part of the body include references to a part surgically constructed (in particular through gender reassignment surgery).

(10) Proceedings for an offence under this section may not be instituted—

(a) in England and Wales, except by or with the consent of the Director of Public Prosecutions; or

(b) [*Northern Ireland*].]

[Exclusion of classified films etc.

31–121 **64.**—(1) Section 63 does not apply to excluded images.

(2) An "excluded image" is an image which forms part of a series of images contained in a recording of the whole or part of a classified work.

(3) But such an image is not an "excluded image" if—

(a) it is contained in a recording of an extract from a classified work, and

(b) it is of such a nature that it must reasonably be assumed to have been extracted (whether with or without other images) solely or principally for the purpose of sexual arousal.

(4) Where an extracted image is one of a series of images contained in the recording, the question whether the image is of such a nature as is mentioned in subsection (3)(b) is to be determined by reference to—

(a) the image itself, and

(b) (if the series of images is such as to be capable of providing a context for the image) the context in which it occurs in the series of images;

and section 63(5) applies in connection with determining that question as it applies in connection with determining whether an image is pornographic.

(5) In determining for the purposes of this section whether a recording is a recording of the whole or part of a classified work, any alteration attributable to—

(a) a defect caused for technical reasons or by inadvertence on the part of any person, or

(b) the inclusion in the recording of any extraneous material (such as advertisements),

is to be disregarded.

(6) Nothing in this section is to be taken as affecting any duty of a designated authority to have regard to section 63 (along with other enactments creating criminal offences) in determining whether a video work is suitable for a classification certificate to be issued in respect of it.

(7) In this section—

"classified work" means (subject to subsection (8)) a video work in respect of which a classification certificate has been issued by a designated authority (whether before or after the commencement of this section);

"classification certificate" and "video work" have the same meanings as in the *Video Recordings Act* 1984;

"designated authority" means an authority which has been designated by the Secretary of State under section 4 of that Act;

"extract" includes an extract consisting of a single image;

"image" and "pornographic" have the same meanings as in section 63;

"recording" means any disc, tape or other device capable of storing data electronically and from which images may be produced (by any means).

(8) Section 22(3) of the *Video Recordings Act* 1984 (effect of alterations) applies for the purposes of this section as it applies for the purposes of that Act.]

[Defences: general

65.—(1) Where a person is charged with an offence under section 63, it is a defence for the person to prove any of the matters mentioned in subsection (2). **31–122**

(2) The matters are—

(a) that the person had a legitimate reason for being in possession of the image concerned;

(b) that the person had not seen the image concerned and did not know, nor had any cause to suspect, it to be an extreme pornographic image;

(c) that the person—

(i) was sent the image concerned without any prior request having been made by or on behalf of the person, and

(ii) did not keep it for an unreasonable time.

(3) In this section "extreme pornographic image" and "image" have the same meanings as in section 63.]

[Defence: participation in consensual acts

66.—(1) This section applies where— **31–123**

(a) a person ("D") is charged with an offence under section 63, and

(b) the offence relates to an image that portrays an act or acts within paragraphs (a) to (c) (but none within paragraph (d)) of subsection (7) of that section.

(2) It is a defence for D to prove—

(a) that D directly participated in the act or any of the acts portrayed, and

(b) that the act or acts did not involve the infliction of any non-consensual harm on any person, and

(c) if the image portrays an act within section 63(7)(c), that what is portrayed as a human corpse was not in fact a corpse.

(3) For the purposes of this section harm inflicted on a person is "non-consensual" harm if—

(a) the harm is of such a nature that the person cannot, in law, consent to it being inflicted on himself or herself; or

(b) where the person can, in law, consent to it being so inflicted, the person does not in fact consent to it being so inflicted.]

[Penalties etc. for possession of extreme pornographic images

67.—(1) This section has effect where a person is guilty of an offence under section 63. **31–124**

(2) Except where subsection (3) applies to the offence, the offender is liable—

(a) on summary conviction, to imprisonment for a term not exceeding the relevant period or a fine not exceeding the statutory maximum or both;

(b) on conviction on indictment, to imprisonment for a term not exceeding 3 years or a fine or both.

(3) If the offence relates to an image that does not portray any act within section 63(7)(a) or (b), the offender is liable—

(a) on summary conviction, to imprisonment for a term not exceeding the relevant period or a fine not exceeding the statutory maximum or both;

(b) on conviction on indictment, to imprisonment for a term not exceeding 2 years or a fine or both.

(4) In subsection (2)(a) or (3)(a) "the relevant period" means—

(a) in relation to England and Wales, 12 months;

(b) in relation to Northern Ireland, 6 months.]

[Special rules relating to providers of information society services

31–125 **68.** Schedule 14 makes special provision in connection with the operation of section 63 in relation to persons providing information society services within the meaning of that Schedule.]

31–126 Sections 63 to 68 come into force on a day to be appointed. The reference to "12 months" in section 67(4)(a) is to be read as a reference to "six months" in relation to an offence committed before the commencement of the *CJA* 2003, s.154(1): 2008 Act, s.148(2), and Sched. 27, para. 23.

31–127 Schedule 14 (not set out in this work) contains special rules relating to providers of information society services (as to which, see para. 6(3)). Paragraph 1 extends the liability of domestic service providers. Paragraph 2 restricts the institution of proceedings against non-UK service providers. Paragraphs 3 to 5 contain exceptions for mere conduits, caching and hosting, and paragraph 6 provides for the interpretation of the schedule.

(7) Customs Consolidation Act 1876

31–128 Section 42 prohibits the importation of "indecent or obscene prints, paintings, photographs, books, cards, lithographic or other engravings, or any other indecent or obscene articles". In relation to this section, see *R. v. Bow Street Magistrates' Court, ex p. Noncyp Ltd* [1990] 1 Q.B. 123, CA (Civ.Div.), and *Wright v. Commrs for Customs and Excise* [1999] 1 Cr.App.R. 69, DC. As to the offence of importation in breach of a prohibition, see the *CEMA* 1979, s.170 (*ante*, § 25–452), and *R. v. Forbes (Giles)* [2002] 2 A.C. 512, HL (*ante*, § 25–464). As to sentence, see *R. v. Hirst* [2001] 1 Cr.App.R.(S.) 44, CA (12 months' imprisonment upheld on plea of guilty by 51-year-old with no convictions to conspiracy to import obscene videos in a "sophisticated operation" in which offender had "important role").

IV. CORRUPTION

A. COMMON LAW

31–129 Where a person in the position of trustee to perform a public duty takes a bribe to act corruptly in discharging that duty, it is an offence in both parties: *R. v. Whitaker* [1914] 3 K.B. 1283, 10 Cr.App.R. 245, CCA. This formulation of the offence is clearly wide enough to embrace those involved in the administration of justice, such as a juror (*R. v. Young* (1801) 2 East 14 at 16), a justice (*R. v. Gurney* (1867) 10 Cox 550), or a coroner (*R. v. Harrison* (1800) 1 East P.C. 382). It also covers the bribery of a privy counsellor: *R. v. Vaughan* (1769) 4 Burr. 2494.

The offer of a bribe is an attempt to bribe, and is also an offence: 3 Co.Inst. 147; *R. v. Vaughan, ante*.

The purchase and sale of public offices is said to be regarded by the common law as bribery. In *R. v. Pollman* (1809) 2 Camp 229n, a conspiracy to obtain money by procuring from the Treasury the appointment of a person to an office in the customs was held to be a misdemeanour at common law. As to this, see also *ante*, § 25–383.

The offence of bribery is punishable by fine and or imprisonment, whether the bribe is accepted or not: 3 Co.Inst. 147; and a financial reporting order may be made: *SOCPA* 2005, s.76 (*ante*, § 5–886a). For sentence in a case of bribing a prison officer, see *R. v. Garner*, 10 Cr.App.R.(S.) 445, CA.

For the purpose of any common law offence of bribery, it is immaterial if the functions of the person who receives or is offered a reward have no connection with the United Kingdom and are carried out in a country or territory outside the United Kingdom: *Anti-terrorism, Crime and Security Act* 2001, s.108(1). This provision came into force on February 14, 2002: *Anti-terrorism, Crime and Security Act 2001 (Commencement No. 3) Order* 2002 (S.I. 2002 No. 228).

B. STATUTE

(1) Representation of the People Act 1983

31–130 As to corrupt practices at elections, see sections 164 to 166 (not printed in this work).

(2) Public Bodies Corrupt Practices Act 1889

Public Bodies Corrupt Practices Act 1889, ss.1, 2

Corruption in office a misdemeanor

1.—(1) Every person who shall by himself or by or in conjunction with any other person, corruptly solicit or receive, or agree to receive, for himself, or for any other person, any gift, loan, fee, reward, or advantage whatever as an inducement to, or reward for, or otherwise on account of any member, officer, or servant of a public body as in this Act defined, doing or forbearing to do anything in respect of any matter or transaction whatsoever, actual or proposed, in which the said public body is concerned, shall be guilty of a misdemeanor. **31-131**

(2) Every person who shall by himself or by or in conjunction with any other person corruptly give, promise, or offer any gift, loan, fee, reward, or advantage whatsoever to any person, whether for the benefit of that person or of another person, as an inducement to or reward for or otherwise on account of any member, officer, or servant of any public body as in this Act defined, doing or forbearing to do anything in respect of any matter or transaction whatsoever, actual or proposed, in which such public body as aforesaid is concerned, shall be guilty of a misdemeanor.

Penalty for offences

2. Any person on conviction for offending as aforesaid shall, at the discretion of the court before which he is convicted, **31-132**

(a) be liable—

(i) on summary conviction, to imprisonment for a term not exceeding *6* [12] months or to a fine not exceeding the statutory maximum, or to both; and

(ii) on conviction on indictment, to imprisonment for a term not exceeding 7 years or to a fine, or to both; and

(b) in addition be liable to be ordered to pay to such body, and in such manner as the court directs, the amount or value of any gift, loan, fee, or reward received by him or any part thereof; and

(c) be liable to be adjudged incapable of being elected or appointed to any public office for five years from the date of his conviction, and to forfeit any such office held by him at the time of his conviction; and

(d) in the event of a second conviction for a like offence he shall, in addition to the foregoing penalties, be liable to be adjudged to be for ever incapable of holding any public office, and to be incapable for five years of being registered as an elector, or voting at an election either of members to serve in Parliament or of members of any public body, and the enactments for preventing the voting and registration of persons declared by reason of corrupt practices to be incapable of voting shall apply to a person adjudged in pursuance of this section to be incapable of voting; and

(e) if such person is an officer or servant in the employ of any public body upon such conviction he shall, at the discretion of the court, be liable to forfeit his right and claim to any compensation or pension to which he would otherwise have been entitled.

[This section is printed as amended by the *Representation of the People Act* 1948, ss.52(7) and 80; and the *CJA* 1988, s.47. In para. (a)(i), "12" is substituted for "6", as from a day to be appointed, by the *CJA* 2003, s.282(2) and (3). The increase has no application to offences committed before the substitution takes effect: s.282(4).]

Public Bodies Corrupt Practices Act 1889, ss.3(2), 4, 7

Savings

3.—(2) A person shall not be exempt from punishment under this Act by reason of the invalidity of the appointment or election of a person to a public office. **31-133**

Restriction on prosecution

4.—(1) A prosecution for an offence under this Act shall not be instituted except by or with the consent of the Attorney General.

(2) In this section the expression "Attorney General" means the Attorney ... General for England, and as respects Scotland means the Lord Advocate.

[This section is printed as repealed in part by the *Statute Law (Repeals) Act (Northern Ireland)* 1954; the *Criminal Jurisdiction Act* 1975, Sched. 6; and the *Law Officers Act* 1997, s.3(2) and Sched.]

Interpretation

31–134 **7.** In this Act—

The expression "public body" means any council of a county or county [*sic*] of a city or town, any council of a municipal borough, also any board, commissioners, select vestry, or other body which has power to act under and for the purposes of any Act relating to local government, or the public health, or to poor law or otherwise to administer money raised by rates in pursuance of any public general Act, and includes any body which exists in a country or territory outside the United Kingdom and is equivalent to any body described above:

The expression "public office" means any office or employment of a person as a member, officer, or servant of such public body:

The expression "person" includes a body of persons, corporate or unincorporate:

The expression "advantage" includes any office or dignity, and any forbearance to demand any money or money's worth or valuable thing, and includes any aid, vote, consent, or influence, or pretended aid, vote, consent, or influence, and also includes any promise or procurement of or agreement or endeavour to procure, or the holding out of any expectation of any gift, loan, fee, reward, or advantage, as before defined.

[The definition of "public body" is printed as amended by the *Anti-terrorism, Crime and Security Act* 2001, s.108(3) (substitution of words beginning "and includes"). This amendment took effect on February 14, 2002: *Anti-terrorism, Crime and Security Act 2001 (Commencement No. 3) Order* 2002 (S.I. 2002 No. 228).]

The definition of "public body" is extended by the *Prevention of Corruption Act* 1916, s.4(2) (*post*, § 31–154). It also includes the Civil Aviation Authority: see the *Civil Aviation Act* 1982, s.19(1). And the *Government of Wales Act* 2006 declares the National Assembly for Wales and the National Assembly of Wales Commission to be public bodies for the purposes of this Act, and of the 1889 and 1916 Acts (*post*).

Indictment

STATEMENT OF OFFENCE

31–135 *Corruption, contrary to section 1(1) of the* Public Bodies Corrupt Practices Act *1889*.

PARTICULARS OF OFFENCE

A B, being a food and drugs inspector of the town council of the borough of ——, on the —— day of ——, 20—, did corruptly solicit [or *receive*] [or *agree to receive*] *for himself the sum of £10 as a fee or reward for forbearing to prosecute for adulteration of milk.*

Where A and B are charged respectively with offering and accepting bribes and are tried separately, the conviction of one and the acquittal of the other does not necessarily render the conviction unsafe on the ground of inconsistency: *R. v. Andrews-Weatherfoil Ltd*, 56 Cr.App.R. 31, CA.

Class of offence and mode of trial

31–136 Offences contrary to section 1 of the 1889 Act are class 3 offences, *ante*, § 2–17, triable either way: s.2, *ante*.

Sentence

31–137 For the maximum penalty and other orders which may be made on conviction, see section 2, *ante*. For cases of corruption, see CSP, B9–1.3.

A person convicted of this offence may be made the subject of a financial reporting order: *SOCPA* 2005, s.76 (*ante*, § 5–886a).

Evidence

31–138 Evidence of system by one defendant may be admissible against another: *R. v. Andrews-Weatherfoil Ltd*, *ante*.

Ingredients of the offence

"corruptly"

31–139 The word "corruptly" means not "dishonestly" but purposely doing an act which the law forbids as tending to corrupt: *Cooper v. Slade* (1858) 6 H.L.Cas. 746; *R. v. Wellburn*, 69 Cr.App.R. 254, CA; and *R. v. Harvey* [1999] Crim.L.R. 70, CA (*post*, § 31–149). Where, therefore, in a case in which the defendant claimed to have offered a bribe with a view to exposing corruption, the judge's direction that "corruptly" meant with intention to corrupt and motive was irrelevant, was correct: *R. v. Smith (John)* [1960] 2 Q.B. 423, 44 Cr.App.R. 55, CCA.

Where a person solicited money from a third party on the basis that it would be paid as a bribe to a public official, it was unnecessary, for the purpose of establishing an offence of corruptly soliciting the bribe, to prove that the public official was aware that an improper offer had been made or a bribe passed. All that was necessary was that the apparent purpose of the transaction was to affect the conduct of such a person corruptly. This was so even where the person soliciting the money had no intention of using it to bribe a public official, but intended to keep it for himself: *Jagdeo Singh v. The State* [2006] 1 W.L.R. 146, PC.

As to a presumption of corruption, see the *Prevention of Corruption Act* 1916, s.2 (*post*, § 31–152).

"reward"

The word "reward" can be given its natural meaning of a "*post facto*" gift for a past favour without there having been any agreement beforehand; any payment will be covered provided it is related to something done or omitted by the recipient in respect of any matter or transaction in which the public body, of which he is a member, officer or servant, is concerned: *R. v. Andrews-Weatherfoil Ltd, ante*; *R. v. Parker (K. R.)*, 82 Cr.App.R. 69, CA (in which the direction of Pain J. to the jury (set out at pp. 72–73) was described as "impeccable … without fault of any kind"). **31–140**

(3) Prevention of Corruption Act 1906

Prevention of Corruption Act 1906, s.1

Punishment of corrupt transactions with agents

1.—(1) If any agent corruptly accepts or obtains, or agrees to accept or attempts to obtain, from any person, for himself or for any other person, any gift or consideration as an inducement or reward for doing or forbearing to do, or for having after the passing of this Act done or forborne to do, any act in relation to his principal's affairs or business, or for showing or forbearing to show favour or disfavour to any person in relation to his principal's affairs or business; or **31–141**

If any person corruptly gives or agrees to give or offers any gift or consideration to any agent as an inducement or reward for doing or forbearing to do, or for having after the passing of this Act done or forborne to do, any act in relation to his principal's affairs or business, or for showing or forbearing to show favour or disfavour to any person in relation to his principal's affairs or business; or

If any person knowingly gives to any agent, or if any agent knowingly uses with intent to deceive his principal, any receipt, account, or other document in respect of which the principal is interested, and which contains any statement which is false or erroneous or defective in any material particular, and which to his knowledge is intended to mislead the principal;

he shall be guilty of a misdemeanour and shall be liable,

(a) on summary conviction, to imprisonment for a term not exceeding *6* [12] months or to a fine not exceeding the statutory maximum, or to both; and

(b) on conviction on indictment, to imprisonment for a term not exceeding 7 years or to a fine, or to both.

(2) For the purposes of this Act the expression "consideration" includes valuable consideration of any kind; the expression "agent" includes any person employed by or acting for another; and the expression "principal" includes an employer. **31–142**

(3) A person serving under the Crown or under any corporation or any borough, county, or district council, or any board of guardians, is an agent within the meaning of this Act.

(4) For the purposes of this Act it is immaterial if—

(a) the principal's affairs or business have no connection with the United Kingdom and are conducted in a country or territory outside the United Kingdom;

(b) the agent's functions have no connection with the United Kingdom and are carried out in a country or territory outside the United Kingdom.

[This section is printed as amended by the *CJA* 1988, s.47; and the *Anti-terrorism, Crime and Security Act* 2001, s.108(4); and as repealed in part by the *Local Authorities, etc. (Miscellaneous Provisions) (No. 2) Order* 1974 (S.I. 1974 No. 595). The amendment effected by the 2001 Act (insertion of subs. (4)) took effect on February 14, 2002: *Anti-terrorism, Crime and Security Act 2001 (Commencement No. 3) Order* 2002 (S.I. 2002 No. 228). In subs. (1)(a), "12" is substituted for "6", as from a day to be appointed, by the *CJA* 2003, s.282(2) and (3). The increase has no application to offences committed before the substitution takes effect: s.282(4).]

Prevention of Corruption Act 1906, s.2

Prosecution of offences

31–143 **2.**—(1) A prosecution for an offence under this Act shall not be instituted without the consent, in England of the Attorney-General ...

(3) Every information for any offence under this Act shall be upon oath.

(6) Any person aggrieved by a summary conviction under this Act may appeal to the Crown Court.

[This section is printed as amended by the *Courts Act* 1971, s.56(1), and Sched. 8, para. 2; the *Criminal Jurisdiction Act* 1975, Sched. 6, Pt II; and the *Law Officers Act* 1997, s.3(2), and Sched. Subss. (2), (4) and (5) were repealed by the *Administration of Justice (Miscellaneous Provisions) Act* 1933, the *Costs in Criminal Cases Act* 1908 and the *CLA* 1967 respectively.]

Indictment

STATEMENT OF OFFENCE

31–144 *Corruption, contrary to section 1 of the* Prevention of Corruption Act *1906.*

PARTICULARS OF OFFENCE

A B, an agent of the —— Assurance Company, on the —— day of ——, 20——, did corruptly accept [or *obtain, etc.*] *from C D for himself the sum of £1,000 as an inducement or reward for doing an act in relation to his principal's affairs, namely for approving the claim of the said C D for payment of £10,000 by the said —— Assurance Company in respect of a fire at the premises of the said C D at 190 High Street, ——.*

Class of offence and mode of trial

31–145 Offences contrary to section 1 of the 1906 Act are class 3 offences, *ante*, § 2–17, triable either way: s.1(1), *ante*.

Sentence

31–146 The maximum sentence on conviction on indictment is seven years' imprisonment or a fine or both, and on summary conviction is six (12, as from a day to be appointed) months' imprisonment or a fine not exceeding the statutory maximum or both: s.1(1), *ante*. The "statutory maximum" means the prescribed sum within the meaning of the *MCA* 1980: *Interpretation Act* 1978, Sched. 1 (Appendix B–28). For section 32 of the 1980 Act, see *ante*, § 1–75aa.

For cases of corruption, see CSP, B9–1.3.

A person convicted of either of the first two offences under section 1 of the 1906 Act may be made the subject of a financial reporting order: *SOCPA* 2005, s.76 (*ante*, § 5–886a).

Evidence

31–147 Evidence of system by one defendant may be admissible against another: *R. v. Andrews-Weatherfoil Ltd*, 56 Cr.App.R. 31, CA (a case on the 1889 Act, *ante*).

Ingredients of the offence

"agent"

31–148 The question in determining whether a person is "serving under the Crown" is not whether he is employed by the Crown but whether the duties he performs are performed by him on behalf of the Crown, it being necessary for the Crown to exercise its functions through human agency: *R. v. Barrett*, 63 Cr.App.R. 174, CA (additional superintendent registrar). A police officer serves under the Crown: *Fisher v. Oldham Corporation* [1930] 2 K.B. 364.

The meaning of "agent" is extended by the *Prevention of Corruption Act* 1916, s.4(3), *post*, § 31–154.

"corruptly"

See generally, *ante*, § 31–139. In *R. v. Harvey* [1999] Crim.L.R. 70, CA, it was held that dishonesty is not an element of the offence; and that the word "corruptly" for the purposes of the section is to be construed as meaning deliberately offering money or other favours, with the intention that it should operate on the mind of the offeree, so as to encourage him to enter into a corrupt bargain. In *R. v. Godden-Wood* [2001] Crim.L.R. 810, CA, it was held that *Harvey* could not be distinguished on the ground that it concerned a public institution; the test for corruption was the same in the private as in the public domain. As to a presumption of corruption, see the *Prevention of Corruption Act* 1916, s.2 (*post*, § 31–152). **31–149**

The prosecution have merely to prove that the defendant received a gift as an inducement to show favour; they are not required to prove that he did actually show favour in consequence of having received the gift: *R. v. Carr*, 40 Cr.App.R. 188, Ct-MAC. Thus, a person who accepts a gift knowing that it is intended as a bribe enters into a corrupt bargain even if he makes a private mental reservation not to carry out his side of the bargain: *R. v. Mills*, 68 Cr.App.R. 154, CA (*obiter*). If the money was received in order to entrap the giver or to provide evidence for police listening or making a tape recording and the acceptor did not intend to keep it, it plainly would not be corrupt: *ibid.* see also Lord Goddard in *R. v. Carr* at p. 189. *Cf. R. v. Smith (John)*, *ante*, § 31–139.

The words of section 1 are by design very wide. If a person uses his position to get commission corruptly it does not matter whether the work in respect of which he gets commission is work to which his duties relate or not: *R. v. Dickinson and De Rable*, 33 Cr.App.R. 5, CCA.

"consideration"

The meaning of the term (which includes "valuable consideration of any kind", see s.1(2) of the 1906 Act) was considered in *R. v. Braithwaite*, 77 Cr.App.R. 34, CA. The meaning of the word must be the legal meaning: see *Currie v. Misa* (1875) L.R. 10 Exch. 153 at 162: "A valuable consideration, in the sense of the law, may consist either in some right, interest, profit or benefit accruing to the one party, or some forbearance, detriment, loss or responsibility, given, suffered or undertaken by the other ...". The word connotes the existence of something in the shape of a contract or a bargain between the parties.

"... in relation to his principal's affairs"

These words fall to be widely construed: *Morgan v. DPP* [1970] 3 All E.R. 1053, DC. **31–150**

Document intended to deceive principal

The third paragraph of section 1(1) applies only to documents which were intended to pass between a principal and a third party. It does not apply to an internal document which was never intended to go to a third party and had not come from one: *R. v. Tweedie* [1984] Q.B. 729, 79 Cr.App.R. 168, CA. But where a third party gives a false document to an agent with a view to deceiving his principal, there is no requirement that the agent knows of the falsity: *Sage v. Eicholz* [1919] 2 K.B. 171, DC (the offence not being limited by the title to the Act or the context of the section). **31–151**

(4) Prevention of Corruption Act 1916

Prevention of Corruption Act 1916, s.2

Presumption of corruption in certain cases

31–152 **2.** Where in any proceedings against a person for an offence under the *Prevention of Corruption Act* 1906, or the *Public Bodies Corrupt Practices Act* 1889, it is proved that any money, gift, or other consideration has been paid or given to or received by a person in the employment of [Her] Majesty or any Government Department or a public body by or from a person, or agent of a person, holding or seeking to obtain a contract from [Her] Majesty or any Government Department or public body, the money, gift, or consideration shall be deemed to have been paid or given and received corruptly as such inducement or reward as is mentioned in such Act unless the contrary is proved.

This section has no application in relation to anything which would not be an offence apart from section 108 or 109 of the *Anti-terrorism, Crime and Security Act* 2001: s.110 of that Act. For the effect of section 108, see *ante*, §§ 31–129, 31–134, 31–142, and *post*, § 31–154. For section 109, see *ante*, § 2–82.

31–153 As to when the presumption arises, see *R. v. Braithwaite*, *ante*. It has no application, however, on an allegation of a statutory conspiracy, for such offence is not an offence under the 1906 Act or the 1889 Act, but is an offence under the *CLA* 1977, s.1: *R. v. Attorney-General, ex p. Rockall* [2000] 1 W.L.R. 882, DC.

The onus of proof lies upon the defendant and may be discharged by evidence satisfying the jury of the probability of that which the defendant is called on to establish. The jury should be so directed: *R. v. Carr-Briant* [1943] K.B. 607, 29 Cr.App.R. 76, CCA.

Prevention of Corruption Act 1916, s.4

Short title and interpretation

31–154 **4.**—(1) This Act may be cited as the *Prevention of Corruption Act* 1916, and the *Public Bodies Corrupt Practices Act* 1889, the *Prevention of Corruption Act* 1906, and this Act may be cited together as the *Prevention of Corruption Acts* 1889 to 1916.

(2) In this Act and in the *Public Bodies Corrupt Practices Act* 1889, the expression "public body" includes in addition to the bodies mentioned in the last-mentioned Act, local and public authorities of all descriptions (including authorities existing in a country or territory outside the United Kingdom) [and companies which in accordance with Part V of the *Local Government and Housing Act* 1989 are under the control of one or more local authorities].

(3) A person serving under any such public body is an agent within the meaning of the *Prevention of Corruption Act* 1906, and the expressions "agent" and "consideration" in this Act have the same meaning as in the *Prevention of Corruption Act* 1906, as amended by this Act.

[The words in round brackets in subs. (2) were inserted as from February 14, 2002 (*Anti-terrorism, Crime and Security Act 2001 (Commencement No. 3) Order* 2002 (S.I. 2002 No. 228)) by the *Anti-terrorism, Crime and Security Act* 2001, s.108(4). The words in square brackets at the end of subs. (2) are inserted as from a day to be appointed by the *Local Government and Housing Act* 1989, s.194(1), and Sched. 11, para. 3.]

The expression "public body" in section 7 of the 1889 Act and sections 2 and 4(2) of the 1916 Act is not restricted to local authorities but refers to any body which has public or statutory duties to perform and which performs those duties and carries out its transactions for the benefit of the public and not for private profit: *DPP v. Holly and Manners* [1978] A.C. 43, HL. Since, however, section 2 distinguishes between the Crown or any government department, on the one hand, and "a public body" on the other, the reference to "public authorities of all descriptions" in the definition of "public body" could not be construed as including either the Crown or a government department: *R. v. Natji* [2002] 2 Cr.App.R. 20, CA.

(5) Honours (Prevention of Abuses) Act 1925

Honours (Prevention of Abuses) Act 1925, s.1

Punishment of abuses in connection with the grant of honours

31–155 **1.**—(1) If any person accepts or obtains or agrees to accept or attempt to obtain from any person, for himself or for any other person, or for any purpose, any gift, money or valuable consideration as an inducement or reward for procuring or assisting or endeavouring to procure the grant of a dignity or title of honour to any person, or otherwise in connection with such a grant, he shall be guilty of an offence.

(2) If any person gives, or agrees or proposes to give, or offers to any person any gift, money or valuable consideration as an inducement or reward for procuring or assisting or endeavouring to procure the grant of a dignity or title of honour to any person, or otherwise in connection with such a grant, he shall be guilty of an offence.

(3) Any person guilty of an offence under this Act shall be liable on conviction on indictment to imprisonment for a term not exceeding two years or to a fine of any amount, or to both such imprisonment and such fine, or on summary conviction to imprisonment for a term not exceeding *three* [12] months or to a fine not exceeding the prescribed sum, or to both such imprisonment and such fine, and where the person convicted (whether on indictment or summarily) received any such gift, money, or consideration as aforesaid which is capable of forfeiture, he shall in addition to any other punishment be liable to forfeit the same to [Her] Majesty.

(4) [*Repealed by* Administration of Justice (Miscellaneous Provisions) Act *1933, Sched. 3 and* Criminal Justice Act (Northern Ireland) *1945, Sched. 4*.]

[This section is printed as amended by the *CLA* 1977 s.32(1); and the *MCA* 1980, s.32(2) (substitution of reference to "the prescribed sum"). In subs. (3), "12" is substituted for "three", as from a day to be appointed, by the *CJA* 2003, s.282(2) and (3). The increase has no application to offences committed before the substitution takes effect: s.282(4).]

As to the current value of "the prescribed sum", see *ante*, § 1–75aa.

CHAPTER 32

MOTOR VEHICLE OFFENCES

I. INTRODUCTION

The primary purpose of this chapter is to cover offences within the first instance jurisdiction of the Crown Court, that is, offences triable on indictment, whether exclusively so triable or not. In addition, this chapter takes in the most serious and frequently charged summary offences, including those which may in certain circumstances be included in an indictment (*CJA* 1988, s.40 (*ante*, § 1–75ai)) or are available as an alternative verdict on a count charging an indictable offence (*RTOA* 1988, s.24 (*post*, § 32–165)). **32–1**

II. DRIVING OFFENCES

A. CAUSING DEATH BY DANGEROUS DRIVING

(1) Statute

Road Traffic Act 1988, s.1

Causing death by dangerous driving

32–2 **1.** A person who causes the death of another person by driving a mechanically propelled vehicle dangerously on a road or other public place is guilty of an offence.

[This section is printed as substituted by the *RTA* 1991, s.1.]

As to the disapplication of this section to authorised motoring events, see the *RTA* 1988, s.13A.

(2) Indictment

STATEMENT OF OFFENCE

32–3 *Causing death by dangerous driving, contrary to section 1 of the* Road Traffic Act *1988*.

PARTICULARS OF OFFENCE

A B, on the —— day of ——, 20—, drove a mechanically propelled vehicle dangerously on a road [or *public place*], *namely ——, and thereby caused the death of CD.*

(3) Class of offence and mode of trial

32–4 This offence is triable only on indictment (*RTOA* 1988, s.9, and Sched. 2, Pt I, *post*, § 32–222). It is a class 3 offence, *ante*, § 2–17.

(4) Alternative verdicts

32–5 As to alternative verdicts generally, see *ante*, §§ 4–453 *et seq*. As to specific alternative verdicts on a charge of causing death by dangerous driving, see the *RTOA* 1988, s.24, *post*, § 32–165.

(5) Sentence

Maximum

32–6 Imprisonment not exceeding 14 years: *RTOA* 1988, s.33, and Sched. 2, Pt 1 (increased from 10 years by the *CJA* 2003, s.285(2) and (3), with non-retrospective effect (s.285(8)), as from February 27, 2004 (*Criminal Justice Act 2003 (Commencement No. 2 and Saving Provisions) Order* 2004 (S.I. 2004 No. 81)). Disqualification for a minimum period of two years and endorsement are obligatory, and the offence carries 3 to 11 penalty points: *ibid.*, ss.28, 34(1), (4), 44 and Sched. 2, Pt I. An order for disqualification until the offender passes an extended driving test is also mandatory: *ibid.*, s.36.

As to disqualification and endorsement generally (including the penalty points system), see *post*, §§ 32–167 *et seq*.

Guidelines

32–7 See Appendix K–185 *et seq.*, for the definitive guideline issued by the Sentencing Guidelines Council which applies to offenders aged 18 or over who fall to be sentenced on or after August 4, 2008.

[The next paragraph is § 32–11.]

(6) Ingredients of the offence

"A person"

32–11 See *Richmond LBC v. Pinn and Wheeler Ltd* [1989] R.T.R. 354, DC, as to whether a corporation may be convicted of an offence an ingredient of which is the act of driving.

"causes the death"

To support a conviction for causing death by dangerous driving, the prosecution need only prove dangerous driving and the fact that driving was a cause of death. There is no need to show that the dangerous driving was the principal, or a substantial, cause of the accident, for the defendant is to be convicted unless the causative nexus between his driving and the accident is "*de minimis*": *R. v. Hennigan*, 55 Cr.App.R. 262, CA. See also *R. v. Skelton* [1995] Crim.L.R. 635, CA, and *R. v. Kimsey* [1996] Crim.L.R. 35, CA. **32–12**

"of another person"

This includes a passenger in the vehicle driven by the person charged under this section: *R. v. Klein*, *The Times*, April 13, 1960, CA. **32–13**

"driving"

Section 192(1) of the *RTA* 1988 provides that "'driver', where a separate person acts as steersman of a motor vehicle, includes (except for the purposes of section 1 of this Act) that person as well as any other person engaged in the driving of the vehicle and 'drive' is to be interpreted accordingly". **32–14**

The test for whether a person is driving a vehicle is whether he is in a substantial sense controlling the movement and direction of the vehicle: *R. v. MacDonagh* [1974] Q.B. 448, 59 Cr.App.R. 55, CA; but the activity must also fall within the ordinary meaning of the word "drive": *ibid.* For particular situations, see *MacDonagh*, *ante* (pushing and steering); *McQuaid v. Anderton* [1981] 1 W.L.R. 154, DC (steering whilst being towed); *R. (Traves) v. DPP*, 169 J.P. 421, QBD (Bean J.) (steering and braking a towed car); *Saycell v. Bool* [1948] 2 All E.R. 83, DC (coasting downhill); *Langman v. Valentine* [1952] 2 All E.R. 803, DC (driving instructor); *Tyler v. Whatmore* [1976] R.T.R. 83, DC (passenger steering the vehicle); *McKoen v. Ellis*, 151 J.P. 60, DC; *Selby v. DPP* [1994] R.T.R. 157, DC; *Gunnell v. DPP* [1994] R.T.R. 151, DC (pushing and steering motorcycle whilst standing astride it); *Leach v. DPP* [1993] R.T.R. 161, DC (sitting in driver's seat with engine on and hands on steering wheel); *May v. DPP* [2000] R.T.R. 7, DC (sitting in driver's seat, with ignition key in the auxiliary position (between "on" and "off") thus engaging the electrical system); *Planton v. DPP* [2002] R.T.R. 9, DC (where vehicle is stationary, it is a question of fact and degree as to whether it has been stopped so long, and in such circumstances, that it could not reasonably be said that the person in the driving seat was driving); and *DPP v. Alderton* [2004] R.T.R. 23, QBD (Harrison J.) (on a grass verge wheel spinning).

Tyler v. Whatmore, *ante* (in which the passenger was held to be driving) may be contrasted with *DPP v. Hastings* [1993] R.T.R. 205, DC, in which a passenger intentionally grabbed the wheel so as to direct the vehicle at a pedestrian. It was held that he was not driving, but interfering with the driving of the vehicle: whether someone was driving in the ordinary sense of the word was a question of fact and degree. **32–15**

A person who causes a vehicle to move by his voluntary act of depressing the accelerator, albeit in the mistaken belief that he is depressing the brake, is "driving" for the purposes of the *RTA* 1988: *Att.-Gen.'s Reference (No. 4 of 2000)* [2001] 2 Cr.App.R. 22, CA.

"mechanically propelled vehicle"

There is no separate definition in the 1988 Act of this expression. If an issue arises as to whether a vehicle was a "mechanically propelled vehicle", it is for the prosecution to prove that it was: *Reader v. Bunyard*, 85 Cr.App.R. 185, DC. **32–16**

For earlier authorities on the meaning of this expression, see *Floyd v. Bush* [1953] 1 W.L.R. 242, DC; *Newberry v. Simmonds* [1961] 2 Q.B. 345, DC; *Smart v. Allen* [1963] 1 Q.B. 291, DC; *McEachran v. Hurst* [1978] R.T.R. 426, DC; and *Chief Constable of Avon and Somerset v. F. (A Juvenile)* [1987] R.T.R. 387, DC.

As to broken-down vehicles, see *Binks v. Department of the Environment* [1975] R.T.R. 318, DC.

"dangerously"

Road Traffic Act 1988, s.2A

Meaning of dangerous driving

32–17 **2A.**—(1) For the purposes of sections 1 and 2 above a person is to be regarded as driving dangerously if (and, subject to subsection (2) below, only if)—

(a) the way he drives falls far below what would be expected of a competent and careful driver, and

(b) it would be obvious to a competent and careful driver that driving in that way would be dangerous.

(2) A person is also to be regarded as driving dangerously for the purposes of sections 1 and 2 above if it would be obvious to a competent and careful driver that driving the vehicle in its current state would be dangerous.

(3) In subsections (1) and (2) above "dangerous" refers to danger either of injury to any person or of serious damage to property; and in determining for the purposes of those subsections what would be expected of, or obvious to, a competent and careful driver in a particular case, regard shall be had not only to the circumstances of which he could be expected to be aware but also to any circumstances shown to have been within the knowledge of the accused.

(4) In determining for the purposes of subsection (2) above the state of a vehicle, regard may be had to anything attached to or carried on or in it and to the manner in which it is attached or carried.

[This section was inserted by the *RTA* 1991, s.1.]

As to the importance of keeping in mind the high threshold set by section 2A, however tragic the outcome, see *R. v. Conteh* [2004] R.T.R. 1, CA.

An allegation of "dangerous" driving cannot be founded on speed alone; the question of speed has to be considered in the context of all the circumstances; but the test of the competent and careful driver when assessing the standard of driving of such a driver is to be applied on an objective, not subjective, basis: *DPP v. Milton* [2006] R.T.R. 21, DC. Distinguishing *R. v. Woodward* (*post*, § 32–20), the court held that section 2A(3) did not permit the court, in determining the issue of dangerousness, to take into account the driver's belief in his own advanced driving skills as a police officer when driving considerably in excess of the speed limit; but, in *Milton v. DPP* [2007] R.T.R. 43, DC, it was held that the *fact* that he has such skills is relevant, because it is a circumstance within his knowledge.

Mistake of fact is irrelevant to the issue of whether the driving in question is dangerous: *R. v. Collins (L.)* [1997] R.T.R. 439, CA (police officer driving across red light in belief that junction being controlled by other officers).

In the context of subsection (2) (dangerous state of vehicle), "obvious to a careful and competent driver" refers to a dangerous state which would be "seen or realised at first glance": *R. v. Strong* [1995] Crim.L.R. 428, CA. *Strong* does not, however, lay down a form of words to be used in every case. "Obvious" is an ordinary English word which has no special meaning in this context and it may be that judges are well advised not to attempt to define it further: *R. v. Marsh* [2002] 2 *Archbold News* 1, CA ([2002] EWCA Crim. 137). If the state of the vehicle is not such as to be obviously dangerous to a competent and careful driver and the driver has no particular knowledge, then no *actus reus* is committed (however dangerous the vehicle is in fact), and nobody can be convicted as a secondary party: *R. v. Loukes* [1996] 1 Cr.App.R. 444, CA; and see *R. v. Roberts and George* [1997] R.T.R. 462, CA. If, however, the alleged secondary party (*e.g.* the owner of a lorry) has actual knowledge of the dangerous state of the vehicle (to be taken into account by virtue of subsection (3)), it is submitted that the ignorance (and innocence) of the driver will not absolve the owner from liability. The driver may be regarded as an innocent agent.

Particular care should be taken in deciding whether it is appropriate to institute a prosecution for dangerous driving based on the "current state" of the vehicle where the alleged danger stems purely from the vehicle's inherent design, rather than from lack of maintenance or positive alteration; the term "current state" implies a state different from what might be termed the "original" or "manufactured" state: *R. v. Marchant* [2004] 1 W.L.R. 442, CA.

For a case of a diabetic driver having been held to have driven dangerously, see *R. v. Marison* [1997] R.T.R. 457, CA (*cf.* the discussion at § 32–22, *post*). See also *R. v. Lowe*

[1997] 2 Cr.App.R.(S.) 324, CA, and *R. v. Akinyeme* [2008] R.T.R. 20, CA (pleas of guilty by epileptics who drove against medical advice or without taking medication).

"road or other public place"

Section 192(1) of the *RTA* 1988 provides that "road", in relation to England and Wales, means "any highway and any other road to which the public has access, and includes bridges over which a road passes". There is no separate definition of public place. **32–18**

Whether a particular area of land is a "road" is a matter of fact; but guidance might be found by considering its physical character and the function which it exists to serve; as a matter of ordinary language a car park does not qualify as a road, the two being distinct in character and function; the proper function of a road is to enable movement along it to a destination; it might incidentally be used for parking; the proper function of a car park is to enable vehicles to stand and wait; a car might be driven across it but that was only incidental to its principal function. While circumstances might occur where an area of land which could reasonably be described as a car park could qualify as a road for the purposes of the legislation, such circumstances would be exceptional; furthermore, it might in certain circumstances be possible to distinguish the carriageway and the parking areas in a car park, but if that is done, it is not then permissible to claim that the car parking areas were an integral part of the carriageway so as to establish the whole as a road: *Clarke v. General Accident Fire and Life Assurance Corporation plc* [1998] 1 W.L.R. 1647, HL. See also *Brewer v. DPP* [2005] R.T.R. 5, DC (railway station car park not a road). The question whether any particular place is a "road" being a question of fact, it was open to justices to find that Trafalgar Square was a "road": *Sadiku v. DPP* [2000] R.T.R. 155, DC.

"Any road may be regarded as a road to which the public have access upon which members of the public are to be found who have not obtained access either by overcoming a physical obstruction or in defiance of a prohibition express or implied": *Harrison v. Hill* [1932] S.C. (J.) 13. The prosecution must show that it is the general public and not a restricted class who have access: *Oxford v. Austin* [1981] R.T.R. 416, DC; and, where the issue was whether a track over a village green was a road, it was held that it was insufficient to show that the public had access to it; it had to be shown that their user of it was *qua* road: *Massey v. Boulden* [2003] 1 W.L.R. 1792, CA (Civ. Div.) (overruled on another point in *Bakewell Management Ltd v. Brandwood* [2004] 2 A.C. 519, HL). Similar considerations apply to "public place". Private land to which the public have access by invitation, express or implied, or by toleration, may be a public place: *Adams v. Commr of Police for the Metropolis* [1980] R.T.R. 289, DC. The prosecution must adduce sufficient evidence of use by the general public in order to establish that the area in question is a public place: *R. v. DPP, ex p. Taussik* [2001] A.C.D. 10, DC (cul-de-sac leading to a local authority block of flats); but justices were entitled to conclude that a public house car park was a public place, even though there was no specific evidence that members of the public used it: *Lewis v. DPP, The Daily Telegraph*, December 23, 2004, QBD (Davis J.). The fact that someone might have authority to require a user of a car park to leave does not prevent it from being a public place: *DPP v. Greenwood* [1997] C.O.D. 278, DC (hospital car park on private land to which public has access day or night); and see *R. v. Spence* [1999] R.T.R. 353, CA (whether a car park is a "public place" would depend on whether it was in fact used by members of the public generally); and *May v. DPP, The Daily Telegraph*, April 28, 2005, DC (car dealership's car park which was accessible from a main road, and in respect of which there were no restrictions on entry by members of the public, albeit that it was intended only for use by customers, was a "public place").

As to the need, in appropriate cases, for the charge to specify "road or other public place", see *Brewer v. DPP, ante*; and *Dunmill v. DPP, The Times*, July 15, 2004, QBD (McCombe J.).

(7) Liability of secondary parties

Where a qualified accompanying driver was charged with aiding and abetting a **32–19** provisional licence holder to drive dangerously, Paull J. directed the jury that if they were satisfied that the car had been driven dangerously by the provisional licence holder for a sufficient time to enable the defendant, if he had acted reasonably, to try to stop the driver from driving dangerously, and that the defendant had not done so, then the defendant was guilty as an aider and abettor: *R. v. Hands and Plant*, unreported, 1966, Staffordshire Assizes. Similarly, in *R. v. Webster* [2006] 2 Cr.App.R. 6, CA, it was held that where a person permitted another whom he knew to be intoxicated to drive his vehicle, an offence of aiding and abetting that other to drive dangerously would only be established where the prosecution proved that, at the time that the driving was permitted, it had been foreseen that the driving was likely to be dangerous, or, alternatively, in the absence of such foresight, that knowledge of the dangerous nature of the driving had been acquired from the manner of the driving itself and that an opportunity to intervene had not been taken.

A company and a director of the company, both being in Scotland, knowing that a vehicle was fitted with a defective tyre, sent an employee with like knowledge to drive the vehicle to England. A fatal accident occurred in England in consequence of its dangerous condition. The driver was found guilty of causing death by dangerous driving. The company and the director were convicted of counselling and procuring the offence. It was held: (a) that even where dangerous driving arose not from the manner of driving, but from some defect in the vehicle, a person could be guilty of procuring the offence; (b) that there might be participation in a crime by a person who was not present at the scene and for that purpose it sufficed if the employers had set the crime in motion by instructing the employee to drive the vehicle when it was in a dangerous condition; and (c) that in the present case it was not right to say that the offence of counselling and procuring was complete at the moment when the driver left the base in Scotland; it was a continuing offence which continued up till the moment of the accident, and was accordingly triable in England: *R. v. Millar* [1970] 2 Q.B. 54, 54 Cr.App.R. 158, CA.

(8) Evidence

Alcohol or drugs

32–20 Evidence that the defendant had consumed alcohol is admissible if it tends to show that the amount of alcohol taken was such as would adversely affect a driver or, alternatively, that the defendant was in fact adversely affected: *R. v. Woodward (T.)* [1995] 2 Cr.App.R. 388, CA; but it cannot by itself prove the offence: *R. v. Webster*, *ante* (condition of driver will be relevant to the issue of danger). A single blood sample, obtained in circumstances where the defendant could not give two samples because of his injuries, was held admissible under the principle in *Woodward*, notwithstanding the *RTOA* 1988, s.15 (*post*, § 32–162), which applies only to offences under sections 3A, 4 and 5 of the *RTA* 1988: *R. v. Ash* [1999] R.T.R. 347, CA.

Woodward was distinguished in *R. v. Pleydell* [2006] 1 Cr.App.R. 12, CA, where it was held that evidence that the defendant had taken cocaine shortly before driving had been admissible notwithstanding that there had neither been evidence as to how much had been consumed, nor as to the defendant having been adversely affected. The court said that the whole purpose of taking such a drug would have been to achieve a material impact.

As to medical evidence as to fitness to drive, see *post*, § 32–72. As to opinion evidence as to whether a person was drunk, see *post*, § 32–73.

Police officer as expert

32–21 A police officer may give evidence as an expert if the subject upon which he gives such evidence is a subject in relation to which he has expert knowledge. His evidence must be restricted to the issues in the case: *R. v. Oakley*, 70 Cr.App.R. 7, CA (evidence as to cause of accident admissible).

As to the use of a retired police officer as an expert witness, see *R. (Doughty) v. Ely Magistrates' Court, CPS (interested party)*, 172 J.P. 259, DC (*ante*, § 10–65).

(9) Defences

Automatism

See generally §§ 17–84 *et seq.*, *ante.* 32–22

In an ordinary case, once it has been proved that the defendant was in the driving seat of a moving car, there is prima facie an obvious and irresistible inference that he was driving it. No dispute or doubt will arise on that point unless and until there is evidence tending to show that by some extraordinary mischance he was rendered unconscious or otherwise incapacitated from controlling the car. If he lapses into a coma, is stunned by a blow on the head or attacked by a swarm of bees, it can be said that he is no longer driving. If he falls asleep it is a question of fact whether driving in the circumstances was reckless: *Hill v. Baxter* [1958] 1 Q.B. 277, 42 Cr.App.R. 51, DC. If his loss of control results from an epileptic fit, a defence of automatism will be tantamount to a plea of insanity: *R. v. Sullivan* [1984] A.C. 156, HL; *R. v. Burgess* [1991] 2 Q.B. 92, 93 Cr.App.R. 41, CA. Similarly, if the loss of control is due to a hyperglycaemic episode caused by diabetes: *R. v. Hennessy*, 89 Cr.App.R. 10, CA. *Per contra* if it is due to a hypoglycaemic episode, caused by taking excessive insulin or insufficient quality or quantity of food to counter-balance the effects of insulin: *Watmore v. Jenkins* [1962] 2 Q.B. 572, DC; *R. v. Quick* [1973] Q.B. 910, 57 Cr.App.R. 722, CA; *R. v. Bingham* [1991] Crim.L.R. 433, CA.

The defence of automatism ought not to be considered at all until the defence has adduced at least prima facie evidence: *Hill v. Baxter*, *ante*. Once a proper foundation is laid for automatism, the matter becomes at large and must be left to the jury. The legal burden comes into play and requires that the jury be satisfied beyond reasonable doubt that the act was a voluntary act: *Bratty v. Att.-Gen. for Northern Ireland* [1963] A.C. 386, HL. In a case concerning a diabetic overcome by coma, the Divisional Court held that the justices could not reasonably find that the defendant had driven five miles on a road which was not straight in a state of automatism: *Watmore v. Jenkins*, *ante*; and see *Broome v. Perkins*, 85 Cr.App.R. 321, DC.

Automatism can only succeed as a defence if it was induced by some factor that could not have been foreseen: *R. v. Quick*, *ante*. Accordingly, it will not avail the victim of a hypoglycaemic attack if he ought to have tested his blood glucose level before embarking on his journey or to have appreciated the onset of symptoms during the journey: *R. v. C.*, unreported, May 23, 2007, CA ([2007] EWCA Crim. 1862).

As to "driving without awareness", see *Att.-Gen's Reference (No. 2 of 1992)*, 97 Cr.App.R. 429, CA, *ante*, § 17–95.

Necessity

See *ante*, §§ 17–127 *et seq.* (many of the cases cited there being driving cases). 32–23

Use of force in making arrest, etc.

Where the conduct alleged to constitute the offence of dangerous driving is also 32–24 capable of amounting to the use of reasonable force for the purpose of assisting in the arrest of an offender, the defendant can properly avail himself of the defence afforded by section 3(1) of the *CLA* 1967 (*ante*, § 19–39): *R. v. Renouf*, 82 Cr.App.R. 344, CA.

Mechanical defect

There is no real distinction between a driver being deprived of all control of the vehi- 32–25 cle by some sudden affliction of his person and being so deprived by some defect suddenly manifesting itself in the vehicle. Cases in which the defence of mechanical defect can successfully be relied on must be rare, and the defence has no application where the defect is known to the driver or should have been discovered by him had he exercised reasonable prudence. The essence of the defence is that the danger was created by a sudden and total loss of control which was in no way due to any fault on the part of the driver. A court should not consider any such special defence unless and until it is raised by the defendant, but once this has been done, the prosecution have to negative it and it must be considered with the rest of the evidence: *R. v. Spurge* [1961] 2 Q.B. 205, 45 Cr.App.R. 191, CA. See also *Rabjohns v. Burgar* [1971] R.T.R. 234, DC; *Wright v. Wenlock* [1971] R.T.R. 228, DC; and *Bensley v. Smith* [1972] R.T.R. 221, DC (justices should not speculate on potential defences).

Emergency calls

32–26 See observations of the Court of Appeal in *R. v. O'Toole*, 55 Cr.App.R. 206; and see also under "special reasons", *post*, § 32–188.

B. DANGEROUS DRIVING

(1) Statute

Road Traffic Act 1988, s.2

Dangerous driving

32–27 **2.** A person who drives a mechanically propelled vehicle dangerously on a road or other public place is guilty of an offence.

[This section is printed as substituted by the *RTA* 1991, s.1.]

As to the disapplication of this section to authorised motoring events, see the *RTA* 1988, s.13A.

As to the requirement of a warning of intended prosecution, see the *RTOA* 1988, s.1 and Sched. 1, *post*, §§ 32–152, 32–166.

(2) Indictment

32–28 An indictment may be framed from the specimen indictment for causing death by dangerous driving (*ante*, § 32–3).

Order of trials where there is an excess alcohol charge

32–29 Whilst it might in some circumstances be oppressive to prosecute for both driving with excess alcohol in one court and, later, for an indictable offence in another, where the charges arise out of the same course of driving, there is no general rule to this effect: *R. v. Arnold* [2008] R.T.R. 25, Ct-MAC (considering *R. v. Forest of Dean JJ., ex p. Farley* [1990] R.T.R. 228, DC, and *R. v. Hartnett* [2003] Crim.L.R. 719, DC (*ante*, § 4–58)).

(3) Class of offence and mode of trial

32–30 This offence is triable either way (*RTOA* 1988, s.9 and Sched. 2, Pt I, *post*, § 32–222), and is a class 3 offence, *ante*, § 2–17.

[The next paragraph is § 32–41.]

(4) Alternative verdicts

32–41 As to alternative verdicts generally, see *ante*, §§ 4–453 *et seq.*

As to specific alternative verdicts on a charge of dangerous driving, see the *RTOA* 1988, s.24, *post*, § 32–165.

(5) Sentence

Maximum

32–42 On conviction on indictment, imprisonment not exceeding two years, or a fine, or both; on summary conviction, imprisonment not exceeding six months or a fine not exceeding the statutory maximum, or both: *RTOA* 1988, s.33 and Sched. 2, Pt I. As from a day to be appointed, the maximum penalty on summary conviction is increased to 12 months' imprisonment: *CJA* 2003, s.282(2) and (3); but the increase has no application to offences committed before it takes effect: s.282(4). Disqualification for a minimum period of 12 months and endorsement are obligatory and the offence carries 3 to 11 penalty points: *ibid.*, ss.28, 34, 44 and Sched. 2, Pt I. In addition an offender convicted of dangerous driving must be disqualified until he passes an extended driving test: *RTOA* 1988, s.36 (*post*, § 32–198).

As to disqualification and endorsement generally (including the penalty points system), see *post*, §§ 32–167 *et seq*.

Guidelines

As to aggravating and mitigating circumstances generally, see the definitive guideline issued by the Sentencing Guidelines Council on causing death by dangerous driving (Appendix K–185 *et seq*.). Whilst this guideline is not expressed to apply to offences under section 2, it is of obvious relevance to the assessment of the seriousness of any offence under section 2. **32–43**

The sentencing bracket for "road rage" cases involving furious driving with intent to cause fear or possible injury, but no accident, consumption of alcohol or injury is six to 12 months: *R. v. Howells* [2003] 1 Cr.App.R. (S.) 61, CA.

(6) Ingredients of the offence

See *ante*, §§ 32–11 *et seq*. The only difference between this offence and the offence under section 1 is the requirement under section 1 that the dangerous driving caused the death of another person. **32–44**

(7) Liability of secondary parties

See *ante*, § 32–19. **32–45**

(8) Evidence

See *ante*, §§ 32–20 *et seq*. **32–46**

(9) Defences

See *ante*, §§ 32–22 *et seq*. **32–47**

It is no defence that the defendant drove at somebody who had no right to be in his way: *R. v. Waterfield and Lynn* [1964] 1 Q.B. 164, 48 Cr.App.R. 42, CCA (driving at policeman who had no right to detain driver).

C. CAUSING DEATH BY CARELESS DRIVING

(1) Statute

Road Traffic Act 1988, s.2B

Causing death by careless, or inconsiderate driving

2B. A person who causes the death of another person by driving a mechanically propelled vehicle on a road or other public place without due care and attention, or without reasonable consideration for other persons using the road or place, is guilty of an offence. **32–47a**

[This section was inserted by the *RSA* 2006, s.20(1) (as from August 18, 2008 (*Road Safety Act 2006 (Commencement No. 4) Order* 2008 (S.I. 2008 No. 1918)). It applies only to driving occurring after it came into force: *RSA* 2006, s.61(4).]

(2) Indictment

STATEMENT OF OFFENCE

Causing death by careless or inconsiderate driving, contrary to section 2B of the Road Traffic Act *1988*. **32–47b**

PARTICULARS OF OFFENCE

A B, on the —— day of ——, 20—, drove a mechanically propelled vehicle without due care and attention on a road [or *public place*], *namely ——, and thereby caused the death of C D.*

(3) Class of offence and mode of trial

32–47c This offence is triable either way (*RTOA* 1988, s.9, and Sched. 2, Pt I, *post*, § 32–222), and is a class 3 offence, *ante*, § 2–17.

(4) Alternative verdicts

32–47d As to alternative verdicts generally, see *ante*, §§ 4–453 *et seq.*

As to specific alternative verdicts on a charge of causing death by careless driving, see the *RTOA* 1988, s.24, *post*, § 32–165.

(5) Sentence

Maximum

32–47e On conviction on indictment, imprisonment not exceeding five years, or a fine, or both; on summary conviction, imprisonment not exceeding 12 months or a fine not exceeding the statutory maximum, or both: *RTOA* 1988, s.33, and Sched. 2, Pt I; but offences committed before the commencement of the *CJA* 2003, s.154(1), are subject to a maximum sentence of six months on summary conviction: *RSA* 2006, s.61(5). Disqualification for a minimum period of 12 months and endorsement are obligatory and the offence carries 3 to 11 penalty points: *RTOA* 1988, ss.28, 34 and 44, and Sched. 2, Pt I.

As to disqualification and endorsement generally (including the penalty points system), see *post*, §§ 32–167 *et seq.*

Guidelines

32–47f See Appendix K–185 *et seq.*, for the definitive guideline issued by the Sentencing Guidelines Council which applies to offenders aged 18 or over who fall to be sentenced on or after August 4, 2008.

(6) Ingredients of the offence

32–47g As to "a person", "causes the death", "of another person", "driving", "mechanically propelled vehicle" and "road or other public place", see *ante*, §§ 32–11 *et seq.*

"without due care and attention, or without reasonable consideration for other persons using the road or place"

Road Traffic Act 1988, s.3ZA

Meaning of careless, or inconsiderate driving

32–47h **3ZA.**—(1) This section has effect for the purposes of sections 2B and 3 above and section 3A below.

(2) A person is to be regarded as driving without due care and attention if (and only if) the way he drives falls below what would be expected of a competent and careful driver.

(3) In determining for the purposes of subsection (2) above what would be expected of a careful and competent driver in a particular case, regard shall be had not only to the circumstances of which he could be expected to be aware but also to any circumstances shown to have been within the knowledge of the accused.

(4) A person is to be regarded as driving without reasonable consideration for other persons only if those other persons are inconvenienced by his driving.

[This section was inserted by the *RSA* 2006, s.30. It applies only to driving occurring after it came into force: *RSA* 2006, s.61(4). To the extent that it applies to sections 3 and 3A, it came into force on September 24, 2007: *Road Safety Act 2006 (Commencement No. 2) Order* 2007 (S.I. 2007 No. 2472). Otherwise, it came into force on August 18, 2008: *Road Safety Act 2006 (Commencement No. 4) Order* 2008 (S.I. 2008 No. 1918).]

32–47i The standard of due care and attention is an objective one, fixed and impersonal, governed by the essential needs of the public, fixed in relation to the safety of other users of the highway: *McCrone v. Riding* [1938] 1 All E.R. 157, DC; *Taylor v. Rogers* [1960] Crim.L.R. 270, DC.

Whether a person was driving carelessly raises only a question of fact. If the defendant was not exercising the degree of care and attention that a reasonable, competent and prudent driver would exercise in the circumstances, he should be convicted. If the circumstances show that his conduct was not inconsistent with that of a reasonably prudent driver he should be acquitted. It is undesirable to complicate these cases by considering whether or not there has been an "error of judgment": *Simpson v. Peat* [1952] 2 Q.B. 24, DC.

Failure to exercise due care and attention may be a deliberate act: *Taylor v. Rogers*, *ante* (overtaking on a curve).

As to subsection (3) of the new section 3ZA, and the need to take account of circumstances within the knowledge of the accused, see *DPP v. Milton* and *Milton v. DPP*, *ante*, § 32–17.

On a charge of driving without reasonable consideration the question at issue is whether other road users were actually inconvenienced by the inconsiderate driving of the defendant: *Dilks v. Bowman-Shaw* [1981] R.T.R. 4, DC (see now s.3ZA(4), *ante*). The "other persons using the road or place" include passengers in the vehicle being driven by the defendant: *Pawley v. Wharldall* [1966] 1 Q.B. 373, DC. **32–47j**

(7) Evidence

See *ante*, §§ 32–20, 32–21. **32–47k**

Although the principle of *res ipsa loquitur* has no application in criminal cases, the facts of a particular case (such as failing to negotiate a bend and hitting a telegraph pole) may be such that, in the absence of any explanation, the only proper inference is that the driving was, at the very least, careless: *Wright v. Wenlock* [1971] R.T.R. 228, DC; *Watts v. Carter* [1971] R.T.R. 232, DC.

(8) Defences

See *ante*, §§ 32–22 *et seq.* **32–47l**

D. CARELESS AND INCONSIDERATE DRIVING

(1) Statute

Road Traffic Act 1988, s.3

Careless, and inconsiderate, driving

3. If a person drives a mechanically propelled vehicle on a road or other public place without due care and attention, or without reasonable consideration for other persons using the road or place, he is guilty of an offence. **32–48**

[This section is printed as substituted by the *RTA* 1991, s.2.]

As to the disapplication of this section to authorised motoring events, see the *RTA* 1988, s.13A.

As to the requirement of a warning of intended prosecution, see the *RTOA* 1988, s.1 and Sched. 1, *post*, §§ 32–152, 32–166.

(2) Mode of trial

This offence is triable only summarily: *RTOA* 1988, s.9 and Sched. 2, Pt I. **32–49**

(3) Sentence

A fine not exceeding level 5 (increased from level 4 with effect from September 24, 2007 (*Road Safety Act 2006 (Commencement No. 2) Order* 2007 (S.I. 2007 No. 2472)) by the 2006 Act, s.23, but only in relation to offences committed on or after that date (2006 Act, s.61(3))) on the standard scale (*ante*, § 5–403): *RTOA* 1988, s.33 and Sched. 2, Pt I. Disqualification is discretionary; endorsement is obligatory; and the offence carries 3 to 9 penalty points: *ibid.*, ss.28, 34, 44 and Sched. 2, Pt I. **32–50**

As to disqualification and endorsement generally (including the penalty points system), see *post*, §§ 32–167 *et seq.*

In *R. v. Simmonds* [1999] 2 Cr.App.R. 18, CA, it was held that it is not wrong in principle to impose an enhanced sentence where death results. The court declined to follow *R. v. Krawec*, 6 Cr.App.R.(S.) 367, CA, in which it had been held that the primary consideration is the degree of culpability and carelessness, and that the unforeseen and unexpected consequences of the carelessness are not in themselves relevant to penalty, although they may sometimes be relevant to an assessment of culpability. *Krawec* had been followed in *R. v. Johnson* [1998] 2 Cr.App.R.(S.) 453, CA; but in *R. v. King* [2001] 2 Cr.App.R.(S.) 114, CA, the court preferred the approach in *Simmonds*. See also *R. v. Morland* [1998] Crim.L.R. 143, CA.

(4) Ingredients of the offence

32–51 As to "a person", "drives", "mechanically propelled vehicle" and "road or other public place", see *ante*, §§ 32–11 *et seq.*

As to "without due care and attention, or without reasonable consideration for other persons using the road or place", see *ante*, §§ 32–47h *et seq.*

[The next paragraph is § 32–55.]

E. CAUSING DEATH BY CARELESS DRIVING WHEN UNDER THE INFLUENCE

(1) Statute

Road Traffic Act 1988, s.3A

Causing death by careless driving when under influence of drink or drugs

32–55 **3A.**—(1) If a person causes the death of another person by driving a mechanically propelled vehicle on a road or other public place without due care and attention, or without reasonable consideration for other persons using the road or place, and—

(a) he is, at the time when he is driving, unfit to drive through drink or drugs, or
(b) he has consumed so much alcohol that the proportion of it in his breath, blood or urine at that time exceeds the prescribed limit, or
(c) he is, within 18 hours after that time, required to provide a specimen in pursuance of section 7 of this Act, but without reasonable excuse fails to provide it, or
(d) he is required by a constable to give his permission for a laboratory test of a specimen of blood taken from him under section 7A of this Act, but without reasonable excuse fails to do so,

he is guilty of an offence.

(2) For the purposes of this section a person shall be taken to be unfit to drive at any time when his ability to drive properly is impaired.

(3) Subsection (1)(b), (c) and (d) above shall not apply in relation to a person driving a mechanically propelled vehicle other than a motor vehicle.

[Section 3A was inserted by the *RTA* 1991, s.3. It is printed as amended, as from September 24, 2007 (*Road Safety Act 2006 (Commencement No. 2) Order* 2007 (S.I. 2007 No. 2472)), by the *RSA* 2006, s.31 (insertion of subs. (1)(d)).]

(2) Indictment

STATEMENT OF OFFENCE

32–56 *Causing death by careless driving when under influence of drink or drugs, contrary to section 3A of the* Road Traffic Act *1988.*

PARTICULARS OF OFFENCE

A B, on the —— day of ——, 20—, caused the death of C D by driving a mechanically propelled vehicle on a road [or *public place*], *namely ——, without due care and attention and when unfit to drive through drink.*

(3) Class of offence and mode of trial

32–57 This offence is triable only on indictment (*RTOA* 1988, s.9, and Sched. 2, Pt I, *post*, § 32–222). It is a class 3 offence, *ante*, § 2–17.

(4) Alternative verdicts

32–58 As to alternative verdicts generally, see *ante*, §§ 4–453 *et seq.*

As to specific alternative verdicts on a charge of causing death by careless driving whilst unfit, see the *RTOA* 1988, s.24, *post*, § 32–165.

(5) Sentence

Maximum

Imprisonment not exceeding 14 years: *RTOA* 1988, s.33, and Sched. 2, Pt 1 (increased from 10 years by the *CJA* 2003, s.285(2) and (4), with non-retrospective effect (s.285(8)), as from February 27, 2004 (*Criminal Justice Act 2003 (Commencement No. 2 and Saving Provisions) Order* 2004 (S.I. 2004 No. 81))). Disqualification for a minimum period of two years and endorsement are obligatory, and the offence carries 3 to 11 penalty points: *ibid.*, ss.28, 34, 44 and Sched. 2, Pt I. **32–59**

As to disqualification and endorsement generally (including the penalty points system), see *post*, §§ 32–167 *et seq.*

Guidelines

See Appendix K–185 *et seq.*, for the definitive guideline issued by the Sentencing Guidelines Council which applies to offenders aged 18 or over who fall to be sentenced on or after August 4, 2008. **32–60**

(6) Ingredients of the offence

As to "a person", "causes the death", "another person", "driving", "mechanically propelled vehicle" and "road or other public place", see *ante*, §§ 32–11 *et seq.* **32–61**

As to "without due care and attention" and "without reasonable consideration for other persons using the road or place", see *ante*, §§ 32–47h *et seq.*

As to being "unfit to drive through drink or drugs", see *post*, §§ 32–71 *et seq.*

As to consuming "so much alcohol that the proportion of it in his breath, blood or urine exceeds the prescribed limit", see *post*, §§ 32–79 *et seq.*

As to failure to provide a specimen, see *post*, §§ 32–93 *et seq.*

"Motor vehicle" (see subs. (3)) in the *RTA* 1988 means "subject to section 20 of the *Chronically Sick and Disabled Persons Act* 1970 (which makes special provision about invalid carriages, within the meaning of that Act), a mechanically propelled vehicle intended or adapted for use on roads": *RTA* 1988, s.185(1).

Whether a vehicle is intended for use on roads does not depend on the intent of the user or the manufacturer. The test is whether a reasonable person looking at the vehicle would say that one of its users would be a road user: *Burns v. Currell* [1963] 2 Q.B. 433, DC (*per* Lord Parker C.J., at p. 440); approved in *Chief Constable of Avon and Somerset v. F.*, 84 Cr.App.R. 345, DC; *DPP v. Saddington* [2001] R.T.R. 15, DC (motorised scooter held to be intended for use on roads); and *DPP v. King*, 172 J.P. 401, DC (an electric scooter (known as a "City Mantis") was a motor vehicle; fact that a reasonable person in ordinary circumstances would not use the scooter on the road because of the dangers involved was not to the point; the exclusion in *Saddington*, *ante*, for "merely isolated use, or use by a man losing his senses" was a narrow one, and would apply only where that was the limit of what the reasonable person might expect; it had no application where the reasonable person would consider that there might well be some general use on roads (albeit only by a limited class of people, such as teenagers)).

In *Chief Constable of Avon and Somerset v. F.*, *ante*, Glidewell L.J. said that if a vehicle was originally manufactured for road use and then was altered, the proper approach might well be to consider whether the degree of alteration was so great as to take the vehicle outside the definition. Once it was established that a vehicle as manufactured was intended or adapted for use on a road, it would require a dramatic alteration for it to be said to be no longer a motor vehicle. **32–62**

(7) Evidence

As to the admissibility of evidence of the proportion of alcohol in a specimen of breath, blood or urine provided by the accused, and the assumption that the proportion of alcohol in his breath, blood or urine at the time of the offence was not less than in the specimen, see section 15 of the *RTOA* 1988, *post*, § 32–162. **32–63**

As to medical evidence of unfitness to drive, see *post*, § 32–72.

A jury are entitled on a prosecution under section 3A to consider evidence that the defendant was adversely affected by drink or that the amount the driver had drunk was such as to affect him adversely: *R. v. Millington* [1996] R.T.R. 80, CA.

F. CAUSING DEATH BY DRIVING: UNLICENSED, DISQUALIFIED OR UNINSURED DRIVERS

(1) Statute

Road Traffic Act 1988, s.3ZB

Causing death by driving: unlicensed, disqualified or uninsured drivers

32–63a **3ZB** A person is guilty of an offence under this section if he causes the death of another person by driving a motor vehicle on a road and, at the time when he is driving, the circumstances are such that he is committing an offence under—

(a) section 87(1) of this Act (driving otherwise than in accordance with a licence),
(b) section 103(1)(b) of this Act (driving while disqualified), or
(c) section 143 of this Act (using motor vehicle while uninsured or unsecured against third party risks).

[This section was inserted by the *RSA* 2006, s.21(1) (as from August 18, 2008 (S.I. 2008 No. 1918 (*ante*, § 32–47a))).]

(2) Indictment

STATEMENT OF OFFENCE

32–63b *Causing death by driving while disqualified, contrary to section 3ZB of the* Road Traffic Act *1988*.

PARTICULARS OF OFFENCE

A B, on the —— day of ——, 20—, caused the death of C D by driving a motor vehicle on a road, namely ——, while disqualified for holding or obtaining a licence to drive.

(3) Class of offence and mode of trial

32–63c This offence is triable either way (*RTOA* 1988, s.9, and Sched. 2, Pt I, *post*, § 32–222), and is a class 3 offence, *ante*, § 2–17.

(4) Alternative verdicts

32–63d As to alternative verdicts generally, see *ante*, §§ 4–453 *et seq.* There are no specific alternative verdicts available under the *RTOA* 1988.

(5) Sentence

32–63e On conviction on indictment, imprisonment not exceeding two years, or a fine or both; on summary conviction, imprisonment not exceeding 12 months, or a fine not exceeding the statutory maximum, or both: *RTOA* 1988, s.33, and Sched. 2, Pt I. Offences committed before the commencement of the *CJA* 2003, s.154(1), are subject to a maximum sentence of six months on summary conviction: *RSA* 2006, s.61(5). Disqualification and endorsement are obligatory; and the offence carries 3 to 11 penalty points: *RTOA* 1988, ss.28, 34, 44 and Sched. 2, Pt.I.

As to disqualification and endorsement generally (including the penalty points system), see *post*, §§ 32–167 *et seq.*

See Appendix K–185 *et seq.*, for the definitive guideline issued by the Sentencing Guidelines Council which applies to offenders aged 18 or over who fall to be sentenced on or after August 4, 2008.

(6) Ingredients of the offence

32–63f As to "a person", "causes the death", "another person", and "driving", see *ante*, §§ 32–11 *et seq.*

As to "motor vehicle", see *ante*, § 32–61.

As to "road", see *ante*, § 32–18.

As to "driving otherwise than in accordance with a licence", see *post*, §§ 32–108 *et seq*.

As to "driving while disqualified", see *post*, §§ 32–114 *et seq*.

As to "using motor vehicle while uninsured or unsecured against third party risks", see *post*, §§ 32–120 *et seq*.

G. Driving, Being in Charge, Whilst Unfit

(1) Statute

Road Traffic Act 1988, s.4

Driving, or being in charge, when under influence of drink or drugs

4.—(1) A person who, when driving or attempting to drive a mechanically propelled vehicle on a road or other public place, is unfit to drive through drink or drugs is guilty of an offence. **32–64**

(2) Without prejudice to subsection (1) above, a person who, when in charge of a mechanically propelled vehicle which is on a road or other public place, is unfit to drive through drink or drugs is guilty of an offence.

(3) For the purposes of subsection (2) above, a person shall be deemed not to have been in charge of a mechanically propelled vehicle if he proves that at the material time the circumstances were such that there was no likelihood of his driving it so long as he remained unfit to drive through drink or drugs.

(4) The court may, in determining whether there was such a likelihood as is mentioned in subsection (3) above, disregard any injury to him and any damage to the vehicle.

(5) For the purposes of this section, a person shall be taken to be unfit to drive if his ability to drive properly is for the time being impaired.

(6)–(8) [*Repealed by* SOCPA *2005, ss.111 and 174(2), Sched. 7, para. 27(1) and (2), and Sched. 17, Pt 2.*]

[This section is printed as amended by the *RTA* 1991, s.4.]

(2) Arrest

A police officer can have reasonable cause to suspect that a person is or has been committing an offence under this section even if he has passed a road side breath test: *DPP v. Robertson* [2002] R.T.R. 22, QBD (Newman J.). **32–64a**

(3) Mode of trial

This offence is triable only summarily: *RTOA* 1988, s.9, and Sched. 2, Pt I. **32–65**

(4) Alternative verdicts

An offence under section 4(1) is an alternative to an allegation of an offence under section 3A of the 1988 Act, and an offence under section 4(2) is an alternative to an allegation of an offence under section 4(1): *RTOA* 1988, s.24, *post*, § 32–165. **32–66**

(5) Sentence

Section 4(1), imprisonment not exceeding six months or a fine not exceeding level 5 on the standard scale, or both: *RTOA* 1988, s.33 and Sched. 2, Pt I (increased to 51 weeks as from a day to be appointed (but only in relation to offences committed after the date on which this amendment takes effect): *CJA* 2003, s.281(4)–(6)). Disqualification and endorsement are obligatory and the offence carries 3 to 11 penalty points: *ibid.*, ss.28, 34, 44 and Sched. 2, Pt I. **32–67**

Section 4(2), imprisonment not exceeding three months (increased to 51 weeks as from a day to be appointed (but only in relation to offences committed after the date on which this amendment takes effect): *CJA* 2003, s.280(2), and Sched. 26, para. 38(1) and (2)), or a fine not exceeding level 4 on the standard scale: *RTOA* 1988, s.33 and Sched. 2, Pt I. Disqualification is discretionary, endorsement is obligatory and the offence carries 10 penalty points: *ibid.*, ss.28, 34 and 44 and Sched. 2, Pt I.

As to disqualification and endorsement generally (including the penalty points system), see *post*, §§ 32–167 *et seq*.

(6) Ingredients of the offence

As to "driving", "mechanically propelled vehicle" and "road or other public place", see *ante*, §§ 32–14 *et seq*. **32–68**

In charge

32–69 This is undefined in the various Acts. It is therefore a question of fact: *R. v. Harnett* [1955] Crim.L.R. 793, CCA. The test was laid down in *Haines v. Roberts* [1953] 1 W.L.R. 309, DC: a person remains in charge of a vehicle until he demonstrates relinquishing control, *e.g.* by handing keys to another or by abandoning it. *DPP v. Watkins* [1989] Q.B. 821, DC, sets out the factors to be taken into account:

(a) whether and where he was in the vehicle or how far he was from it;
(b) what he was doing at the relevant time;
(c) whether he was in possession of the keys;
(d) whether there was evidence of an intention to take or assert control of the car by driving or otherwise;
(e) whether any other person was in at or near the vehicle and if so, the like particulars in respect of that person.

There is no requirement of proof of an intention to drive if the evidence otherwise establishes that the defendant was in charge of the vehicle: *CPS v. Bate*, *The Daily Telegraph*, December 2, 2004, DC.

As to the supervisor of a learner driver, see *DPP v. Janman*, *post*, § 32–81a.

Drink or drugs

32–70 Section 11 of the *RTA* 1988 defines "drug" as including "any intoxicant other than alcohol". In *Armstrong v. Clark* [1957] 2 Q.B. 391, DC, "drugs" was held to include a medicament or medicine.

(7) Evidence

Proof of unfitness

32–71 The prosecution must prove not only the influence of drink or drugs but also that proper control of the vehicle is impaired by drink or drugs: *R. v. Hawkes*, 22 Cr.App.R. 172, CCA. This may be shown by evidence of: (a) the manner of driving; (b) the driver's physical condition; (c) the proportion of alcohol in a specimen of breath, blood or urine, pursuant to section 15 of the *RTOA* 1988. In the case of a specimen, it is assumed (subject to s.15(3)) that the proportion of alcohol in the defendant's breath, blood or urine at the time of the alleged offence was not less than in the specimen: s.15(2). In the case of a high reading, an inference of impairment may be drawn. For section 15, see *post*, § 32–162.

Medical witness

32–72 A surgeon or other doctor summoned by the police to conduct an examination of a person suspected of having committed this offence is to be regarded as an independent medical referee: *R. v. Nowell*, 32 Cr.App.R. 173, CCA, as explained in *R. v. Lanfear* [1968] 2 Q.B. 77, 52 Cr.App.R. 176, CA.

Where evidence from the police and an analyst provided an ample basis for conviction, no inference adverse to the prosecution could result from failure to call the police surgeon: *Leetham v. DPP* [1999] R.T.R. 29, DC.

In *R. v. Payne*, 47 Cr.App.R. 122, CCA, the appellant, who had been arrested for driving while unfit to drive through drink, consented to be examined by a doctor having been told that it was no part of the doctor's duty to examine him in order to give an opinion as to his unfitness to drive. The doctor subsequently gave evidence that he was unfit to drive. It was held that the evidence was admissible, but ought not to have been admitted as the appellant may have refused to allow himself to be examined if he had known that the doctor might have given such evidence. See also *R. v. Palfrey*; *R. v. Sadler*, 54 Cr.App.R. 217, CA.

A medical witness may give evidence as to the quantity of drink the result of any analysis represents and the rate at which alcohol in the body is destroyed. He may also refresh his memory from recognised publications of the British Medical Association: *R. v. Somers*, 48 Cr.App.R. 11, CCA.

Opinion evidence of non-expert

A lay witness giving evidence for the prosecution can give evidence of his opinion that the defendant was drunk if he also states the facts upon which his opinion is based, but he cannot give evidence as to whether the defendant was fit to drive, even if the witness is himself a driver: *R. v. Davies*, 46 Cr.App.R. 292, Ct-MAC. *Cf. R. v. Neal* [1962] Crim.L.R. 698, Ct-MAC, where no objection was taken to such evidence and *R. v. Davies* was distinguished. **32–73**

(8) Defences

A person is deemed not to have been in charge if he proves on a balance of probabilities that at the material time the circumstances were such that there was no likelihood of him driving whilst still unfit: *RTA* 1988, s.4(3) (*ante*). **32–74**

Immobilising a vehicle will not suffice: *Saycell v. Bool* [1948] 2 All E.R. 83, DC; but having it clamped may: *Drake v. DPP* [1994] R.T.R. 411, DC.

H. DRIVING, BEING IN CHARGE, WHILST ABOVE THE PRESCRIBED LIMIT

(1) Statute

Road Traffic Act 1988, s.5

Driving or being in charge of a motor vehicle with alcohol concentration above prescribed limit

5.—(1) If a person— **32–75**

(a) drives or attempts to drive a motor vehicle on a road or other public place, or

(b) is in charge of a motor vehicle on a road or other public place,

after consuming so much alcohol that the proportion of it in his breath, blood or urine exceeds the prescribed limit he is guilty of an offence.

(2) It is a defence for a person charged with an offence under subsection (1)(b) above to prove that at the time he is alleged to have committed the offence the circumstances were such that there was no likelihood of his driving the vehicle whilst the proportion of alcohol in his breath, blood or urine remained likely to exceed the prescribed limit.

(3) The court may, in determining whether there was such a likelihood as is mentioned in subsection (2) above, disregard any injury to him and any damage to the vehicle.

(2) Mode of trial

This offence is triable only summarily: *RTOA* 1988, s.9 and Sched. 2, Pt I. **32–76**

(3) Alternative verdicts

An offence under section 5(1)(a) is an alternative to an allegation of an offence under section 3A of the 1988 Act, and an offence under section 5(1)(b) is an alternative to an allegation of an offence under section 5(1)(a): *RTOA* 1988, s.24, *post*, § 32–165. **32–77**

(4) Sentence

Section 5(1)(a): as for section 4(1), *ante*, § 32–67 (and subject to the same prospective increase: see *CJA* 2003, s.281(4)–(6)). **32–78**

Section 5(1)(b): as for section 4(2), *ante*, § 32–67 (and subject to the same prospective increase: see *CJA* 2003, s.280(2), and Sched. 26, para. 38(1) and (3)).

(5) Ingredients of the offence

As to "drives" and "road or other public place", see *ante*, §§ 32–14, 32–18. As to "motor vehicle", see *ante*, § 32–61. **32–79**

"consuming"

"Consuming" is not limited to intake into the body by the mouth: *DPP v. Johnson* [1995] R.T.R. 9, D.C. **32–80**

"breath"

"Breath" means all that is exhaled, not just deep lung air; the fact that the intoximeter is designed to measure the latter and not the former is irrelevant: *Zafar v. DPP* **32–80a**

[2005] R.T.R. 18, DC; and *Woolfe v. DPP* [2007] R.T.R. 16, DC; but, as to the possibility of establishing special reasons not to disqualify where what is exhaled is not deep lung air, see *post*, § 32–185.

Zafar and *Woolfe* were followed in *McNeil v. DPP* [2008] L.S. Gazette, May 15, 28, DC ([2008] EWHC 1254 (Admin.)), where it was held that a police officer was not entitled to require a specimen of blood or urine under section 7(3)(bb) of the 1988 Act (*post*, § 32–93) on the ground that he had reasonable cause to believe that the reading on the intoximeter was not a reliable indication of the proportion of alcohol in the breath by reason of the specimen having been affected or potentially affected by reflux or regurgitation from the stomach.

"the prescribed limit"

32–81 The limits are: (a) 35 microgrammes of alcohol in 100 millilitres of breath; (b) 80 milligrammes of alcohol in 100 millilitres of blood; (c) 107 milligrammes of alcohol in 100 millilitres of urine: *Road Traffic Act* 1988, s.11(2). Normally prosecutions are not pursued with readings under 40 microgrammes (breath).

"in charge"

32–81a See generally, *ante*, § 32–69.

A person supervising a learner driver was in charge of the vehicle even if the learner was a good driver who had not needed supervision; but if there was no likelihood of the supervisor driving, he might bring himself within subsection (2): *DPP v. Janman* [2004] R.T.R. 31, DC.

(6) Liability of secondary parties

32–82 The prosecution have to prove that the principal offender committed the offence, that the defendant was aware, or was reckless whether the former had consumed excessive alcohol and that the defendant had aided, abetted, counselled or procured the principal to commit the offence: *DPP v. Anderson* [1990] R.T.R. 269, DC. *Blakely v. DPP* [1991] R.T.R. 405, DC, suggests that recklessness will not suffice for a charge of procuring.

(7) Evidence

Specimen of breath, blood or urine

32–83 Sections 15 and 16 of the *RTOA* 1988 (see *post*, §§ 32–162 *et seq.*) provide for the use in evidence of specimens in proceedings for an offence under this section. Evidence of the proportion of alcohol or of a drug in a specimen may be given by means of a printout from an approved device or by evidence of a certificate signed by an authorised analyst.

An approved breath-testing device remains such even though modifications have been made to it; the test is whether, after such modification or alteration, the machine continues to satisfy the description in the approval document; if that description made no reference to the agreement with the manufacturer or the "Guide to Type Approval Procedures for Evidential Breath Alcohol Testing Instruments used for Road Traffic Enforcement in Great Britain", then the device would still be an approved device if the only effect of any modification to it was that it did not comply with one of those documents: *Breckon v. DPP* [2008] R.T.R. 8, DC. See also *Kemsley v. DPP*, 169 J.P. 148, DC (mere fact that there are some differences between the machine used and the approved type does not mean that the particular machine is of an unapproved type; anybody who seeks to argue that a particular machine has been changed so as to be different from the approved type would be well advised to be in a position to demonstrate how and in what respects it differs from the approved type, and how any difference is sufficient to make it of a different type).

Oral evidence may also be given of the results from an approved device, so long as it includes the breath/alcohol reading and the machine's calibration readings: *Owen v. Chesters* [1985] R.T.R. 191, DC; *Greenaway v. DPP* [1994] R.T.R. 17, DC.

Where the defendant has exercised his option, under section 8 of the *RTA* 1988 (see *post*, § 32–100), to provide a sample of blood or urine in substitution for the specimen of breath, the printout may not be relied on for the purposes of proving the reliability of the analysis of a specimen of blood or urine: see s.8(2), and *Carter v. DPP* [2007] R.T.R. 22, DC. Nor can it be relied on if the self-calibration check is outside the limits: *R. v. Kingston-upon-Thames JJ., ex p. Khanna* [1986] R.T.R. 364, DC. Nor may it be relied on in support of a charge of driving with excess alcohol in blood or urine where the alternative sample was unlawfully required: *Evans v. DPP*, *The Times*, May 30, 1996, DC. The printout may, however, be relied on: (i) where the defendant frustrates the proper exercise of the option or, indeed, tampers with his option specimen: *DPP v. Poole* [1992] R.T.R. 177, DC; *Yhnell v. DPP* [1989] R.T.R. 250, DC; (ii) where the only inaccuracy is of the clock, which is not part of the processing function: *DPP v. McKeown*; *DPP v. Jones* [1997] 2 Cr.App.R. 155, HL; (iii) despite minor typographical or printing errors, providing the Intoximeter's computer is working properly: *Reid v. DPP* [1999] R.T.R. 357, DC, applying *DPP v. McKeown*; *DPP v. Jones*; and *DPP v. Barber*, 163 J.P. 457, DC; or (iv) for the purpose of assessing the credibility of the defendant's evidence as to how much alcohol he had consumed: *Carter v. DPP*, *ante*.

Where a prosecution is based on the analysis of a sample of blood provided by the defendant under section 7(3) of the *RTA* 1988 (*post*, § 32–93) on the ground that the constable who had required the specimen of blood had had reasonable cause to believe that a device used to take a specimen of breath from the accused had not produced a reliable result (see s.7(3)(bb)), and there is at trial an issue as to the reliability of the analysis of the blood sample (the defence having raised the issue of contamination), it is open to the prosecution to adduce evidence of the breath test result to prove compatibility, on the basis that if the blood sample had been contaminated, it was remarkable that the result should be entirely compatible with the result given by the breath test, albeit there had been cause to suppose that the breath test device had not given an accurate reading; and if both tests were flawed, it was even more unlikely that the results would, by chance, be the same; but evidence of compatibility should be the subject of expert evidence, for the purpose of identifying and explaining the significance of the relationship between the two results: *Slasor v. DPP* [1999] R.T.R. 432, DC. Equally, where a prosecution is based on the analysis of a specimen of blood, evidence of the result of a pre-release breath test is in principle admissible for the purpose of impugning the reliability of the analysis of the blood specimen: *Parish v. DPP* [2000] R.T.R. 143, DC.

Where the reliability of an approved breath-testing device is challenged, it is not necessary, as a matter of law, to adduce expert evidence: *DPP v. Spurrier* [2000] R.T.R. 60, DC.

The court should only concern itself with the reliability of the particular device used, it being no part of its function to consider whether the type of device used should have received the approval of the Secretary of State; in evaluating any challenge to the reliability of the device, the court should be careful to ensure that the evidence on which the challenge is founded is relevant; where, therefore, it was common ground that at the material time there would not have been mouth alcohol or alcohol vapour in the dead-space of the upper respiratory tract of the defendant, a challenge to the reliability of the device used (an Intoximeter EC/IR) based on evidence as to the effect on the device of mouth alcohol or alcohol vapour was a challenge based on irrelevant evidence where the court was satisfied that the device was otherwise reliable: *DPP v. Brown*; *DPP v. Teixeira* [2002] R.T.R. 23, DC. See also *DPP v. Memery* [2003] R.T.R 18, DC (it had not been open to the Crown Court to find that the Secretary of State in approving the Intoximeter EC/IR for the purposes of section 7(1)(a) of the 1988 Act had acted unlawfully or *Wednesbury* unreasonably (*Associated Provincial Picture Houses Ltd v. Wednesbury Corp* [1948] 1 K.B. 223, CA) on account of the inability of the device to detect mouth alcohol; having regard to the procedural safeguards relating to inaccurate readings due to mouth alcohol, the approval of the device was not irrational; the reading from such a device was admissible; the reliability of the reading was always open to challenge; on the facts, however, the inability of the device to detect mouth alcohol was wholly irrelevant to the issue as to reliability); *Grant v. DPP*, 167 J.P. 459, DC (following *Memery*); and *DPP v. Wood*; *DPP v. McGillicuddy*, 170 J.P.177, DC (*ante*, § 12–59).

In *Gregory v. DPP*, 166 J.P. 400, DC, it was held that where, on a prosecution of a person for driving a motor vehicle whilst over the prescribed limit, it had been established that the capacity of the sample vials was six millilitres, that fluoride was present in the vials as a preservative, that an approximate amount of two millilitres of blood had been put into each vial, and that the method of analysis which had been used to measure the alcohol content of the blood sample retained by the police was headspace gas chromotography (blood is heated/ some of the air above it—the "headspace"—is sucked out and analysed/ amount of alcohol in headspace is proportionate to level of alcohol in blood sample), the evidence of a defence expert to the effect that a failure to fill the vial with blood would mean that there is too much preservative for equilibrium to occur when heated, with the consequence that the result would exaggerate the blood alcohol level by about eight per cent, was not inadmissible as being entirely theoretical. Furthermore, since the evidence was unchallenged, and since the analysis evidence of the prosecution had put the defendant's blood alcohol level at 84 milligrammes per 100 millilitres of blood, it seriously called into question the reliability and accuracy of that analysis; in the absence of any rational basis for rejecting this evidence, it could not be said that the prosecution had discharged the burden of proving a blood alcohol level which exceeded the permitted limit.

Where a person having been lawfully required to provide two specimens of breath pursuant to section 7(1) of the *RTA* 1988, provided two specimens with readings of 48 and 58 microgrammes of alcohol per 100 millilitres of breath, and having been offered the option of providing a specimen of blood pursuant to section 8(2) of the Act, provided such specimen which, upon analysis, was found to be over the prescribed limit, she was properly convicted of an offence contrary to section 5, notwithstanding the finding of the court that the breath testing device was not working properly: *Branagan v. DPP* [2000] R.T.R. 235, DC.

As to continuity evidence in relation to a blood sample, and as to the contents of the label being admissible under sections 24 and 26 of the *CJA* 1988 (see now s.117 of the *CJA* 2003, *ante*, § 11–26), see *Khatibi v. DPP*, 168 J.P. 361, DC.

Back calculation

32–84 The prosecution may rely on the statutory assumption (s.15(2), *post*, § 32–162) to prove that the defendant's alcohol level at the time of the offence was the same as his specimen or they may back calculate to show that it was higher: *Smith v. Geraghty* [1986] R.T.R. 222, DC. This is so even where the specimen alcohol proportion is below the limit and it is back calculation which takes the defendant over the limit. Back calculation is, however, both judicially and medically discouraged due to the inherently unreliable nature of the calculation and should not be relied on unless the evidence is straightforward and would place the defendant clearly over the limit at the time of the offence: *Gumbley v. Cunningham*; *Gould v. Castle* [1987] 3 All E.R. 733, DC.

(8) Defences

32–85 The statutory assumption in section 15(2) of the *RTOA* 1988 (*ante*) shall not be made if the defendant brings himself within section 15(3). As to this, see *post*, § 32–162.

The evidence of the breath test device can be challenged but the scope is narrow. The most fertile source of challenge in the past has been in connection with the calibrations being outside the accepted parameters or the presence of high acetone levels. The approved devices currently in operation have a greater ability (a) to differentiate between various substances contained within a sample, (b) to take account of mouth alcohol in a breath sample, and (c) to deal with differences in samples that exceed certain parameters.

In *Sheldrake v. DPP*; *Att.-Gen.'s Reference (No. 4 of 2002)* [2005] 1 A.C. 264, HL, it was held that section 5(2) imposes a legal burden on the accused; but such a burden is not beyond reasonable limits or in any way arbitrary, notwithstanding that it may infringe the presumption of innocence.

The issue to be addressed under section 5(2) is the likelihood of the defendant having driven the vehicle, not whether he had any intention of doing so: *CPS v. Thompson* [2008] R.T.R. 5, DC.

As to duress and necessity as possible defences, see *ante*, §§ 17–119 *et seq.*

I. FAILURE TO CO-OPERATE WITH PRELIMINARY TEST

(1) Statute

Road Traffic Act 1988, ss.6–6E

Power to administer preliminary tests

6.—(1) If any of subsections (2) to (5) applies a constable may require a person to co-operate with any one or more preliminary tests administered to the person by that constable or another constable. **32–86**

(2) This subsection applies if a constable reasonably suspects that the person—

(a) is driving, is attempting to drive or is in charge of a motor vehicle on a road or other public place, and

(b) has alcohol or a drug in his body or is under the influence of a drug.

(3) This subsection applies if a constable reasonably suspects that the person—

(a) has been driving, attempting to drive or in charge of a motor vehicle on a road or other public place while having alcohol or a drug in his body or while unfit to drive because of a drug, and

(b) still has alcohol or a drug in his body or is still under the influence of a drug.

(4) This subsection applies if a constable reasonably suspects that the person—

(a) is or has been driving, attempting to drive or in charge of a motor vehicle on a road or other public place, and

(b) has committed a traffic offence while the vehicle was in motion.

(5) This subsection applies if—

(a) an accident occurs owing to the presence of a motor vehicle on a road or other public place, and

(b) a constable reasonably believes that the person was driving, attempting to drive or in charge of the vehicle at the time of the accident.

(6) A person commits an offence if without reasonable excuse he fails to co-operate with a preliminary test in pursuance of a requirement imposed under this section.

(7) A constable may administer a preliminary test by virtue of any of subsections (2) to (4) only if he is in uniform.

(8) In this section—

(a) a reference to a preliminary test is to any of the tests described in sections 6A to 6C, and

(b) "traffic offence" means an offence under—

(i) a provision of Part II of the *Public Passenger Vehicles Act* 1981,

(ii) a provision of the *Road Traffic Regulation Act* 1984,

(iii) a provision of the *Road Traffic Offenders Act* 1988 other than a provision of Part III, or

(iv) a provision of this Act other than a provision of Part V.

Preliminary breath test

6A.—(1) A preliminary breath test is a procedure whereby the person to whom the test is administered provides a specimen of breath to be used for the purpose of obtaining, by means of a device of a type approved by the Secretary of State, an indication whether the proportion of alcohol in the person's breath or blood is likely to exceed the prescribed limit. **32–86a**

(2) A preliminary breath test administered in reliance on section 6(2) to (4) may be administered only at or near the place where the requirement to co-operate with the test is imposed.

(3) A preliminary breath test administered in reliance on section 6(5) may be administered—

(a) at or near the place where the requirement to co-operate with the test is imposed, or

(b) if the constable who imposes the requirement thinks it expedient, at a police station specified by him.

Preliminary impairment test

6B.—(1) A preliminary impairment test is a procedure whereby the constable administering the test— **32–86b**

(a) observes the person to whom the test is administered in his performance of tasks specified by the constable, and

(b) makes such other observations of the person's physical state as the constable thinks expedient.

(2) The Secretary of State shall issue (and may from time to time revise) a code of practice about—

(a) the kind of task that may be specified for the purpose of a preliminary impairment test,

(b) the kind of observation of physical state that may be made in the course of a preliminary impairment test,

(c) the manner in which a preliminary impairment test should be administered, and

(d) the inferences that may be drawn from observations made in the course of a preliminary impairment test.

(3) In issuing or revising the code of practice the Secretary of State shall aim to ensure that a preliminary impairment test is designed to indicate—

(a) whether a person is unfit to drive, and

(b) if he is, whether or not his unfitness is likely to be due to drink or drugs.

(4) A preliminary impairment test may be administered—

(a) at or near the place where the requirement to co-operate with the test is imposed, or

(b) if the constable who imposes the requirement thinks it expedient, at a police station specified by him.

(5) A constable administering a preliminary impairment test shall have regard to the code of practice under this section.

(6) A constable may administer a preliminary impairment test only if he is approved for that purpose by the chief officer of the police force to which he belongs.

(7) A code of practice under this section may include provision about—

(a) the giving of approval under subsection (6), and

(b) in particular, the kind of training that a constable should have undergone, or the kind of qualification that a constable should possess, before being approved under that subsection.

Preliminary drug test

32–86c **6C.**—(1) A preliminary drug test is a procedure by which a specimen of sweat or saliva is—

(a) obtained, and

(b) used for the purpose of obtaining, by means of a device of a type approved by the Secretary of State, an indication whether the person to whom the test is administered has a drug in his body.

(2) A preliminary drug test may be administered—

(a), (b) [*identical to s.6B(4)(a), (b)*, ante, *§ 32–86b*].

Arrest

32–86d **6D.**—(1) A constable may arrest a person without warrant if as a result of a preliminary breath test the constable reasonably suspects that the proportion of alcohol in the person's breath or blood exceeds the prescribed limit.

(1A) The fact that specimens of breath have been provided under section 7 of this Act by the person concerned does not prevent subsection (1) above having effect if the constable who imposed on him the requirement to provide the specimens has reasonable cause to believe that the device used to analyse the specimens has not produced a reliable indication of the proportion of alcohol in the breath of the person.

(2) A constable may arrest a person without warrant if—

(a) the person fails to co-operate with a preliminary test in pursuance of a requirement imposed under section 6, and

(b) the constable reasonably suspects that the person has alcohol or a drug in his body or is under the influence of a drug.

(2A) A person arrested under this section may, instead of being taken to a police station, be detained at or near the place where the preliminary test was, or would have been, administered, with a view to imposing on him there a requirement under section 7 of this Act.

(3) A person may not be arrested under this section while at a hospital as a patient.

Power of entry

6E.—(1) A constable may enter any place (using reasonable force if necessary) for the purpose of— **32–86e**

(a) imposing a requirement by virtue of section 6(5) following an accident in a case where the constable reasonably suspects that the accident involved injury of any person, or

(b) arresting a person under section 6D following an accident in a case where the constable reasonably suspects that the accident involved injury of any person.

(2) [*Non-application to Scotland.*]

[Ss.6 to 6E were substituted for the original s.6 by the *Railways and Transport Safety Act* 2003, s.107, and Sched. 7, para.1. S.6D is printed as amended by the *SOCPA* 2005, s.154(1) to (3).]

(2) Mode of trial

The offence contrary to section 6(6) is triable only summarily: *RTOA* 1988, s.9, and Sched. 2, Pt 1. **32–87**

(3) Sentence

A fine not exceeding level 3 on the standard scale: *RTOA* 1988, s.33 and Sched. 2, Pt I. Disqualification is discretionary, endorsement is obligatory and the offence carries 4 penalty points: *ibid.*, ss.28, 34, 44 and Sched. 2, Pt I. **32–88**

(4) Power to stop vehicles

The police have several powers to stop vehicles, including the general one contained in section 163 of the *RTA* 1988 (*post*, § 32–136) and those in the *PACE Act* 1984 (*ante*, §§ 15–49 *et seq.*). To that extent, they may stop vehicles randomly; however, they may not test unless they have reasonable grounds for suspicion/belief, otherwise any arrest may be unlawful and the result of the test excluded: *DPP v. Godwin* [1991] R.T.R. 303, DC. This suspicion may arise before or after the vehicle has been stopped; and it need not be a suspicion that the alcohol level is in excess of the limit: *Blake v. Pope* [1986] 1 W.L.R. 1152, DC. The constable does not need to state his grounds for suspicion: *Williams v. Jones* [1972] R.T.R. 4, DC. The grounds may be based on information from others depending on source and contemporaneity: *Erskine v. Hollin* [1971] R.T.R. 199, DC; *Monaghan v. Corbett, The Times*, June 23, 1983, DC. As to whether any duty to caution a person to whom a test is to be administered arises prior to the administration of the test, see *ante*, § 15–486. **32–89**

(5) Disclosure

The reference to "a specimen of breath" in section 15(2) of the *RTOA* 1988 (use of specimens in proceedings for offence under section 4 or 5 (*post*, § 32–162)) is to a specimen of breath taken under section 7 of the *RTA* 1988 (*post*, § 32–93a); it does not include a preliminary roadside breath test under section 6A; but it would be good practice, and may be required by the *CPIA* 1996, s.3 (*ante*, § 12–54), where the equipment permits this to be done, for the reading in figures obtained from the roadside breath test to be disclosed to the defence; there may be cases in which this could be used to challenge the accuracy of the evidence in relation to the section 7 specimen: *Smith v. DPP* [2007] R.T.R. 36, DC; and *Breckon v. DPP* [2008] R.T.R. 8, DC. **32–89a**

(6) Ingredients of the offence

"in pursuance of a requirement imposed under this section"

A preliminary breath or drug test must be carried out by an approved device, the assembly of which has been carried out in accordance with the manufacturer's instructions: *R. v. Coates* [1971] R.T.R. 74, CA. Failure will not be fatal unless it can be shown to invalidate the result: *Att.-Gen's Reference (No. 1 of 1978)* [1978] R.T.R. 377, CA. The officer may ask for a second test if he believes the first one to be unreliable: *Sparrow v. Bradley* [1985] R.T.R. 122, DC. **32–90**

Where the prosecution rely on section 6(5), they must prove that an accident actually took place. There need be no other vehicle involved: *R. v. Pico* [1971] R.T.R. 500, CA. Nor, conversely, need the defendant's vehicle be involved in the accident, but there must be a direct causal connection between the vehicle's presence on the road and the accident: *M. (A Minor) v. Oxford* [1981] R.T.R. 246, DC.

If a requirement for a preliminary test is not "imposed" in accordance with the provisions of the statute, there can be no conviction of an offence: see *Fox v. Chief Constable of Gwent* [1986] A.C. 281, HL; *Gull v. Scarborough* [1987] R.T.R., DC. But an unlawful arrest will not *per se* invalidate the procedure under section 7: *post*, § 32–97.

"fails"

32–91 The word "fail" includes "refuse": *RTA* 1988, s.11(2). In the absence of an express refusal to supply a specimen or the motorist specifying an outrageous condition prior thereto, it is for the tribunal of fact to decide whether the conduct of a motorist is such as to amount to a refusal: *R. v. Mackey* [1977] R.T.R. 146, CA. See also *R. v. Wagner* [1970] R.T.R. 422, CA (indication of an intention to leave scene temporarily whilst awaiting arrival of breath-test machine); and *DPP v. Swan, The Daily Telegraph*, October 28, 2004, DC (question is one of fact in each case; a motorist's indication of non-cooperation could amount to failure).

A person "fails to provide a specimen of breath" if he blows into an Alcometer testing device so as to illuminate one only of the two lights, when the device operated in such a way that if the "Read" button were pressed, a positive reading would be reliable but a negative reading would be unreliable; section 11(3) of the Act stipulates that a person does not co-operate with a preliminary test or provide a specimen of breath for analysis unless his co-operation or the specimen is sufficient to enable the test to be carried out and is provided in such a way as to enable the objective of the test to be satisfactorily achieved; the objective of the test was to obtain a reliable reading, not to obtain a reading which was reliable in some circumstances but not others: *DPP v. Heywood* [1998] R.T.R. 1, DC.

"without reasonable excuse"

32–92 See *post*, §§ 32–104 *et seq.*

J. FAILING TO PROVIDE EVIDENTIAL SPECIMEN

(1) Statute

Road Traffic Act 1988, s.7

Provision of specimens for analysis

32–93 **7.**—(1) In the course of an investigation into whether a person has committed an offence under section 3A, 4 or 5 of this Act a constable may, subject to the following provisions of this section and section 9 of this Act, require him—

(a) to provide two specimens of breath for analysis by means of a device of a type approved by the Secretary of State, or

(b) to provide a specimen of blood or urine for a laboratory test.

(2) A requirement under this section to provide specimens of breath can only be made—

(a) at a police station,

(b) at a hospital, or

(c) at or near a place where a relevant breath test has been administered to the person concerned or would have been so administered but for his failure to co-operate with it.

(2A) For the purposes of this section "a relevant breath test" is a procedure involving the provision by the person concerned of a specimen of breath to be used for the purpose of obtaining an indication whether the proportion of alcohol in his breath or blood is likely to exceed the prescribed limit.

(2B) A requirement under this section to provide specimens of breath may not be made at or near a place mentioned in subsection (2)(c) above unless the constable making it—

(a) is in uniform, or

(b) has imposed a requirement on the person concerned to co-operate with a relevant breath test in circumstances in which section 6(5) of this Act applies.

(2C) Where a constable has imposed a requirement on the person concerned to co-operate with a relevant breath test at any place, he is entitled to remain at or near that place in order to impose on him there a requirement under this section.

(2D) If a requirement under subsection (1)(a) above has been made at a place other than at a police station, such a requirement may subsequently be made at a police station if (but only if)—

(a) a device or a reliable device of the type mentioned in subsection (1)(a) above was not available at that place or it was for any other reason not practicable to use such a device there, or

(b) the constable who made the previous requirement has reasonable cause to believe that the device used there has not produced a reliable indication of the proportion of alcohol in the breath of the person concerned.

(3) A requirement under this section to provide a specimen of blood or urine can only be made at a police station or at a hospital; and it cannot be made at a police station unless—

(a) the constable making the requirement has reasonable cause to believe that for medical reasons a specimen of breath cannot be provided or should not be required, or

(b) specimens of breath have not been provided elsewhere and at the time the requirement is made a device or a reliable device of the type mentioned in subsection (1)(a) above is not available at the police station or it is then for any other reason not practicable to use such a device there, or

(bb) a device of the type mentioned in subsection (1)(a) above has been used (at the police station or elsewhere) but the constable who required the specimens of breath has reasonable cause to believe that the device has not produced a reliable indication of the proportion of alcohol in the breath of the person concerned, or

(bc) as a result of the administration of a preliminary drug test, the constable making the requirement has reasonable cause to believe that the person required to provide a specimen of blood or urine has a drug in his body, or

(c) the suspected offence is one under section 3A or 4 of this Act and the constable making the requirement has been advised by a medical practitioner that the condition of the person required to provide the specimen might be due to some drug;

but may then be made notwithstanding that the person required to provide the specimen has already provided or been required to provide two specimens of breath.

(4) If the provision of a specimen other than a specimen of breath may be required in pursuance of this section the question whether it is to be a specimen of blood or a specimen of urine and, in the case of a specimen of blood, the question who is to be asked to take it shall be decided (subject to subsection (4A)) by the constable making the requirement.

(4A) Where a constable decides for the purposes of subsection (4) to require the provision of a specimen of blood, there shall be no requirement to provide such specimen if—

(a) the medical practitioner who is asked to take the specimen is of the opinion that, for medical reasons, it cannot or should not be taken; or

(b) the registered health care professional who is asked to take it is of the opinion that there is no contrary opinion from a medical practitioner;

and, where by virtue of this subsection there can be no requirement to provide a specimen of blood, the constable may require a specimen of urine instead.

(5) A specimen of urine shall be provided within one hour of the requirement for its provision being made and after the provision of a previous specimen of urine.

(6) A person who, without reasonable excuse, fails to provide a specimen when required to do so in pursuance of this section is guilty of an offence.

(7) A constable must, on requiring any person to provide a specimen in pursuance of this section, warn him that a failure to provide it may render him liable to prosecution.

[This section is printed as amended by the *CPIA* 1996, s.63(1); the *Police Reform Act* 2002, s.55(1) and (2); the *Railways and Transport Safety Act* 2003, s.107, and Sched. 7, para. 2; and the *SOCPA* 2005, s.154(4) to (6).]

Section 11 of the Act (interpretation) was amended by the *Police Reform Act* 2002, s.55(3) and (4), so as to insert a definition of "registered health care professional" as meaning a person (other than a medical practitioner) who is a registered nurse or a registered member of a health care profession which is designated for the purposes of the section by an order made by the Secretary of State.

(2) Mode of trial

32–94 This offence is triable only summarily: *RTOA* 1988, s.9, and Sched. 2, Pt I.

(3) Alternative verdicts

32–95 An offence under section 7(6) is an alternative to an allegation of an offence under section 3A of the 1988 Act: *RTOA* 1988, s.24, *post*, § 32–165.

(4) Sentence

32–96 Where the specimen was required to ascertain ability to drive or the proportion of alcohol at the time the offender was driving or attempting to drive, six months' imprisonment (increased to 51 weeks as from a day to be appointed (but only in relation to offences committed after the date on which this amendment takes effect): *CJA* 2003, s.281(4)–(6)) or a fine not exceeding level 5 on the standard scale, or both; disqualification and endorsement are obligatory in such a case; and the number of penalty points applicable in such cases is 3 to 11; in any other case, three months' imprisonment (increased to 51 weeks as from a day to be appointed (but only in relation to offences committed after the date on which this amendment takes effect): *CJA* 2003, s.280(2), and Sched. 26, para. 38(1) and (4)) or a fine not exceeding level 4 on the standard scale, or both; disqualification is discretionary and endorsement obligatory; the number of penalty points is 10: *RTOA* 1988, ss.28, 33, 34, 44 and Sched. 2, Pt I.

As to disqualification and endorsement generally (including the penalty points system), see *post* §§ 32–167 *et seq.*

(5) Procedure

Device approvals

32–96a As to challenges to approval orders and to the reliability of approved devices, see *ante*, § 32–83.

Of whom requirement may be made

32–97 The defendant need not have been driving in order for a request to be made so long as it is in the course of an investigation: *Hawkes v. DPP* [1993] R.T.R. 116, DC. Where it is unclear who the driver is, more than one person, if suspected, may be required to give a specimen: *Pearson v. Metropolitan Police Commr* [1988] R.T.R. 276, DC.

Failure to follow guidelines

32–97a A requirement to provide a specimen is not rendered unlawful by virtue of a failure to follow particular police guidelines (*e.g.* a requirement that where an individual indicates during breath test procedure that he has eaten recently, the police officer should wait 20 minutes before continuing with the procedure); whilst it was possible that such a failure could affect the reliability of a specimen, that was of no relevance where no specimen had in fact been provided: *DPP v. Coulter*, *The Daily Telegraph*, July 7, 2005, DC ([2005] EWHC 1533 (Admin.)).

Where, contrary to the instructions issued by the machine, the mouthpiece of a breath testing device is not retained, so as to preclude subsequent testing thereof by the defence, this will not provide a basis for a stay of a prosecution for failure to provide a specimen where the failure is shown to have had nothing to do with any fault in the mouthpiece: *McKeon v. DPP* [2008] R.T.R. 14, DC; *Longstaff v. DPP* [2008] R.T.R. 17, DC.

Warning of consequences of non-compliance

32–98 If there is no warning given under section 7(7) then the requirement is negatived:

Simpson v. Spalding [1987] R.T.R. 221, DC. It also affords a reasonable excuse for failing to provide a specimen: *R. v. Dolan* [1970] R.T.R. 43, CA. See also *Edmond v. DPP, post,* § 32–99.

Blood and urine samples

The issue of whether the officer had reasonable cause to believe that a specimen could not be provided for medical reasons is one to be assessed by the court: *DPP v. Davies* [1989] R.T.R. 391, DC. The following have all been held to be capable of being medical reasons: injuries, *Horrocks v. Binns (Note)* [1986] R.T.R. 202, DC; intoxication, *Young v. DPP* [1992] R.T.R. 388, DC; taking tablets, *Wade v. DPP* [1996] R.T.R. 177, DC. An officer who has required a specimen of blood or urine on the basis that he has reasonable cause to believe that for medical reasons a specimen of breath cannot be provided may, however, change his mind, as where he subsequently obtains the opinion of a medical practitioner that there were no such medical reasons: *Longstaff v. DPP* [2008] R.T.R. 17, DC. **32–99**

Whether the machine is operating reliably is a matter for the officer's judgment. However, this must be a reasonable belief otherwise any subsequent specimen obtained may be excluded: *DPP v. Dixon* [1993] R.T.R. 22, DC. A discrepancy in breath test readings can give rise to such a belief even though the device is in fact working properly: *DPP v. Smith (Robert James)* [2000] R.T.R. 341, DC; but such a belief may not be based on the possibility of the specimen having been affected or potentially affected by reflux or regurgitation from the stomach: *McNeil v. DPP* (*ante,* § 32–80a). Where the constable who made the initial requirement for breath had cause to suppose that the reason for an unreliable indication had nothing to do with the reliability of the machine itself, but was caused by the individual providing two significantly different amounts of breath, he was entitled to offer the individual the opportunity of providing further breath samples; he was, however, under no obligation to do so: *Jubb v. DPP* [2003] R.T.R. 19, QBD (McCombe J.). In *Stewart v. DPP* [2003] R.T.R. 35, DC, the court went further, saying that when McCombe J. had added that the operator could not require two further breath specimens, this was unnecessary to the decision and went too far. It was said that a second requirement could lawfully be made: *sed quaere*. Where a person is invited to provide, or offered the opportunity of providing, a second set of specimens of breath, it would be misleading to give a second warning under section 7(7), and there is no duty to do so: *Edmond v. DPP* [2006] R.T.R. 18, DC.

The procedure to be followed under section 7(4) was laid down by the House of Lords in *DPP v. Warren* [1993] A.C. 319. The constable must tell the driver why breath specimens cannot be taken or used, tell him that he is required to give a specimen of blood or urine, but that it is for the constable to decide which, warn him that failure to provide a specimen may render him liable to prosecution, and then, if the constable has decided to require blood, ask him if there are any reasons why a specimen cannot or should not be taken from him by a doctor. Provided the driver has an opportunity to raise any objection he might have to giving blood on medical grounds or for any other reason which might afford "a reasonable excuse", there is nothing in the language of the statute to justify a procedural requirement that the driver be invited to express his own preference for giving blood or urine.

Subsequent cases initially indicated that the procedure is strict and that deviation therefrom would be fatal to conviction: *Ogburn v. DPP*; *Williams v. DPP*; *DPP v. Duffy*; *DPP v. Nesbitt* [1994] R.T.R. 241, DC. More recent authorities indicated a less strict interpretation of *Warren*. In *Baldwin v. DPP* [1996] R.T.R. 238, DC, it was said that *Warren* was guidance and not a statute. See also *Joiner v. DPP (Note–1995)* [1997] R.T.R. 387, DC; *DPP v. Ormsby (Note)* [1997] R.T.R. 394, DC; and *Gorman v. DPP*; *DPP v. Arnup (Note)* [1997] R.T.R. 409, DC.

The matter eventually came back before the House of Lords in *DPP v. Jackson*; *Stanley v. DPP* [1999] 1 A.C. 406. It was held that: (i) with three exceptions, what was said in *Warren* as to what should be said to a driver where a specimen of blood or urine may be required under section 7(3), or in a case falling within section 8(2) of that Act (*post,* § 32–100), should not be regarded as mandatory; the exceptions being: (a) in a section 7(3) case, the warning as to the risk of prosecution for failure to provide a specimen required by section 7(7); (b) in a section 7(3) case, the reason under that subsection for making the requirement (*e.g.* no breath device available); and (c) in a section 8(2) case, a statement that the specimen of breath with the lower proportion of alcohol did not exceed 50 microgrammes of alcohol in 100 millilitres of breath; (ii) it was, however, desirable that the driver should know that any blood sample taken would be by a doctor, and to this end it would be advisable for police officers to go through the *Warren* formula (at p. 327 for section 8(2), and at p. 328 for section 7(3)); (iii) failure to do so would not, however, be fatal so long as the driver was aware of the fact that a blood sample would be taken by a doctor; (iv) in a section 8(2) case, if the full formula was not given, the question for the court would be whether the omission had deprived the driver of the opportunity to exercise the option or had caused him to exercise it in a way in which he would not have done, had the full formula been used; only exceptionally would justices be able to conclude there had been prejudice in the absence of evidence from the accused on the issue; if, however, they were not satisfied that there had been no prejudice, they should acquit; (v) in neither case is it necessary for the driver to be asked if there are any non-medical reasons for a specimen of blood not being taken; (vi) in a section 8(2) case, however, it is necessary not just to tell the driver that a specimen of blood will be taken by a doctor unless the doctor considers there are medical reasons for not taking blood, but he should also be asked if there are any medical reasons why a specimen could not or should not be taken by a doctor; and (vii) as to statements by the driver about not liking needles (or similar), it was a question of fact for the justices whether what was said raises a medical reason for not providing blood or is tantamount to a refusal.

If there was no reason for choosing a specimen of blood in preference to urine and a valid reason had been given for choosing urine prior to a decision being made, the constable should at least consider whether to opt for urine rather than blood. Opting for a specimen to which the individual objected, without any basis for so doing would be perverse: *Joseph v. DPP* [2004] R.T.R. 21, DC.

Where a requirement to provide a specimen of blood has been properly made at a police station pursuant to section 7(3), the specimen may be taken elsewhere by a medical practitioner: *Russell (RUC Superintendent) v. Devine* [2003] 2 Cr.App.R. 26, HL.

In *Butler v. DPP* [2001] R.T.R. 28, DC, it was held that a constable proposing to require a blood specimen at a hospital is under a duty to inform the medical practitioner of any potential medical objection to giving blood of which he is aware; a failure to give such information renders any resulting blood sample inadmissible, even though the medical practitioner raises no objection to the proposal and would not do so even if he were told of the potential medical objection.

The obligation to inform the person of whom a requirement is made under section 7(3) of the ground for making the requirement may be discharged by a constable other than the constable making the requirement: *Bobin v. DPP* [1999] R.T.R. 375, DC.

The specimen required is usually blood; but if a medical practitioner is of the opinion that for medical reasons a specimen of blood cannot or should not be taken, then the specimen must be urine (s.7(4)). Section 7(4) does not oblige the officer requiring the specimen to make his own assessment of possible medical reasons for not giving blood (see *DPP v. Gibbons*, 165 J.P. 812, QBD (Sullivan J.)). A person provides a blood specimen if and only if he consents to the taking of it, and it is taken by a medical practitioner or, if it is taken in a police station, either by a medical practitioner or by a registered health professional (as to which, see *ante*, § 32–93): RTA 1988, s.11(4).

The only purpose of section 7(5) was to make finite the length of time within which a driver is required to provide a sample. If he did not provide it within that time, he could be charged with failing to provide a sample of urine, contrary to section 7(6); a police officer was not obliged to wait beyond that time, but if he did and a sample was provided, the sample analysis would not be rendered inadmissible on a prosecution under section 3A, 4 or 5: *DPP v. Baldwin* [2000] R.T.R. 314, DC.

Choice of specimens of breath

32–100 Of any two specimens of breath provided in pursuance of section 7, that with the lower proportion of alcohol in the breath shall be used and the other shall be disregarded: *RTA* 1988, s.8(1).

Where the lower reading is no more than 50 microgrammes, the person who provided it may claim that it should be replaced by such specimen as may be required under section 7(4), and, if he then provides such a specimen, neither specimen of breath shall be used: s.8(2) (but see *ante*, § 32–83). As to the procedure to be followed, see *DPP v. Warren* and *DPP v. Jackson*; *Stanley v. DPP*, *ante*. Where the driver elects, the prosecution do not have to show that the breath-testing device was working accurately at the time: *Branagan v. DPP* [2000] R.T.R. 235, DC. In an option case, if the person concerned was required to provide specimens of breath under section 7 at or near a place mentioned in subsection (2)(c), a constable may arrest him without warrant: s.8(2A).

There is no right to legal advice before deciding whether to exercise the option: *R. v. DPP, ex p. Ward* [1999] R.T.R. 11, DC.

Detention until fit

A person required to provide a specimen under section 7 or 7A (*post*, § 32–104a) may be detained at a police station until he is fit to drive or until the officer has determined that there is no likelihood of him driving whilst unfit: *RTA* 1988, s.10; or, if the specimen was provided otherwise than at a police station, may be arrested and detained at a police station, if a constable has reasonable grounds for believing that, were that person then driving or attempting to drive, he would commit an offence under section 4 or 5 of the Act: s.10(1). A person shall not, however, be so detained if it ought reasonably to appear to the constable that there is no likelihood of his driving or attempting to drive whilst his ability to drive properly is impaired or whilst the amount of alcohol in his breath, blood or urine exceeds the prescribed limit: s.10(2). And a person who is at hospital as a patient shall not be arrested and taken from there to a police station in pursuance of subsection (1) if it would be prejudicial to his proper care and treatment as a patient: s.10(2A). **32–101**

(6) Ingredients of the offence

One offence only

The substance of the offence is the refusal made in the course of a general investigation for the purposes of section 3A, 4 or 5, and the question whether the person was driving or in charge of the vehicle is not part of the inquiry whether there was a refusal. Accordingly, there is no need to specify in the charge which if any, specific offence, was being investigated; and it follows that subsection (6) creates one offence only: *DPP v. Butterworth* [1995] 1 A.C. 381, HL. **32–102**

"fails"

Failure includes refusal: see *ante*, § 32–91. It is arguable that once a specimen has been physically handed over to the officer, the requirement is fulfilled. Thus stealing the specimen back was not a failure: *R. v. Rothery* [1976] R.T.R. 550, CA; but dropping it in the process of handing it over, was: *Ross v. Hodges* [1975] R.T.R. 55, DC. Initial refusal followed by later agreement can amount to failure: *Procaj v. Johnstone* [1970] Crim.L.R. 110, DC. It is a matter of fact and degree: see *Smyth v. DPP* [1996] R.T.R. 59, DC (defendant said "No", but asked to change his mind five minutes later; not a failure); and *Burke v. DPP* [1999] R.T.R. 387, DC (where driver's initial response made it plain that she had no intention of providing any specimen, it was not necessary that the officer should continue with the procedure and say to the driver what his decision was as to whether the specimen should be of blood or urine, and make a specific requirement for blood or urine). Only providing one specimen when two are required, even though the first was below the limit, constitutes failure: *Stepniewski v. Commr of Police of the Metropolis* [1985] R.T.R. 330, DC. **32–103**

The printout is admissible to show failure: *Castle v. Cross* [1984] 1 W.L.R. 1372.

"without reasonable excuse"

The defendant has an evidential burden to raise the issue: *McKeon v. DPP* [2008] **32–104**

R.T.R. 14, DC. Once raised the prosecution must disprove it (*Roland v. Thorpe* [1970] 3 All E.R. 195, DC) to the criminal standard: *R. v. Harling* [1970] R.T.R. 441, CA. Whether the facts are capable of amounting to a reasonable excuse is a matter of law. Whether they do so amount is a question of fact and degree: *Law v. Stevens* [1971] R.T.R. 358, DC.

"Reasonable excuse" is undefined in the Act but it has been held that it must arise, "out of a physical or mental inability to provide [a specimen] or a substantial risk to health in its provision": *R. v. Lennard* [1973] 1 W.L.R. 483, CA. There must be a causative link between the inability and the failure to provide: *DPP v. Furby* [2000] R.T.R. 181, DC.

Expert medical evidence would normally be required when such a defence is raised (*DPP v. Crofton* [1994] R.T.R. 279, DC), though the justices may decide without it (*DPP v. Pearman* [1992] R.T.R. 407, DC). In *R. v. Harding* [1974] R.T.R. 325, DC, Lord Widgery C.J. said that no fear short of a medically recognised phobia and supported by medical evidence would excuse the failure. Genuine but unreasonable phobias may still, however, be accepted: *De Freitas v. DPP* [1993] R.T.R. 98, DC.

The evidential burden on the defendant will not be satisfied by evidence to the effect that he was "trying his best"; what is required is evidence of a relevant mental or physical infirmity, which, in "almost every imaginable case" will need medical evidence in support thereof: *DPP v. Simpson*, unreported, January 18, 2000, DC (CO 991 99) (following *Grady v. Pollard* [1988] R.T.R. 316, DC; *DPP v. Eddowes* [1991] R.T.R. 35, DC; and *DPP v. Ambrose* [1992] R.T.R. 285, DC, in disapproving *Cotgrove v. Cooney* [1987] R.T.R. 124, DC).

The language of subsection (6) does not require that the excuse must be communicated to the person requiring the specimen; *dicta* to the contrary in *Teape v. Godfrey* [1986] R.T.R. 213, DC, were *obiter*, and cases in which those *dicta* had been approved were cases where the defendant had deliberately refused or failed to provide a specimen and not where he had made a genuine attempt to do so but had failed in the attempt for some medical (or other) reason; a failure to mention an excuse may, however, be a highly relevant, and even decisive, factor against a defendant when deciding whether an excuse belatedly proffered is a reasonable one or whether there has been, in reality, a wilful refusal to provide a specimen, particularly if the defendant did not mention a medical condition of which he was well aware: *Piggott v. DPP* [2008] R.T.R. 16, DC. To similar effect, see *DPP v. Kinnersley* [1993] R.T.R. 105, DC. For cases in which *Teape v. Godfrey* was followed, see *DPP. v. Lonsdale* [2001] R.T.R. 29, DC (not open to defendant to seek to rely on claimed medical excuse, *viz.* bronchitis, when he had made no attempt to comply with requirement, nor offered any reason for non-compliance), and *R. (Martiner) v. DPP* [2005] A.C.D. 65, QBD (Davis J.).

A "panic attack" may amount to a reasonable excuse: see *DPP v. Falzarano* [2001] R.T.R. 14, DC (the justices were entitled to observe the defendant's demeanour at trial and conclude that she had a reasonable excuse, contrary to the evidence given by the defendant's own GP). An aversion to the sight of blood is not a reasonable excuse for not providing a sample of blood, it being possible to provide such a specimen without seeing blood: *DPP v. Mukandiwa* [2006] R.T.R. 24, DC.

The entitlement of a person in custody to legal advice as enacted in section 58 of the *PACE Act* 1984 (*ante*, § 15–206) does not provide a reasonable excuse for failure to provide a specimen until the person has had such legal advice: *DPP v. Billington*, 87 Cr.App.R. 68, DC; nor does an honest belief that there is such a right: *Grennan v. Westcott* [1988] R.T.R. 253, DC; *DPP v. Varley*, 163 J.P. 443, DC; nor does a willingness to provide a specimen on condition of first being allowed to consult a law book: *Noe v. DPP* [2000] R.T.R. 351, DC. *Billington* has survived the *Human Rights Act* 1998, Article 6(3)(c) of the ECHR (*ante*, § 16–57) not imposing a blanket requirement that each time a person is detained, legal advice must be made available to him before he can be asked to do or say anything: *Campbell v. DPP* [2004] R.T.R. 5, QBD (Goldring J.); *Kennedy v. DPP* [2004] R.T.R. 6, DC. Where, however, a detainee indicates that he wishes to exercise his right to legal advice and it is possible for him to do so without delaying the taking of the specimens to any significant extent, he should be allowed to do so: *Kennedy v. DPP*, *ante*. See also *Kirkup v. DPP* [2004] Crim.L.R. 230,

DC (where legal advice has been requested, it was the duty of the police to act on it without delay, as required by Code C:6.5 (Appendix A–54); whether they have delayed is a question of fact and degree in any given case); and *Whitley v. DPP*, 168 J.P. 350, DC (if there has been a breach of either provision, the question whether it was significant and substantial is also a question of fact and degree; and what is "practicable" has to be judged from the point of view, and the state of knowledge, of those then present).

It is no excuse that the person was not the driver at the time and that the constable was not acting in good faith or that the officer has no power to make the requirement: *McGrath v. Vipas* [1984] R.T.R. 58, DC; *R. v. Reid* [1973] 1 W.L.R. 1283, CA.

K. Failing to Give Permission for Laboratory Test

(1) Statute

Road Traffic Act 1988, s.7A

Specimens of blood taken from persons incapable of consenting

7A.—(1) A constable may make a request to a medical practitioner for him to take a specimen of blood from a person ("the person concerned") irrespective of whether that person consents if— **32–104a**

(a) that person is a person from whom the constable would (in the absence of any incapacity of that person and of any objection under section 9) be entitled under section 7 to require the provision of a specimen of blood for a laboratory test;

(b) it appears to that constable that that person has been involved in an accident that constitutes or is comprised in the matter that is under investigation or the circumstances of that matter;

(c) it appears to that constable that that person is or may be incapable (whether or not he has purported to do so) of giving a valid consent to the taking of a specimen of blood; and

(d) it appears to that constable that that person's incapacity is attributable to medical reasons.

(2) A request under this section—

(a) shall not be made to a medical practitioner who for the time being has any responsibility (apart from the request) for the clinical care of the person concerned; and

(b) shall not be made to a medical practitioner other than a police medical practitioner unless—

(i) it is not reasonably practicable for the request to made [*sic*] to a police medical practitioner; or

(ii) it is not reasonably practicable for such a medical practitioner (assuming him to be willing to do so) to take the specimen.

(3) It shall be lawful for a medical practitioner to whom a request is made under this section, if he thinks fit—

(a) to take a specimen of blood from the person concerned irrespective of whether that person consents; and

(b) to provide the sample to a constable.

(4) If a specimen is taken in pursuance of a request under this section, the specimen shall not be subjected to a laboratory test unless the person from whom it was taken—

(a) has been informed that it was taken; and

(b) has been required by a constable to give his permission for a laboratory test of the specimen; and

(c) has given his permission.

(5) A constable must, on requiring a person to give his permission for the purposes of this section for a laboratory test of a specimen, warn that person that a failure to give the permission may render him liable to prosecution.

(6) A person who, without reasonable excuse, fails to give his permission for a laboratory test of a specimen of blood taken from him under this section is guilty of an offence.

(7) In this section "police medical practitioner" means a medical practitioner who is engaged under any agreement to provide medical services for purposes connected with the activities of a police force.

[This section was inserted by the *Police Reform Act* 2002, s.56(1).]

(2) Mode of trial

32–104b This offence is triable only summarily: *RTOA* 1988, s.9, and Sched. 2, Pt I.

(3) Sentence

32–104c As for the offence under section 7, *ante*, § 32–96.

L. CAUSING DANGER TO ROAD USERS

(1) Statute

Road Traffic Act 1988, s.22A

Causing danger to road-users

32–105 **22A.**—(1) A person is guilty of an offence if he intentionally and without lawful authority or reasonable cause—

(a) causes anything to be on or over a road, or

(b) interferes with a motor vehicle, trailer or cycle, or

(c) interferes (directly or indirectly) with traffic equipment,

in such circumstances that it would be obvious to a reasonable person that to do so would be dangerous.

(2) In subsection (1) above "dangerous" refers to danger either of injury to any person while on or near a road, or of serious damage to property on or near a road; and in determining for the purposes of that subsection what would be obvious to a reasonable person in a particular case, regard shall be had not only to the circumstances of which he could be expected to be aware but also to any circumstances shown to have been within the knowledge of the accused.

(3) In subsection (1) above "traffic equipment" means—

(a) anything lawfully placed on or near a road by a highway authority;

(b) a traffic sign lawfully placed on or near a road by a person other than a highway authority;

(c) any fence, barrier or light lawfully placed on or near a road—

(i) in pursuance of section 174 of the *Highways Act* 1980, or section 65 of the *New Roads and Street Works Act* 1991 (which provide for guarding, lighting and signing in streets where works are undertaken), or

(ii) by a constable or a person acting under the instructions (whether general or specific) of a chief officer of police.

(4) For the purposes of subsection (3) above anything placed on or near a road shall unless the contrary is proved be deemed to have been lawfully placed there.

(5) In this section "road" does not include a footpath or bridleway.

(6) This section does not extend to Scotland.

[This section was inserted by the *RTA* 1991, s.6. It is printed as amended by the *New Roads and Street Works Act* 1991, s.168, and Scheds 8 and 9.]

(2) Class of offence and mode of trial

32–106 This offence is triable either way (*RTOA* 1988, s.9, and Sched. 2, Pt I), and is a class 3 offence, *ante*, § 2–17.

(3) Sentence

32–107 On indictment, imprisonment not exceeding seven years or a fine, or both; on summary conviction, imprisonment not exceeding six months, or a fine not exceeding the statutory maximum, or both: *RTOA* 1988, s.33 and Sched. 2, Pt I. As from a day to be appointed, the maximum penalty on summary conviction is increased to 12 months' imprisonment: *CJA* 2003, s.282(2) and (3); but the increase has no application to offences committed before it takes effect: s.282(4).

(4) Ingredients of the offence

32–107a The "reasonable person" for the purposes of the offence contrary to section 22A(1)(a) is not to be taken as a reasonable and prudent driver who drives at the correct speed, but as a reasonable bystander (who may or may not be a motorist) who is fully aware of the fact that not all drivers drive carefully and well: *DPP v. D.* [2006] R.T.R. 38, DC.

M. DRIVING WITHOUT A LICENCE

(1) Statute

Road Traffic Act 1988, s.87

Drivers of motor vehicles to have driving licences

87.—(1) It is an offence for a person to drive on a road a motor vehicle of any class otherwise than in accordance with a licence authorising him to drive a motor vehicle of that class. **32–108**

(2) It is an offence for a person to cause or permit another person to drive on a road a motor vehicle of any class otherwise than in accordance with a licence authorising that other person to drive a motor vehicle of that class.

[This section is printed as amended by the *Road Traffic (Driver Licensing and Information Systems) Act* 1989, ss.7 and 16, and Scheds 3 and 6; and the *RTA* 1991, s.17.]

(2) Mode of trial

These offences are triable only summarily: *RTOA* 1988, s.9 and Sched. 2, Pt I. **32–109**

(3) Sentence

The offences contrary to both subsections (1) and (2) are punishable by way of a fine not exceeding level 3 on the standard scale (*ante*, § 5–403): *RTOA* 1988, s.33 and Sched. 2, Pt I. The offence contrary to subsection (1) attracts discretionary disqualification and obligatory endorsement in a case where the offender's driving would not have been in accordance with any licence that could have been granted to him; it carries 3 to 6 penalty points: *RTOA*, ss.28, 34, 44 and Sched. 2, Pt I. **32–110**

As to disqualification and endorsement generally (including the penalty points system), see *post*, §§ 32–167 *et seq*.

(4) Interpretation

Road Traffic Act 1988, s.108

108.—(1) In this Part of this Act— **32–111**

...

"British external licence" and "British Forces licence" have the meanings given by section 88(8) of this Act,

...

"counterpart"—

(a) *in relation to a licence under this Part of this Act, means a document in such form as the Secretary of State may determine, issued with the licence, containing such information as he determines and designed for the endorsement of particulars relating to the licence,*

(aa) *in relation to a Northern Ireland licence, has the meaning given by section 109A of this Act (except in the definition of "Northern Ireland counterpart" below), and*

(b) *in relation to a Community licence, has the meaning given by* section 99B *of this Act,*

"disability" has the meaning given by section 92 of this Act,

"disqualified" means disqualified for holding or obtaining a licence (or, in cases where the disqualification is limited, a licence to drive motor vehicles of the class to which the disqualification relates), and "disqualification" is to be interpreted accordingly,

"EEA Agreement" means the Agreement on the European Economic Area signed at Oporto on 2nd May 1992 as adjusted by the Protocol signed at Brussels on 17th March 1993,

"EEA State" means a State which is a Contracting Party to the EEA Agreement,

"exchangeable licence" means a document issued in respect of—

(a) Gibraltar,

(b) a country or territory which is within this paragraph by virtue of an order under subsection (2) below, by an authority of Gibraltar or that country or territory (as the case may be), authorising the holder to drive a motor vehicle, not being a document mentioned in paragraph (b) of the definition of "Community licence" above, "full licence" means a licence other than a provisional licence,

"large goods vehicle" has the meaning given by section 121(1) of the Act,

"licence" (except where the context otherwise requires) means a licence to drive a motor vehicle granted under this Part of this Act,

…

"passenger-carrying vehicle" has the meaning given by section 121(1) of this Act,

…

"prescribed" means prescribed by regulations,

"prospective disability" has the meaning given by section 92 of this Act,

"provisional licence" means a licence granted by virtue of section 97(2) of this Act,

"regulations" means regulations made under section 105 of this Act,

"relevant disability" has the meaning given by section 92 of this Act,

"relevant external law" has the meaning given by section 88(8) of this Act,

…

"test of competence to drive" means such a test conducted under section 89 of this Act,

"approved training course for motor cyclists" and, in relation to such a course, "prescribed certificate of completion" mean respectively any course of training approved under, and the certificate of completion prescribed in, regulations under section 97(3A) of this Act.

(2) If the Secretary of State is satisfied that satisfactory provision for the granting of licences to drive motor vehicles is made by the law of a country or territory which neither is nor forms part of an EEA State, he may by order made by statutory instrument designate that country or territory as a country or territory within paragraph (b) of the definition of exchangeable licence in subsection (1) above.

(3) [*Duty to consult before making order under subs. (2).*]

[Section 108 is printed as amended by the *Road Traffic (Driver Licensing and Information Systems) Act* 1989, s.7 and Sched. 3; the *Driving Licences (Community Driving Licence) Regulations* 1990 (S.I. 1990 No. 144); the *Driving Licenses (Community Driving Licence) Regulations* 1996 (S.I. 1996 No. 1974); and the *Crime (International Co-operation) Act* 2003, s.91, and Sched. 5, para. 25; and as amended, as from a day to be appointed, by the *RSA* 2006, ss.10(1) and (12) and 59, Sched. 3, paras 2 and 14, and Sched. 7(4) (omission of definition of "counterpart"). It should be noted that definitions of the following expressions (which are less important to this work) have been omitted: "agricultural or forestry tractor", "articulated goods vehicle", "Community licence", "maximum gross weight", "maximum train weight", "medium-sized goods vehicle", "Northern Ireland driving licence", "Northern Ireland licence", "permissible maximum weight", "relevant maximum weight", "relevant maximum train weight", "semi-trailer", "small goods vehicle" and "small passenger vehicle".]

For orders having effect under subsection (2), see the *Driving Licences (Exchangeable Licences) Order* 1984 (S.I. 1984 No. 672) (designating Australia, Kenya, New Zealand, Norway, Singapore, Spain, Sweden, Switzerland and the territory of Hong Kong); the *Driving Licences (Exchangeable Licences) Order* 1985 (S.I. 1985 No. 65) (designating Barbados, the Republic of Cyprus, Finland, Malta, Zimbabwe and the territory of the British Virgin Islands); and the *Driving Licences (Exchangeable Licences) (No. 2) Order* 1985 (S.I. 1985 No. 1461) (designating Austria and Japan).

Where there was an issue as to whether a particular vehicle fell within the definition of "agricultural or forestry tractor", the onus was on the defendant to establish on a balance of probabilities that the vehicle in question fell within the definition: *Vehicle and Operator Services Agency v. Greenfarms Ltd* [2006] R.T.R. 20, DC.

(5) Grant and form of licences

Road Traffic Act 1988, s.97

Grant of licences

32–112 **97.**—(1) Subject to the following provisions of this section and section 92 of this Act and, in the case of licences to drive large goods vehicles or passenger-carrying vehicles, to Part IV of this Act, the Secretary of State must grant a licence to a person who—

(a) makes an application for it in such manner and containing such particulars as the Secretary of State may specify and pays the fee (if any) which is prescribed,

(b) provides the Secretary of State with such evidence or further evidence in support of the application as the Secretary of State may require,

(c) surrenders to the Secretary of State—

(i) any previous licence granted to him after 1st January 1976 *and its counterpart,*

(ia) any Northern Ireland licence held by him *together with its Northern Ireland counterpart and its counterpart (if any) issued to him under this Part of this Act,*

(ii) any Community licence *and its counterpart (if any) issued to him*, and

(iii) any British external licence or British Forces licence or exchangeable licence held by him,

or provides the Secretary of State with an explanation for not surrendering them which the Secretary of State considers adequate,

(d) is not, in accordance with section 88(1B) of this Act, subject to a current disqualification which is relevant to the licence he applies for and is not prevented from obtaining it by the provisions of section 89 of this Act or section 4 of or paragraph 6 or 9 of Schedule 1 to the *Road Traffic (New Drivers) Act* 1995.

[(1ZA) Regulations may provide that in prescribed circumstances a licence granted by the Secretary of State may be granted subject to prescribed conditions having effect—

(a) for a prescribed period, or

(b) until the happening of a prescribed event.]

(1A) Where any licence to be granted to an applicant would be in the form of a photocard, the Secretary of State may under subsection (1)(a) and (b) above in particular require him to provide a photograph which is a current likeness of him.

(1AA) Where a licence under this Part of this Act is granted to a person who surrenders under sub-paragraph (ia) of subsection (1)(c) above his Northern Ireland licence *together with the counterparts mentioned in that sub-paragraph* to the Secretary of State—

(a) that person ceases to be authorised by virtue of section 109(1) of this Act to drive in Great Britain a motor vehicle of any class, and

(b) the Secretary of State must send the Northern Ireland licence *and its Northern Ireland counterpart* to the licensing authority in Northern Ireland together with particulars of the class of motor vehicles to which the licence granted under this Part of this Act relates.

(2) If the application for the licence states that it is made for the purpose of enabling the applicant to drive a motor vehicle with a view to passing a test of competence to drive, any licence granted in pursuance of the application shall be a provisional licence for that purpose, and nothing in section 89 of this Act shall apply to such a licence.

(3) A provisional licence—

(a) shall be granted subject to prescribed conditions,

(b) shall, in any cases prescribed for the purpose of this paragraph, be restricted so as to authorise only the driving of vehicles of the classes so prescribed,

(c) may, in the case of a person appearing to the Secretary of State to be suffering from a relevant disability or a prospective disability, be restricted so as to authorise only the driving of vehicles of a particular construction or design specified in the licence,

(d) shall not authorise a person under the age of 21 years, before he has passed a test of competence to drive a motor bicycle—

(i) to drive a motor bicycle without a side-car unless it is a learner motor bicycle (as defined in subsection (5) below) or its first use (as defined in regulations) occurred before 1st January 1982 and the cylinder capacity of its engine does not exceed 125 cubic centimetres, or

(ii) to drive a motor bicycle with a side-car unless its power to weight ratio is less than or equal to 0.16 kilowatts per kilogram, and

(e) except as provided under subsection (3B) below, shall not authorise a person, before he has passed a test of competence to drive, to drive on a road a motor bicycle or moped except where he has successfully completed an approved training course for motor cyclists or is undergoing training on such a course and is driving the motor bicycle or moped on the road as part of the training.

(3A) Regulations may make provision as respects the training in the driving of motor bicycles and mopeds of persons wishing to obtain licences authorising the driving of such motor bicycles and mopeds by means of courses of training provided in accordance with the regulations; and the regulations may in particular make provision with respect to—

(a) the nature of the courses of training;

(b) the approval by the Secretary of State of the persons providing the courses and the withdrawal of his approval;

(c) the maximum amount of any charges payable by persons undergoing the training;

(d) certificates evidencing the successful completion by persons of a course of training and the supply by the Secretary of State of the forms which are to be used for such certificates; and

(e) the making, in connection with the supply of forms of certificates, of reasonable charges for the discharge of the functions of the Secretary of State under the regulations;

and different provision may be made for training in different classes of motor bicycles and mopeds.

(3B) Regulations may prescribe cases in which persons holding a provisional licence are exempt from the restriction imposed by subsection (3)(e) above on their driving under the licence; and the regulations may—

(a) limit the exemption to persons in prescribed circumstances;

(b) limit the exemption to a prescribed period or in respect of driving in a prescribed area;

(c) attach conditions to the exemption; and

(d) regulate applications for, and the issue and form of, certificates evidencing the holder's exemption from the restriction.

(4) Regulations may authorise or require the Secretary of State to refuse a provisional licence authorising the driving of a motor bicycle or moped of a prescribed class if the applicant has held such a provisional licence and the licence applied for would come into force within the prescribed period—

(a) beginning at the end of the period for which the previous licence authorised (or would, if not surrendered or revoked, have authorised) the driving of such a motor bicycle or moped, or

(b) beginning at such other time as may be prescribed.

(5) A learner motor bicycle is a motor bicycle which either is propelled by electric power or has the following characteristics—

(a) the cylinder capacity of its engine does not exceed 125 cubic centimetres,

(b) the maximum net power output of its engine does not exceed eleven kilowatts.

(6) In this section—

"maximum net power output", in relation to an engine, means the maximum net power output measured under full engine load, and

"power to weight ratio" in relation to a motor bicycle with a side-car, means the ratio of the maximum net power output of the engine of the motor bicycle to the weight of the combination with—

(a) a full supply of fuel in the tank,

(b) an adequate supply of other liquids needed for its propulsion and

(c) no load other than its normal equipment, including loose tools.

[This section is printed as amended by the *Road Traffic (Driver Licensing and Information Systems) Act* 1989, ss.6(2), 7 and 16, and Scheds 3 and 6; the *Driving Licences (Community Driving Licence) Regulations* 1990 (S.I. 1990 No. 144); the *RTA* 1991, ss.17(3) and 83 and Sched. 8; the *Road Traffic (New Drivers) Act* 1995, Sched.2, para. 2; S.I. 1996 No. 1974 (*ante*, § 32–111); the *Driving Licences (Community Driving Licence) Regulations* 1998 (S.I. 1998 No. 1420); and the *Crime (International Co-operation) Act* 2003, ss.78(1) and (2), and 91, and Sched. 5, para. 21; and as amended, as from a day to be appointed, by the *RSA* 2006, ss.10(1) and (12), 38(2) and 59, Sched. 3, paras 2 and 6, and Sched. 7(4) (insertion of words in square brackets, omission of italicised words).]

For regulations made or having effect under this section, see the *Motor Vehicles (Driving Licences) Regulations* 1999 (S.I. 1999 No. 2864) (as most recently amended by the *Motor Vehicles (Driving Licences) (Amendment) (No. 5) Regulations* 2008 (S.I. 2008 No. 2508)).

Road Traffic Act 1988, s.97A

[Meaning of "driving record"

97A.—(1) In this Act "driving record", in relation to a person, means a record in relation to the person maintained by the Secretary of State and designed to be endorsed with particulars relating to offences committed by the person under the *Traffic Acts*. **32–112a**

(2)–(4) [*Procedure for exercising powers conferred on Secretary of State to allow certain persons access to information held on a person's driving record.*]

[This section is inserted, as from a day to be appointed, by the *RSA* 2006, s.8.]

Road Traffic Act 1988, s.98

Form of licence

98.—(1) A licence shall be in the form of a photocard of a description specified by the Secretary of State or such other form as he may specify and— **32–113**

(a) the licence shall state whether, apart from subsection (2) below, it authorises its holder to drive motor vehicles of all classes or of certain classes only and, in the latter case, specify those classes,

(b) the licence shall specify (in such manner as the Secretary of State may determine) the restrictions on the driving of vehicles of any class in pursuance of the licence to which its holder is subject by virtue of section 101 of this Act, and any conditions on the driving of vehicles of any class in pursuance of the licence to which its holder is subject by virtue of section 92(7ZA) of this Act, and

(c) *in the case of a provisional licence*, the licence *or its counterpart* shall specify (in such manner as the Secretary of State may determine) *the* [any] conditions subject to which it is granted.

(1A) The Secretary of State may specify different descriptions of photocards, and different forms of licences not in the form of a photocard, for different cases and may determine the form of licence to be granted in any case.

(2) Subject to subsections (3), (4) and (4A) below, a person who holds a licence which authorises its holder to drive motor vehicles of certain classes only (not being—

(a) a provisional licence, or

(b) any other prescribed description of licence)

may drive motor vehicles of all other classes subject to the same conditions as if he were authorised by a provisional licence to drive motor vehicles of those other classes.

(3) Subsection (2) above does not authorise a person to drive—

(a) a vehicle of a class for the driving of which he could not, by reason of the provisions of section 101 of this Act, lawfully hold a licence, or

(b) unless he has either passed a test of competence to drive a motor bicycle or attained the age of 21 years, a motor bicycle which, by virtue of section 97(3)(d) of this Act, a provisional licence would not authorise him to drive before he had passed that test or attained that age (as the case may be), or

(c) unless he has passed a test of competence to drive, a motor bicycle or moped on a road in circumstances in which, by virtue of section 97(3)(e) of this Act, a provisional licence would not authorise him to drive it before he had passed that test.

(4) In such cases or as respects such classes of vehicles as the Secretary of State may prescribe, the provisions of subsections (2) and (3) above shall not apply or shall apply subject to such limitations as he may prescribe.

(4A) Subsection (2) above does not authorise a person on whom a notice under section 92(5)(b) of this Act has been served to drive motor vehicles otherwise than in accordance with the limits specified in the notice.

[This section is printed as amended by the *Road Traffic (Driver Licensing and Information Systems) Act* 1989, ss.5 and 7 and Sched. 3; the *Driving Licences (Community Driving Licence) Regulations* 1990 (S.I. 1990 No. 144); the *RTA* 1991, ss.17(3) and 83 and Sched. 8; S.I. 1996 No. 1974 (*ante*, § 32–111); and S.I. 1998 No. 1420 (*ante*, § 32–112); and as amended, as from a day to be appointed, by the *RSA* 2006, ss.10(1) and (12), 38(3) and 59, Sched. 3, paras. 2 and 7, and Sched. 7(4) and (11) (insertion of word in square brackets, omission of italicised words).]

The "notice under section 92(5)(b) of this Act" referred to in subsection (4A) is a notice in writing to the effect that the Secretary of State is satisfied that the person on whom the notice is served is suffering from a disability such that there is likely to be a danger to the public if he drives a vehicle other than a vehicle of a particular class.

N. OBTAINING A LICENCE, OR DRIVING, WHILE DISQUALIFIED

(1) Statute

Road Traffic Act 1988, s.103

Obtaining licence, or driving, while disqualified

32–114 **103.**—(1) A person is guilty of an offence if, while disqualified for holding or obtaining a licence, he—

(a) obtains a licence, or

(b) drives a motor vehicle on a road.

(2) A licence obtained by a person who is disqualified is of no effect (or, where the disqualification relates only to vehicles of a particular class, is of no effect in relation to vehicles of that class).

(3) [*Repealed by Police Reform Act* 2002, *s.107(1), and Sched. 7, para. 11.*]

(4) Subsection (1) above does not apply in relation to disqualification by virtue of section 101 of this Act.

(5) Subsection (1)(b) above does not apply in relation to disqualification by virtue of section 102 of this Act.

(6) In the application of subsection (1) above to a person whose disqualification is limited to the driving of motor vehicles of a particular class by virtue of—

(a) section 102, 117 or 117A of this Act, or

(b) subsection (9) of section 36 of the *Road Traffic Offenders Act* 1988 (disqualification until test is passed),

the references to disqualification for holding or obtaining a licence and driving motor vehicles are references to disqualification for holding or obtaining a licence to drive and driving motor vehicles of that class.

[This section is printed as substituted by the *RTA* 1991, s.19; and as subsequently amended by S.I. 1996 No. 1974 (*ante*, § 32–111); and the *Police Reform Act* 2002, s.107(1) and Sched. 7, para. 11.]

(2) Class of offence and mode of trial

32–115 Offences contrary to section 103(1)(a) and (b) are summary offences: *RTOA* 1988, s.9 and Sched. 2, Pt I; but an offence contrary to section 103(1)(b) may, in certain circumstances, be joined in an indictment: see the *CJA* 1988, s.40(3)(c), *ante*, § 1–75ai.

(3) Sentence

32–116 Section 103(1)(a), a fine not exceeding level 3 on the standard scale: *RTOA* 1988, s.33 and Sched. 2, Pt I.

Section 103(1)(b), imprisonment not exceeding six months (increased to 51 weeks as from a day to be appointed (but only in relation to offences committed after the date on which this amendment takes effect): *CJA* 2003, s.281(4)–(6)) or a fine not exceeding level 5 on the standard scale (*ante*, § 5–403), or both: *ibid*. Disqualification is discretionary, endorsement is obligatory and the offence carries 6 penalty points: *ibid.*, ss.28, 34, 44 and Sched. 2, Pt I.

As to disqualification and endorsement generally (including the penalty points system), see *post*, §§ 32–167 *et seq.*

(4) Ingredients of the offence

32–117 As to the meaning of "drives", see *ante*, § 32–14; of "motor vehicle", see *ante*, § 32–61; and of "road" see *ante*, § 32–18.

Subsection (1)(b) creates an absolute offence. It is not necessary that the defendant should know that he has been disqualified: *Taylor v. Kenyon* [1952] 2 All E.R. 726, DC; and see *R. v. Lynn*, 55 Cr.App.R. 423, CA, and *R. v. Bowsher* [1973] Crim.L.R. 373, CA. It is no defence that subsequent to the driving the original disqualification was quashed on appeal: *R. v. Thames Magistrates' Court, ex p. Levy*, *The Times*, July 17,

1997, DC, applying *R. v. Lynn* (*ante*). Service of a statutory declaration under the *MCA* 1980, s.14, in relation to proceedings resulting in disqualification, avoids the disqualification from the date of service, but not *ab initio*. Accordingly, it is no defence to a charge of driving while disqualified that subsequent to the driving the defendant served such a declaration: *Singh (Jaspal) v. DPP* [1999] R.T.R. 424, DC.

As to the grant, and form of, licences, see *ante*, §§ 32–112 *et seq*.

For the interpretation of Part III of the Act (ss.87 to 109), see *ante*, § 32–111.

(5) Evidence

It is necessary to prove that the defendant was, at the relevant date, disqualified by reason of a court order. The court order should be proved by a certificate of conviction under section 73 of the *PACE Act* 1984 (*ante*, § 9–80). **32–118**

The certificate should be restricted to the relevant offence for which the defendant was disqualified: *Stone v. Bastick* [1967] 1 Q.B. 74, DC. In *Holland v. Phipp* [1982] 1 W.L.R. 1150, DC, the defendant had been disqualified from driving for five years. On the same occasion he was also disqualified for two-and-a-half years under another section. This period should have been ordered to run consecutively to the five year period. The court register showed them to run concurrently. The defendant drove at the end of the five years and was charged with driving while disqualified. It was held that the certified copy of the register of the original court was admissible as evidence of the earlier adjudication under (what is now) rule 6.4 of the *Criminal Procedure Rules* 2005 (S.I. 2005 No. 384). Although the register disclosed an error of law, it was the only evidence of the earlier adjudication; and, accordingly, since the justices were bound by it, they could only act on the evidence which showed that the defendant had ceased to be disqualified at the expiry of the five years.

Establishing that the defendant was the person disqualified can be achieved in a number of ways: by an admission by or on behalf of an accused pursuant to the *CJA* 1967, s.10; by the defendant's admissions in interview: *Moran v. CPS*, 164 J.P. 562, DC; or by evidence of a person present in court when the accused was convicted. It is not, however, sufficient to prove that the defendant has the same name and date of birth as the details recorded on the certificate of conviction: *R. v. Derwentside JJ., ex p. Heaviside* [1996] R.T.R. 384, DC; and *Bailey v. DPP*, 163 J.P. 518, DC (insufficient to produce a certificate of disqualification in the defendant's name, with his date of birth and an address proved to be that of his sister, even if coupled with evidence that he had been living at his sister's address at the time of the disqualification and that this was a fact known to relatively few people). The combination of a certificate of conviction in the same name as the defendant's and evidence from a police officer that he had arrested the defendant for the offence specified in the certificate was sufficient to raise a prima facie case that the defendant and the person named in the certificate were one and the same: *DPP v. Mansfield* [1997] R.T.R. 96, DC. See also *R. v. Derwentside JJ., ex p. Swift*; *R. v. Sunderland JJ., ex p. Bate* [1997] R.T.R. 89, DC. A reply of "guilty" when charged may be sufficient: *DPP v. Mooney* [1997] R.T.R. 434, DC.

In the absence any such evidence, a prima facie case may normally be established by proof that the personal details of the defendant matched those of the person convicted on the previous occasion; if the names are common and there is material indicative of the possibility of mistake, this will not necessarily follow; where, however, a prima facie case is established by reference to such matching details, it is open to the court in deciding whether the case is proved to have regard, in appropriate circumstances, to a failure of the defendant to give evidence or to a lie told by the defendant when questioned: *Olakunori v. DPP* [1998] C.O.D. 443, DC; *Pattison v. DPP* [2006] R.T.R. 13, QBD (Newman J.); and *R. v. Burns* [2006] 1 W.L.R. 1273, CA (the question of whether names and dates of birth appearing in a certificate of conviction constituted prima facie evidence that the person to whom the certificate related was the accused was not a matter of law, but was fact-specific).

Where, however, the prosecution failed to adduce evidence of the conviction, it was not open to justices to consult their own court records, and, having found a record of a person of the same name, date of birth and address as the defendant having been disqualified on the date put forward, to pronounce themselves satisfied as to that ingredient of the offence; what is required is proof by the prosecution of the conviction and disqualification and proof that the person convicted and disqualified and the defendant are one and the same person: *R. (Kingsnorth and Denny) v. DPP* [2003] 5 *Archbold News* 1, QBD (Mitchell J.).

(6) Defences

32–119 A mistaken belief that the road being driven on was a private road is no defence to a charge under subsection (1)(b): *R. v. Miller* [1975] Crim.L.R. 723, CA.

"Necessity" can be a defence to a charge under subsection (1)(b), where the facts establish "duress of circumstances", *i.e.* where the defendant was constrained by circumstances to drive in order to avoid a threat of death or serious bodily harm to himself or some other person: *R. v. Martin*, 88 Cr.App.R. 343, CA (*ante*, § 17–130).

O. NO INSURANCE

(1) Statute

Road Traffic Act 1988 s.143

Users of motor vehicles to be insured or secured against third-party risks

32–120 **143.**—(1) Subject to the provisions of this Part of this Act—

(a) a person must not use a motor vehicle on a road or other public place unless there is in force in relation to the use of the vehicle by that person such a policy of insurance or such a security in respect of third party risks as complies with the requirements of this Part of this Act, and

(b) a person must not cause or permit any other person to use a motor vehicle on a road or other public place unless there is in force in relation to the use of the vehicle by that other person such a policy of insurance or such a security in respect of third party risks as complies with the requirements of this Part of this Act.

(2) If a person acts in contravention of subsection (1) above he is guilty of an offence.

(3) A person charged with using a motor vehicle in contravention of this section shall not be convicted if he proves—

(a) that the vehicle did not belong to him and was not in his possession under a contract of hiring or of loan,

(b) that he was using the vehicle in the course of his employment, and

(c) that he neither knew nor had reason to believe that there was not in force in relation to the vehicle such a policy of insurance or security as is mentioned in subsection (1) above.

(4) This Part of this Act does not apply to invalid carriages.

[This section is printed as amended by the *Motor Vehicles (Compulsory Insurance) Regulations* 2000 (S.I. 2000 No. 726) (as to which, see *post*, § 32–129).]

(2) Mode of trial

32–121 This offence is triable only summarily: *RTOA* 1988, s.9 and Sched. 2, Pt I.

(3) Sentence

32–122 A fine not exceeding level 5 on the standard scale: *RTOA* 1988, s.33 and Sched. 2, Pt I. Disqualification is discretionary, endorsement is obligatory and the offence carries 6 to 8 penalty points: *ibid.*, ss.28, 34, 44 and Sched. 2, Pt I.

(4) Ingredients of the offence

32–123 As to the meaning of "motor vehicle", see *ante*, § 32–61; and of "road", see *ante*, § 32–18.

"use"

32–124 The term "use" has been held to mean some degree of control, managing or operating the particular vehicle as a vehicle. It is possible for the owner to be using the vehicle although someone else is the driver: *Cobb v. Williams* [1973] R.T.R. 113, DC; *Bennett v. Richardson* [1980] R.T.R. 358, DC; *Jones v. DPP* [1999] R.T.R. 1, DC.

Whether a pillion passenger on a motor-cycle is using it within the meaning of section 143 was considered in *Hatton v. Hall* [1997] R.T.R. 212, CA (Civ. Div.), and *O'Mahony v. Joliffe* [1999] R.T.R. 245, CA (Civ. Div.). *Hatton v. Hall* involved an agreement to travel somewhere on the uninsured vehicle and did not bring the passenger within the meaning of "use" in section 143. *O'Mahony v. Joliffe* concerned a joint venture to go for a drive for the thrill of the drive itself. There were times when the plaintiff was driving the motor-cycle, and, although at the time of the accident, she was not actually driving the motor-cycle, the degree of control, management and operation of the motor-cycle was sufficient to constitute her a user.

"permit"

"Permit" includes honestly but mistakenly allowing a car to be driven by someone who is in fact uninsured: *Lloyd-Wolper v. Moore* [2004] R.T.R. 30, CA (Civ. Div.). **32–124a**

"requirements of the Act"

Road Traffic Act 1988, s.145

Requirements in respect of policies of insurance

145.—(1) In order to comply with the requirements of this Part of this Act, a policy of insurance must satisfy the following conditions. **32–125**

(2) The policy must be issued by an authorised insurer.

(3) Subject to subsection (4) below, the policy—

(a) must insure such person, persons or classes of persons as may be specified in the policy in respect of any liability which may be incurred by him or them in respect of the death of or bodily injury to any person or damage to property caused by, or arising out of, the use of the vehicle on a road or other public place in Great Britain, and

(aa) must, in the case of a vehicle normally based in the territory of another member state, insure him or them in respect of any civil liability which may be incurred by him or them as a result of an event related to the use of the vehicle in Great Britain if—

(i) according to the law of that territory, he or they would be required to be insured in respect of a civil liability which would arise under that law as a result of that event if the place where the vehicle was used when the event occurred were in that territory, and

(ii) the cover required by that law would be higher than that required by paragraph (a) above, and

(b) must, in the case of a vehicle normally based in Great Britain, insure him or them in respect of any liability which may be incurred by him or them in respect of the use of the vehicle and of any trailer, whether or not coupled, in the territory other than Great Britain and Gibraltar of each of the member States of the Communities according to—

(i) the law on compulsory insurance against civil liability in respect of the use of vehicles of the state in whose territory the event giving rise to the liability occurred; or

(ii) if it would give higher cover, the law which would be applicable under this Part of this Act if the place where the vehicle was used when that event occurred were in Great Britain; and

(c) must also insure him or them in respect of any liability which may be incurred by him or them under the provisions of this Part of this Act relating to payment for emergency treatment.

(4) The policy shall not, by virtue of subsection (3)(a) above, be required—

(a) to cover liability in respect of the death, arising out of and in the course of his employment, of a person in the employment of a person insured by the policy or of bodily injury sustained by such a person arising out of and in the course of his employment, or

(b) to provide insurance of more than £250,000 in respect of all such liabilities as may be incurred in respect of damage to property caused by, or arising out of, any one accident involving the vehicle, or

(c) to cover liability in respect of damage to the vehicle, or

(d) to cover liability in respect of damage to goods carried for hire or reward in or on the vehicle or in or on any trailer (whether or not coupled) drawn by the vehicle, or

(e) to cover any liability of a person in respect of damage to property in his custody or under his control, or

(f) to cover any contractual liability.

(4A) In the case of a person—

(a) carried in or upon a vehicle, or

(b) entering or getting on to, or alighting from, a vehicle,

the provisions of paragraph (a) of subsection (4) above do not apply unless cover in respect of the liability referred to in that paragraph is in fact provided pursuant to a requirement of the *Employers' Liability (Compulsory Insurance) Act* 1969.

(5) "Authorised insurer" has the same meaning as in section 95.

(6) [*Person or body ceasing to be member of Motor Insurers' Bureau.*]

[This section is printed as amended by the *Motor Vehicles (Compulsory Insurance) Regulations* 1992 (S.I. 1992 No. 3036); S.I. 2000 No. 726 (*ante*, § 32–120); and the *Financial Services and Markets Act 2000 (Consequential Amendments and Repeals) Order* 2001 (S.I. 2001 No. 3649), art. 313.]

32–126 As to the ambit of the words "any liability" in section 145(3)(a), see *Charlton v. Fisher* [2002] Q.B. 578, CA (Civ. Div.).

As to the requirements in respect of securities, see section 146 of the 1988 Act.

Section 144 contains exceptions to the requirement of third-party insurance or security. Sections 148 and 149 provide for the avoidance of certain exceptions to policies or securities, and of certain agreements as to liability towards passengers. Section 150 stipulates that insurance or security in respect of private use of a vehicle is to cover use under car-sharing arrangements.

Absolute offence

32–127 The offence contrary to section 143 is absolute, even where the allegation is causing or permitting the uninsured use: *Tapsell v. Maslen* [1967] Crim.L.R. 53, DC.

(5) Burden of proof

32–128 The prosecution have to prove that the defendant used a vehicle on a road. Once that is established it is for the defendant to prove that there was a valid policy of insurance in force at the time: *Philcox v. Carberry* [1960] Crim.L.R. 563, DC; *DPP v. Kavaz* [1999] R.T.R. 40, DC (immaterial that no statutory request made for production of documents pursuant to the *RTA* 1988, s.165, but it is desirable for such a request to be made since there is scope for abuse if this is not done).

P. FAILING TO STOP OR REPORT

(1) Statute

Road Traffic Act 1988, s.170

Duty of driver to stop, report accident and give information or documents

32–129 **170.**—(1) This section applies in a case where, owing to the presence of a mechanically propelled vehicle on a road or other public place, an accident occurs by which—

(a) personal injury is caused to a person other than the driver of that mechanically propelled vehicle, or

(b) damage is caused—

(i) to a vehicle other than that mechanically propelled vehicle or a trailer drawn by that mechanically propelled vehicle, or

(ii) to an animal other than an animal in or on that mechanically propelled vehicle or a trailer drawn by that mechanically propelled vehicle, or

(iii) to any other property constructed on, fixed to, growing in or otherwise forming part of the land on which the road or place in question is situated or land adjacent to such land.

(2) The driver of the mechanically propelled vehicle must stop and, if required to do so by any person having reasonable grounds for so requiring, give his name and address and also the name and address of the owner and the identification marks of the vehicle.

(3) If for any reason the driver of the mechanically propelled vehicle does not give his name and address under subsection (2) above, he must report the accident.

(4) A person who fails to comply with subsection (2) or (3) above is guilty of an offence.

(5) If, in a case where this section applies by virtue of subsection (1)(a) above, the driver of a motor vehicle does not at the time of the accident produce such a certificate of insurance or security, or other evidence, as is mentioned in section 165(2)(a) of this Act—

(a) to a constable, or

(b) to some person who, having reasonable grounds for so doing, has required him to produce it,

the driver must report the accident and produce such a certificate or other evidence.

This subsection does not apply to the driver of an invalid carriage.

(6) To comply with a duty under this section to report an accident or to produce such a certificate of insurance or security, or other evidence, as is mentioned in section 165(2)(a) of this Act, the driver—

(a) must do so at a police station or to a constable, and

(b) must do so as soon as is reasonably practicable and, in any case, within twenty-four hours of the occurrence of the accident.

(7) A person who fails to comply with a duty under subsection (5) above is guilty of an offence, but he shall not be convicted by reason only of a failure to produce a certificate or other evidence if, within seven days after the occurrence of the accident, the certificate or other evidence is produced at a police station that was specified by him at the time when the accident was reported.

(8) In this section "animal" means horse, cattle, ass, mule, sheep, pig, goat or dog.

[This section is printed as amended by the *RTA* 1991, s.48 and Sched. 4, para. 72; and S.I. 2000 No. 726 (*ante*, § 32–120).]

The amendment effected by S.I. 2000 No. 726 (insertion of "or other public place" in subsection (1)) was not *ultra vires*: *R. (Parker) v. Crown Court at Bradford* [2007] R.T.R. 30, DC.

(2) Mode of trial

The offences contrary to section 170(4) and (7) are triable only summarily: *RTOA* 1988, s.9, and Sched. 2, Pt I. **32–130**

(3) Sentence

The offence contrary to section 170(4), imprisonment not exceeding six months (increased to 51 weeks as from a day to be appointed (but only in relation to offences committed after the date on which this amendment takes effect): *CJA* 2003, s.281(4)–(6)) or a fine not exceeding level 5 (*ante*, § 5–403), or both; disqualification is discretionary; endorsement is obligatory: *RTOA* 1988, s.33 and Sched. 2, Pt I. The offence carries 5 to 10 penalty points: *ibid*. **32–131**

The offence contrary to section 170(7), a fine not exceeding level 3: *ibid*.

(4) Ingredients of the offences

As to the meaning of "mechanically propelled vehicle", see *ante*, § 32–16; of "motor vehicle", see *ante*, § 32–61; and of "road", see *ante*, § 32–18. **32–132**

Where a driver stopped his car to post a letter, and it rolled off and collided with a wall, causing the wall damage, it was open to the tribunal to find that although not in the car at the time of the collision, he was nevertheless the "driver" for the purposes of section 170: *Cawthorn v. DPP* [2000] R.T.R. 45, DC.

The question of whether the defendant has stopped or not is one of fact and degree, not law: *McDermott v. DPP* [1997] R.T.R. 474, DC.

A driver who gave his solicitor's address was held to have complied with subsection (2) in *DPP v. McCarthy* [1999] R.T.R. 323, DC.

Where a driver collided with another car and was then taken to hospital unconscious, the presence of the police at the scene of the accident (and their failure to request information from the driver due to his unconscious state) did not excuse the driver from his obligation to report the accident within the prescribed time: *DPP v. Hay* [2006] R.T.R. 3, DC.

In relation to subsection (4), the prosecution have to prove that an accident which involved the defendant's vehicle took place and that the accident caused some injury or damage. Once this is proved, it is then for the defendant to prove on a balance of probabilities that he was unaware of the accident: *Selby v. Chief Constable of Somerset* [1988] R.T.R. 216, DC.

For the purposes of subsection (5), a valid international motor insurance card has effect as though it were a certificate of insurance issued by an authorised insurer: see reg. 6 of the *Motor Vehicles (International Motor Insurance Card) Regulations* 1971 (S.I. 1971 No. 972).

Q. FAILING TO GIVE INFORMATION AS TO IDENTITY OF DRIVER

(1) Statute

Road Traffic Act 1988, s.172

Duty to give information as to identity of driver etc in certain circumstances

32–133 **172.**—(1) This section applies—

(a) to any offence under the preceding provisions of this Act except—
(i) an offence under Part V, or
(ii) an offence under section 13, 16, 51(2), 61(4), 67(9), 68(4), 96 or 120, and to an offence under section 178 of this Act,

(b) to any offence under sections 25, 26 or 27 of the *Road Traffic Offenders Act* 1988,

(c) to any offence against any other enactment relating to the use of vehicles on roads, … and

(d) to manslaughter, or in Scotland culpable homicide, by the driver of a motor vehicle.

(2) Where the driver of a vehicle is alleged to be guilty of an offence to which this section applies—

(a) the person keeping the vehicle shall give such information as to the identity of the driver as he may be required to give by or on behalf of a chief officer of police, and

(b) any other person shall if required as stated above give any information which it is in his power to give and may lead to identification of the driver.

(3) Subject to the following provisions, a person who fails to comply with a requirement under subsection (2) above shall be guilty of an offence.

(4) A person shall not be guilty of an offence by virtue of paragraph (a) of subsection (2) above if he shows that he did not know and could not with reasonable diligence have ascertained who the driver of the vehicle was.

(5) Where a body corporate is guilty of an offence under this section and the offence is proved to have been committed with the consent or connivance of, or to be attributable to neglect on the part of, a director, manager, secretary or other similar officer of the body corporate, or a person who was purporting to act in any such capacity, he, as well as the body corporate, is guilty of that offence and liable to be proceeded against and punished accordingly.

(6) Where the alleged offender is a body corporate, or in Scotland a partnership or an unincorporated association, or the proceedings are brought against him by virtue of subsection (5) above or subsection (11) below, subsection (4) above shall not apply unless, in addition to the matters there mentioned, the alleged offender shows that no record was kept of the persons who drove the vehicle and that the failure to keep a record was reasonable.

(7) A requirement under subsection (2) may be made by written notice served by post; and where it is so made—

(a) it shall have effect as a requirement to give the information within the period of 28 days beginning with the day on which the notice is served, and

(b) the person on whom the notice is served shall not be guilty of an offence under this section if he shows either that he gave the information as soon as reasonably practicable after the end of that period or that it has not been reasonably practicable for him to give it.

(8) Where the person on whom a notice under subsection (7) above is to be served is a body corporate, the notice is duly served if it is served on the secretary or clerk of that body.

(9) For the purposes of section 7 of the *Interpretation Act* 1978 as it applies for the purposes of this section the proper address of any person in relation to the service on him of a notice under subsection (7) above is—

(a) in the case of the secretary or clerk of a body corporate, that of the registered or principal office of that body or (if the body corporate is the registered keeper of the vehicle concerned) the registered address, and

(b) in any other case, his last known address at the time of service.

(10) In this section—

"registered address", in relation to the registered keeper of a vehicle, means the address recorded in the record kept under the *Vehicle Excise and Registration Act* 1994 with respect to that vehicle as being that person's address, and

"registered keeper", in relation to a vehicle, means the person in whose name the vehicle is registered under that Act;

and references to the driver of a vehicle include references to the rider of a cycle.

(11) [*Scotland*.]

[This section is printed as substituted by the *RTA* 1991, s.21; and as amended, and repealed in part, by the *Vehicle Excise and Registration Act* 1994, s.63, and Sched. 3; and the *Statute Law (Repeals) Act* 2004, Sched., Pt 14.]

As to the compatibility of this provision with a defendant's privilege against self-incrimination as an aspect of the right to a fair trial under Article 6 of the ECHR, see *Brown v. Stott* [2003] 1 A.C. 681, PC, and *O'Halloran and Francis* (2008) 46 E.H.R.R. 21, ECtHR (*ante*, § 16–69).

No distinction in this regard is to be made as between a requirement under section 172(2)(a) and one under section 172(2)(b): *DPP v. Wilson* [2002] R.T.R. 6, DC. Where the means by which the requisite information is to be given are specified in the requirement, then the information must be given in the manner specified, provided only that the means are reasonable: *Broomfield v. DPP* [2003] R.T.R. 5, QBD (H.H.J. Wilkie Q.C., sitting as a deputy High Court judge). A requirement that the form should be signed was reasonable: *Francis v. DPP*, 168 J.P. 492, DC. See also *Jones v. DPP* [2004] R.T.R. 20, DC (where the defendant had written on a standard form, endorsed to the effect that when replying the form must be used, "Please see accompanying letter" in the space for giving the name of the driver, and had attached a signed letter with the information required); and *R. (Flegg) v. Southampton and New Forest JJ.*, 170 J.P. 373, DC (keeper replied to effect that more than one person could have been driving vehicle on day in question, without identifying the only person, apart from himself, who could have been driving; not only had keeper not identified driver, but had failed to supply such information as was within his power to give; *Jones v. DPP* distinguished).

That a requirement to give information was made "by or on behalf of" a chief officer of police has to be proved by the prosecution, and a statement served under section 9 of the *CJA* 1967 (*ante*, § 10–50) made by a postal clerk, and which merely asserted that a requirement under section 172 was served, without producing a copy, was insufficient for this purpose: *Mohindra v. DPP*; *Browne v. Chief Constable of Greater Manchester Police* [2005] R.T.R. 7, QBD (Moses J.).

If it is properly to be inferred from the evidence that an unsigned section 172 form was completed by the accused, then such form is admissible in evidence as a confession (falling within the definition of "confession" in section 82(1) of the *PACE Act* 1984 (*ante*, § 15–354)); and it would be open to a court to infer that a form had been completed by the defendant from the facts that it had been sent to him at his address, and had been returned bearing detailed information relating to him (name, address, date of birth); further, such a confession would not require to be excluded on the ground that a caution should have been administered, as the case came within the exception provided for by Code C:10.1 (Appendix A–69) for the obtaining of information pursuant to a statutory requirement: *Mawdesley v. Chief Constable of Cheshire Constabulary*; *Yorke v. DPP* [2004] 1 All E.R. 58, QBD (Owen J.).

Just as a formal admission under section 172 is admissible in an excess alcohol trial, so also is an informal admission made at the roadside: *Kemsley v. DPP*, 169 J.P.148, DC.

In *Mohindra v. DPP*; *Browne v. Chief Constable of Greater Manchester Police*, *ante*, Moses J. held, *obiter*, that section 172(3) creates a single offence, and an information need do no more than allege a failure to give information, identifying the particulars of the vehicle and the date of the failure.

In *Hayes v. DPP* [2004] 2 *Archbold News* 2, DC, the court expressed the *obiter* opinion that the burden of proof of the defence under subsection (4) was on the accused.

As to a defendant's entitlement to reasons for rejecting a defence under subsection (4), see *Weightman v. DPP* [2007] R.T.R. 45, DC (*ante*, § 2–202).

(2) Mode of trial

32–134 This offence is triable only summarily: *RTOA* 1988, s.9 and Sched. 2, Pt I.

(3) Sentence

32–135 A fine not exceeding level 3 on the standard scale (*ante*, § 5–403): *RTOA* 1988, s.33 and Sched. 2, Pt I. Disqualification is discretionary and endorsement obligatory if the offence is committed otherwise than by virtue of subsection (5) or (11); and the offence carries 6 penalty points: *ibid.*, ss.28, 34, 44 and Sched. 2, Pt I (as amended, as from September 24, 2007 (*Road Safety Act 2006 (Commencement No. 2) Order* 2007 (S.I. 2007 No. 2472)), by the *RSA* 2006, s.29 (substituting 6 penalty points for 3), but only in relation to offences committed on or after that date (2006 Act, s.61(3))).

R. POLICE POWERS

(1) Power to stop vehicles

(a) *Statute*

Road Traffic Act 1988, s.163

Power of police to stop vehicles

32–136 **163.**—(1) A person driving a mechanically propelled vehicle on a road must stop the vehicle on being required to do so by a constable in uniform or a traffic officer.

(2) A person riding a cycle on a road must stop the cycle on being required to do so by a constable in uniform or a traffic officer.

(3) If a person fails to comply with this section he is guilty of an offence.

(4) [*Repealed by* SOCPA *2005, ss.111 and 174(2), Sched. 7, para. 27(3), and Sched. 17, Pt 2.*]

[This section is printed as amended by the *RTA* 1991, s.48, and Sched. 4, para. 67; the *Police Reform Act* 2002, s.49(1); and the *Traffic Management Act* 2004, s.6(4).]

(b) *Mode of trial*

32–137 This offence is triable only summarily: *RTOA* 1988, s.9 and Sched. 2, Pt I.

(c) *Sentence*

32–138 In the case of a mechanically propelled vehicle, a fine not exceeding level 5 (increased from level 3 with effect from September 24, 2007 (*Road Safety Act 2006 (Commencement No. 2) Order* 2007 (S.I. 2007 No. 2472)) by the 2006 Act, s.27, but only in relation to offences committed on or after that date (2006 Act, s.61(3))) on the standard scale (*ante*, § 5–403); in the case of a cycle, a fine not exceeding level 3 on that scale: *RTOA* 1988, s.33, and Sched. 2, Pt I.

(d) *Ingredients of the offence*

32–139 As to the meaning of "driving", see *ante*, § 32–14; of "mechanically propelled vehicle", see *ante*, § 32–16; and of "road", see *ante*, § 32–18.

The references to a constable in section 163 include a reference to a traffic warden: *Functions of Traffic Wardens Order* 1970 (S.I. 1970 No. 1958) (as amended by the *Functions of Traffic Wardens (Amendment) Order* 2002 (S.I. 2002 No. 2975)).

A person sitting in the driving seat of a stationary car, who switched on the engine and sat erect in his seat with his hands on the steering wheel, could not *per se* be said to be a person "driving" the vehicle within the meaning of section 163: *Leach v. DPP* [1993] R.T.R. 161, DC. But it was open to the justices to find that a request by a constable to such person not to drive off continued to operate on his mind when he set the car in motion seconds later and thus became a person "driving" the vehicle: *ibid.*

(2) Power to require production of licence

(a) *Statute*

Road Traffic Act 1988, s.164

Power of constables to require production of driving licence and in certain cases statement of date of birth

164.—(1) Any of the following persons— **32–140**

(a) a person driving a motor vehicle on a road,

(b) a person whom a constable or vehicle examiner has reasonable cause to believe to have been the driver of a motor vehicle at a time when an accident occurred owing to its presence on a road,

(c) a person whom a constable or vehicle examiner has reasonable cause to believe to have committed an offence in relation to the use of a motor vehicle on a road, or

(d) a person—

(i) who supervises the holder of a provisional licence while the holder is driving a motor vehicle on a road, or

(ii) whom a constable or vehicle examiner has reasonable cause to believe was supervising the holder of a provisional licence while driving, at the time when an accident occurred owing to the presence of the vehicle on a road or at a time when an offence is suspected of having been committed by the holder of the provisional licence in relation to the use of the vehicle on a road,

must, on being so required by a constable or vehicle examiner, produce his licence *and its counterpart* for examination, so as to enable the constable or vehicle examiner to ascertain the name and address of the holder of the licence, the date of issue, and the authority by which *they were* [it was] issued.

(2) A person required by a constable under subsection (1) above to produce his licence must in prescribed circumstances, on being so required by the constable, state his date of birth.

(3) If—

(a) [a person is required to deliver his licence *and its counterpart* to the Secretary of State under section 63 of the *Crime (International Co-operation) Act* 2003 or] the Secretary of State has—

(i) revoked a licence under section 92, 93 or 99 of this Act, or

(ii) revoked or suspended a large goods vehicle driver's licence or a passenger-carrying vehicle driver's licence under section 115 of this Act, or

(iii) served notice requiring the delivery of a licence to him in pursuance of section 99C [, 109B] or 115A of this Act, and

(b) the holder of the licence fails to deliver it *and its counterpart* to the Secretary of State or the traffic commissioner, as the case may be, in pursuance of section 92, 93, 99, 99C, 109B, 115A or 118 [or section 63 of the *Crime (International Co-operation) Act* 2003] (as the case may be),

a constable or vehicle examiner may require him to produce the licence *and its counterpart* and upon *their* [its] being produced may seize *them* [it] and deliver *them* [it] to the Secretary of State.

(4) Where a constable has reasonable cause to believe that the holder of a licence, or any other person, has knowingly made a false statement for the purpose of obtaining the grant of the licence, the constable may require the holder of the licence to produce it *and its counterpart* to him.

(4A) Where a constable to whom a provisional licence has been produced by a person driving a motor bicycle has reasonable cause to believe that the holder was not driving it as part of the training being provided on a training course for motor cyclists, the constable may require him to produce the prescribed certificate of completion of a training course for motor cyclists.

(5) Where a person has been required under section 26 or 27 of the *Road Traffic Offenders Act* 1988, section 40B of the *Child Support Act* 1991, *section 40 of the* Crime (Sentences) Act *1997* [section 301 of the *Criminal Justice Act* 2003], section 146 or 147 of the *Powers of Criminal Courts (Sentencing) Act* 2000 or section 233A or 436A of the *Criminal Procedure (Scotland) Act* 1975 to produce a licence *and its counterpart* to the court and fails to do so, a constable or vehicle examiner may require him to produce *them* [it] and, upon *their* [its] being produced, may seize *them* [it] and deliver *them* [it] to the court.

(6) If a person required under the preceding provisions of this section to produce a licence *and its counterpart* or state his date of birth or to produce his certificate of completion of a training course for motor cyclists fails to do so he is, subject to subsections (7) to (8A) below, guilty of an offence.

(7) Subsection (6) above does not apply where a person required on any occasion under the preceding provisions of this section to produce a licence *and its counterpart*—

(a) produces on that occasion a current receipt for the licence *and its counterpart* issued under section 56 of the *Road Traffic Offenders Act* 1988 and, if required to do so, produces the licence *and its counterpart* in person immediately on *their* [its] return at a police station that was specified on that occasion, or

(b) within seven days after that occasion produces such a receipt in person at a police station that was specified by him on that occasion and, if required to do so, produces the licence *and its counterpart* in person immediately on *their* [its] return at that police station.

32–141 (8) In proceedings against any person for the offence of failing to produce a licence *and its counterpart* it shall be a defence for him to show that—

(a) within seven days after the production of his licence *and its counterpart* was required he produced *them* [it] in person at a police station that was specified by him at the time *their* [its] production was required, or,

(b) he produced *them* [it] in person there as soon as was reasonably practicable, or

(c) it was not reasonably practicable for him to produce *them* [it] there before the day on which the proceedings were commenced,

and for the purposes of this subsection the laying of the information or, in Scotland, the service of the complaint on the accused shall be treated as the commencement of the proceedings.

(8A) Subsection (8) above shall apply in relation to a certificate of completion of a training course for motor cyclists as it applies in relation to a licence.

(9) Where in accordance with this section a person has stated his date of birth to a constable, the Secretary of State may serve on that person a notice in writing requiring him to provide the Secretary of State—

(a) with such evidence in that person's possession or obtainable by him as the Secretary of State may specify for the purpose of verifying that date, and

(b) if his name differs from his name at the time of his birth, with a statement in writing specifying his name at that time,

and a person who knowingly fails to comply with a notice under this subsection is guilty of an offence.

(10) A notice authorised to be served on any person by subsection (9) above may be served on him by delivering it to him or by leaving it at his proper address or by sending it to him by post, and for the purposes of this subsection and section 7 of the *Interpretation Act* 1978 in its application to this subsection the proper address of any person shall be his latest address as known to the person giving the notice.

(11) In this section—

"licence" means a licence under Part III of this Act, a Northern Ireland licence or a Community licence,

"vehicle examiner" means an examiner appointed under section 66A of this Act;

and "Community licence", *"counterpart"*, "Northern Ireland licence", "provisional licence", "training course for motor cyclists" and, in relation to such a course, "the prescribed certificate of completion" have the same meanings as in Part III of this Act.

[This section is printed as amended by the *Driving Licences (Community Driving Licence) Regulations* 1990 (S.I. 1990 No. 144); the *Road Traffic (Driver Licensing and Information Systems) Act* 1989, s.7 and Sched. 3; the *RTA* 1991, ss.48 and 83, and Scheds 4, para. 68, and 8; S.I. 1996 No. 1974 (*ante*, § 32–111); S.I. 1998 No. 1420 (*ante*, § 32–112); the *PCC(S)A* 2000, s.165(1) and Sched. 9, para. 117; the *Child Support, Pensions and Social Security Act* 2000, s.16(4); and the *Crime (International Co-operation) Act* 2003, s.91, and Sched. 5, para. 27(a)(ii) and (iii), and (b); and, as from a day to be appointed, by *ibid.*, para. 27(a)(i) and (iii) (insertion of words in square brackets in subs. (3)); and the *CJA* 2003, s.304, and Sched. 32, para. 51 (substitution of words in square brackets in subs. (5) for reference to s.40 of the *C(S)A* 1997); and the *RSA* 2006, ss.10(1) and (12), and 59, Sched. 3, paras. 2 and 26, and Sched. 7(4) (insertion of all other words in square brackets, omission of italicised words (other than titles of Acts)).]

For sections 146 and 147 of the *PCC(S)A* 2000, see *ante*, §§ 5–844, 5–845.

Persons other than constables

The powers exercisable by a constable or vehicle examiner under subsections (1) and (3) may also be exercised in the case of prescribed classes of goods vehicle and passenger-carrying vehicle by a person authorised for the purpose by a traffic commissioner appointed under the *Public Passenger Vehicles Act* 1981: see s.166 of this Act, *post*, § 32–151. **32–142**

References to a constable are for certain purposes to include references to a traffic warden: see art. 3(4) of S.I. 1970 No. 1958 (*ante*, § 32–139), as substituted by the *Function of Traffic Wardens (Amendment) Order* 1993 (S.I. 1993 No. 1334). The effect is that a traffic warden may exercise the powers conferred on constables by subsections (1), (2) and (6) where he has reasonable cause to believe an offence has been committed by stopping a vehicle on a pedestrian crossing in breach of pedestrian crossing regulations or by leaving a vehicle in a dangerous position. Such powers can also be exercised where a traffic warden is performing custodial functions in respect of vehicles removed under regulations made under section 99 of the *Road Traffic Regulation Act* 1984 or from a parking place pursuant to a street parking order and he has reasonable cause to believe that an offence of obstructing a road, or certain other offences, has been committed in respect of the vehicle.

(b) *Mode of trial*

This offence is triable only summarily: *RTOA* 1988, s.9 and Sched. 2, Pt I. **32–143**

(c) *Sentence*

A fine not exceeding level 3 on the standard scale (*ante*, § 5–403): *RTOA* 1988 s.33 and Sched. 2, Pt I. **32–144**

(3) Power to obtain names and addresses

(a) *Statute*

Road Traffic Act 1988, s.165

Power of constables to obtain names and addresses of drivers and others, and to require production of evidence of insurance or security and test certificates

165.—(1) Any of the following persons— **32–145**

(a) a person driving a motor vehicle (other than an invalid carriage) on a road, or

(b) a person whom a constable or vehicle examiner has reasonable cause to believe to have been the driver of a motor vehicle (other than an invalid carriage) at a time when an accident occurred owing to its presence on a road or other public place, or

(c) a person whom a constable or vehicle examiner has reasonable cause to believe to have committed an offence in relation to the use on a road of a motor vehicle (other than an invalid carriage),

must, on being so required by a constable or vehicle examiner, give his name and address and the name and address of the owner of the vehicle and produce the following documents for examination.

(2) Those documents are—

(a) the relevant certificate of insurance or certificate of security (within the meaning of Part VI of this Act), or such other evidence that the vehicle is not or was not being driven in contravention of section 143 of this Act as may be prescribed by regulations made by the Secretary of State,

(b) in relation to a vehicle to which section 47 of this Act applies, a test certificate issued in respect of the vehicle as mentioned in subsection (1) of that section, and
(c) in relation to a goods vehicle the use of which on a road without a plating certificate or goods vehicle test certificate is an offence under section 53(1) or (2) of this Act, any such certificate issued in respect of that vehicle or any trailer drawn by it.

(3) Subject to subsection (4) below, a person who fails to comply with a requirement under subsection (1) above is guilty of an offence.

(4) A person shall not be convicted of an offence under subsection (3) above by reason only of failure to produce any certificate or other evidence if in proceedings against him for the offence he shows that—

(a) within seven days after the date on which the production of the certificate or other evidence was required it was produced at a police station that was specified by him at the time when its production was required, or
(b) it was produced there as soon as was reasonably practicable, or
(c) it was not reasonably practicable for it to be produced there before the day on which the proceedings were commenced,

and for the purposes of this subsection the laying of the information or, in Scotland, the service of the complaint on the accused shall be treated as the commencement of the proceedings.

(5) A person—

(a) who supervises the holder of a provisional licence granted under Part III of this Act while the holder is driving on a road a motor vehicle (other than an invalid carriage), or
(b) whom a constable or vehicle examiner has reasonable cause to believe was supervising the holder of such a licence while driving, at a time when an accident occurred owing to the presence of the vehicle on a road or at the time when an offence is suspected of having been committed by the holder of the provisional licence in relation to the use of the vehicle on a road,

must, on being so required by a constable or vehicle examiner, give his name and address and the name and address of the owner of the vehicle.

(6) A person who fails to comply with a requirement under subsection (5) above is guilty of an offence.

(7) In this section "owner", in relation to a vehicle which is the subject of a hiring agreement, includes each party to the agreement and "vehicle examiner" means an examiner appointed under section 66A of this Act.

[This section is printed as amended by the *Road Traffic (Driver Licensing and Information Systems) Act* 1989, s.7 and Sched. 3; the *RTA* 1991, ss.48 and 83, and Scheds 4, para. 69, and 8; and S.I. 2000 No. 726 (*ante*, § 32–120).]

Persons other than constables

32–146 The powers exercisable by a constable or vehicle examiner under this section may also be exercised in the case of prescribed classes of goods vehicle and passenger-carrying vehicle by a person authorised for the purpose by a traffic commissioner appointed under the *Public Passenger Vehicles Act* 1981: see s.166 of this Act, *post*, § 32–151.

References in section 165 to a constable are for certain purposes to include references to a traffic warden: see art. 3(3) of S.I. 1970 No. 1958 (*ante*, § 32–142).

(b) *Mode of trial*

32–147 This offence is triable only summarily: *RTOA* 1988, s.9 and Sched. 2, Pt I.

(c) *Sentence*

32–148 A fine not exceeding level 3 on the standard scale (*ante*, § 5–403): *RTOA* 1988, s.33 and Sched. 2, Pt I.

(d) *Documentation*

32–149 For the purposes of this section a valid international motor insurance card has effect as though it were a certificate of insurance issued by an authorised insurer: see reg. 6 of the *Motor Vehicles (International Motor Insurance Card) Regulations* 1971 (S.I. 1971 No. 792).

For the evidence prescribed for the purposes of subsection (2)(a), see regulation 7 of the *Motor Vehicles (Third Party Risks) Regulations* 1972 (S.I. 1972 No. 1217), as amended by S.I.s 1973 No. 1821, 1974 No. 792, 1974 No. 2187 and 1992 No. 1283.

(e) *Visiting forces*

For the application of section 165 to vehicles in the service of a visiting force or an international headquarters, see article 8(2) of the *Visiting Forces and International Headquarters (Application of Law) Order* 1999 (S.I. 1999 No. 1736). **32–150**

(4) Power to seize, etc. vehicles driven without licence or insurance

Section 165A of the *RTA* 1988 (inserted by the *SOCPA* 2005, s.152) creates a new power to seize a vehicle where a driver has failed on request to produce to a uniformed police officer his licence and its counterpart for examination; or evidence that he holds valid insurance; or has failed to stop the vehicle on request to enable the officer to make enquiries. In each case, the officer must also have reasonable grounds for believing that the vehicle is or was being driven in contravention of section 87(1) (no licence) or section 143 of the *RTA* 1988 (no insurance). Where practicable, he must warn the driver that unless he produces immediately his licence and counterpart or evidence of insurance the vehicle will be seized. **32–150a**

Where the above conditions are satisfied, the officer may seize the vehicle and remove it. For the purposes of seizing the vehicle, he may also enter any premises (other than a private dwelling house) on which he has reasonable grounds for believing the vehicle to be and may use reasonable force where necessary. If the officer is unable to seize the vehicle immediately because the person driving the vehicle has failed to stop as requested or has driven off, he may seize it at any time within the period of 24 hours beginning with the time at which the condition in question is first satisfied.

Section 165B provides that the Secretary of State may by regulations make provision as to the removal and retention of vehicles seized under section 165A; and the release and disposal of such vehicles.

(5) Powers in respect of goods vehicles and passenger-carrying vehicles

Road Traffic Act 1988, s.166

Powers of certain officers as respects goods vehicles and passenger-carrying vehicles

166. A person authorised for the purpose by a traffic commissioner appointed under the *Public Passenger Vehicles Act* 1981, may, on production if so required of his authority, exercise in the case of goods vehicles or passenger-carrying vehicles of any prescribed class all such powers as are, under section 164(1) or (3) or 165 of this Act, exercisable by a constable. **32–151**

[This section is printed as substituted by the *Road Traffic (Driver Licensing and Information Systems) Act* 1989, s.7, and Sched. 3; and as amended by the *RTA* 1991, s.48, and Sched. 4, para. 70.]

S. PROCEDURE AND EVIDENCE

(1) Notice of intended prosecution

Road Traffic Offenders Act 1988, s.1

Requirement of warning, etc. of prosecutions for certain offences

1.—(1) Subject to section 2 of this Act, a person shall not be convicted of an offence to which this section applies unless— **32–152**

(a) he was warned at the time the offence was committed that the question of prosecuting him for some one or other of the offences to which this section applies would be taken into consideration, or

(b) within fourteen days of the commission of the offence a summons (or, in Scotland, a complaint) for the offence was served on him, or

(c) within fourteen days of the commission of the offence a notice of the intended prosecution specifying the nature of the alleged offence and the time and place where it is alleged to have been committed, was—

(i) in the case of an offence under section 28 or 29 of the *Road Traffic Act* 1988 (cycling offences), served on him,

(ii) in the case of any other offence, served on him or on the person, if any, registered as the keeper of the vehicle at the time of the commission of the offence.

(1A) A notice required by this section to be served on any person may be served on that person—

(a) by delivering it to him;

(b) by addressing it to him and leaving it at his last known address; or

(c) by sending it by registered post, recorded delivery service or first class post addressed to him at his last known address.

(2) A notice shall be deemed for the purposes of subsection (1)(c) above to have been served on a person if it was sent by registered post or recorded delivery service addressed to him at his last known address, notwithstanding that the notice was returned as undelivered or was for any other reason not received by him.

(3) The requirement of subsection (1) above shall in every case be deemed to have been complied with unless and until the contrary is proved.

(4) Schedule 1 to this Act shows the offences to which this section applies.

[This section is printed as amended by the *RTA* 1991, s.48 and Sched. 4, para. 80; and the *CJPOA* 1994, s.168(1), and Sched. 9, para. 6(3).]

"at the time the offence was committed"

32–153 It is a question of fact and degree whether a warning was given at the time the offence was committed: *Jollye v. Dale* [1960] 2 Q.B. 258, DC (where 100 minutes after the incident was held to be "at the time").

The phrase must be construed sensibly and should not be confined to a matter of seconds after the offence. It embraces the period of time within which a constable appears on the scene and ascertains the facts from witnesses still present: *Shield v. Crighton* [1974] Crim.L.R. 605, DC, where a policeman arrived about 10 minutes after the incident.

"within fourteen days of the commission of the offence"

32–153a The notice must be posted on such a date that it would reach the defendant in the ordinary course of post within 14 days of the commission of the offence. In *Groome v. Driscoll* (1969) 113 S.J. 905, DC, where the notice was posted the day after the offence but failed to arrive within 14 days, it was deemed to have been served within the statutory period. *Cf. Nicholson v. Tapp* [1972] 1 W.L.R. 1044, where on the fourteenth day after the offence the notice of intended prosecution was sent to the defendant by recorded delivery. The dismissal of the information was upheld on appeal to the Divisional Court.

The notice

32–154 The object of the notice is to bring to the defendant's mind, while events are still fresh in his memory, the fact that he is going to be prosecuted. Inaccuracies in the notice served (*e.g.* as to the time of the alleged offence) are immaterial if they are not such as to mislead the defendant: *Pope v. Clarke*, 37 Cr.App.R. 141, DC. The notice of intended prosecution need not specify the precise section of the Act under which proceedings are contemplated: *Russell v. Read*, 113 J.P. 111.

A notice of intended prosecution which is incorrectly addressed is not necessarily bad: *Rogerson v. Edwards*, 95 S.J. 172.

A notice of an intended prosecution of a company is valid notwithstanding that the word "Limited" is omitted from the company's name: *Springate v. Questier*, 116 J.P. 367, DC.

In *Young v. Day*, 123 J.P. 317, a notice of intended prosecution was served on a motorist alleging that he had driven dangerously "along the Hathfield to Bethersden

Road". The road in question was about four miles long, and the dangerous driving alleged was that he had narrowly avoided colliding with a stationary vehicle on the offside of the road. The Divisional Court held that the notice did not sufficiently specify the place where the offence was alleged to have taken place.

Service of notice

The notice may be posted to the defendant's home even if the police know that he is in hospital: *Phipps v. McCormick* [1972] R.T.R. 21, DC. **32–155**

In *Lund v. Thompson* [1959] 1 Q.B. 283, 43 Cr.App.R. 9, DC, L was involved in a traffic incident on February 11, 1958. On February 14, a notice of intended prosecution was served on him. On February 27, the police wrote to L saying that they had decided to take no further action in the matter, but on March 13 the police again wrote to L saying that they had decided to institute proceedings against him after all. The Divisional Court held that the letter of February 27 did not invalidate the notice of intended prosecution.

As to service on the agent of the defendant, see *Burt v. Kirkcaldy* [1965] 1 W.L.R. 474, DC. See also *R. v. Bott and Baker* [1968] 1 W.L.R. 583, Assizes (Veale J.), and *Penman v. Parker* [1986] 1 W.L.R. 882, DC.

A defendant must prove that neither he nor the registered keeper has been served. It is then for the prosecution to prove a posting: *Archer v. Blacker* [1965] Crim.L.R. 164, DC; *Sanders v. Scott* [1961] 2 Q.B. 326, DC.

Road Traffic Offenders Act 1988, s.2

Requirement of warning, etc.: supplementary

2.—(1) The requirement of section 1(1) of this Act does not apply in relation to an offence if, at the time of the offence or immediately after it, an accident occurs owing to the presence on a road of the vehicle in respect of which the offence was committed. **32–156**

(2) The requirement of section 1(1) of this Act does not apply in relation to an offence in respect of which—

(a) a fixed penalty notice (within the meaning of Part III of this Act) has been given or fixed under any provision of that Part, or

(b) a notice has been given under section 54(4) of this Act.

(3) Failure to comply with the requirement of section 1(1) of this Act is not a bar to the conviction of the accused in a case where the court is satisfied—

(a) that neither the name and address of the accused nor the name and address of the registered keeper, if any, could with reasonable diligence have been ascertained in time for a summons or, as the case may be, a complaint to be served or for a notice to be served or sent in compliance with the requirement, or

(b) that the accused by his own conduct contributed to the failure.

(4) Failure to comply with the requirement of section 1(1) of this Act in relation to an offence is not a bar to the conviction of a person of that offence by virtue of the provisions of—

(a) section 24 of this Act, or

(b) any of the enactments mentioned in section 24(6);

but a person is not to be convicted of an offence by virtue of any of those provisions if section 1 applies to the offence with which he was charged and the requirement of section 1(1) was not satisfied in relation to the offence charged.

[This section is printed as amended by the *RTA* 1991, s.48, and Sched. 4, para. 81.]

In subsection (3), "the court" means "the judge" and "reasonable diligence" means reasonable diligence on the part of the officer in charge of the prosecution: *R. v. Bolkis*, 24 Cr.App.R. 19, CCA.

The decision as to whether section 2(1) applies is to be made by the judge and not by the jury: *R. v. Currie* [2007] 2 Cr.App.R. 18, CA. Where the prosecution seek to rely on section 2(1), the burden is on them to prove to the criminal standard that there had been an accident; and as to what amounts to an "accident" for these purposes, the word is to be given a common sense meaning and is not restricted to untoward or unintended consequences having an adverse physical effect: *ibid.* (there had been an "accident" where a police officer had grabbed the open door of a vehicle to prevent the driver from driving off and the driver had nonetheless driven away at speed, causing the police officer to lose her grip; the circumstances would have been sufficiently memorable for it to have been unnecessary for the prosecution to have drawn the driver's attention to it).

Whether an accident has occurred "owing to the presence on the road" of the vehicle in question will depend on whether there is a sufficient causal link between the offence and the accident, such that a driver need not be warned of the risk of prosecution; whilst, in many such instances, the offence will be the, or at least a, cause of the accident, section 2 does not absolutely require that, since what matters is whether the accident is attributable to the presence of a vehicle on the road, rather than to the fact that its driver has committed an offence; where, therefore, the two appellants were driving separate cars dangerously, encouraging each other and a third party, who subsequently crashed his own car fatally, there was a sufficient causal link, the fatal accident occurring owing to the presence on the road of all three dangerously driven vehicles: *R. v. Myers and Ennis-Simpson* [2007] 2 Cr.App.R. 19, CA.

(2) Time limits

Road Traffic Offenders Act 1988, s.6

Time within which summary proceedings for certain offences must be commenced

32–157 **6.**—(1) Subject to subsection (2) below, summary proceedings for an offence to which this section applies may be brought within a period of six months from the date on which evidence sufficient in the opinion of the prosecutor to warrant the proceedings came to his knowledge.

(2) No such proceedings shall be brought by virtue of this section more than three years after the commission of the offence.

(3) For the purposes of this section, a certificate signed by or on behalf of the prosecutor and stating the date on which evidence sufficient in his opinion to warrant the proceedings came to his knowledge shall be conclusive evidence of that fact.

(4) A certificate stating that matter and purporting to be so signed shall be deemed to be so signed unless the contrary is proved.

(5) [*Scotland*.]

(6) Schedule 1 to this Act shows the offences to which this section applies.

For the "period of six months" within subsection (1), see *Radcliffe v. Bartholomew* [1892] 1 Q.B. 161, DC.

A traffic examiner employed by the vehicle inspectorate to investigate traffic offences, but not authorised to decide whether or not to prosecute, is not a "prosecutor" within section 6(1). Accordingly, the six-month period runs from the time when sufficient evidence comes to the attention of a person authorised to prosecute (*e.g.* the *senior* traffic examiner): *Swan v. Vehicle Inspectorate* [1997] R.T.R. 187, DC.

Where this section applies, it also applies to aiding and abetting: *Homolka v. Osmond* [1939] 1 All E.R. 154, DC.

(3) Duty of accused to provide licence

Road Traffic Offenders Act 1988, s.7

Duty of accused to provide licence

32–158 **7.**—(1) A person who is prosecuted for an offence involving obligatory or discretionary disqualification and who is the holder of a licence must—

(a) cause it to be delivered to the proper officer of the court not later than the day before the date appointed for the hearing, or

(b) post it, at such a time that in the ordinary course of post it would be delivered not later than that day, in a letter duly addressed to the clerk and either registered or sent by the recorded delivery service, or

(c) have it with him at the hearing

and the foregoing obligations imposed on him as respects the licence also apply as respects the counterpart to the licence.

(2) In subsection (1) above "proper officer" means—

(a) in relation to a magistrates' court in England and Wales, the designated officer for the court, and

(b) in relation to any other court, the clerk of the court.

[This section is printed as amended by the *Driving Licences (Community Driving Licence) Regulations* 1990 (S.I. 1990 No. 144); the *RTA* 1991, s.48 and Sched. 4, para. 83; the *Access to Justice Act* 1999, s.90(1) and Sched. 13, para. 141; the *Courts Act* 2003, s.109(1), and Sched. 8, para. 310; and as amended, as from a day to be appointed, by the *RSA* 2006, ss.10(1) and (12), and 59, Sched. 3, paras. 30 and 31, and Sched. 7(4) (omission of italicised words).]

(4) Mode of trial

Road Traffic Offenders Act 1988, s.9

Mode of trial

9. An offence against a provision of the Traffic Acts specified in column 1 of Part I of Schedule 2 to this Act or regulations made under such a provision (the general nature of which offence is indicated in column 2) shall be punishable as shown against the offence in column 3 (that is, on summary conviction or on indictment or in either one way or the other). **32–159**

(5) Evidence

Road Traffic Offenders Act 1988, s.11

Evidence by certificate as to driver, user or owner

11.—(1) In any proceedings in England and Wales for an offence to which this section applies, a certificate in the prescribed form, purporting to be signed by a constable and certifying that a person specified in the certificate stated to the constable— **32–160**

(a) that a particular mechanically propelled vehicle was being driven or used by, or belonged to, that person on a particular occasion, or

(b) that a particular mechanically propelled vehicle on a particular occasion was used by, or belonged to, a firm and that he was, at the time of the statement, a partner in that firm, or

(c) that a particular mechanically propelled vehicle on a particular occasion was used by, or belonged to, a corporation and that he was, at the time of the statement, a director, officer or employee of that corporation,

shall be admissible as evidence for the purpose of determining by whom the vehicle was being driven or used, or to whom it belonged, as the case may be, on that occasion.

(2) Nothing in subsection (1) above makes a certificate admissible as evidence in proceedings for an offence except in a case where and to the like extent to which oral evidence to the like effect would have been admissible in those proceedings.

(3) Nothing in subsection (1) above makes a certificate admissible as evidence in proceedings for an offence—

(a) unless a copy of it has, not less than seven days before the hearing or trial, been served in the prescribed manner on the person charged with the offence, or

(b) if that person not later than three days before the hearing or trial or within such further time as the court may in special circumstances allow, serves a notice in the prescribed form and manner on the prosecutor requiring attendance at the trial of the person who signed the certificate.

(3A) *Where the proceedings mentioned in subsection (1) above are proceedings before a magistrates' court inquiring into an offence as examining justices this section shall have effect with the omission of—*

(a) *subsection (2), and*

(b) *in subsection (3), paragraph (b) and the word "or" immediately preceding it.*

(4) In this section "prescribed" means prescribed by rules made by the Secretary of State by statutory instrument.

(5) Schedule 1 to this Act shows the offences to which this section applies.

[This section is printed as amended by the *RTA* 1991, s.48 and Sched. 4, para. 84; and the *CPIA* 1996, s.47, and Sched. 1, para. 35. Subs. (3A) is repealed as from a day to be appointed: *CJA* 2003, ss.41 and 332, Sched. 3, para. 61(1) and (2), and Sched. 37, Pt 4.]

For the prescribed form and manner of service of a certificate admissible under this section, see the *Evidence by Certificate Rules* 1961 (S.I. 1961 No. 248), *ante*, § 10–54.

The reference to a constable in subsection (1) is for certain purposes to include a reference to a traffic warden: see S.I. 1970 No. 1958 (*ante*, § 32–142).

Road Traffic Offenders Act 1988, ss.13, 15, 16

Admissibility of records as evidence

32–161 **13.**—(1) This section applies to a statement contained in a document purporting to be—

(a) a part of the records maintained by the Secretary of State in connection with any functions exercisable by him by virtue of Part III of the *Road Traffic Act* 1988 or a part of any other records maintained by the Secretary of State with respect to vehicles, or

(b) a copy of a document forming part of those records, or

(c) a note of any information contained in those records,

and to be authenticated by a person authorised in that behalf by the Secretary of State.

(2) A statement to which this section applies shall be admissible in any proceedings as evidence (in Scotland, sufficient evidence) of any fact stated in it to the same extent as oral evidence of that fact is admissible in those proceedings.

(3) In the preceding subsections, except in Scotland—

"copy", in relation to a document, means anything onto which information recorded in the document has been copied, by whatever means and whether directly or indirectly;

"document" means anything in which information of any description is recorded; and

"statement" means any representation of fact, however made.

(3A) [*Scotland.*]

(3A) In any case where—

(a) a person is convicted by a magistrates' court of a summary offence under the *Traffic Acts* or the *Road Traffic (Driver Licensing and Information Systems) Act* 1989,

(b) a statement to which this section applies is produced to the court in the proceedings,

(c) the statement specifies an alleged previous conviction of the accused of an offence involving obligatory endorsement or an order made on the conviction, and

(d) the accused is not present in person before the court when the statement is so produced,

the court may take account of the previous conviction or order as if the accused had appeared and admitted it.

(3B) Section 104 of the *Magistrates' Courts Act* 1980 (under which previous convictions may be adduced in the absence of the accused after giving him seven days' notice of them) does not limit the effect of subsection (3A) above.

(4) In any case where—

(a) a statement to which this section applies is produced to a magistrates' court in any proceedings for an offence involving obligatory or discretionary disqualification other than a summary offence under any of the enactments mentioned in subsection (3A)(a) above,

(b) the statement specifies an alleged previous conviction of an accused person of any such offence or any order made on the conviction,

(c) it is proved to the satisfaction of the court, on oath or in such manner as may be prescribed by Criminal Procedure Rules, that not less than seven days before the statement is so produced a notice was served on the accused, in such form and manner as may be so prescribed, specifying the previous conviction or order and stating that it is proposed to bring it to the notice of the court in the event of or, as the case may be, in view of his conviction, and

(d) the accused is not present in person before the court when the statement is so produced,

the court may take account of the previous conviction or order as if the accused had appeared and admitted it.

(5) Nothing in the preceding provisions of this section enables evidence to be given in respect of any matter other than a matter of a description prescribed by regulations made by the Secretary of State.

(6) [*Regulations under this section to be made by statutory instrument.*]

(7) *Where the proceedings mentioned in subsection (2) above are proceedings before a*

magistrates' court inquiring into an offence as examining justices this section shall have effect as if—

(a) *in subsection (2) the words "to the same extent as oral evidence of that fact is admissible in those proceedings" were omitted;*

(b) *in subsection (4) the word "and" were inserted at the end of paragraph (a);*

(c) *in subsection (4), paras (c) and (d) and the words "as if the accused had appeared and admitted it" were omitted.*

[This section is printed as amended by the *Civil Evidence Act* 1995, s.15(1), Sched. 1, para. 15; the *CPIA* 1996, s.47, and Sched. 1, para. 36 (insertion of subs. (7)); the *Magistrates' Courts (Procedure) Act* 1998, s.2 (insertion of second subs. numbered (3A), subs. (3B), and words beginning "other than" at the end of subs. (4)(a)); and the *Courts Act 2003 (Consequential Amendments) Order* 2004 (S.I. 2004 No. 2035). Subs. (7) is repealed as from a day to be appointed: *CJA* 2003, ss.41 and 332, Sched. 3, para. 61(1) and (3), and Sched. 37, Pt 4.]

The *Vehicle and Driving Licences Records (Evidence) Regulations* 1970 (S.I. 1970 No. 1997) have effect as if made under subsection (5).

Use of specimens in proceedings for an offence under section 4 or 5 of the Road Traffic Act.

15.—(1) This section and section 16 of this Act apply in respect of proceedings for an offence under section 3A, 4 or 5 of the *Road Traffic Act* 1988 (driving offences connected with drink or drugs); and expressions used in this section and section 16 of this Act have the same meaning as in sections 3A to 10 of that Act. **32–162**

(2) Evidence of the proportion of alcohol or any drug in a specimen of breath blood or urine provided by or taken from the accused shall, in all cases (including cases where the specimen was not provided or taken in connection with the alleged offence) be taken into account and, subject to subsection (3) below, it shall be assumed that the proportion of alcohol in the accused's breath, blood or urine at the time of the alleged offence was not less than in the specimen.

(3) That assumption shall not be made if the accused proves—

(a) that he consumed alcohol before he provided the specimen or had it taken from him and—

(i) in relation to an offence under section 3A, after the time of the alleged offence, and

(ii) otherwise, after he had ceased to drive, attempt to drive or be in charge of a vehicle on a road or other public place, and

(b) that had he not done so the proportion of alcohol in his breath, blood or urine would not have exceeded the prescribed limit and, if it is alleged that he was unfit to drive through drink, would not have been such as to impair his ability to drive properly.

(4) A specimen of blood shall be disregarded unless—

(a) it was taken from the accused with his consent and either—

(i) in a police station by a medical practitioner or a registered health care professional; or

(ii) elsewhere by a medical practitioner; or

(b) it was taken from the accused by a medical practitioner under section 7A of the *Road Traffic Act* 1988 and the accused subsequently gave his permission for a laboratory test of the specimen.

(5) Where, at the time a specimen of blood or urine was provided by the accused, he asked to be provided with such a specimen, evidence of the proportion of alcohol or any drug found in the specimen is not admissible on behalf of the prosecution unless—

(a) the specimen in which the alcohol or drug was found is one of two parts into which the specimen provided by the accused was divided at the time it was provided, and

(b) the other part was supplied to the accused.

(5A) Where a specimen of blood was taken from the accused under section 7A of the *Road Traffic Act* 1988, evidence of the proportion of alcohol or any drug found in the specimen is not admissible on behalf of the prosecution unless—

(a) the specimen in which the alcohol or drug was found is one of two parts into which the specimen taken from the accused was divided at the time it was taken; and

(b) any request to be supplied with the other part which was made by the accused at the time when he gave his permission for a laboratory test of the specimen was complied with.

[This section is printed as amended by the *RTA* 1991, s.48, and Sched. 4, para. 87; and the *Police Reform Act* 2002, s.57(1)–(4).]

As to the reference to "a specimen of breath" being to a specimen taken under section 7 of the *RTA* 1988, and as not including a preliminary roadside breath test under section 6A, see *Smith v. DPP*, *ante*, § 32–89a.

The assumption under section 15(2) does not infringe Article 6(2) of the ECHR: *Parker v. DPP* [2001] R.T.R. 16, DC.

The assumption shall not be made if the defendant proves:

(a) that he consumed alcohol after he had ceased to drive, attempt to drive or be in charge of a motor vehicle on a road or other public place and before he had provided the specimen; and

(b) that had he not done so the proportion of alcohol in his breath, blood or urine would not have been such as to impair his ability to drive properly: s.15(3).

Section 15(3) imposes a persuasive burden on the defendant; such legislative interference with the presumption of innocence is, however, justified, being no greater than necessary to combat the social evil of driving whilst under the influence of alcohol; first, the offence involves no examination of the mind of the accused; rather it depends on the result of a scientific test intended to be as exact as possible, with any inexactness working in favour of the accused; secondly, it is the act of the accused, by consuming alcohol after driving, that tends to defeat the legislative scheme, the likelihood being that such act is done for such purpose; and thirdly, the evidence necessary to rebut the assumption is all peculiarly within the knowledge of the accused: *R. v. Drummond* [2002] 2 Cr.App.R. 25, CA.

It will usually be necessary to call expert evidence to show the back calculation: *Dawson v. Lunn* [1986] R.T.R. 234, DC, and if such evidence is to be called, the prosecution should be notified in advance.

As to section 15(5), this imposes no requirement that the accused should have been told of his right to be given part of a specimen of blood or urine: *Campbell v. DPP*, unreported, February 28, 2003, QBD (Pitchford J.) ([2003] EWHC 559 (Admin.)).

In *Jones v. CPS*, 167 J.P. 481, DC, it was held that where a specimen of blood had been divided into two parts, the motorist did not "ask" to be provided with a specimen, within section 15(5)(b), by merely pointing with her finger to one of the two parts when a sample was offered to her; an offer to supply a sample, coupled with an acceptance by means of pointing did not amount to a request; but she had in fact been supplied with a part in that the offer of a sample, together with her pointing to one part, amounted to a tender of a sample and its supply, even though she never obtained physical possession of it, both samples having then been placed in the police refrigerator and the motorist having failed to collect it on leaving the police station.

Documentary evidence as to specimens in such proceedings

32–163 **16.**—(1) Evidence of the proportion of alcohol or a drug in a specimen of breath, blood or urine may, subject to subsections (3) and (4) below and to section 15(5) and (5A) of this Act, be given by the production of a document or documents purporting to be whichever of the following is appropriate, that is to say—

(a) a statement automatically produced by the device by which the proportion of alcohol in a specimen of breath was measured and a certificate signed by a constable (which may but need not be contained in the same document as the statement) that the statement relates to a specimen provided by the accused at the date and time shown in the statement, and

(b) a certificate signed by an authorised analyst as to the proportion of alcohol or any drug found in a specimen of blood or urine identified in the certificate.

(2) Subject to subsections (3) and (4) below, evidence that a specimen of blood was taken from the accused with his consent by a medical practitioner or a registered health care professional may be given by the production of a document purporting to certify that fact and to be signed by a medical practitioner or a registered health care professional.

(3) Subject to subsection (4) below—

(a) a document purporting to be such a statement or such a certificate (or both such a statement and such a certificate) as is mentioned in subsection (1)(a) above is admissible in evidence on behalf of the prosecution in pursuance of this section only if a copy of it either has been handed to the accused when the document was produced or has been served on him not later than seven days before the hearing, and

(b) any other document is so admissible only if a copy of it has been served on the accused not later than seven days before the hearing.

(4) A document purporting to be a certificate (or so much of a document as purports to be a certificate) is not so admissible if the accused, not later than three days before the hearing or within such further time as the court may in special circumstances allow, has served notice on the prosecutor requiring the attendance at the hearing of the person by whom the document purports to be signed.

(5) [*Scotland.*]

(6) A copy of a certificate required by this section to be served on the accused or a notice required by this section to be served on the prosecutor may be served personally or sent by registerd post or recorded delivery service.

(6A) *Where the proceedings mentioned in section 15(1) of this Act are proceedings before a magistrates' court inquiring into an offence as examining justices this section shall have effect with the omission of subsection (4).*

(7) In this section "authorised analyst" means—

(a) any person possessing the qualifications prescribed by regulations made under section 27 of the *Food Safety Act* 1990 as qualifying persons for appointment as public analysts under that Act, and

(b) any other person authorised by the Secretary of State to make analyses for the purposes of this section.

[This section is printed as amended by the *CPIA* 1996, s.47, and Sched. 1, para. 37; and the *Police Reform Act* 2002, s.57(5) and (6). Subs. (6A) is repealed as from a day to be appointed: *CJA* 2003, ss.41 and 332, Sched. 3, para. 61(1) and (4), and Sched. 37, Pt 4.]

A failure to serve not later than seven days before the hearing any of the documents specified in section 16(1)(a) cannot be waived: *Tobi v. Nicholas*, 86 Cr.App.R. 323, DC; and the statute providing that the statement and/ or certificate would be admissible "only if" the prescribed steps had been taken, the fact that no objection to the evidence was taken in the magistrates' court until the close of the evidence could not have been held to be a waiver of any right to object: *McCormack v. DPP* [2002] R.T.R. 20, QBD (Maurice Kay J.). Strict proof of service can, however, be waived: *Louis v. DPP* [1998] R.T.R. 354, DC. The court held that once the certificate had been admitted in evidence it was not open to the defence subsequently to challenge the admissibility of the document on the ground that the certificate of service had not been signed as required by section 16.

Section 16(2) is permissive, and proof of consent need not necessarily be by way of documentary or oral evidence from the person who took the sample: *Steward v. DPP* [2004] R.T.R. 16, DC (evidence of police officer, present when surgeon took motorist's blood, was sufficient proof of consent).

Section 16(3)(a) was complied with where the officer conducting the procedure offered one copy of the statement produced by the machine to the accused who refused to accept it, even though there had been no physical transfer of the document to him; "handed to" in this context means "tendered to": *McCormack v. DPP*, *ante*.

Where an analyst's certificate was not served by registered post or recorded delivery in accordance with section 16(6), it was inadmissible: *DPP v. Stephens*, unreported, June 22, 2006, DC ([2006] EWHC 1860 (Admin.)).

(6) Notification of disability

Road Traffic Offenders Act 1988, s.22

Notification of disability

22.—(1) If in any proceedings for an offence committed in respect of a motor vehicle it **32–164**

appears to the court that the accused may be suffering from any relevant disability or prospective disability (within the meaning of Part III of the *Road Traffic Act* 1988) the court must notify the Secretary of State.

(2) A notice sent by a court to the Secretary of State in pursuance of this section must be sent in such manner and to such address and contain such particulars as the Secretary of State may determine.

(7) Alternative verdicts

Road Traffic Offenders Act 1988, s.24

Alternative verdicts: general

32–165 **24.**—(A1) Where

(a) a person charged with manslaughter in connection with the driving of a mechanically propelled vehicle by him is found not guilty of that offence, but

(b) the allegations in the indictment amount to or include an allegation of any of the relevant offences,

he may be convicted of that offence.

(A2) For the purposes of subsection (A1) above the following are the relevant offences—

(a) an offence under section 1 of the *Road Traffic Act* 1988 (causing death by dangerous driving),

(b) an offence under section 2 of that Act (dangerous driving),

(c) an offence under section 3A of that Act (causing death by careless driving when under the influence of drink or drugs), and

(d) an offence under section 35 of the *Offences against the Person Act* 1861 (furious driving).

(1) Where—

(a) a person charged with an offence under a provision of the *Road Traffic Act* 1988 specified in the first column of the Table below (where the general nature of the offences is also indicated) is found not guilty of that offence, but

(b) the allegations in the indictment or information (or in Scotland complaint) amount to or include an allegation of an offence under one or more of the provisions specifies in the corresponding entry in the second column,

he may be convicted of that offence or of one or more of those offences.

Offence charged	*Alternative*
Section 1 (causing death by dangerous driving)	Section 2 (dangerous driving) Section 2B (causing death by careless, or inconsiderate, driving) Section 3 (careless, and inconsiderate, driving)
Section 2 (dangerous driving)	Section 3 (careless, and inconsiderate, driving)
Section 2B (causing death by careless, or inconsiderate driving)	Section 3 (careless and inconsiderate driving)
Section 3A (causing death by careless driving when under influence of drink or drugs)	Section 2B (causing death by careless, or inconsiderate driving) Section 3 (careless, and inconsiderate, driving) Section 4(1) (driving when unfit to drive through drink or drugs) Section 5(1)(a) (driving with excess alcohol in breath, blood or urine) Section 7(6) (failing to provide specimen) Section 7A(6) (failing to give permission for laboratory test)
Section 4(1) (driving or attempting to drive when unfit to drive through drink or drugs)	Section 4(2) (being in charge of a vehicle when unfit to drive through drink or drugs)
Section 5(1)(a) (driving or attempting to drive with excess alcohol in breath, blood or urine)	Section 5(1)(b) (being in charge of a vehicle with excess alcohol in breath, blood or urine)
Section 28 (dangerous cycling)	Section 29 (careless, and inconsiderate, cycling)

(2) Where the offence with which a person is charged is an offence under section 3A of the *Road Traffic Act* 1988, subsection (1) above shall not authorise his conviction of any offence of attempting to drive.

(3) Where a person is charged with having committed an offence under section 4(1) or 5(1)(a) of the *Road Traffic Act* 1988 by driving a vehicle, he may be convicted of having committed an offence under the provision in question by attempting to drive.

(4) Where by virtue of this section a person is convicted before the Crown Court of an offence triable only summarily, the court shall have the same powers and duties as a magistrates' court would have had on convicting him of that offence.

(5) [*Scotland.*]

(6) This section has effect without prejudice to section 6(3) of the *Criminal Law Act* 1967 (alternative verdicts on trial on indictment), sections 61, 63, 64, 312 and 457A of the *Criminal Procedure (Scotland) Act* 1975 and section 23 of this Act.

[This section is printed as substituted by the *RTA* 1991, s.24; and as amended by the *RSA* 2006, ss.20(2), 31(4) and 33.]

In connection with section 24, see *R. v. Griffiths* [1998] Crim.L.R. 348, CA, *ante*, § 4–455; and *DPP v. Smith* [2002] Crim.L.R. 970, QBD (Elias J.). A jury may not return an alternative verdict under this section unless they have first found the defendant not guilty of the original offence: *R. v. Khela*; *R. v. Smith (Tina)* [2006] 1 Cr.App.R. 23, CA.

(8) Offences to which sections 1, 6, 11 and 12 apply

Road Traffic Offenders Act 1988, Sched. 1

SCHEDULE 1

OFFENCES TO WHICH SECTIONS 1, 6, 11 AND 12(1) APPLY

1.—(1) Where section 1, 6, 11 or 12(1) of this Act is shown in column 3 of this Schedule against a provision of the *Road Traffic Act* 1988 specified in column 1, the section in question applies to an offence under that provision. **32–166**

(2) The general nature of the offence is indicated in column 2.

1A. Section 1 also applies to—

(a) an offence under section 16 of the *Road Traffic Regulation Act* 1984 consisting in the contravention of a restriction on the speed of vehicles imposed under section 14 of that Act,

(b) an offence under subsection (4) of section 17 of that Act consisting in the contravention of a restriction on the speed of vehicles imposed under that section, and

(c) an offence under section 88(7) or 89(1) of that Act (speeding offences).

2.–4. [*Not printed.*]

(1)	(2)	(3)
Provision creating offence	*General nature of offence*	*Applicable provisions of this Act*
RTA section 1	Causing death by dangerous driving.	Section 11 of this Act.
RTA section 2	Dangerous driving.	Sections 1, 11 and 12(1) of this Act.
RTA section 2B	Causing death by careless, or inconsiderate, driving.	Sections 11 and 12(1) of this Act.
RTA section 3	Careless, and inconsiderate, driving.	Sections 1, 11 and 12(1) of this Act.
RTA section 3ZB	Causing death by driving: unlicensed, disqualified or uninsured drivers.	Sections 11 and 12(1) of this Act.
RTA section 3A	Causing death by careless driving when under influence of drink or drugs.	Section 11 of this Act.

(1) *Provision creating offence*	(2) *General nature of offence*	(3) *Applicable provisions of this Act*
RTA section 4	Driving or attempting to drive, or being in charge of a mechanically propelled vehicle, when unfit to drive through drink or drugs.	Sections 11 and 12(1) of this Act.
RTA section 5	Driving or attempting to drive, or being in charge of a motor vehicle, with excess alcohol in breath, blood or urine.	Sections 11 and 12(1) of this Act.
RTA section 6	Failing to co-operate with a preliminary test.	Sections 11 and 12(1) of this Act.
RTA section 7	Failing to provide a specimen for analysis or laboratory test.	Sections 11 and 12(1) of this Act.
RTA section 7A	Failing to allow specimen of blood to be subjected to laboratory test	Sections 11 and 12(1).
RTA section 12	Motor racing and speed trials.	Sections 11 and 12(1) of this Act.
RTA section 22	Leaving vehicles in dangerous positions.	Sections 1, 11 and 12(1) of this Act.
RTA section 23	Carrying passenger on motor-cycle contrary to section 23.	Sections 11 and 12(1) of this Act.
RTA section 35	Failing to comply with traffic directions.	Sections 1, 11 and 12(1) of this Act.
RTA section 36	Failing to comply with traffic directions.	Sections 1, 11 and 12(1) of this Act.
RTA section 40A	Using vehicle in dangerous condition etc.	Sections 11 and 12(1) of this Act.
RTA section 41A	Breach of requirement as to brakes, steering-gear or tyres.	Sections 11 and 12(1) of this Act.
[*RTA* section 41C]	[Breach of requirement as to speed assessment detection device.]	[Sections 11 and 12(1) of this Act.]
RTA section 41D	Breach of requirements as to control of vehicle, mobile telephones etc.	Sections 11 and 12(1) of this Act.
RTA section 87(1)	Driving otherwise than in accordance with a licence.	Sections 11 and 12(1) of this Act.
RTA section 92(10)	Driving after making false declaration as to physical fitness.	Sections 6, 11 and 12(1) of this Act.
RTA section 94(3A) and that subsection as applied by *RTA* section 99D(b) or 109C(c)	Driving after such a failure.	Sections 6, 11 and 12(1) of this Act.
RTA section 94A	Driving after a refusal of licence under section 92(3), revocation under section 93 or service of a notice under section 99C or 109B.	Sections 6, 11 and 12(1) of this Act.
RTA section 103(1)(b)	Driving while disqualified.	Sections 6, 11 and 12(1) of this Act.
RTA section 143	Using motor vehicle, or causing or permitting it to be used, while uninsured or uninsured against third party risks.	Sections 6, 11 and 12(1) of this Act.
RTA section 170	Failure by driver to stop, report accident or give information or documents.	Sections 11 and 12(1) of this Act.

[This Schedule is printed as amended by the *Road Traffic Act* 1991, ss.22 and 83 and Scheds 1 and 8; S.I. 1996 No. 1974 (*ante*, § 32–111); the *Police Reform Act* 2002, s.56(4); the *Railways and Transport Safety Act* 2003, s.107 and Sched. 7, para. 7; the *Crime (International Co-operation) Act* 2003, s.91, and Sched. 5, para. 36; and the *RSA* 2006, ss.20(3), 21(2) and 26(3); and as amended, as from a day to be appointed, by *ibid*., s.18(5) (insertion of entry in square brackets).]

NOTE: only those entries in the above Schedule which relate to offences which must or may be tried on indictment or which involve obligatory or discretionary disqualification are included here.

T. DISQUALIFICATION AND ENDORSEMENT

(1) Introduction

The following guidance on sentencing in road traffic cases, including the "convoluted" penalty points system, is taken from *R. v. Kent*, 77 Cr.App.R. 120, CA. It has been updated to reflect the changes introduced by the *RTA* 1991. It is interpolated with editorial notes. **32–167**

(2) Disqualification

At present a person appearing before a court may be disqualified: **32–168**

(a) because the offence of which he is convicted attracts obligatory or discretionary disqualification (*RTOA* 1988, s.34(1), (2) and Sched. 2, *post*, §§ 32–181, 32–222); or

(b) because he has committed repeated offences attracting the imposition of penalty points—the "totting-up" procedure (*RTOA* 1988, s.35(1), *post*, § 32–192); or

(c) under the *PCC(S)A* 2000, s.147 (*ante*, § 5–845) (motor vehicle used by person convicted, or another, for the purpose of committing or facilitating the commission of the offence); or

(d) under section 146 of the 2000 Act (*ante*, § 5–844) (general power to disqualify offender in addition to dealing with him in any other way).

All orders for disqualification take effect from the day on which they are imposed. Accordingly, if an offender is disqualified both under the "totting-up" provisions and under some other provision, the disqualifications will run concurrently.

NOTES: **32–169**

(a) In (a) above, the period of disqualification is 12 months or more for an obligatory offence unless there are special reasons for disqualifying for a lesser period or for not disqualifying at all.

(b) The totting up procedure applies where a person is convicted of an endorseable offence and, taking that offence into account, the number of penalty points which the offender has accumulated over a three-year period totals 12 or more (the qualifying dates for the earlier offences and the current offence being the dates of the offences and not the dates of conviction). In those circumstances, disqualification is obligatory unless there are mitigating circumstances (see s.35(1) and (4) of the 1988 Act), in which case the court may order the offender to be disqualified for a shorter period or not at all.

(c) Where two or more offences were committed on the same occasion, the basic rule is that the number of penalty points to be endorsed is the number attributable to the offence carrying the highest number of points; but the court may disapply this basic rule if it thinks fit (see s.28(4)–(6) of the 1988 Act).

(d) The minimum period of disqualification for a person with 12 or more penalty points varies. The determining factor is whether there have been any previous disqualifications (other than an interim disqualification under section 26 of the 1988 Act, or under section 147 of the *PCC(S)A* 2000, or for an offence of stealing a motor vehicle or an offence under section 12 or section 25 of the *Theft Act* 1968) in the three years preceding the commission of the latest offence in respect of which penalty points are being taken into account. The minimum periods are as follows:

(i) six months if there are no such disqualifications;
(ii) one year if there is one;
(iii) two years if there are two or more.

(e) Where any totting-up disqualification is ordered, the penalty points endorsed on the offender's licence prior to that disqualification cease to be effective. He is not liable to a further totting-up disqualification until a further 12 points for offences within a three-year period have been accumulated.

(f) Where an offender is convicted on the same occasion of more than one offence to which section 35(1) applies, only one totting-up disqualification can be imposed (see s.35(3)(a) of the 1988 Act).

(g) In determining for the purposes of section 35(1) whether the penalty points to be taken into account under section 29(1) of the 1988 Act number 12 or more, it should be borne in mind that, under the changes introduced by the *RTA* 1991,
(i) no account is to be taken of penalty points attributable to an offence in respect of which the court disqualifies the offender under section 34 of the 1988 Act (see ss.29(1)(a) and 34(2) of the Act), and
(ii) disqualification under section 34 no longer has the effect of "wiping the slate clean", *i.e.* of wiping out the record of previously accumulated penalty points (see s.29(1)(b) of the Act).

(h) Where a defendant is convicted of an offence involving discretionary disqualification and by virtue of that conviction is potentially liable to disqualification under the "totting up" procedure, the court is obliged to consider first the question of whether to disqualify for the offence itself under section 34(2) before it considers whether to apply the provisions of section 35; but the court is not limited in considering that question to the provisions and requirements of section 34 alone; in answering the question, the court is entitled to have regard to the prior endorsements on the licence and it is open to the court in its discretion to decide not to impose a disqualification under section 34 with the intent that the totting up provisions should be triggered: *Jones v. DPP* [2001] R.T.R. 8, DC.

(3) Endorsement

32–170 All offences attracting obligatory endorsement must be endorsed on the offender's driving licence or counterpart (licences coming into force after May 31, 1990), unless there are special reasons for not doing so: see *post*, § 32–183. This is irrespective of whether he is disqualified or not: s.44(1) of the 1988 Act, *post*, § 32–210.

NOTES:

(a) The endorseable offences are set out in Schedule 2 to the 1988 Act, *post*, § 32–222.

(b) In the absence of special reasons, if an offender is convicted of an offence involving obligatory endorsement the court must order that the licence or counterpart is endorsed with particulars of:
(i) the conviction; *and*
(ii) the disqualification (if the court orders disqualification), *or*
(iii) the offence and the penalty points awarded (if the court does *not* order disqualification).

(4) Penalty points

32–171 If a court does not disqualify an offender for an offence attracting obligatory or discretionary disqualification, it is bound to endorse his driving licence with the particulars of the offence and with the appropriate number of penalty points, as set out in Schedule 2 to the 1988 Act (*post*, § 32–222), unless there are special reasons for not doing so: s.44(1) and (2) of the 1988 Act. Conversely, if a court does disqualify from driving, it is not able, on the same occasion, to order penalty points to be endorsed: s.44(1) of the 1988 Act (*post*, § 32–210).

If the court's power to disqualify derives solely from section 147 of the *PCC(S)A* 2000 and the court decides not to disqualify, it cannot order the offender's licence to be endorsed either generally or with penalty points: s.35(5) (*post*, § 32–192).

NOTES: 32–172

(a) An order for disqualification made under section 34 of the 1988 Act does not have the effect of "wiping the slate clean", *i.e.* wiping out the record of previously accumulated penalty points: see s.29(1)(b).

(b) The court has no power to reduce the number of points to be endorsed in respect of an offence, although in relation to some offences a range of points is allocated by Schedule 2 to the 1988 Act.

(c) Where two or more offences were committed on the same occasion, the basic rule is that the number of penalty points to be endorsed is the number attributable to the offence carrying the highest number of points; but the court may disapply this basic rule if it thinks fit: see s.28(4)–(6) of the 1988 Act.

(d) *Semble*, where a range of points is allocated to an offence by Schedule 2 to the 1988 Act, the court should have regard primarily to the gravity of the offence in deciding the appropriate number to award.

Difficulties encountered in practice

Their Lordships in *Kent*, *ante*, gave the following examples of Crown Court mistakes resulting in illegal sentences:

(a) ordering consecutive periods of disqualification;

(b) disqualifying and ordering penalty points to be endorsed on the licence;

(c) awarding the incorrect number of penalty points;

(d) disqualifying for repeated offences without allocating the disqualification to a single offence—see section 35(3)(a) of the 1988 Act;

(e) ordering penalty points to be endorsed for more than one offence committed on the same occasion: the correct procedure would be to allocate a number of points to the most serious of the offences (but see now s.28(4)–(6) of the 1988 Act);

(f) failing to disqualify when the points exceeded 12 when there were no mitigating circumstances;

(g) failure to state special reasons or mitigating circumstances, (i) when not ordering disqualification, or ordering disqualification less than the minimum, (ii) when not ordering endorsement of the licence—see section 47(1) of the Act.

Further difficulties had arisen as a result of understandable efforts of court staff who had discovered mistakes. Their Lordships made three matters clear:

First, the order of the court was that pronounced by the judge in open court.

Secondly, the responsibility of the court was to make a record which accurately reflected that pronouncement.

Thirdly, if the court staff were in doubt as to the pronouncement, the judge had to be consulted—for example, where the staff were not clear what it was that the judge said, or where they thought that the judge's order might be faulty.

Special reasons and mitigating circumstances

Where either are found, they must be specified in open court. 32–173

(5) Statutory provisions—general

Road Traffic Offenders Act 1988, ss.27, 28

Production of licence

27.—(1) Where a person who is the holder of a licence is convicted of an offence involving obligatory or discretionary disqualification, and a court proposes to make an order disqualifying him or an order under section 44 of this Act, the court must, unless it has already received *them* [[it]], require the licence [*and its counterpart*] to be produced to it. 32–174

(2) [*Repealed by* RTA *1991*, *Sched. 8*.]

(3) If the holder of the licence has not caused it [*and its counterpart*] to be delivered, or posted it [*and its counterpart*], in accordance with section 7 of this Act and does not produce it [*and its counterpart*] as required under this section or *section 40 of the* Crime (Sentences) Act *1997* [section 301 of the *Criminal Justice Act* 2003], section 146 or 147 of the *Powers of*

Criminal Courts (Sentencing) Act 2000, or section 223A or 436A of the *Criminal Procedure (Scotland) Act* 1975 or if the holder of the licence does not produce it and its counterpart as required by section 40B of the *Child Support Act* 1991, then, unless he satisfies the court that he has applied for a new licence and has not received it—

(a) he is guilty of an offence, and

(b) the licence shall be suspended from the time when its production was required until [it *and its counterpart are*] [[is]] produced to the court and shall, while suspended, be of no effect.

(4) Subsection (3) above does not apply where the holder of the licence—

(a) has caused a current receipt for the licence *and its counterpart* issued under section 56 of this Act to be delivered to the proper officer of the court not later than the day before the date appointed for the hearing, or

(b) has posted such a receipt, at such time that in the ordinary course of post it would be delivered not later than that day, in a letter duly addressed to the proper officer and either registered or sent by the recorded delivery service, or

(c) surrenders such a receipt to the court at the hearing,

and produces the licence *and its counterpart* to the court immediately on *their* [[its]] return.

(5) In subsection (4) above "proper officer" means—

(a) in relation to a magistrates' court in England and Wales, the designated officer for the court, and

(b) in relation to any other court, the clerk of the court.

[This section is printed as amended by the *Driving Licences (Community Driving Licence) Regulations* 1990 (S.I. 1990 No. 144) (insertion of words in single square brackets in subss. (1) and (3) in relation to licences coming into force after May 31, 1990); the *RTA* 1991, ss.48 and 83 and Scheds 4, para. 91, and 8; the *PCC(S)A* 2000, s.165(1) and Sched. 9, para. 120; the *Access to Justice Act* 1999, s.90(1) and Sched. 13, para. 144; the *Child Support, Pensions and Social Security Act* 2000, s.16(5); and the *Courts Act* 2003, s.109(1), and Sched. 8, para. 313; and as amended, as from a day to be appointed, by the *CJA* 2003, s.304, and Sched. 32, paras 52 and 53 (substitution (in subs. (3)) of words in square brackets for reference to s.40 of the *C(S)A* 1997); and the *RSA* 2006, ss.10(1) and (12) and 59, Sched. 3, paras. 30 and 33, and Sched. 7(4) (omission of italicised words other than (i) titles of Acts and (ii) the reference to s.40 of the 1997 Act; and insertion of words in double square brackets).]

For sections 146 and 147 of the *PCC(S)A* 2000, see *ante*, §§ 5–844, 5–845.

Penalty points to be attributed to an offence

32–175 **28.**—(1) Where a person is convicted of an offence involving obligatory endorsement, then, subject to the following provisions of this section, the number of penalty points to be attributed to the offence is—

(a) the number shown in relation to the offence in the last column of Part I or Part II of Schedule 2 to this Act, or

(b) where a range of numbers is shown, a number within that range.

(2) Where a person is convicted of an offence committed by aiding, abetting, counselling or procuring, or inciting to the commission of, an offence involving obligatory disqualification, then, subject to the following provisions of this section, the number of penalty points to be attributed to the offence is ten.

(3) Where both a range of numbers and a number followed by the words "(fixed penalty)" is shown in the last column of Part I of Schedule 2 to this Act in relation to an offence, that number is the number of penalty points to be attributed to the offence for the purposes of sections 57(5) and 77(5) of this Act; and, where only a range of numbers is shown there, the lowest number in the range is the number of penalty points to be attributed to the offence for those purposes.

[(3) For the purposes of sections 57(5) and 77(5) of this Act, the number of penalty points to be attributed to an offence is—

(a) where both a range of numbers and a number followed by the words "(fixed penalty)" is shown in the last column of Part 1 of Schedule 2 to this Act in relation to an offence, that number,

(b) where a range of numbers followed by the words "or appropriate penalty points (fixed penalty)" is shown there in relation to the offence, the appropriate number of penalty points for the offence, and

(c) where only a range of numbers is shown there in relation to the offence, the lowest number in the range.

(3A) For the purposes of subsection (3)(b) above the appropriate number of penalty points for an offence is such number of penalty points as the Secretary of State may by order made by statutory instrument prescribe.

(3B) An order made under subsection (3A) above in relation to an offence may make provision for the appropriate number of penalty points for the offence to be different depending on the circumstances, including (in particular)—

(a) the nature of the contravention or failure constituting the offence,

(b) how serious it is,

(c) the area, or sort of place, where it takes place, and

(d) whether the offender appears to have committed any offence or offences of a description specified in the order during a period so specified.]

(4) Where a person is convicted (whether on the same occasion or not) of two or more offences committed on the same occasion and involving obligatory endorsement, the total number of penalty points to be attributed to them is the number or highest number that would be attributed on a conviction of one of them (so that if the convictions are on different occasions the number of penalty points to be attributed to the offences on the later occasion or occasions shall be restricted accordingly).

(5) In a case where (apart from this subsection) subsection (4) above would apply to two or more offences, the court may if it thinks fit determine that that subsection shall not apply to the offences (or, where three or more offences are concerned, to any one or more of them).

(6) Where a court makes such a determination it shall state its reasons in open court and, if it is a magistrates' court, or in Scotland a court of summary jurisdiction, shall cause them to be entered in the register (in Scotland, record) of its proceedings.

(7)–(9) [*Power of Secretary of State by statutory instrument to amend penalty points to be attributed to an offence.*]

[This section is printed as substituted by the *RTA* 1991, s.27. Subss. (3) to (3B) (in square brackets) are substituted for subs. (3) (in italics) as from a day to be appointed: *RSA* 2006, s.4(1) and (2). The *RSA* 2006, s.9(6), and Sched. 2, paras 2 and 3, provide for the amendment of subs. (3), as from a day to be appointed, by substituting ", 57A(6), 77(5) and 77(8)" for "and 77(5)". The Act does not make clear, however, whether this amendment is intended to bite on the original subs. (3) or the new subs. (3). Presumably, however, the intention is that the section 4 amendment will come into force before the Schedule 2 amendment, in which case the position will be clear. As from a further date to be appointed (which must be later than the date in respect of Sched. 2 (see s.61(8))), the 2006 Act, s.10(1) and (12) and Sched. 3, paras 30 and 34, amend the amendment of subs. (3) by substituting "57A(6)" for "57(5), 57A(6), 77(5)". The reference to the common law offence of incitement in subs. (2) has effect as a reference to the offences in the *SCA* 2007, Pt 2: 2007 Act, s.63(1), and Sched. 6, para. 15(a).]

A person who is convicted of failing to stop after an accident (s.170(2) of the *RTA* 1988) and of failing to report the accident to the police (s.170(3) of that Act) is to be treated for the purposes of subsection (4) as having committed the offences "on the same occasion", since their commission arises from the same accident: *Johnson v. Finbow* [1983] 1 W.L.R. 879, DC.

Road Traffic Offenders Act 1988, s.29

Penalty points to be taken into account on conviction

29.—(1) Where a person is convicted of an offence involving obligatory endorsement, the penalty points to be taken into account on that occasion are (subject to subsection (2) below)— **32–176**

(a) any that are to be attributed to the offence or offences of which he is convicted, disregarding any offence in respect of which an order under section 34 of this Act is made, and

(b) any that were on a previous occasion ordered to be endorsed on *the counterpart of any licence held by him* [*or on* his driving record], unless the offender has since that occasion and before the conviction been disqualified under section 35 of this Act.

(2) If any of the offences was committed more than three years before another, the penalty points in respect of that offence shall not be added to those in respect of the other.

[(2A) Subsection (1)(b) above has effect subject to section 30A(4) of this Act.]

(3) *In relation to licences which came into force before 1st June 1990, the reference in subsection (1) above to the counterpart of a licence shall be construed as a reference to the licence itself.*

[This section is printed as substituted by the *RTA* 1991, s.28. It is printed as amended, and repealed in part, as from days to be appointed, by the *RSA* 2006 as follows: (i) the words in square brackets in subs. (1)(b) are inserted by s.9(6), and Sched. 2, paras 2 and 4; (ii) the italicised words in that paragraph and subsection (3) are repealed by ss.10(1) and (12), Sched. 3, paras 30 and 35, and Sched. 7(4); and (iii) subsection (2A) is inserted by s.34(1) and (2).]

Where a person is convicted of an offence involving obligatory endorsement and sentencing is adjourned, but before the adjournment date he appears before another court and is disqualified, the slate is thereby wiped clean for the purposes of section 29(1)(b): *R. v. Brentwood JJ., ex p. Richardson*, 95 Cr.App.R. 187, DC. The words "on that occasion" in the opening words of the subsection refer to the occasion when the court is considering penalty points, that is the occasion of sentencing rather than conviction in the narrow sense of that word: *ibid.* The case was decided on the original section 29. However, the principle plainly applies to the substituted section.

Road Traffic Offenders Act 1988, s.30

Penalty points: modification where fixed penalty also in question

32–177 **30.**—(1) Sections 28 and 29 of this Act shall have effect subject to this section in any case where—

(a) a person is convicted of an offence involving obligatory endorsement, and

(b) the court is satisfied that [the counterpart of] his licence [[or his driving record]] has been or is liable to be endorsed under section 57 *or 77* [[, 57A, 77 or 77A]] of this Act in respect of an offence (referred to in this section as the "connected offence") committed on the same occasion as the offence of which he is convicted.

(2) … the number of penalty points to be attributed to the offence of which he is convicted is—

(a) the number of penalty points to be attributed to that offence under section 28 of this Act apart from this section, less

(b) the number of penalty points required to be endorsed on [the counterpart of] his licence [[or his driving record]] under section 57 *or 77* [[, 57A, 77 or 77A]] of this Act in respect of the connected offence (except so far as they have already been deducted by virtue of this paragraph).

(3) [*Repealed by* RTA *1991*, *Sched. 8*.]

[This section is printed as amended by S.I. 1990 No. 144 (see the note to s.27, *ante*, § 32–174); and the *RTA* 1991, ss.48 and 83, and Scheds 4, para. 92, and 8. In subss. (1)(b) and (2)(b), the italicised words are omitted, and the words in double square brackets are inserted, as from a day to be appointed, by the *RSA* 2006, s.9(6), and Sched. 2, paras 2 and 5. As from a later day to be appointed (see s.61(8) of the 2006 Act), the 2006 Act, ss.10(1) and (12) and 59, Sched. 3, paras 30 and 36, and Sched. 7(4), repeal the words "the counterpart of his licence or" in subs. (1)(b), substitute "57A" for "57, 57A or 77" in subss. (1)(b) and (2)(b), and repeal the words "on the counterpart of his licence or" in subs. (2)(b).]

Sections 57 and 77 of the *RTOA* 1988 deal with the endorsement of licences in respect of fixed penalty offences, without the requirement of any order from a court.

Road Traffic Offenders Act 1988, s.30A

[Reduced penalty points for attendance on course

32–177a **30A.**—(1) This section applies where—

(a) a person is convicted of a specified offence by or before a court,

(b) penalty points are to be attributed to the offence and the court does not order him to be disqualified, and

(c) at least seven but no more than eleven penalty points are to be taken into account on the occasion of the conviction.

(2) In this section "specified offence" means—

(a) an offence under section 3 of the *Road Traffic Act* 1988 (careless, and inconsiderate, driving),

(b) an offence under section 36 of that Act (failing to comply with traffic signs),

(c) an offence under section 17(4) of the *Road Traffic Regulation Act* 1984 (use of special road contrary to scheme or regulations), or

(d) an offence under section 89(1) of that Act (exceeding speed limit).

(3) But the Secretary of State may by regulations amend subsection (2) above by adding other offences or removing offences.

(4) Where this section applies, the court may make an order that three of the penalty points attributed to the offence (or all of them if three or fewer are so attributed) shall not be taken into account under section 29(1)(b) of this Act on the occasion of any conviction of an offence after the end of the period of twelve months beginning with the date of the order if, by the relevant date, the offender completes an approved course specified in the order.

(5) In subsection (4) above—

"an approved course" means a course approved by the appropriate national authority for the purposes of this section in relation to the description of offence of which the offender is convicted, and

"the relevant date" means such date, no later than ten months after the day on which the order is made, as is specified in the order.

(6) A court shall not make an order under this section in the case of an offender convicted of an offence if—

(a) the offender has, during the period of three years ending with the date on which the offence was committed, committed a specified offence and successfully completed an approved course pursuant to an order made under this section or section 34A of this Act on conviction of that offence, or

(b) the offence was committed during his probationary period.

(7) A court shall not make an order under this section in the case of an offender unless—

(a) the court is satisfied that a place on the course specified in the order will be available for the offender,

(b) the offender appears to the court to be of or over the age of 17,

(c) the court has informed the offender (orally or in writing and in ordinary language) of the effect of the order and of the amount of the fees which he is required to pay for the course and when he must pay them, and

(d) the offender has agreed that the order should be made.]

[This section is inserted, as from a day to be appointed, by the *RSA* 2006, s.34(1) and (3).]

Certificates of completion of courses; approval of courses

As from a day to be appointed, the *RSA* 2006, s.34(1) and (3), insert sections 30B, 30C and 30D into the *RTOA* 1988. Section 30B deals with certificates of completion of courses. Following successful completion, a certificate of completion is sent to the court in order for the reduced penalty points to come into effect. There are provisions concerning the "non-issue" of a certificate by the course organiser which allow the offender to apply to the court for a declaration that the organiser has defaulted in his obligations. If such a declaration is made, then it has the effect of the certificate being issued (s.30B(6), (8)). Section 30C deals with the approval of courses by the appropriate national authority for the purposes of section 30A. Section 30D contains provisions supplementary to sections 30A to 30C, mainly to do with the procedure governing the exercise of his powers by the Secretary of State. Subsection (3) defines various terms in sections 30A to 30C. **32–177b**

Road Traffic Offenders Act 1988, s.30D(3)

[30D.—(3) In sections 30A to 30C of this Act and this section— **32–177c**

"appropriate national authority" means (as respects Wales) the National Assembly for Wales and (otherwise) the Secretary of State;

"course provider", in relation to a course, means the person by whom it is, or is to be, provided;

"probationary period" has the meaning given in section 1 of the *Road Traffic (New Drivers) Act* 1995;

"proper officer" means—

(a) in relation to a magistrates' court in England and Wales, the designated officer for the court, and

(b) otherwise, the clerk of the court;

"relevant local court", in relation to an order made under section 30A of this Act in the case of an offender, means—

(a) in England and Wales, a magistrates' court acting for the local justice area in which the offender resides, and

(b) [*Scotland*].]

Road Traffic Offenders Act 1988, s.31

Court may take particulars endorsed on licence into consideration

32–178 **31.**—(1) *Where a person is convicted of an offence involving obligatory or discretionary disqualification and his licence [and its counterpart are] produced to the court—*

(a) *any existing endorsement on [the counterpart of] his licence is prima facie evidence of the matters endorsed, and*

(b) *the court may, in determining what order to make in pursuance of the conviction, take those matters into consideration.*

[(1) Where a person is convicted of an offence involving obligatory or discretionary disqualification—

(a) any existing endorsement on *the counterpart of his licence or on* his driving record is prima facie evidence of the matters endorsed, and

(b) the court may, in determining what order to make in pursuance of the conviction, take those matters into consideration.]

(2) [*Scotland.*]

[This section is printed as amended by S.I. 1990 No. 144 (see the note to s.27, *ante*, § 32–174); and the *RTA* 1991, s.48 and Sched. 4, para. 93. The words "on licence" in the heading are omitted, and subs. (1) (in square brackets) is substituted for subs. (1) (in italics), as from a day to be appointed, by the *RSA* 2006, ss.9(6) and 59, Sched. 2, paras 2 and 6, and Sched. 7(3). As from a later day to be appointed (see s.61(8) of the 2006 Act), the 2006 Act, ss.10(1) and (12) and 59, Sched. 3, paras 30 and 37, and Sched. 7(4), repeal the italicised words in the substituted subs. (1).]

A court is entitled to take into consideration previous convictions evidenced by endorsements which are no longer "effective" within the meaning of section 45(5) to (7) of this Act: *Chief Constable of West Mercia Police v. Williams* [1987] R.T.R. 188, DC.

Road Traffic Offenders Act 1988, s.33

Fine and imprisonment

32–179 **33.**—(1) Where a person is convicted of an offence against a provision of the Traffic Acts specified in column 1 of Part I of Schedule 2 to this Act or regulations made under any such provision, the maximum punishment by way of fine or imprisonment which may be imposed on him is that shown in column 4 against the offence and (where appropriate) the circumstances or the mode of trial there specified.

(2) Any reference in column 4 of that Part to a period of years or months is to be construed as a reference to a term of imprisonment of that duration.

Consecutive sentences

32–180 In *R. v. Lawrence*, 11 Cr.App.R.(S.) 580, CA, the court rejected the argument that consecutive sentences should not be passed as a matter of practice for motoring offences arising out of the same incident. The court said that the problem is really one of determining what sentence is appropriate for the offences taken as a whole. So, driving while disqualified is not so serious as driving while disqualified with excess alcohol in the bloodstream, which plainly deserves greater punishment. It makes no difference in the end whether the court imposes shorter sentences to run consecutively or longer sentences to run concurrently. In some cases, a long or even the maximum sentence for each offence to run consecutively will be justified, *e.g.* where the defendant drove dangerously with a high blood-alcohol concentration. It will depend upon the circumstances of each individual case whether any and if so what discount should be given for a plea of guilty. In *R. v. Hardy* [2006] 2 Cr.App.R.(S.) 4, CA, it was said that consecutive sentences were appropriate where an offender fell to be sentenced for dangerous driving, failure to provide a breath specimen and driving whilst disqualified.

For a different approach, see *R. v. Kirby* [2008] 2 Cr.App.R.(S.) 46, CA, where the judge had passed concurrent maximum sentences for aggravated vehicle-taking, dangerous driving and driving whilst disqualified, and the Court of Appeal held that notwithstanding the gravity of the offences, the appellant had been entitled to some discount for his pleas of guilty. No reference was made to *Lawrence*. Had it been, the overall sentence could have been upheld, whilst reducing the individual sentences, but making them consecutive.

Road Traffic Offenders Act 1988, s.34

Disqualification for certain offences

34.—(1) Where a person is convicted of an offence involving obligatory disqualification, the court must order him to be disqualified for such period not less than twelve months as the court thinks fit unless the court for special reasons thinks fit to order him to be disqualified for a shorter period or not to order him to be disqualified. **32–181**

(1A) Where a person is convicted of an offence under section 12A of the *Theft Act* 1968 (aggravated vehicle-taking), the fact that he did not drive the vehicle in question at any particular time or at all shall not be regarded as a special reason for the purposes of subsection (1) above.

(2) Where a person is convicted of an offence involving discretionary disqualification, and either—

(a) the penalty points to be taken into account on that occasion number fewer than twelve, or

(b) the offence is not one involving obligatory endorsement,

the court may order him to be disqualified for such period as the court thinks fit.

(3) Where a person convicted of an offence under any of the following provisions of the *Road Traffic Act* 1988, that is—

(aa) section 3A (causing death by careless driving when under the influence of drink or drugs),

(a) section 4(1) (driving or attempting to drive while unfit),

(b) section 5(1)(a) (driving or attempting to drive with excess alcohol),

(c) section 7(6) (failing to provide a specimen) where that is an offence involving obligatory disqualification,

(d) section 7A(6) (failing to allow a specimen to be subjected to laboratory test) where that is an offence involving obligatory disqualification;

has within the ten years immediately preceding the commission of the offence been convicted of any such offence, subsection (1) above shall apply in relation to him as if the reference to twelve months were a reference to three years.

(4) Subject to subsection (3) above, subsection (1) above shall apply as if the reference to twelve months were a reference to two years—

(a) in relation to a person convicted of—

(i) manslaughter, or in Scotland culpable homicide, or

(ii) an offence under section 1 of the *Road Traffic Act* 1988 (causing death by dangerous driving), or

(iii) an offence under section 3A of that Act (causing death by careless driving while under the influence of drink or drugs), and

(b) in relation to a person on whom more than one disqualification for a fixed period of 56 days or more has been imposed within the three years immediately preceding the commission of the offence.

(4A) For the purposes of subsection (4)(b) above there shall be disregarded any disqualification imposed under section 26 of this Act or section 147 of the *Powers of Criminal Courts (Sentencing) Act* 2000 or section 223A or 436A of the *Criminal Procedure (Scotland) Act* 1975 (offences committed by using vehicles) and any disqualification imposed in respect of an offence of stealing a motor vehicle, an offence under section 12 or 25 of the *Theft Act* 1968, an offence under section 178 of the *Road Traffic Act* 1988, or an attempt to commit such an offence.

(4B) Where a person convicted of an offence under section 40A of the *Road Traffic Act*

1988 (using a vehicle in a dangerous condition etc.) has within the three years immediately preceding the commission of the offence been convicted of any such offence, subsection (1) above shall apply in relation to him as if the reference to twelve months were a reference to six months.

(5) The preceding provisions of this section shall apply in relation to a conviction of an offence committed by aiding, abetting, counselling or procuring, or inciting to the commission of, an offence involving obligatory disqualification as if the offence were an offence involving discretionary disqualification.

(6) This section is subject to section 48 of this Act.

[This section is printed as amended by the *RTA* 1991, s.29; the *Aggravated Vehicle-Taking Act* 1992, s.3(2); the *PCC(S)A* 2000, s.165(1), and Sched. 9, para. 121; the *Police Reform Act* 2002, s.56(3); and the *RSA* 2006, s.25(2) (insertion of subs. (4B)). The amendment effected by the 2006 Act came into force on September 24, 2007 (*Road Safety Act 2006 (Commencement No. 2) Order* 2007 (S.I. 2007 No. 2472)), but only in relation to offences committed on or after that date (2006 Act, s.61(3)). The reference to the common law offence of incitement in subs. (5) has effect as a reference to the offences under the *SCA* 2007, Pt 2: 2007 Act, s.63(1), and Sched. 6, para. 15(b).]

Disqualifications under section 34 take effect immediately and cannot be made consecutive to each other: *R. v. Meese*, 57 Cr.App.R 568, CA.

For the relationship between this section and sections 29 and 35, see *Jones v. DPP*, *ante*, § 32–169.

Length of disqualification

32–182 Disqualification for an indefinite period may not be imposed: *R. v. Fowler* [1937] 2 All E.R. 380, CCA. Disqualification for life is for a period certain: *R. v. Tunde-Olarinde*, 51 Cr.App.R. 249, CA; but such a sentence should only be passed in very unusual circumstances: *R. v. North* [1971] R.T.R. 366, CA; *R. v. Tantrum*, 11 Cr.App.R.(S.) 348, CA. It is inappropriate in the absence of either psychiatric evidence or evidence of many previous convictions which indicates that the offender will indefinitely be a danger to the public if he is allowed to drive: *R. v. King*, 13 Cr.App.R.(S.) 668, CA; *R. v. Buckley*, 15 Cr.App.R.(S.) 695, CA.

A man aged 28 was disqualified for life for two groups of offences, including taking and driving away and driving whilst disqualified. In allowing his appeal, the court stated that excessive periods of disqualification were harmful and, in the circumstances, having regard to the appellant's occupation as a driver and to the fact that none of the convictions was for careless or dangerous driving, he should have some hope of being allowed to drive again: *R. v. Bond*, 52 Cr.App.R. 505, CA; and see *R. v. Shirley*, 53 Cr.App.R. 543, CA.

In *R. v. McLaughlin* [1978] R.T.R. 452, CA, a man of 43 was disqualified for 20 years for driving with excess alcohol and failing to provide a specimen. He had a drink problem, although he did not recognise this and previous convictions for drink driving. In dismissing his appeal, the court said that, whilst very long periods of disqualification may be counter-productive, in this case there was a serious risk that the offender would injure or kill someone if allowed to drive.

Where the offender has no previous record of bad driving, the period of disqualification should not impede his rehabilitation after completion of a custodial sentence: *R. v. Lee* [1971] R.T.R. 30, CA; *R. v. Pashley* [1974] R.T.R. 149, CA; *R. v. Davegun*, 7 Cr.App.R.(S.) 110, CA; *R. v. Simpson*, *The Times*, December 14, 1989, CA; *R. v. Marsh* [2002] 2 *Archbold News* 1, CA ([2002] EWCA Crim. 137); and *R. v. Cully* [2006] R.T.R. 32, CA (the purpose of disqualification being to protect the public, in cases of drivers with appalling records, extended periods of disqualification may be appropriate since the offence indicates the risk to the public in the individual continuing to drive; but where the circumstances do not suggest such a risk, whilst a period of disqualification is inevitable in a case of dangerous driving, it should be kept to a minimum; where an offender's job involved driving, absent an apparent risk identified from the particular offence, the financial strains involved would make it too punitive to impose a lengthy disqualification).

The need for courts to bear in mind the undesirability of placing young persons at liberty under long periods of disqualification was referred to in *R. v. Farnes (Note)* [1983] R.T.R. 441, CA. However, in *R. v. Hansel*, 4 Cr.App.R.(S.) 368, CA, the court declined to accept the submission based upon *Farnes*, *ante*, and *R. v. Wright*, 1 Cr.App.R.(S.) 82, CA, that there was a rule that persons who are sent to prison and disqualified at the same time are entitled to have the period of disqualification coincide more or less automatically with the period of sentence which they have to serve. The nature of the offence, the antecedents of the offender and the extent to which he will in fact be handicapped by not being able to drive immediately on his release have to be considered in deciding whether on balance the period of disqualification should coincide with the effective period of his sentence.

While accepting the approach in *Hansel*, that the period of disqualification must depend on all the facts of the particular case, the court emphasised in *R. v. Thomas (K.)*, 78 Cr.App.R. 55, CA, that it is accepted sentencing policy (see *Farnes*, *ante*) in relation to persons who are imprisoned after repeated offences of driving while disqualified and who are incapable of leaving motor vehicles alone, that the court should not impose a period of disqualification extending for a substantial period beyond their release from prison. For the purposes of section 35 of the *RTOA* 1988 (*post*, § 32–192), that policy is a "ground for mitigating the normal consequences of the conviction" where there are 12 or more penalty points to be taken into account under section 29(1) of the Act.

R. v. Thomas was considered in *R. v. Matthews*, 9 Cr.App.R.(S.) 1, CA, and *R. v. Gibbons*, 9 Cr.App.R.(S.) 21, CA. *Gibbons* provides an example of circumstances where departure from the basic principle emphasised in *Thomas* was justified.

When sentencing for an offence for which there may or must be a period of disqualification, the court may take into consideration another offence carrying the possibility of disqualification: *R. v. Jones*, 55 Cr.App.R. 32, CA.

(6) Special reasons

Discretion not to disqualify

See section 34(1) of the *RTOA* 1988, *ante*, § 32–181. The burden of establishing special reasons is on the defendant and the standard is on the balance of probabilities: *Pugsley v. Hunter* [1973] 1 W.L.R. 578, DC. The court may find special reasons exist but nonetheless refuse to exercise the discretion that special reasons give rise to: *R. v. Newton* [1974] R.T.R. 451, CA. This case makes it clear that a two stage process is involved: (a) to determine if special reasons exist; and, if so (b) whether the justices in their discretion should not disqualify or disqualify for less than 12 months. Where "special reasons" are found, it could not be said that it would never be appropriate, in the exercise of the court's discretion, to impose a period of disqualification in excess of the statutory minimum; where, however, it was not suggested that the actual driving undertaken or contemplated could have posed any appreciable risk of danger to anyone it would be hard to justify a period of disqualification in excess of the minimum: *R. v. St Albans Crown Court, ex p. O'Donovan* [2000] 1 Cr.App.R.(S.) 344, DC. As to the proper construction of the statute, see the commentary to this case in *Criminal Law Week* 2000/14/76. **32–183**

In deciding whether to exercise the discretion, the court should take into account matters such as: should the defendant have realised he was not in a fit state to drive (*Pridige v. Gant* [1985] R.T.R. 196, DC)? Was the motorist driving erratically (*Donahue v. DPP* [1993] R.T.R. 156, DC)? What had the defendant been drinking and what was his tolerance to alcohol (*DPP v. Barker* [1990] R.T.R. 1, DC)? The general rule of thumb is that the exercise of the discretion should be used only in "clear and compelling cases": *Vaughan v. Dunn* [1984] R.T.R. 376, DC, following *Taylor v. Rajan* [1974] R.T.R. 304, DC. In *DPP v. Bristow* [1998] R.T.R. 100, DC, it was held that the key question to ask in assessing whether special reasons exist not to disqualify a drink driver is what a sober, reasonable and responsible friend of the defendant, present at the time but himself a non-driver and thus unable to help, would have advised in the circumstances: drive or not drive. The discretion should only be exercised in the defendant's favour if there was a real possibility, as opposed to an off- chance, that the friend would have advised the defendant to drive.

32–184 When a court decides to exercise its discretion not to disqualify or to disqualify for a shorter period, it should state its reasons in open court and, if in the magistrates' court, the reasons must be entered into the register: *RTOA* 1988, s.47(1).

Definition

32–185 There is no statutory definition of special reasons, but the accepted definition is that in *R. v. Crossen* [1939] N.I. 106, as approved in *Whittall v. Kirby* [1946] 2 All E.R. 552, DC, and interpreted in *R. v. Wickens*, 42 Cr.App.R. 236, CCA. From this, four points emerge: it must be a mitigating or extenuating circumstance; it must not amount in law to a defence; it must be directly connected with the commission of the offence; it must be a matter which the court ought properly to take into account when considering sentence.

Reasons such as: the person relies on their transport for work (*R. v. Hart*; *R. v. Jackson* [1970] R.T.R. 165, CA); serious hardship caused to the family (*Reynolds v. Roche* [1972] R.T.R. 282, DC); being just over the limit (*R. v. Anderson* [1972] R.T.R. 113, CA); ignorance of the overnight effect of alcohol (*DPP v. O'Mara* [1989] R.T.R. 24, DC); good driving record (*Lines v. Hersham* [1951] 2 All E.R. 650, DC), cannot amount to special reasons. These are matters which go to mitigation.

Medical conditions, etc.

32–186 Ignorance of a medical condition could amount to a special reason: *R. v. Wickins*, 42 Cr.App.R. 236, CCA (unaware that diabetic and drank beer). This decision was not followed in *Jarvis v. DPP*, 165 J.P. 15, DC, where a distinction was drawn between those circumstances peculiar to the offender and those peculiar to the offence. Unfitness due to lack of food could not amount to a special reason: *Archer v. Woodward* [1959] Crim.L.R. 461, DC; nor could an abnormal alcohol metabolism: *Kinsella v. DPP*, *The Daily Telegraph*, March 21, 2002, DC ([2002] EWHC 545 (Admin.)).

Eructation (*i.e.* belching), leading to an artificially increased reading on a breath specimen, is capable of amounting to a special reason not to disqualify on a charge of driving with excess alcohol, because it goes directly to the commission of the offence: *Ng v. DPP* [2007] R.T.R. 35, QBD (Owen J.), following *Woolfe v. DPP* [2007] R.T.R. 16, DC (defendant suffering from medical condition whereby he regurgitated stomach content into his oesophagus). To succeed, the driver would have to show, (a) that the amount of alcohol consumed was insufficient without more to exceed the limit, (b) that, on each occasion when the breath specimen was provided, alcohol from the stomach had been regurgitated into the mouth, and (c) it was the regurgitated alcohol which caused the readings to exceed the limit: *Woolfe*, *ante* (as to which, see also *ante*, § 32–80a).

Ignorance as to consumption of alcohol

32–186a In *R. v. Cambridge Magistrates' Court, ex p. Wong* [1992] R.T.R. 54, DC, the defendant had consumed some wine and two doses of cough linctus. His reading was 40. He gave evidence that he was unaware that the linctus contained alcohol and called expert evidence to show that the linctus would account for 1.6 microgrammes. It was the prosecution practice not to prosecute cases below a reading of 40. *Held*, the facts were capable of amounting to special reasons.

In *CPS v. Jowle*, 163 J.P. 85, DC, a finding that special reasons applied in the case of a driver who had not knowingly drunk alcohol for 21 years but who was addicted to mouthwash, which unknown to him, contained 26.9 per cent alcohol, was held to be perverse. Special reasons did not apply, as the driver knew that the mouthwash gave him a "lift", albeit he did not associate that with alcohol.

Laced drinks

32–187 Two different situations are to be distinguished. The first is what is commonly known as the laced drink situation—that is, the person does not know he is drinking alcohol. The second situation is where the person knows he is drinking alcohol, but is misled as to the nature of the drink. A plea of special reasons in the latter situation will fail; a person who chooses to combine drinking and driving is under a duty to observe both the quantity and the quality of the drink consumed: *DPP v. Anderson* [1998] C.O.D. 363, DC, following *Adams v. Bradley* [1975] R.T.R. 233, DC.

In cases of laced drinks, the court is entitled to find special reasons where it can be established that: the defendant's drink was laced, that he did not know or suspect that fact, and had it not been laced he would not have been above the legal limit: *Pugsley v. Hunter* [1973] 1 W.L.R. 578, DC; *DPP v. Frost* [1989] R.T.R. 11, DC.

Guidance for the conduct of such cases was given in *DPP v. O'Connor*, 95 Cr.App.R. 135, DC. Expert evidence should be called except in obvious cases where the reading was just above the prescribed limit. Observations were also made about the procedure. Where the defendant intends to call evidence to prove facts or medical opinion in support of special reasons, it is desirable that notice is given to the prosecution in sufficient time before the hearing to enable the prosecution to be prepared to deal with the evidence. Where the defendant has not informed the prosecution of his intention to rely on special reasons, the prosecution may elicit that fact in the course of cross-examination so that the justices can consider whether the defendant's failure to give notice reflected on his bona fides. In *DPP v. Sharma* [2005] R.T.R. 27, QBD, Mitting J. said that, since each case turned on its own facts, it would be unwise to deduce from the guidance given in *O'Connor* a statement of the law which, if not followed by justices to the letter, would categorise their subsequent decision as wrong in law.

Magistrates have a discretion to hear "back calculation" evidence in considering special reasons, but only where the evidence is clear and straightforward: *Smith v. Geraghty* [1986] R.T.R. 222, DC.

Following *DPP v. Anderson* [1990] R.T.R. 269, DC, it is open to the prosecution in appropriate cases to bring proceedings against the person responsible for lacing the drinks. If it is proposed to call evidence in a "laced drink" case in the form of the person who laced the drink then that person should be warned that he could be in danger of being charged with procuring the commission of a criminal offence: *Att.-Gen.'s Reference (No. 1 of 1975)* [1975] Q.B. 733, 61 Cr.App.R. 118, CA.

Emergency

Driving because of an emergency may amount to a special reason only if the defendant had not been intending to drive at the time of drinking and a sudden and unexpected situation arose which compelled him to drive. A court should have regard to: (a) the degree and character of the emergency; (b) the extent to which alternative means of transport were available; and (c) other means of dealing with the emergency: *Jacobs v. Reed* [1974] R.T.R. 81, DC; *DPP v. Goddard* [1998] R.T.R. 463, DC; and should ask itself what a reasonable person faced with the circumstances in question would have done: *DPP v. Ubhi*, unreported, February 11, 2003, QBD (Moses J.) ([2003] EWHC 619 (Admin.)). **32–188**

Two cases illustrate the types of situations which the courts would regard as genuine emergencies. In *DPP v. Upchurch* [1994] R.T.R. 366, DC, the defendant's friends were injured in a disturbance. Unable to get an ambulance or taxi to the nearest hospital, the defendant drove his car.

In *DPP v. Knight* [1994] R.T.R. 374, DC, the defendant, who had been the recipient of threatening telephone calls, drove home after having received a telephone call at a public house from her babysitter that there had been threatening telephone calls at her home. She had tried unsuccessfully to get a taxi or a friend to take her home. Her reading was 44 and there was no evidence of bad driving.

It is essential to determine when the emergency is over. Continued fear and distress as a result of an incident cannot be a special reason: *DPP v. Feeney*, 89 Cr.App.R. 173, DC; *DPP v. Waller* [1989] R.T.R. 112, DC.

Shortness of distance driven

In *Chatters v. Burke* [1986] R.T.R. 396, DC, the court set out matters which should be taken into account when determining if special reasons exist which go beyond the **32–189** mere question of shortness of distance driven. They are: (a) how far the vehicle is driven in fact; (b) the manner in which it was driven; (c) the state of the vehicle; (d) whether the driver intended to drive any further; (e) the road and traffic conditions at the time; (f) whether there was any possibility of danger by contact with other road users; and (g) the reason the vehicle was driven.

The fact that the defendant had driven for only half a mile could not on its own amount to "special reasons": *DPP v. Elsender* [1999] 9 *Archbold News* 1, DC; and the fact that the defendant had only driven a few yards, and was not likely to have driven further (on account of difficulty in getting the vehicle started), was not capable of constituting "special reasons", where it was plain that the defendant had intended to drive the vehicle if he could have got it started: *DPP v. Humphries* [2000] R.T.R. 52, DC. See also *DPP v. Conroy* [2004] 1 Cr.App.R.(S.) 37, DC, and *DPP v. Harrison*, unreported, March 1, 2007, DC ([2007] EWHC 556 (Admin.)) (driving 446 yards on a major road in order to identify youths who had harassed the defendant and damaged his property did not amount to special reasons).

Manner of driving

32–189a In a case of dangerous driving arising from the condition of the vehicle, where no criticism is made of the manner in which the offender drove the vehicle, it is possible to find "special reasons" for not imposing the compulsory disqualification; in the circumstances, it was appropriate to disqualify only for the period that the offender was likely to be in custody: *R. v. Marsh* [2002] 2 *Archbold News* 1, CA ([2002] EWCA Crim. 137).

Failure to provide a specimen

32–190 The following matters have been held to be capable of being special reasons: there being no intent to drive in a case of "being in charge" (*McCormick v. Hitchins* [1988] R.T.R. 182, DC); the fact that the defendant, at the time of the request for a specimen, was pre-occupied with a more serious charge (of theft) for which he had been arrested and of which he had been cleared by the inquiries of the police, although they had not communicated this to the defendant at the time of the request (*Daniels v. DPP* [1992] R.T.R. 140, DC); a genuine fear of contracting AIDS as a result of blowing into the breath test machine (*DPP v. Kinnersley* [1993] R.T.R. 105, DC); an incorrect statement by a police officer to the effect that failing to provide a specimen would not necessarily result in disqualification (*Bobin v. DPP* [1999] R.T.R. 375, DC).

Awaiting legal advice cannot amount to special reasons: *Hosein v. Edmunds* [1970] R.T.R. 51, DC.

Insurance cases

32–191 These cases are largely characterised by the fact that the defendant was misled in some way. The general principle is that ignorance of the law cannot be a special reason (for not ordering endorsement): *Swell v. McKechnie* [1956] Crim.L.R. 423, DC. An honest though groundless belief that a policy covers a particular use is not a special reason: *Rennison v. Knowler* [1947] 1 All E.R. 302, DC; but if, by looking at a policy, it would appear to the layman that the vehicle was covered then this could amount to a special reason: *Carlton v. Garrity* [1964] Crim.L.R. 146, DC.

Thinking insurance was not required for a motorised children's bicycle, regarded as a toy, was held to be a special reason: *DPP v. Powell* [1993] R.T.R. 266, DC.

The shortness of the distance driven is capable of amounting to a special reason even where the prosecution case was not based on "driving" but on the leaving of the vehicle in the road: *DPP v. Heritage*, 166 J.P. 772, QBD (Jackson J.).

Delay

32–191a In *Myles v. DPP* [2004] 2 All E.R. 902, DC, it was held that delay in hearing an appeal in breach of Article 6 of the ECHR (*ante*, § 16–57) did not amount to special reasons so as to allow a mandatory disqualification to be expunged or reduced, but it would be appropriate to quash the appellant's fine.

(7) "Totting" disqualifications

Road Traffic Offenders Act 1988, s.35

Disqualification for repeated offences

35.—(1) Where— **32–192**

(a) a person is convicted of an offence to which this subsection applies, and

(b) the penalty points to be taken into account on that occasion number twelve or more,

the court must order him to be disqualified for not less than the minimum period unless the court is satisfied, having regard to all the circumstances, that there are grounds for mitigating the normal consequences of the conviction and thinks fit to order him to be disqualified for a shorter period or not to order him to be disqualified.

(1A) Subsection (1) above applies to—

(a) an offence involving discretionary disqualification and obligatory endorsement, and

(b) an offence involving obligatory disqualification in respect of which no order is made under section 34 of this Act.

(2) The minimum period referred to in subsection (1) above is—

(a) six months if no previous disqualification imposed on the offender is to be taken into account, and

(b) one year if one, and two years if more than one, such disqualification is to be taken into account;

and a previous disqualification imposed on an offender is to be taken into account if it was for a fixed period of 56 days or more and was imposed within the three years immediately preceding the commission of the latest offence in respect of which penalty points are taken into account under section 29 of this Act.

(3) Where an offender is convicted on the same occasion of more than one offence to which subsection (1) above applies—

(a) not more than one disqualification shall be imposed on him under subsection (1) above,

(b) in determining the period of disqualification the court must take into account all the offences, and

(c) for the purpose of any appeal any disqualification imposed under subsection (1) above shall be treated as an order made on the conviction of each of the offences.

(4) No account is to be taken under subsection (1) above of any of the following circumstances—

(a) any circumstances that are alleged to make the offence or any of the offences not a serious one,

(b) hardship, other than exceptional hardship, or

(c) any circumstances which, within the three years immediately preceding the conviction, have been taken into account under that subsection in ordering the offender to be disqualified for a shorter period or not ordering him to be disqualified.

(5) References in this section to disqualification do not include a disqualification imposed under section 26 of this Act or section 147 of the *Powers of Criminal Courts (Sentencing) Act* 2000 or section 223A or 436A of the *Criminal Procedure (Scotland) Act* 1975 (offences committed by using vehicles) or a disqualification imposed in respect of an offence of stealing a motor vehicle, an offence under section 12 or 25 of the *Theft Act* 1968, an offence under section 178 of the *Road Traffic Act* 1988, or an attempt to commit such an offence.

(5A) The preceding provisions of this section shall apply in relation to a conviction of an offence committed by aiding, abetting, counselling, procuring, or inciting to the commission of, an offence involving obligatory disqualification as if the offence were an offence involving discretionary disqualification.

(6) [*Scotland.*]

(7) This section is subject to section 48 of this Act.

[This section is printed as amended by the *RTA* 1991, s.48 and Sched. 4, para. 95; and the *PCC(S)A* 2000, s.165(1), and Sched. 9, para. 122. The reference to the common law offence of incitement in subs. (5A) has effect as a reference to the offences under the *SCA* 2007, Pt 2: 2007 Act, s.63(1), and Sched. 6, para. 15(c).]

For the relationship between this section and sections 29 and 34, see *Jones v. DPP*, *ante*, § 32–169.

"grounds for mitigating" (s.35(1))

32–193 "Grounds for mitigating" within the meaning of subsection (1) may be wider than "special reasons" under section 34(1) and include the personal circumstances of the offender, as well as circumstances concerned with the offence: *Baker v. Cole* [1971] 1 W.L.R. 1788, DC; *R. v. Preston* [1986] R.T.R. 136, CA. A reduction in the minimum period of disqualification was a just and appropriate remedy for a breach of Article 6 of the ECHR (*ante*, § 16–57) by reason of delay: *Miller v. DPP* [2005] R.T.R. 3, QBD (Richards J.).

"previous disqualification imposed" (s.35(2))

32–194 The word "imposed" means imposed by a court after conviction for a road traffic offence, and accordingly a disqualification by reason of age cannot be described as "imposed" within the meaning of this subsection: *R. v. Scurry*, 13 Cr.App.R.(S.) 517, CA.

"exceptional hardship" (s.35(4)(b))

32–195 The provision that no account is to be taken of hardship, other than exceptional hardship, does not prevent the court from having in mind the offender's rehabilitation: *R. v. Preston*, *ante*.

In *Owen v. Jones*, 9 Cr.App.R.(S.) 34, DC, it was said that although an offender who was liable to disqualification under what is now section 35(1) had to prove that exceptional hardship would result from the normal consequences of conviction if he was to avoid disqualification, it was not always necessary for the offender to give or call evidence to establish this. Justices could rely on information they believed to be true of their own knowledge. However, they should not easily come to the conclusion that their belief was sufficient unless it was well founded on facts known to them. In the vast majority of cases, justices would need evidence to satisfy themselves that exceptional hardship would follow.

"any circumstances which, within three years immediately preceding the conviction ..." etc., (s.35(4)(c))

32–196 The onus of establishing that the mitigating circumstances differ from those previously taken into account where that issue arises is on the defendant: *R. v. Sandbach JJ., ex p. Prescund*, 5 Cr.App.R.(S.) 177, CA.

(8) Interim disqualification

Road Traffic Offenders Act 1988, s.26

Interim disqualification

32–197 **26.**—(1) Where a magistrates' court—

(a) commits an offender to the Crown Court under section 6 of the *Powers of Criminal Courts (Sentencing) Act* 2000 or any enactment mentioned in subsection (4) of that section, or

(b) remits an offender to another magistrates' court under section 10 of that Act,

to be dealt with for an offence involving obligatory or discretionary disqualification, it may order him to be disqualified until he has been dealt with in respect of the offence.

(2) Where a court in England and Wales—

(a) defers passing sentence on an offender under section 1 of that Act in respect of an offence involving obligatory or discretionary disqualification, or

(b) adjourns after convicting an offender of such an offence but before dealing with him for the offence,

it may order the offender to be disqualified until he has been dealt with in respect of the offence.

(3) [*Scotland.*]

(4) Subject to subsection (5) below, an order under this section shall cease to have effect

at the end of the period of six months beginning with the day on which it is made, if it has not ceased to have effect before that time.

(5) [*Scotland.*]

(6) Where a court orders a person to be disqualified under this section ("the first order"), no court shall make a further order under this section in respect of the same offence or any offence in respect of which an order could have been made under this section at the time the first order was made.

(7) Where a court makes an order under this section in respect of any person it must—

(a) require him to produce to the court any licence held by him *and its counterpart*, and

(b) retain the licence *and counterpart* until it deals with him or (as the case may be) cause *them* [it] sent to the proper officer of the court which is to deal with him.

(7A) In subsection (7) above "proper officer" means—

(a) in relation to a magistrates' court in England and Wales, the designated officer for the court, and

(b) in relation to any other court, the clerk of the court.

(8) If the holder of the licence has not caused it *and its counterpart* to be delivered, or has not posted *them* [it], in accordance with section 7 of this Act and does not produce the licence *and counterpart* as required under subsection (7) above, then he is guilty of an offence.

(9) Subsection (8) above does not apply to a person who—

(a) satisfies the court that he has applied for a new licence and has not received it, or

(b) surrenders to the court a current receipt for his licence *and its counterpart* issued under section 56 of this Act, and produces the licence *and counterpart* to the court immediately on *their* [its] return.

(10) Where a court makes an order under this section in respect of any person, sections 44(1), 47(2), 91ZA(7) and 91A(5) of this Act shall not apply in relation to the order, but—

(a) the court must send notice of the order to the Secretary of State, and

(b) if the court which deals with the offender determines not to order him to be disqualified under section 34 or 35 of this Act, it must send notice of the determination to the Secretary of State.

(11) A notice sent by a court to the Secretary of State in pursuance of subsection (10) above must be sent in such manner and to such address and contain such particulars as the Secretary of State may determine.

(12) Where on any occasion a court deals with an offender—

(a) for an offence in respect of which an order was made under this section, or

(b) for two or more offences in respect of any of which such an order was made,

any period of disqualification which is on that occasion imposed under section 34 or 35 of this Act shall be treated as reduced by any period during which he was disqualified by reason only of an order made under this section in respect of any of those offences.

(13) Any reference in this or any other Act (including any Act passed after this Act) to the length of a period of disqualification shall, unless the context otherwise requires, be construed as a reference to its length before any reduction under this section.

(14) *In relation to licences which came into force before 1st June 1990, the references in this section to counterparts of licences shall be disregarded.*

[This section is printed as amended by S.I. 1996 No. 1974 (*ante*, § 32–111); the *Access to Justice Act* 1999, s.90(1) and Sched. 13, para. 143; and the *PCC(S)A* 2000, s.165(1), and Sched. 9, para. 119; the *Courts Act* 2003, s.109(1), and Sched. 8, para. 312; and the *Crime (International Co-operation) Act* 2003, s.91, and Sched. 5, para. 34; and as amended, as from a day to be appointed, by the *RSA* 2006, ss.10(1) and (12) and 59, Sched. 3, paras 30 and 32, and Sched. 7(4) (omission of italicised words, insertion of words in square brackets).]

(9) Disqualification until test is passed

Road Traffic Offenders Act 1988, s.36

Disqualification until test is passed

36.—(1) Where this subsection applies to a person the court must order him to be disqualified until he passes the appropriate driving test. **32–198**

(2) Subsection (1) above applies to a person who is disqualified under section 34 of this Act on conviction of—

(a) manslaughter, or in Scotland culpable homicide, by the driver of a motor vehicle, or

(b) an offence under section 1 (causing death by dangerous driving) or section 2 (dangerous driving) of the *Road Traffic Act* 1988.

(3) Subsection (1) above also applies—

(a) to a person who is disqualified under section 34 or 35 of this Act *in such circumstances or for such period* [for such period, in such circumstances or for such period and in such circumstances] as the Secretary of State may by order *prescribe* [specify], or

(b) to such other persons convicted of such offences involving obligatory endorsement as *may be so prescribed* [the Secretary of State may by order specify].

(4) Where a person to whom subsection (1) above does not apply is convicted of an offence involving obligatory endorsement, the court may order him to be disqualified until he passes the appropriate driving test (whether or not he has previously passed any test).

(5) In this section—

"appropriate driving test" means—

(a) [in such circumstances as the Secretary of State may prescribe] an extended driving test, *where a person is convicted of an offence involving obligatory disqualification or is disqualified under section 35 of this Act,* [and]

(b) [otherwise,] a test of competence to drive, *other than* [which is not] an extended driving test, *in any other case,*

"extended driving test" means a test of competence to drive prescribed for the purposes of this section [by regulations made by the Secretary of State], and

"test of competence to drive" means a test prescribed by virtue of section 89(3) of the *Road Traffic Act* 1988.

(6) In determining whether to make an order under subsection (4) above, the court shall have regard to the safety of road users.

(7) Where a person is disqualified until he passes the extended driving test—

(a) any earlier order under this section shall cease to have effect and

(b) a court shall not make a further order under this section while he is so disqualified.

(8) Subject to subsection (9) below, a disqualification by virtue of an order under this section shall be deemed to have expired on production to the Secretary of State of evidence, in such form as may be prescribed by regulations *under section 105 of the* Road Traffic Act *1988* [made by the Secretary of State], that the person disqualified has passed the test in question since the order was made.

(9) A disqualification shall be deemed to have expired only in relation to vehicles of such classes as may be prescribed in relation to the test passed by regulations *under that section* [made by the Secretary of State].

(10) *Where there is issued to a person a licence on the counterpart of which are endorsed particulars of a disqualification under this section, there shall also be endorsed the particulars of any test of competence to drive that he has passed since the order of disqualification was made.*

[(10A) Where a person's driving record is endorsed with particulars of a disqualification under this section, it shall also be endorsed with the particulars of any test of competence to drive that he has passed since the order of disqualification was made.]

(11) For the purposes of an order under this section, a person shall be treated as having passed a test of competence to drive other than an extended driving test if he passes a corresponding test conducted—

(a) under the law of Northern Ireland, the Isle of Man, any of the Channel Islands, another EEA State, Gibraltar or a designated country or territory, or

(b) for the purposes of obtaining a British Forces licence (as defined by section 88(8) of the *Road Traffic Act* 1988);

and accordingly subsections (8) to (10) above shall apply in relation to such a test as they apply in relation to a test prescribed by virtue of section 89(3) of that Act.

(11A) In subsection (11) above "designated country or territory" means a country or territory designated under section 108(2) of the *Road Traffic Act* 1988.

(12) This section is subject to section 48 of this Act.

(13) [*Order under subs. (3) to be made by statutory instrument.*]

[(13A) *Requirement for Secretary of State to consult.*]

(14) *The Secretary of State shall not make an order under subsection (3) above after the end of 2001 if he has not previously made such an order.*

[This section is printed as substituted by the *RTA* 1991, s.32; as subsequently amended by S.I. 1996 No. 1974 (see *ante*, § 32–111); and as amended, as from days to be appointed, by the *RSA* 2006, ss.10(1) and (12), 37(1) to (7) and 59, Sched. 2 para 7, Sched. 3, paras 30 and 39, and Sched. 7(4) and (10) (omission of italicised words, insertion of words in square brackets).]

The *Driving Licence (Disqualification until Test Passed) (Prescribed Offence) Order* 2001 (S.I. 2001 No. 4051) was made under subsection (3), and prescribes an offence under section 3A of the *RTA* 1988 and any person committing such offence for the purposes of subsection (1).

For endorsement, see section 44, *post*, § 32–210.

Where there is a discharge, see section 46(1), *post*, § 32–216.

An order of disqualification is good although no other penalty is imposed: *R. v. Bignell*, 52 Cr.App.R. 10, CA.

For the provisions relating to a person disqualified under section 36 obtaining a provisional licence, see section 37(3), *post*, § 32–199.

Where the Crown Court omits to make an order under this section, the Court of Appeal has no power to do so on an unsuccessful appeal against sentence, for to do so would result in the appellant being dealt with more severely on appeal than in the court below, contrary to section 11(3) of the *CAA* 1968 (*ante*, § 7–126): *R. v. Murphy*, 89 Cr.App.R. 176, CA; *R. v. Lauder*, 163 J.P. 721, CA (in which the court drew attention to the fact that the mandatory requirement of this section was often overlooked).

Where the court has a discretion as to the making of an order under this section, it is generally inappropriate to make an order against a person convicted as a passenger: *R. v. Wiggins* [2001] R.T.R. 3, CA.

(10) Effect of disqualification

Road Traffic Offenders Act 1988, s.37

Effect of order of disqualification

37.—(1) Where the holder of a licence is disqualified by an order of a court, the licence shall be treated as being revoked with effect from the beginning of the period of disqualification. **32–199**

(1A) Where—

(a) the disqualification is for a fixed period shorter than 56 days in respect of an offence involving obligatory endorsement, or

(b) the order is made under section 26 of this Act,

subsection (1) above shall not prevent the licence from again having effect at the end of the period of disqualification.

(2) Where the holder of the licence appeals against the order and the disqualification is suspended under section 39 of this Act, the period of disqualification shall be treated for the purpose of subsection (1) above as beginning on the day on which the disqualification ceases to be suspended.

(3) Notwithstanding anything in Part III of the *Road Traffic Act* 1988, a person disqualified by an order of a court under section 36 of this Act is (unless he is also disqualified otherwise than by virtue of such an order) entitled to obtain and to hold a provisional licence and to drive a motor vehicle in accordance with the conditions subject to which the provisional licence is granted.

[This section is printed as amended by the *RTA* 1991, ss.33 and 48, and Sched. 4, para. 96.]

On a prosecution for driving while disqualified, the burden is on the defendant to establish the defence provided by section 37(3): *DPP v. Barker*, 168 J.P. 617, DC.

(11) Appeal against disqualification and suspension pending appeal

Road Traffic Offenders Act 1988, ss.38–40

Appeal against disqualification

38.—(1) A person disqualified by an order of a magistrates' court under section 34 or 35 of this Act may appeal against the order in the same manner as against a conviction. **32–200**

(2) [*Scotland.*]

Suspension of disqualification pending appeal

32–201 **39.**—(1) Any court in England and Wales (whether a magistrates' court or another) which makes an order disqualifying a person may, if it thinks fit, suspend the disqualification pending an appeal against the order.

(2) [*Scotland.*]

(3) Where a court exercises its power under subsection (1) or (2) above, it must send notice of the suspension to the Secretary of State.

(4) The notice must be sent in such manner and to such address and must contain such particulars as the Secretary of State may determine.

Power of appellate courts in England and Wales to suspend disqualification

32–202 **40.**—(1) This section applies where a person has been convicted by or before a court in England and Wales of an offence involving obligatory or discretionary disqualification and has been ordered to be disqualified; and in the following provisions of this section—

(a) any reference to a person ordered to be disqualified is to be construed as a reference to a person so convicted and so ordered to be disqualified, and

(b) any reference to his sentence includes a reference to the order of disqualification and to any other order made on his conviction and, accordingly, any reference to an appeal against his sentence includes a reference to an appeal against any order forming part of his sentence.

(2) Where a person ordered to be disqualified—

(a) appeals to the Crown Court, or

(b) appeals or applies for leave to appeal to the Court of Appeal,

against his conviction or his sentence, the Crown Court or, as the case may require, the Court of Appeal may, if it thinks fit, suspend the disqualification.

(3) Where a person ordered to be disqualified has appealed or applied for leave to appeal to the House of Lords—

(a) under section 1 of the *Administration of Justice Act* 1960 from any decision of a Divisional Court of the Queen's Bench Division which is material to his conviction or sentence, or

(b) under section 33 of the *Criminal Appeal Act* 1968 from any decision of the Court of Appeal which is material to his conviction or sentence,

the Divisional Court or, as the case may require, the Court of Appeal may, if it thinks fit, suspend the disqualification.

(4) Where a person ordered to be disqualified makes an application in respect of the decision of the court in question under section 111 of the *Magistrates' Courts Act* 1980 (statement of case by magistrates' court) or section 28 of the *Supreme Court [Senior Courts] Act* 1981 (statement of case by Crown Court) the High Court may, if it thinks fit, suspend the disqualification.

(5) Where a person ordered to be disqualified—

(a) applies to the High Court for an order of *certiorari* to remove into the High Court any proceedings of a magistrates' court or of the Crown Court, being proceedings in or in consequence of which he was convicted or his sentence was passed, or

(b) applies to the High Court for leave to make such an application,

the High Court may, if it thinks fit, suspend the disqualification.

(6) Any power of a court under the preceding provisions of this section to suspend the disqualification of any person is a power to do so on such terms as the court thinks fit.

(7) Where, by virtue of this section, a court suspends the disqualification of any person, it must send notice of the suspension to the Secretary of State.

(8) The notice must be sent in such manner and to such address and must contain such particulars as the Secretary of State may determine.

[The reference to the *Supreme Court Act* 1981 is replaced by a reference to the *Senior Courts Act* 1981 as from a day to be appointed: *Constitutional Reform Act* 2005, s.59, and Sched. 11, para. 1(2).]

The reference to "an order of *certiorari*" in subsection (5) is to be read as a reference to "a quashing order": *Supreme Court [Senior Courts] Act* 1981, s.29(5).

As to the power of a single judge to exercise the powers of the Court of Appeal under subsections (2) and (3), see the *CAA* 1968, ss.31(2A) (*ante*, § 7–231) and 44(2) (*ante*, § 7–336) respectively.

Road Traffic Offenders Act 1988, s.41A

Suspension of disqualification pending determination of applications under section 34B

41A.—(1) Where a person makes an application to a court under section 34B of this Act, the court may suspend the disqualification to which the application relates pending the determination of the application. **32–203**

(2) Where a court exercises its power under subsection (1) above it must send notice of the suspension to the Secretary of State.

(3) The notice must be sent in such manner and to such address, and must contain such particulars, as the Secretary of State may determine.

[This section was inserted by the *RTA* 1991, s.48 and Sched. 4, para. 97.]

Road Traffic Offenders Act 1988, s.41B

[Suspension of certificate pending determination of applications under section 34E

41B.—(1) Where a person given a certificate under subsection (1) of section 34E of this Act makes an application to a court under subsection (5) of that section, the court may suspend the effect of the certificate pending the determination of the application. **32–203a**

(2), (3) [*Identical to s.41A(2) and (3)*, ante, *§ 32–203*.]]

[This section is inserted, as from a day to be appointed, by the *RSA* 2006, s.15(2).]

(12) Rehabilitation courses for drink-drive offenders

Sections 34A to 34C of the *RTOA* 1988 provide for the court to offer the opportunity to those over the age of 17 convicted of drink/driving offences and who face a minimum of 12 months' disqualification, to attend special courses. It is not part of the penalty and is voluntary. There must be a place available and the court must explain the effect of the order, the cost (payable by the offender) and the requirements of the course. The scheme was initially introduced for an experimental period, and was subject to restrictions. The effect of the *Courses for Drink-Drive Offenders (Experimental Period) (Termination of Restrictions) Order* 1999 (S.I. 1999 No. 3130) was to make the scheme permanent and to remove all the restrictions as from December 31, 1999. **32–204**

Section 35 of the *RSA* 2006 substitutes new sections 34A to 34C in the *RTOA* 1988 (as from a day to be appointed), and thereby extends the drink driving offences in respect of which orders of reduced disqualification following attendance on a course may apply.

Road Traffic Offenders Act 1988, s.34A

Reduced disqualification period for attendance on courses

34A.—(1) *This section applies where*— **32–205**

(a) *a person is convicted of an offence under section 3A (causing death by careless driving when under influence of drink or drugs), 4 (driving or being in charge when under influence of drink or drugs), 5 (driving or being in charge with excess alcohol) or 7 (failing to provide a specimen) of the* Road Traffic Act *1988*, *and*

(b) *the court makes an order under section 34 of this Act disqualifying him for a period of not less than twelve months.*

(2) *Where this section applies, the court may make an order that the period of disqualification imposed under section 34 shall be reduced if, by a date specified in the order under this section, the offender satisfactorily completes a course approved by the Secretary of State for the purposes of this section and specified in the order.*

(3) *The reduction made by an order under this section in a period of disqualification imposed under section 34 shall be a period specified in the order of not less than three months and not more than one quarter of the unreduced period (and accordingly where the period imposed under section 34 is twelve months, the reduced period shall be nine months).*

(4) *The court shall not make an order under this section unless*—

(a) *it is satisfied that a place on the course specified in the order will be available for the offender,*

(b) *the offender appears to the court to be of or over the age of 17,*

(c) *the court has explained the effect of the order to the offender in ordinary language, and has informed him of the amount of the fees for the course and of the requirement that he must pay them before beginning the course, and*

(d) *the offender has agreed that the order should be made.*

(5) *The date specified in an order under this section as the latest date for completion of a course must be at least two months before the last day of the period of disqualification as reduced by the order.*

(6) *An order under this section shall name the petty sessions area (or in Scotland the sheriff court district or, where an order has been made under this section by a stipendiary magistrate, the commission area) in which the offender resides or will reside.*

[(1) This section applies where—

(a) a person is convicted of a relevant drink offence or a specified offence by or before a court, and

(b) the court makes an order under section 34 of this Act disqualifying him for a period of not less than twelve months.

(2) In this section "relevant drink offence" means—

(a) an offence under paragraph (a) of subsection (1) of section 3A of the *Road Traffic Act* 1988 (causing death by careless driving when unfit to drive through drink) committed when unfit to drive through drink,

(b) an offence under paragraph (b) of that subsection (causing death by careless driving with excess alcohol),

(c) an offence under paragraph (c) of that subsection (failing to provide a specimen) where the specimen is required in connection with drink or consumption of alcohol,

(d) an offence under section 4 of that Act (driving or being in charge when under influence of drink) committed by reason of unfitness through drink,

(e) an offence under section 5(1) of that Act (driving or being in charge with excess alcohol),

(f) an offence under section 7(6) of that Act (failing to provide a specimen) committed in the course of an investigation into an offence within any of the preceding paragraphs, or

(g) an offence under section 7A(6) of that Act (failing to allow a specimen to be subjected to a laboratory test) in the course of an investigation into an offence within any of the preceding paragraphs.

(3) In this section "specified offence" means—

(a) an offence under section 3 of the *Road Traffic Act* 1988 (careless, and inconsiderate, driving),

(b) an offence under section 36 of that Act (failing to comply with traffic signs),

(c) an offence under section 17(4) of the *Road Traffic Regulation Act* 1984 (use of special road contrary to scheme or regulations), or

(d) an offence under section 89(1) of that Act (exceeding speed limit).

(4) But the Secretary of State may by regulations amend subsection (3) above by adding other offences or removing offences.

(5) Where this section applies, the court may make an order that the period of disqualification imposed under section 34 of this Act ("the unreduced period") shall be reduced if, by the relevant date, the offender satisfactorily completes an approved course specified in the order.

(6) In subsection (5) above—

"an approved course" means a course approved by the appropriate national authority for the purposes of this section in relation to the description of offence of which the offender is convicted, and

"the relevant date" means such date, at least two months before the last day of the period of disqualification as reduced by the order, as is specified in the order.

(7) The reduction made in a period of disqualification by an order under this section is a period specified in the order of—

(a) not less than three months, and

(b) not more than one quarter of the unreduced period,

(and, accordingly, where the unreduced period is twelve months, the reduced period is nine months).

(8) A court shall not make an order under this section in the case of an offender convicted of a specified offence if—

(a) the offender has, during the period of three years ending with the date on which the offence was committed, committed a specified offence and successfully completed an approved course pursuant to an order made under this section or section 30A of this Act on conviction of that offence, or

(b) the specified offence was committed during his probationary period.

(9) A court shall not make an order under this section in the case of an offender unless—

(a) the court is satisfied that a place on the course specified in the order will be available for the offender,

(b) the offender appears to the court to be of or over the age of 17,

(c) the court has informed the offender (orally or in writing and in ordinary language) of the effect of the order and of the amount of the fees which he is required to pay for the course and when he must pay them, and

(d) the offender has agreed that the order should be made.]

[This section was inserted by the *RTA* 1991, s.30. The italicised subss. (1) to (6) are replaced by new subss. (1) to (9) (in square brackets), as from a day to be appointed, by the *RSA* 2006, s.35.]

Following successful completion, a certificate of completion is sent to the court in order for the reduced period to come into effect. There are provisions concerning the "non-issue" of a certificate by the course organiser which allows the offender to apply to the court for a declaration that the organiser has defaulted in his obligations. If such a declaration is made, then it has the effect of the certificate being issued (s.34B(7), (9)). As from a day to be appointed, section 34B is substituted by a new section 34B (by s.35 of the 2006 Act). The foregoing summary applies equally to the new section. **32–206**

Section 34BA (inserted by s.35 of the 2006 Act, as from a day to be appointed) deals with the approval of courses by the appropriate national authority for the purposes of section 34A. Section 34C (replacing the old section 34C) contains provisions supplementary to sections 34A to 34BA, and mainly to do with the procedure governing the exercise of his powers by the Secretary of State. Section 34C(3), however, defines various terms in sections 34A to 34BA, and does so identically to section 30D(3), *ante*, § 32–177c. **32–206a**

(13) Alcohol interlock programme orders

Road Traffic Offenders Act 1988, s.34D

[Reduced disqualification period: alcohol ignition interlock programme orders

34D.—(1) This section applies where— **32–206b**

(a) a person is convicted of a relevant drink offence by or before a court,

(b) he has committed another relevant drink offence at any time during the period of ten years ending with the date of the conviction,

(c) the court makes an order under section 34 of this Act but does not make an order under section 34A of this Act, and

(d) the period stated by the court as that for which, apart from this section, he would be disqualified ("the unreduced period") is not less than two years.

(2) [*Identical to s.34A(2), as substituted by the* RSA *2006, s.35,* ante, *§ 32–205.*]

(3) Where this section applies, the court may specify a lesser period of disqualification ("the reduced period") if it also makes an order (an "alcohol ignition interlock programme order") requiring the offender to comply with the alcohol ignition interlock conditions.

(4) The difference between the unreduced period and the reduced period shall be a period specified in the order of—

(a) not less than 12 months, and

(b) not more than one half of the unreduced period.

(5) If the offender contravenes the alcohol ignition interlock conditions, a further order under section 34 disqualifying him for the rest of the unreduced period is to be treated as having been made by the court immediately before the contravention.

(6) "The alcohol ignition interlock conditions" are that the offender—

(a) must participate fully in an approved alcohol ignition interlock programme specified in the order during such part of the unreduced period as is so specified, and

(b) during the part of that period following the reduced period must not drive a motor vehicle unless it is fitted with an alcohol ignition interlock in good working order and must not drive a motor vehicle which is so fitted when not using the alcohol ignition interlock properly.

(7) A court shall not make an alcohol ignition interlock programme order in the case of an offender unless—

(a) the court is satisfied that a place on the approved alcohol ignition interlock programme specified in the order will be available for the offender,

(b) the offender appears to the court to be of or over the age of 17,

(c) the court has informed the offender (orally or in writing and in ordinary language) of the effect of the order and the amount of the fees which he is required to pay for the programme and when he must pay them, and

(d) the offender has agreed that the order should be made.

(8) For the purposes of this section an "approved alcohol ignition interlock programme" is a programme approved by the appropriate national authority and involving the provision of an alcohol ignition interlock for use by the offender, training in its use and other education and counselling relating to the consumption of alcohol and driving.

(9) For the purposes of this section "alcohol ignition interlock" means a device—

(a) of a type approved by the Secretary of State, and

(b) designed to be fitted to a motor vehicle with the purpose of preventing the driving of the vehicle by a person who does not, both before starting driving the vehicle and at regular intervals while driving it, provide specimens of breath in which the proportion of alcohol is likely not to exceed the limit specified in subsection (10) below.

(10) That limit is 9 microgrammes of alcohol in 100 millilitres of breath or such other proportion of alcohol to breath as the Secretary of State may by regulations prescribe.

(11) For the purposes of this section an offender uses an alcohol ignition interlock properly if (and only if) he is complying with all the instructions given to him about its use as part of the approved alcohol ignition interlock programme.

(12) Where an alcohol ignition interlock is fitted to a motor vehicle as part of an approved alcohol ignition interlock programme relating to an offender, a person commits an offence if—

(a) he interferes with the alcohol ignition interlock with intent to cause it not to function or not to function properly, or

(b) he is a person other than the offender and provides or attempts to provide a specimen of breath for the purposes of the alcohol ignition interlock with intent to enable the driving (or continued driving) of the vehicle by the offender.]

[This section is inserted, as from a day to be appointed, by the *RSA* 2006, s.15(1).]

32–206c Section 34E of the *RTOA* 1988 deals with certificates of failing fully to co-operate with an alcohol ignition interlock programme. An offender shall only be regarded as so failing if a certificate to that effect is received by the proper officer of the supervising court (s.34E(1)). Such a certificate may only be given if the offender has failed (a) to make due payment of fees for the programme, (b) to attend for training, education or counselling forming part of the programme in accordance with the programme provider's reasonable instructions, (c) to attend at a place specified by the programme provider for the monitoring and maintenance of the alcohol ignition interlock, at a time specified by the programme provider or a person with whom the programme provider has made arrangements for its monitoring and maintenance, or (d) to comply with any other reasonable requirement of the programme provider (s.34E(2)). There are provisions concerning the wrongful issue of a certificate by the programme provider which allow the offender to apply to the court for a declaration that the programme provider is in breach of section 34E(2). If such a declaration is made, then it has the effect of the certificate not having been received by the court (s.34E(5), (6)). Section 34F of the *RTOA* 1988 deals with the approval of courses by the appropriate national authority for the purposes of section 34D. Section 34G contains provisions supplementary to sections 34D to 34F, mainly to do with the procedure governing the exercise of his powers by the Secretary of State. Section 34G(3) defines "programme provider", in relation to an alcohol ignition interlock programme, as "the person by whom it is, or is to be, provided"; other terms in sections 34D to 34F are defined identically to the *RTOA* 1988, s.30D(3), *ante*, § 32–177c.

Experimental period for alcohol ignition interlock programme

32–206d Section 15(1) of the *RSA* 2006, which inserts sections 34D to 34G into the 1988 Act, is subject to an experimental period, as stipulated in section 16 of the 2006 Act. During that period, no order under section 34D may be made (a) by virtue of a conviction under the *RTA* 1988, s.3A, or (b) other than by a designated magistrates' court: 2006 Act, s.16(3). The balance of the section is mainly concerned with the procedure governing the exercise of his powers by the Secretary of State.

(14) Removal of disqualification

Road Traffic Offenders Act 1988, s.42

Removal of disqualification

42.—(1) Subject to the provisions of this section, a person who by an order of a court is disqualified may apply to the court by which the order was made to remove the disqualification. **32–207**

(2) On any such application the court may, as it thinks proper having regard to—

(a) the character of the person disqualified and his conduct subsequent to the order,

(b) the nature of the offence, and

(c) any other circumstances of the case,

either by order remove the disqualification as from such date as may be specified in the order or refuse the application.

(3) No application shall be made under subsection (1) above for the removal of a disqualification before the expiration of whichever is relevant of the following periods from the date of the order by which the disqualification was imposed, that is—

(a) two years, if the disqualification is for less than four years,

(b) one half of the period of disqualification, if it is for less than ten years but not less than four years,

(c) five years in any other case;

and in determining the expiration of the period after which under this subsection a person may apply for the removal of a disqualification, any time after the conviction during which the disqualification was suspended or he was not disqualified shall be disregarded.

(4) Where an application under subsection (1) above is refused, a further application under that subsection shall not be entertained if made within three months after the date of the refusal.

(5) If under this section a court orders a disqualification to be removed, the court—

(a) *must cause particulars of the order to be endorsed on the counterpart of the licence, if any, previously held by the applicant, and*

[(a) must—

(i) if particulars of the disqualification were previously endorsed on the counterpart of any licence previously held by the applicant, cause particulars of the order to be endorsed on that counterpart, and

(ii) if particulars of the disqualification were previously endorsed on the driving record of the applicant, send notice of the order to the Secretary of State,]

(b) may in any case order the applicant to pay the whole or any part of the costs of the application.

(5A) Subsection *(5)(a)* [(5)(a)(i)] above shall apply only where the disqualification was imposed in respect of an offence involving obligatory endorsement; and in any other case the court must send notice of the order made under this section to the Secretary of State.

[(5AA) If the disqualification was imposed in respect of an offence involving obligatory endorsement, the Secretary of State must, on receiving notice of an order under subsection (5)(a)(ii) above, make any necessary adjustments to the endorsements on the person's driving record to reflect that order.]

(5B) A notice under subsection [(5)(a)(ii) or] (5A) above must be sent in such manner and to such address, and must contain such particulars, as the Secretary of State may determine.

(6) The preceding provisions of this section shall not apply where the disqualification was imposed by order under section 36(1) of this Act.

[This section is printed as amended by the *Driving Licences (Community Driving Licence) Regulations* 1990 (S.I. 1990 No. 144); and the *RTA* 1991, s.48, and Sched. 4, para. 98. The italicised words are omitted and the words in square brackets are inserted, as from a day to be appointed, by the *RSA* 2006, s.9(6), and Sched. 2, paras 2 and 8. As from a later date (see s.61(8) of the 2006 Act), the following further amendments are effected by the 2006 Act, ss.10(1) and (12) and 59, Sched. 3, paras 30 and 40, and Sched. 7(4): (i) the words "must send notice of the order to the Secretary of State" are substituted as the text of subs. (5)(a); (ii) subs. (5A) is repealed; (iii) "(5)(a)" is substituted for "(5)(a)(ii)" in subs. (5AA); and (iv) "(5)(a)" is substituted for "(5)(a)(ii) or (5A)" in subs. (5B).]

32–208 Section 42 applies irrespective of whether the disqualification was mandatory or discretionary; but a court may, if it thinks fit, regard a mandatory disqualification as one which it is somewhat less ready to remove than a discretionary disqualification: *Damer v. Davison*, 61 Cr.App.R. 232, DC.

The concluding words in section 42(3)—"he was not disqualified shall be disregarded"—are to be construed as if they read "he was not disqualified *by virtue of that order* shall be disregarded": see *R. v. Lambeth Metropolitan Magistrate, ex p. Everett* [1968] 1 Q.B. 446, 51 Cr.App.R. 425, DC.

Subsection (6) does not prevent a person who was disqualified for a period under section 34(1), and who was also disqualified under section 36 until he passed a test, from applying for the removal of the former disqualification: *R. v. Nuttall* (1971) 115 S.J. 489.

The order of disqualification cannot be varied in any other way, for example by requiring the driver to pass a driving test: *R. v. Bentham* [1982] R.T.R. 357, CA.

The possibility of an application being made under this section should be disregarded in fixing the length of a period of disqualification: *Corner v. Southend Crown Court*, 170 J.P. 6, DC.

Road Traffic Offenders Act 1988, s.43

Rule for determining end of period of disqualification

32–209 **43.** In determining the expiration of the period for which a person is disqualified by an order of a court made in consequence of a conviction, any time after the conviction during which the disqualification was suspended or he was not disqualified shall be disregarded.

(15) Endorsement

Road Traffic Offenders Act 1988, s.44

Endorsement of licences [Orders for endorsement]

32–210 **44.**—(1) Where a person is convicted of an offence involving obligatory endorsement, the court must order there to be endorsed on [the counterpart of] any licence held by him particulars of the conviction and also—

(a) if the court orders him to be disqualified, particulars of the disqualification, or
(b) if the court does not order him to be disqualified—
  (i) particulars of the offence, including the date when it was committed, and
  (ii) the penalty points to be attributed to the offence.

(2) Where the court does not order the person convicted to be disqualified, it need not make an order under subsection (1) above if for special reasons it thinks fit not to do so.

(3) [*Scotland*.]

[(3A) Where a person who is not the holder of a licence is convicted of an offence involving obligatory endorsement, subsection (1) above applies as if the reference to the counterpart of any licence held by him were a reference to his driving record.]

(4) This section is subject to section 48 of this Act.

[This section is printed as amended by the *Driving Licences (Community Driving Licence) Regulations* 1990 (S.I. 1990 No. 144) (insertion of words in square brackets (in subs. (1)) in relation to licences which came into force after May 31, 1990). The words in square brackets in the heading are substituted for the current heading, and subs. (3A) is inserted, as from a day to be appointed by the *RSA* 2006, s.9(1) and (2). As from a later date (see s.61(8) of the 2006 Act), the following further amendments are effected by the 2006 Act, ss.10(1) and (2) and 59, and Sched. 7(4): (i) the words "his driving record" are substituted for the words "the counterpart of any licence held by him" in subs. (1); and (ii) subs. (3A) is repealed.]

As to "special reasons" generally, see *ante*, §§ 32–183 *et seq*. See also *Nicholson v. Brown* [1974] R.T.R. 177, DC, and *Hawkins v. Roots*; *Hawkins v. Smith* [1976] R.T.R. 49, DC.

In *R. v. Ashford and Tenterden Magistrates' Court, ex p. Wood* [1988] R.T.R. 178, DC, it was held that even if a "special reason" is made out, the court still has a discretion whether or not to order endorsement.

Where a person is disqualified from driving under section 34 of the *RTOA* 1988 (*ante*, § 32–181) and falls to be dealt with on the same occasion for another offence carrying obligatory endorsement, the order for endorsement required by section 44 should be confined to the particulars of conviction and should not include particulars of the offence or the penalty points attributable to the offence: *Martin v. DPP* [2000] 2 Cr.App.R.(S.) 18, DC.

Road Traffic Offenders Act 1988, s.44A

[Endorsement of driving record in accordance with order

44A.—(1) Where the court orders the endorsement of a person's driving record with any particulars or penalty points it must send notice of the order to the Secretary of State. **32–210a**

(2) On receiving the notice, the Secretary of State must endorse those particulars or penalty points on the person's driving record.

(3) A notice sent by the court to the Secretary of State in pursuance of this section must be sent in such manner and to such address and contain such particulars as the Secretary of State may require.]

[This section is inserted, as from a day to be appointed, by the *RSA* 2006, s.9(1) and (3).]

Road Traffic Offenders Act 1988, s.45

Effect of endorsement [of counterparts]

45.—(1) An order that any particulars or penalty points are to be endorsed on [the counterpart of] any licence held by the person convicted shall, *whether he is at the time the holder of a licence or not*, operate as an order that [the counterpart of] any licence he may then hold or may subsequently obtain is to be so endorsed until he becomes entitled under subsection (4) below to have a licence issued to him [with its counterpart] free from the particulars or penalty points. **32–211**

(2) On the issue of a new licence to a person, any particulars or penalty points ordered to be endorsed on [the counterpart of] any licence held by him shall be entered on [the counterpart of] the licence unless he has become entitled under subsection (4) below to have a licence issued to him [with its counterpart] free from those particulars or penalty points.

(3) [*Repealed.*]

(4) A person [the counterpart of] whose licence has been ordered to be endorsed is entitled to have *a new licence issued to him free from the endorsement if, after the end of the period for which the endorsement remains effective*, [issued to him with effect from the end of the period for which the endorsement remains effective a new licence with a counterpart free from the endorsement if] he applies for a new licence in pursuance of section 97(1) of the *Road Traffic Act* 1988, surrenders any subsisting licence [and its counterpart], pays the fee prescribed by regulations under Part III of that Act and satisfies the other requirements of section 97(1).

(5) An endorsement ordered on a person's conviction of an offence remains effective (subject to subsections (6) and (7) below)—

(a) if an order is made for the disqualification of the offender, until four years have elapsed since the conviction, and

(b) if no such order is made, until either—

(i) four years have elapsed since the commission of the offence, or

(ii) an order is made for the disqualification of the offender under section 35 of this Act.

(6) Where the offence was one under section 1 or 2 of *that Act* [[the *Road Traffic Act* 1988]] (causing death by dangerous driving and dangerous driving) the endorsement remains in any case effective until four years have elapsed since the conviction.

(7) Where the offence was one—

(a) [[under]] section 3A, 4(1) or (5)(1)(a) of that Act (driving offences connected with drink or drugs),

(b) under section 7(6) of that Act (failing to provide specimen) involving obligatory disqualification, or

(c) under section 7A(6) of that Act (failing to allow a specimen to be subjected to laboratory test),

the endorsement remains effective until eleven years have elapsed since the conviction.

[This section is printed as amended, and repealed in part, by the *Road Traffic (Driver Licensing and Information Systems) Act* 1989, ss.7 and 16, and Scheds 3, para. 25, and 6; S.I. 1990 No. 144 (*ante*, § 32–210) (insertion of words in single square brackets—in substitution for italicised words in subs. (4)—in relation to licences which came into force after May 31, 1990); the *RTA* 1991, s.48, and Sched. 4, para. 99; and the *RSA* 2006, ss.14 (insertion of subs. (7)(c) with effect from September 24, 2007 (*Road Safety Act 2006 (Commencement No. 2) Order* 2007 (S.I. 2007 No. 2472)), but only in relation to offences committed on or after that date (2006 Act, s.61(3)) and 59, and Sched. 7(5). As from a day to be appointed, the words in square brackets in the heading, and the words in double square brackets, are inserted, and the italicised words in subss. (1) and (6) are omitted: *RSA* 2006, ss.9(6), 58(3) and 59, Sched. 2, paras 2 and 9, and Sched. 7(3). As from a later date (see s.61(8) of the 2006 Act), the whole section is repealed: *ibid.*, ss.10(1) and (12) and 59, Sched. 3, paras 30 and 41, and Sched. 7(4).]

Road Traffic Offenders Act 1988, s.45A

[Effect of endorsement on driving records

32–211a **45A.**—(1) An order that any particulars or penalty points are to be endorsed on a person's driving record shall operate as an order that his driving record is to be so endorsed until the end of the period for which the endorsement remains effective.

(2) At the end of the period for which the endorsement remains effective the Secretary of State must remove the endorsement from the person's driving record.

(3) *On the issue of a new licence to a person, any particulars ordered to be endorsed on his driving record shall be entered on the counterpart of the licence unless he has become entitled under subsection (4) below to have a licence issued to him with its counterpart free from those particulars or penalty points.*

(4) *A person the counterpart of whose licence has been endorsed under subsection (3) above is entitled to have issued to him with effect from the end of the period for which the endorsement remains effective a new licence with a counterpart free from the endorsement if he applies for a new licence in pursuance of section 97(1) of the* Road Traffic Act *1988, surrenders any subsisting licence and its counterpart, pays the fee prescribed by regulations under Part 3 of that Act and satisfies the other requirements of section 97(1).*

(5) *The period for which an endorsement remains effective is determined in accordance with section 45(5) or (7) of this Act.*]

[[(3) An endorsement ordered on a person's conviction of an offence remains effective (subject to subsections (4) and (5) below)—

(a) if an order is made for the disqualification of the offender, until four years have elapsed since conviction, and

(b) if no such order is made, until either—

(i) four years have elapsed since the commission of the offence, or

(ii) an order is made for the disqualification of the offender under section 35 of this Act.

(4) Where the offence was one under section 1 or 2 of the *Road Traffic Act* 1988 (causing death by dangerous driving and dangerous driving), the endorsement remains in any case effective until four years have elapsed since the conviction.

(5) Where the offence was one—

(a) under section 3A, 4(1) or 5(1)(a) of that Act (driving offences connected with drink or drugs),

(b) under section 7(6) of that Act (failing to provide specimen) involving obligatory disqualification, or

(c) under section 7A(6) of that Act (failing to allow a specimen to be subjected to laboratory test),

the endorsement remains effective until eleven years have elapsed since the conviction.]]

[Section 45A is inserted, as from a day to be appointed, by the *RSA* 2006, s.9(6), and Sched. 2, paras 2 and 10. Subss. (3) to (5) in double square brackets are substituted for subss. (3) to (5) in italics as from a later date (see s.61(8) of the 2006 Act): 2006 Act, s.10(1) and (12), and Sched. 3, paras 30 and 42.]

(16) New drivers

The *Road Traffic (New Drivers) Act* 1995 provides for the revocation of the driving licences of new drivers who accumulate six or more penalty points within a probationary period of two years after the driver first becomes qualified. A driver whose licence is thus revoked must pass a further test to regain the entitlement to drive. **32–212**

Road Traffic (New Drivers) Act 1995, ss.1–3

Probationary period for newly qualified drivers

1.—(1) For the purposes of this Act, a person's probationary period is, subject to section 7, the period of two years beginning with the day on which he becomes a qualified driver. **32–213**

(2) For the purposes of this Act, a person becomes a qualified driver on the first occasion on which he passes—

(a) any test of competence to drive mentioned in paragraph (a) or (c) of section 89(1) of the *Road Traffic Act* 1988;

(b) any test of competence to drive conducted under the law of—

(i) another EEA State;

(ii) the Isle of Man;

(iii) any of the Channel Islands, or

(iv) Gibraltar.

(3) In subsection (2) "EEA State" means a State which is a contracting party to the EEA Agreement but until the EEA Agreement comes into force in relation to Liechtenstein does not include the State of Liechtenstein.

(4) In subsection (3) "EEA Agreement" means the Agreement on the European Economic Area signed at Oporto on 2nd May 1992 as adjusted by the Protocol signed at Brussels on 17th March 1993.

[This section is printed as amended by S.I. 1996 No. 1974 (*ante*, § 32–111).]

Surrender of licences

2.—(1) Subsection (2) applies where— **32–214**

(a) a person is the holder of a licence;

(b) he is convicted of an offence involving obligatory endorsement;

(c) the penalty points to be taken into account under section 29 of the *Road Traffic Offenders Act* 1988 on that occasion number six or more;

(d) the court makes an order falling within section 44(1)(b) of that Act in respect of the offence;

(e) the person's licence shows the date on which he became a qualified driver, or that date has been shown by other evidence in the proceedings; and

(f) it appears to the court, in the light of the order and the date so shown, that the offence was committed during the person's probationary period.

(2) *Where this subsection applies, the court must send to the Secretary of State—*

(a) *a notice containing the particulars required to be endorsed on the counterpart of the person's licence in accordance with the order referred to in subsection (1)(d); and*

(b) *on their production to the court, the person's licence and its counterpart.*

[(2) Where this subsection applies, the court must, together with the notice of the order referred to in subsection (1)(d) required to be sent to the Secretary of State under section 44A of the *Road Traffic Offenders Act* 1988, send the person's licence on its production to the court.]

(3) Subsection (4) applies where—

(a) a person's licence and its counterpart have been sent to the fixed penalty clerk under section 54(7) of the *Road Traffic Offenders Act* 1988 [, retained by a vehicle examiner under that section] or delivered to the *fixed penalty clerk* [appropriate person] in response to a conditional offer issued under section 75 of that Act;

(b) the offence to which the fixed penalty notice or the conditional offer relates is one involving obligatory endorsement;

(c) the *fixed penalty clerk* [appropriate person] endorses the number of penalty points to be attributed to the offence on the counterpart of the licence;

(d) the penalty points to be taken into account by the *fixed penalty clerk* [appropriate person] in respect of the offence number six or more;

(e) the licence shows the date on which the person became a qualified driver; and

(f) it appears to the *fixed penalty clerk* [appropriate person], in the light of the particulars of the offence endorsed on the counterpart of the licence and the date so shown, that the offence was committed during the person's probationary period.

(4) Where this subsection applies, *the fixed penalty clerk*—

(a) [the appropriate person] may not return the licence and its counterpart under section 57(3) or (4) or 77(1) of the *Road Traffic Offenders Act* 1988; but

(b) [unless the appropriate person is the Secretary of State, he] must send them to the Secretary of State.

(5) For the purposes of subsection (3)(d) the penalty points to be taken into account *by the fixed penalty clerk* in respect of the offence are the penalty points which would have been taken into account under section 29 of the *Road Traffic Offenders Act* 1988 if—

(a) the person in question had been convicted of the offence; and

(b) the number of penalty points to be attributed to the offence on that occasion had been determined in accordance with section 28(3) of that Act.

(6) In this section and section 3 "licence" includes a Northern Ireland licence.

[(7) In this section and section 3—

"the appropriate person", in relation to a fixed penalty notice, means—

(a) if it was given by a constable or an authorised person, the fixed penalty clerk, and

(b) if it was given by a vehicle examiner or the Secretary of State, the Secretary of State, and

"the appropriate person", in relation to a conditional offer, means—

(a) where the conditional offer was issued under subsection (1), (2) or (3) of section 75 of the *Road Traffic Offenders Act* 1988, the fixed penalty clerk, and

(b) where it was issued under subsection (1A) or (3B) of that section, the Secretary of State.]

[This section is printed as amended by the *Crime (International Co-operation) Act* 2003, s.91, and Sched. 5, para. 46. The italicised words (other than titles of Acts) in subss. (3) to (5) are omitted, and the words in square brackets in those subsections are inserted, together with subs. (7), as from a day to be appointed by the *RSA* 2006, ss.5 and 59, Sched. 1, paras 24 and 25, and Sched. 7(2). Also as from a date to be appointed (presumably a later date), the 2006 Act, s.10(1) and (12), and Sched. 3, paras 66 and 67, make the following further amendments: (i) subs. (2) (in square brackets) is substituted for subs. (2) (in italics); (ii) in subs. (3)(a), the word "has" is substituted for the words "and its counterpart have"; (iii) in subs. (3)(c), the words "appropriate person endorses the number of" are repealed, and the words "are to be endorsed on the person's driving record" are substituted for the words "on the counterpart of the licence"; (iv) in subs. (3)(f), the words "to be" are inserted before the word "endorsed" and the words "person's driving record" are substituted for the words "counterpart of the licence"; (v) in subs. (4)(a), the words "and its counterpart" are repealed, and the words "57A(3) or (4) or 77A(2)" are substituted for the words "57(3) or (4) or 77(1)"; and (vi) in subs. (4)(b), the words "together with the notice he is required to send under section 57A or 77A of that Act of the particulars to be endorsed on the person's driving record" are inserted at the end.]

Revocation of licences

32–215 **3.**—(1) Where the Secretary of State receives—

(a) a notice sent to him under section 2(2)(a) of particulars required to be endorsed on the counterpart of a person's licence, or

(b) a person's licence and its counterpart sent to him in accordance with section 2(2)(b) or *(4)* [(4)(b)],

the Secretary of State must by notice served on that person revoke the licence.

[(1) Where the Secretary of State receives—

(a) a notice sent to him under section 44A, 57A or 77A of the *Road Traffic Offenders Act* 1988 of particulars required to be endorsed on a person's driving record, and

(b) a person's licence sent to him in accordance with section 2(2) or (4)(b), the Secretary of State must by notice served on that person revoke the licence.]

[(1ZA) Where section 2(4)(a) applies but the appropriate person is the Secretary of State, the Secretary of State must by notice served on the person to whom the fixed penalty notice or conditional offer was given or issued, revoke that person's licence.]

(1A) Where the Secretary of State serves on the holder of a Northern Ireland licence a notice under subsection (1) [or (1ZA)], the Secretary of State must send to the licensing authority in Northern Ireland—

(a) particulars of the notice; and

(b) the Northern Ireland licence.

(1B) Where the Secretary of State is sent by that licensing authority particulars of a notice served on the holder of a licence under a provision of Northern Ireland law corresponding to subsection (1) [or (1ZA)], he must by notice served on the holder revoke the licence.

(2) A revocation under *subsection (1) or (1B)* [this section] shall have effect from a date specified in the notice of revocation which may not be earlier than the date of service of that notice.

(3) In this section references to the revocation of a person's Northern Ireland licence are references to its revocation as respects Great Britain; and, accordingly, the person ceases to be authorised by virtue of section 109(1) of the *Road Traffic Act* 1988 to drive in Great Britain a motor vehicle of any class.

[This section is printed as amended by the *Crime (International Co-operation) Act* 2003, s.91, and Sched. 5, para. 47. The words in square brackets in subss. (1), (1A), (1B) and (2) are inserted, together with subs. (1ZA), and the italicised words in subss. (1) and (2) are omitted, as from a day to be appointed, by the *RSA* 2006, s.5, and Sched. 1, paras 24 and 26. Also as from a date to be appointed (presumably a later date), the 2006 Act, s.10(1) and (12), and Sched. 3, paras 66 and 68, further amend this section by substituting a new subs. (1) (in square brackets).]

Once the licence has been revoked a further licence cannot be issued until the driver has passed a driving test. The test must be passed within two years of the order revoking the licence. If there is an appeal against conviction or the endorsement which formed the basis of the revocation of the licence, then the licence cannot be revoked (ss.4 and 5 of the Act). There are similar provisions for those drivers who hold a provisional licence and a test certificate rather than a full licence.

(17) Miscellaneous and general

Road Traffic Offenders Act 1988, ss.46, 47, 49

Combination of disqualification and endorsement with probation orders and orders for discharge

46.—(1) Notwithstanding anything in section 14(3) of the *Powers of Criminal Courts (Sentencing) Act* 2000 (conviction of offender discharged to be disregarded for the purposes of enactments relating to disqualification), a court in England and Wales which on convicting a person of an offence involving obligatory or discretionary disqualification makes— **32–216**

(a) *[repealed by* CJA *2003, s.304, and Sched. 32, paras 52 and 54*]

(b) an order discharging him absolutely or conditionally,

may on that occasion also exercise any power conferred, and must also discharge any duty imposed, on the court by sections 34, 35, 36 *or 44* [[, 44 or 44A]] of this Act.

(2) A conviction—

(a) in respect of which a court in England and Wales has ordered a person to be disqualified, or

(b) of which particulars have been endorsed on [the counterpart of] any licence held by him [[or on his driving record]],

is to be taken into account, notwithstanding anything in section 14(1) of the *Powers of Criminal Courts (Sentencing) Act* 2000 (conviction of offender discharged to be disregarded for the purpose of subsequent proceedings), in determining his liability to punishment or disqualification for any offence involving obligatory or discretionary disqualification committed subsequently.

(3) [*Scotland*.]

[This section is printed as amended by S.I. 1990 No. 144 (*ante*, § 32–210) (insertion of words in square brackets in relation to licences issued after May 31, 1990); the *CJA*

1991, ss.100, and 101(2), and Scheds 11, para. 38, and 13; and the *PCC(S)A* 2000, s.165(1), and Sched. 9, para. 123. The italicised words (other than titles of Acts) are omitted, and the words in double square brackets are inserted, as from a day to be appointed, by the *RSA* 2006, s.9(6), and Sched. 2, paras 2 and 11. As from a later date (see s.61(8) of the 2006 Act), the words "the counterpart of any licence held by him or on" in subs. (2)(b) are repealed by the 2006 Act, ss.10(1) and (12) and 59, Sched. 3, paras 30 and 43, and Sched. 7(4).]

Supplementary provisions as to disqualifications and endorsements

32–217 **47.**—(1) In any case where a court exercises its power under section 34, 35 or 44 of this Act not to order any disqualification or endorsement or to order disqualification for a shorter period than would otherwise be required, it must state the grounds for doing so in open court and, if it is a magistrates' court or, in Scotland, a court of summary jurisdiction, must cause them to be entered in the register (in Scotland, record) of its proceedings.

(2) Where a court orders the endorsement of [the counterpart of] any licence held by a person it may, and where a court orders the holder of a licence to be disqualified for a period of 56 days or more it must, send the licence [and its counterpart], on *its* [their] being produced to the court, to the Secretary of State, and if the court orders the endorsement but does not send the licence [and its counterpart] to the Secretary of State it must send him notice of the endorsement.

[[(2) Where a court orders the endorsement of a person's driving record it may, and where a court orders a person to be disqualified for a period of 56 days or more it must, send any licence of the person that is produced to the court, to the Secretary of State.]]

(2A) Subsection (2) above is subject to section 2(2) of and paragraph 7(2) of Schedule 1 to the *Road Traffic (New Drivers) Act* 1995 (obligations of court to send licence and its counterpart to the Secretary of State).

(3) Where on an appeal against an order for the endorsement of a licence [[or a driving record]] or the disqualification of a person the appeal is allowed, the court by which the appeal is allowed must send notice of that fact to the Secretary of State.

[[(3A) On receiving such a notice in relation to a person who is not the holder of a licence, the Secretary of State must make any necessary adjustments to the endorsements on the person's driving record to reflect the outcome of the appeal.]]

(4) A notice sent by a court to the Secretary of State in pursuance of this section must be sent in such manner and to such address and contain such particulars as the Secretary of State may determine, and a licence [and the counterpart of a licence] so sent in pursuance of this section must be sent to such an address as the Secretary of State may determine.

[This section is printed as amended by S.I. 1990 No. 144 (*ante*, § 32–210) (insertion of words in square brackets—in substitution for italicised word in subs. (2)—in relation to licences issued after May 31, 1990); the *RTA* 1991, s.48 and Sched. 4, para. 100; and the *Road Traffic (New Drivers) Act* 1995, Sched. 2, para. 4. The words in double square brackets in subs. (3) and subs. (3A) are inserted, as from a day to be appointed, by the *RSA* 2006, s.9(6), and Sched. 2, paras 2 and 12. As from a later date (see s.61(8) of the 2006 Act), subs. (2) (in double square brackets) is substituted for the current subs. (2), and the words "and its counterpart" in subs. (2A), "a licence or" in subs. (3), "in relation to a person who is not the holder of a licence" in subs. (3A) and "and the counterpart of a licence" in subs. (4) are repealed: 2006 Act, ss.10(1) and (12) and 59, Sched. 3, paras 30 and 44, and Sched. 7(4).]

The requirement that a court state the grounds for not disqualifying is directory and not mandatory, and a mere failure to comply is not of itself a ground of appeal by the prosecution: *Brown v. Dyerson* [1969] 1 Q.B. 45; 59 Cr.App.R. 630, DC. *Aliter*, if the court refuses to state the grounds for non-disqualification: *Barnes v. Gevaux* [1981] R.T.R. 236, DC.

Offender escaping consequences of endorseable offence by deception

32–218 **49.**—(1) This section applies where in dealing with a person convicted of an offence involving obligatory endorsement a court was deceived regarding any circumstances that were or might have been taken into account in deciding whether or for how long to disqualify him.

(2) If—

(a) the deception constituted or was due to an offence committed by that person, and

(b) he is convicted of that offence,

the court by or before which he is convicted shall have the same powers and duties regarding an order for disqualification as had the court which dealt with him for the offence involving obligatory endorsement but must, in dealing with him, take into account any order made on his conviction of the offence involving obligatory endorsement.

(18) Interpretation

Road Traffic Offenders Act 1988, ss.96, 97

Meaning of "offence involving obligatory endorsement"

96. For the purposes of this Act, an offence involves obligatory endorsement if it is an offence under a provision of the Traffic Acts specified in column 1 of Part I of Schedule 2 to this Act or an offence specified in column 1 of Part II of that Schedule and either— **32–219**

(a) the word "obligatory" (without qualification) appears in column 6 (in the case of Part I) or column 3 (in the case of Part II) against the offence, or

(b) that word appears there qualified by conditions relating to the offence which are satisfied.

Meaning of "offence involving obligatory disqualification" and "offence involving discretionary disqualification"

97.—(1) For the purposes of this Act, an offence involves obligatory disqualification if it is an offence under a provision of the Traffic Acts specified in column 1 of Part I of Schedule 2 to this Act or an offence specified in column 1 of Part II of that Schedule and either— **32–220**

(a) the word "obligatory" (without qualification) appears in column 5 (in the case of Part I) or column 2 (in the case of Part II) against the offence, or

(b) that word appears there qualified by conditions relating to the offence which are satisfied or obtain.

(2) For the purposes of this Act, an offence involves discretionary disqualification if it is an offence under a provision of the Traffic Acts specified in column 1 of Part I of Schedule 2 to this Act or an offence specified in column 1 of Part II of that Schedule and either—

(a) the word "discretionary" (without qualification) appears in column 5 (in the case of Part I) or column 2 (in the case of Part II) against the offence, or

(b) that word appears there qualified by conditions relating to the offence which are satisfied or obtain.

U. PROSECUTION AND PUNISHMENT OF OFFENCES

In relation to Schedule 2 to the *RTOA* 1988 (*post*), see, in particular the following sections of the Act: 9 (mode of trial) (*ante*, § 32–159), 28 (penalty points) (*ante*, § 32–175), 33 (fine and imprisonment) (*ante*, § 32–179), 34 (disqualification) (*ante*, § 32–181), 44 (endorsement) (*ante*, § 32–210), 96 (meaning of "offence involving obligatory endorsement") (*ante*, § 32–219), and 97 (meaning of "offence involving obligatory disqualification" and meaning of "offence involving discretionary disqualification") (*ante*, § 32–220). **32–221**

In the extract from Schedule 2 set out, *post*, only those entries relating to offences triable on indictment or which carry obligatory or discretionary endorsement or which are dealt with in detail in this chapter are included.

Road Traffic Offenders Act 1988, Sched. 2

Section 9

SCHEDULE 2

PROSECUTION AND PUNISHMENT OF OFFENCES, ETC.

PART I

Offences under the Traffic Acts

(1) *Provision creating offence*	(2) *General nature of offence*	(3) *Mode of prosecution*	(4) *Punishment*	(5) *Disqualification*	(6) *Endorsement*	(7) *Penalty points*
		Offences under the Road Traffic Regulation Act 1984				
RTRA section 16(1)	Contravention of temporary prohibition or restriction.	Summarily.	Level 3 on the standard scale.	Discretionary if committed in respect of a speed restriction.	Obligatory if committed in respect of a speed restriction.	3–6 or 3 (fixed penalty)
RTRA section 17(4)	Use of special road contrary to scheme or regulations.	Summarily.	Level 4 on the standard scale.	Discretionary if committed in respect of a motor vehicle otherwise than by unlawfully stopping or allowing the vehicle to remain at rest on a part of a special road on which vehicles are in certain circumstances permitted to remain at rest.	Obligatory if committed as mentioned in the entry in column 5.	*3–6 or 3 (fixed penalty) if committed in respect of a speed restriction* [2-6 or appropriate penalty points (fixed

(1) *Provision creating offence*	(2) *General nature of offence*	(3) *Mode of prosecution*	(4) *Punishment*	(5) *Disqualification*	(6) *Endorsement*	(7) *Penalty points*
			Offences under the Road Traffic Regulation Act 1984			
						penalty) if committed in respect of a speed limit], 3 in any other case.
RTRA section 25(5)	Contravention of pedestrian crossing regulations.	Summarily.	Level 3 on the standard scale.	Discretionary if committed in respect of a motor vehicle.	Obligatory if committed in respect of a motor vehicle.	3
RTRA section 28(3)	Not stopping at school crossing.	Summarily.	Level 3 on the standard scale.	Discretionary if committed in respect of a motor vehicle.	Obligatory if committed in respect of a motor vehicle.	3
RTRA section 29(3)	Contravention of order relating to street playground.	Summarily.	Level 3 on the standard scale.	Discretionary if committed in respect of a motor vehicle.	Obligatory if committed in respect of a motor vehicle.	2
RTRA section 89(1)	Exceeding speed limit.	Summarily.	Level 3 on the standard scale.	Discretionary.	Obligatory.	*3–6 or 3* [2-6 or appropriate penalty points] (fixed penalty)

(1) *Provision creating offence*	(2) *General nature of offence*	(3) *Mode of prosecution*	(4) *Punishment*	(5) *Disqualification*	(6) *Endorsement*	(7) *Penalty points*
		Offences under the Road Traffic Regulation Act 1984				
RTRA section 115(1)	Mishandling or faking parking documents.	(a) Summarily. (b) On indictment.	(a) The statutory maximum. (b) 2 years.			

(1) *Provision creating offence*	(2) *General nature of offence*	(3) *Mode of prosecution*	(4) *Punishment*	(5) *Disqualification*	(6) *Endorsement*	(7) *Penalty points*
		Offences under the Road Traffic Act 1988				
RTA section 1	Causing death by dangerous driving.	On indictment.	14 years.	Obligatory.	Obligatory.	3–11
RTA section 2	Dangerous driving.	(a) Summarily. (b) On indictment.	(a) *6* [12] months or the statutory maximum or both. (b) 2 years or a fine or both.	Obligatory.	Obligatory.	3–11
RTA section 2B	Causing death by careless, or inconsiderate, driving.	(a) Summarily. (b) On indictment.	(a) 12 months (in England and Wales) or 6 months (in Scotland) or the statutory maximum or both. (b) 5 years or a fine or both.	Obligatory.	Obligatory.	3–11
RTA section 3	Careless, and inconsiderate, driving.	Summarily.	Level 5 on the standard scale.	Discretionary.	Obligatory.	3–9

(1) *Provision creating offence*	(2) *General nature of offence*	(3) *Mode of prosecution*	(4) *Punishment*	(5) *Disqualification*	(6) *Endorsement*	(7) *Penalty points*
Offences under the Road Traffic Act 1988						
RTA section 3ZB	Causing death by driving: unlicensed, disqualified or uninsured drivers.	(a) Summarily. (b) On indictment.	(a) 12 months (in England and Wales) or 6 months (in Scotland) or the statutory maximum or both. (b) 2 years or a fine or both.	Obligatory.	Obligatory.	3–11
RTA section 3A	Causing death by careless driving when under influence of drink or drugs.	On indictment.	14 years or a fine or both.	Obligatory.	Obligatory.	3–11
RTA section 4(1)	Driving or attempting to drive when unfit to drive through drink or drugs.	Summarily.	*6 months* [51 weeks] or level 5 on the standard scale or both.	Obligatory.	Obligatory.	3–11
RTA section 4(2)	Being in charge of a mechanically propelled vehicle when unfit to drive through drink or drugs.	Summarily.	*3 months* [51 weeks] or level 4 on the standard scale or both.	Discretionary.	Obligatory.	10

(1) *Provision creating offence*	(2) *General nature of offence*	(3) *Mode of prosecution*	(4) *Punishment*	(5) *Disqualification*	(6) *Endorsement*	(7) *Penalty points*
			Offences under the Road Traffic Act 1988			
RTA section 5(1)(a)	Driving or attempting to drive with excess alcohol in breath, blood or urine.	Summarily.	*6 months* [51 weeks] or level 5 on the standard scale or both.	Obligatory.	Obligatory.	3–11
RTA section 5(1)(b)	Being in charge of a motor vehicle with excess alcohol in breath, blood or urine.	Summarily.	*3 months* [51 weeks] or level 4 on the standard scale or both.	Discretionary.	Obligatory.	10
RTA section 6	Failing to co-operate with a preliminary test.	Summarily.	Level 3 on the standard scale.	Discretionary.	Obligatory.	4

(1) *Provision creating offence*	(2) *General nature of offence*	(3) *Mode of prosecution*	(4) *Punishment*	(5) *Disqualification*	(6) *Endorsement*	(7) *Penalty points*
Offences under the Road Traffic Act 1988						
RTA section 7	Failing to provide specimen for analysis or laboratory test.	Summarily.	(a) Where the specimen was required to ascertain ability to drive or proportion of alcohol at the time offender was driving or attempting to drive, 6 *months* [51 weeks] or level 5 on the standard scale or both.	(a) Obligatory in case mentioned in column 4(a).	Obligatory.	(a) 3–11 in case mentioned in column 4(a).
			(b) In any other case, 3 *months* [51 weeks] or level 4 on the standard scale or both.	(b) Discretionary in any other case.		(b) 10 in any other case.
RTA section 7A	Failing to allow specimen to be subjected to laboratory test.	Summarily.	(a) Where the test would be for ascertaining ability to drive or proportion of alcohol at the time offender was driving or attempting to drive, 6 *months* [51 weeks] or level 5 on the standard scale or both.	(a) Obligatory in case mentioned in column 4(a).	Obligatory.	3–11, in case mentioned in column 4(a) 10 in any other case.
			(b) In any other case, 3 *months* [51 weeks] or level 4 on the standard scale or both.	(b) Discretionary in any other case.		

(1) *Provision creating offence*	(2) *General nature of offence*	(3) *Mode of prosecution*	(4) *Punishment*	(5) *Disqualification*	(6) *Endorsement*	(7) *Penalty points*
			Offences under the Road Traffic Act 1988			
RTA section 12	Motor racing and speed trials on public ways.	Summarily.	Level 4 on the standard scale.	Obligatory.	Obligatory.	3–11
RTA section 22	Leaving vehicles in dangerous positions.	Summarily.	Level 3 on the standard scale.	Discretionary if committed in respect of a motor vehicle.	Obligatory if committed in respect of a motor vehicle.	3
RTA section 22A	Causing danger to road-users.	(a) Summarily.	(a) *6* [12] months or the statutory maximum or both.			
		(b) On indictment.	(b) 7 years or a fine or both.			
RTA section 23	Carrying passenger on motor-cycle contrary to section 23.	Summarily.	Level 3 on the standard scale.	Discretionary.	Obligatory.	3
RTA section 35	Failing to comply with traffic directions.	Summarily.	Level 3 on the standard scale.	Discretionary, if committed in respect of a motor vehicle by failure to comply with a direction of a constable, traffic officer or traffic warden.	Obligatory if committed as described in column 5	3

(1) *Provision creating offence*	(2) *General nature of offence*	(3) *Mode of prosecution*	(4) *Punishment*	(5) *Disqualification*	(6) *Endorsement*	(7) *Penalty points*
			Offences under the Road Traffic Act 1988			
RTA section 36	Failing to comply with traffic signs.	Summarily.	Level 3 on the standard scale.	Discretionary, if committed in respect of a motor vehicle by failure to comply with an indication given by a sign specified for the purposes of this paragraph in regulations under *RTA* section 36.	Obligatory if committed as described in column 5	3
RTA section 40A	Using vehicle in dangerous condition, etc.	Summarily.	(a) Level 5 on the standard scale if committed in respect of a goods vehicle or a vehicle adapted to carry more than eight passengers. (b) Level 4 on the standard scale in any other case.	(a) Obligatory if committed within three years of a previous conviction of the offender under section 40A. (b) Discretionary in any other case.	Obligatory.	3
RTA section 41A	Breach of requirement as to brakes, steering-gear or tyres.	Summarily.	(a) Level 5 on the standard scale if committed in respect of a goods vehicle or a vehicle adapted to carry more than eight passengers. (b) Level 4 on the standard scale in any other case.	Discretionary.	Obligatory.	3

(1) *Provision creating offence*	(2) *General nature of offence*	(3) *Mode of prosecution*	(4) *Punishment*	(5) *Disqualification*	(6) *Endorsement*	(7) *Penalty points*
			Offences under the Road Traffic Act 1988			
[*RTA* section 41C	Breach of requirement as to speed assessment equipment detection devices.	Summarily.	(a) Level 4 on the standard scale if committed on a special road. (b) Level 3 on the standard scale in any other case.	Discretionary.	Obligatory.	3–6 or 3 (fixed penalty).]
RTA section 41D	Breach of requirements as to control of vehicle, mobile telephones etc.	Summarily.	(a) Level 4 on the standard scale if committed in respect of a goods vehicle or a vehicle adapted to carry more than eight passengers. (b) Level 3 on the standard scale in any other case.	Discretionary.	Obligatory.	3.
RTA section 87(1)	Driving otherwise than in accordance with a licence.	Summarily.	Level 3 on the standard scale.	Discretionary in a case where the offender's driving would not have been in accordance with any licence that could have been granted to him.	Obligatory in the case mentioned in column 5	3–6
RTA section 92(10)	Driving after making false declaration as to physical fitness.	Summarily.	Level 4 on the standard scale.	Discretionary.	Obligatory.	3–6

(1) *Provision creating offence*	(2) *General nature of offence*	(3) *Mode of prosecution*	(4) *Punishment*	(5) *Disqualification*	(6) *Endorsement*	(7) *Penalty points*
			Offences under the Road Traffic Act 1988			
RTA section 94(3A) and that subsection as applied by *RTA* section 99D(b)	Driving after such a failure or 109C(c).	Summarily.	Level 3 on the standard scale.	Discretionary.	Obligatory.	3–6
RTA section 94A	Driving after refusal of licence under section 92(3), revocation under section 93 or service of a notice under section 99C or 109B.	Summarily.	*6 months* [51 weeks] or level 5 on the standard scale or both.	Discretionary.	Obligatory.	3–6
RTA section 96	Driving with uncorrected defective eyesight, or refusing to submit to test of eyesight.	Summarily.	Level 3 on the standard scale.	Discretionary.	Obligatory.	3
RTA section 103(1)(a)	Obtaining driving licence while disqualified.	Summarily.	Level 3 on the standard scale.			

(1) *Provision creating offence*	(2) *General nature of offence*	(3) *Mode of prosecution*	(4) *Punishment*	(5) *Disqualification*	(6) *Endorsement*	(7) *Penalty points*
			Offences under the Road Traffic Act 1988			
RTA section 103(1)(b)	Driving while disqualified.	(a) Summarily, in England and Wales. (b) [*Scotland*.] (c) [*Scotland*.]	(a) *6 months* [51 weeks] or level 5 on the standard scale or both. (b) [*Scotland*.] (c) [*Scotland*.]	Discretionary.	Obligatory.	6
RTA section 143	Using motor vehicle while uninsured or unsecured against third-party risks.	Summarily.	Level 5 on the standard scale.	Discretionary.	Obligatory.	6–8
[Regulations under *RTA* section 160 made by virtue of paragraph 2(4) of Schedule 2A	Contravention of provision of regulations (which is declared by regulations to be an offence) prohibiting making of false or misleading declaration to secure release of vehicle from immobilisation device.	(a) Summarily. (b) On indictment.	(a) The statutory maximum. (b) 2 years or a fine or both.]			

(1) *Provision creating offence*	(2) *General nature of offence*	(3) *Mode of prosecution*	(4) *Punishment*	(5) *Disqualification*	(6) *Endorsement*	(7) *Penalty points*
			Offences under the Road Traffic Act 1988			
[Regulations under *RTA* section 160 made by virtue of paragraph 4 of Schedule 2A	Contravention of provision of regulations (which is declared by regulations to be an offence) prohibiting making of false or misleading declaration to secure possession of vehicle in person's custody.	(a) Summarily. (b) On indictment.	(a) The statutory maximum. (b) 2 years or a fine or both.]			
RTA section 163	Failing to stop mechanically propelled vehicle or cycle when required.	Summarily.	(a) Level 5 on the standard scale if committed by a person driving a mechanically propelled vehicle. (b) Level 3 on the standard scale if committed by a person riding a cycle.			

(1) *Provision creating offence*	(2) *General nature of offence*	(3) *Mode of prosecution*	(4) *Punishment*	(5) *Disqualification*	(6) *Endorsement*	(7) *Penalty points*
			Offences under the Road Traffic Act 1988			
RTA section 164	Failing to produce driving licence *and counterpart, etc.* or to state date of birth, or failing to provide the Secretary of State with evidence of date of birth, etc.	Summarily.	Level 3 on the standard scale.			
RTA section 165	Failing to give ... certain names and addresses or to provide certain documents.	Summarily.	Level 3 on the standard scale.			
RTA section 170(4)	Failing to stop after accident and give particulars or report accident.	Summarily.	*6 months* [51 weeks] or level 5 on the standard scale or both.	Discretionary.	Obligatory.	5–10

(1) *Provision creating offence*	(2) *General nature of offence*	(3) *Mode of prosecution*	(4) *Punishment*	(5) *Disqualification*	(6) *Endorsement*	(7) *Penalty points*
		Offences under the Road Traffic Act 1988				
RTA section 170(7)	Failure by owner of motor vehicle to give police information for verifying compliance with requirement of compulsory insurance security.	Summarily.	Level 4 on the standard scale.			
RTA section 172	Failure of person keeping vehicle and others to give police information as to identity of driver, etc., in the case of certain offences.	Summarily.	Level 3 on the standard scale.	Discretionary, if committed otherwise than by virtue of subsection (5) or (11).	Obligatory, if committed otherwise than by virtue of subsection (5) or (11).	6

(1) *Provision creating offence*	(2) *General nature of offence*	(3) *Mode of prosecution*	(4) *Punishment*	(5) *Disqualification*	(6) *Endorsement*	(7) *Penalty points*
		Offences under the Road Traffic Act 1988				
RTA section 173	Forgery, etc., of licences, *counterparts of Community licences*, test certificates, certificates of insurance and other documents and things.	(a) Summarily. (b) On indictment	(a) The statutory maximum. (b) 2 years			
RTA section 174	Making certain false statements, etc., and withholding certain material information.	(a) Summarily. (b) On indictment	(a) *6* [12] months or the statutory maximum or both (b) 2 years or a fine or both			

PART II

Other Offences

(1)	(2)	(3)	(4)
Offence	*Disqualification*	*Endorsement*	*Penalty points*
Manslaughter or, in Scotland, culpable homicide by the driver of a motor vehicle.	Obligatory.	Obligatory.	3–11
An offence under section 35 of the *Offences against the Person Act* 1861 (furious driving).	Discretionary.	Obligatory if committed in respect of a mechanically propelled vehicle.	3–9
An offence under section 12A of the *Theft Act* 1968 (aggravated vehicle-taking).	Obligatory.	Obligatory.	3–11
Stealing or attempting to steal a motor vehicle.	Discretionary.		
An offence or attempt to commit an offence in respect of a motor vehicle under section 12 of the *Theft Act* 1968 (taking conveyance without consent of owner etc. or, knowing it has been so taken, driving it or allowing oneself to be carried in it).	Discretionary.		
An offence under section 25 of the *Theft Act* 1968 (going equipped for stealing, etc.) committed with reference to the theft or taking of motor vehicles.	Discretionary.		

[This Schedule is printed as amended by the *New Roads and Street Works Act* 1991, s.168(2) and Sched. 9; the *Aggravated Vehicle-Taking Act* 1992, s.3; the *RTA* 1991, ss.26 and 83, and Scheds 2, and 8; the *CJA* 1993, s.67(1); S.I. 1996 No. 1974 (*ante*, § 32–111); the *Police Reform Act* 2002, s.56(5); the *Railways and Transport Safety Act* 2003, s.107, and Sched. 7, para. 8; the *CJA* 2003, ss.285(2)–(4), and 286(1); the *Crime (International Co-operation) Act* 2003, s.91, and Sched. 5, para. 37; the *Traffic Management Act* 2004, s.6(5); and the *RSA* 2006, ss.20(4), 21(3), 23, 25(1), 26(4), 27, 28 and 29; and as amended, as from days to be appointed, by the 2006 Act, ss.10(1) and (12), 17, 18(6), 22(8) and 59, Sched. 3, paras 30 and 63(3) and (4), and Sched. 7(4) (insertion of words, *etc.*, in square brackets, omission of italicised words, *etc.*) (and as to these amendments, see also *post*). There is an apparent error in one of the amendments made by the *Crime (International Co-operation) Act* 2003, in that it would appear that the insertion of the words "or section 109C(c)" at the end of column 2 of the entry relating to section 94(3A) should have been inserted in column 1. For further details in relation to the amendments made by the *CJA* 2003, see *ante*, §§ 32–6, 32–59; and *post*, § 32–227. As from a day to be appointed, the maximum penalty on summary conviction of offences contrary to sections 2, 22A and 174 is increased to 12 months' imprisonment; and the maximum penalty on conviction of offences contrary to sections 4(1), 4(2), 5(1)(a), 5(1)(b), 7, 7A, 94A, 103(1)(b) and 170(4) is increased to 51 weeks' imprisonment (but none of these increases have effect in relation to offences committed before the date that they take effect): *CJA* 2003, ss.280(2), 281(4)–(6) and 282(2)–(4), and Sched. 26, para. 38. As to the amendments made by the 2006 Act, (i) any alteration of penalty applies only to offences committed after the alteration takes effect (s.61(3)); and (ii) the maximum penalty on summary conviction of an offence contrary to s.2B or s.3ZB is six months' imprisonment where the offence was committed before the commencement of the *CJA* 2003, s.154(1) (s.61(5)). As to the details of the dates of commencement of the *RSA* 2006 amendments, see *ante* in this chapter where the individual offences are dealt with in detail.]

NOTE: only those entries in the above Schedule which relate to offences which must or may be tried on indictment or which involve obligatory or discretionary disqualification are included here.

III. DOCUMENT OFFENCES

A. Transport Act 1968

Section 97AA of the Act deals with the forgery of seals on recording equipment installed in or designed for installation in a vehicle. It carries a maximum penalty on indictment of two years' imprisonment and on summary conviction a fine not exceeding the statutory maximum. **32–223**

Section 99(5) covers offences of falsification of records kept or carried for the purposes of relevant Community regulations. The section also carries a power of seizure by an officer who has reason to believe that an offence has been committed in respect of any record or document seized by him.

B. Public Passenger Vehicles Act 1981

Section 65 creates offences of forgery and misuse of certain documents ranging from licences, operators discs to certificates of conformity of vehicles. The provisions are similar to those of section 173 of the *RTA* 1988 (see *post*). **32–224**

Summary proceedings must be brought within six months from the date when evidence comes to the prosecutor's attention which is in his opinion sufficient to warrant a prosecution. No proceedings shall be brought more than three years after the commission of the offence: section 73.

Penalties are as set out at § 32–228, *post*.

C. Road Traffic Regulation Act 1984

The main provisions of section 115 cover the fraudulent use of parking devices, tickets or other authorised devices; possession of forgeries of such items and knowingly making a false statement in order to procure any of the above. Penalties are as set out at § 32–222, *ante*. **32–225**

D. Road Traffic Act 1988

(1) Statute

Road Traffic Act 1988, ss.173, 174

Forgery of documents, etc.

173.—(1) A person who, with intent to deceive— **32–226**

(a) forges, alters or uses a document or other thing to which this section applies, or

(b) lends to, or allows to be used by, any other person a document or other thing to which this section applies, or

(c) makes or has in his possession any document or other thing so closely resembling a document or other thing to which this section applies as to be calculated to deceive,

is guilty of an offence.

(2) This section applies to the following documents and other things—

(a) any licence under any Part of this Act, *or, in the case of a licence to drive, any counterpart of such a licence,*

(aa) *any counterpart of a [Northern Ireland licence or] Community licence,*

(b) any test certificate, goods vehicle test certificate, plating certificate, certificate of conformity or Minister's approval certificate (within the meaning of Part II of this Act),

(c) any certificate required as a condition of any exception prescribed under section 14 of this Act,

(cc) any seal required by regulations made under section 41 of this Act with respect to speed limiters,

(d) any plate containing particulars required to be marked on a vehicle by regulations under section 41 of this Act containing plated particulars (within the meaning of Part II of this Act) or containing other particulars required to be marked on a goods vehicle by section 54 to 58 of this Act or regulations under those sections,

(dd) any document evidencing the appointment of an examiner under section 66A of this Act,

(e) any records required to be kept by virtue of section 74 of this Act,
(f) any document which, in pursuance of section 89(3) of this Act, is issued as evidence of the result of a test of competence to drive,
(ff) any document evidencing the successful completion of a driver training course provided in accordance with regulations under section 99ZA of this Act,
(g) *any badge or certificate prescribed by regulations made by virtue of section 135 of this Act,*
[(g) any document evidencing the passing of an examination (or part of an examination) required by regulations under section 132 of this Act or the successful completion of training provided in accordance with regulations under section 133ZA of this Act,
(ga) any certificate under section 133A of this Act,
(gb) any certificate or other item prescribed under section 135(1)(a) of this Act,]
(h) any certificate of insurance or certificate of security under Part VI of this Act,
(j) any document produced as evidence of insurance in pursuance of Regulation 6 of the *Motor Vehicles (Compulsory Insurance) (No. 2) Regulations* 1973,
(k) any document issued under regulations made by the Secretary of State in pursuance of his power under section 165(2)(a) of this Act to prescribe evidence which may be produced in lieu of a certificate of insurance or a certificate of security,
(l) any international road haulage permit, *and*
(m) a certificate of the kind referred to in section 34B(1) of the *Road Traffic Offenders Act* 1988[; and
(n) any document produced as evidence of the passing of an appropriate driving test within the meaning of section 36 of that Act].

(3) In the application of this section to England and Wales "forges" means makes a false document or other thing in order that it may be used as genuine.

(4) *In this section "counterpart", "Community licence" and "Northern Ireland licence" have the same meanings as in Part III of this Act.*

[This section is printed as amended by the *Driving Licences (Community Driving Licence) Regulations* 1990 (S.I. 1990 No. 144); the *Road Traffic (Driver Licensing and Information Systems) Act* 1989, ss.7 and 16 and Scheds 3 and 6; the *RTA* 1991, ss.48 and 83 and Scheds 4, para. 73, and 8; S.I. 1996 No. 1974 (*ante*, § 32–111); the *Crime (International Co-operation) Act* 2003, s.91, and Sched. 5, para. 29; and the *RSA* 2006, s.41(4). As from a day to be appointed, in subs. (2), paras (g), (ga) and (gb) (in square brackets) are substituted for para. (g) (in italics) and para. (n) is inserted: *RSA* 2006, ss.37(8) and 42, and Sched. 6, paras 1 and 27. Also as from a day to be appointed, the italicised words in subs. (2)(a), the whole of subs. (2)(aa), the italicised word at the end of subs. (2)(l) and the whole of subs. (4) are repealed: *ibid.*, ss.10(1) and (12) and 59, Sched. 3, paras 2 and 28, and Sched. 7(4) and (10).]

False statements and withholding material information.

32–226a **174.**—(1) A person who knowingly makes a false statement for the purpose—
(a) of obtaining the grant of a licence under any Part of this Act to himself or any other person, or
(b) of preventing the grant of any such licence, or
(c) of procuring the imposition of a condition or limitation in relation to any such licence, or
(ca) of obtaining a document evidencing the successful completion of a driver training course provided in accordance with regulations under section 99ZA of this Act, or
(d) of securing the entry or retention of the name of any person in the register of approved instructors maintained under Part V of this Act, or
[(da) of obtaining a document evidencing the passing of an examination (or part of an examination) required by regulations under section 132 of this Act or the successful completion of training provided in accordance with regulations under section 133ZA of this Act, or]
(dd) of obtaining the grant to any person of a certificate under section 133A of this Act, or
(e) of obtaining the grant of an international road haulage permit to himself or any other person,

is guilty of an offence.

(2) A person who, in supplying information or producing documents for the purposes either of sections 53 to 60 and 63 of this Act or of regulations made under sections 49 to 51, 61, 62 and 66(3) of this Act—

(a) makes a statement which he knows to be false in a material particular or recklessly makes a statement which is false in a material particular, or

(b) produces, provides, sends or otherwise makes use of a document which he knows to be false in a material particular or recklessly produces, provides, sends or otherwise makes use of a document which is false in a material particular,

is guilty of an offence.

(3) A person who—

(a) knowingly produces false evidence for the purposes of regulations under section 66(1) of this Act, or

(b) knowingly makes a false statement in a declaration required to be made by the regulations,

is guilty of an offence.

(4) A person who—

(a) wilfully makes a false entry in any record required to be made or kept by regulations under section 74 of this Act, or

(b) with intent to deceive, makes use of any such entry which he knows to be false,

is guilty of an offence.

(5) A person who makes a false statement or withholds any material information for the purpose of obtaining the issue—

(a) of a certificate of insurance or certificate of security under Part VI of this Act, or

(b) of any document issued under regulations made by the Secretary of State in pursuance of his power under section 165(2)(a) of this Act to prescribe evidence which may be produced in lieu of a certificate of insurance or a certificate of security,

is guilty of an offence.

[This section is printed as amended by the *Road Traffic (Driving Instruction by Disabled Persons) Act* 1993, s.6, and Sched., para.10; and the *RSA* 2006, s.41(5); and as amended, as from a day to be appointed, by *ibid.*, s.42, and Sched. 6, paras 1 and 28 (insertion of words in square brackets).]

(2) Class of offence and mode of trial

Offences under either section are triable either way (*RTOA* 1988, s.9, and Sched. 2, Pt 1), and are class 3 offences, *ante*. However, offences contrary to section 174 committed prior to January 29, 2004, are triable only summarily: see the *CJA* 2003, s.286, and the *Criminal Justice Act 2003 (Commencement No. 2 and Saving Provisions) Order* 2004 (S.I. 2004 No. 81). **32–227**

(3) Sentence

On conviction of either offence on indictment, imprisonment not exceeding two years; on summary conviction, a fine not exceeding the statutory maximum (s.173), or six months' imprisonment or a fine not exceeding the statutory maximum, or both (s.174): RTOA 1988, s.33, and Sched. 2, Pt I. However, offences contrary to section 174 committed prior to January 29, 2004, are triable only summarily and subject to a maximum fine not exceeding level 4 on the standard scale: see the *CJA* 2003, s.286, and S.I. 2004 No. 81 (*ante*). **32–228**

(4) Ingredients of the offences

Section 173(1) creates three separate offences, and accordingly a conviction under paragraph (a) was overturned where the defendant had forged a document which resembled, but was not, an international road haulage permit: *Holloway v. Brown* [1978] R.T.R. 537, DC. **32–229**

The production of a driving licence to police officers pursuant to a request unconnected with driving on a road is not "user" of the licence for the purposes of subsection (1)(a): *R. v. Howe* [1982] R.T.R. 45, CA.

Possession of a certificate of insurance which related to a policy which had been cancelled by the insurers was held to be an offence under section 112 of the *RTA* 1930 (*rep.*): *R. v. Cleghorn* [1938] 3 All E.R. 398, CCA.

The question whether the defendant derived gain or advantage from his conduct is immaterial in considering whether an offence has been committed under this section: *Jones v. Meatyard* [1939] 1 All E.R. 140, DC; and see *Welham v. DPP* [1961] A.C. 103, HL (see *ante*, §§ 17–62 *et seq.*); "calculated to deceive" can mean likely to deceive: *R. v. Davison* [1972] 1 W.L.R. 1540, CA.

A "test certificate" within subsection (2)(b) means the printed and serially numbered form, even if incomplete: *R. v. Pilditch* [1981] Crim.L.R. 184 (distinguishing *Holloway v. Brown*, *ante*).

Bogus forms of insurance certificates, even when uncompleted, can constitute documents so closely resembling genuine insurance certificates as to be calculated to deceive within section 173(1)(c): *R. v. Aworinde* [1996] R.T.R. 66, CA, applying *R. v. Pilditch*.

Section 173 applies to Convention driving permits as it applies to licences: see Article 1(9) of the *Motor Vehicles (International Circulation) Order* 1975 (S.I. 1975 No. 1208), as amended by S.I. 1989 No. 993.

(5) Power to seize articles

Road Traffic Act 1988, s.176

Power to seize articles in respect of which offences under sections 173 to 175 may have been committed

32–230 **176.**—(1) If a constable has reasonable cause to believe that a document produced to him—

(a) in pursuance of section 137 of this Act, or

(b) in pursuance of any of the preceding provisions of this Part of this Act,

is a document in relation to which an offence has been committed under section 173, 174 or 175 of this Act or under section 115 of the *Road Traffic Regulation Act* 1984, he may seize the document.

(1A) *Where a licence to drive or a counterpart of any such licence or of any Northern Ireland licence or Community licence may be seized by a constable under subsection (1) above, he may also seize the counterpart, the licence to drive or the Northern Ireland licence or Community licence (as the case may be) produced with it.*

(2) When a document is seized under subsection (1) above the person from whom it was taken shall, unless—

(a) the document has been previously returned to him, or

(b) he has been previously charged with an offence under any of those sections,

be summoned before a magistrates' court or, in Scotland, the sheriff to account for his possession of the document.

(3) The court or sheriff must make such order respecting the disposal of the document and award such costs as the justice of the case may require.

(3A) *An order under subsection (3) above respecting the disposal of a licence to drive or a counterpart of any such licence or of a Northern Ireland licence or Community licence may include an order respecting the disposal of any document seized under subsection (1A) above.*

(4) If a constable, an examiner [*sic*] appointed under section 66A of this Act has reasonable cause to believe that a document or plate carried on a motor vehicle or by the driver of the vehicle is a document or plate to which this subsection applies, he may seize it.

For the purposes of this subsection the power to seize includes power to detach from a vehicle.

(5) Subsection (4) above applies to a document or plate in relation to which an offence has been committed under sections 173, 174 or 175 of this Act in so far as they apply—

(a) to documents evidencing the appointment of examiners under section 66A of this Act, or

(b) to goods vehicle test certificates, plating certificates, certificates of conformity or Minister's approval certificates (within the meaning of Part II of this Act), or

(c) to plates containing plated particulars (within the meaning of that Part) or containing other particulars required to be marked on goods vehicles by sections 54 to 58 of this Act or regulations made under them, or

(d) to records required to be kept by virtue of section 74 of this Act, or

(e) to international road haulage permits.

(6) When a document or plate is seized under subsection (4) above, either the driver or owner of the vehicle shall, if the document or plate is still detained and neither of them has previously been charged with an offence in relation to the document or plate under section 173, 174 or 175 of this Act, be summoned before a magistrates' court or, in Scotland, the sheriff to account for his possession of, or the presence on the vehicle of, the document or plate.

(7) The court or sheriff must make such order respecting the disposal of the document or plate and award such costs as the justice of the case may require.

(8) *In this section "counterpart", "Community licence" and "Northern Ireland licence" have the same meanings as in Part III of this Act.*

[This section is printed as amended by the *Driving Licences (Community Driving Licence) Regulations* 1990 (S.I. 1990 No. 144); the *RTA* 1991, s.48, and Sched. 4, para. 74; S.I. 1996 No. 1974 (*ante*, § 32–111); and the *Crime (International Co-operation) Act* 2003, s.91, and Sched. 5, para. 30; and as amended, as from a day to be appointed, by the *RSA* 2006, ss.10(1) and (12) and 59, Sched. 3, paras 2 and 29, and Sched. 7(4) (omission of subss. (1A), (3A) and (8)).]

E. MOTOR VEHICLES (E.C. TYPE APPROVAL) REGULATIONS 1998

Section 2(2) of the *European Communities Act* 1972 permits the Crown to make regulations implementing European Community law. Such regulations may create new criminal offences punishable with imprisonment for up to two years: see para. 1(1)(d) of Schedule 2 to the Act. The *Motor Vehicles (E.C. Type Approval) Regulations* 1998 (S.I. 1998 No. 2051), made pursuant to section 2(2) of the 1972 Act, deal with the forgery and misuse of E.C. type approval certificates and of E.C. certificates of conformity. The regulations have been amended by a series of sets of regulations, the most recent of which are the *Motor Vehicles (E.C. Type Approval) (Amendment No. 2) Regulations* 2007 (S.I. 2007 No. 3135). **32–231**

Regulation 14(1) to (3) creates an offence relating to an E.C. type approval certificate or an E.C. certificate of conformity which is in identical terms to section 38 of the *Goods Vehicles (Licensing of Operators) Act* 1995 (see *post*, § 32–241). The offence carries the same penalties.

F. VEHICLE EXCISE AND REGISTRATION ACT 1994

(1) Statute

As from September 1, 1994 the *Vehicles (Excise) Act* 1971 was repealed and replaced by the *Vehicle Excise and Registration Act* 1994. By section 64 of, and Schedule 4, para. 2(1) to, the Act, anything done or having effect as done (including the making of subordinate legislation and the issuing of licences) under or for the purposes of any provision repealed by the 1994 Act has effect as if done under or for the corresponding purposes of the 1994 Act. **32–232**

Vehicle Excise and Registration Act 1994, s.44

Forgery and fraud

44.—(1) A person is guilty of an offence if he forges, fraudulently alters, fraudulently uses, fraudulently lends or fraudulently allows to be used by another person anything to which subsection (2) applies. **32–233**

(2) This subsection applies to—

(a) a vehicle licence,

(b) a trade licence,

(c) a nil licence,

(d) a registration mark,

(e) a registration document, and

(f) a trade plate (including a replacement trade plate).

(3) A person guilty of an offence under this section is liable—

(a) on summary conviction, to a fine not exceeding the statutory maximum, and

(b) on conviction on indictment, to imprisonment for a term not exceeding two years or to a fine or (except in Scotland) to both.

[This section is printed as amended by the *Finance Act* 1997, s.18 and Sched. 3, para. 6.]

(2) Class of offence and mode of trial

32–234 This offence is triable either way (s.44(3), *ante*), and is a class 3 offence, *ante*, § 2–17.

(3) Sentence

32–235 See section 44(3), *ante*.

(4) Vehicles for the disabled

32–236 A vehicle is an exempt vehicle under section 5 of, and Schedule 2, para. 19, to the 1994 Act, if it is used or kept for use by a disabled person who satisfies the conditions set out therein.

(5) Ingredients of the offence

32–237 In *R. v. Macrae* [1994] Crim.L.R. 363, CA, it was held that the definition of "forgery" in subsection (1) should be drawn from the definition in the *Forgery and Counterfeiting Act* 1981, s.1 (*ante*, § 22–5). Forgery for the purposes of the 1994 Act is thus committed if the defendant: (a) makes a false vehicle licence (etc.); (b) with the intent that he or another should use it to induce another to accept it as genuine; and (c) by reason of so accepting it to do or not to do some act to his own or another's prejudice as a result of such acceptance of the false licence as genuine in connection with the performance of any duty. For a suggestion that this approach narrows the law, see the commentary at [1994] Crim.L.R. 364; and *cf. R. v. Clayton*, 72 Cr.App.R. 135, CA.

In order to be guilty of fraudulently using a vehicle licence, it is not necessary for the defendant to have intended economic loss to the licensing authority—an intention to deceive a person responsible for a public duty is sufficient. Thus, using vehicle A's licence on vehicle B in an endeavour to avoid being charged with using the vehicle without a licence being exhibited, in breach of section 33(1) of the 1994 Act, is an offence within section 44(1): *R. v. Terry* [1984] A.C. 374, HL, overruling *R. v. Manners-Astley*, 52 Cr.App.R. 5, CA.

In *R. v. Johnson (T.)* [1995] R.T.R. 15, CA, it was held that there can be a conviction for the offence of fraudulently using a vehicle licence only where there is evidence that the vehicle is being or has been used on a public road while displaying the licence. If the vehicle is on private land, it is not enough for the prosecution to show an intention to use it on public land with the offending licence at some future time.

(6) False declarations, etc.

32–238 Section 45 deals with offences of making false or misleading declarations in connection with applications for vehicle or trade licences, rebates, allocation of registration marks, exempt vehicles; supplying false or misleading information in connection with the keeper of vehicles or regulations made under section 60A; forgery, alteration, lending, etc., of certificates under section 61A. As from a day to be appointed, the section is amended by the *RSA* 2006, s.47(11)–(13), so as to broaden the offence to include production of a document known to be false or, in any material respect, misleading. The penalties as the same as under section 44. Section 45 applies to a declaration in connection with an application for a refund of vehicle excise duty under section 20 of the *Finance Act* 2000 as it applies to a declaration in connection with an application for a vehicle licence: s.20(10) of the 2000 Act. It also applies to making a false or misleading declaration in connection with an application for a refund in relation to the reduced rate threshold: *Finance Act* 2001, s.8(9).

Where under section 45, a question arises as to: (a) the number of vehicles used; (b) the character, weight or cylinder capacity of the vehicle; (c) the seating capacity of a vehicle; or (d) the purpose for which a vehicle has been used, the burden of proof lies on the defendant (s.53).

(7) Evidence

Section 52 of the Act (as amended by the *Civil Evidence Act* 1995, s.15(1) and Sched. 1, para. 19) covers records; it is in similar terms to section 13 of the *RTOA* 1988 (*ante*, § 32–161). The *Vehicle and Driving Licences Records (Evidence) Regulations* 1970 (S.I. 1970 No. 1997) prescribe the matters in respect of which evidence may be given under this section. **32–239**

G. MOTOR CYCLES ETC. (E.C. TYPE APPROVAL) REGULATIONS 1999

In the *Motor Cycles Etc. (E.C. Type Approval) Regulations* 1999 (S.I. 1999 No. 2920) (as most recently amended by the *Motor Cycles Etc. (E.C. Type Approval) (Amendment) Regulations* 2007 (S.I. 2007 No. 2656)), made pursuant to the *European Communities Act* 1972, s.2(2), an offence relating to motor cycles, and triable either way, is created dealing with the forgery and misuse of E.C. type approval certificates and of E.C. certificates of conformity. The 1999 regulations are similar in form to S.I. 1998 No. 2051 (*ante*, § 32–231). Regulation 10(1) to (3) of the 1995 regulations is identically worded to regulation 11(1) to (3) of the 1992 regulations. **32–240**

H. GOODS VEHICLES (LICENSING OF OPERATORS) ACT 1995

This Act replaced parts of both the *RTA* 1960 and the *Transport Act* 1968. Section 38 is couched in similar terms to section 173 of the *RTA* 1988 (*ante*, § 32–226) and relates to items such as operators' licences, plates, marks, licences used under an operator's licence and other certification. As to penalties, see *ante*, § 32–228. **32–241**

CHAPTER 33

CONSPIRACY, ENCOURAGEMENT AND ATTEMPT TO COMMIT CRIME

I. CONSPIRACY

A. INTRODUCTION

The *CLA* 1977 replaced common law conspiracy with a statutory offence, preserving only common law conspiracy to defraud (*post*, §§ 33–34 *et seq.*) and conspiracy to do acts tending to corrupt public morals or outrage public decency (*post*, § 33–41). However, many of the old common law rules and concepts remain extant, albeit restated in statutory form: *Report on Conspiracy and Criminal Law Reform*, Law Com. No. 76, paras 1.20 *et seq.* As to the history and evolution of the offence, see *Russell on Crime*, Vol. I, pp. 200 *et seq.*, and Vol. II, pp. 1469 *et seq.* (12th ed.); Holdsworth, *History of English Law*, Vol. III, pp. 400 *et seq.*; Wright, *The Law of Criminal Conspiracies and Agreements* (1873). **33–1**

B. STATUTORY OFFENCE OF CONSPIRACY

(1) Definition

Criminal Law Act 1977, s.1

The offence of conspiracy

1.—(1) Subject to the following provisions of this Part of this Act, if a person agrees with any other person or persons that a course of conduct shall be pursued which, if the agreement is carried out in accordance with their intentions, either— **33–2**

(a) will necessarily amount to or involve the commission of any offence or offences by one or more of the parties to the agreement, or

(b) would do so but for the existence of facts which render the commission of the offence or any of the offences impossible,

he is guilty of conspiracy to commit the offence or offences in question.

(1A), (1B) [*Repealed by* Criminal Justice (Terrorism and Conspiracy) Act *1998, s.9(3)(a) and Sched. 1, para. 4.*]

(2) Where liability for any offence may be incurred without knowledge on the part of the person committing it of any particular fact or circumstance necessary for the commission of the offence, a person shall nevertheless not be guilty of conspiracy to commit that offence by virtue of subsection (1) above unless he and at least one other party to the agreement intend or know that that fact or circumstance shall or will exist at the time when the conduct constituting the offence is to take place. **33–3**

(3) [*Repealed by* Trade Union and Labour Relations (Consolidation) Act *1992, s.300(1) and Sched. 1.*]

(4) In this Part of this Act "offence" means an offence triable in England and Wales, … .

(5), (6) [*Repealed by* Criminal Justice (Terrorism and Conspiracy) Act *1998, s.9(3)(a) and Sched. 1, para. 4.*]

[Subs. (1) was substituted by the *Criminal Attempts Act* 1981, s.5, with effect from August 27, 1981. As to agreements entered into before that date, see section 5(2). The repealed section 1(3) excluded a conspiracy to commit a summary offence where the acts in question were to be done in contemplation or furtherance of a trade dispute. A similar provision is now contained in the *Trade Union and Labour Relations (Consolidation) Act* 1992, s.242. The words omitted from subs. (4) were repealed by the *Criminal Justice (Terrorism and Conspiracy) Act* 1998, s.9(3)(a) and Sched. 1, para. 4.]

As from a day to be appointed, a person subject to service law, or a civilian subject to service discipline, commits an offence if he does any act punishable by the law of England and Wales or, if it were done in England or Wales, any act which would be so punishable: *AFA* 2006, s.42. Section 45 of the 2006 Act modifies sections 1 and 2 of the 1977 Act for the purpose of determining whether an agreement that a course of conduct be pursued is an offence under section 42.

33–4 As to the application of this section in determining guilt of an offence of conspiracy under an enactment other than this Act (*e.g.* the *Explosives Substances Act* 1883, s.3(1)(a), *ante*, § 23–66), see section 5(6), *post*, § 33–34.

Section 1(2) was intended to give effect to the decision of the House of Lords in *Churchill v. Walton* (*post*, § 33–16). Its proper interpretation, which has not proved easy, was considered in *R. v. Saik* [2007] 1 A.C. 18, HL, in relation to a conspiracy to launder the proceeds of crime, contrary to the *CJA* 1988, s.93C, an offence which required proof that the property dealt with was in fact the proceeds of crime (*R. v. Montila* [2005] 1 Cr.App.R. 26, HL). It would be idle to pretend that the reasoning of their Lordships was identical. The following general propositions are based on the speech of Lord Nicholls, with whose reasoning Lord Steyn expressly agreed. Section 1(2) (notwithstanding its language), (a) applies to all offences, an ingredient of which is the existence of a fact or circumstance (*i.e.* even those where knowledge of the fact or circumstance is an ingredient of the substantive offence); (b) the phrase "fact or circumstance necessary for the commission of the offence" is directed at the *actus reus* of the offence, and what the subsection requires is that the conspirator must "intend or know" that this fact or circumstance "shall or will exist" when the conspiracy is carried into effect; (c) the mental element required by the subsection subsumes and renders otiose any lesser mental element that may suffice for the substantive offence; in such a case, any reference to the lesser mental element in the particulars of offence should be avoided as potentially confusing; and (d) any additional mental element required by the substantive offence must also be proved. Lords Hope and Brown, whilst discussing the subsection generally, expressed their conclusions in terms only of the particular conspiracy charged. As to that, they were in broad agreement with Lords Nicholls and Steyn. For this aspect of the decision, see *ante*, § 26–9. Baroness Hale dissented in part.

As to applications for leave to appeal where the applicant was convicted of conspiracy to launder the proceeds of drug trafficking or of criminal conduct before the decision in *R. v. Saik*, and where his conviction would be unsafe in the light of that decision, but not otherwise, see *R. v. R.* [2007] 1 Cr.App.R. 10, CA (*ante*, § 7–182). As to the disposal of such appeals (where leave is granted or the case is referred to the Court of Appeal by the Criminal Cases Review Commission), see *R. v. K*; *R. v. S and R*; *R. v. X* [2008] 1 Cr.App.R. 1, CA (*ante*, §§ 7–46, 7–52).

(2) The ingredients of conspiracy

(a) *Agreement*

General

33–5 The essence of conspiracy is the agreement. When two or more agree to carry their criminal scheme into effect, the very plot is the criminal act itself: *Mulcahy v. R.*

(1868) L.R. 3 H.L. 306 at 317; *R. v. Warburton* (1870) L.R. 1 C.C.R. 274; *R. v. Tibbits and Windust* [1902] 1 K.B. 77 at 89; *R. v. Meyrick and Ribuffi*, 21 Cr.App.R. 94, CCA. Nothing need be done in pursuit of the agreement: *O'Connell v. R.* (1844) 5 St.Tr.(N.S.) 1; repentance, lack of opportunity and failure are all immaterial: *R. v. Aspinall* (1876) 2 Q.B.D. 48. As the essence of conspiracy is agreement, withdrawal therefrom goes to mitigation only: *R. v. Gortat and Pirog* [1973] Crim.L.R. 648, Crown Court (Cusack J.).

It is the course of conduct agreed upon which is critical; if that course involves some act by an innocent party, the fact that he does not perform it and thus prevents the commission of the substantive offence, does not absolve the parties to the agreement from liability: *R. v. Bolton*, 94 Cr.App.R. 74, CA.

It is important to resist the temptation to introduce into the simple concept of agreement to pursue a course of conduct, ideas derived from the civil law of contract. Any number of persons may agree that a course of conduct shall be pursued without undertaking any contractual liability: *R. v. Anderson* [1986] A.C. 27 at 37, HL.

Qualified agreement

An agreement may amount to a conspiracy even if it contains some reservation, express or implied. The question depends largely on the form of the reservation. If, for instance, it is no more than that a pre-arranged crime will not be attempted if a policeman is at the scene, there is an agreement amounting to conspiracy to commit the crime. If, on the other hand, the matters left outstanding or reserved are of a substantial nature, the arrangement may amount only to negotiation falling short of conspiracy: *R. v. Mills* [1963] 1 Q.B. 522, 47 Cr.App.R. 49, CCA; *R. v. O'Brien (P.J.)*, 59 Cr.App.R. 222, CA; and see *R. v. Saik, ante*, § 33–4 (*per* Lord Nicholls (at [5]). **33–6**

In *R. v. Reed* [1982] Crim.L.R. 819, CA, R had been convicted of conspiring to aid and abet suicide. It was argued that an agreement could not amount to a conspiracy if it was capable of a successful conclusion without a crime being committed. It was said that the most that could be inferred about the nature of the agreement was that the other conspirator (L) would visit individuals and either give them faith healing, consolation and comfort while discouraging suicide, or he would actively help them to commit suicide, depending on his assessment of the appropriate course of action. The argument was rejected. Donaldson L.J. gave two examples: **33–7**

> "In the first, A and B agree to drive from London to Edinburgh in a time which can be achieved without exceeding the speed limit, but only if the traffic which they encounter is exceptionally light. Their agreement will not necessarily involve the commission of any offence, even if it is carried out in accordance with their intentions, and they do arrive ... within the agreed time. Accordingly the agreement does not constitute the offence of statutory conspiracy .... In the second example, A and B agree to rob a bank, if when they arrive at the bank it seems safe to do so. Their agreement will necessarily involve the commission of the offence of robbery if it is carried out in accordance with their intentions. Accordingly, they are guilty of the statutory offence of conspiracy. The instant case is an example of the latter type of agreement. If circumstances had permitted and the agreement ... had been carried out in accordance with their intentions L would have aided, abetted, counselled, and procured a suicide" (at p. 820).

Uncommunicated intentions

The offence of conspiracy cannot exist without the agreement, consent or combination of two or more persons: *Mawji v. R.* [1957] A.C. 126, PC; *R. v. Plummer* [1902] 2 K.B. 339. So long as a design rests in intention only, it is not indictable: there must be agreement. Accordingly a secret and uncommunicated intention to join an illegal enterprise, should the occasion arise, does not amount to an agreement: *R. v. Scott (Valerie)*, 68 Cr.App.R. 164, CA. **33–8**

Duration of the agreement

A conspiracy does not end with the making of the agreement; it will continue so long as there are two or more parties to it intending to carry out the design: *DPP v. Doot* [1973] A.C. 807, HL; *R. v. Boyle and Mears*, 94 Cr.App.R. 158, CA. See also, *post*, § 33–25. **33–9**

Agreements with more than one objective or to commit more than one offence

33–10 A statutory conspiracy can comprise one agreement which, if carried out, will necessarily amount to or involve the commission of more than one offence: see ss.1(1) (*ante*, § 33–2), 3 (*post*, § 33–32) and 4 (*post*, § 33–33); and see *R. v. Siracusa*, 90 Cr.App.R. 340, CA (*post*, § 33–18); *R. v. Roberts* [1998] 1 Cr.App.R. 441, CA; *R. v. Hussain* [2002] 2 Cr.App.R. 26, CA. Where the indictment alleges an agreement to commit two or more specific offences, each offence probably constitutes an essential element of the conspiracy so that, unless it is proved that the conspiracy extended to all the offences alleged, the charge will not be made out: *Roberts*, *ante*. Similarly, where a count of conspiracy to defraud alleges an agreement to achieve two or more distinct objectives, each objective is an essential element which must be proved: *R. v. Bennett (Sharon)*, unreported, May 6, 1999, CA (9802782 Z3).

Such multiple objective conspiracies can cause difficulties. For example, where the objectives are consecutive, latecomers who join after the first objective has been achieved do not join that original agreement, but a different conspiracy, one more limited in scope. Where multiple objective conspiracies are pleaded, it is submitted that the safer course is to add alternative counts of conspiracy each alleging but one of the objectives or offences contained in the composite count: *Roberts*, *ante*; and see *post*, § 33–56.

Agreement to pursue course of conduct involving commission "of any offence"

33–11 Conspirators who agree to pursue a course of conduct may not have the commission of a specific offence in mind: see *post*, § 33–17. It may not, however, be necessary to prove that the carrying out of the agreement will necessarily result in the commission of a specific offence, provided that it can be shown that it would, or was intended to, result in the commission of at least one of two identified offences: *R. v. El-Kurd* [2001] Crim.L.R. 234, CA; *R. v. Suchedina* [2007] 1 Cr.App.R. 23, CA. An agreement to commit either one or another crime, although unlikely, is possible and permissible: *R. v. Hussain* [2002] 2 Cr.App.R. 26, CA; and an agreement to commit offences in the alternative (*e.g.* to steal a particular item, by burglary or robbery if necessary) is an agreement to commit all of those offences (*e.g.* theft, burglary and robbery): *R. v. Suchedina*; *Att.-Gen.'s Reference (No. 4 of 2003)* [2005] 1 Cr.App.R. 2, CA.

Agreement to do the impossible

33–12 See section 1(1)(b) of the 1977 Act, *ante*, § 33–2. (For the common law rule, see *DPP v. Nock* [1978] A.C. 979, HL, and the 1994 edition of this work, §§ 33–29 *et seq.*)

Agreement to aid and abet an offence

33–13 An agreement to aid and abet an offence is not in law capable of constituting a criminal conspiracy under section 1 of the 1977 Act: *R. v. Kenning* [2008] 2 Cr.App.R. 32, CA. However, an agreement to commit a substantive offence, the definition of which involves aiding and abetting an act which is not itself an offence, is good in law: see *R. v. Reed*, *ante*, § 33–7.

Proving the agreement

33–14 The agreement may be proved in the usual way or by proving circumstances from which the jury may presume it: *R. v. Parsons* (1763) 1 W.Bl. 392; *R. v. Murphy* (1837) 8 C. & P. 297. Proof of the existence of a conspiracy is generally a "matter of inference, deduced from certain criminal acts of the parties accused, done in pursuance of an apparent criminal purpose in common between them": *R. v. Brisac* (1803) 4 East 164 at 171, cited with approval in *Mulcahy v. R.* (1868) L.R. 3 H.L. 306 at 317. See also, *R. v. Meyrick and Ribuffi*, 21 Cr.App.R. 94 at 99 and 101; *R. v. Brittain and Shackell* (1848) 3 Cox 76 at 77; *R. v. De Berenger* (1814) 3 M. & Sel. 67, cited in *R. v. Gurney* (1869) 11 Cox C.C. 414 at 423–424; *R. v. Parnell* (1881) 14 Cox 508 at 515–516; *R. v. Frost* (1839) 9 C. & P. 129 at 150; *R. v. Hunt* (1820) 1 St.Tr.(N.S.) 171 at

437–438; *R. v. Hardy* (1794) 24 St.Tr. 199 at 473–474. Overt acts which are proved against some defendants may be looked at as against all of them, to show the nature and objects of the conspiracy: *R. v. Stapylton, Esdaile and Brown* (1857) 8 Cox 69.

(b) *Mens rea*

Mens rea is an essential element in conspiracy only in that there must be an intention to be a party to an agreement to do an unlawful act. In *R. v. Anderson* [1986] A.C. 27, HL, Lord Bridge said: **33–15**

> "But, beyond the mere fact of agreement, the necessary *mens rea* of the crime is, in my opinion, established if, and only if, it is shown that the accused, when he entered into the agreement, intended to play some part in the agreed course of conduct in furtherance of the criminal purpose which the agreed course of conduct was intended to achieve. Nothing less will suffice; nothing more is required" (at p. 39E).

The point was emphasised in *Yip Chiu-Cheung v. R.*, 99 Cr.App.R. 406, PC, where an undercover officer who entered into an agreement to export drugs was held to have had the necessary *mens rea* for conspiracy. Lord Griffiths said:

> "The crime of conspiracy requires an agreement between two or more persons to commit an unlawful act with the intention of carrying it out. It is the intention to carry out the crime that constitutes the necessary *mens rea* for the offence. As Lord Bridge pointed out, an undercover agent who has no intention of committing the crime lacks the necessary *mens rea* to be a conspirator" (at p. 410).

Although *Yip Chiu-Cheung* was a common law conspiracy there appears to be no difference on this point between statutory conspiracy in England and common law conspiracy in Hong Kong.

The passages cited above should not be regarded as authority for the proposition that all conspirators must intend to play an active part in the agreed course of conduct. The organiser of a crime who recruits others to carry it out is equally guilty of conspiracy whether or not the organiser intends to play some active part in it thereafter: see *R. v. Siracusa*, 90 Cr.App.R. 340 at 349, *per* O'Connor L.J., *post*, § 33–18. Conversely, a person who intends that the offence should be carried out is guilty of conspiracy even if he has a larger purpose in mind, such as the gathering of evidence for the authorities: *R. v. Jones and Warburton*, unreported, March 1, 2002, CA ([2002] EWCA Crim. 735).

Knowledge of the law and the facts

Knowledge of the law on the part of the defendant is immaterial. If what the alleged conspirators agreed to do was, on the facts known to them, an unlawful act, they cannot excuse themselves by saying that, owing to their ignorance of the law, they did not realise that it was a crime. If, on the facts known to them, what they agreed to do was lawful, they are not rendered artificially guilty by the existence of other facts, not known to them, giving a different and criminal quality to the act agreed upon: *Churchill v. Walton* [1967] 2 A.C. 224, HL, given effect to in section 1(2) of the *CLA* 1977, *ante*, § 33–3. **33–16**

Intention to commit an offence

In *R. v. Anderson* [1986] A.C. 27, HL, it was held that there was no requirement that the prosecution should prove against any particular alleged conspirator that he intended that the offence the subject of the conspiracy should be committed. Thus it would be sufficient for an alleged conspirator who had full knowledge of the plan to have agreed to play a minor role by way of assistance (*e.g.* supplying inside information to intending robbers of a bank), but with a state of mind of complete indifference as to whether the others actually carried out the robbery. What has to be proved, according to Lord Bridge in *Anderson* (at p.37), is that the accused knew that the course of conduct agreed upon involved the commission of an offence (although not the name of the offence: see *R. v. Siracusa*, *ante*). It is doubtful that Lord Bridge intended to suggest that it is necessary that the accused should know that what was agreed upon was criminal, but, to the extent that he did so suggest, it is submitted that this is wrong in principle and contrary to *Churchill v. Walton*, *ante*. What is required is that the **33–17** conspirators should agree on a course of conduct which involves an act or omission by at least one of them which is prohibited by the criminal law (statute or common law), knowing or intending that any fact or circumstance necessary for the commission of the offence shall or will exist at the time when the conduct constituting the offence is to take place, and that the conspirator acting or omitting to act in the prohibited way will do so with any additional mental element appropriate to the offence: *R. v. Saik*, *ante*, § 33–4.

The agreement and the required intention

33–18 The *mens rea* sufficient to support a substantive offence will not necessarily support a charge of conspiracy to commit that offence. An intent to commit grievous bodily harm is sufficient for murder, but is insufficient for conspiracy to murder: *R. v. Siracusa*, 90 Cr.App.R. 340 at 350, CA; for similar considerations relating to money laundering, see *R. v. Saik*, *ante*, §§ 26–9, 33–4. Much depends on the nature of the agreement and the particulars alleged. A conspiracy to steal cannot be proved by a conspiracy to rob: *R. v. Barnard*, 70 Cr.App.R. 28, CA (*post*, § 33–76). Nor can a conspiracy to import heroin (a Class A drug within the *Misuse of Drugs Act* 1971) be established by proving an agreement to import cannabis (a Class B drug at the material time): *R. v. Siracusa*, *ante*. The court pointed out that if the facts suggest that the agreement was to import drugs of more than one class, then that could be appropriately laid in the indictment because section 1(1) of the 1977 Act provides for the agreed course of conduct to involve the commission of more than one offence.

33–19 The effect of *Siracusa* was summarised in *R. v. Patel*, unreported, August 7, 1991, CA (894351 S1), and the summary was specifically approved in *R. v. Taylor* [2002] Crim.L.R. 205, CA. The effect of these decisions is that where a conspiracy count identifies in the particulars of offence a particular controlled drug, it must be proved against any defendant not merely that he knew that the agreement related to the importation, production, supply, etc., of a controlled drug; he must be proved either (i) to have known that it related to the particular drug mentioned in the indictment, or (ii) to have known it related to a drug of the same "Class" (as specified in the *Misuse of Drugs Act* 1971) as the drug mentioned, without having any knowledge or belief as to it involving any particular drug, or (iii) to have believed that it related to another particular drug of the same class, or of a class attracting a greater penalty, or (iv) to have believed that it related to a drug of a class attracting a greater maximum penalty, without having any belief as to any particular drug, or (v) to have not cared at all what particular drug was involved. A defendant would escape liability only where he mistakenly believed that the conspiracy related to a controlled drug of a class attracting a lesser maximum penalty.

33–20 It might be thought that the best course for the Crown to adopt is not to name the drug. The Court of Appeal has, however, discouraged such a practice. When it is "reasonably possible" to identify the drug, this should be done. Furthermore, the naming of the drug will assist the judge when it comes to sentencing: *R. v. Patel*, *ante*.

(3) Jurisdiction

(a) *Summary*

33–21 (a) A conspiracy between a person in England and a person abroad to commit a crime in England is indictable in England: *R. v. Parnell* (1881) 14 Cox 508 at 515, referred to in *R. v. Meyrick and Ribuffi*, 21 Cr.App.R. 94 at 99, CCA, and *R. v. Hammersley*, 42 Cr.App.R. 207 at 217, CCA.

(b) A conspiracy to commit a crime abroad is not indictable at common law unless the contemplated crime is one for which an indictment would lie here: *Board of Trade v. Owen* [1957] A.C. 602, HL. As to the current statutory position, see *post*, § 33–22.

(c) A conspiracy formed abroad to commit an offence within the jurisdiction is indictable even if no acts in futherance of the conspiracy are committed within the jurisdiction: see *post*, § 33–23.

(d) Special rules applied to a conspiracy to murder abroad where the agreement was entered into before September 4, 1998: *CLA* 1977, s.1(4) (as originally enacted). The relevant wording has ceased to have effect (*ante*, § 33–3), and conspiracies to murder abroad are now covered by section 1A of the Act, *post*, § 33–22.

(b) *Conspiracy to commit a crime abroad*

Criminal Law Act 1977, s.1A

Conspiracy to commit offences outside the United Kingdom

1A.—(1) Where each of the following conditions is satisfied in the case of an agreement, this Part of this Act has effect in relation to the agreement as it has effect in relation to an agreement falling within section 1(1) above. **33–22**

(2) The first condition is that the pursuit of the agreed course of conduct would at some stage involve—

(a) an act by one or more of the parties, or

(b) the happening of some other event,

intended to take place in a country or territory outside the United Kingdom.

(3) The second condition is that that act or other event constitutes an offence under the law in force in that country or territory.

(4) The third condition is that the agreement would fall within section 1(1) above as an agreement relating to the commission of an offence but for the fact that the offence would not be an offence triable in England and Wales if committed in accordance with the parties' intentions.

(5) The fourth condition is that—

(a) a party to the agreement, or a party's agent, did anything in England and Wales in relation to the agreement before its formation, or

(b) a party to the agreement became a party in England and Wales (by joining it either in person or through an agent), or

(c) a party to the agreement, or a party's agent, did or omitted anything in England and Wales in pursuance of the agreement.

(6) In the application of this Part of this Act to an agreement in the case of which each of the above conditions is satisfied, a reference to an offence is to be read as a reference to what would be the offence in question but for the fact that it is not an offence triable in England and Wales.

(7) Conduct punishable under the law in force in any country or territory is an offence under that law for the purposes of this section, however it is described in that law.

(8) Subject to subsection (9) below, the second condition is to be taken to be satisfied unless, not later than rules of court may provide, the defence serve on the prosecution a notice—

(a) stating that, on the facts as alleged with respect to the agreed course of conduct, the condition is not in their opinion satisfied,

(b) showing their grounds for that opinion, and

(c) requiring the prosecution to show that it is satisfied.

(9) The court may permit the defence to require the prosecution to show that the second condition is satisfied without the prior service of a notice under subsection (8) above.

(10) In the Crown Court the question whether the second condition is satisfied shall be decided by the judge alone, and shall be treated as a question of law for the purposes of—

(a) section 9(3) of the *Criminal Justice Act* 1987 (preparatory hearing in fraud cases), and

(b) section 31(3) of the *Criminal Procedure and Investigations Act* 1996 (preparatory hearing in other cases).

(11) Any act done by means of a message (however communicated) is to be treated for the purposes of the fourth condition as done in England and Wales if the message is sent or received in England and Wales.

(12) In any proceedings in respect of an offence triable by virtue of this section, it is immaterial to guilt whether or not the acused was a British citizen at the time of any act or other event proof of which is required for conviction of the offence.

(13) References in any enactment, instrument or document (except those in this Part of this Act) to an offence of conspiracy to commit an offence include an offence triable in England and Wales as such a conspiracy by virtue of this section (without prejudice to subsection (6) above).

(14) Nothing in this section—

(a) applies to an agreement entered into before the day on which the *Criminal Justice (Terrorism and Conspiracy) Act* 1998 was passed, or

(b) imposes criminal liability on any person acting on behalf of, or holding office under, the Crown.

[This section was substituted (as to which, see also *post*, § 33–24) by the *Criminal Justice (Terrorism and Conspiracy) Act* 1998, s.5(1), on September 4, 1998.]

As to the common law position, see *ante*, § 33–21.

(c) *Conspiracy formed out of jurisdiction to commit a crime in England*

33–23 A conspiracy formed outside the jurisdiction to commit a crime within the jurisdiction is indictable in England and Wales even though no act in furtherance of the agreement is committed in England or Wales: *Somchai Liangsiriprasert v. Government of the United States of America* [1991] 1 A.C. 225, PC. This applies to both common law and statutory conspiracies: *R. v. Sansom* [1991] 2 Q.B. 130, 92 Cr.App.R. 115, CA. Both cases were decided before the enactment of Part I of the *CJA* 1993, as to which, see *ante*, §§ 2–37 *et seq.*

(d) *Fraud and related offences and sexual offences*

33–24 Special provisions were introduced in relation to conspiracy to commit fraud and related offences abroad by the *CJA* 1993, s.5(1) (inserting s.1A in the 1977 Act, but never brought into force) and in relation to conspiracy to commit sexual offences abroad by the *Sexual Offences (Conspiracy and Incitement) Act* 1996, ss.1 and 3 (from October 1, 1996). These provisions ceased to have effect as from September 4, 1998, and were superseded by the general provisions of the *CLA* 1977, s.1A (*ante*, § 33–22).

(4) Parties

General

33–25 Conspiracy requires the agreement of two or more persons. However it is not necessary to prove that the defendants met to concoct or originate the scheme. A conspiracy may exist between persons who have neither seen nor corresponded with each other: *R. v. Parnell* (1881) 14 Cox 508; *R. v. Meyrick and Ribuffi*, 21 Cr.App.R. 94, CCA; *R. v. Hammersley*, 42 Cr.App.R. 207 at 217, CCA. If a conspiracy is already formed, and a person joins it afterwards, he is equally guilty with the original conspirators: *R. v. Murphy* (1837) 8 C. & P. 297 at 311; see too *DPP v. Doot* [1973] A.C. 807, HL, and the observations of Paull J. in *R. v. Griffiths* [1966] 1 Q.B. 589, 49 Cr.App.R. 279, CCA. Some conspirators may drop out and others join in during the course of the conspiracy but it may nevertheless remain a single conspiracy: *R. v. Simmonds* [1969] 1 Q.B. 685 at 696, 51 Cr.App.R. 316 at 332; *R. v. Hammersley*, *ante*.

Criminal Law Act 1977, s.2

Exemptions from liability for conspiracy

33–26 **2.**—(1) A person shall not by virtue of section 1 above be guilty of conspiracy to commit any offence if he is an intended victim of that offence.

(2) A person shall not by virtue of section 1 above be guilty of conspiracy to commit any offence or offences if the only other person or persons with whom he agrees are (both initially and at all times during the currency of the agreement) persons of any one or more of the following descriptions, that is to say—

(a) his spouse or civil partner;

(b) a person under the age of criminal responsibility; and

(c) an intended victim of that offence or of each of those offences.

(3) A person is under the age of criminal responsibility for the purposes of subsection (2)(b) above so long as it is conclusively presumed, by virtue of section 50 of the *Children and Young Persons Act* 1933, that he cannot be guilty of any offence.

[This section is printed as amended by the *Civil Partnership Act* 2004, s.261(1), and Sched. 27, para. 56.]

As to the modification of this section by the *AFA* 2006, see *ante*, § 33–3.

As to the application of this section in determining whether a person is guilty of conspiracy under an enactment other than this Act (*e.g.* the *Explosives Substances Act* 1883, s.3(1)(a), *ante*, § 23–66), see section 5(6), *post*, § 33–34.

Husbands and wives and civil partners

A husband and wife are not guilty of conspiracy if they alone are parties to the agreement; and the same rule now applies to civil partners: s.2(2)(a), *ante*. As far as concerns married couples, this reflects the common law: see 1 Hawk. c.27, s.8; *Mawji v. R.* [1957] A.C. 126, PC. **33–27**

A wife may conspire with her husband, contrary to section 1(1) of the Act if, knowing that her husband was involved with others in a conspiracy to commit an unlawful act, she agreed with him to join that conspiracy, notwithstanding that the only person with whom she concluded the agreement was her husband: *R. v. Chrastny*, 94 Cr.App.R. 283, CA. Where husband and wife are charged with conspiring with another, the jury should be directed to acquit the husband and wife if they are not satisfied that there was another party to the conspiracy: *R. v. Lovick* [1993] Crim.L.R. 890, CA.

Persons under the age of criminal responsibility

For section 50 of the *CYPA* 1933, see *ante*, § 1–90. **33–28**

Victims

See the *CLA* 1977, s.2(1), (2)(c), *ante*, § 33–26. **33–29**

In *R. v. Drew* [2000] 1 Cr.App.R. 91, CA, the court said that it would be a misuse of language to say that a person to whom controlled drugs were supplied was a "victim" of the offence of unlawful supply; and accordingly, he could be charged with a conspiracy to supply drugs in respect of his agreement with the supplier for the latter to supply him with drugs. This point was, however, conceded, and must remain open to argument.

Persons incapable of committing the substantive offence

Where a substantive offence may be committed only by a person of a particular description, a person not fitting the description may nevertheless be guilty of a conspiracy to commit that offence provided that the course of conduct agreed upon involved the commission of that offence by another conspirator who necessarily fitted the specified description: *R. v. Sherry and El Yamani* [1993] Crim.L.R. 536, CA. See also *ante*, § 19–312. **33–30**

Companies

A company may be convicted of an offence of conspiracy: *R. v. I.C.R. Haulage Co. Ltd* [1944] K.B. 551, 30 Cr.App.R. 31, CCA. Where the sole responsible person in a company is the defendant, an indictment for conspiracy between the defendant and that company will not lie, since there are not two or more persons or minds acting: *R. v. McDonnell* [1966] 1 Q.B. 233, 50 Cr.App.R. 5, Assizes (Nield J.). It may be otherwise if the defendant brings his company into combination with himself in his capacity not as the person solely responsible for his company, but as a person responsible for the acts of another corporation: see the Canadian cases cited in *McDonnell*, *ante*. **33–31**

(5) Penalties

Criminal Law Act 1977, s.3

Penalties for conspiracy

3.—(1) A person guilty by virtue of section 1 above of conspiracy to commit any offence or offences shall be liable on conviction on indictment— **33–32**

(a) in a case falling within subsection (2) or (3) below, to imprisonment for a term related in accordance with that subsection to the gravity of the offence or offences in question (referred to below in this section as the relevant offence or offences); and

(b) in any other case, to a fine.

Paragraph (b) above shall not be taken as prejudicing the application of section 163 of the *Criminal Justice Act* 2003 (general power of court to fine offender convicted on indictment) in a case falling within subsection (2) or (3) below.

(2) Where the relevant offence or any of the relevant offences is an offence of any of the following descriptions, that is to say—

(a) murder, or any other offence the sentence for which is fixed by law;

(b) an offence for which a sentence extending to imprisonment for life is provided; or

(c) an indictable offence punishable with imprisonment for which no maximum term of imprisonment is provided,

the person convicted shall be liable to imprisonment for life.

(3) Where in a case other than one to which subsection (2) above applies the relevant offence or any of the relevant offences is punishable with imprisonment, the person convicted shall be liable to imprisonment for a term not exceeding the maximum term provided for that offence or (where more than one such offence is in question) for any one of those offences (taking the longer or the longest term as the limit for the purposes of this section where the terms provided differ).

In the case of an offence triable either way the references above in this subsection to the maximum term provided for that offence are references to the maximum term so provided on conviction on indictment.

[This section is printed as amended by the *PCC(S)A* 2000, s.165(1) and Sched. 9, para. 55; and the *CJA* 2003, s.304, and Sched. 32, para. 24.]

Where a single criminal enterprise is indicted as a number of conspiracies to commit substantive offences of the same nature, the judge should not regard the upper limit of his sentencing powers as the maximum sentence for any one conspiracy; where consecutive sentences would be appropriate on ordinary sentencing principles, it would be permissible to arrive at an overall sentence in excess of the maximum for any one offence: see *Att.-Gen.'s References (Nos 120 and 121 of 2004) (R. v. Herbert and Beard)* [2006] 1 Cr.App.R.(S.) 7, CA; and *Att.-Gen.'s References (Nos 42, 43 and 44 of 2006) (R. v. Clemow)* [2007] 1 Cr.App.R.(S.) 80, CA.

(6) Restrictions on institution of proceedings

Criminal Law Act 1977, s.4

Restrictions on the institution of proceedings for conspiracy

33–33 **4.**—(1) Subject to subsection (2) below proceedings under section 1 above for conspiracy to commit any offence or offences shall not be instituted against any person except by or within the consent of the Director of Public Prosecutions if the offence or (as the case may be) each of the offences in question is a summary offence.

(2) In relation to the institution of proceedings under section 1 above for conspiracy to commit—

(a) an offence which is subject to a prohibition by or under any enactment on the institution of proceedings otherwise than by, or on behalf or with the consent of, the Attorney General, or

(b) two or more offences of which at least one is subject to such a prohibition,

subsection (1) above shall have effect with the substitution of a reference to the Attorney General for the reference to the Director of Public Prosecutions.

(3) Any prohibition by or under any enactment on the institution of proceedings for any offence which is not a summary offence otherwise than by, or on behalf or with the consent of, the Director of Public Prosecutions or any other person shall apply also in relation to proceedings under section 1 above for conspiracy to commit that offence.

(4) Where—

(a) an offence has been committed in pursuance of any agreement; and

(b) proceedings may not be instituted for that offence because any time limit applicable to the institution of any such proceedings has expired,

proceedings under section 1 above for conspiracy to commit that offence shall not be instituted against any person on the basis of that agreement.

(5) Subject to subsection (6) below, no proceedings for an offence triable by virtue of section 1A above may be instituted except by or with the consent of the Attorney General.

(6) The Secretary of State may by order provide that subsection (5) above shall not apply, or shall not apply to any case of a description specified in the order.

(7) [*Making of order under subs. (6).*]

[Subss. (5) to (7) were added by the *Criminal Justice (Terrorism and Conspiracy) Act* 1998, s.5(2), which came into force on September 4, 1998.]

As to consents generally, see the *Prosecution of Offences Act* 1985, s.25 (*ante*, § 1–278); as to proof of consents, see *ibid.* s.26 (*ante*, § 1–279). Failure to obtain a requisite consent will render the proceedings a nullity: *R. v. Angel*, 52 Cr.App.R. 280, CA; *R. v. Pearce*, 72 Cr.App.R. 295, CA.

Consent to a prosecution for a substantive offence does not extend to a prosecution for a conspiracy to commit such offence: *R. v. Pearce*, *ante*. As to this, see also *ante*, § 29–51.

C. SAVING OF CERTAIN CONSPIRACIES AT COMMON LAW, ETC.

(1) Statute

Criminal Law Act 1977, s.5

Abolitions, savings, transitional provisions, consequential amendments and repeals

5.—(1) Subject to the following provisions of this section, the offence of conspiracy at common law is hereby abolished. **33–34**

(2) Subsection (1) above shall not affect the offence of conspiracy at common law so far as relates to conspiracy to defraud ....

(3) Subsection (1) above shall not affect the offence of conspiracy at common law if and in so far as it may be committed by entering into an agreement to engage in conduct which—

(a) tends to corrupt public morals or outrages public decency; but
(b) would not amount to or involve the commission of an offence if carried out by a single person otherwise than in pursuance of an agreement.

(4), (5) [*Transitional provisions—not printed in this work.*]

(6) The rules laid down by sections 1 and 2 above shall apply for determining whether a person is guilty of an offence of conspiracy under any enactment other than section 1 above, but conduct which is an offence under any such other enactment shall not also be an offence under section 1 above.

(7) [*Repealed by* SCA *2007, ss.63(2) and 92, Sched. 6, para. 54, and Sched. 14.*]

(8) The fact that the person or persons who, so far as appears from the indictment on which any person has been convicted of conspiracy, were the only other parties to the agreement on which his conviction was based have been acquitted of conspiracy by reference to that agreement (whether after being tried with the person convicted or separately) shall not be a ground for quashing his conviction unless under all the circumstances of the case his conviction is inconsistent with the acquittal of the other person or persons in question.

(9) Any rule of law or practice inconsistent with the provisions of subsection (8) above is hereby abolished.

(10) [*Repeals, in part, section 4 of the* Offences against the Person Act *1861*, ante, *§ 19–119.*]

(11) [*Repealed by* Trade Union and Labour Relations (Consolidation) Act *1992, s.300(1) and Sched. 1*]

[This section is printed as amended by the schedule to the *Criminal Attempts Act* 1981; and the *CJA* 1987, s.12.]

As to subsections (8) and (9), see *post*, §§ 33–72 *et seq.*

Criminal Justice Act 1987, s.12

Charges of and penalty for conspiracy to defraud

12.—(1) If— **33–35**

(a) a person agrees with any other person or persons that a course of conduct shall be pursued; and
(b) that course of conduct will necessarily amount to or involve the commission of any offence or offences by one or more of the parties to the agreement if the agreement is carried out in accordance with their intentions,

the fact that it will do so shall not preclude a charge of conspiracy to defraud being brought against any of them in respect of the agreement.

(2) [*Repeal in part of* Criminal Law Act *1977, s.5(2)*.]

(3) A person guilty of conspiracy to defraud is liable on conviction on indictment to imprisonment for a term not exceeding 10 years or a fine or both.

(2) Conspiracy to defraud

The meaning of defraud

33–36 See *ante*, §§ 17–62 *et seq.*

Limitations

33–37 Conspiracy to defraud should not be used to reinstate as a crime that which Parliament thought right to take off the statute book as a crime: *R. v. Zemmel*, 81 Cr.App.R. 279, CA. Nor does it extend to criminalise price-fixing or cartel agreements in restraint of trade, even if they are unreasonable and not in the public interest or void or unenforceable: *Norris v. Government of the United States of America* [2008] 2 W.L.R. 673, HL. Such agreements are not indictable at common law in the absence of fraud, misrepresentation, violence, or intimidation: *ibid.*

Indictment

33–38 See *post*, §§ 33–44 *et seq.*

The Attorney-General has issued guidance (January 9, 2007) to prosecuting authorities as to when it is appropriate to charge a common law conspiracy to defraud instead of a substantive offence, contrary to the *Fraud Act* 2006, or a statutory conspiracy to commit a substantive offence, contrary to section 1 of the 1977 Act. For further details thereof, see Appendix A–272.

Sentence

33–39 10 years' imprisonment or a fine, or both: *CJA* 1987, s.12(3), *ante*, § 33–35.

A financial reporting order may be made in respect of a person convicted of an offence of conspiracy to defraud: *SOCPA* 2005, s.76 (*ante*, § 5–886a).

Jurisdiction

33–40 Where the true object of a conspiracy is to defraud abroad, it is not indictable in England merely because its performance abroad would either cause economic loss and damage to the proprietary interests of a company within the jurisdiction or injure a person or company here by causing him or it damage abroad. Such consequences are incidental and are not the object of the conspiracy: *Att.-Gen.'s Reference (No. 1 of 1982)* [1983] Q.B. 751 (applying the test in *Board of Trade v. Owen* [1957] A.C. 602 and a dictum of Lord Wilberforce in *DPP v. Doot* [1973] A.C. 807 at 818, HL). The court observed that it would be contrary to principle for the courts here to attribute to the defendants a constructive intention to defraud third parties based upon what the defendants should have foreseen as probable or possible consequences.

Conspiracy to defraud is a Group B offence within Part I (ss.1–6) of the *CJA* 1993. Part I came into force on June 1, 1999 (*Criminal Justice Act 1993 (Commencement No. 10) Order* 1999 (S.I. 1999 No. 1189) and *Criminal Justice Act 1993 (Commencement No. 11) Order* 1999 (S.I. 1999 No. 1499)). It is not retrospective: *CJA* 1993, s.78(5) (*ante*, § 2–43). The effect of these provisions is set out at §§ 2–44 *et seq.*, *ante*. For the extended jurisdiction in respect of Group B offences, see *ante*, §§ 2–45 *et seq.*

(3) Conspiracies to do acts tending to corrupt public morals or outrage public decency

General

33–41 There is such an offence as a conspiracy to corrupt public morals: *Shaw v. DPP* [1962] A.C. 220, HL; *Knuller (Publishing, Printing and Promotions) Ltd v. DPP*

[1973] A.C. 435, HL. There is also an offence of conspiracy to outrage public decency: *Knuller (Publishing, Printing and Promotions) Ltd v. DPP*, *ante* (Lords Reid and Diplock dissenting). For further consideration of these offences, see *ante*, §§ 20–238 *et seq.*

Sentence

The punishment for conspiracy at common law is a fine or imprisonment, or both. The only common law restriction is that the punishment should not be inordinate. **33–42**

D. PLEADING, EVIDENCE AND PRACTICE

(1) Time bars and other restrictions on instituting proceedings

Common law conspiracies are not subject to time-limits: see *R. v. Simmonds* [1969] 1 Q.B. 685, 51 Cr.App.R. 316, CA. As to statutory conspiracies, see section 4(4) of the *CLA* 1977 (*ante*, § 33–33). **33–43**

As to certain restrictions on the institution of proceedings for an offence of statutory conspiracy except by or with the consent of the Director of Public Prosecutions or the Attorney-General, see section 4(1) to (3) of the 1977 Act, *ante*, § 33–33.

(2) The indictment

Mens rea

See *R. v. Saik*, § 33–4. **33–44**

Pleading overt acts

The overt acts need not be set out. The conspiracy is the offence, and it is immaterial whether anything has been done in pursuance of it: *R. v. Whitehouse* (1852) 6 Cox 38 at 45, 47; *R. v. Richardson* (1834) 1 M. & Rob. 402; *R. v. Kenrick* (1843) 5 Q.B. 49; *Wright v. R.* (1849) 14 Q.B. 148; and see *post*, § 33–48. **33–45**

Co-conspirators and persons unknown

Where the evidence discloses that the accused conspired with other persons who are not before the court, this should be averred in the indictment. If they cannot be identified, it is sufficient to describe them as "persons unknown". Sometimes, the evidence may be unclear as to which identifiable persons were involved. In such circumstances, there can be no objection either to "other persons unknown", or to "other persons". However, where during the course of the trial the uncertainty is resolved by evidence which is capable of founding the assertion that an identifiable person not before the court was a conspirator with the accused, then the indictment should be amended accordingly. **33–46**

Requests for particulars

On a general count not alleging any overt act, the court can order particulars if satisfied that without them the conduct of the defence will be embarrassed. However, this sort of difficulty will only genuinely arise on rare occasions. The information sought on a request for further and better particulars can usually be found in the evidence, in the Crown's opening, or in both. **33–47**

One of the purposes of particulars is to allow the defence to know precisely the case it has to meet and to stop the Crown shifting its ground during the trial: *R. v. Landy*, 72 Cr.App.R. 237, CA; *R. v. Hancock* [1996] 2 Cr.App.R. 554, CA. However, the particulars given should not be more than necessary, having regard to the need to avoid complex, lengthy and unmanageable trials: *R. v. Cohen*, *The Independent*, July 29, 1992, CA. **33–48**

Particulars and overt acts in conspiracy to defraud

A count of conspiracy to defraud should identify the agreement alleged with the specificity necessary in the circumstances of each case: if the agreement is complex, then **33–49** details of that may be needed and those details will, as in *Bennett* (*ante*, § 33–10), form part of what must be proved. However, reasonable information given in respect of the indictment, such as the general nature of the case which the prosecution seek to prove, and the principal overt acts upon which they rely to invite a jury to infer the existence of the dishonest agreement, form no part of the ingredients of the offence: *Hancock*, *ante*; and *R. v. K.* [2005] 1 Cr.App.R. 25, CA.

Care should be taken to differentiate between particulars which define the agreement which the Crown seek to prove, as in *Bennett*, and those which set out overt acts from which the Crown invite the jury to infer the existence of an agreement. Some counsel have begun to limit the particulars of offence to the terms of the agreement to be proved, followed by voluntary particulars which set out the principal overt acts relied upon. This practice, it is submitted, has the advantage of clarity and precision and was approved by the Court of Appeal in *R. v. K.*, *ante*.

Pleading conspiracy to defraud

33–50 In *R. v. Landy*, *ante*, the Court of Appeal said that in complicated cases, care should be taken to ensure that the indictment does not lack particularity. The court deprecated the use of expressions such as "and by divers other false and fraudulent devices" as being a relic of the past which should never again appear in an indictment. What is wanted is precision and clarity. The court gave an example of the sort of detailed pleading which it would have regarded as appropriate to the facts before it. In the example given, there were five sub-paragraphs (sub-paras (ii) and (iii) are omitted here but are in the same vein as sub-para. (i)) (see pp. 244–245 of the report).

PARTICULARS OF OFFENCE

33–51 [The defendants] on divers days between … and … conspired together and with … to defraud such corporations, companies, partnerships, firms and persons as might lend funds to or deposit funds with [X Bank Ltd] ("the Bank") by dishonestly—

(i) causing and permitting the Bank to make excessive advances to insubstantial and speculative trading companies incorporated in Liechtenstein and Switzerland, such advances being inadequately secured, inadequately guaranteed and without proper provision for payment of interest; …

(iv) causing and permitting the Bank's accounts and Bank of England returns to be prepared in such a way as (a) to conceal the nature, constitution and extent of the Bank's lending and (b) to show a false and misleading financial situation as at the ends of the Bank's accounting years;

(v) causing and permitting the Bank to discount commercial bills when (a) there was no underlying commercial transaction, (b) the documents evidencing the supposed underlying transactions were false, and (c) the transactions were effected in order to transfer funds to the Bank's parent company in Tel Aviv.

Duplicity and "rolled-up charges"

33–52 No more than one offence should be charged in a single count; this rule against duplicity applies to conspiracy as much as to any other offence. Duplicity is a matter of form not evidence (see *R. v. West* [1948] 1 K.B. 709, 32 Cr.App.R. 152, CCA; *R. v. Davey and Davey*, 45 Cr.App.R. 11, CCA; *R. v. Griffiths* [1966] 1 Q.B. 589, 49 Cr.App.R. 279, CCA): *R. v. Greenfield*, 57 Cr.App.R. 849, CA. To ascertain whether a count is bad for duplicity, it is ordinarily unnecessary to look further than the count itself. If particulars have been asked for and provided, those too may be considered. Where particulars have been requested but refused, the judge may look at the evidence to discover the nature of the charge: *R. v. Greenfield*, *ante*.

Where the indictment is perfectly regular on its face, the evidence may nevertheless prove not one but several conspiracies. If, at the close of the case for the prosecution, there is no evidence to support the single conspiracy charged, it is the duty of the judge to withdraw the case from the jury. This is a quite distinct issue from that of duplicity, although the two are frequently confused in practice. It follows, however, that it is particularly important when drafting an indictment to consider both whether the proposed count charges a single offence only on its face, and whether the evidence reveals the existence of a single conspiracy or several conspiracies.

In order properly to found one count, alleging against several people a conspiracy to commit an offence, the evidence would have to show that all had joined in one agreement, each with the others. The principle was considered in *R. v. Griffiths*, *ante* (the "lime fraud" case). Paull J., giving the judgment of the court, said: **33–53**

> "... in law all must join in the one agreement, each with the others, in order to constitute one conspiracy. They may join in at various times, each attaching himself to that agreement; any one of them may not know all the other parties, but only that there are other parties; any one of them may not know the full extent of the scheme to which he attaches himself; but what each must know is that there is coming into existence, or is in existence, a scheme which goes beyond the illegal act which he agrees to do" (at pp. 597, 290).

See also his Lordship's celebrated "accountant" example of a situation where there would be several conspiracies (at pp. 598–599, 291).

If one or more persons are at the centre of the unlawful activity and deal with individuals who do not know, or know of, each other, and each of whom is ignorant of the fact that the activities go beyond his own dealings, then the whole evidence relating to all the individuals does not disclose one single conspiracy. If, however, each individual, although ignorant of the details of the others concerned, knows that there are others and that the activity in which he takes a part extends beyond his own dealings with the person or persons at the centre, then the evidence discloses one conspiracy: *ibid.*, and *R. v. Meyrick and Ribuffi*, 21 Cr.App.R. 94, CCA. The question is always whether there was a common criminal purpose: *ibid.* at p. 102.

The longer a conspiracy is alleged to have lasted, the more important it is to make sure it is one and the same agreement that is being alleged, and not a number of different agreements within that one period: *R. v. Greenfield*, 57 Cr.App.R. 849 at 857, CA. **33–54**

If, at the end of the prosecution case, there is evidence on which, if uncontradicted, a reasonably minded jury could convict the accused of the conspiracy charged, despite evidence of the existence of a different conspiracy, then the judge should let the case go to the jury: *R. v. Greenfield*, *ante*, at p. 857.

Where the appellant had been charged in a single count of conspiracy with three co-defendants and others unknown, but the evidence failed to establish that one of the co-accused was party to any agreement with the appellant and the other two co-accused, albeit it would have supported a separate conspiracy involving that defendant and others unknown, the judge had been correct in ruling that the case should go no further against that defendant on the count charged; and, having rejected a prosecution application to amend the indictment so as to include a second count alleging a separate conspiracy against that defendant "and others unknown" on the basis that it would be unfair to do so, he had been under no obligation to make a similar ruling in respect of the appellant in relation to the original count, where he was not only caused no embarrassment by the acquittal of the co-defendant, but, if anything, was potentially assisted by his disappearance from the case: *R. v. Mintern* (2004) 148 S.J. 146, CA (see also *ante*, §§ 1–140, 1–146).

Wheels and chains

It should be noted that the sentence in the headnote to *Griffiths*, *ante*, which says that the kind of conspiracy, known as a "wheel conspiracy", is not known to law, goes beyond what was decided: see *R. v. Ardalan*, 56 Cr.App.R. 320, CA. Use of the expression "wheel conspiracy" to describe the situation in *Griffiths* is misleading. It was made clear in *R. v. Meyrick and Ribuffi*, *ante*, that what are described as "wheel" conspiracies, or "chain" conspiracies, may be one conspiracy. It is perfectly possible for a number of conspirators to deal only with a person at the hub and all to be members of the same conspiracy. The issue in such a case is whether they were aware that the scheme to which they attached themselves went beyond their agreement with the person at the hub. Equally, it is possible for there to be but one conspiracy where A agrees with B, B agrees with C, C agrees with D (a "chain" conspiracy). In each case, it is a question of fact whether there is one agreement or several agreements. **33–55**

Alternative counts

Where it is uncertain whether there is one or more conspiracy it is advisable to **33–56** lay one count charging the whole as one conspiracy and alternative counts charging each possible constituent part as a separate conspiracy, leaving it to the jury to decide whether there was one conspiracy or more than one conspiracy. As to this, see *R v. Radley*, 58 Cr.App.R. 394, CA, *ante*, § 1–140.

Plot and sub-plots

33–57 If A and B agree to embark on a bombing campaign throughout England, they will be guilty of conspiracy to cause explosions as soon as the agreement is concluded, despite the fact that nothing may have been done to execute the agreement, with no targets identified and no times determined. If thereafter, as a result of detailed planning, they identify a target and determine a time for the placing of their first bomb, it is submitted that this would not constitute a separate offence, the test being whether what was done was done in pursuit of the original agreement (a course of conduct involving the commission of one or more offences by either or both of them—see s.1); but, if they were to recruit C for the specific purpose of placing the first bomb, C having no knowledge of their wider plans, it is submitted that there would now be a second (sub-)conspiracy, with A, B and C as the parties thereto. If A and B were being tried on the wider conspiracy, the sub-conspiracy and any overt acts done in pursuance of it would be admissible. If, on the other hand, C were to be recruited to the wider conspiracy, there would remain one conspiracy only. This, it is submitted, is the effect of *R. v. Coughlan and Young*, 63 Cr.App.R. 33, CA (a decision on the common law), taken together with the provisions of section 1 of the 1977 Act.

Election by prosecution

33–58 Where an indictment contains substantive counts and one or more related conspiracy counts the judge should require the prosecution to justify the joinder. Failing justification the Crown should be required to elect whether to proceed on the substantive counts or on the conspiracy counts. A joinder is justified for this purpose if the judge considers that the interests of justice demand it: *Practice Direction (Criminal Proceedings: Consolidation)* [2002] 1 W.L.R. 2870 (para. IV.34.3, *ante*, § 1–112).

Two problems arise in this context: (a) whether it is appropriate to include a count for conspiracy at all; and (b) if it is, whether counts for substantive offences can properly be included in the same indictment. Of the two, it is the second problem which most frequently arises in court on applications for severance. Applications to sever are invariably made when the substantive counts add nothing to the conspiracy allegation but are simply sample counts relating to the carrying out of the conspiracy. Such applications are usually granted and the Crown elects which limb of the indictment it proposes to proceed upon. It should be remembered, however, that the fact that the substantive counts are sample counts is not *per se* a ground for granting an application to sever. One example of where such an application should be refused is where sample counts do not reflect the overall criminality of the case. A further example arises when (notwithstanding the decision in *DPP v. Shannon* [1975] A.C. 717, HL, *post*, § 33–72, and section 5(8) and (9) of the 1977 Act, *ante*, § 33–34), only two persons are alleged to have conspired together. On the assumption that the conspiracy count is properly included, it is submitted that there can be no objection to sample counts being included to cater for the possibility that one of the alleged conspirators will be acquitted. A similar argument may be advanced where, for example, of three alleged conspirators, two are husband and wife.

Whether to include a count for conspiracy at all

33–59 The question of whether a conspiracy charge is properly included cannot be determined by the application of any rigid rules. Each case must be considered on its own facts: see *R. v. Jones (J.)*, 59 Cr.App.R. 120, CA. Subject to that caveat, the general principles governing the desirability or otherwise of including a count for conspiracy in the indictment may be summarised as follows.

33–60 (1) As a general rule where there is an effective and sufficient charge of a substantive offence, a charge of conspiracy is undesirable: *Verrier v. DPP* [1967] 2 A.C. 195, HL; *R. v. Griffiths* [1966] 1 Q.B. 589, 49 Cr.App.R. 279, CCA; *R. v. Greenfield*, 57 Cr.App.R. 849, CA; *R. v. Jones (J.), ante*; *R. v. Watts, The Times*, April 14, 1995, CA.

(2) There are exceptions which include the following. **33–61**

(a) Cases of complexity in which the interests of justice can only be served by presenting to a jury an overall picture which cannot be achieved by charging a relatively small series of substantive offences: *R. v. Hammersley*, 42 Cr.App.R. 207, CCA; *R. v. Simmonds* [1969] 1 Q.B. 685 at 690, 51 Cr.App.R. 316 at 322, 323, CA. The indictment ought to include charges which simplify the issues, shun complexity and avoid a multiplicity of counts. Sometimes, a charge of conspiracy may be the simpler way of presenting the case or reflecting the overall criminality of the case: *R. v. Jones (J.), ante*, at p. 124.

(b) Cases in which a general conspiracy, *e.g.* to steal, is likely to be inferred by the jury from the evidence but in which the particular acts constituting the thefts may only be supported by rather nebulous evidence: *R. v. Cooper and Compton*, 32 Cr.App.R. 102, CCA. Where there is clear evidence of conspiracy but little evidence that any of the conspirators committed any of the overt acts, a count for conspiracy is both justifiable and necessary. Where there is evidence that some, but not all, of the defendants committed a few, but not all of the overt acts, a count for conspiracy is justified: *R. v. Greenfield, ante*.

(c) Cases where the agreement to commit the offence is itself more wicked than the act. Thus a conspiracy to desecrate a Jewish cemetery (maximum penalty 10 years) could be charged although, when the agreement was carried out, the amount of damage caused rendered the substantive offence of criminal damage triable only summarily (maximum penalty three months): *R. v. Ward* [1997] 1 Cr.App.R.(S.) 442, CA.

(3) A count for conspiracy should not be included with counts charging substantive offences if the inclusion will result in unfairness to the defence. This is an aspect which has to be weighed with other considerations: *R. v. Jones (J.), ante*. Where the prosecution have elected to proceed on substantive counts, they may apply to re-elect and allege conspiracy again if such a course does not cause any prejudice to the defence: *R. v. Findlay and Francis* [1992] Crim.L.R. 372, CA (prosecution re-elected after judge excluded one of the defendant's interviews). **33–62**

(3) Severance

Persons indicted together for conspiracy may be separately tried, and are not entitled to have judgment stayed on conviction until the others are tried: *R. v. Ahearne* (1852) 6 Cox 6 (Ir.). Cases must be rare in which fellow conspirators can properly be granted a separate trial: *per* Devlin J. in *R. v. Miller*, 36 Cr.App.R. 169, Assizes. See generally, *ante*, §§ 1–160 *et seq.* As to severance of a conspiracy count from substantive counts, see *ante*, § 33–58. **33–63**

In complicated cases, the trial judge has the ultimate responsibility for ensuring that the indictment is one on which a manageable trial is possible; he should be robust in using his power of severance to secure this: *R. v. Cohen, The Independent*, July 29, 1992, CA, and see generally, *ante*, §§ 1–167 *et seq.* If a judge, on examination of the material before him, considers that the prosecution's proposed presentation of the case will impose an undue burden on the court and jurors and is therefore contrary to the interests of justice, he has a duty to ask the prosecution to recast their approach, even if it entails an adjournment: *R. v. Simmonds* [1969] 1 Q.B. 685, 51 Cr.App.R. 316, CA.

(4) The trial of a single conspirator

One person alone may be tried for a conspiracy, provided that the indictment charges him with conspiring with others who have not appeared (*R. v. Plummer* [1902] 2 K.B. 339); or who are since dead (*R. v. Nichols, or Nicholls* (1742) 2 Str. 1227); or whose names are unknown. Persons jointly indicted may be severally tried: *R. v. Ahearne, ante*. The death of one or two conspirators does not affect the right to try the other, whether the death happens before indictment or during trial: *R. v. Kenrick* (1843) 5 Q.B. 49. Where two defendants are jointly indicted for conspiracy, and one of them **33–64** pleads guilty, and the other not guilty, the former is admissible as a witness against the latter: *R. v. Gallagher* (1883) 15 Cox 291, CCR; *R. v. Plummer*, *ante*. These authorities are superseded by the general provision as to competence in section 53 of the *YJCEA* 1999 (*ante*, § 8–36a).

As to the proof of the conviction of one conspirator upon the trial of another, under section 74 of the *PACE Act* 1984 (*ante*, § 9–82), see *R. v. Robertson*; *R. v. Golder* [1987] Q.B. 920, 85 Cr.App.R. 304, CA, *ante*, § 9–85.

(5) Acts and declarations in furtherance of the common design

Principle

33–65 Ordinarily, acts done or words uttered by an offender will not be evidence against a co-accused absent at the time of the acts or declarations. However, it is now well established that the acts and declarations of any conspirator made in furtherance of the common design may be admitted as part of the evidence against any other conspirator. Such acts and declarations may provide evidence not only of the existence, nature and extent of the conspiracy, but also of the participation in it of persons absent when those acts or declarations were made. As to the express preservation of this rule by the *CJA* 2003, see section 118(1) thereof, *ante*, § 11–49.

The extent to which declarations made and actions done by a person in furtherance of a conspiracy are admissible is never an easy problem to solve: *R. v. Donat*, 82 Cr.App.R. 179 at 180, CA. However, the authorities are conveniently reviewed in *R. v. Devenport and Pirano* [1996] 1 Cr.App.R. 221, CA; and *R. v. Jones* [1997] 2 Cr.App.R. 119, CA. See also *ante*, § 15–451, and the cases cited at § 25–16, *ante*.

Acts and declarations of any conspirator

33–66 The act or declaration must be made by a conspirator, although it matters not whether the maker is present or absent at the trial. Where a person has been acquitted at an earlier trial or on appeal, that acquittal binds the Crown against the individual only, and the Crown may, at a subsequent trial of co-conspirators, assert that the acquitted person was a party to the agreement: *R. v. Mitchell* [1964] Crim.L.R. 297, CA. In *R. v. Gibbins*, unreported, July 21, 2004, Crown Court at Southwark, Field J. expressed the view that *Mitchell* was authority only for the proposition that the prosecution could give in evidence the acts of the acquitted person (*i.e.* without alleging that he was party to the conspiracy). It is submitted, however, that this reads too much into a single sentence in the judgment in *Mitchell*, and overlooks the rationale of admitting evidence of the conduct of a person not before the court, *viz.* that it evidences a conspiracy to which both he and one or more of the defendants were party. His Lordship's view is also inconsistent with the principles underlying *Shannon v. DPP*, *R. v. Longman and Cribben* and *R. v. Testouri*, *post*, §§ 33–72 *et seq.*

Acts or declarations made by an agent for a conspirator are admissible as acts of the principal. Thus, a document in furtherance of the unlawful agreement and written by an innocent third party but at the dictation of a conspirator was admissible against all other conspirators: *R. v. Devenport and Pirano*, *ante*.

Evidence of a request made by a solicitor's clerk acting for the defendant that "the defendant has asked me to ask you to say that he bought the ring off you" was inadmissible. It could only be admitted if the clerk had the defendant's authority to act. It was not enough that the clerk thought he was, or had said that he was so authorised: *R. v. Evans* [1981] Crim.L.R. 699, CA. Authority is assumed where counsel makes a statement in court on behalf of, and in the presence of, a defendant: *R. v. Turner (B.J.)*, 61 Cr.App.R. 67, CA.

The acts and declarations of co-conspirators made before another joined the association are only admissible against the newly joined conspirator to prove the origin, character and object of the conspiracy, and not his own participation therein: *R. v. Walters*, 69 Cr.App.R. 115, CA; *R. v. Governor of Pentonville Prison, ex p. Osman* [1990] 1 W.L.R. 277 at 316, DC.

In furtherance of the common design

The act or declaration must also be in furtherance of the common design. That means "no more than that the act must be demonstrated to be one forming an integral part of the machinery designed to give effect to the joint enterprise": *R. v. Reeves*, unreported, December 4, 1998, CA (97253251). The rule obviously admits printed handbills or placards of speeches of co-conspirators and resolutions at their meetings: *R. v. Duffield* (1851) 5 Cox 404; *R. v. Hunt* (1820) 1 St.Tr.(N.S.) 171; *R. v. Vincent* (1839) 9 C. & P. 91. **33–67**

Matters recorded by one conspirator for his convenience, mere narratives, descriptions of past events or records made after the conclusion of the conspiracy are not in furtherance of the common design and are thus not admissible against anyone other than the maker: *R. v. Blake* (1844) 6 Q.B. 126; *R. v. Jones, ante*. Usually the question of admissibility will relate to directions, instructions or arrangements or to utterances accompanying acts: *Tripodi v. R.* (1961) 104 C.L.R. 1 at 7, approved by Glidewell L.J. in *R. v. Gray and Liggins* [1995] 2 Cr.App.R. 100, CA; *R. v. Jones, ante*. However, an aide memoire might be admissible if it enabled the author to do something pursuant to the note which was intended to advance the agreement: see *R. v. Reeves, ante*.

Determination of the issue

It is a matter for the trial judge whether any act or declaration is admissible to prove the participation of another. The judge (and not the jury: see *R. v. Platten* [2006] Crim.L.R. 920, CA) must be satisfied that the act or declaration (i) was made by a conspirator, (ii) that it was reasonably open to the interpretation that it was made in furtherance of the alleged agreement, and (iii) that there is some further evidence beyond the document or utterance itself to prove that the other was a party to the agreement: *R. v. Devenport and Pirano, ante*; *R. v. Jones, ante*, § 33–65. **33–68**

In determining whether there is a common purpose so as to render the acts and extra-judicial statements done or made by one party in furtherance of the common purpose evidence against the others, the judge may have regard to such acts and statements, although their admissibility is in issue, as well as to other evidence. It is an example of conditional admissibility in that it makes no difference which is adduced first, but it follows that if in the result there is no other evidence of common purpose, the act or statement will have to be excluded: *R. v. Donat*, 82 Cr.App.R. 173 at 179–180, CA (adopting a passage in *Cross on Evidence*, 6th ed., p. 527; and see *Cross & Tapper on Evidence*, 11th ed., p. 622). See also *Queen Caroline's Case* (1820) 2 B. & B. 284; and *R. v. Brittain* (1848) 3 Cox 76.

The requirement that there should be some further evidence beyond the document or utterance itself to prove that the other was a party to the agreement (condition (iii), *ante*) was considered in *R. v. Smart and Beard*, unreported, March 27, 2002, CA ([2002] EWCA Crim. 772), where there was ample evidence of association and joint activity relating to innominate drugs. It was held that further "direct evidence" against the accused that the drugs were those particularised in the indictment was unnecessary. The evidence identifying the drugs could appear, for example, in notes made by a co-conspirator. Such notes were admissible to prove the "breadth" of the common purpose which had already been established. It is submitted that this approach should not be taken too far. The evidential doctrine of "acts in furtherance" arises at common law, and at common law an accused, to be guilty of conspiracy must at least know the essential matters which constitute the agreement: *Churchill v. Walton, ante*, § 33–16. It is submitted that a person cannot be guilty of conspiracy where the only evidence against him of an essential element of the offence arises from the acts and declarations of another. However, such difficulty did not arise on these facts as a person may be guilty of a drugs conspiracy without having knowledge of the specific drug indicted, provided that he knew that some controlled or "innominate" drug was involved and did not care what drug it was: see *ante*, § 33–19.

Directions to the jury

Any direction must be tailored to the facts of the individual case. However, to avoid **33–69** the danger of a jury rejecting the independent evidence of participation and relying solely upon the acts and declarations of others outside the presence of the accused, a judge should remind them: (i) of any shortcomings in the evidence of the acts and declarations of the others including, if it is the fact, the absence of any opportunity to cross-examine the actor or maker of the statement in question; (ii) if it be the case, the absence of corroborative evidence; and, where appropriate, (iii) not to conclude that an accused is guilty merely upon the say so of another: *R. v. Jones*, *ante*.

In *R. v. Keen*, unreported, November 5, 1999, CA (990571152), the court suggested, in relation to diary entries, that the jury should be directed to consider any explanation proffered by the author and the evidence of the other alleged conspirators. They should be told that if any innocent explanation given by the author might be true, then they should make no further use of the item as evidence against its maker or any other alleged conspirator. If, on the other hand, they did not accept any innocent explanation offered by its author, then they should remember that the entries were made in the absence of the other defendants, and that they should not convict any other defendant on the evidence of those entries alone.

Conspiracy and joint enterprise

33–70 The principle stated in § 33–65 applies when the charge is one of a crime committed in pursuance of a conspiracy, whether the indictment contains a count for conspiracy or not, and whether the co-conspirator be indicted or not, or tried or not: Phillips, *Treatise on Evidence* (4th ed., 1820), pp. 96–100; *Phipson on Evidence* (16th ed.), para. 31–45; *R. v. Jones*, *ante*; *R. v. Murray* [1997] 2 Cr.App.R. 136, CA. The principle does not, however, extend to cases where individual defendants are charged with a number of separate substantive offences and the terms of a common enterprise are not proved or are ill-defined: *R. v. Gray* [1995] 2 Cr.App.R. 100, CA, as explained in *R. v. Murray*, *ante*.

(6) Summing up

33–71 Where an indictment contains counts for substantive offences and also a count for conspiracy to commit those offences (see *ante*, § 33–59), the summing up should deal first with the substantive offences and then proceed to consider whether the count for conspiracy is properly included and how far it is proved: *R. v. Dawson and Wenlock*, 44 Cr.App.R. 87, CCA. As conspiracy involves concert, it is a misdirection to discuss the case of each defendant separately without reference to the alleged concert: *R. v. Bailey and Underwood*, 9 Cr.App.R. 94, CCA; *R. v. Ardalan*, 56 Cr.App.R. 320, CA.

(7) Conviction of one conspirator only

33–72 The enactment of section 5(8) and (9) of the *CLA* 1977 (*ante*, § 33–34) abolished the former requirement that, on a joint trial of the only two alleged conspirators, the jury must be directed to convict both or acquit both: see *Shannon v. DPP* [1975] A.C. 717, HL. It does not follow that such a direction might not be given in proper cases: see the concluding words of subsection (8).

The following approach to the problem was laid down in *R. v. Longman and Cribben*, 72 Cr.App.R. 121, CA:

33–73 "When a trial judge is faced with the task of directing a jury in a case where the charge is that A and B conspired together but with no one else to commit a crime, he will, as in other cases involving two defendants, as a general rule have to tell the jury that they must consider the evidence against each defendant separately.

Where the strength of the evidence against each is markedly different, usually because A has confessed and B has not, he should then go on to explain that because there is that difference in the evidence against each, the jury may come to the conclusion that the prosecution have proved beyond doubt against A that A conspired with B, but have not proved against B that any such conspiracy existed. That may appear to be illogical, but it is the necessary result of the rules of evidence which are designed to ensure fairness. If, therefore, the jury are satisfied that A conspired with B but are not satisfied that there is adequate evidence of B's guilt, they should convict A and acquit B.

Where at the close of the prosecution case the evidence against one of the defendants is such that it would be unsafe to ask any jury to convict, ... the judge should so rule, and the case can then continue against the other defendant.

There will, however, be cases where the evidence against A and B is of equal weight or nearly so. In such a case there may be a risk of inconsistent verdicts, and the judge should direct the jury that because of the similarity of the evidence against each, the only just result would be the same verdict in respect of each.... Hemust be careful to add, however, that if they are unsure about the guilt of one, then both must be found not guilty. Whether he gives such a direction will depend on the way the evidence has emerged. The test is this. Is the evidence such that a verdict of guilty in respect of A and not guilty in respect of B would be, to all intents and purposes, inexplicable and therefore inconsistent? If so, it would be an occasion for the 'both guilty or both not guilty' direction. If not, then the separate verdict direction is required" (at p. 125).

Longman and Cribben was applied in *R. v. Roberts*, 78 Cr.App.R. 41, CA, in which the court emphasised that the judge has to make up his mind on the evidence, whether or not it is possible, as a matter of law, for one of the accused to be convicted and the other to be acquitted. Once the judge has decided, he must direct the jury accordingly. A factor to be considered in arriving at a decision is whether the two cases are different to a substantial degree; that is a matter for the judge's assessment, not the jury's. See also *R. v. Testouri* [2004] 2 Cr.App.R. 4, CA (judge should ask himself, first, whether there is evidence of conspiracy; if not, both should be acquitted; secondly, whether there is evidence admissible against one defendant only which could be critical as against him; if not, the jury should be directed that it is not open to them to return different verdicts; if there is, then they should be directed as to the possibility of different verdicts). **33–74**

It is invariably sensible for the judge to invite submissions from counsel about whether there is a material distinction between the two defendants: only if the judge is satisfied that there is no such distinction can he direct the jury that they must acquit or convict both. The appropriate direction is not a matter of judicial discretion but depends upon the judge's evaluation of the strength of the case against each conspirator: *R. v. Ashton* [1992] Crim.L.R. 667, CA.

(8) Contradictory conspiracy and substantive verdicts

Where counts for conspiracy and substantive offences allegedly committed in carrying out the conspiracy are joined in an indictment, verdicts of not guilty of the conspiracy, but guilty of the specific offences, or vice versa, are not necessarily inconsistent as a matter of principle: *R. v. Sweetland*, 42 Cr.App.R. 62, CCA. Where, however, in such a case the verdict appears to be inconsistent, it is proper for the judge to endeavour to elucidate its meaning by questions to the jury, and it may be desirable that he should give them a further direction on the meaning of conspiracy: *ibid.* As to ambiguous and inconsistent verdicts generally, see *ante*, §§ 4–451 and 7–70 *et seq.* **33–75**

(9) Alternative verdicts

The application of section 6(3) of the *CLA* 1967 (*ante*, § 4–455) to conspiracy counts was canvassed in *R. v. Barnard*, 70 Cr.App.R. 28, CA. B pleaded "not guilty" to a count alleging conspiracy to steal. His defence was that his involvement did not go beyond negotiations from which he eventually withdrew. It was not alleged that he later participated in the robbery at the premises in question. The court held that evidence of the robbery should not have been admitted against B. Rejecting the Crown's contention that conspiracy to steal was a lesser form of a conspiracy to rob and that if there was a conspiracy to steal the fact of the stealing could be used to prove the conspiracy (albeit the stealing occurred in circumstances amounting to robbery), the court held that the two conspiracies involved different agreements: **33–76**

"There has to be another agreement if a conspiracy to steal is to become a conspiracy to rob. ... It necessarily follows that there must have been a separate agreement at some time after the original agreement to steal had been made to substitute robbery for stealing. It also follows that the evidence of the overt acts pursuant to the conspiracy to rob had no relevance to the conspiracy to steal because they showed an intention by those who carried out the agreement to rob to do something other than follow the intentions of those who had started by agreeing to steal" (at p. 33).

It is implicit in this judgment that if the charge upon which a defendant is tried is **33–77** conspiracy to rob, then, notwithstanding that implicit in an allegation of robbery is an allegation of theft, since (a) "agreement" is the essence of conspiracy, and (b) an agreement to steal is a different agreement from the one charged, section 6(3) of the 1967 Act cannot be applied and the jury cannot convict of conspiracy to steal. However, all this judgment actually decides is that where a person is charged with conspiracy to steal, the Crown cannot adduce evidence of the overt acts of others in pursuance of a conspiracy to rob. The remaining observations of the court would appear to be *obiter*. The case is further considered *ante*, at § 21–96.

II. SOLICITING OR INCITING CRIME

(1) Common law

33–78 The common law offence of inciting the commission of another offence was abolished by section 59 of the *SCA* 2007 with effect from October 1, 2008 (*Serious Crime Act 2007 (Commencement No. 3) Order* 2008 (S.I. 2008 No. 2504)). The common law will, however, continue to apply in relation to conduct occurring before that date: 2007 Act, s.91(1), and Sched. 13, paras 5 and 6 (*post*, § 33–118). For the details of the common law offence of incitement, see §§ 33–78 *et seq.* in the supplement. As to jurisdiction in relation to the common law offence, see § 33–81 in the supplement; but as to the extended jurisdiction of the courts in relation to "incitement" (now to be construed as a reference to the offences under Pt 2 of the 2007 Act) to commit certain sexual offences and certain offences of dishonesty, see *ante*, §§ 2–36b *et seq.*

[The next paragraph is § 33–91.]

(2) Statute

33–91 Various statutes create particular offences of "soliciting" or "inciting" particular substantive offences. Whilst these are statutory offences, the concept of solicitation or incitement has generally been construed in accordance with the common law: see, in particular, the *Offences against the Person Act* 1861, s.4, "Soliciting murder", *ante*, § 19–119, the *Official Secrets Act* 1920, s.7, "Inciting, counselling or attempting to procure another to commit an offence against the *Official Secrets Acts* 1911 and 1920", *ante*, § 25–318, the *Misuse of Drugs Act* 1971, s.19, *ante*, § 27–95, and the *Perjury Act* 1911, s.7(2), "Inciting to commit perjury", *ante*, § 28–185.

Apart from the above, the statute book contains many references to the common law offence of incitement. These are converted so that they have effect as references to the offences under Part 2 of the *SCA* 2007 (*post*).

III. ENCOURAGING OR ASSISTING CRIME

(1) Introduction

Serious Crime Act 2007, Pt 2

33–92 Part 2 of the *SCA* 2007 (into force October 1, 2008: S.I. 2008 No. 2504 (*ante*)) introduced new provisions relating to encouraging or assisting crime.

Outline of Part 2

Inchoate offences (ss.44–49)

33–93 Section 44 creates the offence of intentionally encouraging or assisting an offence, and provides that a person is guilty of this offence where he does an act capable of encouraging or assisting the commission of an offence and he intends to encourage or assist its commission. It clarifies what is meant by "intention", by making it clear that foresight of consequences is not sufficient. Section 45 creates the offence of encouraging or assisting an offence believing it will be committed, and provides that a person is guilty of this offence if he does an act capable of encouraging or assisting the commission of an offence and he believes that the offence will be committed and that his act will encourage or assist its commission. Section 46 creates the offence of encouraging or assisting offences believing one or more will be committed, and provides that a person is guilty of this offence if he does an act capable of encouraging or assisting the commission of a number of offences and he believes that one or more of those offences will be committed (but has no belief as to which) and that his act will encourage or assist the commission of one or more of them. It also provides that it is not necessary for a person to have a belief as to which offence will be encouraged or assisted, and that an indictment for this offence must specify the offences that it is alleged the accused believed might be committed (but not necessarily all the offences he did indeed believe might be committed). Section 47 elaborates on the mental element of the offences under sections 44 to 46. In particular, (a) in order to establish that a person intended to encourage or assist the commission of an offence (s.44), it is sufficient to demonstrate that he intended to encourage or assist the doing of an act which would amount to the commission of an offence; (b) if it is alleged under section 45(b) that a person believed that an offence would be committed and that his act would encourage or assist its commission, it is sufficient to prove that he believed that an act would be done which would amount to the commission of that offence; and that his act would encourage or assist the doing of that act; and (c) if it is alleged under section 46(1)(b) that a person believed that one or more of a number of offences would be committed and that his act would encourage or assist the commission of one or more of them, it is sufficient to prove that he believed that one or more of a number of acts would be done which would amount to the commission of one or more of those offences; and that his act would encourage or assist the doing of one or more of those acts (s.47(2)–(4)). If the offence that it is alleged a person intended or believed would be encouraged or assisted requires proof of fault, it must be proved that the person either believed that, were another person to do the act, that person would have the necessary fault, or he was reckless as to whether or not the other person would have the necessary fault, or he himself would have had the necessary fault (if he were to do the act himself) (s.47(5)(a)), and if the last of these is relied upon a person cannot escape liability purely because it is impossible for him to commit the offence (s.47(6)); if the offence that it is alleged a person intended or believed would be encouraged or assisted requires proof of particular circumstances or consequences, it will be necessary to demonstrate that the person either believed [intended or believed (in the case of s.44)], or was reckless as to whether, were another person to do the act, that person would do so in those circumstances or with those consequences (s.47(5)(b), (7)). References in section 47 to doing an act include a failure to act, the continuation of an act and an attempt to do an act (unless that amounts to an offence of attempt) (s.47(8)).

Section 48 makes it clear that, to prove an offence under section 46, it is sufficient to establish that a person who provided encouragement or assistance had the required belief or recklessness in relation to one offence only, but that that offence must be one of those specified in the indictment (subject to the rules allowing for alternative verdicts). Section 49 contains supplemental provisions. In particular, a person may commit an offence under this part whether or not any offence capable of being encouraged or assisted by his act is committed (s.49(1)); if a person's act is capable of encouraging or assisting a number of criminal offences, and he either intends or believes that each of those offences will happen, he can be prosecuted and convicted in relation to every offence that he intends to encourage or assist, or believes will be encouraged or assisted (s.49(2)); a person may, in relation to the same act, commit an offence under more than one provision of this part (s.49(3)); a person cannot be guilty of encouraging or assisting an offence under section 45 or 46 believing that an offence under section 44, 45 or 46 or one of the offences listed in Schedule 3 (generally statutory forms of incitement) will happen (s.49(4), (5)); and the requirement that a person believes that an offence, or a number of offences, be committed is satisfied if he believes that the offence, or that one or more offences, would be committed if certain conditions are met (s.49(7)).

Reasonableness defence (s.50)

33–94 A person is not guilty of an offence under Part 2 if he proves that he acted reasonably in the circumstances he knew to exist or that he acted reasonably in the circumstances he reasonably believed to exist. Factors to be considered when deciding on the reasonableness of a person's actions include (but are not limited to) the seriousness of the anticipated offence, the purpose for which he claims to have been acting and the authority under which he claims to have been acting (s.50(3)).

Limitation on liability of victims (s.51)

33–95 A person cannot be guilty of an offence under Part 2 if, in relation to an offence that is a "protective" offence (one that exists (wholly or in part) for the protection of a particular category of persons), the person who does the act capable of encouraging or assisting that offence falls within the category of persons that the offence was designed to protect and would be considered as the victim.

Jurisdiction and procedure (ss.52–58)

33–96 A person may be convicted of an offence in Part 2, regardless of his own location, if he knew or believed that the act which would amount to the commission of an offence would take place, at least in part, in England and Wales (s.52(1) and (3)), and if it is not possible to establish these circumstances, it may be possible to convict the person if the facts fall within paragraph 1, 2 or 3 of Schedule 4, *viz.* the offence is one for which the perpetrator could be prosecuted in England and Wales even though committed elsewhere, or the act took place in England and Wales and the anticipated offence is an offence in the country where it was anticipated it would be committed (s.52(2)). Where jurisdiction depends on the provisions of Schedule 4, the Attorney-General must give his consent to a prosecution (s.53). Where an offence is covered by provisions that require consent to institute proceedings or that confer a power to institute proceedings, to seize and detain property, or of forfeiture, those provisions apply equally to an offence under Part 2 where the offence covered by those provisions is the anticipated offence (s.54). An offence under section 44 or 45 is triable in the same way as the anticipated offence, and an offence under section 46 is triable on indictment (s.55). A person may be convicted of an offence under this part if an anticipated offence has been committed and it cannot be proved whether that person has either encouraged or assisted the offence on the one hand, or committed the offence as a principal on the other (s.56). Section 57 sets out the offences in relation to which a person may be found guilty as an alternative where he has been prosecuted for an offence under this part, the rules being parallel to those in relation to alternative verdicts in respect of a trial on indictment for the offences encouraged or assisted. The maximum penalty for an offence under this part is the same as the maximum penalty for the anticipated offence (or, if the offence is under section 46 and more than one offence is specified, the maximum penalty for whichever anticipated specified offence has the highest), except that the maximum penalty where the anticipated offence (or one of them) is murder is imprisonment for life, and an unlimited fine may always be imposed for an offence under section 46 where more than one offence is specified (s.58).

(2) Legislation

(a) *Inchoate offences*

Serious Crime Act 2007, ss.44–49

Intentionally encouraging or assisting an offence

33–97 **44.**—(1) A person commits an offence if—

(a) he does an act capable of encouraging or assisting the commission of an offence; and

(b) he intends to encourage or assist its commission.

(2) But he is not to be taken to have intended to encourage or assist the commission of an offence merely because such encouragement or assistance was a foreseeable consequence of his act.

Encouraging or assisting an offence believing it will be committed

33–98 **45.** A person commits an offence if—

(a) he does an act capable of encouraging or assisting the commission of an offence; and

(b) he believes—

(i) that the offence will be committed; and

(ii) that his act will encourage or assist its commission.

Encouraging or assisting offences believing one or more will be committed

46.—(1) A person commits an offence if— 33–99

(a) he does an act capable of encouraging or assisting the commission of one or more of a number of offences; and

(b) he believes—

(i) that one or more of those offences will be committed (but has no belief as to which); and

(ii) that his act will encourage or assist the commission of one or more of them.

(2) It is immaterial for the purposes of subsection (1)(b)(ii) whether the person has any belief as to which offence will be encouraged or assisted.

(3) If a person is charged with an offence under subsection (1)—

(a) the indictment must specify the offences alleged to be the "number of offences" mentioned in paragraph (a) of that subsection; but

(b) nothing in paragraph (a) requires all the offences potentially comprised in that number to be specified.

(4) In relation to an offence under this section, reference in this Part to the offences specified in the indictment is to the offences specified by virtue of subsection (3)(a).

Proving an offence under this Part

47.—(1) Sections 44, 45 and 46 are to be read in accordance with this section. 33–100

(2) If it is alleged under section 44(1)(b) that a person (D) intended to encourage or assist the commission of an offence, it is sufficient to prove that he intended to encourage or assist the doing of an act which would amount to the commission of that offence.

(3) If it is alleged under section 45(b) that a person (D) believed that an offence would be committed and that his act would encourage or assist its commission, it is sufficient to prove that he believed—

(a) that an act would be done which would amount to the commission of that offence; and

(b) that his act would encourage or assist the doing of that act.

(4) If it is alleged under section 46(1)(b) that a person (D) believed that one or more of a number of offences would be committed and that his act would encourage or assist the commission of one or more of them, it is sufficient to prove that he believed—

(a) that one or more of a number of acts would be done which would amount to the commission of one or more of those offences; and

(b) that his act would encourage or assist the doing of one or more of those acts.

(5) In proving for the purposes of this section whether an act is one which, if done, would amount to the commission of an offence—

(a) if the offence is one requiring proof of fault, it must be proved that—

(i) D believed that, were the act to be done, it would be done with that fault;

(ii) D was reckless as to whether or not it would be done with that fault; or

(iii) D's state of mind was such that, were he to do it, it would be done with that fault; and

(b) if the offence is one requiring proof of particular circumstances or consequences (or both), it must be proved that—

(i) D believed that, were the act to be done, it would be done in those circumstances or with those consequences; or

(ii) D was reckless as to whether or not it would be done in those circumstances or with those consequences.

(6) For the purposes of subsection (5)(a)(iii), D is to be assumed to be able to do the act in question.

(7) In the case of an offence under section 44—

(a) subsection (5)(b)(i) is to be read as if the reference to "D believed" were a reference to "D intended or believed"; but

(b) D is not to be taken to have intended that an act would be done in particular circumstances or with particular consequences merely because its being done in those circumstances or with those consequences was a foreseeable consequence of his act of encouragement or assistance.

(8) Reference in this section to the doing of an act includes reference to—

(a) a failure to act;

(b) the continuation of an act that has already begun;

(c) an attempt to do an act (except an act amounting to the commission of the offence of attempting to commit another offence).

(9) In the remaining provisions of this Part (unless otherwise provided) a reference to the anticipated offence is—

(a) in relation to an offence under section 44, a reference to the offence mentioned in subsection (2); and

(b) in relation to an offence under section 45, a reference to the offence mentioned in subsection (3).

Proving an offence under section 46(1)

33–101 **48.**—(1) This section makes further provision about the application of section 47 to an offence under section 46.

(2) It is sufficient to prove the matters mentioned in section 47(5) by reference to one offence only.

(3) The offence or offences by reference to which those matters are proved must be one of the offences specified in the indictment.

(4) Subsection (3) does not affect any enactment or rule of law under which a person charged with one offence may be convicted of another and is subject to section 57.

Supplemental provisions

33–102 **49.**—(1) A person may commit an offence under this Part whether or not any offence capable of being encouraged or assisted by his act is committed.

(2) If a person's act is capable of encouraging or assisting the commission of a number of offences—

(a) section 44 applies separately in relation to each offence that he intends to encourage or assist to be committed; and

(b) section 45 applies separately in relation to each offence that he believes will be encouraged or assisted to be committed.

(3) A person may, in relation to the same act, commit an offence under more than one provision of this Part.

(4) In reckoning whether—

(a) for the purposes of section 45, an act is capable of encouraging or assisting the commission of an offence; or

(b) for the purposes of section 46, an act is capable of encouraging or assisting the commission of one or more of a number of offences;

offences under this Part and listed offences are to be disregarded.

(5) "Listed offence" means—

(a) in England and Wales, an offence listed in Part 1, 2 or 3 of Schedule 3; and

(b) [*Northern Ireland*].

(6) The Secretary of State may by order amend Schedule 3.

(7) For the purposes of sections 45(b)(i) and 46(1)(b)(i) it is sufficient for the person concerned to believe that the offence (or one or more of the offences) will be committed if certain conditions are met.

Listed offences

33–103 Schedule 3 lists the following offences dealt with in this work—

(i) *Offences against the Person Act* 1861

the offences contrary to sections 4, 21 and 22; in the case of sections 21 and 22, so far as they may be committed with the intention of enabling any other person to commit, or assisting any other person in the commission of, an indictable offence, but the reference to "any other person" does not include reference to the person whose act is capable of encouraging or assisting the commission of the offence under section 21 or, as the case may be, section 22;

(ii) *Perjury Act* 1911

an offence contrary to section 1;

(iii) *Aliens Restriction (Amendment) Act* 1919
an offence contrary to section 3(1) consisting in attempting an act calculated or likely to cause sedition or disaffection in contravention of that subsection; or section 3(2) consisting in attempting to promote industrial unrest in contravention of that subsection;

(iv) *Official Secrets Act* 1920
an offence contrary to section 7;

(v) *Incitement to Disaffection Act* 1934
an offence contrary to section 1;

(vi) *Prison Act* 1952
an offence contrary to section 39(1);

(vii) *Criminal Law Act* 1967
an offence contrary to section 4(1) or 5(1);

(viii) *Misuse of Drugs Act* 1971
an offence contrary to section 19 or 20;

(ix) *Immigration Act* 1971
an offence contrary to section 25 or 25B;

(x) *Criminal Law Act* 1977
an offence contrary to section 1(1); or an offence falling within section 5(2) or (3);

(xi) *Criminal Attempts Act* 1981
an offence contrary to section 1(1);

(xii) *Public Order Act* 1986
an offence contrary to section 12(6), 13(9), 14(6) or 14B(3);

(xiii) *Computer Misuse Act* 1990
an offence contrary to section 3A(1), (2) or (3);

(xiv) *Terrorism Act* 2000
an offence contrary to section 1(2), 2(1), 5, 6(1) or (2) or 59; and

(xv) an attempt under "a special statutory provision" (as to which, see the *Criminal Attempts Act* 1981, s.3 (*post*, § 33–123)).

(b) *Reasonableness defence*

Serious Crime Act 2007, s.50

Defence of acting reasonably

50.—(1) A person is not guilty of an offence under this Part if he proves— **33–104**

(a) that he knew certain circumstances existed; and
(b) that it was reasonable for him to act as he did in those circumstances.

(2) A person is not guilty of an offence under this Part if he proves—

(a) that he believed certain circumstances to exist;
(b) that his belief was reasonable; and
(c) that it was reasonable for him to act as he did in the circumstances as he believed them to be.

(3) Factors to be considered in determining whether it was reasonable for a person to act as he did include—

(a) the seriousness of the anticipated offence (or, in the case of an offence under section 46, the offences specified in the indictment);
(b) any purpose for which he claims to have been acting;
(c) any authority by which he claims to have been acting.

(c) *Limitation on liability*

Serious Crime Act 2007, s.51

Protective offences: victims not liable

51.—(1) In the case of protective offences, a person does not commit an offence under this Part by reference to such an offence if— **33–105**

(a) he falls within the protected category; and

(b) he is the person in respect of whom the protective offence was committed or would have been if it had been committed.

(2) "Protective offence" means an offence that exists (wholly or in part) for the protection of a particular category of persons ("the protected category").

This section purports to set out, in statutory form, the common law exemption from liability established in *R. v. Tyrrell* [1894] 1 Q.B. 710, CCR (*ante*, § 18–12).

(d) *Jurisdiction and procedure*

Serious Crime Act 2007, ss.52–58

Jurisdiction

33–106 **52.**—(1) If a person (D) knows or believes that what he anticipates might take place wholly or partly in England or Wales, he may be guilty of an offence under section 44, 45 or 46 no matter where he was at any relevant time.

(2) If it is not proved that D knows or believes that what he anticipates might take place wholly or partly in England or Wales, he is not guilty of an offence under section 44, 45 or 46 unless paragraph 1, 2 or 3 of Schedule 4 applies.

(3) A reference in this section (and in any of those paragraphs) to what D anticipates is to be read as follows—

(a) in relation to an offence under section 44 or 45, it refers to the act which would amount to the commission of the anticipated offence;

(b) in relation to an offence under section 46, it refers to an act which would amount to the commission of any of the offences specified in the indictment.

(4) [*Northern Ireland.*]

(5) Nothing in this section or Schedule 4 restricts the operation of any enactment by virtue of which an act constituting an offence under this Part is triable under the law of England and Wales or Northern Ireland.

For Schedule 4, see *post*, § 33–117.

Prosecution of offences triable by reason of Schedule 4

33–107 **53.** No proceedings for an offence triable by reason of any provision of Schedule 4 may be instituted—

(a) in England and Wales, except by, or with the consent of, the Attorney General; or

(b) [*Northern Ireland*].

Institution of proceedings etc. for an offence under this Part

33–108 **54.**—(1) Any provision to which this section applies has effect with respect to an offence under this Part as it has effect with respect to the anticipated offence.

(2) This section applies to provisions made by or under an enactment (whenever passed or made) that—

(a) provide that proceedings may not be instituted or carried on otherwise than by, or on behalf or with the consent of, any person (including any provision which also makes exceptions to the prohibition);

(b) confer power to institute proceedings;

(c) confer power to seize and detain property;

(d) confer a power of forfeiture, including any power to deal with anything liable to be forfeited.

(3) In relation to an offence under section 46—

(a) the reference in subsection (1) to the anticipated offence is to be read as a reference to any offence specified in the indictment; and

(b) each of the offences specified in the indictment must be an offence in respect of which the prosecutor has power to institute proceedings.

(4) Any consent to proceedings required as a result of this section is in addition to any consent required by section 53.

(5) No proceedings for an offence under this Part are to be instituted against a person providing information society services who is established in an EEA State other than the United Kingdom unless the derogation condition is satisfied.

(6) The derogation condition is satisfied where the institution of proceedings—

(a) is necessary to pursue the public interest objective;

(b) relates to an information society service that prejudices that objective or presents a serious and grave risk of prejudice to it; and

(c) is proportionate to that objective.

(7) The public interest objective is public policy.

(8) In this section "information society services" has the same meaning as in section 34, and subsection (7) of that section applies for the purposes of this section as it applies for the purposes of that section.

For section 34 of the 2007 Act, see *ante*, § 5–876g.

Mode of trial

55.—(1) An offence under section 44 or 45 is triable in the same way as the anticipated offence. **33–109**

(2) An offence under section 46 is triable on indictment.

Persons who may be perpetrators or encouragers etc.

56.—(1) In proceedings for an offence under this Part ("the inchoate offence") the defendant may be convicted if— **33–110**

(a) it is proved that he must have committed the inchoate offence or the anticipated offence; but

(b) it is not proved which of those offences he committed.

(2) For the purposes of this section, a person is not to be treated as having committed the anticipated offence merely because he aided, abetted, counselled or procured its commission.

(3) In relation to an offence under section 46, a reference in this section to the anticipated offence is to be read as a reference to an offence specified in the indictment.

Alternative verdicts and guilty pleas

57.—(1) If in proceedings on indictment for an offence under section 44 or 45 a person is not found guilty of that offence by reference to the specified offence, he may be found guilty of that offence by reference to an alternative offence. **33–111**

(2) If in proceedings for an offence under section 46 a person is not found guilty of that offence by reference to any specified offence, he may be found guilty of that offence by reference to one or more alternative offences.

(3) If in proceedings for an offence under section 46 a person is found guilty of the offence by reference to one or more specified offences, he may also be found guilty of it by reference to one or more other alternative offences.

(4) For the purposes of this section, an offence is an alternative offence if—

(a) it is an offence of which, on a trial on indictment for the specified offence, an accused may be found guilty; or

(b) it is an indictable offence, or one to which section 40 of the *Criminal Justice Act* 1988 applies (power to include count for common assault etc. in indictment), and the condition in subsection (5) is satisfied.

(5) The condition is that the allegations in the indictment charging the person with the offence under this Part amount to or include (expressly or by implication) an allegation of that offence by reference to it.

(6) Subsection (4)(b) does not apply if the specified offence, or any of the specified offences, is murder or treason.

(7) In the application of subsection (5) to proceedings for an offence under section 44, the allegations in the indictment are to be taken to include an allegation of that offence by reference to the offence of attempting to commit the specified offence.

(8) Section 49(4) applies to an offence which is an alternative offence in relation to a specified offence as it applies to that specified offence.

(9) In this section—

(a) in relation to a person charged with an offence under section 44 or 45, "the specified offence" means the offence specified in the indictment as the one alleged to be the anticipated offence;

(b) in relation to a person charged with an offence under section 46, "specified offence" means an offence specified in the indictment (within the meaning of subsection (4) of that section), and related expressions are to be read accordingly.

(10) A person arraigned on an indictment for an offence under this Part may plead guilty to an offence of which he could be found guilty under this section on that indictment.

(11) This section applies to an indictment containing more than one count as if each count were a separate indictment.

(12) This section is without prejudice to—

(a) section 6(1)(b) and (3) of the *Criminal Law Act* 1967;

(b) [*Northern Ireland*].

Penalties

33–112 **58.**—(1) Subsections (2) and (3) apply if—

(a) a person is convicted of an offence under section 44 or 45; or

(b) a person is convicted of an offence under section 46 by reference to only one offence ("the reference offence").

(2) If the anticipated or reference offence is murder, he is liable to imprisonment for life.

(3) In any other case he is liable to any penalty for which he would be liable on conviction of the anticipated or reference offence.

(4) Subsections (5) to (7) apply if a person is convicted of an offence under section 46 by reference to more than one offence ("the reference offences").

(5) If one of the reference offences is murder, he is liable to imprisonment for life.

(6) If none of the reference offences is murder but one or more of them is punishable with imprisonment, he is liable—

(a) to imprisonment for a term not exceeding the maximum term provided for any one of those offences (taking the longer or the longest term as the limit for the purposes of this paragraph where the terms provided differ); or

(b) to a fine.

(7) In any other case he is liable to a fine.

(8) Subsections (3), (6) and (7) are subject to any contrary provision made by or under—

(a) an Act; or

(b) Northern Ireland legislation.

(9) In the case of an offence triable either way, the reference in subsection (6) to the maximum term provided for that offence is a reference to the maximum term so provided on conviction on indictment.

(e) *Interpretation of Part 2*

Serious Crime Act 2007, ss.64–67

Encouraging or assisting the commission of an offence

33–113 **64.** A reference in this Part to encouraging or assisting the commission of an offence is to be read in accordance with section 47.

Being capable of encouraging or assisting

33–114 **65.**—(1) A reference in this Part to a person's doing an act that is capable of encouraging the commission of an offence includes a reference to his doing so by threatening another person or otherwise putting pressure on another person to commit the offence.

(2) A reference in this Part to a person's doing an act that is capable of encouraging or assisting the commission of an offence includes a reference to his doing so by—

(a) taking steps to reduce the possibility of criminal proceedings being brought in respect of that offence;

(b) failing to take reasonable steps to discharge a duty.

(3) But a person is not to be regarded as doing an act that is capable of encouraging or assisting the commission of an offence merely because he fails to respond to a constable's request for assistance in preventing a breach of the peace.

Indirectly encouraging or assisting

33–115 **66.** If a person (D1) arranges for a person (D2) to do an act that is capable of encouraging or assisting the commission of an offence, and D2 does the act, D1 is also to be treated for the purposes of this Part as having done it.

Course of conduct

33–116 **67.** A reference in this Part to an act includes a reference to a course of conduct, and a reference to doing an act is to be read accordingly.

(f) *Extra-territoriality*

Serious Crime Act 2007, Sched. 4

Section 52(2) SCHEDULE 4

EXTRA-TERRITORIALITY

1.—(1) This paragraph applies if— 33–117

(a) any relevant behaviour of D's takes place wholly or partly in England or Wales;

(b) D knows or believes that what he anticipates might take place wholly or partly in a place outside England and Wales; and

(c) either—

(i) the anticipated offence is one that would be triable under the law of England and Wales if it were committed in that place; or

(ii) if there are relevant conditions, it would be so triable if it were committed there by a person who satisfies the conditions.

(2) "Relevant condition" means a condition that—

(a) determines (wholly or in part) whether an offence committed outside England and Wales is nonetheless triable under the law of England and Wales; and

(b) relates to the citizenship, nationality or residence of the person who commits it.

2.—(1) This paragraph applies if—

(a) paragraph 1 does not apply;

(b) any relevant behaviour of D's takes place wholly or partly in England or Wales;

(c) D knows or believes that what he anticipates might take place wholly or partly in a place outside England and Wales; and

(d) what D anticipates would amount to an offence under the law in force in that place.

(2) The condition in sub-paragraph (1)(d) is to be taken to be satisfied unless, not later than rules of court may provide, the defence serve on the prosecution a notice—

(a) stating that on the facts as alleged the condition is not in their opinion satisfied;

(b) showing their grounds for that opinion; and

(c) requiring the prosecution to show that it is satisfied.

(3) The court, if it thinks fit, may permit the defence to require the prosecution to show that the condition is satisfied without prior service of a notice under sub-paragraph (2).

(4) In the Crown Court, the question whether the condition is satisfied is to be decided by the judge alone.

(5) An act punishable under the law in force in any place outside England and Wales constitutes an offence under that law for the purposes of this paragraph, however it is described in that law.

3.—(1) This paragraph applies if—

(a) any relevant behaviour of D's takes place wholly outside England and Wales;

(b) D knows or believes that what he anticipates might take place wholly or partly in a place outside England and Wales; and

(c) D could be tried under the law of England and Wales if he committed the anticipated offence in that place.

(2) For the purposes of sub-paragraph (1)(c), D is to be assumed to be able to commit the anticipated offence.

4. In relation to an offence under section 46, a reference in this Schedule to the anticipated offence is to be read as a reference to any of the offences specified in the indictment.

The provisions of this schedule need to be taken in conjunction with other specific statutory provisions, such as the *Sexual Offences (Conspiracy and Incitement) Act* 1996, s.2 (*ante*, § 2–36b), and the *CJA* 1993, s.1(3)(d) (*ante*, § 2–37).

(g) *Transitional and transitory provisions and savings*

Serious Crime Act 2007, Sched. 13, paras 5, 6

Encouraging or assisting crime

5.—(1) Nothing in any provision of Part 2 affects the operation of— 33–118

(a) any rule of the common law; or

(b) any provision made by or under an Act or Northern Ireland legislation;

in relation to offences committed wholly or partly before the commencement of the provision in Part 2 concerned.

(2) For the purposes of sub-paragraph (1), an offence is partly committed before commencement if—

(a) a relevant event occurs before commencement; and
(b) another relevant event occurs on or after commencement.

(3) In this paragraph "relevant event", in relation to an offence, means any act or other event (including any consequence of an act) proof of which is required for conviction of the offence.

6.—(1) This paragraph applies where, in any proceedings—

(a) a person ("D") is charged in respect of the same act both with an offence under section 44 and with the common law offence of inciting the commission of another offence;
(b) the only thing preventing D from being found guilty of the offence under section 44 is the fact that it has not been proved beyond reasonable doubt that the time when the act took place was after the coming into force of that section; and
(c) the only thing preventing D from being found guilty of the common law offence is that it has not been proved beyond reasonable doubt that that time was before the coming into force of section 59.

(2) For the purpose of determining D's guilt it shall be conclusively presumed that the time when the act took place was before the coming into force of section 44.

Schedule 13 (which is given effect by section 91(1)) came into force on October 1, 2008: *Serious Crime Act 2007 (Commencement No. 3) Order* 2008 (S.I. 2008 No. 2504).

IV. ATTEMPT TO COMMIT CRIME

A. INTRODUCTION

33–119 The *Criminal Attempts Act* 1981 abolished the offence of attempt at common law and any offence at common law of procuring materials for crime: s.6(1). The reference to procuring materials for crime caters for the situation which arose in *R. v. Gurmit Singh* [1966] 2 Q.B. 53, where it was held by McNair J. that procuring an imitation stamp of an Indian magistrate with intent to forge income tax claims constituted an offence at common law.

The Act further provides (s.6(2)) that "references in any enactment passed before this Act which fall to be construed as references to the offence of attempt at common law shall be construed as references to the offence under section 1." Important examples of such references are subsections (3) and (4) of section 6 of the *CLA* 1967, *ante*, § 4–455.

B. STATUTORY OFFENCE OF ATTEMPT

Criminal Attempts Act 1981, ss.1, 1A

Attempting to commit an offence

33–120 **1.**—(1) If, with intent to commit an offence to which this section applies, a person does an act which is more than merely preparatory to the commission of the offence, he is guilty of attempting to commit the offence.

(1A) Subject to section 8 of the *Computer Misuse Act* 1990 (relevance of external law), if this subsection applies to an act, what the person doing it had in view shall be treated as an offence to which this section applies.

(1B) Subsection (1A) above applies to an act if—

(a) it is done in England and Wales; and
(b) it would fall within subsection (1) above as more than merely preparatory to the commission of an offence under section 3 of the *Computer Misuse Act* 1990 but for the fact that the offence, if completed, would not be an offence triable in England and Wales.

(2) A person may be guilty of attempting to commit an offence to which this section applies even though the facts are such that the commission of the offence is impossible.

(3) In any case where—

(a) apart from this subsection a person's intention would not be regarded as having amounted to an intent to commit an offence; but

(b) if the facts of the case had been as he believed them to be, his intention would be so regarded,

then, for the purposes of subsection (1) above, he shall be regarded as having had an intent to commit that offence.

(4) This section applies to any offence which, if it were completed, would be triable in England and Wales as an indictable offence, other than—

(a) conspiracy (at common law or under section 1 of the *Criminal Law Act* 1977 or any other enactment);

(b) aiding, abetting, counselling, procuring or suborning the commission of an offence;

(c) offences under section 4(1) (assisting offenders) or 5(1) (accepting or agreeing to accept consideration for not disclosing information about an arrestable offence) of the *Criminal Law Act* 1967.

[Subss. (1A) and (1B) were inserted by the *Computer Misuse Act* 1990, s.7(3).]

The words in section 1(4), "triable in England and Wales as" are mere surplusage: *R. v. Bristol Magistrates' Court, ex p. E.* [1999] 1 Cr.App.R. 144, DC.

Extended jurisdiction in relation to certain attempts

1A.—(1) If this section applies to an act, what the person doing the act had in view shall be treated as an offence to which section 1(1) above applies. **33–121**

(2) This section applies to an act if—

(a) it is done in England and Wales, and

(b) it would fall within section 1(1) above as more than merely preparatory to the commission of a Group A offence but for the fact that that offence, if completed, would not be an offence triable in England and Wales.

(3) In this section "Group A offence" has the same meaning as in Part I of the *Criminal Justice Act* 1993.

(4) Subsection (1) above is subject to the provisions of section 6 of the Act of 1993 (relevance of external law).

(5) Where a person does an act to which this section applies, the offence which he commits shall for all purposes be treated as the offence of attempting to commit the relevant Group A offence.

[This section was inserted by the *CJA* 1993, s.5(2).]

For the meaning of "Group A offence", see section 1(1) and (2) of the 1993 Act, *ante*, § 2–37. For section 6 of the 1993 Act, see *ante*, § 2–42. In relation to this section, see generally, *ante*, § 2–47.

Criminal Attempts Act 1981, ss.2, 3

Application of procedural and other provisions to offences under s.1

2.—(1) Any provision to which this section applies shall have effect with respect to an offence under section 1 above of attempting to commit an offence as it has effect with respect to the offence attempted. **33–122**

(2) This section applies to provisions of any of the following descriptions made by or under any enactment (whenever passed)—

(a) provisions whereby proceedings may not be instituted or carried on otherwise than by, or on behalf or with the consent of, any person (including any provisions which also make other exceptions to the prohibition);

(b) provisions conferring power to institute proceedings;

(c) provisions as to the venue of proceedings;

(d) provisions whereby proceedings may not be instituted after the expiration of a time limit;

(e) provisions conferring a power of arrest or search;

(f) provisions conferring a power of seizure and detention of property;

(g) provisions whereby a person may not be convicted *or committed for trial* on the uncorroborated evidence of one witness (including any provision requiring the evidence of not less than two credible witnesses);

(h) provisions conferring a power of forfeiture, including any power to deal with anything liable to be forfeited;

(i) provisions whereby, if an offence committed by a body corporate is proved to have been committed with the consent or connivance of another person, that person also is guilty of the offence.

[The italicised words are repealed as from a day to be appointed: *CJA* 2003, ss.41 and 332, Sched. 3, para. 52, and Sched. 37, Pt 4.]

Offences of attempt under other enactments

33–123 **3.**—(1) Subsections (2) to (5) below shall have effect, subject to subsection (6) below and to any inconsistent provision in any other enactment, for the purpose of determining whether a person is guilty of an attempt under a special statutory provision.

(2) For the purposes of this Act an attempt under a special statutory provision is an offence which—

(a) is created by an enactment other than section 1 above, including an enactment passed after this Act; and
(b) is expressed as an offence of attempting to commit another offence (in this section referred to as "the relevant full offence").

(3) A person is guilty of an attempt under a special statutory provision if, with intent to commit the relevant full offence, he does an act which is more than merely preparatory to the commission of that offence.

(4) A person may be guilty of an attempt under a special statutory provision even though the facts are such that the commission of the relevant full offence is impossible.

(5) In any case where—

(a) apart from this subsection a person's intention would not be regarded as having amounted to an intent to commit the relevant full offence; but
(b) if the facts of the case had been as he believed them to be, his intention would be so regarded,

then, for the purposes of subsection (3) above, he shall be regarded as having had an intent to commit that offence.

(6) Subsections (2) to (5) above shall not have effect in relation to an act done before the commencement of this Act.

Criminal Attempts Act 1981, s.4

Trial and penalties

33–124 **4.**—(1) A person guilty by virtue of section 1 above of attempting to commit an offence shall—

(a) if the offence attempted is murder or any other offence the sentence for which is fixed by law, be liable on conviction on indictment to imprisonment for life; and
(b) if the offence attempted is indictable but does not fall within paragraph (a) above, be liable on conviction on indictment to any penalty to which he would have been liable on conviction on indictment of that offence; and
(c) if the offence attempted is triable either way, be liable on summary conviction to any penalty to which he would have been liable on summary conviction of that offence.

(2) In any case in which a court may proceed to summary trial of an information charging a person with an offence and an information charging him with an offence under section 1 above of attempting to commit it or an attempt under a special statutory provision, the court may, without his consent, try the informations together.

(3) Where, in proceedings against a person for an offence under section 1 above, there is evidence sufficient in law to support a finding that he did an act falling within subsection (1) of that section, the question whether or not his act fell within that subsection is a question of fact.

(4) Where, in proceedings against a person for an attempt under a special statutory provision, there is evidence sufficient in law to support a finding that he did an act falling within subsection (3) of section 3 above, the question whether or not his act fell within that subsection is a question of fact.

(5) Subsection (1) above shall have effect—

(a) subject to section 37 of and Schedule 2 to the *Sexual Offences Act* 1956 (mode of trial of and penalties for attempts to commit certain offences under that Act); and
(b) notwithstanding anything—
   (i) in section 32(1) (no limit to fine on conviction on indictment) of the *Criminal Law Act* 1977; or
   (ii) in section *78(1) and (2) (maximum of six months' imprisonment on summary conviction unless express provision made to the contrary) of the* Powers of Criminal Courts (Sentencing) Act *2000* [154(1) and (2) (general limit on magistrates' court's powers to impose imprisonment) of the *Criminal Justice Act* 2003].

[This section is printed as amended by the *PCC(S)A* 2000, s.165(1), and Sched. 9, para. 82; and, as from a day to be appointed, by the *CJA* 2003, s.304, and Sched. 32, para. 33 (substitution of words in square brackets for italicised words).]

"More than merely preparatory"

The 1981 Act is a codifying statute. Attempts to construe it by reference to previous conflicting case law are misconceived; the correct approach is "to look first at the natural meaning of the statutory words": *R. v. Jones*, 91 Cr.App.R. 351, CA, applying *R. v. Gullefer*, 91 Cr.App.R. 356, CA. An accurate paraphrase of the test in section 1(1) is to ask whether the defendant had actually tried to commit the act in question or whether he had only got ready, or put himself in a position, or equipped himself to do so: *R. v. Geddes* [1996] Crim.L.R. 894, CA. "Attempt begins at the moment when the defendant embarks upon the crime proper, as opposed to taking steps rightly regarded as merely preparatory": *R. v. Qadir and Khan* [1998] Crim.L.R. 828, CA. **33–125**

The task of judging where the line falls between acts merely preparatory and the point of embarkation upon the commission of an actual crime always depends upon the circumstances of the case. In deciding whether the act relied upon is capable of being more than merely preparatory, the judge should have in mind the essential nature of the crime alleged to be attempted, *i.e.* the nature of the act upon which the definition of the crime focuses. For example, a wounding usually concentrates on a particular moment in time, whereas an allegation of deception which involves a stratagem is likely to cover a broad course of conduct: *R. v. Qadir and Khan*, *ante*. The creation of a draft will, complete but for the intended testator's signature, could not be said to be more than merely preparatory where there was no evidence of any attempt to have it executed: *R. v. Bowles and Bowles* [2004] 8 *Archbold News* 2, CA ([2004] EWCA Crim. 1608). **33–126**

Where a substantive offence consists of acts preparatory to another substantive offence (*e.g. SOA* 2003, s.14 (*ante*, § 20–85)), it is permissible to charge an attempt to commit the preparatory offence: see *R. v. Robson* [2008] 2 Cr.App.R. 38, CA.

Direction to the jury

In directing a jury on attempt, a judge should restrict himself to the definition of attempt in the Act; it is wholly unnecessary to direct a jury with reference to the law obtaining before the Act: *R. v. Campbell*, 93 Cr.App.R. 350, CA. **33–127**

"With intent to commit an offence"

In *R. v. Khan*, 91 Cr.App.R. 29, CA, the court considered the application of section 1(1) to the element of recklessness in the then definition of rape (no question of attempting to achieve a reckless state of mind arises; the attempt relates to the physical activity; the mental state, in relation to lack of consent, is the same as for the full offence; a man does not recklessly have sexual intercourse, nor does he recklessly attempt it). *Khan* was applied in *Att.-Gen.'s Reference (No. 3 of 1992)*, 98 Cr.App.R. 383, CA (arson). **33–128**

The existence of the requisite intent cannot of itself convert into an attempt, an act which is not more than merely preparatory: *R. v. Rowley*, 94 Cr.App.R. 95, CA. *Cf. R. v. Millard and Vernon* [1987] Crim.L.R. 393, CA.

Attempting the impossible

In *Anderton v. Ryan* [1985] A.C. 567, HL, it was held that notwithstanding the wording of section 1 of the 1981 Act, a woman was not guilty of attempting to handle stolen goods when she purchased a video recorder believing it to be stolen when in fact it was not. That decision was overruled in *R. v. Shivpuri* [1987] A.C. 1, HL (see *ante*, § 25–463 for the facts). **33–129**

The questions which now arise for consideration are the following:

(a) Did the defendant intend to commit the offence which it is alleged he attempted to commit?

(b) Did he, in relation to that offence, do an act which was more than merely

> preparatory to the commission of the *intended* offence? Obviously, if commission of the *actual* offence is impossible no act is going to be more than merely preparatory to the commission of the *actual* offence. Section 1(2) simply requires an act which is more than merely preparatory to the commission of the offence which the defendant intended to commit. If it were otherwise, whenever the facts were such that the commission of the actual offence was impossible, it would be impossible to prove an act more than merely preparatory to the commission of the offence and subsections (1) and (2) would contradict each other: *ibid*.

It is not certain whether a person can be convicted of an attempt if he had merely tried to commit a crime for which he cannot be criminally liable because of a special circumstance applicable to him (*e.g.* prior to the *SOA* 1993, the case of rape by a boy under 14).

Mistake of law

33–130 Where mistake of law is a defence to a charge of committing a specific crime, *e.g.* section 2(1)(a) of the *Theft Act* 1968 (see *ante*, § 21–23), it will also be a defence to a charge of attempting to commit that crime.

Attempting to procure

33–131 In *Chief Constable of Hampshire v. Mace*, 84 Cr.App.R. 40, DC, it was held that section 1(4)(a) of the 1981 Act did not operate to prevent the charging of an attempt to procure the commission of an act of gross indecency under section 1(1) of that Act, because procuring the commission of an act of gross indecency was itself a substantive offence under section 13 of the *SOA* 1956 (*rep.*).

Charging aiders and abettors

33–132 Section 1(4)(b) of the 1981 Act does not preclude an allegation of aiding and abetting an attempt: *R. v. Dunnington* [1984] Q.B. 472, 78 Cr.App.R. 171, CA.

C. JURISDICTION

General rule

33–133 The general rule is that if the completed offence would be triable in England and Wales, an attempt to commit it will be so triable: see s.1(1) and (4) of the 1981 Act, *ante*, § 33–120.

Extended jurisdiction

33–134 For Part I (ss.1–6) of the *CJA* 1993, and the general effect thereof, see *ante*, §§ 2–37 *et seq.* The jurisdiction of the courts over certain offences of attempt is, however, further extended by section 1A of the 1981 Act (*ante*, § 33–121).

D. PLEADING AND PRACTICE

Indictment

33–135 An indictment for the statutory offence of an attempt to commit an offence can be framed on the precedents for the full offence by inserting the words "attempted to" before the words charging the full offence. The statement of offence will be, for example, "Attempted theft, contrary to section 1(1) of the *Criminal Attempts Act* 1981".

Functions of judge and jury

33–136 See section 4(3) and (4) of *Criminal Attempts Act* 1981, *ante*, § 33–124. It is for the judge to rule whether there is any evidence capable of constituting an attempt, and for the jury to say whether they accept it as amounting to an attempt. There should therefore be a careful direction in every case as to the general principle as to what acts constitute attempts: *R. v. Cook*, 48 Cr.App.R. 98, CCA; *DPP v. Stonehouse* [1978] A.C. 55, HL; and see *ante*, § 33–125.

Alternative verdicts

See the *CLA* 1967, s.6(3), (4), *ante*, § 4–455. **33–137**

Sentence

See the *Criminal Attempts Act* 1981, s.4, *ante*, § 33–124, and *R. v. Robson*, unreported, May 6, 1974, where Megaw L.J. observed that it would be "at least unusual that an attempt should be visited with punishment to the maximum extent that the law permits in respect of a completed offence". **33–138**

In *R. v. Ford* [2006] 1 Cr.App.R.(S.) 36, CA, it was held that where the provisions of the *CJA* 2003, s.269, and Sched. 21 (*ante*, §§ 5–239, 5–245), relating to the minimum term to be served by a person convicted of murder, would lead to a higher minimum term (than would have been fixed prior to the commencement of those provisions), then there should be a corresponding increase for corresponding attempted murders; but whatever the minimum term would have been had the offence been completed, it was appropriate to fix the sentence for attempted murder at a level such that the offender would in fact serve about half the minimum term that would have been set for the completed offence. The court added that judges sentencing for attempted murder should bear in mind, also, that provocation and diminished responsibility not being available defences, comparison with manslaughter sentences, rather than minimum terms for murder, would be more appropriate in cases where such defences would have succeeded had the charge been murder. *Ford* was further considered in *R. v. Szypusz and Gaynor* [2007] 1 Cr.App.R.(S.) 49, CA (sentencing by analogy to the principles applicable to the determination of the minimum term in a case of murder, as set out in Schedule 21 to the 2003 Act, may not be appropriate in every case of attempted murder, but sentencing for attempted murder had to bear a proper relationship to sentencing for murder, and such an approach was appropriate for a cold-blooded attempted execution in a public place); *R. v. Clark* [2008] 1 Cr.App.R.(S.) 105, CA (proper approach was to produce a proportional correlation between the determinate sentence for attempted murder and the minimum term for murder had death resulted); and *R. v. Taylor* [2008] 2 Cr.App.R. 9, CA (comparison with Schedule 21 should not result in too mechanistic an approach; a judge should still sit back and ask whether the resulting sentence properly reflects the gravity of the attempted murder in question).

For a statement of the general principle that an attempt normally carries a lesser sentence than the full offence, see *R. v. Joseph* [2001] 2 Cr.App.R.(S.) 88, CA. And, for a practical example, see *R. v. Wolin* [2006] 1 Cr.App.R.(S.) 133, CA (eight years' imprisonment reduced to five for a person who thought she was importing cocaine, but who was in fact in possession of a substance which was not a controlled drug).

INDEX

LEGAL TAXONOMY

FROM SWEET & MAXWELL

This index has been prepared using Sweet and Maxwell's Legal Taxonomy. Main index entries conform to keywords provided by the Legal Taxonomy except where references to specific documents or non-standard terms (denoted by quotation marks) have been included. These keywords provide a means of identifying similar concepts in other Sweet & Maxwell publications and online services to which keywords from the Legal Taxonomy have been applied. Readers may find some minor differences between terms used in the text and those which appear in the index. Suggestions to *sweetandmaxwell.taxonomy@thomson.com*

All references are to paragraph numbers. General cross-references appear at the beginning of certain main headings, referring to entries for specific offences or subjects. Specific cross-references are either to sub-headings elsewhere under the same main heading or to other main headings.